Who's Who in the West®

Who's Who in the West®

2000~2001

Millennium Edition

Since 1899

Including Alaska, Arizona, California, Colorado, Hawaii, Idaho, Montana, Nevada, New Mexico, Oregon, Utah, Washington, and Wyoming; and in Canada, the provinces of Alberta, British Columbia, and Saskatchewan, and the Northwest and Yukon Territories.

27th Edition

MARQUIS
Who's Who®

121 Chanlon Road
New Providence, NJ 07974 U.S.A.
www.marquiswhoswho.com

Who's Who in the West®

Marquis Who's Who®

Table of Contents

Preface

The 27th Edition of *Who's Who in the West* is a compilation of biographical information on men and women of distinction whose influence is concentrated in the western region of North America. Such individuals are of reference interest locally and, to a degree, nationally.

The volume contains approximately 16,000 names from the western region of the United States including Alaska, Arizona, California, Colorado, Hawaii, Idaho, Montana, Nevada, New Mexico, Oregon, Utah, Washington, and Wyoming. Also included are the Canadian provinces of Alberta, British Columbia, and Saskatchewan, and the Northwest and Yukon Territories. In some instances, persons who do not reside in the western region of the United States or Canada have also been included as Biographees. They appear in this edition because they have made significant professional or civic contributions to this region. Reviewed, revised, and amended, the 27th Edition offers current coverage of a broad range of Westerners based on position or individual achievement.

The persons sketched in this volume represent virtually every important field of endeavor. Included are executives and officials in government, business, education, medicine, religion, the press, law, and other fields. This edition also includes significant contributors in such areas as contemporary art, music, and science.

In most cases, Biographees have furnished their own data, thus assuring a high degree of accuracy. In some cases where individuals failed to supply information, Marquis staff members compiled the data through careful, independent research. Sketches compiled in this manner are denoted by an asterisk. As in previous editions, Biographees were given the opportunity to review prepublication proofs of their sketches to make sure they were correct.

The question is often asked, "How do people get into a Marquis Who's Who volume?" Name selection is based on one fundamental principle: reference value.

Biographees of *Who's Who in the West* can be classified in two basic categories: (1) Persons who are of regional reference importance to colleagues, librarians, researchers, scholars, the media, historians, biographers, participants in business and civic affairs, and others with specific or general inquiry needs; (2) Individuals of national reference interest who are also of such regional or local importance that their inclusion in the book is essential.

In the editorial evaluation that resulted in the ultimate selection of the names appearing in this directory, an individual's desire to be listed was not sufficient reason for inclusion; rather it was the person's achievement that ruled. Similarly, neither wealth nor social position was a criterion; only occupational stature or achievement in a field within the western region of North America influenced selection.

A Professional Index is again included in *Who's Who in the West.* Within the index, each Biographee is listed by occupation, and under each occupational category, names are listed alphabetically by country, state, and city. This reference tool will make it easier than ever for interested readers to find Biographees in any given profession or location.

Marquis Who's Who editors exercise the utmost care in preparing each biographical sketch for publication. Occasionally, however, errors occur. Users of this directory are requested to draw the attention of the publisher to any errors found so that corrections can be made in a subsequent edition.

The 27th Edition of *Who's Who in the West* carries on the tradition of excellence established in 1899 with the publication of the first edition of *Who's Who in America*. The essence of that tradition is reflected in our continuing effort to produce reference works that are responsive to the needs of their users throughout the world.

Board of Advisors

Marquis Who's Who gratefully acknowledges the following distinguished individuals who have made themselves available for review, evaluation, and general comment with regard to the publication of the 27th Edition of *Who's Who in the West*. The advisors have enhanced the reference value of this edition by the nomination of outstanding individuals for inclusion. However, the Board of Advisors, either collectively or individually, is in no way responsible for the final selection of names, or for the accuracy or comprehensiveness of the biographical information or other material contained herein.

Standards of Admission

The foremost consideration in selecting Biographees for *Who's Who in the West* is the extent of an individual's reference interest. Such reference interest is judged on either of two factors: (1) the position of responsibility held, or (2) the level of achievement attained by the individual.

Admissions based on the factor of position include:

> *Members of the U.S. Congress*
>
> *Federal judges*
>
> *Governors of states covered by this volume*
>
> *Premiers of Canadian provinces covered by this volume*
>
> *State attorneys general*
>
> *Judges of state and territorial courts of highest appellate jurisdiction*
>
> *Mayors of major cities*
>
> *Heads of major universities and colleges*
>
> *Heads of leading philanthropic, educational, cultural, and scientific institutions and associations*
>
> *Chief ecclesiastics of the principal religious denominations*
>
> *Principal officers of national and international business*

Admission for individual achievement is based on objective qualitative criteria. To be selected, a person must have attained conspicuous achievement.

Key to Information

[1] **ASHTON, HARDY AMES,** [2] lawyer; [3] b. Topeka, Aug. 3, 1934; [4] s. Samuel Taylor and Barbara (Hanson) A.; [5] m. Nancy Richardson, June 20, 1955; [6] children: Marilyn Ashton Heim, Barbara Anne, William Marc. [7] BA, Pa. State U., 1955; JD, Syracuse U.,1960. [8] Bar: Calif.1960, U.S. Supreme Ct. 1968. [9] Assoc. Prine, Belden and Coates, Sacramento, 1960-67; mem. Johnson, Randolph, Sikes and Bord, Sacramento, 1967—, ptnr., 1969-74, sr. ptnr., 1974—; [10] legal cons. Sacramento Urban League. [11] Author: Urban Renewal and the Law, 1975, Changes in California Zoning Laws: A Perspective, 1987. [12] Commr. Sutter County Park Dist., 1971-78; mem. planning com. Arroyo Seco Redevel. Project, Sacramento, 1980—; bd. dirs. Hargrave Inst. [13] Served with U.S. Army, 1956-57. [14] Named Man of the Yr., Sacramento C. of C., 1996. [15] Mem. ABA, Calif. Bar Assn., Sacramento Bar Assn., Am. Judicature Soc., Order of Coif. Clubs: Twelve Trees Country, Tuesday Luncheon. Lodge: Lions (Sacramento). [16] Democrat. [17] Episcopalian. [18] Home: 3080 Grant St Sacramento CA 95814 [19] Office: Johnson Randolph Sikes & Bord 10 Saint Paul St Sacramento CA 95822

KEY

[1] Name
[2] Occupation
[3] Vital statistics
[4] Parents
[5] Marriage
[6] Children
[7] Education
[8] Professional certifications
[9] Career
[10] Career-related
[11] Writings and creative works
[12] Civic and political activities
[13] Military
[14] Awards and fellowships
[15] Professional and association memberships, clubs and lodges
[16] Political affiliation
[17] Religion
[18] Home address
[19] Office address

Table of Abbreviations

The following abbreviations and symbols are frequently used in this book.

*An asterisk following a sketch indicates that it was researched by the Marquis Who's Who editorial staff and has not been verified by the Biographee.

A Associate (used with academic degrees only)

AA, A.A. Associate in Arts, Associate of Arts

AAAL American Academy of Arts and Letters

AAAS American Association for the Advancement of Science

AACD American Association for Counseling and Development

AACN American Association of Critical Care Nurses

AAHA American Academy of Health Administrators

AAHP American Association of Hospital Planners

AAHPERD American Alliance for Health, Physical Education, Recreation, and Dance

AAS Associate of Applied Science

AASL American Association of School Librarians

AASPA American Association of School Personnel Administrators

AAU Amateur Athletic Union

AAUP American Association of University Professors

AAUW American Association of University Women

AB, A.B. Arts, Bachelor of

AB Alberta

ABA American Bar Association

ABC American Broadcasting Company

AC Air Corps

acad. academy, academic

acct. accountant

acctg. accounting

ACDA Arms Control and Disarmament Agency

ACHA American College of Hospital Administrators

ACLS Advanced Cardiac Life Support

ACLU American Civil Liberties Union

ACOG American College of Ob-Gyn

ACP American College of Physicians

ACS American College of Surgeons

ADA American Dental Association

a.d.c. aide-de-camp

adj. adjunct, adjutant

adj. gen. adjutant general

adm. admiral

adminstr. administrator

adminstrn. administration

adminstrv. administrative

ADN Associate's Degree in Nursing

ADP Automatic Data Processing

adv. advocate, advisory

advt. advertising

AE, A.E. Agricultural Engineer

A.E. and P. Ambassador Extraordinary and Plenipotentiary

AEC Atomic Energy Commission

aero. aeronautical, aeronautic

aerodyn. aerodynamic

AFB Air Force Base

AFL-CIO American Federation of Labor and Congress of Industrial Organizations

AFTRA American Federation of TV and Radio Artists

AFSCME American Federation of State, County and Municipal Employees

agr. agriculture

agrl. agricultural

agt. agent

AGVA American Guild of Variety Artists

agy. agency

A&I Agricultural and Industrial

AIA American Institute of Architects

AIAA American Institute of Aeronautics and Astronautics

AIChE American Institute of Chemical Engineers

AICPA American Institute of Certified Public Accountants

AID Agency for International Development

AIDS Acquired Immune Deficiency Syndrome

AIEE American Institute of Electrical Engineers

AIM American Institute of Management

AIME American Institute of Mining, Metallurgy, and Petroleum Engineers

AK Alaska

AL Alabama

ALA American Library Association

Ala. Alabama

alt. alternate

Alta. Alberta

A&M Agricultural and Mechanical

AM, A.M. Arts, Master of

Am. American, America

AMA American Medical Association

amb. ambassador

A.M.E. African Methodist Episcopal

Amtrak National Railroad Passenger Corporation

AMVETS American Veterans of World War II, Korea, Vietnam

ANA American Nurses Association

anat. anatomical

ANCC American Nurses Credentialing Center

ann. annual

ANTA American National Theatre and Academy

anthrop. anthropological

AP Associated Press

APA American Psychological Association

APGA American Personnel Guidance Association

APHA American Public Health Association

APO Army Post Office

apptd. appointed

Apr. April

apt. apartment

AR Arkansas

ARC American Red Cross

arch. architect

archeol. archeological

archtl. architectural

Ariz. Arizona

Ark. Arkansas

ArtsD, ArtsD. Arts, Doctor of

arty. artillery

AS American Samoa

AS Associate in Science

ASCAP American Society of Composers, Authors and Publishers

ASCD Association for Supervision and Curriculum Development

ASCE American Society of Civil Engineers

ASHRAE American Society of Heating, Refrigeration, and Air Conditioning Engineers

ASME American Society of Mechanical Engineers

ASNSA American Society for Nursing Service Administrators

ASPA American Society for Public Administration

ASPCA American Society for the Prevention of Cruelty to Animals

assn. association

assoc. associate

asst. assistant

ASTD American Society for Training and Development

ASTM American Society for Testing and Materials

astron. astronomical

astrophys. astrophysical

ATLA Association of Trial Lawyers of America

ATSC Air Technical Service Command

AT&T American Telephone & Telegraph Company

atty. attorney

Aug. August

AUS Army of the United States

aux. auxiliary

Ave. Avenue

AVMA American Veterinary Medical Association

AZ Arizona

AWHONN Association of Women's Health Obstetric and Neonatal Nurses

B. Bachelor

b. born

BA, B.A. Bachelor of Arts

BAgr, B.Agr. Bachelor of Agriculture

Balt. Baltimore

Bapt. Baptist

BArch, B.Arch. Bachelor of Architecture

BAS, B.A.S. Bachelor of Agricultural Science

BBA, B.B.A. Bachelor of Business Administration

BBB Better Business Bureau

BBC British Broadcasting Corporation

BC, B.C. British Columbia
BCE, B.C.E. Bachelor of Civil Engineering
BChir, B.Chir. Bachelor of Surgery
BCL, B.C.L. Bachelor of Civil Law
BCLS Basic Cardiac Life Support
BCS, B.C.S. Bachelor of Commercial Science
BD, B.D. Bachelor of Divinity
bd. board
BE, B.E. Bachelor of Education
BEE, B.E.E. Bachelor of Electrical
  Engineering
BFA, B.F.A. Bachelor of Fine Arts
bibl. biblical
bibliog. bibliographical
biog. biographical
biol. biological
BJ, B.J. Bachelor of Journalism
Bklyn. Brooklyn
BL, B.L. Bachelor of Letters
bldg. building
BLS, B.L.S. Bachelor of Library Science
BLS Basic Life Support
Blvd. Boulevard
BMI Broadcast Music, Inc.
BMW Bavarian Motor Works (Bayerische
  Motoren Werke)
bn. battalion
B.&O.R.R. Baltimore & Ohio Railroad
bot. botanical
BPE, B.P.E. Bachelor of Physical Education
BPhil, B.Phil. Bachelor of Philosophy
br. branch
BRE, B.R.E. Bachelor of Religious
  Education
brig. gen. brigadier general
Brit. British, Brittanica
Bros. Brothers
BS, B.S. Bachelor of Science
BSA, B.S.A. Bachelor of Agricultural Science
BSBA Bachelor of Science in Business
  Administration
BSChemE Bachelor of Science in Chemical
  Engineering
BSD, B.S.D. Bachelor of Didactic Science
BSEE Bachelor of Science in Electrical
  Engineering
BSN Bachelor of Science in Nursing
BST, B.S.T. Bachelor of Sacred Theology
BTh, B.Th. Bachelor of Theology
bull. bulletin
bur. bureau
bus. business
B.W.I. British West Indies

CA California
CAA Civil Aeronautics Administration
CAB Civil Aeronautics Board
CAD-CAM Computer Aided Design–
  Computer Aided Model
Calif. California
C.Am. Central America
Can. Canada, Canadian
CAP Civil Air Patrol
capt. captain
cardiol. cardiological
cardiovasc. cardiovascular
CARE Cooperative American Relief
  Everywhere
Cath. Catholic
cav. cavalry
CBC Canadian Broadcasting Company
CBI China, Burma, India Theatre of
  Operations
CBS Columbia Broadcasting Company
C.C. Community College
CCC Commodity Credit Corporation
CCNY City College of New York

CCRN Critical Care Registered Nurse
CCU Cardiac Care Unit
CD Civil Defense
CE, C.E. Corps of Engineers, Civil Engineer
CEN Certified Emergency Nurse
CENTO Central Treaty Organization
CEO chief executive officer
CERN European Organization of Nuclear
  Research
cert. certificate, certification, certified
CETA Comprehensive Employment Training
  Act
CFA Chartered Financial Analyst
CFL Canadian Football League
CFO chief financial officer
CFP Certified Financial Planner
ch. church
ChD, Ch.D. Doctor of Chemistry
chem. chemical
ChemE, Chem.E. Chemical Engineer
ChFC Chartered Financial Consultant
Chgo. Chicago
chirurg. chirurgical
chmn. chairman
chpt. chapter
CIA Central Intelligence Agency
Cin. Cincinnati
cir. circle, circuit
CLE Continuing Legal Education
Cleve. Cleveland
climatol. climatological
clin. clinical
clk. clerk
C.L.U. Chartered Life Underwriter
CM, C.M. Master in Surgery
CM Northern Mariana Islands
CMA Certified Medical Assistant
cmty. community
CNA Certified Nurse's Aide
CNOR Certified Nurse (Operating Room)
C.&N.W.Ry. Chicago & North Western
  Railway
CO Colorado
Co. Company
COF Catholic Order of Foresters
C. of C. Chamber of Commerce
col. colonel
coll. college
Colo. Colorado
com. committee
comd. commanded
comdg. commanding
comdr. commander
comdt. commandant
comm. communications
commd. commissioned
comml. commercial
commn. commission
commr. commissioner
compt. comptroller
condr. conductor
Conf. Conference
Congl. Congregational, Congressional
Conglist. Congregationalist
Conn. Connecticut
cons. consultant, consulting
consol. consolidated
constl. constitutional
constn. constitution
constrn. construction
contbd. contributed
contbg. contributing
contbn. contribution
contbr. contributor
contr. controller
Conv. Convention
COO chief operating officer

coop. cooperative
coord. coordinator
CORDS Civil Operations and Revolutionary
  Development Support
CORE Congress of Racial Equality
corp. corporation, corporate
corr. correspondent, corresponding,
  correspondence
C.&O.Ry. Chesapeake & Ohio Railway
coun. council
CPA Certified Public Accountant
CPCU Chartered Property and Casualty
  Underwriter
CPH, C.P.H. Certificate of Public Health
cpl. corporal
CPR Cardio-Pulmonary Resuscitation
C.P.Ry. Canadian Pacific Railway
CRT Cathode Ray Terminal
C.S. Christian Science
CSB, C.S.B. Bachelor of Christian Science
C.S.C. Civil Service Commission
CT Connecticut
ct. court
ctr. center
ctrl. central
CWS Chemical Warfare Service
C.Z. Canal Zone

D. Doctor
d. daughter
DAgr, D.Agr. Doctor of Agriculture
DAR Daughters of the American Revolution
dau. daughter
DAV Disabled American Veterans
DC, D.C. District of Columbia
DCL, D.C.L. Doctor of Civil Law
DCS, D.C.S. Doctor of Commercial Science
DD, D.D. Doctor of Divinity
DDS, D.D.S. Doctor of Dental Surgery
DE Delaware
Dec. December
dec. deceased
def. defense
Del. Delaware
del. delegate, delegation
Dem. Democrat, Democratic
DEng, D.Eng. Doctor of Engineering
denom. denomination, denominational
dep. deputy
dept. department
dermatol. dermatological
desc. descendant
devel. development, developmental
DFA, D.F.A. Doctor of Fine Arts
D.F.C. Distinguished Flying Cross
DHL, D.H.L. Doctor of Hebrew Literature
dir. director
dist. district
distbg. distributing
distbn. distribution
distbr. distributor
disting. distinguished
div. division, divinity, divorce
divsn. division
DLitt, D.Litt. Doctor of Literature
DMD, D.M.D. Doctor of Dental Medicine
DMS, D.M.S. Doctor of Medical Science
DO, D.O. Doctor of Osteopathy
docs. documents
DON Director of Nursing
DPH, D.P.H. Diploma in Public Health
DPhil, D.Phil. Doctor of Philosophy
D.R. Daughters of the Revolution
Dr. Drive, Doctor
DRE, D.R.E. Doctor of Religious Education
DrPH, Dr.P.H. Doctor of Public Health,
  Doctor of Public Hygiene
D.S.C. Distinguished Service Cross

DSc, D.Sc. Doctor of Science
DSChemE Doctor of Science in Chemical
Engineering
D.S.M. Distinguished Service Medal
DST, D.S.T. Doctor of Sacred Theology
DTM, D.T.M. Doctor of Tropical Medicine
DVM, D.V.M. Doctor of Veterinary Medi-
cine
DVS, D.V.S. Doctor of Veterinary Surgery

E, E. East
ea. eastern
E. and P. Extraordinary and Plenipotentiary
Eccles. Ecclesiastical
ecol. ecological
econ. economic
ECOSOC Economic and Social Council (of
the UN)
ED, E.D. Doctor of Engineering
ed. educated
EdB, Ed.B. Bachelor of Education
EdD, Ed.D. Doctor of Education
edit. edition
editl. editorial
EdM, Ed.M. Master of Education
edn. education
ednl. educational
EDP Electronic Data Processing
EdS, Ed.S. Specialist in Education
EE, E.E. Electrical Engineer
E.E. and M.P. Envoy Extraordinary and
Minister Plenipotentiary
EEC European Economic Community
EEG Electroencephalogram
EEO Equal Employment Opportunity
EEOC Equal Employment Opportunity
Commission
E.Ger. German Democratic Republic
EKG Electrocardiogram
elec. electrical
electrochem. electrochemical
electrophys. electrophysical
elem. elementary
EM, E.M. Engineer of Mines
EMT Emergency Medical Technician
ency. encyclopedia
Eng. England
engr. engineer
engring. engineering
entomol. entomological
environ. environmental
EPA Environmental Protection Agency
epidemiol. epidemiological
Episc. Episcopalian
ERA Equal Rights Amendment
ERDA Energy Research and Development
Administration
ESEA Elementary and Secondary Education
Act
ESL English as Second Language
ESPN Entertainment and Sports
Programming Network
ESSA Environmental Science Services
Administration
ethnol. ethnological
ETO European Theatre of Operations
Evang. Evangelical
exam. examination, examining
Exch. Exchange
exec. executive
exhbn. exhibition
expdn. expedition
expn. exposition
expt. experiment
exptl. experimental
Expy. Expressway
Ext. Extension

F.A. Field Artillery
FAA Federal Aviation Administration
FAO Food and Agriculture Organization (of
the UN)
FBA Federal Bar Association
FBI Federal Bureau of Investigation
FCA Farm Credit Administration
FCC Federal Communications Commission
FCDA Federal Civil Defense Administration
FDA Food and Drug Administration
FDIA Federal Deposit Insurance
Administration
FDIC Federal Deposit Insurance Corporation
FE, F.E. Forest Engineer
FEA Federal Energy Administration
Feb. February
fed. federal
fedn. federation
FERC Federal Energy Regulatory
Commission
fgn. foreign
FHA Federal Housing Administration
fin. financial, finance
FL Florida
Fl. Floor
Fla. Florida
FMC Federal Maritime Commission
FNP Family Nurse Practitioner
FOA Foreign Operations Administration
found. foundation
FPC Federal Power Commission
FPO Fleet Post Office
frat. fraternity
FRS Federal Reserve System
FSA Federal Security Agency
Ft. Fort
FTC Federal Trade Commission
Fwy. Freeway

G-1 (or other number) Division of General
Staff
GA, Ga. Georgia
GAO General Accounting Office
gastroent. gastroenterological
GATE Gifted and Talented Educators
GATT General Agreement on Tariffs and
Trade
GE General Electric Company
gen. general
geneal. genealogical
geod. geodetic
geog. geographic, geographical
geol. geological
geophys. geophysical
geriat. geriatrics
gerontol. gerontological
G.H.Q. General Headquarters
GM General Motors Corporation
GMAC General Motors Acceptance
Corporation
G.N.Ry. Great Northern Railway
gov. governor
govt. government
govtl. governmental
GPO Government Printing Office
grad. graduate, graduated
GSA General Services Administration
Gt. Great
GTE General Telephone and
ElectricCompany
GU Guam
gynecol. gynecological

HBO Home Box Office
hdqs. headquarters

HEW Department of Health, Education and
Welfare
HHD, H.H.D. Doctor of Humanities
HHFA Housing and Home Finance Agency
HHS Department of Health and Human
Services
HI Hawaii
hist. historical, historic
HM, H.M. Master of Humanities
HMO Health Maintenance Organization
homeo. homeopathic
hon. honorary, honorable
Ho. of Dels. House of Delegates
Ho. of Reps. House of Representatives
hort. horticultural
hosp. hospital
H.S. High School
HUD Department of Housing and Urban
Development
Hwy. Highway
hydrog. hydrographic

IA Iowa
IAEA International Atomic Energy Agency
IATSE International Alliance of Theatrical
and Stage Employees and Moving Picture
Operators of the United States and Canada
IBM International Business Machines
Corporation
IBRD International Bank for Reconstruction
and Development
ICA International Cooperation Administra-
tion
ICC Interstate Commerce Commission
ICCE International Council for Computers in
Education
ICU Intensive Care Unit
ID Idaho
IEEE Institute of Electrical and Electronics
Engineers
IFC International Finance Corporation
IGY International Geophysical Year
IL Illinois
Ill. Illinois
illus. illustrated
ILO International Labor Organization
IMF International Monetary Fund
IN Indiana
Inc. Incorporated
Ind. Indiana
ind. independent
Indpls. Indianapolis
indsl. industrial
inf. infantry
info. information
ins. insurance
insp. inspector
insp. gen. inspector general
inst. institute
instl. institutional
instn. institution
instr. instructor
instrn. instruction
instrnl. instructional
internat. international
intro. introduction
IRE Institute of Radio Engineers
IRS Internal Revenue Service
ITT International Telephone & Telegraph
Corporation

JAG Judge Advocate General
JAGC Judge Advocate General Corps
Jan. January
Jaycees Junior Chamber of Commerce
JB, J.B. Jurum Baccalaureus

JCB, J.C.B. Juris Canoni Baccalaureus
JCD, J.C.D. Juris Canonici Doctor, Juris
    Civilis Doctor
JCL, J.C.L. Juris Canonici Licentiatus
JD, J.D. Juris Doctor
jg. junior grade
jour. journal
jr. junior
JSD, J.S.D. Juris Scientiae Doctor
JUD, J.U.D. Juris Utriusque Doctor
jud. judicial

Kans. Kansas
K.C. Knights of Columbus
K.P. Knights of Pythias
KS Kansas
K.T. Knight Templar
KY, Ky. Kentucky

LA, La. Louisiana
L.A. Los Angeles
lab. laboratory
L.Am. Latin America
lang. language
laryngol. laryngological
LB Labrador
LDS Latter Day Saints
LDS Church Church of Jesus Christ of Latter
    Day Saints
lectr. lecturer
legis. legislation, legislative
LHD, L.H.D. Doctor of Humane Letters
L.I. Long Island
libr. librarian, library
lic. licensed, license
L.I.R.R. Long Island Railroad
lit. literature
litig. litigation
LittB, Litt.B. Bachelor of Letters
LittD, Litt.D. Doctor of Letters
LLB, LL.B. Bachelor of Laws
LLD, L.L.D. Doctor of Laws
LLM, L.L.M. Master of Laws
Ln. Lane
L.&N.R.R. Louisville & Nashville Railroad
LPGA Ladies Professional Golf Association
LPN Licensed Practical Nurse
LS, L.S. Library Science (in degree)
lt. lieutenant
Ltd. Limited
Luth. Lutheran
LWV League of Women Voters

M. Master
m. married
MA, M.A. Master of Arts
MA Massachusetts
MADD Mothers Against Drunk Driving
mag. magazine
MAgr, M.Agr. Master of Agriculture
maj. major
Man. Manitoba
Mar. March
MArch, M.Arch. Master in Architecture
Mass. Massachusetts
math. mathematics, mathematical
MATS Military Air Transport Service
MB, M.B. Bachelor of Medicine
MB Manitoba
MBA, M.B.A. Master of Business
    Administration
MBS Mutual Broadcasting System
M.C. Medical Corps
MCE, M.C.E. Master of Civil Engineering
mcht. merchant
mcpl. municipal
MCS, M.C.S. Master of Commercial Science

MD, M.D. Doctor of Medicine
MD, Md. Maryland
MDiv Master of Divinity
MDip, M.Dip. Master in Diplomacy
mdse. merchandise
MDV, M.D.V. Doctor of Veterinary
    Medicine
ME, M.E. Mechanical Engineer
ME Maine
M.E.Ch. Methodist Episcopal Church
mech. mechanical
MEd., M.Ed. Master of Education
med. medical
MEE, M.E.E. Master of Electrical
    Engineering
mem. member
meml. memorial
merc. mercantile
met. metropolitan
metall. metallurgical
MetE, Met.E. Metallurgical Engineer
meteorol. meteorological
Meth. Methodist
Mex. Mexico
MF, M.F. Master of Forestry
MFA, M.F.A. Master of Fine Arts
mfg. manufacturing
mfr. manufacturer
mgmt. management
mgr. manager
MHA, M.H.A. Master of Hospital
    Administration
M.I. Military Intelligence
MI Michigan
Mich. Michigan
micros. microscopic, microscopical
mid. middle
mil. military
Milw. Milwaukee
Min. Minister
mineral. mineralogical
Minn. Minnesota
MIS Management Information Systems
Miss. Mississippi
MIT Massachusetts Institute of Technology
mktg. marketing
ML, M.L. Master of Laws
MLA Modern Language Association
M.L.D. Magister Legnum Diplomatic
MLitt, M.Litt. Master of Literature, Master
    of Letters
MLS, M.L.S. Master of Library Science
MME, M.M.E. Master of Mechanical
    Engineering
MN Minnesota
mng. managing
MO, Mo. Missouri
moblzn. mobilization
Mont. Montana
MP Northern Mariana Islands
M.P. Member of Parliament
MPA Master of Public Administration
MPE, M.P.E. Master of Physical Education
MPH, M.P.H. Master of Public Health
MPhil, M.Phil. Master of Philosophy
MPL, M.P.L. Master of Patent Law
Mpls. Minneapolis
MRE, M.R.E. Master of Religious Education
MRI Magnetic Resonance Imaging
MS, M.S. Master of Science
MS, Ms. Mississippi
MSc, M.Sc. Master of Science
MSChemE Master of Science in Chemical
    Engineering
MSEE Master of Science in Electrical
    Engineering

MSF, M.S.F. Master of Science of Forestry
MSN Master of Science in Nursing
MST, M.S.T. Master of Sacred Theology
MSW, M.S.W. Master of Social Work
MT Montana
Mt. Mount
MTO Mediterranean Theatre of Operation
MTV Music Television
mus. museum, musical
MusB, Mus.B. Bachelor of Music
MusD, Mus.D. Doctor of Music
MusM, Mus.M. Master of Music
mut. mutual
MVP Most Valuable Player
mycol. mycological

N. North
NAACOG Nurses Association of the
    American College of Obstetricians and
    Gynecologists
NAACP National Association for the
    Advancement of Colored People
NACA National Advisory Committee for
    Aeronautics
NACDL National Association of Criminal
    Defense Lawyers
NACU National Association of Colleges and
    Universities
NAD National Academy of Design
NAE National Academy of Engineering,
    National Association of Educators
NAESP National Association of Elementary
    School Principals
NAFE National Association of Female
    Executives
N.Am. North America
NAM National Association of Manufacturers
NAMH National Association for Mental
    Health
NAPA National Association of Performing
    Artists
NARAS National Academy of Recording
    Arts and Sciences
NAREB National Association of Real Estate
    Boards
NARS National Archives and Record Service
NAS National Academy of Sciences
NASA National Aeronautics and Space
    Administration
NASP National Association of School
    Psychologists
NASW National Association of Social
    Workers
nat. national
NATAS National Academy of Television
    Arts and Sciences
NATO North Atlantic Treaty Organization
NATOUSA North African Theatre of
    Operations, United States Army
nav. navigation
NB, N.B. New Brunswick
NBA National Basketball Association
NBC National Broadcasting Company
NC, N.C. North Carolina
NCAA National College Athletic Association
NCCJ National Conference of Christians and
    Jews
ND, N.D. North Dakota
NDEA National Defense Education Act
NE Nebraska
NE, N.E. Northeast
NEA National Education Association
Nebr. Nebraska
NEH National Endowment for Humanities
neurol. neurological
Nev. Nevada
NF Newfoundland

NFL National Football League
Nfld. Newfoundland
NG National Guard
NH, N.H. New Hampshire
NHL National Hockey League
NIH National Institutes of Health
NIMH National Institute of Mental Health
NJ, N.J. New Jersey
NLRB National Labor Relations Board
NM New Mexico
N.Mex. New Mexico
No. Northern
NOAA National Oceanographic and
    Atmospheric Administration
NORAD North America Air Defense
Nov. November
NOW National Organization for Women
N.P.Ry. Northern Pacific Railway
nr. near
NRA National Rifle Association
NRC National Research Council
NS, N.S. Nova Scotia
NSC National Security Council
NSF National Science Foundation
NSTA National Science Teachers Association
NSW New South Wales
N.T. New Testament
NT Northwest Territories
nuc. nuclear
numis. numismatic
NV Nevada
NW, N.W. Northwest
N.W.T. Northwest Territories
NY, N.Y. New York
N.Y.C. New York City
NYU New York University
N.Z. New Zealand

OAS Organization of American States
ob-gyn obstetrics-gynecology
obs. observatory
obstet. obstetrical
occupl. occupational
oceanog. oceanographic
Oct. October
OD, O.D. Doctor of Optometry
OECD Organization for Economic
    Cooperation and Development
OEEC Organization of European Economic
    Cooperation
OEO Office of Economic Opportunity
ofcl. official
OH Ohio
OK Oklahoma
Okla. Oklahoma
ON Ontario
Ont. Ontario
oper. operating
ophthal. ophthalmological
ops. operations
OR Oregon
orch. orchestra
Oreg. Oregon
orgn. organization
orgnl. organizational
ornithol. ornithological
orthop. orthopedic
OSHA Occupational Safety and Health
    Administration
OSRD Office of Scientific Research and
    Development
OSS Office of Strategic Services
osteo. osteopathic
otol. otological
otolaryn. otolaryngological

PA, Pa. Pennsylvania

P.A. Professional Association
paleontol. paleontological
path. pathological
PBS Public Broadcasting System
P.C. Professional Corporation
PE Prince Edward Island
pediat. pediatrics
P.E.I. Prince Edward Island
PEN Poets, Playwrights, Editors, Essayists
    and Novelists (international association)
penol. penological
P.E.O. women's organization (full name not
    disclosed)
pers. personnel
pfc. private first class
PGA Professional Golfers' Association of
    America
PHA Public Housing Administration
pharm. pharmaceutical
PharmD, Pharm.D. Doctor of Pharmacy
PharmM, Pharm.M. Master of Pharmacy
PhB, Ph.B. Bachelor of Philosophy
PhD, Ph.D. Doctor of Philosophy
PhDChemE Doctor of Science in Chemical
    Engineering
PhM, Ph.M. Master of Philosophy
Phila. Philadelphia
philharm. philharmonic
philol. philological
philos. philosophical
photog. photographic
phys. physical
physiol. physiological
Pitts. Pittsburgh
Pk. Park
Pky. Parkway
Pl. Place
P.&L.E.R.R. Pittsburgh & Lake Erie
    Railroad
Plz. Plaza
PNP Pediatric Nurse Practitioner
P.O. Post Office
PO Box Post Office Box
polit. political
poly. polytechnic, polytechnical
PQ Province of Quebec
PR, P.R. Puerto Rico
prep. preparatory
pres. president
Presbyn. Presbyterian
presdl. presidential
prin. principal
procs. proceedings
prod. produced (play production)
prodn. production
prodr. producer
prof. professor
profl. professional
prog. progressive
propr. proprietor
pros. atty. prosecuting attorney
pro tem. pro tempore
PSRO Professional Services Review
    Organization
psychiat. psychiatric
psychol. psychological
PTA Parent-Teachers Association
ptnr. partner
PTO Pacific Theatre of Operations, Parent
    Teacher Organization
pub. publisher, publishing, published
pub. public
publ. publication
pvt. private

qnar. quarterly
qm. quartermaster

Q.M.C. Quartermaster Corps
Que. Quebec

radiol. radiological
RAF Royal Air Force
RCA Radio Corporation of America
RCAF Royal Canadian Air Force
RD Rural Delivery
Rd. Road
R&D Research & Development
REA Rural Electrification Administration
rec. recording
ref. reformed
regt. regiment
regtl. regimental
rehab. rehabilitation
rels. relations
Rep. Republican
rep. representative
Res. Reserve
ret. retired
Rev. Reverend
rev. review, revised
RFC Reconstruction Finance Corporation
RFD Rural Free Delivery
rhinol. rhinological
RI, R.I. Rhode Island
RISD Rhode Island School of Design
Rlwy. Railway
Rm. Room
RN, R.N. Registered Nurse
roentgenol. roentgenological
ROTC Reserve Officers Training Corps
RR Rural Route
R.R. Railroad
rsch. research
rschr. researcher
Rt. Route

S. South
s. son
SAC Strategic Air Command
SAG Screen Actors Guild
SALT Strategic Arms Limitation Talks
S.Am. South America
san. sanitary
SAR Sons of the American Revolution
Sask. Saskatchewan
savs. savings
SB, S.B. Bachelor of Science
SBA Small Business Administration
SC, S.C. South Carolina
SCAP Supreme Command Allies Pacific
ScB, Sc.B. Bachelor of Science
SCD, S.C.D. Doctor of Commercial Science
ScD, Sc.D. Doctor of Science
sch. school
sci. science, scientific
SCLC Southern Christian Leadership
Conference
SCV Sons of Confederate Veterans
SD, S.D. South Dakota
SE, S.E. Southeast
SEATO Southeast Asia Treaty Organization
SEC Securities and Exchange Commission
sec. secretary
sect. section
seismol. seismological
sem. seminary
Sept. September
s.g. senior grade
sgt. sergeant
SHAEF Supreme Headquarters Allied
    Expeditionary Forces
SHAPE Supreme Headquarters Allied Powers
    in Europe
S.I. Staten Island

xiv

S.J. Society of Jesus (Jesuit)
SJD Scientiae Juridicae Doctor
SK Saskatchewan
SM, S.M. Master of Science
SNP Society of Nursing Professionals
So. Southern
soc. society
sociol. sociological
S.P.Co. Southern Pacific Company
spkr. speaker
spl. special
splty. specialty
Sq. Square
S.R. Sons of the Revolution
sr. senior
SS Steamship
SSS Selective Service System
St. Saint, Street
sta. station
stats. statistics
statis. statistical
STB, S.T.B. Bachelor of Sacred Theology
stblzn. stabilization
STD, S.T.D. Doctor of Sacred Theology
std. standard
Ste. Suite
subs. subsidiary
SUNY State University of New York
supr. supervisor
supt. superintendent
surg. surgical
svc. service
SW, S.W. Southwest
sys. system

TAPPI Technical Association of the Pulp and Paper Industry
tb. tuberculosis
tchg. teaching
tchr. teacher
tech. technical, technology
technol. technological
tel. telephone
Tel. & Tel. Telephone & Telegraph
telecom. telecommunications
temp. temporary
Tenn. Tennessee
Ter. Territory
Ter. Terrace
TESOL Teachers of English to Speakers of Other Languages
Tex. Texas
ThD, Th.D. Doctor of Theology
theol. theological

ThM, Th.M. Master of Theology
TN Tennessee
tng. training
topog. topographical
trans. transaction, transferred
transl. translation, translated
transp. transportation
treas. treasurer
TT Trust Territory
TV television
TVA Tennessee Valley Authority
TWA Trans World Airlines
twp. township
TX Texas
typog. typographical

U. University
UAW United Auto Workers
UCLA University of California at Los Angeles
UDC United Daughters of the Confederacy
U.K. United Kingdom
UN United Nations
UNESCO United Nations Educational, Scientific and Cultural Organization
UNICEF United Nations International Children's Emergency Fund
univ. university
UNRRA United Nations Relief and Rehabilitation Administration
UPI United Press International
U.P.R.R. United Pacific Railroad
urol. urological
U.S. United States
U.S.A. United States of America
USAAF United States Army Air Force
USAF United States Air Force
USAFR United States Air Force Reserve
USAR United States Army Reserve
USCG United States Coast Guard
USCGR United States Coast Guard Reserve
USES United States Employment Service
USIA United States Information Agency
USMC United States Marine Corps
USMCR United States Marine Corps Reserve
USN United States Navy
USNG United States National Guard
USNR United States Naval Reserve
USO United Service Organizations
USPHS United States Public Health Service
USS United States Ship
USSR Union of the Soviet Socialist Republics
USTA United States Tennis Association

USV United States Volunteers
UT Utah

VA Veterans Administration
VA, Va. Virginia
vet. veteran, veterinary
VFW Veterans of Foreign Wars
VI, V.I. Virgin Islands
vice pres. vice president
vis. visiting
VISTA Volunteers in Service to America
VITA Volunteers in Technical Assistance
vocat. vocational
vol. volunteer, volume
v.p. vice president
vs. versus
VT, Vt. Vermont

W, W. West
WA Washington (state)
WAC Women's Army Corps
Wash. Washington (state)
WATS Wide Area Telecommunications Service
WAVES Women's Reserve, US Naval Reserve
WCTU Women's Christian Temperance Union
we. western
W. Ger. Germany, Federal Republic of
WHO World Health Organization
WI Wisconsin
W.I. West Indies
Wis. Wisconsin
WSB Wage Stabilization Board
WV West Virginia
W.Va. West Virginia
WWI World War I
WWII World War II
WY Wyoming
Wyo. Wyoming

YK Yukon Territory
YMCA Young Men's Christian Association
YMHA Young Men's Hebrew Association
YM & YWHA Young Men's and Young Women's Hebrew Association
yr. year
YT, Y.T. Yukon Territory
YWCA Young Women's Christian Association

zool. zoological

Alphabetical Practices

Names are arranged alphabetically according to the surnames, and under identical surnames according to the first given name. If both surname and first given name are identical, names are arranged alphabetically according to the second given name.

Surnames beginning with De, Des, Du, however capitalized or spaced, are recorded with the prefix preceding the surname and arranged alphabetically under the letter D.

Surnames beginning with Mac and Mc are arranged alphabetically under M.

Surnames beginning with Saint or St. appear after names that begin Sains, and are arranged according to the second part of the name, e.g. St. Clair before Saint Dennis.

Surnames beginning with Van, Von, or von are arranged alphabetically under the letter V.

Compound surnames are arranged according to the first member of the compound.

Many hyphenated Arabic names begin Al-, El-, or al-. These names are alphabetized according to each Biographee's designation of last name. Thus Al-Bahar, Neta may be listed either under Al- or under Bahar, depending on the preference of the listee.

Also, Arabic names have a variety of possible spellings when transposed to English. Spelling of these names is always based on the practice of the Biographee. Some Biographees use a Western form of word order, while others prefer the Arabic word sequence.

Similarly, Asian names may have no comma between family and given names, but some Biographees have chosen to add the comma. In each case, punctuation follows the preference of the Biographee.

Parentheses used in connection with a name indicate which part of the full name is usually deleted in common usage. Hence Chambers, E(lizabeth) Anne indicates that the usual form of the given name is E. Anne. In such a case, the parentheses are ignored in alphabetizing and the name would be arranged as Chambers, Elizabeth Anne. However, if the name is recorded Chambers, (Elizabeth) Anne, signifying that the entire name Elizabeth is not commonly used, the alphabetizing would be arranged as though the name were Chambers, Anne. If an entire middle or last name is enclosed in parentheses, that portion of the name is used in the alphabetical arrangement. Hence Chambers, Elizabeth (Anne) would be arranged as Chambers, Elizabeth Anne.

Where more than one spelling, word order, or name of an individual is frequently encountered, the sketch has been entered under the form preferred by the Biographee, with cross-references under alternate forms.

Who'sWho in the West®

Biographies

AADAHL, JORG, business executive; b. Trondheim, Norway, June 16, 1937; came to U.S., 1966; s. Ottar P. and Gurli (Lockra) A.; MS in Mech. Engring., Tech. U. Norway, 1961; MBA, U. San Francisco, 1973; m. Inger R. Holst, July 13, 1973; children: Erik, Nina. Rsch. fellow Tech. U. Norway, Trondheim, 1961-62; mgr. arc welding devel. NAG, Oslo, 1964-66; mfg. engr. Varian Assocs., Palo Alto, Calif., 1966-67; sr. tech. writerLynch Comm. Sys., 1967-69; indsl. engr., project mgr., 1969-74, bus. mgr. United Airlines, San Francisco, 1974-75, sr. systems analyst, 1976-81; strategic planning specialist Magnex Corp., San Jose, 1981-82; cons. in mgmt., 1982-84; founder, pres. Safeware, Inc., San Mateo, Calif., 1984—; founder, prin. CampuSafe Sys., 1996—; dir. Safeware Sys.Ltd., U.K., 1990—. Developer Safechem Hazardous Chem. Mgmt. Sys. Recipient Cert. of Honor, San Francisco Bd. Suprs., 1973. Mem. Leif Erikson League (pres. 1973), Norwegian Soc. Profl. Engrs. Club: Young Scandinavians (v.p. 1971). Environment and Safety Data Exch. (founding mem., dir.). Author: Strength Analysis, Welded Structures, 1967; contbr. articles in various fields to profl. jours.; editor Nordic Highlights, 1972. Office: Safeware Inc PO Box 6745 2575 Flores St San Mateo CA 94403-2366

AALTO, MADELEINE, library director. BA, Wellesley Coll., 1964; BLS, U. Toronto, 1967. Clerical asst. Toronto Pub. Libr., 1964-66, children's libr. Parkdale br., 1968-69, collection libr. Spaced Out libr., 1969-73, br. head Annette St. br., 1973-74, coord. adult svcs., 1974-75; chief libr. East York Pub. Libr., 1975-84, Greater Victoria Pub. Libr., 1984-88; dir. Vancouver (B.C.) Pub. Libr., Can., 1988—. Contbr. intro. to A Geography for Children (Philippe du Fresnoy), 1968. Recipient Commerative medal 125th Anniversary Confederation Can., 1993. Mem. B.C. Libr. Assn. Office: Vancouver Pub Libr, 350 W Georgia St, Vancouver, BC Canada V6B 6B1

AARON, ALEXANDER, systems analyst, consultant; b. Las Vegas, June 17, 1961; s. Bud and Dina (Prasinos) A.; m. Tsie-Jen Carrie Tu, Sept. 20, 1997. Programmer Bus. Master, Carlsbad, Calif., 1976-86; freelance writer Oceanside, Calif., 1986-91; sys. analyst CheckMaster, Oceanside, 1991—. Author: Upgrading PC's Made Easy, 1991, Treasure Chest Display Fonts, 1993, Treasure Chest Text Fonts. Republican. Jewish. Avocations: woodworking, homebrewing, kayaking, camping, aquaria. Office: CheckMaster 4058 Johnson Dr Oceanside CA 92056-3805

AARON, BUD, systems analyst; b. White Sulphur Springs, Mont., Apr. 27, 1927; m. Dina Aaron, Jan. 10, 1960; children: Alex, Roy, Erica, Bill. Owner Microkits, 1963-67; prodn. mgr. Ednl. Computer Products, 1967-68, mfg. rep., 1968-69; instr. Control Data Inst., 1969-70; supr. ICL, Kidsgrove, England, 1970-73; tech. writer Philips Small Computers, Fontenay aux Rose, France, 1973-74; designer, developer computer programs Hughes, JPL, Lawrence Livermore Labs. and others, 1974-76; programmer, mgr., sales BusinessMaster, Carlsbad, Calif., 1976-86; mgr., writer, programmer CheckMaster Corp., Oceanside, Calif., 1986—.

AARON, ROY HENRY, entertainment company executive; b. Los Angeles, Apr. 8, 1929; s. Samuel Arthur and Natalie (Krakauer) A.; m. Theresa Gesas, Dec. 20, 1953; 1 child, Jill. BA, U. Calif.-Berkeley, 1951; LLB, U. So. Calif., 1956. Bar: Calif. 1957. Mem. Pacht, Ross, Warne, Bernhard & Sears, Inc., L.A., 1957-79, of counsel, 1979-83; sr. v.p., gen. counsel Plitt Theatres, Inc. and Plitt Theatre Holdings, Inc., L.A., 1978-80, pres., COO, 1980-85; pres. Plitt Entertainment Group, Inc., L.A., 1985—; pres., chief exec. officer Showscan Corp., L.A., 1985-93; chmn., CEO Intra-Asia Ent. Corp., 1998—; lectr. Calif. Continuing Edn. of Bar; lectr. continuing legal edn. Loyola U. Law Sch., Los Angeles. Mem. editorial bd. U. So. Calif. Law Rev., 1954-56. Trustee, mem. exec. com. Vista Del Mar Child-Care Svc., 1968-80, Reiss-Davis Child Study Ctr., 1977-80, Plitt So. Theaters Inc., Employees Trust, 1978-97; bd. dirs. Rape Found.; mem. adv. bd. dirs. Rape Treatment Ctr. of Santa Monica, UCLA Med. Ctr.; pres. UCLA Royce Two Seventy, 1986-88; mem. UCLA Found., pres. 1996-98, chmn., 1998—, bd. dirs. Fellow Am. Bar Found. (life), L.A. County Bar Found. (life); mem. ABA, State Bar Calif., L.A. County Bar Assn. (trustee 1977-83, v.p. 1979-80, sr. v.p. 1980-81, pres.-elect 1982-83, pres. 1982-83, Shattuck-Price Meml. award 1996), U. Calif.-Berkeley Alumni Assn., UCLA Alumni Assn., Found. Motion Pictures Pioneers (bd. dirs.), So. Calif. Tennis Assn. (bd. dirs.).

AARONSON, BARBARA HARLAN, interior designer; b. Miami, Fla., May 19, 1956; m. Peter Aaronson, Feb. 14, 1992; children: Jarret, Chase. Diploma in interior design, Art Inst., Ft. Lauderdale, Fla., 1991, UCLA, 1993; diploma in interior design with honors, Interior Design Inst., Las Vegas, Nev., 1994. Prin. designer Oceanview Interiors, Las Vegas, 1991—; instr. Interior Design Inst.; guest host Am. Online Decorating Forum; judge Dream Rm. Competition, Las Vegas. Co-host TV show Designing You, 1997; creator/host model home tour Designer Secrets, 1997; author design column Home and Hearth mag., 1998. Vol. profl. svcs. Downs Syndrome Assn., Muscular Dystrophy Assn., Shade Tree Shelter, Women's Devel. Ctr., Las Vegas. Recipient Blue Chip Enterprise award Mass. Mut./C. of C., 1997, Congl. award Cong. Ensign, 1997. Mem. Am. Soc. Interior Designers (exec. bd.), Nat. Assn. Women Bus. Owners.

AASEN-HULL, AUDREY AVIS, music educator; b. Coquille, Oreg., July 9, 1916; d. John Lawrence and Orra Amy (Kelley) Aasen; m. James Byrne Hull, Sept. 15, 1962. BA, U. Oreg., 1939; MA, Stanford U., 1946. Music tchr. Monroe (Oreg.) H.S., 1939-40, Estacada (Oreg.) Union Sch., 1940-41; performer of solo violin program Sta. KOOS, Coos Bay, Oreg., 1941-43; supr. instrumental music San Francisco Pub. Schs., 1944-45; tchr. violin and piano Menlo Sch. & Coll., Menlo Park, Calif., 1947-48, Sacred Heart Convent Sch., Menlo Park, Calif., 1948-49. Performances of string quartets, trios, quintets and sextets for San Francisco Musical Club and Palo Alto Fortnightly Music Club, 1947-89; performed with People's Symphony, San Francisco, 1945, Calif. Mfrs. Assn., San Francisco, 1950, Palo Alto String quartet, 1958, String Orch. Televised Concert, Innsbruck, Austria, 1982, Queen Elizabeth Hall, Belgium, Internat. String Tchrs. Workshop, Brussels, 1984, and numerous others; soloist at Soroptimist Internat. Conv. for Am. Fedn. Soroptimist Clubs, Can., 1954; concertmistress Penisula Symphony, 1958-59; most recent performances include recital Menlo Park, Calif., 1997, performances at Fortnightly Music Club, 1997, 98, U. Oreg., 1997. Adv. bd. mem. Calif. Summer Music at Pebble Beach, initiating mem., 1996—; patron San Francisco Symphony, underwriter violin chair position, 1989—. Recipient citation for Disting. Svc. USO, 1943-44, 45-46. Mem. Am. Fed. Musicians (life), Am. String Tchrs. Assn., Soroptimist Club (life), Fortnightly Music Club. Avocations: gardening, studying French, dancing, cooking.

ABBOTT, H. PORTER, English language educator; b. Balt., Nov. 21, 1940; s. Horace P. and Barbara Ann (Trueblood) A.; m. Anita Vaivods, June 25, 1966; children: Jason, Byram. BA, Reed Coll., Portland, Oreg., 1962; MA, U. Toronto, Ont., Can., 1964, PhD, 1968. From asst. prof. to assoc. prof. U. Calif., Santa Barbara, 1966-82, prof., 1982—, chair of English, 1983-87, 90, acting dean humanities and fine arts, 1992-94; lectr., instr. Yeats Summer Sch., Sligo, Ireland, 1989. Author: The Fiction of Samuel Beckett, 1973, Diary Fiction, 1984, Beckett Writing Beckett, 1996, (poetry chapbook) Cold Certainties and Changes Beyond Measure, 1988. Pres. Foothill Preservation League, Santa Barbara, 1996—. Recipient William Stafford award Poetry Assn. Wash., 1977. Mem. MLA, Samuel Beckett Soc. (pres. 1962-64). Office: U of Calif Dept English Santa Barbara CA 93106

ABBOTT, PATTI MARIE, middle school educator; b. Lewistown, Mont., Mar. 15, 1942; d. Vernal Hall and Marquerite (Cowen) A. BS, Ea. Mont. Coll., 1963, MS, 1968; postgrad. in adminstrn., Mont. State U., 1980. Tchr. Sch. Dist. No. 1, Glendive, Mont., 1964; tchr. Billings (Mont.) Pub. Schs., 1964—, pub. rels. rep., 1983-87. Contbr. articles to profl. jours. Resource person Girl Scouts U.S., Billings, 1973—, cadet leader, 1976-79; resource person Campfire Girls, Billings, 1978—; vol. Heart Fund, Am. Cancer Soc., Birth Defects Found., 1976—; v.p. Sweet Adelines, Billings, 1981-83. Named Tchr. of Yr., Masonic Order, Billings, 1985, 86. Mem. NEA, ASCD, AAUW (sec. Billings chpt. 1985-87, scholar 1987, essay chairperson 1992-93), Am. Bus. Women's Assn. (pres. Billings chpt. 1980-82, Woman of Yr. award 1980), Harmony Club (pres. 1986-87), Rebeccas, Eagles, Alpha Delta Kappa (mem. internat. exec. bd., grand historian, grand v.p. 1983-87, grand pres. 1993-95, exec. bd. 1995—). Avocations: music, writing, gardening, reading. Home: 701 Torch Dr Billings MT 59102-5925 Office: Lewis and Clark Jr High 1315 Lewis Ave Billings MT 59102-4299

ABBOTT, ROBERT CARL, management company executive; b. Riverside, Calif., Oct. 20, 1955; s. Orville Hancock and Erna Adella (Sparber) Whitney; m. Diane Alicia Sallstrom, Aug. 5, 1978; children: Ryan Christian, Aaron Matthew, Kalen James. MBA, Century U., 1993. Ordained to ministry Calvary Grace Christian, 1976; firefighter, Wash., Emergency Med. Tech., first aid instr. and survival instr.; reg. hypnotherapist Am. Bd. Hypnotherapists, Wash. State Dept. of Health; lic. massage therapist, Oreg. Affirmative action officer State of Wash., Spokane, Wash., 1976-77; personnel supr. Key Tronic Corp., Spokane, 1977-80; personnel mgr. ISC Systems Corp., Spokane, 1980-84; fire chief Millwood Fire Dept., Millwood, Wash., 1982-88; pres. and CEO Total Mgmt. Systems, Inc., Millwood, 1984-88; gen. mgr. Ptarmigan Village, Whitefish, Mont., 1988-91, Unitech Composites, Inc., Hayden Lake, Idaho, 1991-93; CEO Total Mgmt Sys., Rathdrum, Idaho, 1993-94; dir. staffing and employee devel. N.W. Natural Gas Co., 1994-97; human resources mgr. Great Western Chem., Portland, Oreg., 1997—; dir. Northwest Psychic Rsch., Oregon City, Oreg. Mem. Gov.'s Com. of Vet. Bus., Washington, 1983-84; chmn. Whitefish Fire Svcs. Area Commn., 1989-91; mem. CAP. Named Most Influential for the Year, Millwood Fire Dept., 1984. Christian. Avocations: karate (black belt), backpacking, scuba diving, juggling, fishing. Home: 17957 S Greenfield Dr Oregon City OR 97045-7848 Office: 808 SW 15th Ave Portland OR 97205-1907

ABBOTT, RUSSELL JOSEPH, computer scientist; b. Bklyn., Mar. 1, 1942; s. Samuel and Lillian (Ginsberg) A.; children: Michael, Julian, Danielle. BA, Columbia U., 1962; MA, Harvard U., 1963; PhD, U. So. Calif., 1973. Researcher GE Ctr. for Adv. Studies, Santa Barbara, Calif., 1965-69, USC-Info. Scis. Inst., Marina del Ray, Calif., 1975-78; chief scientist Silogic, L.A., 1984-87; prof. Calif. State U., Northridge, 1973-84, L.A., 1987—; mem. tech. staff The Aerospace Corp., El Segundo, Calif., 1978-97. Author: (book) Software Engineer, 1986. Office: Dept of Math/CS CSULA Los Angeles CA 90032

ABBOUD, SAM, investor; b. Jan. 1, 1973. BS, U. So. Calif., 1992; postgrad., Harvard Bus. Sch. Fin. analyst Salomon Bros., L.A., 1992-95; assoc. Freeman Spogli & Co., L.A., 1995-97. Exec. dir. L.A. Street Project, 1992-97. Republican. Avocations: martial arts, basketball, travel.

ABBRUZZESE, CARLO ENRICO, physician, writer, educator; b. Rome, Italy, May 28, 1923; came to U.S., 1951, naturalized, 1959; s. Aurelio and Maria (Sbriccoli) A.; m. Silvia Ramirez-Lemus; children: Marco A., Carlo M., Eric L., Christopher E., Romana S., Kevin R., Alvaro L. Liceo-Ginnasio, Dante Alighieri, Roma, 1935-43; Facoltà di Medicina e Chirurgia, Università di Roma, 1943-49; DSc, London Inst. Applied Rsch., 1973. Lic. med. dr. Italy, European Community, Calif. Resident in tropical subtropical diseases U. Rome, 1950-51; intern Woman's and Highland Park Gen. hosps., Detroit, 1951-53; resident in family practice Saratoga Gen. Hosp., Detroit, Columbus Hosp., Newark, 1953-57; gen. practice occupational and sport medicine Rome, 1949-51, Oakland, Calif., 1958-75, Santa Ana, Calif., 1975-84; dir. emergency and outpatient depts. Drs. Hosp. Santa Ana, Calif., 1975-77; dir. North Bristol Family Med. Clinic, Rsch. and Diagnostic Lab. Author: Storia della Psicologia, 1949, Roma, L'ascoltazione Stetoscopica del cuore, RCA italiana, 1953, L'ascoltazione stetoscopica, 1955, 56, 83, 86, Roma, 1986, Esercitazioni di diagnostica ascoltatoria, 1983, 86; founder, pub., editor-in-chief ESDNA, Rome, 1983, ESDI, Rome, 1986; pub. Med. Newsletter, 1987; contbr. articles to profl. jours. Founder, leader polit. youth movements, Rome, 1943-47; co-founder, nat. chmn. U.S. divorce reforms orgns., 1975; UN rep. on violation of due process and domestic human rights, 1977; exec. officer Men Internat., Calif.; active Nat. Italian Am. Found. Decorated Commendatore di Merito, 1950, Gran Croce Merito del Lavoro, Internat. Bus. Corp., 1981; Fulbright fellow, 1951-53. Fellow Am. Acad. Family Physicians; mem. AMA, Calif. Med. Assn., Orange County Med. Assn., Ordine dei Medici di Roma, Società Italiana di Chirurgia, Union Am. Physicians, Am. Acad. Family Practice (co-founder). Office: 316 N Bristol St Santa Ana CA 92703-3811

ABDALLAH, CHAOUKI TANIOS, electrical engineering educator; b. Rachana, Batroun, Lebanon, July 4, 1959; s. Tanios Youssef and Zoumorrod (Kanaan) A.; m. Catherine Lee Cooper, July 14, 1990. BE, Youngstown State U., 1981; MS, Ga. Inst. Tech., 1982, PhD, 1988. Project mgr. Sawtek Inc., Orlando, Fla., 1984-85; asst. prof. EECE U. N.Mex., Albuquerque, 1988-94, assoc. prof., 1994—. Co-author: Control of Robot Manipulators, 1993, Linear Quadrant Control, 1994; co-editor: Robot Control: Dynamics Motion Planning and Analysis, 1992. Office: U NMex Dept Elec Engring Albuquerque NM 87131

ABDUL, CORINNA GAY, software engineer, consultant; b. Honolulu, Aug. 10, 1961; d. Daniel Lawrence and Katherine Yoshie (Kanada) A. BS in Computer Sci., U. Hawaii, 1984. Programmer, analyst, adminstrv. and fiscal svcs. U. Hawaii, Honolulu, 1982-84, software engr. libr. of divsn. of planetary geoscis., 1984; sys. software engr. II, test systems and software engr. dept space and tech. TRW Inc., Redondo Beach, Calif., 1985-89; systems software engr. II, Sierra On-Line, Inc., Oakhurst, Calif., 1989-90; sr. programmer, analyst Decision Rsch. Corp., Honolulu, 1990-92; ind. computer cons. Honolulu, 1992-94; computer cons. Wailuku, Hawaii, 1994—. Recipient The 20th Century award for achievement, 1994. Avocations: traditional Chinese medicine herbalist, practice Japanese Meridian therapy. Home: 856 W Kaena Pl Wailuku HI 96793-9620

ABDUL-JABBAR, KAREEM (LEWIS FERDINAND ALCINDOR), retired professional basketball player, sports commentator; b. N.Y.C., Apr. 16, 1947; s. Ferdinand Lewis and Cora Alcindor; m. Habiba (Janice Brown), 1971 (div. 1973); children: Habiba, Kareem, Sultana, Amir. B.A., UCLA, 1969. Basketball player with Milw. Bucks, 1969-75, Los Angeles Lakers, 1975-89; owner Kareem Productions; now commentator ESPN, Bristol, Ct. Became NBA all-time leading scorer, 1984; appeared on TV in episodes of Mannix, The Man from Atlantis, Diff'rent Strokes, Tales from the Darkside, Pryor's Place, The ABC Afterschool Spl.; appeared in movies: The Fish that Saved Pittsburgh, 1979, Airplane, 1980, Fletch, 1985; author: (with Peter Knobler) Giant Steps: An Autobiography of Kareem Abdul-Jabbar, 1983, (with Mignon McCarthy) Kareem, 1990. Named Rookie of Year NBA, 1970; recipient Maurice Podoloff Cup; named Most Valuable Player NBA, 1971, 72, 74, 76, 77, 80; player NBA All-Star game, 1970-87, 89; named to NBA 35th Anniversary All-Time Team, 1980; NBA Playoff Most Valuable Player, 1971, 85; mem. NBA Championship Team, 1971, 80, 82, 85, 87, 88, NCAA Championship Team, 1967, 68, 69; named NCAA Tournament Most Outstanding Player, 1967, 68, 69. Muslim. Avocation: jazz. Office: 10100 Santa Monica Blvd Los Angeles CA 90067 also: Kareem Productions Ste 2200 1999 Avenue Of The Stars Los Angeles CA 90067-4699*

ABEL, JAMES CALVIN, JR., financial planner; b. Aurora, Colo., Feb. 27, 1963; s. James C. and Barbara A. (Fruge) A.; m. Elizabeth J. Nelson, Mar. 10, 1989; children: Brooke, Morgan, Hunter. AA, Miramar Coll., 1988. Cert. fin. planner; registered fin. cons. With USN, Hawaii, 1981-88; sr. investment exec. Liberty Securities, Lacey, Wash., 1990-93; investment mgr. Ind. Fin., Lacey, 1993-94; personal investment officer Zions Investment Securities, St. George, Utah, 1994-95; reg. prin. Investment Mgmt. Rsch., St. George, 1995—. Mem. Internat. Assn. Fin. Planners, Internat. Bd. Cert. Fin. Planners, Nat. Assn. Securities Dealers (arbitrator), St. George Kiwanis. Republican. Mem. LDS Ch. Avocations: reading, family activities, travel. Office: Investment Mgmt Rsch Inc 720 S River Rd Ste C215 Saint George UT 84790-5535

ABEL, MICHAEL L., marketing executive; b. New London, Wis., Jan. 15, 1952; s. William A. and Delores R. (Shuey) A.; m. Monica L. Miller, Dec. 18, 1971; children: Richard M., David M. AAS, Joliet (Ill.) Jr. Coll., 1975; BA in Bus. Adminstrn., Lewis U., 1977, MBA, 1979. Lab. technician No. Petrochem. Co., Morris, Ill., 1975-76, tech. specialist, 1976-80; nat. account rep. No. Petrochem. Co., Des Plaines, Ill., 1980-82; product mgr. Enron Chem. Co., Omaha, 1982-85, mktg. mgr., 1985-87; sr. account exec. Quantum Chem. Co., Rancho Mirage, Calif., 1987-89; sr. v.p. N.Am. ops. Intac Automotive Products, Inc., Lemont, Ill., 1989—; pres., chief exec. officer Desert Leisure Devel. Corp., Palm Springs, 1991—, bd. dirs.; bd. dirs. Palm Cts. Assn., Rancho Mirage, 1988-97, The Kids Business, Inc., Rancho Mirage, 1996—. Patentee in chem. engring. field. Pres. Palm Ct. Owners Assn., Rancho Mirage, 1988-97; mem. Rep. Presdl. Task Force, 1990—. Mem. ASTM, Soc. Automotive Engrs., Nat. Assn. Corrosion Engrs. (sec. 1981-82), Internat. Platform Assn. Republican. Lutheran. Home: 36845 Palm Ct Rancho Mirage CA 92270-2206

ABELES, KIM VICTORIA, artist; b. Richmond Heights, Mo., Aug. 28, 1952; d. Burton Noel Wright and Frances Elizabeth (Sander) Hoffman. B.F.A. in Painting, Ohio U., 1974; M.F.A. in Studio Art, U. Calif.-Irvine, 1980. Free-lance artist, Los Angeles, 1975—; lectr. various schs. and art ctrs., 1980—; vis. disting. artist Calif. State U., Fullerton, 1985-87. Author, illustrator: Crafts, Cookery and Country Living, 1976. Author, photographer: Impressions, 1979. Work featured in Artery, 1979, Pacific Poetry and Fiction Review, 1980, Fiction Internat., 1985. One-woman shows include U. Calif.-Irvine, 1979, 80, Mcpl. Art Gallery, L.A., 1981, L.A. City Hall, 1982, Phyllis Kind Gallery, Chgo., 1983, Karl Bornstein Gallery, Santa Monica, Calif., 1983, 85, 87, Pepperdine U., Malibu, Calif., 1985, A.I.R. Gallery, N.Y.C., 1986, Chapman Coll., Orange, Calif., 1986, Mount St. Mary's Coll., Los Angeles, 1987, Atlanta Pavilion, 1990, Calif. Mus. of Sci. and Industry, L.A., 1991, Laguna Art Mus. Satellite Gallery, Costa Mesa, Calif., 1991, Turner-Krull Gallery, L.A., 1992, Lawrence Miller Gallery, N.Y.C., 1992, Santa Monica Mus. of Art (15 yr. survey), L.A., 1993, Nat. Mus. Fine Arts, Santiago, Chile, 1996, Mus. Modern Art, Rio de Janeiro, 1996, Complejo Cultural Recoleta, Buenos Aires, 1996, Centro Cutural Consolidado, Caracus, 1997, Cepa Gallery, Buffalo, 1998, Art, Inc., N.Y.C., 1999. Honored for outstanding student research and creative achievement, U. Calif.-Irvine, 1979; recipient U.S. Steel award Exhibition of the Associated Artists of Pitts., 1977, Clean Air award Air Quality Mgmt. Dist., Calif., 1992; Hand Hollow Found. fellow, 1984, Design Team fellow Panorama City Libr., Calif., 1992-93, J. Paul Getty Trust Fund for the Visual Arts fellow, 1994; Pollock-Krasner Found. grant, 1990, Calif. Arts Coun. grant, 1990, L.A. Cultural Affairs grant, 1991, 95, 96, U.S. Info. Agy. grant, 1995-97; commissioned by Panorama City Pub. Libr., L.A., 1993, Met. Transportation Authority, L.A., 1995.

ABELS, ROBERT FREDERICK, tax consultant; b. West Palm Beach, Fla., Nov. 18, 1926; s. John Frederick and Nelly (Bulfin) A.; m. Shirley Mae Larsen, May 31, 1953; children: Robert Frederick, Steven John, Richard Alan. Student, U. S.C., 1946-47; ed. flight tng. program, Naval Air Sta., Pensacola, Fla., 1947-49; BS, Naval Postgrad. Sch., Monterey, Calif., 1965; MBA in Fin., U. West Fla., 1971. Enlisted USN, 1944, commd. ensign, 1949, advanced through grades to comdr., 1963, radar operator PT boats, 1945-46, radar and radio operator PT Boats World War II; aviator USN, Republic of Korea, 1950-51, 53, Pensacola, Fla., Vietnam, 1962-63, 65-66; ret. USN, 1969; tchr. math. and bus. Skyline H.S., Lemon Grove, Calif., 1971-83, 1983; past ptnr., salesman area real estate co.; enrolled agent IRS, Washington, 1984. Decorated Bronze Star, Air medal, Vietnamese Cross Gallantry. Mem. Nat. Assn. Enrolled Agts., Inland Soc. Tax. Cons., Nat. Assn. Tax Consultors. Republican. Lutheran.

ABERCROMBIE, NEIL, congressman; s. G. Don and Vera June (Giersdorf) A.; m. Nancie Ellen Caraway, July 18, 1981; BA Union Coll., 1959, MA U. Hawaii, 1964, PhD in Am. Studies, 1974; Mem. Hawaii state legislature, 1974-86; elected to U.S. Congress, 1986, 91—, mem. Resources subcom. on Energy & Mineral Resources; mem. Nat. Security Com., Honolulu City Coun., 1988-90. Democrat. Address: US Ho of Reps 1233 Longworth Bldg Washington DC 20515-1101*

ABERLE, DAVID FRIEND, anthropologist, educator; b. St. Paul, Nov. 23, 1918; s. David Winfield and Lisette (Friend) A.; m. Eleanor Kathleen Gough, Sept. 5, 1955 (dec. Sept. 1990); 1 son. A.B. summa cum laude, Harvard U., 1940; Ph.D. in Anthropology, Columbia U., 1950; postgrad., U. N.Mex., summers 1938-40, No. Ariz. U., summers 1971, 73, Harvard U., 1946-47. Instr. dept. social rels. Harvard U., Cambridge, Mass., 1947-50, rsch. assoc. Sch. Pub. Health, 1948-50; vis. assoc. prof. Page Sch., Johns Hopkins U., Balt., 1950-52; assoc. prof., then prof. dept. sociology and dept. anthropology U. Mich., Ann Arbor, 1952-60; fellow Ctr. Advanced Study in Behavioral Scis., Stanford, Calif., 1955-56; Simon vis. prof. and hon. research assoc. dept. social anthropology Manchester U., Eng., 1960-61; prof., chmn. dept. anthropology Brandeis U., Waltham, Mass., 1961-63; prof. dept. anthropology U. Oreg., Eugene, 1963-67; prof. dept. anthropology and sociology U. B.C., Vancouver, Can., 1967-83, prof. emeritus, 1983—; cons. Inst. Devel. Anthropology, Inc., Binghamton, N.Y., 1978-79; cons. to attys. Navajo Tribe, 1976-77; disting. lectr. at ann. meeting Am. Anthrop. Assn., 1986. Author: The Peyote Religion Among the Navaho, 1966, (with Isidore Dyen) Lexical Reconstruction, the Case of the Proto-Athapaskan Kinship System, 1974; contbr. articles on anthropological theory and Navajo Indians to scholarly jours.; rev. editor: Am. Anthropologist, 1952-55. Served with U.S. Army, 1942-46. Recipient Social Sci. Research Council Demobilization award, 1946; Harvard U. Nat. scholar; NIMH grantee; USPHS grantee; Wenner-Gren Found. grantee, 1954-63; NSF grantee, 1965-72; Can. Council grantee, 1969-77; Social Scis. and Humanities Research Council Can., 1978-80, 84-86. Fellow Royal Soc. Can., Royal Anthropol. Inst. of Gt. Britain and Ireland; mem. Am. Anthropol. Assn. (mem. panel on Navajo-Hopi land dispute 1973-95), Am. Sociol. Assn., Soc. Applied Anthropology, Am. Ethnol. Assn., Can. Anthropology Soc., Soc. Lesbian and Gay Anthropologists, Phi Beta Kappa. Jewish. Office: U BC Dept Anthropology, 6303 NW Marine Dr, Vancouver, BC Canada V6T 2B2

ABERNATHY, CHARLES C., museum official. Pres. C.M. Russell Mus., Gt. Falls, Mont. Office: CM Russell Mus 400 13th St N Great Falls MT 59401-1498*

ABERNATHY, SHIELDS B., allergist, immunologist, internist; b. Bronxville, N.Y., Mar. 14, 1951; m. Leslie Abernathy; children: Amelia, Camille, Lant. BA, Ohio Wesleyan U., 1973; MS, Harvard U., 1975; MD, Med. Coll. Pa., 1979. Diplomate Am. Bd. Internal Medicine, Am. Bd. Allergy and Immunology, eligible Am. Preventive Medicine, Nat. Bd. Med. Examiners; Qualified Med. Examiner Calif.; Fed. Aviation Med. Examiner; ACLS Am. Heart Assn. Intern in internal medicine L.A. County/U. So. Calif. Med. Ctr., L.A., 1979-80; resident in internal medicine Hosp. of Good Samaritan, L.A., 1980-81; resident UCLA Wadsworth VA Med. Ctr., 1981-82, fellow allergy and immunology, 1982-84; instr. pub. edn. programs; rschr. in field. Fellow Am. Coll. Allergy and Immunology, Am. Acad. Allergy and Immunology; mem. Am. Med. Health Assn., Am. Pub. Health Assn. (internat. health sect.). Office: 1050 Las Tablas Rd Ste 3 Templeton CA 93465-9792

ABERNATHY, VICKI MARIE, nurse; b. L.A., Feb. 14, 1949; d. James David and Margaret Helen (Quider) Abernathy; m. Dirk Klaus Ernst Wiese, Aug. 15, 1968 (div. 1973); 1 child, Zoe Erde. Student, U. Calif., Riverside, 1966-67, L.A. City Coll., 1968-69; AA in Nursing, Riverside City Coll., 1971-74. RN, Calif.; cert. med.-surg. nurse; cert. ACLS. Staff nurse Riverside (Calif.) County Hosp., 1974, Oceanside (Calif.) Community Hosp., 1974-76; with Scripps Hosp., Encinitas, Calif., 1976—, ambulatory surgery unit and endoscopy coord., 1981-94, staff nurse short stay unit, 1994—. Mem. ACLU, Calif. Nurses Assn., San Diego Zoöl. Soc., San Elijo Lagoon Conservancy. Democrat. Avocations: camping, fishing, travel, reading.

ABERNETHY, ROBERT JOHN, real estate developer; b. Indpls., Feb. 28, 1940; s. George Lawrence and Helen Sarah (McLandress) A. BA, Johns Hopkins U., 1962; MBA, Harvard U., 1968; cert. in real estate fin. and constrn., UCLA, 1974. Asst. to chief scientist Phoenix missile program Hughes Aircraft Co., L.A., 1968-69, asst. program mgr. Iroquois night fighter and night tracker program, 1969-71, asst. to contr. space and comm. group, 1971-72, contr. tech. divsn., 1972-74; pres. Am. Std. Devel. Co., L.A., 1974—, Transit Cmty. Devel. Corp., 1997—; bd. dirs., chmn. audit com. Pub. Storage, Inc., Glendale, Calif., Marathon Nat. Bank, L.A., L.A. Bancorp, Met. Water Dist., So. Calif., Met. Transp. Authority, L.A. County; pres. Self Svc. Storage Assn., San Francisco, 1978-83. Asst. to dep. campaign mgr. Humphrey for Pres., Washington, 1968; commr. L.A. Planning Commn., 1984-88, L.A. Telecom. Commn., 1992-93; vice chmn. L.A. Econ. Devel. Coun., 1988-93; chmn. Ctr. for Study Dem. Inst., Santa Barbara, Calif., 1986—; bd. dirs. Met. Transp. Authority Los Angeles County, South Bay Civic Light Opera, World Children's Transplant Fund, French Found. for Alzheimers Rsch., Pacific Coun. on Internat. Policy; adv. bd. mem. Peabody Conservatory, 1992—, Ctr. Talented Youth, 1992—, Nitse Sch. Advanced Internat. Studies, 1993—, Harvard Ptnrs., 1996—, Inst. Acad. Achievement of Youth, 1999—; bd. vis. Davidson Coll.; bd. dirs. L.A. Theatre Ctr., 1986-92, YMCA; trustee Johns Hopkins U., 1991—; mem. Coun. on Fgn. Rels., L.A. Com. on Fgn. Rels. Lt. USNR, 1962-66. Mem. So. Calif. Planning Congress (bd. dirs.), Parker Found. (bd. dirs.), Californian Club, St. Francis Yacht Club, Jonathan Club, Calif. Yacht Club, Alpha Lambda. Home: 5800 W Century Blvd Los Angeles CA 90009-5600 Office: PO Box 90855 Los Angeles CA 90009-0855

ABRAHAMS, SIDNEY CYRIL, physicist, crystallographer; b. London, May 28, 1924; arrived in U.S., 1948; s. Aaron Harry and Freda (Cohen) A.; m. Rhoda Banks, May 1, 1950; children: David Mark, Peter Brian, Jennifer Anne. BSc, U. Glasgow, Scotland, 1946; PhD, U. Glasgow, 1949, DSc, 1957; Fil. Dr. (hon.), U. Uppsala, Sweden, 1981; D Honoris Causa, U. Bordeaux, 1997. Rsch. fellow U. Minn., Mpls., 1949-50; mem. staff MIT, Cambridge, 1950-54; rsch. fellow U. Glasgow, 1954-57; mem. tech. staff Bell Labs., Murray Hill, N.J., 1957-82; disting. mem. tech. staff AT&T Bell Labs., Murray Hill, 1982-88; Humboldt sr. scientist Inst. Crystallography, U. Tübingen, Fed. Republic Germany, 1989-90; guest scientist Brookhaven Nat. Lab., Upton, N.Y., 1957—; vis. prof. U. Bordeaux, France, 1979, 90; Humboldt sr. scientist U. Tübingen, Germany, 1995; adj. prof. physics So. Oreg. U., 1990—. Mem. editorial bd., Rev. Sci. Instruments, 1963-65; co-editor, Anomalous Scattering, 1975; editor, World Directory of Crystallographers, 1977; editor-in-chief Acta Crystallographica, 1978-87; book rev. editor, Ferroelectrics, 1975—. Recipient Sr. U.S. Scientist award, Alexander von Humboldt Found., 1989-90. Fellow AAAS, Am. Phys. Soc.; mem. Am. Crystallographic Assn. (pres. 1968, mng. editor 1965-90), Royal Soc. Chemistry, Am. Inst. Physics (chmn. pub. policy com. 1981-91), Internat. Union Crystallography (chmn. commn. on crystallographic apparatus 1972-75, commn. on jours. 1978-87, commn. on crystallographic nomenclature 1978—), Internat. Union Pure and Applied Chemistry (rep. interdivsnl. com. on nomenclature and symbols 1984—), Sigma Xi (founding pres. So. Oreg. State Coll. 1993-95). Avocations: photography, hiking. Home: 89 Mallard St Ashland OR 97520-7316 Office: So Oreg State Coll Physics Dept Ashland OR 97520

ABRAMOVITZ, MOSES, economist, educator; b. Bklyn., Jan. 1, 1912; s. Nathan and Betty (Goldenberg) A.; m. Carrie Glasser, June 23, 1937; 1 son, Joel Nathan. A.B., Harvard U., 1932; Ph.D., Columbia U., 1939; Ph.D. (hon.), Uppsala U., Sweden, 1985, U. Ancona, Italy, 1992. Instr. Harvard U., 1936-38; mem. research staff Nat. Bur. Econ. Research, 1938-69; lectr. Columbia U., 1940-42, 46-48; prof. econs. Stanford U., 1948—, Coe prof. Am. econ. history, exec. head dept. econs., 1963-65, 71-74; vis. prof. U. Pa., 1955; prin. economist WPB, 1942, OSS, 1943-44; econ. adviser to U.S. rep. on Allied Commn. on Reparations, 1945-46; econ. adviser to sec.-gen. Orgn. for Econ. Coop. and Devel., 1962-63; vis. fellow All Souls Coll., Oxford, Eng., 1968. Author: Price Theory for a Changing Economy, 1939, Inventories and Business Cycles, 1950, The Growth of Public Employment in Great Britain, 1957, (with Vera Eliasberg) Thinking About Growth, 1989; also articles.; editor: Capital Formation and Economic Growth, 1955; mng. editor Jour. Econ. Lit., 1981-85. Served as lt. AUS, 1944-45. Recipient Nitti prize Accademia Nazionale Dei Lincei, Rome, 1990. Fellow Am. Acad. Arts and Scis., Am. Econ. Assn. (disting., pres. 1980), Am. Statis. Assn.; mem. Am. Econ. History Assn. (pres. 1991-92), Western Econ. Assn. (pres. 1988), Accademia Nazionale dei Lincei (fgn.), Phi Beta Kappa. Home: 762 Dolores St Stanford CA 94305-8428 Office: Stanford U Dept Econs Stanford CA 94305-6072

ABRAMS, OSSIE EKMAN, fundraiser; b. Olofström, Blekinge, Sweden, Jan. 8, 1952; came to the U.S., 1972; d. Ossian B. and Margit A. (Adolfsson) Ekman; m. Howard L. Abrams, Nov. 17, 1973 (div. Sept. 1983); m. David B. Orser, Aug. 1992. Student, Lärarhögskolan, 1972, New Sch. for Social Rsch., 1975; BA (hon.), Rocky Mountain Coll., 1994. Dental asst., sec. Samuel Meyer DDS, N.Y.C., 1973-74; office mgr., adminstr. Irving Peress DDS, N.Y.C., 1974-81; chief adminstr. Allen Kozin DDS, N.Y.C., 1981-87; head devel. Rocky Mountain Coll., Billings, Mont., 1991-92; owner, operator Davoss Ranch, Park City, Mont.; bd. mem. Mental Health Found., Billings, 1991, 92, bd. pres., 1993, 94. Active in Met. Opera Guild, N.Y.C., N.Y.C. Ballet Guild, N.Y. Philharm. Soc.; supporter Alberta Bair Theater, Billings Symphony, Billings Studio Theater; mem. selection com. Orser Chair, Coll. Bus., Mont. State U., Bozeman, 1988-99; fundraiser ann. campaign Yellowstone Art Ctr., Billings, 1989; fundraiser bus. drive Rocky Mountain Coll., Billings, 1990, vol. Rocky Mountain Coll. Black Tie Blue Jeans Ball, mem. auction com. 1990-93, chair auction com. 1994, 95, chair ball, 1996, chair sponsor com., 1997; mem. nat. adv. coun. Rocky Mountain Coll., 1993-98; mem. sponsor com. Salute to Women, YMCA, 1997; mem. subscription dr. Billings Symphony, 1996, 97. Recipient Alumni Hall of Fame award Rocky Mountain Coll., 1993, Leadership award Mental Health Found., Billings, 1994. Home: 1420 Granite Ave Billings MT 59102-0716 Office: Davoss Ranch 804 Valley Creek Rd Park City MT 59063

ABRAMSON, ALBERT, television historian, consultant; b. Chgo., June 9, 1922; s. Joseph David and Minnie Lillian Abramson; m. Arlene Betty Corin, Jan. 8, 1950; children: Jay Allen, Susan Marie. BA, U. So. Calif., 1950. Tchr. L.A. City Schs., 1950-52; TV engr. CBS-TV, Hollywood, Calif., 1952-87; hist. cons. RCA, Princeton, N.J., Ampex Mus., Redwood City, Calif., UCLA/ATAS TV Archives, L.A. Author: Electronic Motion Pictures, 1955, The History of Television, 1880-1941, 1987, Zworykin: Pioneer of Television, 1995—; contbr. articles to profl. jours. With U.S. Army Air Forces. Recipient J.T. Taylor award for preserving history of television, Antique Wireless Assn., 1996. Mem. IEEE, Royal TV Soc. London, Brit. Kinematagraph, Sound and TV Soc., LeComité d'histoire de la Télevision, Acad. TV Arts and Scis., Soc. Motion Picture and TV Engrs. Democrat. Jewish. Developed 2 patents, one for three-dimensional television without glasses and another for a super high brightness television projector that will project television pictures on a 40 foot screen with motion picture brightness. Home: 2224 Beacon Ridge Dr Las Vegas NV 89134-5319

ABRAMSON, TREVA THOMASSON, teacher; b. Midland, Tex., Nov. 26, 1931; d. Wilford Winn and MayLarue (Harp) Thomasson; m. Walter Leroy Hulen, June 16, 1950 (div. Nov. 1960); children: Sandra Lee Kaufmann, Julie Kathleen Wheeler; m. Bernard G. Abramson, Aug. 10, 1963 (div. Aug. 1978); 1 child, David M. BS, U. Tex. (name formerly Tex. Western Coll.), El Paso, 1962; MA, Ariz. State U., 1969. Tchr. El Paso Pub. Schs., 1962-63, Scottsdale (Ariz.) Pub. Schs., 1966-92. Grade level cons. (textbook): Arizona, 1990. Bd. dirs. 1st Ch. Christ Scientist, Scottsdale, 1986-88; tchr. Adventure Unltd. Ranches, Buena Vista, Colo., 1980, 84, 85, 87. Mem. Ariz. Assn. Tchrs. Math., Ariz. Reading Tchrs., Ariz. Assn. for Learning about Environ. (com. chmn. 1990-91, 92-93, sec. 1991-92), Scottsdale Edn. Assn. (sec. 1985-87, treas. 1987-88), Ariz. Sci. Tchrs. Assn., Principia Club (Phoenix chpt., treas. 1976-87, pres. 1974-75), Phi Delta Kappa (com. chmn. 1989-91), Delta Kappa Gamma (sec. 1992-93). Republican. Avocations: landscape painting, gardening, hiking, camping. Home: 8555 E Rose Ln Scottsdale AZ 85250-5837

ABRUMS, JOHN DENISE, internist; b. Trinidad, Colo., Sept. 20, 1923; s. Horatio Ely and Clara (Apfel) A.; m. Annie Louise Manning, June 15, 1947; children: Louanne C. Abrums Sargent, John Ely. BA, U. Colo., 1944; MD, U. Colo., Denver, 1947. Diplomate Am. Bd. Internal Medicine. Intern Wisc. Gen. Hosp., Madison, 1947-48; resident in internal medicine VA Hosp., Albuquerque, 1949-52, attending physician, 1956-80; mem. staff Presbyn. Hosp. Ctr., Albuquerque; cons. staff physician St. Joseph Hosp., Albuquerque, 1957-85; attending physician U. N.Mex. Hosp., Albuquerque, 1954-95; med. dir. Turquoise Lodge, Albuquerque; cons. physician A.T. & S.F. Meml. Hosp., Albuquerque, 1957-83; clin. assoc. in medicine U. N.Mex.; mem. N.Mex. Bd. of Med. Examiners. Bd. dirs. Blue Cross/Blue Shield, 1962-76. Brig. gen. M.C., U.S. Army, ret., N.Mex. Nat. Guard. Fellow ACP (life), AMA, Am. Soc. Internal Medicine (trustee 1976-82, pres. 1983-84), N.Mex. Soc. Internal Medicine (pres. 1962-64), N.Mex. Med. Soc. (pres. 1980-81), Nat. Acads. Practice (disting. practitioner), Albuquerque and Bernalillo County Med. Assn. (bd. govs. 1959-61, chmn. pub. rels. com. 1959-61), Am. Geriatric Soc., 1992—. Brig. gen. M.C., U.S. Army, ret. Republican. Episcopalian. Office: Turquoise Lodge N Mex Dept Health 6000 Isleta Blvd SW Albuquerque NM 87105-6632

ABUGOV, JEFF, scriptwriter; b. Montreal, Que., Can., Dec. 31, 1959; came to U.S., 1986; s. Ben and Ida (Einbinder) A. Diploma, Dawson Coll., 1979; BFA, Concordia U., 1982. Dir., prodr. Transition Films, Montreal, 1983-84; writer Check It Out! Taffner and Assocs., Toronto, Ont., Can., 1985; story editor, writer Cheers Charles-Burrows-Charles/Paramount, L.A., 1986-87; exec. script cons., writer My Two Dads/Tri Star TV, L.A., 1987; exec. story editor, writer The Golden Girls/Witt-Thomas-Harris Prodns., L.A., 1988; sr. prodr./writer Roseanne/Carsey-Werner Prodns., 1990-91, supervising prodr., writer, 1991-92; exec. prodr. Roc-Live/HBO Prodns., 1992-93, Grace Under Fire/Carsey-Werner Prodns., 1994-95; cons. prodr. Caroline in the City/CBS Prodns., 1996, The Tony Danza Show, 1998-99; writer/dir. The Mating Habits of the Earthbound Human, 1996-98. Writer, dir., producer: (films) Harry's Story, 1981 (Best Fiction Film Can. Student Film Festival 1981), The Death Shop, 1982. Mem. Writers Guild Am. West, Assn. Can. TV and Radio Artists.

ABUL-HAJ, ELIZABETH, fine arts and antique appraiser; b. Erie, Pa., Jan. 15, 1924; d. George Elias and Sarah (Muffett) Abood; m. Suleiman K. Abul-Haj, Feb. 11, 1948; children: Charles, Alan, Cary. Student, John Huntington Polytech., Cleve., 1942-45, Cleve. Art Sch., 1945-46, San Francisco Art Inst., 1946-48. Office supr. pub. works dept. Naval Supply Ctr., Oakland, Calif., 1951-52; tech., sec. Bur. of Mines/U. Calif., Berkeley, 1952-53; med. office supr. Cancer Divsn. U. Calif., San Francisco, 1953; office mgr. Henry and Charles Mock, M.D., Chgo., 1955-56; v.p., sec. Path. Svc. Med. Group, Ventura, Calif., 1971-83; v.p. Clin. Path. Svc. Group, Ventura, Calif., 1971-83; owner, appraiser Appraising, Elizabeth Abul-Haj, Ventura, Calif., 1968—. Author: Charles Andre Boulle for ASA, 1970s. Bd. dirs. Am. Cancer Soc., Ventura, 1967-72; bd. dirs., sec. Forum of Arts, Ventura, 1968-70, YWCA, Ventura; bd. dirs., pres. Vis. Nurses Assn., 1970-83, Ventura Med. Soc. Aux., 1978-80; pres., mem. Ventura Med. Soc., 1979-80; mem. Assistance League, Ventura Heart Assn., Children's Home Soc. Recipient Disting. Svc. award Am. Cancer Soc., Ventura. Mem. Am. Soc. Appraisers (bd. dirs. 1971-89, pres. 1971-89, sr. mem. Ventura Santa Barbara br.), World's Affair Coun., Channel Island Club. Republican. Avocations: collecting antiques, books, reading, swimming, tennis. Home: 105 Encinal Way Ventura CA 93001-3317

ABUL-HAJ, SULEIMAN KAHIL, pathologist; b. Palestine, Apr. 20, 1925; came to U.S., 1946, naturalized, 1955; s. Sheik Khalil and S. Buteina (Oda) Abul-H.; m. Elizabeth Abood, Feb. 11, 1948; children: Charles, Alan, Cary. *The roots of the Abul-Haj family date back to the 7th century, A.D. Arab armies invaded North Africa and intermarried with local inhabitants, the Berbers. The Berbers were Barbarian Germanic hords who invaded Rome and then moved into and settled in North Africa. Tarique Bin Ziyad, born to Berber mother and an Arab father, was the founding ancestor. Tarique commanded the Arab armies that conquered Spain in 711 A.D. Jabal Tarique, anglicized to Gibralter, was named after him, which means the Mount of Tarique. The name Abul-Haj, father of the pilgrims, was dubbed in the 12th century following the treaty between Saladdin and the Crusaders.* BS, U. Calif. at Berkeley, 1949; M.S. at San Francisco, U. Calif., 1951, MD, 1955. Intern Cook County Hosp., Chgo., 1955-56; resident U. Calif. Hosp., San Francisco, 1949, Brooke Gen Hosp., 1957-59; chief clin. and anatomic pathology Walter Reed Army Hosp., Washington, 1959-62; assoc. prof. U. So. Calif. Sch. Medicine, Los Angeles, 1963-69; sr. surg. pathologist L.A. County Gen. Hosp., 1963; dir. dept. pathology Cmty. Meml. Hosp., Ventura, Calif., 1964-80, Gen. Hosp. Ventura County, 1966-74; dir. Pathology Service Med. Group, 1970—; cons. Calif. Tumor tissue Registry, 1962-96, Camarillo State Hosp., 1964-70, Tripler Gen. Hosp., Hawaii, 1963-67, Armed Forces Inst. Pathology, 1960-69. Contbr. articles to profl. jours. Bd. dirs. Tri-Counties Blood Bank, Am. Cancer Soc. Served to maj., M.C., U.S. Army, 1956-62. Recipient Borden award Calif. Honor Soc., 1949; Achievement cert. Surgeon Gen. Army, 1962. Fellow Am. Soc. Clin. Pathologists, Coll. Am. Pathologist; mem. Internat. Coll. Surgeons, World Affairs Coun. Achievements include research in cardiovascular disease, endocrine, renal, skin diseases, also cancer. Home and Office: 105 Encinal Way Ventura CA 93001-3317

ABU-MOSTAFA, AYMAN SAID, computer consultant; b. Giza, Egypt, June 1, 1953; came to U.S., 1978; s. Said S. Abu-Mostafa and Faiza A. Ibrahim. BME, Cairo U., 1976; MS in Mech. and Aerospace Engring., Okla. State U., 1980, PhD, 1984. Tchg. asst. Cairo U., Giza, Egypt, 1978; tchg. asst. Okla. State U., Stillwater, 1978-79, rsch. assoc., 1979-81; software engr. SEAM Internat. Corp., Palos Verdes, Calif., 1984-87; computing and networking cons. Calif. State U., Los Alamitos, 1987-92; sr. sys. analyst Allied Signal Aerospace, Torrance, Calif., 1992-93; pres., CEO NeuroDollars, Inc., Huntington Beach, Calif., 1993-97; sr. program analyst Softnet Systems, Irvine, Calif., 1997—. Author papers, articles in field. Undergrad. fellow Ministry of Higher Edn., Cairo, 1971, 72, 76; NASA/Ames grantee, 1979-81. Mem. AIAA, IEEE, Assn. for Computing Machinery. Avocations: reading, computers, languages, music. Office: Softnet Systems 18662 Macarthur Blvd Ste 300 Irvine CA 92612-1215

ACCOMANDO, RAYMOND ANDREW, gambling commission executive, consultant; b. Highland Park, Ill., Dec. 28, 1949; s. Anthony Joseph and Violet Norberta (Neufeldt) A.; m. Delinda Mae Nickels, Mar. 4, 1980 (div. Sept. 1984); 1 child, Alicia Louise; m. Tammy Dee Aaron, Feb. 28, 1998. Security mgr. Tahoe-Crystal Bay (Nev.) Inc., 1979-81; br., ops. mgr. CPP/Pinkertons Inc., Albuquerque, San Antonio, 1982-88; acct. mgr. advanced micro devices Advanced Security - Pinkertons Inc., Austin, Tex., 1988-92; sr. insp. Tulalip Tribes Wash., Marysville, 1993-95; exec. dir. Chehalis Tribal Gaming Commn. Conf. Tribes Che Indian Reservation, Oakville, Wash., 1995—; cons. tribal gambling, software, Aberdeen, Wash., 1992—; software developer Design Data Software, Aberdeen, 1988—. Author: (software) Background Investigation Info. Sys., 1996, Roulette Awareness, 1997; contbr. articles to profl. jours. Ssgt. USAF, 1970-76. Office: Chehalis Tribal Gaming Commn PO Box 536 Oakville WA 98568-0536

ACHEN, MARK KENNEDY, city manager; b. Vancouver, Wash., Apr. 13, 1943; s. George Ben and Marjorie Beth (Pierson) A.; m. Mary Ann Uzzell, Aug. 14, 1971; children: Wyndi Marie, Kara Lynn. BA, U. Wash., 1967; MA, U. Mo., 1981. Asst. to city mgr. City of Ferguson, Mo., 1972-74; city adminstr. City of Mounds View, Minn., 1974-79; city mgr. City of Gladstone, Mo., 1979-84, City of Grand Junction, Colo., 1984—; cons. U.S. Nat. Fire Acad., Emmitsburg, Md., 1990-91, adj. faculty, 1991-92, mem. Supreme Ct. Diisplinary Hearing Bd., 1999—. Gates Found. fellow Harvard U. Sr. Govt. Exec. Program, 1987. Mem. ASPA (Kansas City chpt. Adminstr. of Yr. 1983), Colo. City Mgmt. Assn. (pres. 1988-89, bd. dirs. 1985-91), Internat. City Mgmt. Assn. (chmn. 1988, internat. conf. planning com., co-chmn. 1995, internat. conf. host com.), Rotary (pres. 1983-84, bd. dirs. 1989-90, 92-93, Paul Harris fellow 1991). Avocations: mountain climbing, tennis, backpacking, golf. Home: 3344 Northridge Dr Grand Junction CO 81506-1926 Office: City Grand Junction 250 N 5th St Grand Junction CO 81501-2668

ACHTEL, ROBERT ANDREW, pediatric cardiologist; b. Bklyn., May 5, 1941; s. Murray and Amelia (Ellian) A.; m. Erica Noel Woods, Mar. 10, 1963; children: Bergen Alison, Roland Hugh. BA, Adelphi U., 1963; MD, U. Cin., 1967. Diplomate Am. Bd. Pediatric Cardiology. Intern, Cin. Children's Hosp., 1967-68; resident in pediatrics Yale U., 1968-69, fellow in pediatric cardiology, 1969-71; clin. instr. pediatrics U. Calif.-Davis, 1972-73, clin. asst. prof., 1977-83; asst. prof. pediatrics, U. Ky., 1973-76; dir. pediatric ICU, Sutter Meml. Hosp., Sacramento, 1977-85, dir. pediatric Cardiology, 1982—, chmn. instl. rev. com., 1981-85, 96—; chmn. dept. pediatrics Mercy Hosp., Sacramento, 1981-83, 97—, vice chmn. pediatrics, 1983-85, 95—; dir. pediatric ICU, 1982-83; dir. Laurel Hills Devel. Ctr., 1985-89.; chmn. rsch com. Sutter Inst. for Med. Rsch., 1989—; trustee, mem. exec. com. Sutler Hosps. Found., vice chmn., 1992-93, CEO Access Care, 1994-95, med. dir. FastServe Med. Group, 1995; vice chmn. dept. pediatrics Mercy Hosp., 1995-97, chmn., 1997—. mem. tech. adv. com. pediat. cardiology State of Calif.; CEO AccessCare, 1993-97; chmn. regional instnl. rev. bd. Sutter/CHS Ctrl., 1996, QA com. Omni Heatlh Plan, Pharmacy com.; lectr. Mooney Aircraft Pilots Assn., FAA; bd. dir. Mooney Aircraft Pilots Assn. Safety Found.; mem. FAA Safety Coun. 1997—. Contbr. articles in cardiovascular rsch. Bd. dirs. Sutter Meml. Hosp. Found., 1986—; bd. dirs. Sutter Found., 1989, trustee, 1989—. Maj. M.C., USAF, 1971-73. Recipient grants from Heart Assn., U. Ky. Tobacco and Health Rsch. Found. Mem. Am. Heart Assn. (dir. Sacramento chpt., mem. councils congenital heart disease and atherosclerosis and cardiovascular surgery), Am. Coll. Chest Physicians, Am. Acad Pediatrics, S.W. Pediatric Cardiology Soc., So. Soc. Pediatric Rsch. Office: Perinatal and Pediatric Subspecialist Med Group 5609 J St Ste A Sacramento CA 95819-3948

ACHTERMAN, GAIL LOUISE, lawyer; b. Portland, Oreg., Aug. 1, 1949. AB in Econs. with distinction, Stanford U., 1971; MS in Natural Resource Policy and Mgmt., U. Mich., 1975, JD cum laude, 1974. Bar: Oreg. 1974, U.S. Dist. Ct. Oreg. 1978, U.S. Supreme Ct. 1978, U.S. Ct. Appeals (fed. and 10th cirs.). Atty.-advisor U.S. Dept. Interior, 1975-78; asst. for natural resources Gov. Neil Goldschmidt, 1987-91; mem. Stoel Rives LLP, Portland; adj. prof. Lewis & Clark Law Sch., 1978-83; adj. prof. forest policy, Coll. Forestry, Oreg. State U., 1991-98; adj. prof. pub. adminstrn. Portland State U., 1998—. Mem. Oreg. Water Resources Commn., 1981-85; chair Strategic Water Mgmt. Group, 1987-91, Gov.'s Growth Task Force, 1998. Mem. bd. dirs. Sustainable Ecosystems Inst., Am. Leadership Forum, Oreg. Women's Forum, Portland C. of C. (bd. dirs. 1996—). Office: Stoel Rives LLP 900 SW 5th Ave Ste 2300 Portland OR 97204-1232

ACKER, GEORGE, artist; b. Cleve., Dec. 1, 1934; s. George Brooks Acker and Georgia Mae (Morris) Acker-White; m. Esther Miller, Nov. 30, 1960 (div. Sept. 1975); children: Anita L., G. David; m. Maria Dolores Romo, Sept. 4, 1982; children: Cyndia, Linda. BA, U. San Francisco, 1987. Artist, 1986—; art tchr. Lawndale (Calif.) Sch. Dist., 1994—. Human rights advocate. Avocations: reading, walking, cooking, observing, listening. Home and Office: 3912 W 148th St Hawthorne CA 90250-8304

ACKER, LOREN CALVIN, medical instrument company executive; b. Lamar, Colo., Mar. 3, 1934; s. John C. and Ada M. (Ecton) A.; m. Judy N. Willms, Sept. 17, 1955 (dec. Oct. 1968); children: Cheryl Acker Hoge, Keith B., Karen Acker Kime; m. Darla C. Copeland, July 24, 1976. BS in Mech. Engring., Fresno State Coll., 1956; Bus. and Mgmt. cert., U. Calif., Berkeley, 1961; MBA, U. Santa Clara, 1966. Flight test technician NASA, Edwards, Calif., 1954-56; engring. mgr. Westinghouse, Sunnyvale, Calif., 1956-69; assoc. dir. Kitt Peak Nat. Obs., Tucson, Ariz., 1969-73; chmn., CEO founder SEBRA-Engr. & Rsch. Assocs., Inc. (SEBRA), Tucson, 1973—; gen. ptnr. Winged Foot Assocs., Tucson, 1974—; dir., founder NYPA Inc., Tucson, 1988—. Patentee in field. Chmn. park and recreation City of Cupertino, Calif., 1968, dir. So. Ariz. Leadership Coun., 1997—. Mem. Am. Assn. Blood Banks, Am. Soc. Apherises, Internat. Soc. for Hematotherapy and Graft Engring. Republican. Avocations: skiing, tennis. Home: 4831 E Winged Foot Pl Tucson AZ 85718-1727 Office: 100 N Tucson Blvd Tucson AZ 85716-4412

ACKERLEY, BARRY, professional basketball team executive, communications company executive. Student, U. Iowa, 1956. Exec. v.p. Advan, Inc.; owner Golden West Outdoor Advt., 1968-75; chmn., CEO Ackerley Comm., Inc., 1975—; owner, chmn. bd. dirs. Seattle SuperSonics, 1984—. Office: Seattle SuperSonics 190 Queen Anne Ave N Ste 200 Seattle WA 98109-9711 also: Ackerley Group 1301 5th Ave Ste 4000 Seattle WA 98101-2603*

ACKERMAN, ARLENE ALICE, accountant, business consultant, artist, writer; b. Omaha, Mar. 24, 1936; d. Walter Nelson and Mildred Eleanor (Krimlofski) A. BA in Social Sci. and Econs., San Francisco State U., 1962; MA in Polit. Sci., Purdue U., 1967; grad., U.S. Dept. Def. Info. Sch., 1973, U.S. Army Command-Gen. Staff Coll., 1977. CPA, Ind. Acct., adminstr. Peeples & MacDonald, CPAs, Sacramento, 1961-66; acct. chief acct.'s office Purdue U., West Lafayette, Ind., 1966-67; adj. gen. and info. officer, editor newspaper 123d Army Res. Command, Ind., 1972-75; mng. ptnr. Piano Showcase, Indpls., 1975-83; adminstr. Bennett Thrasher & Co. CPAs, Atlanta, 1983-86, Melvin Belli Law Offices, San Francisco, 1990; bus. cons. Ackerman & Assocs., Indpls., 1986-90; acctg. mgr., acting CFO Lera Dynalectric, San Francisco, 1991-94; CFO Nat. Home Bus. Assn., St. Helena, Calif., 1994-96; prin. Ackerman & Assocs., Fairfax, Calif. Editor Mus. Indian Heritage Newsletter, Indpls., 1971-77; exhibited in group shows at Marin Agrl. Land Trust, San Rafael, Calif., 1993, Marin County Fair & Exposition, San Rafael, 1993, 96, Marin Soc. Artists, Ross, Calif., 1993, 94, Monterey Peninsula Mus. Art Christmas Miniature Show, 1993, Artisans Gallery, Mill Valley, Calif., 1993-95, Sonoma-Marin Fair, Petaluma, Calif., 1993-94, San Mateo (Calif.) County Fair, 1992-94, Sonoma County Fair, Santa Rosa, Calif., 1993-95; contbr. articles to Army profl. jours. Officer U.S. Army, 1956-61, 67-71; col. USAR. Mem. Soc. Children's Book Writers and Illustrators (assoc.), Marin Soc. Artist, San Francisco Early Music Soc., Nat. Assn. Miniature Enthusiasts. Avocations: classical piano, painting, drawing, writing children's stories, miniature artist. Home: 255 Scenic Rd Fairfax CA 94930-1550 Office: Ackerman & Assocs PO Box 663 Fairfax CA 94978-0663

ACKERMAN, GARY EDWARD, artist; b. L.A., May 13, 1941; s. Morey and Alyce (Eig) A.; m. Yeasan Ko, Dec. 13, 1981; children: Alyssa, Camille, Maylan. Student, U. So. Calif., Sorbonne, Paris. Founder, pres. The Grants Pass Art Mus., Oreg. One-man shows include Sutton Galleries, New Orleans, Merrill Chase Galleries, Chgo., Tallman Galleries, N.Y.C., Face Galleries, Houston, Trebor Galleries, San Francisco, Regency Galleries, Atlanta, Gallerie D'tours, Carmel, Calif., Newbern Galleries, Dallas, Two Squares Gallery, Denver, Ira Roberts Galleries, L.A., Mauna Lani Gallery, Hawaii, Brennen Gallery, Palm Desert, Calif., Ackerman Galleries, Hawaii.

E-mail: ack4art@fte.net. Office: Ackerman Galleries Akoni Pule Hwy PO Box 961 Kapaau HI 96755-0961

ACKERMAN, LOWELL J., veterinarian, writer; b. Hamilton, Ont., Can., July 21, 1956; s. H. David and Mary (Glass) A.; m. Susan J. Eisenberg, Dec. 27, 1992; children: Nadia, Rebecca, David. BSc, U. Western Ont., 1977; DVM, Ont. Vet. Coll., 1982; PhD, La Salle U., 1993. Diplomate Am. Coll. Vet. Dermatology. Pres. Dermvet, Inc., Scottsdale, Ariz., 1985—, PHI, Inc., Scottsdale, 1990—; dir. dept. clin. resources Mesa (Ariz.) Vet. Hosp., Ltd., 1998—. Author: Owner's Guide to Dog Health, 1995, Skin & Coat Care for Your Cat, 1996; co-author: Canine & Feline Dermatology; editor: (3 book series) Biology Husbandry & Health Care of Reptiles, 1997. Avocations: genealogy. Office: Mesa Vet Hosp Ltd 858 N Country Club Dr Mesa AZ 85201-4181

ACKLEY, MARJORIE ROSE, health educator; b. Shanghai, China, Nov. 15, 1922; came to U.S., 1926; d. Millard Charles Ackley and Luella Alice (Williams) Scharffenberg; m. Donald Wilton Oswald, Sept. 24, 1942 (dec. 1955); children: Donald Theodore Oswald, Jacklyn Rae Hoiland; m. J. Paul Vaughn. AS, Grossmont Coll., 1977; BS in Allied Health Professions, Loma Linda U., 1987, MPH, 1988. RN, registered dietitian, fitness instr.; lic. M/V operator. Adminstrv. grant sec. Palo Alto (Calif.) Med. Research Found., 1962-67; devel. dir. San Francisco Eye and Ear Hosp., 1967-70; fin. planner Robert W. P. Holstrom Co., San Francisco, 1971-74; health educator San Francisco, 1972-74; registered nurse Groves Registry, San Francisco, 1977-88, Humana Hosp., Anchorage, 1983-85; owner, dir. Profl. Health Svcs., 1984-95; nurse Providence Hosp., Anchorage, 1983-85, 90-95; registered nurse MedPro Nurses Registry, San Diego, 1984-89; cardiac rehab. Providence Hosp., Anchorage, 1990-95; health educator Anchorage, 1983-95; mgr. Providence Kodiak Island Med. Ctr., Kodiak, Alaska, 1995—; nurse mgr. home care and wellness; med. coord. Canvasback Mission, Inc., Benecia, Calif., 1988-97; health educator, Sch. of Pub. Health, Loma Linda, Calif., 1988, Seventh-Day Adventist Ch., San Francisco, 1973, Health Expo, Yucaipa, Calif., 1988; health edn. lectr. 1990-93. Author of numerous articles in field. Vol. Health Expo, Alaska, 1988. Mem. Am. Dietetic Assn. (Eleanor Mitchell Meml. award 1986), Alaska Dietetic Assn., Seventh-Day Adventist Dietetic Assn., Am. Pub. Health Assn. Seventh-Day Adventist. Avocations: music, creative cooking, gardening, boating. Office: 1915 E Rezanof Dr Kodiak AK 99615-6602

ACOSTA, FRANK XAVIER, psychologist, educator; b. L.A., Apr. 2, 1945; s. Gilbert Lascurain and Virginia (Posada) A.; m. MaryAnn Gonzales, June 30, 1979; children: Robert Xavier, Jeanette Marie. BS in Psychology magna cum laude, Loyola U., L.A., 1968; MA, UCLA, 1970, PhD in Clin. Psychology, 1974. Lic. psychologist, Calif. Rsch. asst. Neuropsychiat. Inst., UCLA, 1968-71, vis. assoc. prof., 1984-85; clin. psychology intern VA Outpatient Clinic, L.A., 1971-72, Didi Hirsch Cmty. Mental Health Ctr., Culver City, Calif., 1972-73, Long Beach VA Hosp., Calif., 1973-74; clin. psychologist L.A. County/U. So. Calif. Med. Ctr., L.A., 1974—; dir. Spanish-Speaking Clinic, Adult Psychiat. Clinic, 1975—; from assoc. dir. to dir. clin. psychol. internship tng. prog, 1986-96; asst. prof. psychiatry Sch. Medicine, U. So. Calif., L.A., 1974-80, assoc. prof. clin. psychiatry, 1980-84, assoc. prof. psychiatry and behaviorl scis., 1984—; mem. allied health profl. staff U. So. Calif. Univ. Hosp., 1991—; cons. Spanish Speaking Mental Health Rsch. Ctr., L.A., 1974-88; cons., reviewer NIMH, 1977—; guest lectr. U. Nacional Autonoma de Mexico, Mexico City, 1985, Tulane U. Sch. Medicine, 1985. Author: (with J. Yamamoto and L. Evans) Effective Psychotherapy for Low-Income and Minority Patients, 1982 (Behavioral Sci. Book Club selection 1983); mem. editorial bd. Hispanic Jour. Behavioral Scis., 1981-85; contbr. chpts. to books, articles to profl. jours. Mem. psychol. rev. panel med. svcs. and occupl. health and safety divsns. of pers. dept. City of L.A., 1986-93; cons. Nat. Coalition Hispanic Mental Health and Human Svcs. Orgns., Washington, 1976-88; chair NRC, Evaluation Panel Psychology, Ford Found. Doctoral Fellowships Minorities Program, Washington, 1986-89; asst. scoutmaster, troop com. mem. Troop 31 Boy Scouts Am., 1994—. Rsch. grantee Social Sci. Rsch. Coun., L.A., 1976, NIMH, 1977-84; Ford Found. postdoctoral minorities fellow NRC, 1984; recipient faculty rsch. prize, dept. psychiatry U. So. Calif. Sch. Medicine, 1977; disting. scholar profl. devel. program U. Calif., Berkeley, 1985. Fellow APA (mem. accreditation com. 1977-80), Am. Assn. for Applied and Preventive Psychology; mem. Western Psychol. Assn., Calif. Psychol. Assn., Los Angeles County Psychol. Assn., Alpha Sigma Nu. Office: Univ So Calif Sch Medicine Dept Psy-Beh Sci 1937 Hospital Pl Dept Psy Los Angeles CA 90033-1011

ACQUISTAPACE, KRIS, English language and humanities educator; b. Biloxi, Miss., June 3, 1955; d. Joseph Terence Allen and Charlotte Watson; m. Albrecht Gerhard Acquistapace, June 25, 1976 (div. Jan. 1989); 1 child, Holly Eve; m. David Acquistapace, Mar. 10, 1994. BA in English, Washington U., 1976; MEd in English, U. So. Miss., 1982. Prof. English Chaffey Coll., Rancho Cucamonga, Calif., 1994-97, Crafton Hills Coll., Yucaipa, Calif., 1997—. Bd. dirs. Upland (Calif.) Hist. Preservation Soc., 1991—; advisor Future Tchrs. of Am., 1998—; coord. Bridgewater, Eng. Student Exch., 1997—. Mem. Nat. Coun. Tchrs. of English, Coll. Bd., English Coun. of Calif. Two Year Colls. Office: Crafton Hills Coll 11711 Sand Canyon Rd Yucaipa CA 92399-1742

ADAIR-VERBAIS, TRUDY MAY, early childhood educator; b. Ogden, Utah, June 11, 1954; d. Ned Allain and Marcia Edine (Bacchus) Adair; m. Henry R. Verbais, Jan. 29, 1977; children: Melissa J., Meghan Elena. BA, U. Ariz., 1977. Cert. early childhood tchr., supr., cert. C.C. instr. Cons. Santa Barbara (Calif.) County Edn. Office, 1977, tchr., 1978-83, program specialist, 1983-85, 1983-85, asst. coord., 1986-88, coord., 1989-94, program dir., 1994—; instr. Calif. State U., Long Beach, 1992, Santa Barbara C.C., 1981; coord. U. Calif., Santa Barbara, 1989; owner, dir. Kid's Club, Santa Barbara, 1981-84; presenter in field. Author: Opening the Door: Serving Children with Special Needs in Child Care, 1993. Founder, dir. Holiday Cheer Project, Santa Barbara, 1981—; chair Santa Barbara County Health Tng. Consortium, 1989—; instr. ARC, 1990—; chair Santa Barbara County Child Care Planning Coun., 1991—, Program Improvement Consortium, 1994—. Nat. Def. scholarship U. Ariz., 1974, 75; recipient Cert. of Recognition Santa Barbara Industry Edn. Coun., 1992, Exemplary Leadership award Santa Barbara County Child Care Planning Coun., 1991. Mem. Nat. Assn. for the Edn. of Young Children, Tri-Counties Assn. for the Edn. of Young Children (chair membership 1981-83), Alternative Payment Program Assn., Calif. Child Care Adminstrn. Assn., Family Day Care Assn. Avocations: cross stitch, baking, travel, antique collecting, art. Office: Santa Barbara County Edn Office PO Box 6307 Santa Barbara CA 93160-6307

ADAM, CORNEL See LENGYEL, CORNEL ADAM

ADAMS, BELINDA JEANETTE SPAIN, nursing administrator; b. Rome, Ga., Dec. 5; d. Oscar Joe and Eleanor (Camacho) Spain. Diploma, Ga. Bapt. Hosp. Sch. Nursing, Atlanta, 1974; BS in Nursing, Med. Coll. Ga., Augusta, 1976; MS in Nursing, Ga. State U., Atlanta, 1980, PhD in Human Resource Devel., 1998. Cert. clin. specialist in med.-surg. nursing, intravenous nurse. Critical care flight nurse Critical Care Medflight, Inc., Atlanta, 1984-88; intravenous therapy coord. DeKalb Gen. Hosp., Atlanta, 1974-81; asst. prof. Mercer U., Atlanta, 1981-87; corp. dir. infusion/high tech. svcs. Kimberly Quality Care, Atlanta, 1988-92; cons. Profl. Learning Systems, 1992—; asst. prof. Clayton State Coll., Morrow, Ga., 1992-94, Ga. Bapt. Coll. Nursing, Atlanta, 1994-95; clin. examiner State of N.Y.-Regents Coll., 1995—. Mem. ANA, Intravenous Nurses Soc. (rsch. com., entrepreneur com.), Ga. Nurses Assn. Home: 4542 Ferncroft Rd Mercer Island WA 98040

ADAMS, BRADY, state official; b. Portland, Oreg., Feb. 28, 1945; m. Pat Adams, 1965; children: Ted, Jennifer. B in mktg., Portland State U. With Evergreen Fed. Savings and Loan, Grants Pass, Oreg., 1972—, now pres.; state senator State of Utah, 1992—, now pres. of senate, 1997—. Founder Our Valley Clin.; treas. Grants Pass Cmty. Sculpture Com. mem. Rotary (hon.). Office: Oregon Senate State Capitol Rm S-203 Salem OR 97310*

ADAMS, BYRON, composer, conductor; b. Mar. 9, 1955. BM, Jacksonville U., 1977; MM, U. So. Calif., 1979; DMA, Cornell U., 1984. Composer-in-residence Music Ctr. U. of the South, 1979-84; lectr. Cornell U., N.Y.C., 1985-87; assoc. prof. of music U. Calif., Riverside, 1993; guest composer 26th Warsaw Autumn Festival, 1983, San Francisco Conservatory, 1966. Composer: Quintet for piano and strings, 1979, Concerto for trumpet and string orch., 1983, Sonata for trumpet and piano, 1983, Concerto for violin and orch., 1984, Go Lovely Rose for male chorus, 1984, Missa Brevis, 1988, Three Epitaph, 1988; recordings include Nightingales, 1979, Serenata Aestiva, 1986; contbr. articles to music jours. Vaughan Williams Rsch. fellow Carthusian Trust, 1985; recipient Grand prize Delius Festval Composition Competition, 1977 Am. Soc. Composers, Medly P. Ray Composition award, 1985. Avocations: reading. Office: U Calif Dept Music 900 University Ave Riverside CA 92521*

ADAMS, CAROL ANN, hairstylist; b. Fontana, Calif., June 2, 1970; d. Alfred Floyd and Rita Clara (Boyer) A,. Grad., DeLoux Sch Cosmotology, 1988. Lic. cosmotologist, 1988. Hair designer Duanes Hair Designs, Redlands, Calif., 1988-92; hairstylist Redlands Hair Co., 1992; receptionist H&R Block, Redlands, 1989-95; hairstylist The Rose of Sharon, Redlands, 1992—; fashon show stylist Jr. Assistance League, Redlands, 1994-96; vol. hairstylist Leukemia Soc., Redlands, 1995. Model for hairstyle competitions, 1989-92. Mem. Nat. Cosmotology Assn. Republican. Baptist. Avocations: collecting plates and Marilyn Monroe memorabilia, working out. Office: The Rose of Sharon 101 E Redlands Blvd Ste 130 Redlands CA 92373-4723

ADAMS, CLINTON, artist, historian; b. Glendale, Calif., Dec. 11, 1918; s. Merritt Cooley and Effie (Mackenzie) A.; m. Mary Elizabeth Atchison, Jan. 9, 1943; 1 child, Michael Gerald. Ed.B., UCLA, 1940, M.A., 1942. Instr. art UCLA, 1946-48, asst. prof., 1948-54; prof. art, head dept. U. Ky.; also dir. Art Gallery, 1954-57; prof. art, head dept. U. Fla., 1957-61; dean Coll. Fine Arts U. N.Mex., Albuquerque, 1961-76, asso. provost, dean faculties, 1976-77; dir. Tamarind Inst., 1970-85; asso. dir. Tamarind Lithography Workshop, Los Angeles, 1960-61, program cons., 1961-70. Represented in permanent collections Bklyn. Mus., Art. Inst. Chgo., Brit. Mus., Australian Nat. Gallery, Mus. Modern Art, Los Angeles County Art Mus., and others; author: (with Garo Antreasian) The Tamarind Book of Lithography: Art and Techniques, 1970, American Lithographers, 1900-1960: The Artists and Their Printers, 1983, (with others) Lasting Impressions: Lithography As Art, 1988, Printmaking in New Mexico, 1880-1990, 1991, Crayonstone: The Life and Work of Bolton Brown, 1993, Nineteenth-Century Lithography in Europe, 1998; editor The Tamarind Papers, 1974-90, Second Impressions: Modern Prints and Printmakers Reconsidered, 1996; subject: bibliography Clinton Adams: Paintings and Watercolors 1945-87; exhbn. catalogue Albuquerque: University of New Mexico Art Mus., 1987; biography A Spectrum of Innovation: Color in American Printmaking, 1890-1990, 1990. Recipient Gov.'s award for outstanding contbns. to arts of N.Mex., 1985. Mem. NAD (academician), Nat. Coun. Fine Arts Deans (chmn. 1965-67). Home: 1917 Morningside Dr NE Albuquerque NM 87110-4927

ADAMS, DIANNE F., bank executive; b. Tracy, Calif., Nov. 9, 1956; d. George M. and Faye D. (Klatt) Hanlon; m. Larry A. Adams, May 16, 1978; children: Tiesha Eileen, Jeanice Vonda, Lawrence Alan, Robert Welcome. AS in Liberal Arts, Modesto Jr. Coll., 1978; BSBA, U. Phoenix, 1991. Owner, pres. Adams Express Bookkeeping and Tax Svcs., Stockton, Calif., 1979—; bookkeeper EMAC, Inc., Oakland, Calif., 1982-83, sr. acct., 1983-84, office mgr., 1984-85; controller OFWHC, Inc., Oakland, 1985-85, CFO acct., 1986-89; acting CFO VNA, Stanislaus, Calif., 1989; sr. acct. Tracy (Calif.) Fed. Bank, 1991-92, fin. analyst, 1992-94, mgr. fin. and planning, 1994—; bd. dirs. LL & R Gems, Ms. Petite, Inc., WCFHP Inc.; contracted sr. acct. Calif. Youth Soccer League, Pleasanton, 1989-91, Sta. KPIX, Livermore, Calif., 1989-91, R. Zaballos & Sons Constrn., Hayward, Calif., 1989-91, Stone Bros. Inc., Stockton, 1989-91, Lodi (Calif.) Meml. Hosp., 1989-91. Leader youths and adults Enterprise 4H Club, Escalon, Calif., 1976-78; tchr. teen and adult Sunday Sch., Saron Luth. Ch., Escalon, 1976-92; coach tee ball, mr. sr. boys team, v.p., sec., Montezuma Little League, Stocton Calif., 1992-93. Mem. NAFE (pres., founder Bay Area Networkers 1985-86), Nat. Assn. Tax Cons., Am. Bus. Womens Assn. (bd. dirs. 1981-86, sec., historian, membership com. Oakdale chpt.), Inst. Mgmt. Accts. (membership com. 1991—). Republican. Avocations: gemology, hiking, roller-blading, skiing, music. Office: Tracy Fed Bank PO Box 389 1003 Central Ave Tracy CA 95376-3914

ADAMS, FRANK, education specialist; b. Cleve., Sept. 11, 1948; s. Frank Albin and Helen (Coleman) Kovacevic. BS in Bus. Adminstrn., Bowling Green (Ohio) State U., 1970, MEd in Phys. Edn., 1978. Tech. writer Soldier Phys. Fitness Sch., Ft. Ben Harrison, Ind., 1983-85; edn. specialist Directorate of Tng. and Doctrine, Ft. Huachuca, Ariz., 1985-90, Dept. Tactics Intelligence Mil. Sci., Ft. Huachuca, 1990-93, 111th Mil. Intelligence Brigade, Ft. Huachuca, 1993-97; staff Directorate Continuous Learning U.S. Army Intelligence Ctr., 1998—; mem. steering com. tng. and doctrine command, staff and faculty devel. divsn., El Paso, Tex., 1987. Co-author: (field manual) Physical Fitness Training, 1984, (Internet site) Total Fitness; contbr. articles to profl. jours. and local newspapers. Recipient Civilian Achievement medal Dept. Army, Ft. Huachuca 1993, Comdr.'s award, 1995. Mem. AAHPERD (life), Mil. Intelligence Corp., Self-Realization Fellowship. Avocations: internal martial arts, reading, Reiki master-teacher. Home: 4838 Corte Vista Sierra Vista AZ 85635-5738 Office: Advanced Individual Skills Divsn Fort Huachuca AZ 85613-6000

ADAMS, HILDA CHASKI, public health administrator, epidemiologist; b. Balt., Apr. 14, 1951; d. Milton Sylvester and Marylee (Evans) C.; m. H. Douglas Adams, 1994. BA in Biology, Manhattanville Coll., 1973; MPH, Yale U., 1987. Pub. health sanitarian Del. Dept. Health and Social Svcs., Georgetown, 1974-85; pub. health cons., New Haven, 1987; dep. dir. div. environ. health and epidemiology Mo. Dept. Health, Jefferson City, 1987-94; dir. environ. health Kansas City (Mo.) Dept. Health, 1990-94, Multnomah County, Portland, 1995—; instr. anatomy and physiology Del. Tech. and C.C., Georgetown, 1981-85; adj. faculty St. Louis U. Sch. Pub. Health, 1992-94; mem. Show Me Health Reform Commn., 1993; presenter in field. Contbr. articles to profl. jours. Pres. Del. Environ. Assn., 1977; mem. Columbia (Mo.) Bd. Plumbing Examiners, 1988-90, Columbia Commn. on Bicycling, 1988-91. Recipient letter of commendation State of Del., 1981, 84, Young Careerist award DeVries Bus. and Profl. Women's Club, 1980, cert of appreciation Del. Tech. and C.C.-Calif. Coll. Respiratory Therapy, 1981, Strategic Leadership for State Execs. award Duke U., 1991, Mo. Gov.'s award for productivity, 1993. Mem. APHA, Nat. Environ. Health Assn. (exec. coun. 1977), Mo. Pub. Health Assn. (v.p. Ctrl. Mo. chpt. 1988-89, pres. 1989-90, chair legis. com. 1993). Avocations: cycling, running, birdwatching. Home: 4579 Laclede Ave # 205 Saint Louis MO 63108-2103 Office: Multnomah County Health Dept 426 SW Stark St Fl 3 Portland OR 97204-2347

ADAMS, JACK, film company executive, screenwriter, producer, educator; b. Lakehurst, N.J., Sept. 15, 1952; s. John Carey and Dorothy Jeanne (Conover) A.; m. Shirley Janulewicz, June 28, 1975; children: Carey Miller, Chanine Angelina, Mikael Walter, Jozef Conover. MusB in Music Edn., U. Del., 1974. Pres. Koala Studio, Valencia, Calif., 1977—; v.p. devel. Unifilms, Inc., North Hollywood, Calif., 1984—; instr. film, TV writing and script analysis Coll. of Canyons, Valencia, 1988—, L.A. City Coll., 1989—, EveryWoman's Village, Van Nuys, Calif., 1990—, Info. Exch., L.A., 1990—, Learning Tree U., Chatsworth, Calif., 1990—, U. Wis., Madison, 1991—, U. Hawaii, 1992—, USIA, Washington, 1991—, Info. Network, South Pasadena, Calif., 1990—, Moorpark Coll., 1991—, Oxnard Coll., 1991—, Northwestern U., Evanston, Ill., 1991—, Glendale (Calif.) Community Coll., 1991—; co-founder ScripTip, 1990, Classes Unlimited, 1992—, Johnson County Community Coll., Kansas City, 1993, Univ. Wis., Milwaukee, 1993, Irvine (Calif.) Valley Coll., 1992—, Shenandoah Valley Writer's Guild, Front Royal, Va., 1993—, Rancho Santiago Coll., Santa Ana, Calif., 1993—, Orange Coast Coll., Costa Mesa, Calif., 1993—; script cons. Wis. Screenwriters Forum; mem. KNX Speakers Bur., CBS Radio, 1989—, Story Bd. Devel. Group, Paramount Studios, 1989—; pres. NBC Writers Workshop; mem. Larry Wilson Devel. Workshop, Paramount Studios, Le Group, Paramount Studios; founding mem., officer, bd. dirs. L.A. Filmmakers Workshop, 1989-91; founder Santa Clarita Scriptwriters Workshop, Writers Anonymous, 1988; pres. Entertainment Writers' Workshop, 1990, Adams Entertainment, 1993; ptnr. Flying Cow, 1994; co-founder: Weasels in My Pants Prodns., 1996; mem. Ind. Feature Project West; presenter numerous seminars and workshops. Composer (film) Eat, 1980 (Filmex award 1981, best short film award Cinemagic mag. 1981); writer, co-creator sitcom pilot Lola, Universal Studios, 1991; writer, developer sitcom pilot Fat Farm; writer, producer, dir. sitcom pilot Box # 22; line producer sitcom pilots Zebra, It's Not My Fault; creator: Screenwriting Warriors: Basic Training, 1988; columnist: Creative Screenwriting Mag., 1994—; TV editor Freelance Screenwriters' Forum Newsletter; columnist ScreenWrite Now mag.; creator (audiotapes) Top 50 Script Marketing Tips, Get An Agent to Sell Your Script, Write To Get Past the Script Reader, Pitch Your Film and Television Projects. Mem. Indian Guides/Princesses Program, chief Apache tribe YMCA, 1990—, produced annual haunted house fundraiser for Santa Clarita Family YMCA, 1991-94, participate in annual fundraising campaign, 1990, Am. Youth Soccer Orgn. AYSO, 1988. Mem. Am. Film Inst. (alumni assn. writers workshop), Scriptwriters Network (bd. advisors), Film Artists Network, Ind. Writers So. Calif. Scriptwriters Caucus, Assn. Info. Systems Profls. (bd. dirs. 1983), Freelance Screenwriter's Forum (founding), Comedy Writers Co-op (founding ABC), Wis. Screenwriters Forum (advisor 1989—). Avocations: tennis, still photography, music. Home and Office: 22931 Sycamore Creek Dr Santa Clarita CA 91354-2050

ADAMS, JAMES FREDERICK, psychologist, educational administrator; b. Andong, Korea, Dec. 27, 1927; s. Benjamin Nyce and Phyllis Irene (Taylor) A.; m. Carol Ann Wagner, Jan. 17, 1980; children—James Edward, Dorothy Lee Adams Vanderhorst, Robert Benjamin. B.A. In Psychology, U. Calif.-Berkeley, 1950; Ed.M. in Counseling and Psychology, Temple U., 1951; Ph.D. in Exptl. Psychology, Wash. State U., 1959. Cert. psychologist, Wash., Pa.; lic. psychologist, Pa. Psychometrician Measurement and Research Ctr., Temple U., Phila., 1951-52; asst. prof. psychology Whitworth Coll., Spokane, Wash., 1952-55; teaching and research asst. State U. Wash., 1955-57; research assoc. Miami U., Oxford, Ohio, 1957-59; asst. prof. psychology Coll. Liberal Arts, Temple U., 1959-62, assoc. prof., 1962-66, prof., 1966-80, chmn. dept. counseling psychology, 1969-72; vis. prof. psychology Coll. Soc. Scis., U. P.R., Rio Piedras, 1963-64, Coll. Scis., Cath. U., Ponce, P.R., 1971-72; chmn. dept. counseling psychology Coll. Edn., Temple U., 1973-77, coordinator div. ednl. psychology, 1974-76; grad. dean, prof. psychology Grad. Coll., U. Nev., Las Vegas, 1980-85; acad. (sr.) v.p. Longwood Coll., Farmville, Va., 1985-86. Author: Problems in Counseling: A Case Study Approach, 1962, Instructors Manual for Understanding Adolescence, 1969; (exhbn. catalogue with J. D. Selig) Colonial Spanish Art of the Americas, 1976; (comml. pamphlet with C. L. Davis) The Use of the Vu-graph as an Instructional Aid, 1960; editor: Counseling and Guidance: A Summary View, 1965, Understanding Adolescence: Current Developments in Adolescent Psychology, 1968, 4th edit., 1980, Human Behavior in a Changing Society, 1973, Songs that had to be Sung (by B. N. Adams), 1979; contbr. chpts., articles, tests and book revs. to profl. publs. Served to cpl. USMC, 1945-46. Recipient Alexander Meiklejohn award AAUP, 1984; James McKean Cattell research fund grantee Miami U., Oxford, Ohio, 1958, Bolton fund research grantee Temple U., 1960, 62, faculty research grantee Temple U., 1961, 63, Commonwealth of Pa. research grantee Temple U., 1969, 70, 71, 72, summer research fellow Temple U., 1979; recipient scholarship U. Munich, 1955. Fellow Am. Psychol. Assn. (divs. 26, 17); mem. Eastern Psychol. Assn., Western Psychol. Assn., Interam. Soc. Psychology, Sigma Xi, Psi Chi. Avocations: art collecting; art restoring. Scholarship established in his name at U. Nev., Las Vegas. Home: 130 Palacio Rd Corrales NM 87048-9648

ADAMS, JO-ANN MARIE, lawyer; b. L.A., May 27, 1949; d. Joseph John and Georgia S. (Wein) A.; AA, Pasadena City Coll., 1968; BA, Pomona Coll., 1970; MA, Calif. State U., L.A., 1971; MBA, Pacific Luth. U., 1983; cert. in Telecomm. and Info. Resource Mgmt., U. Hawaii, 1993; JD, Santa Clara U., 1996. Secondary tchr. South Pasadena (Calif.) Unified Schs., 1970-71; appraiser Riverside County (Calif.) Assessor's Office, 1972-74; systems and procedures analyst Riverside County Data Processing Dept., 1974-76, supervising systems analyst, 1976-79; systems analyst computer Boeing Computer Svcs. Co., Seattle, 1979-81; sr. systems analyst Thurston County Central Svcs., Olympia, Wash., 1981-83, data processing systems mgr., 1983-84; data processing systems engr. IBM Corp., 1984-87; realtor-assoc., Dower Realty, 1987-92; corp. sales rep. UniGlobe Met. Travel, 1988-89; project mgr. Servco Pacific, 1989-90, Scott Software Systems, 1990-91; systems analyst Dept. Atty. Gen., 1991-93; cons. in field, 1993—; pvt. practice, 1996—; law clerk HiTech Law, 1995-96, Law Offices Thomas R. Hogan, 1995; instr. Riverside City Coll., 1977-79; vis. lectr. Santa Clara U., 1997—. Chair legis. task force Riverside/San Bernardino chpt. NOW, 1975-76, chpt. co-chair, 1978; mem. ethics com. Calif. NOW Inc., 1978; alt. del. Calif Dem. Caucus, 1978. Mem. ABA, SCCBA, NAFE, Pomona Coll. Alumni Assn., Santa Clara U. Alumni Assn. Home: 1200 Ranchero Way Apt 80 San Jose CA 95117-3155 Office: 19925 Stevens Creek Blvd Cupertino CA 95014-2305

ADAMS, JOHN M., library director; b. Chicago, Ill., June 10, 1950; s. Merlin J. and Esther (Bohn) A.; m. Nancy Ileen Coultas, June 12, 1970; 1 child, Arwen Lee. B.A. in English, U. Ill., 1972, M.L.S., 1973. Grad. asst. U. Ill. Libr., Urbana, 1972-73; libr.-reference Sherman Oaks Libr., L.A., 1973-75; libr. philosophy dept. L.A. Pub. Libr., 1975-77, head gen. reading svc., 1977-78; dir. Moline Pub. Libr., Ill., 1978-83, Tampa (Fla.)-Hillsborough County Pub. Libr. System, 1983-91; dir., county librarian Orange County (Calif.) Public Library System, 1991—; dir. Tampa Bay Libr. Consortium, Fla., 1983-91, Santiago Libr. System, 1991—; mem. adv. com. on pub. libs. OCLC, 1992-95. Contbr. articles to profl. jours. Bd. dirs. Planned Parenthood of Tampa, 1984. Recipient Frontier award ALA Mag., 1981; named Outstanding Young Man, Moline Jaycees, 1983. Mem. ALA (J.C. Dana award 1982, 93), Calif. Libr. Assn., Calif. County Librs. Assn., Orange County C. of C. Avocations: music; tennis. Office: Orange County Pub Libr 1501 E Saint Andrew Pl Santa Ana CA 92705-4930

ADAMS, KENNETH ROBERT, gaming analyst, writer, consultant, historian; b. Carson City, Nev., Sept. 8, 1942; s. Maurice Adams and Gertrude Aloha (Wilson) Burke; children: John Anthony, James. Prin. Ken Adams and Assoc., Sparks, Nev., 1990—; coord. gaming history series of the oral history program U. Nev., continuing edns. gaming mgmt. program adv. com., 1988-97, chmn., 1988. Co-author: Playing the Cards That Are Dealt, 1992, Always Bet on the Butcher, 1994, War Stories, 1995; publ., assoc. editor: Nev. Gaming Almanac, 1991-97, Nev. Gaming Directory, 1993-97, The Adams Report. Chmn. mktg. com. Downtown Improvement Assn., 1994—; steering com., chmn. gaming com. Festival Reno, 1984-86; mem. adv. bd. Leadership Reno Alumni Assn., 1995-97. Mem. Internat. Platform Assn. Fax: (702) 322-7806. Office: Ken Adams and Assocs 210 Marsh Ave Ste 103 Reno NV 89509-1625

ADAMS, LORETTA, marketing executive. BS in Internat. Mktg., Am. U., 1962; postgrad. in Econs., U. Panama, Panama City, 1963-64. Mgmt. trainee Sears Roebuck & Co., Panama City, Panama, 1962-63, mgmt. pers., 1963-65; supr. internat. advertising projects Kenyon & Eckhardt Advertising, Inc., N.Y.C., 1965-68; asst. rsch. dir. divsn. L.Am. and Far E. Richardson-Vicks Internat., Mexico City and Wilton, Conn., 1968-69, rsch. dir. divsn. Mex. and L.Am., 1969-75, mem. top mgmt. strategic planning team, 1975-78; founder, pres. Mkt. Devel., Inc., San Diego, 1978—. Contbr. articles to profl. jours. Mem. Am. Mktg. Assn., European Soc. for Opinion & Market Rsch., Advt. Rsch. Found., Coun. Am. Survey Rsch. Orgns., Market Rsch. Assn. Office: Market Devel Inc 600 B St Ste 1600 San Diego CA 92101-4584*

ADAMS, MARK, artist; b. Ft. Plain, N.Y., Oct. 27, 1925; s. Earl D. and Edith (Wohlgemuth) A.; m. Beth Van Hoesen, Sept. 12, 1953. Student, Syracuse U., 1943-46, Hans Hofmann Sch. Fine Arts, 1946, 48, Jean Lurcat, 1955. Instr. San Francisco Art Inst., 1961; panelist Internat. Symposium on Tapestry, San Francisco, 1976; disting. vis. prof. U. Calif. at Davis, 1978; painter in residence Am. Acad. in Rome, 1963. Book: Mark Adams, 1985; one-man shows include deYoung Mus., San Francisco, 1959, Portland (Oreg.) Mus., 1961, Calif. Palace of Legion of Honor, San Francisco, 1961, retrospective, 1970, San Francisco Mus. Modern Art, 1962, French & Co., N.Y.C., 1964, John Berggruen Gallery, San Francisco, 1978, 80, 82, 83, 85, 87, 90, 94, Graham Modern, N.Y.C., 1981, 84, Jane Haslem Salon, Washington, 1989, Palo Alto (Calif.) Cultural Ctr., 1990; exhibited in numerous group shows including Mus. Contemporary Crafts, N.Y.C., 1957, 58, 62, 65, Dallas Mus., 1958, Internat. Biennial of Tapestry, Lausanne, Switzerland, 1962, 65, St. Louis Art Mus., 1964, Norfolk Mus., 1966; represented in permanent collections San Francisco Mus. Modern Art, Dallas Mus. Fine

Arts, Chase Manhattan Bank, N.Y.C., San Francisco Pub. Library, Legion of Honor Mus., San Francisco; maj. archtl. commns. include tapestries, Bank of Calif., San Francisco, Weyerhauser Co., Tacoma, Wash., Fairmont Hotel, Dallas, San Francisco Internat. Airport, Luth. Brotherhood, Mpls., stained glass, Temple Emanu-el, San Francisco, St. Thomas More Cath. Ch., San Francisco, St. Andrews Episcopal Ch., Saratoga, Calif. Office: care John Berggruen Gallery 228 Grant Ave San Francisco CA 94108-4612*

ADAMS, MICHAEL CHARLES, computer consultant, computer engineer; b. French Camp, Calif., Nov. 17, 1949; s. Lloyd Edward and Olive Bernice (Cheatham) A. AA, AS in Electron Microscopy, San Joaquin Delta Coll., 1970; BS in metall. welding, engring., Calif. Poly. U., 1975; BA, Univ. Without Walls, U. Pacific, 1978; student, Stanford U., 1978-79; MA in computer graphics, Calif. State U. (Sacamento), 1981, MFA in engring. design, product design, 1982; PhD, U. Chgo., 1987. Lic. in explosives and demolition, firearms and blasting, Calif. Intern Sandia Corp., Livermore, Calif., 1967; intern intelligence and security Lawrence Livermore Radiation Lab., Livermore, Calif., 1968-69; intern in reconnaissance ranger, naval enlisted sci. engring. evaluations program, navy seal U. Calif., Berkeley, 1969; commd. 2nd. lt. USMC, 1970, advanced through grades to maj., 1978; prof. art, design Calif. State U. (Sacramento), 1979-82, tchr., artist, 1980-81; Calculus, Chemistry, Physics tchr. Educere Corp., Sacramento, 1981-83; recruitment vol. Atty. Gen's. Office, Sacramento, 1982; postal worker U.S. PO, Stockton, Calif., 1983-85; spl. assignments US Postal Inspection Svc., 1985-87; computer, art design cons. Michael Charles Adams & Assocs. Corp., Stockton, 1990; field ops. supr. Census Bur., Washington, 1990; computer cons., 1990—; CEO, pres. Kafkaesque Inc., 1992—; mem. think tanks, Lawrence U. Calif., Berkeley, 1968-69, Hoover, Stanford U., 1978-79; software developer, numerous elec. and mech. inventions and designs. One-man shows include U. Pacific, 1978-79; exhibited in group shows at the Winslow Nat. Competition, Googenheimer Nat. Competition, U. Pacific, Stanford U., Calif. Poly. U., San Joaquin Delta Coll., Calif. State Coll. (Sacramento), Brown-Stone Coffee & Tea Co., others; inventor, patentee in field. Active Boy Scouts Am. (unit commr., round table commr., Dist. Tng. award, Commrs. Tng. award, Woodbadge Tng. award, Order Arrow Vigil award, Disting. Svc. award, William T. Hornaday Nat. award, Silver Beaver award, Disting. Eagle Scout with Silver Eagle Palms, Gold Life Saving Medal, Cub Scouts and Webloe's Tng. Knots); adult supr. Girl Scouts U.S. (Disting. Svc. award); coord. Am. Conservation Youth Movement. Decorated Purple Heart, Navy Cross; Svc. medal, Occupation medal, Gallantry medal, Medal Honor 1st Class Gold (Vietnam); receipient Crocker Kingley, Croker DeWitt No. Calif. Open Competition Sculpture. Mem. USMC League, U.S. Navy Seal League (exemplary league soc.), Decade Club (hon. mem.). Democrat. Avocations: computers programming, design, animation, exploring, landscape design. Home: 2207 Raymond Ave Stockton CA 95203-1231

ADAMS, ROBERT GRANVILLE, marketing professional; b. Indpls., July 2, 1927; s. Jack and Iris (Trippeer) A.; m. Marilyn Howe (div.); m. Ilona Molnar (div.); children: Lynn, Victoria, Amy. BS, Ind. U., 1953. Capt. USAF, 1945-65; various assignments as pilot Adams Mktg., Inc.; horse rancher Am. Quarter Horse Assn., Scottsdale, Ariz., 1965-88; wholesaler Nat. Home Furnishings Assn., Scottsdale, 1988—; pres. Adams Mktg., Inc., Scottsdale, 1980—. Bd. dirs. Desert Caballeros, Wickenburg, Ariz., Rancheros Visitadores, Santa Barbara, Calif. Mem. Desert Caballeros (Wickenburg, Ariz., bd. dirs.), Rancheros Visitadores (Santa Barbara, Calif.), Sigma Chi (life Loyal Sig). Avocations: horse breeding, training, riding. Office: PO Box 14350 Scottsdale AZ 85267-4350

ADAMS, ROBERT MONROE, retired dermatologist, educator; b. Pasadena, Calif., May 4, 1926; s. Oscar D. and Mamie (Butler) A.; m. Lorene Tassi, Mar. 21, 1948; children: Cynthia, Gregory. AB with distinction, Stanford U., 1946, MD, 1950. Diplomate Am. Bd. Dermatology. Rotating intern San Francisco City and County Hosp., 1949-50; resident in internal medicine Tripler Army Hosp., Honolulu, 1950-52; pvt. practice in family medicine Stockton, Calif., 1952-64; dermatologist Palo Alto (Calif.) Med. Clinic, 1967-75; resident in dermatology Stanford (Calif.) U. Med. Ctr., 1964-67, fellow in dermatology, 1966-67, dir. Contact Dermatitis and Occupational Skin Disease Clinic, 1967-96; from instr. to clin. prof. dermatology Stanford U., 1966-82, clin. prof. dermatology, 1982-96; mem. staff Stanford U. Hosp., 1967-96; pvt. practice in dermatology Menlo Park, Calif., 1975—; ret., 1996; dir. or co-dir. various profl. courses and symposia; guest lectr. many sci. confs. and ednl. instns., most recently Skin and Cancer Found. Seminar, Sidney, Australia, 1992, Cypress Found., Carmel, Calif., 1994, U. Calif., San Francisco, L.A. and Davis, numerous occasions. Author: (textbooks) Occupational Contact Dermatitis, 1969, Occupational Skin Disease, 1983, 2nd edit., 1990; co-author: Color Text of Contact Dermatitis, 1992; editor: Occupational Medicine, State of the Art Reviews, 1986; contbr. 13 chpts. to books; founding editor Am. Jour. Contact Dermatitis, editor-in-chief, 1989-92, mem. editl. bd., 1992—; mem. editl. bd. Jour. Am. Acad. Dermatology, 1986—, Health Hazards of the Workplace Report, 1989; contbr. numerous articles and revs. to sci. jours. Recipient Jean Spencer Felton award for Excellence in Sci. Writing, 1983. Mem. AMA (mem. adv. panel on med. standards 1979-83), Am. Acad. Dermatology (mem. task force on contact dermatitis 1976-91, Gold award for Teaching 1981, bd. dirs. 1989-93), Calif. Med. Assn. (mem. adv. panel on occupational medicine 1975-83), We. Occupational Med. Assn. (pres. 1983-84), Am. Soc. for Contact Dermatitis (pres., founder 1989-91), Am. Conf. Govtl. Indsl. Hygienists, San Francisco Dermatology Soc. (pres. 1985-86), Soc. for Investigative Dermatology, Pacific Dermatol. Assn., Internat. Soc. for Tropical Dermatology, Santa Clara Med. Soc., Brit. Assn. Dermatologist (hon.), Mex. Acad. Dermatology (hon.), Chilean Soc. Dermatology (hon.), Venezuelan Soc. Dermatology (hon.). Avocations: piano playing/accompanying. Home: 555 Laurel Ave Apt 108 San Mateo CA 94401-4157

ADAMS, SARAH VIRGINIA, family counselor; b. San Francisco, Oct. 23, 1955; d. Marco Tulio and Helen (Jorge) Zea; separated; children: Mark Vincent, Elena Giselle, Johnathan Richard. BA, Calif. State U., Long Beach, 1978, MS in Psychology, 1980; MA in Psychology, Fuller Sem., Pasadena, 1996, MA in Christian Leadership, 1997; postgrad., Fuller Sem., 1996—. Lic. marriage, family, child counseling. Tutor math. and sci. Montebello, Calif., 1979-82; behavioral specialist Cross Cultural Psychol. Corp., L.A., 1979-80; psychol. asst. Legal Psychology, L.A., 1980-82, Eisner Psychol. Assocs., L.A., 1982-83; assoc. dir. Legal Psychodiagnosis and Forensic Psychology, L.A., 1982-83; adminstrv. dir. Diagnostic Clinic, Calif., 1983-85; dir. Diagnostic Clinic of West Covina, Calif., 1985-87; owner Adams Family Counseling Inc., Calif., 1987—; with Health Group Psychol. Svcs., 1994—; tchr. piano, Montebello, 1973-84; ins. agent Am. Mut. Life Ins., Des Moines, 1982-84. Fellow Am. Assn. Marriage and Family Therapists, Am. Psychol. Assn.; mem. NAFE, Calif. Assn. Marriage and Family Therapists, Calif. State Psychol. Assn., Calif. Soc. Indsl. Medicine and Surgery, Western Psychol. Assn., Psi Chi, Pi Delta Phi. Republican. Roman Catholic. Avocations: piano, creative writing, drawing, collecting coins. Office: Adams Family Counseling 260 S Glendora Ave Ste 103 West Covina CA 91790-3041

ADAMS, SHAD ARDIS, communication technician; b. Douglas, Wyo., Oct. 4, 1964; s. Douglas Ray Reeves and Mary Ann (Coe) Todd; m. Rebecca Dawn Boone, June 22, 1996. AAS in Comm. Tech., Arapahoe C.C., 1998. Warehouse person Carpet Barn, Prescott, Ariz., 1985-87, warehouse mgr., 1987-90, installation mgr., 1990-92; acct. svc. rep. AT&T, Englewood, Colo., 1992-96; sys. support specialist Lucent Techs., Englewood, 1996-98, sys. application specialist, 1998—. Union rep. Comm. Workers Am., Englewood, 1992-98; vol. Jr. Achievement, Denver, 1998; steering com. mem. Colo. Netdays, Denver, 1996-98, Colo. Tech Corps, Denver, 1998. Mem. Phi Theta Kappa. Democrat. Roman Catholic. Avocations: computers, sports, reading, cooking. Home: PO Box 3669 Englewood CO 80155-3669 Office: Lucent Techs 7200 S Alton Way Englewood CO 80112-2201

ADAMS, SHARRON ANN EMANUEL, business owner, educator; b. Norman, Okla., Sept. [illegible]; d. [illegible] Thomas [illegible] and Theda Belle (Halford) Smethers; m. Jeffrey Inglis Adams, Mar. 21, 1970; children: Adrian H. Inglis, Julia Alison. BS in Edn. cum laude, Abilene Christian U., 1961; MA, Mich. State U., 1972. Tchr. Wichita (Kans.) Pub. Schs., 1961-63, Orlando (Fla.) Pub. Schs., 1963-64; educator U.S. Dept. Def. Schs., Europe, 1964-75, Santa Fe Pub. Schs., 1978-90; v.p. Jeffrey Adams Antiques, Inc., Santa Fe, 1981-91, Carefree, Ariz., 1991—; adj. faculty Prescott (Ariz.) Coll., 1994—. Co-author: A Critical Guide to Dining Out in Santa Fe, 1987. Capt. CAP aux. USAF, 1986-91, comdr. Santa Fe Composite Squadron, 1989-91. Mem. NOW, Carefree/Cave Creek C. of C. (bd. dirs. 1993, v.p. 1994), Kappa Delta Pi, Sigma Tau Delta. Democrat. Unitarian Universalist. Avocations: studying piano, composing music. Office: Jeffrey Adams Antiques Inc PO Box 3155 Carefree AZ 85377-3155

ADAMS, STEPHEN SHAWN, management consultant, hotel caterer; b. Chgo., Apr. 8, 1961; s. Leonard G. Mano and Rose Mary (Sharber) Bassett. Grad. high sch., Palmer, Alaska. Mgr. lounge The Pines Hotel, Anchorage, Alaska, 1979-81; dist. mgr. Pines Corp., Anchorage, 1985-86; mgr. Sheffield Hotels, Valdez, Alaska, 1981-85; project mgr. Global Svcs., Inc., Anchorage, 1986—; pres. Focus Enterprises, Inc., Anchorage, 1988—, Realty Investment Group, Inc., Anchorage, 1989—. Author: A Collection of Shawn, 1988, Uncommon Sense, 1989. Com. leader Valdez Jaycees, 1983; bd. dirs. Valdez Conv. and Visitors' Bur., 1983-84. Named King of Accommodations Mayor of Valdez, 1984. Republican. Home: 200 W 34th Ave Ste 346 Anchorage AK 99503-3969

ADAMS, WARREN ERNEST, security manager, educator; b. Danville, Ark., Dec. 3, 1933; s. Orville Cletus and Mildred Ernestine (Waid) A.; m. Doris Anne Reed, April 9, 1954 (div. June 1974); children: Warren Lynn, Loren Keith, Eric Brian, Alicia Renee. BA in English, U. Ozarks, 1958; MS in Elem. Edn., Northeastern U., 1965; PhD in Edn., Okla. State U., 1971. Tchr. Livermore (Calif.) Sch. Dist., 1958-62; tchr., prin. Delaware County Schs., Jay, Okla., 1962-68; supt. Waurika (Okla.) Pub. Schs., 1968-74, Anderson Sch. Dist., Sands Springs, Okla., 1974-78, Mission Soledad (Calif.) Schs., 1978-82; tchr. Monterey County Sch., Salinas, Calif., 1982-97; security mgr. Natividad Med. Ctr., Salinas, Calif., 1997—; instr. Hartnell Coll., Salinas, 1995—, Nat. Traffic Safety Inst., San Jose, Calif., 1995—. Elvis impersonator, TV and Stage, 1992-96 (best of Monterey County award). Republican. Avocations: private pilot, scuba diving, drove the Alcan Hwy. to Fairbanks. Home: 333 W Laurel Dr 44 Salinas CA 93906 Office: Natividad Med Ctr PO Box 6292 Salinas CA 93912

ADAMSON, GEOFFREY DAVID, reproductive endocrinologist, surgeon; b. Ottawa, Ont., Can., Sept. 16, 1946; came to U.S., 1978, naturalized, 1986; s. Geoffrey Peter Adamson and Anne Marian Allan; m. Rosemary C. Oddie, Apr. 28, 1973; children: Stephanie, Rebecca, Eric. BSc with honors, Trinity Coll., Toronto, Can., 1969; MD, U. Toronto, 1973. Diplomate Am. Bd. Ob-Gyn., Am. Bd. Laser Surgery; cert. Bd. Reproductive Endocrinology. Resident in ob-gyn. Toronto Gen. Hosp., 1973-77, fellow in ob-gyn., 1977-78; fellow reproductive endocrinology Stanford (Calif.) U. Med. Ctr., 1978-80; practice medicine specializing in infertility Los Gatos, Calif., 1980-84; instr. Stanford U. Sch. Medicine, 1980-84; clin. asst. prof. Stanford U. Sch. Medicine, Calif., 1984-92; clin. assoc. prof. Stanford U. Sch. Medicine, 1992-95, clin. prof., 1995—; assoc. clin. prof. Sch. Medicine U. Calif., San Francisco, 1992—; founder, chmn., CEO Advanced Reproductive Care Inc., Palo Alto, Calif., 1997—. Mem. editl. adv. bd. Can. Doctor mag., 1977-83, numerous others; contbr. numerous articles to sci. jours., mags.; editor: (textbook) Endoscopic Management of Gynecologic Disease, 1996. Ontario Ministry of Health fellow, 1977-78. Fellow ACS, Royal Coll. Surgeons Can., Am. Coll. Ob-Gyns.; mem. AAAS, AMA, Am. Assn. Gynecol. Laparoscopists (adv. bd.), Am. Soc. Reproductive Medicine (numerous coms.), Soc. Reproductive Endocrinologists (charter), Soc. Reproductive Surgeons (charter, bd. dirs., sec., treas., v.p., pres., past pres.), Soc. Assisted Reproductive Tech. (treas., dir., v.p., pres.), Pacific Coast Reproductive Soc. (dir., sec., v.p., pres.), Pacific Coast Ob-Gyn. Soc., Soc. Gynecologic Surgeons, San Francisco Ob-Gyn. Soc., Bay Area Reproductive Endocrinologists Soc. (founding pres.), Gynecol. Laser Soc., N.Y. Acad. Scis., Shufelt Gynecol. Soc., Peninsula Gynecol. Soc. (past pres.), Calif. Med. Assn., San Mateo County Med. Assn., Santa Clara County Med. Assn., Am. Fedn. Clin. Rsch., Nat. Resolve (bd. dirs. 1992—, sec., treas.), Can. Assn. Interns and Residents (hon. life, pres. 1977-79, bd. dirs. 1974-79, rep. AMA resident physician sect. 1978-79, rep. Can. Med. Protective Assn. 1975-78, rep. Can. Med. Assn. 1975-78, Disting. Svc. award 1980), Profl. Assn. Interns and Residents Ont. (bd. dirs. 1973-76, v.p. 1974-75, pres. 1975-76), Royal Coll. Physicians and Surgeons Can. (com. exams. 1977-80), Ont. Med. Assn. (sec. interns and residents sect. 1973-74). Avocations: hiking, ice hockey, skiing. Office: 540 University Ave Ste 200 Palo Alto CA 94301-1929

ADCOCK, BETTY-LEE, real estate brokerage executive; b. Waldo, Kans., Nov. 19, 1921; d. Ralph Preston and Hazel (Pangburn) Beatty; m. Charles Warren Adcock, Feb. 17, 1945; 1 dau., Roberta Lee. B.S. in Journalism, Kans. State Coll., 1946; grad. Realtors Inst. Lic. real estate broker, Hawaii; cert. residential specialist, residential broker. Mem. pub. relations staff Boeing Airplane Co., Wichita, Kans., 1942-45; biographical staff AP, N.Y.C., 1945-46; real estate salesman and broker, Honolulu, 1972—; prin. broker, pres., owner Adcock, Ltd., real estate mktg., Honolulu, 1983—. Recipient Girl Scout Award of Merit, Kitzingen, Germany, 1960, spl. award Am. Cancer Soc., Middlebury, Vt., 1956. Mem. Nat. Assn. Realtors. Hawaii Assn. Realtors, Honolulu Bd. Realtors, Honolulu Zool. Soc., Friends of Waikiki Aquarium, Nat. Trust for Historic Preservation, Honolulu Art Acad., Friends of Iolani Palace, Bishop Mus., Hawaii Hist. Soc., Hawaii Humane Soc., Hist. Hawaii Found., Chi Omega. Republican. Episcopalian. Home and Office: Adcock Ltd 2415 Aha Aina Pl Honolulu HI 96821-1001

ADCOCK, MURIEL W., special education educator; b. Chgo.. BA, U. Calif. Sonoma State, Rohnert Park, 1979. Cert. spl. edn. tchr., Calif., Montessori spl. edn. tchr. Tchr. The Concordia Sch., Concord, Calif., 1980-85; tchr., cons. Tenderloin Community Children's Ctr., San Francisco, 1985-86; adminstr. Assn. Montessori Internat.-USA, San Francisco, 1988, tchr., advisor, 1989—; course asst. Montessori Spl. Edn. Inst., San Francisco, 1985-87, tchr. spl. edn., 1990, tchr. cons., 1991—, rschr. 1992—. Contbr. articles to profl. jour. Sec. Internat. Forum World Affairs Coun., San Francisco, 1990-95, program chair, 1993-95. Mem. ASCD, Nat. Assn. Edn. Young Children, Am. Orthopsychiat. Assn., Am. Assn. Mental Retardation, Assn. Montessori Internat., N.Am. Montessori Tchrs. Assn., Assn. Childhood Edn. Internat., Smithsonian Assocs., N.Y. Acad. Scis., Nat. Geog. Soc., Menninger Found. Avocations: cross-cultural communication, sustainable development, educational systems design, human and organizational development. Office: PO Box 424519 San Francisco CA 94142-4519

ADCOCK, RONALD WADE, artist, sculptor; b. Fairbanks, Alaska, U.S., June 18, 1946; s. Ralph Henry and Irma Irene (Fitz) A.; children: Sean Knute Wade Adcock, Laura Alexandra Adcock. BA, U. Washington, 1972, BFA, 1972; MFA, U. of Washington, 1974. scale model maker, Rauda Scale Models, Seattle, 1971-1975, furniture designer, Lundstead Designs, Kent, 1975-1985, landscape architect, freelance, Fayetteville, Tenn. Author: Blue Maze Trilogy, Sculptor: Sunrise/Sunset, 1986. Recipient Commander's award King County Dept. Pub. Safety, 1992, Poncho scholar, Seattle, 1992-94. Avocations: designing and building water falls in butterfly gardens, drummer for

ADDAMS, ROBERT JEAN, finance executive; b. Salt Lake City, Sept. 24, 1942; s. Harvey J. and Virginia (Dutson) A.; m. Elizabeth Addams; children: Ryan, Kelley, Amy, Michael. BS, U. Utah, 1968, MBA, 1969. Dir. budgets & cost control Western Airlines, Inc., L.A., 1976-80; v.p., gen. mgr. Ball Bros., Inc., Everette, Wash., and Anchorage, 1980-82; pres., cons. Addams & Assocs., Woodinville, Wash., 1982-89; contr. Lafayette Fisheries, Seattle, 1990-93; CFO Internat. Inetegrators, Seattle; CFO Mountain High Knitting, Seattle and San Diego, 1995-98; v.p. ISSI Bus. Solutions, Bothell, Wash., 1999—. Author: Care and Handling of Wetsalted Cod Fish, 1984; also articles on budgeting and business plans to nat. monthly newsletter. Scoutmaster, Explorer advisor Gt. Salt Lake and L.A. councils Boy Scouts Am., 1973-75; served 2-yr. mission for Ch. Jesus Christ Latter-day Saints, 1962-64. Served with U.S. Army, 1961-62. Named Outstanding Grad. Coll. Bus. 1969, Beehive Honor Soc. 1969. Mem. U. Utah Alumni Assn. (pres. So. Calif. chpt. 1976-80), U. Utah Coll. of Bus. Alumni (pres. So. Calif. group 1978-79), Alpha Kappa Psi. Republican. Home: 3028 177th Ave NE Redmond WA 98052

ADDIS, RICHARD BARTON, lawyer; b. Columbus, Ohio, April 9, 1929; s. Wilbur Jennings and Leila Olive (Grant) A.; m. Marguerite C. Christjohn, Feb. 9, 1957; children: Jacqueline Carol, Barton David. BA, Ohio State U., 1954, JD, 1955. Bar: Ohio 1956, U.S. Dist. Ct. (no. dist.) Ohio 1957, N.Mex. 1963, U.S. Dist. Ct. N.Mex. 1963, Laguna Pueblo (N.Mex.) Tribal Ct. 1986. Pvt. practice, Canton, Ohio, 1956-63, Albuquerque, 1963—, Laguna Pueblo, Navajo Nation, 1986—. Co-developer The Woodlands Subdivsn., Albuquerque; co-owner Cerro del Oro Mine, Valencia County, N.Mex., 1977—. With USMC, 1946-48, 50-52. Mem. Ohio Bar Assn., N.Mex. Bar Assn. Office: PO Box 25923 Albuquerque NM 87125-0923

ADDIS, THOMAS HOMER, III, professional golfer; b. San Diego, Nov. 30, 1945; s. Thomas H. and Martha J. (Edwards) A.; student Foothill Jr. Coll., 1963, Grossmont Jr. Coll., 1965; degree in profl. golf mgmt. (hon.) Ferris State U.; m. Susan Tera Buckley, June 13, 1966; children: Thomas Homer IV, Bryan Michael. Head golf profl., mgr. Sun Valley Golf Course, La Mesa, Calif., 1966-67; head golf profl., dir. golf Singing Hills Country Club and Lodge, 1969-98, sr. v.p. Golfstar Mgmt., 1998—; pres. PGA of Am., 1994-96; gen. chmn. Nat. Jr. Golf championship U.S. Golf Assn., 1973, 89; lectr.; owner Golf Cons. & Design, Rocky Mountain Chocolate Factory, Mammoth. Pres. Calif. State Open, 1980-84; chmn. Nat. Com. Liaison for Physically Challenged, 1984-88; dir. Cuyamaca Coll. Found. Recipient Retailer award Golf Industry mag., 1985; named to Lady Aztec San Diego State U. Hall of Fame. Mem. PGA (pres. San Diego chpt. 1978-79; pres. sect. 1980-82, bd. dirs. sect. 1974-90, speaker, chmn. mem. svc. com. 1986-87, bd. dirs. San Diego sect. 1974-90, assn. coord. bus. schs. and seminars, named Profl. of Yr. So. Calif. sect. 1979, 89, Horton Smith award So. Calif. sect. 1980-81, 89, PGA Golf Profl. of Yr. 1989, Nat. Horton Smith award 1981, Resort Merchandiser of Yr., So. Calif. sect. 1978, 83, mem. nat. bd. control 1978-85, chmn. nat. bd. control 1991-92, membership com. 1978, 89-90, nat. edn. com. 1980-85, 89-90, nat. bd. dirs., 1986-88, rules com. 1986-90, championship com. 1986—, hon. life mem. So. Calif. sect. and San Diego PGA, sec. PGA Am. 1991, 92, v.p. PGA Am. 1993, 94, pres. 1994-96), So. Calif. PGA Hall of Fame, Nat. Golf Found. (Joe Graffis award, 1988) Nat. Amputee Golf Assn. (hon. mem.), San Diego Jr. Golf Assn. (pres., 1996), Assn. Golf Educators, Golf Collector's Soc., Rotary. Author articles. Office: Golfstar Mgmt 170 S Main St Ste 1600 Salt Lake City UT 84101-1605

ADDISON, ALICE ADAMS, international language educator; b. Washington, Sept. 14, 1946; d. John Bucher and Alvadee (Hutton) Adams; m. William Phillip Deibler, Sept. 3, 1967 (div. 1972); m. Anthony Thomas Addison, Aug. 25, 1973. BA in History, U. Calif., Santa Barbara, 1968; MS, Pepperdine U., 1979; PhD in Linguistics, Georgetown U., 1983. Cert. life std. secondary tchr., cert. life bilingual cross-cultural specialist, cert. life cmty. coll. instr., cert. in adminstrv. svcs., Calif. Clerical positions U.S. senators, reps., lobby orgns., Washington, 1964-69; student tchr. Spanish La Colina Jr. H.S., Santa Barbara, 1969; tchr. humanities, ESL, publs. Santa Barbara H.S., 1970-73; tchr. internat. langs. Santa Maria (Calif.) H.S., 1973—; title VII/migrant dir. Santa Maria H.S. Dist., 1985-90; publs. editl. asst. U. Calif., Santa Barbara, 1964-69, extension instr., 1983—; vis. scholar Georgetown U., 1985; ednl. cons. various schs. and univs., 1972—; ednl. cons., author/editor various docs. Calif. State Dept. Edn., Sacramento, 1990-92; elected mem. coun. Shared Decision Making, Santa Maria H.S., 1997—; editor/advisor yearbooks Santa Barbara H.S., U. Calif. Contbr. articles to various publs. Life mem. South County Hist. Soc., Arroyo Grande, Calif., 1975—. U.S. Dept. Edn. Title VII grantee, 1985-90; recipient Alumni Achievement award Grad. Sch. Georgetown U., 1983, NABE award for Outstanding Dissertations in Bilingual Edn., 1984; Woman Plus publicity honoree Santa Maria Times, 1987. Fellow Am. Bd. Master Educators (disting.); mem. ASCD, AAUW (v.p. Pismo Beach/Arroyo Grande chpt. 1996-97), TESOL (presenter, mem. coms., Summer Inst. fellow), Assn. Calif. Sch. Adminstrs., Calif. Assn. Bilingual Edn. (presenter), Ctrl. Coast Assn. Lang. Profls. (pres., bd. dirs.), Calif. Assn. TESOL (pres., various previous offices), Altrusa (pres., various offices 1982—), Phi Delta Kappa, Kappa Delta Pi. Democratic. Avocations: language, linguistics, and brain rsch. reading, fishing, international travel, gardening, local history.

ADDISON, WALLACE LLOYD, aerospace engineer; b. Greenville, S.C., June 26, 1965; s. Lloyd Brandford and Patricia Ann (Priester) A. BS in Aerospace Engring., U. Ala., 1988; MS in Adminstrn., Cen. Mich. U., 1995. Mgr. reliability cost program ALD/OAF, Wright-Patterson AFB, Ohio, 1989-90; mgr. F-16 reliability/cost program ASD/YPLI, Wright-Patterson AFB, Ohio, 1990-91, mgr. F-16 reliability and maintainability program, 1991-92; mgr. Korean fighter program ASC/YPX-KFP, Wright-Patterson AFB, Ohio, 1993; ASC/YC C-17 lend integrated engr. Wright-Patterson AFB, Ohio, 1994-95; fellow The Boeing Co., Seattle, 1995—. Active Boy Scouts Am., 1975—. Capt. USAF, 1988—. Mem. AIAA, U. Ala. Nat. Alumni Assn., Capstone Engring. Soc., Nat. Eagle Scout Assn., K.C. Roman Catholic. Office: Boeing Def & Space Group M/S:3C-30 PO Box 3999 Seattle WA 98124-2499

ADELEKAN, PATRICIA ANN, school administrator; b. Columbus, Ohio, Mar. 13, 1942; d. Arthur H. and Betty Jane Isbell; children: Adebola, Adetokunbo, Aderemi, Adegboyega. BA, Ohio State U., 1966; MA, U. San Francisco, 1975; PhD, U. Ibadan, 1983. Cert. coll. adminstr., secondary tchr. Tchr. various schs., Hartford, Conn. and Oakland, Calif., 1968-75; v.p. Lagos State Coll. Edn., Nigeria, 1976-80; dept. head Ogun State Poly. U., Nigeria, 1980-84; rsch. specialist Sacramento City (Calif.) Unified Sch. Dist., 1985-87; lectr. Sierra Coll., Rocklin, Calif., 1988-89; founder, pres. Youth-on-the-Move, Inc., Sacramento, 1986—; cons. Gifted and Talented Edn., Sacramento, 1985-86; columnist Sacramento Observer, 1987—; founder Youth-on-the-Move, Inc. Prep. Acad. and Family Learning Ctr., 1992, Youth-on-the-Move, Inc. African Am. Multicultural Hall of Fame, 1993. Author: Hall of Fame Educators, 1993, Multicultural Hall of Fame Educators, 1993, 94, 95; prodr. Youth Talk, a live youth radio program, 1993; editor: Multicultural Hall of Fame Educators, 1995, numerous articles; contbr. articles to profl. jours.; pub./editor Youth-on-the-News, monthly newspaper, 1989—. V.p. YWCA, Sacramento, 1988-89; commr. County Children's Commn., Sacremento, 1989—; mem. Leadership Sacramento, 1988-89; program coord. World Exch., 1991—; chairperson Juneteenth Art & Music Festival, 1991-95. Recipient Cert. of Recognition award, Assemblyman Norman Waters, 1981, Proclamation award City of Sacramento Mayor, 1989, Plaque of Achievement award, 1989, Love and Help Children award, Luminary of the Yr. award Coors, 1992, Outstanding Woman Cmty. Leader YWCA, 1991-95, over 25 awards and honors, 1992—; named to African Am. Educators' Hall of Fame, 1993. Mem. Calif. Tchr.'s Assn., Nat. Assn. French Tchrs., Nat. Mensa Soc., AAUW (chair edn. com.), NAFE, Nat. Coun. of Negro Women, Inc. (life), Friends of Marva Collins (founder), Phi Delta Kappa. Avocations: research, writing, public speaking, youth advocate, travelling. Home: 2340 S Manor Dr Sacramento CA 95822-6138

ADELMAN, CAROL, artist; b. Bronx, NY, June 8, 1960; d. Stanley Murray and Norma (Rabinowitz) A. BFA, Carnegie Mellon U., 1982; MFA, U. Wash., 1997. Edn. staff The Phillips Collections, Washington, 1985-88; dir. gallery accts. Mus. & Arts Washington, 1986-91; dep. dir. The Glass Gallery, Bethesda, Md., 1994-95; instr. Pratt Fine Art Ctr., Seattle, 1998; lectr. U. Wash., 1998—; contbg. writer Sculpture Mag., Seattle, 1999—; GPSS rep. Wash. State Arts Commn., U. Wash. Pub. Art Com., Seattle, 1995-97; lectr. Arts and Learning Ctr., U. Md., College Park, 1997, U. Wash. Sch. Art, 1998; artist resident Vt. Studio Ctr., 1998. Exhbns. include Osuna Gallery, Washington, 1993, Wohlfarth Gallery, Provincetown, Mass., 1993, Emerson Gallery, McLean, Va., 1995, Henry Art Gallery, Seattle, 1997, Bowery Gallery, N.Y.C., 1997. W.W. Stout fellow; U. Wash. Spl. Projects grantee, U. Wash. Sch. Art, 1997, Vt. Studio Ctr. grantee, 1998; Fulbright Finalist, Netherlands, 1998, 99. Mem. Coll. Art Assn., Jackson Art Ctr. (media officer 1994-95). Home: PO Box 45021 Seattle WA 98145-0021

ADELMAN, IRMA GLICMAN, economics educator; b. Cernowitz, Rumania, Mar. 14, 1930; came to U.S., 1949, naturalized, 1955; d. Jacob Max and Raissa (Ettinger) Glicman; m. Frank L. Adelman, Aug. 16, 1950 (div. 1979); 1 son, Alexander. BS, U. Calif., Berkeley, 1950, MA, 1951, PhD, 1955. Teaching assoc. U. Calif., Berkeley, 1955-56; instr. U. Calif., 1956-57, lectr. with rank asst. prof., 1957-58; vis. asst. prof. Mills Coll., 1958-59; acting asst. prof. Stanford, 1959-61, asst. prof., 1961-62; assoc. prof. Johns Hopkins, Balt., 1962-65; prof. econs. Northwestern U., Evanston, Ill., 1966-72, U. Md., 1972-78; prof. econs. and agrl. econs. U. Calif. at Berkeley, 1979-94; prof. emeritus, 1994—; cons. divsn. indsl. devel. UN, 1962-63, AID U.S. Dept. State, Washington, 1963-72, World Bank, 1968—, ILO, Geneva,

1973—. Author: Theories of Economic Growth and Development, 1961, (with A. Pepelasis and L. Mears), Economic Development: Analysis and Case Studies, 1961, (with Eric Thorbecke) The Theory and Design of Economic Development, 1966, (with C.T. Morris) Society, Politics and Economic Development—A Quantitative Approach, 1967, Practical Approaches to Development Planning-Korea's Second Five Year Plan, 1969, (with C.T. Morris) Economic Development and Social Equity in Developing Countries, 1973, (with Sherman Robinson) Planning for Income Distribution, 1977-78, (with C. T. Morris) Comparative Patterns of Economic Growth, 1850-1914, 1987, (J. Edward Taylor) Village Economies: Design, Estimation and Application of Village Wide Economic Models, 1996, Institutions and Development Strategies: Selected Essays of Irma Adelman Vol. I, 1994, Vol. II, 1994, Selected Essays (in Spanish), 1994, (with Irma and Song Byong Nak) The South Korean Miracle: How Replicable Is It?, 1999. Fellow Center Advanced Study Behavioral Scis., 1970-71; named Women's Hall Fame U. Calif., Berkeley, 1994. Fellow Am. Acad. Arts and Scis., Econometric Soc., Royal Soc. Encouragement Arts, Mfgs. & Commerce (Berkeley citation 1996); mem. Am. Econ. Assn. (mem. exec. com., v.p. 1969-71). Office: Univ Calif Dept Agr & Natural Resources 207 Giannini Hall Spc 3310 Berkeley CA 94720-3310

ADELMAN, JONATHAN REUBEN, political science educator, consultant; b. Washington, Oct. 30, 1948; s. Benjamin and Kitty (Sandler) A.; m. Agota Kuperman, Aug. 3, 1997. BA, Columbia U., 1969, MA, 1972, M in Philosophy, 1974, PhD, 1976. Vis. asst. prof. Columbia U., N.Y.C., 1977; vis. asst. prof. U. Ala., Tuscaloosa, 1977-78; asst. prof. Grad. Sch. Internat. Studies U. Denver, 1978-85, assoc. prof., 1985-92, prof. polit. sci., 1992—; sr. rsch. analyst Sci. Applications, Inc., Denver, 1981-87, 96—; hon. prof. People's U., Beijing, 1996—, Beijing U., 1996; cons., 1988-89, 96—, Lady Davis vis. assoc. prof. Hebrew U., Jerusalem, 1986; vis. fellow Soviet Acad. Scis., 1989, 90, Chinese Inst. Contemporary Internat. Rels., Beijing, 1988, People's U., Beijing, 1990, 94, 96, 97, 98; vis. prof. Beijing U., 1989, 98, U. Haifa, Israel, 1990; vis. spkr. Soviet Acad. Scis., 1990, Barcelona (Spain) U. and Complutense U., 1990, Cambridge (Eng.) U., 1991, Nat. Taiwan U., 1998; vis. lectr., Japan, India, Hong Kong, Yugoslavia, Spain, 1990, 91, Germany, 1991, Bulgaria, 1991; vis. spkr. Conf. for Study of European Ideas, Aalborg U., Denmark, 1992; vis. prof. People's U., Beijing, 1990, 97, Janus Pannonius U., Pecs, Hungary, 1981. Author: The Revolutionary Armies, 1980, Revolution, Armies and War, 1986, Prelude to the Cold War: Tsarist, Soviet and U.S. Armies in Two World Wars, 1988, Torrents of Spring: Soviet and Post Soviet Politics, 1994; co-author: The Dynamics of Soviet Foreign Policy, 1988; editor: Communist Armies in Politics, 1982, Terror and Communist Politics, 1984, Superpowers and Revolution, 1986; co-editor: Contemporary Soviet Military Affairs: The Legacy World War II, 1989; contbr. numerous articles in fieod to profl. jours. Charles Phelps Taft fellow U. Cin., 1976-77; Am. Philos. Soc. grantee, 1980. Mem. Am. Polit. Sci. Assn., Am. Assn. Advancement Slavic Studies. Democrat. Jewish. Office: U Denver Grad Sch Internat Studies Denver CO 80208

ADELMAN, RICK, professional basketball coach; b. June 16, 1946; m. Mary Kay Adelman; children: Kathryn Mary, Laura, R.J., David. Master's, Loyola Marymount U. Profl. basketball player San Diego, 1968-70; profl. basketball player Portland (Oreg.) Trail Blazers, 1970-73, asst. coach, 1983-89, head coach, 1989-94; basketball player Chgo., New Orleans, Kansas City, and Omaha, 1973-75; head coach Chemeketa Community Coll., Salem, Oreg., 1975-83, Golden State Warriors, Oakland, Calif., 1995-97. Office: Sacramento Kings ARCO Arena One Sports Parkway Sacramento CA 95834

ADELSMAN, (HARRIETTE) JEAN, newspaper editor; b. Indpls., Oct. 21, 1944; d. Joe and Beatrice Irene (Samuel) A. BS in Journalism, Northwestern U., 1966, MS in Journalism, 1967. Copy editor Chgo. Sun-Times, 1967-75, fin. news editor, 1975-77, entertainment editor, 1977-80, asst. mng. editor features, 1980-84; now mng. editor Daily Breeze, Torrance, Calif. Office: Daily Breeze 5215 Torrance Blvd Torrance CA 90503-4077*

ADELSON, MERV LEE, entertainment and communication industry executive; b. Los Angeles, Oct. 23, 1929; s. Nathan and Pearl (Schwarzman) A.; m. Thea Nesis, May 25, 1993; 1 child, Lexi Rose; children from previous marriage: Ellen, Gary, Andrew. Student, Menlo Park Jr. Coll. Pres. Markettown Supermarket and Builders Emporium, Las Vegas, 1953-63; mng. ptnr. Paradise Devel., Las Vegas, 1958—; pres. Realty Holdings, 1962—, La Costa, Inc., 1963-87; chmn. bd. dirs. Lorimar Inc., Culver City, Calif., 1969-86; chmn. bd. dirs., chief exec. officer Lorimar Telepictures Corp., Culver City, 1986-89; vice chmn. Warner Communications, 1989—; chmn. East-West Capital Assocs., Inc., 1989—; bd. dirs. Time-Warner Inc. Co-founder Nathan Adelson Hospice Found. Recipient Sherill Corwin Human Relations award Am. Jewish Com., 1987. Mem. Am. Film Inst. (trustee), Am. Mus. of Moving Images (trustee), Entertainment Industries Council (trustee), Acad. Motion Pictures Arts and Scis., Acad. TV Arts and Sciences, Nat. Acad. Cable Programming, Alliance for Capital Access (bd. dirs.), Com. Publicly Owned Cos. (bd. dirs.).

ADEY, WILLIAM ROSS, physician; b. Adelaide, Australia, Jan. 31, 1922; s. William James and Constance Margaret (Weston) A.; m. Alwynne Sidney Morris (div. 1970); children: John, Susan, Geoffrey. MB and BS, U. Adelaide, Australia, 1943, MD, 1949. Sr. lectr. and reader, Dept. Anatomy U. Adelaide, Australia, 1947-53; sr. lectr., Dept. Anatomy U. Melbourne, Australia, 1955-56; prof. anatomy and physiology UCLA, 1957-77; dir. Space Biology Lab UCLA Space Biology Lab., 1965-77; dir. rsch. VA Med. Ctr., Loma Linda, Calif., 1977-97; adj. prof. biochemistry U. Calif., Riverside, 1997—; cons. Office of Sci. and Tech. Policy, Washington,. 1964—, NIH, 1961—, NAS, 1965—. Author: Nonlinear Electrodynamics in Biological Systems, 1984, Magnetic Resonance Imaging of the Brain, Head and Neck, 1984. Surgeon lt. Australian Navy, 1944-46, South Pacific. Fellow IEEE, Royal Soc. and Nuffield Found. (London), AAAS, Am. Electroencephalographic Soc., Royal Soc. Medicine (London), Am. Assn. Neurolog. Surgeons. Avocations: radiophysics, radioastronomy, marathon running, backpacking. Home: Rte 1 Box 615 31866 3rd Ave Redlands CA 92374-8237*

ADISA, OPAL PALMER, ethnic studies educator; b. Kingston, Jamaica, Nov. 6, 1954; came to U.S., 1970; d. Orlando and Catherine (James) Palmer; children: Shola Adisa-Farrar, Jawara Adisa-Farrar, Teju Adisa-Farrar. BA in Comm., CUNY-Hunter Coll., 1975; MA in English, San Francisco State U., 1981, MA in Drama, 1986; PhD in Ethnic Studies and Lit., U. Calif., Berkeley, 1992. Head tchr. Booker T. Washington Child Devel. Ctr., San Francisco, 1978-79; tchr., counselor Lucinda Weeks Ctr., San Francisco, 1979-81; instr. poetry City Coll. San Francisco, 1980-84; poet, curriculum writer Oakland (Calif.) Mus., 1986-92; lectr. poetry, lit. studies San Francisco State U., 1981-87, instr. summer writing and reading program, 1987-88, 90, 92-93; lectr. writing English dept. St. Mary's Coll., 1993; lectr. writing and lit. Holy Name's Coll., 1993, 94; lectr. dept. African Studies U. Calif., Berkeley, 1978-93, vis. prof., 1994-96; vis. prof. Stanford U., 1995; assoc. prof., chair ethnic studies/cultural diversity program Calif. Coll. of Arts, Oakland, 1993—; mentor summer rsch. opportunity program U. Calif., Berkeley, summer 1990, Organizer, host poetry tribute to Audre Lorde, 1993, co-chair exhbn. on Jamaica, Doe Libr., 1993; co-organizer, mem. conf. planning com. Calif. Coll. Arts and Crafts, 1994, mem. ednl. adv. bd., 1994, faculty mentor, 1993-96, mem. disting. faculty task force, 1994—, mem. various coms.; writer-in-residence Headlands Ctr for Arts, Sausalito, Calif., 1996; cons., writer Reading for Real lit. project Developmental Studies Ctr., 1991-92; participant tng. Stir Fry Prodn., Berkeley, 1995, Nat. Coalition Bldg. Inst., 1996, Nat. Conf. on Race and Ethnicity in Am. Higher Edn., Atlanta, 1994; presenter, reader various instns., most recently U. Calif., San Francisco, 1995, U. Miami, Coral Gables, 1995, Mills Coll., 1995, Miami Book Fair Internat., 1995, Macy's San Francisco Celebration of Poetry Month, 1996, Buchhandlung Schoningh, Wurzburg, Germany, 1996, Intersection for Arts, San Francisco, 1996, U. Ill., Carbondale, 1997, U. Mo., St. Louis and Columbia, 1997; faculty mentor San Francisco State U., 1983-86; judge ann. fiction competition San Francisco Bay Guardian, 1994, 95; judge artist residency program Villa Montalvo, 1994; judge residency in lit. program Headlands Ctr. for Arts, 1990; judge screenplay competition Black Filmmakers Hall of Fame, 1991. Author: (children's book) Pina The Many-Eyed Fruit, 1985; Bake-Face and Other Guava Stories, 1986, Brit. edit., 1989; (novel) It Begins With Tears, 1997; (poetry collection with D. Major) Traveling Women, 1989; (poetry) Tamarind and Mango Pomen, 1992 (Joseph Miles Lit. award Oakland PEN 1992), video performance edit., 1995; (video poetry performance) Despair Series, 1994; interviewee, contbr. essays, stories, articles, revs. to lit. publs.; included in: Directory of American Poets and Fiction Writers, 1992, Black Authors and Illustrators of Books for Children and Young Adults, 1996, Strong Hearts, Inspired Minds: 22 Interviews with Artists Who are Mothers, 1996; author, performer (poetry/jazz album)Firece Love, 1992; participant visual arts exhbns. at African Am. Hist. Soc., San Francisco, 1983-94, Montgomery Gallery, Pomona (Calif.) Coll., 1995, Lopdell Ho. Gallery, Waitakere City, New Zealand, 1996, Hearts Art Gallery, St. Mary's Coll., 1996. Mem. adv. bd. Defermery Pk., Oakland, 1992-94; chair music com., bd. dirs. Chabot PTA, 1994-95; chair Joseph Henry Jackson and Jane D. Phelan Lit. awards, 1997; mem. Beat Culture consortium Fine Art Mus., San Francisco, 1996; cons. Families Learning Together poetry project Mayhem Prodns., San Francisco, 1995—. Recipient 3rd pl. award ann. poetry contest Am. Poetry Assn., 1982, Merit cert. Jamaica Festival Lit. Competition, 1982, Bronze medal, 1984, Pushcart prize for short story, 1987, Disting. Bay Area Woman Writer award/Calif. Legis. Assembly Cert. of Recognition, Nat. Women's Polit. Caucus, 1991, Daily News prize for best poems in Caribbean Writer, U. V.I., St. Croix, 1995, Canute A. Brodhurst prize for story in Caribbean Writer, 1996; named Master Folk Artist for Storytelling, Calif. Arts Coun., 1991-92; honoree Lit. Women, Pleasant, Calif., 1994; recipient Caribbean Writer Summer Inst., U. Miami, Coral Gables, Fla., summer 1995. Mem. Nat. Assn. for Ethnic Studies, Soc. for Study of Multi-Ethnic Lit. of U.S., No. Assn. African Am. Storytellers, Caribbean Assn. for Feminist Rsch. and Action (diasporic rep. 1991-93), Calif. Poets in Schs. (chair employment com., bd. dirs. 1989-91), Phi Beta Kappa. Home: PO Box 10625 Oakland CA 94610-0625 Office: Calif Coll Arts and Crafts 5212 Broadway Oakland CA 94618-1426

ADKINS, BEN FRANK, management and engineering consultant; b. West Liberty, Ky., Mar. 6, 1938; s. Stuart Kendall Adkins and Dorothy Elizabeth (Shaver) Indes; m. Judith Ann Williams, Mar. 14, 1959; children: Michelle Rene, Lori Lee. BS in Indsl. Engring., Ariz. State U., 1964; MBA, Western New Eng. Coll., Springfield, Mass., 1971; MS in Systems Mgmt., U. So. Calif., 1983. Registered profl. engr. Enlisted USAF, 1955, commd. 2d lt., 1964, advanced through grades to maj., 1975, ret., 1979; internal cons., mgr. State of Wash., Olympia, 1979-87; mgmt. and engring. cons. Olympia, 1987-88; sr. rsch. sci. Battelle Pacific N.W. Labs., Richland, Wash., 1988-89; mng. prin. Ben Adkins & Assocs., Olympia, 1989—. Decorated Bronze star USAF. Mem. Inst. Indsl. Engrs. (sr. mem., bd. dirs. Puget Sound chpt. 1984-86, asst. dir. and dir. govt. div. 1979-83, v.p. Washington chpt. 1969-76). Avocations: skiing, sailing, photography, reading. Home: 6606 Miner Dr SW Olympia WA 98512-7257 Office: Ben Adkins & Assocs PO Box 7613 Olympia WA 98507-7613

ADLER, ADRIENNE EDNA-LOIS, art dealer, gallery owner, publisher; b. Stillwater, Okla., Mar. 9, 1947; d. Wayne L. Brake and Lois K. (Fisk) Kyle; m. Gary G. Wilcox, Aug. 4, 1964 (div. 1974); children: Troy V., Trisha J.; m. Frederick Peter Adler, Oct. 11, 1991. Butler County Jr. Coll., Richland Coll. From asst. to pres. H.J. Gruy & Assocs., Dallas, 1972-75; from asst. to v.p. econs. dept. DeGolyer and MacNaughton, Dallas, 1975-80; sales mgr. Telecom. Specialists, Inc., Dallas, 1980-85; dir. various art galleries in Calif., Wash., Colo., Tex. & Hawaii, 1985-90; owner Genestar Internat., Santa Barbara, Calif., 1990-95, Galerie Adrienne & Adrienne Editions, San Francisco, La Jolla,, San Diego, 1995—. Chmn. tri-counties adv. bd. Jefferson Ctr. Character Edn., Santa Barbara 1993-95; v.p., pres. women's bd. Santa Barbara Mus. Art, 1995; v.p., chmn. of ball Symphony League, Santa Barbara, 1994-95; advocate, mem. Calif. Assn. Mentally Ill, 1993—. Mem. NAFE, The Commonwealth Club Calif., San Francisco Mus. Art, World Affairs Coun. No. Calif., San Diego Mus. Art, Contemporary Art Mus. San Diego. Avocations: walking, reading, theatre, symphony, opera. Office: Galerie Adrienne and Adrienne Editions 377 Geary St San Francisco CA 94102-1801

ADLER, CHARLES SPENCER, psychiatrist; b. N.Y.C., Nov. 27, 1941; s. Benjamin H. and Anne (Greenfield) A.; m. Sheila Noel Morrissey, Oct. 8, 1966 (dec.); m. Peggy Dolan Bean, Feb. 23, 1991. BA, Cornell U., 1962; MD, Duke U., 1966. Diplomate Nat. Bd. Med. Examiners, Am. Bd. Psychiatry and Neurology. Intern Tucson Hosps. Med. Edn. Program, 1966-67; psychiat. resident U. Colo. Med. Sch., Denver, 1967-70; pvt. practice medicine specializing in psychiatry and psychosomatic medicine Denver, 1970—; chief divsn. psychiatry Rose Med. Ctr, 1982-87; co-founder Applied Biofeedback Inst., Denver, 1972-75; prof. pro tempore Cleve. Clinic, 1977; asst. clin. prof. psychiatry U. Colo. Med. Ctr., 1986—, chief psychiatry and psychophysiology Colo. Neurology and Headache Ctr., 1988-95; med. dir. Colo. Ctr. for Biobehavioral Health, Boulder, 1994—; bd. dirs. Acad. Cert. Neurotherapists. Author: (with Gene Stanford and Sheila M. Adler) We Are But a Moment's Sunlight, 1976, (with Sheila M. Adler and Russell Packard) Psychiatric Aspects of Headache, 1987; contbr. (with S. Adler) sect. biofeedback med. and health ann. Ency. Britannica, 1986; chpts. to books, articles to profl. jours.; mem. editorial bd. Cephalalgia: an Internat. Jour. of Headache, Headache Quar. Emeritus mem. Citizen's Adv Bd. Duke U. Ctr. Aging and Human Devel. Recipient Award of Recognition, Nat. Migraine Found., 1981; N.Y. State regents scholar, 1958-62. Fellow Am. Psychiat. Assn.; mem. AAAS (rep. of AAPB to med. sect. com.), Am. Assn. Study Headache, Internat. Headache Soc. (chmn. subcom. on classifying psychiat. headaches), Am. Acad. Psychoanalysis (sci. assoc.), Colo. Psychiat. Soc., Biofeedback Soc. Colo. (pres. 1977-78), Assn. for Applied Psychophysiology and Biofeedback (rep. to AAAS, chmn. ethics com. 1983-87, bd. dirs. 1990-93, Sheila M. Adler cert. honor 1988). Jewish. Office: 955 Eudora St Apt 1605 Denver CO 80220-4341

ADLER, ERWIN ELLERY, lawyer; b. Flint, Mich., July 22, 1941; s. Ben and Helen M. (Schwartz) A.; m. Stephanie Ruskin, June 8, 1967; children: Lauren, Michael, Jonathan. B.A., U. Mich., 1963, LL.M., 1967; J.D., Harvard U., 1966. Bar: Mich. 1966, Calif. 1967. Assoc. Pillsbury, Madison & Sutro, San Francisco, 1967-73; assoc. Lawler, Felix & Hall, L.A., 1973-76, ptnr., 1977-80; ptnr. Rogers & Wells, L.A., 1981-83, Richards, Watson & Gershon, L.A., 1983—. Bd. dirs. Hollywood Civic Opera Assn., 1975-76, Children's Scholarships Inc., 1979-80. Mem. ABA (vice chmn. appellate advocacy com. 1982-87), Calif. Bar Assn., Phi Beta Kappa, Phi Kappa Phi. Jewish. Office: Richards Watson & Gershon 333 S Hope St Bldg 38 Los Angeles CA 90071-1406

ADLER, JACK, writer; b. N.Y.C., Aug. 1, 1940; s. Isidor and Anna (Blosser) A.; m. Barbro Kristina Friberg, June 1972; children: Jason, Gregory. BA, U. Calif., Berkeley, 1963. Feature editor Travel Weekly, N.Y.C., 1969-72; freelance columnist, Travel Sect. L.A. Times, 1978-93; leader, Travel Bull. Bd. Prodigy, 1994—; Sysop N.Am. Excite, 1998—. Author travel books including Southern India, Travel Safety (selected by the Libr. of Congress for translation into Braille), Consumer's Guide to Travel, Exploring Historic California, 9 1-act plays, 2 optioned screenplays. Recipient grant as playright Yaddo Found., Saratoga Springs, N.Y., 1966. Mem. Soc. of Am. Travel Writers. Home and Office: 6122 Shadyglade Ave North Hollywood CA 91606-4636

ADLER, LOUISE DECARL, bankruptcy judge; b. 1945. BA, Chatham Coll., Pitts.; JD, Loyola U., Chgo. Bar: Ill., 1970, Calif., 1972. Practicing atty. San Diego, 1972-84; standing trustee Bankruptcy Ct. So. Dist. Calif., San Diego, 1974-79, chief judge bankruptcy, 1996—. Mem. editorial bd. Calif. Bankruptcy Jour., 1991-92. Fellow Am. Coll. Bankruptcy; mem. San Diego County Bar Assn. (chair bus. law study sect. 1979, fed. ct. com. 1983-84), Lawyers Club of San Diego (bd. dirs. 1972-73, treas. 1972-75, sec. 1972-74, v.p. 1974-75), San Diego Bankruptcy Forum (bd. dirs. 1989-92), Nat. Conf. Bankruptcy Judges (bd. dirs. 1989-91, sec. 1992-93, v.p. 1993-94, pres. 1994-95). Office: US Bankruptcy Ct 325 W F St Rm 2 San Diego CA 92101-6017

ADLER, MICHAEL L., lawyer; b. San Francisco, May 10, 1949. BA in Polit. Sci. summa cum laude, UCLA, 1971, JD, 1976; MA, Columbia U., 1973. Bar: Calif. 1977. Extern to Hon. Matthew O. Tobriner Calif. Supreme Ct., 1975; law clerk to Hon. William B. Enright U.S. Dist. Ct. (so. dist.) Calif., 1976-77; mem. Lichter, Grossman, Nichols & Adler, Inc., L.A., 1977-97, now ptnr., 1997—; mem. entertainment law symposium com. UCLA, 1979—; instr. UCLA Extension, 1980. Woodrow Wilson fellow, 1972; Columbia U. Presdl. fellow, 1973. Mem. ABA, State Bar Calif., L.A. County Bar Assn., Beverly Hills Bar Assn., Phi Beta Kappa, Phi Eta Sigma. Office: Lichter Grossman Nichols & Adler Inc 9200 W Sunset Blvd Ste 1200 Los Angeles CA 90069-3507*

ADMASSU, WUDNEH, chemical engineering educator; b. Dilla, Sidamo, Ethiopia, Sept. 17, 1955; came to U.S., 1974; s. Admassu Shallemo and Manalebish Donsa; m. Elizabeth Lemma, Nov. 19, 1991; children: Zelalem, Wudneh. BS, Oreg. State U., Corvallis, 1979; MS, U. Idaho, Moscow, 1980, PhD, 1984. Vis. asst. prof. U. Idaho, Moscow, 1984-86; sr. rsch. engr. Dow Chem., Walnut Creek, Calif., 1986-87, project leader, 1988-91; asst. prof. U. Idaho, Moscow, 1992-94, assoc. prof., 1995—. Mem. AIChE, Am. Soc. Engring. Edn., N.Am. Membrane Soc. Achievements include 4 patents dealing with innovative development of polycarbonate membranes (hollow fibers) for gas separation, especially for nitrogen and oxygen gases. Home: 254 Sunrise Dr Moscow ID 83843-9249 Office: U Idaho Dept Chem Engring Moscow ID 83844-1021

ADOLPH, MARY ROSENQUIST, financial company executive; b. Springfield, Mass., Oct. 7, 1949; d. Jesse Woodson and Doris May (Marquette) Rosenquist; m. Earl Anthony Soares, Mar. 18, 1972 (div. 1982); m. Joseph Edward Adolph, Oct. 3, 1986. Student San Domenico Sch., 1966-68, Dominican Coll., San Rafael, 1967-69, Calif., San Francisco Conservatory of Music, 1968-70; A.A., Coll. of Marin, 1969. Asst. v.p. Western Travelers Life Ins. Co./Putnam Fin. Services, San Rafael, 1970-80; v.p. Unimarc, Ltd., Novato, Calif., 1980-83; v.p. mktg. Western States Monetary Planning Services, Inc., Newhall, Calif., 1983-88; asst. to pres. Fed. Inventory Wholesale, Inc., 1988-90; v.p. E.W. Richardson & Assocs. Inc., Newhall, Calif., 1991-94; v.p. ops. Tri Telic Inc., Santa Rosa, Calif., 1994—. Prodr. Radio Talk Show Financial Information, 1994—. Mem. exec. com. San Marin Valley Homeowners Assn., 1979-81. Mem. Internat. Assn. Fin. Planners, Life Underwriters Assn. Democrat. Roman Catholic. Home: 1127 Neale Dr Santa Rosa CA 95404-3454 Office: Tri Telic Inc 555 5th St Ste 320 Santa Rosa CA 95401-6342

AEBY, KIM, artist, educator; b. Los Alomos, N.Mex., Mar. 7, 1954; s. Jack Warren and Jeanne (clemens) A.; m. Frances L. Wilmeth. BFA, U. N.Mex., 1977; postgrad., U. Wash., 1977; MFA, Brandeis U., 1986. Asst. lighting designer Santa Fe Opera, 1978, Can. Opera Co., Toronto; resident in set lighting, costume design, tech. dir. Performing Arts Collective, Albuquerque, 1979; lighting and set designer Albuquerque Opera Theater, 1981-83; lighting designer House of Bernarda Alba, U. N.Mex., 1982; lighting and set designer The Am. Shaw Festival, Mt. Gretna, Pa., 1985; lighting designer various prodns. Brandeis U., 1984-86; resident lighting designer, tech. dir. South Fla. Shakespeare Festival, Miami, 1986; set and lighting design U. Del., Newark, 1987-88; lighting designer La Compania, Albuquerque, 1991; adj. prof., prodn. mgr. Highlands U., Las Vegas, N.Mex., 1997—. Home: RR 1 Box 385-a Espanola NM 87532-9706 Office: N Mex Highlands U 901 University Ave Las Vegas NM 87701-4072

AFFLECK, JULIE KARLEEN, accountant; b. Upland, Calif., Dec. 23, 1944; d. Karl W. and Juliette O. (Oppegaard) Hall; m. William J. Affleck, Aug. 29, 1964; children: Stephen, Tamara. BS in Bus., U. Colo., 1967; MBA, U. Denver, 1972. CPA, Colo. Cost acct. IBM, Boulder, Colo., 1967-71; audit supr. Ernst & Young, Denver, 1972-79, Rosemary E. Weiss & Co., Denver, 1979-80; ptnr. Affleck, Melaragno, Gilman & Co., Denver, 1980—; tchr. Colo. Soc. CPA's., U. Denver; dir., corp. sec. Better-Way Electric, Inc. Treas., bd. dirs. Bal Swan Children's Ctr. for Handicapped, Broomfield, Colo. Mem. Am. Inst. CPA's., Colo. Soc. CPA's., Am. Soc. Women Accts. (pres. chpt. 1980-81), Nat. Assn. Women Bus. Owners (treas., dir., pres. 1988-89). Republican. Lutheran. Home: 1270 Elmwood Ct Broomfield CO 80020-7609

AFSARY, CYRUS, artist; b. Oct. 18, 1940; s. Mehraban Afsary and Mehrbanoo Jamasbi; children: Bonnie, Jacqui-Mitra. BA in Art, U. Mid. East, 1962, BA in Interior Design, 1971. Resident artist Grand Gallery, Las Vegas, Nev., 1975-80; freelance artist Las Vegas, 1980-88, Scottsdale, Ariz., 1988—; art tchr., Mid. East, 1967-68; participant Artists of Am., 1988, 92. Works featured in Southwest Art, 1987, Midwest Art, 1988, Arts of the West, 1988. Recipient Exceptional award Pastel Soc. Am., 1986; named Best of Show, C.M. Russell Show, 1985, Best Oil, Amarillo Rotary Club Art Show, 1991, chosen Ofcl. Poster Artist, 1991. Mem. Nat. Acad. Western Art (gold medal 1987, Robert Lougheed gold medal 198, silver medal 1989), N.W. Renedzvous Art (merit award 1987). Avocations: photography, reading, music (new age). Studio: PO Box 3217 Scottsdale AZ 85271-3217

AGARWAL, STEVE (SUDHIR), software company executive; b. India, Feb. 16, 1957. BSEE, Banaras Hindu U., Varanasi, India, 1977; MBA, U. Delhi, India, 1988. Project engr. Siemens, New Delhi, 1977-87; regional mgr. Nelco, New Delhi, 1987-93; dir. sales Forth, Inc., Manhattan Beach, Calif., 1993-98; dir. mktg. and sales Safer Systems, Westlake Village, Calif., 1998. Exec. bd. Neighborhood Coun. #3, Simi Valley, Calif., 1997-98. Office: Safer Systems Ste 350 4265 E Thousand Oaks Blvd Westlake Village CA 91362

AGBEJA, TIMOTHY OMOLAYO, pastor; b. Ilesha, Nigeria, Mar. 27, 1954; came to U.S., 1986; s. Abraham Olayiwola and Lydia 'Funso (Folorunso) A.; m. Agnes Adebomi Adeniji, Jan. 31, 1981; children: Gabriel 'Bukola, Victor Oluwabunmi, Timothy Bolade, Lydia Adebisi. Diploma in theology, Assemblies of God Bible Coll., Eng., 1983; BS, Somerset U., 1984; ThM, Internat. Sem., Plymouth, Fla., 1987, LittD (hon.), 1988; PhD, Internat. Sem., Plymouth, 1991. Ordained to ministry Christ Apostolic Ch. Am., 1984. Asst. pastor Christ Apostolic Ch., 1974-84; head dept. Christian edn. Evang. Tng. Coll., Akure, Nigeria, 1984-86; pastor Christ Apostolic Ch., Miami, Fla., 1986-88, N.Y.C., 1988-90, L.A., 1990—. Author: Christianity: Life Not Religion, 1990. Home: 5612 59th Ave Riverdale MD 20737-2618 Office: Christ Apostolic Ch PO Box 19340A Los Angeles CA 90019-1340

AGERBEK, SVEN, mechanical engineer; b. Soerabaya, Dutch Indies, Aug. 2, 1926; came to U.S., 1958, naturalized, 1964; s. Niels Magnus and Else Heidam (Nielsen) Agerbek-Poulsen; m. Helen Hadsbjerg Gerup, May 30, 1963; 1 child, Jesper. MSME, Tech. U., Denmark, 1952; LLB, LaSalle Ext. U., 1967; postgrad., UCLA, 1969. Registered profl. engr., Calif., Ohio, Fla. With Danish Refrigeration Rsch. Inst., Copenhagen, 1952; engr. B.P. Oil Co., Copenhagen, 1952-54; refrigeration insp. J. Lauritzen, Copenhagen, 1954-56; engr. Danish-Am. Gulf Oil Co., Copenhagen, 1956-58; instr. Ohio U., Athens, 1958-60; asst. prof. Calif. State Poly. U., San Luis Obispo, 1960-62; prin. engr. dept. environ. Ralph M. Parsons Co., L.A., 1962-73; engring. supr. Bechtel Power Co., Norwalk, Calif., 1973-85; pres., owner Woodcraft Cabinets, Inc., Rancho Cordova, Calif., 1985-90; owner Acrebrook Cons., Fair Oaks, Calif., 1990—; exec. v.p. U.S.E., Inc., Incline Village, Nev., 1994—. Past mem. Luth. Ch. coun., pres. Luth. Sch. bd. With Danish underground movement, WWII. Mem. ASHRAE (mem. tech. com., author Guide on Air Conditioning of Nuclear Power Plants), Danish Engring. Soc. Home and Office: Acrebrook Consulting 5201 Vista Del Oro Way Fair Oaks CA 95628-4148 also: USE Inc Engring Office 9244 Old State Hwy Newcastle CA 95658-9998

AGHILI, SHAUN SHAHRIAR, financial consultant, loan specialist; b. Jan. 14, 1962. BA, Cath. U. Am., Wash., D.C., 1985; student, Coll. Financial Planning, 1989-91. CFP; lic. real estate broker, Calif.; lic. ins. broker, Calif. Prin. Shaun Aghili & Assoc., Walnut Creek, Calif., 1987—. Author: No-Nonsense Financial Planning, 1995, The No-Nonsense Credit Manual: How to Repair Your Credit Profile, Manage Personal Debts and Choose the Right Home Loan or Car Lease, 1994-98; contbr. various newspaper columns, 1995—. Mem. Internat. Bd. Cert. Financial Planners, Nat. Assn. Securities Dealers (registered rep.). Avocations: long distance running, martial arts, hiking, skiing. E-mail: shaunaghili@juno.com. Home and Office: Shaun Aghili & Associates 712 Bancroft Rd # 140 Walnut Creek CA 94598-1531

AGLER, DAVID, conductor; b. South Bend, Ind., Apr. 12, 1947; s. Wave Bloom and Doris (Sheeler) A. B.Music, Westminister Choir Coll., Princeton, N.J., 1965-70; postgrad., Phila. Coll. Performing Arts, 1973-75. Mem. faculty Westminster Choir Coll., 1970-72, Acad. Vocal Arts, Phila., 1970-72, Phila. Coll. Performing Arts, 1973-75; adminstrv. dir. Spoleto Fes-

tival, 1974-75, gen. mgr., asso. music dir., 1975-76; mem. faculty San Francisco Conservatory Music, 1980-82; dir. Am. Opera Project.; music dir. Syracuse Opera Theatre, 1978-79; music supr., resident condr. San Francisco Opera, 1979-84; prin. condr. Australian Opera, 1986—; music dir. Vancouver (B.C.) Opera. Named Exxon Arts-Endowment condr., 1979. Office: Vancouver Opera, 845 Cambie St Ste 500, Vancouver, BC Canada V6B 4Z9 Office: care Neil Funkhouser, 62-1386 Nicola St, Vancouver, BC Canada 06G 2G2*

AGNEW, KATHLEEN DIANNE CROSBIE, language educator; b. Tulsa, Okla., June 16, 1946; d. James Conn and Madeline Madge (Baldwin) Crosbie; m. James Alford Tulley, Jan. 28, 1968 (div. 1991); children: Jennifer R., Scott A.; m. David Dutilh Agnew, June 21, 1997. BA, Butler U., 1968. Lic. secondary tchr. Educator East Ladue (Mo.) Jr. H.S., Laude, 1968-74, Sweet Grass County H.S., Big Timber, Mont., 1975—. Mem. Sweet Grass County Task Force At Risk Children, 1985-90; organist, vestry St. Mark's Episcopal Ch., Big Timber, 1991-98. Recipient Milken Educator award Milken Family Found., 1997; Excellence in Tchg. English and Am. Studies award Am. Coun. Tchrs. Russian and Am. Coun. Collaboration in Edn. and Lang. Study, 1998. Mem. NEA, Nat. Coun. Tchrs. English, Mont. Assn. Tchrs. English and Lang. Arts, Mont. Edn. Assn. (pres., sec), Sponsors Sch. Publs. (v.p., pres.). Avocations: piano, writing, photography, painting. Office: Sweet Grass County HS PO Box 886 Big Timber MT 59011-0886

AGOSTI, DEBORAH, judge. Justice Nev. Supreme Court, Carson City. Office: Supreme Ct Capitol Complex 201 S Carson St Carson City NV 89710*

AGTE, LLOYD MARK, adult education educator; b. Plummer, Idaho, Dec. 30, 1938; s. William Frederick and Fern Irene (Campbell) A.; m. Barbara Becker, Sept. 19, 1967 (div. July 1992); m. Barbara Joanne Sixbey, June 20, 1997. BA, U. Idaho; MA, Sul Ross State U.; PhD, Kent State U., 1980. Inspector Boeing Airplane Co., Seattle, 1957-59; tchg. asst. Sul Ross State U., Alpine, Tex., 1964-66; instr. U. Wyo., Laramie, 1966-68; tchg. fellow Kent (Ohio) State U., 1968-72; instr. Casper (Wyo.) Coll., 1973—; adj. prof. U. Wyo., Casper, 1990—; bd. dirs. Artcore, Casper, Casper Film Group. Dir. (video) The Wind River Reservation, 1983; prodn. asst. (movie) Prison, 1987. Mem. MLA, Rocky Mountain MLA, Univ. Film and Video Assn. Home: 2636 E 10th St Casper WY 82609-2824 Office: Casper Coll 125 College Dr Casper WY 82601-4612

AGTHE, DONALD ERWIN, economist; b. Buffalo, Aug. 13, 1940; s. Erwin George and Emily (Hochgrebe) A. BS, Rutgers U., 1962, MS, 1964; PhD, Fla. State U., 1970. Asst. prof. econs. and fin. U. New Orleans, 1970-74; asst. prof. econs. St. Mary U., San Antonio, 1978-80; assoc. prof. U. Nev., Reno, 1983-84; econ. cons. Tucson, 1992—. Contbr. articles to profl. jours. Mem. Am. Econs. Assn., Soc. Govt. Economists, Omicron Delta Epsilon, Delta Tau Kappa. Avocations: master's swimming (3 state age group titles 1978-83), hiking. Home: 2801 E Devon St Tucson AZ 85716-5507

AGUILAR, GLADYS MARIA, counselor, educator; b. Mérida, Mexico, Mar. 16, 1965; came to the U.S., 1968; d. Francisco Javier and Gladys Maria (Salazar) Aguilar; children: Emmanuel, Daniel. BS cum laude, Loyola Marymount U., 1987; MS, Calif. State U., 1990. Cert. in pupil personnel svcs. Youth min. St. Francis of Assisi Parish, L.A., 1987-88; sch. counselor Concern Counseling Svcs., Fullerton, Calif., 1988-89; bilingual behavioral therapist Inst. for Applied Behavioral Analysis, L.A., 1988-89; sch. counselor, tchr. St. Lucy's Priory High Sch., Glendora, Calif., 1989-90; intern Cath. Psychol. Svcs. Cath. Charities of L.A., L.A., 1990-93; bilingual elem. sch. counselor L.A. Unified Sch. Dist., 1993-96; therapist Foothill Cmty. Mental Health Ctr., 1996-97; mental health cons. Plz. de la Raza Preschool Corp., 1996—; bilingual elem. sch. tchr. Ont.-Montclair Sch. Dist., 1997—; marriage, family and child counseling intern Brown & Assocs., Whittier, Calif., 1989-93. Eucharistic min., lector St. Francis of Assisi Cath. Ch., 1986-92. Mem. Soc. Children Book Writers and Illustrators, Calif. Tchrs. Assn., Calif. Assn. Marriage and Family Therapists, Calif. Assn. Bilingual Educators, L.A. Sch. Counselors Assn., Psi Chi, Alpha Sigma Nu. Avocations: travel, folkloric dancing, reading. Home: 836 N Forest Hills Dr Covina CA 91724-3609

AGUILAR, LETICIA (LETICIA R BALLESTERO), artist, graphic designer; b. Irapuato, Guanajuato, Méx., Dec. 16, 1956; came to U.S., 1990.; d. Antonio Aguilar and Cristina Ayala; m. Richard Ballestero. Grad., Atenas Coll., Irapuato, Guanajuato, Méx., 1972; postgrad. studies in Acrylic Painting, Nat. Inst. Fine Arts, Irapuato, Guanajuato, Méx., 1989; postgrad. studies in Graphic Design, Cerritos Coll., Norwalk, Calif., 1992-95. Coord. art exhibit, head dept. investigation Mus. City of Irapuato, Guanajuato, Mex., 1989-90; instr. natural design House of Culture, Irapuato, Guanajuato, Mex., 1989; instr. drawing, painting, free hand, acrylics City of Norwalk Arts and Sports Complex, Calif., 1994-95; featured on TV News Channel 22 ECO, 1995, KMEX, Channel 34, L.A. Al Dia, 1996, Sabado Gigante Internat. Univision, Channel 34, 1996; also featured in Agora Mag., Irapuato City, Guanajuato, Mex., 1996 and in many newspapers in Mex. and Calif. Artist: solo exhibitions include Kiros Gallery, Irapuato, Mex., 1987, City Hall, Salamanca, Mex., 1987, Atenea Gallery, San Miguel Allende, Mex., 1988, House of Culture, Irapuato, Mex., 1989, Zarattini Gallery, Venice, Italy, 1989, Multicity exhbn., Guanajuato, Mex., 1989, Mus. City, Irapuato, Mex., 1989, 94, Multicity exhbn.. Nat. Inst. Fine Arts, Mex., 1990, Mary Paxon Gallery Cultural Arts Ctr., Norwalk, Calif., 1995, Women's History Month, Wilford Michael Libr., Cerritos Coll., Norwalk, Calif., 1996, Echo Park Br., L.A. Pub. Libr., 1998, U. So. Calif. Faculty Ctr., 1998, U. So. Calif. El Chicano Ctr., L.A., 1998, Opening Ceremony Celeb. Latino Heritage Month, L.A., 1998, Latino Bus. Expo. Bkst., 1998, Alhambra (Calif.) City Hall Gallery, 1998; group show appearances include House of Culture Jesus Romero Flores, Cuauhtemoc Dept. Mexico City, 1989, Galeria Atenea, San Miguel Allende, Guanajuato, Mex., House of Culture, Irapuato, Guanajuato, Mex., 1989, Am. Coll., Irapuato, Mex., 1990, Irapuato Mus., Mex., 1990, Fed. Electricity Commn., Irapuato, Mex., 1991, Downey (Calif.) Art Mus. 1993, 94, 95, Coffee House, Cultural Arts Ctr., Norwalk, Calif., 1995, Mary Paxon Gallery, Cultural Arts Ctr., Norwalk, 1995, Windows to the World, Cerritos Coll., Norwalk, Calif., 1996. Recipient Hon. Mention award Art Mus. Downey, Calif., 1993, 94, 95; Recognition for Latina Leadership Network Cerritos Coll. chpt. Fifth Sun Collection which was her work, 1996; work chosen for Latina Entrepeneur Honorees, 1998. Mem. Latin Bus. Assn. Fax: (323) 263-0532. Home and Office: 1346 S Ferris Ave Los Angeles CA 90022-3808

AGUILAR, SCOTT LEE, producer, director, writer; b. Oct. 26, 1954; m. Kwi-Ye Kim, Apr. 14, 1976; children: Matthew, Katie. BA motion picture prodn., Columbia Coll., Hollywood, 1995. RN, Calif. Owner Hyong-Bu Prodns., Whittier, Calif., 1998—. Dir. numerous theatre, feature films, music videos, informercials, pub. svc. announcements. Served with U.S. Army, 1973-79, USAF, 1986-94. Recipient award of excellence Videographer Awards, 1997, Excellence award AEGIS, 1998. Mem. Am. Film Inst., AHA, Nat. Assn. Underwater Instrs., Calif. Ednl. Theatre Assn., Disabled Am. Vets., Emergency Nureses Assn., Ind. Feature Project (W.). E-mail: Hyongbu@aol.com. Office: Hyong-Bu Prodns PO Box 1785 Whittier CA 90609-1785

AGUILERA, DONNA CONANT, psychologist, researcher; b. Kinmundy, Ill.; d. Charles E. and Daisy L. (Frost) Conant; m. George Limon Aguilera; children: Bruce Allen, Craig Steven. B.S., UCLA, 1963, M.S., 1965; Ph.D., U. So. Calif., 1974. Teaching asst. UCLA, 1965, grad. rsch. asst., 1965-66; prof. Calif. State U., L.A., 1966-81; cons. crisis intervention Didi Hirsch Community Mental Health Ctr., L.A., 1967-82; mem. Def. Adv. Com. Women in the Services, 1978-82; originator, project dir. Project Link Lab. U. Author: Crisis Intervention: Theory and Methodology, 1974, 8th edit., 1997 (pub. in 14 langs., braille and tapes), Review of Psychiatric Nursing, 1977, 7th edit., 1978, Crisis Intervention: Therapy for Psychological Emergencies, 1983; contbr. articles to profl. jours. Docent Huntington Libr. San Marino, Calif. 1991—; mem., mgr. disaster mental health svcs. ARC. NIH fellow, 1972-75. Fellow Am. Acad. Nursing (sec. 1976-77, pres. 1977-78), Acad. Psychiat. Nurse Specialists, Internat. Acad. Eclectic Psychotherapists (pres. 1987-89); mem. Am. Nurses Assn., Faculty Women's Assn., Am. Psychol. Assn., Calif. Psychol. Assn., AAUP, Alpha Tau Delta, Sigma Theta Tau. Home: 3924 Dixie Canyon Ave Sherman Oaks CA 91423-4830 Office: 450 N Bedford Dr Ste 210 Beverly Hills CA 90210 4306

AGUIRRE-BATTY, MERCEDES, Spanish and English language and literature educator; b. Cd Juarez, Mex., Dec. 20, 1952; came to U.S., 1957.; d. Alejandro M. and Mercedes (Péon) Aguirre; m. Hugh K. Batty, Mar. 17, 1979; 1 child, Henry B. BA, U. Tex., El Paso, 1974, MA, 1977. Cert. online tchr., Calif. Instr. ESL Paso del Norte- Prep Sch., Cd Juarez, 1973-74; tchg. asst. ESL and English U. Tex., El Paso, 1974-77; instr. ESL English Lang. Svcs., Bridgeport, Conn., 1977-80; instr. Spanish and English, coord. modern lang. Sheridan (Wyo.) Coll., 1980—, pres. faculty senate, 1989-90; pres. faculty senate, chair dist. coun. No. Wyo. C.C. Dist., 1995-96; mem. planning com. No. Wyo. C.C. Dist., 1996-97; mem. advanced placement faculty Spanish cons. Coll. Bd. Ednl. Testing Svc.; adj. prof. Spanish, U. Autonoma Cd Juarez, 1975; adj. prof. Spanish and English, Sacred Heart U., Fairfield, Conn., 1977-80; spkr. in field. Bd. dirs. Wyo. Coun. for the Humanities, 1988-92; translator county and dist. cts., Sheridan; vol. Wmen's Ctr.; translator Sheridan County Meml. Hosp.; del. Citizen Ambassador Program, People to People-India, 1996. NEH fellow, 1991, 92; Wyo. State Dept. Edn. grantee, 1991. Mem. MLA (del. assembly 1998—), Wyo. Fgn. Lang. Tchrs. Assn. (pres. 1990-92), Am. Assn. Tchrs. Spanish and Portuguese (founder, 1st pres. Wyo. chpt. 1987-90), TESOL, Sigma Delta Mu (v.p. 1992—), Sigma Delta Pi (pres. 1974-75). Avocations: traveling, reading, archeology, languages, geography. Office: Sheridan Coll NWCCD 3059 Coffeen Ave Sheridan WY 82801-9133

AHART, ALAN M., bankruptcy judge; b. 1949. AB, U. Calif., Berkeley, 1970; JD, SUNY, 1975; LLM, U. Pa., 1979. Judge U.S. Bankrupty Ct. Cen. Dist. Calif., L.A., 1988—. Contbr. articles to profl. jours. Office: US Bankruptcy Ct Calif Edward R Roybal Bldg 255 E Temple St Ste 1382 Los Angeles CA 90012-3334*

AHERIN, DARREL WILLIAM, lawyer; b. Colfax, Wash., July 11, 1946; s. Don Lewis and Leona Margaret (Edwards) A. m. Freda jean Kieffer, June 27, 1968 (dec.); children: Daniel Winston, Dustin Wynne; m. Michelle Rae Messley, June 26, 1982; children: Alex William. BA, Lewis Clark State Coll., 1969; JD, U. Idaho, 1973. Pvt. practice Lewiston, Idaho, 1973—; ptnr. Aherin, Rice & Anegon (formerly Aherin, Rice & Brown), Lewiston, 1973—. Active Planning & Zoning Com., Genesee, Idaho, 1996—. Mem. ATLA (gov. 1996—), Idaho Trial Lawyers Assn. (sec., treas., pres.), Western Trial Lawyers (gov. 1995—), Lewis Clark State Coll. Alumni (pres.). Home: PO Box 337 Genesee ID 83832-0337 Office: Aherin Rice & Anegon 1212 Idaho St Lewiston ID 83501-1941

AHERN, ARLEEN FLEMING, retired librarian; b. Mt. Harris, Colo., Oct. 15, 1922; d. John R. and Josephine (Vidmar) Fleming; m. George Irving Ahern, June 14, 1944; 1 child, George Irving Jr. BA, U. Utah, 1943; MA, U. Denver, 1962; postgrad. U. Colo., 1967. Library asst. Army Air Force Library, Salt Lake City, 1943-44; library asst. Colo. Women's Coll. Library (now U. Denver/CWC Campus), 1952-60, acquisitions librarian, 1960—, rep. Adult Edn. Council Denver, 1960-90, reference librarian Penrose Library, WEC librarian, assoc. prof. librarianship through 1987, U. Denver Penrose Libr.; prof. emeritus, U. Denver; retired. Committeewoman, Republican Com., Denver, 1958-59; vol., Opera Colo. Guild; treas., bd. dirs. Denver Lyric Opera; bd. dirs. dirs. U. Denver Women's Libr. Assn., 1996-97, Samaritan House Guild, Jeanne Jugan (Little Sisters Poor) Aux., Colo. Symphony Guild, Cinema Study Club Colo., Carson Brierly Dance Libr., bd. dirs. Mem. AAUP, ALA, Mountain Plains Library Assn., Colo. (1st v.p., pres. 1969-70, dir. 1971—), Library Assn., Altrusa Club of Denver (2d v.p. 1968-69, dir. 1971-74, 76, 78), Soc. Am. Archivists, Mountain Plains Adult Edn. Assn., Denver Botanic Gardens. Home: 746 Monaco Pky Denver CO 80220-6041

AHERN, GEOFFREY LAWRENCE, behavioral neurologist; b. N.Y.C., Feb. 20, 1954. BA, SUNY, Purchase, 1976; MS, Yale U., 1978, PhD in Psychology, 1981, MD, 1984. Med. intern Waterbury (Conn.) Hosp., 1984-85; resident in neurology Boston U., 1985-88; fellow in behavioral neurology Beth Israel Hosp., Boston, 1988-90; instr. neurology Harvard Med. Sch., Boston, 1988-90; asst. prof. neurology and psychology U. Ariz., Tucson, 1990-96, assoc. prof., 1996—. Contbr. articles to profl. jours., chpts. to books. Mem. Am. Acad. Neurology, Am. Neurol. Assn. Office: Univ Med Ctr Dept Neurology 1501 N Campbell Ave Tucson AZ 85724-0001

AHN, PETER PYUNG-CHOO, dean; b. Chor-won, Korea, May 21, 1917; came to U.S., 1948; s. Kyung-sam and Ok-bong (Lee) A.; m. Grace Chung, June 10, 1950; children: David Kyu-young and John Avery (twins). Diploma, St. Paul's U., Tokyo, 1944; BD, Garrett Theol. Sem., 1949; MA, Northwestern U., 1951; PhD, Boston U., 1962. Ordained to ministry United Meth. Ch., 1954. Pastor San Francisco Korean Meth. Ch., 1953-60, various United Meth. Chs., Calif., 1965-82; asst. prof. L.A. Pacific Coll., 1963-65; dean Korean Christian Acad., Oakland, Calif., 1986—; trustee Calif.-Nev. annual conf. United Meth. Ch., San Francisco, 1970-73, chair div. higher edn., 1973-76. Compiler: English-Korean and Korean-English dictionaries, 1947-48; translator: New American Standard Bible, 1965-70; chmn. translation project: New Korean Standard Bible, 1989—; rsch. dir. New Am. Standard Bible Exhaustive Concordance, 1970-76. Recipient Outstanding Contbn. award Lockman Found., 1973, Korean-Eng. Bible pub., 1990. Mem. Soc. Biblical Lit. Republican. Home: 608 Princeton Dr Sunnyvale CA 94087-1851 Office: Lockman Found 900 S Euclid St La Habra CA 90631-6893

AHN, SAMUEL SEUNGHAE, vascular surgeon, researcher, consultant; b. Pusan, Korea, Feb. 9, 1954; came to U.S., 1959; s. Chai Ho and Sun Duk A.; m. Mi Ryu, Aug. 20, 1983; children: Justin, Alexander. BA in Biology, U. Tex., 1972-74; MD, U. Tex. Southwestern, 1974-78. Dimplomate Am. Bd. Surgery, Am. Bd. Med. Examiners; lic. Tex., Calif. Gen. surgery intern UCLA Med. Ctr., 1978-79, jr. resident gen. surgery, 1979-80, NIH rsch. fellow in surg. oncology, 1980-82, sr. resident gen. surgery, 1982-83, chief resident gen. surgery, 1983-84, clin. fellwo vascular surgery, 1984-85, rsch. fellow vascular surgery, 1985-86, attending surgeon, 1984—; asst. prof. surgery UCLA Med. Sch., 1986-93, assoc. clin. prof., 1994-98, prof., dir. endovascular surgery, 1999—; attending surgeon Sepulveda (Calif.) VA Med. Ctr., 1985-94; cons. surgeon UCLA Student Health Svcs., 1986—; surg. cons. Endovascular Equipment Cos., 1986-94; organizer facilities and programs in field; task force mem.; numerous com. appointments UCLA, 1985; guest lectr. and rsch. in field. Editor: (with W.S. Moore) Endovascular Surgery, 1989, 2d edit., 1992, (with J. Seeger) Endovascular Surgery for Peripheral Vascular Disease: Surgical Clinics of North America, 1992, (with D. Eton, K. Hodgson) Current Concepts in Endovascular Surgery, 1994; mem. editorial bd. Vascular Forum, 1993-94, Jour. Endovascular Surgery, 1994, Vascular Surgery, 1994; guest reviewer Jour. of Vascular Surgery, 1991-94, Postgraduate Vascular Surgery Jour., 1992-93, Surgery, 1992, Atherosclerosis and Thrombosis, 1992, Jour. of Am. Geriatrics Soc., 1992-93; abstractor Jour. of Vascular Surgery, 1994; contbr. chpts. books, articles to profl. jours. Mem. stroke coun. Am. Heart Assn., 1991—; vol. Korean Med. Missionary, 1969-88, Pub. Edn. of Cancer, 1980-83. East Tex. Chest Found. fellow East Tex. Chest Hosp., Tyler, 1976, Sigvaris award 1986; preceptee Am. Soc. Anestehsiologists, 1976; grantee E.R. Squibb and Sons. 1985-87, 85-86, Olympus Corp., 1985-86, UCLA Med. Aux., 1986, Bio-Quantum Tech., 1986-87, W.L. Gore and Assocs., 1986-87, 94, UCLA Sch. Medicine, 1986-87, NIH, 1987, 88, 93, Boston Scientific/Diasonics, 1989, Quadralogic Tech., Inc., 1990, Endo Vascular Instruments, Inc., 1993-94, Echocath and Acuson, 1993-94. Fellow Am. Coll. Surgeons; mem. AMA, Assn. Academic Surgery , Interant. Soc. Cardiovascular Surgery (N.Am. Chapter, rsch. fellow 1992, 93), So. Calif. Vascular Surg. Soc., Western Vascular Soc., Pacific Coast Surg. Assn., L.A. Surg. Soc., Acad. Surg. Rsch., Peripheral Vascular Surgery soc., Soc. Clin. Vascular Surgery, The Soc. for Vascular Surgery, Longmire Surg. Soc. Office: UCLA Med Ctr Ste 526 200 UCLA Med Plz Los Angeles CA 90024-6992

AHNA, ALICE ALMEDA See NEVILLE-HARRIS, ALICE ALMEDA

AHRENS, PAMELA, state legislator; b. Portland, Oreg., Nov. 15, 1945; m. Steve Ahrens; children: Melissa Ann, Elaine, Annette, Shannon. Grad., Ea. Wash. State U. Mem. Idaho Ho. of Reps., 1983—; dir. Dept. Adminstrn. State of Idaho, Boise; owner equipment rental bus. Chmn. Statewide Safety and Loss Control Com.; bd. dirs. Boise City Club. Named to Hall of Fame, Idaho Rep. Party. Mem. Idaho Hosp. Assn. (dir. polit. activities), Idaho Rep. Women's Fedn. (nat. fedn. rep. v.p.), Idaho Info. Tech. Resource Mgmt. Coun. (chair); mem. Lincoln Day Banquet Assn. (pres.), Rotary (v.p.). Republican. Presbyterian. Home: 5186 S Farmhouse Pl Boise ID 83716-9013 Office: Dept of Adminstrn State of Idaho PO Box 83720 Boise ID 83720-3720

AIELLO, ELIZABETH ANN, public relations liaison; b. Pitts., Apr. 10, 1922; d. Edward Aloysisus and Sarah Marie (Short) Maroney; m. William Peter Aiello, June 4, 1946 (dec. Nov. 1989); children: David Robert, Beverly Ann Aiello Reecer. BA, Chatham Coll., 1943; MA, St. John's Coll., Santa Fe, N.Mex., 1969; postgrad., U. N.Mex., 1970—. Cert. tchr. elem./secondary English, history, social studies, govt., civics. Secondary instr. history Moon Twp. Schs., Coraopolis, Pa., 1943-44; secondary instr. English, Latin Blawnox (Pa.) Schs., 1944-49; elementary instr. upper primary Los Alamos (N.Mex.) Schs., 1949-59, secondary instr. advanced placement English/history, 1959-82; chair English dept. U. N.Mex., Los Alamos, 1982-90, head humanities div., 1986-90, dir. reentry program for women in sci., 1984-89, dir. reentry program for Native Am./Hispanic students, 1987-90; ednl. pub. rels. liaison Los Alamos Nat. Lab., 1984—; Great Books discussion groups coord. No. N.Mex., 1992—; adv. bd. N.Mex. Women in Sci., Santa Fe, 1980-84, Los Alamos Women in Sci., 1984-90; Fulbright teaching fellow U.S. Dept. Edn., Washington, 1971-72. Author: Perigrinations at Pokesdown, 1974, Consumation and Other Poems, 1984, New Hope for Dying Muse, 1986, Perceptions and Reality, 1991, Perceptions I-IV; editor The Main Gate, Los Alamos Nat. Lab. publ. for lab. retirees, 1997—. Phoebe Brashear Soc. scholar, Pitts., 1939-43; Am. Hist. Soc.-NEH joint fellow, 1976, William Robertson Coe fellow, 1981; rsch. grantee AAUW, 1982, Carl Perkins grantee N.Mex. Dept. Vocat.-Tech. Edn., 1986-90; named Outstanding N.Mex. History Tchr., DAR, 1976, One of 80 Women to Watch in 80's, N.Mex. Women's Polit. Caucus, 1980; recipient N.Mex. Women at Work award Nat. Coun. Working Women and Minority Affairs, Washington, 1975, Gov.'s award Gov. N.Mex., N.Mex. Commn. Status of Women, 1986, 89, Pres.'s award Nat. Libr. Poetry, 1996, 98. Mem. NEA, AAUW (dir. adv. bd. 1985-90, nat. adv. bd. 1985-89, June B. West fellow N.Mex. div. 1969, Grace Braker Wilson award 1990), Los Alamos Nat. Edn. Assn. (adv. bd., pres. 1975-80), Delta Kappa Gamma. Office: Los Alamos Nat Lab Box 1663 MS C330 Los Alamos NM 87545

AIKENS, C(LYDE) MELVIN, anthropology educator, archaeologist; b. Ogden, Utah, July 13, 1938; s. Clyde Walter and Claudia Elena (Brown) A.; m. Alice Hiroko Endo, Mar. 23, 1963; children: Barton Hiroyuki, Quinn Yoshihisa. A.S., Weber Coll., 1958; B.A., U. Utah, 1960; M.A., U. Chgo., 1962, Ph.D., 1966. Curator U. Utah Mus. Anthropology, Salt Lake City, 1963-66; asst. prof. U. Nev., Reno, 1966-68; asst. prof. anthropology U. Oreg., Eugene, 1968-72, assoc. prof., 1972-78, prof., 1978—, dir. U. Oreg. Mus. Natural History, 1996—. Author: Fremont Relationships, 1966, Hogup Cave, 1970, Great Basin Archaeology, 1978, The Last 10,000 Years in Japan and Eastern North America, 1981, From Asia to America: The First Peopling of the New World, 1990, Archaeology of Oregon, 1993; co-author: Prehistory of Japan, 1982, Great Basin Numic Prehistory, 1986, Early Human Occupation in Far Western North America, 1988; editor: Archaeological Studies Willamette Valley, 1975; co-editor: Prehistoric Hunter-Gatherers in Japan, 1986, Pacific Northeast Asia in Prehistory, 1992, Archaeological Researches in the Northern Great Basin, 1994. NSF research grantee, 1970, 73, 78-80, 84; NSF Sci. Faculty fellow Kyoto U., Japan, 1971-72; Japan Found. research fellow Kyoto U., 1977-78, Tokyo U., 1986. Fellow Am. Anthrop. Assn., AAAS; mem. Soc. for Am. Archaeology. Home: 3470 Mcmillan St Eugene OR 97405-3317 Office: U Oreg Dept Anthropology Eugene OR 97403-1218

AILOR, KAREN TANA, writer, editor, proposal consultant; b. Seattle, June 1, 1943; d. Dale Ingram and Neva Gail (Houck) A. Student, U. Calif., Berkeley, 1961-63; BA in Journalism, U. Oreg., 1992. Copy editor Physical Review Letters, Brookhaven, N.Y., 1963-65; proposal writer TRW Def. Systems, L.A., 1965-73; mktg. support mgr. TRW Electronics, L.A., 1973-79; proposal cons. TRW, Hughes, Northrop, Logicon, and others, L.A., 1980—; contbg. writer Old Oreg. Mag., Eugene, 1991-94. Editor: Software Project Management: A Unified Approach, 1998. Mem. Phi Beta Kappa (award 1992), Kappa Tau Alpha (award 1991). Democrat. Home and Office: 125 Rosetta Ave Eugene OR 97404-2849

AINGE, DANNY RAY, professional basketball coach; b. Eugene, Oreg., Mar. 17, 1959; m. Michele Ainge; children: Ashlee, Austin, Tanner, Taylor, Cooper, Crew. Grad., Brigham Young U., 1981. Basketball player Boston Celtics, 1981-89, Sacramento, 1989-90, Portland Trailblazers, 1990-92; basketball player Phoenix Suns, 1992-95, head coach, 1996—; player Celebrity Golf Assn. Tour. Active Children's Miracle Network, Spl. Olympics. Holder of record for most 3-pointers mde and attempted in playoffs; one of 4 players in NBA history to make 1,000 or more career 3-pointers. Avocation: golf. Office: Phoenix Suns Am West Arena 201 E Jefferson St Phoenix AZ 85004-2412*

AKAGI, LEORA JEAN, marketing consultant; b. Clarita, Okla., Mar. 14, 1939; d. Percy Alfred and Viola Violet (Lane) Ennis; m. Kaku Akagi, Jan. 24, 1959 (div. May 1985); children: Kay Lynn, Patrick Gregg. Student, Shasta Coll., 1994. Profl. model Touch of Class, Denver, 1958-90; deputy treas. Stanton County, Johnson, Kans., 1970's; sec., bookkeeper Stanton County Schs., Johnson, Kans., 1970's; co-owner Red Tree Farms, Inc., Johnson, Kans., 1961-85; animal nutritionist Continental Grain, N.Y.C., 1986-90; owner, editor Meeting Place for Friends, Redding, Calif., 1990-96; sales mgr. Avanti, Redding, Calif., 1990-92; mktg. dir. Bijan Corp., Redding, Calif., 1992-94; records dept. clk. Calif. Dept. Corrections, Delano, 1995—. Author: Page Day USA, 1980, Single & Fre2beme, 1990, Let the Kids Cook, 1992, I'm One of those Ennis Kids, 1994. Bd. dirs. Shasta County symphony, 1993-94, Tumbleweed Girl Scout Coun., Garden City, Kans., 1970, Southwest Kans. Area Mental Health, Garden City, 1978-85. Mem. VFW Aux. (chmn. Americanism for Kans. 1980-81), Bus. Profl. Women Kans. (dit. dir. 1970-72), Ladies of Moose, Emblem Club Elks, Am. Legion Aux. Republican. Methodist. Avocations: flying, skiing, golf, dancing, stain glass art. Office: Calif Dept Corrections 2737 W Cecil Delano CA 93216

AKAKA, DANIEL KAHIKINA, senator; b. Honolulu, Sept. 11, 1924; s. Kahikina and Annie (Kahoa) A.; m. Mary Mildred Chong, May 22, 1948; children: Millannie, Daniel, Gerard, Alan, Nicholas. BEd, U. Hawaii, 1952, MEdn, 1966. Tchr. Hawaii, 1953-60; vice prin., then prin. Ewa Beach Elem. Sch., Honolulu, 1960-64; prin. Pohakea Elem. Sch., 1964-65, Kaneohe Elem. Sch., 1965-68; program specialist Hawaii Compensatory Edn., 1978-79, from 1985; dir. Hawaii OEO, 1971-74; spl. asst. human resources Office Gov. Hawaii, 1975-76; mem. 95th-101st Congresses from 2d Dist., Hawaii, 1977-90; U.S. senator from Hawaii, 1990—, mem. energy and natural resources com., mem. govt. affairs com., mem. Indian affairs com., mem. Indian affairs com., mem. vets. affairs com., mem. Senate dem. policy com.; chmn. Hawaii Principals' Conf. Bd. dirs. Hanahauoli Sch.; mem. Act 4 Ednl. Adv. Council, Library Adv. Council.; Trustee Kawaiahao Congl. Ch. Served with U.S. Army, 1945-47. Mem. NEA, Musicians Assn. Hawaii. Democrat. Office: US Senate 720 Senate Hart Office Bldg Washington DC 20510-1103*

AKBARIAN, SHAH-ROKH, management consultant; b. Abadan, Khuzestan, Iran, May 20, 1953; came to U.S., 1969; s. Ramezan and Mahin A.; m. Joni Louise Stump, Nov. 1, 1980; 1 child, Katayun Alexandra. BA, Westminster Coll., 1976, BS, 1977; M of Internat. Mgmt., Am. Grad. Sch. Internat. Mgmt., Glendale, Ariz., 1980; postgrad., U. Utah, 1993; Cert. in Advanced Mgmt., The Grad. Sch. of Am., Mpls., 1998. Account exec. Bonneville Rsch., Salt Lake City, 1980-84; prin. Pendar Internat., Salt Lake City, 1984—; bd. dirs. Sports Am, Salt Lake City, 1988—. Pub., editor Commerce Internat. News; contbr. articles to profl. jours. Mem. adv. bd. U. Utah Internat. Ctr., 1992—, mem. chmn. bus. and industry com.; mem. adv. bd. Salt Lake County Cmty. and Econs. Devel., 1994-95, exec. coun. Westminster Coll. Alumni Assn., 1993-96, pres., 1995-96, trustee, 1995, mem. instnl. advancement com., 1994-95; alumni ednl. counselor Am. Grad. Sch. Internat. Mgmt., 1994—; adv. bd. Salvation Army, 1982-84. Mem. Inst. Indsl. Engrs., Assn. MBA Execs., Salt Lake Area C. of C. (mem. export

devel. com., mem. editl. bd. chamber newsletter, pub. rels. coord.). Avocations: tennis, golf.

AKERMAN, JOSEPH LAX, JR., film and television producer; b. Weslaco, Tex., Oct. 29, 1950; s. Joseph Lax and Orfa Mae (Palko) A.; m. Christie Crisp, Mar. 15, 1970 (div. Oct., 1972); m. Nancy Rae Stone, June 5, 1988 (div. Jan. 1996); 1 child: Ethan Wyatt. BA in Mass Communications, U. Cen. Fla., 1972; MFA in Motion Picture Prodn., U. So. Calif., 1979, MFA in Motion Picture Mgmt., 1981. Prodn. exec. Arkoff Internat. Pictures, Los Angeles, 1980-83, New World Pictures, Los Angeles, 1983-85; producer, prodn. exec. Leonard Hill Films, Los Angeles, 1985-86; producer Peregrine Producers Group, Los Angeles, 1986; ind. producer Los Angeles, 1986-88; exec. in charge of prodn. Spirit Entertainment, 1988-90; v.p. prodn. Vidmark Entertainment, 1990-91; ind. producer L.A., 1991—; instr. communication arts Loyola U., Los Angeles, 1981—. Co-producer (TV movie) Prince of Bel-Air, 1985, The Last Fling, 1986; assoc. producer (pilot) Rags and Riches, 1986; exec. producer (film) Ernest Saves Christmas, 1988; exec. in charge of prodn. Black Magic Woman, 1990, Servants of Twilight, 1991, Whore, 1991, Psychic, 1991, Into the Sun, 1991; screenwriter Liars School, 1987, Buried Secrets, 1988, Edge of the Envelope, 1992, Under the Rose, 1996, Broken Rainbow, 1997. Mem. Sierra Club, San Francisco, 1983—, Mus. of Contemporary Art, Los Angeles, 1986—, Mus. Neon Art, 1985—. Mem. Writers Guild Am. West, U. So. Calif. Cinema/TV Alumni Assn., U. So. Calif. Cinema Circulus. Club: Sports Car of Am. (N. Hollywood, Calif.), Into the Night Rallye Team. Avocations: sports car racing, gardening, home computing.

AKINS, GEORGE CHARLES, accountant; b. Willits, Calif., Feb. 22, 1917; s. Guy Brookins and Eugenie (Swan) A.; A.A., Sacramento City Coll., 1941; m. Jane Babcock, Mar. 27, 1945. Accountant, auditor Calif. Bd. Equalization, Dept. Finance, Sacramento, 1940-44; controller-treas. DeVons Jewelers, Sacramento, 1944-73, v.p., controller, 1973-80, v.p., chief fin. officer, dir., 1980-84; individual accounting and tax practice, Sacramento, 1944—. Accountant, cons. Mercy Children's Hosp. Guild, Sacramento, 1957-77. Served with USAAF, 1942. Mem. Soc. Calif. Pioneers, Nat. Soc. Accts., U.S. Navy League, Calif. Hist. Soc., Drake Navigators Guild, Internat. Platform Assn., Mendocino County Hist. Soc. (life), Sacramento County Hist. Soc. (life), Northwestern Pacific Railroad Hist. Soc., Crocker Art Mus. (life). Republican. Roman Catholic. Clubs: Commonwealth of Calif., Comstock. Contbg. author: Portfolio of Accounting Systems for Small and Medium-Sized Business, 1968, rev., 1977. Home and Office: 96 S Humboldt St Willits CA 95490-3539

AKIYAMA, CAROL LYNN, motion picture industry executive; b. Chgo.; d. Makio M. Akiyama and Mary (Uyeda) Maruyama. BA magna cum laude, U. So. Calif., 1968, JD, 1971. Bar: Calif. Atty. NLRB, Los Angeles, 1971-75, ABC-TV, Hollywood, Calif., 1975-79, So. Calif. Edison, Rosemead, 1980-81; asst. gen. atty. CBS Inc., Los Angeles, 1981-82; sr. v.p. Alliance of Motion Picture and TV Producers, Sherman Oaks, Calif., 1982-88; ind. producer and writer TV, motion pictures and multimedia/new techs., Woodland Hills, Calif., 1988—; cons. entertainment industry; founding ptnr. Bierstedt, Akiyama and Assocs., Woodland Hills, 1988—. Mem. Los Angeles County Bar Assn. (chmn. labor law sect. 1981-82, exec. com. 1975-85), Phi Kappa Phi, Phi Beta Kappa.

AKUJUOBI, CAJETAN MADUABUCHUKWU, systems engineer, electrical engineering educator, researcher; b. Umuahia, Abia, Nigeria, Apr. 18, 1950; came to U.S., 1977; s. John Ohiri and Roseline (Amadi) A.; m. Caroline Chioma Njoku, May 8, 1982; children: Obinna Chukwuemeka, Chijoke Eze. BSEE, So. Univ., 1980; MSEE, Tuskegee (Ala.) Inst., 1983; MBA, Hampton U., 1987; PhD, George Mason U., 1995. Asst. prof. elec. engr. Norfolk State U., Va., 1983-96; R&D engr. Austin Product Ctr., Schlumberger Inc., 1996-97; engr. sr. design and devel. Data Race, Inc., San Antonio, 1997—; rsch./systems engr., cons. Advanced Hardware Architectures, Inc., Pullman, Wash., 1998—; assoc. prof., rschr. NASA ctr. space radiation Prairie View A&M U., Prairie View, Tex., 1998—; adj. assoc. prof. U. D.C., 1989-90; rsch. fellow NASA, Langley, Va., 1987; tech. staff AT&T Bell Labs., Holmdel, N.J., 1986, 88, 90, 91; prin. engr. Spectrum Engring. & Tech., Washington, 1991-92; rschr. George Mason U., Fairfax, Va., 1991-94; engr. Intelsat, Washington, 1993; session chmn. Modeling and Simulation Conf., Pitts., 1986-90; judge Tidewater Sci. Fair, Southampton H.S., Courtland, Va., 1994; chief judge sr. engring. design projects Tidewater Sci. Fair, 1996, head jusge, 1995; faculty rsch. participant Argonne Nat. Lab., 1995-96. Mem. SPIE, IEEE (award 1982, 83, counselor 1977—, judge 1986), Instrument Soc. Am. (chmn. digital sys. 1986, session organizer 1986—), Am. Soc. Engring. Edn. (campus rep. 1983—), Soc. Indsl. and Applied Math., Sigma Xi, Alpha Kappa Mu. Roman Catholic. Avocations: soccer, tennis, swinning, volleyball, table tennis. Home: 1050 SW Viento St Pullman WA 99163-2034 Office: Prairie View A&M U Dept Elec Engring PO Box 2117 Prairie View TX 77446-2117

AKUTAGAWA, DONALD, psychologist, educator; b. Grace, Idaho, June 7, 1923; s. Fred T. and Shizue (Oyama) A.; children: Trina Bortko, Murray, Doran. MA, U. Chgo., 1951; PhD, U. Pitts., 1956. Group counselor Orthogenic Sch., U. Chgo., 1951-52; clin. psychologist Inst. Pa. Hosp., Phila., 1959-67; pvt. practice Phila., 1957—, Bellevue, Wash., 1968—; chief community services Eastside Community Mental Health Center, Bellevue, 1968-72; clin. prof. psychology U. Wash., Seattle, 1974-90. Served with AUS, 1944-46. Fellow Am. Orthopsychiat. Assn. Office: Family Treatment Ctr 10845 Main St Bellevue WA 98004-6362

ALAMEDA, RUSSELL RAYMOND, JR., radiologic technologist; b. San Jose, Calif., Oct. 13, 1945; s. Russell Raymond and Rose Margaret (Manzone) A.; m. Gayle Evileen Allison, Feb. 16, 1969 (div. 1975); children: Lynda Rae, Anthony David. Student San Jose City Coll., 1963-65. Served with U.S. Navy, 1966-75; x-ray technician VA Hosp., Palo Alto, Calif., 1975-78; office mgr., radiologic technologist, responsible safety officer Orthopedic Surgery, Mountain View (Calif.), 1978—; owner, operator Ren-Tech, San Jose, 1982-87; radiologic technologist San Jose (Calif.) Med. Clinic, 1982-93; part-time fin. analyst Primerica Fin. Svcs., Newark, Calif., 1998—. Mem. DeFrank Community Ctr. Recipient Mallinckrodt Outstanding Achievement award Mallinckrodt Corp., 1971. Mem. DAV (life), ACLU, NOW, Am. Registry of Radiologic Technologists, Lamda Legal Def., Calif. Soc. Radiologic Technologists, Am. Soc. Radiologic Technologist. Democrat. Lutheran. Home: 165 Blossom Hill Rd Spc 76 San Jose CA 95123-5906 Office: Orthopedic Surgery 2500 Hospital Dr Bldg 7 Mountain View CA 94040-4115 also: Primerica Fin Svcs 39899 Balentine Dr Ste 175 Newark CA 94560-5357

ALARCON, ARTHUR LAWRENCE, federal judge; b. L.A., Aug. 14, 1925; s. Lorenzo Marques and Margaret (Sais) A.; m. Sandra D. Paterson, Sept. 1, 1979; children—Jan Marie, Gregory, Lance. B.A. in Polit. Sci, U. So. Calif., 1949, J.D., 1951. Bar: Calif. 1952. Dep. dist. atty. L.A. County, 1952-61; exec. asst. to Gov. Pat Brown State of Calif., Sacramento, 1962-64, legal adv. to gov., 1961-62; judge L.A. Superior Ct., 1964-78; assoc. justice Calif. Ct. Appeals, L.A., 1978-79; judge U.S. Ct. Appeals for 9th Circuit, L.A., 1979—. Served with U.S. Army, 1943-46, ETO. Office: US Ct Appeals 9th Cir 1607 US Courthouse 312 N Spring St Los Angeles CA 90012-4701*

ALAYETO, OFELIA LUISA, writer, researcher, educator; b. Havana, Cuba, July 24; came to U.S., 1960; d. Pedro O. and Ofelia Luisa (Martinez-Torres) A.; m. Allan W. Solomonow, Oct. 16, 1967; children: Gregory Igal, Seth Rafael. BA, CUNY, 1973, MPhil, 1980, PhD, 1983. Spl. asst. to exec. dir. Sierra Club, San Francisco, 1984-90, assoc. dir. rsch., 1990-93; lectr. U. San Francisco, 1987—, San Francisco, 1987—; rsch. analyst U. Calif., San Francisco, 1994—. Author: Sofia Casanova: Spanish Poet, Journalist and Writer, 1992; contbr. articles to profl. jours. Recipient Humanities award Richmond Coll./CUNY, 1973, Arleigh Williamson award, 1973. Mem. MLA, Am. Assn. Tchrs. Spanish and Portuguese, Sierra Club. Democrat. Roman Catholic. Avocations: opera, ballet, film, modern and classical literatures. Office: Univ of San Francisco Presentation Campus 103 Ignatian Heights San Francisco CA 94117-1080

ALBANESE, THOMAS, minerals company executive; b. Akron, Ohio, Sept. 9, 1957; s. Paul F. Albanese and Rosemarie (Helm) Rovito; m. Mary D. Ross, June 14, 1979; children: Yvonne, Amy. BS in Mining Econs., U. Alaska, 1979, MS in Mining Engring., 1981. Engr. Resource Assocs. Alaska, Fairbanks, 1981-82; various positions to COO, Nerco Minerals Co., Portland, Oreg., 1993; pres. Pikes Peak, Portland, 1993; sr. v.p. Nerco, Inc., Portland, 1993; gen. mgr. Kenncott Gen. Co., Juneau, Alaska, 1993-95; group exploration exec. RTZ, London, 1995-98; v.p. engring. and tech. svcs. Kennecott Utah Copper, Magna, 1998—; bd. dirs. Silver Inst./Silver Trust, N.Y.C., 1988-93. Bd. dirs. Gold Inst., Washington, 1988-93, Alaska Prodrs. Coun., Juneau, 1993-95; pres., chmn. Western States Pub. Lands, Pueblo, Colo., 1991-92. Mem. Utah Mining Assn. (bd. dirs. 1998—). Office: Kennecott Utah Copper PO Box 6001 Magna UT 84044-6001

ALBANESE, THOMAS, food industry executive, consultant; b. Passaic, N.J., June 27, 1930; s. Charles and Viola (Gueritey) A.; m. Theresa Mary Perez, Aug. 8, 1953; children: Thomas II, John, Theresa Lynn, Richard Charles, Michael Quintin. Grad. high sch., Garfield, N.J., 1948. Pres. Thomas Albanese Inc., Clifton, N.J., 1958-60; founder, pres. Alabanese Products Inc., Las Vegas, Nev., 1960—; exec. cons. The Norlen Co., Las Vegas, 1971—; exec. dir. The Las Vegas Chili Co., Las Vegas, 1982—; owner The Chef Tomal Co., Las Vegas, 1995—. Creator Gourmet Chili Meals and Desserts-La Chilafesta, 1982, Mr. B's Hang All Kit, 1971; patentee plumbing sys. Founder Double TT Rancho, dir., 1986—. Airman 1st class USAF, 1951-55. Mem. United Assn. Plumbers and Pipefitters, Plumbers and Pipefitters Local 525. Avocations: designing, inventing. Home and Office: 700 Sunny Pl # 804 Las Vegas NV 89106-3632

ALBANO, ANDRES, JR., real estate developer, real estate broker; b. Honolulu, Apr. 16, 1941; s. Andres Pacis and Florence (Paglinawan) A.; m. Sandra Kam Mee Ymas, Nov. 29, 1961; children: Cheryl Ann, Denise Lynn. BEE, U. Hawaii, 1965, MBA, 1972. Engr. nuclear power USN, 1965-67; elec. engr. U.S. Aviation Adminstrn., Honolulu, 1967-69, Honolulu Bd. Water Supply, 1969-79; exec. v.p. MidPac Devel. Ltd., Honolulu, 1979-84; pres. Albano & Assocs., Honolulu, 1984—; prin. broker Gen. Growth Mgmt. of Hawaii, Inc., 1993-96; real estate devel. cons. CB Richard Ellis, Inc., Honolulu, 1998—. Mem. NSPE, Hawaii Soc. Profl. Engrs. (pres. 1979-80), Devel. Assn. Hawaii (pres. 1992-93), Nat. Assn. Realtors, Hawaii Developers Coun. (pres. 1995-96), Rotary, Beta Gamma Sigma. Roman Catholic. Avocations: tennis, karate, weight lifting. Home: 748 Kokomo Pl Honolulu HI 96825-1603 Office: Albano & Assocs Inc 3322 Campbell Ave Honolulu HI 96815-3856

ALBERGHINI, CHRISTOPHER ROBERT, producer, writer, actor; b. Plymouth, Mass., Sept. 27, 1965; s. Robert and Beverly-Ann (Busi) A. Writer, actor The Nanny, Murphy Brown, Style and Substance, The Love Boat, Ink, Love and War, Life with Louie, All Good Children: The Women of the Manson Family.

ALBERS, LUCIA BERTA, land developer; b. Guatemala, Feb. 10, 1943; d. Jose Luis De Leon Polanco and Maria Marta (Vasquez) De Leon; m. Ray Cisneros, Nov. 2, 1968 (div. 1972); 1 child, Elizabeth Ann Albers Cisneros; m. Monte Dean Albers, June 12, 1974; 1 child, Monte Roberto. Grad. in Acctg., Sacred Heart, Guatemala, 1963; student in Econs., San Carlos, Guatemala, 1964; student, Diablo Valley Coll., 1975, 76. Chief acct. Discovery Bay, Byron, Calif., 1971-76; asst. fin. dir. City of Pittsburg, Calif., 1976-78; corporate contr. Conco Cement, Concord, Calif., 1981-90; land developer Contra Costa County, Calif., 1990—. Mem. adv. coun. City of Byron, Calif., 1991-94; dir. Ctr. for New Ams., Concord, 1994—. Mem. Nat. Assn. Accts., Nat. Assn. Exec. Women, Nat. Assn. Women, Mex.-Am. Polit. Assn. Home: 9601 Deer Valley Rd Brentwood CA 94513-4907

ALBERT, N. ERICK, urologist; b. West Frankfort, Ill., July 27, 1945; s. Norman and Dorothy Dean (Trout) A.; m. Julie L. Wuorisalo, June 18, 1977; children: Alexander, Jillian. BS with honors, Tulane U., 1967; MD, U. Ill., 1971. Resident in surgery UCLA, 1971-73; resident in urology Yale U., New Haven, Conn., 1973-77; ptnr. Lodi (Calif.) Urol. Med. Group, Inc., 1980—; dir. Found. Med. Care, Stockton, Calif., 1985-88; chief dept. surgery Lodi Meml. Hosp., 1989-90; CEO ARTEL Med. Devel. Inc., Lodi, 1990-95; dir. Lodi Ind. Practice Orgn., 1994—; bd. dirs. ARTEL Med. Devel. Inc., Lodi, 1985—. Contbr. articles to profl. jours. Maj. U.S. Army, 1977-79. Yale U. fellow, 1975-76. Fellow ALS, Am. Urol. Assn.; mem. Calif. Med. Soc. Avocations: fly fishing, hunting, scuba diving. Office: Lodi Urol Med Group Inc 830 S Ham Ln Ste 26 Lodi CA 95242-7510

ALBERTS, DAVID, artistic director, mime; b. Akron, Ohio, Nov. 14, 1946; married (div. 1972); 1 child, Morgan Elizabeth; married (div. 1992); children: Sarah Aimee, Samantha Kaitlin Wynne. BA in Music, Kent State U., 1972; MA in Theatre, West Va. U., 1978; PhD in Theatre, Bowling Green State U., 1989. Instr. Akron (Ohio) U., 1970-71, W.Va. U., 1978, Va. Commonwealth U., Richmond, 1979-81, Calif. State U., Turlock, Calif., 1981-83, Kent (Ohio) State U., 1986-87, Bowling Green (Ohio) State U., 1987-89; artistic dir. Theatre of the One Actor, San Diego, 1995—; mime artist in field. Author: Pantomime: Exercises and Elements, 1971, Talking About Mime, 1994 (San Diego Book award 1994), Rehearsal Management for Directors, 1995, The Expressive Body: Physical Characterization for the Actor, 1997, (play) Death by Arrangement, 1981; contbr. articles to profl. jours. Recipient Founders award Internat. Thespian Soc., 1972, Directing award Am. Coll. Theatre Festival, 1982. Mem. Internat. Mimes and Pantomimes, Assn. for Theatre in Higher Edn., Speech Comms. Assn.

ALBERTSON, DAVID, food products executive. V.p., treas. Ballantine Produce Co. Inc., Sanger, Calif., 1971—. Office: Ballatine Produce Co Inc 325 L St Sanger CA 93657-2122*

ALBINO, JUDITH ELAINE NEWSOM, university president; b. Jackson, Tenn.; m. Salvatore Albino; children: Austin, Adrian. BJ, U. Tex., 1967, PhD, 1973. Mem. faculty sch. dental medicine SUNY, Buffalo, 1972-90, assoc. provost, 1984-87, dean sch. arch. and planning, 1987-89, dean grad. sch., 1989-90; v.p. acad. affairs and rsch, dean system grad. sch. U. Colo., Boulder, 1990-91, pres., 1991-95, pres. emerita, prof. psychiatry, 1995-97; pres. Calif. Sch. Profl. Psychology, San Francisco, 1997—. Contbr. articles to profl. jours. Acad. Adminstrn. fellow Am. Coun. on Edn., 1983; grantee NIH. Fellow APA (treas., bd. dirs.); mem. Behavioral Scientists in Dental Rsch. (past pres.), Am. Assn. Dental Rsch. (bd. dirs.). Office: Calif Sch Profl Psychology Office of the Pres 2748 Hyde St San Francisco CA 94109-1223

ALBRECHT, ALBERT PEARSON, electronics engineer, consultant; b. Bakersfield, Calif., Aug. 23, 1920; s. Albert Waldo and Elva (Shuck) A.; m. Muriel Elizabeth Grenell, June 15, 1942 (dec. Apr. 1943); m. Edith J. Dorner, July 18, 1944. BSEE, Calif. Inst. Tech., 1942; MSEE, U. So. Calif., L.A., 1947. Registered profl. engr., Calif. Rsch. assoc. radiation lab. MIT, Cambridge, 1942-43; chief engr. Gilfillan Bros., L.A., 1943-58; v.p. Space Gen. Corp., El Monte, Calif., 1958-68; exec. v.p. Telluran Cons., Santa Monica, Calif., 1968-72; dir. systems evaluation Office of Asst. Sec. of Def. for Intelligence, Washington, 1972-76; assoc. adminstr. FAA, Washington, 1976-86; cons., prin. AP Albrecht-Cons., Bellingham, Wash., 1986—; bd. dirs. Air Traffic Control Assn.; mem. exec. bd. RADIO Tech. Commn. for Aeronautics, Washington, 1980-86; mem. aeronautics adv. com. NASA, Washington, 1980-90. Co-author: Electronic Designers Handbook-Design Compendium, 1957, 2d edit., 1974; editor Air Traffic Control Quar. Fellow AIAA (adv. com. Aerospace Am. 1984—), IEEE (Engr. Mgr. of the Yr. 1989). Achievements include technical leadership of the replacement and automation of the nation's air traffic control system. Home and Office: 3224 Eagleridge Way Bellingham WA 98226-7821

ALBRECHT, JOIE, television and film producer, director, writer; b. Denver; d. Alfred Emil and Virginia Lee Albrecht; m. Scott N. Garen, Sept. 17, 1979 (div. Aug. 1989). Student, U. Colo., 1976-78, U. Calif., Bakersfield, 1979. V.p. Garen/Albrecht Prodns. Inc., Santa Monica, Calif., 1980-88; owner, pres. Albrecht & Assocs., Inc., Topanga, Calif., 1989—; guest lectr. Am. Film Inst., L.A., 1981, Women's Image Network, L.A., 1994; judge Emmy awards, L.A., 1985—; producer, writer, dir. Scandals, pilot for ABC/Stephen J. Cannell Prodns.; producer, dir., writer CBS Comedy Bloopers; author Adam's Guide to Eve. Prodr. (nat. syndication) The Cliffwood Avenue Kids'; prodr., dir. Up Close HBO series; co-creator, developer, prodr.: (TV spl.) Sixty Years of Seduction, cable spl. Carole King: One to One; prodr., writer TV's Bloopers and Practical Jokes--NBC; developer, prodr., writer: (TV spls.) Television's Greatest Commercials; creator, prodr., writer, dir.: Down and Out with Donald Duck, 1987; prodr., writer, co-dir.: Mickey's 60th Birthday, Totally Minnie--Disney/NBC; prodr., writer, dir.: (TV spl.) Comedy Bloopers. Recipient Belding Bowl for outstanding contbn. to advt. Belding Awards, 1984, gold award for Smart Investing, N.Y. Film Festival, 1986, bronze award for outstanding achievement in film and TV music video category Cindy Awards,; talent scholar U. Colo. Mem. AFTRA, ASCAP, SAG, Dirs. Guild Am. (women's com. 1991—), Writers Guild Am., Women in Film, Topanga Assn. for Scenic Cmty., Old Topanga Homeowners Assn. Democrat. Avocations: spiritual pursuits, crafts, travel. Office: PO Box 8626 Calabasas CA 91372-8626

ALBURGER, JAMES REID, audio production specialist, director, entertainer; b. Los Angeles, Aug. 7, 1950; s. James Reid Sr. and Alys (Shannon) A. AA, Pasadena City Coll., 1970; BS, San Diego State U., 1972. Rec. engr. Bell Sound Studios, Hollywood, Calif., 1972-73; audio supr. Sta. NBC 7-39 (KNSD-TV), San Diego, 1973-98; audio prodn specialist Shannon-Reid, Ltd., San Diego, 1983—; producer, dir. Shannon-Reid Illusions Unlimited, San Diego, 1986—; owner, producer, dir., engr. James Alburger Sound Design, San Diego, 1992—; freelance magician, San Diego, 1974—. Author: Get Your Act Together, 1978, Voice Actor and Voice-Over Teacher, 1996—, the Art of Voice Acting, 1998. Recipient 9 Emmy awards, 1990—. Mem. NATAS, Soc. Am. Magicians (best stage technician 1970, 72, best supernatural act 1970, best novelty act 1973), Internat. Brotherhood Magicians. Home and Office: Shannon-Reid Ltd 13639 Freeport Rd San Diego CA 92129-3210

ALCANTARA, DONNA L., political organization administrator. Chairwoman Rep. Party Hawaii, Honolulu. Fax: (808) 593-7742. Office: Rep Party Hawaii 1946 N King St Honolulu HI 96819*

ALCINDOR, LEWIS FERDINAND See ABDUL-JABBAR, KAREEM

ALCONE, MATT, advertising executive; b. 1953. BS in Biology, U. Calif., Irvine, BA in Bus. Adminstrn. CEO Alcone Mktg. Group, Irvine, Calif., 1975—, also chmn. bd. dirs. Office: Alcone Mktg. Group 15 Whatney Irvine CA 92618-2808

ALCOSSER, SANDRA, English language educator; b. 1944. Assoc. editor Mademoiselle, N.Y.C., 1966-69; dir. Poets-in-the-Park, N.Y.C., 1975-77; instr. La. State U., 1982-85, asst. prof. English,, 1985-87; dir. creative writing program San Diego State U., 1988-91, assoc. prof. English,, 1986-89, prof., 1990—; writer-in-residence, workshop dir. various locations, 1973-85; vis. prof. creative writing U. Mich., 1994; guest spkr. Nat. Pub. Radio and Pub. TV programs. Author: (poetry) Each Bone a Prayerpoetry, 1982, A Fish to Feed All Hunger, 1986, Sleeping Inside the Glacier, 1997, Except by Nature, 1998; contbr. to books and jours. Grantee NEA.

ALCOTT TEMPEST TEMPLE, LESLIE, artist; b. Oklahoma City, 1951; d. William Joseph and Gretta Atkinson; m. George Arthur Carlson, July 18, 1974 (div. Feb. 1981); children: Solon Emil Carlson, Andra Sean Carlson. Student, Colo. Women's Coll., 1969-70; BS, Oklahoma City U., 1973; postgrad., Cen. State U., Edmond, Okla., 1973-74; studied with, Bruno Lucchesi, Jon Zahourek. Cert. in concrete work City of Denver and State of Colo.; cert. tchr. elem. edn., Okla. Artist, 1965—; adult reading tchr. Oscar Rose Jr. Coll., Midwest City, Okla., 1971; art tchr. Oklahoma City Fine Arts Mus., 1972; bus. mgr. and mktg. dir. for artist George Carlson Elizabeth and Frankton, Colo., 1974-80; pres. S L A Arch/Couture, Inc., Denver, 1981—; tchr. art and art history 2d grade Our Lady of Lourdes Sch., 1988; mem. adv. com. Colo. Dept. Transp., 1991-92. Author: The Tarahumara, 1976, 78, Body of Work, 1982: exhibited in shows including Catherine Lorillard Wolfe 92d Ann., N.Y.C., N.Am. Sculpture Exhbn., High Plains Sculpture Exhbn., Greely Invitation (Best of Show 1983), Am. Artists Profl. League 60th Grand Nat. Exhbn., Salmagundi Club, N.Y., 1988; represented in corp. and pvt. collections including Nat. Jewish Med. and Rsch. Ctr., JRS Exploration Co. LTD, Calgary, Geoevalaciones, So. America, Founders Corp., N.Y.C., J. Serrano, Mexico City & Fla., The Andrews Group Internat., Inc., Houston, No. Geophys., Inc., Anchorage, Patricia Ellison, MD, Denver, others, World Summit of the Eight, Denver, 1997, others; featured in permanent collection monumental sculptor Western history dept. Denver Pub. Libr., Mus. Outdoor Art; contbr. to Nat. Libr. Poetry. Mem. audience devel. and pub. rels. coms. Denver Art Mus., 1993—; founder, pres. Am. Assn. for Benefit of Tarahumara Indian Tribe, 1997-98; vol. Denver Safe House, Oklahoma City Fine Arts Mus., Spkr.'s Bur. of Heart Paths, Head Start Program, Denver Indian Ctr., Denver Pub. Sch. Sys., Denver Christian H.S., others; trustee Denver Art Mus., 1993-94, audience devel. com.; tribal diplomat govt. offices and Native Am. tribal leaders; mem. mktg. com. Artists of Am. Exhbn., 1999. Summer scholar Oklahoma City U. Mem. Museo de las Ams., Denver Art Mus., Denver Art Students League, Natural History Mus., Women Constrn. Owners and Execs. (founding mem., officer), Artists of Am. (mktg. com. 1999). Avocations: art philosophy as life, research in psychology, physics, symbolism, ethnology and ethnography. Home and Studio: 2088 S Pennsylvania Denver CO 80210 Office: Am Assn For Benefit Of Tarahumara Indian Tribe 2075 S University Blvd Denver CO 80210-4300

ALDAG, RICHARD JEFFREY, composer, educator; b. N.Y.C., Aug. 8, 1955; s. Russell Thomas and Emily (Carro) A.; m. Maria Celi, July 2, 1977 (div.); m. Astrid Juárez, Dec. 30, 1989. B.A., Queens Coll., 1977, M.A., 1979; Ph.D., CUNY, 1990. Music events coordinator CUNY Grad. Ctr., N.Y.C., 1981-84; chmn. dept. theory Bklyn. Conservatory Music, Flushing, N.Y., 1981-92; exec. dir. Musica Poetica Publs., 1992—; adj. asst. prof. Fordham U., Bronx, 1984-92; bd. dirs. Am. New Music Consortium, N.Y.C., 1985-86, Access Chamber Ensemble, N.Y.C., 1987-90; dir. Silicon Valley Youth Conservatory, 1994-98; lectr. music San Jose (Calif.) State U., 1993—; vis. prof. composition Shanghai Conservatory of Music, 1993-94; exec. dir. Los Lupenos de San Jose, 1998. Composer numerous vocal and instrumental works. CUNY fellow, 1980, 84. Mem. League of Composers/Internat. Soc. for Contemporary Music (bd. dirs. 1988-91), Internat. Alban Berg Soc. (sec.-treas. 1982-86), Roger Sessions Soc. (v.p. 1988). Avocation: Mexican cooking.

ALDERMAN, MINNIS AMELIA, psychologist, educator, small business owner; b. Douglas, Ga., Oct. 14, 1928; d. Louis Cleveland Sr. and Minnis Amelia (Wooten) A. AB in Music, Speech and Drama, Ga. State Coll., Milledgeville, 1949; MA in Supervision and Counseling Psychology, Murray State U., 1960; postgrad. Columbia Pacific U., 1987—. Tchr. music Lake County Sch. Dist., Umatilla, Fla., 1949-50; instr. vocal and instrumental music, dir. band, orch. and choral Fulton County Sch. Dist., Atlanta, 1950-54; instr. English, speech, debate, vocal and instrumental music, dir. drama, band, choral and orch. Elko County Sch. Dist., Wells, Nev., 1954-59; tchr. English and social studies Christian County Sch. Dist., Hopkinsville, Ky., 1960; instr. psychology, counselor critic prof. Murray (Ky.) State U., 1961-63, U. Nev., Reno, 1963-67; owner Minisizer Exercising Salon, Ely, Nev., 1969-71, Knit Knook, Ely, 1969—, Minimimeo, Ely, 1969—, Gift Gamut, Ely, 1977—; prof. dept. fine arts Wassuk Coll., Ely, 1986-91, assoc. dean, 1986-87, dean, 1987-90; counselor White Pine County Sch. Dist., Ely, 1960-68; dir. Child and Family Ctr., Ely Indian Tribe, 1988-93, Family and Cmty. Ctr., Ely Shoshone Indian Tribe, 1988-93, Family Resource Ctr., Great Basin Rural Nev. Youth Cabinet, 1996—; adv. Ely Shoshone Tribal Youth Coun., 1990-93, Budge Stanton Meml. Scholarship, 1991-93, Budge Stanton Meml. Living Mus. and Cultural Ctr., 1991-93; fin. aid contracting officer Ely Shoshone Tribe, 1990-93; instr. No. Nev. C.C., 1995—; supr. testing Ednl. Testing Svc., Princeton, N.J., 1960-68, Am. Coll. Testing Program, Iowa, 1960-68, U. Nev., Reno, 1960-68; chmn. bd. White Pine Sch. Dist. Employees Fed. Credit Union, Ely, 1961-69; psychologist mental hygiene div. Nev. Pers., Ely, 1969-75, dept. employment security, 1975-80; sec.-treas. bd. dirs. Gt. Basin Enterprises, Ely, 1969-71; speaker at confs.; rep. Ely/East Ely Bus. Coun., 1997—; mem. Econ. Devel. Bd., 1998—. Author various news articles, feature stories, pamphlets, handbooks and grants in field. Pvt. instr. piano, violin, voice and organ, Ely, 1981—; dir. Family Resource Ctr. (Great Basin Rural Nev. Youth Cabinet), 1996—; bd. dirs. band Sacred Heart Sch., Ely, 1982—; mem. Gov.'s Mental Health State Commn., 1963-65, Ely Shoshone Tribal Youth Camp, 1991-92, Elys Shoshone Tribal Unity Conf., 1991-92, Tribal Parenting Skills Coord., 1991; bd. dirs. White Pine County

Sch. Employees Fed. Credit Union, 1961-68, pres., 1963-68; 2d v.p. White Pine Community Concert Assn., 1965-67, pres., 1967, 85—, treas., 1975-79, dr. chmn., 1981-85; chmn. of bd., 1984; bd. dirs. White Pine chpt. ARC, 1978-82; mem. Nev. Hwy. Safety Leaders Bd., 1979-82; mem. Gov.'s Commn. on Status Women, 1968-74, Gov.'s Nevada State Juvenile Justice Adv. Commn., 1992-94, White Pine Overall Econ. Devel. Plan Coun., 1992-94; sec.-treas. White Pine Rehab. Tng. Ctr. for Retarded Persons, 1973-75; mem. Gov.'s Commn. on Hwy. Safety, 1979-81, Gov's. Juvenile Justice Program; sec.-treas. White Pine County Juvenile Problems Cabinet, 1994—; dir. Ret. Sr. Vol. Program, 1973-74; vice chmn. Gt. Basin Health Coun., 1973-75, Home Extension Adv. Bd., 1977-80; sec.-treas. Great Basin chpt. Nev. Employees Assn.; bd. dirs. United Way, 1970-76; vice chmn. White Pine Coun. on Alcoholism and Drug Abuse, 1975-76, chmn., 1976-77; grants author 3 yrs. Indian Child Welfare Act; originator Community Tng. Ctr. for Retarded People, 1972, Ret. Sr. Vol. Program, 1974, Nutrition Program for Sr. Citizens, 1974, Sr. Citizens Ctr., 1974, Home Repairs for Sr. Citizens, 1974, Sr. Citizens Home Assistance Program, 1977, Creative Crafters Assns., 1976, Inst. Current World Affairs, 1989, Victims of Crime, 1990-92, grants author Family Resource Ctr., 1995; bd. dirs. Family coalition, 1990-92, Sacred Heart Parochial Sch., 1982—, dir. band, 1982—; candidate for diaconal ministry, 1982-93; dir. White Pine Community Choir, 1962—, Ely Meth. Ch. Choir, 1960-84; choir dir., organist Sacred Heart Ch., 1984—. Precinct reporter ABC News 1966; speaker U.S. Atty. Gen. Conf. Bringing Nev. Together; bd. dirs. White Pine Juvenile Cabinet, 1993—, Ely/East Ely Bus. Coun., 1997—, Econ. Devel. Bd., 1998—. Recipient Recognition rose Alpha Chi State Delta Kappa Gamma, 1994; mem. adv. com. William Bee Ririe Hosp., 1996—, Ea. Nev. Child and Family Svcs., 1996—. Fellow Am. Coll. Musicians, Nat. Guild Piano Tchrs.; mem. NEA (life), UDC, DAR, Nat. Fedn. Ind. Bus. (dist. chair 1971-85, nat. guardian coun. 1985—, state guardian coun. 1987—), AAUW (pres. Wells br. 1957-58, pres. White Pine br. 1965-66, 86-87, 89-91, 93—, bd. dirs. 1965-87, rep. edn. 1965-67, implementation chair 1967-69, area advisor 1969-73, 89-91), Nat. Fedn. Bus. and Profl. Women (1st v.p. Ely chpt. 1965-66, pres. Ely chpt. 1966-68, 74-76, 85—, bd. dirs. Nev. chpt. 1966—, 1st v.p. Nev. Fedn. 1970-71, pres. Nev. chpt. 1972-73, nat. bd. dirs. 1972-73), White Pine County Mental Health Assn. (pres. 1960-63, 78—), Mensa (supr. testing 1965—), Delta Kappa Gamma (br. pres. 1968-72, 94—, state bd. 1967—, chpt. parliamentarian 1974-78, state 1st v.p. 1967-69, state pres. 1969-71, nat. bd. 1969-71, state parliamentarian 1971-73, 95—, chmn. state nominating com. 1995-97, workshop presenter on aging S.W. Regional Conf. San Francisco 1995), White Pine Knife and Fork Club (1st v.p. 1969-70, pres. 1970-71, bd. dirs. 1979—), Soc. Descendants of Knights of Most Noble Order of Garter, Nat. Soc. Magna Charta Dames, Delta Kappa Gamma. Office: PO Box 150457 East Ely NV 89315-0457

ALDERMAN, WILLIAM FIELDS, lawyer; b. Hamilton, Ohio, 1945. AB summa cum laude, Miami U., 1967; JD, Yale U., 1970. Bar: Calif. 1971. Ptnr. Orrick, Herrington & Sutcliffe, San Francisco, 1976—; ct. apptd. arbitrator, mediator and evaluator, 1988—. Dir. Lawyers Com. for Civil Rights of the San Francisco Bay Area, 1985—, St. Thomas More Soc. San Francisco, 1987-94, pres. 1993; dir. San Francisco Neighborhood Legal Assistance Found., 1995—. Mem. Phi Beta Kappa. Office: Orrick Herrington & Sutcliffe Old Federal Reserve Bank Bldg 400 Sansome St San Francisco CA 94111-3143

ALDRICH, DAVID LAWRENCE, public relations executive; b. Lakehurst Naval Air Sta., N.J., Feb. 21, 1948; s. Clarence Edward and Sarah Stiles (Andrews) A.; m. Benita Susan Massler, Mar. 17, 1974. BA in Communications, Calif. State U.-Dominguez Hills, 1976. Pub. info. technician City of Carson (Calif.), 1973-77; pub. rels. dir./adminstrv. asst. Calif. Fed. Savs., L.A., 1977-78; v.p., group supr. Hill & Knowlton, L.A., 1978-81; v.p., mgr. Ayer Pub. Rels. western div. N.W. Ayer, L.A., 1981-84; pres. Aldrich and Assocs. Inc., L.A., 1984—; bd. dirs., exec. com. Drum Corps Internat. Bd. dirs. Long Beach (Calif.) Housing Devel. Co.; mayor's task force for strategic planning Long Beach. Home: 25 15th Pl Unit 704 Long Beach CA 90802-6061 Office: Aldrich & Assocs 110 Pine Ave Ste 620 Long Beach CA 90802-4423

ALDRICH, DELL STANLEY, orthodontist; b. Southgate, Calif., July 31, 1938; s. Adelbert Carl and Marian Grace (Carlson) A.; m. Joanne Emily VanderByl, June 30, 1962 (div. 1976); children: Cheryl Marlene, Michelle Renee. AA, Glendale Coll., 1959; DDS, U. So. Calif., 1963, MS in Orthodontics, 1970. Intern U.S.C. Med. Ctr., L.A.; resident U.S.C. Sch. Dentistry, L.A.; clin. instr. fixed prosthetic dept. U. So. Calif., L.A., 1962-63, 66-68; pvt. practice instr. Swiss Dental Assn., Geneva and Zurich, Switzerland, 1970-71; instr. Internat. Post Doctorate Program, 1989-96; pvt. practice Descanso Med. Ctr., La Canada, Calif., 1972-93, Flintridge, Calif., 1993—. Author: Differential Response Incident to Tooth Movement, 1970; contbr. articles to profl. jours.; inventor, developer ultrasonic and fiber optic instruments; patentee in field. Mem. Rep. Presdl. Task Force, 1984. Capt. U.S. Army, 1963-66, Fed. Republic Germany. Mem. Am. Assn. Orthodontists, Pacific Coast Soc. Orthodontics, Am. Dental Assn., Calif. Dental Soc., Kiwanis, Tournament of Roses Assn., Omicron Kappa Epsilon Alumni Assn., Phi Kappa Phi. Avocations: antique restoration, photography, scale model railroading. Address: 241 W Wilson St Apt 20 Costa Mesa CA 92627-5634

ALDRICH, MICHAEL RAY, library curator, health educator; b. Vermillion, S.D., Feb. 7, 1942; s. Ray J. and Lucile W. (Hamm) A.; AB, Princeton, 1964; MA, U. S.D., 1965; PhD, SUNY, 1970; m. Michelle Cauble, Dec. 26, 1977. Fulbright tutor Govt. Arts and Commerce Coll., Indore, Madhya Pradesh, India, 1965-66; founder Lemar Internat., 1966-71; mem. faculty Sch. Critical Studies, Calif. Inst. Arts, Valencia, 1970-72; workshop leader Esalen Inst., San Francisco, 1972; co-founder AMORPHIA, Inc., The Cannabis Coop., Mill Valley, Calif., 1969-74; curator Fitz Hugh Ludlow Meml. Libr., San Francisco, 1974—. Freelance writer, photographer, lectr., cons. on drug rsch., and sociolegal reform specializing in drug laws and history to various colls., drug confs., publishers, svc. groups; cons. Commn. of Inquiry into Non-Med. Use of Drugs, Ottawa, Ont., 1973; rsch. aide, select com. on control marijuana Calif. Senate, 1974. Bd. dirs. Ethno-Pharmacology Soc., 1976-83, Nat. Assn. Ethnography & Social Policy, 1997—, Exotic Dancers Alliance, 1997—, Calif. Helping Alleviate Med. Problems, 1997—. Calif. Marijuana Initiative, 1971-74; mem. nat. adv. bd. Nat. Orgn. for Reform of Marijuana Laws, 1976-86; mem. Princeton working group Future of Drug Policy, 1990-93; asst. dir. Nat. Inst. on Drug Abuse AIDS Project Menu, Youth Environment Study, San Francisco, 1987-88; project adminstr. YES Tng. Ctr., 1989, program coord. Calif. AIDS Intervention Tng. Ctr. Inst. for Cmty. Health Outreach, 1990—. Author: The Dope Chronicles 1850-1950, 1979, Coricancha, The Golden Enclosure, 1983; co-author: High Times Ency. of Recreational Drugs, 1978, Fiscal Costs of California Marijuana Law Enforcement, 1986, YES Tng. Manual, 1989, Methods of Estimating Needle Users at Risk for AIDS, 1990; editor: Marijuana Review, 1968-74, Ludlow Library Newsletter, 1974-81; contbg. author: Cocaine Handbook, 1981, 2d edit., 1987, Cannabis in Medical Practice, 1997; mem. editorial rev. bd. Jour. Psychoactive Drugs, 1981—, marijuana theme issue editor, 1988; research photographer Life mag., 1984; contbg. editor High Times, 1979-85; contbr. articles to profl. publs. Office: PO Box 640346 San Francisco CA 94164-0346

ALDRICH, ROBERT EARLE, optical engineer; b. Ithaca, N.Y., Jan. 11, 1963; s. Angus John and Joan Shirely (Earle) A. BS in Optics, U. Rochester, 1985; MS in Optics, U. Ariz., 1995. Lead optical design engr. Tex. Instruments, Dallas, 1985-92; sr. optical engr. Flir Sys. Inc., Portland, Oreg., 1992-96; sr. staff engr. Hughes/Raytheon Aircraft, Tucson, Arlington, Va., and El Segundo, Calif., 1996—; divsn. rep. to corp. optics coun. Hughes Electronics-GM, Tucson, 1996-97. Mem. Internat. Soc. for Optical Engring., Optical Soc. Am. Republican. Achievements include design of single element diffractive optical eyepiece, two and three element wide field of view infrared lenses, three element two position infrared lenses; research in diffractive optics, infrared lens design. Home: 13606 Marina Pointe Dr Apt D503 Marina Del Rey CA 90292-9235 Office: Bldg El MS D109 2000 E El Segundo Blvd El Segundo CA 90245-4501

ALDRIDGE, CYNTHIA LOU, credit reporting agency executive; b. Torrance, Calif., Oct. 27, 1959; d. Orville Raymond Balcom, Jr. and Mary Lou (Graves) Hunt; children: Alicia Giuliani, Nicholas Giuliani; m. Jan. 16, 1999. Treas., v.p. Nat. Credit Svc. Ctr., Ft. Worth, Tex., 1981-84; pres. Compunet Credit Svcs., Lake Havasu City, Ariz., 1984—. Pres. Lake Havasu City Town Hall, 1994-98; mem. adv. bd. Lake Havasu Samaritan Regional Hosp., 1996-98; mem. Ariz. Town Hall, Phoenix, 1994—; treas. Partnership for Econ. Devel., Lake Havasu, 1996-97; campaign chmn. United Way, Lake Havasu City, 1998. Mem. Nat. Acctg. and Fin. Coun., Truckload Carriers Assn., Intermodal Coun. Office: Compunet Credit Svcs PO Box 710 Lake Havasu City AZ 86405-0710

ALDRIDGE, GEANIE BLACK, bank executive; b. Holyoke, Mass., July 6, 1942; d. Edward Dewey and Mary Virginia (Johnson) Black; m. Robert Patten Aldridge, Jan. 16, 1969; 1 child, Ruth Johnson. Student, U. N.C., 1960-61, Gonzaga U., 1977-81; grad., Pacific Coast Banking Sch., 1983. Asst. cashier N.C. Nat. Bank, Chapel Hill, 1967-69; mgmt. trainee Seafirst Bank, Spokane, 1976-78, br. mgr., 1978-82; v.p., mgr. Seafirst Bank, Moses Lake, Wash., 1982-85, Wenatchee, Wash., 1985-89; v.p., mgr. Seafirst Bank, Yakima, Wash., 1989-92, sr. v.p., mgr., 1992-95, regional sr. v.p., divsn. mgr., 1995—; mem. steering com. Wash. State Agrl. Showcase, Yakima, 1992—. Bd. dirs. Yakima County Devel. Assn., 1994—, vice chmn., 1997; mem. sel. jury Freedom Found., Valley Forge, Pa., 1986; pres. coun. Heritage Coll., Toppenish, Wash., 1996; bd. dirs. United Way Yakima County, 1996. Mem. Am. Bus. Women's Assn. (nat. pres. 1985-86, nat. sec.-treas. 1984-85, dist. v.p. 1982-83), Rotary. Presbyterian. Avocations: travel, bridge, golf. Office: Seafirst Bank 101 N 2nd St Yakima WA 98901-2613

ALECKSICH-AKEY, SUSAN C., political organization administrator. Chairwoman Mont. Rep. State Ctrl. Com., Helena. Fax: (406) 442-3293. Office: Mont Rep State Ctrl Com 1419-B Helena Ave Helena MT 59601*

ALENIKOV, VLADIMIR, motion picture director and writer; b. Leningard, Russia, Aug. 7, 1948; came to U.S., 1990; s. Michael and Stella (Alenikova) Volkenshtein; 1 child, Philip; m. Tamara Karpovitch; 1 child, Anastassia. Student, Leningrad State U., 1965-67, Leningrad Inst. Theatre, 1967-69, Moscow State U., 1969-72. Tchr. Russian lit. and french, dep. prin. Secondary Sch. 2, Moscow, 1969-72; dir. Gorky Film Studios, Moscow, 1974-78, 88-89, Odessa Film Studio, 1982-84; dir. music Ekran TV Studio, Moscow, 1979-81, dir., 1985-87; dir., pres. Aquilon Co., Moscow, 1989—; dir., owner Destiny Films, L.A., 1992—; lectr. at film showing; mem. 1st Soviet del. of cinematographers, Cyprus, Greece. Author: The White Page, 1972, The Mysteries of a Women's Heart, 1975, also articles, poems and short stories; Dir. and writer of feature films: The Garden, 1973, The Composer Comitas, 1974, The Room of Laughter, 1975, What a Mess, 1976, There Lived a Piano-Tuner, 1979, The Adventures of Petrov and Vasechkin, Ordinary and Extraordinary, 1982, The Hooligan, 1983, The Knight, 1983, Unique, 1986, Valuable Friends, 1987, The Drayman and the King, 1989, The Time of Darkness, 1991, The Awakening, 1991, Monique, 1993; Dir. and writer of stage plays: The Locals, 1976, The Adventures of d'Artagnan, 1986, (with David Wolcomb), Peace Child, 1985, The Hooligan is Coming, 1986, The Tale of the Warrior, 1987, The Tower, 1988, White Mercedes, 1992; Screen plays include: August Weather Forecast, 1984, A Night Story, 1985, To Kill and be Alive, 1990, The Incredible Adventures of Ricky Plim, 1992, Without Past, 1993, War of Princess, 1993. Pres. Russian-Am. Art Ctr., L.A., 1992—. Recipient 1st prize for best TV film 22d Internat. Festival Children and Youth Films Gijon Spain 1984, award for best film dir.'s debut Internat. Festival TV Films Montreux Switzerland 1979, Danube prize 8th Internat. Festival Childrens' TV Films Bratislava Czechoslovakia 1985, Grand Prix Soviet Nat. Festival Youth-83 1983, Grand Prix First Moscow Film Festival of Children's Scetches 1987, prize for funniest movie 10th Internat. Festival Children's Films Moscow 1987, AFI Film Internat. Festival award L.A. 1990, Jerusalem Film Festival award 1990, Toronto Festival of Festivals diploma 1990, Moscow Internat. Film Festival award 1991; also others. Mem. Russian Film Makers, Russian Guild Scriptwriters, Russian Guild Dir., Moscow Guild Diirs., L.A. Press Club. Jewish. Avocations: reading, writing. Home and Office: Apt 122 1274 N Crescent Heights Blvd West Hollywood CA 90046-5059

ALESZKA, JAMES CHARLES, metallurgical and corrosion engineer; b. Oakland, Calif., June 9, 1949; s. Benjamin John and Virginia Zeeb (Schonbein) A. BS in Engring., UCLA, 1971, MS in Engring., 1973. Registered profl. metall. engr., Calif., corrosion engr., Calif. Prin. investigator U.S. Army Constrn. Engring. Rsch. Lab., Champaign, Ill., 1974-75; supr. fracture mechanics lab. Gen. Rsch. Corp., Santa Barbara, Calif., 1975-79; engring. specialist Gen. Dynamics Corp., San Diego, 1979-92; owner Fracture Investigations, San Diego, 1987—; presenter in field. Contbr. articles to Metall. Transactions, Jour. Testing and Evaluation. Blood donor San Diego Blood Bank, 1979—; vol. Wine and Roses Charity Event, San Diego. Sea Grant fellow U.S. Dept. of Interior, UCLA, 1971. Mem. ASTM, Nat. Assn. Corrosion Engrs., Am. Soc. Metals, Convair Sailing Club (treas.). Avocations: running, sailing, wine collecting. Home and Office: 4718 Renovo Way San Diego CA 92124-2451

ALEVY, SCOTT DAVID, telecommunications company executive; b. Long Beach, Calif., Aug. 7, 1950; s. Herman Solomon and Pauline Sarah (Selikowitz) A.; m. Mitzi Gay Stone, Feb. 18, 1981; children: Lauren, Shea. AA in Radio/TV, Long Beach City Coll., 1970; BA in Broadcast Journalism, U. So. Calif., 1976; honor grad., Def. Info. Sch., 1974. Mgr. pub. rels., passenger svc. Pacific S.W. Airlines, San Diego, San Francisco, 1973-86; acct. exec. Calif. Radio Group, San Diego, 1986-92; dir. sales mktg. Ad Mail Direct Mktg., San Diego, 1993-95; assoc. Nelson Comm. Group, San Diego, 1995-97; dir. external affairs Pacific Bell, San Diego, 1997—. Contbr. articles to airline mags; co-writer (TV comml. series) Jeep Shots, 1992. Vice chair Parks Recreation Commn., Chula Vista, 1992-95; councilman City of Chula Vista, 1995-97; bd. dirs. S. Bay Family YMCA, Chula Vista, Calif., 1996—, World Trade Ctr., San Diego, 1997—, San Diego Convention-Visitors Bur., 1997—. With USAF, 1974-77, Korea. Mem. Chula Vista C. of C. (v.p., chmn. econ. devel., pub. policy com. 1996—, bd. dirs. 1997—, Legis. of Yr. 1996), Greater San Diego C. of C. (pub. policy com. 1997—), Chula Vista Men's Golf Club (bd. dirs. 1991-97). Republican. Jewish. Avocations: golfing, concerts. Office: Pacific Bell External Affairs 101 W Broadway Ste 1440 San Diego CA 92101

ALEXANDER, AMY JILL, computer-video artist, art educator; b. Phila.. BA, Rowan U., 1991; MFA, Calif. Inst. of Arts, Valencia, 1996. Freelance video prodr. Phila., 1991-93; freelance digital artist, programmer L.A., 1996—; faculty U. So. Calif., L.A., 1997, Calif. Inst. of Arts, 1996—. Office: Calif Inst of Arts 24700 Mcbean Pkwy Valencia CA 91355-2397

ALEXANDER, CHRISTOPHER, architecture educator; b. Vienna, Austria, Oct. 4, 1936; married; two children. BA in Architecture, Cambridge (Eng.) U., MA in Math.; PhD in Architecture, Harvard U. Research asst. Joint Ctr. for Urban Studies of MIT and Harvard, 1959-60; instr. Harvard U., 1960-61; research assoc. Ctr. for Cognitive Studies, Harvard U., 1960-61; cons. village devel. planning Govt. of Gujarat, India, 1962; cons., researcher MIT Civil Engring. Systems Lab., 1960-63; from asst. prof. to full prof. architecture U. Calif., Berkeley, 1963—; dir. Ctr. for Environ. Structure, Berkeley, 1967—; advisor or cons. architect Govts. of Israel, Mexico, Spain, other nat. and city govts. and orgns. internationally; vis. prof. or lectr. univs. worldwide; invited artist at Forum Design, Linz, Austria, 1982; chief architect The Eishin Sch., Tokyo, 1980-82; advisor to Nordic Council of Ministers, 1985. Principal works include: (with Janet Johnson) Village School, Bavra, Gujarat, India, 1962; Master Plan for U. Oreg., 1969; (with Murray Silverstein and Nacht and Lewis, Sacramento) Community Mental Health Ctr., Modesto, Calif., 1972; Experiments in Sprayed Concrete, U. Calif., Berkeley, 1978; The Linz Cafe, 1980, Fresno Farmers Market, 1983; (with Hajo Neis, Gary Black, Ingrid King, others) The New Eishin Univ., 1985; also pvt. residences, low cost housing projects, factories, and numerous decorative works. Author: (with Serge Chermayeff) Community and Privacy, 1963; Thick Wall Pattern, 1967, Tres Aspectos de Matematica Y Diseqno, 1969; (with Ronald Walkey, Murray Silverstein and others) A Human City, 1970, La Estructura del Medio Ambiente, 1971, (with Howard Davis and Halim Abdelhalim) People Rebuilding Berkeley, 1975; The Oregon Experiment, 1975; (with S. Ishikawa, M. Silverstein, M. Jacobson, I. Fiksdahl-King, S. Angel) A Pattern Language, 1977; The Timeless Way of Building, 1979, The Linz Cafe, 1981; (with Howard Davis, Julio Martinez, Don Corner) The Production of Houses, 1985; (with Hajo Neis, Gary Black and Ingrid King) Battle: The Story of a Historic Clash Between World System A and World System B, 1985; Very Early Turkish Carpets, 1985, Sketches of a New Architecture, 1985; (with Hajo Neis, Artemis Anninou, Ingrid King) A New Theory of Urban Design, 1985; The Nature of Order, 1985; also numerous articles to profl. jours. Numerous of his works translated into Japanese, German, Spanish, French, others. His works and writings the subject of numerous studies. Fellow, Soc. of Fellows, Harvard U., 1961; vis. fellow Rockefeller Found., Villa Servelloni, Italy, 1965; recipient Research medal AIA, 2d prize for Best Bldg. in Japan, Japan Inst. Architects, 1985, Disting. Prof. award Assn. Collegiate Schs. of Architecture, 1987. Mem. Swedish Royal Acad. Office: U Calif Coll of Environ Design 232 Wurester Hall Berkeley CA 94720*

ALEXANDER, DEAN, museum director. Supt. Kalaupapa (Hawaii) Nat. Hist. Park. Office: Kalaupapa Nat Hist Park 7 Puahi St PO Box 2222 Kalaupapa HI 96742-2222*

ALEXANDER, GERRY L., state supreme court justice; b. Aberdeen, Wash., Apr. 28, 1936. BA, U. Wash., 1958, JD, 1964. Bar: Wash. 1964. Pvt. practice Olympia, Wash., 1964-73; judge Wash. Superior Ct., Olympia, 1973-85, Wash. Ct. Appeals Divsn. II, Olympia, 1985-95; justice Wash. Supreme Ct., Olympia, 1995—. Lt. U.S. Army, 1958-61. Mem. ABA, Am. Judges Assn., Wash. State Bar Assn., Thurston-Mason County Assn. (pres. 1973), Puget Sound Inn of Ct. (pres. 1996). Office: Temple of Justice PO Box 40929 Olympia WA 98504-0929

ALEXANDER, JAMES ENOS, race horse trainer; b. Miamisburg, Ohio, June 27, 1927; s. Joseph Edward and Adora (Butrick) A.; m. Arlene May Stanley (div. 1979); children: Beckly Lee, James Enos Jr.; m. Janis Ellen McFarland. Bull rider RCA, 1946-61. With U.S. Army, 1954-58. Avocations: writing, painting, collecting and trading artifcacts, horses. Home: PO Box 123 Maxwell NM 87728-0123

ALEXANDER, JASPER D., publishing executive; m.; 1 child. BA in English and history, Wake Forest U., 1966. Reporter Winston-Salem (N.C.) Jour., 1958-59; dir. info. Bowman Gray Sch. Medicine, Winston-Salem, 1960; from copy editor to asst. nat. editor Washington Post, 1967-74; exec. asst. to publ. N.Y.C., 1975-76; mng. editor San Diego Union, 1977-86; exec. editor Seattle Post-Intelligencer, 1986-93, editor, publ., 1993—; lectr. in field. Founding dir. Calif. Soc. Newspaper Editors; past chmn. journalism edn. com. Pacific N.W. Newspaper Assn.; trustee Corp. Coun. for the Arts; dir., vice chair TVW, 1999—. With USAF, 1965-65. Mem. Am. Soc. Newspaper Editors, Allied Daily Newspapers (bd. dirs.), Greater Seattle C. of C. (trustee), Wash. State Hist. Soc. (trustee). Office: Seattle Post Intelligencer 101 Elliott Ave W Seattle WA 98119-4295*

ALEXANDER, JOHN BRADFIELD, scientist, retired army officer; b. N.Y.C., Nov. 21, 1937; m. Victoria Lacas Alexander; children: Marc Bradfield, Joshua John. BGS in Sociology, U. Nebr., 1971; MA in Edn., Pepperdine U., 1975; PhD in Edn., Walden U., 1980; postgrad., UCLA, 1990, MIT, 1991, Harvard U., 1993; attended various milit. schs. Pvt. U.S. Army, 1956, advanced through grades to col., 1986; comdr. Army Spl. Forces Teams U.S. Army, Thailand, Vietnam, 1966-69; chief human resources divsn. U.S. Army, Ft. McPherson, Ga., 1977-79; inspector gen. Dept. of Army U.S. Army, Washington, 1980-82; chief human tech. Army Intelligence Command U.S. Army, Arlington, Va., 1982-83; mgr. tech. integration Army Materiel Command U.S. Army, Alexandria, Va., 1983-85; dir. advanced concepts U.S. Army Lab. Command U.S. Army, Adelphi, Md., 1985-88; ret. U.S. Army, 1988; mgr. nonlethal weapons def. tech. Los Alamos (N.Mex.) Nat. Lab., 1988-95 (ret.), mgr. anti-materiel tech. Def. Initiatives Office, 1988-91, program mgr. contingency missions tech. Conventional Def. Tech., 1991-92; dir. for sci. liaison Nat. Inst. for Discovery Sci., Las Vegas, Nev., 1995—; vis. scientist Los Alamos, 1995-96; panelist Nat. Inst. Justice, Washington, 1994; adj. prof. Grad. Sch. Union Inst., Cin., 1992-97; U.S. del. to NATO adv. group aerospace R&D, 1994-97; chmn. NonLethal Def. Conf. Johns Hopkins Applied Physics Lab., 1993, NonLethal Def. Conf. II, 1996, III, 1998; mem. tech. panel Advanced Weapons Conf., 1992, tech. opportunities in low intensity conflict panel LIC Tech. Conf., RAND Corp., 1992; cons. Office Sec. of Def., 1996—; spkr., presenter in field. Author: Future War: Non-Lethal Weapons in Modern Warfare, 1999; co-author: The Warrior's Edge, 1990; contbr. numerous articles to profl. jours. Bd. dirs., past v.p. Children's Hospice Internat., Alexandria, 1982-96. Recipient Nat. Award for Volunteerism by Pres. Reagan, 1987, Aerospace Laureate award Aviation Week, 1993, 94, Weapons Program recognition of excellence, 1994; decorated numerous milit. awards; inducted into Laureate Hall of Fame U.S. Air and Space Mus., 1997. Mem. Soc. Sci. Exploration. Home: 9521 Grand Canal Dr Las Vegas NV 89117-0860

ALEXANDER, JOHN CHARLES, editor, writer; b. Lincoln, Nebr., Jan. 25, 1915; s. John Merriam Alexander and Helen (Abbott) Boggs; m. Ruth Edna McLane, Aug. 20, 1955. Student, U. Nebr., 1933-37, Chouinard Art Inst./Ben Bard Playhouse Sch., L.A., 1937-38, Pasadena Playhouse, 1939-42, UCLA, 1945-47. Aircraft assembler N. Am. aviation, Inglewood, Calif., 1941-42; engring. writer Lockheed-Vega Aircraft, Burbank, Calif., 1942-45; prodn. mgr/actor Gryphon Playhouse, Laguna Beach, Calif., 1947-49; asst. producer/writer Young & Rubicam/ABC, Hollywood, Calif., 1949-51; editor-in-chief Grand Cen. Aircraft, Tucson, 1952-53; sr. writer/editor various cos., Calif., 1953-60; sr. editor/writer, sec. Sci. Guidance Rsch. Coun. Stanford Rsch. Inst., U.S. Army Combat Devel. Command, Menlo Park, Calif., 1962-66; editor-in-chief Litton Sci. Support Lab. USACDC, Fort Ord, Calif., 1966-70; editorial dir./sec. The Nelson Co., Film and Video Prodn., Tarzana, Calif., 1971—; editorial cons., dir. Human Resources Rsch. Office, George Washington U., The Presidio, Monterey, Calif., 1960-62; book editor The Dryden Press, Hinsdale, Ill., 1971-72; book editor/adaptor Gen. Learning Press, Silver Burdette Co., Morristown, N.J., 1972-74; contbg. editor West Coast Writers Conspiracy mag., Hollywood, Calif., 1975-77; contbg. editor/book reviewer Santa Ynez Valley Times, Solvang, Calif., 1976-77; participant Santa Barbara Writers Conf., Montecito, Calif., 1974, 75. Author: (TV plays) Michael Has Company for Coffee, 1948, House on the Hill, 1958, (radio drama) The Couple Next Door, 1951; co-author nine films for U.S. Dept. Justice: Under the Law, Parts I and II, 1973; co-author 10 films for Walt Disney Ednl. Media Co.: Lessons in Learning, Parts I and II, 1978-81; author: (with others) The American West Anthology, 1971; editorial cons. Strangers in Their Land: CBI Bombardier, 1939-45, 1990-92. Recipient award for short story, Writer's Digest, 1960, 61, Gold award, The Festival of the Americas, Houston Internat. Film Festival, 1977. Mem. Nat. Cowboy Hall of Fam, Nat. Geog. Soc., Nat. Soc. Lit. and Arts, Soc. Tech. Writers and Pubs., Western Hist. Soc., Calif. Acad. Sci., Nat. Air and Space Mus., Smithsonian Instn., Woodrow Wilson Internat. Ctr. for Scholars, Aircraft Owners and Pilots Assn., Air Force Assn., U. Nebr.-Lincoln Alumni Assn., Stanford Rsch. Internat. Alumni Assn., Sigma Nu, Alpha Phi Omega. Avocations: scale model building, environmental/wildlife conservation, aviation, science, foreign affairs, intelligence. Home: 23123 Village 23 Camarillo CA 93012-7602

ALEXANDER, JOHN DAVID, JR., college administrator; b. Springfield, Tenn., Oct. 18, 1932; s. John David and Mary Agnes (McKinnon) A.; m. Catharine Coleman, Aug. 26, 1956; children: Catharine McKinnon, John David III, Julia Mary. BA, Southwestern at Memphis, 1953; student, Louisville Presbyn. Theol. Sem., 1953-54; DPhil (Rhodes Scholar), Oxford (Eng.) U., 1957; LLD, U. So. Calif., Occidental Coll., 1970, Centre Coll. of Ky., 1971, Pepperdine U., 1991, Albertson Coll. Idaho, 1992; LHD, Loyola Marymount U., 1983; LittD, Rhodes Coll., 1986, Pomona Coll., 1996. Assoc. prof. San Francisco Theol. Sem., 1957-65; pres. Southwestern at Memphis, 1965-69, Pomona Coll., Claremont, Calif., 1969-91; Am. sec. Rhodes Scholarship Trust, 1981-98; mem. commn. liberal learning Assn. Am. Colls., 1966-69; mem. commn. instl. affairs, 1971-74; mem. commn. colls. So. Assn. Colls. and Schs., 1966-69; mem. Nat. Commn. Acad. Tenure, 1971-72; dir. Am. Coun. on Edn., 1981-84, Nat. Assn. Ind. Colls. and Univs., bd. dirs. Children's Hosp. L.A., chair Rsch. Inst., 1997—; trustee Tchrs. Inst. and Annuity Assn., 1970—, Woodrow Wilson Nat. Fellowship Found., 1978—, Seaver Inst., 1992—, Phi Beta Kappa Assocs., 1993—, Wenner-Gren Found. for Anthrop. Rsch., 1995—, Webb Schs. Calif., 1995—; bd. overseers Huntington Libr., 1991—. Editor: The American Oxonian, 1997—. Decorated Comdr. of the Order of Brit. Empire (hon.).

Mem. Soc. Bib. Lit., Soc. Religion in Higher Edn., Phi Beta Kappa Alumni in So. Calif. (pres. 1974-76), Century Club, Calif. Club, Bohemian Club, Phi Beta Kappa, Omicron Delta Kappa, Sigma Nu. Office: Pomona Coll 333 N College Way Claremont CA 91711-4429

ALEXANDER, RICHARD, lawyer; b. Cleve., Sept. 26, 1944; m. Nancy L. Biebel, Mar. 16, 1968; children: Marshall, Meredith. BA, Ohio Wesleyan U., 1966; JD (Nat. Honor scholar), U. Chgo., 1969. Bar: Mich. 1969, U.S. Dist. Ct. (ea. and we. dists.) Mich. 1970, U.S. Dist. Ct. (so. dist.) Ind. 1970, Calif. 1971, U.S. Dist. Ct. (no. dist.) Calif. 1971, U.S. Ct. Appeals (9th cir.) 1971, U.S. Dist. Ct. (cen. dist.) Calif. 1972, U.S. Dist. Ct. (ea. dist.) Calif. 1973, U.S. Dist. Ct. D.C. 1980. Diplomate Nat. Bd. Trial Advocacy; cert. specialist in trial law. Asst. prof. Grad. Sch. Bus., Mich. State U., 1969-71; assoc. Belli, Ashe, Ellison, Choulos & Lieff, San Francisco, 1971-72, Lieff, Alexander, Wilcox & Hill, San Francisco, 1972-74, Boccardo, Lull, Niland & Bell, San Francisco and San Jose, Calif., 1974-80; ptnr. Boccardo Law Firm, San Jose, 1980-87; Alexander & Bohn, San Jose, 1987-91; The Alexander Law Firm, San Jose, 1992—; v.p. State Bar Calif., 1987-88, bd. govs. 1985-88; mem. Santa Clara County Criminal Justice Adv. Bd., 1978-82, chmn., 1978-80; mem. Santa Clara County Jail Over-crowding Task Force, 1978-81; mem. Santa Clara County Pub. Defender Charter Amendment Task Force, 1980; judge pro tem Santa Clara County Superior Ct., 1976-83, 85-90, arbitrator, 1976-96; co-chmn. Superior Ct. Arbitration Adminstrn. Com., 1979—; spl. master State Bar Calif., 1980—, lectr. continuing edn., 1975, 78, 81-89, bd. govs. 1985—, mem. com. profl. ethics, 1977-80; speaker legal seminars. Pub. The Consumer Law Page; contbr. articles to profl. jours. Mem. Palo Alto (Calif.) Unified Sch. Dist. Task Force on Spl. Edn., 1975-79; vice chmn. sch. improvement program Palo Alto Unified Sch. Dist., 1977-78, mem. found. exploration com., 1984; mem. Santa Clara County Data Confidentiality Commn., 1976-78, chmn., 1977-78; mem. Santa Clara County Democratic Central Com., 1978-80; bd. dirs. Japanese Am. Environ. Conf., 1979-81. Recipient Santa Clara County Youth Commn. medal, 1980, Man of Yr. Women's Fund.; commendation for disting. service Mayor San Jose, 1982; Roscoe Pound fellow; named one of Outstanding Young Men of Am., Man of Yr. The Women's Found., 1989; recipient Pro Bono award Ctr. Occupl. Safety Health, 1993. Mem. San Francisco Bar Assn., Nat. Bd. Trial Advocacy (cert. civil adv. 1980, 85, 90, 95), Nat. Bar Register of Preeminent Lawyers, Santa Clara County Bar Assn. (pres. 1984), Calif. Attys. for Criminal Justice (founding; treas. 1972-74, gov. 1972-75), Calif. Trial Lawyers Assn. (recognized trial lawyer 1980-89, bd. govs. 1989-94, v.p. 1994-96), Nat. Assn. Consumer Advocates (founding), Consumer Attys. Calif. (v.p. 1995), State Bar Calif. (bd. govs., 1985—, v.p. 1987—), Assn. Trial Lawyers Am., NAACP, Stanford Alumni Assn., Alexander Graham Bell Assn. for Deaf, Nat. Trust Hist. Preservation. Clubs: U. Chgo. Alumni, Silicon Valley Capital. Office: The Alexander Law Firm # 600 152 N 3d San Jose CA 95112

ALEXANDER, ROBERT C., lawyer; b. Clarksville, Tenn., Aug. 7, 1947; s. Donald C. and Margaret S. Alexander; m. Rosalie Bailey, June 14, 1969. BA cum laude, Yale Coll., 1969; JD magna cum laude, Harvard U., 1972. Bar: Calif. 1972, D.C. 1973. Law clk. to Hon. Alfred T. Goodwin U.S. Ct. Appeals, 9th cir., San Francisco, 1972-73; shareholder Heller, Ehrman, White & McAuliffe, San Francisco, 1973-86, 88—; prin. Babcock & Brown, San Francisco, 1986-87; writer in field. Mem. ABA, State Bar Calif., D.C. Bar, Internat. Fiscal Assn., Equipment Leasing Assn. Office: Heller Ehrman White & McAuliffe 333 Bush St San Francisco CA 94104-2806

ALFARO, FELIX BENJAMIN, physician; b. Managua, Nicaragua, Oct. 22, 1939; came to U.S., 1945, naturalized, 1962; s. Agustin Jose and Amanda Julieta (Barillas) A.; student (State scholar) U. San Francisco, 1958-59, 61-62; M.D., Creighton U., 1967; m. Carmen Heide Meyer, Aug. 14, 1965; children—Felix Benjamin, Mark. Clk., Pacific Gas & Electric Co., San Francisco, 1960-61; intern St. Mary's Hosp., San Francisco, 1967; resident Scenic Gen. Hosp., Modesto, Calif., 1970; practice family medicine, Watsonville, Calif., 1971—; active staff Watsonville Community Hosp., 1971—. Served to capt., M.C., U.S. Army, 1968-69. Lic. physician, Nebr., La., Calif. Diplomate Am. Bd. Family Practice. Fellow Am. Acad. Family Practice; mem. AMA, Calif. Med. Assn., Santa Cruz County Med. Soc., 38th Parrallel Med. Soc. of Korea, Nat Rifle Assn., VFW. Republican. Roman Catholic. Office: 30 Brennan St Watsonville CA 95076-4303

ALHADEFF, DAVID ALBERT, economics educator; b. Seattle, Mar. 22, 1923; s. Albert David and Pearl (Taranto) A.; m. Charlotte Pechman, Aug. 1, 1948. B.A., U. Wash., 1944; M.A., Harvard U., 1948, Ph.D., 1950. Faculty U. Calif.-Berkeley, 1949-87, prof. bus. adminstrn., 1959-87, prof. emeritus, 1987—, assoc. dean Sch. Bus. Adminstrn., 1980-82, 85-86. Author: Monopoly and Competition in Banking, 1954, Competition and Controls in Banking, 1968, Microeconomics and Human Behavior, 1982; Contbr. articles to profl. jours., chpts. to books. Served with AUS, 1943-46. Recipient The Berkeley Citation U. Calif.-Berkeley, 1987. Mem. Am. Econ. Assn., Western Econ. Assn., Am. Fin. Assn. Home: 2101 Shoreline Dr Apt 456 Alameda CA 94501-6209 Office: Haas Sch Bus Berkeley CA 94720

ALIA, VALERIE, humanities educator, writer; b. N.Y.C., Dec. 20, 1942; d. Julius Abraham and Bertha (Fenyves) Graber; m. Sal P. Restivo, 1967 (div. 1984); children: David Owen Restivo, Daniel Olam Restivo; m. Pete Steffens, 1998. BA, U. Cin., 1965; MA, Mich. State U., 1967; PhD, York U., Toronto, Ont., 1989. Dance critic Boston Herald Traveller, 1971-72; dance and music critic Capital Newspapers, Albany, N.Y., 1974-79; reporter, photographer Rutland (Vt.) Herald, 1979-81; instr. U. Toronto, summer 1989; broadcast coord., prof. U. Western Ont., London, 1989-96; Disting. prof. Can. culture Western Wash. U., Bellingham, 1996-98; cons. faculty of environ. studies York U., 1987-88; cons. Inst. Environ. Rsch., Toronto, Yukon Govt., Whitehorse, 1990-91. Royal Commn. on Electoral Reform and Party Financing, Can., 1990-92; mem. awards panel NSF, Washington, 1997-99. Author: Names, Numbers & Northern People, 1994, Deadlines & Diversity, 1996, Un/covering the North, 1999. spkr., panelist U. Haifa, Israel, 1997; spkr. Investiture of Fed. Judge Susan P. Graber, Portland, Oreg., 1998. Strategic grantee in media ethics Social Scis. and Humanities Rsch. Coun. of Can., 1994-96, Workshop grantee Western Wash. U. Diversity Fund, 1998, Ethics/Values Studies and Arctic Social Sci. Program grantee NSF, 1998—; rsch. fellow Fairhaven Coll., Belllingham, 1998-99. Mem. Can. Fedn. for Humanities Women's Caucus (co-chair 1994-96), The Writers' Union of Can., Native News Network of Can. (founding, bd. dirs. 1990-95, mem. adv. bd.), Arctic Inst. N.Am., Internat. Arctic Social Scis. Assn. (founding), Internat. Coun. Onomastic Scis. Jewish. Avocations: travel, gardening.

ALINDER, MARY STREET, writer, lecturer; b. Bowling Green, Ohio, Sept. 23, 1946; d. Scott Winfield and McDonna Matlock (Sitterle) Street; m. James Gilbert Alinder, Dec. 17, 1965; children: Jasmine, Jesse, Zachary. Student, U. Mich., 1964-65, U. N.Mex., 1966-68; BA, U. Nebr., 1976. Mgr. The Weston Gallery, Carmel, Calif., 1978-79; chief asst. Ansel Adams, Carmel, 1979-84; exec. editor, bus. mgr. The Ansel Adams Pub. Rights Trust, Carmel, 1984-87; freelance writer, lectr., curator, Gualala, Calif., 1989—; ptnr. The Alinder Gallery, Gualala, 1990—; selector and writer biographies Focal Press Ency., 3d edit., 1993; curator Ansel Adams: 80th Birthday Retrospective, Friends of Photography, Carmel, Acad. Sci., San Francisco, Denver Mus. Natural History; co-curator One With Beauty, M.H. deYoung Meml. Mus., 1987, Ansel Adams: American Artist, The Ansel Adams Ctr., San Francisco; lectr. Nat. Gallery Art, Barbican Ctr., M.H. deYoung Meml. Mus., Stanford U., L.A. County Mus., U. Mich.; vis. artist and lectr. Nebr. Art Assn., 1997; Wallace Stegner meml. lectr. Peninsula Open Space Inst., Mountainview, Calif., 1998, Assn. Internat. Photographic Art Dealers, N.Y.C., 1999. Author: Picturing Yosemite (Places), 1990, The Limits of Reality: Ansel Adams and Group f/64 (Seeing Straight), 1992, Ansel Adams, A Biography (Henry Holt), 1996, Mabel Dodge Luhan, 1997 (ViewCamera), (with others) the Scribner Encyclopedia of American Lives, 1998; co-author: Ansel Adams: An Autobiography, 1985; co-editor: Ansel Adams: Letters and Images, 1988; columnist Coast and Valley Mag., 1993-98; columnist (Internet site) biz travel.com, 1996-98; contbr. articles to jours. and popular mags. Office: Alinder Gallery PO Box 1146 Gualala CA 95445-1146

ALIOTTI, GILLI, singer, songwriter; b. Milan, Italy, Mar. 29, 1969; came to U.S., 1996; d. Claude and Bronwyn Mary (White) A. BEd, Australian Cath. U., 1991. Cert. tchr., Australia. Prin., owner Aliotti Media, Sydney, Australia, 1994-97; singer, songwriter, producer Indigo Moon Records, L.A., 1996—; prin., owner Songsalive!, Sydney and L.A., 1997—; cons. various music artists, L.A., 1996-98. Composer, artist (CD) Shamballa, 1995, Gilli Moon, 1996, Girl in the Moon, 1998. Mem. adv. bd. Pacific Circle Music, Sydney, Australia, 1998. Mem. FID, Nat. Acad. Songwriters, Australian Performing Rights Assn. (Sydney chpt.). Roman Catholic. Avocations: music, art, water sports, creative writing, travel.

ALISKY, MARVIN HOWARD, political science educator; b. Kansas City, Mo., Mar. 12, 1923; s. Joseph and Bess June (Capp) A.; m. Beverly Kay, June 10, 1955; children: Sander Michael, Joseph. BA, U. Tex., 1946, MA, 1947, PhD, 1953; cert., Instituto Tecnologico, Monterey, Mex., 1951. News corr. S.W. and Latin Am. NBC, 1947-49, news corr. Midwest, 1954-56; news corr. NBC and Christian Sci. Monitor, Latin Am., 1957-72; asst. prof. Ind. U., 1953-57; assoc. prof. journalism and polit. sci. Ariz. State U., Tempe, 1957-60; prof. polit. sci. Ariz. State U., 1960—, founding chmn. dept. mass communication (now Sch. Journalism and Telecommunications), 1957-65, founding dir. Ctr. Latin Am. Studies, 1965-72; vis. fellow Princeton U., 1963-64, Hoover Inst., Stanford, 1978; Fulbright prof. Cath. U., Lima, Peru, 1958, U. Nicaragua, 1960; researcher U.S.-Mex. Interparliamentary Conf., Baja, Calif., 1965, Latin Am. Inst., Chinese Acad. Social Scis., Beijing, 1986, European Inst. Def. and Strategic Studies, London, 1985, Politics Inst., Copenhagen, Denmark, 1987, U. So. Calif., 1982—; U.S. del. UNESCO Conf., Quito, Ecuador, 1960; dir. Gov.'s Ariz.-Mex. Commn., 1975—; U.S. State Dept. lectr., Costa Rica, Peru, Argentina, Chile, 1983, 88; bd. dirs. Goldwater Inst. Pub. Policy Rsch., 1989—. Author: Governors of Mexico, 1965, Uruguay: Contemporary Survey, 1969, The Foreign Press, 1964, 70, Who's Who in Mexican Government, 1969, Political Forces in Latin America, 1970, Government in Nuevo Leon, 1971, Government in Sonora, 1971, Peruvian Political Perspective, 1975, Historical Dictionary of Peru, 1979, Historical Dictionary of Mexico, 1981, Latin American Media: Guidance and Censorship, 1981, Global Journalism, 1983; co-author: Political Systems of Latin America, 1970, Political Parties of the Americas, 1982, Yucatan: A World Apart, 1980, (with J.E. Katz) Arms Production in Developing Nations, 1984, Mexico: Country in Crisis, 1986, (with Phil Rosen) International Handbook of Broadcasting Systems, 1988, Dictionary Latin American Political Leaders, 1988, (with W.C. Soderlund) Mass Media and the Caribbean, 1990; columnist Thompson Corp. Newspapers in ariz., 1999—; contbr. numerous articles to profl. jours. and mags. Bd. dirs. Phoenix Com. on Fgn. Res., 1975—, Ariz. Acad. Town Hall, 1981, Tempe Pub. Libr., 1974-80; mem. U.S. Bd. Fgn. Scholarships Fulbright Commn. Bd., 1984—, Acad. Coun. Goldwater Inst. of Pub. Policy, 1989—. Ensign USNR, 1944-45. NSF grantee, 1984, Ariz. State U. rsch. grantee, 1962, 65, 70, Southwestern Studies Ctr. rsch. grantee, 1983, Latin Am. Rsch. in China grantee, 1986, World Media Rsch. in Soviet Union grantee, 1989, rsch. grantee, London, 1992, 94, Edinburgh, 1994, 97, Vancouver, 1998. Fellow Hispahic Soc. Am.; mem. Am. Polit. Sci. Assn., Western Polit. Sci. Assn., Latin Am. Studies Assn., Pacific Coast Coun. Latin Am. Studies (bd. dirs.), Inter-Am. Press Assn., Inter-Am. Broadcasters Assn. (rsch. assoc.), Assocs. Liga de Municipios de Sonora, Friends of Mex. Art, Southwestern Polit. Sci. Assn. (chmn. 1976-77), Nat. Assn. Scholars, Soc. Profl. Journalists (life), Tempe Rep. Men's Club, Knights of Sq. Roundtable, Sigma Delta Chi. Home: 44 W Palmdale Dr Tempe AZ 85282-2139 Office: Ariz State U Dept Polit Sci Tempe AZ 85287-2001

ALKANA, LOUIS DAVID, writer, editor; b. Bklyn., Aug. 29, 1955; s. Samuel and Mildred Carol (Matorin) A.; m. Lisa Ann Haggard, Mar. 28, 1992. AA, West Los Angeles Coll., 1975; BA, Calif. State U., Northridge, 1979. Freelance sportswriter Seattle, 1980-82; editor Frames Publs., Newport Beach, Calif., 1982-84; assoc. editor Lets Live Mag., L.A., 1984-85; mgr. employee comm. Nat. Med. Enterprises, L.A., 1985-88; acct. exec. Russell Comm. Group, L.A., 1988-92; pvt. practice cons. corp. comm. Culver City, Calif., 1992-97; acct. exec. Silverman Heller Assocs., L.A., 1997—. Author: (short stories) A Spy Alone, 1994, The Fifth Down, 1995. Recipient Citizen's award Seattle Police Dept., 1981, Award of Excellence, Greater L.A. Press Club, 1986, Bronze Quill award Internat. Assn. Bus. Communicators (L.A. chpt.), 1987, Maggie award Western Publs. Assn., 1988, 1st pl. award Am. Bus. Communicators Ann. Report Competition, 1996. Avocations: writing fiction, sport fishing, woodworking, reading. E-mail: lalkana@msn.com.

ALKANA, RONALD LEE, neuropsychopharmacologist, psychobiologist; b. L.A., Oct. 17, 1945; s. Sam Alkana and Madelyn Jane Davis; m. Linda Anne Kelly, Sept. 12, 1970; children; Alexander Philippe Kelly, Lorna Jane Kelly. Student, UCLA, 1963-66; PharmD, U. So. Calif., 1970; PhD, U. Calif., Irvine, 1975. Postdoctoral fellow Nat. Inst. Alcohol Abuse and Alcoholism, U. Calif., Irvine, 1974-76; resident asst. dir. div. neurochemistry, dept. psychiatry and human behavior U. Calif., Irvine, 1976; asst. prof. pharmacy (pharmacology) U. So. Calif., L.A., 1976-82, assoc. prof. pharmacy (pharmacology and toxicology), 1982-89, prof. molecular pharmacology and toxicology, 1989—, asst. dean grad. affairs, 1995-98, asst. dean interdisciplinary programs Sch. Pharmacy U. So. Calif., 1998—. Editl. bd. Alcoholism: Clinical and Experimental Research, 1989-94, assoc. editor, 1994-98; contbr. chpts. to books, articles to profl. jours. Recipient various scholarships and grants. Mem. AAAS, Soc. Neurosci., Am. Soc. Pharmacology and Exptl. Therapeutics, Internat. Soc. Biomed. Research on Alcoholism, Research Soc. Alcoholism, Internat. Brain Rsch. Organizational World Fedn. Neuroscientists, Soc. of Toxicology, Western Pharmacology Soc., QSAD (bd. dirs. 1998—), Sigma Xi, Phi Delta Chi (bd. dirs. Omicron alumni 1997—, Omicron chpt., Outstanding Alumnus of Yr. 1996—). Office: U So Calif Sch Pharmacy Dept Molecular Pharmacolgy Toxicology 1985 Zonal Ave Los Angeles CA 90033-1039

ALKHALILI, OUSSAMA AHMAD, adult education educator, consultant, director; b. Beirut, Sept. 2, 1960; came to U.S., 1981; s. Ahmad Abdu El Rhaman and Dalal (Damaj) A.; m. Darleen Ishahara, 1993; children: Bassam, Zayna. Baccalaureate Tech. 1 and Tech. 2, Amelich Tech. Sch., Beirut, 1980; AA, Coll. Sequoias, 1993; BS, Calif. State U. (Fresno), 1996. Mgr. Florsheim Shoes, L.A., 1982-86; sales mgr. F.G.A. Trading, Lodi, Calif., 1986-89; instr. Full Force Kick Boxing, Visalia, Calif., 1990-92; math., engring., sci. achievement dir. Coll. Sequoias, Visalia, Calif., 1996—; dir. MESA program, Visalia, 1996—; adv. Calif. State U.-Alliance for Minority Participation programs, Fresno, Calif., 1996—; cons. Pipeline project, Visalia, 1996—. Mem. Nat. Assn. of Minority Engring. Adminstrs. (com. mem. 1997—), Soc. for Advancement of Chicanos and Native Americans in Sci. Democrat. Islamic. Avocations: basketball, table tennis (San Joaquin Valley champion, 1993), raquetball, music, martial arts (black belt in kickboxing). Home: 3741 W Coppola Ave Visalia CA 93277-5804 Office: College of the Sequoias 915 S Mooney Blvd Visalia CA 93277-2234

ALKIRE, JOHN D., lawyer, mediator, arbitrator; b. Seattle, Nov. 15, 1948; s. Durwood Lee and Dorys (Maryon) A.; m. Karen A. Heerensperger, May 6, 1994; children: Lauren M., Kevin G. Student, U. Calif., Berkeley, 1967-68; BA, Principia Coll., Elsah, Ill., 1970; JD, U. Wash., 1975. Bar: Wash. 1975, Washington 1977, U.S. Dist. Ct. (we. dist.) Wash., U.S. Ct. Appeals (4th, 9th and D.C. cirs.), U.S. Supreme Ct. Budget analyst Office Mgmt. and Budget, Seattle, 1970-72; law clk 9th cir. Honorable Eugene A. Wright, Seattle, 1975-76; assoc. Jones, Grey & Bayley, Seattle, 1976-77, Steptoe & Johnson, Washington, 1977-80; assoc. Perkins Coie, Seattle, 1980-85, ptnr., 1985—. Mem. ABA, Wash. State Bar Assn. Avocations: outdoor sports, major league baseball, travel, music, volunteer mediation. Office: Perkins Coie 1201 3rd Ave Fl 40 Seattle WA 98101-3000

ALLAMANDOLA, LOUIS JOHN, low temperature chemist/astrophysicist; b. N.Y.C., Aug. 28, 1946; s. Louis John Allamandola and Santina (Nella) Nicoletti; m. Mary Ellen Scott, June 8, 1968; children: Monica, Patrick, David Kees, Anthony. BSc, St. Peter's Coll., Jersey City, 1968; PhD in Phys. Chemistry, U. Calif., Berkeley, 1974. Rsch. assoc. chem. dept. Oreg. State U., Corvallis, 1974-76; asst. prof. lab. astrophysics Leiden (the Netherlands) U., 1976-79, assoc. prof. lab. astrophysics, 1979-83; NRC sr. assoc. NASA Ames Rsch. Ctr., Mountain View, Calif., 1983-85, astrochemistry lab. group leader, 1985—; mem. adv. panels NASA, Washington, 1988-95; mem. sci. adv. coun., Ames; mem. grad. rsch. fellows panel NSF, 1995-97; co-chair IAU Symposium 135 on Interstellar Dust, Santa Clara, 1988; chmn. sci. meeting ESA-Comet project, Monterey, Calif., 1991; mem. sci. organizing com. numerous internat. meetings. Editor: Interstellar Dust, 1989; contbr. over 150 articles to profl. jours., including Science, Astrophysics Jour. and Jour. Chem. Physics, Nature. Vol. with teenage youth ministry, 1987—. NASA Ames Assoc. fellow, 1996-97, recipient Nat. Medal for Exceptional Scientific Achievement, NASA, 1992, H. Julian Allen award NASA, 1987; NRC sr. fellow, 1983-85, NSF-Energy Related fellow, 1976. Mem. ACS, Am. Astron. Soc., Internat. Astron. Union (co-chmn. sci. meeting 1988), Friends of Berkeley Chemistry. Roman Catholic. Achievements include pioneering the new fields of laboratory astrophysics, astrochemistry and astrobiology in which low temperature, solid state chemistry in interstellar space, comets and distant moons and planets are simulated to interpret data from telescopes and design spacecraft; demonstrated that polycyclic aromatic hydrocarbons (PAHs) are ubiquitous in space; research on identifying frozen molecules on interstellar grains, comets and planets and investigating their relevance to the origin of life. Office: NASA Ames Rsch Ctr Ms 245 # 6 Mountain View CA 94035-1000

ALLAN, DAVID LEWIS, artist, researcher, educator; b. Pasadena, Calif., Nov. 29, 1949; s. Robert Moffat and Harriet (Spicer) A. BA, U. Calif., Santa Barbara, 1972. Cert. tchr., Calif. Tchr. Robert Louis Stevenson sch., Pebble Beach, Calif., 1976-77; art tchr. various, Calif., 1977-78, Fort Ord (Calif.) Arts and Crafts Ctr., 1978-90; pvt. practice Big Sur, Calif., 1989—; recreation specialist Presidio of Monterey (Calif.) Recreation, 1990-93; art tchr. City of Carmel (Calif.) By The Sea, 1993—, Pacific Valley Sch., Big Sur, Calif., 1993—; cons. in field. One-man shows include Artist Response Gallery, 1976, Artist's Palette Gallery, D. Logan Hill Gallery, Fort Ord, Presidio of Monterey Galleries, 1979-93, Seaside City Hall, 1981; group shows include Monterey Bay Co. Gallery, Cannery Row, others. Founder Carmel By the Sea Cmty. Program, Calif., 1993—. Lt. USN, 1972-75, Vietnam. Recipient Carnegie medal for heroism, 1996, U.S. Coast Guard Silver Lifesaving medal and Resolution Pebble Beach Cmty. Svcs. District for heroism, 1996. Mem. Central Coast Art Assn. Home: PO Box 3073 Carmel CA 93921-3073

ALLAN, ROBERT MOFFAT, JR., corporate executive, educator; b. Detroit, Dec. 8, 1920; s. Robert M. and Jane (Christman) A.; m. Harriet Spicer, Nov. 28, 1942; children: Robert M. III, Scott, David, Marilee. BS, Stanford U., 1941; postgrad. Stanford Grad. Sch. Bus., 1941-42; MS, UCLA, 1943; postgrad. Loyola Law Sch., 1947-50. Economist research dept. Security First Nat. Bank, 1942; exec. Marine Ins., 1946-53; asst. to pres., work mgr. Zinsco Elec. Products, 1953-55, v.p., dir., 1956-59; asst. to pres. The Times-Mirror Corp., 1959-60, corp. v.p., 1961-64; pres., dir. Cyprus Mines Corp., 1964-67; pres. Litton Internat., 1967-69; pres. U.S. Naval Postgrad. Sch. Found., prof. internat. mgmt. 1969-85. Bd. dirs., advisor U.S. Naval Acad.; trustee Boys Republic, Pomona Grad. Sch., Claremont Grad. Sch., Del Monte Forest Homeowners; vis. prof. of internat. mgmt. grad. schs. of bus. MBA Stanford, Harvard, U. of Chgo., UCLA, USA and Internat. Inst. Fgn. Studies, Monterey; adv. trustee Monterey County Sheriff, 1982—. Capt. USAF, 1942-45. Recipient award Helms Athletic Found., 1947, 49, Navy Cross of Merit, 1976, Plaque of Merit USCG, 1990, Medal for Heroism, 1990; named Outstanding Businessman of Yr., L.A., Nat. Assn. Accts., 1966; elected to Sailing Hall of Fame, 1969; named Monterey Inst. Fgn. Studies trustee and sr. fellow, 1976. Mem. Mchts. and Mfrs. Assn. (dir.), Intercollegiate Yachting Assn. (regional dir. 1940-55), Phi Gamma Delta, Phi Delta Phi. Clubs: Newport Harbor Yacht (commodore 1962), Trans-Pacific Yacht, Carmel Valley Country. Home: 167 Del Mesa Carmel CA 93923

ALLAN, ROBERT OLAV, lawyer; b. Albuquerque, Dec. 22, 1960; s. Alexander Olav and Angeline Elsie (Whipple) A.; m. Dawn Marie Gourneau, Aug. 8, 1986; children: Gabrielle, Joshua, Robert. BA, Dartmouth Coll., 1985; JD, U. Colo., 1991. Bar: Navajo Nation 1985, N.Mex. 1994, U.S. Dist. Ct. N.Mex. 1995. Tribal ct. advocate I Navajo Nation Dept. Justice, Window Rock, Ariz., 1985-86, tribal ct. advocate II, 1986-87, tribal ct. advocate III, 1987-88; title examiner II Navajo Land Dept., Window Rock, 1992-94, atty., 1994-95; atty. Navajo Nation Divsn. Natural Resources, Window Rock, 1995—; project dir. Intergovtl. Land Consolidation Project Tri-Party Coop. Agreement Orgn. and Workgroups, 1987-88; pro bono legal counsel Navajo Nation Cts., Window Rock, 1991—; rep. Alliance to Protect Native Rights in Natural Parks Navajo Nation, L.A., 1996—. Mem. Dartmouth Native Am. Coun., Hanover, N.H., 1980-84, Apache County Dems., Window Rock, 1993-96. Am. Indian Grad. Ctr. fellow, 1988-91. Fellow N.Mex. First; mem. Navajo Nation Bar Assn., N.Mex. Bar Assn. Home: 3209 Grey Hills Ave Gallup NM 87301-6928

ALLARD, A. WAYNE, senator, veterinarian; b. Ft. Collins, Colo., Dec. 12, 1943; m. Joan Malcolm, Mar. 23, 1967; children: Cheryl, Christie. D.V.M., Colo. State U., 1968. Veterinarian, Allard Animal Hosp.; mem. Colo. State Senate, 1982-91, chmn. health, environment and instn. com., chmn. senate majority caucus; mem. 102nd-104th Congresses from 4th dist., Colo., 1991-96; mem. agrl. com., 1991-92, 93-94, 95-96, mem. small bus. com., 1991-92, mem. interior and insular affairs com., 1991-92, mem. com. on coms., 1991-92, 93-94, mem. budget com., 1993-94, 95-96, mem. natural resources com., 1993-94, 95-96, mem. joint com. on reorganization of Congress, 1993-94, 95-96, chmn. subcom. of agr. conservation, forest and water, 1995-96; senator 105th Congress, 1997—, mem. banking, urban affairs com., 1997—, environment and pub. works com., 1997—, intelligence select com., 1997—, Senate armed svcs. com., banking, housing and urban affairs com., select com. on intelligence; health officer Loveland, Colo.; mem. regional adv. council on vet. medicine Western Interstate Commn. Higher Edn.; mem. Colo. Low-level Radioactive Waste Adv. Com. Chmn. United Way; active 4-H Found. Mem. Loveland C. of C., AVMA, Colo. Vet. Medicine Assn., Larimer County Vet. Medicine Assn. (past pres.), Bd. Vet. Practitioners (charter mem.), Am. Animal Hosp. Assn., Nat. Conf. State Legislatures (vice chmn. human resources com. 1987—, healthcare cost containment com.). Republican. Methodist. Home: PO Box 2405 Loveland CO 80539-2405 Office: US Senate 513 Hart Bldg Washington DC 20510

ALLAWAY, WILLIAM HARRIS, retired university official; b. Oak Park, Ill., Mar. 31, 1924; s. William Horsford and Helen Margaret (Harris) A.; m. Olivia Woodhull Foster, June 28, 1952; children: William Harris Jr., Ben Foster, Eve Olivia. BS, U. Ill., 1949; postgrad., U. Grenoble, France, 1950-51; MA, U. Ill., 1951; EdD, U. Denver, 1957. Traveling sec. World Student Svc. Fund, 1947-48; spl. asst. to chmn. U.S. Nat. Commn. for UNESCO, 1949; asst. to field dir. World U. Svc. attached to Internat. Refugee Orgn., Salzburg, Austria, 1951; field rep. Inst.of Internat. Edn., Chgo. and Denver, 1952-54; gen. sec. U. Kans. YMCA, 1954-57; asst. dean of men and dir. Wilbur Hall Stanford (Calif.) U., 1957-61; dir. edn. abroad program U. Calif., Santa Barbara, 1961-89, spl. asst. to chancellor, 1990-93; cons. and lectr. in field; mem. ednl. assoc. adv. com. Inst. Internat. Edn., 1984-87; mem. Pres.'s Coun. for Internat. Youth Exch., 1982-85; mem. U.S. Del. to conf. on ednl. exch. between U.S. and U.K., 1970, 1974. Co-chair Peace and Justice Com., Goleta Presbyn. Ch., chair steering com. PAX 2100; mem. Nuclear Age Peace Found., Santa Barbara, Internat. Peace Rsch. Assn., Yellow Springs, Ohio; mem. Coun. on Internat. Ednl. Exch., 1961—, chmn. bd. dirs. 1978-83; past bd. dirs., hon. trustee Am. Ctr. for Students and Artists, Paris; bd. advisors Hariri Found., 1987—; exec. sec. Internat. Com. for Study of Edn. Exch., 1970-95, exec. com. Inter-Univ. Ctr. Postgrad. Studies, Dubrovnik, 1988-96, bd. dirs., 1996—. With USAAF, 1943-46. Hon. DHC, U. Sussex, Eng., 1992; PhD h.c. U. Bergen, Norway, 1990; DHC, U. Bordeaux, France, 1988; Hon. Dr. of U. of Stirling, Scotland, 1981; recipient Scroll of Appreciation Leningrad State U., 1989, Award for Svc. to Internat. Ednl. Exch. Council on Internat. Ednl. Exch., 1989, Silver medal U. Lund, Sweden, 1990, Alumni Achievement award Coll. Liberal Arts and Sci. Alumni Assn. U. Ill., 1990, Gold Medal of Honor of the Complutense U. of Madrid, Spain, 1991. Mem. NAFSA Assn. Internat. Educators (hon. life mem.), Internat. Assn. Univs. (dep. mem., adminstrv. bd. 1995—, chair task force on internationalization of higher edn.), La Cumbre Golf and Country Club. Democrat. Presbyterian. Avocations: golf, skiing, choir, reading. Fax: (805) 687-5779. E-mail: boallaway@aol.com. Home: 724 Calle De Los Amigos Santa Barbara CA 93105-4439

ALLBEE, SANDRA MOLL, real estate broker; b. Reading, Pa., July 15, 1947; d. Charles Lewars and Isabel May (Ackerman) Frederici; m. Thomas J. Allbee, Oct. 18, 1975 (div. 1987). Exec. sec. Hamburg (Pa.) State Sch. and Hosp., 1965-73; regional mgr. Am. Bus. Service Corp., Newport Beach, Calif., 1973-78; v.p. T.A.S.A., Inc., Long Beach, Calif., 1978-86; realtor Very

Important Properties, Inc., Rolling Hills Estates, Calif., 1986-90, Re/Max Palos Verdes Realty, Rolling Hills Estates, Calif., 1990—. Bd. dirs., v.p. Nat. Coun. on Alcoholism, Torrance, Calif., 1987-96; pres. Rollingwood Homeowners Assn., Rolling Hills Estates, Calif., 1985-92. Mem. Palos Verdes Rep. Women's Club (bd. dirs. 1989-94). Office: Re/Max Palos Verdes Realty 4030 Palos Verdes Dr N Ste 104 Rolling Hills CA 90274-2526

ALLEN, BONNIE LYNN, optometrist; b. L.A., Oct. 2, 1957; d. David and Lucille M. (Scott) A. B.A. summa cum laude, UCLA, 1979, OD, U. Calif., Berkeley, 1998. Math. tutor, L.A., 1971—; reader math. dept. UCLA, 1977-79; pension actuary Martin E. Segal Co., L.A., 1980-92. Author short stories and poetry. Active mentor program UCLA Alumni Assn., 1978-79, bd. dirs. Westside Bruins. Mem. Math. Assn. Am., Am. Optometric Assn., Am. Math. Soc., L.A. Film Tchrs'. Assn., Acad. Sci. Fiction, Fantasy and Horror Films, U. Calif. Berkeley Optometry Alumni Assn., UCLA Alumni Assn. (life), Westside Bruin Club (bd. dirs.), L.A. Actuarial Club, Beta Sigma kappa, Phi Beta Kappa, Golden Key.

ALLEN, BRIAN R., insurance company executive, state legislator; b. Salt Lake City, May 20, 1957; s. Ralph K. and Ruby L. A.; m. Velene Esplw, Aug. 10, 1983; children: Jared, Josh, Chantel, Scott. Student, U. Utah, 1986-89. Owner Key Ins. Svcs., Murray, Utah, 1986-91; acct. exec. 1st Security Ins., Salt Lake City, 1991-96; v.p. Zions Ins. Agy., Salt Lake City, 1996—. Bd. dirs. Vols. of Am., Salt Lake City, 1988—; mem. Utah Ho. of Reps., Salt Lake City, 1995—; mem. Utah Opera Chorus. Republican. Mem. LDS Ch. Avocation: professional baritone vocalist. Home: 7386 Banbury Cir Salt Lake City UT 84121-4106 Office: Zions Ins Agy 310 S Main St Ste 308 Salt Lake City UT 84101-2127

ALLEN, BRUCE JOHN, writer, activist; b. Buffalo, Apr. 16, 1960; s. John Edgar and Isabel Sarah (Nicholson) A.; m. Sarah Bragg Lindsley, Mar. 31, 1992; 1 child, John Edgar. BA in English Lit. magna cum laude, U. Colo., 1985. Columnist Colo. Daily, Boulder, 1985; field mgr. Colo. Pub. Interest Rsch. Group, Boulder, 1985-86; editor Nat. Student News Svc., Boston, 1986-88; writer The New Paper, Providence, 1988-91; comm. dir. Save the Bay, Providence, 1990-92, Ctr. for Econ. Conversion, Mountain View, Calif., 1993-96; publs. cons. Calif. Abortion Rights Action League, San Francisco, 1993. Mem. Save El Dorado Mountain Campaign, Boulder, 1985; advisor People Against the CIA, Providence, 1989; co-founder Preserve the Presidio Campaign, San Francisco, 1994; bd. dirs. Calif. Peace Action, 1996—. Home: 560 Crestlake Dr San Francisco CA 94132-1325

ALLEN, CHARLES RICHARD, retired financial executive; b. Cleve., Mar. 10, 1926; s. Charles Ross and Jennie (Harmon) A.; m. Marion Elizabeth Taylor, Aug. 17, 1946; children: Kathleen Allen Templin, Jeanne Allen Duffy, Kenneth. Student, Occidental Coll., 1942-43; BS, UCLA, 1945. Acctg. supr. N.Am. Aviation, Inc., Los Angeles, 1946-55; div. controller TRW, Inc., Los Angeles, 1955-61, dir. fin., 1961-64; assoc. controller TRW, Inc., Cleve., 1964-66, controller, 1966-67, v.p., 1967-77, exec. v.p., 1977-86, chief fin. officer, 1967-86; advisor New Court Ptnrs., N.Y.C.; bd. dirs. Titan Corp., San Diego. Trustee Maritime Mus. San Diego; mem. San Diego World Affairs Coun. Served with USNR, 1943-46. Mem. Fin. Execs. Inst., Univ. Club, City Club of San Diego. Home: 1730 Avenida Del Mundo Coronado CA 92118-3021

ALLEN, CRYSTAL DEEAN, producer, actress; b. Seattle, Apr. 17, 1970; d. Wilbert and Winnifred (Bascomb) A. BA, Wash. State U., 1992; MFA magna cum laude, U. San Diego, 1992. Job svc. specialist Wash. State Dept. Employment Security, Seattle, 1993-95; actress Brooks-Atkinson Theatre-Broadway, N.Y.C., 1997; CEO, Cryst-Like Prodns., Atlanta, Ga., 1997—; creative writer A-Tac Prodns., L.A. Fellow Old Globe Theatre, San Diego, 1995-98; acad. scholar U. San Diego, 1995-98, Dramatic Arts scholar Ms. Seattle Pageant, Seattle, 1992. Mem. New Birth Ministries.

ALLEN, CYNTHIA L., personnel executive; b. Mpls.. Tng. coord. US Airlines, Phoenix, 1975-92; recruiter Roberson & Co., Scottsdale, Ariz., ARC Ptnrs., Inc., Scottsdale. Recipient Silver Target award Nat. Personnel Assocs. Placement Gen. Fedn., 1994, Top Med/Net Cons., 1994, Top 10 Cons., 1994, Top MED/NET Cons., 1996. Mem. Gen. Fedn. Women's Club (chairwoman pub. affairs 1990, v.p. fundraising 1991, Clubwoman of Yr. 1991, Ariz. Clubwoman 1991), Scottsdale Jrs. (chairperson dept. edn.). Republican. Fax: (602) 951-2082. Office: ARC Ptnrs INC 6441 E Beverly Ln Scottsdale AZ 85254-1475

ALLEN, DAVID CHARLES, computer science educator; b. Syracuse, N.Y., Jan. 15, 1944; s. Charles Robert and Jane Loretta (Doolittle) A.; m. Mary Ann Stanke, June 15, 1968 (div. Mar. 1994); children: Meredith Rae, Amelia Kathrine, Carl James; m. Barbara Ann Riis, Mar. 14, 1994. B.Tech. Edn., Nat. U., San Diego, 1983, MA in Human Behavior, 1984. Dir. retail sales Nat. U. Alumni Assn., 1981-83; audiovisual technician Grossmont Union H.S. Dist., La Mesa, Calif., 1983-84; spl. project instr. San Diego C.C., 1985-91; instr. computer tech. Coleman Coll., 1991-98, sr. instr. computer applications and networking, 1998—. Mem. Presdl. Task Force; mem. Congl. Adv. Com. on Vets. Benefits for congressmen 44th. With USN, 1961-81. Mem. DAV, VFW, Am. Legion, Vietnam Vets. Am., Fleet Reservation Assn., Nat. U. Student and Alumni Assn., Am. Tech. Edn. Assn., Beta Sigma Phi (hon.). Republican. Roman Catholic. Home: 3156 Lamar Ct Spring Valley CA 91977-2650 Office: Coleman Coll Computer Applications & Networking 7380 Parkway Dr La Mesa CA 91942-1532

ALLEN, DAVID HARLOW, business educator, logistician, consultant; b. Lynn, Mass., May 26, 1930; s. Donald H. and Miriam Ellsworth (Harlow) A.; m. Roberta Arlene Miller, July 15, 1952; children: Donald Bruce, Richard Leroy, William David. BS in Gen. Edn., U. Nebr., Omaha, 1967; MBA, N.Mex. Highlands U., 1978. Cert. profl. logistician, cost analyst. Commd. 2d lt. USAF, 1955, advanced through grades to lt. col., 1970; instr., planner, aircraft maintenance, staff, prodn. control officer, squadron comdr., wing asst. dep. comdr. maintenance SAC, 1948-74; dir. aircraft maintenance, dir. material Air Force Inspection and Safety Ctr., San Bernardino, Calif., 1969-72; dep. dir. logistics Air Force Test and Evaluation Ctr., Albuquerque, 1974-78; ret., 1978; sr. sys. analyst, space sys. project leader Arinc Rsch. Corp., 1978-84; airborne missile system dep. program mgr. for logistics, logistics project mgr. Ventura divsn. Northrop Corp., 1984-91; assoc. prof. West Coast U. Coll. Bus. and Mgmt., L.A., 1988—; asst. dean West Coast U., L.A., 1988-90; com. chmn. So. Calif. Logistics Conf. and Workshop, 1989-93; v.p., mem. bd. govs., trustee Logistics Edn. Found., 1993-96. Contbr. articles to profl. jours. Active state and nat. Rep. orgns., 1978—; mem. Ventura County-Santa Barbara County Planning Com. for Nat. Engring. Week, 1990—. Decorated Bronze Star. Mem. Soc. Logistics Engrs. (chmn. chpt. 1988-90, Pres.'s award for merit 1994), Logistics Edn. Found. (v.p., bd. trustees 1993-95, Pres.'s award for merit 1996), Soc. Cost Estimating and Analysis, Air Force Assn., Ret. Officers Assn., Am. Assn. Ret. Persons, Phi Kappa Phi. Avocations: racquetball, golf, swimming. Home and Office: 428 Moondance St Thousand Oaks CA 91360-1209

ALLEN, DONALD VAIL, investment executive, writer, concert pianist; b. South Bend, Ind., Aug. 1, 1928; s. Frank Eugene and Vera Irene (Vail) A.; m. Betty Dunn, Nov. 17, 1956. BA magna cum laude, UCLA, 1972, MA, 1973, D (hon.), 1973. Pres., chmn. bd. dirs. Cambridge Investment Corp.; music editor and critic Times-Herald, Washington; music critic L.A. Times; lectr. George Washington U., Am. U., Washington, Pasadena City Coll. Transl. works of Ezra Pound from Italian into English; author of papers on the musical motifs in the writings of James Joyce and Stravinsky; mem. Steinway Roster of Concert Artists; specialist in works of Beethoven, Chopin, Debussy and Liszt; premiere performances of works of Paul Creston, Norman dello Joio, Ross Lee Finney, appearances in N.Y., L.A., Washington; represented by William Matthews Concert Agy., N.Y.C. Pres. Funds for Needy Children, 1974-76. Mem. Ctr. for Study of Presidency, Am. Mgmt. Assn., Internat. Platform Assn., Nat. Assn. Securities Dealers, Am. Guild Organists, Chamber Music Soc., Am. Mus. Natural History. Avocations: languages, music, travel, writing, stock market. Home: 670 W Via Rancho Pkwy Escondido CA 92029-7313

ALLEN, EDGAR BURNS, records management professional; b. L.A., Sept. [illegible] Gregory, July 24, 1960; children: Linda Marie, Lisa Ann. AA, L.A. City Coll., 1958; student, Calif. State U., L.A., 1958, 81; BS, UCLA, 1985. Supr. records ctr. L.A. Dept. Water and Power, 1958-67, records mgr., 1967-76; records mgmt. officer City of L.A., 1976-85; records mgmt. cons. L.A., 1985—; profl. creator records mgmt. systems, tax preparer, L.A., 1990—; established City Records Ctr. and City Archives. Chmn. Leimert Pk. Community Assn., L.A., 1972-75. Mem. Assn. Records Mgrs. and Administrs. (bd. dirs. 1975-76), Soc. Calif. Archivists, All Yr. Figure Skating Club (bd. dirs. 1970-79). Democrat. Roman Catholic. Avocations: bowling, walking, travel.

ALLEN, EDWARD RAYMOND, retired business educator, accountant; b. Indpls., Sept. 30, 1913; s. Edward L. and Emmeline (Rice) A.; BS in Commerce, Drake U., 1950, MA in Accounting, 1951; m. Norma D. M. Brennan, May 10, 1941. CPA, Idaho. Asst. prof. bus. adminstrn. Parsons Coll., Fairfield, Iowa, 1952-56; faculty Coll. of Idaho, Caldwell, 1956-73, prof. bus. adminstrn., 1956-73, head dept., 1962-70, chmn. social sci. divsn., 1972-73, emeritus, 1973—, vis. lectr., 1973-74; practicing CPA, Caldwell, 1958-92; ret., 1992. Contbr. articles to profl. jours. Served to capt. AUS, 1942-46; lt. col. Res. ret. Decorated Bronze Star with 1 palm, Med. Badge. Mem. AICPA, AAUP (past pres. Coll. of Idaho chpt.), Idaho Soc. CPAs (dir., regional v.p. 1958-61, mem. standards of practice com. 1974-83, chmn. com. 1980-83, chmn. relations with ednl. instns. com. 1984-86, mem. 1993—), Elks, Pi Kappa Phi. Home: PO Box 336 Caldwell ID 83606-0336

ALLEN, FLOYD E., secondary education educator; b. Hadley, N.Y., Jan. 8, 1949; s. Floyd E. and Leona e. (LaPier) A.; m. Clarissa K. Schultz, July 29, 1972; children: Melissa, Matthew, Meredith. Diploma, Hadley-Luzerne Ctrl. U., 1967; BS in Edn., SUNY, Plattsburgh, 1971; MA in History, SUNY, Potsdam, 1976. Faculty Brushton-Moira Ctrl. U., Brushton, N.Y., 1971-76; office mgr. Funny Shirts, Phoenix, 1976-82; asst. prof. N.W. Christian Acad., Glendale, Ariz., 1982-94; dept. chair upper divsn. Paradise Valley Christian Sch., Phoenix, 1994—; bd. dirs. The Covenant Group, Phoenix; adv. bd. Am. Christian Writers, Nashville, 1996—. Author: The Ananias Precedent, 1987. Deacon Paradise Hills Christian Ctr., Phoenix, 1984-90.

ALLEN, GARY, association executive; b. Lockport, N.Y., Apr. 7, 1942; m. Elaine Irene, June 13, 1964; 3 children. BSEE, Cornell U., 1965; PhD, SUNY, 1969. Asst. prof. lab. neurobiology, dept. physiology SUNY, Buffalo, 1971-76, dir. lab. neurobiology, 1975-76; dir. internat. student ministry devel. base U. Calif., Campus Crusade for Christ, Berkeley, 1976-79; dir. UN ministry Christian Embassy of Campus Crusade for Christ, 1979-83; pres. co-founder Christian Mission UN Cmty., 1983—; lectr. dept. physiology & anatomy U. Calif., 1976-79; adj. asst. prof. dept. physiology N.Y. Med. Coll., 1981-85; spkr. & lectr. in field. Author: Building a Democratic Society: Principles for Nation Building; contbr. articles to profl. jours. Bd. dirs. Christian Heritage Sch., 1991-93. Vis. scholar U. Calif., 1976-79, Kappa Delta Rho Nat. Found. scholar, 1963. Mem. Am. Physiol. Soc., Internat. Brain Rsch. Orgn., Soc. Neurosci., Phi Eta Sigma, Kappa Kappa Psi, Eta Kappa Nu. Avocations: snorkeling, sailing, reading, early American history, swimming. Home: PO Box 2752 Carlsbad CA 92018-2752 Office: PO Box 2703 Carlsbad CA 92018-2703

ALLEN, GORDON KELLEY, communications company executive; b. Oklahoma City, July 4, 1957; s. Vincent H. Jr. and Carole Ann (Koch) A.; m. Kimberly Ann Hulse, July 15, 1995; children: Gordon Luke, Haley Lynne, Jacob Michael. BS in Econs. and Bus. Adminstrn., Westminster Coll., 1980. V.p. Vince Allen & Assoc., Denver, 1980-94, pres., 1994-95; v.p. CTG Telecom., Denver, 1987-93; pres. CTG Telecom., 5, 1993-95; mng. ptnr. Data Choice Network Svcs., LLC, Littleton, Colo., 1996—. Republican. Avocations: sports, reading, traveling, family activities. Office: Data Choice Network Svcs LLC 9200 W Cross Dr Ste 313 Littleton CO 80123-2238

ALLEN, HOWARD NORMAN, cardiologist, educator; b. Chgo., Nov. 19, 1936; s. Herman and Ida Gertrude (Weinstein) A.; children: Michael Daniel, Jeffrey Scott. BS, U. Ill., Chgo., 1958, MD, 1960. Diplomate Am. Bd. Internal Medicine, Am. Bd. Cardiovascular Disease, Nat. Bd. Med. Examiners. Intern Los Angeles County Gen. Hosp., L.A., 1960-61; resident in internal medicine Wadsworth VA Med. Ctr., L.A., 1961, 64-66; fellow in cardiology Cedars-Sinai Med. Ctr., L.A., 1966-67, dir. cardiac care unit Cedars of Lebanon Hosp. div., 1968-74, dir. Pacemaker Evaluation Ctr., 1968-89, dir. Cardiac Noninvasive Lab., 1972-88; Markus Found. fellow in cardiology St. George's Hosp., London, 1967-68; attending physician cardiology svc. Sepulveda (Calif.) VA Med. Ctr., 1972-86; pvt. practice Beverly Hills, Calif., 1988—; asst. prof. medicine UCLA, 1970-76, assoc. prof., 1976-84, adj. prof., 1984-88, clin. prof., 1988—; cons. Sutherland Learning Assocs., Inc., L.A., 1970-75; cardiology cons. Occidental Life Ins. Co., L.A., 1972-86. Contbr. articles to med. jours., chpts. to books. Commr. L.A. County Emergency Med. Svcs., 1989-91. Capt. M.C., U.S. Army, 1962-63, Korea. Fellow NSF, 1958, NIH, 1966-67. Fellow ACP, Am. Coll. Cardiology; mem. Am. Heart Assn. (fellow coun. on clin. cardiology, pres. Greater L.A. affiliate 1987-88, bd. dirs. 1979-94, Heart of Gold award 1994), U. Ill. Alumni Assn. (life, Loyalty award 1996), Big Ten Club So. Calif. (bd. dirs.), Alpha Omega Alpha, Pi Kappa Epsilon. Office: 414 N Camden Dr Ste 1100 Beverly Hills CA 90210-4532

ALLEN, JOSE R., lawyer; b. Panama, Sept. 8, 1951; arrived in U.S., 1956; s. Joseph R. and Grace A. (Osborne) A.; m. Irvenia E. Waters, July 20, 1986; 1 child, Jeffrey Richard Allen. BA, Yale U., 1973; JD, Boston Coll., 1976. Bar: Mass. 1977, Calif. 1986. Asst. atty. gen. Mass. Atty. Gen. Office, Boston, 1976-79; trial atty. U.S. Dept. Justice, Washington, 1979-80, asst. sect. chief, 1980-82, sect. chief, 1982-85; of counsel Orrick, Herrington & Sutcliffe, San Francisco, 1985-88; ptnr. Skadden, Arps, Slate, Meagher & Flom LLP, San Francisco, 1988—; mem. adv. com. Practicing Law Inst., N.Y.C., 1992—. Bd. dirs. San Francisco Bay Area Lawyers' Com. Urban Affairs, 1990, Legal Aid Soc. San Francisco, 1993. Mem. ABA, Bar Assn. San Francisco, Charles Houston Bar Assn., State Bar Calif. (mem. environ. law sect.). Office: Skadden Arps Slate Meagher & Flom LLP Four Embarcadero Ctr San Francisco CA 94111

ALLEN, LOUIS ALEXANDER, management consultant; b. Glace Bay, N.S., Oct. 8, 1917; s. Israel Nathan and Emma (Greenberg) A.; m. Ruth Graham, Aug. 24, 1946; children: Michael, Steven, Ace, Terry Allen Beck, Deborah Allen. BS cum laude, Wash. State U., 1941. Cert. mgmt. cons. Asst. to dean of men Wash. State U., Pullman, 1940-42; tng. supr. Aluminum Co. Am., Pitts., 1946-49; mgr. pers. adminstrn. Koppers Co. Inc., Pitts., 1949-53; dir. rsch. projects The Conf. Bd., N.Y.C., 1953-56; dir. orgnl. planning Booz, Allen & Hamilton, Chgo., 1956-58; pres., chmn. emeritus Louis Allen Assocs., Los Altos, Calif., 1958—; lectr. on bus. mgmt. Stanford U., U. Chgo., NYU, Japan, China, Australia, Africa and Europe. Author: Improving Staff and Line Relationships, 1956, Preparing the Company Organization Manual, 1957, Organization of Staff Functions, 1958, Management and Organization, 1958, The Management Profession, 1964, Professional Management: New Concepts and Proven Practices, 1973, Time before Morning: Art and Myth of the Australian Aborigines, 1975, Making Managerial Planning More Effective, 1982, The Allen Guide for Management Leaders, 1989, Common Vocabulary for Management Leaders, 1989, The Louis Allen Leader's Handbook, 1995, The New Leadership, 1996; (mus. catalog) Australian Aboriginal Art, 1972; translated into Japanese, German, French, Finnish, Swedish, Dutch, Spanish, Portuguese, Bahasa; contbr. numerous articles and monographs to profl. jours. on mgmt., primitive art; exhibitor primitive art major mus. worldwide, 1969—. Maj. USAF, 1942-55, PTO. Decorated Legion of Merit; recipient McKinsey award Acad. Mgmt. Mem. Inst. Mgmt. Cons. (sr. assoc., regional pres. 1985). Avocations: hiking, theater, opera, gardening. Office: Louis Allen Rsch PO Box 11 Palo Alto CA 94302-0011

ALLEN, LOUISE, writer, educator; b. Alliance, Ohio, Sept. 21, 1910; d. Earl Wayne and Ella Celesta (Goodall) Allerton; m. Benjamin Yukl, June 27, 1936; children: Katherine Anne Yukl Johnston, Kenneth Allen, Richard Lee, Margaret Louise Yukl Border. Student, Cleve. Coll. Western Res. U., 1963, Lakeland C.C., 1981-84. Co-founder Sch. Writing, Cleve., 1961-62; founder, dir. Allen Writers' Agy., Wickliffe, Ohio, 1963-84; editorial assoc. criticism service Writer's Digest mag., 1967-69; instr. Cuyahoga C.C., 1963-[illegible] Author: (poems) Confetti, 1987; contbr. articles to mags.; composer (hymn) The Foot of the Cross. Mem. AAUW, Mensa, Assn. Mundial de Mujures Periodistas y Escritoras, Women in Communications, Nat. League Am. Pen Women, DAR, Shore Writers Club (founder), Euclid Three Arts Club, Women's City Club (Cleve.). Republican. Congregationalist. Home: 4632 W Laredo St Chandler AZ 85226-6034

ALLEN, MERRILL JAMES, marine biologist; b. Brady, Tex., July 16, 1945; s. Clarence Francis and Sara Barbara (Finlay) A. BA, U. Calif., Santa Barbara, 1967; MA, UCLA, 1970; PhD, U. Calif., San Diego, 1982. Cert. jr. coll. tchr., Calif. Asst. environ. specialist So. Calif. Coastal Water Rsch. Project, El Segundo, 1971-77; postdoctoral assoc. Nat. Rsch. Coun., Seattle, 1982-84; oceanographer Nat. Marine Fisheries Svc., Seattle, 1984-86; sr. scientist MBC Applied Environ. Scis., Costa Mesa, Calif., 1986-93; prin. scientist So. Calif. Coastal Water Rsch. Project, Long Beach and Westminster, Calif., 1993—; tech. adv. com. Santa Monica Bay Restoration Project, Monterey Park, Calif., 1989—; steering com. So. Calif. Bight Pilot Project, 1993-98, So. Calif. Bight 1998 Regional Marine Survey, 1998—; affiliate asst. prof. sch. fisheries U. Wash., Seattle, 1985-89; mem. sci. rev. panel for ecol. reserves rsch. program Calif. Sea Grant Coll., 1996-97; adj. prof. dept. biology Calif. State U., Long Beach, 1996—. Mem. AAAS, Am. Inst. Fisheries Rsch. Biologists (dir. So. Calif. dist. 1991-93), Am. Fisheries Soc., Am. Soc. Ichthyologists and Herpetologists. Achievements include development of most comprehensive atlas of marine fishes from Bering Sea to Mexico; description of state of contamination of Santa Monica Bay. Office: So Calif Coastal Water Rsch Project 7171 Fenwick Ln Westminster CA 92683-5218

ALLEN, PAUL, computer executive, professional sports team owner. Student, Wash. State U. Co-founder Microsoft Corp., Redmond, Wash., 1975, exec. v.p., 1975-83; founder Asymetrix Corp., Bellevue, Wash., 1985—, Starwave Corp., Bellevue; founder, chmn. Intervas Rsch., Palo Alto, Calif.; owner, chmn. bd. Portland (Oreg.) Trail Blazers, 1988—; bd. dirs. Egghead Discount Software, Microsoft Corp., Darwin Molecular, Inc.

ALLEN, RICK (FREDERICK ALLEN KLYCINSKI), magician, advertising and publicity consultant; b. Detroit, Nov. 4, 1941; s. Chester Bruno and Johana Jean (Guzdzial) Klycinski; m. Marie DeLeon, Nov. 2, 1965 (div. Mar. 1985); children: John Paul, Marie Louise, Diane Lynn, Mark Frederick; m. Sasikanch Adulchit, July 21, 1998. AA, Pasadena Coll., 1961. Account exec. Knight Ridder Newspapers, Long Beach, Calif., 1966-68, advt. mgr., 1969-71; advt. mgr. Copley Newspapers, Torrance, Calif., 1972-73; cons. Scripps Newspapers, Napa, Calif., 1974-75; founder, owner, mgr. Creative Advt. Svc., Vallejo, Calif., 1976—; dir. mail advt. cons. Vallejo, 1980—; profl. magician for fund-raising orgns., 1976—. Author: Public Relations and Publicity for Entertainers, 1978; editor: Stick to the Cash Register, 1970; contbr. articles to various publs. Founder Anti-Grafitti Task Force. Named top fund raiser United Way, L.A., Long Beach, 1971; recipient awards for creative advt. Calif. Advt. Assn., Calif. Pubs. Assn., Am. Assn. Advt. Agys. Mem. Soc. Am. Magicians, Internat. Brotherhood Magicians, Pacfic Coast Assn. Magicians, Lions Club Internat. Avocations: international travel, collecting books and entertainment memorabilia. Home and Office: 917 Bradford Way Benicia CA 94510-3616

ALLEN, ROBERT EDWARD, JR., physician assistant; b. Omaha, Mar. 27, 1950; s. Robert Edward and Virginia (Connor) A.; m. Christine Ann Rahm, July 16, 1985; children: Sean Edward, Erin Christine. Student, Brooke Army Hosp., San Antonio, 1968-69, St. Anthony Ctrl. Hosp., Denver, 1984, 86. Cert. Nat. Bd. Orthopaedic Physician Assts.; cert. EMT, vocat. tchr., Colo.; lic. physician asst., Colo.; cert. BLS. Mem., patroller, instr. Nat. Ski Patrol, 1974-90; orthopaedic physician asst., orthopaedic technician Luth. Med. Ctr., Wheatridge, Colo., 1980-85, instr. EMT program, 1983-89; physician asst., mem. staff St. Joseph Hosp., Denver, 1985-87; physician asst. Denver Orthopedic Clinic and Inst. for Limb Preservation, 1987-96, Advanced Orthopedics Assoc., 1996—; part-time EMT, Golden, Colo., 1980-84; lectr. continuing med. edn. Colo. Emergency Med. Svcs. Sys., also nursing staffs; manuscript reviewer William and Wilkins, Balt., 1993—; splty. lectr. oncology Clinicians Rev., Clifton, N.J., 1993—; insvc. lectr. in field. Exec. prodr. instrnl. videos; contbr. articles to profl. publs.; designer saw blade for arthroscopic anterior crucial ligament reconstrn.; co-designer antibiotic bead maker. Vol. Toys for Tots, Denver, 1992—. With Spl. Forces, U.S. Army, 1968-71, Vietnam. Recipient 2nd place in best case study for alkaptonuria/ochrunosis Advance PA mag., 1997. Fellow Am. Soc. Orthopedic Physician Assts.; mem. Am. Acad. Physician Assts., NRA. Lutheran. Avocations: scuba diving, hunting, fishing, water and snow skiing. Home: 14650 E Floyd Ave Aurora CO 80014-3803 Office: Advanced Orthopedics Assocs 360 S Garfield St Ste 630 Denver CO 80209-3136 also: 4500 E 9th Ave Ste 150S Denver CO 80220-3932

ALLEN, ROBERT EUGENE BARTON, lawyer; b. Bloomington, Ind., Mar. 16, 1940; s. Robert Eugene Barton and Berth R. A.; m. Cecelia Ward Dooley, Sept. 23, 1960 (div. 1971); children: Victoria, Elizabeth, Robert, Charles, Suzanne, William; m. Judith Elaine Hecht, May 27, 1979 (div. 1984); m. Suzanne Nickolson, Nov. 18, 1995. BS, Columbia U., 1962; LLB, Harvard U., 1965. Bar: Ariz. 1965, U.S. Dist. Ct. Ariz. 1965, U.S. Tax Ct., 1965, U.S. Supreme Ct. 1970, U.S. Ct. Customs and Patent Appeals 1971, U.S. Dist. Ct. D.C. 1972, U.S. Ct. Appeals (9th cir.) 1974, U.S. Ct. Appeals (10th, and D.C. cirs.) 1984, U.S. Dist. Ct. N.Mex., U.S. Dist. Ct. (no. dist.) Calif., U.S. Dist. Ct. (no. dist.) Tex. 1991, U.S. Ct. Appeals (fed. cir.) 1992, U.S. Dist. Ct. (ea. dist.) Wis. 1995. Ptnr., dir. Allen & Price, Phoenix; spl. asst. atty. gen. Ariz. Ct. Appeals, 1978, judge pro-tem, 1984, 92, 99; Nat. pres. Young Dems. Clubs Am., 1971-73, mem. exec. com. Dem. Nat. Com., 1972-73, Ariz. Gov.'s Kitchen Cabinet working on a wide range of state projects, bd. dirs. Phoenix Bapt. Hosp., 1981-83, Phoenix and Valley of the Sun Conv. and Visitors Bur., United Cerebral Palsy Ariz., 1984-89, Planned Parenthood of Cen. and No. Ariz., 1984-90, Ariz. Aviation Futures Task Force, chmn. Ariz. Airport Devel. Criteria Subcom., mem. Apache Junction Airport Rev. Com., Am. rep. exec. bd. Atlantic Alliance of Young Polit. Leaders, 1973-77, 77-80, trustee Am. Counsel of Young Polit. Leaders, 1971-76, 81-85, mem. Am. delegations to Germany, 1971, 72, 76, 79, USSR, 1971, 76, 88, France, 1974, 79, Belgium, 1974, 77, Can., 1974, Eng., 1975, 79, Norway, 1975, Denmark, 1976, Yugoslavia and Hungary, 1985, Am. observer European Parlimentary elections, Eng., France, Germany, Belgium, 1979, Moscow Congrssional, Journalist delegation, 1989, NAFTA Trade Conf., Mexico City, 1993, Atlantic Assembly, Copenhagen, 1993, Internat. Coun. Ariz. Heart Inst. Found., 1998—, trustee Environ. Health Found., 1994-97, Friends of Walnut Canyon, 1994-97, Cordell Hull Found., 1996—, spkr. seminars and profl. assns. *Founder of the law firm Allen & Price, Allen practices in the areas of intellectual property and technology, health care, patent and trade secret litigation, antitrust and securities litigation, and general business and personal counseling. The firm of Allen & Price has been the subject of newspaper and magazine articles emphasizing the firm's use of technology to provide prompt and timely business representation at lower cost than the traditional large law firms.* Contbr. articles on comml. litigation to profl. jours. Mem. ABA, Ariz. Bar Assn., Maricopa County Bar Assn., N.Mex. State Bar, D.C. Bar Assn., Am. Judicature Soc., Fed. Bar Assn., Am. Arbitration Assn., Phi Beta Kappa, Harvard Club. Democrat. Episcopalian (lay reader). Office: Allen & Price 2850 E Camelback Rd Phoenix AZ 85016-4311

ALLEN, ROY VERL, life insurance company executive; b. Hyrum, Utah, Aug. 3, 1933; s. Winfrd A. and Sarah Ann (Nielsen) A.; m. Judith Green, Aug. 11, 1961; children: Ann Marie Allen Webb, Michael R., Blair J. BS, Utah State U., 1958. CLU, Chartered Fin. Cons. Mgr. employee benefits Thiokol Chem. Corp., Brigham City, Utah, 1959-61; employment interviewer Hercules, Salt Lake City, 1962-63; agy. mgr. Standard Ins. Co., Salt Lake City, 1963—. Maj. U.S. Army Res., 1962-79. Mem. CLUs (bd. mem. 1973-75), Estate Planning Coun. (bd. mem. 1979-81), Utah Gen. Agts. and Mgrs. [illegible] Utah Assn. Life Underwriters (pres. 1988-89) Exchange Club. Republican. Mormon. Avocations: fishing, hunting, basketball. Home: 2526 Olympus Dr Salt Lake City UT 84124-2916 Office: Standard Ins Co 525 3rd Ave Salt Lake City UT 84103-2973

ALLEN, RUSSELL LAWTON, pharmaceutical executive; b. Jamaica, N.Y., June 8, 1946, s. George Howard and Virginia A. (Russell) A.; m. Claudette L. Ruiz de Luzuriaga, July 19, 1972; children: Philip E., Matthew C. BA,

Amherst Coll., 1968; MBA, Harvard Bus. Sch., 1970. Tng. assoc. Ford Found., Manila, Philippines, 1970-72; prof. brand mgr. Procter & Gamble, Cin., 1973-80; mktg. product group dir. Bristol-Myers-Squibb, Evansville, Ind., 1980-85; v.p. bus. devel., strategic analysis Eastman Kodak Co./ Sterling Winthrop, Inc., N.Y.C., 1985-94; gen. mgr. Ctrl. Am. Sanofi Winthrop, San Jose, Costa Rica, 1994-96; v.p. corp. devel. & strategic planning Ligand Pharms., San Diego, 1997—. Avocations: jazz, gardening. Office: Ligand Pharms 10275 Science Center Dr San Diego CA 92121-1117

ALLEN, SAM RAYMOND, organization development specialist; b. Cody, Wyo., Oct. 6, 1953; s. Robert Sam and Jerrine (Cross) A.; m. Melinda Jo Daniels, Oct. 23, 1979; children: Eric Samuel, Andrew William. BS, U. Wyo., 1976, MBA, 1986; postgrad., George Washington U., 1977-79, Hastings Coll., Nebr., 1972-74. Accredited pub. rels. cert. Teller Bank of Va., Rosslyn, Va., 1978-79; legis. asst. U.S. Senate/Alan K. Simpson, Washington, 1979-81; bus. mgr. Coors Brewing Co., Golden, Colo., 1986-87; vol. prog. mgr. Coors Brewing Co., 1987-90, tng. mgr., 1990-96; exec. dir. tng. svcs. Red Rocks Inst., Lakewood, Colo., 1996—. Editor V.I.C.E. Activity Guide newsletter, 1987-90. Bus. advisor Jr. Achievement, Denver, 1988-90; corp. mem. Assn. for Vol. Adminstrn., Boulder, 1987-90; elder Shepherd of the Hills Presbyn. Ch., 1986-89. Named Outstanding Corp. Coord., Adopt-A-School, Denver, 1987. Mem. ASTD, U. Wyo. Alumni Assn., Pub. Rels. Soc. Am., Rotary (community svc. dir. 1989), Alpha Kappa Psi. Republican. Presbyterian. Avocations: nature photography, public speaking, skiing. Home: 11636 W 74th Way Arvada CO 80005-3274 Office: Red Rocks Institute c/o Red Rocks Cmty College 13300 W 6th Ave Lakewood CO 80228-1213

ALLEN, SHEILA HILL, nursing executive, counselor, consultant; b. Imperial, Nebr., Sept. 28, 1935; d. Roger William and Lois Marion (Clayton) Hill; children: Steven Morgan, Lee-Ann Hill, Todd Everett, Andrew James. R.N., St. Lukes Sch. Nursing, 1958; BS, U. Denver, 1959. Cert. alcohol drug counselor, Calif. Asst. head nurse St. Lukes Hosp., Denver, 1959-62; dir. nursing Ridge Vista Mental Health, San Jose, Calif., 1973-75; dir. nursing svcs. Westwood Mental Health Facility, Fremont, Calif., 1975-89, dir. nursing svcs. Chem. Dependency Inst. No. Calif., Campbell, 1989-90; program dir. O'Connor Hosp. Recovery Ctr., San Jose, 1991-94; health facilities evaluator nurse State of Calif. Dept. Health Svcs. Licensing and Certification, 1995—. Bd. dirs., sec., Health Acctg. Svcs., Calif., 1984-89; co-founder, partner Health Acctg. Svcs., Fremont, 1984-89; co-owner Westwood Mental Health, 1984-89. Contbr. articles to profl jours. Mem. Calif. Assn. Alcoholism and Drug Abuse Counselors, Nat. Consortium Chem. Dependency Nurses, Brookridge Inst. Serving Addiction and Consciousness Profls., San Francisco Acad. Hypnosis, Nat. Coun. Alcoholism and Drug Dependence, Delta Gamma.

ALLEN, STEPHEN VALENTINE PATRICK WILLIAM, television comedian, author, pianist, songwriter; b. N.Y.C., Dec. 26, 1921; s. Carroll and Isabelle (Donohue) A.; m. Dorothy Goodman, Aug. 23, 1943; children: Stephen, Brian, David; m. Jayne Meadows, July 31, 1954; 1 child, William Christopher. Student journalism, Drake U., 1941, State Tchrs. Coll., Ariz., 1942. Radio announcer Sta. KOY, Phoenix, 1942, Stas. KFAC and KMTR, Los Angeles, 1944; comedian MBS, 1945; entertainer CBS, 1948-50; wrote narration and appeared in movie: Down Memory Lane; also appeared in motion pictures Warning Shot, The Benny Goodman Story, Amazon Women on the Moon, Great Balls of Fire, The Player, after 1950; appeared in Broadway play The Pink Elephant, 1953; creator, host Tonight Show, NBC, 1953-57; host TV shows Steve Allen Show, NBC, 1956-60, WBC syndicate, 1961-64, I've Got A Secret, 1964-67, Laughback, 1976-77, Meeting of Minds, 1977-81; composer over 7,000 songs including Picnic, Impossible, This Could Be The Start; author 43 books including Fourteen for Tonight, 1955, Bop Fables, 1955, The Funny Men, 1956, Wry on the Rocks, 1956, The Girls on the Tenth Floor, 1958, The Question Man, 1959, Mark It and Strike It; autobiography, 1960, Not All of Your Laughter, Not All of Your Tears, 1962; Letter to a Conservative, 1965, The Ground is Our Table, 1966, Bigger Than A Breadbox, 1967, A Flash of Swallows, 1969, The Wake, 1972, Princess Snip-Snip, 1973, Curses!, 1973, Schmock-Schmock!, 1975, What To Say When It Rains, 1974, Meeting of Minds, 1978, Chopped Up Chinese, 1978, Ripoff, 1979, Explaining China, 1980, Funny People, 1981, The Talk Show Murders, 1982, More Funny People, 1982 Beloved Son: A Story of the Jesus Cults, 1982, More Funny People, 1982, How To Make a Speech, 1986, How To Be Funny, 1987, Murder on the Glitter Box, 1989, (with Bill Adler Jr.) The Passionate Nonsmoker's Bill of the Rights, 1989, Dumbth: And 81 Ways to Make Americans Smarter, 1989, The Public Hating, 1990, Murder in Manhattan, 1990, Steve Allen and The Bible: Religion and Morality, 1990, Murder in Vegas, 1991, Hi-Ho, Steverino! My Adventures in the Wonderful Wacky World of TV, 1992, How to be Funny, 1992, The Murder Game, 1993, More Steve Allen on the Bible, Religion & Morality, Book Two, 1993, Make 'Em Laugh, 1993, Reflections, 1994, Murder on the Atlantic, 1995, The Man Who Turned Back the Clock and Other Short Stories, 1995, The Bug and The Slug in The Rug, 1995, But Seriously..., 1996, Wake Up to Murder, 1996, Die Laughing, 1998, Dumbth: The Lost Art of Thinking, 1998. Recipient Grammy award for Gravy Waltz, 1964; named to TV Acad. Hall of Fame, 1986. Address: Ste B 15201 Burbank Blvd Van Nuys CA 91411-3532

ALLEN, WILLIAM MERLE, university administrator, museum director; b. San Luis Obispo, Calif., Oct. 9, 1939; s. Lloyd Marion and Berwyn Rose (Palmer) A.; m. Janet Laurentine Clayton, June 11, 1963; children: Barbara, Gregory. BA in Chemistry, La Sierra Coll., 1961; PhD in Organic Chemistry, U. Md., 1967. From instr. to asst. prof. chemistry Andrews U., Berrien Springs, Mich., 1966-68; from asst. prof. to prof. chemistry Loma Linda U., Riverside, Calif., 1968-84; sr. v.p. acad. adminstrn. So. Coll. Seventh Day Aventists, Collegedale, Tenn., 1984-87; dean grad. sch. Loma Linda U., 1987-88; dir. ctr. lifelong learning La Sierra U., Riverside, 1988-98, dir. World Mus. Nat. History, 1988—, dir. devel., 1998—; chair chemistry dept. Loma Linda U., 1971-79, dir. divsn. natural sci., 1977-81; sec., trustee So. Coll. Seventh Day Adventists, 1984-87. Internet website developer. Trustee Smyrna Hosp., Atlanta, 1986-87. Republican. Avocations: gardening, racquetball, collecting autographed books. Office: La Sierra U World Museum Natural History 4700 Pierce St Riverside CA 92505-3332

ALLERY, KENNETH EDWARD, air force officer; b. Holyoke, Mass., Mar. 3, 1925; s. Alfred Edward and Anne (Millen) A.; m. Constance DuFresne, June 22, 1946; children—Katherine Ann, Kenneth Scott, Bryan Keith, David Edward. B.A., Park Coll., 1965; M.S., George Washington U., 1969; grad., Air Command and Staff Coll., 1961, Nat. War Coll., 1969. Commd. 2d lt. U.S. Army Air Force, 1944; advanced through grades to brig. gen. U.S. Air Force, 1972; insp. with Insp. Gen. Team 17th Air Force; exec. officer, ops. officer 526th Fighter Interceptor Squadron, Ramstein Air Base, Germany, 1961; sr. Air Force adviser Oreg. Air N.G., Portland Internat. Airport, 1965-67; dir. ops. and tng. 1st Air Force, Stewart AFB, N.Y., 1967-68; mem. N.Am. br. Directorate Plans and Programs, Orgn. Joint Chiefs of Staff, 1969-71; asst. dep. chief of staff for plans Aerospace Def. Command, Ent AFB, Colo., 1971-72; asst. dep. chief of staff for plans N.Am. Air Def. Command/Continental Air Def. Command, 1972-73, asst. dep. chief of staff for ops., 1973-74; also dep. chief of staff for ops. Aerospace Def. Command; command insp. gen. NORAD/CONAD/ADC, 1974-76; ret.; asst. to v.p. Syscon Corp., Colorado Springs, 1976-85; bus. devel. mgr. Litton Computer Services, Colorado Springs, 1985-96; founder Allery Enterprises, Inc., Colorado Springs, 1996—; bd. govs. Nat. Coll., Colorado Springs, 1993-94. Decorated D.S.M., D.F.C., Air medal with 4 oak leaf clusters, Meritorious Service medal with oak leaf cluster, Air Force Commendation medal. Office: Allery Enterprises Inc PO Box 15123 Colorado Springs CO 80935-5123

ALLIO, ROBERT PAUL, management consultant; b. Troy, N.Y., Nov. 3, 1956; s. Robert John and Barbara Maria (Littauer) A.; m. Beate Barbara Freter, Nov. 28, 1981 (div. Oct. 31, 1997); children: Christopher, Devon, Nicole. BA, York U., Toronto, Can., 1979; postgrad., Am. Univ., 1980. Bus. mgr. Planning Rev., Cambridge, Mass., 1981-83; v.p. Robert J. Allio and Assocs., Cambridge, 1982-89; tchg. fellow Harvard U., Cambridge, 1984-88; dir. corp. mktg. Paul C. Rizo & Assocs., Pitts., 1990-92; chief adminstrv. officer Nicholson Constrn. Corp., Atlanta, 1993-96; sr. v.p. Robert J. Allio and Assocs., Santa Fe, N.Mex., 1997—. Mem. Strategic Leadership Forum, Strategic Planning Soc., Brit. Am. Bus. Group. Avocations: tennis, Tae Kwon Do (instructor). Home: 58 Circle Drive Compound Santa Fe NM 87501-9594 Office: Robert J Allio & Assocs Inc 125 Lincoln Ave Ste 213 Santa Fe NM 87501-2057

ALLISON, LAIRD BURL, business educator; b. St. Marys, W.Va., Nov. 7, 1917; s. Joseph Alexander and Opal Marie (Robinson) A.; m. Katherine Louise Hunt, Nov. 25, 1943 (div. 1947); 1 child: William Lee; m. Genevieve Nora Elmore, Feb. 1, 1957 (dec. July 1994). BS in Personnel and Indsl. Relations magna cum laude, U. So. Calif., 1956; MBA, UCLA, 1958. Chief petty officer USN, 1936-51, PTO; asst. prof. to prof. mgmt. Calif. State U., L.A., 1956-83; asst. dean Calif. State U. Sch. Bus. and Econs., L.A., 1971-72, assoc. dean, 1973-83, emeritus prof. mgmt., 1983—; vis. asst. prof. mgmt. Calif. State U., Fullerton, 1970. Co-authored the Bachelors degree program in mgmt. sci. at Calif. State U., 1963. Mem. U.S. Naval Inst., Navy League U.S. Ford Found. fellow, 1960. Mem. Acad. Mgmt., Inst. Mgmt. Sci., Western Econs. Assn. Internat., World Future Soc., Am. Acad. Polit. Social Sci., Calif. State U. Assn. Emeriti Profs., Calif. State U. L.A. Emeriti Assn. (program v.p. 1986-87, v.p. adminstrn. 1987-88, pres. 1988-89, exec. com. 1990-91, treas. 1991—), Am. Assn. Individual Investors, Am. Assn. Ret. Persons, Ret. Pub. Employees Assn. Calif. (chpt. sec. 1984-88, v.p. 1989, pres. 1990-92), Am. Legion, Phi Kappa Phi, Beta Gamma Sigma, Alpha Kappa Psi. Avocations: history, travel, photography, hiking. Home: 2176 E Bellbrook St Covina CA 91724-2346 Office: Calif State U Dept Mgmt 5151 State University Dr Los Angeles CA 90032-4226

ALLISON, REBECCA ANNE, cardiologist, writer; b. Greenwood, Miss., Dec. 21, 1946; d. Errol Ward and Mabel Irene (Blackwell) Atkinson. BS, U. Miss., 1968, MD, 1971. Diplomate Am. Bd. Internal Medicine. Intern. Parkland Meml. Hosp., Dallas, 1971-72; res. U. Miss. Med. Ctr., 1972-74, chief res., 1974-75, fellowship (cardiology), 1985-87; physician in internal medicine Physicians and Surgeons Clinic, Amory, Miss., 1975-79, Amory Internal Medicine Clinic, 1980-85; staff cardiologist Vets. Hosp., Jackson, Miss., 1987-89; physician in cardiology Cardiology Group Miss., Jackson, 1989-93, Cigna Healthcare, Phoenix, 1994—. Author: The Real Life Test, 1996; author (column) The Grace and Lace Letter, 1992-98. Fellow Am. Coll. Cardiology, Am. Coll. Physicians; mem. N.Am. Soc. Pacing and Electrophysiology, Harry Benjamin Internat. Gender Dysphoria Assn. Episcopalian. Avocations: travel, music, Internet web site. Home: 10636 N 11th St Phoenix AZ 85020-1180 Office: 755 E Mcdowell Rd Phoenix AZ 85006-2506

ALLRED, KEITH JOHNS, naval officer; b. El Paso, Tex., Jan. 4, 1955. BA with high honors, Brigham Young U., 1979; student, Univ. Wash., 1982-85; JD, U. Wash., 1985; student, DePaul Univ., Chicago, 1994-95; LLM, DePaul U., 1995. Bar: Wash. 1985, Ct. Mil. Appeals 1987. Gunnery officer, navigator USS Towers (DDG-9), 1979-82; trial lawyer San Diego, 1985-89; attorney Commander Fleet Air, Carribbean, Puerto Rico, 1989-92; staff judge advocate Battle Force Seventh Fleet, Yokosuka, Japan, 1991-92, Carrier Strike Force U.S. Seventh Fleet, Yokosuka, Japan, 1992-94; gen. counsel Naval Med. Ctr., San Diego, 1995-97; exec. officer Naval Legal Svc. Office Southwest, San Diego, 1997-99; instr. Keller Grad. Sch. Mgmt., San Diego, 1997-99. Contbr. articles to profl. jours.; asst. case note editor: Jour. Health & Hosp. Law, 1994-95. ensign, US Navy, 1979, lieutenant, 1981, lieutenant, 1984, lieutenant commander, 1990, commander, 1985. Office: Naval Legal Svc Office Southwest 3205 Senn Rd San Diego CA 92136-5090

ALM, STEVE, prosecutor; m. Haunani Ho; 1 child. MEd, U. Oreg., 1979; JD, U. Pacific, 1983. Editor West Pub. Co., 1983-85; dep. prosecuting atty. City and County of Honolulu, 1985-87, line-dep., then felony team supr., 1987-90, dir. dist. and family ct. divsn., 1990-94; U.S. atty. for Hawaii U.S. Dept. Justice, Honolulu, 1994—; adj. prof. Richardson Sch. Law U. Hawaii. Mem. ABA (mem. gov. com. on crime), Hawaii State Bar Assn. (ex-officio mem. domestic violence coordinating coun., v.p. criminal justice and corrections sect.). Office: US Dept Justice Box 50183 300 Ala Moana Blvd Rm 6-100 Honolulu HI 96850-0001*

AL MALEK, AMIR ISA, entrepreneur, business consultant, actor, musician; b. Shreveport, La., Apr. 2, 1951; s. Samuel Leroy and Evelyn Cynthia (Jones) K. AA Arts and Humanities, Laney Coll., 1981, AA Social Sci., 1983, AA Language Arts, 1985, AA Theater Arts, 1989, AA in Music, 1995; student, Columbia Sch. Broadcasting, Radio & T.V. Announcing, 1986; male modeling student, Barbizon Sch. Modeling, 1994; cert., Founds. of Faith Theology, 1994. Assoc. The Heritage Group, Walnut Creek, Calif., 1974—; pres., CEO Magnetic Phi Artists, Oakland, Calif., 1988—; supervisor Loomis Armored Inc, Oakland, Calif., 1991—; coach San Francisco Generals; coord.-backfields and lineman Am. Athletic League; musician, poet free-lance, Oakland, 1970—; model, actor, Laney Coll., Yosson Enterprises, Oakland, San Francisco, 1981—; actor, dir. The Mahdi Theater, Oakland, 1989—; rschr., dir., The Oil Bandana, Oakland, 1989—. Author (book of poetry) Africa Sweet Africa Me Africa Me, 1991, (short story) Three Coins for the Fisherman, 1990; composer: Tally of the Leaves, 1994. Min. Imam Nation of Islam, San Francisco, 1975—; min.-in-tng. Allen Temple Bapt. Ch., 1981; fruit of Islam, Nation of Islam Mosque 26; asst. coach Peralta Coll. Dist., Oakland, 1986-87; active spl. svcs. Rainbow Coalition Calif., 1984; del. Students for Jesse Jackson Campaign, Calaif., 1989; candidate for mayor City of Oakland, 1994. With U.S. Army, 1975-76. Named Citizen of Yr., recipient Ambassador award Principality of the Hutt River Province, Queensland, Australia. Mem. Internat. Platform Assn., Pre-Paid Legal Svcs. (assoc., license), The Fed. Bear Sports Club (diploma), Nirvana Found. for Psychic Rsch. (life), Am. Legion (life), Smithsonian Inst., Knight of the Realm (ambassador, Citizen of Yr. 1995, Principality of Hutt River Province Australia), Phi Beta Lambda, Epsilon Alpha Phi (past pres., past v.p. state chpt.). Republican. Islam. Avocations: martial arts, weight lifting, yoga, wrestling. Home and Office: 9437 Olive St Oakland CA 94603-1725

ALMOND, ELIZABETH ANNE, professional association administrator; b. Miller, S.D., May 16, 1972; d. James Richard and Sandra Marie (Feeley) A. BA in Journalism, U. Mont., 1994, BA in Polit. Sci., 1994. From alumni coord. to media & alumni rels. dir. Billings (Mont.) Cath. Schs., 1994-96; comms. coord. Mont. Stockgrowers Assn., Helena, 1996—. Block leader Sen. Conrad Burns Campaign, Billings, 1994. Mem. Nat. Soc. Fundraising Execs. (newsletter chair 1995-96). Republican. Roman Catholic. Avocations: hiking, camping, writing. Office: Mont Stockgrowers Assn 420 N California St Helena MT 59601-4968

ALMORE-RANDLE, ALLIE LOUISE, special education educator; b. Jackson, Miss., Apr. 20; d. Thomas Carl and Theressa Ruth (Garrett) Almore; m. Olton Charles Randle, Sr., Aug. 3, 1974. *Great-great grandfather, Major Eugene Gatlin, fathered one child, Martha, to his Indian housekeeper Alice Rice. He and his sister, Elizabeth, educated Martha. Great-grandfather Solomon Ward, rose as a politician, teaching citizens to vote in an area now known as Terry, Mississippi. He later married Martha Gatlin, and built the Ward Line school so that their ten children could be educated. Grandparents, on mother's side, Joseph and Louise Almore, raised their sons, Rodney and Thomas, in Jackson Mississippi. Her father, a postman for forty-seven years, and her mother, a teacher, saw to it that all eight of their children received a college education, and reached their professional goals.* BA, Tougaloo (Miss.) Coll., 1951; MS in Edn., U. So. Calif., L.A., 1971; EdD, Nova Southeastern U., 1997. Recreation leader Pasadena (Calif.) Dept. Recreation, 1954-56; demonstration tchr. Pasadena Unified Schs., 1956-63; cons. spl. edn. Temple City (Calif.) Sch. Dist., 1967; supr. tchr. edn. U. Calif., Riverside, 1971; tchr. spl. edn. Pasadena Unified Sch. Dist., 1955-70, dept. chair spl. edn. Pasadena H.S., 1972—, also adminstrv. asst. Pasadena H.S., 1993—; supr. Evelyn Frieden Ctr., U. So. Calif., L.A., 1970; mem. Coun. Exceptional Children, 1993—. Organizer Northwest Project, Camp Fire Girls, Pasadena, 1963; leader Big Sister Program, YWCA, Pasadena, 1966; organizer, dir. March on The Boys' Club, the Portrait of a Boy, 1966; pub. souvenir jours. Women's Missionary Soc., AME Ch., State of Wash. to Mo.; mem. NAACP, Ch. Women United, Afro-Am. Quilters L.A., established Dr. Allie Louise Almore-Randle Scholarship Award, Pasadena H.S., 1998; co-established Theressa Garrett Almore Music Scholarsip award Jackson State U., Jackson, Miss., 1989. Recipient Cert. of Merit, Pasadena City Coll., 1963, Outstanding Achievement award Nat. Coun. Negro Women, Pasadena, 1965, Earnest Thompson Seton award Campfire Girls, Pasadena, 1968, Spl. Recognition, Outstanding Community Svc. award The Tuesday Morning Club, 1967, Dedicated Svc. award AME Ch., 1983, Educator of Excellence award Rotary Club of Pasadena, 1993, Edn. award Altadena NAACP, 1994; named Tchr. of Yr., Pasadena Masonic Bodies, 1967, Woman of the Yr. for Community Svc. and Edn., Zeta Phi Beta, 1992; grad. fellow U. So. Calif., L.A., 1970, recognition Uniformly Excellent Work and Exceptional Commitment and Dedication to Altadena/ Pasadena Communities, Pasadena African Amer. Sch. Administr., 1998, Cert. Achievment in Educational Leadership, First AME Ch., 1998, Fran Cook Salute Great Inspiring Educator Award, United Tchrs. of Pasadena, 1998, Named Outstanding Educator, Nat. Sorority Phi Delta Kappa, 1998. Mem. NAACP (bd. mem., chmn. ch. workers com. 1955-63, Fight for Freedom award West Coast region 1957, NAACP Edn. award Altadena, Calif. chpt. 1994), ASCD, Calif. Tchrs. Assn., Calif. African Am. Genealog. Soc., Nat. Coun. Negro Women, Phi Delta Gamma (hospitality chair 1971—), Phi Delta Kappa, Alpha Kappa Alpha (membership com.), Phi Delta Phi (founder, organizer 1961), Phi Delta Kappa. Democrat. Mem. AME Ch. Avocations: wedding director, photography, gardening, arts and crafts, sewing, sports. Fax: 626-797-5549. E-mail: akainger@acninc.net. Home: 1710 La Cresta Dr Pasadena CA 91103-1261

ALPEN, EDWARD LEWIS, biophysicist, educator; b. San Francisco, May 14, 1922; s. Edward Lawrence and Margaret Catherine (Shipley) A.; m. Wynella June Dosh, Jan. 6, 1945; children: Angela Marie, Jeannette Elise. B.S., U. Calif., Berkeley, 1946, Ph.D., 1950. Br. chief, then dir. biol. and med. scis. Naval Radiol. Def. Lab., San Francisco, 1952-68; mgr. environ. and life scis. Battelle Meml. Inst., Richland, Wash., 1968-69, assoc. dir., then dir. Pacific N.W. div., 1969-75; dir. Donner Lab., U. Calif., Berkeley; also assoc. dir. Lawrence Berkeley Lab., 1975-87; prof. biophysics emeritus U. Calif., Berkeley, 1975—; prof. radiology emeritus U. Calif., San Francisco, 1976—; dir. study ctr. U. Calif., London, 1988-90; councillor, dir. Nat. Council Radiol. Protection, 1969-92; exec. v.p., tech. dir. Neutron Tech. Corp., Berkeley, 1990-93; mem. Gov. Wash. Council Econ. Devel., 1973-75; bd. dirs. Wash. Bd. Trade, 1973-76. Author books, papers, abstracts in field. Served to capt. USNR, 1942-46, 50-51. Recipient Navy Sci. medal, 1962, Disting. Service medal Dept. Def., 1963, Sustaining Members medal Assn. Mil. Surgeons, 1971; fellow Guggenheim Found., 1960-61; sr. fellow NSF, 1958-59. Fellow Calif. Acad. Scis.; mem. Bioelectromagnetics Soc. (pres. 1979-80), Radiation Rsch. Soc., Soc. Exptl. Biology and Medicine, Biophys. Soc., Brit. Inst. Radiology, Am. Philatelic Soc., Sigma Xi (nat. lectr. 1994-96). Episcopalian. Home: 1182 Miller Ave Berkeley CA 94708-1755

ALPERS, EDWARD ALTER, history educator; b. Phila., Apr. 23, 1941; s. Bernard Jacob and Lillian (Sher) A.; m. Ann Adele Dixon, June 14, 1963; children: Joel Dixon, Leila Sher. AB magna cum laude, Harvard U., 1963; PhD, U. London, 1966. Lectr. history Univ. Coll., Dar es Salaam, Tanzania, 1966-68; from asst. prof. to prof. history UCLA, 1968—, dean div. honors Coll. Letters and Sci., 1985-87, dean honors and undergrad. programs, 1987-96. Author: Ivory and Slaves in East Central Africa, 1975; editor: Walter Rodney: Revolutionary and Scholar, 1982, (newsletter) Assn. Concerned Africa Scholars, 1983-85; contbg. editor: Comparative Studies of South Asia, Africa and the Middle East, 1997; contbr. articles to scholarly jours. Fellow Ford Found., 1972-73, NEH, 1978-79, Fulbright Found., 1980; Conf. fellow Humanities Rsch. Ctr., Nat. Australia U., Canberra, 1998; Fundacao Calouste Gulbenkian grantee, Lisbon, Portugal, 1975. Mem. Am. Hist. Assn. (mem. com. Joan Kelly Meml. prize 1998—), Africa Studies Assn. (bd. dirs. 1985-88, v.p. 1992-93, pres. 1993-94), Assn. Concerned Africa Scholars (bd. dirs. 1983-93), Alliance for Undergrad. Edn. (UCLA rep. 1987-95, co-chair 1989-92), Hist. Abstracts (adv. bd. 1994—). Office: UCLA Dept History Los Angeles CA 90095-1473

ALPERT, DEDA WHITTLETON (DEDE ALPERT), state legislator; b. N.Y.C., Oct. 6, 1945; d. Harry Mark and Dorothy (Lehn) Whittleton; m. Michael Edward Alpert, Jan. 1, 1964; children: Lehn, Kristin, Alison. Student, Pomona Coll., 1963-65; LLD (hon.), Western Am. U., 1994. Mem. from 78th dist. Calif. State Assembly, Sacramento, 1990-96; mem. from 39th dist. Calif. Senate, Sacramento, 1997—; chairwoman Women's Legislators Caucus, Sacramento, 1993, Assembly Edn. Com., 1995, Senate Revenue and Taxation Com.; active Calif. Tourism Commn., Sacramento, 1990—, Calif. Libr. Allocations Bd., Sacramento, 1993—; com. mem. Edn. Standards and Teaching Training, Appropriations Subcom. on Fiscal Oversight, Joint Com. on Fisheries and Aquaculture, Pacific Fisheries Legis. Task Force, Calif. Commission on Status of Women. Author: Mammography Quality Assurance Act 1992, Assembly Bill 114 of 1993, Workplace Violence Safety Act, 1994, Battered Women's Protection Act, 1994, ABC, 1995, California Assessment Academic Achievement Act, 1995. Spl. advocate Voices for Children, San Diego, 1982-90; mem. bd. Solana Beach (Calif.) Sch. Bd., 1983-90, also pres.; pres. beach and county guild United Cerebral Palsy, San Diego, 1986. Recipient Legis. award Calif. Regional Occupation Program, 1991-92, Am. Acad. Pediats., 1991-92, San Diego Psychol. Assn., 1993-94, Commitment to Children award Calif. Assn. for Edn. of Young Children, 1991-92, Legis. Commendation award Nat. Assn. for Yr.-Round Edn., 1991-92, State Commn. on Status of Women, 1993-94, Friend of Public Edn. award Calif. Sch. Bds. Assn., 1997-98; named Friend of Yr., Children's PKU Network, 1991-92, Woman of Yr., Nat. Women's Polit. Caucus San Diego, 1991-92, Orgn. for Rehab. through Tng., 1993-94, High Tech Legislator of Yr., Am. Electronics Assn., 1991-92, 1993-94, 1997, Calif. Sch.-Age Consortium, 1993-94, Women of Distinction, Soropimists Internat. of La Jolla, 1993-94, Assemblymember of Yr., Calif. Assn. Edn. Young Children, 1993-94, Calif. Tourism Hall of Fame, 1997. Mem. Charter 100 of San Diego, Calif. Elected Women's Assn. for Edn. and Rsch. (pres. 1995-96). Democrat. Mem. Congregation Ch. Avocations: golf, reading. Office: State Capitol District 39 Sacramento CA 95814 also: 1557 Columbia St San Diego CA 92101-2934

ALSAKER, ROBERT JOHN, information systems specialist; b. Los Angeles, June 15, 1945; s. Lauris Ronald and Hazel Mildred (Danz) A.; m. Cynthia Ann Gillesvog, Feb. 25, 1984; children: Troy R., Erik G., Karlee A. AA, Fullerton (Calif.) Jr. Coll., 1966; BS, Moorhead (Minn.) State Coll., 1970. Project mgr. Jet Propulsion Lab., Pasadena, Calif., 1970-80; mgr. mgmt. info. systems Kroy Inc., Scottsdale, Ariz., 1980-85; adminstr. City of Pasadena, 1985-86; mgr. tech. cons. U.S. West Info. Systems, Phoenix, 1986-88; v.p. MIS ACB Cos., Phoenix, 1988-95; dir. MIS Midwest Pub., Inc., Phoenix, 1995-97; v.p. MIS Santa Fe Natural Tobacco Co., 1997—. Served in U.S. Army, 1968-69, Vietnam. Republican. Lutheran. Office: 1368 Cerrillos Rd Santa Fe NM 87505-3507

ALSTROM, SVEN ERIK, architect; b. Emporia, Kans., July 27, 1951; s. William E. and Willa M. (Russell) A.; m. Lynn M. Mathews, June 22, 1974 (div. June 1983). B. Gen. Studies, U. Kans., 1975; student evening div. U. Denver Coll. Law, 1984. Registered architect, Calif., Colo., Kans., Mo., N.Mex., Ariz., Tex. (non-active); cert. Nat. Council Archtl. Registration Bds. Architect, PGAV Architects, Kansas City, Mo., 1972-74, Horner Blessing, Kansas City, 1977-79, MSFS Architects, Kansas City, 1979-80, Marshall & Brown, Kansas City, 1980-81, Urban Design, Denver, 1981-82, Dominick Assocs., Denver, 1983-84; with C. Welton Anderson & Assocs., Aspen, Colo., 1989-90; pvt. practice Alstrom Group, Aspen, 1990—. Mem. AIA, Colo. AIA, Zen-Presbyterian. Home: PO Box 551 Aspen CO 81612-0551 Office: Alstrom Group PC 121 S Galena St Ste B Aspen CO 81611-1960

ALTER, EDWARD T., state treasurer; b. Glen Ridge, N.J., July 26, 1941; s. E. Irving and Norma (Fisher) A.; m. Patricia R. Olsen, 1975; children: Christina Lyn, Ashly Ann, Darci Lee. B.A., U. Utah, 1966; M.B.A., U. Utah, 1967. C.P.A., Calif., Utah. Sr. acct. Touche Ross & Co., Los Angeles, 1967-72; asst. treas. U. Utah, Salt Lake City, 1972-80; treas. State of Utah, Salt Lake City, 1981—; pres. Nat. Assn. State Treas., 1987-88. Bd. dirs. Utah Housing Fin. Agy., Utah State Retirement Bd., pres., 1984-93; mem. Utah State Rep. Cen. Com., 1981—, Anthony Com. on Pub. Fin., 1988-92. Sgt. USAR, 1958-66. Named to All-pro Govt. Team, City and State Mag., 1988; recipient Jesse M. Uhruh Award for Svc. to State Treas.', 1989. Mem. Am. Inst. CPAs, Nat. Assn. State Treas. (past sr. v.p., pres. 1987), Delta Sigma Pi, Delta Phi Kappa. Club: Utah Bond (pres. 1981-82). Office: State Capitol 215 State Capitol Building Salt Lake City UT 84114-1202

ALTER, GERALD L., real estate executive; b. Rensselaer, Ind., Aug. 24, 1910; s. Leslie and Lettie (Willis) A.; m. Margaret A. Davis, Sept. 15, 1939

(dec. Nov. 13, 1996); children: Judith Ann (dec.), John Edward. Student Bus. Coll., 1927-28. Clk. and office mgr., 1929-35; bldg. contractor, 1936-45; real estate broker, 1946—; officer Torrance Police Res., 1948-63; pres. Alter Realty & Ins., Alter Ins. Agy., Inc., REMCO Real Estate Mgmt. Co., Alter Devel. Co.; pres. Developers & Builders. Planning commr. City of Torrance, 1966-83, chmn. Torrance Planning Commn. 1982-83; water commr. City of Torrance, 1982-91, chmn. 1987-88; former bd. dirs. Harbor Area United Way. With Calif. State Guard, 1942-43; U.S. Army, 1945-46. Mem. Torrance-Lomita-Carson Bd. Realtors (pres. 1978, v.p. 1980-81), Calif. Assn. Realtors (hon., dir. 1978-81), Nat. Assn. Realtors, Torrance C. of C. (past dir.), Am. Legion, Rotary (recipient Torrance Rotary 40 yr. perfect attendance pin 1998), OX-5 Club (pioneer airman). Republican. Home: 1337 Engracia Ave Torrance CA 90501-2603 Office: 2305 Torrance Blvd Torrance CA 90501-2520

ALTHEIMER, BRIAN P. See TUTASHINDA, A.K. KWELI

ALTMAN, ADELE ROSENHAIN, radiologist; b. Tel Aviv, Israel, June 4, 1924; came to U.S., 1933, naturalized, 1939; d. Bruno and Salla (Silberzweig) Rosenhain; m. Emmett Altman, Sept. 3, 1944; children: Brian R., Alan L., Karen D. Diplomate Am. Bd. Radiology. Intern Queens Gen. Hosp., N.Y.C., 1949-51; resident Hosp. for Joint Diseases, N.Y.C., 1951-52, Roosevelt Hosp., N.Y.C., 1955-57; clin. instr. radiology Downstate Med. Ctr., SUNY, Bklyn., 1957-61; asst. prof. radiology N.Y. Med. Coll., N.Y.C., 1961-65, assoc. prof., 1965-68; assoc. prof. radiology U. Okla. Health Sci. Ctr., Oklahoma City, 1968-78; assoc. prof. dept. radiology U. N.Mex. Sch. Medicine, Albuquerque, 1978-85. Author: Radiology of the Respiratory System: A Basic Review, 1978; contbr. articles to profl. jours. Fellow Am. Coll. Angiology, N.Y. Acad. Medicine; mem. Am. Coll. Radiologist, Am. Roentgen Ray Soc., Assn. Univ. Radiologists, Radiol. Soc. N.Am., B'nai B'rith Anti-Defamation League (bd. dirs. N.Mex. state bd.), Hadassah Club.

ALTMAN, ROBERT CHARLES, apparel designer; b. Waterbury, Conn., Aug. 30, 1964; s. Marvin and Lillian Anne (Bacy) A. AA, Harbor Coll., Wilmington, Calif., 1985; BFA, UCLA, 1989. Draftsman Strand Century, San Dominquez, Calif., 1986; draftsman Strand Lighting, San Dominquez, 1987; owner fashion co. AnyDay, Kula, Hawaii, 1991—. Designer miscellaneous computer art, 1991—. Home and Office: 229 Kahoea Pl Kula HI 96790-9413

ALTSCHILLER, IRA RICHARD, artist, desktop publishing and Internet consultant; b. N.Y.C., May 25, 1945; s. William and Minna (Spielvogel) A.; m. Phyllis E Rose. MFA, San Francisco Art Inst., 1972. Artist, 1972—. Exhibited in Stephen Wirtz Gallery, Meridian Gallery, Museo Nacional De Bellas Artes, Chile, Salmagundi Club, Alonzo Gallery, N.Y.C., D.P. Fong, San Jose; represented in permanent collections Sanyo Corp., Oakland Mus.; contbr. author: (book) Digital Design: The New Computer Art, 1998. Recipient Best Internet Art Installation award Oakland Mus., 1998; Painting grantee John F. and Anna Lee Stacey Found., 1978, Contemporary Art Ctr. grantee, 1996. Jewish. E-mail: fineart@kagi.com.

ALTSCHUL, DAVID EDWIN, record company executive, lawyer; b. N.Y.C., Apr. 8, 1947; s. Norbert and Grace (Aderer) A.; m. Margaret Berne, July 4, 1969; children: Jonathan, Jared, Eric, Emily. BA summa cum laude, Amherst Coll., 1969; JD, Yale U., 1974. Bar: Calif. 1974. Law clerk U.S. Dist. Ct. Conn., Hartford, 1974-75; assoc. Tuttle & Taylor, Los Angeles, 1975-76, Pryor, Cashman, Sherman & Flynn, Beverly Hills, Calif., 1976-77, Hardee, Barovick, Konecky & Braun, Beverly Hills, 1977-79; prin. Rosenfeld, Kassoy & Kraus, Beverly Hills, 1979-80; dir. bus. affairs Warner Bros. Records, Inc., Burbank, Calif., 1980-83, v.p. bus. and legal affairs, 1983-88, sr. v.p. bus. and legal affairs, 1988-93, gen. counsel and sr. v.p. bus. affairs, 1993-95, vice chmn., gen. counsel, 1995—; bd. dirs. Rec. Industry Assn. Am., Reprise! Broadway's Best in Concert, 1998—, L.A. Jewish Fedn. Music Industry Divsn.; mem. Millenium Coun., Save Ams. Treasures, 1998—. Bd. dirs. Los Encinos Sch., Encinos, Calif., 1986-93, treas., 1986-87, pres., 1987-92; bd. dirs. People for the Am. Way, 1991—, vice chmn., 1996-97, chmn., 1998—; bd. dirs. People for the Am. Way Found., 1991—, bd. dirs. exec. com., 1993—; bd. dirs. San Fernando Valley Neighborhood Legal Svcs., Inc., 1989-90, Rock the Vote, 1997—. Mem. Phi Beta Kappa. Democrat. Jewish. Avocations: photography, reading. Office: Warner Bros Records Inc 3300 Warner Blvd Burbank CA 91505-4694

ALTSHILLER, ARTHUR LEONARD, secondary education educator; b. N.Y.C., Aug. 12, 1942; s. Samuel Martin and Betty Rose (Lepson) A.; m. Carol Heiser, Aug. 16, 1980. BS in Physics, U. Okla., 1963; MS in Physics, Calif. State U., Northridge, 1971. Elec. engr. Garrett Corp., Torrance, Calif., 1963-64, Volt Tech. Corp., Phoenix, 1965; engr., physicist Aerojet Gen. Corp., Azusa, Calif., 1966-68; elec. engr. Magnavox Rsch. Labs., Torrance, 1968-69; sr. engr. Litton Guidance & Control, Canoga Park, Calif., 1969; physics tchr. L.A. Unified Sch. Dist./Van Nuys Math/Sci. Magnet High Sch., 1971—; math. instr. Valley Coll., Van Nuys, Calif., 1986—; part-time physics and chemistry tchr. West Coast Talmudical Sem., L.A., 1978-88; foster tchr. Seti Inst. and NASA Ames Rsch. Ctr., 1994; coach Van Nuys (Calif.) H.S. Nat. Championship Sci. Bowl Team, 1995; tchr. mem. U.S. Olympic Physics Team, 1996. Mesa Club sponsor Math.-Engring. Sci. Achievement L.A. High Sch. and U. So. Calif., 1984-87, Van Nuys H.S., 1997-98, Calif. State U. Northridge, 1997-98. Recipient Cert. of Honor Westinghouse Sci. Talent Search, 1990. Mem. AAAS, Am. Assn. Physics Tchrs., Nat. Coun. Tchrs. Math., N.Y. Acad. Scis., Am. Meteorol. Soc., So. Calif. Striders, Santa Monica Astron. Soc., United Tchrs. L.A. Avocations: cycling, tennis, weight lifting, track and field, swimming. Home: 6776 Vickiview Dr Canoga Park CA 91307-2751 Office: Van Nuys High Sch 6535 Cedros Ave Van Nuys CA 91411-1599

ALVARADO, REBECCA JANE, secondary education educator; b. LeMars, Iowa, Apr. 17, 1955; d. Robert Joseph and Beverly Anne (Smith) Meylor; m. John Frederick Clair, June 10, 1974 (div. June 24, 1987); 1 child, Christopher L. Clair; m. Hector Abel Alvarado, Sept. 5, 1987; children: David M. Strait, Randee M. Alvarado. BS in Edn., Ea. Mont. Coll., 1985. Cert. K-12 tchr., Mont. Pharmacy technician St. Anthony Hosp., Denver, Colo., 1972-78; sec. to pharmacy dir. Mercy Med. Ctr., Denver, 1980; with radio sales advt. Sta. KLYC, Laurel, Mont., 1981; realtor ERA Leuthold, Billings, Mont., 1981-84; art tchr. gifted and talented Lockwood (Mont.) Intermediate Sch., 1985-86; substitute tchr. Billings (Mont.) Pub. Schs., 1986-87; art tchr. Hardin (Mont.) Mid. Sch., 1987—, art-dist. curriculum coord., 1993—; cons., judge Jailhouse Art Gallery, Hardin, 1991; postal stamp cancellation designer Little Big Horn Days, Hardin, 1993—. Watercolor, photography exhibited in Metrapark Art Gallery, 1985-94, Nothcutt Gallery, 1985, Jailhouse Art Gallery, 1994; Appeared in film: Son of the Morningstar, 1990. Tchr. Upward Bound Ea. Mont. Coll., Billings, 1991-94; acting cmty. theatre Der Schwartzwald Dinner Theatre, Billings Studio Theatre, Alberta Bair Theatre, Eastern Mont. Coll. Katoya Players, E.M.C. FIne Arts Festival; coach: Odyssey of the Mind, 1992-93, 95—; advisor photography and layout Hardin Mid. Sch. Yearbook, 1987-98; bd. dirs. Big Horn County Planning Bd., 1998—. Mem. NEA, Mont. Edn. Assn. (rep. 1996-97), Nat. Art Edn. Assn., Kappa Delta Epsilon (hon.), Alpha Psi Omega (hon.). Avocations: river rafting, horseback riding, quilting, art endeavors, remodeling, gardening. Home: RR 1 Box 1223C Hardin MT 59034-9721 Office: Hardin Mid Sch 611 5th St W Hardin MT 59034-1613

ALVAREZ, OFELIA AMPARO, medical educator; b. Havana, Cuba, Mar. 29, 1958; d. Alvaro Venancio and Lydia Caridad (Folgueras) A.; m. Manuel Sanabria, Mar. 9, 1985; children: Marian Paola, David Manuel, Gabriel Jesus. BS, U. Puerto Rico, 1978, MD, 1982. Diplomate Nat. Bd. Med. Examiners, Am. Bd. Pediat., Sub-bd. Pediatric Hematology-Oncology. Pediatric residency Univ. Children's Hosp., San Juan, P.R., 1982-85; fellow pediatric hematology oncology Children's Hosp. L.A., 1985-88; asst. prof. pediat. Loma Linda (Calif.) U., 1988-95, assoc. prof., 1995—; med. advisor Candlelighter, Inland Empire, 1988—. Contbr. articles to profl. jours. Bd. mem., med. advisor Make A Wish Found., Inland Empire, 1994-95. Clin. oncology fellow Am. Cancer Soc., 1985-86; pediatric rsch. fund Loma Linda U., 1993-95. Fellow Am. Acad. Pediat.; mem. Am. Soc. Clin. Oncology, Am. Soc. Pediatric Hematology/Oncology, Calif. Med. Assn., AAUW, Histiocyte Soc., Beta Beta Beta. Roman Catholic. Office: Loma Linda Children's Hosp 11175 Campus St Loma Linda CA 92350-1700

ÁLVAREZ, RODOLFO, sociology educator, consultant; b. San Antonio, Oct. 23, 1936; s. Ramon and Laura (Lobo) A.; m. Edna Rosemary Simons, June 25, 1960 (div. 1984); children: Ánica, Amira. *Daughter Ánica Álvarez Nishio, BA Yale 1988, and her husband, Yoshi Nishio, BA and MA Oxford 1987, MFA University of California Los Angeles 1992, expect their first child March 1999. They reside in London (Kensington), England where Ánica commissions and edits non-fiction books and Yoshi is an international investment consultant. Daughter Amira Álvarez, BA University of California Berkeley 1992, resides in Berkeley, California where she is a corporate relocations consultant to major business corporations.* BA, San Francisco State U., 1961; cert. European Studies, Inst. Am. Univs., Aix-en-Provence, France, 1960; MA, U. Wash., 1964, PhD, 1966. Teaching fellow U. Wash., Seattle, 1963-64; asst. prof. Yale U., New Haven, 1966-72; assoc. prof. sociology UCLA, 1972-80, prof., 1980—, dir. Chicano Studies Rsch. Ctr., 1972-74, chair undergrad. coun., 1995-97; vis. lectr. Wesleyan U., Middletown, Conn., 1970; founding dir. Spanish Speaking Mental Health Research Ctr., 1973-75. Author: Discrimination in Organizations: Using Social Indicators to Manage Social Change, 1979; Racism, Elitism, Professionalism: Barriers to Community Mental Health, 1976; mem. editorial bd. Social Sci. Quar., 1971-86. Pres. ACLU So. Calif., 1980, 81, sec., treas. 1999, Westwood Dem. Club, Calif., 1977-78; trustee Inst. for Am. Univs., Aix-en-Provence, France, 1968—; bd. dirs. Mex. Am. Legal Def. and Ednl. Fund, 1975-79, 88-92; mem. adv. commn. on housing 1984 Olympic Organizing Com., 1982-84; chmn. bd. dirs. Narcotics Prevention Assn., L.A., 1974-77; mem. bilingual adv. com. Children's TV Workshop, N.Y.C., 1979-82; candidate rep. Nat. Dem. Platform Com., Washington, 1976; alt. del. Nat. Dem. Conv., N.Y.C., 1976; bd. dirs. Univ. Credit Union, 1985-92, chmn. strategic plan com., 1987-92. Sgt. USMC, 1954-57. Pres. Mgmt. fellow U. Calif., 1994-95; recipient citation meritorious service for devel. Nat. Fed. Offenders Rehab. and Rsch. Program, State of Wash., 1967. Mem. Internat. Sociol. Honor Soc. (pres. 1976-79), Am. Sociol. Assn. (mem. coun. 1982-85, chairperson sect. racial and ethnic minorities 1989-90, assoc. editor Am. Sociol. Rev. 1989-91, chairperson sect. on sociol. practice 1990-91), Soc. Study of Social Problems (bd. dirs. 1982-87, pres. 1985-86), Pacific Sociol. Assn. (mem. coun. 1979-83, 87-89, v.p. 1991-93, pres. 1996-97), Marines Meml. Club, Rotary. Office: UCLA Dept Sociology 405 Hilgard Ave Los Angeles CA 90095-1551

ALVI, KHISAL AHMED, chemist; b. Karachi, Pakistan, Mar. 15, 1958; came to U.S., 1989; s. Wisal Ahmed Alvi and Abida Begum; m. Tanvir Sultana, July 4, 1989; children: Rida, Rohail. BS with honors, U. Karachi, 1981, MS, 1983, PhD, 1987. Rsch. asst. U. Southhampton, Eng., 1988-89; rsch. fellow U. Calif., Santa Cruz, 1989-91, sr. rsch. fellow, 1991-92; sr. scientist MDS-PANLABS, Inc., Bothell, Wash., 1993-99, The Tagen, Bothell, Wash., 1999—; presenter in field. Contbr. articles to profl. jours. Spl. predoctoral scholar U. Grant Commn. Pakistan, 1986, postdoctoral scholar U. Calif. Cancer Rsch. Coordinating Com., 1989. Mem. AAAS, Am. Chem. Soc., Am. Soc. Pharmocognosy, Soc. Indsl. Microbiology, N.Y. Acad. Scis. Office: The Tagen 11804 N Creek Pkwy S Bothell WA 98011-8801

ALZOFON, FREDERICK ELLIS, retired optics engineer; b. Detroit, July 18, 1919; s. Samuel and Kate (Moltner) A.; m. Norma Dorothy Shaw, 1947 (div. 1970); children: David, Rebecca, Julia, Daniel. AB in Math., UCLA, 1941; MA in Physics, U. Calif., Berkeley, 1948, PhD in Math., 1956. From staff to physicist Santa Barbara Rsch. Ctr., Goleta, Calif., 1953-56; sr. mathematician Stanford Rsch. Inst., Menlo Park, Calif., 1956-57; aeronaut. rsch. engr. Ames Aeronaut. Lab. (now NASA), Moffett Field, Calif., 1957-58; asst. prof. San Jose (Calif.) State Coll., 1961-62; tchr. math. U. Calif. Ext. Divsn., 1962-67; engr. Lockheed Missiles and Space Co., Sunnyvale, Calif., 1958-69, Houston Aerospace Divsn./Lockheed Electronics Co., 1969-76, Rockwell Internat. Corp., 1976-78, Boeing Aerospace Co., Seattle, 1978-84. Contbr. articles to profl. jours. Mem. AAAS, Optical Soc. Am., Am. Assn. Physics Tchrs., Soc. Photo-Optical Instrumentation Engrs., Sigma Xi, Pi Mu Epsilon. Achievements include originating a unified field theory readily tested by experiment; first to demonstrate feasibility of thermography for structural materials; generalized Sommerfeld's method of solving diffraction problems by multi-valued functions and showed the method could be applied to many kinds of surfaces; rsch. in high optical background radiation for instruments mounted on missiles and satellites for the USAF, transition from laminar to turbulent flow in viscous fluids.

AMALSAD, MEHER DADABHOY, financial consultant; b. Karachi, Pakistan, Sept. 12, 1958; s. Dadabhoy and Nancy A.; m. Katayoon Amalsad; 1 child, Anahita Meher. BS in Engring., Nadirshaw Edulgee Dinshaw Engring. Univ., Karachi, Pakistan, 1982; MS in Engring., Northrop Univ., 1987. Program mgr. Hughes Aircraft Co., Rancho Santa, Calif., 1988-95; dist. mgr. ICM Sun Am. Securities, Garden Grove, Calif., 1995-97; pres., CEO Starmasters, Garden Grove, Calif., 1997—; mem. acad. svcs. com. The Pegasus Sch., Huntington Beach, Calif., 1991-98. Author: Gifts That Lift, Shift and Uplift, 1996, Bread for the Head, 1997, In Search of Your Quest, How to Be Your Best, 1995, Love Grows and Shows Only When it Flows, 1995; co-author: (with Shahriar Shahriari) SOUL (Success Out of Understanding Love), 1998, Bread for the Parents' Head, 1997; inventor. Chairperson First World Zoroastrian Youth Congress, 1993, First North Am. Zoroastrian Youth Congress, 1987, Helping Hands Com. of Fedn. of Zoroastrian Assns. N.Am., 1987-93; pres. Hughes Toastmasters, 1995. Mem. Profl. Speakers Network, Relationship Building Network (sponsor), Leads Club. Avocations: music, writing, dancing, speaking, inventing, creative cooking. Home: 15842 Villanova Cir Westminster CA 92683-7616

AMAN, REINHOLD ALBERT, philologist, publisher; b. Fuerstenzell, Bavaria, Apr. 8, 1936; came to U.S., 1959, naturalized, 1963; s. Ludwig and Anna Margarete (Waindinger) A.; m. Shirley Ann Beischel, Apr. 9, 1960 (div. 1990); 1 child, Susan. Student, Chem. Engring. Inst., Augsburg, Germany, 1953-54; B.S. with high honors, U. Wis., 1965; Ph.D., U. Tex., 1968. Chem. engr. Munich and Frankfurt, Ger., 1954-57; petroleum chemist Shell Oil Co., Montreal, Que., Can., 1957-59; chem. analyst A. O. Smith Corp., Milw., 1959-62; prof. German U. Wis., Milw., 1968-74; editor, pub. Maledicta Jour., Maledicta Press Publs., Santa Rosa, Calif., 1976—; pres. Maledicta Press, Santa Rosa, 1976—; dir. Internat. Maledicta Archives, Santa Rosa, 1975—. Author: Der Kampf in Wolframs Parzival, 1968, Bayrisch-oesterreichisches Schimpfwoerterbuch, 1973, 86, 96, Talking Dirty, 1993, Opus Maledictorum, 1996, Hillary Clinton's Pen Pal, 1996; gen. editor Mammoth Cod (Mark Twain), 1976, Dictionary of International Slurs (A. Roback), 1979, Graffiti (A. Read), 1977; editor Maledicta: The Internat. Jour. Verbal Aggression, 1977—, Maledicta Monitor, 1990-92; contbr. articles to profl. jours. U. Wis. scholar, 1963-65; U. Wis. research grantee, 1973, 74; NDEA Title IV fellow, 1965-68. Mem. Internat. Maledicta Soc. (pres.), Am. Dialect Soc., Am. Name Soc., Dictionary Soc. N.Am. Home and Office: PO Box 14123 Santa Rosa CA 95402-6123

AMATO, CAROL JOY, writer, anthropologist; b. Portland, Oreg., Apr. 9, 1944; d. Sam Lawrence and Lena Dorothy (Dindia) A.; m. Neville Stanley Motts, Aug. 26, 1967 (div. 1978); children: Tracy, Damon. BA, U. Portland, 1966; MA, Calif. State U., 1986. Freelance writer, Westminster, Calif., 1969—; human factor cons. Design Sci. Corp., L.A., 1979-90; dir. software documentation Trans-Ed Communications, Westminster, 1980-84, pres. Advanced Profl. Software, Inc., Westminster, 1984-86, Systems Rsch. Analysis, Inc., Westminster, 1986-95, pres. Stargazer Pub. Co., Westminster, 1995—. Author: The Earth, 1992, Astronomy, 1992, The Human Body, 1992, Inventions, 1992, Inside Out: The Wonders of Modern Technologies Explained, 1992, 50 Nifty Science Fair Projects, 1993, The Super Science Project Book, 1994, The World's Easiest Guide to Using the APA, 1995, 2nd edit., 1998, The Earth, 1995, Creepy Crawlies, 1995, The World's Easiest Guide to Using the MLA, 1999; editor, Cultural Futuristics, 1975-80, numerous articles and short stories; participant in numerous radio and TV interviews. Sec. bd. dirs. Am. Space Meml. Found., L.A., 1986-87; bd. dirs. Orange County Acad. Decathalon, 1986-94. Mem. Ind. Writers of So. Calif. (bd. dirs. Orange County sect. 1986-93), Profl. Writers Orange County (bd. dirs. 1993—, pres. 1994-97), Writers' Club of Whittier, Inc. (bd. dirs. 1991—), Internat. Pen. E-mail: bestseler1@aol.com. Office: Stargazer Pub Co PO Box 10084 Westminster CA 92685-0084

AMAVISCA, EDWARD DEAN, electrical engineer; b. Yuma, Ariz., Aug. 12, 1965; s. Robert Manuel and Anna-Teresa (Mendoza) A.; m. Jamie Sue Felkins, July 7, 1995; stepchildren: Candice Cruz, Jesse Cruz. BSEE, U. Ariz., 1988, MS, 1991. Rsch. engr. asst. Allied Signal Aerospace, Phoenix, 1984-90; elec. engr. II Ariz. Pub. Svc. Co., Phoenix, 1992-99; computer engr. Info. Tech., 1997—. Mem. Soc. Hispanic Profl. Engrs. Republican. Roman Catholic. Avocations: running, swimming, hiking, skiing, music. Home: 20275 N 51st Dr Glendale AZ 85308-9319 Office: Ariz Pub Svc Co PO Box 52034 Phoenix AZ 85072-2034

AMBER, SHARMAI, writer; b. St. Paul, July 14, 1956. Spiritual tchr. Sambershar, O'ahu, Hawaii, 1986—. Author: The Melding, 1998. Mem. NAPRA, NWU. Avocations: spiritual growth, cats, birds, fish, crystals. E-mail: heal@lava.net. Fax: (808) 239-9128. Home and Office: Sambershar 47 660 Melekula Rd Kaneohe HI 96744

AMBROSE, THOMAS CLEARY, communications executive; b. Kalispell, Mont., Mar. 6, 1932; s. William Patrick and Anne Marie (Cleary) A.; m. Joyce Leona Demco, Aug. 13, 1960; children: Thomas Neal, John Alan, Bridget Sharon. BA in Journalism, U. Mont., 1952. Editor Choteau (Mont.) Acantha, 1952; reporter Daily Chronicle, Spokane, Wash., 1954-57, bus. editor, 1957-64; rep., mgr. media rels. Weyerhaeuser Co., Tacoma, 1964-74, dir. external communications, 1974-91; prin. Ambrose & Assocs., Seattle and Sun Valley, 1991—. Author, editor: Where The Future Grows, 1989. Pres. Spokane Editorial Soc., 1963-64, Spokane Press Club, 1959-60; dir. Federal Way C. of C., 1968-71, Ketchum/Sun Valley Hist. Soc., 1995-96. 1st lt. U.S. Army, 1952-54, Korea.

AMBROSE, WILLIAM WRIGHT, JR., college dean, accounting educator, tax researcher; b. Norfolk, Va., Oct. 13, 1947; s. William Wright and Charlotte Gertrude (Williamson) A.; m. Marcelia A. Conerly, Aug. 7, 1971 (div. Dec. 1986); children: William Wright III, Xandrea M., Mark S.; m. Jacqueline D. Woodard, Dec. 28. 1998. BSBA, Norfolk State U., 1974; MBA, Pepperdine U., 1982, postgrad. Enrolled agt. IRS; lic. ins. broker, notary pub., cmty. coll. teaching credential, Calif.; cert. tax profl. Quality assurance mgr. mfg. Corning (N.Y.) Glass Co., 1974-78; contr., plant mgr. Phillip Morris, Auburn, N.Y., 1978-79; sr. exec. mgr. Kerr Glass Corp., L.A., 1979-84; instr. Nat. Edn. Corp., Anaheim, Calif., 1985-87; assoc. prof., chmn. dept. acctg. and bus. DeVry Inst. Tech., Univ. Ctr., Pomona, Calif., 1987—; entrepreneur dba The Tax Inst., 1990; cons. Protrans, Santa Ana, Calif., 1985—, Castillo Electronics, Los Alamitos, Calif., 1986, Heriberto Constrn., Santa Ana, 1985—. Co-patentee polarized contaminate viewer. Sgt. Army Security Agy., U.S. Army, 1967-71, Vietnam. Mem. AAUP, Am. Assn. Higher Edn., Nat. Assn. Acad. Affairs Adminstrs., Nat. Assn. Accts., Nat. Bus. Edn. Assn., Am. Acctg. Assn., Am. Mgmt. Assn., Am. Prodn. and Inventory Control Soc., Nat. Soc. Tax Profls., Nat. Soc. Pub. Accts., Phi Beta Lambda, Sigma Beta Delta. Avocations: computer programming, golf, writing, investing. E-Mail: wambrose@admin.pom.devry.edu. Home: 795 S Pampas Ave Rialto CA 92376-2102 Office: DeVry Inst Tech 901 Corporate Center Dr Pomona CA 91768-2642

AMDAHL, KENN, writer; b. Richmond, Calif., May 4, 1949; m. Cheryl Amdahl; children: Paul, Scott, Joey. Student, St. Olaf Coll., Northfield, Minn., 1967, U. Colo., 1967-71; BA, Regis U., Denver, 1992. bd. dirs. Colo. Authors League. Author: There Are No Electrons, 1991, Land of Debris and Home of Alfredo, 1997; co-author: Algebra Unplugged, 1996. Mem. Rocky Mountain Fiction Writers, Mountains and Plains Booksellers, Rocky Mountain Book Pub. Assn., Colo. Ind. Pub. Assn. Avocations: guitar, gardening. Home: PO Box 778 Broomfield CO 80038-0778

AMERINE, ANNE FOLLETTE, aerospace engineer; b. San Francisco, Sept. 27, 1950; d. William T. and Wilma (Carlson) F.; m. Jorge Armando Verdi D'Eguia, July 4, 1970 (div.); m. Donald Amerine, Dec. 18, 1983. AA, Coll. Marin, 1977; BA in Math. with honors, Mills Coll., 1979; MS in System Mgmt. U. So. Calif., 1990. Sr. computer operator Bank of Am. Internat. Services, San Francisco, 1972-74; mathematician Pacific Missile Test Ctr., Pt. Mugu, Calif., 1979-80; engr. Grumman Aerospace Corp., Pt. Mugu, 1979-83; engr. Litton Guidance and Control Systems, 1984-86, product support and assurance dept. project mgr., 1986-97, project engr., 1997—. Chmn. Marina West Neighborhood Council, 1982-84; mem. NOW; chmn. subcom. Ventura County Community Coll. Dist. Citizen's Adv. Com. on Status of Women, 1983-84. Aurelia Henry Reinhart scholar, 1978-79; recipient Project Sterling award Grumman Aerospace Corp., 1982. Mem. Nat. Assn. Female Execs., Soc. Women Engrs. (chmn. career guidance com. and speaker Ventura County sect.), Litton Women's Enhancement Orgn. (founder, v.p. and chmn. info. and edn. com. 1985-86, editor newsletter 1986-87), Mills Coll. Alumni, Litton Mgmt. Club (sec. 1990), Alpha Gamma Sigma (life). Office: Litton Guidance & Control Systems 5500 Canoga Ave # 80 Woodland Hills CA 91367-6698

AMERMAN, JOHN W., toy company executive; b. 1932; married. BA, Dartmouth Coll., 1953, MBA, 1954. With Colgate-Palmolive Co., 1958-64, Warner-Lambert Co., 1965-80; v.p. Du Barry Cosmetics, 1971-72, v.p. internat. group, 1972-77, from v.p. to pres. Am. Chicle divsn., 1977-80; pres. Mattel Internat., from 1980; chmn., CEO Mattel, Inc., El Segundo, Calif., 1987-96; also bd. dirs. Mattel Inc., El Segundo, Calif.; bd. dirs. Unocal Corp., Vanstar, Phoenix House Calif., Amos Tuck Sch. Dartmouth Coll. Bd. govs. Hugh O'Brian Youth Found. Served with U.S. Army, 1954-57. Office: Mattel Inc 333 Continental Blvd El Segundo CA 90245-5012

AMES, KENNETH CARL, hydrologist, geology educator; b. Seattle, Dec. 20, 1965; s. Robert Kenneth and Janet Ann (Haltom) A. BA in Geology, Whitman Coll., 1988; MS in Geology, U. Idaho, 1992; postgrad. in soil chemistry, U. Wash., 1994—. Cons. Radon Detection Sys., Boise/Moscow, Idaho, 1989-91; chief Wash. metals in soils program U.S. Geol. Survey, Tacoma, 1991—; chief Midnite Mine groundwater quality monitoring program U.S. Geol. Survey, 1995—; dir. field svc. unit/water quality lab., mgr. investigations U.S. Geol. Survey, Tacoma, 1994—, chief Midnite Mine groundwater quality monitoring program; spkr. Am. Inst. Hydrology, Austin, 1994, Geol. Soc. Am., Seattle, 1994, U. Wash., Seattle, 1994-95. Contbr. articles to profl. jours. Mem. Magnolia Chorale, Seattle, 1992-94. Whitman scholar, Welch scholar Whitman Coll., 1985-88, Coll. of Mines scholar U. Idaho, 1989-90. Mem. AAAS, Soil Sci. Soc. Am., Geol. Soc. Am., Am. Soc. Agronomy, Nat. Eagle Scout Assn. Episcopalian. Achievements include the establishment of baseline concentrations of metals in soils for the state of Washington, determined changes in bulk chemistry of soil immediately below the 1980 Mt. St. Helens ash horizon. Avocations: hiking, running, music. Office: US Geol Survey 1201 Pacific Ave Ste 600 Tacoma WA 98402-4384

AMICO, CHARLES WILLIAM, management consultant; b. Boston, May 6, 1942; s. William Charles and Marie Josephine (Nicholas) A. Assoc. in Engring., Franklin Inst., 1962; BS, Suffolk U., 1968. Jr. chem. technician Avco Corp., Lowell, Mass., 1963-64; advanced vacuum tech. technician Nat. Rsch. Corp., Newton, Mass., 1964-68; semicondr. engr. IBM, Essex Junction, Vt., 1968-72, semicondr. mfg. engring. mgr., 1972-76, mgmt. devel. cons., 1976-86; founder, pres., CEO Creative Directions, Inc., San Francisco, Burlington, Vt., 1982—; bd. dirs. Holiday Project, 1987-88. State chmn. Vt. Hugh O'Brian Youth Leadership Seminar; bd. dirs. Vt. Hugh O'Brian Youth Seminars, Inc., CEO, 1984-85; corp. pres. Hugh O'Brian Youth Found., No. Calif., 1994-95. Recipient Hugh O'Brian Outstanding State Chmn. in Nation award, 1984, 85. Office: Creative Directions Inc PO Box 10101 Zephyr Cove NV 89448-2101

AMIDEI, L. NEAL, public relations counselor; b. Chgo., Oct. 22, 1933; s. Joseph Gabriel and Marilyn Jean (Ruddy) A.; m. M. Joan Powers, Sept. 5, 1961; children: Christopher Paul, Geoffrey Neal, Brian Joseph. AB, Loyola U., Chgo., 1954. Account exec. P.J. McCarthy & Assocs., Chgo., 1960-63; dir. pub. rels. Fulton Morrissey Co., Chgo., 1963-68; Hoefer, Dieterich & Brown, San Francisco, 1970-73; mgr. communication svcs. Chevron, San Francisco, 1968-70; pres. Amidei & Co., San Francisco, 1973-89; pres., mng. dir. Dorf & Stanton/West, San Francisco, 1989-91; pres. The Amidei Group, San Francisco, 1991—; pres. The Pinnacle Group, 1979; instr. San Francisco State U., 1985. Bd. dirs. Laguna Honda Hosp., San Francisco, 1978-86. Mem. Pub. Rels. Soc. Am. (accredited, pres. San Francisco chpt. 1984, dist. chmn. 1987, com. chmn. 1989, mem. exec. com. Counselors Acad. 1985-89). Office: The Amidei Group 230 California St San Francisco CA 94111-4301

AMIN, MASSOUD, executive, systems science and mathematics educator; b. Tabriz, Iran, July 4, 1961; came to U.S., 1978; s. Mohammad Shafi and Nahid (Loghman-Adham) A.; m. Elizabeth Ambrose, May 28, 1994. BSEE, U. Mass., 1982, MS in Elec. and Computer Engring., 1985; MSc, Washington U., 1986, DSc, 1990. Rsch. assoc. elec. and computer engring. U. Mass., Amherst, 1982-84, tchg. assoc. elec. and computer engring. dept. math, 1983-85; lectr., rsch. assoc. systems sci. and math. Washington U., St. Louis, 1987-92, sr. fellow Ctr. for Optimization and Semantic Control, 1990-94, asst. prof. systems sci. and math., 1992-97, assoc. prof., 1997-98, assoc. dir. Ctr. for Optimization and Semantic Control, 1994-98; mgr. math., info. sci. Electric Power Rsch. Inst., Palo Alto, Calif., 1998—; co-chair conf. Internat. Fedn. Operational Rsch. Soc., St. Louis, 1995; advisor grad. theses and sr. projects Washington U., 1990-98; referee, reviewer jours. in field. Guest editor Math. and Computer Modelling, 1995, 98, Internat. Transactions in Operational Rsch., 1998; editl. bd. of four acad. jours.; contbr. numerous articles to profl. jours. Vol. Orgn. for Aged in St. Louis, 1988-91; vol. instr. Washington U. Kenpo Club, 1992-96. Mem. AIAA (Young Profl. award 1990), IEEE (liaison to neural network coun., assoc. editor Control Systems mag. 1998, Best Session Paper Presentation awards Am. Control Conf. 1997), Inst. Ops. Rsch. & Mgmt. Scis., Sigma Xi, Eta Kappa Nu, Tau Beta Pi (chief advisor Mo. Gamma chpt. 1994-98). Achievements include work as principal investigator or co-principal investigator on several collaborations with industry and government, original contributions to research and design of decision-aiding system for advanced tactical aircraft as well as cross-disciplinary contributions in intelligent control and optimization, research on development and application of the Semantic Control Paradigm. Avocations: books, travel, athletics, Kenpo karate. E-mail: mamin@epri.com. Office: EPRI 3412 Hillview Ave Palo Alto CA 94304-1395

AMIOKA, WALLACE SHUZO, retired petroleum company executive; b. Honolulu, June 28, 1914; s. Tsurumatsu and Reye (Yoshimura) A.; BA, U. Hawaii, 1966, MBA, 1968; m. Ellen Misao Honda, Aug. 9, 1942; children: Carol L. Amioka Price, Joanne M. Amioka Chikuma. With Shell Oil Co., 1931-77, fin. svcs. mgr., Honolulu, 1962-77; pub. affairs cons., Honolulu, 1977-87; gen. ptnr. Pub. Affairs Cons. Hawaii, 1988-94; ret., 1994; lectr. econs. U. Hawaii, 1969-79. Mem. Honolulu Police Commn., 1965-73, vice chmn., 1966, 68, chmn., 1971; U.S. civil adm. Ryuku Islands, 1950-52. Mem. City and County of Honolulu Charter Commn., 1981-82; bd. dirs. Honolulu Symphony Soc., 1968. With M.I., AUS, 1944-48. Mem. M.I. Svc. Vets. (pres. 1981-82), Hawaii C. of C. (chmn. edn. com. 1963-64, chmn. pub. health com. 1966-67), Hui 31 Club, Hui Aikane Club, Honolulu Police Old Timers Club, Phi Beta Kappa, Phi Kappa Phi. Home: 46-310 Kamehameha Hwy Kaneohe HI 96744-4045

AMMON, MARY LOUISE, artist; b. Riverside, Calif., Sept. 25, 1969; d. Robert George and Isabelle Mary (Given) A. AA in Liberal Arts, Ohlone Coll., 1990; BA in Film, San Francisco State U., 1992. Med. records clk. Fremont (Calif.) Med. Clinic, 1987-88; receptionist Dutra Realty, Fremont, 1989-92; asst. mgr. Super Saver Cinema, Fremont, 1992; stock assoc. Macy's, Newark, Calif., 1992-93; compliance and quality control specialist Fremont Bank, 1994-96; video prodr. Wohlmut Media Svcs., Union City, Calif., 1996-97; quality control specialist Coast Comml. Bank, Santa Cruz, Calif., 1997—, Fremont Bank, 1997—. Assoc. prodr. (documentary video) The Spirit of Mission San Jose, 1997 (Joey award 1997, Telly award 1998). Mem. Am. Film Inst., Tri-Cities Scottish Assn. Calif. (Tartan Day Pub. chair 1996—), Rosicrucian Order, A.M.O.R.C. Avocations: fencing, researching ancient cultures, arts and crafts. Home: 41759 Higgins Way Fremont CA 94539-4614

AMOAKO, JAMES KWAKU, transportation services executive, financial analyst; b. Nkwatia, Ghana, Dec. 4, 1951; came to U.S., 1970; s. Kwame and Amma (Nyame) A.; m. Rose Tiokor; children: James Jr., Nicole, Jennifer. AS, Cosumnes River Coll., 1977; BS, Calif. State U., Sacramento, 1978; MBA, Golden Gate U., 1979; PhD, LaSalle U., 1997. Bank examiner Calif. State Banking Dept., San Francisco, 1979-80; fin. analyst Artec Internat. Corp., Mountain View, Calif., 1980-83; cost acct. Sun Microsystems, Mountain View, Calif., 1983-88; pres., CEO Alpha Transp. Corp., Phoenix, Ariz., 1988—. Recipient Svc. award Am. Field Svc., 1970. Home: 8826 W Encanto Blvd Phoenix AZ 85037-3619 Office: Alpha Transp Corp 4024 S 16th St Phoenix AZ 85040-1315

AMOR, SIMEON, JR., photographer; b. Lahaina, Hawaii, Apr. 24, 1924; s. Simeon and Victoria Amor. Grad. high sch., Hilo, Hawaii. Post commdr. Engrs. Post #22, Am. Legion, Honolulu, 1952-53; approp. acct. Hawaii Air Nat. Guard, Honolulu, 1953-64; prodn. control supr. Svc. Bur. Corp., Honolulu, 1964-73; prodn. control computer ops. Bank of Hawaii, Honolulu, 1973-86; owner, propreitor Image Engring., Honolulu, 1986—; historian VFW Dept. Hawaii, Honolulu, 1987-90, 96-97, First Filipino Infantry Regiment Hawaii Connection; treas. DAV Dept. Hawaii, Honolulu. Tech. advisor: (film documentary) Untold Triumph, Saga of the American Filipino Soldier. Cpl. U.S. Infantry, 1943-46, master sgt. USNG, 1952-64. Recipient Disting. Svc. award Nat. Disabled Am. Vet., 1992-94, Oahu chpt. Disabled Am. Vet., 1992-94. Mem. Am. Photographer's Internat., VFW. Home: 1634 Kino St Honolulu HI 96819-2651

AMORY, THOMAS CARHART, management consultant; b. N.Y.C., Oct. 29, 1933; s. George Sullivan and Marion Renee (Carhart) A.; m. Elisabeth Andrews Jackson, June, 1956 (div. Mar. 1969); children: Renee Elizabeth, Caroline Carhart, Gillian Brookman; m. Carolyn Marie Pesnell, May 10, 1969 (div. Nov. 1987) ; m. Doris Ruth Mack, Mar. 18, 1989. A.B., Harvard U., 1956. Comml. mgr. N.Y. Telephone Co., N.Y.C., 1957-60; sales mgr. Royce Chem. Co., East Rutherford, N.J., 1960-62; asst. to chmn. Seatrain Lines, Inc., Edgewater, N.J., 1963-65; mgmt. cons. Booz Allen & Hamilton, N.Y.C., 1966-67; ptnr. William H. Clark Assocs., Inc., N.Y.C., 1967-75, pres., 1975-79, chmn., 1979-88; mgmt. cons. Montecito, Calif., 1989—. Trustee Mus. City, N.Y., 1971-92, Santa Barbara Mus. Art, 1990-95, Santa Barbara Chamber Orch., 1991-96, United Boys' and Girls' Clubs of Santa Barbara County, 1995-96. Mem. Santa Barbara Club, Birnam Wood Golf Club, Coral Beach Club (Bermuda). Republican. Roman Catholic. Office: 1187 Coast Village Rd Ste 1-386 Santa Barbara CA 93108-2761

AMOS, STANLEY EDD, minister; b. Jackson, Miss., Dec. 18, 1956; m. Gladys Anes; m. Arlinda Staley, Aug. 15, 1987; 1 child, Preston Charles. BA in Polit. Sci. and Sociology, Tougaloo (Miss.) Coll., 1985; MDiv, Andover Newton Theol. Sch., Boston, 1988. Ordained to ministry Nat. Bapt. and Am. Bapt. Chs., 1983. Asst. pastor Zion Travelers Missionary Bapt. Ch., Jackson, Miss., 1983-85; chaplain Boston City Hosp., 1986; instl. chaplain Southeastern Correctional Ctr., Bridgewater, Mass., 1987-89; interim pastor Ebenezer Bapt. Ch., Boston, 1988-89; pastor Trinity Missionary Bapt. Ch., Honolulu, 1989—. Founder, exec. dir. The Hawaii African-Am. Unity Orgn., Honolulu, 1990—; advisor Martin Luther King Jr. Commn., 1990-91, apptd. chmn., 1991—. Fellow Afro-Am. Ministerial Alliance, The Afro-Am. Assn. of Hawaii; mem. NAACP, Hawaii Assn. Am. Bapt. Chs. (exec. bd. 1989—), African Am. C. of C. Hawaii (exec. bd.), Afro-Am. C. of C. (fellow mem.). Home: 500 Mananai Pl Apt 17C Honolulu HI 96818-5303 Office: Trinity Missionary Bapt Ch PO Box 31182 Honolulu HI 96820-1182

AMOS, WALLY, entrepreneur; b. Tallahassee, Fla., July 1, 1936; s. Wallace Sr. and Ruby Amos; m. Maria LaForey (div.); children: Michael, Gregory; m. Shirlee Ellis (div.); 1 child, Shawn; m. Christine Amos, 1979; 1 child, Sarah. Stockroom clk. Saks Fifth Ave., N.Y.C., 1957-58, stockroom supr., 1958-61; mail room clk. William Morris Agy., N.Y.C., 1961, sec., 1961-62, asst. agt., 1962; talent agt., 1962-67; ind personal mgr. L.A., 1967-75; founder Famous Amos Chocolate Chip Cookie Corp., Hollywood, Calif., 1975-89, Wally Amos Presents: Chip and Cookie, 1991-92, UNCLE Noname Cookie Co., 1992—. Author: The Famous Amos Story: The Face That Launched a Thousand Chips, 1983, The Power In You: Ten Secret Ingredients for Inner Strength, 1988, Mau with No Name: Turn Lemons Into Lemonade, 1994. Nat. spokesman Literacy Vols. of Am., 1979. With USAF, 1953-57. Recipient Pres.' award for Entrepreneurial Excellence, 1986, Horatio Alger award 1987, Nat. Literacy Honors award 1990. Home and Office: UNCLE Noname Cookie Co PO Box 897 Kailua HI 96734*

AMUNDSON, EVA DONALDA, civic worker; b. Langdon, N.D., Apr. 23, 1911; d. Elmer Fritjof and Alma Julia (Nelson) Hultin; m. Leif Amundson, Mar. 1, 1929 (dec. 1974); children: Constance, Eleanor, Ardis, Priscilla. Bd. dirs. Opportunity Workshop, Missoula, Mont., 1950—, Rockmont Group Homes, Missoula, 1976—, Bethany L'Arche (group home for girls), 1976—; sec. bd. dirs. Opportunity Industries, 1990-91, pres. 1991—; mem. Missoula Sr. Citizen's Ctr., 1980-82, 88—, pres., 1982-85, bd. dirs., 1988—; tchr. Norwegian cooking and baking, 1954-56, Norwegian Rosemaling, 1975-79; treas. Sacakawea Homemakers Club, 1979-81; mem. Am. Luth. Ch. Women St. Pauls' Lutheran Ch., 1951—; active Easter Seal Program, Heart Fund, March of Dimes, United Way, Campfire Girls; mem. adv. council Area Agy. on Aging, Missoula, 1984—. Recipient Outstanding Sr. award Missoula Jr. C. of C., 1984, IDEA-PTA award, 1998, Lyle Heath award Missoula Sentinel Kiwanis Club, 1998, Golden Rule award J.C. Penney, 1998; Eva Amunson, Missoula Vol. Day proclaimed by city mayor and county commr., 1998. Mem. Sons of Norway (sec. 1989—), Orchard Homes Country Club (mem. art judging com.), Order of Eastern Star, Elks. Avocations: rosemaling, oil painting, poetry. Home: 324 Kensington Ave Missoula MT 59801-5726

ANAND, SURESH CHANDRA, physician; b. Mathura, India, Sept. 13, 1931; came to U.S., 1957, naturalized, 1971; s. Satchit and Sumaran (Bai) A. m. Wiltrud, Jan. 29, 1966; children: Miriam, Michael. MB, BS, King George's Coll., U. Lucknow (India), 1954; MS in Medicine, U. Colo., 1962. Diplomate Am. Bd. Allergy and Immunology. Fellow pulmonary diseases Nat. Jewish Hosp., Denver, 1957-58, resident in chest medicine, 1958-59, chief resident allergy-asthma, 1960-62; intern Mt. Sinai Hosp., Toronto, Ont., Can., 1962-63, resident in medicine, 1963-64, chief resident, 1964-65, demonstrator clin. technique, 1963-64, U. Toronto fellow in medicine, 1964-65; rsch. assoc. asthma-allergy Nat. Jewish Hosp., Denver, 1967-69; clin. instr. medicine U. Colo., Denver, 1967-69; internist Ft. Logan Mental Health Ctr., Denver, 1968-69; pres. Allergy Assocs. & Lab., Ltd., Phoenix, 1974—; mem. staff Phoenix Bapt. Hosp., chmn. med. records com., 1987; mem. staff St. Joseph's Hosp., St. Luke's Hosp., Human Hosp., John C. Lincoln Hosp., Good Samaritan Hosp., Phoenix Children's Hosp., Tempe St. Luke Hosp., Desert Samaritan Hosp., Mesa Luth. Hosp., Scottsdale Meml. Hosp., Phoenix Meml. Hosp., Chandler (Ariz.) Regional Hosp., Valley Luth. Hosp., Mesa, Ariz.; pres. NJH Fed. Credit Union, 1967-68. Contbr. articles to profl. jours. Mem. Camelback Hosp. Mental Health Ctr. Citizens Adv. Bd., Scottsdale, Ariz., 1974-80; mem. Phoenix Symphony Coun., 1973-90; mem. Ariz. Opera Co., Boyce Thmpson Southwestern Arboretum; mem. Ariz. Hist. Soc., Phoenix Arts. Mus., Smithsonian Inst. Fellow ACP, Am. Coll. Chest Physicians (crit. care com.), Am. Acad. Allergy, Am. Assn. Cert. Allergists, Am. Coll. Allergy and Immunology (aerobiology com., internat. com., pub. edn. com. 1991-94); mem. AAAS, AMA, Internat. Assn. Allergy and Clin. Immunology, Ariz. Med. Assn., Ariz. Allergy Soc. (v.p. 1988-90, pres. 1990-91), Maricopa County Med. Soc. (del. ariz. Med. Assn., bd. dirs. 1996-98, exec. com. 1996-98), West Coast Soc. Allergy and Immunology, Greater Phoenix Allergy Soc. (v.p. 1984-86, pres. 1986-88, med. adv. team sports medicine Ariz. State U.), Phoenix Zoo, N.Y. Acad. Scis., World Med. Assn., Internat. Assn. Asthmology, Assn. Care of Asthma, Ariz. Thoracic Soc., Nat. Geog. Soc., Ariz. Wild Life Assn., Village Tennis Club. Office: 1006 E Guadalupe Rd Tempe AZ 85283-3044 also: 6553 E Baywood Ave Ste 201 Mesa AZ 85206-1754 also: 7331 E Osborn Dr Ste 340 Scottsdale AZ 85251-6422

ANANG, KOFI, artistic director, educator, dancer; b. Pakro, Ghana. Degree, U. Ghana, 1971. Lead dancer Profl. OBOADE African Music and Dance Co., 1972-77; instr. African dance and music U. Washington, 1973-74; instr. African games and music Everybody's Creative Arts Ctr., Oakland, Calif., 1978; instr. W. African dance and drumming Madrona Dance Studio, 1978; instr. W. African games and drumming Langston Hughes Cultural Arts Ctr., Seattle, 1978-80; artistic dir., master drummer, dancer Ocheami-Afrikan Dance Co., Seattle, 1978—; rschr. devels. in music and dance, Ghana and Nigeria; founder Internat. Directory Black and African Choreographers; African music instr. Prescott (Ariz.) Coll., 1993, 94; dance accompanist Cornish Coll. Arts, Seattle, 1993—. Creative designer, musician (play) Sigi- Three W. African Stories, 1994; numerous appearances worldwide. Inst. African Studies scholar. Office: Ocheami Afrikan Dance Co PO Box 31635 Seattle WA 98103-1635

ANAPOL, BERTE, artist; b. Chgo., Oct. 10, 1912. BAE, Sch. of Art Inst. Chgo., 1958; MSAE, Ill. Inst. Tech., Chgo., 1962. Tchr. art Carl Schurz H.S., Chgo. One woman shows include The Little Gallery, Esquire theatre, Chgo., 1950, Robert North Gallery, Chgo., 1952, 53, 54, 55, Mandel Bros. Gallery, Chgo., 1954, Cromer and Quint Galleries, Chgo., 1956, 57, John M. Smythe Michigan Ave., Chgo., 1958, Riccardo Restaurant Galleries, Chgo., 1961, Lyons Twp. Coll. Gallery, Lyons, Ill., 1962, Monroe Galleries, Chgo., 1963, 71, 72, 73, Chgo. Soc. Artists Gallery, 1974, Downtown Gallery, N.Y.C., 1974, Nelson Meml. Mus., Kansas City, Mo., 1975, Village Gallery, San Diego, 1977, Hery Fine Arts Gallery, San Diego, 1978; group shows include Art Inst. Chgo., Art Rental of Art Inst., Springfield (Ill.) Art Mus., The 1020 Art Ctr. with Artists Equity, Chgo., Sherman Hotel Galleries, Chgo., Kalamazoo Art Ctr., Evanston (Ill.) Art Ctr., Krock and Brentano Gallery, Helpern Art Gallery, N.Y.C., Rockford (Ill.) Art Ctr., Fisher Hall Galleries, Chgo., Covenant Club Galleries, Chgo., Hillel Gallery, Northwestern U., Evanston, Univ. Club, Chgo., Art Inst. of San Diego, Village Gallery, San Diego, Southwestern County Fair, Del Mar, 1977, 78, 79, Fine Arts Mus. Rental, San Diego. Recipient 1st prize Spectrum Soc. of the Arts, Mandel Bros. Galleries, 1953, Chgo. Soc. Artists Internat. Calendar of Block Prints, 1965, others. Mem. Chgo. Soc. Artists, Am. Jewish Arts Club, Artists Equity Assn., Art Rental, Art Inst. of Chgo., Clairemont Art Guild, San Diego Art Inst., Art Rental at Fine Arts Mus. San Diego. Home and Office: 2601 Point Del Mar Ave Corona Del Mar CA 92625

ANARGYROS, NEDRA HARRISON, cytotechnologist; b. N.Y.C., Dec. 3, 1915; d. Leverette Roland and Florence Martha (Pickard) Harrison; student Emerson Coll., 1936; cert. in cytology U. Calif., San Francisco, 1957; m. Spero Drosos Anargyros, Oct. 21, 1940 (div. 1969). Supr. cytology San Francisco Gen. Hosp., 1957-88; ret. 1988. Mem. Am. Soc. Clin. Pathologists (affiliate mem.), Am. Soc. for Cytotech. (affiliate mem., cert. cytologist), Women Flyers of Am., DAR (past regent, 1990-91, 1st vice regent La Puerta de Ora chpt., San Francisco), Nat. Soc. Colonial Dames of Am. in Calif., Huguenot Soc. of Calif. Republican. Christian Scientist. Club: Presidents of Mercer U. (Macon, Ga.). Home: 2503 Clay St San Francisco CA 94115-1810 also: 1400 Geary Blvd Apt 5N San Francisco CA 94109-6555

ANASTASI, MICHAEL ANTON, journalist; b. Kitzbuhel, Tirol, Austria, Sept. 15, 1965; s. Antone Frank and Waltraud (Salinger) A; m. Julie Hibbs Anastasi, Nov. 18, 1995; 1 child, Grace Antonia. BA in Internat. Rels., U. Calif., Davis, 1988; Journalism, Calif. State U., Long Beach. Reporter The Daily Democrat, Woodland, Calif., 1984-85, dep. sports editor, 1985-87; sports editor The Davis (Calif.) Ent., 1987-93; asst. sports editor L.A. Daily News, 1993-95, sports editor, 1995—. Recipient 1st prize best sports sect. Calif. Newspaper Pubrs. Assn., 1990, APSE award, (Best Dailey News section, 1995, honorable mention, Best spl. section under 175,000, 1993, 1st place and honorable mention, Best interprise reporting, under 50,000, 1993, 4th place columnist under 50,000, honorable mention, 1989);Best sports columns award (Nat. Newspaper Assn., 2nd, 1992, hon. mention, 1993),Best sports pages, (3rd 1993, N.M., 1992). Mem. Soc. Profl. Journalists (1st place best columnist, 1991, 93, 94,), AP Sports Editors. Roman Catholic. Avocation: history. Office: LA Daily News 21221 Oxnard St Woodland Hills CA 91367-5015

ANAWALT, PATRICIA RIEFF, anthropologist; b. Ripon, Calif., Mar. 10, 1924; d. Edmund Lee and Anita Esto (Capps) Rieff; m. Richard Lee Anawalt, June 8, 1945; children: David, Katherine Anawalt Arnoldi, Harmon Fred. BA in Anthropology, UCLA, 1957, MA in Anthropology, 1971, PhD in Anthropology, 1975. Cons. curator costumes and textiles Mus. Cultural History UCLA, 1975-90, dir. Ctr. for Study Regional Dress, Fowler Mus. Cultural History, 1990—; trustee S.W. Mus., L.A., 1978-92; rsch. assoc. The San Diego Mus. Man, 1980—, UCLA Inst. Archaeology, 1994—; trustee Archaeol. Inst. Am., U.S., Can., 1983-95, 98—; traveling lectr., 1975-86, 94-96, Pres.'s Lectureship, 1993-94, Charles E. Norton lectureship, 1996-97; cons. Nat. Geog. Soc., 1980-82, Denver Mus. Natural History, 1992-93; apptd. by U.S. Pres. to Cultural Property Adv. Com., Washington, 1984-93; fieldwork Guatemala, 1961, 70, 72, Spain, 1975, Sierra Norte de Puebla, Mex., 1983, 85, 88, 89, 91. Author: Indian Clothing Before Cortés: Mesoamerican Costumes from the Codices, 1981, paperback edit., 1990; co-author: The Codex Mendoza, 4 vols., 1992 (winner Archaeol. Inst. Am. 1994 James Wiseman Book award), The Essential Codex Mendoza, 1996; mem. editl. bd.: Ancient Mesoamerica, 1999; contbr. articles to profl. jours. Adv. com Textile Mus., Washington, 1983-87. Grantee NEH, 1990, 96, J. Paul Getty Found. 1990, Nat. Geog. Soc., 1983, 85, 88, 89, 91, Ahmanson Found., 1996; Guggenheim fellow, 1988. Fellow Am. Anthrop. Assn.; mem. Centre Internat. D'Etude Des Textiles Anciens, Am. Ethnol. Soc., Soc. Am. Archaeology, Soc. Women Geographers (Outstanding Achievement award 1993), Textile Soc. Am. (bd. dirs. 1992-96, co-coord. 1994 biennial symposium). Avocations: ballet, reading, hiking. Office: Fowler Mus Cultural History Ctr Study of Regional Dress Los Angeles CA 90095-1549

ANCELL, WILLIAM JOSEPH, civil and environmental engineer; b. Chgo., Oct. 17, 1937; s. Marion and Linda (Walker) A.; m. Judith Anne Weeks, Oct. 1, 1961; children: William, Brian, Mark. AD in Bus., Lansing C.C., 1972; BS, Tri-State U., 1958. Diplomate Am. Acad. Environ. Engrs.; profl. engr., Idaho. Asst. county engr. Muskegon County, Mich., 1962-66, county engr., 1966-68; asst. dir. pub. svc. Lansing (Mich.) Pub. Svc. Dept., 1968-72; dir. pub. works Boise (Idaho) Pub. Works Dept., 1972—. Fellow Inst. Water Resources Am. Pub. Works Assn. (pres. 1983-84); mem. Am. Acad. Environ. Engrs., Idaho Soc. Profl. Engrs. (pres. 1989-90), Assn. Met. Sewage Agys. (Pres.'s award).

ANCHIE, TOBY LEVINE, health facility administrator; b. New Haven, Conn., Jan. 21, 1944; d. Solomon and Mary (Karlins) Levine; m. Alonzo C. Moreland III; children: Michael D. Anchie, Robert P. Anchie. BSN, U. of Conn., 1966; MA in Edn. magna cum laude, Nor. Ariz. U., 1984. RN Ariz., Conn. Coord. spl. projects, nurse coord., adult day hosp. Barrow Neurol. Inst. of St. Joseph's Hosp. and Med. Ctr., Phoenix, 1984-87, mgr., 1985-92, mgr. adminstrv. and support svcs., neuroscis., 1992-94, mgr. rsch. adminstrn., 1994-97, dir. rsch. adminstrn., 1997—; cons.; presenter in field; mem. faculty U. Phoenix; adv. bd. mem. Myasthenia Gravis Assn.; mem. adv. coun. Office Disability Prevention Ariz. Dept. Health Svcs., mem. strategic planning com. Contbr. articles to profl. jours., chpts. Mem. NAFE, Am. Assn. Neurosci. Nurses (bd. dirs., pres.), Assn. Clin. Rsch. Profls., Am. Bd. Neurosci. Nursing (treas. 1995-96), World Fedn. Splty. Nursing Orgn. (chair membership com. 1993-95), Assn. Clin. Rsch. Coords. (Ariz. chpt.), Ariz. Assn. Neurosci. Nurses. Home: 3112 S Los Feliz Dr Tempe AZ 85282-2854

ANCIER, GARTH RICHARD, television broadcast executive; b. Perth Amboy, N.J., Sept. 3, 1957; s. Sherman and Jean A. BA, Princeton U., 1979. Exec. producer syndicated program Am. Focus, 1975-79; v.p. comedy programs NBC Entertainment, N.Y.C. and Burbank, Calif., 1979-86; pres. entertainment Fox TV Network, L.A., 1986-89; pres. network TV Walt Disney Studios, Burbank, 1989-90; corp. officer, producer Fox, Inc., L.A., 1991-92; pres. The WB TV Network, 1994—; TV cons. Dem. Nat. Com., Washington, 1991-92; trustee Nat. Coun. Families and TV, 1991—; creator, exec. producer (TV show) Ricki Lake, The Garth Ancier Co., 1992-97, exec. cons., 1997—. Mem. Hollywood TV & Radio Soc. (trustee 1996—). Democrat. Office: The WB TV Network 4000 Warner Blvd Burbank CA 91522-0001

ANDARY, THOMAS JOSEPH, biochemist; b. Sault Sainte Marie, Mich., Oct. 8, 1942; s. Joseph Boula and Marion (Schwifetti) A. BS, No. Mich. U., 1966, MA, 1968; PhD, Wayne State U., 1974. Instr. biology No. Mich. U., Marquette, 1967-69; rsch. assoc. physiology Wayne State U., Detroit, 1973-76; sr. rsch. scientist, mgr. coagulation research Hyland Labs., Costa Mesa, Calif., 1976-83; dir. quality control Hyland Therapeutics, Glendale, Calif., 1983-90; dir. quality assurance and regulatory affairs Baxter/Hyland Div., Glendale, 1990-91, v.p. quality assurance and regulatory affairs, 1991—, responsible head, 1993-96; cons. in regulatory affairs/quality assurance to biopharmaceutical industry, 1996—; lectr. in field. Mem. Parenteral Drug Assn. NDEA fellow, 1969-72. Mem. Am. Chem. Soc., N.Y. Acad. Sci., Internat. Assn. Biol. Standardization, Drug Info. Assn., Sigma Xi (Rsch. award 1973). Roman Catholic. Contbr. over 25 articles to profl. publs. Home and Office: 531 N Canyon Blvd Monrovia CA 91016-1707

ANDERMANN, GREG, producer, director, consultant. BA in TV and Film Prodn., San Francisco State U., 1977. Dir., camera operator Video Image, Inc., San Francisco, 1977-78; creative dir. Cleland Advt., Inc., Los Angeles, 1978-79; prin., producer, dir. Telemar, Hollywood, Calif., 1980-84; comml. dir. Sta. KITV, Honolulu, 1984, Hawaii Prodn. Ctr., Honolulu, 1984-85; creative producer Am. TV Corp., Honolulu, 1985-86; mgr. TV and film producer GTE Hawaii, Honolulu, 1986—; cons. 80/20 Mktg. Inc., Beverly Hills, Calif., 1980-82, Fawcett McDermott Cavanagh Advt., Inc., Honolulu, 1984-86. dir. (TV campaign) Sheraton Islands, 1984 (Pele award 1984), (videos) Hall of Fame Sports, 1984 (Pele award 1985); dir., dir. photography (music video) Reflections, 1986; assoc. producer (TV campaign) Aloha United Way, 1986 (Telly award 1986). Field producer Jerry Lewis Muscular Dystrophy Assn. Nat. Telethon, 1990. Recipient Pele Merit awards, 1985, 2, 1997, Star Award Nat. Cable Mktg. Assn., 1985, Gecko award, Hawaii Cable TV Assn., 1985, Telly award, TV campaign, 1986, Long Format TV, 1997, Cable Advt., Promotion award, 2, 1986, Ilima award Interna. Assn. Bus. Communicators, 1986, 94, 96, 97 (2), Silver Monitor award Internat. TV Assn., 1986, 87, 88, 89, Gold Monitor award Internat. TV Assn., 1987, 89, Silver Six Regional Internat Assn. Bus. Communicators, 1988 (2), Angel award L.A. Viedo Festival, 1988, 1st pl. Pub. Rels Soc. Am., 1994, 95 (2), Excellence award Internat. Assn. Bus. Communicators, 1997, award of honor, Pub. Rels. Soc. Am., 1997. Mem. Am. Film Inst., Dirs. Network, Soc. for Motion PIcture and TV Engrs., Internat. TV Assn., Am. Advtg. Fedn., Photographic Soc. Am., Honolulu Advt. Fedn., Film and Video Assn. Hawaii, Internat. Assn. Bus. Communicators. Avocations: swimming, surfing, sailing, all water sports.

ANDERS, DARRILL JAMES, sales professional; b. Evanston, Ill., Jan. 13, 1967; s. Donald and Dorothy (Delacoma) A.; m. Vicki Howard, Nov. 13, 1993. BA in Art, San Diego State U., 1990. Cert. Nat. Coun. for Interior Design Qualification, kitchen designer. Designer Form and Function, San Diego, 1989-93; designer and sales profl. Home Depot, San Diego, 1993-97; sales profl., designer Kraftmaid Cabinetry, San Diego, 1997—; kitchen designer Nat. Kitchen and Bath Assn., Hackettstown, N.J., 1996—. Mem. ASID. Avocations: golf, swimming, songwriting. Home: 8560 Lemon Ave La Mesa CA 91941-5366

ANDERS, WILLIAM ALISON, aerospace and defense manufacturing executive; b. Hong Kong, Oct. 17, 1933; s. Arthur Ferdinand and Muriel Florence (Adams) A.; m. Valerie Elizabeth Hoard, June 26, 1955; children: Alan Frank, Glen Thomas, Gayle Alison, Gregory Michael, Eric William, Diana Elizabeth. BS, U.S. Naval Acad., Annapolis, 1955; MS in Nuclear Engring., U.S. Inst. Tech., Wright-Patterson AFB, 1962. Commnd. 2d lt. U.S. Air Force, 1955, pilot, engr., 1955-69; astronaut NASA-Johnson Space Ctr., Houston, 1963-69, Apollo 8, 1st lunar flight, 1968; exec. sec. Nat. Aero. and Space Council, Washington, 1963-72; commr. AEC, Washington, 1973-74; chmn. Nuclear Regulatory Commn., Washington, 1975-76; U.S. Ambassador to Norway, 1976-77; v.p., gen. mgr. nuclear energy products div. Gen. Electric Co., 1977-80; v.p., gen. mgr. aircraft equipment div. Gen. Electric Co., DeWitt, N.Y., 1980-84; sr. exec., v.p. ops. Textron Inc., Providence, R.I., 1984-89; vice chmn. Gen. Dynamics, St. Louis, 1990-91; chmn., CEO Gen. Dynamics, 1991-93; chmn. bd. dirs. N000, 1993-94; pres. Apogee Group. Trustee Battell Meml. Inst., Reno Air Races Unltd. Class, 1997-98. Maj. gen. USAFR, 1983-88. Decorated various mil. awards; recipient Wright, Collier, Goddard and Arnold flight awards; co holder several world flight records. Mem. Soc. Exptl. Test Pilots , Nat. Acad. Engring., Tau Beta Pi. Office: Apogee Group PO Box 1630 Eastsound WA 98245-1630

ANDERSEN, LUBA, electrologist, electropigmentologist; b. Germany, Mar. 29, 1945; came to U.S., 1955; d. Osyp and Justyna (Drozd) Nahorniak; m. Roger A. Andersen, Dec. 9, 1989. A in Bus. and Acctg., DePaul U., 1977; BS in Commerce and Social Studies, LaSalle U., 1978; postgrad., U. Mich., 1984; cert., Ariz. Inst. Electrolysis, 1993. Cert. profl. electrologist, clin. electropigmentologist. From analyst to contr. Fed. Home Loan Bank,

Chgo., 1965-83, v.p., contr., 1985-92; owner The Electrolysis Connection, Tucson, 1993—. Mem. NAFE, Am. Soc. Women Accts. (chair bylaws com. 1981), Am. Electrology Assn., Electrologists Assn. Ariz., Internat. Guild Profl. Electrologists, Inc., Fin. Mgrs. Soc., Soc. Cosmetic Profls., Assn. Clin. Electropigmentologists. Republican. Roman Catholic. Avocation: creating tapestries. Office: Electrolysis Connection 3131 N Country Club Rd Ste 110 Tucson AZ 85716-1637

ANDERSON, ARTHUR LEE, sculptor, writer; b. Washington, Nov. 28, 1952; s. Kenneth Arthur and Marjorie Ruth (Anderson) A.; m. Marion Mann, Oct. 18, 1981 (div. Nov. 1987); 1 child, Tanya Leah. Grad., Gemological Inst. Am., Santa Monica, Calif., 1986. Importer Washington, 1971-75; contractor New Orleans, 1976-80; deckhand Chotin Shipping Co., New Orleans, 1980-81; gem cutter, sculptor Speira Gems, Ashland, Oreg., 1984—; vol. spkr. on gemstone-related topics, pub. schs., Ashland, 1990—; bd. mem. Gemartists N.Am., 1996; judge Am. Gem Trading Assn. cutting edge competition, 1996. Editor Gemartists N.Am. Newsletter, 1995, 96; contbr. tech. articles to Gems and Gemology, Lapidary Jour. Recipient 1st pl. for creative gem cut Am. Gem Trade Assn., 1992, 1st pl. for objet d'art, 1993, 2d pl. fancy gem cut, 1994, 3d pl. pairs and suites, 1994, 1st pl. pairs and suites, 1995, 1st pl. German award for precious stones and jewelry, 1997, 1st pl. faceting, 1998, others. Libertarian. Avocations: music (guitar), Writing. E-mail: zliff@aol.com. Home: Speira Gems 680 Alton Alston Rd Pittsboro NC 27312 Office: Speira Gems PO Box 976 Carrboro NC 27510-0976

ANDERSON, ARTHUR SALZNER, publishing company executive, marketing executive; b. Boise, Idaho, Jan. 17, 1923; s. Howard Ballantyne and Mildred Ina (Salzner) A.; m. Janice Virginia Jacobsen, June 21, 1948; children: Roger Bruce, Gregory Bryan, Julie Janice Olsen, Lane Jacobsen, Margaret Virginia Ence, Heidi Gail Eldredge, Steven Jacobsen. B.A., U. Utah, 1947. Sales promotion asst. Internat. Harvester Co., 1947-48, zone mgr., 1948-51; sr. v.p., dir., chmn. exec. com. Evans Communications, Inc., Salt Lake City, 1977-84, dir., chmn. exec. com., 1984-87, pres., 1984-87; chmn. bd. Panoram Prodns., 1977-82; pres. Deseret Book Co., 1975-80, dir., 1975-92; pres., chief exec. officer Anderson Mktg. Inc., Salt Lake City, 1987—. Author By Example, 1961. Vice-pres. Salt Lake Area United Fund, 1977-80; mem. governing bd. Primary Children's Med. Ctr., 1975—, vice chmn., 1981-83, chmn., 1982-83; bd. dirs. Osmond Found., 1982-83. Served with AUS, 1943-46. Mem. Utah Advt. Fedn. (pres. 1967-68), Sales and Mktg. Execs. Utah (pres. 1965-66). Mem. LDS Ch. Home: 2242 Kensington Ave Salt Lake City UT 84108-2310 Office: Anderson Mktg Inc 925 Executive Park Dr Ste E Salt Lake City UT 84117-3541

ANDERSON, AUSTIN GILMAN, economics research company consultant; b. Mpls.; s. Clifford Hawkins and Katharine (Irving) A.; m. Marilyn Wheeler, Mar. 17, 1968; children: Guy, Alisa, Michael, Emily. BS, Stanford U., 1964, MBA, 1966. Systems analyst Jet Propulsion Lab., Pasadena, Calif., 1966-68; assoc. Econs. Rsch. Assoc., L.A., 1968-72; sr. v.p., 1977-88, pres., chief exec. officer, 1988—; dir. rsch. Property Rsch. Corp., L.A., 1972-73; prin. Levander, Partridge & Anderson, Beverly Hills, Calif., 1973-77; instr. Grad. Sch. Mgmt. UCLA, 1989, extension, 1987; bd. dirs. Crown Iron Works Co., Mpls., 1983—; mem. bd. counselors Sch. Urban and Regional Planning U. So. Calif., L.A., 1984-95; mem. bd. trustees Real Estate Investment Trust of Calif., 1994—. Mem. Urban Land Inst. Avocations: sculpting, golf. Home: 328 17th St Manhattan Beach CA 90266-4636 Office: Econs Rsch Assocs 10990 Wilshire Blvd Ste 1600 Los Angeles CA 90024-3913*

ANDERSON, BARBARA JANE, songwriter, singer; b. Ill., Feb. 21, 1952; d. Thomas Pond and Elaine Mary (Fitzwilson) A.; m. Loyal E. Leavenworth, Oct. 29, 1981 (div. Jan. 1991); children: Thatcher Leavenworth, Loyal E. Leavenworth. Student, Stephens Coll. Songwriter: (recs.) Naked Truth, 1993; performer; produced and wrote CD to benefit the Nat. Coalition for the Homeless, Washington. Home: PO Box 370079 Montara CA 94037-0079

ANDERSON, BARBARA LOUISE, retired library director; b. San Diego, Jan. 5, 1933; d. Lorenzo and Louise (Morgan) A.; 1 child, Sean Allen. BS, San Diego State U., 1954; MLS, Kans. State Teachers Coll., 1955. Br. librarian L.A. Pub. Library, 1956-59; br. librarian, reference, young adult librarian San Diego Pub. Library, 1959-64; librarian U.S. Army, Europe, 1964-69; coordinator Serra Reference Project, Serra Regional Library System, San Diego, 1969-71; head readers services Riverside (Calif.) City and County Pub. Library, 1972-74; county librarian San Bernardino County (Calif.) Library, 1974-94; ret. 1994; del. White House Conf. on Libraries and Info. Services, 1979. Bd. dirs. Inland Empire Symphony, 1982-84, Riverside Mental Health Assn., 1975-79; mem. citizens adv. bd. San Bernardino YWCA, 1988-89; Riverside County Archives Commn., 1996—; Riverside County Libr. Adv. Bd., 1997—, Lake Elsinore Womans Club, 1997—. Mem. ALA, Calif. Library Assn., Black Caucus of Calif. Library Assn., Congress of Pub. Library Systems (pres. 1984), Calif. County Librarians Assn., Calif. Soc. Librarians (pres. 1974-75, mem. OCLС Users Council 1984-88), AAUW (pres. Riverside Br. 1976-77), NAACP, Bus. and Profl. Women San Bernardino. Democrat. Baptist. Contbr. articles to publs. in field.

ANDERSON, BRUCE MORGAN, computer scientist; b. Battle Creek, Mich., Oct. 8, 1941; s. James Albert and Beverly Jane (Morgan) A.; m. Jeannie Marie Hignight, May 24, 1975; children: Ronald, Michael, Valerie, John, Carolyn. BEE, Northwestern U., 1964; MEE, Purdue U., 1966; PhD in Elec. Engring., Northwestern U., 1973. Rsch. engr. Zenith Radio Corp., Chgo., 1965-66; assoc. engr. Ill. Inst. Tech. Rsch. Inst., Chgo., 1966-68; sr. electronics engr. Rockwell Internat., Downers Grove, Ill., 1973-75; computer scientist Argonne (Ill.) Nat. Lab., 1975-77; mem. group tech. staff Tex. Instruments, Dallas, 1977-88; sr. scientist BBN Systems and Techs., Cambridge, Mass., 1988-90; systems engr. Lockheed Martin, Denver, 1990-94; sr. scientist CTA Inc., Englewood, Colo., Colo., 1994-97; sr. program mgr. SAIC, Englewood, 1997-98; sr. tech. mgr. TRW, Denver, 1998—; lectr. computer sci. U. Tex.-Arlington and Dallas; adj. prof. computer sci. N. Tex. State U.; vis. indsl. prof. So. Meth. U.; computer systems cons. Info. Internat., Culver City, Calif., HCM Graphic Systems, Gt. Neck, N.Y.; computer cons. depts. geography, transp., econs., sociology and computer sci. Northwestern U., also instr. computer sci.; expert witness for firm Burleson, Pate and Gibson. Contbr. articles to tech. jours. NASA fellow Northwestern U., 1973. Mem. IEEE Computer Soc. (chmn. Dallas 1984-85), Am. Assn. Artificial Intelligence, Assn. Computing Machinery (publs. chmn. 1986 fall joint computer conf. IEEE and Assn. Computing Machinery), Toastmasters Internat., Sigma Xi, Eta Kappa Nu, Theta Delta Chi. Home: 3473 E Euclid Ave Littleton CO 80121-3663 Office: 1999 Broadway Denver CO 80202-3025

ANDERSON, CAROL RUTH, secondary school educator; b. Conewango, N.Y., Aug. 24, 1926; d. Maynard William and Hila Martha (Kent) Phillips; m. George Boyer, Mar. 27, 1948 (div. July 1967); children: Gregory, Gail, Martha; m. Donald Anderson, Jan. 13, 1978 (div. Jan. 1981). Assoc. BS, Jamestown (N.Y.) Community Coll., 1962; BEd, U. Buffalo, 1966; MS in Edn., SUNY, Fredonia, 1971; postgrad., Ariz. State U., 1980-81. Cert. secondary tchr., N.Y., Ariz. Sec. Jamestown Metal Corp., 1957-61; sec. to judge Cattaraugus County, Little Valley, N.Y., 1961-66; bus. educator Jamestown High Sch., 1966-82, Phoenix Union High Sch. Dist., 1982-88; ret., 1988. Rep. committeewoman Cattaraugus County, 1960-62. Mem. N.Y. State Ret. Tchr.'s Assn., U. of Buffalo Alumni Assn., NEA, Jamestown High Sch. Tchrs. Club (sec., treas. 1967-82), Ariz. State Ret. Tchrs. Assn., Am. Legion, VFW, Women of Moose. Republican. Methodist. Avocations: golf, bowling, skiing, reading, gardening.

ANDERSON, CATHERINE, artist; b. Chgo., Aug. 12, 1947; d. William Joseph and Dorothy Virginia Anderson; 1 child, Scott Russell. Student, Am. Acad. Art, Chgo., 1967-70, Il. Cin., 1970-77, Acad. Art Coll., San Francisco, 1982-85. Represented by Trailside Americana Fine Art Galleries, Carmel, Calif., 1992-95, Quast Gallery, Taos, N.Mex., Breckenridge (Colo.) Galleries, Howard Portnoy Gallerie, Carmel, Calif.; juror various art shows. Exhbns. include Elk Grove Village (Ill.) Art Festival, 1980, 81, 24th Gold Coast Art Fair, Chgo., 1981, Mill Valley City Hall, 1986, Westamerica Bank, Sausalito, Calif., 1990-95, Marin County Fair, San Rafael, Calif., 1990, 92, 93, 94, Lenten Arts Festival, San Anselmo,

Calif., 1991. Spirit Wings de Santa Fe, 1991. Artisans Gallery, Mill Valley, Calif., 1991, 94, 96, Sausalito Arts Festival, 1991, 92, 93, 94, 95, JCC, San Rafael, 1991, Green Gulch Farm, Muir Beach, Calif., 1991, Gallery One, Petaluma, Calif., 1991, Poudre Valley Art League, Ft. Collins, Colo., 1992, Saratoga (Calif.) Rotary Art Show, 1992, La Quinta (Calif.) Arts Festival, 1993, Canessa Gallery, San Francisco, 1993, Santa Barbara Mus. of Natural History, Santa Barbara, Calif., 1993, Art Concepts Gallery, Walnut Creek, Calif., 1993, Scottsdale (Ariz.) Arts Festival, 1994, CCC, Tiburon, Calif., 1994, Blue Heron Gallery, Yountville, Calif., 1994, Buena Vista Winery, Sonoma, Calif., 1994, Watercolof USA Springfield (Mo.) Art Mus., 1995, 96, Rocky Mountain Nat. Foothills Art Ctr., Golden, Colo., 1995, Calif. Watercolor Assn. Gallery Concord, Concord, Calif., 1995, 96, Catharine Lorillard Wolfe Art Club, N.Y., 1995, Am. Water Color Soc. The Salmagundi Club, N.Y.C., 1995, Neville Pub. Mus., Green Bay, Wis., 1996, Denver Rotary Club Artists of Am. (AOA) Invitational Show, 1996, Colo. History Mus., Denver, No. Colorado Artists Assn. Nat. Art Exhibit, GAA Exhibit, Cin. Mus. Ctr., Great Artists of Am. Invitational Show, 1996, Cin. Mus. Ctr., Midwest Watercolor Soc. Neville Pub. Mus., Green Bay, Wis., 1996, Watercolor USA Springfield Art Mus., Mo., 1996, Triton Mus. Art, Santa Clara, Calif., 1996, Watercolor West Ann. Exhibition XXVIII, Brea, Calif., 1996, Knickerbocker Show Joan Cauley Gallery, Scottsdale, Ariz., 1997, Artist's Am. Denver Rotary's Invitational Exhibit, 1997, Great Am. Artists Invitational Exhibit, Cin., 1997, and numerous others; and numerous pvt. collections; columnist Watercolor Magic; author: Basic Watercolor Answer Book. Recipient Tony Couch award Western Colo. Watercolor Soc., 1991, 1st Pl. award Affaire in the Gardens, 1993, Blue ribbon Santa Barbara Mus. Natural History, 1994, 1st Pl. award Scottsdale Arts Festival, 1994, 1st Pl. award Marin County Fair, 1994, 95, 1st Pl. award Rocky Mountain Nat. Watermedia Exhibit, 1995, Anna Hyatt Huntington Bronze medal Catharine Lorillard Wolfe Art Club, 1995, Nat. Galleries Endowment award, 1995, Nat. Watercolor Soc. 75th Ann. Exhibit, 1995, Mary and Ben Rabe Soft Colors award Watercolor West, 1996, Best of Show Napa Valley Studio Tours, 1996, Helga's Palette Workshop award Midwest Watercolor Soc., 1996. Mem. Am. Watercolor Soc. (Winsor-Newton award), Nat. Watercolor Soc., Calif. Watercolor Assn. (Gold medal 1996). Home: 4900 Trinity Rd Glen Ellen CA 95442-9718

ANDERSON, CHARLES MICHAEL, accountant; b. Londonderry, N. Ireland, England, July 15, 1944; came to U.S. 1946; s. Albert and Elizabeth (McDaid) A.; m. Terri Lynn Good, Oct. 6, 1981; children: Sean Michael, Kevin Patrick, Kelli Marie. BS, Northern Ill. U., 1966; MBA, U. Southern Calif., 1970. CPA; CFP. Staff acct. Price Waterhouse Co., Chgo., 1966-69; mgmt. cons. Price Waterhouse Co., L.A., 1970-72; pvt practice, Manahttan Beach, Calif., 1972-73; mgr. corp. budgets Great Southwest Corp., L.A., 1973-76; dir. internal audit Standard Brands Paint, Torrance, Calif., 1976-86; dir. control systems Standard Brands Paint, 1986-87; chief fin. officer One-Day Paint & Body, Torrance, 1988-89; fin. planner, registered rep., investment adv. The Equitable Life Agent. Contbr. articles to profl. jours. Chmn. city budget rev. com. Torrance Area C. of C., 1990-93; pres. Joie De Vive Homeowners Assn. Manhattan Beach, 1979-82, treas., 1985—; pres., chmn. Calif. Mus. Sci. & Industry, L.A., 1975-78; mem. Cath. Big Bros., Torrance, 1973-84 (Ten Yr. award 1984). Fellow AICPA, Calif. Soc. CPAs, Am. Inst. Profl. Bookkeepers; mem. Irish Network So. Calif., Le Tip Internat. (treas./sec. 1991-98), Rotary (bd. dirs. 1989—). Democrat. Roman Catholic. Avocations: sports, photography, reading, travel. Email: cma1944@earthlink.net. Home: 1220 9th St Manhattan Beach CA 90266-6018

ANDERSON, CHARLES ROSS, civil engineer; b. N.Y.C., Oct. 4, 1937; s. Biard Eclare and Melva (Smith) A.; m. Susan Breinholt, Aug. 29, 1961; children: Loralee, Brian, Craig, Thomas, David. BSCE, U. Utah, 1961; MBA, Harvard U., 1963. Registered profl. engr.; cert. land surveyor. Owner, operator AAA Engring. and Drafting, Inc., Salt Lake City, 1960—; mem. acad. adv. com. U. Utah, 1990-91, chmn. civil engring. adv. bd., 1995—. Mayoral appointee Housing Devel. Com., Salt Lake City, 1981-86; bd. dirs., vice chmn., cons. Met. Water Dist., Salt Lake City, 1985—; bd. dirs., pres., v.p., sec. bd. Utah Mus. Natural History, Salt Lake City, 1980-92; asst. dist. commr. Sunrise Dist. Boy Scouts Am., Salt Lake City, 1985-86; fundraising coord. architects and engrs. United Fund; mem. Sunstone Nat. Adv. Bd., 1980-88; bd. dirs. Provo River Water Users Assn., 1986—. Fellow Am. Gen. Contractors, Salt Lake City, 1960; recipient Hamilton Watch award, 1961. Mem. ASCE, Am. Congress on Surveying and Mapping, U. Utah Alumni Assn. (bd. dirs. 1989-92), Harvard U. Bus. Sch. Club (pres. 1970-72), The Country Club (bd. dirs. 1998—), Rotary (v.p. Club 24 1990-91, chmn. election com. 1980-81, vice chmn. and chmn. membership com. 1988-90, 1st. v.p. 1997-98, pres. 1998-99), U. Utah Crimson Club (bd. dirs. 1996-99), Pi Kappa Alpha (internat. pres. 1972-74, trustee endowment fund 1974-80, Outstanding Alumnus 1967, 72, mem. Hall of Fame 1995), Phi Eta Sigma, Chi Epsilon, Tau Beta Pi. Avocations: fly fishing, golfing, foreign travel. Home: 2689 Comanche Dr Salt Lake City UT 84108-2846 Office: AAA Engring & Drafting Inc 1865 S Main St Salt Lake City UT 84115-2045

ANDERSON, CHRISTINA SUSANNE, speech and language therapist; b. Long Beach, Calif., Mar. 15, 1950; d. John Edwin and Mary Belle (Olson) Hockett; m. Robert George Anderson, June 9, 1973; children: Michelle, Marc, Brian. BS, Ariz. State U., 1972, MS, 1976. Speech therapist Rio Linda Sch. Dist., Sacramento, 1973-76, Washington Elem. Sch. Dist., Phoenix, 1976—; pvt. practice speech therapy Phoenix, 1978—. Active St. Helen's Ch., Glendale, Ariz., 1980-86, St. Paul's Ch., 1986—. Elks Found. scholar, 1968-71. Mem. NEA, Am. Speech and Hearing Assn. (Clin. Competency Cert.), Washington Dist. Edn. Assn., Maricopa County Bar Assn. (Womans Aux. Club), Sigma Alpha Eta, Alpha Lambda Delta, Phi Kappa Phi. Democrat. Roman Catholic. Avocations: skiing, aerobics, needlecrafts. Home: 215 W Kathleen Rd Phoenix AZ 85023-3652

ANDERSON, CLIFTON EINAR, writer, communications consultant; b. Frederic, Wis., Dec. 17, 1923; s. Andrew John and Ida Louise (Johnson) A.; m. Phyllis Mary Nolan, Oct. 5, 1943; children: Kristine, Craig. BS, U. Wis., 1947; MA, U. Calif., Berkeley, 1954. News editor Chgo. Daily Drover's Jour., 1943-45; asst. editor The Progressive, Madison, Wis., 1946-47; dir. publs. Am. Press, Beirut, 1948-53; mgr. rural programs Houston C. of C., 1957-62; faculty Tex. A&M U., College Station, 1962-65; rsch. fellow U. Tex., Austin, 1965-68; faculty Southwestern Okla. U., Weatherford, 1968-72; extension editor U. Idaho, Moscow, 1972-97, prof. emeritus, 1997—; speaker John Macmurray Centennial Conf. Marquette U., 1991; speaker Nat. Conf. on Peacemaking and Conflict Resolution, 1993, moderator the UN at 50 seminar, 1995; moderator Korea Today and Tomorrow Symposium Wash. State U., 1995. Editor: The Horse Interlude, 1976; author: History of the College of Agriculture at the University of Idaho, 1998, (with others) Ways Out: The Book of Changes for Peace, 1988, The Future: Opportunity Not Destiny, 1989, The Years Ahead: Perils, Problems and Promises, 1993, Eating Agendas: Food and Nutrition as Social Problems, 1995, Futurevision: Ideas, Insights, and Strategies, 1996; contbr. articles to profl. jours. and mags. Treas. Moscow Sister City Assn., 1986—; founding mem. Coalition for C.Am., Moscow, 1986; chmn. U. Idaho Affirmative Action Com., 1990; mem. coun. on home and cmty. care Area Agy. on Aging, 1995; writer campaign staff Senator R.M. La Follette, Jr., Madison, Wis., 1946; on senatorial campaign staff of Hubert H. Humphrey, Mpls., 1948; chmn. Borah Found. for Outlawry of War, U. Idaho, 1986-87, chmn. Borah Symposium, 1986-87. Recipient Rsch. award Fund for Adult Edn., 1954-55, U.S. Office Edn., 1965-68, 1st prize in newswriting competition Assn. Am. Agrl. Coll. Editors, 1976, merit award Agrl. Rels. Coun., 1995, Nat. Svc. award Washington Times Found., 1996. Fellow Martin Inst. Peace Studies and Conflict Resolution; mem. World Future Soc. (speaker 6th gen. assembly 1989, 7th gen. assembly 1993), Agr., Food and Social Values Soc., Assn. for Humanistic Psychology, Assn. for Religion and Intellectual Life, Profs. World Peace Acad., World Constn. and Parliament Assn. Democrat. Avocations: gardening, photography, writing poetry. Home: 234 N Washington St Moscow ID 83843-2757 Office: U Idaho Agrl Communications Ctr Moscow ID 83844-2332

ANDERSON, DAVID CHARLES, librarian, writer; b. Oakland, Calif., 1931 or 1934; s. Charley Leon Jr. and Inez Christian (Turner) A.; m. Hess, June 8, 1957; children: Alan R., David Christian, Gregory Leon, Bradley Ross, Lisa Louise. BA in Liberal Arts, U. Calif., Berkeley, 1952; BLS, 1953. Libr. State Office of Local Planning, Sacramento, 1957-62, Calif. State Dept. of Fin., Sacramento, 1960-62; serials cataloger gen. libr. U. Calif.,

Davis, 1962-69, head health scis. cataloging pool, 1969-71, head tech. svcs. Carlson Health Sci. Libr., 1971-91, part-time info. specialist Ctr. Animal Alternatives Sch. Vet. Medicine, 1992-98. Editor: Veterinary Serials, A Union List, 2d edit., 1988, Humans and Other Species (quar. resource jour. on the human-animal relationship), 1990—; author poetry; contbr. articles to profl. jours. Served with U.S. Army, 1953-56. Mem. Med. Libr. Assn. (chair vet. med. librs. sect. 1988-89, chair union list com. 1981-95, chair pub. and info. industries rels. com. 1984-85), No. Calif. Med. Libr. Group, Spl. Librs. Assn. E-mail: rockydel@quiknet.com.

ANDERSON, DAVID E., zoological park administrator. Student, Pfeiffer Coll., 1964-65; BS in Zoology/Psychology, Duke U., 1972, postgrad., 1973. Colony supervisor Primate Ctr. Duke U., Durham, N.C., 1972-77, asst. dir. Primate Ctr., 1977-78; curator of mammals San Francisco Zool. Gardens, 1978-81, gen. curator, 1981-87, assoc. dir., gen. curator, 1987-90, dir., 1990—; tech. advisor Nature Conservancy La. 1987-90; animal tech. cons., mem. advisement com. La. State U.; mem. animal care com. Tulane U.; chmn. steering com. Madagascar Fauna Captive Propagation Group. Revs. editor Zoo Biology, 1982-88; contbr. articles to profl. publs. With USMC, 1965-69, Vietnam. Mem. Am. Assn. Zool. Parks and Aquariums (grad. mgmt. sch. 1982, ethics com., long range planning com., accreditation com., program chmn. Nat. Conf. 1981, others), Internat. Union Dirs. Zool. Gardens (captive breeding specialist group). Office: San Francisco Zool Gardens 1 Zoo Rd San Francisco CA 94132-1098*

ANDERSON, DEE, government relations and management consultant; b. Fresno, Calif., Dec. 23, 1953; d. Calvin Carroll Coolidge and Gonvella (Parrish) A.; 1 child, Shakibria Shauntae. BA, U. Wash., 1978, MPA, 1987. Cert. secondary tchr., 1978. Bus. tchr. Seattle and Renton, Wash., 1983-84; bus. edn. instr. Seattle Cen. Community Coll., 1984-86; grad. teaching asst. U. Wash., Seattle, 1985-87; program specialist Wash. State Office of Minority and Women's Bus. Enterprises, Olympia, 1987-89; exec. dir. Operational Emergency Ctr., Seattle, 1989-93; dir. Ctrl. Area Youth Assn., Seattle, 1993-94; bus. advisor/cons. U.S. Peace Corps/Ukraine, 1996—; legis. asst. Seattle City Coun., 1984. Dep. dir. Mondale-Ferraro Presdl. campaign, Seattle, 1984; mem. World Affairs Coun., Seattle; Seattle King County Pvt. Industry Coun., 1990-96—; U.S. del. Seattle Goodwill Games Women's Conf., 1990; USSR/U.S./G.B./Ireland/Japan Internat. Women's Forum in Soviet Union; mem. Dem. Nat. Com., 1992-96; U.S. del., White House Conf. on Small Bus., 1995. Mem. Nat. Women's Politic Caucus (honored as Wash. state woman leader 1989), Alpha Kappa Alpha. Democrat. Baptist. Avocation: tennis. Office: Continental Profl Enterprs PO Box 28368 Seattle WA 98118-8368

ANDERSON, DOROTHY FISHER, social worker, psychotherapist; b. Funchal, Madeira, May 31, 1924; d. Lewis Mann Anker and Edna (Gilbert) Fisher (adoptive father David Henry Fisher); m. Theodore W. Anderson, July 8, 1950; children: Robert Lewis, Janet Anderson Yang, Jeanne Elizabeth. BA, Queens Coll., 1945; AM, U. Chgo., 1947. Diplomate Am. Bd. Examiners in Clin. Social Work; lic. clin. social worker, Calif.; registered cert. social worker, N.Y. Intern Cook County (Ill.) Bur. Pub. Welfare, Chgo., 1945-46, Ill. Neuropsychiat. Inst., Chgo., 1946; clin. caseworker, Neurol. Inst. Presbyn. Hosp., N.Y.C., 1947; therapist, Mental Hygiene Clinic VA, N.Y.C., 1947-50; therapist, Child Guidance Clinic Pub. Elem. Sch. 42, N.Y.C., 1950-53; social worker, counselor Cedarhurst (N.Y.) Family Service Agy., 1954-55; psychotherapist, counselor Family Service of the Midpeninsula, Palo Alto, Calif., 1971-73, 79-86, George Hexter, M.D., Inc., 1972-83; clin. social worker Tavistock Clinic, London, 1974-75, El Camino Hosp., Mountain View, Calif., 1979; pvt. practice clin. social work, 1978-92, ret., 1992; cons. Human Resource Services, Sunnyvale, Calif., 1981-86. Hannah G. Solomon scholar U. Chgo., 1945-46; Commonwealth fellow U. Chgo., 1946-47. Fellow Soc. Clin. Social Work (Continuing Edn. Recognition award 1980-83); mem. Nat. Assn. Social Workers (diplomate in clin. social work). Avocations: sculpture, tennis, travel, drawing, pastels.

ANDERSON, DUANE, anthropologist; b. Norton, Kans., Nov. 21, 1943; s. Charles Raymond and Leta Marie (Stapp) A.; m. Carol Sue Haloin, Jan. 25, 1944; 1 child, Diana Sue Anderson Mann. BA, U. Colo., 1965, MA, 1967, PhD, 1972. Dir. Sanford Mus. and Planetarium, Cherokee, Iowa, 1966-75; state archaeologist U. Iowa, Iowa City, 1975-86; exec. dir. Dayton (Ohio) Mus. Natural History, 1986-92; v.p. Sch. Am. Rsch., Santa Fe, N.Mex., 1992—. Co-editor, author: The Cherokee Excavations, 1980, All That Glitters, 1997, 1999; editor: Legacy, 1999. Pres. Iowa Acad. Scis., Cedar Falls, 1983-84, Plains Anthropol. Soc., Lincoln, Nebr., 1985-86, Coun. for Mus. Anthropology, Arlington, Va., 1992-94; mem. exec. com. U. Iowa Mus. Natural History, 1977-86; mem., chair Iowa State Preserves Bd., Des Moines, 1976-86; bd. dirs. N.Mex. Mus. Natural History Found., Albuquerque, 1994-97. NDEA grad. fellow, 1970; grantee NSF, 1976-77, NEH, 1976, 80, 88. Mem. Am. Anthropol. Assn., Soc. Am. Archeology, Am. Assn. Mus. (sr. examiner, accreditation), Plains Anthropol. Soc. (pres. 1985-86), Coun. for Mus. Anthropology (pres. 1992-94), Ctrl. States Anthropol. Soc. (sec. 1987-90). Avocations: travel, jewelry making.

ANDERSON, EDWARD VIRGIL, lawyer; b. San Francisco, Oct. 17, 1953; s. Virgil P and Edna Pauline (Pedersen) A.; m. Kathleen Helen Dunbar, Sept. 3, 1983; children: Elizabeth D., Hilary J. AB in Econs., Stanford U., 1975, JD, 1978. Bar: Calif. 1978. Assoc. Pillsbury Madison & Sutro, San Francisco, 1978—, ptnr., 1987-94; ptnr., mem. firm mgmt. com. Skjerven Morrill MacPherson Franklin and Friel, San Jose, Calif., 1994—. Editor IP Litigator, 1995—; mem. bd. editors Antitrust Law Devel., 1983-86. Trustee Lick-Wilmerding H.S., San Francisco, 1980—, pres.; trustee Santa Clara Law Found., 1995—, Hamlin Sch. for Girls, San Francisco, 1999—. Mem. ABA, Calif. Bar Assn., San Francisco Bar Assn., Santa Clara Bar Assn. (counsel), City Club San Francisco, Stanford Golf Club, Phi Beta Kappa. Republican. Episcopal. Home: 330 Santa Clara Ave San Francisco CA 94127-2035 Office: Skjerven Morrill MacPherson Franklin and Friel 25 Metro Dr Ste 700 San Jose CA 95110-1349

ANDERSON, ERIC EDWARD, architect, planner; b. N.Y.C., Aug. 30, 1957; s. Robert Edward Anderson and Grace Anne (Cinquemani) Olson. BArch, Carnegie-Mellon U., 1979; MA, W.Va. Univ., 1989. Vista vol. Design and Planning Assistance Ctr., Albuquerque, 1980-82; archl. asst. W.Va. U., Morgantown, 1982-84, asst. dir., 1984-88, interim dir. 1988-90; campus arch. SUNY, Stony Brook, 1990-95; dir. planning & constrn. U. Nev., Las Vegas, 1995—. Mem. AIA, Assn. Univ. Architects, Soc. Coll. & Univ. Planners, Rotary. Roman Catholic. Avocations: reading, drawing, website designer, model railroading. Home: 2110 Los Feliz St Unit 2011 Las Vegas NV 89115-8016

ANDERSON, GARRY MICHAEL, diagnostic radiologist; b. Houston, May 17, 1955; s. Dan Luther and Marcella Marie (Hanel) A. BS in Biology, Tarleton State U., Stephenville, Tex., 1977; BS in Medicine, Tex. A&M U., 1979, MD, 1981. Diplomate Nat. Bd. Med. Examiners, Am. Bd. Radiology. Intern in pathology Scott & White Hosp., Temple, Tex., 1981-82, resident in diagnostic radiology, 1982-86; fellow in imaging UCLA Ctr. of the Health Scis., 1986-87, asst. attending clin. prof., 1987-88; diagnostic radiologist Long Beach (Calif.) Cmty. Hosp., 1987—. Mem. Second Decade Coun., Am. Film Inst., L.A., 1993—. Named Outstanding Young Alumnus, Tarleton State U., 1991. Mem. Am. Coll. Radiology, Radiol. Soc. N.Am. Roman Catholic. Avocation: tennis. Home: 1813 Termino Ave Apt 8401 Long Beach CA 90815-2674 Office: Cmty Radiology Med Group 1703 Termino Ave Ste 107A Long Beach CA 90804-2126

ANDERSON, GERALD VERNE, retired aerospace company executive; b. Long Beach, Calif., Oct. 25, 1931; s. Gordon Valentine and Aletha Marian (Parkins) A.; m. Judith B. Marx, May 14, 1992; children by previous marriage: Lori Jean Anderson Fronk, Gregory Verne, David Harman, Lynn Elaine Anderson Lee (dec.), Brian Earl, Michael Gordon. AA, Long Beach City Coll., 1952; BS, U. Calif., Berkeley, 1958. Registered profl. engr., Calif. Tech. specialist N. Am. Aviation Co., L.A., 1958-65; tech. specialist McDonnell Douglas Astronautics, Huntington Beach, Calif., 1965-84; mgr. mfg. engring. process methods and control McDonnell Douglas Aerospace, Huntington Beach, 1987-94; cons. Mitsubishi Heavy Industries, Nagoya, Japan, 1972-73, Aeritalia, Turin, Italy, 1975-76. Patentee portable vacuum chamber, electron beam welding device. Mem. Westminster (Calif.) Planning Com., 1974, Huntington Beach Citizens

Adv. Com., 1975, Westminster Bicentennial Com., 1976, L.A. Classical Ballet Guild, 1992—. Mem. Soc. Mfg. Engrs., Soc. Automotive Engrs., Aerospace Industries Assn., AIAA. Republican. Avocations: photography, skiing, backpacking, snorkeling. Home: 3452 Falcon Ave Long Beach CA 90807-4814

ANDERSON, HERSCHEL VINCENT, librarian; b. Charlotte, N.C., Mar. 14, 1932; s. Paul Kemper and Lillian (Johnson) A. B.A., Duke U., 1954; M.S., Columbia U., 1959. Library asst. Bklyn. Public Library, 1954-59; asst. bookmobile librarian King County Public Library, Seattle, 1959-62; asst. librarian Longview (Wash.) Public Library, 1962-63; librarian N.C. Mus. Art, Raleigh, 1963-64; audio-visual cons. N.C. State Library, Raleigh, 1964-68; dir. Sandhill Regional Library, Rockingham, N.C., 1968-70; asso. state librarian Tenn. State Library and Archives, Nashville, 1970-72; unit dir. Colo. State Library, Denver, 1972-73; state librarian S.D. State Library, Pierre, 1973-80; dir. Mesa (Ariz.) Public Library, 1980—; dir. Bibliographical Ctr. for Rsch., Denver, 1974-80, v.p. 1977; mem. Western Coun. St. Librs., 1975-80, v.p., 1978, pres., 1979; mem. Ariz. LSCA Adv. Coun., 1981-84, pres., 1982-83; mem. Ariz. Libr. Devel. Coun., 1991-93, Ariz. State Libr. Adv. Coun., 1998—; mem. libr. technician tng. adv. com. Mesa C.C., 1982-85, mem. commn. for excellence, 1993—; chmn. Serials On-Line in Ariz. Consortia, 1985-86. Jr. warden St. Mark's Episcopal Ch., Mesa, 1985-87, vestryman, 1987-90, 95-98, sr. warden, 1996-98; del. ann. conv. Episcopal Diocese of Ariz., 1989-92, 94-98, mem. archives com., 1990-97, mem. Diocesan Coun. Episcopal, Diocese of Ariz., 1996-98; mem., treas. Maricopa County Libr. Coun., 1981—, pres., 1983, 93; mem. Valley Citizens League, 1991—. With U.S. Army, 1955-57. Recipient Emeritus Honors Ariz. Library Friends, 1987. Mem. ALA, S.D. Libr. Assn. (hon. life, Libr. of Yr. award 1977), Mountain Plains Libr. Assn. (pres. 1974, bd. dirs. 1974-77, 86-87, Intellectual Freedom award 1979), Ariz. Libr. Assn. (exe. com. 1986-87), Chief Officers of State Libr. Agys. (bd. dirs. 1974-76), Kiwanis (bd. dirs. Mesa 1981-86, v.p. 1983, pres. 1985-86), Phi Kappa Psi. Office: Mesa Pub Libr 64 E 1st St Mesa AZ 85201-6768

ANDERSON, HOLLY GEIS, women's health facility administrator, commentator, educator; b. Waukesha, Wis., Oct. 23, 1946; d. Henry H. and Hulda S. Geis; m. Richard Kent Anderson, June 6, 1969. BA, Azusa Pacific U., 1970. CEO Oak Tree Antiques, San Gabriel, Calif., 1975-82; pres., founder, CEO Premenstrual Syndrome Treatment Clinic, Arcadia, Calif., 1982—, Breast Healthcare Ctr., 1986-89, Hormonal Treatment Ctrs., Inc., Arcadia, 1992-94; lectr. radio and TV shows, L.A.; on-air radio personality Women's Clinic with Holly Anderson, 1990—. Author: What Every Woman Needs to Know About PMS (audio cassette), 1987, The PMS Treatment Program (video cassette), 1989, PMS Talk (audio cassette), 1989. Mem. NAFE, The Dalton Soc., Am. Hist. Soc. of Germans from Russia. Republican. Avocations: writing, genealogy, travel, hiking, boating. Office: PMS Treatment Clinic 150 N Santa Anita Ave Ste 755 Arcadia CA 91006-3148

ANDERSON, IRIS ANITA, retired secondary education educator; b. Forks, Wash., Aug. 18, 1930; d. James Adolphus and Alma Elizabeth (Haase) Gilbreath; m. Donald Rene Anderson, 1951; children: Karen Christine, Susan Adele, Gayle Lynne, Brian Dale. BA in Teaching, U. Wash., 1969; MA in English, Seattle U., 1972. Cert. English tchr., adminstr., Calif. Tchr. Issaquah (Wash.) Sr. High Sch., 1969-77, L.A. Sr. High Sch., 1977-79. Contbr. article to Skeptic mag. Nutrition vol. Santa Monica (Calif.) Hosp. Aux., Jules Stein Eye Inst., L.A.; mem. Desert Beautiful, Palm Springs Panhellenic; mem. Rancho Mirage Reps. W-Key activities scholar U. Wash. Mem. NEA, DAR (1st vice regent Cahuilla chpt.), AAUW (Anne Carpenter fellow 1998), LEV, Wash. Speech Assn., Nat. Thespians, Bob Hope Cultural Ctr., Palm Springs Press Women, Desert Music Guild, Coachella Valley Hist. Soc., Palm Desert Womens Club, Skeptics Soc., Calif. Ret. Tchrs. Assn., CPA Wives Club, Desert Celebrities, Rancho Mirage Womens Club, Round Table West, World Affairs Coun., Living Desert Wildlife and Bot. Preserve. Republican.

ANDERSON, J. WILLIAM, management consultant; b. Boise, May 15, 1936; s. Ira Antone and Ruth Elizabeth (Eichenberger) A.; m. Anita May Gregory, Apr. 23, 1960; children: Judith Louise, Kimberly Anne. BA, Linfield Coll., 1958; MBA, U. Chgo., 1971. Cert. mgmt. cons. Gen. mgr. Rodgers Organ Co., Hillsboro, Oreg., 1961-69; v.p. mktg. Hammond Organ, Chgo., 1969-72; nat. divsn. mgr., musical instruments Yamaha, Internat., Buena Park, Calif., 1973-75; divsn. v.p. CBS, Inc., N.Y.C., 1975-79; mng. assoc. Theodore, Barry & Assocs., L.A., 1980-86; sr. cons. Mgmt. Analysis Co., San Diego, Calif., 1986-88; dir. of corp. planning Sacramento Mcpl. Utility Dist., Sacramento, 1988-91; dir. of mgmt. svcs. R.W. Beck, Inc., Seattle, 1991-98; prin. NUtility Cons., Elk Grove, Calif., 1998—. Mem. Rotary. Republican. Avocations: sacred music, model railroad, travel. Home: 9471 Wadena Way Elk Grove CA 95758-1070

ANDERSON, JACK JOE, retired communications and multimedia training consultant; b. Lipan, Tex., Oct. 22, 1928; s. William Amon and Tommie Lucille Anderson; BA, San Jose Sta U., 1965, MA, 1967; postgrad. in bus. adminstrn. Pepperdine U., Los Angeles; m. Maria I. Kamantauskas, Mar. 13, 1976; children: Mark, Douglas, Craig. Asst. mgr. edn. systems Lockheed Missiles & Space Co., Sunnyvale, Calif., 1966-69; v.p. Learning Achievement Corp., San Jose, Calif., 1969-74; mgr. instrnl. systems Ford Aerospace & Communications Corp., Pasadena, Calif., 1974-83; pres. Anderson & Assocs., Alta Loma, Calif., 1983-98; cons. tng. programs and systems, 1969-98. With USAF, 1946-66. Recipient Nat. award for tng. program design Indsl. TV Assn., 1974. Mem. Am. Mgmt. Assn., ASTD. Contbr. tech. and gen. instrnl. materials in field.

ANDERSON, JAMES ARTHUR, research laboratory administrator; b. Montgomery, Ala., July 18, 1948; s. John Arthur and Jessie Jean (Smith) A. BA in Secondary Edn., Carroll Coll., Helena, Mont., 1970; JD, Gonzaga U., 1975. Cert. secondary sch. tchr., Mont.; registered stockbroker, registered investment advisor; lic. health ins. agt., Wash., lic. life ins. agt., Wash. Legal intern U.S. Atty., Spokane, Wash., 1973-75; atty./contracts specialist Spokane County, 1975-80; contracts mgr./exec. dir. Wash. Energy, Spokane, 1980-82; sr. contracts assoc./atty. Battelle Pacific N.W. Nat. Lab., Richland, Wash., 1982-90, contracting officer, 1994—; fin. planner Am. Express Co., Kennewick, Wash., 1990-91; registered investment advisor James A. Anderson, Kennewick, Wash., 1992-93. Case law editor Gonzaga Law Rev., 1974-75; contbr. articles to profl. jours. Bd. trustees Richland Players Theater, 1984, treas., 1985, chmn. bd. trustees, 1986; mem. Vanderpoole Trust Com., Richland, 1985-89. With U.S. Army, 1970-71. David Sullivan Meml. scholar Carroll Coll., 1969-70, Gonzaga U. Law Coun. scholar, 1973-74, Law Rev. scholar, 1973-74, 74-75. Fellow Nat. Contract Mgmt. Assn. (cert. assoc. contract mgr., Columbia Basin chpt. awards chmn., ednl. v.p., N.W. Region Golden Nugget award 1991); mem. Wash. Bar Assn., Delta Epsilon Sigma. Office: Battelle Pacific Northwest Nat Lab Battelle Blvd Richland WA 99352

ANDERSON, JANET ALM, librarian; b. Lafayette, Ind., Dec. 20, 1952; d. Charles Henry and Lenore Elaine Alm; m. Jay Allan Anderson, May 21, 1983. BS, Bemidji State U., 1975; MA in Folklore, Western Ky. U., 1981, MSLS in Libr. Sci., 1982; PhD in Recreation Resources Mgmt., Utah State U., 1994. Cert. elem. tchr., sch. libr. and media specialist. Storyteller, puppeteer North Country Arts Coun., Bemidji, Minn., 1975-76; head children's libr. Bemidji State U., 1976-77; mid. sch. libr. Custer County Sch. Dist., Miles City, Mont., 1977-79; tchr. of gifted and talented Custer County Sch. Dist., Miles City, 1979-80; folklore archivist Western Ky. U., Bowling Green, 1981-83; head children's and young adults' svcs. Bowling Green Pub. Libr., 1983-85; head of serials Utah State U., Logan, 1986-91, campus svcs. libr., 1991—, adj. asst. prof. forestry, 1995—, chmn. adv. bd. Women's Ctr., 1988-92; adj. instr. Miles Community Coll., 1978-80; cons. to various Am. outdoor museums; speaker Utah Endowment for the Humanities Speakers Bur., Salt Lake City, 1987-90; mem. acad. freedom and tenure com. Utah State U., 1995-97, chair, 1997-98. Author: Old Fred, 1972, A Taste of Kentucky, 1986 (Ky. State Book Fair award), Bounty, 1990, (with others) Advances in Serials Management, Vol. 3, 1989, Vendors and Library Acquisitions, 1991; contbr. to Ency. of Am. Popular Beliefs and Superstitions, articles on folklore, librarianship, museology, and natural resource mgmt. to mags. and periodicals; assoc. editor: (jour.) InterpEdge; delivered radio and TV presentations on folklore and librarianship. Co-founder, past pres. Rosebud chpt. Nat. Audubon Soc., Miles City, Mont., 1978-80; mem. Providence/River Hts. Libr. Bd.; trustee Cache County Libr. Bd.; bd. dirs. Denzil Stewart Nature Park; mem. adv. panel Hardware Ranch Wildlife Mgmt. Area; invited author Ky. State Book Fair, 1986, Utah Arts Festival, 1991; life mem. Women and Gender Rsch. Inst., Friends of Brooks Free Libr. Recipient Exhibit and Program Grant Nat. Endowment for the Arts, Bowling Green, Ky., 1984-85. Mem. ALA, Nat. Audubon Soc. (trustee Bridgerland chpt. 1994-97), Nat. Assn. Interpretation, John Muir Assn. (founding mem. environ. ctr.), Utah Libr. Assn., Consortium of Utah Women in Higher Edn. (campus coord. 1989-91), Am. Folklore Soc., Utah Folklore Soc., Assn. Living Hist. Farms and Agrl. Mus., Visitor Studies Assn., Women and Gender Rsch. Inst. (life), Am. Assn. Mus., Assn. Coll. and Rsch. Librs., Old Main Soc., Xi Sigma Pi. Democrat. Lutheran. Home: 1090 S 400 E Providence UT 84332-9461 Office: Utah State U Merrill Libr Logan UT 84322-3000

ANDERSON, JOHN DAVID, architect; b. New Haven, Dec. 24, 1926; s. William Edward and Norma Vere (Carson) A.; m. Florence A. Van Dyke, Aug. 26, 1950; children—Robert Stewart, David Carson. A.B. cum laude, Harvard U., 1949, M.Arch., 1952. Draftsman John K. Monroe, Architect, Denver, 1952-54; draftsman, designer, assoc. Wheeler & Lewis, Architects, Denver, 1954-60; prin. John D. Anderson, Denver, 1960-64; ptnr. Anderson, Barker Rinker, Architects, Denver, 1965-69, A-B-R Partnership, Architects, Denver, 1970-75; prin., CEO Anderson Mason Dale P.C., Denver, 1975-96, sr. v.p., 1997—; vis. lectr. U. Colo., U. N.Mex., U. Nebr., U. Cape Town, Colo. State U., Plymouth Polytech., Eng.; chmn. Denver Bldg. Dept. Bd. Appeals, 1974-75; chmn. Colo. Gov.'s Task Force on Removal of Archtl. Barriers, 1972-74; vice chmn. Colo. Bd. Non-Residential Energy Conservation Stds., 1978-80. Prin. works include: Community Coll. Denver, North campus, Westminster, 1977, Solar Energy Rsch. Inst., Golden, 1980 (award winning solar heated structures). Served with USNR, 1944-46. Fellow AIA (pres. Colo. chpt. 1967, Western Mountain region dir. 1995-97, nat. v.p. 1999, Silver medal, 1984, Firm of Yr. award 1986 Western Mountain region); mem. Colo. Soc. Archs. (Arch. of Yr. award 1987, pres. 1971), Internat. Solar Energy Soc., Council Ednl. Facility Planners (internat. chmn. energy com. 1980). Republican. Congregationalist. Home: 57 S Rainbow Trail Golden CO 80401-8341 Office: Anderson Mason Dale PC 1615 17th St Denver CO 80202-1293

ANDERSON, JOHN DAVID, astronomer, researcher; b. Moscow, Idaho, Mar. 5, 1934; s. Elmer Fridolph and Jean Fife (Little) A.; m. Betty Williamson, July 7, 1956 (div. Sept. 1972); children: David W., Norman C., Marilyn L. Anderson Benoit; m. Lillian Yuriko Takemoto, Jan. 8, 1977; 1 child, Michelle Miki. BA, UCLA, 1956, MA, 1962, PhD, 1967. Mem. tech. staff Sys. Lab. Corp., L.A., 1956-60; mem. tech. staff Jet Propulsion Lab., Pasadena, Calif., 1960-67, group supr., 1967-77, staff scientist, 1977-80, sr. rsch. scientist, 1980—; vis. prof. Stanford (Calif.) U., 1971, Monash U., Australia, 1985-98. Contbr. articles to Astrophys. Jour., Planetary Report, Space Sci. Revs., Icarus, Jour. Geophys. Rsch., Astron. Jour., Sci., Nature, Phys. Rev. Letters. With USAFR, 1957-65. Recipient Exceptional Sci. Achievement award NASA, 1974. Mem. Am. Astron. Soc., Am. Geophys. Union, European Geophys. Soc., Japanese Am. Nat. Mus. Republican. Episcopalian. Achievements include principal investigator of NASA missions Mariner 6/7, Mariner 5 and Pioneer 10/11; science team leader NASA Galileo Mission; science team member NASA missions Mariner 10, Voyager, Cassini, Stardust and ESA missions Rosetta, SMART 1. Office: Jet Propulsion Lab Mail Stop 301-230 4800 Oak Grove Dr Pasadena CA 91109-8001

ANDERSON, JON M., architect; b. Lewiston, Idaho, May 11, 1962; s. Don LeAnder and Kay LaNeve (White) A.; m. Martha Jane Potter, June 8, 1985 (div. April 1994); m. Kimberly Sue Pelett, June 20, 1997; 1 child, Julia Kay. BArch, U. Oreg., 1988. Registered architect, Oreg., Wash., and Ohio. Mngr. Dolle/Swatosh Partnership, Vancouver, Wash., 1988-89; architect Jon R. Jurgens & Assoc., Beaverton, Oreg., 1989-92, NBBJ, Columbus, Ohio, 1992-94; Sen. Assoc. Jon R. Jurgens & Assoc., Beaverton, Oreg., 1994—. mem. AIA, Nat. Coun. Archtl. Registration Bd. Democrat. Lutheran. Avocations: family, golf, dragon boat racing, computers, design. Home: 1805 SE Ml King Blvd Portland OR 97214-4540 Office: Jon F. Jurgens & Assoc. 15455 NW Greenbrier Pkwy Beaverton OR 97006-5766

ANDERSON, KARL RICHARD, aerospace engineer, consultant; b. Vinita, Okla., Sept. 27, 1917; s. Axel Richard and Hildred Audrey (Marshall) A.; B.S., Calif. Western U., 1964, M.A., 1966; Ph.D., U.S. Internat. U., 1970; m. Jane Shigeko Hiratsuka, June 20, 1953; 1 son, Karl Richard. Engr. personnel subsystems Atlas Missile Program, Gen. Dynamics, San Diego, 1960-63; design engr. Solar divsn. Internat. Harvester, San Diego, 1964-66, sr. design engr., 1967-69, project engr., 1970-74, product safety specialist, 1975-78; aerospace engring. cons., 1979-86; cons. engring., 1979—; lectr. Am. Indian Sci. and Engring. Soc. Served to maj. USAF, 1936-60. Recipient Spl. Commendation award San Diego County Bd. Supervisors, 1985, Spl. Commendation award San Diego City Council, 1985, Spl. Commendation award City of San Diego, 1994, Grace "Peter" Sargent award San Diego City Natural Park, 1994. Registered profl. engr., Calif. Home: 5886 Scripps St San Diego CA 92122-3212

ANDERSON, KATHERYN LUCILLE, language arts educator and author; b. Aberdeen, Md., Aug. 17, 1949; d. Boyd Frederick and Lucy Charlotte Anderson. BS in Edn., U. Md., 1973; MA in Spl. Edn., Adams State Coll., Alamosa, Colo., 1977; MA in Ednl. Tech., U. Colo., 1986. Lic. profl. tchr., Colo. Mental health paraprofl. Prince George's County Mental Health, Landover, Md., 1970-73; spl. edn. tchr. Fountain/Ft. Carson (Colo.) Sch. Dist., 1973-75; instr. mil. program Pikes Peak Cmty. Coll., Colorado Springs, Colo., 1977-78; spl. edn. tchr. Harrison Sch. Dist., Colorado Springs, 1978-88, tchr. lang. arts, 1988—, team leader lang. arts, 1989—, dept. chair, 1992—; lectr. in field. Author: English and American Culture, 1991, English and American Culture 6, 1993, English and American Culture 7, 1993, A Writing Companion, 1993; co-author: The Sound of the Apple IIe, 1986, The Shape of the Apple IIe, 1986. Chpt. II Ednl. Program Devel. grantee Harrison Sch. Dist., 1991, 92, 93; recipient 1996 Colo. State A World of Difference Educator of Yr. award. Mem. AAUW, ASCD, Colo. Assn. Middle Level Educators, Colo. Lang. Arts Soc., Nat. Coun. Tchrs. English, Nat. Women's History Project Network, Tenn. Walking Horse Assn. (rep., stock show and horse exposition 1993-94), Tenn. Walking Horse Breeders and Exhibitors Assn. Democrat. Avocations: riding, breeding and showing Tennessee walking horses, reading, computers, authoring. Office: Carmel Middle Sch 1740 Pepperwood Dr Colorado Springs CO 80910-1599

ANDERSON, KATHLEEN GAY, mediator, hearing officer, arbitrator, educator; b. Cin., July 27, 1950; d. Harold B. and Trudi L. (Chambers) Briggs; m. J.R. Carr, July 4, 1988; 1 child, Jesse J. Anderson. Student, U. Cin., 1971-72, Antioch Coll., 1973-74; cert., Nat. Jud. Coll., U. Nev., Reno, 1987, Inst. Applied Law, 1987, Acad. Family Mediators, 1991. Cert. Am. Arbitration Assn. Comml. Arbitration Panel, Nat. Assn. Securities Dealers Arbitration and Mediation Panels, Lemmon Mediation Inst., Acad. Family Mediators. Paralegal Lauer & Lauer, Santa Fe, 1976-79, Wilkinson, Cragun & Barker, Anchorage, 1981-82; employment law paralegal specialist Hughes, Thorsness, Gantz, Powell & Brundin, Anchorage, 1983-91; investigator, mediator Alaska State Commn. Human Rights, 1991; mediator, arbitrator, trainer The Arbitration and Mediation Group, Anchorage, 1987—; hearing officer Municipality of Anchorage, 1993—; State of Alaska, 1994—; mem. faculty nat. Jud. Coll., U. Nev., Reno, 1988-89; adj. prof. U. Alaska, Anchorage, 1985—, Alaska Pacific U., 1990-96, Chapman U., 1990; mem. Alaska Supreme Ct. Mediation Task Force, 1991-96; adv. com. Am. Arbitration Assn. for Alaska, 1995—, ADR subcom. Supreme Ct. Civil Justice Reform task force, 1998—, panel comml. arbitrators: trainer mediation svcs. pvt. profit and nonprofit groups, pub. groups, U.S. mil., state and fed. govt.; arbitrator Anchorage Bd. Realtors, 1997—. Author, editor: Professional Responsibility Handbook for Legal Assistants and Paralegals, 1986; contbr. articles to profl. jours. Lectr. Alaska Bar Assn., 1989—, NLRB, Anchorage, 1986, Alaska Assn. Bus. and Profl. Women, 1988—, Coun. on Edn. and Mgmt., 1993—, Small Bus. Devel. Coun., various employers and bus. groups. Mem. ABA (ethics com., alt. dispute resolution sect.), Am. Arbitration Assn. (cert. comml. arbitration panel 1996—), Soc. Profls. in Dispute Resolution, Acad. Family Mediators (practitioner mem.), Nat. Inst. Dispute Resolution, Nat. Fedn. Paralegal Assn. (edn. task force coord. 1988-89, adminstrv. v.p. 1988-91), Alaska Bar Assn. (assoc., employment, alt. dispute resolution, family law sect.), Bus. and Profl. Women, Alaska Dispute Settlement Assn. (v.p. 1992-93, chair com. on credentialing and stds. of practice, pres. 1997-98). Avocations: diving, gourmet cooking, entertaining. Home: PO Box 100098 Anchorage AK 99510-0098 Office: PO Box 240783 Anchorage AK 99524-0783

ANDERSON, KATHRYN D., surgeon; b. Ashton-Under-Lyne, Lancashire, Eng., Mar. 14, 1939; came to U.S., 1961; m. French Anderson, June 24, 1961. BA, Cambridge (Eng.) U., 1961, MA, 1964; MD, Harvard U., 1964. Diplomate Am. Bd. Surgery. Intern in pediat. Children's Hosp., Boston, 1964-65; resident in surgery Georgetown U. Hosp., Washington, 1965-69, chief resident in surgery, 1969-70, attending surgeon, 1972-74, vice chmn. surgery, 1984-92; chief resident in pediat. surgery Children's Hosp., Washington, 1970-72, sr. attending surgeon, 1974-84; surgeon-in-chief Children's Hosp., L.A., 1992—; prof. surgery U. So. Calif. Fellow ACS (sec. 1992—), Am. Acad. Pediatrics (sec. surg. sect. 1982-85, chmn. 1985-86), Am. Pediatric Surg. Assn. (sec. 1988-91); Am. Surg. Assn., Soc. Univ. Surgeons. Avocations: opera, yoga. Office: Childrens Hosp 4650 W Sunset Blvd Los Angeles CA 90027-6062

ANDERSON, KENNETH CHARLES, data processing executive; b. San Francisco, July 17, 1947; s. Delbert Clarence and Vera Virginia (Asaro) A. BA, U. Calif., Berkeley, 1970. Programmer/analyst Glen Slaughter and Assocs., Oakland, Calif., 1976-85, 86—; systems analyst 1st Nationwide Bank, Daly City, Calif., 1985-86. Contbr. to American Poetry Anthology, Vol. VIII, No. 3, 1989, Best New Poets of 1988, 1989. Avocation: poetry. Home: 47 Haight St San Francisco CA 94102-5801 Office: Glen Slaughter and Assocs 1999 Harrison St Ste 500 Oakland CA 94612-3586

ANDERSON, KENNETH JEFFERY, family financial planner, accountant, lawyer; b. Daytona Beach, Fla., May 7, 1954; s. Kenneth E. and Petronella G. (Jeffer) A.; m. Susan Wagner, Aug. 19, 1978; children: Melissa, Kiersten. BSBA, Valparaiso U., 1976, JD, 1979. CPA, Ill. Prof. staff, mgr. Arthur Andersen & Co., Chgo., 1979-84; mgr. Arthur Andersen & Co., L.A., 1984-90, ptnr., 1990—, dir. individual tax fin. svcs., western region; founding mem., mem. adv. bd. U. So. Calif. Family and Closely-Held Bus. Inst. Bd. govs., treas. Idyllwild (Calif.) Arts, 1990—; bd. dirs. Boy Scouts Am. W. L.A. County Coun.; mem. L.A. Philanthropic Found., 1995; profl. adv. bd. Children's Bur., 1995; adv. bd. L.A. Philharmonic, 1996—; mem. assocs. bd. Chgo. Lung Assn., 1980-84; vol. Hospice of North Shore, Winnetka, Ill., 1981. Mem. AICPA, Fla. Bar Assn., Ill. Bar Assn., Ill. CPA Soc., Calif. CPA Soc. (apptd. to state com. on personal fin. planning), Soc. CPA-Fin. Planners (bd. dirs. 1987-89), Sports Lawyers Assn., Calif. Club. Republican. Avocations: sports, sailing, music, golfing. Home: 28 Cinch Rd Bell Canyon CA 91307-1003 Office: Arthur Andersen & Co 633 W 5th St 26th Flr Los Angeles CA 90071-2005

ANDERSON, KEVIN J., writer; b. Racine, Wis., Mar. 27, 1962; s. Andrew James and Dorothy Arloah (Cooper) A.; m. Mary Esther Franco, Nov. 7, 1984 (div. June 1987); m. Rebecca Moesta, Sept. 15, 1991; 1 stepchild, Jonathan Cowan. BS, U. Wis., 1983. Tech. writer Lawrence Livermore (Calif.) Nat. Lab., 1983-95; pres. Word Fire, Inc., Monument, Colo., 1995—. Author: Star Wars: Jedi Search, 1994, X-Files: Ground Zero, 1995, Darksaber, 1995, Ignition, 1997. Mem. Sci. Fiction Writers Am., Horror Writers Am. Avocations: hiking, microbrew beers.

ANDERSON, LINDA (LYNN ANDERSON), radio executive; b. Detroit, Dec. 24; d. Robert A. and Lucille A. Tower; children: Kierstyn R. Anderson, Gretchen N. Anderson. BA in Bus., Mich. State U., 1968; postgrad., UCLA, 1968-70. Cert. radio mktg. cons. Tchr. pub. schs. L.A. and Chgo., 1968-70; mgr. display ads Frontier Publs., 1970-71; broadcaster Sta. WVVX, Chgo., 1971-72; account exec. Metromedia Radio, Sta. WDHF, Chgo., 1972-76; v.p. sales Metro Radio Sales Metromedia Radio, L.A., 1976-79; sr. account exec. RKO Radio/Sta. KHJ, L.A., 1979-80; with Gannett Radio/Sta. KIIS AM-FM, L.A., 1980-90, v.p. sales, 1984-85, v.p., sta. mgr., 1986, v.p., gen. mgr., 1986-87, pres., 1987-90; exec. v.p. mktg. and sales worldwide Radio Express, L.A., 1991-95; v.p., gen. mgr. Southwestern region Metro Networks, L.A., 1995, v.p. internat. devel., 1996; v.p. nat. sales Chancellor Media, San Francisco, 1996; v.p., gen. mgr. KYFX and KFGY, 1997; v.p. Training Radio Advt. Bur., 1998—. Mem. bd. visitors Southwestern Coll. Law, Los Angeles, 1987. Recipient Jim Dunkan awards 1987, 88; named Gen. Mgr. Yr. Poe Music Survey, 1989. Mem. Nat. Assn. Broadcasters (steering com. 1987—), Am. Women Radio & TV (Broadcaster of Yr. 1990), Hollywood Radio & TV Soc. (IBA awards chair), Hollywood Arts Com. (bd. dirs. 1986—), So. Calif. Broadcasters Assn. (sec. 1989, bd. dirs. 1986—), Hollywood Women's Polit. Com., Hollywood C. of C. (spl. events com. 1987—). Clubs: Los Angeles Ad; Calif. Yacht; Santa Monica Yacht. Avocation: goldsmith.

ANDERSON, LOIS M., artist, librarian; b. Milw., Jan. 1, 1927; d. Melvin Anderson and Agnes Luisier. BS in Edn., Wis. State Coll., 1949; MLS, U. Calif., Berkeley, 1960. Head sch. librarian Lagunitas (Calif.) Sch. Dist., 1963-74; substitute librarian Many County Librs., Calif., 1974-84; ref. librarian Sausalito (Calif.) Pub. Libr., 1984-94; ref. librarian substitute Marin County Sys., Calif., 1994—; cons., library freelance, Marin County, 1982-93; juror 3 arts shows, San Francisco and Marin County, 1985-91. Exhibited in group shows at Bedford Gallery, Walnut Creek, Calif., 1997, Wilson Gallery, Santa Rosa, Calif., 1996, Mill Valley Calif., 1995, Falkirk Mus., San Rafael, Calif., 1992, Oakland Mus., Oakland, Calif., 1990, and numerous others. Recipient award NEA, 1978, award San Francisco Art Commn., 1987, award Art Matters, Inc., 1989. E-mail: scAltavant@ad.com. Avocations: reading, gardening, hunting for art materials. Home: 50 Catalpa Ave Mill Valley CA 94941

ANDERSON, LOUISE STOUT, crime analyst; b. Wellsville, N.Y., Aug. 11, 1952; d. Carlton C. and Mary (Gasdik) Stout; m. Leonard M. Anderson, June 2, 1973. BA in German Lit., Polit. Sci., Mt. Holyoke Coll., 1974; MA in Polit. Sci., San Diego State U., 1977; MS Human Resources and Organizational Devel., 1994. Cert. C.C. tchr., Calif. Statistician Grossmont Coll., El Cajon, Calif., 1976-78; crime analyst San Diego Police Dept., 1978-80; crime analyst Career Criminal Apprehension Program, Marin County Sheriff's Office, San Rafael, Calif., 1980-83; crime analyst CCAP Unit, Sonoma County Sheriff's Office, Santa Rosa, Calif., 1983-85; mgr. mktg. svcs. Command Data Systems, Dublin, Calif., 1985-87, client svcs. mgr., 1988-92; contracts mgr. Tiburon Inc., 1992; mgr. field svcs. OCS Techs., 1992-95, v.p. nat. customers support, 1994-95; project mgr. IBM Global Svcs., 1995—; cons. Search Group Inc. for Automated Crime Analysis. Contbr. articles in field. Owner Acacia Assocs., public safety cons. and training orgn.; project mgmt. profl. Project Mgmt. Inst., 1994; bd. dirs. Mt. Holyoke Club So. Calif., 1996-98. Mem. Antioch Police Commn.; alumna recruiter Mt. Holyoke Club No. Calif., 1981-86.

ANDERSON, MARILYN NELLE, elementary education educator, librarian, counselor; b. Las Animas, Colo., May 5, 1942; d. Mason Hadley Moore and Alice Carrie (Dwyer) Coates; m. George Robert Anderson, Sept. 4, 1974; children: Lisa Lynn, Edward Alan, Justin Patrick. BEd magna cum laude, Adams State Coll., 1962, postgrad., 1965; MEd, Ariz. State U., 1967; postgrad., Idaho State U., 1971, 86, Columbia Pacific U., 1991—. Cert. elem. tchr., K-12 sch. counselor. Tchr. Wendell (Idaho) Sch. Dist. 232, 1962-66, Union-Endicott (N.Y.) Sch. Dist., 1967-68; counselor, librarian West Yuma (Colo.) Sch. Dist., 1968-69; elem. sch. counselor Am. Falls (Idaho) Sch. Dist. 381, 1969-73; project dir. Gooding County (Idaho) Sr. Citizens Orgn., 1974-75; tchr. Castleford (Idaho) Sch. Dist. 417, 1982-92; placement specialist, referral counselor Idaho Child Care Program South Ctrl. Idaho Community Action Agy., Twin Falls, 1992—; mem. Castleford Schs. Merit Pay Devel. program, 1983-84, Accreditation Evaluation com., 1984-85, Math. Curriculum Devel. com., 1985-86. Leader Brownie Scouts, Endicott, 1967-68; chmn. fundraising com. Am. Falls Kindergarten, 1971-73. Recipient Leader's award Nat. 4-H Conservation Natural Resources Program, 1984. Mem. NEA, ASCD, Nat. Assn. Edn. Young Children, Assn. Childhood Edn. Internat., Idaho Edn. Assn., So. Idaho Assn. for Childhood Edn. Internat. (pres.), Idaho Coun. Internat. Reading Assn., Magic Valley Reading Assn., Support Unltd. Providers and Parents. Republican. Baptist. Avocations: reading, painting, writing short stories, photography. Home: 1675 BBH Wendell ID 83355-9801 Office: South Ctrl Idaho Community Action Agency Twin Falls ID 83301

ANDERSON, MARILYN WHEELER, English language educator; b. Tulsa, Mar. 18, 1946; d. Robert Leslie and Lola Madelene (Offutt) Wheeler; m. Austin Gilman Anderson, Mar. 17, 1968; children: Guy, Lisa, Michael, Emily. BA, Calif. State U., L.A., 1968; MA, UCLA, 1972, Calif. State U., Dominguez Hills, 1989. Actress and dir. L.A., 1977-83; cons. Redondo Beach (Calif.) Beach City Schs., 1981-83; prof. of English El Camino Coll., Torrance, Calif., 1986—; fine arts com. mem. El Camino Coll., 1992—, affirmative action officer, 1995-96; presenter in field. Author: (textbook) Keys to Successful Writing, 1998; contbr. articles to profl. jours. Vol. 1736 House/Crisis Ctr., Hermosa Beach, Calif., 1985-86. Mem. MLA, Nat. Coun. Tchrs. of English. Democrat. Avocations: jogging, travel, hiking, book club membership. Office: El Camino Coll 10067 Crenshaw Blvd Torrance CA

ANDERSON, MARK ALEXANDER, lawyer; b. Santa Monica, Calif., Nov. 15, 1953; s. William Alexander and Christina (Murray) A.; m. Rosalie Louise Movius, Nov. 28, 1986; 1 child, Morgan Anderson Movius. AB, U. So. Calif., 1974; JD, Yale U., 1978. Bar: Calif. 1979, U.S. Dist. Ct. (no. dist.) Calif. 1979, U.S. Ct. Appeals (9th cir.) 1979, Oreg. 1982, U.S. Dist. Ct. Oreg. 1982, Wash. 1985, U.S. Dist. Ct. (we. dist.) Wash. 1986, U.S. Supreme Ct. 1989. Law clk. U.S. Ct. Appeals (9th cir.), San Francisco, 1978-79, U.S. Dist. Ct. Oreg., Portland, 1980-82; atty. Miller, Nash, Wiener, Hager & Carlsen, Portland, 1983-92; gen. counsel, asst. sec. Dark Horse Comics, Inc., Milwaukie, Oreg., 1992-98. Chair Raleigh Hills-Garden Home Citizen Participation Orgn., 1992-93. Mem. N.W. Lawyers and Artists (pres. 1988-90), State Bar Calif., Wash. State Bar Assn., Oreg. State Bar (chair antitrust, trade regulation and unfair bus. practices sect. 1991-92), City Club of Portland (chair arts and culture standing com. 1990-92). Home: PO Box 8154 Portland OR 97207-8154

ANDERSON, MARK EUGENE, specialized truck driver, safety inspector; b. Richland Center, Wis., Oct. 9, 1952; s. Harold Eugene and Laila Marie (Jacobson) A.; m. Marilyn Jones, June 22, 1972 (div. 1984); children: Michael, Kenneth, Thomas; m. Georgina Therese Scinta, Sept. 29, 1984. Grad., Mich. Ctr. for Design Driving, 1993, Mich. Ctr. Decision Driving. Enlisted U.S. Army, 1970, ret., 1977; mgr. Taco Bell, Farmington, N.Mex., 1977-78; truck driver Farmington Meat Processors, 1978-80, Nobel/Sysco, Albuquerque, 1980-89; specialized truck driver transuranic nuclear waste Dawn Enterprises Inc., Farmington, 1989-95, Steere Tank Lines, 1995, ABF Freight Sys. Inc., 1995—; truck driver, cert. safety inspector Comml. Vehicle Safety Alliance, Oreg., 1991; truck driver transp. safeguards div. U.S. Dept. Energy, Albuquerque, 1989. Mem. Mich. Truck Safety Commn., 1993. Named N.Mex. State Truck Driving Champion N.Mex. Motor Carriers, 1988, Grand Champion Truck Driving Championship, N.Mex. Motor Carriers, 1994. Avocations: classic cars, woodworking, motorcycling, home improvement. Home: 5201 Chuckwagon Trl NW Albuquerque NM 87120-2889 Office: Dawn Enterprises Inc PO Box 204 Farmington NM 87499-0204

ANDERSON, MARK ROBERT, data processing executive, biochemist; b. Oak Park, Ill., Aug. 11, 1951; s. Robert Hugo and Marilyn Pettee (Johnson) A.; m. Mary Jane Helsell, June 6, 1980; children: Berit Bracken, Evan Robert. BS, Stanford U., 1972; MS, Stanford U., Hopkins Marine Sta., 1973; postgrad., U. Brit. Columbia, Vancouver, 1973. Publisher Potlatch Press, Friday Harbor, Wash., 1974-77; assoc. prof. Western Wash. U., Bellingham, 1977, Harvard U., Boston, 1978; chief scientist Ocean Research & Edn. Soc., Boston, 1978; v.p. Moclips Cetological Soc., Friday Harbor, 1979-81; founder, exec. dir. The Whale Mus., Friday Harbor, 1979-81; pres. The Oikos Co., Friday Harbor, 1980—, San Juan Software, Friday Harbor, 1983-84; pres., bd. dirs. Island Tech. Inc., Friday Harbor, 1984—; founder, pres. Tech. Alliance Ptnrs., 1989—; bd. dirs. Worldesign, PreText, Inc., Wa. Software Assn.; bd. advisors HIT Lab., U. Wash., 1991—; founder, pres. Strategic News Svc. LLC, 1995—; founder WSA Investment Forum; CEO, bd. dirs. Carrier Wave, Inc., 1996—; program chair Online Advantage 96; founder, exec. dir. Orca Relief Citizens Alliance, 1998—. Author: Nineteen Fathers, 1971, (software) The Agent's Advantage, 1983; producer TV film Survivors, 1980; editor, founder Jour. Cetus, 1981; discoverer Resonance Theory, 1981. Founder San Juan Musicians Guild, 1974-78, Anti-Spray Coalition, 1977. Mem. Wash. Software Assn. (bd. dirs. 1988-90, chair pres.'s group 1989—), Database Standards Com., Am. Electronics Assn. Avocations: theoretical physics, musical composition, skiing.

ANDERSON, MARTIN CARL, economist; b. Lowell, Mass., Aug. 5, 1936; s. Ralph and Evelyn (Anderson) A.; m. Annelise Graebner, Sept. 25, 1965. AB summa cum laude, Dartmouth Coll., 1957, MS in Engring., MSBA; PhD in Indsl. Mgmt., MIT, 1962. Asst. to dean, instr. engring. Thayer Sch. Engring. Dartmouth Coll., Hanover, N.H., 1959; research fellow Joint Ctr. for Urban Studies MIT and Harvard U., Cambridge, 1961-62; asst. prof. fin. Grad. Sch. Bus. Columbia U., N.Y.C., 1962-65, assoc. prof. bus., 1965-68; sr. fellow Hoover Inst. on War, Revolution and Peace Stanford (Calif.) U., 1971—; spl. asst. to Pres. of U.S. The White House, 1969-70, spl. cons. for systems analysis, 1970-71, asst. for policy devel., 1981-82; mem. Pres.' Fgn. Intelligence Adv. Bd., 1982-85, Pres.' Econ. Policy Adv. Bd., 1982-88, Pres.' Gen. Adv. Com. on Arms Control and Disarmament, 1987-93; pub. interest dir. Fed. Home Loan Bank San Francisco, 1972-79; mem. Commn. on Crucial Choices for Ams., 1973-75, Def. Manpower Commn., 1975-76, Com. on the Present Danger, 1977—. Author: The Federal Bulldozer: A Critical Analysis of Urban Renewal, 1949-62, 1964, Conscription: A Select and Annotated Bibliography, 1976, Welfare: The Political Economy of Welfare Reform in the U.S., 1978, Registration and the Draft, 1982, The Military Draft, 1982, Revolution, 1988, Impostors in the Temple, 1992; columnist Scripps-Howard News Svc., 1993-94. Dir. research Nixon presdl. campaign, 1968; policy adviser Reagan presdl. campaign, 1976, 80; del. Rep. Nat. Conv., 1992-96; policy adviser Dole Presdl. Campaign, 1996; trustee Ronald Reagan Presdl. Found., 1985-92; mem. Calif. Gov.'s Coun. Econ. Advisors, 1993—, chmn. Congl. Policy Adv. Bd., 1998—. 2d lt. AUS, 1958-59. Mem. Am. Econ. Assn., Mont Pelerin Soc., Phi Beta Kappa. Club: Bohemian. Office: Stanford U Hoover Instn Stanford CA 94305-6010

ANDERSON, MICHAEL GEORGE, marketing and advertising executive; b. Boulder, Colo., Aug. 3, 1951; s. George Martin and Annette Elizabeth (Girmann) A.; m. Susan Elliott, Mar. 19, 1977; children: Gregory Michael, Richard Charles. BS in Aero. Engring., U. Colo., 1973, MBA in Fin., 1978. Design engr. Beech Aircraft, Boulder, 1976-78, liaison engr., 1978-79; mech. engr. Dieterich Standard, Boulder, 1979-80, mgr. engring. design, 1980-84, quality assurance mgr., 1984-87, mgr. advt., mktg. strategic planning and quality assurance, 1987-90, mgr. regional mktg., advt. mgr., 1990-96; product group mgr. Advanced Forming Tech., Longmont, Colo., 1996—. Author (computer software) Tektronix Header Program, 1982. V.p. Luth. Ch. Coun.,1 988-91; asst. scoutmaster Troop 161 Boy Scouts Am.; football and basketball coach Niwot Youth Sports. Recipient NPT Stamp and Cert., ASME, Boulder, 1986. Mem. Instrument Soc. Am., Boulder Flycasters Club, U. Colo. Alumni Assn. (bd. dirs. 1985-87, v.p. bd. dirs. Boulder chpt. 1985-86), Buff Club (v.p., bd. dirs. 1985-87, pres. 1988-90), Moose. Republican. Avocations: running, fly fishing. Home: 7400 Mount Meeker Rd Longmont CO 80503-7143 Office: PCC/Advanced Forming Technology 7040 County Road 20 Longmont CO 80504-9423

ANDERSON, MICHAEL ROBERT, marketing representative; b. Mpls., Nov. 3, 1953; s. Arthur Robert Anderson and Patricia Roberta Carlson; divorced; children: Jenna Courtney, Evan Brendan. BSEE, U. Minn., 1976; MS in Sys. Mgmt., U. So. Calif., 1981. Microelectronics engr. Hughes Aircraft Co., Fullerton, Calif., 1977; mktg. rep. Hewlett Packard, Orange County, Calif., 1977-81; regional mgr. Group III Elec., Orange County, 1981-85; mktg. rep. Lisp Machines Inc., L.A., 1985-87, Sun Microsys., Inc., Orange, Calif., 1987-91; mktg.rep. Auspex Sys., Inc., Santa Clara, Calif., 1992-95, Raptor Systems, Waltham, Mass., 1995—. Active Big Brother, Big Bros. Inc., Orange, Calif., 1979-81. Fellow AAAS, Am. Assn. Artificial Intelligence, Planetary Soc. Avocations: reading, piano, family activities, bicycling, travel. Home: PO Box 5199 San Clemente CA 92674-5199 Office: Maxager Sys Inc Ste. #200 302 N El Camino Real San Clemente CA 92672

ANDERSON, MICHAEL ROBERT, computer forensics specialist; b. Salt Lake City, May 16, 1948; s. Robert Louis and Shannon Corrine (Harding) A.; m. Alyda LaRae Fuit, Aug. 12, 1967 (div. Nov. 1985); children: Summer Lee, Ryan M,; m. Lorraine L. Cox, Feb. 17, 1996. BS, Weber State U., 1970. Spl. agt. criminal investigation divsn. IRS, Las Vegas, Portland, 1971-96; pres., CEO New Technologies, Inc., Gresham, Oreg., 1996—; lectr., adviser U. New Haven Ctr. for Judicial Tech., Info. Mgmt. and Pub. Policy, West Haven, Conn., 1998—; tng. advisor Nat. White Collar Crime Ctr., 1996-99; cons. and spkr. in field. Contbr. articles to profl. jours. Recipient Letter of Commendation from the Under Sec. of Treasury, 1995-96. Office: New Tech Inc 2075 NE Division Gresham OR 97030

ANDERSON, MITCHELL, chiropractor; b. L.A., Aug. 9, 1963; s. Charles Terry and Anita Louise (Rose) A.; m. Patricia Elaine Evora, June 10, 1989. AA, Cerritos Coll., 1983; BS, Cleveland Chiropractic Coll., L.A., 1985; D of Chiropractic, Cleveland Chiropractic Coll., 1987; sports cert., L.A. Chiropractic Coll., 1988. Cert. chiropractor Nat. Bd. Chiropractic Examiners; diplomate Am. Bd. Chiropractic Sports Physicians; lic. chiropractor, Calif., Hawaii. Massage therapist/owner Body Work by Mitch, Downey, Calif., 1983-87; chiropractor Anderson Chiropractic Ctr., Los Alamitos, Calif., 1987—; referal doctor/owner Anderson Worker's Referal Svc., Orange, Calif., 1991—; physician Bretheren Christian High Sch., Cypress, Calif., 1988—; team chiropractor Anaheim Bullfrogs, 1993—; pres. Calif. Chiropractic Coun. on Sports Injuries and Phys. Fitness; physician 1992 Olympic Games, Barcelona, Spain, Profl. Rodeo, 1992—, 1996 Olympic Games, Atlanta. Mem. Am. Chiropractic Assn. (sports cert. 1989, coun. sports injuries 1988—), Fed. Internat. Chiropractic Sportive, Calif. Chiropractic Assn., Rotary, Masons (3 degree), Scottish Rite (32 degree). Republican. Baptist. Avocations: weight lifting, woodworking, skiing. Home: PO Box 1039 Los Alamitos CA 90720-1039 Office: Anderson Chiropractic Ctr 10671 Los Alamitos Blvd Los Alamitos CA 90720-2137

ANDERSON, NED, SR., Apache tribal chairman; b. Bylas, Ariz., Jan. 18, 1943; s. Paul and Maggie (Rope) A.; m. Delphina Hinton; children—Therese Kay, Linette Mae, Magdalene Gail, Ned, Sean. AA, Ea. Ariz. Coll., 1964, AAS in computer sci., 1989; BS, U. Ariz., 1967, JD, 1973. Field dir. Nat. Study Indian Edn., dept. anthropology U. Ariz., Tucson, 1968-70; tech. asst. Project Head Start, Ariz. State U., Tempe, 1970; ethnographer Smithsonian Instn., Washington, 1970-73; dir. Jojoba Project, Office of Arid Land Studies, U. Ariz. Tucson, 1973-76; with Jojoba devel. project San Carlos Apache Tribe, Ariz., 1976-78, tribal councilman, 1976-78, 93—, tribal chmn., 1978-86, gen. mgr. spl. housing projects, 1991—. Contbr. articles to profl.jours. Bd. dirs. Southwestern Indian Devel., Inc., 1971; mem. affirmative action com. City of Tucson, 1975-76; bd. dirs. Indian Enterprise Devel. Corp., 1976-78; mem. study panel NAS, 1975-77; pres. Inter-Tribal Coun. Ariz., 1979—; mem. supervisory bd. Ariz. Justice Planning Commn., 1978—, Indian adv. bd. Intergovtl. Personnel Program, 1978—; pres. bd. Ft. Thomas High Sch. Unified Dist., 1987—, clk. bd., 1989—; trustee Bacone Coll., 1986—; mem. adv. bd. Am. Indian Registry for Performing Arts, 1985—, San Carlos Fish and Game Commn., 1975—, chmn., 1976—; mem. exec. com. San Carlos Apache Tribal Coun., 1976-78, budget, fin. com., 1976—, constn. and ordinance com. 1976-78, investment com. 1997—, chmn. law and order com., 1976-78, 98—; adv. bd. Gila Pueblo Community Coll. extension Ea. Ariz. Coll., 1979—; mem. sch. bd. Ft. Thomas High Sch. Unified Dist., 1977—, clk., 1987—, pres. sch. bd., 1992—; mem. County Govt. Study Commn. State Ariz., 1981-84; adv. bd. Indian Edn., Ariz. State U., Tempe, 1978—, U. Ariz., Tucson, 1978—; bd. dirs. San Carlos Lake Devel., 1994—, Western Apache Constrn. Co., 1994—, Apache Gold Resort Public Authority, 1997—; mem. reinvention mgmt. lab. workgroup Nat. Housing Improvement Program, 1995-96. Recipient Outstanding Community Coll. Alumni award Ariz. Community Coll. Bd./Ea. Ariz. Coll., 1982, Outstanding Cooperation award U.S. Secret Svc., 1984, A.T. Anderson Meml. scholarship, 1989, Univ. Rels. award AT&T, 1989, Outstanding 20-yr. Svc. award to Ft. Thomas Unified Sch. Dist. State of Ariz., 1998. Mem. Nat. Tribal Chmn.'s Assn. (bd. edn. 1978—, adv. bd. 1978—), Ariz. Acad., Globe C. of C., Phi Theta Kappa.

ANDERSON, PARKER LYNN, editorial columnist, playwright; b. Wickenburg, Ariz., Apr. 19, 1964; s. Harry Milton and Darla Raejean (Hangartner) A. Mem. prodn. com. Prescott (Ariz.) Fine Arts Assn., 1993-95, 98—, adv. mem., 1987—; columnist, theatre critic The Prescott News, 1995-96; with Cath. Social Svc. of Yavapai, 1983—; mem. adv. com. The Blue Rose Theatre Co., Prescott, 1994—; guest on talk shows Sta. KUSK-TV, 1991—. Author: (plays) The Startled Cowboys, 1991, Voices From the Past, 1995, The Sleeping Toad, 1997, Virgil Earp, 1998; freelance guest columnist and letters of comment in numerous Ariz. publs., 1990—; pub. Roasting Roderick. Home: PO Box 1285 Prescott AZ 86302-1285

ANDERSON, PAUL NATHANIEL, oncologist, educator; b. Omaha, May 30, 1937; s. Nels Paul E. and Doris Marie (Chesnut) A.; BA, U. Colo., 1959, MD, 1963; m. Dee Ann Hipps, June 27, 1965; children: Mary Kathleen, Anne Christen; Diplomate Am. Bd. internal Medicine, Am. Bd. Med. Mgmt. Intern Johns Hopkins Hosp., 1963-64, resident in internal medicine, 1964-65; rsch. asso., staff assoc. NIH, Bethesda, Md., 1965-70; fellow in oncology Johns Hopkins Hosp., 1970-72, asst. prof. medicine, oncology Johns Hopkins U. Sch. Medicine, 1972-76; attending physician Balt. City Hosps., Johns Hopkins Hosp., 1972-76; dir. dept. med. oncology Penrose Cancer Hosp., Colorado Springs, Colo., 1976-86; clin. asst. prof. dept. medicine U. Colo. Sch. Medicine, 1976-90, clin. assoc. prof., 1990—; dir. Penrose Cancer Hosp., 1979-86, chief dept. medicine, 1985-86; founding dir. Cancer Ctr. of Colorado Springs, 1986-95, founding dir., Pikes Peak Forum for Health Care Ethnics, 1996—; dir. Rocky Mountain Cancer Ctr., Colorado Springs, 1995—; med. dir. So. Colo. Cancer Program, 1979-86; pres., chmn. bd. dirs. Preferred Physicians, Inc., 1986-92; mem. Colo. Found. for Med. Care Health Standards Com., 1985, sec., exec. com., 1990, bd. dirs., pres. 1992-93; mem., chmn. treatment com. Colo. Cancer Control and Rsch. Panel, 1980-83; prin. investigator Cancer Info. Svc. of Colo., 1981-87. Editor Advances in Cancer Control; editorial bd. Journal of Cancer Progam Management, 1987-92, Health Care Management Review, 1988—. Mem. Colo. Gov.'s Rocky Flats Employee Health Assessment Group, 1983-84; mem. Gov.'s Breast Cancer Control Commn. Colo., 1984-89; pres., founder Oncology Mgmt. Network, Inc., 1985-95; founder, bd. dirs. Timberline Med. Assocs., 1986-87; founder, dir. So. Colo. AIDS project 1986-91; mem. adv. bd. Colo. State Bd. Health Tumor Registry, 1984-87; chmn., bd. dirs. Preferred Physicians, Inc., 1986-92; bd. dirs. Share Devel. Co. of Colo. Share Health Plan of Colo., 1986-90, vice chmn., 1989-91; bd. dirs., chmn. Preferred Health Care, Inc., 1991-92; founding dir. Pikes Peak Forum for Health Care Ethics, 1996—; mem. health care standards com., trustee Colo. Found. for Med. Care (PRO); mem. nat. bd. med. dirs. Fox Chase Cancer Ctr. Network, Phila., 1987-89; mem. tech. expert panel Harvard Resource-Based Relative Value Scale Study for Hematology/Oncology, 1991-92; founding dir. Colo. Health-care Improvement Found., 1994-95, Pike's Peak Forum Health Care Ethics, 1996—. Served with USPHS, 1965-70. Diplomate Am. Bd. Internal Medicine, Am. Bd. Med. Oncology. Mem. Am. Soc. Clin. Oncology (chmn. subcom. on oncology clin. practice standards, mem. clin. practice com., rep. to AMA 1991—, mem. healthcare svcs. rsch. com., chmn. clin. guidelines subcom. 1993—), Am. Assn. Cancer Rsch., Am. Assn. Cancer Insts. (liaison mem. bd. trustees 1980-92), Am. Coll. Physician Execs., Am. Hospice Assn., Am. Soc. Internal Medicine, Nat. Cancer Inst. (com. for community hosp. oncology program evaluation 1982-83), Colo. Soc. Internal Medicine, Assn. Community Cancer Ctrs. (chmn. membership com. 1980, chmn. clin. rsch. com. 1983-85, sec. 1983-84, pres.-elect 1984-85, pres. 1986-87, trustee 1981-88), AAAS, N.Y. Acad. Scis., Johns Hopkins Med. Soc., AMA (mem. practice parameters forum 1989—, adv. com. to HCFA on uniform clin. data set), Colo. Med. Soc., Am. Mgmt. Assn., Am. Assn. Profl. Cons., Am. Soc. for Quality Control, Am. Acad. Med. Dirs., Am. Coll. Physician Execs., El Paso County Med. Soc., Rocky Mountain Oncology Soc. (chmn. clin. practice com. 1989-94, pres.-elect 1990, pres. 1993-95), Acad. Hospice Physicians, Coalition for Cancer, Colo. Springs Clin. Club, Alpha Omega Alpha. Contbr. articles to med. jours. Office: Rocky Mountain Cancer Ctr PO Box 7148 Colorado Springs CO 80933-7148 also: 32 Sanford Rd Colorado Springs CO 80906-4233

ANDERSON, RICHARD ERNEST, agribusiness development executive, rancher; b. North Little Rock, Ark., Mar. 8, 1926; s. Victor Ernest and Lillian Josephine (Griffin) A.; m. Mary Ann Fitch, July 18, 1953; children: Vicki Lynn, Lucia Anita. BSCE, U. Ark., 1949; MSE, U. Mich., 1959. Registered profl. engr., Mich., Va., Tex., Mont. Commd. ensign USN, 1952, advanced through grades to capt., 1968, ret., 1974; v.p. Ocean Resources, Inc., Houston, 1974-77; mgr. maintenance and ops. Holmes & Narver, Inc., Orange, Calif., 1977-78; pres. No. Resources, Inc., Billings, Mont., 1978-81; v.p. Holmes & Narver, Inc., Orange, Calif., 1981-82; owner, operator Anderson Ranches, registered Arabian horses and comml. Murray Grey cows, Pony, Mont., 1982—; pres., dir. Carbon Resources Inc., Butte, Mont., 1983-88, Agri Resources, Inc., Butte, Mont., 1988-95, Anderson Holdings, Inc., Pony, Mont., 1995—. Trustee Lake Barcroft-Virginia Watershed Improvement Dist., 1973-74; pres. Lake Barcroft-Virginia Recreation Center, Inc., 1972-73. With USAAF, 1944-45. Decorated Silver Star, Legion of Merit with Combat V (2), Navy Marine Corps medal, Bronze Star with Combat V, Meritorious Service medal, Purple Heart; Anderson Peninsula in Antarctica named in his honor. Mem. ASCE, Soc. Am. Mil. Engrs. (Morrell medal 1965). Republican. Methodist. Office: Anderson Holdings Inc PO Box 266 Pony MT 59747-0266

ANDERSON, ROGER BANKS, retired surgeon; b. Albert Lea, Minn., June 13, 1918; s. Joseph Leonard and Exine Pearl (Robertson) A.; m. June Beverly Green, Sept. 1, 1939 (dec. 1986); 1 child, David Roger; m. Emily Agnes Sheldorf, Feb. 5, 1988. Student, Macalester Coll., 1936-38; D of Osteopathy, Des Moines Still Coll. Osteopathy, 1942. Diplomate Am. Osteopathic Bd. of Surgery, 1962. Intern Des Moines Gen. Hosp., 1943-44, resident, 1944-45; founder Manning (Iowa) Gen. Hosp., 1949, chmn. dept. surgery, 1951-64; staff mem. Gordon Meml. Hosp., Sioux City, Iowa, 1956-64, chmn. dept. surgery, 1957-64; staff mem. Davenport (Iowa) Osteopathic Hosp., 1964-69, chmn. dept. surgery, 1969-74; staff mem. St. Luke Hospital, Davenport, 1974-81; staff mem. dept. surgery Mercy Hosp., Davenport, 1974-81, ret., 1981; fellow in surgery Coll. Osteo. Physicians and Surgeons, L.A., 1954-55; cons. Dickinson County Meml. Hosp., Spitit Lake, Iowa, 1958-64; clin. assoc. prof. surgery Kirksville Coll. Osteopathy, 1969-77; with Iowa State Bd. Osteopathic Examiners, 1953-56, chmn., 1956-62; Iowa State Bd. Med. Examiners, 1963-75; mem. founding and adv. com. Illowa Health Planning Coun., 1967. Contbr. articles to profl. jours. Recipient Boss of the Yr. award Am. Bus. Women's Assn., 1969; recipient Disting. Svc. award West Ctrl. Iowa Healthcare Found., 1992. Fellow Am. Coll. Osteopathic Medicine and Surgery (surg.); mem. AMA, Am. Osteop. Assn. (life, del., mem. profl. affairs com. 1968-69, mem. hosp. inspection team), Nat. Alumnae Assn. (pres. 1965-66), Iowa Soc. Osteopathic Physicians and Surgeons (dist. V chmn. 1950, mem. legal and legislative com. 1952-75, chmn. legal and legislative com. 1960-75, mem. M.D.-D.O. com. 1958-75, chmn. M.D.-D.O. liaison com. 1960-75, ann. conclave chmn. 1964, pres. 1965-66), Iowa Osteopathic Med. Assn. (life), Iowa Med. Soc. (life), Scott County Med. Soc. (life, exec. com. 1979-80), Masons (32 degrees), Psi Sigma Alpha (scholar 1942). Avocations: golf, computer science. Address: 12442 Marble Dr PO Box 5048 Sun City West AZ 85376-5048

ANDERSON, ROGER WILLIAM, chemistry educator; b. Fargo, N.D., Jan. 9, 1943; s. Carl William and Ruth Anderson; m. Eva Menger, Sept. 4, 1964 (div. Aug. 1976); m. Myrna Britton, Aug. 8, 1982; children: Kirsten, Lenore. BA, Carleton Coll., Northfield, Minn., 1964; MS, Harvard U., 1965, PhD, 1968. Asst. prof. U. Calif., Santa Cruz, 1969-75, assoc. prof., 1975-90, prof. chemistry, 1991—; chair planning and budget com. U. Calif., 1995-96; cons., Calif., Ariz., 1985—. Pub. Molecular Dynamics News, 1990—. Chair Local Agy. Formation Com., Santa Cruz, Calif., 1996—; mem. Air Pollution Adv. Bd., Monterey, Calif., 1989—; mem. City Coun., Scotts Valley, Calif., 1984-88. Home: 311 Dickens Way Santa Cruz CA 95064-1065 Office: U Calif Dept Chemistry Santa Cruz CA 95064

ANDERSON, ROSS, columnist. Editorial writer, columnist The Seattle Times. Recipient Pulitzer Prize for nat. reporting, 1990. Office: The Seattle Times PO Box 70 Seattle WA 98111-0070*

ANDERSON, ROY A., aerospace company executive; b. Ripon, Calif., Dec. 15, 1920; s. Carl Gustav and Esther Marie (Johnson) A.; m. Betty Leona Boehme, 1948; 4 children. Grad. Humphrey's Sch. Bus., Stanford U. Mgr. factory acctg. Westinghouse Electric Corp., 1952-56; mgr. acctg. and fin., dir. mgmt. controls Lockheed Missiles and Space Co., 1956-65; dir. finance Lockheed Ga. Co., 1965-68; asst. treas. Lockheed Aircraft Corp. (now Lockheed-Martin Corp.), 1968-69, v.p., controller, 1969-71, sr. v.p. finance, 1971-75, vice chmn. bd. dirs., chief fin. adminstrv. officer, 1975-77, chair, CEO, 1977-85, dir., chair exec. com., 1985-88, chair emeritus, 1991—; chair, CEO Weingart Found., 1994-98; chair Oversight Bd., State of Calif., 1997-98. Avocations: tennis, golf, gardening. Office: Lockheed-Martin Corp 606 S Olive St Fl 23 Los Angeles CA 90014-1604

ANDERSON, STEPHEN HALE, federal judge; b. 1932; m. Shirlee G. Anderson. Student, Eastern Oreg. Coll. Edn., Brigham Young U.; LLB, U. Utah, 1960. Bar: Utah 1960, U.S. Claims Ct. 1963, U.S. Tax Ct. 1967, U.S. Ct. Appeals (10th cir.) 1970, U.S. Supreme Ct. 1971, U.S. Ct. Appeals (9th cir.) 1972, various U.S. Dist. Cts. Tchr. South H.S., Salt Lake City, 1956-57; trial atty. tax div. U.S. Dept. Justice, 1960-64; ptnr. Ray, Quinney & Nebeker, 1964-85; judge U.S. Ct. Appeals (10th cir.), Salt Lake City, 1985—; spl. counsel Salt Lake County Grand Jury, 1975; chmn. fed.-state jurisdiction com. Jud. Conf. U.S., 1995-98; mem. Nat. Jud. Coun. State and Fed. Cts., 1992-96; mem. ad hoc. com. on bankruptcy appellate panels 10th Cir. Jud. Coun., 1995-97; mem. various coms. U.S. Ct. Appeals (10th cir.). Editor-in-chief Utah Law Rev. Cpl. U.S. Army, 1953-55. Mem. Utah State Bar (pres. 1983-84, various offices), Salt Lake County Bar Assn. (pres. 1977-78), Am. Bar Found., Salt Lake Area C. of C. (bd. govs. 1984), U. Utah Coll. Law Alumni Assn. (trustee 1979-83, pres. 1982-83), Order of Coif. Office: US Ct Appeals 4201 Fed Bldg 125 S State St Salt Lake City UT 84138-1102

ANDERSON, STUART, retired restaurant owner, retired rancher, writer; b. Tacoma, Wash., Nov. 27, 1922; s. Roger Smedburg and Susan (Carver) A.; m. Marilyn Smith McKenzie, Sept. 1947 (div. 1957); m. Helen Elaine Fisher, Dec. 29, 1982; children: Christopher Carol, Susan Quincy. BA, U. Wash., 1947. Founder Stuart Anderson's Black Angus and Cattle Co. Restaurants, 1964-86; rancher Black Angus Cattle Co., Thorp, Wash., 1966-90, ret.; pub. spkr. Author: Here's the Beef, 1997. Bd. dirs. Wash. State 4-H Club. With U.S. Army, 1942-45. Recipient Grand Marshall award Ellensburg Rodeo, Wash., 1978. Mem. Roundtable West Literary Club. Avocations: reading, travel, golf.

ANDERSON, WILLAM CRAIG, television writer, producer; b. Ogden, Utah, July 17, 1946; s. William Glen and Margery Doris (Gorman) A.; m. Mary Lee Pearson, Dec. 22, 1970 (div. 1997); children: William Wyatt, Katharine Diane. BS in TV, Radio and Film, U. Tex., 1968, postgrad., 1968-70. Instr. U. Tex., Austin, 1970-71; film dir. Richard Kidd Prodns., Austin, 1971-72; filmmaker Lyndon B. Johnson Library, Austin, 1972-73; news cameraman, editor Sta. KERA-TV, Dallas, 1973-75; film dir. Dallas County Community Coll. Dist., 1975-81; communications mgr. May Co., Los Angeles, 1982—; prodr., dir. Not Bothered by Tigers Productions, 1996—; mem. Ind. Features Project, West. Writer, dir. (TV series): In Our Image, 1976 (Bronze award), American Government, 1979 (Silver award); writer (TV program) Divorce Court, 1984-86. Recipient Ohio State award Ohio State U., 1980, Gold Cindy Internat. Film Producers, 1977, Silver awards Internat. Film and TV Festival of N.Y., 1977, 78, 79, 80. Office: May Co 6160 Laurel Canyon Blvd North Hollywood CA 91606-3247

ANDERSON, WILLIAM, retail company executive, business education educator; b. L.A., May 21, 1923; s. William Bert and Marie (Novotney) A.; m. Margaret Lillian Phillips, Aug. 16, 1951; children: Margaret Gwen, Deborah Kay, William Keven, Denise Marie. BA in Econs., UCLA, 1948, MEd, 1957. Cert. secondary tchr. (life), Calif. Tchr. bus. edn. Big Bear Lake (Calif.) High Sch., 1949-52, Ventura (Calif.) Unified Sch. Dist. Buena High Sch., 1952-89; chief exec. officer Day's Aircraft Inc., Santa Paula, Calif., 1967—; cons. micro computers Calif. State Dept. Edn., 1983-85; pres. "Dollars for Schollars", Ventura. Crew chief Olympic Games basketball stats., 1984, basketball stats. World Games for the Deaf, 1985, U.S. Olympic Festival, 1991, vol. Calif. Police Olympics, 1989. With USAAF, 1943-45, PTO. Mem. NEA (life), Calif. Bus. Edn. Assn. (pres. So. sect. 1959-60, state sec. 1960-61, hon. life 1991), Internat. Soc. Bus. Edn. (voting del. to Soc. Internat. pour l'Enseignement Comml., Western rep. 1988-89, apptd. historian 1991, 1st Medal for Outstanding Svc. 1997), Am. Aviation Hist. Soc., Calif. Assn. Work Experience Educators (life), Air Force Assn. (life), So. Calif. Badminton Assn. (past bd. dirs.), Phi Delta Kappa, Delta Pi Epsilon (hon. life). Democrat. Lutheran. Avocations: photography, aviation history, badminton, UCLA basketball stats. Home: 334 Manzanita Ave Ven-

tura CA 93001-2227 Office: Day's Aircraft Co Inc PO Box 511 Santa Paula CA 93061-0511

ANDERSON-GRAM, JANICE, publishing executive; married; children: Zachary, Braden. BA, U. Calif., Berkeley, 1967. Lic., Nat. Assn. Securities Dealers. Securities rep. Capital Funding Corp., 1967-69; v.p. Cert. Portfolios, Inc. & Trust Cons., Inc., 1969-71; mem. corp. and regional staff, mktg. rep. IBM, 1971-78; account supr. D'Arcy, MacManus & Masius, 1978-80; prin. Coopers & Lybrand, 1980-87; freelance non-fiction writer, 1988-96; pub. Waters Edge Press, Tiburon, Calif., 1996—; arbitrator Bar Assn. San Francisco, Am. Arbitration Assn.; presenter profl. confs., instns. including Data Processing Mgrs. Assn., Am. Bankers Assn., Innovation Devel. Inst., Santa Clara County Bar Assn., San Francisco Barristers' Panels, San Francisco State U., U. Utah. Author: Poinsettias: Myth & Legend—History & Botanical Fact, 1998; contbr. articles to various publs.; guest Nancy Graham Show, Sta. WTVU-TV, and others nationwide. Mem. adv. bd. dirs. San Francisco Shakespeare, Young Audiences of Bay Area; founding chair Bay Area Children's Media Awards; mem. exec. bd. Peninsula Libr. Found., Tiburon Arts & Garden Ctr.; past bd. dirs. Children's Media Lab. Finalist Giving Something Back award Mgmt. Ctr. and Bank of Calif., Benjamin Franklin award Best New Voice, Pubs. Mktg. Assn. Mem. Am. Assn. Bot. Gardens and Arboretum, Garden Writers Assn., Bay Area Ind. Pubs. Assn. Fax: 415-435-2402. E-mail: books@watersedgepress.com. Home: 8 Venado Dr Tiburon CA 94920 Office: Waters Edge Press 98 Main St # 527 Tiburon CA 94920-2566

ANDERSSON, MARI LOUISE, writer, editor, consultant; b. Remsen, Iowa, Mar. 24, 1918; d. David and Florence (Johnson) A.; 1 child, Robert. Student, Northwestern U. Writer/editor United Meth. Pub. House, Chgo., 1961-68; mag. editor Am. Soc. Safety Engrs., 1968-69; asst. Latin Am. affairs, protocol officer State of Ill., Chgo., 1969-72; freelance writer newspapers, mags. Editor: The Spruce Goose, Seekers of the Spring, The Gladiator, The Galloping Swede, The Greek Portico, China Adventure, Antarctic Adventure; author: Wry Goods, Fancy Notions, Altercations to Suit; contbr. articles to newspapers, mags. Named Writer of Yr., Christian Writers Guild, 1985, Calif. Press Women, 1985. Mem. Nat. Fedn. Press Women, Conn. Press Club (1st pres., Woman of Achievement 1979), Mensa (assoc. editor, OWL award). Methodist. Avocations: writing, reading. Home and Office: PO Box 1521 Carlsbad CA 92018-1521

ANDRASICK, JAMES STEPHEN, agribusiness company executive; b. Passaic, N.J., Mar. 27, 1944; s. Stephen Adam and Emily (Spolnik) A.; children: Christopher J., Gregory O.; m. Ginger Michael Simon, Feb. 22, 1997. BS, USCG Acad., 1965; MS, MIT, 1971. Commd. ensign USCG, 1965, advanced through grades to lt., 1968; assigned to Vietnam, 1967-68; resigned, 1969; sys. analyst Jamesbury Corp., 1970; corp. fin. and product devel. staffs Ford Motor Co., 1971-74; mgr. corp. devel. IU Internat. Corp., Phila., 1974-78; from v.p. planning, contr. to exec. v.p. C. Brewer & Co., Ltd., Honolulu, 1978-92, pres., 1992—, also bd. dirs.; chmn. bd., mng. gen. ptnr. ML Macadamia Orchards LP, 1986-88; chmn. bd. HCPC, Olokele Sugar Co., Hawaiian Sugar and Transp. Coop., 1993-96; chmn. Hawaiian Sugar Planters Assn., 1992-93; bd. dirs. Wailuku Agribus. Co. Bd. dirs. Aloha United Way, Honolulu, 1983-89; treas., bd. dirs. ARC, Hawaii, 1983-94, 96—, chmn., 1989-90; bd. dirs. Hawaii Employers Coun., 1992-98, chmn., 1995-98; trustee UH Found., 1988-94, vice chmn., 1992-93, chmn., 1993-94; trustee Hawaii Maritime Ctr., 1993-98; bd. dirs. Coast Guard Found., chmn., 1994. Office: C Brewer & Co Ltd PO Box 1826 Papaikou HI 96781-1826

ANDREASEN, STEVEN W., lawyer; b. Salt Lake City, Sept. 17, 1948. BA, U. Utah, 1970, JD, 1974. Bar: Washington 1974. Mem. Davis Wright Tremaine, Seattle, 1974—. Comment Editor: Utah Law Review 1973-74. Mem. Seattle Estate Planning Coun., Order of Coif, Am. Coll. Trust and Estate Counsel. Office: Davis Wright Tremaine LLP 2600 Century Sq 1501 4th Ave Ste 2600 Seattle WA 98101-1688*

ANDREASON, SHARON LEE, sculptor; b. Lebanon, Oreg., Mar. 20, 1937; d. LeRoy and Galdys Edwina (Wells) A.; m. Raymond Locke Eller, Aug. 30, 1957 (div. 1981); 1 child, Jordan Lee; m. Stoddard Pintard Johnston, Dec. 21, 1985 (div. 1998). Student, UCLA, 1983. Performing artist Screen Extras Guild, Hollywood, Calif., 1962-70; profl. artist, Carmel, Calif., 1981—, Gaucín, Spain, 1998—. Sculptor: solo shows include Pacific Grove Art Ctr., 1984, Zantman Art Gallery, Carmel, 1989, Highlands Sculpture Gallery, Carmel, 1991, 92, 93, Galeria Brisamar, Marbella, Spain, 1993, Smith Cosby Gallery, Carmel, 1995, Silver Light Gallery, Carmel, 1996, 97, 98, 99, Marin-Price Galleries, 1997, Linnemann Gallery, Chgo., 1998, Galerie de Sculpture, Paris, 1999; group exhbns. include Monterey County (Calif.) Mus. Art, 1984, Gallery Mack, Seattle, 1993, Am. Acad. Equine Art, Ky. Horse Park, Lexington, 1993, 94, 95, Galeria Seris, Madrid, 1993, Galeries Kriesler, Madrid, 1994, 95, Galeria Brisamar, Marbella, 1995, Galeria Sculpture, Paris, 1995, 96, 98, Signature Gallery, Del Mar, Calif., 1995, Signature Gallery, San Diego, 1995, Galeria Iris Ryman, Marbella, 1996, Nova Galeria De Arte, Malaga, Spain, 1996, 97, 98, 99, Ky. Derby Mus., Louisville, 1996, 97, Klausner/Cooperage Gallery, Louisville, 1995-97, 98, Perry House Gallery Competitives, Alexandria, 1997, Harpe Galeria, Galeria de Sculptures, Marbella, Spain, 1997, 98, 99, Gallery 444 Post, San Francisco, 1997, 98, 99, Reflections Gallery, Santa Fe, 1997, 98, 99, Linnemann Gallery, Chgo., 1997-98, Montecito Art and Frame Gallery, Santa Barbara, 1998, 99; most of her works are reproduced in bronze and sold for pvt. and pub. collections; represented in collections internationally. Pres., founder Horse Power Internat., Inc., 1989-97; founder Horse Power Sanctuaries, Inc.; founder Horse Power Protection Projects, Inc., 1991-97; authored horse protection legislation Sacramento, Calif., 1993-94. Recipient Gwendolyn May award, Monterey County SPCA, Monterey, Calif., 1994. Mem. Artists Equity, Women's Mus. of Art, Conv. on the Welfare and Protection of Animals in Transit (N.Am. Free Trade Agreement animal legis. group), Internat. Sculpture Ctr., Pacific Rim Sculptors Group, Monterey Peninsula Mus. of Art, Sculpture Soc. Ireland. Avocations: horse riding and related activities, ancient art and civilizations, travel. E-mail: andreasons@aol.com. Studios: PO Box 998 Carmel CA 93921-0998 also: Apartado 65 Gaucin, 29480 Malaga Spain

ANDREOPOULOS, SPYROS GEORGE, writer; b. Athens, Greece, Feb. 12, 1929; came to U.S., 1953, naturalized, 1962; s. George S. and Anne (Levas) A.; m. Christiane Loesch Loriaux, June 6, 1958; 1 child, Sophie. AB, Wichita State U., 1957. Pub. info. specialist USIA, Salonica, Greece, 1951-53; asst. editorial page editor Wichita (Kans.) Beacon, 1955-59; asst. dir. info. svcs., editor The Menninger Quar., The Menninger Found., Topeka, 1959-63; info. officer Stanford U. Med. Ctr., 1963-83; dir. comm., editor Stanford Medicine, 1983-93, dir. emeritus comm., editor emeritus, 1993—; editor Sun Valley Forum on Nat. Health, Inc. (Idaho), 1972-83, 85-95. Co-author, editor: Medical Cure and Medical Care, 1972, Primary Care: Where Medicine Fails, 1974, National Health Insurance: Can We Learn from Canada? 1975, Heart Beat, 1978, Health Care for an Aging Society, 1989; contbr. articles to newspapers and profl. jours. With Royal Hellenic Air Force, 1949-50. Mem. AAAS, Assn. Am. Med. Colls., Nat. Assn. Sci. Writers, Am. Med. Writers Assn., Am. Hosp. Assn., Am. Soc. Hosp. Mktg. and Pub. Rels., Coun. for Advancement and Support of Edn. Home: 1012 Vernier Pl Stanford CA 94305-1027

ANDRESS, CATHY, psychologist, educator; b. Akron, Ohio, June 17, 1960; d. Samuel Coe and Joan (Ferguson) A. BA, Randolph-Macon Woman's Coll., 1982; MA, So. Ill. U., Edwardsville, 1985; PsyD, Chgo. Sch. Profl. Psychology, 1991. Child and family therapist No. Wyo. Mental Health Ctr., Newcastle, 1988-89; sr. therapist Tri-City Community Mental Health Ctr., East Chicago, Ind., 1990; part-time instr. Oakton C.C., Des Plaines, Ill., 1989-91, adj. counselor, 1991; part-time instr. Northeastern Ill. Univ., Chgo., 1990-91; instr. psychology Big Bend C.C., Moses Lake, Wash., 1991-97. Mem. AAUW, Assn. for Humanistic Psychology, Assn. for Transpersonal Psychology.

ANDREW, JANE HAYES, non-profit organization executive; b. Phila., Jan. 1, 1947; d. David Powell and Vivian Muriel (Saeger) Hayes; m. Brian David Andrew, June 14, 1977; 1 child, Kevin Hayes. AB, Barnard Coll., 1968, grad., Harvard Arts Administrn. Instit., 1972; MBA, U. Wash., 1994. Mgr. theater Minor Latham Playhouse, Barnard Coll., N.Y.C., 1970-74; co. mgr. Houston Ballet, 1974-77, Ballet West, Salt Lake City, 1978-83; gen. mgr. Pacific N.W. Ballet, Seattle, 1983-87; organizer non-profit consortium nat. ballet cos. and nat. presenting orgns., 1987; pres., exec. dir. Ballet/America, 1988-91; ind. cons. arts mgmt., 1991-94; dir. Found. for Internat. Understanding Through Students, 1995-97; panelist NEA Dance Program Presentors, 1987-88, 88-89, 89-90, Seattle Arts Commn. dance grants, 1989, 90; cons. Ariz. Arts Commn., Phoenix, 1985-86; com. mem. 25th Anniversary of World's Fair, Seattle, 1986-87; panelist NEA Local Programs, 1987; vol. Interlace H.S., 1997. Editor (directory) Philadelphia Cultural Orgns., 1977. Bd. dirs. Good Shepherd Adv. Bd., Seattle, 1985-87. Recipient Dorothy D. Spivack award Barnard Coll., N.Y.C., 1972. Mem. Dance/USA (chmn. Mgrs. Coun. 1986). Home and Office: 7706 146th Ave NE Redmond WA 98052-4105

ANDREWS, AARON JOHN, recreational facility executive; b. Merced, Calif., July 12, 1941; s. B.P. and Pearline Alice (Kuhlman) A.; m. Sandra Jean Coile, Oct. 3, 1963; children: Kimberly Aaron, Kevin Scott. AA, Merced Coll., 1970. Gen. mgr. Pine Lane/Branding Iron, Merced, 1957-87, Merced Golf and Country Club, 1987-96; contr. Allco Mfg., Merced, 1997-98; gen. mgr. Yuma (Ariz.) Golf and Country Club, 1998—; cons. A.J. Consulting, Merced, 1993—. Bd. dirs. Prop Warner Football, pres., 1974-75; bd. dirs. Merced Coll., v.p., 1986-87; bd. dirs. Jurinor Golf, pres., 1988-96. Republican. Roman Catholic. Avocations: cycling, weight lifting, painting, golf, volunteer work. Home: 3210 Kernland Ave Merced CA 95340-1644 Office: Yuma Golf and Country Club PO Box 2048 Yuma AZ 85366-2048

ANDREWS, CAROL LYNN, producer, writer; b. Ladysmith, Wis., Sept. 14, 1940; d. Clarence G. and Bessie (Andrews) Christopherson. BA, U. Wash., 1962; MA, U. Pa., 1963. Writer Seven Keys, Hollywood, Calif., 1963; assoc. prodr. Let's Make a Deal, Hollywood, 1964-84; freelance writer L.A., 1984-93; assoc. prodr. Hallet St. Prodns., Beverly Hills, Calif., 1993—. Mem. Writers Guild of Am.

ANDREWS, DONALD L., performing arts company executive. Pres., CEO Utah Symphony, Salt Lake City. Office: Utah Symphony Maurice Abravanel Hall 123 W South Temple Salt Lake City UT 84101-1496*

ANDREWS, FREDERICK M., marketing analyst; b. Lafayette, Ind., June 30, 1942; s. Frederick Newcomb and Gertrude Evelyn (Martin) A.; m. Angelika Bartels, July 23, 1971; 1 child: Sandra Claire. BS in Indsl. Mgmt., Purdue U., 1965; postgrad., U. London, 1968-69, 71-72. With sales dept. Boeing Co., Seattle, 1973-78, mktg. analyst, 1978—; contract mgr. Ctrl. Navigation and Trading Co., Saigon, Vietnam, 1969-71. Trustee Young Reps. (King County), Seattle, 1976; chmn. Rep. 35th Dist., 1977-79, 11th Dist., 1986-88. Capt. USAR, 1965-68. Named Bd. Mem. of Yr., King County Rep. Club, Seattle, 1984. Mem. AIAA (sr.), USAF Assn. (life), Wash. State Mainstream Reps. (bd. dirs. 1988-89). Avocations: skiing, sailing, politics. Office: Boeing MC 21-36 PO Box 3707 Seattle WA 98124-2207

ANDREWS, LEROY MILES, architect; b. Hughesville, Calif., May 20, 1921; s. Miles Charles and Mollie Ursula (Guinter) A.; m. Margaret Eva Day, Apr. 25, 1943; children: Donald Fred, Dean Allen. AA, Ventura Coll., 1956. Registered architect, Calif., Ariz.; cert. Nat. Coun. Archtl. Registration Bds. Aeronautical engr. Lycoming Divsn. Avco, Williamsport, Pa., 1942-43, Bell Aircraft, Marietta, Ga., 1943-46, Northrop Aircraft, Hawthorne, Calif., 1948-50; engr. E E Co. of Calif., Pt. Mugu, 1950-53; pres. LeRoy Andrews Architects, Inc., Ventura, 1953—. Inventor in field. Mem. AIA (chpt. pres. 1996), Am. Fedn. Musicians, Masons, Rotary (Paul Harris fellow 1991-92, club pres. 1991-92). Republican. Methodist. Avocations: piano, band leading, composing. Office: LeRoy Andrews Architects Inc 2319 Alameda Ave Ste 2A Ventura CA 93003-6675

ANDREWS, RALPH HERRICK, television producer; b. Chgo., Dec. 17, 1927; s. Henry Karl and Sylvia Angelica (Lorenzen Barth; m. Margaret Ann Belt, Feb. 5, 1951 (div. 1977); m. Aleksandra Vaz vel Wezykowska, June 1, 1986; children: William, Herrick, Phyllis, Patrice, Peter, James, Jakub, Matthew. Announcer, disc jockey, salesman radio stas. WSAM and WKNX, Saginaw, Mich.; page NBC, Hollywood; with Don Fedderson Prodns., Ralph Edwards Prodns.; dir. live programming Desilu; prin. Ralph Andrews Prodns.; co-founder, bd. dirs. Entertainment Industries Coun. Producer: Divorce Hearing, By the Numbers, Zoom, Show Me, You Don't Say, I'll Bet, Wedding Party, The Family Game, It Takes Two, It's Your Bet, Liars Club, The Mickie Finn Show, Celebrity Sweepstakes, 50 Grand Slam, Lingo, (movies) Silent Treatment, Skyjacked; producer, host: Lie Detector. Cand. for Congress, 1972; nat. dir. edn. and tng. Rep. Nat. Com., Washington, 1972 (Presidential commendation). Republican. Roman Catholic. Avocations: skiing, flying, skating, running, sailing. Home and Office: 5449 Paradise Valley Rd Hidden Hills CA 91302-2435

ANDREWS, WILLIAM SCOTT, investment advisor; b. Miami, Fla., June 22, 1955; s. George Allen and Jeanette Ann (Kronen) A. CFP, Coll. for Fin. Planning, 1982; BS in Mktg., Fla. Internat. U., 1991. Agt. Union Cen. Life, Cin., 1979-82; pres. Andrews & Assocs., Miami, 1982-88; gen. mgr. Lombard Ins. Brokers, Miami, 1988-90; registered rep. Mktg. One Securities Inc., Portland, Oreg., 1990—; mem. securities sales task force Am. Savs. and Loan, Miami, 1992. Patron Camilus House for the Homeless, Miami, 1991-92; sponsor St. Louis Cath. Ch., Miami, 1990-92. Home: 9530 Windrose Ln Granite Bay CA 95746-6486

ANDRIANO-MOORE, RICHARD GRAF, naval officer; b. Petaluma, Calif., May 25, 1932; s. Norvel Moore and Thelma Elizabeth (Cook) Koch-Andriano Atkins; m. Janice Lynn Hironaka, Jan. 10, 1976 (div. Feb. 1990); children: Erika Lynn, Stephen Albert. BA, San Jose State U., 1956; MBA, Pepperdine U., 1977; B in Metaphysical Sci., U. Metaphysics, 1993. Commd. ens. USN, 1957, advanced through grades to comdr.; 1st lt., and gunnery officer U.S.S. Jefferson Count LST1068, 1957-60; 7th grade tchr. Oasis Sch., Riverside County, Calif., 1960-63; pers. and legal officer U.S.S. Maury AGS-16, 1963-65; commdg. officer Naval & Marine Corps reserve Training Ctrl., Port Arthur, Tex., 1965-68; ops. officer U.S.S. Muliphen LKA 64, 1968-69; ASW & surface program officer 11th Naval Dist., San Diego, 1970-74; commdg. officer Naval Reserve Ctrl., Hunters Point, Calif., 1974-75, Army, Navy & Marine Corps Reserve Ctr, San Bruno, Calif., 1975-79; dir. of adminstrn. Nat. Com. for Employer, Washington, 1979-82; comdr., regional recruiting coord. for 10 western states, Alameda, Calif., 1982-84; chief of staff N.R. Readiness comdr., Treasure Island, Calif., 1984-85; tchr. Shoreline Unified Sch. Dist., Tomales, Calif., 1985-92, 94-99. Editor-in-chief: California Compatriot, 1976-80. Insp. Precinct Bd., Petaluma, Calif., 1987-90; scoutmaster Boy Scouts Am., 1989-92, dist. exec., 1992-94. Decorated Defense Meritorious Svc. medal Sec. of Def., Washington, 1982; recipient Ancestral Coat of Arms of the Counts of Andriano, Wappenrolle, Austria, 1985, Rome, Italy, 1994, Disting. Alumni award San Jose State U., 1991; knighted Order St. John of Jerusalem Knights Hospitaller, 1991. Mem. The Augustan Soc. Inc. (v.p. 1990-93, bd. dirs. 1995-99), Calif. Soc. SAR (state pres. 1986-87, San Francisco chpt. pres. 1976-77, Silver Good Citizenship medal 1978, Patriot medal 1985, Meritorious Svc. medal 1987, oak leaf cluster 1996), Mil. Order of Loyal Legion of U.S. (Calif. comdr. 1982-88), Naval Order U.S. Avocations: reading, hiking, biking, traveling, abstract artist. Office: 1253 Bertha Ln Santa Rosa CA 95405-7003

ANDRING, RONALD PAUL, protective services official; b. Yakima, Wash., Apr. 17, 1953; s. Richard Joseph and JeRene Estelle (Krienke) A.; m. Margaret Anne Yount, Jan. 13, 1978; children: Margaret Ann, Ronald Paul Jr. BA in Criminal Justice, Ea. Wash. U., 1990, MPA, 1995. Enforcement officer Wash. State Patrol, Kennewick, 1975-78, Walla Walla (Wash.) Police Dept., 1978-79; correctional officer Wash. State Penitentiary, Walla Walla, 1979-89, adminstrv. asst., 1990-91, correctional sgt., 1991-98, correctional lt., 1998—; mem. regional adv. com. Dept. Corrections, Olympia, Wash., 1991-93, trainer, 1988-97; adj. faculty Ea. Wash. U., Cheney, 1997—. Contbr. articles to profl. jours. and mags. Organizer Jr. Achievement awards, Walla Walla, 1991-93, Kid's Classic Fun Run, Walla Walla, 1991-93; candidate 14th legis. dist. Dem. Cen. Com., Wash., 1972; vol. Friends and Families of Violent Crime Victims, 1989-92; chair publs. com. Blue Ridge PTA, 1989-91. Recipient Pub. Adminstrn. Honors Student award Ea. Wash. U., 1995. Mem. Am. Correctional Assn. (adv. com. 1991—, del. assembly 1994—, coord. mid-winter conf., 1995, 96, 125th congress of corrections, vice chair mem. com. 1996-97, com. mem. coun. congress programs 1996-99, chair com. congress program planning 1999), Wash. Correctional Assn. (exec. bd. 1989—, treas. 1994-95, Spl. Svc. award 1993, pres. 1996—), Western Correctional Assn., Am. Criminological Soc., Am. Platform Assn., Masons (master 1992-93), Scottish Rite. Congregationalist. Avocations: reading, gardening, outdoor recreation, travel, woodworking. Home: 502 W Chestnut St Walla Walla WA 99362-3963 Office: Washington State Penitentiary 1313 N 13th St Walla Walla WA 99362-0520

ANDRUS, CECIL DALE, academic administrator; b. Hood River, Oreg., Aug. 25, 1931; s. Hal Stephen and Dorothy (Johnson) A.; m. Carol Mae May, Aug. 27, 1933; children: Tana Lee, Tracy Sue, Kelly Kay. Student, Oreg. State U., 1948-49; LLD (hon.), Gonzaga U., U. Idaho, U. N.Mex., Coll. Idaho, Idaho State U., Whitman Coll. State gen. mgr. Paul Revere Life Ins. Co., 1969-70; gov. State of Idaho, 1971-77, 87-95; sec. of interior, 1977-81; chmn. Andrus Ctr. for Pub. Policy, Boise (Idaho) State U., 1995—; bd. dirs. KeyCorp., Albertson's, Inc., Coeur d'Alene Mines; mem. Idaho Senate, 1961-66, 69-70; mem. exec. com. Nat. Gov.'s Conf., 1971-72, chmn., 1976; chmn. Fedn. Rocky Mountain States, 1971-72. Chmn. bd. trustees Coll. of Idaho, 1985-89; bd. dirs. Sch. Forestry, Duke U. With USN, 1951-55. Recipient Disting. Citizen award Oreg. State U., 1980, Collier County Conservancy medal, 1979, Ansel Adams award Wilderness Soc., 1985, Audubon medal, 1985, Statesman of the Yr. award Idaho State U., 1990, Torch of Liberty award B'nai B'rith, 1991; named Conservationist of Yr. Nat. Wildlife Fedn., 1980, Idaho Wildlife Fedn., 1972, Man of Yr., VFW, 1959. Mem. VFW, Idaho Taxpayers Assn. (bd. dirs. 1964-66). Democrat. Office: Boise State U Andrus Ctr Pub Policy 1910 University Dr Boise ID 83725-0399*

ANDURI, CARL ENOCH, JR., lawyer; b. Visalia, Calif., Sept. 2, 1946; s. Carl Enoch Sr. and Mary Elizabeth (Starns) A.; m. Sharon Louise Woodnutt, June 28, 1970; children: Eric Carl, Lauren Mary. AB, Stanford U., 1968; JD, Yale U., 1974. Bar: Calif. 1974, N.Y. 1983. Assoc. Morrison & Foerster, San Francisco, 1974-80, ptnr., 1980-82; mng. ptnr. Hong Kong office Morrison & Foerster, Hong Kong, 1982-86; mng. ptnr. Tokyo office Morrison & Foerster, Tokyo, 1986-91; ptnr., coord. internat. practice Morrison & Foerster, San Francisco, 1991—. Mem. Inter-Pacific Bar Assn. (pres. 1995-96), Japan Soc. of Northern Calif., (pres., 1999—). Office: Morrison & Foerster LLP 425 Market St Ste 3100 San Francisco CA 94105-2482

ANGEL, ARMANDO CARLOS, rheumatologist, internist; b. Las Vegas, N.Mex., Mar. 25, 1940; s. Edmundo Clemente and Pauline Teresa (Flores) Sanchez A.; m. Judith Lee Weedin, Aug. 5, 1961; children: Stephanie, Renee. BA, San Jose State U., 1963; MS, U. Ariz., 1970, PhD, 1971, M.D., 1977. Chemist Tracerlab, Inc., Richmond, Calif., 1963-67; prof. chemistry Pima Coll., Tucson, Ariz., 1971-74; intern U. N.Mex., Albuquerque, 1977-78, resident, 1978-80; resident VA Hosp., Lovelace Med. Ctr., Albuquerque, 1978-80; practice medicine specializing in internal medicine, Las Cruces, N.Mex., 1980-88; pvt. practice, El Paso, Tex., 1990—; dir. pain program Rio Vista Rehab. Hosp., 1992; med. dir. Ctr. for Rehab. and Evaluation, 1992—; chief of staff Rio Vista Rehab. Hosp., 1997—; with Estrella Cons. Group, 1999—; cons. minority biomed. sci. project NIH, Washington, 1970-74, Ednl. Assocs., Tucson, 1971-74. Author: Llevve Tlaloc No. 2, 1973. Treas. Nat. Chicano Health Orgn., Los Angeles, 1974-75; v.p. Mexican-Am. Educators, Tucson, 1973-74; pres. N.Mex. affiliate Am. Diabetes Assn., Albuquerque, 1983-85. Fellow U. Ariz., 1988-90. Fellow Am. Coll. Rheumatology; mem. AMA, Tex. Med. Soc., El Paso County Medical Soc., Am. Diabetes Assn., ACP, Dona Ana County Med. Soc. (pres. 1983), Am. Coll. Rheumatology, Am. Assn. Internal Medicine, Alpha Chi Sigma.

ANGEL, STEVEN, musician; b. Bklyn., Aug. 2, 1953; s. Morris and Rosalyn (Sobiloff) A. Grad. H.S., L.I. Pres. Daystar Records, Santa Monica, Calif., 1991—; profl. drummer, 1960—; lectr. The Whole Life Expo, Pasadena, 1992-95, Inst. for the Advanced Studies of Human Sexuality, San Francisco; drum therapist, 1998—; drum therapist, 1998—. Author (music and book) Angels Rejoice, 1976-80; wrote music for tv show Another World, 1987-91; wrote, recorded, produced three songs for Playboy album Music for Lovers, 1993; wrote, recorded, produced album The Erotic God, 1993; editor Unity and Difference Jour., 1994-97. Avocations: tennis, hiking, running. Home and Office: Daystar Records 2132 Montana Ave Apt B Santa Monica CA 90403-2017

ANGELE, ALFRED ROBERT, police labor union executive; b. N.Y.C., Dec. 9, 1940; s. Alfred Otto and Alma Margaret (Branda) A.; m. Barbara Ann Chavez, Sept. 30, 1961; children: Cynthia Lynn, Lynda Renee. AA, L.A. Valley Coll., 1968. Cert. tchr. community coll. police adminstrn. Patrolman Burbank (Calif.) Police Dept., 1963-67, detective, 1967-74, sgt., dept. self def. instr., 1974-78; gen. mgr. Calif. Orgn. Police and Sheriffs, Sacramento, 1978-89, exec. dir., 1989—; internat. sec./treas. Internat. Union Police Assns. AFL-CIO, Alexandria, Va., 1985-90; internat. sec./treas. emeritus Internat. Union Police Assns. AFL-CIO, Alexandria, 1990-92; Govt. appt. commr. on Peace Officer Standards/Tng., Sacramento, 1979-84; mem. AFL-CIO observer team sent to Nicaragua to monitor presdl. election, 1990, Police Adv. Coun. on Car Clubs, 1967-70; mem. exch. progrm with German Police Union, 1987. Contbr. articles to profl. jours. including USA Today. Mem. L.A. Host committee for nat. tour Bill of Rights, 1991. Recipient Mike Maggiora Meml. Humanitarian award Maggiora family, 1980, Commendations, Letters of Appreciation Burbank Bar Assn., Elks, Calif. Hwy. Patrol, Mayor's Drug and Alcohol Abuse Com., L.A. County Dist. Atty.'s Office, Houston Police Patrolmans Union, Calif. Dept. Corrections, Mayor of L.A., numerous others; named 1st Officer of the Month Jaycees, 1977. Mem. Burbank Police Officers Assn. (pres. 1976-81, named dir. of yr. 1972, commendation award), Internat. Union Police Assns. AFL-CIO (sec.-treas. 1985—, dir. 1981-85, named law enforcement editor of the yr. 1987), Calif. Narcotics Officers Assn., Calif. Orgn. Police/Sheriffs (gen. mgr. 1978—, sec. 1976-78, commendation award), Calif. Narcotics Info. Network. Democrat. Roman Catholic. Avocations: home remodeling, music, restoring cars. Office: 301 E Olive Ave Ste 224 Burbank CA 91502-1216

ANGELO, CHRISTOPHER EDMOND, lawyer, consultant; b. L.A., Dec. 19, 1949; s. Edmond James and Shirley Ann (Richards) A.; m. Patrice Lonnette Brown, Apr. 26, 1980; 1 child, Alexander Bradshaw. BA, U. Calif., Riverside, 1972; JD, Loyola U., 1975. Bar: Calif. 1976, U.S. Dist. Ct. Calif. 1976. Trial atty. Spray, Gould & Bowers, L.A., 1976-78, Harrington, Foxx, Dubrow & Canter, L.A., 1978-83, Gage & Mazursky, Beverly Hills, Calif., 1983-85; trial atty., ptnr. Gage, Mazursky, Schwartz, Angelo & Kussman, Beverly Hills, Calif., 1986-88; trial atty., gen. ptnr. Mazursky, Schwartz & Angelo, L.A., 1988—; faculty lectr. Calif. Judges Assn., 1989; mem. Loyola Law Sch. Law Review, L.A., 1974-75. Author books and articles in field of tort and ins. bad faith liability. Cons. Bet Tzedak Legal Aid Found., L.A., 1992; counsel Christopher Sampson Non-Profit Found. for Catastrophically Injured, L.A., 1991, dir., founder. Recipient Highlander scholarship U. Calif., 1968-72. Mem. ABA, Italian Am. Lawyers Assn. (bd. govs. 1979-83), Calif. Trial Lawyers Assn. (lectr. 1983—, Cert. of Appreciation), Calif. Bar Assn., Consumer Attys. Assn. L.A. (lectr. 1983—, Cert. of Appreciation). Office: Mazursky Schwartz & Angelo 10990 Wilshire Blvd Ste 1200 Los Angeles CA 90024-3927

ANGELOV, GEORGE ANGEL, pediatrician, anatomist, teratologist; b. Bulgaria, May 12, 1925; came to U.S., 1978; s. Angel Christov and Maria Angelov; m. Olga Valerie Minkova, Dec. 21, 1952; 1 child, Angel. MD, Sch. of Medicine, Sofia, Bulgaria, 1952. Pediatrician Distric Hosp., Bulgaria, 1952-53; asst. prof. Sch. of Medicine, Sofia, Bulgaria, 1953-64; prof. anatomy and anthropology Sch. of Biology, Sofia, Bulgaria, 1964-77; mgr. reproductive toxicology Lederle Labs., Pearl River, N.Y., 1979-89; cons. reproductive toxicology pvt. practice, Laguna Niguel, Calif., 1989—; assoc. dean Sch. of Biology, Sofia, 1970-72; vis. scientist Sch. of Medicine, Geneva, 1971, 74. Author: (textbook) Anatomy, 1970; mem. glossary com. Teratology Glossary, 1987-89; reviewer several sci. jours.; contbr. numerous sci. publs. on anatomy, teratology, and growth and devel. of adolescents to profl. jours. Mem. Teratology Soc. USA, European Teratology Soc., Human Biology Coun. USA, Free Union of Univ. Profs. of Anatomy. East Orthodox. Avocations: bridge, chess, 20th century history.

ANGOTTI, ANTONIO MARIO, international merchant, banker; b. Whittier, Calif., Jan. 15, 1958; s. Anna Maria (Massei) Angotti. BA, U. Calif.,

Berkeley, 1981; postgrad., Cambridge U., Eng., 1981-82. With Paul H. Nitze Sch. Advanced Internat. Studies, Johns Hopkins U., 1982-84; assoc. Citicorp Investment Bank, N.Y.C., 1984-85; v.p. Bear Stearns & Co., Inc., N.Y.C., 1985-87; v.p., dir. sovereign debt Security Pacific Mcht. Bank, N.Y.C., 1987-89; White House fellow, spl. asst. to Sec. of State U.S. Dept. State, Washington, 1989-90; chmn. bd. Calif. World Trade Ctrs., Inc., Long Beach, 1991-93; mem. adv. bd. Bologna Ctr., Johns Hopkins, Washington, coll. letters and sci. U. Calif. Mem. Fgn. Policy Assn., 1987; co-chair U. Calif. Berkeley, N.Y.C. campaign com., Coun. of 1000, Nat. Italian Am. Found., The Asia Found., Friends of the Philippines, Robert Scalapino Scholarship Fund, U. Calif.; Leadership So. Calif., 1993; presdl. appt. The White House, 1989. Walter Haas Meml. scholar, 1980-81; named Brit.-Am. Successor Generation, 1990, U.S.-Italy Next Generation Leaders, 1988. Mem. Acad. Polit. Sci., U. Calif. Alumni Assn., Johns Hopkins U. Alumni Assn. Roman Catholic. Office: Calif World Trade Ctrs Inc 7825 Fay Ave Ste 200 La Jolla CA 92037-4270

ANJARD, RONALD PAUL, SR., business and industry executive, consultant, educator, technologist, importer, author; b. Chgo., July 31, 1935; s. Auguste L. and Florence M. (Byrne) A.; m. Marie B. Sampler; children: Ronald Paul Jr., Michael P., Michele M., John R. BS in Metall. Engring., Carnegie Mellon U., 1957; MS/MBA in Indsl. Adminstrn., Purdue U., 1968; AS in Supervision, Ind. U., 1973; BS, U. State of N.Y., 1978; PDE, U. Wis., 1976; BA in Humanities, USNY, 1979; PhD in Edn., Columbia Pacific U., 1981, PhD in Metall. Engring., 1982; postgrad., Ind. U. Law Sch., 1975, La. State U., 1978, U. Calif., 1978; MS in Computer Resource Mgmt., Webster U., 1992; postgrad., U. Calif. Berkeley, 1978, La State U., 1979. Metallurgist U.S. Steel Corp., Braddock, Pa., 1956-57; metall. engr. Crucible Steel Co., Pitts., 1957-58; process engr. Raytheon Mfg. Co., Newton, Mass., 1958-59; program mgmt. engr. Delco Electronics div. GM, Kokomo, Ind., 1959-81; div. quality mgr. AVX Materials Div. Delco Electronics div. GM, Kokomo, 1981-82, div. quality mgr., JMI Electronic Materials div., 1982-83; v.p. engring. AG Tech, 1983—; pres. Anjard Internat. Cons., 1983, 86—, Anjard Solder Paste Tech., 1983—, Anjard Solder and Mfg. Tech., 1987—; corp. dir. quality Kaypro Corp., 1983-87; pres. Anjard Imports, 1965-80, 92—; sr. bank officer Mission Viejo (Calif.) Nat. Bank, 1986-87; v.p. mktg. Alpha Cast Products, 1987-93; v.p. adminstrn. Triage Network, 1988-93; sr. exec. broker Futures Investment Firm, 1983; quality cons. Gen. Dynamics, Convair, 1987, 92; SPC coord. Gen. Dynamics Electronics Div., 1989-94; distbr. Vertical Computer System, 1987; free-lance writer, photographer, 1966—; retail salesman Nurseryland, 1987-88; prof. Calif. Nat. U., 1993—, U. United States, 1995—; instr. Ball State U., 1970-71, 75-76, Kokomo Apprentice Program, 1971-81, Ind. Vocat. Tech. Coll., 1978-81, U. Phoenix, 1983, U. So. Calif., 1985-90, U. La Verne, 1985-92, Ala. A&M U., 1983, Chapman Coll., 1983-92, Nat. U., 1982-83, San Diego Community Coll., 1984—, U. Calif. San Diego, 1986-92, Golden State U., 1986-92, U. La Jolla, San Diego Job Corps, Union of Experimental Colls. and Univs., 1987—, Karanovich Counseling Ctr., Cen. Tex. Coll., 1987-92, numerous others; thesis mentor Columbia Pacific U., 1981—. Rev. editor Solid State Tech., rev. edit. Microelectronics and Reliability, 1982—, Ceram, 1985—, IEEE Circuits and Devices, 1985-93; contbr. to tech. and non-tech. publs. Pres. Greater Kokomo Assn. Chs., 1972-74; chmn. Diocesan Pastoral Council, Diocese Layfayette, Ind., 1977-78, diocesan ecumenical officer, 1972-78, diocesan impact coordinator, 1972-81; mem. Ascension Council, 1984—; active Ind. Council Chs., 1971-81; mem. San Diego Ecumenical Coun., 1995—; mem. Tierra Santa Town Council, 1988-90; councilman Howard County Council, Ind., 1981; trustee Clay Twp., 1970-75; dir. 5th dist. Ind. Twp. Trustees Assn.; vice chmn. Ind. State U. Young Republicans; del. Rep. State Conv., 1970, 74, 78, 80, dep. registration officer, 1970, 72, 74, 76, 80; mem. Rep. Nat. Com., 1970-75, mem. San Diego Rep. Cen. Com.; resolutions chmn. Young Reps. Conv., 1969; state minority chmn., dir. Howard County Young Reps.; regional dir. Leadership Tng. Sch.; chmn. 5th Dist. Young Reps.; mem. San Diego Rep. Cen. Com., 1985—; mem. Ind. State Com. for Med. Assistance, Ind. Citizens Adv. Council on Alcoholism, Ind. Citizens Council on Addictions, Mayor's Human Rights Com.; active Meshingomesia council Boy Scouts Am.; chmn. Clay Twp. Bicentennial Com., 1974-76; mem. exec. com. Kokomo Bicentennial Com., 1974-76; govt. agys. chmn. Howard County Bicentennial Com., 1974-76; capt. capital fund drive Sangralea Valley Boys Home Campaign, 1968; mem. San Diego Rep. Cen. Com., 1985—; regional bd. dirs. Drug Abuse Council, Howard County; bd. dirs., membership chmn. Mental Health Assn.; lector Ascension, San Diego, 1984—, mem. council, 1985-91, also numerous other civic activities. Served to capt., Ordnance Corps U.S. Army, 1957-66. Recipient Ind. Mental Health citations, 1969, 70, Howard County Mental Health citations, 1969, 70, Nat. Young Rep. Hard Charger award, 1970, Gen. Motors Community Service award, 1970, Jaycee Disting. Service award, 1970, Disting. Service award Ind. Young Reps., 1971, Layman of Year award K.C., 1971, Ind. Mental Health award, 1971-72, Heart Fund award, 1973, Ind. Gov.'s Vol. Action commendation, 1975, 78, award Greater Kokomo Council of Chs., 1975; named Outstanding Ind. Young Rep., 1970; fellow Harry S. Truman Library, 1974—. Fellow Internat. Soc. for Hybrid Microelectronics (Midwest regional dir., charter state pres., treas., v.p., publicity chmn., program chmn., others 1970), mem. Semicondr. Materials Soc., Am. Soc. Quality Control (editor non-periodic publs., electronics div.), Am. Soc. Metals, ABA, ASTM (chmn. subcoms. 1963-68), AIME, Kokomo Engring. Soc., Internat. Platform Assn., Internat. Brick Collectors Assn. (pres., gov. bd. 1983-93), Am. Indian Assn., Ind. Chess Assn., Nat. Hist. Soc., Ind. Hist. Soc., Howard County Hist. Soc. (bd. dirs.), Tippecanoe County Hist. Assn., Found. Ill. Archeology, Epigraphic Soc., Nat., Fla., Clearwater Audubon socs., N.Am. Acad. Ecumenists, Soc. Investigation of Unexplained, Ancient Astronaut Soc., Internat. Assn. for Investigation Ancient Civilizations (internat. dir. 1980—), Napoleonic Soc. Am., Internat. UFO Registry, Kokomo Fine Arts Assn., Nat. Wilderness Soc., Whitewater Valley R.R. Assn., Kokomo Mgmt. Club (auditor 1970), Am. Hort. Soc., Nat. Greentown Glass Assn., San Diego Hist. Soc., San Diego Archeol. Soc., Calif. Archeol. Soc., San Diego Zool. Soc., Soc. for Hist. Archaeology, Soc. for Calif. Archaeology, San Diego Cymbidium Soc., San Diego Orch. and Soc., Nat. Acad. Ecumenists, Internat. Order St. Luke the Physician, Sigma Xi, others. Clubs: Kokomo Photo Guild, Ind. Chess, Donora Sportsman, Sycamore Racquet, Kokomo Rose Soc., Kokomo Astronomy, Kokomo Poetry, Kokomo Swim, East County Rep., Orion. Home: PO Box 420950 San Diego CA 92142-0950

ANNO, KIM, artist, art educator; b. L.A., Dec. 19, 1958; d. George Harold and Jacqulin Faye (Robertson) A. BA, San Francisco State U., 1982; MFA, San Francisco Art Inst., 1985. Lectr. Ohio State U., Columbus, 1989-90; asst. prof. painting La. State U., Baton Rouge, 1991; lectr. U. Calif., Berkeley, 1992-96, Stanford U., Palo Alto, Calif., 1994-95; asst. prof. painting Calif. Coll. Arts and Crafts, Oakland, 1996—; vis. asst. prof. painting Stanford U., Palo Alto, Calif., 1994-95; lectr. U. Calif., Berkeley, 1992-96; vis. faculty San Francisco Art Inst., 1993-96. Exhibited in solo shows at San Francisco State U. Gallery, San Francisco Art Inst., Mus. of the Rockies, Bozeman, Mont., C.N. Gorman Mus., Davis, Calif., San Jose State U. Gallery, Meridian Art Gallery, San Francisco, Ebert Gallery, San Francisco, Patricia Correia Gallery, Santa Monica, Calif., others; group shows include Chgo. Art Inst., Galeria De La Raza, San Francisco, Wayne State U., Detroit, Sherman Gallery, Columbus, Ohio, San Jose Art League, Peter Miller Gallery, Chgo., Mus. Modern Art, Rio de Janeiro, Berkeley (Calif.) Art Ctr., Patricia Correia Gallery, Gallery 128, N.Y.C., Richmond (Calif.) Art Ctr., Armory Ctr. for the Arts, Pasadena, Calif.; designer Fruitvale Streetscape Banners, City of Oakland, 1997, Women Artists of Am. West (website gallery) Purdue U., 1998; lead artist mural Unfinished Bus., 1991, also numerous comms.; subject of numerous articles. Mem. Cultural Arts Master Panel, Oakland, 1986, Bedford Gallery Coun., Walnut Creek, Calif., 1994-98; mem. jury Pub. AASF Arts Commn., San Francisco, 1998. Recipient Flintridge Found. award, 1995, others; Individual Artist fellow Nat. Endowment for Arts, 1996. Mem. Coll. Art Assn., Asian Women's Art Assn. Avocations: films, camping, cooking, yoga. Home: 626 66th St Oakland CA 94609-1004 Office: Calif Coll Arts and Crafts 5212 Broadway Oakland CA 94618-1426

ANSCHUTZ, PHILIP F., transportation executive; b. 1939. BS, Univ. Kansas, 1961. Former pres. Anschutz Corp., now chmn. bd., CEO, dir.; chmn. bd. So. Pacific Rail Corp., San Francisco; vice chmn. Union Pacific, San Francisco. Office: Southern Pacific Rail Corp 1 Market Plz San Francisco CA 94105 also: CEO 555 17th St Ste 2400 Denver CO 80202-3941

Office: Los Angeles Kings 3900 W Manchester Blvd Inglewood CA 90305-2200*

ANSELL, GEORGE STEPHEN, retired metallurgical engineering educator, academic administrator; b. Akron, Ohio, Apr. 1, 1934; s. Frederick Jesse and Fanny (Soletsky) A.; m. Marjorie Boris, Dec. 18, 1960; children: Frederick Stuart, Laura Ruth, Benjamin Jesse. B. in Metall. Engring., Rensselaer Poly. Inst., 1954, M. in Metall. Engring., 1955, PhD, 1960; DEng (hon.), Coll. Sch Mines, 1998. Physical metallurgist USN Research Lab., Washington, 1957-58; mem. faculty Rensselaer Poly. Inst., Troy, N.Y., 1960-84, Robert W. Hunt prof., 1965-84, chmn. materials div., 1969-74, dean engring., 1974-84; pres. Colo. Sch. Mines, Golden, 1984-98; bd. dirs. Cyprus Amax Minerals Co., OEA, Inc. Editor books; patentee in field; contbr. over 100 articles to profl. jours. Served with USN, 1955-58. Recipient Hardy Gold Medal AIME, 1961, Curtis W. McGraw award Am. Soc. Engring. Edn., 1971, Souzandrade Gold Medal of Univ. Merit Fed. U. Maranhao, 1986. Fellow Metall. Soc. (pres. 1986-87), Am. Soc. Metals (Alfred H. Geisler award 1964, Bradley Stoughton award 1968), Am. Soc. Engring. Edn. (Curtis W. McGraw award 1971), Sigma Xi, Tau Beta Pi, Phi Lambda Upsilon.

ANSELL, PHIL BARRY, social services professional; b. L.A., Feb. 7, 1960; s. Herbert Murray Ansell and Helene Sharon (Hurov) Goodman; m. Silvia Battigalli, Sept. 23, 1984; children: David, Daniel. BA with honors and distinction, Stanford U., 1982. Anthropol. rsch. asst. Stanford U., 1982; law clk. Ansell & Ansell, 1982-84; sr. field rep. Social Svcs. Union, 1984-95; intergovtl. rels. dir. L.A. County Dept. Cmty. and Sr. Svcs., L.A., 1995-96; welform reform spl. asst. L.A. County Dept. Pub. Social Svcs., L.A., 1996-97; chief divsn. strategic planning and govtl. rels. L.A. County Dept. Pub. Social Svcs., City of Industry, 1997—. Host radio show Labor Scene, Sta. KPFK-FM, L.A., 1988-94. Office: LAC Dept Pub Social Svcs 12860 Crossroads Pkwy S City Of Industry CA 91746-3411

ANSLEY, JULIA ETTE, educator, poet, writer, consultant; b. Malvern, Ark., Nov. 10, 1940; d. William Harold and Dorothy Mae (Hamm) Smith; m. Miles Ansley, Nov. 8, 1964 (div. June 1976); children: Felicia Dianne, Mark Damon. BA in Edn., Calif. State U., Long Beach, 1962; postgrad., UCLA Ext. Early childhood edn., life, gen. elem., kindergarten/primary, Miller-Unruh reading specialist credentials, Calif. Elem. tchr. L.A. Unified Sch. Dist., 1962—; coord. Proficiency in English Program, L.A., 1991-93, 98—; mem., advisor P.E.P. instrnl. tchrs. network, 1993—, workshop presenter, staff devel. leader, and classroom demonstration tchr. in field; also poetry presentations, L.A., 1989—; owner Poetry Expressions, L.A.; self-markets own poetry posters; creator, presenter KidChess integrated lang. arts program, 1987—. Author: (poetry vols.) Out of Heat Comes Light, From Dreams to Reality. Bd. dirs. New Frontier Dem. Club, L.A., 1990-93; mem. exec. bd. L.A. Panhellenic Coun., rec. sec., 1993-95; vol., cmty. orgns. Greater South L.A. Affirmative Action Project, 1995-96; elected tchr. rep. Ten Schs. Leadership Team, 1992-93. Honored by Teacher mag., 1990; recipient Spirit of Edn. award Sta. KNBC-TV, L.A., 1990, Shiny Apple award L.A. Tchr. Ctr., 1992, Dedicated Tchr. award Proficiency in English Program, 1994; grantee L.A. Ednl. Partnership, 1985, 87, 89, 93. Mem. L.A. Alliance African-Am. Educators (exec. bd. 1991-94, parliamentarian 1992-94), Black Women's Forum, Black Am. Polit. Assn. (edn. co-chair 1993-95), Sigma Gamma Rho. Mem. FAME Ch. Avocations: reading, listening to music, writing, playing chess (cert. chess instr. for grades K-3), political involvement. Home: 3828 Sutro Ave Los Angeles CA 90008-1925

ANTHONY, ELAINE MARGARET, real estate executive, interior designer; b. Mpls., Apr. 23, 1932; d. Jerome Pius and Adeline (Shea) Clarkin; m. Ronald Carl Anthony, Aug 28, 1954 (div. 1977); children: Richard, Lisa, Laura. Student, U. Minn., 1950-51; AA, Diablo Valley Coll., 1978; postgrad., San Jose (Calif.) State U., 1979, U. Calif., Berkeley, 1983-91. Agt., broker Sycamore Realty, Danville, Calif., 1972-75; broker, project sales mgr. Crocker Homes, Dublin, Calif., 1975-80; exec. v.p. BlackHawk Properties, Danville, 1980-82; broker, project sales mgr. Harold W. Smith Co., Walnut Creek, Calif., 1982-86; pres. Elaine Anthony & Assocs., Inc., Oakland, Calif., 1986—. Mem. vol. coun. San Francisco Symphony, 1986. Mem. Bldg. Industry Assn. (Outstanding Sales Person of Yr. No. Calif. chtp. 1983), Inst. Residential Mktg., Calif. Assn. Realtors, Contra Costa Assn. of Realtors, Nat. Assn. Realtors, Oakland Assn. Realtors, Bellevue Club Oakland, Commonwealth Club (San Francisco.). Republican. Roman Catholic. Avocations: traveling, food, theater. Home and Office: 1875 Grand View Dr Oakland CA 94618-2339

ANTHONY, HARRY ANTONIADES, city planner, architect, educator; b. Skyros, Greece, July 28, 1922; came to U.S., 1951, naturalized, 1954; s. Anthony G. and Maria G. (Ftoulis) Antoniades; m. Anne C. Skoufis, Sept. 23, 1950; children: Mary Anne Anthony Smith, Kathryn Harriet. B.Arch., Nat. Tech. U., Athens, Greece, 1945; student, Ecole Nat. Supérieure des Beaux Arts, Paris, 1945-46; M.City Planning, U. Paris, 1947; Docteur de l'Université, Sorbonne, Paris, 1949; Ph.D. in Arch. and Urban Planning, Columbia, 1955. Architect-planner with Constantinos A. Doxiadis, Athens, 1943-45, LeCorbusier, Paris, 1946-47, ECA, Paris, 1949-51; city planner with Maurice E.H. Rotival, N.Y.C., 1951-52; chief planner Brown & Blauvelt, N.Y.C., 1952-54; city planner, urban designer Skidmore, Owings & Merrill, N.Y.C., 1954-56; prin. planning cons. Brown Engrs. Internat., N.Y.C., 1956-60; prin. Brown & Anthony City Planners, Inc., N.Y.C., 1960-69; v.p. Doxiadis Assocs., Inc., Washington, 1971-72; mem. faculty Columbia U., 1953-72, from asst. to assoc. prof., 1956-63, prof. urban planning, 1963-72, dir. grad. div. urban planning Grad. Sch. Architecture and Planning, 1962-65; prof. urban planning Calif. State Poly. U., Pomona, 1972-83, prof. emeritus urban and regional planning, 1983—; chmn. dept. Calif. State Poly. U., 1972-76; vis. prof. urban design Tulane U., 1967-68; vis. lectr. U. Calif. at Berkeley, Stanford U., Dartmouth, San Diego State U., CUNY, U. Okla., Ohio U., Auburn U., Salk Inst. Biol. Studies, U.S. Internat. U.; lectr. urban studies and planning U. Calif., San Diego, 1980-82; scholar-in-residence U. B.C., Vancouver, 1978; planning, zoning, urban renewal and urban design cons. to several cities, U.S. and abroad; also cons. to UN, Am. Med. Bldg. Guild, corps. and pvt. firms, to govts. and univs.; planning commr., Leonia, N.J., 1958-64; master planner, cons. arch. for Ss. Constantine and Helen Greek Orthodox Ch. and Village for the Elderly, Cardiff-by-the-Sea, Calif., 1983-97 (AIA design awareness program orchid award 1997). Author, co-author, contbr.: Four Great Makers of Modern Architecture: Gropius, Le Corbusier, Mies Van Der Rohe, Wright, Dictionary of American History, The Challenge of Squatter Settlements-With Special Reference to the Cities of Latin America, La Défense à Paris et le Quartier d'Affaires de Vancouver: Une Comparaison Urbaine, New Orleans Air Rights Study, Woodstock Growth Plan and Land Use Controls, Mt. Vernon Planning Study, Corning Area, N.Y.: Conditions and Prospects, Metairie Shore, La.: Lakefront Recreation and Comty. Devel., U.S. Navy Multiple Activity Master Plan: Norfolk Complex, Aqaba, Jordan: Future Devel., Lands of Kapua, Hawaii: Feasibility Study for Urban, Agricultural and Recreational Devel.; several master plans, city and regional planning reports, urban design plans and programs, environ. impact reports, zoning ordinances, educational videocassettes on urban planning subjects; contbr. articles to profl. jours., mags., newspapers; acad. profl. writings, awards, plans, designs and reports included in Spl. Collections Libr., U. Calif. (San Diego), 1998. Recipient Premier Grand Prix Internat. Exhbn. Housing and City Planning, Paris, 1947; William Kinne Fellows travelling fellow in planning N.Am., 1956, French Govt. fellow, 1945-47; research award Urban Center of Columbia U., 1969; named Outstanding Prof. Calif. State Poly. U., 1975; founder Met. Opera House, Lincoln Ctr. for the Performing Arts, N.Y.C. Mem. AIA (Arnold W. Brunner scholar 1958), Am. Inst. Cert. Planners (bd. examiners), Am. Planning Assn. (Disting. Svc. award 1984, San Diego Cmty. Design Awareness Program Orchid award 1997), Order of Am. Hellenic Ednl. Progressive Assn., Hellenic Cultural Soc., Internat. Land Econs. Soc. of Lambda Alpha (Richard T. Ely Disting. Educator award 1988), Univ. Calif. San Diego Faculty Club. Home: 7665 Caminito Avola La Jolla CA 92037-3956

ANTHONY, JAMES PATRICK, state program administrator, artist; b. Chgo., Apr. 7; s. Rudolph Alvin and Margaret Mary A.; m. Janice Kay Moore (div.); 1 child, Jordanna; m. Linda Jean Gorton, Oct. 23, 1993. BA in Design, So. Ill. U.; cert. in real estate, Miramar Coll.; cert. in real estate devel., U. Calif., San Diego. Lic. real estate broker Ariz., Calif. Sales/leasing administr. real estate assets dept. City San Diego, 1985-92; retail svc. bus. owner, operator Mesa, Ariz., 1992-95; land sale adminstr. Ariz. State Land Dept., Phoenix, 1993-95; land use planner cons. Scottsdale, Ariz., 1995-96; sr. planner Salt River Indian Cmty., Scottsdale, Ariz., 1996-98; sr. program assoc. Main St. program Ariz. Dept. Commerce, Phoenix, 1998—; bd. dirs. Friends of Ariz. Main St. Group art exhbns. include Parkerburg (W.Va.) Art Ctr.'s "Realism", 1996, San Diego Art Inst. (hon. mem. ann. internat. juried exhbn.), Chgo.'s Formost Liquor Stores (1st place ann. wine art competition). Mem. Desert Preservation Task Force, Scottsdale, 1996-97; mem. adv. com. State Growing Smarter Commn., State of Ariz., 1999. Lt. USN, 1977-81, 85-87. Recipient top purchase prize So. Ill. U. First Ann. Undergrad. Art Show, award of excellence Manhattan Arts Internat. Fifth Ann. Art competition, 1996, 1st Pl. Chgo.'s Formost Liquor Stores Ann. Wine Art competition. Mem. Am. Planning Assn., Bldg. Owners & Mgrs. Assn. (cert. real property adminstr.). Avocations: hiking, archaeology. Home: 8311 E Via de Ventura #2010 Scottsdale AZ 85258 Office: Ariz Dept Commerce Main St Program 3800 N Central Ave Ste 1400 Phoenix AZ 85012

ANTIN, MICHAEL, lawyer; b. Milw., Nov. 30, 1938; s. David Boris and Pauline (Mayer) A.; m. Evelyne Judith Hirsch, June 19, 1960; children: Stephanie, Bryan, Randall. BS, Univ. Calif., 1960; JD, U. Calif., 1963. Bar: Calif. 1963; cert. tax specialist. Tax atty. Cruikshank, Antin & Grebow, Beverly Hills, Calif., 1963-81, Antin, Litz & Grebow, Beverly Hills, 1981-91, Antin & Taylor, L.A., 1993—; bd. dirs. Small Bus. Counsel Am., Washington, The Group, Inc.; speaker in field; instr. Solomon S. Heubner Sch. CLU Studies, 1977-86. Author: How to Operate Your Trust or Probate, 1983; contbr. articles to profl. jours. With U.S. Air Force, 1959-67. Fellow Am. Coll. Tax Counsel, Am. Coll. of Trust & Estate Counsel, L.A. County Bowlers Assn. (bd. dirs. 1996). Avocations: jogging, tennis, cross country skiing, bowling. Office: Antin & Taylor 1875 Century Park E Ste 700 Los Angeles CA 90067-2508

ANTOCH, ZDENEK VINCENT, electrical engineering educator; b. Prague, Czechoslovakia, Oct. 16, 1943; came to U.S., 1950; s. Zdenek Antoch and Marta (Smidova) Frank; m. Maureen O. Shaw, June 24, 1968 (div.); 1 child, Anna Marie. BS, Portland State U., 1971, postgrad. in Engring., 1971-73, postgrad. in Physics, 1973-75, MS, 1989, postgrad., 1989—. Research asst. Portland (Oreg.) State U., 1972-75; electronics instr. Portland (Oreg.) Community Coll., 1975-80, 81—. Mem. IEEE, Am. Soc. Engring. Edn. Democrat. Avocation: sailing. Office: Portland Community Coll 12000 SW 49th Ave Portland OR 97219-7199

ANTON, CAROL J., small business owner, writer; b. Rice Lake, Wis., June 12, 1949; d. Edward Burton and Clementine Emma (Kuhrt) McManus; m. Jimmy Eugene Anton, Oct. 31, 1965; children: David E., Brandi J. Grad. high sch., Dora, N. Mex. Cert. marine mechanic; ceramics instr. Beauty councilor Vanda Beauty Councilors, Fla., 1967-69; owner Sunshine Ceramics, Elephant Butte, N. Mex., 1980-94; freelance writer, 1994-96, Sierra County Sentinel, T-or-C, N. Mex., 1995—; co-owner, office mgr. Anton's Marine, Elephant Butte, 1969—. Cub scout leader, 1976; scout leader Rio Grande Girl Scout Coun., N. Mex., 1981-83; project chmn. children's grant T-or-C community theater, N. Mex., 1997, theater dir., 1991—, sec., treas. Recipient Hearts and Hands Acting Out award N.Mex. Arts Coun., 1997. Mem. Sierra Shooters's Club (sec., treas.). Democrat. Baptist. Avocations: reading, writing, crocheting, theater projects. Office: Anton's Marine PO Box Aa Elephant Butte NM 87935-7525

ANTON, FRANCIS MATTHEW, JR., software engineer; b. Cut Bank, Mont., June 4, 1966; s. Francis Matthew Anton Sr. and Mina Adeline (Paradis) Salsbery; m. Gail Lynn Tulach, May 27, 1989. BS in Pure Math., U. Chgo., 1988; PhD in Religion, ULC, Modesto, Calif., 1998. Devel. engr. Hewlett-Packard, Cupertino, Calif., 1988-89; sys. designer file sys. Transarc Corp., Pitts., 1989-90, sys. designer transaction processing, 1990-93; sr. mem. tech. staff Computer Scis. Corp., Mountain View, Calif., 1993; sr. engr. Taligent, Inc., Cupertino, 1993-96; project mgr. Apple Computer, Cupertino, 1996-97; chief arch., mgr. sys. devel. iPass Inc., Mountain View, 1997—; contbr. IETF, 1997-98, ETSI, 1997-98; spkr. in field. Republican. Roman Catholic. Avocations: sports, computers, electronics, motorcycle racing. E-mail: butch@zaphod.uchicago.edu. and butch@ipass.com. Fax: 650-237-7321. Home: 1838 Charmeran Ave San Jose CA 95124-3644 Office: iPass Inc 650 Castro St Ste 500 Mountain View CA 94041-2057

ANTONIUK, VERDA JOANNE, secondary school educator; b. Moline, Ill., Sept. 10, 1936; d. Joe Oscar and Verda Mathilde (Oakberg) Butts; m. Vladimir Antoniuk, Sept. 1, 1972; children: Daniel Sean, Stephen Dwight. Diploma in missions, Moody Bible Inst., 1957; BS in Edn., Ea. Ill. U., 1960; MA in Internat. Rels., Calif. State U. Stanlslaus, Turlock, 1981, cert. in ESL, 1989. Cert. tchr., ESL tchr., bilingual, crosscultural, lang. and acad. devel. cert., Calif. Tchr. Wheatridge (Colo.) H.S., 1960-61, Modesto (Calif.) City Schs., 1971-73, Modesto Jr. Coll., 1979-80, 84-89, Turlock Christian H.S., 1980-83, Turlock H.S., 1989—; part-time faculty edn. dept. Chapman U., 1995; missionary Oversease Missionary Fellowship, Littleton, Colo., 1961-69; tchr. Turlock Adult Sch., 1969-79, 84-89, program dir. ESL, 1976-79, amnesty coord., 1986-89; cons. Britannica-ARC Project, Oakland, Calif. and Boston, 1993-94; ednl. cons. Valley Fresh, Turlock, 1987-88. Translator multi-media U.S. Constitution, Britannica, 1993; cons. to book on amnesty, 1987; contbt. to book Intervarsity Christian Fellowship, 1965. Sunday sch. supt. Evang. Free Ch., Turlock, 1979-82; cons. Spanish work Turlock Covenant Ch., 1990—; mem. Malaysian Youth Coun., Kuala Lumpur, 1967-68. Mem. Calif. Tchrs. English to Spkrs. of Other Langs., Nat. Assn. Bilingual Educators, Tchrs. of English to Spkrs. of Other Langs. Republican. Avocations: reading, MacIntosh computers, writing, collecting stamps and coins. Home: 553 South Ave Turlock CA 95380-5606

ANTREASIAN, GARO ZAREH, artist, lithographer, art educator; b. Indpls., Feb. 16, 1922; s. Zareh Minas and Takouhie (Daniell) A.; m. Jeanne Glascock, May 2, 1947; children: David Garo, Thomas Berj. BFA, Herron Sch. Art, 1948; DFA (hon.), Ind. U.-Purdue U. at Indpls., 1972. Instr. Herron Sch. Art, 1948-64; tech. dir. Tamarind Lithography Workshop, Los Angeles, 1960-61; prof. art U. N.Mex., 1964-87, chmn. dept. art, 1981-84; tech. dir. Tamarind Inst., U. N.Mex., 1970-72; vis. lectr., artist numerous univs.; Bd. dirs. Albuquerque Mus., 1980-90; printmaker emeritus Southern Graphics Coun., 1994. Prin. author: The Tamarind Book of Lithography: Art and Techniques, 1970; one-man shows include Malvina Miller Gallery, San Francisco, 1971, Marjorie Kauffman Gallery, Houston, 1975-79, 84, 86, U. Colo., Boulder, 1972, Calif. Coll. Arts & Crafts, Oakland, 1973, Miami U., Oxford, Ohio, 1973, Kans. State U., 1973, Atlanta Coll. Art, 1974, U. Ga., Athens, 1974, Alice Simsar Gallery, Ann Arbor, 1977-79, Elaine Horwich Gallery, Santa Fe, 1977-79, Mus. of N.Mex., Santa Fe, 1979, Robischon Gallery, Denver, 1984, 86, 90, Moss-Chumley Gallery, Dallas, 1987, Rettig-Martinez Gallery, Santa Fe, 1988, 91, 92, U. N.Mex. Art Mus., 1988, Albuquerque Mus., 1988, Louis Newman Gallery, L.A., 1989, Expositum Gallery, Mexico City, 1989, State U. Coll., Cortland, N.Y., 1991, Mus. Art, U. Ariz., Tucson, 1991, Indpls. Mus. Art, 1994, Ruschmon Gallery, Indpls., 1994, Mitchell Mus. Art, Vernon, Ill., 1995, Cline-Lewallen Gallery, Santa Fe, 1997, Anderson Gallery, Albuquerque, 1997, Feenix Gallery, Taos, NM State U., Las Crucis, 1998; exhibited group shows Phila. Print Club, 1960-63, Ind. Artists, 1947-63, White House, 1966, Nat. Lithographic Exhbn. Fla. State U., 1965, Library Congress, 1961-66, Bklyn. Mus., 1958-68, 76, U.S. Pavilion Venice Biennale, 1970, Internat. Biennial, Bradford, Eng., 1972-74, Internat. Biennial, Tokyo, 1972, City Mus. Hong Kong, 1972, Tamarind UCLA, 1985, Roswell Mus., 1989, Pace Gallery, 1990, Worcester (Mass.) Art Mus., 1990, Amon Carter Mus., Ft. Worth, 1990, Albuquerque Mus., 1991, 92, Art Mus. U. N.Mex., 1991, 92; represented in permanent collections: Bklyn. Mus., Guggenheim Mus., N.Y.C., Cin. Mus., Chgo. Art Inst., Ind. State Mus., Mus. Modern Art, N.Y.C., Library of Congress, Met. Mus., N.Y.C., N.Y. Pub. Libr., Mus. Fine Arts, Santa Fe, also, Albuquerque, Boston, Indpls., Seattle, Phila., San Diego, Dallas, N.Mex., Worcester Art Museums, Los Angeles County Mus., Roswell Mus. and Art Ctr., Tucson Mus., murals, Ind. U., Butler U., Ind. State Office Bldg. Fulbright vis. lectr. U. São Paulo and Found. Armando Alvares Penteado, Brazil, 1985. Combat artist with USCGR, World War II, PTO. Recipient Distinguished Alumni award Herron Sch. Art, 1972, N.Mex. Annual Gov.'s award, 1987; Grantee Nat. Endowment for Arts, 1983. Fellow NAD; mem. World Print Coun. (bd. dirs. 1980-87), Nat. Print

Coun. Am. (co-pres. 1980-82), Coll. Art Assn. Am. (bd. dirs. 1977-80). Home: 6004 Torreon Dr NE Albuquerque NM 87109-3819

ANTRIM, MINNIE FAYE, residential care facility administrator; b. Rochester, Tex., June 30, 1916; d. Charles C. Montandon and Myrtle Caldona (Brown) Montandon Taylor; m. Cecil C. Antrim, Jan. 1, 1938; children—Linda Faye Antrim Hathway, Cecil C. Student Central State Tchrs. Coll., Edmond, Okla., 1937. Asst. purchasing agt. Scenic Gen. Hosp., Modesto, Calif., 1955-68, Health Dept., Probation Dept., Stanislaus, Calif., 1955-68; owner, adminstr. Sierra Villa Retirement Home, Fresno, Calif., 1968-77, Mansion Home, Fresno, 1977—. Mem. Am. Coll. Health Care Adminstrs., Calif Bus. and Profl Club. Methodist. Club: Garden. Avocation: glee clubs. Home: 6070 E Townsend Ave Fresno CA 93727-5617

AOUN, JOSEPH, linguistics educator, researcher; b. Beirut, Mar. 26, 1953; came to U.S., 1978; s. Elie and Josephine (Kikano) A.; m. Zeina El-Imad, June 22, 1979; children: Joseph K., Adrian M. PhD, MIT, 1981. Asst. prof. linguistics U. So. Calif., L.A., 1982-86, assoc. prof., 1986-89, prof., 1989—, dean Faculty Letters, Arts and Sci., 1994—. Author: A Grammar of Anaphora, 1985, Generalized Binding: The Syntax and LF of Interrogatives, 1986; co-author: The Syntax of Scope, 1993. Mem. Linguistic Soc. Am., Phi Kappa Phi. Office: U So Calif University Park ADM 304 Los Angeles CA 90089-4012

APGOOD, ROBERT D., financial consultant; b. Idaho Falls, Idaho, Feb. 20, 1941; s. Dale Marvin and Esther (Palmer) A.; m. Marsha Foreman; children: Allyson, Anthony, Richard. BA, Brigham Young U., 1965, U. Utah, 1980; MBA, U. Utah, 1967, PhD, 1985. Cert. pub. acct. CPA Peat Marwick, L.A., 1965-67; asst. prof. Weber State U., Ogden, Utah, 1970-75; v.p. KUTV, Salt Lake City, 1975-77; pvt. practice Utah, 1977—; prof. San Francisco State U., 1985-86. Home: 2195 Parleys Ter Salt Lake City UT 84109-1509

APODACA, MICHAEL, elementary educator; b. Downey, Calif.; s. David Gomez Apodaca and Virginia Mae (Russell) Miller; m. Deborah Denise Mobly, June 18, 1983; children: Nicole Michelle, Jeremy Christopher. BA, Pacific Christian Coll., 1984; MA, Fuller Sem., 1988; tchg. credential, Chapman U., 1992. Cert. tchr., Calif.; ordained minister. Min. North Bellflower (Calif.) Christian Ch., 1978-88; tchr. New Life Christian Sch., Hesperia, Calif., 1988, Hesperia (Calif.) Unified Schs., 1989—. Author: Deadly Forecast, 1995, INCA!, 1996. E-mail: MrDaca@aol.com.

APPELBAUM, BRUCE DAVID, physician; b. Lincroft, N.J., Apr. 24, 1957; s. John S. and Shirley B. (Wolfson) A. BS in pharmacy, Rutgers Coll., 1980; MS in pharmacy, Emory U., 1983, PhD in pharmacology, 1985; MD, Medical Coll. Ga., 1989. Diplomate Nat. Bd. Med. Examiners, Am. Bd. Psychiatry and Neurology. Rsch. assoc. Emory U. Dept. Pharmacology, Atlanta, 1985; resident physician U. Calif. Dept. Psychiatry, Irvine, Calif., 1989-93; pvt. practice Pacifica Therapists, Huntington Beach, Calif., 1993—; med. dir. Coll. Health Ptnrs., Santa Ana, Calif., 1995—. Contbr. articles to profl. jours. Recipient Nat. Rsch. Svc. award Nat. Inst. Health, 1982-83, Ea. Student Rsch. Forum U. Miami Medical Sch., 1984, Nat. Student Rsch. Forum, 1987. Mem. AMA, Am. Psychiat. Assn., Orange County Psychiat. Soc., N.Y. Acad. Scis., Sigma Xi. Avocations: traveling, photography, bicycling, reading. Home: 29681 Monarch Dr San Juan Capistrano CA 92675-1425 Office: 18811 Huntington St Ste 200 Huntington Beach CA 92648-6003

APPLEGATE, (HAROLD) REED, retired graphic designer, advertising executive; b. Chico, Calif., Mar. 26, 1943; s. Michael and Jean (Shear) A. BFA, Chico State U., 1967. Advt. account exec. Butte County Bugle Newspaper, Chico, 1970-77; graphic designer Chico Enterprise-Record, 1983-87; prin. Chico, D, 1977-93; advisor Chico Symphony Bd., 1994-96, Annie Awards Visual Arts Com., Chico, 1995—; rsch. libr. Janet Turner Print Gallery, Chico State U., 1995—. Contr. articles on area artists to local newspaper, 1993—. Mem. Chico Art Ctr. Avocations: art collecting (No. Calif. artists). Home: 319 W Lincoln Ave Chico CA 95926-4520

APPLEHANS, TROY SCOT, animal scientist; b. Denver, June 19, 1967; s. Wayne Roger and Marlene Joyce (Summers) Cozzie; m. Kerri Beth Thornton, May 31, 1997; 1 child, Taylor Brooke. AA, Northeastern Okla. A&M, 1987; BS, Okla. State U., 1990. Animal scientist, dir. advt. and field svcs. Cattle Today, Inc., Fayette, Ala., 1990-97; regional mgr. Am. Gelbvieh Assn., Westminster, Colo., 1997—; livestock judging cons. Okla. State Livestock Team, 1989. Author: (video) Keys to Oral Reasons, 1988. Mem. Nat. Champion Livestock Team Nat. Juco Judging Team, 1986, 87, Nat. Champion Sr. Coll. Judging Team, 1988. Avocations: livestock evaluation, coaching 4-H livestock team, auctioneering, team roping, auto racing.

APPLETON, JAMES ROBERT, university president, educator; b. North Tonawanda, N.Y., Jan. 20, 1937; s. Robert Martin and Emma (Mollnow) A.; m. Carol Koelsch, Aug. 8, 1959; children: Steven, Jon, Jennifer. AB in Social Sci., Wheaton Coll., 1958; MA, PhD, Mich. State U., 1965. Lectr. Mich. State U., East Lansing, 1969-72; assoc. dean students Oakland U., Rochester, Mich., 1965-68, dean student life, 1968-72, assoc. prof. behavioral scis., 1969-72, v.p., 1969-72; v.p. student affairs U. So. Calif., L.A., 1972-82, v.p. devel., 1982-87; pres., Univ. prof. U. Redlands, Calif., 1987—. Author: Pieces of Eight: Rights, Roles & Styles of the Dean; guest editor Nat. Assn. Student Pers. Adminstrs. Jour., 1971; contbr. articles to profl. jours. Bd. dirs. So. Calif. Ind. Colls., Nat. Assn. Ind. Colls. and Univs. Exec. Com., Inland Empire Econ. Partnership, Tuition Exch.; trustee San Francisco Presbyn. Sem. 1st lt. U.S. Army, 1958-60. Named One of 100 Emerging Young Leaders in Higher Edn., Am. Council Edn./Change, 1978; recipient Fred Turner award Nat. Assn. Student Personnel Adminstrs., 1980. Mem. NCAA (pres.'s commn.), Assn. Ind. Calif. Colls. & Univs. (govtl. rels. com., natural exec. com. tuition exch.), Am. Assn. Higher Edn., Western Coll. Assn. (past pres.). Avocations: music performance and appreciation, athletics. Home: 1861 Rossmont Dr Redlands CA 92373-7219 Office: U of Redlands 1200 E Colton Ave PO Box 3080 Redlands CA 92373-0999*

APPLETON, STEVEN R., electronics executive. BBA, Boise State U., 1982. Fab supr., prodn. mgr., dir. mfg., v.p. mfg. Micron Tech., Inc., Boise, Idaho, 1983-91, pres., COO, 1991, now chmn., CEO, pres.; chmn., CEO Micron Semiconductor, 1992. bd. dirs. Semiconductor Industry Asssn., St. Luke's Hosp.; trustee Boise State U.; mem. Coll. Bus. Adv. Coun., Semiconductor Tech. Coun. Office: Micron Tech PO Box 6 8000 Federal Way Boise ID 83707-0006*

APURON, ANTHONY SABLAN, archbishop; b. Agana, Guam, Nov. 1, 1945; s. Manuel Taijito and Ana Santos (Sablan) P. BA, St. Anthony Coll., 1969; MDiv, Maryknoll Sem., 1972, M Theology, 1973; MA in Liturgy, Notre Dame U., 1974. Ordained priest Roman Catholic ch., 1972, ordained bishop, 1984, installed archbishop, 1986. Chmn. Diocesan Liturgical Commn., Agana, 1974-86; vice chmn. Chamorro Lang. Commn., Agana, 1984-86; aux. bishop Archdiocese of Agana, 1984-85, archbishop, 1986—; chmn. Interfaith Vols. Caregivers, Agana, 1984—; mem. Civilian Adv. com., Agana, 1986—; pres. Cath. Bishops' Conf. of Pacific, 1990—; v.p. Cath. Bishops' Conf. of Aceania, 1990—. Author: A Structural Analysis of the Content of Myth in the Thought of Mircea Eliade, 1973. Chmn. Cath. Ednl. Radio. Named Most Outstanding Young Man, Jaycees of Guam, 1984. Avocations: jogging, walking, swimming. Office: Archbishop's Office 196B Cuesta San Ramon Hagatna GU 96910*

ARABIAN, ARMAND, arbitrator, mediator, lawyer; b. N.Y.C., Dec. 12, 1934; s. John and Aghavnie (Yalian) A.; m. Nancy Arabian, Aug. 26, 1962; children: Allison Ann, Robert Armand. BSBA, Boston U., 1956, JD, 1961; LLM, U. So. Calif., L.A., 1970; LLD (hon.), Southwestern Sch. Law, 1990, Pepperdine U., 1990, U. West L.A., 1994, We. State U., 1997, Thomas Jefferson Sch. of Law, 1997. Bar: Calif. 1962, U.S. Supreme Ct. 1966. Dep. dist. atty. L.A. County, 1962-63; pvt. practice law Van Nuys, Calif., 1963-72; judge Mcpl. Ct., L.A., 1972-73, Superior Ct., L.A., 1973-83; assoc. justice U.S. Ct. Appeal, L.A., 1983-90, U.S. Supreme Ct. Calif., San Francisco, 1990-96; ret., 1996. 1st lt. U.S. Army, 1956-58. Recipient Stanley Litz Meml. award San Fernando Valley Bar Assn., 1986, Lifetime Achievement award San Fernando Valley Bar Assn., 1993/. Republican. Fax no.: (818) 781-6002; e-mail: honarabian@AOL.com. Office: 6259 Van Nuys Blvd Van Nuys CA 91401-2711

ARAI-ABRAMSON, LUCY, freelance artist; b. Tokyo, Mar. 3, 1956; came to U.S., 1956; d. Lucian Ford Robinson and Masuko Arai; m. William John Abramson, Dec. 31, 1975. Student, Ea. Mich. U., 1974-75; BFA cum laude, U. S.C., 1979; MFA, U. Mich., 1983, grad. cert. of mus. practices, 1986. Copy editor U. Mich. Microfilms, Ann Arbor, 1979-80; mus. shop asst. mgr. U. Mich. Mus. of Art, 1983, membership coord., 1984; asst. curator Cranbrook Art Acad./Mus., Bloomfield Hills, Mich., 1985-86; cons. archives and exhbns., 1987—, freelance instr., 1987—, artist/designer, 1987—; archive cons. Wente Bros. Winery, Livermore, Calif., 1989-92; Japanese stitching instr. nat. quilting orgs., 1989—; lectr./panelist Am. Acad. Religion, San Francisco, 1997; lectr. Holy Name Coll., Oakland, Calif., 1998. Designer/contbr.: (artist biography/slidebooks) Of Our Own Voice: Asian American Women Artists, 1996, 98; designer: (one of a kind garments) Kasuri Dyeworks, 1994—; author: (monograph) Mirrors of the Soul, 1992, Sashiko: Innovations & Refinement of a Japanese Stitchery Technique, 1994. Vol. instr. Hawes and Jack London Schs., Redwood City and Antioch, Calif., 1992, 93, 94, 95; vol. arranger Calif. wildflower exhbn., Oakland, Calif., 1995, 96, 97, 98; garden designer/vol. coord. Dearborn (Mich.) Hist. Mus., 1997; vol. instr. Sansei Legacy Project, Alameda, Calif., 1991. Work judged Best in Show U. S.C., 1979; recipient grad. fellowship U. Mich., 1980, 81, 82, 83, art scholarship U. Mich. Sch. Art, 1980, 81, 82, 83, curatorial internship grant Cranbrook Acad. Art/Mus., 1984-85. Mem. Coll. Art Assn., Asian Am. Women Artists Assn. Avocations: hiking, Calif. wildflowers, camping, travel, reading. Fax: 925-679-0506. Office: PO Box 683 Oakley CA 94561-0683

ARANDA, MARY KATHRYN, state legislator; b. Nassawadox, Va., Sept. 28, 1945; d. John McCallister and Frances Esther (Mausteller) Copper; m. Ronald William Meyer, Dec. 28, 1965 (dec. June 1966); m. Rembert Aranda, Feb. 4, 1973; 1 child, Olivia Kathryn. BA, Goucher Coll., 1969. Jr. planner Balt. Regional Planning Coun., 1968-71; asst. planner edn. sect. N.Y.C. Dept. City Planning, 1971-74, assoc. dir. edn. and social svcs. sect., 1974-76; rep. Gen. Ct. State of N.H., Concord, 1993-96. Commr. Derry House and Devel. Authority, 1983-95; incorporator Alexander-Eastman Found., Derry and Concord, 1993-96; mem. Derry Planning Bd., 1984-88. Mem. Nat. Orgn. Women Legislators, Internat. Platform Assn. Republican. Avocations: sewing, gardening.

ARBUTHNOT, JEANETTE JAUSSAUD, educator, researcher; b. Walla Walla, Wash., Feb. 17, 1934; d. Andre P. and Lena Mae (Fox) Jaussaud; m. Alfred Harold Arbuthnot, Aug. 20, 1953 (div. July 1981); children: Kristi Noel Arbuthnot Bronkema, Lisa Gaye, Douglas Randal. BS, Fla. Internat. U., Miami, 1980; MS, Colo. State U., Ft. Collins, 1984; PhD, Okla. State U., 1990. Sect. mgr. The Treasury Dept. Store divsn. J.C. Penney, Miami, 1980-81; dept. mgr. The Denver, Boulder, Colo., 1981-82; lectr. U. Nev.-Reno, 1984-85; asst. prof. Utah State U., Logan, 1988-96, assoc. prof., 1996—, dir. grad. rsch., 1990—, coord. apparel merchandising and design program, 1990—; reviewer for pubs. McMillan, Fairchild and Delmar, 1994, 95. Contbr. articles to profl. jours. Bd. dirs. Utah State U./Cmty. Assocs., Logan, 1995—; mem. exec. bd. Citizens Agains Phys. and Sexual Abuse, Logan, 1995—. Named Advisor of Yr., Coll. Family Life, Utah State U., 1990, 92; USDA rsch. grantee, 1993—. Mem. Internat. Textile and Apparel Assn. (strategic planning com. 1991-93), Costume Soc. Am. (membership adv. com. 1992-93), Am. Collegiate Retailing Assn., Am. Assn. Family and Consumer Scis., Internat. Fedn. Home Econs., Soroptimists Internat., Phi Upsilon Omicron, Kappa Omicron Nu. Episcopalian. Avocations: writing, fashion, silversmithing, travel, women's issues. Home: 242 N 200 E Logan UT 84321-4035 Office: Utah State U 303A Coll of Family Life Logan UT 84322-2910

ARBUTHNOT, ROBERT MURRAY, lawyer; b. Montreal, Quebec, Can., Oct. 23, 1936; s. Leland Claude and Winnifred Laura (Hodges) A.; m. Janet Marie O'Keefe, Oct. 6, 1968; children: Douglas, Michael, Mary Kathleen, Allison Anne. BA, Calif. State U., San Francisco, 1959; JD, U. Calif., San Francisco, 1966. Bar: Calif. 1967, U.S. Dist. Ct. (no. and cen. dists.) Calif. 1967, U.S. Ct. Appeals (9th cir.) 1967, U.S. Supreme Ct. 1975. Assoc. trial lawyer Rankin & Craddick, Oakland, Calif., 1967-69; assoc. atty. Ericksen, Arbuthnot, Brown, Kilduff & Day, Inc., San Francisco, 1970-73, ptnr., 1973-80, chmn. bd., mng. dir., 1980—; gen. counsel CFS Ins. Svcs., San Francisco, 1990—; pro tem judge, arbitrator San Francisco Superior Ct., 1990—; lectr. in field. Bd. regents St. Mary's Coll. High Sch., Berkeley, Calif., 1988-91. With U.S. Army, 1959-62. Recipient Honors plaque St. Mary's Coll. High Sch., 1989. Mem. Internat. Assn. of Ins. Counsel, No. Calif. Assn. of Def. Counsel, Def. Rsch. Inst., Assn. Trial Lawyers Am., San Francisco Lawyers Club. Avocations: boating, family activities. Office: Ericksen Arbuthnot Brown Kilduff & Day Inc 260 California St Ste 1100 San Francisco CA 94111-4300*

ARCADI, JOHN ALBERT, urologist; b. Whittier, Calif., Oct. 23, 1924; s. Antonio and Josephine (Ramirez) A; m. Doris M. Bohanan, Apr. 11, 1951; children: Patrick, Michael, Judith, Timothy, Margaret, William, Catherine. BS cum laude, U. Notre Dame, 1947; MD, Johns Hopkins U., 1950; LHD (hon.), Whittier Coll., 1998. Diplomate Am. Bd. Urology. Intern Johns Hopkins Hosp., Balt., 1950-51, resident, 1951-52, 53-55; instr. urology Johns Hopkins U., Balt., 1953-55, U. So. Calif., L.A., 1955-60; research assoc. Whittier (Calif.) Coll., 1957-70, research prof., 1970—; coord. prostate cancer rsch. Huntington Med. Rsch. Inst., Pasadena, Calif., 1993—; emeritus staff mem. urology sect. Presbyn. Hosp., Whittier, 1960-97, dir. emeritus hosp. bd. Fellow AAAS, ACS; mem. Endocrine Soc., Am. Urology Assn., Am. Micros. Soc., Internat. Urol. Soc., Am. Assn. Clin. Anatomy, Am. Assn. Anatomists, Soc. for Basic Urologic Rsch., Soc. for Invertebrate Pathology. Republican. Roman Catholic. Avocations: photography, stamp and coin collecting, fishing. Home: 6202 Washington Ave Whittier CA 90601-3640

ARCHBOLD, RICHARD, newspaper editor; m. Pat Archbold; children: Kelly, Katie. Degree in polit. sci., U. Ill., 1960. Statehouse reporter UPI, Lincoln, Nebr.; govt. reporter Omaha World-Herald; pub. affairs reporter, city editor, mng. editor Broward County Bur.-Miami Herald, Ft. Lauderdale, Fla.; exec. editor Press-Telegram, Long Beach, Calif., 1978—. Co-chmn. Long Beach (Calif.) Pub. Safety Summit I, 1995, II, 1996, III, 1997; active Leadership Long Beach. Mem. AP Mng. Editors Assn. (past pres. 1994). Office: 604 Pine Ave Long Beach CA 90844-0003*

ARCHER, STEPHEN HUNT, economist, educator; b. Fargo, N.D., Nov. 30, 1928; s. Clifford Paul and Myrtle Mona (Blair) A.; m. Carol Rosa Mohr, Dec. 29, 1951 (div. Feb. 1971); children—Stephen Paul, Timothy William, David Conrad; m. Lana Jo Urban, Sept. 23, 1972. B.A., U. Minn., 1949, M.S., 1953, Ph.D., 1958; postdoctoral student (Ford Found. grantee), U. Calif. at Los Angeles, 1959-60. Mgr. trader J.M. Dain Co., Mpls., 1950; account exec. J.M. Dain Co., 1952-53; instr. econs. U. Minn., Mpls., 1954-56; asst. prof. fin. U. Wash., Seattle, 1956-60; assoc. prof. U. Wash., 1960-65, prof., 1965-73, chmn. dept. fin., bus. econs. and quantitative methods, 1966-70; dean Grad. Sch. Adminstrn. Willamette U., Salem, Oreg., 1973-76, 83-85; prof. Willamette U., 1976-79, Guy F. Atkinson prof., 1979-96; Fulbright sr. lectr. Bocconi U., Milan, Italy, 1982; v.p. Hinton, Jones & Co., Inc. (investment brokers), Seattle, 1969-70; cons. Wash. Bankers Assn., 1971-72, Weyerhaeuser Co., 1971, Bus.-Econs. Adv. & Research Inc., 1969-77, State of Oreg., 1984, 86, 88, 91; vis. prof. Manchester Bus. Sch., Manchester, Eng., 1990-91. Author: Introduction to Mathematics for Business Analysis, 1960, Business Finance: Theory and Mgmt, 1966, revised edit., 1972, The Theory of Business Finance, 1967, 2d revised edit., 1983, Portfolio Analysis, 1971, revised edit., 1979, Introduction to Financial Management, 1979, revised edit., 1983, Cases and Readings in Corporate Finance, 1988; editor Jour. Fin. and Quantitative Analysis, 1966-70, Economic Perspectives, Economica Aziendale, Jour. Bus. and Entrepreneurship. Served with USNR, 1950-52. Mem. Fin. Mgmt. Assn. (pres. 1973-74), Western Fin. Assn., Am. Fin. Assn., Phi Beta Kappa, Beta Gamma Sigma.

ARCHIBEQUE, CHARLENE PAULLIN, music educator; b. Mt. Sterling, Ohio, July 15, 1935; d. Howard Samuel and Roberta Mae (Miller) Paullin; 1 child, Melissa. BME, U. Mich., 1957; MA, San Diego State Coll., 1965; DMA, U. Colo., 1969. Tchr. San Diego Unified Sch. Dist., 1957-69; dir. choral activities San Jose (Calif.) State U., 1970—; cons., guest lectr. many univs.; conductor choirs in 42 states and Can. Contbr. articles to profl. jours. Dir. chorus San Jose Symphony, 1970—, bd. dirs. 1993—. Named Woman of Vision Career Ctr., Disting. Alumni U. Colo., 1986, Woman of Achievement in Arts San Jose Mercury News and Women's Fund, 1998; recipient Pen award, 1996, numerous others. Mem. Am. Choral Dirs. Assn. (state pres. 1971-73, nat. chair 1973-75), Music Educators Nat. Conf., Internat. Choral Fedn. Avocations: travel, reading, cooking, entertaining. Home: 11511 Summit Wood Rd Los Altos Hills CA 94022-4512 Office: Sch of Music and Dance San Jose State U 1 Washington Sq San Jose CA 95112-3613

ARCHIBOLD, JOHN EWING, lawyer, consultant; b. Denver, Mar. 15, 1933; s. Robert French and Eleanor Eileen (Ewing) A.; m. Mary Ellen Ogelsby, Sept. 12, 1964; children: John Christopher, Stephen Ewing, Mary Elizabeth Eileen, Sarah Ellen Dean. AB, Princeton U., 1955; LLB, U. Denver, 1959; LLM, Georgetown U., 1965. Bar: Colo. 1960, D.C. 1964, U.S. Supreme Ct. 1965. Spl. liaison asst. U.S. Dept. State, Washington, 1960; trial atty. U.S. Dept. Justice, Washington, 1960-66; assoc. Grant, Shafroth, Toll & McHendrie, Denver, 1966-68; ptnr. Casey, Klene, Horan & Archibold, Denver, 1968-69; asst. atty. gen. Colo. Dept. Law, Denver, 1970-72; assoc. counsel Colo. Pub. Utilities Commn., Denver, 1972-74, chief counsel, 1974-90; of counsel Kelly, Stanfield & O'Donnell, Denver, 1991-1993; v.p. Info-Media, Inc., Denver, 1990—. Contbr. articles to legal pubs. Precinct committeeman Denver Rep. Party, 1958-59; chmn. Citizenship Day Com., Denver, 1967; dir. Rude Park Nursery, 1957-59; chancellor Anglican Cath. Ch. 1979-80, Diocese of Holy Trinity, 1977-90. Col. U.S. Army, 1955-86. Mem. Denver Bar Assn., Colo. Bar Assn. Avocations: reading, travel. Home: 1624 S Steele St Denver CO 80210-2940

ARCHIE, CAROL LOUISE, obstetrician and gynecologist, educator; b. Detroit, May 18, 1957; d. Frank and Mildred (Barmore) A.; m. Edward Louis Keenan III, Mar. 7, 1993. BA in History, U. Mich., 1979, postgrad. in Pub. Health Adminstrn., 1979-83; MD, Wayne State U., 1983. Diplomate Am. Bd. Ob-Gyn., Am. Bd. Maternal-Fetal Medicine. Resident ob-gyn. Wayne State U., Detroit, 1983-87; fellow in maternal fetal medicine UCLA, 1987-89, asst. prof. ob-gyn., 1989-97, asst. prof. dept of cmty. health scis., 1995-97, assoc. prof. ob-gyn. and cmty. health scis., 1997—; cons. Office Substance Abuse Prevention, Washignton, 1989—, NIH, Bethesda, Md., 1990—, RAND, 1995—. Peer reviewer jours. Obstetrics and Gynecology, 1989—, Am. Jour. Pub. Health, 1994—, Am. Jour. Obstetrics and Gynecology, 1993—; contbr. chpts. to books. Mem. internal rev. bd. Friends Med. Rsch., 1991—; bd. dirs. Matrix Inst. on Addictions, L.A., 1993—; bd. dirs., vice chair Calif. Advocates for Pregnant Women, 1993—; bd. dirs., asst. v.p. med. svcs. Venice (Calif.) Free Clinic, 1994—, v.p. svcs., 1998—. Clin. Tng. grantee UCLA, 1993—; recipient Faculty Devel. award Berlex Found., 1992. Fellow ACOG; mem. AMA, APHA, Soc. Perinatal Obstetricians, Royal Soc. of Medicine (Eng.), Assn. Profs. of Gynecology and Obstetrics. Office: Dept Ob-gyn UCLA Sch Medicine Rm 22-132 10833 Le Conte Ave Los Angeles CA 90095-3075

ARCHULETA, KEITH ANTHONY, arts administrator, consultant, educational administrator; b. Denver, Mar. 13, 1955; s. Willie M. and Judith Ruth (Archuleta) Suggs; m. Iris Curtis, May 27, 1995; 1 child, Dorian. *Keith Archuleta has provided over 20 years of service to schools, businesses, agencies and nonprofits throughout the U.S. as a consultant, executive director and board member. Wife Iris Archuleta, is a recognized expert in community reinvestment, she is often called upon to advise on the economic condition of inner city communities and has contributed to youth and business development in the Bay Area for over 15 years. Son, Dorian, a college student planning to become a teacher, interns with the family business, Emerald Consulting which combines their skills and training with a love and faith in God to develop whole people, healthy organizations and sustainable communities.* BA in Comm., Stanford U., 1978, BA in African and African Am. Studies, 1978; MA, U. San Francisco, 1992. Founder, bus. mgr. Stanford Black Media Inst., 1976; dir. So. Africa Media Ctr., San Francisco, 1979-80; program coord. Student Arts at Stanford (Calif.), 1982-84; asst. dir. Stanford Residential Edn., 1984-88; founder/dir. Black Cmty. Svcs. Ctr., Stanford, 1987-92; exec. dir. Oakland (Calif.) Youth Chorus, 1993; project adminstr. Arts Edn. Funders Collaborative, San Francisco, 1994—; site adminstr. Young African Am. Achievers Program, San Francisco, 1995-97; interim exec. dir. LEAP...Imagination in Learning, San Francisco, 1996, Oakland Asian Cultural Ctr., Oakland, 1998; founder/pres. Emerald Consulting, Hayward, Calif., 1992—; mem. adv. bd. CIIS MBA Program, San Francisco, 1994-97; mem. bd. devel./mktg. chair LEAP...Imagination in Learning, San Francisco, 1995-97; rev. panelist Arts Coun. Santa Clara County, San Jose, Calif., 1996-97. Author: (play) Their Spirits are Free, 1982; prodr., editor (ednl. video) Song for Melvin Truss, 1986. Fellow Calif. State Legislature, Sacramento, 1978-79; vol. Crossroads Africa, Liberia, West Africa, 1979, San Francisco Sch. Vols., 1995—; founder Kuumba Arts Ensemble, 1979, East Palo Alto Youth Theatre Project, 1985; congrl. dist. coord./del. Jesse Jackson for Pres., Santa Clara County, Calif., 1984, 88; bd. emeritus Theatre Works, Palo Alto, Calif., 1991—; interim exec. dir. Oaklnd Asian Cultural Ctr., 1998. Mem. ASCD, Calif. Alliance Arts Edn., Calif. Assn. Non-Profits, Co-Op Am. Bus. Network, Fellowship Cos. Christ Internat., Bus. Social Responsibility (founder), San Francisco Christian Ctr., Youth for Christ (mem. nat. adv. bd. 1997—). Avocations: poetry writing, theatre, music, cinema, travel. Office: Emerald Consulting Ste 154 665 Dartmore Ln Hayward CA 94544-6785

ARCINIEGA, TOMAS ABEL, university president; b. El Paso, Tex., Aug. 5, 1937; s. Tomas Hilario and Judith G. (Zozaya) A.; m. M. Concha Ochotorena, Aug. 10, 1957; children: Wendy M. Heredia, Lisa, Judy, Laura. BS in Tchr. Edn., N. Mex. State U., 1960; MA, U. N. Mex., 1966, PhD, 1970; postdoc., Inst. for Ednl. Mgmt., Harvard U., 1989. Asst. dean Grad. Sch. U. Tex.-El Paso, 1972-73; co-dir. Southwestern Schs. Study, U. Tex.-El Paso, 1970-73; dean Coll. Edn. San Diego State U., 1973-80; v.p. acad. affairs. Calif. State U., Fresno, 1980-83; pres. Calif. State U., Bakersfield, 1983—; prof. ednl. adminstrn. and supervision U. N.Mex., U. Tex.-El Paso, San Diego State U., Calif. State U., Fresno, Calif. State U., Bakersfield; cons. in edn. to state and fed. agys., instns.; USAID advisor to Dominican Republic U.S. Dept. State., 1967-68; dir. applied rsch. project U. N.Mex., 1968-69, dep. chief party AID Project, Colombia, 1969-70; cons. in field. Author: Public Education's Response to the Mexican-American, 1971, Preparing Teachers of Mexican Americans: A Sociocultural and Political Issue, 1977; co-author: Chicanos and Native Americans: The Territorial Minorities, 1973; guest editor: Calif. Jour. Tchr. Edn., 1981; editor Commn. on Hispanic Underrepresentation Reports, Hispanic Underrepresentation: A Call for Reinvestment and Innovation, 1985, 88; contbr. articles to profl. jours. Trustee emeritus Carnegie Corp. N.Y.; trustee Ednl. Testing Svc., Princeton, N.J., The Aspen Inst.; bd. dirs. Math., Engring., Sci. Achievement, Berkeley, Calif.; mem. bd. dirs. Air U., Nat. Hispanic Scholarship Fund; mem. Am. Coun. on Edn.; founding mem., trustee Tomas Rivera Policy Studies Ctr.; dir. Civic Kern Citizens Effective Local Govt.; mem. adv. bd. Beautiful Bakersfield; advisor Jr. League Bakersfield. Vis. scholar Leadership Enrichment Program, 1982; recipient Legis. commendation for higher edn. Calif. Legislature, 1975-78, Meritorious Svc. award Am. Assn. Colls. Tchr. Edn., 1977-78, Meritorious Svc. award League United L.Am. Citizens, 1983, Pioneer award Nat. Assn. Bilingual Edn., 1994; named to Top 100 Acad. Leaders in Higher Edn. Change Mag., 1978. Mem. Am. Ednl. Rsch. Assn. (editl. com. 1979-82), Am. Assn. State Colls. and Univs. (bd. dirs.), Hispanic Assn. Colls. and Univs. (bd. dirs.), Assn. Mexican Am. Educators (various commendations), Am. Assn. Higher Edn. (instl. rep.), Western Coll. Assn. (past pres.), Rotary, Stockdale Country Club, Bakersfield Petroleum Club. Democrat. Roman Catholic. Home: 2213 Sully Ct Bakersfield CA 93311-1560 Office: Calif State U 9001 Stockdale Hwy Bakersfield CA 93311-1022

ARDANTZ, HENRI, agricultural products executive; b. 1936. Student, Fresno State Coll. With Ferini & Ardantz, Santa Maria, Calif., 1958-63; ptnr. Betteravia Farms, Santa Maria, Calif., 1963—. Office: Betteravia Farms PO Box 5079 Santa Maria CA 93456*

ARENA, THOMAS, writer; b. Chgo., May 27, 1959; s. Charles C. and Virginia Alleria (Jones) Nardi. BA, U. Calif., Berkeley, 1981; MA, San Francisco State U., 1987. lectr. in field. Author Life Sentences, 1994 (1995 Am. Book

award), Dream of Order, 1997 (1994 Joseph Heary Jackson Literary award), Jerome: After the Pageant, 1996, numerous poems. Office: PO Box 422820 San Francisco CA 94142-2820

ARENBERG, IRVING KAUFMAN KARCHMER, ear surgeon, educator, entrepeneur; b. East Chicago, Ind., Jan. 10, 1941; s. Harry and Gertrude (Field) Kaufman; divorced; children: Daniel Kaufman, Michael Harrison, Julie Gayle. BA in Zoology, U. Mich., Ann Arbor, 1963; MD, U. Mich., 1967. Diplomate Am. Bd. Otolaryngology. Intern Chgo. Wesley Meml. Hosp., 1967-68; resident Barnes and Allied Hosps., St. Louis, 1969-74; asst. prof. surgery U. Wis., Madison, 1976-80, chief otolaryngology, 1976-80; clin. assoc. prof. otolaryngology U. Colo., Denver, 1980—; pres., CEO Ear Ctr. PC, Englewood, Colo., 1989-96; pres., chmn. bd., CEO IntraEar, Neurobiometrix Inc., IEMDS, Inc., 1994—; dir., founder Internat. Meniere's Disease Rsch. Inst., Denver, 1971—; guest of honor 39th Chinese Nat. ENT Congress, Taipei, 1985, U. Antwerp, 1995, West German ENT Soc., 1996; vis. scientist Swedish Med. Rsch. Coun., 1975-76, vis. surgeon, 1987; vis. prof. U. Mich., Ann Arbor, 1988, 94, St. Mary's Hosp. and Med. Sch., London, 1988, U. Verona (Italy) Med. Sch., 1989, U. N.C., Chapel Hill, 1989, U. Wurzburg (Germany) Med. Sch., 1989, 90, 92, U. Ark., Little Rock, 1990, 95, U. Innsbruck, Austria, 1991, U. Sydney, Australia, 1992, U. Tex., Dallas, 1993. Editor: Meniere's Disease, 1983, Inner Ear Surgery, 1991, Dizziness and Balance Disorders, 1993; assoc. editor AMA Archives of Otolaryngology, 1968-81; mem. editorial bd. Am. Jour. Otology, 1978-91, Head and Neck Surgery Jour., 1992—, Jour. Club Jour., 1993; guest editor Otolaryngologic Clinics N.Am., 1980, 83, Neurologic Clinics N.Am., 1990; editor Inner Ear Surgery, 1991; mem. rev. bd. Rev. de Laryngologie et Otology (France), 1984—; contbr. over 100 articles to profl. jours. Recipient Pietro Caliceti prize and Gold Medal Honor award U. Bologna, Italy, 1983, Spl. Tchr. Investigation Tng. award NIH; fellow Barnes and Allied Hosps., 1968-69, 75, NIH, 1971-76, U. Uppsala-Royal Acad. Hosp., Sweden, 1975-76; grantee NIH, 1971-77, Deafness Rsch. Found., 1971-73. Fellow ACS, Am. Acad. Otolaryngology, Am. Soc. Neurophysiologic Monitoring; mem. AMA, Am. Neurotology Soc., Am. Soc. Laser Medicine and Surgery, Am. Acad. Otolaryngic Allergy, N.Y. Acad. Scis., Colo. Orologic Rsch. Ctr. (pres., bd. dirs. 1980-88), Internat. Meniere's Disease Rsch. Inst. (founder, dir. 1971—), Internat. ECoG Monitoring Correspondence Group (founder), Internat. Electric Response Audiometry Study Group, Assn. Rsch. in Otolaryngology, Barany Soc., Triological Soc., Politzer Soc., Prosper Meniere Soc. (founder, exec. dir. 1981—), Children's Deafness Found. (pres., bd. dirs. 1983-88), Acoustical Soc. Am., Von Bekesy Soc., N.Am. Skull Base Soc. (founder), Ogura Soc., Sigma Xi. Avocations: skiing, golf, biking, tennis. Office: IntraEar Inc #110 7995 E Prentice Ave Ste 110 Greenwood Village CO 80111

ARENDS, VERNONICA JOAN, artist, painter; b. Phila., Jan. 16, 1943; d. Albin Blanton Fowler and Rosemary Veronica (Howell) Kreibick; m. Carl Florin Arends, Jan. 12, 1986. BA, Sonoma State U., 1993; MFA, Ctrl. Wash. U., 1998. Tchg. asst. Ctrl. Wash. U., Ellensburg, 1997—. One-woman shows include Ctrl. Wash. Artists Exhibn., 1996, 97. Catherine Hall Moe scholar, 1996. Avocations: music, dance, gardening, reading. Home and Office: 412 S Matthews Rd Ellensburg WA 98926-9059

ARENOWITZ, ALBERT HAROLD, psychiatrist; b. N.Y.C., Jan. 12, 1925; s. Louis Isaac and Lena Helen (Skovron) A.; m. Betty Jane Wiener, Oct. 11, 1953; children: Frederick Stuart, Diane Helen. BA with honors, U. Wis., 1948; MD, U. Va., 1951. Diplomate Am. Bd. Psychiatry, Am. Bd. Child Psychiatry. Intern Kings County Gen. Hosp., Bklyn., 1951-52; resident in psychiatry Bronx (N.Y.) VA Hosp., 1952-55; postdoctoral fellow Youth Guidance Ctr., Worcester, Mass., 1955-57; dir. Ctr. for Child Guidance, Phila., 1962-65, Hahnemann Med. Service Eastern State Sch. and Hosp., Trevose, Pa., 1965-68; dir., tng. dir. Child and Adolescent Psychiat. Clinic, Phila. Gen. Hosp., 1965-67; asst. clin. prof. psychiatry Jefferson Med. Coll., Phila., 1974-76; exec. dir. Child Guidance and Mental Health Clinics, Media, Pa., 1967-74; med. dir. Intercommunity Child Guidance Ctr., Whittier, Calif., 1976—; cons. Madison Pub. Schs., 1957-60, Dane County Child Guidance Ctr., Madison, 1957-62, Juvenile Ct., Madison, 1957-62; clin. asst. prof. child psychiatry Hahnemann Med. Coll., Phila., 1966-74; asst. clin. prof. psychiatry U. Wis., Madison, 1960-62, clin. asst. prof. psychiatry, behavioral scis. and family medicine U. So. Calif., L.A., 1976—; mem. med. staff Presbyn. Intercommunity Hosp., Whittier, 1976—. Pres. Whittier Area Coordinating Coun., 1978-80; chmn. ethics com. Presbyn. Intercommunity Hosp. Flight officer, navigator USAF, 1943-45. Decorated Air medal, POW medal. Fellow Am. Psychiat. Assn., Am. Acad. Child Psychiatry; mem. AAAS, Los Angeles County Med. Assn., So. Calif. Psychiat. Soc., So. Calif. Soc. Child Psychiatry, Phila. Soc. Adolescent Psychiatry (pres. 1967-68), Peace Sci. Soc. Avocations: study of violence and aggression, ethnic travels, ethnic folk music, photography. Office: Intercommunity Child Guidance Ctr 8106 Broadway Ave Whittier CA 90606-3118

ARGYS, RICHARD JAMES, secondary education English and social studies educator; b. Sacramento, Calif., Feb. 25, 1952; m. Laura Mesplé; children: Ian Daniel, Colin Patrick. BA in English, Calif. State U., Sacramento, 1978; teaching cert., U. Colo., 1985. Cert. tchr. English, Colo. English and social studies tchr. Adams County Sch. Dist. 12, Northglenn, Colo., 1986—; basketball coach Thornton (Colo.) H.S., 1986-89; vol. mentor, advisor Sch. Substance Abuse and At-risk Intervention Coms., Adams County, Colo., 1987-89, 91-92. Dem. precinct com. mem., Weld County, Colo., 1992—. Mem. Nat. Coun. Tchrs. of English. Office: Northglenn HS 106 W 100th Pl Northglenn CO 80221

ARIAS, JOE, agricultural products company executive. With subsidiaries of Valley Fresh Foods, Inc., 1966—; pres., chmn. bd. Valley Fresh Foods, Inc., Turlock, Calif., 1991—. Office: Valley Fresh Foods Inc 3600 E Linwood Ave Turlock CA 95380-9109

ARIDI, SOUHAIL KAMAL, literature educator; b. Beyssour, Aley, Lebanon, May 5, 1950; came to U.S., 1976; s. Kamal Salim and Widad (Abbass) A.; m. Maha Aridi, Aug. 3, 1986; children: Sanaa, Fadi, Samar. BA in Arabic Lit., U. Lebanon, Beirut, 1976; BA in Polit. Sci., U. Tex., Dallas, 1984. Part-time lectr. Arabic lit. Universal Coll., Aley, 1972-76; v.p. Sarah Cosmetic Co., Dallas, 1980-83; dit. mgr. United Yellow Pages, L.A., 1983-86; pres. Aridi Internat. Pub. and Translation, Monterey, Calif., 1990—; asst. prof. Def. Lang. Inst., Monterey, 1987—. Translator: By Way of Deception, 1995. Regional leader Nat. Polit. Party, Lebanon, 1968-75. Sgt. M.I., U.S. Army, 1977-80. Avocations: reading, writing, translation, music, walking. Office: PO Box 5794 Monterey CA 93944-0794

ARISS, DAVID WILLIAM, SR., real estate developer, consultant; b. Toronto, Ont., Can., Nov. 29, 1939; s. William H. and Joyce Ethel (Oddy) A.; m. Lillie Ariss, Jan. 26, 1962 (div. 1989); m. Debra Ann Nocciolo, Nov. 17, 1990 (div. 1998); children: Katherine Joyce, David William Jr., Dylan William. BA, Claremont Men's Coll., 1961. Lic. real estate broker. Real estate broker Coldwell Banker, Torrance, Calif., 1971-75; v.p. The Lusk Co., Irvine, Calif., 1975-77; pres. DAL Devel. Co., Corona, Calif., 1977-84; mng. dir. Calif. Commerce Ctr. at Ontario, Ontario, Calif., 1984—. Chmn. Inland Empire Econ. Coun., Ontario, Calif., 1991-92; pres., adv. com. Chaffey Coll., Ontario, 1989; apptd. Calif. World Trade Commn., 1993, 95, 97. Maj. USMC, 1961-70, Vietnam. Decorated Silver Star, Disting. Flying Cross, two Purple Hearts, numerous Air medals. Mem. Urban Land Inst., Nat. Assn. Fgn. Trade Zone, Nat. Assn. Indsl. and Office Parks. Republican. Avocations: skiing, music, reading. Office: PIB Realty Advisors 3200 Inland Empire Blvd Ste 235 Ontario CA 91764-5513

ARITA, GEORGE SHIRO, biology educator; b. Honolulu, Oct. 9, 1940; s. Ichimatsu and Natsu (Kimoto) A.; m. Harriet Yooko Ide, Dec. 26, 1964; children: Laurie Reiko, Daren Shizuo. BA, U. Hawaii, 1962, MS, 1964; MS, U. B.C., Vancouver, 1967; postgrad. U. Calif., Santa Barbara, 1967-71. Cert. community coll. tchr., Calif. Prof. biology Ventura (Calif.) Coll., 1971—, curator fish collection, 1976—, head dept. biology, 1989—. Author: (with others, lab. manual) Basic Concepts in Biology, 1981, Study Guide to Accompany Biology: Today and Tomorrow, 2d edit., 1984; contbr. articles on ichthyology to profl. jours. Fushiminomiya Meml. scholar U. Hawaii, 1961-62, Fisheries Assn. B.C. scholar U. B.C., 1964-65; NSF grad. trainee U. Calif. Santa Barbara, 1969-71. Mem. AAAS, Am. Soc. Ichthyologists and Herpetologists, Western Soc. Naturalists, Sigma Xi. Avocations: fishing, hiking, long distance running, photography. Home: 94 Howard Ave Oak View CA 93022-9524 Office: Ventura Coll Dept Biology Ventura CA 93003

ARMANTROUT, RAE, poet; b. Vallejo, Calif., Apr. 13, 1947; d. John William and Hazel Maud (Hackett) A.; m. Charles Matos Korkegian, Aug. 21, 1971; 1 child, Aaron Mark. A.B., U. Calif.-Berkeley, 1970; M.A., San Francisco State U., 1975. Lectr. San Diego State U., 1979-82, U. Calif., San Diego, 1982—. Author: (poetry) Extremities, 1978; The Invention of Hunger, 1979; Precedence, 1985, Necromance, 1991, Made To Seem, 1995. Mem. Poets and Writers. Democrat. Office: 4774 E Mountain View Dr San Diego CA 92116-2256

ARMENTROUT, STEVEN ALEXANDER, oncologist; b. Morgantown, W.Va., Aug. 22, 1933; s. Walter W. and Dorothy (Gasch) A.; m. Johanna Ruszkay; children—Marc, Susan, Sandra, Nancy. A.B., U. Chgo., 1953, M.D., 1959. Intern U. Hosp., Cleve., 1959-60; resident in medicine, fellow Am. Cancer Soc. Western Res. U. Hosp., 1960-63; project dir. USPHS, 1963-65; asst. prof. Case Western Res. U. Med. Sch., 1965-71; mem. faculty U. Calif. Med. Sch., Irvine, 1971—; prof. medicine, chief divsn. hematology-oncology U. Calif. Med. Sch., 1978—, also dir. program in oncology.; pres. med. staff U. Calif.-Irvine Med. Ctr., 1983-85; researcher in multiple sclerosis. Mem. Am. Assn. Cancer Research, AAUP, ACP, Am. Cancer Soc. (chmn. bd. 1973, pres. Orange County chpt. 1985-86), AMA, Am. Soc. Clin. Oncology, Am. Soc. Hematology, Orange County Med. Assn., Am. Soc. Internal Medicine, Calif. Med. Assn., Cen. Soc. Clin. Research, Leukemia Soc. Am., Orange County Chief of Staff Council. Office: 101 The City Dr S Orange CA 92868-3201

ARMEY, DOUGLAS RICHARD, investment consultant; b. Fresno, Calif., Oct. 23, 1948; s. Wilbur Rutter and Mildred (Broadbent) A.; m. Jennifer Louise Armey, Sept. 23, 1972; children: Laura Elizabeth, Andrew Douglas. AA, Fresno (Calif.) City Coll., 1969; BS summa cum laude, Calif. State U., Fresno, 1971; MA, Mennonite Brethren Sem., Fresno, 1976. Ordained to ministry, Ch. of Brethren, 1973. Intern pastor The Peoples Ch. of Fresno, 1972-73; founding chaplain Fresno County Juvenile Hall, 1973; pres. Precision Parts Distbrs., Inc., Fresno, 1973-80, Rutter Armey Engine Co., Inc., Bakersfield, Calif., 1980-88; sr. pastor Fresno Ch. of the Brethren, 1988-97; investment cons., 1997—; radio broadcaster Fresno Fellowship of Christian Athletes/KIRV Radio, 1987-96. Contbr. articles to profl. jours. and mags. Bd. dirs. Fresno Youth for Christ, 1985-87. With Calif. Air N.G., 1968-74. Mem. Nat. Assn. Evangelicals, Rotary, Sigma Alpha Epsilon. Republican. Ch. of the Brethren. Avocations: martial arts, snow skiing, tennis. Office: 3901 E Clinton Ave Fresno CA 93703-2517

ARMINANA, RUBEN, academic administrator, educator; b. Santa Clara, Cuba, May 15, 1947; came to U.S., 1961; s. Aurelio Ruben and Olga Petrona (Nart) A.; m. Marne Olson, June 6, 1954; children: Cesar A. Martino, Maria G. Arminana. AA, Hill Jr. Coll., 1966; BA, U. Tex., 1968, MA, 1970; PhD, U. New Orleans, 1983; postgrad. Inst. of Applied Behavioral Scis., Nat. Tng. Labs., 1971. Nat. assoc. dir. Phi Theta Kappa, Canton, Miss., 1968-69; dir. ops. and tng. Inter-Am. Ctr., Loyola U., New Orleans, 1969-71; administrv. analyst City of New Orleans, 1972, administrv. analyst and organizational devel. and tng. cons., 1972-78; anchor and reporter part time STA. WWL-TV, New Orleans, 1973-81; v.p. Commerce Internat. Corp., New Orleans, 1978-83; exec. asst. to sr. v.p. Tulane U., New Orleans, 1983-85, assoc. exec. v.p., 1985-87, v.p., asst. to pres., 1987-88; v.p. fin. and devel. Calif. State Poly U., Pomona, 1988-92; pres. Sonoma State U., 1992—; TV news cons., New Orleans, 1981-88; lectr. Internat. Trade Mart, New Orleans, 1983-89, U.S. Dept. Commerce, New Orleans. Co-author: Hemisphere West-El Futuro, 1968; co-editor: Colloquium on Central America-A Time for Understanding, Background Readings, 1985. Bd. dirs. Com. on Alcoholism and Substance Abuse, 1978-79, SER, Jobs for Progress, Inc., 1974-82, Citizens United for Responsive Broadcasting, Latin Am. Festival Com; dir., bd. advisors Sta. WDSU-TV, 1974-77; mem. Bus. Govt. Rsch., 1987-88, Coun. Advancment of Support to Edn.; mem. League of United Latin Am. Citizens, Mayor's Latin Am. Adv. Com., Citizens to Preserve the Charter, Met. Area Com., Mayor's Com. on Crime. Kiwanis scholar, 1966, Books scholar, 1966. Mem. Assn. U. Related Rsch. Prks., L.A. Higher Edn. Roundtable, Soc. Coll. and U. Planning, Nat. Assn. Coll. and U. Bus. Officers Cou., Am. Econ. Assn., Assn. of Evolutionary Econs., Am. Polit. Sci. Assn., AAUP, Western Coll. Assn. (pres. 1994-95), Latin Am. C. of C. (founding dir. New Orleans and River Region 1976-83), Cuban Profl. Club, Phi Theta Kappa, Omicron Delta Epsilon, Sigma Delta Pi, Delta Sigma Pi. Democrat. Roman Catholic. Avocation: mask collecting. Office: Sonoma State U 1801 E Cotati Ave Rohnert Park CA 94928-3609

ARMISTEAD, KATHERINE KELLY (MRS. THOMAS B. ARMISTEAD, III), interior designer, travel consultant, civic worker; b. Pitts., Apr. 14, 1926; d. Joseph Anthony and Katherine Arnold (Manning) Kelly; grad. Finch Jr. Coll., 1946; m. Thomas Boyd Armistead, III, Nov. 29, 1952; children: Katherine Kelly (Mrs. W. Michael Roark), Thomas Boyd IV. Editor news Sta. WOR, N.Y.C., 1946-51; with Dumont TV, 1951-52; editor Social Service Rev., L.A., 1956-57; interior designer, L.A., 1963—; travel cons. Gilner Internat. Travels, Beverly Hills, Calif., 1980—. Editorial bd. Previews Mag., 1984-87. Pres. Jrs. Social Svc., L.A., 1962-64; nat. chpt. chmn. Associated Alumnae of Sacred Heart, 1960-66; pres. Las Floristas, 1967-68; pres. L.A. Orphanage Guild, 1969-70; coord. Jr. Mannequin Assisteens, Assistance League So. Calif., 1971-72; pres. docent coun. L.A. County Mus. Art, 1976-77, pres. decorative arts coun., 1977-80, chmn. Am. Antiques Conf., 1979-81, mem. costume coun., mem. past pres.' coun., 1981—, mem. capital gifts campaign com.; bd. dirs. L.A. Orphanage Guild, 1970—; Cert. travel cons. Recipient Eve award Assistance League So. Calif. Mem. Am. Soc. Travel Agts., Inst. Cert. Travel Agts. (cert.), Lady Comdr. with star Equestrian Order of the Holy Sepulchre of Jerusalem. Republican. Roman Catholic. Clubs: Birnam Wood Golf (Santa Barbara, Calif.), Bel Air Garden.

ARMSTRONG, BILLIE BERT, retired highway contractor; b. Roswell, N.Mex., Apr. 18, 1920; s. Gayle G. and Murphy (Shannon) A.; m. Betty-Ellen Wilcox, Aug. 16, 1941: children: Billie B. Jr., Judith C., Robert G., Riley A. Student, N.Mex. Mil. Inst., 1935-39, Washington & Lee U., 1939-41. Mng. ptnr. Armstrong & Armstrong Ltd., Roswell, 1950—, G.G. Armstrong & Son, Ltd., Roswell, 1950—; chmn. bd. dirs. Sunwest Nat. Bank of Roswell, 1967-84; pres. Assoc. Gen. Contractors Am., Washington, 1966-67, Assoc. Contractors N.Mex., Santa Fe, 1952-53, 63; bd. dirs. Southwestern Pub. Svc. Co., Sunwest Fin. Svcs., Inc. Pres. Conquistador Coun. Boy Scouts Am., Roswell, 1981-82, bd. regents N.Mex. Mil. Inst., Roswell, 1960-62. Major U.S. Army, 1942-45. Named Citizen of Yr. Realtors N.Mex., 1969, Roswell, 1968, Jaycees, 1964; recognized for svc. to mankind Sertoma, 1966. Mem. Masons, Shriners, Jesters. Methodist. Avocation: golf. Home: 2619 Coronado Dr Roswell NM 88201-3404 Office: Armstrong & Armstrong Ltd PO Box 1873 Roswell NM 88202-1873

ARMSTRONG, DALE P., plastic surgeon; b. Detroit, July 25, 1933; s. Clifford Earl and Lauretta Marie (Wilson) A.; m. Margaret Charlotte Goebel, June 16, 1956; children: Karen, Clifford, Douglas. BS, U. Mich., 1958, MD, 1958. Diplomate Am. Bd. Plastic Surgery. Intern U. Mich., Ann Arbor, 1958-59, resident gen. surgery, 1959-62; resident plastic surgery Duke U., 1962-65; pvt. practice plastic and reconstructive surgery Denver, 1965-66, Ventura, Calif., 1966—; presenter in field. contbr. articles to books and med. jours. chmn. United Way Ventura County Physician's Campaign, 1981-83, bd. trustees 1981-83; chief of staff Cmty. Meml. Hosp., 1984, bd. trustees 1984-85; clin. faculty mem. UCLA, 1985—; bd. dirs. Ventura Meml. Healthcare Found., chmn. svcs. assessment com., 1984—. Fellow ACS; mem. Am. Soc. Plastic and Reconstructive Surgeons, Am. Soc. Aesthetic Plastic Surgery, Calif. Med. Assn., Ventura County Med. Soc. (sec. 1972-73), L.A. Soc. Plastic Surgeons (pres. 1980-81), Soc. Clin. Aesthetic Surgery. Republican. Avocations: golf, music, travel. Home: 1051 Rancho Vista Ln Santa Paula CA 93060-9743 Office: 168 N Brent St Ste 403 Ventura CA 93003-2824

ARMSTRONG, DAVID MICHAEL, biology educator; b. Louisville, July 31, 1944; s. John D. and Elizabeth Ann (Horine) A.; children: John D., Laura C. BS, Colo. State U., 1966; MA in Teaching, Harvard U., 1967; PhD, U. Kans., 1971. From asst. prof. to prof. natural sci. U. Colo., Boulder, 1971-85, prof. environ., population, and organismic biology, 1993—, assoc. chair, 1997—; sr. scientist Rocky Mountain Biol. Lab., Gothic, Colo., 1977, 79; resident naturalist Sylvan Dale Ranch, Loveland, Colo., 1984—; acting dir. Univ. Mus., 1987-88, dir., 1989-93; cons. ecologist. Author: Distribution of Mammals in Colorado, 1972, Rocky Mountain Mammals, 1975, 87, Mammals of the Canyon Country, 1982; co-author: Mammals of the Northern Great Plains, Mammals of the Plains States, Mammals of Colorado. Mem. non-game adv. council Colo. Div. Wildlife, 1972-76, Colo. Natural Areas Council, 1975-80. Mem. Am. Soc. Mammalogists (editor 1981-87), Southwestern Assn. Naturalists (editor 1976-80), Rocky Mountain Biol. Lab. (trustee 1979-83), The Nature Conservancy (Colo. chpt. trustee 1989—, chair 1996-98). Avocations: draft horses, conservation activities, writing. Office: U Colo EPO Biology PO Box 334 Boulder CO 80309-0334

ARMSTRONG, GENE LEE, systems engineering consultant, retired aerospace company executive; b. Clinton, Ill., Mar. 9, 1922; s. George Dewey and Ruby Imald (Dickerson) A. m. Lael Jeanne Baker, Apr. 3, 1946; children: Susan Lael, Roberta Lynn, Gene Lee. BS with high honors, U. Ill., 1948, MS, 1951. Registered profl. engr., Calif. With Boeing Aircraft, 1948-50, 51-52; chief engr. astronautics divsn., corp. dir. Gen. Dynamics, 1954-65; chief engr. Def. Sys. Group TRW, Redondo Beach, Calif., 1956-86; pvt. cons. sys. engring. Def. Sys. Group TRW, 1986—; Mem. NASA Rsch. Adv. Com. on Control, Guidance & Navigation, 1959-62. Contbr. chpts. to books, articles to profl. publs. 1st lt. USAAF, 1942-45. Decorated Air medal; recipient alumni awards U. Ill., 1965, 77;. Mem. Am. Math. Soc., AIAA, Nat. Mgmt. Assn., Am. Def. Preparedness Assn., Masons. Home: 5242 Bryant Cir Westminster CA 92683-1713 Office: Armstrong Sys Engring Co PO Box 86 Westminster CA 92684-0086

ARMSTRONG, JOANNA, education educator; b. Vienna, Austria, Feb. 3, 1915; came to U.S., 1946; m. David B. Armstrong, Mar. 12, 1946 (dec. Feb. 1992). Diploma, Kindergarten Tchr. State Coll., Vienna, 1933; diploma French Lit., Sorbonne, Paris, 1935; MA, U. Utah, 1951; EdD, U. Houston, 1959. Caseworker, interpreter Czech Refugee Trust Fund, London, 1939-41; tchr. French Gt. Missenden, Bucks, Eng., 1941-43; sec., translator-interpreter U.S. Army, England and France, 1943-46; instr. Coll. William and Mary, Williamsburg, Va., 1951-55, U. St. Thomas, Houston, 1957-59; chmn. langs. sect. South Tex. Coll., Houston, 1961-62; assoc. prof. fgn. langs. Tex. So. U., Houston, 1962-68; dir. NDEA Inst. U. Tex. at Houston, Houston, summer 1964, 65; assoc. prof. sch. edn. tng. Headstart tchrs. U. Tex., El Paso, 1968-71; cons. office Child Devel. HEW, Kansas City, Mo., 1973-75; ret., 1975; cons. Tex. Edn. Agy., Austin, 1965; sec. U.S. Forest Svc., Ely, Nev., 1948; dir. summer programs U. Bordeaux at Pau, U. Zaragoza at Jaca. Author: (book) A European Excursion-From the Mediterranean to the Alps, 1967, Surprising Encounters, 1994; contbr. articles to profl. publs. Vol. Long Beach (Calif.) Symphony, 1978-81, Long Beach Opera, 1982-88, Long Beach Cambodian Scs., 1983-85; mem. Normandy Found. (participant 50th D-Day anniversary 1994). Decorated chevalier Ordre des Palmes Academiques, 1969; recipient award Heart Start, 1971, Pres. plaque Alliance Francaise El Paso, 1971, Commemorative Medal of Freedom, Coun. of Normandy, France, 1994. Mem. Long Beach Women's Music Club (program chmn. 1986-88, mem. choral sect. 1989-96, 1st v.p. 1990-92, rec. sec., chmn. opera sect. 1993-94), U.S.-China Peoples Friendship Assn. (rec. sec. 1987—), W.A.C. (Queen City chpt. 57). Avocations: walking, swimming, travel, photography, opera. Home: 215 Long Beach Blvd Ste 206 Long Beach CA 90802-3136

ARMSTRONG, JOHN, newspaper editor. Exec. editor Contra Costa (Calif.) Times. Office: 2640 Shadelands Dr Walnut Creek CA 94598-2513*

ARMSTRONG, LINDA JEAN (GENE), writer, artist; b. L.A., Feb. 23, 1947; d. Charles Fred and Mary Eugenia (Gentry) Keck; m. Alden Arthur Armstrong, July 28, 1966; 1 child, Amy Alice. BA, Calif. State Coll., 1969. Tchr. elem. sch. L.A. Unified Sch. Dist., 1970-86; writer, artist, 1986—. Author: Early Tigers, 1995, Tanya's Desert Star, 1997. Fellow Woodstock (N.Y.) Sch. Art, 1993. Mem. Soc. Children's Book Writers and Illustrators. Home: PO Box 3151 Grand Junction CO 81502-3151

ARMSTRONG, LLOYD, JR., university official, physics educator; b. Austin, Tex., May 19, 1940; s. Lloyd and Beatrice (Jackson) A.; m. Judith Glantz, July 9, 1965; 1 son, Wade Matthew. BS in Physics, MIT, 1962; PhD in Physics, U. Calif., Berkeley, 1966. Postdoctoral physicist Lawrence Berkeley (Calif.) Lab., 1965-66, cons., 1976; sr. physicist Westinghouse Research Labs., Pitts., 1967-68, cons., 1968-70; research asso. Johns Hopkins U., 1968-69, asst. prof. physics, 1969-73, assoc. prof., 1973-77, prof., 1977-93, chmn. dept. physics and astronomy, 1985-87, dean Sch. Arts and Scis., 1987-93; provost, sr. v.p. for acad. affairs U. So. Calif., L.A., 1993—, prof. physics, 1993—; assoc. rsch. scientist Nat. Ctr. Sci. Rsch. (CNRS), Orsay, France, 1972-73; vis. fellow Joint Inst. Lab. Astrophysics, Boulder, Colo., 1978-79; program officer NSF, 1981-83, mem. adv. com. for physics, 1985-87, mem. visitors com. physics divsn., 1991; chmn. com. atomic and molecular scis. NAS/NRC, 1985-88, mem. bd. physics and astronomy, 1989-96; mem. adv. bd. Inst. for Theoretical Physics, Santa Barbara, 1992-96, chmn., 1994-95, Inst. Theoretical Atomic and Molecular Physics, Cambridge, Mass., 1994-97, Rochester Theory Ctr. for Optical Sci. and Enging., 1996—, chmn., 1997—; bd. dirs. So. Calif. Econ. Partnership, 1994—, Calif. Coun. on Sci. and Tech., 1994—, Pacific Coun. on Internat. Policy, 1996—. Author: Theory of Hyperfine Structure of Free Atoms, 1971; contbr. articles to profl. jours. NSF grantee, 1972-90; Dept. Energy grantee, 1975-82. Fellow Am. Phys. Soc. Office: U So Calif Office Provost University Park Los Angeles CA 90089-4019

ARMSTRONG, ORVILLE, judge; b. Austin, Tex., Jan. 21, 1929; s. Orville Alexander and Velma Lucille (Reed) A.; m. Mary Dean Macfarlane; children: Anna Louise Glenn, John M., Paul Jefferson. BBA, U. Tex., Austin, 1953; LLB, U. So. Calif., 1956. Bar: Calif., 1957, U.S. Ct. Appeals (9th cir.) 1958, U.S. Supreme Ct. 1980. Ptnr., Gray, Binkley & Pfaelzer, 1956-61, Pfaelzer, Robertson, Armstrong & Woodard, L.A., 1961-66, Armstrong & Lloyd, L.A., 1966-74, Macdonald, Halsted & Laybourne, L.A., 1975-88, Baker & McKenzie, 1988-90; judge Superior Ct. State of Calif., 1991-92, assoc. justice ct. appeal State of Calif., 1993—; lectr. Calif. Continuing Edn. of Bar. Served with USAF, 1946-49. Fellow ABA, Am. Coll. Trial Lawyers; mem. State Bar Calif. (gov. 1983-87, pres. 1986-87), L.A. County Bar Assn. (trustee 1971-72), Chancery Club (pres. 1988), Calif. Club. Baptist. Office: 300 S Spring St Los Angeles CA 90013-1230

ARMSTRONG, ROBERT ARNOLD, petroleum company executive; b. Chgo., Feb. 17, 1928; s. Arnold Gustave and Lillian (Laver) A.; m. Jane Victoria Colestock, May 13, 1951 (dec. 1964); children: Michael, Richard, Patricia, Casey; m. Margaret Soden, Nov. 17, 1973; children: Gregory, Jennifer. Student, Mo. Sch. Mines, 1946-48; B.S., Stanford U., 1951; postgrad., Colo. Sch. Mines, 1956-58; M.S., U. So. Calif., 1961, postgrad., 1961-64. Petroleum engr. S.Am.; with Standard Oil Co. of Calif., 1951-58; research engr. Chevron Research Labs., La Habra, Calif., 1958-61; sr. evaluation engr. Union Oil Co., Los Angeles, 1961-63; v.p. Lee Keeling & Assocs., Los Angeles, 1963-65; pres. Armstrong Petroleum Corp., Newport Beach, Calif., 1965—; pres. West Newport Oil Co., 1983—, also bd. dirs.; pres. Los Amigos de Aviones, Tram Tower Comm. Assn.; bd. dirs. Armstrong Petroleum, Calif. Ind. Oil Producers; dir., pres. West Newport Oil Co., Newport Beach, Calif., Angel Flight; vis. prof. engring. U. So. Calif., Los Angeles, 1960-65. patentee in field of subsea prodn. systems. Mem. adv. bd. Stanford Bus. Sch.; chmn. U.S. Internat. U., Africa, chmn., San Diego. Mem. AAAS, Ind. Oilman's Assn., Calif. Conservation Commn., Am. Inst. Mining Engrs. (pres. jr. group, petroleum br. 1960-61), Am. Petroleum Inst., Orange County Petroleum Assn. (bd. dirs.). Office: 2244 W Coast Hwy Newport Beach CA 92663-4724

ARMSTRONG, R(OBERT) DEAN, entertainer; b. Serena, Ill., July 2, 1923; s. Francis Robert and Viola D. (Thompson) A.; m. Ardith Roberta Taylor, Jan. 10, 1943; 1 child, Larry Dean. Grad. high sch., Serena, Ill.; student, Joliet (Ill.) Conservatory of Music, 1942. Host Dean Armstrong Show Sta. KOLD-TV, Tucson, 1953-75; leader, owner Ariz. Dance Hands, Tucson, 1946—. Served with U.S. Mil., 1943-45, ETO, PTO. Recipient Jefferson award Am. Inst. for Pub. Svc., 1992; inducted into Tucson Area Music Assn. Hall of Fame, 1994. Mem. Tucson Musicians Assn. (meritorious svc. award 1981), VFW, Western Music Assn. (charter mem.), Profl. Western Music

Assn. Democrat. Methodist. Lodges: Elks, Eagles. Home and Office: 4265 N Avenida Del Cazador Tucson AZ 85718-7005

ARMSTRONG, SAUNDRA BROWN, federal judge; b. Oakland, Calif., Mar. 23, 1947; d. Coolidge Logan and Pauline Marquette Brown; m. George Walter Armstrong, Apr. 18, 1982. B.A., Calif. State U.-Fresno, 1969; J.D. magna cum laude, U. San Francisco, 1977. Bar: Calif. 1977, U.S. Supreme Ct. 1984. Policewoman Oakland Police Dept., 1970-77; prosecutor, dep. dist. atty. Alameda County Dist. Atty., Oakland, 1978-79, 80-82; staff atty. Calif. Legis. Assembly Com. on Criminal Justice, Sacramento, 1979-80; trial atty. Dept. Justice, Washington, 1982-83; vice chmn. U.S. Consumer Product Safety Commn., Washington, 1984-86; commr. U.S. Parole Commn., Washington, 1986-89; judge Alameda Superior Ct., 1989-91, U.S. Dist. Ct. (no. dist.) Calif., San Francisco, 1991—. Recipient commendation Calif. Assembly, 1980. Mem. Nat. Bar Assn., ABA, Calif. Bar Assn., Charles Houston Bar Assn., Black C. of C., Phi Alpha Delta. Republican. Baptist. Office: US Dist Ct 1301 Clay St Oakland CA 94612-5217

ARMSTRONG, WALLACE DOWAN, JR., data processor; b. Los Angeles, Feb. 9, 1926; s. Wallace Dowan and Vina Edith (Kreinbring) A.; BS cum laude, U. So. Calif., 1951; postgrad. U. Oslo (Norway), 1955; 1 son, Erik Bentung. Supr. accounting Ramo Wooldridge Corp., 1955-60; mgr. programmers, systems analyst Aerospace Corp., El Segundo, Calif., 1960-80, mgr. bus. systems, 1980—. Mem. Common Cause, Handgun Control, Inc. With USMCR, 1944-46, sgt., 1951-53, WWII, PTO, Korea. Mem. Data Processing Mgmt. Assn., Marine Corp. Assn., Am. Legion, VFW. Home: 25713 Crest Rd Torrance CA 90505-7022 Office: Aerospace Corp 2350 E El Segundo Blvd El Segundo CA 90245-4691

ARNBERGER, ROBERT, federal administrator. Supt. Grand Canyon Nat. Park, Ariz. Office: Grand Canyon Nat Park PO Box 129 Grand Canyon AZ 86023-0129*

ARNELL, WALTER JAMES WILLIAM, mechanical engineering educator, consultant; b. Farnborough, Eng., Jan. 9, 1924; came to U.S., 1953, naturalized, 1960; s. James Albert and Daisy (Payne) A.; m. Patricia Catherine Cannon, Nov. 12, 1955; children—Sean Paul, Victoria Clare, Sarah Michele Arnell. Aero. Engr., Royal Aircraft Establishment, 1946; BSc, U. London, 1953, PhD, 1967; MA, Occidental Coll., L.A., 1956; MS, U. So. Calif., 1958. Lectr. Poly. and Northampton Coll. Advance Tech., London, 1948-53; instr. U. So. Calif., L.A., 1954-59; asst. prof. mech. engring. Calif. State U., Long Beach, 1959-62, assoc. prof., 1962-66, prof., 1966-71, chmn. dept. mech. engring., 1964-65, acting chmn. divsn. engring., 1964-66, dean engring., 1967-69; rschr. Calif. State U. Ctr. Engring. Rsch., Long Beach; affiliate faculty dept. ocean engring. U. Hawaii, 1970-74; adj. prof. systems and insdl. engring. U. Ariz., 1981—; pres. Lenra Assocs. Ltd., 1973—; chmn., project mgr. Hawaii Environ. Simulation Lab., 1971-72. Contbr. articles to profl. jours. Trustee Rehab. Hosp. of the Pacific, 1975-78. Mem. Royal Aero. Soc., AIAA, IEEE Systems Man and Cybernetics Soc., AAUP, Am. Psychol. Assn., Soc. Engring., Psychology, Human Factors Soc., Ergonomics Soc., Psi Chi, Alpha Pi Mu, Tau Beta Pi, Phi Kappa Phi, Pi Tau Sigma. Home: 4491 E Fort Lowell Rd Tucson AZ 85712-1106

ARNEY, JAMES DOUGLAS, forestry biometrics consultant; b. Hoquiam, Wash., Dec. 9, 1941; s. James Dennis and Martha (Wylam) A.; m. Jo Ann Joyce Loehrke, Febr. 14, 1991; children: Michael, BettiJean. BS in Forest Mgmt., U. Mont., 1965; MS in Forest Mensuration, Oreg. State U., 1968, PhD in Forest Biometrics, 1971. Forest mensurationist U.S. Forest Svc. Expt. Sta., Portland, 1965-66; rsch. scientist Canadian Forestry Svc., Victoria, B.C., 1970-72; rsch. mgr. Weyerhaeuser Co., Centralia, Wash., 1973-80; mgr. forest dept. Reid, Collins & Assocs., Vancouver, B.C., 1980-81; rsch. forester Potlatch Corp., Lewiston, Idaho, 1982-84; forestry cons. Applied Biometrics, Spokane, Wash., 1985-88, Mason, Bruce & Girard, Inc., Portland, 1989-94, Forest Biometrics, Gresham, Oreg., 1995—. Mem. Soc. Am. Foresters, We. Forestry Assn. Avocations: hiking, snow skiing, pacific NW history, golf, scuba diving. Home: 3486 SW Tegart Ave Gresham OR 97080-5433 Office: Forest Biometrics 3486 SW Tegant Ave Gresham OR 97080

ARNOLD, MICHAEL NEAL, real property appraiser, consultant; b. Madera, Calif., June 6, 1947; s. John Patrick and Patricia (Neal) A.; m. Suzanne Elizabeth Badal, Aug. 31, 1968; children: C. Matthew Neal Arnold, Nathaniel T. Badal Arnold, Andrew T. White Arnold, Thomas A. Badal Arnold. BA in Geography, U. Calif., Santa Barbara, 1974. Cert. appraiser. Assoc. R.W. Raymond & Co., Santa Barbara, 1974; appraiser Madera County Assessor Office, 1975; assoc. Pickthorne & Assocs., San Bruno, Calif., 1975-76; ptnr. Hammock, Arnold, Smith, Santa Barbara, 1976—; instr. Santa Barbara City Coll., 1980-85, 99. Contbr. articles to profl. jours. Coach AYSO, Santa Barbara, 1978—; cub master Boy Scouts Am., Santa Barbara, 1985. Mem. Appraisal Inst., Vieja Valley Site Coun., Santa Barbara Coun. Real Estate Appraisers (founder, sec., speaker bur.), Appraisal Inst. (instr. 1990—, grader, com. chair, officer, chpt. pres.), Amateurs Club, Santa Barbara City Coll. (adv. coun. mem.). Anglican-Episcopalian. Avocations: reading, walking, skiing, talking, genealogy. Home: 3707 Hitchcock Ranch Rd Santa Barbara CA 93105-3177 Office: Hammock Arnold Smith & Co 215 W Figueroa St Fl 2 Santa Barbara CA 93101-3602

ARNOLD, RALPH LEO, III, valuation analyst, consultant; b. Butte, Mont., Oct. 22, 1949; s. Ralph L. Jr. and Annie B. (Baker) A. BS in Acctg., Calif. State U., Hayward, 1973. Auditor Calif. State Controller's Office, San Francisco, 1973-76, chief auditor, 1976-79; assoc. Holton Accountancy Corp., San Francisco, 1979-83; sr. valuation analyst Willamette Mgmt. Assocs., Portland, Oreg., 1983-92; valuation cons. Arnold & Olds, LLC, Portland, 1992—; instr. Portland State U., 1986-87. Contbr. chpt. to book, articles to profl. jours. Mem. Am. Soc. Appraisers (accredited sr. appraiser, pres. 1987-88), Fin. Analysts Fedn., Inst. Mgmt. Accts. Office: Arnold & Olds LLC 610 SW Alder St Ste 918 Portland OR 97205-3610

ARNOLD, RONALD HENRI, nonprofit organization executive, consultant; b. Houston, Aug. 8, 1937; s. John Andrew and Carrie Virginia (Henri) A.; m. Phoebe Anne Trogdon, Oct. 12, 1963 (dec. Feb. 1974); 1 child, Andrea; m. Janet Ann Parkhurst, Aug. 8, 1974; stepchildren: Andrea Wright, Rosalyn Wright. Tech. publ. Boeing Co., Seattle, 1961-71; cons. Northwoods Studio, Bellevue, Wash., 1971—; exec. v.p. Ctr. for Def. of Free Enterprise, Bellevue, 1984—; advisor Nat. Fed. Lands Conf., 1988-92. Author: James Watt and the Environment, 1981, Ecology Wars, 1987, The Grand Prairie Years, 1987, (with Alan Gottlieb) Trashing the Economy, 1993, Politically Correct Environment, 1996, Ecoterror, 1997, Battered Communities, 1998; editor: Stealing the National Parks, 1987; contbg. editor Logging Mgmt. mag., 1978-81, Western Conservation Jour., 1974-81. Recipient Editorial Achievement award Am. Bus. Press, 1981. Mem. AFTRA, Forest History Soc. Republican. Avocation: music. Home: 12605 NE 2nd St Bellevue WA 98005-3206

ARNOLD, ROY GARY, academic administrator, food science and technology educator; b. Lyons, Nebr., Feb. 20, 1941; m. Jane Kay Price, 1963; children: Jana Lynn, Julie Kay. BS, U. Nebr., 1962; MS, Oreg. State U., 1965, PhD in Food Sci. and Tech., 1967. Research and devel. project leader Fairmont Foods Co., Omaha, 1962-63; asst. prof. food sci. and tech. U. Nebr., Lincoln, 1967-71, assoc. prof., 1971-74, asst. dir. resident instrn., 1971-72, acting dir. resident instrn., 1972-73, prof., 1974-87, head dept. food sci. and tech., 1973-79, coordinator food protein research group, 1975-79, dean, dir. agrl. expt. sta., 1980-82, vice chancellor inst. agr. and natural resources, 1982-87; dean Coll. Agrl. Scis. Oregon State U., Corvallis, 1987-91, provost, exec. v.p., 1991—; cons. in field; interviewer Sta. KRVN-AM; participant numerous workshops, 1977—; del., devel. com. Imo (Nigeria) State U., 1981; mem. Ralston Purina Grad. Food Sci. Fellowship com., 1976-78, rev. team dept. food sci. U. Ill., 1979, adminstrv. site visit com. to Mid-Am. Internat. Agriculture Consortium Agy. for Internat. Devel. Morocco project, 1983, exec. com. agr. 2001 com. U. Nebr. Bd. Regents, 1982-83; program chmn. corn and sorghum industry research conf. Am. Seed Trade Assn., 1985. Mem. editorial bd. Jour. Dairy Sci., 1976-82, Jour. Agrl. and Food Chemistry, 1978-81; contbr. numerous articles to profl jours.; patentee in field. Mem. adminstrv. bd. St. Mark's United Meth. Ch., Lincoln, 1975-78, chmn. long range planning com., 1977-78, chmn. bldg. com. 1978-82. Recipient William V. Cruess award Inst. Food Technologists, 1980; grantee Nutrition Found., FDA, Nebr. Soybean Bd., Am. Soybean Assn. Research Found., Am. Egg Bd; Gen. Foods fellow, 1963-66. Fellow AAAS; mem. Inst. Food Technologists (nat. orgn. chmn. forward planning subco. of exec. com. 1976-79, expert panel food safety and nutrition 1979-82, chmn. 1980-81, nominations and elections com. 1981-83, exec. com. 1985—, William V. Cruess award 1980; Ak-Sar-Ben sect. past treas., sec., chmn.-elect, chmn. nat. councilor), Am. Chem. Soc., Nat. Assn. Colls. and Tchrs. Agr., Univ. Assn. Adminstrv. Devel. (exec. com. 1973-74, 76-77, pres. 1978-79), MidAm. Internat. Agrl. Consortium (bd. dirs. 1982—, chmn.-elect. 1985-86), N. Cen. Adminstrv. Heads Agr. (chmn.-elect 1985-86), Nat. Assn. State Univs. and Land Grant Colls. (div. agr.council adminstrv. heads agr. exec. com. 1985-87), Coll. Agr. Alumni Assn. (v.p. 1977-79), Innocents Soc. (pres. 1961-62), Sigma Xi (Nebr. chpt. sec. 1979-81), Phi Kappa Phi, Alpha Zeta, Gamma Sigma Delta (Nebr. chpt. past treas., sec., v.p., pres., Merit Teaching award 1975), Phi Tau Sigma, FarmHouse Frat. (Doane award Nebr. chpt. 1962). Club: Crucibles (Lincoln). Office: Oreg State U Office Acad Affairs 624 Herr Adminstrn Bldg Corvallis OR 97331-2153*

ARNOLD, SAMUEL P., restauranteur, writer; b. Pitts., June 28, 1926; s. Samuel and Katherine (Nissley) A.; m. Karen L. Forman, May 2, 1971; children: Keith, Holly. BA, Yale U., 1947; student, U. Denver, 1966-68. Mem. staff Koppers Co., Pitts., 1947-48, KVSF-CBS, Santa Fe, N. Mex., 1948-49; prin., owner Arnold & Co., Denver, Colo., 1954—, The Fort Restaurant, Denver, Colo., 1963—. Author: Frying Pans West, 1959, The Fort Restaurant: The New Foods of the Old West, 1997, Eating Up the Santa Fe Trail, Sam Arnold's Feast of Life, The View from Mt. Moorison; co-editor: A Taste of the West from Coors; radio shows include Food for Thought, Sam Arnold's Feast of Life, A Traveler's Treasury of Food and Drink; TV prodns. include Fryingpans West, Sam Arnold's Feast of Life. Office: The Fort Restaurant 2221 S Fillmore St Denver CO 80210-4821

ARNOLD, SEVERIN GRUNDVIG, JR., software company executive; b. Price, Utah, Nov. 22, 1948; s. Arnold Severin and Lorraine (Dowd) G.; m. Barbara Swain, Aug. 15, 1975; children: Brigitte, Jeremy Michael, Nicholas Christian. BS in Psychology, U. Utah, 1970; MBA, U. Phoenix, 1989. Sr. fin. analyst Dun & Bradstreet, Inc., Salt Lake City, 1971-77; mgr. credit dept. First Interstate Bank, Salt Lake City, 1977-83; turn-around cons. Salt Lake City, 1983-85; fin. analyst Petro Source Corp., Salt Lake City, Houston, 1985-89; contr. Weider Health & Nutrition, Salt Lake City, Houston, 1990-92; pres., CEO A-Systems Corp., Salt Lake City, Houston, 1993—; sec.-treas., dir. Bonanza Gold Corp., Salt Lake City, 1990-97, Atomic Energy Corp., Salt Lake City, 1983-90, Atomic Western Corp., Salt Lake City, 1975-77. Author: The Fountain of Youth, 1993. Referee adminstr. area 9B, Am. Youth Soccer Orgn., Salt Lake City, 1990—, referee instr. sect. 126, 1991—; vice chmn. Ednl. Equipment Found., Brigham City, Utah, 1997—; vol. Cmty. Emergency Response Group, Salt Lake City, 1997—. Republican. Mem. Ch. of Jesus Christ of Latter Day Saints. Avocations: youth soccer, computer programming.

ARNOLD, TERRY SUTTON, security engineer executive; b. Colorado Springs, Colo., Jan. 13, 1945; s. Robert Elwyn and Frances (Sutton) A.; m. Martha Welch, Oct. 6, 1976. MSCS, West Coast U., 1978. Statistician County of San Bernardino, San Bernardino, Calif., 1965-66; tech. staff TRW Inc., San Bernardino, 1966-67; sect. head TRW Inc., Redondo Beach, Calif., 1967-72; chief scientist Merdan Group Inc, San Diego, 1972—; assoc. prof. computer sci. West Coast U., 1979-96; cons. NASA, 1971, U.S. Postal Svc., 1971; bd. dirs. Merdan Group, San Diego. Contbr. articles to profl. jours.; patentee in field. Named Rookie of Yr. Sports Car Club Am., 1969, Pacific Divsn. Champ, 1970, Nat. Champ Mexico Rally Fedn., 1971. Mem. IEEE (vice chmn. P1363 standard com. 1995—), Assoc. Computer Machinery, Western Soc. Malacologists (sec. 1993—), San Diego Shell Club (v.p. 1992-93, 95-96, pres. 1997-99). Democrat. Avocations: paleontology, scuba diving. Office: Merdan Group 4617 Ruffner St San Diego CA 92111-2280

ARNOW, EDWARD, retired reporter; b. N.Y.C., July 18, 1923; s. Robert and Ida (Pike) A.; m. Joanna Spinney, Dec. 14, 1949 (dec. 1971); m. Gracia Anne Alkema, Jan. 1, 1978 (div. Oct. 1989); m. Jo Ann Cosmo, Nov. 15, 1990; children: Joanna, Stephanie, Doe. BA, Syracuse U., 1946; MA, Stanford U., 1948; MBA, San Francisco State U., 1983. Reporter Stockton (Calif.) Record, 1947-49; newswriter/corres. NBC News, various, 1949-65; prof. U. Calif., Berkeley, 1965-70; Fulbright prof. U. Ankara (Turkey), 1969-70; news corres. ABC News, Turkey, Cyprus, 1969-70; reporter Sta. KPIX-TV, San Francisco, 1970-83, Sta. KRON-TV, San Francisco, 1984-85; cons. Cyprus Broadcasting Corp., Nicosia, 1970. Reporter/prodr. TV news documentary Managua Earthquake, 1973 (Emmy award); corres. TV news documentary Your Invisible Neighbor, 1974 (Emmy award); author: Rogue Reporter, 1997. Pvt. U.S. Army Air Corps, 1943-45. Mem. Broadcast Legends (founding). Avocations: jazz trumpet, travel, boating. Home: 2231 Biscay Ct Discovery Bay CA 94514-9115

ARO, GLENN SCOTT, environmental and safety executive; b. Balt., Jan. 18, 1948; s. Raymond Charles Sr. and Elizabeth Virginia (Coppage) A.; m. Marlene Rose Lefler, Jan. 8, 1972 (div. June 1987); children: Vincent Wade, Marlena Irene; m. Rosie Ann Lucero, Nov. 22, 1994. BS in Mech. Engring., Gen. Motors Inst., Flint, Mich., 1972; MBA in Fin., Wayne State U., 1980. Registered environmental assessor, Calif. From engr. to supr. GM, Detroit, Balt., L.A., 1966-84; environ. specialist New United Motor, Fremont, Calif., 1984-86; environ. engring. mgr. Def. Systems FMC Corp., San Jose, Calif., 1986-89; cons./exec. sales rep. Gaia Systems, Menlo Park, Calif., 1990; corp. environ. & safety mgr. Ampex Corp., Redwood City, Calif., 1990-92; gen. ops. mgr. Hughes Environ. Systems, El Segundo, Calif., 1992-98; corp. EHS mgr. Hughes Electronics Corp., El Segundo, Calif., 1998—; lectr. colls. and seminars Environ. Regulatory Issues, 1988—. Author: Developing a National Environmental Policy in a Global Market, 1989; contbd. articles to profl. jours. Panel mem. Toxics Awareness Project, San Francisco, 1989—; com. mem. Environ. Working Group, Sacramento, 1986-88. Mem. Peninsula Indsl. & Bus. Assn. (bd. dirs., v.p. 1988-91). Republican. Roman Catholic. Avocations: running, reading, travel, baseball, basketball. Home: 241 Palos Verdes Dr W Apt 203 Palos Verdes Estates CA 90274

ARONOWITZ, JOEL ALAN, plastic and reconstructive surgeon; b. Memphis, Dec. 5, 1956. MD, Baylor Coll. Medicine, 1982. Intern in gen. surgery Baylor Coll. Medicine, 1982-83, resident in plastic surgery, 1983-87; attending plastic surgeon Cedars Sinai Med. Ctr., 1987—, vice chmn. plastic surgery divsn., 1997—. Office: 8635 W 3rd St Ste 1170W Los Angeles CA 90048-6104

ARONSON, JONATHAN DAVID, international relations educator; b. St. Louis, Oct. 28, 1949; s. Adam and Judith (Spector) A.; m. Joan Abrahamson, May 28, 1984; children: Adam Brody, Zachary Alden, James Dillon (dec.). BA, Harvard U., 1971; MA in Polit. Sci., Stanford U., 1973, MA in Applied Econs., 1975, PhD in Polit. Sci., 1977. Asst. prof. internat. relations U. So. Calif., Los Angeles, 1976-82; internat. economist rep. Office of U.S. Trade, Washington, 1982-83; assoc. prof. Sch. of Internat. Relations U. So. Calif., 1982-88, prof., 1988, dir., 1995—. Author: Money and Power, 1977; editor: Debt and the Less Developed Countries, 1979; author (with others): Trade Talks, 1986, When Countries Talk, 1988, Managing the World Economy, 1993. Fellow Ctr. Internat. Affairs; mem. Coun. Fgn. Rels. Jewish. Office: U Southern Calif Sch Internat Rels Los Angeles CA 90089-0043

ARREGUIN, ALFREDO MENDOZA, artist; b. Morelia, Mex., Jan. 20, 1935; came to U.S., 1956; s. Felix Velez and Maria Martinez (Mendoza) A.; m. Susan Ridgely Lytle, Jan. 7, 1979; children: Lesley, Rialto Lytle-Arreguin. BFA, U. Wash., 1967, MFA, 1969. Tchrs. asst. art dept U. Wash., Seattle, 1960-69. One-man shows include The Polly Friedlander Gallery, Seattle, 1971-77, The Mex. Mus., San Francisco, 1977, Mocha Mus. Contemporary Hispanic Art, N.Y.C., 1978, Kiku Gallery, Seattle, 1979, Winn Galleries, Seattle, 1980-81, The Bellevue Art Mus., Wash., 1981, The Boise Gallery Art, Idaho, 1982, The Diane Gilson Gallery, Seattle, 1983, Viking Union Gallery, Bellingham, Wash., 1984, Fine Arts Ctr. Tempe, Ariz., 1985, MARS Art Gallery, Phoenix, 1986, Foster/White Gallery, Seattle, 1987, Gallery 76, Wenatchee, Washington, 1988, North Ctrl. Wash. Mus. Gallery, 1989, Fresno Met. Mus., Calif., 1990, Tacoma art Mus., 1992, Everett Cultural Commn., Wash., 1993, Nat. Assn. Chicano Studies, Cheney, Wash., 1994, Kans. State U., Manhattan, 1995, Sinrise Mus., W.Va., 1996, others; group shows include Seattle Art Mus., 1971-72, Nat. Drawing Exhbn., Potsdam, N.Y., 1973, Grand Galleria Nat. Exhbn., Seattle, 1974-75, Galeria De La Raza, San Francisco, 1978, Line Art Ctr., Arlington, Va., 1980, Suzanne Brown Gallery, Scottsdale, Ariz., 1981, Gallery 1330, McLean, Va., 1984, Portland Design Ctr., 1987, Ethnographic Mus., Warsaw, Poland, 1991, Steens Land Art Mus., Northfield, Minn., 1994, Wichita Art Mus., 1997, others; represented in permanent collections at Nat. Acad. Scis., Washington, Smithsonian Inst., Washington, Tucson Mus. Art, Ariz., Sea Mar Cmty. Health Ctrs., San Francisco Mus. Art, Denter Art Mus., Guadalupe Cultural Arts Ctr., Denver, Morris Art Mus., Morristown, N.J., Cralin & Co., N.Y.C., Boeing Hdqrs., Seattle, Met. Ptnrs., Chgo., Graphic Gallery, Calgary, Alberta, Can., others. Commr. Seattle Arts Commn., 1980-82. With U.S. Army, 1957-59, Korea. Recipient Humanitarian award Wash. State Legislature, Olympia, 1989, Cmty. award Wash. State Hispanic Bar Assn., Seattle, 1993. Avocation: hiking. Home: 2412 NE 80th St Seattle WA 98115-4632

ARRINGTON, HARRIET ANN HORNE, historian, biographer, researcher, writer; b. Salt Lake City, June 22, 1924; d. Lyman Merrill and Myrtle (Swainston) Horne; m. Frederick C. Sorensen, Dec. 22, 1943 (div. Dec. 1954); children: Annette S. Rogers, Frederick Christian, Heidi S. Swinton; m. Gordon B. Moody, July 26, 1958 (div. Aug. 1963); 1 child, Stephen Horne; m. Leonard James Arrington, Nov. 19, 1983. BS in Edn., U. Utah, 1957. Cert. tchr., Utah, Ga. Supr. surg. secs. Latter-day Sts. Hosp., Salt Lake City, 1954-58; tchr. Salt Lake City Schs., 1957-58, Glynn County Schs., Brunswick, Ga., 1958-59, 60—; from med. sec. to office mgr. Dr. Horne, Salt Lake City, 1962-83; tchr. Carden Sch., Salt Lake City, 1973-74, women's history rschr., tchr.; mem. Utah Women's Legis. Coun.; co-establisher Arrington Archives, Utah State U. Author: Heritage of Faith, 1988, (essay) Worth Their Salt, 1997; contbr. chpts. to books and articles to profl. jours., biog. encys. and confs. Dist. chmn. Utah Rep. Com., 1972-76; mem. art com. Salt Lake City Bd. Edn.; chmn. art exhibit Senator Orrin Hatch's ann. Utah Women's Conf., 1987; past pres. L.D.S. Women's Relief Soc., Twin Falls, cultural refinement and/or spiritual living tchr.; chmn. Utah Women Artists' Exhbns., AAUW, Utah divsn., 1986-87, Springville Mus. of Art. Recipient Vol. Action award Utah Women Artists' Exhbn., 1987, resolution of appreciation Utah Arts Coun., 1989. Mem. AAUW (Utah state cultural refinement chmn., cert. of appreciation 1988), DAR (Regent Princess Timpanogos Utah Chpt. Utah State U., Friends of Humanities, Arts, Scis. and Social Sci. award 1995); Old Main Soc. Utah State U., Chi Omega, Xi Alpha, (past pres. alumni chpt.). Avocations: art, writing, gourmet cooking. Home and Office: 2236 S 2200 E Salt Lake City UT 84109-1135

ARROSSA, MOLLY, middle school educator; b. Boise, Idaho, Oct. 30, 1950; d. John P. and Eileen (Killoran) Molitor; m. George P. Arrossa, Oct. 21, 1972; children: Tracy, Rich. BA in English Edn., Idaho State U., 1972. Tchr. Kimberly (Idaho) H.S., 1973-77; tchr. Robert Stuart Jr. H.S., Twin Falls, Idaho, 1988—, dept. chair for lang. arts, 1991—; mem. lang. arts curriculum bd. Twin Falls Sch. Dist., 1995—. Mem. Booster Club-Athletics, Kimberly H.S., 1990—. Mem. Nat. Coun. Tchrs. English, Reader's Guild (pres. 1973-74), Delta Kappa Gamma. Avocations: reading, golfing, tennis, traveling. Office: Robert Stuart Jr HS 644 Caswell W Twin Falls ID 83301

ARROW, KENNETH JOSEPH, economist, educator; b. N.Y.C., Aug. 23, 1921; s. Harry I. and Lillian (Greenberg) A.; m. Selma Schweitzer, Aug. 31, 1947; children: David Michael, Andrew. BS in Social Sci., CCNY, 1940; MA, Columbia U., 1941, PhD, 1951, DSc (hon.), 1973; LLD (hon.), U. Chgo., 1967, CUNY, 1972, Hebrew U. Jerusalem, 1975, U. Pa., 1976, Washington U., St. Louis, 1989; D. Social and Econ. Scis. (hon.), U. Vienna, Austria, 1971; LLD (hon.), Ben-Gurion U. of the Negev, 1992; D. Social Scis. (hon.), Yale, 1974; D (hon.), Université René Descartes, Paris, 1974, U. Aix-Marseille III, 1985, U. Cattolica del Sacro Cuore, Milan, Italy, 1994, U. Uppsala, 1995; Dr.Pol., U. Helsinki, 1976; MA (hon.), Harvard U., 1968; DLitt, Cambridge U., Eng., 1985. Rsch. assoc. Cowles Commn. for Research in Econs., 1947-49; asst. prof. econs. U. Chgo., 1948-49; acting asst. prof. econs. and stats. Stanford, 1949-50, assoc. prof., 1950-53, prof. econs., stats. and ops. rsch., 1953-68; prof. econs. Harvard, 1968-74, James Bryant Conant univ. prof., 1974-79; exec. head dept. econs. Stanford U., 1954-56, acting exec. head dept., 1962-63, Joan Kenney prof. econs. and prof. ops. rsch., 1979-91, prof. emeritus, 1991—; economist Coun. Econ. Advisers, U.S. Govt., 1962; cons. RAND Corp.; Fulbright prof. U. Siena, 1995; vis. fellow All Souls Coll., Oxford, 1996. Author: Social Choice and Individual Values, 1951, Essays in the Theory of Risk Bearing, 1971, The Limits of Organization, 1974, Collected Papers, Vols. I-VI, 1983-85; co-author: Mathematical Studies in Inventory and Production, 1958, Studies in Linear and Nonlinear Programming, 1958, Time Series Analysis of Inter-industry Demands, 1959, Public Investment, The Rate of Return and Optimal Fiscal Policy, 1971, General Competitive Analysis, 1971, Studies in Resource Allocation Processes, 1977, Social Choice and Multicriterion Decision Making, 1985. Served as capt. AUS, 1942-46. Recipient Alfred Nobel Meml. prize in econ. scis. Swedish Acad. Scis., 1972, Kempé de Feriet medal, 1998, medal U. Paris, 1998; Social Sci. Rsch. fellow, 1952; fellow Ctr. for Advanced Study in the Behavioral Scis., 1956-57, Churchill Coll., Cambridge, Eng., 1963-64, 70, 73, 86; Guggenheim fellow, 1972-73. Fellow AAAS (chmn. sect. K. 1983), Am. Acad. Arts and Scis. (v.p. 1979-81, 91-93), Econometric Soc. (v.p. 1955, pres. 1956), Am. Statis. Assn., Inst. Math. Stats., Am. Econ. Assn. (exec. com. 1967-69, pres. 1973, John Bates Clark medal 1957), Internat. Soc. Inventory Rsch. (pres. 1983-90); mem. NAS (mem. coun. 1990-93), Internat. Econs. Assn. (pres. 1983-86), Am. Philos. Soc., Inst. Mgmt. Scis. (pres. 1963, chmn. coun. 1964, Von Neumann prize 1986), Finnish Acad. Scis. (fgn. hon.), Brit. Acad. (corr.), Western Econ. Assn. (pres. 1980-81), Soc. Social Choice and Welfare (pres. 1991-93), Pontifical Acad. Social Scis. Fax: (650) 725-5700. E-mail: arrow@leland.stanford.edu.que. Office: Stanford U Dept Econs Stanford CA 94305-6072

ARTAUD-WILD, SABINE MARIE, retired research dietitian; b. Marseille, France, Jan. 25, 1928; came to U.S., 1953; d. Charles Marie and Jane Virginie (Millaud) Artaud; m. John B. Wild; children: Anne Wild Mozell, Phillip Charles, Paul James. BS in Pharmacy, U. Aix-Marseille, 1950, BS in Dietetic, 1958. Lic. dietitian; registered Am. Dietetic Assn. Pharmacist Ciotat, France, 1950-52; rsch. dietitian Inst. Gustave Roussy, Villejuif, France, 1952-53; adminstrv. dietitian Children's Hosp., Iowa City, 1954-55; cons. dietitian Weight Mgmt., Portland, Oreg., 1985-94, Health Mgmt. Resources, Portland, 1987-91; rsch. dietitian Lipid Atherosclerosis Oreg. Health Scis. U.-Lab., Portland, 1977-92. Editor: Simply Nutritious, 1985; first author and contbr. of articles to profl. jours. Pres. Reed Coll. Women Com., Portland, 1974-75; docent Portland Art Mus., 1971-77, Oreg. Hist. Soc., Portland, 1976-78; sec. Alliance Francaise, Portland, 1986; mem. City Club of Portland, 1983—; mem., v.p. Profl. Woman's League, 1990—; mem. program com., archivist, historian Native Am. Art Coun. Portland Art Mus., 1992—; mem. house of dels. Am. Dietetic Assn. (pres. 1989-90, newsletter editor 1986-87, historian 1992, career guidance 1985). Fullbright scholar, 1952-53. Mem. Oreg. Dietetic Assn. (pres. 1989-90, newsletter editor 1986-87, historian 1992, career guidance 1985), Profl. Women League Portland (v.p. 1994-95). Avocations: book discussions, chamber music, art history. Home: 2309 SW 1st Ave Apt 545 Portland OR 97201-5074

ARTHUR, GREER MARTIN, maritime container leasing firm executive; b. Champaign, Ill., Feb. 15, 1935; s. Greer Martin and Olive Loretta (Simard) A.; m. Veronica Lattman, Nov. 30, 1968; children: Alexandra, Vincent, Tanya, Greer III. BA, Lafayette Coll., 1956; JD, Columbia U., 1961. Bar: N.Y. 1961. Account exec. tng. program Young & Rubicam, 1957-58; firm assoc. Havens, Wandless, Stitt & Tighe, N.Y.C., 1961-62; mgmt. cons. McKinsey & Co., 1962-67; asst. to v.p. internat. Scovil Mfg. Co., Waterbury, Conn.; internat. market mgr. Scovil France, Paris, market mgr. Hamilton Beach div. Scovil, Waterbury, 1967-69; pres., CEO SSI Container Corp., subs. Itel Corp., San Francisco, 1969-73; founder, chmn., pres., CEO, dir. Trans Ocean Ltd, San Bruno, Calif., 1973—; founder, dir., bd. dirs. Inst. Internat. Container Lessors, 1970-73, dir., 1977—, pres. 1982-84, 89-90, 94—. Treas., trustee Phillips Brooks Sch., Menlo Park, Calif., 1980-83; bd. dirs. Alzheimer's Assn., 1994—; dir. San Francisco Opera; active Lafayette Coll. Nat. Coun., 1981-83. Mem. Assn. Corp. Growth, Chief Exec. Orgn. (bd. dirs. 1988-91), World Pres. Orgn. (No. Calif. chpt. chmn. 1991-92, bd. dirs. 1994—). Clubs: Bankers, World Trade (San Francisco); Club at World

Trade Center (N.Y.C.); Family, Commonwealth. Office: Trans Ocean Distribution Greer Arthur 2500 Sand Hill Rd Ste 215 Menlo Park CA 94025

ARTHUR, PAUL KEITH, electronic engineer; b. Kansas City, Mo., Jan. 14, 1931; s. Walter B. and Frieda J. (Burckhardt) A.; m. Joy N. Lim, Apr. 26, 1958; children: Gregory V., Lia F. Student Ohio No. U., 1947, Taylor U., Upland, Ind., 1948-49; BSEE, Purdue U., 1956; postgrad. N.Mex. State U., 1957-78. Registered profl. engr., N.Mex.; cert. army acquisition profl.; cert. Naval engrng. duty officer, Navy material profl. With White Sands Missile Range, N.Mex., 1956—, electronic engr. field engrng. group missile flight surveillance office, 1956-60, chief field engrng. group, 1960-62, project engr. Pershing weapon system Army Missile Test and Evaluation Directorate, 1962-74, chief high altitude air def. projects br., 1974-82, chief air def. materiel test div., 1982-91, dep. dir. Materiel Test Directorate, 1991-95, dir., 1995-98, exec. dir. Nat. Range, 1998—; spl. asst. to WSMR comdr. for Space Programs, 1994—; mem. N.Mex. Spaceport Commn., Southwest Regional Space Task Force, Metro Planning Orgn.; past pres. missile range pioneer group; bd. dirs. Dagupan Electric Corp. of the Philippines. Chmn. adminstrv. bd. Meth. Ch., 1992-95. Served with USN, 1949-53, USNR, 1954-87, rear adm. and, sr. engrng. duty officer, 1984-87. Decorated Legion of Merit, Meritorious Svc. medal, Navy Achievement medal, Mil. Order St. Barbara, others. Mem. Internat. Test and Evaluation Assn., Am. Def. Preparedness Assn. (past pres.), AIAA (past vice chmn.), Assn. Old Crows, Naval Res. Assn., Res. Officers Assn. (pres. 1983-85), United Vets. Council (chmn. 1984-85), Am. Soc. Naval Engrs., Naval Inst., Navy League, Surface Navy Assn., Assn. U.S. Army, U.S. Field Arty. Assn., Purdue Alumni Assn. (past pres.), N.Mex. State U. Alumni Assn., Mesilla Valley Track Club, Bujutsukan Acad. Martial Arts. Author numerous plans and reports on weapon systems test and evaluation and topics in naval engrng. Home: 2050 San Acacio St Las Cruces NM 88001-1570 Office: Nat Range White Sands Missile Range NM 88002-1121

ARTHUR, WILLIAM LYNN, environmental foundation administrator; b. Spokane, Wash., May 22, 1954; s. Robert Cyril and Mabel Mildred (Collison) A.; m. Debora Lee Donovan, Feb. 2, 1975; children: Kathleen, Jonathan. BA in Econs., Wash. State U., 1976, postgrad., 1982-83. Rsch. asst. Wash. State U., 1976-77; project mgr. Ctr. Environ. Understanding, Cheney, Wash., 1977-78; program dir. Wash. Energy Extension Svc., Spokane, 1978-79; econs. instr. Spokane Falls Community Coll., 1977-81; economist, cons. Biosystems Analysis Inc., Spokane, 1983; assoc. N.W. rep. Sierra Club, Seattle, 1983-87, N.W. rep., 1987-91, N.W. regional dir., 1992—; also mem. nat. wildlands campaign com. Sierra Club, —; chmn. bd. N.W. Conservation Act Coalition, Seattle, 1982-83; adv. com. N.W. Renewable Resources Ctr., Seattle, 1987-91; cons. energy workshops N.W. Regional Found., Spokane, 1982; mem. exec. com. Save Our Wild Salmon Coalition, 1991-95 (bd. dirs. 1999—); mem. adv. com. Inland Empire Pub. Lands Coun., 1990—; mem. steering com. Campaign for the Northwest, 1998—. hmn., mem. city commn. Environ. Quality Commn., Pullman, Wash., 1976-77; bd. di rs. Ryegrass Sch., Spokane, 1978-81; conservation rep. Internat. Mountain Caribou Tech. Com., 1978-81; bd. dirs. Wash. Citizens for Recycling, Seattle, 1980-82; chair Wash. State Environmentalists for Clinton/Gore Com., 1992, 96; environ. rep. N.W. Forest Conf. convened and chaired by Pres. Clinton, Apr. 2, 1993; mem. steering com. on No Initiative 164 Coalition, 1995; mem. Wash. State Steering Com. to Re-elect Clinton/Gore, 1996. Avocations: hiking, rafting, fishing, playing guitar. Office: Sierra Club NW Office 180 Nickerson St Ste 103 Seattle WA 98109-1631

ARUNDEL, JAMES D., lawyer; b. Omaha, July 30, 1947. BA, U. Nebr., 1969; JD, U. Chgo., 1972. Bar: Nebr. 1972, Colo. 1981. Vice chmn. Kutak Rock, Denver. Mem. Nebr. State Bar Assn., Colo. State Bar Assn., Omaha Bar Assn., Denver Bar Assn., Phi Beta Kappa. Office: Kutak Rock 717 17th St Ste 2900 Denver CO 80202-3329

ARVIN, JOANIE IDA, artist, consultant; b. Cin., Nov. 29, 1934; d. Porter Lawrence and Donitza (Widowich) A.; m. Harold C. Stewart, 1956 (div. 1959). BA, Ariz. State U., 1973; postgrad., Phoenix Coll., 1994-98. Clk. typist Am. Tool Work, Cin.; recreation artist Gibson Art Greeting Card Co., Cin.; art dir. Mead Paper Co., Cin.; tech. illustrator GE, Cin.; staff artist U. Cin. Alumni Mag.; owner Cin. Chili Parlor, Phoenix, 1981-84, Arvin Arts, Phoenix, 1984—; cons. Phoenix, 1988—. Mem. Nat. Assn. Fine Artists, Nat. Mus. Women in the Arts, Ariz. Artists Guild. Roman Catholic. Avocations: caring for cats, cooking, music, tennis, swimming. Office: Arvin Arts 9426 N 17th St Phoenix AZ 85020-2306

ARVIZU, CHARLENE SUTTER, elementary education educator; b. San Jose, Calif., Mar. 1, 1947; d. Joseph Carl and Marjorie Loreen (Nylin) Sutter; m. Ambrose Emanuel Arvizu, Apr. 7, 1980; children: Joseph Todd Nottingham, Matthew Sutter. BA in Art, San Jose State U., 1964, lifetime tchg. credential grades K-9, 1969, lifetime spl. edn. grades K-14, 1969, specialist/learning handicapped, 1969. Tchr. edn. mentally retarded class grades K-12 Berryessa Union Sch. Dist., 1969-71, resource ctr. dir. grades K-5, 1971-73, kindergarten tchr. Ruskin Sch., 1974—; instr. Ohlone Coll., Fremont, Calif., 1980-89, Chapman Coll., 1985-88, San Jose County Office Edn., 1985-94; nat. lectr., cons. and presenter in field. Author: Read It Again, 1990, Whole Language Strategies in the Classroom, 1991, Strengthening Your Kindergarten Using Thrmatic, Integrate Literature Based Strategies, 1993, Kindergarten 5 Day Institute Book, 1994. Recipient Disting. Sch. award Office of Mayor of San Jose, Calif., 1987, Award Bur. of Edn. and Rsch., 1998. Mem. Internat. Reading Assn., Calif. Reading Assn., Internat. Book Assn. for Young Readers, Children's Book Coun. Inc., Calif. Sch. Age Consortium, Planetary Citizens-One World-One People, Soc. Children's Book Writers, Delta Kappa Gamma. Avocations: animals, horseback riding. Home: 3010 Daurine Ct Gilroy CA 95020-9552 Office: Ruskin Sch 1401 Turlock Ln San Jose CA 95132-2399

ARZOO, EMIL J., electronics engineer; b. Esfahan, Iran, 1963; s. Karapet and Hasmik (Stepanian) A.; 1 child, Derek; m. Pailik T. Arzoo, Feb. 5, 1949; 1 child, Andre I. BS, Univ. S. Calif., 1958; MS, UCLA, 1968. Tchr. Calif. Cmty. Coll., 1978-80; real estate broker, 1980—; lead engr. Bendix Oceaonix, Sylmar, Calif.; mem. tech. staff The Aerospace Corp., El Segundo, Calif.; elect. specialist Northrop Corp., Hawthorne, Calif.; mem. tech. staff Hugh Aircraft, L.A. Author: Armenians in Iran, 1994-95, The Satanic Rulers of Middle-East, 1996, AtaTurk, 1997. Pres. The Armenian Societ of L.A., 1963, 68. Recipient Hughes fellowship Scholarship 1966, 1966. Mem. Armenia Scientists and Engrs., The Armenian Engrs. Home: 1501 W Kenneth Rd Glendale CA 91201-1423

ASADI, ROBERT SAMIR, high school principal; b. Salt Lake City, Dec. 21, 1953; s. Abdul-Aziz and Wilma (Craig) A.; m. Karen Lee Schenk, June 16, 1990; children: Scott, Ryan. BS, U. Wyo., 1986; MEd, No. Ariz. U., 1994. Cert. tchr. and adminstr. Tchr., coach Cactus H.S., Glendale, Ariz., 1986-89, Holbrook (Ariz.) H.S., 1989-91; tchr., adminstrv. asst., coach Agua Fria Union H.S. South, Avondale, Ariz., 1991-94; prin. Agua Fria Union H.S.-North, Goodyear, Ariz., 1994-98, Millennium H.S., 1998—. mem. West Valley Fine Arts Coun., Avondale, 1995-96, Leadership West II, Avondale, 1995-96. Mem. ASCD, Tri City West C. of C., Ariz. Sch. Adminstrs., Nat. Assn. of Secondary Sch. Prins. Avocations: computers, golf, backpacking, spectator sports. Home: 9139 W Evans Dr Peoria AZ 85381-3784 Office: Millennium High Sch 14802 W Wigwam Blvd Goodyear AZ 85338

ASAM, MICHAEL EVANS, credit union administrator; b. Honolulu, Mar. 27, 1948; s. Francis Peter and Annie Ealani (Copp) A.; m. Chu Cha Yang, Aug. 22, 1974. BBA in Mgmt., U. Hawaii, 1974. Cert. credit union exec. V.p. Hawaii Credit Union league, Honolulu, 1975-83; exec. v.p. AFL-CIO Hotel Workers Fed. Credit Union, 1983-85; v.p. Kona Community Fed. Credit Union, Kealakekua, Hawaii, 1985-87, pres., 1987—; chmn. bd. dirs. Pacific Corp. Fed. Credit Union, Honolulu. Chief lobbyist Hawaii Credit Union League, Honolulu, 1981-83; dir. Kana Adult Day Ctr., 1989—, chmn. mktg. com., 1990. Sgt. U.S. Army, 1968-71, Vietnam. Mem. Credit Union Exec. Soc., Hawaii Coun. Credit Union Exec. Soc., Big Island Credit Union Exec. Assn. (pres. 1985—), Lions (fin. chmn. Kona chpt. 1985-87, v.p. 1986-87, pres. 1989-90). Democrat. Lutheran. Avocations: reading, exercising, golf, softball. Office: Kona Community Fed Credit Union PO Box 747 Kealakekua HI 96750-0747

ASANO, HISAKO, fine arts educator; b. Osaka City, Japan, Jan. 5, 1944; came to the U.S., 1960; d. Denzo and Matsuko Asano; m. Michael B. Gould, Feb. 12, 1972 (div. 1981). BFA, U. So. Calif., 1966, MFA, 1971. Educator U. So. Calif., L.A., 1970—; adj. prof. Loyola Marymount U., L.A., 1971-72, L.A. County High Sch., 1986, South Bay Adult Sch., Manhattan Beach, Calif., 1977-88, L.A. County Mus. Art, 1989, Palos Verdes (Calif.) Art Ctr., 1989-90, Torrance (Calif.) Art Ctr., 1990—, So. Coast Botanic Garden, Rolling Hills, Calif., 1987—, L.A. Harbor Coll., 1976—, L.A. County Mus. Art, 1997; Japanese brush painting instr. L.A. County Mus. Art, 1996. Exhibited works in numerous shows including U. So. Calif., 1971, Malone Gallery, L.A., 1975, L.A. Mus., 1974-75, So. Coast Botanic Garden, 1989. Mem. Printmaking Soc., Women Archtl. League, L.A. Jr. Chamber Com., Friends of Fine Arts. Avocations: painting, reading, playing koto, gardening. Home: 27838 Palos Verdes Dr E Rancho Palos CA 90275-5151 Office: U So Calif University Park Los Angeles CA 90089-0292

ASARCH, ELAINE, interior designer, anthropologist; b. Des Moines, Nov. 4, 1944; d. Morris and Rose (Sherman) Feintech; m. Richard Asarch, Aug. 17, 1965; children: Deborah, Chad, Jonathan, Adam, David. BA, U. Iowa, 1966; postgrad., U. Colo., 1992—. Tchr. spl. edn. Univ. Hosp. Schs., Iowa City, 1966-69; tchr. Raleigh Hill Elem. Sch., Portland, Oreg., 1969; learning therapist Psychol. & Guidance Ctr., Devner, 1974; interior designer Sipple/Asarch Design, Denver, 1981-83, Elaine Asarch Design Assocs., Englewood, Colo., 1983—. Contbr. articles, photographs to Better Homes and Garden, 1980. Mktg. chmn. Jr. League of Denver, 1985-87; mem. com. Rose Found., Denver, 1997—; Pres., chmn. women's campaign Allied Jewish Fedn. of Denver, 1990-93; chmn. cmty. rels. com., 1994-96; mem. steering com. Harvard Womens Studies in Religion, 1994-99; founder Cmty. Help and Abuse Info. Agy. Recipient ann. award Yeshiva Toras Chaim, Denver, 1994, Tree of Life award Herzl Day Sch., Denver, 1997. Mem. Am. Soc. Interior Designers (cert.). Achievements include research in relationship between environment and healing with relationship to medical practices. Avocations: hiking, snowshoeing, cross country skiing, painting, golf. Home: 1000 E Tufts Ave Englewood CO 80110-5931

ASARO, V. FRANK, lawyer; b. San Diego, July 28, 1935; s. Frank B. and Josephine (Quinci) A.; m. Barbara A. Mansfield, Aug. 16, 1958 (div. Mar., 1988); children: Dean, Valerie, Stephanie, Audrey. BA, San Diego State U., 1957; postgrad., Loyola U., L.A., 1957-60; JD, LLB, Southwestern U., L.A., 1961. Bar: Calif. 1962; U.S. Dist. Ct. (so. dist.) Calif. 1962, U.S. Dist. Ct. Ala. 1990; U.S. Ct. Appeals (9th cir.) 1965, U.S. Ct. Appeals (6th cir.) 1983. Clk. to the Hon. Justice Coughlin Calif. Dist. Ct. Appeal (4th dist.), San Diego, 1961-62; assoc. atty. Jenkins & Perry, San Diego, 1962-65, partner, 1965-70; partner Gant & Asaro, San Diego, 1970-80; sr. partner Asaro, Gattis & Sullivan, San Diego, 1980-82, Asaro & Long, San Diego, 1982-85, V Frank Asaro and Assocs., San Diego, 1985—; judge pro-tem San Diego Superior Ct., 1975—; arbitrator, San Diego Superior Ct., 1975, 1997; lectr. Practicing Law Inst. Author: Balance Between Order and Chaos, 1988, A Primal Wisdom, 1997; contbr. columnist Dicta County Bar Journal, 1965-70. Chairman Harborview Redevelopment Com., San Diego, 1975-85; mem. County Airport relocation SANPAT Com., San Diego County, 1970-75, City Center Planning Com., San Diego, 1986-90. Recipient citation for pub. svc., Mayor San Diego, 1989. Mem. Calif. State Bar Assn. (del.), San Diego County Bar Assn., Rotary Club (program chair 1996—, pres. 1998—), Barristers Club San Diego (dir.). Achievements include patent for avalanche rescue markers. Avocations: writing, music, philosophy. Office: Ste 400 4370 La Jolla Village Dr San Diego CA 92122-1249

ASCHAFFENBURG, WALTER EUGENE, composer, music educator; b. Essen, Germany, May 20, 1927; came to U.S., 1938, naturalized, 1944; s. William Arthur and Margarete (Herz) A.; m. Nancy Dandridge Cooper, Aug. 14, 1951 (div.); children: Ruth Margareta, Katherine Elizabeth; m. Rayna Klatzkin Barroll, Aug. 5, 1987. Diploma, Hartford Sch. Music, 1945; BA, Oberlin Coll., 1951; MA, Eastman Sch. Music, 1952. Prof. composition and music theory, former chmn. composition dept. Oberlin (Ohio) Coll. Conservatory of Music, prof. emeritus, 1987—, also former chmn. dept. music theory., 1952-87. Composer: TRIO for piano, violin, cello, 1951, Divertimento for Trumpet, Horn Trombone 1952, Chaconne for Brass Ensemble, 1952, Ozymandias-Symphonic Reflections for Orch., 1952, cello Sonata, 1953, Sonata for Solo Violin, 1954, Piano Sonatina, 1954, String Quartet, 1955, Bartleby-opera, 1962, Elegy for Strings, 1961, The 23d Psalm for chorus, tenor solo, and oboe, 1963, Three Dances for Orch., 1966, Three Shakespeare Sonnets for tenor and piano, 1967, Quintet for Winds, 1967, Proem for Brass and Percussion, 1969, Blossom Music Ctr. Fanfare, 1970, Duo for Violin and Cello, 1971, Conversations-Six Pieces for Piano, 1973, Summit Records, 1994, Libertatem Appellant for Tenor, Baritone and Orch., 1976, Carrousel—24 Pieces for Piano, 1980, Concertino for Violin, Ten Winds and Contrabass, 1982, Laughing Time for Mixed Chorus, 1983, Festive Fanfare and Hymn for Brass and Percussion, 1983, Concerto for Oboe and Orch., 1985, New World Records, 1997. From South Mountain for Brass Quintet, 1988, Coalescence for Oboe and Cello, 1989, Sonata for the Fortepiano or Pianoforte, 1990, Parings for Clarinet and Piano, 1993. Served with AUS, 1945-47. Recipient award Fromm Music Found., 1953; Nat. Inst. Arts and Letters award, 1966; Cleve. arts prize, 1980; Guggenheim fellow, 1955-56, 73-74. Mem. ASCAP, Soc. Composers, Am. Music Ctr., Soc. Music Theory. Home: 4639 E Monte Way Phoenix AZ 85044-7517

ASCHENBRENNER, FRANK ALOYSIOUS, former diversified manufacturing company executive; b. Ellis, Kans., June 26, 1924; s. Philip A. and Rose E. Aschenbrenner; m. Gertrude Wilhelmina DeBie, Nov. 15, 1946; children: Richard David, Robert Wayne, Mary Lynne. BS with high honors, Kans. State U., 1950; PhD in Physics, M.I.T., 1954. Mgr. physics and math. Gen. Electric, Cin., 1958-61; asst. dir. space div. Rockwell Internat., Downey, Calif., 1961-69; corp. dir. tech. Rockwell Internat., Pitts., 1969-71; v.p., gen. mgr. div. yarn machinery Rockwell Internat., Charlotte, N.C., 1971-75; pres. COR, Inc., Charlotte, 1975-77; v.p. research and devel. and engrng. Ball Corp., Muncie, Ind., 1977-86; pvt. bus. cons. Poway, Calif., 1986—; chmn. bd. RAMZ Corp., Dunkirk, Ind., 1985—; nat. bd. advisors Rose-Hulman Inst., Terre Haute, Ind., 1984—, U. Tenn. Space Inst., Tullahoma, 1982—. Served with USN, 1943-47. Mem. AIAA, Am. Phys. Soc., Naval Res. Assn., San Diego Venture Group. Achievements include design of measurement technique which was needed to determine threshold energy for nuclear fission in order to improve efficiency of nuclear bombs; pioneering of computerized nuclear radiation shielding design and analysis for nuclear reactors. Home and Office: 14258 Palisades Dr Poway CA 92064-6443

ASH, LAWRENCE ROBERT, public health educator, administrator; b. Holyoke, Mass., Mar. 5, 1933; s. Lawrence Clifton and Alice (Sartini) A.; m. Luana Lee Smith, Aug. 4 1960; 1 child, Leigh I. BS in Zoology, U. Mass., 1954, MA in Zoology, 1956; PhD in Parasitology, Tulane U., 1960. Asst. parasitologist U. Hawaii, Honolulu, 1960-61; instr. Tulane U., New Orleans, 1961-65; med. parasitologist South Pacific Commn., Noumea, New Caledonia, 1965-67; asst. prof. pub. health UCLA Sch. Pub. Health, 1967-71, assoc. prof., 1971-75, prof., 1975-94, chmn. dept., assoc. dean, 1979-84, prof. emeritus, 1994—; panelist U.S. Panel on Parasitic Diseases, U.S.-Japan Program, Washington, 1972-78, chmn., 1978-84; cons. Naval Med. Rsch. Unit # 2 Taipei, China, Manila, 1970-80. Sr. author: Atlas of Human Parasitology, 1980, 4th rev. edit., 1997, Parasites: A Guide to Laboratory Procedures and Identification, 1987; co-author: Parasites in Human Tissues, 1995. NIH grantee, 1970-84. Fellow Royal Soc. Tropical Medicine and Hygiene; mem. Am. Soc. Tropical Medicine and Hygiene (councilor 1974-77), Am. Soc. Parasitologists (councilor 1972-75, 88-92, v.p. 1982-83). Home: 10400 Northvale Rd Los Angeles CA 90064-4332 Office: UCLA Sch Pub Health Los Angeles CA 90095-1772

ASH, WALTER BRINKER, lawyer; b. Wichita, Kans., June 8, 1932; s. Walter Bonsall and Gladys Elvira (Brinker) A.; m. Fern Ostrom, Sept. 16, 1986; children: Paul B., Allison L., Carolyn A. BA, U. Kans., 1955, BL, 1957. Bar: Kans. 1957, Colo. 1959. Personal asst. to Solicitor Gen. U.S. Dept. Justice, Washington, 1957-58; trial atty., 1958-59; assoc. Davis Graham & Stubbs, Denver, 1959-63, ptnr., 1964-82; ptnr. Wade Ash Woods Hill & Guthery P.C., Denver, 1982-91, Wade Ash Woods & Hill P.C., Denver, 1991-93, Wade Ash Woods Hill & Farley, P.C., Denver, 1993—. Fellow Am. Coll. Trust and Estate Counsel; mem. ABA, Colo. Bar Assn., Denver Bar Assn., Internat. Acad. Estate and Trust Law. Home: 6814 N Trailway Cir Parker CO 80134-6200 Office: Wade Ash Woods Hill & Farley 360 S Monroe St Ste 400 Denver CO 80209-3709

ASHBY, DENISE STEWART, speech educator, communication consultant; b. Charleston, W.Va., Aug. 15, 1941; d. Dennison Elmer and Marie Juanita (Queripel) Ellis; m. Rudolph Krutzner III, Dec. 6, 1958 (div. 1961); m. Garth Rodney Ashby, Feb. 15, 1976; children: Kevin Krutzner, Kevin Ashby, Lisa Ashby, Scott Ashby. AA with highest honors, Diablo Valley Coll., Pleasant Hill, Calif., 1981; BA in Speech summa cum laude, Calif. State U., Hayward, 1982; MA in Speech and Communication summa cum laude, Calif. State U., 1983. Lic. beautician N.J. Bd. Cosmetology. Owner Salon 105, Somerville, N.J., 1964-66; pres. Second Hand Rose, New Providence, N.J., 1966-76, The Place to be Beauty Salon, New Providence, 1966-76, The Place to be Boutique, New Providence, 1966-76; mgr. LaTortuga Boutique, 1977-81; instr. Los Positas Coll., Livermore, Calif., 1985-90; tenured instr. Diablo Valley Coll., Pleasant Hill, 1982—; pres. Ashby & Assocs., Danville, Calif.; AAUW liaison Ctr. for Higher Edn., San Ramon, 1988-90. Vice pres. Danville United Presbyn. Women, 1978-79. Recipient Pres.'s award, Calif. State U., 1983. Mem. AAUW (bd. dirs. 1988-90), NAFE, Speech Comm. Assn., Pi Lambda Theta, Pi Kappa Delta (pres. 1982). Home: 82 Cumberland Ct Danville CA 94526-1819 Office: Diablo Valley Coll Golf Club Rd Pleasant Hill CA 94523

ASHBY, LINDSEY GORDON, railroad transportation executive; b. Pittsburg, PA, Dec. 7, 1933; s. James Lindsey and Nina Gordon (Johnson) A.; m. Rosa Lee Frost, Dec. 27, 1961; 1 child, Leah. BS in Petroleum Engr., La. State U., 1956; MS in Basic Sci., U. Colo., 1967. Gas engr. Peoples Gas Light & Coke, Chicago, IL, 1956-58, Pub. Svc. Co. Colo., Denver, 1960-63; petroleum engr. Marathon Oil Co., Littleton, Colo., 1963-85; pres. Georgetown (Colo.) Loop R.R., 1973—, Canon City & Royal George R.R., 1998—; v.p. Tourist Rwy. Assn., N.Y.C., 1989-97, pres. 1997—; v.p. Colo. R.R. Mus., Golden, 1996—. Democrat. Avocations: railroads, jeeping, photography, computers. Office: Georgetown Loop RR Inc PO Box 217 Georgetown CO 80444-0217

ASHDOWN, FRANKLIN DONALD, physician, composer; b. Logan, Utah, May 2, 1942; s. Donald and Theresa Marie (Hill) A. BA, Tex. Tech. U., 1963; MD, U. Tex., 1967. Chief of med. Holloman Air Force Base, New Mexico, 1971-73; chief of staff Gerald Champion Mem. Hosp., Alamogordo, N.M., 1976, 91, 92; pvt. practice Alamogordo, 1978—; pres. Otero County Concerts Assn., Alamogordo, 1985-94, Otero County Med. Soc., Alamogordo, 1986; cons. New Mexico Sch. for Visually Handicapped, Alamogordo, 1973-76. Composer of more than 60 published and recorded works. Bd. dirs. Otero County Mental Health Assn., Alamogordo, 1973-77, Flickinger Found. for Performing Arts, 1995; bd. trustees Gerald Champion Meml. Hosp., 1992. Mem. Gerald Champion Mem. Hosp., N.M. Med. Soc., Am. Soc. Internal Med., ASCAP. Republican. Office: 1301 Cuba Ave Alamogordo NM 88310-5727*

ASHER, JAMES EDWARD, forestry consultant, engineer, arborist, forensic expert; b. L.A., July 22, 1931; s. John Edward and Dorothy (Ingraham) A.; m. Marilyn Lee Struebing, Dec. 28, 1953; children: Lynne Marie, Laure Ann. Student Pasadena City Coll., 1949-50; BS, Oreg. State U., 1954. Certs. continuing forestry edn. Soc. of Am. Foresters. With U.S. Forest Svc., San Bernardino (Calif.) Nat. Forest, summers 1950-53, forester, 1956-57; prin. James E. Asher, ACF, Cons. Forester, 1957—; capt., bn. chief, asst. chief, fire prevention officer Crest Forest Fire Protection Dist., Crestline, Calif., 1960-69, chief, 1969-71; forester Big Bear div. Golden State Bldg. Products, Redlands, 1972, timber mgr., 1972-74; mem. profl. foresters exam. com. Calif. Bd. Forestry, 1978-90, vice chmn., 1982-90; mem. Calif. Bd. Forestry Resolution of Gratitude, 1990—; mem. Calif. Forest Pest Control Coun.; mem. Forest Adv. Com., 1982—; chmn. Profl. Foresters Ad Hoc Task Force, 1983-90. Vol. firewarden State of Calif., 1967—; mem. adv. com. Range Mgmt. Program, 1986-90; chmn. Tree Conservation Subcom., First Dist. Suprs. Ad Hoc Com. on Soil Erosion and Sediment Control, County of San Bernardino, 1984—; forensic expert witness. With AUS, 1954-56. Recipient Certificate of Merit Nat. Fire Protection Assn., San Bernardino Mountains Assn.; Resolution of Commendation, County Bd. Suprs.; Forester of Year award So. Calif. sect. Soc. Am. Foresters, 1977, Superior Continuing Forestry Edn. accomplishment Soc. Am. Foresters, 1996; others. Registered profl. forester, registered profl. engr., Calif.; lic. pest control advisor, pest control applicator, Calif. Mem. Internat. Soc. Arboriculture (cert. arborist 1988—), So. Calif. Assn. Foresters and Fire Wardens, Soc. Am. Foresters (cert., chmn. licensing and ethics com. So. Calif. sect., chmn. So. Calif. 1983), Assn. Cons. Foresters, Internat. Soc. Arboriculture, Calif. Urban Forests Coun., Calif. Agrl. Prodn. Cons. Assn., Pesticide Applicators Profl. Assn., Masons, Tau Kappa Epsilon. Presbyterian. Author: (with others) A Technical Guide for Community and Urban Forestry in Washington, Oregon and California. Contbr. 72 articles to profl. jours.; presenter in field. Office: PO Box 2326 Lake Arrowhead CA 92352-2326

ASHER, JAMES JOHN, psychology educator; b. Detroit, Aug. 10, 1929; s. James Joseph and Antoinette Marie (Abdo) Asher; m. Virginia Lee Gardner, Apr. 20, 1954; children: Jeffrey John Asher, Melissa Marie Smith. BA, U. N.Mex., 1951; MA, U. Houston, 1955, PhD, 1957; postdoctoral, various univs. Instr. dept. psychology U. Houston, 1956-57; asst. prof. dept. psychology San Jose (Calif.) State U., 1957-60, assoc. prof., 1961-65, prof., 1965—, assoc. dean sch. of social scis., 1976-78; lectr. in psychology U. Calif., Berkeley, 1960-61, U. Santa Clara, Calif., 1964, Monterey Peninsula Coll., 1964; vis. lectr. NYU, 1966, 67 summer, UCLA, 1971, U. Calif., Santa Barbara, 1971. Author: Learning Another Language Through Actions, 5th edit., Brainswitching, 1988, The Super School of the 21st Century, 1995; contbr. numerous articles to profl. jours. With U.S. Army, 1951-54. Rsch. grantee U.S. Office of Edn., Office of Naval Rsch., Office of Postal Rsch. and Engring., Dept. of Def., Def. Lang. Inst., State of Calif. Mem. Am. Psychol. Assn., Western Psychol. Assn., Am. Speech-Lang. Hearing Assn. (editl. bd. 1994). Avocations: traveling, fishing, playing with grandchildren. Home: PO Box 1102 Los Gatos CA 95031-1102

ASHER, ROBERT BERNARD, aerospace engineer, educator, academic administrator; b. Chgo., June 15, 1941; s. Ben and Edwina R. (Deutschle) A.; m. Linda L. Parker, May 15, 1965; children—Christina Dawn, Kimberly Diane, Heidi Darlene. B.S., Okla. State U., 1969, M.S., 1971, Ph.D. in Engring., 1974. Commd. 2d lt. U.S. Air Force, 1969, advanced through grades to capt., 1972; computer analyst AF Satellite Control Facility, Sunnyvale, Calif., 1964-66; tech. mgr. AF Avionics Lab., Wright Patterson AFB, Ohio, 1971-74; vis. scientist Info. Scis. Lab., Stanford U., Calif., 1975; research assoc. F.J. Seiler Research Lab., USAF Acad., Colo., 1974-77; resigned, 1977; cons. Optical Scis. Co., Placentia, Calif., 1977-78; asst. prof. dept. elec. engring. Tex. Tech U., Lubbock, 1978; program mgr. Orincon Corp., San Diego, 1978-79; sr. staff scientist, tech. supr. optics group Lockheed Palo Alto Research Labs., Calif., 1979-81; program dir. Sandia Nat. Labs., Albuquerque, 1981-85; assoc. dir. Space Flight Systems Lab., U. Colo.-Colorado Springs, 1985-86; mem. tech. staff Sandia Nat. Labs., 1986-92, mgr., 1992—; prof. Old Testament and semitics Albuquerque Bible Coll., 1992—, acad. dean, 1995—. Contbr. articles to profl. jours. Elder, Pulpit Rock Ch., Colorado Srings, Colo., 1976-77; adult edn. dir. Grace Bible Ch., Albuquerque, 1981-83, Hope Evangelical Free Ch., 1997—. Decorated Meritorious Service medal, others. Mem. IEEE, Optical Soc. Am. Republican. Evangelical. Home: 5410 Candlewood Ct NE Albuquerque NM 87111-1614 Office: Sandia Nat Labs Albuquerque NM 87111

ASHLEY, LADELL CAROL, transportation executive; b. Monterey Park, Calif., Aug. 27, 1962; d. Bernard Eugene and Barbara Marie (Roksa) A. Diploma, Rosemead (Calif.) H.S., 1980. Firefighter Calif. Conservation Corps, Klamath, 1980-81; foreperson, deckhand Sterling Seafoods, Sitka, Alaska, 1982-84; deckhand Glacier Bay Lodge, Seattle, 1984; relief capt., chief mate Exploration Cruise lines, Seattle, 1985-88; relief capt. Pacific N.W. Explorer, Prince William Sound, Alaska, 1989; capt. Yachts Around, Seattle, 1990, YachtShip CruiseLines, Seattle, 1991-94; capt. Americas Cup Races, San Diego, 1992, Alaska Sea Charters, Valdez, Alaska, 1992. Democrat. Roman Catholic. Avocations: travel, photography, prose, recreational athletics.

ASHLEY, MICHAEL HAROLD, systems engineer; b. New Castle, Ind., Dec. 7, 1956; s. Richard Harold and Nancy Helen (Hueston) A. BSBA, U.

Fla., 1978; postgrad., Claremont Grad. U. Cost analyst Gen. Foods Corp., Dover, Del., 1978-80; sr. rsch. engr. Gen. Dynamics Corp., Pomona, Calif., 1984-86; project engr. mil. aircraft sys. divsn. Northrop Grumman, Pico Rivera, Calif., 1986—. Lt. USN, 1980-84. Mem. VFW, Northrop Grumman Mil. Aircraft Sys. Divsn. Mgmt. Club, Beta Gamma Sigma, Beta Alpha Psi. Home: 960 E Bonita Ave Apt 83 Pomona CA 91767-2013 Office: Northrop Grumman Mil Aircraft Sys Divsn 8900 E Washington Blvd Pico Rivera CA 90660-3765

ASHLEY, SHARON ANITA, pediatric anesthesiologist; b. Goulds, Fla., Dec. 28, 1948; d. John H. Ashley and Johnnie Mae (Everett) Ashley-Mitchell; m. Clifford K. Sessions, Sept. 1977 (div. 1985); children: Cecili, Nicole, Erika. BA, Lincoln U., 1970; postgrad., Pomona Coll., 1971; MD, Hahnemann Med. Sch., Phila., 1976. Diplomate Am. Bd. Pain Mgmt., Am. Bd. Anesthesiologists. Intern pediatrics Martin Luther King Hosp., L.A., 1976-77, resident pediatrics, 1977-78, resident anesthesiology, 1978-81, mem. staff, 1981—. Named Outstanding Tchr. of Yr., King Drew Med. Ctr., Dept. Anesthesia, 1989, Outstanding Faculty of Yr., 1991. Mem. Am. Soc. Anesthesiologists, Calif. Med. Assn., L.A. County Med. Soc., Soc. Regional Anesthesia, Soc. Pediatric Anesthesia. Democrat. Baptist. Avocations: reading, crocheting, sailing. Office: Martin Luther King Hosp 12021 Wilmington Ave Los Angeles CA 90059-3099

ASHLEY-FARRAND, MARGALO, lawyer, mediator, private judge; b. N.Y.C., July 26, 1944; d. Joel Thomas and Margalo (Wilson) Ashley; m. Marvin H. Bennett, Mar. 5, 1964 (div. June 1974),; children: Marc, Aliza; m. Thomas Ashley-Farrand, Dec. 11, 1981. Student, UCLA, 1962-63, U. Pitts., 1972-74; BA cum laude, NYU, 1978; JD, Southwestern U., 1980. Bar: D.C. 1981, Md. 1981, Calif. 1983, U.S. Dist. Ct. (ctrl. and no. dists.) Calif. 1984; cert. family law specialist Calif. State Bar. Pvt. practice law Washington, 1981-82; ptnr. Ashley-Farrand & Smith, Glendale, Calif., 1983-87; pvt. practice law, 1987-95; pvt. practice Pasadena, Calif., 1995—; v.p. Legal Inst. Fair Elections, 1995—; pvt. judge pro tem L.A. Mcpl. Ct., 1989—, settlement officer, 1990—; judge pro tem L.A. Mcpl. Ct., 1989—, L.A. Superior Ct., 1993—. Convenor, pres. East Hills chpt. NOW, 1972-74, mem. Pa. state bd., 1972-74, pres. Hollywood chpt. 1974-75, mem. bd. N.Y.C. chpt. 1975-78; convenor, coord. L.A. Women's Coalition for Better Broadcasting, 1974-75; Dem. nominee Calif. State Assembly, 1994. Themis soc. scholar, 1980; named one of Outstanding Young Women of Am., 1980. Mem. ABA, ACLU, LWV, NOW, NWPC, Calif. Women Lawyers, Women Lawyers Assn. L.A., Pasadena Interracial Women's Club (pres. 1993-94). Office: 215 N Marengo Ave Fl 3 Pasadena CA 91101-1504

ASHMAN, STUART, museum director; b. N.Y.C., Apr. 10, 1948. BA, CUNY, 1972. Mus. intern in mus. studies and cinematography Staten Island (N.Y.) Inst. Arts and Scis., 1970-72; with Apeiron Workshops in Photography, Rochester Inst. Tech., 1972-78; gallery dir., visual arts coord. Armory for the Arts, Santa Fe, 1978-80; art instr. Santa Fe Preparatory Sch., 1980-82; artist in residence N.Mex. rural pub. schs., 1982-84; art instr. Penitentiary of N.Mex., 1984-86; studio artist Santa Fe, 1986-90; founder, coord. Mus. on Wheels program Santa Fe Children's Mus., 1990-92; Art with Elders coord. Open Hands Inc., 1990-92; artist in residence N.Mex. Arts Divsn., Santa Fe, 1990-92; curator/dir. The Gov.'s Gallery Mus. Fine Arts, Mus. N.Mex., Santa Fe, 1992-95, dir., 1995—; chmn. acquisitions com. Mus. N.Mex.; adv. bd. Georgia O'Keeffe Mus., SITE Santa Fe; bd. dirs. N.Mex. Counseling and Therapy Bd., Art Therapy Standards Com., Capitol Arts Found., Santa Fe Children's Mus. Mem. Am. Assn. Muss., Am. Fedn. Arts, Mus. N.Mex. Found., Friends of Contemporary Art, Folk Art Soc. Am. Home: RR 4 Box 16K Santa Fe NM 87501-7021 Office: Mus Fine Arts PO Box 2087 Santa Fe NM 87504-2087

ASHMEAD, ALLEZ MORRILL, speech, hearing, and language pathologist, orofacial myologist, consultant; b. Provo, Utah, Dec. 18, 1916; d. Laban Rupert and Zella May (Miller) M.; m. Harvey H. Ashmead, 1940; children: Harve DeWayne, Sheryl Mae Harames, Zeltha Janeel Henderson, Emma Allez Broadfoot. BS, Utah State U., 1938; MS summa cum laude, U. Utah, 1952, PhD summa cum laude, 1970; postgrad., Idaho State U., Oreg. State Coll., U. Denver, U. Utah, Brigham Young U., Utah State U., U. Washington, U. No. Colo. Cert. secondary edn., remedial reading, spl. edn., learning disabilities; cert. ASHA clin. competence speech pathology and audiology; profl. cert. in orofacial myology. Tchr. pub. schs. Utah, Idaho, 1938-43; speech and hearing pathologist Bushnell Hosp., Brigham City, Utah, 1943-45; sr. speech correctionist Utah State Dept. Health, Salt Lake City, 1945-52; dir. speech and hearing dept. Davis County Sch. Dist., Farmington, Utah, 1952-65; clin., field supr. U. Utah, Salt Lake City, 1965-70, 75-78; speech pathologist Box Elder Sch. Dist., Brigham City, 1970-75, 78-84; teaching specialist Brigham Young U., Provo, 1970-73; speech pathologist Primary Children's Med. Ctr., Salt Lake City, 1975-77; pvt. practice speech pathology and orofacial myology, 1970-88; del. USSR Profl. Speech Pathology seminar, 1984, 86; participant numerous internat. seminars. Author: Physical Facilities for Handicapped Children, 1957, A Guide for Training Public School Speech and Hearing Clinicians, 1965, A Guide for Public School Speech Hearing Programs, 1959, Impact of Orofacial Myofunctional Treatment on Orthodontic Correction, 1982, Meeting Needs of Handicapped Children, 1975, Relationship of Trace Minerals to Disease, 1972, Macro and Trace Minerals in Human Metabolism, 1971, Electromotive Potential Differences Between Stutterers and Non-stutterers, 1970, Learning Disability, An Educational Adventure, 1969, New Horizons in Special Education, 1969, Developing Speech and Language in the Exceptional Child, 1961, Parent Teacher Guidance in Primary Stuttering, 1951, numerous others; contbr. research articles to profl. jours. Student Placement chair Am. Field Service, Kaysville, Utah, 1962-66; ednl. del. Women's State Legis. Council, Salt Lake City, 1958-70; chairwoman fund raising Utah Symphony Orch., Salt Lake City, 1970-71; sec., treas. Utah chpt. U.S. Council for Exceptional Children, 1958-62, membership com. chair, 1962-66, program com. chair, 1966-68. Recipient Scholarship award for Higher Edn. U. Utah, Salt Lake City, 1969; Phi Kappa Phi scholar, Delta Kappa Gamma scholar, 1968; rsch. grantee Utah Dept. Edn., 1962. Mem. NEA, Utah Ednl. Assn., Am. Speech, Lang. Hearing Assn. (life, continuing edn. com. 1985, Ace award for Continuing Edn. 1984), Western Speech Assn., Internat. Assn. Orofacial Myology (life, bd. examiners, Sci. Contribution award 1982), Utah Speech, Hearing and Lang. Assn. (life, sec., treas. 1956-60), AAUW (Utah state bd. chair status of women 1959-62, Kaysville br. 1957-60, bd. dirs. Kaysville-Davis br. 1987-92, chair internat. rels. 1987-91, chair cultural interests Kaysville-Davis br. 1991-92), Delta Kappa Gamma (state scholarship award 1968, del. Woman's State Legis. Coun. 1958-70, profl. affairs chair 1963-67, tchr. of yr. award 1978), AAUW (bd. dirs. internat. rels. Kaysville-Davis br., 1988-91), Daus. Utah Pioneers (parliamentarian Kaysville 1980-92, historian 1974-80, lesson leader 1992-95, capt. 1996-98), Soroptimists (charter, bd. dirs. 1954-56, pres. Davis County chpt. 1965-69, Rocky Mountain regional bd. dirs. 1965-70, cmty. svc. award 1968, pub. svc. award 1970), Sigma Alpha Eta, Theta Alpha Phi, Psi Chi, Zeta Phi Eta, Phi Kappa Phi. Republican. Mem. LDS Ch. Avocations: international travel, reading, boating, sports, fine and performing arts. Home: 719 E Center St Kaysville UT 84037-2138

ASHPOLE, WILLIAM EMORY, minister; b. Buffalo Center, Iowa, June 3, 1929; s. Harold Lester and Emily Jane (Hays) A.; m. Bonnie Lou Mundale, Oct. 16, 1950; children: Bryan Lee, Brenda Kay, Bradley Chris, Brent Harold. BA in Theology, N. Cen. Bible Coll., Mpls., 1971; student, Ark. Stte Coll. Lic. to ministry Assemblies of God, 1950, ordained, 1956. Pastor Horatio (Ark.) Assembly of God, 1950-51, Montevideo (Minn.) Assembly of God, 1954-59, Redwood Falls (Minn.) Assembly of God, 1959-60, Portia (Ark.) Assembly of God, 1960-62, Bay Village (Ark.) Assembly of God, 1962-64, Montevideo Assembly of God, 1964-67, Aloha Assembly of God, Lihue, Hawaii, 1967-78, Faith Assembly of God, Mililani, Hawaii, 1978—; dir., teen challenge pres. Home Mission, Mililani, 1978—; asst. supt. Hawaii Assemblies of God, Honolulu, 1978—, Christian Edn. dir., 1969-78, presbyter (Kauai), 1967-69; evangelist, dir. Youth with a Mission, 1964-65; short-term missionary evangelist Philippines, Guam, P.R., Tonga, Samoa, Ponape; coord. Hawaii Coll. Fund, 1978—; contact pastor Mil. Ministry, 1978—. Chaplain (Maj.) Civil Air Patrol, 1969-74; precinct chmn. Rep. Party, Wahiawa, 1988. Mem. Chi Alpha (com. mem. 1978—). Home: 57 Ilima St Wahiawa HI 96786-1611 Office: Faith Assembly of God 95-121 Waimakua Dr Mililani HI 96789-3238

ASHTON, RICK JAMES, librarian; b. Middletown, Ohio, Sept. 18, 1945; s. Ralph James and Lydia Marie (Thornbery) A.; m. Marcia K. Zuroweste, Dec. 23, 1966; children: Jonathan Paul, David Andrew. AB, Harvard U., 1967; MA, Northwestern U., 1969, PhD, 1973; MA, U. Chgo., 1976. Instr., asst. prof. history Northwestern U., Evanston, Ill., 1972-74; curator local and family history Newberry Libr., Chgo., 1974-77; asst. dir. Allen County Pub. Libr., Ft. Wayne, Ind., 1977-80, dir., 1980-85; city libr. Denver Pub. Libr., 1985—; mem. Ind. Coop Libr. Svcs. Authority, 1980-85, pres., 1984-85; cons. NEH, Nat. Ctr. Edn. Stats., Northwestern U. Office Estate Planning, Snowbird Leadership Inst. Author: The Life of Henry Ruiter, 1742-1819, 1974, The Genealogy Beginner's Manual: A New Edition, 1977, Stuntz, Fuller, Kennard and Cheadle Ancestors, 1987 (with others) Trends in Urban Library Management, 1989. Bd. dirs. Cmty. Coordinated Child Care, Evanston, 1972-74, Three Rivers Montessori Sch., Ft. Wayne, 1977-80; bd. dirs., sec. Allen County-Ft. Wayne Hist. Soc., 1977-83; conscientious objector. Recipient Old City Hall Hist. Svc. award, 1985, Phil Milstein award Denver AIA, 1998; NDEA fellow, 1967-69, Downtown Denver award, 1996, 97; Woodrow Wilson fellow, 1971-72. Mem. ALA, Colo. Libr. Assn., Colo. Alliance Rsch. Librs. (pres. 1987-88, sec. 1993-95, chmn. 1995—), Cactus Club. Home: 2974 S Verbena Way Denver CO 80231-4219 Office: Denver Pub Libr 10 W 14th Avenue Pkwy Denver CO 80204-2731

ASHWORTH, BRENT FERRIN, lawyer; b. Albany, Calif., Jan. 8, 1949; s. Dell Shepherd and Bette Jean (Brailsford) A.; m. Charlene Mills, Dec. 16, 1970; children: Amy, John, Matthew, Samuel (dec.), Adam, David, Emily, Luke, Benjamin. BA, Brigham Young U., 1972; JD, U. Utah, 1975. Bar: Utah 1977. Asst. county atty. Carbon County, Price, Utah, 1975-76; assoc. atty. Frandsen & Keller, Price, 1976-77; v.p. legal affairs, sec., gen. counsel Nature's Sunshine Products, Provo, Utah, 1977—; bd. mem., gen. counsel Carbon County Nursing Home, Price, 1976-77; mem. Provo Landmarks Commn., 1997—, co-chair sesquicentennial com., 1998—. Chmn. Utah County Cancer Crusade Com., 1981-83; chmn. Provo LCOC Arts subcom.; city councilman Payson City, Utah, 1980-82, mem. planning commn., 1980-82, mayor pro tem, 1982; bd. dirs. ARC, Utah County chpt., 1988-94; pres. Deseret Village Spani Fork, Utah, 1988-90; gen. counsel Brigham Young Acad. Found., 1995—. Mem. ABA, SAR (pres. Utah County chpt. 1989-90, state chpts. 1st v.p. 1990-91, state soc. pres. 1991-92, chancellor, 1992-94), ATLA, Southeastern Utah Bar Assn. (sec. 1977), Utah State Bar, Am. Corp. Counsel Assn. (sec. Intermountain chpt. 1990-91), Emily Dickinson Soc. Utah (pres. 1995-97), Sons Utah Pioneers, Kiwanis Club (v.p. 1995-96, pres. 1997-98), Phi Kappa Phi, Phi Eta Sigma. Home: 1965 N 1400 E Provo UT 84604-2106 Office: Natures Sunshine Products 1655 N Main St Spanish Fork UT 84660-1007

ASIELLO, ROBERT MICHAEL, manufacturing executive, retired military officer; b. Corning, N.Y., Feb. 3, 1945; s. Dominic John and Jean Marie (Swallow) A.; m. Margaret Frances Baldau, Feb. 24, 1968; children: Robin Michele Crump, Douglas James. BA, Niagara U., 1966; MA, U. Ky., 1979. Commd. 2nd lt. U.S. Army, 1966, advanced through grades to col., 1989; asst. prof. U.S. Mil. Acad., West Point, N.Y., 1979-83; dir. pers. 24th Inf. Divsn., Ft. Stewart, Ga., 1983-86, U.S. Army-Europe, Heidelberg, Germany, 1987-92; prof. U.S. Army War Coll., Carlisle, Pa., 1992-93; ret. U.S. Army, 1993; exec. v.p. Sci. Imaging, Beaverton, Oreg., 1993—. Author: (reference text) Army Command, Leadership, and Management: Theory and Practice, 1992-93. Bd. dirs. Washington County (Oreg.) Hist. Soc., 1994—. Mem. Ret. Officers Assn., Res Vineyard and Golf Club (mem. adv. bd. 1997—). Republican. Roman Catholic. Avocations: golf, fishing, skiing. Home: 4130 NW 152nd Ter Portland OR 97229-7897 Office: Sci Imaging Techs Inc PO Box 569 Beaverton OR 97075-0569

ASKANAS-ENGEL, VALERIE, neurologist, educator, researcher; b. Poland, May 28, 1937; came to U.S., 1969, naturalized, 1975; d. Marian and Leontyne Hornik; m. W. King Engel; 1 dau., Eve Monique Kerr. MD, Warsaw Med. Sch., Poland, 1960, PhD, 1967; Doctor honoris causa, U. d'Aix-Marseille, France, 1987. Rotating intern Univ. Hosp. Warsaw Med. Sch., 1960-61, resident in neurology, 1961-64, fellow in neuromuscular diseases, 1964-65; asst. prof. neurology Warsaw Med. Sch., 1965-69; assoc. mem. Inst. Muscle Diseases, N.Y.C., 1969-73; asst. prof. NYU Med. Sch., 1973-77; sr. investigator NIH, Bethesda, Md., 1977-81; prof. neurology and pathology U. So. Calif., L.A., 1981—; co-dir. Neuromuscular Ctr. at Hosp. Good Samaritan, 1981—, Muscular Dystrophy Assn. Clinic, 1981—, The Jerry Lewis ALS Clin. and Rsch. Ctr., 1988—; v.p. 6th Internat. Congress on Neuromuscular Diseases, 1986, 7th, 1990, 8th, 1994; vis. prof. internat. congresses, Europe, S.Am., Can., Far East. Contbr. numerous articles, chpts., abstracts to med. publs. Recipient Dean's prize for outstanding research, 1967; Premio Associazione Stampa Medica Italiana Di Giurnal Italianalsmo Medico, 1980; grantee NIH, 1974-77, 83—, Muscular Dystrophy Assn., 1969-77, 81—. Fellow Am. Acad. Neurology, L.A. Acad. Medicine; mem. Soc. for Neurosci., Am. Neurol. Assn., d'Honneur de la Soc. Francaise de Neurologie, Am. Soc. Cell Biology, Am. Assn. Neuropathology, Histochem. Soc., Uruguayan Neurological Assn. (hon. mem.), L.A. County Med. Assn., Polish Neurol. Assn. (hon.). Home: 527 S Arden Blvd Los Angeles CA 90020-4737 Office: U So Calif Neuromuscular Ctr Good Samaritan Hosp 637 Lucas Ave Los Angeles CA 90017-1912

ASKIN, RICHARD HENRY, JR., entertainment company executive; b. Flushing, N.Y., Feb. 11, 1947; s. Richard H. and Anne Margaret A.; children: Jennifer Leigh, Michael Richard. BA in Econs., Rutgers Coll., 1969; MA in Comm., U. Tex., 1971; MBA in Fin., Fordham U., 1976. Sales rep. Proctor & Gamble Distbg. Co., Jericho, N.Y., 1969; account exec. CableRep, Inc., N.Y.C., 1973-74, WNBC-TV Nat. Broadcasting Co., N.Y.C., 1974-75, NBC-TV, NBC, N.Y.C., 1975-76, sales mgr. KNBC-TV, Los Angeles, 1976-79, dir. sales, 1979-85; v.p. domestic sales Fries Distbn. Co., Los Angeles, 1985-86, sr. v.p. distbn., 1986-87; pres. TV, The Samuel Goldwyn Co., L.A., 1987-96, pres., CEO Tribune Entertainment Co., 1996—; pres. The Breckford Group, Inc.; trustee Entertainment Industry Coun. Served to 1st lt. Adj. Gen. Corps, U.S. Army, 1971-73. Decorated Army Commendation medal; Alcoa fellow, 1969-70. Mem. Hollywood Radio and TV Soc., Advt. Industry Emergency Fund (pres., bd. dirs.), Acad. of TV, Arts and Scis. (bd. govs. telecomm. exec. br.), Sierra Club, Alpha Rho Alumni Assn., Chi Psi. Home: 1520 Aldercreek Pl Westlake Vlg CA 91362-4211 Office: Tribune Entertainment 5800 W Sunset Blvd Los Angeles CA 90028-6607

ATAIE, ATA JENNATI, oil products marketing executive; b. Mashad, Iran, Mar. 15, 1934; s. Hamid Jennati and Mohtaram (Momeni) A.; came to U.S., 1957, naturalized, 1969; B.S. in Agr., Fresno (Calif.) State U., 1964; B.A. in Econs., San Francisco State U., 1966; m. Judith Garrett Bush, Oct. 7, 1961; children—Ata Jennati, Andrew J. Mktg. exec. Shell Oil Co., Oakland, Calif., 1966-75; pres. A.J. Ataie & Cos., Danville, Calif., 1975—; Am. Value Inc., 1976—. Served as 2d lt. Iranian Army, 1953. Mem. Nat. Petroleum Retailers Assn. Democrat.

ATCHER, ROBERT WHITEHILL, chemist, educator; b. Chgo., June 12, 1951; s. Robert O. and Marguerite (Whitehill) A.; m. Lisa Laidlaw, 1990 (div. 1995); 1 child, Robert Andrew Laidlaw Atcher; m. Sharon Ciessau, 1998. BA, Washington U., St. Louis, 1972; MS, U. Rochester (N.Y.), 1974, PhD, 1980; MA, U. Mo., 1976. Rsch. assoc. radiology Harvard Med. Sch., 1982-83, Brigham & Women's Hosp., 1982-83; rsch. affiliate Nuclear Reactor Lab. MIT, 1982-83; cancer expert, radiation oncology br. div. cancer treatment Nat. Cancer Inst., NIH, Bethesda, Md., 1983-86; adj. prof. dept. chemistry U. Md., College Park, 1984-86; group leader nuclear medicine rsch. chemistry div. Argonne (Ill.) Nat. Lab., 1986-93; radiochemist Michael Reese/U. Chgo. Ctr. Radiation Therapy, 1986-94; asst. prof. radiation oncology dept. U. Chgo., 1986-94; assoc. prof. medicine, assoc. prof. radiation oncology U. Ala., Birmingham, 1994-97; tech. staff mem. Los Alamos (N.Mex.) Nat. Lab., 1997—; prof. Coll. Pharmacy U. N.Mex., Albuquerque, 1997—; teaching asst. dept. chemistry U. Rochester, 1972-74; teaching asst. Sch. Journalism, U. Mo., 1974-75; advisor lab. grad. participant program Argonne Nat. Lab., 1986-93, advisor undergrad. student rsch. program, 1986-93; cons. Cytogen Corp., Princeton, N.J., 1986-90, NeoRx Corp., Seattle, 1987—, Sterling Drug, 1989-93; mem. task force Isotope Prodn./Distbn., U.S. Dept. Energy, Washington, 1990—. Bd. reviewers Jour. Nuclear Medicine, 1989—; editorial bd. Bioconjugate Chemistry, 1989-93. Fellow Am. Inst. Chemists; mem. AAAS, Radiation Rsch. Soc., Soc. Nuclear Medicine (pres. radiopharm. sci. coun.), Am. Chem. Soc., Fedn. Am. Scientists, N.Y. Acad. Scis., Sigma Xi. Roman Catholic. Office: Chem Sci Tech Div MS J514 Los Alamos NM 87545

ATCHESON, SUE HART, business educator; b. Dubuque, Iowa, Apr. 12; d. Oscar Raymond and Anna (Cook) Hart; m. Walter Clark Atcheson (div.); children: Christine A. Hischar, Moffet Zoe, Claye Williams. BBA, Mich. State U.; MBA, Calif. State Poly. U., Pomona, 1973. Cert. tchr. and adminstr. Instr. Mt. San Antonio Coll., Walnut, Calif., 1968-90; bd. dirs. faculty assn. Mt. San Antonio Coll.; mem. acad. senate Mt. San Antonio Coll.; originator vol. income tax assistance Mt. San Antonio Coll.; speaker in field. Author: Fractions and Equations on Your Own, 1975. Charter mem. Internat. Commn. on Monetary and Econ. Reform; panelist infrastructure funding reform, Freeport, Ill., 1989. Mem. Cmty. Concert Assn. Inland Empire (bd. dirs.), Scripps Coll. Fine Arts Found., Recyclers Club (pres. 1996).

ATCHITY, KENNETH JOHN, producer, literary manager/producer; b. Eunice, La., Jan. 16, 1944; s. Fred J. and Myrza Marie (Aguillard) A.; m. Kathleen Dillon, 1964 (div. 1972); children: Vincent, Rosemary. BA, Georgetown U., 1965; PhD in Comparative Lit., Yale U., 1971. Prof. comparative lit. Occidental Coll., L.A., 1970-87; disting. instr. writers program UCLA, 1971-87; Fulbright prof. Am. Lit. U. Bologna; pres., exec. prodr. L.A. House Romances, L.A. and Montreal, 1986-89; pres. Atchity Editl./Entertainment Internat., Inc., L.A., N.Y.C., 1990—; regular reviewer The L.A. Times, 1970-87; founder, co-editor Dreamworks Mag., N.Y.C., 1980-86; v.p., yearbook editor L.A. P.E.N., 1982-83. Author: Sleeping with an Elephant, 1978, A Writer's Time: A Guide to the Creative Process From Vision Through Revision, 1995, The Mercury Transition, 1995, Cajun Household Wisdom, 1995; co-author: (with Chi Li Wong) Writing Treatments That Sell, 1997; editor: Italian Literature: Roots and Branches, 1976, Homer: Critical Essays, 1987, The Renaissance Reader, 1997, The New Classical Roman Reader, 1997, The New Classical Greek Reader, 1997; movie prodr. Falling Over Backwards, Shadow of Obsession, The Amityville Horror, The Rose Cafe, The Emerald Tear/Meg, Henry's List of Wrongs, The Kill Martin Club, Life, or Something Like It, Dante's Inferno. Libr. assoc. Georgetown U., 1995—. Mem. Am. Comparative Lit. Assn. (membership chair). Roman Catholic. Avocations: tennis, travel, collecting autographed books. Office: Atchity Editl/Entertainment Internat Box 1202 9601 Wilshire Blvd Beverly Hills CA 90210-5213

ATEN, FREDRICK PARK, helicopter pilot, instructor, television engineer; b. Springfield, Mo., Nov. 1, 1951; s. Georgia Eldred (Baker) Aten. Student electronics engring., De Vry Inst., Phoenix, 1969-70; student electronics, Glendale (Ariz.) C.C., 1974-75, Phoenix Coll., 1975-76; student robotics and fine arts, Ariz. State U., 1982-83. Lic. comml. helicopter pilot, cert. flight instr., FCC 1st Class Radar-Endorsed lic. Studio engr. KPHO-TV, Phoenix, 1976-81; maintenance engr. R&D Image Transform, Universal City, Calif., 1981-85; maintenace engr. AME, Burbank, Calif., 1985-87, Unimedia, Inc., Phoenix, 1987-93; instr. pilot Aero Helicopters, Scottsdale, Ariz., 1994-98; factory instr., pilot The Boeing Co., Mesa, Ariz., 1998—; cons., advisor Davenport Aviation Group, Scottsdale, 1997—; R&D cons. Unimedia, Inc., Phoenix, 1997—. Inventor: numerous inventions, 1970—; editor flight tng. manuals, 1994—. Nominee Flight Instr. of Yr., FAA, Phoenix, 1998. Mem. Nat. Broadcast Pilots Assn. Avocations: desert horticulture, inventing, blacksmithing. Office: The Boeing Co MW45-051 5000 E Mcdowell Rd Mesa AZ 85215-9707

ATENCIO, J(OSEPH) ANDREW, computer systems official, computer designer; b. Canon City, Colo., May 26, 1965; s. Joseph Andrew Atencio and Carol Lynn (Gordon) Pross; m. Kimberly Ann Maritz, Aug. 8, 1992. AS in Applied Techs., Phoenix Inst. Tech., 1988; BS in Bus. Info. Sys., U. Phoenix, 1996. Cert. AUTOCAD technician; Microsoft cert. sys. engr. Designer, drafter Fine Line Designs, Tempe, Ariz., 1987-89; tchr. Phoenix Inst. Tech., 1989-90; computer aided designer, computer system mgr. PRC Environ. Mgmt., Inc., Denver, 1990-91; mgr. computer systems RUST Environ. and Infrastructure (formerly SEC Donohue), Englewood, Colo., 1991-92, regional info. sys. mgr., 1992-95, applications and sys. devel. engr., 1995—; computer aided drafter Greeley & Hansen Engrs., Phoenix, 1988-90; owner, designer, cons. Midnight Wind Design Svcs., Phoenix and Denver, 1990—. Mem. Am. Design Drafting Assn. Democrat. Avocations: comic books, football, snow skiing, camping, reading. Office: RUST Environ-Infrastructure 5575 Dtc Pkwy Ste 200 Englewood CO 80111-3016

ATHERTON, WILLIAM GERARD, marketing professional; b. Chgo., Jan. 25, 1956; s. William George and Carole Ann (Simpson) A.; m. Karen Irene Roders, June 15, 1987 (div. Sept. 1991); m. Elizabeth Irene Gutierrez, July 15, 1995. BS in Mktg., U. Nevada, 1979. Prin. W.G. Atherton & Assoc., L.A., 1980-82; sales Johnson & Staley, L.A., 1982-84, K&M co., L.A., 1984-85; prin., owner Atherton & Assoc., San Diego, Phoenix, 1985-92; prin., owner, founder Atherton Pacific, Honolulu, 1992—. mem. Plaza Club, Honolulu Club. Republican. Catholic. Avocations: surfing, music, weight lifting, softball. Home: 41 020 Hilu St Waimanalo HI 96795

ATKINS, HONEY JEAN, retired business executive; b. Chgo., Mar. 6, 1932; d. Anthony Theophane and Mary Jean (Barrett) Shelvis; m. Robert Claremore Atkins, Aug. 30, 1975; stepchildren: Brett, Cary, Dean, Dana, Christopher, Mary Clare, Patrick. Grad., Rome City H.S., Rome City, Ind., 1948. Mgr. Pacific Telesis, Santa Ana, Calif., 1956-82. Commr. cultural commn. City of La Quinta (Calif.), 1994-98; mem. adv. com. Riverside County Free Libr., La Quinta, 1995-97; mem. adv. bd. CVC Concert Assn., 1995—; bd. dirs. Friends of Libr., v.p., 1993—. Named Citizen of Yr., La Quinta C. of C., 1996, Woman of Distinction, Soroptimists, 1995. Mem. La Quinta Arts League (pres., 1995-97), La Quinta Arts Found. (bd. dirs. 1995—), La Quinta Hist. Soc. (fundraising chair 1994-95), Round Table West (founder Desert chpt., chair), La Quinta On Stage (pres.). Home: 52470 Avenida Madero La Quinta CA 92253-3315

ATKINS, WILLIAM THEODORE, insurance company executive; b. Chgo., Nov. 20, 1950; s. William Theodore and Katherine Malinda (Shank) A.; m. Cathleen Ann Connelly, May 27, 1978; 1 child, William T. BBA, Wash. State U., 1972. CPCU, Am. Inst. Property and Liability Underwriters, Inc.; cert. ins. counselor Soc. Cert. Ins. Counselors; assoc. in risk mgmt., assoc. in mgmt., assoc. in underwriting, assoc. in reins. Ins. Inst. Am. Underwriter/mktg. rep. Unigard Ins. Co., Spokane, Wash., 1972-77; underwriting mgr. Unigard Ins. Co., Spokane, Fresno, Calif. and Portland, Oreg., 1977-81, North Pacific Ins. Co., Portland, 1981-84, United Pacific/Reliance Ins. Co., Portland, 1984-89; br. mgr. North Pacific Ins. Co., 1989-93, asst. v.p., 1993-95, v.p. underwriting, 1995—; chmn. Oreg. Ins. Coun. Western Ins. Info. Inst., Portland, 1991; mem. Wash. State U. Risk Mgmt. and Ins. Adv. Bd., Pullman, Wash., 1995—; spkr. in field. Mem. deacon bd. Village Bapt. Ch., 1987-90; mem. Agt.'s Lic. Exam Review Com., Salem, Oreg., 1990-93; mem. Mayor's Auto Theft Task Force, Portland, 1992-93. Mem. CPCU Soc. (nat. pub. rels. com. 1995—, Oreg. chpt. pres. 1987). Republican. Avocations: boating, skiing. Office: CGU-North Pacific Ins Co 1675 SW Marlow Ave Portland OR 97225-5103

ATKINS-MERSEREAU, JAMES MARVIN, accountant, educator; b. Toledo, Mar. 14, 1964; s. Marilyn Louise (Brown) Atkins. BBA, U. Toledo, 1984; MS in Acctg., Tex. A&M U., 1987; postgrad., U. Ky., 1989-93, No. Ariz. U., 1995-96. Instr. Blinn Coll., Bryan, Tex., 1986-87, Alice Lloyd Coll., Pippa Passes, Ky., 1987-89; asst. prof. S.E. C.C., Middlesborough, Ky., 1989-91; assoc. prof. acctg. Jefferson C.C., Louisville, 1991-94; instr. acctg., chmn. acctg. dept. Yavapai Coll., Clarkdale, Ariz., 1994-96; trainer CYMA Sys., Tempe, Ariz., 1997; acctg., bus. mgr., human resources dir. U-Pull-It Self Svc. Salvage, Phoenix, 1997—; cons. Atkins-Mersereau Consulting, Phoenix, 1991-98. Chair Knott County Rep. Party, Hindman, Ky., 1986-87; pres. Yavapai Coll. Faculty Assn., Clarkdale, 1996. Libertarian. Avocations: reading, music, theatre, opera. E-mail: jimmers@psn. Office: U-Pull-It PO Box 6310 Phoenix AZ 85005-6310

ATKINSON, JOHN CHRISTOPHER, magazine editor, critic, writer; b. Hitchin, Eng., June 12, 1948; came to U.S., 1987; s. Harry Archer and Jacqueline Ellen (Elliott) A.; m. Maree Froy, Dec. 12, 1970 (div. 1981); m. Pamela Margaret Edwards, June 19, 1982 (div. 1987); 1 child, Heather Louise; m. Laura Jean LoVecchio, Nov. 28, 1987; children: Henry Joseph, Emily Claire. BSc in Chemistry and Physics, U. London, 1972; grad. cert. in

edn., 1974. Sci. officer Warren Spring Lab., Stevenage, Eng., 1969-72; freelance bass guitarist, London, 1972-76; news editor Hi-Fi News and Record Rev. mag., Croydon, Surrey, Eng., 1976-78, dep. editor, 1978-82, editor, 1982-86; internat. editor Stereophile UK Ltd., London, 1986-87; editor Stereophile mag., Santa Fe, 1987—. Prodn. compact discs Hi-Fi News Test Disc, 1985, Poem (flute/piano music), 1989, Stereophile Test Disc, 1990, Intermezzo (Brahms piano music), 1991, Stereophile Test CD 2, 1992, Concert (piano recital), 1994, Stereophile Test CD 3, 1995, Festival (orchestral works by Copland, Kohjiba, Milhaud), 1995, Sonata (Liszt piano music), 1996, Serenade (chamber works by Mozart, Brahms, Dvorak), 1996, Encore (works by Brahms, Mendelssohn), 1997, Rhapsody (works by Gershwin), 1997, Duet (violin sonatas by Janacek, Schulhoff e Enesco), 1998; contbr. numerous articles and revs. of hi-fidelity components to music mags. Avocations: playing recorder, photography. Office: 208 Delgado St Santa Fe NM 87501-2728

ATKINSON, PERRY, political organization administrator. Chair Oreg. Rep. Party, Beaverton. Fax: (503) 644-0210. Office: Oreg Rep Party PO Box 1450 Beaverton OR 97075*

ATKINSON, RICHARD CHATHAM, university president; b. Oak Park, Ill., Mar. 19, 1929; s. Herbert and Margaret (Feuerbach) A.; m. Rita Loyd, Aug. 20, 1952; 1 dau., Lynn Loyd. Ph.B., U. Chgo., 1948; Ph.D., Ind. U., 1955. Lectr. applied math. and stats. Stanford (Calif.) U., 1956-57, assoc. prof. psychology, 1961-64, prof. psychology, 1964-80; asst. prof. psychology UCLA, 1957-61; dep. dir. NSF, 1975-76, acting dir., 1976, dir., 1976-80; chancellor, prof. cognitive sci. U. Calif., San Diego, 1980-95; pres. U. Calif., 1995—. Author: (with Atkinson, Smith and Bem) Introduction to Psychology, 12th edit., 1996, Computer Assisted Instruction, 1969, An Introduction to Mathematical Learning Theory, 1965, Contemporary Developments in Mathematical Psychology, 1974, Mind and Behavior, 1980, Stevens' Handbook of Experimental Psychology, 1988. Served with AUS, 1954-56. Guggenheim fellow, 1967; fellow Ctr. for Advanced Study in Behavioral Scis., 1963; recipient Distinguished Research award Social Sci. Research Council, 1962. Fellow APA (Disting. Sci. Contbn. award 1977, Thorndike award 1980), AAAS (pres. 1989-90), Am. Psychol. Soc. (William James fellow 1985), Am. Acad. Arts and Scis.; mem. NAS, Soc. Exptl. Psychologists, Am. Philos. Soc., Nat. Acad. Edn., Inst. of Medicine, Cosmos Club (Washington), Explorer's Club (N.Y.C.). Home: 70 Rincon Rd Kensington CA 94707-1047 Office: U Calif Office of Pres 1111 Franklin St Oakland CA 94607-5200*

ATKINSON, SALLY JO, writer; b. Cherry Point, N.C., June 25, 1953; d. Russell Berdean and Lois Gladene (Myers) McGregor; m. Donald John Atkinson, July 20, 1980. Graphic artist Alfred M. Gordan Design, Costa Mesa, Calif., 1972-75; cashier Longs Drug Store, Kahului, Maui, Hawaii, 1976-79; ad writer Longs Drug Store, Carson City, Nev., 1979-96, bookkeeper, 1990—. Author: (children's books) The Tales of Tango: The Brave Lesson, 1996, The Tales of Tango: The Sticky Situation, 1998. Avocations: snow skiing, reading, travel. Home: 1561 Walker Dr Carson City NV 89701-2910 Office: Tangos Grove Pub PO Box 20074 Carson City NV 89721-0074

ATKINSON, SHERIDAN EARLE, lawyer; b. Oakland, Calif., Feb. 14, 1945; s. Arthur Sheridan and Esther Louise (Johnson) A.; m. Margie Ann Lehtin, Aug. 13, 1966. 1 son, Ian Sheridan. BS, U. Calif.-Berkeley, 1966, MBA, 1971; JD, U. San Francisco, 1969. Bar: Calif. 1970. Prin. Atkinson & Assocs., fin. and mgmt. cons., corp. and bus. valuations, San Francisco, 1968—; assoc. Charles O. Morgan, Jr., San Francisco, 1972-76; pvt. practice, San Francisco Bay Area,1976—. With USAR, 1970-76. Mem. Calif. Bar Assn. Republican.

ATTIG, JOHN CLARE, secondary education educator, consultant; b. Chgo., Apr. 2, 1936; s. Clare McKinley and Elsie Bertha (Nagel) A.; m. Harriet Jane Rinehart, June 13, 1959; children: Laura, Victoria. BA, DePauw U., 1958; MA, U. Chgo., 1961. Cert. tchr., Calif. Social studies tchr. Lyons Twp. H.S., LaGrange, Ill., 1961-65, Henry Gunn H.S., Palo Alto, Calif., 1965-72, 78—; univ. faculty assoc. Simon Fraser U., Burnaby, Canada, 1972-73; social studies tchr. Jordan Jr. H.S., Palo Alto, 1973-75, Cubberley Sr. H.S., Palo Alto, 1975-78; lectr., demonstrator, pub. simulation games for classes in history and govt. various univs. and sch. dists. in U.S. and Can. Contbr. numerous articles to profl. jours.; author numerous simulation games; dir. simulation games pub. History Alive. With USAR, 1958-64. NEH fellow, 1983, 87, 89, Tchr. fellow St. Andrews U., Scotland, 1993. Mem. NEH (project dir. Masterworks Seminar 1991), Western History Assn. Methodist. Avocations: travel, reading, wine. E-mail: jcahista@televar.com.

ATTIYEH, ROBERT S., retired biotechnology executive; b. Oak Park, Ill., June 10, 1934; s. Semeer M. and Dorothy Lydia Attiyeh; m. Linda Helen Harden, Jul. 20, 1963; children: Robert, Jenny. BSEE, Cornell Univ., 1956; MBA, Harvard Univ., 1961. Gen. mgr. TRW Elec., El Segundo, Calif., 1961-67; dir. McKinsey & Co., L.A., 1967-94; sr. v.p., fin. & corp. devel., CFO Amgen, Inc., Thousand Oaks, Calif., 1994-98. Contbr. numerous articles to profl. jours. Pres., chmn. bd. L.A. Philharmonic Assn., 1994—; chmn. bd. House Ear Inst., 1991-96; pres., chmn. bd. Natural History Mus., L.A.,, 1990-96; dir. Fed. Res. Bank of San Francisco, 1997—. With US Navy, 1956-59. Mem. Calif. Club, L.A. Club. Avocations: ranching, restoring and preserving historical properties, reading. Home: 210 S Canyon View Dr Los Angeles CA 90049-3810 Office: Amgen Inc One Amgen Ctr Thousand Oaks CA 91320

ATWELL, JAMES D., venture capitalist; b. San Luis Obispo, Calif., June 13, 1955. BS, Santa Clara U., 1977. Sr. assoc. Coopers & Lybrand, San Jose, Calif., 1983-85; mgr. Coopers & Lybrand, San Jose, 1985-90, ptnr., 1990-96, mng. ptnr., 1996-98; global tech. leader for venture capital and pvt. equity Pricewaterhouse Coopers, San Jose, 1998—; mem. adv. bd. Silicon Valley Bank, San Jose, 1996—, Frontier Ventures, Redwood City, Calif., 1997—; dir. Bd. of Fellows, Santa Clara, 1994—. Office: Pricewaterhouse Coopers 10 Almaden Blvd Ste 1600 San Jose CA 95113-2238

ATWOOD, KELLY PALMER, insurance agency executive; b. Portland, Oreg., Jan. 7, 1946; s. Baird Ewing and Lelia Claire (Donham) McNeese A.; m. Regina Louise Hamilton, July 30, 1983; children: Derek, Lynn, Jason, Beri, Courtney. Student, U. Oreg., 1964-66, Chemeketa Community Coll., 1976-78. Pres., chief exec. officer Group Ins. Mktg., Inc., Salem, Oreg., 1970-85, Contractors Ins. Svcs. Inc., Lake Oswego, Oreg., 1985—; also bd. dirs. Metro Ins. Agy., Inc., Lake Oswego, Oreg. Contbr. articles on ins. to profl. jours. Former mem. Reagan Task Force, Washington, 1985-86, Denny Smith Task Force on Crime, Salem, 1988. Served with USN, 1967-69. Named Sr. Agt. of Yr. Salem Life Underwriters Assn., 1980, 81. Mem. Nat. Assn. Life Underwriters, Nat. Assn. Home Builders, Oreg. State Home Builders Assn., Home Builders Assn. Met. Portland (bd. dirs. 1985—). Republican. Avocations: water skiing, snow skiing, steelhead fishing. Home: 3300 River Woods Pl Lake Oswego OR 97034-5115 Office: Contractors Ins Svcs Inc PO Box 2267 Lake Oswego OR 97035-0071

ATWOOD, MARY SANFORD, writer; b. Mt. Pleasant, Mich., Jan. 27, 1935; d. Burton Jay and Lillian Belle (Sampson) Sanford; B.S., U. Miami, 1957; m. John C. Atwood, III, Mar. 23, 1957. Author: A Taste of India, 1969. Mem. San Francisco/N. Peninsula Opera Action, Hillsborough-Burlingame Newcomers, Suicide Prevention and Crisis Center, DeYoung Art Mus., Internat. Hospitality Center, Peninsula Symphony, San Francisco Art Mus., World Affairs Council, Mills Hosp. Assos. Mem. AAUW, Suicide Prevention Aux. Republican. Club: St. Francis Yacht. Office: 40 Knightwood Ln Hillsborough CA 94010-6132

AU, LAWRENCE, minister; b. Nanjing, Peoples Republic of China, Jan. 14, 1938; came to U.S., 1967; s. Kaying and Waichun (Lee) A.; married; 1 child, Lorenzo. BTh, Hong Kong Bapt. Theol. Seminary, 1963; MA, MDiv., Golden Gate Bapt. Theol. Seminary, Mill Valley, Calif., 1969, 1972, D of Ministry, 1975; BS, U. San Francisco, 1979; postgrad., U. Vienna, 1985; MPA, U. San Francisco, 1993. Cert. counselor, adminstr., Calif.; ordained to ministry Chinese Bapt. Ch., 1967; cert. chaplain FBI/SFHQ, 1993—. Pastor First Bapt. Ch., Macao, 1963-65, Ipoh, Malaysia, 1965-67; pastor First Chinese So. Bapt. Ch., San Francisco, 1967-84; pres. Christian Witness Theol. Seminary, Berkeley, Calif., 1984-88; pastor San Bruno (Calif.) Chinese Bapt. Ch., 1988—; adv. pastor San Francisco Mandarin Bapt. Ch., 1984-88; moderator San Francisco So. Bapt. Assn, 1978-80; com. chmn. Calif. So. Bapt. State Conv., Fresno, 1979-82, teller, L.A., 1981; trustee/chmn. San Francisco Chinese Childrens Choir, 1984-90; commd. chaplain San Francisco Police Dept., 1983—; vis. prof. Hong Kong Bapt. Seminary, 1982, Singapore Bible Seminary, 1986, Russian Bapt. Seminary, Ufa, 1995. Author/translator: Baptist Church Manual, 1982; translator Calif. Bar, 1991. com. chmn. Calif. State Ednl. Dept., Sacramento; diplomate World Jewish Congress, 1990—; leader San Francisco Internat. Airport Aircrash Team, 1989—; chaplain-in-residence FBI Acad., Quantico, Va., 1995, 97; advisor San Francisco Youth Ct. Recipient certs. Appreciation, Fgn. Mission Bd./So. Bapt. Conv., Richmond, Va., 1970, 81, Civil Air Patrol/USAF, San Francisco, 1978, San Francisco Police Acad., 1982, Calif. State Edn. Dept., Sacramento, 1988, San Franciso So. Bapt. Assn., 1990. Mem. Internat. Conf. Police Chaplains, Am. Assn. Christian Counselors, Am. Counseling Assn. Home: 639 38th Ave San Francisco CA 94121-2617 Office: San Bruno Chinese Bapt Church 250 Courtland Dr San Bruno CA 94066-4025

AUBERY, STEPHEN R.E., film producer; b. Kingston Upon Hull, Yorkshire, Eng., July 4, 1951; came to U.S., 1964; s. Gerald Royston and Doreen (Stevens) A.; m. Rose Marie Marks, Feb. 23, 1973 (div. Dec. 1991); children: Suzanne Marie, Julia Dawn, Wendy Lynn, Katrina Rose; m. Tamara Phizacklea, Oct. 4, 1994. Student, U. Utah, 1968-70, Brigham Young U., 1974-75. Sound dept. mgr. Brigham Young U. Motion Picture Studio, Provo, Utah, 1972-76; film prodr., ptnr. Linton Prodns., Salt Lake City, 1976-79; prodr., gen. ptnr. Seven Star Pictures, Salt Lake City, 1979-82; news editor KUTV Inc., Salt Lake City, 1982-84; film prodr., mgr. LDS Audiovisual, Salt Lake City, 1984-94; film prodr., owner Encore Prodns., Salt Lake City, 1995-96; film prodr. Mountain Prodns., Inc., Draper, Utah, 1997—; film prodr. Challenger Schs., Salt Lake City, 1984-85; film dept. instr. U. Utah, Salt Lake City, Brigham Young U., Provo. Co-author, prodr., cinematographer (screenplay, book, feature motion picture) Knocking at Heaven's Door, 1980; film prodr. (internat. film) Temple Open House, 1992 (Telly award 1993); film prodr., dir. (ednl. film) Phonics Fun, 1993 (two Telly awards 1994); prodr., dir. (motivational film) From Thoughts to Things, 1997 (Telly Communicator award 1997); author, contbg. editor Super 8 Filmaker Mag., 1975-80. Bd. dirs. World Firefighters Assistance League, Salt Lake City. Mem. Internat. TV Assn., Soc. Motion Picture and TV Engrs. (presenter tech. paper L.A. conv. 1974-80, cert. presentation 1995), Sandy (Utah) Area C. of C. (video historian 1997—). Avocations: vocal performing, playing guitar, computers, member top 40 soft rock dance band 1980-97. E-mail: captainvideo@tvspec.com. and steve@mountain-productions.com. Fax: 801-571-9699. Home: 1042 Fort Union Blvd #445 Midvale UT 84047-1894 Home: 7870 Promontory Way H-301 Sandy UT 84094-0789 Office: Mountain Prodn Group 1061 East 13200 South Draper UT 84020-9399

AUBIN, BARBARA JEAN, artist; b. Chgo., Jan. 12, 1928; d. Philip Theodore and Dorothy May (Chapman) A. BA, Carleton Coll., 1949; B Art Edn., Sch. Art Inst. Chgo., 1954, M Art Edn., 1955. Lectr. Centre D'Art & Haitian Am. Inst., Port-Au-Prince, Haiti, 1958-60; asst. prof. Sch. Art Inst. Chgo., 1960-67, Loyola U., Chgo., 1968-71; lectr. Calumet Coll., Hammond, Ind., 1971-75; prof. art Chgo. State U., 1971-91; ret., 1991; vis. prof., artist Wayne State U., Detroit, Mich., 1965; vis. artist St. Louis C.C., Forest Park, Mo., 1980, 81, U. Wis., Green Bay, 1981; co-curator Art for the Next Millennium Kimo Theatre Gallery, Albuquerque, 1997. One-woman shows include Countryside Arts Ctr., Arlington Heights, Ill., 1954, Avant Arts Gallery, Chgo., 1954, Riccardo's Restaurant and Gallery, Chgo., 1956, Evanston (Ill.) Twp. H.S., 1958, Centre d'Art, Port-au-Prince, Haiti, 1960, Chgo. Pub. Libr., 1960, Chgo. Acad. Fine Arts, 1965, Oxbow Summer Sch. Fine Arts, 1965, Lewis Towers Gallery, Loyola U., Chgo., 1970, Chgo. State U., 1971, 74, 85, North River Cmty. Gallery, Northeastern Ill. U., Chgo., 1974, Ill. Arts Coun., Chgo., Crossroads-Jr. Mus., Art Inst. Chgo., 1976, Fairweather Hardin Gallery, Chgo., 1978, 80, 85, 90, U. Wis., 1981, Illini Union Gallery, U. Ill., Urbana, 1986, Countryside Art Ctr., Arlington Heights, 1987, Artemisia Gallery, Chgo.; exhibited in group shows at Art Inst. Chgo., 1960, 78, 80, 85, 89, Vanderpoel Art Assn., Beverly Art Ctr., Chgo., 1992, Ancient Echoes, Chgo., 1992, Renaissance Ct., Chgo. Cultural Ctr., 1993, Artemisia Gallery, Chgo., 1994, Art Place Gallery, Chgo, 1994, Chgo. State U., 1994, Chgo. Women's Caucus for Art, 1994, 98 Eastern Ill. U., Charleston, 1994, ARC Gallery, Chgo., 1995, 97, N.Mex. Art League, Albuquerque, 1996, Mirage Gallery, Albuquerque, Barrington Arts Coun., 1997, Meridian Ctr., Washington, 1997, Chgo. Women's Caucus for Art No. Ill. U., 1998; represented in permanent collections at Art Inst. Chgo., Ill. State Mus., Ball State Mus., Calumet Coll., Hammond, Ind., Shimer Coll., Waukegon, Ill., Kemper Group Collection, Long Grove, Ill., State of Ill. Bldg., Chgo., Seyfarth, Shaw, Fairweather & Geraldson, Washington, Ernst & Ernst, Chgo., Foote, Cone & Belding, Chgo., U.S. League of Savs. and Loans, Chgo., Northside Industries, Chgo., Keck, Cushman, Mahin & Cate, Chgo., Gould, Inc., Rolling Meadows, Ill., First Nat. Bank Chgo., Ill. Tool Works, Chgo., Internat. Mineral and Chem., Skokie, Ill.; reporter Women Artists News, 1977, 80, 83-86; pvt. collections. V.p. Midwest region Womens Caucus for Art, Chgo., 1982-88; founding mem. local chpt. Chgo. Women's Caucus for Art, 1973; bd. dirs. Chgo. Artists Coalition, 1992-94. Recipient George D. Brown Fgn. Travel fellowship Sch. Art Inst. Chgo., 1955-56, Art grant Fulbright Found., 1958-60, grant Huntington Hartford Fedn., 1963, Project Completion grant Ill. Arts Coun., 1978, 79. Mem. Arts Club Chgo., Chgo. Artists' Coalition, Chgo. Womens Caucus for Art, Albuquerque United Artists. Home: 5101 Glenwood Pointe Ln NE Albuquerque NM 87111-2976

AUERBACK, SANDRA JEAN, social worker; b. San Francisco, Feb. 21, 1946; d. Alfred and Molly Loy (Friedman) A. BA, U. Calif., Berkeley, 1967; MSW, Hunter Sch. Social Work, 1972. Diplomate clin. social work. Clin. social worker Jewish Family Services, Bklyn., 1972-73; clin. social worker Jewish Family Services, Hackensack, N.J., 1973-78; pvt. practice psychotherapy San Francisco, 1978—; dir. intake adult day care Jewish Home for the Aged, San Francisco, 1979-91. Mem. NASW (cert., bd. dirs. Bay Area Referral Svc. 1983-87, chmn. referral svc. 1984-87, state practice com. 1987-91, regional treas. 1989-91, rep. to Calif. Coun. Psychiatry, Psychology, Social Work and Nursing, 1987-95, chmn. 1989, 93, v.p. cmty. svcs. 1991-93, chair Calif. polit. action com. 1993-95), Am. Group Psychotherapy Assn., Mental Health Assn. San Francisco (trustee 1987—). Home: 1100 Gough St Apt 8C San Francisco CA 94109-6638 Office: 450 Sutter St San Francisco CA 94108-4206

AUGUSTON, MIKHAIL, computer scientist; b. Riga, Latvia, Apr. 16, 1948; came to U.S., 1992; s. Isay and Sofia (Levina) A.; m. Tatyana Dimanstein; children: Ilana, Maria. BS in Math., U. Latvia, 1971; PhD in Computer Sci., Glushkov Cybernetics Inst., Kiev, Russia, 1983. Rschr. Inst. Math. and Computer Sci. U. Latvia, 1971-92; assoc. prof. computer sci. N.Mex. State U., Las Cruces, 1992—. Co-author: (in Russian) Programming in PL/1, 1979, 2d edit., 1984, Polish translation, 1988; contbr. articles to profl. jours. Office: NMex State Univ PO Box 30001 Las Cruces NM 88003-8001

AULT, PHILLIP HALLIDAY, author, editor; b. Maywood, Ill., Apr. 26, 1914; s. Frank W. and Bernda (Halliday) A.; m. Karoline Byberg, June 5, 1943 (dec. Jan. 1990); children: Frank, Ingrid, Bruce; m. Jane Born, May 1, 1993. AB, DePauw U., 1935. Reporter LaGrange (Ill.) Citizen, 1935-37; corr. editor UPI, Chgo., N.Y.C., Iceland, North Africa, London, 1938-48; bur. chief UPI, London, 1944-45; asst. mng. editor, dir. editorial page Times-Mirror Co., L.A., 1948; editorial page editor L.A. Mirror-News, 1948-57; exec. editor Associated Desert Newspapers, 1958-68; assoc. editor South Bend (Ind.) Tribune, 1968-79, cons. editor, 1979—. Author: This Is the Desert, 1950, News Around the Clock, 1960, How to Live in California, 1961, Home Book of Western Humor, 1967, Wonders of the Mosquito World, 1970, These Are The Great Lakes, 1972, Wires West, 1974, All [illegible] 1982, co-author: Springboard to Berlin, 1943, Reporting and Writing the News, 1983, Introduction to Mass Communications, 1960, Public Relations: Strategies and Tactics, 1986; editor: Santa Maria Historical Photo Album, 1987. Named to Ind. Journalism Hall of Fame, 1998. Mem. Am. Soc. Newspaper Editors, Assn. Edn. in Journalism, Western Writers Am. (Spur award 1977), Sigma Nu. Home: 21408 157th Dr Sun City West AZ 85375-6626

AUNG-THWIN, MICHAEL ARTHUR, history educator; b. Rangoon, Burma, 1946. BA, Doane Coll., 1969; MA, U. Ill., Urbana, 1971; PhD, U. Mich., 1976. Asst. prof. Asian history Elmira (N.Y.) Coll., 1980-87; assoc. prof. history No. Ill. U., DeKalb, 1987-95; dir. Ctr. S.E. Asian Studies No. Ill. U., DeKalb, Ill., 1987-95; prof. Asian Studies U. Hawaii, Honolulu, 1995—; vis. prof. Cornell U., 1981; vis. scholar Ctr. for S.E. Asian Studies, Kyoto, Japan. Contbr. articles to profl. jours. NEH fellow, 1977-80. Mem. Assn. for Asian Studies (bd. dirs. 1980-83, mem. S.E. Asia Coun.), Burma Studies Found. (sec.-treas.). Office: U Hawaii Sch Hawaiian Asian Studies 413 Moore Hall Honolulu HI 96822

AURAND, CHARLES HENRY, JR., music educator; b. Battle Creek, Mich., Sept. 6, 1932; s. Charles Henry and Elisabeth Dirk (Hoekstra) A.; m. Donna Mae Erb, June 19, 1954; children: Janice, Cheryl, Sandra, Charles III, William. MusB, Mich. State U., 1954, MusM, 1958; PhD, U. Mich., 1971. Cert. tchr., Mich., Ohio. Asst. prof. music Hiram Coll., Ohio, 1958-60; dean, prof. music Youngstown State U., 1960-73; dean No. Ariz. U., Flagstaff, 1973-88, prof. music, 1988-94, prof. emeritus, 1994—; chmn. Ariz. Alliance for Arts Edn., 1974-77; solo clarinetist Flagstaff Symphony; solo, chamber music and orch. musician, 1973-86; fine arts cons. Miami U. of Ohio, 1982. Author: Selected Solos, Methods, 1963. Elder Presbyterian Ch., 1965; chmn. Boy Scouts Am., Coconino dist., 1974-78; bd. dirs. Ariz. Com. Arts for the Handicapped, 1982-88, Flagstaff Symphony Orch., 1973-85, Flagstaff Festival of Arts, 1973-89; bd. dirs. Sedona Chamber Mus. Soc., 1989—, Sedona Med. Ctr., 1998—; conf. dir. Internat. Clarinet Soc., 1991; pres. Citizens for an Alt. Rt., 1995—. Served to 1st lt. USAF, 1955-57. Recipient award of merit Boy Scouts Am., 1977; cert. appreciation John F. Kennedy Ctr. Performing Arts, 1985. Mem. Am. Assn. Higher Edn., Ariz. Humanities Assn., Music Educators Nat. Conf., State Adminstrs. of Music Schs. (chmn. 1971-73), Internat. Clarinet Soc./ClariNetwork Internat. (conf. dir. 1991), No. Ariz. U. Retirees Assn. (pres. 1997-98). Republican. Presbyterian. Lodge: Kiwanis (pres. 1984-85). Avocations: golf, tennis, bridge. Home: 140 Fairway Oaks Ln Sedona AZ 86351-8835 Office: No Ariz U Box 6040 Flagstaff AZ 86011

AUSTEN, SHELLI OETTER, radio news anchor, consultant; b. Tulsa, Sept. 8, 1954; m. Fred Chris Sorenson, Dec. 31, 1984 (div. Oct. 1988); 1 child, Kristen Amara; m. John R. Oetter, May 16, 1998. BA, U. Calif., Santa Barbara, 1974. Actress Starlight Theatre, Pasadena Playhouse, 1974; with various improvisational acting troupes, 1974-80; news dir. Sta. KMVI, Maui, Hawaii, 1980-83; v.p. Bill Baker Advt., Honolulu, 1983-85; advt. dir. Ground Swell Mag., Haleiwa, 1985-87; prodr., reporter, anchor Sta. KHVH, Honolulu, 1987-92; dir. adv. Beachcomber Mag., 1992-93; disc jockey Sta. KGY, Olympia, Wash., 1994—; reporter Alameda (Calif.) Times Star, 1994-96; morning news anchor KSRO AM Radio, Santa Rosa, Calif., 1996—; pres. In House Prodns. Media Consulting Firm, 1997-98; pres., news anchor KSSK-AM Radio, Honolulu, 1998—; media cons. Rep. Party of Hawaii, Honolulu, 1987—; actress Altarina Playhouse, 1994-95, News Anchor KSSK, Honolulu. Contbr. articles to profl. jours. Media coord. Merimed found., Honolulu, 1988; del. Rep. Party, Honolulu, 1989, mem. presdl. task force, Honolulu, 1989-90. Christian. Home: 58-032 Kapuai Pl Haleiwa HI 96712-9730

AUSTIN, DAVID LEONARD, II, bishop; b. Tampa, Fla., Nov. 19, 1928; s. David Leonard Sr. and Lula (Thompson) A.; m. Elnora Sanders, Sept. 22, 1956; children: Susan, David Leonard III, Kathy, Bernadett. Student, CCNY, 1948-50; D in Evangelism, Fuller Theol. Sem., 1960. Mem. dept. Evangelism Gen. Ch., 1950, exec. sec., 1950-65, 1st conv. chmn. Evangelism dept., 1969—, 1st v.p.; founder Maranatha Ch., L.A., 1976—, Assemblies of God in Christ, L.A., 1989—; founder 14 other chs. and missions, 1953—; bishop Cen. Ky. Chs. of God in Christ, 1966-71. Author: Doing the Work of an Evangelism; contbr. articles to profl. jours.; composer ch. music. First presiding bishop, Assemblies of God in Christ.

AUSTIN, JAMES W., architect, artist; b. Cleve., Feb. 11, 1950; s. Allan Stewart and Winifred Austin; m. Rosy Moore, 1998. BA, Yale U., 1972; postgrad., Archtl. Assn., London, 1977; MArch, U. Calif., Berkeley, 1978. Lic. arch., Calif. Draftsman Copper, Wade & Copper, Cleve.; staff arch. Caisse Nat., Kinshasa, Zaire, 1973; project arch. Govt. Zaire, Uvira, 1973-74; designer Hood Chathman, Arch., San Francisco, 1978, Crosby, Thornton & Marshal, San Francisco, 1979; assoc. Mahar & Moulton, San Francisco, 1981; prin. James Austin Arch., San Francisco and Nicasio, Calif., 1982—; co-chmn. Design Rev. Bd., Nicasio, 1990-97. Prin. works include foam house prototype, central market place, Uvira, his. restoration, rural devel., watercolors. Mem. Calif. Watercolor Assn.

AUSTIN, JOHN NORMAN, classics educator; b. Anshun, Kweichow, China, May 20, 1937; s. John Alfred and Lillian Maud (Reeks) A. B.A., U. Toronto, Ont. Can., 1958; M.A., U. Calif.-Berkeley, 1959, Ph.D., 1965. Vis. lectr. Yale U., New Haven, 1971; asst. prof., then assoc. prof. UCLA, 1966-76; Aurelio prof. Greek Boston U., 1976-78; prof., chmn. dept. classics U. Mass., Amherst, 1978-80; prof. classics U. Ariz., Tucson, 1980—, acting dean humanities, 1987-88, head, dept. classics, 1995—. Author: Archery at the Dark of the Moon, 1975, Meaning and Being in Myth, 1990, Helen of Troy and Her Shameless Phantom, 1994; editor: (with others) The Works of John Dryden, vol. III; sr. editor Calif. Studies Classical Antiquity, vols. VI and VII. Jr. fellow Ctr. for Hellenic Studies, 1968-69, J.S. Guggenheim Found. fellow, 1974-75. Mem. Am. Philol. Assn. (bd. dirs. 1983-86). Episcopalian. Home: 2939 E 3rd St Tucson AZ 85716-4122 Office: U Ariz Dept Classics PO Box 210067 Tucson AZ 85721-0067

AUSTIN, JOYCE CAROLINE, cake decorator, artist; b. Bussum, Netherlands, Nov. 3, 1943; came to U.S., 1956; d. Antonie C. and Lida J. Schatborn; divorced; children: Cynthia, Cameron. AA, Fresno City Coll., 1964; BA, Fresno State U., 1967. Artist freelance, Merced, Calif., 1987-94; cake decorator Anna's Fairview Bakery, Santa Barbara, Calif., 1994-95, Vons Co., Santa Barbara, 1995—. Recipient Discovery award Art of Calif. mag., 1993. Mem. Pastel Soc. Am. (award 1991), Soc. Western Artists (signature mem.), Pastel soc. West Coast (signature mem.). Avocations: showing cats in cat shows, painting, reading. Home: 4326 Calle Real Spc 96 Santa Barbara CA 93110-3049

AUSTIN, MARY JANE, small business owner; b. Autauga, Ala., Aug. 17, 1955; d. Henry and Janie Ella (Lewis) A.; 1 child, Keith Roderick. AA, Ala. State U., 1983; student, San Diego State U., 1990—. Ptnr. Bobbie's & Marcie's, Prattville, Ala., 1982-85; office asst. Montgomery (Ala.) Area Skills, 1987-88; clk. Am. Svc. Life, Montgomery, 1986-89; ptnr. Say What? Distbrs., Chula Vista, Calif., 1994; owner M.J. Austin Distbg. Co., Chula Vista, 1994—. Author: Secret of Our Ancestors, 1993, Black Men Are Their Own Worst Enemies, 1996; contbr. articles to popular publs. Fundraiser Day of the Young Child, Chula Vista, 1996; co-chair Carol Bower Organ Transplant, Chula Vista, 1996, Hillcrest Home for Abused Children, Chula Vista, 1996; docent Old Town State Hist. Park, San Diego, 1996; vol. Bob Filner for Congress, National City, Calif., 1996; coord. docent tng. San Diego Hist. Soc. Mem. NOW, NAFE, Chi Epsilon. Democrat. Avocations: art, walking, traveling, reading, antiques. Home: 272 Kennedy St Apt 56 Chula Vista CA 91911-3222 Office: MJ Austin Distbg Co PO Box 121671 Chula Vista CA 91912-6371

AUTOLITANO, ASTRID, consumer products executive; b. Havana, Cuba, Aug. 25, 1938; came to U.S., 1966; d. Manuel and Efigenia (Giquel) Rodriguez; m. Dominick Autolitano, July 23, 1977; children: Astrid Martinez, Manuel Martinez. Student, U. Havana, 1962-64, El Camino Coll., Torrance, Calif., 1968-71, UCLA, Westwood, 1973-75, Columbia U., 1983. [illegible] sales, 1969-73, mgr. Pan Am. sales, 1973-78, dir. export sales and licensees, 1978-83, v.p. Latin Am., 1983-89; sr. v.p. Latin Am. Mattel Toys, El Segundo, Calif., 1989-95, exec. v.p. Latin Am., 1995-96, exec. v.p. Ams., 1996; pres. internat. Mattel Toys, 1996—. Office: Mattel Toys 333 Continental Blvd El Segundo CA 90245-5012

AVAKOFF, JOSEPH CARNEGIE, medical and legal consultant; b. Fairbanks, Alaska, July 15, 1936; s. Harry B. and Margaret (Adams) A.; m. Teddy I. Law, May 7, 1966; children: Caroline, Joey, John. AA, U. Calif., Berkeley, 1956, AB, 1957; MD, U. Calif., San Francisco, 1961; JD, Santa Clara U., 1985. Bar: Calif. 1987; diplomate Am. Bd. Surgery, Am. Bd. Plastic Surgery. Physicist U.S. Naval Radiol. Def. Lab., San Francisco, 1957, 59; intern So. Pacific Gen. Hosp., San Francisco, 1961-62; resident in surgery Kaiser Found. Hosp., San Francisco, 1962-66; resident in plastic surgery U. Tex. Sch. Medicine, San Antonio, 1970-72; pvt. practice specializing in surgery Sacramento, 1966-70; pvt. practice specializing in plastic surgery Los Gatos and San Jose, Calif., 1972-94; cons. to med. and legal professions, 1994—; clin. instr. surgery U. Calif. Sch. Medicine, Davis, 1967-70; chief dept. surgery Mission Oaks Hosp., Los Gatos, 1988-90; chief divsn. plastic surgery Good Samaritan Hosp., San Jose, 1989-91; expert med. reviewer Med. Bd. Calif., 1995—; spl. cons. Calif. Dept. Corps., 1997—; presenter numerous med. orgns. Contbr. numerous articles to med. jours. Mem. San Jose Adv. Commn. on Health, 1975-82; bd. govs. San Jose YMCA, 1977-80. Mem. AMA, Calif. Med. Assn., Santa Clara County Bar Assn., Santa Clara County Med. Assn., Union Am. Physicians and Dentists, Phi Beta Kappa, Phi Eta Sigma. Republican. Presbyterian. Avocations: music, photography, computer programming. Home: 6832 Rockview Ct San Jose CA 95120-5607

AVERETT, ROBERT LEE, educator, information system professional; b. Richfield, Utah, Dec. 4, 1952; s. Robert Elmo and Patsy (Meyer) A.; m. Alice Greenhalgh, Mar. 23, 1972; children: Nathan Christopher, Rachel Leah, Christian Alexander, Jeduthan William. BA, Brigham Young U., 1975, MLS, 1976; MA, Ball State U., 1979; D of Pub. Adminstrn., George Mason U., 1991. Cert. computer profl.; cert. secondary tchr., counselor, Utah. Commd. 2d lt. U.S. Army, 1976, advanced through grades to lt. col., 1993, ret., 1996; chief personnel info. system dept. Mil. Personnel Ctr., Alexandria, Va., 1982-84; info. systems project mgr. Orgn. of Joint Chiefs of Staff, The Pentagon, 1984-85; mgmt. info. systems officer Hqrs. Dept. of Army, The Pentagon, 1985-87; comdr. 201st Signal Co., Seoul, Republic of Korea, 1987-89, Mil. Entrance Process Sta., Amarillo, Tex., 1989-92; asst. prof. mil. sci. Brigham Young U., Provo, Utah, 1992-93; chair, prof. mil. sci. U. Utah, Salt Lake City, 1993—, 1993-96; asst. prin. Granite Sch. Dist., Salt Lake City, 1995-98, 1998—; Cons., adj. Amarillo Coll., 1989-92, Limestone Coll., 1979-82; treas. Utah Sch. Counselor Assn., 1995. Leader Boy Scouts Am., Nat. Capitol Coun., Alexandria, 1982-87, Golden Spread Coun., Amarillo, 1987-89. Recipient Meritorious Svc. award N.G. Bur., 1987, Armed Forces Comm-Elec Assn., 1989. Mem. ASPA. Avocations: running, artistry. Home: 484 Rocky Mouth Ln Draper UT 84020-7665

AVERY, KEITH WILLETTE, artist, educator; b. Lansing, Mich., Dec. 3, 1921; s. Norton Louis and Ruby Mae (Willette) A.; m. Carol Joyce Haddan, Oct. 10, 1946; children: Carleton Louis, David Keith, Jane Ellen Avery Gray. BS, N.Mex. State U., 1955, LittD, 1986. Cert. secondary edn. tchr., N.Mex., Ariz., Mich. Horse trainer and exhibitor A.B. Johnson Chevrolet Co., Grand Rapids, Mich., 1946-47; ranch foreman and horse trainer Lazy U Ranch, Bartlesville, Okla., 1949-50, Mill Iron Lazy 3 Ranch, Carrizozo, N.Mex., 1950-51; artist N.Mex. State U., Las Cruces, 1951-55; instr. and calf roping coach Judson Sch., Scottsdale, Ariz., 1955-59; instr. Lowell (Mich.) High Sch., 1961-74; artist horseman Springer, Roswell, N.Mex., 1974—; dir. alumni rels. N.Mex. State U., Las Cruces, 1959-60. Author: Ridden Hard and Put Up Wet, 1990, Campfire Echoes, 1994, (biography) Trails of a Wanderer, 1995. With U.S. Air Force, 1942-46. Recipient Champion Working Stock Horse Nat. Horse Show Assn., Chgo., 1946, Gold, Silver and Bronze medals Phippen Invitational Art Show, Prescott, Ariz., 1978, Stetson Hat award Tex. Cowboy Artists Gold Medal Exhibit, San Angelo, Tex., 1983, Best of Show Painting award S.W. Regional Art Show Roswell, 1982, Gov.'s award of Excellence and Achievement in the Arts as the dean of N.Mex. cowboy poets and premier painter of the working cowboy, 1994; rep. N.Mex. Cowboy Poetry gathering Nat. Endowment for the Arts, Elko, Nev., 1986. Republican. Methodist. Home: 2809 S Graves Rd Roswell NM 88201-9024

AVERY, RONALD DENNIS, school psychologist; b. Passaic, N.J., Oct. 24, 1940; s. George Anthony and Ethel (Nikovits) A.; children: George Anthony Jr., Ronald Dennis. BA in English, Calif. State U., 1970, MA in Secondary Edn., 1972; MS in Psychology, U.S. Internat. U., 1978, PhD in Profl. Psychology, 1977. Cert. psychologist, tchr., Calif. Tchr. reading Lynwood (Calif.) H.S., 1971-78, Lynwood Adult Sch., 1972-74; instr. bus. English and comm. L.A. C.C., 1973-84; tchr., reading specialist Hosler Jr. H.S., Lynwood, 1984-86, 88-94; tchr. Roosevelt Elem. Sch., Lynwood, 1986-87; sch. psychologist Lynwood Unified Sch. Dist., 1994—; instr. psychology U.S. Internat. U., San Diego, 1975, Calif. Am. U., San Diego, 1976-77; pvt. practice clin. psychology, L.A., 1978—; clin. psychologist Claif. Youth Authority, Southern Reception Ctr., Norwalk, L.A., 1978, 94, Calif., 1980-82; sch. psychologist, Nellis, Whittier and Norwalk, 1993-94; expert witness Calif. Jud. Sys., L.A. and Orange Counties, 1978—. With USAF, 1960-61. Mem. Calif. Assn. Sch. Psychologists (Outstanding Sch. Psychologist Los Angeles County/Region V), Lynwood Tchrs. Assn. (chmn. grievance com. 1974, pres. 1975), KC, Phi Delta Kappa. Republican. Roman Catholic. Avocations: beach activities, fishing, hiking. Home: 1321 S Bromley Ave West Covina CA 91790-2453 Office: Lynwood Unified Sch Dist 11321 Bullis Rd Lynwood CA 90262-3666

AVERY, STEPHEN NEAL, playwright, author; b. Hot Springs, Ark., Mar. 20, 1955; s. Leo A. Avery and Dedette Carol (Miles) Denatale; m. Kathleen Annette Twin, Sept. 7, 1979. Free-lance reporter Hot Springs Sentinel-Record and New Era, 1970-73. Author: Hungry: 3 Plays, 1991, Because, 1991, Insidious, 1992, Burning Bridges, 1999. With USN, 1973-77. Mem. Dramatists Guild Inc., Authors League of Am. Avocations: museum and gallery exhbns.

AVOLIO, WENDY FREEDMAN, speech and language pathologist; b. Phila., Feb. 24, 1953; d. Harold Stanley and Phyllis Maxine (Broodno) Freedman; m. Michael Howard Strauss, Aug. 31, 1975 (div. 1981); children: Nicole Erin, Mallary Blair; m. Mark Richard Avolio, Mar. 24, 1985. BS, Bradley U., 1973; MA, No. Ill. U., 1975. Speech-lang. pathologist Bartlett (Ill.) Sch. Dist., 1975-76, Proviso Area for Exceptional Children, Maywood, Ill., 1976-77, Cen. Reading and Speech Clinic, Mt. Prospect, Ill., 1977-78, Tucson Unified Sch. Dist., 1978-79, Handmaker Jewish Geriatric Ctr., Tucson, 1981; mgr. speech-lang. therapy program Dept. Econ. Security/Div. Devel. Disabilities, Tucson, 1981-86, So. Ariz. Spl. Edn. Coop., Vail, 1986-92, Amphitheater Sch. Dist., 1992-95; therapeak Life Care Ctr.-Tucson, 1993-95; speech-lang. pathologist Sundance Rehab. Corp., Tucson, 1995-97; pvt. practice Tuscon, 1997—; cons. speech-lang. Parent Support Group, Tucson, 1981-87, Ariz. Adv. Com. For Deaf-Blind, Tucson, 1983-87; lang. cons. Community Outreach Program for Deaf, Tucson, 1983. Active youth and children com. Jewish Comty. Ctr., Tucson, 1986-88, Tucson Classics, 1989-94; bd. dirs. Tucson Residence Found., 1993—. Mem. Am. Speech Lang. and Hearing Assn. (cert.), Ariz. Speech and Lang. Assn. Avocations: dancing, aerobics, travel. Home and Office: 3532 N Fiesta Del Sol Tucson AZ 85750

AWALT, BARBARA J(ANE), public relations company executive; b. Balt., Dec. 29, 1951; d. Robert Francis and Jane Rosalee (Kriete) A.; m. Paul Fisher Rhetts, Mar. 13, 1981; stepchildren: Joanna Katherine, Alexandra Copeland. BS, Towson (Md.) State U., 1973; MS, Johns Hopkins U., 1976. Cert. tchr., Md. Microfilmer, editor Md. Blue Cross and Blue Shield, Towson, 1969-70; mfr.'s rep. Hutzler's Dept. Stores, Towson, 1971-74; regional mktg. rep. Pierce Trends Internat., Ft. Lauderdale, Fla., 1980-81; U.S. distbr. and mktg. mgr. Mayan Rubbings, Inc., Columbia, Md., 1980-83; creative dir. R & R Assocs., Inc., Columbia, 1982-85; graphics dir. Galaxy Graphics, Columbia, 1985-86; exec. v.p. Laser Pub. & Design, Columbia, 1986—; tchr. Howard County Pub. Sch. System, Ellicott City, Md., 1973-87; tchr. art Md. Scy. for Blind, Balt., 1972-73; art supr. summer sch. Howard County Dept. Parks and Recreation, Ellicott City, 1973-78. Illustrator Fin. Independence/Money Dynamics Letter, Reston (Va.) Pub. Co., 1982-83. Mem. citizens adv. com. Howard Cable TV Co., Ellicott City, 1978-79; dir. pub. rels. Columbia Community Band, 1979-81; bd. dirs., newsletter editor Lakeside Assn., 1985-89. Mem. Nat. Sch. Pub. Rels. Assn. (leader regional and nat. seminars and workshops on publs. design and electronic pub.), Am. Bus. Women's Assn. (newsletter editor 1985-89, v.p. 1986-89), Nat. Press Women, Md. Press Women, Howard County C. of C., Columbia Bus. Exchange. Democrat. Home and Office: 925 Salamanca St NW Albuquerque NM 87107-5647

AXELSON, JOSEPH ALLEN, professional athletics executive, publisher; b. Peoria, Dec. 25, 1927; s. Joseph Victor Axelson and Florence (Ealen) Massey; m. Malcolm Rae Smith, Oct. 7, 1950 (dec.); children: David Allen, Mark Stephen, Linda Rae. B.S., Northwestern U., 1949. Sports info. dir. Ga. So. U., Statesboro, 1957-60, Nat. Assn. Intercollegiate Athletics, Kansas City, Mo., 1961-62; tournament dir. Bowling Proprs. Assn. Am., Park Ridge, Ill., 1963-64; asst. exec. sec. Nat. Assn. Intercollegiate Athletics, Kansas City, Mo., 1964-68; exec. v.p., gen. mgr. Cin. Royals Profl. Basketball Team, Cin., 1969-72; mgr. Cin. Gardens, 1970-72; pres., gen. mgr. Kansas City Kings Profl. Basketball Team, Kansas City, Mo., 1972-79, 82-85; pres., gen. mgr. Sacramento Kings Profl. Basketball Team, 1985-88, exec. v.p., 1988-90; pres. Arco Arena, Sacramento, 1985-88; exec. v.p. Sacramento Sports Assn., Arco Sports Complex, 1988-90, Profl. Team Publs., Inc., Stamford, Conn., 1991-92; pub. Between The Vines Newsletter, 1993—; exec. v.p. ops. NBA, N.Y.C., 1979-82, chmn. competition and rules com., 1975-79; trustee Naismith Basketball Hall of Fame; co-host The Sports Page, Sta. KFMB-AM, San Diego, 1994-97. Author: Basketball Basics, 1987. Mem. Emil Verban Meml. Soc., Washington. Capt. Signal Corps. AUS, 1949-54. Named Nat. Basketball Exec. of Yr. The Sporting News, St. Louis, 1973, Sportsman of Yr., Rockne Club, Kansas City, 1975; recipient Annual Dirs. award Downtown, Inc., Kansas City, Mo., 1979, Nat. Assn. Intercollegiate Athletics Frank Cramer Nat. Svc. award, 1983, Man of Yr. award Sacramento (Calif.) C. of C., 1986; named to Ga. So. U. Sports Hall of Fame, 1990. Mem. Am. Philatelic Soc., Phi Kappa Psi. Republican. Presbyterian. Office: 1112 1st St Ste 410 Coronado CA 92118-1407

AXON, DONALD CARLTON, architect; b. Haddonfield, N.J., Feb. 27, 1931; s. William Russell Sr. and Gertrude L. (Ellis) A.; m. Rosemary Smith, Sept. 1952 (div. Oct. 1967); children: Donald R., James K., Marianne Axon Flannery, Darren H., William R. II; m. Janice Jacobs, Mar. 16, 1968; stepchildren: Jonathan Lee, Elise Marie. BArch, Pratt Inst., 1954; MS in Arch., Columbia U., 1966. Registered architect, N.Y., Pa., Calif. Designer, drafter Keith Hibner, Assoc., Hicksville, N.Y., 1954-56; designer Charles Wood, Riverhead, N.Y., 1956-59; architect, prin Donald C. Axon, Assoc., Wantaugh, N.Y., 1959; ptnr. Bailey-Axon & Assoc., Long Beach, N.Y., 1960-66; project mgr. Caudill Rowlett Scott, Houston, 1966-69; in-house architect Kaiser Permanente Hosp., L.A., 1969-75; dir. med. facilities Daniel Mann Johnson Mendenhall, L.A., 1975-78, Lyon Assocs., L.A., 1979-80; pres. Donald C. Axon, FAIA, Inc., L.A., 1980—; tchr. bldg. sci. program U. So. Calif., 1978-82; lectr. in field; profl. advisor dept. architecture U. Tex., 1968-69; advisor to chmn. Sch. Architecture Rice U., Houston, 1968-69; profl. dir. Future Architect Am., 1965-66. Mem. Crestwood Hills Assn., bd. dirs. 1971-75, pres., 1973-75, archtl. rev. com., 1987—; bd. dirs. Brentwood Community Fedn., 1973-75, v.p., 1974-75. Recipient L.A. Beautiful award KPH Norwalk Hosp. Fellow AIA (Calif. regional bd. dirs. 1987-89, mem. various subcoms., chair steering com. 1980, liaison 1991—, bd. dirs. L.A. chpt. 1983-84, pres. 1986, chair com. on architecture for health 1974, chair health facilities com. Calif. coun. 1975, Disting. Svc. citation 1992), Royal Soc. Health, Health Facilities Inst., Hosp. Facilities Inst.; mem. Archtl. Found. L.A. (founding, v.p. 1985-89, pres. 1989-90), Internat. Conf. Bldg. Ofcls., Am. Hosp. Assn., Forum for Health Care Planning (bd. dirs. 1982—, pres. 1993-94). Fax: 949 360 8112. E-mail: donaxon@aol.com. Office: 24302 Carlton Ct Laguna Niguel CA 92677-3718

AYLESWORTH, JOHN BANSLEY, writer, television producer; b. Toronto, Ont., Can., Aug. 18, 1928; s. Fredrick Allen and Marie Thelma (Bansley) A.; (divorced); children: Linda, Robert, John, Cynthia, William, Thomas. Writer The Perry Como Show, N.Y.C., 1960-63; headwriter Judy Garland show ABC, L.A., 1963-64; headwriter Hullabaloo NBC, N.Y.C., 1965-66; headwriter Frank Sinatra - A Man and His Music CBS, L.A., 1966; headwriter Kraft Music Hall NBC, N.Y.C., 1967-68; producer, writer Jonathan Winters Show CBS, L.A., 1968-69; creator, exec. producer Hee Haw CBS, L.A., Nashville, 1968-85; headwriter Julie Andrews Show, L.A., 1972-73; cons. Dolly Parton Show ABC, L.A., 1987-88. Author: Fee-Fi-Fo-Fum, 1961, theatre musical: Durante, 1990, Palm Springs Confidential, 1998. Recipient Peabody award, 1967; named Man of Yr., Country Music Assn., 1970. Mem. Writers Guild Am., Assn. TV and Radio Actors. Home: 1137 S La Verne Way Palm Springs CA 92264-9251

AYLSWORTH, WENDY LYNN, technology executive; b. Detroit; m. Dana Willis Alden. BS in computer scis., Univ. Mich., 1974; MS in mgmt. scis., Univ. Southern Calif., 1981. Software engr. Lockhead Aircraft Co., Burbank, Calif., 1975-80; systems engr. Honeywell Training Systems, West Corina, Calif., 1980-83, mgr. software R&D, 1983-89; mgr. software Walt Disney Imagineering, Burbank, Calif., 1989-90; dir. engring. Walt Disney Feature Animation, Burbank, Calif., 1990-94; dir. tech. Warner Bros. Feature Animation, Burbank, Calif., 1994-95, v.p. tech., facilities, 1995—. Chairperson Klimke Endowment Fund, Pasadena, Calif., 1989-97; v.p., bd. trustees High Point Acad., 1990—, v.p. bd. dirs. Honeywell West Coast Credit Union, West Corina, Calif., 1985-89. Mem. Assn. of Computing Machinery, YWCA (Woman of Yr. in Engring. 1978). Office: Warner Bros Feature Animation 4000 Warner Blvd Burbank CA 91522

AYRES, JANICE RUTH, social service executive; b. Idaho Falls, Idaho, Jan. 23, 1930; d. Low Ray and Frances Mae (Salem) Mason; m. Thomas Woodrow Ayres, Nov. 27, 1953 (dec. 1966); 1 child, Thomas Woodrow Jr. (dec.). MBA, U. So. Calif., 1952, M in Mass Comms., 1953. Asst. mktg. dir. Disneyland, Inc., Anaheim, Calif., 1954-59; gen. mgr. Tamasha Town & Country Club, Anaheim, Calif., 1959-65; dir. mktg. Am. Heart Assn., Santa Ana, Calif., 1966-69; state exec. dir. Nev. Assn. Mental Health, Las Vegas, 1969-71; exec. dir. Clark Co. Easter Seal Treatment Ctr., Las Vegas, 1971-73; mktg. dir., fin devel. officer So. Nev. Drug Abuse Coun., Las Vegas, 1973-74; exec. dir. Nev. Assn. Retarded Citizens, Las Vegas, 1974-75; assoc., cons. Don Luke & Assocs., Phoenix, 1976-77; program dir. Inter-Tribal Coun. Nev., Reno, 1977-79; exec. dir. Ret. Sr. Vol. Program, Carson City, Nev., 1979—; chair sr. citizen summit State of Nev., 1996; presenter in field. Bd. suprs. Carson City, Nev., 1992—; commr. Carson City Parks and Recreation, 1993—; obligation bond com., legis. chair Carson City; bd. dirs. Nev. Dept. Transp., 1993; active No. Corp. for Nat. and Cmty. Svc. by Gov., 1994, V&TRR Commn., 1993, chair, 1995, vice-chair, chair pub. rels. com., bd. dirs. Hist. V&TRR Bd., chair PR Cmty./V&RR Commn., vice-chair Carson City Gen. Obligation Bond Commn., Nev. Home Health Assn.; appointed liaison Carson City Sr. Citizens Bd., 1995; chair summit Rural Nev. Sr. Citizens, Carson City; pres. No. Nev. R.R. Found., 1996—; chair Tri-Co-R.R. Commn., 1995; chair Gov.'s Nev. Commn. for Corp. in Nat. and Cmty. Svc., 1997—, pres. 1998., Carson City Pub. Transp. Commn., 1998—, Carson City Commn. for Clean Groundwater Act, 1998—. Named Woman of Distinction, Soroptimist Club, 1988, Outstanding Dir. of Excellence, Gov. State of Nev., 1989, Outstanding Dir., Vol. Action Ctr., J.C. Penney Co., Outstanding Nev. Women's Role Model Nev. A.G., 1996. Mem. AAUW, Am. Mgmt. Assn. (bd. dirs.), Am. Mktg. Assn., Internat. Platform Assn., Pub. Rels. Soc. Am. (chpt. pres., Silver Spike award 1996), Women Radio and TV, Nat. Soc. Fund Raising Execs., Nev. Fair and Rodeo Assn. (pres.), Nev. Assn. Transit Svcs. (bd. dirs., legis. chmn.), Nev. Women's Polit. Caucus, Nat. Women's Polit. Caucus, Am. Soc. Assn. Execs., No. Nev. Railroad found. (pres. 1996). Home: 1762 Montelena Ct Carson City NV 89703-7383 Office: Ret Sr Vol Program 501 E Caroline St Carson City NV 89701-4054

AYRES, JEFFREY JOHN, chemistry educator; b. Des Moines, Iowa, Sept. 20, 1959; s. John Edward and Joleen Diane (Story) Dubois A.; m. Caroline Sulzberger Stephenson, Nov. 21, 1980 (div. June 1982). BS, Univ. South Fla., 1987; MS, Calif. State Univ., 1996. Tutor chem. Calif. State, Hayward, 1994-96, teaching asst., 1995, student researcher, 1995-96; sub. tchr. Oakland (Calif.) Unified Sch. Dist., 1995-96; chem., math. tutor Yavapai Cmty. Coll., Prescott, Ariz., 1997—; adj. faculty Mesa Cmty. Coll., Mesa, Ariz., 1997—, Yavapai Cmty. Coll., Prescott, 1998—; tutor chem., math. Academic Assistance Access, 1997—. Author: Gibbs Free Energy of Annealing of Dinucleotide Dimers, 1996. Recipient Selby grant Selby Found., 1977. Mem. Computational Chemistry List, Am. Assn. Clinical Chem. Avocations: web page development, rock climbing, fishing, golfing. Home: 555 Dameron Dr Apt 1 Prescott AZ 86301-2446

AZARNOFF, DANIEL LESTER, pharmaceutical company consultant; b. Bklyn., Aug. 4, 1926; s. Samuel J. and Kate (Asarnow) A.; m. Joanne Stokes, Dec. 26, 1951; children: Rachel, Richard, Martin. BS, Rutgers U., 1947, MS, 1948; MD, U. Kans., 1955. Asst. instr. anatomy U. Kans. Med. Sch., 1949-50, research fellow, 1950-52, intern, 1955-56, resident, Nat. Heart Inst. research fellow, 1956-58, asst. prof. medicine, 1962-64, assoc. prof., 1964-68, dir. clin. pharmacology study unit, 1964-68, assoc. prof. pharmacology, 1965-68, prof. medicine and pharmacology, 1968, dir. Clin. Pharmacology-Toxicology Ctr., 1967-78, Disting. prof., 1973-78, also prof. medicine, 1965-67, pres. Sigma Xi Club, 1968-69, clin. prof. medicine, 1982-96; Nat. Inst. Neurol. Diseases and Blindness spl. trainee Washington U. Sch. Medicine, St. Louis, 1958-60; asst. prof. medicine St. Louis U. Sch. Medicine, 1960-62; vis. scientist, Fulbright scholar Karolinska Inst., Stockholm, Sweden, 1968; sr. v.p. worldwide research and devel. G.D. Searle & Co., Skokie, 1978; pres. Searle Research and Devel., Skokie, 1979-85, Azarnoff Assocs., Inc., Evanston, Ill., 1986—, D.L. Azarnoff Assocs., So. San Francisco, Calif., 1987—; prof. pathology, clin. prof. pharmacology Northwestern U. Med. Sch., 1978-85; commr. Nat. Commn. on Orphan Diseases, 1985-87; chmn. bd. dirs. Alpha RX Corp., South San Francisco, Calif., 1992-94; clin. prof. med. Stanford U. Sch. Med., 1998—; professorial lectr. U. Chgo., 1978-86; dir. Second Workshop on Prins. Drug Evaluation in Man, 1970; chmn. com. on problems of drug safety NRC-NAS, 1972-76; bd. dirs. Oread, Inc., Lawrence, Kans., chmn., 1998—; CEO Cibus Pharms., Burlingame, Calif.; cons. numerous govt. agys.; chmn. bd. dirs. Cibus Pharm., Inc., 1996-97; bd. dirs. Entropin, Inc., De Novo, Inc., Menlo Park, Calif. Editor: Devel. of Drug Interactions, 1974-77, Yearbook of Drug Therapy, 1977-79; series editor: Monographs in Clin. Pharmacology, 1977-84; mem. editorial bd. Drug Investigation, 1989—, others. Served with U.S. Army, 1945-46. Recipient Ginsburg award in phys. diagnosis U. Kansas. Med. Ctr., 1953, Outstanding Intern award, 1956, Ciba award for gerontol. rsch., 1958, Rectors medal U. Helsinki, 1968; named Disting. Med. Alumnus, U. Kans. Coll. Health Sci., 1995; John and Mary R. Markle scholar, 1964, William N. Creasy vis. prof. clin. pharmacology Med. Coll. Va., 1975; Bruce Hall Meml. lectr. St. Vincents Hosp., Sydney, 1976, 7th Sir Henry Hallett Dale lectr. Johns Hopkins U. Med. Sch., 1978. Fellow ACP, N.Y. Acad. Scis., Am. Assn. Pharm. Scientists (Rsch. Achievement award in clin. scis. 1995); mem. Am. Soc. Clin. Nutrition, Am. Nutrition Instn., Am. Soc. Pharmacology and Exptl. Therapeutics (chmn. clin. pharmacology divsn. 1969-71, mem. exec. com. 1966-73, 78-81, del. 1975-78, bd. publ. trustees), Am. Soc. Clin. Pharmacology and Therapeutics (Oscar B. Hunter Meml. award 1995), Am. Fedn. Clin. Rsch., Brit. Pharmacol. Soc., AMA (vice chmn. coun. on drugs 1971-72, editl. bd. jour.), Ctrl. Soc. Clin. Rsch., Royal Soc. for Promotion Health, Inst. Medicine of Nat. Acad. Scis., Soc. Exptl. Biology and Medicine (councillor 1976-80), Internat. Union Pharmacologists (sec. clin. pharmacology sect. 1975-81, internat. adv. com. Paris Congress 1978), GPIA (blue ribbon com. on generic medicine 1990), Sigma Xi.

BAAB, CARLTON, advertising executive. COO, CFO CKS Ptnr., Cupertino, Calif. Office: CKS Partners 10443 Bandley Dr Cupertino CA 95014-1912*

BAACK, BRET ROLYN, plastic surgeon; b. Albuquerque, July 27, 1958; s. Rolyn Ernest and Karen Lee (Engelbert) B.; m. Elena Lisa Sandoval, Feb. 14, 1987; children: Amy, David. BS in Chemistry, U. N.Mex., 1979, BA in Biology, 1979, MD, 1983. Diplomate Am. Bd. Plastic Surgery. From asst. to assoc. prof. U. N.Mex., 1990—. Fellow ACS; mem. Am Soc. Plastic and Reconstructive Surgeons (socioecon. com. 1993—), Alpha Omega Alpha, Phi Beta Kappa. Luth. Avocations: keyboards, golf. Office: Univ Hosp Dept Surg 2211 Lomas Blvd NE Albuquerque NM 87106-2745*

BAAS, JACQUELYNN, art historian, museum administrator; b. Grand Rapids, Mich., Feb. 14, 1948. BA in History of Art, Mich. State U.; Ph.D. in History of Art, U. Mich. Registrar U. Mich. Mus. Art, Ann Arbor, 1974-78, asst. dir., 1978-82; editor Bull. Museums of Art and Archaeology, U. Mich., 1976-82; chief curator Hood Mus. Art, Dartmouth Coll., Hanover, N.H., 1982-84, dir., 1985-89; dir. U. Calif. Berkeley Art Mus. and Pacific Film Archive, Calif., 1989—; cons. in field; organizer exhbns. Contbr. articles to jours. and catalogues. NEH fellow, 1972-73; Nat. Endowment Arts fellow, 1973-74, 87-88. Mem. Coll. Art Assn. Am., Am. Assn. Museums, Assn. Art Mus. Dirs.. Office: U Calif Berkeley Art Mus and Pacific Film Archive 2625 Durant Ave Berkeley CA 94720-2250

BABAYANS, EMIL, financial planner; b. Tehran, Iran, Nov. 9, 1951; came to U.S., 1969; s. Hacob and Jenik (Khatchatourian) B.; m. Annie Ashjian. B.S., U. So. Calif., 1974, M.S., 1976; Cert. fin. planner; chartered life underwriter, fin. cons. Pres. Babtech Internat., Inc., Sherman Oaks, Calif., 1975-85; sr. ptnr. Emil Babayans & Assocs., Woodland Hills, Calif., 1985—. Mem. Am. Mgmt. Assn., Nat. Assn. Life Underwriters, Inst. Cert. Fin. Planners, Internat. Assn. Fin. Planners, Am. Soc. CLU and Chartered Fin. Cons., Million Dollar Round Table. Armenian Orthodox. Office: 21700 Oxnard St Ste 1100 Woodland Hills CA 91367-7574

BABBIE, EARL ROBERT, sociologist, educator; b. Detroit, Mich., Jan. 8, 1938; s. Earl Nicolas Arbuckle and Marion Evelyn (Towle) Babbie-Burch; m. Sheila Trimble, May 17, 1965; 1 child, Aaron Robert Babbie. AB cum laude, Harvard Coll., 1960; MA, U. Calif., Berkeley, 1966, PhD, 1969. From asst. prof. to prof. U. Hawaii, Honolulu, 1968-79; prin., owner Babbie Enterprises, Inc., Honolulu, Hawaii, 1976—; writer Babbie Enterprises, Inc., Mill Valley, Calif., 1980-86; prof. Chapman U., Orange, Hawaii, 1987—; vis. prof. U. Calif., Berkeley, 1980. Author: Survey Research Methods, 1973, 90, The Practice of Social Research, 1975, 79, 83, 86, 89, 92, 95, 98, Society by Agreement, 1977, 80, 83, You can Make a Difference, 1985, What is Society, 1993, Adventures in Social Research, 1993, 95 (with Fred Halley), Research Methods for Criminal Justice and Criminology, 1995 (with Michael Maxfield), Adventures in Criminal Justice Research, 1996 (with George Dowdall and Fred Halley), Exploring Social Issues , 1996 (with Joseph Healey and Fred Halley), others. Chmn. The Hunger Project, San Francisco, 1979-84; bd. dirs. The Holiday Project, San Francisco, 1980-87, Zero Population Growth, Washington, 1980-82, The Inst. Applied Physics, Orange, Calif., 1997—. 1st Lt. USMC, 1960-63, Okinawa, Japan. Calif. State U. scholar, Bakersfield, 1994, 96, Santa Clara (Calif.) U. scholar, 1998; Hua-cheng Wang fellow Chapman U., Orange, Calif., 1994-95. Mem. Am. Sociological Assn. (council mem., Calif. chpt. pres. 1995-96), Am. Assn. Pub. Opinion Rsch. (council mem., com. mem.). Democrat. Avocations: computers, photography. E-mail: babbie@chapman.edu. Fax: (714) 281-6213. Home: 6640 E Paseo Fiesta Anaheim CA 92807-4212 Office: Chapman U 333 N Glassell St Orange CA 92866-1099

BABBUSH, HARVEY EDWARD, university administrator, consultant; b. Detroit, Dec. 4, 1928; s. David Charles and Edith Judith (Finegood) B.; m. Elaine Joyce Karasick, Sept. 17, 1950; children: Randall Mark, Wendy Jo, Robert Allan. BS, Mich. State U., 1952; MS, Calif. State U., Long Beach, 1957; postgrad., UCLA, 1962. Tchr. Long Beach Schs., 1953-56; tng. adminstr. N.Am. Aviation, Downey, Calif., 1956-57; personnel adminstr. Calif. State U., Long Beach, 1957-59, writer chancellor's office, 1960-61, career devel. adminstr., 1961-92; cons., pres. Babbush & Thronson, Long Beach, 1991—; pres. Coll. Placement Coun., 1990. Author: Job Finders—Seekers, 1981, College Relations & Recruiting, 1982; editor: Putting Drugs out of Business, 1988; contbr. over 35 articles to profl. jours. Sgt. U.S. Army, 1946-48, Korea. Dir. Western Coll. Placement Assn. (hon. life), pres. Nat. Assn. of Colls. and Employers, chmn. Long Beach Comty. Action Agy. Avocations: writing, woodwork, travel, babysitting grandchildren. Home and Office: 6521 El Roble Long Beach CA 90815

BABCOCK, JEFF CHARLES, financial planner; b. Fontana, Calif., Dec. 9, 1960; s. Charles R. and Sherrill R. (Griffin) B.; m. Kathy J. Myers, Apr. 30, 1982; children: Chantal, Devin. BS in Fin. Planning, Brigham Young U., 1983. CFP. Rep. Mony Fin. Svc., Carlsbad, Calif., 1985-87; pres., CFP Babcock Fin. Svc., Vista, Calif., 1987—; owner Together Forever Bookstore, Escondido, Calif., 1989-95; practice mgmt. cons. Abacus Data Systems, Del Mar, Calif., 1983-85. Contbr. articles to profl. jours. Mem. Inst. of Cert. Fin. Planners, Nat. Assn. Life Underwriters, Nat. Assn. of Health Underwriters. Mormon. Avocations: softball, scuba diving, weight lifting. Office: Babcock Fin Svcs 138 Escondido Ave Ste 207 Vista CA 92084-6057

BABCOCK, LEWIS THORNTON, federal judge; b. 1943. BA cum laude, U. Denver, 1965, JD, 1968; LLM, U. Va., 1968. Ptnr. Mitchell and Babcock, Rocky Ford, Colo., 1968-76; atty. City Las Animas, Colo., 1969-74, City Rocky Ford, 1970-76; asst. dist. atty. 11th Jud. Cir., La Junta, Colo., 1973-76, dist. judge, 1978-83; judge Colo. Ct. Appeals, 1983-88, U.S. Dist. Ct. Colo., Denver, 1988—; escrow and loan closing agt. FHA, Rocky Ford, 1973-76. Bd. dirs. Colo. Rural Legal Svcs. Inc., 1974-76. With Colo. N.G., 1968-74. Named to Order St. Ives. Mem. ABA, Colo. Bar Assn., Denver Bar Assn., Colo. Bar Found., North Ind. Dist. Bar Assn. Office: US Dist Ct 1929 Stout St Rm C550 Denver CO 80294-0001

BABCOCK, WALTER CHRISTIAN, JR., membrane company executive; b. Oakland, Calif., Oct. 20, 1947; s. Walter Christian and Beatrice Alice (Sommerfield) B.; m. Jacqueline Ann Mills, Dec. 30, 1971; children: Jennifer Suzanne, Rebecca Christine. BS, U. Calif., San Diego, 1969; MS, U. Oreg., 1970, PhD, 1976. V.p. Rsch. Cons. and Design, La Jolla, Calif., 1970-71; rsch. chemist Bend (Oreg.) Rsch. Inc., 1976-81, dir. separations div., 1981-86, v.p., 1983-87, pres., 1987—, chief oper. officer, 1987-89, chief exec. officer, 1989—, pres.; bd. dirs. Consep Membranes, Bend. Contbr. articles to profl. jours. Bd. dirs. St. Charles med. Ctr., Bend, 1986. Mem. Am. Chem. Soc., N.Am. Membrane Soc., Oreg. Biotech. Assn. (bd. dirs. 1990-91). Republican. Avocations: sailing, horseback riding. Office: Bend Rsch Inc 64550 Research Rd Bend OR 97701-8599*

BABEL, DEBORAH JEAN, social worker, paralegal; b. Fulton, N.Y., Oct. 12, 1959; d. Sheldon Rowell and Mary Jane (Dimon) Ford; m. Charles Jacob Babel III, Sept. 7, 1984 (seperated); children: Casandra Jane, Stefan Michael (dec.). BA in Acctg., Aurora (Colo.) C.C., 1981; BS in Social Wk., U. Boulder, 1982, MS in Social Work, 1984; cert., Denver Paralegal Inst., 1995. Cert. respite care for abused children; paralegal cert. Denver Paralegal Inst., 1986. Acct. Dale Conklin and Assocs. CPA Firm, Englewood, Colo., 1981-84, Beechcraft Aviation Inc., Denver, 1985-92; pres., founder The Parents Help Network, Aurora, 1993—; adv. Adoptive Families of Am., Mpls., 1989—, Colo. Coalition for Children, Denver, 1989—, Fedn. of Families for Childrens Mental Health, Alexandria, Va., 1989—; parent rep. N.Am. Coun. on Adoptable Children. Contbr. articles to profl. jours. Mem. NAFE, NASW, Nat. Com. on the Prevention of Child Abuse, Attachment Disorder Parents Network (v.p. 1988—, Parent Advocacy award 1989), N.Am. Coun. on Adoptable Children (Warmline and Parent Advocate). Democrat. Roman Catholic. Avocations: adoption and foster care legislation, abuse and neglect issues in children, swimming, crafts, spending time with children. Home and Office: Parents Help Network 10555 W Jewell Ave #4-208 Lakewood CO 80232

BABICK, DON, newspaper executive; b. Montreal, Que., Can., Jan. 18, 1942; s. George and Elizabeth (Ferguson) B.; m. Jacqueline, Oct. 30, 1966; children: Nancy, Todd. Student, Ryerson Poly Inst. Pres., pub. Southam Inc., 1996—; advt. mgr. Montreal Gazette, 1969-77; advt. dir. Montreal Star, 1977-79; advt. mgr. Vancouver Sun, 1980-83; mktg. dir. Calgary Herald, 1983-88; v.p. mktg. Southam Newspaper Group, Toronto, 1988-90; pres., pub. Edmonton Jour., 1990-92, Pacific Press, 1992—. Office: Vancouver Province, 200 Granville St, Vancouver, BC Canada V6H 3N3

BABOW, IRVING PAUL, sociologist, researcher; b. Kiev, Russia, Aug. 12, 1913; came to U.S., 1914; s. Paul Louis and Rose (Millman) B.; m. Frances Sona Silberstein, Nov. 19, 1945; 1 child, Robin Lynn Babow Rowe. BA in Social Theory, U. Calif., Berkeley, 1936, PhD in Sociology, 1954. Rsch. dir., civil rights inventory Coun. Civic Unity, San Francisco, 1954-55; lectr. social welfare U. Calif., Berkeley, 1954-63; rsch. dir. Calif. Cancer Patient Study Am. Cancer Soc. Calif. Divsn., San Francisco, 1962-63; sociologist nursing rsch. U.S. Pub. Health Svc., San Francisco, 1964; rsch. social scientist Calif. Dept. Mental Hygiene, Imola, 1965-70; prof. sociology Calif. Poly. State U., San Luis Obispo, 1971-78; ind. rsch. sociologist Mill Valley, Calif., 1979—; rsch. dir. health & rehab. study United Cmty. Fund San Francisco, 1959-60, Alameda County mental health study Mental Health Assn. & East Bay Coun. Social Planning, Oakland, Calif., 1961. Contbr. articles to profl. jours. Med. field agent U.S. Selective Svc., San Francisco, 1942-44; mem. cons. intercultural edn. Calif. Dept. Edn. Primary Schs. Divsn., Sacramento, 1945-48. Psychiat. fellow Grad. Sch. Jewish Social Work, N.Y.C., 1936-38. Mem. NASW, Am. Sociol. Assn., Am. Assn. Suicidology. Democrat. Jewish. Avocations: travel, music, writing satire. Home: 139 Seminary Dr Apt D Mill Valley CA 94941-3140

BACA, JOSEPH FRANCIS, state supreme court justice; b. Albuquerque, Oct. 1, 1936; s. Amado and Inez (Pino) B.; m. Dorothy Lee Burrow, June 28, 1969; children: Jolynn, Andrea, Anna Marie. BA in Edn., U. N.Mex., 1960; JD, George Washington U., 1964; LLM, U. Va., 1992. Asst. dist. atty. 1st Jud. Dist., Santa Fe, 1965-66; pvt. practice Albuquerque, 1966-72; dist. judge 2d Jud. Dist., Albuquerque, 1972-88; justice N.Mex. Supreme Ct., Santa Fe, 1989—; spl. asst. to atty. gen. Office of N.Mex. Atty. Gen., Albuquerque, 1966-71. Dem. precinct chmn., albuquerque, 1968; del. N.Mex. Constl. Conv., Santa Fe, 1969; bd. dirs. State Justice Inst., 1994—. Recipient Judge of Yr. award Peoples Commn. for Criminal Justice, 1989, Quincentennial Commemoration Achievement award La Hispanidad Com., 1992, Luchando por la Justicia award Mex. Am. Law Students Assn. U. N.Mex. Law Sch., 1993; J. William Fulbright Disting. Pub. Svc. award George Washington U. Alumni Assn., 1994, Recognition and Achievement award Commn. on Opportunities for Minorities in the Profession, 1992, others; named one of 100 most influential Hispanics Hispanic Bus. Mag., 1997, 98. Mem. ABA, Hispanic Nat. Bar Assn., N.Mex. Bar Assn. (outstanding jud. svc. award 1998), Am. Law Inst., Scribes, Am. Jud. Soc., Albuquerque Bar Assn., Santa Fe Bar Assn., N.Mex. Hispanic Bar Assn., Alumni Assn. (pres. 1980-81), Kiwanis (pres. Albuquerque chpt. 1984-85), KC (dep. grand knight 1968). Roman Catholic. Avocation: reading history. Office: Supreme Ct NMex Supreme Court Bldg PO Box 848 Santa Fe NM 87504-0848

BACA, MARY FRANCES, mental health therapist; b. Sante Fe, N. Mex., Aug. 31, 1963; d. Alfred Cylde and Rita Martha (Padilla) B.; m. Leslie L. Lopez, Oct. 7, 1995. BA, U. N. Mex., 1986; MA, Webster U. St Louis, 1989. Lic. Profl. Clin. Counselor. Mental health worker Bernalillo City Mental Health Ctr., Albuquerque, 1984-86; child devel. spl. U. N. Mex., Albuquerque, 1986-87; mental health worker Heights Psychiat. Hosp., Albuquerque, 1986-87; soc. worker III, investigator Child Protective Svcs., Albuquerque, 1988-89; therapist, case mng. Genesis Womens Ctr., Albuquerque, 1989-90; residential dir. Teen Parent Residence, Albuquerque, 1990-92; instr. U. N. Mex., Albuquerque, 1993—, rsch. asst., 1995—; therapist, pvt. practice Odyssey Counseling Svcs., Albuquerque, 1990—. Mem. Assn. for Counseling & Devel. Avocations: pets, outdoors, camping, hiking. Office: Odyssey Counseling Svcs 120 Madeira Dr NE Ste 224 Albuquerque NM 87108-1525

BACANI, NICANOR-GUGLIELMO VILA, civil and structural engineer, consultant; b. Dagupan City, Pangasinan, Philippines, Jan. 10, 1947; s. Jose Montero and Felisa Lomibao (Vila) B.; m. Julie Bacani, June 24, 1972; children: Julinor, Jazmin. BCE, U. Philippines, 1968, MCE, 1973. Registered profl. engr., Philippines. Structural engr. FR Estuar, PhD. Assocs., Quezon City, Philippines, 1970-72; civil structural engr. BestPhil Cons., Dagupan City, 1972-73; engring. mgr. Supreme Structural Products, Inc., Manila, 1974; chief engr. Tecphil Cons., Quezon City, 1974-76; v.p. Erectors, Inc., Makati, Philippines, 1977-81; pres. NGV Bacani & Assocs., various locations, 1981—; advisor, cons. Met. Manila Office of Commr. Planning, 1980-85; profl. lectr. U. Manila Grad. Sch., 1982-83; resource person Nat. Engring. Ctr. U.P., Quezon City, 1983—; cons. Geo. J. Fosdyke Assocs., L.A., 1985-86, Victor Constrn. & Devel., 1986-87, Stanley Assocs. Internat., 1988, H.A. Simons Internat., 1988-90, Azlon Devel. Corp., 1990—; pres. Mgmt. Design & Investment Co., 1987—; sr. structural cons. Seismic Engring. Ltd., 1990—; sr. cons. Davey Gibson Cons., 1991-92; pres. Bestphil Can., 1992—, Seismic Cons., 1993—; cons. Chemetics Internat., 1994—. Author: A Reference for Engineers and Builders, 1983. Mem. Internat. Assn. Bridge and Structural Engrs. Switzerland, Assn. Structural Engrs. Philippines (life, bd. dirs. 4 terms), U. Philippines Alumni Engrs. Assn. (life), Nat. Geog. Soc., Tri-City C. of C. Avocations: guitar playing, choir. Office: PO Box 3856 Blaine WA 98231-3856

BACH, CYNTHIA, educational program director, writer; b. Oct. 28. BA in Art Edn., UCLA, 1955; MPA, U. So. Calif., 1978; LDS, Calif. Luth., 1993. Cert. gen. elem., spl. secondary art, and gen. jr. h.s. tchr. Staff asst. L.A. Unified Sch. Dist., 1976; rainbow tchr., gifted coord. Trinity Elem. Sch., L.A., 1978-81; field worker/in-svc. for parents and staff educator Hubbard Elem. Sch., Sylmar, Calif., 1981-90; student observer Liggett Elem. Sch., Panorama City, Calif., 1990-92; tng. tchr. Calif. State U. (Northridge)-Vena Sch., Arleta, Calif., 1992-93; pres. Comprehensive Learning Systems; rsch. bd. advisors Am. Biograph. Inst., Inc. Author: Alternatives to Retail Marketing for Seniors (Bur. of Consumer Affairs). Lectr. Sr. Citizens Bur of Consumer Affairs, City Hall; past pres. local PTA; lay eucharistic min., 1998; del. Children's Def. Fund Conf., 1998; sch. bd. mem. St. Martin-in-the-Fields Parish Sch. Nat. Art scholar, Chouinard Art Inst. scholar., Special Recognition, 79 State Evaluation Mar Team-outstanding educator, Phi Alpha Alpha, Nat. Acad. Hon. Soc. Pub. Affairs Admin., Order of Internat. Fell.(-500 persons worldwide)-Edn., Nat. Div. Research Brd. Advisors Amer. Biographical Inst., elected assoc. mem., Nat. Mus. Women in Arts, elected Internat. Platform Assn., 21st Century Award for Achievement. Mem. NAFE, AAUW, 1st Century Soc. UCLA, Nat. Mus. Women in Arts (assoc.), Internat. Platform Com., Phi Alpha Alpha. Avocations: reading, theology, old movies, writing, gardening. Home: 5140 White Oak Ave Apt 214 Encino CA 91316-2435

BACH, MARTIN WAYNE, stockbroker, owner antique clock stores; b. Milw., Mar. 30, 1940; s. Jack Baer and Rose (Weiss) B.; m. Roberta Sklar, Aug. 19, 1962; children: David Louis, Emily Elizabeth. BA, U. Wis., 1963. Stockbroker J. Barth & Co., Oakland, Calif., 1966-72, v.p., 1970-72; sr. v.p., stockbroker Dean Witter & Co., Oakland, 1972—; founder The TimePeace, Carmel, Calif., 1972-83, San Francisco, 1975-83, La Jolla, 1977-83; instr. fin. San Leandro, Lafayette and Hayward (Calif.) Adult Sch., 1970—. Chmn. bd. dirs. Diablo Light Opera Co., 1985-87; bd. dirs. East Bay Hosp., 1985-90. 1st lt. U.S. Army, 1963-65. Mem. Calif. Thoroughbred Breeders Assn., Calif. Thoroughbred Assn., Nat. Assn. Clock and Watch Collectors, Am. Horse Coun., East Bay Brokers Club, Blackhawk Country Club, Dean Witter Chairmen's Club, B'nai B'rith. Avocations: breeder, owner thoroughbred race horses. Home: 4431 Deer Ridge Rd Danville CA 94506-6019 Office: 2 Theatre Sq Ste 322 Orinda CA 94563-3346

BACHMAN, SALLYANNE, opera singer, educator, coach; b. Rushville, Nebr., Jan. 31, 1934; d. Ernest Randolph and Malena (Johnson) Werner; m. Lanell Blaine Bachman; children: Blaine Lanell, Kirk Werner, Vaughn Joseph, Honey Marlena, Garth Ernest. BS, Utah State U., 1957. Cert. elem., secondary tchr. Tchr. Norwalk/La Mirada Sch. Dist., 1958-63; resident cast mem. Medolyland Theatre, Anaheim, Calif., 1963-68; tchr., resource developer Corona (Calif.) Sch. Dist., 1969-74; artist, performer Cmty. Concert Assn., N.Y.C., 1974-94; concert artist, 1981—. Performances include Amneris in Aida, Rosina in The Barber of Sevile, title role in Carmen, Dorabella Cosi fan Tutte, Giulietta Tales of Hoffman, Ann Glawari on The Merry Widow; soloist Mormon Tabernacle Choir. Ch. Jesus Christ Latter Day Saints. Home: 8402 Aztec Rd NE Albuquerque NM 87111-4502

BACHRACH, CHARLES LEWIS, advertising agency executive; b. N.Y.C., Feb. 22, 1946; s. Herbert and Lilla Clare (Blumberg) B.; m. Lois Susan Davis, Sept. 12, 1968; 1 dau., Jennifer Leigh. B.S., Ithaca (N.Y.) Coll., 1968. Assoc. producer MPO Sports Co., N.Y.C., 1968-69; unit mgr. NBC, N.Y.C., 1969; with Ogilvy & Mather, Inc., N.Y.C., 1969—; sr. v.p. broadcast Ogilvy & Mather, Inc., 1978-83, dir. Network and Programming Dept; sr. v.p. network and programming Western Internat. Media, 1983-89, exec. v.p., 1989—; pres. Western Internat. Syndication, 1983—; sr. v.p., dir. network and program purchasing Rubin Postaer & Assocs., L.A., 1990-92, exec. v.p., dir. media and resources and programming, 1992—; vis. prof. Ithaca Coll. Sch. Communications; vis. lectr. New Sch.; guest lectr. UCLA, Calif. State, L.A., Marymount Coll.; guest commentator NPR, CNN, NBC. Contbr. articles to profl. publs. Judge Internat. Emmy Awards.; Lobbyist N.Y. State pvt. colls.; bd. dirs. Caption Ctr., 1992. Recipient Disting. Alumni award Ithaca Coll., 1980, Aid to Advt. Edn. award Am. Advt. Fedn., 1986, Media Maven award Advt. Age, 1996; named One of Top 100 Young People in Advt., 1985. Mem. AAAA (com. broadcast network and programming), TV Acad. Arts and Scis., L.A. Advt. Club (bd. dirs. 1989). Home: 3121 Dona Marta Dr Studio City CA 91604-4327 Office: Rubin Postaer and Assocs 1333 2d St Santa Monica CA 90401-1100*

BACHTEL, ANN ELIZABETH, educational consultant, researcher, educator; b. Winnipeg, Man., Can., Dec. 12, 1928; d. John Wills and Margaret Agnes (Gray) Macleod; m. Richard Earl Bachtel, Dec. 19, 1947 (dec.); children: Margaret Ann, John Macleod, Bradley Wills; m. Louis Philip Nash, June 30, 1978 (div. 1987). AB, Occidental Coll., 1947; MA, Calif. State U.-L.A., 1976; PhD, U. So. Calif., 1988. Cert. life tchr., adminstr., Calif. Elem. tchr. pub. and pvt. schs. in Calif., 1947-50, 64-77; dir. Emergency Sch. Aid Act program, spl. projects, spl. arts State of Calif., 1977-80; leader, mem. program rev. team Calif. State Dept. Edn., 1981-85; cons. Pasadena Unified Sch. Dist., 1981-86; teaching asst., adj. prof. U. So. Calif.; cons. sch. dists., state depts. internat. edn.; presenter workshops/seminars; mem. legis. task forces. Chair resource allocation com. City of Pasadena, 1982-90, Pasadena-Mishima (Japan) Sister Cities Internat. Com., 1983-87; asst. chair Pasadena-Jarvenpaa, Finland, 1990-92, chair, 1992-95; asst. chair Pasadena-Mishima, 1996-97; mem. L.A. World Affairs Coun., Bonita Unified Sch. Dist. Curriculum Coun., 1990-93, Dist. Task Force Fine Arts, 1990-93, Dist. Task Force Tech., 1990-93, Dist. Handwriting Task Force, 1993; active Pasadena Hist. Soc., Pasadena Philharm. Com., Women's Com. Pasadena Symphony Assn.; deacon Pasadena Presbyn. Ch., 1989-92, elder 1997—. Emergency Sch. Aid Act grantee, 1977-81. Named to Hall of Fame Bonita Unified Sch. Dist., 1990-91. Mem. World Coun. Gifted and Talented Children, Internat. Soc. Edn. Through Art, Nat. Art Educators Assn. (dels. assembly 1988-92), Clan MacLeod Soc. (bd. dirs. So. Calif. chpt.), Phi Delta Kappa, Kappa Delta Pi, Pi Lambda Theta (Ella Victoria Dobbs Nat. Rsch. award 1989, pres. L.A chpt. 1991-95, nat. rsch. awards com. 1989-91, chair 1991-95, co-pres. region V 1993-95, 95-97, Outstanding Pi Lambda Thetan in region V 1993-95), Assistance League of Pasadena. Contbr. articles to publs.; writer/editor: Arts for the Gifted and Talented, 1981; author Nat. Directory of Programs for Artistically Gifted and Talented Students, K-12.

BACHUS, BENSON FLOYD, mechanical engineer, consultant; b. LeRoy, Kans., Aug. 10, 1917; s. Perry Claude and Eva Pearl (Benson) B.; m. Ruth Elizabeth Beck, May 31, 1942; children: Carol Jean Schueler, Bruce Floyd, Linda Ruth Gadway. Degree, Hemphill Diesel Sch., Chgo., 1937; student, Sterling Coll., 1937-39; BSME, Kans. State U., 1942; postgrad., Ohio State U., 1961, Stevens Inst., 1964; MBA, Creighton U., 1967. Registered profl. engr., Ariz., Ill., Nebr. Researcher, mech. engr. Naval Ordnance Rsch. Lab., Washington, 1942-43; jr. product engr. Western Electric Co., Inc., Chgo. and Eau Claire, Wis., 1944-46; sr. devel. engr. Western Electric Co., Inc., Chgo., 1946-56; devel. engr. Western Electric Co., Inc., Omaha, 1960-66; product engr. mgr. Century Electronics and Instruments, Inc., Tulsa, Okla., 1956-60; sr. staff engr. Western Electric Co. div. AT&T Techs., Phoenix, 1966-85; cons. in field, Phoenix, 1985—; chmn. energy conservation AT&T Techs., Inc., 1973-85; advisor to student engrs. Ariz. State U., 1967-87. Patentee in field (9). Trustee Village of Westchester (Ill.), 1949-53; sec.-treas. Westchester Broadview Water Commn., 1949-53; Sunday Sch. supr. Westchester Cmty. Ch., 1949-56; vol. campaign worker, precinct committeeman, capt. Phoenix Rep. Party, 1986—. Named Westchester Family of Yr., Westchester Cmty. Ch., 1952; recipient Centennial medal Am. Soc. Engrs., 1979, Recognition and Appreciation award Sterling Coll., 1996; inducted Kans. State U. Coll. Engring. Hall of Fame, 1995. Fellow ASME (state legis. coord. 1985-86, 88-93, treas. Ariz. sect. 1971-72, sec. 1972-73, vice chmn. 1973-74, chmn. 1974-75, 50-Yr. Membership award, President's Dedicated Svc., Devotion, Leadership, Performance award 1992, Dedicated Svc. award 1993); mem. TAPPI, NSPE (Engr. of Yr. award 1979), Soc. Profl. Engrs. (editor mag. 1972-86), Ariz. Coun. Engring. and Sci. Assn., Am. Security Coun., Soc. Plastics Engrs., Weoma Sci. Club (pres. 1963-66), Tel. Pioneers Am., Order of Engrs., Elks, Airstream Wally Byam Caravan Club Internat Trailer Club. Avocations: woodworking, hiking, fishing, tennis, writing. Home and Office: 5229 N 43d St Phoenix AZ 85018-1671

BACON, ELIZABETH MORROW, librarian, writer, editor, educator; b. L.A., Sept. 15, 1914; d. James Edwin and Elizabeth Margaret (Hodenpyl) Morrow; m. George Richards Bacon, Sept. 7, 1939 (div. June 1963); children: David Nathaniel, Daniel Carl. BA, Bryn Mawr Coll., 1935; MLS, U. Calif., Berkeley, 1958. Children's book editor various publishing firms, N.Y.C., 1935-52; ctrl. children's svcs. librarian Contra Costa County Libr., Pleasant Hill, Calif., 1959-70; dir. children's svcs. Solano County Libr., Vallejo, Calif., 1970-78; lectr., Sch. of Libr. and Info. Studies U. Calif., Berkeley, 1978-84; lectr. extension classes Calif. State U. Sonoma, Solano Cmty. Coll., U. Calif. Berkeley, 1970-82. Author: See Through the Sea, 1955, See Up the Mountain, 1958, Jewish Holidays, 1967, A Great Miracle, 1968, People at the Edge of the World, 1991; editor: How Much Truth Do We Tell the Children?, 1988; contbr. articles and book revs. to profl. jours. Mem. exec. com. Friends Com. on Legis., Sacramento, Calif., 1974—; mem. adv. com. Criminal Justice Project, Am. Friends Svc. Com., Oakland, Calif., 1994—; vol. organizer Am. Fedn. Tchrs. AFL-CIO, Berkeley, 1979-86. Recipient spl. recognition Bay Area Storytelling Festival, Berkeley, 1994, Tribute of a Lifetime Com. of Correspondence, San Francisco, 1994. Mem. Assn. Children's Librarians (book rev. chair 1971), Soc. Children's Book Writers (spkr. 1977), Calif. Libr. Assn. (various coms. 1968-78). Mem. Soc. of Friends. Avocations: travel, bird watching, needlepoint, archeology. Home: 1320 Addison St Apt C-232 Berkeley CA 94702-1738

BACON, LEONARD ANTHONY, accounting educator; b. Santa Fe, June 10, 1931; s. Manuel R. and Maria (Chavez) Baca; m. Patricia Balzaretti; children—Bernadine M., Jerry A., Tiffany A. B.E., U. Nebr.-Omaha, 1965; M.B.A., U. of the Americas, Mexico City, 1969; Ph.D., U. Miss., 1971. CPA; cert. mgmt. acct., internal auditor. Commd. 2d lt. U.S. Army, 1951, advanced through grades to maj., 1964, served fin. and acctg. officer mainly Korea, Vietnam; ret., 1966; asst. prof. Delta State U., Cleveland, Miss., 1971-76; assoc. prof. West Tex. State U., Canyon, 1976-79; prof. acctg. Calif. State U., Bakersfield, 1979—; cons. Kershen Co. (now Atlantic Richfield Oil Co.), Canyon, 1979-80. Contbr. articles to profl. jours. U.S., Mex., Can., papers to profl. confs. Leader Delta area Boy Scouts Am., Cleveland, 1971-76; dir. United Campus Ministry, Canyon, 1976-79; min. Kern Youth Facility, Bakersfield, 1983—, Christians in Commerce, 1990—. Paratrooper Brazilian Army, 1955. Mem. Am. Acctg. Assn., Am. Inst. CPA's, Am. Assn. Spanish Speaking CPA's, Inst. Mgmt. Accts. (pres. Bakersfield chpt. 1981-82, Most Valuable Mem. award 1981), Am. Mgmt. Assn., Inst. Mgmt. Acctg., Calif. Faculty Assn., Acad. Internat. Bus., Inst. Internal Auditors, Inst. Cost Estimators and Analysts, Alpha Kappa Psi (Dedicated Service award 1979). Omicron Delta Epsilon, Beta Gamma Sigma. Clubs: Jockey (Rio de Janeiro). Lodges: Lions (v.p. Cleveland 1971-73), Kiwanis (v.p. 1974-79, A Whale of a Guy award, Cleveland 1975, Plaque of Appreciation, 1992-93). Office: Calif State U 9001 Stockdale Hwy Bakersfield CA 93311-1022

BACON, ROGER LEE, English educator, consultant; b. Boise, Idaho, Oct. 23, 1939; s. Russell C. and Uvonna (Royle) B.; m. Christine Lee Wright, Dec. 18, 1965; children: Kim Bacon Stanger, Bryan Lee Bacon, Eric Lee Bacon, Melissa Lee Bacon Magelsen, Jill Leeann Bacon. BA in English, Bus., U. Oreg., 1964, MA in English, 1965; PhD in English, U. Utah, 1972, PhD in Cultural Founds. Edn., 1976. Asst. prof. So. Oreg. Coll., Ashland, 1965-69; tchg. fellow U. Utah, Salt Lake City, 1969-72; assoc. prof. English, coord. tech. writing program No. Ariz. U., Flagstaff, 1972-98, coop. edn. intern dir., 1975—; vis. prof. U. Utah, Salt Lake City, 1973-77, U. Wash., Seattle, 1982; cons. Franklin Covey & Shipley Assocs., Salt Lake City, Utah, 1980—, Law Sch. Adminstrn. Test Board, 1980—. Cons. editor various textbooks Prentice Hall Publishers, Wadsworth Publishers, 1978—. Merit Badge Counselor Boy Scouts Am., Flagstaff, Ariz., 1973—; Bishop Ch. Latter Day Saints, Flagstaff, 1994-97. Col. USAFR, 1958-98, chaplain. Mem. Assn. Tchrs. Tech. Writing, Soc. Tech. Comm., Reserve Officer Assn., Phi Kappa Phi. Avocations: Christmas story collecting, environmental writing. Office: No Ariz U English Dept Box 6032 Flagstaff AZ 86011

BACON, URSULA A., publisher; b. Breslau, Germany, Oct. 6, 1932; arrived in U.S., 1947; d. Martin and Frieda (Julius Burger) B.; m. Wolf L. Lansing, Mar. 26, 1948 (dec. Jan. 1970); children: Ron S., Marly Joan Speros. Co-author: Shuage Shadows, 1995, contbr. author: Chocolate For A Women's Soul, 1997, Chocolate For A Women's Heart, 1998. Mem. Nat. Speakers Assn., Oregon Speakers Assn. (v.p. 1996). Avocations: music, people, travel, reading. Home: PO Box 922 Wilsonville OR 97070-0922 Office: Bookpartners Inc 10955 SW Commerce Cir Wilsonville OR 97070-9627

BACON, VICKY LEE, lighting services executive; b. Oregon City, Oreg., Mar. 25, 1950; d. Herbert Kenneth and Lorean Betty (Boltz) Rushford; m. Dennis M. Bacon, Aug. 7, 1971; 1 child, Randene Tess. Student, Portland Community Coll., 1974-75, Mt. Hood Community Coll., 1976, Portland State Coll., 1979. With All Electric Constrn., Milwaukie, Oreg., 1968-70, Lighting Maintenance Co., Portland, Oreg., 1970-78; svc. mgr. GTE Sylvania Lighting Svcs., Portland, 1978-80, br. mgr., 1980-83; div. mgr. Christenson Electric Co. Inc., Portland, 1983-90, v.p. mktg. and lighting svcs., 1990-91, v.p. svc. ops. and mktg., 1991—; chmn. Oreg. Ltd. Energy Com., 1993—; vice chmn. to labor commr. Oreg. State Apprenticeship Coun., 1996—. Mem. Energy Contractors Assn., Illuminating Engring. Soc., Nat. Elec. Contractors Assn. (bd. dirs. Oreg. Columbia chpt. 1997—), Nat. Assn. Lighting Maintenance Contractors, Elec. Contractors Assn.,. Office: Christenson Electric Co Inc 111 SW Columbia St Ste 480 Portland OR 97201-5886

BADGLEY, JOHN ROY, architect; b. Huntington, W. Va., July 10, 1922; s. Roy Joseph and Fannie Myrtle (Limbaugh) B.; m. Janice Atwell, July 10, 1975; 1 son, Adam; children by previous marriage: Dan, Lisa, Holly, Marcus, Michael. AB, Occidental Coll., 1943; MArch, Harvard, 1949; postgrad., Centro Internazionale, Vincenza, Italy, 1959. Pvt. practice, San Luis Obispo, Calif., 1952-65; chief architect, planner Crocker Land Co., San Francisco, 1965-80; v.p. Cushman & Wakefield Inc., San Francisco, 1980-84; pvt. practice, San Rafael, Calif., 1984—; tchr. Calif. State U. at San Luis Obispo, 1952-65; bd. dirs. Ft. Mason Ctr., Angel Island Assn. Served with USCGR, 1942-54. Mem. AIA, Am. Arbitration Assn., Golden Gate Wine Soc. Home and Office: 1356 Idylberry Rd San Rafael CA 94903-1074

BAEHR, THEODORE, religious organization administrator, communications executive; b. May 31, 1946; m. Liliana Milani, 1975; children: Thedore Peirce, James Stuart Castiglioni, Robert Gallatin, Evelyn Noelle. Student in French lit. U. Bordeaux and Toulouse, France, 1967; student English lit. Cambridge (Eng.) U., 1967; student German lit. U. Munich, 1968; BA in Comparative Lit. with high distinction, Dartmouth Coll., 1969; JD, NYU, 1972; postgrad. Inst. Theology, Cathedral St. John the Divine, N.Y.C., 1978-80. Rsch. engr. Precision Sci. Co., Chgo., 1964-65; legal cons. firm Dandeub, Fleissig & Assocs., N.Y.C., 1970-71; law student asst. U.S. Atty.'s Office, So. Dist. N.Y., 1971-72; pres. Agape Prodns., N.Y.C., 1972-79, chmn. bd., 1979-82; exec. dir. Good News Comms., Inc., N.Y.C., 1978-80, chmn. bd., 1980—; pres. Episc. Radio-TV Found., Inc., Atlanta, 1981-82, Trinity Concepts, 1982; cons. media; dir. TV Center, CUNY at Bklyn. Coll., 1979-80, 82—; Episc. Communicators, 1981-84; exec. prodr. Ch.'s Presence at World's Fair, Knoxville, Tenn., 1982; dir. Am. Theater Actors, Episc. Comms. Editor, Commentator, NYU Law Sch. newspaper, 1969-72, Contemporary Drug Problems, 1971-72, Atlanta Area Christian News; creator, coord. Communicate Workshops, 1979; creator, writer, editor Episc. Ch. Video Resource Guide and Episcopal Video/TV Newsletter, 1979; prodr., dir., writer various TV and radio programs including Movieguide, Joy of Music, Perspectives, PBS, 1981-82, Religionwise on WGST, CBS, 1981— (Religion in Media award), Searching, 1978-80, others; editor, writer various books, including TV and Reality, Asking the Right Questions, Tangled Christian Communications, Getting the Word Out (Wilbur award), Movie and Video Guide for Christian Families (Religion in Media award), Hollywood's Reel of Fortune, 1991, The Media-Wise Family, 1998; dir. Runaways (Chgo. Intercom Gold Plaque and Religion in Media award 1989); prodr. In Their Own Words, Was It Love (Religion in Media award). V.p. Ctr. for TV in Humanities, 1982; chmn. bd. Christian Film & TV Commn., 1990—; bd. dirs. Celebrate Life, Christian Conciliation Svc., Dorsey Theatre, SUP, Inc., Coalition on Revival, Habitat for Humanity; mem steering com. Theol. Summit Conf. Mem. Nat. Assn. TV Arts and Scis., Nat. Religious Broadcasters (dir., chmn. TV com.), Bishop in Ind. Christian Chs. Internat., Seawanhaka Corinthian Yacht Club, Nat. Press Club.

BAER, PETER ERIC, architect; b. Bend, Oreg.; s. William Joseph and Marilyn Lynn (Waterman) Baer; m. Patrice Marie Cecil, Aug. 1, 1987; children: Maxwell, Elizabeth. BArch, U. Oreg., 1987. Draftsman J.L. Ward Constrn., Bend, Oreg., 1987; project mgr. Pennbrook Devel. Co., Bend, Oreg., 1987-90; instr. Ctrl. Oreg. C.C., Bend, 1988-92; prin. Pinnacle

Architecture, Bend, 1990—. Mem. AIA, Urban Land Inst., Bend C. of C. Republican. Roman Catholic. Office: Pinnacle Architecture 141 SE 3d St Bend OR 97702

BAERWALD, SUSAN GRAD, television broadcasting company executive producer; b. Long Branch, N.J., June 18, 1944; d. Bernard John and Marian Grad; m. Paul Baerwald, July 1, 1969; children: Joshua, Samuel. Degre des Arts and Lettres, Sorbonne, Paris, 1965; BA, Sarah Lawrence Coll., 1966. Script analyst United Artists, L.A., 1978-80; v.p. devel. Gordon/Eisner Prodns., L.A., 1980-81; mgr. mini-series and novels for TV, NBC, Burbank, Calif., 1981-82, dir. mini-series and novels for TV, 1982, v.p. mini-series and novels for TV, 1982-89; exec. producer NBC Prodns., 1989-95, Savoy Pictures TV, 1995-96, Citadel Entertainment, 1996-97. Producer TV mini-series: Blind Faith, 1990, Lucky Chances (Jackie Collins), 1990, One Spl. Victory, 1991, Cruel Doubt, 1993, A Time to Heal, 1994, Inflammable, 1995. Bd. dirs. The Paper Bag Players, N.Y.C., 1974—; vol. L.A. Children's Mus., 1978-80; mem. awards com. Scott Newman Found., 1982-84; bd. dirs. L.A. Goal, 1996—. Recipient Vol. Incentive award NBC, 1983. Mem. ATAS (bd. govs. 1993-97, nat. awards chmn. 1997-98), Am. Film Inst., Hollywood Radio and TV Soc.

BAEZ, JOAN CHANDOS, folk singer; b. S.I., N.Y., Jan. 9, 1941; d. Albert V. and Joan (Bridge) B.; m. David Victor Harris, Mar. 1968 (div. 1973); 1 son, Gabriel Earl. Appeared in coffeehouses, Gate of Horn, Chgo., 1958, Ballad Room, Club 47, 1958-68, Newport (R.I.) Folk Festival, 1959-69, 85, 87, 90, 92, 93, 95, extended tours to colls. and concert halls, 1960s, appeared Town Hall and Carnegie Hall, 1962, 67, 68, U.S. tours, 1970—, concert tours in Japan, 1966, 82, Europe, 1970-73, 80, 83-84, 87-90, 93—, Australia, 1985; rec. artist for Vanguard Records, 1960-72, A&M, 1973-76, Portrait Records, 1977-80, Gold Castle Records, 1986-89, Virgin Records, 1990-93, Grapevine Label Records (UK), 1995—, Guardian Records, 1995—, European record albums, 1981, 83, award 8 gold albums, 1 gold single; albums include Gone From Danger, 1997, Rare, Live & Classic (box set), 1993; author: Joan Baez Songbook, 1964, (biography) Daybreak, 1968, (with David Harris) Coming Out, 1971, And a Voice to Sing With, 1987, (songbook) An Then I Wrote, 1979. Extensive TV appearances and speaking tours U.S. and Can. for anti-militarism, 1967-68; visit to Dem. Republic of Vietnam, 1972, visit to war torn Bosnia-Herzegovina, 1993; founder, v.p. Inst. for Study Nonviolence (now Resource Ctr. for Nonviolence, Santa Cruz, Calif.), Palo Alto, Calif., 1965; mem. nat. adv. coun. Amnesty Internat., 1974-92; founder, pres. Humanitas/Internat. Human Rights Com., 1979-92; condr. fact-finding mission to refugee camps, S.E. Asia, Oct. 1979; began refusing payment of war taxes, 1964; arrested for civil disobedience opposing draft, Oct., Dec., 1967. Office: Diamonds & Rust Prodns PO Box 1026 Menlo Park CA 94026-1026

BAGAN-PROCHELO, BARBARA ELLEN, psychotherapist; b. Sioux City, Iowa, Jan. 15, 1939; d. Elmer Emanuel and Minerva Lucille (Henry) Bagan; divorced; children: L. Charles, Joseph, Gary, Michael, Thomas, Mari Jo. BA in Psychology/Art, Buena Vista Coll., 1981; MA in Art Therapy, Ariz. Inst. Art Therapy, 1983; PhD in Psychology, Walden U., 1986. Registered art therapist; cert. sandplay therapist; cert. substance abuse counselor; cert. sex therapist. Family programs coord. Phoenix Gen. Hosp., 1983-86; pvt. practice therapist C.A.R.E. Assocs., Scottsdale, Ariz., 1986-89, Psychol. Counseling Svcs., Scottsdale, 189—; adj. faculty Ottawa U. Phoenix, 1990—; trainer, tchr. of therapists Ludwig Tng. Inst., Phoenix, 1991—; cons. Draw From Within, Inc., Scottsdale, 1990—. Author: Draw from Within, 1990, (with others) Sexual Addiction: Case Studies and Treatment, 1994. Fellow Am. Bd. Sexology (clin. diplomate); mem. Am. Psychol. Assn., Am. Art Therapy Assn. (registered), Internat. Soc. of Sandplay Therapists (cert.), Ariz. Bd. of Alcohol and Drug Counselors (cert.). Avocations: hiking, jogging, writing, art (painting, paper making). Office: Psychol Counseling Svcs 7530 E Angus Dr Scottsdale AZ 85251-6410

BAGDIKIAN, BEN HAIG, journalist, emeritus university educator; b. Marash, Turkey, Jan. 30, 1920; came to U.S., 1920, naturalized, 1926; s. Aram Theodore and Daisy (Uvezian) B.; m. Elizabeth Ogasapian, Oct. 2, 1942 (div. 1972); children: Christopher Ben, Frederick Haig; m. Betty L. Medsger, 1973 (div.); m. Marlene Griffith, 1983. A.B., Clark U., 1941, LittD, 1963; LHD, Brown U., 1961, U. R.I., 1992. Reporter Springfield (Mass.) Morning Union, 1941-42; assoc. editor Periodical House, Inc., N.Y.C., 1946; successively reporter, fgn. corr., chief Washington corr. Providence Jour., 1947-62; contbg. editor Saturday Evening Post, 1963-67; project dir. study of future U.S. news media Rand Corp., 1967-69; asst. mng. editor for nat. news Washington Post, 1970-71, asst. mng. editor, ombudsman, 1971-72; nat. corr. Columbia Journalism Review, 1972-74; prof. Grad. Sch. Journalism U. Calif., Berkeley, 1976-90, dean, Grad. Sch. Journalism, 1985-88, prof. emeritus, Grad. Sch. Journalism, 1990—. Author: In the Midst of Plenty: The poor in America, 1964, The Information Machines: Their Impact on Men and the Media, 1971, The Shame of the Prisons, 1972, The Effete Conspiracy, 1972, Caged: Eight Prisoners and Their Keepers, 1976, The Media Monopoly, 1983, 5th edit., 1997, Double Vision: Reflections on My Heritage, Life and Profession, 1995; also pamphlets; contbr.: The Kennedy Circle, 1961; editor: Man's Contracting World in an Expanding Universe, 1959; bd. editors Jour. Investigative Reporters and Editors, 1980-88. Mem. steering com. Nat. Prison Project, 1974-82; trustee Clark U., 1964-76; bd. dirs. Nat. Capital Area Civil Liberties Union, 1964-66, Com. to Protect Journalists, 1981-88, Data Ctr., Oakland, Calif., 1990-97; pres. Lowell Mellett Fund for Free an Responsible Press, 1965-76; acad. adv. bd. Nat. Citizens Com. for Broadcasting, 1978—; judge Ten Most Censored Stories, 1976-98. Recipient George Foster Peabody award, 1951, Sidney Hillman Found. award, 1956, Most Perceptive Critic citation Am. Soc. Journalism Adminstrs., 1978, Career Achievement award Soc. Profl. Journalists, John and Catherine Zenger award, 1996, James Madison award ALA, 1998; named to R.I. Journalism Hall of Fame, 1992; fellow Ogden Reid Found., 1956, Guggenheim fellow, 1961-62. Mem. ACLU. Home: 25 Stonewall Rd Berkeley CA 94705-1414

BAGG, GERALD DAVID, health foundation administrator; b. Des Moines, Nov. 1, 1946; s. Robert Harry Sr. and Jacquline Helen (Gillespie) B. BA, St. Thomas Seminary, 1969, ThM, 1973. Dir. Colo. govs. office of vols. State of Colo., Denver, 1978-82; dir. of vols. Penrose Hosp., Colorado Springs, 1982-84; dir. of gift planning Penrose-St. Francis Found., Colorado Springs, 1984-86, chief operating officer, 1986-89, v.p., 1989-97, pres., 1997—; exec. v.p. Centura Hosp., Denver, 1997—. Vocation dir. Diocese of Pueblo, Colo., 1975-79; bd. dirs. Samaritan Counseling Svcs., Colorado Springs, 1998, Franciscan Family Wellness, Colorado Springs, 1993-96. Recipient Showcase award Assn. of Healthcare Philanthropy, 1989, 90, 91. Democrat. Home: 9815 Raygor Rd Colorado Springs CO 80908-4821 Office: Penrose St Francis Health Found 825 E Pikes Peak Ave Colorado Springs CO 80903-3635

BAGLEY, JAMES W., executive. CEO Lam Rsch., Fremont, Calif. Office: 4650 Cushing Pkwy Fremont CA 94538-6401

BAGNULL, GARY LYNN, accountant; b. Jefferson City, Mo., June 24, 1956; s. Paul Edward and Irma Marie (Mueller) B.; m. Julie Anne Brown, May 12, 1990. Student, Mesa C.C., San Diego, 1974-76; BS in Bus. Adminstrn. and Mgmt., U. Phoenix, San Diego, 1995. Warehouseman Navy Exch., San Diego, 1974-76; drafting aide Archtl. div. County of San Diego, 1976-77; account clk. Probation Dept., County of San Diego, 1978-80; night auditor Best Western Inn, Jefferson City, 1981-82; night auditor Sheraton Harbor Island Hotel, San Diego, 1983-85, income auditor, 1986-87, project contr., 1990-91; chief acct. Sheraton San Diego Hotel & Marina, 1988-97; asst. controller Sheraton Seattle Hotel and Towers, Seattle, 1997—. Avocations: travel, photography, reading.

BAHN, GILBERT SCHUYLER, retired mechanical engineer, researcher; b. Syracuse, N.Y., Apr. 25, 1922; s. Chester Bert and Irene Eliza (Schuyler) B.; m. Iris Cummings Birch, Sept. 14, 1957 (dec.); 1 child, Gilbert Kennedy. BS, Columbia U., 1943; MS in Mech. Engring., Rensselaer Poly. Inst., 1965; PhD in Engring., Columbia Pacific U., 1979. Chem. engr. GE Co., Pittsfield, Mass., 1946-48, devel. engr., Schenectady, 1948-53; sr. thermodynamics engr. Marquardt Co., Van Nuys, Calif., 1953-54, rsch. scientist, 1954-64, rsch. cons., 1964-70; engring. specialist LTV Aerospace Corp., Hampton, Va., 1970-88; ret.; freelance rsch. FDR at Nadir, 1988—. Mem. JANNAF performance standardization working group, 1966-83, Thermochemistry Working Group, 1967-72; propr. Schuyler Tech. Libr., 1952—. Air raid warden, 1941-43; active Boy Scouts Am., 1958-78. Served to capt. USAAF, 1943-46. Recipient Silver Beaver award Boy Scouts Am., 1970. Registered profl. engr., N.Y., Calif. Mem. ASME, Combustion Inst. (sec. western states sect. 1957-71), Soc. for Preservation Book of Common Prayer. Episcopalian (vestryman 1968-70). Author: Reaction Rate Compilation for the H-O-N System, 1968, Blue and White and Evergreen: William Byron Mowery and His Novels, 1981, Oliver Norton Worden's Family, 1981, Studies in American Historical Demography to 1850, Vol. 1, 1987, Overall Population Trends, Age Profiles, and Settlement, Vol. 2, 1987, The Wordens, Representative of the Native Northern Population, Vol. 3, 1994, Computerized Treatment and Statistical Evaluation of the 1790 Federal Census for the Northern Half of the State of New York, The Ancient Worden Family in America: A Story of Growth and Migration, 1988, FDR at Nadir: 1937 & 1938, 1993, Senator Alva B. Adams of Colorado, 1993, Senator Bennett Champ Clark of Missouri, 1993, Senator Walter F. George of Georgia, 1993, Senator Guy Mark Gillette of Iowa, 1993, Senator Augustine Lonergan of Connecticut, 1993, Senator Frederick Van Nuys of Indiana, 1993, Senator Patrick Anthony Mc Carran of Nevada, 1994, Senator Ellison D. Smith of South Carolina, 1995, Senator Millard E. Tydings of Maryland, 1996, Franklin D. Roosevelt's Appointments and Itineraries for the New Deal Years in Alphabetical Fashion, 1996, Infestation of Yankees: Reference Guide to Union Troops In Confederate Territory, 1998, American Place Names of Long Ago, 1998; founding editor Pyrodynamics, 1963-69; proceedings editor Kinetics, Equilibria and Performance of High Temperature Systems, 1960, 63, 67; contbr. articles to profl. jours.; discoverer free radical chem. species diboron monoxide, 1966. Home: 4519 N Ashtree St Moorpark CA 93021-2156

BAHORSKI, JUDY ANN WONG, computer specialist, learning strategist; b. Pueblo, Colo., Oct. 15, 1949; d. Yen Gim and Ngon (Mah) Wong. BA, So. Colo. State U., 1971; MEd, U. Nev., Las Vegas, 1976. Cert. tchr., Nev. 2d grade tchr. Sunrise Acres Elem. Sch., Las Vegas, 1971-77; 2d grade tchr. Myrtle Tate Elem. Sch., Las Vegas, 1977-84, 3d grade tchr., 1984-85; reading specialist Martin Luther King Jr. Elem. Sch., Las Vegas, 1988-90; reading specialist Charlotte Hill Elem. Sch., Las Vegas, 1990-91, computer specialist, 1991-93; learning specialist Mable Hoggard Math./Sci. Magnet Sch., Las Vegas, 1993—, mem. elem. tech. com., 1991-92, mem. supt. tech. study com., 1989-90; computer tchr. trainer Clark County Sch. Dist., Las Vegas, 1984—. Life mem. PTA, 1986—. Mem. Internat. Reading Assn., Reading Improvement Coun., Clark County Classroom Tchrs. Assn., Nev. Edn. Assn., Computer Using Educators (pres. 1991-92), Phi Delta Kappa. Democrat. Roman Catholic. Avocations: boating, reading, computer activities. Office: Mabel Hoggard Math/Sci Magnet Sch 950 N Tonopah Dr Las Vegas NV 89106-1902

BAHR, EHRHARD, Germanic languages and literature educator; b. Kiel, Germany, Aug. 21, 1932; came to U.S., 1956; s. Klaus and Gisela (Badenhausen) B.; m. Diana Meyers, Nov. 21, 1973; stepchildren: Gary, Timothy, Christopher. Student, U. Heidelberg, Germany, 1952-53, U. Freiburg, Germany, 1953-56; M.S. Ed. (Fulbright scholar), U. Kans., 1956-58; postgrad., U. Cologne, 1959-61; Ph.D., U. Calif., Berkeley, 1968. Asst. prof. German UCLA, 1968-70, assoc. prof., 1970-72, prof., 1972—, chmn. dept. Germanic langs., 1981-84, 93-98, chair grad. council, 1988-89; Author: Irony in the Late Works of Goethe, 1972, Georg Lukacs, 1970, Ernst Bloch, 1974, Nelly Sachs, 1980; editor: Kant, What is Enlightenment?, 1974, Goethe, Wilhelm Meister's Journeyman Years, 1982, History of German Literature, 3 vols., 1987-88; co-editor: The Internalized Revolution: German Reactions to the French Revolution, 1789-1989, 1992; commentary: Thomas Mann: Death in Venice, 1991; contbr. articles to profl. jours. Author: Irony in the Late Works of Goethe, 1972, Georg Lukacs, 1970, Ernst Bloch, 1974, Nelly Sachs, 1980; editor: Kant, What is Enlightenment, 1974, Goethe, Wilhelm Meister's Journeyman Years, 1982, History of German Literature, 3 vols., 1987-88, 2nd edit., 1998-99, The Novel as Archive: The Genesis, Reception and Criticism of Goethe's Wilhelm Meisher Waudlkjalike, 1998; co-editor: The Internalized Revolution: German Reactions to the French Revolution, 1789-1989, 1992; commentary: Thomas Mann: Death in Venice, 1991; contbr. articles to profl. jours. Recipient Disting. Teaching award UCLA, 1970, Humanities Inst. award, 1972, summer stipend NEH, 1978. Mem. MLA, Am. Soc. 18th Century Studies, Am. Assn. Tchrs. German, Western Soc. 18th Century Studies, German Studies Assn. (pres. 1987-88), Philol. Assn. Pacific Coast, Lessing Soc., Goethe Soc. N.Am. (exec. sec. 1979-89, pres. 1995-97). Office: UCLA Dept Germanic Langs Los Angeles CA 90095-1539

BAHR, HOWARD MINER, sociologist, educator; b. Provo, Utah, Feb. 21, 1938; s. A. Francis and Louie Jean (Miner) B.; m. Rosemary Frances Smith, Aug. 28, 1961 (div. 1985); children: Bonnie Louise, Howard McKay, Rowena Ruth, Tanya Lavonne, Christopher J., Laura L., Stephen S., Rachel M.; m. Kathleen Slaugh, May 1, 1986; children: Alden Keith, Jonathan Andrew. B.A. with honors, Brigham Young U., 1962; M.A. in Sociology, U. Tex., 1964, Ph.D., 1965. Research asso. Columbia U., N.Y.C., 1965-68; vis. lectr., summer 1968; lectr. in sociology N.Y. U., 1967-68, Bklyn. Coll., City U. N.Y., 1967; asso. prof. sociology Wash. State U., Pullman, 1968-73; prof. Wash. State U., 1972-73, chmn. dept. rural sociology, 1971-73; prof. sociology Brigham Young U., Provo, Utah, 1973—; dir. Family Research Inst., 1977-83; fellow David M. Kennedy, 1992; vis. prof. sociology U. Va., 1976-77, 84-85. Author: Skid Row: An Introduction to Disaffiliation, 1973, Old Men Drunk and Sober, 1974, Women Alone: The Disaffiliation of Urban Females, 1976, American Ethnicity, 1979, Sunshine Widows: Adapting to Sudden Bereavement, 1980, Middletown Families, 1982, All Faithful People: Change and Continuity in Middletown's Religion, 1983, Life in Large Families, 1983, Divorce and Remarriage: Problems, Adaptations and Adjustments, 1983, Social Science Research Methods, 1984, Recent Social Trends in the United States 1960-90, 1991, Dine' Bibliography to the 1990's, 1999; contbr. articles to profl. jours.; asso. editor: Rural Sociology, 1978-83, Jour. Marriage and the Family, 1978-83. NIMH grantee, 1968-70, 71-73; NSF grantee, 1971-72, 76-80. Mem. Soc. Applied Anthropology, Rural Sociol. Assn., Nat. Coun. Family Rels. Mem. LDS Ch. Office: Brigham Young U Dept Sociology 842 SWKT Provo UT 84602*

BAILEY, CHARLES-JAMES NICE, linguistics educator; b. Middlesborough, Ky., May 2, 1926; s. Charles Wise and Mary Elizabeth (Nice) B. AB in Classical Philology with highest honors, Harvard U., 1950, MTh, 1955; DMin, Vanderbilt U., 1963; AM, U. Chgo., 1966, PhD, 1969. Mem. faculty dept. linguistics U. Hawaii, Manoa, 1968-71, Georgetown U., 1971-73; prof. Technische U. Berlin, 1974-91, univ.-prof. emeritus, 1991—; vis. prof. U. Mich., Ann Arbor, 1973, U. Witwatersrand, Johannesburg, 1976, U. Brunei, Darussalam, 1990; Forcheimer prof. U. Jerusalem, 1986; proprietor Orchid Land Publs.; hon. col. Staff Gov. of Ky. Fellow Netherlands Inst. Advanced Study (life), Internat. Soc. Phonetic Scis.; mem. AAAS, Linguistic Soc. Am. (life), European Acad. Scis., Arts and Letters (corr.), N.Y. Acad. Scis., Soc. Linguistica Europaea, Am. Dialect Soc., Internat. Palm Soc.

BAILEY, DAVID H., computer scientist; married; 4 children. BS in Math., Brigham Young U., 1972; PhD in Math., Stanford U., 1976. Computer scientist U.S. Govt., Fort Meade, Md., 1976-80, TRW/ESL, Inc., Sunnyvale, Calif., 1980-82, SRI Internat., Menlo Park, Calif., 1982-84, NASA Ames Rsch. Ctr., Moffett Field, Calif., 1984-98, Lawrence Berkeley Lab., Berkeley, Calif., 1998—; mem. editl. bd., referee numerous profl. jours.; presenter in field; contbr. articles to profl. jours. Recipient Chauvenet prize Math. Assn. Am., 1993, Merten Hasse prize, 1993. Mem. IEEE Computer Soc. (Sidney Fernbach award 1993), Soc. Indsl. and Applied Math., Assn. for Computing Machinery. Office: Lawrence Berkeley Lab Mail Stop 50B-2239 Berkeley CA 94720

BAILEY, EXINE MARGARET ANDERSON, soprano, educator; b. Cottonwood, Minn., Jan. 4, 1922; d. Joseph Leonard and Exine Pearl (Robertson) Anderson; m. Arthur Albert Bailey, May 5, 1956. B.S., U. Minn., 1944; M.A., Columbia U., 1945; profl. diploma, 1951. Instr. Columbia U., 1947-51; faculty U. Oreg., Eugene, 1951—, prof. voice, 1966-87, coordinator voice instrn., 1969-87, prof. emeritus, 1987—; faculty dir. Salzburg, Austria, summer 1968, Europe, summer 1976; vis. prof., head vocal instrn. Columbia U., summers 1952, 59; condr. master classes for singers, developer summer program study for h.s. solo singers, U. Oreg. Sch. Music, 1988—, mem. planning com. 1998-99 MTNA Nat. Convention. Profl. singer, N.Y.C.; appearances with NBC, ABC symphonies; solo artist appearing with Portland and Eugene (Oreg.) Symphonies, other groups in Wash., Calif., Mont., Idaho, also in concert; contbr. articles, book revs. to various mags. Del. fine arts program to Ea. Europe, People to People Internat. Mission to Russia for 1990. Recipient Young Artist award N.Y.C. Singing Tchrs., 1945, Music Fedn. Club (N.Y.C.) hon. award, 1951; Kathryn Long scholar Met. Opera, 1945. Mem. Nat. Assn. Tchrs. Singing (lt. gov. 1968-72), Oreg. Music Tchrs. Assn (pres. 1974-76), Music Tchrs. Nat. Assn. (nat. voice chmn. high sch. activities 1970-74, nat. chmn. voice 1973-75, 81-85, NW chmn. collegiate activities and artists competition 1978-80, editorial com. Am. Music Tchr. jour. 1987-89), AAUP, Internat. Platform Assn., Kappa Delta Pi, Sigma Alpha Iota, Pi Kappa Lambda. Home: 17 Westbrook Way Eugene OR 97405-2074 Office: U Oreg Sch Music Eugene OR 97403

BAILEY, KATHERINE CHRISTINE, artist, writer; b. Glendale, Calif., Dec. 1, 1952; d. Carl Leonard and Anna Alice (Dzamka) Abrahamson; m. David Francis Bailey, Sept. 27, 1975. BA, Calif. State U., L.A., 1974, MA, 1975; PhD, U. N.Mex., 1982. Exhbns. include Miniature Painters Sculptors & Gravers Soc., Washington, Oil Pastel Assn., N.Y.C., Mont. Miniature Art Soc. Internat., many others; author: (novel) Brush With Death; also numerous short stories; participant in Cyberspace Exhbn. on internet. Recipient hon. mention in mixed media category Nat. Western Small Painting Show, Bosque Art Gallery, N.Mex., 1985, 2d pl. award in pastels, 1986, Cert. of Merit award 4th Ann. Holiday Exhbn. of Oil Pastel Assn., 1994; tuition fellow U. N.Mex., 1977; Alpha Gamma Sigma scholar, 1972. Mem. Oil Pastel Assn., Nat. Mus. Women in Arts, Mont. Miniature Art Soc., Laramie Art Guild, N.W. Pastel Soc., Phi Kappa Phi, Alpha Gamma Sigma. Avocations: playing piano, photography, hiking. Home and Studio: PO Box 301 Daggett CA 92327-0301

BAILEY, PAUL LEROY, career officer; b. Miami, Fla., Nov. 17, 1952; s. Edward Legare and Paula Marie (Foster) B.; m. Deborah Land Denison, Dec. 27, 1974; children: Scott Denison, Jillian Marie. BS, Fla. State Univ., 1974; MA, Webster Univ., 1977; MS, Def. Intelligence Coll., Washington, 1991. Commd. USAF, 1974, advanced through ranks to lt. col., 1995; missile crew commdr. USAF, Little Rock, 1974-79; intelligence officer USAF, various, 1979-86; intelligence specialist pentagon USAF, Washington, 1989-93; intelligence specialist U.S. Army, Washington, 1986-89; intelligence officer USAFR, Peterson AFB, Colo., 1986—; intelligence plans specialist U.S. Space Command, Peterson AFB, 1993—. Leader, Boy Scouts Am., Va., 1989-92, 4-H, Va., 1991-93. Decorated Meritorious Svc. medal, 1986, Performance awards, 1993, 94, 95, 96, Joint Svc. Commendation medal Def. Intelligence Agy., 1993; recipient Mil. Outstanding Vol. Svc. medal USAF, 1996. Mem. Res. Officer Assn. (dept. pres. 1995-96), Nat. Mil. Intelligence Assn. (chpt. v.p. 1991-93), Masonic Knights Templar (jr. warden 1996—), Masonic Royal Arch Chpt. (prin. 1995-96), Masonic Tejon 104 Lodge, Grand Chpt. Colo. (grand ambassador, rep.), Assn. Old Crows. Presbyterian. Avocations: bowling, skiing, hiking, camping. Home: 3640 Windjammer Dr Colorado Springs CO 80920-4435 Office: HQ USSpacecom/J5I 250 S Peterson Blvd Ste 116 Colorado Springs CO 80914-3060

BAILEY, ROBERT C., opera company executive; b. Metropolis, Ill., Dec. 28, 1936; m. Sally McDermott, July 13, 1958. BA in Speech, U. Ill., 1958, MA in English, 1960; BM in Applied Voice, Eastman Sch. Music, 1965; MM in Applied Voice, New Eng. Conservatory Music, 1969. Music producer Nat. Pub. Radio, Washington, 1971-73, dir. cultural programming, 1973-75; mgr. Western Opera Theater, San Francisco, 1975-79; instr. arts mgmt. Golden Gate U., San Francisco, 1977-82; cons. arts mgmt., San Francisco, 1980-82; gen. dir. Portland Opera Assn., Oreg., 1982—; dir. Oreg. Advocates Arts, Portland, 1982-97; cons. On-Site Program Nat. Endowment Arts, Washington, 1982—; judge Met. Opera Auditions, 1977—. Mem. Bohemian Club (San Francisco), City Club (Portland), Arlington Club, Rotary. Office: Portland Opera Assn Inc 1515 SW Morrison St Portland OR 97205-1814

BAILEY, STEPHEN FAIRCHILD, museum director and curator, ornithologist; b. Stamford, Conn., Feb. 7, 1948; s. Edwin Montgomery and Frances (Sherman) B.; m. Karen Lynn Burtness Bailey, Aug. 18, 1971 (div. July 1987); divorced. BA in Biology magna cum laude, Beloit Coll., 1971; PhD in Zoology, U. Calif., Berkeley, 1978. Museum dir. and curator Pacific Grove Mus. of Natural Hist., Calif., 1992—; collections mgr. for ornithology and mammalogy Calif. Acad. Scis., San Francisco, 1984-92; biological cons., 1979-92; adj. prof. biology San Francisco State U., 1986—; teaching Albany Adult Sch., Calif., 1979-85. Co-author Atlas of the Breeding Birds of Monterey County, 1993; co-author, photographer Audubon Society Master Guide to Birding 3 vols., 1983; regional editor Field Notes, 1985-88; contbr. articles to profl. jours. Rsch. fellowship Christensen Rsch. Inst., Papua New Guinea, 1989. Mem. Am. Birding Assn. (elected), Ecological Soc. Am. (life), Am. Ornithologists Union, Cooper Ornithological Soc. (life), Pacific Seabird Group, Soc. Preservation of Natural Hist. Collections, Phi Eta Sigma, Phi Beta Kappa. Avocations: birding, travel, nature study, military history. Home: 830 Sunset Dr Apt J Pacific Grove CA 93950-4729 Office: Pacific Grove Museum Natural History 165 Forest Ave Pacific Grove CA 93950-2612

BAIN, JENNIFER, artist; b. N.Y.C., Nov. 24, 1955; d. Conrad Staford and Monica Margorie (Sloan) B.; m. Michael Kerry Mew, May 6, 1989. BFA, Calif. Coll. Arts and Crafts, 1982; MFA, San Francisco Art Inst., 1985. One-woman shows include Fiberworks Gallery, Berkeley, Calif., 1983, Southern Exposure Gallery, San Francisco, 1987, San Francisco Mus. Modern Art Rental Gallery, 1991, Joan Roebuck Gallery, Lafayette, Calif., 1994, Erickson & Elins Gallery, San Francisco, 1994, 97, Erickson & Elins, 1999, Napa City-County Libr., 1999; exhibited in group shows at Polytechnic U., San Luis Obispo, Calif., 1983, Crocker Art Mus., Sacramento, 1985, 98, Koret Gallery, Palo Alto, Calif., 1987, Southern Exposure Gallery, 1987, Design Ctr., L.A., 1987, San Mateo Arts Coun., Calif., 1987, Matrix Gallery, Sacramento, 1988, 89, Gallery Route One, Point Reyes, Calif., 1988, 93, Lillian Paley Ctr. Visual Arts, Oakland, Calif., 1989, Calif. Mus. Art, Santa Rosa, 1989, Kaiser Conv. Ctr., Oakland, 1990, Calif. Craft Mus., San Francisco, 1990, San Francisco Craft and Folk Art Mus., 1990, Oakland Ctr. Visual Arts, 1991, Beaverton Arts Commn., Oreg., 1992, Butchess County Art Assn., Poughkeepsie, N.Y., 1992, Gallery Ten, Rockford, Ill., 1993, Berkeley Art Ctr., 1993, Gallery Viva, Kawasaki City, Japan, 1994, Butler Inst. Am. Art, Youngstown, Ohio, 1994, Erickson & Elins Gallery, 1995, 97, Alexandria Mus. Art, La., 1995, Chuck Levitan Gallery, N.Y.C., 1995, Modesto Jr. Coll., Calif., 1996, Joan Roebuck Gallery, 1996, Silvia White Comtemporary, L.A., 1996, Takara Gallery, Houston, 1997, Visual Arts Ctr. Boise State U., Boise, Idaho, 1999; represented in permanent collections Security Pacific, Nordstrom's, Kaiser Permanente, Sony, Inc., J.P. Morgan Co., Merrill Lynch Inc., Helm Fin. Corp., Cooley, Godward, Castro and Tatem Inc., SAP Tech. Inc., Sun Chase Internat. Group (China); named in several catalogues and reviews.

BAINES, DAVID RAY, family physician, health education educator; b. Mt. Edgecumbe, Alaska, Apr. 26, 1955; s. Raymond George and Carolyn (Fenton) B.; m. Pamela Kay Sellers, Dec. 30, 1975 (div. Oct. 1981); m. Catherine Ann Panfilio, July 6, 1985. BS in Zoology, Ariz. State U., 1978; med. degree, Mayo Med. Sch., 1982. Bd. cert. in family practice, recert. Intern King Drew Med. Ctr., L.A., 1982-83; family practice resident Cheyenne (Wyo.) Family Practice Residency, 1983-85; staff family physician St. Maries (Idaho) Family Medicine, 1985—; clin. faculty U. Wash., Seattle, 1992-94, U. Nev., Reno, 1994—; affiliate faculty family practice program Idaho State U., Pocatello, 1996—; clin. asst. prof. dept. family practice U. Wash., Seattle, 1996—; mem. environ. justice com. Inst. Medicine, NAS, Washington, 1996-98; mem. polar rsch. bd. Nat. Rsch. Coun., 1995-97; mem. clin. lab. improvement adv. com. Ctrs. for Disease Control and Prevention, Atlanta, 1995-99; chair ad hoc com. for minority populations Nat. Heart Lung and Blood Inst., NIH, Bethesda, Md., 1991—. Author: (book chpts.) Principles and Practice of Clinical Prevention Medicine, 1992, Behavioral Medicine for Women: A Comprehensive Handbook, 1997; contbr. articles and papers to profl. publs. Recipient Gentle Giant of Medicine award G.D. Searle and Co., 1992, Founders award for comty. svc. in health and medicine Nat. Med. Fellowships, 1997; Merit scholar Henry J. Kaiser Found., 1982. Fellow Am. Acad. Family Physicians (chair com. on minority health affairs 1990-91); mem. AMA, Assn. Am. Indian Physicians (bd. dirs. 1986-92, Outstanding Am. Indian Med. Student award 1981), Idaho Acad.

Family Physicians (bd. dirs. 1990-92), Idaho Med. Assn. Avocations: archery hunting, blackpowder muzzleloader hunting, motorcycle riding, pow wow dancing. Home: 311 S 14th St Saint Maries ID 83861-1408 Office: St Maries Family Practice 229 S 8th St Saint Maries ID 83861-1813

BAIRD, ALAN C., screenwriter; b. Waterville, Maine, Jan. 5, 1951; s. Chester A. and Beverly E. B. BA, Mich. State U., 1973. Pres. Souterrain Teeshirts, Nice, France, 1977-78; page NBC, N.Y.C., 1979-80; producer, dir. Random Prodns., Hollywood, Calif., 1981; writer, producer Preview STV, N.Y.C., 1982-83, Sta. KCOP-TV, Hollywood, 1983-84; writer Vidiom Prodns., Hollywood, 1985-95; screenwriter, 1995—. Author: ATS Operations, 1976, Writes of Passage, 1992, Nine Time Zones, 1998; prodr. TV script Live at the Palomino, 1981; designer Screenwright Screenplay Formatting Software, 1985; writer TV scripts Night Court, 1986, 20/60, 1986, Golden Girls, 1986, Family Ties, 1986, Max Headroom, 1987, Dave's World, 1993, movie scripts Trading Up, 1988, Merlinsky, 1989, Eleven Thousand Virgins, 1994, The Fall in Budapest, 1997; play script Twisted Pair, 1998. Crisis counselor San Francisco Suicide Prevention, 1975; prodn. asst. March of Dimes Telethon, Hollywood, 1985; escort, host, vol. Verdugo Hills Hosp., 1994-96. Recipient Harvard Book prize Harvard U., Cambridge, Mass., 1969. Avocations: flying, running, scuba diving, parachuting, competitive driving.

BAIRD, BRIAN N., congressman; b. Chama, N.Mex., Mar. 7, 1956; m. Mary Baird; 2 stepchildren. BS, U. Utah, 1977; MS, U. Wyo., 1980, PhD, 1984. Mem. faculty dept. psychology Pacific Luth. U., 1986—; mem. 106th Congress from 3d Wash. dist., 1999—; mem. transp. and infrastructure and small bus. coms.; cons. clin. psychologist St. Charles Med. Ctr., 1994-96. Mem. NOW, APA, Wash. State Psychol. Assn., Amnesty Internat. *

BAIRD, DOROTHY SCROGGY, retired librarian, educator, consultant; b. Winfield, Kans., July 9, 1927; d. Clair B. and Shirley M. (Calvin) Scroggy; m. John S. Baird; children: John Scott, Jo Lise, Shirley Nan, Peter Miles. BA, U. Kans., 1949; MA, Calif State U., Long Beach, 1967. Cert. sch. libr., jr. coll. tchr., Calif. mem and chair Edn. Innovation and Planning Commn., Sacramento, Calif., 1979-82. Editor (newsletter) Good Ideas, 1991-95, curriculum guides, 1980-89; author: Handbook for Curriculum Review and Materials Selection k-12, 1989. Mem., chair Human Svcs. Commn., Dana Point, Calif., 1992-93. Recipient Hon. Svc. award Los Alamitos Dist. PTA, 1989; cited for outstanding contbrn. to edn. in Orange County, Orange County Dept. Edn., 1990. Mem. LWV (pres. Capistrano Bay chpt. 1995-97), Am. Libr. Assn., Am. Assn. Sch. Librs. (nat. libr. program of yr. 1977), Calif. Assn. Sch. Librs. (chair conf., hon. mem. 1989)), Phi Beta Kappa. Avocations: piano, sketching. Home: 24732 Dana Point Dr Dana Point CA 92629-1813

BAIRD, LOURDES G., federal judge; b. 1935. BA with highest honors, UCLA, 1973, JD with honors, 1976. Asst. U.S. atty. U.S. Dist. Ct. (ctrl. dist.) Calif., L.A., 1977-83, U.S. atty., 1990-92; ptnr. Baird & Quadros, 1983-84, Baird, Munger & Myers, 1984-86; judge East L.A. Mcpl. Ct., 1986-87; adj. prof. law Loyola U., L.A., 1986-90; judge L.A. Mcpl. Ct., 1987-88, L.A. Superior Ct., 1988-90; U.S. atty. ctrl. dist. Calif., 1990-92; judge U.S. Dist. Ct. (ctrl. dist.) Calif., L.A., 1992—; faculty civil RICO program Practicing Law Inst., San Francisco, 1984-85, western regional program Nat. Inst. Trial Advocacy, Berkeley, Calif., 1987-88; adj. prof. trial advocacy Loyola U., L.A., 1987-90. Recipient Silver Achievement award for the professions YWCA, 1994; named Woman of Promise, Hispanic Womens' Coun., 1991, Alumnus of Yr., UCLA Sch. Law, 1991. Mem. Mexican-Am. Bar Assn., Calif. Women Lawyers, Hispanic Nat. Bar Assn., UCLA Sch. Law alumni Assn. (pres. 1984). Office: US Dist Ct Ctrl Dist Calif Edward R Roybal Bldg 255 E Temple St Ste 770 Los Angeles CA 90012-3334

BAIRD, MELLON CAMPBELL, JR., electronics industry executive; b. Corsicana, Tex., Feb. 24, 1931; s. Mellon Campbell and Katherine (Wasson) B.; m. Mary Beth Norman, Dec. 27, 1956. BBA, North Tex. State U., 1957, MBA, 1961. Adminstrv. asst. VARO Inc., Garland, Tex., 1957-59; western region mgr. VARO Inc., Los Angeles, 1959-61; dir. mktg. VARO Inc., Santa Barbara, Calif., 1961-63; exec. v.p., pres. F&M Systems Co., Dallas, 1963-74; pres., bd. dirs. fed. systems group Sanders Assocs. Inc., Nashua, N.H., 1974-81; pres. def. and electronics group Eaton Corp., Cleve., 1981-86; pres., chief oper. officer, bd. dirs. Tracor Inc., Austin, 1986-87, pres., CEO, 1988-89; pres., CEO, chmn. bd. dirs. Delfin Systems, Sunnyvale, Calif., 1990—; pres., CEO TITAN Techs. and Info. Sys. Corp., San Diego, 1998—; bd. dirs. Software Spectrum Inc., Dallas, EDO Corp., College Point, N.Y., Hawker Pacific Aerospace, Sun Valley, Calif. Served with USN, 1951-55. Mem. Nat. Security Indsl. Assn. (trustee 1974—), Navy League U.S. (life), Armed Forces Communications & Electronics Assn., Assn. Old Crows (life, tech. symposium chmn. 1987), Security Affairs Support Assn. (bd. dirs. 1988-91), Tex. Assn. Taxpayers (bd. dirs. 1988-91). Home: 4204 Green Cliffs Rd Austin TX 78746-1241 Office: TITAN Corp 3033 Science Park Rd San Diego CA 92121-1199

BAIRD, SUSAN ELIZABETH, secondary education educator, writer; b. L.A., May 7, 1954; d. Thomas Alva Baird and Sarah Ann (Mott) Durand; m. David Patrick Hogan, Apr. 5, 1980; 1 child, Adam Michael Hogan. BA in Secondary Edn./English Media Endorsement, So. Oreg. State Coll., 1982, MA in Humanities, 1989. Cert. Oreg. std. tchr. secondary edn. media endorsement. Tchr. English Ashland (Oreg.) Mid. Sch., 1983—; advisor Speech and Theatre Clubs, Ashland Mid. Sch., 1989—; lectr. human rights Ashland Sch. Dist., 198—8. Contbr. articles to mags. Spkr. Common Ground Conf., Ashland, 1991; adminstr. Rogue Valley Coalition Cultural Diversity Conf., Ashland, 1992, Nat. Coalition Bldg. Inst., Ashland, 1994; people to people citizen amb. del. to So. Africa, 1998. Miss. Project grantee So. Oreg. R&D, 1988, Mark Twain Prodn. grantee, 1989. Mem. NEA, Nat. Coun. Tchrs. English, So. Poverty Law Ctr., N.W. Coalition Against Malicious Harassment. Avocations: theatre, travel, dogs, water sports. E-mail: susan.baird!ashland.k12.or.us. Office: Ashland Mid Sch 100 Walker Ave Ashland OR 97520-1399

BAKEMAN, CAROL ANN, travel and administrative services manager, singer; b. San Francisco, Oct. 27; d. Lars Hartvig and Gwendolyne Beatrice (Zimmer) Bergh; student UCLA, 1954-62; m. Delbert Clifton Bakeman, May 16, 1959; children: Laurie Ann, Deborah Ann. Singer, Roger Wagner Chorale, 1954-92, L.A. Master Chorale, 1964-86, The Wagner Ensemble, 1991—; libr. Hughes Aircraft Co., Culver City, Calif., 1954-61; head econs. libr. Planning Rsch. Corp., L.A., 1961-63; corp. libr. Econ. Cons., Inc., L.A., 1963-68; head econs. libr. Daniel, Mann, Johnson & Mendenhall, archs. and engrs., L.A., 1969-71, corporate libr., 1971-77, mgr. info. svcs., 1978-81, mgr. info. and office svcs., 1981-83, mgr. adminstrv. svcs., 1983-96, sr. assoc., 1996-98, assoc. v.p., 1998—; travel mgr. AECOM Tech. Corp., 1996—; pres., Creative Libr. Sys., L.A., 1974-83; libr. cons. ArchiSystems, divsn. SUMMA Corp., L.A., 1972-81, Property Rehab. Corp., Bell Gardens, Calif., 1974-75, VTN Corp., Irvine, Calif., 1974, William Pereira & Assos., 1975; mem. office sys. and bus. edn. adv. bd. Calif. State U. Northridge, 1992. Mem. Assistance League, So. Calif., 1956-86, nat. auxilaries com. 1968-72, 75-78, nat. by laws com. 1970-75, assoc. bd. dirs., 1966-76. Mem. AFTRA, SAG, Am. Guild Musical Artists, Adminstrv. Mgmt. Soc. (v.p. L.A. chpt. 1984-86, pres. 1986-88, internat. conf. chmn. 1988-89, internat. bd. dirs. 1988-90, internat. v.p. mgmt. edn. 1990-92), L.A. Master Chorale Assn. (bd. dirs. 1978-83), L.A. Bus. Travel Assn. (bd. dirs. 1995, sec. 1997, v.p. 1998, pres. 1999), Nat. Bus. Travel Assn. (nat. conv. seminar com. 1994-95). Office: DMJM 3250 Wilshire Blvd Los Angeles CA 90010-1577

BAKENHUS, AUGUST ANTHONY, mathematics educator, computer specialist; b. Houston, Feb. 22, 1958; s. August Frederick and Velia (Mancilla) B. AA, Deanza Jr. Coll., Cupertino, Calif., 1983; BA in Physical Scis., San Jose (Calif.) State U., 1985; MA in Ednl. Adminstrn., Calif. State U., L.A., 1994. cert. secondary school tchr. of physical scis., Calif. Tchr. San Jose Unified, 1987-89, L.A. Unified, Tarzana, Calif., 1989—. Mem. Nat. Coun. Tchrs. Math., L.A. City Tchrs. Math. Assn., Calif. Math. Coun., United Tchrs. L.A., Internat. Coun. Computers in Edn. Tennis, chess, sailing, reading, golf. Home: PO Box 571356 Tarzana CA 91357-1356 Office: Portola Jr H S 18720 Linnet St Tarzana CA 91356-3392

BAKER, ALLISON PAIGE, photographer, musician, educator; b. Bend, Oreg., Aug. 21, 1950; s. Franklyn Lyle and Juanita Ellen (Martin) B.; m. Brenda Sue Anderson, Sept. 20, 1996. BA in Edn. and Music, Ctrl. Wash. U., 1978; postgrad., U. Portland, 1978-82. Cert. tchr., Wash. Comml. fisherman, Oreg., Wash., and Alaska, 1968-83, profl. musician and sound engr., Wash. and Oreg., 1971-84; part-time tchr., grad. asst. U. Portland, 1978-84; prof. music Mt. Hood C.C., Gresham, Oreg., 1978-84; membership and mktg. mgr. Costco Wholesale, Alaska, 1984-86; mgr. membership and adminstrn. Costco Wholesale, Clackamas, Oreg., 1986-88, supervising field engr. computer sys. N.W. region, 1988-93; receiving and front end mgr. Costco Wholesale, Tualatin, Oreg., 1993-95; computer sys. mgr. Citizens Graphic Arts, Portland, Oreg., 1995—; profl. photographer, 1995—. Bd. dirs. Oreg. Repertory Singers, Portland, 1994-96, singer, 1st tenor, 1980-83, 93—; mem. Mazamas, 1993—. Named Outstanding Musician Nat. Assn. Jazz Educators, 1974. Democrat. Avocations: mountain climbing, singing, swimming, travel. Office: Citizens Graphic Arts 709 SE 7th Ave Portland OR 97214-2235

BAKER, ARNOLD BARRY, economist; b. N.Y.C., Feb. 3, 1946; s. Max Michael and Sue (Feingold) B.; m. Wendy Glaus, 1990. BA in History, Va. Poly. Inst., 1968; MA, in Econs., 1970, PhD, 1972. Spl. asst. to undersec. for monetary affairs U.S. Dept. Treasury, Washington, 1977-79; sr. cons. Atlantic Richfield Co., L.A., 1979-82; mgr. planning info. analysis Arco Exploration Co., Dallas, 1983; mgr. strategic planning Arco Oil & Gas Co., Dallas, 1983-85, dir. energy market analysis, L.A., 1986-89, dir. pub. issues, 1989-94, dir. polit. econ. analysis, 1994-95; mgr. energy and critical infrastructure policy & planning Sandia Nat. Labs., Albuquerque, 1996—. Contbr. articles to profl. jours., chpts. to books. Mem. Nat. Assn. Bus. Econs., Internat. Assn. Energy Econs. Avocation: jogging. Office: Sandia Nat Labs PO Box 5800/MS 0749 Albuquerque NM 87185

BAKER, BRIDGET DOWNEY, newspaper executive; b. Eugene, Oreg., Sept. 14, 1955; d. Edwin Moody and Patricia B.; m. Guy Dominique Wood, June 30, 1977 (div. Oct. 1981); m. Rayburn Keith Kincaid, June 27, 1987; stepchildren: Benjamin, Jacob. BA in English, French and Theatre, Lewis and Clark Coll., 1977; MA in Journalism, U. Oreg., 1985. Circulation dist. supr. The Register-Guard, Eugene, 1978-80, pub. relations coordinator, 1980-83, promotion dir., 1983-86, mktg. dir., 1986-88; corp. pub. rels. dir., 1989—; bd. dirs. Guard Pub. Co., Eugene. Bd. dirs. Wilani Coun. Camp Fire, 1982-88, pres. bd. dirs., 1986-88; bd. dirs. Lane County United Way, 1982-88, community info. com. chairperson, 1982-84; chair planning com., 1987-88; bd. dirs. Eugene Opera, 1988-91, pres. bd. dirs., 1990-91. Recipient 1st pl. advt. award Editor and Pub. Mag., N.Y.C., 1984, also 1st pl. TV promotion, 1st pl. newspaper rsch. award, 1988, Best Mktg. Idea/Campaign award Oreg. Newspaper Pub. Assn., 1984, 85; named Woman of Yr., Lane County Coun. of Orgns., 1994. Mem. Internat. Mktg. Assn. (bd. dirs. Western region 1986-88, internat. bd. dirs. 1995—, 8 1st pl. Best in the West awards 1983-91), Pub. Rels. Soc. Am. (pres. Greater Oreg. chpt. 1995-96, Spotlight award 1986), Eugene C. of C. (bd. dirs. 1989-92), U. Oreg. Alumni Assn. (bd. dirs. 1990-93), Lane C.C. Found. (bd. dirs. 1995-97), Town Club (bd. dirs. 1995-97), Downtown Athletic Club, Eugene Yacht Club, Zonta Internat. (pres. Eugene Club 1994-96, area dir. 1997-98, lt. gov. Dist. 8, 1998—). Republican. Avocations: sailing, folk dance, outdoor activities, piano. Office: Guard Pub Co PO Box 10188 Eugene OR 97440-2188

BAKER, C. B., retired day care director, organizer, communicator; b. Ft. Wayne, Ind.; d. James Edwin Doelling Sr. and Susie Mae Nutter; m. Gerald R. Baker, June, 1962 (div. 1966); 1 child, Erin Lee; m. Jeffrey E. Baker, June, 1967 (div. 1972); 1 child, Shannon Rae. Student, Internat. Bus. Coll., Ft. Wayne, 1961. Expeditor Wayne Fabricating, Ft. Wayne, 1971; county adminstr. Champaign (Ill.) County Bd., 1974-76; sec. WICD-TV, Champaign, 1976-77; ops. chmn. 40 Plus of Colo., Inc., Denver, 1983, v.p., 1984-85, pres., 1985-86; co-dir. St. Anne's Extended Day Program, Denver, 1986-88; self-employed organizer Denver, 1988—. Editor The Village Voice newsletter, Savoy, Ill., 1974. Chmn. Winfield Village Swimming Pool Com., Savoy, 1975; dir. Mich. Sugar Festival, Sebewaing, 1991. Mem. Am. Bus. Women's Assn., Colo. Women's C. of C. Avocations: reading, horseback riding, weights, walking.

BAKER, CAROLYN ELIZABETH ELLIOTT, educator, writer; b. Eureka, Kans., Apr. 18, 1952; d. William Hill and Janice Elizabeth (Crouch) Elliott; 1 child, Marissa Elizabeth. BA, U. Northern Colo., 1974, MA, 1977. Licensed principal, Colo., cert. tchr., Colo. Tchr. Bozeman (Mont.) Pub. Schs., 1974, Boulder (Colo.) Valley Pub. Schs., 1977—. Editor Boulder-Westminster (Colo.) tchr. newspaper, 1984-85. Chmn. Broomfield (Colo.) High program for gifted, 1980-88; mem., presenter Colo. Dept. Edn. Instrnl. Design Cadre, 1986-88. Recipient Exemplary Tchr. of Yr. award KCNC Channel 4 News, Denver, 1991. Best Shot Tchr. award Centaurus High Sch., Colo. Nuggets, Denver Post, Lafayette and Denver, Colo., 1992. Mem. Nat. Edn. Assn. (Colo. chpt., Boulder Valley chpt.), Nat. Council Tchrs. English, Phi Delta Kappa. Avocations: reading, writing, taking adventures with my daughter, listening to music. Home: 913 Arapahoe Cir Louisville CO 80027-1088 Office: Centaurus H S 10300 South Boulder Rd Lafayette CO 80026-2853

BAKER, CHARLES DEWITT, research and development company executive; b. Dayton, Ohio, Jan. 5, 1932; s. Donald James and Lillian Mae (Pund) B.; m. June Thordis Tandberg, June 25, 1954; children: Charles, Robert, Thomas, Michael. AA in Elec. Engring., Long Beach City Coll., 1953; ed., Boston U., 1954, Pacific Coast U., 1963, U. Utah, 1980. Registered profl. mfg. engr., Calif. Chemist Shell Oil, Torrance, Calif., 1957-60; materials and process engr. Northrop Corp., Hawthorne, Calif., 1960-63; packaging engr. Jet Propulsion Lab., Pasadena, Calif., 1963-71; med. design engr. Utah Biomed. Test Lab., Salt Lake City, 1971-78, sect. mgr., 1978-83; v.p. Tech. Rsch. Assocs., Salt Lake City, 1983-88, pres., 1988—; pres. Thordis Corp., 1980—. Contbr. articles to profl jours.; 20 patents in field. Chmn. bd. dirs. Care Holder Group, 1996—; mem. cmty. adv. com. Heart and Lung Inst., spl. study sect rev. NIH, Tech. Transfer Forum, U. Utah, 1984. Recipient Cost Reduction award NASA, 1969, New Tech. award, 1969, 71, 75. Mem. ASME, Soc. Mfg. Engrs., Utah Mfg. Assn., Acad. of Tech., Entrepreneurs and Innovators. Republican. Avocations: teaching, reading, car rebuilding.

BAKER, CHARLES LYNN, management consultant; b. Dallas, Mar. 17, 1934; s. Leonard Allan and Nellie (Boals) B.; m. Joan Heverly, June 1, 1968; 1 child, Annette Lynn. BS in Internat. Rels. summa cum laude, Syracuse U., 1967; MA in Polit. Sci. cum laude, Auburn U., 1975. Commd. USAF, advanced through grades to col.; dep. inspector gen. USAF, Washington, 1975-80; retired USAF, 1980; mng. ptnr. T.Z. Assocs., Balt., 1980-83; pres. McDermott Internat. Trading A.G., Zurich, 1983-88; mng. dir. McDermott Internat. Gen. Svcs., Hong Kong, 1983-88; pres. Baker Assocs., Redlands, Calif., 1988—; bd. dirs. T.Z. Assocs., Balt., Environ. Scis., San Diego, Broadleaf Industries, San Diego; adj. prof. U. Redlands Grad. Bus. Sch. Author: Strategic Planning, 1987. Pres. Redlands Ballet Co., 1987-89; chmn. Redlands Cultural Art Commn., 1988—. Mem. Am. C. of C. (v.p. Hong Kong br. 1984-86), Rotary (pres. Redlands chpt. 1989-90, bd. dirs. internat. chpt. in Hong Kong 1983-85), Pres.'s Assn. (chmn. 1988—), Calif. Cultural Arts Commn. Republican. Episcopalian. Avocations: golf, tennis, reading. Office: Baker Assocs 16047 Via Galan Rancho Santa Fe CA 92091-4014

BAKER, CHRISTINE MARIE, secondary education educator; b. Tucson, Sept. 19, 1951; d. Howard Harold and Dorathy (Rice) B.; m. Steven Edward Willhoite, Aug. 24, 1968 (div. Dec. 1995); children: Stacey Leigh Rubalcava, Michael Edward Willhoite. BA, U. Calif., Berkeley, 1990; tchg. credential, San Francisco State U., 1991. Cert. tchr. secondary social sci., govt. and introductory English, Calif. Tchr. social sci. Franklin Jr. H.S., Vallejo, Calif., 1993—, mentor tchr., 1997—, dir. after sch. homework club, 1996—; dept. chair social sci. Franklin Jr. H.S., Vallejo, 1994—; mem. newspapers in edn. adv. bd. San Francisco Newspaper Agy., 1995-96; mem. instrnl. improvement coun. Franklin Jr. H.S., Vallejo, 1995—, mem. leadership coun., 1994-95. Democrat. Office: Franklin Jr H S 501 Starr Ave Vallejo CA 94590-7154

BAKER, DANIAL EDWIN, director, consultant, pharmacy educator; b. Whitefish, Mont., May 25, 1955; s. Arby E. and Cathy Lee (Yarroll) B.; m. Patricia Samuelson, Aug. 28, 1976 (div.); 1 child, Kristin Nicole. B in Pharmacy, Wash. State U., 1978; PharmD, U. Minn., 1980. Lic. pharmacist, Wash. Instr. in pharmacology for respiratory therapist St. Paul Tech. Vocat. Inst., 1980; asst. prof. U. Okla., 1980-83; asst. prof. Wash. State U., Spokane, 1983-88, dir. Drug Info. Ctr., 1983—, assoc. prof., 1988-95; prof. Wash. State U., 1995—, dir. clin. pharmacy programs, interim chmn. pharmacy dept., 1994-95, 96-97, dir. continuing edn., 1997—; mem. drug formulary adv. com. divsn. med. assistance Wash. Dept. Social and Health Svcs., Olympia, 1990, chmn., 1990-92; mem. cons. panel The Upjohn Co., Kalamazoo, 1990-93; mem. adv. panel on drug info. sci. U.S. Pharmacopeial Conv., Inc., Rockville, Md., 1990-95; mem. Inst. for Safe Medication Practices, Inc., Huntington Valley, Pa., 1990—, Inst. Rev. Bd., Spokane, 1992—, Wash. State U., 1993—; mem. adv. bd. Syntex Area Adv. Bd., Denver, 1994-96; cons., mem. pharmacy and therapeutics com. Merck Medco Managed Care, Montvale, N.J., 1995—; mem. pharmacy and therapeutics com. Whatcom Med. Bur., Bellingham, Wash., 1996—. Mem. Nat. Ski Patrol, 49 degree North Chewelah, Wash., 1994—. Recipient Pharmacist Achievement award Merck Sharp and Dohme, 1993. Fellow Am. Soc. Cons. Pharmacists, Am. Soc. Hosp. Pharmacists; mem. Am. Assn. Colls. Pharmacy, Am. Coll. Clin. Pharmacy, Am. Diabetes Assn., Am. Pharm. Assn., Wash. Pharmacists Assn. (senator 1991-95, continuing edn. com. 1988—, award com. 1989-95, co-chmn. undergrad. affairs com. 1990-92, del. quinquinnel conv. 1987—, Pharmacist of Yr. award 1992), Wash. Soc. Hosp. Pharmacists (coun. edn. and manpower 1989-92, chmn. 1990-92, bd. dirs. 1989-93, pres. Spokane chpt. 1992-93), Wash. Pharmacy Coun. Republican. Avocations: skiing, white water rafting, photography, cycling. Office: Wash State U 601 W 1st Ave Spokane WA 99201-3825

BAKER, DAVID J., multimedia communications executive, educator; b. La Junta, Colo.; s. Galen R. and Nancy Joan (Inge) B. BA, U. Denver, 1991. Announcer Colo. Pub. Radio, 1989-91; prodn. technician Walt Disney Entertainment Prodn. Svcs., Orlando, Fla., 1991-93; multimedia cons. U. Calif., L.A., 1993-94; multimedia devel. Joint IBM/UCLA Partnership, L.A., 1994-96; multimedia cons. S.W. Colo. Interactive Learning Network, Durango, Colo., 1996-98; comms. planner U. Calif., L.A., 1998—; comm. planner UCLA, 1998—; dir. Multimedia Computer Camp, L.A. and La Junta, Colo., 1996—. Founding mem. Internet Soc., L.A. chpt., 1998. Vol. Heart of L.A. For Youth, 1996-97; vol. Civil Air Patrol USAF Auxillary, Colo., Calif., 1986-98; contbr. Koshare Indian Mus. With USMC, 1984-88. Mem. Koshare Indian Mus. Avocations: the arts, nat. state and local pub. policy, electronic media and entertainment bus., higher edn., physical fitness. Office: UCLA PO Box 951557 Los Angeles CA 90095-1557

BAKER, DON ROBERT, chemist, inventor; b. Salt Lake City, Apr. 6, 1933; s. Ralph H. and Ruth Eve (Thalmann) B.; m. Shirley May Nelson, Nov. 20, 1954 (dec. 1993); children: Robert, David, George, Barbara; m. Shirlee Ann Call, Sept. 17, 1994. AA, Sacramento City Coll., 1953; AB, Calif. State U., Sacramento, 1955; PhD, U. Calif., Berkeley, 1959. Sr. rsch. chemist Stauffer Chem. Co., Richmond, Calif., 1958-72, rsch. assoc., 1970-74, supr., 1974-85; sr. rsch. assoc. ICI Ams. Inc. Zeneca Ag Products, Richmond, 1985-98; cons. in chemistry and chem. safety, 1998—. Editor Calif. Chemists Alert, 1986—, Synthesis and Chemistry of Agrochems., 1987, 90, 92, 95, 98; contbr. articles to profl. jours.; holder more than 200 U.S. patents. Recipient Zeneca Patent award, 1996. Fellow Am. Chem. Soc. (chmn. Calif. sect. 1973, councilor 1971—, chmn. nat. divsn. profl. rels. 1980, coordinating com. Calif. sects. 1970—, vice-chmn. agrochem. divsn. 1993, chmn. agrochems. divsn. 1995, Walter Petersen award 1991, ACS Internat. award for agrl. rsch. 1999); mem. Plant Growth Regulator Soc., Orchid Soc. Calif. (pres. 1979-80), Oakland Family History Ctr. (libr. 1967—). Republican. Mormon. Avocations: orchid growing, mineralogy, genealogy. Home: 15 Muth Dr Orinda CA 94563-2805 Office: Zeneca Ag Products 15 Muth Dr Orinda CA 94563-2805

BAKER, DUSTY (JOHNNIE B. BAKER, JR.), professional baseball team manager; b. Riverside, Calif., June 15, 1949. Student, Am. River Coll. Player Atlanta Braves, 1968-75, L.A. Dodgers, 1976-83, San Francisco Giants, 1984, Oakland A's, 1985-86; coach San Francisco Giants, 1988-92, mgr., 1993—; mem. Nat. League All-Star Team, 1981-82. Recipient Silver Slugger award, 1980-81, Gold Glove, 1981; named to Sporting News All-Star Team, 1980. Office: San Francisco Giants 3 com park at Candlestick Point San Francisco CA 94124*

BAKER, EDWIN MOODY, retired newspaper publisher; b. Cleve., Dec. 20, 1923; s. Alton Fletcher and Mildred Elizabeth (Moody) B.; m. Patricia Petersen, 1954 (dec. 1983); children: Bridget Baker Kincaid, Amanda Baker Barber, Jonathan; m. Marie Kottkamp Randall, 1984; step children: Steven, Mark, Bruce Randall. B.S. in Bus. Adminstrn., U. Oreg., 1948. With Eugene (Oreg.) Register-Guard, 1948-88, successively advt. mgr., bus. mgr., gen. mgr., pub., pres., chmn. bd. Guard Pub. Co. Mem. exec. bd. Oreg. Trail Council, Boy Scouts Am., 1953—, pres. 1960-61, chmn. Region XI Area I (Northwest) 1971, pres., 1972, mem. nat. exec. bd., 1971-72, nat. adv. council, 1972-82; trustee U. Oreg. Found., 1975-90, Lane C.C. Found. Bd.; bd. dirs. Oreg. Community Found., 1982-90; Oreg. Hist. Soc., 1988-92; trustee Eugene Arts Found., 1980-85; pres. Oreg. Pacific Econ. Devel. Corp., 1984-85; 2d v.p. Eugene Springfield Met. Ptnrship.; mem., chmn. Kakegawa Sister City com., 1986-88; co-chmn. Birth to Three Capital Campaign, 1997; chmn. United Way Leadersip, 1997-98. Served with AUS, World War II. Decorated Bronze Star, Purple Heart; recipient Silve r Beaver award, Boy Scouts Am., 1962, Silver Antelope, 1965, Pioneer award U. Oreg., 1982, Disting. Eagle Scout, 1982, Awbrey Watzig award Lewis and Clark Coll., 1988; named Eugene First Citizen, 1983. Mem. Am. Newspaper Pubs. Assn. (research inst. lab. com. 1978-79), Oreg. Newspaper Pubs. Assn. (dir. 1982-90, pres. 1988-89), U. Oreg. Pres. Assocs., Nat. Assn. Fund Raising Execs. (vol. 1994 Oreg. chpt., Fund Raiser of Yr. 1993), Rotary, Eugene Country Club. Home: 2121 Kimberly Cir Eugene OR 97405-5821 Office: PO Box 10188-2188 Eugene OR 97401-3204

BAKER, EDWIN STUART, retired computer consultant; b. Ottumwa, Iowa, Feb. 14, 1944; s. Edwin Moore and Geraldine Vivian (Irby) B; m. Wilma Jeanne Parker, 1968 (div. 1970). Student, Whitman Coll., 1962-64; BS, Oreg. State U., 1978. Programmer agrl. engring. dept. Oreg. State U., Corvallis, 1977-78, rsch. asst., 1979-83, sr. rsch. asst., 1984-89; measurement standards specialist Oreg. Dept. Agr., Salem, 1990-93; cons. in field. Mem. IEEE, Assn for Computing Machinery, Am. Legion, DAV, NRA, Nat. Intercollegiate Rodeo Assn., 59ers Svc. Club. Avocations: photography, horses. Home: PO Box 68 Fairview OR 97024-0068 Office: Oreg Dept Agr Measurements Standards Divsn Salem OR 97310

BAKER, JAMES BRUCE, publishing company executive, writer; b. Darrovzuett, Tex., Dec. 17, 1925; s. Rufus Limon Guy and Lola (Allen) B. BA, U. San Francisco, 1954. Real estate salesman various, 1955-84; cashier Taco Bell, Sacramento, Calif., 1985-91, Shell Oil, Sacramento, 1991-97; owner, editor, pub. Promart Writing Lab., Sacramento, 1995—. Pub. several anthologies including The 6th Senses, Just Because. Pfc. U.S. Army, 1944-46, ETO. Mem. MENSA, Internat. Soc. Poets (life). Avocations: bowling, biking, pool, chess, cards. Office: Promart Writing Lab PO Box 1094 Sacramento CA 95608

BAKER, JEFFREY CHARLES, telecommunications executive; b. Springfield, Ohio, Feb. 23, 1952; s. Robert Jones and Elizabeth (Hunt) B.; m. Linnea Liane Strehlow, May 14, 1977 (div. Mar. 1985); m. Maryanne Elise Lubresky, Mar. 24, 1986; children: Megan Elisabeth, Kelle Marie. BFA in Comms., U. Cin., 1976. Acct. exec., sta. mgr. Continental Cablevision, Springfield, 1976-78; spl. projects mgr. Tele-Communications, Inc., Middletown, Ohio, 1978; dir. mktg. Viacom Inc., Dayton, Ohio, 1978-80, gen. mgr., 1980-82; gen. mgr. Viacom Inc., Everett, Wash., 1982-86, v.p., bus. & mktg. ops., 1986; v.p., gen. mgr. Viacom Inc., Tacoma, Wash., 1986-90; pres. Sound Comms., Inc., Sky Comms., Inc., Bellevue, Wash., 1991-; v.p., gen. mgr. Supershuttle, Phoenix, 1994-95; v.p. S.W. region Cornell Bokelmann, Phoenix, 1995-97; pres. ICS of Ariz., Phoenix, 1997—; mem. bd. dirs. Wash. State Cable Comms. Assn., Seattle, 1985-90; mem. Women in Cable, Seattle, 1984-90; com. chair Ohio Cable TV Assn., Columbus, Ohio, 1976-80. Republican. Presbyterian. Avocations: collecting vintage American-made electric guitars from 1950's and 60's. Home: 30223 N 51st Pl Cave Creek AZ 85331-2909 Office: Gainey Ranch Town Ctr Ste 200 7702 E Doubletree Ranch Rd Scottsdale AZ 85258-2132

BAKER, JOHN FRANKLIN, III, retired educational administrator, author; b. El Centro, Calif., May 28, 1925; s. John Franklin Jr. and Kaylah Rae (Ames) Baker. AA, L.A. C.C., 1946; BA in Psychology, U. Calif., Berkeley,

1947, MA in Psychology, 1949. Tchg. credential, Calif. Lectr., staff U. Calif., Sacramento, 1950-51; tchr., adminstr. various primary schs., 1952-64; primary tchr. local sch. dist. Gabbs, Nev., 1965-67; tchr. Page Mil. Acad., Claremont, Calif., 1968, Calif. Sch. for Boys, Inglewood, 1969-74; adminstr. U. So. Calif., L.A., 1975; free-lance writer L.A., 1976—. Author: Love Gems, 1981; co-author: The Brain Jogger, 1986; co-inventor: (bd. game) Brain Jogger Game, 1975, (internet game) Bombastics Game, 1997. Avocations: personality theory, developing intelligencer creativity.

BAKER, JOSEPH RODERICK, III, aviculturist; b. Middletown, Ohio, Sept. 26, 1947; s. Joseph Roderick and Lois Patricia (Barnhart) B. BS in Math., Rensselaer Poly. Tech., 1969. Systems rep. Burroughs Corp., Honolulu, 1973-80; mgr. data processing Kenault Inc., Honolulu, 1980-81; v.p. Software Solutions Inc., Honolulu, 1982-83; br. mgr. DataPhase Corp., Honolulu, 1983-88; pres. Birds of Paradise, Kurtistown, Hawaii, 1987—. Lt. (j.g.) USN, 1969-73. Mem. Am. Fedn. Aviculture, Nat. Cockatoo Soc., Macaw Soc. Am., Eclectus Soc., Am. Contract Bridge League, Pionus Breeders Assn., Amazona Soc. Avocation: bridge.

BAKER, KAREN, newspaper editor. Mng. editor Idaho Statesman, Boisie, exec. editor. Office: Idaho Statesman 1200 N Curtis Rd PO Box 40 Boise ID 83706-0040*

BAKER, KENT ALFRED, broadcasting company executive; b. Sioux City, Iowa, Mar. 22, 1948; s. Carl Edmund Baker and Miriam M. (Hawthorn) Baker Nye. Student, Iowa State U., 1966-70. Editor Iowa State Daily, 1969-70; mem. U.S. Peace Corps., 1971-72; editor The Glidden (Iowa) Graphic, 1973-75; bureau chief The Waterloo (Iowa) Courier, Iowa, 1975; state editor The Des Moines Register, 1976-77; news dir. Sta. WQAD-TV, Moline, Ill., 1978; Sunday editor The Des Moines Sunday Register, 1979; news dir. Sta. KHON-TV, Honolulu, 1980-95; v.p., gen. mgr. KHON-TV, Honolulu, 1996—; chmn. Hawaii Freedom of Info. Coun., 1992-94. Recipient news writing awards Iowa Press Assn., 1973-74. Mem. Radio and TV News Dirs. Assn., Bishop Mus. Assn., Hoover Libr. Assn., Iowa State U. Alumni Assn. Office: Sta KHON-TV 1170 Auahi St Honolulu HI 96814-4917

BAKER, LUCINDA, writer; b. Atlanta, Ill., July 10, 1916; d. Hazle Howard and Adah Rebecca (Mason) B.; m. Willard Alan Greiner, June 27, 1946. Student, Ariz. State Coll., 1934-38. Author: Place of Devils, 1976, Walk the Night Unseen, 1977, Memoirs of First Baroness, 1978, The Painted Lady, 1998; contbr. short stories to mags. Mem. Author's Guild, Mystery Writers Am., Romance Writers Am.

BAKER, MALCOLM, marketing executive. Pres. BRS Group Inc., Calif. Office: BRS Group Inc Ste B-325 100 Shoreline Hwy Mill Valley CA 94941-3645*

BAKER, MARIA, zoological park administrator. Dir., CEO Sacramento Zoo, Calif. Office: Sacramento Zoo 3930 W Land Park Dr Sacramento CA 95822-1123*

BAKER, MICHAEL J., lawyer; b. Lexington, Ky., Apr. 14, 1947. AB cum laude, Harvard U., 1969; JD, U. Calif., Berkeley, 1973. Bar: Calif. 1973. Ptnr. Jackson, Tufts, Cole & Black, San Francisco, 1981—; chief legal divsn., litigation dir. Calif. Fair Political Practices Com., 1976-78. Contbr. articles to profl. jours. Mem. ABA. Office: Jackson Tufts Cole & Black 650 California St Fl 32 San Francisco CA 94108-2702*

BAKER, PAT ELLEN, artist, educator; b. Butte, Mont., Dec. 1, 1943; d. Laurence Aldred and June Marjorie (Adams) Dempsey; m. Merle Eugene Baker, Nov. 30, 1968; children: Terri Lynn Montes, Patrick Eugene. Grad. H.S., Coeur d'Alene, Idaho, 1963. Recipient 28 different awards for various art works including Best Western People's Choice award for poster, 1991, 93, 95, 97, 98, People's Choice award Trails West Oreg., 1989, 90, 91, 92, 93, Richlands, Wash. Western Reflections award for poster, 1997, Pres.'s Choice award St. Paul (Oreg.) Wild West Art Show, 1995. Mem. Pheasant Forever, Rocky Mt. Elk Found., Mural Soc. Toppinish, Wash. (mural artist 1995-98). Democrat. Avocations: framing, going to art shows, travel, walking, mornings. Home: 275 Hansen Ave S Salem OR 97302-4517 Office: Baker Fine Arts 275 Hansen Ave S Salem OR 97302-4517

BAKER, PHILLIP WILSON, psychologist; b. Culver City, Calif., Mar. 5, 1942; s. Eugene F. and Bette Belle (Stewart) B.; m. Wendy Catherine Warren, Aug. 3, 1974; children: Ian, Colin. BS, San Jose State U., 1965, MBA, 1967; EdS, Vanderbilt U., 1978, EdD, 1982. Diplomate Am. Coll. Forensic Examiners; lic. clin. psychologist. Mgr., tng. and devel. Memorex Corp., Santa Clara, Calif., 1967-71; clin. supr. Island Counseling Ctr., Fairbanks, Alaska, 1971-74; instr. U. Alaska, Fairbanks, 1974-76; staff psychologist Manchester (N.H.) Mental Health Ctr., 1982-86; clin. supr., employee assistance program Human Affairs of Alaska, Anchorage, 1987-89; staff psychologist South Cen. Counseling Ctr., Anchorage, 1989; pvt. practice Anchorage, 1989—; adj. faculty U. Alaksa, Anchorage. Mem. APA, Alaska Psychol. Assn. (sec. 1990-91, pres. elect 1998—). Avocations: skiing, hiking, water sports, jogging. Office: 4325 Laurel St Ste 215 Anchorage AK 99508-5338

BAKER, RICHARD EARL, business management educator; b. Inglewood, Calif., Sept. 22, 1928; s. Glyn Maynard and Ruth Elizabeth (Norton) B.; m. Dorotha Jean Mayo; children: Mary K. Walton, Thomas P., Kimberlee S. Tillman, Scott R. BS, U. So. Calif., L.A., 1951, MBA, 1956; postgrad., U. Calif., Berkeley, 1958-60. Various mgmt. positions AT&T Co., 1952-76; cons. Graves & Campbell, L.A., 1974-79; prof. U. LaVerne (Calif.), 1976-79, Calif. State Poly. U., Pomona, 1976-80; cons. Kingman, Ariz., 1980—; instr. Mohave Community Coll., Kingman, 1980—; bd. dirs. Profession Sales Gen. Motors Dealership, Kingman, 1987; adj. prof. Prescott (Ariz.) Coll., 1982—; sr. cons. Roberts & Heck Assocs., L.A., 1974-78; cons. Svc. Corps of Retired Execs. SBA, 1980—. Editor: Stress/Assertiveness, 1981; contbr. articles to profl. jours. Foster parent Foster Parent Assn., L.A., 1965-78; counselor Teenage Drug Rehab., L.A. 1970-78; coun. commr. Boy Scouts Am., L.A., 1975, scoutmaster, 1965-74; coord. Vocat. Adv. Coun., 1980-90. Lt. comdr. USN, 1945-48, PTO, 1950-52. Mem. Kingman C. of C., Kiwanis, Beta Gamma Sigma. Republican. Avocations: photography, marksmenship-gun collecting, landscaping, electronics. Home: 4909 Scotty Dr Kingman AZ 86401-1077 Office: Mohave Community Coll 1971 Jagerson Ave Kingman AZ 86401-1238

BAKER, RICHARD W., structural and architectural engineer; b. Glendale, Calif., Aug. 16, 1945; s. Elwood V. and Eleanor J. (Vickers) B.; m. Judith K. Fields, July 5, 1969; children: Carrie A., Brian R. AA, Pasadena City Coll., 1965; BS in Archtl. Engring., Calif. State Poly. Coll., San Luis Obispo, 1968. Naval architect Long Beach (Calif.) Naval Shipyard, 1968-69; stress engr. Lockheed Aero. Systems Co., Burbank, Calif., 1969-73, 75-87, Rockwell Internat., Downey, Calif., 1974; group engr. Lockheed Advanced Devel. Co., Burbank, Calif., 1987-89, project structures engr., 1989-90; dep. chief engr. Lockheed Advanced Devel. Co., Burbank, 1991-93; dir. engring. Lockheed Martin Skunk Works, Palmdale, Calif., 1994-96; program mgr. Lockheed Martin Skunk Works, Palmdale, 1996—; archtl. cons., Cerritos, Calif., 1972-. Editor: Aircraft Stress Analysis, 1987. Mgr. Frontier Little League, Cerritos, 1985-92; coach City of Cerritos Parks & Recreation Dept., 1982-87. Mem. AIAA. Republican. Methodist. Avocations: sports, baseball, basketball, football. Office: Lockheed Martin Skunk Works Dept 72-34 Bl 611 Plant 10 1011 Lockheed Way Palmdale CA 93599-0001

BAKER, ROSALYN HESTER, economic development administrator; b. El Campo, Tex., Sept. 20, 1946. BA, Southwest Tex. State U., 1968; student, U. Southwestern La., 1969. Lobbyist, asst. dir. Govt. Rels. Nat. Edn. Assn., Washington, 1969-80; owner, retail sporting goods store Maui, Hawaii, 1980-87; legis. aide to Hon. Karen Honita Hawaii Ho. of Reps., Honolulu, 1987, mem., 1989-93, house majority leader, 1993, state senator Hawaii, 1993-98, majority leader, 1995-96; dir. office econ. devel. County of Maui, Hawaii, 1996—; co-chair ways and means com.; mem. econ. devel. com., water, land and Hawaiian affairs com.; co-chair rules com. Hawaii State Dem. Conv., 1990, resolutions com. 1994. Del.-at-large Dem. Nat. Conv., 1984, 92, 96; mem. exec. com. Maui County Dem. Com., 1986-88; vice chmn. Maui Svc. Area Bd. om Mental Health and Substance Abuse; unit pres. Am. Cancer Soc. Democrat. Home: 2180 Vineyard Wailuku HI 96793 Office: 200 S High St # 612 Wailuku HI 96793

BAKER, SUSAN LEIGH, manufacturing company executive; b. Inglewood, Calif., Sept. 24, 1962; d. Richard Leigh and Betty Ann (Payne) B. BS, U. Calif., Irvine, 1990. Computer operator Screening Systems, Inc., Laguna Hills, Calif., 1980-85, systems analyst, 1985-87, acctg. supr., 1987, fin. mgr., 1987-90, corp. sec., 1989—, v.p. fin., 1991—; pres. NB Networks, 1995. Republican. Office: Screening Systems Inc 7 Argonaut Aliso Viejo CA 92656-1423

BAKER, TIMOTHY ALAN, healthcare administrator, educator, consultant; b. Myrtle Point, Oreg., July 30, 1954; s. Farris D. and Billie G. (Bradford) B.; 1 child, Amanda Susann. BS in Mgmt. with honors, Linfield Coll., McMinnville, Oreg., 1988; MPA in Health Adminstrn. with distinction, Portland State U., 1989, PhD in Pub. Adminstrn. and Policy, 1992. Registered emergency med. technician. Gen. mgr. Pennington's, Inc., Coos Bay, Oreg., 1974-83; dep. dir. Internat. Airport Projects Med. Svcs., Riyadh, Saudi Arabia, 1983-87; adminstrv. intern Kaiser Sunnyside Hosp., Portland, Oreg., 1988-89; grant mgr. Oreg. Health Sci. U., Portland, 1989-90; dir. health sci. program Linfield Coll., Portland, Oreg., 1992—, asst. prof. health scis.; rsch. assoc. Portland State U., 1990—; instr. S.W. Oreg. C.C., Coos Bay, 1980-83; pres. Intermed. Inc., Portland, 1987—; sr. rschr. small area analysis Oreg. Health Sci. U., 1990, The Oreg. Health Plan Project, 1990-91; developer, planner, prin. author trauma sys. devel. S.W. EMS and Trauma Sys., 1991-93, regional adminstr., Vancouver, 1990—; cons. ednl. def. Min. Civil Def., Riyadh, Saudi Arabia, 1992. Author: TQ·EMS: Total Quality Emergency Medical Services, 1996, TQ-EMS: The Tools of Total Quality, 1996; pub. Jour. Family Practice, Internat. Jour. Pub. Adminstrn., Internat. Jour. Emergency Med. Svcs., 1997. Planner mass disaster plan King Khaled Internat. Airport, 1983; EMS planner Emergency Med. Plan, Province of Cholburi, Thailand, 1985; bd. dirs. Coos County Kidney Assn., 1982, Coos Bay Kiwanis Club, 1979; regional adv. com. EMS and Trauma, State Wash. Dept. Health, 1990—. Recipient Pub. Svc. award Am. Radio and Relay League, 1969, Med. Excellence award KKIA Hosp., 1985; named Fireman of Yr. Eastside Fire Dept., 1982, Adminstr. of Yr., Wash. Dept. Health, 1993. Mem. Am. Mgmt. Assn., Am. Soc. Pub. Adminstrn. (doctoral rep. to faculty senate Portland State U. 1990), Am. Pub. Health Assn., Am. Coll. Healthcare Execs. Avocations: flying, scuba diving, photography, racquetball, amateur radio. Home: 608 N Hayden Bay Dr Portland OR 97217-7964 Office: Linfield Coll Portland Campus 2255 NW Northrup St Portland OR 97210-2952

BAKER, VINCENT LAMONT, basketball player; b. Lake Wales, Fla., Nov. 23, 1971. Grad., Hartford U., 1993. Player Milw. Bucks, 1993-97, Seattle Supersonics, 1997—. Named to NBA All-Rookie First Team, 1994, All-NBA Third Team, 1996-97, All-NBA Second Team, 1997-98, NBA All Star, 1995-97. Avocation: singing. Office: c/o Seattle Supersonics 190 Queen Anne Ave N Ste 200 Seattle WA 98109-4926*

BAKER, WARREN J(OSEPH), university president; b. Fitchburg, Mass., Sept. 5, 1938; s. Preston A. and Grace F. (Jarvis) B.; m. Carol Ann Fitzsimons, Apr. 28, 1962; children: Carrie Ann, Kristin Robin, Christopher, Brian. B.S., U. Notre Dame, 1960, M.S., 1962; Ph.D., U. N.Mex., 1966. Research assoc., lectr. E. H. Wang Civil Engring. Research Facility, U. N.Mex., 1962-66; assoc. prof. civil engring. U. Detroit, 1966-71, prof., 1972-79, Chrysler prof., dean engring., 1973-78, acad. v.p., 1976-79; NSF faculty fellow M.I.T., 1971-72; pres. Calif. Poly. State U., San Luis Obispo, 1979—; mem. Bd. Internat. Food and Agrl. Devel., USAID, 1983-85; mem. Nat. Sci. Bd., 1985-94, Calif. Bus. Higher Edn. Forum, 1993-98; founding mem. Calif. Coun. on Sci. and Tech., 1989—; trustee Amigos of E.A.R.T.H. Coll., 1991-96; bd. dirs. John Wiley & Sons, Inc., 1993—; bd. regents The Am. Archtl. Found., 1995-97; co-chair Joint Policy Coun. on Agr. and Higher Edn., 1995—. Contbr. articles to profl. jours. Mem. Detroit Mayor's Mgmt. Adv. Com., 1975-76; mem. engring. adv. bd. U. Calif., Berkeley, 1984-96; bd. dirs. Calif. Coun. for Environ. and Econ. Balance, 1980-85; trustee Nat. Coop. Edn. Assn.; chmn. bd. dirs. Civil Engring. Rsch. Found., 1989-91, bd. dirs., 1991-94. Fellow Engring. Soc. Detroit; mem. ASCE (chmn. geotech. div. com. on reliability 1976-78, civil engring. edn. and rsch. policy com. 1985-89), NSPE (pres. Detroit chpt. 1976-77), Am. Soc. Engring. Edn., Am. Assn. State Colls. and Univs. (bd. dirs. 1982-84). Office: Calif Poly State U Office of Pres San Luis Obispo CA 93407

BAKER, WILLIAM P. (BILL BAKER), former congressman; b. Oakland, Calif., June 14, 1940; m. Joanne Atack; children: Todd, Mary, Billy, Robby. Grad. in Bus. and Indsl. Mgmt., San Jose State Coll. Budget analyst State Dept. Fin., Calif.; assemblyman 15th dist. State of Calif., 1980-92; mem. of Congress from 10th Calif. dist., 1993—; vice chmn. budget writing Ways and Means Com., 1984-91. Exec. v.p. Contra Costa Taxpayers Assn.; active Contra Costa County Farm Bur. With USCG Res., 1958-65. Republican. Address: 7 Way Points Rd Danville CA 94526-3221

BAKKE, LESLIE RONICA (COOKIE), editor; b. Detroit, July 31, 1947; d. Ben and Eva (Katzman) Garrison; m. Robert Leroy Stearns, Oct. 31, 1966 (div. 1973); children: Shannan, Steven, Susan, Scott; m. Merlin Russell Bakke, Apr. 7, 1985; 1 child, Kimberly Evanna. Grad. h.s., Grand Rapids, Mich. Cert. fraud examiner. Underwriter to v.p. B.G.U. Inc., Grand Rapids, 1962-74; agent, owner Woodland Ins. Agy., Wyoming, Mich., 1974-83; freelance writer Las Vegas, Nev., 1983-85; assorted fraud worker Hull & Co., Balboa Ins., Home Ins. Co., Orange County, Calif., 1986-93; editor Alikim Media, Orange, Calif., 1994—; assoc. editor Am. Mensa, Ft. Worth, 1988—. Editor The Oracle, 1987; contbr. articles to profl. jours. Mem. Am. Mensa Ltd. (assoc. editor 1988—), So. Calif. Fraud Investigation Assn. Jewish. Avocations: cooking, writing, travel, education, shoes. Office: PO Box 4847 Orange CA 92863-4847

BAKKEN, GORDON MORRIS, law educator; b. Madison, Wis., Jan. 10, 1943; s. Elwood S. and Evelyn A. H. (Anderson) B.; m. Erika Reinhardt, Mar. 24, 1943; children: Angela E., Jeffrey E. B.S., U. Wis., 1966, M.S., 1967, Ph.D., 1970, J.D., 1973. Asst., then assoc. prof. history Calif. State U.-Fullerton, 1969-74, dir. faculty affairs, 1974-86, prof. history, 1974—; cons. Calif. Sch. Employees Assn., 1976-78; cons. Calif. Bar Commn. Hist. Law., 1985—; mem. mgmt. task force on acad. grievance procedures Calif. State Univ. and Colls. Systems, 1975; mem. Calif. Jud. Coun. Com. Trial Ct. Records Mgmt., 1992—. Placentia Jusa referee coordinator, 1983. Russell Sage resident fellow law, 1971-72; Am. Council Learned Socs. grantee-in-aid, 1979-80; Am. Bar Found. fellow in legal history, 1979-80, 84-85. Mem. Orgn. Am. Historians, Am. Soc. Legal History, Law and Soc. Assn., Western History Assn., Calif. Supreme Ct. Hist. Soc. (v.p.), Phi Alpha Theta (v.p. 1994-95, pres. 1996-97). Democrat. Lutheran. Author 5 books on Am. legal history; contbr. articles to profl. jours. Office: Calif State U 800 N State College Blvd Fullerton CA 92831-3547

BAKKENSEN, JOHN RESER, lawyer; b. Pendleton, Oreg., Oct. 4, 1943; s. Manley John and Helen (Reser) B.; m. Ann Marie Dahlen, Sept. 30, 1978; children: Michael, Dana, Laura. AB magna cum laude, Harvard U., 1965; JD, Stanford U., 1968. Bar: Oreg. 1969, Calif. 1969, U.S. Dist. Ct. Oreg. 1969. Ptnr. Miller, Nash, Wiener, Hager & Carlsen, Portland, Oreg., 1968—; lawyer del. 9th Cir. Jud. Conf., San Francisco, 1980-82. Author: (with others) Advising Oregon Businesses, 1979. Past bd. dirs. Assn. for Retarded Citizens, Portland; advisor Portland Youth Shelter House; mem. and counsel to bd. dirs. Friends of Pine Mountain Observatory, Portland. Mem. ABA (forum on constrn. industry and sect. pub. contract law and sci. and tech.), Fed. Comm. Bar Assn., Oreg. State Bar, Oreg. Assoc. Gen. Contractors (legal com. 1991, counsel to bd. dirs. 1992), Multnomah Athletic Club. Avocation: astronomy. Office: Miller Nash Wiener Hager & Carlsen 111 SW 5th Ave Portland OR 97204-3699

BALAGURA, SAUL, neurosurgeon; b. Cali, Colombia, Jan. 11, 1943; s. Itco and Sara (Zieghelboim) B.; M.D., U. Calle (Colombia), 1964; M.A., Princeton U., 1966, Ph.D., 1967; m. Ursula Lowy, Aug. 15, 1964. Intern, Univ. Hosp., Cali, Colombia, 1963-64; resident in gen. surgery SUNY Downtate Med. Ctr., Bklyn., 1974-76, Albert Einstein Sch. Medicine, N.Y.C., 1976-80; asst prof. biopsychology U. Chgo., 1967-71; assoc. prof. bio-psychology U. Mass., Amherst, 1971-74; asst. prof. neurosurgery and anatomy Emory U., Atlanta, 1980-81; attending neurosurgeon Watson Clinic, Lakeland, Fla., 1981-82; neurosurgeon Carle Clinic, Urbana, Ill., 1983—; clin. assoc. prof. surgery U. Ill., 1984—, pvt. prac., Victoria, Tex., 1988-94, neurosurgical cons., 1994—. Fellow Am. Psychol. Assn.; mem. AMA, Soc. Neurosci, Physiol. Soc., Am. Bd. Neurol. Surgery. Jewish. Author: Hunger: A Biopsychological Analysis, 1973; contbr. articles to profl. jours. Office: PO Box 508 Tesuque NM 87574-0508

BALASH, JEFFREY LINKE, investment banker; b. N.Y.C., Nov. 2, 1948; s. George Everett and Jeanne Marie (Linke) B. BA in Econs. summa cum laude, Princeton, 1970; MBA, Harvard U., 1974, JD cum laude, 1974. Bar: N.Y. 1974. Asst. to chmn. Louis-Dreyfus Corp., N.Y.C., 1974-76; dir. Avon Products, N.Y.C., 1976-79; mng. dir. Lehman Bros., N.Y.C., 1979-85, Drexel Burnham Lambert, Beverly Hills, Calif., 1985-90; founding ptnr. Anthem Ptnrs., L.A. and N.Y.C., 1991-92; chmn. Comstock Ptnrs., L.L.C., Beverly Hills, Calif., 1992—, JL Furnishings, L.L.C., Gardena, 1997—. Bd. dirs. Joffrey Ballet, N.Y.C., and L.A., 1986-89; mem. alumni coun. Harvard U. Bus. Sch., Boston, 1989-92; major gifts com. Princeton U. Class 1970. Baker scholar Harvard U. Sch. Bus. Adminstrn., 1974. Mem. Harvard Bus. Sch. Assn. So. Calif. (bd. dirs.), Phi Beta Kappa. Republican. Roman Catholic. Avocations: golf, weight training, wine, jazz, art. Home: 9430 Readcrest Dr Beverly Hills CA 90210-2552

BALBAS, CHRISTINE, social services administrator; b. Madera, Calif., May 23, 1958; d. Anthony and Rose (Gomez) B.; m. Ricky Lynn Brincefield, Nov. 21, 1978 (dir. Nov. 1987); children: Timothy Brincefield, Kristen Brincefield, Elizabeth Brincefield, Eric Brincefield; m. Rolando G. Mendiola, Aug. 24, 1996. BA in Agrl. Edn., Calif. State U., Fresno, 1980, MPA, 1998. Youth counselor Madera County Dept. Edn., 1980, substitute tchr., 1981-82; eligibility worker Madera County Dept. Pub. Welfare, 1982-83; eligibility worker Fresno County Dept. Social Svcs., 1982-87, supr. social svcs. program, 1987-91, staff analyst, 1991-96, sr. staff analyst, 1996—; dir. child care program Dept. Employment & Temporary Assistance Fresno County Human Svcs. Sys. Mem. Am. Pub. Welfare Assn., Fresno County Child Devel. Consortium, Calif. Dept. Edn. Legal Compliance Review Com., Toastmasters Internat. (v.p. publicity 1996). Fax: 559-453-3782. E-mail: cbalbas@fresno.ca.gov. Home: 27337 Ellist St Madera CA 93638-1707 Office: Fresno County Human Svcs Sys Dept Employment & Temp Asst Fresno CA 93750

BALCH, PAMELA MAE, education educator; b. Uniontown, Pa., June 4, 1950; d. James E. and Grace L. (Springer) Jubin; m. Patrick Eugene Balch, June 30, 1972; children: Paul James, Julie Lynn. BA in Edn., W.Va. Wesleyan Coll., 1971; MA in Edn., W.Va. U., 1973, EdD in Curriculum and Instrn., 1977. Elem. edn. tchr. Cen. Sch., Weston, W.Va., 1971-72; middle sch. tchr. Evansdale Elem., Morgantown, W.Va., 1972-78; asst. and assoc. prof. of edn. W.Va. Wesleyan Coll., Buckhannon, W.Va., 1978-85; assoc. and full prof. edn., dir. grad. program tchr. edn. W.Va. Wesleyan Coll., Buckhannon, 1985-88; assoc. and full prof. edn., dir. tchr. edn. Imperial Valley Campus San Diego State Univ., Calexico, Calif., 1988-91, assoc. dean acad. affairs Imperial Valley Campus, 1991—. Author: (textbook) The Cooperative Teacher, 1987; contbr. articles to profl. jours. Mem. AAUW (bd. dirs., pres. 1992-93), Am. Assn. for Higher Edn., Phi Kappa Phi, Kappa Delta Pi, Phi Delta Kappa (v.p. Imperial Valley chpt. 1990—). Avocations: playing piano, collecting antiques, traveling. E-maill: p.balch@mail.bethanywv.edu. Home: 2202 Desert Gardens Dr El Centro CA 92243-9421 Office: Bethany Coll VP Acad Affairs/Dean Bethany WV 26032-0417

BALCOM, ORVILLE, engineer; b. Inglewood, Calif., Apr. 20, 1937; s. Orville R. and Rose Mae (Argo) B.; B.S. in Math., Calif. State U., Long Beach, 1958, postgrad., 1958-59; postgrad. UCLA, 1959-62; m. Gloria Stadtmiller, July 23, 1971; children—Cynthia, Steven. Engr., AiResearch Mfg. Co., 1959-62, 64-65; chief engr. Meditron, El Monte, Calif., 1962-64; chief engr. Astro Metrics, Burbank, Calif., 1965-67; chief engr., gen. mgr. Varadyne Power Systems, Van Nuys, Calif., 1968-71; owner, chief engr. Brown Dog Engring., Lomita, Calif., 1971—. Mem. IEEE Computer Group, Independent Computer Cons. Assn. Patentee in field. Club: Torrance Athletic. Home: 24521 Walnut St Lomita CA 90717-1260 Office: PO Box 427 Lomita CA 90717-0427

BALDASSARRE, JOSEPH ANTHONY, musician, musicologist, music educator; b. Cleve., Oct. 16, 1950; s. Antonio Saverio and Mary Jane (Fondale) B.; children: Genya Marie, Leyla Noelle, Stephen Joseph. B of Music Edn., Baldwin-Wallace Coll., 1972; MA, Kent State U., 1979; D of Mus. Arts, Cleve. Inst. Music, 1986. Cert. music tchr., Ohio. Freelance musician, rec. artist Cleve., 1965-75; prof. music Boise (Idaho) State U., 1975—; classical guitar soloist; designer early string instruments; performer early music. Contbr. music revs. to Idaho Statesman, 1985-88, Soundboard mag., 1987. Founding mem. Idaho Camerata Baroque Music Ensemble. Mem. Guitar Found. Am., Am. Lute Soc., Am. Musicol. Soc., Early Music Am., Boise Early Music Soc. (founder), Soc. for Am. Baseball Rsch., Phi Kappa Phi. Roman Catholic. Avocations: flintlock firearms, recording music, racquetball, baseball. Home: 1309 Rand St Boise ID 83709-2147 Office: Boise State U Dept Music 1910 University Dr Boise ID 83725-0399

BALDOCK, BOBBY RAY, federal judge; b. Rocky, Okla., Jan. 24, 1936; s. W. Jay and S. Golden (Farrell) B.; m. Mary Jane (Spunky) Holt, June 2, 1956; children: Robert Jennings, Christopher Guy. Grad., N.Mex. Mil. Inst., 1956; JD, U. Ariz., 1960. Bar: Ariz. 1960, N.Mex. 1961, U.S. Dist. Ct. N.Mex., 1965. Ptnr. Sanders, Bruin & Baldock, Roswell, N.Mex., 1960-83; adj. prof. Eastern N.Mex. U., 1962-81; judge U.S. Dist. Ct. N.Mex., Albuquerque, 1983-86, U.S. Ct. Appeals (10th cir.), 1986—. Mem. N.Mex. Bar Assn., Chaves County Bar Assn., Ariz. Bar Assn., Phi Alpha Delta. Office: US Ct Appeals PO Box 2388 Roswell NM 88202-2388*

BALDON, CLEO, interior designer; b. Leavenworth, Wash., June 1, 1927; d. Ernest Elsworth and Esther Jane (Hannan) Chute; m. Lewis Smith Baldon, Nov. 20, 1948 (div. July 1961); 1 child, Dirk; m. Ib Jørgen Melchior, Jan. 18, 1964; 1 stepson, Leif Melchior. BS, Woodbury Coll., 1948. Ptnr. Interior Designs Ltd., Los Angeles, 1948-50; freelance illustrator Los Angeles, 1952-54; prin. Cleo Baldon & Assocs., Los Angeles and Venice, Calif., 1954—; ptnr. Galper/Baldon Assocs., Landscape Archs., Venice, 1970—. Co-author: Steps and Stairways, 1989, Reflections on the Pool, 1997; contbr. articles to profl. jours.; patentee in field. Recipient City Beautification awards L.A., 1974-77, 80, 83, 85-90, 92, Beverly Hills, 1982, Calif. Landscape Contbr., 1975, 79, Pacifica award Resources Coun., CAlif., 1979, Honor awards Landscape Archs. Fund, 1988, 89, Award of Excellence, Landscape Archs. Fund, 1990. Avocations: photography, collecting Colonial Am. documents. Home: 8228 Marmont Ln West Hollywood CA 90069-1624 Office: Galper/Baldon Assocs 723 Ocean Front Walk Venice CA 90291-3270

BALDRIDGE, CHARLENE, writer; b. Evanston, Ill., Apr. 26, 1934; d. Charles Edward and Thelma Marie (Good) S.; m. Charles S. Baldridge, Jan. 1963 (div. Apr. 1993); children: Charles E. Ortego, Robert J. Ortego (dec.), Laura Costales. Student, Mesa Coll., Grossmont Coll. Bank teller Bank of N.Mex., Albuquerque, 1956-62; note teller, opers. various banks, San Diego, 1962-76; freelance writer San Diego, 1975-84, 95—; pub. rels. dir. Old Globe Theatre, San Diego, 1981-95. Author: (books) Zingers, 1990, Drawing in Chocolate, 1995, (theatre piece) Winter Roses, 1986; contbr. articles to jours. Recipient 1st place award in column writing, San Diego Press Club, 1997, 2d place critical writing, 1997, Outstanding Alumna award Mesa Coll., 1990. Mem. San Diego Press Club, Poets and Writers. Home: 4435 Hamilton St #5 San Diego CA 92116

BALDWIN, BETTY JO, computer specialist; b. Fresno, Calif., May 28, 1925; d. Charles Monroe and Irma Blanche (Law) Inks; m. Barrett Stone Baldwin Jr. (dec. 1998); two daughters. AB, U. Calif., Berkeley, 1945. With NASA Ames Rsch. Ctr., Moffett Field, Calif., 1951-53, math tech. 14' Wind Tunnel, 1954-55, math analyst 14' Wind Tunnel, 1956-63, supr. math analyst Structural Dynamics, 1963-68, supervisory computer programmer Structural Dynamics, 1968-71, computer programmer Theoretical Studies, 1971-82, adminstrv. specialist Astrophys. Experiments, 1982-85, computer specialist, resource mgr. Astrophysics br., 1985—; v.p. B&B Baldwin Farms, Bakersfield, Calif., 1978-98. Mem. IEEE, Assn. for Computing Machinery, Am.

Geophys. Union, Am. Bus. Womens Assn. (pres., v.p. 1967, one of Top 10 Women of Yr. 1971). Presbyterian. Avocations: reading, bridge, hiking. Office: NASA Ames Rsch Ctr Mail Stop 245-6 Moffett Field CA 94035-1000

BALDWIN, EMORY RIEGEL, architect, woodworker; b. Providence, R.I., Nov. 23, 1969; s. Gunnar Ives and Leila Edmonston (Emory) B.; m. Helena Frances Fox, Dec. 26, 1994. BA, Tufts U., 1991; MArch, U. Wash., 1997. Registered profl. architect, Wash. Wildlife mgr., trail clearer Squam Lakes Assn., Holderness, N.H., 1988-90; ski instr. Waterville (N.H.) Valley, 1991-93; carpenter Ravenna Springs Arboretum, Seattle, 1996; arcthl. intern Dyer/Brown & Assocs., Boston, 1994; architect LMN Architects, Seattle, 1997-98, Mithun Ptnrs., Seattle, 1998—; conf. presenter Internat. Conf. Universal Design, N.Y., 1998. Avocations: woodworking, skiing, hiking. Home: 1717 N 35th St Apt 10 Seattle WA 98103-9048

BALDWIN, HUGH JOHN, dean; b. Ashern, Man., Can., Feb. 24, 1940; came to the U.S., 1964; s. George Herbert and Margaret Edith (Mackey) B.; m. Marilyn Jean Halloran, Nov. 17, 1973 (dec. Nov. 1991). BSc in Pharmacy, U. Man., 1962; MS, Purdue U., 1967, PhD, 1969. Pharmacist Gurvey's Pharmacies, Winnipeg, Man., 1962-64; tchg. asst., instr. Purdue U., West Lafayette, Ind., 1964-68; asst. prof. pharmacy U. Mo., Kansas City, 1968-72, Ohio State U., Columbus, 1973-74; from assoc. prof. to prof., dept. chair W.Va. U., Morgantown, 1974-85; dean Sch. Pharmacy U. Wyo., Laramie, 1985—; bd. dirs. Pharmat, Lawrence, Kans. Co-editor: Pharmacy Ethics, 1991; contbr. articles to profl. jours. Amb. Laramie C. of C. Recipient Appreciation award Wyo. State Bd. Pharmacists, Jackson, 1993. Mem. Am. Assn. Colls. Pharmacy (sect. chair, sec.-treas. 1975-77), Am. Inst. History Pharmacy, Am. Soc. Health-Sys. Pharmacy, Am. Pharm. Assn., Wyo. Pharmacists Assn., Laramie Country Club (bd. dirs.). Avocations: golf, bridge, reading. Office: Univ Wyo Sch Pharmacy PO Box 3375 Laramie WY 82071-3375

BALDWIN, MARK ALAN, communications consultant, writer; b. Sheboygan, Wis., June 13, 1958; s. Robert Franklin and Lucille Bertha (Karstedt) B. BA, U. Wis., La Crosse, 1980. Pub./client rels. specialist Cap-Rock-Walworth, Janesville, Wis., 1981-82; energy advisor Madison (Wis.) Gas & Electric, 1982-85; devel. specialist WHA-TV, Madison, 1985-89; devel. assoc., editor San Francisco AIDS Found., 1989-92; dir. found. rels. Sierra Club Legal Def. Fund, San Francisco, 1992-94; devel. dir. Marin Cons. Corps, San Rafael, Calif., 1995-96; dir. comms. Merritt Cmty. Capital Corp., Oakland, Calif., 1996—; pub. rels. cons. Bay Area Cmty. Svcs., Oakland, 1997—; fundraising cons. Brothertown Indian Nation, Woodruff, Wis., 1980—. Author: (brochure) Winds of Change, 1987. Home: 1935 Clay St Apt 102 San Francisco CA 94109-3432 Office: Merritt Cmty Capital Corp 1736 Franklin St Ste 600 Oakland CA 94612-3423

BALKANSKI, ALEXANDRE, executive. Pres, CEO C-Cube Micrisystems, Milpitas, Calif. Office: 1778 McCarthy Blvd Milpitas CA 95035-7421

BALL, CURT, actor, writer; b. Corydon, Ky., Sept. 14, 1931; s. Gobel Miller and Nannie Hugh Pirtle (King) B.; m. Belle Schnabel, Dec. 11, 1960. BA, Univ. Evansville, 1965; MA, Ill. State Univ., 1970. Producer, dir. J.B. Rogers Prod. Co., Fostoria, Ohio, 1957-61; freelance actor/writer, 1951—; teaching assoc. Ill. State Univ., Normal, 1969-70; comml. broadcast coach/instr. Mel Blanc & Assocs., Beverly Hills, Calif., 1975. Actor in numerous plays including The Merchant of Venice, The Inspector General, The Man Who Came to Dinner, Summer and Smoke, Idiots Delight, Witness for the Prosecution, Waltz of the Torreadores, Apple of His Eye, Nude With Violin, Once More with Feeling, The Phantom, The Rainmaker, Twelth Night, Antigone, The Goodwoman of Setzuan, The Gazebo, Banners of Steel, The Male Animal, Mary Mary, Barefoot in the Park, Arms and the Man, Marat Sade, Summer Tree, Death of a Salesman, Bus Stop, A Midsummer Night's Dream, Days of Wine and Roses, others; author: poems, fiction and reportage; announcer, actor numerous radio and TV commls; model number mags.; soundtrack recording work; dramatic reader with jazz groups. With USAF, 1951-53. Avocations: sports car racing. Office: PO Box 2435 Winnetka CA 91396-2435

BALL, DONALD EDMON, architect; b. Evansville, Ind., July 18, 1942; s. Harvey and Myrl (Norris) B. BA in Design, So. Ill. U., 1967. Registred architect Ariz., Calif., Colo., Nev.; cert. Nat. Coun. Archtl. Registration Bd. With design dept. Leo A. Daly Co., Architects and Engrs., Omaha, 1968; project mgr. Buetow & Assocs., St. Paul, 1969-70; ptnr. Comprehensive Design, Mpls., 1971-73; with Caudill Assocs., Aspen, Colo., 1973-76, Hagman Yaw, Ltd., Aspen, 1977; project mgr. Hauter Assocs., Aspen, 1978; pres. Jacobs, Ball & Assocs., Architects, Aspen and Denver, 1978-85; project mgr. Moshe Safdie & Assocs., Boston, 1985-87; dir. design Dwayne Lewis Architects, Inc., Phoenix, 1987-88; prin. Donald Ball and Assocs., Scottsdale, Ariz., 1988—. Mem. Aspen Bldg. Insp. Selection Com., 1982, Pitkin County Housing Authority Bd., Aspen, 1984. Mem. AIA (chmn. Colo. West chpt., documents com.), Ariz. Soc. Architects (profl. practice com.). Avocations: golf, old cars. Home and Office: 7702 E Sutton Dr Scottsdale AZ 85260-4031

BALL, EVERETT L., artist, advertising executive; b. L.A.; m. Jane Eklund, 1951 (dec. 1992); children: Tevvy, Francesca, Jocelyn. BA in English cum laude, UCLA, 1939. Writer, dir. UN, N.Y.C., 1946-48, Paris, 1950-54; pres. Ball Advt., Palm Springs, 1956-64; ptnr. Anderson, Morgan, DeSantis and Ball (Ball, Morgan Assocs.), Palm Springs, Calif., 1965-70; creative dir., v.p. Ball, Morgan Assocs., Hollywood, Calif., 1973-85; distbr., designer Lindal Cedar Homes, Seattle, 1977-84. Author: A Painting for Isolde, 1952; one-man shows include MacQuarie Gallery, Sydney, Australia, 1946, Bonestell Gallery, N.Y.C., 1947, Paideia Gallery, L.A., 1966, Galerie St. Germain des Pres, Paris, France, 1971, Galleria Acropoli, Milan, 1973, Hoover Gallery, San Francisco, 1973, Fresno (Calif.) Arts Center, 1974, Speaker Gallery, L.A., 1981, Vorpal Galleris, N.Y.C. and San Francisco, 1985, 86, Grossman Gallery, Lompoc, 1990, Foyer Gallery, Pacific Asia Mus., Pasadena, 1991, 1996-97, Faulkner Gallery East, Santa Barbara, 1994; exhibited in group shows at Contemporary Arts Gallery, N.Y.C., 1962-64, Cooper Gallery, Beverly Hills, Calif., 1973-74, Ankrum Gallery, L.A., 1987, Grossman Gallery, 1988, 1996, Faulkner Gallery, 1990; contbr. Voice of the Turtle, Dear Ruth, Melbourne, Australia, 1945, 46. Sch. bd. Unified Sch. Dist., Palm Springs, Calif., 1960-64. Recipient Peabody awards UN, 1947, 48. Avocations: painting, sculpting, writing, classical music announcing, manuscript editing. Studio: 415 Powers Ave Santa Barbara CA 93103 Office: 42 Helena Ave Santa Barbara CA 93101-2318

BALL, JAMES HERINGTON, lawyer; b. Kansas City, Mo., Sept. 20, 1942; s. James T. Jr. and Betty Sue (Herington) B.; m. Wendy Anne Wolfe, Dec. 28, 1964; children: James H. Jr., Steven Scott. AB, U. Mo., 1964; JD cum laude, St. Louis U., 1973. Bar: Mo. 1973. Asst. gen. counsel Anheuser-Busch, Inc., St. Louis, 1973-76; v.p., gen. counsel, sec. Stouffer Corp., Solon, Ohio, 1976-83; sr. v.p., gen. counsel Nestle Enterprises, Inc., Solon, 1983-91; gen. counsel, sr. v.p. Nestle USA, Inc., Glendale, Calif., 1991—. Editor-in-chief St. Louis U. Law Jour., 1972-73. Bd. dirs. Alliance for Children's Rights, L.A., 1992—, Am. Swiss Found., N.Y.C., 1996—. Lt. comdr. USN, 1964-70, Vietnam. Mem. Mo. Bar Assn. Office: Nestle USA Inc 800 N Brand Blvd Rm 1045 Glendale CA 91203-3213

BALL, JOHN PAUL, publishing company executive; b. N.Y.C., Dec. 15, 1946; s. William Emil and Else (Schmidt) B.; m. Jayne Barbara Irwin, Jan. 30, 1970 (div. 1991); m. Eileen M. Mitchell, Oct. 25, 1997. Student, N.Y. Sch. Printing, 1964. Prodn. assoc. Macmillan Co., N.Y.C., 1964-65; asst. to pres. Frederick Fell, Inc., N.Y.C., 1965-69; v.p., dir. prodn. William Morrow & Co., Inc., N.Y.C., 1969-86; sr. v.p. mfg. and paper purchasing Macmillan Pub. Co., N.Y.C., 1986-94; pub. and graphic arts cons., chmn. bd. Electronic Pub. Ctrs. Inc., N.Y.C., 1994—, exec. v.p., sec. IDG Books, Foster City, Calif., 1996—. Recipient Comet Press award graphic arts, 1964, Columbia Scholastic Press Assn. Best Editorial Writing award, 1965. Office: IDG Books Worldwide Inc 919 E Hillsdale Blvd Foster City CA 94404-4247

BALL, LAWRENCE, retired physical scientist; b. Albion, N.Y., Aug. 10, 1933; s. Harold Witheral and Gladys (Gibbs) B.; m. Caroline Moran, June 21, 1957; children: Daniel Lawrence, Logan Edward, Stacey Laura Ball Lucero, Ryan Laird (dec.). Diploma, Williston Acad., 1952; BSME, Antioch Coll., 1957; MSc in Elec. Engring., Ohio State U., 1962. Engring. aid Wright Air Devel. Ctr., Dayton, Ohio, 1957-60; engr. Deco Electronics Inc., Boulder, Colo., 1962-66; sr. engr. Westinghouse Rsch. Labs., Boulder, 1966-73, Westinghouse Ocean Rsch. Lab., Annapolis, Md., 1973-74; program mgr. div. geothermal energy U.S. Dept. Energy, Washington, 1974-79; lab. dir. U.S. Dept. Energy, Grand Junction, Colo., 1979-93; ret., 1993; pres. Liberty Cons. Co., Grand Junction, 1984—; emergency coord. dist. 3 Amateur Radio Emergency Svcs., 1995-97. Co-inventor coal mine communications; contbr. articles to profl. jours. Mem. various vol. fire depts., 1954-79; mem., sr. patroller Nat. Ski Patrol Sys., Md., Colo., 1973-92; mem. Amateur Radio Emergency Svcs., 1995—; bd. dirs. Colo. Head Injury Found., chpt. pres., 1989-91. Named Profl. Govt. Employee of Yr., Western Colo. Fed. Exec. Assn., 1991. Mem. Toastmasters Internat. (area gov. 1991-92, divsn. gov. 1992-93, Toastmaster of Yr. Western Colo. 1990, DTM & ATM-S 1994), West Slope Wheelman (charter bd. dirs. 1992-93), Western Colo. Amateur Radio Club, Inc. (pres. 1994-96, bd. dirs. 1996—, emergency coord. Amateur Radio Emergency Svcs. 1995-97). Avocations: bicycling, scuba diving, woodworking, amateur radio (extra class), Bible archaeology.

BALL, WILLIAM PAUL, physicist, engineer; b. San Diego, Nov. 16, 1913; s. John and Mary (Kajla) B.; m. Edith Lucile March, June 28, 1941 (dec. 1976); children: Lura Irene Ball Raplee, Roy Ernest. AB, UCLA, 1940; PhD, U. Calif., Berkeley, 1952. Registered profl. engr. Calif. Projectionist, sound technician studios and theatres in Los Angeles, 1932-41; tchr. high sch. Montebello, Calif., 1941-42; instr. math. and physics Santa Ana (Calif.) Army Air Base, 1942-43; physicist U. Calif. Radiation Lab., Berkeley and Livermore, 1943-58; mem. tech. staff Ramo-Wooldridge Corp., Los Angeles, 1958-59; sr. scientist Hughes Aircraft Co., Culver City, Calif., 1959-64; sr. staff engr. TRW-Def. Systems Group, Redondo Beach, Calif., 1964-83, Hughes Aircraft Co., 1983-86; cons. Redondo Beach, 1986—. Contbr. articles to profl. jours.; patentee in field. Bd. dirs. So. Dist. Los Angeles chpt. ARC, 1979-86. Recipient Manhattan Project award for contbn. to 1st atomic bomb, 1945. Mem. AAAS, Am. Phys. Soc., Am. Nuclear Soc., N.Y. Acad. Scis., Torrance (Calif.) Area C. of C. (bd. dirs. 1978-84), Sigma Xi. Home and Office: 209 Via El Toro Redondo Beach CA 90277-6561

BALLAINE, JERROLD CURTIS, artist; b. Seattle, Feb. 16, 1934; s. Jerrold Felch and Elizabeth (Maxson) B.; m. JoAnn Heinbaugh, Dec. 3, 1960 (div. June 1972); children: Theresa, Peter; m. Nancy Carroll, May 24, 1980; children: Danielle, Emily. Student, U. Wash., 1955, Art Ctr. Sch., L.A., 1956-58; BFA, San Francisco Art Inst., 1958, MFA, 1961. One-person shows include Zabriskie Gallery, N.Y.C., 1960, Scott Gallery, Seattle, 1964, 65, Richmond (Calif.) Art Ctr., 1966, San Francisco Mus. Art, 1970, Gallery Reese-Palley, San Francisco, 1971, Stephen Wirtz Gallery, San Francisco, 1977, San Jose Mus. Art, 1981, Joseph Chownig Gallery, San Francisco, 1986, Erickson and Elins Gallery, San Francisco, 1988, Malton Gallery, Cin., 1990, Ebert Gallery, San Francisco, 1991, 92, 93, Al-Adwani Gallery, Kuwait, 1995, Trosa, Sweden, 1998; exhibited in group shows San Francisco Mus. Art, 1960, Calif. Palace of Legion of Honor, 1962, Berkeley Gallery, San Francisco, 1966, Univ. Art Mus., U. Calif., Berkeley, 1967, Portland Art Mus., Seattle, 1968, Deane Coll., Crete, Nebr., 1969, Jewish Mus., N.Y.C., 1970, Seattle Art Mus., 1970, others; represented in pub. collections San Francisco Mus. Modern Art, Seattle Art Mus., Whitney Mus. Am. Art, N.Y.C., Denver Art Mus., Joslyn Art Mus., Omaha, also numerous pvt. collections; subject of 2 documentaries Sta. KQED, 1971. With U.S. Army, 1956-58. Recipient Award San Francisco Mus., 1960, 4th Internat. award Japanese Govt., 1967; fellowship U. Calif. Berkeley, 1969, rsch. fellowship, 1980.

BALLANTINE, MORLEY COWLES (MRS. ARTHUR ATWOOD BALLANTINE), newspaper editor; b. Des Moines, May 21, 1925; d. John and Elizabeth (Bates) Cowles; m. Arthur Atwood Ballantine, July 26, 1947 (dec. 1975); children—Richard, Elizabeth Ballantine Leavitt, William, Helen Ballantine Healy. AB, Ft. Lewis Coll., 1975; LHD (hon.), Simpson Coll., Indianola, Iowa, 1980. Pub. Durango (Colo.) Herald, 1952-83, editor, pub., 1975-83, editor, chmn. bd., 1983—; dir. 1st Nat. Bank, Durango, 1976—, Des Moines Register & Tribune, 1977-85, Cowles Media Co., 1982-86. Mem. Colo. Land Use Commn., 1975-81, Supreme Ct. Nominating Commn., 1984-90; mem. Colo. Forum, 1985—; trustee Choate/Rosemary Hall, Wallingford, Conn., 1973-81, Simpson Coll., Indianola, Iowa, 1981—, U. Denver, 1984—, Fountain Valley Sch., Colorado Springs, 1976-89, trustee emerita, 1993—; mem. exec. com. Ft. Lewis Coll. Found., 1991—. Recipient 1st place award for editorial writing Nat. Fedn. Press Women, 1955, Outstanding Alumna award Rosemary Hall, Greenwich, Conn., 1969, Outstanding Journalism award U. Colo. Sch. Journalism, 1967, Disting. Svc. award Ft. Lewis Coll., Durango, 1970, named to Colo. Cmty. Journalism Hall of Fame, 1987; named Citizen of Yr. Durango Area Chamber Resort Assn., 1990, Athena award Female Cmty. Leader, 1997. Mem. Nat. Soc. Colonial Dames, Colo. Press Assn. (bd. dirs. 1978-79), Colo. AP Assn. (chmn. 1966-67), Federated Women's Club Durango, Mill Reef Club (Antigua, W.I.) (bd. govs. 1985-91). Episcopalian. Address: care Durango Herald PO Drawer A Durango CO 81302

BALLARD, CLYDE, state legislator; b. Batesville, Ark., June 8, 1936; s. Jeffery C. and Monnie F. Ballard; m. Ruth L. Guthrie, Feb. 6, 1955; children: Jeff, Shawn, Scott. Store mgr., gen. mgr. Peter Rabbit Stores, Wenachee, Wash., 1955-66; owner Ballard Svcs., Wenachee, 1967-87; caucus chmn., minority leader Wash. Ho. Rep., Olympia, 1985-94, spkr. house, 1995-98, co-speaker house, 1999—. Republican. Methodist. Home: 1790 N Baker Ave East Wenatchee WA 98802-4157 Office: PO Box 40600 Olympia WA 98504-0600*

BALLARD, LORREN LEE, fire protection official; b. Denver, May 8, 1939; s. David Crockett and Dorothy (Canter) B.; m. Barbara Ballard, Feb. 15, 1961 (div. 1967); children: Lorren Jr., Christopher; m. Donna Mae Veenstra, Dec. 30, 1988; 1 child, Erika Rasmussen. BS, Regis Coll., 1987. From firefighter to divsn. chief City of Denver, 1963-89; fire chief City of Billings, Mont., 1989—; active Comm. Ctr. Adv. Bd., Billings, 1989—. Chmn. Local Emergency Planning Com., Billings, 1989—; v.p. adv. bd. Salvation Army, 1989—; chmn. adv. bd. Critical Incident Stress Debriefing Team, 1989—. Avocations: golf, tennis, fishing. Office: Billings Fire Dept PO Box 1178 Billings MT 59103*

BALLARD, RONALD MICHAEL, lawyer, political consultant; b. Covina, Calif., Apr. 17, 1958; s. Gonzy Steven and Eleanor (Guarino) B.; m. Jamie S. Kemmerer, Aug. 17, 1980; children: Nathaniel, Kaitlyn, Nolan, Devin, Casadei, Cameron, Aliza, Damian. BA, Claremont McKenna Coll., 1980; JD, UCLA, 1983. Bar: Calif. 1983, U.S. Dist. Ct. (cen. dist.) Calif. 1984. Assoc. Reid and Hellyer, San Bernardino, Calif., 1984-85; pvt. practice law Irvine, Calif., 1985-95, Lake Forest, CA, 95—. Mem., v.p. Charter Oak Unified Sch. Dist. Bd. Edn., Covina, 1977-81; mem., sec. 62d A.D. Rep. Cen. Com., Covina, 1978-81; lector, commentator St. Elizabeth Ann Seton Ch., Irvine, 1987-92; nat. sec. Caths. Respect Life, Westminster, Calif., 1990. Mem. State Bar Calif. (bus. law, estate, probate and trusts sect.), South Orange County C. of C. Office: 22996 El Toro Rd Lake Forest CA 92630-4961

BALLENTINE, LEE KENNEY, writer, publishing company executive; b. Teaneck, N.J., Sept. 4, 1954; s. George Kenney and Veda Avis Maxine (Havens) B.; m. Jennifer Ursula Marie Moore, Aug. 20, 1983; 1 child, Philip Alden Emerson. Student, Harvey Mudd Coll., 1972-73; BS in Computer Sci., SUNY, Albany, 1976; postgrad., U. Colo., 1976-77, U. Calif., Berkeley, 1977-78. Software engr. Osborne & Assocs. Pubs., Berkeley, 1978-80, Triad Systems Corp., Sunnyvale, Calif., 1981-84; group leader, operating systems and communications Daisy Systems Corp., Sunnyvale, 1984-85; software applications engr. mgr. Fairchild Clipper Div., Palo Alto, Calif., 1985-87; cons. numerous electronic and pub. industry clients, 1987-88; pres. Ocean View Tech. Publs., Mountain View, Calif., 1989-91, Profl. Book Ctr., Denver, 1991—; pub. Ocean View Books, Denver, 1986—; seminar presenter Willamette Writer's Conf., Portland, Oreg., 1990, Rocky Mountain Book Festival, 1993, Rocky Mountain Book Publishers, 1993, Denver Book Mall, 1994, Tattered Cover Book Store, 1993, 94, Boulder Pub. Libr., 1995; cons. Prentice-Hall Pub. Co., Englewood Cliffs, N.J., 1989-90, Amdahl Corp., Sunnyvale, 1988-90; mem. New Eng. Book Show, 1991. Author: Directional Information, 1981, Basements in the Music Box, 1986, Dream Protocols, 1992, Phase Language, 1995; editor: Poly: New Speculative Writing, 1989, An Anatomy of wonder, 1995; pub. Phi Beta Kappa newsletter, San Francisco, 1987-89; art editor High Fantastic: Colorado's Fantasy, Dark Fantasy and Science Fiction, 1996. Presenter Mount View Pub. Libr., 1990. Recipient Ednl. Explorations award Reader's Digest, 1975, Outstanding Scholarly Book award Am. Pub. Assn., 1995; Nat. Merit scholar, 1972. Mem. Am. Book Producers Assn., Sci. Fiction Writers of Am., Sci. Fiction Poetry Assn., USR Group Unix Profl. Assn., Book Builder's West (cert. of merit), The Am. Booksellers Assn., Small Press Book Ctr., Poeisis (adv. bd. 1993), PEN West. Avocations: rare books, poetry. Office: Profl Book Ctr PO Box 102650 Denver CO 80250-2650

BALLESTEROS, JUVENTINO RAY, JR., minister; b. L.A., June 27, 1953; s. Juventino Ray and Esther Marie (Mendoza) B.; m. Rebecca Ann Williamson, Dec. 30, 1978. BA, Birmingham South Coll., 1977; MA, Presbyn. Sch. Christian Edn., 1979; D Ministry, Union Theol. Sem., 1982. Intern minister Crystal Cathedral, Garden Grove, Calif., 1978, Philippi Presbyn. Ch., Raeford, N.C., 1980-81; assoc. minister 1st Presbyn. Ch., Fayetteville, N.C., 1982-84, Orlando, Fla., 1984-92; pastor, Christian Edn. Crystal Cathedral, Garden Grove, Calif., 1992—; chmn. Div. Edn., Fayetteville, 1982-84, Nat. Tchr. Edn. Program, Fayetteville, 1983-84. Bd. dirs. Cumberland County Clean Community Council, Fayetteville, 1982-84, Nat. Tchr. Ednl. Program, Durham, N.C.; bd. advisors Jr. League, Fayetteville, 1983-84; v.p. Spouse Abuse Inc., Orlando, 1984-86; bd. trustees Union Theol. Sem./Presbyn. Sch. Christian Edn., 1996—. Mem. Religious Educators Assn., Assn. Presbyn. Ch. Educators. Republican. Avocation: all sports. Office: Crystal Cathedral 12141 Lewis St Garden Grove CA 92840-4699

BALLING, CHRISTINE, venture capitalist; b. Boston, Jan. 20, 1968; d. Ludwig Christian and Livia Marta (Rubulis) B. BA cum laude, Columbia U., 1990. MIS trainee Morgan Stanley, N.Y.C., 1990, Lehman Bros., N.Y.C., 1991-92; writer Creative Artists Agy., L.A., 1993-96; exec. v.p. Page One Bus. Prodns., L.A., 1996-98; bd. dirs. CD World Corp., Geneva, Radio World Corp., N.Y.C. Big Sister for Big Sisters/Big Bros., N.Y.C., 1986-90. Mem. Andover Alumni Assn. of So. Calif. (bd. dirs., sec. 1997).

BALLING, ROBERT C., JR., geography educator; b. 1952. Asst. prof. geography U. Nebr., 1979-84; mem. faculty Ariz. State U., 1985—, assoc. prof.; dir. Office of Climatology; lectr. greenhouse effect debate, Australia, New Zealand, Can., Kuwait, U.S. Author: The Heated Debate: Greenhouse Predictions Versus Climate Reality, 1992; contbr. articles to sci. jours. Office: Ariz State U PO Box 871508 Tempe AZ 85287-1508*

BALLINGER, CHARLES KENNETH, information specialist; b. Johnstown, Pa., July 28, 1950; s. Delores Jean (Cool) B.; m. Deb C. Delger, Sept. 14, 1985. Programmer analyst Cowles Pub. Co., Spokane, Wash., 1975-78; systems analyst Old Nat. Bank, Spokane, 1978-82; software engr. ISC System, Spokane, 1982; micro computer analyst Acme Bus. Computers, Spokane, 1982-85; info. ctr. analyst Wash. Water Power Co., Spokane, 1985-92; office automation analyst EDS Corp., Spokane, 1992-96, software engr.-mini/micro, 1996-98, info. analyst for client-server human resources info. sys., 1998—; cons. IDP Co., Spokane, 1978—. Contbr. articles to profl. jours. Served with Signal Corps, U.S. Army, 1968-71. Mem. IEEE (assoc.), Spokane Health Users Group (pres. 1979-83). Avocations: software development, motorcycling, boating, shooting, amateur radio. Home: 3810 S Havana St Spokane WA 99223-6006 Office: EDS-I/S Avista Corp 1411 E Mission Ave Spokane WA 99202-2617

BALLINGER, JAMES K., art museum executive; b. Kansas City, Mo., July 7, 1949; s. Robert Eugene and Yvonne (Davidson) B.; m. Nina Lundgaard, Aug. 21, 1971; children—Erin, Cameron. B.A., U. Kans., 1972, M.A., 1974. Gallery coordinator Tucson Art Ctr., 1973; registrar U. Kans., Lawrence, 1973-74; curator collections Phoenix Art Mus., 1974-81, asst. dir., 1981, dir., 1982—. Author: (exhbn. catalogues) Beyond the Endless River, 1980, Visitors to Arizona 1846 to 1980, 1981, Peter Hurd, 1983, The Popular West, 1982, Thomas Moran, 1986, Frederick Remington, 1989. Bd. dirs. Balboa Art Conservation Ctr. Fellow Am. Assn. Mus. Dirs. (bd. dirs.), Western Assn. Art Museums; mem. Central Ariz. Mus. Assn. (v.p. 1983). Avocations: hiking; basketball; traveling. Home: 5002 E Calle Tuberia Phoenix AZ 85018-4425 Office: Phoenix Art Mus 1625 N Central Ave Phoenix AZ 85004-1685*

BALLINGER, KATHRYN ANNETTE (PHELPS), mental health counseling executive, consultant; b. Creswell, Oreg., Aug. 1, 1940; d. Henry Wilbur and Lake Ilene (Wall) M.; children: David Bryan (dec.), Derek Alan, Darla Ailene; m. Ray Ballinger, June 27, 1998. BS in edn., Western Oreg. State Coll., 1962; MSW, Columbia State U., 1992, PhD, 1993. Tchr. Germany, Thailand, U.S., 1962-88; acct. exec. ins. industry; weight-loss counselor, alchohol/drug abuse prevention/intervention counselor teens, 1990-93; counselor Eugene, 1989-94; sr. exec. v.p., edn. dir. Light Streams, Inc., Eugene, 1993—; sr. exec. v.p., therapist Comprehensive Assessment Svcs./The Focus Inst., Inc., Eugene, 1994—; mental health counselor in pvt. practice; ednl. cons. specializing in learning disability testing Comprehensive Assessment Svcs., Eugene, 1995—; CEO Comprehensive Assessment Svcs., LLC, 1995—; cons. consumer edn.; mem. Am. Bd. Disability Analysts. Author: Easy Does It, books 1 & 2; hosted weekly TV cooking segment, Portland and U.S. Guardian Jobs Daughters, 1980-82; bd. dirs., den mother Cub Scouts, Boy Scouts, Kansas, Oreg., 1974-82; coach girls volleyball, 1974-80; vol. in orphanages, elderly nursing homes, Thailand, Germany, U.S., 1954-95; sunday sch. tchr., 1956-90; sponsored exchange student, 1984-88. Mem. Am. Bd. Disability Analysts, Eastern Star, Nat. Assn. Social Workers, Am. Counseling Assn., Columbia State U. Alumni Assn., Women's Internat. Bowling Conf. Avocations: cooking, gardening, reading, walking, car races, bowling. Home: 770 18th Ave Coos Bay OR 97420

BALLON, IAN C., lawyer, writer, educator; b. Montreal, Que., Can., June 4, 1962; m. Camille Smith. BA, Tufts U.; JD, George Washington U.; LLM, Georgetown U. Of counsel Couvert Bros., San Jose, Calif., Brown & Bain, Palo Alto, Calif., 1996; ptnr. Finnegan Henderson, Palo Alto, Calif., 1997—; adj. prof. Santa Clara U. Law Sch., 1998; spkr. in field. Author: The Law of the Internaet, 1998; mem. editl. bd. The Cyberspace Lawyer, Jour. Internet Law, Intellectual Lawcast; contbr. articles to profl. jours. Mem. ABA (chair intellectual property 1998). Office: Finnegan Henderson 700 Hansen Way Palo Alto CA 94304-1016

BALLSUN, KATHRYN ANN, lawyer; b. Calif., May 8, 1946; d. Zan and Doris (Pratt) B. BA, U. So. Calif., 1969, MA, 1971; JD, Loyola U., L.A., 1976. Bar: Calif. 1976, U.S. Dist. Ct. (cen. dist.) Calif. 1977. Ptnr. Sherer, Bradford, Lyster & Ballsun, L.A.; vis. prof. UCLA Law Sch., Loyola U. Law Sch., L.A.; adj. prof. U. So. Calif. Law Sch.; mem. planning com. U. So. Calif. Progate and Trust Conf., 1985-87; lectr. various schs. Author: (with others) Estate Planning for the General Practitioner; editor: How to Live and Die with California Probate; contbr. articles to profl. jours. Mem. graphic arts coun. L.A. County Mus. Art, Children's Coun., Westwood Meth. Ch.; co-chmn. for Class of 1976 Greater Loyola Law Sch. Devel. Program, 1983; advisor Am. Cancer Soc. Program; radio vol. sta. KUSC; bd. dirs. Planned Protective Svcs. Inc.; bd. dirs. L.A. Philharm. Orch., com. profl. women, treas. 1985-86. Fellow Am. Coll. Probate Counsel; mem. ABA (real property, probate and trust law, taxation sects., pre-death planning com.), State Bar Calif. (resolutions com., exec. com., co-vice chair estate planning techniques, post death, pre-death com., trust and probate, bus. law, taxation sects., law revision study team 1983-85), L.A. County Bar Assn. (trustee, exec. com., trust and probate, taxation sects.), Beverly Hills Bar Assn. (treas. 1985-86, bd. govs. 1982-84, 84-86, probate and trust com., taxation com., sr. vice chair resolutions com., del. State Bar Conv. 1981-85, v.p. 1987-89, pres.-elect, pres. 1989—, panelist), Nat. Acad. Elder Law Attys., Inc., Calif. Women Lawyers, L.A. Women Lawyers, Women in Business (sec., polit. action com.), Beverly Hills Estate Planning Com., Estate Counselor's Forum (past pres., v.p., bd. dirs.), Los Angeles County Mus. Art, L.A. C. of C., ACLU (L.A. chpt.), UCLA Ctr. for Study of Women, ACLU (L.A. chpt.), Kappa Alpha Theta. Office: Sherer Bradford Lyster & Ballsun 11th Fl 1901 AVe of the Americas Los Angeles CA 90067

BALLWEG, RUTH MILLIGAN, physician assistant, educator; b. Feb. 29, 1944. BS in Sociology, So. Oregon State Coll., 1969; grad. MEDEX N.W.

physician asst. program, U. Wash., Seattle, 1978, postgrad. study, present. Cert. State Bd. Med. Examiners, Oregon, Wash.; cert. Nat. Commn. on Cert. of Physician Assts. Asst. to dirs. honors program So. Oregon State Coll., Ashland, Ore., 1968; social worker and clinical asst. M. Kirk Gooding MD and William Sammons MD, Ashland, Ore., 1971-78; physician asst. M. Kirk Gooding MD, Ashland and Medford, 1978-80; childbirth educator Childbirth Education Assn. So. Oregon, Ashland and Medford, Ore., 1971-79; physician asst. Bremerton Kitsap County Health Dept., Bremerton, Wash., 1980-81; asst. program dir. MEDEX Northwest, Wash., 1984-85; dir. physician asst. program MEDEX Northwest, U. Wash. Sch. Med., 1985—; cons. N. Mex. State Policy Commn. on Physician Assts. Program Devel, 1993, Oregon Office Rural Health on Physician Assts. Program Feasibilty, 1992, Physician Asst. Program Devel, Oregon Health Scis. U., Portland, Ore., 1993, 1994, Nat. Health Svc. Corps. James Bowman and Assocs., San Francisco, 1992, 93, Stanford U. Fed. Contract on Deployment of Physician Assts. Nurse Practicioners and CNM's to Underserved Populations, 1992-93; mem. Nat. Adv. Bd. Nat. Health Svc. Corps, 1994-96, mem. Alaska Workgroup on Primary Care Planning, Dept. Health, Rural Alaska Health Edn. Ctr., 1994; co-dir. Sugarloaf Leadership Inst., Sugarloaf, Maine, 1993; lectr. Seattle Midwifery Sch. 1984-88, cons. 1984—, MEDEX Northwest, 1981-84; commr. PEW Commn. on the Health Professions, 1997—. Co-Editor: Physician Assistant: A Guide to Clinical Practice, 1994; mem. editl. bd. Clinician Reviews, 1996, Physician Assistant, 1989-90; contbr. articles to profl. jours. adv. com. Northwest AIDS Edn. Ctr, U. Wash., 1991-92; mem. People to People USSR Rural Health Project, Sch. Pub. Health, Sch. Medicine, U. Wash 1986-88. Primary Care Health Policy fellow, Bureau Health Professions, 1992; Recipient Disting. Svc. award Nat. Indian Health Bd. 1987. Grantee MEDEX Northwest Fed. Tng. , Wash., Alaska, Mont. Ore. Idaho, 1985-94, Health Careers Opportunity award, 1987, 90, Model Edn. Projects Health Professions, 1990. Mem. Assn. Physician Asst. Programs (pres. elect 1989-90, pres. 1990-91, 91-92, chair external rels. com. 1991—, co-dir. new program devel. project, bd. mem.-at-large 1993-95, UPJOHN Presidential award 1991), Am. Acad. Physician Assts.(ho. dels. alt. 1984-87, cons. to edn. coun.1989-90, mem. health reform task force, 1994), Wash. Acad. Physician Assts. (bd.mem. 1984-86, v.p. 1986-88, chair health policy coun. 1993—, pres.-elect. 1993-94, pres. 1994-95, spl. recognition award, 1988), Oregon Soc. Physician Assts.(MEDEX northwest liason bd. dirs. 1981-92), Nat. Rural Health Assn. (mem. task force Barriers to Practice Non Physician providers, 1991-92, frontier constituency), Wash. Rural Health Assn. Office: MEDEX NW UWMC Roosevelt 4245 Roosevelt Way NE Seattle WA 98105-6008

BALMUTH, BERNARD ALLEN, retired film editor; b. Youngstown, Ohio, May 19, 1918; s. Joseph and Sadie (Stein) B.; m. Rosa June Bergman, Mar. 2, 1952; children: Mary Susan, Sharon Nancy. BA in English, UCLA, 1942. Postal clk. U.S. Postal Svc., L.A., 1946-55; asst. and apprentice film editor, film editor L.A., 1955-90; ret., 1990; instr. film editing dept. of the arts UCLA Extension, 1979—; film editing cons. Am. Film Inst., L.A., 1982-92. Author: (manual) The Language of the Cutting Room, 1979, (text) Introduction to Film Editing, 1989. Initiator petition STOP Save TV Original Programming and Stop Excessive Reruns, 1971-75. Sgt. U.S. Army, 1942-46. Recipient Honor Cert. for Contribution Acad. TV Arts and Scis., 1974, Emmy nomination Best Editing, 1982. Mem. Am. Cinema Editors (life, bd. dirs. 1982-85, 97—, sec. 1985-87, v.p. 1987-91, chmn. spl. awards com. 1988—, hon. historian 1993—), Hollywood Film and Labor Coun. (rep. for Editors Guild 1972—), Stage Soc. (bd. dirs., sec. 1949-54). Democrat. Jewish. Avocations: cinema, theatre, dancing, cinema books, tennis. Address: care Rosallen Publs PO Box 927 North Hollywood CA 91603-0927

BALOG (GILLETTE), DAWN LOIS, motivational therapist, nutritionist; b. Lansing, Mich., May 5, 1940; d. Harold James and Edna Alice (Richmond) Gilpin; m. John Francis Balog, June 22, 1963; children—Monica Marie, Teresa Alice. B.A., Immaculate Heart Coll., 1974; M.S., Donsbach U., 1981, Ph.D., 1983. Cert. biofeedback therapist. Program dir. Life Fitness Center, Pasadena, Calif., 1980-83; program dir., co-founder Lifestyle Dynamics, Pasadena, 1983-94; founder Awareness in Action, Kapalua, Hawaii. Bd. dirs. Immaculate Heart Coll., Los Angeles. Mem. Calif. Inst. Tech. Assocs. (Pasadena). Office: Awareness In Action 500 Bay Dr # 35b2 Lahaina HI 96761-9034

BALOIAN, EDWARD, food products executive; b. 1921. With Charles Baloian Co., Fresno, Calif., 1946-86; v.p. Balo Packing Co., Inc., Fresno, 1978—; chmn. bd. dirs. Baloian Packing Co., Fresno, 1985—. Office: Baloian Packing Co 324 N Fruit Ave Fresno CA 93706-1420*

BALOIAN, TIMOTHY, food products executive; b. 1952; s. Edward Baloian. Pres. Balo Packing Co., Fresno, 1978—, Baloian Packing Co., Fresno, 1985—. Office: Baloian Packing Co Inc 324 N Fruit Ave Fresno CA 93706-1420*

BALSWICK, JACK ORVILLE, social science educator. Asst. prof. sociology Wis. State U., 1967; asst. prof. sociology U. Ga., 1968-71, assoc. prof., 1972-78, prof., 1978-82; prof. sociology and family devel. Fuller Theol. Sem., Pasadena, Calif., dir. rsch. marriage and family ministries. Author (with wife, Judith K. Balswick): The Family, 1989, Social Problems, 1990. Office: Fuller Theol Sem 135 N Oakland Ave Pasadena CA 91182*

BALTAKE, JOE, film critic; b. Camden, N.J., Sept. 16; s. Joseph John and Rose Clara (Bearint) B.; m. Susan Shapiro Hale. BA, Rutgers U., 1967. Film critic Gannett Newspapers (suburban), 1969, Phila. Daily News, 1970-85; movie editor Inside Phila., 1986—; film critic The Sacramento Bee, 1987—; leader criticism workshop Phila. Writer's Conf., 1977-79; film critic. Contbg. editor: Screen World, 1973-87 ; author: The Films of Jack Lemmon, 1977, updated, 1986; contbr. articles to Films in Rev., 1969—, broadcast criticism for Prism Cable TV, 1985; cons. Jack Lemmon: American Film Institute Life Achievement Award, 1987, Jack Lemmon: A Life in the Movies, 1990. Recipient Motion Picture Preview Group award for criticism, 1986, citation Phila. Mag., 1985, First Pl. commentary award Soc. of Profl. Journalists, 1995. Mem. Nat. Soc. Film Critics. Office: Sacramento Bee 2100 Q St Sacramento CA 95816-6899

BALTIMORE, DAVID, academic administrator, microbiologist, educator; b. N.Y.C., N.Y., Mar. 7, 1938; s. Richard I. and Gertrude (Lipschitz) B.; m. Alice S. Huang, Oct. 5, 1968; 1 dau., Teak. BA with high honors in Chemistry, Swarthmore Coll., 1960; postgrad., MIT, 1960-61; PhD, Rockefeller U., 1964. Research assoc. Salk Inst. Biol. Studies, La Jolla, Calif., 1965-68; assoc. prof. microbiology MIT, Cambridge, 1968-72, prof. biology, 1972-95; Ivan R. Cottrell prof. molecular biology and immunology MIT, 1994-97; inst. prof. MIT, Cambridge, 1995-97, Am. Cancer Soc. prof. microbiology, 1973-83, 94-97, dir. Whitehead Inst. Biomed. Rsch., 1982-90; pres. Rockefeller U., N.Y.C., 1990-91, prof., 1990-94; pres. Calif. Inst. Tech., Pasadena, 1997—. Mem. editorial bd. Jour. Molecular Biology, 1971-73, Jour. Virology, 1969-90, Sci., 1986-98, New Eng. Jour. Medicine, 1989-94. Bd. govs. Weizmann Inst. Sci., Israel; bd. dirs. Life Sci. Rsch. Found.; co-chmn. Commn. on a Nat. Strategy of AIDS; ad hoc program adv. com. on complex genome, NIH; mem. office AIDS rsch. adv. coun. NIH, chair vaccine adv. com., 1997—. Recipient Gustav Stern award in virology, 1970; Warren Triennial prize Mass. Gen. Hosp., 1971; Eli Lilly and Co. award in microbiology and immunology, 1971; Nat. Acad. Scis. U.S. Steel award in molecular biology, 1974; Gairdner Found. ann. award, 1974; Nobel prize in physiology or medicine, 1975. Fellow AAAS, Am. Med. Writers Assn. (hon.), Am. Acad. Microbiology; mem. NAS, Am. Acad. Arts and Scis., Inst. Medicine, Pontifical Acad. Scis., Royal Soc. (Eng.) (fgn.). Office: Calif Inst Tech 1200 E California Blvd Pasadena CA 91125-6301

BALTZ, ANTONE EDWARD, III, journalist, writer, academic administrator; b. Memphis, Aug. 23, 1965; s. Antone Edward Jr. and Mary (Tobin) B.; m. Kristine Lynn Harrison, Mar. 16, 1996. BA, U. Notre Dame, 1987; M in Liberal Studies, U. Denver, 1997. News editor The Observer, Notre Dame, Ind., 1986-87; intern Notre Dame Mag., 1987; reporter City News Bur., Chgo., 1987-88; legal writer DuPage Press Svc., Wheaton, Ill., 1988-90; staff writer Chgo. Daily Law Bull., 1990-92; staff corr. Bur. Nat. Affairs, Washington, 1992—; dir. liberal studies dept. U. Coll. U. Denver; instr. Coll. DuPage, Glen Ellyn, Ill., 1990-92; freelance writer Chgo. Sun-Times, 1990-92, DuPage Press, Elmhurst, Ill., 1990-91. Contbr. articles to legal jours. Mem. student adv. bd. U. Denver, 1994-96; pres. St. Vincent's Single Adults, Denver, 1994. Recipient Media award for sensitivity to Asian Americans, Asian-Am. Bar Assn., 1991, Achievement award Chgo. Bar Assn., 1992. Mem. Soc. Profl. Journalists. Roman Catholic. Avocations: rock climbing, backpacking, skiing, fly fishing, harmonica.

BAMBERGER, ALAN STUART, writer; b. Cleve., Oct. 3, 1950; s. Leo S. and Myrtle S. (Sokolsky) B.; m. Louise Rush, May 9, 1987; children: Elliot, Nicholas. BA, Kenyon Coll., 1972. Author: Buy Art Smart, 1990, Art for All, 1994; columnist Art Talk, 1986, Art Business Questions, 1991. Mem. Antiquarian Booksellers Assn. Am., Internat. League Antiquarian Booksellers. E-mail: alanb@artbusiness.com. Home: 2510 Bush St San Francisco CA 94115-3002

BAMBURG, MARVIN A., architect; b. Chgo., Sept. 19, 1935; s. Leslie Harold and Rose May (Abrahams) B.; m. Bonnie Lee, May 1, 1960; children: Marvin Jr. and Heidi F. Tucker. BArch, U. Ill., 1958. Draftsman Miller & Steiner Arch., San Mateo, Calif., 1963-64; arch. Wlm. Hedley Jr. Arch., Campbell, Calif., 1964-68; prin. Marvin A. Bamburg Arch., San Jose, Calif., 1968-78; pres. MBA Arch., San Jose, Calif., 1978—. Designed Temple Altar, SCAIA, 1979. Chpt. pres. local AIA, 1983 and 1991; chmn. Code Enforcement Appeals Bd., San Jose, Calif., 1992—; chmn. Willow Glen beautification com.; dir. Chai Care, 1995—; pres. Rotary Club of Campbell. Avocations: tennis, skiing. Office: MBA Arch 1176 Lincoln Ave San Jose CA 95125-3001

BAME, JAMES EDWIN, English educator; b. Findlay, Ohio, Aug. 25, 1948. BS in Edn., Ashland (Ohio) U., 1970; MA in English, San Francisco State U., 1983. Vol. Peace Corps, Sana'a, Yemen, 1976-78, tchr., materials developer Ea. Mich. U./USAID, Sana'a, 1979-80; lang. instr. U. San Francisco, 1982-83, King Saud U., Riyadh, Saudi Arabia, 1983-84, N.Mex. State U./USAID, Las Cruces, 1984-86; internat. edn. specialist U. Ky./USAID, Lexington, 1987-90; prof. Intensive English Lang. Instrn./Utah State U., Logan, 1990—; presenter Tchrs. of English to Spkrs. of Other Langs., Washington, 1993-98; faculty senator Utah State U., 1995—. Author, contbr.: New Ways Series/TESOL, 1993-98, Tasksin Independent Language Learning, 1996; mem. editl. adv. bd. Collegiate Press, Alta Loma, Calif., 1996-97; reviewer Fund for Improvement of Post-Secondary Edn., Washington, 1996, Cambridge (Eng.) U. Press, 1996. Mem. Intermountain Tchrs. of English to Spkrs. of Other Langs. (chair higher edn. interest sect. 1993-94, Prof. Devel. award 1994, sec. bd. dirs. 1998—). Avocations: hiking, gardening, nurturing children, camping. Office: IELI 715 University Blvd Logan UT 84322-0715

BANAS, EMIL MIKE, physicist, educator; b. East Chicago, Ind., Dec. 5, 1921; s. John J. and Rose M. (Valcicak) B.; m. Margaret Fagyas Welton, Oct. 9, 1948; children: Mary K., Barbara A. BA, Benedictine Univ., 1943; student (U.S. Rubber fellow), U. Notre Dame, 1954, PhD, 1955. Mem. Pres. Assocs. of Benedictine U., 1997—. Home: 1426 SE Fancy Free Dr Pullman WA 99163-5522

BANCROFT, PAUL, III, investment company executive; b. N.Y.C., Feb. 27, 1930; s. Paul and Rita (Manning) B.; m. Monica M. Devine, Jan. 2, 1977; children by previous marriage: Bradford, Kimberly, Stephen, Gregory. BA, Yale U., 1951; postgrad., Georgetown Fgn. Svc. Inst., 1952. Account exec. Merrill Lynch Pierce Fenner & Smith, N.Y.C., 1956-57; assoc. corp. fin. dept. F. Eberstadt & Co., N.Y.C., 1957-62; ptnr. Draper, Gaither & Anderson, Palo Alto, Calif., 1962-67; with Bessemer Securities Corp., Palo Alto, Calif., 1967-92; ind. venture capitalist N.Y.C., 1988—; v.p. Venture Capital Investments, 1967-74, sr. v.p. securities investments, 1974-76, pres., CEO, dir., 1976-87; cons. Bessemer Securities Corp., 1988-92; bd. dirs. Unova, Inc., Scudder Securities Trust, Scudder Value Equity Trust, Scudder Internat. Fund, Scudder Global/Internat. Fund, Scudder New Asia Fund, Scudder New Europe Fund, Inc.; founder, past pres. and chmn. Nat. Venture Capital Assn. 1st lt. USAF 1952-56. Mem. Yale Club, Pacific Union Club, Bohemian Club. Home and Office: PO Box 6639 Snowmass Village CO 81615-6639

BANDER, CAROL JEAN, German and English language educator; b. N.Y.C., Jan. 5, 1945; d. Frank Samuel and Susie Ruth Heimberg; m. Myron Bander, Aug. 20, 1967. BA, Queens Coll., 1966; MA, U. So. Calif., L.A., 1968, PhD, 1972. Cert. life commun. coll. credential, life standard secondary credential, ESL cert. Assoc. faculty Orange Coast Coll., Costa Mesa, Calif., 1974-77, North Orange Community Coll., Fullerton, Calif., 1974-77; prof. German and English as second lang. Saddleback Coll., Mission Viejo, Calif., 1977—, dept. chair English as a second lang., 1989-92, 96-98. NDEA Title IV fellowship U.S. Govt., 1966-70. Mem. Calif. Assn. of Tchrs. of English to Speakers of Other Langs. (pres.-elect 1998—, sec. 1992-93, bd. dirs. 1988-90, chpt. chair 1989-90, coord. Orange County chpt. 1988-90), Am. Assn. Tchrs. of German, Tchrs. of English to Speakers of Their Langs., Phi Beta Kappa. Avocations: travel, music, theatre, movies, cooking. Home: 39 Northampton Ct Newport Beach CA 92660-4206 Office: Saddleback Coll 28000 Marguerite Pky Mission Viejo CA 92692-3635

BANDT, PAUL DOUGLAS, physician; b. Milbank, S.D., June 22, 1938; s. Lester Herman and Edna Louella (Sogn) B.; m. Mary King, Aug. 26, 1962 (div. Feb. 1974); children: Douglas, Peggy; m. Inara Irene Von Rostas, Apr. 1, 1974; 1 child, Jennifer. BS in Edn. with distinction, U. Minn., 1960, BS in Medicine, 1966, D in Medicine, 1966. Diplomate Am. Bd. Diagnostic Radiology, Am. Bd. Nuclear Medicine. Intern U.S. Pub. Health Svc., San Francisco, 1966-68; physician U.S. Pub. Health Svc., Las Vegas, 1968-69; resident Stanford U., Palo Alto, Calif., 1969-72; physician Desert Radiologists, Las Vegas, 1972—; vice chief med. staff Desert Springs Hosp., Las Vegas, chmn. dept. radiology; past chief of staff U. Med. Ctr. So. Nev., Las Vegas. Contbr. articles on diagnostic radiology to profl. jours. With USPHS, 1966-69. Recipient Nev. Physician Yr. award, 1998. Mem. Am. Coll. Radiology, Am. Coll. Nuclear Medicine, Clark Med. Soc., Nev. State Med. Soc. Avocations: skiing, scuba diving, photography. Office: Desert Radiologists 2020 Palomino Ln Las Vegas NV 89106-4812

BANDY, AMANDA MCNEILL, anthropologist, educator; b. Houston, Sept. 15, 1944; d. I. Eugene and Edith Amanda (Richards) McNeill; children: Matthew Sebastian, Robin Emmanuel, Lysandra Amanda Nicole. BS, U. Houston, 1968; postgrad., Regis U., 1993—. Edn. coord. Family/Child Resources Ctr., Towaoc, Colo., 1977-79; child welfare worker Ute Mountain Ute Tribe, Towaoc, 1979-88, gen. assistance supr., child welfare worker, 1988-90, dept. ct. liaison, child welfare worker, 1990-92; senator State of Colo. Senate Dist. 6, 1994-95; educator Crow Canyon Archeol. Ctr., Cortez, Colo., 1995—. Pres. Episcopal Ch. Women, St. Barnabas of the Valley, Cortez, 1979-80, mem. vestry, 1981-84, 93-97, founding coord. Good Samaritan Ctr., 1982-83, lic. lay reader, 1997; bd. dirs. Sunrise Youth Shelter, Towaoc, 1982-87, Colo. Am. Indian Found., Denver, 1993-96; mem. Ute Mountain Ute Tribal Election Com., Towaoc, 1983-88; mem. Gov.'s Traffic Safety Com., 1987-91, chmn., 1990-91; mem. State Merit Sys. Coun., Denver, 1990-96, chmn., 1995-96; mem. adv. bd. Women's Resource Ctr., Dolores, Colo., 1991-93, bd. dirs., 1993-94, co-chair bd. dirs., 1994; mem. Four Corners (Colo.) Heritage Coun., 1996—; active Colo. Dems., Denver and Montezuma County Dems., Cortez, 1983—. Mem. AAUW, Am. Indian Coll. Fund (hon. alumni), Archeol. Conservancy, Cortez U. Colo. Ctr., Friends of the Ute Mus., Nat. Mus. Am. Indian-Smithsonian (charter) Natural Resources Def. Coun., S.W. Natural and Cultural Heritage Assn., Alpha Lamda Delta, Alpha Chi. Episcopalian.

BANDY, JACK D., lawyer; b. Galesburg, Ill., June 19, 1932; s. Homer O. and Gladys L. (Van Winkle) B.; m. Betty McMillan, Feb. 18, 1956; children: Jean A. Bandy Abramson, D. Michael, Jeffery K. *Great-great grandparents, Reuben and Sibby Adkisson Bandy were among the first settlers of Know County, Illinois in 1837. They bought 160 acres near Galesburg, and started the family farm. After Reuben's death (1861), it was operated by their son, George, and his wife, Narcissa Holland Bandy. When George retired, his son, George Albert "Burt" and his wife Mattie Mears Bandy, continued the farm until 1907 when they sold it and moved to Galesburg. Their son, Homer Oliver, married Gladys Lillian Winkle Bandy. They were parents of Jack D. Bandy, subject of this biography.* B.A., Knox Coll., 1954; LL.B., U. La Verne, 1967. Bar: Calif. 1972. Safety engr. Indsl. Indemnity Co., L.A., 1960-65, sr. safety engr., 1965-69, resident safety engr., 1969-72; trial atty. Employers Ins. of Wausau, L.A., 1972-79; mng. atty. Wausau Ins. Cos., L.A., 1979-92; arbitrator, mediator L.A. Superior Mcpl. Ct., 1992—. Contbr. articles to profl. jours. Youth leader YMCA, Mission Hills, Calif., 1965-72. Served with U.S. Army, 1954-56. Mem. Calif. State Bar, Am. Soc. Safety Engrs. (cert. safety profl.).

BANERJEE, PRANAB K., engineer, researcher, consultant; b. Calcutta, India; came to U.S., 1985; s. Kanty Pada and Anima (Chakravarty) B. B in Tech. with honors, Indian Inst. Tech., Kharagpur, 1985; MS in Computational Physics, Kans. State U., 1988. Programmer analyst Lab. NeuroImaging UCLA, 1989-93, Crump Inst. Biol. Imaging UCLA, 1993-96; mem. info. sys. and computing sci. staff NASA Jet Propulsion Lab., Pasadena, Calif., 1997—; cons. D&P Cons., L.A., 1998—. Contbr. articles to profl. jours. Achievements include research in scientific data visualization, 3D computer graphics, scientific computing. Avocations: tennis, travel, hiking, photography, music concerts. Office: NASA Jet Propulsion Lab MS 169-237 4800 Oak Grove Dr Pasadena CA 91109

BANGS, JOHN WESLEY, III, law enforcement administrator; b. Phila., Dec. 26, 1941; s. John Wesley Jr. and Sarah Emily (Morcom) B.; m. Donna Louise McClanahan, June 1, 1963; children: Louis M., Terry M., John W. IV. AA summa cum laude, E. Los Angeles Coll., 1976. Calif. Commn. on Peace Officer Standards and Training: Basic, Intermediate, Advanced, Supervisory, Mgmt. Police officer Los Angeles Police Dept., 1964-70, sgt., 1970-74, lt., 1974-84; chief spl. officer I L.A. Dept. Airports Police, 1988—; lectr. U. So. Calif., 1978-79. Author: Narcotics Overview, 1983, Psychological Evaluation for Police Candidates, 1969. Cub master Cub Scouts Am., Ontario, Calif., 1968; scout master Boy Scouts Am., Ontario, 1971; explorer leader Explorer Scouts Am., Los Angeles, 1976; mem. Greater Los Angeles Scouting Council, 1976. Sgt. U.S. Army, 1959-62. Mem. Internat. Assn. Chiefs of Police, Calif. Peace Officers Assn., Calif. Narcotics Officers, Los Angeles Police Protective League, Los Angeles Police Relief Assn. Republican. Episcopalian. Avocations: fishing, boating, breeding German shepherd dogs. Office: LA Airport Police 1 World Way Los Angeles CA 90045-5803

BANIK, GAUTAM GOUR, biochemical engineer; b. Bombay, Dec. 14, 1967; came to U.S., 1989; s. Gour Gopal and Rani (Sarkar) B. B of Chem. Engring., U. Bombay, 1989; PhD, Dartmouth Coll., 1995. Process technologist Shamrit Assocs. and Cons., Bombay, 1989; rsch. asst. Thayer Sch. Engring. Dartmouth Coll., Hanover, N.H., 1989-94; rsch. assoc. dept. chem. engring. U. Colo., Boulder, 1995-97; assoc. scientist Cell Genesys Inc., Foster City, Calif., 1997—. Contbr. articles to profl. jours. Govt. India scholar, 1985-89; Morgan Parker fellow Dartmouth Coll., 1989-90. Mem. AIChE, Am. Chem. Soc. (Biot fellow 1995). Achievements include process development, T-cell expansion, T-cell transduction, adenoviral vector production, AAV vector production, gene therapy. Office: Cell Genesys Inc 322 Lakeside Dr Foster City CA 94404-1146

BANKS, CHERRY ANN MCGEE, education educator; b. Benton Harbor, Mich., Oct. 11, 1945; d. Kelly and Geneva (Smith) McGee; m. James A. Banks, Feb. 15, 1969; children: Angela Marie, Patricia Ann. BS, Mich. State U., 1968; MA, Seattle U., 1977, EdD, 1991. Tchr. Benton Harbor Pub. Sch., 1968; staff assoc. Citizens Edn. Ctr. N.W., Seattle, 1984-85; edn. specialist Seattle Pub. Schs., Seattle, 1985-87; pres. Edn. Material and Svcs. Ctr., Edmonds, Wash., 1987—; asst. prof. edn. U. Wash., Bothell, 1992-96, assoc. prof. edn., 1996—; cons. Jackson (Miss.) Pub. Schs., 1988, Seattle Pub. Schs., 1988-90, Little Rock Pub. Schs., 1989, Scott Foreman Pub. Co., Glenview, Ill., 1992—; vis. asst. prof. Seattle U., 1991-92. Co-author: March Toward Freedom, 1978, Teaching Strategies for the Social Studies, 1999; co-editor: Multicultural Education: Issues and Perspectives, 1989, rev. edits., 1993, 97; assoc. editor Handbook of Rsch. on Multicultural Edn.; contbr. chpts. to books. Mem. Jack and Jill Am., Seattle, 1978-94, First AME Headstart Bd., Seattle, 1981-83; trustee Shoreline C.C., Seattle, 1983-95; bd. dirs. King County Campfire, Seattle, 1985-88. Recipient Outstanding Commitment and Leadership of C.C. award Western Region Nat. Coun. on Black Am. Affairs, 1989. Mem. ASCD, Nat. Coun. for Social Studies Programs Com. (vice chairperson Carter G. Woodson Book award com. 1991-92, chair person 1992-93, mem. nominating com.), Am. Rsch. Assn., The Links, Inc., Phi Delta Kappa (founding, Seattle U. chpt.), Alpha Kappa Alpha. Avocations: tennis, swimming, reading, traveling. Office: U Wash Edn Program 22011 26th Ave SE Bothell WA 98021-4900

BANNER, BOB, television producer, director; b. Ennis, Tex., Aug. 15, 1921; s. Robert James and Viola (Culbertson) B.; m. Alice Jane Baird, Jan. 14, 1946; children—Baird Allen, Robert James, Charles Moore. B.B.A., So. Meth. U., 1943; M.A., Northwestern U., 1948. Pres. Bob Banner Assocs., 1958—; vis. prof. So. Meth. U. Dir. Garroway-at-Large, NBC-TV; producer, dir. Fred Waring Show, CBS-TV; dir. Omnibus; TV producer, pres., Bob Banner Assos.; TV shows include (series) The Uptown Comedy Club, It's Showtime at the Apollo, Garroway At Large, Fred Waring Show, Don Ho, Omnibus, Jr. Almost Anything Goes, Almost Anything Goes, Candid Camera, Carol Burnett Show, Garry Moore Show, Dinah Shore Chevy Show, Kraft Summer Music Hall, Solid Gold, Star Search, It's Showtime at the Apollo, The Uptown Comedy Club; (spls.) Perry Como Holiday Spls., Carnegie Hall Salutes Jack Benny, Peggy Fleming Holiday Spl., Amazing Music Spls., Happy Birthday, George Gershwin, 1996, Julie & Carol at Carnegie Hall, Ford Motor Co.'s 75th Ann., Am. West of John Ford, A Spl. Sesame St. Christmas; spls. starring Bob Hope, Julie Andrews, Andy Williams; (movies) My Sweet Charlie, My Husband is Missing, Warning Shot, Journey from Darkness, The Darker Side of Terror, If Things were Different, Yes Virginia There Is A Santa Claus, 1991, Crash Landing, 1992, With Murder In Mind, 1992, The Sea Wolf, 1993. Recipicient 15 Emmy awards, 11 Christopher awards, 3 Peabody awards. Mem. Acad. of TV Arts and Scis. Presbyn. Office: 535 S Curson Ave Apt 9L Los Angeles CA 90036-5297

BANNER-BACIN, LINDA LENORE, program analyst; b. Greenville, S.C., Jan. 7, 1956; d. John Lewis and Stella (Nidock) Banner; m. Mark Stephen Bacin, June 25, 1994. AAS in Horticulture, SUNY, Cobleskill, 1976; Ba in Humanities, SUNY, Stonybrook, 1979; MBA, Pepperdine U., 1995. Jr-sr. h.s. tchr. U.S. Peace Corps, Liberia, W. Africa, 1980-82; adaptive aquatics instr. City of Oxnard, Calif., 1983; flight coord. Air Camarillo, Calif., 1984-85; police dispatcher City of Oxnard, 1985-86; program analyst Naval Surface War Ctr., Port Hueneme, Calif., 1987—; chairperson Fed. Women's Program, Port Hueneme, 1990-94; mem. Equal Employment Opportunity Com., Port Hueneme, 1992-94. Vol. Focus on the Masters, 1996; mem. Carnegie Art Mus., 1994—, Banner Elk Hist. Soc., 1989—. Recipient Beyond War award Beyond War Award Found., 1987. Mem. Am. Soc. Mil. Comptrollers, Am. Rose Soc. Ventura, Ventura County Maritime Mus., Carnegie Art Mus. Avocations: gardening, painting, antique restoration, golf, historic sites. Home: 461 S F St Oxnard CA 93030-5949

BANUELOS, BETTY LOU, rehabilitation nurse; b. Vandergrift, Pa., Nov. 28, 1930; d. Archibald and Bella Irene (George) McKinney; m. Raul, Nov. 1, 1986; children: Patrice, Michael. Diploma, U. Pitts., 1951; cert., Loma Linda U., 1960. RN, Calif.; cert. chem. dependency nurse. Cons. occupational health svcs. Bd. Registered Nurses, 1984—; lectr., cons. in field. Recipient Scholarship U. Pitts. Mem. Dirs. of Nursing, Calif. Assn. Nurses in Substance Abuse. Home and Office: 15 Oak Spring Ln Laguna Hills CA 92656-2980

BAO, JOSEPH YUE-SE, orthopedist, microsurgeon, educator; b. Shanghai, Feb. 20, 1937; s. George Zheng-En and Margaret Zhi-De (Wang) B.; m. Delia Way, Mar. 30, 1963; children: Alice, Angela. MD, Shanghai First Med. Coll., 1958. Intern affiliated hosps. Shanghai First. Med. Coll.; resident Shanghai Sixth People's Hosp., orthopaedist, 1958-78, orthopaedist-in-charge, 1978-79, vice chief orthopaedist, 1979-84; rsch. assoc. orthop. hosp. U. So. Calif., L.A., 1985-90, 94—, vis. clin. assoc. prof. dept. orthopedics, 1986-89; coord. microvascular svcs. Orthopaedic Hosp., L.A., 1989-91; clin. assoc. prof. dept. orthopedics U. So. Calif., L.A., 1989—, clin. assoc. prof. plastic surgery, 1997—; attending physician Los Angeles County and U. So. Calif. Med. Ctr., L.A., 1986, 90—, Orthopaedic Hosp., L.A., 1998—; cons. Rancho Los Amigos Med. Ctr., Downey, Calif., 1986. Contbr. articles to profl. jours., chpts. to books. Mem. Internat. Microsurg. Soc., Am. Soc. for Reconstructive Microsurgery, Am. Soc. for Peripheral Nerve, Orthop. Rsch. Soc., Societe Internationale de Chirurgie Orthopedique et de Traumatologie.

Home: 17436 Terry Lyn Ln Cerritos CA 90703-8522 Office: 11741 Telegraph Rd Ste G Santa Fe Springs CA 90670 3687

BARAB, MARVIN, financial consultant; b. Wilmington, Del., July 16, 1927; s. Jacob and Minnie (Press) B.; m. Gertrude Klein, June 13, 1951; children: Jordan, Neal, Caryn. BS with distinction, Ind. U., 1947, MBA, 1951. Dir. mktg. Edward Weiss & Co., Chgo., 1951-56; dir. bus. rsch. Parker Pen Co., Janesville, Wis., 1956-59; dir. mktg. rsch. packaging and graphics Mattel Inc., Hawthorne, Calif., 1959-65; pres. Barcam Pub. Co., Rolling Hills Estates, Calif., 1959-70, Rajo Publs., Rolling Hills Estates, 1967-70, So. Calif. Coll. Med. & Dental Careers, Anaheim, 1970-81, Barbrook, Inc., Rolling Hills Estates, 1981-86; cons. Marvin Barab & Assocs., Rolling Hills Estates, Calif., 1981—. Editor: Rand McNally Camping Guide, 1967-70; contbr. articles to various publs., 1982-87. Treas. Harbor Free Clinic, 1990-92; bd. dirs. So. Bay Contemporary Art Mus., 1993-94, sec., 1994. Mem. Nat. Assn. Trade and Tech. Schs. (hon. life, sec. 1977-79, pres. 1979-81, bd. dirs.), Calif. Assn. Paramed. Schs. (pres. 1973-77). Avocations: travel, music, art. Office: 904 Silver Spur Rd Ste 110 Palos Verdes Peninsula CA 90274-3800

BARAD, JILL ELIKANN, toy company executive; b. N.Y.C., May 23, 1951; d. Lawrence Stanley and Corinne (Schuman) Elikann; m. Thomas Kenneth Barad, Jan., 28, 1979; children: Alexander David, Justin Harris. BA English and Psychology, Queens Coll., 1973. Asst. prod. mgr. mktg. Coty Cosmetics, N.Y.C., 1976-77, prod. mgr. mktg., 1977; account exec. Wells Rich Greene Advt. Agy., L.A., 1978-79; product mgr. mktg. Mattel Toys, Inc., L.A., 1981-82, dir. mktg., 1982-83, v.p. mktg., 1983-85, sr. v.p. mktg., 1985-86, sr. v.p. product devel., from 1986, exec. v.p. product design and devel., exec. v.p. mktg. and worldwide product devel., 1988-89; pres. girls and activity toys div. Mattel Toys, Inc (name now Mattel Inc.), L.A., 1989-90; pres. Mattel USA, El Segundo, Calif., 1990-92; pres., COO Mattel, Inc., El Segundo, Calif., 1992-97, pres., CEO, 1997, chmn., CEO, 1997—; former bd. dirs. Bank of Am., bd. dirs. Microsoft Corp., Claremont U. Ctr., Arco Toys Ltd., Mattel Inc., Pixar Animation Studios. Bd. govs. Town Hall of Los Angeles; trustee Queens Coll.; chair exec. adv. bd. Children Affected by AIDS Found., Mattel Found, catalyst The For All Kids Found., bd. advs. Children's Scholarship Fund, catalyst The For All Kids Found., Inc. Exec. bd. Med. Scis. UCLA,. Office: Mattel Inc 333 Continental Blvd El Segundo CA 90245-5012

BARAN, SHIRLEY WALTERS, artist, sculptor; b. New Orleans; d. Harmon Jesse and Willa Mae Walters; m. Helko Eli Baran; 3 children. Student, Corcoran Mus. Sch. Art, 1943-45, U. Ark., 1945-48, Pratt Inst., 1945-48. Co-owner, illustrator Baran-Walters Advt., Tulsa, Okla., 1949-65; free lance illustrator, painter, sculptor Greenville, S.C., 1966-81; art coord. Her Majesty Industries, Greenville, S.C.; illustrator, layout artist Millbrae (Calif.) Sun, Boutique Villager, Burlingame, Calif., Foster City (Calif.) Progress, Millbrae Leader, San Carlos (Calif.) Inquirer, Belmont (Calif.) Courier Bull., 1981-93; freelance designer Clay Art Co., San Francisco, 1987—; doll designer Friends Forever, Windsor, Calif., 1987—. Recipient Merit award S.C. Watercolor Soc., 1978, Best in Category Original Sculpture Doll award Doll Artisan Guild, 1987, 89, Internat. Doll Expo, 1995. Office: Friends Forever PO Box 691 Windsor CA 95492-0691

BARANEK, ROBERT R., writer, dockworker; b. Anaheim, Calif., May 12, 1959; s. James Allen Baranek Sr. and Donna Darlene (Adams) Baranek Webster. BA in Liberal Arts, Western Ill. U., 1991; MA in Christian Apologetics, Simon Greenleaf U., 1992. Author: Kingdom Discipleship: Living and Discipleship in Post-Christian Age. Republican. Presbyterian.

BARASHKOV, NICKOLAY NICKOLAYEVICH, polymer chemist, researcher; b. Kimry, Russia, May 11, 1952; came to U.S., 1993; s. Nikolay A. and Klavdia A. (Gorshkova) B.; m. Irina I. Barashkova, Jan. 11, 1975; 1 child, Andrew N. MS, Lomonosov Inst. Chem. Tech., Moscow, 1975; 1st PhD, Karpov Inst. Phys. Chemistry, Moscow, 1978, sr. scientist, 1983, 2d PhD (DSc), 1990. Head chemistry group Karpov Inst. Phys. Chemistry, 1989-93; vis. scientist Fermi Nat. Lab., Batavia, Ill., 1993; vis. assoc. prof. Tex. Tech. U., Lubbock, 1993-94; rsch. scientist U. Tex., Dallas, 1994-97; sr. rsch. chemist Radiant Color, Richmond, Calif., 1997—; mgr. internat. (U.S.-Russian) project, Internat. Sci. and Tech. Ctr., Batavia and Moscow, 1995-96. Adv. bd. Jour. Chemistry and Life, Moscow, 1994-97; author: Polymer Composites, 1984, Structurally-Colored Polymers, 1987, Optically Transparent Polymers, 1992, Fluorescent Polymers, 1994, 2 other books. Recipient 1st prize Mendeleev's Chem. Soc., 1983. mem. Am. Chem. Soc., N.Y. Acad. Scis. Achievements include 25 patents in field of colored and fluorescent polymers. Office: Radiant Color Co 2800 Radiant Ave Richmond CA 94804

BARBAKOW, JEFFREY, health facility administrator; b. 1944. BS, San Jose U.; MBA, U. So. Calif. With Merrill Lynch Capital Mkts. and several additional affiliates, 1972-88, MGM/UA Communications Inc., 1988-91, Donaldson, Lufkin & Jenrette Securities Corp., 1991; dir. Tenet Healthcare, Santa Barbara, Calif., 1990—, chmn. bd., CEO, 1993—. Office: Tenet Healthcare Inc 3820 State St Santa Barbara CA 93105-3112*

BARBAS, JEFFREY LAWRENCE, finance company executive; b. Detroit, Oct. 22, 1947; s. Sidney and Betty (Rosenberg) B.; m. Lynne Goodstein, Feb. 15, 1974 (div. Mar. 1990); children: Sean, Christopher. BA in Journalism, Calif. State U., Northridge, 1973. Dist. mgr. CIT Group, L.A., 1974-79; v.p., mgr. Cmty. Bank, L.A., 1979-85; v.p., gen. mgr. Mazak Corp., Gardena, Calif., 1985-91; pres. C D Financing, Inc., Anaheim, Calif., 1991—; cons. Fine CNC Sys., Anaheim. Author: (poem) Poem for the Living, 1991; author Fin. Forum, 1984—. Comdr. Club L.A. Rescue Mission; medallion mem. Orange (Calif.) County Rescue Mission; pacesetter CFIDS Assn. Am. With mil. intelligence U.S. Army, 1965-69, Vietnam. Avocations: sports, writing, reading. Office: C D Financing Inc 2735 Saturn St Brea CA 92821-6705

BARBEE, BOB, administrator. Seasonal naturalist Rocky Mountain Nat. Park, 1958; various positions Yosemite Nat. Park, Carlsbad Caverns Nat. Park, Big Bend Nat. Park, Point Reyes Nat. Park; supt. Cape Lookout and Cape Hatteras Nat. Seashores, Hawaii Volcanoes Nat. Park, Redwood Nat. Park, Yellowstone Nat. Park; regional dir. Klondike Gold Rush Nat. Hist. Park, Skagway, Alaska, 1994—. Office: PO Box 517 Skagway AK 99840-0517

BARBEE, JOE ED, lawyer; b. Pharr, Tex., Feb. 27, 1934; s. Archie Allen and Concha (Leal) B.; m. Yolanda Margaret Atonna, Feb. 17, 1962; children—Cynthia M., Adam A., Walter J. BSEE, U. Ariz., 1961; JD, Western New Eng. Coll., 1973. Bar: Mass. 1973, U.S. Patent Office 1973, U.S. Ct. Appeals (fed. cir.) 1982. Engr. Gen. Electric Co., Pittsfield, Mass., 1961-73; patent atty. Fort Wayne, Ind., 1973-75, Magnavox, Fort Wayne, 1975-76, Motorola, Inc., Phoenix, 1976—. Sgt. U.S. Army, 1953-56. Recipient Outstanding Performance award U.S. Civil Svc., 1960. Mem. ABA, Am. Patent Law Assn., Am. Intellectual Property Law Assn. Republican. Methodist. Avocations: tennis, hunting, fishing. Home: 7611 N Mockingbird Ln Paradise Valley AZ 85253-3126 Office: Motorola Inc 8220 E Roosevelt St # B3 Scottsdale AZ 85257-3804

BARBER, CLARENCE LYLE, economics educator; b. Wolseley, Sask., Can., May 5, 1917; s. Richard Edward and Lulu Pearl (Lyons) B.; m. Barbara Anne Patchet, May 10, 1947; children—Paul Edward, Richard Stephen, David Stuart, Alan Gordon. BA, U. Sask., 1939; MA, Clark U., 1941; postgrad., U. Minn., 1941-43, PhD, 1952; LLD (hon.), U. Guelph, 1988. With Stats. Can., 1945-48; mem. faculty McMaster U., 1948-49, U. Man., Winnipeg, Can., 1949-85; prof. econs. U. Man., 1956-85, disting. prof., 1982-85, emeritus, 1985—, head dept., 1963-72; vis. prof. Queen's U., 1954-55, McGill U., 1964-65; Commr. Royal Commn. on Farm Machinery, 1966-71; spl. adviser on nat. income Phillipines Govt., 1959-60; commr. for study welfare policy in Man., 1972; mem. Nat. Commn. on Inflation, 1979, Royal Commn. Econ. Union and Devel. Prospects for Can., 1982-85. Author: Inventories and the Business Cycle, 1958, The Theory of Fiscal Policy as Applied to a Province, 1966, (with others) Inflation and Unemployment: The Canadian Experience, 1980, Controlling Inflation: Learning from Experience in Canada, Europe and Japan, 1982, False Promises: The Failure of Conservative Economics, 1993. Served with RCAF, 1943-45. Named Officer in Order of Can., 1987; Can. Coun. Profl. Leave fellow, 1970-71. Fellow Royal Soc. Can.; mem. Canadian Assn. U. Tchrs. (pres. 1958-59), Canadian Econ. Assn. (pres. 1971-72), Am. Econ. Assn., Royal Econ. Soc., Social Sci. Research Council Can. (mem. exec. 1972-73), U. Victoria Faculty Club. Home: 766 Richmond Ave, Victoria, BC Canada V8S 3Z1

BARBER, DIANE L., adult education educator; b. Bakersfield, Calif., Apr. 29, 1952; d. Leo and Helen (Garabedian) B.; m. A. Richard Ellis, June 9, 1984; children: Claire, Lauren. BS, U. Calif., Davis, 1975, MS, 1977; PhD, U. Calif., L.A., 1985. Postdoctoral fellow U. Mass., Worcester, 1985-87; asst. prof. Yale U., New Haven, Conn., 1987-91; asst. prof. U. Calif., San Francisco, 1991-95, assoc. prof., 1995—; established investigator Am. Heart Assn., 1996—. Office: U Calif HSW604 513 Parnassus Ave San Francisco CA 94122-2722

BARBER, JAMES P., lawyer; b. Berkeley, Calif., Nov. 11, 1944. BA, U. Calif., Santa Barbara, 1967; JD, U. Calif., 1973. Bar: Calif. 1973. Ptnr. Hancock, Rothert & Bunshoft LLP, San Francisco, 1980—. Articles editor Hastings Law Jour., 1972-73. Mem. ABA, State Bar Calif., Bar Assn. San Francisco, Def. Rsch. Inst., Thurston Soc., Order of the Coif. Office: Hancock Rothert & Bunshoft LLP 4 Embarcadero Ctr Ste 300 San Francisco CA 94111-4106*

BARBER, KATHLEEN ANN STARKS, software developer, public relations consultant; b. Phoenix, Nov. 24, 1950; d. Ross Owen and Maribel Louise (Barnes) Starks; m. H. Bradford Barber, Nov. 17, 1984; 1 child. Student, Phoenix Coll., 1970; BS in Liberal Arts, U. Ariz., 1972, M.S. in Mgmt. Info. Systems, 1992. Lic. pilot. Retail Tucson, 1972-75, freelance pub. rels., 1972-78; from campaign mgr., legis. aide State Senator Morris Farr, Tucson, 1975-78; from consumer info. specialist to exec. dir. crime victim compensation program Office of Pima County Atty., Tucson, 1978-92; software developer Avalon Software, Inc., Tucson, 1992—. Sec. bd. dirs. Crime Prevention League, Tucson, 1987-96; v.p. bd. dirs. Ariz. Consumers Coun., Phoenix, 1974—; bd. dirs. Headline Prodns., 1993-95; exec. com. bd. dirs. Ariz. Coalition Victim Svcs., Phoenix, 1987-92; Dem. precinct committeeman Pima County, 1974—, state committeeman, 1974-98, state vice chair, Ariz., 1978-80, Pima County, 1980-82; del. Dem. Nat. Conv., 1980. Mem. Nat. Women's Polit. Caucus (chpt. pres. state office 1974—), Assn. Computing Machinery, Soaring Assn., Am. Women's Soaring Pilots Assn., Ninety Nines, Ariz. Sonora Desert Mus. Avocations: skiing, scuba, gardening, reading, ethics in computing. Office: Indsl & Fin Sys 3716 E Columbia St Tucson AZ 85714-3414

BARBER, NORMA ANN, secondary education educator; b. Emmett, Idaho, June 22, 1953; d. Willard Andrus and Theo Elaine (Garner) Jensen; m. Clinton Earl Barber, Mar. 17, 1979; children: Laura Ann, Janet Marie, Susan Elaine. AA, Treasure Valley C.C., 1973; BS in Edn., Ea. Oreg. State Coll., 1975; MEd, Ea. Oreg. U., 1998. Cert. secondary tchr., Oreg. Owner, mgr. Gen. Store, Ukiah, Oreg., 1988—; tchr. Ukiah Sch. Dist., 1991—; tchr., rschr. Oreg. Writing Project at Eastern, LaGrande, 1997—, co-dir., 1999—; instr. student writers workshop, Ukiah, 1992-98; mem. crisis interventin flight team Unatilla-Morrow Schs., 1999—. Vol. EMT Ukiah Quick Response Team, 1984—; adv. com. Umatilla County Health Dept., Pendelton, Oreg., 1986-88; sch. bd. mem. Ukiah Sch. Dist., 1981-83. Named Homemaker of Yr., Umatilla County, 1986. Mem. ASCD, Assn. Rural Tchrs. English, Oreg. Tchrs. English. Avocations: quilting, cooking, reading, writing, gardening.

BARBER, WILLIAM HAROLD (BILL), artist, sculptor, motion picture producer; b. Glendale, Calif., Oct. 23, 1940; s. Julius Rideout and Lillian Carmel (McCarthy) B.; m. Janice McPheeters, Oct. 13, 1941; children: Brian, Scott, Michael, Jesse, Heather, Justin. Grad. H.S., Pico Rivera, Calif. Money courier, clk., carrier P.O. Dept., Pico-Rivera and Provo, Utah, 1960-75; prodn. mgr. Natures Way Herbs, Provo, 1975-76; movie stunt driver Sun Classic Pictures, Heber, Utah, 1982; set designer LDS Motion Picture Studios, Provo, 1989—. Art dir., props tech. advisor, prodr., actor, visionary, writer Golden Apple Prodns., Majestic Entertainment, Films for Familes, IMAX, others; actor, prodr. (motion picture) The Butterchurn, 1995 (silver award 1995). Del. Rep. party, Daniel, Utah, 1988; rep. Freeman Inst., Salt Lake City, 1982; 1st sgt., survival trainer State Def., State of Utah, Camp Williams, 1985, mem. Merrill Cook election com., 1989. Recipient Silver Spur award, 1986, Grand Champion Best Artist of Show award, 1995, cert. of achievement Pyzell Sch. Navigation, Santa Barbara, Calif., 1982. Mem. LDS Ch. Avocations: horseman, sailing, archery, navigator, healing arts. Home and Office: PO Box 243 Heber City UT 84032-0243

BARB MINGO, ARTURO, romance literature and languages educator; b. Fla., Jan. 20, 1944; s. Willie Arthur and Jeanette (Mingo) Barb; m. Marleny Paredes. BA, Dillard U., 1965; MA, Tulane U., 1968; PhD, Internat. Inst. Advanced Study, 1980. Cert. in higher edn., Calif. Chair modern and classical langs. Chapman U., Orange, Calif., 1972-75; prof. modern langs. Santa Ana (Calif.) Coll., 1977-97; chair langs. dept. Santiago Canyon Coll., Orange, 1997—. Author: Poesias, 1972, 78, Grandma's Up, 1990. Mem. Am. Coun. on the Tchg. of Fgn. Langs., Assn. of Depts. of Fgn. Langs. Avocations: bodybuilding, vocal music coach. Office: Santiago Canyon Coll 8045 E Chapman Ave Orange CA 92869-4512

BARBORKA, CLIFFORD JOSEPH, III, broadcaster, marketing consultant; b. Chgo., Aug. 31, 1950; s. Clifford Joseph Jr. and Melva (Niles) B.; m. Karen Diane Judd, Aug. 8, 1996; children: Jason, Tara, Brett, Christopher. A, Ricks Coll., Rexburg, Idaho, 1973; student, Brigham Young U., 1973-74. Dir. student devel. assn. Ricks Coll., 1974-75; account exec. WHO-TV, Des Moines, 1976-80, KSL-TV and Radio, Salt Lake City, 1980-87; v.p. Advt. Mgmt. Svcs., Salt Lake City, 1987-89; sales mgr. KBCK Radio, Salt Lake City, 1989-90; broadcaster KBBK Radio, Rupert, Idaho, 1990-93; broadcaster, cons. Tri-Market Broadcasting, Rupert, 1993—; mktg. cons. Minidoka Meml. Hosp., Rupert, 1992—. Mem. Iowa Advt. Fedn., Utah Advt. Fedn., Utah Sales and Mktg. Assn., Kiwanis, Rupert C. of C. Avocations: baseball, racquetball, poetry, music. Home: PO Box 612 Burley ID 83318-0612 Office: Tri-Market Broadcasting Inc 120 S 300 W Rupert ID 83350-9667

BARCA, GEORGE GINO, winery executive, financial investor; b. Sacramento, Jan. 28, 1937; s. Joseph and Annie (Muschetto) B.; m. Maria Sclafani, Nov. 19, 1960; children—Anna, Joseph, Gina and Nina (twins). A.A., Grant Jr. Coll.; student LaSalle U., 1963. With United Vintners, U.S.A., St. Helena, Napa Valley, Calif., 1960—; pres., gen. mgr. Barcamerica U.S.A., Barca Wine Cellars, Calif. Wine Cellars, U.S.A., Calif. Grape Growers, U.S.A., Calif. Vintage Wines, U.S.A., Am. Vintners, U.S.A. Gen. trustee Barca Investment Trust, U.S.A. Named Best Producer of Sales and Fin. Investments, United Vintners, U.S.A. Roman Catholic. Club: KC. Developer wine trademarks and brands.

BARCA, KATHLEEN, marketing executive; b. Burbank, Calif., July 26, 1946; d. Frank Allan and Blanch Irene (Griffith) Barnes; m. Gerald Albino Barca, Dec. 8, 1967 (dec. May 1993); children: Patrick Gerald, Stacia Kathleen. Student, Pierce Coll., 1964; B in Bus., Hancock Coll., 1984. Teller Security Pacific Bank, Pasadena, Calif., 1968-69, Bank Am., Santa Maria, Calif., 1972-74; operator Gen. Telephone Co., Santa Maria, Calif., 1974-83, supr. operator, 1983-84; account exec. Sta. KRQK/KLLB Radio, Lompoc, Calif., 1984-85; owner Advt. Unltd., Orcutt, Calif., 1986-88; regional mgr. A.L. Williams Mktg. Co., Los Alamos, Calif., 1988-89; supr. Matol Botanical Internat., 1989-91; account exec. Santa Maria Times, 1989-95. Author: numerous local TV and radio commercials, print advt. Activist Citizens Against Dumps in Residential Environments, Polit. Action Com., Orcutt and Santa Maria; chmn. Community Action Com. Santa Maria Workshop EPA, Calif. Div., Dept. Health Svcs. State of Calif.; vice coord. Toughlove, Santa Maria, 1988-89; parent coord., mem. steering com. ASAP and Friends, 1988-89; mem. Sloco Access, 1997—; mem. Friends San Luis Obispo Bot. Gardens, 1997—. Mem. NAFE, Womens Network-Santa Maria, Ctrl. Coast Ad (recipient numerous awards), Santa Maria C. of C. (amb. representing Santa Maria Times 1990-94, asst. chief amb. 1993-94). Democrat. Avocations: raising exotic birds, writing childrens books. Home: 850 Golf Club Rd Lake Almanor CA 96137-9524

BARCLAY, JOHN ALLEN, lawyer; b. L.A., Feb. 14, 1951; s. George H. and Shirley Iris (Handler) B. AA, L.A. Valley Coll., 1970; BA, U. Southern Calif., 1972, JD, 1975. Bar: Calif. 1975, U.S. Dist. Ct. (cen., ea., and no. dists.) Calif. 1976, U.S. Ct. Appeals (9th cir.) 1976, U.S. Tax Ct. 1976, U.S. Ct. Claims, 1995. Prin. Barclay & Brestoff, Encino, 1978-80, Barclay & Moskatel, Beverly Hills, Calif., 1980-82, Barclay Law Corp., Newport Beach, Calif., 1982—; instr. U. Calif.-Irvine, 1985-87, UCLA, 1982-85, L.A. Valley Coll., Van Nuys, 1980-82. Author: Exchanging in the '80's, 1986, Accumulating Wealth, 1987, Insurance for Environmental Claims Against Bankruptcy Estates, 1992, Deducting Your Down Payment, 1984; contbr. articles to profl. jours. Mem. adv. bd. Calif. State U.; dir., sec. Orange County Nat. Conf. Christians and Jews; dir. Parent Help USA. Mem. ABA, Legion Lex (bd. dirs. Orange County chpt. 1987-95, pres. 1992), Masons (master Hollywood chpt. 1982). Jewish. Avocations: sailing, scuba. Office: Barclay Law Corp 5000 Birch St Ste 2900 Newport Beach CA 92660-2139

BARDACH, SHELDON GILBERT, lawyer; b. Holyoke, Mass., Sept. 4, 1937; s. Arthur Everett and Ruth (Goodstein) B.; m. Martha Robson, June 7, 1970; 1 child, Noah Arthur. AB, Bklyn. Coll., 1958; JD, UCLA, 1961. Bar: Calif. 1962. Pvt. practice Beverly Hills, Calif., 1962-67, Century City, Calif., 1967-85; sr. mem. Law Offices Sheldon G. Bardach, L.A., 1969—; bd. dirs. Mambo Films, Inc.; arbitrator L.A. Superior Ct., 1979—; gen. counsel Century Artists, Ltd.; mem. nat. and internat. panels arbitrators Am. Arbitration Assn. Bd. editors Law in Transition Quar., 1967; contbr. articles to profl. jours. Bd. govs. Studio Watts Workshop, 1963-71; founder, bd. dirs. UCLA Sch. Law, 1968. Recipient Lubin award Sch. Law UCLA, 1961, Bancroft-Whitney award UCLA Sch. Law, , 1961. Mem. ABA, Calif. Bar Assn., Beverly Hills Bar Assn. (bd. govs. varristers 1964-69), Am. Arbitration Assn., UCLA Law Sch. Alumni Assn. (bd. dirs. 1991-94), L.A. County Bar Assn., Assn. Trial Lawyers Am., Comml. Law League Am., Vikings of Scandia, Zeta Beta Tau, Phi Alpha Delta. Democrat. Jewish. Office: 11755 Wilshire Blvd Ste 1450 Los Angeles CA 90025-1543*

BARDSLEY, KAY, historian, archivist, dance professional; b. Port Said, Egypt, Apr. 17, 1921; came to U.S., 1929; d. Chris and Helen (Jones) Lanitis; m. James Calvert Bardsley, May 30, 1947 (wid. Sept. 1978); children: Wendy Jane, Amy Kim; m. Donald Marshall Kuhn, Feb. 25, 1990. Student, Duncan Dance Tng./Carnegie, Hall, Steinway Hall Studios, N.Y.C., 1931-42; BA cum laude, Hunter Coll., 1942. Dance debut Maria-Theresa Duncan, N.Y.C., 1934; soloist Maria-Theresa Heliconiades, N.Y.C., 1936-42; Duncan tchr. Maria-Theresa Sch., N.Y.C., 1937-46; tchr. Creative Dance for Children, N.Y.C., 1960-66, Isadora Duncan-Maria-Theresa Heritage Group, N.Y.C., 1977-81; fashion editor Woman's Day, N.Y.C., 1943-45; TV work WPIX Gloria Swanson Hour, 1948-49; writer TV Guide, 1949; writer/producer ABC Network/Don Ameche Langford Show, 1949-50; syndicated film series producer, 1950-60; producer video documentation of Duncan Repertory, 1976-80. Writer, lectr. in field; prodr.: (documentary) The Last Isadorable, 1988, re-issued, 1997; contbr. articles to profl. dance jours. and publs. including Dance Scope, 1977, Ballet Rev., 1991, 94; most recent works in field include ReAnimations of Duncan Masterworks, A Four-year Project, presented at Dance ReConstructed Conf., Rutgers U., 1992, numerous conf. presentations and documentation of Isadora Duncan's 1st sch.; pub. by Congress for Rsch. in Dance Ann., 1979; resident dancer scholar U. Oreg., Eugene, 1997-98. Trustee Coun. for the Arts in Westchester, N.Y., 1973-76; bd. dirs. Bicentennial Com., Chappaqua, N.Y., 1973-76; co-chmn. Community Day, 1973, 75. Grantee NEA, N.Y.C., 1980; pioneer NYU/Master Tchr. Dance Tng. Inst., 1987; recipient 1997-98 Creativity award in Dance U. Oreg. Mem. Soc. Dance History Scholars, Am. Dance Guild, World Dance Alliance, Dance Critics Assn. (bd. dirs. 1997—), Isadora Duncan Internat. Inst. (dir., founder 1978-99). Office: Isadora Duncan Internat. Inst. 6305 S Geneva Cir Englewood CO 80111-5437

BAREFOOT, LINDA, pharmaceutical company manager; b. Pensacola, Fla., Jan. 10, 1953; d. Paul and Emma Louise (Barnard) B. AA, Jacksonville (Fla.) C.C., 1973; student, Fla. Atlantic U., 1976; BS summa cum laude, U. North Fla., 1981. Med. staff asst. Shands Tchg. Hosp., U. Fla., Gainesville, 1974-76; med. asst. Edwin A. Sapp, MD, Jacksonville, Fla., 1976-81; hosp. sales specialist Eli Lilly & Co., Jacksonville and Gainesville, Fla., 1981-85, Am. Critical Care, Jacksonville and Gainesville, Fla., 1985-86; hosp. sales rep. specialist DuPont Merck Pharm. Co., Jacksonville and Gainesville, Fla., 1986-90; clin. liaison in clin. devel. and edn. DuPont Merck Pharm. Co., Fla., Ga., N.C., S.C., 1990-92; dist. sales mgr. DuPont Merck Pharm. Co., Knoxville, 1992-94; govt. affairs mgr. DuPont Merck Pharm. Co., Farmington, Conn., 1994—; lobbyist for med. industry; mem. healthcare reform coms. Singer in choir Congl. Ch. of Christ. Avocations: golf, snow skiing, travel, reading, singing. Home and Office: 562 Brainard Cir Lafayette CO 80026-3407

BARELA, BERTHA CICCI, elementary education educator, artist; b. McKeesport, Pa., June 13, 1913; d. James and Julia (Kolesar) Faix; m. John Slebodnik, June 23, 1934 (dec. 1967); children: Dolores S. Garvis, James, John, Judith Greene, Jane Minda, William, Cynthia Lombardi, Rosemary Lewis, Martha Williams; m. Amerigo Cicci, May 25, 1974 (dec. 1975); m. Abran Barela, Dec. 8, 1984 (div. Nov. 1992). BA, Seton Hill Coll., 1970. Elem. tchr. Blessed Sacrament Sch., Greensburg, Pa., 1967-74; ind. artist, clown Phoenix, 1985—; asst. pre-sch. tchr. Sunnyslope Ctr.; guest art tchr. various schs., 1980-90; Westmoreland (Pa.) County Girl Scout Leader; internat. del. St. Louis; tchrs. aide, 1996-98. Formerly news and mag. writer; numerous commissioned art works. Dep. registrar Maricopa County, Phoenix, 1983-86, election bd. worker, 1980-97; Dem. committeewoman, election worker, Pa., 1960-73, Phoenix, 1980—. Mem. Sunnyslope Recreation Ctr. (adv. bd. 1998). Avocation: performing as Lollipop the Clown. Home: 841 E Cinnabar Ave Phoenix AZ 85020-1732

BARGER, LOUISE BALDWIN, religious organization administrator; b. Mexia, Tex., Nov. 7, 1938; d. Curtis Arthur and Vada Irene (Barker) Baldwin; m. Billy Joe Barger, June 15, 1957; children: Kenneth Gene, Keith Dean, Kimberly Ann Barger Moeller. BS, Tex. Woman's U., 1961; MS in Nursing, St. Louis U., 1974, PhD in Higher Edn., 1981; MRE, So. Bapt. Theol. Sem., 1982. Ordained to ministry Am. Bapt. Chs. in U.S.A., 1986. Faculty Mo. Bapt. Hosp. Sch. Nursing, 1973, St. Louis U., 1974-80; min. Christian edn., mem. pastoral staff 3d Bapt. Ch., St. Louis, 1980-86; dir. leader devel. Am. Bapt. Chs. Pa. and Del., Valley Forge, Pa., 1986-93; interim dir. evangelism and social concern Am. Bapt. Chs. Pa. and Del., Valley Forge, 1989-91; exec. min. Am. Bapt. Chs. of the Rocky Mountains, 1993—; mem. Christian edn. com., Area V, Gt. Rivers region, Am. Bapt. Chs. Mo., and Am. Bapt. Chs. U.S.A., 1981-86; Handicapped Ministry, Home Mission Bd. So. Bapt. Conv., 1983; mem. Mins. Coun., Am. Bapt. Conv., U.S.A., Am. Bapt. Chs., U.S.A. Author: Growing through the Sunday School: A Sourcebook for Sunday School Growth, 1988; co-author: New and Renewed Churches: A Time of Prayer and Preparation for Invitation to New Life, 1991, New and Renewed Churches: A Time of Invitation ti New Life, 1992; contbr. Bapt. Leader. Mem. Handicapped Ministry Home Mission Bd., So. Bapt. Conv., 1983. Recipient Richard Hoiland citation Am. Bapt. Chs. U.S.A.; grantee Fund of Renewal Am. Bapt. Chs. U.S.A., 1980, Hazle Fund, 1984. Mem. Religious Edn. Assn., Assn. Profs. and Researchers in Religious Edn. Office: Am Bapt Ch Rocky Mts 3900 S Wadsworth Blvd Ste 365 Denver CO 80235-2220

BARKER, CELESTE ARLETTE, computer scientist; b. Redding, Calif., Apr. 19, 1947; d. Edwin Walter Squires and Rachel (Kinkead) Layton; m. Julius Jeep Chernak, Sept. 13, 1970, (div. 1980); children: Sean Matthew, Bret Allen; m. Jackson Lynn Barker, Oct. 8, 1988. BA in Art, San Francisco State U., 1970; AA in Engring. Tech., Coll. Marin, 1980; MBA in Mgmt., Golden Gate U., 1988. Cert. netware engr. Art tchr. San Rafael (Calif.) Schs., 1971-75; owner, photographer Julius Chernak Photography, Novato, Calif., 1970-76; draftsman Donald Foster Drafting, San Rafael, 1975-76; surveyor Parks Dept. State Calif., Inverness, 1976; electric draftsman Pacific Gas & Electric, San Rafael, 1976-78, electric engring. estimator, 1978-79; mktg. rep. Pacific Gas & Electric, Santa Rosa, 1980-85; valuation analyst Pacific Gas & Electric, San Francisco, 1985-86, budget analyst, 1986-88, budget system project mgr., 1988-89; fin. asset mgr. Pacific Gas & Electric, Vallejo, Calif., 1989-90; ops. mgr. San Francisco Mus. Modern Art, 1990-91; cons. CB Cons., Atlanta, 1991-93; computer local area network mgr. Ga. Inst. Tech., Atlanta, 1993-94; systems integrator Bank South, Atlanta, 1994-95; mgmt. info. sys. mgr. Dinwiddie Constr., San

Francisco, Calif., 1995-96; process/project mgr. Sybase, Inc., Emeryville, Calif., 1996-98; Wintel delivery mgr. Fair-Isaac Cos., San Rafael, Calif., 1998—. Dir. Mariner Green Townhomes Assn., treas. 1987-88. Mem. Sierra Club. Avocations: photography, painting, backpacking. Home: 114 Mariner Green Dr Corte Madera CA 94925

BARKER, DOUGLAS P., food products executive; b. 1935. With Sunkist Growers, Van Nuys, Calif., 1961-78, Sun World Internat. Inc., Bakersfield, Calif., 1978-81, 84—, Blue Anchor, Sacramento, Calif., 1981-84. Office: Sun World Internat Inc PO 80298 Bakersfield CA 93380-0298*

BARKER, ELVER AMOS, artist, educator, social change activist; b. Newcastle, Wyo., Jan. 2, 1920; s. Jessie Amos and Opal Rhoada (Roadifer) B. AB, U. Denver, 1943; studied with, Arthur W. Palmer, Thomas Leighton, San Francisco, Daniel Greene, Merlin Enabnit, Ben Konis, Mel Fillerup, George Cherepov. Former elem. sch. tchr.; formerly with Am. Friends Svc. Com., Fellowship of Reconciliation, United World Federalists; instr. art, 1962—. Author: Finger Painting in Oils, 1968. Bd. dirs., mem. editl. bd. Mattachine Soc., San Francisco, 1954-60. Mem. Fellowship of Reconciliation, War Resisters League, Rocky Mountain Skeptics, Human Rights Campaign, Rainbow Vegetarians. Home and Studio: Timberline Art Studio 1315 Columbine St Apt 105 Denver CO 80206-2350

BARKER, ROBERT WILLIAM, television personality; b. Darrington, Wash., Dec. 12, 1923; s. Byron John and Matilda Kent (Tarleton) B.; m. Dorothy Jo Gideon, Jan. 12, 1945 (dec. Oct. 1981). BA in Econs. summa cum laude, Drury Coll., 1947. Master of ceremonies: Truth or Consequences, Hollywood, Calif., 1957-75, Price is Right, 1972—, Miss Universe Beauty Pageant, 1966-87, Miss U.S.A. Beauty Pageant, 1966-87, Pillsbury Bake-Off, 1969-85, Bob Barker Fun and Games Show, 1978—; host: Rose Parade, CBS, 1969-88; appeared in (feature film) Happy Gilmore, 1996. Served to lt. (j.g.) USNR, 1943-45. Recipient Emmy award for Best Audience Participation Host, 1981-82, 82-83, 86-87, 87-88, 89-90, 90-91, 91-92, 93-94, 94-95, 95-96. Mem. AGVA, AFTRA, Screen Actors Guild. Office: The Price is Right care CBS TV 7800 Beverly Blvd Los Angeles CA 90036-2112

BARKER, VERLYN LLOYD, retired minister, educator; b. Auburn, Nebr., July 25, 1931; s. Jack Lloyd and Olive Clara (Bollman) B. AB, Doane Coll., 1952, DD, 1977; BD, Yale U., 1956, STM, 1960; postgrad., U. Chgo., 1960-61; PhD, St. Louis U., 1970. Ordained to ministry United Ch. of Christ, 1956. Instr. history, chaplain Doane Coll., Crete, Nebr., 1954-55; pastor U. Nebr., 1956-59; sec. ministry higher edn. United Ch. Bd. Homeland Ministries, N.Y.C., 1961-96; ret. United Ch. Bd. Homeland Ministries, Cleve., 1996. Author: Health and Human Values: A Ministry of Theological Inquiry and Moral Discourse, 1987; editor: The Church and the Public School, 1980, Science, Technology and the Christian Faith, 1990; contbg. author: Campus Ministry, 1964; mem. editorial adv. com. Jour. Current Social Issues; contbr. articles to various publs. Pres. United Ministries in Higher Edn., N.Y.C., 1971-77. Mem. AAAS, ACLU, Am. Assn. Higher Edn., Am. Studies Assn., Acad. Polit. Sci., Am. Acad. Polit. and Social Sci., Soc. Health and Human Values, Doane Coll. Alumni Assn. (pres. 1957-58), Nat. Assn. for Sci., Tech. and Soc., Yale Club.

BARKIN, ELAINE RADOFF, composer, music educator; b. N.Y.C., Dec. 15, 1932; m. George J. Barkin, Nov. 28, 1957; 3 children. BA in Music, Queens Coll., 1954, MFA in Composition, 1956; PhD in Composition and Theory, Brandeis U., 1971; Cert. in Composition and Piano, Berlin Hochschule Musik, 1957; studied with Karol Rathaus, Irving Fine, Boris Blacher, Arthur Berger. Lectr. in music Queens Coll., 1964-70, Sarah Lawrence, 1969-70; from asst. to assoc. prof. music theory U. Mich., 1970-74; from asst. prof. to prof. composition and theory U. Calif., L.A., 1974-97; vis. asst. prof. Princeton (N.J.) U., 1974; lectr. in field. Asst. to co-editor: Perspectives of New Music, 1963-85; composer String Quartet, 1969, Sound Play for violin, 1974, String Trio, 1976, Plein Chant, alto flute, 1977, Ebb Tide, 2 vibraphones, 1977, ...the Supple Suitor...for soprano and five players, 1978, (chamber mini opera) De Amore, 1980, Impromptu for violin, cello, piano, 1981, (theatre piece) Media Speak, 1981, At the Piano, piano, 1982, For String Quartet, 1982, Quilt Piece graphic score for 7 instruments, 1984, On The Way To Becoming for 4-track Tape Collage, 1985, Demeter and Persephone for violin, tape, chamber ensemble, dancers, 1986, 3 Rhapsodies, flutes and clarinet, 1986, Encore for Javanese Gamelan Ensemble, 1986, Out of the Air for Basset Horn and Tape, 188, To Whom It May Concern 4 track tape collage, reader and 4 players, 1989, Legong Dreams, oboe, 1990, Gamélange for harp and mixed gamelan band, 1992, Five Tape Collages, Open Space CD #3, 1993, "for my friends' pleasure," soprano and harp, 1994, numerous improvised group and duo sessions on tape; produced cassette and video: New Music in Bali, 1994; "touching all bases" for electronic bass, electronic percussion, and Balinese gamelan, 1996, e: an anthology (music, texts and graphics) 1975-95, (Chamber Music Improvisations) Open Space, 1999. Recipient Fulbright award, 1957, awards NEA, 1975, 79, awards Rockefeller Found., 1980, Meet the Composer award, 1994. Home: 12533 Killion St Valley Village CA 91607

BARKLEY, THIERRY VINCENT, lawyer; b. Paris, Mar. 21, 1955; s. Jacques and Michéline Marié (Rossi) B.; came to U.S., 1967, naturalized, 1974; m. Mary Ellen Gamble, June 18, 1983; children: Richard A., Robert V., Marriah E., Christopher R. BA in Polit. Sci., UCLA, 1976; JD, Calif. Western Sch. Law, San Diego, 1979. Bar: Nev. 1980, U.S. Dist. Ct. Nev. 1982, U.S. Supreme Ct. 1986. Intern, Calif. Ct. Appeals 4th Circuit, San Diego, 1978-79; law clk. Nev. Dist. Ct., 7th Jud. Dist., Ely, 1979-81; assoc. firm C.E. Horton, Ely, 1982-83; asst. city atty. Ely, 1982-83; assoc. firm Barker, Gillock & Perry, Reno, 1983-87, Perry & Spann, 1987-89, ptnr., 1990—. Editor Internat. Law Jour., 1979. Mem. Internat. Moot Ct. Team, 1978; recipient Dean's award Calif. Western Sch. Law, 1979. Mem. Rep. Presdl. Task Force, 1990. Mem. Nev. Bar Assn., Washoe Bar Assn., U.S. Jaycees (past pres. White Pine, Nev.). Republican. Roman Catholic. Lodge: Elks (past treas. Ely club). Office: Perry & Spann 6130 Plumas St Reno NV 89509-6041

BARKLEY, WILLIAM DONALD, museum executive; b. New Westminster, B.C., Can., Apr. 4, 1941; s. Donald MacMillan and Ethel Margaret (Mines) B.; m. Helen Gayle Alanson, Aug. 29, 1964; children: Warren Vincent, Colleen Michelle. BS, U. B.C., 1964, MA, 1971. Cert. tchr. Can. Tchr. Salmon Arm (B.C.) Sr. Secondary Sch., 1965-68; wildlife biologist Wye Marsh Wildlife Ctr., Midland, Ont., Can., 1968-72; chief interpretation Can. Wildlife Svc., Ottawa, Ont., 1972-77; asst. dir. B.C. Provincial Mus., Victoria, 1977-84; CEO Royal BC Mus., Victoria, 1984—; advisor cultural resource mgmt. program U. Victoria, 1985—; lectr. univs. Contbr. articles to Nat. History Interpretation mag., 1965—. Bd. dirs. Tourism Victoria, 1985—. Recipient Disting. Svc. award Interpretation Can., Ottawa, 1983, Can. 125 award for svc. to mus. cmty. Fellow Can. Mus. Assn.; mem. Can. Mus. Assn. (pres. 1987-89), B.C. Mus. Assn., Internat. Coun. of Mus.-Can., Can. Pks. and Wilderness Soc., Can. Nature Fedn., Victoria A.M. Tourism Svcs. Assn. (treas.). Mem. United Ch. Can. Avocations: design and production stained glass, backpacking, skiing, wind surfing, numismatics. Office: Royal BC Mus, PO Box 9815 Stn Prov Govt, Victoria, BC Canada V8W 9W2

BARLOW, JOHN ADEN, lawyer; b. Columbus, Ohio, June 8, 1942; s. William Willard and Eleanore (Johnson) B.; m. Patricia Ann Mowry, Oct. 17, 1970 (div. Aug. 1982); children: William P., Allison J., Jonathan A.; m. Patricia Marion Palmer, Sept. 3, 1982. BSc in Edn., Ohio State U., 1963, JD cum laude, 1968. Bar: Ohio 1969, Wash. 1969, U.S. Dist. Ct. (we. dist.) Wash. 1969. Assoc. Skeel McKelvey Henke Evenson & Betts, Seattle, 1968-70; ptnr. Walstead Mertsching Husemoen Donaldson & Barlow, Longview, Wash., 1970—; mem. Wash. State Ins. Commr.'s Tort Reform Com., 1987. Contbg. author to 2 books. Named Boss of Yr., Cowlitz County Legal Secs. Assn., 1989. Mem. Wash. State Trial Lawyers Assn. (bd. dirs. 1981-90, v.p. for west 1989-90), Cowlitz County Bar Assn. (pres. 1974-75), Longview C. of C. (bd. dirs. 1977-80), Kiwanis (pres. Longview 1973). Democrat. Avocations: golf, antiques. Home: 1506 23d Ave Longview WA 98632-3616 Office: 1000 12th Ave Ste 2 Longview WA 98632-2500

BARLOW, WILLIAM PUSEY, JR., accountant; b. Oakland, Calif., Feb. 11, 1934; s. William P. and Muriel (Block) B.; student Calif. Inst. Tech., 1952-54. AB in Econs., U. Calif.-Berkeley, 1956. CPA, Calif. Acct. Barlow, Davis & Wood, San Francisco, 1960-72, ptnr., 1964-72; ptnr., J.K. Lasser & Co., 1972-77, Touche Ross & Co., San Francisco, 1977-78; self employed acct., 1978-89; ptnr. Barlow & Hughan, 1990—. Co-author: Collectible Books: Some New Paths, 1979, The Grolier Club, 1884-1984, 1984; editor: Book Catalogues: Their Varieties and Uses, 2d edit., 1986, Officially Sealed Notes, 1996—; contbr. articles to profl. jours. Fellow Gleeson Libr. Assocs., 1969, pres., 1971-74; mem. Coun. Friends Bancroft Libr., 1971-98, chmn., 1974-79; bd. dirs. Oakland Ballet, 1982—, pres. 1986-89, chmn. 1995-98. Recipient Sir Thomas More medal Gleeson Libr. Assocs., 1989; named to Water Ski Hall of Fame, 1993. Mem. Am. Water Ski Assn. (bd. dirs., regional chmn. 1959-63, pres. 1963-66, chmn. bd. 1966-69, 77-79, hon. v.p. 1969—), Internat. Water Ski Fedn. (exec. bd. 1961-71, 75-78), Bibliog. Soc. Am. (coun. 1986-92, pres. 1992-96), Grolier Club (N.Y.C.), Roxburghe Club (San Francisco), Book of Calif. Club (bd. dirs. 1963-76, pres. 1968-69, treas. 1971-83). Home: 1474 Hampel St Oakland CA 94602-1346 Office: 449 15th St Oakland CA 94612-2821

BARMAN, ROBERT JOHN, home electronics company executive; b. Glendale, Calif.; s. Robert Grant and Geraldine (Howe) B.; m. Jean Ann Crane, June 19, 1965; children: John Robert, Jeffrey Wynn. BS in Mktg., Calif. State U., L.A., 1965. Sales coord. Teledyne Packard Bell, L.A., 1965-67; dist. mgr. Teledyne Packard Bell, Fresno, L.A., 1968-71; regional sales mgr. Teledyne Packard Bell, Boston, 1971-73; major accounts sales mgr. Quasar Co., L.A., 1973-75, regional sales mgr., 1975-76, sales mgr., 1976-77, zone mgr., 1985—; v.p., br. mgr. Quasar Co., Seattle, 1977-84; gen. mgr. Matsushita, L.A., 1985-95; mem. mgmt. com. Matsushita Elec. Corp. of Am. West; mem. distbg. coun. Quasar Co., Chgo.; mgr. spl. markets, region mgr., gen. mgr. Panasonic Co. West, 1995—. Bd. dirs. Irvine (Calif.) Aquatics Swim Team, Bellevue (Wash.) Athletic Club Swim Team. Office: Panasonic Co W 6550 Katella Ave Cypress CA 90630-5102

BARNARD, ANNETTE WILLIAMSON, elementary school educator; b. Phoenix, Nov. 29, 1948; d. Water Albert and Geraldine Williamson; m. Richard W. Heinrich, Sept. 1969 (div.); 1 child, Jennifer Anne; m. Charles Jay Barnard, June 6, 1981. AA, Mesa C.C., 1979; BA in Spl. Edn., Elem. Edn., Ariz. State U., 1981, postgrad., 1989; M in Edn. Leadership, 1996, No. Ariz. U., 1996. Cert. tchr., prin., Ariz. Tchr. spl. edn. Tempe (Ariz.) Sch. Dist., 1981-83, tchr. Indian community, 1983-84; tchr. elem. sch. Kyrene Sch. Dist., Tempe, 1984-97; sch. dist. mentor coord., 1994-96; tchr. Chandler (Ariz.) Sch. Dist., 1986-89; v.p. Pendergast Elem. Sch., Phoenix, 1997-98; chair profl. stds. and cert. com. Ariz. Bd. Edn., Phoenix, 1990-94; chair facilitator Kyrene Legis. Action Community, 1991-94; mentor Kyrene Sch. dist., 1990—; commencement spkr. Ariz. State U., 1981; design. team. mem. Quality Cert. Employee Appraisal System; speaker in field. Contbg. author: Environmental Education Compendium for Energy Resources, 1991, System of Personnel Development, 1989; contbr. articles to profl. jours. Bd. dirs. Ariz. State Rep. Caucus, Phoenix, 1990-93, precinct committeewoman, Tempe, 1990-92. Recipient Profl. Leadership award Kiwanis Club Am., Tempe, 1984; nominee to talent bank Coun. on Women's Edn. Programs U.S. Dept. Edn., 1982; named Tchr. of Yr., local newspaper, 1993. Mem. ASCD, Kyrene Edn. Assn. (chair legis. com. 1990-94), Kappa Delta Pi, Phi Kappa Phi, Phi Theta Kappa, Pi Lambda Theta. Featured in PBS Cornerstones video, 1994. Home: 3221 W Jasper Dr Chandler AZ 85226-1421

BARNARD, ROLLIN DWIGHT, retired financial executive; b. Denver, Apr. 14, 1922; s. George Cooper and Emma (Riggs) B.; m. Patricia Reynolds Bierkamp, Sept. 15, 1943; children: Michael Dana, Rebecca Susan (Mrs. Paul C. Wulfestieg), Laurie Beth (Mrs. Kenneth J. Kostelecky). B.A., Pomona Coll., 1943. Clk. Morey Merc. Co., Denver, 1937-40; ptnr George C. Barnard & Co. (gen. real estate and ins.), Denver, 1946-47; v.p. Foster & Barnard, Inc., 1947-53; instr. Denver U., 1949-53; dir. real estate U.S. P.O. Dept., Washington, 1953-55, dep. asst. postmaster gen., bur. facilities, 1955-59, asst. postmaster gen., 1959-61; pres., dir. Midland Fed. Savs. & Loan Assn., Denver, 1962-84; vice chmn. Bank Western Fed. Savs. Bank, 1984-87; vice chmn., pres. Western Capital Investment Corp., 1985-87. Mayor City of Greenwood Village, Colo., 1989-93, chmn. Planning and Zoning Commn., 1969-73, mem. coun., 1975-77; pres. Denver Area coun. Boy Scouts Am., 1970-71, mem. exec. bd., 1962-73; mem. adv. bd. Denver Area coun. Boy Scouts Am., 1973—; bd. dirs. Downtown Denver Improvement Assn., pres., 1965; bd. dirs. Bethesda Found., Inc., 1973-82, Children's Hosp., 1979-84, treas., 1983-84; bd. dirs. Children's Health Corp., Inc., 1982-93; trustee Mile High United Fund, 1969-72, Denver Symphony Assn., 1973-74; bd. dirs. Colo. Coun. Econ. Edn., 1971-80, chmn. 1971-76; trustee, v.p., treas. Morris Animal Found., 1969-81, pres., chmn. 1974-78, trustee emeritus, 1981—; trustee Denver Zool. Found., 1994—, exec. v.p. 1996—; mem. acquisitions com. Friends Found. Denver Pub. Libr., 1994—; mem. dir. Wings over the Rockies Air & Space Mus. Found., 1998—. Nominated One of Ten Outstanding Young Men in Am., U.S. Jaycees, 1955, 57; recipient Disting. Svc. award Postmaster Gen. U.S., 1960; Silver Beaver award Boy Scouts Am., 1969; named Outstanding Citizen of Yr., Sertoma, 1982, Colo. Citizen of Yr., Colo. Assn. Realtors, 1982, Citizen of West, Nat. Western Stockshow, 1994. Mem. Greater Denver C. of C. (pres. 1966-67), U.S. League Savs. Instns. (bd. dirs. 1972-77, vice chmn. 1979-80, chmn. 1980-81, mem. nat. legis. com., exec. com. 1974-77), Savs. League Colo. (exec. com. 1969-73, pres. 1971-72), Colo. Assn. Commerce and Industry (dir. 1971-76), Fellowship Christian Athletes (Denver area dir. 1963-76), Western Stock Show Assn. (dir. 1971—, exec. com. 1982-94, 1st v.p. 1985-94), Mountain and Plains Appaloosa Horse Club (pres. 1970-71), Roundup Riders of the Rockies (bd. dirs. 1979—, treas. 1980-87, v.p. 1987-89, pres.-elect 1989-91, pres. 1991-93). Republican. Presbyterian. Home: 3151 E Long Rd Greenwood Village CO 80121-1716

BARNARD, WILLIAM MARION, psychiatrist; b. Mt. Pleasant, Tex., Dec. 17, 1949; s. Marion Jaggers and Med (Cody) B. BA, Yale U., 1972; MD, Baylor U., 1976. Diplomate Am. Bd. Psychiatry and Neurology. Resident NYU/Bellevue Med. Ctr., 1976-79; liaison, consultation fellow L.I. Jewish/Hillside Med. Ctr., 1979-80; chief, liaison, consultation psychiatrist Queens (N.Y.) Med. Ctr., 1980-83; liaison, consultation psychiatrist Mt. Sinai Med. Ctr., N.Y.C., 1983-84; clin. asst. prof. NYU Med. Sch., N.Y.C., 1984-87; emergency psychiatrist VA Med. Ctr., N.Y.C., 1984-87; pvt. practice Pasadena, Calif., 1987—; chief psychiat. svc. Las Encinas Hosp., Pasadena, 1989, chief staff, 1990, med. dir. gen. adult. psychiat. svc., 1990-92, asst. med. dir., 1992; med. dir. BHC Alhambra Hosp., Rosemead, Calif., 1992—. Chmn. mental health com. All Saints AIDS Svc. Ctr., Pasadena, 1990-94, bd. dirs., 1991-94; bd. dirs. Pasadena Symphony, 1989-97, v.p., 1996-97; bd. dirs. Whiffenpoof Alumni, New Haven, 1991—, haberdasher, 1995—. Wilson scholar Yale U., 1973. Mem. NYU-Bellevue Psychiat. Assn., Am. Soc. Addiction Medicine, Calif. Med. Assn., So. Calif. Psychiat. Soc., Acad. Psychosomatic Medicine, L.A. County Med. Assn., Amateur Comedy Club N.Y.C., Met. Opera Club, Yale Club N.Y.C., Univ. Glee Club of N.Y.C., Order of St. John (knight). Republican. Episcopalian. Office: 2810 E Del Mar Blvd Ste 11B Pasadena CA 91107-4323

BARNDOLLAR, DONALD LEE, engineering professional; b. Urbana, Ill., May 23, 1954; s. James Walter and Betty Mae (Matsler) B. Student, Ill. State U., 1972-75; Assoc. degree, Heald Bus. Coll., Concord, Calif., 1993. Head danish dept. Epplers Bakery, San Francisco, 1981-89; lab. supr. Smith-Emery Co., San Francisco, 1993—. Recipient tuition award Senator Weaver, Ill., 1972. Avocations: collecting art, movies, reading, auctions, Egyptology. Office: Smith-Emery Co Hunters Point Shipyard 114 San Francisco CA 94188

BARNER, C. HENRY, confectioner; b. Jackson Center, Pa., Jan. 14, 1935; s. Charles Walter and Henrietta (Turner) B. BS, Pa. State U., 1961; MHA, Med. Coll. Va., 1963. Staff assoc. Am. Hosp. Assn., Chgo., 1963-66; cons. Booz, Allen & Hamilton, Chgo., 1966-68, assoc., 1968-75, v.p., 1975-76; owner Liled's Candy Kitchen, Vallejo, Calif., 1976—. Pres. Black Point Improvement Club, Novato, Calif., 1980—; bd. dirs. Novato Fire Protection Dist., 1989-97; mem. Marin Local Agy. Formation Commn., San Rafael, Calif., 1995-97. With USN, 1954-58. Fellow Royal Soc. Health; mem. No. Calif. Ice Cream Mfg. Assn. (pres. 1979-80), Calif. Ice Cream Assn. (pres. 1980-81). Republican. Episcopalian. Avocations: local politics, hiking, reading, gardening. Home: 427 Grandview Ave Novato CA 94945-3518 Office: Liled's Ice Cream & Candy Kitchen 1318 Tennessee St Vallejo CA 94590-4625

BARNES, CLOYD RAY, sculptor, retired engineer; b. Hartford, Ark., July 18, 1934; s. Cloyd Hiram and Esta Elizabeth (McCafferty) B.; m. Wanda Jean Carlton, Oct. 17, 1954; children: Mark E., Stephanie Barnes Veasman. BS in Physics, Tulsa U., 1968. Mem. tech. staff N.Am. Rockwell, Tulsa, 1964-68; sr. aerosystems engr. Gen. Dynamics, Alamogordo, N.Mex., 1968-72; mgr. project engrng. Dynalectron Corp., Alamogordo, 1972-77; mgr. ops. dept. Dynalectron Corp., Alamagordo, 1977-80, tech. dir. radar backscatter divsn., 1980-84, tech. dir., site mgr., 1984-86; mgr. radio frequency test ops. Martin Marietta Denver Aerospace, 1986-89, dept. staff engr., 1989-91; represented by numerous galleries, including Fenn Galleries, Santa Fe, Knox Galleries, Vail and Beaver Creek, Colo.; interim instr. Denver Art Students League, 1994. Exhibited in group shows at Southeastern Wildlife Expo, Charleston, S.C., Nat. Acad. Design, N.Y.C., Audubon Show, N.Y.C., Am. Artists Profl. League, N.Y.C., (Helen G. Oehler award), 1991, Nat. Wildlife Show, Kansas City, 1993 (Best of Show), Cantigny Park, Chgo., BCCFA Show, Clifton, Tex. (Best of Show award), Western Regional Show, Cheyenne, Wyo., N.Am. Sculpture Exhibit, Golden, Colo., Rough Rider Art Show, Williston, N.D., 1993 (Grand Prize 1993), Ho. Reps. Office Bldg.-Rotunda, Washington, 1994, Am. Artists Profl. League, 1994 (Leila G. Sawyer award), Visual Individualists United, Bklyn., 1995 (Grumbacher Gold Medallion award), Pacific Rim Wildlife Art Show, Seattle, Wash.; commissioned works include life-size bronze portrait figure of C.L. Tutt, Colo. Coll., Colorado Springs, 1992, monumental bronze running buffalo Buffalo Run Golf Course, Adams County, Colo., 1996. Mem. IEEE, Rocky Mountain Elk Found. (assoc.), Allied Artists Am. (assoc.), Knickerbocker Artists (assoc.). Avocations: hunting, hiking, travel, reading. Home and Studio: 7425 S Milwaukee Way Littleton CO 80122-1951

BARNES, GEORGE E., investment company executive. Co-founder, ptnr. Wayne Hummer & Co., 1932—. Author: Personal Security, 1932. Developer internat. women's tennis competition, 1923; pres. Chgo. Tennis Assn. 1945-46, Nat. Tennis Ednl. Found, 1958-66, River Forest Tennis Club, 1960-61; pres., co-founder Chgo. Tennis Patrons; v.p. We. Tennis Assn., 1947-48; co-creator George E. Barnes Family Tennis Ctr. of San Diego. Recipient Samuel Hardy award Internat. Hall of Fame, 1961; named Sportsman of Yr., Chgo. Press, 1961, Citizen of Yr., 1996, City of San Diego, 1996. Mem. U.S. Tennis Assn. (pres. 1960-61, 50 Years Svc. award 1996). N.Y. Stock Exchange (oldest living mem.). also: 46730 Amir Dr Palm Desert CA 92260

BARNES, GERALD R., bishop; b. Phoenix, Ariz., June 22, 1945. Grad., St. Leonard Sem., Dayton, Ohio; student, Assumption-St. John's Sem., San Antonio. Ordained priest Roman Cath. Ch., 1975, titular bishop of Monte Fiascone. Aux. bishop San Bernardino, Calif., 1992-95, bishop, 1996—; Chmn. com. Hispanic affairs Nat. Conf. Cath. Bishops. Office: 1201 E Highland Ave San Bernardino CA 92404-4607

BARNES, JOANNA, author, actress; b. Boston, Nov. 15, 1934; d. John Pindar and Alice Weston (Mutch) B. BA, Smith Coll., 1956. Actress appearing in motion pictures: Auntie Mame, 1958, B.S. I Love You, 1971, Spartacus, 1963, The Parent Trap, 1961, The War Wagon, 1971, The Parent Trap, 1998; TV appearances include What's My Line, The Tonight Show with Johnny Carson, Merv Griffin Show, Trials of O'Brien, Dateline: Hollywood, Murder She Wrote; book reviewer L. A. Times, syndicated columnist Chgo. Tribune, N.Y. News Syndicate, 1963-65; author: Starting from Scratch, 1968, The Deceivers, 1970, Who Is Carla Hart, 1973, Pastora, 1980, Silverwood, 1985. Mem. Phi Beta Kappa.

BARNES, LARRY BURDETTE, career officer; b. Velasco, Tex., Jan. 25, 1946; s. Earle Burdette and Lucile (Seamster) B.; m. Cynthia Grace Hill, Oct. 1, 1972; children: Benjamin Earle, Laura Grace. BS in Biology & Chemistry, Tex. Christian U., 1968; postgrad., Baylor Coll. Medicine, 1972. Commd. 2d lt. USMC, 1975, advanced through grades to col., 1996; retired, 1998; sr. analyst Kapos Assocs. Inc., San Diego, Calif., 1998—. Decorated Bronze Star, Defense Meritorious Svc. medal, Meritorious Svc. medal, Legion of Merit Armed Forces Expeditionary medal. Mem. VFW, Marine Corps Assn., Amateur Radio Relay League. Avocations: amateur radio, aviation, scuba diving, astronomy, history. Home: 3988 Syme Dr Carlsbad CA 92008-3569 Office: Kapos Assoc Inc San Diego CA 92108

BARNES, RAYMOND EDWARD, fire department official; b. Denver, Colo., May 1, 1950; s. Carroll E. and Margaret A. (Minckler) B.; m. Katherine Michele Sanchez, Jan. 3, 1970; 1 child, Tamara Adrienne. BS in Aerospace Tech., Bus., Edn., Met. State Coll., 1971; postgrad., Red Rocks C.C., 1974-75, U. No. Colo., 1976; grad. exec. fire officer program, Nat. Fire Acad., 1990; MPA, U. Colo., 1991. With City of Aurora (Colo.) Fire Dept., 1971—, paramedic and rescue technician, 1976-79, lt., 1979-82, capt., 1982-85, battalion chief, suppression, 1985-87, dir. tng., 1987-91, fire chief, 1991—; adj. instr. Nat. Fire Acad., Md., 1987—; co-dir. Rocky Mountain Fire Acad.; metro co-chair Region VIII Tng. Resources and Data Exch. Active Aurora Gang Task Force; past committeeman, del. to county, state polit. assemblies;. Mem. Internat. Assn. Fire Chiefs (com. on terrorism), Internat. Assn. Metro Fire Chiefs (bd. mem.), Internat. Soc. Fire Svc. Instrs., Internat. Assn. Firefighters (occupl. safety and health com.), Instn. Fire Engrs., Soc. Nat. Fire Acad. Instrs., Soc. Exec. Fire Officers, Fire Dept. Safety Officers Orgn., State Fire Chiefs, Denver Metro Fire Chiefs, Aurora C. of C. (bd. dirs. leadership forum), Homeowners Assn. (past pres. bd. dirs.). Avocations: whitewater rafting, mountain biking, world travel, skiing, golf. Home: 3966 S Sable Cir Aurora CO 80014-5176 Office: City of Aurora Fire Dept 1470 S Havana St Aurora CO 80012-4090

BARNES, ROBERT JAMES, small business owner, cosmetologist; b. Washburn, Ill., Jan. 10, 1934; s. John William and Margaret Gladys (Imhoff) B.; m. Norene Davis, Sept. 4, 1955 (div. Jan. 1975); 1 child, Annette. Student, Ill. State U., 1952-53, Bradley U., 1953-56, Denver U., 1973, Purdue U., 1973. Registered cosmetologist, Ill., Tex., Colo.; cert. ins. agt. and broker, Colo. Operator attendant Std. Oil Svc., Washburn, summer 1948; carpenter Barnes Constrn. Co., Washburn, summers 1949-52; with coll. tng. program Caterpillar Tractor Co., Peoria, Ill., 1953-57; pvt. practice registered cosmetologist various locations, 1958-71, pvt. practice profl. model, 1958-73; ins. broker Barnes Ins. Agy., Denver and Salido, Colo., 1973-79; owner Log Cabin Ct. Motel, Salida, 1973—; treas. Colo. Cosmetologist Assn., 1967-72; pres. Denver Cosmetologist Assn., 1968-71; mem. trade and indsl. edn. adv. com. Denver Pub. Schs., 1971-73; Gov. apptd. mem. State Bd. Cosmetology, State of Colo., 1971-73. Sr. ptnr. Ptnrs. Inc., Denver, 1972-73; precinct com. man Rep. Party, Salida, Colo., 1974-80; mem. Chaffee County Ctrl. Com. Rep. Party, 1974-80; pres., adv. Alliance Against Domestic Abuse, Chaffee County, 1993-95. Sgt. U.S. Army, 1953-61. Recipient Cmty. Leadership awards Nat. Hairdressers and Cosmetologist Assn., 1971, Colo. Cosmetologist Assn., 1971, Denver Cosmetologist Assn., 1971, Cert. for Outstanding Advocacy, Alliance Against Domestic Abuse, Chaffee County, 1993, 93, 94, 95, Cert. for Exemplary Svc. and Dedication, Alliance Against Domestic Abuse, 1995. Mem. Nat., State and Local Parents Families and Friends of Lesbians and Gays, Chaffee County Lodgeing Assn., Columbine Gem and Mineral Soc., So. Colo. Consistory (32nd degree), Washburn Lodge #421 AF and AM (3rd degree), Al Kaly Temple (Shrine of N.Am.), SAR (Fla. Soc. SAR ctrl. Fla. chpt.). Avocations: genealogist, leather tooling, gardening, rock hunting. Office: 536 E 1st St Salida CO 81201-2806 also: 6190 Jibway Ct Orlando FL 32807-2928

BARNES, WILLIAM ANDERSON, real estate investment executive; b. Cin., Mar. 11, 1944; s. Frederick Walter and Catherine Gardner (Bowden) B.; m. Sara Winkler, Dec. 13, 1980; children: Tucker, Charlie, Hanne. BA, Yale U., 1966; MBA, Harvard U., 1970; postgrad. in Internat. Econs., Inst. D'Etudes Politiques, Paris, 1993. Adminstrv. asst. to pres. Boise Cascade Corp., Palo Alto, Calif., 1970-71; project gen. mgr. Boise Cascade Corp., Incline Village, Nev., 1971-73; sr. devel. dir. The Rouse Co., Columbia, Md., 1973-76; exec. dir. Pa. Ave. Devel. Corp., Washington, 1977-82; mng. dir. Edward Plant Co., San Francisco, 1982-87; pres. Broadacre Pacific Corp., San Francisco, 1987-92, Barnes and Co., San Francisco, 1992-96; CEO Stapleton Devel. Corp., Denver, 1996—; guest lectr. Harvard Bus. Sch., Cambridge, Mass.; faculty mem. Profl. Devel. Sem.; dist. coun. exec. com. Urban Land Inst.; lectr. Smithsonian Instn., U. San Francisco, mem. adv. coun.; chair Am. Russian Tech. Assn. Trustee Navy Meml. Found., Brichard Properties Trust, S.H. Children's Svcs., Inc., Columbia Interfaith Housing Corp., 1974-76; mem. U.S./USSR Trade Mission, 1975, Bay Area

Coun. Housing Action Task Force, 1983-85, Mill Valley City Gen. Plan Com.; treas. Yale U. Class of 1966. U.S. White House fellow, Washington, 1976, German Marshall Fund fellow, 1979; recipient Presdl. Design award, 1988. Home: 1450 Wynkoop St Denver CO 80202-1116 Office: Barnes and Co Ste 860 One Embarcadero Ctr San Francisco CA 94111

BARNES, WILLIAM DAVID, non-profit charities consultant, publisher; b. Gary, Ind., July 14, 1938; s. Frank J. and Marie M. (Jasorka) B.; m. Suzanne Frost Barnes, June 10, 1961 (div. June 1977); children: Adam Frost, Eric Earl; m. Ellen M. Vager, Dec. 30, 1997. BA in Edn., Ariz. State U., 1960; Cert., Northwestern U., Chgo., 1965. Asst. editor The Arizonian Newspaper, Scottsdale, 1960-61; asst. v.p. First Security Bank, Mesa, Ariz., 1962-65; dir. mktg., v.p. Great Western Bank, Phoenix, 1966-67; dir. alumni fund Ariz. State U., Tempe, 1967-71; pres., sr. editor Barnes Assocs., Inc., Phoenix, Sacramento and Modesto, Calif., 1971—. Author: How to Build Your Development Program, 1973, More on How to Build Your Development Program, 1974, Fund Raiser's Planning and Budgeting Guide, 1976. V.p. United Way, Mesa, 1962; Ariz. bus. chmn. Com. to Re-elect Pres., 1972; cons. to 68 local, state and nat. polit. campaigns, 1960-84 (62 victories); chair pub. rels. com. Ariz. Bankers Assn., 1968. Recipient Nat. 1st pl. award in mktg. Chrysler Corp. Young and Rubicam, 1974, Silver Triange award Am. Advt. Assn., 1977, Exec. Leaders Inst. award Lilly Endowment/Nat. Soc. Fund Raising Execs., 1990, Man of Yr. award for vol. work Rainbow Acres Ranches for Developmentally Challenged, 1982. Mem. Nat. Soc. Fund Raising Execs. (cert., nat. bd. dirs. 1975-78, One of 25 Authors Worldwide Contributing Most to Profession 1985, Outstanding Fund Raising Exec. No. Calif. 1987). Roman Catholic. Avocations: tennis, gardening. Office: Barnes Assocs Inc 1400 K St Ste D1 Modesto CA 95354-1018

BARNETT, CHARLES RADCLIFFE, film writer, producer, director; b. N.Y.C., Feb. 23, 1934; s. Carlyle Reginald and Anne Nathalie (Mooney) B.; m. Noel Ray Phillips, Feb. 3, 1963 (div. 1963). BA, Columbia Coll., 1956; PhD, Union Inst., Cin., 1980. Cert. profl. geologist. Health physicist U. Calif., Los Alamos, N.Mex., 1962-69, writer, producer, dir., 1975-90, head motion picture prodn., 1977-90; video producer, 1990—; lab. assoc. U. Calif., Los Alamos, 1990-94; adj. prof. N.Mex. Highlands U., 1990-93; pvt. practice geol. cons., Woodstock, N.Y., 1971-73; dir., v.p. Anthrop. Film Found., Santa Fe, 1978— ; dir. audio-visuals Albuquerque Mus. Maya Project, 1983-87; Writer, producer, dir. more than 60 documentary films, 1975—, (90 awards); editorial bd. Explorers Jour., 1988-89; contbr. Smithsonian mag., various jours. Mem. N.Mex. Arts Commn. Media Panel, 1978, chmn., 1979, 80. With U.S. Army, 1956-58, Fed. Republic Germany. Recipient film awards, France, Belgium, Italy, Yugoslavia, Fed. Republic Germany, Great Britain, Czechoslovakia, Poland, Egypt, Brazil, 1978—, 19 CINE Golden Eagle awards, Coun. on Internat. Non-theatrical Events, 1978—. Mem. Univ. Film Assn., Am. Film Inst., Rio Grande Producers Assn., Ind. Video and Filmmakers, Am. Inst. Profl. Geologists, Edouard Manet Soc. (Paris, regional v.p. 1967—), Explorers Club of N.Y. (elected to carry flag on expeditions to Guatemala 1985 and Greenland 1988), Quien Sabe Club. Roman Catholic. Home and Office: 331 Calle Loma Norte Santa Fe NM 87501-1256

BARNETT, FILA, artist, executive recruiter; b. Bklyn., Feb. 6, 1945; d. Irwin and Pearl (Geller) Cohen. BA, Keane U., Union, N.J., 1967; student, N.Y. Sch. Interior Design, N.Y.C., 1967-68. Interior/visual designer N.Y.C., 1968-79; pub. Resources, San Diego, 1980-82; video producer San Diego, 1982-85; yoga/stress mgmt. Stress Break, Inc., San Diego, 1985-90; western dir. mktg. Cancer Treatment Ctrs. Am., Brea, Calif., 1991-93; artist, 1993—; exec. recruiter Exec. Search Profls., Inc., Laguna Beach, Calif., 1998—. Mem. docent coun. Orange County Mus. Art. Mem. The Inside Edge. Avocations: swimming, reading, culture, hiking, travel. Home: 330 Cliff Dr Apt 309 Laguna Beach CA 92651-1697

BARNETT, JOHN ARTHUR, art educator, artist; b. Seattle, July 23, 1943; s. Arthur and Virginia Barnett; m. Suellen Wailani Kanapea, Aug. 23, 1966 (div. 1978); children: Malia Anne, Michael John; m. Maria Letitia Gudde, Jan. 17, 1987; children: James Roel William. BA in Art, Western Washington U., 1967; MFA in Art Sculpture, U. Washington, 1971. Instr., asst. prof. visual art U. Puget Sound, Tacoma, Wash., 1971-76; with Kapiolani Cmty. Coll., Honolulu, 1977-78; instr., asst. prof. U. Hawaii-Manoa, Honolulu, 1979-81; technician, vis. lectr. sculpture San Jose (Calif.) State U., 1981-84; asst. prof. visual art Calif. State U., Turlock, 1984-85, prof., 1987—; asst. prof. Chico (Calif.) State U., 1985-86; art foundry mgr. Nordhammer Art, Oakland, Calif., 1986-87; carpenter M.A.K. Builders, Honolulu, 1976-78; judge art shows, 1971-98; design cons. Turlock City Arts Comm., 1996—. Exhibited in one-man and group shows, 1971-98. Mem. State Arts Commn. Calif. State U. Summer Arts, Long Beach, 1977, 98, Art Commn. Turlock, Calif., 1997, 98, Internat. Art com MDSTD Russia Arts, 1997. Mem. Pacific Rim Sculpt Group. Avocations: high mountain fly fishing. Home: 600 W Greenway Ave Turlock CA 95380-6423

BARNETT, MICHAEL, sports agent, business manager; b. Olds, Alta., Can., Oct. 9, 1948; came to U.S., 1988; s. Terence R. and Mary M. Barnett; m. Dalyce M. Giordano, Apr. 2, 1988; children: Jesse, Joey, Justin, Janie, Jenna. Student, St. Lawrence U., 1968-70; BS in Health and Phys. Edn., U. Calgary, 1973. Registered agent Nat. Hockey League Players Assn. Profl. hockey player, 1973-75; founder, CEO Corpsport Internat.; agent, bus. mgr. Wayne Gretzky, 1981—; internat. v.p. Internat. Mgmt. Group; gen. mgr. Ninety-Nine All Stars; pres. Internat. Mgmt. Group Hockey, 1990. Active H.E.L.P., L.A. Named one of Top 100 Most Powerful in Sports, The Sporting News, 1994, 95, 96, Oe of Twelve Most Powerful in Hockey, Hockey News, 1995. Mem. U.S.A. Hockey, U.S. Golf Assn., Edmonton Klondike Days Assn. (dir.). Avocations: golfing, running. Home: PO Box 50 Lake Arrowhead CA 92352-0050 Office: PO Box 565 Ste 01-270 28200 Hwy 189 Lake Arrowhead CA 92352

BARNHART, JACK HARMON, purchasing agent; b. Mt. Vernon, Ohio, Mar. 12, 1939; s. John Harmon and Esther Elizabeth (Conard) B.; m. Sharon Dawn Johnston, Apr. 15, 1961 (div.); children: Shannon, Eric; m. Eileen Mary Doyle, Jan. 9, 1970; 1 child, Adam. Student, Calif. State U., Fullerton. Salesman Metal Source, Downey, Calif., 1982-84; product specialist MetalCenter, Inc., Cerritos, Calif., 1984-86; cons. Barnhart Consulting, Long Beach, Calif., 1986-90; purchasing agt. Endura Steel, Hesperia, Calif., 1990-92; product specialist Tomen Am., L.A., 1992-95; asst. br. mgr. Southstar Steel, Buena Park, Calif., 1995-96; product specialist EMJ, Brea, Calif., 1996-97; purchasing officer CD Assocs., Irvine, Calif., 1997—. Scientologist. Avocations: shooting, tinkering, genealogy, computers. E-mail: barndoyl@pacbell.net. Fax: 562-799-9351. Home: 2521 Ladoga Ave Long Beach CA 90815-2308 Office: CD Assocs 15 Marconi Ste A Irvine CA 92618-2781

BARNHILL, KENNETH SMALTZ, JR., lay worker; b. Mesilla, N.Mex., Aug. 2, 1928; s. Kenneth S. and Rega (Ragan) B.; m. Patricia Jean Boney, Aug. 10, 1950; children: Jane Ann, Martha Jean Barnhill-Martin. BS in Engring., N.Mex. Coll. Agrl. and Mech. Arts, 1952. Exec. dir. Episcopal Charities of the Rio Grande, Albuquerque, 1987—; adminstr./treas. Cathedral Ch. of St. John, Albuquerque, 1988—; bd. dirs. United Episcopal Charities, N.Y.C.; regional chair Diocesan Stewardship Commn., Albuquerque, 1983—; mem. Companion Diocese Commn., Albuquerque, 1983—; dir. Camp Stoney (Episcopal), Santa Fe, 1977-83. Holder 2 mineral process patents. Bd. Dirs. New Heart of Albuquerque, 1989—, N.Mex. Mining Assn., Santa Fe, 1976-83, Cibola County C . of C., 1976-82; advisor N.Mex. Sch. Mines Mining Dept., Socorro, 1977-83. With U.S. Army, 1946-48, Korea. Mem. AIME, Am. Inst. Chem. Engrs., Can. Inst. Mining and Metallurgy, Nat. Assn. Christian Bus. Adminstrs., Masons (master 1984, 87), Shriners. Home: 7223 Chickadee Ln NE Albuquerque NM 87109-6013 Office: Cathedral Ch of St John PO Box 1246 Albuquerque NM 87103-1246

BARNHOUSE, LILLIAN MAY PALMER, retired medical surgical nurse, researcher, civic worker; b. Canton, Ohio, Sept. 26, 1918; d. Frank Barnard and Jenny Mildred (Leggett) Shear; m. Arnold Barnhouse, June 26, 1940 (dec. Nov. 1996); 1 child, James Wilson. Diploma, Aultman Hosp. Sch. Nursing, Canton, 1939. RNCC, Ohio, obstetrics specialty. Supr., 1943-44; nurse physician's office Canton, Ohio, 1943-49; ind. critical care nursing local hosps., 1953-68. Instr., blood bank worker ARC, 1940-70; mem. Rep. Nat Com., 1980—; vol. genetic rschr., 1972—; bd. dirs. Canton Cemetery Assn., 1990-97; vol. mem. Valley Health Svcs., 1997—. Mem. Ohio Nurses Assn. (past v.p., past chmn. dist. legis. com.), First Families of Ohio, Ladies Oriental Shrine.

BARNHURST, CHRISTINE LOUISE, broadcast executive; b. Salt Lake City, Sept. 3, 1949; d. Joseph Samuel and Luana Jean (Jackson) B. BS, U. Utah, 1971. From account exec. to mktg. specialist Bonneville Internat. Corp. KSL TV, Salt Lake City, 1972-84; mgr. corp. media funding U. Utah, Salt Lake City, 1985-86; dir. advt. Larry H. Miller Group, Salt Lake City, 1986-89; dir. mktg. and promotion Sta. KXIV TV Am. TV of Utah, Salt Lake City, 1989-92; gen. sales, mktg. and promotion mgr. Sta. KJZZ TV Larry H. Miller Comms., Salt Lake City, 1993-96; owner, developer Cruisin' Cards, 1997—; cons., dir. Cause Mktg. KSL-TV, 1997—; freelance producer of corp. sales and tng. videos, TV documentary. Bd. dirs., telethon producer March of Dimes; bd. dirs. YWCA, Relief Soc. LDS Ch. Gen. Bd.; mem. Salt Lake Conv. Bur. Recipient Nat. Print Ad award Athena, 1990, Walt Disney Top Mktg. and Promotion award, 1992, INTV Indy award, 1991, BPME Gold/Silver/Bronze awards, 1989-93, Telly awards, 1992, 93, 94, 95, 96, Gold/Silver/Bronze Addy award Utah Advt. Fedn., Emmy award, 1992, 94, March of Dimes Recognition Svc. award, 1982. Mem. Am. Mktg. Assn. (exec. mem.), Promax.

BARNSTONE, TONY DIMITRIOS, English writing educator; b. Middletown, Conn., May 29, 1961; s. Willis Robert and Helle Phaedra (Tzalopoulou) B.; m. Ayame Fukuda, Sept. 4, 1994. BA, U. Calif., Santa Cruz, 1985; MA, U. Calif., Berkeley, 1990, PhD, 1998. From reader to coord. Holloway poetry series U. Calif., Berkeley, 1987-93; coord. poetry and fiction series Whittier (Calif.) Coll., 1993—, asst. prof. English, 1995—; instr. English dept. Beijing Fgn. Studies U., 1984. Editor, co-translator: The Art of Writing: Teachings of the Chinese Masters, 1996, Laughing Lost in the Mountains: Poems of Wang Wei, 1991; co-editor: Literatures of Asia, Africa and Latin America, 1998; editor: Out of the Howling Storm: The New Chinese Poetry, 1993. Recipient Chester H. Jones Found. award, 1989, 94, Milton Dorfman Poetry prize Rome Art and Cmty. Ctr., 1994, J.B. Speed Gallery award, 1985. Mem. MLA, Poetry Soc. Am., William Carlos Williams Soc. Avocations: theatre, swimming, salsa dancing, art, pool. Office: Whittier Coll English Dept PO Box 634 Whittier CA 90608-0634

BARON, FREDERICK DAVID, lawyer; b. New Haven, Dec. 2, 1947; s. Charles Bates and Betty (Leventhal) B.; m. Kathryn Green Lazarus, Apr. 4, 1982; children—Andrew K. Lazarus, Peter D. Lazarus, Charles B. B.A., Amherst Coll., 1969; J.D., Stanford U., 1974. Bar: Calif. 1974, D.C. 1975, U.S. Supreme Ct. 1978, U.S. Dist. Ct. D.C. 1979, U.S. Ct. Appeals (D.C. cir.) 1979, U.S. Dist. Ct. (no. dist.) Calif. 1982, U.S. Ct. Appeals (9th cir.) 1982. Counsel select com. on intelligence U.S. Senate, Washington, 1975-76; spl. asst. to U.S. atty. gen., Washington, 1977-79; asst. U.S. atty. for D.C., 1980-82; assoc. dep. atty. gen., dir Exec. Office for Nat. Security, U.S. Dept. of Justice, 1995-96; atty. Clark, Baron & Korda, San Jose, Calif., 1982-83; ptnr. Cooley, Godward, Castro, Huddleson & Tatum, San Francisco, 1983—; lectr. U.S. Info. Service, 1979-80; pres. bd. trustees Keys Sch., Palo Alto, Calif., 1983-87; bd. dirs. Retail Resources Inc., 1987-88. Co-author, editor U.S. Senate Select Com. on Intelligence Reports, 1975-76; also articles. Issues dir. election com. U.S. Senator Alan Cranston, 1974, Gov. Edmund G. Brown Jr., 1976; mem. transition team Pres. Carter, 1976-77, Pres. Clinton, 1992; del. Calif. Dem. Conv., 1989-90. Mem. ABA, Calif. Bar Assn., D.C. Bar Assn., Santa Clara County Bar Assn. Club: University. Office: Cooley Godward Castro Huddleson & Tatum 5 Palo Alto Sq Palo Alto CA 94306-2122

BARON, MELVIN FARRELL, pharmacy educator; b. L.A., July 29, 1932; s. Leo Ben and Sadie (Bauchman) B.; m. Lorraine Ross, Dec. 20, 1953; children: Lynn Baron Friedman, Ross David. PharmD, U. So. Calif., 1957, MPA, 1973. Lic. pharmacist, Calif. Pres. Shield Health Care Ctrs., Van Nuys, Calif., 1957-83; dir. externship program U. So. Calif., L.A., 1981; v.p. Shield Health Care Ctrs., Inc. (C.R. Bard, Inc. subsidiary), 1983-86; pres. Merit Coll., 1988-92, PharmCom., L.A., 1990—; asst. prof. clin. pharmacy U. So. Calif., L.A., 1991—, assst. dean pharm. care programs, 1995—, dir. PharmD/MBA program, asst. dean programmatic advancment, 1998; prin. New Horizon Pharmacy Cons.; adj. asst. prof. U. Without Walls, Shaw U., Raleigh, N.C., 1973; project dir. Hayne Found. Drug Rsch. Ctr. U. So. Calif., L.A., 1973; assoc. dir. Calif. Alcoholism Found., 1973-75; adj. asst. prof. clin. pharmacy Sch. of Pharmacy U. So. Calif., L.A., 1981-91; cons. Topanga Terr. Convalescent Hosp., 1970-80, Calif. Labor Mgmt. Plan for alcoholism programs and coords., 1974, Office of Alcoholism, State of Calif., Nat. In-Home Health Svc., 1975, Continuity of Life Team, 1975, Triad Med., Longs Drug Stores, HealthTek, others; vis. prof. Tokyo Coll. Pharmacy, 1994, Sandoz Pharm Co., 1995; lectr. Meijo U., Nagoya U., Japan, 1994; presenter Nat. Pharmacy Dir. Conf., 1995; cons., mem. sci. adv. bd. Leiner Health Products, 1998; cons. Prime Care Pharmacy, 1998—, Jackson Meml. Hosp., 1998. Adv. bd. Pharmacist Newsletter, 1980—. Chmn. Friends of Operation Bootstrap, 1967-77; svc. chmn. tng. coord. Am. Cancer Soc., San Fernando Valley, Calif., 1980; mem. adv. bd. L.A. VNA, 1982; bd. dirs. pres. QSAD, 1987-88; pres. bd. Everywoman's Village, 1988-89; bd. dirs. Life Svcs., 1988—; pres. bd. counselors, U. So. Calif., 1988-92, mem. Calif. State Bd. Pharmacy Com. on Student/Preceptor Manual, 1991-93. Named Disting. Alumnus of Yr., U. So. Calif., Sch. of Pharmacy Alumni Assn., 1979, U. So. Calif. Torchbearer, 1990-91, Hon. Tchr. of Yr. U. So. Calif. Sch. Pharmacy, 1997. Fellow Am. Coll. Apothecaries; mem. Am. Pharm. Assn., Am. Soc. Health Sys. Pharmacists, Calif. Pharmacist Assn. (chair edn. com.), Am. Soc. Pub. Adminstrn., Am. Assn. Colls. of Pharmacy, Phi Kappa Phi, Phi Lambda Sigma (hon., faculty advisor), Rho Chi. Home: 323 San Vicente Santa Monica CA 90402-1629 Office: U So Calif 1985 Zonal Ave Los Angeles CA 90033-1039

BARON, ROBERT CHARLES, publishing executive; b. L.A., Jan. 26, 1934; s. Leo Francis and Marietta (Schulze) B.; m. Faye Helen Rogers, Jan. 28, 1961 (div. 1984); m. Charlotte Rose Persinger, Nov. 29, 1986; stepchildren: Brett, Kristen. BS in Physics, St. Joseph's Coll., 1956. Registered profl. engr., Mass. Engr. RCA, Camden, N.J., 1955-57, Computer Control Co., Framingham, Mass., 1959-61; program mgr. Mariner II and IV space computers Computer Control Co., Framingham, 1961-65, engring. mgr., 1965-69; worldwide systems mgr. Honeywell Minicomputer, Framingham, 1970-71; founder, pres., CEO Prime Computer, Framingham, 1971-75; pvt. practice Boston, 1976-83; founder and pres. Fulcrum Pub., Golden, Colo., 1984—; bd. dirs. Prime Computer, Framingham, Mass., Alling-Lander, Cheshire, Conn., Oxion, Hugoton, Kans., Fulcrum Pub., Golden Colo. Author: Digital Logic and Computer Operations, 1966, Micropower Electronics, 1970, America in the Twentieth Century, 1995; editor: The Garden and Farm Books of Thomas Jefferson, 1987, Soul of America: Documenting Our Past, 1492-1974, 1989, Colorado Rockies: The Inaugural Season, 1993, Thomas Hornsby Ferril and the American West, 1996. Trustee Lincoln Filene Ctr., Tufts U., Medford, Mass., 1982-84; vice chmn. bd. dirs. Mass. Audubon Soc., Lincoln, 1980-85; bd. dirs. Rocky Mountain Women's Inst., Denver, 1987-90; bd. dirs. Denver Pub. Libr. Friends Found., 1989-96, pres., 1994-96. Mem. Am. Antiquarian Soc. (bd. dirs., chmn. 1993—), Internat. Wilderness Leadership Found. (bd. dirs. 1990—, chmn. 1994—), Thoreau Soc., Mass. Hist. Soc., Western History Assn., Grolier Club, Hakluyt Soc. Avocations: writing, reading, sports, gardening, collecting clocks. Office: Fulcrum Pub 350 Indiana St Ste 350 Golden CO 80401-6567

BARON, WAYNE DAVID, engineering executive; b. Phila., Feb. 22, 1954; s. Jerome and Blossom Baron. BSEE, MIT, 1977, MSEE in Computer Sci., 1977. Mem. tech. staff HP Labs., Palo Alto, Calif., 1977-80, project mgr., 1981-83; v.p. engring. Galil Motion Control, Mountain View, Calif., 1983—. E-mail: Wayneb@galilmc.com. Home: 11600 Old Ranch Ln Los Altos CA 94024-6343 Office: Galil Motion Control Inc 203 Ravendale Dr Mountain View CA 94043-5216

BARONE, ANGELA MARIA, artist, researcher; b. Concesio, Brescia, Italy, June 29, 1957; came to U.S., 1983; d. Giuseppe and Adelmina (D'Ercole) B. Laurea cum laude in geol. scis., U. Bologna, Italy, 1981; PhD in Marine Geology, Columbia U., 1989. Cert. in profl. photography, N.Y. Inst. Photography, N.Y.C., 1992; cert. in the fine art of painting and drawing North Light Art Sch., Cin., 1993. Collaborative asst. Marine Geology Inst., Bologna, 1981-83, Inst. Geology and Paleontology, Florence, Italy, 1982-83, Sta. de Geodynamique, Villefranche, France, 1982; grad. rsch. asst. Lamont-Doherty Geol. Obs., Palisades, N.Y., 1983-89; postdoctoral rsch. asst. Lamont-Doherty Geol. Obs., Palisades, 1989; postgrad. rschr. Scripps Instn. of Oceanography, La Jolla, Calif., 1990-92; artist San Diego, 1993—. Contbr. articles to profl. jours. Mem. Am. Geophys. Union (co-pres. meeting session 1990), Nat. Mus. Women in Arts (assoc.). Home: 7540 Charmant Dr Apt 1222 San Diego CA 92122-5044

BARR, JAMES NORMAN, federal judge; b. Kewanee, Ill, Oct. 21, 1940; s. James Cecil and Dorothy Evelyn (Dorsey) B.; m. Trilla Anne Reeves, Oct. 31, 1964 (div. 1977); 1 child, James N. Jr.; m. Phyllis L. DeMent, May 30, 1986. BS, Ill. Wesleyan U., 1962; JD, Ill. Inst. Tech., 1971. Bar: Ill. 1972, Calif. 1977. Assoc. Pretzel, Stouffer, Nolan & Rooney, Chgo., 1974-76; claims counsel Safeco Title Ins. Co., L.A., 1977-78; assoc. Kamph & Jackman, Santa Ana, Calif., 1978-80; lawyer pvt. practice Law Offices of James N. Barr, Santa Ana, 1980-86; judge U.S Bankruptcy Ct. Ctrl. Dist. Calif., Santa Anna, 1987—; adj. prof. Chapman U. Sch. Law, 1996—. Lt. (s.g.) USN, 1962-67, Vietnam. Mem. Orange County Bankruptcy Forum (bd. dirs. 1989—), Peter M. Elliott Inn Ct. (pres. 1990-91). Office: US Bankruptcy Ct 411 West 4th St Santa Ana CA 92701-4593

BARR, ROBERT EDWARD, computer company executive; b. Neosho, Mo., July 29, 1956; s. Donald A. and Cecilia K.; m. Aileen Conlon, Nov. 10, 1978; children: Stephanie E., Dacia K., Marysia S. BS, U. S.C., 1978; MBA, U. Pa., 1984. Cert. systems profl., cert. in prodn. and inventory mgmt. Analyst Hanes Hosiery, Winston-Salem, N.C., 1978-80; project leader Cryovac div. WR Grace, Duncan, S.C., 1980-82; mktg. dir. Cullinet Software, Westwood, Mass., 1984-86, Online/Database Software, Pearl River, N.Y., 1986-88; info. resource mgmt. mgr. S.C. Tax Commn., Columbia, 1988-92; v.p. govt. programs Intuit Inc., San Diego, 1995-96; mem. adj. faculty Midlands Tech. Coll., Columbia, 1989-92; instr. APICS, Westwood, Mass., 1985; mem. IRS Commr.'s Adv. Group, 1994-96, IRS Info. Returns Program Adv. Com., 1995—. Co-author: Employee Relations..., 1987; contbr. articles to profl. jours. Capt. March of Dimes, Columbia, 1989, 90, 91; steering com. Mainstreet Celebrates Edn., Columbia, 1990; mem. PTO, Columbia, 1989, 90, 91; pres. Hotspurs Soccer Club, 1996—, pres., 1996—; v.p. PTA, 1996—; mem. Cmty. Planning Group, San Diego, 1996—. Mem. Am. Prodn. and Inventory Control Soc. (sec. 1981-82, Svc. award 1982, 85), Am. Payroll Assn. (svc. award 1993, 96), Am. Nat. Stds. Inst. (accredited stds. com. x12, subcom. chair 1991-92), Cert. Electronic Trade Profls. Assn. (chmn. 1991-92), Coun. for Electronic Revenue Comm. Advancement (pres. 1994-96), Columbia Forum, U. S.C. Alumni Assn., Wharton Alumni Assn. Avocations: running, writing, reading. Home: 6511 Rockland Dr Clifton VA 20124-2415 Office: Intuit Inc 6220 Greenwich Dr San Diego CA 92122-5913

BARR, SUE, secondary education educator. Tchr. S. Eugene High Sch., Oreg. Named Spl. Recognition adviser Journalism, 1990, Disting. adviser Journalism Dow Jones Newspaper Fund, 1992. Office: South Eugene H S 400 E 19th Ave Eugene OR 97401-4190

BARRAD, CATHERINE MARIE, lawyer; b. Moscow, Idaho, Dec. 12, 1953; d. Richard Gary and Hazel Mae (Hollon) Morrison; m. Mark William Barrad, Dec. 29, 1974 (div. June 1997); children: Joshua, Samuel, Rachel. Student, Saddleback Coll., 1971-72, UCLA, 1972-73, U. Calif., Irvine, 1973-74, Calif. State U., Long Beach, 1976-77; BS in Law, JD, Western State U., 1980. Bar: Calif. 1980, Hawaii 1993. Pvt. practice Law Offices of Catherine M. Barrad, Long Beach, 1980-93, Maui, 1993—; arbitrator court annexed arbitration program 2d Cir. Ct. Hawaii, 1993—. Del. Coun. Jewish Fedns., Long Beach, 1990, bd. dirs., 1983-93; del. Jewish Community Rels. Coun., 1987, 92; cubmaster Pack 111 Boy Scouts Am., Long Beach, 1989-93; v.p. Jewish Arts and Edn. Maui, 1994-97. Recipient Neuberger Young Leadership award Jewish Fedn. Long Beach, 1990, Chai Vol. award Jewish Community Ctr., Long Beach, 1990. Mem. Women Lawyers of Long Beach (sec. 1981-82, pres. 1982-83), Hawaii State Bar Assn, Hawaii Women Lawyers, Maui County Bar Assn., Aloha House (bd. dirs. 1996-97), Rotary Maui Upcountry (pres. 1994-96, bd. dirs. 1994-97). Democrat. Jewish. Fax: 808-573-0853. Office: PO Box 1591 Makawao HI 96768-1591

BARRERA, JOE OSCAR, JR., composer, music producer, music publisher; b. Alice, Tex., Oct. 11, 1949; s. Joe Oscar and Tommie (Pena) B.; m. Lynn Ann Dodd, Apr. 25, 1985; children: Jessica Leah, Ryan Jay. MusB, U. North Tex., 1974, MusM, 1976. Cert. music instr., Calif. Artist in residence N.C. State U., Raleigh, 1976-77; composer, music dir. Sonrisas TV Prodns., Austin, Tex., 1977-79; prodn. staff Sta. KHJ-TV, Hollywood, Calif., 1979-82; instr. asst. East L.A. Coll., Monterey Pk., Calif., 1984-86; asst. to pres. New Zoo Revue TV, Beverley Hills, Calif., 1986-88; composer, pres. Bar Scoring Prodns., Glendale, Calif., 1989—; adj. prof. music Del Mar Coll., Corpus Christi, 1998-99; mem. com. NARAS, Santa Monica, Calif., 1996—. Composer various TV features including Sonrisas, 1977-79, A Rainy Day, 1995, El Artista, 1997. Recieved Emmy nomination, NATAS, Austin, Tex., 1979, Peadody nomination, Austin, 1979; recipient Cert. Achievement, Billboard Contest, Tulsa, Okla., 1988, ASCAP award, N.Y.C., 1996, 97, 98. Mem. ASCAP (writer, pub.), NARAS, Soc. Composers Lyricists, Profl. Musicians Local 47. Democrat. Roman Catholic. Home: 520 W Wilson Ave Apt 104 Glendale CA 91203-2426

BARRETO, KATHLEEN ANNE COOGAN, technical writing consultant; b. New London, Conn., Sept. 5, 1954; d. Eugene Aloysius and Germaine Marie (Hangley) Coogan; m. Oscar Eduardo Barreto, May 28, 1972 (separated 1980); 1 child, Victoria Anne. AA in Tech. Writing magna cum laude, De Anza Coll., 1988. Banker, 1974-80; tech. recruiter Menlo Svc. Corp., Sunnyvale, Calif., 1980-84; tech. writer Textron-Singer-Dalmo Victor, Belmont and Fremont, Calif., 1984-87; tech. writing cons., Sunnyvale, 1987—, design cons., 1988—; cons. Tech. for Communications Internat., Fremont, 1987—, Ultra Systems, Sunnyvale, 1988, cisco Systems, Menlo Park, Calif., 1990—. Author, co-producer High-Tech for Ind. Living, PBS-TV, 1988 (Waveform award 1988, Bay Area Cable Excellence award for Best Docudrama 1989); writer, producer, host On the Move, Able Cable TV, 1988—. Mem. Soc. for Tech. Communications, Writer's Connection, Mensa. Libertarian. Roman Catholic. Avocations: photography, cross-country skiing.

BARRETT, BRUCE RICHARD, physics educator; b. Kansas City, Kans., Aug. 19, 1939; s. Buford Russell and Miriam Aileen (Adams) B.; m. Gail Louise Geiger, Sept. 3, 1961 (div. Aug. 1969); m. Joan Frances Livermore, May 21, 1979. BS, U. Kans., 1961; postgrad., Swiss Poly., Zurich, 1961-62; MS, Stanford U., 1964, PhD, 1967. Research fellow Weizmann Inst. Sci., Rehovot, Israel, 1967-68; postdoctoral research fellow, research assoc. U. Pitts., 1968-70; asst. prof. physics U. Ariz., Tucson, 1970-72, assoc. prof., 1972-76, prof., 1976—, assoc. chmn. dept., 1977-83, mem. faculty senate, 1979-83, 88-90, 91-97, program dir. theoretical physics NSF, 1985-87, mem. tech. transfer com., 1996-97, 98—; chmn. adv. com. Internat. Scholars, Tucson, 1985-96; chmn. rsch. policy com. U. Ariz. Faculty Senate, 1993-94, 95-96. Woodrow Wilson fellow, 1961-62; NSF fellow, 1962-66; Weizmann Inst. fellow, 1967-68; Andrew Mellon fellow, 1968-69; Alfred P. Sloan Found. research fellow, 1972-74; Alexander von Humboldt fellow, 1976-77; Japanese Soc. for Promotion of Sci. rsch. fellow, 1998; NSF grantee, 1971-85, 87—; Netherlands F.O.M. research fellow Groningen, 1980; recipient sr. U.S. scientist award (Humboldt prize) Alexander von Humboldt Found., 1983-85. Fellow Am. Phys. Soc. (publs. com. divsn. nuclear physics 1983-86, program com. 1993-94, chmn. steering com. for Nuclear Physics Summer Sch. 1996-98), Phi Beta Kappa (pres. Alpha Ariz. chpt. 1992), Sigma Xi, Sigma Pi Sigma, Omicron Delta Kappa, Beta Theta Pi. Office: U Ariz Dept Physics PO Box 210081 Tucson AZ 85721

BARRETT, CANDICE, museum administrator. BS, Northwestern U.; postgrad., U. Minn. Past dir. theatre in edn. program So. Meth. U., Dallas; past acting and directing instr. San Francisco State U.; past exec. dir. Acad. Media and Theatre Arts, San Francisco; past live entertainment dir. Disneyland, Anaheim, Calif.; past prodr., writer, actress Children's Audio Svc., Chapel Hill, N.C.; dir., curator L.A. Children's Mus., 1998—; past guest instr. audio prodn. tchrs. seminar Stephens Coll., Columbia, Mo.; past guest instr. Nat. Summer Drama Inst. So. Ill. U., Edwardsville; past panelist children's media NEH, Washington; past on-site reviewer theatre arts NEA, Washington; past West Coast rep. Action Children's TV; past children's

media reviewer Corp. Pub. Broadcasting; past adj. prof. directing dept. theatre U. So. Calif.; past asst. agent Writers and Artists. Past edn. program cons. Joseph Campbell Found. Home: 3720 Tilden Ave Los Angeles CA 90034 Office: LA Children's Mus 310 N Main St Los Angeles CA 90012-2830

BARRETT, CRAIG R., computer company executive; b. 1939. Assoc. prof. Stanford U., 1965-74; with Intel Corp., Chandler, Ariz., 1974—, v.p. components tech. and mfg. group, sr. v.p., gen. mgr. components tech. and mfg. group, exec. v.p., mgr. components tech., now pres., COO. Office: Intel Corp 5000 W Chandler Blvd Chandler AZ 85226-3699

BARRETT, DOROTHY, performing arts administrator; b. L.A.; d. Lester Arnold and Kathryn (Halverson) Silvera; m. Robert A.H. Cochrane, May 20, 1949 (div. Feb. 1965); 1 stepchild, Michele Cochrane Shaw. Student, LA C.C., 1937-38. Adminstrv. dir. Am. Nat. Acad. of Performing Arts, 1964—; founder, dir. Acad. Children's Workshop, 1964—; produced, choreographed 30 Christmas shows, 1964—; tchr. of dance Barrett Sch. of the Arts, North Hollywood, 1948, Am. Nat. Acad., Studio City, 1964—, tchr. of acting, 1964—; tchr. of speech UCLA Extension, West Hollywood, 1972. Actress, dancer: (motion pictures) A Damsel in Distress, 1937, The Great Waltz, 1938, Gone with the Wind, 1939, Frisco Sal, Wizard of Oz, 1939, Juke Box Soundies, 1942, Hot Money, 1944, Monsieur Beaucaire, 1945, The Imperfect Lady, 1947, Perils of Pauline, 1945, The Stork Club, 1945, Mildred Pierce, 1945, A Bell for Adano, 1945, Weekend at the Waldorf, 1945, Blue Skies, 1946, Connecticut Yankee in King Arthur's Court, 1947, California, 1947, Samson and Delilah, 1948, The Babe Ruth Story, 1948; (Broadway stage productions) Earl Carroll's Vanities, 1939, Buddy De Sylva's Louisiana Purchase, 1940, Billy Rose's Diamond Horseshoe, 1943, George Abbott's Beat the Band, 1942, others; (TV) co-star KTLA's Secrets of Gourmet, 1946; prodr., dir.: A Touch of Broadway, 1996, 97, (on tour) 1998; author: (poetry) Between the Bookends, 1942, The Tolucan, The Legal Journal, 1959, Valley Green Sheet & Van Nuys News; contbr. articles to jours. Active Am. Women's Vol. Svc., 1942. Named Miss Culver City, 1937; recipient award ARC, 1943, Humanitarian award for work with children City of L.A., 1994. Office: Am Nat Acad Performing Arts 10944 Ventura Blvd Studio City CA 91604-3340

BARRIOS, JOHN ANTHONY, bank official; b. Tucson, Nov. 15, 1969; s. Frank Valenzuela and Maria Christina (Lujan) B. Student, U. Ariz., 1987-90; BA in Mgmt., U. Phoenix, 1992. Ops. clk. Valley Nat. Bank, 1986-87; customer sales rep. III Gt. Am. Bank, Tucson, 1988-91, ops. supr., 1991—. Mem. Am. Philatelic Soc. Republican. Roman Catholic. Avocations: stamp collecting, computers. Home: 332 E Vaquero Pl Tucson AZ 85706-2511 Office: Gt Am Bank 3640 S 16th Ave Tucson AZ 85713-6001

BARRON, MICHAEL JAMES, interior designer; b. Morristown, N.J., June 28, 1963; s. Joseph Edward Barron and Shirley (Harris) Boralsky; life ptnr. Luis Corona. Degree in Applied Sci. Interior Design, Phoenix Coll., 1995. Registered archtl. draftsman, Ariz. Owner, prin. designer Casa Del Encanto, Scottsdale, Ariz., 1989—. Contbg. designer Showcase of Interior Design, 1996. Adv. bd. mem. Phoenix Coll., 1995—; cpl. USMC, 1981-85. Recipient 1st Place Residential House award, Am. Soc. Interior Design, 1994, 1st Place Showcase House award, Am. Soc. Interior Design, 1994, Best of Show, 1st Place Commercial House awards, Am. Soc. Interior Design, 1997. Mem. Am. Soc. Interior Design. Avocations: performance cars, classic Mustangs. Office: Casa Del Encanto 6939 E 1st Ave Scottsdale AZ 85251-4301

BARROW, THOMAS FRANCIS, artist, educator; b. Kansas City, Mo., Sept. 24, 1938; s. Luther Hopkins and Cleo Naomi (Francis) B.; m. Laurie Anderson, Nov. 30, 1974; children—Melissa, Timothy, Andrew. B.F.A., Kansas City Art Inst., 1963; M.S., Ill. Inst. Tech., 1965. With George Eastman House, Rochester, N.Y., 1966-72; asst. dir. George Eastman House, 1971-72; assoc. dir. Art Mus., U. N. Mex., Albuquerque, 1973-76; assoc. prof. U. N.Mex., 1976-81, prof., 1981—, Presdl. prof., 1985-90. Author: The Art of Photography, 1971; sr. editor: Reading into Photography, 1982; contbr. to Brit. Ency. Am. Art, 1973, A Hundred Years of Photographic History: Essays in Honor of Beaumont Newhall, 1975, Experimental Vision, 1994; forward The Valiant Knights of Daguerre, 1978; contbr. articles to profl. jours.; one-man shows include Light Gallery, N.Y.C., 1974-76, 79, 82, Amarillo Art Ctr., 1990, Andrew Smith Gallery, Santa Fe, 1992, Laurence Miller Gallery, N.Y.C., 1996, U. N.Mex. Art Mus., 1997; exhibited in group shows including Pace Gallery, N.Y.C., 1973, Hudson River Mus., Yonkers, N.Y., 1973, Internat. Mus. Photography, Rochester, 1975, Seattle Art Mus., 1976, Mus. Fine Arts, Houston, 1977, Retrospective exhbn. L.A. County Mus. Art, 1987—; represented in permanent collections Nat. Gallery Can., Mus. Modern Art, Getty Ctr. for Arts and Humanities. Nat. Endowment for Arts fellow, 1971, 78. Office: U NMex Dept Art Albuquerque NM 87131

BARRY, HENRY FORD, chemical company executive; b. Detroit, June 25, 1923; s. William H. and Antoinette (Griese) B.; m. Helen A. Sasso, Aug. 27, 1947 (dec. Dec. 1983); children: Henry V., John M., Robert C., Christine M., Elizabeth M., Catherine A. BS in Chemistry, Stanford U., Palo Alto, Calif., 1950; MS in Chem. Engring., U. Mich., 1952, MBA in Mktg., 1978. Registered profl. engr., Ind., Colo. Researcher Amoco Oil Co., Whiting, Ind., 1952-59; tech. dir. Haviland Products Co., Grand Rapids, Mich., 1960-62; supr. Climax Molybdenum Co., Detroit, 1962-66; mgr. chem. rsch. Climax Molybdenum Co., Ann Arbor, Mich., 1967-76, dir. chem. devel., 1977-82; v.p. tech. Shattuck Chem. Co., Denver, 1983—. Editor: Chemistry/Uses of Mo., Vol. III, 1979, Vol. IV, 1982. With U.S. Army, 1943-46. Mem. Am. Chem. Soc., Nat. Assn. Corrosion Engrs., Soc. Tribology and Lubrication Engrs. Achievements include 6 U.S. and 4 foreign patents. Avocation: swimming. Home: 2714 Antietam Ct Ann Arbor MI 48105-1457 Office: Shattuck Chem Co Inc 1805 S Bannock St Denver CO 80223-3699

BARRY, RICK (RICHARD FRANCIS DENNIS BARRY, III), sportscaster, retired professional basketball player, marketing professional; b. Elizabeth, N.J., Mar. 28, 1944; s. Richard Francis and Alpha Monique (Stephanovich) B.; m. Pamela Hale, June 1965 (div.); children: Richard Francis IV, Jon Alan, Brent Robert, Drew William, Shannon Leigh; m. Pamela Stenesen, Sept. 1981 (div.); m. Lynn Norenberg, Aug. 1991; 1 child, Canyon Shane. Student, U. Miami, 1961-65. Basketball player San Francisco Warriors, NBA, 1965-67, Oakland Oaks, Am. Basketball Assn., 1967-69, Washington, Am. Basketball Assn., 1969-70, Virginia Squires, 1970, N.Y. Nets, Am. Basketball Assn., 1970-72, Golden State Warriors, NBA, 1972-78, Houston Rockets, NBA, 1978-80; sports broadcaster, basketball analyst CBS Sports, 1974-81; NBA color analyst Turner Sports, 1984-91; dir. mktg. Profl. Logistics Mgmt. Inc., Lafayette, Calif., 1994—. Mem. Am. Basketball Assn. All-Star Team, 1968-72, NBA All-Star Team, 1966-67, 73-78, NBA Championship Team, 1975; named Rookie of Yr., NBA, 1966, Most Valuable Player All Star Game, 1966, Most Valuable Player Championship Series, 1975; inducted into Basketball Hall of Fame, 1986. Only player to lead NCAA, NBA and Am. Basketball Assn. in scoring; all-time leader in free throw shooting NBA. *

BARRY(-BRANKS), DIANE DOLORES, podiatrist; b. Cornwall, Ont., Can., Apr. 3, 1958; d. George Henry and Dolores Angeline (Latulippe) Barry; m. Paul Lloyd Branks, Sept. 19, 1987; children: Katherine Ann Branks, Andrew Joseph Branks, Annemarie Elizabeth Branks. BS, U. San Diego, 1980; B in Med. Sci., Calif. Coll. Podiatric Medicine, 1983, D in Podiatric Medicine, 1985. Lab technician Scripps Rsch. Inst., La Jolla, Calif., 1980, Salk Inst., La Jolla, 1981, Quidel Labs., La Jolla, 1982; dry waller Barry Drywall, San Diego, 1985; med. office mgr. Bay Harbor Podiatry Group, Harbor City, Calif., 1985; podiatry resident VA West L.A., 1986; podiatrist Bay Harbor Podiatry Group, 1987-88, Southeast Med. Ctr., Huntington Park, Calif., 1987-88; podiatrist Kaiser Permanente, Fontana, Calif., 1988-97, Baldwin Park, Calif., 1997—. NIH grantee, 1997. Fellow Am. Coll. Foot and Ankle Surgeons, Am. Coll. Foot and Ankle Orthops.; mem. Am. Podiatric Med. Soc., Am. Diabetic Assn., Calif. Podiatric Med. Soc. (alt. 1994, 96, del. 1995), So. Calif. HMO Podiatric Med. Soc. (founder, pres. 1989-91, 97-98). Republican. Roman Catholic. Avocation: weight lifting. Office: Kaiser Permanente Med Ctr 1011 Baldwin Park Blvd Baldwin Park CA 91706-5806

BARSAN, RICHARD EMIL, oral and maxillofacial surgeon; b. Selma, Ala., Dec. 18, 1945; s. Emil and Letitia Barsan; m. Sandra Sherrick, June 22, 1974; children: Kelly Lynn, Robert Scott. BS in Chem. Engring., U. Cin., 1968; DDS, Ohio State U., 1979. Diplomate Am. Bd. Oral and Maxillofacial Surgeons. Chem. engr. various cos., 1968-76; resident VA Hosp., Sepulveda, Calif., 1979-80; resident in oral and maxillofacial surgery La. State U., New Orleans, 1980-84; pvt. practice, La Jolla and El Centro, Calif., 1985—. Chrysler scholar U. Cin., 1964. Fellow Am. Assn. Oral and Maxillofacial Surgeons; mem. ADA, Calif. Dental Assn., San Diego County Dental Soc. (bd. dirs. 1988-92), San Diego County Oral Surgeons (pres. 1990), So. Calif. Soc. Oral and Maxillofacial Surgeons, Imperial Valley Dental Soc. (pres. 1993), Paul Revere Study Club (pres. 1988), Toastmasters (pres. La Jolla chpt. 1988), Omicron Kappa Upsilon. Republican. Avocations: computers, swimming, diving. Home: 3211 Via Marin La Jolla CA 92037-2937 Office: 1745 S Imperial Ave Ste 107 El Centro CA 92243-4243

BART, PETER BENTON, newspaper editor, film producer, novelist; b. N.Y.C., July 24, 1932; m. Leslie Cox; children: Colby, Dilys. BA, Swarthmore Coll., 1954; MA, London Sch. Econs., 1956. Staff reporter The Wall Street Jour., N.Y.C., 1956-57, The N.Y. Times, N.Y.C., 1957-67; v.p. Paramount Pictures, Los Angeles, 1967-74; pres. Bart Palevsky Prodn., L.A., 1974-77, Lorimar Film Co., Los Angeles, 1977-82; sr. v.p., film producer Metro Goldwyn Mayer/United Artists, L.A., 1982-85; v.p., editorial dir. Variety and Daily Variety, L.A., 1989-, editor-in-chief. Author: Destinies, 1980, Thy Kingdom Come, 1983, Fade Out: The Calamitous Final Days of MGM, 1990; prodr.: (films) Fun with Dick and Jane, Islands in the Stream, Youngblood. Office: Variety 5700 Wilshire Blvd Ste 120 Los Angeles CA 90036-3659*

BARTANEN, KRISTINE MARIE, communications educator; b. Silverton, Oreg., Feb. 16, 1953; d. Leonard Charles and Patricia Ann (Thompson) Dieker; m. Michael David Bartanen, June 7, 1984; children: Peter Andrew, Brendan Patrick. BA in Speech, Pacific U., 1974; MA in Speech Comm., U. Iowa, 1975, PhD in Speech Comm., 1978. Grad. tchg. asst. U. Iowa, Iowa City, 1974-77; instr. H.S. Forensics Inst. Western Wash. U., summer 1982, 84; asst. prof. comm., dir. forensics, coord. comm. activities U. Puget Sound, 1978-84, assoc. prof. comm., dir. forensics, 1984-90, prof. comm., dir. forensics, 1990—, comm. and theatre arts dept. chair, 1986-93; workshop leader; invited speaker profl. confs.; mem. Dist. II Nat. Debate Tournament, 1980-87; exec. com. N.W. Forensics Conf., 1988-90, chair awards com., 1992—; proposal screener CEDA Assessment Conf., 1990; participant Nat. Ctr. Post Secondary Tchg., Learning and Assessment Project, 1993-94. Contbr. papers to conf. procs., revs. and articles to profl. jours.; mem. editorial rev. bd. CEDA Yearbook, 1991—; assoc. editor The Forensic, 1993—, mem. editorial bd., 1987-91. Bd. dirs., sec. Harbor Montessori Sch., 1991-92; forum moderator Tacoma Little Theatre, 1991. Thomas J. Watson Nat. Merit scholar, 1971-74; NEH summer seminar fellow, 1983; U. Puget Sound rsch. grantee, 1989; named Faculty Marshall, 1992. Mem. Speech Comm. Assn., Western States Comm. Assn., Am. Forensic Assn. (pub. rels. com. 1986-88), Cross Examination Debate Assn. (chair ethics com. 1988-90, N.W. region rep. 1994—)), Nat. Forensic Assn., Guild Am. Forensic Educators (task force chair 1992—, charter mem.), Phi Kappa Phi, Pi Kappa Delta (John Shields award 1992, conf. work group chair 1991, charter and standards com. 1989-91, pub. rels. com. 1987-89, nominations com. 1987, 89, 91, lt. gov. N.W. Province 1982-84, gov., 1984-88).

BARTEL, ARTHUR GABRIEL, educational administrator, city official; b. San Francisco, Oct. 20, 1934; s. Irving Peter and Elian Leah (Barker) B.; m. Dottie Lu Smith, Dec. 14, 1963 (dec. Apr. 1972); children: Brian Blake, Scott Michael, m. Suzane M. Loftis, Feb. 14, 1989. Student, San Jose State Coll., 1952-54; BS, U. Calif., Berkeley, 1957; postgrad., U. So. Calif., 1968-70; MA, Pepperdine U., 1973, Calif. State U., Fresno, 1995. Cert. FAA air traffic controller, 1957-77, naval flight officer, 1965; lic. standard tchr., life standard svc., life cmty. coll. life chief coll. adminstrv. officer, life cmty. coll. supr., life cmty. coll. instr., spl. edn. svcs. credential, Calif. Enlisted USMC, 1954, commd. 2d lt., 1957, advanced through grades to maj., 1967; comdg. officer VMFA-314 Fighter-Attack Squadron USMC, El Toro, Calif., 1970-72; ret. USMC, 1977; gen. mgr. Nieuport 17 Restaurant, Santa Ana, Calif., 1977-78; pres., chief exec. officer High Flight Inc., Hanford, San Diego, Calif., 1978-81; teaching vice prin. Armona (Calif.) Union Elem. Sch., 1982-84, tchr. sci. and lang. arts., 1981-84; curriculum cons. Kings County Office Edn., Hanford, 1984-86; program specialist Kings County Supt. Schs., Hanford, 1986-91; prin. Kings County Cmty. Sch., Hanford, 1994-98, ret., 1998; councilman City of Hanford, 1986-90, mayor, 1988-90; mem. adv. bd. San Joaquin Valley Writing Project, 1984-86, 92—. Vice chmn. Hanford Planning Commn., 1982-86; vice chmn. bd. trustees Sacred Heart Hosp., 1987-93; bd. dirs. Navy League, 1992—. Decorated Air medal, Vietnam Cross of Gallantry; fellow internat. writing project U. Calif., Irvine, 1985. Mem. Assn. Calif. Sch. Adminstrs., Calif. Soc. Program Specialists, Hanford C. of C., DAV (life), Ret. Officers Assn., Navy League (v.p. 1993-95), Delta Upsilon (life). Avocations: hunting, fishing, coin collecting, gun and knife collecting, domestic and foreign traveling, antiques.

BARTELS, ALOYSIA DE BESSIERÉS, mariculturist, seafood producer; b. Victoria, B.C., Can., Aug. 11, 1923; d. Jean Marie de Hedouville and Aloysia Theresa van Goidtsoven (Sant Anna); m. Jay Murray Bartels; m. George P. Meade III; m. Karl L. Agricola; children: Joseph W., William L. II; m. Jay Bartels. Owner shrimp fishing boats Fla., Tex., 1972-86; pres., dir. W.I. Sea Farms Ltd., Carriacore, Grenada, 1986-92. Author: (poem) Navaho, 1993 (Best of 1993 award); co-author: Pageant of Eight Flags, 1993. Mem. Fernandina Beach Fla. Hist. Soc. (past pres., head restoration commn.). Republican. Avocations: travel, history, painting, writing, poetry. Home: 3917 Saint Andrews Dr SE Rio Rancho NM 87124-2151

BARTELS, BRIAN LOWELL, electronics engineer, consultant; b. Glendale, Calif., July 26, 1958; s. Lowell Dean and Dixie Lee (Whitlock) B.; m. Sally Annette Romo, Aug. 25, 1979; children: Cathy, Mike, Scott. AS in Electronics Tech., Citrus C.C., Glendora, Calif., 1987; BS in Electronics Engring., Calif. State Poly. U., Pomona, 1994. Computer svc. ctr. mgr., sr. customer engr. Computer Svcs. divsn. Tandy Corp. Radio Shack, L.A. area, 1979-86; systems engr. B-2 divsn. Northrop Grumman, Pico Rivera, Calif., 1986-97; lead design engr. Mil. Aircraft Systems divsn. Northrop Grumman, El Segundo, Calif., 1997—; prin. engr. Bartels Microengring., Glendora, 1982-94. Republican. Christian. Avocations: hiking and camping, reading science fiction. Office: Northrop Grumman Corp MASD 30/8E10/W5 One Hornet Way El Segundo CA 90245

BARTH, DAVID VICTOR, computer systems designer, consultant; b. Tulsa, Sept. 23, 1942; s. Vincent David and Norma (Bell) B. BS summa cum laude, Met. State Coll., Denver, 1977; MS, U. No. Colo., 1982; PhD, Kennedy-Western U., Boise, Idaho, 1995. Programming mgr. Am. Nat. Bank, Denver, 1967-72; cons. Colo. Farm Bur. Ins. Corp., Denver, 1972; systems analyst Mid-Continent Computer Services, Denver, 1972-73; programming mgr. Bayly Corp., Denver, 1973-75; project leader Cobe Labs. Inc., Denver, 1976-84; part-time tchr. Met. State Coll., 1982-83; systems analyst Affiliated Banks Service Co., Denver, 1985-87; real estate broker Van Schaack & Co., Denver, 1985; tech. supr. Affiliated Banks Svc. Co., Denver, 1987-89; software engr. Computer Data Systems, Inc., Aurora, Colo., 1990-91, 94-98; sr. computer systems designer Martin Marietta Corp., Golden, Colo., 1991-92; owner, operator Computer Shop, Lakewood, Colo., 1992-93; cons. Ross Co., Denver, 1993-95; sr. software engr. Perot Systems, Englewood, Colo., 1998—; freelance flight instr., 1977—. Vol. Am. Red Cross, 1987—; Served with USN, 1961-66. Mem. Soc. for Info. Mgmt. (editor newsletter 1983), Exptl. Aircraft Assn. (editor newsletter chpt. 660, 1989-91), Aircraft Owners and Pilots Assn., Flying Circus Skating Club, Air West Flying Club (editor newsletter 1997—). Republican. Avocations: ice skating, flying, creative writing. Home: 509 S Cody St Lakewood CO 80226-3047 Office: Perot Systems Corp Ste 350 5990 Greenwood Plaza Blvd Englewood CO 80111-4743

BARTHOLD, EDWARD A., physician; b. San Francisco, May 3, 1926; s. Edward A. B.; widowed; children: Gordon, Lara, Christine, Jeff Leslie, Jim, Holly; m. Connie Hitte, May 31, 1987. AB, U. Calif., 1946, MD, 1950. Diplomate Am. Bd. Internal Medicine. Chief resident VA Hosp., San Francisco, 1955-56; ptnr. Menlo Med. Clinic, Menlo Park, Calif., 1956-90; chief of staff Palo Alto-Stanford Hosp., Palo Alto, Calif., 1960-61; CEO, pres. PenMed Lab to Diagnostic Lab, Inc., 1965-94; pres. bd. dirs. Charles Armstrong Found., Menlo Park. Recipient Gold Headed Cane, U. Calif. San Francisco Med. Sch., 1950. Mem. Am. Soc. Internal Medicine (chmn. comms. 1970—), Menlo Circus Club, Palo Alto Club, World Trade Club. Avocations: tennis, dominoes. Office: 1188 Chestnut St Menlo Park CA 94025

BARTLETT, ARTHUR EUGENE, franchise executive; b. Glens Falls, N.Y., Nov. 26, 1933; s. Raymond Ernest and Thelma (Williams) B.; m. Collette R. Bartlett, Jan. 9, 1955; 1 dau., Stacy Lynn. Sales mgr. Forest E. Olson, Inc., 1960-64; co-founder, v.p. Four Star Realty, Inc., Santa Ana, Calif., 1964-71, v.p., sec., 1964-71; founder, pres. Comps, Inc., Tustin, Calif., 1971-81; co-founder, chmn. of bd., pres., CEO Century 21 Real Estate Corp., Tustin, 1980—; pres. Larwin Sq. LLC Shopping Ctr, Tustin, Calif., 1979—. Chmn. bd. United Western Med. Ctrs., 1981-87. Named to Internat. Franchise Assn. Hall of Fame, 1987. Mem. Internat. Franchise Assn. (v.p., bd. dirs. 1975-80). Lodge: Masons. Office: 275 Centennial Way Ste 209 Tustin CA 92780-3709

BARTLETT, DEBORAH ANN, financial management consultant; b. Aberdeen, Md., Aug. 4, 1953; d. James L. and Theresa A. (Leskowits) Taylor; m. Michael J. Bartlett, July 23, 1986. Cert. investment mgmt. analyst, U. Pa., 1992. Adminstrv. asst. Merrill Lynch, Everett, Wash., 1981-84, fin. cons., 1984-92, sales mgr., 1992—. Contbr. articles to bus. jours. Donor, patron Everett Cmty. Theater. Mem. Nat. ESOP Assn., Investment Mgmt. Cons. Assn., Nat. Ctr. for Employee Ownership, Chmn.'s Club Merrill Lynch. Avocations: travel, reading, scuba diving. Office: Merrill Lynch 2707 Colby Ave Ste 1401 Everett WA 98201-3568

BARTLETT, THOMAS ALVA, educational administrator; b. Salem, Oreg., Aug. 20, 1930; s. Cleave Wines and Alma (Hanson) B.; m. Mary Louise Bixby, Mar. 20, 1954; children: Thomas Glenn, Richard A., Paul H. Student, Willamette U., 1947-49, DCL (hon.), 1986; A.B., Stanford U., 1951, Ph.D., 1959; M.A. (Rhodes scholar), Oxford U., 1953; L.H.D. (hon.), Colgate U., 1977, Mich. State U., 1978, Union Coll., 1979; D.C.L. (hon.), Pusan Nat. U., Korea, 1985, U. Ala., 1983. Mem. U.S. Permanent Mission to UN, 1956-63; advisor Gen. Assembly Dels., 1956-63; pres. Am. U., Cairo, 1963-69, Colgate U., Hamilton, N.Y., 1969-77, Assn. Am. Univs., Washington, 1977-82; chancellor U. Ala. System, 1982-89, Oreg. State System of Higher Edn. Office, Eugene, 1989-94, SUNY, 1994-96; ret.; mem. UAR-U.S. Ednl. Exch. Commn., 1966-69; mem. Task Force on Financing Higher Edn. in N.Y. State (Keppel Commn.), 1972-73; chmn. Commn. Ind. Colls. and Univs. N.Y., 1974-76; bd. dirs. Nat. Assn. Ind. Colls. and Univs., 1975-76; trustee Univs. Field Staff Internat., 1985-87; mem. NASA Comml. Space Adv. Com., 1988-90. Mem. nat. bd. examining Chaplains Episcopal Ch., 1978-91; trustee Gen. Theol. Sem., 1977-82, Am. U. in Cairo, 1978— (vie chair 1998—), U.S.-Japan Found., 1988— (chm. 1996—), bd. mem. Internat. Assn. of Univs., 1995—. Mem. Coun. Fgn. Rels., Phi Beta Kappa, Century Assn. Home: 2550 Fairmount Blvd Eugene OR 97403

BARTOK, MICHELLE, cosmetic company executive; b. Youngstown, Ohio, Feb. 18, 1961; d. Albert James and Judith Ann (Phillips) Bartok; m. John Anthony Garruto, Apr. 2, 1988 (div. 1997); children: Catherine Michelle, Gabrielle Bartok. BS in Physiol. Psychology, U. Calif., Santa Barbara, 1983. EMT, Calif. Asst. to phys. therapist Santa Barbara Phys. Therapy, 1983-84, Escondido (Calif.) Phys. Therapy, 1984-85; regional sales rep. Ft. Dodge Labs., San Francisco, 1985-87; owner North Coast Therapeutics, Oceanside, Calif., 1987-92; CEO, Innovative Bioscis. Corp., Carlsbad, Calif., 1992—. Mem. Nat. Women's Fitness Assn., Women's Enterprise Network, Soc. Cosmetic Chemists, Beauty Industry West (pub. rels. dir. 1991-92, chair symposium 1996), Internat. Spa and Fitness Assn. (sponsor Ironman competition 1989). Avocations: surfing, scuba diving, yoga. Home: 178 Grandview St Encinitas CA 92024-1009 Office: Innovative Bioscis Corp 2724 Loker Ave W Carlsbad CA 92008-6603

BARTON, ANN ELIZABETH, retired financial executive; b. Long Lake, Mich., Sept. 8, 1923; d. John and Inez Mabel (Morse) Seaton; m. H. Kenneth Barton, Apr. 3, 1948; children: Michael, John, Nancy. Student Mt. San Antonio Coll., 1969-71, Adrian Coll., 1943, Citrus Coll., 1967, Golden Gate U., 1976, Coll. Fin. Planning, 1980-82. CFP. Tax cons., real estate broker, Claremont, Calif., 1967-72, Newport Beach, Calif., 1972-74; v.p., officer Putney, Barton, Assocs., Inc., Walnut Creek, Calif., 1975-94, ret., 1997; bd. dir. Fin. Svc. Corp. Cert. fin. planner. Mem. Internat. Assn. Fin. Planners (registered investment advisor), Calif. Soc. Enrolled Agts., Nat. Assn. Enrolled Agts., Inst. CFP.

BARTON, BILLIE JO, artist, educator; b. Childress, Tex., June 23, 1926; d. Robert Douglas and Erma Ada (Collier) Perry; m. Hudson James Barton, June 28, 1947; 1 child, David Douglas. Student, Frank Wiggins Sch., 1944-45, ABC Sch. Dist., 1956-86; studied with Ken Decker, Mary Bugher. Art instr. Smithys Art Gallery, Orange, Calif., 1976-77, Internat. Studio, Cerritos, Calif., 1978-79, Lakewood, Calif., 1980—; juror Fine Art Commn., Buena Park, Calif., 1993-96. Author: The Guidebook for Oil Painters, 1993; work pub. in books: Artists of California, 1993, Encyclopedia of Living Artist, 1997; editor Buena Park Art Guild newsletter, 1993; group exhibits and juried shows include The La Mirada (Calif.) Art Gallery, 1993-94, Art Assocs. Gallery, Huntington Beach, Calif., 1994, Calif. Coun. Art League, 1992, 93, 94, Knott's Berry Farm Artist Round-Up, Buena Park, 1992, 93, 94, Fine Art Inst. San Bernardino County Mus., Redlands, Calif., 1992, 93, 94, Santa Barbara 6th Ann. Festival Art, 1994, Festival Whales Dana Point Harbor, Dana Point, Calif., 1995, Newport Beach Festival Art, Newport, Calif., 1995, Tall Ships Show, Dana Point, 1995, 21st Ann. Juried Art Exhibit, Cypress, Calif., 1996, Sunday Arts Delight, Cypress, 1996, Ann. Father's Day Celebration, Dana Point, 1996. Parent aide PTA, Lakewood, 1959-64; den mother Cub Scouts Am., Lakewood, 1961; precinct worker Los Angeles County Elections, Norwalk, Calif., 1949, Lakewood, 1965-86. Fellow Nat. Mus. Women in Arts, Niguel Art Assn., Nat. Assn. Fine Art, Buena Art Guild (recording sec. 1992-96, Best of Show award 1992), Ea. Star Lodge (hostess 1966-67); mem. La Palma Art Assn. (news editor, v.p. 1975-76, Artist of Yr. award 1976). Republican. Avocations: travel, gardening. Home and Studio: 11720 207th St Lakewood CA 90715-1331

BARUA, DIBAKAR, English language and literature educator, writer; b. Chittagong, Bangladesh, Oct. 17, 1951; came to U.S., 1977; s. Rajendra Binode and Mallika (Choudhury) B.; m. Carol Ann Wester, Oct. 23, 1982 (div. Feb. 1997); m. Rupa Ward, Dec. 18, 1998. MA, U. Dhaka (Bangladesh), 1972; diploma in Language, Lit., Edinburgh (Scotland) U., 1977; PhD, SUNY (Stony Brook), 1982. Asst. prof. SUNY (Stony Brook), 1982-83; lectr. UCLA, 1983-89; English prof. Golden West Coll., Huntington Beach, Calif., 1989—, chair English dept., 1996—. Author short stories; contbr. articles to profl jours. Coord. Puente Project Golden West Coll., 1991-92; faculty adv. Buddhist Student Club, Golden West Coll., 1993-97; v.p. acad. senate, Golden West Coll., 1994-95; adv. bd. mem. Collegiate Handbook, Collegiate Press, San Diego, 1997—. Brit. Coun. scholar, London, 1976; SUNY Intercampus Doctoral fellow, 1979. Democrat. Office: Golden W Coll 15744 Golden West St Huntington Beach CA 92647-3103

BARUSCH, AMANDA SMITH, social welfare educator, researcher; b. Long Beach, Calif., Sept. 8, 1955; d. Gilbert T. and Helen (Dauphine) Smith; m. Lawrence Roos Barusch, Aug. 7, 1983; children: Ariana Grace, Nathaniel Morris. BA, Reed Coll., Portland, Oreg., 1977; M in Social Welfare, U. Calif., Berkeley, 1981, D in Social Welfare, 1985. Planner Govt. of Guam, Agana, 1980-82, supr. Title XX, 1983-84; teaching asst. U. Calif., Berkeley, 1982-83; asst. prof. U. Guam, Mangilao, 1984-85; asst. prof. grad. sch. social work U. Utah, Salt Lake City, 1985-90, assoc. prof. grad. sch. social work, 1990-94, prof. grad. sch. social work, 1994—; chmn. rev. bd. Salt Lake City Alcohol/Drug Abuse Services, 1985—; tng. cons. Sr. Companion Program, Salt Lake City, 1985—; mem. Gov.'s Task Force, Agana, 1984, Gov.'s Commn., Agana, 1984-85. Contbr. articles on social work and psychology to profl. jours. Mem. Hospice Adv. Bd. Named Regent's fellow U. Calif., Berkeley, 1982, 83. Mem. Guam Assn. Social Workers (pres. 1984-85), Nat. Assn. Social Workers, Nat. Council on Aging, Am. Soc. on Aging, Gerontol. Soc. Am. Democrat. Office: U Utah Social Work Bldg 1 University of Utah Salt Lake City UT 84112

BARVILLE, REBECCA PENELOPE, elementary school educator; b. Tulare, Calif., Nov. 7, 1936; m. David Leopold Barville, June 8, 1958; children: Mark, Becky, Curtis. BA, Simpson Coll., San Francisco, 1958; MA summa cum laude, Fresno State U., 1974. Cert. reading specialist, edn. adminstr., elem. tchr., Calif. Social worker Tulare County Welfare Dept., Porterville, Calif., 1961-63, San Bernadino Welfare, Ontario, Calif., 1963-65; tchr., reading specialist Pleasant View Sch., Porterville, 1969—; instr. Porterville Coll., 1993—. Pres. PTA, Lindsay, Calif., 1966-67. Fellow Delta Kappa Gamma; mem. AAUW (bd. dirs. 1974-83), Calif. Reading Assn. (sec. 1974), Pleasant View Educators Assn. (past pres., sec. 1985—). Republican. Presbyterian. Club: P.E.O. (v.p. 1986-87). Avocations: cross country skiing, swimming, hiking, biking, reading.

BASCH, REVA, information services company executive; b. Chgo., Aug. 1, 1947; d. Victor Hugo and Hertha (Levi) B.; m. Jerrald C. Shifman, Apr. 17, 1982. BA in English Lit. summa cum laude, U. Pa., 1969; MLS, U. Calif., Berkeley, 1971. Head libr. Cogswell Coll., San Francisco, 1971-72; tech. info. specialist Gilbert Assocs. Inc., Reading, Pa., 1973-79; tech. libr. NuTech, San Jose, Calif., 1980-81; rsch. assoc. Info. on Demand, Berkeley, Calif., 1981-82, asst. dir. rsch., 1982-83, dir. rsch., 1983-86, v.p., dir. rsch., 1985-86; software designer Mead Data Ctrl., Personal Computer Sys. Group, Menlo Park, Calif., 1986-88; pres. Aubergine Info. Svcs., The Sea Ranch, Calif., 1986—. Author: Secrets of the Super Searchers, 1993, Electronic Information Delivery: Ensuring Quality and Value, 1995, Secrets of the Super Net Searchers, 1996, Researching Online for Dummies, 1998; columnist Online mag., CyberSkeptic's Guide to Internet Rsch.; contbr. articles to profl. jours. Recipient award for best paper UMI/Data Courier, 1990, Online Champion award Dun & Bradstreet. Mem. Assn. of Ind. Info. Profl.(pres.1991-92), Spl. Librs. Assn. , Assn. Info. and Dissemination Ctrs., Info. Bay Area, So. Calif. Online Users Group. Avocations: online communications, reading, travel, cooking.

BASCOM, JOHN UPTON, surgeon; b. Richmond, Va., June 6, 1925; s. Kellog F. and Lillian (Paulson) B.; m. Ruth Fenton, June 4, 1950; children: Lucinda, Ellen, Rebecca, Thomas, Paul, Mary. BS, Kans. State U., 1948, MS, 1949; MD, Northwestern U., Chgo., 1953; PhD in Surgery, U. Minn., 1960. Diplomate Am. Bd. Surgery. Intern Cook County Hosp., Chgo., 1953-54; resident in surgery Mpls. Gen. Hosp., 1954-60; pvt. practice, Eugene, Oreg., 1960—; mem. surg. staff Sacred Heart Med. Ctr., Eugene, 1960—; mem. Oreg. Bd. Med. Examiners, Salem, 1972-77, sec.-treas., 1974, chmn., 1976. Fellow ACS (pres. Oreg. chpt. 1982); mem. N.W. Soc. Colon and Rectal Surgeons (pres. 1995), Pacific Coast Surg. Soc., North Pacific Surg. Assn., Lane County Med. Soc. (pres. 1971). Avocation: tree farming. Office: 655 E 11th Ave Ste 5 Eugene OR 97401-3621

BASCOM, RUTH F., retired mayor; b. Ames, Iowa, Feb. 4, 1926; d. Frederick Charles and Doris Hays Fenton; m. John U. Bascom, June 14, 1950; children: Lucinda, Rebecca, Ellen, Thomas, Paul, Mary. BS, Kans. State U., Manhattan, 1946; MA, Cornell U., 1949. Tchr. Dickinson County Cmty. H.S., Kans., 1946-48, Nat. Coll. Edn., Chgo., 1949-51; co-chair Cascadia High Speed Rail, 1995-98. Chair City and State Bicycle Com., 1971-83; mem., chair Met. Park Bd., Eugene, 1972-82; past bd. pres. Youth Symphony; city councilor City of Eugene, Oreg., 1984-92, coun. v.p., pres., 1988-90, mayor, 1993-97; v.p., pres. LWV, Eugene, 1967-69; adv. coun. Willamette Valley Passenger Rail, 1997—. Recipient Gold Leaf award Internat. Soc. Arboriculture, 1993. Democrat. Congregational. Avocations: music, tree farm, bicycling. Fax: 541-683-4717. Home: 2114 University St Eugene OR 97403-1542 Office: City of Eugene 777 Pearl St Ste 105 Eugene OR 97401-2720

BASCONCILLO, LINDY, insurance and financial services company executive; b. Honolulu, Dec. 11, 1943; s. Catalino M. and Primitiva (Barientos) B.; children: Lisa M., Rod Alan. BA, Pacific Union Coll., 1965; MA, Azusa Pacific U., 1979. CLU. Tchr., vice prin. Santa Monica (Calif.) Jr. Acad., 1965-68; tchr. Temple City (Calif.) Unified Schs., 1968-79; sales agent N.Y. Life Ins. Co., Eugene, Oreg., 1980-81, tng. mgr., 1981-87; sales mgr. MONY Fin. Svcs., Eugene, 1987-88; sr. mktg. cons. Prudential Ins. and Fin. Svcs., Woodland Hills, Calif., 1988-89; sales mgr. Prudential Ins. and Fin. Svcs., Sacramento, 1989-91; bus., estate, retirement specialist John Deere Life Ins. Co., Calif. and Nev., 1991-94; dist. sales mgr. Mut. of Omaha, 1994-95; mng. dir. Elite Consulting, Lincoln, Calif., 1994—; brokerage dir. Nat. Life of Vt., 1995-96; reg. rep., agy. tng. dir. MassMutual, Sacramento, 1996—; bus. cons. Jr. Achievement, Eugene, 1986; pres.-elect Eugene Life Underwriters Assn., 1988, v.p., 1987; chairperson Life Underwriter Tng. Coun., 1987, moderator, 1984-86. Mem. coun. for minority edn. U. Oreg., Eugene, 1986-88; mem. Lane County Tng. and Devel. Com., Eugene, 1985-87. Mem. Sacramento Chpt. CLU's (bd. dirs.), Sacramento Life Underwriters Assn. Avocations: snow skiing, golfing. Home: 1812 5th St Lincoln CA 95648-2328 Office: 2180 Harvard St Ste 375 Sacramento CA 95815-3324

BASEMAN, SANDRA LIBBIE, editor, financial advisor; b. Detroit, Nov. 22, 1949; d. Jerome Sylvan and Mildred (Zaff) B.; m. Carl A. Keene, May 23, 1971; children: Jerome, Rachel. AB, U. Mich., 1971, AM, 1976. Admitted Registry of Fin. Planning Practitioners; CFP. Asst. editor Great Lakes Basin Commn., Ann Arbor, Mich., 1974-76; grad. student tchg. asst. U. Mich., Ann Arbor, 1976-78; mktg. asst. Caz Co., Santa Clara, Calif., 1978-79; pvt. practice fin. advisor San Jose, Calif., 1979-93; fin. advisor, mktg. coord. Reinhardt Werba Bowen, San Jose, 1993-94, dir. corp. comm., 1994—; bd. mem., membership dir. Inst. CFP, Silicon Valley Chpt., 1984-87; bd. mem. Internat. Assn. for Fin. Planning, Santa Clara County Chpt., San Jose, 1986-87. Phone counselor, trainer Women's Crisis Ctr., Ann Arbor, 1973-76; precinct leader Dem. Party, San Jose, 1992; bd. mem. pub. rels. East Hills Elem. Sch., San Jose, 1992-94; vol. clinic def. Planned Parenthood, San Jose, 1993. Office: Reinhardt Werba Bowen 1190 Saratoga Ave Ste 200 San Jose CA 95129-3433

BASHA, CLAUDIA ANN, language and theater arts educator; b. Chgo., Feb. 14, 1948; d. Richard Robert and Marion Frances (Millizen) Johnson; m. Leroy Conrad Basha, Dec. 27, 1969. BA in English, U. Ill., 1969; Hautes Etudes et Lettres, Ctr. Universitaire, Avignon, France, 1984; MS in Curriculum and Instrn., Okla. State U., 1985; postgrad., Calif. State U., San Bernardino, 1990—. French instr. Okla. State U., Stillwater, 1983-85; part-time instr. French and English Victor Valley Coll., Victorville, Calif., 1986-88, prof. French and English, 1988—. Bd. dirs. Victor Valley Symphony Assn., Victorville, 1996—. Mem. NEA, Nat. Coun. Tchrs. English. Avocation: breeding quarter paint horses. Office: Victor Valley Coll Langs Dept 18422 Bear Valley Rd Victorville CA 92392-5850

BASICHIS, GORDON ALLEN, author, screenwriter; b. Phila., Aug. 23, 1947; s. Martin and Ruth (Gordon) B.; m. Marcia Hammond; 1 child, Casey James. BS, Temple U., 1969. Reporter Phila. Bull., 1969; writer, reporter Santa Fe News, 1971-72; with advt., pub. relations Jay Bernstein Pub. Relations, Los Angeles, 1978-80; screenwriter Metro Goldwyn Mayer Feature Films, Culver City, Calif., 1982-83; ind. writer, 1983—; pres. Moonlight, Inc., L.a., 1982—; exec. v.p. Antigua Rd. Prodns., 1996. Author: Beautiful Bad Girl: The Vicki Morgan Story, 1985, (novel) Constant Travelers, 1978; producer, dir. (video documentary) Jerry: One Man's Triumph, 1980; co-prodr. (TV series) Frank and Jesse; screenwriter Breach of Trust, 1994, Princess Pamela, 1998-99; co-writer Shysters, 1996; exec. prodr. Land of Dreams, 1999—. Mem. Dem. Nat. Com. Mem. Writers Guild Am. West, Am. Film Inst., Simon Wiesenthal Inst., Statue of Liberty/Ellis Island Found. Office: PO Box 1511 Beverly Hills CA 90213-1511

BASILE, PAUL LOUIS, JR., lawyer; b. Oakland, Calif., Dec. 27, 1945; s. Paul Louis and Roma Florence (Paris) B.; m. Linda Lou Paige, June 20, 1970; m. 2d Diane Chierichetti, Sept. 2, 1977. BA, Occidental Coll., 1968; postgrad., U. Wash., 1969; JD, UCLA, 1971. Bar: Calif. 1972, U.S. Dist. Ct. (cen. dist.) Calif. 1972, U.S. Dist. Ct. (no. dist.) Calif. 1985, U.S. Ct. Appeals (9th cir.) 1972, U.S. Tax Ct. 1977, U.S. Ct. Claims. 1978, U.S. Customs Ct. 1979, U.S. Ct. Customs and Patent Appeals 1979, U.S. Ct. Internat. Trade 1981, U.S. Supreme Ct. 1977; cert. specialist in taxation law Bd. of Legal [illegible] & O'Hara, L.A., 1971-72; corp. counsel TFI Cos., Inc., Irvine, Calif., 1972-73; pvt. practice L.A., 1973-80, 90-96, 98—; mem. Basile & Siener, L.A., 1980-86, Clark & Trevithick, L.A., 1986-90; ptnr. Wolf, Rifkin & Shapiro, L.A., 1990, of counsel, 1990-92; ptnr. Basile & Lane, LLP, L.A., 1996-97; of counsel Shaffer, Gold & Rubaum, L.L.P., L.A., 1996—; gen. counsel J.W. Brown, Inc., L.A., 1980—, asst. sec., 1984-92; sec., gen. counsel Souriau, Inc., Valencia, Calif., 1981-90; v.p., sec., dir., gen. counsel Pvt. Fin. Assocs., L.A., 1983-94; gen. counsel Quest Relocation Group, Toluca Lake, Calif., 1994-97, v.p. real estate, 1996—. Trustee, sec. Nat. Repertory Theatre Found., 1975-94, mem. exec. com., 1976-94, chmn. bd. dirs., 1991-94; mem. fin. com., bd. dirs. Calif. Music Theatre, 1988-92; bd. dirs. March of Dimes Birth Defects Found., Los Angeles County, 1982-87, mem. exec. com., 1983-86, sec., 1985-86; dist. fin. chmn. L.A. Area coun. Boy Scouts Am., 1982-83; trustee Occidental Coll., L.A., 1989-94; active L.A. Olympic Organizing Com., Ketchum Downtown YMCA, Vols. Am. L.A., others. Mem. ABA (taxation sect., corp. tax com., vice chmn. closely held bus. com. 1992-94, chair, 1994-96, chmn. subcom. on continuing legal edn. 1990-94, chmn. subcom. on estate planning 1992, sec. 1996-97, small firm lawyers com., bus. law sect., real property sect., probate and trust law sect., spl. problems of bus. owners com., estate planning and drafting, pre-death planning issues com.), State Bar Calif. (bus. law sect., nonprofit and unicorporated orgns. com. 1989-92, taxation sect., estate planning, trust and probate sect., taxation law adv. commn. 1994-97, vice chmn. 1995-96, chair 1996-97, mem. bd. legal specialization 1996-97), L.A. County Bar Assn. (taxation sect., com. on closely-held and pass-through entities, bus. and corps. law sect., sole practitioner section exec. com. 1995—), Beverly Hills Bar Assn. (probate, trust & estate planning section, taxation section, vice chmn. Estate and Gift Tax Com., 1998—, law practice mgmt. section), Can. Calif. C. of C. (dir. 1980-89, 2d v.p. 1983-84, 1st v.p. 1984-85, pres. 1985-87), L.A.-Vancouver Sister City Assn. (dir., exec. com. 1987-92, treas. 1987-89, pres. 1989-92), French-Am. C. of C. (councilor 1979-84, v.p. 1980, 82-84), L.A. Area C. of C. (dir. 1980-81), Occidental Coll. Alumni Assn. (pres. 1979-80, v.p. 1978-79, alumni bd. govs. 1977-81, chmn. annual fund campaign 1990-91), Grand People (bd. dirs. 1985-92, chmn. bd. 1986-92), Rotary Club of L.A. (dir. 1994-96, sergeant-at-arms 1986-87, chmn. gateway com. 1993-94, chmn. world cmty. svc. com. 1991-93, chmn. vols. Am. of L.A. com. 1988-90, chmn. golf com. 1986-87, vice-chmn. pres. com. 1985-86), Rotary Internat. (chmn. club extension com. 1995-96, cmty. svc. dir. 1993-95, chmn. gift of life com. 1992-93), Small Bus. Coun. of Am., Inc. (legal adv. bd. 1989—), The Group, Inc., Attorneys for Family Held Enterprises. Democrat. Baptist. Home: 3937 Beverly Glen Blvd Sherman Oaks CA 91423-4404 Office: 11400 W Olympic Blvd Ste 350 Los Angeles CA 90064-1558

BASINGER, RICHARD LEE, lawyer; b. Canton, Ohio, Nov. 24, 1941; s. Eldon R. and Alice M. (Bartholomew) B.; m. Rita Evelyn Gover, May 14, 1965; children: David A., Darron M. BA in Edn., Ariz. State U., 1963; postgrad. Macalester Coll., 1968-69; JD, U. Ariz., 1973. Bar: Ariz. 1973, U.S. Dist. Ct. Ariz. 1973, U.S. Tax Ct. 1977, U.S. Ct. Appeals (6th cir.) 1975, U.S. Ct. Appeals (9th cir.) 1976, U.S. Supreme Ct. 1977; cert. arbitrator. Assoc. law offices, Phoenix, 1973-74; pvt. practice, Scottsdale, Ariz. 1974-75; pres. Basinger & Assocs., P.C., Scottsdale, 1975—, also bd. dirs. Contbr. articles to profl. jours. Bd. dirs. Masters Trail Ventures, Scottsdale, 1984-85, Here's Life, Ariz., Scottsdale, 1976—; precinct committeeman Republican Party, Phoenix, 1983—; bd. dir. Ariz. Coll. of the Bible, 1992-93. NSF grantee, 1968-69. Mem. ABA, Ariz. Bar Assn., Maricopa County Bar Assn., Ariz. State Horseman's Assn. (bd. dirs. 1984-86, 1st v.p. 1986), Scottsdale Bar Assn., Western Saddle Club (bd. dirs. 1983-86, pres. 1985-86), Scottsdale Saddle Club, Saguaro Saddle Club. Baptist. Office: Mohave County Atty Dep County Atty Civil Divsn PO Box 7000 Kingman AZ 86402-7000

BASKERVILLE, TIM, marketing executive; b. Burbank, Calif., July 31, 1949; s. David Ross and Roberta Mildred (Hollis) B.; m. Carol Kahler, Jan. 19, 1974 (div. June 1983); 1 child, Robin Ann. BA in Theatre Arts, TV, UCLA, 1971. Assoc. producer Sta. KNXT/CBS News, Hollywood, Calif., 1967-71; reporter Radio News West, Los Angeles, 1972; news producer Sta. KTVU Cox Broadcasting, Oakland, Calif., 1972-73; dep. bur. chief TV News, Inc., Los Angeles, 1973-74; pres. Media Service Corp., Hollywood, 1975-80, Video Mktg. (name now Vidmar Communications, Inc.), Hollywood, 1980-93, Baskerville Comm., L.A., 1993—; cons. ABC, CBS, Metro-Goldwyn-Mayer/United Artists, Eastman Kodak, 20th Century Fox, IBM, Tribune Co., Young and Rubicam, J. Walter Thompson, Grey Advt., and others. Editor: (newsletters) Job Leads, 1977, Video Mktg., 1980— (also pub.); creator (TV documentary) Alien and Illegal, 1971 (Emmy award nomination 1972); contbr. articles to Los Angeles Times. Mem. Newsletter Assn. (founder, pres. So. Calif. chpt. 1981-82), Radio TV News Assn. So. Calif., Radio TV News Dirs. Assn., Writers Guild Am. West. Club: Overseas Press of Am.

BASKIN, CATHRYN, magazine editor. BA in English, SUNY, Albany; MEd, North Adams State Coll. Feature editor Popular Computing; mng. editor Byte, Lotus, New Eng. Living, PC World, San Francisco; editor-in-chief, 1996—. McAllister Editl. fellow Am. Bus. Press, 1995. Office: PC World 501 2d St Ste 600 San Francisco CA 94107-1496*

BASKIN, OTIS WAYNE, business educator; b. Houston, Oct. 26, 1945; s. Samuel and Ollie Estell (Key) B.; m. Maryan Kay Patrick, Dec. 26, 1970. BA, Okla. Christian Coll., 1968; MA, U. Houston, 1970; PhD, U. Tex., 1975. Asst. prof. Tex. Luth. Coll., Seguin, 1970-75; prof. U. Houston, 1975-87; prof., acad. dir. Ariz. State U., Phoenix, 1987-91; prof., dean Memphis State U., 1991-92, prof., dir. family bus., 1992-95; dean George L. Graziadio Sch. Bus. and Mgmt. Pepperdine U., Malibu, Calif., 1995—; vis. faculty U. Md., London, 1979, Oxford U., 1994; dir. Durham Found., Memphis, 1992-95; cons. Ministry Trade, Sophia, Bulgaria, 1990, Utara U., Malaysia, 1992. Author: Guidelines for Research in Business Communication, 1977, (With Craig Aronoff) Interpersonal Communication in Organizations, 1980, Getting Your Message Across, 1981, Public Relations: The Profession and the practice, 1983, (with Grover Starling) Issues in Business and Society: Capitalism and Public Purpose, 1985; contbr. articles to profl. jours. Bd. dirs. Jr. Achievement Memphis, 1991-92, Econ. Club Memphis, 1991-94, Theatre Memphis, 1992-95, Margurite Pizza Gala for St. Jude's Hosp., Memphis, 1992-95. Recipient Advancing Pub. Rels. Through Rsch. award Tex. Pub. Rels. Soc., Houston, 1983. Mem. Acad. Mgmt. (divsn. chair 1985), Rotary, Sigma Iota Epsilon (bd. dirs. 1986—), Beta Gamma Sigma. mem. Ch. of Christ. Avocations: reading, travel. Office: George L Graziadio Sch Bus & Mgmt Pepperdine Univ Malibu CA 90263

BASLER, RICHARD ALAN, medical consultant; b. San Francisco, Sept. 12, 1939; s. Henry Edwin and Margaret Henrietta (Cooper) B.; m. Carol Audrey Foster, Aug. 4, 1962; children: Rodney Giles, Eric Richard. BA, U. Calif., Berkeley, 1960; MBA, U. Phoenix, Irvine, Calif., 1983. Indsl. engr., prodn. supr. Standard Register, Oakland and Corcoran, Calif., 1967-72; knitting supt. Duplan Knits West, Carson, Calif., 1972-75; prodn. supr. Am. Edwards Labs., Irvine, 1976-78, chief indsl. engr., 1978-80, supr. mfg. engring., 1980-86, with engring. systems devel., 1986-87; mgr. quality assurance/quality control Cardiovascular Devices Inc., 1987-88; dir. quality assurance/quality control Applied Vascular Devices Inc., 1988-90, dir. compliance, 1990-94; dir. compliance Micro Therapeutics, Inc., 1994-96; v.p. ops. Laurus Med. Corp., Irvine, Calif., 1996-97; pres. Med-Visory Cons., Irvine, 1997—; owner Internat. Numismatics, Irvine, 1974—. Editor Calif. Engr. mag., 1959, ASQ Scope mag., 1998; contbr. articles to mags. Bd. dirs. UNCAP, Inc., L.A., 1980-82; pres. Colonnade of History, 1990—. Recipient Kenneth Brainard Meml. Literary award, George Bennett Meml. Literary award. Mem. Am. Soc. Quality, U.S. Kerry Blue Terrier Club (gov. 1983-85), Gt. Western Terrier (bd. dirs. 1979-92). Republican. Avocations: ancient numismatics, breeding show dogs. Office: Med-Visory Cons 15412 Verdun Cir Irvine CA 92604

BASS, AUDREY, commodities trader; b. 1946. With Berger & Plate Co., San Francisco, 1966-74, Berger & Co., San Francisco, 1974-88; asst. sec., treas. Berdex Internat. Inc., San Francisco, 1988—. Office: Berdex Internat Inc 1050 Sansome St Ste 300 San Francisco CA 94111-1325*

BASS, HAROLD NEAL, pediatrician, medical geneticist; b. Chgo., Apr. 14, 1939; s. Louis A. and Minnie (Schachter) B.; m. Phyllis Appell, June 25, 1961; children: Laura Renee, Alana Suzanne. Student, U. Ill., 1956-59; MS in Pharmacology, U. Chgo., 1963, MD, 1963. Diplomate Am. Bd. Pediatrics, Am. Bd. Med. Genetics, Nat. Bd. Med. Examiners. Intern Children's Meml. Hosp., Chgo., 1963-64; resident Children's Meml. Hosp., 1964-65, chief resident, 1965-66, fellow in med. genetics, 1965-66; chief pediatrics and profl. svcs. Norton AFB Hosp., Calif., 1966-68; attending pediatrician/med. geneticist Kaiser Permanente Med. Ctr., Panorama City, Calif., 1968—; dir. med. genetics prog. Kaiser Permanente Med. Care Program So. Calif., 1987—; clin. prof. pediatrics and genetics UCLA Med. Sch., 1970—; pres. med. staff Kaiser Permanente Med. Ctr., 1989; bd. dirs. So. Calif. Permanente Med. Group, 1998—; adj. prof. biology Calif. State U., Northridge, 1995—. Contbr. articles to profl. jours. Mem. mayor's adv. com. San Fernando Valley, City of L.A., 1973-78. Capt. M.C., USAF, 1966-68. Fellow Am. Coll. Human Genetics, Western Soc. Pediat. Rsch., L.A. Pediats. Soc., San Fernando Valley Interfaith Coun., Pacific S.W. Regional Genetics Network, Handgun Control, ACLU, Am. Soc. Human Genetics, Amnesty Internat., Physicians for Social Responsibility. Democrat. Jewish. Avocations: civic affairs, music, writing. Home: 11922 Dunnicliffe Ct Northridge CA 91326-1324 Office: Kaiser Permanente Med Ctr 13652 Cantara St Panorama City CA 91402-5423

BASS, KENNETH LEE, radio broadcast consultant; b. St. Louis, Jan. 28, 1944; s. Orville E. and Elsie Ruth (Lancaster) B.; m. Myra L. Wiesenthal, Oct. 28, 1970; children: Tiffany L. Medlin, Kierstan L. Bass. Cert., Nat. Tech. Inst., 1960, RCA Tech. Inst., 1974. FCC lifetime gen. radiotelephone lic. Announcer, news dir. Sta. KWRE Radio, Warrenton, Mo., 1962-66; owner, operator K&M Field Svc., St. Peters, Mo., 1970-81; pres., gen. mgr., chief exec. Lynnlee Broadcasting Co. Inc., Monroe City, Mo., 1981-85; chief engr. Sta. KBCQ-KCKN Radio, Roswell, N.Mex., 1985-89, Sta. KBIM Radio, Roswell, 1989-93; owner, operator K&M Consulting, Alamogordo, N.Mex., 1993—; chmn. Emergency Comms. Com., Roswell, 1990-95. Staff sgt. USAF, 1966-70. Mem. Am. Assn. Ret. Persons, Masons (Roswell Lodge # 18). Avocations: photography, computers, travel. Home: PO Box 1109 Alamogordo NM 88311-1109

BASS, NANCY AGNES, airport executive; b. Beaver Falls, Pa., Feb. 26, 1937; d. John Joseph and Kathleen Lillian (Retzer) Paff; m. Lee Herbert Bass, Jan. 10, 1959; children: Thomas Andrew, Marilee, Laura Kathleen. Student, Clarion State Coll., 1954-56. Purchasing clk. Orange County Purchasing Dept., Santa Ana, Calif., 1957-60; bookkeeper Cal Gas, Ridgecrest, Calif., 1975-78; interline mgr. C and M Airlines, Inyokern, Calif., 1978-82; mgr. CLC Engring and Surveying, Ridgecrest, Calif., 1982-86; gen. mgr. Indian Wells Valley Airport Dist., Inyokern, Calif., 1985—, Ridgecrest (Calif.) Redevel. Agy., 1989-90; chair Kern County Aviation Transp. Tech. Adv. Com., Bakerfield, Calif., 1989, 92; mem. tech. adv. com. for aeronautics State of Calif. Transp. Commn., 1994—. Bd. dirs. Ridgecrest Bd. of Appeals, 1986-90, dir. High Desert Child Abuse Prevention Coun., Ridgecrest, 1985-87, Am. Cancer Soc., Ridgecrest, 1988—, sec. Airport Dist. Formation Com., Ridgecrest, 1983-85; planning commr. City of Ridgecrest, 1990—, vice-chair, 1992-94, chair 1995—; dir., treas. Ridgecrest Area Conv. & Visitor Bur., 1992-94, chair., 1995—. Mem. Calif. Assn. Airport Execs., Am. Assn. Airport Execs. (cert.), Altrusa. Home: 600 W Coral Ave Ridgecrest CA 93555-5214 Office: IWV Airport Dist PO Box 634 Inyokern CA 93527-0634

BASSETT, JOHN WALDEN, JR., lawyer; b. Roswell, N.Mex., Mar. 21, 1938; s. John Walden Sr. and Evelyn (Thompson) B.; m. Patricia Lubben, May 22, 1965 (dec. Apr. 22, 1995); children: John Walden III, Loren Patricia; m. Nolana Knight, May 2, 1998. AB in Econs., Stanford U., 1960; LLB with honors, U. Tex., 1964. Bar: Tex. 1964, N.Mex. 1964. Assoc. Atwood & Malone, Roswell, 1964-66; White House fellow, spl. asst. to U.S. atty. gen., Washington, 1966-67; ptnr. Atwood, Malone, Mann & Turner and predecessors, P.A., Roswell, 1967-95, Bassett & Copple, LLP, 1995—; bd. dirs. A.H. Belo Corp., Dallas, AMMA Found., Washington. Assoc. editor: U. Tex. Law Review, 1962; mem. N.Mex. State Bd. of Edn., 1987-91. Pres., chmn. bd. United Way of Chaves County, N.Mex., 1973; bd. dirs. Ednl. Achievement Found., Roswell, 1992—. 1st lt. U.S. Army, 1961-68. Mem. ABA, Tex. Bar Assn., N.Mex. Bar Assn., Chaves County Bar Assn., Order of Coif, Rotary (pres. 1976, Roswell), N.Mex. Amigos, Phi Delta Phi. Republican. Episcopalian. Home: 5060 Bright Sky Rd Roswell NM 88201-8800 Office: Bassett & Copple 400 N Pennsylvania Ave Ste 250 Roswell NM 88201-4788

BASTINE, PAUL ARTHUR, judge; b. Laramie, Wyo., June 1, 1939; s. Arthur Bastine and Anne S. (McLay) Hedge; m. Janet E. Harris, Feb. 19, 1966; children: Patricia Anne, Kenneth McLay. JD, Gonzaga U., 1964. Bar: Wash. 1964. Dep. prosecuting atty. Spokane, Wash., 1966; pvt. practice, Spokane, 1966-95; prin. Lukins, Annis & Bastine, P.S. and predecessors, Spokane, 1966-78, Bastine, Carroll & Iverson, P.S. and predecessors, Spokane, 1978-95; judge dept. 8 Superior Ct. of Spokane County, Spokane, 1995—; mem. Spokane County Legal Svcs. Bd., 1971-76; incorporator Evergreen Legal Svcs., 1976, treas., 1976-78, bd. apptd. by Wash. state bar bd. govs., 1976-80; apptd. mem. Legal Svcs. Adv. Coun. for Wash. State, 1976; apptd. bd. trustees Legal Found. Wash., 1987-90, pres., 1990; co-chair Spokane County Law and Justice Coun., 1990-95; mem. Access to Justice Bd., 1994—. Vol. Peace Corps, vol. leader, Brazil, 1964, 65; mem. N.E. br. Children's Home Soc. Washington, 1979-88, chmn., 1982-84, state trustee, 1984-90; bd. advisors Gonzaga U. Sch. Law, 1985—; mem. Valley Hosp. Found. Bd., 1985-95, sec., 1990; mem. Valley Hosp. Comty. Bd., 1986-95; trustee Gonzaga Law Sch. Found., 1986—. Recipient Disting. Alumni Svcs. award Gonzaga U. Law Sch., 1995, Goldmark award for promoting civil legal svcs. for the disadvantaged Legal Found. Wash. State, 1998. Mem. Wash. State Bar (resolutions com. 1973-75, ethics com. 1973-74, mem. legal aid com. 1974-76, chmn. legal aid com. 1975-76, chmn. spl. task force on statewide legal svcs. 1976, pro bono svcs. task force 1 1980, Spokane chmn. local adminstrv. com. 1981-82, disciplinary bd. 1982-84, family law task force 1990, access to justice task force 1992, jud. recommendation com. 1991-94), Spokane County Bar Assn. (trustee 1978-80, pres. 1984-85, co-chair vol. lawyer program com. 1994-95). Avocations: building and remodeling lake home, traveling, gardening. Fax: 509-477-5714. E-mail: pbastine@spokanecounty.org. Office: Spokane County Superior Ct 1116 W Broadway Ave Spokane WA 99201-2004

BATAILLARD, STEPHAN MARC, film and commercial producer; b. Washington, Aug. 15, 1961; s. Jean Alphonse and Suzanne (Ghiotti) B. BA, U. Calif., Berkeley, 1984; MFA, U. So. Calif., L.A., 1989. Prodr. Velvet Glove Prodns., L.A., 1990-91, Eden West Pictures, L.A., 1991-92, White Noise Prodns., L.A., 1992-96, 3-Oh!-5 Creative Advt., L.A., 1997—. Prodr. (short film) Red Mambo, 1992. Home: 5932 Manola Way Los Angeles CA 90068-3041

BATAILLE, GRETCHEN, academic administrator. B of English, Calif. Polytech. State U., M of English Edn.; D, Drake U. Provost, acad. v.p. Wash. State U., Pullman. Office: Wash State U French Adminstrn 422 Pullman WA 99164-1046

BATCHELOR, JAMES KENT, lawyer; b. Long Beach, Calif., Oct. 4, 1934; s. Jack Morrell and Edith Marie (Ottinger) B.; m. Jeanette Lou Dyer, Mar. 27, 1959; children: John, Suzanne; m. Susan Mary Leonard, Dec. 4, 1976. AA, Sacramento City Coll., 1954; BA, Calif. State U., Long Beach, 1956; JD, Hastings Coll. Law, U. Calif., 1959. Bar: Calif. 1960, U.S. Dist. Ct. (cen. dist.) Calif. 1960, U.S. Supreme Ct. 1968; cert. family law specialist Calif. Bd. Legal Specialization, 1980. Dep. dist. atty., Orange County, Calif., 1960-62; assoc. Miller, Nisson, Kogler & Wenke, Santa Ana, Calif., 1962-64; ptnr. Batchelor, Cohen & Oster, Santa Ana, 1964-67, Kurilich, Ballard, Batchelor, Fullerton, Calif., 1967-72; pres. James K. Batchelor, Inc.; tchr. paralegal sect. Santa Ana City Coll.; judge pro-tem Superior Ct., 1974—; lectr. family law Calif. Continuing Edn. of Bar, 1973—. Contbr. articles to profl. jours. Fellow Am. Acad. Matrimonial Lawyers (pres. So. Calif. chpt. 1989-90); mem. ABA, Calif. State Bar (placque chmn. family law sect. 1975-76, advisor 1976-78), Orange County Barristers (founder, pres., placque 1963), Calif. State Barristers (placque 1965, v.p.), Orange County Bar Assn. (plaque sec. 1977, pres. family law sect. 1968-71, Best Lawyers in Am. 1989-90, 91-92, 93-94, 95-96, 97-98, 99—). Republican. Methodist. Office: 765 The City Dr S Ste 270 Orange CA 92868-4942

BATCHELOR, KAREN LEE, English language educator; b. Oregon City, Oreg., June 17, 1948; d. Jewel Elaine Durham; m. Luis Moncado, Mar. 17, 1978 (div. Aug. 1988); children: Virginia, Travis. BA in English, San Fransicso State U., 1971, MA in English, 1980. Vol. U.S. Peace Corps, Andong, South Korea, 1972-74; tchr. English as second lang. City Coll. San

Francisco, 1975—; tchr. trainer U. Calif., Berkeley, 1986—; acad. specialist USIA, 1991—; speaker in field. Co-author: (textbooks) Discovering English, 1981, In Plain English, 1985, More Plain English, 1986, The Writing Challenge, 1990, The English Zone, Books 1-4, 1998; contbr. articles to profl. jorus. Mem. Tchrs. English to Speakers of Other Langs., Calif. Tchrs. English to Speakers of Other Langs. Office: City Coll San Francisco 50 Phelan Ave San Francisco CA 94112-1821

BATCHELOR, LYNNE, vice principal; b. Kingsville, Tex., Aug. 22, 1943; d. Richard Earl and Carolyn Louise (Knowles) B. BA, Tex. Wesleyan U., 1964; MA, Pepperdine U., 1978. Tchr. San Diego Unified Schs., 1966-95, vice-prin., 1996—; Fulbright exch. tchr. Bishop Hedley H.S., Merthyr Tydfil, Wales, 1978-79, Alloa Acad., Stirling, Scotland, 1983-84, Bournville Further Edn. Coll., Birmingham, Eng., 1993-94. Contbr.: Merthyr Tydfil Now & Then, 1978. Mem., officer Chula Vista (Calif.) Jr. Women's Club, 1965-77; mem. LWV, Chula Vista, 1970-75. Mem. AAUW (moderator pub. forums 1985-98), Calif. Assn. Dir.'s Activities (state bd., Associated Student Body Advisor of Yr. 1993), Calif. Exch. Tchrs. Orgn. (v.p.), San Diego Edn. Assn., Calif. Tchrs. Assn., Natl. Edn. Assn. Methodist. Avocations: travel, reading, bridge, antiques. Home: 16048 Caminito Aire Puro San Diego CA 92128-3557 Office: San Diego Unified Schs 6811 Bisby Lake Dr San Diego CA 92119

BATEMAN, MERRILL JOSEPH, university president; b. Lehi, Utah, June 19, 1936; s. Joseph Fredric and Belva (Smith) B.; m. Marilyn Scholes, Mar. 23, 1959; children: Michael, Mark, Michele, Melisa, Merilee, Matthew, McKay. BA, U. Utah, 1960; PhD, MIT, 1965. Exec. Mars, Inc., 1971-75; dean Sch. Mgmt. Brigham Young U., Provo, Utah, 1975-79, pres. Brigham Young U., 1996—; mgmt. cons. Provo, 1979-92; mem. 2d Quorum of 70 LDS Ch., Salt Lake City, 1992-94, presiding bishop, 1994-95, mem. 1st Quorum of 70, 1996—; pres. Deseret Mgmt. Corp., Salt Lake City, 1993-95. 1st lt. USAF, 1964-67. Danforth fellow, 1960-64, Woodrow Wilson fellow, 1960-61. Mem. Am. Assn. Presidents of Colls. and Univs. (pres.), Mountain West Conf. Coun. of Presidents, Phi Kappa Phi, Phi Beta Kappa. Office: Brigham Young U PO Box 21346 Provo UT 84602-1346

BATES, CHARLES WALTER, human resources executive, lawyer; b. Detroit, June 28, 1953; s. E. Frederick and Virginia Marion (Nunneley) B. BA in Psychology and Econs. cum laude, Mich. State U., 1975, M in Labor and Indsl. Rels., 1977; postgrad., DePaul U., 1979-80; JD, William Mitchell Coll. Law, 1984. Bar: Wash. 1990, U.S. Dist. Ct. (we. dist.) Wash. 1992; cert. sr. profl. in human resources. Vista vol., paralegal Ventura County Legal Aid Assn., Calif., 1975-76; job analyst Gen. Mills, Inc., Mpls., 1977-78; asst. plant pers. mgr. Gen. Mills, Inc., Chgo., 1978-80; plant pers. asst. mgr. Gen. Mills Inc., Chgo., 1980-81; pers. mgr. consumer foods mktg. Gen. Mills, Inc., Mpls., 1981-82; pers. mgr. consumer foods mktg. divns. Saluto Pizza, Mpls., 1982-84; human resources mgr. Western divsn. Godfather's Pizza, Inc., Costa Mesa, Calif., 1984-85; human resources mgr. western U.S. and Can. Godfather's Pizza, Inc., Bellevue, Wash., 1985-91; dir. human resources Royal Seafoods, Inc., Seattle, 1991-92, dir. human resources, employee rels. counsel, 1992-94, dir. human resources, counsel, 1994-95; sr. internal auditor PACCAR, Inc, Bellevue, Wash., 1995-97; dir. field human resources PACCAR Automotive, Inc., Renton, Wash., 1997, dir. human resources, 1997—; instr. employee labor rels. Lake Washington Tech. Coll., 1992-94. Mem. editl. adv. bd. Recruitment Today mag., 1990-91. Candidate for lt. gov. of Minn., 1982; asst. scoutmaster Boy Scouts Am., 1971—, asst. advisor activities Order of Arrow, 1989-92, 96-97; Sammamish Cmty. Councilman, Bellevue, 1990-93; mem. East Bellevue Transp. Study Adv. Group, 1989-92; mem. Bellevue Civil Svc. Commn., 1997—, vice chair, 1999—. Recipient Scouter's Tng. award Boy Scouts Am., 1979, Dist. award of merit, 1991, Nat. Vantage Recruiting award, 1990, VigilHonor, 1990. Mem. ABA (labor and employment law), Wash. State Bar Assn., King County Bar Assn. (labor law sect.), Nat. Eagle Scout Assn., N.W. Human Resources Mgmt. Assn., Soc. for Human Resources Mgmt. Home: 232 168th Ave NE Bellevue WA 98008-4522 Office: PACCAR Automotive Inc 1400 N 4th St Renton WA 98055-1535

BATES, CRAIG DANA, curator, ethnographer, government official; b. Oakland, Calif., Aug. 2, 1952; s. Dana Raymond and June (Robinson) B.; m. Jennifer Dawn Bernido, May 12, 1973 (div. 1987); 1 child, Carson Dana. Park technician Nat. Park Svc., Yosemite National Park, Calif., 1973-76, Indian cultural specialist, 1976-80, asst. curator, 1980-82, curator ethnography, 1982—; rsch. assoc. Santa Barbara (Calif.) Mus. Natural History, 1983—; cons. Calif. Indian exhbn. SW Mus., L.A., 1985, Culin exhbn. Bklyn. Mus., 1988-89, Lowie Mus. Anthropology, U. Calif., Berkeley, 1990. Co-author: (with Martha Lee) Tradition and Innovation: A Basket History of the Indians of the Yosemite Mono Lake Area, 1990; contbr. more than 100 articles on Am. Indian culture to profl. jours. Office: Nat Park Svc Yosemite Mus PO Box 577 Yosemite National Park CA 95389-0577

BATES, DWIGHT LEE, mechanical engineer; b. Miles City, Mont., Aug. 19, 1943; s. Edmond Russell and Verna Elizabeth (Johnson) B.; m. Diane Marie Seppi, Aug. 19, 1967. BSME, U. Wyo., 1966; MBA in Mktg., Seattle U., 1971. Registered profl. engr., Wash. Rsch. engr. comml. airplane div. Boeing Co., Seattle, 1966-70; product devel. engr. internat. mktg. div. Warn Industries, Seattle, 1972-73, 1972-73; prin. engr. Heath Tecna, Kent, Wash., 1973-74; mech. design engr. Puget sound naval shipyard U.S. Dept. Def., Bremerton, Wash., 1974-78; supervisory indsl. engr. Supship Seattle, 1978-85; sr. specialist engr. Comml. Airplane div. Boeing Co., Seattle, 1985—; cons. in field. Contbr. publs. in field. Pres. Melrose E. Condo Assn., Seattle, 1978-81; bus. adv. coun. Resource Ctr. for Handicapped. With USCG Aux. Recipient 2 letters of appreciation and 2 letters of commendation U.S. Dept. Def., award Am. Mktg. Assn., 1973; honored as grad. with successful career U. Wyo. Coll. Engring., 1993. Mem. Resource Ctr. for Handicapped Bus. Adv. Coun. (7 letters of commendation, Mus. Flight award, Seattle Block Capt. award), AIAA (pres. Laramie, Wyo. chpt. 1966), NSPE, Wash. State Profl. Engrs. Soc., Wash. State Power Squadron, Am. Inst. Indsl. Engrs., Seattle U. MBA Assn.. Democrat. Lutheran. Avocations: skiing, hiking, climbing, photography, computers. Home: 1912 E Mcgraw St Seattle WA 98112-2629 Office: Boeing Co PO Box 707 Seattle WA 98111-0707

BATES, GEORGE E., oil industry executive; b. 1943. BS, U. Hawaii, 1967, MBA, 1981. With Gasco, Inc., Honolulu, 1967-91; v.p. environ. and govt. affairs BHP Hawaii, Inc., Honolulu, 1991—. Office: BHP Hawaii Inc 733 Bishop St Ste 2700 Honolulu HI 96813-4022

BATES, JAMES ROBERT, newspaper editor; b. Great Bend, Kans., Dec. 12, 1954; s. Robert Lane and Phyllis Fern (Koltermann) B.; m. Jennifer Petkus, Nov. 7, 1986. BS, U. Kans., 1977; postgrad., U. Colo., 1979-80. Copy editor Springfield (Mo.) Daily News, 1977-78; reporter Colo. Springs (Colo.) Sun, 1978-79, news editor, 1980-86; copy editor, asst. news editor Denver Post, 1986-87, news editor, 1987-89, exec. news editor, 1989—. Recipient design and editing awards Colo. Press Assn., Colo. AP, 1986—. Mem. Soc. Newspaper Design. Office: The Denver Post 1560 Broadway Denver CO 80202-5177*

BATES, MARY PATRICIA, art educator; b. Billings, Mont., Jan. 30, 1951; d. Kermit Wilson and Priscilla Louise (Jenkins) Beal; children: Devin Patrick, Megan Ann. BFA, Colo. State U., 1973; MFA in Sculpture, Ind. U., 1981. Artist, technician Art Castings of Colo., Loveland, 1973-75; assoc. instr. art Ind. U., Bloomington, 1979-80; head dept. Johnson Atelier Tech. Inst. for Sculpture, Princeton, N.J., 1981-82; chmn. dept. art Sonoma State U., Rohnert Park, Calif., 1986-89, prof. sculpture, 1982—; exch. prof., Fulbright fellow Anglia U., Cambridge, Eng., 1994-98; prof. Sch. Art Ariz. State U., Tempe, 1996—. Commd. works include Trigon, Triangulum, 1992; prin. works include 1 person exhbn. Implement Series, Barclay Simpson Gallery, 1991, 92, Balanced Terrain, RHA Gallery, Dublin, 1988, Fabricated Works, Calif. Artists Who Are Educators, San Francisco Internat. Airport, 1989, L.A. Art Fair, 1990, Loveland Mus. of Art, Pub. Commn. Trigon, City of Loveland, Colo., 1990, Kyle Belding Gallery, Denver, 1992, Charleston Heights Arts Ctr., Las Vegas, Nev., 1993, Michael Dunev Fine Arts, San Francisco, 1993, Calif. Crafts Mus., 1993, Univ. Gallery Eastern Wash. U., 1994, Corvallis (Oreg.) Art Ctr., 1994, Charles Winston Mus., 1994, Betty Rymer Gallery Art Inst. Chgo., 1994, Michael Dunev Gallery, San Francisco, 1995, McHenry County Coll. Art Gallery, Crystal Lake, Ill., 1997, Meml. Union Gallery, U. Ariz., Tucson, 1998; guest artist Cast, Ltd. Art Foundry, Dublin, 1991. Ford fellow, 1980, 81. Mem. Internat. Sculpture Conf., Internat. Conf. Cast Iron Art (steering com.). Democrat. Avocation: reading. Fax: (602) 965-8338. E-mail: mbates@asuvm.inre.asu.edu. Office: Ariz State U Sch of Art PO Box 1505 Tempe AZ 85280-1505

BATINIC, MARYANNE FRANCES, accountant, volunteer; b. San Jose, Calif., Nov. 1, 1953; d. James Howard and Frances (Ivicevich) Banich; m. Mark Steven Ross, Mar. 2, 1974 (div. Jan. 1980); 1 child, James Steven Ross; m. Stevan Batinic, Oct. 20, 1990; 1 stepchild, Sean. Cosmetologist, LaVonnes Acad., Arvada, Colo., 1980, San Francisco, 1984. Cert. cosmetologist. Acct. Orrison Distbg., Glenwood Springs, Colo., 1979-80; cosmetologist McCauleys Salon, Denver, 1980-83; acct. Daisy Sys., Mountain View, Calif., 1984, Particular Man, Sunnyvale, Calif., 1986, Exec. Cuts, Sunnyvale, 1987, Sandoz Crop Protection, Palo Alto, Calif., 1988-89, Applied Immune Scis., Menlo Park, Calif., 1989-91, Tibco Software, Palo Alto, 1992—. Gen. svc. rep. Freedom Fellowship-AA, Mountain View, Calif., 1989, co-chairperson, 1992; coord. hosps. and instns. facilities Monte Villa Hosp. for AA, San Jose, Calif., 1991; meeting sec. hosps. and instns. for AA meetings Elmwood Women's Prison, Milpitas, Calif., 1992-93, 95—; mem. Silicon Valley Toxics Coalition, 1995-97. Recipient 1st Place mens hair design Nat. Beauty Show, 1980, 3rd Place women's hair design, 1980, 12 Yr. award AA, 1997. Mem. Peninsula Astronom. Soc. Republican. Avocations: computer programming in C, snow skiing, camping, walking. Fax: (408) 985-2537. E-mail: kcom2@pacbell.net, mbatinic@tibco.com. Home: 2623 Pebble Beach Dr Santa Clara CA 95051-1130 Office: Tibco Software 3165 Porter Dr Palo Alto CA 94304-1213

BATSON, RAYMOND MILNER, retired cartographer; b. Lincoln, Nebr., July 8, 1931; s. Avery A. and Margaret Elizabeth (Milner) B.; m. Rhoda May Meier, Aug. 31, 1955; children: Beverly Ann Batson Platten, Frederick Avery, Thomas Raymond. Student, U. Colo., 1953-57, BA, 1962. Field engr., photogrammetrist U.S. Geol. Survey, Denver, 1957-63; rsch. cartographer U.S. Geol. Survey, Flagstaff, Ariz., 1963-94, chief planetary cartography, 1963-92; ret., 1994; mem. planetary cartography working group NASA, Washington, 1978-94, mem. planetary geol. and geophys. working group, 1982-92, expert mem. U.S./USSR joint working group for planetary data exch., 1988-92. Author, editor: Planetary Mapping, 1990, NASA Atlas of the Solar System, 1997. Staff sgt. USAF, 1951-52. Fellow Am. Soc. for Photogrammetry; mem. Am. Soc. Photogrammetry (chmn. extraterrestrial sci. com. 1981-88), Astron. Soc. of the Pacific (hon.), Internat. Soc. PHotogrammetry (chmn. working group 3 com. IV 1982-85), Internat. Astron. Union (working group for planetary system nomenclature com. 16, 1991-94).

BATT, PHILIP E., former governor; b. Wilder, Idaho, Mar. 4, 1927; m. Jacque Fallis, 1948; children: Bill, Rebecca, Leslie. Attended, U. Idaho, 1944-48. Elected mem. Idaho State Legislature, 1965-77; lt. gov. State of Idaho, 1978-82, gov., 1995-99. First pres. Idaho Food Producers; co-chmn. Wilder United Charity Auction; mem. Idaho Potato Growers Commn.; mem. bd. dirs. Wilder Farm Labor Com.; mem. bd. trustees Coll. Idaho; past pres. Idaho Hop Growers Assn., Hop Growers of Am., Homedale PTA. *

BATTY, HUGH KENWORTHY, physician; b. Kansas City, Kans.; s. James Jacob and Genevieve Adeline (Johnston) B.; m. Mercedes Aguirre, Mar. 17, 1979; 1 child, Henry Briton. BS in Zoology, U. Wash., 1970; PhD in Anatomy, U. Utah, 1974; MD, Ciudad Juárez, Mex., 1977. Intern, asst. resident St. Vincent's Med. Ctr., Bridgeport, Conn., 1977-78, resident, 1978-79, chief resident, 1979-80; pvt. practice Sheridan, Wyo., 1980—; chmn. dept. medicine Meml. Hosp. Sheridan, 1989, 91, 93, 96, 97, 98, chmn. ICU, 1995. Contbr. articles to profl. jours. Del. Citizen Ambassador Program, India. Eleanor Roosevelt Cancer Rsch. Found. grantee, 1972. Mem. ACP, Wyo. Med. Soc., Sheridan County Med. Soc. Avocations: archeology, reading, hiking, wrestling, fishing. Office: 1260 W 5th St Sheridan WY 82801-2702

BAUCH, THOMAS JAY, lawyer, educator, former apparel company executive; b. Indpls., May 24, 1943; s. Thomas and Violet (Smith) B.; m. Ellen L. Burstein, Oct. 31, 1982; children: Chelsea Sara, Elizabeth Tree. BS with honors, U. Wis., 1964, JD with highest honors, 1966. Bar: Ill. 1966, Calif. 1978. Assoc. Lord, Bissell & Brook, Chgo., 1966-72; lawyer, asst. sec. Marcor-Montgomery Ward, Chgo., 1973-75; spl. asst. to solicitor Dept. Labor, Washington, 1975-77; dep. gen. counsel Levi Strauss & Co., San Francisco, 1977-81, sr. v.p., gen. counsel, 1981-96, counsel, 1996—; pvt. practice, Tiburon, Calif., 1996—; cons. prof. Stanford (Calif.) U. Law Sch., 1997—; ptnr. Ika Enterprises; mng. dir. Domghnet.com Inc.; mng. dir., gen. counsel Marine Desalinazation Corp. Mem. U. Wis. Law Rev., 1964-66. Bd. dirs. Urban Sch., San Francisco, 1986-91, San Francisco Psychoanalytic Inst., Gateway H.S., San Francisco, Charles Armstrong Sch., Belmont, Calif.; bd. visitors U. Wis. Law Sch., 1991-95. Mem. Am. Assn. Corp. Counsel (bd. dirs. 1984-87), Bay Area Gen. Counsel Assn. (chmn. 1994), Univ. Club, Villa Taverna Club, Corrinthian Yacht Club, Order of Coif, San Francisco Yacht Club. Office: 49 Main St Tiburon CA 94920-2507

BAUCUS, MAX S., senator; b. Helena, Mont., Dec. 11, 1941; s. John and Jean (Sheriff) B.; m. Wanda Minge, Apr. 23, 1983. BA, Stanford U., 1964, LLB, 1967. Bar: D.C. 1969, Mont. 1972. Staff atty. CAB, Washington, 1967-68; lawyer SEC, Washington, 1968-71; legal asst. to chmn. SEC, 1970-71; sole practice Missoula, Mont., 1971-74; mem. Mont. Ho. of Reps., 1973-74; mem. 94th-95th congresses from 1st Dist. Mont., 1975-79, mem. com. appropriations; U.S. senator from Mont., 1979—, ranking minority mem., mem. environ. and pub. works com., mem. fin. subcom. on internat. trade, mem. health com., taxation and IRS oversight com., mem. agrl./nutrition and forestry coms., mem. intelligence/joint com. on taxation, mem. Senate Dem. steering and coordination com. Office: US Senate 511 Hart Senate Bldg Washington DC 20510-2602*

BAUER, A(UGUST) ROBERT, JR., surgeon, educator; b. Phila., Dec. 23, 1928; s. A(ugust) Robert and Jessie Martha-Maynard (Monie) B.; BS, U. Mich., 1949, MS, 1950, MD, 1954; M Med. Sci.-Surgery, Ohio State U., 1960; m. Charmaine Louise Studer, June 28, 1957; children: Robert, John, William, Anne, Charles, James. Intern Walter Reed Army Med. Ctr., 1954-55; resident in surgery Univ. Hosp., Ohio State U., Columbus, also instr., 1957-61; pvt. practice medicine, specializing in surgery, Mt. Pleasant, Mich., 1962-74; chief surgery Ctrl. Mich. Community Hosp., Mt. Pleasant, 1964-65, vice chief of staff, 1967, chief of staff, 1968; clin. faculty Mich. State Med. Sch., East Lansing, 1974; mem. staff St. Mark's Hosp., Salt Lake City, 1974-91; pvt. practice surgery, Salt Lake City, 1974-91; clin. instr. surgery U. Utah, 1975-91. Trustee Rowland Hall, St. Mark's Sch., Salt Lake City, 1978-84; mem. Utah Health Planning Coun., 1979-81. Served with M.C., U.S. Army, 1954-57. Diplomate Am. Bd. Surgery. Fellow ACS, Southwestern Surg. Congress; mem. AMA, Salt Lake County Med. Soc., Utah Med. Assn. (various coms.), Utah Soc. Certified Surgeons, Salt Lake Surg. Soc., Pan Am. Med. Assn. (affiliate), AAAS (affiliate), Sigma Phi Epsilon, Phi Rho Sigma. Episcopalian. Club: Zollinger. Contbr. articles to profl. publs., researcher surg. immunology. Office: PO Box 17533 Salt Lake City UT 84117-0533

BAUER, HENRY LELAND, lawyer; b. Portland, Oreg., June 7, 1928; s. Henry and Emma L. (Peterson) B.; m. Doris Jane Philbrick, Sept. 11, 1952 (dec.); children: Henry Stephen, Thomas Leland. BS in Bus., Oreg. State U., 1950; JD, U. Oreg., 1953. Bar: Oreg. 1953, U.S. Dist. Ct. Oreg., 1956; U.S. Ct. Appeals (9th cir.), 1960. Mem. Bauer & Bauer, Portland, Oreg., 1955-70, Bauer, Murphy, Bayless & Fundingsland, and successor firms, Portland, 1970-75; prin. Henry L. Bauer & Assocs. P.C., Portland. Past mem. adv. council Oreg. State U. Coll. Bus.; past bd. dirs., vice chmn. St. Vincent Hosp. and Med. Ctr.; mem., past pres. council of trustees St. Vincent Med. Found.; lifetime trustee Kappa Sigma Endowment Fund; bd. dirs., past pres. Nat. Interfrat. Conf.; trustee Nat. Interfrat. Found.; past pres. Columbia Pacific council Boy Scouts Am.; past pres. Portland Civic Theatre; bd. visitors U. Oreg. Sch. Law, 1979-83; trustee Oreg. State U. Found.; chmn. Oreg. State U. Pres's. Club. 1st lt. USAF, 1953-55. Recipient Silver Antelope award Boy Scouts Am.; named Disting. Alumnus, Oreg. State U., 1994. Mem. ABA, Oreg. Bar Assn., Multnomah County Bar Assn., Am. Judicature Soc., Lang Syne Soc., German-Am. Soc., Oreg. State U. Alumni Assn. (bd. dirs.), Delta Theta Phi, Kappa Sigma (past nat. pres.). Republican. Presbyterian. Clubs: Multnomah Athletic, Arlington, Masons. Office: 25-3 NW 23rd Ave Portland OR 97210-3517

BAUER, JAY S., architect. AB, Washington U., 1970, MArch, 1972. Fellow AIA. Office: Bauer and Wiley 2507 W Coast Hwy Ste 202 Newport Beach CA 92663-4755*

BAUER, JEROME LEO, JR., chemical engineer; b. Pitts., Oct. 12, 1938; s. Jerome L. and Anna Mae (Tucker) B.; children from previous marriage: children: Lori, Trish, Jeff. BSChemE, U. Dayton, 1960; MSChemE, Pa. State U., 1963; postgrad., Ohio State U., 1969. Registered profl. engr., Ohio. Asst. prof. chem. engring. U. Dayton, Ohio, 1963-67; mgr. advanced composites dept. Ferro Corp., Cleve., 1967-72; engring. material and process specifications mgr. Lockheed Missiles & Space Co., Inc., Sunnyvale, Calif., 1972-74; gen. dynamics design specialist Convair Div., San Diego, 1974-76, project devel. engr., 1976-77; dir. research Furane div. M&T Chems. Inc., Glendale, Calif., 1980-82; mem. tech. staff Jet Propulsion Lab., Calif. Inst. Tech., Pasadena, Calif., 1977-80, 82-90; mem. tech. staff mfg. engring. The Aerospace Corp., El Segundo, Calif., 1990—, engring. specialist, 1997—. Editor: Materials Sciences for Future, 1986, Moving Foreward With 50 Years of Leadership in Advanced Materials, 1994, Materials and Processes Challenges, 1996, Evolving & Revolutionary Technologies for the New Millennium, 1999; contbr. articles to profl. jours. Jr. warden St. Luke Episcopal Ch., La Crescenta, Calif., 1980, sr. warden 1981. Fellow Internat. Electronics Packaging Soc. (pres. L.A. chpt. 1982), Soc. Advancement of Material Process Engring. (membership chmn. no. Calif. sect. 1973-74, sec. San Diego sect. 1974-75, vice chmn. 1975-76, chmn. 1976, chmn. L.A. sect. 1977, nat. treas. 1978-82, gen. chmn. 31st internat. symposium exhbn., Las Vegas, Nev., 1986, Meritorious Achievement award 1983, internat. v.p. 1987-89, internat. pres. 1989-90); mem. Am. Inst. Chem. Engrs. (founder, chmn. Dayton sect. 1964-66, spl. projects chmn. Cleve. sect. 1968-69), Phi Lambda Upsilon, Delta Sigma Epsilon. Republican. Avocations: carpentry, photography, camping. Home: PO Box 3298 El Segundo CA 90245-8398 Office: The Aerospace Corp 2350 E El Segundo Blvd El Segundo CA 90245-4691

BAUER, MARK DAVID, educator; b. Mt. Clemens, Mich., Apr. 23, 1951; s. Walter Roy and Irene Lucille (Hotchkiss) B.; m. Kathleen Ann King, Aug. 11, 1973; children: Benjamin, Jackson. BA in English, Calif. Lutheran Coll., 1973; MA in English, Ctrl. Mich. U., 1975. Cert. tchr., Calif. Graduate asst. Ctrl. Mich. U., Mt. Pleasant, Mich., 1973-75; adj. tchr. Moorpark (Calif.) Coll., 1975-76; english instr. Hawaii Pacific U., Honolulu, 1986—. Scoutmaster Boy Scouts Am., Honolulu, 1996—; com. mem. Boy Scouts Am., Honolulu, 1990—; chief Indian Guides, Oak View, Calif., 1979-82. Mem. Nat. Council Tchrs. English, Hawaii Pacific U. english coord. Democrat. Lutheran. Avocations: swimming, boogie boarding, snorkeling, fishing, playing saxaphone. Home: 1777 Ala Moana Blvd Apt 1410 Honolulu HI 96815-1610 Office: Hawaii Pacific U 1188 Fort Street Mall # 329 Honolulu HI 96813-2713

BAUER, RALPH LEROY, business executive; b. Evansville, Ind., Dec. 19, 1925; s. John George and Elfrieda Louise (Gresser) Huber; m. Margaret Ellen Masters, Sept. 11, 1948 (div. 1975); children: Clinton L., Warren L., Brian E., Scott A.; m. Anna Mae Cooke, Nov. 9, 1984. BSEE, U. Evansville, 1950; postgrad., U. Calif., Riverside, 1956-58, UCLA, 1960, 65, U. Mich., 1969. Ordnance engr. Internat. Harvester Co., Evansville, Ind., 1950-54; test & product design Naval Ordnance Lab., Silver Springs, Md., 1954-55; test engr. Naval Ordnance Lab., Carona, Calif., 1955-57, br. head, 1957-61, div. head, 1961-70; div. head Naval Weapons Ctr., China Lake, Calif., 1970-82, assoc. dept. head, 1982-83; pres. RB Assocs. Inc., Lake Arrowhead, Calif., 1983-95; retired, 1996; cons. to major aerospace firms in missile guidance/fuzing and electronic counter-countermeasures. Inventor in field. Elder, local sec. Presbyn. Ch., U.S.A., 1994-96; elected alumni bd. dirs. U. Evansville, 1996—. With U.S. Army Air Corps, 1944-46, radar operator-VH Bomb Group. Mem. IEEE (life mem., sect. chmn. 1968, sect. vice chmn. 1967, sect. sec.-treas. 1966), Am. Def. Preparedness Assn., Assn. Old Crows. Home: PO Box 2172 987 LeMont Way Lake Arrowhead CA 92352

BAUER, RANDY MARK, management training firm executive; b. Cleve., Sept. 2, 1946; s. Ralph I. and Gloria P. Bauer; B.S. summa cum laude, Ohio State U., 1968; M.B.A., Kent State U., 1971; m. Sue Dellva, July 4, 1975; children—Sherri, Kevin. Mgmt. auditor Peat Marwick Mitchell & Co., Cleve., 1971-72; mgmt. devel. specialist GAO, Denver, 1972-80; adj. prof. mgmt. Columbia Coll., Denver, 1979—; pres. Leadership Tng. Assos., Denver, 1979—; condr. exec. devel. workshops U. Colo., Denver, 1979—. Recipient Best in 1976 award GAO. Mem. Am. Soc. for Tng. and Devel., Beta Gamma Sigma. Address: 10022 Oak Tree Ct Lone Tree CO 80124-9714

BAUER, STEVEN MICHAEL, cost containment engineer; b. Hemet, Calif., Nov. 8, 1949; s. Donald Richard and Jeanne Patricia (Lamont) B.; m. Myung-Hee Min, Sept. 10, 1983; children: Claudia Margaret, Monica Anne. BA in Physics, Calif. State U., San Bernardino, 1971, BS in Physics, 1984, cert. in acctg., 1980, cert. in computer programming, 1986; postgrad., U. Calif., 1974, Calif. State U., 1982-87; cert. in counseling skills, U. Calif. extension, 1991., cert. in alcohol and other drug studies, 1992; Cert. in Micro Computer Applications, U. Calif. Ext., 1996. Registered engr. in tng., Calif., 1976. Asst. nuclear engr. So. Calif. Edison Co., Rosemead, 1973-76, assoc. nuclear engr., 1976-88, cost containment engr., 1988—; cons. rsch. dept. Jerry L. Pettis Meml. Vets. Hosp., 1978-79, Calif. State U., San Bernardino, 1983-84; cons. planning San Bernardino County, 1975-76; cons. alumni rels. Calif. State U., San. Bernardino, 1989-90. Supporter St. Labre Indian Sch., 1984, Asian Relief Fund, 1985—, So. Poverty Law Ctr., Amnesty Internat., Freedom Writer, 1988; mem. Greenpeace, Wilderness Soc., Internat. Platform Assn.; supporter United Negro Coll. Fund, 1985, vol., 1988; vol. counselor San Bernardino Girls' Juvenile Hall, ARC, 1990—; fellow Casa Colina Hosp.; mem. Robert V. Fullerton Art Mus.; campaign vol. Congressman George E. Brown, 1986; block capt. Neighborhood Watch Assn., sec., 1991-92, v.p., 1992-93, pres., 1994-96. Mem. Am. Nuclear Soc. (assoc.), Calif. State U. San Bernardino Alumni Assn. (sec. bd. 1979-80, rep. food com. 1980-82), Nat. Assn. Accts., Astron. Soc. Pacific, Assn. Computing Machinery (assoc.), Ams. for Energy Independence (bd. dirs. 1990-93), KC (sec., recorder 1989, cmty. dir. Outstanding Svcs. award 1989), Toastmasters, UCLA Alumni (life), Calif. State U. Fullerton Computer Club, Sierra Club (sec. San Gorgonio chpt. 1992). Avocations: personal computers, reading, working out, gardening. Home and Office: 131 Monroe Ct San Bernardino CA 92408-4137

BAUGH, L. DARRELL, financial executive; b. Prairie Grove, Ark., Oct. 7, 1930; s. Lacey D. and Mary Grace (Brown) B.; BBA, U. Ark., 1954; MBA, U. Colo., 1960; CLU, Am. Coll., 1967. Chartered fin. cons.; cert. estate planner. m. Wileeta Claire Gray, June 15, 1958; children: Adrienne Leigh Calvo, John Grayson. With Penn Mut. Life Ins. Co., 1961-71, gen. agt., Sacramento, 1968-71; pres. Nat. Estate Planning Inst., Boulder, Colo., 1974—; faculty estate planning seminars Colo. State U.; dir. Nat. Assn. Estate Planner/Coun., 1992-95; cons. U. Colo. Center for Confs. Mgmt./Tech. Programs, 1975-80; sponsor ednl. programs for profl. estate planners and estate owners. Bd. dirs. Boulder Men's Christian Fellowship. With U.S. Army, 1954-56. Mem. Boulder C. of C., Soc. of Profl. Fin. Advisors, Boulder County Estate Planning Coun. (pres. 1972-73), Sacramento Estate Planning Coun., Soc. Fin. Svc. Profls., Nat. Registry Fin. Planners (interview com.), Nat. Assn. Estate Planners (planners accreditation com., mem. Denver study group), Student Venture (bd. dirs.). Contbr. articles to profl. jours. Club: Flatirons Country. Office: 4770 Baseline Rd Boulder CO 80303-2666

BAUGHN, ALFRED FAIRHURST, lawyer; b. Florence, Ariz., May 1, 1912; s. Otis James and Mary Holman (Fairhurst) B.; m. Barbara Hobbs, June 17, 1935; children: Brent F., Barbara E. AB, U. So. Calif., 1935, JD, 1938. Bar: Calif. 1938, U.S. Dist. Ct. (so. dist.) Calif. 1939, U.S. Ct. Appeals (9th cir.) 1945, U.S. Dist. Ct. Ariz. 1948, Ariz. 1959, U.S. Supreme Ct. 1967. With Title Guarantee & Trust, L.A., 1937-41; corp. counsel Pacific Western Oil Co., 1942-43; pvt. practice law, L.A. and Hollywood, Calif., 1943-56; head Ariz. atty. Signal/Garrett Co., 1956-77, ret., 1977; pvt. practice law, Ariz. and Calif., 1977-94; Ariz. Assn. Industries spl. atty. utility rate hearings Ariz. Corp. Commn., 1977-80; bd. dirs. EPI-HAB, Inc., 1974-90. Adopted by Hopi Indian Chief Seletstewa and Squaw (2d Mesa), 1967; Pres. scholar U. So. Calif., 1931-35. Mem. L.A. Philanthropic Found. (life), Skull and Scales (U. So. Calif.), Phi Alpha Delta (chpt. pres. 1938), Kappa Sigma (pres. L.A. alumni 1945, pres. Phoenix Alumni 1960). Republican. Mem. Christian Ch. Clubs: Hollywood Exch. (pres. 1947); Kiwanis (Phoenix pres.

club 1965); Hopi Kachina Klub (organizer, charter v.p. 1974), Hon. Order Ky. Cols. (pres. Phoenix chpt. 1980—), Phoenix Teocali of Order Quetzalcoatl (pres. 1984), Ariz. Bola Tie Soc., Masons (Master 1953), Shriners (Potentate 1971), Jesters (head Phoenix Ct. 1969), Internat. Gorillas (chief 1971—).

BAUM, CARL EDWARD, electromagnetic theorist; b. Binghamton, N.Y., Feb. 6, 1940; s. George Theodore and Evelyn Monica (Bliven) B. BS with honors, Calif. Inst. Tech., 1962, MS, 1963, PhD, 1969. Commd. 2d lt. USAF, 1962, advanced through grades to capt., 1967, resigned, 1971; project officer Air Force Rsch. Lab. (formerly Phillips Lab.), Kirtland AFB, N.Mex., 1963-71, sr. scientist for electromagnetics, 1971—; pres. SUMMA Found.; U.S. del. to gen. assembly Internat. Union Radio Sci., Lima, Peru, 1975, Helsinki, Finland, 1978, Washington, 1981, Florence, Italy, 1984, Tel Aviv, 1987, Prague, Czechoslovakia, 1990, Kyoto, Japan, 1993, Lille, France, 1996; mem. Commn. B U.S. Nat. Com., 1975—, Commn. E, 1982—, Commn. A, 1990—. Author: (with others) Transient Electromagnetic Fields, 1976, Electromagnetic Scattering, 1978, Acoustic, Electromagnetic and Elastic Wave Scattering, 1980, Fast Electrical and Optical Measurements, 1986, EMP Interaction: Principles, Techniques and Reference Data, 1986, Lightning Electromagnetics, 1990, Modern Radio Science, 1990, Recent Advances in Electromagnetic Theory, 1990, Direct and Inverse Methods in Radar Polarimetry, 1992, (with A.P. Stone) Transient Lens Synthesis: Differential Geometry in Electromagnetic Theory, 1991; editor: (with H.N. Kritikos) Electromagnetic Symmetry, 1995, (with L. Carin and A.P. Stone) Ultra-Wideband, Short-Pulse Electromagnetics 3, 1997, Detection and Identification of Visually Obscured Targets, 1998; contbr. articles to profl. jours. Recipient award Honeywell Corp., 1962, R&D award USAF, 1970, Harold Brown award Air Force Systems Command, 1990; Air Force Rsch. fellow, 1996; Electromagnetic pulse fellow. Fellow IEEE (Harry Diamond Meml. award, 1987, Richard R. Stoddart award, 1984); mem. Electromagnetics Soc. (pres. 1983-85), Electromagnetics Acad., Sigma Xi, Tau Beta Pi. Roman Catholic. Home: 5116 Eastern Ave SE Apt D Albuquerque NM 87108-5618 Office: AFRL/DEHP 3550 Aberdeen Ave SE Bldg 909 Albuquerque NM 87117-5748

BAUM, KERRY ROBERT, retired military officer; b. LaGrande, Oreg., May 25, 1939; s. Guy Hiatt B. and Niola (Anderson) Jones; m. Lynda Sue Christian, Dec. 18, 1964; children: Kerry Jr., Tatia D., Christian H., Buffy Jo, Patrick H., Britta Sue, Natalie A. BA in History, Brigham Young U., 1967; MBA in Mktg., Murray State U., 1978; postgrad., Webster Coll., St. Louis, 1979-80. Commd. 2d lt. U.S. Army, 1957, advanced through grades to col., 1990, ret., 1991; mgr. emergency preparedness Brigham Young U., 1993—; U.S. rep. to Major NATO Comdrs. Alert Conf., 1987-90; joint staff rep LIVE OAK, 1986-90. Author, editor: NATO Alert Procedures for Joint Staff, 1988, Transfer of U.S. Forces to NATO Command, 1990, Focal Point Procedures Manual, 1989. Bishop Mormon Ch., Hopkinsville, Ky., 1974-78, councilor, bishopric, Newport, R.I., 1985-86; bishop Mormon Ch. BYU 185th Ward, 1996—; mem. Utah Campus Safety Assn. (pres. elect). Decorated Bronze Star, Army Commendation medal, Air Force Commendation medal, Defense Superior Service Medal. Mem. Res. Officers Assn., Assn. Contingency Planners (treas. Utah chpt.). Home: 10938 N 5870 W Highland UT 84003-9487

BAUM, PHYLLIS GARDNER, travel management consultant; b. Ashtabula, Ohio, Dec. 13, 1930; d. Charles Edward Schneider and Stella Elizabeth (Schaefer) Gardner; m. Kenneth Walter Baum, Oct. 21, 1948 (div. July 1971); children: Deidre Adair, Cynthia Gail; m. Dennis Carl Marquardt, Sept. 22, 1979 (dec. 1991). Grad. high sch., Cleve. Am. Soc. Travel Agents. Travel cons. Fredo Travel Svc., Ashland, Ohio, 1960-66; sales mgr. Travelmart, Willoughby, Ohio, 1966-68; br. mgr. Travelmart, Mentor, Ohio, 1966-68, Diners Fugazy Travel, Sun City, Ariz., 1968-69; travel cons. Jarrett's Travel Svc., Phoenix, 1969-72; sr. cons. Loyal Travel, Phoenix, 1972-74; co-mgr. Phil Carr Travel, Sun City, 1974-77; tour ops. mgr. ASL Travel, Phoenix, 1978-79; owner, mgr. Travel Temporaries, Glendale, Ariz., 1979—; cons. and lectr. in field. Adv. bd. mem. Small Bus. Devel. Ctr., Phoenix, 1986—. Mem. Pacific Asia Travel Assn. Ariz. (bd. dirs. 1986—), Ariz. Women in Travel, NAFE, Altrusa. Republican. Avocations: music, travel, tatting, knitting, horseback riding. Home and Office: Travel Temps 10249 N 45th Ave Glendale AZ 85302-1901

BAUMAN, STEPHEN ADRIAN, lawyer; b. L.A., Jan. 25, 1935. BS in Bus. Adminstrn., UCLA, 1956; JD, Stanford U., 1959; LLM, Harvard U., 1960. Bar: Calif. 1960; cert. taxation specialist Calif. State Bar Bd. Legal Specialization. Ptnr. Seyfarth, Shaw, Fairweather & Geraldson, L.A., 1987—; lectr. tax law and estate planning U. So. Calif. Law Ctr. Advanced Profl. Program; U. So. Calif. Tax Inst., Calif. Continuing Edn. of Bar, Practising Law Inst. Mem. State Bar Calif. Office: Seyfarth Shaw Fairweather & Geraldson 2029 Century Park E Ste 3300 Los Angeles CA 90067-3019*

BAUMANN, ERNST FREDERICK, college president; b. N.Y.C., Oct. 4, 1943; s. Ernst and Grace (Crowley) B.; m. Kathleen Ann Brennan, June 17, 1967; children: Ernst Frederick Jr., Lori Ann, Macushla, Katrinka, Victoria, Greta. BA, Harvard U., 1967; postgrad., Colo. U. Observer, rsch. asst. High Altitude Obs., Nat. Ctr. for Atmospheric Rsch., Boulder, Colo., 1967-69; uranium geologist, grade control engr. Kerr-McGee Corp., Casper, Wyo., 1969-71; mine geologist engr. Am. Smelting and Refining Co., Leadville, Colo., 1975; chief geologist, engr. Leadville (Colo.) Lead Corp., 1977-86; dir. adult basic edn. and gen. ednl. devel., counselor Upper Ark. Area Coun. Govts., Cañon City, Colo., 1980-87; corr. officer, supr. C.T.C.F./D.O.C., Cañon City, 1987-96; pres., chmn. Coll. of the Cañons, Cañon City, 1979—; officer Colo. Territorial Correctional Facility, Dept. Corrections, Cañon City; recruiter Harvard U., Cañon City; pres., chmn. bd. Working in SETI Search for Extra-Terrestrial Intelligence. Co-author: Toward a New World: Powerful Proof of the Existence of God, 1995; patentee mil. mountaineer's collapsible ski. Mayoral candidate City of Cañon City, 1983, 85. Maj. CAP, USAF Aux., 1980-98. Mem. K. of C. (scribe). Republican. Roman Catholic. Home: 1101 Phay Ave Canon City CO 81212-2248 Office: Coll of the Cañons Forge Rd/Indsl Park Canon City CO 81212

BAUMANN, THEODORE ROBERT, aerospace engineer, consultant, army officer; b. Bklyn., May 13, 1932; s. Emil Joseph and Sophie (Reiblein) B.; m. Patricia Louise Drake, Dec. 16, 1967; children: Veronica Ann, Robert Theodore, Joseph Edmund. B in Aerospace Engring., Poly. U., Bklyn., 1954; MS in Aerospace Engring., U. So. Calif., L.A., 1962; grad., US Army C&GS Coll., 1970, Indsl. Coll. of Armed Forces, 1970, US Army War Coll., 1979, Air War Coll., 1982. Structures engr. Glenn L. Martin Co., Balt., 1954-55; structural loads engr. N.Am. Rockwell, L.A., 1958-67; dynamics engr. TRW Systems Group, Redondo Beach, Calif., 1967-71, systems engr., 1971-75, project engr., 1975-84, sr. project engr., 1984-92; cons. SAAB-Scania Aerospace Div., Linkoping, Sweden, 1981-82; asst. dir. Dir. Weapons Systems, U.S. Army, Washington, 1981-85, staff officer Missile & Air Def. System div., 1975-81. Contbr. articles to Machine Design, tech. publs., tech. symposia. Asst. scoutmaster Boy Scouts Am., Downey, Calif., 1985-93; instr. Venice Judo Boys Club, 1966-86. Served from 2d lt. U.S. Army to col. USAR, 1954-88. Decorated Legion of Merit. Mem. AIAA; mem. Soc. Am. Mil. Engrs (life), Am. Legion, Res. Officers Assn. (life), U.S. Judo Fedn., Nat. Rifle Assn, Knights of Columbus. Republican. Roman Catholic. Achievements include developing a new method for the analysis and classification of random data; contbr. to air force ballistic missile program; devel. procedure for design of prestressed joints and fittings. Office: Theodore R Baumann & Assoc 7732 Brunache St Downey CA 90242-2206

BAUMER, EDWARD FERDINAND, financial services executive; b. Irvington, N.J., Dec. 5, 1913; s. Ferdinand Fred and Augusta Baumer (Wagemann) B.; m. Elizabeth Karl, Feb. 10, 1940; children: Edward K. (dec.), Richard Eaton, Jane Elizabeth Woodman. Liberal arts, Rutgers Univ., 1934, JSD, LLB, 1937. Commd. U.S. Army, 1934, advanced through grades to brig. gen., 1973, ret., 1973; dir. adv.,pub. rels. Prudential Ins. Co. Am., L.A., 1934-55; v.p. McCann Erickson Comm., N.Y.C., 1955-59, Union Bank, L.A., 1959-61; sr. v.p. Great Western Fin. Corp., Beverly Hills, Calif., 1961-65; pres., CEO E.F. Baumer & Co., L.A., 1965-87; chmn. Baumer FIn. Publ., L.A., 1987; chmn., pres., CEO World-Wide Super Sr. Sports, 1999—; chmn. emeritus Baumer Fin. Publ., Chgo., 1997— (affiliate Imagination Publ. Chgo.). Mem. Calif. Club, La Jolla Beach & Tennis Club, L.A. Tennis Club. Republican. Protestant. Avocations: won 14 sr. European Tennis Championships and World ITF Tennis Championship (doubles), 1998. Home: 1820 Avenida del Mundo 1504 Coronado CA 92118

BAUMGARTNER, ANTON EDWARD, automotive sales professional; b. N.Y.C., May 18, 1948; s. Hans and Carmen Maria (Figueroa) B.; m. Brenda Lee Lemmon, May 24, 1969 (div. 1990); 1 child, Anton Nicholaus; m. Virginia Thiele, 1992; 1 child, Bree Alexandra. BS, Woodbury U., 1970. Sales mgr. Maywood Bell Ford, Bell, Calif., 1966-69, O.R. Haan, Inc., Santa Ana, Calif., 1969-72; pres. Parkinson Volkswagen, Placentia, Calif., 1972-77; exec. v.p. United Moped, Fountain Valley, Calif., 1975-82; pres. Automobili Intermeccanica, Fountain Valley, 1975-82; gen. mgr. Bishop (Calif.) Volkswagen-Bishop Motors, 1982-85, Beach Imports-Irvine Imports, Newport Beach, Calif., 1985-88; chmn. bd. Stan and Ollie Ins. Co., Santa Ana, Calif., 1989—; exec. v.p. Asterism, Inc., 1992-96; chmn. Marich Acceptance Inland Empire, 1996—; mem. faculty, Automotive World Congress, Detroit, 1980. Contbr. articles to weekly serial publs. Mem. Coachbuilders Assn. N.Am. (sec. 1975-78). Office: Marich Acceptance 6 Satinbush Aliso Viejo CA 92656-1827

BAUMRIND, DIANA, research psychologist; b. N.Y.C., Aug. 23, 1927. A.B., Hunter Coll., 1948; M.A., U. Calif., Berkeley, 1951, Ph.D., 1955. Cert. and lic. psychologist, Calif. Project dir. psychology dept. U. Calif., Berkeley, 1955-58; project dir. Inst. of Human Devel., 1960—, also rsch. psychologist and prin. investigator family socialization and devel. competence project; lectr. and cons. in field; referee for rsch. proposals Grant Found., NIH, 1970—, NSF, 1970—. Contbr. numerous articles to profl. jours. and books; author 2 monographs; mem. editorial bd. Devel. Psychology, 1986-90. Recipient Rsch. Scientist award, NIMH; grantee NIMH, 1955-58, 60-66, Nat. Inst. Child Health and Human Devel., 1967-74, MacArthur Found., Grant Found., 1967-92. Fellow Am. Psychol. Assn., Am. Psychol. Soc. (G. Stanley Hall award 1988); mem. Soc. Research in Child Devel. Office: U Calif Inst of Human Devel 1217 Tolman Hall Berkeley CA 94720-1691*

BAUTISTA, ANTHONY HERNANDEZ, biomedical company executive; b. Palo Alto, Calif., Sept. 19, 1955; s. Anthony Hernandez and Velma Rose (Morinan) B.; m. Jill Davis, June 17, 1978; children: Evan Thomas, Laura Anne. AA in Electronic Tech., Coll. of San Mateo, 1976; BSEE, San Jose (Calif.) State U., 1994. Elec. engr. Hewlett Packard, Palo Alto, Calif., 1976-86; mfg. engring. mgr. Molecular Devices Corp., Menlo Park, Calif., 1986-91; ops. v.p. LJL Biosystems, Inc., Sunnyvale, Calif., 1991—. Mem. Toastmasters (adminstrv. v.p. 1990), Tau Beta Pi.

BAWDEN, GARTH LAWRY, museum director; b. Truro, Eng., Dec. 31, 1939; s. Richard Thomas and Susan Elizabeth Olga (Lawry) B.; m. Margaret Ruth Greet, Dec. 21, 1963 (div. Mar. 1978); children: Michael Greet, Teona Mary, Kerenza Elizabeth; m. Elaine Louise Comack, Oct. 26, 1978; children: Jonathan Richard, Rebecca Lawry. Diploma in phys. medicine, West Middlesex Sch. Phys. Medicine, Isleworth, Eng., 1961; BA in Art History, U. Oreg., 1970; PhD in Anthropology, Harvard U., 1977. Assoc. in archaeology Harvard U., Cambridge, Mass., 1977-81, instr., 1980-85, asst., acting dir. Peabody Mus., 1980-85; assoc. prof. U. N.Mex., Albuquerque, 1985-91; prof. U. Mex., Albuquerque, 1991—; dir. Maxwell Mus. U. N.Mex., Albuquerque, 1985—; dir. field research project Harvard U., Galindo, Peru, 1971-74, dir. field survey Peabody Mus., Saudi Arabian Archaeol. Survey, 1978-80; field supr. Cuntisuyu Project, Moquegua, Peru, 1983-86; dir. U. N.Mex. Acheol. Project, So. Peru, 1985—. Author: (with G. Conrad) The Andean Heritage, 1982; contbr. articles on archaeology to profl. jours. Fellow Woodrow Wilson, U. Oreg., 1970, Tinker, Harvard U., 1983. Mem. Soc. Am. Archaeology, Assn. Field Archaeology, Assn. Sci. Mus. Dirs., Current Anthropology (assoc.), Phi Beta Kappa, Sigma Xi. Home: 6 Applewood Ln NW Albuquerque NM 87107-6404 Office: Univ NMex Maxwell Mus Anthropology Albuquerque NM 87131-1201*

BAXTER, BETTY CARPENTER, educational administrator; b. Sherman, Tex., 1937; d. Granville E. and Elizabeth (Caston) Carpenter; m. Cash Baxter; children: Stephen Barrington, Catherine Elaine. AA in Music, Christian Coll., Columbia, Mo., 1957; MusB in Voice and Piano, So. Meth. U., Dallas, 1959; MA in Early Childhood Edn., Tchrs. Coll., Columbia, 1972, MEd, 1979, EdD, 1988. Tchr. Riverside Ch. Day Sch., N.Y.C., 1966-71; headmistress Episcopal Sch., N.Y.C., 1972-87, headmistress emeritus, 1987—; founding head Presbyn. Sch., Houston, 1988-94; dir. Chadwick Village Sch., Palos Verdes Peninsula, Calif. Author: The Relationship of Early Tested Intelligence on the WPPSI to Later Tested Aptitude on the SAT. Mem. ASCD, Nat. Assn. Episcopal Schs. (former gov. bd., editor Network publ.), Nat. Assn. Elem. Sch. Prins., Ind. Schs. Assn. Admissions Greater N.Y. (former exec. bd.), Nat. Assn. for Edn. of Young Children, L.A. Assn. Sch. Heads, Nat. Assn. Elem. Sch. Prins., Assn. Supervision and Curriculum Devel., Kappa Delta Pi, Delta Kappa Gamma. Republican. Presbyterian. Home and Office: 26800 Academy Dr Palos Verdes Peninsula CA 90274-3980

BAXTER, GENE KENNETH, mechanical engineer, company executive; b. Emmett, Idaho, Sept. 4, 1939; s. Glen Wilton Sr. and Mable Velhelmina (Casper) B.; m. Laraine Marie Mitchell, Jan. 20, 1968; children: Gretchen Lynn, Aaron Gregory. AA in Mech. Engring. (scholar), Boise Jr. Coll., 1959; BS in Mech. Engring., U. Idaho, 1961; MS in Aero. Engring. (NDEA fellow), Syracuse U., 1966, PhD in Mech. Engring., 1971. Registered profl. engr., N.Y., Ariz. Engr. Pratt & Whitney Aircraft Co., East Hartford, Conn., 1961; tchng. and rsch. asst. Syracuse (N.Y.) U., 1962-67; engr. Galson & Galson Cons. Engrs., Syracuse, 1968; sr. mech. engr., staff engr. electronic systems div. Gen. Electric Co., Syracuse, 1968-77, advanced project mgr. mech. design engring. mgr., space div. Daytona Beach, Fla., 1977-82; engring. dept. head Schlumberger Tech. Corp., Rosharon, Tex., 1982-83; mgr. engring., downhole svcs. div. Exploration Logging, Inc. div. Baker Internat. Corp., Sacramento, 1983-85; mgr. handling qualities sect. engring. and tng. simulation systems dept. McDonnell Douglas Helicopter Co., Mesa, Ariz., 1985-87, mgr. projects mgmt., 1987-88, project mgr. Advanced Apache Simulation projects, 1988-91; pres. Exodyne Electric Motors, Inc., Tempe, Ariz., 1991-93, Baxter Engring., Mesa, 1993—; dir. mech. projects creating visual simulation and tng. systems, nuclear power controls, shipboard digital control systems; dir. equipment for measurement, analysis and control of wellhead, formation and drilling parameters for oil well services industry; dir. hardware systems and software models of flight, avionics, displays, controls and aircraft subsystems for helicopter simulation and training systems; director for design and manufacture of submersible electric motors and accessories for indsl. turbine pumping applications; director of mechanical engineering consulting for forensic applications; tchr. refresher course N.Y. State Profl. Engrs., Syracuse, 1975-76. Chmn. fin. and stewardship com. United Ch. of Christ, Liverpool, N.Y., 1974-77, chmn. bd. trustees, 1977; ruling elder Ormond Beach (Fla.) Presbyn. Ch., 1979-82, chmn. stewardship com., 1979-80, pres. corp., 1980-82, chmn. fin. com., 1981-82; pres. bd. dirs. Hope Women's Ctr., 1995—. Recipient design award Machinery Mag., 1961; Raymond J. Briggs award Idaho Bd. Engring. Examiners, 1961. Mem. IEEE (sr., treas. Daytona sect. 1978-79, chmn. 1979-80, treas. Phoenix Area Cons. Network, 1995—), ASME, SAE, ASHRAE, NSPE, NAFE, Nat. Assn. Profl. Accident Reconstruction Specialists, Southwestern Assn. Tech. Accident Investigators, Ariz. Soc. of Profl. Engrs., Phi Kappa Phi, Tau Beta Pi. Speaker numerous profl. confs.; contbr. over 30 research papers in field. Home: 1243 N Norwalk Mesa AZ 85205-4038

BAXTER, MARVIN RAY, state supreme court justice; b. Fowler, Calif., Jan. 9, 1940; m. Jane Pippert, June 22, 1963; children: Laura, Brent. BA in Econs., Calif. State U., 1962; JD, U. Calif.-Hasting Coll. Law, 1966. Bar: Calif. 1966. Appointments sec. to Gov. George Deukmejian, 1983-88; dep. dist. atty. Fresno County, Calif., 1967-68; assoc. Andrews, Andrews, Thaxter & Jones, 1968-70, ptnr., 1971-82; apptd. sec. to Gov. George Deukmejian, 1983-88; assoc. justice Calif. Ct. Appeal (5th dist.), 1988-90, Calif. Supreme Ct., 1991—; mem. Jud. Coun. of Calif., chmn. policy coord. and liaison com., 1996—. Mem. Fresno County Bar Assn. (bd. dirs. 1977-82, pres. 1981), Calif. Young Lawyers Assn. (bd. gov. 1973-76, sec.-treas. 1974-75), Fresno County Young Lawyers Assn. (pres. 1973-74), Fresno County Legal Svcs., Inc. (bd. dirs. 1973-74), Fresno State U. Alumni Assn. (pres. 1970-71), Fresno State U. Alumni Trust Coun. (pres. 1970-75). Office: Calif Supreme Ct 350 McAllister St San Francisco CA 94102-3600

BAXTER, MILLIE MCLEAN, business owner, educator; b. Denver, Mar. 14, 1926; d. Stanley Allan and Jessie (Brown) McL.; m. Glenn A. Hettler, Dec. 28, 1949 (div. Mar. 1969); children: Douglass Kent, Linda Horn, Joni Birdsall; m. Jack Stanley Baxter, Feb. 4, 1977; children: David, Fred. Grad., Dickenson Bus. Sch., 1944; student, U. Colo., 1944-46; grad., McConnell Modeling Sch., 1946, Jones Real Estate Coll., 1971. With sales and mktg. The Arnold Corp., Denver, 1973-84; broker, mgr. Evergreen (Colo.) Properties, 1984-87; broker, owner Century 21 Evergreen Real Estate, 1987-92; ind. mgr. Real Estate Tng. Ctr., Evergreen, 1987-91; personal life history tchr. Sr. Resource Ctr., Evergreen, 1992—; distbr. Bay Formula D Products, Evergreen, 1993—; vol. computer instr. for srs., 1991—. Author: How to Write Your Life History for a Family Legacy, 1994. Mem. Denver Bd. Realtors (Salesperson of Yr. 1978), Denver Brokers Council, Evergreen Bd. Realtors, Jefferson County Bd. Realtors, Sales and Mktg. Council (Salesperson of Yr. 1979, Golden Medallion award 1978, 79, 80, 81, 82, 83). Republican. Avocations: writing children's and self-help books, walking, swimming. Office: Bax Products Inc PO Box 733 Evergreen CO 80437-0733

BAXTER, RALPH H., JR., lawyer; b. San Francisco, 1946. AB, Stanford U., 1968; MA, Cath. U. Am., 1970; JD, U. Va., 1974. Chmn. Orrick, Herrington & Sutcliffe LLP, San Francisco, 1990—; mem. adv. bd. nat. Employment Law Inst. Author: Sexual Harassment in the Workplace: A Guide to the Law, 1981, 2nd. rev. edit., 1989, 94, Manager's Guide to Lawful Terminations, 1983, rev. edit., 1991; mem. editorial bd. Va. Law Rev., 1973-74; mem. editorial adv. bd. Employee Rels. Law Jour. Mem. ABA (mgmt. co-chair com. on employment rights and responsibilities in workplace labor and employment law sect. 1987-90). Office: Orrick Herrington & Sutcliffe LLP Old Fed Res Bank Bldg 400 Sansome St San Francisco CA 94111-3143*

BAYER, WILLIAM, writer; b. Cleve., Feb. 20, 1939; s. Leo Bayer and Eleanor (Rosenfeld) Perry; m. Paula Wolfert, Aug. 10, 1983. BA, Harvard U., 1960. Fgn. svc. officer USIA, Washington and Saigon, Republic of Vietnam, 1963-68; freelance documentary filmmaker, 1968-72; freelance writer San Francisco, 1972—. Author: In Search of a Hero, 1966, Stardust, 1974, Visions of Isabelle, 1976, Tangier, 1978, Punish Me With Kisses, 1980, Peregrine, 1981 (Edgar award 1982), Switch, 1984, Pattern Crimes, 1987, Blind Side, 1989, Wallflower, 1991, Mirror Maze, 1994, (as David Hunt) The Magician's Tale, 1997, Trick of Light, 1998, Breaking Through, Selling Out, Dropping Dead, 1971, The Great Movies, 1973; (teleplay) Internal Affairs, 1988, Murder X Seven, 1991, When Love Kills, 1993; contbr. articles to profl. jours. Mem. PEN, Writers Guild Am. West, Authors Guild, Internat. Assn. Crime Writers (pres. 1991-93), Mystery Writers of Am. Avocations: photography, book collecting. Home and Office: 1201 Greenwich St Apt 900 San Francisco CA 94109-1584

BAYLESS, BETSEY, state official; b. Phoenix. BA in Latin Am. Studies and Spanish, U. Ariz., 1966; MPA, Ariz. State U., 1974. V.p. pub. fin. Peacock, Hislop, Staley & Given, Inc., Phoenix, Ariz.; asst. dir. Ariz. Bd. Regents; acting dir. dept. revenue State of Ariz., dir. dept. adminstrn., sec. of state, 1997—; bd. suprs. Maricopa County, 1989-97, chmn. bd., 1992, 94, vice chair, 1997. Nat. bd. advisors U. Ariz. Coll. Bus. & Pub. Adminstrn.; adv. bd. Ariz. State U. West; bd. dirs. Xavier Coll. Preparatory Found., Ariz. Ctr. for the Book; commr. Gov.'s Commn. Violence Against Women; mem. Ariz. Town Hall, Charter 100, Valley Leadership Class VI, Ariz. Rep. Caucus, Ariz. Women's Forum. Named to Hall of Fame, Ariz. State U. Coll. Pub. Programs; recipient Disting. Citizen award U. Ariz. Alumni Assn., Woman of Yr. award Capitol chpt. Bus. and Profl. Women, Disting. Achievement award NEH Fellowship, Achievement award Nat. Assn. Counties, 1993, Citizen award Bur. Reclamation, 1993, Woman of Achievement award Xavier Coll. Preparatory, 1995. Mem. Phi Beta Kappa (Freeman medal 1966). Office: State Capitol 1700 W Washington St Fl 7 Phoenix AZ 85007-2814

BAYLIFF, WILLIAM HENRY, fishery biologist; b. Annapolis, Md., Aug. 29, 1928; s. William Howard and Nelle (Jones) B.; m. Norma Jean York, Jan. 2, 1969. AB, Western Md. Coll., 1949; MS, U. Wash., 1954, PhD, 1965. Biologist Wash. Dept. Fish, Seattle, 1952-54, 57-58; scientist Inter-Am. Tropical Tuna Commn., Republic of Panama, 1958-63, La Jolla, Calif., 1963-67, 1969—; biologist FAO U.N., Republic of Panama, 1967-68; cons. in field. Contbr. articles to profl. jours. Served with U.S. Army, 1955-56. Fellow Am. Inst. Fishery Research Biologists (W.F. Thompson award, 1969); mem. Sigma Xi. Office: Inter-Am Tropical Tuna Commn La Jolla CA 92037-1508

BAYLOR, DON EDWARD, professional baseball manager; b. Austin, Tex., June 28, 1949; s. George Edward and Lillian Joyce B.; m. Rebecca Giles, Dec. 12, 1987; 1 child by previous marriage, Don Edward. Student, Miami-Dade Jr. Coll., Miami, Fla., Blinn Jr. Coll., Brenham, Tex. With Balt. Orioles, 1970-76, Oakland Athletics, 1976, 88, California Angels, 1976-82, N.Y. Yankees, 1983-86, Boston Red Sox, 1986-87, Minnesota Twins, 1987; mem. World Series Championship Team, 1987; mgr. Colorado Rockies, Denver, CO, 1992—; Set new career record for hit by pitches; hit safely in 12 consecutive Am. League Championship Series games. Author: (with Claire Smith) Don Baylor, Nothing But the Truth: A Baseball Life, 1989. Chmn. nat. sports Cystic Fibrosis Found. Recipient Designated Hitter of Yr. award, 1985, 86, Roberto Clemente award, 1985; named Am. League's Most Valuable Player, 1979, Sporting News Player of Yr., 1979; player All-Star Game, 1979; named Nat. League Mgr. of Yr. Sporting News, 1995, Baseball Writers Assn. Am., 1995. Holder Am. League playoff record most RBI (10), 1982, Am. League single season record most times hit by pitch (35), 1986. Office: Colorado Rockies 2001 Blake St Denver CO 80205-2000 Office: Major League Baseball Players Assn 805 3d Ave New York NY 10022-7513*

BAYLOR, ELGIN GAY, professional basketball team executive; b. Washington, Sept. 16, 1934; m. Elaine; 1 dau., Krystle. Ed., Coll. Idaho, Seattle U. Profl. basketball player Los Angeles (formerly Minneapolis) Lakers, 1958-72; asst. coach New Orleans Jazz, NBA, 1974-76, coach, 1976-79; exec. v.p., gen. mgr. Los Angeles Clippers, 1986—, v.p. basketballops. Most Valuable Player, NCAA Tournament, 1958; mem. NBA All-Star Team, 1959-65, 67-70; Rookie of the Yr., NBA, 1959; co-Most Valuable Player, NBA All-Star Game, 1959; named to NBA 35th Anniversary All-Time Team, 1980. Office: LA Clippers 3939 S Figueroa St Los Angeles CA 90037-1200*

BAZERMAN, CHARLES, English language educator, writing researcher; b. Bklyn., June 30, 1945; s. Solomon and Miriam (Kirschenberg) B.; m. Shirley Geok-lin Lim, Nov. 24, 1972; 1 child, Gershom Kean. BA, Cornell U., 1967; MA, Brandeis U., 1968, PhD, 1971. Asst. prof. English Baruch Coll., CUNY, 1971-78, assoc. prof., 1979-84, prof., 1985-90; prof. lit., communication and culture Ga. Inst. Tech., Atlanta, 1990-94; prof. English and edn. U. Calif., Santa Barbara, 1994—; vis. prof. Nat. U. Singapore, 1985-86' Watson disting. vis. prof. composition U. Louisville, 1997. Co-author: Reading Skills Handbook, 1978; author: Informed Writer, 1981, Shaping Written Knowledge, 1988, Constructing Experience, 1994, Textual Dynamics of the Professions, 1991, Landmark Essays in Writing across the Curriculum, 1995, Involved, 1997. NEH grantee, 1989; recipient McGovern medal Am. Writers' Assn., 1990, NCTE Award of Excellence, 1990. Mem. MLA, Soc. for Lit. and Sci., Conf. Coll. Composition and Comm., Soc. for Social Studies Sci. (coun. 1989-92), CUNY Assn. Writing Suprs. (chmn. 1978-80). Democrat. Home: 574 Calle Anzuelo Santa Barbara CA 93111-1721 Office: U Calif Santa Barbara Dept English Santa Barbara CA 93106

BAZIGOS, MARY, English as a secong language speech and writing educator; b. Pitts., Jan. 30, 1951; d. Spyros P. and Julia (Zahariadis) Metropoulasi; m. Michael Bazigos; children: Julia, Eugenia. BA, U. Calif., Berkeley, 1973; Master, San Francisco State U., 1976. Cert. tchr., Calif. Tchr. ESL Heald Engring. Coll., San Francisco, 1976-77, Lincoln U., San Francisco, 1978-82; ESL lab program City Coll. San Francisco, 1983-84; tchr. ESL intermediate reading/writing, 1983-84; tchr. ESL intermediate writing Jefferson Adult Sch., Paly City, Calif., 1987-90; tchr. ESL advanced listening/speaking, writing Cañada Coll., Redwood City, Calif., 1990-91; tchr. ESL intermediate, speech, writing Coll. San Mateo, Calif., 1991—; ESL tutor Lang. Program Designs, San Francisco, 1977, Linda Arrillaga and Assocs.,

Mountain View, 1997-98. Mem. Calif. Assn. TESOL, Calif. Scholastic Fedn. (life). Home: 2624 Sequoia Way Belmont CA 94002-1450

BEACH, ARTHUR O'NEAL, lawyer; b. Albuquerque, Feb. 8, 1945; s. William Pearce and Vivian Lucille (Kronig) B.; BBA, U. N.Mex., 1967, JD, 1970; m. Alex Clark Doyle, Sept. 12, 1970; 1 son, Eric Kronig. Bar: N.Mex. 1970. Assoc. Smith & Ransom, Albuquerque, 1970-74; assoc. Keleher & McLeod, Albuquerque, 1974-75, ptnr., 1976-78, shareholder Keleher & McLeod, P.A., Albuquerque, 1978—; teaching asst. U. N. Mex., 1970. Bd. editors Natural Resources Jour., 1968-70. Mem. ABA, State Bar N.Mex. (unauthorized practice of law com., adv. opinions com., med.-legal panel, legal-dental-osteo.-podiatry com., jud. selection com., specialization bd.), Albuquerque Bar Assn. (dir. 1978-82). Democrat. Mem. Christian Sci. Ch. Home: 2015 Dietz Pl NW Albuquerque NM 87107-3240 Office: Keleher & McLeod PA PO Drawer AA Albuquerque NM 87103

BEACH, JOHN LAURENCE, storyteller, writer; b. Almy, Wyo., Sept. 20, 1939; s. Laurence Edwin Beach and Marguerite (Bowns) Kennedy; m. Judith Anne Roylance, Dec. 16, 1966; children: Kristen, Carrie, Corey. BA, U. Wyo., 1963; postgrad., Utah State U., 1966-89. Cert. speech, drama and English tchr., Wyo. Announcer/program dir. KIXX Radio, Provo, Utah, 1959-61, KLME Radio, Laramie, Wyo., 1963-65; tchr. Sch. Dist. # 1, Rock Springs, Wyo., 1965-95; part-time disc jockey KRKK-KQSW Radio, Rock Springs, Wyo., 1973-83; program dir./news dir. KSIT Radio, Rock Springs, Wyo., 1984-94; part-time instr. Western Wyo. C.C., Rock Springs, Wyo., 1995—; freelance storyteller/writer Books Without Covers, Rock Springs, Wyo., 1989—; writing assessment dir. Sch. Dist. # 1, Rock Springs, 1995-97; storytelling festival coord. Wyo. Territorial Prison Pk., Laramie, 1997—; pageant dir. Sweetwater County Pageant Com., Rock Springs, 1997. Author: Many Voices: True Tales of Americas Past, 1995; author (rec.) Children of the Journey, 1996. Mem. City Planning and Zoning, Rock Springs, 1990-95; storyteller Nat. Mormon Trail Wagon Train, Split Rock, Wyo., 1997. Mem. Nat. Coun. Tchrs. English, Nat. Storytelling Assn., Soc. Children's Book Writers and Illustrators, Wyo. Writer's Inc. Mem. LDS Ch. Avocations: gardening, music, reading, traveling. Home and Office: 1315 Kimberly Ave Rock Springs WY 82901-7412

BEACH, LEE ROY, psychologist, educator, academic administrator; b. Gallup, N.Mex., Feb. 29, 1936; s. Dearl and Lucile Ruth (Krumtum) B.; m. Barbara Ann Heinrich, Nov. 13, 1971. B.A., Ind. U., 1957; M.A., U. Colo., 1959, Ph.D., 1961. Aviation psychologist U.S. Sch. Aviation Medicine, Pensacola, Fla., 1961-63; human factors officer Office of Naval Research, Washington, 1963-64; postdoctoral research U. Mich., Ann Arbor, 1964-66; faculty dept. psychology U. Wash., Seattle, 1966-89; faculty mgmt. & policy, psychology U. Ariz., Tucson, 1990—, McClelland chair mgmt. & policy, 1989—, vice dean Sch. Bus., 1998—. Contbr. articles to profl. jours. Recipient Feldman rsch. award, 1981, Disting. Tchr. award U. Wash., 1986, Prof. of Yr. award State of Wash., 1989, nat. teaching award Coun. for Advancement and Support Edn., 1989; fellow NIMH, 1964-66. Fellow Am. Psychol. Soc.; mem. Soc. for Orgnl. Behavior. Office: Univ Arizona Coll Bus & Pub Adminstrn Tucson AZ 85721

BEACH, ROGER C., oil company executive; b. Lincoln, Nebr., Dec. 5, 1936; s. Melvin C. and L. Mayme (Hoham) B.; m. Elaine M. Wilson, Oct. 1954 (div. 1972); children: Kristi, Mark, Anne; m. Karen Lynn Ogden, July 27, 1974. BS, Colo. Sch. Mines, 1961. Profl. petroleum refining engr., Calif. With Unocal Corp., L.A., 1961—; mgr. spl. projects Unocal Corp., Los Angeles, 1976-77, dir. planning, 1977-80, v.p. crude supply, 1980-86, pres. refining and mktg., 1986-92, corp. sr. v.p., 1987-1992, pres., 1992-94, CEO, 1994—, now chmn. and COO, 1994-98, CEO, 1998—. Chmn. bd. trustees Nat. 4-H Coun. Mem. Pres.'s Interchange Exec. Alumni Assn. Office: Unocal Corp 2141 Rosecrans Ave Ste 4000 El Segundo CA 90245-4746*

BEAGLE, JOHN GORDON, real estate broker; b. Spokane, Wash., Dec. 31, 1943; s. Gordon Avril and Sylvia Alberta (Dobbs) B.; m. Shihoko Ledo, Nov. 14, 1964; children: James, Steven, Kevin, Melanie. BS, Mont. State U., 1970; GRI, Realtors Inst., Helena, Mont. Cert. real estate broker. Instr. Kalispell (Mont.) High Sch., 1970-71; gen. mgr. Equity Coop. Assn., Harlem, Mont., 1971-76; owner, operator Howards Pizza, Livingston, Mont., 1976-79; broker, owner Beagle Properties, Sidney, Mont., 1979—. Appointed to Mont. Bd. Realty Regulation, 1995. With USN, 1963-67. Mem. Mont. Assn. Realtors (v.p. ea. dist. 1982-84, 90-94), Gateway Bd. Realtors (pres. 1987-88), Kiwanis, Masons (past master). Republican. Mem. Ch. of Christ. Avocations: computers, readings, fishing. Office: ERA Beagle Properties 120 2nd Ave SW Sidney MT 59270-4018

BEAL, GRAHAM WILLIAM JOHN, museum director; b. Stratford-on-Avon, Eng., Apr. 22, 1947; came to U.S., 1973; s. Cecil John Beal and Annie Gladys (Barton) Tunbridge; m. Nancy Jane Andrews, Apr. 21, 1973; children: Priscilla Jane, Julian William John. BA, Manchester U., Eng., 1969; MA, U. London, 1972. Acad. asst. to dir. Sheffield City (Eng.) Art Galleries, 1972-73; gallery dir. U. S.D., Vermillion, 1973-74, Washington U., St. Louis, 1974-77; chief curator Walker Art Ctr., Mpls., 1977-83; dir. Sainsbury Ctr. for Visual Arts, Norwich, Eng., 1983-84; chief curator San Francisco Mus. Modern Art, 1984-89; dir. Joslyn Art Mus., Omaha, 1989-96, Los Angeles County Mus. Art, 1996—; mem. Fed. Adv. Com. on Internat. Exhbns., 1991-94. Author: (book, exhbn. catalog) Jime Dine: Five Themes, 1984; co-author: (book, exhbn. catalog) A Quiet Revolution, 1987, David Nash: Voyages and Vessels, 1994, Joslyn Air Museum: Fifty Favorities; contbr. to Apollo Mag., London, 1989-91; contbg. author: Joslyn Art Musuem: A Building History, 1998. Trustee Djerassi Found., Woodside, Calif., 1987-89. Mem. Assn. Art Mus. Dirs. Avocations: history, cooking, music. Office: LA County Mus Art 5905 Wilshire Blvd Los Angeles CA 90036-4504

BEAL, MARY EVELYN, radio show personality, foundation administrator; b. Jerome, Ariz., Oct. 18, 1947; d. Edwin Beall and Dorothy (Wombacher) Starkey; m. Robert L. Beal, Feb. 11, 1977 (div. Mar. 1986); children: Alison Marie, Robert L. III. Student, Ariz. State U., 1965-68, U. Nebr. and Bellevue Coll., 1972-73. Promoter Lincoln/Mercury Tennis Classic, 1983-85; mgr. sales, owner Ariz. Fitness mag., 1986; pvt. practice cons., 1985-88; dir. mktg. New West Radio, Inc., Wichita, 1986-89; sta. mgr., talk show hostess Sta. KNSS AM, 1989—; program mgr. WOKV, Jacksonville, Fla., 1994-95; talk show host KNST, Tuscon, 1996-97. Bd. dirs. Fan Kane Fund for Brain Injured, 1977-87, 3HO Drug Alcohol Rehab., 1985-86, St. Jospeh Hosp. Classic/Emerald Ball, 1988—, Parallax, Inc. Drug & Alcohol Rehab., 1988-91, Wichita Symphony Decorator Showhouse, 1988; mem. Sedgwick County Planning Commn., 1990; mem. drunk under influence adv. bd. YWCA, 1990—, bd. dirs., 1992, Oliver Elliott Sch. Comm. Wichita State U., 1992; exec. dir. Ctr. for Preservation and Edn. Ancient Western Civilization Art and Artifacts, 1998—; mem. adv. bd. Assistance League of Wichita, 1992; pres. Brian D. Higby Fund, Wichita, Kan., 1994—. Mem. Nat. Assn. Radio Talk Show Hosts (pres. 1991—). Avocations: collecting pre Columbian art. Home: 1275 Canyon Rd Santa Fe NM 87501-6166 Office: 1275 Canyon Rd Santa Fe NM 87501-6166

BEALL, BURTCH W., JR., architect; b. Columbus, Ohio, Sept. 27, 1925; s. Burtch W. and Etta (Beheler) B.; m. Susan Jane Hunter, June 6, 1949; children: Brent Hunter, Brook Waite. Student, John Carroll U., 1943; BArch, Ohio State U., 1949. Draftsman Brooks & Coddington, Architects, Columbus, 1949-51, William J. Monroe, Architects, Salt Lake City, 1951-53, Lorenzo Young, Architect, Salt Lake City, 1953-54; prin. Burtch W. Beall, Jr., Architect, Salt Lake City, 1954—; vis. lectr. Westminster Coll., 1955; adj. prof. U. Utah, 1955-85, 92-97; treas. Nat. Coun. Archtl. Registration Bds., 1982-84. Restoration architect Salt Lake City and County Bldg; contbr. projects to: A Pictorial History of Architecture in America, America Restored, This Before Architecture. Trustee Utah Found. for Arch., 1985, pres., 1987-91; mem. Utah State Bd. Fine Arts, 1987-95, chmn., 1991-93; chmn. Utah State Capitol Adv. Com., 1986-90, Western States Art Fedn., Bd. trustees, 1991-94; mem. exec. residence com. State of Utah, 1991-97; mem. Utah: A Guide to the State Found. With USN, 1943-45. Recipient several merit and honor awards; Found. fellow Utah Heritage Found., 1985. Fellow AIA; mem. Masons, Sigma Alpha Epsilon. Methodist. Home: 4644 Brookwood Cir Salt Lake City UT 84117-4908 Office: Burtch W Beall Jr Arch 2188 Highland Dr Salt Lake City UT 84106-2896

BEALL, DENNIS RAY, artist, educator; b. Chickasha, Okla., Mar. 13, 1929; s. Roy A. and Lois O. (Phillips) B.; 1 son, Garm. Musician,, Okla. City U., 1950-52; B.A., San Francisco State U., 1953, M.A., 1958. Registrar Oakland (Calif.) Art Mus., 1958; curator Achenbach Found. for Graphic Arts, Calif. Palace of the Legion of Honor, San Francisco, 1958-1965; asst. prof. art San Francisco State U., 1965-69, assoc. prof., 1969-76, prof. art, 1976-92; prof. emeritus, 1992—. Numerous one-man shows of prints, 1957—, including: Award Exhbn. of San Francisco Art Commn., Calif. Coll. Arts and Crafts, 1978, San Francisco U. Art Gallery, 1978, Los Robles Galleries, Palo Alto, Calif.; numerous group shows 1960— including Mills Coll. Art Gallery, Oakland, Calif., Univ. Gallery of Calif. State U., Hayward, 1979, Marshall-Meyers Gallery, 1979, 80, Marin Civic Ctr. Art Galleries, San Rafael, Calif., 1980, San Francisco Mus. Modern Art, 1985; touring exhibit U. Mont., 1987-91; represented in numerous permanent collections including Libr. of Congress, Washington, Mus. Modern Art, N.Y.C., Nat. Libr. of Medicine, Washington, Cleve. Mus., Whitney Mus., Phila. Mus., U.S. embassy collections, Tokyo, London and other major cities, Victoria and Albert Mus., London, Achenbach Found. for graphic Arts, Calif. Palace of Legion of Honor, San Francisco, Oakland Art Mus., Phila. Free Libr., Roanoke (Va.) Art Ctr., Worcester (Mass.) Art Mus., Whitney Mus. Am. Art, Cleve. Mus., various colls. and univs. in U.S. Served with USN, 1947-50, PTO. Office: San Francisco State Univ Art Dept 1600 Holloway Ave San Francisco CA 94132-1722

BEALL, DONALD RAY, multi-industry high-technology company executive; b. Beaumont, Calif., Nov. 29, 1938; s. Ray C. and Margaret (Murray) B. BS, San Jose State Coll., 1960; MBA, U. Pitts., 1961; postgrad., UCLA; D of Engring (hon.), GMI Engring. and Mgmt. Inst., 1994, Milw. Sch. Engring., 1994. With Ford Motor Co., 1961-68; fin. mgmt. positions Newport Beach, Calif., 1961-66; mgr. corp. fin. planning and contracts Phila., 1966-67; controller Palo Alto, Calif., 1967-68; exec. dir. corp. fin. planning N.Am. Rockwell, El Segundo, Calif., 1968-69, exec. v.p. electronics group, 1969-71; exec. v.p. Collins Radio Co., Dallas, 1971-74; pres. Collins Radio Group, Rockwell Internat. Corp., Dallas, 1974-76; corp. v.p., pres. Electronic Ops., Dallas, 1976-77; exec. v.p. Rockwell Internat. Corp., Dallas, 1977-79; pres., chief operating officer Rockwell Internat. Corp., Pitts., 1979-88; chmn. bd., chief exec. officer Rockwell Internat. Corp., Costa Mesa, Calif., 1988-98; chmn. Rockwell Internat. Corp., Seal Beach, 1997-98, chmn. of exec. com. of bd., 1998—; mem. bd. overseers and Grad. Sch. of Mgmt.; bd. visitors U. Calif., Irvine, 1988—; trustee Calif. Inst. Tech.; bd. dirs. Procter & Gamble Co., Amoco Corp., Times-Mirror Corp., L.A. World Affairs Coun.; mem. Bus. Higher Edn. Forum, Bus. Coun., Bus. Roundtable, SRI Adv. Coun., Coun. on Competitiveness. Recipient Exemplary Leadership in Mgmt. award John E. Anderson Sch. Mgmt., UCLA, 1991, Excellence in Tech. award Gartner Group, 1991, Spirit of Achievement award Jr. Achievement of So. Calif., 1993, Adm. Chester W. Nimitz award Navy League's Fleet, 1995, Inaugural Front and Ctr. award Calif. State U., Fullerton, 1996, Human Rels. award Am. Jewish Com., Orange County, 1996; named hon. chmn. Nat. Engrs. Week, 1994. Fellow AIAA, Soc. Mfg. Engrs.; mem. Navy League U.S., Young Pres.'s Orgn., Sigma Alpha Epsilon, Beta Gamma Sigma. Office: Rockwell Internat Corp 2201 Seal Beach Blvd Seal Beach CA 90740*

BEAR, GREGORY DALE, writer, illustrator; b. San Diego, Aug. 20, 1951; s. Dale Franklin and Wilma (Merriman) B.; m. Astrid May Anderson, June 18, 1983; children: Erik William, Alexandra. AB in English, San Diego State U., 1973. Tech. writer, host Reuben H. Fleet Space Theater, 1973; freelance writer, 1975—. Author: Hegira, 1979, Psychlone, 1979, Beyond Heaven's River, 1980, Strength of Stones, 1981, The Wind From a Burning Woman, 1983, The Infinity Concerto, 1984, Blood Music, 1985, Eon, 1985, The Serpent Mage, 1986, The Forge of God, 1987, Eternity, 1988, Tangents, 1989, Heads, 1990, Queen of Angels, 1990, Anvil of Stars, 1992, Moving Mars, 1993 (Nebula award 1994), Songs of Earth and Power, 1993, Legacy, 1995, Slant, 1997, Dinosaur Summer, 1998, Foundation and Chaos, 1998, Darwin's Radio, 1999; short stories: Blood Music (Hugo and Nebula awards), 1983, Hardfought (Nebula award), 1993, Tangents (Hugo and Nebula awards), 1987; editor: New Legends, 1995. Cons. Citizen's Adv. Council on Nat. Space Policy, Tarzana, Calif., 1983-84. Mem. Sci. Fiction Writers of Am. (editor Forum 1983-84, chmn. grievance com. 1985-86, v.p. 1987, pres. 1988-90). Avocations: book collecting; science; music; movies, history. Home: 506 Lakeview Rd Lynnwood WA 98037-2141

BEAR, JEFFREY WARREN, construction executive; b. Amittyville, N.Y., Mar. 18, 1945. BA, San Diego State U., 1972, MFA, 1975; postgrad., Harvard U., 1985; PhD with honors, Coll. of Edassea, Mararastra, India, 1978. Pres. Orion Fin. Fund, San Diego, 1972-83; bus. mgr. Matlines, Inc., San Diego, 1983-87; priest Good Samaritans, National City, Calif., 1978—; chief adminstrv. officer Phoenix Cos., San Diego, 1987—; chmn. Svc. Benefit Corp. of Am., San Diego, 1987—; cons. Arts Counsel, Reno, 1975—; bd. dirs. J. Christopher Enterprises, Reno. Author: American Contemporary Pottery, 1974; contbr. articles to profl. jours. Bd. dirs. Soc. St. Thomas, San Diego, 1978—; floor runner Dem. Conv., L.A., 1960. Mem. Am. Mgmt. Assn., Am. Bldg. Contractors, Assoc. Bldg. Contractor Assn., Internat. Assn. Concrete Repair Specialists (bd. dirs.), Nat. Restoration Contractors Assn. Eastern Catholic. Avocations: art, pottery, hypnotherapy. Address: 3029 Broadway Apt 18 San Diego CA 92102-2340

BEARD, ANN SOUTHARD, government official, travel company executive, art framing company executive; b. Denver, Jan. 13, 1948; d. William Harvey and Cora Alice Cornelia (Caldwell) Southard; m. Terrill Leon Beard, Dec. 20, 1970 (div. Oct. 1980); 1 son, Jeffery Leon; m. Rainer G. Froehlich, Feb. 12, 1988 (div. 1992). BA, Willamette U., 1970; postgrad U. Calif.-San Diego, 1981-82. Exec. asst. Kidder Peabody & Co., San Francisco, 1970-72; adminstrv. aide Arthur Anderson & Co., Portland, Oreg., 1972-73; owner, mgr. Beard's Frame Shoppes, Inc., Portland, 1973-80; dir. mktg. Multnomah County Fair, Portland, 1979; owner, CEO Ann Beard Spl. Events, San Diego, 1980-82; pres. Frame Affair, Inc., San Diego, 1982-86, Jack Oil Co., Inc., Greeley, 1982—; co-owner, v.p. Froehlich Internat. Travel, La Jolla, Calif., 1987-92; chief of protocol Mayor Susan Golding's Office, City of San Diego, 1993—; v.p. 146 Co., Inc., Greeley, pres., 1970-88; lectr., cons. SBA, San Diego, 1980-85. Mem. Civic Light Opera, Old Globe Theatre; bd. dirs. San Diego Master Chorale, 1981-92; mem. state bd. Miss Calif. Pageant/Miss Am., 1982-87; mem. citizens adv. bd. Drug Abuse Task Force/Crime Prevention Task Force, San Diego, 1983-87; campaign coord. Bill Mitchell for City Coun., 1985; candidate for Congress; staff aide to dep. mayor, 1987; mem. Lead San Diego Alumni, 1988, Scripps Hosp. Aux., 1992—, Internat. Visitors Coun., 1993—, San Diego County Commn. on the Status of Women, 1993-96; mem. Internat. Affairs Bd., San Diego, 1993—; bd. dirs. La Jolla Rep. Women Fedn., 1992—. Mem. Am. Mktg. Assn., World Affairs Coun., San Diego C. of C., Save Our Heritage Orgn., Charter 100 San Diego, San Diego 1988 Alumna Willamette U., 1909 Univ. Club (bd. dirs. 1992—, pres. 1996—), Univ. Club San Diego (mktg., devel. and social dir. 1987-88), Delta Gamma. Home and Office: 934 Santa Helena Park Ct Solana Beach CA 92075-1543

BEART, ROBERT W., JR., surgeon, educator; b. Kansas City, Mo., Mar. 3, 1945; s. Robert Woodward and Helen Elizabeth (Wamsley) B.; m. Cynthia Anne, Jan. 23, 1971; children: Jennifer, Kristina, Amy. AB, Princeton U., 1967; MD, Harvard U., 1971. Diplomate Am. Bd. Surgery, Am. Bd. Colon and Rectal Surgery. Intern U. Colo., 1971-72, resident, 1972-76; prof. surgery Mayo Clinic, Scottsdale, Ariz., 1976-87, 1987-92; prof. surgery U. So. Calif., L.A., 1992—. Maj. USMC, 1972-83. Fellow Am. Soc. Colon and Rectal Surgery (pres. 1994); mem. Commn. on Cancer (chmn.). Office: U So Calif Dept Surgery 1450 San Pablo St # 5400 Los Angeles CA 90033-1042

BEARWALD, JEAN HAYNES, company executive; b. San Francisco, Aug. 31, 1924; d. Joseph Robert and Edna Haynes (Goudey) Bearwald; m. William Henry Sherburn, Apr. 12, 1969 (dec. 1970); 1 child by previous marriage, David Richard Cross. BA, Stephens Coll., Columbia, Mo., 1945. Adminstrv. asst. Bearwald & Assocs., Sacramento, 1966-78; acct. Truck Parts Co., Sand City, Calif., 1979-80; pres., chief exec. officer Bearwald and Assocs., Fresno, Calif., 1980-89, Las Vegas, N.Mex., 1989-91; owner Traditions D'Elegance, Santa Fe, 1991-96; program dir. hosp. and institution State of Calif. Ann. Conf., Carmel, 1980-82. Chmn. Sunset Serenade Gala, Santa Fe Opera Guild, 1993-94. Republican. Episcopalian. Avocations: golf, polo. Home and Office: PO Box 788 Santa Fe NM 87504-0788

BEARY, SHIRLEY LORRAINE, retired music educator; b. New Albany, Kans., Feb. 4, 1928; d. Howard Warren and Bertha Adelia (Wilcox) Froelsanger; children: Stephanie Beary Johnson, Susan Beary Maloney. BA, Andrews U., 1949; MusM, U. Redlands, 1967; D Mus. Arts, Southwestern Bapt. Theol. Sem., 1977. Tchr. music Nevada, Iowa, 1949-50; prof. music Southwestern Adventist Coll., Keene, Tex., 1959-84, lectr. Christian ethics, 1978-84; prof. music Oakwood Coll., Huntsville, Ala., 1984-94; ret., 1994; ch. organist Seventh-day Adventist Ch., Kalamazoo, 1951-59, Keene, 1959-80, organist, min. music, 1980-82. Mem. bd. advisors Am. Biog. Inst., Raleigh, N.C. Mem. Coll. Music Soc., Am. Hymn Soc., Internat. Adventist Music Assn. Democrat. Avocations: travel, flower gardening, stamps and records collecting, gospel singing. Home: 2615 Oak Valley Dr Yreka CA 96097-9744

BEASLEY, BRUCE MILLER, sculptor; b. L.A., May 20, 1939; s. Robert Seth and Bernice (Palmer) B.; m. Laurence Leaute, May 21, 1973; children: Julian Bernard, Celia Beranice. Student, Dartmouth Coll., 1957-59; BA, U. Calif., Berkeley, 1962. One-man shows include Everett Ellin Gallery, L.A., 1963, Kornblee Gallery, N.Y.C., 1964, Hansen Gallery, San Francisco, 1965, David Stuart Gallery, L.A., 1966, Andre Emmerich Gallery, N.Y.C., 1971, DeYoung Mus., San Francisco, 1972, Santa Barbara Mus. Art, 1973, San Diego Mus. Art, 1973, Fuller-Goldeen Gallery, San Francisco, 1981, Hooks-Epstein Gallery, Houston, 1990, 93, 95, Pepperdine U., L.A., 1990, So. Oreg. State U., 1991, Sonoma State U., Rhonert Park, Calif., 1991, Fresno Art Mus., 1992, Oakland Mus., 1992, Utermann Gallery, Dortmund, Germany, 1993, Scheffel Gallery, Bad Homberg, Germany, 1993, Galerie Rudolfinum, Prague, 1994, Kunsthalle Mannheim, Germany, 1994, Harcourts Gallery, San Francisco, 1994, Galerie Wirth, Zurich, Switzerland, 1995, Yorkshire Sculpture Park, Eng., 1995, City Ctr., Dortmund, Germany, 1996, Atrium Gallery, St. Louis, 1997, Purdue U., West Lafayette, Ind., 1997, Solomon-Dubnick Gallery, Sacramento, 1997, Gwenda Jay Gallery, Chgo., 1998; exhibited in group shows at San Francisco Mus. of Modern Art, 1961, Mus. of Modern Art, N.Y.C., 1961,62, Dallas Mus. Contemporary Art, 1962, Musee d'Art Moderne, Paris, 1963, U. Art Mus., Berkeley, 1964, Fine Arts Museums, San Francisco, 1965, Guggenheim Mus., 1966, Krannert Art Mus., Ill., 1969, Jewish Mus., N.Y.C., 1970, Milw. Art Ctr., 1970, Expo '70, Osaka, Japan, Stanford Art Mus., 1972, Musee d'Art Moderne, Paris, 1973, Nat. Mus. Am. Art, 1980, Musee d'Art Contemporain Bordeaux, France, 1984, Kunsthalle Mannheim, 1984, Palace of Exhbns., Budapest, Hungary, 1987, Middleheim Sculpture Park, Belgium, 1987, Yorkshire Sculpture Park, Eng., 1984, 87, Hakone Open-Air Mus., Japan, 1993, 95, Landesgartenschau, Germany, 1994, Sculpture '97, Bad Homberg, Germany, Pier Walk '97, 98, Chgo., Galerie Wirth, Zurich, Switzerland, 1997, Darmstadt (Germany) Sculpture Biennale, 1998, Cairo Biennale, Egypt, 1998; represented in permanent collections Mus. Modern Art, N.Y.C., Guggenheim Mus., N.Y.C., Musee d'Art, Paris, Nat. Mus. Am. Art, Washington, Kunsthalle Mannheim, Germany, San Franciso Mus. Modern Art, L.A. County Mus. Art, Sheldon Mem. Art Gallery, Lincoln, Nebr., Hood Mus. Art, Spencer Mus. Art, Lawrence, Kans., Laguna Art Mus., Franklin D. Murphy Sculpture Garden, UCLA, Crocker Art Mus., Sacramento, Bellevue Art Mus., Fresno Art Mus., Xantus Janos Mus., Hungary, Fine Art Mus., San Francisco, Oakland Mus. Calif., Santa Barbara Mus. Art, San Jose (Calif.) Mus. Art, Dartmouth Coll., N.H., Grounds for Sculpture, Hamilton, N.J., Nora Eccles Harrison Mus., Utah State U., Logan; commissions include State of Calif., Oakland Mus., City San Francisco, Miami Internat. Airport, San Francisco Internat. Airport, Fed. Home Loan Bank, San Francisco, Stanford U., City Anchorage, City Salinas, Calif., Fresno Art Mus. Bd. dirs. Internat. Sculpture Ctr., Washington. Home: 322 Lewis St Oakland CA 94607-1236

BEATON, ROY HOWARD, retired nuclear industry executive; b. Boston, Sept. 1, 1916; s. John Howard and Mary Beaton (LaVoie) B.; m. Margaret Marchant, July 22, 1939 (dec. Oct. 4, 1978); m. Leora Lauer Schier, June 26, 1982; children: Constance Beaton Fegley, Roy Howard, Patricia Schier Briselden, Susan Schier Carter, Mary Schier Rieber. BS, Northeastern U., 1939, DSc (hon.), 1967; DEng, Yale U., 1942. Registered profl. engr., Wash., Wis., Fla., Calif. With E.I. DuPont, 1942-46, plant tech. supr. Manhattan (Nuclear Bomb) Project, 1943-44; chief chem. devel., chief engr., gen. mgr. constrn. engring. GE, Richland, Wash., 1946-56; gen. mgr. neutron devices dept. GE, Milw., 1957-63; gen. mgr. Apollo Systems, Daytona Beach, Fla., 1964-68; v.p., gen. mgr. electronics systems div. GE, Syracuse, N.Y., 1968-74; v.p., gen. mgr. energy systems and tech. div. GE, Fairfield, Conn., 1974-75; sr. v.p. Nuclear Energy Group, San Jose, Calif., 1975-81. Chmn. industry div. United Way Campaign, Santa Clara County, Calif., 1978-79. Fellow Am. Inst. Chemists, AAAS; mem. NSPE, Nat. Acad. Engring., Am. Ordnance Assn., Am. Nuclear Soc., Am. Inst. Chem. Engrs., IEEE, AIAA, Navy League U.S., Air Force Assn., Soc. Mil. Engrs., Santa Clara County Mfg. Group, Sigma Xi, Tau Beta Pi. Home: 12 Fawn Ln Sequim WA 98382-3887

BEATON-HOLLINGSWORTH, MEREDITH, enterostomal therapy clinical nurse specialist; b. Danvers, Mass., Oct. 5, 1941; d. Allan Cameron and Arlene Margaret (Jerue) Beaton; m. William Paul Hollingsworth, Nov. 19, 1983 (div.); 1 stepchild, Brendon R. Diploma, R.I. Hosp. Sch. Nursing, Providence, 1968; BS in Nursing, U. Ariz., 1976; MS in Human Resource Mgmt., Golden Gate U., 1984; postgrad., U. Tex., 1988; EdD, U. N.Mex., 1995; MS in Nursing, U. Phoenix, 1998. Cert. enterostomal therapy nurse, health edn. specialist. Commd. ensign USN, 1968, advanced through grades to lt. comdr., 1979; charge nurse USN, USA, PTO, 1968-88; command ostomy nurse, head ostomy clinic Naval Hosp. Portsmouth, Va., 1985-88; pres., chief exec. officer Enterostomal Therapy Nursing Edn. and Tng. Cons. (ETNetc), Rio Rancho, N.Mex., 1989—; mgr. clin. svcs. we. area Support Systems Internat., Inc., Charleston, S.C., 1990-92; pres., CEO Paumer Assocs. Internat., Inc., Rio Rancho, N.Mex., 1992—; sr. cons. enterostomal therapy nursing, edn., & tng. cons.; dir./provost N.Mex. Sch. Enterostomal Nursing, Rio Rancho, 1996—; enterostomal therapy nurse, clin. nurse specialist, educator Presbyn. Health Care Svcs., Albuquerque, 1992-95; sr. cons. Enterstomal Therapy Nursing Edn. & Tng. Cons. A Divsn. of Paumer Assocs., Rio Rancho, N. Mex., 1995—; dir./provost N.Mex. Sch. ET Nursing, Rio Rancho, 1995—; lectr. in field. Mem. adminstrv. bd. Baylake United Meth. Ch., Virginia Beach, 1980-83; chmn. bd. deacons St. Paul's United Ch., Rio Rancho; active Am. Cancer Soc. Mem. Wound, Ostomy and Continence Nurses Soc. (nat. govt. affairs com., govt. affairs com. Rocky Mountain region, newsletter editor, pub. rels. com., regional pres. 1989-93, nat. sec. 1994-95), United Ostomy Assn., World Coun. Enterstomal Therapists, N. Mex. Health Care Assn., N. Mex. Assn. for Home Care, N. Mex. Assn. for Continuity of Care. Republican. Avocations: hot air ballooning, gourmet cooking, flower arranging, interior design. Office: PO Box 44395 Rio Rancho NM 87174-4395

BEATTIE, GEORGE CHAPIN, orthopedic surgeon; b. Bowling Green, Ohio, Sept. 24, 1919; s. George Wilson and Mary Turner (Chapin) B.; m. Nancy U. Fant, Mar. 1, 1947; children: Michael, Suzanne, Eric. BA, Bowling Green U., 1939; MD, U. Chgo., 1943. Diplomate Am. Bd. Orthopaedic Surgery. Commd. lt. (j.g.) MC USN, 1943, advanced through grades to lt. comdr., 1951; med. officer, intern U.S. Naval Hosp., Great Lakes, Ill., 1943-44; resident, fellow in orthopaedic surgery Lahey Clinic, Boston, 1944; ward med. officer orthopaedic services Naval Hosp., Guam, 1944-46; sr. med. officer USN, Manus Island, Papua New Guinea, 1946; resident tng. in orthopaedic surgery U.S. Naval Hosp. St. Albans, N.Y.C., 1947-48; resident in orthopaedic surgery Children's Hosp., Boston, 1949; asst. chief orthopaedic surgery U.S. Naval Hosp. Oak Knoll, Oakland, Calif., 1950-52; comdg. officer med. co. 1st Marine Div. Med. Bn., Republic of Korea, 1952-53; chief orthopaedic service Dept. Phys. Medicine and Navy Amputee Ctr. U.S. Naval Hosp., Phila., 1954; resigned USN, 1954; practice medicine specializing in orthopaedic surgery San Francisco, 1954—; co-chmn. handicapping conditions com. Health Action Study San Mateo County, 1965; 1st chmn. orthopaedic sect. surg. dept. Peninsula Hosp. and Med. Ctr., Burlingame, Calif., 1967, chmn. rehab. service, 1967-71, chmn. phys. therapy and rehab. com., 1956—, vice chmn. orthopaedic dept., 1973-76, chmn., 1977-79; med. dir. research and rehab. ctr. San Mateo (Calif.) County Soc. Crippled Children and Adults, 1958-63; mem. exec. com. Harold D. Chope Community Hosp., San Mateo, 1971-76, chief, co-chmn. orthopaedic sect., 1971-76; chief orthopaedic surg. sect. Mills Meml. Hosp., San Mateo, 1976-78; others. Contbr. articles to profl. jours. Active Indian Guides, 1972-77; pres. Calif. Easter Seal Soc., 1969-71. Decorated Bronze Star. Fellow Am. Acad. Orthopaedic Surgeons (exhibit com. 1979-86); mem.

AMA (Billings Bronze medal 1954), Western Orthopaedic Assn. (pres., bd. dirs. 1986), Leroy Abbott Orthopaedic Soc. U. Calif. San Francisco (assoc. clin. prof.), Alpha Omega Alpha. Office: 1663 Rollins Rd Burlingame CA 94010-2301

BEATTIE, LANE, state senator; b. Sept. 29, 1951; m. Joy Hadlow; 3 children. Student, U. Utah. Mem. Utah State Senate, 1988—, majority leader, 1993-94, pres., 1995-96; owner Lane Realty, West Bountiful, Utah; co-chair state strategic planning com.; mem. various coms. including retirement, transportation and pub. safety. Toll fellow Coun. of State Govt., 1991; recipient Colleen M. Bangerter award, 1992. Mem. Utah Assn. Realtors, Nat. Assn. Realtors, Bountiful Area C. of C. Republican. Office: Lane Realty 1313 N 1100 W West Bountiful UT 84087-1830*

BEAUMONT, MONA, artist; b. Paris; d. Jacques Hippolyte and Elsie M. (Didisheim) Marx. m. William G. Beaumont; children: Garrett, Kevin. Postgrad., Harvard U., Fogg Mus., Cambridge, Mass. One-woman shows include Galeria Proteo, Mexico City, Gumps Gallery, San Francisco, Palace of Legion of Honor, San Francisco, L'Armitiere Gallery, Rouen, France, Hoover Gallery, San Francisco, San Francisco Mus. Modern Art, Galeria Van der Voort, San Francisco, William Sawyer Gallery, San Francisco, Palo Alto (Calif.) Cultural Ctr., Galerie Alexandre Monnet, Brussels, Honolulu Acad. Arts; group shows include San Francisco Mus. Modern Art, San Francisco Art Inst., DeYoung Meml. Mus., San Francisco, Grey Found. Tour of Asia, Bell Telephone Invitational, Chgo., Richmond Art Ctr., L.A. County Mus. Art, Galerie Zodiaque, Geneva, Galerie Le Manoir, La Chaux de Fonds, Switzerland, William Sawyer Meml. Exhibit, San Francisco, others; represented in permanent collections Oakland (Calif.) Mus. Art, City and County of San Francisco, Hoover Found., San Francisco, Grey Found., Washington, Bulart Found., San Francisco, 1st Internat. Trevi (Italy) Flash Art Mus. Exhbn.; also numerous pvt. collections. Mem. Soc. for Encouragement of Contemporary Art, Bay Area Graphic Art Coun., San Francisco Art Inst., San Francisco Mus. Modern Art, Capp Street Project, San Diego Mus. Contemporary Art, L.A. Mus. Contemporary Art. Recipient ann. painting award Jack London Square, 2 ann. awards San Francisco Women Artists, One-man Show award San Francisco Art Festival; purchase award Grey Found., San Francisco Women Artists (2), San Francisco Art Festival; included in Printworld Internat., Internat. Art Diary, Am. Artists, N.Y. Art Rev., Calif. Art Rev., Art in San Francisco Bay Area. Address: 1087 Upper Happy Valley Rd Lafayette CA 94549-2805

BEAUMONTE, PHYLLIS ILENE, secondary school educator; b. Seattle, Dec. 15; d. Albert Hendrix and Bessie Dorothy (Buford) Ratcliff; m. Pierre Marshall Beaumonte, Mar. 12, 1962 (div. Aug. 1974). BA, U. Wash., 1973, MPA, 1975; postgrad., N.W. Theol. Union, Seattle, 1990-92, Seattle U., 1995—. Cert. tchr. K-12, Wash. Adminstrv. intern Office of the City Coun., Seattle, 1974; guest lectr. Pacific Luth. U., Tacoma, Wash., 1975; tchr. The Hebrew Acad., Seattle, 1979; instr./tchr. Seattle Ctrl. C.C., 1988; tchr. Seattle Pub. Schs., 1980—; coord. h.s. Bus. Ptnrs. in Pub. Edn., Seattle, 1989-92; social studies chairperson Rainier Beach H.S., Seattle, 1992—; cons. RA Beau Enterprises, Seattle, 1987—; participant Ctr. for Rsch. and Devel. in Law-Related Edn., Wake Forest U., Winston-Salem, N.C., 1994; adv. com. Wash. State Commn. on Student Learning, Social Studies Acad. Learning Requirements, 1994—; part-time faculty South C.C., Seattle, 1998-99. Author: (poetry) Satyagraha, 1992; author/editor: Roses and Thorns, 1994. Mem. King County Women's Polit. Caucus, Seattle, 1993—; mem. candidate evaluation com. Seattle Mcpl. League, 1972-74; Seattle edn. sch. rep. Seattle Tchrs. Union, 1983-85; v.p. Ch. Women United, State of Wash. and N. Idaho, 1976-78; alumni advisor Grad. Sch. Pub. Affairs, U. Wash., 1994—; v.p. Black Heritage Assn. of Wash. State, Inc. Recipient Internat. Poet of Merit award Internat. Soc. Poets, 1993; U. Wash. minority journalism scholar, 1972. Mem. Mus. of History and Industry, Nat. Coun. for History Edn. (Cert. of Appreciation 1993), Internat. Soc. Poets (life), Nat. Coun. for the Social Studies, Sigma Gamma Rho. Baptist. Avocations: singing, writing, reading, teaching. Home: Apt 402 9030 Seward Pk Ave S Seattle WA 98118

BEBOUT, ELI DANIEL, oil executive; b. Rawlings, Wyo., Oct. 14, 1946; s. Hugh and Dessie Bebout; m. Lorraine J. Tavares; children: Jordan, Jentry, Reagen, Taggert. BEE, U. Wyo., 1969. With U.S. Energy Co., Riverton, Wyo., 1972-75; field engr. Am. Bechtel Corp., Green River, Wyo., 1975-76; pres. NUPEC Resources, Inc., Riverton, 1976-83, Smith-Collins Pharm. Inc., Riverton, 1976-83; cons. Nucor Inc., Riverton, 1984-87; v.p. Nucor Drilling, Inc., Riverton, 1987—. Mem. Wyo. Ho. of Reps., mem. rules com. mgmt. coun., majority floor leader, spkr. Republican. Office: Nucor Inc PO Box 112 Riverton WY 82501-0112*

BECERRA, AUGUSTO ANTONIO, geologist; b. Lima, Peru, Sept. 28, 1955; s. Antonio Armando and Lucrecia Carmen (Florez) B.; m. Angela Alvarez, Aug. 11, 1978; children: Jorge, Roberto, Miguel, Paola. BS in Geol. Scis., U. San Marcos, 1978. Registered profl. engr., Peru. From geol. asst. to geologist Occidental Peruana, Lima, 1978-87; sr. geologist Occidental Peru, Lima, 1987-91, Occidental Internat. Exploration Products, Bakersfield, Calif., 1991-94, Occidental Peruana, 1994—. Mem. Am. Assn. Petroleum Geologists, Soc. Petroleum Engrs., Am. Inst. Mining, Metallurgical and Petroleum Engrs. Office: Occidental Peruana 1200 Discovery Dr Bakersfield CA 93309-7007

BECERRA, XAVIER, congressman, lawyer; b. Sacramento, Jan. 26, 1958; s. Manuel and Maria Teresa B.; m. Carolina Reyes, 1987. AB, Stanford U., 1980, JD, 1984. Atty., 1984—; dir. dist. office State Senator Art Torres, L.A.; dep. atty. gen. dept. justice, Calif., 1987-90; assemblyman, 59th dist. State of Calif., 1990-93; mem. 105th Congress from 30th Calif. dist., 1993—; mem. ways and means com.; chmn. Congl. Hispanic Caucus. Mem. Mexican-Am. Bar Assn., Calif. Bar Assn., Assn. Calif. State Attys. and Adminstrv. Law Judges. Democrat. Avocations: reading, carpentry, golf. Office: Ho of Reps 1119 Longworth Bldg Washington DC 20515-0530

BECHTEL, RILEY PEART, engineering company executive; s. Stephen Davison Bechtel, Jr. BA in Polit. Sci., Psychology, U. Calif., Davis, 1974; JD, MBA, Stanford U., 1979. Bar: Calif. 1979. With Bechtel Group, Inc., San Francisco, 1966-79, 81—; Thelen, Marrin, Johnson & Bridges, San Francisco, 1979-81; bd. dirs. Bechtel Corp. (formerly Bechtel Group Inc.), 1987—, pres., coo, 1989-1990, chmn. exec. com., ceo, 1990—, CEO, 1993—; mem. Bus. Coun., Bus. Roundtable policy com., Calif. Bus. Roundtable, J.P. Morgan Internat. Adv. Coun.; adv. coun. Stanford U. Grad. Sch. of Bus.; dean's adv. coun. Stanford Law Sch. Trustee Thacher Sch., Ojai, Calif. Mem. ABA. Office: Bechtel Corp PO Box 193965 San Francisco CA 94119-3965*

BECHTEL, STEPHEN DAVISON, JR., engineering company executive; b. Oakland, Calif., May 10, 1925; s. Stephen Davison and Laura (Peart) B.; m. Elizabeth Mead Hogan, June 5, 1946; 5 children. Student, U. Colo., 1943-44; BS, Purdue U., 1946, D. in Engring. (hon.), 1972; MBA, Stanford U., 1948; DSc (hon.), U. Colo., 1981. Registered profl. engr., N.Y., Mich., Alaska, Calif., Md., Hawaii, Ohio, D.C., Va., Ill. Engring. and mgmt. positions Bechtel Corp., San Francisco, 1941-60, pres., 1960-73, chmn. of cos. in Bechtel group, 1973-80; chmn. Bechtel Group, Inc., 1980-90, chmn. emeritus, 1990—; bd. dirs. Remington Arms, former chmn., mem. bus. coun., emeritus life councillor, past chmn. conf. bd.; chmn. emeritus Fremont Group, Inc., Sequoia Ventures, Inc., 1995—. Trustee, mem., past chmn. bldg. and grounds com. Calif. Inst. Tech.; mem. pres.'s coun. Purdue U.; adv. coun. Inst. Internat. Studies, bd. visitors, former charter mem., adv. coun. Stanford U. Grad. Sch. Bus. With USMC, 1943-46. Decorated officer French Legion of Honor; recipient Disting. Alumnus award Purdue U., 1964, U. Colo., 1978, Ernest C. Arbuckle Disting. Alumnus award Stanford Grad. Sch. Bus., 1974, Disting. Engring. Alumnus award 1979, Beta Theta PI Oxford Cup award 1997; named Man of Yr. Engring. News-Record, 1974, Outstanding Achievement in Constrn. award Moles, 1977, Chmn.'s award Am. Assn. Engring. Soc., 1982, Washington award Western Soc. Engrs., 1985, Nat. Medal Tech. from Pres. Bush, 1991, Golden Beaver award 1992, Herbert Hoover medal 1980. Mem. ASCE (hon., engring. mgmt. award 1979, pres. award 1985), AAAS, Inst. Chem. Engrs. (U.K., hon.); mem. AIME, NSPE (hon. chmn. Nat. Engrs. Week 1990), Nat. Acad. Engring. (past chmn.), Calif. Acad. Scis. (hon. trustee), Am. Soc. French Legion Honor (bd. dirs., disting. achievement medal 1994), Royal Acad. Engring. (U.K., fgn. mem.), Pacific Union Club, Bohemian Club, San Francisco Golf Club, Claremont Country Club, Cypress Point Club, St. Francis Yacht Club, Bear River Club (Utah), Wild Goose Club (Calif.), Chi Epsilon, Tau Beta Pi. Office: Bechtel Group Inc PO Box 193965 San Francisco CA 94119-3965

BECHTLE, ROBERT ALAN, artist, educator; b. San Francisco, May 14, 1932; m. Nancy Elizabeth Dalton, 1963 (div. 1982); children: Max Robert, Anne Elizabeth; m. Whitney Chadwick, 1982. B.A., Calif. Coll. Arts and Crafts, Oakland, 1954, M.F.A., 1958; postgrad., U. Calif.-Berkeley, 1960-61. Graphic designer Kaiser Industries, Oakland, 1956-59; instr. Calif. Coll. Arts and Crafts, 1957-61, assoc. prof. to prof.; lectr. U. Calif.-Berkeley, 1965-66; vis. artist U. Calif.-Davis, 1966-68; assoc. prof. San Francisco State U., 1968-76, prof., 1976—. One-man shows Mus. of Art, San Francisco, 1959, 64, Berkeley Gallery, 1965, Richmond Art Ctr. (Calif.), 1965, U. Calif.-Davis, 1967, O.K. Harris Gallery, N.Y.C., 1971, 74, 76, 81, 84, 87, 92, 96, Berggruen Gallery, San Francisco, 1972, E.B. Crocker Art Mus., Sacramento, 1973, Univ. Art Mus., U. Calif.-Berkeley, 1979, Daniel Weinberg Gallery, Santa Monica, 1991, Gallery Paul Anglim, San Francisco, 1991, San Francisco Mus. Modern Art, 1991; exhibited in group shows San Francisco Art Inst., 1966, Whitney Mus. N.Y.C., 1967, Milw. Art Ctr., 1969, Mus. Contemporary Art, Chgo., 1971, Serpentine Gallery, London, 1973, Toledo Mus. Art, 1975, San Francisco Mus. Modern Art, 1976, Pushkin Fine Arts Mus., Moscow, 1978, Pa. Acad. Fine Arts, Phila., 1981, San Antonio Mus. Art, 1981, Pa. Acad. Fine Arts, Phila, 1981, Calif. Palace of Legion of Honor, San Francisco, 1983, Mus. Contemporary Art, L.A., 1984, San Francisco Mus. Modern Art, 1985, Univ. Art Mus., U. Calif., Berkeley, 1987, Whitney Mus., N.Y.C., 1991, Fine Arts Mus. San Francisco, 1995; represented in permanent collections Achenbach Found. for Graphic Arts, San Francisco, Chase Manhattan Bank, N.Y.C., E.B. Crocker Art Mus., Sacramento, Gibbes Art Gallery, S.C., High Mus. Art, Atlanta, Hunter Art Mus., Chattanooga, Library of Congress, Washington, Lowe Art Mus.-U. Miami, Coral Gables, Fla., Mills Coll., Oakland, Mus. Modern Art, N.Y.C., Met. Mus., N.Y.C., Neue Gal der Stadt Aachen, West Germany, Oakland Mus., San Francisco Mus. Modern Art, Univ. Art Mus.-U. Calif-Berkeley, Fine Arts Mus. of San Diego, Rose Art Mus., Brandeis U., Waltham, Mass., U. Nebr.-Lincoln, Whitney Mus., N.Y.C., Guggenheim Mus., N.Y.C., Nat. Academician, Nat. Acad. Design, 1993. Served with U.S. Army, 1954-56. Recipient James D. Phelan award, 1965, Acad. award Am. Acad. Arts and Letters, 1995; named Nat. Academician, Nat. Acad. Design, 1993; Nat. Endowment for Arts grantee, 1977, 83, 89, Guggenheim grantee, 1986. Office: San Francisco State U Dept Art 1600 Holloway Ave Dept Art San Francisco CA 94132-1722

BECHTOLD, PAULA MILLER, judge; b. San Luis Obispo, Calif., Oct. 18, 1946; d. Leland F. and Barbara M. (Stallcup) Milller;m. Robert D. Laird, Oct. 23, 1976; children: Deven M., Brenna C. BS, Lewis and Clark Coll., 1967; JD, Northwestern Sch. Law, Portland, Oreg., 1975. Tchr. Milwaukie (Oreg.) H.S., 1969-71; office mgr. Met. Pub. Defender, Portland, 1972-75; law clk. Oreg. Supreme Ct., Salem, 1975-76; assoc. Bechtold & Laird, P.C., Coos Bay, Oreg., 1976-94; judge Oreg. Jud. Dept., North Bend, 1995—; chair Oreg. State Bar Task Force on Lawyer Competency, 1996; sec.-treas. Oreg. Law Found., 1987. V.p. Local Alcohol and Drug Abuse Planning Com., Coos County, Oreg., 1996—; mem. Family Violence Coun., Coos County, 1994—; mem. benchmark com. Commn. on Children & Families, Coos County, 1995—; treas. Mingus Park Pool Mgmt., Coos Bay, 1996—; mem. adv. coun. Coos County Retired Sr. Vol. Program; mem. Coos County Women's Health Coalition. Mem. Oreg. City Attys. Assn. (pres. 1988), Oreg. State Bar (chair legal aid com. 1981), Zonta Internat. (dist. 8 gov. 1992-94, club pres. 1984-86, 98-99). Democrat. Unitarian. Avocations: reading, hiking. Office: Coos County Cir Ct PO Box 865 North Bend OR 97459-0033

BECK, DORIS OLSON, retired library media director; b. Kingsville, Tex., June 4, 1930; d. Thomas Leon and Estelle (Fosselman) Olson; m. John Roland Beck, Feb. 9, 1951; children: Elizabeth Joan, Thomas Roland, Patricia Lind, John William. BS in Chemistry, Tex. A & I Coll., 1949, BSChemE, 1950; MLS, Wayne State U., 1975. Cert. secondary educator with libr. endorsement, Ariz. Chemist Patterson's Lab., Harlingen, Tex., 1950-51; asst. libr. Tex. A & I Coll., Kingsville, Tex., 1951; chemist U.S. Geol. Svc., Stillwater, Okla., 1951-53; bookkeeper, nurse's aide McKenzie Co. Hosp., Watford City, N.D., 1953-54; math. tchr. Prescott Jr. High, Corpus Christi, Tex., 1954; chemist U.S. Geol. Svc., Columbus, Ohio, 1957-58; math. tchr. Christiansberg (Va.) High Sch., 1967-69; sci. tchr. East Jr. High Sch., Farmington, Mich., 1969-70; sci./math. tchr. Jane Addams Jr. High Sch., Royal Oak, Mich., 1970-78; math support Oakland Vocat. Sch., Royal Oak, 1978-79; head libr. S.W. Bapt. Coll., Pontiac, Mich., 1977-79; libr. media dir. Humboldt (Ariz.) Jr. High, 1979-87, Bradshaw Mt. Jr. High, Dewey, Ariz., 1987-95; ret., 1995; site based com. Bradshaw Mt. Jr. High Sch., Dewey, Ariz., 1992-95. Vol. ch. libr., 1994—; trustee Prescott Valley Pub. Libr. Mem. Ariz. Libr. Assn., Ariz. Ednl. Media Assn., Alpha Delta Kappa. Republican. Baptist. Avocations: reading, needlework, travel. Home: PO Box 25824 3829 N Valorie Dr Prescott Valley AZ 86312

BECK, GORDON EUGENE, art history educator, consultant; b. Goshen, Ind., Mar. 23, 1929; s. Ralph Lea and Lydia Elizabeth (Greenlee) B.; m. Elizabeth Alice Arnholt, Mar. 22, 1951; children: Anne Elizabeth, Susan Elizabeth, Stephen Lea, John Lyons. BA, Bowling Green State U., 1951; MA, Western Res. U., 1952; PhD, U. Ill., 1964; postdoctoral student, Cini Found., Venice, Italy, 1979. Founder Studio 16, Washington, 1953-54; asst. instr. U. Ill., Urbana, 1954-56; instr. Bowling Green (Ohio) State U., 1956-57; instr., dir. univ. theatre U. Kans., Lawrence, 1957-65; asst. prof., dir. univ. theatre Cornell U., Ithaca, N.Y., 1965-71; prof. art history Evergreen State Coll., Olympia, Wash., 1971-94, prof. emeritus art history and archaeology, 1994—; cons. European travel, Euro-Files, Olympia; dir. U. Kans. Theatre, 1957-65, Cornell U. Cinema, 1965-70, Mus. and Monuments Program, Olympia, 1975—; vis. prof. cinema Am. U. Rome, 1973-74; del. Cannes Internat. Film Festival, 1996, 97, 98. Editor, Players Mag., 1961-67; contbr. articles to Theatre Ann., 1964-69, Ency. World Drama, 1969; producer feature film, Branches, 1970. Cpl. M.C., U.S. Army, 1952-54. Mem. Coll. Art Assn., Mediaeval Acad. Am., Am. Soc. Aesthetics. Democrat. Home: 2406 18th Ave NW Olympia WA 98502-4119 Office: Evergreen State Coll 3602 Library Bldg Olympia WA 98505

BECK, JEROME JOSEPH, health care administrator, biomedical technologist; b. Mesa, Ariz., Nov. 7, 1957; s. Robert Leon and Marie Margaret (Curry) B.; m. Catherine Elizabeth Williams, June 27, 1981; 1 child, John Robert. BSBA, U. Phoenix, 1989. Cert. hemodialysis technologist Bd. of Nephrology Examiners Nursing & Tech. Dialysis unit housekeeper Good Samaritan Hosp., Phoenix, 1976-78, dialysis equipment technician, 1978-81, dialysis sr. equipment technician, 1981-83, coord. tech. staff devel., 1983-88, mgr. dialysis tech. svcs., 1988-89; dir. tech. svcs. East Valley Dialysis Svcs., Mesa, 1989-91, program dir., 1991-93; ops. mgr., dir. ops. Renalwest L.C. (formerly East Valley Dialysis Svcs.), Mesa, 1993—; dir. ops.; bd. dirs. Bd. Nephrology Examiners, Madison, Wis., 1990-92; mem. renal disease and detoxification com. Assn. for the Advancement of Med. Instrumentation, 1989-93; mem. technicians com. ESRD Network VI, Albuquerque, 1984-85; nephrology conf. lectr. nationwide. Mem. editl. adv. bd. Nephrology News and Issues, 1996—; contbr. articles to profl. jours. Mem. Nat. Assn. Nephrology Technologists (bd. dirs., western v.p. 1989-91, Torchbearer award 1994). Republican. Avocations: bicycling, swimming, golf, camping, scuba diving. Office: Renalwest LC 1750 S Mesa Dr Ste 110 Mesa AZ 85210-6213

BECK, JOHN CHRISTEN, sociologist, educator; b. Provo, Utah, Dec. 7, 1959; s. Jay Vern and Allida Faye (Ellison) B.; m. Martha Nibley, June 21, 1983; children: Katherine, Adam, Elizabeth. BA, Harvard U., 1983, MA, 1988, PhD, 1989. Pub. The Asian Century Bus. Report, Provo, 1991-97; prof. Am. Grad. Sch. of Internat. Mgmt., Glendale, Ariz., 1994-98; sr. strategic advisor Royal Govt. of Cambodia, 1994—; prin. Anderson Cons., Phoenix, 1997—; prof. UCLA Anderson Sch., L.A., 1998. Author: Breaking the Cycle of Compulsive Behavior, 1990, The Change of a Lifetime, 1994; contbr. articles to profl. jours. Harvard Bus. Sch. grantee, 1988, fellow, 1984-89; recipient Hoopes Rsch. prize Harvard U., 1983; Rotary scholar, 1983-84. Office: PO Box 55870 Phoenix AZ 85078-5870

BECK, JOHN CRAIG, industrial hygienist; b. Sioux Falls, S.D., Oct. 30, 1934; s. James Joseph and Marjorie Lorraine (Beaty) B.; m. Emilie Owen Wheeler, July 31, 1985 (div. Oct. 1986). BS, Colo. State U., 1980, MS summa cum laude, 1985. Cert. indsl. hygienist Am. Bd. Indsl. Hygiene. Indsl. hygienist State of Colo., Denver, 1983-84; environ. engr. Digital Equipment Corp., Colorado Springs, Colo., 1984-86; sr. indsl. hygienist Morrison Knudsen Corp., Denver, 1986-88; regional health and safety mgr., 1995—, Dames & Moore, Denver, 1988-90; health and safety mgr. Australia and S.E. Asia Dames & Moore, Sydney, NSW, Australia, 1990-94; regional health and safety mgr. Dames & Moore, Seattle, 1994-95. Mem. Am. Indsl. Hygiene Assn., Am. Acad. Indsl. Hygiene. Avocations: backpacking, bicycling. Office: Morrison Knudsen Corp 7100 E Belleview Ave Ste 300 Englewood CO 80111-1636

BECK, TIMOTHY DANIEL, human resources specialist, consultant; b. Santa Monica, Calif., Mar. 21, 1953; s. James Daniel and Bettye June (Cisler) B.; m. Marcia Ann Smith, Jan. 16, 1977; children: Tracy Beth and Erica Brandy (twins), Jenna Michelle. AA, El Camino Community Coll., 1974; BA, Calif. State U., Northridge, 1979. Registered health underwriter, registered employee benefits cons. Candidate cert. employee benefit specialist, group claims supr. Prudential Ins. Co. Am., L.A., 1973-79; employee benefits cons. Olanie, Hurst & Hemrich, L.A., 1979-81; v.p. policyholder svc. dept. Health Maintenance Life Ins. Co., Fountain Valley, Calif., 1981; v.p. Robert E. French Ins. Svcs., Inc., Huntington Beach, Calif., 1981-85; v.p., mng. cons. employee benefits Warren, McVeigh & Griffin, Inc., Newport Beach, Calif., 1985-91; mng. cons. employee benefits A. Foster Higgins and Co., Inc., 1991-96; prin. Buck Cons., Inc., L.A., 1996—; mem. Kaiser Permanente Orange County Consumer Coun., 1987—; mem. pub. edn. com. Calif. Health Decision, 1988—; mem. bus. and health adv. panel Am. Health Pub.; speaker to confs. and profl. socs.; cons. Healthnet Adv. Coun., 1996—, Orange County Bus. Coun., Town Hall, 1996—; mem. Healthnet Cons. Adv. Coun., 1997—. Creator, contbg. editor Employee Benefits Mgmt. Letter, 1985-91; contbr. articles to profl. publs. Mem. Internat. Found. Employee Benefits, Nat. Assn. Health Underwriters, Calif. Assn. Health Underwriters, Employee Benefit Planning Assn. So. Calif. (bd. dirs. 1992-93), So. Calif. Assn. Benefit Plan Adminstrs., Orange County Assn. Health Underwriters (founder, 1st v.p. 1987-88), Orange County Bus. Coun., Orange County Employee Benefit Coun., Calif. State U. Northridge Alumni Assn. Avocations: fishing, hiking, backpacking, rock climbing.

BECKER, DONALD PAUL, surgeon, neurosurgeon; b. Cleve., 1935. MD, Case Western Res. U., 1961. Diplomate Am. Bd. Neurol. Surgery. Intern U. (Cleve.) Hosps., 1961-62, resident in surgery, 1962-63, resident in neurol. surgery, 1963-67; fellow in neurosurgery NIH, Bethesda, Md., 1966; prof. UCLA Med. Ctr., 1967-71; prof., chmn. divsn. neurol. surgery Med. Coll. Va., Richmond, 1971-85; chief neurosurgery UCLA Med. Ctr., 1985—; prof., chmn. divsn. neurol. surgery Med. Coll. Va., Richmond, 1971-85. Mem. ACS, AMA. Office: UCLA Med Ctr Divsn Neurosurgery PO Box 957039 Los Angeles CA 90095-7039

BECKER, ELISABETH MARIA, artist, educator; b. Paris, Nov. 1, 1942; came to U.S., 1987; d. Henri Georges and Irene Maria (Tobler) B.; children: Mariette Schlegel, Natalie Schlegel Barker, Pascale Schlegel, Claudine Cariezel. Diploma, Internat. Acad. Arts, Basel-Bern, 1964. Tchr. Handecapt Sch., St. Gallen, CH, 1974-76; artist City Theater, St Gallen; substitute tchr. Internat. Orphin Coll., Pestalozzi Village, Trogen, CH, 1973; lectr. U. St. Gallen, CH, 1986-88; freelancer Elisabeth Maria Becker Fine Art Gallery, Taos, N.Mex, 1991—. Exhibited in group show Art Expo, N.Y., 1998. Mem. Soc. Suriss Painter Sculpter. Home: 212 Siler 5198 NDCBU Taos NM 87571-6108 Office: Elisabeth Maria Becker Fine Art Gallery 212 Siler Rd Taos NM 87571-6108

BECKER, KATHARINE ELIZABETH, special education educator; b. Madison, Wis., Nov. 30, 1952; d. Robert Mettler Becker and Katharine Jane (Morris) Bruère; m. Lyle Franklin Strehlow, Mar. 29, 1986. BS in Elem. Edn., U. Wis., 1976; MS in Speech and Hearing, Washington U., St. Louis, 1978; EdD, Nova Southeastern U., 1995. Cert. elem. tchr., hearing handicapped tchr., Ariz. Tchr., evaluator, cons. hearing impaired program Cartwright Sch. Dist., Phoenix, 1979—, mem. spl. edn. adv. com., 1992—; mem. hearing impaired stds. working com. Dept. Edn., Phoenix, 1992-93. State chmn. Better Hearing and Speech Month, Ariz., 1991. Mem. Alexander Graham Bell Assn. for the Deaf (co-founder Ariz. chpt. 1986, bd. dirs., sec. 1986-87, pres. 1987-88), Phi Delta Kappa. Avocations: walking, gardening, reading. Home: 2528 Commonwealth Ave Madison WI 53711-1913

BECKER, LESLEE, English language and creative writing educator; b. Plattsburgh, N.Y., May 10, 1945; d. John Herman and Mary Veronica (George) B. BA, Cortland Coll., 1966; MA, U. Vt., 1972, Hollins Coll., 1980; MFA, U. Iowa, 1984. Jones lectr. in fiction Stanford U., Palo Alto, Calif., 1987-90; asst. prof. English Colo. State U., Ft. Collins, 1990-96, assoc. prof. English, 1996—, dir. creative writing program, 1996—. Author: The Sincere Cafe, 1996 (Mid-List Press Fiction prize 1996). Recipient Wallace Stegner Writing fellowship Stanford U., 1984, James Michener Writing fellowship Iow Writers' Workshop, 1985, Pirate's Alley Faulkner award Pirate's Alley Faulkner Soc., 1992. Home: 318 Starboard Ct Fort Collins CO 80525-3137 Office: Colo State Univ Dept English 359 Eddy Hall Fort Collins CO 80523

BECKER, NANCY ANNE, state supreme court justice; b. Las Vegas, May 23, 1955; d. Arthur William and Margaret Mary (McLoughlin) B. BA, U.S. Internat. U., 1976; JD, George Washington U., 1979. Bar: Nev. 1979, D.C. 1980, Md. 1982, U.S. Dist. Ct. Nev. 1987, U.S. Ct. Appeals (9th cir.) 1987. Legis. cons. D.C. Office on Aging, Washington, 1979-83; assoc. Goldstein & Ahalt, College Park, Md., 1980-82; pvt. practice Washington, 1982-83; dep. city atty., prosecutor criminal div. City of Las Vegas, 1983; judge Las Vegas Mcpl. Ct., 1987-89, Clark County Dist. Ct., Las Vegas, 1989—; cons. MADD, Las Vegas, 1983-87. Contbr. articles to profl. publs. Pres. Clark County Pro Bono Project, Las Vegas, 1984-88. Mem. So. Nev. Assn. Women Attys. (past officer), Am. Businesswomen's Assn. (treas. Las Vegas chpt. 1985-86), NCCJ, Las Vegas and Latin C. of C., Vietnam Vets Am., Soroptimist Internat. Office: Nevada Supreme Court Capital Complex 201 S Carson St Carson City NV 89701-4702*

BECKER, STEPHEN ARNOLD, museum administrator; b. Redwood City, Calif., Aug. 24, 1951; s. Leo H. and May B. (Goldberg) B.; m. Beverly Nichols-Fredotovich, July 31, 1977; 1 child, Joseph Nikola. Asst. curator mus. Ind. U., Bloomington, 1973-77, lectr. folklore dept., 1975-77; historian Sacramento History Ctr., 1977-78; dir. history divsn. County Pks. Dept., Riverside, Calif., 1979-85; asst. dir. Mus. Internat. Folk Art, Santa Fe, 1985-89; dir. Mus. Indian Arts and Culture/Lab. Anthropology, Santa Fe, 1989-95; pres., CEO, Turtle Bay Mus. and Arboretum, Redding, Calif., 1995-98; mus. cons. Redding, 1998—; deputy dir. devel. & external affairs Lindsay Wildlife Mus., Walnut Creek, Calif., 1998—. Mem. Am. Assn. Museums, Am. Folklore Soc. e-mail: sbecker@wildlife-museum.org. Office: 1931 First Ave Walnut Creek CA 94596

BECKER, WENDY JEANNE, music and drama educator; b. Milw., July 26, 1956; d. Arthur Becker and Muriel Jeanne (Mark) Sweet; m. David Gordon Tucker, July 13, 1981 (div.). BFA, U. Wis., 1979. Registered music therapist. Music dir. Camp Hess Kramer, L.A., 1976-81; music tchr., dir. schs. and synagogues, L.A., 1981-90; music and choir dir. Stephen Wise Cmty. H.S., L.A., 1987-94; drama dir. Milken Cmty. H.S., L.A., 1992-97; music specialist Congregation Ohr Ha Torah, L.A., 1997-98; v.p. Merrie Way Cmty., non-profit org.; producer Morphing of Am. Actress: Days of Our Lives, My Work is Blessed, Getting Back, Blithe Spirit. Recipient Tchr. of the Yr. award Morphing of Am., 1997. Mem. Nat. Assn. Music Therapy, SAG, AFTRA, Actors Equity Assn., Delta Omicron. Avocations: singing, dancing.

BECKET, BRUCE DAVID, architect; b. L.A., Sept. 16, 1941; s. Welton David and Fay (Kastner) B.; m. Sharon Good, Sept. 6, 1963; children: Mark Christopher, Alisa Christina, Alexander Tiffany. BArch, Calif. State Polytech U., 1965. Project architect Welton Becket & Assocs., L.A., 1966-73; pres. Turnkey Projects, Inc., L.A., 1973, Bruce Becket & Assocs., L.A., 1973—, Becket Devel. Corp., L.A., 1973—. Mem. AIA, Med. Arbitration Assn., L.A. Country Club, Eldorado Country Club. Republican. Avoca-

tions: photography, landscape & gardening, stock market, travel. Office: Bruce Becket & Assocs 1516 Pontius Ave Los Angeles CA 90025-3306

BECKET, JOHANNA NINA, special education educator; b. Bronx, N.Y., Dec. 14, 1949; d. Vincent Angelo and Jenny (Filippino) Vecchione; children from previous marriage: Jenny, Victoria; m. Lee Hatton, Nov. 8, 1991. BA, Adelphi U., 1964, MA, 1968; MS, Barry U., 1981. Art tchr. Syosset (N.Y.) Pub. Schs., 1964-74; art therapist Jackson Meml. Hosp., Miami, 1978-81; brain mapping technician St. Francis Hosp., Miami, 1981-83, head nuerometrics dept., 1981-83; tchr. severely emotionally disturbed Dade County Pub. Schs./Miami Sunset Sr. High, 1983—, dept. head, spl. edn., 1988—; psychotherapist Christian Counseling Ctr, Meml. Med. Ctr. East Tex., 1992-93, Four Corners Mental Health-Green River High Sch., 1992-93. Editor Counselor Assn. newspaper, 1980-81. Co-chmn. Very Spl. Arts, 1988. Recipient Found. for Excellence grant, Miami, 1988, Citicorp Success Fund grant, 1988; named region VI finalist, Tchr. of the Yr., Dade County Pub. Schs., 1991-92. Mem. Coun. Exceptional Edn., United Tchrs. Dade. Democrat. Roman Catholic. Avocations: art, music, cooking, dancing. Home: 455 W Ferron Creek Dr Ferron UT 84523 Address: 501 E Marco Polo Rd Phoenix AZ 85024-1028

BECKETT, TED, commercial land developer; b. Oakland, Calif., Mar. 31, 1936; s. Theodore Temple Beckett and Kathryn L. Sweetland; m. Marjory May Beckett, Dec. 28, 1958 (div. May 1986); children: Ted Jr., Shaun, Casey, Brenda, Brigette, Mark, Bethany; m. Audrey Clair Beckett, July 27, 1986. Student, U. Nev., 1957, 58, Santa Ana Coll., 1979, 80. With southwest regional sales staff Kaiser Gypsum Co., San Antonio, 1959-61; co-owner Beckett Constrn., San Antonio, 1962 65; owner Comml. Investment Realty, Irving (Tex.), Dallas, 1966-78, R.E. Brokerage, Santa Ana, Calif., 1978-86; co-owner Crest Mobile Estates, Fountain, Colo., 1986-97; founder, owner Beckett Devel. LLP, Colorado Springs, Colo., 1995—; founder Douglas Meml. Children HOme, Port Au Prince, Haiti, 1970; co-founder Bridges for Peace, Jerusalem, 1976—; founder, pres. Found. for Israel, Colorado Springs, 1986—; founder, dir. Christian Friends of Israeli Cmtys., Colorado Springs, 1995—. Prodr. (video) Israel at 40, 1988, West Bank Settlements: Holy Land or Holy War, 1997; author: The Domino Effect, 1991, The Time of Jacobs Trouble, 1995. With USMC, 1954-57. Republican. Office: PO Box 16050 Colorado Springs CO 80935-6050

BECKMAN, JAMES WALLACE BIM, economist, marketing executive; b. Mpls., May 2, 1936; s. Wallace Gerald and Mary Louise (Frissell) B. BA, Princeton U., 1958; PhD, U. Calif., 1973. Pvt. practice, Berkeley, Calif. 1962-67; cons. Calif. State Assembly, Sacramento, 1967-68; pvt. practice, Laguna Beach, Calif., 1969-77; cons. Calif. State Gov.'s Office, Sacramento 1977-80; pvt. practice real estate cons., L.A. 1980-83; v.p. mktg. Gold-Well Investments, Inc., L.A. 1982-83; pres. Beckman Analytics Internat., econ. cons. to bus. and govt., L.A. and Lake Arrowhead, Calif., 1983—, East European/Middle East Bus. and Govt., 1992—; adj. prof. Calif. State U. Sch. Bus., San Bernardino, 1989—, U. Redlands, 1992—; cons. E European, environmental issues. Contbr. articles to profl. jours. Ordained elder, commr. Maj. USMC 1958-67. NIMH fellow 1971-72. Fellow Soc. Applied Anthropology; mem. Am. Econs. Assn., Am. Statis. Assn., Am. Mktg. Assn. (officer), Nat. Assn. Bus. Economists (officer). Democrat. Presbyterian. Office: PO Box 1753 Lake Arrowhead CA 92352-1753

BECKMAN, KENNETH OREN, film and video specialist, researcher; b. Detroit, Nov. 26, 1948; s. Aron J. Beckman; children: Oren Rigel, Sienna Grace. BA in Theater, Mich. State U., 1970; MA in Film, San Francisco State U., 1982. Freelance prodr., 1969-74; tech. dir. Center for Contemporary Music, Oakland, Calif., 1974-76; prodr. Optic Nerve, San Francisco, 1976-78; dir. video lab. Xerox/Parc, Palo Alto, Calif., 1978-86; founding ptnr. SIRIUS Comms. Group, La Honda, Calif., 1984-90; sr. comms. mgr. R&D., mgr. video lab. Sys. Rsch. Ctr. Digital Equipment Corp., Palo Alto, 1986-98; founder Foton Factory, La Honda, 1991; sr. comm. dir. Compaq Computer Corp./SRC; cons. Apple Computer, Multi-Media Group, Oceanic Inst. Dir. video art including A Man With an Idea, Reach Out, 1986, Clean Machine, 1987, Song of the Street of the Singing Chicken, 1982 (1st place award Santa Cruz Video Festival 1982, Am. Film Inst. Nat. Winner 1982); patentee in field. Recipient Hometown USA Video Festival award, Denver, 1984. Fellow Photon Factory (dir. 1984-87, Wave/Particle award 1986); mem. Music Video Dirs. Guild (dir. 1985-87, Deep Purple Music TV award 1985), Soc. Motion Picture TV Engrs. Achievements include patent on TV/computer design, a device for viewing numerous channels of cable traffic simultaneously. Office: Sys Rsch Ctr 130 Lytton Ave Palo Alto CA 94301-1044

BECKMAN, LEEANN MARIE, researcher; b. Le Sueur, Minn., Aug. 7, 1971; d. William Paul and Sherry Marlene B. BA, Mont. State Univ., 1994; MA in internat. affairs, U.S. Internat. Univ., 1997. Adminstrv. asst. U.S. Internat. Univ., San Diego, 1996, dir.'s asst., 1996-97, office mgr., 1997-98; human rels. mgr. MacKenzie N.W., Inc., Bozeman, Mont., 1998—; participant Internat. Studies Assn., 1996. Contbr. articles to profl. jours. Student amb. U.S. Internat. Univ., 1996-97. Mem. Women In Internat. Security, World Affairs Coun. Office: MRPC Belgrade 409 W Main St Belgrade MT 59714-3458

BECKMAN, PATTY ZOE, special education educator, consultant; b. L.A., Mar. 2, 1941; d. Alson Collins Peckham and Doris Lee (Baker) White; m. Bruce William Beckman, Aug. 18, 1962; children: Brenda, Robert, Jeffrey, Janine. BA, Whittier Coll., 1963; MEd, U. Utah, 1988. Cert. gen. edn., spl. edn. tchr., Utah. Tchr. East Whittier (Calif.) Sch. Dist., 1967-69, Santee (Calif.) Sch. Dist., 1969-77, Jordan Sch. Dist., Sandy, Utah, 1982—; cons. Jordan Sch. Dist., 1995—; instr. U. Utah, Salt Lake City, 1996—. Contbr. articles to profl. jours. Pres. Utah Fedn. Coun. for Exceptional Children. Mem. ASCD, NEA, CEC (Snowbird chpt. pres. 1995-96, pres.-elect Utah Fedn.), Utah Divsn. Learning Disabilities (pres. 1997—), Utah Edn. Assn. (Utah Disting. Educator 1997), Jordan Edn. Assn. (Tchr. of Month 1993, 95). Avocations: music, writing, gardening. Home: 8706 Alta Canyon Dr Sandy UT 84093-1957

BECKS, RONALD ARTHUR, film producer; b. N.Y.C., July 9, 1953; s. Wellington and Vivian (Newkirk) B. Student, York Coll., 1969-71; cert. for prodrs., Cintel Corp., 1974-75; cert., Ch. Religious Sc., 1975-77; D of Religious Communication (hon.), Temple Faith, 1974. Owner, pres., chmn. Ronald A. Becks Internat. Theatre Soc., N.Y.C., 1978-90; v.p. Miracle Prodns., N.Y.C., 1978-90; pres. Magic Circle Players, Australia and Hong Kong, Sodeko Films, Australia and Hong Kong; mktg. dir. V.R.B. Enterprises, Australia and Hong Kong, Multi-Media Svcs., Australia and Hong Kong; pres. Noduki Films, Australia and Hong Kong, 1990, Face Affair, Beverly Hills, Calif., 1991, Film Gods Prodns., Beverly Hills, 1991—; founder, pres. STN TV Network, 1994; prodr. Blues TV, Century Cable, 1996, Inside Press TV, 1997, MASC TV, 1997; artistic dir. Beverly Hills Cmty. Theatre, 1997; v.p. BBH Cosmetics Labs., Beverly Hills, 1994; mem. adv. coun. Internat. Biog. Ctr., Cambridge, Eng., 1995, Inside Press TV Show, Blues TV; pres. Sir Ronald Blues Band, 1996; artistic dir. Beverly Hills Cmty. Theatre Co., 1997; exec. dir. United Citizens Com. Am., 1997. Author: The 3rd Testament, 1990, Legend of Billy Blue, 1988, Black Diamond, 1989, Come and Get It, 1991, Say a Little Prayer, 1991, Stagecoach Mary, 1993, Gigi and the Bogey-Man, 1993; prodr.: You Bring Out the Best in Me, 1984 (top 40 song); inventor phone device; songwriter Perfume in My Coffee; prodn. coord. Asian Belle, 1995. Dep. chmn. UN Assn., 1979, dep. amb., 1979, chmn. Song Quest, 1979; entertainment coord. Keep Australia Beautiful, 1980; prodr. children's show Consulate of Peru, 1979; prodr. and host I Love New York, N.Y.C., 1978; mem. notary pub. commn., 1996. Recipient Internat. Order of Merit, Cambridge. Fellow Highlander Club (life); mem. Prodrs. and Dirs. Guild, Prodrs. Assn., PEN Internat., Am. Soc. Notaries, NAACP, Internat. Platform Assn., Rainbow Coalition, Writers Guild, Journalists Club, Hollywood Press Club, Noetic Scis. Avocations: sports, writing, martial arts, horses, farming. Home and Office: 264 S La Cienega Blvd Ste 364 Beverly Hills CA 90211

BECK-VON-PECCOZ, STEPHEN GEORGE WOLFGANG, artist; b. Munich, Oct. 18, 1933; came to U.S., 1937; s. Wolfgang Anton Willibald Maria and Martha Jeanette (Morse) Beck-von-P.; m. Dorothy Ann Freytag, June 16, 1956 (div. 1971); m. Michele Marie Perry, Jan. 8, 1972; children: Stephen Jr., David, Kenneth, Lisa. BEE, Cornell U., 1956; MA in Art, Calif. State U., San Diego, 1974. Electronic engr. Stromberg Carlson Co., San Diego, 1958-60; project mgr. Control Data Corp., San Diego, 1960-65, Digital Devel. Corp., San Diego, 1965-66; project engr. Stromberg Datagraphix, Inc., San Diego, 1966-69; project mgr. Digital Sci. Corp., San Diego, 1969-71; artist San Diego, 1974—; cons. elec. engring., San Diego, 1974-78. Served to 2d lt. USAF, 1956-58. Mem. Internat. Sculpture Ctr., Kappa Alpha Soc. Avocations: art, travel. Home and Studio: 636 Nardito Ln Solana Beach CA 92075-2306

BECKWITH, CHARLES ALLAN, healthcare administrator, consultant; b. L.A., Feb. 15, 1940; s. Harry Spencer and Mary Dorothy (Riley) B.; m. Roberta Louise Sommerdorf, Nov. 27, 1963 (dec. Jan. 1966); m. Susan Ann Robinson, Aug. 24, 1969; 1 child, Mary Aileen. BS in Psychology, Loyola-Marymount U., 1962; cert., George Washington U., 1989; M of Profl. Studies: Hosp. and Health Svcs. Adminstrn., Cornell U., 1976. Adminstr. Grover M. Hermann divsn. Comty. Gen. Hosp. Sullivan County, Callicoon, N.Y., 1976-77; assoc. dir. Comty. Gen. Hosp. Sullivan County, Harris, N.Y., 1977-78; adminstr. for ambulatory care USPHS Hosp., Balt., 1978-81; program cons. Office Ambulatory Care Bur. Med. Svcs., Hyattsville, Md., 1981; adminstr. area contract health svcs., program/internal auditor Albuquerque Area Indian Health Svc., 1981-84, internal auditor Office of Area Dir., 1984; sr. internal auditor Calif. Area Indian Health Svc., Sacramento, 1984-89, spl. adminstrv. asst., 1989—; mem. health svcs. adminstrn. adv. bd. Sch. Pub. Adminstrn., U. So. Calif., 1988-93; adminstrv. residency preceptor for M. of Healthcare Adminstrn. students Sacramento campus U. So. Calif., 1992-94; presenter profl. papers ann. meeting USPHS Profl. Assn., Scottsdale, Ariz., 1988, 93; mem. Sloan Program Hosp. and Health Svcs. Adminstrn., Grad. Sch. Bus. and Pub. Adminstrn., Cornell U., 1976; presenter in field. Contbr. articles to profl. publs. Alumni admissions interviewer Johnson Grad. Sch. Mgmt., Cornell U., 1985—; co-master of ceremony duties for commemorative awards Indian Health Svcs. Honor Awards Ceremony, Rockville, Md., 1989, 91. Capt. USPHS, 1978—. Decorated Bronze Star medal; recipient Calif. Area Dir.'s award for Managerial Excellence for leadership in advancement of healthcare adminstrn., 1994, award of appreciation Combined Fed. Campaign Coord., 1993, award for Area Office with Best Overall Performance, U.S. Savs. Bond Campaign Coord., 1994, PHS Outstanding Svc. medal, 2 PHS Commendation medals, PHS Citation and Unit Citation. Fellow Am. Coll. Healthcare Execs. (membership examiner); mem. Commd. Officers Assn. Roman Catholic. Achievements include initiation and coordination of first epidemiology study of California Indian health status. Avocations: reading, gardening, golf, travel, genealogy. Office: Calif Area Indian Health Svcs 1825 Bell St Ste 200 Sacramento CA 95825-1020

BEDSWORTH, O. DIANE, retail executive; b. Detroit, Nov. 30, 1942; d. William H. and Olive Emily (Ludwig) Goodson; m. Gary J. Bedsworth, Apr. 4, 1964 (div. Feb. 1983); children: Jay William, Pamela Diane. Student, Mich. State U., 1961-64. Interior designer Dayton-Hudson Corp., Mpls., 1973-85; pres. Bedsworth Design Internat., Blackhawk, Calif., 1985—; owner Bedsworth Style, Danville, Calif., 1989—; cons. San Souci Hotel, Taipei, Taiwan, 1980—, Hotel Group, Inc., 1982-83, Corp. Homes, Damman, Saudi Arabia, residential homes, Hawaii, Calif., Ariz., 1986—. Mktg. dir. Sta. KTCA-TV Pub. Auction, Mpls., 1979-83, chairwoman, 1983, 84. Mem. Am. Soc. Interior Designers (profl.). Republican. Episcopalian. Avocations: dancing, cruising. Office: Bedsworth Style 1822 Whitecliff Way Walnut Creek CA 94596-6235

BEEBE, DONALD PAUL, financial planner, consultant, editor; b. Portland, Oreg., Jan. 28, 1966; s. Donald Jack and Anna Marie (Blickenstaff) B. BA, Portland State U., 1989; MA in Religion, Yale U., 1991, MPhil, 1993, MA, 1996, PhD, 1998. Editl. cons. and series mgr. Harry N. Abrams, N.Y.C., 1997—; fin. advisor Am. Express, Portland, 1998—; tchg. fellow Yale U., 1994-96; Andrew Mellon curatorial asst. Yale U. Art Gallery, 1993-94; intern So. Renaissance painting Nat. Gallery of Art, Washington, 1992; intern edn. dept. Art Inst. of Chicago, 1992. Curator. (exhbn.) A Renaissance Requiem, 1998. Recipient Bridwell Libr. Rsch. fellowship So. Meth. U., 1997-98, Yale U. Dissertation fellowship, 1995-96, Italian Cultural Inst. scholarship, N.Y.C., 1993, Religion and Arts prize Yale Divinity Sch., 1991. Mem. Coll. Art Assn., Renaissance Soc., Yale Alumni Assn. of Oreg., Phi Sigma Iota (chpt. pres. 1988-89), Mu Phi Epsilon (chpt. pres. 1986-87), Beta Gamma Sema, Phi Kappa Phi. Episcopalian. Avocations: travel, hiking, ballroom dancing, music. Home: 10025 SE Eastview Dr Portland OR 97266-6951 Office: Am Express Fin Advisors 8800 Sunnyside Rd Ste 300 Portland OR 97222

BEEBE, JOHN E., psychiatrist; b. Washington, June 24, 1939; s. John Eliott, Jr. and Patricia Eloise (Boden) B. AB, Harvard Coll., 1961; MD, U. Chgo., 1965. Intern USPHS, San Francisco, 1965-66; resident in psychiatry Stanford U. Hosp. Med. Ctr., Calif., 1968-71; chief resident in psychiatry Adult Psychiatry Clinic, Stanford, 1970-71; pvt. practice Stanford Hosp., San Francisco, 1971—; clin. asst. prof. U. Calif. Med. Ctr., San Francisco, 1973—; candidate C.G. Jung Inst. of San Francisco, 1970-78; mem. analyst C.G. Jung Inst. of San Francisco, 1978—, pres.-elect, 1998—. Editor: The San Francisco Jung Inst. Libr. Jour., 1979-99; co-editor: The Journal of Analytical Psychology, London, 1990-97; co-editor/co-author: (book) Psychiatric Treatment: Crisis, Clinic, and Consultation, 1975; editor: (books) Money, Food, Drink, Fashion and Analytic Training, 1983, C.G. Jung's Aspects of the Masculine, 1989; author: Integrity in Depth, 1992. Surgeon USPHS, 1965-68. Mem. No. Calif. Psychiat. Soc., APA, Internat. Assn. for Analytical Psychology. Independent. Avocations: film, songwriting, Chinese philosophy, criticism, non-vernacular music. Office: 337 Spruce St San Francisco CA 94118-1830

BEEBE, MARY LIVINGSTONE, curator; b. Portland, Oreg., Nov. 5, 1940; d. Robert and Alice Beebe. B.A., Bryn Mawr Coll., 1962; postgrad. Sorbonne, U. Paris, 1962-63. Curatorial asst. Fogg Art Mus., Harvard U., Cambridge, Mass., 1966-68; Apprentice Portland Art Mus., 1963-64, Boston Mus. Art, 1964-65; exec. dir. Portland Ctr. for Visual Arts, 1973-81; dir. Stuart Collection U. Calif.-San Diego, La Jolla, 1981—; cons. in field. Mem. art steering com. Portland Devel. Commn., 1977-80; bd. dirs. Henry Gallery, U. Wash., Seattle, 1977-80; project cons. Nat. Rsch. Ctr. for Arts, N.Y.C., 1978-79; bd. dirs. Western Assn. Art Museums, Art Mus. Assn. San Francisco, 1978-84; bd. dirs., trustee Art Matters Inc., 1985-96; trustee Russell Found., 1982-94; hon. mem. bd. dirs. Portland Ctr. for Visual Arts, 1984-91; mem. arts adv. bd. Centre City Devel. Corp., San Diego, 1982-94; arts adv. bd. Port of San Diego; panel mem., cons. Nat. Endowment Arts; juror numerous art shows and exhbns. Nat. Endowment Arts fellow, 1979. Recipient Allied Professions award AIA, 1992. Contbr. articles to profl. jours. Office: U Calif San Diego The Stuart Collection 9500 Gilman Dr La Jolla CA 92093-0010

BEEBE, SANDRA E., retired English language educator, artist, writer; b. March AFB, Calif., Nov. 10, 1934; d. Eugene H. and Margaret (Fox) B.; m. Donald C. Thompson. AB in English and Speech, UCLA, 1956; MA in Secondary Edn., Calif. State U., Long Beach, 1957. Tchr. English, Garden Grove (Calif.) High Sch., 1957-93, attendance supr., 1976-83, ret., 1993; tchr. watercolor courses, Asilomar, Calif., 1997; jury chmn. N.W.S., 1997. Contbr. articles to English Jour., chpts. to books; watercolor artist; exhbns. include AWS, NWS, Okla. Watercolor Soc., Watercolor West, Midwest Watercolor Soc., Butler Inst. Am. Art, Youngstown, Ohio, Kings Art Ctr., Audubon Artists N.Y.; cover artist Exploring Painting, 1990, title page Understanding Watercolor, American Artist, 1991. mem. faculty Asilomar, 1997; chmn. of jurors N.W.S. Open, 1997. Named one of the Top Ten Watercolorists The Artists Mag., 1994; recipient Best Watercolors award Rockport Press, 1995; chosen for Design Poster selection, 1995, 97. Mem. Am. Watercolor Soc. (dir. 1999—), Nat. Watercolor Soc., Midwest Watercolor Soc., Watercolor West, Allied Artists N.Y., Knickerbocker Artists N.Y., Audubon Artists N.Y., West Coast Watercolor Soc., Rocky Mountain Nat. Watermedia Honor Soc., Jr. League Long Beach, Kappa Kappa Gamma. Republican. Home: 7241 Marina Pacifica Dr S Long Beach CA 90803-3899 Studio: B-Q Gallery 3920 E 4th St Long Beach CA 90814-1656 also: 239 Mira Mar Ave Long Beach CA 90803-6153

BEECHER, EARL STEPHENS, financial educator, consultant; b. Montpelier, Idaho, Jan. 20, 1928; s. Paul Edwin and Artel (Stephens) B.; m. Marguerite Harriet Garner, Oct. 2, 1952; children: Stephen Paul, Marguerite Blanche, James Earl. BA, U. Utah, 1949; MBA, UCLA, 1956, PhD, 1965. CLU, CFA. Prof. fin. Calif. State U., Long Beach, 1961-94; staff asst., sr. estimator bus. controls dept. navigation systems autonetics N.Am. Aviation, Anaheim, Calif., 1962-63; sales mgr., tng. dir. Fin. Security Corp., Long Beach, 1967-70; owner Outstanding Records, Huntington Beach, Calif., 1968—; syndicated columnist Knight-Ridder Newspapers, Long Beach, 1983; with Outstanding Records Prodn. Co., 1968—. Producer, host: (radio shows) Dr. Beecher's Business Forum, 1979-81, Southern California Business Focus, 1991-94, (TV shows) Earl Beecher Interviews, 1984-88, Adventures In Life, 1996—. Chaplain U.S. Army, 1952-63, Korea. Recipient Wall St. Jour. award UCLA, 1957; Isaias Hellman fellow UCLA, 1958. Mem. Inst. Chartered Fin. Analysts, L.A. Fin. Analysts Soc. LDS. Avocation: script-writing. Office: Outstanding Records PO Box 2111 Huntington Beach CA 92647-0111

BEEGLE, EARL DENNIS, family physician; b. Ashland, Ohio, July 24, 1944; s. Ray Benjamin and Alice Mae (Imhoff) B.; m. Isabel Sloan-Kerr Adamson, Sept. 3, 1964; children: Ryan Benjamin, Kevin Ian. BA, Manchester Coll., 1967; MS, Purdue U., 1970; MB BChir, MD, BAO, Queen's U., Belfast, No. Ireland, 1978. Diplomate Am. Bd. Family Practice. Life scis. tchr. Elkhart (Ind.) Schs., 1967-72; house officer Nat. Health Svc. of U.K., 1978-79; resident in family practice Riverside Hosp. Med. Coll. Ohio, Toledo, 1979-81, chief resident, 1981-82; pvt. practice Everett, Wash., 1982-93; med. dir. Providence Primary Care Network, Everett, 1993-96; v.p., med. dir. Medalia Healthcare, Seattle, 1997-98, exec. v.p. managed care, 1998-99; CEO Medalia Med. Group N.W. Wash., 1999—; credentials com. Providence Gen. Med. Ctr., 1996—, physician well-being com., 1997—; med. dir. Planned Parenthood, Everett, 1983-86; chmn. utilization Providence Hosp., Everett, 1987-90, chmn. quality assurance, 1991-92; chmn. dept. family practice Providence-Gen. Med. Ctr., Everett, 1993-94; dir. Sisters of Providence Health Plans, Seattle, 1993-98. Active Friends of the Somme, No. Ireland, 1991—. NSF fellow, 1967-70. Fellow Am. Acad. Family Practice; mem. Irish and Am. Pediatric Soc., Snohomish County Med. Soc., Associated Physicians of Snohomish County (bd. dirs.), Internat. Soc. Travel Medicine. Avocations: international travel, period furniture, antiquities. Office: Providence Claremont Clinic 5007 Claremont Way Everett WA 98203-3321

BEEL, LORRAINE KUHN, tutor; b. Bklyn., July 9, 1921; d. Harold Edmond and Regina Hermenia (Doscher) Kuhn; m. Samuel Lee Painter, July 11, 1942 (dec. July 1961); children: Karen Melfi, Patricia Murphy, Pamela Brown, Thomas Painter, Susan Peterson, Laurie Pace; m. Lawrence Samuel Ronald, Apr. 19, 1968 (dec. 1980);. BS, Cornell U., 1942; MA, U. N.Mex., 1957. Cert. tchr. of handicapped, Calif., elem. tchr., Calif., N.Mex. Asst. supr. Daysch., tchr. home econs. Norwood (Ohio) Schs., 1942-44; elem. tchr. Dep. Schs. Overseas, Linz, Austria, 1949-50; supr. kindergarten day nursery Sandia Base, Albuquerque, 1955-56, Albuquerque Pub. Schs., 1959-61; tchr. pre-kindergarten Monzano Day Sch., Albuquerque, 1962-63; elem. tchr., spl. edn. tchr. Palo Alto (Calif.) Unified Schs., 1963-82; tutor pvt. and pub. schs., Albuquerque, 1982—. Fellow Albuquerque Assn. Ednl. Retirees (v.p. 1994—), Delta Kappa Gamma (v.p. 70s, scholarship 1974), Alpha Delta Kappa (v.p. 1977-78, pres. 1978-79), Pi Lambda Theta (v.p. 1958, 1985, regional treas. 1992-94). Avocations: choral music, internat. rels. study group, fgn. cuisine, dancing.

BEEMAN, ANNA MARIE, volunteer; b. Woodland, Calif.; d. Frank and Anna Marie (Williams) Sieferman; widowed, Jan. 1992; children: Sue Ann, Kevan, Donald, Michael, Betsy, Howard. Grad., Margaret Place Sec. Sch., 1942. Pres., bd. dirs. Yolo County Hist. Mus., Woodland, Calif., 1983—; mem. Yolo County Fair Bd., 1990—. Mem. Elks Club, Omega Nu (past pres.). Republican. Episcopalian. Office: Yolo County Fair Bd Fair Grounds Woodland CA 95695

BEEMAN, MALINDA MARY, artist, program administrator; b. Pomona, Calif., Jan. 23, 1949; d. Earl Wilson and Mary (Alvey) B. BA, San Diego State U., 1971; MFA, San Francisco Art Inst., 1973. Area coord. printmaking U. Houston, 1985-92; program dir. Anderson Ranch Art Ctr., Snowmass Village, Colo., 1992—. Recipient Visual Artists award Nat. Endowment for Arts, 1988, 96, Covision Recognition award Colo. State Arts Coun., 1992. Office: Anderson Ranch Arts Ctr 5263 Owl Creek Rd Snowmass Village CO 81615*

BEEN, HANS HENRIK, finance executive; b. Copenhagen, Aug. 30, 1949; came to U.S., 1976; s. Borge and Tove (Hansen) B.; m. Helle Nymann Eriksen, Jan. 16, 1971; children: Louise, Henriette. BA in Econs., U. Copenhagen, 1970; MBA, Copenhagen Sch. Econs., 1973; MSc in Fin., Calif. State U., Northridge, 1979. Fin. planner Novo Pharms., Ltd., Copenhagen, 1972-74; asst. gen. mgr. Sadolin & Holmblad, Ltd., Copenhagen, 1974-76; comml. officer Danish Fgn. Svc., Royal Danish Consulate Gen., L.A., 1976-80; mgr. corp. banking Den Danske Bank, Copenhagen, 1980-81; mgr. proj. fin. Bank of Montreal, Toronto, Ont., 1981-85, N.Y.C., 1985-86; v.p. Bechtel Financing Svcs., Inc., San Francisco, 1986-89, Bechtel Enterprises, Inc., San Francisco, 1989—; lectr. fin. U. So. Calif., St. Mary's Coll., 1977-91. Mem. Danish-Am. C. of C., L.A., 1976-79. Recipient Pathfinder Leadership award Applied Energy Svcs., Washington, 1990. Mem. Nat. Assn. Securities Dealers (registered rep. 1989). Avocations: tennis, skiing, jogging, sailing. Home: 1869 Countrywood Ct Walnut Creek CA 94598-1013 Office: Bechtel Enterprises Inc 50 Beale St San Francisco CA 94105-1813

BEENE, RICHARD STUART, editor; b. Knoxville, Tenn., June 11, 1951; s. William Wolbach and Julia (Swysgood) B.; m. Dianne Elise Klein, May 29, 1983; children: Lauren Elizabeth, Hannah Julia. BA in History, Ga. So. U., 1973. Reporter Fort Lauderdale (Fla.) Sentinel, 1978-80; state mgr. UPI, N.Y.C., Miami & Atlanta, 1980-84; bur. chief UPI, Cairo, 1983; L.Am. corr. Dallas Times Herald, 1984-87; city editor L.A. Times, 1987-94; exec. editor Bakersfield (Calif.) Californian, 1994-98, pres., CEO, 1998—. Recipient Pulitizer, L.A. Times, 1995. Mem. Am. Soc. Newspaper Editors, Calif. Soc. Newspaper Editors, Sigma Delta Chi. Avocation: bicycle racing. Office: Bakersfield Californian 1707 Eye St Bakersfield CA 93302-5299*

BEER, JOSEPH ERNEST, telecommunications manager; b. Pasadena, Calif., June 5, 1959; s. Joseph Andrew and Pauline Sylvia (Micciche) B.; m. Amy Shun-Fong Wu, Oct. 13, 1984. BS in Internat. Bus., Calif. State U., L.A., 1982; MBA in Info. Tech. Mgmt., U. So. Calif., 1987. Asst. engr. ARCO-Electronics & Telecommunications, L.A., 1979-83, sr. coord., 1983-84, project engr., 1984-85, sr. project engr., 1985-87; mgr. Ernst & Young, L.A., 1987-91; dir. telecommunications and network svcs. South Coast Air Quality Mgmt. Dist., L.A., 1991-94; mgr. info. tech. svcs. Tosco Northwest Co., Seattle, 1994-96; dir. profl. svcs. Mosaix Inc., Seattle, 1996-98; sr. mgr. Ernst & Young, Seattle, 1999—. Recipient scholarship, Ebell Found., L.A., 1981, Bank Am. scholarship, Bank Am. Found., 1981. Mem. Soc. Telecommunications Consultants, Project Mgmt. Inst. Republican. Avocations: biking, hiking, antique car and telephone collecting and restoration. Home: 24012 SE 37th Pl Issaquah WA 98029-6320 Office: Ernst & Young 999 3d St Ste 3500 Seattle WA 98101

BEERBOHM, ELISA NEWELL, advertising professional; b. Palo Alto, Calif., May 15, 1960; d. Harry S. and Dorothy L. (Perkins) B. BA, UCLA, 1984; MBA, U. So. Calif., 1994. Sr. account mgr. Tribune Newspapers, L.A., 1987-96; gen. mgr., pub. Std. Rate and Data Svc., L.A., 1996—. Bd. dirs. Advt. Industry Emergency Fund, 1996—. Recipient Pres. award for Outstanding Achievement, Advt. Ind. Emergency Fund, 1996. Mem. Am. Mktg. Assn., L.A. Advt. Club. Avocations: gardening, hiking, gourmet cooking, writing. Office: Std Rate and Data Svc 11500 W Olympic Blvd Ste 385 Los Angeles CA 90064-1554

BEERS, SUSAN ALICE, dean; b. Tucson, July 21, 1946; d. Laverne G. and Claire M. (Liles) B. BA, Chapman U., 1968; MA, Calif. State U., Long Beach, 1972; EdD, Pepperdine U., 1997. Cert. tchr., Calif. Tchr. Norwalk (Calif.) H.S., 1969-74; realtor assoc. Nolan Real Estate, Laguna Beach, Calif., 1988-90; prof. Fullerton (Calif.) Coll., 1974-89, athletic dir., dept. chair, 1989-92, dean phys. edn./athletics, 1992—, interim dean counseling/student devel., 1995—; mem. dist. mgmt. negotiation team Fullerton Coll., 1994-95, pres. Orange Empire Conf. Com., 1995—, Title IX officer, 1994—; presenter in field. Editor Scope newsletter, 1992-96. Mem. Dept. Social Svc., Orange, Calif., 1992; Scope rep./presenter State Legis. Conf., 1994;

prsenter Calif. Assn. Health, Sacramento, 1995. Mem. AAHPERD, State Commn. on Athletics, State Cmty. Coll. Orgn. of Phys. Educators (pres. 1993-95, spkr. 1995). Democrat. Avocations: snow skiing, swimming, travel. Home: 607 Fontana Way Laguna Beach CA 92651-4053 Office: Fullerton Coll 321 E Chapman Ave Fullerton CA 92832-2011

BEERY, ROGER LEWIS, II, risk management consultant; b. San Antonio, Apr. 9, 1957; s. Roger Lewis Sr. and Margaret (Dorrill) B.; m. Donna M. Hodgkinson. BBA, U. Tex., 1979, MBA, 1981. Founder, pres. Austin (Tex.) Cons. Group, Inc., Breckenridge, Colo., 1980—; lectr. U. Tex., Austin, 1979-87, Rice U., Houston, 1986-88; expert witness in ins. related lawsuits; speaker in field; guest cons. Rice U. Entrepeneur's Conf., 1986-88; speaker Nat. Automobile Dealers Assn. Conv., 1990. Author: Dealership Risk Mgmt. Newsletter; contbr. articles to profl. jours. including Automotive Exec., Automobile Dealer Mag. Founder Exec. Level Mgmt., Ltd., Bermuda, 1991—; bd. dirs. Summit Sch. Dist. RE-1, 1997—. Republican. Avocations: skiing, hiking, mountain biking. Office: Austin Cons Group Inc 130 Ski Hill Rd #140 Breckenridge CO 80424

BEESON, MARY A., sculptor; b. Noble, Okla., Oct. 12, 1924; d. Emsley M. and Ollie Jane (Donnell) Hitchcock; widowed; children: J. Bradley, Donald D., Nancy Kay Beeson Hurley. Student, Riverside City Coll., 1960-61. Sculptor Encinitas, Calif., 1965-72; gallery owner Sculpture Gallery, Del Mar, Calif., 1970-72, Art Ctr. Fine Arts Gallery, Rancho Santa Fe, Calif., 1973-74, Prime Time Fine Arts, Napa, Calif., 1975-76; sculpting tchr. Napa Coll., Yountville, Calif., 1976-80; juror fine arts Napa State Fair, 1975-80. Sculpting commns. include: 4 1/2-ft. cast cement "Sermon on the Mount", Bloomington, Calif. Cemetery, 1960, 72x60 bronze for Marin County Calif./ Meml. to Vietnam and Korean Wars at Civic Ctr., 1985. Mem. Nat. Artists Assn., Nat. League of Am. Pen Women, La Jolla, Calif., 1970-74; counselor Riverside County Peer Counselling, 1995; hospice vol. Eisenhower Hosp. Seventh Day Adventist. Avocations: painting in watercolor, sewing, reading, travel. Home: 69530 Dillon Rd Spc 63 Desert Hot Springs CA 92241-9333

BEESTON, JOSEPH MACK, metallurgist; b. Fillmore, Utah, Aug. 12, 1918; s. Joseph W. and Florence (Swallow) B.; m. Blanche Weight, Dec. 20, 1946; children: Miriam, Jolynn. BChEng, U. Utah, 1949; postgrad., Oreg. State U., 1949-50; PhD in Metall. Engring., U. Utah, 1953. Asst. prof. Wash. State U., Pullman, 1953-58; sr. metallurgist Phillips Pet Atomic Energy Div., Idaho Falls, Idaho, 1958-61, leader irr. material group, 1961-64; chief materials tech. sect. Idaho Nuclear, Idaho Falls, 1964-71; chief irradiation material engring. Aerojet Gen., Idaho Falls, 1971-78; sci. specialist EG&G Idaho Inc., Idaho Falls, 1978-85; cons. metallurgist Garrison, Utah, 1985—. Contbr. over 100 articles to profl. jours. With USAF, 1941-45. Mem. ASTM (com. nuclear tech. and applications), Am. Soc. Metals. Home and Office: 625 Circle Dr Garrison UT 84728-9600

BEEZER, ROBERT RENAUT, federal judge; b. Seattle, July 21, 1928; s. Arnold Roswell and Josephine (May) B.; m. Hazlehurst Plant Smith, June 15, 1957; children: Robert Arnold, John Leighton, Mary Allison. Student, U. Wash., 1946-48, 51; BA, U. Va., 1951, LLB, 1956. Bar: Wash. 1956, U.S. Supreme Ct. 1968. Ptnr. Schweppe, Krug, Tausend & Beezer, P.S., Seattle, 1956-84; judge U.S. Ct. Appeals (9th cir.), Seattle, 1984-96, sr. judge, 1996—; alt. mem. Wash. Jud. Qualifications Commn., Olympia, 1981-84. 1st lt. USMCR, 1951-53. Fellow Am. Coll. Trust and Estate Counsel, Am. Bar Found.; mem. ABA, Seattle-King County Bar Assn. (pres. 1975-76), Wash. Bar Assn. (bd. govs. 1980-83). Clubs: Rainier, Tennis (Seattle). Office: US Ct Appeals 802 US Courthouse 1010 5th Ave Seattle WA 98104-1130*

BEGGS, HARRY MARK, lawyer; b. Los Angeles, Nov. 15, 1941; s. John Edgar and Agnes (Kentro) B.; m. Sandra Lynne Mikal, May 25, 1963; children: Brendan, Sean, Corey, Michael. Student, Ariz. State U., 1959-61, Phoenix Coll., 1961; LL.B., U. Ariz., 1964. Bar: Ariz. 1964, U.S. Dist. Ct. Ariz. 1964, U.S. Ct. Appeals (9th cir.) 1973, U.S. Ct. Appeals (fed. cir.) 1995, U.S. Supreme Ct. 1991. Assoc. Carson Messinger Elliott Laughlin & Ragan, Phoenix, 1964-69, ptnr., 1969-93; mem., mng. lawyer Carson Messinger Elliott Laughlin & Ragan, P.L.L.C, Phoenix, 1994—. Mem. editorial bd. Ariz. Law Rev. 1963-64; contbr. articles to profl. jours. Recipient award for highest grade on state bar exam. Atty. Gen. Ariz., 1964; Fegtly Moot Ct. award, 1963, 64; Abner S. Lipscomb scholar U. Ariz. Law Sch., 1963. Fellow Ariz. Bar Found. (founder); mem. State Bar Ariz., Ariz. Acad., Maricopa County Bar Assn. Office: PO Box 33907 Phoenix AZ 85067-3907

BEHAN, PETER, computer company executive; b. Manchester, England, June 23, 1949; came to U.S., 1984; s. Patrick James and Florence May (Furness) B.; m. Ellen Marie Mendoza (div. Oct. 1993); children: Shontal, Patrick. BSc, St. Johns Coll., 1971. Exec. dir. CoSystems Inc., Sunnyvale, Calif., 1994-98. Avocations: squash, archeology, golf. Home: 22141 Knox Rd Twain Harte CA 95383-9602

BEHDAD, ALI, English language educator; b. Sabzevar, Khorasan, Iran, May 22, 1961; came to U.S., 1979; s. Hassan and Fatimeh (Oskoui) H.; m. Laura E. Pélez, May 29, 1990 (div. May 1995). BA, U. Calif., Berkeley, 1983; MA, U. Mich., 1986, Middlebury (Vt.) Coll., 1988; PhD, U. Mich. 1990. Asst. prof. U. Rochester, N.Y., 1990-93; asst. prof. UCLA, 1993-95, assoc. prof. English, 1995—; mem. adv. bd. Jouvert, N.C., 1995. Author: Belated Travelers: Orientalism in the Age of Colonial Dissolution, 1994; contbr. articles to profl. jours. Recipient Humanities Rsch. Inst. fellowship U. Calif., Irvine, 1996, Rockham predoctoral fellowship U. Mich., Ann Arbor, 1989-90, Rockham rsch. partnership U. Mich., Ann Arbor, 1988-89, U. Calif. Pres. fellowship, 1999—. Mem. MLA, Middle Ea. Scholars Assn. Democrat. Muslim. Avocations: skiing, tennis, swimming. Office: UCLA English Dept 405 Hilgard Ave Los Angeles CA 90095-9000

BEHLE, J. GREGORY, educator; b. L.A., Sept. 7, 1958; s. James G. and Carolyn Jean (Summitt) B.; m. Kelly Therese Behle, June 7, 1986; children: John Gregory, Brittany Megan. BA, Biola U., 1982; ThM, Dallas Theol. Sem., 1986; PhD, U. So. Calif., 1996. Prof. The Master's Coll., Santa Clarita, Calif., 1986—. Mem. Am. Ednl. Rsch. Assn., N.Am. Assn. Profs. Christian Edn., Evangel. Theol. Soc., History of Edn. Soc., Phi Delta Kappa.

BEHLENDORF, BRIAN EUGENE, chief technology officer; b. Burbank, Calif., Mar. 30, 1973; s. Robert Paul and Becky Lynn (Johnson) B.; m. Laura Lee La Gassa, Sept. 14, 1995. Student, U. Calif., Berkeley, 1991-94. Chief engr. Hotwired Mag., San Francisco, 1993-95; chief tech. officer Organic Online, San Francisco, 1993—; co-founder, software engr. Apache Group, Calif., 1995—; spkr. in field. Author: Running a Web Server with Apache, 1996; contbr. articles to profl. jours. Avocations: travel, dance, music. Office: Organic Online 510 3d St Ste 540 San Francisco CA 94107-3803

BEHLMER, RUDY H., JR., director, writer, film educator; b. San Francisco, Oct. 13, 1926; s. Rudy H. and Helen Mae (McDonough) B.; 1 child by previous marriage, Curt; m. Stacey Endres, Oct. 1992. Student, Pasadena Playhouse Coll., 1946-49, Los Angeles City Coll., 1949-50. Dir. Sta. KLAC-TV, Hollywood, Calif., 1952-56; network TV dir. ABC-TV, Hollywood, 1956-57; TV comml. producer-dir., Assoc. Grant Advt., Hollywood, 1957-60; exec. producer-dir. Sta. KCOP-TV, Hollywood, 1960-63; v.p., TV comml. producer-dir. Hollywood office Leo Burnett USA, 1963-84; lectr. film Art Ctr. Coll. of Design, Pasadena, Calif., 1967-92, Calif. State U., Northridge, 1984-92, UCLA, 1988. Author: Memo from David O. Selznick, 1972, (with Tony Thomas) Hollywood's Hollywood, 1975, America's Favorite Movies-Behind the Scenes, 1982, Inside Warner Bros., 1985, Behind the Scenes: The Making of ..., 1990, Memo From Darryl F. Zanuck, 1993, W.S. Van Dyke's Journal-White Shadows in the South Seas, 1996; co-author: The Films of Errol Flynn, 1969; text on Warner Bros. Fifty Years of Film Music, 1973; editor: The Adventures of Robin Hood, 1979, The Sea Hawk, 1982 (Wis./Warner Bros. Screenplay series), Warner Bros. 75 Years of Film Music, 1998; contbr. articles on film history, booklets for film music CDs; writer and narrator for laserdiscs and video documentaries. Served with AC, USNR, 1944-46. Mem. Dirs. Guild Am.

BEHNEY, CHARLES AUGUSTUS, JR., veterinarian; b. Bryn Mawr, Pa., Nov. 30, 1929; s. Charles Augustus and Victoria Parks (Wythe) B.; B.S., U. Wyo., D.V.M., Colo. State U., 1961; m. Judith Ann Boggs, May 26, 1979;

children—Charles Augustus III, Keenan F. Owner, Cochise Animal Hosp., Bisbee, Ariz., 1961- ; veterinarian, dir. S.W. Traildust Zoo, Bisbee, 1966- ; owner Kazam Arabians, Bisbee, 1969—; asso. prof. Cochise Coll. Chmn., Comprehensive Health Planning, Cochise County, Ariz., 1968. Mem. Am. Vet. Med. Assn., Soc. for Breeding Soundness, Internat. Platform Assn. Republican. Episcopalian. Rotarian, Elk. Patentee ultrasound device and eye cover for treating infections, apparatus to alter equine leg conformation, external vein clamp, equine sanitation instrument; developer ear implant instrumentation system. Home and Office: PO Box 4337 Bisbee AZ 85603-4337

BEHNKE, DONNA BETH, counselor; b. Burbank, Calif., May 19, 1957; d. Frank Michael and Dorothy Eva (Dubis) Behnke; m. Sherman Voorhies, Mar. 22, 1980 (div. Dec. 1985); children: Paul, Daniel; m. Neil Art Jones, Apr. 7, 1990 (div. Aug. 1995); children: Neil, Jr., Jimmy, Joshua Jones. BA in English, Calif. State Univ., L.A., 1980, MA in Ednl. Adminstrv. Svcs., 1990; student, Calif. Luth. Univ., Thousand Oaks, 1996. Cert. counselor, English, speech, drama instr., secondary adminstr. Tchr. L.A. Unified Sch. Dist., 1985-88, tchr., forensics dir., 1988-94, counselor, 1994—; table leader, testing coord., scorer Calif. Assessment Program Ednl. Testing Svcs., Berkeley, 1986-94. Parent connection counselor Huntington Meml. Hosp. Mem. Nat. Tchrs. Assn., Nat. English Tchrs. Assn., Counselors Assn. Roman Catholic. Avocations: acting, directing, reading, volunteer work, sewing, cooking. Home: 4750 Rosebank Dr La Canada CA 91011-1524 Office: San Fernando Mid Sch 130 N Brand Blvd San Fernando CA 91340-2901

BEHR, TED ARTHUR, religious organization administrator; b. L.A., May 28, 1934; s. Arthur William and Veta Felcia (Turner) B.; m. Barbara Jean Prevol, June 8, 1963; children: Robert Arthur, John William. AA, Santa Monica City Coll., 1954. Fellow in ch. bus. adminstrn., 1979. Exec. producer Lloyd Ogilvie Ministries, Hollywood, Calif., 1978-86; ch. adminstr. First Presbyn. Ch., Hollywood, 1975—; chmn. bd. advs. Templeton prize, Nassau, Bahamas, 1985; vice-chmn. So. Calif. Presbyn. Homes, Glendale, 1984—. Bd. dirs. Hollywood YMCA, 1972-73; deacon First Presbyn. Ch., Hollywood, 1969-71, elder, 1973-75. Quartermaster USCG, 1954-56. Mem. Nat. Assn. Ch. Bus. Adminstrs. (pres. So. Calif. chpt. 1979-80), Christian Ministry Mgmt. Assn. (bd. dirs. 1984-85), Jaycees (pres. Hollywood chpt. 1963), Rotary (pres. Hollywood chpt. 1970), Hollywood C. of C. (bd. dirs. 1975-78). Republican. Home: 619 Avenida Acapulco San Clemente CA 92672-2404 Office: First Presbyterian Church 1760 N Gower St Los Angeles CA 90028-5498

BEHREND, DONALD FRASER, university administrator; b. Manchester, Conn., Aug. 30, 1931; s. Sherwood Martin and Margaret (Fraser) B.; m. Joan Kirkland, Nov. 9, 1957; children: Andrew Fraser, Eric Hemingway, David William. BS with honors and distinction, U. Conn., 1958, MS, 1960; PhD in Forest Zoology, SUNY, Syracuse, 1966. Forest game mgmt. specialist Ohio Dept. Natural Resources, Athens, 1960; res. asst. Coll. Forestry, SUNY, Newcomb, 1960-63, res. assoc., 1963-67; dir. Adirondack ecol. ctr. Coll. Environ. Science and Forestry, SUNY, Newcomb, 1968-73; acting dean grad. studies Syracuse, 1973-74; asst. v.p. research programs, exec. dir. Inst. Environ. Program Affairs, 1974-79, v.p. acad. affairs, prof., 1979-85, prof. emeritus, 1987—; asst. prof. wildlife mgmt. U. Maine, Orono, 1967-68; provost, v.p. acad. affairs U. Alaska Statewide System, Fairbanks, 1985-87, exec. v.p., provost, 1988; chancellor U. Alaska, Anchorage, 1988-94, chancellor emeritus, 1994—; mem. patent policy bd. SUNY, 1983-85, chmn. Res. Found. com. acad. res. devel., 1984-85; chmn. 6-Yr. planning com. U. Alaska, 1985-86; bd. dirs. Commonwealth North, 1991-92, Alaska Internat. Ednl. Found., 1997; mem. selection com. Harry S. Truman Scholarship Found.; mem. Pres.'s Commn., NCAA, 1992-95; chmn. spl. com. on student athlete welfare access and equity, 1993-95; chmn. 20th Great Alaska Shootout, 1997. Contbr. numerous articles and papers to profl. jours. Mem. Newcomb Planning Bd., 1967-69; mem., pres. Bd. Edn. Newcomb Cent. Sch., 1967-73; chmn. governing bd. N.Y. Sea Grant Inst., 1984-85; trustee U. Ala. Found., 1990-94. Served with USN, 1950-54. Mem. Alaska Internat. Edn. Found. (bd. dirs. 1997—), Wildlife Soc., Soc. Am. Foresters, AAAS, Phi Kappa Phi (hon.), Sigma Xi, Gamma Sigma Delta, Sigma Lambda Alpha (hon.). Lodges: Rotary (bd. dirs. Fairbanks club 1985-86), Lions (bd. dirs. Newcomb club 1966-67). Avocations: reading, writing, photography, fishing, bagpiping. Home: 333 M St Apt #403 Anchorage AK 99501-1902

BEHRENDSEN, ARDEN EUGENE, interior designer, history educator; b. Gilmore City, Iowa, Dec. 20, 1931; s. Frank Henry and Vera Doris (Lynch) B.; m. Ruth Ann Floy, Aug. 18, 1956; children: Erik, Burr, Brooke (Carpenter) Gunnar. BA, U. Iowa, 1953, MA, 1958. Cert. tchr. Colo. Pres. Behrendsen/Interiors, Denver, 1960-65; dir. Denver Dry Goods Co., 1965-72; sr. designer Hartley House Interiors, Denver, 1972—; adj. prof. Arapahoe C.C., Littleton, Colo., 1988—, Adams State Coll., Alamosa, Colo., 1996-98; chmn., prof., lectr. Behrensen Tours LLC, Denver, 1991—. Designer palace Saudi Arabia; contbr. articles to mags. Chmn. Dem. Precinct, Denver, 1958-68, county and state del. Dem. Convention, Denver, 1965-68; dir. interiors Humphrey for Pres., Denver, 1968. With U.S. Army, 1953-55. Avocations: collecting books, European travel. Home: 1470 S Quebec Way Apt 163 Denver CO 80231-2660 Office: Hartley House Interiors Ltd 290 S Franklin St Denver CO 80209-2607

BEHRENS, BARBARA BLAUTH, healthcare administrator; b. Bkln., Apr. 20, 1937; d. Robert James and Theresa (Enriquez) Blauth; m. Herbert Harry Behrens, Mar. 21, 1959 (div. July 1986); children: Christopher Charles, Catherine Ann. RN grad., Bellevue Sch. Nursing, N.Y.C., 1957; BA with distinction, U. of Redlands, 1976, MA in Mgmt. Human Resources with distinction, 1979. RN, Hawaii, Calif., N.Y.; cert. advanced cardiac life support, basic cardiac life support instr./trainer, cert. emergency nurse, mobile intensive care nurse. Staff nurse med.-surg. and critical care depts. U. Calif., Moffett Hosp., San Francisco; staff nurse with Bellevue Hosp., N.Y.C.; relief nurse all units Stanford (Calif.) Univ. Hosp., 1962-69, staff nurse IV, acting insvc. instr., 1972-76, ednl. coord., 1976-78, clin. nursing coord., 1978-82, asst. dir. dept. emergency svcs., 1982-86; dir. critical care and emergency svcs. Queen's Med. Ctr., Honolulu, 1986-89; exec. dir. Queen's Heart Inst., 1989—. Mem. ACCA, ACC. Cardiovascular Adminstrs. (state dir. Hawaii chpt.), Am. Acad. Med. Adminstrs. (state dir. Hawaii chpt.), Am. Heart Assn. (Hawaii ACLS faculty, bd. dirs. exec. com. Hawaii affiliate), Am. Orgn. Nurse Execs. (chair nominating com., legis. com.), Emergency Nurses Assn, Nat. League of Nursing (bd. dir. Hawaii affiliate). Avocations: reading, dancing, performing arts. Home: Redwood Shores 16 Cape Hatteras Ct Redwood City CA 94065-1263

BEHRENS, BEREL LYN, physician, academic administrator; b. New South Wales, Australia, 1940. MB, BS, Sydney (Australia) U., 1964. Cert. pediatrics, allergy and immunology. Intern Royal Prince Alfred Hosp., Australia, 1964; resident Loma Linda (Calif.) U. Med. Ctr., 1966-68; with Henrietta Egleston Hosp. for Children, Atlanta, 1968-69, T.C. Thompson Children's Hosp., Chattanooga, 1969-70; instr. pediatrics Loma Linda U., 1970-72, with dept. pediatrics, 1972—, dean Sch. Medicine, 1986-91, pres., 1990—. Office: Loma Linda U Office of the Pres Loma Linda CA 92350

BEHRENS, ROBERT KARL, sculptor, architectural designer, urban planner; b. Teaneck, N.J., May 12, 1939; s. George Henry and Gaetanina (Idarolla) B.; m. Elizabeth Carroll Jackson, Apr. 22, 1966 (div. 1976); 1 child, Francis Gaeta. BFA, Kans. City Art Inst., 1965; postgrad., U. Wis.; MA in Sculptor, U. Denver, 1972. Instr. design Denver U., 1969-72; project architect G. Cabell Childress Architects, Denver, 1968-75; prin. Behrens/ Friberg Site Specific Art/Design, Santa Sonoma, Calif., 1985-; vis. lectr. U. Colo. Grad. Sch. Archtecture, Denver, 1979-83. Prin. works include pub. site sculptures, Cambridge, Mass.- Boston, New Orleans, Denver, Fairbanks, Alaska, Oxnard, Calif., Stanford U., U. Colo., Beaver Creek, Colo., Vancouver B.C. Can, U So Colo, Davis Calif, Sonoma Calif. Coord. Green Belt Alliance, Santa Rosa, Calif., 1995; chmn. Broadway Landscape Improvement Com., Sonoma, 1989; pres. Mountain Area Planning Coun., Evergreen, Colo., 1965; mem. adv. bd. Wright Ingram Inst., 1967-79; pres. North Mission Assn., 1997-98; bd. dirs. Sonoma Citizen Coalition, 1998; mem. adv. bd. Am. Sculpture Soc., 1985-87; mem. Sonoma Town Design Task Force, 1998. Recipient citation AIA, 1973, award of excellence Calif. Coun. Landscape Architects, 1987, Yolo County Bd. Realtors, 1987, Am. Planning Assn. Ednl. award, 1992, Sonoma League Hist. Preservation award

of Excellence, 1995; 1993 NEA grantee, 1975-95. Home and Office: 302 1st St E Sonoma CA 95476-5705

BEHRING, KENNETH E., professional sports team owner; b. Freeport, Ill., June 13, 1928; s. Elmer and Mae (Priewe) B.; m. Patricia Riffle, Oct. 16, 1949; children: Michael, Thomas, David, Jeffrey, Scott. Student, U. Wis., 1947. Owner Behring Motors, Monroe, Wis., 1953-56, Behring Corp., Ft. Lauderdale, Fla., 1956-72; owner Blackhawk Corp., Danville, Calif., 1972—, also chmn. bd. dirs.; owner Seattle Seahawks, NFL, 1988-97; Calif. land developer; mem. policy adv. bd. real estate and urban econs. U. Calif. Berkeley.; chmn. bd. dirs. Behring-Hofmann Ednl. Inst., Inc. U. Calif. Trustee U. Calif., Berkeley; regent St. Mary's Coll., Moraga, Calif., Holy Name Coll., Oakland, Calif.; hon. trustee Mt. Diablo Hosp. Found., Concord, Calif.; hon. chmn. Seattle Art Mus., Am. Cancer Soc., Muscular Dystrophy, Silverado Concours. Named Man of Yr. Boys Town Italy, Entrepreneur of Yr. INC mag. Mem. Am. Acad. Achievement (honoree 1989), Assn. Wash. Bus., Seattle Master Builders Assn., Blackhawk Club, Vintage Club, Seattle Yacht Club, Wash. Athletic Club. Office: Blackhawk Corp PO Box 807 Danville CA 94526-0807*

BEIGHLE, DOUGLAS PAUL, electric power industry executive; b. Deer Lodge, Mont., June 18, 1932; s. Douglas Paul Beighle and Clarice Janice (Driver) Kiefer; m. Gwendolen Anne Dickson, Oct. 30, 1954 (dec. Jan. 1996); children: Cheryl, Randall, Katherine, Douglas J. B.S. in Bus. Adminstrn., U. Mont., 1954; J.D., U. Mont, 1958; LL.M., Harvard U., 1960. Bar: Mont. 1958, Wash. 1959, U.S. Supreme Ct. 1970. Assoc. Perkins & Coie, Seattle, 1960-67, ptnr., 1967-80; v.p. contracts Boeing Co., Seattle, 1980-81, v.p. contracts, gen. counsel, sec., 1981-86; sr. v.p. Boeing Co., 1986-97; chief legal counsel Puget Sound Energy Co., Bellevue, Wash., 1970-80, also bd. dirs., 1981—; exec. dir. Wash. State, U.S. West Comm., Denver, 1990-95; bd. dirs. Peabody Holding Co., St. Louis, 1982-90, Washington Mut. Inc., Seattle, 1989—, KCTS-9 TV, 1995—, chair 1996—. Nat. bd. dirs. Jr. Achievement, Colorado Springs, 1981-95; bd. dirs. Greater Puget Sound Jr. Achievement, 1983—, Intiman Theatre, Seattle, 1991-93; trustee Mcpl. League Seattle, 1983-88, U. Mont. Found., Missoula, 1983-91, Mansfield Found., Missoula, 1990-95, Pacific Sci. Ctr., Seattle, 1992—, pres. 1996; trustee Corp. Coun. for the Arts, Seattle, 1994—, chair, 1995-96; active Voice Corp., 1998—. 1st lt. USAF, 1954-56. Harvard U. Law Sch. fellow, 1959. Mem. ABA, Mont. Bar Assn., Wash. State Bar Assn. (chmn. adminstrv. law sect. 1959-60), Seattle-King County Bar Assn., Nat. Assn. Mfrs. (bd. dirs., regional vice chmn. 1988-93), Greater Seattle C. of C. (chair 1994-95), Rainier Club Seattle, Seattle Yacht Club, Poulsbo Yacht Club. Republican. Presbyterian. Office: 1000 2nd Ave Ste 3700 Seattle WA 98104-1053

BEILENSON, ANTHONY CHARLES, former congressman; b. New Rochelle, N.Y., Oct. 26, 1932; s. Peter and Edna (Rudolph) B.; m. Dolores Martin, June 20, 1959; children: Peter, Dayna, Adam. B.A., Harvard Coll., 1954; LL.B., Harvard U., 1957. Bar: Calif. 1957. Mem. Calif. Assembly from 59th Dist., 1963-66, Calif. Senate from 22d Dist., 1967-76, 95th-104th Congresses from 23rd (now 24th) Calif. Dist., 1977-96; ranking minority mem. subcom. on Rules & Orgn. of Ho. Democrat. Home: 8109 Kerry Ln Chevy Chase MD 20815-4811*

BEIMAN, NANCY ROBIN, animator; b. Jersey City, N.J., Sept. 20, 1957; d. Melvyn B. and Frances Marion. BFA, Calif. Inst. Arts, 1979. Animator, designer Zander's Animation Parlour, N.Y.C., 1979-82; freelancer, 1983-88; prodr., dir. Caged Beagle Animation, N.Y.C., 1986-88; dir., animator Gerhard Hahn Filmproduction GMBH, Berlin, 1988-89; supervising animator Amblimation Studio, London, 1989-90; dir. Warner Bros. TV Animation, N.Y.C., 1990-92, Phillips Sidewalk Studio, Santa Monica, Calif., 1992-93; supervising animator Walt Disney TV Animation, Burbank, Calif., 1993-95; supervising animator, devel. artist Walt Disney Feature Animation, Burbank, Calif., 1995—. Supervising animator: (animated feature film) An American Tale: Feivel Goes West, 1990, (animated feature film) A Goofy Movie, 1994, (animated feature film) Hercules, 1997; dir. (animated video) Bugs Bunny's Lunar Tunes, 1991. Donor CARE, Habitat for Humanity. Mem. Nat. Cartoonists Soc. (Reuben category award Best in Animation 1985, membership chmn. 1984-86), Cartoon Artists Profl. Soc., Sons of the Desert (Laurel and Hardy Club). Fax: (818) 563-2859. Office: Walt Disney Feature Animation Box 4985 500 S Buena Vista St Burbank CA 91521-0004

BEIZER, LANCE KURT, lawyer; b. Hartford, Conn., Sept. 8, 1938; s. Lawrence Sidney and Victoria Merriam (Kaplan) B. BA in Sociology, Brandeis U., 1960; MA in English, San Jose State U., 1967; JD, U. San Diego, 1975. Bar: Calif. 1975. Selective svc. affairs coord. U. Calif., 1969-73, vet. affairs coord., 1973-75; vet. outreach coord. San Diego Community Coll. Dist., 1975-76; dep. dist. atty. Santa Clara County, Calif. 1976—. Bd. mgrs. Santa Clara Valley S.W. YMCA, Saratoga, Calif., 1988—, chair, 1991-93; bd. dirs. The Lumen Found., San Francisco, 1985—. Bd. dirs. Fedn. Cmty. Ministries, Calif., 1992—, chair, 1996—. South Bay Homeless Teenagers Alliance, 1997—, chair, 1997—. Lt. USNR, 1961-65. Mem. Calif. Dist. Attys. Assn., Santa Clara County Bar Assn., Am. Profl. Soc. on Abuse of Children, Nat. Assn. Counsel for Children, Am. Weil Soc., Mensa, Commonwealth Club. Republican. Episcopalian. Home: 1197 Capri Dr Campbell CA 95008-6002 Office: Santa Clara County Dist Atty 70 W Hedding St San Jose CA 95110-1768

BEKAVAC, NANCY YAVOR, academic administrator, lawyer; b. Pitts., Aug. 28, 1947; d. Anthony Joseph and Elvira (Yavor) B. BA, Swarthmore Coll., 1969; JD, Yale U., 1973. Bar: Calif. 1974, U.S. Dist. Ct. (cen. dist.) 1974, (no. dist.) Calif. 1975, (so. dist.) Calif. 1976, U.S. Ct. Appeals (9th cir.) 1975, (8th cir.) 1981, U.S. Supreme Ct. 1979. Law clk. at large U.S. Ct. Appeals (D.C. cir.), Washington, 1973-74; assoc. Munger, Tolles & Rickershauser, L.A., 1974-79, ptnr., 1987-88; counselor to pres. Dartmouth Coll., Hanover, N.H., 1988-90; pres. Scripps Coll., Claremont, Calif., 1990—; adj. prof. law UCLA Law Sch., 1982-83; mem. Calif. Higher Edn. Roundtable, 1996—; trustee Am. Coun. Edn., 1994-97. Bd. mgrs. Swarthmore Coll., 1984—; trustee Wenner-Gren Found. for Anthr. Rsch. 1987-94; bd. trustees Am. Coun. Edn., 1994-97; chair Assn. Ind. Colls. and Univs., 1996-97. Recipient Human Rights award L.A. County Commn. on Civil Rights, 1984; Woodrow Wilson fellow, Thomas J. Watson fellow, 1969. Mem. Assn. Ind. Calif. Colls. and Univs. (chair 1996), Sierra Club. Avocations: hiking, reading, traveling. Office: Scripps Coll Office of Pres 1030 N Columbia Ave Claremont CA 91711-3948*

BEKEY, SHIRLEY WHITE, psychotherapist; b. L.A.; d. Lawrence Francis and Alice (King) White; m. George Albert Bekey, June 10, 1951; children: Ronald S., Michelle E. BA in Psychology, Occidental Coll., L.A., 1949; MSW in Psychiat. Social Work, UCLA, 1954; PhD in Edn. Psychology, U. So. Calif., 1980. Lic. clin. social worker, Calif.; cert. in pupil pers., parent-child edn. Caseworker outpatient svcs. Calif. State Dept. Mental Health, Montebello; caseworker Lowman Sch. for Handicapped, L.A. Unified Sch. Dist., North Hollywood, Calif., 1971-72; psychotherapist Hofmann Psychiat. Clinic, Glendale (Calif.) Adventist Hosp., 1973-75; pvt. practice Encino, Calif., 1980—; sprk. in field; TV expert on children's emotional problems. 1st hosp. vol. candystriper in U.S., Hollywood Pres. Hosp., 1942; mem. World Affairs Coun., L.A., 1960—. Fellow Soc. for Clin. Social Work; mem. NASW, APA, Am. Ednl. Rsch. Assn., Nat. Assn. Gifted Children, Assn. Transpersonal Psychology, Inst. Noetic Sci., Assn. Ednl. Therapists, So. Calif. Soc. for Clin. Hypnosis, Analytical Psychology Club L.A., Nat. Assn. Poetry Therapy, Calif. Assn. for Gifted. Avocations: clinical hypnosis, gifted and talented, learning disabilities. Office: 4924 Balboa Blvd # 199 Encino CA 91316-3402

BEKIR, NAGWA ESMAT, electrical engineer, educator, consultant; b. Cairo, Dec. 31, 1944; came to U.S. 1972; s. Mohammed Ragab Shalaby and Kamla (Abdel Megeed) Mahmood; m. Esmat Ghobi, Sept. 23, 1971; children: Ahmad C., Badr E. BSEE, Cairo U., Egypt, 1966; MSEE, U. So. Calif., 1975, PhD in EE, 1978. Rsch. and hardware engr. Egyptian Indsl. Rsch. Inst., Cairo, 1966-69; quality control engr. Nat. Egyptian Co. for TV and Electronics, Cairo, 1969-72; mem. tech. staff Axiomatics, L.A., 1978; sr. staff engr. Hughes Aircraft Co., Canoga Park, Calif., 1985, mem. tech. staff, 1978-80; assoc. prof. elec. and computer engring. dept. Calif. State U., Northridge, 1980-83, prof., 1984—, chair elec. and computer engring. dept., 1997—;

mem. tech. staff ITT Gilfillan, Van Nuys, Calif., 1984; cons. aircraft divsn. Northrop Co., El Segundo, Calif., 1987; cons. Budlong & Assocs., Inc., Agoura Hills, Calif., 1992-93; rschr. Northrop Grumman Co., El Segundo, 1994-95. Contbr. articles to profl. jours. Recipient Meritorious Performance and Profl. Promise award Calif. State U., Northridge, 1989, Outstanding Faculty awards Sch. of Engring. and Computer Sci., 1990. Mem. IEEE (sr.), Health and Tennis Corp. Am., Eta Kappa Nu, Tau Beta Pi. Avocations: swimming, racquet ball. Office: Calif State U 18111 Nordhoff St Northridge CA 91330-0001

BELALIA, ABDELKADER, computer consultant; b. Bir-El-Djir, Algeria, Nov. 29, 1957; came to U.S., 1993; s. Mohamed and Lalia B.; children: Henia, Nadia. Degree in mech. engring., IPSA, Paris, 1983; B of Mech. Engring., U. Paris VI, 1982. Software engr. Sligos, Paris, 1984-86; support engr. Metrologie, Paris, 1986-88, Aenix Infomatique, Paris, 1988-90; sr. cons. Tandem Computers, Cupertino, Calif., 1990—. Vol. ARC, France, 1975—. Moslem. Avocations: photography, social work. Home: 866 Bruce Dr Palo Alto CA 94303-3643

BELGRADER, ANDREI, director, writer; b. Romania, Mar. 31, 1946; s. Tiberiu and Magdalena (Gross) B.; m. Dora Belgrader, 1976 (div. 1983). MFA, Romanian Inst. Theatre and Film, 1972. Tchr. Yale Sch. Drama, 1979-92; prof. U. Calif., San Diego, 1992—. Stage dir. Woyzeck, 1978, As You Like It, 1979, Ubu Rex, 1980, About Face, 1983, Waiting for Godot (Boston Theatre Critics Circle award), 1983, Measure for Measure, 1984, What the Butler Saw, 1985, Bald Soprano and the Chairs, 1990; dir. episodes TV series Coach, 1993-95; author, dir.: Happy Days, 1986, The Miser, 1986, Rameau's Nephew, 1988, Scapin, 1989, Servant of Two Masters, 1991, Ubu Rock, 1995, The Imaginary Invalid, 1998;. Mem. Soc. for Stage Dirs. and Choreographers, Dirs. Guild Am., Screen Actors Guild.

BELIĆ WEISS, ZORAN, artist, educator; b. Beograd, Srbija, Yugoslavia, Apr. 24, 1955; came to the U.S., 1989; s. Milan and Ljubinka (Vidosavljević) Belić; m. Mila Djermanović, 1999. BFA in Painting, U. Arts, Beograd, Yugoslavia, 1981; BA in Philosophy, U. Beograd, 1985; MFA in Multimedia, Rutgers U., 1991. Pvt. practice Mission Viejo, Calif.; art dir. D'Arcy, Masius, Benton & Bowles, Inc., New York City, 1991-93; prof. Miss. State (Miss.) U., 1993-96, U. Denver, Colo., 1996-97, Art Inst. So. Calif., Laguna Beach, 1997—, U. Calif., Irvine, 1998—; dir. gen. Imperium DeSign, Cosmopolis, Calif., 1998—. Exhibited in 16 one-man shows; exhibited in 125 group shows; Author: Academy of Arts and Sciences Dictionary of Visual Arts, 1989; lectr. in field; contbr. articles to profl. jours. Tchr. Internat. Aikido Fedn., Mission Viejo, Calif., 1988—. Recipient II award Internat. Drawing Triennial, Wroclaw, Poland, 1981, IV award, Internat. Drawing Biennial, Rijeka, Yugoslavia, 1988; ULUS fellow Beograd, Yugoslavia, 1986-87, Rsch. grantee U.S. Dept. Interior, Washington, 1996. Mem. Internat. Assn. Aesthetics, Internat. Aikido Fedn., Coll. Art Assn., Udruzenje Likovnih Umetnika Srbije (v.p. 1989). Avocations: contemplation. E-mail: zbelic@pacbell.net. Home: 21622 Marguerite Pkwy Apt 144 Mission Viejo CA 92692-4409

BELILLE, RONALD, safety and security coordinator; b. Portland, Nov. 22, 1947; s. Frank and Geraldine (Kron) B. AA in Law Enforcement, Portland Community Coll., 1970; student, Fed. Law Enforcement Tng. Ctr., Glynco, Ga., 1978; BS in Adminstrn. Justice, Portland State U., 1979; AA in Occupational Safety and Health, Mt. Hood Community Coll., 1985; grad., Police Reserve Acad., Oregon City, Oreg., 1985; grad. Intermediate Security Acad., Clackamas Community Coll., 1987; AA in Mgmt. and Supervisory Devel., Portland Community Coll., 1988; postgrad., Portland State U., 1985. Cert. emergency med. technician 1. Correctional officer State Penitentiary, Salem, Oreg., 1972; fed. protective officer Fed. Protective Svcs., Portland, 1978; safety/security officer Precision Castparts, Portland, 1979-83, security coordinator, 1983-93; security coordinator Portland Gen. Elec., 1995-96, Tri-Met Transit System, 1997—; CPR instr., first aid instr., portable fire extinguishers instr. Precision Castparts, 1983-85; chmn. steering com. Intermediate Security Acad. Clackamas Community Coll., 1987; project coord.City of Portland Office of the City Auditor, 1993, project asst. City of Portland Office of the Mayor, 1994. Vol. asst. counselor Multiple County Adult Probation/Parole, Portland, Oreg., 1975; vol. asst. recognizance Officer Multiple County Ct., Oreg., 1982; mem. police and law enforcement task force Citizen's Crime Commn., 1989-93); vice chair Citizens Bur. Adv. Coordinating Com. City of Portland; mem. Portland bur. adv. com. Portland Police Bureau; bd. dirs. Ryles Med. Ctr. Evaluation and Treatment. With USAF, 1966-68. Mem. Am. Soc. for Indsl. Security (chmn. legis. com. 1989-90, treas. 1990-91), Am. Soc. Safety Engrs., Nat. Assn. Chiefs Police, Portland Police Athletic Assn., Masons, Elks, Phi Theta Kappa. Avocations: racquetball, chess, reading. Home: 1238 SE 47th Ave Portland OR 97215-2512

BELKNAP, JODI PARRY, graphic designer, writer, business owner; b. New Canaan, Conn., June 4, 1939; d. Corliss Lloyd and Joan (Pike) Parry; m. William Belknap III, Feb. 20, 1970 (div. Nov. 1982). AB in English and Writing, Barnard Coll., 1962; MA in Drama and Theater, U. Hawaii at Manoa, Honolulu, 1988. Life elem. tchr. credential, Calif. Tchr. grade 6 Ruth Fyfe Sch., Las Vegas, Nev., 1963-64; tchr. grades. 2,3 Schilling Sch., Hayward, Calif., 1964-69; master tchr. U. Calif., Hayward, 1967-69; editor Island Heritage Ltd., Honolulu, 1970-73; Pacific bur. chief OAG Pubis. (Dun and Bradstreet), Honolulu, 1972-82; freelance writer, columnist various mags. and publs., 1976-88; owner Belknap Pub. and Design, Honolulu, 1987—. Author: (books) Majesty, The Exceptional Trees of Hawaii, 1982, Kaanapali, 1981, Halekulani, 1982, (children's book) Felisa and the Magic Tikling Bird, 1973; prin. design projects for Gray Line Hawaii, 1993-95, Sheraton Hotels in Hawaii, 1988—, others; Hawaiian corr. Sr. Travel Tips, 1997. Pro bono pub. Friends of Honolulu Bot. Gardens, 1996—. Recipient Gold award Hospitality Mktg. Assn. Internat., 1995, award Hawaii chpt. Pub. Rels. Soc. Am., 1993, 94, Ilima award of excellence Internat. Assn. Bus. Communicators, 1989, 90. Mem. Am. Inst. Graphic Arts, Soc. Children's Book Writers, Small Bus. Hawaii. Avocations: swimming, hiking, family trips. Address: Belknap Pub PO Box 22387 Honolulu HI 96823-2387

BELL, ALAN, publishing company executive; b. L.A., Mar. 14, 1945. BA in Sociology, UCLA, 1969; postgrad., NYU, 1972-73; BS in Bus., SUNY, 1985; postgrad., Calif. State U., L.A., 1991. Psychiat. social worker dept. forensic psychiatry NYU Med. Ctr., Bellevue Hosp. Prison Ward, 1969-71; exec. asst. to vice chancellor adminstrv. affairs CUNY, 1971-72; pres. Intertypographics, N.Y.C., 1973-79; product mgr. Graphic Products, Inc., L.A., 1986-89; prodn. mgr. Hi-Speed Advt. Typography, Inc., L.A., 1979-89; film critic L.A. Sentinel, 1985-94; pres. Blk Pub. Co., Inc., L.A., 1988—; film reviewer Motion Picture Assn. Am., 1986—. Appt. to Coun. on Intergroup Rels., 1979. Recipient Martin Luther King. Jr. grant, 1973, 73-74, N.Y. State Scholar Incentive award, 1972-74, Francis Emory Fitch Meml. award Printing Industries of Met. N.Y., 1975. Office: 6709 La Tijera Blvd # 402 Los Angeles CA 90045-2017

BELL, DANIEL CARROLL, realtor, community association, ranch and land manager; b. Chgo., July 17, 1940; s. Daniel Gregory and Inez Margarite (Carroll) B.; m. Elaine Paula Rhody, Feb. 1, 1960; children: Tana Lou, Daniel Arden, Andrea Jane. Student, Colo. State U., 1958-62, Reisch Coll. Auctioneering, Mason City, Iowa, 1983. Cert. assn. mgmt. specialist, ind. cmty. mgr. Mgr. ptnr. Three Bell Ranch, Ft. Collins, Colo., 1958-69; sales rep. Pacific Vegetable Oil Co., San Francisco, 1969-70; mng. dir. Paveoor A.G. subs. PVO Internat., Rotterdam, Netherlands, 1970-71; nat. sales mgr. PVO Internat., San Francisco, 1971-72; v.p. commodity trading San Pablo Mfg. Co. subs. PVO Internat., Manila, Philippines, 1972-74; v.p. Rothschild Brokerage Co., San Francisco, 1975-76; owner, prin. Feed, Etc., Harbor, Oreg., 1976-79; commodity specialist Shearson Loeb Rhodes, Medford, Oreg., 1979-80; exec. v.p., gen. mgr. Superior Credit Assocs., Inc., Medford, 1981-86; mng. ptnr. Three Bell Land Co., Pierce, Colo., 1986—; ptnr. Legacy Transp. Co., 1986-93; v.p. Bell & Assocs. Ltd., 1993—; gen. mgr. Greenfield Village RV Resort Assn., 1994-98. Mem. Medford (Oreg.) Planning Commn., 1981-84, Medford Sister Cities Commn., 1984; treas. Jackson County Rep. Ctrl. Com., Medford, 1982-84; arbitrator Better Bus. Bur., Medford and Ft. Collins, Colo., 1984-89; candidate Oreg. Ho. Reps., 1984; mem. Mesa (Ariz.) Human Svcs. Adv. Bd., 1994-95; grad. Mesa Citizens Police Acad., 1995, v.p., 1996, pres., 1998—, facilitator, 1997-98; mem. Housing and Human Svcs. Adv. Bd., Mesa, 1998-99. With USAR, 1958-63, Colo. Air N.G., 1963-65. Mem. NRA, Nat. Assn. Recreational Vehicle Parks and Campgrounds (cert. park operator), Cmty. Assn. Inst. (cert. assn. mgmt. specialist), Inst. Cmty. Mmgt. (cert. ind. cmty. mgr.), Ariz. Travel Parks Assn. (bd. dirs. 1997-99, treas.), Elks. Republican. Presbyterian. Avocations: fishing, golf. Office: 5434 E Calypso Cir Mesa AZ 85206-2246

BELL, DENISE LOUISE, newspaper reporter, photographer, librarian; b. Washington, Nov. 27, 1967; d. Richard Keith Bell and Kay Lorraine (Sutherland) Reynolds. Student, Inst. Adventiste du Saleve, Collonges, France, 1988; BA in French, Loma Linda U., 1990. Yearbook editor Loma Linda U., La Sierra, Calif., 1989-90; desk technician Loma Linda U., Loma Linda, Calif., 1990-92; staff writer Inland Empire Cmty. Newspapers, Colton, Calif., 1990-91; city editor Inland Empire Cmty. Newspapers, San Bernardino, Calif., 1991-94; asst. circ. supr. Del Webb Meml. Libr. Loma Linda (Calif.) U., 1994—; reporter City Newspaper Group, Colton, Calif., 1995—. Asst. leader Girl Scouts U.S., Walla Walla, Wash., 1986; co-leader Girl Scouts Switzerland, Geneva, 1987, Girl Scouts U.S., Loma Linda, 1988-93. Mem. Toastmasters. Avocations: photography, writing, archery. Home: 9 Crooks St Loma Linda CA 92354-1935

BELL, DONALD RAY, civil engineer; b. Shawnee, Okla., Apr. 23, 1935; s. Ray L. and Mary Ruth (Wilson) B.; m. Jimmie S., Sept. 1, 1957 (div. 1976); children: Jeri, Johnna, Nolan, Charles, Mary; m. Joy Miller, Aug. 17, 1996; children: Richard L., R. Lee Berlemann. BS in Civil Engring., N. Mex. State U., 1966. Registered profl. engr., N. Mex. Estimator Burn Construction, Las Cruces, N. Mex., 1959-62; engring. tchr. N. Mex. State U., Las Cruces, 1962-66; county engr. Los Alamos (N. Mex.) County, 1966-68; dir. pub. works Hobbs (N. Mex.) City, 1968-69; asst. dir. pub. works City of Las Cruces, 1970-71, dir. pub. works, 1971-82; profl. civil engr. U.S. Dept. Defense, White Sands Missile Range, N. Mex., 1982—; dir. Bell, Inc., Las Cruces, 1997—. Pres. Dona Ana County Horseman's Assn., Las Cruces, 1972; mem. Dona Ana Dem. Party, Las Cruces, 1990—. With USMC, 1957-59. Mem. Nat. Assn. Retired Federal Employees, Pub. Employees Retirement Assn. N. Mex. Methodist. Avocations: writing, playing harmonica and guitar. Office: Bell Inc 4633 Lamar Rd Las Cruces NM 88005 Office: Bell Inc PO Box 577 Las Cruces NM 88004

BELL, DONALD WILLIAM, experimental psychologist; b. L.A., Apr. 28, 1936; s. Samuel Chamblis and Betty M. (Welz) B. BA, U. So. Calif., 1959, MA, 1963, PhD, 1966. Rsch. assoc. Subcom. on Noise Rschr. Ctr., L.A., 1962-66; postdoctoral fellow Stanford (Calif.) U., 1966-68; rsch. psychologist SRI Internat., Menlo Park, Calif., 1968-76, sr. rsch. psychologist, 1976-82, program mgr., 1982-83, dir. speech rsch. program, 1983-89, dir., sensory sci. and tech. ctr., 1989-93; pres. Digital Voice Corp., 1982—; prin., dir. Security Group Inc., 1996—; pres. Digital Voice Corp., 1982—; prin., dir. Security Group, Inc., 1996—. Contbr. articles to profl. jours. Mem. planning commn. Town of Portola Valley, Calif., 1980-92. Mem. IEEE, Acoustical Soc. Am., Psychonomic Soc., Am. Voice I/O Soc. (dir.). Republican. Home and Office: 1288 Spring Rd Montecito CA 93108-2831

BELL, ELOUISE MILDRED, English language educator, writer, speaker; b. Scranton, Pa., Sept. 10, 1935; d. Alexander Hurlow and Esther Myra (Beppler) B. BA magna cum laude, U. Ariz., 1957; MA, Brigham Young U., 1959. Instr. English Brigham Young U., Provo, Utah, 1959-60, 63-73, asst. prof., 1973, assoc. prof., 1981, prof., 1989, assoc. dean honors and gen. edn., 1989-92, prof. emeritus, 1994; prof. English Berzenyi Coll., Hungary, 1992-93; field dir. Brigham Young U. Washington, D.C. Seminar, 1981; pub. spkr. Utah Humanities Coun., Salt Lake City, 1994-97. Author: (essays) Only When I Laugh, 1990; author (monthly column) Network mag., 1979-95, assoc. editor, 1983-95; editor: Shall I Ever Forget This Day?, 1980; columnist Salt Lake Tribune, 1995—. Mem. Gov.'s Commn. on Child Abuse, Salt Lake City, 1989-92; mem. gen. bd. of young women LDS Ch., 1973-78. Named Outstanding Young Woman of Utah, 1970; recipient Woman of Achievement award Gov.'s Commn. for Women and Families, 1997. Mem. Utah Women's Forum, Assn. for Mormon Letters (life), Women's Studies Assn. (editl. assoc.). Democrat. E-mail: Bellabell@aol.com. Home: 827 N 435 E Orem UT 84097-3359

BELL, GENE, newspaper publishing executive. Pres. and ceo San Diego Union-Tribune, San Diego, 1992—. Office: San Diego Union-Tribune 350 Camino De La Reina San Diego CA 92108-3003*

BELL, LARRY STUART, artist; b. Chgo., Dec. 6, 1939; s. Hyman David and Rebecca Ann (Kriegmont) B.; three children. Student, Chouinard Art Inst., L.A., 1957-59. One man exhbns. include Stedelijk Mus., Amsterdam, 1967, Pasadena (Calif.) Art Mus., 1972, Oakland (Calif.) Mus., 1973, Ft. Worth Art Mus., 1975, Santa Barbara (Calif.) Mus. Art, 1976, Washington U., St. Louis, 1976, Art Mus. So. Tex., Corpus Christi, 1976, Erica Williams, Anne Johnson Gallery, Seattle, 1978, Hayden Gallery, MIT, Cambridge, Mass., 1977, Hudson River Mus., Yonkers, N.Y., 1981, Newport Harbor Art Mus., 1982, Marian Goodman Gallery, N.Y.C., 1982, Ruth S. Schaffner Gallery, Santa Barbara, Calif., Arco Ctr. Visual Arts, L.A., 1983, Unicorn Gallery, Aspen, Colo., 1983, Butler Inst. Am. Art, Youngstown, Ohio, 1984, Leigh Yawkey Woodson Art Mus., Wausau, Wis., 1984, Colorado Springs, Colo. Fine Arts Ctr., 1987, Cleve. Ctr. for Contemporary Art, Ohio, 1987, Mus. Contemporary Art, L.A., 1987, Am. Acad. and Inst. Arts and Letters, N.Y.C., 1987, Boise (Idaho) Gallery Art, 1987, Gilbert Brownstone Gallery, Paris, 1987, Braunstein/Quay Gallery, San Francisco, 1987, 89, Fine Arts Gallery, N.Mex. State Fairgrounds, 1987, Laguna Art Mus., Laguna Beach, Calif., 1987, High Mus. Art, Atlanta, 1988, Sena Galleries West, Santa Fe, 1989, Kiyo Higashi Gallery, L.A., 1989, 90, 94, Musee D'Art Contemporain, Lyon, France, 1989, Contemporary Art Ctr., Kansas City, Mo., 1989, San Antonio Art Inst., 1990, New Gallery, Houston, 1990, Braunstein/Quay Gallery, San Francisco, 1990, Galerie Rolf Ricke, Koln, Fed. Republic Germany, 1990, Galerie Montenay, Paris, 1990, 95, The Works Gallery, L.A., 1990, Galerie Kammer, Hamburg, Germany, 1990, Tony Shafrazi Gallery, N.Y.C., 1991, Tucson Mus. Art, 1991, New Gallery, Houston, 1991, Janus Gallery, Santa Fe, 1992, Kiyo Higashi Gallery, L.A., 1992, 93, New Gallery, Houston, 1992, Tampa Mus. Art, 1992, Kiyo Higashi Gallery, L.A., 1993, 94, New Directions Gallery, Taos, N.M., 1993, Dartmouth St. Gallery, Albuquerque, 1994, Braunstein/Quay Gallery, San Francisco, 1994, Leedy/Voulkos Gallery, Kansas City, 1994, Kiyo Higashi Gallery, L.A., 1994, U. Wyo. Art Mus., Laramie, 1995, Denver Art Mus., 1995, Indigo Gallery, Boca Raton, Fla., 1995, Harwood Mus. U. N. Mex., Taos, 1995, Galerie Montenay, Paris, 1995, Joy Tash Gallery, Scottsdale, Ariz., 1996, Kiyo Higashi Gallery, L.A., 1996, Boulder Mus. Contemporary Art, 1996, Braunstein/Quay Gallery, San Francisco, 1996, Art et Industrie Gallery, N.Y.C., 1996, The Albuquerque Mus., 1997, The Reykjavik Mcpl. Art Mus., Iceland, 1997, Bergen (Norway) Kunstmus., 1998, Seljord (Norway) Art Assn., 1998, group exhbns. include Mus. Modern Art, N.Y.C., 1965, 79, Jewish Mus., N.Y.C., 1966, Whitney Mus. Am. Art, 1966, Guggenheim Mus., N.Y.C., 1967, Tate Gallery, London, 1970, Hayward Gallery, London, 1971, Detroit Inst. Arts, 1973, Nat. Collections Fine Arts, 1975, San Francisco Mus. Modern Art, 1976, Museo de Arte Contemporaneo de Caracas, Venezuela, 1978, Aspen Ctr. for Visual Arts, 1980, Fruit Market Gallery, Edinburgh, Scotland, 1980, Albuquerque Mus., 1980, Art Inst. Chgo., 1982, Santa Barbara Art Mus., 1984, The Rufino Tamayo Mus., Mexico City, 1985, Colorado Springs Fine Art Ctr., 1986, Mus. Comtemporary Art, 1986, AAAL, 1986, Ariz. State U., Tempe, 1987, Phoenix Art Mus., 1987, Braunstein/Quay Gallery, 1987, The Works Gallery, Long Beach, 1987, Davis/McClain Gallery, Houston, 1987, Basel (Switzerland) Art Fair, 1989, Galerie Joan Prats, Barcelona, Spain, 1989, Musee d'Art Contemporain, Lyon, 1989, Harcus Gallery, Boston, 1989, Colorado Springs Gallery Contemporary Art, 1990, Mus. Contemporary Art, L.A., 1990, Musee de Grenoble, France, 1990, L.A. County Mus. Art, 1991, U. So. Calif. Fisher Gallery, L.A., 1991, Espace Lyonnais d'Art Contemporain, France, 1991, Galerie Montenay, Paris, 1991, Galerie Rolf Ricke, Köln, Germany, 1991, Arolsen, Germany, 1992, Leedy/Voulkos Gallery, Kansas City, Mo., 1993, Musee du Palais du Luxembourg, Paris, 1993, Denver Art Mus., 1993, New Gallery, Houston, 1993, Whitney Mus. Am. Art, N.Y.C., 1993, Conn., 1994, Parrish Art Mus., Southampton, N.Y., 1994, Kiyo Higashi Gallery, L.A., 1994, Madison (Wis.) Art Ctr., 1994, Whitney Mus. Am. Art, 1995, Galerie Ncht St. Stephen, Vienna, 1995, Galerie Rolf Ricke, Cologne, 1996, Colorado Springs Fine Art Ctr., 1996, Mus. N.Mex., Santa Fe, 1996, Orange County Mus. Art, Newport Beach, Calif., 1997, Harwood Mus. U. N.Mex., Taos, 1997, Louisiana Mus. Modern Art, Humlebaek, Denmark, 1997, Milw. Art Mus., 1997, Whitney Mus. Am. Art, N.Y., 1997, San Jose (Calif.) Mus. Art, 1997; represented in permanent collections including Nat. Collection Fine Arts, Musee de Art Contemporaine, Lyon, France, Mus. of Fine Arts, Santa Fe, N.Mex., Whitney Mus. Am. Art, N.Y.C., 1994, Laguna Gloria Mus., Austen, 1994, H & W Bechtler Gallery, Charlotte, 1994, Calif. Crafts Mus., San Francisco, 1994, Parrish Art Mus., Southampton, 1994, Tate Gallery, London, Gallery New South Wales, Australia, Albright-Knox Gallery, Buffalo, Art Inst. Chgo., Denver Art Mus., Dallas Mus. Fine Arts, Guggenheim Mus., Houston, L.A. County Mus., Victoria and Albert Mus., London, San Antonio Mus. Art, The Menil Collection, Houston, Mpls. Inst. Arts, Mus. Ludwig, Koln, Albuquerque Mus., Mpls. Inst. Arts, others; instr. sculpture, U. South Fla., Tampa, U. Calif., Berkeley, Irvine, 1970-73, So. Calif. Inst. of Architecture, 1988, Taos (N.Mex.) Inst. of Art, 1989-94. Copley Found. grantee, 1962; Guggenheim Found. fellow, 1970; Nat. Endowment Arts grantee, 1975; recipient Gov.'s award for excellence in visual arts, N.Mex., 1990. Office: PO Box 4101 Taos NM 87571-9998

BELL, LEE PHILLIP, television personality, television producer; b. Chgo.; d. James A. and Helen (Novak) P.; m. William Joseph Bell, Oct. 23, 1954; children: William J., Bradley, Lauralee. B.S. in Microbiology, Northwestern U., 1950. With CBS-TV, Chgo., 1952-86; pres. Bell-Phillip TV Prodns., 1985—; bd. dirs. William Wrigley, Jr. Co., Chgo. Bank Commerce, Phillips Flowers Inc. TV and radio shows include Lee Phillip Show, Chgo., from 1952, Lady and Tiger Show WBBM Radio, from 1962, WBBM TV from 1964; hostess Noon Break, numerous TV Spls. including Forgotten Children, The Rape of Paulette (nat. Emmy award, duPont Columbia award); Children and Divorce (Chgo. Emmy award) co-creator: (with William Bell) The Young and the Restless CBS-TV daytime drama, 1973 (Emmy award); co-creator, exec. producer The Bold and the Beautiful, 1987—. Bd. dirs. United Cerebral Palsy, Chgo. Unlimited, Northwestern U. Hosp., Chgo. Heart Assn., Nat. Com. Prevention of Child Abuse, Mental Health Assn., Children's Home and Aid Soc., Salvation Army (L.A. bd. dirs.), Family Focus; mem. Chgo. Maternity Ctr.; life mem. Northwestern U. Bd. Trustees. Recipient 16 Chgo. Emmys; Top Favorite Female award TV Guide mag., 1956, Outstanding Woman of Radio and TV award McCall's mag., 1957-58, 65, bd. govs. award Chgo. chpt. Nat. Acad. TV Arts and Scis., 1977, William Booth award for community svc. Salvation Army, 1990; named Person of Yr. Broadcast Advt. Club, Chgo., 1980. Mem. Am. Women Radio and TV (Golden Mike award 1968, Broadcaster of Yr. 1993), Acad. TV Arts and Scis. (bd. dirs.), Chgo. chpt. Acad. TV Arts and Scis., Women's Athletic Club of Chgo., Comml. Club, Delta Delta Delta. Office: CBS-TV City 7800 Beverly Blvd Los Angeles CA 90036-2188

BELL, LEO S., retired physician; b. Newark, Nov. 7, 1913; s. Alexander M. and Marie (Saxon) B.; AB, Syracuse U., 1934; MD, 1938; m. Edith Lewis, July 3, 1938; children: Jewyl Linn, David Alden. Intern, N.Y.C. Hosp., 1938, Bklyn. Hosp., 1939-40; resident in pediatrics Sea View Hosp., N.Y.C., 1940-41, N.Y.C. Hosp., 1941-42; practice medicine specializing in pediatrics, San Mateo, Calif., 1946-86; mem. staff Mills Meml. Hosp., San Mateo, Peninsula Hosp. & Med. Ctr., Burlingame, Children's Hosp., San Francisco; assoc. clin. prof. pediatrics U. Calif. Med Sch., San Francisco, prof. clin. emeritus Stanford Med. Sch., Palo Alto; mem. curriculum & ednl. affairs comm. U. San Francisco Med. Sch., adminstv. coun.; med. columnist San Mateo Times. Bd. dirs. Mills Hosp. Found., San Mateo, U. Calif. San Francisco Hosp., San Mateo County Heart Assn., Hillsborough Schs. Found. (Calif.), 1980-83. Capt. as flight surgeon USAAF, 1942-46. Recipient bronze and silver medals Am. Heart Assn. Diplomate Am. Bd. Pediatrics. Fellow Am. Acad. Pediatrics, Am. Pub. Health Assn.; mem. Clin. Faculty Assn. (pres.), Calif. Fedn. Pediatric Socs. (pres.), Am. Fedn. Pediatric Socs. (pres.), Calif. Med. Assn., Am. Pub. Health Assn., Air Force Assn., AMA (alt. del. to ho. of dels.), Calif. Med. Assn. (ho. of dels.), San Mateo County Med. Assn., Internat. Snuff Bottle Soc., Hong Kong Snuff Bottle Soc., San Francisco Gem and Mineral Soc., World Affairs Coun. San Francisco, U. San Francisco Med. Sch. Clin. Faculty Assn. (coun., pres.), Peninsula Golf and Country Club, Commonwealth Club. Contbr. articles to profl. jours. Home: 220 Roblar Ave Burlingame CA 94010-6846 Office: PO Box 1877 San Mateo CA 94401-0946

BELL, LESLIE ANN, sculptor, moldmaker; b. Billings, Mont., Dec. 29, 1960; d. Robert Burns and Farrell Jane (Coffman) Stewart; m. Bruce E. Bell, Dec. 18, 1996. BA, Eastern Mont. Coll., 1987; MA, Eastern Ill. U., 1988. Asst. mgr. KMART Corp., Billings, Mont., 1977-87; foundry Ariz. Bronze, Tempe, Ariz., 1988-90; prin., pres. LASH Quality Molds & Sculpture Supplies Inc., Portland, Oreg., 1990—; moldmaker Fredric Remington Art Mus., Ogdensburg, N.Y., 1997, personal work specializing in figurative abstraction and bronze skulls cast from life. Mem. Investment Club (v.p. 1996—), Portland Art Mus. Avocations: motorcycling, windsurfing, canoeing, fishing. Home: 7615 NE 156th Ave Vancouver WA 98682 Office: LASH Quality Molds 4702 NE 102nd Ave Portland OR 97220

BELL, M. JOY MILLER, financial planner, real estate broker; b. Enid, Okla., Dec. 29, 1934; d. H. Lee and M.E. Madge (Hatfield) Miller; m. Richard L.D. Berlemann, July 21, 1957 (div. Nov. 1974); children: Richard Louis, Randolph Lee; m. Donald R. Bell, Aug. 17, 1996; children: Jeri Lynn, Johnna Kay, Nolan Ray, Charles, Mary. BSBA, N.Mex. State U., 1956. CFP; grad. Realtors Inst.; fellow Life Underwriting Tng. Coun. Tchr. of bus. and mathematics Alamogordo (N.Mex.), Las Cruces (N. Mex.) and Omaha Pub. Schs., 1956-63; tchr., dir. Evelyn Wood Reading Dynamics Southern N.Mex. Inst., 1967-68; registered rep. Westamerica Fin. Corp., Denver, 1968-76; gen. agt. Security Benefit Life, Topeka, 1969—, Delta Life & Annuity, Memphis, 1969—; registered rep. Am. Growth Fund Sponsors, Inc., Denver, 1976—; pres., broker Fin. Design Corp. R.E. (name changed to Bell, Inc. 1997), Las Cruces, 1977—; ofcl. goodwill amb. U.S. Treasury, U.S. Savs. Bond Divsn., Washington, 1968-70. Contbr. articles to profl. jours. Vice pres. Dona Ana County Fedn. Rep. Women. Recipient Top Sales Person award Investment Trust and Assurance, 1976-77. Mem. Nat. Assn. Realtors, Nat. Assn. Life Underwriters, Nat. Assn. Ret. Fed. Employees (program chmn. local chpt.), Internat. Assn. Registered Fin. Planners, S.W. N.Mex. Assn. Life Underwriters (treas. 1990-91, pres.-elect 1991-92, pres. 1992-93), Las Cruces City Alumnae Panhellenic, Altrusa, Order Ea. Star, Delta Zeta. Methodist. Home: 4633 Lamar Rd Las Cruces NM 88005-3558 Office: Bell Inc PO Box 577 Las Cruces NM 88004-0577

BELL, RICHARD G., lawyer; b. Billings, Mont., Sept. 16, 1947; s. George A.W. and Mary Helen (Sharp) B.; m. Linda Carol Riggs, June 21, 1969; children: Stephen, Geoffrey. AB, Stanford U., 1969; JD, U. Calif., San Francisco, 1972. Bar: Calif.; U.S. Supreme Ct., 1990; U.S. Ct. Appeals Calif. (9th cir.) 1973; U.S. Dist. Ct. Calif. (no. dist., 1972, cen. dist., 1976). Assoc. Finch, Sauers, Player & King, Palo Alto, Calif., 1972-76; ptnr. Finch, Sauers, Player & Bell, Palo Alto, 1976-83; gen. counsel Watkins-Johnson Co., Palo Alto, 1983-90; v.p., gen. counsel Watkins-Johnson Co., 1990-97; ptnr. Corp. Advisory Law Group, Los Altos, Calif., 1998—. Bd. dirs. Family Svc. Assn., Palo Alto, 1981-87; trustee Mountain View Los Altos Union H.S. Dist., 1990-98; pres. bd. Los Altos Conservatory Theater, 1991-95. Mem. ABA, Calif. Bar Assn., Santa Clara County Bar Assn., Palo Alto Area Bar Assn. Republican. Episcopalian. Office: Corp Adv Law Group 40 Main St Los Altos CA 94022-2902

BELL, W. DONALD, electronics company executive. Pres., CEO, chmn. Bell Microproducts, San Jose. Office: Bell Microproducts 1941 Ringwood Ave San Jose CA 95131-1721*

BELL, WAYNE STEVEN, lawyer; b. L.A., June 24, 1954; s. Joseph and Jane Barbara (Barsook) B.; m. M. Susan Modzelewski, Apr. 1, 1989; 1 child, Seth Joseph Bell. BA magna cum laude, UCLA, 1976; JD, Loyola U., L.A., 1979; Advanced Mgmt. Program, Rutgers U., 1992. Bar: Calif. 1980, U.S. Dist. Ct. (cen. dist.) 1981, U.S. Tax Ct. 1981, U.S. Ct. Appeals (9th cir.) 1981, U.S. Dist. Ct. (so. and no. dists.) Calif. 1983, U.S. Supreme Ct. 1984, D.C. 1986, Tex. 1995; lic. real estate broker, Calif. Intern office of gov. State of Calif., Sacramento, summer 1976; assoc. Levinson, Rowen, Miller, Jacobs & Kabrins, L.A., 1980-82; sr. assoc. Montgomery, Gascou, Gemmill & Thornton, L.A., 1982-84; counsel, project developer Thomas Safran & Associates, L.A., 1984-85; of counsel Greenspan, Glasser & Medina, Santa Monica, Calif., 1984-86; assoc. gen. counsel Am. Diversified Cos., Costa Mesa, Calif., 1985-88; legal cons. Project Atty., L.A., 1988-89; sr. counsel, asst. sec. Ralphs Grocery Co., L.A., 1989—; judge pro tem Mcpl. Ct. South

Bay Jud. Dist., 1987, L.A. Superior Ct., 1991, 94, 97; settlement officer L.A. Mcpl. Ct., Settlement Officer Program, 1990-92; spl. master State Bar Calif., 1991-92. Chief note and comment editor Loyola U. Law Rev., 1978-79; contbr. articles to profl. jours. and gen. pubs. Vol. atty. Westside Legal Svcs., Santa Monica, 1982-87; legal ombudsman Olympics Ombudsman Program L.A. County Bar Assn., 1984; gov. apptd. mem. Calif. adv. coun. Legal Svcs. Corp., 1982-88, Autism Soc. Am., Amnesty Internat.; contbg. mem. Dem. Nat. Com.; mem. leadership coun. So. Poverty Law Ctr.; charter mem. presdl. task force Ams. for Change; bd. dirs. Am. Theatre Arts, Hollywood, Calif., 1983-84; pres., exec. com., bd. dirs. Programs for the Developmentally Handicapped, Inc., L.A., 1987-92; chmn. bd. appeals handicapped accommodations City of Manhattan Beach, 1986-88; bd. dirs. The Foodbank of So. Calif., 1991-94, sec., 1993; legal oversight com. Legal Corps L.A., 1995-97; sec. bd. trustees The Ralphs/Food 4 Less Found., 1995—; vol. L.A. County Bar Assn., Barristers Homeless Shelter Advocacy Project, 1996—. Mem. Calif. Bar Assn. (legal svcs. sect. standing com. legal problems of aging 1983-86, chmn. legis. subcom. 1984-86, conf. dels. alternate 1987), D.C. Bar Assn. (real estate sect. com. on comml. real estate), Legal Assistance Assn. Calif. (bd. dirs., mem. exec. com., legis. strategy com. 1984-86), Loyola Law Sch. (advocate), Los Angeles County Bar Assn. (mem. exec. com. labor and employment law sect. 1997—). Democrat. Avocations: sailing, hiking, human behavior study, photography, travel. Office: Ralphs Grocery Co PO Box 54143 Los Angeles CA 90054-0143

BELL, WILLIAM JAMES, music educator; b. East Moline, Ill., July 12, 1936; s. William David and Lottie Mae (Rush) B.; m. Gale Jean Norman, Dec. 26, 1959; children: Deborah Bell Cole, David William, Thomas Norman. BA in Music Edn., U. Iowa, 1958, MA in Music Edn., 1963. H.s. band dir. Traer (Iowa) Cmty. Schs., 1960-63; dir. jr. h.s. band Oakland (Calif.) Pub. Schs., 1963-69; piano accompanist The Supremes Motown Prodns., 1970; music instr. Peralta C.C., Oakland, 1970—; adj. prof. U. Calif., Berkeley, 1995—. Composer: Right On, 1973, East Meets West, 1978; prodr.: Basically Bill Bell, 1981, The Jazz Professor, 1995. Mem. Sigma Pi Phi. Home: 6612 Hagen Blvd El Cerrito CA 94530-1717

BELLAH, LINDA RUTH, design consultant; b. Dallas, Nov. 8, 1944; d. Glover Bee and Ola Moss (Rogers) B.; m. Larry Hurtado, 1965 (div. 1975); 1 child, Tiffany Lynn Hurtado Cerasoli; m. Theodore Buder, 1980 (div. 1988); m. Bob Cote, 1990 (div. 1992). BA in Edn., Ctrl. Bible Coll., 1966. Min. Assemblies of God, Lewisville, Tex., 1959-63; youth pastor Assemblies of God Ch., Akron, Ohio, 1967-68; youth pastor, tchr. Assemblies of God Ch., Cleve., 1968-69; activities coord. Assemblies of God Ch., Glenview, Ill., 1970-74; sales rep. King & Leslie, Denver, 1976-78; pres. Bellah Enterprises, Canon City, Colo., 1978-96. Founder Women's Retreats (Nat.) Assemblies of God, Chgo., 1974; pres. No. Ill. Assemblies of God Women's Missionary Coun., Chgo., 1974-75; co-founder Rocky Mt. Singles, Denver, 1978-81; coord. Cancun (Mex.) Disaster Relief, 1987; mem. Valley Bible Ch., 1990-96; co-tchr. Bible Study Group, 1996. Named Vol. of Yr. Step 13, 1990, Pres. Bush 1000 Points of Lights, 1991. Mem. Nat. Assn. Bus. Women, Christian Bus. Women, Colo. Hist. Soc., Great Books Discussion Program, Rotary Internat. (fund raiser 1995). Republican. Avocations: camping, reading, travel. Home: 1226 Elm Ave Canon City CO 81212-4830 Office: Deweese Lodge Bed & Breakfast 1226 Elm Ave Canon City CO 81212-4830

BELLAH, ROBERT NEELLY, sociologist, educator; b. Altus, Okla., Feb. 23, 1927; s. Luther Hutton and Lillian Lucille (Neelly); m. Melanie Hyman, Aug. 17, 1949; children: Jennifer, Harriet. BA, Harvard U., 1950, PhD, 1955. Rsch. assoc. Inst. Islamic Studies, McGill U., Montreal, Can., 1955-57; with Harvard U., Cambridge, Mass., 1957-67, prof., 1966-67; mem. faculty dept. sociology U. Calif., Berkeley, 1967-97, Elliott prof. emeritus, 1997—. Author: Tokugawa Religion, 1957, Beyond Belief, 1970, The Broken Covenant, 1975 (Sorokin award Am. Sociol. Assn. 1976), (with Charles Y. Glock) The New Religious Consciousness, 1976, (with Phillip E. Hammond) Varieties of Civil Religion, 1980, (with others) Habits of the Heart, 1985, (with others) The Good Society, 1991. With U.S. Army, 1945-46. Fulbright fellow, 1960-61; recipient Harbison award Danforth Found., 1971. Mem. Am. Acad. Arts and Scis., Am. Sociol. Assn., Am. Acad. Religion, Am. Philos. Soc. Episcopalian. Office: U Calif Dept Sociology Berkeley CA 94720-1980

BELLANICH, ALICE MARIE, sales representative, minister; b. Seattle, May 31, 1956; d. Neil Carr and Marlene Rae (Pederson) Gemmill; m. Larry K. Bellanich, Aug. 30, 1981; children: Sean, Austin, Beau. BS in Bus. Mgmt., U. Redlands, 1997. Ordained to ministry, 1998. Prin., owner LA-Z-Boy Gallery, Rancho Mirage, Calif., 1985-94; sales rep. LAAGCO Sales, Burbank, Calif., 1997-98, Sebastian Internat. Inc., Woodland Hills, Calif., 1998—; teen minister Ch. Religious Sci., Palm Desert, Calif., 1992—. Avocations: watercolor painting, teen and youth work, soccer, my children, public speaking. Office: Sebastian Internat Inc 6109 DeSoto Ave Woodland Hills CA 91367

BELLER, GERALD STEPHEN, professional magician, former insurance company executive; b. Phila., Aug. 6, 1935; s. Nathan and Adelaide B. (Goldfarb) B.; m. Nancy R. Nelson, June 8, 1968; children: Fay A., Mark S., Royce W., Merrilee A., Marie A., Frank A. CLU, Am. Coll., Bryn Mawr, Pa., 1972. Spl. agt. Prudential Ins. Co., San Bernardino, Calif., 1959-62, div. mgr., 1962-66; agy. supr. Aetna Life & Casualty, L.A., 1966-69, gen. agt., 1969-77; rsch. analyst Investigative Svcs. Bur. San Bernardino County Sheriff's Dept., 1991-95; capt. specialized svcs. bur. San Bernardino County (Calif.) Sheriff's Dept.; profl. magician, 1982—; mem. Magician Magic Castle, Hollywood, Calif. mem. sheriff's coun. San Bernardino County Sheriff's Dept., Apple Valley sheriff's adv. bd. Served with USAF, 1953-57. Recipient Man of Year award, 1961; Manpower Builders award, 1966-69; Agy. Builders award, 1970-72; Pres.'s Trophy award, 1973-74. Mem. Am. Soc. CLUs, Golden Key Soc., Internat. Exec. Svc. Corps. (vol.), Acad. Magical Arts, Internat. Brotherhood of Magicians (Outstanding Magic Lectr. of Yr. 1989-90, Aldini Meml. award 1990), Soc. Am. Magicians. Home: 20625 Tonawanda Rd Apple Valley CA 92307-5736

BELLES, DONALD ARNOLD, pastoral therapist, mental health counselor; b. Sayre, Pa., Mar. 7, 1948; s. William and Alice (Arnold) B.; m. Linda Scheel, July 9, 1981. BA, St. Martin's U., 1973; MDiv, Fuller Theol. Sem., 1977; PhD, Calif. Grad. Sch. Theology, 1981; MBA, City U. Bellevue, 1994; postgrad., Seattle Pacific U., 1997—. Lic. amateur radio operator; ordained to ministry Worldwide Congl. Fellowship, 1989; cert. c.c. tchr., Calif., mental health counselor, Wash., profl. stage hypnotist. Chaplain Vols. of Am., L.A., 1976-78; therapist Greater life Found., Seattle, 1979-81; industrial engr. commercial airplane divsn. Boeing, 1979-80, program planner aerospace divsn., 1980-86, sr., lead program planner electronics divsn., 1986-97, systems analyst, contract tech. mgr., 1989-92, analyst software engring. practices, mgr. total quality improvement project, 1992-95, lead, mgr. computing infrastructure archtl. design team, 1995—, mgr. computing infrastructure design, 1996-97; therapist, dir. clinic Creative Therapies, Seattle, 1982-83; clin. dir. Applied Hypnosis, Tacoma, 1984-87; dir. Active Therapy Assoc., Tacoma, 1988-89; dean of students Coll. Therapeutic Hypnosis, Puyallup, Wash., 1989-93; cons. theological issues, abduction rsch., psychic phenomena, paranormal events; adult edn. instr. Tacoma C.C., 1987-88, Pierce Coll., 1990-92; mem. U.S. Acad. Team to CIS, U. St. Petersburg, Russia, 1994; presenter, lectr. in field; instr. Olympia Diocese Sch. of Theology, 1995; adv. bd. mem. Software Support Profls. Orgn.; cons. Wash. State Offices Supr. of Pub. Instrn. Contbr. articles to profl. jours., prodr. hypnosis, mental health videos in field. Exec. dir. Nat. Assn. to Prevent and Eliminate Child Abuse, Tacoma, 1987-89. Maj. U.S. Army, 1969-75, USAR, 1975—. Fellow Am. Assn. Profl. Hypnotherapists; mem. Nat. Assn. Clergy Hypnotherapists (bd. dirs. 1987-88, editor jour. 1987), Internat. Med. Dental Hypnotherapy Assn., Wash. State Head Injury Found. Avocations: backpacking, swimming, reading, amateur radio.

BELLIS, CARROLL JOSEPH, surgeon, educator; b. Shreveport, La.; s. Joseph and Rose (Bloome) B.; m. Mildred Darmody, Dec. 26, 1939; children: Joseph, David. BS summa cum laude, U. Minn., 1930, MS in Physiology, 1932, PhD in Physiology, 1934, MD, 1936, PhD in Surgery, 1941. Diplomate Am. Bd. Surgery. Fellow in physiology U. Minn., Mpls., 1930-34; resident in surgery U. Minn. Hosps., Mpls., 1937-41; pvt. practice surgery, Long Beach, Calif., 1945-87; mem. staff St. Mary Med. Ctr., Long Beach; prof., chmn. dept. surgery Calif. Coll. Medicine, 1962—; surg. cons. to surgeon gen. U.S. Army; adj. prof. surgery U. Calif. Author: Fundamentals of Human Physiology, A Critique of Reason, Lectures in Medical Physiology; contbr. numerous articles on surgery and physiology to profl. jours. Served to col. M.C. AUS, 1941-46. Recipient Charles Lyman Green prize in physiology, 1934, prize Mpls. Surg. Soc., 1938, ann. award Mississippi Valley Med. Soc., 1955; Alice Shevlin fellow U. Minn., 1932-34. Fellow ACS, Royal Soc. Medicine, Internat. Coll. Surgeons, Am. Coll. Gastroenterology, Am. Med. Writers Assn., Internat. Coll. Angiology (sci. council), Gerontol. Soc., Am. Soc. Abdominal Surgeons, Nat. Cancer Inst., Phlebology Soc. Am., Internat. Acad. Proctology, Peripheral Vascular Soc. Am. (founding); mem. AAAS, Am. Assn. Study Neoplastic Diseases, Mississippi Valley Med. Soc., N.Y. Acad. Scis., Hollywood Acad. Medicine, Am. Geriatrics Soc., Irish Med. Assn., Am. Assn. History Medicine, Pan Pacific Surgical Assn., Indsl. Med. Assn., L.A. Musicians Union (hon.), Pan Am. Med. Assn. (diplomate), Internat. Bd. Surgery (cert.), Internat. Bd. Proctology (cert.), Phi Beta Kappa, Sigma Xi, Alpha Omega Alpha. Home: 904 Silver Spur Rd Ste 804 Rolling Hills Estates CA 90274-3800

BELLOWS, ROBERT ALVIN, research physiologist; b. Bozeman, Mont., Aug. 22, 1934; s. Alvin O. and Lucy E. (Norman) B.; m. Laura Mae Pasha, Dec. 27, 1957; children: Donna Kay, William, Norman, David. BS, Mont. State U., 1956, MS, 1958; PhD, U. Wis., 1962. Registered profl. animal scientist. Rsch. physiologist USDA-Agrl. Rsch. Svc., Miles City, Mont., 1962-67, rsch. physiologist, investigations leader, 1967-71, rsch. physiology supr., 1971-79, rsch. leader, 1979-84, rsch. physiologist, 1984—; reviewer, cons. State Expt. Stas., USDA-Agrl. Rsch. Svc., Can., Mex., Egypt, Soviet Union, Kazakhstan, Kyrgyzstan, Nat. Cattleman's Assn., Angus, Hereford, Charolais and Simmental Breed Assn., 1971—; adj. prof. Mont. State U.; mem. rsch. adv. team Farmland Industries, 1998. Reviewer Agriculture Can., 1996. Recipient internat. honor award Office of Internat. Coop. and Devel., 1993. Mem. Am. Soc. Animal Sci. (western dir. 1967, sec., pres. elect, pres. western sect. 1989-91, disting. svc. award 1983, animal mgmt. award 1993, sr. scientist of yr. North Gt. Plains area 1994, sect. editor Jour. Animal Sci. 1979-81, 94-96, mem. editl. bd. 1972-82), Coun. Agrl. Sci. and Tech., Alpha Zeta. Avocations: reading, fishing, hunting, rock collecting. Office: US Dept Agr Agrl Rsch Svc Livestock & Range Rsch Lab RR 1 Box 2021 Miles City MT 59301-9200

BELLUOMINI, FRANK STEPHEN, accountant; b. Healdsburg, Calif., May 19, 1934; s. Francesco and Rose (Giorgi) B.; m. Alta Anita Gifford, Sept. 16, 1967; 1 child, Wendy Ann. AA, Santa Rosa Jr. Coll., 1954; BA with honors, San Jose State U., 1956. CPA, Calif. Staff acct. Hood, Gire & Co., CPA's, San Jose, Calif., 1955-60, ptnr., 1960-66; ptnr. Touche Ross & Co., CPA's, San Jose, 1967-89, ptnr.-in-charge San Jose office, 1971-85, sr. ptnr. San Jose office, 1985-89; ptnr. Deloitte & Touche, San Jose, 1989-95. Bd. dirs. Santa Clara Valley chpt. ARC, 1993-99, chmn. bd. dirs. 1995-97; mem. adv. bd. Salvation Army, San Jose, 1979-85, San Jose Children's Coun., 1982-89; mem. citizens adv. coun. Via Rehabilitation Svcs., Inc., 1989-94, bd. dirs., 1995—, sec./treas., 1996-98, vice chair, 1998—; trustee Santa Clara County (Calif.) United Way, 1979-95, v.p. planning and allocations, 1981-83, vice chmn., 1985-87, chmn. 1987-89; bd. dirs. San Jose Mus. Art, 1984-86; mem. Presentation High Sch. Devel. Bd., 1989-92; mem. dean's adv. coun. San Jose State U. Bus. Sch., 1990-95, mem. adv. bd. The Acad. of Fin., 1992-94. Named Disting. Alumnus, San Jose State U. Sch. Bus., 1978. Mem. Santa Clara County Estate Planning Council (pres. 1979-80), Calif. Soc. CPA's (pres. chpt. 1968-69, state v.p. 1976-77), Am. Inst. CPA's (chmn. state and local govt. com. 1976-79), San Jose State Alumni Assn. (treas. 1960-61, dir. 1961-62, exec. com. 1961-62), San Jose State Acctg. Round Table (bd. dirs., treas. 1982-87, 92-97, pres. 1994-95), Beta Alpha Psi (San Jose State U. Outstanding Alumnus award 1986). Clubs: San Jose Rotary (dir. 1979-81, trustee and treas. San Jose Rotary Endowment 1976-83).

BELLUS, RONALD JOSEPH, marketing and communications executive; b. Travis AFB, Calif., Feb. 25, 1951; s. Vincent Joseph and Katherine Veronica (Giudice) B.; m. Beth Ann Johnson, June 26, 1976 (div.); children: Veronica Lee, Joseph Vincent, Kenneth James; m. Gina Jean Prom, Aug. 9, 1990; children: Anthony Taylor, Andrew Tyler. BA in Communications, Brigham Young U., 1977. Lic. FCC radio telephone operator, 1979. Sports dir. Sta. KGUY-AM, Palm Desert, Calif., 1979; news, sports dir. Sta. KBLQ-AM/FM, Logan, Utah, 1979-80; gen. sales mgr. Sta. KSTM-FM/KVVA-AM, Phoenix, 1980-84, Sta. KLFF-AM/KMZK-FM, Phoenix, 1984-85; media cons. Mediacorp Planning & Buying, Phoenix, 1985-86; press sec. Gov. of Ariz., Phoenix, 1986-87; asst. dir. Ariz. Office of Tourism, Phoenix, 1987-88; media cons. Bellus Media, Phoenix, 1988-93; pres. Taska Ltd. (formerly Bellus Media), Phoenix, 1993—; ptnr. Desertwest Media Group, Inc., Phoenix, 1988-96; v.p. Nat. Restaurant Group, Inc., Phoenix, 1990-91; media cons. Mecham for Gov. com., Glendale, Ariz., 1986; host cable TV show Arizona-Now and Then, Cox Cable, 1990—; v.p. Infosystems, Tempe, 1991-94, Green Valley Health Group, Phoenix, 1992-98; co-founder Cinema Concepts Found., Scottsdale, 1994—; co-founder, CEO Bronze Memories Ltd., Phoenix, 1994—; co-founder, pres. Taurus, Inc., 1998—; assoc. dir. Southwest Ctr. for Ethics, Scottsdale C. C., 1998—. Author: Mecham: Silence Cannot Be Misquoted, 1988, Ariz. Tourism Travel Planner, 1988. Comm. mem. Phoenix Boys Choir, 1988; precinct committeeman Rep. State Com., Phoenix, 1987-89, del., 1988; candidate for state senate, Phoenix, 1988; bd. dirs. Cinema Concepts Found., 1994—; mem. Gilbert Anti-Gang Task Force, 1994—, Gilbert Action Inter-Faith Network, 1994—; chmn. adv. bd. Original Kids TV, Inc. Named one of Outstanding Young Men Am., 1987. Mem. Phoenix Press Box Assn. (treas. 1984-85, exec. dir. 1985-86). Ch. of Latter Day Saints. Avocations: golf, travel, reading. Office: 15812 N 32d St Ste 9 Phoenix AZ 85032-3857

BELLUZZO, RICHARD E., executive. BS in Acctg., Golden Gate U. Chmn., CEO Silicon Graphics, Mountain View, Calif. Office: 2011 N Shoreline Blvd Mountain View CA 94043-1342*

BELNAP, NORMA LEE MADSEN, musician; b. Tremonton, Utah, Dec. 2, 1927; d. Doyle Franklin and Cleo (Crawforth) Madsen; m. H. Austin Belnap, Jan. 19, 1980; 7 stepchildren. Student, Brigham Young U., summer 1947, San Francisco Conservatory of Music, summer 1949; B.S., U. Utah, 1951; postgrad., Aspen Inst. Music, 1953, Music Acad. of West, Santa Barbara, Calif., 1962. Sec.-treas., dir., mem. faculty Treasure Mountain Festival of Arts, 1965, 66; mem. nat. adv. com. Nat. Black Music Colloquium and Competition, 1951-93; instr., 1965, adj. asst. prof. music, 1969-73, adj. assoc. prof., 1973-77, adj. prof., 1977-93; exec. v.p. LOZO Pub. Co., 1991-94. Violinist, Utah Symphony, 1944-93, ret. 1993; asst. concert master Utah Symphony, 1977-93, mem., Utah Opera Theatre Orch., 1951-54, Utah Ballet Theatre Orch., 1953-93; assoc. concertmaster Southwest Symphony St. George, Utah, 1994—, Melody Maids, 4 violins and piano, 1943-49; active in chamber music circles, 1946-81, concert mistress, U. Utah Symphony, 1947-58, prin. violist, 1958-62, soloist, Utah Artist Series, 1964, mem., Treasure Mountain String Quartet, Park City, Utah, 1964, 65, 66; appeared as violin soloist, U. Utah Symphony and Ballet Theatre Orch., 1954, 56, 57, 82; 2d violinist (affiliated with Young Audiences, Inc.) Utah String Quartet, 1958-68; Quartet-in-residence U. Utah, 1968-81, Idaho State U., 1967; with Bach Festival Orch., Carmel, Calif., 1963, 69, Sunriver Festival Orch., summer 1988, Utah-ASTA Faculty Quartet, 1970-79, tour of Europe with Utah Symphony, 1966, 77, 81, 86, S. and Cen. Am., 1971, Brit. Isles, 1975, Hawaii, 1979, concertizing throughout Western states, frequent festival adjudicator; numerous solo recitals. Recipient Tchr. Recognition award Music Tchrs. Nat. Assn., 1971, 72, 73. Mem. Music Educators Nat. Conf., Utah String Tchrs. Assn. (state membership chmn. 1969-73), Utah Music Tchrs. Assn. (state cert. bd. 1968-94), Utah Fedn. Music Clubs (1st v.p.), Am. String Tchrs. Assn. (dir. Utah nat. string conf. ann. 1970-79), Mortar Bd., Mu Phi Epsilon (founder, 1st pres. U. Utah chpt. 1950, compiler Mu Phi Epsilon Composers and Their Works 1956, nat. v.p., music adv., province gov. 1954-58, chpt. honoree for 30 yrs. of dedicated svc. 1981, chpt. honoree for 50 yrs. as mem. with Utah Symphony, honoree for 43 yrs of svc. 1994), Alpha Lambda Delta, Phi Kappa Phi, Alpha Xi. Delta, Lambda Delta Sigma. Mem. LDS Ch. Home: 2809 Connor St Salt Lake City UT 84109-1909

BELSHE, JUDY BERNICE, casting director; b. Compton, Calif., Sept. 7, 1946; d. Kenneth Eugene and Aline Laverne (Smith) Sessions; children: Adam Wayne Belshe, Yvette Janda Marie Chassé, Erick Jason Belshe, Jeremy Aaron Matthew Belshe. Grad. H.S., Torrance, Calif. Casting dir. ind. films and commls., 1978—. Author: The Long Schmooze: Everything the Gatekeeper to Hollywood Don't Have Time to Tell You Again, It's a Freeway Out There!: The Parents Guide to the Film and Comml. Industry (So. Calif. Publicists Irwin award, 1997). Recipient Best Actress award Torrance Cmty. Theater, 1962. Republican. Avocations: writing, playing music and guitar, singing, swimming.

BELSON, PATRICIA A., artist; b. Sn Francisco, Apr. 5, 1932; d. Joseph Patrick and Norma Stephanie (Bole) Gleeson; m. Dogan E. Belson, Sept. 2, 1961 (dec. July 1991); children: Linda, Susan. Office mgr. Psychiat. Group Offices, Seattle, 1958-63; pub. rels., brochure designer, English sec. Istanbul Hilton Hotel, Turkey, 1963-64; office mgr. Psychiat. Outpatient Facility, San Francisco, 1973-76; owner Wadyacallit, Sequim, Wash., 1980-85; corp. ptnr., mktg. dir. Fantasy Prodns., Inc., Seattle, 1985-90; self employed fine artist Seattle, Sequim, 1990—; vol. treas. Blue Whole Gallery, Sequim, 1997-98, artists' coop. mem., charter mem., 1997—. Exhbns. include Bechtel Corp., 1976, Juan de Fuca Festival of Arts, 1994, Clallam Art League, 1995, Northwest Watercolor Soc., 1994, Blue Whole Gallery, Sequim, Wash., 1997—, Clallam Art League Sr. Show, 1998; one-woman shows include Istanbul (Turkey) InterContinental Hotel, 1978, Galerie du Soleil, Sequim, 1996; group shows include A Contemporary Theater Gallery, Seattle, 1992. Vol. tourist info. ctr. Sequim/Dungeness Valley C. of C., 1994-96; pub. rels. vol. Sequim Arts, 1996-97; vol. tutor Seattle Sch. Dist., 1991-92; vol. Sequim Arts Treas., 1997-99. Recipient Best of Show award Clallam Art League Sr. Show, 1995, 1st Pl. Sequim Arts Mem. Show, 1995, Best Still Live award Clallam Sr. Show, 1998. Avocations: sailing, canoeing, tennis, skiing, hiking. Home: 101 Wilcox Ln Sequim WA 98382-8904

BELTRÁN, ANTHONY NATALICIO, military non-commissioned officer, deacon; b. Flagstaff, Ariz., Aug. 17, 1938; s. Natalicio Torres and Mary Mercedes (Sandoval) B.; m. Patricia Emily Cañez, Nov. 18, 1962; children: Geralyn P., Bernadette M., Albert A., Catherine M., Elizabeth R., Michael J., Theresa R., Christopher M. AA, Phoenix Jr. Coll., 1971, C.C. of Air Force, 1992; grad., Def. Equal Oppty. Mgmt. Inst., 1991. Gen. clk. Blue Cross Blue Shield, Phoenix, 1958-61; enlisted Air N.G., advanced through ranks to chief master sgt.; unit clk. Ariz. Air N.G., Phoenix, 1961, personnel technician, 1962-65, adminstrv. supr., 1965-81, support services supr., 1981-88, equal employment specialist, 1988-95, state sr. enlisted advisor, 1995-98, ret., 1998; with St. Matthew Cath. Ch., Phoenix. Bd. dirs. Friendly House, Phoenix, 1982-86, mem. aux. bd., 1989-97; mem. Alma de la Gente, Phoenix, 1982-92, Chiefs Police Community Adv. Group, Phoenix, 1984-85, Mayor's Task Force on Juvenile Crime, Phoenix, 1979-81; pres. IMAGE de Phoenix, 1985-87. Staff sgt. USAF, 1961-62. Recipient Community Service award Phoenix C. of C., 1982. Mem. Fed. Exec. Assn. (sec., treas. Phoenix chpt. 1985-86, 1st v.p. 1987, pres. 1987-88, Community Svc. award 1986), Am. GI Forum (sec. Sylvestre Herrera chpt. 1995-96, comdr. 1996—), Ariz. Hispanic Employment Program Mgrs. (treas. 1980-81, v.p. 1981-82, pres. 1982-84, named Outstanding Mem. of Yr. 1981, 83), Enlisted Assn. N.G. Ariz. (pres. Copperhead chpt. 1987-90), Non-Commd. Officers Acad. Grad. Assn. (chpt. 46 v.p. 1992-94). Democrat. Avocations: permanent Deacon Roman Cath. Diocese assigned to ministry for the Spanish speaking. Home: 4109 W Monte Vista Rd Phoenix AZ 85009-2005 also: St Matthew Cath Ch 320 N 20th Dr Phoenix AZ 85009-3819

BELYEA, PAMELA JILL, art association administrator; b. Ottawa, Ont., Can., July 21, 1954; d. James Louis and Muriel Myra Belyea; m. Gary David Faigin, Oct. 6, 1976; children: Sarah Jane Faigin, Benjamin James Faigin. Tech. diploma, Nat. Theater Sch., Montreal, 1976; etudiate libre, Ecole des Beaux Arts, Paris, 1978-79; BArch, Cooper Union, N.Y.C., 1985. Registered architect, N.Y. Curatorial asst. Mies Van der Rohe Archive Mus. Modern Art, N.Y.C., 1980; architect Steven Robinson Architects, N.Y.C., 1986-89, Larry Rouche & Co., Seattle, 1989, deMehil Architects, N.Y.C., 1989; exec. dir., co-founder Acad. Realist Art/Young Artists Acad., Seattle, 1989—; patent cons. Randolph-Rand Inc., N.Y.C., 1994-95. conceptual artist pub. art project for Arts Ballard Denisons of the Deep, 1998 (neighborhood matching grant 1998). Recipient Excellence in Total Design award N.Y. Soc. Architects, 1985, Peter W. Bruder Meml. prize for Excellence in Structures Cooper Union, 1985, Abraham E. Kazan prize for Excellence in Urban Design Cooper Union, 1985, Dr. Martin J. Water prize for Excellence in Humanities Cooper Union, 1984. Mem. Greater Seattle C. of C., Univ. Heights Cmty. Center, Center on Contemporary Art, Arts Ballard, Frye Art Mus., Seattle Art Mus. E-mail: www.realistart.com. Office: Acad Realist Art 5004 6th Ave NW Seattle WA 98107-3511

BELZBERG, LESLIE CAROL, film and television producer; b. Calgary, Alta., Can., Apr. 5, 1953; d. Hyman and Jenny (Lavin) B.; 1 child, Sophie Bennett. BA, York U., 1974; MBA, Fordham U., 1979. Prodr. (films) Oscar, 1990, Innocent Blood, 1991, Beverly Hills Cop III, 1993, The Stupids, 1994, Blues Brothers 2000, 1997, Susan's Plan, 1998; assoc. prodr. (film) Genocide, 1981 (Acad. award), Spies Like Us, 1985, Three Amigos, 1986, Into the Night, 1984; exec. prodr. (film) Coming to Am., 1987, (TV) Here Come the Munsters, 1995, The Munsters' Scary Little Christmas, 1996, Campus Cops, 1996, (HBO comedy series) Dream On, 1991, (weekly series) Weird Science, 1996, (weekly series) Sliders, 1995, Honey I Shrunk the Kids, 1996; asst. to prodr. (film) Trading Places, 1982; prodn. coord., auditor (film) Thriller, 1983. Mem. steering com. Access Now for Gay and Lesbian Equality, L.A., 1992—, OutThere, L.A., 1996—; bd. dirs. Nat. Gay and Lesbian Task Force, Washington, 1996—. Mem. Am. Film Inst., Am. Cinematheque, Acad. TV Arts and Scis., Acad. Motion Picture Arts and Scis. (prodr.'s br.). Avocations: travel, gourmet dining, wine collector, athletics. Office: St Clare Entertainment 1875 Century Park E Ste 1100 Los Angeles CA 90067-2512

BENACH, SHARON ANN, physician assistant; b. New Orleans, Aug. 28, 1944; d. Wilbur G. and Freda Helen (Klaas) Cherry; m. Richard Benach, Dec. 6, 1969 (div. Oct. 1976); children: Craig (dec.), Rachel. Degree, St. Louis U., 1978. Physician asst. VA Hosp., St. Louis, 1982-84, Maricopa County Health Svcs., Phoenix, 1984—. Served with USPHS, 1978-82. Recipient Outstanding Performance award HHS. Mem. Maricopa Faculty Assn. (div. internal medicine), Mensa. Jewish. Avocation: pre-Columbian archaeology. Home: 5515 N 7th St Apt 5-600 Phoenix AZ 85014-2531

BEN-ASHER, M. DAVID, physician; b. Newark, June 18, 1931; s. Samuel Irving and Dora Ruth (Kagan)B.; m. Bryna S. Zeller, Nov. 22, 1956. BA, Syracuse U., 1952; MD, U. Buffalo Sch. Med., 1956. Intern E.J. Meyer Mem. Hosp., Buffalo, N.Y., 1956-57; resident Jersey City Med. Ctr., 1957-58; asst. chief med. service U.S. Army Hosp., Ft. McPherson, Ga., 1958-60; resident Madigan Gen. Hosp., Tacoma, Wash., 1960-62; chief gen. med. service Walson Army Hosp., Ft. Dix, N.Y., 1962-64; attending staff St. Mary's Hosp., Tucson, Ariz., 1964—; pvt. practice Tucson, 1964—. Bd. dirs. Tucson Symphony, 1971-73; mem. Ariz. State Bd. Med. Examiners, 1978-88, joint bd. for regulation of physicians' assts., 1990-97; bd. trustees United Synagogue Am., 1981-87, nat. adv. bd., 1987-91. Fellow ACP; mem. Pima County Med. Soc. (bd. dirs. 1971-77, pres. 1976), Ariz. Med. Assn., AMA. Democrat. Avocations:health club, music, computers. Home: 3401 N Tanuri Dr Tucson AZ 85750-6735 Office: So Ariz Med Specialists 4711 N 1st Ave Tucson AZ 85718-5610

BENAVIDES, MARY KATHLEEN, anesthesiologist, nutritional consultant; b. Alhambra, Calif., Sept. 10, 1958; d. Duane Joseph B. and Janet Leona Johnson; m. John Gerard Migliori, May 27, 1946. BS, U. Calif., 1980, MD, 1985. Diplomate Nat. Bd. Med. Examiners, Am. Bd. Anesthesiology. Intern Wadworths-VA Adminstrn. Hosp., Los Angeles, Calif., 1985-86; resident Loma Linda (Calif.) Med. Ctr., 1986-89; Attending physician L.A. Children's Hosp., 1989-90; anesthesiologist Inland Valley Regional Med. Ctr., Wildomar, Calif., 1990-91, Mission Bay Hosp., San Diego, 1991-96, Treasure Valley Hosp., Boise, 1996—; nutritional cons. BodyWise Internat., San Diego, 1994—, Boise, 1996—. Fellow Am. Bd. Anesthesiology; mem. Am. Soc. Anesthesiologists, Soc. Ambulatory Care Anesthesiology, Idaho State Soc. Anesthesiology. Avocations: running, skiing, reading, personal improvement. Home: PO Box 418 Boise ID 83701-0418

BENBOW, RICHARD ADDISON, psychological counselor; b. Las Vegas, Dec. 27, 1949; s. Jules Coleman and Bonnie Ray B. BBA, U. Nev. 1972, MS in Counseling, 1974; AAS in Bus. Mgmt. and Real Estate, Clark County

Community Coll., 1980; PhD in Clin. Psychology, U. Humanistic Studies, 1986. Cert. tchr., Nev.; cert. clin. mental health counselor, secondary sch. counselor, Nev., substance abuse counselor, Nev., substance abuse program adminstr., Nev.; nat. cert. counselor. Jud. svcs. officer Mcpl. Ct. City of Las Vegas, 1983-88, pretrial program coord., 1988—; inmate classification technician Detention and Correctional Svcs., 1982-83; stress mgmt. cons. Mem. Biofeedback Soc. Am., Assn. Humanistic Psychology, Nat. Assn. Psychotherapists, Am. Counseling Assn., Am. Mental Health Counselors Assn., Am. Acad. Crisis Interveners, Jr. C. of C., U.S. Jaycees (presdl. award of honor 1978-79), Delta Sigma Phi. Democrat. Christian Scientist. Office: Mcpl Ct Intake Svcs City of Las Vegas 400 Stewart Ave Las Vegas NV 89101-2927

BENDER, EDWARD ERIK, geology educator, researcher; b. Bronxville, N.Y., Dec. 9, 1962; s. Edward Joseph and Mae Virgina (Camera) B.; m. Linda Dee Young, June 8, 1964; 1 child, Alexandra Dominique. BS in Geology, Rider U., 1985; MS, Vanderbilt U., 1990; PhD, U. So. Calif., 1994. Instr. Calif. State U., Fullerton, 1991-92; asoc. prof. Orange Coast Coll., Costa Mesa, Calif., 1994—; adj. prof. Chaffey Coll., Alta Loma, Calif., 1991—, Mt. San Antonio Coll., Walnut, Calif., 1992-93, Pasadena (Calif.) City Coll., 1992-94; adv. com-edn. So. Calif. Earthquake Ctr., L.A., 1995—; spkr. Earthquake Awareness Orange Coast Coll., 1996, Costa Mesa Mineral Soc., 1995. Contbr. articles to profl. jours. Mem. Seismological Soc. Am., Geol. Soc. Am. (Penrose grant 1986), Am. Geophys. Union, Mineralog. Soc. Am. Achievements include examination of growth of North American continent, mechanisms and timing; discovery that many terranes of California have not travelled as previously believed. Office: Orange Coast Coll 2701 Fairview Rd Costa Mesa CA 92626-5563

BENDER, MICHAEL LEE, state supreme court justice, lawyer; b. N.Y.C., Jan. 7, 1942; s. Louis and Jean (Waterman) B.; m. Judith Jones, Feb. 27, 1967 (div. Mar. 1977); children: Jeremy, Aviva; m. Helen H. Hand, Sept. 10, 1977; children: Maryjean Hand-Bender, Tess Hand-Bender, Benjamin Hand-Bender. BA in Philosophy, Dartmoutn Coll., 1964; JD, U. Colo., 1967. Bar: Colo. 1967, D.C. 1967, U.S. Supreme Ct. 1980. Pub. defender City and County Denver, 1968-71; assoc. regional atty. EEOC, 1974-75; pub. defender Colo. State Pub. Defender, Denver, 1975-78; atty. Gibson, Dunn & Crutcher, L.A., 1978-79; ptnr. Bender & Treece P.C., Denver, 1979—; also pres. Bender & Treece P.C.; chair. ABA Criminal Justice sect., Washington, 1990-91, NACD Lawyers Assistant Com., 1989-90; dir. Nat. Assn. Criminal Def. Lawyers, 1984-90; mem. practitioner's adv. com. U.S. Sentencing Com., 1990-91. Contbr. articles to profl. jours. Bd. govs. Colo. Bar, 1989-91. Recipient Fireman award Colo. State Pub., 1990; Heeney Meml. award Nat. Assn. Criminal Def. Lawyers, 1990; named Vol. of Yr. Denver Bar Assn., 1988. Mem. Colo. Bar Assn. (ethics com. 1980—). Democrat. Jewish. Avocations: aerobics, skiing, bicycling, camping. Office: Colo Supreme Ct Colo State Jud Bldg 2 E 14th Ave, 4th Fl Denver CO 80203

BEN-DOR, GISÈLE, conductor, musician; b. Montevideo, Uruguay; came to U.S., 1982; m. Eli Ben-Dor; children: Roy, Gabriel. Student, Acad. of Music, Tel Aviv; artist diploma, Rubin Acad. Music, Tel Aviv; M, Yale Sch. of Music, 1982. Music dir. Annapolis Symphony, Md., Pro Arte Chamber Orch. of Boston; condr. Norwalk (Conn.) Youth Symphony; conducting fellow L.A. Philharm. Inst., 1984, Tanglewood Music Ctr., 1985; resident condr. Houston Symphony, 1991; music dir. Santa Barbara Symphony, Calif., 1994—; resident condr. Houston Symphony, condr. variety conducting activities including prestigious summer festivals, competitions, 1983-87, Hungarian Nat. Symphony, Budapest Philharm., others; guest condr. orchs. in Uruguay, Ea. Europe, Israel and U.S. including Barvarian Radio Orch., Boston POPS, New World Symphony, Women's Philharm, San Francisco, Minn. Orch. in Summerfest Festival, 1986, N.Y. Philharm., 1993, 95, Orquestra del Teatro Nacional, Brazil, Ulster Orch., Israel Philharm., 1991, Carnegie Hall, 1991, others; past music dir. Houston Youth Symphony; past acting orch. dir. Shepherd Sch. Music Rice U.; music dir. Boston ProArte Chamber Orch., Annapolis Symphony. Condr. Israel Philharm. Orch. (play) The Rite of Spring; recs. with London Symphony, Israel Chamber Orch., (CD) London Symphony Orch., Sofia Soloists, Boston ProArte Chamber Orch.; numerous TV appearances. Am.-Israel Cultural Found scholar, Frances Wickes scholar; Leonard Bernstein fellow; recipient Bartók prize Hungarian TV Internat. Condrs. Competition, 1986. Office: Santa Barbara Symphony Orch Arlington Theatre 1900 State St Ste G Santa Barbara CA 93101-8424 Office: Del Rosenfield Assoc 714 Ladd Rd Bronx NY 10471-1204

BENEDICT, MONSEIGNEUR, priest, religious researcher; b. Bay City, Mich., Dec. 29, 1917. BA in Psychology, Chapman Coll., 1971; postgrad., U. So. Calif., U. Calif., Long Beach, 1972-80. Ordained priest Ch. of Antioch, 1971, consecrated monsignor, 1991. Pastor, minister Chapel of the Chimes, Orange, Calif., 1972-81; researcher Apostle Thomas Gnostics, Malabar Rite, Thousand Oaks, Calif., 1981—. Research on the cosmological connection, synaptology and brain waves, gnostic cybernetics, altered states of consciousness and varieties of religious experiences. Home and Office: 887 St Charles Dr Apt 16 Thousand Oaks CA 91360-4028

BENEDICT, DEBORAH ANKLAM, English language educator; b. Ventura, Calif., Sept. 11, 1957; d. James Richard and Markie Anklam; m. Jeff Scott Benedict, June 3, 1979; children: Katie, J.P., Jason, Rowan. BA, Univ. Ariz., 1979. Tchr. Providence H.S., San Antonio, Tex., 1981-83, Kitty Hawk Jr. High, Converse, Tex., 1983-84, Judson High, Converse, Tex., 1984-85, Oscar Smith, Chesapeake, Va., 1985-87, Tempe (Ariz.) High., 1988-95, Mountain Pointe H.S., Phoenix, 1992-95, Desert Vista H.S., Phoenix, 1995—; chair North Cen. Desert Vista H.S., 1996—, site base chair, 1995—, Tempe Sister Cities Exchange Tchr., Regensburg, Germany, 1992. V.p. Desert Aquatics Swim Bd., 1993-94; treas. PTA, Phoenix, 1988-89. Recipient Outstanding Creative Educator Cox Communications, 1996-97, J. Morton Award Excellence, 1995, Milken Nat. Educator award, 1998, Tchr. Venture grant, 1993-94. Mem. Nat. Coun. Tchrs. Eng., Ariz. Tennis Assn., PEO, Alpha Delta Kappa (treas.). Republican. Presbyterian. Avocations: tennis, art, reading. Home: 17002 S 34th Pl Phoenix AZ 85044-7816 Office: Desert Vista H S 16440 S 32d St Phoenix AZ 85044-7807

BENEDICT, MARGARET ROSE (PEGGY BENEDICT), English language and speech educator; b. Sheridan, Wyo., Jan. 4, 1948; d. Francis William and Carlotta Hamilton (Whitney) B.; m. Robert Morrell Dorsey, June 26, 1994. BA, U. No. Colo., 1970; Masters, U. Colo., 1978. Master cert. tchr., Colo. Comms. specialist Union Oil of Calif., L.A., 1970-72; tchr. English and drama Pacific Palisades (Calif.) Sch., 1972-74; tchr. English John Dewy Jr. H.S., Thornton, Colo., 1974-75, Highland H.S., Thornton, 1975-79; tchr. speech/debate, asst. coach speech team Cherry Creek H.S., Englewood, Colo., 1980-90, head coach debate team and forensics team, 1992—. Sec., bd. dirs. Nat. Abortion Rights Action League, 1991—; head coach state champion debate team, Colo., 1982—; asst. forensics coach nat. champion team, 1992. Head coach state champion debate team, Colo., 1982—; asst. forensics coach nat. champion team, 1992; named Colo. Educator of Yr. Nat. H.S. Assn., 1998. Mem. NOW, NEA, Nat. Coun. Tchrs. English, Nat. Forensics League (One Diamond Coach award 1993), Colo. Edn. Assn. (state rep. 1972—), Colo. Lang. Arts Soc., Mapleton Edn. Assn. (pres. 1974-76), Cherry Creek Tchrs. Assn. (faculty rep. 1979—), Phi Delta Kappa. Democrat. Episcopalian. Avocations: reading, gardening, travel. Home: 730 Humboldt St Denver CO 80218-3512 Office: Cherry Creek Schs 9300 E Union Ave Englewood CO 80111-1306

BENES, ANDREW CHARLES, professional baseball player; b. Evansville, Ind., Aug. 20, 1967. Student, U. Evansville. With San Diego Padres, 1988-95, Seattle Mariners, 1995, St. Louis Cardinals, 1996-98, Ariz. Diamondbacks, 1998—; mem. U.S. Olympic Baseball Team, 1988, Nat. League All-Star Team, 1993. Named Sporting News Rookie Pitcher of Yr., 1989. Office: care Ariz Diamondbacks Bank One Ballpark 401 E Jefferson Phoenix AZ 85004*

BENEŠ, NORMAN STANLEY, meteorologist; b. Detroit, July 1, 1921; s. Stanley and Cecelia (Sereneck) B.; m. Elinor Simson, May 5, 1945 (div. Feb. 1972); children: Gregory, Heather, Michelle, Francine; m. Celia Sereneck, Mar. 3, 1972. BS, U. Wash., 1949; postgrad., U. Calif., Davis, 1963, U. Mich., 1966. Chief meteorologist Hawthorne Sch. of Aero., Moultrie, Ga., 1951-55; meteorologist U.S. Weather Bur., Phoenix, 1955-57, 59-60; meteorologist in charge NSF, Hallett, Antarctica, 1958; sta. sci. leader NSF, Byrd, Antarctica, 1960-61; meteorologist Nat. Weather Service, Sacramento, Calif., 1962-84; mem. Exec. Com. Range Benes Peak, Antarctica. Contbr. articles to profl. jours. Pres. local chpt. PTA, 1965. With USN, 1943-46, PTO. Mem. AAAS, Am. Meteorol. Soc., Am. Geophys. Union, Nat. Weather Assn., Masons. Avocation: model trains. Home: 3311 Holiday Ln Placerville CA 95667-9076

BENET, LESLIE ZACHARY, pharmacokineticist; b. Cin., May 17, 1937; s. Jonas John and Esther Racie (Hirschfeld) B.; m. Carol Ann Levin, Sept. 8, 1960; children: Reed Michael, Gillian Vivia. AB in English, U. Mich., 1959, BS in Pharmacy, 1960, MS in Pharm. Chemistry, 1962; PhD in Pharm. Chemistry, U. Calif., San Francisco, 1965; PharmD (hon.), Uppsala U., Sweden, 1987; PhD (hon.), Leiden U., The Netherlands, 1995; DSc (hon.), U. Ill., Chgo., 1997, Phila. Coll. Pharm. & Sci., 1997, L.I. U., 1999. Asst. prof. pharmacy Wash. State U., Pullman, 1965-69; asst. prof. pharmacy and pharm. chemistry U. Calif., San Francisco, 1969-71, assoc. prof., 1971-76, prof., 1976—, vice chmn. dept. pharmacy, 1973-78, chmn. dept. pharmacy, 1978-96, dir. drug studies unit, 1977—, dir. drug kinetics and dynamics ctr., 1979—, chmn. dept. biopharm. scis., 1996-98; mem. pharmacology study sect. NIH, Washington, 1977-81, chmn., 1979-81, mem. pharmacol. scis. rev. com., 1984-88, chmn., 1986-88; mem. generic drugs adv. com. FDA, Washington, 1990-94, mem. Sci. Bd., 1992—; mem. sci. adv. bd. SmithKline Beecham Pharms., 1989-92, Pharmetrix, 1989-92, Alteon, Inc., 1993—, TheraTech, Inc., 1993-96, Roche Biosci., 1998—; chmn. bd. AvMax, Inc., 1994—; bd. dirs. Oxon Medica, Inc., InforMedix, Inc., Josman Labs., Inc. Editor Jour. Pharmacokinetics and Biopharmaceutics, 1976-98; assoc. editor Pharmacology and Therapeutics, 1995—; editl. bd. Pharmacology, 1979-98, Pharmacy Internat., 1979-82, Pharmaceutical Rsch., 1983-95, ISI Atlas of Sci.: Pharmacology, 1988-89, Pharmaceutical News, 1994—, The Effect of Disease States on Drug Pharmacokinetics, 1976, Pharmacokinetic Basis for Drug Treatment, 1984, Pharmacokinetics: A Modern View, 1984, ISI Atlas of Sci.: Pharmacology, 1988-89, Integration of Pharmacokinetics, Pharmacodynamics and Toxicokinetics in Rational Drug Development, 1992, Clinical Applications of Mifepristone (RU486) and Other Antiprogestins, 1993; contbr. more than 380 articles to profl. jours. Appt. to Forum on Drug Devel. and Regulation, 1988. Fellow Acad. Pharm. Scis. (pres. 1985-86, chmn. basic pharmaceutics sect. 1976-77, mem.-at-large exec. com. 1979-83, Rsch. Achievement award 1982), AAAS (mem.-at-large exec. com. pharm. scis. sect. 1978-81, 91-95, chair 1996-97), Am. Assn. Pharm. Scientists (pres. 1986, treas. 1987, bd. dirs. 1988-93, Disting. Pharm. Scientist award 1989, Disting. Svc. award 1996); mem. Inst. Medicine NAS (forum on drug devel. and regulation 1988-94, chmn. com. on antiprogestins, 1993, membership com. 1994-97, chmn. other health professions sect. 1995-97, chmn. com. pharmacokinetics & drug interactions in elderly 1996-97, mem. Round Table R & D Drugs, Biologics & Med. Devices 1997—), AAUP, Am. Found. for Pharm. Edn. (bd. dirs. 1987—, Disting. Svc. "Profile" award 1993), Am. Coll. Clin. Pharmacology (Disting. Svc. award 1988), ISSX (councillor 1992-96, treas. 1998—), Am. Pharm. Assn., Am. Soc. Clin. Pharmacology and Therapeutics (Rawls-Palmer award and lectureship 1995), Am. Soc. for Pharmacology and Exptl. Therapeutics, Generic Pharm. Industry Assn. (mem. blue ribbon com. on generic medicines 1990), Internat. Pharm. Fedn. (bd. pharm. scis. 1988, chair 1996—), Drug Info. Assn., Am. Coll. Clin. Pharmacy (therapeutic frontiers lectr. 1995), Am. Assn. Colls. Pharmacy (Volwiler Rsch. Achievement award 1991, pres. 1993-94, bd. dirs. 1992-95), Sigma Xi, Rho Chi (Ann. Lecture award 1990), Phi Lambda Sigma. Home: 53 Beach Rd Belvedere CA 94920-2364 Office: U Calif San Francisco Dept Biopharm Scis San Francisco CA 94143

BENGEL, BERYL KENNEY, retired elementary education educator; b. Brooksville, Ky., Oct. 18, 1911; d. Lewis Wadsworth and Nicie Elizabeth (Kirk) Kenney; m. Joseph Nichlas Bengel, Aug. 15, 1942. BA, U. Ky., 1941; MS, U. So. Calif., 1954. Tchr. art, sci. Bracken County Schs., Brooksville, 1935-43; tchr. art, linguistics Lynwood (Calif.) Unified Sch. Dist., 1946-76. Moderator of deacons Oceanside, Calif. Presbyn. Ch., 1990-92, elder, 1995-98; 1st v.p. Oceanside Dem. Club, 1991-92; pres. Stars of Palomar, 1987-89, Oceanside chpt. AARP, 1992-94, San Luis Rey Sr. Ctr., 1985-87, 94-95. Winner 3 top awards for watercolor painting Oceanside Festival of Arts, state, nat. convs. Gen. Fedn. Woman's Clubs. Mem. NEA, AAUW (pres. Huntington Park chpt. 1959-60), AARP (chaplain 1995-99), Calif. Tchrs. Assn. (life), PTA (life), Calif. Red. Tchrs. Assn., Woman's Club of Carlsbad (pres. 1982-84, Woman of Yr. 1984), North County Art Assn., Calrsbad Oceanside Art Assn., San Diguito Art League, Parliamentary Law Club, Palomar Orchid Soc., Cymbidium Soc. Am., Am. Orchid Soc., Epsilon Sigma Omicron, Delta Kappa Gamma (pres. chpt. 1862-67, 86-88). Democrat. Presbyterian. Avocations: painting watercolors and oils, reading, walking. Home: 2730 MacDonald St Oceanside CA 92054-4421

BENHAM, JAMES H., state official; b. Twin Falls, Idaho, July 14, 1944; s. James Henry and Matilda (Riggs) B.; m. Ann Elizabeth McIntosh, Mar. 27, 1965; 2 children. BA in Polit. Sci., Idaho State U., 1990, MPA, 1992. From police officer to chief of police Pocatello (Idaho) Police Dept., 1988-94; U.S. marshal dept. justice U.S. Dist. Idaho, Boise, 1994—. Contbr. articles to profl. jours. Bd. dirs. Nat. Criminal Justice Assn., 1992-93. Mem. Idaho Peace Officers Assn. (pres. 1986), Idaho Chief of Police Assn. (pres. 1990-91), Pocatello Police Relief Assn., Lions, Phi Kappa Phi. Methodist. Avocations: golf, fishing, exercizing, hunting, gardening. Office: US Marshal for Dist Idaho 550 W Fort St # 010 Boise ID 83724-0101

BENHAMOU, ERIC A., computer company executive. MSEE, Stanford U.; diplome d'Ingenieur, Ecole Nationale Superieure d'Arts et Metiers, Paris. Project mgr., software mgr., design engr. Zilog, Inc.; v.p. Bridge Comm., 1981; chmn., chief exec. officer 3Com Corp., Santa Plz., Calif., 1990—; bd. dirs. Smart Valley Inc., Cypress Semiconductor, Legato, Santa Clara U. Sch. Bus.; chair Am. Electronics Assn. Nat. Info. Infrastructure Task Force. Recipient Pres. Environ. and Conservation Challenge award, 1992. Office: 3COM Corp 5400 Bayfront Plz Santa Clara CA 95052-3600*

BENJAMIN, LORNA SMITH, psychologist; b. Rochester, N.Y., Jan. 7, 1934; d. Lloyd Albert and Esther (Tack) Smith; children: Laureen, Linda. AB, Oberlin Coll., 1955; PhD, U. Wis., 1960. NIMH fellow dept. psychiatry U. Wis., 1958-62, clin. psychology intern, 1960-64, asst. prof., 1966-71, assoc. prof., 1971-77, prof. psychiatry, 1977-88; prof. psychology U. Utah, 1988—; research asso. Wis. Psychol. Inst., Madison, 1962-66. Contbr. articles to profl. jours. Mem. Am. Psychol. Assn., Soc. Psychotherapy Research, Phi Beta Kappa. Office: Univ Utah Dept Psychology 390 S 1530 E Dept Salt Lake City UT 84112-8936

BENNER, MICHAEL, broadcast journalist, consultant; b. Lansing, Mich., Nov. 29, 1947; s. Gregg Donald Benner and Mary Eleanor (Waters) Morris; m. Doreen Key, April 23, 1995. BA in TV Radio Mgmt., Mich. State U., 1970. Broadcast news talk, commentator WILS AM&FM, Lansing, Mich., 1968-71, WDRQ-FM, Detroit, 1971, WRIF-FM, Detroit, 1971-72, WWWW-FM, Detroit, 1972-75, KABC-AM, KLOS-FM, L.A., 1977-87, KLSX-FM, L.A., 1991-95, KCBS-FM, L.A., 1997—; prin., owner Personal Devel. Strategies, Glendale, Calif., 1987—; adv. bd. L.A. County Bd. Edn. Radio Broadcast, 1996—, Pasadena (Calif.) City Coll. Broadcast, 1996—; cons. U. So. Calif., L.A., 1993, Burbank (Calif.) High Sch., 1997-98. City radio officer Glendale (Calif.) Emergency Amateur Radio Svc., 1997—; chmn. disaster svcs. Am. Red Cross, Glendale, Calif., 1997—; bd. dirs. Glendale (Calif.) Family YMCA, 1991-96, Am. Red Cross, Glendale, 1997—. Recipient Certificate of Appreciation Leukemia Broadcast Council, 1981, Certificate of Appreciation L.A. County Bd. of Suprs., 1984, Beacon award Live and Learn Found., Sherman Oaks, Calif., 1985, Certificate of Appreciation United Nations Assn., 1995. Mem. Glendale C. of C. (chair emergency preparedness com. 1997—). Avocations: amateur radio operations. Office: Personal Devel Strategies PO Box 867 Glendale CA 91209-0867

BENNER, RICK, professional basketball team executive; m. Diann Benner. Grad. magna cum laude, U. Mo., Columbia, 1978. CPA. Acct. Coopers and Lybrand, Kansas City, 1978-83; contr., pres. fin., exec. v.p. bus. ops. King ARCO Arena, Sacramento, 1983-89; pres. Capital Sports and Entertainment, Sacramento, 1989—. Mem. adv. bd. Salvation Army, People Reaching Out. Mem. Sacramento Metro C. of C. (mem. adv. bd.), Rotary Club. Office: Sacramento Kings One Sports Pkwy Sacramento CA 95834

BENNETT, CHARLES LEON, vocational and graphic arts educator; b. Salem, Oreg., Feb. 5, 1951; s. Theodore John and Cora Larena (Rowland) B.; m. Cynthia Alice Hostman, June 12, 1976 (div.); m. Lynn Marie Toland, Aug. 12, 1977 (div.); children: Mizzy Marie, Charles David; m. Christina M. Crawford, Dec. 19, 1987 (div.). AS in Vocat. Tchr. Edn., Clackamas C.C., 1977; AS in Gen. Studies, Linn Benton C.C., 1979; BS in Gen. Studies, Ea. Oreg. State Coll., 1994. Tchr. printing Tongue Point Job Corps, Astoria, Oreg., 1979-80; tchr., dept. chmn. Portland (Oreg.) pub. schs., 1980—; owner, mgr. printing and pub. co., Portland, 1981-87. With AUS, 1970-72. Mem. NRA, Oreg. Vocat. Trade-Tech. Assn. (dept. chmn., pres. graphic arts div., Indsl. Educator of Year 1981-82), Oreg. Vocat. Assn. (Vocat. Tchr. of Yr. 1982-83), Graphic Arts Tech. Found., In-Plant Printing Mgmt. Assn., Internat. Graphic Arts Edn. Assn. (v.p. N.W. region VI), Oreg. Assn. Manpower Spl. Needs Personnel, Oreg. Indsl. Arts Assn., Internat. Platform Assn. Nat. Assn. Quick Printers, Am. Vocat. Assn., Pacific Printing & Imaging Assn., Inplant Printing Mgmt. Assn., Portland Club Lithographers and Printing House Craftsmen. Republican. Home: 20295 S Unger Rd Beavercreek OR 97004-8884 Office: 546 NE 12th Ave Portland OR 97232-2719

BENNETT, GARY LEE, physicist, consultant; b. Twin Falls, Idaho, Jan. 17, 1940; s. Joseph Albert and Adelaide Phillipa (Leonard) B.; m. Cleo Sue Guetschow McMurtrie, Sept. 14, 1961. AA, Boise State U., 1960; BS, U. Idaho, 1962, M of Nuclear Sci., 1966; PhD, Wash. State U., 1970. Physicist, engr. Idaho Nat. Engring. and Environ. Lab., Idaho Falls, 1962-66; mgr. project Lewis Rsch. Ctr., Cleve., 1970-71; mgr. safety U.S. Atomic Energy Commn., Germantown, Md., 1971-74; br. chief U.S. Nuclear Regulatory Commn., Silver Spring, Md., 1974-79; dir. nuclear ops. U.S. Dept. Energy, Germantown, 1980-85, dep. office dir., 1985-88; program mgr. advanced technology NASA, Washington, 1988-91, deputy div. dir., 1992-94, aerospace cons., 1994—. Author: The Star Sailors, 1980; contbr. articles and papers to profl. jours. Served as staff sgt. ANG, 1957-63. Recipient numerous profl. and govt. awards including Dist. Alumnus award Boise State U., 1990, Silver & Gold award U. Idaho Alumni Assn., 1994, Schreiber-Spence Space Achievement award, 1996. Fellow AIAA (Aerospace Power Systems Award, 1995), Brit. Interplanetary Soc., Am. Phys. Soc.; mem. AAAS, Fedn. Am. Scientists, Am. Astronaut. Soc., Am. Assn. Physics Tchrs., Planetary Soc., Space Studies Inst., Com. Sci. Investigation Claims Paranormal, Sci. Fictions Writers Am., Nat. Space Soc., Sigma Xi, Sigma Pi Sigma. Home and Office: 5000 Butte Rd Emmett ID 83617-9500

BENNETT, GENEVIEVE, artist; b. Chgo., Feb. 11, 1927; d. Joseph and Mary Sieczka; m. William A. Bennett, Jan. 31, 1953; children: William George, J. Daniel, Gordon Dean. BA, Calif. State U., Fullerton, 1974; MA, Calif. State U., Long Beach, 1978. Artist Anaheim, Calif.; part-time tchr. art Ebell Club Anaheim, 1985-97, art tchr. Whittier and Anaheim, Calif.; lectr. on N.Am. temple mound builders. One-woman shows include Calif. Poly. U., Ponoma, 1995, Orange County Fair, Calif., 1995, Anaheim Mus., 1997. Mem. Nat. League Am. Pen Women (state v.p. 1997-98, Orange County br. pres. 1997-98, recipient Women of Achievement award, 1998), Calif. State U. Art Alliance, So. Calif. Women's Caucus for Art, Orange County Fine Arts, Phi Delta Gamma (Phi chpt.). Avocations: archaeology, piano, music, travel, art meetings. Home: 2026 W Judith Ln Anaheim CA 92804-6511

BENNETT, HAROLD EARL, physicist, optics researcher; b. Missoula, Mont., Feb. 25, 1929; s. Edward Earl and Linda Queen (McCoy) B.; m. Jean Louise McPherson, Aug. 17, 1952 (div. Nov. 1984); m. Dorothy Jean Searles, Nov. 17, 1984; children: Jeanie Nybo, Dorothy Ann Picking. BA, U. Mont., 1951; MS, Pa. State U., 1953, PhD, 1955. Instrument-rated pilot. Grad. asst. Pa. State U., State College, 1951-55; physicist Wright Air Devel. Ctr., Dayton, Ohio, 1955-56; physicist Naval Air Warfare Ctr. (name Naval Weapons Ctr. 1964-93), China Lake, Calif., 1956-62, rsch. physicist, 1962-95, ret., 1995, assoc. head rsch. dept. physics div., 1972-91; cons. optical physics Quoin Inc., Ridgecrest, Calif., 1995—; pres. Bennett Optical Rsch. Inc., Ridgecrest, 1995—, chair Space Applications Com., IWV 2000 Orgn., Ridgecrest, Calif., 1996—; co-chmn. Laser Induced Damage in Optical Materials Conf., Boulder, Colo., 1979-96. Adv. editor Optics Communications, 1969-86; contbr. over 100 articles on optics to profl. jours., chpts. to books; patentee on optical instruments. Pres. Indian Wells Valley Community Concert Assn., Ridgecrest, Calif., 1974-75; sr. fellow Naval Weapons Ctr., 1990; mem. Calif. Rep. State Ctrl. Com. Recipient LTE Thompson award Naval Weapons Ctr., 1974, Tech. Dir.'s award, 1983; Capt. Robert Dexter Conrad award Dept. Navy, 1979, Dep. Comdr.'s award for R & D, 1995, Tech. Leadership award Navy High Energy Laser Project, 1995, Navy Meritorius Civilian Svc. award, 1995. Fellow Optical Soc. Am. (assoc. editor Jour. 1968-79, bd. dirs. 1972-75), Internat. Soc. for Optical Engring. (bd. dirs. 1985-87, v.p. 1987, pres. 1988, Tech. Achievement award 1983, organizer and chair Laser Power Beaming II Conf. 1995, chair Free Electron Laser Challenges Conf. 1997), Maturango Mus. (life). Republican. Achievements include research in interferometry, large optics, optical testing, thin film optics, laser power beaming to space. Home: 916 N Randall St Ridgecrest CA 93555-3007 Office: 201 N Sanders St Ridgecrest CA 93555-3867

BENNETT, JAMES CHESTER, computer consultant, real estate developer; b. Chico, Calif., May 14, 1932; s. George Clerk and Georgia Mae (James) B.; m. Grace M. Schutrum, Feb. 14, 1955 (div. 1967); children: Ronald, Becky Ann, Todd Bryant. BA in Bus., Calif. State U., Long Beach, 1965. Sgt. USAF, 1947-62; customer engr. IBM, L.A., 1962-70; mgr. computer systems Continental Airlines, L.A., 1970-82; instr. ITT Tech. Inst., Buena Park, Calif., 1982-84; dir. Ramasat Comm., LTD, Bangkok, Thailand, 1984-89; instr. ITT Tech. Inst., San Diego, 1989-90; pres. The Systems Group, Inc., Ramona, Calif., 1990—. Avocations: computer graphics, amature radio. Home: PO Box 2032 1446 Cedar St Ramona CA 92065-1326

BENNETT, JAMES P., construction executive; b. 1936. Pres. J.A. Jones Co. SA, Tenn., 1959-78, Rogers Cons., Nashville, 1978-87; with PCL Enterprises Inc., Denver, 1987—, now pres. Office: PCL Enterprises Inc 2000 S Colorado Blvd Ste 400 Denver CO 80222-7907*

BENNETT, KENNETH R., oil company executive, school board executive; b. Tucson, Aug. 1, 1959; s. Archie Roy and Donna Lucille (Bulechek) B.; m. Jeanne Tenney Bennett, Mar. 13, 1982; children: Ryan, Dana, Clifton. BS, Ariz. State U., 1984. Ceo Bennett's Oil Co., 1984—; mem. Ariz. State Bd. Edn., Phoenix, 1992—, pres., 1996-97; Ariz. State Bd. for Charter Schs., Phoenix, 1994—, Governor's Task Force Edn. Reform, Phoenix, 1991-92. Mayor Pro Tempore City of Prescott (Ariz.), 1988; councilman City of Prescott (Ariz.), 1985-89; scoutmaster Boy Scouts of Am., 1993—. Republican. LDS. Home: 1826 Oaklawn Dr Prescott AZ 86305-1159 Office: Bennett Oil Co 810 E Sheldon St Prescott AZ 86301-3214*

BENNETT, LISA COHEN, psychologist; b. Phila., Oct. 21, 1957; d. Edwin and Shirley Jane (Korz) Cohen; m. Terrence Raymond Bennett, June 14, 1987; 1 child, Noah. BA, U. Ill., 1978; MA, Calif. Inst. Integral Studies, 1984, PhD, 1989. Lic. psychologist, Calif. Psychotherapist Integral Counseling Ctr., San Francisco, 1983-85, supr. therapists, 1986-89; facilitator Therapy Groups, San Francisco Bay Area, 1984—; regional outreach coord. Union Am., Hebrew Congregations, San Francisco, 1987-90; mental health specialist La Cheim Residential Treatment Facility, Richmond, Calif., 1990-93; instr. San Francisco, Contra Costa County Foster Care, 1992—; clin. psychologist AB3632 Children's Mental Health Ctr., Contra Costa County, Calif., 1994-98; psychologist pvt. practice, Lafayette, Calif., 1992—; clin., directoral cons. Xanthos, Inc., Alameda Calif., 1987; intermarriage cons. Jewish Cmtys., San Francisco, 1987—; supr., cons. The Wright Inst., Berkeley, Calif., 1994-96. Co-author: Reaching Adolescents: Interdating, Intermarriage, Jewish Identity, 1990; contbr articles to profl. jours. Mem. Calif. Psychol. Assn., Orthopsychiatric Assn., Mt. Diablo Psychologist Info. Referral Svc. Jewish. Avocations: reading, going to movies, walking, going to baseball games. Office: 919 Village Ctr Ste 2 Lafayette CA 94549-3541

BENNETT, PAUL GROVER, agribusiness executive; b. Ancon, C.Z., Panama, Sept. 1, 1940; s. Arden Lamont and Mercedes (Reluz) B.; m. Diane Huarte, Dec. 17, 1967; children: Courtney, Kimberly, Christopher, Michael. BA, Northwestern U., 1962; MBA, Stanford U., 1968. Fin. analyst, research supt. Standard Fruit Co. (Dole Food Co.), Limon, Costa Rica, 1968-70, research dir., La Ceiba, Honduras, 1970-72, asst. gen. mgr., Guayaquil,

Ecuador, 1972-73; v.p., regional controller Castle & Cooke Foods (Dole Food Co.), San Francisco, 1973-74, v.p., gen. mgr., Davao, Philippines, 1974-76, v.p., gen. mgr., Medellin, Colombia, 1977-78; v.p., gen. mgr. Mauna Loa Macadamia Nut Corp., Hilo, Hawaii, 1978-81, pres., 1981-83; group v.p. diversified services Internat. Air Service Co. Ltd., Foster City, Calif., 1983-86; pres. Hawaiian Holiday Macadamia Nut Co., Honolulu, 1986-89; sr. ptnr. Agricon Hawaii, Honolulu, 1989-91; pres., CEO Calif. Ammonia Co., Stockton, Calif., 1991-93, pres., CEO, Naturipe Berry Growers, Watsonville, Calif., 1993-96; mng. ptnr. Agri-Food Internat., 1996-97; pres., CEO Sakata Seed Am., Inc., Morgan Hill, Calif., 1997—; dir. Agrl. Coun. of Calif.; alt. dir. Calif. Strawberry Commn.; mem. adv. bd. Agribus. Inst., Sta. Clara U. Served to lt. comdr. USN, 1962-66. Mem. Stanco, Stanford Alumni Assn., Phi Gamma Delta. Republican.

BENNETT, ROBERT F., senator; b. Salt Lake City, Utah, 1933; s. Wallace F. Bennett; m. Joyce McKay; 6 children. BS, U. of Utah, 1957. Various staff positions U.S Ho. of Reps., U.S. Senate, Washington; CEO Franklin Quest, Salt Lake City, 1984-90; U.S. senator from Utah, 1993—; chmn. legis. br. appropriations subcom. Senate GOP, chmn. fin. instns. subcom.; chmn. spl. com. Yr. 2000 Tech. Problem; mem. banking, housing, urban affairs com., appropriations com., environ. and pub. works com., joint economic com., small bus. com.; chmn. task force Senate reorganization; lobbyist various orgns., Washington; head Dept. Transp.'s Congl. Liaison. Author: Gaining Control. Chmn. Education Strategic Planning Commn. Utah State Bd. Edn. (mem. Edn. Strategic Planning Com.). Recipient Light of Learning award for Outstanding Contbns. to Utah edn., 1989; named Entrepreneur of Yr. for Rocky Mtn. region INC. magazine, 1989. Republican. Office: US Senate Office Of Senate Mems Washington DC 20510

BENNETT, ROBERT LEROY, computer software development company executive; b. Salt Lake City, May 16, 1937; s. Edward L. and Helen (Hofheins) B.; m. Linda Lou Anderson, Aug. 25, 1961; children: Keri Lynn, Troy, Nicole, Jessica, Candice, Chelsea. *Daughter Keri Lynn, MD and board certified psychiatrist and child psychiatrist, is clinical director of pediatric psychiatry at Utah State Hospital. Keri Lynn and her husband Kurt Herrmann, have five children. Son Troy, BA 1988 BYU, teacher and coaches high school history and volleyball, respectively , in Skokie, IL. Troy and his wife Elizabeth have three children. Daughter Nicole, BA 1991, MA 1994 BYU, teacher in the English Department at Brigham Young University. Nicole and her husband Brian Wistisen, have three children.* BA, Brigham Young U., 1962; JD, UCLA, 1965. Bar: Calif. 1966, U.S. Supreme Ct. 1969. Atty., advisor CIA, Washington, 1965-70; exec. v.p., chief operating officer Mead Data Central, Inc. (now Lexis-Nexis), Washington and N.Y.C., 1970-81; assoc. Heidrick and Struggles, Inc., N.Y.C., 1982-83; pres., chief exec. officer Mirror Systems, Inc., Cambridge, Mass., 1983-92; prin. Bennett, Fisher, Giuliano and Gottsman: The Electronic Publishing Group, N.Y.C., 1993—; bd. dirs. Raytech Corp., Trumbull, Conn., ADVOCAST, Provo, Utah. Mem. ABA. Mormon.

BENNETT, ROBERT ROWLAND (BOB), commercial photographer; b. Burlington, Vt., Oct. 16, 1951; s. Robert T. and Margaret (Mathews) B.; 1 child, Madeleine Grace Bennett Patton. Student, Am. Univ., 1969-71, North Va. C.C., 1973-75. Adv. art dir. Earle Palmer Brown, Bethesda, Md., 1976-82; archtl. photographer Washington, 1982-91; photo illustrator, fine art photographer, 1986—. Photography exhibits include Laguna Gloria Art Mus., Austin, Tex., 1991, Sacramento (Calif.) Fine Arts Ctr., 1993, 94, 95, 8th St. Gallery, Albuquerque, 1994, Bayfront Gallery, Fort Mason, Calif., 1995, others. Avocations: music, computers, camping, hiking. Home and Office: 575 12th Ave San Francisco CA 94118

BENNETT, RONALD THOMAS, photojournalist; b. Portland, Oreg., Nov. 6, 1944; s. E.E. Al and Donna Mae (Thomas) B.; children: R. Thomas, Gardinas. Student, Portland State U., 1964-67; student in photojournalism, U. Wash., 1965; student pre-law and bus. mgmt, Multnomah Coll., Portland, 1963-64. Lab. technician, photographer Sta. KATU-TV, Portland, 1963-65; staff photographer Oreg. Jour., Portland, 1965-68, UPI Newspictures, L.A., 1968-70; staff photojournalist UPI at White House, 1970-88; sr. photo editor The San Diego Union, 1988-89; owner, CEO Capital TV, La Jolla, Calif., 1989-97; graphic artist, illustrator, 1997—; internat. launch svcs. mission integrator, 1998—; instr. photojournalism Portland State U., 1967; mem. standing com. U.S. Senate Press Photographers Gallery, 1980-89, sec.-treas.; CEO, Ronald T. Bennett Photography Frameable Original Photos & Note Cards, 1995—. Photographer: Assassination, 1968; one-man show Lake Oswego, Oreg., 1979; group exhbns. Libr. of Congress, 1971-89; exhibited in juried art shows in Calif. and Ariz., show photography, Offtrack Gall. Mem. coun. Town of La Jolla, Calif., active Associated Volume Buyers, chmn. Brown Goods. Recipient 1st prize World Press Photo Assn., 1969, Calif. Press Photographers, 1968, 69, Gold Seal competition, 1968, 69; nominated for Pulitzer prize, 1968, 76, 77, 78, first prize, Internatl. Exhibition of Photography, 1996-97. Mem. White House News Photographers (bd. dirs. photo exhbn. com. 1974-78, 1st prize 1976, 77, 78, 80, 84, 86, 87), Nat. Headliner Club (1st prize 1969, 78), Nat. Press Photographers Assn. (1st prize 1972), San Diego Art Guild and Colo. Art Assn., Calif. Press Photographers Assn., Rotary (staff photographer La Jolla chpt., Achievement award Am. Project 1992, 93), German Shepherd Dog Club. Baptist. e-mail: RonPhoto@worldnet.att.net. Home: 12907 La Tortola San Diego CA 92129-3057

BENNETT, RONALD V., communications educator, writer; b. Rigby, Idaho, Oct. 11, 1946; s. Charles S. and Pearl A. (Scott) B.; m. Lylene Scott, July 9, 1965; children: Kendall, Michael, Matthew, Greg, Jennifer, Breanna. BA, Brigham Young U., 1969; MA in Edn., Idaho State U., 1982. Instr. Bonneville H.S., Idaho Falls, Idaho, 1970-91, Hillcrest H.S., Idaho Falls, Idaho, 1992-94; journalism educator Ricks Coll., Rexburg, Idaho, 1994—; cons., tchr. Dow Jones Newspaper Fund IJW, Bloomington, Ind., 1992-98; instr. various profl. summer workshops, 1989—. Contbr. articles to mags. and newspapers. Recipient Dist. Advisor award Dow Jones Newspaper Fund, 1991, Excellence Tchg. award Brigham Young U., 1993, Outstanding Tchr. award Idaho Falls Jaycees; named Idaho Journalism Tchr. Yr. Idaho Journalism Advisor's Assn., 1989. Mem. LDS Ch. Office: Ricks Coll Spori Bldg 525 S Center St Rexburg ID 83460

BENNETT, SHOSHANA STEIN, post partum counselor, consultant, lecturer; b. N.Y.C., Sept. 5, 1954; . Herman David and Charmion Kerr (Goldfarb) S.; m. Henry Joseph Bennett, May 24, 1981; children: Elana Michelle, Aaron Daniel. BA, Grinnell Coll., 1975; MA, San Francisco State U., 1977; PhD in Clin. Psychology, Calif. Coast U., Santa Ana, 1998. Cert tchr. learning handicapped, multiple subjects, Calif.; cert. c.c. tchr., Calif.; cert. in clin. hypnotherapy. Founder, coord. Postpartum Assistance for Mothers, Castro Valley, Calif., 1987—; instr. in handling postpartum depression Hayward (Calif.) Adult Sch., 1988-90; group leader Acalanes Adult Sch., Walnut Creek, Calif., 1988-90; guest spkr., cons. Western Regional Postpartum Support Internat. Seminar, Oakland (Calif.) Children's Hosp., 1990, ASPO Lamaze Conf., Walnut Creek, Calif., 1990, Nat. Assn. Postpartum Care Svcs. Conf., Oakland, 1992, Ob.Gyn. Conf., Kaiser Oakland Med. Ctr., 1992, 95, Calif. Healthy Mothers, Healthy Babies Conf., Oakland, 1993, Calif. Diabetes and Pregnancy Program, Warrack Hosp., Santa Rosa, Calif., 1994, San Joaquin County Comprehensive Perinatal Svc. Program, Stockton, Calif., 1995, Family Practitioner Grand Rounds, San Joaquin Gen. Hosp., Stockton, 1995, Dept. Psychiatry Kaiser Permanente Med. Group, Redwood City, Calif., 1995, Walnut Creek, Calif., 1998, Kaiser Lactation Assocs. Conf., Hayward Med. Ctr., 1996, others. Speaker on People are Talking TV program, 1987, KLOK radio From Birth and Beyond, 1992; author hosp. manuals on postpartum depression. Mem. Sch. Site Coun., Castro Valley, Calif., 1995—. Mem. Am. Counseling Assn., Postpartum Health Alliance (v.p.), Postpartum Support Internat. (bd. dirs.), Depression After Delivery. Office: Postpartum Assistance for Mothers PO Box 20513 Castro Valley CA 94546-8513

BENNETT, WILLIAM GORDON, casino executive; b. Glendale, Ariz., Nov. 16, 1924. Gen. mgr. Del Webb Corp., Las Vegas, 1965-70; with Western Equities Inc., Reno, Nev., 1971-78; chmn. Circus Circus Enterprises Inc., 1974—, dir.; pres. Circus Circus Enterprises, 1995—. Office: c/o Sierra Hotel Casino 2535 Las Vegas Blvd S Las Vegas NY 89109-1137*

BENNINGTON, LESLIE ORVILLE, JR., insurance agent; b. Sedalia, Mo., Dec. 29, 1946; s. Leslie Orville Sr. and Eunice May Marguerite (Cole) B.; m. Susan Frances Grotha, June 1, 1968; children: Leslie O. III, Jeremy Lawrence. BSME, U. Mo., Rolla, 1968; postgrad., U. Tenn. Space Inst., 1969; ChFC, Am. Coll., 1988. CLU; chartered fin. cons.; registered profl. engr., Wash., Wyo. Design engr. Arnold Research Orgn., Tullahoma, Tenn., 1968-70; engr. Pacific Power & Light, Glenrock, Wyo., 1973-75; agt., asst. gen. agt. Am. Nat. Ins. Co., Casper, Wyo., 1975-85; gen. agt. Ins. Sales, Glenrock, 1985—; pres. Cen.Wyo. Estate Planning Coun., Casper, 1985-86. Mem. Glenrock Vol. Fire Dept., 1973—, asst. chief, 1982, pres., 1993-97; pres., v.p. Converse County Recreation Bd., Douglas, Wyo., 1980-90; judge dist. h.s. speech contests, Glenrock; bd. dirs. Converse County Sch. Dist. 2, 1976; bd. dirs. Glenrock Cmty. Recreation Dist., 1990-97, pres., 1992-94; guide Helluva Hunt for physically disabled hunters, 1986—, bd. dirs., 1991—; bd. dirs. Nat. Bow Hunt, Glenrock, 1994—; baseball coach Little League and Babe Ruth, 1983-93. Mem. Nat. Assn. Life Underwriters (Nat. Quality award, Health Ins. Quality award, Nat. Sales Achievement award), Cen. Wyo. Life Underwriters (pres. 1978-80), Wyo. Life Underwriters Assn. (chmn. membership com. 1985-87, nat. com. 1982-87, v.p. 1986-87, bd. dirs. 1980-90, Ins. Agt. of Yr., 1980, pres. 1988-89), West Cen. Wyo. CLUs (pres. 1986-88), Million Dollar Round Table, Nat. Pony Express Assn. (pres. Ea. Wyo. div. 1985—, v.p. Wyo. div. 1989-97, pres. 1997—), KC (grand knight, faithful navigator). Republican. Roman Catholic. Avocations: cattle, livestock. Home: 6 Shannon Dr Glenrock WY 82637 Office: PO Box 2049 1260 East US Hwy 20-26-87 Glenrock WY 82637-2049

BENNION, JOHN STRADLING, engineering educator, consultant; b. Salt Lake City, Sept. 19, 1954; s. Mervyn S. Jr. and LaRee (Stradling) B. BS in Chemistry, U. Utah, 1987, BSChemE, 1987, MS in Nuclear Engring., 1990, PhD in Nuclear Engring., 1996. Lic. profl. engr., Utah, Idaho; registered radiation protection technologist Nat. Registry of Radiation Protection Technologists; lic. sr. reactor operator U.S. Nuclear Regulatory Commn.; cert. health physicist. Carpenter various cos. Utah, 1974-86; sr. reactor engr. U. Utah Nuclear Engring. Lab., Salt Lake City, 1987-93; instr. mech. engring. dept. U. Utah, Salt Lake City, 1992—; asst. prof. Coll. Engring. Idaho State U., Pocatello, 1995—; reactor adminstr. Idaho State U. Coll. Engring., 1996—. Author tech. papers and reports. Mem. AAAS, ASME, NSPE, IEEE, Am. Chem. Soc., Am. Soc. Engring. Edn., Am. Nuclear Soc., Am. Soc. Quality Control, Am. Acad. Health Physics, N.Y. Acad. Scis., Health Physics Soc., Internat. Soc. Radiation Physics, Utah Acad. Arts and Scis., Phi Kappa Phi, Alpha Nu Sigma, Pi Tau Sigma, Tau Beta Pi, Sigma Xi. Republican. Mem. LDS Church. Office: Idaho State U Coll of Engring Campus Box 8060 Pocatello ID 83209

BENNION, JOHN WARREN, urban education educator; b. Salt Lake City, Nov. 25; s. M. Lynn and Katherine Bennion; m. Sylvia Lustig; children: Philip, Stanford, David, Bryan, Grant, Andrew. BS in Philosophy, English, U. Utah, 1961, MA in Edn. Adminstrn., 1962; PhD in Edn. Adminstrn., Ohio State U., 1966. Tchr. Granite High Sch., Salt Lake City, 1961-63; asst. instr. Ohio State U., Columbus, 1963-64, adminstrv. asst., 1965-66; adminstrv. intern Parma (Ohio) Sch. Dist., 1964-65; asst. supt. Elgin (Ill.) Pub. Schs., 1966-68; asst. prof. edn. adminstrn. Ind. U., Bloomington, 1968-69; supt. Brighton Cen. Schs., Rochester, N.Y., 1969-79, Bloomington (Minn.) Pub. Schs., 1979-80, Provo (Utah) Sch. Dist., 1980-85, Salt Lake City Schs., 1985-94; prof. urban edn., dir. Utah Edn. Consortium U. Utah, Salt Lake City, 1994—. Recipient Nat. Superintendent of the Yr. award, Utah, Am. Assn. of School Administrators, 1992. Mem. Assn. Supervision and Curriculum Devel., Assn. Early Childhood Edn., Am. Assn. Sch. Adminstrs., Phi Delta Kappa, Rotary. Home: 1837 Harvard Ave Salt Lake City UT 84108-1804 Office: Univ Utah Grad Sch of Edn 1705 E Campus Ctr Dr Rm 225 Salt Lake City UT 84112-9251*

BENNIS, WARREN GAMELIEL, business administration educator, author, consultant; b. N.Y.C., Mar. 8, 1925; s. Philip and Rachel (Landau) B.; m. Clurie Williams, Mar. 30, 1962 (div. 1983); children: Katharine, John Leslie, Will Martin; m. Mary Jane O'Donnell, Mar. 8, 1988 (div. 1991); m. Grace Gabe, Nov. 29, 1992. AB, Antioch Coll., 1951; hon. cert. econs., London Sch. Econs., 1952; PhD, MIT, 1955; LLD, Xavier U., Cin., 1972, George Washington U., 1977; LHD (hon.), Hebrew Union Coll., 1974, Kans. State U., 1979; DSc (hon.), U. Louisville, 1977, Pacific Grad. Sch. Psychology, 1987, Gov.'s State U., 1991; LHD (hon.), Doan Coll., 1993. Diplomate Am. Bd. Profl. Psychology. Asst. prof. psychology MIT, Cambridge, 1953-56, prof., 1959-67; asst. prof. psychology and bus. Boston U., 1956-59; prof. Sloan Sch. Mgmt., 1959-67; provost SUNY-Buffalo, 1967-68, v.p. acad. devel., 1968-71; pres. U. Cin., 1971-77; U.S. prof. corps. and soc. Centre d'Etudes Industrielles, Geneva, Switzerland, 1978-79; exec.-in-residence Pepperdine U., 1978-79; George Miller Disting. prof.-in-residence U. Ill., Champaign-Urbana, 1978; Disting. prof. Bus. Adminstrn. Sch. Bus., U. So. Calif., L.A., 1980-88; univ. prof. U. So. Calif., L.A., 1988—; vis. lectr. Harvard U., 1958-59, Indian Mgmt. Inst., Calcutta; vis. prof. U. Lausanne (Switzerland), 1961-62, INSEAD, France, 1983; bd. dirs. The Foothill Group. Author: Planning of Change, 4th edit., 1985, Interpersonal Dynamics, 1963, 3d and 4th edits., 1975, Personal and Organizational Change, 1965, Changing Organizations, 1966, repub. in paperback as Beyond Bureaucracy, 1974, The Temporary Society, 1968, Organization Development, 1969, American Bureaucracy, 1970, Management of Change and Conflict, 1972, The Leaning Ivory Tower, 1973, The Unconscious Conspirary: Why Leaders Can't Lead, 1976, Essays in Interpersonal Dynamics, 1979; (with B. Nanus): Leaders, 1985, On Becoming a Leader, 1989, (with I. Mitroff) The Unreality Industry, 1989, Why Leaders Can't Lead, 1989, Leaders on Leadership, 1992, An Invented Life: Reflections on Leadership and Change, 1993, Beyond Bureaucracy, 1993, (with J. Goldsmith) Learning to Lead, 1994, (with M. Mische) Reinventing the 21st Century, 1994, Beyond Leadership, 1994, Herding Cats: Bennis on Leadership, 1996, Organizing Genius, 1997, The Temporary Society, 1998, Co-Leaders, 1999, Old Dogs, New Tricks, 1999; co-headers, 1999, cons. editor Calif. Mgmt. Rev., Mgmt. Series Jossey-Bass Pubs. Mem. Pres.' White House Task Force on Sci. Policy, 1960-70; mem. FAA study task force U.S. Dept. Transp., 1975; mem. adv. com. N.Y. State Joint Legis. Com. Higher Edn., 1970-71; mem. Ohio Gov.'s Bus. and Employment Coun., 1972-74; mem. panel on alt. approaches to grad. edn. Coun. Grad. Schs. and Grad. Record-Exam Bd., 1971-73; chmn. Nat. Adv. Commn. on Higher Edn. for Police Officers, 1976-78; adv. bd. NIH, 1978-84; trustee Colo. Rocky Mountains Sch., 1978-82; bd. dirs. Am. Leadership Forum, 1984-89; mem. vis. com. for Humanities MIT, 1975-81; trustee Antioch Coll., Salk Inst. Capt. AUS, World War II. Decorated Bronze Star, Purple Heart; recipient Dow Jones award, 1987, McKinsey Fedn. award, 1967, 68. Mem. Am. Acad. Arts and Scis. (co-chmn. policy coun. 1969-71), Am. Mgmt. Assn. (dir. 1974-77), U.S. C. of C. (adv. group scholars). Office: U So Calif Sch Bus University Park Los Angeles CA 90089-1421

BENSCH, KLAUS GEORGE, pathology educator; b. Miedar, Germany, Sept. 1, 1928; married; 3 children. M.D., U. Erlangen, Germany, 1953. Diplomate: Am. Bd. Pathology. Intern U. Hosps. of Erlangen, 1953-54; resident in anat. pathology U. Tex. and; M.D. Anderson Hosp., Houston, 1954-56, Yale, 1956-57; instr. pathology Yale Med. Sch., 1958-61, asst. prof., 1961-64, assoc. prof., 1964-68; prof. pathology Stanford Med. Sch., 1968—, acting chmn. dept. pathology, 1984-85, chmn. dept. pathology, 1985—. Office: Stanford U Med Sch Dept Pathology 300 Pasteur Dr Palo Alto CA 94304-2203

BENSKY, LAWRENCE MARTIN, journalist; b. Bklyn., May 1, 1937; s. Eli and Sarah (Davidson) B. BA, Yale U., 1958. Reporter Mpls. Star-Tribune, 1958-59; assoc. editor Random House Pub., N.Y.C., 1960-63; Paris editor Paris Rev., 1964-66; asst. editor N.Y. Times Book Rev., N.Y.C., 1966-68; mng. editor Ramparts mag., San Francisco, 1968; news reporter, anchor Sta. KSAN, San Francisco, 1969-70, 77-79; gen. mgr. Sta. KPFA, Berkeley, Calif., 1974-77; news dir. Sta. KBLX, Berkeley, 1981-82; mng. editor Calif. Pub. Radio, San Francisco, 1982-83; nat. affairs corr. Pacifica Radio, Washington, Berkeley, 1987—; co-founder, bd. dirs. Media Alliance, San Francisco, 1975—; vis. lectr. Stanford U., 1989, 91, 93-94, 98, U. Calif., Berkeley, 1991; lectr. Calif. State U., Hayward, 1992—. Bd. dirs. Am. Youth Hostels, San Francisco, 1991-96. Recipient George Polk award L.I. U., 1987, Golden Gadfly award Media Alliance, 1988, Golden Reel award Nat. Fedn. Cmty. Broadcasters, 1988, 91-93, 95, Thomas M. Storke award World Affairs Coun., San Francisco, 1991, Career Achievement award No. Calif. Soc. Profl. Journalists, 1997. Avocations: bicycling, hiking. Office: 1929 Martin Luther King Jr Way Berkeley CA 94704-1037

BENSON, DEE VANCE, federal judge; b. Salt Lake City, Aug. 25, 1948; s. Gilbert and Beryl Butler (Despain) B.; children: Angela, Natalie, Lucas, Katherine. BA, Brigham Young U., 1973, JD, 1976. Bar: Utah 1976, U.S. Dist. Ct. Utah 1976, U.S. Ct. Appeals (10th cir.) 1976, U.S. Supreme Ct. 1984, U.S. Ct. Appeals (5th cir.) 1988. Ptnr. Snow, Christensen & Martineau, Salt Lake City, 1976-84; legal counsel Senate Judiciary Com., Washington, 1984-86; chief of staff Senator Orrin Hatch's Office, Washington, 1986-88; legal counsel U.S. Senate Select Com., Washington, 1987; assoc. dep. atty. gen. U.S. Dept. Justice, Washington, 1988; U.S. atty. dist. Utah U.S. Dept. Justice, Salt Lake City, 1989-91; judge U.S. Dist. Ct., Salt Lake, 1991—; legal counsel Iran-Contra Congl. Investigating Com., Washington, 1987. Contbg. author univ. law rev. Mem. ABA, Utah State Bar (com. on cts. and judges), Salt Lake County Bar Assn., Phi Alpha Delta. Mem. LDS Ch. Avocations: soccer, skiing, mountain biking, basketball, running. Office: US Dist Ct 350 S Main St Ste 253 Salt Lake City UT 84101-2153

BENSON, DONALD EDWARD, landscape designer; b. Taos, N.Mex., Nov. 11, 1949; s. Reo Jack and Mary Veilla B. BS in Geography, N.Mex. State U., 1971; BS in Landscape Architecture, Wash. State U., 1978. Planner, designer Philip M. Botch & Assocs., Bellevue, Wash., 1979-84, Hedges and Roth Engring., Kirkland/Payallup, Wash., 1984-94; sr. planner, landscape designer URS Greiner, Seattle, 1994—. Mem. Wash. chpt. Am. Soc. Landscape Architects (visibility com. chair 1996-97, pres. 1998-99), Am. Planning Assn., Profl. Geographers Puget Sound. (pres. 1996-98). Avocations: cross country skiing, hiking, camping. Home: 539 NE Ravenna Blvd Apt 4 Seattle WA 98115-6453

BENSON, FRANCIS M., production engineer, radio producer; b. Bklyn., Oct. 7, 1958; s. Francis Gerald Benson and Grace Angela (Superty) Brothers; children: Megan Kristine, Lindsey Nicole; m. Lucena Arcila, Feb. 14, 1998. Student, Palmdale High Sch., Calif. Cert. Airframe & Powerplant Mechanic, Calif. Structure mechanic B Lockheed Aircraft Co., Palmdale, Calif., 1979-80, final assembly mechanic, 1980-83, structure mechanic B, 1985-86, mfg. supr., 1986-87; structure mechanic B Rockwell Internat., Palmdale, Calif., 1983-85, hydraulic checkout mechanic, 1985; structure mechanic A Northrop B-2 Division, Palmdale, Calif., 1987-88, mfg. supr., 1988, mfg. planner, 1988-89, mfg. engr., 1989-92; program coord., prodr. Disney/ABC, 1992-94, prodn. coord./prodr., 1994-97; computer and audio-visual technician Palos Verdes Peninsula Unified Sch. Dist., Palos Verdes Estates, Calif., 1998—; union steward Internat. Assn. Machinists & Aerospace, Palmdale Calif. Democrat. Roman Catholic. Avocations: snow skiing, running, triathlon, golf, camping. Home: 3520 Maricopa St Unit 19 Torrance CA 90503-4994 Office: 3801 Via La Selva Palos Verdes Estates CA 90274

BENSON, GREGORY DOUGLAS, video engineer; b. Balt., Apr. 26, 1963; s. Paul Robert and Joanne Nadeen (McSparron) B. AA in Drafting Tech., N. Harris County C.C., Houston, 1987. Purchasing agt. and draftsman Component Video, Inc., Van Nuys, Calif., 1989-93; video engr. Vidfilm Svcs., Inc., Glendale, Calif., 1994—. Mem. Soc. Motion Picture and TV Engrs. Avocations: designing and building loud speakers, music, reading, playing bagpipes. Home: 9026 Hillrose St Sunland CA 91040-1713 Office: Vidfilm Svcs Inc 1631 Gardena Ave Glendale CA 91204-2713

BENSON, JAMES BERNARD, JR., criminologist, educator; b. Phila., May 8, 1930; s. James Bernard Benson and Elizabeth (Smeaton) Caswell; m. Hiroko Nakamura, Apr. 14, 1955. LLD (hon.), Nat. Law Enforcement Acad., 1968; BA in Police Sci., Pacific Coll., 1976; PhD (hon.), St. John's U., Springfield, La., 1988. Cert. behavioral therapist, Calif. Chief criminal investigator U.S. Marine Corps, 1947-66; corp. officer Bank of Am., L.A., 1966-85; pvt. practice Anaheim, Calif., 1985-93; instr. police sci. St. John's U., Springfield, La. Editor: (poetry) Devotion in Blue, 1973, Lawman's Lament, 1974; contbr. articles to police mags. Fellow Am. Assn. Profl. Hypnotherapists, Am. Assn. Criminologists; mem. Nat. Soc. Clin. Hypnotherapists. Republican. Avocations: photography, writing. Home and Office: 1400 S Sunkist St Ste 199 Anaheim CA 92806-5624

BENSON, JOAN, musician, music educator; b. St. Paul; d. John Raymond and Frances (Ostergren) B. MusM, U. Ill., 1952; performer's cert., Ind. U., 1953; pvt. studies with Edwin Fischer, Switzerland, 1953-57; pvt. studies with Fritz Neumeyer, Fed. Republic Germany, 1958-59; pvt. studies with Santiago Kastner, Portugal, 1960. Concert musician worldwide, 1962—; lectr. early keyboard Stanford U., Palo Alto, Calif., 1970-76; asst. prof. U. Oreg., Eugene, 1976-82; mem. artist faculty Aston Magna Acad., Mass., 1980, 82; adj. prof. U. Oreg., 1982—; artistic advisor Boston Clavichord Soc., 1996—. Albums: Repertoire, 1962, Music of C. P. E. Bach for Piano and Clavichord, 1972, Pasquini and Haydn on Clavichords of the Boston Museum of Fine Arts, 1982, Kuhnau and C.P.E. Bach on Clavichord, 1988; contbr. music notes to Titanic and Focus record labels; contbr. articles to internat. profl. jours. Recipient Kate Nell Kinley award. Mem. Am. Musicol. Soc. Home: 2795 Central Blvd Eugene OR 97403-2528

BENSON, JOHN ALEXANDER, JR., physician, educator; b. Manchester, Conn., July 23, 1921; s. John A. and Rachel (Patterson) B.; m. Irene Zucker, Sept. 29, 1947; children: Peter M., John Alexander III, Susan Leigh, Jeremy P. BA, Wesleyan U., 1943; MD, Harvard Med. Sch., 1946. Diplomate Am. Bd. Internal Medicine (mem. 1969-91, sec.-treas. 1972-75, pres. 1975-91, pres. emeritus 1991—), Subsplty. Bd. Gastroenterology (mem. 1961-66, chmn. 1965-66). Intern Univ. Hosps., Cleve., 1946-47; resident Peter Bent Brigham Hosp., Boston, 1949-51; fellow Mass. Gen. Hosp., Boston, 1951-53; rsch. asst. Mayo Clinic, Rochester, Minn., 1953-54; instr. medicine Harvard U., 1956-59; head divsn. gastroenterology U. Oreg. Med. Sch., Portland, 1959-75, prof. medicine, 1965-93; prof. emeritus Oreg. Health Sci. U., Portland, 1993—; interim dean Sch. Medicine Oreg. Health Sci. U., 1991-93, dean emeritus, 1993—; cons. VA Hosps., Madigan Gen. Army Hosp., John A. Hartford Found. Editorial bd.: Am. Jour. Digestive Diseases, 1966-73; Contbr. articles to profl. jours. Mem. Oreg. Med. Ednl. Found., 1967-73, dir., 1967-73, pres., 1969-72; bd. dirs. N.W. Ctr. for Physician-Patient Comm., 1994—, Am. Acad. on Physician and Patient, 1994-99; bd. dirs. Found. for Med. Excellence, 1996—, pres., 1998—. With USNR, 1947-49. Mem. AAS, AMA, ACP (master), Am. Gastroenterol. Assn. (sec. 1970-73, v.p. 1975-76, pres.-elect. 1976-77, pres. 1977-78), Am. Clin. and Climatol. Assn. (v.p. 1997), Am. Soc. Internal Medicine, Western Assn. Physicians, North Pacific Soc. Internal Medicine, Am. Fedn. Clin. Rsch., Federated Coun. for Internal Medicine, Am. Assn. Study Liver Disease, Western Soc. Clin. Investigation, Soc. Health and Human Values, Assn. Health Svcs. Rsch., Inst. Medicine NAS (sr.), Phi Beta Kappa, Sigma Xi, Alpha Omega Alpha. Office: Oreg Health Scis U Sch Medicine L102 Portland OR 97201

BENSON, KAREN A., nursing educator; b. Havre, Mont., Sept. 10, 1946; d. William Duncan and Norma Evelyn (Erickson) Ross; children: Alice, Evan, David, Marc. BSN, Mont. State U., 1968; MS in Biology, Wash. State U., 1978, PhD in Vet. Sci., 1983; MS in Nursing, Oreg. Health Scis. U., 1986. Lectr. Seattle U. Contbr. articles to profl. publs. Dr. Lynn A. George scholar; Sigma Xi rsch. grantee. Mem. ANA, Wash. State Nurses Assn., Am. Holistic Nurses Assn., Sigma Theta Tau, Phi Kappa Phi. Home: 17103 25th Ave NE Seattle WA 98155-6124

BENSON, M. (BOB), artist, drama educator; b. Chgo., July 22, 1951; s. Eva Ann (Japuntich) Benson; children: Amber K., Aaron D. MA in Lit., Composition, Theatre Prodn., Humboldt State U., Calif., 1982-95. Staff drama dept. Ariz. State U., Tempe; disk jockey KHSU Radio , Arcata, Calif., 1985-96; acad. advisor, Shakespeare tchr., Upward Bound, Arcata, Calif., 1991-96. Writer, producer, dir.; (art pieces) Into the Clinic, 1994, A Walk in Old Town, 1995, Lot 59, 1997, Eureka, 1997. Recipient Calif State U. Forgiveble Loan Program, Arcata, Calif., 1993-94. Mem. MLA, Am. Alliance for Theatre Edn., Calif. Artists for Edn. Avocations: jester, fool, arbiter of words. Home: PO Box 2142 Tempe AZ 85280-2142 Office: Ariz State U Dept of Theatre Tempe AZ 85287

BENSON, STEPHEN R., editorial cartoonist. BA in Polit. Sci. cum laude, Brigham Young U., 1979. With Senate Rep. Policy Com., 1979-80;

cartoonist The Ariz. Republic, Phoenix, 1980-90, 91—, The Morning-News Tribune, Tacoma, Wash., 1990-91. Author: Fencin' with Benson, 1984, Evanly Days, 1988, Back at the Barb-B-Cue, 1991, Where Do You Draw the Line?, 1992. Recipient Nat. Headliner award, 1984, 1st Place Best of the West, 1991, 92, 93, Pulitzer Prize finalist editorial cartooning, 1984, 89, 92, 94, Pulitzer Prize for editorial cartooning, 1993. Office: The Ariz Republic 200 E Van Buren St Phoenix AZ 85004-2238*

BENSON, STEVEN DONALD, sheet metal research and marketing executive, sheet metal mechanic, programmer, author; b. Longview, Wash., Oct. 11, 1953; s. Steven Hughes Benson and Donna Ruth (Johnson) McKinney; m. Patricia Joyce Krauss, Feb. 14, 1982; children: Steven William, Patricia Ann. AA in Drafting, South Salem Indsl. Arts Coll., 1973; AA in Robotics, AMADA Sch., Buena Park, Calif., 1997. Precision sheet metal mechanic Ariz. Precision Sheet Metal, Phoenix, 1980-86, Neilson Mfg. Inc., Salem, Oreg., 1986—; owner, operator Time Honored Gifts, Salem, 1988—; pres. Advanced Sheet Metal Applications, Salem, 1986—; instr. Oreg. Advanced Tech. Consortium, Wilsonville, 1990—; sheet metal instr. Clackamas C.C., Oregon City, Oreg., 1997—; editor, pub. Precision Sheet Metal Chronicle, electronic mag., 1998—. Author: (textbooks) Introduction to Precision Press Brake, 1991, Intermediate Press Brake, 1992, Advanced Precision Press Brake, 1994, Press Brake Technology, 1997, (software) Advanced Sheet Metal Applications (ASMA 4.0), 1982, 90, 92, 95, 97. Sec., treas. Bike PAC of Oreg., Salem, 1988—, lobbyist, 1992; mem. A Brotherhood Against Totalitarian Enactments (ABATE), Oreg., Inc. Mem. Fabricators and Mfrs. Assn. (mem. adv. com. precision sheet metal adv. 1997—, mem. coun.), Soc. Mfg. Engrs., Internat. Sheet Metal Workers (local #16). Avocations: family activities, children, politics, Indian moto-cycles, British sports cars. Fax: 206-727-8729. E-mail: steve@asmachronicle.com. Home: 395 23d St NE Salem OR 97301-4440 Office: Advanced Sheet Metal Applications 398 Rose St NE Salem OR 97301-4468

BENSON, TIMOTHY OLIVER, curator, educator; b. Utica, N.Y., May 9, 1950; s. Donald Robert and Martha Jo Benson; m. Susan Ellen Annett, Aug. 14, 1976. BA, Grinnell Coll., 1972; MA, U. Iowa, 1976, PhD, 1985. Lectr. Drake U., Des Moines, 1982, 84, U. Nebr., Omaha, 1985; asst. prof. U. Nebr., Lincoln, 1985-86; assoc. curator Rifkind Ctr. L.A. County Mus. Art, 1986-97, curator Rifkind Ctr. for German Expressionist Studies, 1997—; adj. instr. Simpson Coll., Indianola, Iowa, 1981-82; adj. prof. U. So. Calif., L.A., 1996—. Co-author: (exhbn. catalog) Emil Nolde: The Painter's Prints, 1995; author, editor: (exhbn. catalog) Expressionist Utopias, 1993; author: (book) Raoul Hausmann & Berlin Dada, 1989. Recipient German Order of Merit, 1997, Alexander von Humboldt stipend, 1991, 97, German Acad. Exch. stipend, 1980; Kress Found. travel grantee, 1981. Mem. Am. Assn. Mus., Coll. Art Assn. of Am., German Studies Assn., Print Coun. of Am., Historians of German and Ctrl. European Art and Arch., Carl Einstein Soc. Office: LA County Mus Art 5905 Wilshire Blvd Los Angeles CA 90036

BENTLEY, JOSHUA MARK, lawyer; b. San Francisco, Feb. 27, 1965; s. John Martin and Ruth Catherine (Marshall) B.; m. Emily Elaine Blanchard, Aug. 15, 1990; children: Kaitlin Meredith, Olivia Roxanne. BA, U. Calif., Santa Barbara, 1983-88; JD, U. Santa Clara, Calif., 1991. Bar: Calif. 1991, U.S. Dist. Ct. Calif. 1991. Dep. dist. atty. San Mateo County Dist. Atty.'s Office, Redwood City, Calif., 1991-93; gen. ptnr. Smith, Bentley & Hartnett, Redwood City, 1993—. Recipient Congl. Recognition, Congresswoman Anna Eshoo, 1996. Mem. ABA, Calif. State Bar. Republican. Roman Catholic. Office: Smith Bentley & Hartnett 777 Marshall St Redwood City CA 94063-1818

BENTLEY, JUDY, english educator, writer; b. Beech Grove, Ind., Apr. 8, 1945; d. Robert Edward and Luella Kathleen (Hart) McBride; m. Allen Russell Bentley, June 6, 1970; children: Anne, Peter. BA, Oberlin Coll., 1967; MA, NYU, 1969, NYU, 1973. Asst. editor Saturday Review, NY, 1970-72; copy editor Newsweek Books, NY, 1973-74; adjunct instructor N.Y.C. C.C., 1975-77; preceptor The Dalton Sch., NY, 1977-79; instructor S Seattle C.C., 1984—. Author: State Government, (The American Government Series), 1978, The National Health Care Controversy, 1981, American Immigration Today: Pressures, Problems, Policies, 1981, Busing, The Continuing Controversy, 1982, Justice Sandra Day O'Connor, 1983, The Nuclear Freeze Movement, 1984, Refugees: Search for a Haven, 1986, Archbishop Tutu of South Africa, 1988, Harriet Tubman, Moses of Her People, 1990, Fidel Castro of Cuba, 1991, Speakers of the House, 1994; series editor and author: Explorers, Furtrappers, and Guides, Brides, Midwives, and Widows, 1995, "Dear Friend," Thomas Garrett & William Still, Collaborators on the Underground Railroad, 1997. Parent rep. Elem. Sch. Study Steering Com. Bellevue Sch. Dist. 1986-89; chair E Bellevue Transp. Adv. Com., 1989-92, chairwoman bd., sec., treas., Peace Action of Washington, 1995—. hiking. E-mail: jbentley@.sccd.ctc.edu. Office: S Seattle C.C. 6000 16th Ave SW Seattle WA 98106

BENTLEY, SARA, newspaper publishing executive. Pres. Gannett Northwest Newspaper Group, Salem, Oreg., 1988—. Office: Statesman-Jour Co Inc 280 Church St NE Salem OR 97301-3762

BENTLY, DONALD EMERY, electrical engineer; b. Cleve., Oct. 18, 1924; s. Oliver E. Bently and Mary Evelyn (Conway) B.; m. Susan Lorraine Pumphrey, Sept. 1961 (div. Sept. 1982); 1 child, Christopher Paul. BSEE with distinction, U. Iowa, 1949, MSEE, 1950; DS (hon.), U. Nev., 1987. Registered profl. engr., Calif., Nev. Pres. Bently Nev. Corp., Minden, 1961-85, chief exec. officer, 1985—; chief exec. officer Bently Rotor Dynamics and Research Corp., Minden, 1985—; also chmn. bd. dirs. Bently Nev. Corp., Minden; chief exec. officer Gibson Tool Co., Carson City, Nev., 1978—; bd. dirs. Sierra Pacific Resources, 1982-83. Contbr. articles to profl. jours.; developer electronic instruments for the observation of rotating machinery, and the algorithm for rotor fluid-induced instability; inventor in field. Trustee Inst. World Politics. With USN, 1943-46, PTO. Named Inventor of Yr., State of Nev. Innovation and Tech. Coun., 1983; recipient first Decade award Vibration Inst., Myklestad award; inducted to Jr. Achievement of Northern Nev. Bus. Leaders' Hall of Fame. Mem. ASME (industry adv. bd.), Am. Petroleum Inst., St. Petersburg (Russian Fedn.) Acad. Engring., Sigma Xi, Eta Kappa Nu, Tau Beta Pi, Sigma Alpha Epsilon. Episcopalian. Avocations: skiing, hiking, biking. Office: Bently Nev Corp 1711 Orbit Way Minden NV 89423-4114

BENTON, FLETCHER, sculptor; b. Jackson, Ohio, 1931. BFA, Miami U., Oxford, Ohio, 1956, DFA (hon.), 1993; DFA (hon.), Rio Grande U., 1994. Mem. faculty Calif. Coll. Arts and Crafts, 1959, San Francisco Art Inst., 1964-67; prof. art Calif. State U., San Jose, 1967-81; prof. Calif. State U., 1981-86. One-man shows include, San Francisco Mus. Modern Art, 1965, Albright-Knox Mus., Buffalo, 1970, Galeria Bonino, N.Y.C., 1969, Galerie Francoise Mayer, Brussels, San Francisco Mus. Modern Art, 1970, London Arts Gallery, Detroit, 1970, Galeria Bonino, Buenos Aires, Estudio Actual, Caracas, Venezuela, 1970, Landry-Bonino Gallery, N.Y.C., 1972, Phoenix Mus. Art, 1973, Galeria Bonino, Rio de Janiero, 1973, Calif. State U.-Berkeley, 1973, Neuberger Mus., N.Y., 1974, Hirshhorn Mus., 1974, Phila. Art Alliance, 1974, Elvehejem Mus. Art, Wis., 1976, San Francisco Modern Mus. Art, 1976, Huntsville Mus. Modern Art, Ala., 1977, Alrich Mus. Contemporary Art, Conn., John Berggruen Gallery, San Francisco, 1978, 84, 89, 96, Am. Acad. and Inst. Arts and Letters, N.Y.C., 1979, Chgo. Arts Club, 1979, Milw. Art Ctr., 1980, Suermondt-Ludwig Mus., Asschen, Fed. Republic Germany, Klingspor Mus., Offenbach, Fed. Republic Germany, 1981, 96, Kunsthandling Brigitte Haasner, Wiesbaden, Fed. Republic Germany, 1987, 92, 96, Sung Dem Fine Arts, Seoul, Korea, 1991, Dorothy Goldeen Gallery, Santa Monica, Calif., 1988, 93, Gallerie Simone Sterne, New Orleans, 1990, 93, Riva Yares Gallery, Scottsdale, 1991, Miami U., Oxford, 1993, Gallery Camino Real, Boca Raton, Fla.; group shows include San Francisco Art Inst., 1964, San Francisco Modern Mus. Art, 1964, Calif. Pal. of Legion of Honor, 1964, Whitney Mus. Am. Art, N.Y.C., 1966, 68, Los Angeles County Mus., 1967, Phila. Art Mus., 1967, Walker Art Ctr., Mpls., 1968, Art Inst. Chgo., 1968, Internat. Mus. Fine Arts, Osaka, Japan, 1970, Hayward Gallery, London, 1970, Stanford (Calif.) Mus., 1971, Am. Acad. and Inst. Arts and Letters, N.Y.C., 1981, Amerika Haus, Frankfurt, 1981, Whitney Mus. Am. Art, N.Y.C., 1981, Oakland Mus., 1982, John Berggruen Gallery, 1983, Olympic Arts Festival, Los Angeles, France, Fed. Republic Germany, Eng., Norway, 1984, John Berggruen Gallery, 1985, 89, 92, Chapman Coll. (Calif.), 1985, The Adrich Mus. Contemporary Art, Conn., 1985, Centro de Arte Moderna, Lisbon, Portugal, 1986, Kleinewefers, Krefeld, Fed. Repbulic Germany, 1987, Kundsthandlung Brigitte Haasner, Wiesbaden, Fed. Republic Germany, 1987, 88, Dorothy Goldeen Gallery, Santa Monica, Calif., 1988, Andre Emmerich Gallery, 1991, 92, Rio Grande (Ohio) U., 1994, Miami Art Mus., Oxford, Ohio, 1996, others; major collections Euroclear Hdqs. Brussels, Belgium, 1993, Modernesstadt Cologne, 1993, Gothaer, Cologne, Top Gallant, 1994, Pauling, N.Y., 1994; subject of book, Fletcher Benton by Paul Karlstrom and Edward Lucie-Smith, 1990. Served with USN, 1949-50. Recipient Disting. Svc. award to arts Am. Acad. and Inst. Arts and Letters, 1979, Career award Ohioana Libr. Assn., 1994; Pres.'s Scholar award San Jose State U., 1980. *

BENTON, LEE F., lawyer; b. Springfield, Ohio, Feb. 18, 1944. AB, Oberlin Coll., 1966; JD, U. Chgo., 1969. Bar: Calif. 1970. Mng. ptnr. Cooley Godward LLP, Palo Alto, Calif.; teaching fellow Stanford Law Sch., 1969-70. Mem. Order Coif, Phi Beta Kappa. Office: Cooley Godward LLP 5 Palo Alto Sq 3000 El Camino Real Palo Alto CA 94306-2120

BENTZ, PENNY LENNEA, special education educator; b. Fremont, Nebr., Nov. 29, 1949; d. Edward Earl and June Lorraine (Larson) B.; 1 child, Nikole Lorraine. BA in Edn., Wayne State Coll., 1972. Cert. tchr., Wash., Nebr. Tchr. grades K-2 Sch. Dist. 23, Valley, Nebr., 1972-74; tchr. Sch. Dist. 90, Scribner, Nebr., 1976-77; substitute tchr. Westside Sch. Dist., Millard Pub. Schs., Omaha, 1974-88; spl. edn. tchr. Lake Washington Sch. Dist., Kirkland, 1988-89, 91-96, Renton (Wash.) Schs., 1989-90, CHILD Inst., Bellevue, Wash., 1990-91; mem. adv. com. Comprehensive Sys. of Pers. Devel., Olympia, Wash., 1993-95; mem. Lake Washington Sch. Dist. Leadership Com. Severe Behavior Disabled Edn. grantee Seattle U., 1993. Mem. NEA, Wash. Edn. Assn. spl. edn. commn. 1992-95, spl. edn. cert. prarprofl. task force), Lake Washington Edn. Assn. (bldg. rep. 1991-95), Delta Kappa Gamma (pres. 1994-96). Methodist. Avocations: spectator sports, reading. also: 12911 87th Ave NE Kirkland WA 98034

BENZING, DAVID WARREN, semiconductor equipment company executive; b. Perth Amboy, N.J., Feb. 11, 1953; s. Walter Charles and Ruth E. (McBride) B.; m. Pamela Jean Drummond, Dec. 28, 1972 (div. 1982); 1 child, Thor A.; m. Cathleen Lynn Hays, Sept. 12, 1985 (div. 1988); 1 child, Allison G. BSChemE, U. Calif., Berkeley, 1974; PhD in Chem. Engring., Princeton U., 1978. Sr. engr. Signetics Corp., Sunnyvale, Calif., 1978-81, Applied Materials, Inc., Santa Clara, Calif., 1981-82; dir. research and devel. Anelva Corp., San Jose, Calif., 1982-84; pres., founder Benzing Technologies, Inc., Santa Clara, 1984—; v.p., gen. mgr. Direction Inc., Sunnyvale, 1994-97; lectr. Sci. and Tech. Inst., Mountain View, Calif., 1981-83; cons. Ube Industries, Ltd., Tokyo, 1984-87, Plasma Sys. Corp., Tokyo, 1993-96. Contbr. articles to profl. jours.; patentee in field. Mem. Electrochem. Soc., Thin Film Soc., Semiconductor Equipment and Materials Inst. Republican. Avocations: wine, home remodeling, gardening. Office: Benzing Techs Inc 1203 Foxworthy Ave San Jose CA 95118-1212

BERAN, CAROL LOUISE VIERTEL, English language educator; b. Bklyn., Jan. 29, 1944; d. Maurice and Olive H.B. Viertel; m. Rudolf Beran, Aug. 24, 1968; children: Rudolf, Gregory. BA, Susquehanna U., 1966; MA, Johns Hopkins U., 1967; PhD, U. Calif., Berkeley, 1977. English tchr. Patapsco H.S., Dundalk, Md., 1967-68; English prof. St. Mary's Coll., Moraga, Calif., 1977—. Author: Living Over the Abyss: Margaret Atwood's Life Before Man, 1993; contbr. articles to profl. jours. Grantee Can. Embassy, 1985-96. Mem. Assn. Can. Studies in U.S., Western Social Sci. Assn., Margaret Laurence Soc., Margaret Atwood Soc. Lutheran. Office: St Mary's Coll PO Box 4336 Moraga CA 94575

BERARD, STEPHEN ALFRED, foreign language educator; b. Boston, Feb. 8, 1948; s. Alfred Adelard and Helen Isabel (Williams) B. BA in Classics, UCLA, 1970; MA in Latin, U. Calif., Berkeley, 1975, Candidatus Philosophiae in Classics, 1981; postgrad., Monterey Peninsula Coll., 1981-82, U. Trier, Germany, 1983, Albert-Ludwigs-U., Freiburg, Germany, 1986-87; MA in German Studies with distinction, Monterey (Calif.) Inst. Intern, 1987; PhD in Germanic Philology, U. Mass., 1993. Tchg. assoc. dept. classics U. Calif., Berkeley, 1975-77, acting instr., 1977-78; vis. instr. dept. classics U. Mass., Amherst, 1978-80, tchg. asst., 1985-86, 87-88; instr., head of Latin dept. Santa Catalina Sch., Monterey, 1981-85; instr. Internat. Lang. Inst., Northampton, Mass., 1986, 87-89; prof. Wenatchee (Wash.) Valley Coll., 1989—; chair humanities divsn. Wenatchee Valley Coll., 1994-96; guest spkr. dept. Germanic langs. and lits. U. Ill., Urbana, 1989; translator Internat. Lang. Inst., Northampton, 1987-89. Contbr. articles to profl. jours. Grantee Kontaktstipendium, Fed. Republic of Germany, 1986-87; recipient 1st pl. award Latin Translation Contest, Berkeley, 1974, 75; Regents fellow U. Calif., Berkeley, 1974-75, Spl. Career fellow, 1973-74, Woodrow Wilson designate, 1970. Mem. MLA, Am. PHilol. Assn., Soc. for Germanic Philology, Pacific N.W. Coun. for Lang., Classical Assn. of Pacific Coast, N.Am. Inst. for Living Latin Studies, Phi Beta Kappa, Alpha Mu Gamma. Avocations: writing poetry and fiction, collecting classical CDs. Office: Wenatchee Valley Coll 1300 5th St Wenatchee WA 98801

BERARDINI, JACQUELINE HERNANDEZ, lawyer; b. Pueblo, Colo., Sept. 16, 1949; d. Basilio Hernandez and Lorenza (Huerta) Zamarripa; stepfather John E. Zamarripa; m. Jose A. Soliz, Aug. 1971 (div. 1980); 1 child, Christopher A.; m. Brian J. Berardini, Oct. 17, 1981; 1 child, Michael J. BA in Psychology, U. Colo., 1971; MA in Counseling, U. No. Colo., 1973; JD, U. Denver, 1980. Bar: Colo. 1980, U.S. Dist. Ct. Colo. 1980, U.S. Ct. Appeals (10th cir.) 1990, U.S. Supreme Ct. 1991. Sr. rehab. counselor divsn. rehab. Colo. Dept. Social Svcs., 1974-77; assoc. Jeffrey A. Springer, P.C. law firm, 1980-85; dep. atty. gen. Office of Colo. Atty. Gen., 1985-91; asst. to dir., dir. multi-media focal group Office of Environment, Colo. Dept. of Health, Denver, 1991-93; dir. environ integration group Colo. Dept. Health and Environment, Denver, 1993-96, dep. dir. Office Policy and Pub./Pvt. Initiatives, 1997—; adj. prof. U. Denver; apptd. to superfund rev. subcom. Nat. Adv. Com. on Environ. and Policy and Tech., EPA; apptd. to subcom. on transport and opening of waste isolation pilot plant Western Govs.' Assn.; mem. subcom. on federal facilities compliance Nat. Govs.' Assn.; apptd. Pueblo Army Depot Chem. Demilitarization Citizen Rev. Com.; alt. mem. high-level radioactive waste com. Western Interstate Energy Bd.; presenter in field; lead negotiator Colo. Rocky Flats cleanup, 1996; mem. Dialogue for Assembled Chem. Weapons Assessment. Contbr. articles to profl. jours. Mem. Colo. Bar Assn., Denver Bar Assn., Colo. Hispanic Bar Assn., Colo. Hispanic League. Avocations: hiking, cross-country skiing, reading. Office: Colo Dept Pub Health and Environment OPPI/A5 4300 Cherry Creek S Dr Denver CO 80246-1523

BERCEL, DANIELLE SUZANNE, software engineer, artist; b. L.A., Mar. 5, 1951; d. Joseph Irwin Bleeden and Barbara Elaine Simons; stepfather Albert Simons. BA in Music, Antioch Coll., Yellow Springs, Ohio, 1976. Cons. D.S. Bercel and Assoc., Beverly Hills, Calif., 1983-85; sr. engr. Sun Microsystems, Mountain View, Calif., 1985-88; sr. engr. software The Wollongong Group, Palo Alto, Calif., 1988-89; R&D software design Hewlett Packard, Palo Alto, 1989-98; R&D protocol arch. BMC Software, Sunnyvale, Calif., 1998—. Artist: Fractal Cosmos, 1993, The Art of Fractals, 1995, 96; art featured on 6 greeting cards; contbr. articles to profl. jours.; author short stories. Mem. Hewlett Packard E-mail Mentor Program. Mem. IEEE, NOW, Assn. Computing Machinery, Scrug, Interex, Internat. Midi Assn. Avocations: electronic music, fractal art, writing. Office: BMC Software 965 Stewart Dr Sunnyvale CA 94086-3913

BERDAHL, ROBERT MAX, academic administrator, historian, educator; b. Sioux Falls, S.D., Mar. 15, 1937; s. Melvin Oliver and Mildred Alberta (Maynard) B.; m. Margaret Lucille Ogle, Aug. 30, 1958; children—Daphne Jean, Jennifer Lynne, Barbara Elizabeth. B.A., Augustana Coll., 1959; M.A., U. Ill., 1961; Ph.D., U. Minn., 1965. Asst. prof. history U. Mass., Boston, 1965-67; asst. prof. history U. Oreg., Eugene, 1967-72; assoc. prof. U. Oreg., 1972-81, prof., 1981-86; dean U. Oreg. (Coll. Arts and Scis.), 1981-86; prof. U. Ill., 1986-93, vice chancellor academic affairs, 1986-93; pres. U. Tex., Austin, 1993-97; chancellor U. Calif., Berkeley, 1997—; research asso. Inst. for Advanced Study, Princeton, 1972-73. Author: The Politics of Prussian Nobility, 1988; (with others) Klassen und Kultur, 1982; contbr. articles to profl. jours. Fulbright fellow, 1975-76; Nat. Endowment Humanities fellow, 1976-77. Office: U Calif at Berkeley 200 California Hall Berkeley CA 94720-7464

BERENDT, PAUL, political party administrator; b. July 16, 1956; m. Beth Berendt. BA, Evergreen State Coll., 1987. Chmn. Wash. State Dem. Party, 1995—. Roman Catholic. Home: 1702 Sulenes Dr SE Olympia WA 98501-7042 Office: PO Box 4027 Seattle WA 98104-0027*

BERETTA, GIORDANO BRUNO, computer scientist, researcher; b. Brugg, Aargau, Switzerland, Apr. 14, 1951; came to U.S., 1984; PhD, ETH, Zurich, Switzerland, 1984. Mem. rsch. staff Xerox Palo Alto (Calif.) Rsch. Ctr., 1984-90; charter mem., sr. scientist Canon Info. Systems, Palo Alto, 1990-93; mem. tech. staff Hewlett-Packard Labs., 1994—; chmn. various confs. Contbr. articles to profl. jours.; patentee digital color reprodn. and colorimetry. Mem. The Internat. Soc. for Optical Engring., Inter-Soc. Color Coun., Soc. for Imaging Sci. and Tech. (svc. award 1998), Swiss Math. Soc., Alumni Orgn. of Swiss Fed. Inst. of Tech. Zurich. Office: Hewlett-Packard Labs 1501 Page Mill Rd Palo Alto CA 94304-1100

BERG, FREDERICKS, audiology educator; b. Butte, Montana, Oct. 13, 1928; s. Nils and Maurina Josephine (Berggren) B.; m. Edna Myrtle Clawson, May 18, 1959; children: Sven, Louis, Glenn, Leonard, Karen, Nathan. BS, Washington U., St. Louis, 1952; MS in Speech Pathology and Audiology, So. Ill. U., 1956, PhD in Speech Pathology and Audiology, 1960. CCC-Audiology Am. Speech-Lang.-Hearing Assn. Tchr. deaf Spokane, Wash., 1952-53; listening specialist So. Ill. U., Carbondale, 1955-56; speech specialist Carterville, Ill., 1955-57; tchr. deaf and hearing aid specialist Oregon Sch. Deaf, Salem, 1959-60; asst. prof. communicative disorders Oregon Coll. Edn., Monmouth, 1960-61; assoc. prof. Wayne State U., Detroit, 1961-65; assoc. prof. Utah State U., Logan, 1965-70, prof., 1970-91, prof. emeritus, 1991—; preschool hearing specialist Wayne State U., 1961-65, aural rehab. specialist Detroit Hearing Hearing, 1961-65; projects dir. U.S. Dept. Edn. and Utah State U., 1966-92, projects evaluator, 1972-75, projects cons., 1992-93; project evaluator Roane County Pub. Schs., Spencr, W.Va., 1974-75. Author: Educational Audiology, 1976, Listening and Speech Package, 1976, Facilitating Classroom Listening, 1987, Acoustics and Sounds Systems in Schools, 1993; (with others) How the Student with Hearing Loss Can Succeed in College, 1990, Rehabilitive Audiology, 1995, Audiology in Education, 1996; Editor: The Hard of Hearing Child: Hearing and Speech Management, 1970, Educational Audiology for the Hard of Hearing Child, 1986; contbr. articles to profl. jours. fundraising United Fund, Smithfield, Utah, 1983, Boy Scouts Am., 1983; petty officer 3rd class USN, 1946-48. Recipient The Frederick S. Berg Ednl. Audiology award Ednl. Audiology Assn., 1992. Fellow Am. Speech-Lang.-Hearing Assn.; mem. Nat. Sound and Communication Assn., Edn. Audiology Assn. (pres. 1984-85), Acad. Rehabilitative Audiology, Alexander Graham Bell Assn. Deaf, Am. Instructors Deaf. Republican. Mem. LDS Ch. Avocations: gardening, fishing, geneology, writing, intalling sound equipment, church work. Home: 516 Summit Dr Smithfield UT 84335-1106

BERG, LINDA THOMS, real estate broker; b. Englewood, N.J., May 27, 1948; d. Arthur W. and Lois A. (Sommerhalter) Thoms; m. Max R. Berg, May 14, 1967; children: Lisa, Darren. BS, Ariz. State U., 1992; M. in Counseling, U. Phoenix, 1995. Grad. Realtor Inst.; cert. residential specialist; cert. residential broker; cert. real estate appraiser, N.J. Founder, CEO Triton Ho. Sr. Citizens Residential Living, 1972-78; pres., ptnr., broker Berg, Brown & Lewis Real Estate, Point Pleasant Beach, N.J., 1984-86; mgr. Diane Turton Realtors, Sea Girt, N.J., 1986-89, Coldwell Banker Success Realty, Tempe, Ariz., 1992—. Editor/pub. Point Pleasant Beach Guidebook, 1976-79. Commr. Dept. Law and Pub. Safety, N.J., 1986-89; v.p., chmn. fundraising Ariz. State U. Adult re-Entry Connection, 1990-92; v.p. Point Pleasant Beach C. of C., 1978-81; mem. profl. stds. com. South Monmouth Bd. Realtors, Manasquan, N.J., 1984-86; vol. counselor Salvation Army ARC. Mem. ACA, AAUW, NAFE, Tempe C. of C., Ariz. State U. Alumni Assn., S.E. Valley Regional Assn. Realtors, Golden Key, Gamma Beta Phi. Avocations: skiing, hiking, scuba diving. Home: 601 E Citation Ln Tempe AZ 85284-1449 Office: Coldwell Banker Success 655 W Warner Rd Ste 101 Tempe AZ 85284-2924

BERG, MARGARETE CLAIRE, banker; b. Seattle, Feb. 21, 1948; d. Orville Clarence and Margaretha Katharina (Hanz) B. BA in Edn., Western State U., Bellingham, Wash., 1970, BA in French/German, 1972; MA in Germanics, U. Wash., 1979, PhD in Comparative Lit., 1994. Banker Seattle First Nat. Bank, 1972—. Mem. MLA, Am. Comparative Lit. Assn., Western State U. Alumni Assn., Am. Conf. on Romanticism, U. Wash. Alumni Assn. Democrat. Lutheran. Avocations: literary research, drawing, classical music, gardening. Home: 129 NE 161st St Seattle WA 98155-5727

BERG, PAUL, biochemist, educator; b. N.Y.C., June 30, 1926; s. Harry and Sarah (Brodsky) B.; m. Mildred Levy, Sept. 13, 1947; 1 son, John. BS, Pa. State U., 1948; PhD (NIH fellow 1950-52), Western Res. U., 1952; DSc (hon.), U. Rochester, 1978, Yale U., 1978, Wash. U., St. Louis, 1986, Oreg. State U., 1989, Pa. State U., 1995. Postdoctoral fellow Copenhagen (Denmark) U., 1952-53; postdoctoral fellow sch. medicine Washington U., St. Louis, 1953-54; Am. Cancer Soc. scholar cancer research dept. microbiology sch. medicine Washington U., 1954-57, from asst. to assoc. prof. microbiology sch. medicine, 1955-59; prof. biochemistry sch. medicine Stanford U., 1959—, Sam, Lulu and Jack Willson prof. biochemistry sch. medicine, 1970-94; Robert W. Cahill prof. cancer rsch., 1994—; chmn. dept. sch. medicine Stanford U., 1969-74; dir. Stanford U. Beckman Ctr. for Molecular and Genetic Medicine, 1985—, Affymetrix, 1993—, Nat. Found. Biomed. Rsch., 1994—; non-resident fellow Salk Inst., 1973-83; adv. bd. NIH, NSF, MIT; vis. com. dept. biochemistry and molecular biology Harvard U.; bd. sci. advisors Jane Coffin Childs Found. Med. Rsch., 1970-80; chmn. sci. adv. com. Whitehead Inst., 1984-90; bd. sci. adv. DNAX Rsch. Inst., 1981—; internat. adv. bd. Basel Inst. Immunology; chmn. nat. adv. com. Human Genome Project, 1990-92. Contbr. profl. jours.; Editor: Biochem. and Biophys. Research Communications, 1959-68; editorial bd.: Molecular Biology, 1966-69. Trustee Rockefeller U., 1990-92. Served to lt. (j.g.) USNR, 1943-46. Recipient Eli Lilly prize biochemistry, 1959; V.D. Mattia award Roche Inst. Molecular Biology, 1972; Henry J. Kaiser award for excellence in teaching, 1969, 72; Disting. Alumnus award Pa. State U., 1972; Sarasota Med. awards for achievement and excellence, 1979; Gairdner Found. annual award, 1980; Lasker Found. award, 1980; Nobel award in chemistry, 1980; N.Y. Acad. Sci. award, 1980; Sci. Freedom and Responsibility award AAAS, 1982; Nat. Medal of Sci., 1983; named Calif. Scientist of Yr. Calif. Museum Sci. and Industry, 1963; numerous disting. lectureships including Harvey lectr., 1972, Lynen lectr., 1977, Priestly lectrs. Pa. State U., 1978, Dreyfus Disting. lectrs. Northwestern U., 1979, Lawrence Livermore Dir.'s Disting. lectr., 1983, Linus Pauling lectr., 1993. Fellow AAAS; mem. NAS, Inst. Medicine, Am. Acad. Arts and Scis., Am. Soc. Biol. Chemists (pres. 1974-75), Am. Soc. Cell Biology (chmn. pub. policy com. 1994—), Am. Soc. Microbiology, Am. Philos. Soc., Internat. Soc. Molecular Biology, Japan Biochem. Soc. (elected fgn. mem. 1978), French Acad. Sci. (elected fgn. mem. 1981), Royal Soc. (elected fgn. mem. 1992). Office: Stanford Sch Medicine Beckman Ctr B-062 Stanford CA 94305-5425*

BERGÉ, CAROL, author; b. N.Y.C., 1928; d. Albert and Molly Peppis; m. Jack Bergé, June 1955; 1 child, Peter. Asst. to pres. Pendray Public Relations, N.Y.C., 1955; disting. prof. lit. Thomas Jefferson Coll., Allendale, Mich., 1975-76; instr. adult degree program Goddard Coll. at Asilomar, 1976; tchr. fiction and poetry U. Calif. Extension Program, Berkeley, 1976-77; assoc. prof. U. So. Miss., Hattiesburg, 1977-78; vis. prof. Honors Ctr. and English dept. U. N.Mex., 1978-79, 87; vis. lectr. Wright State U., 1979, SUNY, Albany, 1980-81; tchr. Poets and Writers, Poets in the Schs. (N.Y. State Council on Arts), 1970-72, Poets in the Schs. (Conn. Commn. Arts); propr. Blue Gate Gallery of Art and Antiques, 1988-99. Author: (fiction) The Unfolding, 1969, A Couple Called Moebius, 1972, Acts of Love: An American Novel, 1973 (N.Y. State Coun. on Arts CAPS award 1974), Timepieces, 1977, The Doppler Effect, 1979, Fierce Metronome, 1981, Secrets, Gossip & Slander, 1984, Zebras, or, Contour Lines, 1991; (poetry) The Vulnerable Island, 1964, Lumina, 1965, Poems Made of Skin, 1968, The Chambers, 1969, Circles, as in the Eye, 1969, An American Romance, 1969, From a Soft Angle: Poems About Women, 1972, The Unexpected, 1976, Rituals and Gargoyles, 1976, A Song, A Chant, 1978, Alba Genesis, 1979, Alba Nemesis, 1979, (reportage) The Vancouver Report, 1965; editor Ctr. Mag., 1970-84, pub., 1991—; editor Miss. Rev., 1977-78, Subterraneans, 1975-76, Paper Branches, 1987, LIGHT YEARS: The N.Y.C. Coffeehouse Poets of the 1960's, 1999; contbg. editor Woodstock Rev., 1977-81,

Shearsman mag., 1980-82, S.W. Profile, 1981; editor, pub. CENTER Press, 1991-93; pub.: Medicine Journeys (Carl Ginsburg), Coastal Lives (Miriam Sagan), 1991; co-pub.: Zebras (Carol Berge). Nat. Endowment Arts fellow, 1979-80. Mem. Authors' League, Poets and Writers, MacDowell Fellows Assn., Nat. Press Women. Home: 2070 Calle Contento Santa Fe NM 87505-5406

BERGEN, CANDICE, actress, writer, photojournalist; b. Beverly Hills, Calif., May 9, 1946; d. Edgar and Frances (Westerman) B.; m. Louis Malle, Sept. 27, 1980 (dec. 1995); 1 dau., Chloe. Ed., U. Pa. Model during coll. Films include The Group, The Sand Pebbles, The Day the Fish Came Out, Live for Life, The Magus, Soldier Blue, Getting Straight, The Hunting Party, Carnal Knowledge, T.R. Baskin, The Adventurers, 11 Harrowhouse, Bite the Bullet, The Wind and the Lion, The Domino Principle, The End of the World in Our Usual Bed in a Night Full of Rain, Oliver's Story, Starting Over, Rich and Famous, Gandhi, 1982, Stick, 1985; TV series: Murphy Brown, 1988-98 (Emmy award, Leading Actress in a Comedy Series, 1988-89, 89-90, 91-92, 93-94, 94-95); TV films Arthur the King, 1985, Murder by Reason of Insanity, 1985, Mayflower Madam, 1987, Tim, 1996; TV miniseries Hollywood Wives, 1985, Trying Times, Moving Day; author Knockwood; photojournalist credits include articles for Life, Playboy; dramatist: (play) The Freezer (included in Best Short Plays of 1968). Recipient Emmy awards for lead actress in a comedy series, 1989, 90, 92, 94, 95. *

BERGENFIELD, LAWRENCE, consumer products company executive; b. Smithtown, N.Y., June 26, 1970; s. Allan and Patricia Wendy B. BS in bus. mgmt., consumer studies, U. Md., 1992. V.p. merchandising, mktg. Midatlantic Mfrs. Brokers, Inc., Potomac, Md., 1987-97; pres., CEO Focused Foods Inc., Las Vegas, Nev., 1997—. Active Bnai Tzedak, Potomac, 1995-97. Mem. Nat. Product Assn. Republican. Jewish. Avocations: tennis, golfing, roller blading, travelling, reading. Office: Focused Foods Inc 3172 N Rainbow Blvd Ste 316 Las Vegas NV 89108-4534

BERGER, DUANE W. (DEWEY BERGER), technical coordinator; b. Dickinson, N.D., Aug. 1, 1952; s. Eugene J. and Johanna A. (Huschka) B.; m. Cindy A. Gilmore, Jan. 4, 1956; children: Josh, Emmie. BS in chem., Dickinson State, 1975. Tchr., coach Bismarck St. Mary's, Bismarck, N.D., 1974-77, Bismarck Pub. Sch., Bismarck, N.D., 1977-80; sales rep. Nalco Chem. Comp., Gillette, Wyo., 1980-83; tech. rockies Nalco Chem. Corp., Cody, Wyo., 1983-86; tech. gulf coast Nalco Chem. Corp., Slidell, La., 1987-89; tech. sales Nalco Chem. Corp., Kenai, Alaska, 1989-93; demulsifer rsch. Nalco Chem. Corp., Houston, 1993-94; tech. coord. Alaska Champion Tech. Inc., Anchorage, Alaska, 1994-95; tech. coord. rockies Champion Tech. Inc., Gillette, 1995—; product devel. chemist, 1983—. Recipient numerous awards for teaching, coaching. Fellow Knights of Columbus, Eagles, Soc. Petroleum Engrs. Republican. Roman Catholic. Avocations: softball, fishing, golf, skiing. Office: Champion Tech Inc 3412 2d St Gillette WY 82718-8234

BERGER, JAY VARI, executive recruiter; b. San Francisco, Aug. 31, 1944; s. Jack Vari and Ruth (Wasserman) B.; m. Margareta Ahlberg, June 14, 1969; children: Karin Britta Margareta, John Vari Sten. BS, U. So. Calif., 1966, MS, 1967, PhD, 1971. Assoc. dean admissions U. So. Calif., L.A., 1969-76, dir. admissions, 1976-82, asst. v.p. devel., 1982-86; prin. ptnr. Morris & Berger, Pasadena, Calif., 1986—. Author: (juvenile) Willie the Worm, 1986; columnist Venture Connections, 1988. Bd. dirs. The Sycamores, Pasadena, 1985-94, chair, 1992-94; bd. dirs. Foothill Friends of Music, 1989-92; bd. dirs. Covenant House Calif., 1992-99, pres., trustee Chandler Sch., Pasadena, 1993-89, chmn. bd., 1987-89; trustee Flintridge Preparatory Sch., 1992-98, chmn. bd. dirs. 1996-98; bd. councilors U. So. Calif. Coll. Letters, Arts & Scis. Mem. Calif. Exec. Recruiters Assn., Calif. Assn. Ind. Schs. (bd. trustees 1988-91), Annandale Golf Club, Rotary (bd. dirs. Pasadena chpt. 1988-92). Avocations: golf, traveling, fishing, reading, writing. Home: 1550 Arroyo View Dr Pasadena CA 91103-1903 Office: Morris & Berger Cons Exec Search 201 S Lake Ave Ste 700 Pasadena CA 91101-3019

BERGER, JOHN MILTON, state agency administrator; b. Marysville, Ohio, June 24, 1943; s. John Howard and Betty Louise (Mossbarger) B. BSBA, Franklin U., 1971; postgrad., Ohio State U., 1972. Cert. hazard control mgr., assoc. Ins. Inst. Am. risk mgmt. designation. Claims adjuster State Compensation Ins. Fund, Denver, 1974-78, loss control cons., 1978-84; adminstrv. officer Indsl. Commn., Denver, 1984-86; self-ins. adminstrn. Colo. Div. Labor, Denver, 1986-91; ins. complaince mgr. divsn. workers' compensation Colo. Dept. Labor and Employment, Denver, 1991-97, mgr. employer svcs. divsn., 1997—; mem. legis. com. Colo. Div. Ins., Denver, 1989-91; mem. self-ins. subcom. of Internat. Assn. Indsl. Accident Bds. and Commns. Author: Workers' Compensation Loss Prevention and Loss Control Manual, 1990; contbr. article to profl. jour. With USN, 1961-64. Recognized for Outstanding Svc. to State Govt., 1986. Mem. Colo. Self-Insurers Assn. Republican. Avocations: scuba diving, photography, fishing, bicycling. Home: 675 Dudley St Lakewood CO 80215-5406 Office: Colo Dept Labor & Employment Employer Svcs Divsn 1515 Arapahoe St Ste 300 Denver CO 80202-3150

BERGER, NEWELL JAMES, JR., security professional; b. Pitts., Oct. 26, 1926; s. Newell James and Marjorie Ikler (Herndon) B.; m. Darlene Ingram, Sept. 6, 1950 (dec. Nov. 1990). BS, Mich. State U., 1958; grad., U.S. Army Command and Gen. Staff Coll., 1963, U.S. Army War Coll., 1972; MA, Webster U., 1993. Enlisted man U.S. Army, 1944, advanced through grades to staff sgt., 1948, commd. 2d lt., 1948, advanced through grades to col., 1970; chief corrections hdqrs. U.S. Army, Washington, 1970-72, dir. security Office Surgeon Gen., 1972-73; dir. security Health Svcs. Command U.S. Army, Ft. Sam Houston, Tex., 1973-78; ret. U.S. Army, 1978; security cons. Phoenix and San Diego, 1979-84; chief plant security Teledyne Ryan Aero. Co., San Diego, 1985-86; dep. dir. security Marconi Intergrated Systems, Inc., San Diego, 1986—. Decorated Legion of Merit with two oak leaf clusters. Mem. (life) Internat. Assn. Chiefs Police, Am. Soc. for Indsl. Security (cert. protection profl.). Republican. Episcopalian. Avocations: music, history. Home: 11872 Caminito Corriente San Diego CA 92128-4550 Office: Marconi Integrated Sys Inc PO Box 1198 Poway CA 92074-1198

BERGER, PAUL ERIC, artist, photographer; b. The Dalles, Oreg., Jan. 20, 1948; s. Charles Glen and Virginia (Nunez) B. B.A., UCLA, 1970; M.F.A., SUNY-Buffalo, 1973. Vis. lectr. U. Ill., 1974-78; prof. art U. Wash.-Seattle, 1978—. Exhibited one-man shows, photographs, Art Inst. Chgo., 1975, Light Gallery, N.Y.C., 1977, Seattle Art Mus., 1980, Light Gallery, N.Y.C., 1982, Univ. Art Mus., Santa Barbara, Calif., 1984, Cliff Michel Gallery, 1989, Seattle Art Mus., 1990, Fuel Gallery, 1993, Galerie Lichtblick GFFK, Cologne, Germany, 1996. NEA Photographer's fellow, 1979, NEA Visual Artist's fellow, 1986; recipient Artist's Commn., Wash. State Arts Commn., 1990. Mem. Soc. Photographic Edn. Office: U Wash Sch Art PO Box 353440 Seattle WA 98195-3440

BERGER, ROBERT DALE, communications company executive; b. Burlingame, Kans., Dec. 13, 1937; s. Dale and Anna (Hotchkiss) B.; m. Gwen Barnthouse, Aug. 7, 1965; 1 child, Andrea Lynn. BA, U. Md., 1960. Dist. mgr. Xerox Corp., Rochester, N.Y., 1964-84; sr. v.p. Cable Investments, Inc., Englewood, Colo., 1984-93, Comm. Equity Assn., Denver, Colo., 1993—; bd. dirs. Digital Cable, Inc., Jacksonville, Fla.; editl. adv. bd. Pvt. Cable & Wireless, Houston, 1996-97. Office: Comm Equity Assocs 4582 S Ulster St Ste 402 Denver CO 80237-2634

BERGERA, CLIFFORD HREINSON, art educator, artist; b. Helper, Utah, Mar. 2, 1944; s. James Joseph and Grace (Hreinson) B.; m. Janet Gail Jackson, Dec. 25, 1968; 1 child, Lis Bergera Jorgensen. BFA, Utah State U., 1967, MFA in Drawing and Painting, 1969. Staff artist Hansen Planetarium, Salt Lake City, 1970-73; mgr. Helper Merchantile Co., 1973-88; prof. art Coll. of Ea. Utah, Price, 1988—. Exhibited in group shows Utah State Fair, 1968, Fossat's Studio, Helper, 1970, Sylvester Gallery, Salt Lake City, 1981, [illegible] Gallery, Salt Lake City, 1984, Alliance Gallery, Salt Lake City, 1985, The Wing Gallery, Sherman Oaks, Calif., 1986-87, The Kneeland Gallery, Sun Valley, Idaho, 1986, 87, 88, The LA Artcore Gallery, L.A., 1988, others. Home: 403 E St Helper UT 84526-1302 Office: Coll Ea Utah 451 E 400 N Price UT 84501-2626

BERGERON, SHEILA DIANE, retired science educator, educational consultant; b. Decatur, Ill., Aug. 17, 1940; d. Lewis F. and Elizabeth A. (Hoff) Brown; m. Richard A. Bergeron, Sept. 25, 1965; 1 child, Cynthia Diane. BS in Spl. Edn., Ill. State U., 1962; MA in Counseling, U. Colo., 1980. Tchr. Villa Park (Ill.) Dist. # 45, 1962-68, Jefferson County Schs. R-1, Golden, Colo., 1968-98; ret., 1998; cons. in field; adj. instr. U. No. Colo., Greeley, 1980-86, Met. State U., 1986-88, U. Colo., Denver, 1986-88, Colo. Christian U., 1998; staff devel. cons. Denver Pub. Schs., Summit County Schs., Dillon, Colo., Dallas Pub. Schs., Lake City Schs., Colo., 1982-93; team mem. North Ctrl. Accreditation Assn., 1978, 90. Steering com. mem., pres. Leadership Golden, 1986-98; emergency communicator ARC, Denver, 1990-98; vol. Pub. TV, KRMA-TV, Denver, 1991-98, Golden Civic Found., 1986-94. Named A-Plus Tchr. Rocky Mountain News and KCNC-TV, 1992; recipient Presdl. Excellence in Sci. Teaching award, 1995. Mem. ASCD, NSTA (Nat. Sci. Tchrs. Assn.), Nat. Staff Devel. Coun. Avocation: amateur radio operator. Home: 606 Alaska St Golden CO 80403-1308

BERGESON, MARVIN ERNEST, pediatrician; b. Seattle, Feb. 28, 1950; s. Ernest Axel Eugene and Martha Bergeson; m. Cindy Lewanne Little, Aug. 21, 1971; children: Bo Eric, Jon Carl, Will Ernst. BA, Augustana Coll., 1972; MD, U. Ill., Peoria, 1977. Diplomate Am. Bd. Pediat.; lic. physician, Wash., Alaska. Tchg. asst. biol. scis. U. Ill., 1972-73; intern, then residen in pediat. Madigan Army Med. Ctr., Tacoma, 1977-80; fellow in developmental pediat. Med. Sch. Harvard U., Boston, 1982; pvt. practice Tanana Valley Clinic, Fairbanks, Alaska, 1984—; chmn. dept. pediat. Fairbanks Meml. Hosp., 1985-87; mem. drug utilization rev. State of Alaska, 1992-98. Co-contbr. articles to profl. jours. Bd. dirs. Alaska Crippled Children's Assn., 1983-89, v.p., 1984-85, 87, pres., 1985-87, 87-89; bd. dirs. Fairbanks Counseling and Adoption, 1985-93, v.p., 1986-87, pres., 1990-92, treas., 1992-93; mem. exec. com. Fairbanks Child Sexual Abuse Task Force, 1985-87, Midnight Sun coun. Boy Scouts Am., 1989-92; founding mem. Youth at Risk Multidisciplinary Team, 1990-93, Super Substance Use, Pregnancy, Edn. and Resources, 1990—; hon. bd. dirs. Resource Ctr. for Parents and Children, 1987—; pres. bd. dirs. Samaritan Counseling Ctr., 1996—; bd. dirs. Alaska Health Care Network, 1997—; treas. Christ Luth. Ch., 1981-88, mem. ch. coun., 1982-85. Maj. U.S. Army, 1977-84. Recipient Leadership award Ill. Alumni Assn., 1977, Granville A. Bennett award for contbns. to med. edn., 1977, Pediat. award for Excellence, Ross Labs., 1977, Friends of Edn. award Beta chpt. Delta Kappa Gamma, 1988, award for Outstanding Cmty. Work, Resource Ctr. for Parents and Children, 1988, award for Vol. Svc. to Fairbanks Cmty., Arctic Alliance for People, 1988, Parent Support Group Cert. of Svc. award City of Fairbanks, 1993. Fellow Am. Acad. Pediat.; mem. AMA, North Pacific Pediat. Soc., Alaska State Med. Assn. (councilor 1989-91), Fairbanks Counseling and Adoption-Bishop Whelan Soc., Omicron Delta Kappa, Beta Beta Beta. Home: 1621 Gonzaga Way Fairbanks AK 99709-6764 Office: Tanana Valley Med Clinic 1001 Noble St Fairbanks AK 99701-4922

BERGH, DAVID MORGAN, entrepreneur; b. Boise, Idaho, Aug. 8, 1947; s. Rolfe Roald and Margaret Rose (Morgan) B.; m. Jan K. Seda, May 17, 1975; children: Hillary Lauren, Benjamin Morgan, Salle Alberta. BS in Mgmt., U. Idaho, 1972. Chpt. cons., then dir. expansion, asst. exec. dir. Kappa Sigma Internat. Fraternity, Charlottesville, Va., 1972-75; propr. Morgan's Exchange, Boise, 1975-79, Strato Lanes, Mountain Home, Idaho, 1979—; concessionaire various recreational concerns, Alaska and Idaho; supr. com. P.F. Credit Union. Chmn. Cen. Dist. Health, Idaho, 1983—; pres. Mountain Home Mil. Affairs Com., 1985—; sec., treas. Silver City Hist. Soc. Mem. Nat. Restaurant and Beverage Assn., Kappa Sigma (dist. prs. 1975—), Elks. Republican. Roman Catholic. Home and Office: PO Box 9 Mountain Home ID 83647-0009

BERGHOLZ, RICHARD CADY, political writer; b. Corvallis, Oreg., Apr. 13, 1917; s. William Orville and Mabel (Cady) B.; m. Elizabeth True Jamison, Feb. 22, 1941; children: Barbara Bergholz Stacy, Richard J., Elizabeth S.J. BA, U. Wash., 1938. Reporter Ventura (Calif.) Star-Free Press, 1938-41, AP, 1941-44; war corr. New Guinea, Philippines, China, Manchuria, 1944-46; reporter Glendale (Calif.) News-Press, 1946-47; polit. editor San Diego Evening Tribune, 1947-54, L.A. Mirror, 1954-62; polit. writer L.A. Times, 1962-83. Bd. dirs. Calif. First Amendment Coalition. Mem. Soc. Profl. Journalists, Pi Kappa Alpha. Home: 929 Crestview Dr Pasadena CA 91107-1950

BERGIN, ALLEN ERIC, clinical psychologist, educator; b. Spokane, Wash., Aug. 4, 1934; s. Bernard F. and Vivian Selma (Kullberg) B.; m. Marian Shafer, June 4, 1955; children: David, Sue, Cyndy, Kathy, Eric, Ben, Patrick, Daniel, Michael. BS, Brigham Young U., 1956, MS, 1957; PhD, Stanford U., 1960. Diplomate Am. Bd. Profl. Psychology. Postdoctoral fellow U. Wis., Madison, 1960-61; prof. psychology and edn. Tchrs. Coll., Columbia U., N.Y.C., 1961-72; prof. psychology Brigham Young U., Provo, Utah, 1972—, dir. Values Inst., 1976-78, dir. clin. psychology, 1989-93; sr. rsch. fellow Nat. Inst. Health Care Rsch., 1992—; assessment officer Peace Corps, Washington, 1961-66; cons. NIMH, Rockville, Md., 1969-75, 90. Co-author: Changing Frontiers in Psychotherapy, 1972; co-editor: Handbook of Psychotherapy, 1971, 4th edit., 1994 (citation classic 1979). Bishop LDS Ch., Emerson, N.J., 1970-72, Provo, 1981-84, stake pres., 1992-95; mem. steering com. Utah Gov.'s Conf. on Families, Salt Lake City, 1979-80. Recipient Biggs-Pine award Am. Assn. Counseling and Devel., 1986, Maeser rsch. award Brigham Young U. Alumni Assn., 1986, exemplary paper award Templeton Found., 1996. Fellow APA (Disting. Contbn. to Knowledge award 1989, William James award div. 36, 1990); mem. Soc. for Psychotherapy Integration (adv. bd.), Soc. for Sci. Study Religion, Soc. for Psychotherapy Rsch. (pres. 1974-75, Disting. Career award 1998), Am. Psychiat. Assn. (Pfister award 1998), Assn. Mormon Counselors (pres. 1979-80). Republican. Avocations: world travel, water sports, gardening. Office: Brigham Young U 285 Tlrb Provo UT 84602-1052*

BERGMAN, RAYMOND LOUIS, art supply executive; b. Salt Lake City, May 9, 1918; s. A. Louis and Abel Louise Bergman; m. Betty Jean Cottle, Dec. 8, 1954; children: Anita Louise, Dorothy Ann, Dean Louis. BA, U. Utah, 1939; MBA, Northwestern U., 1945. Continuity and promotion mgr. Sta. KSL, Salt Lake City, 1945-48; radio dir. Francom Advertising, 1948-50; yearbook dept. mgr. Wheelwright Lithographing, Salt Lake City, 1950-60; owner The 65 Shop, Holladay, UT, 1961-64; pres. Key Tng. of Salt Lake, UT, 1965-67; owner, mgr. Ray's Art & Frame, Salt Lake City, 1968-87; lectr. mktg. U. Utah, 1946-48. Author: Roadshows Are Fun, 1954, The Children Sang-The Life and Music of Evan Stephens, 1992; contbr. articles to mags. and newspapers. Recipient 3d prize Evans Manuscript Competition Utah State U., 1991, 1st prize State of Utah Healthy Aging Letter-Writing Competition U.S Post Office and Ednl. TV Network, 1997. Mem. League Utah Writers (state historian, chpt. treas., 1st prize Full Length Book 1991). Democrat. Mem. LDS Ch. Avocations: writing novels, freelance writing, traveling, attending elderhostel programs. Home: 7319 Union Village Cir Midvale UT 84047-2261

BERGMAN, TERRIE, psychic consultant; b. Phila., Mar. 4, 1942; d. Harry Bernard and Berthe Rose (Simons) Goldberg; m. Clifford Coulston, May 4, 1960 (div. 1967); 1 child, Lori Coulston; m. Joel David Bergman, Dec. 22, 1979. B Metaphys. Sci., D Metaphys. Counseling, U. Metaphysics, 1994. Ordained to metaphys. ministry, 1994. Indsl. trainer, vocat. evaluator, mktg. mgr. Atlantic County Opportunity Ctr. for Handicapped, Atlantic City, N.J., 1971-74; job developer, vocat. evaluator, counselor Narcotics Addicts Rehab. Orgn., Atlantic City, 1974-75; psychic cons. Atlantic City & Las Vegas, 1973—; seminar facilitator on death and dying Las Vegas, 1990—; 1st, 2d, and 3d degree Reiki healer, Atlantic City and Las Vegas, 1984—. Appeared on TV programs, including People Are Talking, Hour Mag., others, 1974—; contbr. articles to mags. and newspapers. Vol. Nathan Adelson Hospice, 1989-94. Named 1 of 83 People to Watch, Atlantic City Mag., 1983; recipient Dynamics of Leadership cert. of achievement Human Factors, Inc., 1981, 82, 86. Mem. Network of Exec. Women in Hospitality. Home and Office: 208 Desert View St Las Vegas NV 89107-2355

BERGMAN, YAACOV, performing company executive; m. Joan Behrens. Degree in conducting and composition, Rubin Acad., Hebrew U., Jerusalem; studied with Richard Westenburg, Mannes Coll. Music; studied with Charles Bruck, Leonard Bernstein. Music dir. Colorado Springs (Colo.) Symphony; music dir. Walla Walla (Wash.) Symphony; founder, music dir., condr. Heritage Orch. N.Y.; condr. Osaka (Japan) Opera Co., 1996. Office: Colorado Springs Symphony PO Box 1692 Colorado Springs CO 80901-1692*

BERGMANN, PETER JAY, television director and producer, educator; b. N.Y.C., Oct. 2, 1949; s. Otto Bergmann and Rose Marie Wasserman. AB, NYU, 1966, MFA, 1968, PhD, 1975; PhD, U. Pa., 1969. V.p. ABC Cir. Films, L.A., 1973-75; asst. pres. ABC Network, L.A., N.Y.C., 1975-78; assto to COB ABC Inc., L.A., N.Y.C., 1978-81; pres. Film Co., L.A., N.Y.C., 1981-86, Odyssey Filmakers, Hollywood, Calif., 1986-90, Bergmann Films, L.A., 1990—; prof. electronic filmmaking Fairleigh Dickinson U., Madison, N.J., 1994—; cons. CBS, L.A., N.Y.C., 1987. Prodr. (film) Boys in Band; (TV movie) Eleanor & Franklin, 1976, Victory at Entebbe, 1976; dir. The Great Stone Balloon, 1987. Bd. dirs. Make-A-Wish Found., L.A., 1990-94, Starlight, L.A., N.Y.C., 1993-95. Mem. Dirs. Guild Am., nat. Acad. TV Arts & Scis. Avocations: fencing, sailing, riding, tennis. Office: Film Co 520 Washington Blvd Marina Del Rey CA 90292-5442

BERGSMA, DERKE PETER, minister, religious studies educator; b. Racine, Wis., Aug. 29, 1927; s. John Sietze and Johanna Jacoba (Vlaardingerbroek) B.; m. Doris Elaine Bielema, Oct. 28, 1950; children: Deborah, Derk, Diann, Danette. AB, Calvin Coll., 1951; BD, Calvin Sem., 1954; MA, Northwestern U., 1962; DTh, Free-U.-Amsterdam, 1964; D Religion, Chgo. Theol. Sem., 1968. Ordained to ministry Christian Reformed Ch. in Am., 1954. Instr. Calvin Coll., Grand Rapids, Mich., 1950-52; pastor Christian Reformed Ch., Grand Rapids, 1954-62; prof. Trinity Christian Coll., Palos Heights, Ill., 1968-81, Westminster Theol. Sem., Escondido, Calif., 1981—; co-founder Christian Counseling Ctr., Palos Heights, 1974-76; trustee Bd. Publs., Christian Reformed Ch., Grand Rapids, 1970-76. Author: Voices, 1976, Predestination: Islam and Calvinism, 1984, Redemption: The Triumph of God's Great Plan, 1988; contbr. articles to profl. jours. Trustee Calvin Theol. Sem., 1989-92. Capt. USN. (Ret.). Chgo. Ch. Fedn. grantee, 1977. Mem. Evang. Theol. Soc., DAV, Lions. Home: 8975 Lawrence Welk Dr Spc 424 Escondido CA 92026-6423 Office: Westminster Theol Sem 1725 Bear Valley Pky Escondido CA 92027-4128

BERGUM, CHRISTIAN OLSON, architect, educator; b. L.A., Nov. 3, 1953; s. Jarle Albert B. Cert., U. dé Geneva, 1972; BArch, U. Oreg., 1976; MArch, U. Wash., 1978; PhD, U. Pa., 1981. Fulbright prof. U. Jordan, Amann, Jordan, 1981-82; vis. scholar Harvard U., Cambridge, Mass., 1983-84; asst. prof. U. Tex., Austin, 1986-87; adj. assoc. prof. Mont. State U., Bozeman, 1983-94; Fulbright prof. Jerusalem, 1984; pvt. practice Victorville, Calif., 1991—. Editor Mont. Archtl. Rev., 1983-86. Graham Found. grantee, Chgo., 1984. Mem. AIA, Nat. Assn. Home Builders (dir. 1995—, Builder of Yr. 1996). Office: 14455 Park Ave Ste B Victorville CA 92392-2344

BERK, AMY LYNNE, artist, educator; b. Bklyn., Aug. 3, 1967; d. George Howard and Barbara Sue (Hillson) B. BA, Wesleyan U., 1989; MFA, San Francisco Art Inst., 1995. Instr. So. Exposure Artist in Edn. Program, San Francisco, 1995-96; program assoc. So. Exposure, San Francisco, 1996; instr. San Francisco Art Inst. Extension Edn., 1994-98; instr./supr. Meridian Interns Program, San Francisco, 1996-98; co-dir. Push! Artspace, San Francisco, 1996-97. Contbr. articles to profl. publs.; exhibited in groups shows at San Francisco Arts Commn. Gallery, 1997, So. Exposure, 1995-98, Ctr. for the Arts, 1998, Traywick Gallery, 1997-98. Recipient Gerbode Purchase award Gerbode Found., 1998. Mem. San Francisco Art Inst. (chair artists com. 1997—). Home: 67 29th St San Francisco CA 94110-4910

BERKE, JUDIE, publisher, editor; b. Mpls., Apr. 15, 1938; d. Maurice M. and Sue (Supak) Kleyman; student U. Minn., 1956-60, Mpls. Sch. Art, 1945-59. Free lance illustrator and designer, 1959—; pres. Berke-Wood, Inc., N.Y.C., 1971-80, Manhattan Rainbow & Lollipop Co. subs. Berke-Wood, Inc., 1971-80; pres. Get Your Act Together, club act staging, N.Y.C., 1971-80; pres. Coordinator Pubs.,Inc., 1982-87; pres., chief exec. officer, Health Market Communications, 1987—; pres. Pub. and Media Services, Burbank, 1987—; pub., editor Continuing Care Coordinator, Health Watch mags.; pres. Continuing Care Coordinator Convs. and Seminars; pres. Rainbow and Lillipop Prodns., 1994—; cons. to film and ednl. cos.; guest lectr. various colls. and univs. in Calif. and N.Y., 1973—; cons., designer Healthy Lifestyles mag.; writer, illustrator, dir. numerous ednl. filmstrips, 1972—, latest being Focus on Professions, 1974, Focus on the Performing Arts, 1974, Focus on the Creative Arts, 1974, Workstyles, 1976, Wonderworm, 1976, Supernut, 1977; author, illustrator film Fat Black Mack (San Francisco Ednl. Film Festival award, part of permanent collection Mus. Modern Art, N.Y.C.), 1970; designer posters and brochures for various entertainment groups, 1963—; composer numerous songs, latest being Time is Relative, 1976, Love Will Live On in My Mind, 1976, My Blue Walk, 1976, You Make Me a Baby, 1982, Let's Go Around Once More, 1983, Anytime Anyplace Anywhere, 1987, Bittersweet, 1987, Sometimes It Pays, 1987, Gimme Back My Money Blues, Everybody Wants Me But the One I Love, Skin to Skin, It's Your Turn to Sing the Blues, Deny Till You Die, Men Just Call It Woman Talk, Poor Me, Women's Work is Never Done, 1993; composer/author off-Broadway musical Street Corner Time, 1978; producer: The Real Estate TV Shows 1988-89; contbr. children's short stories to various publs., also articles. Trustee The Happy Spot Sch., N.Y.C., 1972-75. Mem. Nat. Fedn. Bus. and Profl. Women, NAFE, Am. Acad. Polit. and Social Sci., Women in Animation.

BERKE, WILLIAM MICHAEL, production editor, writer; b. L.A., June 11, 1956; s. Lester William Berke and Elaine Mickey Selwyn; m. Debra Renée Bradshaw, Sept. 1, 1995. BA in English Lit., San Diego State U., 1985. Prodn. artist Am. Film Techs., San Diego, 1987-90; copy editor Nat. Steel and Shipbuilding Co., San Diego, 1991; proof reader (part time) KPBS Radio On Air Mag., San Diego, 1988—; prodn. editor Harcourt Brace & Co., San Diego, 1991—. Avocation: drawing. Home: 1775 Diamond St # 1-115 San Diego CA 92109-3319 Office: Harcourt Brace & Co 525 B St Ste 1900 San Diego CA 92101-4495

BERKES, LESLIE JOHN, psychologist, management consultant; b. Simbach, Bavaria, Fed. Republic of Germany, Aug. 18, 1946; came to U.S., 1949; naturalized; s. Leslie Michael and Marie Gizella (Villanyi) B.; m. Cheryl Kaye Stelter, Dec. 28, 1968; children: Adrienne Villanyi, Andrew Stelter, Kathryn Fowlkes. BS, U. So. Calif., 1968; MS, U.S. Naval Portgrad. Sch., 1969; postgrad., Union coll., 1971, SUNY, 1971-72; PhD, U. Calif., 1976; postgrad., Wright State U., 1983. Lic. psychologist, Ohio, Calif. Mgmt. auditor U.S. Gen. Acctg. Office, L.A., 1972-73; asst. rsch. specialist Pub. Policy Rsch. Orgn. U. Calif., Irvine, 1974-76; faculty rsch. assoc. Program Study Crime and Delinquency Ohio State U., Columbus, 1980-82; asst. prof. mgmt. sci. Ohio State U., Columbus, 1976-82; clin. psychologist Psychol. Cons. Inc., Columbus, 1981-82; psychologist Mgmt. Health & Devel. Corp., Malibu, Calif., 1983-86; v.p., chief tech. officer Netmap Internat. Inc., San Francisco, 1986-90; pres. Mgmt. Tech. Inc., San Francisco, 1990—; mng. dir. pacific region Nolan Norton & Co., 1994-97; dir. JM Perry Corp., Palo Alto, Calif., 1997—; adj. faculty Grad. Sch. Mgmt. U. Calif., Irvine, 1985-86, St. Mary's Coll. of Calif., 1987—; clin. assoc. prof. psychology Wright State U.; cons., presenter in field. Contbr. articles to profl. jours. Chair St. Monica's Town Hall, Moraga, Calif., 1988-89; mem. parish coun., St. Monica's, 1991-92; co-dir. 7th grade edn. St. Monica's, 1988-89; police reserve officer, Columbus, 1979-81; reserve firefighter Moraga Fire Dist., 1991-96; softball coach Lafayette Moraga Youth Assn., 1989-94. With USN, 1968-72, Vietnam; with USNR Med. Svc. Corps, 1978-87. Mem. Acad. Mgmt., Am. Inst. Decision Scis., Am. Med. Joggers Assn., Am. Phychological Assn., Am. Soc. Pub. Adminstrn., Calif. Psychol. Assn., Internat. Assn. Applied Psychology, Soc. Indsl. and Orgnl. Psychology, Soc. Psychol. Study Social Issues, Beta Gamma Sigma. Democrat. Roman Catholic. Avocations: neural network programming, cognitive science. Home: 203 Calle La Montana Moraga CA 94556-1642 Office: Delta Cons Group 275 Battery St Ste 2940 San Francisco CA 94111

[illegible] s. Joseph Omer and Gertrude Madelyn (Thompson) B. m. Janice Lark Keirstead, Dec. 19, 1966; children: Krista Lynn, Jay Olin. AA, Santa Rosa Jr. Coll., 1951, AB, U. Calif., Berkeley, 1958; MS, San Jose State U., 1964; postgrad., U. Calif., Davis, 1969-72. Registered geologist, Calif.; cert. engring. geologist, Calif. Psychiat. tech. Sonoma State Hosp., 1951-57; with U.S.

Geol. Survey, 1958-64; engring. geologist U.S. Bur. Reclamation, 1964-69, cons. geologist, 1969-72; asst. prof. Appalachian State U., Boone, N.C., 1972-73; county geologist Santa Clara County, San Jose, Calif., 1973-94; ret., 1994; mem. geotech. adv. com. San Jose; adj. prof. San Jose State U., 1973-75, lectr. Gen. Edn. Conf., Sci. and Tech. Soc., 1985-89, coord. com. Calif. Conv., 1978; mem. evening faculty San Jose City Coll.; mem. West Valley Legis. Com., 1979-90; lectr. ann. deposit receipt seminar San Jose Real Estate Bd., 1980-85; discoverer in field; featured spkr. Keynote Speakers, Inc.; role model San Jose Sch. Dist., 1995-97. Contbr. numerous articles to profl. jours.; originator seismic window theory for earthquake prediction, 1974; TV and radio appearances including PBA, Frontline, Evening Mag., People are Talking, 48 Hours, Sightings, You Bet Your Life, Science Faction, Science Fiction Cable, Two on the Town, CNN News, WGN, KIRO, KSL, KIEV, KGO, KCBS, KNYV, KOA, KOGO, KVEN, KSCO, KOMO, KPFK, Two at Noon, KPFA-FM Radio, The Other Side, Northwest Afternoon, Art Bell's Coast to Coast, Town Meeting, Ron Owens Show, Laura Lee Show, Art Bell Show, Kathi Gori Show, Extra, Strange Universe; articles on work featured in OMNI, STERN, Wall St. Jour., Bergen's Tidende, San Francisco Examiner, San Francisco Chronicle, L.A. Times, Nat. Geog., Am. Health, The Astrology Ency., Old Farmers Almanac, 1991, Gilroy Dispatch, Bakersfield Californian, San Jose Mercury News, Sonoma Index Tribune, Intuition, Farmers Almanac, others; editor: SYZYGY-An Earthquake Newsletter, 1990—; co-founder Quakeline. Treas. Creekside/Park Place Homeowners Group; v.p. West Coast Aquatics, Creekside/Park Place Swim Team; mem. various city and county adv. bds.; mem. Ctr. for Study Early Man, East Valley YMCA, legis. com. West Valley, 1980—, Route 85 Task Force, Earthquake Watch, 1979-82, New Weather Observer, Nat. Wildlife Fedn.; mem. Found. for the Study of Cycles, invited lectr. monthly and ann. meeting; active Statue of Liberty Found; mem. tech. and soc. San Jose Sch. Dist., 1980—, mem. role model program, 1996-97; mem. Sonoma Land Trust; active The Nature Conservancy, Nat. Wildlife Fed.; charter mem. The Dolphin Inst. Recipient Resolution of Commendation Santa Clara Bd. Suprs., 1994. Mem. Smithsonian Inst. (assoc.), Ret. Pub. Employee Assn. Calif., Alumni Assn. San Jose State U. Democrat. Home: 5317 Knights Estate San Jose CA 95135-1211

BERKLEY, ROBERT JOHN, federal agency professional; b. Albion, Mich., Oct. 2, 1933; s. Paul Clifford and Ina Muriel (Burroughs) B.; m. Sharon Irene Haynes, Sept. 9, 1955 (div. 1965); children: Thomas Alan, Richard Jon, Luann Michele; m. Jacquelyn Jane (Lewis) Ballou, Jan. 14, 1966. AA, Jackson (Mich.) Jr. Coll., 1953; BS in Police Adminstrn., Calif. State U., L.A., 1962. Police officer City of Claremont, Calif., 1959-62, 63-66; investigator U.S. Civil Svc. Commn., Washington and L.A., 1962-63, 66-72; spl. agt. FAA, Seattle, 1972—, office mgr., 1973—. Local chmn. Selective Svc. Bd., Wash., 1981—. Sgt. USMC, 1953-56, Korea. Mem. SAR (chpt. pres. 1989-90, state sec. 1989-91, state pres. 1992, Patriots medal 1990, Law Enforcement medal 1991, 92), Am. Legion, Eastern Star (patron 1989-90), Masons (master 1984, life), Scottish Rite, Shriners. Avocations: computers, photography, camping, travel. Home: 4403 192d Pl SE Issaquah WA 98027-9708 Office: FAA SEA-CASFO 1601 Lind Ave SW Rm 230 Renton WA 98055-4099

BERKLEY, SHELLEY, congresswoman; b. N.Y.C., Jan. 20, 1951. BA, U. NEv., 1972; JD, U. San Diego, 1976. Mem. 106th Congress from 1st Nev. dist., 1999—. Office: 1505 Longworth House Office Bldg Washington DC 20515 also: 2340 Paseo Del Prado Ste D 106 Las Vegas NV 89102*

BERKLEY, STEPHEN MARK, computer peripherals manufacturing company executive; b. N.J., 1944; s. Irving S. and Goldie A. Berkley; student London Sch. Econs., 1964-65; BA in Econs., Colgate U., 1966; MBA, Harvard U., 1968; children: David, Michael.Mgmt. cons. Boston Cons. Group, 1968, 71-73; mgr. strategic planning Potlatch Corp., 1973-77; v.p. bus. devel. Qume Corp. subs. ITT, Hayward, Calif., 1977-80, v.p., gen. mgr. memory products div., 1980-81; v.p. mktg. Quantum Corp., Milpitas, Calif., 1981-83, chmn., CEO, 1987-92, chmn., 1992-93, 95-98; chmn., CEO Coactive Computing Corp., 1993-94; pres. Plus Devel. Corp. (Quantum subs.), 1983-87, chmn., CEO, 1987-92; pres., The Rosewood Found., 1991—; bd. dirs. Quantum Corp., Edify Corp., Coactive Computing Corp.; instr. bus. and econs. E. Carolina U., 1969-71. Served to lt. USNR, 1968-71. Mem. Corp. Planners Assn. (dir.), Harvard Bus. Sch. Club No. Calif., Phi Beta Kappa. Office: Quantum Corp 500 McCarthy Blvd Milpitas CA 95035-7909

BERKMAN, SAMUEL A., internist; b. Dayton, Ohio, Dec. 21, 1945; s. Sydney and Edna (Cohen) B.; m. Michele Ehrlich; children: Lauren, Jacqueline. BA, Syracuse U., 1967; MD, Tufts U., 1971. Cert. in internal medicine, hematology, med. oncology. Intern Cedars-Sinai Med. Ctr., L.A., 1971-72; resident Cedars-Sinai Med. Ctr., 1972-74; fellow U.C.L.A., 1974-76; fellow med. oncology NIH, Bethesda, Md., 1976-78; pvt. practice. Contbr. articles to profl. jours. including Hosp. Practice, Blood Reviews, Annals of Internal Med. Avocation: foreign languages. Office: 9400 Brighton Way Beverly Hills CA 90210

BERKUS, DAVID WILLIAM, venture capitalist; b. Los Angeles, Mar. 23, 1941; s. Harry Jay and Clara S. (Widess) B.; m. Kathleen McGuire, Aug. 6, 1966; children: Eric, Matthew, Amy. BA, Occidental Coll., 1962. Pres. Custom Fidelity Inc., Hollywood, Calif., 1958-74, Berkus Compusystems Inc., Los Angeles, 1974-81; pres., CEO, Computerized Lodging Systems Inc. and subs., Los Angeles, 1981-93; pres. Berkus Tech. Ventures, venture capital, L.A., 1993—; mng. dir. worldwide lodging Sulcus Computer Corp., 1998—. Author: Better Than Money, 1994; author software Hotel Compusystem, 1979; creator 1st artificial intelligence-based yield mgmt. sys., 1987. Chmn. bd. Boy Scouts Am., San Gabriel Valley, 1986, v.p. area IV, 1993-94, pres. 1995-98, v.p. western region, 1998—; trustee Occidental Coll., L.A. Lt. USNR, 1963-72. Recipient Disting. award of Merit, Boy Scouts Am., 1986, INC. mag. 500 award, 1986, Silver Beaver award Boy Scouts Am., 1988, Silver Antelope award, 1997; inducted into hospitality industry Hall of Fame, 1998. Mem. Am. Hotel-Motel Assn., Audio Engring. Soc. (chmn. Los Angeles sect. 1973-74). Office: 1430 Glencoe Dr Arcadia CA 91006-1909

BERMAN, HOWARD LAWRENCE, congressman; b. L.A., Apr. 15, 1941; s. Joseph M. and Eleanor (Schapiro) B.; m. Janis Berman, 1979; children: Brinley Ann, Lindsey Rose. BA, UCLA, 1962, LLB, 1965. Bar: Calif. 1966. Vol. VISTA, Balt., San Francisco, 1966-67; assoc. Levy, Van Bourg & Hackler, L.A., 1967-72; mem. Calif. State Assembly from 43d dist., 1972-82 (majority leader); with 98th-105th Congresses from 26th Calif. dist.; freshman rep. steering and policy com., 1983, ranking mem. com. standards of ofcl. conduct, mem. jud. com., internat. law, immigration and refugees, intellectual property and jud. adminstrn., mem. internat. rels. com. Asia and Pacific. Pres. Calif. Fedn. Young Democrats, 1967-69 (budget com.); mem. adv. bd. Jewish Fund for Justice. Office: US Ho of Reps Rm 2330 Rayburn House Office Bldg Washington DC 20515*

BERMAN, JEROME, museum director, curator. Exec. dir., curator Calif. Mus. Ancient Art, Beverly Hills, 1983—. Office: Calif Mus Ancient Art PO Box 10515 Beverly Hills CA 90213-3515*

BERMAN, SANFORD SOLOMON, motion picture sound designer, composer, arranger, artist; b. Long Branch, N.J., Nov. 14, 1951; s. Jerome Sidney and Marion (Solomon) B. BFA, Phila. Coll. Art, 1974. Freelance sound designer, record prodr./arranger, musician/composer. Sound designer, supr. (features) Brokedown Palace, Neil Simon's Odd Couple 2, Hard Rain, Hush, Multiplicity, Jade, Virtuosity, Wings of Courage, Bad Girls, Tombstone, Striking Distance Aladdin (Golden Reel winner, FX Editl., Oscar nomination), Love Field, Unlawful Entry, J.F.K. (FX Editl., Brit. Acad. award, Golden Reel nominee), Hot Shots!, Back to the Future (The Ride), Revenge (Golden Reel nominee), Immediate Family, Oliver & Company (Golden Reel winner), The Princess Bride (Golden Reel nominee), The Seventh Sign (Golden Reel nominee), da, Big Bad John, Going Under Cover, Mac & Me, Weeds, Jaws III, Cloak & Dagger, The Stone Boy, Wolfen, Strange Invaders, That Championship Season, The Sword & The Sorcerer, History of the World Part I, Miss Lonelyhearts, Ten to Midnight, The House on Sorority Row, Evilspeak, Q, Summerspell, Suburbia, Roar, Sweet Sixteen, The Fatal Game, Radioactive Dreams, The Glory of Khan, (short subjects) A Hard Rain, Ballet Robotique (Oscar nomination), The Wizard of Change, The Quest, A Trip to Tomorrow, Bird & The Robot, The Water Engine, Lean Machine, Wind Tunnel, Environmental Effects, New Magic, The Collector, Niagara, Lets Go!, Tour of the Universe, Runaway Train, Zargon, Deep Water Rescue, Rollercoaster, Monte Carlo Race, Alpine Highway, Toyota, Chevrolet, Jet Helicopter, Call from Space; keyboardist for James Brown "Static", 1996; creator comic effects Eat It (Grammy nomination), Like a Surgeon (Grammy nomination), New Duck (Grammy nomination); prodr., arranger, keyboardist Secret Smiles; composer (feature film scores) Screamers, Cataclysm, (commls.) Toyota, 1986, Celica, 1986; appeared with Bruce Springsteen, Steel, Hall & Oates, Chuck Berry, Dwayne Eddy, Jr. Walker & The All-Stars, James Brown, others. Mem. ACLU, So. Calif., 1985—, People for the Am. Way, So. Calif., 1985—, Am. Jewish Congress, 1982—. Recipient Brit. Acad. award Brit. Acad. of Film and TV Arts, Gt. Britain, 1992. Mem. Motion Picture Sound Editors (pres. 1992—, Golden Reel award 1988, 92), Acad. of Motion Picture Arts and Scis., Nat. Acad. Recording Arts and Scis., Am. Soc. Music Arrangers and Composers, Motion Picture Editors Guild. Democrat. Avocations: drawing, antique and classic automobiles, books.

BERMAN, SAUL JAY, strategic consultant; b. Phila., Jan. 1, 1946; s. Sherwood and Leona (Habelson) B.; m. S. Jann Gillen, June 6, 1980; 1 child, Ashley Scott. BS in Econs., U. Pa., 1967; MBA, Columbia U., 1969, PhD, 1973. Asst. prof. U. So. Calif., L.A., 1972-77; divisional v.p. Broadway Dept. Stores, L.A., 1977-82; case leader Boston Consulting Group, L.A., 1982-86; mng. ptnr. Price Waterhouse Strategic Change Group, 1986-98; global and Ams. leader corp. and ops. strategy PricewaterhouseCoopers, 1998—; active Strategic Leadership Forum, 1986—. Bd. dirs. Love is Feeding Everyone, L.A., 1988-89; mem. L.A. County Beach Commn., 1978-80, Planning Forum, L.A., 1987—, Town Hall, L.A., 1987-94. Mem. U. Pa. Alumni Club (bd. dirs. 1986-88, So. Calif. assoc. alumni trustee 1990—), Columbia Bus. Sch. Club of So. Calif. (bd. dirs. 1992-95). Avocations: tennis, running. Office: PriceWaterhouseCoopers 1880 Century Park E Ste 1200 Los Angeles CA 90067-1600

BERMAN, SKY, art educator, photographer; b. Phila., Sept. 25, 1965; d. Herbert Bergman and Evelyn (Ricciuti) Gordon. AA in Fine Arts, Broward C.C., 1984; BS in Fin., U. South Fla., 1987; MFA in Photography, U. Calif., Santa Barbara, 1991. Lectr. Ventura (Calif.) Coll., 1993-94, El Camino Coll., Torrance, Calif., 1994, U. Calif., Santa Barbara, summer 1995; asst. prof. Calif. Poly. State U., San Luis Obispo, 1995—. One-person shows include UCEN Gallery, U. Calif., Santa Barbara, 1991, Jaffe/Baker Gallery, Boca Raton, Fla., 1991, Contemporary Arts Forum, Santa Barbara, 1992, Level Three Gallery, Phila., 1992, Deadalus Gallery, Venice, Calif., 1993, Ro Snell Gallery, Santa Barbara, 1993, 97, Women's Ctr., U. Calif., Santa Barbara, 1993, Allan Hancock Coll., Santa Maria, Calif., 1994, Maryhill Mus. Art, Goldendale, Wash., 1994, C.A.G.E. Gallery, Cin., 1994, Sarah Moody Art Gallery, U. Ala., Tuscaloosa, 1995, Carnegie Mus. Art, Oxnard, Calif., 1995, N.Y. Acad. Art, N.Y.C., 1995, U. Kans., 1996, The F-STOPs here, Santa Barbara, 1997; exhibited in group shows Women's Ctr., U. Calif., Santa Barbara, 1991, 92, 93, Contemporary Arts Forum, Santa Barbara, 1992, 97, Laguna Art Mus., Laguna Beach, Calif., 1993, Atkinson Gallery, Santa Barbara City Coll., 1993, Griffin Fine Art, Costa Mesa, Calif., 1994, Scheinbaum & Russek, Santa Fe, 1994, L.A. County Mus. of Art, 1994, Visions Gallery, San Francisco, 1995, Calif. Poly. State U., San Luis Obispo, 1996. Office: Calif Poly State U Dept Art and Design San Luis Obispo CA 93407

BERMAN, STEVEN RICHARD, software engineer; b. N.Y.C., Dec. 30, 1947; s. Harold and Norma (Bystock) B.; m. Susan Segall, Aug. 3, 1969; 1 child, Russell T. BS in Meteorology, CCNY, 1968; postgrad., U. Chgo., 1968-69; MS in Tech. Mgmt., Pepperdine U., 1993. Programmer, analyst Logicon, Inc., San Pedro, Calif., 1970-73, 75-78, Hughes Aircraft Co., Culver City, Calif., 1973-75; sr. analyst Argosystems, Inc., Sunnyvale, Calif., 1978-80; mgr. software support Ultrasystems, Inc., Irvine, Calif., 1981-86; sr. rsch. engr. Northrop Grumman Inc., Hawthorne, Calif., 1986-98; sr. software engr. TRW Inc., L.A., 1998—. Author (computer programs) Recording Input-Output, 1983, Batch Jobs from Fortran, 1988, Marking Files No Backup, 1988. NDEA Title IV fellow, Chgo., 1968. Mem. Am. Contract Bridge League, Mensa. Avocations: bridge, travel. Home: 17336 Flame Tree Cir Fountain Valley CA 92708

BERMOY, EMILIANO SIMACIO, minister, church administrator; b. Bohol, The Philippines, June 30, 1946; came to U.S., 1985; s. Roman and Antonia (Simacio) B.; m. Amelia Gomez, July 5, 1975; children: Emil II, Jerusalem, Kathrine, Greg. BS in Edn., U. Philippines, 1972, MEd, 1975; Ma in Missiology, Fuller Theol. Sem., 1988, postgrad. Ordained to ministry Christian Cath. Ch. of The Philippines, 1985. Dean acad. affairs Febias Coll. Bible, The Philippines, 1982-83; founding pastor U. The Philippines Bliss Christian Fellowship, 1982-85; dir. crusades and counseling Asian Christian Outreach, The Philippines, 1983-85; founding pres. Christian Fellowship Ministries, The Philippines, 1985—; founding pastor Bible Christian Fellowship, L.A., 1986—; founding pres. Igniting Light Around the World, Pasadena, 1987—; bd. dirs. Christian Fellowship Found. for Mindanao, Sunnyvale, Calif. Office: Bible Christian Fellowship 2701 Beverly Blvd Los Angeles CA 90057-1007

BERMUDEZ, MARI PAZ TIANGCO, interior designer; b. Quezon City, The Philippines, July 27, 1955; came to U.S., 1989; d. Joel Paglinawan and Crisanta Espino (Torres) Tiangco; m. Lordito Jun de Guzman Bermudez, Jan. 5, 1983; 1 child, Jaemi Cheri Tiangco. B in Interior Design, U. of The Philippines, Quezon City, 1976, BS in Landscape Arch., 1986, M in Environ. Planning, 1989. Cert. kitchen designer; cert. bathroom designer Nat. Kitchen and Bath Assn. of U.S. and Can. Furniture plant mgr. Nat. Housing Corp., The Philippines, 1976-82, comml. and indsl. estate mgr., 1982-90; mgr. Colorel Bunds, Tukwila, Wash., 1990-93; mgr. kitchen and bath dept. Home Depot, Seattle, 1993—; pres. XCLNT Design, Kent, Wash., 1992-98. Mem. Christian Faith Ctr., Wash. Recipient Best Kitchen Design award St. of Dreams, 1993, 94, Best Bath Design award, 1993, 94. Mem. Nat. Kitchen and Bath Assn. (sec., bd. edn. 1996-98), Am. Soc. Interior Design, Filipino Archs. in Wash. Home: 13506 SE 239th St Kent WA 98042-3280

BERNAL, JOLENE CHRISTINE, education educator; b. Lewiston, Idaho, Nov. 13, 1971; d. Dennis Duaine and Mary Belle (Dyer) Cartwright; m. Leon Antonio Bernal, Mar. 22, 1997. BA in English, Northwest Nazarene Coll., Nampa, Idaho, 1994, MEd in Curriculum and Instrn., 1995; postgrad., Boise State U. Cert. tchr., Idaho. Tchr. Homedale (Idaho) Sch. Dist., 1994—; mem. sch. to work com. Homedale Sch. Dist., 1996—, advisor, acad. bowl, 1994-98. Mem. NEA, Idaho Edn. Assn., Nat. Coun. Tchrs. English. Democrat. Nazarene. Avocations: reading, writing, photography, gardening. Home: 2625 Sunflower Dr Nampa ID 83686-7133 Office: Homedale Sch Dist 203 E Idaho Ave Homedale ID 83628-3216

BERNARD, ALEXANDER, airport police official; b. L.A., Apr. 23, 1952; s. Louis and Hannah (Bergman) B.; m. Diana LoRee Winstead, Dec. 17, 1976; children: Michael Alexander, Andrew Alexander. AA magna cum laude, L.A. Valley Coll., 1976; BS summa cum laude, Calif. State U., L.A., 1989. Parking meter collector L.A. City Clk.'s Office, 1973-79; police officer L.A. Airport, 1979-95; sgt. police svcs. divsn. L.A. Airport, Ontario, Calif., 1995—. Contbr. articles to profl. jours. Active Boy Scouts Am. Mem. NRA (life), Internat. Police Assn. (life), Indsl. Rels. Rsch. Assn., Calif. Peace Officers Assn., Peace Officers Rsch. Assn. Calif. (chpt. pres. 1982-84, 85-87, state bd. dirs. 1984-85, 88—, ethnic rels. com. 1993-94, exec. com. 1994—, sec. 1999—), L.A. Airport Peace Officers Assn. (pres. 1981-89, 94-95, bd. dirs. 1992-94), Airport Supervisory Police Officers' Assn. L.A. (bd. dirs. 1996, v.p. 1997-98, pres. 1999—), Fraternal Order of Police, Calif. Rifle and Pistol Assn. (life), Golden Key (life), Phi Kappa Phi (life). Democrat. Mem. Assemblies of God Ch. Avocations: travel, record collecting. Office: Police Svcs Divsn Ontario Internat Airport 1070 S Vineyard Ave Ontario CA 91761-8007

BERNARD, CHRISTOPHER WILLIAM, writer, consultant, editor; b. Burlington, N.J., May 6, 1950; s. Glenn Thompson and Joan (Sproul) B. BA in Humanities, New Coll. Calif., 1981. Pvt. practice San Francisco, Phila., 1973—; editorial cons. San Francisco, 1984—; editor Caveat Lector, San Francisco, 1989—. Author: Kafka's Smile, 1984, Isman, 1986, The Dilettate of Cruelty: Deserts, 1996. Named Temple U. poetry contest winner, Phila., 1972. Mem. Bay Area Editors Forum. Avocations: music, dance, photography, swimming. Home and Office: 400 Hyde St Apt 606 San Francisco CA 94109-7445

BERNARD, JONATHAN WALTER, music educator; b. Portsmouth, N.H., June 27, 1951; s. Walter J. and Claire J. (Laflamme) B.; m. Molly Schubert, June 3, 1984; 1 child, Nina Rose. AB, Harvard Coll., 1972; PhD, Yale U., 1977. Asst. prof. Amherst (Mass.) Coll., 1976-79, Yale U., New Haven, 1979-87; assoc. prof. U. Wash., Seattle, 1987-93, prof., 1993—; com. examiners GRE Music Test, Princeton, N.J., 1992-98. Author: The Music of Edgard Varèse, 1987; editor: Elliott Carter: Collected Essays & Lectures, 1937-95, 1997; co-editor: Music Theory in Concept and Practice, 1997; editor Music Theory Spectrum, 1988-91; mem. editl. bd. Perspectives of New Music, 1992—. Mem. Am. Musicol. Soc., Soc. for Music Theory (Young Scholar award 1988). Avocations: reading, running. Office: Univ Wash Sch Music PO Box 353450 Seattle WA 98195-3450

BERNARD, THELMA RENE, property management professional; b. Phila.; d. Michael John and Louise Thelma (Hoffman) Campione; m. Gene Bernard (div.). Sec. Penn. Mut. Life Ins. Co., Phila., Suffolk Franklin Savs. Bank, Boston, Holmes and Narver, Inc., Las Vegas; constrn. site office mgr. Miles R. Nay, Inc., Las Vegas; adminstrv. asst to pres. N.W.S. Constrn. Corp., Inc., Las Vegas, 1982-86, corp. sec., 1982-86; gen. mgr., corp. sec. D.A.P., Inc. property mgmt. com, Las Vegas, 1991-97, pres., 1991—. Author: Blue Marsh, 1972, Winds of Wakefield, 1972, Moonshadow Mansion, 1973, 2d edit., 1976, Spanish transl., 1974, German transl., 1977; contbr. articles to Doll Reader, Internat. Doll World, other mags.; past editor Cactus Courier; editor, pub. The Hoyer Enthusiastic Ladies Mail Assn., 1980-90, 96—; Friendly Tymes, 1991—, Lady Charleen, 1995—; writer song lyrics. Mem. Keats-Shelley Assn. Am. Inc., Broadcast Music Inc., Nat. League Am. Pen Women (v.p. Red Rock Canyon br. 1986-88), Original Paper Doll Artists Guild, Heritage Rose Soc., Bookmark Collector Club, Seed Savers Exch. Office: PO Box 14002 Las Vegas NV 89114-4002

BERNARD, TIMOTHY HENRY, sculptor, designer; b. San Francisco, Aug. 8, 1956; s. Harold Dewey Dinning and Margaret Andrews B.; m. Melinda Hornby, July 25, 1998. BMF, Stanford U., 1976; BA, Denison U., 1977; BFA, R.I. Sch. Design, 1980. Tech. asst. R.I. Sch. Design Foundry, Providence, 1978-79; prin., owner T. Barny Designs, Healdsburg, Calif., 1978—; cons. Stewart Construction, Healdsburg, Calif., 1990—, Dane Schieber Designs, San Francisco, 1995-97; judge Marin Soc. Art, San Rafael, Calif., 1997. Titled sculptures include Effleurage, 1982 (1st place award), Dalliance, 1982 (1st place award), Nautilus, 1983 (best of show award), Running Brook, 1992. Bd. dirs. Healdsburg (Calif.) Arts Council, 1992-95, Geyserville (Calif.) Fire District, 1994—, Alexander Valley Assn., Healdsburg, 1994—; EMT Emergency Medical Svcs., Sonoma County, Calif.; firefighter Geyserville Fire Dept., Calif. Recipient Best New Artist award Bay Area Arts Council, San Mateo, Calif., 1980, Best of Show award Calif. State Fair, Sacramento, 1984, First Place Sculpture award Ctrl. Calif. Biennial, Monterey, 1985; fellow Woodstock (N.Y.) Sch. Art, 1995. Mem. Calif. Lawyers for Arts, Calif. Stone Sculptors, Santa Rosa Arts Guild, Bohemian Club. Avocations: river rafting, skiing, tennis, hunting, mountain biking. Office: T Barny Designs 4370 Pine Flat Rd Healdsburg CA 95448-9015

BERNASCONI, CLAUDE FRANÇOIS, chemistry educator; b. Zürich, Switzerland, Feb. 17, 1939; came to U.S., 1967; s. Oscar Antonio and Jeanne Marie (Borel) B.; m. Regula Luchsinger, Sept. 15, 1962 (div. Mar. 1979); children: Andrea K., Marc P.; m. Anastassia Kanavarioti, Sept. 10, 1983. MS, Swiss Fed. Inst. Tech., Zürich, 1963, PhD, 1965. Postdoctoral fellow Max Planck Inst. for Phys. Chemistry, Göttingen, Fed. Republic Germany, 1966-67; asst. prof. chemistry U. Calif., Santa Cruz, 1967-72, assoc. prof., 1972-77, prof., 1977—. Author: Relaxation Kinetics, 1976; editor: Investigation of Rates and Mechanisms of Reactions, 1986; contbr. over 160 articles to profl. jours. Grantee NSF, 1969—; Alfred P. Sloan fellow, 1971-73. Mem. AAAS, Am. Chem. Soc. (grantee 1970—). E-mail: bernasconi@chemistry.ucsc.edu. Home: 101 Hillcrest Ter Santa Cruz CA 95060-2012 Office: U Calif Dept Chemistry Santa Cruz CA 95064

BERNHARD, HARVEY, producer; b. Seattle, Mar. 5, 1924; s. Moe and Rose Minnie (Cohn) B.; m. Lillian Vera Kramer, June 23, 1962; 1 child, Craig Allen. BA, Stanford U., 1947. In charge of prodn. Wolper Prodns., Los Angeles, 1961-68, Metromedia Producers Assoc., Los Angeles, 1968-70. Producer: (films) The Mack, Oakland, Calif., 1972, The Omen, London, 1975, Omen II: Damien, Chgo., 1977, Omen III: Final Conflict, London, 1979, Goonies, 1985, The Lost Boys, 1987, Omen IV, 1991; exec. producer Lady Hawke, Italy, 1983. Served with USNR, 1943-45, ETO. Republican. Jewish. Avocations: tennis, horses, golfing, fishing, bicycling. Home: 21211 Happy Valley Rd Stanwood WA 98292-5734 Office: Allen Susman Rosenfeld Meyer & Susman 9601 Wilshire Blvd Beverly Hills CA 90210-5213

BERNHEIMER, MARTIN, music critic; b. Munich, Germany, Sept. 28, 1936; came to U.S., 1940, naturalized, 1946; s. Paul Ernst and Louise (Nassauer) B.; m. Lucinda Pearson, Sept. 30, 1961 (div. Feb. 1989); children: Mark Richard, Nora Nicoll, Marina and Erika (twins); m. Linda Winer, Sept. 27, 1992. MusB with honors, Brown U., 1958; student, Munich Conservatory, 1958-59; MA in Musicology, NYU, 1961. Free-lance music critic, 1958—; contbg. critic N.Y. Herald Tribune, 1959-62; mem. music faculty NYU, 1959-62; contbg. editor Mus. Courier, 1961-64; temporary music critic N.Y. Post, 1961-65; N.Y. corr. for Brit. Publ. Opera, 1962-65, L.A. corr., 1965—; corr. West Coast Brit. Opera Mag., 1965—; asst. to music editor Saturday Rev., 1962-65; mng. editor Philharmonic Hall Program, N.Y.C., 1962-65; music editor, chief critic L.A. Times, 1965-96; mem. faculty U. So. Calif., 1966-71, music faculty UCLA, 1969-75, Calif. Inst. Arts, 1975-82, Calif. State U., Northridge, 1978-81, Rockefeller Program for Tng. of Music Critics; mem. Pulitzer Prize Music Jury, 1984, 86, 90; L.A. corr. for Swiss publ. Opernwelt, 1984—. Contbg. author New Groves Dictionary; contbr. liner notes for recordings; appearances on radio and TV, Met. Opera Broadcasts; contbr. articles to Vanity Fair, Music Quar., The Critic, Opera News, Mus. Am., Fin. Times, London, Sidewalk N.Y. (internet), others. Recipient Deems Taylor award ASCAP, 1974, 78, Headliners award, 1979, Pulitzer Prize for disting. criticism, 1981, Lifetime Achievement award Svc. to Music, Calif. Assn. Profl. Music Tchrs., 1990. Mem. Nat. Opera Inst. (ind. selection com. 1980), Pi Kappa Lambda (hon.).

BERNHOFT, FRANKLIN OTTO, psychotherapist, psychologist; b. Fargo, N.D., Aug. 12, 1944; s. Otto and Irene Bernhoft; m. Dorothy Ann Larsen, Aug. 11, 1973; children: Kimberley, Brady, Heather. BA in English, N.D. State U., 1966; MA in Counseling Psychology, U. N.D., 1970; MA in English, Calif. State U., 1978; PhD in Counseling Psychology, Brigham Young U., 1985. Cert. therapist, hypnotherapist, counselor, secondary tchr.; lic. psychologist, marriage, family and child counselor, edn. psychologist. Instr. Chapman Coll., Brigham Young U., U. N.D., U.S. I.U.; staff trainer Sacramento (Calif.) County Office Edn., 1977-82; therapist Lodi and Stockton, Calif., 1985—; therapist, family fitness trainer, master trainer systematic helping skills, devel. capable people trainer U. Pacific Behavioral Medicine Clinic; co-founder prevention/intervention project, Sacto County, 1977; presenter in field. Contbr. articles to profl. jours. Lt. U.S. Army, 1967-69. H.H. Kirk R. Askanase scholar; cert. achievement Ft. Carson; decorated Bronze star, combat med. badge Nat. Def. Svc. Vietnam. Mem. ASCD, Children with Attention Deficit Disorders, Nat. Assn. Sch. Psychologists, Assn. Mormon Counselors and Psychotherapists, Calif. Assn. Marriage and Family Therapists, Calif. Psychol. Assn., Sacramento Area Sch. Psychologists Assn., Calif. Continuation Edn. Assn. (past treas.), Calif. Assn. Lic. Edn. Psychologists, Mensa, Eye Movement Desensitization and Reprocessing Internat. Assn., Calif. Assn. Psychologists, Am. Assn. Christian Counselors. Office: Creative Therapy 2000 W Kettleman Ln Ste 103 Lodi CA 95242

BERNIER, EMILY S., English literature educator; b. Farmington, N.Mex., Nov. 27, 1963; d. Phil H. Barck and Miriam Lorraine Martin Deen; m. Steven C. Bernier, Dec. 21, 1989. BA in Bus. Adminstrn., Eastern N.Mex. U., 1986, MA in English, 1991. Pers. mgmt. officer 40th Pers. Svc. Co., Sacramento, 1991-94, detachment comdr., 1994-96; HHD comdr. Hdqrs. 100th Troop Command, Fairfield, Calif., 1996—; instr. tech. writing Embry-Riddle Aero. U., Travis AFB, Calif., 1993—; English instr. Solano Coll.,

Suisun, Calif., 1992—; program coord., English instr. Chapman U., Fairfield, 1991—. Mem. mil. affairs com. USAF, Travis AFB, 1998. Recipient Red Ribbon for Cmty. Svc., Solano County, 1996, Young Leadership award Chapman U., 1997. Mem. Soc. for Human Resources Mgmt., Fairfield/ Suisun C. of C., N.G. Assn. Calif., Calif. Tchrs. Assn. Avocations: humani diversity, Southwestern writers, human rights, river rafting. Office: Chapman U 450 Chadbourne Rd Suisun City CA 94585-9647

BERNING, PAUL WILSON, lawyer; b. Marceline, Mo., Apr. 22, 1948; s. Harold John and Doris (Wilson) B. BJ, U. Mo., 1970; JD with honors, U. San Francisco, 1986. Bar: Calif. 1986, U.S. Dist. Ct. (no. dist., ea. dist., so. dist.) Calif. 1986, U. S. Dist. Ct. (cen. dist.) Calif. 1989, U.S. Ct. Appeals (9th cir.) 1986, U.S. Ct. Claims 1992, U.S. Supreme Ct. 1992. Copy editor Chgo. Sun-Times, 1970-74, nat., fgn. editor, 1974-78; asst. news editor San Francisco Examiner, 1978-83; law clerk San Francisco dist. atty. Consumer Fraud Divsn., 1984; extern Calif. Supreme Ct., San Francisco, 1985, San Francisco Superior Ct., 1986; assoc. Thelen, Marrin, Johnson & Bridges, San Francisco, 1986-94, ptnr., 1995-98; ptnr. Thelen Reid & Priest, San Francisco, 1998—. Co-author: (book chpt.) Proving and Pricing Construction Claims, 1990; contbr. speeches and papers to profl. confs. Mem. ABA (forum on constrn. industry 1986—), State Bar Assn. Calif., Bar Assn. San Francisco (coord. legal assistance for mil. pers. 1991-92, assoc. liaison to San Francisco lawyers com. for urban affairs 1987-92), High Speed Ground Transp. Assn., Modern Transit Soc. Avocations: horseback riding, sailing, reading. Office: Thelen Reid & Priest LLP 2 Embarcadero Ctr Ste 2100 San Francisco CA 94111-3995

BERNOCO, DOMENICO, immunogeneticist, educator; b. Cherasco, Cuneo, Italy, Apr. 6, 1935; s. Giuseppe and Lucia (Merlo) D.; m. Marietta Magdelene von Diepow, July 20, 1972. DVM, U. Torino, Italy, 1959; lic. vet. medicine, Rome, 1961; Libera Docenza, Ministry Pub. Instrn., Rome, 1971. Asst. prof. med. genetics U. Torino, 1961-70; mem. staff Basel (Switzerland) Inst. Immunology, 1970-76; assoc. rsch. immunologist dept. surgery UCLA, 1977-81; assoc. prof. vet. medicine reproduction U. Calif., Davis, 1981-94, prof. emeritus, 1994—. Contbr. 105 articles to profl. jours. Fellow Italian Nat. Coun. Rsch., 1962-63, Italian Ministry for Pub. Instrn., 1963-64, fellow for fgn. countries NATO, 1967-68. Mem. Am. Assn. Immunologists, Internat. Soc. Animal Genetics, Am. Soc. Histocompatibility and Immunogenetics. Avocations: gardening, bicycling, hiking, wildlife photography, travel. Home: 1002 Deodara Ct Davis CA 95616-5037 Office: U Calif Sch Vet Medicine Dept Population Health & Reproduction Davis CA 95616-8743

BERNS, PAMELA MARIE, English language and literature educator; b. Baldwin, Kans., Jan. 13, 1953; d. Warren Frank and Helen Elizabeth Schmidt. AS, York Christian Coll., 1973; BA in Edn., Wayne State Coll., 1976, MA in Edn., 1978; AAS in Animal Health Tech., Colo. Mountain Coll., 1986. Secondary English speech instr. David City (Nebr.) H.S., 1979-82; lang. arts instr. Revere Sr. H.S., Ovid, Colo., 1982-83; instr. English speech and lit. Colo. Mountain Coll., Glenwood Springs, 1984-88, No. Jr. Coll., Sterling, Colo., 1988—; English instr. Am. Indian Satellite C.C., Winnebago, Nebr., 1978; English instr. Navajo C.C., Tsaile, Ariz., 1985. Mem. Faculty Assn. Northeastern Jr. Coll. Avocations: reading, gardening, piano. Office: Northeastern Jr Coll 100 College Dr Sterling CO 80751-2344

BERNSTEIN, CHARLES HARRY, composer; b. Mpls., Feb. 28, 1943. Student, Juilliard Sch. Music, 1963-64; BA, UCLA, 1966, BA (Outstanding Grad. award), 1966, postgrad., 1966-69. Freelance composer various studios including Universal, Warner Bros., Columbia, Lorimar, Paramount, 20th Century, Los Angeles, 1972—; grad. faculty in film music, U. So. Calif., 1995; extension faculty, UCLA, 1990. Composer: (films) White Lightning, 1973, Mr. Majestyk, 1974, Gator, 1976, Foolin' Around, 1979, Love at First Bite, 1980, The Entity, 1981, Cujo, 1983, A Nightmare on Elm Street, 1984, The Allnighter, 1987, Dudes, 1987, Excessive Force, 1994, Rumplestiltskin, 1995, (TV mini-series) Scruples, 1980, Sadat, 1983, The Long Hot Summer, 1985, Drug Wars, 1990, Love, Lies and Murder, 1991, Drug Wars II, 1991, Trial: The Price of Passion, 1992, (TV films) Women at West Point, Are You in the House Alone?, 1978, Katie: Portrait of a Centerfold, 1978, The Winds of Kitty Hawk, 1978, The House on Garibaldi Street, 1979, Secret Weapons, 1985, Malice in Wonderland, 1985, Chase, 1985, The Last Fling, 1986, Ghost of a Chance, 1987, Love and Betrayal, 1989, Caroline, 1990, The Man Who Broke 1,000 Chains, 1988 (Ace award nomination), Too Young to Die, 1990, The Last Elephant, 1990, She Said No, 1990, The Love She Sought, 1990, Fall From Grace, 1990, Sophie and the Moonhanger, 1995, Dead Ahead, The Ticket, 1996, Whena Stranger Follows You Home, 1997, Bloodhounds II, 1997, Out of Auswies Past, 1994, My Name is Nate, 1991, Finale Appeal, 1991, Guilty Until Proven Innocent, 1992, Payoff, 1990, Between Love and Hate, 1991, Yes, Virginia There is a Santa Claus, 1991, Somebody's Daughter, 1993, (documentaries) Czechoslavakia, 1968 (Oscar award 1970), Soutine (Golden Lion award), Rose Kennedy: A Lite Remembered, 1994, Maya Lin: A Strong Clear Vision, 1995 (Acad. award), Return With Honor, 1999. Bd. govs. Acad. of Motion Pictures, 1995—; bd. dirs. ASCAP Found., 1998—. Chancellors Teaching fellow UCLA, 1966, Woodrow Wilson fellow, 1966. Mem. Acad. Motion Picture Arts and Scis. (exec. com. 1978—), Acad. TV Arts and Scis. (Emmy award 1987), Acad. Rec. Arts and Scis., ASCAP, Soc. Composers and Lyricists (bd. dirs. 1986—, v.p. 1997-99). Office: Turnstyle Music PO Box 11413 Beverly Hills CA 90213-4413

BERNSTEIN, GERALD WILLIAM, management consultant, researcher; b. Boston, Nov. 25, 1947; s. Alan Irwin and Anne (Fine) B.; m. Kathleen Ann Chaikin, Jan. 12, 1985. BS in Aero. Engring., Rensselaer Poly. Inst., 1969; MS in Engring., Stanford U., 1978. Transp. engr., dept. transp. State of N.Y., Albany, 1969-70; transp. planner Kennebec Regional Planning Com., Winslow, Me., 1974-77; dir. transp. dept. SRI Internat., Menlo Park, Calif., 1979-95; v.p. BACK Mgmt. Svcs., San Francisco, 1995-98; mng. dir. Stanford Transp. Group, San Francisco, 1998—; session chmn. aviation workshop NSF, 1985, 91; profl. conf. chmn.; bd. dirs. GlobTran Corp., 1993-98. Contbr. articles to profl. jours. Chmn. transp. com. Glenn Park Neighborhood Assn., San Francisco, 1982-85; dir. Balboa Terrace Neighborhood Assn., San Francisco, 1986-88; trustee Congregation Beth Israel-Judea, 1991-93. With U.S. Army, 1970-72. Recipient Cert. Appreciation City of Waterville, Maine, 1977. Mem. Am. Inst. Aeronautics and Astronautics (sr. mem.), Transp. Research Bd. of Nat. Research Council. Democrat. Jewish. Club: Toastmasters (Menlo Park, pres. 1986). Avocations: flying, skiing. Office: Stanford Transp Group 236 W Portal Ave Ste 359 San Francisco CA 94127-1423

BERNSTEIN, GIORA, artistic director; b. Vienna, Austria. Studied with Igor Markevitch; doctorate, Boston U. Mem. Boston Symphony; founder, dir. Boston Chamber Orch., Claremont (Calif.) Music Festival; founding music dir., condr. Colo. Music Festival; guest condr. Liege Philharmonic, Stuttgart Philharmonic, Netherlands Chamber Orch., Tonkunstler Orch. Vienna, Berlin Symphony Orch., Basel Radio Orch., St. Gallen Symphony, San Remo Symphony, Haifa Symphony Orch., Seattle Symphony Orch., Colo. Symphony Orch. Recipient Westinghouse Debut Recital award, City of Claremont commendation, County of L.A. commendation, Calif. Fedn. of Music Club award, Nat. Fedn. of Music Club award, Coleman Chamber Music award, six ASCAP awards, Excellence in the Arts award Gov. of Colo.; Internat. Acad. at Mozarteum fellow, Salzburg, Austria; Juilliard Sch. of Music scholar, Brandeis U. scholar, Boston U. scholar. Office: Colo Music Festival Orch 1525 Spruce St Ste 101 Boulder CO 80302-4256*

BERNSTEIN, JACK BARRY, film company executive, producer; b. N.Y.C., May 6, 1937. BA in Sociology, SUNY, Bklyn., 1962. V.p., gen. mgr. S.I.B. Prodns./Paramount Pictures, N.Y.C., L.A., 1962-64, C.P.I. Prodns., N.Y.C., L.A., 1964-66; freelance prodn. mgr., asst. dir. worldwide, 1966-73, freelance producer, 1973-86; v.p. worldwide prodn. Walt Disney Pictures, Burbank, Calif., 1983-86; sr. v.p. worldwide prodns. United Artist Pictures, Culver City, Calif., 1987-88, MGM Pictures/ MGM/UA, Culver City, Calif., 1988-90. Exec. producer: (films) North Dallas Forty, 1979, The Beast Within, 1981; assoc. producer: (films) Unfaithfully Yours, 1983, The Other Side of Midnight, 1977; co-producer: (film) The Mambo Kings, 1991, Under Siege, 1992. Served with U.S. Army, 1956-58. Mem. Dirs. Guild Am., Acad. Motion Picture Arts and Scis., Acad. TV Arts and Scis., Am. Film Inst. Club: Friars (N.Y.C. and Beverly Hills).

BERNSTEIN, SOL, cardiologist, educator; b. West New York, N.J., Feb. 3, 1927; s. Morris Irving and Rose (Leibowitz) B.; m. Suzi Maris Sommer, Sept. 15, 1963; 1 son, Paul. AB in Bacteriology, U. Southern Calif., 1952, MD, 1956. Diplomate Am. Bd. Internal Medicine. Intern Los Angeles County Hosp., 1956-57, resident, 1957-60; practice medicine specializing in cardiology L.A., 1960—; staff physician dept. medicine Los Angeles County Hosp. U. So. Calif. Med. Center, L.A., 1960—, chief cardiology clinics, 1964, asst. dir. dept. medicine, 1965-72; chief profl. services Gen. Hosp., 1972-74; med. dir. Los Angeles County-U So. Calif. Med. Center, L.A., 1974-94; med. dir. central region Los Angeles County, 1974-78; dir. Dept. Health Services, Los Angeles County, 1978; assoc. dean Sch. Medicine, U. So. Calif., L.A., 1986-94, assoc. prof., 1968—; med. dir. Health Rsch. Assn., L.A., 1995—; cons. Crippled Childrens Svc. Calif., 1965—. Contbr. articles on cardiac surgery, cardiology, diabetes and health care planning to med. jours. Served with AUS, 1946-47, 52-53. Fellow A.C.P., Am. Coll. Cardiology; mem. Am. Acad. Phys. Execs., Am. Fedn. Clin. Research, N.Y. Acad. Sci., Los Angeles, Am. heart assns., Los Angeles Soc. Internal Medicine, Los Angeles Acad. Medicine, Sigma Xi, Phi Beta Phi, Phi Eta Sigma, Alpha Omega Alpha. Home: 4966 Ambrose Ave Los Angeles CA 90027-1756 Office: 1640 Marengo St Los Angeles CA 90033-1036

BERRING, ROBERT CHARLES, JR., law educator, law librarian, former dean; b. Canton, Ohio, Nov. 20, 1949; s. Robert Charles and Rita Pauline (Franta) B.; m. Barbara Rust, June 20, 1975; children: Simon Robert, Daniel Fredrick. B.A. cum laude, Harvard U., 1971; J.D., U. Calif.-Berkeley, 1974, M.L.S., 1974. Asst. prof. and reference librarian U. Ill. Law Sch., Champaign, 1974-76; assoc. librarian U. Tex. Law Sch., Austin, 1976-78; dep. librarian Harvard Law Sch., Cambridge, Mass., 1978-81; prof. law, law librarian U. Wash. Law Sch., Seattle, 1981-82; prof. law, law librarian Boalt Hall Law Sch., Berkeley, Calif., 1982—, dean sch. library and info. scis., 1986-89; mem. Westlaw Adv. Bd., St. Paul, 1984-91; cons. various law firms; mem. on Legal Exch. with China, 1983—, chmn., 1991-93.; vis. prof. U. Cologne, 1993. Author: How to Find the Law, 8th edit., 1984, 9th edit., 1989, Great American Law Revs., 1985, Finding the Law, 1995; co-author: Authors Guide, 1981; editor Legal Reference Svc. Quar., 1981—; author videotape series Commando Legal Rsch., 1989. Chmn. Com. Legal Ednl. Exch. with China, 1991-93. Robinson Cox fellow U. Western Australia, 1988; named West Publishing Co. Acad. Libr. of Yr., 1994. Mem. Am. Assn. Law Libraries (pres. 1985-86), Calif. Bar Assn., ABA, ALA. Office: Boalt Hall Rm 345 Berkeley CA 94720

BERRY, GLENN, educator, artist; b. Glendale, Calif., Feb. 27, 1929; s. B. Franklin and Heloise (Sloan) B.; BA magna cum laude, Pomona Coll., 1951; BFA (Honnold fellow), MFA, Sch. Art Inst. Chgo., 1956. Faculty, Humboldt State U., Arcata, Calif., 1956-81, prof. art, 1969-81, emeritus, 1981—. Exhibited one-man shows Ingomar Gallery, Eureka, Calif., 1968, Ankrum Gallery, L.A., 1970, Esther Bear Gallery, Santa Barbara, Calif., 1971, Coll. Redwoods, Eureka, Calif., 1989; exhibited in group shows Palace of Legion of Honor, San Francisco, Pasadena (Calif.) Art Mus., Rockford (Ill.) Coll., Richmond (Calif.) Art Mus., Henry Gallery U. Wash., Seattle; represented in permanent collections at Storm King Art Center, Mountainville, N.Y., Kaiser Aluminum & Chem. Corp., Oakland, Calif., Palm Springs (Calif.) Desert Mus., Hirshhorn Mus., Washington, others; mural Griffith Hall, Humboldt State U., 1978. Mem. Phi Beta Kappa. Home: PO Box 2241 Mckinleyville CA 95519-2241

BERRY, GREGORY WAYNE, language arts educator; b. La Grande, Oreg., Oct. 31, 1963; s. Charles Duane Berry and Carolyn Ann (Vickers) Shaw. BA in Secondary Edn., English, Ea. Oreg. U., 1986, MS in Edn., 1990. Cert. tchr., Oreg. Instr. lang. arts Ontario (Oreg.) Jr. H.S., 1986-89; instr. English, drama Ontario H.S., 1989-98; instr. English Treasure Valley C.C., Ontario, 1994-98, South Salem (Oreg.) H.S., 1998—. Mem. Malheur Citizens for Democracy, Ontario, 1992—; participant Gov.'s Summit on Hate-Free Oreg., 1993; precinct committeeman Oreg. Dem. Party, Malheur County, 1998. Mem. Nat. Coun. Tchrs. English, Oreg. Edn. Assn. (Ontario Assn. sec. 1993-94). Avocations: reading, theatre, music.

BERRY, JOHN CHARLES, clinical psychologist, educational administrator; b. Modesto, Calif., Nov. 29, 1938; s. John Wesley and Dorothy Evelyn (Harris) B.; A.B., Stanford, 1960; postgrad. Trinity Coll., Dublin, Ireland, 1960-61; Ph.D., Columbia, 1967; m. Arlene Ellen Sossin, Oct. 7, 1978; children—Elise, John Jordan, Kaitlyn. Research assoc. Judge Baker Guidance Center, Boston, 1965-66; psychology asso. Napa State Hosp., Imola, Calif., 1966-67, staff psychologist, 1967-75, program asst., 1975-76; program dir. Met. State Hosp., Norwalk, Calif., 1976-77; asst. supt. Empire Union Sch. Dist., Modesto, Calif., 1977-93, dep. supt., 1993—. Mem. Am. Psychol. Assn., Assn. Calif. Sch. Adminstrs., Sigma Xi. Contbg. author: Life History Research in Psychopathology, 1970. Home: 920 Eastridge Dr Modesto CA 95355-4672 Office: Empire Union Sch Dist 116 N Mcclure Rd Modesto CA 95357-1329

BERRY, JOHN JOSEPH, educational administrator; b. Chgo., Mar. 6, 1953; s. Richard Martin and Dorothy Mae (Lyke) B. BA, Marquette U., Milw., 1975; MA, U. San Francisco, 1985. Cert. tchr. spl. edn., sch. adminstrn. Tchr. Kelseyville (Calif.) Unified Sch. Dist., 1980-88, adminstr., 1988—. Golf columnist On the Links, 1993—. Commr., Lake County Athletic League, Lakeport, Calif., 1990—; exec. dir. Lake County Jr. Golf Coun., Loch Lomand, Calif., 1989—. Mem. Assn. Calif. Sch. Adminstrs., Calif. Golf Writers Assn. Democrat. Roman Catholic. Avocations: golf, coaching basketball, audiophile. Home: 2904 Buckingham Dr Kelseyville CA 95451-7003 Office: Mount Vista Mid Sch PO Box 308 Kelseyville CA 95451-0308

BERRY, KENNETH J., sociology educator. Prof. dept. sociology Colo. State U. Recipient Banner I. Miller award Am. Meteorol. Assn., 1994. Office: Colorado St Univ Dept Sociology B258 Clark Fort Collins CO 80523*

BERRY, PHILLIP SAMUEL, lawyer; b. Berkeley, Calif., Jan. 30, 1937; s. Samuel Harper and Jean Mobley (Kramer) B.; m. Michele Ann Perrault, Jan. 16, 1982; children: David, Douglas, Dylan, Shane, Matthew. AB, Stanford U., 1958, LLB, 1961. Bar: Calif. 1962. Ptnr., Berry, Davis & McInerney, Oakland, Calif., 1968-76; owner Berry & Berry, Oakland, 1976—, pres., 1977—. Mem. adv. com. Coll. Natural Resources, U. Calif., Berkeley; mem. Calif. State Bd. Forestry, 1974-86, vice-chmn., 1976-86; trustee So. Calif. Ctr. for Law in Pub. Interest, 1970-87, Sierra Club Legal Def. Fund, 1975-90, Pub. Advs., 1971-86, chmn. bd., 1980-82; dir. Pacific Environment Resources Ctr., 1997—. Served with AUS, 1961-67. Mem. ABA, Calif. State Bar Assn., Sierra Club (nat. pres. 1969-71, 91-92, v.p. conservation law 1971—, v.p. polit. affairs 1983-85, John Muir award), Am. Alpine Club. Office: Berry & Berry 1300 Clay St Fl 9 Oakland CA 94612-1425

BERRY, ROBERT WORTH, lawyer, educator, retired army officer; b. Ryderwood, Wash., Mar. 2, 1926; s. John Franklin and Anita Louise (Worth) B. B.A. in Polit. Sci., Wash. State U., 1950; J.D., Harvard U., 1955; M.A., John Jay Coll. Criminal Justice, 1981. Bar: D.C. 1956, U.S. Dist. Ct. (D.C.) 1956, U.S. Ct. of Appeals (D.C. cir.) 1957, U.S. Ct. Mil. Appeals 1957, Pa. 1961, U.S. Dist. Ct. (ea. dist.) Pa. 1961, U.S. Dist. Ct. (ctrl. dist.) Calif. 1967, U.S. Supreme Ct. 1961, Calif. 1967, U.S. Ct. Claims 1975, Colo. 1997, U.S. Dist. Ct. Colo. 1997, U.S. Ct. Appeals (10th cir.) 1997. Research assoc. Harvard U., 1955-56; atty. Office Gen. Counsel U.S. Dept. Def., Washington, 1956-60; staff counsel Philco Ford Co., Phila., 1960-63; dir. Washington office Litton Industries, 1967-71; gen. counsel U.S. Dept. Army, Washington, 1971-74, civilian aide to sec. army, 1975-77; col. U.S. Army, 1978-87; prof., head dept. law U.S. Mil. Acad., West Point, N.Y., 1978-86; ret. as brig. gen. U.S. Army, 1987; mil. asst. to asst. sec. of army, Manpower and Res. Affairs Dept. of Army, 1986-87; asst. gen. counsel pub. affairs Litton Industries, Beverly Hills, Calif., 1963-67; chair Coun. of Def. Space Industries Assns., 1968; resident ptnr. Quarles and Brady, Washington, 1971-74; dir., corp. sec., treas., gen. counsel G.A. Wright, Inc., Denver, 1987-92, dir., 1987—; pvt. practice law Fort Bragg, Calif., 1993-96; spl. counsel Messner & Reeves LLC, Denver, 1997—; foreman Mendocino County Grand Jury, 1995-96. Served with U.S. Army, 1944-46, 51-53, Korea. Decorated Bronze Star, Legion of Merit, Disting. Service Medal; recipient Disting. Civilian Service medal U.S. Dept. Army, 1973, 74, Outstanding Civilian Service medal, 1977. Mem. FBA, Bar Assn. D.C., Calif. Bar Assn., Pa. Bar Assn., Colo. State Bar Assn., Army-Navy Club, Army-Navy Country Club, Phi Beta Kappa, Phi Kappa Phi, Sigma Delta Chi, Lambda Chi Alpha. Protestant.

BERSIN, ALAN DOUGLAS, school system administrator, lawyer; b. Bklyn., Oct. 15, 1946; s. Arthur and Mildred (Laikin) B.; m. Elisabeth Van Aggelen, Aug. 17, 1975 (div. Dec. 1983); 1 child, Alissa Ida; m. Lisa Foster, July 20, 1991; children, Madeleine Foster, Amalia Rose. AB magna cum laude, Harvard U., 1968; student, Oxford U., 1968-71; JD, Yale U., 1974. Bar: Calif. 1975, U.S. Dist. Ct. (ctrl. dist.) Calif. 1975, U.S. Ct. Appeals (9th cir.) 1977, Alaska 1983, U.S. Dist. Ct. Alaska 1983, U.S. Dist. Ct. Hawaii 1992, U.S. Dist. Ct. (so. dist.) Calif. 1992, U.S. Supreme Ct., 1996. Exec. asst. Bd. Police Commrs., L.A., 1974-75; assoc. Munger, Tolles & Olson, L.A., 1975-77, ptnr., 1978-92; spl. dep. dist. atty. Counties of Imperial and San Diego, Calif., 1993—; supt. pub. edn. San Diego City Schs.; adj. prof. of law U. So. Calif. Law Ctr.; vis. prof. Sch. Law U. San Diego, 1992—; named spl. rep. for U.S. s.w. border by U.S. Atty. Gen., 1995—; mem. Atty Gen.'s adv. com. of U.S. Attys.,tech. adv. panel Nat. Inst. of Justice Law Enforcement, adv. com. FCC/NTIA Pub. Safety Wireless; founder U.S./Mex. Binat. Lab. Program; chmn. bd. dirs. U.S. Border Rsch. Tech. Ctr., S.W. Border Coun. Named Rhodes scholar 1968; recipient Resolution of Merit award Mayor and City Coun. L.A., 1991, Spl. Achievement award Hispanic Urban Ctr., 1992. Mem. Assn. Bus. Trial Lawyers (bd. govs. 1986-88), Inner City Law Ctr. (chmn. bd. dirs. 1987-90). Democrat. Jewish. Avocations: scuba diving, skiing, travel. E-mail: abersin@mail.sandi.net. Office: Office of US Atty 880 Front St Ste 6293 San Diego CA 92101-8897 also: U San Diego Sch Law 5998 Alcala Park San Diego CA 92110-2429

BERTAGNOLE, SUZANNE BONACCI, customer service administrator, writer, artist; b. Salt Lake City, June 4, 1953; d. Joseph A. and Mary Helen (Darrow) Bonacci; m. Harold Lee Bertagnole, Feb. 14, 1982 (div. Aug. 1988); children: Shane Andrew, Vanessa Lee, Vincent Leon. BS in Comms., Westminster U., Salt Lake City, 1982. Freelance writer for mass media, Salt Lake City, 1980—; writer UPS, Salt Lake City, 1993—; designer, layout, advt. Westminster Profl. Bus., Salt Lake City; adminstrv. asst. UPS. Artist/ writer Black Ministry, 1982. Christian.

BERTAIN, G(EORGE) JOSEPH, JR., lawyer; b. Scotia, Humboldt County, Calif., Mar. 9, 1929; s. George Joseph and Ellen Veronica (Canty) B.; m. Bernardine Joy Galli, May 11, 1957; 1 child, Joseph F. AB, St. Mary's Coll. Calif., 1951; JD, Cath. U. Am., 1955. Bar: Calif. 1957. Assoc. Hon. Joseph L. Alioto, San Francisco, 1955-57, 59-65; asst. U.S. Atty. No. Dist. Calif., 1957-59; pvt. practice of law San Francisco, 1966—; panel mem. Theodore Granik's Am. Forum of The Air, Washington, 1955. Editor-in-Chief, Law Rev. Cath. U. Am. (vol. 5), 1954-55. Mem. bd. regents St. Mary's Coll. Calif., 1980—; chmn. San Francisco Lawyers Com. for Ronald Reagan, 1966-78, San Francisco lawyers com. for elections of Gov./U.S. Pres. Ronald Reagan, 1966, 70, 80, 84; spl. confidential advisor to Gov. Reagan on jud. selection, San Francisco, 1967-74; chmn. San Francisco Lawyers for Better Govt., 1978—; confidential advisor to Senator Hayakawa on judicial selection, 1981-82, to Gov. Deukmejian, 1983-90, to Gov. Wilson, 1991-92; bd. dirs. St. Anne's Home, Little Sisters of the Poor, San Francisco. Recipient De La Salle medal St. Mary's Coll. Calif., 1951, Signum Fidei award, 1976. Mem. ABA, Calif. Bar Assn., Fed. Bar Assn. (del. to 9th cir. jud. conf. 1967-76), St. Thomas More Soc. San Francisco, U.S. Supreme Ct. Hist. Soc., Assn. Former U.S. Attys and Asst. U.S. Attys. No. Calif. (past pres.), Commonwealth Club, Wester Assn., Knights of Malta, KC. Republican. Roman Catholic. Office: 22 Battery St Ste 1100 San Francisco CA 94111-5525

BERTHELSDORF, SIEGFRIED, psychiatrist; b. Shannon County, Mo., June 16, 1911; s. Richard and Amalia (Morschenko) von Berthelsdorf; m. Mildred Friederich, May 13, 1945; children: Richard, Victor, Dianne. BA, U. Oreg., 1934, MA, MD, 1939. Lic. psychiatrist, psychoanalyst. Intern U.S. Marine Hosp., Staten Island, N.Y., 1939-40; psychiat. intern Bellevue Hosp., N.Y.C., 1940-41; psychiat. resident N.Y. State Psychiat. Hosp., N.Y.C., 1941-42; research assoc. Columbia U. Coll. Physicians and Surgeons, N.Y.C., 1942-43; asst. physician Presbyn. Hosp. and Vanderbilt Clinic, N.Y.C., 1942-51; supervising psychiatrist Manhattan (N.Y.) State Hosp., 1946-50; asst. adolescent psychiatrist Mt. Zion Hosp., N.Y.C., 1950-52; psychiat. cons. MacLaren Sch. for Boys, Woodburn, Oreg., 1952-84, Portland (Oreg.) Pub. Schs., 1952-67; clin. prof. U. Oreg. Health Scis. Ctr., 1956—; tng. and supervising analyst Seattle Psychoanalytic Inst., 1970—. Author: Treatment of Drug Addiction in Psychoanalytic Study of the Child, Vol. 31, 1976, Ambivalence Towards Women in Chinese Characters and Its Implication for Feminism, American Imago, 1988, (with others) Psychiatrists Look at Aging, 1992. Bd. dirs., v.p. Portland Opera Assn., 1960-64, Portland Musical Co., 1987-92; bd. dirs., pres. Portland Chamber Orch., 1964-70, 92-94, 96-97. Maj. USAF, 1943-46. Recipient Henry Waldo Coe award U. Oreg. Med. Sch., Portland, 1939, citation Parry Ctr. for Children, Portland, 1970, Child Advocacy award ORAPT, 1998. Fellow Am. Psychiat. Assn. (life), Am. Geriatrics Soc. (founding fellow); mem. Am. Psychoanalytic Assn. (life), Portland Psychiatrists in Pvt. Practice (charter, pres. 1958), Mental Health Assn. (bd. dirs., chmn. med. adv. com. 1952-60), Multnomah County Med. Soc. (pres.'s citation 1979), Oreg. Psychoanalytic Found. (founding mem.), Am. Rhododendron Soc. (bd. dirs., v.p. Portland chpt. 1956-58, Bronze medal and citation 1974), Am. Rhododendron Species Found. (bd. dirs. 1960-75), Phi Beta Kappa, Sigma Xi, Phi Sigma. Avocations: farming, music. Home and Office: 1125 SW St Clair Ave Portland OR 97205-1127

BERTHIAUME, MARC ANDRE, screenwriter, director, cinematographer; b. Montreal, Que., Can., Apr. 30, 1956; s. Paul and Helen Patricia (Monty) B.; m. Wendy Ann Rittermal, Dec. 20, 1990 (div. Dec. 1996); 1 child, Monique Erin. BFA in Film Prodn., Concordia U., Montreal, 1990. Dir., cinematographer Push One Stop Films Prodns., Montreal, Que., 1982—. Screenwriter, dir. film Prenons La Mer, 1983; screenwriter, dir., cinematographer, producer FORCIER "en attendant", 1984-87; cinematographer The Elder, Little Corey Gorey, 1990, Ride Me, 1991, Printemps Incertains, 1991, Nelson Symonds Quartet, 1992, L'Attente, 1992, Merry Widows, 1993, If These Walls, 1994; screenwriter MTL-Three River Aller Simple, 1989, Personne M'a Dit Comment, 1990; producer, dir. A Bee Story, 1991, Nobody Told Me How, 1995; writer The Gun, 1994. Recipient Panavision award Concordia U., 1982, Mel Hoppenheim award Panavision, 1983. Mem. Acad. Can. Cinema and TV, Assn. Realisateurs et Realisatrices Que., Syndicat des Techniciens et Techniciennes en Cinema et Video du Quebec, Syndicat des Techniciens en Cinéma du Québec. Avocations: photography, horses, sailing, music, travel. Office: Push One Stop Film Prodns 1527 11th St Apt 3 Santa Monica CA 90401-2924

BERTHOLF, NEILSON ALLAN, JR., aviation executive; b. Morristown, N.J., Jan. 6, 1933; s. Neilson Allan Sr. and Marion Edna (Tiger) B.; m. Geraldine Henrietta Crabtree, Aug. 6, 1955; children: Mark Allan, Karen Jo. BS in Bus. Mgmt., Fairleigh Dickinson U., Rutherford, N.J., 1960, MBA, 1966. Flight dispatcher Lockheed Aircraft Svc., Inc., Atlantic City, N.J., 1958-59; chief airport ops. and safety Fed. Aviation Agy., Atlantic City, 1959-64; airport ops. mgr. City of Kansas City, Mo., 1965-67, asst. dir. aviation, 1967-79; airport dir. County of Milw., 1979-82; aviation dir. Sky Harbor Airport, Phoenix, 1982—. V.p. programs Boy Scouts Am., Phoenix, 1983—; com. mem. Fiesta Bowl Com., Phoenix, 1983—. With USN, 1951-55. Mem. Am. Assn. Airport Execs. (accredited; bd. dirs. S.W. chpt. 1988—), Airport Operators Coun. Internat. (official rep.; bd. dirs. 1981-84), Ariz. Airport Assn. (pres. 1983-84). Avocations: bowling, sports. Home: 3804 E Briarwood Ter Phoenix AZ 85044-7956 Office: Phoenix Aviation Dept 3400 E Sky Harbor Blvd Phoenix AZ 85034-4403

BERTIGER, KAREN LEE, real estate broker, asset manager, consultant; b. Louisville, Aug. 25, 1951; d. Joseph Henry and Phyllis June (Hupp) Dickhaus; m. Paul Robert Kastensmith, June 3, 1978 (div. June 1980); children: Christine, Jennifer; m. Bary Robert Bertiger, Dec. 28, 1985; stepchildren: Karen, Jeff. Student, Miami U., 1972-73, U. Cin., 1973-75, Am. Open U., 1986-88. Pres. Seville Realty and Investment Co., Phoenix, 1983-84; realtor Realty Execs., Scottsdale, Ariz., 1984-89; CEO Landvest Securities, Ltd., Scottsdale, 1987 , Landvest, Ltd., 1989-92, Golden Desert Capital Corp., Scottsdale, 1992—; designated broker Landvest Ltd., Scottsdale, 1989-92, Golden Desert Capital Corp., Scottsdale, 1992—. Leader

Ariz. Cactus-Pine Girl Scouts, Phoenix, 1985-86; co-founder The McDowell Sonoran Land Trust, 1991—, dir., treas., 1991-92. Mem. Nat. Assn. Realtors (grad. Realtor's Inst. 1986, cert. residential specialist 1989), Ariz. Assn. Realtors (registered lobbyist, chair fin., taxation subcom. 1995—, vice chair legis. com. 1996-97, chair 1997—), Urban Land Inst., World Future Soc., Scottsdale Assn. Realtors (grievance com. 1989-96, commun. rels. com. 1989-91, local city govt. com. 1988-89, govt. affairs com. 1989-90). Republican. Avocations: photography, hiking, music, reading. Office: Golden Desert Capital Corp 8711 E Pinnacle Peak Rd # 247 Scottsdale AZ 85255-3517

BERTOLINO, JAMES D., English language educator; b. Pence, Wis., Oct. 4, 1942; s. James and Doris (Robbins) B.; m. Lois Ann Behling, Nov. 29, 1966. BS, U. Wis., 1970; MFA, Cornell U., 1973. Lectr. Cornell U., Ithaca, N.Y., 1973-74; assoc. prof. U. Cin., 1974-84; sr. lectr. West Wash. U., Bellingham, 1991-98; vis. prof. Willamette U., Salem, Oreg., 1998—. Author: (poetry) Snail River, 1995, First Credo, 1986, New and Selected Poems, 1978, Precinct Kali, 1982. Mem. adv. bd. Skagit Valley Herald, Mt. Vernon, Wash., 1997. Fellowship Nat. Endowment for the Arts, 1974; writers grant Ohio Arts Coun., 1981; recipient Internat. Merit award Atlanta Rev., 1997. Shinto. Home: PO Box 1157 Anacortes WA 98221-6157

BERTRAM, JACK RENARD, information systems company executive; b. Lincoln, Nebr., Nov. 20, 1943; s. John Lewis and Emma Louise (Doerr) B.; m. Ingrid Frieda Reschke, Feb. 14, 1975; children: Deborah Geniene, Kenneth Brian. BS, Stanford U., 1966, MA, 1971; MS, Santa Clara U., 1988. Scientific programming specialist Lockheed Missles & Space Co., Sunnyvale, Calif., 1980-92; pres. Hansatech Internat., Redwood City, Calif., 1993—. Mem. AIAA, IEEE Computer Soc., Am. Assn. for Artificial Intelligence, Am. Astronautical Soc., Assn. for Computing Machinery, Computer Profls. for Social Responsibility, Inst. Cert. Profl. Mgrs. (cert. mgr.). Democrat. Home: 1580 Alameda De Las Pulgas Redwood City CA 94061-2404 Office: Hansatech Internat PO Box 554 Redwood City CA 94064-0554

BESHUR, JACQUELINE E., pet training consultant, writer; b. Portland, Oreg., May 8, 1948; d. Charles Daniel and Mildred (Domreis) Beshears. BA, UCLA, 1970; MBA, Claremont Grad. Sch., 1980; postgrad., City U., Seattle, 1989-90. Dir. and founder L.A. Ctr. for Photog. Studies, 1972-76; precious gem distbr. Douglas Group Holdings, Australia, 1976-78; small bus. owner BeSure Cleaning, 1981-90; animal trainer, exotic livestock farmer, 1990—. Author: Good Intentions Are Not Good Enough, 1992. Dir. County Citizens Against Incineration, 1987—, Ames Lake Protection Com., 1989—. Mem. Bridges for Peace, Nature Conservancy, Wash. Wilderness Coalition, Issaquah Alps Club, Inland Empire Pub. Lands Coun. Republican. Fundamentalist. Office: BeSure Tng PO Box 225 Carnation WA 98014-0225

BEST, MICKEY D., educator; b. Duncan, Okla., Aug. 25, 1957; s. Charles William and Barbara Colleen (Wylder) B.; m. Cynthia Wryn Anderson, Aug. 14, 1982; 1 child, Seth William. BA, Southwest Okla. Univ., 1980; MFA, TTU, 1990. Dir. student svcs. Coll. of the SW, Hobbs, N.Mex., 1984-87; tchr. Lovington (N.Mex.) Pub. Schs., 1987-89; instr. New Mex. Jr. Coll., Hobbs, 1989—, dept. chair, 1990—. Author (play): Voices, 1985. V.p. auditions SW Theatre Assn., 1995-97, v.p. Theatre New Mex., 1996-97, pres., 1997—; mem. Art in Pub. Places, 1984. Recipient Outstanding Acting award ACTF, 1977. Republican. Methodist. Avocation: Native Am. artifact documentation. Office: NMex Jr Coll 5317 N Lovington Hwy Hobbs NM 88240-9121

BEST, REED WAYNE, quality assurance professional; b. Provo, Utah, Dec. 30, 1953; s. Joseph and Elaine (Park) B.; m. Katherine Ann Hale, Jan. 12, 1953 (dec. June 1997); Steven Patrick, Richard Joseph, Christopher Michael, Helaine Ann, Aucia Maria. Assoc. in Drafting and Design, UVSC, Orem/Provo, Utah. Draftsman, designer Horrocks & Assocs., Salt Lake City, 1975-76; with coke and coal chems. Geneva, Orem, 1977-87; quality profl. Novell, Provo, 1987-90; quality supr. Procitho, Provo, 1990-92; lead assessor BSI/RRD-Stream, Provo, 1992-94; quality mgr. Stream Modus Media, Lindon, Utah, 1995—. CContbr. articles to profl. jours. Missionary LDS Ch., Salt Lake City, 1973-75; mem. Utah Regional Ballet, American Fork, Utah, 1986-96. Home: 261 Clegg Cir American Fork UT 84003-2625 Office: Modus Media Internat Lindon UT 84042

BEST, ROGER NORMAN, real estate investment manager; b. L.A., Apr. 16, 1949; s. Norman Frank and Muriel Noreen (Atkinson) B.; m. Sheri Lyn Kruyer, Oct. 16, 1982. BA, U. Wash., 1971. Lic. Real Estate Broker, Calif., 1985. Musician, entertainer, 1963-69; pres. Best Enterprises, L.A., 1969—; head electronic media svcs. Cedars-Sinai Med. Ctr., L.A., 1971-73; pres. Tazio Prodns., L.A., 1973-76; v.p. Video Disco & Assocs., L.A., 1975-76, DSL Constrn. Corp., L.A., 1977-85; v.p., chief operating officer Scott Properties, Inc., L.A., 1978-85; pres., chief exec. Tazio Properties, Inc., L.A., 1980—. Inventor correctable typewriter ribbon; creator original music videos concept with Visual Music, 1974; featured columnist Apt. Age Mag., L.A., 1989—. Mem. Van Nuys Airport Adv. Coun., 1987-94. Citation of Appreciation, City of L.A., 1988, 89, 94. Avocations: boating, skiing, flying, target shooting. Office: Tazio Properties Inc 3580 Wilshire Blvd Fl 17 Los Angeles CA 90010-2501

BEST, SUSAN KIMBERLY, gifted education educator; b. Tonasket, Wash., Dec. 17, 1954; d. Hubert Edward and Bertha Alberta (Michel) Matt; m. Dennis Eugene Best, Nov. 23, 1979; children: Devin Gene, Danyal Denise. BE, Heritage Coll., 1987, MEd, 1994. Cert. tchr., Wash. Tchr. Paschal Sherman Indian Sch., Omak, Wash., 1987—, coord. gifted program, 1991—. Contbr. poetry to anthologies. Lifetime mem. Okanagan/Lakes Band Enrollment # 1721-C, Colville Confederated Tribes, Colville Indian Reservation. Mem. ASCD, Nat. Assn. for Gifted Children, Colville Tribal Artists. Avocations: poetry, oil painting, drawing, design, Native American history. Home: PO Box 1149 181 Haley Creek Rd Omak WA 98841-9443 Office: Paschal Sherman Indian Sch Soaring Eagles Gifted Program Omak Lake Rd Omak WA 98841

BETANCOURT, HECTOR MAINHARD, psychology scientist, educator; b. Chile, Sept. 1, 1949; came to U.S. 1979; s. Hector and Eleonora (Mainhard) B.; m. Bernardita Sahli; children: Paul, Daniel. BA, Cath. U., Santiago, Chile, 1976; MA, UCLA, 1981, PhD in Psychology, 1983. From asst. prof. to assoc. prof. psychology Cath. U., Santiago, Chile, 1977-79, 83-85; from assoc. prof. to prof. of psychology Loma Linda U., Riverside, Calif., 1985-93, chmn., 1990-93; prof. psychology Grad. Sch. Loma Linda U., Calif., 1993-98; chmn. Grad. Sch. Loma Linda U., 1993-98; internat. cons. in grad. edn./tng. in psychology, 1997—. Editor Interam. Psychologist, 1982-86; mem. edit. bd. Jour. Cmty. Psychology, 1986-89, Spanish Jour. Social Psychology, 1986—, Conflict and Peace, 1993—, Jour. Personality and Social Psychology, 1997-98; contbr. articles to profl. jours. Recipient Rotary Found. award for Internat. Understanding, Rotary Internat., 1976-77; Fulbright fellow, UCLA, 1979-80. Mem. APA (exec. com. and chmn. task force on ethnicity, divsn. 48 peace psychology 1994-95, pres. 1997-98), Internat. Soc. Polit. Psychology, Internat. Soc. Cross-Cultural Psychology (exec. com. 1984-86), Interam. Soc. Psychology (sec.-gen. 1983-87), Soc. for Psychol. Study Social Issues, Soc. Personality and Social Psychology. Avocations: internat. politics, literature, philosophy. Office: Loma Linda U Dept Psychology Grad S Loma Linda CA 92350

BETTERIDGE, FRANCES CARPENTER, retired lawyer, mediator; b. Rutherford, N.J., Aug. 25, 1921; d. James Dunton and Emily (Atkinson) Carpenter; m. Albert Edwin Betteridge, Feb. 5, 1949 (div. 1975); children: Anne, Albert Edwin, James, Peter. A.B., Mt. Holyoke Coll., 1942; J.D., N.Y. Law Sch., 1978. Bar: Conn. 1979, Ariz. 1982. Technician in charge blood banks Roosevelt Hosp., N.Y.C. and Mountainside Hosp., Montclair, N.J., 1943-49; substitute tchr. Greenwich High Sch. (Conn.), 1978-79; intern and asst. to labor contracts office Town of Greenwich, 1979-80; vol. referee Pima County Juvenile Ct., Tucson, 1981-85, judge Pro Tempore Pima County Justice Cts., 1988-91; sole practice immigration law, Tucson, 1982-87; commr. Juvenile Ct., Pima County Superior Ct., Tucson, 1985-87; hearing officer Small Claims Ct., Pima County Justice Cts., Tucson, 1982; mediator Family Crisis Svc., Tucson, 1982-85. Pres. High Sch. PTA, Greenwich, 1970, PTA Council, 1971; mem. Greenwich Bd. Edn., 1971-76, sec., 1973-76; com. chmn. LWV Tucson, 1981, bd. dirs., 1984-85; bd. dirs., sec. Let The Sun Shine Inc., Tucson, 1981—; vol. referee Pima County Superior Ct., 1981-85; lectr. Tucson Mus. Art, 1994—; part time site coord. Elderhostel, Oaxaca, Mex., 1995. Mem. ABA, Conn. Bar Assn., Ariz. Bar Assn., Pima County Bar Assn., Tucson Sr. Acad., Point o'Woods Club. Republican. Congregationalist. Avocation: imports folk art from Oaxaca, Mex. Home and Office: 5320 N Campbell Ave Tucson AZ 85718-4908

BETTIGA, FLOYD H., artist, painter, educator; b. Ferndale, Calif., May 31, 1932; s. Emilio J. and Mary (Scalvini) B. BA, Humboldt State U., Arcata, Calif., 1954, MA, 1966. Art tchr. Fontana (Calif) Unified H.S., 1957-58, Jacobs Jr. H.S., Eureka, Calif., 1958-59, Eureka (Calif.) H.S., 1959-64, Coll. of the Redwoods, Eureka, 1964-91; planner, organizer Art Gallery at Coll. of the Redwoods, 1972. Artist: one-person exhbns. Candystick Studio, Ferndale Calif., Tuomala Gallery, Fort Bragg, Calif., Carter House, Eureka, Calif., Jacksonville (Oreg.) Gallery, Humboldt Gallery, San Francisco, Red Barn, Eureka, Humboldt State U., Arcata, Calif., Mezzanine Gallery, San Francisco, Calif., Humboldt Fed. Savings and Loan, Arcata, Calif.; group exhbns. Carter House, Eureka, Calif., Ankrum Gallery, L.A., Henry Gallery, U. Wash., Seattle, Coll. of the Redwoods, Eureka, Calif., Calif. Jr. Colls. Exhbn., San Mateo, Calif., Humboldt Cultural Ctr., Redwood Art Assn. ann. exhbns., Percival Galleries, Des Moines, Iowa, Am. House Tubingen, Germany, Phelan Awards Exhbn. Calif. Palace of the Legion of Honor, San Francico, Gumps Gallery San Francisco, Crocker Art Gallery, Kinsley Ann. Exhbn., Sacramento, Calif., Mus. of Art, Santa Barbara; represented in over 400 private and pub. collections . Art talks, fund raiser KZPN Radio, Eureka, 1997—; bd.dirs. Humboldt Arts Coun., Eureka, 1997-98; mem. friends of Clarke Mus., Eureka; past mem. NAACP, Nat. Trust for Historic Preservation, Humboldt County Hist. Soc., Soc. Archtl. Historians. With U.S. Army, 1956-57, Europe. Recipient Humboldt Art Coun. award, 1971, 1989, KEET-TV award, 1977, Outstanding Alumni award Humboldt State U., 1989. Roman Catholic. Avocations: travel, swimming, reading, working with charitable organizations. Home and Studio: PO Box 56 Bayside CA 95524-0056

BETTIS, JOHN GREGORY, songwriter; b. Long Beach, Calif., Oct. 24, 1946; s. Wayne Douglas and Nellie Jane (House) B. Songwriter, music pub. Warner/Chappel Music, 1976-82; songwriter, pub. John Bettis Music, Santa Monica, Calif., 1982—. Lyricist: (songs) Yesterday Once More, 1973 (Gold Record), Top of the World, 1974 (Gold Record), Heartland, Can You Stop the Rain, 1991, (Grammy nominee 1991), Promise Me You'll Remember, 1990 (acad. awards nominee 1991), One Moment In Time, 1988 (Emmie 1989), Crazy for You, 1985 (Gold Record), Slow Hand, 1981 (Gold Record), Human Nature, 1983 (Grammy cert.-Album of Yr. 1984); lyricist songs for movies including Say Anything, Star Trek V, Cocktail, Nothing in Common, Godfather Part III; lyricist TV theme songs. Recipient Top TV Series award for Growing Pains, ASCAP, 1986, for Just the Ten of Us, ASCAP, 1987, for Empty Nest, ASCAP, 1990, 34 Gold Records, Rec. Industry Assn. Am., 1970-90, 7 Platinum Records, Rec. Industry Assn. Am., 1970-90, 32 Performance awards ASCAP, 1970-90. Mem. ASCAP (bd. rev. 1982-88, bd. dirs. 1995—), Nat. Acad. Songwriters (bd. dirs. 1980-94, chmn. bd. dirs. 1985-87). Avocations: scuba diving, sailing. Office: John Bettis Music PO Box 668 Sunset Beach CA 90742-0668

BETTS, BARBARA LANG, lawyer, rancher, realtor; b. Anaheim, Calif., Apr. 28, 1926; d. W. Harold and Helen (Thompson) Lang; m. Roby F. Hayes, July 22, 1948 (dec.); children: John Chauncey IV, Frederick Prescott, Roby Francis II; m. Bert A. Betts, July 11, 1962; 1 child, Bruce Harold; stepchildren: Bert Alan, Randy W., Sally Betts Joynt, Terry Betts Marsteller, Linda Betts Hansen, LeAnn Betts Wilson. BA magna cum laude, Stanford U., 1948; LLB, Balboa U., 1951. Bar: Calif. 1952, U.S. Supreme Ct. 1978. Pvt. practice Oceanside, Calif., 1952-68, San Diego, 1960—, Sacramento, 1962—; ptnr. Roby F. Hayes & Barbara Lang Hayes, 1952-60; city atty. Carlsbad, Calif., 1969-68; v.p. Isle & Oceans Marinas, Inc., 1970-80, W.H. Lang Corp., 1964-69; sec. Internat. Prodn. Assocs., 1968—, Margaret M. McCabe, M.D., Inc., 1977-78. Co-author: (with Bert A. Betts) A Citizen Answers. Chmn. Traveler's Aid, 1952-53; pres. Oceanside-Carlsbad Jr. Chambrettes, 1955-56; vice chmn. Carlsbad Planning Commn., 1959; mem. San Diego Planning commn., 1959; v.p. Oceanside Diamond Jubilee Com., 1958; candidate Calif. State Legislature, 77th Dist., 1954; mem. Calif. Dem. State Ctrl. Com., 1958-66, co-chmn. 1960-62; co-chmn. 28th Congl. Dist.; alt. del. Dem. Nat. Conv., 1960; co-sponsor All Am. B-24 Liberator Collings Found. Named to Fullerton Union H.S. Wall of Fame, 1986; recipient Block S award Stanford U. Mem. ABA, AAUW (legis. com. 1958-59, local pres. 1959-60, asst. state legis. chmn. 1958-59), DAR (regent Oceanside chpt. 1960-61), DFC Soc. (assoc.), Am. Judicature Soc., Nat. Inst. Mcpl. Officers, Calif. Bar Assn., San Diego County Bar Assn., Oceanside C. of C. (sec. 1957, v.p. 1958, dir. 1953-54, 57-59), Heritage League (2d divsn. 8th Air Force), No. San Diego County Assn. Cs. of C. (sec.-treas.), Bus. and Profl. Women's Club (so. dist. legislation chmn. 1958-59), San Diego C. of C., San Diego Hist. Soc., Fullerton Jr. Assistance League, Calif. Scholarship Fedn. (life), Loyola Guild of Jesuit H.S., Soroptimist Internat. (pres. Oceanside-Carlsbad 1958-59, sec. pub. affairs San Diego and Imperial Counties 1954, pres. pres.'s coun. San Diego and Imperial Counties, Mex. 1958-59), Barristers (Stanford, Sacramento), Disting. Flying Cross Soc. (assoc.), Stanford Mothers, Phi Beta Kappa. Home: 441 Sandburg Dr Sacramento CA 95819-2559 Office: Betts Ranch PO Box 306 Elverta CA 95626-0306 also: 1830 Avenida Del Mundo Coronado CA 92118-4026

BETTS, BARBARA STOKE, artist, educator; b. Arlington, Mass., Apr. 19, 1924; d. Stuart and Barbara Lillian (Johnstone) Stoke; m. James William Betts, July 28, 1951; 1 child, Barbara Susan (dec.). BA, Mt. Holyoke Coll., 1946; MA, Columbia U., 1948. Cert. tchr., N.Y., Calif., Hawaii. Art tchr. Walton (N.Y.) Union Schs., 1947-48, Presidio Hill Sch., San Francisco, 1949-51; free-lance artist San Francisco, 1951; art tchr. Honolulu Acad. Arts, summer 1952, 59, 63, 85, spring 61, 64; libr. aide art rm. Libr. of Hawaii, Honolulu, 1959; art tchr. Hanahauoli Sch., Honolulu, 1961-62, Hawaii State Dept. Edn., Honolulu, 1958-59, 64-84; owner Ho'olaule'a Designs, Honolulu, 1973—. Illustrator: Cathedral Cooks, 1964, In Due Season, 1986; exhibited in Hawaii Pavilion Expo '90, Osaka, Japan, State Found. of Culture and Arts, group shows since 1964, one person shows 1991, 96; represented in Arts of Paradise Gallery, Waikiki, 1990—; traveling exhbns. include Pacific Prints, 1991, Printmaking East/West, 1993-95, Hawaii/Wis. Watercolor Show, 1993-94. Mem. Hawaii Watercolor Soc. (newsletter editor 1986-90), Nat. League Am. Pen Women (art chmn. 1990-92, sec. 1992-94, nat. miniature art shows 1991, 92, 93, 95), Honolulu Printmakers (dir. 1986, 87), Assn. Hawaii Artists. Republican. Episcopalian. Avocations: art, travel, writing, photography. Home: 1434 Punahou St Apt 1028 Honolulu HI 96822-4740

BETTS, JAMES WILLIAM, JR., financial analyst, consultant; b. Montclair, N.J., Oct. 11, 1923; s. James William and Cora Anna (Banta) B.; m. Barbara Stoke, July 28, 1951; 1 child, Barbara Susan (dec.). BA, Rutgers U., 1946; postgrad. New Sch. for Social Rsch., 1948-49; MA, U. Hawaii, 1957. With Dun & Bradstreet, Inc., 1946-86, svc. cons., 1963-64, reporting and svc. mgr., 1964-65, sr. fin. analyst, Honolulu, 1965-86; owner Portfolio Cons. of Hawaii, 1979—; cons. Saybrook Point Investments, Old Saybrook, Conn., 1979—; owner James W. Betts and Co., 1996—. Contbr. articles to mag. Served with AUS, 1943. Mem. Am. Econ. Assn., Nat. Assn. Bus. Economists, Western Econ. Assn., Atlantic Econ. Soc., Col. Henry Rutgers Soc., Internat. Inst. Forecasters, Transp. Rsch. Forum. Republican. Episcopalian. Office: Portfolio Cons Hawaii 126 Queen St Ste 222 Honolulu HI 96813-4411

BETZ, RICHARD, agricultural products executive; b. 1943. Sec.- treas. Royal Pak Produce Inc., Hermiston, Oreg., 1968-74; with Bud-Rich Potato Inc., Hermiston, 1974—, now pres./treas. With U.S. Army, 1964-68. Office: Bud-Rich Potato Inc 78049 Hwy 207 Hermiston OR 97838*

BEUDERT, MARK CHRISTOPHER, opera singer, voice educator; b. Mineola, N.Y., June 4, 1961; s. Hubert J. and Margery J. (Lozier) B.; m. Jennifer L. Knapp, Jun. 26,1982; children: Katherine, Sarah, Nicholas. BA, Columbia U., N.Y.C., 1982; MM, U. Mich., 1991, MusD, 1994. Singer N.Y.C. Opera, 1985—, Scottish Opera, Glasgow, 1988-89, English Nat. Opera, London, 1988-89, Opera Ovecnsland, 1987-91; chmn. dept. voice U. Oreg., Eugene, 1995—; singer Opera No. Ireland, Torino, 1994-98, Cleveland Orchestra, 1993. Office: U Oreg Dept Music Eugene OR 97403

BEUMLER, HENRY WEBER, lawyer; b. Douglas, Ariz., May 27, 1913; s. Henry Conrad Andrew and Susan Alberta (Weber) B.; m. Mary Estelle Collins, June 11, 1939; children: Henry Collins, Timothy Collins, Edward Collins, Candyce Collins. BA, U. Ariz., 1934, JD, 1936; postgrad., U. Mex., 1937, Ariz. State U., 1960. Bar: Ariz. 1936, U.S. Dist. Ct. (Ariz.) 1936. Ptnr. Beumler & Beumler, Douglas, 1936-58; pvt. practice Douglas, 1958-78, Portal, Ariz., 1978—; tchr. Douglas High Sch., 1958-78; mayor City of Douglas, 1950-60; city atty. Douglas, 1939-42; dep. atty. Cochise County, Ariz., 1940-42; commr. U.S. Dist. Ct., Tucson, 1948-68. Mem. Ariz. Devel. Bd., 1954-58, Ariz. Civil Rights Commn., 1956-58, San Simon Unified Dist. Sch. Bd., pres., 1985-88. Served to lt. col. AUS, 1942-46. Mem. ABA, Ariz. Bar Assn., Cochise County Bar Assn., Ret. Tchrs. Assn., Masons, Phi Delta Kappa. Address: PO Box 16166 Portal AZ 85632-1166

BEURMAN, ALBERT LEROY, retired corrections officer; b. Pueblo, Colo., Sept. 18, 1935; s. William Franklin and Mildred Leona (Smith) B.; children: Leann, Bert, Frank, Chris, Connie, Richard. Student, Midwest Bus. Coll., 1968-69. Usher Mesa Drive Theater, Pueblo, Colo., 1951-53; meat cutter Pueblo Meat and Provisions, 1953-54; rolling mill laborer Colo. Fuel and Iron, Pueblo, 1955-68; clk. Farmers Union Coop., Belt, Mont., 1970-72; corrections officer Ariz. Dept. Corrections, Florence, 1972-76; security officer Transp. Test Ctr., Pueblo, 1977-82; corrections officer Colo. Dept. Corrections, Canon City, 1982-88, ret. Author: (book) The Ride of a Lifetime, 1995. Recipient Cert. of Recognition, U.S., 1995. Avocations: motorcycle touring, fishing, writing, video camera photography, pilot. Home: 1104 Beulah Ave Pueblo CO 81004-2728

BEVERETT, ANDREW JACKSON, marketing executive; b. Midland City, Ala., Feb. 21, 1917; s. Andrew J. and Ella Levonia (Adams) B.; m. Martha Sophia Landgrebe, May 26, 1951; children: Andrew Jackson III, James Edmund, Faye A. BS, Samford U., 1940; MBA, Harvard U., 1942. Various exec. positions in corporate planning and mgmt. United Air Lines, Chgo., 1946-66; dir. aviation econs., sr. mktg. and econ. cons. Mgmt. and Econs. Research, Inc., Palo Alto, Calif., 1966-71; sr. economist Stanford Research Inst., Menlo Park, 1971-72; pres. Edy's on the Peninsula stores, 1973-78; real estate broker, fin. and tax cons., Saratoga and San Jose, Calif., 1979—. Ensign to lt. USNR, 1942-46. Mem. Nat. Assn. Enrolled Agts., Nat. Assn. Realtors, Pi Gamma Mu, Phi Kappa Phi. Home: 6325 Whaley Dr San Jose CA 95135-1447

BEVERNICK, MARY BICKERT, school district administrator; b. N.Y.C., June 24, 1948; d. Gordon William and Patricia Louise (Clinton) Bickert; m. Alexander Heywood Bevernick, June 22, 1968; children: Anna Christina, Alexandra Louise. Student, Bennington Coll., 1968; BA, U. Calif. (Santa Cruz), 1980; MA in Counseling, Santa Clara (Calif.) U., 1994. Cert. resource specialist, pupil pers. credential, learning handicapped credential. Instrnl. aide Santa Cruz County Office Edn., Capitola, Calif., 1971-77, substitute tchr., 1981-85; tchr. San Lorenzo Valley H.S., Felton, Calif., 1987-92, counselor, 1994-97; counselor San Lorenzo Jr. H.S., Felton, 1992-94; dir. spl. svcs. San Lorenzo Valley Unified Sch. Dist., Felton, 1998—. Recipient We Honor Ours award Calif. Tchrs. Assn., 1992. Mem. Calif. Tchrs. Assn. (state coun. rep. 94-97), Ctrl. Coast Svcs. Ctr. Calif. Tchrs. Assn. (sec. 1996-97, mem. steering com.). Avocations: blue water cruising, skiing, gardening. Home: 13490 Debby Ln Boulder Creek CA 95006-9356

BEVERSDORF, ANNE ELIZABETH, astrologer, author, educator; b. Houston, Tex., Aug. 14, 1949; d. S. Thomas and Norma (Beeson) B. BA, U. Tex., 1972; MLS, Ind. U., 1974. jyotishi. Founding librarian Social Studies Devel. Ctr. Ind. U., Bloomington, 1975-79, info. specialist, 1980-82; co-founder Ind. Clearinghouse for Computer Edn., Indpls., 1983-86; Calif. mktg. rep. Minn. Ednl. Computing Corp., San Marcos, Calif., 1986-88; pres., chief exec. officer Beversdorf Assocs., Ltd., Vista, Calif., 1988-93; writer, lectr., astrologer Vista, Calif., 1993—; cons. Procter & Gamble Ednl. Services, Cin., 1981-85, Brazil Office of Tech. Edn., Rio de Janeiro, Porto Alegre, 1986; mem. faculty Ind. U., Indpls., 1986, San Diego State U., 1988-91. Contbr. over 30 articles to U.S. and internat. profl. jours. Mem. Am. Coun. Vedic Astrology, Am. Fedn. Astrologers, San Diego Astrol. Soc. Avocations: reading, weaving, needlework, piano music. Home and Office: 1119 Anza Ave Vista CA 92084-4517

BEY, EVERETT EDWARD, newspaper editor, publisher; b. LaCrosse, Wis., May 15, 1918; s. Edward Christ and Leonora Mathilda Bey; m. Faye June Schaller, July 27, 1946 (dec. Nov. 1993); 1 child, Keri Ruth Bey Taborski; m. Rose Alexandra Dillberger-Bey, Jan. 1, 1995. Advtg. salesman LaCrosse Tribune, 1936-42; advtg. mgr., editor San Bruno (Calif.) Herald, 1946-49; retail advtg. mgr. San Luis Obispo (Calif.) Telegram-Tribune, 1949-52; co-pub., editor Millbrae (Calif.) Sun, 1952-69; editor-pub. Feather River Bull., Quincy, Calif., 1969-83; pub. emeritus Feather Publs., Quincy, 1983—; founding dir. Plumas Bank, Quincy, 1980-90. Com. mem. Rep. County Ctrl. Com., Plumas County, Calif., 1980-90; pres. Sun Cities West Valley Art Mus., 1996-97, life mem. With U.S. Army, 1942-46. Mem. AARP, Nat. Newspaper Assn. (dir. 1976-85), Suburban Newspapers Am., Internat. Newspaper Promotion Assn., Am. Forests Soc., Nat. Kidney Found., Am. Assn. Kidney Patients, Am. Cribbage Congress (pres. 1993—, Hall Fame 1985), Calif. Newspaper Pubs. Assn. (pres. 1984), Calif. Press Assn. (Pub. Yr. award 1984), Ex-Press Club Sun Cities (founder, pres. 1989-90), Calif. Soc. Newspaper Editors, Calif. Club Sun Cities, Wis. Club Sun Cities, Wis. Badger Men's Club, Mo. Club Sun Cities, Soc. Profl. Journalists, Soc. Weekly Newspaper Editors, Investigative Reporters & Editors, Quincy Rotary Club (Paul Harris award 1984), Order Ea. Star (Lodge 246), Masons (Lodge 70), Am. Legion (Post 304), Symphony West Valley, Sun Cities Chamber Music Soc., Plumas County Arts Commn., Plumas County Mus. Assn. (life), Plumas County Hist. Soc. (life), Plumas County C. of C. (Merchant Yr. award 1980), Smithsonian Instn. (assoc.), Friends Plumas County Libr., Palo Verde Artists, Sun City Taxpayers Club, Eagle Lake Assn., E Clampus Vitus, Lakes Club Sun City. Avocations: cribbage, travel, art. Home: 10826 W Thunderbird Blvd Sun City AZ 85351-2646 Office: Feather Pub Co Inc 555 W Main St PO Box B Quincy CA 95971

BEYER, RICHARD MICHAEL, communications company executive; b. N.Y.C., Oct. 12, 1948; s. Thomas Robert Sr. and Madeline Frances B.; m. Nikki Cole Greene, Nov. 5, 1983; children: Laura, Christopher. BS in Russian, Georgetown U., 1970, MS in Russia, 1974; MBA, Columbia U., 1977. V.p. mktg. ITT, Raleigh, N.C., 1984-86, v.p., gen. mgr. PABX sys. divsn., 1986-87; v.p., gen. mgr. PABX sys. divsn. Alcatel, Alexandria, Va., 1987-89; v.p., gen. mgr. Rockwell Internat., Downers Grove, Ill., 1989-93; pres. comm. and computing group Nat. Semiconductor, Sunnyvale, Calif., 1993-95, exec. v.p., COO, 1995-96; pres., COO, bd. dirs. VSLI Tech. Inc., San Jose, Calif., 1996-98; pres., CEO, FVC.COM, Inc., Santa Clara, Calif., 1998—. Bd. dirs. San Jose Symphony, 1995-96. 1st lt. USMCR, 1970-73. Mem. Am. Electronics Assn. (bd. dirs. 1997—). Republican. Methodist. Avocations: skiing, bicycling, reading, tennis, wine. Office: FVC.COM Inc 3393 Octavius Dr Santa Clara CA 95054-3004

BEYERS, WILLIAM BJORN, geography educator; b. Seattle, Mar. 24, 1940; s. William Abraham and Esther Jakobia (Svendsen) B.; m. Margaret Lyn Rice, July 28, 1968. B.A., U. Wash., 1962, Ph.D., 1967. Asst. prof. geography U. Wash., Seattle, 1968-74, assoc. prof., 1974-82, prof., 1982—, chmn. dept. geography, 1991-95. Mem. Assn. Am. Geographers, Regional Sci. Assn., Am. Econs. Assn., Western Regional Sci. Assn. Home: 7159 Beach Dr SW Seattle WA 98136-2077 Office: U Wash Dept Geography DP 10 PO Box 353550 Seattle WA 98195-3550

BEYERSDORF, MARGUERITE MULLOY, educator; b. Terry, Mont., Apr. 20, 1922; d. John William and Laura Agnes (Mahar) Mulloy; m. Curtis Alexander Beyersdorf, 1946; 1 child, Mary Jo Wright. Kindergarten-Primary Cert., Coll. St. Catherine, St. Paul, 1942; PhB, Marquette U., 1945; postgrad., Gonzaga U., Spokane, Wash., 1957-62, Ea. Wash. State U., 1977-79. Tchr. grade 3 Sacred Heart Sch., Oelwein, Iowa, 1942-43; tchr. grades 1 and 2 Jr. Mil. Acad., Chgo., 1943-44; tchr. history, English Fairfield (Wash.) High Sch., 1945-46; substitute tchr. Riverside High Sch., 1957; tchr. Mead (Wash.) Sch. Dist., 1958-75; owner/mgr. First Ave. Parking Lot, Spokane, Wash., 1957—. Vol. Spokane N.W. Communities Found., 1982—; active United Way Spokane, 1950, ARC, Am. Cancer Soc., Multiple Sclerosis Soc., others; vol. coord. Dominican Outreach Found. to Domicile Single Parent Families; canteen vol. Spokane Blood Bank, 1981—; vol. Miryam's House of

Transition, 1989—. Recipient Vol. of Yr. Golden Rule award J.C. Penney Co., 1993; grantee NSF, Whitworth Coll., 1967. Mem. NEA, APGA, AAUW (bd. dirs. Spokane br., chmn. scholarship com.), Wash. Edn. Assn.-Retired (del. rep. assembly, mem. comm. com 1993—, chmn. comm. commn. 1993—), Mead Edn. Assn. (sec., exec. bd., former bldg. rep., mem. curriculum com.). Avocations: golf, travel, reading, needlepoint, walking.

BEYLKIN, GREGORY, mathematician; b. St. Petersburg, USSR, Mar. 16, 1953; came to U.S., 1980; naturalized citizen, 1985; s. Jacob and Raya (Pripshtein) B.; m. Helen Simontov, 1974; children: Michael, Daniel. Diploma in Math., U. St. Petersburg, Leningrad, 1975; PhD in Math., NYU, 1982. Assoc. rsch. sci. NYU, 1982-83; mem. profl. staff Schlumberger-Doll Research, Ridgefield, Conn., 1983-91; prof. dept. applied math. U. Colo., Boulder, 1991—. Contbr. articles to profl. jours. Mem. Am. Math. Soc., Soc. for Indsl. and Applied Math., Soc. Exptl. Geophysicists. Home: 3897 Promontory Ct Boulder CO 80304-1053 Office: U Colo Dept Applied Math PO Box 526 Boulder CO 80309-0526

BEYMER, DALE ALLEN, manufacturing executive; b. Van Nuys, Calif., July 31, 1957; s. Lawrence Elmos and Patricia Anne (Bryce) B.; m. Anna Louise Beverage, June 3, 1984. Foreman Ronlo Engring. Ltd., Camarillo, Calif., 1975-79; gen. mgr. prodn. Alonian Enterprises Inc., Newbury Park, Calif., 1979-87; v.p. ops. J.M. Precision Inc., Chatsworth, Calif., 1987-88; mgr. machine shop Crane Co. Hydro-Aire Divsn., Burbank, Calif., 1988—; owner, pres. Dycal Systems, Newbury Park, 1982-92. Patentee torque limiting vise handle, 1985. Recipient Geometric Dimensioning and Tolerancing award Tech. Cons., Inc., 1993. Mem. Assn. for Integrated Mfg. Tech. Avocations: computers, golf, auto racing. Home: 11 E Avenida De Las Flores Thousand Oaks CA 91360-3104 Office: Crane Co Hydro-Aire Divsn PO Box 7722 Burbank CA 91510-7722

BEYSTER, JOHN ROBERT, engineering company executive; b. Detroit, July 26, 1924; s. John Frederick and Lillian Edith (Jondro) B.; m. Betty Jean Brock, Sept. 8, 1955; children: James Frederick, Mark Daneil, Mary Ann. B.S. in Engring., U. Mich., 1945, M.S., 1948, Ph.D., 1950. Registered profl. engr., Calif. Mem. staff Los Alamos Sci. Lab., 1951-56; chmn. dept. accel. physics Gulf Gen. Atomic Co., San Diego, 1957-69; pres., chmn. bd. Sci. Applications, Inc., La Jolla, Calif., from 1969, now chmn. bd., chief exec. officer; mem. Joint Strategic Target Planning Staff, Sci. Adv. Group, Omaha, 1978—; panel mem. Nat. Measurement Lab. Evaluation panel for Radiation Research, Washington, 1983—; dir. Scripps Bancorp, La Jolla, 1983. Co-author: Slow Neutron Scattering and Thermalization, 1970. With USN, 1943-46. Fellow Am. Nuclear Soc., Am. Phys. Soc.; mem. NAE. Republican. Roman Catholic. Home: 9321 La Jolla Farms Rd La Jolla CA 92037-1126 Office: Science Applications Inter Corp 10260 Campus Point Dr San Diego CA 92121-1522*

BHAGWAN, SUDHIR, computer industry and research executive, consultant; b. Lahore, West Pakistan, Aug. 9, 1942; came to U.S., 1963; s. Vishan and Lakshmi Devi (Arora) B.; m. Sarita Bahl, Oct. 25, 1969; children: Sonia, Sunil. BSEE, Punjab Engring. Coll., Chandigarh, India, 1963; MSEE, Stanford U., 1964; MBA with honors, Golden Gate U., 1977. Engr. Gaylor Products, North Hollywood, Calif., 1964-68, Burroughs Corp., Pasadena, Calif., 1968-70; engring. mgr. Burroughs Corp., Santa Barbara, Calif., 1970-78; engring. mgr. Intel Corp., Hillsboro, Oreg., 1978-81, chmn. strategic planning, 1981-82, gen. mgr., 1983-88; pres., exec. dir., bd. dirs. Oreg. Advanced Computing Inst., Beaverton, 1988-90; strategic bus. mgr. INTEL Corp., Hillsboro, Oreg., 1990-92, gen. mgr. bus. multimedia products, 1992-93, bus. area mgr., 1993-94, dir. internat. mktg., 1995—; spkr. to high tech. industry, Oreg., 1988—; mem. organizing com. Distributed Memory Computing Conf., 1989-90, gen. chmn., 1990-91; chmn. computer tech. adv. bd. Oreg. Mus. Sci. and Industry, 1991-93; bd. dirs. II-Tracker Inc. Cons. Oreg. Econ. Devel. Dept., 1988-91; bd. dirs. St. Mary's Acad., Portland,, 1989-92. Mem. Am. Electronics Assn. (higher edn. com. Oreg. chpt. 1989-90, exec. com. 1990). Avocations: electronics, photography, tennis, art. Home: 13940 NW Harvest Ln Portland OR 97229-3653 Office: INTEL Corp 5200 NE Elam Young Pkwy Hillsboro OR 97124-6497

BHANU, BIR, computer information scientist, educator, director university program; b. Etah, India, Jan. 8, 1951; came to U.S., 1975; naturalized, 1987.; s. Rameshwar Dayal and Omwati Devi; m. Archana Bhanu Bhatnagar, Dec. 21, 1982; children: Shiv Bir, Ish Bir. BS with honors, Inst. Tech., Banaras Hindu U., Varanasi, India, 1972; M in Engring. with distinction, Birla Inst. Tech. and Sci., Pilani, India, 1974; SM and EE, MIT, 1977; PhD Image Processing Inst., U. So. Calif., 1981; MBA, U. Calif., Irvine, 1984; diploma in German, B.H.U., India, 1971. Lectr. in elec. engring. Birla Inst. Tech. and Sci., Pilani, 1974-75; acad. assoc. IBM Research Lab., San Jose, Calif., 1978; research fellow INRIA, Rocquencourt, France, 1980-81; engring. specialist Ford Aerospace and Communications Corp., Newport Beach, Calif., 1981-84; asst./assoc. prof. and dir. grad. admissions, dept. computer sci. U. Utah, Salt Lake City, 1984-87; staff scientist, Honeywell fellow, sr. Honeywell fellow Honeywell Systems and Rsch. Ctr., Mpls., 1986-91; prof. electrical engring., computer sci., program leader electrical engring. U. Calif., Riverside, 1991-94; dir. Visualization and Intelligent Systems Lab, U. Calif., Riverside, 1991—; cons. U. Calif., Irvine, 1983-84, Evolving Tech. Inst., San Diego, 1983-85, Bonneville Sci. Co., Salt Lake City, 1985-86, TRW, L.A., 1991—; pres. Internat. Student Assn. U. So. Calif., 1978-79; prin. investigator grants from DARPA, NSF, NASA, AFOSR, ARO, Rockwell, Ford, others. Co-author: Qualitative Motion Understanding, Kluwer, 1992, Genetic Learning for Adaptive Image Segmentation, Kluwer, 1994, Computational Learning for Adaptive Computer Vision, 1998; assoc. editor Jour. Math. Imaging and Vision, Pattern Recognition Jour., Internat. Jour. Machine Vision Applications; guest editor, co-editor IEEE Computer, 1987, Jour. Robotic Systems, 1992, Internat. Jour. Machine Vision and Applications, 1994, IEEE Transactions on Pattern Analysis and Machine Intelligence, 1994, IEEE Transactions on Robotics and Automation, 1994, IEEE Transactions on Image Processing, 1997; 10 patents in field; contbr. numerous reviewed publs. on subject of image processing, computer vision, artificial intelligence, machine learning and robotics. Recipient Outstanding Paper award Pattern Recognition Soc., 1990, Honeywell Motec and Alpha team awards, 1989, Project award Outstanding contbn. IBM Corp., 1978. Fellow IEEE (gen. chair IEEE workshop applications computer vision 1992, chair DARPA Image Understanding Workshop 1994, gen. chmn. IEEE conf. on computer vision and pattern recognition 1996), AAAS; mem. Assn. Computing Machinery, Soc. Photo-Optical and Instrumentation Engrs., Pattern Recognition Soc., Sigma Xi. Avocations: swimming, skiing, tennis, table tennis, writing. Home: 6733 Canyon Hill Dr Riverside CA 92506-5672 Office: U Calif Coll Engring Riverside CA 92521

BHATIA, PETER K., editor, journalist; b. Pullman, Wash., May 22, 1953; s. Vishnu N. and Ursula Jean (Dawson) B.; m. Elizabeth M. Dahl, Sept. 27, 1981; children: Megan Jean, Jay Peter. BA, Stanford U., 1975. Polit. reporter, asst. news editor Spokesman Rev., Spokane, Wash., 1975-77; news editor Dallas Times Herald, 1980-81; asst. news editor San Francisco Examiner, 1977-80, news editor, 1981-85, dep. mng. editor/news, 1985-87; mng. editor Dallas Times Herald, 1987-88; editor York Dispatch, York, Pa., 1988-89; mng. editor The Sacramento Bee, 1989-93; exec. editor The Fresno Bee, 1993; mng. editor The Oregonian, Portland, 1993-97, exec. editor, 1997—; Pulitzer Prize juror, 1992-93, 98. Mem. Stanford U. Alumni Assn. (bd. dirs. 1998—), Am. Soc. Newspaper Editors (bd. dirs. 1997—), AP Mng. Editors (bd. dirs. 1991-97), Asian Am. Journalists Assn., Nat. Assn. Minority Media Execs., Sigma Delta Chi, Theta Delta Chi. Office: The Oregonian 1320 SW Broadway Portland OR 97201-3499

BHATTACHARJEE, SUBRATA, mechanical engineering educator; b. Habiganj, Bangladesh, Apr. 1, 1961. BTech in Mech. Engring., Indian Inst. Tech., Kharagpur, 1983; MS in Mech. Engring., Wash. State U., 1985, PhD in Mech. Engring., 1988. Tchg. and rsch. asst. Wash. State U., Pullman, 1983-88; postdoctoral fellow NASA, Lewis Rsch. Ctr. and Miss. State U., 1988-90; asst. prof. mech. engring. San Diego State U., 1991-94, assoc. prof., 1994—; lectr. various univs., 198[illegible]—, presenter tech. meetings. Contbr. numerous articles to profl. jours., including Combustion and Flame, Jour. Heat Transfer, Combustion Sci. and Tech., Internat. Jour. Heat and Mass Transfer., AIAA Jour. also others, chpt. to book. Rsch. grantee NASA, 1991-93, San Diego State U., 1991-94, Calif. State U., 1994-96. Mem. ASME, Combustion Inst. (session chmn. 1989), Tau Beta Pi. Office: San Diego State U Dept Mech Engring San Diego CA 92182-0191

BHELA, HARVINDER SINGH, computer software company executive; b. Bombay, India, Jan. 20, 1971; s. Balwant Singh and Rajinder Kaur (Saini) B. B of Engring., U. Bombay, 1992; MS, U. Minn., 1995. Software engr. Harmonix Corp., Woburn, Mass., 1995-96, Interse Corp., Sunnyvale, Calif., 1996-97; devel. lead Microsoft Corp., Redmond, Wash., 1997-98, devel. mgr., 1998—. Fellowship U. Minn., 1994-95. Mem. Assn. for Computing Machinery, Phi Kappa Phi. Sikh. Avocations: mountain biking, skiing. Home: 15606 NE 40th St Apt S370 Redmond WA 98052-7016 Office: Microsoft Corp One Microsoft Way Redmond WA 98052

BIALIK, JEFFREY VINCENT, treasurer, academic administrator; b. Port Angeles, Wash., Oct. 15, 1956; s. Vencelaus William and Hazel Frances (Samson) B.; m. Sharon Bravo, Sept. 20, 1975 (div. June, 1981); m. Mabel Morozumi, Oct. 8, 1982; children: Adam Michael, Eleen Mariko. BA in Acctg., Bus., U. Wash., 1981; MBA, U. Calif., Berkeley, 1989. Fin. analyst Exxon Western Prodn. Divsn., L.A., Thousand Oaks, Calif., 1981-84; fin. coord. Exxon Western Prodn. Divsn., Thousand Oaks, 1984-85; acctg. mgr. U. Calif., Berkeley, 1985-88, gen. acctg. mgr., 1988-90, dir. acctg. svcs., 1990-91; v.p. adminstrv and fiscal affairs Dominican Coll., San Rafael, Calif., 1991-95; exec. v.p., treas. Dominican Coll., San Rafael, 1995—. Bd. dirs. ARC, San Francisco, 1996—, chmn. Marin County, San Rafael, Calif., 1997—; bd. alt. N. Bay Coun., Novato, Calif. With U.S. Army, 1975-78, Korea. Bd. dirs. San Rafael C. of C. Democrat. Avocations: music, golf. Home: 12 Salvador Way San Rafael CA 94903-1819 Office: Dominican Coll 50 Acacia Ave San Rafael CA 94901-2230

BIANCHI, RICHARD, food products executive; b. 1947. With Bianchi Land Co., Merced, Calif., 1968—, v.p., 1971—, now v.p., sec., CFO. Office: Bianchi Land Co 201 Elliott Ave W Ste 400 Seattle WA 98119*

BIANCHI, ROBERT STEVEN, author, lecturer, TV personality; b. N.Y.C., Nov. 30, 1943; s. Robert and Bessie (Litrakis) B.; 1 child, Kyria Marcella Osborne. PhD, N.Y. Inst. Fine Arts, 1976. Dir. acad. and curatorial affairs The Bklyn. Mus., 1976-92; author, lectr., TV personality; dir. acad. and curatorial affairs Broughton Internat. Inc., 1997—; guest curator Daily Life of Ancient Egypt, Fundacio La Cairo, Barcelona, Spain, 1997—. Author: Inside the Tomb of Nefertari, 1993, Nubians, 1994, Splendors of Ancient Egypt, 1995; book rev. editor Jour. Am. Rsch. Ctr. in Egypt, 1995—; co-host: (BBC-TV series) BBC Channel 4 and TLC, Pharoahs and Kings: A Biblical Quest, 1995. Mem. Internat. Assn. Egyptologists (Am. rep. 1989-95), Explorers Club. Home and Office: 522 Valley Vista Blvd Lewiston ID 83501-6705

BIANCO, JAMES A., research and development executive; b. 1956. BS cum laude with honors, NYU, 1979; MD, Mt. Sinai Sch. of Medicine, 1983. Intern, then resident Mt. Sinai Med. Ctr., N.Y.C., 1983-87; fellow in oncology U. Wash., Seattle, 1987-91, asst. prof. medicine, 1991-92; dir. bone marrow transplant program VA Med. Ctr., Seattle, 1990-92; asst. mem. Fred Hutchinson Cancer Rsch. Ctr., Seattle, 1991-92; pres., CEO Cell Therapeutics, Inc., Seattle, 1992—. Mem. Alpha Omega Alpha. Office: Cell Therapeutics Inc 201 Elliott Ave W Ste 400 Seattle WA 98119*

BIBBIE, NELLIE BRASSFIELD, retired eligibility professional; b. Leavenworth, Kans., Jan. 31, 1913; d. Joseph Henry and Hattie (McClanahan) Johnson; m. William Lloyd Bibbie, June 1, 1933; children: Lee-Roy, Carol Ann Bibbie Lewis. AA, Pasadena City Coll., 1964; post-grad., Calif. State U., 1974. Cert. eligibility worker, L.A. County. Key punch operator L.A. County, L.A., 1947-48, Dept. Water and Power, L.A., 1948-56; outside sales profl. Fuller Products, Pasadena, Calif., 1956; eligibility profl. L.A. County, Pasadena, 1956-96; ret., 1996. Author: Duty's Castle, 1997. Mem. Nat. Humane Soc. Democrat. Avocations: reading, collecting classic books. Home: PO Box 20422 2123 Clayne St Oxnard CA 93034

BIBEAULT, DONALD BERTRAND, turnaround executive, investor; b. Woonsocket, R.I., Nov. 14, 1941; s. George Bertrand and Renee (Herbert) B.; m. Gigi Loving, June 18, 1994; 1 child, Zachary James. BSEE, U. R.I., 1963; MBA, Columbia U., 1965; PhD, Golden Gate U., 1979. COO Pacific States Steel, Union City, Calif., 1975-78, PLM Internat., San Francisco, 1979-81; turnaround advisor Varity Corp., 1981-82; pres., CEO Best Pipe and Steel Co., San Francisco, 1983-86; workout advisor Bank of Am., 1987-89; chmn. Am. Nat. Petrol, Houston, 1990-91; chmn., CEO Tyler Dawson Supply Co., Tulsa, 1990-91, Iron Oak Supply Co., Sacramento, 1990-93; pres. Bibeault and Assocs., Inc., Mill Valley, Calif., 1976—; bd. trustees Golden Gate U., San Francisco, 1986-97; bd. advisors U. R.I. Bus., Kinston, 1993—; bd. overseers Columbia Grad. Sch. Bus., N.Y.C., 1994—. Author: Corporate Turnaround, 1982 (Fortune award 1982); contbr. articles to profl. jours. Mem. adv. bd. on trade Dept. of Commerce, Washington, 1988-92. Lt. U.S. Army, 1963-65. Mem. Turnaround Mgmt. Assn. (founding dir. 1987-91), Bankers Club San Francisco, Assn. for Corp. Growth (dir. 1985-90). Home and Office: Bibeault Assocs 60 Peacock Dr San Rafael CA 94901-1505

BIBLE, FRANCES LILLIAN, mezzo-soprano, educator; b. Sackets Harbor, N.Y.; d. Arthur and Lillian (Cooke) B. Student, Juilliard Sch. Music, 1939-47. Artist-in-residence Shepherd Sch. of Music Rice U., Houston, 1975-91. Appeared throughout U.S., Australia, Europe including Vienna Staatsoper, Karlsruhe Staatsoper, Dublin Opera Co., N.Y.C. Opera, NBC-TV Opera, San Francisco Opera, Glyndebourne Opera, San Antonio Opera Festival, New Orleans Opera, Houston Grand Opera, Miami Opera, Dallas Opera; appeared in concer with major symphonies; world premiers (opera): The Ballad of Baby Doe, The Crucible, The Troubled Island, The Dybuk. Named Woman of the Yr. in Opera, Mademoiselle, 1949. Mem. Am. Guild Mus. Artists (past 3d v.p., bd. dirs. 1989-91), Sigma Alpha Iota (hon.), Beta Sigma Pi (hon.). Episcopalian. Home: 2377 Thata Way Hemet CA 92544-7009

BICE, SCOTT HAAS, lawyer, educator; b. Los Angeles, Mar. 19, 1943; s. Fred Haas and Virginia M. (Scott) B.; m. Barbara Franks, Dec. 21, 1968. B.S., U. So. Calif., 1965, J.D., 1968. Bar: Calif. bar 1971. Law clk. to Chief Justice Earl Warren, 1968-69; successively asst. prof., assoc. prof., prof. law., Carl Mason Franklin prof. U. So. Calif., Los Angeles, 1969—; assoc. dean U. So. Calif., 1971-74, dean, 1980—; vis. prof. polit. sci. Calif. Inst. Tech., 1977; vis. prof. U. Va., 1978-79; bd.dirs. Western Mut. Ins. Co., Residence Mut. Ins. Co., Imagine Films Entertainment Co., Jenny Craig, Inc. Mem. editl. adv. bd. Calif. Lawyer, 1989-93; contbr. articles to law jours. Bd. dirs. L.A. Family Housing Corp., 1989-93, Stone Soup Child Care Programs, 1988—. Affiliated scholar Am. Bar Found., 1972-74. Fellow Am. Bar Found.; mem. Am. Law Inst., Calif. Bar, Los Angeles County Bar Assn., Am. Law Deans Assn. (pres. 1997—), Am. Judicature Soc., Calif. Club, Chancery Club, Long Beach Yacht Club. Home: 787 S San Rafael Ave Pasadena CA 91105-2326 Office: U So Calif Sch of Law 699 Exposition Blvd Los Angeles CA 90007-4003

BICHETTE, ALPHONSE DANTE, professional baseball player; b. West Palm Beach, Fla., Nov. 18. Student, Palm Beach C.C. With Calif. Angels, 1988-90, Milw. Brewers, 1991-92; outfielder Colo. Rockies, 1993—. Named Nat. Leagye All-Star Team, 1994-96. Achievements include led nat. leagye in runs batted in (RBI) with (128), hone rums (40), 1995, tied with Tony Gwynn for most hits (197), 1995. Office: Colo Rockies 2001 Blake St Denver CO 80205-2008*

BICKART, THEODORE ALBERT, university president; b. N.Y.C., Aug. 25, 1935; s. Theodore Roosevelt and Edna Catherine (Pink) B.; m. Carol Florence Nichols, June 14, 1958 (div. Dec. 1973); children: Karl Jeffrey, Lauren Spencer; m. Frani W. Rudolph, Aug. 14, 1982; 1 stepchild, Jennifer Anne Cumming. B. Engring. Sci., Johns Hopkins U., 1957, MS, 1958, DEng, 1960; D Univ. (hon.), Dneprodzerzhinst State Tech. U, Ukraine, 19956. Asst. prof. elec. and computer engring. Syracuse (N.Y.) U., 1963-65, assoc. prof., 1965-70, prof., 1970 89, assoc. to vice chancellor for acad. affairs for computer resources devel., 1983-85, dean L.C. Smith Coll. Engring., 1984-89; prof. elec. engring., dean engring. Mich. State U., East Lansing, 1989-98; pres. Colo. Sch. Mines, Golden, 1998—; vis. scholar U. Calif., Berkeley, 1977; Fulbright lectr. Kiev Poly Inst., USSR, 1981; vis. lectr. Nanjing Inst. Tech., China, 1981; hon. disting. prof. Taganrog Radio Engring. Inst., Russia, 1992—; mem. Accreditation Bd. for Engring. and Tch., Engring. Accreditation Commn.; chmn. Engring. Workforce Commn., 1996-98. Co-author: Electrical Network Theory, 1969, Linear Network Theory, 1981; contbr. numerous articles to profl. jours. Served to 1st lt. U.S. Army, 1961-63. Recipient numerous rsch. grants. Fellow IEEE (best paper awards Syracuse sect. 1969, 70, 73, 74, 77, chmn. com. on engring. accreditation activities 1996-98); mem. Am. Soc. Engring. Edn. (v.p. 1997—), Am. Math. Soc., Assn. for Computing Machinery, Soc. for Indsl. and Applied Math., N.Y. Acad. Scis., Ukrainian Acad. Engring. Scis.), Internat. Higher Edn. Acad. Scis. (Russia), Internat. Acad. Informatics (Russia). Avocations: bicycling; hiking; gardening. Home: 1722 Illinois St Golden CO 80401-1836 Office: Colo Sch Mines Office of Pres 1500 Illinois St Golden CO 80401-1887*

BICKEL, NANCY KRAMER, writer; b. Phoenix, Feb. 23, 1941; d. Sidney David and Miriam (Zales) Kramer; m. Peter John Bickel, Mar. 2, 1964; children: Amanda Sidney, Stephen Eliezer. BA with high honors, Swarthmore Coll., 1962; MA, U. Calif., Berkeley, 1965. Acting instr. English dept. U. Calif., Berkeley, 1974; bd. dirs., v.p., writer LWV, Berkeley, 1977-84; TV producer LWV, Oakland, Calif., 1978-86; writer, producer LWV, Calif., 1985—; ind. writer, prodr., 1991—; assoc. prodr. CPS Assocs., Video Prodn., 1997—; chair bd. dirs. Berkeley Cmty. Media, Inc., 1993-98; assoc. prodr. CPS Assocs. Video Prodn., 1997—. Author and co-prodr. TV documentary Can I Drink the Water, 1986 (Silver Apple award 1987), Toxic Chemicals: Information is the Best Defense, 1 & 2, 1984 (Blue Ribbon award 1985); author, prodr.: Cleaning Up Toxics at Home and Cleaning Up Toxics in Business, 1990 (Bronze Apple award 1991), Teaming Up for the Bay and Delta, 1993, Where Does It Go?, 1994, Hold on to Your Dirt: Preventing Erosion from Construction Sites (Silver Apple award 1998), Keet It Clean: Preventing Pollution from Construction Sites (awrd of distinction The Communicator awards 1998). V.p., trustee Berkeley Pub. Lib., 1983-85; chair Cable TV Task Force, Berkeley, 1988-91, LWV. Recipient commendation by City of Berkeley; Woodrow Wilson fellow. Mem. Alliance for Cmty. Media, Bay Area Video Coalition, Assn. Ind. Video & Filmmakers, Inc., Phi Beta Kappa. Office: 1522 Summit Rd Berkeley CA 94708-2217

BICKEL, PETER JOHN, statistician, educator; b. Bucharest, Romania, Sept. 21, 1940; came to U.S., 1957, naturalized, 1964; s. Eliezer and P. Madeleine (Moscovici) B.; m. Nancy Kramer, Mar. 2, 1964; children: Amanda, Stephen. AB, U. Calif., Berkeley, 1960, MA, 1961, PhD, 1963; PhD (hon.), Hebrew U. Jerusalem, 1988. Asst. prof. stats. U. Calif., Berkeley, 1964-67, assoc. prof., 1967-70, prof., 1970—, chmn. dept. stats., 1976-79, dean phys. scis., 1980-86, chmn. dept. stats., 1993-97; vis. lectr. math. Imperial Coll., London, 1965-66; fellow J.S. Guggenheim Meml. Found., 1970-71, J.D. and Catherine T. MacArthur Found., 1984-89; NATO sr. sci. fellow, 1974. Author: (with K. Doksum) Mathematical Statistics, 1976, (with C. Klaassen, Y. Ritov and J. Wellner) Efficient and Adaptive Estimation in Semiparametric Models, 1993; assoc. editor Annals of Math. Stats., 1968-76, 86-93; contbr. articles to profl. jours. Fellow J.D. and Catherine T. MacArthur Found., 1984-89. Fellow AAAS (chair sect. U 1996-97), Inst. Math. Stats. (pres. 1980), Am. Statis. Assn.; mem. NAS, Royal Statis. Soc., Internat. Statis. Inst., Am. Acad. Arts and Scis., Royal Netherlands Acad. Arts and Scis., Bernoulli Soc. (pres. 1990). Office: U Calif Dept Stats Evans Hall Berkeley CA 94720

BICKNELL, BARBARA ANN, mechanical engineer, executive, consultant; b. Elyria, Ohio, Mar. 18, 1958; d. Joseph Robert and Doris Genevieve (Urig) Lach; m. Kris D. Bicknell, July 2, 1983. BS in Mech. Engring., U. Notre Dame, 1981; MS in Engring., U. Colo., 1993. Engring. mgr. Lockheed Martin, Denver, 1981-92; prers. Bicknell Consulting, Inc., Golden, Colo., 1992—; adj. instr. U. Denver, 1992—. Contbg. author: Basic Statistics, 1993; co-author: The Road Map to Repeatable Success, 1995. Mentor Asian Am. Corp. Experience Devel., Denver, 1992-95. Recipient Tech. award NASA, 1989. Mem. AIAA, Internat. Coun. Sys. Engrs. Achievements include experiments in low-gravity. Avocations: hiking, volleyball. Office: Bicknell Consulting Inc 433 Park Point Dr Ste 200 Golden CO 80401-5752

BIDDLE, DONALD RAY, aerospace company executive; b. Alton, Mo., June 30, 1936; s. Ernest Everet and Dortha Marie (McGuire) B.; m. Nancy Ann Dunham, Mar. 13, 1955; children: Jeanne Kay Biddle Bednash, Mitchell Lee, Charles Alan. Student El Dorado (Kans.) Jr. Coll., 1953-55, Pratt (Kans.) Jr. Coll., 1955-56; BSME, Washington U., St. Louis, 1961; postgrad. computer sci. Pa. State U. Extension, 1963; cert. bus. mgmt. Alexander Hamilton Inst., 1958. Design group engr. Emerson Elec. Mfg., St. Louis, 1957-61; design specialist Boeing Vertol, Springfield, Pa., 1962; cons. engr. Ewing Tech. Design, Phila., 1962-66; chief engr. rotary wing Gates Learjet, Wichita, Kans., 1967-70; dir. engring./R & D BP Chems., Inc. Advanced Materials Div., Stockton, Calif., 1971-93; prin. Biddle & Assocs., Consulting Engrs., Stockton, 1993—; pres., CEO Big Valley Aviation, Inc., Stockton, Calif., 1997—. Guest lectr. on manrated structures, devel. proprietary designs, small bus. devel. to various univs. and tech. socs. Cons. engr. Scoutmaster , counselor, instl. rep. Boy Scouts Am., St. Ann, Mo., 1958-61; mem. Springfield Sch. Bd., 1964. Mem. ASME, ASTM, AIAA, Am. Helicopter Soc. (sec.-treas. Wichita chpt. 1969), Am. Mgmt. Assn., Exptl. Pilots Assn., Soc. for Advancement of Metals and Process Engring. Republican. Methodist (trustee, chmn. 1974-76, 84-86, staff parish 1987-90, fin. 1991-96, video and interiors 1990—). Patentee landing gear designs, inflatable rescue system, glass retention systems, adjustable jack system, cold weather start fluorescent lamp, paper honeycomb core post-process systems. Home: 1140 Stanton Way Stockton CA 95207-2537 Office: Big Valley Aviation Inc ESOP/T 7535 Lindbergh St Stockton CA 95206-3914

BIDWILL, WILLIAM V., professional football executive; s. Charles W. and Violet Bidwill; m. Nancy Bidwill; children: William Jr., Michael, Patrick, Timothy, Nicole. Grad., Georgetown U. Co-owner St. Louis Cardinals Football Team (now Ariz. Cardinals), 1962-72, owner, 1972—, also chmn., 1972—, pres. Office: Ariz Cardinals PO Box 888 Phoenix AZ 85001-0888*

BIEDERMAN, DONALD ELLIS, lawyer; b. N.Y.C., Aug. 23, 1934; s. William and Sophye (Groll) B.; m. Marna M. Leerburger, Dec. 22, 1962; children: Charles Jefferson, Melissa Anne. AB, Cornell U., 1955; JD, Harvard U., 1958; LLM in Taxation, NYU, 1970. Bar: N.Y. 1959, U.S. Dist. Ct. (so. dist.) N.Y. 1967, Calif. 1977. Assoc. Hale, Russell & Stentzel, N.Y.C., 1962-66; asst. corp. counsel City of N.Y., 1966-68; assoc. Delson & Gordon, N.Y.C., 1968-69; ptnr. Roe, Carman, Clerke, Berkman & Berkman, Jamaica, N.Y., 1969-72; gen. atty. CBS Records, N.Y.C., 1972-76; sr. v.p. legal affairs and adminstrn. ABC Records, L.A., 1977-79; ptnr. Mitchell, Silberberg & Knupp, L.A., 1979-83; exec. v.p., gen. counsel bus. affairs Warner/Chappell Music Inc. (formerly Warner Bros. Music), L.A., 1983—; adj. prof. Sch. Law Southwestern U., L.A., 1982—, Pepperdine U., Malibu, Calif., 1985-87, Loyola Marymount U., L.A., 1992; lectr. Anderson Sch. Mgmt. UCLA, 1993, U. So. Calif. Law Ctr., 1995-97. Editor: Legal and Business Problems of the Music Industry, 1980; co-author: Law and Business of the Entertainment Industries, 1987, 2nd edit., 1991, 3d edit., 1995. Bd. dirs. Calif. Chamber Symphony Soc., L.A., 1981-92; dir. Entertainment Law Inst. U. So. Calif., 1993—. 1st lt. U.S. Army, 1959. Recipient Hon. Gold Record, Recording Industry Assn. Am., 1974, Trendsetter award Billboard mag., 1976. Mem. N.Y. Bar Assn., Calif. Bar Assn., Riviera Country Club, Cornell Club. Democrat. Jewish. Avocations: golf, skiing, travel, reading. Home: 2406 Pesquera Dr Los Angeles CA 90049-1225 Office: Warner/Chappell Music Inc 10585 Santa Monica Blvd Los Angeles CA 90025-4921

BIELAGUS, JOSEPH BRUCE, mechanical engineer; b. Jacksonville, Fla., Oct. 24, 1952; s. Joseph Francis and Frances Blanche (Lugin) B.; m. Barbara Jo Carroll, Sept. 4, 1976; children: Kate Elizabeth, Melissa Anne. BSME, Portland State U., 1980. Registered profl. engr. Oreg., Calif. Draftsman FMC Corp., Portland, Oreg., 1976-77; designer Moore Internat., Portland, 1977-78; design engr. Rader Industries, Portland, 1978-79; mgr. R&D Rader Cos., Portland, 1979—; owner, cons. engr. Innotech Industries, Portland, 1990—. Patentee in field. Mem. ASME, TAPPI. Avocations: baseball, fishing, biking, hiking, reading. Home: 21308 SW Christensen Ct Tualatin OR 97062-8910 Office: Rader Cos 6005 NE 82nd Ave Portland OR 97220-1301

BIELE, HUGH IRVING, lawyer; b. Bridgeport, Conn., July 28, 1942; s. Ray James and Blanche (McClellan) B.; m. Pamela Althea Johnson, Aug. 21, 1965 (div.); children: Jonathan Christopher, Melissa Lynne. BA, St. Lawrence U., Canton, N.Y., 1965; JD, U. Utah, 1968. Bar: Utah 1968, U.S. Dist. Ct. Utah 1968, Calif. 1972, U.S. Dist. Ct. Calif. 1972, U.S. Ct. Appeals (9th and 10th cirs.). Instr. San Francisco Law Sch., 1971-73; atty. United Calif. Bank, San Francisco, 1971-74; v.p., sr. counsel First Interstate Bank, L.A., 1974-81; ptnr. Biele & Stuehrmann, L.A., 1981-83; sr. ptnr. Biele, Stuehrmann & Lapinski, L.A., 1983-84; founding ptnr. Biele & Lapinski, L.A., 1985-89; ptnr. Barton, Klugman & Detting, L.A., 1989-91; ptnr., dir. comml. law and litigation Grace, Skocypec, Cosgrove & Schirm, L.A., 1992-95; bd. govs. Fin. Lawyer Conf., L.A., 1976—, pres. 1984-85, original developer, ptnr. Engine Co. No. 28 rehabilitation, 1982—, ptnr. Engine Co. No. 28 Restaurant, 1988—, owner Biele Enterprises, bd. dirs. Vege-Kurl, Inc., 1990—. Author screenplay: Corporate Cancer, 1989, Hedge of Thorns, 1990. Bd. dirs. Community Counseling Svc., L.A., 1989—, pres., 1993-95, chmn. bd. dirs., 1995—; bd. dirs. Casa de Rosa and the Sunshine Mission, 1997—; bd. dirs., v.p., sec. Project New Hope, Inc., L.A., 1990-92; commr. Episc. Diocese AIDS Ministry, L.A., 1988-93; chmn. Vols. in Parole, L.A., 1979-80, 89-90, Lawyers for Human Rights, 1988—, co-pres. elect, 1999. Maj. U.S. Army, 1968-70. Decorated Bronze Star with oak leaf cluster, Army Commendation medal. Mem. ABA, Fed. Bar Assn., Internat. Bar Assn., L.A. County Bar Assn. (internat. sect. exec. com. 1978-97, chmn. 1981-82, exec. com. comml. law and bankruptcy sect. 1986—, chair 1992-93), Calif. State Bar (fin. inst. com.), Internat. Bankers Assn. Calif., St. Lawrence U. Alumni Assn. (pres. 1979-91). Republican. Episcopalian. Avocations: skiing, jogging, aerobics, travel. Home and Office: 3016 Hollycrest Dr Los Angeles CA 90068-1802

BIENVENU, JOHN CHARLES, lawyer; b. Modesto, Calif., Sept. 11, 1957; s. Robert Charles and Martha Louise (Beard) B.; m. Sarah Luciene Brick, May 10, 1983; children: Reed Charles, Loren John. Student, U. Calif., Berkeley, 1975-78; BA summa cum laude, U. N.Mex., 1985; JD with distinction, Stanford U., 1988. Bar: Calif., 1988, N.Mex., 1990; U.S. Ct. Appeals (9th cir.) 1988, U.S. Ct. Appeals (10th cir.) 1990; U.S. Ct. Fed. Claims, 1991. Assoc. Brobeck, Phleger & Harrison, San Francisco, 1988-90, Rothstein, Walther, Donatelli, Hughes, Dahlstrom & Cron, Santa Fe, N.Mex., 1990-93; prin. Santa Fe, 1993—. Mem. N.Mex. State Bar (legal svcs. com.), Am. Trial Lawyers Assn., ACLU (cooperating atty. N.Mex.). Democrat. Home: 1580 Cerro Gordo Rd Santa Fe NM 87501-6143 Office: PO Box 2455 310 Mckenzie St Santa Fe NM 87501-1883

BIERBAUM, JANITH MARIE, artist; b. Evanston, Ill., Jan. 14, 1927; d. Gerald Percy and Lillian (Sullivan) Turnbull; m. J. Armin Bierbaum, Apr. 17, 1948; children: Steve, Todd, Chad, Peter, Mark. BA, Northwestern U., 1948; student, Mpls. Art Inst., 1964; postgrad., St. Paul Art Inst., 1969-70. Rsch. asst. AMA, Chgo., 1948-49; tchr. Chgo. high schs., 1949-51; freelance artist Larkspur, Colo., 1951—. Exhibited in group shows at Foot Hills Art Ctr., 1985, 86, 87, Palmer Lake (Colo.) Art Assn., 1986-87, 88-89, Gov.'s Mansion, Bismarck, N.D., 1960; oil painting appeared in 1989 Women in Art Nat. calendar pub. by AAUW. Recipient 1st Place Purchase award U. Minn., Mpls., 1966, Coors Classic award Coors Beer, Golden, Colo., 1987. Mem. Colo. Artist Assn. Republican. Avocations: cross-country skiing, swimming, hiking. Home and Office: 7787 S Perry Park Blvd Larkspur CO 80118-9005

BIERLY, SHIRLEY ADELAIDE, communications executive; b. Waterbury, Conn., Jan. 19, 1924; d. Samuel and Frances Ada (Bogorad) Brown; m. Leroy Elwood Bierly, Jan. 19, 1946 (div. 1951); children: Lee Jr., Dennis Ray, David Lincoln. Student, Orange Coast Coll., 1963-66, L.A. City Coll., 1967-69. Mgr. Pacific Telephone, San Francisco, Calif., 1953-82; exec. dir. Sr. Power Office, San Francisco, 1982—. Pres. Calif. Legis. Coun. for Older Am., San Francisco, 1984—, treas. Calif. Assn. of Older Am., 1984—, sec., bd. mem. Sr. Action Network, San Francisco, 1991—, Congress of Calif. Sr., Sacramento, 1994—; bd. trustees Agape Found., policy bd. Nat. Coun. Sr. Citizens, 1995—; commr. San Francisco Residential Arbitration and Stabilization Bd., 1997—. Mem. Am. Civil Liberties Union, Older Women's League, Gray Panthers. Avocations: photography, theatre, reading, philately. Fax: 415-541-9630. Office: Calif Assn for Older Ams 325 Clementina St San Francisco CA 94103-4104

BIERMAN, SANDRA L., artist; b. Bklyn., N.Y., 1938; d. John Charles Riesberg and Martha Lee Blair; m. Arthur Bierman, Oct. 1, 1983; children: Cheryl, Steven, James. Represented by Moondance Gallery, Santa Fe, N.Mex., 1992-94, Galerie du Bois, Aspen, Colo., 1994-97, Contemporary S.W. Gallery, Santa Fe, 1994—, Merrill Gallery, Denver, 1995—, David Haslam, Boulder, Colo., 1992—, Gallery East, Loveland, Colo., 1996—, Suzanne Brown Gallery, Scottsdale, Ariz., 1997—, Jack Meier Gallery, Houston, Tex., 1997—; instr. workshop Am. Acad. Women Artists, Wickenburg, Ariz., 1997. One-person shows include Nat. Ctr. for Atmospheric Rsch., Boulder, 1992, David Haslam Gallery, 1993, 94, 95, Columbine Gallery, Loveland, Colo., 1995, Contemporary S.W. Galleries, 1996, Lincoln Ctr. for the Arts, Ft. Collins, Colo., 1998, Jack Meier Gallery, 1998—; group shows include C.S. Lewis Summer Inst. Show on Tour, 1994, Queens Coll. Art Gallery, Cambridge, Eng., 1994, 99th Nat. Exhbn. Nat. Arts Club, N.Y.C., 1995, 67th Grand Nat. Show, Salmagundi Club, N.Y.C., 1995, Artistes Americaines, Maison du Terroir, Genouilly, France, 1996, Colo. History Mus., 1996, Clymer Mus., Ellensburg, Wash., 1996, Desert Caballeros Mus., Wickenburg, Ariz., 1997, Colo. Gov.'s Invitational Show, Loveland (Colo.) Mus., 1997, 98, 99, Art Expo, N.Y.C., 1998, Art Meets Entertainment, Roar Found., Beverly Hills, Calif., 1998, Palm Desert (Calif) Art Gallery, 1998; works in permanent collections at City of Loveland, CSI Ltd., Cambridge, Eng., El Pomar Found., Colorado Springs, Colo., Gilford, Inc., N.Y.C., Herzog & Adams, N.Y.C., Harlow Club Hotel, Palm Springs, Calif., Loveland Mus., Telluride Gallery of Fine Art, Colo., Kaiser Permanente, Denver, Kohn Family Trust, Balt., Mfrs.-Hanover trust, N.Y.C., Mayo Women's Clinic, Scottsdale, Penrose Conf., Ctr., Colorado Springs, Philip Chamberlan Inc., Madison, Conn.; featured in Southwest Art Mag., Art Trends Mag., Mountain Living mag., Woman's Mag., Radiance mag., Sun Storm Fine Art Mag., others. Recipient Colo. Gov.'s Purchase award, Loveland, 1988, Best of Show award Western Images, Boulder, 1993, medal of honor award Am. Artists Profl. League, N.Y.C., 1995. Mem. Am. Artist s Profl. League, Nat. Mus. of Women in the Arts, Katharine Lorillard Wolfe Art Club, Am. Acad. Women Artists (nominating juror, exec. bd. dirs. 1997—). Studio: 542 Arapahoe Ave Boulder CO 80302-5827

BIERSTEDT, PETER RICHARD, lawyer, entertainment industry consultant; b. Rhinebeck, N.Y., Jan. 2, 1943; s. Robert Henry and Betty (MacIver) B.; m. Carol Lynn Akiyama, Aug. 23, 1980 (div. Oct. 1995). AB, Columbia U., 1965, JD cum laude, 1969; cert., U. Sorbonne, Paris, 1966. Bar: N.Y. 1969, U.S. Supreme Ct. 1973, Calif. 1977. Atty. with firms in N.Y.C., 1969-74; pvt. practice cons. legal and entertainment industry, 1971, 75-76, 88—; with Avco Embassy Pictures Corp., L.A., 1977-83; v.p., gen. counsel Avco Embassy Pictures Corp., 1978-80, sr. v.p., 1980-83, dir., 1981-83; gen. counsel New World Entertainment (formerly New World Pictures), L.A., 1984-87, exec. v.p., 1985-87, sr. exec. v.p. Office of Chmn., 1987-88, also bd. dirs.; pres. subs. New World Prodns. and New World Advt. New World Pictures, 1985-88; guest lectr. U. Calif., Riverside, 1976-77, U. So. Calif., 1986, 91, UCLA, 1987, 95, 96; bd. dirs. New World Pictures (Australia) Ltd., FilmDallas Pictures, Inc., Cinedco, Inc. Exec. prodr. (home video series) The Comic Book Greats. Mem. Motion Picture Assn. Am. (dir. 1980-83), Acad. Motion Picture Arts and Scis. (exec. br.), N.Y. State Bar Assn., L.A. Copyright Soc., ACLU. Democrat. Avocations: astronomy, literature, tennis, scuba diving. Home and Office: 6201 Quebec Dr Los Angeles CA 90068-2219

BIESPIEL, DAVID, poet, educator; b. Tulsa, Okla., Feb. 18, 1964; s. Stephen Edwin Biespiel and Rosalyn Borg; m. Tricia Snell, May 16, 1987; 1 child, Lucas. BA, Boston U., 1986; MFA, U. Md., 1986. Adj. prof. U. Md., College Park, 1989-91, Mount Vernon Coll., Washington, 1992, George Washington U., Washington, 1992; Richard H. Thornton writer in residence Lynchburg (Va.) Coll., 1993; adj. prof. Stanford U., Palo Alto, Calif., 1995. Author: Shattering Air; editor: Artists' Communities, 1996. Springboard and platform diving coach Tualatin Hills Dive Club, Portland, Oreg., 1995—. Recipient Poets prize Acad. Am. Poets, 1989, Ind. Artist award Md. Arts Coun., 1992; Wallace Stegner fellow Stanford U., 1993-95, Creative Writing fellow NEA, 1997. Home: 1418 SE 43rd Ave Portland OR 97215-2407

BIGGERS, WALTER DAVID, mechanical engineer; b. Boise, Idaha, Sept. 6, 1927; s. Birdie and Lena (Chilcot) B.; m. Helen Hammond, Dec. 16, 1949; children: David, Karen, Mark, Ann, Laura. BSME, Calif. Inst. Tech., Pasadena, 1955. Design engr. Holly Mfg. Co., Pasadena, 1953-59; chief prodn. engr. Endevco, Pasadena, 1959-68, prodn. mgr. inertial ins. divsn., 1968-70; from emissions lab. mgr. to v.p. advanced planning Subaru of Am., Garden Grove, Calif., 1971-90; cons. Fuji Heavy Industries, Shin Juku, Japan, 1991-95. Mem. Soc. Automotive Engrs. Episcopalian.

BIGGS, THOMAS WYLIE, chemical company executive; b. Seattle, Oct. 28, 1950; s. Ray Wylie and Mildred Virginia (Ramsey) B.; m. Marcia Jean Holts, Aug. 4, 1973; children: Jennifer Tamar, Jordan Wylie. BA, U. Wash., 1972. Chemisty tchr. Samammish High Sch, Bellevue, Wash., 1972-74; sales rep. Litton Industries, Seattle, 1974-75; sales rep. Van Waters & Rogers, Kent, Wash., 1975-80, area chem. mgr., 1988-90, br. mgr., 1990-94; nat. raw materials mgr. Van Waters & Rogers, Kirkland, 1995-97; field sales mgr. Van Waters & Rogers, Kent, Wash., 1980-85; sales mgr. Van Waters & Rogers, South Bend, Ind., 1985-86; mgr. chem. dept. Van Waters & Rogers, Indpls., 1986-88; comml. dir. internat. dept. URECO (subs. Royal Pakhoed Co.), 1997—. 1st lt. USAR, 1973-80. Mem. Chgo. Drug and Chem. Assn., N.W. Paint and Coating Assn., Nat. Petroleum Refiners Assn. Avocations: skiing, golf, travel, fishing. Office: Van Waters and Rogers 6100 Carillon Pt Kirkland WA 98033-7357

BILBRAY, BRIAN P., congressman; b. Coronado, Calif., Jan. 28, 1951; m. Karen; 5 children. Supr.ctrl. and so. coastal regions San Diego County, Calif.; mem. now 106th Congress from 49th Calif. dist., 1994—; mem. commerce com.; mem. commerce, fin. & hazardous materials, health & environment, oversight & investigations coms. Avocations: sailing, surfing, horseback riding. Office: US Ho of Reps 1530 Longworth HOB Washington DC 20515-0549*

BILBRAY, JAMES HUBERT, former congressman, lawyer, consultant; b. Las Vegas, May 19, 1938; s. James A. and Ann E. (Miller) B.; m. Michaelene Mercer, Jan. 1960; children: Bridget, Kevin, Erin, Shannon. Student, Brigham Young U., 1957-58, U. Nev., Las Vegas, 1958-60; BA, Am. U., 1962; JD, Washington Coll. Law, 1964. Bar: Nev. 1965. Staff mem. Senator Howard Cannon U.S. Senate, 1960-64; dep. dist. atty. Clark County, Nev., 1965-68; mem. Lovell, Bilbray & Potter, Las Vegas, 1969-87; mem. Nev. Senate, 1980-86, chmn. taxation com., 1983-86, chmn. interim com. on pub. broadcasting, 1983; 100th-103d U.S. Congresses from 1st Nev. dist.; mem. 100th-103rd Congresses from 1st Nev. dist., 1987-95; mem. fgn. affairs com., 1987-88, mem. house armed svs. com., subcom. procurement, mil. contracts, sea power, mem. small bus. com., chmn. procurement, taxation and tourism subcom., 1989-95; ptnr. Alcalde & Fay, Arlington, Va., 1995—; mem. Spl. Panel on NATO and North Atlantic Alliance, fgn. affairs com., select com. on hunger, 1987-88, select com. on aging, 1988-93, subcoms. Africa, trade exports and tourism, select com. on intelligence, 1993-95; alt. mcpl. judge City of Las Vegas, 1987-89; del. North Atlantic Alliance, 1989-95; bd. visitors U.S. Mil. Acad., West Point, 1995—, vice chmn., 1996-97; mem. adv. bd. Ex-Import Bank of U.S., 1996—. Bd. regents U. Nev. Sys., 1968-72; mem. Nat. Coun. State Govts. Commn. on Arts and Historic Preservation; mem. bd. visitors USAF Acad., 1991-93; mem. Dem. Nat. Com., 1996—. Named Outstanding Alumnus U. Nev., Las Vegas, 1979, Man of Yr. Am. Diabetes Assn., 1989, Man of Yr. Haddassah (Nev.), 1990. Mem. Nev. State Bar Assn., Clark county Bar Assn., U. Nev.-Las Vegas Alumni Assn. (pres. 1964-69, Humanitarian of Yr. 1984), Phi Alpha Delta, Sigma Chi, KC. Democrat. Roman Catholic. Lodges: Elks, Rotary.

BILBRUCK, DANIEL WAYNE, investment company executive; b. Portland, Sept. 22, 1946; s. William Wayne Bilbruck and JoAnn Irene (Black) Bellomy; m. Jodell Girrard, 1966 (div. 1968); m. Sue Cox, 1998; children: Curtis, Scott. Pres., CEO Azaru Corp., Washougal, Wash., 1989-94, Global Tech. Group, Vancouver, Wash., 1993—; CEO Global Tech. Group, Plymouth, Eng., 1995—, Global Advanced Recycling, Plymouth, 1995—; pres., CEO Global Tech. Group, Port Moresby, New Guinea, 1993—; gen. mgr. Rootco, Inc., Kent, Wash., 1990-95; v.p. D&S Devels. Internat. Ltd., 1998—. editor Foc'sle Hints by Captain Dan, 1976-78. Served with USN, 1965. Mem. Moose. Avocations: sailing, Native American art, fishing, humanitarian projects, research. Home and Office: 1910 SE 96th Ct Vancouver WA 98664-3734

BILBY, RICHARD MANSFIELD, federal judge; b. Tucson, May 29, 1931; s. Ralph Willard and Marguerite (Mansfield) B.; m. children: Claire Louise, Ellen M. Moore; m. Elizabeth Alexander, May 25, 1996. BS, U. Ariz., 1955; JD, U. Mich., 1958. Bar: Ariz. 1959. Since practiced in Tucson; law clk. to Chief Judge Chambers, 9th Circuit Ct. Appeals, San Francisco, 1958-59; mem. firm Bilby, Thompson, Shoenhair & Warnock, 1959-79, partner, 1967-79; judge U.S. Dist. Ct., Dist. Ariz., Tucson, 1979-96; chief judge U.S. Dist. Ct., Dist. Ariz., 1984-90, sr. judge, 1996—; conscientious objector hearing officer Dept. Justice, 1959-62; chmn. Pima County Med.-Legal panel, 1968-70; Mem. Tucson Charter Revision Com., 1965-70. Chmn. United Fund Profl. Div., 1968; chmn. Spl. Gift Div., 1970, St. Joseph Hosp. Devel. Fund Drive, 1970; Republican state chmn. Vols. for Eisenhower, 1956; Rep. county chmn., Pima County, Ariz., 1972-74; Past pres. Tucson Conquistadores; bd. dirs. St. Josephs Hosp., 1969-77, chmn., 1972-75. Served with AUS, 1952-54. Fellow Am. Coll. Trial Lawyers; mem. Ariz. Acad., Town Hall (dir. 1976-79). Office: care US Dist Ct US Courthouse Rm 301 44 E Broadway Blvd Tucson AZ 85701-1711

BILEK, WENDY HOLLY, lobbyist; b. Greenville, Pa., Dec. 26, 1953; d. Robert Paul and Shirley Jane (Kerr) Lowe; m. David John Frueauf, Nov. 20, 1980 (div. Apr. 1989); 1 child, Allyson Jean Frueauf; m. Jerry Bilek, July 9, 1992. B in Polit. Sci., Coll. of Wooster, 1976. Intern Ohio Ho. of Reps., Columbus, 1976-77; legis. aide Ohio Senate, Columbus, 1977-80; assoc. dir. Petroleum Assn. Wyo., Casper, 1982-91; mineral lobbyist Casper, 1991—; store owner Blue Heron Books, Casper, 1995—. Mem. Wyo. Mining Assn. (chmn. pub. affairs com. 1993-98, chmn. legis. affairs com.), Petroleum Assn. Wyo., Wyo. Taxpayers Assn., Casper C. of C. (chmn. govt. affairs com. 1994-95), Wyo. Capital Club (pres. 1998—). Republican. Mem. Christian Ch. (Disciples of Christ). Avocations: reading, walking, fishing, gardening. Office: Blue Heron Books 201 E 2nd St Casper WY 82601-2576

BILEZIKJIAN, EDWARD ANDREW, architect; b. Los Angeles, Mar. 29, 1950; s. Andrew and Alice (Dardarian) B. BSArch, U. So. Calif., 1973, MArch, 1977. Registered architect, Calif. Project mgr. RMA Archtl. Group, Inc., Costa Mesa, Calif., 1977-78; dir. architecture Donald De Mars Assocs., Inc., Van Nuys, Calif., 1978-85; prin. architect EAB Architects, Sepulveda, Calif., 1985-87, Laguna Hills, Calif., 1988—; architect, planner III Trammell Crow Co., Irvine, Calif., 1986-88; prin. architect Fluor Daniel, Inc., Irvine, Calif., 1989—. Chmn. parish coun. Armenian Apostolic Ch. Newport Beach, 1988-91, 94-95. Mem. AIA, Triple-X Fraternity of Calif. (corresponding sec. 1984-85), Nat. Coun. Archtl. Registration Bds. (cert.). Democrat. Mem. Armenian Apostolic Ch.

BILLING, RONALD JAMES, immunologist, researcher; b. U.K., July 23, 1943; came to U.S., 1970; s. James Jackson and Margaret Isobel (O'Connor) B.; m. Angela Mary Gillett, July 9, 1965; children: Peter, Michael, Janet. BS, U. Liverpool, 1965; PhD, U. Glasgow, 1969. Postdoctoral fellow Cal Inst. Tech., Pasadena, 1970-72; asst. prof., assoc. prof. UCLA, 1972-85; rsch. dir. C V Cancer Ctr., San Marcos, Calif., 1985—; rschr. in field. Patentee in field; contbr. numerous articles to profl. jours. Gosney fellow, 1970-72; grantee NIH, 1974-77, 77-88. Avocations: tennis, chess, backpacking, fishing, golf. Office: C V Cancer Ctr PO Box 456 San Marcos CA 92079-0456

BILLINGS, BECKY LEIGH, nurse; b. Provo, Utah, Aug. 19, 1964; d. Laird Dean and Helen Virginia (Jack) B. Orem high sch., Utah, 1982; Cert. Lic. Practical Nurs, Utah Tech. Coll., Provo, 1985. On call-practical nurse Utah Valley regional Med. Ctr., Provo, 1985-86, staff nurse, 1986; head nurse Westside Care Home, Lexington, Nebr., 1987; case coord. Universal Home Care, Lexington, Nebr., 1988; staff nurse chem. dependancy unit Richard Young Hosp., Kearney, Nebr., 1989-91; staff nurse cardiac unit Good Samaritan Hosp., Kearney, Nebr., 1991, North Suburban Med. Ctr., Denver, 1992-94; office nurse, pediatrics, 1994—. Vol. Co-Therapeutic Riding Ctr. Handicapped Children. Avocations: volleyball, softball, racquetball, quarterhorses. Home: 841 E 85th Ave Denver CO 80229-4922

BILLINGS, KATHY, national monument official. Supt. USS Arizona Meml., Honolulu. Office: USS Arizona Meml #1 USS Arizona Meml Pl Honolulu HI 96818*

BILLINGS, THOMAS NEAL, computer and publishing executive, management consultant; b. Milw., Mar. 2, 1931; s. Neal and Gladys Victoria (Lockard) B.; m. Barta Hope Chipman, June 12, 1954 (div. 1967); children: Bridget Ann, Bruce Neal; m. Marie Louise Farrell, Mar. 27, 1982. AB with honors, Harvard U., 1952, MBA, 1954. V.p. fin. and adminstrn. and technol. innovation Copley Newspapers Inc., La Jolla, Calif., 1957-70; group v.p., dir. tech. Harte-Hanks Comm. Inc., San Antonio, 1970-73; exec. v.p. United Media, Inc., Phoenix, 1973-75; asst. to pres., dir. corp. mgmt. systems Ramada Inns, Inc., Phoenix, 1975-76; exec. dir. NRA, Washington, 1976-77; pres. Ideation Inc., N.Y.C., 1977-81; chmn. Bergen-Billings Inc., N.Y.C., 1977-80; pres. The Assn. Svc. Corp., San Francisco, 1978—; pres. Recorder Printing and Pub. Co. Inc., San Francisco, 1980-82; v.p. adminstrn. Victor Techs. Inc., Scotts Valley, Calif., 1982-84; mng. dir. Saga-Wilcox Computers Ltd., Wrexham, Wales, 1984-85; chmn. Thomas Billings & Assocs., Inc., Reno, 1978—, Intercontinental Travel Svc. Inc., Reno, 1983-88, Oberon Optical Character Recognition, Ltd., Hemel-Hemstead, Eng., 1985-86; bd. dirs. 5M Corp., San Francisco, Intercontinental Rsch. Coun., London, Corp. Comm. Coun., Alameda; dir., CEO Insignia Software Solutions group, High Wycombe, Eng., Cupertino, Calif., 1986-89; chmn. Intercontinental News Svc. Inc., London and Alameda, Calif., 1989—; v.p. Cromer Equipment Co., Oakland, Calif., 1991-94; chmn. Newton Group of Cos., Las Vegas, 1993—, Info. Integrity Internat., Inc., Las Vegas, London, 1994—, WordMaster Corp., Reno, 1995—, GolfDoctor!Inc., Las Vegas, 1998—; bd. dirs. Digital Broadcasting Corp., Mountain View, Calif., Lenny's Restaurants Inc., Wichita, Kans., Tymyndr Corp., Dover, Del., Zzyzzyx Corp., Reno, Harrod's Hotel & Casino Corp., Las Vegas, Pandemonium Pictures, Inc., San Mateo, Calif., Bonanza Enterprises, Inc., Virginia City, Nev., Quillmill Ltd., London, Better Betting Systems, Inc., Alameda, Calif., Video Stream, Inc., Cupertino, Calif., ResuMaster Corp., Walnut Creek, Calif., ProcessMaster Corp., Pleasanton, Calif., Enterprise House, Alameda, People Finders, Inc., Walnut Creek, Calif., Chut! Cheri's Chic Chit Choppe, S.A., Laguna Beach, Calif., Waters Equipment Co., Inc., San Francisco, Goldstein Miller and Assocs. Inc., San Bruno, Calif., Silicon World Search Group, Inc., Alameda, Calif., Knickers' Ltd., Reno; speaker and seminar leader; co-inventor Strok-Savr Software, 1994. Bd. dirs. Nat. Allergy Found., 1973—, The Wilderness Fund, 1978—, San Diego Civic Light Opera Assn., 1965-69; chief exec. San Diego 200th Anniversary Expn., 1969; founder, exec. dir. Am. Majority Party, 1993—. The Millenium Three Found., 1996—, The Rememberance Soc., 1996—, People Finders' Inc., 1996—, Corp. Comm. Counsel Inc., 1996—. Served with U.S. Army, 1955-57. Recipient Walter F. Carley Meml. award, 1966, 69. Fellow U.K. Inst. Dirs.; mem. Am. Newspaper Pubs. Assn., Inst. Execs. Inc. (dir.), Inst. Newspaper Fin. Officers, Sigma Delta Chi. Clubs: West Side Tennis, LaJolla Country; Washington Athletic; San Francisco Press; Harvard (N.Y.C.); Elks. Author: Creative Controllership, 1978, Our Credibility Crisis, 1983, Non-Euclidean Theology, 1987, Ruminations on Meta Mentality, 1990, Fixing our Broken System, 1992, (series) The Ethnic Epicure, 1995—; editor: The Vice Presidents' Letter, 1978-92; pub. The Microcomputer Letter, 1982-94, Synthetic Hardware Update, 1987-93, Windows on Tomorrow Magazine, 1994—; editor: Intercontinental News Svc., London and Alameda, Calif., 1985—. Office: PO Drawer I Alameda CA 94501-0262 also: 100 W Grove St Ste 360 Reno NV 89509-4028

BILLINGSLEY, MICHAEL J., producer; b. El Paso, Tex., Dec. 31, 1966; s. Phillip N. and Mary G. (Judd) B.; m. Stephanie Anne Kokes, Aug. 2, 1968. BS in Comm. and Broadcast Mgmt., Northern Ariz. U., 1990. Dir. mktg., prodn. Sta. KZIA, Las Cruces, N.M., 1990-91; prodr. Sta. KVBA-TV, Vail, Colo., 1991; station mgr. Vail Valley TV, Colo., 1991-92; pres., owner Video Graphic West, Vail; presenter in field, 1993-98. Contbr. articles to mags. Recipient Best 30 Second Commerical award FAST Multimedia, 1996, Best 30 Minute Program award, 1996. Mem. Colo. Film and Video Assn. Republican. Methodist. Avocations: golf, skiing, music, reading. Office: Video Graphic West PO Box 1093 Avon CO 81620-1093

BILLS, ROBERT HOWARD, political party executive; b. North Conway, N.H., Jan. 13, 1944; s. Howard William and Mary Catherine (Jackson) B.; m. Donna Gail Florian; children: Emily Ida, Katherine Mary. Staff writer Weekly People Newspaper, Bklyn., 1970-74, Palo Alto, Calif., 1974-76; nat. sec. Socialist Labor Party, Sunnyvale, 1980—; mem. nat. exec. subcom. Socialist Labor Party, 1976-79. Office: Socialist Labor Party of Am PO Box 218 Mountain View CA 94042-0218

BINDER, GORDON M., health and medical products executive; b. St. Louis, 1935. Degree in elec. engring., Purdue U., 1957; MBA, Harvard U., 1962. Formerly with Litton Industries, 1962-64; various fin. mgmt. positions Ford Motor Co., 1964-69; CFO Sys. Devel. Corp., 1971-81; v.p., CFO Amgen, Thousand Oaks, Calif., 1982-88, CEO, 1988—, chmn. bd., 1990—. Baker scholar Harvard U. Office: Amgen 1 Amgen Center Dr Thousand Oaks CA 91320-1799*

BINDER, JAMES KAUFFMAN, computer consultant; b. Reading, Pa., Nov. 20, 1920; s. Paul Burdette and Edna (Kauffman) B.; B.A., Lehigh U., 1941; M.A., Johns Hopkins U., 1952; profl. cert. in systems mgmt. U. Calif.-San Diego, 1976; A.S. in Data Processing, San Diego Evening Coll., 1979, A.A. in Fgn. Lang., 1979; A.A. in Spanish, Mira Costa Coll., Oceanside, Calif., 1981. Instr. English, Notre Dame U., South Bend, Ind., 1948-49; prof. English, Athens (Greece) Coll., 1950-51; CARE rep., Greece, 1951-52; reporter, staff writer Athens News, 1952-53; dir. lang. tng. World Council Chs. Refugee Service, Athens, 1953-54; co-editor Am. Overseas Guide, N.Y., West Berlin, 1957-58; lectr. English, U. Md. Overseas Program, European and Far East divs., 1958-66; successively supr. Cen. Info. Ctr., supt. documents, sr. systems analyst GA Techs., Inc., La Jolla, Calif., 1968-85. Recipient Williams Prize, Lehigh U., 1939, 41; Johns Hopkins U. Grad. Sch. Pres. scholar, 1945-48. Roman Catholic. Clubs: Tudor and Stuart, Automobile of So. Calif. Author: The Correct Comedy, 1951; contbg. translator Modern Scandinavian Poetry, 1948; editor: (with Erwin H. Tiebe) American Overseas Guide, 1958.

BINGAMAN, JEFF, senator; b. El Paso, Tex., Oct. 3, 1943; s. Jesse and Beth (Ball) B.; m. Anne Kovacovich, Sept. 13, 1968. BA in Govt., Harvard U., 1965; JD, Stanford U., 1968. Bar: N.Mex. 1968. Asst. atty. gen., 1969; atty. Stephenson, Campbell & Olmsted, 1971-72; ptnr. Campbell, Bingaman & Black, Santa Fe, 1972-78; former atty. gen. State of N.Mex.; now U.S. senator from N.Mex. 106th Congress; mem. armed svcs. com., mem. joint econ. com., mem. Senate Dem. steering and coordination com. State of N.Mex., mem. Senate Den. tech. and comm. com., ranking minority mem., mem. energy and natural resources subcom. of energy prodn. and regulation, mem. labor and human resources com. U.S. Army 1968-74. Democrat. Methodist. Home: PO Box 5775 Santa Fe NM 87502-5775 Office: US Senate 703 Hart Senate Bldg Washington DC 20510*

BINGHAM, PARIS EDWARD, JR., electrical engineer, computer consultant; b. Aurora, Colo., Sept. 26, 1957; s. Paris Edward and Shirley Ann (Blehm) B.; m. Laurie Sue Piersol, May 9, 1981 (div. Sept. 1987); m. Helen Naef, Aug. 7, 1993. BS in Elec. Engring. and Computer Sci., U. Colo., 1979. Mem. tech. staff Western Electric Co., Aurora, 1979-81, system engr., 1981; mem. electronic tech. staff Hughes Aircraft Co., Aurora, 1981-83, staff engr., 1983-86, sr. staff engr., 1986-93, scientist, engr., 1993-94; area systems support engr. Sun Microsystems, Inc., Englewood, Colo., 1994—; cons. RJM Assocs., Huntington, N.Y., 1987-91; cons. Aurora, 1988—. Mem. IEEE, Assn. for Computing Machinery. Republican. Presbyterian. Achievements include research on artificial intelligence applications, distributed networking and computing, next generational software technologies. Office: Sun Microsystems Inc 5251 Dtc Pkwy Ste 500 Englewood CO 80111-2700

BINNIE, NANCY CATHERINE, retired nurse, educator; b. Sioux Falls, S.D., Jan. 28, 1937; d. Edward Grant and Jessie May (Martini) Larkin; m.

Charles H. Binnie. Diploma, St. Joseph's Hosp. Sch. Nursing, Phoenix, 1965; BS in Nursing, Ariz. State U., 1970, MA, 1974. Intensive care charge nurse Scottsdale (Ariz.) Meml. Hosp., 1968-70, coordinator critical care, 1970-71; coordinator critical care John C. Lincoln Hosp., Phoenix, 1971-73; prof. nursing GateWay Community Coll., Phoenix, 1974-96; coord. part-time evening nursing programs Gateway Community Coll., 1984-97, interim dir. nursing, 1989, 91. Mem. Orgn. Advancement of Assoc. Degree Nursing, Practical and Assoc. Coun. Nursing Educators, Ariz. Coun. Nurse Educators. Avocations: gardening, golf, sewing. Office: Gateway C C 104 N 40th St Phoenix AZ 85034-1704

BIRCHER, ANDREA URSULA, psychiatric-mental health nurse, educator, clinical nurse specialist; b. Bern, Switzerland, Mar. 6, 1928; came to U.S., 1947; d. Franklin E. Bircher and Hedy E. Bircher-Rey. Diploma, Knapp Coll. Nursing, Santa Barbara, Calif., 1957; BS, U. Calif., San Francisco, 1961, MS, 1962; PhD, U. Calif., Berkeley, 1966. RN, Calif., Ill. Staff nurse, head nurse Cottage Hosp., Santa Barbara, 1957-58; psychiatric nurse, jr., sr. Langley-Porter Neuropsychiatric Inst., San Francisco, 1958-66; asst. prof. U. Ill. Coll. Nursing, Chgo., 1966-72; prof. U. Okla. Coll. Nursing, Oklahoma City, 1972-93, prof. emeritus, 1993—. Contbr. articles and papers to profl. jours. Recipient award for Outstanding Contributions to Faculty Governance U. Okla. Faculty Senate 1985, 93, others. Mem. AAUP, ANA, AAUW, Am. Psychotherapy Assn. (cert. diplomate), Soc. for Edn. and Rsch. in Psychiat. Nursing, Nat. League for Nursing, N.Am. Nursing Diagnosis Assn., Calif. Assn. of Psychiat. Nurses in Advanced Practice, Ventura County Writers Club, Sigma Theta Tau, Phi Kappa Phi. Republican. Avocations: indoor gardening, cooking, reading, yoga, writing. Home: 1161 Cypress Point Ln Apt 201 Ventura CA 93003-6074

BIRD, MARGARET DUERING, writer; b. Phila., Nov. 12, 1942; d. Henry Alexander and Margaret Helen (Donahoo) D.; m. Charles Benjamin Bird, June 6, 1964 (div. Dec. 1981); 1 child, Margaret Bird Stern; m. Robert Lane Friedenwald, Sept. 16, 1989. Diploma, Hosp. U. Pa., 1963; BS, Portland State U., 1976. RN, Pa., Oreg. Nurse various orgns., 1963-71; legis. asst. Oreg. Ho. of Reps., Portland, 1975-80; cons. Don Barney & Assocs., Portland, 1980-84; exec. dir. Pacific N.W. Waterways Assn., Vancouver, Wash., 1984-89; cons. Barney & Worth Inc., Portland, 1989-93; freelance writer, 1994—. Contbr. to book: An Ear to the Ground, 1997, also essays to popular jours. Pres. bd. dirs. New Rose Theater, Portland, 1980-84; vol. hospice program, Portland, 1997—; reading tutor Portland Sch. Dist., 1995-97; mem. com. City Club of Portland, 1989-94; mem. Clackamas County Youth Svcs. Commn., Oreg., 1980-84; mem. adv. com. ARC, Portland, 1991-93. Democrat. Lutheran. Avocations: reading, needlework.

BIRDSALL, BRIAN, food products executive; b. 1956. Grad., Wash. State U., 1979. With Pannell Kerr Foster Acctg., Wenatchee, Wash., 1979-88; pres., treas. Chief Wenatchee, 1988—. Office: Chief Wenatchee 1705 N Miller St Wenatchee WA 98801-1585*

BIREN, RICHARD LEE, elementary school counselor, writer; b. Fargo, N.D., Feb. 27, 1947; s. Edward Michael and Augusta Mary (Hamerlinck) B.; m. Cynthia Susan Brook, July 26, 1978; children: Rebecca, Jimmy. BS in Psychology, N.D. State U., 1969, MS in Counseling, 1970; cert. elem. counseling, Colo. State U., 1981. Lic. counselor, Colo. Sports editor Spectrum N.D. State U., Fargo, 1968-69, grad. asst., 1969-70; sch. counselor Stephen (Minn.) Sch. Dist., 1970-73, Hope (N.D.) Sch. Dist., 1974-76, Page (N.D.) Sch. Dist., 1975-76; elem. sch. counselor Brush (Colo.) Sch. Dist., 1976—. Pres. Stephen Edn. Assn., 1973; chmn. meet and conf. team Brush Edn. Assn., 1989; tchr. St. Mary's Religious Edn., Brush, 1977—; mem. BOCES-Drug Free Com., Ft. Morgan, Colo., 1995-97. Grantee State N.D., 1976. Mem. Colo. Sch. Counselors Assn., NEA (advisor profl. libr. 1987-98), Colo. Edn. Assn., N.D. State U. Alumni Assn., Shanley Grow Club, Kappa Delta Pi. Roman Catholic. Avocations: travel, sports, writing. Home: 315 Ray St Brush CO 80723-2423

BIRKBY, WALTER HUDSON, forensic anthropologist, consultant; b. Gordon, Nebr., Feb. 28, 1931; s. Walter Levy and Margery Hazel (Moss) B.; m. Carmen Sue Gates, Aug. 18, 1955; children: Jeffrey Moss, Julianne. BA, U. Kans., 1961, MA, 1963; PhD, U. Ariz., 1973. Diplomate Am. Bd. Forensic Anthropology (pres. 1985-87, exec. com. 1980-87). Med. and X-ray technician Graham County (Kans.) Hosp., Hill City, 1955-58; phys. anthropologist Ariz. State Mus., Tucson, 1968-85; lectr. anthropology U. Ariz., Tucson, 1981-90, adj. rsch. prof. anthropology, 1990-96, emeritus prof., 1996—; curator phys. anthropology Ariz. State Mus., Tucson, 1985-96; forensic anthropologist Pima County Med. Examiner's Office, Tucson, 1981—, Recovery of Victims of Alfred G. Packer party (1874), Lake City, Colo., 1989; dental cons. USAF Hosp., Davis Monthan AFB, Tucson, 1984-96; human osteologist U. Ariz.-Republic of Cyprus Archaeol. Expdn., 1985-87, Lugnano in Teverina (Italy) Expdn., 1990-91; dir. dept. anthropology masters program in forensic anthropology, 1983-96; cons. to Chief Armed Svcs. Graves Registration Office U.S. Army, 1987-93 97—, UN Internat. Criminal Tribunal for Yugoslavia, 1997-98; mem. disaster mortuary team Nat. Disaster Med. Sys., 1994—. Mem. editorial bd. (jour.) Cryptozoology, 1982—; bd. editors Am. Jour. Forensic Medicine and Pathology, 1992-97; co-author video tng. film Identification of Human Remains, 1980; contbr. articles to profl. jours. Served as sgt. USMCR, 1951-52, Korea. Recipient Achievement medal for meritiorious svc. Pima County Sheriff's Dept., 1992, Spl. Recognition award, 1995; NIH fellow U. Ariz., 1966-68. Fellow Am. Acad. Forensic Scis. (exec. com. 1978-81, T. Dale Stewart award in anthropology 1991); mem. Am. Assn. Phys. Anthropologists, Calif. Assn. Criminalists, Ariz. Identification Coun. of the Internat. Assn. for Identification, Ariz. Homicide Investigators Assn., Sigma Xi (pres. local chpt. 1984-85). Republican. Avocations: photography, hunting, fishing. Home: 7349 E 18th St Tucson AZ 85710-4904 Office: Forensic Sci Ctr 2825 E District St Tucson AZ 85714-2081

BIRKINBINE, JOHN, II, philatelist; b. Chestnut Hill, Pa., Mar. 29, 1930; s. Olaf Weimer and Gertrude Marie (Tyson) B.; m. Ausencia Barrera Elen, Dec. 19, 1969; children: John III, Bayani Royd. Chmn., CEO Am. Philatelic Brokerages, Tucson, 1946—; chmn. bd. dirs. Ariz. Philatelic Rangers, Tucson, 1987—; bd. dirs. Postal History Found. Chmn. bd. 1869 Pictorial Rsch. Assn., 1969, bd. dirs., 1970-76, chmn. Baha'i Faith Adminstrv. Body, Pima County, Ariz., 1977-81, 83-91; sheriff, chmn. Santa Catalina Corral of Westerners Internat., Tucson, 1986. Recipient Large Gold and Spl. award Spanish Soc. Internat., San Juan, P.R., 1982, New Zealand Soc. Internat., Auckland, 1990, Large Internat. Gold award Australian Soc. Internat., Melbourne, 1984, Swedish Soc. Internat., Stockholm, 1986, Singapore Soc. Internat., 1995, U.S. Soc. Internat., San Francisco, 1997, Internat. Gold award U.S. Soc. Internat., Chgo., 1986, Bulgarian Soc. Internat., Sofia, 1989. Mem. Am. Philatelic Soc. (U.S. Champion of Champions award 1985), U.S. Philatelic Classics Soc. (disting. philatelist award 1995), Am. Philatelic Congress (McCoy award 1969, 97), Scandinavian Collectors Club, Collectors Club N.Y., Western Cover Soc. Avocations: swimming, tennis, travel, music, western U.S. historical research. Office: Am Philatelic Brokerages PO Box 36657 Tucson AZ 85740-6657 Address: PO Box 36657 Tucson AZ 85740-6657

BIRMAN, ALEXANDER, physicist, researcher; b. Moscow, May 23, 1946; came to U.S., 1994; s. Yakov and Rozaliya (Krimerman) B.; m. Emily Freydman, Dec. 25, 1980; children: Igor, Eugene. MSc, Moscow Physico-Tech. Inst., 1970; PhD, Inst. Applied Physics, Moscow, 1975. Sr. rsch. scientist Inst. Applied Physics, Moscow, 1970-85; leading rsch. scientist Astrophysics Corp., Moscow, 1985-93; sr. optical scientist Dicon Fiberoptics, Inc., Berkeley, Calif., 1995—; lectr. Moscow Physico-Tech. Inst., 1987-92. Contbr. articles to profl. jours. Mem. IEEE, Optical Soc. Am., Internat. Soc. for Optical Engring. Achievements include work on theory of waves diffraction in ring lasers; contribution to design of laser and fiber-optic gyroscopes; development of passive fiberoptic components for advanced communication systems. Home: 535 Pierce St Apt 2105 Albany CA 94706-1055 Office: Dicon Fiberoptics 1331 8th St Berkeley CA 94710-1453

BIRNBAUM, JANE ELLEN, writer; b. N.Y.C., May 26, 1955; d. Owen and Claire Birnbaum. BA, Harvard U., 1978. Scheduler Jerry Brown re-election campaign, Calif., 1978; editl. writer Press Telegram, Long Beach, Calif., 1980-83; columnist Herald Examiner, L.A., 1984-89; freelance writer, 1989—. Contbg. writer Worth Mag., N.Y.C., 1994—.

BIRNBAUM, STEVAN ALLEN, investment company executive; b. L.A., Apr. 21, 1943; s. Eugene David and Bessie (Holtzman) B.; m. Barbara Patricia Ostroff, June 29, 1971 (div. Aug. 1991); children: Marc, Jill; m. Bonnie Lynn Baehr, Jan. 2, 1999. BS in Engring., UCLA, 1965; MBA, Harvard U., 1967. Dir. advanced programs Whittaker Corp., L.A., 1967-69; v.p. Hohenberg & Assocs., Beverly Hills, Calif., 1969-74; dir. adminstrv. mgmt. Dames & Moore, L.A., 1974-77; prin. Xerox Venture Capital, L.A., 1977-81; venture capitalist, L.A., 1981-83; ptnr. Oxford Ptnrs., Santa Monica, Calif., 1983-95; pres. Oxcal Venture Corp., Santa Monica, 1981—; founder, bd. dirs. Brentwood Savs. Bank, 1982; bd. dirs. Quintar Corp., Torrance, Calif. Republican. Jewish.

BISHOP, BETTY JOSEPHINE, lawyer, expert witness mortgage banking; b. Seattle, Wash., Feb. 27, 1947; d. Arthur Joseph and Julia Teresa (Azzolina) Lovett; children: Deborah, Scott. BS, Wash. State U., 1969; postgrad., Ohio State U., 1983; JD, Santa Barbara Coll. of Law, 1995. Cert. real estate appraiser, Calif. Tchr. Seattle Sch. Dist., 1973-75; appraiser Pacific First Fed., Tacoma, 1977-78, asst. v.p., mgr., secondary market ops., 1978-82; regional exec. United Guaranty, Westlake Village, Calif., 1982-83; sr. v.p. comml. secondary mktg. FCA Am. Mortgage Corp./ Am. Savs., Santa Monica, Calif., 1983-85; v.p., mgr. secondary market ops. County Savs. Bank, Santa Barbara, Calif., 1985-88; pres., fin. cons. SMC Fin. Svcs., Montecito, Calif., 1988-97; mem. conf. subcom., sec. mktg. com. Calif. Savs. and Loan League, L.A., 1985-88; document subcom., sec. mktg. subcom. U.S. Savs. and Loan League, Chgo., 1987-88. Contbr. articles to profl. jours. Fund drive chmn. Easter Seal Soc., Olympia, 1972. Mem. Calif. Bar, Los Angeles County Bar, Orange County Bar, Beverly Hills Bar, Santa Barbara Assocs., Conejo Ski Club (past woman of yr.), Santa Barbara Ski Club (past pres., past L.A. coun. rep.). Republican. Roman Catholic. Avocations: snow ski racing, water skiing, softball, golf.

BISHOP, C. DIANE, state agency administrator, educator; b. Elmhurst, Ill., Nov. 23, 1943; d. Louis William and Constance Oleta (Mears) B. BS in Maths., U. Ariz., 1965, MS in Maths., MEd in Secondary Edn., 1972. Lic. secondary educator. Tchr. math. Tucson Unified Sch. Dist., 1966-86, mem. curriculum council, 1985-86, mem. maths. curriculum task teams, 1983-86; state supt. of pub. instrn. State of Ariz., 1987-95, gov.'s policy advisor for edn., 1995-97, dir. gov.'s office workforce devel. policy, 1996—; asst. dep. dir. Ariz. Dept. Commerce, 1997—; exec. dir. Gov.'s Strategic Partnership for Econ. Devel., 1997—; mem. assoc. faculty Pima C.C., Tucson, 1974-84; adj. lectr. U. Ariz., 1983, 85; mem. math. scis. edn. bd. NRC, 1987-90, mem. new standards project governing bd., 1991; dir. adv. bd. sci. and engring. ednl. panel, NSF; mem. adv. bd. for arts edn. Nat. Endowment for Arts. Active Ariz. State Bd. Edn., 1984-95, chmn. quality edn. commn., 1986-87, chmn. tchr. crt. subcom., 1984-95, mem. outcomes based edn. adv. com., 1986-87, liaison bd. dirs. essential skills subcom., 1985-87, gifted edn. com. liaison, 1985-87; mem. Ariz. State Bd. Regents, 1987-95, mem. com. on preparing for U. Ariz., 1983, mem. high sch. task force, 1984-85; mem. bd. Ariz. State Community Coll., 1987-95; mem. Ariz. Joint Legis. Com. on Revenues and Expenditures, 1989, Ariz. Joint Legis. Com. on Goals for Ednl. Excellence, 1987-89, Gov.'s Task Force on Ednl. Reform, 1991, Ariz. Bd. Regents Commn. on Higher Edn., 1992. Woodrow Wilson fellow Princeton U., summer 1984; recipient Presdl. Award for Excellence in Teaching of Maths., 1983, Ariz. Citation of Merit, 1984, Maths. Teaching award Nat. Sci. Research Soc., 1984, Distinction in Edn. award Flinn Found., 1986; named Maths. Tchr. of Yr. Ariz. Council of Engring. and Sci. Assns., 1984, named One of Top Ten Most Influential Persons in Ariz. in Field of Tech., 1998. Mem. AAUW, NEA, Nat. Coun. Tchrs. Math., Coun. Chief State Sch. Officers, Women Execs. in State Govt. (bd. dirs. 1993), Ariz. Assn. Tchrs. Math., Women Maths. Edn., Math. Assn. Am., Ednl. Commn. of the States (steering com.), Nat. Endowment Arts (adv. bd. for arts edn.), Nat. Forum Excellence Edn., Nat. Honors Workshop, Phi Delta Kappa. Republican. Office: Ariz Dept Commerce 3800 N Central Ave Bldg D Phoenix AZ 85012-1908

BISHOP, DAVID STEWART, clergyman; b. Thunder Hawk, S.D., May 13, 1933; s. Joel Lewis and Grace Miriam (Peterson) B.; m. Shirley Yvonne Orndorff, July 15, 1941 (dec. Nov. 1964); children: Sheryl Ann Bishop Walker, Mellanie Kay Bishop Hunt; m. Sandra Alyn Reasy, Mar. 20, 1967; children: Shannon Dee, David Stewart. AA, Lee Coll., Cleveland, Tenn., 1955; BA magna cum laude, Birmingham So. Coll., 1958; PhD, Calif. Grad. Sch. Theology, 1978. Ordained to ministry Ch. of God, 1960. Tchr. West Coast Bible Coll., Fresno, Calif., 1958-59, dean coll., 1960-62, supt., 1962-65; coord./tchr. Bible Inst. for Ministry/Lay Enrichment, L.A., 1971-73, Yakima and Pasco, Wash., 1975-77, 79; founder, dir., tchr. Yakima Sch. Christian Ministries, 1977—; chaplain's staff St. Joseph's Hosp., Burbank, Calif., 1970-72; pastor North Hollywood (Calif.) Ch. of God, 1969-73; sr. pastor Christian Life Ctr. Ch. of God, Yakima, 1973—; sec. Yakima Pentecostal Fellowship, 1975-76, pres., 1975-77; v.p. Yakima Full Gospel Minister's Fellowship, 1982; mem. Mayor's Prayer Breakfast Com., Yakima, 1986, 88; dist. overseer Ch. God, Yakima, 1983—, mem. Wash. state coun., 1974-78, 80-84, 86-90, trustee Wash. state, 1974—, chmn. state edn. bd. 1978-79, mem. state ministers' examining bd., 1984-86; mem. gen. exec. coun. Ch. God, 1986-90, com. internationalization, 1986-90, motions com. gen. assembly, 1990; com. rev. N.W. Bible Coll., 1986; mem. task force on edn. Ch. of God, 1991—. Author: Effective Communication, 1977, Into His Presence, 1988; contbr. articles to profl. jours., chpts. to books; chalk artist in ministry and fine art in several media; composer several songs; producer teaching tapes and Bible study outlines and materials; founder, minister Alive Through the Word, daily radio broadcast, 1974-87, Alive in the Spirit, weekly TV ministry, 1979—. Bd. dirs. West Coast Christian Coll., 1960-69, 87—; bd. govs., Calif. Theol. Sem., Fresno, Calif., 1984-86, chmn., 1990—. Recipient Vision Found. Golde Mike award Ch. of God, 1980. Mem. Phi Beta Kappa. Home: 3811 Woodcrest Ave NW Cleveland TN 37312-3814 Office: Christian Life Ctr Ch God 716 N 40th Ave Yakima WA 98908-2671

BISHOP, FORREST FREDERICK, engineering executive; b. Portland, Oreg., July 25, 1955; s. Alexander T. and Elizabeth (Griesel) B. Student, U. Wash., 1973-92. Pres. Sound Works, Seattle, 1986-89, Eigen Design, Seattle, 1991-95; embedded sys. developer, mgr. Interworld Prodns. LLC, Seattle, 1998—; chmn. Inst. Atomic-Scale Engring., Seattle, 1996—. Contbr. articles to profl. publs.; prodr. documentary video series Nanotechnology: Machines Alive, 1998; inventor in field. Mem. Nat. Space Soc., Extropy Inst., Mensa, Foresight Inst. (sr. assoc.). Office: Interworld Prodns LLC PO Box 30121 Seattle WA 98103-0121

BISHOP, JAMES E., biotechnologist, research scientist; b. Malvern, Ark., Aug. 16, 1951; s. Kenneth L. and Ada L. (Van Cleave) B.; m. Alexandra Lee Stanton White, Feb. 6, 1982. BS, U. Minn., 1975; MS, U. Mich., 1977, PhD, 1981. Postdoct. researcher U. Mich., Ann Arbor, 1981-82, U. Cape Town (South Africa), 1982-84; postdoct. researcher U. Md., Balt., 1984-87, asst. prof., 1987-89; product devel. scientist Becton Dickinson Immunocytometry Sys., San Jose, Calif., 1990-91; rsch. scientist Becton Dickinson Immunocytometry Sys., San Jose, 1991—. Contbr. articles to profl. jours.; patentee in field. Mem. Am. Chem. Soc., Internat. Soc. for Analytical Cytology. Democrat. Avocations: swimming, backpacking, mountaineering, writing. Office: Becton Dickinson Immunocytometry Sys 2350 Qume Dr San Jose CA 95131-1807

BISHOP, JOHN MICHAEL, biomedical research scientist, educator; b. York, Pa., Feb. 22, 1936; married 1959; 2 children. AB, Gettysburg Coll., 1957; MD, Harvard U., 1962; DSc (hon.), Gettysburg Coll., 1983. Intern in internal medicine Mass. Gen. Hosp., Boston, 1962-63, resident, 1963-64; rsch. assoc. virology NIH, Washington, 1964-66, sr. investigator, 1966-68; from asst. prof. to assoc. prof. U. Calif. Med. Ctr., San Francisco, 1968-72, prof. microbiology and immunology, 1972—, prof. biochemistry and biophysics, 1982—; dir. G.W. Hooper Rsch. Found. G.W. Hooper Rsch. Found., 1981—; Univ. prof. U. Calif. Med. Ctr., San Francisco, 1994, chancellor U. Calif. Med. Ctr., San Francisco, 1998—. Recipient Nobel prize in physiology or medicine, 1989, Biomed. Rsch. award Am. Assn. Med. Colls., 1981, Albert Lasker Basic Med. Rsch. award, 1981, Armand Hammer Cancer award, 1984, GM Found. Cancer Rsch. award, 1984, Gairdner Found. Internat. award, Can., 1984, Medal of Honor, Am. Cancer Soc., 1984; NIH grantee, 1968—. Fellow Salk Inst. (trustee 1991—); mem. NAS, Inst. Medicine, Nat. Cancer Adv. Bd. Achievements include research in biochemistry of animal viruses, replication of nucleic acids, oncogenesis, control of cell growth, and molecular genetics. Office: U Calif Med Ctr Dept Microbiology Box 0552 San Francisco CA 94143-0552

BISHOP, ROB, political party executive. Chmn. Utah State Rep. Party, 1997—. Office: 117 E South Temple Salt Lake City UT 84111-1101*

BISHOP, ROBERT CHARLES, architect, metals and minerals company executive; b. Butte, Mont., June 6, 1929; s. Lester Farragut and Helen Katherine (Bauman) B.; m. B. Jean Rausch, June 29, 1957; children: Desta Fawn Bishop O'Connor, Valerie Dawn. BS in Gen. Engring., Mont. State U., 1958, BArch., 1960. Assoc. architect various firms, Mont., 1960-64; owner, architect R.C. Bishop & Assocs., Butte, Great Falls and Missoula, Mont., 1965-69; owner, chief exec. officer Val-Desta 4M, Butte, 1980—, Val-Desta Mines and Minerals, Louisville, Ky., 1985—; prin. Archtl. Assocs., 1969—; chief exec. officer, pres. Cove-Lock Log Home Mfrs., Inc., Butte, 1968-72, Busy Beaver Enterprises, Great Falls, 1968-72, New Horizon Homes, Missoula, 1968-72; asst. contracts adminstr. Davy-McKee Constrn. Engrs., Butte, 1982-83. Developer 9 major and 2 minor algorithms for mineral prospecting, valid for over 100 areas in Mont. and Idaho; discoverer 100 to 300 million tons of high grade bull quarts and rock crystal, copper and molybdenum, potential world class deposits; discoverer naturally occurring minerals that when infused in a water medium are capable with electrolysis to produce 3.5 times the hydrogen as available from the electrolysis of sea water; co-patentee in field. Advisor, Kiwanis, Jaycees, Nat. Res., 1960-72, Am. Legion, 1976. With U.S. Army, 1953-55. Named One of 2,000 Men of Achievement Melrose Press, 1970, 73. Mem. Internat. Platform Assn., Nat. Hist. Soc. (founding assoc. 1971), Elk Bow Hunting Club (bugle tchr. 1970-84), Butte Mulitlist Club (real estate tchr. 1978-84), Nat. Coun. Archtl. Registeration Bds. (registered architect seismic design 1965—). Presbyterian. Achievements include research in hydraulic trompe technology to retrofit existing hydroelectric generation in a Co-generation format to increase electrical production performance, to reduce fuel consumption and reduce particulate air emissions; research in contaminated waste-water remediation; development of radial dihedral stressed skin roof lens system. Home and Office: 1008 W Galena St Butte MT 59701-1420

BISHOP, RODNEY PHILIP, physician; b. London, Mar. 22, 1932; came to U.S., 1993; s. Reginald Henry and Eileen Gertrude (Hill) B.; m. Ann Frances Margaret Swindale, July 17, 1965; children: James, Sarah, Amy. BA in Natural Sci., Cambridge (Eng.) U., 1955, MA in Natural Sci., 1959; MD, London Royal Coll., Eng., 1960; D in Pub. Adminstrn., Pacific Western U., 1988. Diplomate English Med. Bd., Can. Med. Bd. Intern Salvation Army Hosp., Winnipeg, Can., 1960-61; surg. tng. Salvation Army Hosp., Nagercoil, South India, 1962-64; maternity tng. Maternity Hosp., Aberdeen, Scotland, 1964-65; pvt. practice Bedforshire, Eng., 1966-73, New Westminster, B.C., Can., 1974—; med. dir. Queens Park Extended Care Hosp., New Westminster, 1977-86; pres., rsch. Rodney Bishop Mgmt. Co., Inc., 1980—. Readership and youth group leader Episcopalian Ch., London, 1956-73. Lt. British Army, 1950-55. Mem. AMA, Brit. Med. Assn., Can. Med. Assn., N.Y. Acad. Sci. Episcopalian. Avocation: sailing. Home: 4126 Matia Dr Ferndale WA 98248-9539 Office: 211-301 E Columbia St, New Westminster, BC Canada V3L 3W5

BISHOP, TILMAN MALCOLM, state senator, retired college administrator; b. Colorado Springs, Jan. 1, 1933; B.A., M.A., U. No. Colo.; m. Pat Bishop, 1951; 1 son, Barry Alan. Retired adminstr., dir. student services Mesa State Coll., Grand Junction, Colo.; mem., pres. pro tem Colo. Senate. World series com. Nat. Jr. Coll. Baseball. Served with U.S. Army. Mem. Am. Sch. Counselors Assn., Nat. Assn. for Counseling and Devel., Colo. Assn. for Counseling and Devel. Republican. Methodist. Lodges: Elks, Lions. Avocations: fishing, small game hunting. Office: State Capitol Bldg Denver CO 80203 Home: 2697 G Rd Grand Junction CO 81506-8367

BISHOP, VIRGINIA WAKEMAN, retired librarian and humanities educator; b. Portland, Oreg., Dec. 28, 1927; d. Andrew Virgil and Letha Evangeline (Ward) Wakeman; m. Clarence Edmund Bishop, Aug. 23, 1953; children: Jean Marie Bishop Johnson, Marilyn Joyce. BA, Bapt. Missionary Tng. Sch., Chgo., 1949, Linfield Coll., McMinnville, Oreg., 1952; MEd, Linfield Coll., McMinnville, Oreg., 1953; MA in Librarianship, U. Wash., 1968. Ch. worker Univ. Bapt. Ch., Seattle, 1954-56, 59-61, pre-sch. tchr. parent coop presch., 1965-66; libr. N.W. Coll., Kirkland, Wash., 1968-69; undergrad. libr. U. Wash., Seattle, 1970; libr., instr. Seattle Cen. Community Coll., 1970-91. Leader Totem coun. Girl Scouts U.S., 1962-65; pres. Wedgwood Sch. PTA, Seattle, 1964-65; chair 46th Dist. Dem. Orgn., Seattle, 1972-73; precinct com. officer Dem. Party, 1968-88, 96—; candidate Wash. State Legislature, Seattle, 1974, 80; bd. dirs. Univ. Bapt. Children's Ctr., 1989-95, chair, 1990-95; vol. Ptnrs. in Pub. Edn., 1992-96. Recipient Golden Acorn award Wedgwood Elem. Sch., 1966. Mem. LWV of Seattle (2d v.p. 1994-96), U. Wash. Grad. Sch. Libr. and Info. Sci. Alumni Assn. (1st v.p. 1986-87, pres. 1987-88). Baptist. Avocations: swimming, hiking, reading. Home: 3032 NE 87th St Seattle WA 98115-3529

BISHOP-GRAHAM, BARBARA, secondary school educator, journalist; b. Angwin, Calif., Apr. 22, 1941; d. Will Francis and Esther Clara (Blissérd) Bishop; children: Gregory Mark, Steven Bishop. BA in Journalism, U. Hawaii, 1975, BA in English, 1975, BA in Art History, 1975, BFA in Painting and Drawing, 1975; nat. cert. in journalism, Kans. State U., 1994; MA in Tech. Curriculum & Instrn., Calif. State U., Sacramento, 1999. Cert. tchr., Hawaii. Photography instr., art tchr. Hawaii Sch. for Girls, Honolulu, 1974-76; substitute tchr. English State Dept. Edn., Oahu, 1977-78; English and grammar instr. Hawaii Sch. for Bus., Honolulu, 1979-80; media dir., exec. asst., historian Oriental Treasures and Points West, Honolulu, 1981-82; legal asst. Goodsill, Anderson, Quinn, Honolulu, 1983-84; lang. arts and photography tchr. Lodi (Calif.) H.S., 1984-88, writing and lang. arts tchr., 1988-93, journalism adviser, 1993-95, lang. arts tchr., 1993-96, Brit. lit. tchr., 1996—; mem. curriculum coun. Lodi Unified Sch. Dist., 1989-92, 97—; liaison to PTSA Lodi H.S., 1991-92, mentor tchr., 1991-94, 97—; student literary mag. advisor Lodi H.S., 1989-98. Sportswriter Oakland Tribune, 1957-60, Author Three Poems, 1998; contbr. articles to profl. publs. Fundraiser chmn. Big Bros. of Am., San Francisco, 1967; media dir. Clements (Calif.) Cmty. Cares, 1985-89. Recipient Edn. Contbn. award Masons 1988-92; grantee Nat. Endowment of Arts, rsch. Japanese Lit. 1989; social rschr. grantee Brazil, U. So. Calif., 1992, grantee, 1992; grantee S. Joaquin County Office Edn., 1996-97; champion Hawaii State barrel racing, 1980. Mem. NEA, Calif. Tchrs. Assn. (mem. state coun. rep. 1996-97), Lodi Edn. Assn. (conf. fund chair 1989-97). Republican. Seventh-Day Adventist. Avocations: writing, dressage riding and showing, growing and testing roses. Office: Lodi HS 3 S Pacific Ave Lodi CA 95242-3020

BISMUT, ALAIN GEORGES, video sales and international film licensing executive, writer, producer, editor; came to U.S., 1986; s. Georges Ange and Maryvonne (Le Corre) B. Student, Charles V U., Paris, 1985, NYU, 1987-89. Head of devel. NS Prodns., L.A., 1991-93; segment prodr. Kingworld/ Prodr.'s Resource, Miami, Fla., 1993-95; dir. prodn. Prodr.'s Resource, Miami Beach, Fla., 1993-97; head of devel. Sales Inc. for Video, Beverly Hills, Calif., 1996—; author, assoc. prodr. The Turk, Inc., Paris, 1997—. Internat. editor-at-large The Link, 1996-97. Office: Sales Inc Ste 250 9424 Dayton Way Beverly Hills CA 90210

BITTERMAN, MELVIN LEE, real estate developer; b. Yankton, S.D., Dec. 9, 1938; s. Edward Phillip and Amanda Bertha (Moke) B.; m. Constance Winfried Mann, Nov. 7, 1970; 1 child, Janet Amanda. BA, N. Tex. State U., 1967. Librarian City of Glendale, Calif., 1967-71; sales rep. Allstate Ins. Co., Glendale, 1971-86; property mgr./developer Glendale, 1986—. With U.S. Army, 1961-64. Mem. Rotary (sec. 1985), Alpha Beta Alpha. Republican. Roman Catholic. Avocations: amateur radio, fishing, tennis, trap shooting, ping pong. Address: 1400 Beaudry Blvd Glendale CA 91208-1708

BITTERMAN, MORTON EDWARD, psychologist, educator; b. N.Y.C., Jan. 19, 1921; s. Harry Michael and Stella (Weiss) B.; m. Mary Gayle Foley, June 26, 1967; children—Sarah Fleming, Joan, Ann. B.A., NYU, 1941; M.A., Columbia U., 1942; Ph.D., Cornell U., 1945. Asst. prof. Cornell U., Ithaca, N.Y., 1945-50; assoc. prof. U. Tex., Austin, 1950-55, mem. Inst. for Advanced Study, Princeton, N.J., 1955-57; prof. Bryn Mawr Coll., Pa., 1957-70, U. Hawaii, Honolulu, 1970—; dir. Békésy Lab. Neurobiology, Honolulu,

1991—. Author: (with others) Animal Learning, 1979; editor: Evolution of Brain and Behavior in Vertebrates, 1976; co-editor: Am. Jour. Psychology, 1955-73; cons. editor Jour. Animal Learning and Behavior, 1973-76, 85-88, Jour. Comparative Psychology, 1988-92. Recipient Humboldt prize Alexander von Humboldt Found., Bonn, W.Ger., 1981; Fulbright grantee; grantee NSF, Office Naval Research, NIMH, Air Force Office Sci. Research, Deutsche Forschungsgemeinschaft. Fellow Soc. Exptl. Psychologists (Warren medal 1997), Am. Psychol. Assn., AAAS; mem. Psychonomic Soc. Home: 229 Kaalawai Pl Honolulu HI 96816-4435 Office: Univ Hawaii Bekesy Lab of Neurobiology 1993 E West Rd Honolulu HI 96822-2321

BITTERS, CONRAD LEE, biological sciences educator; b. Waco, Tex., Jan. 2, 1946; s. E. Conrad and Margaret Lee (Miles) B.; m. Karen Kay, May 1, 1970; children: Rebecca, Brian. BA, Calif. State U., Fresno, 1969. Life Credential, Biol./Phys. Sciences, Calif. Biology/zoology tchr. Clovis (Calif.) High Sch., 1970—, science dept. chmn., 1973-80, biology coordinator, 1980—; founder, sponsor Clovis (Calif.) High Ecology club, 1970—, Clovis High Fgn. Studies Club, 1978-87, 92-97; jr. div. judge Cen. Valley Sci. Fair, Fresno, Calif., 1975—; coach-sr. div. Cen. Valley Sci. Fair, Fresno, 1972—; dist. rep. Jr. Sci. and Humanities Symposium, Berkeley, Calif., 1974—; Calif. Ednl. Initiatives Fund Grant Dir., 1986. Recipient Faculty award Eastman Kodak Co., 1980, Nat. Jr. Sci. and Humanities Symposium, 1985, 93, 94, Merit award Rotary Club Fresno, 1985, 88, 93-94, Faculty Commendation Lawrence Hall of Sci., 1985, 87, 94, John D. Isaacs Scholarship Com., 1985, Outstanding Sci. Tchrs. Fresno County, Dow Chem. Co., 1986, Presdl. award in sci. tchg. Calif. State Dept. Edn., 1986, Faculty Commendation award Calif. Sci. Fair, 1988, 94, commendation Internat. Sci. Engring. Fair, 1982, 93-94, Commendation for Dept. Energy award, 1993. Mem. Nat. Sci. Teachers' Assn. Republican. Mem. LDS Ch. Avocations: hiking, fishing, cross-country skiing, paleontology, international travel. Home: 2695 Armstrong Ave Clovis CA 93611-4167 Office: Clovis HS 1055 Fowler Ave Clovis CA 93611-2099

BITTING, KEVIN NOEL, pediatric craniofacial orthotist, researcher; b. Kenmore, N.Y., Dec. 18, 1957; s. Harry Lincoln Jr. and Shirley Ann (Smith) B. BA, Villanova U., 1980; Degree in Prosthetics, Northwestern U., 1989. Cert. orthotist, Md. Rsch. asst. Villanova (Pa.) U., 1979; orthotist-prosthetist S.W. Lab., Burbank, Calif., 1988—; chief pediatric craniofacial orthotist Cranial Therapies, Inc., Burbank, 1991—. Avocations: Alpine skiing, physical fitness/swimming, computers. Office: Cranial Therapies Inc 1023 N Hollywood Way Ste 103 Burbank CA 91505-2539

BJORKLUND, JANET VINSEN, speech and language pathologist; b. Seattle, July 31, 1947; d. Vernon Edward and Virginia Lea (Rogers) B.; m. Dan Robert Young, Dec. 04, 1971; children: Emery Allen, Alanna Vinsen, Marisa Rogers. Student, U. Vienna, Austria, 1966-67; BA, Pacific U., 1969; student, U. Wash., 1970-71; MA, San Francisco State U., 1977. Cert. clin. speech pathologist, audiologist. Speech pathologist, audiological cons. USN Hosp., Rota, Spain, 1972-75; traineeship in audiology VA Hosp., San Francisco, 1976; speech pathologist San Lorenzo (Calif.) Unified Schs., 1975-77, 78-81; dir. speech pathology St. Lukes Speech and Hearing Clinic, San Francisco, 1977-78; audiologist X.O. Barrios, M.D., San Francisco, 1977-81; cons. Visually Impaired Infant Program, Seattle, 1981-82; speech pathologist Everett (Wash.) Schs., 1982-94; speech-lang. pathologist, supr. Sultan (Wash.) Schs., 1995—; supr. pediat. programs speech pathology Group Health Coop. Puget Sound, Seattle, 1994; rep. profl. edn. adv. com. Office of Supt. of Pub. Instrn., 1995—, Speech-Language Pathologist/Audiologist adv. com., 1995—; cons. Providence Hosp. Childrens Ctr., Everett, 1985-93, Pacific Hearing and Speech, 1988-93. Author: (with others) Screening for Bilingual Preschoolers, 1977, (TV script), Clinical Services in San Francisco, 1978, Developing Better Communication Skills, 1982. Chair Washington Mid. Sch. Site Coun., 1995—. Mem. Am. Speech-Lang. and Hearing Assn., Wash. Speech and Hearing Assn. (regional rep. 1985-86, chair licensure task force 1986-88, rep. Birth to Six Project 1988-91, pres. 1993, speech pathology/audiology adv. com. rep. 1995), Phi Lambda Omicron (pres. Pacific U. chpt. 1968). Congregationalist. Avocations: traveling, needlework, cooking.

BLACHER, JOAN HELEN, psychotherapist, educator; b. L.A., Aug. 10, 1928; d. Albert Scribner and Isabel (Marriott) Oakholt; m. Norman Blacher, July 27, 1973; stepchildren: Eric, Steven, Mark. BA, U. Calif., Berkeley, 1950; MEd, U. So. Calif., 1971, PhD, 1981. Lic. ednl. psychologist, Calif.; lic. marriage, family and child counselor, Calif. Elem. tchr. L.A. Unified Sch. Dist., 1962-71, sch. psychologist, 1971-72, 73-74; sch. psychologist Pasadena (Calif.) Unified Sch. Dist., 1972-73; sch. psychologist Ventura (Calif.) County Supt. Schs., 1974-79, prin., 1979-86; assoc. prof. sch. edn., dir. counseling and guidance program Calif. Luth. U., Thousand Oaks, 1987-98, prof. emerita, 1998—; pvt. practice, Ventura, 1984—. Bd. dirs. Coalition Against Household Violence, Ventura, 1984-85, Camarillo Hosp., 1994—. Mem. APA, Am. Counselors Assn., Am. Ednl. Rsch. Assn., Calif. Assn. Counselors, Educators, Suprs. (past pres.), Calif. Assn. Marriage and Family Therapists, Calif. Assn. Counseling Devel., Phi Delta Kappa. Republican. Avocations: tennis, traveling.

BLACK, BARBARA CROWDER, educational consultant; b. Woodbine, Iowa, Feb. 11, 1922; d. John Hershel and Elsie May (Jenkins) Crowder; m. (Estel) Eugene Black, Sept. 1, 1944; 1 child, (Estel) Eugene Jr. (dec. 1993). AB, N.Mex. Western U., 1946; teaching credential, UCLA, 1964; cert. in reading, math., Calif. State U., 1969, 72; postgrad., Sacramento State U., 1977-89. Cert. tchr., Calif. Tchr. Chavez County Schs., Roswell, N.Mex., 1942-44; tchr. ESL 6th St. Elem. Sch., Silver City, N. Mex., 1946-47; girls athletic coach Silver City Jr. High Sch., Silver City, N. Mex., 1946-47; tchr. Lovington (N.Mex.) Pub. Schs., 1950-51, Long Beach (Calif.) Unified Sch. Dist., 1951-58, Santa Maria (Calif.) Elem. Sch. Dist., 1958-59; tchr. spl. edn. Bellflower (Calif.) Unified Sch. Dist., 1959-67; instr. Sacramento Unified Sch. Dist., 1968-79; co-owner, v.p. El Paso Southwestern R.R. Ednl. Consultants, Sacramento, 1985—; demonstration tchr. Long Beach Unified Sch. Dist., 1952-59; master tchr. to student tchrs. Calif. State U., Long Beach, 1954-59, Sacramento, 1972-73; supr. tchr. aides Sacramento Unified Sch. Dsit., 1969-79; co-editor revision of math. testing materials, 1977; English instr. Jian Ping Middle Sch., Shanghai, China, 1992; pvt. tutor to elem. students in computers, math. and reading, 1994—; seminar coord. China New Renaissance Soc., U. Calif., Sacramento, geneal. rschr. and historian, 1996—. Co-author tchr. manuals in sci. and arithmetic, tchrs. guide for social studies; cons., editor: Barking at Shadows (Gene Black, Jr.), 1994, Effing the Ineffible (Gene Black, Jr.), 1995. Elder Westminster Presbyn. Ch., Sacramento, 1973—; Bd. dirs. Calif. State R.R. Mus. Docents, Sacramento, 1981-89; vol. Jed Smith Sch. Computer Class, Sacramento, 1989, Habitat for Humanity, 1994; mem. Friends of Sacramento Pub. Libr., Calif. State Libr. Found. Grantee Sacramento County Office Edn., 1969, Calif. Dept. Edn., 1972-73, Study-Miller Math Specialists; recipient cert. spl. commendation Calif. Dept. Parks, 1988. Mem. Calif. Tchrs. Assn., Calif. Ret. Tchrs. Assn., Calif. State Libr. Found., Sacramento State Parks Docent Assn. (membership chair 1981-87, Outstanding Svc. award 1983, 86, 87, 89, Silver cert. for 15 yrs. Vol. Svc. Calif. State Railroad Mus.), Renaissance Soc. (Calif. State U. Sacramento), Sigma Tau Delta (pres. 1944-46). Avocations: travel, computers, swimming, genealogy. Office: El Paso Southwestern R R 1500 7th St Sacramento CA 95814-5444

BLACK, EILEEN MARY, elementary school educator; b. Bklyn., Sept. 20, 1944; d. Marvin Mize and Anne Joan (Salvia) B. Student, Grossmont Coll., El Cajon, Calif., 1964; BA, San Diego State U., 1967; postgrad., U. Calif., San Diego, Syracuse U. Cert. tchr., Calif. Tchr. La Mesa (Calif.)-Spring Valley Sch. Dist., 1967—. NDEA grantee Syracuse U., 1968; recipient 30 Yrs. Svc. award La Mesa-Spring Valley Sch. Dist., 1997. Mem. Calif. Tchrs. Assn., Greenpeace, San Diego Zoological Soc., Wilderness Soc. Roman Catholic. Avocations: reading, baseball, walking. Home: 9320 Earl St Apt 15 La Mesa CA 91942-3846 Office: Lemon Ave Elem Sch 8787 Lemon Ave La Mesa CA 91941-5459

BLACK, LAVONNE PATRICIA, special education educator; b. West Palm Beach, Fla., Sept. 28, 1924; d. Harvey Francis Paul and Elsie Marguerite (Theegarten) B. Diploma, Palm Beach Jr. Coll., 1945; BA in Edn., Fla. State Coll. for Women, 1947; MA in Edn., George Peabody Coll. Tchrs., 1964. Cert. tchr. elem. edn. reading, hearing disabilities, motor disabilities, Fla.; cert. tchr. social studies, elem. edn., Kans.; cert. elem. edn. spl. hard of hearing-orthopedic, Ky. Tchr. physically handicapped Bd. Pub. Instr., West Palm Beach, 1947-58; tchr. deaf and hard of hearing Royal Palm Sch., West Palm Beach, 1952-58; tchr. physically handicapped/learning disorders Bd. Pub. Instrn. Exceptional Child Ctr., Ft. Lauderdale, Fla., 1958-69; dir., tchr. Scenicland Sch., Chattanooga, 1969-70; occupational edn. tchr. John Currie Jr. High Sch., Jacksonville, Fla., 1970-71; substitute tchr. Iliff Pre-Sch., Denver, 1972, University Park Coop., Denver, 1973, Austin Presch., 1973; house mother Sigma Alpha Epsilon Fraternity, U. Denver, 1971—; organizer, mgr. Sigma Alpha Epsilon Summer Rental Program, 1976—. Inventor portable sound chart for Lang., reading, speech, 1964. Active Jr. Welfare League, Inc., Palm Beach and Ft. Lauderdale.; secret spl. messenger Morrison Field, West Palm Beach, World War II, summer 1942. Recipient Thomas G. Goodale award for disting. svc. U. Denver, 1991. Mem. Coun. Exceptional Children, PEO, Palm Beach Jr. Coll. Alumni Assn., Kappa Alpha Theta. Democrat. Methodist. Avocations: swimming, dancing, backgammon, walking, travel. Home and Office: Sigma Alpha Epsilon 2050 S Gaylord St Denver CO 80210-4306

BLACK, LEE ROY, investment professional, consultant; b. Chgo.; s. Lee Roy and Christine (Gray) B. BBA with highest honors, Long Beach Coll., 1995. Cons., advisor to pvt. bus. orgns. Calif., 1998—; cons., advisor to pvt. bus. orgns., Calif., 1998—. Author: The Four Elements of Success, 1998. Mem. Phi Beta Kappa. Democrat/Libertarian. Avocations: tennis, bicycling, art, weight lifting, basketball. Home: 15220 Ocaso Ave # H207 La Mirada CA 90638-5063

BLACK, NOEL ANTHONY, television and film director; b. Chgo., June 30, 1937; s. Samuel Abraham and Susan (Quan) B.; m. Catherine Elizabeth Cownie, June 1, 1988; children: Marco Eugene, Nicole Alexandra, Carmen Elizabeth, Catherine Ellen. BA, UCLA, 1959, MA, 1964. Ind. fil, TV dir., 1966—; asst. prof. grad. program Inst. Film and TV, Tisch Sch. of Arts, NYU, 1992-93. Dir. (TV films) Trilogy: The American Boy, 1967 (Outstanding Young Dir. award Monte Carlo Internat. Festival of TV, Silver Dove award Internat. Cath. Soc. for Radio and TV), I'm a Fool, 1977, Mulligan's Stew, 1977, The Golden Honeymoon, 1979, The Electric Grandmother, 1981 (George Foster Peabody award 1982), The Other Victim, 1981, prime Suspect, 1981, Happy Endings, 1982, Quarterback Princess, 1983, Deadly Intentions, 1985, Promises to Keep, 1985, A Time to Triumph, 1985, My Two Loves, 1986, Conspiracy of Love, 1987, The Town Bully, 1988, Hollow Boy, 1991, (short films) Skaterdater, 1966 (Grand Prix award Cannes XX Film Festival, Grand Prix Tech. Cannes XX Internat. Film Festival, awards Cork Film Festival, Silver medal Moscow Internat. Film Festival, others), Riverboy, 1967 (Lion of St. Mark awrad Venice Internat. Film Festival, 1st prize Vancouver Internat. Film Festival), (feature films) Pretty Poison, 1968, Mirrors, 1974, A Man, A Woman and A Bank, 1978; screenwriter, exec. prodr. Mischief, 1984. Mem. Writers Guild Am., Dirs. Guild Am., Acad. Motion Picture Arts and Scis., Acad. TV Arts and Scis. Office: Starfish Prodns 126 Wadsworth Ave Santa Monica CA 90405-3510

BLACK, PETE, retired state legislator, educator; b. Ansbach, Germany, Sept. 16, 1946; came to U.S., 1948; s. Howard and Kadi (Fietz) B.; m. Ronda Williams, July 12, 1970; 1 child, Darin. BS, Idaho State U., 1975, MEd, 1998. Cert. elem. tchr. Tchr. Pocatello (Idaho) Sch. Dist., 1975—; mem. Idaho Ho. Reps., Boise, 1983-96, asst. minority leader, 1987-96; tech. tng. specialist Sch. Dist. 25, 1996—; mem. edn. tech. coun.; mem. adv. coun. chpt. II ESEA. Bd. dirs. Arts for Idaho. With USNR, 1964. Mem. NEA, Idaho Edn. Assn. (bd. dirs.), Idaho Libr. Assn. (state libr. bd.). Democrat. Home: 2249 Cassia St Pocatello ID 83201-2059 Office: Idaho House of Reps Statehouse Mail Boise ID 83720

BLACK, RICHARD BRUCE, business executive, consultant; b. Dallas, July 25, 1933; s. James Ernest and Minerva Iantha (Braden) B.; children: Kathryn Braden, Paula Anne (dec.), Erica Lynn. BS in Engring., Tex. A&M U., 1954; MBA, Harvard U., 1958, postgrad., Northwestern U., 1960-62; PhD (hon.), Beloit Coll., 1967. With Vulcan Materials Co., Birmingham, Ala., 1958-62; v.p. fin. Warner Electric Brake & Clutch Co., Beloit, Wis., 1962-67, dir., 1973-85; pres. automotive group, exec. v.p. corp. Maremont Corp., Chgo., 1967-72, pres. corp., COO, 1972-76, pres., chmn., CEO, 1976-79; pres., CEO, dir. Alusuisse of Am., Inc., N.Y.C., 1979-81; chmn., CEO, dir. AM Internat., Inc., Chgo., 1981-82; owner R. Black & Assocs., 1983—; chmn. ECRM, Boston, 1983—; pres., dir. Oak Technology, Inc., Sunnyvale, Calif., 1998—; bd. dirs. Gabelli Funds, Inc., Gen. Scanning Corp., Morgan Group Inc., Benedetto Gartland, Inc., Grand Eagle Cos., Inc.; lectr. econs. Beloit (Wis.) Coll., 1964-67. Author: (with Jack Pierson) Linear Polyethylene-Propylene: Problems and Opportunities, 1958. Trustee Beloit Coll., Am. Indian Coll. Fund., N.Y.C., Teton Sci. Sch., Bard Coll. Ctr. for Curatorial Studies, Inst. for Advanced Study, Princeton, N.J., Snake River Conservancy Found. 1st lt. USAF, 1954-56. Recipient Flame of Hope Lifetime Achievement award, Am. Indian Coll. Fund, 1998. Mem. Am. Alpine Club, Harvard Club (N.Y.C.).

BLACK, ROBERT CLIFFORD, III, history educator; b. N.Y.C., Feb. 11, 1914; s. Robert Clifford and Beatrice (Cluett) B.; B.A., Williams Coll., 1937; M.A., U. Denver, 1947; Ph.D., Columbia U., 1951; m. Regina Ann Maleham, Sept. 5, 1939; children: Maleham C., R. Clifford, Beatrice (Mrs. Rolland W. Hoverstock), John N., Peter N., James A. Instr. history Rensselear Poly. Inst., Troy, N.Y., 1945-48; instr. history Trinity Coll., Hartford, Conn., 1950-52, assoc. prof., 1952-66; prof. history Colo. Women's Coll., Denver, 1965-79, emeritus, 1979—; lectr. in field. Dist. committeeman West Hartford Republican Com., 1954-66; bd. dirs. Hist. Denver Inc., 1974-76. Served to capt. AUS, 1942-45. Recipient Merit award Am. Assn. State and Local History, 1970. Mem. Am., Can., Conn., Colo. hist. assns., Assn. Am. Historians, Colo. Hist. Soc. (dir. 1969-88), Friends of Denver Pub. Library, Alpha Delta Phi., Pi Gamma Mu. Episcopalian. Clubs: Denver Country, Denver, Williams. Author: The Railroads of The Confederacy, 1952, The Younger John Winthrop, 1966, Island in the Rockies, 1969, Railroad Pathfinder, 1988. Home: 1510 E 10th Ave Apt 8E Denver CO 80218-3105

BLACK, RONALD ROSS, educator, basketball coach; b. Clovis, N.Mex., July 2, 1942; s. Ralph Ross and Laura Pearl (Smiley) B.; m. Carol Jan Simmons, Aug. 25, 19`'; children: Kevin R., Karla Black Crow, Shannon D. BA, Eastern N.Mex. U., 1964, MA, 1965. Instr. Cameron State Coll., Lawton, Okla., 1965-66; prof. N.Mex. Jr. Coll., Hobbs, 1966—, head basketball coach, 1978—. Named Prof. of Yr., N.Mex. Jr. Coll., 1978, Coach of Yr., Western Jr. Coll. Athletic Conf., 196,87, 92, 95, Region V/Nat. Jr. Coll. Athletic Assn., 1995, 96. Mem. Nat. Jr. Coll. Coaches Assn., S.W. Basketball Coaches Assn. (v.p. 1990-91). Republican. Baptist. Avocations: golf, travel, sailing. Office: NMex Jr Coll 5317 N Lovington Hwy Hobbs NM 88240-9121

BLACK, ROSA VIDA, writer, educator; b. Lovell, Wyo., Sept. 18, 1903; d. Robert John Bischoff and Rose Ann Jensen; m. Clinton Melford Black, June 4, 1925 (dec. May 1989); children: Harvey, Jean, Homer, John, Evelyn, Merrill, Francis, Carol. Student, U. Wyo., 1922-24, U. Utah, 1946. Tchr. Converse Sch. Dist., Douglas, Wyo., 1922-23, Granite Sch. Dist., Salt Lake City, 1946, Granger Camp Daus. of Utah Pioneers, Salt Lake City, 1950—; speech dir. Kearns 13th ward L.D.S. Ch. Young Women Mut. Improvement Assn., 1968, pres., 1924-25; writer, narrator script Kearns North Stake Relief Soc. Singing Mothers Concert, 1967, 68; lectr. on womanhood and patriotic subjects to girls' groups; writer, presenter tribute to builders of Lovell Canal, 1993; program chmn. Basin (Wyo.) Woman's Club, 1942. Author: Mother of the Year, 1969, Mother Stood Tall, 1971, Open Door to the Heart, 1986, Meet My Wonderful Family, 1993, Pioneer Stories of Yesterday for Children of All Ages of Today and Tomorrow, 1997; (essays) I Believe, 1996; (histories) Under Granger Skies, 1963 (award), Proud of Kearns, 1979 (award), Lovell, Our Pioneer Heritage, 1986, Pioneer Stories of Yesterday for Children of Today and tomorrow, 1997; co-author: Living Testimonies, Personal Histories, 1967. Panel advisor PTA, Salt Lake City, 1950; judge of election Rep. Party, Lovell, 1924; reader Relief Soc., Granger, Utah, 1953, pres., 1934-41, organist, 1957-60, social sci. tchr., 1952-54, theology tchr., 1954; mem. Young Women Orgn., pres., 1944; missionary, Australia, 1971-73, Nauvoo, Ill., 1975-77; asst., planner children's parade, Laramie, Wyo., 1932; counselor Stake Relief Soc., Laramie, 1931; pres. Children's Primary Orgn., Basin, Wyo., 1941-42. Recipient Cert. of Merit, Am. Mothers com., 1969. Mem. Daus. of the Utah Pioneers (capt. 1968—, pres. 1988-89, tchr. 1992—). Democrat. Mormon. Avocations: reading, writing, visiting with friends and family. Office: Daus of Utah Pioneers 330 N Main St Salt Lake City UT 84103-1632

BLACK, SUSAN EASTON, religious studies educator, writer; b. Long Beach, Calif., Nov. 9, 1944; m. Harvey Black. EdD, Brigham Young U., 1978. Prof. church history and doctrine Brigham Young U., Provo, Utah, 1978-97. Author: Nauvoo, 1997, Who's Who in the Doctrine and Covenants, 1997, Impressions of Joseph Smith, 1998. Recipient Sundberg Rsch. and Writing award, 1978, Joseph Fielding Smith fellowship, 1986, Utah Heritage award Calif. Utah Women, 1995.

BLACK, WILLIAM REA, lawyer; b. N.Y.C., Nov. 4, 1952; s. Thomas Howard and Dorothy Chambers (Dailey) B.; m. Kathleen Jane Owen, June 24, 1978; children: William Ryan, Jonathan Wesley. BSBA, U. Denver, 1978, MBA, 1981; JD, Western State U., Fullerton, Calif., 1987. Bar: Calif., U.S. Ct. Appeals (fed. cir.), U.S. Dist. Ct.; lic. real estate broker. Bus. mgr. Deere & Co., Moline, Ill., 1979-85; dir. Mgmt. Resource Svcs. Co., Chgo., 1985-86; sr. v.p. Geneva Corp., Irvine, Calif., 1986-91; pvt. practice Newport Beach, Calif., 1991-92; gen. counsel Sunclipse, Inc., 1992-98; spl. counsel Amcor, Ltd., 1992-98; dir. gen. Amcor de Mex., S.A. de C.V., 1993-98; secretario KHL de Mex. S.A. de C.V., 1995-98; CEO Kuroi Kiku Corp., Kuroi Ryu Corp., First Reconnaissance Co.; exec. v.p., dir., gen. counsel, sec. LL Knickerbocker Co., Inc., 1997—, Mann-Craft, Inc., Pyraponic Industries, Arkenol Asia, Inc.; dir. Anle Paper Co.; sec. Krasner Group, TCJC, Inc., Charisma Mfg. Co., Inc., KGI Fashions, Inc., Dermasci. Labs., Inc., Raymark Container, Inc., Georgetown Collection, Inc., Magic Attic Press, Inc., The LL Knickerbocker Co. (Thailand), Ltd., Harlyn Internat. Co., Ltd., S.L.S. Trading Co., Ltd., Am. Employers Def., Inc. Mng. editor Western State U. Law Rev., Fullerton, 1984-87. Instr. Pai Lum Kung Fu Karate, Hartford, Conn., 1970-75, U.S. Judo Assn., Denver, 1975-80, United Senpo, L.A., 1995—. Recipient Am. Jurisprudence award Bancroft-Whitney Co., 1984, 85, 86; Pres.'s scholar full acad. merit scholarship, 1983. Mem. ABA, Am. Soc. Appraisers, Inst. Bus. Appraisers, Assn. Productivity Specialists, Am. Employment Law Coun., Profls. in Human Resources Assn., Am. Mgmt. Assn., Orange County Bar Assn., L.A. County Bar Assn., Mu Kappa Tau. Avocations: karate (2d degree black belt), skiing, scuba, golf. Office: The LL Knickerbocker Co Inc 25800 Commercentre Dr Lake Forest CA 92630-8804

BLACKBURN, CHARLES EDWARD, manufacturing executive; b. Detroit, June 19, 1939; s. Wallace Manders and Elva Jean (Beetham) B.; m. Judith Ann Brady, June 30, 1979. BS, Baldwin-Wallace Coll., 1961; MBA, Pepperdine U., 1990. Assoc. rsch. chemist Parke-Davis and Co., Ann Arbor, Mich., 1963-71; mgr. Mallinckrodt Chem. Works, St. Louis, 1971-74; sr. product mgr. Packard Instrument Co., Downers Grove, Ill., 1974-77; product mktg. mgr. Beckman Instruments, Fullerton, Calif., 1977-80; gen. sales mgr. Wahl Instruments, Culver City, Calif., 1980-84; v.p. Signet Sci. Co., El Monte, Calif., 1984-91; chmn., CEO "C" Enterprises, San Marcos, Calif., 1991—. Contbr. articles to profl. jours. Mem. Rotary Internat. (sec. 1983, pres. 1984). Avocation: boating. Office: "C" Enterprises 540 S Pacific St San Marcos CA 92069-4056

BLACKBURN, FRANK THOMAS, emergency water supply executive; b. San Francisco, Mar. 4, 1933; s. Frank Paul and Sylvia Josephine (Rosenlund) B.; m. Irmgard Knitt, Dec. 1, 1968 (div. 1978); children: Ingrid, Matthew. Student, Cogswell Poly., San Francisco, 1951-52, San Francisco State U., 1960-62; AA, City Coll. San Francisco, 1966. Asst. fire chief San Francisco Fire Dept., 1956-91; instr. City Coll. San Francisco, 1978-83; dir. earthquake preparedness City of San Francisco, 1986-88; pres. Portable Water Supply System Co., Ltd., Redwood City, Calif., 1989—; dir. ops. PWSS Rescue Operation, U.S. Army, Zaire, 1994-95; mem. Nat. Std. Com. State of Calif. Inventor portable hydrant; co-author tech. studies. With USN, 1951-59. Recipient commendations Bd. Suprs. San Francisco, 1986, 89, City of Erie, Pa., 1990, U.S. Senator Diane Feinstein, 1994; Commander award U.S. Army, 1994, Humanitarion award M.L. King Jr. Civic Com. San Francisco, 1995. Fellow U.S. Naval Inst., San Francisco Fire Chiefs Assn., Dolphin Swimming & Rowing Club. Republican. Lutheran. Avocations: skiing, swimming, hiking. Office: PWSS Co Ltd 7 Balhi Ct San Francisco CA 94112-3205

BLACKETER, JAMES RICHARD, artist; b. Laguna Beach, Calif., Sept. 24, 1931; s. Cleo Toby and Ida Hattie (Renter) B.; m. Gloria Jean Blacketer, June 20, 1971 (div. Aug. 1975); children: Susan Elizabeth Glover, Mary Jane Kelsey; m. Frances Blacketer. Owner Blacketer Sign Co., Laguna Beach, 1950-53; designer/art dir. Fed. Sign and Signal Corp., Santa Ana, Calif., 1953-73; owner The Studio Antiques, Laguna Beach, 1973-95. Exhibited in group shows at Showcase 21, L.A., 1959, The Studio Gallery, Laguna Beach, Ferguson Gallery, La Jolla, Long Beach Art Mus., Porth Gallery, Laguna Beach, Pasadena Art Mus., Los Angeles County Fair, Laguna Beach Art Festival, Fresno Art Mus., Ebell Club, L.A., Wells Gallery, Laguna Beach, others; represented in permanent collections at Norton Simon Art Mus., Laguna Beach Art Assn., South Coast Med. Ctr. Bd. dirs. festival of Arts, Laguna Beach, 1965-66. Recipient Nat. Award for Outdoor Advertising, Nat. Elec. Sign Assn., 1970, 71, 72, Nat. Award for Design, Nat. Interscholastic Art Assn., Pitts., 1950, Calif. Award for poster design Am. Legion, State of Calif., 1946; winner various painting awards, 1950—. Mem. Laguna Beach Art Assn. (art dir. 1968-69, bd. dirs. 1969-70). Avocations: antique and art collecting, antique automobiles, designing historical home interiors. Home: 266 Canyon Acres Dr Laguna Beach CA 92651-1106

BLACKFIELD, CECILIA MALIK, civic volunteer, educator; b. Oakland, Calif., Jan. 18, 1915; d. Benjamin Malik and Mollie Saak; m. William Blackfield, Dec. 25, 1941; children: Leland Gregory, Pamela Esther, Karen Ann. BA, U. Calif., Berkeley, 1936; MEdn., San Francisco State Tchrs. Coll., 1937. cert. elem. tchr. Calif. (lifetime). Tchr. Albany (Calif.) Sch. Dist., 1938-43; rep. NEA, Alameda County, Calif., 1938-43. Pres. Calif. Tchrs. Assn., Alameda County, Calif., 1939; mem. (charter) Territorial Hosp. Aux., Kauikeolani Children's Hosp. (bd. dirs.); bd. dirs. Hastings Law Sch. Found., San Francisco, Calif., McCoy Pavilion Park, Honolulu, Hi., Daughters of the Nile, Honolulu, Temple Emmanuel; mem. Mayor's Citizen Advisory Com. for Diamond Head, Wakiki, Honolulu, Mayor's Adv. Com. for Community & Urban Renewal, Beautification Com., League of Women Voters; chmn. Hawaii Cancer Fund Crusade and many more; mem. master planning com. Vision for Waikiki 2020; mem. Preservation Rev. Com. Hist. Hawaii. Named Woman of the Year for Nat. Brotherhood Week, Honolulu, 1972. Mem. Nat. Assn. Home Builders (pres. Hawaii chpt. women's aux.), Outdoor Circle (pres.), Friends of Foster Gardens, Washington Palace State Capitol, Hadassah (past pres. Oakland chpt.), Women's Com. Brandeis U. (life mem.). Avocations: bridge, orchidist. Home: 901 Kealaolu Ave Honolulu HI 96816-5416

BLACKHAM, LEONARD MOYLE, state senator; b. Mt. Pleasant, Utah, Aug. 26, 1949; m. Laura Bagley, Feb. 20, 1970; 6 children. AS, Snow Coll., 1969; BS, Utah State U., 1971. Turkey prodr. agrl. co-op bus.; mem. Utah Ho. of Reps., 1992-94; mem. Utah State Senate, 1994—, majority whip, 1995-96, mem. legis. exec. appropriations com., mem. legis. tax and revenue standing com.; chmn. bd. dirs. Moroni Feed Co.; bd. dirs. Norbest; mem. various coms. including energy, natural resources, agrl. standing. Past county commr. Republican. Office: PO Box 394 Moroni UT 84646-0394

BLACKMAN, DAVID LEE, research scientist; b. Chgo., Jan. 4, 1948; s. Sol and Carol Edith (Rothman) B. BS in Maths., U. Ariz., 1973; student, Laney Coll., Oakland, Calif., 1977-79; MS in Chemistry, San Francisco State U., 1983. Lic. technician. Rsch. cons. Detox Assn., San Bernadino, Calif., 1973-74; peer counselor Laney Coll., 1977-79; lectr. San Francisco State U., 1979-83; staff rsch. assoc. U. Calif., Berkeley, 1984—; speaker PEW Found., N.Y., 1989. Author: Flourescent Spectroscopy..., 1983; contbr. articles to profl. jours. Mem. adv. bd. P.P. Land Conservancy, Berkeley, 1984-86; bd. dirs. Cmty. Svcs. United, Berkeley, 1985-86; vol. No. Alameda ARES/RACES, Berkeley, 1992-95. NSF grantee, 1989, 91. Mem. AAAS, Am. Assn. Physics Tchrs., Am. Radio Relay League, Co-op. Am., N.Y. Acad. Sci., Golden Gate Nat. Park Assn., Sierra Club, Mensa. Democrat. Jewish. Avocations: photography, computers, water coloring, swimming, non-linear dynamics. Home: 307 W 2nd St Phoenix OR 97535-0514

BLACKMAN, HAROLD STABLER, research scientist; b. Phoenix, June 13, 1953; s. Robert D. and Mollie D. (Wusich) B.; m. Marsha H., Nov. 8, 1975; 1 child, Allison M. BAE in Secondary Edn. Biology, Ariz. State U., 1975, MA in Ednl. Psychology, 1979, PhD in Ednl. Psychology, 1980. Biology tchr. Carl Hayden H.S., Phoenix, 1975-77; rsch. and evaluation staff mem. Mesa (Ariz) Pub. Schs., 1979-81; asst. prof. Idaho State U., Pocatello, 1981—; scientist Idaho Nat. Engring. Lab EG&G Idaho, Idaho Falls, 1982-86, unit mgr. human factors, 1986-91, group mgr. risk assessment and applied math., 1991-94; dept. mgr. engring. analysis Idaho Nat. Engring. Lab. Lockheed Martin Idaho, Idaho Falls, 1994-98; chief engr. Techs. Co., Idaho Falls, 1998—. Author: User Computer Interface in Process Control, 1989, Human Reliability and Safety Analysis, 1993; editor: (book) Human Reliability Models, 1998, (jour.) Internat. Jour. Cognition, 1997—. Fellow Human Factors Soc.; mem. Am. Psychol. Assn., Nat. Rsch. Coun. Program (mem. tech. rev. com.). Home: 2754 Waterford Ct Idaho Falls ID 83404-7366 Office: Idaho Nat Engring Lab PO Box 1625 Idaho Falls ID 83415-0001

BLACKMAN, JEFFREY WILLIAM, lawyer; b. L.A., Oct. 24, 1948; s. Ralph Leonard and Judith Esther (Glantz) B. BA, U. Ariz., 1970, JD, 1976. Bar: Ariz. 1976, U.S. Dist. Ct. Ariz. 1977, U.S. Ct. Appeals (9th cir.) 1980, U.S. Supreme Ct. 1980, U.S. Dist. Ct. (no. dist.) Calif. 1988. Pvt. practice law Oracle, Ariz., 1977-85; assoc. with several law firms Phoenix, Tucson, 1986-87; pvt. practice law Tucson, 1988—. Participant March for the Animals, Washington, 1990, 96. 2d lt. ROTC, U.S. Army, 1968-69. Recipient Cert. of Appreciation, Ctr. for Environ. Edn. Whale Protection Fund, 1984, UNICEF, Defenders of Wildlife, Nat. Humane Edn. Soc., ASPCA, Nation of Israel, Wine Diploma, San Francisco Wine Inst. Wine Adv. Bd., 1964; named Ptnr. for Life, Cal Farley's Boy Ranch, Amarillo, Tex., 1982. Mem. State Bar Ariz., Mensa, Alliance Francaise. Democrat. Jewish. Avocations: rock drummer, tennis, desert hiking, gardening, animal welfare. Office: PO Box 41624 Tucson AZ 85717-1624

BLACKMAN, WILLIAM HENRY, artist, educator; b. San Diego, Feb. 2, 1930; s. Phillip Jackson and Mary Kathrine (Blankenship) B.; m. Shirley Lorraine Ramos, June 11, 1955; children: William James, Denise Marie. BA, Woodbury Coll., L.A., 1954. Advt. prodn.mgr. Lennen & Newell/EWRR BBDO, L.A., 1958-65; fine artist self employed, Thousand Oaks, Calif., 1965—. Author, illustrator: Oil Painting the Easy Way, 1995, II, 1996, Lighted Windows and Gardens, 1997; exhibited works at Pomeroy Gallery Fine Art, Carmel, Calif., Kobayashi's Art Enterprise, Honolulu, Copenhagen Gallery, Solvang, Calif., Houstonian Art Gallery, Spring, Tex., Austin St. Gallery, Rockport, Tex. Served with USN, 1949-50. Avocations: tennis, golf. Home and Studio: 2369 Magda Cir Thousand Oaks CA 91360-1829

BLACKMAN-BUCKOUT, JOANN LOUISE, accountant; b. Culver City, Calif., July 29, 1938; d. William Henry Blackman and Ann Marie (Chandler) Sobodos; m. Robert W. Beardslee, Oct. 5, 1975 (div.); m. Daniel Bryan Buckout, Feb. 22, 1992; children: Gregory, Gary, Robert, Alan, Bradley, William. D in Hosp. Adminstrn., U. Saskatchewan, 1981. Bus. mgr. Del Amo Psychiat. Hosp., Torrance, Calif., 1972-78, Comp. Care Corp., Kirkland, Wash., 1978-80; asst. adminstr. Comp. Care Corp., St. Louis, 1980-82; regional coord. Comp. Care Corp., Newport Beach, Calif., 1982-85; adminstr. Comp. Care Corp., Portland, Oreg., 1985-87; exec. dir. McMinnville (Oreg.) Hosp., 1987-89; exec. dir. Heritage Health Corp., Melbourne, Fla., 1989-90, v.p., COO, 1990-91; cons., 1991-92; finance dir. Devils Lake Rock Co., Lincoln City, Oreg., 1992-96; staff acct. Harrison & Trope, Newport, Oreg., 1996—; cons., 1980—. Author: ABC's of Workshop Presentations, 1992, Producing Community Theater, 1994; prodr. Porthole Players, 1995—. Chair Jobs Plus Adv. Coun, Newport, 1993-96; pres. Lincoln County Devel. Corp., Newport, 1993-95; bd. dirs. Cmty. Svcs. Consorrium, 1994-95, Oreg. Coast Coun. Arts, Newport, 1997—. Mem. Lincoln City C.C. (chair econ. devel. 1994-95, named Woman of Yr. 1995), Newport C.C. (ambassdor 1996—), Delphos (sec./treas. 1994—), Toastmasters (v.p. 1992-95), Kiwanis (v.p. 1987—). Avocations: writing, artist. Office: Harrison & Trope CPAs 157 NW 15th St Newport OR 97365-2367

BLACKSTOCK, JOSEPH ROBINSON, newspaper editor; b. L.A., Dec. 8, 1947; s. Joseph Richard McCall and Doris Louise (Robinson) B.; m. Nancy Ruth Frederiksen, Feb. 9, 1974; children: Miriam, Susan, Cynthia, Catherine. BA, Calif. State U., L.A., 1970, MA, 1977. Sports writer Monterey Park Californian, 1967-72; sports and news writer, mng. editor San Gabriel Valley Tribune, West Covina, Calif., 1972-89; exec. editor Pasadena (Calif.) Star-News, 1989-93; layout editor Riverside (Calif.) Press-Enterprise, 1993-98; asst. city editor Inland Valley Daily Bull., Ontario, Calif., 1998—. With USAR, 1970-78.

BLACKSTOCK, VIRGINIA HARRIETT, artist; b. St. Louis; d. Charles William Valentine and Ruth (Winn) Arnott; m. Ross Holcomb Blackstock, June 13, 1953; children: Susan, Kathleen, Julianne, Brian. BS, Mo. U., 1950; MA, U. Wis., 1952. Cert. tchr. Mo. Tchr. Ctrl. Mo. State U., U. of the South, Tenn., We. State Coll., Colo.; instr. watercolor painting and drawing workshops. Artist in watercolors; exhibited in 35 one person month-long gallery and mus. exhibits; group shows in Watercolor Soc. Exhbns. include Ariz., Colo., Kans., Ky., Mont., N.Mex., La., Okla., Pa. and San Diego Nat. Watercolor Soc., Rocky Mountain Nat. Exhbn., Nat. Watercolor Soc., Audubon Artists, Inc., N.Y., Allied Artists of Am., Adirondacks Nat., C.M. Russell Mus. Auction; paintings in books include Creative Watercolor A Step by Step Guide, Beckwith, The Artistic Touch I and III, Unwin, Abstracts in Watercolor, Schlemm, Exploring Color (revised edit.), Leland. She was commissioned to do a painting for the cover of Ouray Summer Guide, '94, and a poster for the Ouray (Colo.) Chamber Music Festival; She created a 17' by 40' mural for the city of Delta, Colo. honoring the cattle industry. Quick draw artist at several fund raising auctions for non-profit orgns. and worthy causes. Winner Am. Artist Mag. Preserving Our Nat. Resources Contest, 1990, hon. mention Artist's Mag. Mem. Colo. Watercolor Soc. (signature mem.), N. Mex. Watercolor Soc. (signature mem.), Pa. Watercolor Soc. (signature mem.), Mont. Watercolor Soc. (signature mem.), We. Colo. Watercolor Soc. (signature mem., exhbn. chair 1991, 92, 93, 98), La. Watercolor Soc. (signature mem.), Am. Watercolor Soc. (assoc.), Midwest Watercolor Soc. (assoc.), Kans. Watercolor Soc. (signature mem.), N.W. Watercolor Soc. (assoc.), Audubon Aritsts (assoc.), Allied Artists of Am. (assoc.). Episcopalian. Avocations: skiing, biking, hiking, photography. E-mail: ruthhb@dmea.net. Home and Studio: 3101 L Rd Hotchkiss CO 81419-9409

BLACKWELL, SAVANNAH ROSE, journalist; b. Austin, June 3, 1969; d. Michael George Hauty and Rose Ann Blackwell. BA with honors, U. Va., 1991; MS with honors, Columbia U., 1992. Reporter Daily News, N.Y.C., 1992, Phila. Inquirer, 1993-94, Tallahassee (Fla.) Dem., 1994-95, Valley Times, Pleasanton, Calif., 1996, San Francisco Bay Guardian, 1996—; correspondent TCI/SF Newshour, 1998—. Recipient 1st place Peninsula Press Club, 1997; 3d place Nat. Newspapers Assn., 1997, hon. mention, 1997; 2d place Calif. Newspapers Pubs. Assn., 1998; Pulitzer Traveling fellow, 1992-93. Mem. Soc. Profl. Journalists, Investigative Reporters & Editors. Avocations: archaeology, piano, painting. Home: 330 Parnassus Ave Apt 102 San Francisco CA 94117-3735 Office: San Francisco Bay Guardian 520 Hampshire St San Francisco CA 94110-1417

BLADEK, PAUL THOMAS, computer science educator, shop owner; b. Spokane, Wash., Apr. 5, 1955; s. Francis A. and Beatrice K. (Koontz) B.; m. Jacqueline Mae (Wentz) Jensen, July 18, 1996. BA with honors, Gonzaga U., 1977, MFA, U. Ky., 1980; MS, Eastern Wash. U., Cheney, 1989. Cert. state tchg., Wash. Owner, operator Personal Video Graphics, Spokane, 1987—; chair computing dept. Spokane Falls C.C., 1991—. Grad. fellow U. Ky., 1978. Fax: 509-533-3856. E-mail: paulb@sfcc.spokane.cc.wa.us. Home: PO Box 38 Spokane WA 99210 Office: Spokane Falls C C 3410 W Fort George Wright Dr Spokane WA 99224

[illegible faded entry]
BLAIR, ROMAN [...] and [...] (Rodriguez) B. [...] studies guitar, Calif., Colo., Utah, Wyo. Writer, performer various popular music revues, Calif., Colo., Utah, N.Mex., Wyo., 1979—; lead The Small, Glowing Loverock band, 1984—; co-writer, performer, mus. dir. A Day in the Night of Adam Starr U. Wyo., Laramie. Composer: (recordings) Marla Slaine,

1981, Feigned Love, 1981, Beginning Goodbye, 1982, Heart of Rock, 1983, A Ring of Soul, 1983, A Changing Grace, 1984, Damnasty Lee Sway, 1984, Up to Now, 1985, Live from 2929, 1986, Queen Exchanger, 1987, There, With Faith by Your Side, 1985, Heavy Day, Heavy Night, 1988, Certain Magic, 1989—, Neoteric, 1993, Generation Z, 1995. Vol. United Way Sr. Ctr., Laramie, 1980-93; producer fundraising concert A.C.E., 1988-89. Mem. Internat. Platform Assn., Performing Artists Soc. Am. Avocation: tennis. Home and Office: PO Box 474 Laramie WY 82073-0474

BLAIR, EDWARD PAYSON, theology educator; b. Woodburn, Oreg., Dec. 23, 1910; s. Oscar Newton and Bertha (Myers) B.; m. Vivian Krisel, Sept. 13, 1934; children: Phyllis, Sharon. BA, Seattle Pacific U., 1931; S.T.B., N.Y. Theol. Sem., 1934; PhD, Yale U., 1939. Ordained to ministry Free Meth. Ch., 1939; transferred to Meth. Ch., 1950. Prof. Bible Seattle Pacific U., 1939-41, dean Sch. of Religion, 1940-41; prof. Old Testament N.Y. Theol. Sem., N.Y.C., 1941-42; prof. Bibl. interpretation Garrett-Evang. Theol. Sem., Evanston, Ill., 1942-60, Harry R. Kendall prof. New Testament interpretation, 1960-71, adj. prof. New Testament interpretation, 1971-75; lectr. in field; archaeol. excavator in Israel at Anata, 1936, Herodian Jericho, 1951, Mt. Gerizim, 1966, 68. Editor Bibl. Rsch., 1964-65; co-editor, author (with others): Illustrated Family Encyclopedia of Living Bible, 1967; author: Jesus in the Gospel of Matthew, 1960, Deuteronomy and Joshua, 1964, Abingdon Bible Handbook, 1975, Illustrated Bible Handbook, 1987. Two Brothers' fellow Yale U., Jerusalem, 1935-36; recipient citation Laymen's Nat. Bible Com., 1975; named Alumnus of Yr., Seattle Pacific U., 1981. Mem. Am. Schs. of Oriental Rsch., Am. Acad. Religion, Soc. Bibl. Lit. Home and Office: 299 N Heather Dr Camano Island WA 98292

BLAIR, FREDERICK DAVID, interior designer; b. Denver, June 15, 1946; s. Frederick Edward and Margaret (Whitely) B. BA, U. Colo., 1969; postgrad. in French, U. Denver, 1981-82. Interior designer The Denver, 1969-76, store mgr., 1976-80; v.p. Hartley House Interiors, Ltd., Denver, 1980-83; pvt. practice interior design, Denver, 1983—; com. mem. Ice House Design Ctr., Denver, 1985-86, Design Directory Western Region, Denver, 1986; edn. com. for ASID Nat. Conf., Denver, 1991. Designs shown in various mags. Mem. Rep. Nat. Com.; bd. dirs. One Day, orgn. for children with AIDS, Very Spl. Arts, 1993; bd. dirs. Supporters of Children, 1996—, mem. steering com., 1994, pres.-elect, 1996-97; pres., bd. dirs. Supporters of Children, 1999. Mem. Am. Soc. Interior Designers (co-chmn. com. profl. registration 1986, edn. com. nat. conf. 1991, bd. dirs. Colo. chpt. 1990—, Humanist award 1997), Denver Art Mus., Nat. Trust Hist. Preservation, Hist. Denver. Christian Scientist. Avocations: skiing, painting, tennis.

BLAIRE, STEPHEN E., bishop; b. L.A., Dec. 22, 1941. Grad., St. John's Sem., Camarillo, Calif. Ordained priest Roman Cath. Ch., 1967, titular bishop of Lamzella, Aux. bishop L.A., 1990—. Office: Our Lady of Angels Pastoral Ctr 2636 S Mansfield Ave Los Angeles CA 90016-3512

BLAIS, MATTHEW P., graphic designer; b. Muskegon, Mich., Jan. 27, 1956; s. George Arthur and Patricia Jane (Dexterhouse) B. BFA, Ill. State U., 1979. Artist, designer Mudlen Originals, Temelula, Calif., 1985-88; prin. graphics tech. City of Riverside (Calif.), 1988—. Avocations: woodworking, golf, tennis, dancing. Office: City of Riverside Pub Works 3900 Main St Riverside CA 92522

BLAIS, ROBERT HOWARD, lawyer; b. Muskegon, Mich., May 14, 1955. BA with high honors, Mich. State U., 1977; JD cum laude, U. Notre Dame, 1980. Ptnr. Bogle & Gates, Seattle, 1988-93; shareholder Gores & Blais, Seattle, 1993—; adj. prof. estate and tax planning Seattle U., 1982-83; chairperson Wash. State U. Planned Giving Adv. Bd., 1989-96. Mem. ABA, Wash. State Bar Assn. (real property, probate and trust coun. 1987-88), Seattle-King County Bar Assn., Estate Planning Coun. Seattle (pres. 1996-97), Am. Coll. Trust and Estate Counsel. Office: Gores & Blais 1420 5th Ave Ste 2600 Seattle WA 98101-1357

BLAKE, D. STEVEN, lawyer; b. Saginaw, Mich., June 2, 1940. BA, Mich. State U., 1963; JD, U. Calif., Davis, 1971. Bar: Calif. 1972. Sr. ptnr. Downey, Brand, Seymour & Rohwer, Sacramento, 1990—; adj. prof. law U. Pacific, 1983. Co-author: California Real Estate Finance and Construction Law, 1995. Mem. ABA (bus. law sect.), Am. Arbitration Assn. (arbitrator), State Bar Calif. (chair corp. com., sec., fin. instns. com., bus. law sect., panelist, presenter numerous seminars Calif. State Bar Continuing Edn. Bar 1981-91, co-chair corps. com. bus. law sect. 1997), Yolo County Bar Assn. Office: Downey Brand Seymour & Rohwer 555 Capitol Mall Ste 1050 Sacramento CA 95814-4601

BLAKE, RACHELLE S., writer, editor, medical transcription educator; b. L.A., Nov. 14, 1964; d. John Arthur and Lettie Annette (Craddock) Scott; m. Richard Blake, Aug. 29, 1987; children: Ashleigh, Angelique. BS in Mass Comms., U. Denver, Boulder, 1987; MA in Health Adminstrn., Boulder Coll., 1988. Med. transcriptionist Mercy Hosp., Denver, 1983-86; med. transcription dir. H. Patrick Carr, M.D., Aurora, Colo., 1987-97; health professions instr. Denver Tech. Coll., 1989-91; founder, dept. head, instr. The Transcription Inst., 1989-93; mgr. med. transcription dept. The Polyclinic, Seattle, 1997; founder, exec. dir. Internat. Med. Transcription Assn., 1989—; CEO, Alphascribe, Inc., Seattle, 1991—; dir. edn. Transcription Inst., Denver. Author: (textbook) The Medical Transcriptionist's Handbook, 1993, 2nd edit., 1997, The Blake Method of Medical Terminology, 1994; editor: Delmar's Medical Assisting Textbook, 1995; contbg. editor: Delmar Publs., Albany, N.Y., 1994—; developmental editor, chief corr. editor Laramide Publs., Aurora, Colo., 1994—; chief editor: Mapletree Med. Transcription, Columbia, S.C., 1998—. Del. Rep. State Convention, Denver, 1995; alt. del. White House Commn. on Small Bus., Washington, 1994; co-dir. Zoo-Two Found. Zool. Found., Denver, 1994-95; vol. coord. 1984 Olympics, L.A. Opening Ceremonies. Recipient Gold Medal Calif. Mem. Internat. Med. Transcriptionists Assn. (exec. dir., Award of Excellence 1995), Internat. Assn. Travel Agents, Minority Bus. Enterprises (mem. econs. com. 1989—), Med. Transcription Svc. Owners, Internat. Med. Transcription Assn. (founder, exec. dir. 1989—), Am. Health Info. Mgmt. Assn., Soc. Hon. Francaise (life). Republican. Lutheran. Avocations: travel, numismatics, angel collecting, beach combing. Fax: (360) 874-0381. E-mail: blakeworld@sinclair.net. Home: 3377 Bethel Rd SE Port Orchard WA 98366-5608

BLAKE-INADA, LOUIS MICHAEL, cardiologist, researcher; b. Osaka, Japan, June 4, 1956; came to U.S. 1959; s. Edward Kneeland, Sr. and Setsuko (Inada) Blake. BA in Biochemistry and Molecular Biology, U. Calif., Santa Barbara, 1979; MD, Case Western Res. U., 1983. Diplomate Am. Bd. Internal Medicine, Am. Bd. Nuc. Medicine. Intern in gen. surgery Letterman Army Med. Ctr., San Francisco, 1983-84; resident in internal medicine Sch. Medicine Stanford U., Calif., 1988-90, resident in nuc. medicine, 1990-92, chief resident in nuc. medicine, 1991-92; fellow in cardiology Calif. Pacific Med. Ctr., San Francisco, 1992-93; fellow in cardiology, cardiac imaging U. Calif., San Francisco, 1993-95; fellow in invasive cardiology U. N.Mex. Health Sci. Ctr., 1997-98; asst. prof. medicine (cardiology), asst. prof. radiology U. Nev. Sch. of Medicine, Reno, 1998—. Contbr. articles to med. jours. including Am. Jour. Radiology, Jour. Nuc. Medicine, others; contbr. editor Jour. Am. Coll. Cardiology, 1993-95. Capt. U.S. Army, 1991-98. Evelyn Neizer rsch. fellow Stanford U., 1992. Fellow Am. Coll. Angiology; mem. ACP, Am. Coll. Cardiology, Am. Coll. Nuc. Physicians, Am. Heart Assn. (coun. on cardiovascular radiology), Soc. Nuc. Medicine, Assn. Military Surgeons of the U.S. Republican. Roman Catholic. Avocations: stocks and bonds, skiing, running, piano, languages. Home: 1855 Joy Lake Rd Reno NV 89511-8718 Office: U Calif Med Ctr San Francisco CA 94110

BLAKELY, EDWARD JAMES, economics educator; b. San Bernardino, Calif., Apr. 21, 1938; s. Edward Blakely and Josephine Elizabeth (Carter) Proctor; m. Maaike C. Vander Sleesen, July 1, 1971; children: Pieta C., Brita R. BA, U. Calif. Riverside, 1960; MA, U. Calif., L.A., 1965; MBA, Pasadena Nazarene Coll., 1967; EdD in Edn. and Mgmt., UCLA, 1971. Mgr. Pacific Telephone Co., Pasadena, Calif., 1960-65; exec. dir. Western Community Action Tng., Los Angeles, 1965-69; spl. asst. U.S. Dept. State, Washington, 1969-71; asst. chancellor, assoc. prof. U. Pitts., 1971-74; assoc. dean and prof. applied econs. and behavioral scis. U. Calif.,

Davis, 1974-77; asst. v.p. U. Calif., Berkeley, 1977-85, prof., chmn. dept. city and regional planning, 1985—; expert advisor Orgn. Econ. Cooperation and Devel., asst. to Mayor Elihu Harris, City of Oakland. Author: Rural Communities in Advanced Industrial Society, Community Development Research, Taking Local Development Initiative, Planning Local Economic Development SAGE, 1988, Separate Societies: Poverty and Inequality in U.S. Cities (Paul Davidoff award 1993), 1992, Fortress America: Gated Communities in the U.S., 1998. Chmn. fin. com. Pvt. Industry Council of Oakland (Calif.), 1978-85; vice chmn. Ecole Bilingue Sch., Berkeley, 1982-85, chmn., 1988—; chmn. bd. Royce Sch., Oakland, Calif., 1988—; sec., treas. Econ. Devel. Corp., Oakland, 1983; expert advisor Orgn. Econ. Corp. and Devel., Paris, 1986; apptd. to pres. trust Pres. Bill Clinton, 1997—; mayoral candidate City of Oakland, Calif., 1998. Served to 1st lt. USAF, 1961-63. Recipient San Francisco Found. award, 1991, Paul Davidoff award, 1993; Guggenheim fellow, 1995-96, fellow Urban Studies Australian Inst. Urban St., 1985, German Acad. Exch., 1984; Fulbright St. scholar Internat. Exch. of Scholars, 1986, John Simon Guggenheim fellow, 1995-96; named to Athlete Hall of Fame, U. Calif. Riverside Alumni Press, 1992, 125th Anniversay Prof. U. Calif. at Riverside Berkeley Campus, 1992; apptd. by Pres. Bill Clinton to the Pres. Trust, 1997. Mem. Cmty. Devel. Soc. (bd. dirs 1980-84, svc. award 1983, disting. svc. award 1990), Calif. Local Econ. Devel. (standing com. 1980-81), Am. Planning Assn. (accreditation com.), Am. Assn. Collegiate Schs. of Planning, Nat. Assn. State and Land Grant Colls. (exec. com. 1987), Phi Delta Kappa, Lambda Alpha. Club: Rueful Order. Home: 652 Orange Grove Ave # 0 South Pasadena CA 91030-2353 Office: Univ So Calif Sch Urban Reg Planning & Devel Los Angeles CA 90089-0042

BLAKEMORE, PAUL HENRY, JR., retired publishing executive; b. Des Moines, Mar. 7, 1925; s. Paul Henry and Mabel (Evstace) B.; m. Barbara Jane Spargur, Oct. 24, 1952; children: Paul H. III, John E. BSBA, Northwestern U., 1950. Regional dir. First Fin. Group, Brookline, Mass., 1955-62; sr. v.p. TV/Radio Age, N.Y.C., 1963-87, cons., 1987—. Capt. USMC, 1943-47. Mem. Lions. Republican. Avocations: jazz, classic cars, model railroading. Home: PO Box 4024 Malibu CA 90264-4024

BLAKEMORE, PAUL RUSSELL, sound recording engineer, producer; b. Fort Worth, Tex., Jan. 11, 1954; s. William S. Jr. and Annelle (Frazier) B.; m. Jenifer MacConnell, Nov. 24, 1984; children: Addison G., Sally R., Lucien S. Student, U. Tex., 1972-75, Eastman Sch. of Music, 1976-77. Audio technician Univ. Tex., Dept. Music, Austin, Tex., 1976-78; broadcast-recording technician Nat. Pub. Radio, Washington, 1978-79; audio engr. Nat. Pub. Radio, Washington, 1978-82; dir. prodn., recording Sta. WJHU-FM, Balt., 1983-86; sales Bradley Broadcast Sales, Gaithersburg, Md., 1988-89; audio engr. Sta. WETA-FM/TV, Washington, 1989-93; owner, engr. Paul Blakemore Audio, Santa Fe, 1994—; faculty Corp. for Pub. Broadcasting, Washington, 1980-92, Coll. Santa Fe, 1994-95. Tech. dir. Jazz Alive, 1980-82, Jazzmobile Sunday Special, 1982 (Peabody award); audio prodr. Sass and Brass, 1987, In Perfomance at the White House, 1981, Music From Washington, 1989 (Gold medal award Internat. Radio Festival); record, mix, edit master (CD) Peace Pieces, 1995, Celebration - Live at the Blue Note, 1996; edit, mix master (CD) Timothy Leary Beyond Life, 1997; sound design (film) One River Many Voices, 1996. Mem. Nat. Acad. Recording Arts and Sci., Audio Engring. Soc. Avocations: cooking, canoeing, bicycling. Home: 3545 28th St Apt 203 Boulder CO 80301-1575 Office: Paul Blakemore Audio 1808 2nd St Ste H Santa Fe NM 87505-3881

BLAKENEY, ALLAN EMRYS, Canadian government official, lawyer; b. Bridgewater, N.S., Can., Sept. 7, 1925; s. John Cline and Bertha (Davies) B.; m. Mary Elizabeth Schwartz, 1950 (dec. 1957); m. Anne Louise Gorham, May 1959; children: Barbara, Hugh, David, Margaret. BA, Dalhousie U., 1945, LLB, 1947, LLD (hon.); BA (Rhodes scholar), Oxford U., 1949, MA, 1955; DCL (hon.), Mount Allison U.; LLD (hon.), York U., Toronto, U. Western Ont., London, 1991, U. Regina, 1993, U. Sask., 1995. Bar: N.S. 1950, Sask. 1951. Queen's counsel, 1961; sec. to govt. fin. office Govt. Sask., 1950-55; chmn. Sask. Securities Commn., 1955-58; ptnr. Davidson, Davidson & Blakeney, Regina, Sask., 1958-60, Griffin, Blakeney, Beke, Koskie & Lueck, Regina, 1964-70; premier of Sask., 1971-82; Mem. Sask. Legislature, 1960-88; Officer of the Order of Can., 1992; leader of the opposition Sask. Legislature, 1970-71, 82-87; prof. Osgoode Hall Law Sch., York U., 1988-90, U. Sask., 1990—; minister of edn., Sask., 1960-61, provincial treas., 1961-62, minister pub. health, 1962-64; mem. Royal Commn. on Aborginal Peoples, 1991-93. Home: 1752 Prince of Wales Ave, Saskatoon, SK Canada S7K 3E5 Office: U Saskatchewan Coll Law, 15 Campus Dr, Saskatoon, SK Canada S7N 5A6

BLAKESLEE, DIANE PUSEY, financial planner; b. West Chester, Pa., Apr. 12, 1933; d. Norman S. and Leona (Ruth) Pusey; m. Earle B. Blakeslee, June 11, 1954; children: Samuel N., Barbara Blakeslee Porteous, David E., Ruth D. Blakeslee Overton. BA, Hood Coll., 1988. CLU; cert. fin. planner. Dist. mgr. Tchrs. Mgmt. and Investment Corp., Newport Beach, Calif., 1972-78, Walt Becker, Inc., Fresno, Calif., 1978-80; pres. Blakeslee & Blakeslee, San Luis Obispo, Calif., 1980—. Author: (column for Sr. Mag. and syndicated for radio) Dollars and Sense; co-editor: How to Survive on $50,000 to $150,000 a Year, 1984; host monthly TV program Welcome to The World of Financial Planning, 1984-87. Bd. dirs., treas. Pvt. Industry Coun., 1979-84; bd. dirs., treas. Child Devel. Ctr., 1980-83; bd. dirs. Cuesta Coll. Found., 1985—; bd. dirs., 1st v.p. San Luis Obispo Art Assn.; 1st v.p. San Luis Obispo Estate Planning Coun.; bd. dirs. Cert. Fin. Planners Bd. of Standards, Ethics and Profl. Rev., 1993-97; regent Coll. Fin. Planning, 1980-85; chmn. planned giving com. Cuesta Coll., 1984-86, pres. found. Named bd. mem. of Yr., Econ. Opportunity Coun., San Luis Obispo County, 1983, Woman of Achievement of Yr. cen. Calif. region Bus. and Profl. Women, 1985-86, Nat. Cert. Fin. Planner of Yr. 1986; recipient Disting. Alumni award George Sch., 1991. Mem. Internat. Assn. Fin. Planners, Inst. Cert. Fin. Planners (chmn. pub. relations, bd. dirs. 1978-82), Nat. Life Underwriters Assn., Bur. Nat. Affairs Tax Mgmt. (bd. advisors 1986—). Republican. Mem. Soc. of Friends. Club: Womens' Network (San Luis Obispo). Avocations: hiking, gardening, sketching. Home: 88 Country Club Dr San Luis Obispo CA 93401-8908 Office: Blakeslee & Blakeslee 299 Madonna Rd San Luis Obispo CA 93405-5430

BLAKEY, SCOTT CHALONER, journalist, writer; b. Nashua, N.H., Nov. 19, 1936; s. Elmer F. and Mildred Livingstone (Chaloner) B.; m. Lone Erting, July 18, 1970 (div.); 1 child, Nicholas Scott; m. Caroline M. Scarborough, June 28, 1985 (div.); children: Alexandra Scarborough, Susannah Chaloner. BA, U. N.H., 1960. Reporter, photographer Nashua (N.H.) Telegraph, 1960-62, polit. reporter, 1963-64; legis. asst. Congressman James C. Cleveland, Washington, 1963; mng. editor Concord (N.H.) Monitor, 1964-68; urban affairs corr. San Francisco Chronicle, 1968-70, reporter, asst. city editor, 1979-84, TV corr., 1985-87; corr., asst. news dir. KQED-TV, San Francisco, 1970-74; free-lance writer San Francisco, 1974-79; news editor KRON-TV (NBC), San Francisco, 1987-89; nationally syndicated columnist KidVid L.A. Times Syndicate, 1990—; sr. news rep. div. corp. communications Pacific Gas & Electric Co. San Francisco, 1991—, nat. video revs. editor Brainplay.com, Denver, 1998—; writer, field prodr. TV documentary 2251 Days, 1973 (2 Emmy awards 1974); author (books) San Francisco, 1976, Prisoner at War, 1978, Kid Vid, 1995; contbr. articles to profl. jours. Recipient Best Polit. Writing award New Eng. AP News Editors Assn., 1965, Dupont Columbia award, 1974. Mem. Nat. Soc. Newspaper Columnists, Authors Guild, Am. Air Mail Soc., Audubon Soc. Democrat. Avocations: philately, ornithology, photography, backpacking. Home: 1801 Turk St Apt 17 San Francisco CA 94115-4429 Office: Pacific Gas & Electric 77 Beale St Ste 2935A San Francisco CA 94105-1814

BLALOCK, ANN BONAR, policy analyst, evaluation researcher; b. Parkersburg, W.Va., Apr. 16, 1928; d. Harry and Fay (Conley) Bonar; m. Hubert Morley Blalock, Jr., 1951 (dec. 1991); children: Susan Blalock Lyon, Kathleen Blalock McCarrell, James M.; m. Gerhard E. Lenski, 1996. AB, [...] Admiralty Inlet Consulting, Hansville, Wash. Sr. author: Introduction to Social Research, 2d edit., 1982; co-editor: Methodology in Social Research, 1968; editor: Evaluation Forum, 1986-97, Evaluating Social Programs, 1990. Recipient research award Partnership for Employment and Tng. Careers. Mem. NASW (past pres. Wash. State chpt.), Am. Eval. Assn. (past com.

chair), Assn. Pub. Policy Analysis and Mgmt. Home: PO Box 409 Hansville WA 98340-0409

BLANC, MAUREEN, public relations executive. Ptnr. Blanc & Otus Pub. Rels., Inc., San Francisco. Office: Blanc & Otus Pub Rels Inc 135 Main St Fl 12 San Francisco CA 94105-1812*

BLANCHARD, WILLIAM HENRY, psychologist; b. St. Paul, Mar. 25, 1922; s. Charles Edgar and Ethel Rachael (Gurney) B.; m. Martha Ida Lang, Aug. 11, 1947; children: Gregory Marcus, Mary Lisa. Diploma in Sci. Mason City Jr. Coll., 1942; BS in Chemistry, Iowa State U., 1944; PhD in Psychology, U. So. Calif., 1954. Lic. clin. psychologist, Calif. Shift chemist B.F. Goodrich Chem. Co., Port Neches, Tex., 1946-47; court psychologist L.A. County Gen. Hosp., 1954-55; psychologist, dir. rsch. So. Reception Ctr. and Clinic, Calif. Youth Authority, Norwalk, 1955-58; social scientist Rand Corp., 1958-60, System Devel. Corp., 1960-70; mem. faculty Calif. State U.-Northridge, L.A., 1970; assoc. prof. UCLA, 1971; faculty group leader urban semester U. So. Calif., L.A., 1971-75; sr. rsch. assoc. Office of Chancellor, Calif. State U., L.A., 1975-76; sr. fellow Planning Analysis and Rsch. Inst., Santa Monica, Calif., 1976-96; pvt. practice psychologist, Calif., 1976-96; clin. assoc. dept. psychology U. So. Calif., 1956-58. Author: Rousseau and the Spirit of Revolt, 1967; Aggression American Style, 1978; Revolutionary Morality, 1984; Neocolonialism American Style, 1996; contbr. articles to profl. jours. Mem. com. on mental health West Area Welfare Planning Council, L.A., 1960-61; bd. dirs. L.A. County Psychol. Assn., 1969; commr. Bd. Med. Examiners, Psychology Exam. Com., State of Calif., 1969; v.p. Parents and Friends of Mentally Ill Children, 1968-69, pres., 1966-68, trustee, 1968-69. Mem. APA, AAAS, Internat. Soc. Polit. Psychology. Home: 4307 Rosario Rd Woodland Hills CA 91364-5546

BLANCHE, JOE ADVINCULA, aerospace engineer, consultant, educator; b. Rizal, Santa, Ilocos Sur, Philippines, Sept. 11, 1954; came to U.S. 1976; s. Emilio Peralta and Concepcion (Advincula) B.; m. Albine Selerio Lansangan, Oct. 9, 1982; children: Emmanuel Joseph, Earl Jordan. Cert. in mil. sci., U. Philippines, 1973; BS in Math., Adamson U., Manila, 1976; postgrad., Calif. State U., Long Beach, 1982-85; AAS in Avionics Systems Tech., C.C. Air Force, Maxwell AFB, Ala., 1990; cert. in mgmt., Cen. Tex. Coll., 1990; PhD in Mgmt., Pacific Western U., 1993; MA in Orgnl. Mgmt., U. Phoenix, 1995. Lic. real estate broker, Calif.; registered tax preparer, Calif. Assoc. engr., scientist McDonnell Douglas Corp., Long Beach, Calif., 1981-84, engr., scientist, 1984-86, engr., scientist specialist, 1987-88, sr. engr., scientist, 1988-94; lead aerospace engr. Sikorsky Aircraft-UTC, Stratford, Conn., 1986-87; founder, pres. J. & A. Blanche Ventures', Inc., Corona Hills, Calif., 1990-96; avionics maint. inspector USAFR, 1983-97, ret., 1997; sr. engr., cons. McDonnell Douglas Tech. Svcs. Co./Shin Maywa, 1996-97; sr. engr., scientist Boeing Co., Delta Rockets Divsn., Huntington Beach, Calif. Eucharistic min. St. Edward's Ch., Corona. With USAF, 1976-80. Bur. Forestry grantee and scholar U. Philippines, 1971-73; USVA scholar Calif. State U., 1982-85. Mem. AIAA (sr.), Nat. Notary Assn., NRA, So. Calif. Profl. Engrs. Assn., Corona-Norco Bd. Realtors, Internat. Soc. Allied Weight Engrs. (sr.), Adamson U. Alumni Assn. So. Calif. (pres., chmn. bd. 1997-98), Santanians USA Inc. (bd. dirs. 1984-87, pres. 1994-96, pres., chmn. bd. 1997-98), Marinduque Assn. So. Calif. (press rels. officer 1998—), Fil-Am. Assn. Corona (auditor 1993-94, bd. dirs. 1995-96, parliamentarian 1997-98). Republican. Office: J & A Blanche Ventures Inc 420 N Mckinley St Ste 111-333 Corona CA 91719-6504

BLAND, DOROTHY ANN, construction executive, real estate agent; b. Black Township, Pa., Jan. 12, 1945; m. Jonathan Lee Sharp, Sept. 28, 1963 (dec. Dec. 31, 1979); children: Deborah, Todd, Wade; m. Brian C. Bland, Nov. 2, 1985; stepchildren: Paulette, Kelli. Lic. Real Estate Agent, Utah. Beauty coll. recruiter, sec. Continental Coll. of Beauty, Salt Lake City, 1968-72; exec. sec. Vaughn Hansen Assoc., Salt Lake City, 1973-82; v.p., co-owner Bland Bros., Inc., West Jordan, Utah, 1985—; co-owner Blands Sand & Gravel, Utah, 1990 ; real estate agent Preferred Properties, Salt Lake City, 1982-90, Mansell, Salt Lake City, 1990—. Avocations: golf, travel. Office: Bland Brothers Inc 8630 Redwood Rd West Jordan UT 84088-9226

BLAND, JANEESE MYRA, editor; b. Evanston, Ill., Feb. 20, 1960; d. James Milton and Jeanette Malisa (Bryant) B. BA, U. Ark., 1980. Cert. tchr., Ark., Ill. Tutor counselor U. Ark., Pine Bluff, 1979; tchr. Pine Bluff High Sch., 1980, Chgo. Bd. Edn., 1981-84; editor, author, columnist, creator Beautiful Images Hollywood (Calif.) Gazette Newspaper, 1985—; VIP organizer People's Choice Awards, Beverly Hills, 1984—; exec. prodr. stas. Chgo. Access Corp., Century Cable Comms., L.A., BH-TV, Beverly Hills; hostess The Janeese Bland Show. Proof editor: Nursing Rsch. Jour., 1989. Polit. vol. Rep. Party, Santa Monica, 1988—; vol. organizer Windfeather, Inc., Beverly Hills, 1983—, United Negro Coll. Fund, L.A., 1984—, Sickle Cell Disease Rsch. Found., L.A., 1985—; pres., founder June Maria Bland Scholarship Found. Recipient Image award Fred Hampton Scholarship Found., 1983, Wiley W. Manuel award State Bar Calif., Cert. Merit, Bet Tzedek Legal Svcs., Ill. Cmty. Leader of the Yr. award Nat. Coun. Negro Women and Quaker Oats, 1998. Mem. SBA (pres.). Republican. Baptist. Office: Sta Century Cable TV JMB Show PO Box 1387 Beverly Hills CA 90213-1387

BLANKENBURG, HEINZ HORST, vocalist, director; b. N.Y.C., Jan. 15, 1931; 3 children from a previous marriage; m. Gayle Cameron-McComb, Dec. 14, 1986. D in Performing Arts (hon.), Calif. State U., 1977, U. Calif., 1986. Operatic debut San Francisco Opera, 1955, leading baritone, 1955-66; leading baritone Glyndenbourne Festival Opera, 1957-70, as Papageno and Figaro, Rimbaud, Arlecchino, Hamburg (Germany) State Opera, 1959-79, as Beckmesser, Schaunard, Fra Melitone in La Forza del Destino, Paolo in Simon Boccanegra; sang in Brit. premiere Die Frau ohne Schatten, Hamburg State Opera, 1966; guest baritone opera cos. in Munich, Berlin, Vienna, Paris, Frankfurt, Met., Amsterdam, Rome, Brussels, Lausanne, Basle, Strasbourg, Naples, N.Z., St. Louis, Portland, numerous others; recordings include CD's, TV, radio for BBC, RAI, ZDF. Recipient Kammersänger Hamburg State Opera, 1966, Maori Welcome, N.Z., 1971. Office: Guild Opera Co of LA Opera Theatre 201 South Lake Ave #409 Pasadena CA 91101*

BLANKENSHIP, JUANITA CHAPMAN, court administrator; b. Miles City, Mont., Feb. 25, 1935; d. Terry Stilson Chapman and June Harriet (Brown) Shelden; m. Thomas Hall Blankenship, June 5, 1956 (div. July 1974). BA, U. Mont., 1956; postgrad., U. Hawaii, 1966-67; MA, U. Nev., Las Vegas, 1970. Mgmt. asst nuc. propulsion office U.S. AEC/NASA, Jackass Flats, Nev., 1962-65; adminstrv. analyst Clark County, Las Vegas, 1970-73, staff dir., criminal justice planner So. Dist. Allocation com., 1973-80; asst. dir. juror svcs. L.A. Superior Ct., 1981-88, dir. juror svcs., 1988-92, adminstr. litigation support, 1992—; mem. adv. com. Voir Dire Calif. Jud. Coun., 1992-93, Am. Bar Assn. Making Jury Svc. Accessible, Washington, 1994; mem. planning com. workshop jury mgrs., 1985; mem., vice chair adv. com. Criminal Justice Tng. Ctr. U. So. Calif., L.A., 1977-81. Co-author: Handbook for Court Specialists, 1976. Bd. dirs., pres. Andalucia Townhomes Com. Assn., Covina, 1989-93, treas. 1996—; charter mem. L.A. Mus. Contemporary Art, 1985—. Recipient Cmty. Svc. award Covina Coord. Coun., 1990, Achievement award Jury Edn. & Mgmt. Forum, 1992, Adminstrn. of Justice award ASPA-SCJA, 1983. Mem. AAUW (br. treas. 1992-93, membership treas. 1995-97, grant honoree 1986), ASPA (chpt. pres. 1972-73, nat. coun. 1974-77, sect. chair 1978-79, exec. com. 1974-80, 96—, criminal justice sect., Pub. Adminstr. of Yr. award Las Vegas br. 1978), Nat. Assn. State Cts., Phi Kappa Phi. Democrat. Avocations: tennis, concerts, theatre, art museums & galleries. Office: LA Superior Ct 111 N Hill St Los Angeles CA 90012-3117

BLANKFORT, LOWELL ARNOLD, newspaper publisher; b. N.Y.C., Apr. 29, 1926; s. Herbert and Gertrude (Butler) B.; m. April Pemberton; 1 child, Jonathan. BA in History and Polit. Sci., Rutgers U., 1946. Reporter, copy editor L.I. (N.Y.) Star-Jour., 1947-49; columnist London Daily Mail, Paris, 1949-50; copy editor The Stars & Stripes, Darmstadt, Germany, 1950-51, Wall St. Jour., N.Y.C., 1951; bus., labor editor Cowles Mags., N.Y.C., 1951-53; pub. Pacifica (Calif.) Tribune, 1954-59; free-lance writer, Europe, Asia, 1959-61; co-pub., editor Chula Vista (Calif.) Star-News, 1961-78; co-owner Paradise (Calif.) Post, 1977—, Monte Vista (Colo.) Jour., Ctr. (Colo.) Post-Dispatch, Del Norte (Colo.) Prospector, 1978-93, Plainview (Minn.) News, St. Charles (Minn.) Press, Lewiston (Minn.) Jour., 1980—, Summit (Colo.) Sentinel, New Richmond (Wis.) News, 1981-87, Yuba City Valley Herald, Calif., 1982-85, TV Views, Monterey, Calif., 1982-87, Summit County Jour., Colo., 1982-87, Alpine (Calif.) Sun, 1987-93. Columnist, contbr. articles on fgn. affairs to newspapers. Mem. Calif. Dem. Cen. Com., 1963. Named Outstanding Layman of Yr. Sweetwater Edn. Assn., 1966, Citizen of Yr. City of Chula Vista, 1976, Headliner of Yr. San Diego Press Club, 1980. Mem. ACLU (pres. San Diego chpt. 1970-71), Calif. Newspaper Pubs. Assn., World Affairs Council San Diego (pres. 1996—), Ctr. Internat. Policy (bd. dirs. 1991—), Internat. Ctr. Devel. Policy (nat. bd. 1985-90), UN Assn. (pres. San Diego chpt. 1991-93, nat. coun. 1992—, nat. bd. 1997—), World Federalist Assn. (nat. bd., pres. San Diego chpt. 1984-86), Soc. Profl. Journalists, East Meets West Found. (nat. v.p. 1992—), Inst. of the Ams. (assoc. 1989—, mem. internat. coun. 1994—). Awards: Best Editorials in California, non-dailies, 1st or 2nd place seven consecutive years (California Newpaper Publishers Association); Best editorial in United States (National Newspaper Association); Best editorial U.S. suburban newspapers (Suburban Publishers Newspapers of America); Headliner of Year (San Diego Press Club); John Swett award (California Education Association) and Citizen of the Year (Sweetwater Education Association); Special Media award (National Conference of Christians and Jews) for articles on South America. Widely travelled writer: more than 100 nations on all continents. Has interviewed many heads of state including Fidel Castro in Cuba; Li Peng and Li Ziannin in China, Benezir Bhutto in Pakistan, Kim Dae Jung in Korea. Home: Old Orchard Ln Bonita CA 91902 Office: 315 4th Ave Ste S Chula Vista CA 91910-3816

BLANTON, JOHN ARTHUR, architect; b. Houston, Jan. 1, 1928; s. Arthur Alva and Caroline (Jeter) B.; m. Marietta Louise Newton, Apr. 10, 1954 (dec. 1976); children: Jill Blanton Milne, Lynette Blanton Rowe, Elena Diane. BA, Rice U., 1948, BS in Architecture, 1949. With Richard J. Neutra, L.A., 1950-64; pvt. practice architecture, Manhattan Beach, Calif., 1964—; lectr. UCLA Extension, 1967-76, 85, Harbor Coll., Los Angeles, 1970-72. Archtl. columnist Easy Reader newspaper, 1994-96. Mem. Capital Improvements Com., Manhattan Beach, 1966, city commr. Bd. Bldg. Code Appeals; chmn. Zoning Adjustment Bd., 1990; active Planning Commn., 1993, chmn., 1996. Served with Signal Corps, U.S. Army, 1951-53. Recipient Best House of Year award C. of C., 1969, 70, 71, 83, Preservation of Natural Site award, 1974, design award, 1975, 84. Mem. AIA (contbr. book revs. to jour. 1972-76, recipient Red Cedar Shingle/AIA nat. merit award 1979). Designed nine bldgs. included in L.A.: An Architectual Guide; works featured in L'architettura mag., 1988; design philosophy included in American Architects (Les Krantz), 1989. Office: John Blanton AIA Architect 1456 12th St # 4 Manhattan Beach CA 90266-6113

BLANTON, WALTER JAMES, composer, musician, educator; b. Kent, Wash., Sept. 4, 1944; s. Harry LeRoy and Lovs Maude (McIntosh) B.; m. Carol Helene Blanton, Dec. 14, 1968. BA, Western Wash. State Coll., Bellingham, 1966; M Mus, Ind. U., 1968, performer's cert. in trumpet, 1968. Lectr. Ind. U., Bloomington, 1988-89; asst. prof. U. Ky., Lexington, 1989-92; mem. faculty U. Nev., Las Vegas, 1981-89, 95—; touring artist Western State Arts Fedn., Santa Fe, 1982-86; music specialist Allied Arts Coun., Las Vegas, 1985-90; pres. Las Vegas Jazz Soc., 1991-94. Composer orchestral works, solo and chamber works, jazz works including Audio Art Ensemble, Bleecker Street Romance, Sonant Voyage, Idigo Blues, The Body of a House, Rite of Passage; founding mem. New World Brass Quintet; soloist, composer Las Vegas Chamber Players; prin. trumpet Nev. Symphony Orch.; composer, toured with Woody Herman Orch., Henry Mancini, Andy Williams, Shirley Bassey, Nancy Wilson, others; past mem. Tropicana, Sands, Stardust, Frontier and Desert Inn hotel orchs., Las Vegas. Named Composer of Yr. Music Tchrs. Nat. Conf., 1985; recipient Gov.'s arts award Nev. State Coun. Arts, 1987, artist fellowship, 1996. Mem. Musicians Union Local 369. Office: U Nev Las Vegas Music Dept 4505 S Maryland Pkwy Las Vegas NV 89154-9900

BLASE, NANCY GROSS, librarian; b. New Rochelle, N.Y.; d. Albert Philip and Elsie Wise (May) Gross; m. Barrie Wayne Blase, June 19, 1966 (div.); 1 child, Eric Wayne. BA in Biology, Marietta (Ohio) Coll., 1964; MLS, U. Ill., 1965. Info. scientist brain info. svc. Biomed. Libr., UCLA, 1965-66; libr. Health Sci. Libr., U. Wash., Seattle, 1966-68, Medlars search analyst, 1970-72, coord. Medline, 1972-79, head Natural Scis. Libr., 1979—; mem. libr. adv. com. Elizabeth C. Miller Libr., Ctr. for Urban Horticulture, Seattle, 1986-90. Contbr. articles to profl. jours. NSF fellow interdept. tng. program for sci. info. specialists U. Ill., 1964-65. Mem. Am. Soc. for Info. Sci. (pres. personal computer spl. interest group 1993-94, chair constn. and bylaws com. 1994-97, rsch. grantee Pacific N.W. chpt. 1984-85), Internat. Tng. in Comm. (pres. Pacific N.W. region 1994-95), Phi Beta Kappa (pres., of Univ. of Wash. chpt. 1993-97), Bet Chaverim (pres. 1998—). Avocations: walking, golf, reading. Home: 10751 Durland Ave NE Seattle WA 98125-6945 Office: U Wash Natural Scis Libr PO Box 352900 Seattle WA 98195-2900

BLASOR-BERNHARDT, DONNA JO, screenwriter, poet, author, photographer; b. Pittsburg, Kans., May 8, 1944; d. Donald Archie and Bessie Beryl (Tatham) Blasor; m. Richard Wayne Bernhardt, Oct. 29, 1964 (dec. Feb. 1987); children: Erik Wayne, Katherine Elizabeth. Student, U. Alaska, Anchorage, 1963-64. Reporter, poet Mukluk News Paper, Tok, Alaska, 1977—; interior, coord., technical advisor Alaska Nitty Gritty Dirty Band Alcan Caravan, 1992—; interior coord. Up With People Internat. Show, 1992, 94, 96; interior Alaska coord. and tech. advisor Nitty Gritty Dirt Band Alcan Caravan TV spl., 1992, regional rep. Internat. Women's Writing Guild, 1996, 97; field editor Birds & Blooms Mag., 1996, 97. Author: (books) A Tent in Tok, 1980, More...A Tent in Tok, 1982, Friends of the Tent in Tok, 1987, (short story) K'hann De G'hann, 1989 (1st pl. adult writing 1989), (book) Beyond the Tent in Tok, 1990, The Tent, 1991, Before the Tent in Tok, 1992, Love and the Tent in Tok, 1994, Tok-The Real Story, 1996, Recipes From the Tent in Tok, 1998, Recipes of the Goldfields, 1998, What Color is Alaska?, 1999, Going to the End of the World, 1992, (audio tape mus. drama) Gettysburg, Fields of Love and Honor, 1993, (radio show play) The River, 1997, (book) Angela's Raincoat, 1998; writer featured story (TV) Paul Harvey's News and Commentary, 1978; featured writer Alaska's S.W. Regional Newsletter, Juneau, 1985, Sta. WAMU Pub. Radio, 1990; featured profile writer Fairbanks (Alaska) Northland News, 1985; featured guest Senator Frank Murkowski's Show, 1988, CBS TV Night Watch, 1989, Tok River Fire Exhibit Dedication, 1992, Channel 11-TV News, Anchorage, 1992, KTVA-TV Norma Goodman Show, Anchorage, 1992, 10th Ann. show Highway Daze, 1992; featured in Outhouses of Alaska, 1996-97, featured in North to Alaska web pages, 1998—; featured profiles in various publs.; contbr. articles, short stories and poetry pub. in Anchorage Times, Anchorage News, Haiku Highlights, Copper River Jour., Delta News, Mukluk News, Fairbanks Northland News, State of Alaska Newsletter, Divsn. of Forestry, Country mag., Fireweed Jour., Bell's Alaska/Yukon Travel Guide, Alaska Mag., The S.C. Observer, Seattle Times, Santa Monica Daily Breeze, Ark. Dem. Gazette, Chgo. Daily News, Angoon Yearbook, Gettysburg Times, RV Today, Fairbanks Heartland Newspaper, Dawson City, Yukon Guide to the Goldfields. Named winner of Alaska State Diving Championship, 1958-62, Poet Laureate, 1990, Internat. Woman of Yr., Internat. Biol. Ctr., 1991-92, Poet Laureate of the Alaska Hwy., 1994; recipient 1st pl. Tok River Fire Writing Competition, 1990, 1st pl. Tok River Wildfire Photo Competition, 1990. Named Poet Laureate of the Alaska Highway, 1990, 1994, 96; winners of Alaska State Diving Championship, 1958-62, Internat. Biological Ctr. Internat. Woman of Yr., 1991-92; recipient 1st pl. Tok River Fire Writing Competition, 1990, 1st pl. Tok River Wildfire Photo Competition, 1990. Avocations: swimming, painting, fishing. Office: A Tent in Tok Winter Cabin Prodns Winter Cabin Bed & Breakfst PO Box 110 Tok AK 99780-0110

BLATT, MORTON BERNARD, medical illustrator; b. Chgo., Jan. 9, 1923; s. Arthur E. and Hazel B. Student Central YMCA Coll., 1940-42, U. Ill., 1943-46. Tchr., Ray-Vogue Art Schs., Chgo., 1946-51; med. illustrator VA Center, Wood, Wis., 1951-57, Swedish Covenant Hosp., Chgo., 1957-76; med. illustrator Laidlaw Bros., River Forest, Ill., 1956-59; cons., artist health textbooks, 1956-59; illustrator Standard Edn. Soc., Chgo., 1960; art editor Covenant Home Altar, 1972-83, Covenant Companion, 1958-82. Served with USAAF, 1943-44. Mem. Art Inst. Chgo. Club: Chgo. Press. Illustrator: Atlas and Demonstration Technique of the Central Nervous System, also numerous med. jours.; illustrator, designer Covenant Hymnal, books, record jackets. Address: 373 Eliseo Dr Greenbrae CA 94904-1326

BLATTNER, MEERA MCCUAIG, computer science educator; b. Chgo., Aug. 14, 1930; d. William D. McCuaig and Nina (Spertus) Klevs; m. Minao Kamegai, June 22 1985; children: Douglas, Robert, William. BA, U. Chgo., 1952; MS, U. So. Calif., 1966; PhD, UCLA, 1973 . Rsch. fellow in computer sci. Harvard U., 1973-74; asst. prof. Rice U., 1974-80; assoc. prof. applied sci. U. Calif. at Davis, Livermore, 1980-91, prof. applied sci., 1991—; adj. prof. U. Tex., Houston, 1977—; vis. prof. U. Paris, 1980; program dir. theoretical computer sci. NSF, Washington, 1979-80. Co-editor: (with R. Dannenberg) Multimedia Interface Design, 1992. NSF grantee, 1977-81, 93—. Mem. Soc. Women Engrs., Assn. Computing Machinery, IEEE Computer Soc. Contbr. articles to profl. jours. Office: U Calif Davis/Livermore Dept Applied Sci Livermore CA 94550

BLAU, EDWARD, lawyer; b. N.Y.C., Aug. 3, 1922. BBA, CCNY, 1948; JD, Harvard U., 1951. Bar: N.Y. 1951, Calif. 1955, U.S. Dist. Ct. (so. dist.), Calif., 1955, U.S. Supreme Ct. 1961. Assoc. Sargoy and Stein, N.Y.C., 1951-52; counsel MCA TV, Ltd., N.Y.C., 1952-54; ptnr. Pacht, Ross and Assocs., L.A., 1954-85, Shea and Gould, L.A., 1985-89; of counsel Richman, Lawrence, Mann & Greene, 1989-92. Served to 1st lt. USAAF, 1943-46. Mem. ABA, Calif. State Bar Assn., Los Angeles County Bar Assn., Beverly Hills Bar Assn., Century City Bar Assn., Calif. Copyright Conf., Los Angeles Copyright Soc., Acad. TV Arts and Scis., Acad. Motion Picture Arts and Scis. Avocations: tennis, racquetball, movies, gym, reading. Office: Law Offices of Edward Blau 10100 Santa Monica Blvd Ste 250 Los Angeles CA 90067-4100

BLAWIE, JAMES LOUIS, law educator; b. Newark, Mar. 26, 1928; s. Louis Paul and Cecelia Ruth (Grish) B.; m. Marilyn June Beyerle, May 30, 1952; children: Elias J., Cecelia R., Christiana L. BA, U. Conn., 1950; AM, Boston U., 1951, PhD, 1959; JD, U. Chgo., 1955. Bar: Conn. 1956, Calif. 1965, U.S. Dist. Ct. (no. dist.) Calif. 1965, U.S. Ct. Appeals (9th cir.) 1967, U.S. Supreme Ct. 1968. Instr. polit. sci. Mich. State U., East Lansing, 1955; assoc. prof. U. Akron, Ohio, 1956-57, Kent State U., 1956-57; asst. prof. bus. law U. Calif., Berkeley, 1958-60; assoc. prof. law Santa Clara U., Calif., 1960-63, prof. law, 1963—; vis. prof. polit. sci. Calif. State U., Hayward, 1966-67; adminstrv. law judge U.S. Equal Employment Opportunity Commn., Washington, 1982-85; complaints examiner U.S. Equal Employment Opportunity Agy., Office Equal Employment Opportunity; cons. in field. Author: (handbook) The Michigan Township Board, 1957; contbr. articles to profl. jours. Mem. Citizen's Adv. Com. on Capital Improvements, 1962-65; bd. dirs. Washington Hosp., 1964-68. Maj. U.S. Army, 1963-74. Boston U. Faculty fellow, 1951-53; U. Chgo. Law Sch. scholar, 1953-55; grantee Mich. State U. grantee, 1955-56, Helsinki Govt. Ministry Edn. grantee, 1980-81. Mem. ABA, Fairfield County Bar Assn., Mensa. Republican. Avocations: computers, photography, travel, rare diseases databases. Home: 41752 Marigold Dr Fremont CA 94539-4779 also: PO Box 1102 Fremont CA 94538-0110 Office: Santa Clara U Sch Law Santa Clara CA 95053

BLEIBERG, LEON WILLIAM, surgical podiatrist; b. Bklyn., June 9, 1932; s. Paul Pincus and Helen (Epstein) B.; m. Beth Daigle, June 7, 1970; children: Kristina Noel, Kelley Lynn, Kimberly Ann, Paul Joseph. Student, L.A. City Coll., 1950-51, U. So. Calif., 1951, Case Western Res. U., 1951-53; DSc with honors, Temple U., 1955; PhD, U. Beverly Hills, 1970. Served rotating internship various hosps., Phila., 1954-55; resident various hosps., Montebello, L.A., 1956-58; surg. podiatrist So. Calif. Podiatry Group, Westchester (Calif.), L.A., 1956-75; health care economist, researcher Drs. Home Health Care Svcs., 1976—; chmn. bd. Unltd. Healthcare, Metro Manila, Philippines; v.p. pub. rels. Bilboa Wellness Found., Upland, Calif.; podiatric cons. U. So. Calif. Athletic Dept., Morningside and Inglewood (Calif.) High Schs., Internet Corp., Royal Navy Assn., Long Beach, Calif. Naval Sta.; exec. cons. Thomas Med. Group, Pomona, Calif., 1995, Cardiotel, Van Nuys, Calif., 1995; lectr. in field; healthcare affiliate Internat. divsn. CARE/ASIA, 1987; pres. Medica, Totalcare, Cine-Medics Corp., Strategic World-Wide Health Care Svcs.; exec. dir. Internat. Health Trust, developer Health Banking Program; adminstr. Orthotic Concepts, 1993; prof. health care econs. and med. rehab. Global U., Ontario, Calif., chmn. dept. health care econs., chmn. dept. biomechanics and phys. rehab.; CEO Integrated Wellness Ctrs.; exec. dir. wellness divsn. Crown Golden Eagles. Producer (films) The Gun Hawk, 1963, Terrified, Day of the Nightmare; contbr. articles to profl. jours. Hon. Sheriff Westchester 1962-64; commd. mem. Rep. Senatorial Inner Circle, 1984-86; co-chmn. health reform com. United We Stand Am., Thousand Oaks, Calif.; mem. exec. coun. State of Calif., United We Stand Am.; active 1st Security and Safety, Westlake Village, Calif., 1993—; lt. comdr. med. svcs. corps Brit.-Am. Sea Cadet Corps, 1984—; track coach Westlake High Sch., Westlake Village; exec. sec. Nat. Coalition Parents for Anti-Drug/Violence Corp., Inc. L.A. World Affairs Coun. With USN, 1955-56. Recipient Medal of Merit, U.S. Presdl. Task Force. Mem. Philippine Hosp. Assn. (Cert. of Appreciation 1964, trophy for Outstanding Svc. 1979), Calif. Podiatry Assn. (hon.), Am. Podiatric Med. Assn. (hon.), Acad. TV Arts and Scis., Royal Soc. Health (Eng.), Western Foot Surgery Assn., Am. Coll. Foot Surgeons, Am. Coll. Podiatric Sports Medicine, Internat. Coll. Preventive Medicine, Hollywood Comedy Club, Sts. and Sinners Club, Westchester C. of C., Hals Und Beinbruch Ski Club, Beach Cities Ski Club, Orange County Stamp Club, Las Virgenes Track Club, Masons, Shriners. Home: 30856 Agoura Rd Apt J16 Agoura Hills CA 91301-4363

BLENCOWE, PAUL SHERWOOD, lawyer; b. Amityville, N.Y., Feb. 10, 1953; s. Frederick Arthur and Dorothy Jeanne (Ballenger) B.; m. Mary Frances Faulk, Apr. 11, 1992; 1 child, Kristin Amanda. BA with honors, U. Wis., 1975; MBA, U. Pa., 1976; JD, Stanford U., 1979. Bar: Tex. 1979, Calif. 1989. Assoc. Fulbright & Jaworski, Houston, 1979-86; assoc. Fulbright & Jaworski, London, 1986-87, ptnr., 1988-89; ptnr. Fulbright & Jaworski L.L.P., L.A., 1989—. Editor: China's Quest for Independence: Policy Evolution in the 1970s, 1980; editor-in-chief Stanford Jour. of Internat. Law, 1978-79; contbr. articles on U.S. securities and corp. law to profl. jours. Mem. ABA, The Calif. Club, Phi Beta Kappa, Phi Kappa Phi, Beta Theta Pi. Office: Fulbright & Jaworski LLP 865 S Figueroa St Fl 29 Los Angeles CA 90017-2543

BLESSING-MOORE, JOANN CATHERINE, physician; b. Tacoma, Wash., Sept. 21, 1946; d. Harold R. and Mildred (Benson) Blessing; m. Robert Chester Moore; 1 child, Ahna. BA in Chemistry, Syracuse U., 1968; MD, SUNY, Syracuse, 1972. Diplomate Am. Bd. Pediatrics, Am. Bd. Allergy Immunology, Am. Bd. Pediatric Pulmonology. Pediatric intern, then resident Stanford U. Sch. Medicine, Palo Alto, Calif., 1972-75, allergy pulmonology fellow, 1975-77; co-dir. pediatric allergy pulmonology dept. Stanford U. Children's Hosp., Palo Alto, Calif., 1977-84; clin. asst. prof. dept. pediatrics Stanford U. Sch. Medicine, Palo Alto, Calif., 1977-84, co-dir. pediatric pulmonology lab., 1977-84; clin. asst. prof. dept. immunology Stanford U. Hosp., 1984—; allergist Palo Alto Med. Clinic, 1984-90; pvt. practice allergy immunology-pediatric-pulmonary Palo Alto, Calif., 1990—; dir. edn. program for children with asthma Camp Wheeze, Palo Alto, 1975—; cons. FDA, 1992-97; cons. in field. Author handbooks, camp program manuals; co-editor jour. supplements; mem. edit. bd. Allergy jours.; contbr. articles to sci. publs. Fellow Am. Acad. Allery, Asthma, Immunology (various offices 1980—, task force parameters of care asthma and allergy 1989-98), Am. Coll. Chest Physicians (com. mem. 1980—), Am. Coll. of Asthma, Allergy and Immunology (regent 1995-98); mem. Am. Thoracic Soc., Am. Lung Assn., No. Calif. Allergy Found. (bd. dirs., pres.), Peninsula Women's Assn., Santa Clara and San Mateo County Med. Soc., Chi Omega. Republican. Presbyterian. Avocations: music, swimming, cooking, horseback riding, scuba diving. Office: 780 Welch Rd #204 Palo Alto CA 94304-1514 also: 101 S San Mateo Dr #310 San Mateo CA 94401-3931 also: Stanford Univ Hosp Dept Immunology Palo Alto CA 94304

BLETHEN, FRANK A., newspaper publisher; b. Seattle, Apr. 20, 1945. B.S. in Bus., Ariz. State U. Pub. Walla Walla Union-Bulletin, Wash., 1975-79; circulation mgr. Seattle Times, 1980-81, v.p. sales and mktg., 1982-85, chair, pub., chief exec. officer, 1985—; chmn. Walla Walla Union-Bull., Yakima (Wash.) Herald Republic; pres. Blethen Corp. Mem. pres.' adv. bd. Wash. State U., campaign chmn., mem. steering com., chair maj. gifts divsn.;

campaign chair United Way King County, 1996, 97, bd. dirs., 1996—; bd. dirs. Md. Inst. for Minority Journalism Edn., 1994—; mem. pres.' adv. group U. Wash. Recipient Pulitzer prize (2) for best newspaper reporting and investigative reporting, 1997, Ida B. Wells award for lifetime achievement in advancement of minority employment, 1997. Mem. Nat. Assn. of Minority Media Execs., Am. Newspaper Pubs. Assn. (bd. dirs., chmn. telecomm. com.), Bellevue Athletic Club, Sigma Delta Chi. Office: Seattle Times Fairview Ave N & John St PO Box 70 Seattle WA 98111-0070*

BLEVINS, LEAFORD LEVEN, JR., architect, consultant; b. Texarkana, Ark., Feb. 13, 1948; s. Leaford Leven and Genevia (Darken) B.; m. Carla Bates (dec. Aug. 1990); children: Haven, Adrienne. BArch, U. Okla., 1971, MArch, 1973. Registered arch., Calif. Pres., arch. Blevins & Spitz, Inc., Shawnee, Okla., 1975-78, B.N.A.C., Inc., Shawnee, 1978-82; project arch. Stearns-Roger World Corp., Denver, 1982-86; pvt. practice Coronado, Calif., 1986-90; chief arch., v.p. arch. United Engrs. and Constructors, Denver, 1991-93; cons. arch. Raytheon Engrs. and Constructors, Phila., 1993-97; assoc. dean New Sch. Arch., San Diego, 1992-95, mgr. design clinic, 1995. Prin. works include Tinker Burger F.F.F., 1976, Family Life Ctr., 1979, Konana Performing Arts Bldg., 1980, Gen. Mail Facility, 1987. Capt. USAF, 1971-75. Fellow Victoria U. Wellington, New Zealand, 1989. Mem. Constrn. Specialist Inst. Presbyterian. Avocations: sailing, antique cars, traveling. Office: Platt Whitelaw Architects 3653 Goldfinch St San Diego CA 92064

BLEVINS, WILLARD AHART, electrical engineer; b. Jonben, W.Va., Nov. 20, 1949; s. Oakley Cameron and Peggy Jane (Agee) B.; m. Nancy Phyllis Bailey, June 26, 1971; children: Maria Dawn, Teresa Lynn. AA in Elec. Tech. with honors, N.D. State Sch. Sci., 1974; BSEE with honors, Ariz. State U., 1988. Technician Sperry Flight Systems, Phoenix, 1974-88; engr. Sperry/Honeywell, Phoenix, 1988—. Patentee out of lock detector. With USAF, 1968-72. Recipient Honeywell Tech. Achievement award, 1995; named Parent of Yr., Phoenix Children's Chorus, 1985. Avocation: playing bass guitar with pop group. Home: 15810 N 47th Ln Glendale AZ 85306-2602 Office: Honeywell PO Box 21111-w33C Phoenix AZ 85036

BLEWETT, PATRICK ALAN, clergyman; b. Lewiston, Idaho, Aug. 31, 1956; s. Pierce Nurse and Grace Johnette (Peters) B.; m. Jana Lee Tureman, July 29, 1978; children: Sheila Marie, Kraig Alan, Amanda Joy. BA in Bibl. Studies, Mont. Inst. Bible, 1978; MA in Ch. Edn., Western Conservative Bapt. Sem, 1981, MDiv, 1990, postgrad., 1990—. Ordained to ministry Community Ch., 1982. Instr. religious edn. Big Sky Bible Coll., Lewistown, Mont., 1981-82; edn. pastor First Federated Ch., Des Moines, 1982-83; edn. pastor, adminstr. First Bapt. Ch., Sheridan, Wyo., 1983-85; assoc. pastor, adminstr. Orchards Community Ch., Lewiston, Idaho, 1985-90; family ministries pastor Cole Community Ch., Boise, Idaho, 1990—; instr. Bibl. studies Cole Ctr. Bibl. Studies, Boise, 1990—; cons. Scripture Press Publs., Wheaton, Ill., 1983—; adminstrv. chaplain Lewiston (Idaho) Police Dept., 1985-90. Mem. instl. rev. bd. St. Joseph's Regional Med. Ctr., Lewiston, 1988-90; bd. mem. Lewis-Clark Coun. on Youth, Lewiston, 1988-90, Lewis-Clark Coalition on At-Risk Youth, Lewiston, 1989-90, Treasure Valley Christian Workers Conf., Boise, 1990—. Recipient Cert. of Excellence in Environ. Protection, Pres. U.S., 1973. Mem. Internat. Conf. Police Chaplains, Conservative Bapt. Assn. Am., Nat. Assn. Evangelicals, Profl. Assn. Christian Educators, Idaho Assn. Pastoral Care (bd. mem. 1988-90), Lewis-Clark Ministerial Assn. (v.p. 1988-90), Rotary (pres. 1989-90). Republican. Home: 11029 Gunsmoke St Boise ID 83713-3855 Office: Cole Community Ch 8775 Ustick Rd Boise ID 83704-5643

BLIESNER, JAMES DOUGLAS, municipal/county official, consultant; b. Milw., Mar. 19, 1945; s. Milton Carl and Dorothy (St. George) B.; m. Phyllis Jean Byrd, June 15, 1966 (div. 1985); children: Tris, Cara. BA in Philosophy, Ea. Nazarene Coll., 1968; MA in Social Ethics, Andover, Newton Theol. Sch., 1973; postgrad., Boston U., 1969-70; student, N.Y. Studio Sch./Decordoua, Mus. Sch., Milw. Tech. Art Sch. Exec. dir. San Diego Youth and Community Svcs., 1974-78; cons., analyst San Diego Housing Commn., 1979-84; dir. San Diego City-County Reinvestment Task Force, 1984—; bd. dirs. Calif. Cmty. Reinvestment Corp.; vice chmn. Calif. Reinvestment Com., 1989—; founder, chmn. City Heights Cmty. Devel. Corp., San Diego, 1980-89; fin. com. chairperson Mid-City Revitalization Com., San Diego, 1988; founding bd. dirs. Neighborhood Nat. Bank; instr. San Diego State U. Author monographs, 1979; visual arts exhbns. include San Diego Arts Inst., Soc. Western Artists, Santa Barbara Contemporary Arts Forum, Calif. Coun. for Humanities; films exhibited in Centro Cultural, Tijuana, Mex.; exhibited in group shows in Venice, Paris, Jerusalem, Mex., Eng., China. Coun. appointee City of San Diego Com. on Reapportionment, 1990, Com. on Growth and Devel., San Diego, 1989; gov. appointee Gov.'s Office of Neighborhoods, Calif., 1987; mem. City Heights Redevel. Project Com., San Diego, 1992; pres. San Diego Housing Consortium. U.S.-Mex. Fund for Culture grantee; recipient Award of Honor, Am. Planning Assn., 1987, Spl. Project award, 1987, Merit award, 1989, Lifetime Achievement award Non-Profit Fedn. San Diego; named Citizen of Yr. Mid-City C. of C., 1986, award Calif. Coun. Humanities. Methodist. Avocation: visual arts. Home: 4106 Manzanita Dr San Diego CA 92105-4508 Office: City County Reinvestment Task Force 3989 Ruffin Rdwy Rm A6 San Diego CA 92123

BLINDER, JANET, art dealer; b. L.A., Sept. 21, 1953; d. Joseph and Margaret (Nadel) Weiss; m. Martin S. Blinder, Dec. 10, 1983. Founder Nationwide Baby Shops, Santa Monica, Calif., 1976-82; adminstr. Martin Lawrence Ltd. Editions, Van Nuys, Calif., 1982-90; art dealer L.A., 1990—. Mem. benefit com. AIDS Project L.A., 1988, prin. sponsor ann. fundraiser, 1990; mem. benefit com. Art Against AIDS, L.A., 1989; patron, sponsor Maryvale Orphanage, Rosemead, Calif., 1984—; patron Scottsdale Ctr. for the Arts. Recipient Commendation for Philanthropic Efforts City of L.A. Mayor Tom Bradley, 1988. Mem. Mus. Modern Art, Whitney Mus. Am. Art, Guggenheim Mus., Palm Springs (Calif.) Mus. Art, Mus. of Contemporary Art, Scottsdale (Ariz.) Ctr. for the Arts.

BLINDER, MARTIN S., business consultant, art dealer; b. Bklyn., Nov. 18, 1946; s. Meyer and Lillian (Stein) B.; m. Janet Weiss, Dec. 10, 1983. BBA, Adelphi U., 1968. Account exec. Bruns, Nordeman & Co., N.Y.C., 1968-69; v.p. Blinder, Robinson & Co., Westbury, N.Y., 1969-73; treas. BHB Prodns., L.A., 1973-76; pres. Martin Lawrence Ltd. Edits., Van Nuys, Calif., 1976-94, chmn., 1986-94, bd. dirs., 1994—; pres., dir. Corp. Art Inc., Visual Artists Mgmt. Corp., Art Consultants Inc.; pres., owner, founder MSB Fine Art, Phoenix, 1994—; lectr. bus. symposia. Contbr. articles to mags. and newspapers; appeared on TV and radio. Mem. Dem. Nat. Com.; mem. benefit com. AIDS project, L.A., 1988; bd. dirs. Very Spl. Arts, 1989—, chmn. visual arts Internat. Very Spl. Arts Festival, 1989; patron Guggenheim Mus., N.Y.C., Mus. Modern Art, N.Y.C., L.A. County Mus. Art, L.A. Mus. Contemporary Art (hon. founder), Whitney Mus. Am. Art, Palm Springs Mus. Art, Hirschhorn Mus., Washington, Skirball Mus., L.A., Diabetes Found. of City of Hope, B'nai B'rith Anti-Defamation League, Very Spl. Arts, Scottsdale (Ariz.) Ctr. for the Arts, Scottsdale Mus. Contempory Art; mem. Citizens for Common Sense; bd. dirs., pres. Rsch. Found. for Crohns Disease; mem. benefit com. Art Against AIDS, 1989; co-chair artists com. for Don't Bungle the Jungle Companions of Arts and Nature, 1989; prin. sponsor, ann. fundraiser AIDS Project, L.A., 1990. Read into Congl. Record, 1981, 83, 86, 88, 91; recipient resolution of commendation L.A. City Coun., 1983, State of Calif. resolution for contbn. to arts in Calif., 1983, Merit award Republic Haiti for contbn. to arts, 1985, U.S. Senate commendation, 1983, County of L.A. Bd. Suprs. resolution for Contbn. to arts in So. Calif., 1983, Gov. of R.I. resolution for contbns. to arts, 1985, commendation County of Los Angeles-Supr. Ed Edelman, 1991, commendation for contbns. to the arts and the healing arts City of L.A., 1991, commendation for contbns. to arts and philanthropy Mayor David Dinkins, N.Y.C., 1992; Nov. 18, 1985 declared Martin S. Blinder Day in L.A. in his honor by Mayor Tom Bradley, spl. award San Diego Youth and Cmty. Svcs., Bruin Bear award for helping to establish Blinder Rsch. Found., 1991. Mem. Fine Art Pub.'s Assn. (bd. dirs. 1990-94), Med. Art Assn. at UCLA.UCLA. Office: MSB Fine Art 9135 N 70th St Scottsdale AZ 85253-1961

BLISH, EUGENE SYLVESTER, trade association administrator; b. Denver, Oct. 9, 1912; s. George Joseph and Lillian Lenox (O'Neill) B.; m. Susan M. Monti, Feb. 21, 1950, children: Eugene A., Mary, Susan Blish Clarke, Julia Blish Gordon. BSC, U. Notre Dame, 1934. Advt. dir. Colo. Milling and Elevator Co., Denver, 1934-45; advt. and mktg. cons., Denver, 1945-57; asst. exec. dir. Am. Sheep Producers Council, Denver, 1957-74; merchandising rep. Nat. Potato Bd., Denver, 1974-87. Mem. alumni bd. dirs. U. Notre Dame, 1947-49. Mem. Soc. Mayflower Desc., Barnstable Hist. Soc. (Mass.). Clubs: Denver Athletic, Mt. Vernon Country, Denver Notre Dame. Home and Office: 1370 Madison St Denver CO 80206-2613

BLISS, MARIAN ALICE, information systems professional; b. Burlington, Wis., Feb. 15, 1943; d. Charles Homer and Mabel Alice (Mantz) Jackson; m. Robert L. McDill, Feb. 13, 1965 (div.); children: Kimberly Ann, Scott Daniel; m. Erlan Shelly Bliss, Nov. 17, 1982. BA, U. Colo., 1965; MBA, Golden Gate U., 1985; MS in Systems Mgmt., U. Denver, 1991. Cert. Inst. for Cert. Computer Profls.; cert. Project Mgmt. Inst., project mgmt. profl. Cardiopulmonary technician Rancho Los Amigos Hosp., Downey, Calif., 1965-66; cardiology technologist William Beaumont Hosp., Royal Oak, Mich., 1966-67; pulmonary technologist Dallas County Hosps., 1967-68; with Pacific Bell, 1980-96, account exec., 1985; sys. design analyst Pacific Bell, San Ramon, Calif., 1986, staff analyst, 1988-90, sr. systems analyst, 1988-90, mgr. software configuration mgmt., 1990-92; graphical user interface devel. Pacific Bell, 1993, info. sys. project mgr. on line text retrieval, 1994, project mgr. phase 1 data warehouse, 1995, project mgr. strategic sys. engring., 1996—; Y2K program mgmt., software devel. & implementation cons. Interim Tech., 1997—. Treas. Greenbrook Sch. PTA, Danville, 1978, pres., 1979. Mem. AAUW. Episcopalian. Avocations: golf, bridge, photography. Home: 357 Conway Dr Danville CA 94526-5511 Office: 444 Market St Ste 760 San Francisco CA 94111-5327

BLITMAN, JOE, doll dealer; b. Englewood, N.J., Nov. 12, 1949; s. Louis and Jane (MacMillan) B. BA, Oberlin Coll., 1971. Vintage doll dealer Joe's Barbies, L.A., 1989—. Author: The Mod, Mod, Mod, World of Barbie Fashion, 1996, The Mod, Mod, Mod, Mod World of Francie Fashion, 1996. Office: Joe's Barbies 5163 Franklin Ave Los Angeles CA 90027-3601

BLITS, STANLEY E., television music director; b. New Rochelle, N.Y., Aug. 23, 1956; s. Jacques and Flora (Pezarro) B. BA, U. So. Calif., 1977. Page CBS, L.A., 1978-79; prodn. asst. Goodson-Todman Prodns., L.A., 1979-82; TV music dir. The Price is Right Mark Goodson Prodns., L.A., 1982—. Avocations: cartooning, cooking. Office: The Price Is Right 5757 Wilshire Blvd Los Angeles CA 90036-3635

BLITT, RITA LEA, artist; b. Kansas City, Mo., Sept. 7, 1931; d. Herman Stanley and Dorothy Edith (Sofnas) Copaken; m. Irwin Joseph Blitt, Apr. 18, 1951; 1 child, Chela Connie. Student, U. Ill., 1948-50; BA, Kansas City U., 1952; postgrad., Kansas City Art Inst., 1952-54. Freelance painter, sculptor Leawood, Kans., 1958—. *In 2000, Rita Blitt: Drawings, Paintings, and Sculpture will be published in conjunction with a traveling exhibit which will include the showing of the 1984 film of dancing hands: Visual Arts of Rita Blitt, followed by a workshop which encourages everyone to draw with one hand or two.* Author: Nessie the Sculpture, 1978; collaborations with dancers and musicians such as dancer/choreographer David Parsons, 1996, and cellist Yehuda Hanani, 1986; creator of words and paintings for internat. distributed posters "Kindness is Contagious, Catch It!", led to the founding of the Kindness Program sponsored by The Stop Violence Coalition; One-woman exhbns. include Unitarian Gallery, Kansas City, Mo., 1965, Spectrum Gallery, N.Y.C., 1969, Angerer Gallery, Kansas City, Mo., 1974, Battle Creek (Mich.) Civic Art Ctr., 1975, Harkness Gallery, N.Y.C., 1977, Martin Schweig Gallery, St. Louis, 1977, Gargoyle Gallery, Aspen, Colo., 1978, Tumbling Waters Mus., Montgomery, Ala., 1978, St. Louis U., 1980, Leedy-Voulkos Gallery, Kansas City, Mo., 1987, Joy Horwich Gallery, Chgo., 1987, Goldman Gallery, Haifa, Israel, 1989, Bet Shmuel, Jerusalem, 1989, Goldman Kraft Gallery, Chgo., 1990, Singapore Nat. Mus., 1991, Albrecht-Kemper Mus., St. Joseph, Mo., 1991, Aspen (Colo.) Inst., 1992, Foothills Art Ctr., Golden, Colo., 1992, Mackey Gallery, Denver, 1992, U. Ill., Urbana, 1994, Kennedy Mus. U. Ohio, Athens, 1994, Krasl Art Ctr., St. Joseph, Mich., 1994, Baker U., Baldwin, Kans., 1995, Ctrl. Exch., Kansas City, Mo., 1995, Atchison (Kans.) Muchnik Gallery, 1996, Marines Meml. Theater, San Francisco, 1997, Resourceful Women, San Francisco, 1997, City Ctr., N.Y., 1998; group exhbns. include Kansas City (Mo.) Mus., 1959, Ringling Mus., Sarasota, Fla., 1967, Springfield (Mo.) Mus., 1967, Joslyn Mus., Omaha, 1972, Doug Drake Gallery, Kansas City, 1975, Conry Gallery, Kansas City, Mo., 1976, Cyvia Gallery, New Haven, 1977, Gargoyle Gallery, Aspen, Colo., 1979, Putney Gallery, Aspen, 1979, Carrefour Gallery, N.Y.C., 1979, Elaine Benson Gallery, Bridgehampton, N.Y., 1980, Tall Grass Fine Arts Gallery, Kansas City, Mo., 1980, 81, Art and Design Gallery, N.Y.C., 1982, Winter Manhattan (Kans.), Streker, Gallery, 1983, Joanne Lyons Gallery, Aspen, 1984, Banaker Gallery, 1987, 88, Andrea Ross Gallery, Santa Monica, Calif., 1990, LA 90, L.A., 1990, Eva Cohon, Chgo., 1995, Obere Galerie, Berlin, 1995, Din Deutsches Inst., Berlin, 1995, Dance Aspen, Colo., 1997; permanent collections include Albrecht-Kemper Mus., St. Joseph, Mo., Ga. Inst. Tech., JFK Libr., Cambridge, Mass., Kennedy Mus. Ohio U., Athens, Nat. Mus. Singapore, Skirball Mus., L.A., Spertus Mus., Chgo., Kansas City (Mo.) Children's Mus., Kennedy Mus., Ohio U., Ga. Tech. Ctr. for the Arts, and other numerous pvt. and pub. collections; sculptures in numerous pub. places including, Calif., Ill., Kans., Mo., Md., N.J., N.Y., Japan. Mem. Soc. Fellow The Nelson Gallery Found., The Aspen Inst.; bd. dirs. Trio Found.; mem. The Stop Violence Coalition; rsch. assoc. The Internat. Rsch. on Jewish Women. Mem. Internat. Sculpture Ctr., Kansas City Artists Coalition. Avocations: music, dance, travel, hiking.

BLITZ, CHARLES AKIN, lawyer; b. Honolulu, Sept. 2, 1949; s. Howard Samuel and Marjorie C. (Cooke) B.; m. Karen Lee Sherwood, May 6, 1976; children: C. Tyler, Derek A., Colby S. BA, Willamette U., 1972; JD, Lewis & Clark Coll., 1975; LLM in Labor and Employment, Georgetown U., 1979. Bar: Ore. Supreme Ct., 1975, U.S. Dist. Ct. (Ore.), 1975, U.S. Dist. Ct. (9th cir.), 1975, U.S. Mil. Ct. Appeals, 1976, U.S. Ct. Appeals (4th cir.), 1977, U.S. Ct. Appeals (DC cir.), 1978, U.S. Supreme Ct., 1979. Assoc. Cass Scott Woods & Smith, Eugene, Oreg., 1979-82; asst. atty. gen. Oreg. Dept. Justice, Salem, 1982-83; assoc. Spears Lubersky Law Firm, Portland, 1983-85; ptnr. Lane Powell Spears Lubersky, Portland, 1985-98, Bullard Korshoj Smith & Jernstedt, Portland, 1998—. Author: Model Policies and Procedures for Special Districts, Including Administrative Rules, 1994, 2nd edit., 1996. Chmn. Civil Svc. Reform Task Force for the City of Portland, 1985-86, Enhanced Sheriff's Patrol Dist. Bd., Washington County Sheriff's Office, Hillsboro, Oreg., 1988-91; asst. scoutmaster, coun. chmn. risk mgmt. and Butte Creek Ranch com. Cascade Pacific Coun., Boy Scouts Am., Portland, 1988—; mem. Citizens Crime Commn., Portland, 1992—; exec. bd. mem. Cascade Pacific Coun., Boy Scouts Am., Portland, 1993—; trustee Charitable Trust Rotary Club Portland, 1994-97; ski patroller Mount Hood Ski Patrol, Portland, 1996—. Capt. USMC, 1975-79, maj. USMCR, 1982. Recipient Vigil Honor, Boy Scouts Am.-Cascade Pacific Coun., Portland, 1996, Silver Beaver award Boy Scouts Am., Portland, 1998; James E. West fellow Boy Scouts Am., Portland, 1996, Paul Harris fellow Rotary Internat., Portland, 1994, 97. Mem. Oreg. State Bar (chmn. labor law sect. 1995-96), Oreg. Assn. Chiefs of Police and Oreg. State Sheriff's Assn. (legal counsel 1987—, Presdl. award of merit 1990, 91, 93), Rotary Club Portland (dir. 1995-98). Republican. Episcopalian. Avocations: skiing, western trail riding. E-mail: ablitz@bksjlaw.com. Fax: 503-224-8851. Office: Bullard Korshoj Smith & Jernstedt Ste 800 1000 SW Broadway Ste 1900 Portland OR 97205

BLITZ-WEISZ, SALLY, speech pathologist; b. Buffalo, Nov. 9, 1954; d. Isaac and Paula (Goldstein) Blitz; m. Andrew Weisz, Dec. 16, 1984; 1 child, Naomi Ariel Weisz. BA in Speech Pathology, Audiology, SUNY, Buffalo, 1976, MA in Speech Pathology, 1978; MS Sch Counseling, pupil pers credential, U. LaVerne, 1991. Lic. speech/lang. pathologist, Calif. Speech, lang. pathologist Lang. Devel. Program, Tonawanda, N.Y., 1978-82, Bailey and Drown Assocs., La Habra, Calif., 1982-83; speech, lang. specialist, cons. Pasadena (Calif.) Unified Schs., 1983-94, L.A. Unified Schs., 1996—. Active Anti-Defamation League, San Fernando Valley, 1985-86; mem. 2d Generation Holocaust Survivors, Los Angeles, 1986—. Recipient Excellence in Studies award Temple Sharey Zedek, Buffalo, 1969. Mem. Am. Speech-Lang.-Hearing Assn. Democrat. Club: Jewish Young Adults. Lodge: B'nai Brith. Avocations: exercise workouts, bicycling. Home: 11671 Amigo Ave Northridge CA 91326-1849 Office: L A Unified Sch Dist Mid City-SESU Los Angeles CA 90051

BLOCH, DORIS BERYL, charitable organization administrator; b. L.A., May 12, 1935; d. Theodore and Eva Lillan (Blockman) Weiner; m. Alfred M. Bloch, June, 1961 (div. Aug., 1973); children: Jeffrey Donner, Laura Jennifer, Lisa Suzanne. Student, U. Calif., Berkeley, L.A. Asst. v.p. RelaxAcizor, Inc., L.A., 1956-61; info. coord. Office of City Atty., L.A., 1973-75; cons. State of Calif. Dept. Bus. and Transp., L.A., 1975-76; cons. to charitable orgns. L.A., 1976-83; exec. dir. L.A. Regional Food Bank, 1983—. Bd. dirs. Auxiliary of So. Calif. Psycho-analytic Soc., 1971-74, Sr. Health and Peer Counseling Ctr., 1981-83, Bay Area Multi-Svc. Ctr., 1981-83, 2d Harvest Nat. Food Bank Network, 1986-91, W. L.A. Police and Comty. Together, 1990-93, Interfaith Hunger Coalition, 1993-96, Emergency Network L.A., 1995—, chair, 1996; pub. mem. L.A. County Bar Assn. Spl. Com. on Lawyer Advtg., 1977-79, edn. com. Ctr. for Early Edn., 1978-80; mem. Private Industry Coun. City of Los Angeles, 1994—, Calif. Assn. Food Banks, 1995—; mayoral appointee L.A. Food Security and Hunger Partnership, 1997. Named Hunger Fighter, Calif. Hunger Action Com., Sacramento, 1988. Mem. Town Hall, Women in Pub. Affairs, UCLA Art Coun., L.A. Libr. Found. Avocations: art, literature, classical music, travel. Office: LA Regional Food Bank 1734 E 41st St Los Angeles CA 90058-1502

BLOCK, MICHAEL KENT, economics and law educator, public policy association executive, former government official, consultant; b. N.Y.C., Apr. 2, 1942; s. Philip and Roslyn (Klein) B.; m. Carole Arline Polansky, Aug. 30, 1964 (div.); children: Robert Justin, Tamara Nicole; m. Olga Vyborna, Dec. 1, 1996. A.B., Stanford U., 1964, A.M., 1969, Ph.D., 1972. Research analyst Bank of Am., San Francisco, 1965-66; research assoc. Planning Assocs., San Francisco, 1966-67; asst. prof. econs. U. Santa Clara, 1969-72; asst. prof. econs. dept. ops. research and adminstrv. sci. Naval Postgrad. Sch., Monterey, Calif., 1972-74, assoc. prof., 1974-76; research fellow Hoover Instn., Stanford U., 1975-76, sr. research fellow, 1976-87; dir. Center for Econometric Studies of Justice System, 1977-81; ptnr. Block & Nold, Cons., Palo Alto, Calif., 1980-81; assoc. prof. mgmt., econs. and law U. Ariz., Tucson, 1982-85, prof. econs. and law, 1989—; mem. U.S. Sentencing Commn., Washington, 1985-89; exec. v.p. Cybernomics, Tucson, 1991—; pres. Goldwater Inst. for Pub. Policy, Phoenix, Ariz., 1992—; sr. policy adviser State of Ariz. Gov. Symington, 1996-97; mem. Ariz. Residential Utility Consumer Bd., 1995-96, chmn. Ariz. Constl. Def. Coun., 1994-97, Ariz. Juvenile Justice Adv. Coun., 1996-97; seminar dir. Econ. Devel. Inst./World Bank, 1992-95; cons. in field. Author: (with H.G. Demmert) Workbook and Programmed Guide to Economics, 1974, 77, 80, (with James M. Clabault) A Legal and Economic Analysis of Criminal Antitrust Indictments:, 1955-80; contbr. articles to profl. publs. Fellow NSF, 1965, Stanford U. Fellow Progress and Freedom Found.; mem. Am. Econ. Assn., Phi Beta Kappa. Office: U Ariz Econ Dept McClelland Hall Tucson AZ 85721

BLODGETT, ELSIE GRACE, association executive; b. Eldorado Springs, Mo., Aug. 2, 1921; d. Charles Ishmal and Naoma Florence (Worthington) Robison; m. Charles Davis Blodgett, Nov. 8, 1940; children: Carolyn Doyel, Charleen Bier, Lyndon Blodgett, Daryl (dec.). Student Warrensburg (Mo.) State Tchrs. Coll., 1939-40; BA, Fresno (Calif.) State Coll., 1953. Tchr. schs. in Mo. and Calif., 1940-42, 47-72; owner, mgr. rental units, 1965—; exec. dir. San Joaquin County (Calif.) Rental Property Assn., Stockton, 1970-81; prin. Delta Rental Property Owners and Assocs., 1981-82; propr. Crystal Springs Health World, Inc., Stockton, 1980-86; bd. dirs. Stockton Better Bus. Bur. Active local PTA, Girl Scouts U.S., Boy Scouts Am.; bd. dirs. Stockton Goodwill Industries; active Vols. in Police Svc., 1993; capt. Delaware Alpine Neighborhood Watch, 1994—. Named (with husband) Mr. and Mrs. Apt. Owner of San Joaquin County, 1977. Mem. Nat. Apt. Assn. (state treas. women's div. 1977-79), Calif. Ret. Tchrs. Assn. Republican. Methodist. Lodge: Stockton Zonta. Home and Office: 2285 W Mendocino Ave Stockton CA 95204-4005

BLODGETT, FORREST CLINTON, economics educator; b. Oregon City, Oreg., Oct. 6, 1927; s. Clinton Alexander and Mabel (Wells) B.; m. Beverley Janice Buchholz, Dec. 21, 1946; children: Cherine (Mrs. Jon R. Klein), Candis Melis, Clinton George. BS, U. Omaha, 1961; MA, U. Mo., 1969; PhD, Portland State U., 1979. Joined C.E. U.S. Army, 1946, commd. 2d lt., 1946, advanced through grades to lt. col., 1965, ret., 1968; engring. assignments U.S. Army, Japan, 1947-49, U.K., 1950-53, Korea, 1955-56, Alaska, 1958-60, Vietnam, 1963; staff engr. 2d Army Air Def. Region U.S. Army, Richards-Gebaur AFB, Mo., 1964-66; base engr. Def. Atomic Support Agy., Sandia Base, N.Mex., 1966-68; bus. mgr., trustee, asst. prof. econs. Linfield Coll., McMinnville, Oreg., 1968-73, assoc. prof., 1973-83, prof., 1983-90, emeritus prof. econs., 1990—; pres. Blodgett Enterprises, Inc., 1983-85; founder, dir. Valley Community Bank, 1980-86, vice chmn. bd. dirs., 1985-86. Commr., Housing Authority of Yamhill County (Oreg.), chmn., 1980-83; mem. Yamhill County Econ. Devel. Com., 1978-83; bd. dirs. Yamhill County Found., 1983-91, Oreg. Internat. Coun., 1995—. Decorated Army Commendation medal with oak leaf cluster; recipient Joint Service Commendation medal Dept. of Def. Mem. Soc. Am. Mil. Engrs. (pres. Albuquerque post 1968), Am. Econ. Assn., Western Econ. Assn. Internat., Nat. Ret. Officers Assn., Res. Officers Assn. (pres. Marion chpt. 1976), SAR (pres. Oreg. soc. 1985-86, v.p. gen. Nat. Soc. 1991-93), Urban Affairs Assn., Soc. for The History of Tech., Am. Law and Econs. Assn., Pi Sigma Epsilon, Pi Gamma Mu, Omicron Delta Epsilon (Pacific NW regional dir. 1978-88), Rotary (pres. McMinnville 1983-84). Republican. Episcopalian. Office: Linfield Coll 1300 NE 16th Ave #1020 Portland OR 97232-1487

BLODGETT, JULIAN ROBERT, small business owner; b. Honolulu, Nov. 21, 1919; s. Harry Hoagland and Esther Julia (Lyons) B.; m. Eleanor Anne Fischer, Nov. 4, 1941 (dec. 1983); children: Eric, Julie, Byron, Paul. BA, UCLA, 1940. Stock clk. Northrop Aircraft Co., Hawthorne, Calif., 1941-42; spl. agt. FBI, Washington, 1942-44, 46-57, Standard Oil Calif., San Francisco, 1945-46; gen. mgr. Western Indsl. Security Co., L.A., 1961-63; chief bur. investigation L.A. Dist. Atty., 1957-61; owner, operator Julian R. Blodgett Investigations, L.A., 1961—, Grey Fox Ltd., 1995—. Chmn., commr. L.A. City Housing Authority, 1963-65. Mem. Former Agts. FBI. Office: PO Box 49658 Los Angeles CA 90049-0658

BLOEBAUM, ROY DRAKE, biologist educator, bioengineering researcher; b. St. Charles, Mo., July 19, 1946; s. August E. and Joan Fay (Drake) B.; m. Lois Dawn Miller, Sept. 27, 1975; children: Drake, Megan, Andrew. AA in Liberal Arts magna cum laude, St. Mary's Coll., O'Fallon, Mo., 1972; BS in Biology cum laude, Lindenwood Coll., 1974; BSc in Anatomy with honors, U. Western Australia, Perth, 1976, PhD in Anatomy, 1981. Youth activities dir. St. Louis, 1971-74; assoc. dean students, student counselor St. Mary's Coll., O'Fallon, Mo., 1974-76, 75-76; lectr. in gross anatomy, human biology, emergency medicine U. Western Australia, Perth, 1976-80; postgrad. rsch. fellow Divsn. Orthopaedic Surgery UCLA, 1978; rsch. assoc. Orthopaedic Hosp., Dept. Orthopaedics U. So. Calif., L.A., 1981-82, lectr. in gross anatomy Dept. Orthopaedics, 1981-84, asst. prof. rsch. orthopaedics, 1982-84; adj. assoc. prof. bioengring. Ariz. State U., Tempe, 1984-87; cons. UCLA-VA Sys., 1986; co-dir. Bone and Joint Rsch. Lab. VA Med. Ctr., Salt Lake City, 1987—; dir. basic sci. Divsn. Orthopedic Surgery U. Utah Sch. Medicine, Salt Lake City, 1987—, rsch. assoc. prof., rsch. prof. Divsn. Orthopaedic Surgery, 1987-92, 92—; rsch. assoc. prof., rsch. prof. biology U. Utah, Salt Lake City, 1989-91, 92—, rsch. assoc. prof. bioengring., rsch. prof., 1988-91, 92—; NIH reviewer and proposal reviewer NIDCD, Bethesda, Md., 1993—; lectr. on tissue response to biomaterials Ariz. State U., Tempe, 1984-87, lectr. in gross anatomy and synovial joint ultrastructure for residents Divsn. Orthopaedic Surgery, U. Utah Sch. Medicine, 1987—, lectr. in biomaterials interaction in tissue, 1987—, lectr. in backscattered electron imaging of bone histology, 1987—; cons. to America's Cup, 1983-89; dir. biol. response analysis group U. Soc. Calif., 1984; dir. basic sci. divsn. Harrington Arthritis Rsch. Ctr., Phoenix, 1984-87; cons. to UCLA-VA Sys., 1986; co-dir. bone and joint rsch. labs. VA Med. Ctr., Salt Lake City, 1987—; dir. basic scis. orthopaedic residency program U. Utah Sch. Medicine, 1987—; guest lectr. in field. Mem. editorial bd. Jour. of Histotechnology, Orthopaedics and Related Scis.; reviewer Clin. Orthopaedics and Related Rsch., Jour. Biomaterials Applications, Jour. of Biomed. Materials Rsch., Scanning Microscopy, Jour. of Transplantation, Jour. of Investigative Surgery; contbr. numerous articles and abstracts to profl. jours. Recipient Air medal (13 Oak Leaf Clusters), 1968-69, Disting. Flying Cross (2 Oak Leaf Clusters), 1969, Sister Theresa Weber Leadership scholarship, 1970, Avant Garde-For Scholarship, Svc. to Univ. and Cmty., 1971, Rotary Internat. scholarship, 1975-76, Otto E. AuFranc award (Basic Rsch.-Orthopaedic Surgery), Hip Soc., 1979, Superior Performance award Dept.

Vets. Affairs Med. Ctr., Salt Lake City, 1989, SIROT Internat. prize Basic Rsch.-Orthopaedic Surgery, 1990; patent Knee Prosthesis, 1987, Hypertonic Solution for Arthroscopic Surgery, 1989, Tibial Componenet for a Knee Prosthesis, 1989, Knee Prosthesis, 1990; grantee Johnson & Johnson Products, Inc., 1981-82, 1988-90, Del E. Webb Found., 1983-85, Intermedics Orthopaedics, Inc., 1983-86, 89-90, Hexcel Med., 1983-86, Good Samaritan Hosp., 1984, Pennwalt Pharm. Corp., 1985-86, Orthopaedic Rsch. and Edn. Found., 1986, AVORE, 1986, Greyhound Assn., 1985-86, Whitaker Found., 1987-90, Life Core/Biomet, 1987-89, 89-92, Zimmer Corp., 1988-91, Dow Corning Wright, 1990-93, 93-97. Mem. Orthopaedic Rsch. Soc., Soc. for Biomaterials, Nat. Soc. for Histotechnology (First Place Med. Photography Contest 1988), Am. Acad. Orthopaedic Surgeons (assoc.). Home: 1643 Wasatch Cir Salt Lake City UT 84105-1740 Office: VA Med Ctr Bone & Joint Lab 500 Foothill Dr Salt Lake City UT 84148-0001

BLOEDE, VICTOR CARL, lawyer, academic executive; b. Woodwardville, Md., July 17, 1917; s. Carl Schon and Eleanor (Eck) B.; m. Ellen Louise Miller, May 9, 1947; children—Karl Abbott, Pamela Elena. A.B., Dartmouth Coll., 1940; J.D. cum laude, U. Balt., 1950; LL.M. in Pub. Law, Georgetown U., 1967. Bar: Md. 1950, Fed. Hawaii 1958, U.S. Supreme Ct. 1971. Pvt. practice Balt., 1950-64; mem. Goldman & Bloede, Balt., 1959-64; counsel Seven-Up Bottling Co., Balt., 1958-64; dep. atty. gen. Pacific Trust Ter., Honolulu, 1952-53; asst. solicitor for ters. Office of Solicitor, U.S. Dept. Interior, Washington, 1953-54; atty. U.S. Justice, Honolulu, 1955-58; assoc. gen. counsel Dept. Navy, Washington, 1960-61, 63-64; spl. legal cons. Md. Legislature, Legis. Council, 1963-64, 66-67; assoc. prof. U. Hawaii, 1961-63, dir. property mgmt., 1964-67; house counsel, dir. contracts and grants U. Hawaii System, 1967-82; house counsel U. Hawaii Research Corp., 1970-82; legal counsel Law of Sea Inst., 1978-82; legal cons. Rsch. Corp. and grad. rsch. divsn. U. Hawaii, 1982-92; spl. counsel to Holifield Congl. Commn. on Govt. Procurement, 1970-73. Author: Hawaii Legislative Manual, 1962, Maori Affairs, New Zealand, 1964, Oceanographic Research Vessel Operations, and Liabilities, 1972, Hawaiian Archipelago, Legal Effects of a 200 Mile Territorial Sea, 1973, Copyright-Guidelines to the 1976 Act, 1977, Forms Manual, Inventions: Policy, Law and Procedure, 1982; writer, contbr. Coll. Law Digest and other publs. on legislation and pub. law. Mem. Gov.'s Task Force Hawaii and The Sea, 1969, Citizens Housing Com. Balt., 1952-64; bd. govs. Balt. Cmty. YMCA, 1954-64; bd. dirs. U. Hawaii Press, 1964-66, Coll. Housing Found., 1968-80; appointed to internat. rev. commn. Canada-France Hawaii Telescope Corp., 1973-82, chmn., 1973, 82; co-founder, incorporator First Unitarian Ch. Honolulu. Served to lt. comdr. USNR, 1942-45, PTO. Grantee ocean law studies NSF and NOAA, 1970-80. Mem. ABA, Balt. Bar Assn., Fed. Bar Assn., Am. Soc. Internat. Law, Nat. Assn. Univ. Attys. (founder & 1st chmn. patents & copyrights sect. 1974-76). Home: 635 Onaha St Honolulu HI 96816-4918

BLOG, GLORIA DELOSH, retired property administrator; b. Norfolk, N.Y., May 13, 1931; d. Leo George and Bernice Fredricka (Gooshaw) DeLosh; m. Orville Allen Bush, July 26, 1948 (dec. 1955); m. Lawrence Blog, Apr. 20, 1970. Attended, Syracuse U., 1956-60, Syracuse Beauty Sch., 1961, New Haven Tech. Sch., 1963-65. Bus. contr. Mega Engring., Lancaster, Calif., 1964-84; property adminstr. Bayco Fin. Corp., Sherman Oaks, Calif., 1984-88, Rodin-Lawson Mgmt. Co., Inc., Sherman Oaks, 1988-97. Sec. Pacific Art Guild, 1989-90. Avocation: oil and acrylic painting.

BLOMQUIST, CARL ARTHUR, medical and trust company executive, insurance executive; b. L.A., Feb. 2, 1947; s. Carl Arthur and Delphine Marie (Forcier) B.; m. Diane Leslie Nunez, May 5, 1973 (div. Dec. 1979); 1 child, Kristin; m. Patricia Marie Johnson, Feb. 3, 1984 (div. Dec. 1988), m. Sharon Elaine Fromwiller, Oct. 14, 1995. BS, U. San Diego, 1969; MPH, UCLA, 1973. Auditor Naval Area Audit Svc., San Diego, 1969-71; trainee USPHS, Washington, 1971; asst. adminstr. Northridge (Calif.) Hosp., 1973-76; asst. adminstr. fin. and facilities St. Vincent Med. Ctr., L.A., 1976-77; asst. v.p. 1st Interstate Mortgage, Pasadena, Calif., 1977-79; chief exec. officer Coop. Am. Physicians/Mut. Protection Trust, L.A., 1979-94; spl. dep. Calif. ins. commr. Exec. Life Ins. Co., L.A., 1991-94, acting CEO, 1991-92; prin. Carl A. Blomquist Cons., Playa Del Rey, Calif., 1994-95; mgr., CEO Head Injury Rehab. Svcs., LLC, 1995—; mem. instl. review bd. Motion Picture Hosp. Woodland Hills, Calif., 1993—; bd. dirs. Risk Mgmt. Assurance Corp., Dallas, 1996—; profl. adv. com. L.A. Posada Home Health, Pasadena, 1996—. Mem. Calif. Health Facilities Financing Authority, Sacramento, 1981—; co-chmn. Adv. Commn. on Malpractice Ins., Calif. Senate, Sacramento, 1984-92, mem. Commn. on Cost Containment in State Govt., 1984—; bd. dirs. Chaminade Coll. Prep. Sch., West Hills, Calif., 1988. Journalism grantee Helms Found., 1965. Mem. Am. Coll. Healthcare Execs., Am. Hosp. Assn., President's Assn. of Am. Mgmt. Assn., Health Care Execs. So. Calif., Hosp. Coun. So. Calif., UCLA Health Care Mgmt. Alumni Assn. (bd. dirs. 1987-94), Case Mgmt. Soc. Am., Am. Congress of Rehab. Med., Big Brothers Am. Republican. Roman Catholic. Avocations: sailing, skiing, golf. Office: Carl A Blomquist Cons 6641 Vista Del Mar Playa Del Rey CA 90293-7545

BLOMQUIST, ROBIN ALICE, artist, elementary education educator; b. Dinuba, Calif., May 14, 1913; d. Joseph Samuel and Lotta D. (Kennedy) Johnson; m. Carl Leonard Blomquist, Aug. 28, 1937; children: Robin John C., Carla May, Victoria, Alson, Mary, Joseph, Valanne. Student, San Diego Acad. Fine Arts, 1932-37, San Diego State Coll., 1936-37; BA, Chico State Coll., 1962, postgrad., 1963—; student, Calif. Sch. Arts Craft, Oakland, 1967. Cert. (life) elem., secondary tchr., Calif.; spl. cert. reading, Calif. State Dept. Edn. Artist, demonstrator Fed. Art Project, San Diego, 1936-37; adult edn. tchr. San Joaquin County Schs., Escalon, Calif., 1949-50, Kern County Schs., Taft, Shafter, Calif., 1950-52; adult edn. tchr. Shasta Coll., Redding, Calif., 1953-58, adult art tchr., 1973-81; art, mech. drawing tchr. Corning (Calif.) H.S., 1953-62; art tchr. Corning (Calif.) Elem. Sch., 1953-54; spl. reading, math tchr. Gerber (Calif.) Elem., 1963-74; substitute, home tchr. Tehama Schs., Red Bluff, Calif., 1973-93; ptnr., conservator, restorer Selected Arts Gallery, Chico, Calif., 1963-72; conservator Los Molinos (Calif.) Antiques, 1963-90; mem. Internat. Reading Conf., Eng., 1969, Alaska, 1970, Scotland, 1971. Troop leader Girl Scouts U.S., 1945-50, Camp Fire Girls, 1928-36, 4-H, 1938-41, Cub Scouts, 1953-55; mem. Tehama County (Calif.) Gen. & Hist. Soc., Hist. Commn., 1976-96, Arts Coun., 1982-85; pres. Tehama County Tchrs. Orgn., 1954-55, pres. Bus. Profl. Women, Corning, Calif., 1962-63, pres. United Meth. Women, Corning, 1964, 90; host Exch. Student Program, Sweden, Morocco, 1958-59, 74-75, Internat. Christian Youth Exch.; active PTA, Calif. Recipient 2nd Internat. Art Schs. award Internat. Latham Found., 1934, scholar San Diego Acad. Fine Arts, 1932-35. Mem. Am. Assn. Ret. Persons (scholarship chmn., citizen of the year, 1995), AAUW, Women in the Arts, Calif. Ret. Tchrs., No. Calif. Doll Club, United Fedn. of Doll Clubs, Corning Friends of Libr., Delta Kappa Gamma (v.p. 1980-81, pres. 1981-82). Democrat. Methodist. Avocations: photography, doll collecting, needlework, history, church. Home: 1417 Colusa St Corning CA 96021-2411

BLOMSTROM, BRUCE A., healthcare executive; b. Salem, Mass., July 4, 1937; m. Anne Blomstrom; children: Jeffrey, Kristin. BS, MIT, 1959, MS in Indsl. Mgmt., 1962. Asst. sec. Ministry of Commerce and Industry, Govt. of Uganda, Kampala, 1962-64; regional dir., Far East dir., internat. product mgmt., Libby McNeil & Libby, Chgo., 1965-73; dir. corp. planning, exec. mng. dir. Nippon Abbott; gen. mgr. South Africa Abbott Labs., North Chicago, Ill., 1973-82; v.p. Alpha Therapeutic, L.A., 1982-84; v.p.corp. devel. Whittaker Corp., L.A., 1984-85; pres., CEO Guardian Products divsn. Sunrise Med., Arleta, Calif., 1985-90; pres., CEO, dir. Clinishare, Inc. divsn. Unihealth, Chatsworth, Calif., 1991-97; pres., dir. NMC Homecare divsn. Fresenius Med. Care, 1997—; pres., dir. Unihealth Investment, Burbank, Calif., 1995-97; bd. dirs. Cedaron, Davis, Calif. Contbr. articles to profl. jours. Mem. alumni fund bd. MIT, 1996—; bd. dirs., v.p. Pasadena (Calif.) Symphony Assn., 1985-97; mem. Pacific Coun. on Internat. Policy, L.A., 1996—. 1st lt. USAR, 1959-67. Mem. Calif. Assn. for Health Svcs. at Home (legis. com. 1992-97), San Marino (Calif.) City Club (bd. dirs. 1994-96), Japan Am. Soc., Delta Tau Delta. Avocations: tennis, swimming, travel, foreign affairs.

BLOOM, JULIAN, artist, editor; b. Cleve., May 6, 1933; s. John Bernard and Lillian Judith (Finkel) B.; m. Shirley Ann Harper, Nov. 29, 1954; children: Sandra Layne Walker, Andrea Sue Wells. AA, Cypress Coll., 1972; student, U. LaVerne (Calif.), 1983-86. Lab tech. Harvey Aluminum, Torrance, Calif., 1956-64, foreman, 1964-66; sr. draftsman Northrop Corp., Anaheim, Calif., 1966-67; designer Northrop Aircraft, Anaheim, Calif., 1967-69, facilities engr., 1969-81, design to corp. cost designer, 1982-84; mfg. engring. mgr. Northrop Aircraft, Anaheim, 1984-85, mfg. mgr., 1985-92; artist, owner Realistic Watercolors, Cypress, 1992—; instr. watercolor Huntington Beach Art Ctr., 1997—. Featured in The Best of Watercolor, 1995; columnist Event Newspapers, 1998—. Co-chmn. Cypress (Calif.) Cultural Arts Planning Com., 1993-95; pres. Cypress Art Art League, 1993-96; commr. Cypress Cultural Arts, 1999—. Served with U.S. Army, 1954-56. Fellow Am. Artists Profl. League (Signature award 1993); mem. Nat. Watercolor Soc. (assoc. mem. 1989—, editor newsletter 1994-97). Republican. Jewish. Avocations: travel, computers, photography. Home and Office: 4522 Cathy Ave Cypress CA 90630-4212

BLOOM, LINDA SUSAN, art historian; b. Phila., Aug. 6, 1958; d. Irving Isadore and René (Perlmutter) Weiner; m. Brad Lane Bloom, Aug. 30, 1981; 1 child, Leah Aliza. BFA, Ohio State U., 1980, B Art Edn., 1980; MA in Art Edn., U. Cin., 1984; MA in Art History, U. Ill., 1995. Cert. tchr., Ohio; lic. real estate salesperson, Calif. Art educator Cin. Pub. Schs., 1980-84; educator Hebrew Union Coll. Skirball, Cin., 1983-84; founder, chair Koret Judaica Gallery, Palo Alto, Calif., 1984-87; mus. asst. World Heritage Mus., Champaign, Ill., 1988-89; grad. teaching asst. U. Ill., Champaign, 1989-92; family educator Sinai Temple, Champaign, 1993-95; educator children's program Parkland Coll., Champaign, 1989; advisor art/acquisitions com. Sinai Temple, Champaign, 1987-95. Worker Meals-on-Wheels, Champaign-Urbana; bd. mem. Women's Health Ctr., Champaign-Urbana, 1987-88; v.p., bd. Sisterhood Sinai, Champaign-Urbana, 1993-94. Recipient Leadership award Jewish Fedn./Jewish Cmty. Ctr., Palo Alto, 1987, Derber Svc. award Hadassah, Champaign-Urbana, 1993, nat. leadership award Hadassah, 1993. Mem. Am. Assn. Museums, Midwest Art Hist. Soc., Ohio Art Edn. Assn. (v.p. bd. Cin. chpt. 1980-84), Hadassah (v.p. bd. Champaign-Urbana chpt. 1984-94), Phi Delta Kappa. Jewish. Address: 11725 Old Eureka Way Gold River CA 95670-8355 Office: Cong B'nai Israel 3600 Riverside Blvd Sacramento CA 95818-4098

BLOOM, MICHAEL EUGENE, consulting executive; b. Pittsburg, Calif., Jan. 16, 1947; s. Benjamin Bernard and Mildred (Haims) B.; m. Deborah Ann Bresler, Aug. 6, 1977; children: Benjamin Solomon Bresler, Miriam Hannah Bresler. BA in Sociology, U. Calif.-Santa Barbara, 1969, postgrad. elec. engring., 1969-71; MBA, Stanford U., 1979. Broadcaster, Sta. KCSB-FM, Santa Barbara, 1964-68, gen. mgr., 1968-69; broadcaster KKIS-AM, Pittsburg, Calif., 1965, KMUZ-FM, Santa Barbara, 1965-67, KTMS-AM-FM, Santa Barbara, 1967-69; mem. tech. staff Gen. Rsch. Corp., Santa Barbara, 1970-72; mgmt. scientist, cons. Sci. Applications, Inc., LaJolla, Calif., 1973-74, Planning and Mgmt. Cons. Corp., Cleve., 1974, Bloom Enterprises, Santa Monica, Calif., 1975-77; project team leader, sr. programmer Bendix Field Engring. Corp., Sunnyvale, Calif., 1977; retail product planner Crocker Nat. Bank, San Francisco, 1978; dir. corp. devel. Am. TV & Communications Corp., Englewood, Colo., 1979-82, dir. new bus. devel., 1983-84, dir. bus. and tech. devel., 1984-85; dir. video svcs. devel. Pacific Bell, San Francisco, 1985-86, dir. product strategy and devel., San Ramon, Calif., 1986-87, dir. market strategy group, 1986-88, dir. customer premises Broadband Mktg. div., 1988-90, dir. customer premises Broadband Applications div., 1990-92, Japan task force, 1988-92; dir. business devel. Kaleida Labs, Inc., 1992-94, co-founder, v.p., gen. mgr. Power TV Inc., 1994-95, founder, pres. Comm. Strategies and Planning, Inc., 1995—; chmn. comm., bd. U. Calif.-Santa Barbara; v.p., bd. dir. Intercollegiate Broadcasting System, Inc., 1967-70; founder, dir. U. Calif. Radio Network, 1967-69; chmn. systems standards task force on teletext Nat. Cable TV Assn., 1980-81. Adv. coun. Coll. Info. Studies, U. Denver, 1982-85; treas. Camp Arazim, Inc. 1993—; mem. tech. com. The Coll. Prepatory Sch., 1993—. Recipient Pres.'s Merit award U. Calif., 1965. Mem. IEEE, Soc. Cable TV Engrs., Nat. Cable TV Assn., U. Calif.-Santa Barbara Alumni Assn. (life), Stanford U. Bus. Sch. Alumni Assn. (program chmn. Rocky Mountain chpt. 1982-85), Stanford U. Alumni Assn. (life). Author: (with L.A. Sibley) Carrier Current System Design, 1967. E-mail: mebloom@CommsVens.com. Office: Comm Strategies and Planning Inc PO Box 717 San Ramon CA 94583-5717

BLOOMFIELD, ARTHUR JOHN, music critic, food writer; b. San Francisco, Jan. 3, 1931; s. Arthur L. and Julia (Mayer) B.; m. Anne Buenger, July 14, 1956; children: John, Cecily, Alison. AB, Stanford U., 1951. Music and art critic San Francisco Call-Bull., 1958-59, San Francisco News Call-Bull., 1962-65; co-music and art critic San Francisco Examiner, 1965-79; corr. Mus. Am. mag., 1958-61, 63-64, Opera mag., 1964-89; restaurant critic Focus mag., San Francisco, 1979-83; program note writer Mus. and Arts Records, 1996. Author: The San Francisco Opera, 1923-61, 61, Fifty Years of the San Francisco Opera, 1972, Guide to San Francisco Restaurants, 1975, The San Francisco Opera 1922-78, 1978, Arthur Bloomfield's Restaurant Book, 1987. With AUS, 1953-55. Home: 2229 Webster St San Francisco CA 94115-1820

BLOOMQUIST, RODNEY GORDON, geologist; b. Aberdeen, Wash., Feb. 3, 1943; s. Verner A. and Margaret E. (Olson) B.; m. Linda L. Lee, Dec. 19, 1964 (div. July 1968); m. Bente Brisson Jørgensen, Aug. 4, 1977; 1 child, Kira Brisson. BS in Geology, Portland State U., 1966; MS in Geology, U. Stockholm, 1970, PhD in Geochemistry, 1977. Rschr. U. Stockholm, 1974-77; asst. prof. Oreg. Inst. Tech., Klamath Falls, 1978-80; geologist Wash. State Energy Office, Olympia, 1980-96; sr. scientist Wash. State U., Olympia, 1996—; vis. prof. Internat. Sch. Geothermics, Pisa, Italy, 1990—; adj. prof. Evergreen State Coll., Olympia, 1996—; cons. U.S. Dept. Energy, Washignton, 1990, Govt. of Can., 1984, Aesa-Stal Geoenergy, Lund, Sweden, 1985-86, City and County of San Francisco, 1988-89, Lake County, Calif., 1992, San Francisco State U., 1993, Internat. Geoenergy Consortium, Springfield, Mo., 1996—, Portland GE, 1997-98, GeothermEx, Oakland, Calif., 1998. Author: Regulatory Guide to Geothermics, 1991; mem. editl. bd. Geothermics, 1985-88; also numerous books and articles. Smitts fellow, Sweden, 1974, Royal Rsch. fellow, Sweden, 1975-77; rsch. grantee U. Stockholm, 1975-77. Mem. Geothermal Resources Coun. (bd. dirs. 1985-92, pres. 1989, pres. Pacific N.W. sect. 1982-85), Internat. Dist. Energy Assn. (western sect. bd. dirs. 1990—, bd. dirs. 1994-97, chmn. com. gov. rels. 1997—), Internat. Geothermal Assn. (bd. dirs. 1988-92, 95—, chmn. edn. com. 1988—), N.Am. Dist. Heating and Cooling Inst. (bd. dirs. 1986-88), Am. Blade Smith Soc. (bd. dirs. 1989—). Democrat. Lutheran. Avocations: skiing, backpacking, fishing, hunting. Office: Wash State Univ 925 Plum St SE Olympia WA 98501-1529

BLOW, JOHN NEEDHAM, social services educator; b. Whitby, Ont., Can., Nov. 30, 1905; came to U.S., 1952; s. Ezekiel Richard and Edith May (Correll) B.; m. Emma Jane White, June 6, 1942; children: Carol Anne, Brenda Jane, Mary Roberta, Elizabeth Diane. BA, McMaster U., 1939; MSW, U. Toronto, Ont., 1948. Cert. elem. tchr., Toronto, community colls. instr., Calif. Exec. sec. Community Welfare Planning Council Ont., Toronto, 1948-52; exec. v.p. Motel Corp., Las Vegas, Nev., 1952-54; exec. dir. Nev. div. Am. Cancer Soc., 1954-56, assoc. exec. dir. Los Angeles County br., 1956-70; program assoc. Am. Heart Assn., Los Angeles, 1970-74; project dir., coordinator sr. community service employment program Orange County, Calif., 1974-75; instr. community service programs for adults North Orange County Community Coll. Dist. and Coastline Coll., 1976-79, Mira Costa and Palomar Community Colls., 1979-85. Author: (poems) New Frontiers, 1984. Vol. Arthritis Found.; asst. commr. tng. Boy Scouts Can., Ottawa, 1934-41; Chaplain Tri-City Coun. Navy League. Wing comdr. RCAF, 1941-46. Recipient Commendation for Outstanding Svc. to Srs., Orange County Sr. Citizens Coun., 1977, Gold award Orange County United Way, 1977, Golden Poet award, 1991, World of Poetry, 1989, 90; named to Internat. Poetry Hall of Fame, 1996. Mem. Nat. Assn. Social Workers, Acad. Cert. Social Workers, San Luis Rey Officers Club, Valley Sr. Ctr., North County Concert Assn., So. Calif. McMaster U. Alumni Assn. (past pres., inducted Alumni Gallery 1986), Can. Soc. Los Angeles (charter, past pres.), U. Toronto Alumni Assn. (exec. com., past pres. So. Calif. br.). Presbyterian. Lodge: Elks. Home: 3725 Sesame Way Oceanside CA 92057-8328

BLOXOM, DAVID MEGRATH, electrical and control systems engineer; b. Yakima, Wash., Apr. 17, 1958; s. John Megrath and Connie (Jones) B.; m. Nancy Lynn Tharp, Aug. 4, 1984; children: Ashley, Addison. Grad. degree, Perry Tech. Inst., Yakima, Wash., 1981. Registered profl. engr., Wash., Oreg. Technician Chevron Chem., Kennewick, Wash., 1981-83; field technician City of Eugene, Oreg., 1983-85; engr. Brown & Caldwell, Seattle, 1985-89, S & B Inc., Bellevue, Wash., 1989-91; prin. engr. Casne Engring., Bellevue, Wash., 1991-95; pres., CEO ECS Engring., Inc., Mill Creek, Wash., 1995—; mem. sect. bd., pres. Internat. Soc. Measurement and Control, Seattle, 1992—; adv. bd. Perry Tech. Inst., Yakima, Wash., 1993—; speaker in field. Mem. Internat. Soc. Measurement and Control (pres. 1994—, sr.), Consulting and Engring. Coun. Wash. Office: ECS Engring Inc PO Box 12884 Mill Creek WA 98082-0884

BLOYD, STEPHEN ROY, environmental manager, educator, consultant; b. Alameda, Calif., Aug. 17, 1953; s. William Allen and Alice Louella (Scott) B. Grad. high sch., Reedley, Calif., 1971. Cert. environ. mgr., Nev.; registered hazardous substances specialist. Reagent tech. Tenneco Corp., Gold Hill, Nev., 1982; environ. tech. Pierson Environ. Drilling, Modesto, Calif., 1982-84; pres. Bloyd and Assocs., Dayton, Nev., 1986—. Author: Hazardous Waste Site Operations for General Site Workers, 1992; editor: (newsletter) Pumper, 1991. Firefighter Dayton Vol. Fire Dept., 1975, capt., 1976-78, chief, 1978-83, tng. officer, 1984-96; mem. Silver City (Nev.) Fire Dept., 1996—; coord. Ctrl. Lyon County Hazardous Materials, 1997—; asst. prof. Dodd/Beals Fire Protection Tng. Acad. U. Nev., Reno, 1990-96; instr. chemistry hazardous materials Nat. Fire Acad., Emmitsburg, Md., 1989—, instr. hazardous materials incident mgmt., 1996—; mem. bylaw com. Dayton Regional Adv. Coun., 1989. Named Firefighter of Yr., City of Dayton, 1992. Mem. NRA, Nat. Environ. Tng. Assn., Nat. Environ. Health Assn., Nev. State Firemen's Assn. (1st v.p. 1992-93, 2d v.p. 1991-92, pres. 1993-94, chmn. hazardous materials com. 1987-93, legis. com. 1991, bylaws com. 1986), Nev. Fire Chief's Assn., Internat. Platform Assn., Soc. Nat. Fire Acad. Instrs. Libertarian. Avocations: fishing, motorcycles, firearms, camping, reading. Office: PO Box 113 Silver City NV 89428-0113

BLUE, JAMES GUTHRIE, retired veterinarian; b. Flora, Ind., Oct. 22, 1920; s. Van C. and Florence A. (Guthrie) B. AB, Wabash Coll., 1943; postgrad., Northwestern U., 1943; DVM, Ohio State U., 1950; AA in Labor Negotiation/Rels., L.A. Trade Tech. Coll., 1989. Pvt. practice cons., 1950-80; field vet. City of L.A., 1980—, acting chief vets., 1992, chief vets., 1992-95; rsch. project cons. Calif. State U. Northridge, 1980-87; pro med. svcs. sec.-negtiator AFSCME, L.A., 1983-96; sec. Ariz. Bd. Vet. Med. Examiners, 1973-79. Mem. wellness com. Drug Free Work Place, 1989-99. Lt. comdr. USN, 1943-46, USNR, 1946-65. Mem. AMVA, N.Y. Acad. Scis., Am. Soc. Lab. Animal Practitioners, L.A. World Affairs Coun., San Diego Vet. Med. Assn., So. Ariz. Vet. Med. Assn., Calif. Vet. Med. Assn. (environ. and pub. health ecology com. 1986-99, state ethics com. 1986-98, wellness com. 1988-99), So. Calif. Vet. Med. Assn. (coun. mem., polit. action com., continuing edn. com. 1980-99), Am. Legion, Navy League, Shriners, Mil. Order World War, U.S. Naval Rsch. Assn., Navy League Coun. Tucson, Rep. Club Tucson (treas. 1996-99), Res. Officers Assn. Republican. Home: 2121 E 2nd St Tucson AZ 85719-4928

BLUM, JOAN KURLEY, fundraising executive; b. Palm Beach, Fla., July 27, 1926; d. Nenad Daniel and Eva (Milos) Kurley; m. Robert C. Blum, Apr. 15, 1967; children: Christopher Alexander, Martha Jane, Louisa Joan, Paul Helmuth, Sherifa. BA, U. Wash., 1948. Cert. fund raising exec. U.S. dir. Inst. Mediterranean Studies, Berkeley, Calif., 1962-65; devel. officer U. Calif. at Berkeley, 1965-67; pres. Blum Assocs., Fund-Raising Cons., San Anselmo, Calif., 1967-92, The Blums of San Francisco, 1992—; mem. faculty U. Calif. Extension, Inst. Fund Raising, S.W. Inst. Fund-Raising U. Tex., U. San Francisco, U.K. Vol. Movement Group, London, Australasian Inst. Fund Raising. Contbr. numerous articles to profl. jours. Recipient Golden Addy award Am. Advt. Fedn.; Silver Mailbox award Direct Mail Mktg. Assn., Best Ann. Giving Time-Life award, others; decorated commdr. Sovereign Order St. Stanislas. Mem. Nat. Soc. Fund-Raising Execs. (dir.), Nat. Assn. of Hosp. Devel., Women Emerging., Rotary (San Francisco), Fund Raising Inst. (Australia), Tahoe Yacht Club. Office: 202 Evergreen Dr Kentfield CA 94904-2708 also: Ste 103, 781 Pacific Hwy, Chatswood NSW 2067, Australia

BLUMBERG, NATHAN(IEL) BERNARD, journalist, educator, writer and publisher; b. Denver, Apr. 8, 1922; s. Abraham Moses and Jeannette Blumberg; m. Lynne Stout, June 1946 (div. Feb. 1970); children: Janet Leslie, Jenifer Lyn, Josephine Laura; m. Barbara Farquhar, July 1973. B.A., U. Colo., 1947, M.A., 1948; D.Phil. (Rhodes scholar), Oxford (Eng.) U., 1950. Reporter Denver Post, 1947-48; assoc. editor Lincoln (Nebr.) Star, 1950-53; asst. to editor Ashland (Nebr.) Gazette, 1954-55; asst. city editor Washington Post and Times Herald, 1956; from asst. prof. to assoc. prof. journalism U. Nebr., 1950-55; assoc. prof. journalism Mich. State U., 1955-56; dean, prof. Sch. Journalism, U. Mont., 1956-68, prof. journalism, 1968-78, prof. emeritus, 1978—; pub. Wood FIRE Ashes Press, 1981—; vis. prof. Pa. State U., 1964, Northwestern U., 1966-67, U. Calif., Berkeley, 1970; Dept. State specialist in Thailand, 1961, in Trinidad, Guyana, Surinam and Jamaica, 1964. Author: One-Party Press?, 1954; The Afternoon of March 30: A Contemporary Historical Novel, 1984, also articles in mags. and jours.; co-editor: A Century of Montana Journalism, 1971; editor: The Mansfield Lectures in International Relations, Vols. I and II, 1979; founder: Mont. Journalism Rev, 1958—; editor, pub. Treasure State Rev., 1991—. Served with arty. U.S. Army, 1943-46. Bronze Star medal. Mem. Assn. Am. Rhodes Scholars, Brasenose Soc., Kappa Tau Alpha (nat. pres. 1969-70). Home: PO Box 99 Bigfork MT 59911-0099

BLUME, JAMES BERYL, financial advisor; b. N.Y.C., Apr. 9, 1941; s. Philip Franklin Blume and Mary Kirschman Asch; m. Kathryn Weil Frank, Jan. 20, 1984; 1 child, Zachary Thomas Philip. BA, Williams Coll., Williamstown, Mass., 1963; MBA, Harvard U., Boston, 1966; M. Psychology, The Wright Inst., Berkeley, Calif., 1983, PhD in Psychology, 1986. Security analyst Faulkner, Dawkins & Sullivan, N.Y.C., 1966-68; sr. v.p. Faulkner, Dawkins & Sullivan Securities, Inc., N.Y.C., 1968-73; ptnr. Omega Properties, N.Y.C., 1973-74; exec.v.p. Arthur M. Fischer, Inc., N.Y.C., 1974-77; psychotherapist in pvt. practice Berkeley, 1985-91, fin. cons., 1987—; pres. James B. Blume, Inc., fin. counsel and mgmt., Berkeley, 1993-94; bd. dirs. Ploughshares Fund. Bd. dirs. ACLU No. Calif., San Francisco, 1988-94, treas., 1993-94; bd. dirs. East Bay Clinic for Psychotherapy, Oakland, Calif., 1981-85, Marin Psychotherapy Inst., Mill Valley, Calif., 1986-87; trustee The Wright Inst., 1981-85. Mem. Berkeley Tennis Club, Williams Club (bd. govs. 1968-72). Democrat. Jewish. Avocations: tennis, piano, political science. Office: 1708 Shattuck Ave Berkeley CA 94709-1700

BLUME-JENSEN, PETER, molecular biologist; b. Nykøbing, Denmark, Apr. 16, 1962; came to the U.S., 1995; s. Tage and Ruth (Madsen) Blume-J. MD, Copenhagen U., 1989; PhD in Molecular Cell Biology, Uppsala (Sweden) U., 1995. Rsch. fellow Ludwig Inst. for Cancer Rsch., Uppsala U., 1989-95; post-doctoral fellow molecular biology and virology lab. The Salk Inst., La Jolla, Calif., 1995—; spkr. in field. Contbr. chpts. to books and articles to profl. jours. Candidate and sr. fellow Danish Cancer Soc., 1991-95; sr. fellow The Med. Rsch. Coun., 1995-98, Leukemia Soc. Am., 1998—. Mem. AAAS, Danish Med. Assn., Danish Cancer Soc., Swedish Med. Assn., Biol. Soc. Avocations: running, sports, music, film, travel. Home: 8138 Regents Rd #303 San Diego CA 92122 Office: The Salk Inst 10010 N Torrey Pines Rd La Jolla CA 92037

BLUMENAUER, EARL, congressman; b. Portland, Oreg., Aug. 16, 1948. BA, Lewis and Clark Coll., 1970, JD, 1976. Asst. to pres. Portland State U., 1971-73; mem. Oreg. Ho. of Reps., 1973-79; county commr. Multnomah County, Portland, 1979-87; mem. Portland City Coun., 1987-96, 104th-106th Congresses from 1st Maine dist., 1996—; mem. transp. com., 1996—; mem. early childhood and oversight subcoms. Econ. and Ednl. Opportunities Com. Avocations: bicycling, running, basketball. Office: US House of Reps 1113 Longworth HOB Washington DC 20515-3703 also: 516 SE MorrisonSte 250 Portland OR 97214*

BLUMENKRANZ, MARK SCOTT, surgeon, researcher, educator; b. N.Y.C., Oct. 23, 1950; s. Edward and Helene (Cymberg) B.; m. Recia Kott, June 10, 1975. AB, Brown U., 1972, MD, 1975, MMS, 1976; postgrad., Stanford U., 1975-79, U. Miami, 1979-80. Intern, resident Stanford (Calif.) U. Med. Ctr., 1975-79; fellow Bascom Palmer Eye Inst. U. Miami, Fla., 1979-80; asst. prof. Bascom Palmer Eye Inst., Miami, 1980-85; assoc. prof. Wayne State U., Detroit, 1985-92; clin. prof. Stanford U., 1992—, dir. of retina, 1992—, chmn. dept. ophthalmology, 1997—; assoc. examiner Am.

Bd. Ophthalmology. Mem. editl. bd. Ophthalmology, Retina; contbr. chpts. to books and articles to profl. jours.; Inventor ophthalmic devices. Mem. bd. overseers Brown U. Sch. Medicine. Recipient Visual Scis. medal in Visual Scis. Rosenthal Found., 1990, Heed award Heed Found., 1988, Manpower award Rsch. to Prevent Blindness. Mem. Am. Acad. Ophthalmology (mem. preferred practice com., others), Macula Soc. (chmn. rsch. com. 1986-90), Assn. Rsch. in Vision and Ophthalmology (chmn. retina sect. 1987-90), Retina Soc. (mem. membership com.), Maimonodes Soc. (mem. exec. com.). Avocations: tennis, sailing, electronic music, fitness. Office: Stanford Univ Dept Ophthalmology Boswell A-157 Stanford CA 94305 also: 1225 Crane St Menlo Park CA 94025-4257

BLUMENTHAL, JOHN FREDERICK, screenwriter, author; b. Middletown, N.Y., Jan. 5, 1949; s. Fritz Frederick and Marianne (Leiter) B.; m. Ingrid Van Eckert, June 20, 1982; children: Julia Anne, Elizabeth Jane. BA cum laude, Tufts Coll., 1971. Asst. editor Esquire mag., N.Y.C., 1973; from asst. editor to assoc. editor Playboy mag., Chgo., 1974-79; staff writer L.A., 1980-81, contbg. editor, 1981-85, freelance screenwriter, author, 1986—; devel. teleplays and pilots for Aaron Spelling Prodns., ABC and Universal TV, 1985—. Author: Official Hollywood Handbook, 1984, Hollywood High, 1988, Tinseltown Murders, 1985, Case of the Hardboiled Dicks, 1985; (with others) Loves Reckless Rash, 1984; co-screenwriter: Short Time, 1990; other screenplays for Columbia Pictures, 1990, Twentieth Century Fox, Warner Bros. and Universal Studios, 1991, NBC, 1996, Tristar, 1995. Mem. Writers Guild Am. Home and Office: 2853 Rikkard Dr Thousand Oaks CA 91362-4614

BLUMENTHAL, RICHARD CARY, construction executive, consultant; b. Bklyn., Dec. 18, 1951; s. Mervin Harold and Barbara June Blumenthal; m. Ginnilyn Hawkins; children: Aaron Joseph, Meredith Taylor. BS, U. N.H., 1974. Planner RECON Assocs., Hamilton, Mont., 1976-77; project mgr. Grizzly Mfg., Hamilton, 1977-78; profl. carpenter Ed Brown Constrn., Bainbridge Island, Wash., 1978-79; pres. Richard Blumenthal Constrn., Inc., Bainbridge Island, 1979—; instr. Bainbridge Island Community Sch., 1993—. Mem. pk. bd. coun. City of Winslow, 1989-90; bd. dirs. Bainbridge Island Pub. Libr., 1992-99; mem. Land Use Profls. Forum, 1992—; mem. advisory com. Bainbridge Island Park & Rec. Gymnastics Com., 1993-98. Mem. Ind. Bus. Assn., C. of C. Avocations: bicycling, hiking, rock climbing, music. Home and Office: 330 Nicholson Pl NW Bainbridge Island WA 98110

BLUMER, HARRY MAYNARD, architect; b. Stillwater, Okla., Aug. 27, 1930; s. Harry H. and Nona A. (Ftizpatrick) B.; m. C. Sue Linebaugh, Sept. 2, 1952; children: Eric W., Laura B., Martha L. BArch, Okla. State U., 1953; BS in Bus., Ariz. State U., 1976. Registered arch., Ariz., landscape arch., Ariz., arch., U.S. Govt.; cert. constrn. specifier, fallout shelter analyst, U.S. Dept. Def. Designer, draftsman Norman Byrd Architect, Oklahoma City, Okla., 1952, Overend & Boucher Architects, Wichita, Kans., 1953-54; archtl. designer, draftsman Louis G. Hesselden Architect, Albuquerque, 1956; project designer, planner, constrn. & contract adminstr. Flatow, Moore, Bryan & Fairburn Architects, Albuquerque, 1956-61; regional architect U.S. Forest Svc., Albuquerque, 1961-62; v.p. prodn. Guirey, Srnka, Arnold & Sprinkle, Phoenix, 1962-82; prin. arch. H. Maynard Blumer, FAIA, FCSI, Consulting Arch., Scottsdale, Ariz., 1982—; lectr. architecture Ariz. State U., Tempe, 1968-69; rep. specifications consulting projects for various stuctures including Chandler Med. Office bldg., 1982, Ariz. State U. w. campus utility tunnel, 1986, Mayo Clinic consourse and parking structure, 1993, City of Tempe, Ariz. Comm. Tech. Ctr., 1997, numerous others; speaker in field. Contbr. articles to profl. publs. Bd. dirs., camping com., camp master plan design Maricopa County Coun. Campfire Girls, 1962-69; pres. N.Mex. Cactus and Succulent Soc., 1959-60; sec. Advancement Mgmt., Phoenix, 1972-73, dir., 1971-72; bd. govs. Amateur Athletic Union U.S., 1972-75, chmn. nat. conv. registration com., 1975; v.p. Ariz. Assn. Bd. MGrs., 1972-73, pres., 1973; treas. Pop Warner Football Assn., 1975; pres. parents club Scottsdale YMCA Judo Club, 1970-80; chairperson materials testing lab. citizens' rev. com. City of Phoenix, 1978, mem. arch. selection com., 1990, constrn. mediation panelist, 1995; commr. planning and zoning commn. Town of Paradise Valley, Ariz., 1994-97, mem. Hillside bldng. rev. com. rotation, 1994—, mem. spl. use permit rev. com. rotation, 1994—; . 1st lt. U.S. Army Corps Engrs., 1954-56, Korea. Recipient Valley Beautiful Citizens Coun. Cmty. Recognition award 1964, 68, Outstanding Use Masonry award, Ariz. Masonry Guild, 1968, Ariz. Aggregate Assn. Spl. Recognition award, 1986, Edn. Commendation award Constrn. Specifications Inst., 1980. Fellow AIA (Honor award Ctrl. Ariz. chpt. 1967, Oustanding Svc. to Profession award 1986), Constrn. Specification Inst. (Phoenix chpt., mem. chpt. fellows com. 1973—, round-table chair, moderator 1981—, Pres.'s Disting. Svc. cert. 1968, Disting. Leadership plaque Phoenix chpt. 1968, Oustanding Profl. Mem. award, 1981, Pres.'s cert. Appreciation 1985, numerous others); mem. ASTM. Office: 8517 N 49th St Paradise Valley AZ 85253-2002*

BLUMHARDT, JON HOWARD, college official; b. Ft. Benning, Ga., Oct. 3, 1951; s. Howard Jerome and Joan (Tisdal) B.; m. Lisette Susan Vinet, Jan. 26, 1973; children: Matthew, Malia, Mark. BA in History, U. Hawaii, 1973, MA in Sociology, 1978, MEd, 1979, postgrad.; EdS, U Va., 1984; EdD in Edn., LaSalle U., 1998. Media specialist U.S. Army JAG Sch., Charlottesville, Va., 1980-85; adminstr. officer OPM Fed. Exec. Inst., Charlottesville, 1985-86; chief resources mgmt. IRS Honolulu Dist., 1986-87; dir. ednl. media svcs. Honolulu C.C., 1987—; owner Media Works, 1996—. Unit commr., Koolau dist., Aloha coun. Boy Scouts Am., 1996. Named one of Outstanding Young Men in Am., 1989, Eagle Scout, 1965; recipient Mahalo award Mayor of Honolulu, 1978, Cert. of Merit Aloha Coun. Boy Scouts Am., 1978, Wood Badge, 1978 Scoutmaster award of Merit Nat. Eagle Scout Assn., 1990, Boy Scout Leader's Tng. award, 1998. Mem. DAV (life), German Benevolent Soc. (Honolulu), Am. Legion, U. Va. Alumni Assn. (life), Pan Pacific Distance Learning Assn. (bd. dirs.), Am. Legion (post 0009). Republican. Roman Catholic. Avocations: gardening, camping, sailing, fishing, woodworking. E-mail: jon@hcc.hawaii.edu. Home: 694 Waraao Rd Kailua HI 96734-4065 Office: Honolulu CC 874 Dillingham Blvd Honolulu HI 96817-4505

BLUMMER, KATHLEEN ANN, counselor; b. Iowa Falls, Iowa, Apr. 17, 1945; d. Arthur G. and Julia C. (Ericson) Thorsbakken; m. Terry L. Blummer, Feb. 13, 1971 (dec. 1980); 1 child, Emily Erica. AA, Ellsworth Coll., Iowa Falls, 1965; BA, U. Iowa, 1967; postgrad., Northeastern Ill. U., 1969-70, U. N.Mex., 1980—; MA, Western N.Mex. U., 1973. Asst. buyer Marshall Field & Co., Chgo., 1967-68; social worker Cook County Dept. Pub. Aid, Chgo., 1968-69; tchr. Chgo. Pub. Schs., 1968-69; student fin. aid counselor Western N.Mex. U., Silver City, 1971-72; family social worker, counselor Southwestern N.Mex. Svcs. to Handicapped Children and Adults, Silver City, 1972-74; career edn. program specialist Galluo McKinley County (N.Mex.) Schs., 1974-76; dir. summer sch. Loving (N.Mex.) Mcpl. Schs., 1977; counselor, dept. chmn. Carlsbad (N.Mex.) Pub. Schs., 1977-82; counselor Albuquerque Pub. Schs., 1982—. Mem. AAUW (topic chmn. Carlsbad chpt., v.p. Albuquerque chpt.), N.Mex. Personnel and Guidance Assn., Theos Club, Highpoint Swim and Racquet Club (Albuquerque), Elks. Democrat. Lutheran.

BOADO, RUBEN JOSE, biochemist; b. Buenos Aires, Argentina, Feb. 8, 1955; came to U.S., 1985; s. Osvaldo Ruben and Lucia B.; m. Adriana Graciela Swiecicki, Jan. 11, 1980; children: Augusto Ruben, Lucrecia Adriana. MS, U. Buenos Aires, 1979, Diploma in Biochemistry, 1980, PhD, 1982. Rsch. fellow endocrinology Nat. Coun. Scientific Rsch., Buenos Aires, 1979-81, postdoctoral rsch. fellow in endocrinology, 1981-83, established investigator, 1983-89; internat. fellow UCLA Sch. Medicine, 1985-88, asst. rsch. endocrinologist, 1988-91, asst. prof. medicine, 1991-97, assoc. prof. medicine, 1997—. Author numerous scientific publs. Recipient Best Scientific Paper award Internat. Assn. Radiopharmacology, Chgo., 1981, Cross-Town Endocrine Soc., L.A., 1988. Mem. AAAS, European Neurosci. Assn., Argentine Soc. Clin. Rsch., Am. Thyroid Assn. (travel award 1987), Endocrine Soc. (travel award 1984), Brain Rsch. Inst., Soc. Neurosci., Controlled Release Soc. Inc. Office: UCLA Dept Medicine/Endocrin Rsch Labs C-Lot Rm 104 Los Angeles CA 90024-1682

BOARDMAN, DAVID, newspaper editor; m. Barbara Winslow; children: Emily, Madeline. BS in Journalism, Northwestern U., 1979; M in Comm., U. Wash., 1983. Copy editor Football Weekly, Chgo., 1977-79; reporter Anacortes (Wash.) American, 1979-80, Skagit Valley Herald, Mt. Vernon, Wash., 1980-81; reporter, copy editor The News Tribune, Tacoma, 1981-83; copy editor The Seattle Times, 1983, editor, reporter, 1984, nat. editor, 1984-86, local news editor, 1986-87, asst. city editor, 1987-90, regional editor, 1990-96, metro. editor, 1997—, asst. mng. editor, 1997—; vis. faculty Poynter Inst. Media Studies, St. Petersburg, Fla. Recipient Goldsmith Prize in Investigative Reporting JFK Sch. Govt. Harvard U., 1993, Worth Bingham prize, 1993, Investigative Reporters and Editors award, 1993, AP Mng. Editors Pub. Svc. award, 1992, 1st place nat. reporting Pulitzer Prize, 1990, lead editor Pulitzer Prize in investigative reporting, 1997; named finalist Pulitzer Prize for Pub. Svc., 1993; fellow Japan-IBCC fellowship Ctr. Fgn. Journalists, 1995. E-mail: dboa-new@seatimes.com. Office: The Seattle Times PO Box 70 1120 John St Seattle WA 98109-5321

BOAS, FRANK, lawyer; b. Amsterdam, North Holland, The Netherlands, July 22, 1930; came to U.S., 1940; s. Maurits Coenraad and Sophie (Brandel) B.; m. Edith Louise Bruce, June 30, 1981 (dec. July 1992); m. Jean Scripps, Aug. 6, 1993. *Frank's father Maurits Boas was a pioneer for the International Business Machines Corporation in Europe. He brought the Hollerith Punched Card System, first used in the United States for the 1890 census, to Holland and Belgium after World War I and he founded the IBM organizations in those countries.* AB cum laude, Harvard U., 1951, JD, 1954. Bar: U.S. Dist. Ct. D.C. 1955, U.S. Ct. Appeals (D.C. cir.) 1955; U.S. Supreme Ct. 1958. Atty. Office of the Legal Adviser U.S. State Dept., Washington, 1957-59; pvt. practice, Brussels and London, 1959-79; of counsel Patton, Boggs & Blow, Washington, 1975-80; pres. Frank Boas Found., Inc., Cambridge, Mass., 1980—. Mem. U.S. delegation to UN confs. on law of sea, Geneva, 1958, 60; vice chmn. Commn. for Ednl. Exch., Brussels, 1980-87; mem. vis. com. Harvard Law Sch., 1987-91, Ctr. for Internat. Affairs, 1988—; dir. Found. European Orgn. for Research and Treatment of Cancer, Brussels, 1978-87, Paul-Henri Spaak Found., Brussels, 1981—, East-West Ctr. Found., Honolulu, 1990—, Law of the Sea Inst., Honolulu, 1992-97, Pacific Forum CSIS, Honolulu, 1996—, Honolulu Acad. Arts, 1997—; hon. sec. Am. C. of C. in Belgium, 1966-78. With U.S. Army, 1955-57. Decorated Officer of the Order of Leopold II, comdr. Order of the Crown (Belgium), comdr. Order of Merit (Luxembourg); recipient Tribute of Appreciation award U.S. State Dept., 1981, Harvard Alumni Assn. award, 1996. Mem. ABA, Fed. D.C. Bar Assn., Pacific and Asian Affairs Coun. (pres.), Honolulu Com. Fgn. Relations, Pacific, Outrigger Canoe (Honolulu), Travellers (London), Am. and Common Market (Brussels pres. 1981-85), Honolulu Social Sci. Assn. Home: 4463 Aukai Ave Honolulu HI 96816-4858

BOAT, RONALD ALLEN, business executive; b. Dayton, Ohio, Nov. 16, 1947; s. Robert Mallory and Elvetta June (Smith) B. Student, Naval Acad./Army Sch. Music, Norfolk, Va., 1968-69, Ariz. State U., 1966-68. Pres. Prodn. Svcs., Phoenix, 1968—, Greek Specialties Corp., Phoenix, 1980-94; v.p. Am. Baby Boomers, San Diego, 1984-93; co-founder, v.p. Internat. Food Network, San Diego, 1985-90; founder, pres. AMC Food Svcs. Corp., 1991-94; pres. The Natural Light Co., 1994-96; ind. prodr. Intel, Honeywell, Best Western, Sperry, Phoenix, 1985—, Phoenix Health Plan, B.P.I., Maricopa Refining Co., P.A.R. Techs., Profitmax, Cycle-Masters, PMH Found.; mem. Lund Team Real Estate Adv. Bd., 1991-95; bd. dirs. Lund Real Estate Corp., 1990-95. Founder, pres. Group AMC, Inc., 1995—. With U.S. Army, 1968-71. Named Outstanding sales rep. Club Am., Dallas, 1972-73, Top Distbr. Club Am., Dallas, 1973; recipient Top Restaurant award Am. Heart Assn., Phoenix, 1988, Best of Phoenix restaurant award, 1991. Mem. Am. Radio Relay League, Internat. Platform Assn., Phi Mu Alpha Sinfonia. Republican. Avocations: amateur radio, music, travel. E-mail: ronb@psa-video.com. Office: P S A 14628 N 48th Way Scottsdale AZ 85254-2203

BOBRICK, STEVEN AARON, executive management assistant; b. Denver, Apr. 11, 1950; s. Samual Michael and Selma Gertrude (Birnbaum) B.; m. Maria Diane Boltz, Oct. 5, 1980. Attended, U. Colo., 1968-72. Registered apt. mgr. Owner Bobrick Constrn., Denver, 1969-72; with Bell Mtn. Sports, Aspen, Colo., 1972-75; mgr. Compass Imports, Denver, 1975-80, Aurora (Colo.) Bullion Exch., 1980-81; contr. Bobrick Constrn., Aurora, 1981-85; appraiser Aurora, 1985—; property mgr. Aurora (Colo) Cmty. Mental Health, 1989-98, active real estate and constrn., facilities mgr., 1989-98; exec. mgmt. asst. E-470 Pub. Hwy. Authority, 1998—. Co-author: Are You Paying Too Much in Property Taxes, 1990. Coun. mem. City of Aurora, 1981-89; chmn. Explore Commercial Opportunities, Aurora, 1986-89, bd. dirs.; bd. dirs. Adam County Econ. Devel. Commn., Northglenn, Colo., 1985-89; vice chair Aurora Urban Renewal Authority, 1982-89; chmn. Aurora Enterprise Zone Found., 1991—; bd. dirs. Aurora Community Med. Clinic, 1987-88. Avocations: skiing, mountain biking, exercise. Office: 7600 E Orchard Rd Ste 370 Aurora CO 80011

BOBROW, SUSAN LUKIN, lawyer; b. Cleve., Jan. 18, 1941; d. Adolph and Yetta (Babkow) Lukin; m. Martin J. Bolhower, Nov. 28, 1986 (div. Dec. 1988); children from previous marriage: Elizabeth Bobrow Pressler, Erica, David. Student, Antioch Coll., Yellow Springs, Ohio, 1958-61; BA, Antioch Coll., L.A., 1975; JD, Southwestern U., L.A., 1979. Bar: Calif. 1980. Pvt. practice Beverly Hills, Calif., 1983-88; assoc. Schulman & Miller, Beverly Hills, 1988-89; staff counsel Fair Polit. Practices Commn., Sacramento, Calif., 1990-96; sr. counsel Calif. State Lottery, Sacramento, 1996-98, Employment Tng. Panel, Sacramento, 1998—; panel for paternity defense L.A. Superior Ct., 1984. Exhibited paintings at Death and Trasnfiguration Show, Phantom Galleries, Sacramento, 1994; exhibited photography U. Calif.-Davis Women's Art Collaborative, Phantom Galleries, Sacramento, 1997, Camera Arts, Sacramento, 1998, Viewpoint Gallery Exhibit, Sacramento, 1998. Bd. dirs. San Fernando Valley Friends of Homeless Women and Children, North Hollywood, Calif., 1985-88, Jewish Family Svcs., 1997; mem. adv. bd. Project Home, Sacramento Interfaith Svc. Coun., 1990-91; v.p. cmty. affairs B'nai Israel Sisterhood, Sacramento, 1991-93; bd. dirs. Sacramento Jewish Family Svcs., 1997-98. Recipient commendation Bd. Govs. State Bar of Calif., 1984. Mem. Inst. Noetic Scis., Sacramento Inst. Noetic Scis. (steering coun. 1994), Los Angeles County Bar Assn. (Barristers com. on adminstrn. of justice 1985), Sacramento County Bar Assn. (com. on profl. responsibility 1993-94, alt. del. to state bar conv. 1991), Sacramento Women Artists, Sacramento Valley Photographic Arts Ctr. Democrat. Office: Employment Tng Panel 1100 J St Sacramento CA 95814

BOCHY, BRUCE, professional sports team manager, coach; b. Landes de Boussac, France, Apr. 16, 1955; m. Kim B.; children: Greg, Brett. Coach San Diego Padres, 1993-94, mgr., 1994—. Office: San Diego Padres PO Box 2000 San Diego CA 92112-2000*

BOCK, RUSSELL SAMUEL, author; b. Spokane, Wash., Nov. 24, 1905; s. Alva and Elizabeth (Mellinger) B.; m. Suzanne Ray, Feb. 26, 1970; children: Beverly A. Bock Wunderlich, James Russell. B.B.A., U. Wash., 1929. Part-time instr. U. So. Calif., UCLA, 1942-50; with Ernst & Ernst, CPAs, Los Angeles, 1938, ptnr., 1951-69; cons. Ernst & Young, 1969—. Author: Guidebook to California Taxes, annually, 1950—, Taxes of Hawaii, annually, 1964—; also numerous articles. Dir., treas. Cmty. TV So. Calif., 1964-74; dir., v.p., treas., So. Calif. Symphony-Hollywood Bowl Assn., 1964-70; bd. dirs. Cmty. Arts Music Assn., 1974-76, 78-84, Santa Barbara Symphony Assn., 1976-78, Santa Barbara Boys and Girls Club, 1980-93, UCSB Affiliates, 1983-85, Santa Barbara Civic Light Opera, 1995-97. Mem. Am. Inst. C.P.A.s (council 1953-57, trial bd. 1955-58, v.p. 1959-60), Calif. Soc. C.P.A.s (past pres.), Los Angeles C. of C. (dir. 1957-65, v.p. 1963), Sigma Phi Epsilon, Beta Alpha Psi, Beta Gamma Sigma. Clubs: Birnam Wood Golf, Santa Barbara Yacht. Office: 300 Hot Springs Rd Apt 190 Santa Barbara CA 93108-2069

BODDIE, LEWIS FRANKLIN, obstetrics and gynecology educator; b. Forsyth, Ga., Apr. 4, 1913; s. William F. and Lucitta T. (Sams) B.; m. Marian Bernice Claytor, Dec. 27, 1941; children: Roberta Boddie Miles, Lewis Jr., Bernice B. Jackson, Pamela, Kenneth, Fredda, Margaret. BA, Morehouse Coll., 1933, MD, Meharry Med. Sch., 1938. Diplomate Am. Bd. Ob-Gyn (proctor parti exam Los Angeles area 1955-63). Intern Homer-Phillips Hosp., St. Louis, 1938-39, resident in ob-gyn, 1939-42; mem. attending staff Grace Hosp., Detroit, 1944-48, Parkside Hosp., Detroit, 1944-48, Los Angeles County Gen. Hosp., 1952-79; sr. mem. attending staff Queen of Angels Hosp., Los Angeles, 1964-91, chmn. dept. ob-gyn, 1968-70; asst. clin. prof. U. So. Calif. Sch. Medicine, L.A., 1953-79, asst. clin. prof. emeritus, 1979—; assoc. clin. prof. U. Calif., Irvine, 1956-81; sec. Verndro Med. Corp., 1952-90. vice chmn. bd. mgrs. 28th St. YMCA, Los Angeles 1960-75; steward African Meth. Episc. Ch., Los Angeles, 1949—. Fellow ACS (life), Am. Coll. Ob-Gyn (life), Los Angeles Ob-Gyn Soc. (life): mem. Los Angeles United Way (priorities and allocations coms., 1985-95, standards com. 1987-95, new admission com. 1988-95), Children's Home Soc. (bd. dirs. 1952-89, trustee 1989—, v.p. 1963-68, pres. 1968-70), Child Welfare League Am. (bd. d irs. 1969-76). Republican.

BODENSIECK, ERNEST JUSTUS, mechanical engineer; b. Dubuque, Iowa, June 1, 1923; s. Julius Henry and Elma (Sommer) B.; BSME, Iowa State U., 1943; m. Margery Elenore Sande, Sept. 9, 1943; children: Elizabeth Bodensieck Eley, Stephen. Project engr. TRW Inc., Cleve., 1943-57; supr. rocket turbomachinery Rocketydyne div. Rockwell Internat., Canoga Park, Calif., 1957-60, supr. nuclear turbomachinery Rocketydyne div., 1964-70; advance gear engr. Gen. Electric Co., Lynn, 1960-64; asst. mgr. engine components Aerojet Nuclear Systems Co., Sacramento, 1970-71; gear and bearing cons. AiResearch div. Garrett Corp., Phoenix, 1971-81; transmission cons. Bodensieck Engring. Co., Scottsdale, Ariz., 1981—. Registered profl. engr., Ariz. Mem. ASME, AIAA, Soc. Automotive Engrs. (various coms.), Aircraft Industries Assn. (various coms.), Am. Gear Mfrs. Assn. (mem. aerospace, gear rating and enclosed epicyclic coms.), Nat. Soc. Profl. Engrs., Pi Tau Sigma. Lutheran. Patentee in field. Home: 7133 N Via De Alegria Scottsdale AZ 85258-3812

BODEY, BELA, immunomorphologist; b. Sofia, Bulgaria, Jan. 18, 1949; came to U.S., 1985, naturalized, 1994; s. Joseph and Rossitza (Derebeeva) B.; m. Victoria Psenko, Aug. 29, 1979; children; Bela Jr., Vivian. MD, Med. Acad., Sofia, 1973; PhD in Immuno-Biology, Inst. Morphology, Bulgarian Acad. Sci., Sofia, 1977. Lic. physician, exptl. pathologist, embryologist, immuno-morphologist, thymologist, exptl. oncologist. Asst. prof. Semmelweis Med. U., Budapest, 1977-80; prof. Inst. Hematology, Budapest, 1980-83; rsch. assoc. Tufts U., Boston, 1985; rsch. fellow immuno-pathology Mass. Gen. Hosp./Harvard U., Boston, 1986; rsch. fellow Childrens Hosp. L.A., 1987-90, rsch. scientist, 1991-92; asst. prof. rsch. pathology, Sch. of Medicine Univ. Southern Calif., 1992—, prof. pathology Sch. Medicine, 1995—; vis. prof. Alexander von Humboldt Found., Ulm, Fed. Republic Germany, 1984. Mem. Am. Assn. Cancer Rsch., Am. and Can. Acad. Pathology, French Soc. Cell Biology, French Soc. Electronmicroscopy, Internat. Soc. Exptl. Hematology, Internat. Soc. Comparative Oncology, N.Y. Acad. Scis., Free Masons. Roman Catholic. Avocations: travel, swimming, dancing. Home: 15745 Saticoy St Van Nuys CA 91406-3155 Office: U So Calif Sch Medicine 2011 Zonal Ave Los Angeles CA 90033-1034

BOERSMA, JUNE ELAINE (JALMA BARRETT), writer, photographer; b. N.Y.C., Apr. 27, 1926; d. Arthur Oscar and Gertrude Ann (Connolly) Schiefer; m. Kenneth Thomas McKim, June 8. 1946 (div. 1957); chldren: Kenneth Thomas Jr., Mark Rennie; m. Lawrence Allan Boersma, Nov. 22, 1962; children: Juliana Jaye, Dirk John. Student, Edgewood Park Jr. Coll., 1944-46. Writer non-fiction; co-owner, photographer Allan/The Animal Photographers, San Diego, 1980—. Author: (series) Wildcats of North America-Bobcat, Cougar, Feral Cat, Lynx, 1998, The Dove Family Tale, A True Story, 1998; contbr. articles to Ladies' Home Jour., Horse Illus., Cat Fancy, Dog Fancy, others. Address: 3503 Argonne St San Diego CA 92117-1009

BOERSMA, LAWRENCE ALLAN, animal welfare administrator; b. London, Ont., Can., Apr. 24, 1932; s. Harry Albert and Valerie Kathryn (DeCordova) B.; m. Nancy Noble Jones, Aug. 16, 1952 (div. 1962) children: Juliana Jaye, Dirk John; m. June Elaine Schiefer McKim, Nov. 22, 1962; children: Kenneth Thomas McKim, Mark Rennie McKim. *Wife June, is a photographer and writes non-fiction under the pen name Jalma Barrett. She wrote a series of four books: Wildcats of North America-Bobcat, Cougar, Feral Cat, Lynx, 1998, and The Dove Family Tale, A True Story, 1998. She's written for Ladies' Home Journal, Dog Fancy, Cat Fancy, Dog World, Horse Illustrated, Popular Photography, MotoFocus, Petersen's Photographic, Studio Photography, and others. She is co-owner, photographer of Allan/The Animal Photographers, San Diego, 1980—; and served as VP/Board Member of The Photographic Institute International, 1982-86. She has addressed the national convention of the Professional Photographers of America, Western States Professional Photographers Association, and the Professional Photographers of Nevada and New Mexico.* BA, U. Nebr., Omaha, 1953, MS, 1955; PhD, Sussex U., 1972; postgrad., U. Oxford, Eng., 1996. Journalism tchr. Tech. High Sch., Omaha, Nebr., 1953-55; dir. pub. rels., chair journalism dept. Adams State Coll., Alamosa, Colo., 1955-59; advt. sales analyst, advt. salesman Better Homes and Gardens, Des Moines, N.Y.C., 1959-63; advt. account exec. This Week Mag., N.Y.C., 1963-66; eastern sales dir., mktg. dir. Ladies' Home Jour., N.Y.C., 1966-75; v.p. assoc. pub., v.p. pub. Saturday Evening Post and The Country Gentleman, N.Y.C., 1975; v.p., dir. mktg. and advt. sales Photo World Mag., N.Y.C., 1975-77; advt. mgr. LaJolla (Calif.) Light, 1977-80; owner, photographer Allan/The Animal Photographers, San Diego, 1980—; pres., CEO The Photographic Inst. Internat., 1982-86; dir. comty. rels. San Diego Humane Soc./Soc. for Prevention Cruelty to Animals, 1985-94; assoc. exec. dir. The Ctr. for Humane Edn. for So. Calif., 1994-98; adj. asst. prof. Grad. Sch. Bus., Pace U., N.Y.C., 1964-65; adj. instr. N.Y. Inst. of Advt., 1974-77, others; adj. prof. Sch. Bus. Mesa Coll., San Diego, 1981-84, City Coll., San Diego, 1982-86; adj. prof. Coll. Bus. Adminstrn. U. LaVerne, San Diego, 1985; pres., CEO United Animal Welfare Found., San Diego, 1992-94; bd. dirs. Escondido Humane Soc. Found., 1994—; chmn., CEO Internat. Dolphin Project, 1995. Author: Strange Events at the House on Park Avenue: A Jack and Jimmy Mystery, 1996; photographer: (as Larry Allan) Wildcats of North America book series, 1998; contbr. photography and articles to mags.; photographer calendars, books, and greeting cards. Spokesperson Coalition for Pet Population Control, San Diego, 1990, 93, Com. Against Proposition C-Pound Animals for Med. Rsch., San Diego, 1990; spokesperson Spay-Neuter Action Project, 1991, mem. steering com., 1991, bd. dirs., 1992-93; mem. evaluation subcom. County of San Diego Dept. Animal Control Adv. Com.; founder, chair Feral Cat Coalition of San Diego County, 1992-93; vol. in pub. info. San Diego/Imperial Counties chpt. ARC, 1993—, mem. chpt. centennial com., 1996-97; mem. pub. info. officers San Diego County Emergency Svcs. Orgn., 1993-95; vol. photographer Julian (Calif.) World Preserve, 1999—. Fellow Royal Photog. Soc. Gt. Britain, Profl. Photographers Am. (Master of Photography award 1985, Photog. Craftsman award 1986), Profl. Photographers of Calif.; mem. PRSA (chmn. So. Tier N.Y. chpt. 1972), Soc. Animal Welfare Adminstrs., Nat. Soc. Fund Raising Execs. (cert., bd. dirs. 1988-89, treas. San Diego chpt. 1990-91, mem. nat. faculty 1992-93), Shriners (pres. Al Bahr chpt., Businessmen's Club), Masons. Republican. Presbyterian. Home: 3503 Argonne St San Diego CA 92117-1009

BOESPFLUG, JOHN FRANCIS, JR., lawyer; b. 1944. AB, Whitman Coll., 1966; JD, U. Wash., 1969. Bar: Wash. 1969. Of counsel Bogle & Gates, Bellevue, Wash., 1994—. Mem. ABA. Office: Bogle & Gates 10500 NE 8th St Ste 1500 Bellevue WA 98004-4398*

BOGANDOFF, MICHAEL A., new-technology vehicle engineer; b. Huntington Park, Calif., Aug. 12, 1946; s. Alex M. and Stella (Kasimoff) B.; m. Darlene J. Probst, Dec. 7, 1974; children: Amy A., Jonathan A., Alicia B., Carrie S. BS in Engring., UCLA, 1968. With Calif. Dept. Transp., L.A., 1968-75; engr. Calif. Air Resources Bd., El Monte, Calif., 1976-91, South Coast Air Quality Mgmt. Dist., Diamond Bar, Calif., 1992—. With U.S. Army, 1969-71, Viet Nam. Mem. Soc. Automotive Engrs. Avocation: coll. soccer referee. Office: S Coast AQMD 21865 E Copley Diamond Bar CA 91765

BOGART, FRANK JEFFREY, system and product planning engineer; b. Johnson City, Tenn., May 17, 1942; s. Frank Lavon and Mary Stein (Hattan) B.; m. JoAnne Ruth Hodgson, Aug. 1, 1964; children: Christopher Alan, Timothy Andrew. BS, U. R.I., 1963; MS, Rutgers U., 1965; postgrad., U. Colo., 1970-74. Mem. tech. staff Lucent Techs. Bell Labs., Holmdel, N.J., 1963-65, 68-69; disting. mem. tech. staff Lucent Techs. Bell Labs., Denver, 1969-98, tech. mgr., 1998—, participant Career Awareness Program, AT&T, Denver, 1985—. Patentee in field. Various positions Boy Scouts Am., 1951—; treas. 1st Congl. Ch., United Ch. of Christ, 1994-96;

moderator 1st Congrl. Ch., UCC, 1997-99. Served to capt. U.S. Army, 1965-67, Vietnam. Decorated Bronze Star; recipient God and Svc. award United Ch. of Christ, 1990, Silver Beaver award Boy Scouts Am., 1976, Disting. Commr. award Boy Scouts Am., 1991. Mem. Telephone Pioneers Am. Avocations: travel, camping, wine-making. Home: 4796 Devonshire St Boulder CO 80301-4137 Office: Lucent Technologies Bell Labs 11900 Pecos St Denver CO 80234-2797

BOGDAN, JAMES THOMAS, secondary education educator, electronics researcher and developer; b. Kingston, Pa., Aug. 14, 1938; s. Fabian and Edna A. (Spray) B.; m. Carolyn Louetta Carpenter, May 5, 1961; 1 child, Thomas James. BS in Edn., Wilkes U., Wilkes-Barre, Pa., 1960. Cert. chemistry and physics tchr., Calif. Tchr. Forty Fort (Pa.) Sch. Dist., 1960-63; tchr., chmn. sci. dept. L.A. Unified Sch. Dist., 1963-96; owner, mgr. Bogdan Electronic Rsch. & Devel., Lakewood, Calif., 1978—; cons. Lunar Electronics, San Diego, 1978-83, T.E. Systems, L.A., 1988-89. Author, pub. The VHF Reporter newsletter, 1967-76. Tng. officer Los Angeles County Disaster Comm., 1968-91, UHF and microwave sys. staff officer, 1991-94, dep. chief comm. officer, 1994-98, chief comm. officer,1998—; pin chmn. Tournament of Roses Comm. Group, Pasadena, Calif., 1985-98, tournament liaison, 1998—. Mem. IEEE. Republican. Achievements include development of specialized electronic test equipment for automotive and marine magneto ignition systems, of electronic bomb disposal equipment, of portable military satellite communication antenna, design and manufacture of aircraft/commercial direction finding antenna; development of direction finding antenna for aircraft/commercial use. Office: PO Box 62 Lakewood CA 90714-0062

BOGDANOWICZ, LORETTA MAE, artist; b. West Palm Beach, Fla., Aug. 11, 1940; d. James Paul and Bessie Margaret (Smith) Cone; m. Lawrence Robert Bogdanowicz, July 18, 1959; children: Laura June Ford, Michael David, Denise Ann Pharris. AA, Ocean County Coll., 1982; BFA, U. Ariz., 1996. Cert. art tchr., Ariz. Art instr. Ariz. Theatre Co., Tucscon, 1997—, Catalina Foothills Cmty. Sch., Tucscon, 1997—, Tucson Mus. Art, 1997—. Exhibited in group shows at The Liquitex Art Gallery, 1996 (Paint Exch. award). Vis. artist Devon Gables Health Care Ctr., Tucson, 1997—; instr. neighborhood classes. Mem. Nat. Assn. Artists Orgn., Womens Caucus for the Arts, Phi Kappa Phi. Avocations: hiking, photography, gardening, reading, travel.

BOGGS, GEORGE ROBERT, academic administrator; b. Conneaut, Ohio, Sept. 4, 1944; s. George Robert and Mary (Mullen) B.; m. Ann Holladay, Aug. 8, 1969; children: Kevin Dale, Ian Asher, Micah Benjamin. BS in Chemistry, Ohio State U., 1966; MA in Chemistry, U. Calif., Santa Barbara, 1968; postgrad. in ednl. adminstrn., natural scis., and edn., Calif. State U., 1969-72; PhD in Ednl. Adminstrn., U. Tex., 1984. Cert. standard teaching specialization in jr. coll. teaching, C.C. supvr., C.C. chief adminstrv. officer. Instr. chemistry Butte Coll., Oroville, Calif., 1968-85, divsn. chmn. nat. sci. and allied health, 1972-81, assoc. dean of instrn., 1981-85; pres., supt. Palomar C.C. Dist., San Marcos, Calif., 1985—; speaker SCCCIRA, Calif., 1985; adj. instr. Austin (Tex.) C.C., 1982; guest lectr. Calif. State U., Chico, 1970, 83, 84, panelist, 1975; tchg. asst. U. Calif., Santa Barbara, 1966-68, Ohio State U., 1965-66; mem. numerous coms. for colls. and univs., Calif., 1968—; cons. U. Calif., Berkeley, 1995—, U. Wis., Madison, 1997—, Pellissippi State Tech. Coll., 1995, El Camino Coll., 1994, U. Hawaii C.C., 1994, Dept. Nat. Edn., Rep. South Africa, 1993, San Joaquin Delta C.C. Dist., 1986, Marin C.C. Dist., 1985. Contbr. articles to profl. jours.; cons. editl. adv. bd. Jour. Applied Rsch. in the C.C., 1993—; mem. editl. bd. C.C. Rev., 1997—. Presenter Nat. Conf. Teaching Excellence and Conf. of Pres.'s, 1983, 93, 95, presenter, mem. coordinating com., 1984, chmn. steering com., 1985; presenter Profl. and Orgl. Devel. Network, 1984; ad hoc com. CPEC/FIPSE/Chancellor's Office, 1984; mem. steering com. Learning Assessment Retention Com., 1983—, pres.-elect 1985-86; mem. instl. research design team No. Calif. Higher Edn. Council, 1984, mission charrette writing team, 1985. Richardson fellow 1982-83; scholar Gen. Ohio State U., 1963, Stadium Dormitory, 1962-65, Scholastic R., 1962, Nat. Honor Soc., 1962; recipient Stanley A. Mahr Cmty. Svc. award Past Pres.' Coun. San Marcos C. of C., Calif., 1994, cert. of Achievement in Recognition of Leadership Excellence and Cmty. Svc. Congress of U.S. Ho. of Reps., 1994, San Diego Hall of Success, 1988, Pacific Region CEO award Assn. C.C. Trustees, Victoria, B.C., Can., 1993, Recognition award Nat. Coun. for Rsch. and Planning Mgmt., 1997, Marie Y. Martin CEO award Assn. C.C. Trustees, 1996, Harry Buttimer Disting. Adminstrs. award Assn. Calif. C.C. Trustees, 1994; named hon. elder Nat. Coun. on Black Am. Affairs, 1993; proclamation of Jan. 14, 1994 as Dr. George R. Boggs Day in Vista, Calif., 1994. Mem. NSF (mem. adv. com. to directorate for edn. and human resources 1995-97, evaluator 1992, 93, 98), Nat. Rsch. Coun. (mem. undergrad. sci. edn. com. 1993-95, chmn. subcom. tchg. and learning 1993-95), Assn. Calif. Coll. Tutorial and Learning Assistance (presenter 1984), Calif. Assn. C.C. (conf. presenter 1984, com. on research 1985—), Assn. Calif. C.C. Adminstrs. (commn. membership devel. 1985), C.C. League Calif. (bd. dirs. 1990-92, presenter confs. 1990-98), Faculty Assn. Calif. C.C., Calif. C.C. Chief Exec. Officers' Assn. San Diego and Imperial Counties C.C. Assn., Am. Assn. Cmty. and Jr. Colls. (presenter 1989, 90, 91, 94, 95, bd. dirs. 1990-95, fed. rels. com. 1990-91, 94-95, chair elect 1993—, chair bd. dirs. 1993-94, exec. com. 1993-95, chair bd. nominating com. 1994-95), So. Calif. C.C. Chief Exec. Officers Assn. (sec., treas. 1990—), Phi Kappa Phi, Upsilon Pi Upsilon (pres. 1965-66), Phi Rho Pi. Lodge: Rotary (pres. Durham club 1980-81, dist. sec. Calif., 1983-84, various other offices and com. positions held locally and nationally). Home: 521 Cassou Rd San Marcos CA 92069-9711 Office: Palomar Coll 1140 W Mission Rd San Marcos CA 92069-1415

BOGGS, STEVEN EUGENE, lawyer; b. Santa Monica, Calif., Apr. 28, 1947; s. Eugene W. and Annie (Happe) B. BA in Econ., U. Calif., Santa Barbara, 1969; D of Chiropractic summa cum laude, Cleveland Chiropractic, L.A., 1974; PhD in Fin. Planning, Columbia Pacific U., 1986; JD in Law, U. So. Calif., 1990. Bar: Calif. 1990, U.S. Dist. Ct. (cen. dist.) Calif. 1990, Hawaii 1991, U.S. Ct. Appeals (9th cir.); CFP; lic. chiropractor Hawaii, Calif.; lic. radiography X-ray supr. and operator. Faculty mem. Cleveland Chiropractic Coll., 1972-74; pres. clinic dir. Hawaii Chiropratic Clinic, Inc., Aiea, 1974-87; pvt. practice Honolulu, 1991—; mem. faculty Hawaii Pacific U., 1997—; cons. in field; seminar presenter 1990—. Contbr. articles to profl. jours. Recipient Cert. Appreciation State of Hawaii, 1981-84. Fellow Internat. Coll. of Chiropractic; mem. ABA, Am. Trial Lawyers Assn., Consumer Lawyers of Hawaii, Am. Chriopractic Assn., Hawaii State Chiropractic Assn. (pres. 1978, 85, 86, v.p. 1977, sec. 1979-84, treas. 1976, other coms., Valuable Svc. award 1984, Cert. Appreciation 1986, Cert. Achievement 1986, Chiropractor of Yr. 1986, Outstanding Achievement award 1991), Consumer Lawyers of Hawaii (bd. dirs.). Democrat. Avocations: sailing, scuba, snorkling, boogie boarding, bicycling. Office: 1188 Bishop St Ste 1705 Honolulu HI 96813-3307

BOGGS, WILLIAM S., lawyer; b. Toledo, Ohio, May 17, 1946. AB summa cum laude, Wittenberg U., 1968; JD cum laude, Harvard U., 1972. Bar: Calif. Ptnr. Gray, Cary, Ware & Freidenrich, San Diego, 1979—. Mem. ABA, San Diego County Bar Assn., Internat. Assn. Defense Counsel, Assn. So. Calif. Defense Counsel, San Diego Defense Lawyers, Lincoln's Inn. Office: Gray Cary Ware & Freidenrich 401 B St Ste 1700 San Diego CA 92101-4240*

BOGUES, TYRONE CURTIS (MUGGSY BOGUES), professional basketball player; b. Balt., Jan. 9, 1965; m. Kimberly Bogues; children: Tyeisha, Brittany, Tyrone Jr. Student, Wake Forest U., 1983-87. Guard Washington Bullets, 1987-88, Charlotte (N.C.) Hornets, 1988-97, Golden State Warriors, Oakland, Calif., 1997—. Founder "Reading and Roundball" charity basketball game, Balt.; dir. numerous basketball camps. Recipient Inspirational Trophy Jim Thorpe Pro Sports Awards, 1995; number retired at Wake Forest; all-time leader assists and steals Atlantic Coast Conf., assist to turnoer ratio NBA, assists Charlotte Hornets; named Belt/WBTV Hornets Player of Yr., 1993-94. Avocations: softball, golf. Office: Golden State Warriors 1011 Broadway Oakland CA 94607*

BOHANNON-KAPLAN, MARGARET ANNE, publisher, lawyer; b. Oakland, Calif., July 6, 1937; d. Thomas Morris and Ruth Frances (Davenport) Bohannon; m. Melvin Jordan Kaplan, Feb. 2, 1961; children: Mark Geoffrey, Craig Andrew, Stephen Joseph, David Benjamin, Jonathan Michael. *Ms. Bohannon-Kaplan is the niece of the late David D. Bohannon, a noted community planner and developer who was well known for his contributions to civic affairs in northern California. Husband, Melvin J. Kaplan, has been a philanthropist and entrepreneur since 1962. He is an alumnus of MIT and the University of California at Berkeley and is currently an investment banker concerned primarily with commercial real estate. Entrepreneurial sons founded two real estate companies and a software company. Combined contributions to the community include service in the Coast Guard, Air Force, Fire Department, and in the fields of health, education and law.* Student, Smith Coll., 1955-56, U. Cin., 1956; B.A. in Philosophy, U. Calif.-Berkeley, 1960; LL.B., LaSalle Extension U., 1982, Coll. Fin. Planning, 1985. Bar: Calif. 1982. Engaged in property mgmt., real estate investment Kaplan Real Estate, Berkely and San Francisco, 1961-77; investment exec. Wellington Fin. Group, San Francisco, 1977—; cons. fin. planning and law San Francisco and Carmel, Calif., 1982—; pres. Wellington Publs., Carmel, 1983—, Exec. Advt., Carmel, 1983—. *Ms. Bohannon-Kaplan has concentrated on pro-bono activities since 1984 when she began promoting social security reform. She directs the 501(c) 3 Harry Singer Foundation whose mission is to promote responsibility nationally. Projects include annual essay contests, online activities (www.singerfoundation.org) and Another Way, which focuses on three undervalued assets (the young, the old and new technology) on local problems. It engages the educational system in experiential learning and efficiently locates and connects resources in a community. Another Way is NOT a new program; it enhances existing programs and encourages people to assume responsibility.* Carmel, 1983—. Author: Another Way, 1997, (pseudonym Helen P. Rogers), Everyone's Guide to Financial Planning, 1984, Social Security: An Idea Whose Time Has Passed, 1985, The American Deficit: Fulfillment of a Prophecy?, 1988, The Election Process, 1988, The Deficit: 12 Steps to Ease the Crisis, 1988, (series) Taking A Stand On, 1991, Alternatives, 1992; editor: What Role if Any, Should Government's Role be Regarding Child Care in the United States?, 1991, What if Any, Should Governments Role Be Regarding Health Care in the United States, 1992, What Role Does, And What Role Should Media Play in Choosing Our Candidates for National Office?, 1993, Doesn't Anyone Care About the Children?, 1994, Responsibility: Who Has It and Who Doesn't and What That Means to The Nation, 1994, 97, White Hats: People Who Try To Make A Difference, 1994, Governments Struggling with Limited Resources, 1995, Should Government Intervene to Help Children and Teens In Trouble, If so How?, 1996, Excerpts From the Harry Singer Foundation High School Essay Contests, 1996, 97, 98. Co-founder The Harry Singer Found., Carmel, Calif., 1988; ind. candidate for U.S. Senate, 1992. Dir. Singer Online internat. programs, 1993—. Mem. ABA, Calif. Bar Assn., Calif. Real Estate Assn., Internat. Assn. Fin. Planners, Inst. Cert. Fin. Planners, Ind. Sector, Philanthropy Round Table Civicus. Club: Commonwealth (San Francisco). Office: PO Box 223159 Carmel CA 93922-3159

BOHN, DENNIS ALLEN, electrical engineer, executive; b. San Fernando, Calif., Oct. 5, 1942; s. Raymond Virgil and Iris Elouise (Johnson) B.; 1 child, Kira Michelle; m. Patricia Tolle, Aug. 12, 1986. BSEE with honors, U. Calif., Berkeley, 1972, MSEE with honors, 1974. Engring. technician GE Co., San Leandro, Calif., 1964-72; research and devel. engr. Hewlett-Packard Co., Santa Clara, Calif., 1973; application engr. Nat. Semicondr. Corp., Santa Clara, 1974-76; engring. mgr. Phase Linear Corp., Lynnwood, Wash., 1976-82; v.p. rsch. and devel., ptnr. Rane Corp., Mukilteo, Wash., 1982—; founder Toleco Systems, Kingston, Wash., 1980. Suicide and crisis ctr. vol., Berkeley, 1972-74, Santa Clara, 1974-76. Served with USAF, 1960-64. Recipient Am. Spirit Honor medal USAF, 1961; Math. Achievement award Chem. Rubber Co., 1962-63. Editor: We Are Not Just Daffodils, 1975; contbr. poetry to Reason mag.; tech. editor Audio Handbook, 1976; contbr. articles to tech. jours.; columnist Polyphony mag., 1981-83; 2 patents in field. Fellow Audio Engring. Soc.; mem. IEEE, Tau Beta Pi. Office: Rane Corp 10802 47th Ave W Mukilteo WA 98275-5098

BOHN, JACK RICHARD, engineering technology manager; b. St. Paul, June 13, 1930; s. Fred Norman and Mona Claire (Studer) B.; m. Marjorie Anne Bleich, July 15, 1954; children: Daniel, Mark, Barbara, Michael, Paul. BSME, Iowa State Coll., 1955; MS in Nuclear Engring., Iowa State U., 1960. Rsch. assoc. Iowa State U., Ames, 1956-61; mem. tech. staff TRW, Space & Defense, Redondo Beach, Calif., 1961-63, sect. head, 1963-75, asst. dept. mgr. materials tech., 1975-80, sr. staff mgr., 1980-89; advanced tech. mgr. TRW, Space & Electronics, Redondo Beach, Calif., 1989-92; cons. Air Force Wright Labs., Dayton, Ohio, 1992—; ceramic processing panel Nat. Acad. of Sci., Washington, 1970-72; space coord. of rsch. Space Def. Initiative Office U.K./USA, Washington, 1988-91; cons. MANTECH, USAF Wright Lab., Dayton, 1992, cons. materials directorate, 1993-95; tech. advisor to space sys. support effort USAF Rsch. Lab, 1995-98. Contbr. numerous articles to profl. jours. Fleet capt. King Harbor Yacht Club, Redondo Beach, 1978. Mem. AIAA, ASME, Am. Soc. for Metals, Am. Ceramic Soc. Republican. Achievements include patents for Thermal Shock Resistant Rocket Nozzle; thermal processing to improve thermal stress resistance; Pressure Swing Recovery for Mineral Deposits; control of retorting methods for oil shale; thermal mechanical fracture system for oil shale; devel. process for recovering petroleum from viscous crude or tar sands; Fiber reinforced viscoelastic composites for passive damping; processes and rocket science for U.S. ballistic missiles, lasers, launch and reentry vehicles; spacecraft design for communication and survialence satelites for DOD and NASA. Home: 27504 Larchbluff Dr Palos Verdes Peninsula CA 90275-3923

BOHN, PAUL BRADLEY, psychiatrist, psychoanalyst; b. Santa Monica, Calif., Apr. 11, 1957; m. Pamela Summit, Nov. 17, 1990. BA in Pharmacology, U. Calif., Santa Barbara, 1980; MD, U. Calif., Irvine, 1984; postgrad. in Psychoanalysis, L.A. Psychoanalytic Inst., 1988-93; PsyD, Grad. Inst. Contemporary Psychoanalysis, 1995. Diplomate Am. Bd. Psychiatry and Neurology, added qualifications in addiction psychiatry. Psychiat. resident UCLA, 1984-88, assoc. dir. anxiety disorders clinic, 1989-95; assoc. clin. prof. psychiatry, 1989—; dir. social anxiety clinic UCLA, 1993-95; fellow U. So. Calif., L.A., 1988-89; v.p. Pacific Psychopharmacology Rsch. Inst., Santa Monica, 1990—; pvt. practice psychiatry Santa Monica, 1988—; expert reviewer, Med. Bd. Calif.; diplomate Am. Bd. Addiction Psychiatry, 1997. Grantee Ciba-Geigy, Santa Monica, 1992. Fellow Am. Psychiat. Assn.; mem. So. Calif. Psychiat. Assn., Anxiety Disorders Assn. of Am., Obsessive Compulsive Found. Office: 2730 Wilshire Blvd Ste 325 Santa Monica CA 90403-4747

BOHN, ROBERT HERBERT, lawyer; b. Austin, Tex., Sept. 2, 1935; s. Herbert and Alice B.; m. Gay P. Maloy, June 4, 1957; children: Rebecca Shoemaker, Katherine Bernat, Robert H., Jr.. BBA, U. Tex., 1957, LLB, 1963. Bar: Tex. 1963, Calif. 1965. Ptnr. Boccardo Law Firm, San Jose, Calif., 1965-87, Alexander & Bohn, San Jose, 1987-91; Bohn, Bennion & Niland, 1992-97, Bohn & Bohn, 1998—; spkr. Calif. Continuing Edn. of Bar; judge pro tem Superior Ct. of Calif., San Jose, 1975-96. Mem. Consumer Attys. Calif., Am. Bd. Trial Advocates, ATLA, Santa Clara County Bar Assn., Calif. State Bar Assn., Trial Lawyers Pub. Justice, Santa Clara County Trial Lawyers Assn. (pres.), Roscoe Pound Found., Million Dollar Advocates Forum, Lawyers Arbitration Mediation Svc. (pres.), Commonwealth Club Calif., Santa Clara County Trial Lawyers Assn. (pres. 1999), Silicon Valley Capital Club, Exec. Golfers (dir. gen.), Texas Cowboys Assn., Phi Gamma Delta. Home: 14124 Pike Rd Saratoga CA 95070-5380 Office: 152 N Third St Ste 200 San Jose CA 95112

BOHNEN, MOLLYN VILLAREAL, nurse, educator; b. Balete, Aklan, Philippines, Nov. 1, 1941; came to the U.S., 1964; d. Wenceslao and Amparo Villareal; m. Robert Frank Bohnen, MD, June 20, 1965; children: Sharon Kay Taylor, Scott Owen David, Paul Alan. BSN, U. Philippines, 1962; MSN, U. Utah, 1971; EdD, U. San Francisco, 1984. Staff nurse U. Philippines Med. Ctr., Manila, 1962-64, St. Lukes Hosp., N.Y.C., 1964-65, Greystone Park Hosp., Morristown, N.J., 1965, Buffalo (N.Y.) Children's Hosp., 1965-66; vol. staff nurse Peace Corps, Cebu City, Philippines, 1966-68; asst. prof. Calif. State U., Sacramento, 1973-76, 82-84, lectr., 1979-82, assoc. prof., 1984-87, prof., 1987—; instr. Am. River Coll., Sacramento, 1977-78; medicolegal cons. Calif. law firms, 1975—; internat. nursing edn. cons. B/B Creation, Rancho Cordova, Calif., 1988—. Contbr. various articles in national and international profl. jours. Recipient J.V. Sotejo Medallion of Honor for national and international innovation and leadership in Nursing, U. Philippines, 1994. Mem. NAFE, ANA Calif., Golden Key, U. Philippines Nursing Alumni Assn. Internat., Sigma Theta Tau (treas. Zeta Eta chpt. 1982-84, rsch. award 1984), Phi Delta Kappa. Democrat. Roman Catholic. Avocations: travel, matchbook and music box collecting, reading, sports. Home: 1441 Wild Plum Ct Klamath Falls OR 97601-1983 Office: Calif State U 6000 J St Sacramento CA 95819-2605

BOHRER, RICHARD WILLIAM, religious writer, editor, educator; b. N.Y.C., June 17, 1926; s. Jacob William and Elsie Marie (Wahlstad) B.; m. Elizabeth Anne Spencer, July 8, 1955; children: Joel Stephen, Janice Joy Bohrer Pruitt. BA, Westmont Coll., 1947; MSc, U. So. Calif., L.A., 1956; MA, Calif. State U., Long Beach, 1962. Tchr. grades 3, 4, 5 Haile Selassie I Elem. Sch., Gondar, Ethiopia, 1947-50; tchr. grades 9, 10, 11 Alhambra (Calif.) High Sch., 1954-55; tchr. grade 6 Maple Ave. Sch., Fullerton, Calif., 1955-56; tchr. grades 9, 10, 11 Orange (Calif.) High Sch., 1956-63; news editor Anaheim (Calif.) Gazette, 1961-62; prof., dir. journalism Multnomah Sch. of the Bible, Portland, Oreg., 1963-79; broker Dick Bohrer Realty Inc., Portland, 1968-81; sr. editor, mng. editor Moody Monthly mag., Chgo., 1979-83; pub. Glory Press, 1981—; prof. Liberty U., Lynchburg, Va., 1983-89, 91-94; asst. prof., head mag. sequence Ball State U., Muncie, Ind., 1989-90; dir. Maranatha Writers Conf., Muskegon, Mich., 1980-89; prof. Inst. Bibl. Studies, Lake Grove, Oreg., 1996-97. Author: Easy English, 1977, Edit, Yourself and Sell, 1980, They Called Him Shifta, 1981, 21 Ways to Write Stories for Christian Kids, 1980, 3d edit., 1997, John Newton, 1983, Bill Borden, 1984, How to Write What You Think, 1985, How to Write Features Like a Pro, 1986, Be an Editor Yourself, 1987, J. Edgar Beanpole: Football Detective, 1991, J. Edgar Beanpole: Volleyball Spy, 1991, J. Edgar Beanpole: Soccer Sleuth, 1991, J. Edgar Beanpole: Night Watcher, 1991, No Frills Editing Skills, 1993, John G. Mitchell: Lion of God, 1994, J. Edgar Beanpole: Stage Snoop, 1999, J. Edgar Beanpole: Basketball Hawkeye, 1999; editor: The Battle for Your Faith (Willard M. Aldrich), The Schemer and the Dreamer (Luis Palau), Down to Earth (John Lawrence), Parables by the Sea (Pamela Reeve), An Everlasting Love (John G. Mitchell), Plague in Our Midst (Gregg Albers, MD), Right With God (John G. Mitchell), What Do You Say When.... (Nellie Pickard), Counseling the Terminally Ill (Gregg Albers, MD), The Self-Study of Liberty University, Maranatha, Our Lord, Come! (Renald Showers), Let's Revel in John's Gospel (John G. Mitchell), Let's Revel in Romans (John G. Mitchell), Priceless Pearls (John and Esther Nader Smit); acting editor Moral Majority Report, 1983-85, copy editor, 1985-88. Recipient Pres.'s Svc. award Liberty U., 1985, Tchr. of Yr. award, 1987, 89. Mem. Northwest Assn. of Book Publ. Republican. Mem. Plymouth Brethren Ch. Avocations: oil painting, cooking, swimming. Home: PO Box 624 West Linn OR 97068-0624

BOISSONEAU, ROBERT ALLEN, health management conusultant, educator; b. Detroit, Sept. 23, 1937; s. Sylvester Napoleon and Dorothea Verjean (DeLamarter) B.; m. JoEllen Marie Fitzgerald, Oct. 15, 1960; children: Mark N., Deborah Jean, Keith Allen. BA, Ea. Mich. U., 1960; M in Hosp. Adminstrn., Med. Coll. Va., 1965; PhD, Ohio State U., 1974; DS, Ind. Grad. Sch. Profl. Mgmt., Fort Wayne, 1979. Asst. adminstr. Detroit-Macomb Hosps., Detroit, 1965-67, Ohio State U. Hosps., Columbus, 1967-72; asst. prof. U. Mo., Columbia, 1972-75; dean Ea. Mich. U., Ypsilanti, 1975-80; prof. Ariz. State U., Tempe, 1980-89; dean S.E. Mo. State U., Cape Girardeau, 1989-94; cons. RBI Consulting, Chandler, Ariz., 1995—; vis. prof. Ctrl. Mich. U., Mount Pleasant, 1994-95; cons. Mich. Dept. Mental Health, 1973, Affiliated Support Enterprises, Phoenix, 1982-88, Pinal Gen. Hosp., Florence, Ariz., 1988-89. *Robert Boissoneau completed a 40-year career as University Health and Human Services Executive, professor, consultant, researcher, grantsman, writer and editorial board member. As start-up manager, served as organizing administrator of Means Hall in the Ohio State University Hospitals system and first dean of the Colleges of Health and Human Services, Eastern Michigan University and Southeast Missouri State University, both colleges becoming among largest of their kind in the U.S. Culminating his teaching career as tenured professor in the College of Business, Arizona State University, Boissoneau totaled more than 200 professional publications and presentations. Areas of expertise included health organizational behavior and design.* Author: (books) Continuing Education in the Health Professions, 1980, Health Care Organization and Development, 1986; also articles in profl. jours. Mem. adult edn. adv. com. Near Northside Comty. Action Ctr., Columbus, Ohio, 1971-72, planning com. adv. bd. St. Joseph Mercy Hosp., Ann Arbor, Mich., 1976-77, adv. bd. Desert Samaritan Hosp., Mesa, Ariz., 1981-83; bd. dirs. ARC, Cape Girardeau, Mo., 1990-92. Capt. U.S. Army, 1960-62. Grantee: Health Svc. Mgmt. Tng., Kellogg Found., Battle Creek, Mich., 1975, HEW Divsn. of Assn. Health Svc. Profls., Washington, 1978; recipient Allen award in nursing rsch. S.E. Mo. State U., Cape Girardeau, 1990. Mem. Acad. of Mgmt, Am. Hosp. Assn. Avocations: tennis, running, reading. Home and Office: 843 N Rita Ct Chandler AZ 85226

BOLAND, MARGARET CAMILLE, financial services administrator, consultant; b. Washington, Feb. 20, 1929; d. Harvey Alvin and Margaret Estelle (Head) Jacob; m. Robert Edgar Hollingsworth, July 14, 1960 (div. July 1980); children: William Lee, Robert Edgar Hollingsworth Jr., Barbara Camille, Bradford Damion; m. James Aldo Boland, Sept. 12, 1998. AA, Va. Intermont Coll., 1949. Bookkeeper Fred A. Smith Real Estate, Washington, 1949-53; adminstrv. mgr. Airtronic, Inc., Bethesda, Md., 1953-61; pers. adminstr. Sears Roebuck, Washington, 1973-74; adminstrv. mgr., communication mgr. Garvin GuyButler Corp., San Francisco, 1980-88, exec. sec., pers. mgr., 1989-95, adminstrv. cons., ret., 1996; adminstrv. cons., Concord, Calif.; assoc. Robert Hollingsworth Nuclear Cons., Walnut Creek, Calif., 1975-79. Bd. dirs. Civic Arts, Walnut Creek, 1975-98; bd. dirs., mem. pub. rels. com. Valley Art Ctr., Walnut Creek, 1997—. Recipient Spl. Recognition award AEC, 1974. Mem. Internat. Platform Assn., Commonwealth Club, Beta Sigma Phi (pres. 1954). Democrat. Presbyterian. Avocations: travel, art appreciation, investments, hiking, reading. Home: 1108 Limeridge Dr Concord CA 94518-1923

BOLDON, ALLIFEE, aerospace company executive; b. Streetman, Tex., July 27, 1941; s. James Paul and Izora (English) B.; children: Latrina, Dwyane, Keith. BA, Dominguez Hills U., 1969; JD, Loyola U., 1975. Mgr. McDonnell Douglas, Santa Monica, Calif., 1962-69, Edison, Rosemead, Calif., 1969-75, Hughes Aircraft, El Segundo, Calif., 1975-79; dir. TRW, Redondo Beach, Calif., 1979—. Bd. dirs. GLAAACC, L.A., 1997, Compton (Calif.) Coll. Exec. Bd., 1997, BBA, L.A., 1997. Recipient Black Profl. of Yr. award Black Engr. Award Select Com., 1998. Mem. Nat. Soc. Am. Indians (dir., Cert. 1997), Nat. Tech. Assn. (dir., Cert. 1996), NASA Prime Contractor Round Table (dir. 1993-97, Cert. 1997). Democrat. Methodist. Avocations: sports, tennis, basketball, fishing, traveling.

BOLDREY, EDWIN EASTLAND, retinal surgeon, educator; b. San Francisco, Dec. 8, 1941; s. Edwin Barkley and Helen Burns (Eastland) B.; m. Catherine Rose Oliphant, Oct. 20, 1973; children: Jennifer Elizabeth, Melissa Jeanne. BA with honors, De Pauw U., 1963; MD, Northwestern U., Chgo., 1967. Diplomate Am. Bd. Ophthalmology. Rotating intern U. Wash., Seattle, 1967-68; resident in gen. surgery U. Minn., Mpls., 1968-69; resident in ophthalmology U. Calif., San Francisco, 1971-74; Heed Found. fellow in retinal and vitreous surgery Washington U., St. Louis, 1974-75; mem. staff dept. ophthalmology Palo Alto (Calif.) Med. Clinic, 1975-91; dept. chmn., 1989-91; pvt. practice, San Jose, Mountain View, Calif., 1991—; clin. instr. Stanford (Calif.) U. Med. Sch., 1975-79, asst. clin. prof., 1979-87, assoc. clin. prof., 1987—; cons. VA Hosp., Palo Alto, Calif., 1976—; vice chmn. dept. ophthalmology Good Samaritan Hosp., San Jose, 1993-95, chmn., 1995-97. Contbr. articles to med. jours., chpt. to book. Lt. comdr. M.C., USNR, 1969-71. Recipient Asbury award dept. ophthalmology U. Calif., San Francisco, 1973. Fellow ACS, Am. Acad. Ophthalmology (honor award 1989); mem. AMA, Retina Soc., Vitreous Soc. (charter), Peninsula Eye Soc. (pres. 1987-88), Western Retina Study Club (charter, exec. sec.-treas. 1983-95), Cordes Eye Soc. (pres. 1995-96), also others. Avocations: skiing, hiking, travel. Office: Retina Vitreous Assocs Inc 2512 Samaritan Ct Ste A San Jose CA 95124-4002

BOLDYREV, PETER MATVEEVICH, Russian language and culture educator, writer; b. Leningrad/St. Petersburg, USSR, Dec. 12, 1936; came to U.S., 1977; MA equivalent in History of Philosophy, Leningrad State U., 1975. Tchr. Russian lang. and culture Def. Lang. Inst., Monterey, Calif., 1981—. Author: Introduction to Soviet Period of Russian History, 1992, Russia's Lessons, 1993; mem. editorial bd. quar. mag. Contemporary, Toronto, 1979-80; author articles and essays. Founding mem. exec. bd.

Russia Without Colonies, N.Y.C., 1977-80. Mem. Internat. PEN Club, Am. Philos. Assn. Home: PO Box 1362 Marina CA 93933-1362

BOLEN, TERRY LEE, optometrist; b. Newark, Ohio, Sept. 16, 1945; s. Robert Howard and Mildred Irene (Hoover) B.; BS, Ohio U., 1968; postgrad. Youngstown State U., 1973; O.D. Ohio State U., 1978; div. Quality control inspector ITT Grinnell Corp., Warren, Ohio, 1973, jr. quality control engr., 1974; pvt. practice optometry, El Paso, Tex., 1978-80, Dallas, 1980-81, Waco, Tex., 1981-85, Hewitt, Tex., 1983-89; comdr. U.S. Pub. Health Svc., 1989—; bd. dirs. Am. Optometric Student Assn., 1977-78; pres. Am. Optometric Student Assn., 1977-78; pres. El Paso Optometric Soc., 1980; adj. prof. clin. optometry Pacific U. Coll. Optometry, So. Calif. Coll. Optometry. Vol. visual examiner, Juarez, Mex., 1979—; chmn. Westside Recreation Ctr. Adv. Com., El Paso, 1979, Lions Internat. Sight Conservation and Work With the Blind Chmn. award, 1989. Served to lt. USN, 1969-72; capt. USAIRNG, 1987-89. Recipient pub. svc. award, City of El Paso, 1980. Mem. Am. Optometric Assn., Tex. Optometric Assn., Assn. Mil. Surgeons of U.S. (life, USPHS HSO liaison 1990-94, edn. coord. optometry section, 1992), Res. Officers Assn. (sec. chpt. # 1 Nev. 1994-96, sr. v.p. Navy Nev. 1995-96, life), Ret. Officers Assn., Optometric Assn. (clin. assoc. Optometric Extension Program Found. 1978-89), Heart of Tex. Optometric Soc. (sec.-treas. 1984-85, pres.-elect 1986, pres. 1987), North Tex. Optometric Soc., USPHS (pres. No. Nev. chpt. Commd. Officers Assn. 1989-91), Epsilon Psi Epsilon (pres., 1977-78), Lions (3rd v.p. Coronado El Paso, svc. award, 1978, 79, Hewitt pres. 1985, v.p. W.Tex. Lions Eye Bank, 1980, 2d v.p. Cen. Tex. Lions Eye Bank, 1988, Hewitt Lion of Yr. 1987). Republican. Mem. Christian Ch. (Disciples of Christ). Home: PO Box 209 Schurz NV 89427-0209

BOLGER, BRENNA M., executive; b. Toledo, Ohio. BA, Santa Clara U. Pres. PRx, Inc., San Jose, Calif., 1974—. Office: PRx Inc 97 S 2d St Ste 300 San Jose CA 95113

BOLIN, RICHARD LUDDINGTON, industrial development consultant; b. Burlington, Vt., May 13, 1923; s. Axel Birger and Eva Madora (Luddington) B.; m. Jeanne Marie Brown, Dec. 18, 1948; children: Richard Luddington, Jr., Douglas, Judith, Barbara, Elizabeth. BSChemE, Tex. A&M U., 1947; MSChemE, MIT, 1950; postgrad. advanced mgmt. program Harvard Bus. Sch., 1969. Jr. rsch. engr. Humble Oil & Refining Co., Baytown, Tex., 1947-49; staff mem. Arthur D. Little, Inc., Cambridge, Mass., 1950-56, Caribbean office mgr. San Juan, 1957-61, gen. mgr., Mex., 1961-72; pres. Internat. Parks, Inc., Flagstaff, Ariz., 1973-94, chmn., 1995—; bd. dirs. Parque Indsl. de Nogales, Nogales, Sonora, Mex.; dir. The Flagstaff Inst., 1976—; Secretariat World Export Processing Zones Assn., 1985—; mem. adv. bd. Lowell Obs., Flagstaff, 1993-94. With U.S. Army, 1942-46. Mem. Univ. Club of Mex. Office: PO Box 986 Flagstaff AZ 86002-0986

BOLIN, VERNON SPENCER, microbiologist, consultant; b. Parma, Idaho, July 9, 1913; s. Thadeus Howard Bolin and Jennie Bell Harm; m. Helen Epling, Jan. 5, 1948 (div. 1964); children: Rex, Janet, Mark; m. Barbara Sue Chase, Aug. 1965; children: Vladimir, Erik. BS, U. Wash., 1942; MS, U. Minn. 1949. Teaching asst. U. Minn.-Mpls., 1943-45; rsch. assoc. U. Utah, Salt Lake City, 1945-50, fellow in surgery, 1950-52; rsch. virologist Jensen-Salsbery Labs., Inc., Kansas City, Mo., 1952-57; rsch. assoc. Wistar Inst. U. Pa., 1957-58; rsch. virologist USPHS, 1958-61; founder Bolin Labs., , Phoenix, 1959—, also bd. dirs. Contbr. articles to profl. jours. Served with U.S. Army, 1931-33. Mem. N.Y. Acad. Scis., Phi Mu Chi. Home: 36629 N 19th Ave Phoenix AZ 85027-9143

BOLIN, VLADIMIR DUSTIN, chemist; b. Inglewood, Calif., Feb. 25, 1965; s. Vernon Spencer and Barbara Sue (Chase) B.; m. Elizabeth Lynne Boswood, May 18, 1985; children: Ragnar Spencer, Roark Morgan. BS, U. Ariz., 1987. Chemist, microbiologist Bolin Labs., Inc., Phoenix, 1987-93; bd. dirs., pres. Aerotech Labs., Inc., Phoenix, 1993—, pres., 1993—; pres. Kalmar Labs., Inc., Phoenix, 1993—, also bd. dirs.; v.p. lab ops. Aqualab Inc., Phoenix, 1996—; bd. dirs., pres. Kalmar Labs., Inc., Phoenix; bd. dirs. Aqualab Inc., v.p., 1996—; bd. dirs. Ariz. Indoor Quality Coun., v.p. 1995—. Mem. ASTM, AAAS, Am. Water Works Assn. (pres.), Assn. Official Analytical Chemists, Am. Soc. Microbiolgoy, Am. Chem. Soc., N.Y. Acad. Scis. Home: 2020 W Lone Cactus Dr Phoenix AZ 85027-2624 Office: Aerotech/Kalmar Labs Inc 2020 W Lone Cactus Dr Phoenix AZ 85027-2624

BOLINGBROKE, RICHARD, artist; b. Southsea Hampshire, Eng., Feb. 28, 1952; s. Johnathan and Ruth (Taylor) B.; partner Steven Gaynes. BSc in geography, London Univ., 1970. Represented by Rivaga Gallery, Wash. Pres. Artspan, San Francisco, 1997. Recipient award Coconut Grove Art Festival, 1997, Gasparilla Festival, 1998. Mem. San Francisco Artist Guild, San Francisco Open Studios, Gay and Lesbian Artists Alliance (founder). Avocations: gardening, carpentry. Home: 2356 15th St San Francisco CA 94114-1224

BOLLES, CHARLES AVERY, librarian; b. Pine Island, Minn., Aug. 10, 1940; s. Arthur Marston and Clarice Ione (Figy) B.; B.A., U. Minn., 1962, M.A. in Library Sci., 1963, M.A. in Hum. Studies, 1969, Ph.D. in Library Sci., 1975; m. Marjorie Elaine Hancock, May 17, 1964; children: Jason Brice, Justin Brian. Catalog and serials librarian U. Iowa, Iowa City, 1964-67; asst. prof. Emporia (Kans.) State U., 1970-76; dir. library devel. div. State Library, 1976-78; dir. Sch. Library Sci., Emporia State U., 1978-80; state librarian State of Idaho, Boise, 1980—. Mem. ALA, Chief Officers State Library Agys., Western Council State Libraries (chmn. 1985-86, 98—), Pacific N.W. Library Assn. (pres. 1990-91), Idaho Library Assn. Office: Idaho State Libr 325 W State St Boise ID 83702-6014

BOLLINGER, KENNETH JOHN, aerospace engineer, computer and space scientist; b. Warren AFB, Wyo., Nov. 6, 1954; s. John Henry and Charleen Edna (Wallick) B.; m. Christine Faye Ferguson, May 11, 1973; children: Kelly Raun, Orion Grant, Sara Selene. BS, Calif. Poly. U., 1987. AER, ops. engr., dep. team chief Voyager project Jet Propulsion Lab., Pasadena, Calif., 1986-89; asst. mgr., PDS Rings Node NASA Ames, Moffett Field, Calif., 1993—; web svcs. mgr. NASA Ames, Moffett Field, 1993—, project mgr., lunar prospector, space directorate; pres. Web Frontiers, Space Frontiers San Jose, Calif., 1993—. Mem. Amateur Radio Civil Emergency Svc., 1988. Mem. Amateur Radio Club, NASA Ames.

BOLOCOFSKY, DAVID N., lawyer, psychology educator; b. Hartford, Conn., Sept. 29, 1947; s. Samuel and Olga Bolocofsky; m. Debra Stein, June 25, 1994; children: Vincent, Daniel, Charly. BA, Clark U., 1969; MS, Nova U., 1974, PhD, 1975; JD, U. Denver, 1988. Bar: Colo. 1988; cert. sch. psychologist, Colo. Tchr. high sch. Univ. Sch., Ft. Lauderdale, Fla., 1972-73; ednl. coord. Living and Learning Ctr., Ft. Lauderdale, 1972-75; asst. prof. U. No. Colo., Greeley, 1975-79, assoc. prof., 1979-90, dir. sch. psychology program, 1979-82; assoc. Robert T. Hinds Jr. & Assocs., Littleton, Colo., 1988-93; hearing officer State of Colo., 1991—; pres. David N. Bolocofsky, P.C., Denver, 1993—; psychol. cons. Clin. Assocs., Englewood, Colo., 1978—. Author: Enhancing Personal Adjustment, 1986, (chpts. in books) Children and Obesity, 1987, Obtaining and Utilizing a Custody Evaluation, 1989; contbr. numerous articles to profl. jours. Mem. Douglas-Elbert Bar Assn., Arapahoe Bar Assn., Nat. Assn. Sch. Psychologists (ethics com. 1988-91), Colo. Soc. Sch. Psychologists (bd. dirs. 1978-96, treas. 1993-96), Interdisciplinary Commn. on Child Custody (pro bono com. 1988-93), Colo. Bar Assn. (family law sect., sec. juvenile law sect. 1990-92), Colo. Soc. Behavioral Analysis Therapy (treas. 1990-96), Arapmhc (bd. mem. 1993—, bd. pres.1995-97). Avocations: sailing, golf, skiing. Home: 9848 E Maplewood Cir Englewood CO 80111-5401 Office: 7887 E Belleview Ave Ste 1275 Englewood CO 80111-6094

BOLSTAD, ROOD IRENE, singer, songwriter; b. Ayrshire, Iowa, Sept. 6, 1927; d. Grover Cleveland and Myrtle Irene (Dannewitz) Maiden; m. Bernard Austin Bolstad, June 17, 1950; children: Gordon Bernard, Margot Rose. BA, U. No. Iowa, 1948; MA, Ctrl. Wash. U., 1972. El. music, sub. music tchr. Bremerton (Wash.) Sch. Dist.; tchr. kindergarten, second grade tchr. Port Orchard (Wash.) Sch. Dist., 1964-67; secondary sch. tchr. Bremerton Sch. Dist., 1967-80, Port Orchard Sch. Dist., 1983-84; pvt. voice and piano tchr., Bremerton, 1969-74. Choir dir. Navy Chapel, Bremerton,

1972-74, First Meth. Ch., Bremerton, 1950-52; dir. orch. First Bapt. Ch., Bremerton, 1969-74; organist Navy Chapel, 1979-83. Mem ASCAP, Women in the Arts. Democrat. Baptist. Home: PO Box 4197 Bremerton WA 98312-0197

BOLTON, MARTHA O., writer; b. Searcy, Ark., Sept. 1, 1951; d. Lonnie Leon and Eunice Dolores Ferren; m. Russell Norman Bolton, Apr. 17, 1970; children: Russell Norman II, Matthew David, Anthony Shane. Grad. high sch., Reseda, Calif. Freelance writer for various comedians, 1975-86; newspaper columnist Simi Valley Enterprise, Simi, Calif., 1979-87; staff writer Bob Hope, 1986—, The Mark and Kathy Show, 1995-96. Author: A Funny Thing Happened to Me on My Way Through the Bible, 1985, A View from the Pew, 1986, What's Growing Under Your Bed?, 1986, Tangled in the Tinsel, 1987, So. How'd I Get To Be in Charge of the Program?, 1988, Humorous Monologues, 1989, Let My People Laugh, 1989, If Mr. Clean Calls Tell Him I'm Not In, 1989, Journey to the Center of the Stage, 1990, If You Can't Stand the Smoke, Get Out of My Kitchen, 1990, Home, Home on the Stage, 1991, TV Jokes and Riddles, 1991, These Truths Were Made for Walking, 1991, When the Meatloaf Explodes It's Done, 1993, Childhood Is a Stage, 1993, Honey, It's Time To Weed the Carpets Again, 1994, Walk A Mile in His Truths, 1994, The Cafeteria Lady on the Loose, 1994, On the Loose, 1994, If the Pasta Wiggles, Don't Eat It, 1995, Bethlehem's Big Night, 1995, Club Family, 1995, When the Going Gets Tough, The Tough Start Laughing, 1995, Who Put The Pizza in the VCR?, 1996, And Now a World from Our Maker, 1997, A Lamb's Tale, 1998, (lyrics) Mouth in Motion, Sermon on the Stage, 1998, Never Ask Delilah For A Trim, 1998, (with Mark Lowry) Piper's Night Before Christmas, (with Gene Perret) Talk About Hope. Pres. Vista Elem. Sch. PTA, Simi, 1980-81. Recipient Emmy nomination for outstanding achievement in music and lyrics, 1988, Internat. Angel award, 1991, Amb. award Media Fellowship Internat., 1995. Mem. ASCAP, NATAS, Nat. League Am. Pen Women (pres. Simi Valley br. 1984-86, 96-98, Woman of Achievement award 1984, Pen Woman of Yr. award 1995, pres. 1996-98), Writers Guild Am. West.$d c. Children's Book Writers. Avocation: traveling. Office: PO Box 1212 Simi Valley CA 93062-1212

BOLTON, ROBERT FLOYD, construction executive; b. Dunlap, Iowa, Oct. 18, 1942; s. Russel J. And Mary Jane (Lacey) B.; m. Mary Louise Hartman, May 15, 1988. Lic. residential/comml. gen. bldg. contractor. Sole practice farming Dunlap, Iowa, 1967-72; supr. Phillips Constrn. Co., Cottonwood, Ariz., 1972-84; contractor Bolton Bldg. and Devel. Co., Sedona, Ariz., 1984—; cons. in field. With U.S. Army, 1964-66. Mem. Nat. Assn. Home Builders, Am. Soc. Home Inspectors, C. of C., VFW, Meth. Mens Fellowship Club. Republican. Methodist. Avocations: reading, hiking, woodworking. Home & Office: 90 Evening Glow Pl Sedona AZ 86351-7912

BONAR, CLAYTON LLOYD, minister; b. Washington County, Kans., Nov. 5, 1934; s. Earl Albert and Violet May (Doane) B.; m. Helen Ann Harmaning, Sept. 12, 1958; children: Renee, Scott. BA, N.W. Nazarene Coll., 1960; postgrad., Fuller Theol. Sem., 1974-75; MA, Point Loma Coll., 1975; postgrad. Rosemead Grad. Sch., 1975. Ordained to ministry Ch. of the Nazarene, 1963. Pastor Ch. of the Nazarene, Caldwell, Idaho, 1961-63, Pocatello, Idaho, 1963-68, Inglewood, Calif., 1968-73, Alhambra, Calif., 1973-78, Richland, Wash., 1978-89, Bremerton, Wash., 1990—; del. Gen. Nazarene World Missionary Soc., Conv. Nazarene Ch., Kansas City, 1968; regent N.W. Nazarene Coll., Nampa, Idaho, 1967-68; dist. sec. Ch. of the Nazarene, L.A., 1976-78; mem. adv. bd. N.W. Dist. 1984—; commitment Nazarene Fed. Credit Union, Whittier, Calif., 1974-78; mem. curriculum com. The Enduring World Series. Author: From Behind Closed Doors, 1981, The Spoken Law, 1985; (with others) Tough Questions: Christian Answers, 1982; contbr. articles to profl. jours. With USAF, 1953-56. Mem. Wesleyan Theol. Soc., Speakers and Writers Ink, Kiwanis. Republican. Avocation: photography. Home: PO Box 5662 Twin Falls ID 83303-5662 Office: 1st Ch of the Nazarene 924 Sheridan Rd Bremerton WA 98310-2730

BONASSI, JODI, artist, marketing consultant; b. L.A., Aug. 22, 1953; d. Julian and Sara (DeNorber) Feldman; m. Raymond Gene Bonassi, June 7, 1986; 1 child, Spencer. Student, Otis Art Inst., L.A., 1972, Calif. State U., L.A., 1983-85, Calif. State U., Northridge, 1985-86. participating artist Concern Found. and World Cup Soccer Gala Event for Cancer Rsch., Beverly Hills, Calif., 1994; lectr., guest spkr. L.A. Pub. Libr., Canoga Park, 1999; mem. adv. bd. Park LaBrea Art Coun. Artist: Creative With Words Publications, 1987; artist, pub. various greeting cards, 1994—; one-woman shows include Pt. Adesa Gallery, Rancho Mirage, Calif., 1996, Showtime TV Film Trust Me, 1997, Orlando Gallery, 1999; exhibited in group shows at Bowles-Sorokko Gallery, Beverly Hills, 1994, ChaChaCha, Encino, Calif., 1994—, Lyn/Bassett Gallery, L.A., 1994, Topanga (Calif.) Canyon Gallery, 1994, Hartog Fine Art Gallery, L.A., 1995, Charles Hecht Gallery, Tarzana, Calif., 1995, New Canyon Gallery, Topanga, 1995, Made With Kare, West Hills, Calif., 1995, Gail Michael Collection, Northridge, 1995, Mythos Gallery, Burbank, 1995-96, Nicole Brown Simpson Found., 1996, Orlando Gallery, Sherman Oaks, Calif., 1998, West Gallery, U. Calif., Fullerton, 1998, The Century Gallery at Mission Coll., 1998, Orlando Gallery, 1998-99; represented in pvt. collections; illustrator All About Us, 1996; featured in various articles and art revs. Art tchr. K-12 West Valley Christian Ch. Schs., 1997—. Recipient Best Banner 2d prize L.A. County Mus. Art, Park LaBrea Arts Coun. for PLB/LACMA Family Art Fund, 1997, World Peace Tour, 1997, Orlando Gallery. Spl. Judges Art award Park LaBrea Art Coun., 1998, L.A. County Mus. of Art. Mem. Calif. Women Bus. Owners, L.A. Mcpl. Art Gallery Registry, So. Calif. Women's Caucus for Art, Soc. Children's Bookwriters and Illustrators. Avocations: hiking, reading, swimming. Studio: 22647 Ventura Blvd Ste 160 Woodland Hills CA 91364-1416

BONATH, JOHN PAUL, graphic designer, educator; b. Bedford, Ohio, Feb. 9, 1951. BFA, Cleve. Inst. Art, 1974; MFA, Western Mich. U., 1978; student, Kyoto (Japan) English Ctr., 1988, Red Rocks C.C. 1991. Tchr. Cooper Sch. Art, Cleve., 1974-76, Cuyahoga C.C. Parma, Ohio, 1975-76, Western Mich. U., Kalamazoo, 1976-78; mem. staff Colo. State U., Bellvue, Colo., 1978-87; performer Storm Mountain Folkdancers, Fort Collins, Denver, Colo., 1981-87; art dir. Poudre Mag., Fort Collins, Colo., 1981-82; prin., owner John Bonath, Bellvue, Colo., 1985-86; mem. staff America Eigo Gakuin, Wakayama-Ken, Tokyo, Japan, 1988-90, Lucas Photographs, Denver, Colo., 1991; photographer, graphic designer MADDOG Studio, Denver, Colo., 1991—; tchr. Rocky Mt. Coll. Art & Design, Denver, 1997. One-man shows include Denver City & County Bldg., The Lincoln Ctr., Aguilar Sch., The Print Ctr., Mizel Mus. of Judaica; group shows include Cleve. Inst. Art, U. Denver Driscoll Ctr. Gallery, Colorado Springs Fine Arts Ctr., One West Art Ctr., The Colo. Gallery of the Arts Arapahoe C.C., Denver Art Mus., Spark Gallery. Selection panelist Project Art Grants, Colo. Council on the Arts, 1994, 95. Recipient Henry Keller Drawing award Cleve. Inst. Art, Cleve., 1972, 1983 Outstanding Young Man Am. award U.S. Jaycees, Montgomery, Ala., 1983, People's Choice award Salina (Kans.) Art Ctr., 1997, Purchase award Colo. Springs (Colo.) Fine Arts Ctr., 1998; featured in articles in Graphics #308, 1997, View Camera Mag., 1997, ZOOM, 1997; rsch. grantee Ford Found., Kalamazoo, Mich., 1976, 78, Colo. Council on the Arts, 1996; Ernest Haas photography scholar Anderson Ranch, Snowmass, Colo., 1997. Mem. Soc. Photographic Edn. E-mail: jbonath@aol.com. Fax: 303-477-1987. Home and Studio: 3556 Osage St Denver CO 80211

BONCHER, JOANNE BARRY, language, speech and hearing specialist; b. Riverside, Calif., June 14, 1938; d. John Henry Barry and Margaret Victoria (Gilman) Hanna; m. Hector Wilfred Boncher, July 2, 1960; children: John, Elizabeth, Philip, Brett. BA, Whittier Coll., 1960; MA, San Diego State U., 1986. Lang./speech/hearing, curriculum resource tchr., lang. arts La Mesa (Calif.) Spring Valley Schs., 1986—; speech, lang. pathologist Marlowe K. Fischer and Assocs., San Diego, 1986—; lectr. San Diego State U., 1987-94; cons., lectr. sch. dists. and confs. in field, 1988—. Mem. Am. Speech, Lang. and Hearing Assn., Calif. Speech, Lang. and Hearing Assn. (adv. bd. 1989-92, 93-95, nominating com. 1991-92, social chmn. 95 CSHA conf. 1994-95, Outstanding Svc. award 1993, Outstanding Achievement 1997), Nat. Tchrs. Pub. Schs. Caucus (chmn. Van Hattum fund 1992), Phi Delta Kappa, Delta Kappa Gamma. Avocations: travel, theater, lit., phys. fitness. Home: 6672 Hemingway Dr San Diego CA 92120-1616 Office: La Mesa Spring Valley Schs 4750 Date Ave La Mesa CA 91941-5214

BONDE, STEVEN ELLING, contract management company executive; b. San Francisco, Oct. 20, 1948; s. Clifton S. and Marion Belke) B.; m. Rhonda Lee Richardson, Sept. 14, 1983; children: Eric, Ian. AB, U. Calif., Berkeley, 1971; MA, SUNY, Stony Brook, 1974. Grant writer Ctr. Ind. Living, Berkeley, 1976-77; contracts specialist U.S. Dept. Energy, Oakland, Calif., 1977-81; contracts supr. Bechtel, San Francisco, 1981-87; contracts mgr., 1987-89; dir. contracts ICF Kaiser Internat., Oakland, Calif., 1989—; cons. govt. and internat. contracting, Alameda, Calif., 1991—; bd. dirs. Krize Lakeside Fed. Credit Union. Mem. Nat. Contracts Mgmt. Assn. Avocations: swimming, bicycling, hiking, history, reading. Office: ICF Kaiser Internat 2101 Webster St Oakland CA 94612-3429

BONDI, BERT ROGER, accountant, financial planner; b. Portland, Oreg., Oct. 2, 1945; s. Gene L. and Elizabeth (Poynter) B.; m. Kimberley Kay Higgins, June 18, 1988; children: Nicholas Stone, Christopher Poynter. BBA, U. Notre Dame, 1967. CPA, Colo. Calif., Wyo. Sr. tax acct. Price Waterhouse, Los Angeles, 1970-73; ptnr. Valentine Adducci & Bondi, Denver, 1973-76; sr. ptnr. Bondi & Co., Englewood, Colo., 1976—; 50 for Colo.-1998 dir. Citizens Bank. Bd. govs. Met. State Coll. Found.; bd. dirs. Am. Cancer Soc. Denver; mem. adv. bd. Jr. League of Denver. Served with U.S. Army, 1968-70. Mem. C. of C., Community Assns. Inst., Govt. Fin. Officers Assn., Colo. Soc. Assn. Execs. (edn. com.), Home Builders Assn., Am. Inst. CPAs, Colo. Soc. CPAs, Wyo. Soc. CPAs., Rotary (Denver), Notre Dame Club, Metropolitan Club (Denver), Castle Pines Country Club. Roman Catholic. Home: 49 Glenalla Pl Castle Rock CO 80104-9026 Office: Bondi & Co 44 Inverness Dr E Englewood CO 80112-5410

BONDOC, ANTONIO C., physician assistant; b. Bataan, Philippines, June 13, 1956; s. Modesto and Teodula C. (Caragay) B.; m. Grace L. Lee, Apr. 16, 1983; children: Lizette, Antonette. MD, Cebu Drs. Coll. Medicine, Cebu City, Philippines, 1983; AS in Primary Care, Foothill Coll., 1996; Cert. Clin. Proficiency, Stanford U., 1997. Cert. physician asst., Calif. Med. intern So. Is. Med. Ctr., Cebu City, Philippines, 1984-84; asst. health svcs. adminstr., supervisory physician asst. Fed. Correctional Instn., Dublin, Calif., 1990-91; physician asst. Fed. Correctional Instn., Dublin, 1991-93, South of Market Health Ctr., San Francisco, 1995—; Calif. Pacific Med. Ctr., San Francisco, 1997-97; nephrology physician asst. East Bay Nephrology Med. Group, Berkeley, Calif., 1997—. Vol. Filipino Task Force on AIDS, San Francisco, 1994-95; mem. Bay Area Non Docs, San Francisco, 1997. Capt. USAFNG, 1996—. Scholar Physician Asst. Found., 1996, Bernice Mitchell Meml. scholar Stanford U. med. Ctr. Aux., 1996. Mem. Am. Acad. Physician Assts. (assoc.), Calif. Acad. Physician Assts., Bay Area Non Docs, Cebu Drs. Coll. of Medicine Alumni Assn. (alumni mem.). Republican. Roman Catholic. Avocations: reading, biking, walking. Fax: (510) 848-9970. E-mail: TBondoc@aol.com. Home: 2107 42nd Ave San Francisco CA 94116-1520 Office: East Bay Nephrology Med Group 2905 Telegraph Ave Berkeley CA 94705-2017

BONDS, BARRY LAMAR, professional baseball player; b. Riverside, Calif., July 24, 1964; s. Bobby B. Student, Ariz. State U. With Pitts. Pirates, 1985-92, San Francisco Giants, 1992—. Named MVP Baseball Writers' Assn. Am., 1990, 1992, 1993, Maj. League Player Yr. Sporting News, 1990, Nat. League Player Yr. Sporting News, 1990, 91, mem. Sporting News Coll. All-Am. team, 1985, mem. All-Star team, 1990, 1992-96; recipient Gold Glove award, 1990-94, 96, Silver Slugger award, 1990-96. Led Nat. League in intentional walks, 1992-94. Office: San Francisco Giants Candlestick Point 3 Com Park San Francisco CA 94124*

BONELL, PAUL IAN, credit union executive; b. Melbourne, Victoria, Australia, June 8, 1961; came to U.S., 1980; s. Eric and Jean Mary (Sunderland) B.; m. Carol Lynn Calloway, Oct. 5, 1986; 1 child, Lindsay M. BSM, U. Pacific, 1990; postgrad., U. Phoenix. Sr. v.p. Great Basin Credit Union, Reno, Nev., 1982-87; pres. Schs. Credit Union, Stockton, Calif., 1987—. Com. mem. Micke Grove Zoo, Stockton, 1992, Pixie Woods, Stockton, 1992. Mem. Credit Union Exec. Soc. (bd. dirs. cen. Calif. chpt. 1989—, Golden Mirror award 1991, 92), Calif. Credit Union League (pres. bd. dirs. San Juaquin chpt. 1987—), Internat. Lions Club (bd. dirs., v.p. 1991). Office: Schs Credit Union PO Box 8929 Stockton CA 95208-0929

BONFIELD, ANDREW JOSEPH, tax practitioner; b. London, Jan. 26, 1924; s. George William and Elizabeth Agnes B.; came to U.S., 1946, naturalized, 1954; m. Eleanor Ackerman, Oct. 16, 1955; children: Bruce Ian, Sandra Karen. Gen. mgr. Am. Cushion Co., Los Angeles, 1948-50, Monson Calif. Co., Redwood City, 1951-58; mfrs. mktg. rep., San Francisco, 1958-62; tax practitioner, bus. cons., Redwood City, San Jose, Los Gatos, Carmel Calif., Kihei, Hawaii, 1963—. Past treas., dir. Northwood Park Improvement Assn.; mem. exec. bd. Santa Clara County council Boy Scouts Am., 1971—, past council pres.; mem. Nat. council; mem. Santa Clara County Parks and Recreation Commn., 1975-81, 82-86; mem. County Assessment Appeals Bd., 1978-86; mem. Hawaii Bd. Taxation Review, 1992-98. Served with Brit. Royal Navy, 1940-46. Decorated King George VI Silver Badge; recipient Silver Beaver award, Vigil honor award Boy Scouts Am.; enrolled to practice before IRS. Mem. Nat. Assn. Enrolled Agts., Calif. Soc. Enrolled Agts., Hawaii Assn. Pub. Accts., Hawaii Soc. Enrolled Agrs., Royal Can. Legion (past state parliamentarian, past state 1st vice comdr.). Club: Rotary (pres. San Jose E. 1977-78, pres. Kihei-Wailea 1993-94). Home: 181 Hacienda Carmel Carmel CA 93923

BONGARTEN, HAROLD, retired business executive, consultant; b. Warsaw, Poland, July 16, 1922; came to U.S., 1925; s. Samual and Kaite (Kupersmith) B.; children: Randall D., Bruce C., Karl J., Elaine K. MS in Mech. Engring., Northeastern U., 1947; MBA, U. Pitts., 1952; student Advanced Mgmt. Program, Harvard U., 1972-73. Gen. mgr. Gen. Electric Co., Schenectady, N.Y., 1947-85; cons. Bongarten Assocs., Schenectady and Tucson, 1985-97; ret., 1997; cons. Burlington No. S.F. R.R., Ft. Worth, 1985-95, CSX R.R., Jacksonville, Fla., 1988-92, Amtrak, Phila., 1990-94, Union Pacific/South Pacific R.R., Omaha and Denver, 1994-97. Pres. Jewish Cmty. Found., Tucson, 1995—; v.p. Hillel, Tucson, 1994-96. With U.S. Army, 1943-45, ETO. Mem. B'nai B'rith (trustee 1997-98, lodge pres. 1993-94). Avocations: fishing, golf. Home: 7273 N Cathedral Rock Rd Tucson AZ 85718-1381

BONNELL, VICTORIA EILEEN, sociologist; b. N.Y.C., June 15, 1942; d. Samuel S. and Frances (Nassau) B.; m. Gregory Freidin, May 4, 1971. B.A. Brandeis U., 1964; M.A., Harvard U., 1966, Ph.D., 1975. Lectr. politics U. Calif.-Santa Cruz, 1972-73, 74-76; asst. prof. sociology U. Calif.-Berkeley, 1976-82, assoc. prof., 1982-91, prof., 1991—; chair Berkeley Ctr. for Slavic and East European Studies, U. Calif.-Berkeley 1994—. Recipient Heldt prize in Slavic women's studies, 1991; AAUW fellow, 1979; Regents faculty fellow, 1978; Fulbright Hays faculty fellow, 1977; Internat. Research and Exchanges Bd. fellow, 1977, 88; Stanford U. Hoover Instn. nat. fellow, 1973-74; Guggenheim fellow, 1985; fellow Ctr. for Advanced Study in Behavioral Scis., 1986-87; Pres.' Rsch. fellow in humanities, 1991-92; grantee Am. Philos. Soc., 1979, Am. Council Learned Socs., 1976, 90-91. Mem. Am. Sociol. Assn., Am. Assn. Advancement Slavic Studies, Am. Hist. Assn. Author: Roots of Rebellion: Workers' Politics and Organizations in St. Petersburg and Moscow, 1900-1914, 1983; editor: The Russian Worker: Life and Labor under the Tsarist Regime, 1983, (with Ann Cooper and Gregory Freidin) Russia at the Barricades: Eyewitness Accounts of the August 1991 Coup, 1994, Iconography of Power: Soviet Political Posters Under Lenin and Stalin, 1997; editor Identities in Transition: Eastern Europe and Russia after the Collapse of Communism, 1996, Beyonf the cultural Turn: New Directions in the Study of Society and Culture, 1999; contbr. articles to profl. jours.

BONNER, ETHEL MAE, religious education educator, advocate; b. N.Y.C., Mar. 1, 1918; d. Herbert John and Grace Marie (Jones) Smith; m. William Lee Bonner, Nov. 18, 1944; children: Ethel Mae Bonner, Archer William Lee Jr. BA, Hunter Coll. 1941; MA, Wayne State U., 1956; DSL, Am. Wesleyan Coll., 1960. Cert. sexual assault victim counselor, Calif. Mgr. Mrs. Bonner's Kitchen, 1946-50; secondary tchr. Detroit Pub. Schs., 1941-61, high sch. tchr. 1961-63 tchr. for multi admitted Abington Sch. Joint Dept. Higher Edn., 1961-63; receptionist Area 4 Agy. on Aging, 1989, office asst., 1993; telephone team Phys. Corp. Am., Inc., 1990-93; intake paralegal for sr. legal hotline Legal Svcs. No. Calif., 1994; founder, dir. Potters Pl. Dir. secular edn. Ch. of Our Lord Jesus Christ of the Apostolic Faith, Inc.;

founder Citadel of Hope Child Devel. Ctr., R.C. Lawson Inst. Lab. Sch. Liberia, West Africa; prin. R.C. Lawson Inst., Southern Pines, N.C.; counselor, instr. Sacramento Christian Helpline. Recipient Spirit of Detroit award The City Coun. of Detroit, 1987, Cert. of Appreciation, Mayor Coleman A. Young, 1987, Spl. Recognition award Pres. Rep. of Liiberia. Home: 600 I St Apt 1410 Sacramento CA 95814-2484

BONNER, KATHLEEN SHEPPARD CLEARY, interior designer; b. Montclair, N.J., Apr. 19, 1940; d. Edward John and Adelaide (Rogers) Cleary; m. Paul Edward Bonner, Aug. 11, 1962 (div. 1980); children: Christopher James, Elizabeth Bonner Rutishauser. AB, Middlebury Coll., 1961; MA, Calif. State U., 1979. Program dir. Calif. Internat. Arts Found., L.A., 1982-84; dir. Inst. of the Arts Calif. State U., Long Beach, 1984-86; dir. ACAN Art Ctr. Coll. of Design, Pasadena, Calif., 1986-89; dept. chmn. LTU Univ., Chatsworth, Calif., 1990-92; designer/owner Kathleen Sheppard Design, Westlake Village, Calif., 1992—. Author art criticism articles, Artweek, 1976-78; artist: L.A. City Exhbn., 1979, Santa Barbara City Coll., Calif., 1979. Grantee Calif. Coun. for Humanities, 1980, Calif. State U. Found., 1979-80. Mem. Conejo Valley Assn. Profl. Interior Designers (bd. dirs., program chmn. 1997-98). Home: 833 Rim Crest Cir Westlake Village CA 91361-2042

BONNER, ROBERT CLEVE, lawyer; b. Wichita, Kans., Jan. 29, 1942; s. Benjamin Joseph and Caroline (Kirkwood) B.; m. Kimiko Tanaka, Oct. 11, 1969; 1 child, Justine M. BA, Md. U., 1963; JD, Georgetown U., 1966. Bar: D.C. 1966, Calif. 1967, S. Ct. Appeals (4th, 5th, 9th, 10th cirs.), U.S. Supreme Ct. Law clk. to judge U.S. Dist. Ct., L.A., 1966-67; asst. U.S. atty. U.S. Atty's Office (cen. dist.) Calif., L.A., 1971-75, U.S. atty., 1984-89; judge U.S. Dist. Ct. (cen. dist.) Calif., L.A., 1989-90; ptnr. Kadison, Pfaelzer, et al, Los Angeles, 1975-84; dir. Drug Enforcement Adminstrn., Washington, 1990-93; ptnr. Gibson, Dunn & Crutcher, L.A., 1993—; chair Calif. Commn. on Jud. Performance, 1997—. Served to lt. comdr. USN, 1967-70. Fellow Am. Coll. Trial Lawyers, Fed. Bar Assn. (pres. Los Angeles chpt. 1982-83). Republican. Roman Catholic. Office: Gibson Dunn & Crutcher 333 S Grand Ave Ste 4400 Los Angeles CA 90071-3197

BONNER, THOMAS NEVILLE, history and higher education educator; b. Rochester, N.Y., May 28, 1923; s. John Neville and Mary (McGowan) B.; children by previous marriage: Phillip Lynn, Diana Joan; m. Sylvia M. Firnhaber, Dec. 28, 1984. AB, U. Rochester, 1947, MA, 1948; PhD, Northwestern U., 1952; LLD, U. N.H., 1974, U. Mich., 1979. Acad. dean William Woods Coll., 1951-54; prof. history, chmn. dept. social sci. U. Omaha, 1955-62; Fulbright lectr. U. Mainz, Germany, 1954-55; prof., head history dept. U. of Cin., 1963-68, v.p. acad. affairs, provost, 1967-71; pres. U. N.H., Durham, 1971-74, Union Coll.; chancellor Union U., Schenectady, 1974-78; pres. Wayne State U., Detroit, 1978-82, disting. prof. history and higher edn., 1983-97; vis. scholar Ariz. State U., Tempe, 1997—; vis. prof. U. Freiburg, Fed. Republic Germany, 1982-83. Author: Medicine in Chicago, 1957, 91, The Kansas Doctor, 1959; (with others) The Contemporary World, 1960, Our Recent Past, 1963, American Doctors and German Universities, 1963, 87, To the Ends of the Earth: Woman's Search for Education in Medicine, 1992, Becoming a Physician: Medical Education in Great Britain, France, Germany and the United States, 1750-1945, 1995; editor, translator: Journey Through the Rocky Mountains, 1959. Democratic candidate for Congress, 1962; legis. aide to Senator McGovern, 1962-63. Served with Radio Intelligence Corps AUS, 1942-46, ETO. Guggenheim fellow, 1958-59, 64-65. Mem. Am. Hist. Assn., Orgn. Am. Historians, Am. Assn. for History Medicine, Phi Beta Kappa, Pi Gamma Mu, Phi Alpha Theta. Home: 10970 E San Salvador Dr Scottsdale AZ 85259-5726

BONNEY, JOHN DENNIS, retired oil company executive; b. Blackpool, Eng., Dec. 22, 1930; s. John P. and Isabel (Evans) B.; four children from previous marriage; m. Elizabeth Shore-Wilson, Aug. 1986; two children. B.A., Hertford Coll., Oxford U., Eng., 1954, M.A., 1959; LL.M., U. Calif., Berkeley, 1956. Oil adviser Middle East, 1959-60; fgn. ops. adviser, asst. mgr., then mgr. Chevron Corp. (formerly Standard Oil Co. of Calif.), San Francisco, 1960-72, v.p., from 1972, vice chmn., dir., 1987-95. Clubs: Commonwealth; World Affairs Coun. of No. Calif., World Trade (San Francisco); Oxford and Cambridge (London). Office: 555 Market St San Francisco CA 94105-2801

BONNY, BLAINE MILAN, retired accountant; b. Midvale, Utah, Oct. 5, 1909; s. Frederick Fritz and Amelia (Poulson) B.; m. Helen Matilda Bolognese, Nov. 3, 1938 (dec. Nov. 18, 1988); children: Brent G., Basche Bonny. Grad. West high sch., Salt Lake City, 1928; mem. U Utah Alumni, 1950-96. Corp. acct. Utah Pr. and Lt. Co., Salt Lake City, 1929-74; ret., 1974—. Patentee in field, 11 copyrights. Mem. Rep. N.H. Com., 1992. Mem. ASCAP, Copper Golf Club, Mason-Acacia Lodge #17, U.S. English, Inc., Rep. N.H. Committee (1992-96). Avocation: acapella solo tenor. Home: 847 S 7th E Salt Lake City UT 84102-3505

BONO, ANTHONY SALVATORE EMANUEL, II, data processing executive; b. N.Y.C., Nov. 24, 1946; s. Anthony S.E. and Lola M. (Riddle) B. BA in Polit. Sci., Hartwick Coll., 1969; cert. in info. systems analysis, UCLA, 1985. Mgmt. trainee Mfrs. Hanover Trust Co., N.Y.C., 1973-74; supr. client services Johnson & Higgins of Calif., Los Angeles, 1974-77, account exec. comml. accounts, 1977-80, coordinator internal systems, 1981-83, mgr. systems devel., 1983-89, v.p., mgr. systems devel., 1989—. Deacon Westwood Presbyn. Ch., 1982-85. Served with USAF, 1969-73. Named Airman of Yr., San Bernadino C. of C., 1970. Mem. Assn. Systems Mgmt. (dir. publicity and awards 1982-84, corr. sec. 1984-85), Channel Island Mensa, Alpha Sigma Phi. Republican. Home: 15010 Reedley St Moorpark CA 93021-2518 Office: Johnson & Higgins 777 S Figueroa St Ste 2200 Los Angeles CA 90017-5820

BONSER, QUENTIN, surgeon; b. Sedro Wooley, Wash., Nov. 1, 1920; s. George Wayne and Kathleen Imogene (Lynch) B.; BA in Zoology, UCLA, 1943; MD, U. Calif., San Francisco, 1947; m. Loellen Rocca, Oct. 20, 1945; children: Wayne, Gordon, Carol, Patricia (Mrs. Martin Sanford). Intern U. Calif. Hosp., San Francisco, 1947-49, resident gen. surgery, 1949-56; practice gen. surgery, Placerville, Calif., 1956—; ret.; surgeon King Faisal Splty. Hosp., Saudi Arabia, Sept.-Oct., 1984; vis. prof. surgery U. Calif., San Francisco, 1968. Capt. M.C., USAF, 1950-51. Vol. physician, tchr. surgery Vietnam, 1971, 72, 73. Diplomate Am. Bd. Surgery. Fellow A.C.S.; mem. H.C. Naffziger Surg. Soc. (pres. 1974-75). Home: 2590 Northridge Dr Placerville CA 95667-3416

BOOCHEVER, ROBERT, federal judge; b. N.Y.C., Oct. 2, 1917; s. Louis C. and Miriam (Cohen) B.; m. Lois Colleen Maddox, Apr. 22, 1943; children: Barbara K., Linda Lou, Ann Paula, Miriam Deon. AB, Cornell U., 1939, JD, 1941; HD (hon.), U. Alaska, 1981. Bar: N.Y. 1944, Alaska 1947. Law clk. Nordlinger, Riegel & Cooper, 1941; asst. U.S. atty. Juneau, 1946-47; partner firm Faulkner, Banfield, Boochever & Doogan, Juneau, 1947-72; asso. justice Alaska Supreme Ct., 1972-75, 78-80, chief justice, 1975-78; judge U.S. Ct. Appeals (9th cir.), Pasadena, Calif., 1980-86; sr. judge U.S. Ct. Appeals, Pasadena, Calif., 1986—; mem. 9th cir. rules com. U.S. Ct. Appeals, 1983-85, chmn. 9th cir. libr. com., 1995—; chmn. Ala. Jud. Coun., 1975-78; mem. appellate judges seminar NYU Sch. Law, 1975; mem. Conf. Chief Justices, 1975-79, vice chmn., 1978-79; mem. adv. bd. Nat. Bank of Ala., 1968-72; guest spkr. Southwestern Law Sch. Disting. Lecture Series, 1992. Contbr. articles to profl. jours. Chmn. Juneau chpt. ARC, 1949-51, Juneau Planning Commn., 1956-61; mem. Alaska Devel. Bd., 1949-52, Alaska Jud. Qualification Commn., 1972-75; mem. adv. bd. Juneau-Douglas Community Coll. Served to Capt. U.S. Army, 1941-45. Named Juneau Man of Year, Rotary, 1974; recipient Disting. Alumnus award Cornell U., 1989. Fellow Am. Coll. Trial Attys.; mem. ABA, Alaska Bar Assn. (pres. 1961-62), Juneau Bar Assn. (pres. 1971-72), Am. Judicature Soc. (dir. 1970-74), Am. Law Inst., Juneau C. of C. (pres. 1952, 55), Alaskans United (chmn. 1972). Clubs: Marine Meml., Cornell Club of L.A., Altadena Town and Country. Office: US Ct Appeals PO Box 91510 125 S Grand Ave Pasadena CA 91105-1652*

BOOKIN, DANIEL HENRY, lawyer; b. Ottumwa, Iowa, Oct. 16, 1951. BA, U. Iowa, 1973; JD, Yale U., 1976. Bar: Calif. 1978. Law clk. U.S. Dist. Ct. (no. dist.) Calif., 1976-77; asst. U.S. atty. U.S. Dist. Ct. (so. dist.) N.Y., 1978-82; ptnr. O'Melveny & Myers, San Francisco, 1982—. Mem. bd. editors Yale Law Jour., 1975-76. Fellow Am. Coll. Trial Lawyers, Phi Beta Kappa. Office: O'Melveny & Myers Embarcadero Ctr W Tower 275 Battery St San Francisco CA 94111-3305

BOOLOOTIAN, RICHARD ANDREW, communications executive; b. Fresno, Calif., Oct. 17, 1927; s. Vanig and Vivian (Ohannesian) B.; m. Mary Jo Blue, Oct. 20, 1945 (div. 1980); children: Mark, Alan, Craig; m. Yvonne Morse Daniels (div. 1994). BA, Calif. State U., Fresno, 1951, MA, 1953; PhD, Stanford U., 1957. Cert. tchr. (life) Calif. Assoc. prof. UCLA, 1957-67; cons. U. Colo., Boulder, 1967-68; pres. Sci. Software Systems Inc., Sherman Oaks, Calif., 1969—, Boolootian & Assocs.; dir. sci. curriculum Mirman Sch. Gifted, L.A., 1974—, chmn. sci. dept., 1986—. Author 21 textbooks; contbr. articles to profl. jours. Fellow Lalor Found., 1963-64, NIH, 1965; nominee excellence in tchg. Presdl. award, 1992-93. Fellow AAAS; mem. Challenger Soc. Avocations: stamp collecting, skiing, Scuba, flying. Office: Sci Software Systems Inc 3576 Woodcliff Rd Sherman Oaks CA 91403-5045

BOONE, EARLE MARION, business executive; b. Panama City, Fla., Apr. 25, 1934; s. Earle Alpha and Lucy Marian (Jerkins) B.; m. Birthe Schnohr Kristensen Boone, Oct. 16, 1979; children: Tina Boone Broderick, Darlene Boone Moseley, Earle Marion Jr. BS in Aviation Mgmt., So. Ill. U., 1977; MS in Pub. Adminstrn., Calif. State U., 1983. Lic. airline transport pilot. USAF pilot, 1954-75; corp. pilot pvt. practice, 1975-78, aviation mgmt. cons., 1978-80; mktg. dir. Northrop Corp., Hawthorne, Calif., 1980-92; v.p. mktg. Cognitive Neurometrics, Scottsdale, Ariz., 1992-95; pres., CEO Cognitive Neurometrics Inc., Scottsdale, Ariz., 1995—; SR-71 pilot 9th Strat Recon Wing, Beale AFB, Calif., 1966-68; F4-E combat fighter pilot 388 Tactical Fighter Wing, Thailand, 1970-71; mktg. dir. Northrop Corp., Hawthorne, 1980-92. lt. col. USAF, 1954-75, Vietnam. Recipient The Disting. Flying Cross, The Air medal, Bronze Star medal, Meritorious Svc. medal, Sec. Air Force, Vietnam, 1970-71,. Mem. Ret. Officers Assn., Order of Daedalians, Sierra Club, Phi Alpha Alpha. Republican. Avocations: reading, hiking, foreign travel, language study, computers. Home: 7508 Orrick Dr Austin TX 78749-2607 Office: Cognitive Neurometrics Inc Scottsdale AZ 85255

BOORSTYN, NEIL, lawyer, educator; b. N.Y.C., Oct. 11, 1931; m. Debbie Boorstyn. LLB, Bklyn. Law Sch., 1954. Of counsel McCutchen, Doyle, Brown & Enersen, San Francisco, 1989—; adj. prof. Hastings Coll. of the Law, 1975—, Golden Gate Sch. of Law, 1976—. Author: Copyright Law, 1981, Boorstyn on Copyright, 2d edit., 1994; author, editor The Copyright Law Jour., 1984.

BOOTH, FORREST, lawyer; b. Evanston, Ill., Oct. 31, 1946; s. Robert and Florence C. (Forrest) B.; m. Louise A. Hayes, June 14, 1980; 1 child, Kristin A. BA, Amherst Coll., 1968; JD, Harvard U., 1975. Bar: D.C. 1976, U.S. Ct. Appeals (D.C. cir.) 1976, Calif. 1977, U.S. Dist. Ct. (no. dist.) Calif. 1977, U.S. Ct. Appeals (9th cir.) 1977, U.S. Supreme Ct. 1979. Assoc. Graham & James, Washington, 1975-76, Mccutchen, Doyle, Brown & Emersen, San Francisco, 1976-78; ptnr. Hancock, Rothert & Bunshoft, San Francisco, 1978-89; sr. ptnr. Booth Banning LLP, San Francisco, 1990—; faculty mem. S.E. Admiralty Law Inst., Savannah, Ga., 1990; chmn. Pacific Admiralty Seminar, San Francisco, 1983-97; advisor U. San Francisco Maritime Law Jour., 1992—. Contbr. articles to profl. jours. Lt. USN, 1968-72, Vietnam. Mem. Maritime Law Assn. U.S. (proctor), World Trade Club of San Francisco, Marine Club London, Assn. Average Adjusters U.K., St. Francis Yacht Club. Avocations: sailing, photography, skiing. Office: Booth Banning LLP 275 Battery St Fl 27 San Francisco CA 94111-3305*

BOOTH, GEORGE EDWIN, facilities engineering manager; b. Visalia, Calif., Jan. 4, 1951; s. Carl Eugene and Mary Elizabeth Booth; m. Lisa Ann Booth, Jan. 5, 1986; children: James Joseph, George Gerst, Courtney Marie. AS, Coll. Sequoia, 1979; BS, Calif. Poly., 1982. Facilities engr. Trilogy Sys., Cupertino, Calif., 1982-84; facilities engring. supr. VLSI Tech., San Jose, Calif., 1984-93; facilities engr. mgr. Linear Tech. Corp., Milpitas, Calif., 1993—; com. mem. ednl. task force Silicon Valley (Calif.) Mfg. Group, 1997-98. Contbr. articles to tech. jours. Cubmaster, asst. scoutmaster Boy Scouts Am., 1995 ; Sgt. U.S. Army, 1971-73. Recipient Cubmaster award, Scouter of Yr. award Boy Scouts Am., 1997. Mem. NRA, Internat. Assn. Scientologists (vol. 1986—, Patron with Honors). Avocations: camping, fishing, mechanics, shooting, scientology. Home: 3635 Tankerland Ct San Jose CA 95121-1244 Office: Linear Tech Corp 1630 Mccarthy Blvd Milpitas CA 95035-7487

BOOTH, JOHN LOUIS, service executive; b. Danville, Va., May 15, 1933; s. William Irvine and Melba (Harvey) B.; m. Ann Fennell, May 23, 1959; children: Mark, Robin. BA, U. Richmond, 1958; ThM, Dallas Theol. Sem., 1962, ThD, 1965, PhD, 1993; postgrad., Ariz. State U., 1972, 79. Pastor Skyway Bible Ch., Seattle, 1964-66, Mount Prospect (Ill.) Bible Ch., 1966-71, Camelback Bible Ch., Paradise Valley, Ariz., 1971-78; counselor Camelback Counseling Ctr., Phoenix, 1978-79; dir. Paradise Valley Counseling, Inc., Phoenix, 1980—; chmn. bd. Paradise Valley Counseling, Inc., 1980—; chmn. bd. Paradise Valley Counseling Found., Inc., Phoenix, 1982—; adj. prof. Grand Canyon U., 1981-96, Southwestern Coll., Phoenix, 1979-97, Talbott Theol. Sem. Phoenix Ext., 1983-85; seminar speaker frequent engagements, 1965—. Author: Understanding Today's Problems, 1980, Marriage by the Master Plan, 1980, Equipping for Effective Marriage, 1983, 95, (tape series) Starting Over, 1982, Enjoying All God Intended, 1988, 95, 96. Precinct committeeman Rep. Party, Phoenix, 1983-84, 87-88, 90-91; chaplain Ariz. State Senate, Phoenix, 1973. Mem. Am. Psychol. Soc., Christian Assn. for Psychol. Studies, Am. Assn. Christian Counselors. Baptist. Avocations: numismatics, antique publications, oil painting, photography. Office: Paradise Valley Counseling Inc 10210 N 32nd St Ste 211 Phoenix AZ 85028-3848

BOOTH, LEO W., priest, author; b. Manchester, Eng., Aug. 22, 1946; s. Leonard and Maud Mary (Bett) B. BD, King's Coll., London, 1970; ThM, St. Augustine's Coll., Canterbury, Eng., 1971. Cert. addictions counselor, cert. eating disorders counselor. Pres. edn. Spiritual Concepts, Long Beach, Calif., 1984—; spkr. in field of addictive behavior. Author: When God Becomes a Drug, 1991, The God Game-It's Your Move, 1994, Meditations for Compulsive People, 1995, The Angel and the Frog, 1997, Spirituality and Recovery, 1997, Say Yes to Life, 1997, Healing Thoughts, 1998. Asst. priest St. Mark's Ch., Downey, Calif., 1984-94; vicar St. George's Ch., Hawthorne, Calif., 1990—. Recipient Sam Shoemaker award Nat. Epis. Coalition on Alcohol and Drug, 1998. Episcopalian. Office: Spiritual Concepts 2700 Saint Louis Ave Long Beach CA 90806-2026

BOOZE, THOMAS FRANKLIN, toxicologist; b. Denver, Mar. 4, 1955; s. Ralph Walker and Ann (McNatt) B.; children: Heather N., Ian T. BS, U. Calif., Davis, 1978; MS, Kans. State U., 1981, PhD, 1985. Registered environ assessor, Calif. Asst. instr. Kans. State U., Manhattan, 1979-85; consulting toxicologist Chevron Corp., Sacramento, 1985-92; sr. toxicologist Radian Internat., Sacramento, 1992—; cons. in field, Manhattan, Kans., 1981-83. contbr. articles to profl. jours. Vol. Amigos de las Americas, Marin County, Calif., 1973, Hospice Care, Manhattan, 1985. Mem. N.Y. Acad. Sci., Soc. Toxicology, Soc. for Risk Analysis, Sigma Xi. Home: 8338 Titian Ridge Ct Antelope CA 95843-5627 Office: Radian Corp 10389 Old Placerville Rd Sacramento CA 95827-2506

BORCHERT, WARREN FRANK, elementary education educator; b. Faribault, Minn., Mar. 5, 1948; s. Harold C. and Beata J. (Hoffmann) B.; m. Mari L. Runquist, Aug. 7, 1971 (div. Oct. 1985); children: Nicholas, Kyle, Megan. BA, Gustavus Adolphus Coll., 1971; postgrad., Boise State U., 1975—, U. Idaho, 1979—; MEd, Coll. Idaho, 1983; cert. instr. leader level, Nat. Fedn. Interscholastic Coaches Edn. Program-Am. Coaching Effectiveness Program, 1991. Cert. advanced elem. and phys. edn. tchr. Phys. edn. tchr. Hopkins (Minn.) Sch. Dist., 1972-73; elem. tchr., phys. edn. tchr. Mountain Home (Idaho) Sch. Dist. 193, 1974-84, phys. edn. tchr., 1984—; coach boys basketball Mountain Home Jr. High Sch., 1986—; coach girls softball Mountain Home High Sch., 1993-97; instr. Intermountain Environ. Edn. Tng. Team, Salt Lake City, 1979—. Instr., mgr. ARC-pool, Mountain Home, 1975-83; pres. Men's Slo Pitch Softball Assn., Mountain Home, 1975-79; bd. dirs., coach Elmore County Youth Baseball Assn., Mountain Home, 1989-92; treas., bd. dirs. Grace Luth. Ch., Mountain Home, 1991-95. Mem. AAHPERD, Idaho Assn. Health, Phys. Edn, Recreation and Dance, Idaho ASCD, Idaho Soc. for Energy and Environ. Edn. (treas. 1985-87). Democrat. Avocations: reading, racquetball, fishing, hunting, horseback tour guide. Office: Base Primary Sch 100 Gunfighter Ave Mountain Home AFB ID 83648-1022

BORDA, RICHARD JOSEPH, management consultant; b. San Francisco, Aug. 16, 1931; s. Joseph Clement and Ethel Cathleen (Donovan) B.; m. Judith Maxwell, Aug. 30, 1953; children: Michelle, Stephen Joseph. AB, Stanford U., 1953, MBA, 1957. With Wells Fargo Bank, San Francisco, 1957-70; mgr. Wells Fargo Bank, 1963-66, asst. v.p., 1966-67, v.p., 1967-70; exec. v.p. adminstrn. Wells Fargo Bank, San Francisco, 1973-85; asst. sec. Air Force Manpower Res. Affairs, Washington, 1970-73; vice chmn., chief fin. officer Nat. Life Ins. Co., Montpelier, Vt., 1985-90, also bd. dirs.; chmn., chief exec. officer Sentinal Group Funds, Inc., 1985-90, also bd. dirs.; mgmt. cons., 1990—. Former pres. Air Force Aid Soc., Washington; trustee Monterey Inst. Internat. Studies (chmn. bd. dirs.); govs. coun. Boys and Girls Club of Monterey Peninsula; bd. dirs. Sunset Ctr. for the Arts Found.; mem. internat. adv. bd. Ctr. for Nonproliferation Studies. Recipient Exceptional Civilian Svc. award, 1973, 95. Mem. USMC Res. Officers Assn., Air Force Assn., Bohemian Club, Monterey Peninsula Country Club, Old Capital Club, Air Force Aid Soc. (disting. counselor), Phi Gamma Delta. Republican. Episcopalian.

BORDEAUX, JEAN-LUC, art expert, consultant, art historian; b. Laval, France, Feb. 13, 1937; came to U.S., 1963; s. Comte Jacques Bordeaux de Noyant and Andrée Bordeaux Le Pecq; m. Mary-Kaye Quackenbush, Dec. 21, 1965; 1 child, Vanessa. PCB, U. Paris, 1959; BS in journalism, Iowa State U., 1964; MA in Art History, Ariz. State U., 1966; PhD in Art History, U. Calif., L.A., 1969. Curatorial asst. J. Paul Getty Mus., Malibu, Calif., 1969-72; dir. fine arts gallery Calif. State U., Northridge, 1972-81, prof. dept. art history, 1972—; guest curator Mus. of the Legion of Honor, San Francisco, 1975; guest curator Musée du Louvre, Paris, 1979-80; dir. Dept. Old Master paintings and Drawings, Christie's, France, Monaco, 1989-93. Author: Francois Le Moyne and His Generation (1688-1737), 1984 (Paribas publ. award, J. Paul Getty Trust publ. award); contbr. scholarly studies to profl. jours., organizer, curator exhbns. 18th century French painting. Lt. Commando Artillery, 1960-62. Franco-Algerian war. Palmes Academiques officer Minister de la Culture, France, 1987; Kress fellow N.Y., 1970-71. Mem. Coll. Art Assn Am., L.A. County Mus. of Art, Les Amis du Louvre, Paris, Archives of Am. Art, Smithsonian Instn., Mus. Contemporary Art, L.A. Republican. Roman Catholic. Avocations: former jr. Davis Cup, played Monte Carlo, Roland Garros in the 1950's.

BORDNER, GREGORY WILSON, chemical engineer; b. Buffalo, Aug. 16, 1959; s. Raymond Gordon and Nancy Lee (Immegart) B.; m. Margaret Patricia Toon, June 14, 1981; children: Eric Lawrence, Heather Rae. BSChemE, Calif. State Poly. U., 1982; MS in Sys. Mgmt., U. So. Calif., 1987. Registered profl. engr., Calif., environ. assessor. Commd. 2nd lt. USAF, 1983, advanced through grades to capt., 1987; engr., mgr. various air launched missile, anti-satellite and strategic def. initiative projects Air Force Rocket Propulsion Lab., Edwards AFB, Calif., 1983-86; asst. mgr. space transp. Air Force Astronautics Lab., Edwards AFB, 1986-87; chief small intercontinental ballistic missiles ordnance firing system br. Hdqrs. Ballistic Missile Orgn., San Bernardino, Calif., 1987-90; sr. plant environ. engr. Filtrol Corp./Akzo Chems. Inc., L.A., 1991-92; water/soils project engr. TABC, Inc., Long Beach, Calif., 1992-98; prodn. engr. TABC, Inc., Long Beach, 1998—. Author: (manual) Pyrotechnic Transfer Line Evaluation, 1984, (with others) Rocket Motor Heat Transfer, 1984. Mem. AIChE, Am. Water Works Assn. Avocations: jogging, weight lifting, bowling. Home: 10841 Ring Ave Alta Loma CA 91737-4429

BORDY, MICHAEL JEFFREY, lawyer; b. Kansas City, Mo., July 24, 1952; s. Marvin Dean and Alice Mae (Rostov) B.; m. Marjorie Enid Kanof, Dec. 27, 1973 (div. Dec. 1983); m. Melissa Anne Held, May 24, 1987; children: Shayna Robyn, Jenna Alexis, Samantha Falyn. Bar: Calif., 1986, U.S. Dist. Ct. (cen. dist.) Calif., 1986, (so. dist.) Calif., 1987, U.S. Ct. Appeals (9th cir.), 1986. Tchg. asst. biology U. Kans., Lawrence, 1975-76, rsch. asst. biology, 1976-80; post-doctoral fellow Johns Hopkins U., Balt., 1980-83; tchg. asst. U. So. Calif., L.A., 1984-86; assoc. Thelen, Marrin, Johnson & Bridges, L.A., 1986-87, Wood, Lucksinger & Epstein, L.A., 1987-89, Cooper, Epstein & Hurewitz, Beverly Hills, Calif., 1989-93; ptnr. Jacobson, Runes & Bordy, Beverly Hills, 1994-96, Jacobson, Sanders & Bordy, LLP, Beverly Hills, 1996-97, Jacobson White Diamond & Bordy, LLP, Beverly Hills, 1997—. Bd. govs. Beverly Hills (Calif.) Bar Barristers, 1988-90, Cedars-Sinai Med. Ctr., L.A., 1994—; bd. dirs. Sinai Temple, 1998—; cabinet United Jewish Fund/Real Estate, L.A., 1995—; mem. planning com. Am. Cancer Soc., 1996—; mem. Guardians of the Jewish Home for the Aging, 1995—, Fraternity of Friends, 1997—; active Lawyers Against Hunger, 1995—. Pre-Doctoral fellow NIH, Lawrence, 1977-80, post-doctoral fellow Mellon Found., Balt., 1980-83. Mem. ABA, State Bar Calif., L.A. County Bar Assn., Beverly Hills Bar Assn. (gov., barrister 1988-92, chair real estate sect. 1998—), Profl. Network Group. Democrat. Jewish. Avocations: running, reading. Office: Jacobson White Diamond & Bordy LLP 9777 Wilshire Blvd Ste 718 Beverly Hills CA 90212-1907

BOREL, JAMES DAVID, anesthesiologist; b. Chgo., Nov. 15, 1951; s. James Albert and Nancy Ann (Sieverson) B. BS, U. Wis., 1973; MD, Med. Coll. of Wis., 1977. Diplomate Am. Bd. Anesthesiology, Nat. Bd. Med. Examiners, Am. Coll. Anesthesiologists. Research asst. McArdle Lab. for Cancer Research, Madison, Wis., 1972-73, Stanford U. and VA Hosp., Palo Alto, 1976-77; intern. The Cambridge (Mass.) Hosp., 1977-78; clin. fellow in medicine Harvard Med. Sch., Boston, 1977-78, clin. fellow in anesthesia, 1978-80, clin. instr. in anaesthesia, 1980; resident in anesthesiology Peter Bent Brigham Hosp., Boston, 1978-80; anesthesiologistt Mt. Auburn Hosp., Cambridge, 1980; fellow in anesthesiology Ariz. Health Scis. Ctr., Tucson, 1980-81; research assoc. U. Ariz. Coll. Medicine, Tucson, 1980-81, assoc. in anesthesiology, 1981—; active staff Mesa (Ariz.) Luth. Hosp., 1981—; courtesy staff Scottsdale (Ariz.) Meml. Hosp., 1982—; vis. anaesthetist St. Joseph's Hosp., Kingston, Jamaica, 1980. Contbr. numerous articles to profl. jours. Mem. AMA, AAAS, Ariz. Anesthesia Alumni Assn., Ariz. Soc. Anesthesiologists, Am. Soc. Regional Anesthesia, Can. Anesthestists' Soc., Internat. Anesthesia Rsch. Soc., Am. Soc. Anesthesiologists. Office: Valley Anesthesia Cons 2200 N Central Ave Ste 203 Phoenix AZ 85004-1431

BOREN, KENNETH RAY, endocrinologist; b. Evansville, Ind., Dec. 31, 1945; s. Doyle Clifford and Jeannette (Koerner) B.; m. Rebecca Lane Wallace, Aug. 25, 1967; children: Jennifer, James, Michael, Peter, Nicklas, Benjamin. BS, Ariz. State U., 1967; MD, Ind. U., Indpls., 1972; MA, Ind. U., Bloomington, 1974. Diplomate Am. Bd. Endocrinology, Am. Bd. Nephrology, Am. Bd. Internal Medicine. Intern in pathology Ind. U. Sch. Medicine, Indpls., 1972; intern in medicine Ind. U. Sch. Medicine, 1972-73, resident in medicine, 1975-77, fellow in endocrinology, 1977-79, fellow nephrology, 1979-80, instr., 1980; physician East Valley Nephrology, Mesa, Ariz., 1980—; chief medicine Mesa Luth Hosp., 1987-89, chief staff, 1990-91; med. dir. RenalWest, 1996—. regional med. dir. RenalWest, 1996—. Bd. dirs. Ariz. Kidney Found., Phoenix, 1984—, pres. 1993-94. Lt. USN, 1973-75. Fellow ACP, Am. Coll. Clin. Endocrinology; mem. AMA, Maricopa County Med. Assn., Ariz. Med. Assn., Am. Soc. Nephrology, Internat. Soc. Nephrology, Am. Diabetes Assn. Republican. Latter Day Saints. Home: 4222 E Mclellan Rd Ste 10 Mesa AZ 85205-3119 Office: East Valley Nephrology 560 W Brown Rd Ste 3006 Mesa AZ 85201-3225

BORER, ANTON JOSEPH, priest; b. Buesserach, Switzerland, Aug. 16, 1916; s. Arnold and Mathilda (Jeker) B. BA, Bruder Klausen Sem., 1939, BA in Theology, 1943. Ordained priest Roman Cath. Ch., 1943. Missionary China, 1946-48; asst. pastor local ch. Denver, 1949-66; founder Bethlehem Ctr., Broomfield, Colo., 1966, dir., 1966-78, spiritual dir., 1978-90; co-founder Shepherds of Bethlehem, Denver, 1991—; dist. superior Bethlehem Fathers USA, 1959-80; dir. Paepl Vols. in Denver, 1968-74; Newman chaplain Dever colls., 1969-90; personal rep. of archbishop to charismatic community in Archdiocese of Denver, 1974-81; bd. dirs. Spirit's Runway, Denver, 1970-76. Co-author: New Life: Preperation of Religious for Retirement, 1973; editor Bethlehem Call, 1974—; contbr. articles to religious jours. Office: 12550 Zuni St Denver CO 80234-2206 Home: Sheperds of Bethlehem 1045 Maple Dr Broomfield CO 80020-1050

BORESI, ARTHUR PETER, author, educator; b. Toluca, Ill.; s. John Peter and Eva B.; m. Clara Jean Gordon, Dec. 28, 1946; children: Jennifer Ann Boresi Hill, Annette Boresi Pueschel, Nancy Jean Boresi Broderick. Student, Kenyon Coll., 1943-44; BSEE, U. Ill., 1948, MS in Mechanics, 1949, PhD in Mechanics, 1953. Research engr. N. Am. Aviation, 1950; materials engr. Nat. Bur. Standards, 1951; mem. faculty U. Ill., Urbana, 1953—, prof. theoretical and applied mechanics and nuclear engring., 1959-79; prof. emeritus U. Ill. at Urbana, Urbana, 1979; Disting. vis. prof. Clarkson Coll. Tech., Potsdam, N.Y., 1968-69; NAVSEA research prof. Naval Postgrad. Sch., Monterey, Calif., 1978-79; prof. civil engring. U. Wyo., Laramie, 1979-95, head, 1980-94, prof. emeritus, 1995—; vis. prof. Naval Postgrad. Sch., Monterey, Calif., 1986-87.; cons. in field. Author: Engineering Mechanics, 1959, Elasticity in Engineering Mechanics, 3d edit., 1987, Advanced Mechanics of Materials, 5th edit., 1993, Approximate Solution Methods in Engineering Mechanics, 1991; also articles. Served with USAAF, 1943-44; Served with AUS, 1944-46. Fellow ASME, ASCE, Am. Acad. Mechanics (founding, treas.); mem. Am. Soc. Engring. Edn. (Archie Higdon Disting. Educator award 1993), Soc. Exptl. Mechanics, Sigma Xi. Office: U Wyo Box 3295 Univ Station Laramie WY 82071

BORG, MARCUS JOEL, theologian, theology educator; b. Fergus Falls, Minn., Mar. 11, 1942; s. Glenn F. and Esther (Stortroen) B.; m. Marianne Wells, Aug. 24, 1985; children: Dane, Julie. BA, Concordia Coll., Moorhead, Minn., 1964; diploma in Theology, U. Oxford, Eng., 1966; D.Phil., U. Oxford, 1972; postgrad., Union Theol. Sem., U. Tübingen, Fed. Republic Germany. Prof. religion Carleton Coll., Northfield, Minn., 1976-79; prof. religion and culture Oreg. State U., Corvallis, 1979—; Disting. vis. prof. U. Puget Sound, Tacoma, Wash., 1986-87; vis. prof. N.T. Pacific Sch. Religion, Berkeley, Calif., 1989-91. Author: Year of Luke, 1976, Conflict and Social Change, 1971, Conflict, Holiness and Politics in the Teaching of Jesus, 1984, Jesus: A New Vision, 1987, Meeting Jesus Again for the First Time, 1994, Jesus in Contemporary Scholarship, 1994, Jesus at 2000, 1996, The God We Never Knew, 1997, Jesus and Buddha, 1997, The Meaning of Jesus: Two Visions, 1998; contbr. articles to religious jours. Recipient Burlington-No. Teaching award Oreg. State U., 1986, Faculty Excellence award Oreg. State Legislature, 1987. Fellow The Jesus Sem.; mem. Soc. Bibl. Lit., Cath. Bibl. Assn., Am. Acad. Religion. Office: Oreg State U Dept Philosophy Corvallis OR 97331

BORGES, WILLIAM, III, environmental scientist; b. Long Beach, Calif., Nov. 21, 1948; s. William Borges Jr. and Dorothy Mae (Raymond) Morris; m. Rosalind Denise Marye, Nov. 23, 1968; children: William IV, Blake Austin. BA in Geography, Calif. State U., Sonoma, 1973; MBA, U. Phoenix, 1997. Environ. planner Mendocino County Planning Dept., Ukiah, Calif., 1976; project mgr. Engring. Sci., Inc., Berkeley, Calif., 1976-79, Santa Clara County Planning Dept., San Jose, Calif., 1979-81, Internat. Tech. Corp., San Jose, 1985-88; mgr. sales ops. Adac Labs., Milpitas, Calif., 1983-85; prin. WT Environ. Cons., Phoenix, 1988-91; project mgr. Dynamac Corp., Newport Beach, Calif., 1991-93; prin. environ. scientist Midwest Rsch. Inst., Scottsdale, Ariz., 1993-96. Contbr. photographs to various mags. Coord. pub. rels. Stellar Acad. for Dyslexics, Fremont, Calif., 1988. With M.I., U.S. Army, 1967-70. Mem. Am. Mensa. Avocations: photography, traveling.

BORGMAN, SYLVIA, artist, activist; b. Clinton, Iowa, Oct. 10, 1952; d. Bernard and Sien (Frik) B.; m. Peter Siczewicz, Oct. 6, 1978 (div. Apr. 1982). BS in Psychology and Sociology, Ill. State U., 1974; postgrad., Boston Coll., 1978, San Francisco Art Inst., 1987. Cert. Women in Politics and Government Boston Coll., 1978. Child and family intake worker Ill. Dept. Child and Family Welfare, Springfield, 1973; youth specialist Sangamon County Juvenile Ct., Springfield, 1974; adminstr., educator MIT, Cambridge, Mass., 1978; ednl. cons. Chrysler Corp., Detroit, 1980, Am. Internat. Tng., San Rafael, Calif., 1984; planner govs. discretionary fund Mass. Dept. Econ. Affairs, Boston, 1976-79; lobbyist women's issues, 1975—. Interviewer WGBH-TV, Bus. Week Mag.; exhibited art in various group shows. Creator sexual harrassment legislation Alliance Against Sexual Harrassment, Boston, 1978-79; intern Women's Polit. Census, Boston, 1977-79, Gov.'s Task Force on Women and Work, Boston, 1977-79; fundraiser Mel King for Gov., Boston, 1977-79. San Francisco Art Inst. scholar, 1989. Mem. Ctrl. Coast Art Inst. Democrat. Avocations: art, music. Home: 463 Reeside Ave Monterey CA 93940-1826

BORGMANN, CAROL A., fundraising executive; b. St. Louis, Mar. 9, 1960; d. Ralph E. and Marilyn E. (Schmitt) B.; m. Steve D. Sorensen, July 27, 1985; 1 child, Lynn Heather. Grad. h.s., St. Louis. Dancer Calif. Festival Ballet, L.A., 1978-81, Pacific Northwest Ballet, Seattle, 1981-82; ann. fund mgr. Seattle Symphony, 1982-90, capital campaign dir., 1990-92; assoc. artistic dir. Spectrum Dance Theater, Seattle, 1985-96; dir. devel. Northwest AIDS Found., Seattle, 1992-98; assoc. dir. Music Works Northwest, Bellevue, Wash., 1998—; treas. bd. dirs. Spectrum Dance Theater, Seattle, 1991-95; pres. bd. Dance Coalition, Seattle, 1986-88. Choreographer various musicals, dance works, 1988-91. Mem. Northwest Devel. Officers Assn.

BORIN, BORIS MICHAYLOVITCH, writer, publisher; b. Kamenets-Dodolsky, Ukraine, June 25, 1935; came to U.S., 1980; s. Meshilim Shlemovitch and Maria Shoel (Keiser) Oykhman; m. Galina Israilovna Goykhenberg, Sept. 19, 1946; children: Marat, Felix (twins). Diploma in mech. engring., Tech. Coll., Tchernovits, Ukraine, 1952-57; diploma in history, St. Petersburg U., St. Petersburg, Leningrad, 1962-67. Tchr., instr. Indsl. coll., Semiluki, Russia, 1968-71; tchr. high sch. Surgut, Russia, 1971-80, Kurganinsk, Russia, 1981-86; tchr., instr. Russian lang. Def. Lang., San Antonio, Tex., 1986—; writer L.A., 1995—; publisher Borin B.M. Publs., L.A., 1995—. Author: Volens and Nolens, 1993, Aesop, 1995; inventor exercise and portable grill. Avocations: writing humor stories, improving inventions, reading, opera music, herb medicine. Home: 7545 Hampton Ave Apt 314 Los Angeles CA 90046-5549

BORMAN, GREGORY STEVEN, artist; b. Pensacola, Fla., Feb. 11, 1968; s. Walter Charles and Kathryn (Matey) B. Student, Pratt Inst., Bklyn., 1986-87, Calif. Coll. Arts & Crafts, Oakland, 1992-93; BFA, U. Cin., 1992. Asst. to artist Alexander Osipov, Cin., 1992; asst. to craftsperson Aron Rosenburg, Oakland, Calif., 1993-94; custom framer N.P.F.C., Inc., San Francisco, 1997; mem. clerical/office support staff Cert. Pers., San Francisco, 1998—; mem., vol. Artwork Gallery, San Francisco, 1996-98, New Langton Arts, San Francisco, 1997-98, Ansel Adams Ctr., San Francisco, 1997-99, Refusalon Gallery, San Francisco, 1997. Co-curator with Johnny Davis Artbeat exhbn., Artbeat Artwork Gallery, 1996; author, rschr. exhbn. Tangeman Gallery, 1992; curator Artwork Gallery, 1999, Crucible Steel Gallery, 1999. Donor U. Calif., San Francisco AIDS Health Project/San Francisco AIDS Found., 1998, The Lab Gallery, San Francisco, 1997-98, Artspan, San Francisco, 1997. Grantee San Francisco Art Inst., 1998—, U. South Fla., 1998—, Calif. Coll. Arts and Crafts, 1993, U. Cin., 1992. Avocations: building picture frames, volunteering for arts organizations. Home: 110 Capp St Apt M San Francisco CA 94110-1293

BORNSTEIN, ELI, artist, sculptor; b. Milw., Dec. 28, 1922; dual citizen, U.S. and Can.; m. Christina Bornstein; children: Sarah, Thea. BS, U. Wis., 1945, MS, 1954; student, Art Inst. Chgo., U. Chgo., 1943, Academie Montmartre of Fernand Leger, Paris, 1951, Academie Julian, 1952; DLitt, U. Sask., Can., 1990. Tchr. drawing, painting and sculpture Milw. Art Inst., 1943-47; tchr. design U. Wis., 1949; tchr. drawing, painting, sculpture, design and graphics U. Sask., Can., 1950-90; prof. U. Sask., 1963-90, prof. emeritus, 1990—, head art dept., 1963-71. Painted in France, 1951-52, Italy, 1957, Holland, 1958; exhibited widely, 1943—; retrospective exhbn. (works 1943-64), Mendel Art Gallery, Saskatoon, 1965, one man shows, Kazimir Gallery, Chgo., 1965, 67, Saskatoon Pub. Library, 1975, Can. Cultural Center, Paris, 1976, Glenbow-Alta. Inst. Art, Calgary, 1976, Mendel Art Gallery, Saskatoon, 1982, York U. Gallery, Toronto, 1983, Confedn. Ctr. Art Gallery, Charlottetown, P.E.I., 1983, Owens Art Gallery, Mt. Allison U., Sackville, N.B., 1984, Fine Arts Gallery, U. Wis.-Milw., 1984, Mendel Art Gallery, Saskatoon, 1996; represented in numerous art collections; executed marble sculpture now in permanent collection, Walker Art Center, Mpls., 1947, aluminum constrn. for Sask. Tchrs. Fedn. Bldg., 1956, structurist relief in painted wood and aluminum for, Arts and Scis. Bldg., U. Sask., 1958, structurist relief in enamelled steel for, Internat. Air Terminal, Winnipeg, Man., Can., 1962, four-part constructed relief for Wascana Pl. Wascana Ctr. Authority, Regina, Sask., 1983; also structurist reliefs exhibited, Mus. Contemporary Art, Chgo., Herron Mus. Art, Indpls., Cranbrook Acad. Art Galleries, Mich., High Mus., Atlanta, Can. House, Cultural Centre Gallery, London, 1983, Can. Cultural Ctr., Paris, 1983, Brussels, 1983, Milw. Art Mus., 1984, Bonn, 1985; model of aluminium construction, 1956 and model version of structurist relief in 5 parts, 1962, now in collection, Nat. Gallery, Ottawa, Ont., others in numerous collections.; Co-editor: periodical Structure, 1958; founder, editor: The Structurist, ann. publ. 1960-72, biennial, 1972—; Contbr. articles, principally on Structurist art to various pubs. Recipient Allied Arts medal Royal Archtl. Inst. Can., 1968; honorable mention for 3 structurist reliefs 2d Biennial Internat. Art Exhbn., Colombia, S.Am., 1970. Fax: (306) 966-8670. E-mail: eli.bornstein@usask.ca. Address: 3625 Saskatchewan Cres S, Corman Park, SK Canada S7T 1B7 Office: U Sask, Box 378 RPO U, Saskatoon, SK Canada S7N 4J8

BORREGO, JESUS GARCIA, engineer; b. El Paso, Tex., Nov. 12, 1953; s. Jesus F. and Maria Luisa (Garcia) B.; m. Maria Magdalena Ornelas, Dec. 18, 1972; children: Maria M., Cristina, Jesus Jr. BSEE, Calif. State U., Fullerton, 1984; BS in Computer Sci., Calif. State U., Dominguez Hills, 1987; MS in Computer Sci., Loyola Marymount, L.A., 1992. Cert. tchr., Calif. Enlisted USMC, 1972-83; mem. tech. staff Logicon, Inc., San Pedro, Calif., 1983-87; tech. lead Advanced Tech., Inc., El Segundo, Calif., 1987-88; staff engr. Hughes Aircraft, El Segundo, Calif., 1988-89; sr. prin. engr. Arinc Rsch. Corp., Fountain Valley, Calif., 1989-94; prof. Webster U., Colorado Springs, Colo., 1995—; sr. mgr. Arinc Inc., Colorado Springs, 1994—; prof. Regis U., Colorado Springs, Colo., 1995—; adj. faculty El Camino Coll., Torrance, Calif., 1988-94; cons. JMB Cons., Gardena, Calif., 1988-94. Contbr. articles to profl. jours. With USMC Res., 1983-92. Mem. IEEE, IEEE Computer Soc., Assn. for Computer Machinery. Republican. Roman Catholic. Avocations: teaching, reading, racquetball, camping, travel. Office: Arinc Inc 1925 Aerotech Dr Ste 212 Colorado Springs CO 80916-4221

BORSCH, FREDERICK HOUK, bishop; b. Chgo., Sept. 13, 1935; s. Reuben A. and Pearl Irene (Houk) B.; m. Barbara Edgeley Sampson, June 25, 1960; children: Benjamin, Matthew, Stuart. AB, Princeton U., 1957; MA, Oxford U., 1959; STB, Gen. Theol. Sem., 1960; PhD, U. Birmingham, 1966; DD (hon.), Seabury Western Theol. Sem., 1978, Gen. Theol. Sem., 1988; STD (hon.), Ch. Div. Sch. of Pacific, 1981, Berk Div. Sch. Yale U., 1983. Ordained priest Episcopal Ch., 1960; curate Grace Episcopal Ch., Oak Park, Ill., 1960-63; tutor Queen's Coll., Birmingham, Eng., 1963-66; asst. prof. N.T. Seabury Western Theol. Sem., Evanston, Ill., 1966-69, assoc. prof. N.T., 1969-71; prof. N.T. Gen. Theol. Sem., N.Y.C., 1971-72; pres., dean Berk Div. Sch. Yale U., Berkeley, Calif., 1972-81; dean of chapel, prof. religion Princeton U., 1981-88; bishop Episc. Diocese, L.A., 1988—; rep. Faith and Order Commn., Nat. Coun. Chs., 1975-81; mem. exec. coun. Episc. Ch., 1981-88, Anglican Cons. Coun., 1984-88; chair bd. govs. Trinity Press Internat., 1989—; bd. adv. UCLA Sch. Pub. Policy & Social Rsch., 1998—; trustee Princeton U., 1998—. Author: The Son of Man in Myth and History, 1967, The Christian and Gnostic Son of Man, 1970, God's Parable, 1976, Introducing the Lessons of the Church Year, 1978, Coming Together in the Spirit, 1980, Power in Weakness, 1983, Jesus: The Human Life of God, 1987, Many Things in Parables, 1988, Christian Discipleship and Sexuality, 1993, Outrage and Hope, 1996; editor: Anglicanism and the Bible, 1984, The Bible's Authority in Today's Church, 1993. Trustee Princeton U., 1998—. Keasbey scholar, 1957-59. Fellow Soc. Arts, Religion and Contemporary Culture; mem. Am. Acad. Religion, Soc. Bibl. Lit., Studiorum Novi Testamenti Societas, Phi Beta Kappa. Home: 2930 Corda Ln Los Angeles CA 90049-1105 Office: Episcopal Diocese of LA PO Box 512164 Los Angeles CA 90051-0164

BORSON, DANIEL BENJAMIN, physiology educator, inventor, researcher, lawyer; b. Berkeley, Calif., Mar. 24, 1946; s. Harry J. and Josephine F. (Esterly) B.; m. Margaret Ann Rheinschmidt, May 22, 1974; children: Alexander Nathan, Galen Michael. BA, San Francisco State Coll., 1969; MA, U. Calif., Riverside, 1973; PhD, U. Calif., San Francisco, 1982; JD, U. San Francisco, 1995. Bar: Calif. 1997, U.S. Dist. Ct. (no. dist.) Calif. 1997, U.S. Patent and Trademark Office 1998; lic. comml. pilot, flight instr. FAA. Musician Composer's Forum, Berkeley, San Francisco, 1961-70; flight instr. Buchanan Flying Club, Concord, Oakland, Calif., 1973-77, pres., 1975-77; physiology U. Calif., San Francisco, 1984-92, asst. rsch. physiologist Cardiovascular Rsch. Inst., 1988-92; assoc. Fliesler Dubb Meyer and Lovejoy, 1997—; vis. scientist Genentech Inc., South San Francisco, Calif., 1990-92. Contbr. articles, rev. chpts. and abstracts to profl. jours., legal periodicals and law rev. Fellow NIH, 1976-84, grantee, 1988-93; fellow Cystic Fibrosis Found., 1985, grantee, 1989-91; fellow Parker B. Francis Found., 1985-87; grantee Am. Lung Assn., 1985-87. Mem. ABA, Am. Physiol. Soc. (editl. bd. Am. Jour. Physiology 1990-92), Am. Soc. Cell Biology, Am. Chem. Soc., Am. Intellectual Property Law Assn., San Francisco Intellectual Property Law Assn., Fed. Cir. Bar Assn., Bay Flute Club (pres. 1978). Avocations: mountain climbing, aviation, music. Home: 23 Warford Ter Orinda CA 94563-2811

BORTON, GEORGE ROBERT, retired airline captain; b. Wichita Falls, Tex., Mar. 22, 1922; s. George Neat and Travis Lee (Jones) B.; m. Anne Louise Bowling, Feb. 5, 1944 (dec.); children: Trudie T., Robert B., Bruce M. AA, Hardin Coll., Wichita Falls, 1940. Cert. airline transport pilot, FAA flight examiner. Flight sch. operator Vallejo (Calif.) Sky Harbor, 1947-48; capt. S.W. Airways, San Francisco, 1948-55; check capt. Pacific Airlines, San Francisco, 1955-68, Hughes Air West, San Francisco, 1968-71; capt. N.W. Airlines, Mpls., 1971-82, ret., 1982. Col. USAF, 1943-73, ret. Decorated Air medal. Mem. Airline Pilots Assn., Res. Officers Assn., Air Force Assn., Horseless Carriage Club, Model T of Am. Club (San Jose, Calif.). Republican. Home: 325 Denio Ave Gilroy CA 95020-9203

BORUCHOWITZ, STEPHEN ALAN, health policy analyst; b. Plainfield, N.J., Sept. 24, 1952; s. Robert and Earla Louise (Sloat) B.; m. Linda Susan Grant, Sept. 16, 1989; 1 child, Grant Stephen. BA in Internat. Affairs, George Washington U., Washington, 1974; MA in Sci., Tech. and Pub. Policy, George Washington U., 1981. Food prog. specialist U.S. Food & Nutrition Svc., Washington, 1978-81; internat. affairs specialist Office Internat. Cooperation & Devel., Washington, 1981-87; legis. analyst Wash. State Senate, Olympia, 1986-89; project dir. Wash. 2000 Project, Olympia, 1989-92; sr. health policy analyst Wash. Dept. Health, Olympia, 1992—; mem. Pew Commn. task force on regulation of health professions, 1994-95. Editor newsletter: Project Update, 1990-92. Study team mem. Gov.'s Efficiency Commn., 1990-91; com. mem. Coun. of State Govts. Strategic Planning Subcom., Lexington, Ky., 1990-92; chmn. Montclair Divsn. IV Neighborhood Assn., 1989-92, Shadywood Homeowner's Assn., 1992-94; bd. dirs. Classical Music Supporters, Seattle, 1987-89. Recipient Superior Performance award, U.S. Dept. Agr., 1986. Mem. World Future Soc., Internat. Health Futures Network, Internat. Soc. of Tech. Assessment in Health Care, Health Svcs. Rsch. Assn. Avocations: writing, travel, cooking, classical music. Office: Wash Dept Health PO Box 47851 Olympia WA 98504-7851

BOS, JOHN ARTHUR, aircraft manufacturing executive; b. Holland, Mich., Nov. 6, 1933; s. John Arthur and Annabelle (Castelli) B.; m. Eileen Tempest, Feb. 15, 1974; children: John, James, William, Tiffany. BS in Acctg., Calif. State Coll., Long Beach, 1971. Officer 1st Nat. Bank, Holland, Mich., 1954-61; dir. bus. mgmt. Boeing Airlift and Tanker Programs, Long Beach, 1962—. Mem. Inst. Mgmt. Accts. (cert. mgmt. acct. 1979), Nat. Assn. Accts. Avocations: automobile marketing, golf, consulting. Office: Boeing Airlift and Tanker Programs 2401 E Wardlow Rd Long Beach CA 90807-5309

BOSKOVICH, GEORGE, JR., food products executive; b. 1946. Chmn. Boskovich Farms. Office: Boskovich Farms Inc 711 Diaz Ave Oxnard CA 93030-7247*

BOSMAJIAN, HAIG ARAM, [illegible] Calif., Mar. 26, 1928; s. Aram and Aurora (Keosheyan) B.; m. Hamida Just, Feb. 27, 1957; 1 child, Harlan. BA, U. Calif., Berkeley, 1949; MA, U. of Pacific, 1951; PhD, Stanford U., 1960. Instr. U. Idaho, Moscow, 1959-61; asst. prof. U. Conn., Storrs, 1961-65; prof. speech comm. U. Wash., Seattle, 1965—. Author: Language of Oppression (Orwell award), 1983; editor: Censorship, Libraries and the Law, 1983; Justice Douglas, 1980, Freedom of Speech, 1983, First Amendment in the Classroom Series, 1987: vol. 1, The Freedom to Read, 1987, vol. II, The Freedom of Religion, 1987, vol. III, Freedom of Expression, 1988, vol. IV, Academic Freedom, 1989, vol. V, Freedom to Publish, 1989, Metaphor and Reason in Judicial Opinions, 1992, The Freedom Not to Speak, 1994. Recipient Bicentennial of the Bill of Rights award Western States Communication Assn., 1991. Mem. Nat. Coun. Tchrs. of English, Speech Comm. Assn.

BOSSERT, PHILIP JOSEPH, information systems executive; b. Indpls., Feb. 23, 1944; s. Alfred Joseph and Phyllis Jean (Cashen) B.; m. Jane Elisabeth Shade, June 29, 1968 (div. Dec. 1990); m. ChaoYing Deng, May 22, 1992; 1 child, Lian Brittni. BA in Econs., Rockhurst Coll., 1968; cert. in Philosophy, U. Freiburg, Fed. Republic Ger., 1970; MA in Philosophy, Washington U., St. Louis, 1972, PhD in Philosophy, 1973. Asst. prof. philosophy Hawaii Loa Coll., Honolulu, 1973-76, pres., 1978-86; dir. Hawaii com. for the humanities Nat. Endowment for the Humanities, Honolulu, 1976-77; dir. long range planning Chaminade U., Honolulu, 1977-78; pres. Strategic Info. Solutions, Honolulu, 1986—; mgr. strategic info. systems GTE Hawaiian Telephone, Honolulu, 1987-91; asst. supt. info. & telecom. svcs. Hawaii State Dept. Edn., 1991-94; project dir. Hawaii Edn. and Rsch. Network, 1994-97; chmn. bd. dirs., dir. Media Design & Devel., Inc., 1996—; chmn. bd. dirs., CEO Baden Wines Internat., Ltd., 1997—; cons. Sangyong Bus. Group, Seoul, Korea, 1987-90, Nat. Assn. Colls. Univs. and Bus. Officers, Washington, 1980-90. Author: Strategic Planning and Budgeting, 1989; author, editor numerous books on philosophy; contbr. articles to profl. jours. Bd. dirs. Hawaii Childrens Mus.; bd. dirs. Friends of the East West Ctr.; bd. dirs. Hawaii Alliance for the Arts. Fulbright-Hays fellow, 1968-70, Woodrow Wilson fellow, 1972-73, Nat. Endowment for Humanities fellow, 1976. Mem. Data Processing Mgmt. Assn., Pacific Telecom. Coun. (bd. dirs.), Honolulu Com. on Fgn. Relations, Honolulu Rotary Club. E-mail: pbossert@sis.net. Office: Strategic Info Solutions Inc 239 Merchant St Honolulu HI 96813-2923

BOSWELL, SUSAN G., lawyer; b. El Paso, Tex., June 26, 1945. BA, U. Ariz., 1972, JD, 1976. Bar: Ariz. 1977, Nev. 1992. Dir. Tuscon (Ariz.) office Streich & Lang P.C., Phoenix, 1987—; instr., faculty mem. Nat. Inst. Trail Advocacy, 1991; bd. vis. U. Ariz. Coll. of Law. Fellow Am. Coll. Bankruptcy; mem. State Bar of Ariz. (peer review com., assistance com.), Ariz. Women Lawyers Assn, Phi Kappa Phi. Office: Streich Lang PC 1 S Church Ave Ste 1700 Tucson AZ 85701-1630*

BOSWORTH, BRUCE LEIGHTON, school administrator, educator, consultant; b. Buffalo, Mar. 22, 1942; s. John Wayman and Alice Elizabeth Rodgers; children: David, Timothy, Paul. BA, U. Denver, 1964; MA, U. No. Colo., 1970; EdD, Walden U., 1984. Elem. tchr. Littleton (Colo.) Pub. Schs., 1964-67, 70-81; bldg. prin. East Smoky Sch. Div. 54, Valleyview, Alta., Can., 1967-70; pres., tchr. Chatfield Sch., Littleton, 1981—; adoption cons. hard-to-place children; ednl. cons. spl. needs children. St. Andrew Presbyn. Ch. (USA). Mem. ASCD, Council Exceptional Children, Masons, Shriners, York Rite. Home and Office: 3500 S Lowell Blvd Apt 316 Denver CO 80236-6168

BOSWORTH, THOMAS LAWRENCE, architect, educator; b. Oberlin, Ohio, June 15, 1930; s. Edward Franklin and Imogene (Rose) B.; m. Abigail Lumbard, Nov. 6, 1954 (div. Nov. 1974); children: Thomas Edward, Nathaniel David; m. Elaine R. Pedigo, Nov. 23, 1974; stepchildren: Robert Haden Pedigo, Kevin Ian Pedigo. BA, Oberlin Coll., 1952, MA, 1954; postgrad., Princeton U., 1952-53, Harvard U., 1956-57; MArch, Yale U., 1960. Draftsman Gordon McMaster AIA, Cheshire, Conn., summer 1957-58; resident planner Tunnard & Harris Planning Cons., Newport, R.I., summer 1959; designer, field supr. Eero Saarinen & Assocs., Birmingham, Mich., 1960-61, Hamden, Conn., 1961-64; individual practice architecture Providence, 1964-68, Seattle, 1968—; asst. instr. architecture Yale U., 1962-65, vis. lectr., 1965-66; asst. prof. R.I. Sch. Design, 1964-66, asso. prof., head dept., 1966-68; prof. architecture U. Wash., Seattle, 1968-98; prof. emeritus U. Wash., 1998—; chmn. dept. U. Wash., Seattle, 1968-72; chief architecture Peace Corps Tng. Program, Tunisia, Brown U., summers 1965-66; archtl. cons., individual practice Seattle, 1972—; dir. multidisciplinary program U. Wash., Rome, Italy, 1984-86; vis. lectr. Kobe U., Japan, Oct., 1982, Nov., 1990, Apr., 1993, May, 1995, June, 1998; Pietro Belluschi Disting. Vis. Prof. U. Oreg., 1996; dir. arch. in Rome program U. Wash., Rome, 1996. Bd. dirs. N.W. Inst. Arch. and Urban Studies, Italy, 1983-90, pres., 1983-85; dir. Pilchuck Glass Sch., Seattle, 1977-80, trustee, 1980-91, adv. coun., 1993—; mem. Seattle Model Cities Land Use Rev. Bd., 1969-70, Tech. Com. Site Selection Wash. Multi-Purpose Stadium, 1970, Medina Planning Commn., 1972-74, steering adv. com. King County Stadium, 1972-74, others; chmn. King County (Wash.) Environ. Devel. Commn., 1972-74, King County Policy Devel. Commn., 1974-77; mem. Rome Ctr. adv. bd. U. of Wash., 1998—; bd. mgrs. YMCA Camping Sv cs., 1998—. With U.S. Army, 1954-56. Winchester Traveling fellow Greece, 1960; assoc. fellow Ezra Stiles Coll. Yale U.; mid-career fellow in arch. Am. Acad. in Rome, 1980-81, vis. scholar, Spring 1988. Fellow AIA; mem. AAUP, Archtl. Inst. Japan, Soc. Archtl. Historians, Rainier Club, Monday Club, Tau Sigma Delta. Home: 4532 E Laurel Dr NE Seattle WA 98105-3839 Office: U Wash Dept Architecture PO Box 355720 Seattle WA 98195-5720

BOTELHO, BRUCE MANUEL, state attorney general, mayor; b. Juneau, Alaska, Oct. 6, 1948; s. Emmett Manuel and Harriet Iowa (Tieszen) B.; m. Guadalupe Alvarez Breton, Sept. 23, 1988; children: Alejandro Manuel, Adriana Regina. Student, U. Heidelberg, Federal Republic of Germany, 1970; BA, Willamette U., 1971, JD, 1976. Bar: Alaska 1976, U.S. Ct. Appeals (9th cir.), U.S. Supreme Ct. Asst. atty. gen. State of Alaska, Juneau, 1976-83, 87-90, dep. commr., acting commr. Dept. of Revenue, 1983-86; mayor City, Borough of Juneau, 1988-91, dep. atty. gen., 1991-94; atty. gen. State of AK, 1994—. Editor: Willamette Law Jour., 1975-76; contbr. articles profl. jours. Assembly mem. City, Borough of Juneau, 1983-86; pres. Juneau Human Rights Commn., 1978-80, Alaska Coun. Am. Youth Hostels, 1979-81, Juneau Arts and Humanities Coun., 1981-83, SE Alaska Area Coun. Boy Scouts Am., 1991-93, coun. commr., 1993—; bd. dirs. Found. for Social Innovations, Alaska, 1990-93, Alaska Econ. Devel. Coun., 1985-87, Alaska Indsl. Devel. Corp., 1984-86, Juneau World Affairs Coun.; chair adminstrv. law sect. Alaska Bar Assn., 1981-82; chair Alaska Resources Corp., 1984-86, Gov.'s Conf. on Youth and Justice, 1995-96; trustee Alaska Children's Trust, 1996—; mem. exec. com. Conf. of Western Attys. Gen., 1997—; co-chair Alaska Justice Assessment Commn., 1997—, chair Gov. Task Force on Confidentiality of Chldns. Proceedings, 1998—. Mem. Nat. Assn. Attys. Gen. (exec. com. 1998—). Democrat. Methodist. Avocation: international folk dance. Home: 401 F St Douglas AK 99824-5353 Office: State Alaska Dept Law PO Box 110300 Juneau AK 99811-0300

BOTELLO, TROY JAMES, arts administrator, educator; b. Long Beach, Calif., Sept. 2, 1953; s. Arthur P. and Jayme Alta (McBride) B. AA in Spl. Edn., Cerritos Coll., 1979; BA in Music Therapy, Calif. State U., Long Beach, 1984; cert. in arts adminstrn., U. So. Calif., Orange County, 1988; MA in Adminstrn., Calif. Polytech. Inst., Pomona, 1992. Cert. tchr., Calif. Asst. music dir. St. John Bosco High Sch., Bellflower, Calif., 1969-72; music dir. Bellflower Unified Schs., 1971-74; tchr. severely handicapped L.A. County Office of Edn., 1974-88; vocat. rehab. counselor Tesseler Counseling Group, Anaheim, Calif., 1988-91; dir. edn. Orange County Performing Arts Ctr., Costa Mesa, Calif., 1991—; exec. dir., co-founder Project: Arts in Motion, Bellflower, 1983-92; ednl. cons. Edn. Div. Music Ctr., L.A., 1986—; vice chmn. La Mirada (Calif.) Community Concerts, 1976-79; v.p. grants Master Symphony Orch., Norwalk, Calif. Chairperson La Mirada Hist. Com., 1977-78; rep. Edn. Adv. Com., L.A., 1981; exec. prod., bd. dirs. Imagination Celebration of Orange County, 1991—, pres. Anaheim Cultural Arts Found., 1993-95; state pres., bd. dirs Very Special Arts Calif., 1992—. Mem. Assn. for Music Therapy Profls., So. Calif. Band and Field Judges, [illegible] Schwelrk, Young Composers of Am., Alumni of Drum Corps Internat. Avocations: cultural events, gourmet cooking. E-mail: tbotello@olpac.org. Home: 14216 Neargrove Rd La Mirada CA 90638-3854 Office: Orange County Performing Arts Ctr 600 Town Center Dr Costa Mesa CA 92626-1007

BOTHELL, LISA JEAN, graphic designer; b. Seattle, Aug. 4, 1965; d. Bruce Eslebe and Diane June (Stevens) B. BA, U. Wash., 1987. Publ. Three-Stones Publ. Ltd., Seattle, 1986-96, Bast Media, Inc., Seattle, 1996-98; project asst. Providence Health Plans, Seattle, 1996-97; graphic designer Highline C.C., Seattle, 1998—. Office: Bast Media Inc 17650 1st Ave S Box 291 Seattle WA 98148

BOTIMER, ALLEN RAY, retired surgeon, retirement center owner; b. Columbus, Miss., Jan. 30, 1930; s. Clare E. and Christel J. (Kalar) B.; m. Dorris LaJean, Aug. 17, 1950; children: Larry Alan, Gary David. BS, Walla Walla Coll., 1951; MD, Loma Linda U., 1955. Diplomate Am. Bd. Surgery. Intern U.S. Naval Hosp., San Diego, 1955-56, surg. resident, 1955-60; asst. chief surgery U.S. Naval Hosp., Guam, 1960-62, Bremerton, Wash., 1962-64; chief surgery Ballard Community Hosp., Seattle, 1970, chief of staff, 1972, chief surgery, 1986-87; pvt. practice Seattle, 1964-87; ret., 1987; ptnr. Heritage Retirement Ctr., Nampa, Idaho, 1972-82, owner, 1982—. Lt. comdr. USN, 1955-64. Fellow ACS, Seattle Surg. Soc.; mem. Wash. State Med. Soc., King County Med. Soc. Avocations: golf, personal computers. Home and Office: 1319 Torrey Ln Nampa ID 83686-5665

BOTSAI, ELMER EUGENE, architect, educator, former university dean; b. St. Louis, Feb. 1, 1928; s. Paul and Ita May (Cole) B.; m. Patricia L. Keegan, Aug. 28, 1955; children: Donald Rolf, Kurt Gregory.; m. Sharon K. Kaiser, Dec. 5, 1981; 1 dau., Kiana Michelle. AA, Sacramento Jr. Coll., 1950; AB, U. Calif.-Berkeley, 1954. Registered architect, Hawaii, Calif. Draftsman, then asst. to architect So. Pacific Co., San Francisco, 1953-57; designer J.H. Ferguson Co., San Francisco, 1955; project architect Anshen & Allen Architects, San Francisco, 1957-63; prin. Botsai, Overstreet & Rosenberg, Architects and Planners, San Francisco, 1963-79, Elmer E. Botsai FAIA, Honolulu, 1979—; of cousnel Groupe 70 Internat., 1998—; chmn. dept. architecture U. Hawaii, Manoa, 1976-80, dean Sch. Architecture, 1980-90, prof., 1990-98; lectr. U. Calif., Berkeley, 1976, dir. Nat. Archtl. Accrediting Bd., 1972-73, 79; adminstrv. and tech. cons. Wood Bldg. Rsch. Ctr., U. Calif., 1985-90, mem. profl. preparation project com. at U. Mich., Ann Arbor, 1986-87; co-author water infiltration seminar series for Bldg. Owners and Mgrs. Rsch. Ctr., 1986-87; chief investigator effects of Guatemalan earthquake for NSF and AIA, Washington, 1976; steering com. on structural failures Nat. Bur. Standards, 1982-84; chmn., dir. gen. svcs. Adv. Com. State of Calif. Co-author: Architects and Earthquake, Research Needs, 1976, ATC Seismic Standards for National Bur. of Standards, 1976, Architects and Earthquakes: A Primer, 1977, Seismic Design, 1978, Wood-Detailing for Performance, 1990, Wood as a Building Material, 2d edit., 1991; contbr. articles and reports to profl. jours.; prin. works include expansion of Nuclear Weapons Tng. Facility at Lemoore Naval Air Sta., Calif., LASH Terminal Port Facility Archtl. Phase, San Francisco, Incline Village (Nev.) Country Club, 1365 Columbus Ave. Bldg., San Francisco, modernization Stanford Ct. Hotel, San Francisco; monument area constrn. several Calif. ceneteries. With U.S. Army, 1946-48. Recipient Cert. Honor Fedn. Archtl. Colls. Mex. Republic, 1984; named to Wisdom Hall of Fame; NSF grantee for investigative workshop project, San Diego, 1974-80. Fellow AIA (bd. dirs., 1966-71, treas. No. Calif. chpt. 1968-69, pres. 1971, nat. v.p., 1975-76, nat. pres. 1978, pres. Hawaii 1985); hon. fellow Royal Can. Inst. Architects, N.Z. Inst. Architects, Royal Australian Inst. Architects, La Societed de Arquitectos Mexicano; mem. Archtl. Secs. Assn. (hon.), Soc. Wood Sci. and Tech., Internat. Conf. Bldg. Ofcls. Home: 321 Wailupe Cir Honolulu HI 96821-1524 Office: 925 Bethel St Fl 5 Honolulu HI 96813-4393

BOTTEL, HELEN ALFEA, columnist, writer; b. Beaumont, Calif.; d. Alpheus Russell and Mary Ellen (Alexander) Brigden; m. Robert E. Bottel; children: Robert Dennis, Rodger M., R. Kathryn Bottel Bernhardt, Suzanne V. Bottel Peppers. AA, Riverside Coll. Calif.; student, Oreg. State U., 1958-59, So. Oreg. Coll., 1959. Writer, editor Illinois Valley News, Cave Junction, Oreg., 1950-56; writer Grants Pass (Oreg.) Courier, Portland Oregonian, Medford (Oreg.) Mail Tribune, 1952-58; daily columnist Helen Help Us and Generation Rap King Features Syndicate, N.Y.C., 1958-83, columnist (with Sue Bottel), 1969-83; adv. bd. Internat. Affairs Inst., N.Y.C., Tokyo, 1986—; freelance mag. writer, author, lectr., 1956—. Author: To Teens with Love, 1969, Helen Help Us, 1970, Parents Survival Kit, 1979; contbg. editor, columnist Real World mag., 1978-84; weekly columnist Yomiuri Shimbun, Tokyo, 1982-90; thrice weekly columnist Sacramento Union, 1986-88; newspaper and mag. columnist Look Who's Aging (with dau. Kathy Bernhardt), 1992-96; contbr. nonfiction to books and nat. mags. Staff mem. ACT Handicapped Children Games, Sacramento, 1986—; bd. dirs. Ill. Valley Med. Ctr., 1958-62, Childrens Ctr., Sacramento, 1969, Family Support Programs, Sacramento, 1991-95; active Grants Pass Br. Oreg. Juvenile Adv. Com., 1960-62, Nat. Spina Bifida Assn.; charter patron Cosumnes River Coll., Sacramento, 1972—; nat. adv. bd. Nat. Anorexic Aid Soc., 1977-83; scholarship com. judge Exec. Women Internat., 1985. Recipient Women's Svc. Cup Riverside Coll., citation for aid to U.s. servicemen in Vietnam Gov. Ga., 1967, Disting. Merit citation NCCJ, 1970, 1st place award for books Calif. Press Women, 1970, Sacramento Regional Arts Coun. Lit. Achievement award, 1974, Alumna of Yr. award Riverside Coll., 1987, Gold and Silver medals Calif. Sr. Games (tennis), 1990-91. Mem. Am. Soc. Journalists and Authors, Internat. Affairs Inst. Presbyterian. Clubs: Calif. Writers, Southgate Tennis. Home: 2060 56th Ave Sacramento CA 95822-4112

BOTTENBENDEV, BRAD JAMES, environmental safety and health administrator; b. Kalamazoo, Dec. 4, 1948; s. Don J. and Thelma Lu (Bacon) B.; m. Patricia Stahl Hubbell, June, 1992. BS, Western Mich. U., 1972; Cert. Hazardous Material Mgmt., U. Calif., Irvine, 1987; Cert. Environ. Auditing, Calif. State U., Long Beach, 1992. Cert. safety profl. of the Ams.; cert. hazardous materials mgr. Supr. mfg. Am. Cyanamid, Kalamazoo, 1973-77; supr. mfg. Productol Chem. div. Ferro Corp., Santa Fe Springs, Calif., 1977-79, environ. adminstr., 1979-80; sr. environ. engr. Ferro Corp., Los Angeles, 1980-87; mgr. environ. safety and indsl. hygiene dept. Composites divsn. Ferro Corp., Los Angeles, 1988-91, Structural Polymer Systems, Inc., Montedison, Calif., 1991-95; dir. environ. safety and health dept. Culver City (Calif.) Composites Corp., 1996-98; mgr. safety, health and environ. dept. Cyte Fiberite-Calif. Divsn., L.A., 1998—; bd. dirs., mem. adv. bd. safety and health extension program U. Calif. Irvine, 1985-91. Bd. dirs. adv. com. hazardous materials Community Right to Know, Culver City, Calif., 1987—; mem. Calif. Mus. Found., L.A., 1985-90, Mus. Contemporary Art, L.A., 1985—; founding sponsor Challenger Ctr. Mem. Am. Inst. Chem. Engrs., Nat. Assn. Environ. Mgmt., Acad. Cert. Hazardous Materials Mgrs., Suppliers of Advanced Composites Materials Assn. (mem. environ. health and safety com. 1989-92), Am. Indsl. Hygiene Assn., Am. Soc. Safety Engrs., Nat. Fire Protection Assn., Beta Beta Beta. Republican. Presbyterian. Avocations: camping, mountaineering, skiing, distance running, reading. Home: 215 Everett St Wrentham MA 02093 Office: Cytec Fiberite-Calif Divsn 5915 Rodeo Rd Los Angeles CA 90016-4312

BOTTI, RICHARD CHARLES, association executive; b. Brockton, Mass., May 1, 1939; s. Alfred Benecchi and Elizabeth Savini; stepson Ernest Botti; student Pierce Jr. Coll., 1959, Orange Coast Coll., 1964; m. Gwen Botti; children—Randolph K., Douglas S., Richard II. Pres., Legis. Info. Services Hawaii, Inc., Honolulu, 1971—; exec. dir., profl. lobbyist Hawaii Food Industry Assn., Honolulu, Hawaii Automotive & Retail Gasoline Dealers Assn., Inc., Honolulu, Hawaii Bus. League, Retail Liquor Dealers Assn. Hawaii, Liquor Dispensers of Hawaii, Hawaii Pubs. Assn., Automotive Body and Painting Assn.; gen. mgr. Hawaii Fashion Industry Assn. Mem. Food Industry Assn. Execs., Am. Soc. Assn. Execs., Aloha Soc. Assn. Execs. (dir. Hawaii Foodbank). Address: Legis Info Services 677 Ala Moana Blvd Ste 815 Honolulu HI 96813-5417

BOTTOMS, BILL, executive. CEO, chmn. Credence Systems Corp., Santa Clara, Calif. Office: 4950 Patrick Henry Dr Santa Clara CA 95054-1822*

BOTWINICK, MICHAEL, museum director; b. N.Y.C., Nov. 14, 1943; s. Joseph and Helen (Shlisky) B.; m. Harriet Maltzer, Aug. 14, 1965; children: Jonathan Seth, Daniel Judah. B.A., Rutgers Coll., 1964; M.A., Columbia U., 1967. Instr. Columbia U., N.Y.C., 1968-69, CCNY, CUNY, 1969; asst. curator medieval art Cloisters Met. Mus. Art, N.Y.C., 1969; asso. curator medieval art Cloisters Met. Mus. Art, 1970, asst. curator-in-chief, 1971—; asst. dir. art Phila. Mus. Art, 1971-74; dir. Bklyn. Mus., 1974-83, Corcoran Gallery Art, 1983-87; sr. v.p. Knoedler-Modarco, S.A., N.Y.C., 1987-88; pres. Fine Arts Group, Chgo., 1989-91; dir. Newport Harbor Art Mus., Newport Beach, Calif., 1991-97; dir. Ctr. Orange County Regional Studies U. Calif., Irvine, 1997—; pres. Cultural Instns. Group, 1975-76; mem. N.Y.C. Adv. Commn. Cultural Affairs, 1975-76, N.Y.C. Urban Design Coun., 1975; mem. adv. bd. WNET, N.Y.C., 1979-83; mem. Nat. Conservation Adv. Coun., 1979-80, exec. com. U.S. Com.-Internat. Coun. Mus., 1982-87, Yale U. Coun. Com. on the Art Gallery, 1983-88, Internat. Rsch. and Exch. Bd., fine arts com. German Dem. Republic, 1984-87, fine arts com. U.S. State Dept. Arts in Embassies Program, 1986-88; arts adminstrn. adv. com. U. Calif.-Irvine, 1993—. Mem. Assn. Art Mus. Dirs., Am. Assn. Museums, Coll. Art Assn., Steppenwolf Theater Co., Chgo. (bd. dirs. 1990-91). Office: U Calif PO Box 6050 Irvine CA 92616-6050

BOUCHARD, PAUL EUGENE, artist; b. Providence, Sept. 26, 1946; s. Marcel Paul and Anna Theresa (Dullea) B., m. Ann Marie Jones, Nov. 18, 1972 (div. 1977); 1 child Michael Paul; m. R. Jane Bouchard, Apr. 11, 1997. BFA, Calif. State U., Long Beach, 1978. bd. dir, Angeles Gate Cultural Ctr., San Pedro, Calif., 1983-85. One-man show at Rogue Coll., Grants Pass, Oreg., 1996, El Camino Coll., 1997, City of Carlsbad, Calif. 1998; exhibited in group shows at Rental Gallery, Oakland Mus., 1984, Rental Gallery, L.A. County Mus. of Art, 1985, Sixth St. Gallery, San Pedro, Calif., Aquarius Gallery, Cambria, Calif., 1986, St. Andrew's Priory, Valyermo, Calif., Riverside (Calif.) Art Mus., Rental Gallery, 1987, Vietnam Vet.'s Art Exhibit, 1988, Coos Art Mus., Coos Bay, Oreg., 1989, Grants Pass Mus. of Art, 1991, Eastern Wash. U., 1992, Dept. Vets. Affairs Hdqrs., Sydney, Australia, 1992-93, Australian Nat. Gallery, Brisbane County Hall Gallery, Nat. Vietnam Vets. Art Mus., Chgo., others. Recipient Contribution to the Arts, City of Torrance, Calif., 1985; grantee Franklin Furnace, N.Y.C., 1989-90, Artist Space, N.Y.C., 1989-90. Home and Studio: 30268 Mersey Ct Temecula CA 92591-3820

BOUKIDIS, CONSTANTINE MICHAEL, lawyer; b. Burbank, Calif., Nov. 16, 1959; s. Michael A. and Frances (Mavros) B.; m. Eugenia Demetra Rodinos, May 17, 1987; children: Michael Constantine, Frances Anastasia, Katherine Elizabeth, Evan Constantine. BA in Econs., Northwestern U., 1981; JD, Loyola Law Sch., L.A., 1984. Bar: Calif. 1985, U.S. Dist. Ct. (cen. dist.) Calif. 1985, U.S. Ct. Appeals (9th cir.), 1985. Investigator Harney & Moore, L.A., 1980-82; assoc. Law Offices of David M. Harney, L.A., 1985-92; pvt. practice, 1992—. Treas., chmn. cathedral planning com. St. Sophia Greek Orthodoc Cathedral Cmty., L.A., 1989, pres. cmty., 1994-96; apptd. St. Sophia Cathedral Found., asst. sec., 1997—; bd. dirs. Glendale (Calif.) YMCA, 1997—, Glendale Bar Assn. Lawyer Referral Svc., 1995—. Mem. ABA, Glendale Bar Assn., Phi Kappa Sigma (treas. 1980-81). Democrat. Avocations: golf, reading, travel. Home: 1641 Country Club Dr Glendale CA 91208-2038 Office: 144 N Glendale Ave Ste 101 Glendale CA 91206-4903

BOUKNIGHT, ROBERT MICHAEL, television executive; b. Columbia, S.C., Aug. 11, 1957; s. James Edward and Vanessa Ann (Dickert) B.; m. Leslie Ellen Suba, May 5, 1985; children: Shannon, Casey, Taylor. BA, UCLA, 1979. Writer, prodr. Showtime Network, N.Y.C., 1979-87; sr. v.p. Fox Broadcasting Co., L.A., 1987—. Recipient Gold medallion Broadcast Promotion & Mktg. Execs., 1991. Home: 25820 Vaquero Ct Valencia CA 91355-2119 Office: Fox Broadcasting Co 10201 W Pico Blvd Los Angeles CA 90064-2606

BOULDEN, JUDITH ANN, bankruptcy judge; b. Salt Lake City, Dec. 28, 1948; d. Douglas Lester and Emma Ruth (Robertson) Boulden; m. Alan Walter Barnes, Nov. 7, 1982; 1 child, Dorian Lisa. BA, U. Utah, 1971, JD, 1974. Bar: Utah 1974, U.S. Dist. Ct. Utah 1974. Law clk. to A. Sherman Christianson U.S. Cts., Salt Lake City, 1974; assoc. Roe & Fowler, Salt Lake City, 1975-81, McKay Burton Thurman & Condie, Salt Lake City, 1982-83; trustee Chpt. 7, Salt Lake City, 1976-82, Standing Chpt. 12, Salt Lake City, 1987-88, Standing Chpt. 13, Salt Lake City, 1979-88; sr. ptnr. Boulden & Gillman, Salt Lake City, 1983-88; U.S. Bankruptcy judge U.S. Cts., Salt Lake City, 1988—. Mem. Utah Bar Assn. Avocations: gardening, golf. *

BOULEY, JOSEPH RICHARD, pilot; b. Fukuoka, Japan, Jan. 7, 1955; came to U.S., 1955; s. Wilfrid Arthur and Minori Cecelia (Naraki) B.; m. Sara Elizabeth Caldwell, July 6, 1991; children: Denise Marie, Janice Elizabeth, Eleanor Catherine. BA in English, U. Nebr., 1977; MAS, Embry Riddle Aeronautical U., 1988. Commd. 2d lt. USAF, 1977; advanced through grades to lt. col. USAFR, 1998; F-117A Stealth Fighter pilot USAF, Persian Gulf, 1991; pilot United Airlines, 1992—. Ct. apptd. spl. advocate Office of Guardian Ad Litem, Salt Lake City, 1996—. Decorated Disting. Flying Cross, 4 Air medals, 3 Meritorious Svc. medals, 2 Aerial Achievement medals, Joint Svc. commendation medal, 3 Air Force Commendation medals, Air Force Achievement medal; recipient Alumni Achievement award U. Nebr., 1998. Mem. VFW, Am. Legion, Disting. Flying Cross Soc., Airline Pilots Assn., Red River Valley Fighter Pilots Assn., Aircraft Owners & Pilots Assn. Republican. Roman Catholic. Avocations: flying, golf, running, photography. Home: 1544 Emerson Ave Salt Lake City UT 84105-2728

BOULWARE, JAMES L., minister; b. Duncan, Okla., Feb. 5, 1921; s. John Lafayett and Opal (Sprouse) B.; m. Virginia Lou Hanson, Feb. 5, 1943; children: Jane Lee, Melody Ann. Grad., LIFE Bible Coll., L.A., 1944; BA in Religious Edn., Coll. of Rockies, 1960; MA in Communication, Assemblies of God Sem. Grad. Sch., 1976; PhD in N.T., Calif. Grad. Sch. Theol., 1983. Ordained to ministry Assemblies of God, 1945. Pastor Assemblies of God, Osawatomie and Hutchinson, Kans., 1944-58, Aurora, Colo., 1959-75; missionary Assemblies of God, Belgium, Fed. Republic Germany, Eng., 1976-80; prof. Am. Indian Bible Coll., Phoenix, 1981-83; pastor Assemblies of God, Montrose, Colo., 1984-86, 1st Assemblies of God Ch., Golden, Colo., 1989—; sectional yourth dir. Kans. Assemblies of God, Osawatomie, 1947-51; dist presbyter Kans. Assemblies of God, Hutchinson, 1954-58; exec. presbyter, asst. supt., men's dir. and missionary Rocky Mountain Dist., 1961-91. Co-founder Ministerial Fellowship, Aurora, Colo., 1960-75; chaplain CAP, Aurora, Denver, 1965-67; founded Aurora Christian Acad., 1965—; mem. Pres.'s Coun. Trinity Bible Coll., 1973-75; bd. dirs. Am. Indian Bible Coll., 1988—; civilian chaplain U.S. Army, Augsburgh, Fed. Republic Germany, 1976-79 (numerous awards). Office: Assemblies of God 16800 W 9th Ave Golden CO 80401-3755

BOUMANN, ROBERT LYLE, lawyer; b. Holdrege, Nebr., June 9, 1946; s. John G. (dec.) and Loretta M. (Eckhardt) B. BS, U. Nebr., 1968, JD, 1974. Bar: Nebr. 1974, Colo. 1987; CPA, Nebr. Sr. acct. Peat, Marwick, Main and Co., Denver, 1968-71; atty., asst. sec. K N Energy, Inc., Lakewood, Colo., 1974-96; pvt. practice Golden, Colo., 1996—; bd. dirs. Consolidated Motor Freight, Inc., Consolidated Cartage, Inc., G&H Transfer, Inc., CMF Rentals, LLC, all Hastings, Nebr. Treas. YMCA, Hastings, 1979-80. Mem. Nebr. Soc. CPAs, Nebr. State Bar Assn., Colo. State Bar Assn., ABA, Jaycees (treas. Hastings chpt. 1977-78), Phi Eta Sigma, Beta Gamma Sigma, Pi Kappa Alpha. Republican. Roman Catholic. Avocations: racquetball, golf. Office: 14118 W 1st Ave Golden CO 80401-5353

BOUQUIN, JAMES RICHARD, healthcare facility executive; b. Detroit, July 12, 1958; s. Richard Hughes and Elaine Grace (Lesniak) B.; m. Yvonne Mary Veronin, Aug. 2, 1992; children: Jevana, Samuel, Alyssa. BA, Stanford U., 1982. Asst. dean for campus affairs Stanford (Calif.) U., 1983-90; exec. dir. Eagle Lake Children's Charities, Sacramento, 1990-92; CEO Crisis Intervention, Walnut Creek, Calif., 1992-96, New Connections, Concord, Calif., 1996—. Mem. cmty. leadership bd. United Way, Concord, 1995—; pres. Inst. on Alcohol, Durgs and Disability, Palo, Alto, Calif.; bd. dirs. Recording for the Blind. Mem. Calif. Assn. Postsecondary Educators (pres.). Office: New Connections 1760 Clayton Rd Concord CA 94520-2700

BOURG, PAMELA WILKINSON, emergency nurse; b. New Orleans, Sept. 17, 1949; d. John Stephen and Melonie Louise (Costello) Wilkinson; m. Wilson Charles Bourg III, Dec. 17, 1971; children: Wilson Charles IV, Dominique, Noel. BSN, La. State U., New Orleans, 1971; MS, Boston U., 1975. RN; cert. adult nurse practitioner; cert. emergency nurse; cert. ACLS. Staff nurse emergency rm. Charity Hosp., New Orleans, 1971-73, Boston City Hosp., 1973-74, Univ. Hosp., Denver, 1976-77; head nurse-emergency U Colo. Med. Sch., Denver, 1977-78; asst. dir. nursing Denver Gen. Hosp., 1978-88, nursing supr., 1988-89; asst. clin. prof. U. Colo. Health Sci. Ctr., Denver, 1979—; med. office adminstr. Kaiser Permanente Health Plan, Denver, 1989-91, area adminstr., med. ctr. adminstr., 1991-96; clin. nurse splst. trauma svc. Centura St. Anthony Ctrl., Denver, 1996—; bd. dirs. Jefferson Ctr. Mental Health; nurse host Copper Mountain (Colo.) Ski Patrol, 1990—; emergency nurse cons. to pvt. attys. *Served on National level for Emergency Nurses Association. Extensively publishedin field of Emergency and Trauma Nursing.* Mem. Fitness Fair Bd., Our Lady of Fatima Sch., Lakewood, Colo., 1990-96; ameteur triathlete offical for USA Swimming. Mem. Emergency Nurses Assn., Sigma Theta Tau. Avocations: swimming, skiing, running, biking. Home: 10909 W 30th Ave Lakewood CO 80215-7300 Office: Centura St Anthony Hosp 4231 W 16th Ave Denver CO 80204-1335

BOURKE, LYLE JAMES, electronics company executive, small business owner; b. San Diego, May 28, 1963; s. Robert Victor and Virginia (Blackburn) B. Cert. in electronics, Southwestern Coll., San Diego, 1984; cert. in microelectronics, Burr Brown, Miramar, Calif., 1985; student, NACS, Scranton, Pa., 1988; AA in Econs., Cuyamaca Coll., 1991, postgrad., 1991-92; student, Wendelstedt Umpire Sch., 1992-93. Counselor Dept. Parks and Recreation City of Imperial Beach, Calif., 1979-80; warehouse worker Seafood Cannery, Cordova, Alaska, 1981, Nat. Beef Packing, Liberal, Kans., 1983; night mgr. Southland Corp., San Diego, 1983-85; tech. developer Unisys Corp., San Diego, 1985-92; process technician Ben & Jerry's Homemade, Inc., Springfield, Vt., 1994-95; technician Laser Power Corp, San Diego, Calif., 1996-98; founder Sparrells Ltd., 1992; instr. Harmonium Enrichment Program, 1993. Editor (handbook) College Policies, 1991; contbr. Cleanrooms mag., 1992; inventor Jacuzzi pillow, no-sit snowboard bindings. Vol. United Way, San Diego, 1987—; donor Imperial Beach Boys and Girls Club, 1988-98, Cal Farley's Boys Ranch, 1985-93, Assn. Handicapped Artists, 1988—, San Diego Jr. Theatre, 1992, Cabrillo Elem. Sch. Found., 1992. Chulsa Vista Lit. Team, 1996-99. Named Most Valuable Player Mex. Amateur Baseball League, San Diego-Tijuana, 1990. Mem. Am. Assn. Ret. Persons, Am. Mgmt. Assn. (charter), Prognosticators Club. Democrat. Avocation: computer tech., writing, Olympics. Office: Unisys 8011 Fairview Ave La Mesa CA 91941-6416

BOURLAND, ROGER, music educator, composer; b. Evanston, Ill., Dec. 13, 1952; s. James Roger and JoAnn (Rhodes) B.; life ptnr. Daniel Marc Gatan Shiplacoff. BM, U. Wis., 1976; MM, New Eng. Conservatory, 1978; AM, Harvard U., 1981, PhD, 1983. Prof. dept. music UCLA, 1983—; publ. Yelton Rhodes Music, L.A., 1994—. Composer: Seven Pollock Paintiings (Koussevitzky award 1978), Dickinson Madrigals, Hidden Legacies. Founding mem. Composers in Red Sneakers, Boston, 1980-83; chmn. bd. Gay Mens Chorus of L.A., 1994-96. Meet the Composer Grants, 1979-98; John Knowles Paine Travelling fellow Harvard U., 1981; recipient Young Composer award ASCAP, 1980, 82. Democrat. Avocations: comparative religion, bicycling, birds, internet publishing. Office: UCLA Dept Music 405 Hilgard Ave Los Angeles CA 90095-9000

BOURQUE, LINDA ANNE BROOKOVER, public health educator; b. Indpls., Aug. 25, 1941; d. Wilbur Bone and Edna Mae (Eberhart) Brookover; m. Don Philippe Bourque, June 3, 1966 (div. Nov. 1974). BA, Ind. U., 1963; MA, Duke U., 1964, PhD, 1968. Postdoctoral researcher Duke U., Durham, N.C., 1968-69; asst. prof. sociology Calif. State U., Los Angeles, 1969-72; asst. prof. to assoc. prof. pub. health UCLA, 1972-86, prof. pub. health, 1986—, acting assoc. dir. Inst. for Social Sci. Research, 1981-82, vice chair dept. community health scis., 1991-94. Author: Defining Rape, 1989, (with Virginia Clark) Processing Data: The Survey Example, 1992, (with Eve Fielder) How to Conduct Self-Administered and Mail Surveys, 1995; contbr. articles to profl. jours. Violoncellist with Santa Monica (Calif.) Symphony Orch., 1978—, Los Angeles Doctors' Symphony, 1981—. Mem. AAAS, Am. Sociol. Assn. (mem. med. sociology sect. council 1975-78, co-chmn. com. freedom research and teaching, 1975-78, cert. recognition 1980), Pacific Sociol. Assn. (co-chmn. program com. 1982, v.p. 1983), Am. Pub. Health Assn. (mem. standing com. on status of women 1974-76), Sociologists for Women in Society, Am. Assn. Pub. Opinion Rsch., Assn. Rsch. in Vision and Ophthalmology, Delta Omega, Phi Alpha Theta. Avocation: playing the violoncello. Office: UCLA Sch Pub Health PO Box 957220 Los Angeles CA 90095-7220

BOUSFIELD, EDWARD LLOYD, biologist; b. Penticton, B.C., Can., June 19, 1926; s. Reginald H. and Marjory F. (Armstrong) B.; m. Barbara Joyce, June 20, 1953 (dec. Apr. 1983); children: Marjorie Anne, Jessie Katherine, Mary Elizabeth, Kenneth Lloyd; m. Joyce Burton, Feb. 11, 1994. BA, U. Toronto, 1948, MA, 1948; PhD, Harvard U., 1954. Invertebrate zoologist Nat. Mus. of Natural Sci., Ottawa, Ont., Can., 1950-64, chief zoologist, 1964-74, sr. scientist, 1974-86; curator emeritus Nat. Mus. of Natural Sci., Ottawa, 1986-90; rsch. assoc. Royal Ont. Mus., Toronto, 1984—, Royal B.C. Mus., Victoria, 1990-95. Author: Canadian Atlantic Sea Shells, 1960, Shallow-water Gammaridean Amphipoda of New England, 1973, History of the Canadian Society of Zoologists: The First Decade, 1974, Cadborosaurus, Survivor from the Deep, 1995; mng. editor: Amphipacifica, 1994-98; contbr. articles to profl. jours. Recipient Outstanding Achievement award Civil Service Can., 1985. Fellow Royal Soc. Can.; mem. Ottawa Field Naturalists Club (hon., pres. 1959-61), Can. Soc. Zoologists (hon., pres. 1979-80, archivist 1971-91, hon. mem. 1993—), Crustacean Soc., New Eng. Estuarine Rsch. Soc., RA Curling Club (pres. 1972-73) (Ottawa), Victoria Curling Club, Highland Park Lawn Bowling Club (pres. 1978-79, 89-90), Victoria Lawn Bowling Club, Sigma Xi. Mem. Reform Party Can. Avocations: musical instruments (Victoria Melody Makers Orch.), lawn bowling, curling. E-mail: elbousf@islandnet.com. Home: 611-548 Dallas Rd, Victoria, BC Canada V8V 1B3

BOUSHEY, DAVID L., stunt coordinator, fight master, educator; b. Everett, Wash., July 22, 1942; s. Kelly W. and Frances A. (Thomason) B.; m. Carmen Dobson, July 1, 1972; 1 child, Ian; m. Kathleen M. Reilly, July 15, 1988; 1 child, Brittany. BA, Ctrl. Wash. State U., 1969; BFA, East 15 Acting Acad., London, 1974. Fight dir. theatre industry USA, 1974—; instr. U. Wash., Seattle, 1974—, Cornish Coll. of Arts, Seattle, 1977-85, Soc. Am. Fight Dirs., Las Vegas, 1980—; stunt coord. film industry USA, 1980—; instr. United Stuntmens Assn., Seattle, 1985—. Prod. (video series) The Fight Master, 1977—. Inducted into Hollywood Stuntmen's Hall of Fame, 1993. Mem. Soc. Am. Fight Dirs. (founder, past pres., Fight Master 1998), United Stuntmen's Assn. (pres. 1985), Screen Actors Guild (regional coun. 1997). Avocation: sailing. Home: 2723 Saratoga Ln Everett WA 98203-1425

BOUVIER, MARSHALL ANDRE, lawyer; b. Jacksonville, Fla., Sept. 30, 1923; s. Marshall and Helen Marion B.; m. Zepha Windle, July 11, 1938; children: Michael A., Debra Bouvier Williams, Mark A., Marshall André III, Suzanne, John A. (dec.), Wendy Bouvier Clark, Jennifer Lynn. AB, Emory U., LLB, 1949. Bar: Ga. 1948, Nev. 1960. Commd. USN, 1949; naval aviator, judge advocate; ret., 1959; atty. State of Nevada, 1959-60; pvt. practice, Reno, 1960-82, 88—; dist. atty. County of Storey, Nev., 1982-88, spl. cons. to Nev. Dist. Attys., 1991-95; pres., CEO A.G.E. Corp., 1997—. Mem. Judge Advocates Assn., Am. Bd. Hypnotherapy, Ancient and Honorable Order Quiet Birdmen, Rotary, E Clampus Vitus, Phi Delta Phi, Sigma Chi.

BOVEN, DOUGLAS GEORGE, lawyer; b. Holland, Mich., Aug. 11, 1943. BSE, U. Mich., 1966, JD, 1969. Bar: Calif. 1970. Dir. Crosby, Heafy, Roach & May PC, San Francisco, 1989—; arbitrator Fed. and Superior Ct. Panel of Arbitrators, 1980—; panelist Superior Ct. Early Settlement Program, 1987. Mem. ABA (mem. bus. bankruptcy, Chpt. 11 and secured creditors coms.), Am. Bankruptcy Inst., Comml. Law League Am., State Bar Calif. (insolvency law and real estate sects.), Alameda County Bar Assn., Sonoma County Bar Assn., Bay Area Bankruptcy Forum, Bar Assn. San Francisco (comml. law and bankruptcy sect., mem. arbitrator fee disputes com. 1973—), Tau Beta Pi. Office: Crosby Heafey Roach & May PC 1999 Harrison St Oakland CA 94612

BOVEY, TERRY ROBINSON, insurance executive; b. Oregon, Ill., May 13, 1948; s. John Franklin and Frances (Robinson) B.; m. Diana Carmen Rodriguez, Aug. 29, 1970 (div. 1980); 1 child, Joshua; m. Kathy Jo Johnston, Sept. 14, 1985; children: Courtney, Taylor. Student, Ariz. Western Coll., 1966-68, Grand Canyon Coll., 1968-69; BBA, U. Ariz., 1972. Salesman All-Am. Dist. Co., Yuma, Ariz., 1972-76; dist. asst. mgr. Equitable

Life Ins., Yuma, 1976-81; gen. sales mgr. Ins. Counselors, Yuma, 1981-83; mng. gen. agt. First Capital Life Ins. Co., Ariz., Calif., Nev., N.C., 1983-90; master gen. agt. Comml. Union Life Ins. Co., Tucson, 1990—; regional commr. Ariz. Interscholastic Assn., Yuma, 1972-88; umpire Nat. League, Major League Baseball, 1979, 95, crew chief, 95, Nat. League playoffs, 1984, baseball supr. Ariz. C.C. Athletic Conf., 1992-97. mem. Century Club, Boy's Club of Yuma. Mem. Million Dollar Round Table, Nat. Assn. Life Underwriters (numerous sales achievement awards, Nat. Quality awards), Life Underwriters Polit. Action Com., Tucson City Assn. Republican. Presbyterian.

BOVITZ, CAROLE JONES, psychotherapist; b. Tulsa, July 9, 1936; d. John Wesley Jones and Vada L. (Dailey) Friesen; m. Richard Stanley Bovitz, May 28, 1959; children: J. Scott, Jennifer Jean. BA in Psychology, Calif. State U., Northridge, 1969; MA in Psychology, Pepperdine U., 1982. Lic. marriage, family, child therapist; cert. employee assistance profl. Ptnr. Personnel Research Assocs., Chatsworth, Calif., 1979-82; pres. Carole Bovitz & Assocs., Huntington Beach and Torrance, Calif., 1982-88; provider rels. mgr. Personal Performance Consultants Inc., Irvine, Calif., 1988-92; pvt. practice Long Beach and Cerritos, Calif., 1992—; dir. presenting services Am. Bus. Concepts, Torrance, 1986-87; seminar cons., trainer Children's Hosp., Orange, Calif., 1986-87; cons. mgmt. seminars C. of C., Riviera Village Assocs., Redondo Beach, Calif., 1988. Pres. Calif. Legis. Roundtable, Sacramento, 1985-86; trustee governing bd. Sch. Dist., Goleta, Calif., 1976; bd. dirs. Calif. Ednl. Congress, Sacramento, 1984-86, Calif. Coalition Fair Sch. Fin., 1984-86. Mem. AAUW (vol. community leadership trainer 1985-88, state pres. 1984-86, state rep. to nat. bd. dirs. 1978-82, state dir. leadership 1988-89, pres. Orange County interbr. council pres.'s 1987-88, Calif. state fellowship endowment named in her honor 1986 in perpetuity, research grant named in her honor 1986 in perpetuity, gift honoree local chpts. 1976, 86, 94), Calif. Assn. Marriage and Family Therapists. Democrat. Avocations: movies, traveling, reading. Office: 10929 South St Ste 103B Cerritos CA 90703-5351

BOW, STEPHEN TYLER, JR., insurance and computer industry consultant; b. Bow, Ky., Oct. 20, 1931; s. Stephen Tyler Sr. and Mary L. (King) B.; m. Kathy O'Connor, July, 1982; children: Jerry, Jon; children by previous marriage: Sandra Bow Morris, Deborah Bow Goodin, Carol, Clara. BA in Sociology, Berea (Ky.) Coll., 1953; grad. exec. program bus. adminstrn., Columbia U., 1976. CLU. With Met. Life Ins. Co., 1953-74, 76-89; agt. Lexington, Ky., 1953-55; sales mgr. Birmingham, Ala., 1955-58, field tng. cons., 1958-59; territorial field supr., 1959-60; dist. sales mgr. Frankfort, 1960-64, Lexington, 1964-66; exec. asst. field tng. N.Y.C., 1966-67; regional sales mgr. North Jersey, 1967-72; agy. v.p., officer-in-charge Can. hdqrs., 1972-74; exec. v.p., chmn., chief exec. officer Capital Holding Corp., Louisville, 1974-76; officer-in-charge Midwestern hdqrs. Met. Life Ins. Co., Dayton, 1976-83, sr. v.p., officer-in-charge Western Hdqrs., 1983-89; chmn., CEO Southeastern Group, Inc., Louisville, 1993-94; pres., CEO Anthem Life of Ind., Indpls., 1993-95; chmn., CEO Anthem Life Ins. Cos., 1995-96; exec. v.p. Assoc. Ins. Cos., Inc., Indpls., 1993-96; chmn. Acordia of San Francisco, 1993-96; pres., CEO Delta Dental Ky., Louisville, 1989-94, Blue Cross and Blue Shield Ky., Louisville, 1989-93; vice chmn. DeHayes Group, 1996—; pres. Steve Bow and Assocs., Inc., 1996—; chmn. Victory Tech., Inc., 1998—; past chmn. Dayton Power and Light Audit Com. Past bd. dirs. San Francisco Visitors and Conv. Bur., 1985-87, Ind. Coll. of No. Calif., Bay Area Coun., Lindsey Wilson Coll.; bd. dirs. Bay Area Boy Scouts Am., Bay Area Council, U. San Francisco; mem. adv. bd. Hugh O'Brian Youth Found.; bd. dirs. Calif. Legis. Adv. Commn. on Life and Health Ins., Metro United Way, Ky. Health Care Access Found., Greater Louisville Econ. Devel. Coun., Leadership Ky., Greater Louisville Fund for the Arts; mem. corp. council San Francisco UN Assn.; mem. bd. dirs. Ky. Home Mut., Ky. Forward, Asian Bus. League, McLaren Coll. of Bus.; past mem. San Francisco Pvt. Industry Council; past chmn. United Negro Coll. Fund of San Francisco, 1985-86; mem. exec. com. bd. dirs., v.p. county ops. United Way of San Francisco Bay Area, 1985-87; vol. chmn. U.S. Savs. Bond Campaign, Bay Area, 1987; trustee Ky. Ind. Coll. Fund, Berea Coll.; bd. dirs. Boy Scouts Am., My Old Ky. Home Coun. Recipient Outstanding Sales Mgmt. award N.Y. Sales Congress, 1972, Frederick D. Patterson award United Negro Coll. Fund San Francisco, 1986, Outstanding County Ops. Vol. award United Way of Bay Area, 1987, Bus. Appreciation award Jeffersontown, Ky. C. of C., 1993, Pres.'s award, 1993, Leadership award Internat. Women's Forum, Washington, 1993; named Citizen of Yr. Wright State U. Med. Sch., Dayton, 1982. Mem. Nat. Assn. Life Underwriters, Gen. Agts. and Mgrs. Assn., Calif. Bus. Roundtable, Nat. Assn. Corp. Dirs. (founder, former pres.), Calif. C. of C. (bd. dirs.), Ky. C. of C., Ky. Home Life Exec. Com., Am. Cancer Soc. Republican. Methodist. Club: Lincoln of Northern Calif.; San Francisco Bankers. Avocations: golf, oil painting, reading. Home: 20 Grand Miramar Dr Henderson NV 89011-2202 Office: 772 W Napa St Sonoma CA 95476-6452

BOWE, ROGER LEE, small business owner; b. Pueblo, Colo., Aug. 30, 1954; s. William Roy and Ruth Ann (Penn) B.; 1 child, Patrick William; m. Wendy C. Kempf, June 5, 1981. Grad. high sch., Denver. Mechanic Crest Motors, Denver, 1970-74; svc. mgr. Grand Prix Imports, Denver, 1974-76; line tech. Kerlin & Son, Denver, 1976-80; owner, operator Wheels of Fortune, Inc., Littleton, Colo., 1981—. Past mem. Vat. Fedn. Ind. Bus., 1988. Mem. Z Car Club Colo. (tech. advisor), Better Bus. Bur. Avocations: boating, bicycling, collecting classic records, creating modern art from auto parts, scuba diving. Office: Wheels of Fortune Inc 2659 1/2 W Main St Littleton CO 80120-1914

BOWEN, CLOTILDE MARION DENT, retired army officer, psychiatrist; b. Chgo., Mar. 20, 1923; d. William Marion Dent and Clotilde (Tynes) D.; m. William N. Bowen, Dec. 29, 1945 (dec.). *Dr. Bowen's paternal grandfather, Thomas Marshall Dent, was born on a Georgia plantation, graduated from Atlanta University and Howard University Law, and was employed at U.S. Commerce Department for 50 years. His son, William Marion, graduated from Dartmouth College in 1913, on a Latin and Greek scholarship. He was the first accountant for the Supreme Liberty Life Insurance Company, Chicago. Uncle Francis M. graduated Amherst, with a law degree from Howard University. Uncle Thomas M. (Jr.) graduated Howard University, and during WWI, he received a battlefield promotion to Captain for bravery in 1918. Dr. Bowen's mother, Clotilde (Tynes), was a fashion designer and business owner in Chicago. Dr. Bowen was raised in Columbus by her aunt Maude (Tynes) and 1st Lt. Stephen Brady Barrows.* BA, Ohio State U., 1943, MD, 1947. Intern Harlem Hosp., N.Y.C., 1947-48; resident and fellow in pulmonary diseases Triboro Hosp., Jamaica, L.I., 1948-50; resident in psychiatry VA Hosp., Albany N.Y., 1959-62; asst. resident in psychiatry Albany Med. Ctr. Hosp., 1961-62; pvt. practice N.Y.C., 1950-55; chief pulmonary disease clinic N.Y.C., 1950-55; asst. chief pulmonary disease svc. Valley Forge Army Hosp., Pa., 1956-59; chief psychiatry VA Hosp., Roseburg, Oreg., 1962-66, acting chief of staff, 1964-66; ast. chief neurology and psychiatry Tripler Gen. Hosp., Hawaii, 1966-68; psychiatr. lcons. and dir. Rev. Br. Office Civil Health and Med. Program Uniform Svcs., 1968-70; commd. capt. U.S. Army, 1955, advanced through ranks to col., 1968; neuropsychiat. cons. U.S. Army, Vietnam, 1970-71; chief dept. psychiatry Fitzsimons Army Med. Ctr. U.S. Army, 1971-74, chief dept. psychiatry Tripler Army Med. Ctr., 1974-75; assoc. clin. prof. psychiatry U. Hawaii, 1974-75; comdr. Hawley Army Clin. U.S. Army, Ft. Benjamin, Harrison, Ind., 1977-78; chief dept. primary care and cmty. medicine U.S. Army, 1978-83, chief psychiat. consultation svc. Fitzsimons Army Med. Ctr., 1983-85; chief psychiatry svc. med./regional office ctr. VA, Chyenne, Wyo., 1987-90; staff psychiatrist Denver VA Satellite Clin., Colorado Springs, Colo., 1990-96; ret., 1996; Locum Tenens practice psychiatry, 1996—; surveyor Joint Commn. on Accreditation Healthcare Orgns., 1985-92; assoc. prof. psychiatary U. Colo. Med. Ctr., Denver, 1971—. Decorated Legion of Merit, several other medals; recipient Colo. Disabled Am. Vets. award, 1994-95, Pres.'s 300 Commencement award Ohio State U., 1987, Profl. Achievement award Ohio State U. Alumni Assn., 1998. Fellow Am. Psychiat. Assn. (life), Acad. Psychosomatic Medicine; mem. AMA, Nat. Med. Assn., Menninger Found (charter), Ctrl. Neuropsychiatric Assn. (councilor at-large). Home: 1020 Tarl Dr Colorado Springs CO 80921-2257

BOWEN, PETER GEOFFREY, arbitrator, investment advisor, business management educator; b. Iowa City, Iowa, July 10, 1939; s. Howard Rothmann and Lois Berntine (Schilling) B.; m. Shirley Johns Carlson, Sept. 11, 1960; [illegible] Boone Johns. BA in Govt. and Econs., Lawrence Coll., 1960; postgrad. U. Wis., 1960-61, U. Denver. cert. expert witness, Denver Dist. Ct., 1987. Dir. devel. Mobile Home Communities, Denver, 1969-71; v.p. Perry & Butler, Denver, 1972-73; exec. v.p., dir. Little & Co., Denver, 1973; pres. Builders Agy. Ltd., Denver, 1974-75; pres. The Investment Mgmt. Group Ltd., Denver, 1975-87; independent investor, writer, Vail, Colo., 1987—; arbitrator NASD Regulation, Inc., 1996—, Am. Arbitration Assn., 1996—; gen. ptnr. real estate ltd. ptnrships.; bus. faculty mem. Colo. Mt. Coll., 1994—; continuing legal edn. lectr. on real estate syndications, 1983. Contbr. articles to profl. publs. Mem. Colo. Coun. Econ. Devel., 1964-68; vice-chmn. Greenwood Village (Colo.) Planning and Zoning Commn., 1983-85; mem. Vail Planning and Environ. Commn., 1992-96; dir. Vail Partnership Environ. Edn. Programs, Inc., 1993—; elected mem. City Council Greenwood Village, 1985-86, also mayor pro tem, 1985-86; trustee Vail Mountain Sch. Found., 1987-88; bd. dirs. Colo. Plan for Apportionment, 1966; speaker Forward Metro Denver, 1966-67. Mem. Rotary Club (bd. dirs. Vail chpt., named Rotarian of Yr. 1992), Lawrence U. Alumni Assn. (bd. dirs. 1966-72, 82-86). Home: 4950 S Beeler St Greenwood Village CO 80111-1312

BOWEN, RICHARD LEE, academic administrator, political science educator; b. Avoca, Iowa, Aug. 31, 1933; s. Howard L. and Donna (Milburn) B.; m. Connie Smith Bowen, 1976; children: James, Robert, Elizabeth, Christopher; children by previous marriage—Catherine, David, Thomas. B.A., Augustana Coll., 1957; M.A., Harvard, 1959, Ph.D., 1967. Fgn. service officer State Dept., 1959-60; research asst. to U.S. Senator Francis Case, 1960-62; legis. asst. to U.S. Senator Karl Mundt, 1962-65; minority cons. sub-com. exec. reorgn. U.S. Senate, 1966-67; asst. to pres., assoc. prof. polit. sci. U. S.D., Vermillion, 1967-69, pres., 1969-76; pres. Dakota State Coll., Madison, 1973-76; commr. higher edn. Bd. Regents State S.D., Pierre, 1976-80; Disting prof. polit. sci. U. S.D., 1980-85; pres. Idaho State U., Pocatello, 1985—. Served with USN, 1951-54. Recipient Outstanding Alumnus award Augustana Coll., 1970; Woodrow Wilson fellow, 1957, Congl. Staff fellow, 1965; Fulbright scholar, 1957. Office: Idaho State U Office of Pres Campus Box 8310 Pocatello ID 83209-0009

BOWEN-FORBES, JORGE COURTNEY, artist, author, poet; b. Queenstown, Guyana, May 16, 1937; came to U.S., 1966; s. Walter and Margarita V. (Forbes) Bowen. BA, Queens Coll., Eve Leary, Guyana, 1969; MFA, Chelsea (Eng.) Sch. Design, 1972. Comml. artist Guyana Litographic, Georgetown; art dir. Corbin Advt. Agy., Bridgetown, Barbados; tech. advisor Ministry of Info. and Culture, Georgetown; nat. juror Nat. Arts Club, N.Y.C., 1985, Nat. Soc. Painters in Casein and Acrylic. Major exhbns. include Expo 67, Can., Nat. Acad. Design, N.Y., Frye Mus., El Paso (Tex.) Mus., Wichita (Kans.) Centennial, Caribbean Festival of the Arts, Newark Mus.; 10-one-man exhbns. worldwide; works in collections including Nat. and Colgrain Collections, Guyana, El Paso Mus. Art, Kindercare Internat., Leon Loards Gallery, The McCreery Cummings Fine Art Collection, Bomani Gallery, San Francisco; poetry and articles pub. various jours.; author: Best Watercolors, 1996, Creative Watercolor, 1996; published in Best in Watercolor, Best in Oil Painting, Best in Acrylic Painting, Creative Watercolor, Splash 11, Best Contemporary Watercolors, American Poetry Annual. Recipient Silver medal of honor Allied Artists of N.Y., 1978, Gold medal of honor, 1975. Mem. Nat. Watercolor Soc. (signature mem.), Nat. Soc. Painters in Casein and Acrylics, Audubon Artists, Knickerbocker Artists (Gold Medal of Honor 1977, 79), Am. Watercolor Soc. (signature mem., High Winds medal 1984).

BOWER, DONALD EDWARD, author; b. Lockport, N.Y., July 19, 1920. BA, U. Nebr., 1942. D.E. Bower & Co., Inc., Denver, 1945-60; editor, pub. Arapahoe Tribune, 1960-62; editor Adams County Almanac, Adams County Dispatch, Jefferson County Herald, 1962-65; freelance staff Writer Fawcett Publs., 1962-64, lit. cons., 1962-67; editor, pub. Buyer's Showcase mag. and FURN Club News 1965-66; exec. editor Colo. mag., 1966-69; editor-in-chief, v.p., dir. Am. West Pub. Co., editor Am. West mag., 1970-74; pres. Colo. Authors League, 1975-76; dir. Nat. Writers Club, Denver, 1974-86; dir. Assoc. Bus. Writers Am., 1978-86, also pres. Assn. Hdqrs., 1978-86; editorial dir. Nat. Writers Press, 1982-86; lit. agent Don Bower Lit. Agy., 1991—. Author: Roaming the American West, 1970; Ghost Towns and Back Roads, 1972; intro. to The Magnificent Rockies, 1972; Fred Rosenstock: A Legend in Books and Art, 1976; The Professional Writers' Guide, 1984, rev. edition, 1990;Ten Keys to Writing Success, 1987, Sex and Espionage, 1990; also 4 paperback detective novels, 1960-64; editor: Living Water, Living Earth, 1971; Anasazi: Ancient People of the Rock, 1973; The Great Southwest, 1972; Edge of a Continent, 1970; The Mighty Sierra, 1972; The Magnificent Rockies, 1972; The Great Northwest, 1973; Gold and Silver in the West, 1973; Steinbeck Country, 1973; contbr. Western Writers Handbook, 1988, articles to mags. Mem. Authors Guild Am., Western Writers Assn. Am., Friends of Denver Pub. Libr., Sigma Delta Chi. Office: 3082 S Wheeling Way Apt 209 Aurora CO 80014-5611

BOWER, JANET ESTHER, writer, educator; b. National City, Calif., Apr. 14, 1943; d. Murvel and Esther Eva (Clark) Newlan; m. Robert S. Bower Jr., Nov. 23, 1968; children: Llance Clark, Esther Elizabeth. BA in History and Psychology, Calif. Western U., San Diego, 1965; MA in History, UCLA, 1966; MA in Edn., U.S. Internat. U., San Diego, 1970. Std. jr. coll. credential, elem. credential, Calif. Instr., mem. adj. faculty San Diego C.C. Dist., 1969—, Grossmont/Cuyamaca Coll. Dist., El Cajon, Calif., 1973, 97—, Palomar Coll. Dist., San Marcos, Calif., 1993, 97—, Midlands Tech. Coll., Columbia, S.C., 1995-96. Contbg. author: Women in the Biological Sciences, 1997; contbr. articles to periodicals; editor Friends of the Internat. Ctr. Newsletter, U. Calif., San Diego, 1984-85. Bd. dirs. Women of St. Paul's Episcopal Ch., San Diego, 1983-86, Oceanids, U. Calif., San Diego, 1980-85. Grantee U.S. Dept. Edn., 1968-69. Mem. Am. Hist. Assn., Calif. Hist. Soc., Project Wildlife (hon. life mem.). Republican. Avocations: cooking, travel.

BOWES, FLORENCE (MRS. WILLIAM DAVID BOWES), writer; b. Salt Lake City, Nov. 19, 1925; d. John Albreckt Elias and Alma Wilhelmina (Jonasson) Norborg; student U. Utah, 1941-42, Columbia, 1945-46, N.Y. U., 1954-55; grad. N.Y. TV Workshop, 1950; m. Samuel Ellis Levine, July 15, 1944 (dec. July 1953); m. William David Bowes, Mar. 15, 1958 (dec. 1976); 1 son, Alan Richard. Actress, writer Hearst Radio Network, WINS, N.Y.C., 1944-45; personnel and adminstrv. exec. Mut. Broadcasting System, N.Y.C., 1946-49, free-lance editor, writer, 1948-49; freelance writer NBC and ABC, 1949-53; script editor, writer Robert A. Monroe Prodns., N.Y.C., Hollywood, Calif., 1953-56; script and comml. dir. KUTV-TV, Salt Lake City, 1956-58; spl. editor, writer pub. relations dept. U. Utah, Salt Lake City, 1966-68, editor, writer U. Utah Rev., 1968-75; author: Web of Solitude, 1979; The MacOrvan Curse, 1980; Interlude in Venice, 1981; Beauchamp, 1983. Mem. Beta Sigma Phi. Home: 338 K St Salt Lake City UT 84103-3562

BOWIE, GEORGE HENRY, university official, public relations consultant; b. Aberdeen, Scotland, Nov. 25, 1945; came to U.S., 1971; s. Joseph and Florence (Patterson) B.; m. Lorna A. Andrew, June 15, 1968; children—Mark George, Lisa Ann. BA, Brigham Young U., 1976, MA, 1990. Income tax officer Inland Revenue Service, Aberdeen, Scotland, 1962-67; officer Aberdeen City Police, 1967-71; dir. pub. affairs Brigham Young U., 1976-82, mng. dir. pub. relations, 1982-85; exec. dir. pub. affairs, 1985-92, asst. advancment v.p., 1992—; ptnr. Darais, Bowie & McIlroy, Provo, 1983-85. Bd. dirs. Utah Valley Indsl. Devel. Assn., Provo, 1976-79; v.p. pub. relations United Way of Utah County, Provo, 1984. Recipient Outstanding Achievement award Utah Valley Indsl. Devel. Assn., 1977, 78; Exec. of Yr. award Profl. Secs. Internat., 1983. Mem. Pub. Relations Soc. Am. (accredited Silver Anvil award 1987), Internat. Pub. Relations Assn., Council for Advancement and Support of Edn., Provo Area C. of C. (bd. dirs. 1985-88); Provo/Orem C. of C. (chmn. bd.). Mem. Ch. of Jesus Christ of Latter-day Saints. Home: 2254 N 390 E Provo UT 84604-1785 Office: Brigham Young Univ Office Alumni House Provo UT 84602

BOWKETT, GERALD EDSON, editorial consultant, writer; b. Sacramento, Sept. 6, 1926; s. Harry Stephen and Jessie (Fairbrother) B.; m. Norma Orel Swain, Jan. 1, 1953; children: Amanda Allyn, Laura Anne. B.A., San Francisco State Coll., 1952; postgrad., Georgetown U., 1954. Radio wire editor UP, Washington, 1956-57; reporter, columnist Anchorage Daily Times, 1957-64; spl. asst., press sec. to Gov. William A. Egan, 1964-66; pub. Alaska Newsletter, 1966-68; Juneau bur. chief Anchorage Daily News, 1967-68, editor S.E. Alaska Empire, Juneau, 1969-71; dir. info. svcs. U. Alaska, 1971-82; prof. English Shanghai Inst. of Tourism, 1992-93. Author: Reaching for a Star: The Final Campaign for Alaska Statehood, 1989. Served with USMC, 1944-46, PTO. Cited for outstanding news and feature writing, editorial works Alaska Press Club. Mem. Alpha Phi Gamma. Home and Office: 14604 W Horizon Dr Sun City West AZ 85375-2764

BOWLAN, NANCY LYNN, elementary and secondary school educator; b. Walla Walla, Wash., Jan. 16, 1946; d. Ralph Reighard and Irene Elizabeth (Fisher) Nowlen; m. Buel Nathan Bowlan; children: Ronald, Sarah, Sandra, Michelle, John. BA, Ariz. State U., 1968. Cert. reading specialist. Tchr. Seligman (Ariz.) Schs., 1968-71, Page (Ariz.) Schs., 1976-87; tchr., ESL coord. Gila Bend (Ariz.) Schs., 1988-94; tchr. Tucson Unified Sch. Dist., Tucson, 1994—. Leader Girl Scouts Am., Page, Ariz., 1974-75. Mem. Delta Kappa Gamma (chmn. state fin. com. Ariz. 1987—, Alpha Zeta chpt. Casa Grande, Ariz. 1993, treas. Tau chpt., Flagstaff, Ariz. 1992, Lambda chpt., Tucson, 1995—), Ea. Star (Worthy Matron 1990). Republican. Avocations: auto rec. driving, computers, planting, reading. Home: 112 N Players Club Dr Tucson AZ 85745-8916

BOWLEN, PATRICK DENNIS, holding company executive, lawyer, professional sports team executive; b. Prairie du Chien, Wis., Feb. 18, 1944; s. Paul Dennis and Arvella (Woods) B. B.B.A., U. Okla., 1966, J.D., 1968. Bar: Alta. 1969. Read law Saucier, Jones, Calgary, Alta., Can., assoc., 1969-70; asst. to pres. Regent Drilling Ltd., 1970-71; pres. Batoni-Bowlen Enterprises Ltd., 1971-79, Bowlen Holdings Ltd., Edmonton, Alta., Can., 1979—; pres., chief exec. officer, owner Denver Broncos, 1984—. Mem. Law Soc. Alta., Can. Bar Assn., Young Presidents Orgn. Roman Catholic. Clubs: Mayfair Golf and Country; Edmonton Petroleum; Outrigger Canoe (Honolulu). Avocations: golf, skiing, surfing. Office: Denver Broncos 13655 Broncos Pkwy Englewood CO 80112-4150*

BOWLES, NANCY RAE, English language educator, registered nurse; b. Olney, Ill., Apr. 5, 1949; d. I. Ray and Herma Belle (Jenner) Dycus; m. Robert Dennis Bowles, Sept. 7, 1969; children: Robert Jason, Jennifer Leigh, Benjamin Dycus, Nathan Bradford, Alison Leigh. AS, Olney Ctrl. Coll., 1969; ADN, Eastern N.Mex. U., 1983, BS in Edn., 1992, MS in Edn., 1998. RN, N.Mex., licensed tchr., N.Mex. RN St. Mary's Hosp., Roswell, N.Mex., 1983-93; tchr. Roswell Ind. Schs., Roswell, N.Mex., 1993—; coord. conflict mediation Roswell Ind. Schs., 1994—. Contbr. articles to jour. Fellow Nat. Writing Hign Plain Writing Project (Writing grant 1996); mem. NEA, Nat. Coun. Tchrs. English. Republican. Protestant. Avocations: running, aerobics, shopping. Home: 2517 N Cambridge Ave Roswell NM 88201-3460

BOWLIN, MICHAEL RAY, oil company executive; b. Amarillo, Tex., Feb. 20, 1943; m. Martha Ann Rowland; 1 child, John Charles. BBA, North Tex. State U., 1965, MBA, 1967. Scheduler prodn. and transp. A. Brant Co., Ft. Worth, 1965-66; mktg. rep. R.J. Reynolds Tobacco Bo., 1967-68; personnel generalist Atlantic Richfield Co., Dallas, 1969-71; coll. relations rep. Atlantic Richfield Co., Los Angeles, 1971-72, mgr. internal profl. placement, 1973, mgr. corp. recruiting and placement, 1973-75, mgr. behavioral sci. services, 1975, sr. v.p. ARCO resources adminstrn., 1985, sr. v.p. ARCO internat. oil and gas acquisitions, 1987, sr. v.p., 1987—; employee relations mgr. Atlantic Richfield Co., Alaska, 1975-77; v.p. employee relations Anaconda Copper Co. (div. Atlantic Richfield Co.), Denver, 1977-81; v.p. employee relations ARCO Oil & Gas (div. Atlantic Richfield Co.), Dallas, 1981-82, v.p. fin. planning and control, 1982-84; sr. v.p. Atlantic Richfield Co., 1985-92; pres. ARCO Coal Co., 1985-87, ARCO Internat. Oil & Gas Co., 1987-92; CEO Atlantic Richfield Co., 1994—, chmn., CEO, 1998—; pres., COO ARCO Internat. Oil & Gas Co., 1993, 1993, pres., CEO, 1994-95, chmn., CEO, 1995—. Office: Atlantic Richfield Co 515 S Flower St Los Angeles CA 90071-2295*

BOWLING, LANCE CHRISTOPHER, record producer, publisher; b. San Pedro, Calif., May 17, 1948; s. Dan Parker and Sylvia Lois (Van Devander) B. BA in Polit. Sci. and History, Pepperdine U., 1966-70, MPA, 1973. Owner, founder Cambria Master Recordings, Palos Verdes, Calif., 1972—. Editor: Joseph Wagner: A Retrospective of Composer-Conductor 1900-74, 1976, Hazards Pavilion, Jour of Soc for Preservation of South Calif. Mus. Heritage, 1985—; author: Eugene Hemmer: Composer-Pianist, 1983; producer over 125 classical records including works by Charles W. Cadman, Madeleine Dring, Mary Carr Moore, John Crown, Ed Bland, Florence Price, Elinor Remick Warren, Miklos Rozsa, Erich W. Korngold, Max Steiner, Ernst Gold, William Grant Still, Arthur Lange, also classical music radio station documentaries. Active allocation com. Region V, United Way, L.A., 1978-85; bd. dirs. Elinor Remick Warren Found., Soc. for the Preservation of Film Music, Hollywood, Calif., New World Ctr. for Arts, L.A., L.A. Ballet. Recipient Golden Rose award Pi Iota chpt. Phi Beta, 1988. Mem. ASCAP, Assn. Recorded Sound Collections, Music Libr. Assn., Soc. for Preservation of Film Music, Sonneck Soc., Variety Arts Club (L.A.), Mus. Arts Club (Long Beach, Calif.), Zamorano Club (L.A.). Episcopalian. Avocations: collecting early Calif. books and ephemera, restoration of 78 RPM recording and antique automobiles. Home: 2625 Colt Rd Palos Verdes Peninsula CA 90275-6578 Office: Cambria Records and Pub 1659 W 7th St San Pedro CA 90732-3421

BOWLINGER, JOHN C., state senator; b. Bozeman, Mont., Apr. 21, 1936; s. John G. and Aileen (Ellison) B.; m. Bette J. Cobetto, April 9, 1963; children: Jeanne, Jan, Mark, Jolynn, Nick, John. BA, U. Mont., 1959. Small bus. owner Women's Apparel Store, Billings, Mont., 1961-92; state rep. Mont. Ho. of Reps., Helena, 1992-96; state senator Mont. Senate, Helena, 1998—. Pres., bd. chmn. Yellowstone Art Mus., Billings, 1965-66, Billings Symphony, 19967-68, MSU Billings Found., 1991-93, St. Vincent de Paul Soc., Billings, 1990-92. With USMC, 1955-61. Republican. Roman Catholic. Avocations: golf, tennis, swimming, fishing, reading. Home: 2233 Remington Sq Billings MT 59102-2489

BOWMAN, A. BLAINE, electronics company executive. Pres., CEO Dionex, Sunnyvale, Calif. Office: Dionex PO Box 3603 1228 Titan Way Sunnyvale CA 94088-3603*

BOWMAN, BRUCE, art educator, writer, artist; b. Dayton, Ohio, Nov. 23, 1938; s. Murray Edgar Bowman and Mildred May (Moler) Elleman; m. Julie Ann Gosselin, 1970 (div. 1980); 1 child, Carrie Lynn. AA, San Diego City Coll., 1962; BA, Calif. State U.-Los Angeles, 1964, MA, 1968. Tchr. art North Hollywood Adult Sch., Calif., 1966-68; instr. art Cypress Coll., Calif., 1976-78, West Los Angeles Coll., 1969—; tchr. art Los Angeles City Schs., 1966—; seminar leader So. Calif., 1986—. Author: Shaped Canvas, 1976; Toothpick Sculpture and Ice Cream Stick Art, 1976; Ideas: How to Get Them, 1985, (cassette tape) Develop Winning Willpower, 1986, Waikiki, 1988. Contbr. articles to profl. jours. One-man shows include Calif. State U.-Los Angeles, 1968, Pepperdine U., Malibu, Calif., 1978; exhibited in group shows McKenzie Gallery, Los Angeles, 1968, Trebor Gallery, Los Angeles, 1970, Cypress Coll., Calif., 1977, Design Recycled Gallery, Fullerton, Calif., 1977, Pierce Coll., Woodland Hills, Calif., 1978, Leopold/Gold Gallery, Santa Monica, Calif., 1980. Served with USN, 1957-61. Avocation: karate (black belt Tang Soo Do). Home: 28322 Rey De Copas Ln Malibu CA 90265-4463

BOWMAN, FAY LOUISE, artist; b. L.A., Feb. 8, 1936; d. Winfield John and Dorothy Ethel (Lane) Michalsky; m. George Arthur Bowman; children: John Winfield, David Lawrence. BA, UCLA, 1958; BFA, Art Inst. So. Calif., 1987. Elem. tchr. Alhambra, Calif., 1958-59, Costa Mesa, Calif., 1959-63. One-woman show includes Art Inst. So. Calif., 1987; exhibited in group show at Irvine Valley Coll., 1991; numerous pvt. collections. Sec. President's Club Art Inst., Laguna Beach, Calif., 1990; discussion leader of Worldwide Bible Study Fellowship Laguna Beach Presbyn. Ch., 1994-95; active Ebell Club, 1973—. Mem. Designing Women of Art Inst., Assocs. Art Inst. So. Calif. (pres. 1988—).

BOWMAN, JEAN LOUISE, lawyer, civic worker; b. Albuquerque, Apr. 3, 1938; d. David Livingstone and Charlotte Louise (Smith) McArthur; student U. N.Mex., 1956-57, U. Pa., 1957-58, Rocky Mountain Coll., 1972-74; B.A. in Polit. Sci. with high honors, U. Mont., 1982, J.D., 1985; children—Carolyn Louise, Joan Emily, Amy Elizabeth, Eric Daniel. Dir. Chris-

tian edn. St. Luke's Episcopal Ch., 1979-80; law clk. to assoc. justice Mont. Supreme Ct., 1985-87; exec. v.p. St. Peter's Community Hospital Found., 1987-91; exec. dir. Harrison Hosp. Found., Bremerton, Wash., 1991-93, St. Patrick Hosp. and Health Found., 1993—, Missoula Symphony Bd., 1993—; pres. Missoula Symphony Assn., 1996-98; dir. 1st Bank West. Bd. trustees Rocky Mountain Coll., 1972-80; bd. dirs. Billings (Mont.) Area C. of C., 1977-80; mem. Internat. Women's Forum, 1996—, City-County Air Pollution Control Bd., 1969-74, chmn., 1970-71; del. Mont. State Constnl. Conv., 1971-72, sec. conv., 1971-72; chmn. County Local Govt. Study Commn., 1973-76; mem. Billings Sch. Dist. Long Range Planning Com., 1978-79; former pres. Billings LWV, dir., 1987-91, pres. Helena LWV, 2d v.p. Mont. LWV; former pres. Silver Run Ski Club. Named one of Billings' most influential citizens, Billings Gazette, 1977; Bertha Morton Scholar, 1982. Rotary (pres. 1997-98). Republican. Home: 1911 E Broadway St Missoula MT 59802-4901

BOWMAN, JEFFREY R., protective services official; b. Akron, Ohio, Apr. 24, 1952; s. Roger Heath and Ruth Ann (Corrigan) B.; divorced; children: Katie, Andrew, Brian. BS in Orgnl. Behavior, U. San Francisco, 1986. Firefighter Anaheim (Calif.) Fire Dept., 1973-75, paramedic, 1975-79, capt., 1979-83, battalion chief, 1983-85, div. chief, 1985-86, fire chief, 1986—. Pres. bd. dirs. Anaheim Boys and Girls Club, 1988—; chmn. fundraising Boy Scouts Am., Anaheim, 1988. Mem. Internat. Assn. Fire Chiefs, Calif. Fire Chiefs Assn. Office: Anaheim Fire Dept 201 S Anaheim Blvd Ste 301 Anaheim CA 92805-3858*

BOWMAN, JON ROBERT, editor, film critic; b. Spokane, Wash., Nov. 9, 1954; s. Donald Ken and Carolyn Joyce (Crutchfield) B.; m. Geraldine Maria Jaramillo, Jan. 27, 1979 (div. Dec. 1985); m. Amy Farida Siswayanti, May 23, 1992 (div. Jan. 1994). BA, U. N.Mex., 1976. Reporter, arts editor, news editor N.Mex. Daily Lobo, Albuquerque, 1972-76; film critic Albuquerque Jour., 1974-76; reporter Alamogordo (N.Mex.) Daily News, 1976; sci. writer, editor Los Alamos (N.Mex.) Monitor, 1976-81; reporter, arts editor New Mexican, Santa Fe, 1981-86, film critic, 1987—; editor New Mexico Mag., Santa Fe, 1986—; guest lectr. U. N.Mex., Coll. Santa Fe, 1976—. Author: (with others) Explore New Mexico, 1988, A New Mexico Scrapbook, 1990, Day Trip Discoveries: Selected New Mexico Excursions, 1993, The Allure of Turquoise, 1995; contbr. articles to mags. and newspapers; author salutes for Greer Garson, James Coburn, Ben Johnson, and John Huston for festivals honoring them. Vol. tchr. Albuquerque pub. schs., 1972-76; organizer film festivals Albuquerque and Santa Fe. 1972-91, benefits including Ctr. for Contemporary Arts, Santa Fe; program cons. Taos Talking Picture Festival, 1995—. Recipient Sci. Writing award AP, 1978, citation AP, 1979, others. Avocations: movies, baseball, travel. Home: 335 W Manhattan Ave Santa Fe NM 87501-2650 Office: NMex Mag Lew Wallace Bldg 495 Old Santa Fe Trl Santa Fe NM 87501-2750*

BOWMAN, LEONARD WAYNE, fine arts expert and appraiser; b. Albion, Wash., July 7, 1920; s. Frank J. and Belle (Griffin) B.; m. Elizabeth Palmer, 1954 (dec.). AAS, Spokane Coll. Pres. Fidelity Appraisal, L.A., 1958-68; pres., owner L. Bowman Appraisers, San Francisco, 1968—. Mem. Univ. Club (San Francisco), World Trade Club (San Francisco). Unitarian. Home and Office: 2324 Market St San Francisco CA 94114-1547

BOWMAN, RAYMOND DEARMOND, SR., writer, music critic; b. Rockingham, Va., Sept. 4, 1917; s. Rawleigh David and Vesta Virginia (Ratliff) B.; m. Lita Salgado Santos, June 1, 1960; children: R. Christian Anderson, Leslieanne Dreith, Raymond DeArmond Jr. Student in History, Columbia U., 1945-47. Classical violinist Calif. Jr. Symphony, Long Beach Symphony, 1936-38, Long Beach Jr. Coll. Trio-Broadcasts, 1938-40; enlisted Calif. N.G., 1939; advanced through grades to master sgt. U.S. Army, 1955; lit. critic Daily Mirror News, L.A., 1949-50; classical impresario mgr./dir. West Coast Artists, Hollywood, Calif., 1954-75; co-owner Bowman-Mann Art Gallery, Beverly Hills, Calif., 1963-66; impresario "Ice House" Monday Night Concerts, Pasadena, Calif., 1966-83; writer, music critic South Bay Daily Breeze News, Torrance, Calif., 1969-87. Violinist (movie) They Shall Have Music, 1939; contbr. articles to newspapers, books and mags. Adminstr. Hollywood Am. Legion, 1953-60; coord. Civilian Def., L.A., 1950s; vol. L.A. Philharmonic Promotion, 1966-87. Recipient Eistedford medal, 1927, numerous art awards. Mem. Pearl Harbor Survivors Assn. (life). Avocations: painting, writing, book collector, reading, sports. Home: Country Club Estates 2024 Fuerte Ln Escondido CA 92026-1640

BOWNE, MARTHA HOKE, publishing consultant; b. Greeley, Colo., June 9, 1931; d. George Edwin and Krin (English) Hoke; children: Gretchen, William, Kay, Judith. BA, U. Mich., 1952; postgrad., Syracuse U., 1965. Tchr. Wayne (Mich.) Pub. Schs., 1953-54, East Syracuse and Minoa Cen. Schs., Minoa, N.Y., 1965-68; store mgr. Fabric Barn, Fayetteville, N.Y., 1969-77; store owner Fabric Fair, Oneida, N.Y., 1978-80; producer, owner Quilting by the Sound, Port Townsend, Wash., 1987—, Quilting by the Lake, Cazenovia, N.Y., 1981—; organizer symposium Am. Quilters Soc.; founder, pres. Quilter's Quest Video Prodns., 1994. Mem., pres. Minoa Library, 1960-75; mem. Onondaga County Library, Syracuse, 1968-71. Mem. Nat. Quilting Assn., Am. Quilters Soc. (editor Am. Quilter mag. 1985-95), new Eng. Quilt Mus. Avocations: reading, hiking, cross-country skiing, travel, bridge. Home: 4445 Oden Bay Rd Sandpoint ID 83864-9499

BOWS, ROBERT ALAN, television producer, writer, director; b. N.Y.C., Apr. 6, 1949; s. Symon Waldman and Mildred (Solomon) B.; m. Mary Elizabeth Lawrence, June 26, 1974 (div. Jan. 1991); children: Joshua Eagle, Jennifer Laura Amrita. Student, Stanford U., 1967-70. Town mgr. Ward, Colo., 1974-78; bus. mgr. Sta. KBDI-TV, Broomfield, Colo., 1978-81, sta. mgr., 1981-82; exec. producer Scripps-Howard Cable Co., Longmont, Colo., 1983-84; producer, dir. United Cable of Colo., Englewood, 1985; producer, writer, dir. Sta. KRMA-TV, Denver, 1985-91; exec. prodr. Amrita Prodns., Denver, 1991—; multimedia applications mgr. Teletech Holdings, Denver, 1996-98; instrnl. designer IPX, Boulder, 1999—. Producer, writer, dir. (TV spl.) The International: A New Golfing Tradition, 1987; producer, writer, host (TV spl.) Arts at Risk, 1989; exec. producer (TV spl.) Peter Kater at Chautauqua, 1991; staff writer Colo. Golf Jour., 1990-95, Desert Golf Mag., 1998—; TV host PGA's Golf Almanac, 1991; radio host Backspin on Tee To Green, 1992-93; theater reviewer KUVO-FM, Denver, 1996—. Commr. Colo. Baseball Commn., 1989-95. Mem. Nat. Acad. TV Arts and Scis. Avocations: competitive amateur golfing, hiking, skiing, gardening.

BOWYER, JANE BAKER, science educator; b. Dayton, Ohio, Mar. 16, 1934; d. Homer Kenneth and Helen Elizabeth (Brown) Baker; m. Charles Stuart Bowyer, Feb. 27, 1957; children: William Stuart, Robert Baker, Elizabeth Ann. BA, Miami U., Oxford, Ohio, 1956; MA, U. Calif., Berkeley, 1972, PhD, 1974. Abbie Valley prof. Mills Coll., Oakland, Calif., 1974—, head dept. edn., 1985—; cons. Lawrence Hall Sci., U. Calif., Berkeley, 1975—, Nat. Assn. Ednl. Progress, 1975-78, Utah State Bd. Edn., 1985-86; mem. Calif. Round Table's Math/Sci. Task Force, 1983-85; dir. ednl. research Industry Initiatives in Sci. and Math Edn., 1985-86, bd. dirs., 1985—; dir. Mills Coll./Oakland Unified Sch. Dist. Partnership, 1985—; dir. midcareer math. and sci. tchr. R&D, NSF, 1987—, prin. investigator and dir. systemic reform program, 1994—, Leadership Inst. Teaching Elem. Sci., Mills and Oakland, Calif., 1994—. Author: Science and Society, 1984, Science and Society Activity Book, 1984; contbr. articles to profl. jours. Bd. dirs. Oakland Sci. and Art Sch., 1979-82, Eric Erickson Sch., San Francisco, 1983-85; prin. investigator Projects in Sci. Edn.; cons. UNESCO, Paris Div. Sci. Edn., 1989-90, 93. Fulbright Research fellow, Germany, 1982-83. Mem. AAAS, Nat. Assn. Research in Sci. Teaching (mem. editorial bd. 1980-82, bd. dirs. 1985-88, Outstanding Paper award, 1979, 81), Am. Ednl. Research Orgn., Mortar Bd. Home: 34 Seacape Dr Muir Beach CA 94965

BOXER, ALAN LEE, accountant; b. Denver, Sept. 9, 1935; s. Ben B. and Minnette (Goldman) B.; m. Gayle, Dec. 21, 1958; children: Michael E., Jodi S., Richard S. BSBA in Acctg., U. Denver, 1956. CPA, Colo. Audit mgr. Touche, Ross & Co. CPAs, Denver, 1956-60, Ballin, Milstein & Feinstein CPAs, Denver, 1960-61; prin. Alan L. Boxer, CPA, Denver, 1961-69; v.p and treas. Pawley Co., Denver, 1969-78; pres. Sci-Pro Inc., Denver, 1978-82; regional mgr. A.T.V. Systems, Inc., Denver, 1982-83; prin. The Enterprise Group, Denver, 1983-86; shareholder, pres. Allerdice, Baroch, Boxer & Co., CPAs, Denver, 1986-87; prin. Alan L. Boxer, CPA, Denver, 1987-97; dir. Boxer & Assocs. CPAs PC, 1997—. Bd. dirs. Anti-Defamation League, Denver, 1986-90, BMH Congregation, Denver, 1986-90, treas. 1990-93, v.p. 1993-98. Mem. Am. Inst. CPAs, Colo. Soc. CPAs, Bnai Brith #171 (pres. 1982, trustee 1983-89). Democrat. Jewish.

BOXER, BARBARA, senator; b. Bklyn., Nov. 11, 1940; d. Ira and Sophie (Silvershein) Levy; m. Stewart Boxer, 1962; children: Doug, Nicole. BA in Econ., Bklyn. Coll., 1962. Stockbroker, econ. rschr. N.Y. Securities Firm, N.Y.C., 1962-65; journalist, assoc. editor Pacific Sun, 1972-74; congl. aide to rep. 5th Congl. Dist. San Francisco, 1974-76; mem. Marin County Bd. Suprs., San Rafael, Calif., 1976-82; mem. 98th-102d Congresses from 6th Calif. dist., mem. armed services com., select com. children, youth and families; majority whip at large, co-chair Mil. Reform Caucus, chair subcom. on govt. activities and transp. of house govt. ops. com., 1990-93, U.S. senator from Calif., 1993—, mem. banking, housing and urban affairs com., mem. budget com., mem. environ. and pub. works com. Pres. Marin County Bd. Suprs., 1980-81; mem. Bay Area Air Quality Mgmt. Bd., San Francisco, 1977-82, pres., 1979-81; bd. dirs. Golden Gate Bridge Hwy. and Transport Dist., San Francisco, 1978-82; founding mem. Marin Nat. Women's Polit. Caucus; pres. Dem. New Mems. Caucus, 1983. Recipient Open Govt. award Common Cause, 1980, Rep. of Yr. award Nat. Multiple Sclerosis Soc., 1990, Margaret Sanger award Planned Parenthood, 1990, Women of Achievement award Anti-defamation League, 1990. Jewish. Office: US Senate 112 Hart Senate Office Bldg Washington DC 20510-0505*

BOXER, JEROME HARVEY, computer and management consultant, vintner, accountant; b. Chgo., Nov. 27, 1930; s. Ben Avrum and Edith (Lyman) B.; AA magna cum laude, East L.A. Coll., 1952; m. Sandra Schaffner, June 17, 1980; children by previous marriage: Michael, Jodi. AB with honors, Calif. State U., L.A., 1954. CPA, Calif; cert. computing profl. Lab. instr. Calif. State U., L.A., 1953-54; staff acct. Dolman, Freeman & Buchalter, L.A., 1955-57; sr. acct. Neiman, Sanger, Miller & Beress, L.A., 1957-63; ptnr. firm Glynn and Boxer, CPAs, L.A., 1964-68; v.p., sec. Glynn, Boxer & Phillips Inc., CPA's, L.A.and Glendale, 1968-90, pvt. practice cons., 1990—; owner Oak Valley Vineyard; pres. Echo Data Svcs., Inc., 1978-90; instr. data processing L.A. City Adult Schs.; tchr. lectr., cons. wines and wine-tasting; instr. photography. Mem. ops. bd. Everywoman's Village; bd. dirs., v.p. So. Calif. Jewish Hist. Soc., v.p. Jewish Hist. Soc. of the Ctrl. Coast; founding pres. Congregation Ohr Tzafon; co-founder Open Space Theatre; former officer Ethel Josephine Scantland Found.; past post adviser Explorer Scouts, Boy Scouts Am., also Eagle Scout. Recipient Youth Svc. award Mid-Valley YMCA, 1972-73; Mem. Am. Inst. CPAs, Calif. Soc. CPAs, Assn. for Systems Mgmt., Data Processing Mgmt. Assn., Am. Fedn. Musicians, Am. Jewish Hist. Soc., Friends of Photography, L.A. Photog. Ctr., Acad. Model Aeros., Nat. Model Railroad Assn., Maltese Falcons Home Brewing Soc., San Fernando Valley Silent Flyers, San Fernando Valley Radio Control Flyers, Associated Students Calif. State U., Los Angeles (hon. life), Acad. Magical Arts, Internal Brotherhood of Magicians, Soc. Preservation of Variety Arts, Am. Wine Soc., Knights of the Vine, Soc. Wine Educators, Napa Valley Wine Libr. Alumni Assn., L.A.-Bordeaux Sister City Affiliation, Soc. Bacchus Am., Paso Robles Dem. Club (pres. 1993), Ctrl. Coast Winegrowers Assn., Wines and Steins, Cellarmasters, Paso Robles Vintners and Growers Assn., German Shepherd Dog Club Am., German Shepherd Dog Club Los Angeles County, Blue Key, Alpha Phi Omega. Clubs: Verdugo, Exchange, Kiwanis (pres. Sunset-Echo Park 1968), Braemar Country, Pacific Mariners Yacht, S.Coast Corinthian Yacht (former dir., officer), B'nai B'rith. Cons., contbr. Wine World Mag., 1974-82. Home and Office: 1660 Circle B Rd Paso Robles CA 93446-9595

BOXER, LESTER, lawyer; b. N.Y.C., Oct. 19, 1935; s. Samuel and Anna Lena (Samovai) B., m. Frances Barenfeld, Sept. 17, 1961; children: Kimberly Brett, Allison Joy. AA, UCLA, 1955, BS, 1957; JD, U. So. Calif., 1961. Bar: Calif. 1962; U.S. Dist. Ct. (cen. dist.) Calif. 1962. Assoc. Bautzer & Grant, Beverly Hills, Calif., 1961-63; pvt. practice Beverly Hills, 1963-65, 69—; ptnr. Boxer & Stoll, Beverly Hills, 1965-69. Mem. Calif. Bar Assn., L.A. County Bar Assn., Beverly Hills Bar Assn. Office: 1875 Century Park E Ste 2000 Los Angeles CA 90067-2521

BOXLEITNER, LINDA SCHRAUFNAGEL, secondary education educator; b. Orofino, Idaho, Mar. 25, 1949; d. Gilbert Leonard and Edna Cecelia (Kempf) S.; m. Warren James Boxleitner, Aug. 23, 1969; 1 child, Kirk Lee. BA in English, U. Idaho, 1971; MEd in Social Sci., Ea. Washington U., 1986. Cert. secondary tchg. cert., Idaho, Mo., Mass., Wash. Author, freelance writer Schlier, Germany, 1979-81, Spokane, Wash., 1981-86; tchr., English Methuen (Mass.) H.S., 1987-95; tchr., dept. head Internat. Sch., Bellevue, Wash., 1995—. Author: (book) Reading Emily's, 1996; contbr. articles to profl. jour. Pres. League of Women Voters, Spokane, 1976-78; del. Wash. State Presdl. conv., Seattle, 1976; pres., treas. Equal Rights Coalition, Seattle, 1976-79; mem. 208 Water Adv. Com., Seattle. Fellow Tokugawa Japan, Rocky Mt. Social Scis. Consortium, Boudler, Colo., 1996, Emily Dickinson, NEH, Amherst, Mass., 1990; named Young Tchr. of Yr. Am. Fedn. of Tchrs. of Kans. City, 1972. Mem. NEA, AAUW, Phi Beta Kappa, Phi Kappa Phi. Avocations: travel, reading, theater, world music. Home: 304 10th St Kirkland WA 98033-6354 Office: The Internat Sch 301 151st Pl NE Bellevue WA 98007-5061

BOYAJIAN, TIMOTHY EDWARD, public health officer, educator, consultant; b. Fresno, Calif., Feb. 22, 1949; s. Ernest Adam and Marge (Medzian) B.; m. Tassanee Bootdeesri, Apr. 23, 1987. BS in Biology, U. Calif., Irvine, 1975; M of Pub. Health, UCLA, 1978. Registered environ. health specialist, Calif. Rsch. asst. UCLA, 1978-81; lectr. Chapman U., 29 Palms, Calif., 1982-84, 88-89; refugee relief vol. Cath. Relief Svcs., Surin, Thailand, 1985-86; lectr. Nat. Univ., L.A., 1989-91; environ. health specialist Riverside County Health Svcs. Agy., Palm Springs, Calif., 1991-96; mem. adj. faculty U. Phoenix, 1998—; cons. parasitologist S. Pacific Commn., L.A., 1979; pub. health cons. several vets. groups, L.A., 1981-84, 97—; cons. Learning Link, Inc. 1999—, Assn. S.E. Asian Nations, Bangkok, Thailand, 1988. Veterans rights advocate, Vietnam Vet. Groups, L.A., 1981-84. With USMC, Vietnam, 1969-71. Recipient U.S. Pub. Health Traineeship, U.S. Govt., L.A., 1977-81. Mem. VFW, So. Calif. Pub. Health Assn., Calif. Environ. Health Assn. Avocation: writing. E-mail: Timothy 300@aol.com. Home: PO Box 740 Palm Springs CA 92263-0740

BOYARSKI, ADAM MICHAEL, physicist; b. North Bank, Alberta, Can., Apr. 14, 1935; came to U.S., 1963; s. Albert and Mary (Roskiewich) B.; m. Lorretta Sramek, June 1, 1968; children: Lisa A., Mike A. BA in Sci., U. Toronto, 1958; PhD, M.I.T., 1962. Rsch. assoc. M.I.T., Cambridge, 1962-63; staff physicist Stanford (Calif.) Linear Accelerator Ctr., 1963—; cons. in field; mem. team discovering psi family of elem. particles. Author: (software) HANDYPAK, A Histogram and Display Package, 1980; contbr. articles to scientific jours. Mem. Am. Phys. Soc. Avocations: woodworking, camping, computers, mechanics. Office: SLAC 2575 Sand Hill Rd Menlo Park CA 94025-7015

BOYD, CHRIS M., elementary educator, consultant, writer; b. Phoenix, Aug. 16; s. Marion Orville and Ruth M. Smyth; children: Micah, Jacob, Sarah. BA, U. Ariz., 1971; MA, Ariz. State U., 1976. Cert. elem. tchr., Ariz. Tchr. Tucson Dist. # 1, 1971-72, Phoenix Dist. # 1, 1972-73, Cartwright Sch. Dist., Phoenix, 1973-76, Washington Sch. Dist., Phoenix, 1976—; instr. Ariz. State U., Ariz. State U. West, Phoenix, 1987-92; cons. Madison Sch. Dist., Phoenix, 1980's, Fair Oaks (Calif.) Sch., 1990-93. Contbr. articles to profl. jours. Mem. com. Young Life Urban, Phoenix, 1990—; pres. Ariz. Kindergarten Tchr.'s Assn. Recipient State Literacy Site award Ariz. State Dept. Edn. Mem. Nat. Coun. Tchrs. English (presenter nat. conventions), Internat. Reading Assn., Ctr. for Establishing Dialog. E-mail: cmboyd@netvalue.net. Office: Lookout Mountain Sch 15 W Coral Gables Dr Phoenix AZ 85023-3697

BOYD, EDWARD HASCAL, retired career officer; b. Kevil, Ky., Sept. 4, 1934; s. Lloyd E. and D. Irene (Steinbeck) B.; m. D. Ann Creecy, Jan. 13, 1956 (dec. Mar. 1970); children: Lawrence H., Debra A.; m. Margaret Lorene Hogan, Nov. 7, 1970; 1 child, Laura Irene. AA, Phoenix Coll., 1954; BS, Ariz. State U., 1956, MBA, 1972. Cert. secondary tchr., Ariz. Commd. 2d lt. USMC, 1956, advanced through ranks to col., 1980, exec. officer Marine Detachment USS Helena, 1959-60; assigned Marine Corps Recruit Depot, San Diego, 1961-63; instr. ops. and intelligence Landing Force Tng. Command USMC, 1963-65, mem. 1st Bn. 4th Marines, 1966-67, instr. Amphibious Warfare Sch., 1967-70, Hdqrs. USMC, 1973-76; assigned to Devel. Ctr. Marine Corps Devel. and Edn. Command, 1977-80; comdr. Hdqrs. Bn., Camp Pendleton, Calif., 1981-84; ret. USMC, 1984; substitute tchr. Mesa (Ariz.) Unified Sch. Dist., 1984-86. Mem. Marine Corps Assn., Ret. Officers Assn., SAR, Magna Charta Barons, Alta Mesa Country Club, Alpha Tau Omega. Avocations: hunting, fishing, hiking. Home: 5851 E Elmwood St Mesa AZ 85205-5833

BOYD, HERCHELL A., career officer; b. Wurzburg, Germany, June 25, 1954; came to U.S., 1955; s. Allen Owsley and Ann (Thomason) B.; m. Julie Ann Pflughaupt, Oct. 2, 1976; children: James O., William C. BS in Aero. Engring., Ga. Inst. Tech., 1976, MSEE, 1988; MA in Nat. Security Studies, U.S. Naval War Coll., 1996. Commd. 2nd lt. U.S. Army, 1976, advanced through grades to col.; comdr. 102nd MI Bn., Republic of Korea, 1983-84; dep. dir. Emergency Ops. Ctr., White Ho., Washington, 1984-86; program mgr. Nat. Security Agy., Ft. Meade, Md., 1989-92; exec. officer 205th MI Brig., Frankfurt, Germany, 1992-93; comdr. 302nd MI Bn., Frankfurt, 1993-95; dir. Battle Tech. Lab. Army Intelligence Ctr., Ft. Huachuca, Ariz., 1996-97, dir. futures, 1997—. Decorated Legion of Merit. Mem. Armed Forces Comm. and Electronics Assn., Am. Legion, VFW.

BOYD, J. MICHAEL, dentist; b. Charlotte, N.C., Oct. 13, 1943; s. James Marion and Alice Purcell Boyd; m. Sharyl McCoy, Dec. 29, 1967; children: Michael Brent, Erin Elizabeth. BS in Dentistry, Ind. U., 1965; DDS, Ind. U., Indpls., 1968. Lic. dentist, Ind., Calif. Dentist Manteca (Calif.) Dental Group, 1970-71; pvt. practice Modesto, Calif., 1971—; regional cons. Delta Dental, San Francisco, 1990—, Stanislaus Dental Found., Modesto, 1990—, v.p., 1988—, bd. dirs., 1985—, continuing edn. chmn. 1985-88; hosp. staff Meml. Hosp. Med. Ctr., 1975-85, Drs. Med. Courtesy, 1975-85, Stanislaus Med. Ctr., 1993-95. Bd. dirs. Am. Cancer Soc., Modesto, 1973-75, chmn. oral cancer screening, 1977; asst. dir. commr. Boy Scouts Am., Modesto, 1974-75; bishop's warden St. Dinstan's Episc. ch., 1972-73, 87-90, bishop's com., 1987-90, 94-96, stewardship chmn., 1995-97; diocesan coun. Diocese of San Joaquin, 1980-85. Capt. USAF, 1968-70. Pierre Fauchard Acad. fellow, 1995. Fellow Internat. Coll. Dentists, Am. Coll. Dentists; mem. ADA (alt. del. 1984, del. 1995-97), Acad. Gen. Dentistry, Calif. Dental Assn. (trustee 1990-96, del. 1983-84, screening com. 1992-95, chmn. 1994-95), Midvalley Dental Health Found. (bd. dirs. 1979-87), Stanislaus Dental Soc. (pres. 1984, v.p. 1983, sec. 1982, treas. 1981, bd. dirs. 1981-85, 90-96, adv. com. 1989-93, peer rev. chmn. 1979, ethics com. 1988-89, dental liaison chmn. 1974), Ind. U. Alumni Assn., Input Dental Study Club, North Modesto Kiwanis (sec. 1989, Disting. Sec. award 1990, chmn. Pre Concours Party 1980-90), Delta Sigma Delta, Omicron Kappa Upsilon, Delta Upsilon. Republican. Episcopalian. Avocations: skiing, fly fishing, gardening. Home: 3712 Almond Blossom Ct Modesto CA 95356-1805 Office: 2813 Coffee Rd Ste B2 Modesto CA 95355-1755

BOYD, JEANNE ROSWELL, classic languages and literature educator; b. Frazee, Minn., Feb. 15, 1920; d. Solomon F. and Lillian Ann Anderson; children: Bonnie, Connie and Larry Boyd. AA, Pierce Coll., Woodland Hills, Calif., 1969; BA, Calif. State U., Northridge, 1971, MA, 1974. Cert. tchr., Calif. Formerly with Walt Disney Corp., MGM, ATC Rosemount/Rockwell; formerly mem. faculty UCLA. Author (poetry) Rainy Day Poems, 1994. Violin player San Fernando Valley Symphony; mem. Reseda Symphony, UCLA Symphony, others; deacon, Stephen min. St. James Ch., Tarzana, Calif., 1990-94. Democrat. Presbyterian. Avocations: classical music, reading, swimming, travel, visiting the sick. Home: 6217 Corbin Ave Tarzana CA 91356-1012

BOYD, JOHN MARVIN, broadcasting executive; b. Pasadena, Calif., Mar. 6, 1943; children: John Matthew, Grace Christina. BA in Oral Communications, U. Redlands, 1966; PhD in Communication, U. So. Calif., 1977. Chmn., chief exec. officer, owner Am. Sunrise Communications, Idyllwild, Calif., 1983—; media rep. Christian Rsch. Inst., San Juan Capistrano, 1977-86, Southwest Radio Ch., Oklahoma City, 1977-86, Billy Graham, Anaheim, Calif., 1985; mem. fin. com. First Bapt. Ch., Huntington Beach, Calif., 1982-89. Producer, writer video series Kingdom of the Cults, 1986 (Angel award 1987), The Gods in Paradise, 1990. Oak Knoll fellow, L.A., 1973; telecommunications scholar RCA, 1973. Mem. Nat. Religious Broadcasters, Theta Alpha Phi, Alpha Epsilon Rho. Republican. Office: Am Sunrise Communications 3935 E Broadway # 410 Long Beach CA 90803-6108

BOYD, LEONA POTTER, retired social worker; b. Creekside, Pa., Aug. 31, 1907; d. Joseph M. and Belle (McHenry) Johnston. Grad. Ind. (Pa.) State Normal Sch., 1927, student Las Vegas Normal U., N.Mex., 1933, Carnegie Inst. Tech. Sch. Social Work, 1945, U. Pitts. Sch. Social Work, 1956-57; m. Edgar D. Potter, July 16, 1932 (div.); m. Harold Lee Boyd, Oct. 1972. Tchr. Creekside (Pa.) Pub. Schs., 1927-30, Papago Indian Reservation, Sells, Ariz., 1931-33; caseworker, supr. Indiana County (Pa.) Bd. Assistance, 1934-54, exec. dir., 1954-68, ret. Bd. dirs. Indiana County Tourist Promotion, hon. life mem.; former bd. dirs. Indiana County United Fund, Salvation Army, Indiana County Guidance Ctr., Armstrong-Indiana Mental Health Bd.; cons. assoc. Community Rsch. Assocs., Inc.; mem. Counseling Ctr. Aux., Lake Havasu City, Ariz., 1978-80; former mem. Western Welcome Club, Lake Havasu City, Sierra Vista Hosp. Aux., Truth or Consequences, N.Mex. Recipient Jr. C. of C. Disting. Svc. award, Indiana, Pa., 1966, Bus. and Profl. Women's Club award, Indiana, 1965. Mem. Am. Assn. Ret. Persons, Daus. Am. Colonists. Lutheran. Home: 444 S Higley Rd Apt 219 Mesa AZ 85206-2186

BOYD, MALCOLM, minister, religious author; b. Buffalo, June 8, 1923; s. Melville and Beatrice (Lowrie) B.; life ptnr. Mark Thompson. B.A., U. Ariz., 1944; B.D., Ch. Div. Sch. Pacific, 1954; postgrad., Oxford (Eng.) U., 1955; S.T.M., Union Theol. Sem., N.Y.C., 1956; DD (hon.), Ch. Div. Sch. of Pacific, 1995. Ordained to ministry Episcopal Ch., 1955. V.p., gen. mgr. Pickford, Rogers & Boyd, 1949-51; rector in Indpls., 1957-59; chaplain Colo. State U., 1959-61, Wayne State U., 1961-65; nat. field rep. Episcopal Soc. Cultural and Racial Unity, 1965-68; resident fellow Calhoun Coll., Yale U., 1968-71, assoc. fellow, 1971—; writer-priest in residence St. Augustine-by-the Sea Episcopal Ch., 1982-95; chaplain to commn. on AIDS Ministries of Episcopal Diocese of L.A., 1993—; lectr. World Council Chs., Switzerland, 1955, 64; columnist Pitts. Courier, 1962-65; resident guest Mishkenot Sha'ananim, Jerusalem, 1974; chaplain AIDS Commn. Episcopal Diocese L.A., 1989—; poet-in-residence Cathedral Ctr. of St. Paul, L.A., 1996—. Host: TV spl. Sex in the Seventies, CBS-TV, Los Angeles, 1975; author: Crisis in Communication, 1957, Christ and Celebrity Gods, 1958, Focus, 1960, If I Go Down to Hell, 1962, The Hunger, The Thirst, 1964, Are You Running with Me, Jesus?, 1965, rev. 25th anniversary edit., 1990, Free to Live, Free to Die, 1967, Book of Days, 1968, As I Live and Breathe: Stages of an Autobiography, 1969, The Fantasy Worlds of Peter Stone, 1969, My Fellow Americans, 1970, Human Like Me, Jesus, 1971, The Lover, 1972, When in the Course of Human Events, 1973, The Runner, 1974, The Alleluia Affair, 1975, Christian, 1975, Am I Running with You, God?, 1977, Take Off the Masks, 1978, rev. edit. 1993, Look Back in Joy, 1981, rev. edit., 1990, Half Laughing, Half Crying, 1986, Gay Priest: An Inner Journey, 1986, Edges, Boundaries and Connections, 1992, Rich with Years, 1993, Go Gentle Into That Good Night, 1998; plays Boy, 1961, Study in Color, 1962, The Community, 1964, others; editor: On the Battle Lines, 1964, The Underground Church, 1968, Amazing Grace: Stories of Gay and Lesbian Faith, 1991; book reviewer: Los Angeles Times.; contbg. editor The Episcopal News; contbr. articles to numerous mags. including Newsday, Parade, Modern Maturity, The Advocate, also newspapers. Active voter registration, Miss., Ala., 1963, 64; mem. Los Angeles City/County AIDS Task Force. Malcolm Boyd Collection and Archives established Boston U., 1973; Recipient Integrity Internat. award, 1978; Union Am. Hebrew Congregations award, 1980. Mem. Nat. Council Chs. (film awards com. 1965), P.E.N. (pres. PEN Ctr. U.S. West 1984-87), Am. Center, Authors Guild, Integrity, Nat. Gay Task Force, Clergy and Laity Concerned (nat. bd.), NAACP, Amnesty Internat., Episc. Peace Fellowship, Fellowship of Reconciliation (nat. com.). Office: PO Box 2164 Los Angeles CA 90051-0164

BOYD, SANDRA HUGHES, priest, librarian; b. Council Bluffs, Iowa, Dec. 29, 1938; d. Floyd Earl and Elizabeth Jane (Sturtevant) Hughes; m. J. Hayden Boyd, Dec. 28, 1963 (div. 1984); children: Jane Elizabeth, Anne Marie. BA, Colo. Coll., 1961; MALS, U. Minn., 1966; MDiv, Episcopal Divinity Sch., 1978. Ordained priest Episcopal Ch., 1979. Lay leader

various Episcopal chs., Columbus, Ohio, Rochester, N.Y., Arlington, Va. and Troy, Mich., 1966-76; parish assoc. Christ Ch., Cambridge, Mass., 1978-86; interim rector St. John's Ch., Charlestown, Mass., 1983-84; parish assoc. St. Barnabas Ch., Denver, 1991—; libr. pub. svcs. Regis U., Denver, 1990—; mem. adj. faculty, libr. Episcopal Divinity Sch., Cambridge, 1978-86; bd. dirs. , v.p., editor Episcopal Women's History Project, N.Y.C., 1981—; dir. Deaconess History Project, 1983-88. Editor: Cultivating Our Roots, 1984; co-author: Women in American Religious History, 1986. Mem. Am. Acad. Religion, Am. Theol. Libr. Assn.

BOYDSTON, JAMES CHRISTOPHER, composer; b. Denver, July 21, 1947; s. James Virgal and Mary June (Wiseman) B.; m. Ann Louise Bryant, Aug. 20, 1975. BA in Philosophy, U. Tex., 1971. Lutenist and guitarist Collegium Musicum, U. Tex., Austin, 1968-70; tchr. classical guitar Extension div. The New Eng. Conservatory of Music, Boston, 1972-73. Arranger music: S. Joplins, "The Entertainer," 1976; arranger/composer/performer cassette recording: Wedding Music for Classical Guitar, 1988; inventor classical guitar bridge-saddle, 1990; author original poetry included in: The World of Poetry Anthology, 1991. Avocations: astronomy, reading, building clavichords, camping. Home: 4433 Driftwood Pl Boulder CO 80301-3104

BOYER, CARL, III, non-profit organization executive, former mayor, city official, secondary education educator; b. Phila., Pa., Sept. 22, 1937; s. Carl Boyer Jr. and Elizabeth Campbell Timm; m. Ada Christine Kruse, July 28, 1962. Student, U. Edinburgh, Scotland, 1956-57; BA, Trinity U., 1959; MEd in Secondary Edn., U. Cin., 1959; postgrad., Calif. State U., Northridge, 1964-72. Tchr. Edgewood High Sch., San Antonio, Tex., 1959-60; libr. U. Cin., Cincinnati, Ohio, 1960-61; tchr. Eighth Avenue Elem. Sch., Dayton, Ky., 1961-62, Amelia High Sch., Amelia, Ohio, 1962-63; instr. Kennedy San Fernando Comm. Adult Sch., San Fernando, Calif., 1964-74, Mission Coll., San Fernando, 1971; tchr. San Fernando High Sch., San Fernando, Calif., 1963-98; faculty chmn. San Fernando High Sch., dept. chmn.; cons. Sofia (Bulgaria) City Coun., 1991; key spkr. World Mayors' Conf., Jaipur, India, 1998. Author, compiler 15 books on genealogy and family history; contbr. articles to profl. jours. Councilman City of Santa Clarita, Calif., 1987-98, mayor pro tem, 1989-90, 94-95, mayor, 1990-91, 95-96; mem. Nat. League Cities Internat. Mcpl. Consortium, 1992-98; mem. revenue and taxation com. League Calif. Cities, 1992-95; sec. Calif. Contract Cities Assn., 1992-93; trustee Santa Clarita C.C. Dist., 1973-81, pres., 1979-81; bd. dirs. Castaic Lake Water Agy., 1982-84, pres. Newhall-Saugus-Valencia Fedn. Homeowners Assn., 1969-70, 71-72; pres. Del Prado Condo. Assn., Inc., Newhall, Calif.; exec. v.p. Canyon County Formation Com.; chmn. Santa Clarita City Formation Com., 1987; pres. Santa Clarita Valley Internat. Program, 1991-97; treas. Healing the Children Calif., 1994-96, pres., 1996-99, nat. pres., 1999—. Mem. United Tchrs. L.A., New Eng. Hist. Geneal. Soc. Republican. Methodist. Avocations: travel, photography. Home: PO Box 220333 Santa Clarita CA 91322-0333

BOYER, FORD SYLVESTER, relationship consultant, minister; b. Cadet, Mo., Jan. 12, 1934; s. Wilford Robert and Mary Elizabeth (DeClue) B.; m. Juelle-Ann Rupkalvis, May 2, 1970. BA in Psychology, USAF Inst., 1957; DD, Am. Bible Inst., Kansas City, Mo., 1977; MA, John F. Kennedy U., 1994. Cert. alcohol specialist. Adminstr. Getz Bros., San Francisco, 1969-73; supr. word processing U.S. Leasing Corp., San Francisco, 1977-82, dir. tng. and applications-word processing, 1982-84; computer cons Petaluma, Calif., 1984-87; massage therapist Petaluma, 1985-87; pvt. practice hypnotherapy Alameda, Calif., 1987—; cons. for chem. dependency Alameda, 1987—. Contbr. articles to profl. publs.; writer, pub.: (newsletter) Starfire, 1988—; participant (TV show) Right Human Relations, San Francisco. Vol. min. Pathways Hospice, Oakland, Calif. With USAF, 1953-57, Korea. Mem. Am Coun. Hypnotist Examiners, Nat. Assn. Alcohol and Drug Abuse Counselors, Calif. Assn. Alcohol and Drug Abuse Counselors, Calif. Assn. Alcohol Recovery Homes. Avocations: writing, volunteering, music, esotericism. Home and Office: Starfire Servers 3327 Cook Ln Alameda CA 94502-6939

BOYKIN, WILLIAM EDWARD, principal; b. Clarendon, Tex., June 27, 1932; s. Garland Lester and Lucy Edna (Matthews) B.; m. Bobby Jo Irving, July 26, 1958 (dec. Apr. 1992); children: Martha Anne, Douglas Irving, Kenneth Garland; m. Jane Ellen Larson, Mar. 1, 1996; stepchildren: Mike, Todd, Phillip Woods. BA in Journalism, N.Mex. State U., 1954, MA in English, 1964, ednl. adminstr., 1976. Tchr., coach, adminstr. Las Cruces (N.Mex.) H.S., 1958-70; asst. football coach N.Mex. State U., Las Cruces, 1970-73; agt., state dir. Fidelity Union Life Ins. Co., Albuquerque, 1973-76; vice-prin., prin. Farmington (N.Mex.) H.S., 1976-86; adminstr. Mesilla Valley Christian Sch., Las Cruces, 1996-98. Author: The Principal of the Thing, The Journal of a High School Principal; contbr. articles to profl. jours. Capt. USAF, 1954-58. Recipient Secondary Adminstr. of Yr. N.Mex. Adminstrs. Assn., 1986, Leadership award, 1986. Mem. NRA, Am. Legion, Aggie Scholarship Assn., N.Mex. State U. Alumni Assn. (life), People for the West, Phi Delta Kappa, Tau Kappa Epsilon. Republican. Methodist. Avocations: travel, fishing, reading, do-it-yourself, writing. Home: 3035 Hillrise Dr Las Cruces NM 88011-4703 Office: Mesilla Valley Christian Sch 3850 Stern Dr Las Cruces NM 88001-7637

BOYLAN, RICHARD JOHN, psychologist, hypnotherapist, researcher, behavioral scientist, educator; b. Hollywood, Calif., Oct. 15, 1939; s. John Alfred and Rowena Margaret (Devine) B.; m. Charnette Marie Blackburn, Oct. 26, 1968 (div. June 1984); children: Christopher J., Jennifer April, Stephanie August; m. Judith Lee Keast, Nov. 21, 1987; stepchildren: Darren Andrew, Matthew Grant. BA, St. John's Coll., 1961; MEd, Fordham U., 1966; MSW, U. Calif., Berkeley, 1971; PhD in Psychology, U. Calif., Davis, 1984. Cert. clin. hypnotherapist. Assoc. pastor Cath. Diocese of Fresno, 1965-68; asst. dir. Berkeley (Calif.) Free Ch., 1970-71; psychiat. social worker Marin Mental Health Dept., San Rafael, Calif., 1971-77; dir. Calaveras Mental Health Dept., San Andreas, Calif., 1977-85; prof., coord. Nat. U., Sacramento, 1985-86; lectr. Calif. State U., Sacramento, 1985-90, 98—; instr. U. Calif., Davis, 1984-88; assoc. prof. Chapman U., Sacramento, 1997—; dir. U.S. Behavioral Health, Sacramento, 1988-89; pvt. practice psychotherapy, Sacramento, 1974-95; hypnotherapy practice, Sacramento, 1996—. Author: Extraterrestrial Contact and Human Responses, 1992, Close Extraterrestrial Encounters, 1994, Labored Journey to the Stars, 1996, Project Epiphany, 1997. Bd. dirs. Marin Mcpl. Water Dist., 1975-77; cons. Calif. State Legis., Sacramento, 1979-80; chmn. Calaveras County Bd. Edn., Angels Camp, Calif., 1981-84. Recipient Geriatric Medicine Acad. award NIH, 1984, Experiment Station grant USDA, Calif., 1983. Mem. APA, ACA, Am. Assn. for Spiritual/Ethical Values in Counseling, Nat. Bd. Hypnotherapy and Med. Anaesthesiology, Calif. Psychol. Assn., Sacramento Valley Psychol. Assn. (past pres.), Sacramento Soc. Profl. Psychologists (past pres.), Nat. Resources Def. Coun., Acad. Clin. Close-Encounter Therapists (founder, sec., treas.). Democrat. Avocations: hiking, jogging, UFO/ET research, camping. Office: 2826 O St Ste 2 Sacramento CA 95816-6400

BOYLE, ANTONIA BARNES, audio producer, writer; b. Detroit, May 21, 1939; d. James Merriam and Florence (Maiullo) B.; 1 child, Caitlin Merriam. BS in Speech, Northwestern U., 1962. Staff announcer WEFM-FM, Chgo., 1975-78; pres. Boyle Communications, Chgo., 1978-85; exec. producer Nightingale-Conant Corp., Chgo., 1985-90, Cassette Prodns. Unltd., Irwindale, Calif., 1990-92; pres. Antonia Boyle & Co., 1992—; v.p. content Youachieve.com, Inc., 1997—. Author: The Optimal You, 1990, Taping Yourself Seriously, 1991; co-author: (with Jay Gordon) Good Food Today, Great Kids Tomorrow, 1994 (with Scott McKain) Just Say Yes, 1994, (with William McCurry) Guerrilla Managing for the Imaging Industry, 1997. Chmn., bd. dirs. Horizons for the Blind, Chgo., 1984. Mem. Am. Fedn. Radio, TV Artists, Com.100 Northwestern U., NU Club, San Francisco. Home: 2526 39th Ave San Francisco CA 94116-2751 Office: Interactive Achievement Ctr 236 W Portal Ave San Francisco CA 94127-1423

BOYLE, BETSY H., educational administrator; b. Cleve., Feb. 18, 1946; d. John J. Jr. and Lois Frances (Hale) B. BA, Loretto Heights Coll., Denver, 1968; MA, U. No. Colo., 1978, postgrad. Cert. adminstr., Colo. Tchr. Archdiocese of Denver, prin. Presentation of Our Lady Sch., Denver, dir. instrnl. programs Office Cath. Schs., Denver, now assoc. supt., exec. dir. Cath. edn. cons. svcs. Contbr. articles to profl. jours. Mem. ASCD, Nat. Cath. Edn. Assn. (profl. presenter, spc. adv. com.), Cath. Urban Educators, Schs. in Urban Neighborhoods.

BOYLE, CAROLYN MOORE, public relations executive, marketing communications manager; b. Los Angeles, Jan. 29, 1937; d. Cory Orlando Moore and Violet (Brennan) Baldock; m. Robert J. Ruppelt, Oct. 8, 1954 (div. Aug. 1964); children: Cory Robert, Traci Lynn; m. Jerry Ray Boyle, June 1, 1970 (div. 1975). AA, Orange Coast Coll., 1966; BA, Calif. State U., Fullerton, 1970; student, U. Calif., Irvine, 1970-71. Program coord. Newport Beach (Calif.) Cablevision, 1968-70; dir. pub. rels. Fish Communications Co., Newport Beach, 1970-74; mktg. rep. Dow Pharm. div. Dow Chem. Co., Orange County, Calif., 1974-77, Las Vegas, Nev., 1980-81; mgr. product publicity Dow Agrl. Products div. Dow Chem. Co., Midland, Mich., 1977-80; mgr. mktg. communications Dowell Fluid Services Region div. Dow Chem. Co. Houston, 1981-84; adminstr. mktg. communications Swedlow, Inc., Garden Grove, Calif., 1984-85; cons. mktg. communications, 1985-86; mgr. mktg. communications Am. Convertors div. Am. Hosp. Supply, 1986-87; mgr. sales support Surgidev Corp., Santa Barbara, Calif., 1987-88; owner Barrel House, Victorville, Calif., 1988-91, Saratoga Fences, Las Vegas, 1991; pub. info. officer Clark County Comprehensive Planning, Las Vegas, 1992-96; pub. info. officer, mgmt. analyst II Clark County, Las Vegas, 1996—; guest lectr. Calif. State U., Long Beach, 1970; seminar coordinator U. Calif., Irvine, 1972; mem. Western White House Press Corps, 1972; pub. relations cons. BASF Wyandotte, Phila., 1981-82. Author: Agricultural Public Relations/Publicity, 1981; editor Big Mean AG Machine (internal mag.), 1977; contbr. numerous articles to trade publs.; contbg. editor Dowell Mktg. Newsletter, 1983; creator, designer Novahistine DMX Trial Size nat. mktg. program, 1977. Com. mem. Dow Employees for Polit. Action, Midland, 1978-80; bd. dirs. Dowell Employees for Polit. Action Com., Houston, 1983-84. World Campus Afloat scholar, U. Seven Seas, 1966-67; recipient PROTOS award, 1985. Mem. Pub. Relations Soc. Am. (cert.), Soc. Petroleum Engrs., Internat. Assn. Bus. Communicators. Episcopalian. Recipient first rights to televise President Nixon in Western White House. Office: 6340 Lanning Ln Las Vegas NV 89108-2605

BOYLE, (CHARLES) KEITH, artist, educator; b. Defiance, Ohio., Feb. 15, 1930. Student, Ringling Sch. Art; B.F.A., U. Iowa. Prof. painting and drawing Stanford U., Calif., 1962-88. Group shows include Stanford U. Mus., 1964, San Francisco Mus. Art, 1965, Ann Arbor, Mich., 1965, Joslyn Art Mus., Omaha, 1970, San Jose Mus. Art, Calif., 1978; represented in permanent collections: San Francisco Mus. Art, Stanford U. Mus., Mead paper Corp., Atlanta, Nat. Fine Arts Collection, Washington, Oakland Mus., Continental Bank, Chgo., Seton Med. Ctr., Daily City, Calif., Schneider Mus., Ashland, Oreg. Grantee NEA, 1981-82, Pew Meml. Trust, 1986-87. Address: 6285 Thompson Creek Rd Applegate OR 97530-9639

BOYLE, LARRY MONROE, federal judge; b. Seattle, June 23, 1943; s. Thomas L. and Winona (Green) B.; m. Beverly Rigby, Jan 31, 1969; children: Brian, Jeffery, Bradley, David, Melissa, Layne. BSc, Brigham Young U., 1968; JD, U. Idaho, 1972. Bar: Idaho 1973, U.S. Dist. Ct. Idaho 1973. Atty. Hansen, Boyle, Beard & Martin, P.A., Idaho Falls, Idaho, 1973-86; dist. judge 7th Jud. Dist., Idaho Falls, 1986-89; judge U.S. Supreme Ct. Idaho, Boise, 1989-92; magistrate judge U.S. Dist. Ct. Idaho, Boise, 1992—. Office: US Courthouse 550 W Fort St Rm 518 Boise ID 83724-0101

BOYLES, PETER GUTHRIE, radio talk show host; b. Pitts., Oct. 17, 1943; s. Ward Guthrie and Eva Rose (Stitt) B.; m. Judy Alee Thoreson, Dec. 16, 1968 (div. 1972); children: Shannon, Morgan; m. Kathleen Elaine Philbrook, Feb. 1, 1992. BA in History, Metro State U.; postgrad. in History, Denver U., 1974. Talk show host KHOW-Radio, Denver, 1994—. Office: KHOW Radio 1380 Lawrence St Denver CO 80204-2029

BOYNTON, DONALD ARTHUR, title insurance company executive; b. Culver City, Calif., Sept. 6, 1940; s. A.A. and Margaret Lena (Slocum) B.; m. Jean Carolyn Ferrulli, Nov. 10, 1962; children: Donna Jean, Michael Arthur; m. Sharon C. Burns, Nov. 18, 1984; children: Cynthia, David, Sharie. Student, El Camino Jr. Coll., 1960-62, Antelope Valley Jr. Coll., 1963-64, Orange Coast Coll., 1969-72; BA, Bradford U., 1977. With Title Ins. & Trust Co., 1958-63; sales mgr. Title Ins. & Trust Co., Santa Ana, Calif., 1980-81; dep. sheriff County of Los Angeles, 1963-65; with Transamerica Title Ins. Co., L.A., 1965-69, state coord., 1981-82; sr. title officer Calif. Land Title Co., L.A. and Orange Counties, 1969-72; asst. sec., systems analyst Lawyers Title Ins. Corp., 39 states, 1972-77; county mgr. Am. Title Co., Santa Ana, Calif., 1977-79; v.p., mgr. Orange County ops. Chgo. Title Ins. Co., Tustin, Calif., 1979-80; pres. Stewart Title Co. of Fresno County, 1985-86; supr. builder svcs. Orange Coast Title Co., Santa Ana, San Diego, 1986-89; sr. title officer TSG dept. Orange Coast/Record Title, Whittier and La Mirada, Calif., 1990-94; sr. title officer, So. Calif. TSG Manager (5 County) State of Calif. for Orange Coast Title, 1993; sr. nat. coord. Chgo. Title and Ins., Irvine, Calif., 1993-96; title officer, claims officer N.Am. Title Ins., Orange, Calif., 1996; nat. underwriter/coord. 50 states and Canada LandAmerica/Lawyers Title Ins. Corp., L.A., 1997—. Mem. Calif. Trustees Assn., Orange County Escrow Assn., Optimists (sec.-treas.), Elks (life, chaplain), Rotary. E-mail: dboynton@landam.com. Home: 9061 Bermuda Dr Huntington Beach CA 92646-7812 Office: 888 W 6th St Fl 4 Los Angeles CA 90017-2703

BOYNTON, ROBERT GRANVILLE, computer systems analyst; b. North Bend, Oreg., Aug. 11, 1951; s. Granville Clarence Jr. and Leatrice Anne (Yoder) B.; m. Sandra Lynn Harrold, Aug. 17, 1991. Student, Central Oreg. Community Coll., 1969-70. cert. career data processing Heald Coll. Bus., 1972. Computer operator Coca-Cola Bottling Co. Calif., San Francisco, 1973-76, data processing mgr., 1977-78; computer operator Warn Industries, Milwaukie, Oreg., 1979-81, computer programmer, 1981-85, analyst, 1983-85, computer systems analyst, 1985-90, info. systems team leader, 1990—, sr. bus. analyst, 1993—. Vol. Oreg. Spl. Olympics, 1985-86. Democrat. Avocations: camping, hunting, fishing, reading. Home: 5712 SE 130th Pl Portland OR 97236-4175 Office: Warn Industries 13270 SE Pheasant Ct Portland OR 97222-1297

BOYNTON, WILLIAM LEWIS, electronic manufacturing company official; b. Kalamazoo, May 31, 1928; s. James Woodbury and Cyretta (Gunther) B.; ed. pub. schs.; m. Kei Ouchi, Oct. 8, 1953. Asst. mgr. Speigel J & R, Kalamazoo, 1947-48; with U.S. Army, 1948-74, ret., 1974; with Rockwell/Collins div., Newport Beach, Calif., 1974-78, supr. material, investment recovery coord., 1974-81, coord., 1981-88; investment recovery supr., coord. Rockwell/CDC, Santa Ana, Calif., 1981-88, coord. investment recovery, 1982-86, shipping supr., investment recovery, environ. coord., 1982-88, 1987-88, material coord., 1988, environ. coord. Rockwell/DCD, Newport Beach, 1988-89, ret.; mem. faculty Western Mich. U., 1955-58. Trustee Orange County Vector Control Dist., 1980—, bd. sec. 1991, bd. v.p. 1992—; pres., 1993. Trustee Corp. Bd., 1993, pres., 1993-94, mem. exec. bd. dirs., 1994, mem. bd.; mem. adv. panel for bus./econ. devel. Calif. State Legislature, 1979-86. Decorated Bronze Star. Mem. Assn. U.S. Army, Assn. U.S. Army, Non-Commd. Officers Assn., Mosquito and Vector Control Assn. Calif. (v.p. 1992, pres. 1993), Nat. Geog. Soc. Republican. Roman Catholic. Home and Office: 5314 W Lucky Way Santa Ana CA 92704-1048

BOYTIM, MICHAEL J., surgical nurse; b. Pitts., Sept. 17, 1958; s. Michael Nicholas and Dolores Marie (Danko) B. BSN, U. Pitts., 1981; M in Nursing, UCLA, 1990. Certified registered nurse anesthetist, Am. Assn. Nurse Anesthetists. Registered nurse Presby. Hosp., Pitts., 1981-82; from certified registered nurse anesthetist to asst. dir. Kaiser Permanente, Pasadena, Calif., 1984-96, asst. dir., 1996—. Author: (with others) Pediatric Anesthesia, 1998. Docent Gamble House, Pasadena, Calif., 1998. Mem. Calif. Assn. Nurse Anesthetists. Avocations: running, cooking, reading. Home: 1290 Fairlawn Way Pasadena CA 91105-1042 Office: Kaiser Permanente 100 S Los Robles Ave # 550 Pasadena CA 91101-2453

BOZAJIAN, JAMES ROBERT, lawyer; b. Inglewood, Calif., Oct. 4, 1965; s. Robert Paul and Frances (Amerian) B. BA in history, UCLA, 1987; JD, U. So. Calif., 1990. Dep. dist. atty. L.A. County, L.A., 1990—. Mayor City of Calabasas, 1998-99; mem. city coun., 1997—; mem. Calabasas Cmty. Policing Commn., 1993-97; mem. Calabasas C. of C., Conejo/Las Virgenes Future Found., St. Peter Armenian Ch.; bd. dirs. UCLA John Wooden Ctr., 1994-97. Mem. Calif. Dist. Attys. Assn., L.A. County Assn. Dep. Dist. Attys. (pres. 1996, 97, bd. dirs. 1993—), UCLA Alumni Assn., U. So. Calif. Sch. Law Alumni Assn. (bd. dirs. 1995-97). Republican. Am. Orthodox. Avocations: writing polit. commentaries, reading, tennis, rollerblading, watching "Columbo" re-runs (has every episode on tape). Office: Calabasas City Hall 26135 Mureau Rd Calabasas CA 91302-3182

BOZARTH, GEORGE S., historian, musicologist, pianist; b. Trenton, N.J., Feb. 28, 1947. MFA, Princeton U., 1973; PhD, Princeton U., 1978. Prof. music history U. Wash.; dir. Brahms Archive, Seattle, Internat. Brahms Conf., Washington, 1983; co-artistic dir. Gallery Concerts, Seattle. Editor: Johannes Brahms, Orgelwerke, The Organ Works, Munich, G Henle, 1988, J.S. Bach Cantata, Ach Gott vom Himmel sieh darein, BWV2, Neue Bach Augabe, 1/16, 1981, 84, The Correspondence of Johannes Brahms and Robert Keller, 1996, articles on Brahms' Lieder and Duets, the genesis and chronology of Brahms's works, Brahms' piano sonatas and First Piano Concerto, editl. problems, questions of authenticity, Brahms's pianos and piano music. Fullbright-Hayes scholar to Austria, 1975-77; fellow ACLS, 1982; NEH Rsch. Conf. grantee, 1983; grantee Am. Philos. Soc., 1999. Mem. Am. Brahms Soc. (exec. dir.), Am. Musicol. Soc., Early Music Am., Classical Consort. Office: U Wash Sch Music PO Box 353450 Seattle WA 98195-3450

BRACCO, GLORIA JEAN, elementary education educator; b. Modesto, Calif., Dec. 20, 1946; d. Charlie and Ida Lena (Morandi) B.; m. Ed Rusca, July 11, 1992. AA, Modesto Jr. Coll., 1967; BA, Chico State Coll., 1970. Cert. elem. edn. tchr. Tchr. first grade Cardozo Elem. Sch., Riverbank, Calif., 1970-73; tchr. first and second grade Rio Altura Sch., Riverbank, 1973-90; tchr. first grade Calif. Ave. Sch., Riverbank, 1990—; speaker Elem. Sch. Sci. Assn., Modesto and Vallejo, Calif., 1983-84; cons. steering com. for outdoor edn. curriculum, Modesto, 1980-82, Mi Wok adv. com., Modesto, 1981-82; presentor Poetry Anthology, Modesto, 1981-82. Co-editor: (periodical) Scenes, 1980-82; contbg. tchr. Frank Schaffer's School Days mag., 1994, 95. Patron Modesto Performing Arts, 1989; assoc. Modesto Symphony, 1991—; mem. Yosemite (Calif.) Assn., 1986—. Recipient Cert. of Recognition, Assemblyman C. Perrino, Sacramento, 1980. Mem. AAUW (gift honoree for ednl. found. 1986, pres. 1982-83), Stanislaus Reading Coun. (sec. 1985-87), Parent/Tchr. Club (treas. 1992-93, VIP award 1993), Stanislaus County Commn. for Women (Outstanding Woman award 1994), Modesto Ski Club (pres. 1984-85, Wagoner trophy 1986), Delta Kappa Gamma. Avocations: tennis, skiing, travel, bicycling, gardening.

BRACEY, EARNEST NORTON, political science educator; b. Jackson, Miss., June 8, 1953; s. Willard and Odessa Manola (Ford) B.; m. Atsuko Konuma, Apr. 2, 1995; children: Dominique, Princess, Omar. MPA, Golden Gate U., 1979; MA, Cath. U., Washington, 1983; D of Pub. Adminstrn., George Mason U., 1993. Commd. 2d lt. U.S. Army, 1975, advanced through grades to lt. col., 1992; ret., 1995; instr. polit. sci. C.C. of So. Nev., Las Vegas, 1996—; adj. prof. Ctrl. Tex. Coll., Camp Zama, Japan, 1993-95; mem. Nev. faculty alliance C.C. of So. Nev., Las Vegas, 1996—. Author: Choson, 1994. Mem. NAACP, Am. Soc. of Mil. Comptrs., Assn. of the U.S. Army, Retired Officer Assn. Avocations: jazz trumpeter, marathon runner, writing, poetry, American historian.

BRACHER, GEORGE, radiologist; b. Portland, Oreg., Mar. 20, 1909; s. George Michael and Anna (Ris) B.; m. Helen Arndt, Oct. 6, 1936; children: Randall W., Ann Louise. BS, U. Oreg., 1932, MD, 1934. Diplomate Am. Bd. Radiology. Intern St. Vincent's Hosp., Portland, 1935; resident fellow U. Chgo., 1936-38; asst. prof. radiology U. Oreg. Med. Sch., Portland, 1938-39; radiologist King County Hosp. System, Seattle, 1939-41, Hilo (Hawaii) Hosp., 1960-85, Lucy Henriques Med. Ctr., Kamuela, Hawaii, 1985—; pvt. practice Seattle and Spokane (Wash.), 1941-60; cons. radiologist Honokaa (Hawaii) Hosp., 1960—, Kohala (Hawaii) Hosp., 1960—, Kau Hosp., Pahala, Hawaii, 1960—; attending physician U. Hawaii Peace Corps Project, 1962-70. Pres. Hawaii County unit Am. Cancer Soc., Hilo, 1970, Hawaii Pacific div. Honolulu, 1972, chmn. Pacific and related islands com., 1975; founder Hawaii County Med. Soc. Scholarship Fund, Cancer Care Trust, Hilo. Mem. AMA, Hawaii Med. Assn., Hawaii County Med. Soc. (pres. 1969), Am. Coll. Radiology, Hawaii Radiologic Soc., Wash. Athletic Club, Hilo Yacht Club. Avocation: woodworking with Hawaii koa. Home: 134 Puako Beach Dr Kamuela HI 96743-9709

BRACKNER, JAMES WALTER, accounting educator, consultant; b. Selma, Ala., Aug. 6, 1934; s. James Oscar and Ruby Belle (Langston) B.; m. Gayle Linton, Sept. 11, 1959; children: James L., Betsy, Joseph L., David L., Susan, Daniel L., Nancy. *Mr. Branckner's progenitors were American Indian (Cherokee), Scotch, English and German. The European progenitors came to America during the 1700s and settled in South Carolina, Georgia, Alabama and Mississippi. Grandfather, James Wesley Brackner and his wife Dovie Lou Jean Acker, raised a family in McCalla, Alabama. Each July 4th week-end the descendants of this couple meet at "Papa Brackner's Park" (where a pavilion has been built on the grandparent's old farm and home site) in McCalla, Alabama for a family reunion. In 1997 there were over 400 descendants of James Wesley Brackner's family and over 350 persons attended the 1997 family reunion.* BS in Acctg., Brigham Young U., 1961, MS in Acctg., 1962; PhD in Accountancy, U. Ala., 1984. CPA; cert. mgmt. acct., cert. in fin. mgmt. Staff acct. Arthur Andersen, L.A., 1962-65; controller, asst. sec. Teledyne-WIW, L.A., 1965-68; CFO Phaostron Electronics, South Pasadena, Calif., 1968-69; instr., asst. prof. Brigham Young U., Provo, Utah, 1969-78; CFO Deseret Mgmt. Corp.-Farms Divsn., Salt Lake City, 1978-81; from asst. prof. to assoc. prof. Utah State U., Logan, 1981-93, prof., 1993—; cons., expert witness Richards Brandt Miller Nelson, Salt Lake City, 1988-91; cons. Latvian and Russian Fin. Ministries, 1993, Ministry of Labour and Social Welfare, Govt. of Thailand, 1998-99. Author: Management Accounting/Manufacturing Excellence, 1996; contbr. more than 40 articles to profl. jours., chpt. to book. Scout leader, merit badge counselor Boy Scouts Am., Logan, 1982—. With U.S. Army 1954-56. Mem. AICPA, Inst. Mgmt. Accts. (nat. v.p. 1996-97, bd. regents 1995-96, edn. com. 1994-95, ethics com. 1991-94, acad. rels. co. 1998, 99, bd. dirs. 1997—), Am. Acctg. Assn., Nat. Contract Mgmt. Assn. (cert. fraud examiners), Utah Assn. CPAs (chpt. pres. 1995-96). Republican. Mormon. Avocations: fishing, travel, genealogy. Home: 760 Stewart Hill Dr Logan UT 84321-5690 Office: Utah State Univ Sch Accountancy Logan UT 84322-3540

BRADEN, GEORGE WALTER, II (BARRON OF CARRIGALINE), company executive; b. L.A., Sept. 1, 1936; s. Paul Sumner and Evelyn Widney (Traver) B.; m. Trina Rose Thomas, July 3, 1964; children: Barbara Diane, Beverly Eileen Braden Christensen. BS, Calif. State U., 1963; grad. cert., U. So. Calif., 1990, Harvard U., 1991; postgrad., UCLA, 1990—; MBA, Chadwick U.; JA, Blackstone Law Sch. Mgr. western region vet. div. Bristol-Myers, Syracuse, N.Y., 1970-79; pres. Braden Sales Assocs. Internat., Apple Valley, Calif., 1980—. Mem. Friends of Hoover Inst., Stanford, Calif.; charter mem. Rep. Presdl. Task Force, Washington, 1989—; commr. Rep. Presdl. Adv. Com., Washington, 1991—; active Nat. Rep. Senatorial Com. Capt. USMB, 1985-93, maj., 1993—. Recipient Presdl. order of Merit, Heritage Found., Rep. Presdl. award, 1994; numerous awards Boy Scouts of Am.; named Lord of North Bovey, Lord of Newton Bushel. Mem. Am. Mktg. Assn., Tex. A&M U. Internat. Assn. of Agri-Bus., Curia Baronis Guild for Barons, Lords of Manor, Pres.'s Club. Mem. LDS Ch.

BRADEN, WARREN RAMSEY, SR., health administrator, educational consultant; b. Chgo., Mar. 25, 1963; s. Joseph and Alberta (Ramsey) B.; m. Yvette Mitchell, May 2, 1995 (div. Oct. 1997); 1 child, Warren R. Jr. BA, St. Olaf Coll., 1985; MS in Edn., No. Ill. U., 1989, EdD, 1993. Asst. dir. Chgo. Area Health Career Program, 1985-89; health educator Ill. Cancer Coun., Chgo., 1989; project counselor Project Upward Bound, Chgo., 1989-90; regional mgr. Kumon Mathematex, Arlington Heights, Ill., 1991-92; assoc. project dir. Wis. AHEC Sys., Milw., 1992-97; exec. dir. Ke Anuenue Area Health Edn. Ctr., Hilo, Hawaii, 1997—; cons./trainer MIE, Hilo, 1993—. V.p. Hilo Jaycees, 1997—; mem. Am. Cancer Soc., 1993-97, Boy Scouts Am., 1995-97; bd. dirs. St. Olaf Alumni, 1993-96. Named one of Outstanding Young Men of Am., 1986; Ill. Consortium for Edn. Opportunity fellow, 1989-93. Mem. Soc. Tchrs. Family Medicine, Phi Delta Kappa. Avocations: reading, basketball, soccer, sailing. Home: HC 1 Box 5502 Keaau HI 96749-8500 Office: Ke Ave Area Health Edn Ctr 1190 Waianuenue Ave Hilo HI 96720-2020

BRADFORD, DAVID PAUL, judicial assistant; b. Lynwood, Calif., Mar. 23, 1955; s. William H. and Barbara E. (O'Leary) Johnson. AA, Citrus Coll., Azusa, Calif., 1975; BA in Polit. Sci., UCLA, 1978; postgrad., Calif. State U., L.A., 1984-85, U. West L.A., 1990-91. Prin. clerk UCLA Brain

Rsch. Inst., 1977-81; adminstrv. asst., supr. UCLA Hosp. and Clinics, 1977-81; dep. to atty. in residence matters office of registrar UCLA, 1981-85; office of clerk L.A. County Bd. Suprs., L.A., 1987-88; judicial asst., ct. clerk L.A. Superior Ct., L.A., 1988—; founder Bradford & Assocs., L.A., 1987—; rsch. dir. citizens Protection Alliance, Santa Monica, 1992—. Active L.A. County Domestic Violence Coun. Recipient Cert. of Appreciation, Domestic Violence Coun., 1990, commendation Los Angeles County Bd. Suprs., 1993, L.A. Police Dept. and Assn. Threat Assessment Profls. award, 1994. Mem. N.Y. Acad. Scis., Los Angeles County Superior Ct. Clks. Assn. (local 575 AFSCME pres. 1993, 94), N.Y. Acad. Polit. Scis. Office: Bradford & Assocs 3921 Wilshire Blvd Ste 303V Los Angeles CA 90010-3317

BRADFORD, DIANE GOLDSMITH, multimedia marketing and product consultant; b. Provo, Utah, Apr. 20, 1951; d. Howard and Roxey Faye (Rosenbaum) B.; 1 child, Tamara. BS, U. Utah, 1973, MS, 1976, PhD, 1980. Instructional design intern InterWest Regional Med. Edn. Ctr., Salt Lake City, 1979; instr. Algebra divsn. continuing edn. U. Utah, Salt Lake City, 1980-81; project tng. coord. Automated Mfg. Resource Planning Project, O.C. Tanner Co., Utah, 1981-83; data processing dir. VA Med. Ctr., Salt Lake City, 1983-85; asst. dir. tng. and publs. IHC Affiliated Svcs. Inc., Salt Lake City, 1985-88; asst. dir. edn. and tng. GTE Health Systems Inc., Moss Rehab. Hosp., Phila., 1988-89; dir. edn. Wharton exec. edn. U. Pa., Phila., 1989-92; pres. Prime Resources Inc., Aspen, Colo., 1993—. Contbr. articles to profl. jours. Awards judge Coun. Internat. Nontheatrical Events. Mem. Am. Prodn. and Inventory Control Soc. (cert., edn. v.p. 1983-84). Avocations: hiking, skiing, cycling, reading. Home: 1145 Black Birch Dr Aspen CO 81611-1003 Office: 1145 Black Birch Dr Aspen CO 81611-1003 also: 255 S 38th St Philadelphia PA 19104-3706

BRADFORD, LEE TYLER, writer; b. Newton, Mass., Mar. 14, 1929; d. Arthur Bromley and Katherine (Brush) T.; m. Robert Brady, 1960 (div. 1967); m. Richard P. Bradford, July 3, 1970 (wid. May 1973). Student, Briarcliff Coll., 1948. Society writer Boston Herald, 1948-50; travel writer Am. Express Co., N.Y.C., 1950-52; publicity dir. Pacific Area Travel Assn., San Francisco, 1952-59; asst. publicity dir. Matson Lines, San Francisco, 1959-62; travel editor San Jose (Calif.) Mercury News, 1962-77; freelance golf writer Burlingame, Calif., 1977—; golf travel columnist GolfWeb, Burlingame, 1996—. Author: (novel, as Lee Tyler) The Clue of the Clever Canine, 1994. Mem. Sisters in Crime, Mystery Writers of Am., Peninsula Tennis Club, Crystal Springs Golf Club. Avocations: tennis, golf, swimming, reading, old movies.

BRADFORD, SUSAN ANNE, political consultant, writer; b. Pasadena, Calif., Dec. 2, 1969; d. Wesley Gene and Nancy Cornelia (Dixon) B. Student, Coll. Cevenol, Le Chambon Sur Lignon, France, 1985, St. Andrews U., Scotland, 1989-90; BA in English, U. Calif., Irvine, 1992; MA in Internat. Rels., Essex U., Eng., 1996, postgrad. Editor-in-chief Gandalf's Gazette, Irvine, Calif., 1987-88; news editor New Univ., Irvine, Calif., 1987-88; intern Sta. CBS-TV News, L.A., 1989; host, exec. producer Witness the News TV show, Irvine, 1990-92; prodn. asst. PBS Red Car Film Project, L.A., 1992-93; intern in news writing Sta. KNX News, L.A., 1993; reporter City News Svc., L.A., 1994-95; founder/editor European Review, 1995-98; sr. rsch. fellow, polit. cons. Atlantic Coun., 1996-98; polit. cons. UK Shadow Fgn. Sec. Michael Howard, 1998. Author poems; contbr. articles to profl. jours.; founding editor: European Rev., 1995—; co-pub. European publs., 1999—. Bd. dirs. HWPC Scholarship Found., Hollywood, Calif., 1992-93; mem. NATO Univs. Adv. Com., 1996—; mem. com. European Movement, 1995—. Recipient Writing awards Palos Verdes Nat. Bank, 1987, AFL-CIO, 1987, 3d Pl. award Nat. Fedn. Press Women, 1992. Mem. Calif. Press Women (pub. rels. chair 1991-92), Hollywood Women's Press Club (bd. dirs. 1989-94), European Movement (committee member/London strategy group media coord.) 1995—, NATO Universities Advisory Committee, 1996—, Irvine Women's Crew (founder, pres.). Mem. United Ch. of Christ. Avocation: studying Japanese language, travel, skiing. Office: PO Box 7000-245 Rolling Hills Estates CA 90275

BRADKIN, TANIA SZLAVIK, foundation administrator; b. Phila., Sept. 11, 1970; d. Joseph and Matilde (Soto) Szlavik; m. David Criscitelli Bradkin, June 7, 1997. BA, The Am. U., 1992, BA in Polit. Sci., 1992. Pub. rels. asst. ACHNA Cultural Ctr., Madrid, Spain, 1990; legis. asst. Sen. Arlen Spector, Washington, 1990-91; nat. sales coord. WASHFM-97.1/WTOP News, Washington, 1992-94; reporter WTOP News Radio - 1500AM, Washington, 1993-94; acct. exec. DC101-FM/WWDC-AM, Washington, 1994-95; comml. agr. Commls. Unltd., Beverly Hills, Calif., 1995-96; exec. dir. The Gonda Family Found., Beverly Hills, Calif., 1996—; publicist, agt. Inger Martens, Beverly Hills, 1997-98. Campaign coord. The Leukemia Soc. Team in Tng., 1998. Mem. NAFE, So. Calif. Assn. Philanthropy, Coun. Founds., Assn. Small Founds., Humane Soc. U.S. (assoc.), Women in Film. Avocations: disco dancing, flag football, Spanish, Hungarian. Office: Leukemia Soc 100 Corporate Point Culver City CA 90230

BRADLEY, CHARLES WILLIAM, podiatrist, educator; b. Fife, Tex., July 23, 1923; s. Tom and Mary Ada (Cheatham) B.; m. Marilyn A. Brown, Apr. 3, 1948 (dec. Mar. 1973); children: Steven, Gregory, Jeffrey, Elizabeth, Gerald. Student, Tex. Tech., 1940-42; D. Podiatric Medicine, Calif. Coll. Podiatric Medicine U. San Francisco, 1949, MPA, 1987, D.Sc. (hon.). Pvt. practice podiatry Beaumont, Tex., 1950-51, Brownwood, Tex., 1951-52, San Francisco, San Bruno, Calif., 1952—; assoc. clin. prof. Calif. Coll. Podiatric Medicine, 1992-98; chief of staff Calif. Podiatry Hosp., San Francisco; mem. surg. staff Sequoia Hosp., Redwood City, Calif.; mem. med. staff Peninsula Hosp., Burlingame, Calif.; chief podiatry staff St. Luke's Hosp., San Francisco; chmn. bd. Podiatry Ins. Co. Am.; cons. VA; assoc. prof. podiatric medicine Calif. Coll. Podiatric Medicine. Mem. San Francisco Symphony Found.; mem. adv. com. Health Policy Agenda for the Am. People, AMA; chmn. trustees Calif. Coll. Podiatric Medicine, Calif. Podiatry Coll., Calif. Podiatry Hosp.; mem. San Mateo Grand Jury, 1989. Served with USNR, 1942-45. Mem. Am. Podiatric Med. Assn. (trustee, pres. 1983-84), Calif. Podiatry Assn. (pres. No. div. 1964-66, state bd. dirs., pres. 1975-76, Podiatrist of Yr. award 1983), Nat. Coun. Edn. (vice-chmn.), Nat. Acads. Practice (chmn. podiatric med. sect. 1991-96, sec. 1996—), Am. Legion, San Bruno C. of C. (bd. dirs. 1978-91, v.p. 1992, bd. dir. grand jury assoc. 1990), Olympic Club, Commonwealth Club Calif., Elks, Lions. Home: 2965 Trousdale Dr Burlingame CA 94010-5708 Office: 560 Jenevein Ave San Bruno CA 94066-4408

BRADLEY, JEAN ELEANOR, newspaper executive, public relations consultant; b. North York, Ontario, Can., Apr. 14, 1928; d. Archer and Eleanor (Aitkin) Wardle; m. Kenneth Gordon Bradley, Nov. 26, 1949; children: Jill (dec. 1964), Anne Marjorie Bradley Jaeger. Grad., Earl Haig Coll., North York, Ont., Can., 1945; student bus. mgmt., Portland (Oreg.) C.C., 1981-85; student computer sci., U. Oregon, Rock Creek, 1987-88. Underwriter, office mgr. A.B. Ferguson, Ins., Toronto, Ont., Can., 1946-55; asst. editor, co-owner Estevan (Sask., Can.) Mercury, 1964-66; pub. rels. mgr. Kaiser Permanente N.W. region, Portland, Oreg., 1968-88; v.p., co-owner Daily Shipping News, Portland, 1985-95; pres. Braeward Pub., Portland, 1996—; exec. com. Kaiser Permanente Retirees, Portland, 1989—. Contbg. author: Oregon Writers Colony Anthology, 1993; author: A Home Across the Water, 1996; contbr. articles to various newspapers and mags. Bd. Dirs. Vol. Ctr., Portland, 1989-95. Named Outstanding Profl. of Yr., Women in Comms., Portland, 1986. Mem. Pub. Rels. Soc. Am. (accredited, chpt. pres. 1980, dist. chmn. 1985, president's citation 1985, William Marsh lifetime achievement award Columbia River chpt. 1988), Oreg. Press Women (various coms.), Oreg. Writers Colony (bd. dirs. 1994), Daus. Brit. Empire (v.p. state bd. dirs. 1989-93). Avocations: painting, poetry, fiction and nonfiction writing.

BRADLEY, JOSEPH, lawyer; b. St. Louis, Aug. 29, 1954; s. Steven J. and Karen (Mertz); m. Kelli Fowler, May 7, 1980; children: Joseph, Melissa. BA in Polit. Sci., U. Mo., Kansas City, 1975, JD, 1981. Bar: Mo. 1982, U.S. Dist. Ct. Mo. 1982, Colo. 1986. Atty. Martin, Payne & Assocs., St. Louis, 1982-91; ptnr. Werik, Sherman & Bradley, Denver, 1991—. Vol. worker Denver Humane Soc., 1993—. Mem. Colo. Assn. Trial Attys., Colo. Bar Assn., Denver Bar Assn. Democrat. Avocations: hunting, fishing, horseback riding, reading. Office: Werik Sherman & Bradley 8751 E Hampden Ave Ste C-5 Denver CO 80231-4914

BRADLEY, THOMAS LEE, sales and marketing executive, management consultant; b. Clinton, Iowa, Apr. 20, 1946; s. Max J. and Dolores Bradley. BBA, Western Ill. U., 1969; MBA, St. Ambrose U., 1991; D of Internat. Mgmt., Nova Southeastern U., 1997. Owner, mgr. Bradco Investments, Belleville, Ill., 1968-74; gen. mgr. Internat. Funding, Denver, 1974-80, Suncatcher, Sacramento, 1980-83; owner, mgr. Colortec Images, San Diego, 1985—, Bradley Internat., Sacramento and San Diego, 1980—; v.p. Realty Group Investments, San Diego, 1986—; owner Bradco Investment Co., 1988—; prof. mgmt. Nat. U., 1996; cons. Artisianes Titicaca, La Paz, Bolivia, 1976-85, Dept. Energy and Land, Sacramento, 1980-82, Trade Union Kovrov Russia, 1992-94; U.S. liaison Robert Lehrer Exports, Lima, Peru, 1975-84; bd. dirs. Satori Enterprises, San Diego, Aries, Denver, Reforming Econs. Rsch. Inst. Author: Iowa Poems, 1978 (Iowa poetry Assn. award 1978), Starting Business--A Primer, 1985, A Moment in Time, 1995, Hofstede's Cultural Dimensions in Ukraine, Russia, Belarus, 1996; contbr. articles and photographs to jours. and newsletters. Vol. fund raising Heart Assn., Belleville, Ill., 1970; asst. chmn. Democratic presdl. election, 1972, chmn. voter registration, 1986; chmn. fund raising Photo Products Assn., 1986. Mem. Am. Internat. Mktg. Assn., Acad. Internat. Bus., San Diego Bd. Realtors, San Diego Life Underwriters, Photo Products Assn. (founder 1986), Toastmasters. Democrat. Avocations: photography, golf, camping, travel. Home: 4360 Campus Ave #15 San Diego CA 92103-2461

BRADLEY, WADE HARLOW, acquisitions specialist; b. Mpls.; s. Robert Douglas and Florence (Wells) B.; m. Alessandra Maria Benitez, June 30, 1984; children: Isabella Andrea, Francesca Alessandra. BS, U. Minn., 1983; postgrad., LaJolla Acad. Advt., 1984. Bus. cons. A.B.A. Investment Corp., La Jolla, Calif., 1987-88; pres. The Harlow Co., San Diego, 1987—; acquisitions specialist Pacific Capital Ptnrs., San Diego, 1989-90; sr. v.p. corp. devel. Sundance Resources Inc., San Diego, 1990-95, sr. v.p., 1995—; sr. analyst La Jolla Securities Corp, San Diego, 1995-97; pres. Elliott Capital Ptnrs., Inc., San Diego, 1997—. Republican. Roman Catholic. Avocations: photography, furniture design. Office: Elliott Capital Ptnrs Inc 12625 High Bluff Dr Ste 300A San Diego CA 92130-2054

BRADLEY, WALTER D., lieutenant governor, real estate broker; b. Clovis, N.M., Oct. 30, 1946; s. Ralph W. and M. Jo (Black) B.; m. Debbie Shelly, Sept. 17, 1977; children: Tige, Lance, Nicole, Kristin. Student Eastern N.M. U., 1964-1967. Supr. Tex. Instruments, Dallas, Tex. 1967-73; mgr., salesman Nat. Chemsearch, Irving, Tex., 1973-76; real estate broker Colonial Real Estate, Clovis, 1976; real estate broker Realtors Assn. N.Mex., Clovis, N.Mex., 1976—; state senator Curry County, State of N.Mex., 1989-93; Lt. Governor State of N.Mex., Santa Fe, N. Mex., 1995—. mem. N.Mex. Senate, 1989-92, 99—; lieutenant governor State N.Mex., 1995—. V.p., bd. dirs. Clovis Indsl. Commn., 1983-86, pres. econ. devel., 1987; bd. dirs. United Way, Clovis, 1984-86, Curry County Blood Adv. Bd., Clovis, 1980-85; chmn. Curry County Reps., Clovis, 1984-88; Cosmos Soccer, Clovis, 1984. Recipient Albuquerque NAACP Disting. Leadership award, 1997, Disting. Svc. award N.Mex. Farm and Livestock Bur., 1997; named Man of Yr., Progressive Farmer Mag., 1998. Mem. Realtors Assn. N.Mex. (v.p., bd. dirs. 1982-85, v.p. 1987-88), Clovis Bd. Realtors (pres. 1982, 93), Clovis C. of C., Curry County Jaycees, N.M. Jaycees. Baptist. Lodge: Lions. Office: Office of Lt Gov State Capitol Bldg Ste 417 Santa Fe NM 87503

BRADLEY, WILLIAM BRYAN, cable television regulator; b. Charleston, W.Va., Feb. 12, 1929; s. Floyd England and Florence Clara (O'Bryan) B.; m. Virginia Vanderhoof Logan, Oct. 27, 1951; children: Christopher, Thomas, Michael, John, Mary Clare (dec.), Mary Ellen, Ann. BA in Journalism cum laude, U. Notre Dame, 1950. Supr., indsl. engr. Martin Co., Denver, 1958-61, 62-65; cons. Reynolds, Ward & Carey, Denver, 1961-62; analyst Denver City Coun., 1965-69, staff dir., 1969-82; dir. Office of Telecommunications, Denver, 1982-94; sr. assoc. Media Mgmt. Svcs., Inc., 1994—; co-founder, dir., vice-chmn. Greater Metro Cable Consortium, 1992; initiated joint city-industry cable TV Tech. Stds., 1987, adopted by FCC, 1992. Participant Japanese-Am. conf. on Globalization and Cable TV, Suwa, Japan, 1991. Co-founder Nat. Assn. Telecomm. Officers and Advisors, Washington, 1980, bd. dirs., 1983-88, pres., 1985-87; chmn. telecomm. subcom. Colo. Mcpl. League, Denver, 1985-86; bd. dirs. Denver Cmty. TV, 1996-98. Line Officer USN, 1950-53. Roman Catholic. Avocations: chess, books.

BRADLEY, WILLIAM GUERIN, radiologist, researcher, educator; b. L.A., July 30, 1948; s. William Guerin and Shirley Ann (Premack) B.; m. Sara Jane Smith Sewall, Nov. 6, 1976 (div. Sept. 1988); children: David, Kristin; m. Rosalind Kaye Brown Dietrich, Oct. 20, 1988; children: India, Felicity. BS, Calif. Inst. Tech., 1970; PhD, Princeton Univ., 1974; MD, U. Calif., San Francisco, 1977; FACR (hon.), Am. Coll. Radiology, Restin, Va. Diplomate Am. Bd. Radiology. Intern U. Calif., San Francisco, 1977-78, resident radiology, 1978-81; dir. MRI Huntington Meml. Hosp. and Huntington Med. Rsch. Inst., Pasadena, Calif., 1982-89; prof. radiology U. Calif., Irvine, 1984-98; dir. MRI Long Beach Meml. Med. Cntr., Calif., 1990 ; bd. trustees Radiol. Soc. of N.Am. Rsch. and Edn. Fund, Chgo., 1996—; chmn. com. on standards and accreditation for neuroradiology and MRI Am. Coll. Radiology, Restin, Va., 1992—; pres. Soc. for MRI, Chgo., 1988-89. Author: (multimedia CD ROM) Mastering MRI: Neuroradiology, 1996; co-author: Advandced MRI Techniques, 1997, MRI: The Basics, 1997; co-editor: Magnetic Resonance Imaging, 1988, 1992 (award best new book by profl. and scholarly pub.). Recipient gold medal Clin. MRI, Eng., 1994. Fellow Am. Coll. Radiology; mem. Am. Soc. Neuroradiology, Jonathon Club, Twilight Club. Republican. Presbyterian. Avocations: skiing, tennis, travel. Office: Long Beach Meml MRI Ctr 403 E Columbia St Long Beach CA 90806-1620

BRADSHAW, JERALD SHERWIN, chemistry educator, researcher; b. Cedar City, Utah, Nov. 28, 1932; s. Sherwin H. and Maree (Wood) B.; m. Karen Lee, Aug. 6, 1954; children: Donna M. Webster, Melinda C. BS, U. Utah, 1955; PhD, UCLA, 1963. Postdoctoral Calif. Inst. Tech., Pasadena, 1962-63; chemist Chevron Research, Richmond, Calif., 1963-66; asst. prof. chemistry Brigham Young U., Provo, Utah, 1966-69, assoc. prof., 1969-74, prof., 1974—, asst. chmn. chemistry dept., 1980-86; vis. prof. Nat. Acad. Sci., U. Ljubljana, Yugoslavia, 1972-73, 82, U. Sheffield, England, 1978, James Cook U., Townsville, Australia, 1988. Author 2 books; contbr. over 350 articles to profl. jours.; patentee in field. Served with USNR, 1955-59. Recipient Gov.'s medal in sci. and tech., 1991. Mem. Am. Chem. Soc. (Utah award 1989, nat. award for separations sci. and tech. 1996), Internat. Soc. Heterocyclic Chemistry (bd. advisors 1980-82), Utah Acad. Sci., Sigma Xi (ann. lectr. 1988). Republican. Mem. LDS Ch. Avocations: stamp collecting, church activities. Office: Brigham Young U Dept Chemistry-Biochemistry Provo UT 84602

BRADSHAW, RALPH ALDEN, biochemistry educator; b. Boston, Feb. 14, 1941; s. Donald Bertram and Eleanor (Dodd) B.; m. Roberta Perry Wheeler, Dec. 29, 1961; children: Christopher Evan, Amy Dodd. BA in Chemistry, Colby Coll., 1962; PhD, Duke U., 1966. Asst. prof. Washington U., St. Louis, 1969-72, assoc. prof., 1972-74, prof., 1974-82; prof., chair dept. U. Calif., Irvine, 1982-93, prof., 1993—; study sect. chmn. NIH, 1979, mem., 1975-79, 80-85; mem. sci. adv. bd. Hereditary Disease Found., 1983-87, ICN Nucleic Acids Rsch. Inst., 1986-87; rsch. study com. physiol. chem. Am. Heart Assn., 1984-86, mem. Coun. on Thrombosis, 1976-90; fellowship screening com. Am. Cancer Soc. Calif., 1984-87; chmn. adv. com. Western Winter Workshops, 1984-88; dir., chmn., mem. organizing com. numerous symposia, confs. in field including Proteins in Biology and Medicine, Shanghai, Peoples Republic of China, 1981, Symposium Am. Protein Chemists, San Diego, 1985, mem. exec. com. Keystone Symp. Mol. Cell Biol., 1991-97, chmn., 1991-94, bd. dirs., 1997—, treas., 1997—; trustee Keystone Ctr., 1991-97; mem. exec. com. Internat. Union Biochem. Mol. Biol., 1991-97, U.S. Nat. Commn. Biochem., 1987-96, chmn., 1992-96; bd. dirs. Fed. Am. Soc. Exptl. Biology, 1992-96, v.p., 1994-95, pres., 1995-96. Mem. editl. bd. Archives Biochemistry and Biophysics, 1972-88, Jour. Biological Chemistry, 1973-77, 78-79, 81-86, assoc. editor, 1989—, Jour. Supramolecular Structure/Cellular Biochemistry, 1980-91, Bioscience Reports, 1980-87, Peptide and Protein Reviews, 1980-86, Jour. Protein Chemistry, 1980-90, IN VITRO Rapid Communication in Cell Biology, 1984—; editor Trends in Biochemical Sciences, 1975-91, editor-in-chief, 1986-91, J. Neurochem, 1986-90, Proteins: Structure, Functions & Genetics, 1988-92; assoc. editor: Growth Factors, 1989—; assoc. editor: Protein Science, 1990-92, 97—, mem. editl. bd., 1992—; mem. editl. bd. Biotech. Appl. Biochem., 1995—; co-editor-in-chief Mol. Cell Biol.-Res. Comm., 1998—; contbr. numerous articles to scientific jours. Recipient Young Scientist award Passano Found., 1976. Fellow AAAS; mem. Am. Chem. Soc. (Sect. award 1979), Am. Soc. Biochem. Molecular Biologists (coun. 1987-90, treas. 1991-97), Am. Peptide Soc., N.Y. Acad. Scis., Protein Soc. (acting pres. 1986-87), Am. Soc. for Cell Biology, Soc. for Neuroscience, The Endocrine Soc., Am. Soc. Bone Mineral Rsch., Assn. Biomolecular Rsch. Facilities, Sigma Xi. Home: 25135 Rivendell Dr Lake Forest CA 92630-4134 Office: U Calif Irvine Coll Medicine Dept Physiol & Biophysics D238 Med Sci I Irvine CA 92697

BRADY, JOHN PATRICK, JR., electronics educator, consultant; b. Newark, Mar. 20, 1929; s. John Patrick and Madeleine Mary (Atno) B.; m. Mary Coop, May 1, 1954; children: Peter, John P., Madeleine, Dennis, Mary G. BSEE, MIT, 1952, MSEE, 1953. Registered profl. engr., Mass. Sect. mgr. Hewlett-Packard Co., Waltham, Mass., 1956-67; v.p. engring. John Fluke Mfg. Co., Inc., Mountlake Terrace, Wash., 1967-73; v.p. engring. Dana Labs., Irvine, Calif., 1973-77; engring. mgr., tech. advisor to gen. mgr. Metron Corp., Upland, Calif., 1977-78; ptnr. Resource Assocs., Newport Beach, Calif., 1978-86; prof. electronics Orange Coast Coll., Costa Mesa, Calif., 1977-99, emeritus, 1999, faculty fellow, dean technology, 1983-84, chmn. electronics tech. dept., 1994-96, chmn. academic rank com., 1988-98; instr. computers and electrinc engring. Calif. State U., Long Beach, 1982-84. Mem. evaluation team Accrediting Commn. for Community and Jr. Colls., 1982-92; mem. blue ribbon adv. com. on oversees technology transfer U.S. Dept. of Commerce, 1974-76. With USN, 1946-48. Mem. Measurement Sci. Conf. (dir. 1982-83), MIT (L.A.). Contbr. articles in field to profl. jours.; mem. Eta Kappa Nu, Tau Beta Pi, Sigma Xi. Office: Orange Coast Coll Costa Mesa CA 92626

BRADY, MARY ROLFES, music educator; b. St. Louis, Nov. 26, 1933; d. William Henry and Helen Dorothy (Slavick) Rolfes; m. Donald Sheridan Brady, Aug. 29, 1953; children: Joseph William, Mark David, Douglas Sheridan, John Rolfes, Todd Christopher. Student, Stanford U., 1951-54, UCLA, 1967, U. So. Calif., 1972-73; pvt. studies with, Roxanna Byers, Dorothy Desmond, and Rudolph Ganz. Pvt. practice tchr. piano L.A., 1955—; TV and radio performer; pres. Jr. Philharmonic Com. L.A., 1975-76; legis. coord., bd. dirs. Philharmonic Affiliates, L.A., 1978-80. Life mem. Good Samaritan Hosp., St. Vincent Med. Ctr., L.A.; trustee St. Francis Med. Ctr., 1984-88; bd. dirs. Hollygrove-L.A. Orphans Home, Inc. Mem. Am. Coll. Musicians Club, Stanford Women's Club (past bd. dirs., pres. L.A. chpt. 1977—), The Muses, Springs Country Club.

BRADY, RODNEY HOWARD, holding company executive, broadcast company executive, former college president, former government official; b. Sandy, Utah, Jan. 31, 1933; s. Kenneth A. and Jessie (Madsen) B.; m. Carolyn Ann Hansen, Oct. 25, 1960; children: Howard Riley, Bruce Ryan, Brooks Alan. BS in Acctg. with high honors, U. Utah, MBA with high honors, 1957; DBA, Harvard U., 1966; postgrad., UCLA, 1969-70; PhD (hon.), Weber State Coll., 1986, Snow Coll., 1991, Univ. Utah, 1997. Missionary Ch. Jesus Christ of Latter-day Saints, Great Britain, 1953-55; teaching assoc. Harvard U. Bus. Sch., Cambridge, Mass., 1957-59; v.p. Mgmt. Systems Corp., Cambridge, 1962-65, Center Exec. Devel., Cambridge, 1963-64; v.p., dir. Center Exec. Devel., Boston, 1964-65; v.p. Tamerand Reef Corp., Christiansted, St. Croix, V.I., 1963-65; v.p., dir. Am. Inst. Execs., N.Y.C., 1963-65; v.p., mem. exec. com. aircraft div. Hughes Tool Co., Culver City, Calif., 1966-70; asst. sec. adminstrn. and mgmt. Dept. HEW, Washington, 1970-72; chmn. subcabinet exec. officers group of exec. br., 1971-72; exec. v.p., chmn. exec. com., dir. Bergen Brunswig Corp., Los Angeles, 1972-78; chmn. bd. Uni-mgrs. Internat., Los Angeles, 1974-78; pres. Weber State Coll., Ogden, Utah, 1978-85; pres., CEO Bonneville Internat. Corp., Salt Lake City, 1985-96, also dir.; pres., CEO Deseret Mgmt. Corp., Salt Lake City, 1996—; bd. dirs. Bergen Brunswig Corp., 1st Security Bank Corp., Mgmt. and Tng. Corp., Deseret Mut. Benefit Assn., chmn.; bd. dirs. Maximum Svc. Television, Inc., Intermountain Health Care Found., Nat. Assn. Broadcasters TV Bd., Utah Opera Co.; bd. advisors Mountain Bell Telephone, 1983-87; chmn. Nat. Adv. Com. on Accreditation and Instl. Eligibility, 1984-86, mem., 1983-87; chmn. Utah Gov.'s Blue Ribbon Com. on Tax Recodification, 1984-90; cons. Dept. Def., Dept. State, Dept. Commerce, HEW, NASA, Govt. of Can., Govt. of India (and indsl. firms), 1962—. Author: An Approach to Equipment Replacement Analysis, 1957, Survey of Management Planning and Control Systems, 1962, The Impact of Computers on Top Management Decision Making in the Aerospace and Defense Industry, 1966, (with others) How To Structure Incentive Contracts—A Programmed Text, 1965, My Missionary Years in Great Britain, 1976, An Exciting Start Along an Upward Path, 1978; contbr. articles to profl. jours. Mem. exec. com. nat. exec. bd. Boy Scouts Am., 1977—; chmn. nat. Cub Scout commn., 1977-81, pres. Western region, 1981-83, chmn. nat. ct. of honor, 1984-88; mem. adv. com. program for health sys. mgmt. Harvard U., 1973-78, mem. nat. adv. coun. U. Utah, 1971—, chairperson, 1974-76, nat. adv. bd. Coll. Bus., 1985—, chmn., 1989-93, mem. adv. com. Brigham Young U. Bus. Sch., 1972—; mem. dean's round table UCLA Grad. Sch. Mgmt., 1973-78; trustee Ettie Lee Homes for Boys, 1973-79; mem. gov. bd. McKay Dee Hosp., Ogden, Utah, 1979-87; bd. dirs. Utah Endowment for Humanities, 1978-80, Nat. Legal Ctr. for the Pub. Interest, 1991—, vice chmn., 1994-95, chmn., 1995-97, Utah Shakespeare Festival, 1992—, Ogden C. of C., 1978-83; bd. dirs. Utah Opera Co., 1997—. 1st lt. USAF, 1959-62. Recipient Silver Antelope award Boy Scouts Am., 1976; recipient Silver Beaver award Boy Scouts Am., 1979, Silver Buffalo award Boy Scouts Am., 1982, Disting. Alumni award U. Utah, 1990. Mem. Nat. Assn. TV Broadcasters (bd. dirs.), Am. Mgmt. Assn. (award 1969), L.A. C. of C. (tax structure com. 1969-70), Salt Lake Area C. of C. (bd. dirs. 1985-88), SAR (pres. Utah chpt. 1986-87), Sons of Utah Pioneers, Freedoms Found. at Valley Forge (nat. bd. dirs. 1986—), L.A. Country Club, Alta Club, Rotary, Phi Kappa Phi, Tau Kappa Alpha, Beta Gamma Sigma. Mem. LDS Ch. (past pres. L.A. stake). Office: Deseret Mgmt Corp Eagle Gate Tower 60 E South Temple Ste 575 Salt Lake City UT 84111-1016

BRADY, STEPHEN R.P.K., physician; b. New London, Conn., Oct. 13, 1955; s. Richard Harris and Jeanne Margaret (Halpin) B.; m. Marsha Anne Erickson, June 18, 1978 (div. Jan. 1993); 1 child, Ericka Anuhea; m. Elizabeth Ada Rewick, Dec. 27, 1994. AB cum laude, Harvard U., 1977; MPH, U. Hawaii, 1978, postgrad., 1979; MD, U. Pa., 1982. Diplomate Am. Bd. Internal Medicine. Intern U. Hawaii, 1982-83, resident in internal medicine, 1983-85; physician Kaiser Clinics, Honolulu, 1985-86; physician, med. dir. Kokua Kalihi Valley, Honolulu, 1986-89; clin. instr. U. Hawaii Sch. Medicine, Honolulu, 1986—, co-chair dept. continuing med. edn., 1993—; physician Waianae (Hawaii) Coast Health Svc., 1989-94; asst. med. dir., physician Am. Hawaii Cruises, Honolulu, 1989—; physician Straub Clinic & Hosp., Honolulu, 1984—; founding chair Hawaii Consortium for Continuing Med. Edn. U. Hawaii Sch. of Medicine, 1993—. Host weekly Ask the Dr. program KHON-Fox 2 News, Hawaii, 1996—. Cubmaster Boy Scouts Am., Kailua, Hawaii, 1995—. Comdr. U.S. Merchant Marine, 1989—. Recipient Po'okela awards, 1991, 93, 95; rsch. grantee Kuakini Med. Rsch. Inst., Honolulu, 1971, Pacific Health Rsch. Inst., Honolulu, 1972-78, Children's Hosp., Phila., 1979; Paul Harris fellow, 1995; named Scot of the Yr. State of Hawaii, 1999. Mem. AMA, Am. Coll. Physicians, Am. Soc. Internal Medicine, Am. Pub. Health Assn, Am. Statistical Assn., Hawaii Soc. Internal Medicine, Hawaii Med. Assn. (chair continuing med. edn. com. 1987—), Soc. Epidemiologic Rsch., Rotary, Soroptimist (pres.), Aumoana Cmty. Assn., (v.p. 1996—); Kaneohe Yacht Club, Plaza Club. Congregationalist. Avocations: singing, running, sailing, scuba diving, music. Home: 758 Kapahulu Ave # 309 Honolulu HI 96816-1196 Office: Straub Clinic & Hosp 888 S King St Honolulu HI 96813-3083

BRAGG, DARRELL BRENT, nutritionist, consultant; b. Sutton, W.Va., May 24, 1933; s. William H. and Gertrude (Perrine) B.; m. Elizabeth Hosse, Dec. 28, 1957; children: Roger, Larry, Teresa. BSc, W.Va. U., 1959, MSc, 1960; PhD, U. Ark., 1966. Instr. dept. animal sci. U. Ark., Fayetteville, 1965-67; asst. prof. U. Man., Winnipeg, Can., 1967-68, assoc. prof., 1968-70; assoc. prof. dept. poultry sci. U. B.C., Vancouver, Can., 1970-74, prof., head dept., 1975-86; industry cons., Vancouver, 1986-89; nutritionist, dir. quality assurance Rangen Aquaculture Feeds, Buhl, Idaho, 1990-92; sr. rsch. scientist Rangen Aquaculture Rsch. Ctr., Hagerman, Idaho, 1991-92; indsl. biochem. cons. Deutrel Labs. Inc., Palmdale, Calif., 1991—. Contbr. numerous articles to sci. jours. With U.S. Army, 1954-56. Recipient numerous rsch. grants from industry, univs. and govts. Mem. Poultry Sci.

Assn. (nat. bd. dirs., v.p., pres. 1978-84), World Poultry Sci. Assn. (bd. dirs., v.p. 1975-86), Sigma Xi, numerous others. Avocations: hunting, fishing, travel. Home: PO Box 38 Payette ID 83661-0038

BRAHMS, KATHERYN ANN, educator; b. San Francisco, May 24, 1939; d. Earl Fred and Verne Maxine (Rees) Melluish; m. Bevan Andre Brahms, June 1, 1958; children: Lani Jo Brahms Melton, Sheri Lynn. AS in Early Childhood Edn., Yuba Coll., 1986; BA in Child Devel., Calif. State U., Sacramento, 1988; MA in Human Devel., Pacific Oaks Coll., 1997. Adult edn. credential; cert. lifetime supervision. Head tchr. presch. Jewish Cmty. Ctr., Belmont, Calif., 1967-69; tchr. Head Start San Mateo (Calif.) City Sch. Dist., 1969-78; dir. Head Start Presch. Placer Cmty. Action, Grass Valley, Calif., 1981-90; area dir. Kids on Kampus, Sacramento, 1991, 92; lead tchr. San Juan Unified Sch. Dist., Carmichael, Calif., 1994—; treas., newsletter com. Nat. Assn. Edn. Young Children, 1985-88; bd. mem. Nevada County Coalition, 1986-88; workshop presenter Nat. Head Start Assn., 1994. Author: (project/book) A Mobile Preschool Environment for Homeless Children, 1997. Bd. mem., treas., publicity com. mem. Welcome Wagon Club, Redwood City, Calif., 1963-65; troop leader Girl Scouts, Redwood City, 1966-76; adv. for children Child Action, Sacramento, 1996. Mem. Orgn. for Rehab. and Tng. (bd. mem., treas. 1965-68, membership chair 1965-68, publicity chair 1965-68, placque 1966-68, cert. 1966-68). Democrat. Jewish. Avocations: genealogy, bicycling, downhill skiing, golf, travel. Home: 1285 Fall Creek Way Sacramento CA 95833-2890 Office: San Juan USD/ECE Dept 5309 Kenneth Ave Carmichael CA 95608-4716

BRAILSFORD, JUNE EVELYN, musician, educator; b. Wiergate, Tex., Apr. 11, 1939; d. Lonnie and Jessie (Coleman) Samuel; m. Marvin Delano Brailsford, Dec. 23, 1960; children: Marvin Delano, Keith, Cynthia. BA in Music, Prairie View A & M U., Tex., 1960; MA in Music, Trenton (N.J.) State Coll., 1981; postgrad., Jacksonville State U., summer 1971, Lamar U., Beaumont, Tex., summer 1963, Juilliard Sch., summer 1994. Jr. high music tchr. Lincoln Jr. High Sch., Beaumont, Tex., 1960-61; organist/choir dir. various chs., various locations, 1962-82; dir. adult edn. Morris County Human Resources, Dover, N.J., 1980-82; band and choral dir. Zweibruecken Am. High Sch., Ger., 1982-84; vocal soloist and pianist Am. Women's Activities, Ger., 1986-87; dir. female choir U.S. Army War Coll., 1978-79, U.S. Air Force Skylarks, Sembach, Ger., 1976-77. Hostess/fundraiser Quad City Symphony Guild 75th Ur., Rock Island, 1989, Links, Inc. Beautillion Scholarship, 1989, Installation Vol. Coord. Cons., Ft. Belvoir, Va., 1990-91; minister music First Bapt. Ch., Vienna, Va., 1995; active numerous charitable orgns. Recipient Molly Pitcher award U.S. Army F.A. Officers, 1986, Outstanding Civilian Svc. award Dept. Army, 1990, Disting. Civilian Svc. award Dept. Army, 1992. Mem. AAUW, NAACP (life mem. No. Va. Fairfax County chpt.), Music/Etude Club, Rock Island Arsenal Hist. Soc. (hon. mem.), Colo. Internat. Club, Quad City Symphony Guild (USO com.). Baptist. Avocations: bridge, bit whist, antiques, traveling, reading. Home: 15865 W Bayaud Dr Golden CO 80401-5055

BRAITHWAITE, WALT WALDIMAN, aircraft manufacturing company executive; b. Kingston, Jamaica, Jan. 19, 1945; s. Ivanhoe Alexander and Ivy Mary (Green) B.; m. Edwina Gerell Patrick, Apr. 7, 1967 (div. Mar. 1976); 1 child, Charlene Maria; m. Rita Cecelia Wood, May 4, 1974; children: Catherine Cecelia, Rachel Christine. BS in Electromech. Engring., Am. Inst. Engring. & Tech., Chgo., 1965; MS in Computer Sci., U. Wash., Seattle, 1975; SM in Mgmt., MIT, Cambridge, 1981. Cert. computer tech. Systems engr. engring. div. The Boeing Co., Renton, Wash., 1979-80; Sloan fellow MIT The Boeing Co., 1980-81; program mgr. bus. planning and commitments 7/7/7 div. The Boeing Co., Renton, Wash., 1981-82, mgr. CAD/CAM integration engring. div., 1982-83; dir. program tech. mgmt. Nat. Airspace Systems Co. div. Boeing/Lockheed, Kent, Wash., 1983-84; chief engr. CAD/CAM integration engring. div. The Boeing Co., Renton, Wash., 1984; chief engr. engring. ops. 747/767 div. The Boeing Co., Everett, Wash., 1984-85, dir. computing systems 747/767 div., 1985-86; dir. program mgmt. 707/737/757 div. The Boeing Co., Renton, 1986-91, v.p. info. systems Boeing Comml. Airplane Group, 1991—, v.p. info., support svcs., 1996—, v.p. co. offices adminstrn., 1997—; initial graphics exchange specification Nat. Bur. Standards, Calif., 1980. Author: Design and Implementation of Interpreters, 1978. Bd. dirs. City Art Works, Seattle, 1981-85. Recipient Joseph Marie Jacquare Meml. award Am. Inst. Mfg. Tech., Mass., 1987, leadership award Computer and Automated Systems Assn., Seattle, 1987, Black Achievers award YMCA, Seattle, 1990. Mem. Soc. Mfg. Engrs., Greater Renton C. of C. (pres. 1990-91), Boeing Mgmt. Assn. (pres. 1994, Black Engr. of Yr. 1995). Episcopalian. Avocations: boating, flying. Office: The Boeing Co PO Box 3707 Seattle WA 98124-2207

BRAKHAGE, JAMES STANLEY, filmmaker, educator; b. Kansas City, Mo., Jan. 14, 1933; s. Ludwig and Clara (Dubberstein) B.; m. Mary Jane Collom, Dec. 28, 1957 (div. 1987); children: Myrrena, Crystal, Neowyn, Bearthm, Rarc; m. Marilyn Jull, Mar. 30, 1989; children: Anton, Vaughn. Ph.D., San Francisco Art Inst., 1981; Doctorate (hon.), Calif. Arts, 1994. Lectr. Sch. Art Inst. Chgo., 1969-81; prof. U. Colo., Boulder, 1981; mem. Filmmakers Coop., N.Y.C., Canyon Cinema Coop., San Francisco, London Filmmakers Coop., Can. Filmmakers' Distbn. Ctr., Toronto, Lightcome, Paris, France; Faculty lectr. U. Colo., 1990-91. Films include Interim, 1952, Anticipation of the Night, 1958, The Dead, 1960, Blue Moses, 1962, Dog Star Man, 1964, Songs in 8mm, 1964-69, Scenes from Under Childhood, 1967-70, The Weir Falcon Saga, 1970, The Act of Seeing with One's Own Eyes, 1971, The Riddle of Lumen, 1972, Sincerity and Duplicity, 1973-80, The Text of Light, 1974, Desert, 1976, The Governor, 1977, Burial Path, 1978, Nightmare Series, 1978, Creation, 1979, Made Manifest, 1980, Salome, 1980, Murder Psalm, 1980, Roman Numeral Series, 1979-81, the Arabic series, 1980-82, Unconscious London Strata, 1982, Tortured Dust, 1984, The Egyptian Series, 1984, The Loom, 1986, Nightmusic, 1986, The Dante Quartet, 1987, Faust, parts I-IV, 1987-89, Marilyn's Window, 1988, Visions in Meditation, 1989-90, City Streaming, 1990, Glaze of Cathexis, 1990, Babylonian Series, 1989-90, Passage Through: A Ritual, 1990, A Child's Garden and the Serious Sea, 1991, Delicacies of Molten Horror Synapse, 1991, Christ Mass Sex Dance, 1991, Crack Glass Eulogy, 1992, Boulder Blues and Pearls and For Marilyn, Interpolations 1-5, 1992, Blossom Gift Favor, The Harrowing, Tryst Haunt, Study in Color and Black and White, Stellar, Atumnal, 1993, Three Homerics, 1993, Naghts, Chartres Series, Ephemeral Solidity, Elementary Phrases, Black Ice, First Hymn to the Night—Novalis, 1994, In Consideration of Pompeii, 1994, The Mammals of Victoria, 1994, Paranoia Corridor, 1994, Can Not Exist, 1994, Can Not Not Exist, 1994, I Take These Truths, 1994, We Hold These, 1994, I..., 1995, Earthen Aerie, 1995, Spring Cycle, 1995, The Lost Films, 1995, The B Series, 1995, Preludes 1-24, 1995, 96, The Fur of Home, 1996, Preludes 13-18, 1996, Preludes, 19-24, 1996, Beautiful Funerals, 1996, Polite Madness, 1996, Shockingly Hot, 1996, Sexual Saga, 1996, The Lost Films, 1996, Comingled Containers, 1996, Yggdrasill Whose Roots Are Stars in the Human Mind, 1997, Last Hymn to the Night - Novalis, 1997, I...Sleeping, 1989, Selfsong/Deathsong, 1998, "..." Reels #1,2,3, 1998; author: Metaphors on Vision, 1963, A Moving Picture Giving and Taking Book, 1971, The Brakhage Lectures, 1972, Seen, 1975, Film Biographies, 1977, Brakhage Scrapbook, 1982, Film at Wits End, 1989, Phillip Taffee: A Long Conversation with Stan Brakhage, 1998, "..." Reels # 1,2,3,4, 1998, The Birds of Paradise, 1999, The Lion and the Zebra Made God's Raw Jewels, 1999, The Earth Song of the Cricket, 1999. Recipient Brussels Worlds Fair Protest award, 1958, Brandeis citation, 1973, Colo. Gov.'s award for arts and humanities, 1974, Jimmy Ryan Morris Meml. Found. award, 1979, Telluride Film Festival medallion, 1981, Maya Deren award Am. Film Inst., 1986, medal U. Colo., 1988, Outstanding Achievement award Denver Internat. Film Festival, 1988, MacDowell medal, 1989, Libr. Congress Nat. Film Registry, 1992, Anthology Film Archives honor, 1993, The Colo. 100 Cert. of Recognition, 1993, Disting. Prof. award U. Colo., 1994; retrospective Mus. Modern Art, 1995; grantee Avon Found., 1965-69, NEA, 1974-75, 77, 80, 83, 88, U. Colo. Coun. Rsch. and Creative Work, 1983, Rocky Mountain Film Ctr., 1985; Rockefeller fellow, 1967-69, Guggenheim fellow, 1978. Democrat. Home: 2142 Canyon Blvd Apt 203 Boulder CO 80302-4517 Office: U Colo Film Studies Hunter 102 PO Box 316 Boulder CO 80309-0316

BRALY, DAVID DUANE, writer; b. Prineville, Oreg., Aug. 4, 1949; s. Emmett Lee and Carrie Audean (Meek) B. BAA, Reed Coll., 1981. Researcher Sumpter Valley R.R. Hist. Dist. Project, Bend, Oreg., 1985; researcher cultural survey City of Klamath Falls, Oreg., 1985. Writer fiction and nonfiction. Mem. Western Writers of Am. Home: 1004 Ochoco Ave Prineville OR 97754-1333

BRAME, MARILLYN A., hypnotherapist; b. Indpls., Sept. 17, 1928; d. David Schwalb and Hilda (Riley) Curtin; 1 child, Gary Mansour. Student, Meinzinger Art Sch., Detroit, 1946-47, U. N.Mex., 1963, Orlando (Fla.) Jr. Coll., 1964-65, El Camino Coll., Torrance, Calif., 1974-75; PhD in Hypnotherapy, Am. Inst. Hypnotherapy, 1989. Cert. and registered hypnotherapist. Color cons. Pitts. Plate Glass Co., Albuquerque, 1951-52; owner Signs by Marillyn, Albuquerque, 1952-53; design draftsman Sandia Corp., Albuquerque, 1953-56; designer The Martin Co., Orlando, 1957-65; pres. The Arts, Winter Park, Fla., 1964-66; supr. tech. publs. Gen. Instrument Corp., Hawthorne, Calif., 1967-76; pres. Camart Design, Westminster, Calif., 1977-86, Visual Arts, El Toro, Calif., 1978—; mgr. tech. publs. Archive Corp., Costa Mesa, Calif., 1986-90; adj. instr. Orange Coast Coll., Costa Mesa, 1985-90; hypnotherapist, Lake Forest, 1986—; bd. dirs. Orange County chpt. Am. Bd. Hypnotherapy. Author: Lemon and Lime Scented Herbs, 1994, (textbook) Folkdancing is for Everybody, 1974, Innovative Imagery, 1996, Changing Your Mood, 1997; inventor, designer dance notation sys. MS Method. Mem. bd. govs. Lake Forest II Showboaters Theatre Group, 1985-88; mem. cultural arts com. City of Mission Viejo, 1995—. Mem. Soc. Tech. Communication (v.p. programs, 1987, newsletter editor 1986-87, newsletter prodn. editor 1985-86). Avocations: folkdancing, rock collecting, community theater, metaphysics.

BRAMWELL, MARVEL LYNNETTE, nurse, social worker; b. Durango, Colo., Aug. 13, 1947; d. Floyd Lewis and Virginia Jenny (Amyx) B. Diploma in lic. practical nursing, Durango Sch. Practical Nursing, 1968; AD in Nursing, Mt. Hood Community Coll., 1972; BS in Nursing, BS in Gen. Studies cum laude, So. Oreg. State Coll., 1980; cert. edn. grad. sch. social work, U. Utah, 1987, cert. counselor alcohol, drug abuse, 1988, MSW, 1992; M in Social Work, 1992. RN, Utah, Oreg., Ind., Nev.; cert. social worker, Utah, Ind., Nev.; cert. clin. social worker, Ind. Staff nurse Monument Valley (Utah) Seventh Day Adventist Mission Hosp., 1973-74, La Plata Cmty. Hosp., 1974-75; health coord. Tri County Head Start Program, 1974-75; nurse therapist, team leader Portland Adventist Med. Ctr., 1975-78; staff nurse Indian Health Service Hosp., 1980-81; coord. village health services North Slope Borough Health and Social Svc. Agy., Barrow, Alaska, 1981-83; nurse, supr. aides Bonneville Health Care Agy., 1984-85; staff nurse LDS Adolescent Psychiat. Unit, 1985-86; coord. adolescent nursing CPC Olympus View Hosp., 1986-87, 91; charge and staff nurse adult psychiatry U. Utah, 1987-88; nurse MSW Cmty. Nursing Svc., Salt Lake City, 1989-90, Willow Springs Ctr., Reno, Nev., 1996—; resident scvs. coord. Arden Cts., Reno, 1998—; med. social worker Meth. Home Health, Indpls., 1994-96; psychiat. nurse Willow Springs Ctr., 1996—; DON, resident svc. coord. Arden Cts., Reno, 1998—; per diem nurse Reno VA Med. Ctr.; assisted with design and constrn. 6 high tech. health clinics in Alaska Arctic, 1982-83; psychiat. nurse specialist Cmty. Nursing Svc. Contbr. articles to profl. jours. Active Mothers Against Drunk Driving, Program U. Alaska Rural Edn., 1981-83. Recipient cert. of appreciation Barrow Lion's Club, 1983, U.S. Census Bur., Colo., 1970, other awards and scholarships. Mem. NOW, Nat. Assn. Social Workers, Assn. Women Sci. Avocations: water color painting, photography, hiking, horseback riding. Home: Apt 150 6200 Meadow Wood Cir Reno NV 89502

BRANCH, ROBERT HARDIN, radio and television educator, broadcast executive; b. L.A., Oct. 12, 1939; s. C.H. Hardin and Erma Mae (Smith) B.; m. Judy Nilsson, Mar. 1965 (div. June 1980); children: Kirsten Giard, Kelley R.H.; m. Carol Bussy, Mar. 1990. BA, Antioch U., 1990. Radio personality Sta. KSL, Salt Lake City, 1970-73; asst. news dir. Sta. KOGO, San Diego, 1973-80; reporter Sta. KSDO, San Diego, 1980-84; show host Sta. KTMS, Santa Barbara, Calif., 1984-86; news dir. Sta. KVSD, Vista, Calif., 1986-88; news anchor Sta. KSDO, San Diego, 1988-90; assoc. prof. radio and TV Palomar Coll., San Marcos, Calif., 1990—; gen. mgr. KKSM, San Marcos, 1990—. Staff sgt. U.S. Army, 1958-68. Recipient Golden Mike award So. Calif. Press Assn., L.A., 1974, Alumni of Yr. award Antioch U., Santa Barbara, 1995. Mem. MADD, Soc. Profl. Journalists, Radio and TV News Dirs. Assn., San Diego Press Club (bd. dirs. 1974-76, VIP award 1976, Spot News Feature award 1976). Amnesty Internat., Smithsonian Instn., Holocaust Mus. (charter mem.). Home: 7170 Rock Valley Ct San Diego CA 92122-2737 Office: Sta KKSM-AM 1140 W Mission Rd San Marcos CA 92069-1415

BRANDENBURG, CARLOS HENRY, clinical psychologist; b. Crisobal Colon, Panama, May 17, 1948; s. James Gilbert and Aura Raquel (Mayorga) B.; 1 child, Frank. BA, U. Nev., Las Vegas, 1969, MA, 1971; PhD, U. Nev., Reno, 1975. Psychologist Lakes Crossing Ctr., Sparks, Nev., 1975-78; dir. Forensic Svcs., Sparks, 1978-95; adminstr. Divsn. Mental Hygiene and Mental Retardation, Carson City, Nev., 1995—; mental health cons. Sierra Nevada Corp., 1978-84. Bd. dirs. Juvenile Justice Com., Reno, 1991—; mem. Criminal Justice Com., Reno, 1992—; mem. United Way, Reno, 1991—. Recipient Leadership award NAMI, 1996, Am. Bd. Mental Health, 1996. Mem. APA, Internat. Coun. Psychologists, Am. Soc. Clin. Psychologists. Democrat. Roman Catholic. Avocation: gardening. Home: 7390 Pinehurst Cir Reno NV 89502-9739 Office: Divsn MH/MR Kinkead Bldg 505 E King St Carson City NV 89710*

BRANDES, STANLEY HOWARD, anthropology educator, writer; b. N.Y.C., Dec. 26, 1942; s. Emanuel Robert and Annette (Zalisch) B.; divorced; children: Nina Rachel, Naomi Clara. BA, U. Chgo., 1964; MA, U. Calif., Berkeley, 1969, PhD, 1971. Asst. prof. anthropology Mich. State U., East Lansing, 1971-75; asst. prof. anthropology U. Calif., Berkeley, 1975-78, assoc. prof., 1978-82, prof. anthropology, 1982—, chmn. dept., 1990-93, 97—; dir. Barcelona Study Ctr., U. Calif. and Ill., Spain, 1981-82, Mexico City Study Ctr., 1995—, U. Calif. Author: Migration, Kinship and Community, 1975, Metaphors of Masculinity, 1980, Forty: The Age and the Symbol, 1985, Power and Persuasion, 1988; co-editor: Symbol as Sense, 1980. NIH fellow, 1967-71; NICHD Rsch. fellow, 1975-77; fellow John Carter Brown Libr., 1994; Am. Council Learned Socs. grantee, 1977. Fellow Am. Anthrop. Assn.; mem. Am. Ethnological Soc., Soc. for Psychol. Anthropology. Office: U Calif Dept Anthropology Berkeley CA 94720

BRANDHORST, CURT W., graphic designer; b. Kingston, N.Y., June 10; s. Curt Werner and Janice Carolyn (Ortmeyer) B.; m. Bonnie Syneva Moller, Feb. 22, 1961. Student, Concordia Tchrs. Coll., 1981-82, Lincoln U., 1991-93. Graphic designer, owner Brandywine Prodns., Lincoln, Nebr., 1978-83; graphic designer Thel Aurther Studios, Woodland Hills, Calif., 1983-84; graphic designer, owner Brandywine Prodns., Jefferson City, Mo., 1984-91, Concord, Calif., 1993—. Avocations: modeling, painting. Office: Brandywine Prodns 2470 Hemlock Ave Concord CA 94520-1724

BRANDON, KATHRYN ELIZABETH BECK, pediatrician; b. Salt Lake City, Sept. 10, 1916; d. Clarence M. and Hazel A. (Cutler) Beck; MD, U. Chgo., 1941; BA, U. Utah, 1937; MPH, U. Calif., Berkeley, 1957; children: John William, Kathleen Brandon McEnulty, Karen (dec.). Intern, Grace Hosp., Detroit, 1941-42; resident Children's Hosp. Med. Center No. Calif., Oakland, 1953-55, Children's Hosp., L.A., 1951-53; pvt. practice, La Crescentia, Calif., 1946-51, Salt Lake City, 1960-65, 86—; med. dir. Salt Lake City public schs., 1957-60; dir. Ogden City-Weber County (Utah) Health Dept., 1965-67; pediatrician Fitzsimmons Army Hosp., 1967-68; coll. health physician U. Colo., Boulder, 1968-71; student health physician U. Utah, Salt Lake City, 1971-81; occupational health physician Hill AFB, Utah, 1981-85; child health physician Salt Lake City-County Health Dept., 1971-82; cons. in field; clin. asst. U. Utah Coll. Medicine, Salt Lake City, 1958-64; clin. asst. pediatrics U. Colo. Coll. Medicine, Denver, 1958-72; active staff emeritus Primary Children's Hosp., LDS Hosp., and Cottonwood Hosp., 1960-67. Diplomate Am. Bd. Pediatrics. Fellow Am. Pediatric Acad., Am. Pub. Health Assn., Am. Sch. Health Assn., mem. Utah Coll. Health Assn. (pres. 1978-80), Pacific Coast Coll. Health Assn., AMA, Utah Med. Assn., Salt Lake County Med. Soc., Utah Public Health Assn. (sec.-treas. 1960-66), Intermountain Pediatric Soc. Home and Office: PO Box 38482 Salt Lake City UT 84158-0482

BRANDON-WATSON, KIM, digital and electronic art company executive; b. L.A., Jan. 10, 1959; d. Edwin L. and Irene M. (Gustin) B.; m. Mike S. Watson, Mar. 5, 1954; 1 child, Kelly. Student, El Camino, 1979, Art Ctr., 1983. Computer artist Subia, Hawthorne, Calif., 1983-84, production mgr., 1984-86; sales exec. Graphic Solution, Irvine, Calif., 1986-88; gen. mgr. Gp Color, L.A., 1988-89; divsn. dir. Killingsworth Presentation, Long Beach, Calif., 1989-95; pres. Interactive Digital Electronic Art, Manhattan Beach, Calif., 1995—. Office: Internat Digital Electronic Art 1334 Parkview Ave # 300 Manhattan Beach CA 90266

BRANDT, BLANCH MARIE, health care facility administrator; b. Dryden, Ont., Can., Apr. 12, 1937; came to U.S., 1964; d. Frederick William and Mary Elizabeth (Gamble) Morton; m. Les W. Brandt, Dec. 12, 1958. BA, Southwestern Bapt. Bible Coll., Tucson, 1983; MA in Psychology, Southwest U., 1991, PhD, 1993. Dir., proprietor SOI Learning Ctr., Riverside, Calif., 1991—; dir. SOI/Vision Clinic Twin Pines Ranch/Van Horn Youth Ctr., Riverside County Probation, 1994—; ednl. and career cons. Recipient Outstanding Project award Am. Pub. Health Assn., Nat. Jewel Young award, 1990, Outstanding Svc. award San Bernardino County Probation, 1995. Mem. Am. Correctional Health Svcs., Am. Probation and Parole Assn., Universal Ch. of the Master Mins. Avocation: writing. Home: 2686 W Mill St # 13 San Bernardino CA 92410-2019 Office: 5051 Canyon Crest Dr Ste 102 Riverside CA 92507-6035

BRANDT, LEVERNE W., healty facility administrator; b. Loganville, Wis., Mar. 20, 1935; s. Herman William and Emma E. (Erdmann) B.; m. Stella Ann Myers, June 3, 1954 (div. Apr. 1983); children: Varney Ray, Kerri LaVerne; m. Barbara Ann Patterson, Nov. 21, 1983. Seismograph labor Continental Oil Co., Roswell, N.Mex., 1956-58; refrigeration svc. Ellis Equipment, Roswell, N.Mex., 1958-59; plant ops. 550 Land Co., Roswell, N.Mex., 1959-66; plant maintenance Osteopathic Hosp., Roswell, N.Mex., 1966-75, adminstr., 1975-76; dir. plant ops. St. Mary;s Hosp., Roswell, N.Mex., 1976—. With U.S. Army, 1954-56, Korea. Mem. Am. Soc. Healthcare, Nat. Fire Protection Assn., N.Mex. Soc. Healthcare Engring., Refrigeration Svc. Engring. Soc. Home: 1508 S Kenrucky Roswell NM 88201

BRANKOVICH, MARK J., restaurateur; b. Rijeka, Yugoslavia, Mar. 4, 1922; came to U.S., 1951; s. Joseph M. and Rose (Haydin) B.; m. Marilyn J. Severin, Jan. 4, 1957; children: Mark, Laura. BA in Philosophy, U. Zurich, 1944; student, U. Geneva, 1945, U. Padua, Italy, 1947. Owner The Golden Deer, Chgo., 1953-55; mgr. Gaslight Club, N.Y.C., 1955-57; gen. mgr., exec. v.p., dir. Gaslight Club, Chgo., 1959-63; owner, mgr. Franchise Gaslight Club, L.A., 1963-66; owner Monte Carlo Italian Deli, Burbank, Calif., 1969—, Pinocchio Restaurant, Burbank, 1970—, Pinocchio West, Santa Monica, 1972—, Pinocchio Westwood (Calif.), 1978, Italia Foods Wholesale, Burbank, 1972. Mem. Presdl. Task Force, Washington, 1980—, Rep. Senatorial Inner Circle, 1986. Mem. Internat. Platform Assn. Serbian Orthodox. Home: 1250 Hilldale Ave West Hollywood CA 90069-1826 Office: Monte Carlo Italia Foods Inc 3103 W Magnolia Blvd Burbank CA 91505-3046

BRANN, ALTON JOSEPH, manufacturing company executive; b. Portland, Maine, Dec. 23, 1941; s. Donald Edward and Marjorie Margaret (Curran) B. BA, U. Mass., 1969. Mgr. advanced programs Dynamics Research Corp., Wilmington, Mass., 1969-73; dir. engring. Litton Guidance & Control Systems, L.A., 1973-79, dir. program mgmt., 1979-81, v.p. engring., 1981-83, pres., 1983-86; group exec. Navigation Guidance and Control Systems Group, Beverly Hills, Calif., 1986-88; sr. v.p. Components and Indsl. Products Group Litton Industries, Beverly Hills, 1988-90, pres., COO, 1990-92, CEO, 1992-94, chmn., 1994-96; chmn., CEO Western Atlas Inc., Beverly Hills, 1994-97, UNOVA Inc., Beverly Hills, 1997—; trustee Mfrs. Alliance Productivity and Innovation, coun. fgn. diplomacy, U.S.-Russia bus. coun. Mem. IEEE (sr. mem.), Optical Soc. Am., L.A. World Affairs Coun., Town Hall of L.A. Avocations: skiing, sailing. Office: UNOVA 360 N Crescent Dr Beverly Hills CA 90210-4802

BRANNEN, JEFFREY RICHARD, lawyer; b. Tampa, Fla., Aug. 27, 1945; s. Jackson Edward and Tobiah M. (Lovitz) B.; m. Mary Elizabeth Strand, Nov. 24, 1972; 1 child, Samuel Jackson. BA in English, U. N.Mex., 1967, JD, 1970. Bar: N.Mex. 1970, U.S. Dist. Ct. N.Mex. 1970, U.S. Ct. Appeals (10th cir.) 1976, U.S. Supreme Ct. 1978. Law clk. N.Mex. State Supreme Ct., Santa Fe, 1970-71; from assoc. to pres., shareholder Montgomery & Andrews, pa, Santa Fe, 1972-93; pres. Jeffrey R. Brannen, P.A., Santa Fe, 1993—; of counsel Carpenter, Comeau, Maldegan, Nixon & Templeman, Santa Fe, 1995—; faculty Nat. Inst. Trial Advocacy, Hastings Ctr. for Trial & Appellate Advocacy, 1980-93; co-chmn. Pers. Injury Inst., Hastings, 1992. Mem. ABA, Am. Bd. Trial Advocates, Assn. Def. Trial Attys. (state chmn. 1992—), Def. Rsch. Inst. (Exceptional Performance Citation 1989), N.Mex. Def. Lawyers Assn. (pres. 1989). Democrat. Avocations: skiing, soccer, fly fishing, travel. Office: Carpenter Comeau Maldegan Nixon & Templeman 141 E Palace Ave Santa Fe NM 87501-2041*

BRANSON, ALBERT HAROLD (HARRY BRANSON), magistrate judge, educator; b. Chgo., May 20, 1935; s. Fred Brooks and Marie (Vowell) B.; m. Siri-Anne Gudrun Lindberg, Nov. 2, 1963; children: Gunnar John, Gulliver Dean, Hannah Marie, Siri Elizabeth. BA, Northwestern U., 1957; JD, U. Chgo., 1963. Bar: Pa. 1965, Alaska 1972. Atty. Richard McVeigh law offices, Anchorage, 1972-73; ptnr. Jacobs, Branson & Guetschow, Anchorage, 1973-76, Branson & Guetschow, Anchorage, 1976-82; pvt. practice Law Offices of Harry Branson, Anchorage, 1982-84, 85-89; atty. Branson, Bazeley & Chisolm, Anchorage, 1984-85; U.S. magistrate judge U.S. Dist. Ct., Anchorage, 1989—; instr., adj. prof. U. Alaska Justice Ctr., 1980-93; U.S. magistrate, Anchorage, 1975-76. Mem. steering com. Access to Civil Justice Task Force, 1997-98. With U.S. Army, 1957-59. Mem. Alaska Bar Assn. (bd. dirs., v.p. bd. govs. 1977-80, 83-86, pres. bd. govs. 1986, Disting. Svc. award 1992, Spl. Svc. award 1988, editor-in-chief Alaska Bar Rag 1978-86), Anchorage Bar Assn. (bd. dirs., bd. govs. 1982-86), Anchorage Inn of Ct. (pres. 1995). Democrat. Avocations: book collecting, cooking, poetry. Office: US Dist Ct 222 W 7th Ave Unit 33 Anchorage AK 99513-7504

BRANSON, HELEN KITCHEN, writer; b. Boise, Idaho, Dec. 19, 1919; d. Carl Clayton and Nora Jane (Goslow) Kitchen; children: Lyn Hamamura, Sharon Stuckey. AB, Pasadena Coll., 1955; MA, U. So. Calif., L.A. Co-di8r. Branson Found., Pasadena, 1941-61. Contbr. numerous articles to profl. jours. Nat. Newspaper Fund fellow, 1968; named Idaho Journalism Tchr. of the Yr., 1965. Mem. Idaho Press Women (Achievement award 1973, 1st place in non-fiction 1997), Nat. Fedn. Press Women (1st prize for non-fiction book 1997, 98). Democrat. Episcopalian. Avocations: gardening, reading by tape. Home: 4496 Malia St Honolulu HI 96821-1155

BRANTING, ROBERT A., SR., marketing specialist; b. Weymouth, Mass., Aug. 7, 1954; s. Morten B. Jr. and Adrienne R. (Bove) B.; m. Helen E. Smith, Feb. 16, 1980; children: Richard, Christopher, Jennifer, Robert, Jr. Student, Boston Coll., 1972-73. Pres. Branting Assocs., Abington, Mass., 1974-80; cons. various, 1983-87; regional v.p. Tax Reduction Inst., Washington, 1987-89; nat. mktg. dir. TRI Seminars, Inc., Bethesda, Md., 1989-93; pres., CEO TRI Western Group, Inc., Washington, 1993-96; exec. v.p. Am. Profitlink, Inc., Edmonds, Wash., 1996-97; mgr. Sundance Cars & Trucks,, 1997-98; pvt. practice cons., trainer, broker, 1998—; devel. cons. Ministry of Tourism, Barbados, Brit. W.I., 1986-87; cons. Am. Internat., Ltd., Boston, 1985; adv. bd. CDG, Inc., Lynnwood, Wash., 1989-91; speaker in field. Author: (books) The Coordinator's Handbook, 1991, The Speaker's Handbook, 1995; contbr. articles to profl. jours. Avocations: speaking, tchg., drama, family.

BRATTON, HOWARD CALVIN, federal judge; b. Clovis, N.Mex., Feb. 4, 1922; s. Sam Gilbert and Vivian (Rogers) B. BA, U. N.Mex., 1941, LLB, 1971; LLB, Yale U., 1947. Bar: N.Mex. 1948. Law clk. U.S. Cir. Ct. Appeals, 1948; ptnr. Grantham & Bratton, Albuquerque, 1949-52; spl. asst. U.S. atty. charge litigation OPS, 1951-52; assoc., then ptnr. Hervy, Dow & Hinkle, Roswell, N.Mex., 1952-64; judge U.S. Dist. Ct. N.Mex., Albuquerque, 1964-67; chief judge U.S. Dist. Ct. N.Mex., Las Cruces, 1978-87, sr. judge, 1987—; chmn. N.Mex. Jr. Bar Assn., 1952; pres. Chaves County (N.Mex.) Bar Assn., 1962; chmn. pub. lands com. N.Mex. Oil and Gas Assn., 1961-64, Interstate Oil Compact Commn., 1963-64; mem. N.Mex. Commn. Higher Edn., 1962-64, Jud. Conf. of U.S. Com. on Operation of Jury Sys., 1966-72, 79-85, Jud. Conf. U.S. Com. on Ethics, 1987-92; mem.

Ad Hoc Com. on Internat. Jud. Rels., 1992-94; 10th cir. rep. Jud. Conf. U.S., 1984-86. Bd. regents U. N.Mex., 1958-68, pres., 1963-64; bd. dirs. Fed. Jud. Ctr., 1983-87. Served to capt. AUS, 1942-45. Mem. Trial Judges Assn. 10th Circuit (pres. 1976-78), Nat. Conf. Fed. Trial Judges (exec. com. 1977-79), Sigma Chi. Home: 6760 Via Emma Dr Las Cruces NM 88005-4977 Office: US Dist Ct 200 E Griggs Ave Las Cruces NM 88001-3523

BRATZLER, MARY KATHRYN, desktop publisher; b. Albuquerque, Sept. 16, 1960; d. William James and Nancy Jane (Hobbs) Colby; m. Zim Emig, May 30, 1987 (div. Nov. 1990); 1 child, Aeriel Kaylee Emig; m. Steven James Bratzler, Mar. 16, 1996, 1 child, Cody Benjamin. B of Univ. Studies, U. N.Mex., 1995. Comml. artist Modern Press, Albuquerque, 1978-80; asst. composition supr. Graphic Arts Pub., Albuquerque, 1980-84, composition supr., 1984-85, asst. plant mgr., 1985-86; typesetter Universal Printing and Graphics, Albuquerque, 1986-87, Bus. Graphics, Albuquerque, 1988-90; office asst. UNM Gen. Honors, Albuquerque, 1992-93; desktop pub., 1990—; computer specialist NEDA Bus. Cons., Inc., 1996-98; cons. Mary Kay Cosmetics, 1991-96. Participant N.Mex. Pub. Utilities Commn., Santa Fe, 1993; coord. clothing bank PTA, Zia Elem. Sch., 1995-96; parent rep. Unified Student Centered Classroom, 1996-98. Mem. Golden Key, Phi Beta Kappa. Avocations: piano playing, bicycling, hiking, camping.

BRAUDY, DOROTHY MCGAHEE, artist, educator; b. L.A., Dec. 10, 1930; d. Clarence Leland and Dorothy (Shacker) Wood; m. George Harbeson Fitzgerald, May 23, 1951 (div. 1965); children: George Fitzgerald, David Fitzgerald; m. Leo Beal Braudy, Dec. 24, 1974. BA, U. Ky., 1952; MA, NYU, 1963; ABD, Tchr.'s Coll. Columbia, 1975. Asst. prof. art edn. Pratt Inst., Bklyn., 1972-78; asst. prof. visual arts Goucher Coll., Towson, Md., 1977-83; guest beijing, Xian, Shanghai, China, 1990. One-person shows include 2d Story Spring St. Soc., Soho, N.Y., 1975, Viridian Gallery, N.Y., 1977-78, B.R. Kornblatt Gallery, Balt., 1979, MAson County Mus., Maysville, Ky., 1982, Clark County C.C., Las Vegas, Nev., 1985, Orlando Gallery Sherman Oaks, Calif., 1986, 88, Pvt. View, L.A., 1991, 871 Fine Arts Gallery, San Francisco, 1993, Fisher Gallery, U. So. Calif., L.A., 1994; exhibited in group shows Pratt-Phoenix Gallery, N.Y.C., 1975, Pratt Inst. Gallery, 1977, Goucher Coll., 1982, 84, UPB Gallery, Berkeley, 1986, 871 Fine Arts Gallery, San Francisco, 1989, 90, 92; represented in pub. collections Am. Embassy, Vienna, Jane Zimmerli Mus. Art, Rutgers U., New Brunswick, N.J., Fed. Res. Bank, Richmond, Va., Mason County Mus., Maysville; represented in pvt. collections Carol Muske and David Dukes, L.A., Albert J. LaValley, Hanover, N.H., John Irwin, Balt., Md.; commd. portraits include Dorothy Lyman and Vincent Malle, L.A., David Brooks family, London, Ira Brind family, Phila.; featured in publs. Atlas of Southern Californa; contbr. revs. and articles to periodicals.

BRAULT, G(AYLE) LORAIN, healthcare executive; b. Chgo., Jan. 3, 1944; d. Theodore Frank and Victoria Jean (Pribyl) Hahn; m. Donald R. Brault, Apr. 29, 1971; 1 child, Kevin David. AA, Long Beach City Coll., 1963; BS, Calif. State U.-Long Beach, 1973, MS, 1977. RN, Calif; cert. nurse practitioner. Dir. nursing Canyon Gen. Hosp., Anaheim, Calif., 1973-76; dir. faculty critical care masters degree program Calif. State U., Long Beach, 1976-79; regional dir.. nursing and support svcs. Western region Am. Med. Internat., Anaheim, Calif., 1979-83; v.p. Hosp. Home Care Corp. Am., Santa Ana, Calif., 1983-85; pres. Hosp. Home Health Care Agy. Calif., Torrance, 1986-92; v.p. Healthcare Assn. So. Calif., L.A., 1993—; invited lectr. China Nurses Assn., 1983; cons. AMI, Inc., Saudi Arabia, 1983; advisor dept. grad. nursing Calif. State U., L.A., 1988, advisor Nursing Inst., 1990-91; guest lectr. dept. pub. health UCLA, 1986-87; assoc. clin. prof. U. So. Calif., 1988—; lectr. Calif. State U., L.A., 1996-97; editl. advisor RN Times, Nurseweek, 1988—, chmn. editl. adv. bd.; bd. dirs. Health and Human Svcs., City of Long Beach, Calif., 1997—. Contbr. articles to profl. jours., chpts. to books. Commr. HHS, Washington, 1988; bd. of Health & Humas Svcs. City of Long Beach, Calif., 1997—. HEW advanced nurse tng. grantee, 1978. Mem. Women in Health Adminstrn. (sec. 1989, v.p. 1990), Nat. Assn. Home Care, Am. Orgn. Nursing Execs., Calif. Assn. Health Svcs. at Home (task force chmn. 1988, bd. dirs. 1988-93, chmn. bd. dirs. 1990-93), Calif. League Nursing (bd. sec. 1983, program chmn. 1981-82), Am. Coll. Health Care Execs., ASAE, AONE, Phi Kappa Phi, Sigma Theta Tau. Republican. Methodist. Home: 1032 E Andrews Dr Long Beach CA 90807-2406

BRAUN, JEROME IRWIN, lawyer; b. St. Joseph, Mo., Dec. 16, 1929; s. Martin H. and Bess (Donsker) B.; children: Aaron, Susan, Daniel; m. Dolores Ferriter, Aug. 16, 1987. AB with distinction, Stanford U., 1951, LLB, 1953. Bar: Mo. 1953, Calif. 1953, U.S. Dist. Ct. (no. dist.) Calif., U.S. Tax Ct., U.S. Ct. Mil. Appeals, U.S. Supreme Ct., U.S. Ct. Appeals (9th cir.). Assoc. Long & Levit, San Francisco, 1957-58, Law Offices of Jefferson Peyser, San Francisco, 1958-62; founding ptnr. Farella, Braun & Martel (formerly Elke, Farella & Braun), San Francisco, 1962—; instr. San Francisco Law Sch., 1958-69; mem. U.S. Dist. Ct. Civil Justice Reform Act Adv. Com., 1991—; spkr. various state bar convs. in Calif., Ill., Nev., Mont.; requent moderator/participant continuing edn. of bar pgorams; past chmn. 9th Cir. Sr. Adv. Bd., past chmn. lawyer reps. to 9th Cir. Jud. Conf.; mem. appellate lawyers liaison com. Calif. Ct. Appeals 1st dist.; jud.conf. U.S. Com. Long Range Planning; founder Jon Samuel Abramson Scholarship Endowment Stanford U. Law. Revising editor: Stanford U. Law Rev.; contbr. articles to profl. jours. Mem. Jewish Community Fedn. San Francisco, The Peninsula, Marin and Sonoma Counties, pres., 1979-80; past pres. United Jewish Community Ctrs. 1st lt. JAGC, U.S. Army, 1954-57, U.S. Army Res., 1957-64. Recipient Lloyd W. Dinkelspiel Outstanding Young Leader award Jewish Welfare Fedn., 1967. Fellow Am. Acad. Appellate Lawyers; mem. ABA, Am. Bar Found., Calif. Bar Assn. (chmn. adminstrn. justice com. 1977), Bar Assn. San Francisco (spl. com. on lawyers malpractice and malpractice ins.), San Francisco Bar Found. (past trustee), Calif. Acad. Appellate Lawyers (past pres., mem. U.S. Dist. Ct. Civil Justice Refomr Act adv. com., Calif. Ct. of Appeals 1st Dist. Appellate Lawyers liaison com., jud. conf. of the U.S., com. on long-range planning, panelist 1994); Am. Judicature Soc. (past dir.), Stanford Law Sch. Bd. of Visitors, Am. Coll. Trial Lawyers (teaching trial and appellate advocacy com.), U.S. Dist. Ct. of No. Dist. Calif. Hist. Soc. (past pres., bd. dirs.), 9th Cir. Ct. of Appeals Hist. Soc. (past. pres.), Mex.-Am. Legal Def. Fund (honoree), Order of Coif.

BRAUN, STEPHEN BAKER, academic administrator; b. Cleve., Nov. 3, 1942; s. William B. and Louise M. (Baker) B.; m. Retta F. Kriefall, June 16, 1974; children: Elizabeth Rachel, Christopher Baker. BS, Xavier U., 1964; MBA, Fairleigh Dickinson U., 1976; postgrad., Imperial Coll., U London, 1996—. Regional mgr. Northwest Airlines, Inc., St. Paul, Minn., 1967-72; v.p. Inflight Motion Pictures, Inc., N.Y.C., 1972-78; v.p., gen. mgr. Columbia Pipe & Supply, Inc., Portland, Oreg., 1978-79; exec. v.p. Golby Mfg. Co., Portland, 1979-80; v.p. fin. Timberline Software, Inc., Portland, 1980-82; pres., founder Computer Systems Supplyware, Inc., Portland, 1982-87; dean Coll. Bus. Concordia U., Portland, 1987-92, exec. v.p., 1993—; COO Concordia U. Found., Portland, 1993—, vice chmn., dir., 1985—; mem. bd. regents Concordia U., 1986-87, 92—; bd. dirs. Alameda Resources Co., Tigard, Oreg. Com. chmn. United Way, Boston, 1966; bd. dirs. German Am. Found., 1990—. With USN, 1964-67. Mem. Oreg. Ctr. for Entrepreneurship (pres., founder, 1986), Am. Mktg. Assn. (panelist 1985-88), Assn. Data Processing Systems Orgn., Rotary (long-range planning com. 1985-96, judge Oreg. Enterprise Forum, Entrepreneur of Yr. award 1998). Lutheran. Office: Concordia U 2811 NE Holman St Portland OR 97211-6099 also: Imperial Coll/Mgmt Sch, 53 Princes Gate Exhibition Rd, London SW7 2PG, England

BRAUTBAR, NACHMAN, physician, educator; b. Haifa, Israel, Oct. 22, 1943; came to U.S., 1975; s. Pinhas and Sabine (Lohite) B.; m. Ronit Aboutboul, Mar. 25, 1968; children: Sigalit, Shirley, Jaques. MD, Med. Sch. Jerusalem, 1968. Diplomate Am. Bd. Internal Medicine, Am. Bd. Nephrology. Intern, Rambam Hosp., Haifa, 1968-69; resident in internal medicine Hadassah Med. Center, Jerusalem, 1972-75; fellow in nephrology UCLA Med. Sch., 1975-77, asst. prof. medicine, 1977-78; asst. prof. medicine U. So. Calif., Los Angeles, 1978-80, assoc. prof. medicine, pharmacology and nutrition, 1980-87, clin. prof. medicine, 1987—, dir. Ctr. for Toxicology and Chem. Exposure; chmn. nephrology sect. Hollywood Presbyn. Med. Center, 1980—. Author: Cellular Bioenergetics, 1985; editor Internat. Jour. Occupl. Medicine and Toxicology; contbr. numerous articles, papers to scientific publs. Chmn. research com., pub. relations com. Kidney Foundation Los Angeles, 1980—. Named Hon. Citizen, Los Angeles City Council, 1984; Grantee Am. Heart Assn., 1980—, NIH, 1983. Mem. Am. Soc. Nephrology, Am. Soc. Bone and Mineral Rsch., Am. Physiol. Soc., Am. Chem. Soc., Am. Soc. Parenteral Nutrition, Am. Coll. Nutrition, Israeli Soc. Nephrology (hon.). Address: 6200 Wilshire Blvd Ste 1000 Los Angeles CA 90048-5811

BRAVERMAN, DONNA CARYN, fiber artist; b. Chgo., Apr. 4, 1947; d. Samuel and Pearl (Leen) B.; m. William Stanley Knopf, Jan. 21, 1990. Student, U. Mo., 1965-68; BFA in Interior Design, Chgo. Acad. Fine Arts, 1970. Interior designer Ascher Dental Supply-Healthco., Chgo., 1970-72, Clarence Krusinski & Assocs. Ltd., Chgo., 1972-74, Perkins & Will Architects, Chgo., 1974-77; fiber artist Fiber Co-op Fibrecations, Chgo., 1977, Scottsdale, Ariz., 1977—. Exhibited in group shows at Mus. Contemporary Crafts, N.Y.C., 1977, James Prendergast Library Art Gallery, Jamestown, N.Y., 1981, Grover M. Herman Fine Arts Ctr., Marietta, Ohio, 1982, Okla. Art Ctr., 1982, Middle Tenn. State U., Murfreesboro, 1982, Redding (Calif.) Mus., 1983, Tucson Mus. Art, 1984, 86, The Arts Ctr., Iowa City, 1985, The Wichita Nat., 1986; in traveling exhibitions Ariz. Archtl. Crafts, 1983, Clouds, Mountains, Fibers, 1983; represented in permanent collections Phillips Petroleum, Houston, Metro. Life, Tulsa, Directory Hotel, Tulsa, Keys Estate Ariz. Biltmore Estates, Phoenix, Sohio Petroleum, Dallas, Reichold Chem., White Plains, N.Y., Rolm Telecommunications, Colorado Springs, Mesirow & Co., Chgo., Exec. House Hotel, Chgo., Cambell Estate, Ariz., Dictaphone Worldhead Quarters, Stratford, Conn., Davenport Bldg., Boston; contbr. articles to profl. jours. Avocation: photography. Home and Office: 1041 E Glenrosa Ave Phoenix AZ 85014-4435

BRAXTON, BONNIT D., former transportation planner, music producer; b. New Orleans; d. John Henry and Thelma Doretha (Bass) James; m. James Carrold Braxton, Mar. 9, 1947; 1 child, Terrence Enrico Hariston. BSBA, San Francisco State U., 1975. With Caltrans, Sacramento, Calif., Yo Momma's Records, Vallejo, Calif. Mem. NAFE. Baptist. Avocations: jewelry, crocheting. Office: Yo Mommas Records PO Box 4684 Vallejo CA 94590-6684

BRAY, JAMES WALLACE, II, minister; b. Fresno, Calif., Aug. 5, 1952; s. James Wallace and Alma Jean (Higgins) B.; m. Diana Sue Rendleman, Sept. 9, 1972; 1 child, Jaime Grace. BA, Calif. Bapt. Coll., Riverside, 1974; M.Ch. Music, Golden Gate Sem., Mill Valley, Calif., 1977. Ordained to ministry, So. Bapt. Conv., 1978. Assoc pastor music and edn. Trinity Bapt. Ch., Vacaville, Calif., 1977-81; missionary So. Bapt. Fgn. Mission Bd., Costa Rica, 1981-82; assoc. pastor Canoga Park (Calif.) Bapt. Ch., 1987-89; assoc. pastor music and edn. First Bapt. Ch., Campbell, Calif., 1982-87, First So. Bapt. Ch., Apple Valley, Calif., 1989—; associational music dir. High Desert Bapt. Assn., Hesperia, Calif., 1990—; state music specialist Calif. So. Bapt. Conv., Fresno, 1980—. Mem. Calif. Singing Churchmen, Western Bapt. Religious Educators Assn. Office: First So Bapt Ch 12345 Navajo Rd Apple Valley CA 92308-7252

BRAY, MARIAN LOUISE, writer, secondary education educator; b. Witchita Falls, Tex., Oct. 19, 1957; d. John Robert and Mary Joan (Jacobus) Flandrick; m. Jeffrey Fred Bray, Oct. 30, 1980; 1 child, Piper Camille. BA, Calif. Poly. Inst., 1979. Cert. EMT, Calif. Reporter The Cambrian, Cambria, Calif., 1978; rschr., paste-up artist The Thoroughbred of Calif., Arcadia, 1979-80; libr. asst. Orange County (Calif.) Pub. Libr., 1983-97; substitute tchr. Santa Ana (Calif.) Unified Sch. Dist., 1997—; freelance writer, 1980—; tchr. of writing various confs. and colls., 1983—. Author: Stay True: Short Stories for Strong Girls, 1998; author over 150 short stories and articles; 17 novels pub. to date. Vol. EMT Orange County Search and Rescue, 1993—. Avocations: horseriding, raising guinea pigs, training dogs. Home and Office: 1603 Brenda Rd SE Rio Rancho NM 87124-2723

BRAY, R(OBERT) BRUCE, music educator; b. La Grande, Oreg., July 24, 1924; s. Ernest C. and Leta M. (Haight) B.; m. Donna Marie Siegman, July 2, 1949 (div. 1980); children: Stephen Louis, Ruth Elizabeth, Katherine Ernestine, Anne-Marie. BA, U. Oreg., 1949, MMus, 1955; postgrad., U. Strasbourg, France, 1949-50, U. Wash., 1960-61. Music tchr. Helen McCune Jr. High Sch., Pendleton, Oreg., 1951-54; dir. choral music Albany (Oreg.) Union High Sch., 1954-56; elem. music supr. Ashland (Oreg.) Public Schs., 1956-57; asst. prof. music Cen. Wash. U., Ellensburg, 1957-60; from asst. to prof. U. Idaho, Moscow, 1961-89, prof. emeritus, 1989—; sec. faculty U. Idaho, Moscow, 1968-88, sec. emeritus, 1988—. Editor: Oreg. Music Educator, 1954-57, Wash. Music Educator, 1957-60, U. Idaho Music, 1961-68, Idaho Music Notes, 1963-68, U. Idaho Register, 1974-88 ; editorial bd. Music Educators Jour., 1964-68. With USNR, 1942-46. Mem. Music Educators Nat. Conf. (bd. dirs., pres. N.W. divsn. 1963-65, nat. exec. com. 1964-66), Phi Mu Alpha Sinfonia. Democrat. Episcopalian. Home and Office: 2614 E Everett Ave Spokane WA 99207-6210

BRECHBILL, SUSAN REYNOLDS, lawyer, educator; b. Washington, Aug. 22, 1943; d. Irving and Isabell Doyle (Reynolds) Levine; B.A., Coll. William and Mary, 1965; J.D., Marshall-Wythe Sch. Law, 1968; children—Jennifer Rae, Heather Lea. Admitted to Va. bar, 1969, Fed. bar, 1970; atty. AEC, Berkeley, Calif., 1968-73, indsl. relations specialist AEC, Las Vegas, 1974-75; atty. ERDA, Oakland, Calif., 1976-77; atty. Dept. Energy, Oakland, 1977-78, dir. procurement div. San Francisco Ops. Office, 1978-85, asst. chief counsel for gen. law, 1985-93, acting asst. mgr. environ. mgmt. and support, 1992, acting asst. mgr. def. programs, 1993; chief counsel Dept. Energy Richland Ops. Office, 1994—; mem. faculty U. Calif. Extension; speaker Nat. Contract Mgmt. Assn. Ann. Symposiums, 1980, 81, 83, 84, 88; speaker on doing bus. with govt. Leader Girl Scouts U.S.A., San Francisco area; bd. dirs. Am. Heart Assn. Eastern Wash., 1997—, Sexual Assault Response Ctr., Tri Cities, Wash., 1997—. Named Outstanding Young Woman Nev., 1974; recipient Meritorious Svc. award Dept. Energy, 1992. Mem. NAFE, Va. State Bar Assn., Fed. Bar Assn., Nat. Contract Mgmt. Assn. (pres. Golden Gate chpt. 1983-84, N.W. regional v.p. 1984-86). Republican. Contbr. articles to profl. jours.

BREDDAN, JOE, systems engineering consultant; b. N.Y.C., Sept. 18, 1950; s. Hyman and Sylvia (Hauser) B. BA in Math. and Psychology, SUNY, Binghamton, 1972; MS in Ops. Research, U. Calif., Berkeley, 1975; PhD in Systems Engring., U. Ariz., 1978. Teaching and research assoc. Dept. Systems and Indsl. Engring. U. Ariz., Tucson, 1975-79; project engr. B.D.M. Services Co., Tucson, 1979-80; mem. tech. staff Bell Labs., Am. Bell, AT&T Info. Systems, Denver, 1980-86; staff mgr. AT&T, Denver, 1986-91; pvt. practice cons. Boulder, Colo., 1991—. Patentee in field. Bd. dirs. Colo. Environ. Coalition, 1996—. bd. dirs. Colo. Environ. Coalition, 1996—. Home and Office: 2120 Goddard Pl Boulder CO 80303-5616

BREISCH, KENNETH ALAN, architectural educator; b. Chgo., Aug. 20, 1949; s. Walter Ernest and La Verne (Ahern) B.; m. Judith Florence Keller, Apr. 28, 1977; 1 child, William Rush Clinger. AB, Univ. Mich., 1975, MA, 1977, PhD, 1982. Dir. survey and planning Tex. Historical Commn., Austin, 1981-86; vis. asst. prof. Univ. Del., Newark, 1986-87; prof. Southern Calif. Inst. of Architecture, L.A., 1987—; adj. assoc. prof. Univ. Southern Calif. Sch. Architecture, L.A., 1997—. Author: Henry Hobson Richardson and the Small Public Library, 1997; editor: Perspectives in Vernacular Architecture. Chair Planning Commn., Santa Monica, Calif., 1995-96, planning commissioner, 1993—. Mem. Am. Studies Assn., Coll. Art Assn., Soc. Arch. Historians, Vernacular Arch. Forum (bd. dirs. 1985-88, 96—), Nat. Trust for Historic Preservation. Office: Southern Calif Inst Arch 5454 Beethoven St Los Angeles CA 90066-7017

BREITENBACH, MARY LOUISE MCGRAW, psychologist, chemical dependency counselor; b. Pitts., Sept. 26, 1936; d. David Evans McGraw and Louise (Schoch) Neel; m. John Edgar Breitenbach, Apr. 15, 1960 (dec. 1963); m. Joseph George Piccioli III, Aug. 15, 1987; children: Cary P. Frye and Douglas (twins), Kirstin Amethyst. Postgrad., Oreg. State Coll., 1960-61; BA, Russell Sage Coll., Troy, N.Y., 1958; MEd, Harvard U., 1983. Lic. profl. counselor, chem. dependency specialist, Wyo.; cert. addiction specialist level III; nat. cert. addiction counselor II, master addiction counselor. Paraprofessional psychologist St. John's Episc. Ch., Jackson, Wyo., 1963-94; pvt. practice Wilson, Wyo., 1983—; counselor Curran/Seeley Found. Addiction Svcs., Jackson, 1989-91, Van Vleck House/Tri-County Group Home, Jackson, 1986-89, others; provider multiple employee assistance programs local and nat. cos.; mem. adv. com. The Learning Ctr., 1997—. Trustee Teton Sci. Sch., Kelly, Wyo, 1960-76; pres. bd. govs. Teton County Mus., 1989-91, Jackson; vestry mem. St. John's Ch., Jackson. Mem. APA, LWV, Wyo. Psychol. Assn., Wyo. Assn. Counseling and Devel., Wyo. Assn. Addiction Specialists, Nat. Assn. Alcohol and Drug Addiction Counselors. Democrat. Episcopalian. Avocations: horseback riding, racquetball. Home and Office: Star Rte # 2 Cheney Ln Wilson WY 83014

BREITWEISER, JAMES RUSSELL, insurance company executive; b. Ogden, Utah, Oct. 19, 1936; s. Elmer Ellsworth and Helen (Russell) B.; m. Rose Mary Holley; children: J. Curtis, Tricia R., Cherise H., Marci A. ASBA, Weber State U., 1958; BSBA, Utah State U., 1960; MSBA, Calif. State U., Sacramento, 1965; CLU, Am. Coll. Life Underwriters, 1975. Sales rep. Procter & Gamble, Stockton, Calif., 1960-62, J.B. Roerig (Div. of Pfizer Labs), Stockton, Calif., 1962-66; dist. sales mgr. Allstate Ins. Co., Bakersfield, Calif., 1966-68; ins. agt. N.Y. Life, New Eng. Life, Ogden, 1968-71; v.p. First Security Ins., Inc., Salt Lake City, 1971-77; pres. Integrated Fin. Mktg., Inc., Ogden, 1987—; owner, ins. agt. Breitweiser Ins. Svcs., Ogden, 1977-92; adj. instr. Weber State U., 1977-87; ins. cons. Ogden First Fed. Savs. and Loan, 1977—. Bd. dirs. Hospice No. Utah, 1993—. Served with USN, 1955-57. Mem. Ogden Exch. Club (pres. 1984-85), Ogden Assn. CLU (pres. 1984-85), Ogden Assn. Ind. Ins. Agts. (pres. 1980-81), Ind. Ins. Agts. of Utah Assn. (pres. 1990-91), Greater Ogden C. of C., Pi Kappa Alpha (hon.). Republican. Mem. LDS Ch. Avocations: hunting, fishing, boating. Home: 5278 S 1300 E Ogden UT 84403-4557 Office: Breitweiser Ins Svcs 4155 Harrison Blvd Ste 202 Ogden UT 84403-2463

BREITWIESER-STACEY, DIANE LOUISE, artist; b. San Diego, Apr. 24, 1948; d. Charles John and Irene (Kellman) B.; m. Robert Harrison Stacey, Apr. 7, 1989. Student, Dr Bakers Coll., Herts, Eng., 1977, Art Sch., 1966-67, Art Sch., 1993-94. cons. for understanding self with Asholoical charts. Exhibited in solo & group shows in various galleries. Leader Moon-Group Medatation, 1991—. Avocations: human rights, inner awareness. E-mail: dianst@cart.net. Home: 576 Stratford Dr Encinitas CA 92024-4544

BRENDLINGER, JACK ALLEN, broadcast executive; b. Denver, Feb. 9, 1933; s. Elmer Lincoln Brendlinger and Catherine Louise (Allen) England; m. Marsha Ann Bray, Mar. 19, 1960; children: Kurt, Eric, Dina, Kira. BS in Business, U. Colo., 1956. Mgr. Standard Oil Calif., El Segundo, 1957-59; area mgmt. Snow Basin Ski Area, Ogden, Utah, 1959-60; adminstrn., pub. relations Martin-Marietta, Denver, 1960-64; proprietor Applejack Inn, Aspen, Colo., 1964-73; assoc. producer Freewheelin' Films, Ltd., Aspen, 1973-76; pub. relations dir. Aspen Skiing Co., 1976-85, co-dir. mktg., 1982-85; pres. New Visions, Inc., Aspen, 1985—; pres. Echo Radio Prodns., 1994—, exec. prodr. "Radio Jeopardy", "Secrets of Success". Exec. producer (films) Love Affair with Aspen, 1979, Welcome to Aspen, 1984, Aspen in January, 1980; co-producer: Visions of Speed, 1975, (TV spls.) Travelin' On, 1987, Colorado...Picture Perfect, 1988, (films) Skiing with Style I: The Parallel Turn, 1988, Skiing with Style II: Mastering the Mountain, 1988; producer The World of Four Wheeling, 1988, Golf...The Perfect Passion, 1989. Bd. dirs. Aspen Resort Assn., 1980-85, Aspen Theater Group, 1973-75, Aspen Council for the Arts, 1979-80. Mem. Aspen C. of C.; assoc. mem. Nat. Assn. TV Program Executives, Nat. Assn. Broadcasters, U.S. Ski Writers Assn., Rotary (dir. 1987-89, 91—, v.p. 1991-92, pres. 1992-93). Club: Aspen Ski (pres. 1969-72). Lodge: Rotary (dir. 1987—). Avocations: skiing, golf, fly fishing, sculpting, hunting. Office: Freewheelin' Films/New Visions Inc New Visions Inc PO Box 599 Aspen CO 81612-0599

BRENEMAN, DAVID CLINTON, II, audio producer, director; b. Tacoma, Feb. 13, 1959; s. Robert Weldon and Jane Harriet (Hill) B. BA in Econs., U. Puget Sound, 1985. Segment producer Photo N.W. Video, Tacoma, 1986-87; dir. Spud Goodman Radio Show, Tacoma, 1986-87; owner Rosedale Audio Prodns., Gig Harbor, Wash., 1986—; dir. program syndicated in the N.W. Spud Goodman Radio-Radio Show, Tacoma, 1987-89; asst. dir. & editor The Other Spud Goodman Show, 1991; data systems adminstr. Tacoma Screw Products, Inc., 1989-93; audio dir., editor The Spud Goodman Show, KTZZ-TV, Seattle, 1992-95; audio dir., editor, cinematographer The Spud Goodman Show, Fox Net, 1996-98; sr. Unix sys. adminstr. AT&T Wireless Svcs., 1995-97; distributed systems software analyst Airborne Freight Corp., 1998—; bd. dirs. Seattle Unix Group, 1991-93. Commn. Pierce County (Wash.) Rev. Com. Charter Rev. Commn., 1987; precinct committeeman Rosedale (Wash.) Reps., 1986-92; mem. Pierce County Rep. Exec. Com., 1989-92; v.p. Rosedale Cmty. Hall Assn., 1996-98. Home: 8520 86th Ave NW Gig Harbor WA 98332-6750 Office: Rosedale Audio Prodns 8520 86th Ave NW Gig Harbor WA 98332

BRENKEN, HANNE MARIE, artist; b. Duisburg, Germany, July 6, 1923; arrived in U.S., 1977; d. Hermann and Luise (Werth) Tigler; m. Hans Brenken, Mar. 28, 1942 (div. 1985); children: Karin Brenken Schneider-Henn, Berndt; m. Ricardo Wiesenberg, May 20, 1986. Grad., Landschulheim, Holzminden, Germany, 1941; studied in pvt. art schs., Munich and Bonn, Germany. One-person shows include Contra Kreis Gallery, Bonn, Germany, 1958, Galerie Junge Kunst, Fulda, Germany, 1959, Universa-Galerie, Nurenberg, Germany, 1960, Galleria Monte Napoleone, Milan, Italy, 1961, Galerie Niedlich, Stuttgart, Germany, 1961, 63, Galerie am Jakobsbrunnen, Stuttgart, 1964, 67, Kunst und Kunstverein Mus., Pforzheim, Germany, 1969, Kunstverein Mus., Munich, 1972, Galerie Dorothea Leonhart, Munich, 1974, I.C.L. Gallery, East Hampton, N.Y., 1980, Anne Reid Gallery, Princeton, N.J., 1981, Adagio Gallery, Bridgehampton, N.Y., 1982, 84, Queens Mus., N.Y., 1983, Ericson Gallery, N.Y.C., 1984, 85, Benton Gallery, Southampton, N.Y., 1986, Vered Gallery, East Hampton, N.Y., 1988, Gallery Rodeo, Lake Arrowhead, Calif., Taos, N.Mex., Beverly Hills, Calif., 1990, Brian Logan Art Space, Washington, 1991, The Gallery, Leesburg, Va., 1992, Amerika Haus, Frankfurt, Germany, 1993, Ganser Haus Gallery, Wasserburg, Germany, 1993, Ann Norton Sculpture Gardens, West Palm Beach, Fla., 19943, Jean Chisholm Gallery, West Palm Beach, 1994, Okuda Internat. Gallery, Washington, 1995, Misia Broadhead Studio/Gallery, Middleburg, Va., 1996, Millennium Gallery, East Hampton, N.Y., 1997, Reynolds Gallery Westmont Coll., Santa Barbara, Calif., 1998; group shows include Duisburg (Germany) Mus., 1959, Baden-Baden Mus., Germany, 1961, 62, Haus der Kunst, Munich, 1963, 64, 69, 70, 71, 72, 73, Kunstgebäude, Stuttgart, 1963, 71, Acad. Fine Arts, Berlin, 1964, 73, Forum Stadtpark, Graz, Austria, 1965, Folkwang Mus., Essen, Germany, 1965, Munich City Mus., 1967, Karlsruhe (Germany) Kunstverein, 1967, Galerie Heseler, Munich, 1968, Hannover (Germany) Mus., 1969, Modern Art Mus., Munich, 1969, Bonn Mus., 1970, Kunstkreis Gallery, Wasserburg, Germany, 1972, 73, Kunstverein Mus., Rosenheim, Germany, 1972, Mainz Mus., 1974, Kunstverein Mus., Frankfurt, Germany, 1977, Guild Hall Mus., East Hampton, N.Y., 1979, 80, 81, 82, 83, Parrish Art Mus., Southampton, N.Y., 1979, 80, 81, Elaine Benson Gallery, Bridgehampton, N.Y., 1980, 81, Kunstverein Mus., Munich, 1982, Ericson Gallery, 1984, Vered Gallery, East Hampton, 1985, 86, 87, 89, Franz Bader Gallery, Washington, 1989, Ganser Haus, Wasserburg, 1992, Reynolds Gallery Westmont Coll., Santa Barbara, Calif., 1998; permanent collections include Solomon R. Guggenheim Mus., N.Y.C., The Queens (N.Y.) Mus., Phoenix Art Mus., Guild Hall Mus., various mus. in Europe; author: (book) Firlefranz, 1969. Avocations: travel, visiting galleries and musuems, reading. Home and Studio: 184 Middle Rd Montecito CA 93108-2446

BRENNAN, CIARAN BRENDAN, accountant; b. Dublin, Ireland, Jan. 28, 1944; s. Sean and Mary (Stone) B. BA with honors, Univ. Coll., Dublin, 1966; MBA, Harvard U., 1973; MS in Acctg., U. Houston, 1976. Lic. real estate broker, Calif.; CPA, Tex. Auditor Coopers & Lybrand, London, 1967-70; sr. auditor Price Waterhouse & Co., Toronto, Ont., Can., 1970-71; project acctg. specialist Kerr-McGee Corp., Oklahoma City, 1976-80; contr. Cummings Oil Co., Oklahoma City, 1980-82; CFO Red Stone Energies, Ltd., 1982, Leonoco, Inc., 1982-87; treas., chief fin. officer JKJ Supply Co., 1983-87, Saturn Investments Inc., 1983-87, JFL Co., 1984-87, Little Chief Drilling & Energy Inc., 1984-85; pres. Ciaran Brennan Corp., 1990, Rathgar Securities, Inc., 1989-90; CFO Nationwide Industries, 1991-93; bd. dirs., cons. small oil cos.; adj. faculty Oklahoma City U., 1977-86; vis. faculty Ctrl. State U., 1977-86. Contbr. articles to profl. jours. Mem. AICPA, Inst. Chartered Accts. Eng. and Wales, Inst. Chartered Accts. Can. Democrat. Roman Catholic.

BRENNAN, JERRY MICHAEL, economics educator, statistician, researcher, clinical psychologist; b. Grosse Pointe, Mich., July 17, 1944; s. Walter X. and Aretta May (Gempler) B. Student Kalamazoo (Mich.) Coll., 1962-64, Pasadena (Calif.) City Coll., 1966-67; B.A., UCLA, 1969; M.A., U. Hawaii, 1973, Ph.D., 1978. Researcher, UCLA, 1968-69; researcher U. Hawaii, 1972, 74-78, cons., 1975, 77, 78, data analyst and statis. cons., 1979-80, lectr., 1976-80, asst. prof. econs., 1980-83; pres. Sugar Mill Software, 1986-97; cons. WHO; v.p. Forest Inst. Profl. Psychology. Light scholar, 1964-66. Mem. Am. Psychol. Assn., Soc. Multivariate Exptl. Psychology, Psychometric Soc., Western Psychol. Assn., AAUP, Hawaii Ednl. Research Assn. Contbr. psychol. articles to profl. jours. Address: 651 Kaumakani St Honolulu HI 96825-1827

BRENNAN, JOAN STEVENSON, federal judge; b. Detroit, Feb. 21, 1933; d. James and Betty (Holland) Stevenson; m. Lane P. Brennan, June 26, 1954 (div. 1970); children: Suzanne, Steven, Clayton, Elizabeth, Catherine. BA, Skidmore Coll., 1954; JD, Santa Clara U., 1973. Bar: Calif. Dep. dist. atty. Dist. Attys. Office, Santa Clara, Calif., 1974-78; legal counsel U.S. Leasing Internat., San Francisco, 1978-79; asst. U.S. atty. U.S. Dist. Ct. (no. dist.) Calif., San Francisco, 1980-82, U.S. Magistrate judge, 1982—. Mem. Nat. Assn. Women Judges, Nat. Assn. Magistrate Judges. Democrat. Office: US Dist Ct PO Box 36054 450 Golden Gate Ave Ste 36052 San Francisco CA 94102-3482*

BRENNAN, PETER JOSEPH, journalist; b. Heidelberg, West Germany, July 1, 1959; came to U.S., 1959; s. William Hubert and Marianne (Enig) B.; m. Cynthia Maria Castillo; 1 child, Nicole. BA in Journalism, San Francisco State U., 1984, BA in English, 1984; MA in Journalism, Ohio State U., 1997. Intern The San Francisco Examiner, 1984; copy editor, reporter The Daily Jour., Caracas, Venezuela, 1984-86; copy editor The Stockton (Calif.) Record, 1987; with The Tico Times, San Jose, 1988-96; editor, reporter Bus. Costa Rica, San Jose, 1992-96; fellow Ohio State U., Columbus, 1996-97; reporter The Orange County Bus. Jour., Newport Beach, Calif., 1997—. Contbr. articles to profl. jours. Mem. Investigative Reporters. E-mail: brennan@ocbj.com. Home: 30 Pinestone Irvine CA 92604-4723

BRENNER, ANITA SUSAN, lawyer; b. Los Angeles, Aug. 18, 1949; d. Morris I. and Lillian F. Brenner; m. Leonard E. Torres, Aug. 19, 1973; children—Andrew Jacob, Rachel Elizabeth. B.A., UCLA, 1970, J.D., 1973. Bar: Calif. 1974, U.S. Dist. Ct. (cen. dist.) Calif. 1974. Atty. Greater Watts Justice Ctr., Los Angeles, 1974-75; sole practice, Los Angeles, 1975; dep. pub. defender Los Angeles County, 1975-84; assoc. Tyre and Kamins, Los Angeles, 1979; ptnr. Torres-Brenner, Pasadena, Calif., 1984—; lectr. criminal law. Mem., assoc. editor UCLA Law Rev., 1971-73. Editor FORUM mag., 1980-83. Contbr. articles to profl. jours. Bd. dirs. One Stop Immigration, 1979-81; vol. Los Angeles Area Council on Child Passenger Safety, 1981; mem. Los Angeles County Med. Assn. joint com. on med.-legal issues, 1983. Mable Wilson Richards scholar, 1971-72. Mem. Calif. Attys. for Criminal Justice (bd. govs. 1980-86), Continuing Edn. of Bar (criminal law sub-com.). Office: Torres-Brenner 301 E Colorado Blvd Ste 614 Pasadena CA 91101-1918

BRENNER, CHARLES FREDERICK, architect; b. Chgo., Sept. 22, 1943; s. William Otto and Evelyn Marie (Schroeder) B.; m. Sharon Ann Lindh, Jan. 5, 1951. BArch, Mont. State U., 1969. Registered arch., Colo. Draftsman Scott, Louie & Browning, Salt Lake City, 1972-76, Grand Junction, Grant Junction, Colo., 1976-78, 1978-81, ptnr., 1981-84; arch. Sun Designs Archs., Glenwood Springs, Colo., 1984-87; pvt. practice C. F. Brenner Inc. Arch., Glenwood Springs, Colo., 1987-94; prin. Brenner Harr PC Arch., Glenwood Springs, Colo., 1994—. Author: Your Architect and the Building Process, 1983. Mem. Bd. Examiners ARch., Colo., 1997-. Recipient Citation Colo. Gov.'s Outstanding Efforts in Smart Growth and Devel., 1995. Mem. AIA (chmn. govt. affairs com.. 1985), AIA West Slope Chpt., (pres. 1952, sec. 1983-84), AIA Colo. Chpt. (treas. 1991-92, sec. 1993), Glenwood Springs Kiwanis Club (pres. 1989, 1991, disting. pres. 1989, Kiar Builders Medallion 1995), Glenwood Springs Chamber Resort Assn. Republican. Methodist. Avocations: golfing, fishing, hunting, hiking. Office: Brenner Harr PC Architecture 826 1/2 Grand Ave Glenwood Springs CO 81601-3404

BRES, PHILIP WAYNE, automotive executive; b. Beaumont, Tex., Mar. 6, 1950; s. Roland Defrance Bres and Edna Gene (Griffith) Seale; m. Janet Vivian Meyer, May 16, 1987; children: Rachel Elizabeth, Rebecca Claire. BA, Lamar U., Beaumont, Tex., 1972; MBA, Stephen F. Austin State U., 1973. Distbn. mgr., bus. mgmt. mgr. Mazda Motors of Am., Houston, 1973-75; analyst, cons. C.H. McCormack and Assocs., Houston, 1975-76; assoc. Frank Gillman Pontiac/GMC/Honda, Houston, 1976-79, David Taylor Cadillac Co., Houston, 1979-80; pres. Braintrust Inc., Houston, 1980-83; sales mgr. Mossy Oldsmobile, Inc., Houston, 1983-84; gen. mgr. Mossy Nissan/Ford, Bellevue, Wash., 1984-86; dir. ops. Mossy Co., Encinitas, Calif., 1986-91; gen. mgr. Performance Nissan, Duarte, Calif., 1991—; seminar lectr. Rice U., Houston, 1980-83. Author: The Entrepreneurs Guide for Starting a Successful Business., 1982; contbr. (book) Business Planning for the Entrepreneur, 1983. Mem. Houston C. of C. (small bus. coun.), Opt Astron. Soc., Univ. Club, Phi Eta Sigma, Phi Kappa Phi. Office: Performance Nissan PO Box 1500 Duarte CA 91009-4500

BRESLAUER, GEORGE WILLIAM, political science educator; b. N.Y.C., Mar. 4, 1946; s. Henry Edward and Marianne (Schaeffer) B.; m. Yvette Assia, June 5, 1976; children: Michelle, David. BA, U. Mich., 1966, MA, 1968, PhD, 1973. Asst. prof. polit. sci. U. Calif., Berkeley, 1971-79, assoc. prof., 1979-90, prof., 1990—, Chancellor's prof., 1998—, chmn. dept., 1993-96, chmn. Ctr. for Slavic and East European Studies, 1982-94; vice chmn. bd. trustees Nat. Coun. for Soviet and East European Rsch., Washington, 1988-91. Author: Khrushchev and Brezhnev as Leaders, 1982, Soviet Strategy in the Middle East, 1989; editor: Can Gorbachev's Reforms Succeed?, 1990, Learning in U.S. and Soviet Foreign Policy, 1991. Grantee Ford Found., 1982-84, Carnegie Corp., 1985-94. Mem. Am. Assn. for Advancement Slavic Studies (bd. dirs., exec. com. 1990-93). Office: U Calif Dept Polit Sci 210 Barrows Hall Berkeley CA 94720-1950

BRESSAN, ROBERT RALPH, accountant; b. Yonkers, N.Y., Feb. 8, 1945; s. Alfred D. and Antionette (Desivo) B.; m. Florence L. Vigna, June 9, 1968 (dec.); children: Anne Marie, Robert A., Tiffany L. BBA in Acctg., Iona Coll., 1967. CPA, Colo.; cert. tax profl. Am. Inst. Tax Studies. Staff to sr. Coopers & Lybrand, N.Y.C., 1967-70; sr. to audit mgr. Fox & Co., Colorado Springs, 1970-80; ptnr., owner Robert R. Bressan, Colorado Springs, 1980-98, Farmer, Bressan & Co, CPA, LLC (formerly Robert R. Bressan), 1998—; mem. exec. com. GAO Intergovtl. Audit Forum. Mem. charity rev. com. BBB. Mem. AICPA, Sertoma, Inst. Mgmt. Accts., Govtl. Fin. Officers Assn., Colo. Govtl. Fin. Officers, Nat. Assn. Counties. Avocations: coins, golf, dancing. Office: 829 N Circle Dr Ste 214 Colorado Springs CO 80909-5008

BREST, PAUL A., law educator; b. Jacksonville, Fla., Aug. 9, 1940; s. Alexander and Mia (Deutsch) B.; m. Iris Lang, June 17, 1962; children: Hilary, Jeremy. AB, Swarthmore Coll., 1962; JD, Harvard U., 1965; LLD (hon.), Northeastern U., 1980, Swarthmore Coll., 1991. Bar: N.Y. 1966. Law clk. to Hon. Bailey Aldrich U.S. Ct. Appeals (1st cir.), Boston, 1965-66; atty. NAACP Legal Def. Fund, Jackson, Miss., 1966-68; law clk. Justice John Harlan, U.S. Supreme Ct., 1968-69; prof. law Stanford U., 1969—, Kenneth and Harle Montgomery Prof. pub. interest law, Richard E. Lang prof. and dean, 1987—. Author: Processes of Constitutional Decisionmaking, 1992. Mem. Am. Acad. Arts and Scis. Home: 814 Tolman Dr Palo Alto CA 94305-1026 Office: Stanford U Sch Law 559 Nathan Abbott Way Stanford CA 94305-8610*

BRET, DONNA LEE, elementary education educator; b. Pottsville, Pa., Dec. 18, 1950; d. S. Allen and Georgene Katherine (Heiser) Zimmerman; m. Donald Louis Bret, Oct. 11, 1969; 1 child, Thomas Donald. AA, Glendale [illegible] Cert. tchr. [illegible] Ariz. Kindergarten tchr. Glendale (Ariz.) Elem. Dist., 1991-92, 1st grade ESL tchr., 1992-93, multi-age ESL tchr., 1993—; rep. Glendale Elem. Assn., 1998-99. Mem. NEA, Ariz. State U. Alumni Assn., Bilingual Club. Office: Glendale Elem Sch Dist 7301 N 58th Ave Glendale AZ 85301-1893

BRETERNITZ, CORY DALE, archaeological company executive, consultant; b. Tucson, Apr. 9, 1955; s. David Alan and Barbara Blair (Myers) B.; m. Adrian Sue White, May 21, 1981; children: Jessie Lynn, Dylan Blair. BA, U. Ariz., 1978; MA, Wash. State U., 1982. Archaeologist Mus. No. Ariz., Flagstaff, 1973; lab. technician Lab. of Tree-Ring Rsch., Tucson, 1973-78; archaeologist Ariz. State Mus., Tucson, 1978, Nat. Pk. Svc., Albuquerque, 1976-79, Dolores (Colo.) Archaeol. Program, 1980-81; project dir. Navajo Nation Archaeology Program, Window Rock, Ariz., 1981-82, Profl. Svc. Industries, Inc., Phoenix, 1982-84; pres. Ctr. for Indigenous Studies in Ams., Phoenix, 1991—; pres., owner Soil Systems, Inc., Phoenix, 1984—. Mem. Ariz. Archaeol. Coun. (exec. com. 1976, editor 1989-94), N.Mex. Archaeol. Coun., Am. Cultural Resources Assn. (bd. dirs. 1995—), Colo. Coun. Profl. Archaeologists, Utah Profl. Archaeol. Coun., Am. Quaternary Assn., Soc. for Am. Archaeology (chmn. 1996—), Am. Anthrop. Assn. Office: Soil Systems Inc 1121 N 2nd St Phoenix AZ 85004-1862

BREUER, STEPHEN ERNEST, temple administrator; b. Vienna, Austria, July 14, 1936; s. John Hans Howard and Olga Marion (Haar) B.; came to U.S., 1938, naturalized, 1945; BA cum laude, UCLA, 1959, gen. secondary credential, 1960; m. Gail Fern Breitbart, Sept. 4, 1960 (div. 1986); children: Jared Noah, Rachel Elise; m. Nadine Bendit, Sept. 25, 1988. *Stephen Breuer's grandparents, Felix and Marie Breuer, perished with dozens of family members in the Holocaust. Stephen's parents, Hans and Olga Breuer, fled Vienna, with him at the age of two, along with his Uncle Fred and Aunt Gisela Ehrlich, on the eve of "kristalnacht," the nazi program against German and Austrian Jews in November 1938. The family settled in Los Angeles, where Stephen's grandparents Helen and Henry Haar joined them in 1941. Stephen's brother, Robert, now a college administrator living in Berkeley, California with his wife Fredericka and their son Noah, was born in 1944. Stephen's cousins Bill Ehrlich and Shirley Ehrlich Kouffman are Los Angeles natives and residents* Tchr. L.A. City Schs., 1960-62; dir. Wilshire Blvd. Temple Camps, L.A., 1962-86; exec. dir. Wilshire Blvd. Temple, 1980—; dir. Edgar F. Magnin Religious Sch., Los Angeles, 1970-80. Instr. Hebrew Union Coll., Los Angeles, 1965-76, 92—, U. Judaism, 1991; field instr. San Francisco State U., 1970-80, Calif. State U., San Diego, Hebrew Union Coll., 1977-81, U. of Judaism UCLA extension. Vice pres. L.A. Youth Programs Inc., 1967-77; youth adviser L.A. County Commn. Human Rels., 1969-72. Bd. dirs. Cmty. Rels. Conf. So. Calif., 1965-85; bd. dirs. Alzheimer's Disease and Related Disorders Assn., 1984-95, v.p. L.A. County chpt., 1984-86, pres., 1986-88, nat. exec. com., 1987-95, nat. devel. chair, 1992-95, Calif. state coun. pres. 1987-92, chmn. of Calif. gov.'s adv. com. on Alzheimer's disease, 1988-97; mem. goals program City of Beverly Hills, Calif., 1985-91; bd. dirs. Pacific SW regional Union Am. Hebrew Congregations, 1985-88, mem. nat. bd. , exec. com., 1993-97; bd. dirs. Echo Found., 1986-88, Mazon-Jewish Response to Hunger, 1993-97, Wilshire Stakeholders, exec. com., 1987-94; treas. Wilshire Community Prayer Alliance, 1986-88; active United Way. Recipient Service awards Los Angeles YWCA, 1974, Los Angeles County Bd. Suprs., 1982, 87, Ventura County Bd. Suprs., 1982, 87, Weinberg Chai Lifetime Achievement award Jewish Fed. Council Los Angeles, 1986, Nat. Philanthropy Day L.A. Medallion, 1993, L.A. County Redevel. Agy. recognition, 1994, L.A. Bus. Coun. award, 1997; Steve Breuer Conference Ctr. in Malibu named in his honor Wilshire Blvd. Temple Camps, 1990. Mem. So. Calif. Camping Assn. (dir. 1964-82), Nat. Assn. Temple Adminstrs. (nat. bd. dirs. 1987—, v.p. 1991-93, pres. 1993-97, Svc. to Judaism award 1989, Svc. to the Community award 1990), Nat. Assn. Temple Educators (Kaminker award 1973), Los Angeles Assn. Jewish Edn. (dir.), Profl. Assn. Temple Adminstrs. (pres. 1985-88), Jewish Communal Profls. So. Calif., Assn. Supervision and Curriculum Devel., Am. Mgmt. Assn., So. Calif. Conf. Jewish Communal Workers, Jewish Profl. Network, Amnesty Internat., Jewish Resident Camping Assn. (pres. 1976-82), World Union for Progressive Judaism, UCLA Alumni Assn., Wilderness Soc., Center for Environ. Edn., Wildlife Fedn., Living Desert, Maple Mental Health Ctr. of Beverly Hills, Los Angeles County Mus. Contemporary Art, People for the Am. Way, Assn Reform Zionists Am. (bd. dirs. 1993—). Office: Wilshire Blvd Temple 3663 Wilshire Blvd Los Angeles CA 90010-2798

BREUER, WERNER ALFRED, retired plastics company executive; b. Sinn, Hessia, Germany, Jan. 30, 1930; came to U.S., 1959; s. Christian and Hedwig (Cunz) B.; m. Gertrud Ackermann, June 21, 1950 (dec. 1998); children: Patricia, Julia, Eva-Maria. BS in Human Rels. and Orgnl. Behavior, U. San Francisco, 1983; MS in Bus. Mgmt., U. La Verne, 1985, DPA, 1988. Musician, bandleader BBT Dance Orch., various cities, Germany, 1950-54; lab. technician Firma E. Leitz GMBH, Wetzlar, Germany, 1954-59; lab. supr. Dayco Corp. (Am. latex divsn.), Hawthorne, Calif., 1959-65; tech. ops. mgr. Olin Corp., Stamford and New Haven, Conn., 1965-69; gen. mgr., exec. v.p. Expanded Rubber and Plastics Corp., Gardena, Calif., 1969-96; ret., 1996; gen. mgr. Schlobohm Co. Inc., Dominguez Hills, Calif., 1989-96; ret.; cons. human resources Stabond Corp., Gardena, 1988-95. Author/composer various popular and sacred recordings, 1970s; contbr. articles to jours. Recipient William of Orange Gymnasium scholarship, Dillenburg, Germany, 1940, Portfolio award U. San Francisco, 1983-84. Mem. ASTM, ASCAP, Am. Soc. for Metals, Soc. for Plastics Engrs., N.Y. Acad. Scis., U. La Verne Alumni Assn. Republican. Avocations: play music, writing, horseback riding, composing, sketching. Achievements include pioneering use of plastics especially polyurethanes in defense missiles and space and communication aviation industry. Home: 564 Sage Cir Highlands Ranch CO 80126-2118

BREWER, DAVID L., sociologist; b. Tucson, Mar. 11, 1933; s. Leslie O. and Nina (Brinkerhoff) B.; m. Sue Mansfield; children: Phillip, Brent, Robin. BS, Brigham Young U., 1957; MS, Purdue U., 1959; PhD in Sociology, U. Utah, 1966. Various teaching and rsch. positions including Fresno (Calif.) State U., Calif. State U./Hayward, Newark State Coll, others, 1964-71; rsch. analyst Calif. Dept. Corrections, Chino, 1972-82; various to assoc. govtl. program analyst Calif. Dept. Corrections, Sacramento, 1982-88, correctional counselor, 1988-89; correctional counselor Calif. Dept. Corrections, Chino, 1989-90, clin. sociologist, 1990-92, correctional counselor, 1992-94; rsch. assoc. Dem. Processes Ctr., Tucson, 1995—. Contbr. articles to profl. jours., publs. Mem. Am. Sociol. Assn., Assn. Criminal Justice Rsch., Soc. for Study of Symbolic Interaction, Calif. Sociol. Assn., Sociol. Practice Assn. Office: Dem Processes Ctr 4349 N Linda Lee Dr Tucson AZ 85705-2399

BREWSTER, RUDI MILTON, federal judge; b. Sioux Falls, S.D., May 18, 1932; s. Charles Edwin and Wilhemina Therese (Rud) B.; m. Gloria Jane Nanson, June 27, 1954; children: Scot Alan, Lauri Diane (Alan Lee), Julie Lynn Yahnke. AB in Pub. Affairs, Princeton U., 1954; JD, Stanford U., 1960. Bar: Calif. 1960. From assoc. to ptnr. Gray, Cary, Ames & Frye, San Diego, 1960-84; judge U.S. Dist. Ct. (so. dist.) Calif., San Diego, 1984—. Served to capt. USNR, 1954-82 Ret. Fellow Am. Coll. Trial Lawyers; mem. Am. Bd. Trial Advs., Internat. Assn. Ins. Counsel, Am. Inns of Ct. Republican. Lutheran. Avocations: skiing, hunting, gardening. Fax: (619) 702-9927. Office: US Dist Ct 940 Front St San Diego CA 92101-8994*

BREZZO, STEVEN LOUIS, museum director; b. Woodbury, N.J., June 18, 1949; s. Louis and Ella Marie (Savage) B.; m. Dagmar Grimm, Aug. 10, 1975. B.A., Clarion State Coll., 1969; M.F.A., U. Conn., 1973. Chief curator La Jolla Mus. Contemporary Art, Calif., 1974-76; asst. dir. San Diego Mus. Art, 1976-78, dir., 1978—. Mem. Am. Assn. Mus. (del. to China 1981, to Italian mus. study trip 1982), Calif. Assn. Mus. (pres. 1992—), La Jolla Library Assn. (pres. 1980). Club: University (San Diego). Lodge: Rotary. Office: San Diego Museum of Art PO Box 122107 San Diego CA 92112-2107*

BRIAN, BRAD D., lawyer; b. Merced, Calif., Apr. 19, 1952. BA, U. Calif., Berkeley, 1974; JD magna cum laude, Harvard U., 1977. Bar: Calif. 1977, U.S. Ct. Appeals (3d cir.) 1978, U.S. Dist. Ct. (ctrl. dist.) Calif. 1978, U.S. Ct. Appeals (9th cir.) 1980. Law clk. to Hon. John J. Gibbons U.S. Ct. Appeals (3d cir.), 1977-78; asst. U.S. atty. Office U.S. Atty. (ctrl. dist.) Calif., 1978-81; hearing examiner L.A. City Police Commn., 1982; atty. Munger, Tolles & Olson, L.A., 1981—; lectr. in law U. So. Calif. Law Ctr., 1983; instr. Nat. Inst. Trial Advocacy, 1980; guest instr. Harvard Law Sch. Trial Advocacy Program, 1983. Bd. editors Harvard Law Rev., 1975-77, mng. editor and treas., 1976-77. Mem. ABA (chmn. pre-trial practice and discovery, litigation sect. 1987-89, liaison with fed. jud. confs. 1989-91, chair task force on civil justice reform act of 1990), State Bar Calif., L.A. County Bar Assn. (mem. fed. practice standards com. 1980-82). Office: Munger Tolles & Olson 355 S Grand Ave Fl 35 Los Angeles CA 90071-1560*

BRICE, CHARLES STEVEN, airline executive; b. Columbus, Ohio, Feb. 13, 1951; s. Charles Simonton Jr. and Rita Eva (Kuder) B.; m. Darlene Lynn Call, Sept. 13, 1978 (div. June 1986); m. Sally Ann Minard, Sept. 20, 1997; children: Marissa Kay and Jessica Victoria (twins). BA, San Francisco State U., 1974. Lic. FAA airframe and power plant. Ops. mgr. Lockheed Aircraft Co., San Francisco, 1979-83; mgr. ramp svcs. Northwest Airlines, San Francisco, 1983-88, mgr. passenger svcs., 1988-92, dir. customer svc. and ground ops., 1992—; vice-chmn. bd. dirs. San Francisco Fgn. Flag Carriers, 1997—; chmn. Sta. Mgrs. Am. Transport/SFO, San Francisco, 1994, chmn. security com., 1995. Bd. dirs. March of Dimes, San Mateo County, Calif., 1994-95; mem., airline advisory bd. Calif. Dept. Agr., Sacramento, 1991-92; mem. adv. bd. San Francisco City Coll., 1988—. Mem. Commonwealth Club. Avocations: skiing, hiking, golf, tennis. Home: # 410 153 N San Mateo Dr Apt 410 San Mateo CA 94401-2775 Office: NW Airlines San Francisco Inter Airport San Francisco CA 94128

BRICKEN, GORDON LEONARD, acoustical engineer; b. Louisville, Nov. 1, 1936; s. William Wathen and Kathleen (Easley) B.; m. Maureen Barbara Mulligan, May 11, 1963; children: Barbara, Mary, Patricia, Victoria. BSEE, Loyola U., L.A., 1959; MSEE, UCLA, 1961; postgrad., U. Calif., Irvine, 1972. Mem. tech. staff Hughes Aircraft, Fullerton, Calif., 1961-68; sr. engr. Northrop Corp., Fullerton, 1968-72, environ. mgr. Olson Labs., 1972-76; ptnr., v.p. Hilliard & Bricken, Santa Ana, Calif., 1976-81; owner, pres. Gordon Bricken & Assocs., Inc., Santa Ana, 1981—. Councilman City of Santa Ana, 1974-84, mayor, 1981-83. Recipient svc. commendation Calif. Senate and Assembly, 1983, Pres. of U.S., 1983. Mem. Inst. Noise Control Engrs., Nat. Coun. Acoustical Engrs., Elks, Rotary. Republican. Roman Catholic. Avocations: antique cars, collecting camera, historical travel. Home: 2424 Oakmont Ave Santa Ana CA 92706-2028 Office: 1621 E 17th St Ste K Santa Ana CA 92705-8518

BRICKNER, DAVID, organization executive, consultant; b. Beverly, Mass., Sept. 29, 1958; s. Avi Stanley and Leah Esther (Kendal) B.; m. Patrice Anne Vasataro, Dec. 29, 1979; children: Isaac, Ilana. Diploma in Jewish Studies, Moody Bible Inst., 1981; BA in Jewish Studies, Northeastern Ill. U., 1986; MA in Jewish Studies, Fuller Sem., 1994. Ordained min. Bapt. Gen. Conf., 1993. Mobile team leader Jews for Jesus, USA, 1981-84; chief of station Jews for Jesus, Chgo., 1985-89; min.-at-large Jews for Jesus, San Francisco, 1989-95; chief of station Jews for Jesus, N.Y.C., 1995-96; exec. dir. Jews for Jesus, San Francisco, 1996—; portfolio holder Jews for Jesus South Africa, 1988-96, bd. dirs., 1989—; pres. bd. dirs. Jews for Jesus USA, San Francisco, 1996—; bd. dirs. Jews for Jesus Europe, London, 1996—. Author: Mishpochah Matters, 1996. Mem. Lausanne Consultation on Jewish Evangelism. Office: Jews for Jesus 60 Haight St San Francisco CA 94102-5895

BRIDGES, EDWIN MAXWELL, education educator; b. Hannibal, Mo., Jan. 1, 1934; s. Edwin Otto and Radha (Maxwell) B.; m. Marjorie Anne Pollock, July 31, 1954; children: Richard, Rebecca, Brian, Bruce. BS, U. Mo., 1954; MA, U. Chgo., 1956, PhD, 1964. English tchr. Bremen Community High Sch., Midlothian, Ill., 1954-56; asst. prin. Griffith (Ind.) High Sch., 1956-60, prin., 1960-62; staff assoc. U. Chgo., 1962-64, assoc. prof., 1967-72; assoc. dir. Univ. Coun. for Edn. Adminstrn., Columbus, Ohio, 1964-65; asst. prof. Washington U., St. Louis, 1965-67; assoc. prof. U. Chgo., 1967-72; prof. U. Calif., Santa Barbara, 1972-74; prof. edn. Stanford (Calif.) U., 1974—; mem. nat. adv. panel Ctr. for Rsch. on Ednl. Accountability and Tchr. Evaluation, 1990-95; external examiner U. Hong Kong, 1990-92; vis. prof. Chinese U., Hong Kong, 1976, 96; cons. World Bank, China, 1986, 89; dir. Midwest Adminstrn. Ctr., Chgo., 1967-72. Author: Managing the Incompetent Teacher, 1984, 2d edit., 1990, The Incompetent Teacher, 1986, 2d edit., 1991, Problem Based Learning for Administrators, 1992; co-author: Introduction to Educational Adminstration, 1977, Implementing Problem-based Leadership Development, 1995. Recipient of the R.F. Campbell Lifetime Achievement award, 1996; named Outstanding Young Man of Ind., C. of C., 1960; named hon. prof. and cert. of honor So. China Normal U., 1989, Citation of Merit for Outstanding Achievement and Meritorious Svc. in Edn., U. Mo. Coll. Edn., 1999. Mem. Am. Ednl. Rsch. Assn. (v.p. 1974-75). Office: Stanford U Sch Edn Stanford CA 94305

BRIDGES, GERALD DEAN, religious organization executive; b. Tyler, Tex., Dec. 4, 1929; s. Rufus Emmett and Lillian Ruth (Reeves) B.; m. Eleanor Louise Miller, Oct. 19, 1963 (dec. Nov. 1988); children: Kathleen Louise, Daniel Mark; m. Jane Bertha Mollet, Nov. 24, 1989. BS in Gen. Engr., U. Okla., 1951. Dept. supr. The Navigators, Colorado Springs, Colo., 1955-59, asst. to overseas dir., 1963-64, office mgr., 1965-69, sec., treas., 1969-79, v.p. for corp. affairs, 1979-94; adminstrv. asst. to Europe dir. The Navigators, Hague, The Netherlands, 1960-63; Bible tchr. The Navigators Collegiate Ministry, 1995—; bd. dirs. Evang. Coun. for Fin. Accountability, Washington, chmn. bd., 1991-92; ruling elder Grace Presbyn. Ch., Colorado Springs, 1972—. Author: (books) The Pursuit of Holiness, 1978, The Practice of Godliness, 1983, The Crisis of Caring, 1985, Trusting God, 1988, Transforming Grace, 1991, The Discipline of Grace, 1994, The Joy of Fearing God, 1998. Chaplain Sertoma, Colorado Springs, 1979-80. Ensign USN, 1951-53. Republican. Office: The Navigators PO Box 6000 Colorado Springs CO 80934-6000

BRIDGES, ROBERT MCSTEEN, mechanical engineer; b. Oakland, Calif., Apr. 17, 1914; s. Robert and Josephine (Hite) B.; BS cum laude in Mech. Engring., U. So. Calif., 1940; postgrad. UCLA; m. Edith Brownwood, Oct. 26, 1945; children: Ann, Lawrence, Robert. Registered profl. engr., Calif. Engr. Nat. Supply Co., Torrance, Calif., 1940-41; design engr. landing gear and hydraulics Lockheed Aircraft Corp., Burbank, Calif., 1941-46; missile hydraulic controls design engr. Convair, San Diego, 1946-48; sr. staff engr. oceanic systems mech. design Bendix Corp., Sylmar, Calif., 1948—; adv. ocean engring. U.S. Congress. Com. chmn. Boy Scouts Am., 1961. Recipient award of Service Am. Inst. Aero. Engrs., 1965. Mem. Marine Tech. Soc. (charter; com. cables, connectors 1969), Tau Beta Pi. Republican. Patentee in field of undersea devices (54 internat., 14 U.S.), including deep ocean rubber band moor; inventor U.S. Navy sonobuoy rotochute; contbr. articles to profl. jours. and confs. Home: 10314 Vanalden Ave Northridge CA 91326-3326 Office: L-3 Communications Ocean Sys 15825 Roxford St San Fernando CA 91342-3537

BRIDGFORTH, ROBERT MOORE, JR., aerospace engineer; b. Lexington, Miss., Oct. 21, 1918; s. Robert Moore and Theresa (Holder) B.; student Miss. State Coll., 1935-37; BS, Iowa State Coll., 1940; MS, MIT, 1948; postgrad. Harvard U., 1949; m. Florence Jarnberg, November 7, 1943; children: Robert Moore, Alice Theresa. Asst. engr. Standard Oil Co., of Ohio, 1940; teaching fellow M.I.T., 1940-41, instr. chemistry, 1941-43, research asst., 1943-44, mem. staff div. indsl. cooperation, 1944-47; asso. prof. physics and chemistry Emory and Henry Coll., 1949-51; rsch. engr. Boeing Airplane Co., Seattle, 1951-54, rsch. specialist 1954-55, sr. group engr., 1955-58, chief propulsion systems sect. Systems Mgmt. Office, 1958-59, chief propulsion rsch. unit, 1959-60; founder, chmn. bd. Rocket Rsch. Corp., 1960-69, Explosives Corp. Am., 1966-69. Fellow AIAA (assoc.), Brit. Interplanetary Soc., Am. Inst. Chemists; mem. AAAS, Am. Astronautical Soc. (dir.), Am. Chem. Soc., Am. Rocket Soc. (pres. Pacific NW 1955), Am. Ordnance Assn., Am. Inst. Physics, Am. Assn. Physics Tchrs., Tissue Culture Assn., Soc. for Leukocyte Biology, N.Y. Acad. Scis., Combustion Inst., Sigma Xi. Achievements include U.S. patents for rocket tri-propellants and explosives. Home: 4325 87th Ave SE Mercer Island WA 98040-4127

BRIDGMAN, RICHARD DARRELL, lawyer; b. Madison, S.D., Mar. 1, 1929; s. Lloyd Alton and Fay Catherine (Turner) B.; m. Marilyn Elizabeth Smith, May 25, 1952 (div. June 1987); 1 child, Richard Darrell. AB, U. Calif., 1951; JD, Golden Gate U., 1958. Bar: Calif, 1958, U.S. Dist Ct. (no. dist.) Calif. 1958, U.S. Dist. Ct. (ea. dist.) Calif. 1982, U.S. Dist Ct. (cen. dist.) Calif. 1985, U.S. Ct. Appeals (9th cir.) 1978. [illegible] Kincaid & Bridgman, Oakland, Calif., 1959-69; ptnr. O'Neill & Bridgman, Oakland, Calif., 1969-86, San Francisco, 1986-88; pvt. practice Richard D. Bridgman, San Francisco, 1988-92; ptnr. Bridgman & Bridgman, San Francisco, 1992—; mem., bd. dirs. Lawyer's Mutual Ins. Co., Burbank, Calif., 1978-88; faculty Golden Gate U., San Francisco, 1963-69, Hastings

Coll. Trial & Appellate Advocacy, San Francisco, 1978-91. Co-author: Legal Malpractice-Suing & Defending Lawyers, 1984; contbr. articles to profl. jours. Lt. U.S. Navy, 1951-54, Korea. Named Lawyer of Yr. Lawyers Club of Alameda Co., 1980. Mem. Inner Cir. Advocates, Am. Bd Trial Advocates, Am. Bd. Profl. Liability Attys. (diplomate), Calif. Trial Lawyers Assn. (bd. govs. 1976-83, sec. 1978-81), Alameda Conta Costa Trial Lawyers Assn. (pres. 1982). Office: Bridgman & Bridgman 5 Marietta Dr San Francisco CA 94127-1839

BRIERRE, MICHELINE, artist; b. Jeremie, Haiti; d. Luc Brierre and Simone Lataillaide; m. Charles Lopez (div.); children: Liza Lopez Camus, Charles Lopez; m. Barry Kaplan. Studied with, Mr. Ramponeau, Haiti, 1951-53; student, Academie Nehemie Jean, Haiti, 1958-60, Miraflores Art Ctr., Peru. Author: I am Eve, 1980, Spanish translation, 1980; solo show Commonwheel, Manitou Springs, Colo., 1995; exhibited in group shows at Galerie Hotel Rancho, Haiti, 1961, Galerie Brochette, Haiti, 1962, Onze Femmes peintres, Haiti, 1963, Gallerie Brochette, Haiti, 1964, Brierre/Castera, Haiti, 1965, Musee d'Art, Haiti, 1980, Galeria 70, Bogota, Colombia, S. Am., 1980, Galeria San Diego, Colombia, 1980, Woman's Way, Miami, Fla., 1982, Un Regard Soleil, Port-au-Prince, Haiti, 1983, Reflection On The Past, Aureus, Miami, 1983, Un Mundo Para Compartir, Lima, Peru, 1983, Festival Arts Gallery, Port-au-Prince, 1984, An Evening With The Artists, Naples, Fla., 1986, 87, Art in Jewelry, Island House, Bayside, Fla., 1987, Mixed Media Studio Show, Miami, 1989, 91, Collective Show, Commonwheel, Manitou Spings, Colo., 1994, Douglas County Art Ctr., Roby Mills Gallery and Bus. of Art Ctr., 1995. Mem. Fine Arts Ctr. Colo. Springs, Bus. of Art Ctr., Commonwheel Co-op. Home and Studio: All Things Beautiful 8050 Woody Creek Dr Colorado Springs CO 80911-8332

BRIESE, LEONARD ARDEN, inventor; b. Mpls., Mar. 21, 1933; s. Leonard Albert and Wilma Mrytle (Richards) B.; m. Joan Elaine Ramsay, Dec. 12, 1953; children: Linda Briese Johnson, Leonard Anthony, Leslie Briese Dietlin. Grad. high sch., El Segundo, Calif. Tooling mgr. Altamil Corp., El Segundo, 1954-60; owner, founder Len Briese & Co., El Segundo, 1960-65; pres., chmn., founder Lenco Mfg. Corp., El Segundo, 1965-70; v.p. engring. R & D, Wescal Industries, Inc., El Segundo, 1968-70; v.p., bd. dirs., founder Minipet Electronics Corp., Carson, Calif., 1972-74; pres., chmn., founder Cutters Unltd. Inc., Gardena, Calif., 1975-82; v.p. R & D and engring. Rotary Techs. Corp., Gardena, 1982-86; owner, founder L.A. Briese Co., Gardena, 1960—, Breeze Tool Co., Gardena, CA, 1992-94; v.p. R&D, founder Briese Industrial Tools, Inc., Harbor City, CA, 1994-95, Briese Industrial Technologies, Inc., 1995—; rsch. cons. Innovative Techs. Inc., Long Beach, Calif., 1986-98, Motivation Inc., Key West, Fla., 1986-98, Mel Fisher, Key West, 1987-98, Mel Fisher Exploration Inc., Key West, 1988-98. Numerous U.S. patents issued or granted in over 50 countries. With USAF, 1952--54, Korea. Mem. VFW (life), Soc. Mfg. Engrs. (sr.), Am. Soc. for Metals, Soc. for Advancement Material and Process Engring, Soc. for Mining, Metallurgy and Exploration, Soc. Plastics Engrs. Republican. Episcopalian. Avocations: motorhome travel, fishing, boating. Home and Office: 1400 240th St # D Harbor City CA 90710-1307

BRIGGS, DINUS MARSHALL, agriculturist; b. Stillwater, Okla., Mar. 5, 1940; s. Hilton Marshall and Lillian (Dinusson) B.; m. June Elaine Wolf, Sept. 2, 1962; children: Denise, Deborah. BS, S.D. State U., 1962; MS, Iowa State U., 1969, PhD, 1971. Asst. pastor Stroudsburg (Pa.) Meth. Ch., 1962-64; grad. asst. Iowa State U., Ames, 1964-66, research assoc., 1966-70; asst. prof. N.C. State U., Raleigh, 1970-75; asst. dir. Ark. Agrl. Expt. Sta., Fayetteville, 1976-82; assoc. dir. N.Mex. Agrl. Expt. Sta., Las Cruces, 1982—. Co-author: Modern Breeds of Livestock, 1980. Mem. Poultry Sci. Assn. (resolutions com. 1972-73), Am. Assn. Animal Sci., World's Poultry Sci., Sigma Xi. Lodge: Rotary. Avocation: horses. Home: 1927 Francine Ct Las Cruces NM 88005-5509 Office: NMex Agrl Experiment Sta PO Box 30003 # 3bf Las Cruces NM 88003-8003

BRIGHAM, SAMUEL TOWNSEND JACK, III, lawyer; b. Honolulu, Oct. 8, 1939; s. Samuel Townsend Jack, Jr. and Betty Elizabeth (McNeil) B.; m. Judith Catherine Johnson, Sept. 3, 1960; children: Robert Jack, Bradley Lund, Lori Ann, Lisa Katherine. B.S. in Bus. magna cum laude, Menlo Coll., 1963; J.D., U. Utah, 1966. Bar: Calif. 1967. Asso. firm Petty, Andrews, Olsen & Tufts, San Francisco, 1966-67; accounting mgr. Western sales region Hewlett-Packard Co., North Hollywood, Calif., 1967-68; atty. Hewlett-Packard Co., Palo Alto, Calif., 1968-70; asst. gen. counsel Hewlett-Packard Co., 1971-73, gen. atty., asst. sec., 1974-75, sec., gen. counsel, 1975-82, v.p., gen. counsel, 1982-85, v.p. corp. affairs, gen. counsel, mgr./dir. law dept., 1985—, sr. v.p. corp. affairs, gen. counsel, mgr./dir. law dept., 1994—; lectr. law Menlo Coll.; speaker profl. assn. seminars. Bd. dirs. Palo Alto Area YMCA, 1974-81, pres., 1978; bd. govs. Santa Clara County region NCCJ; trustee Menlo Sch. and Coll.; bd. dirs. Just Say No. Served with USMC, 1957-59. Mem. ABA, Calif. Bar Assn., Peninsula Assn. Gen. Counsel, MAPI Law Council, Am. Corp. Counsel Assn. (chmn. 1985, bd. dirs. 1983—), Am. Soc. Corp. Secs. (pres. No. Calif. Chpt. 1983—), Assn. Gen. Counsel (sec.-treas. 1991—). Home: 920 Oxford Dr Los Altos CA 94024-7032 Office: Hewlett-Packard Co 3000 Hanover St Palo Alto CA 94304-1181*

BRILL, JESSE M., publishing executive. JD, Yale Law Sch. Publisher-editor The Corporate Counsel, The Corporate Executive, 1978—; owner Exec. Press, Concord, Calif.; securities counsel Dean Witter. Mem. Nat. Assn. Stock Plan Profls. (chair). Office: Exec Press PO Box 21639 Concord CA 94521-0639

BRILL, MARK, lawyer; b. N.Y.C., Feb. 26, 1941; s. David and Beverly (Elpus) B. BS in English, Columbia U., 1965, LLB, 1969. Computer programmer Atlantic Mut. Ins. Co., N.Y.C., 1961-65; copywriter/analyst Young & Rubicam Advt., N.Y.C., 1965-66; corp. legal asst. Grey Advt., N.Y.C., 1966-68; asst. corp. counsel Random House, N.Y.C., 1968-73; gen. counsel, Internat. Divsn. Time, Inc., N.Y.C., Paris, Amsterdam, 1973-75; legis. counse., Corp. Divsn. U.S. & Fgn. Comms., N.Y.C., Toronto, 1976-87; cons. atty. N.Y.C., Washington, L.A., 1987-91; pub. interest atty. Legal Aid Soc., N.Y.C., 1991-96; corp. counsel Datagate, Inc., Reno, Nev., 1996—. Coord. counsel Gramercy Park Rep. Club, N.Y.C., 1992; pro bono vol. Advocates to End Domestic Violence, Carson City, Nev., 1996; advisor Washoe Indian Coord. Coun., Carson City, 1996-98. Lt. (j.g.) USN. Recipient Legal Ethics in Academia award Marymount Manhattan Coll., N.Y.C., 1993, Pro Bono award Legal Aid Soc., 1995. Mem. VFW. Republican. Avocations: flying, skiing, golf, dancing, reading, rock climbing. Home: 216 S Carson Meadows Dr Carson City NV 89701-6300 Office: Datagate Inc 6490 S Mccarran Blvd # B-14 Reno NV 89509-6118

BRIMMER, CLARENCE ADDISON, federal judge; b. Rawlins, Wyo., July 11, 1922; s. Clarence Addison and Geraldine (Zingsheim) B.; m. Emily O. Docken, Aug. 2, 1953; children: Geraldine Ann, Philip Andrew, Andrew Howard, Elizabeth Ann. BA, U. Mich., 1944, JD, 1947. Bar: Wyo. 1948. Pvt. practice law Rawlins, 1948-71, mcpl. judge, 1948-54; U.S. commr., magistrate, 1963-71; atty. gen. Wyo. Cheyenne, 1971-74; U.S. atty., 1975; chief judge U.S. Dist. Ct. Wyo., Cheyenne, 1975-92, dist. judge, 1975—; mem. panel multi-dist. litigation, 1992—; mem. Jud. Conf. U.S., 1994-97, exec., 1995-97. Sec. Rawlins Bd. Pub. Utilities, 1954-66; Rep. gubernatorial candidate, 1974; trustee Rocky Mountain Mineral Law Found., 1963-75. With USAAF, 1945-46. Mem. ABA, Wyo. Bar Assn., Laramie County Bar Assn., Carbon County Bar Assn., Am. Judicature Soc., Masons, Shriners, Rotary. Episcopalian. Office: US Dist Ct PO Box 985 Cheyenne WY 82003-0985*

BRINEGAR, CLAUDE STOUT, retired oil company executive; b. Rockport, Calif., Dec. 16, 1926; s. Claude Leroy Stout and Lyle (Rawles) B.; m. Elva Jackson, 1950 (div.); children: Claudia, Meredith, Thomas; m. Mary Katharine Potter, 1983 (dec. 1993); m. Karen Bartholomew, 1995. BA, Stanford U., 1950, MS, 1951, PhD, 1954; LLD (hon.), Elmira Coll., 1997. V.p. econs. and planning Union Oil (now Unocal), L.A., 1965; pres. Pure Oil divsn. Union Oil (now Unocal), Palatine, Ill., 1965-69; sr. v.p., pres. refining and mktg. Union Oil (now Unocal), L.A., 1969-73; U.S. Sec. of Transp. Washington, 1973-75; sr. v.p. adminstr. Unocal Corp., L.A., 1975-85, mem. exec. com., 1968-73, 75-92, exec. v.p., CFO, 1985-91, also bd. dirs., 1968-73, 75-95, vice chmn. bd., 1990-95; founding dir. Conrail, Inc., 1974-75, 90-98; bd. dirs. Maxicare Health Plans, Inc., CSX Corp.; vis. scholar Stanford U., 1992-97. Author: monograph on econs. and price behavior, 1970; contbr. articles to profl. jours. on statistics and econs. Chmn. Calif. Citizens Compensation Commn., 1990—; mem. regional selection panel White House Fellows Program, 1976-83, chmn., 1983. Mem. Am. Petroleum Inst. (bd. dirs. 1976-85, 88-91, hon. life dir. 1992), Georgetown Club, Boothbay Harbor Yacht Club, Southport Yacht Club, Phi Beta Kappa, Sigma Xi. Avocation: collecting first editions of Mark Twain. Home and Office: PO Box 4346 Stanford CA 94309-4346

BRINGARDNER, JOHN MICHAEL, lawyer, clergyman; b. Columbus, Ohio, Nov. 7, 1957; s. John Krepps and Elizabeth (Evans) B.; m. Emily Presley, June 19, 1982; children: John Taylor, Michael Steven, Malee Elizabeth. BA, U. Central Fla., Orlando, 1979; postgrad., Mercer U., 1979; JD, Fla. State U., 1981. Bar: Fla. 1982, Calif. 1994, U.S. Dist. Ct. (mid. dist.) Fla., U.S. Dist. Ct. (no. dist.) Fla., U.S. Ct. Appeals (11th cir.). Assoc. McFarlain, Bobo, Sternstein, Wiley & Cassidy, Tallahassee, Fla., 1982-87, Finley, Kumble Wagner, Tallahassee, 1987; minister Boston Ch. of Christ, 1987-90; evangelist Bankok Christian Ch., 1990-92, Metro Manila Christian Ch., 1992-93; gen. counsel Internat. Chs. of Christ, L.A., 1993—; bd. dirs. Eye Care Corp., Orlando, Fla., Quality Coffee Corp., Tallahassee. Mem. ABA, Fla. Bar Assn. Avocations: football, basketball, triathalons, hiking, music. Office: International Churches of Christ 3530 Wilshire Blvd Ste 1750 Los Angeles CA 90010-2238

BRINKERHOFF, DERICKSEN MORGAN, art history educator; b. Phila., Oct. 4, 1921; s. Robert Joris and Marion (Butler) B.; m. Mary Dean Weston, Dec. 20, 1946; children: Derick W., Elizabeth, Jonathan D., Caroline. BA, Williams Coll., 1943; AM, Yale U., 1947; postgrad., U. Zurich, Switzerland, 1948-49; Ph.D., Harvard U., 1958. Teaching fellow Harvard U., 1949-50; instr. Brown U., 1952-55; assoc. prof., head history dept. R.I. Sch. Design, 1955-59, chmn. div. liberal arts, 1956-59; asso. prof. Pa. State U., 1961-62, Tyler Sch. Art, Temple U., Phila., 1962-1965; chmn. dept. art U. Calif. Riverside, 1965-71, 80-85, prof., 1967-92, prof. emeritus, 1992—; vis. prof. U. Calif. Berkeley, U. So. Calif. Author monograph on classical and early medieval art; contbr. articles to profl. jours. Trustee Riverside Art Assn., 1968-72. Served with AUS, World War II. Recipient U. Calif. Humanities Inst. award, 1971-72; Summer fellow Belgian Am. Ednl. Found., 1959; sr. fellow classical studies Am. Acad. in Rome, 1959-61; Am. Philos. Soc. grantee, 1960-61. Mem. Archaeol. Inst. Am., Art Historians So. Calif. (pres. 1982-83, co-pres. 1998-99), Coll. Art Assn. Am. Home: 4985 Chicago Ave Riverside CA 92507-5859

BRINTON, RICHARD KIRK, marketing executive; b. Hanover, Pa., Apr. 21, 1946; s. James Henry and Mabel (Adelung) B.; m. Joan Marita Ayo, Mar. 21, 1970; children: Katherine, Mark, Michael. BA in Liberal Arts, BS in Indsl. Engring., Pa. State U., 1968. Registered profl. engr., Ohio. From systems engr. to dir. mktg. AccuRay/ABB, Columbus, Ohio, 1968-82; group mktg. dir. AccuRay/ABB, London, 1982-84; internat. sales mgr. Flow Systems, Seattle, 1984, v.p. sales and mktg., 1985-87; dir. mktg. and bus. devel. UTILX Corp., Seattle, 1987-90, v.p. mktg. and bus. devel., 1990-93, v.p. internat. ops., 1993-96; chmn. Nippon FlowMole, Tokyo, 1991-93; dir. worldwide mktg. and sales Lamb-Grays Harbor, Hoquiam, Wash., 1996-97; pres. BBD Internat., Edmonds, Wash., 1997—; sr. mgmt. advisor, dir. mktg. Pacific N.W. Advisors, Seattle, 1997—. Mem. World Trade Club Seattle (bd. dirs. 1993-95). Home: 541 Pine St Edmonds WA 98020-4028 Office: 541 Pine St Edmonds WA 98020-4028

BRISBIN, ROBERT EDWARD, insurance agency executive; b. Bklyn., Feb. 13, 1946; m. Sally Ann Tobler-Norton. BSBA, San Fancisco State U., 1968. Cert. safety exec. Field rep. Index Research, San Mateo, Calif., 1969-82; mgr. loss control Homeland Ins. Co., San Jose, Calif., 1982-87; ins. exec. Morris and Dee Ins. Agy., San Luis Obispo, Calif., 1987—; prin., cons. Robert E. Brisbin & Assocs., Pismo Beach, Calif., 1972—; mgt. cons.; pres. Profl. Formulas Amino Acid Food Supplements, 1987-90. Author: Amino Acids, Vitamins and Fitness, 1986, Loss Control for the Small- to Medium-Sized Business, 1989, (with Carol Bayly Grant) Workplace Wellness, 1992; composer: Country Songs and Broken Dreams, 1978, America the Land of Liberty, 1980. Mem. Am. Soc. Safety Engrs., World Safety Orgn. (cert. safety exec.), UN Roster Safety Cons. Republican. Avocations: photography, flying, scuba diving, musical composition. Office: PO Box 341 Pismo Beach CA 93448-0341

BRISCOE, JOHN, lawyer; b. Stockton, Calif., July 1, 1948; s. John Lloyd and Doris (Olsen) B.; divorced; children: John Paul, Katherine. JD, U. San Francisco, 1972. Bar: Calif. 1972, U.S. Dist. Ct. (no., ea. and ctrl. dists.) Calif. 1972, U.S. Supreme Ct. 1978, U.S. Ct. Appeals (9th cir.) 1981. Dep. atty. gen. State of Calif., San Francisco, 1972-80; ptnr. Washburn and Kemp, San Francisco, 1980-88, Washburn, Briscoe & McCarthy, San Francisco, 1988—; bd. dirs. San Francisco Bay Planning coalition, chmn., 1990-93; vis. scholar U. Calif., Berkeley, 1990—; spl. adviser UN Compensation Commn., Geneva, Switzerland, 1998—. Author: Surveying the Courtroom, 1984, Falsework, 1997; editor: Reports of Special Masters, 1991; contbr. articles to profl. and lit. jours. Mem. ABA, San Francisco Bar Assn., Law of the Sea Inst. Roman Catholic. Office: Washburn Briscoe & McCarthy 55 Francisco St San Francisco CA 94133-2122

BRISCOE, MARIANNE GRIER, development professional, educator; b. Orange, Calif., Nov. 25, 1945; d. Nelson Borland and Anne Kathryn Grier; m. Alden Frank Briscoe, Aug. 10, 1968; 1 child, Stacy Anne. AB cum laude, Goucher Coll., 1967; cert. in medieval studies, Cath. U. Am., 1972; PhD, Cath. U., 1975. Cert. fund raising exec. Lectr. English lit. U. Mich., Flint, 1973; pub. info. officer Flint Charter Revision Commn., 1974-75; devel. officer The Newberry Library, Chgo., 1975-78, dir. devel., 1978-81; prin. The Briscoe Co., Chgo., 1981-84; assoc. dir. devel. U. Chgo., 1984-85, dir. corp. rels., 1985-89; centennial campaign dir. Sierra Club, San Francisco, 1989-91; sr. cons. Staley/Robeson/Ryan/St Lawrence, 1989-91; v.p. advancement St. Mary's Coll. Calif., Moraga, 1992-94; founding prin. Hayes Briscoe Assocs., San Mateo, Calif., 1994—. Author, co-editor: Contexts of Early English Drama, 1989; author: Artes Praedicandi, 1992; author, editor: Ethics and Fundraising; Putting Values into Practice, 1994; contbr. articles to profl. jours. Founder Washington Sq. Consortium, Chgo., 1978-81; grant reviewer NEH, Washington, 1979-82. Brit. Acad. fellow, 1978-80, Newberry Library fellow, 1981, Med. Acad. fellow, 1974; Am. Philos. Soc. grantee, 1981. Mem. MLA, Internat. Diplomacy Coun. (v.p. bd. dirs.), Nat. Soc. Fund Raising Execs. (nat. bd. dirs. 1984-93, vice chmn. found. 1989-91), Internat. Women's Forum, Women's Forum West.

BRISCOE, TERRY LEE, marketing executive; b. Oregon City, Oreg., Aug. 28, 1948; s. Ervin E. and Marguerite L. (Penne) B.; m. Kathleen Sue Mauro, June 14, 1986. BSME, U. Portland, 1970. Registered profl. engr., Oreg. Land survey Bert Mason Jr. Surveyors, Oregon City, 1967-69; design engr. ESCO Corp., Portland, 1970-72, project engr., 1972-76, engring. mgr. capital products, 1976-84, engring. mgr. new product devel., 1984-89, mgr. sales engring., 1989-92, mktg. mgr. capital products, 1992—; cons. ALCOA Sandow Mine, Rockdale, Tex., 1990. 15 patents in field including mech. pin lock, 1982, chain connecting link, 1983, dragline dump block, 1987, dragline bucket, 1988, mining tooth point, 1990, universal wear element, 1991, reverse spade dragline lip, 1992, others. Team leader Jr. Achievement, Portland, 1985; vol. Boys Scouts Am., Portland, 1987-92; citizen ambassador People to People, USSR, 1991. With U.S. Army N.G., 1970-76. Named Hon. Inventor of the Yr. Intellectual Property Owners, 1990. Mem. Soc. Mining Engrs., Rocky Mountain Coal Mining Inst. Avocations: golf, skiing, trap and skeet shooting. Home: 11399 NW Ridge Rd Portland OR 97229-4070 Office: ESCO Corp 2141 NW 25th Ave Portland OR 97210-2597

BRITTON, DENNIS A., newspaper editor, newspaper executive; b. Santa Barbara, 1940; m. Theresa Romero Britton; children: Robert, Patrick, Anne. Attended, San Jose State U. Joined L.A. Times, 1966, various positions, including copy editor, reporter, news editor, asst. nat. editor, nat. editor, 1977-83, then dep. mng. editor; editor Chgo. Sun-Times, 1989-96, also exec. v.p., until 1996; now editor-in-chief Denver Post, 1996—. Mem. Nat. Assn. Hispanic Journalists. Office: Denver Post 1560 Broadway Denver CO 80202-5177*

BRITTON, EVE MARCHANT, newspaper reporter; b. N.Y.C., June 25, 1965; d. Donald Robison and Susan Harriet (Marchant) B. Student, Allegheny Coll., 1983-85; BA in Journalism, San Francisco State U., 1990; postgrad., Monterey Coll. Law, 1995—. Reporter city coun. Carmel (Calif.) Pine Cone, 1990; reporter youth issues Monterey (Calif.) County Herald, 1990—; mem. newsroom task force Monterey County Herald, 1992-94. Mem. steering com. Beacon House 10K Run, Pacific Grove, Calif., 1986-94, 1st Night Monterey, 1993-96; tutor Seaside (Calif.) Homework Ctr., 1993-94; commr. Monterey County Juvenile Justice Commn. and Deliquency Prevention Commn.; choir mem., lector All Sts. Episcopal Ch., Carmel, 1994—. Named Woman of Distinction, Soroptomists Internat., 1995; recipient 1st pl. honor Monterey County Literacy Assn., 1994, HIV Cmty. Action award Monterey County AIDS Project. Mem. Student Bar Assn., Humane Soc. U.S., Women's Golf Connection, Richard Nixon Meml. Libr., Ctrl. Coast Press Club. Avocations: golf, skiing, tennis, singing. Home: PO Box 221639 Carmel CA 93922-1639 Office: Monterey County Herald PO Box 271 Monterey CA 93942-0271

BRITTON, MATT J., special effects company manager; b. San Jose, Calif., May 22, 1964; s. Alfred B. Britton and Charlotte Louise (Ely) Britton-Anderson; m. Alice Rodriguez, July 25, 1992. BA, Santa Clara U., 1986. Prodn. asst. Smith-Hemion Prodn., L.A., 1986; prodn. coord. Vic Kaplan Prodn., L.A., 1987-88; robotics specialist Landmark Entertainment, N. Hollywood, Calif., 1990-91; effects shop supr. Cinovation, Inc., Glendale, Calif., 1988-90, 91-94; creature shop gen. mgr. Jim Henson's Creature Shop, Burbank, Calif., 1994—; exec. cons. Brats of the Lost Nebula, Warner Bros. TV, 1998. Film projects include: Gremlins 2, Matinee, Baby's Day Out, Wolf, Ed Wood, The Phantom, George of the Jungle, Dr. Doolittle, Frost. Avocations: scuba, music composition, custom toy construction. Office: Jim Hensons Creature Shop 2821 Burton Ave Burbank CA 91504

BRITTON, THOMAS WARREN, JR., management consultant; b. Pawhuska, Okla., June 16, 1944; s. Thomas Warren and Helen Viola (Haynes) B.; BS in Mech. Engring., Okla. State U., 1966, MS in Indsl. Engring. and Mgmt., 1968; m. Jerlyn Kay Davis, 1964 (div. 1970); 1 child, Natalie Dawn; m. Deborah Ann Mansour, Oct. 20, 1973; 1 child, Kimberly Ann. Cons., Arthur Young & Co., Los Angeles, mgr., 1972-76, prin., 1976-79, ptnr., 1979-87, office dir. mgmt. svcs. dept., Orange County, Calif., 1979-88; ptnr. Price Waterhouse; ptnr.-in-charge west coast mfg. cons. practice, Nat. Aero space and Def. Industry, 1988-95; part-in-charge west coast products and logistics practice, 1995—, Price Waterhouse Coopers mng. ptnr. west region MCS Products Practice, chmn. US MCS Tech. Industry Practice, chmn. Global MCS Tech. Industry Practice; lectr. in field. Mem. City of San Dimas Creative Growth Bd., 1976-77, chmn. planning commn., 1977-83; trustee World Affairs Council of Orange County, 1980; benefactor, founders com., v.p. ann. fund, pres., chair long range planning, trustee South Coast Repertory Theater, 1982-92; trustee Providence Speech and Hearing Ctr., 1985-90, Spl. Olympics of So. Calif., 1995-97; mem. devel. com. U. Calif.-Irvine Med. Sch.; chmn. Costa Mesa Arts Council. Served to capt. USAR, 1971-86. Cert. mgmt. cons. Mem. Los Angeles Inst. CPAs, Mgmt. Adv. Svcs. Com., Am. Prodn. and Inventory Control Soc., Am. Inst. Indsl. Engrs., Greater Irvine Indsl. League, Okla. State Alumni Assn., Kappa Sigma Alumni Assn. Clubs: Jonathan, Ridgeline Country, Santa Ana Country. Home: 18982 Wildwood Cir Villa Park CA 92861-3137

BRIXEY, SHAWN ALAN, digital media artist, media educator, director; b. Springfield, Mo., Jan. 23, 1961; s. Alan M. and Mary Lou (Peters) B.; m. Sonja Max, 1998. BFA in New Media, Kansas City Art Inst., 1985; MS in Advanced Visual Studies, MIT, 1988. Grad. tchg. asst. dept. arch. MIT, Cambridge, 1985-87; Leonardo fellow, inaugural vis. fellow Leonardo Project U. Mich., Ann Arbor, 1988; adj. faculty, lectr. CAVS dept. arch. MIT, Cambridge, 1989; asst. prof., dir. media arts program art U. Ky., Lexington, 1990, grad. faculty, assoc. mem. Coll. Fine Arts, 1991; asst. prof., chair cross-disciplinary arts program Sch. Art U. Wash., Seattle, 1994, grad. faculty Coll. Arts and Scis., 1995-98; disting. fellow Inst. for New Media San Francisco State U., 1997-98; asst. prof. digital media/new genre U. Calif., Berkeley, 1998—, dir. Ctr. Digital Art and New Media Rsch., 1998—; dir. exptl. media lab. dept. art U. Ky., Lexington, 1992; dir. studio for media arts rsch. and techs. lab U. Wash., Seattle, 1994-98, co-dir. lab animation for arts, 1995-98, acting dir. Ctr. Advanced Rsch. Tech. in the Arts and Humanities, 1996-97; Disting. mentor in multimedia San Francisco State U., 1997; keynote spkr. Mayor's Internat. Tech. Summit, San Francisco, 1998; mem. U. Calif., Pres.'s Planning Group on Digital Art, 1998. Exhbns. include Documenta 8, Kassel, Germany, 1987, 85th Anniversary of the German Art Union, Badischer, Kunstverein, Karlsruhe, Germany, 1988, Cranbrook Acad. Art Mus., Bloomhill Hills, Mich., 1990, Contemporary Art Ctr., Cin., 1991, State Mus., Columbia, S.C., 1992, MIT Mus., Cambridge, Mass., 1995, Del. Ctr. Contemporary Art, Wilmington, 1996, Internat. Symposium Electronic Art ISEA 97, Chgo., Cultural Olympiad, 1998, Winter Olympics Nagano, Japan. Mentor advanced placement new media and digital video/audio courses Fayette County H.S. Sys., Lexington, Ky., 1990-93; bd. dirs. Ctr. for Contemporary Art, Seattle; keynote spkr. Seattle-Northshore Sch. Dist. Leadership Conf., 1998. Recipient Major Equip. award Silicon Graphics Industries, 1994, Apple Computer Inc., 1994, Newport/Klinger, 1996, Intel Corp., 1997. Democrat. Episcopalian. Avocations: scuba diving, tennis, collecting old film, media electronics, electric toys. Office: Univ Calif Digital Media/New Genre 345 Kroeber Hall Berkeley CA 94720

BROAD, ELI, financial services executive; b. N.Y.C., June 6, 1933; s. Leon and Rebecca (Jacobson) B.; m. Edythe Lois Lawson, Dec. 19, 1954; children: Jeffrey Alan, Gary Stephen. BA in Acctg. cum laude, Mich. State U., 1954. CPA, Mich. 1956. Co-founder, chmn., pres., CEO SunAmerica Life Ins. Co. (formerly Kaufman & Broad, Inc.), L.A., 1957; chmn. SunAmerica Life Ins. Co., Anchor Nat. Life Ins. Co., First SunAmerica Life Ins. Co.; chmn. Kaufman and Broad Home Corp., L.A., 1986-93, chmn. exec. com., 1993-95, founder, chmn., 1993—; chmn. Stanford Ranch Co.; mem. exec. com. adv. bd. Fed. Nat. Mortgage Assn., 1972-73; active Calif. Bus. Roundtable, 1986—; co-owner Sacramento Kings and Arco Arena, 1992—; trustee Com. for Econ. Devel., 1993-95; mem. real estate adv. bd. Citibank, N.Y.C., 1976-81. Mem. bd. dirs. L.A. World Affairs Coun., 1988—, chmn., 1994—, DARE Am., 1989-95, hon. mem. bd. dirs. 1995—; founding trustee Windward Sch., Santa Monica, Calif., 1972-77; bd. trustees Pitzer Coll., Claremont, Calif., 1970-82, chmn. bd. trustees, 1973-79, life trustee, 1982—, Haifa U., Israel, 1972-80, Calif. State U., 1978-82, vice chmn. bd. trustees, 1979-80, trustee emeritus, 1982—, Mus. Contemporary Art, L.A., 1980-93, founding chmn., 1980, Archives Am. Art, Smithsonian Instn., Washington, 1985—, Am. Fedn. Arts, 1988-91, Leland Stanford Mansion Found., 1992—, Calif. Inst. Tech., 1993—, Armand Hammer Mus. Art and Cultural Ctr. UCLA, 1994—; pres. Calif. Non-Partisan Vote Registration Found., 1971-72; chancellor's assoc. UCLA, 1971—, mem. vis. com. Grad. Sch. Mgmt., 1972-90, trustee UCLA Found., 1986—, exec. com. bd. visitors Sch. of the Arts & Architecture, 1997—; assoc. chmn. United Crusade, L.A., 1973-76; chmn. Mayor's Housing Policy Com., L.A., 1974-75; del., spkr. Fed. Econ. Summit Conf., 1974, State Econ. Summit Conf., 1974; mem. contemporary coun. L.A. County Mus. Art, 1973-79, bd. trustees acquisitions com., 1978-81, trustee, 1995—; bd. fellows, mem. exec. com. The Claremont (Calif.) Colls., 1974-79; nat. trustee Balt. Mus. Art, 1985-91; mem. adv. bd. Boy Scouts Am., 1982-85, L.A. Bus. Jour., 1986-88; mem. adv. coun. Town Hall of Calif., 1985-87; trustee Dem. Nat. Com. Victory Fund, 1988, 92, 96; mem. painting and sculpture com. Whitney Mus., N.Y.C., 1987-89; chmn. adv. bd. ART/LA, 1989; bd. overseers The Music Ctr. of L.A. County, 1991-92, mem. bd. govs., 1996—; mem. contemporary art com. Harvard U. Art Mus., Cambridge, Mass., 1992—; mem. internat. dirs. coun. Guggenheim Mus., N.Y.C., 1993—; active Nat. Indsl. Pollution Control Coun., 1970-73, Maeght Found., St. Paul de Vence, France, 1975-80, Mayor's Spl. Adv. Com. on Fiscal Adminstrn., L.A., 1993-94; bd. dirs. UCLA/Armand Hammer Mus. Art And Cultural Ctr., 1994—. Recipient Man of Yr. award City of Hope, 1965, Golden Plate award Am. Acad. Achievement, 1971, Housing Man of Yr. award Nat. Housing Coun., 1979, Humanitarian award NCCJ, 1977, Am. Heritage award Anti Defamation League, 1984, Pub. Affairs award Coro Found., 1987, Honors award visual arts L.A. Arts Coun., 1989; Eli Broad Coll. Bus. and Eli Broad Grad. Sch. Bus. named in his honor Mich. State U., 1991; knighted Chevalier in Nat. Order Legion of Honor, France, 1994. Mem. Beta Alpha Psi, Regency Club and Hillcrest Country Club (L.A.). Home: 75 Oakmont St Los Angeles CA 90049-1901 Office: SunAmerica Inc 1 Sun America Ctr Los Angeles CA 90067-6022*

BROADHEAD, RONALD FRIGON, petroleum geologist, geology educator; b. Racine, Wis., July 22, 1955; s. Ronald Leslie and Thereise (Frigon) B. BS, N.Mex. Tech. U., 1977; MS, U. Cin., 1979. Geologist, Cities Svc. Oil Co., Oklahoma City and Tulsa, 1979-81; sr. petroleum geologist N.Mex. Bur. Mines, Socorro, 1981—, asst. dir., 1994-98; mem. adj. faculty N.Mex. Tech. Coll., 1983—; mem. potential gas com. Potential Gas Agy. Union Oil Co. summer fellow Duke U. Marine Lab., 1977. Mem. Am. Assn. Petroleum Geologists (Ho. of Dels.), Soc. Econ. Paleontologists and Mineralogists, N.Mex. Geol. Soc. (past pres.) , Roswell Geol. Soc., Four Corners Geol. Soc., West Tex. Geol. Soc., Sigma Xi. Office: NMex Bur Mines Campus Sta Socorro NM 87801

BROADHURST, NORMAN NEIL, foods company executive; b. Chico, Calif., Dec. 17, 1946; s. Frank Spencer and Dorothy Mae (Conrad) B.; BS, Calif. State U., 1969; MBA, Golden Gate U., 1975; m. Victoria Rose Thomson, Aug. 7, 1976; 1 child, Scott Andrew. With Del Monte Corp., San Francisco, 1969-76, product mgr., 1973-76; product mgr. Riviana Foods, Inc., div. Colgate Palmolive, Houston, 1976-78; new products brand devel. mgr. foods div. Coca Cola Co., Houston, 1978-79, brand mgr., 1979-82, mktg. dir., 1982-89, v.p. mktg. Beatrice Foods Co., Chgo., 1983-86; pres., COO Famous Amos Chocolate Chip Cookie Co., Torrance, Calif., 1986-88; corp. sr. v.p., gen. mgr. Kerr Group Inc., L.A., 1988-92, corp. sr. v.p., pres. Kerr Group Consumer Products, 1992-95; chmn. dir. Double Eagle Holdings, Inc., 1995—; chmn., pres. and CEO Trusted Brands, Inc., 1995-98. Chmn. youth soccer program Cystic Fibrosis Found., Houston, 1982-83; chmn., pres. South Coast Symphony, 1985-88; mem. nat. bd. Literacy Vols. Am., 1988—, vice chmn. 1993-95, chmn. 1997—); bd. dirs. Human Options, 1997—. Mem. Am. Mktg. Assn., Am. Mgmt. Assn.

BROCCHINI, RONALD GENE, architect; b. Oakland, Calif., Nov. 6, 1929; s. Gino Mario and Yoli Louise (Lucchesi) B.; m. Myra Mossman, Feb. 3, 1957; 1 child, Christopher Ronald. B.A. in Architecture with honors, U. Calif., Berkeley, 1953, M.A. in Architecture with honors, 1957. Registered architect, Calif., Nev. Architect, designer SMP, Inc., San Francisco, 1948-53, designer, assoc., 1956-60; assoc. architect Campbell & Wong, San Francisco, 1961-63; prin. architect Ronald G. Brocchini, Berkeley, Calif., 1964-67, Worley K Wong & Ronald G Brocchini Assocs., San Francisco, 1968-87, Brocchini Architects, Berkeley, 1987—; lectr. Calif. Coll. Arts and Crafts, Oakland, 1981-83; commr. Calif. Bd. Archtl. Examiners, 1961-89; mem. exam. com. Nat. Coun. Archtl. Registration Bds., 1983-85. Author: Long Range Master Plan for Bodega Marine Biology, U. Calif., 1982; prin. works include San Simeon Visitor Ctr., Hearst Castle, Calif., Mare Island Med.-Dental Facillity, IBM Ednl. and Data Processing Hdqrs., San Jose, Calif., Simpson Fine Arts Gallery, Calif. Coll. Arts, Ceramics and Metal Crafts, Emery Bay Pub. Market Complex, Analytical Measurement Facility, U. Calif., Berkeley, Bodega Marine Biology Campus, U. Calif., Berkeley, Fromm & Sichell (Christian Bros.) Hdqrs., The Nature Co., Corp. Offices, Berkeley, Merrill Coll., Athletic Facilities, U. Calif., Santa Cruz, Coll. III Housing, U. Calif., San Diego, Ctr. Pacific Rim Studies, U. San Francisco, married student housing Escondido II, III, IV, Stanford (Calif.) U. With U.S. Army, 1953-55. Recipient Bear of Yr. award U. Calif., Berkeley, 1987, Alumni Citation, 1988; recipient 18 Design Honor awards for architecture, Design award State of Calif. Dept. Rehab., 1995. Fellow AIA (bd. dirs. Calif. coun., pres. San Francisco chpt. 1982); mem. Bear Backers Club (bd. dirs. U. Calif.-Berkeley athletic coun.), Berkeley Breakfast Club (bd. govs.), Order of the Golden Bear, Chi Alpha Kappa. Republican. Roman Catholic. Avocations: auto restoration; photography; sports; art. Office: Brocchini Architects Inc 2748 Adeline St Berkeley CA 94703-2251

BROCKETT, DAN D., video producer; b. Glendale, Calif., Feb. 2, 1963; s. Dale Gene Brockett and Susan Charmain (Paige) Collins; m. Elizabeth Ann Sarzotti, Dec. 1, 1984; 1 child, Elise Angeline. Student, Moorpark Coll., 1989-91. Waiter Port Royal Restaurant, Oxnard, Calif., 1982-83; store mgr. Circuit City Stores, Inc., Ventura, Calif., 1984-92; producer, dir. Videogenics Video Prodn., Camarillo, Calif., 1992—. Recipient Crystal award Internat. Communicator Awards, Irving, Tex., 1997. Mem. NRA, Internat. TV Assn., Channel Islands Underwater Photographic Soc., Osai Valley Gun Club. Republican. Avocations: scuba, shooting, camping, photography. Office: Videogenics Video Productions 1136 Saddleback Cir Camarillo CA 93012-4414

BRODERICK, DONALD LELAND, electronics engineer; b. Chico, Calif., Jan. 5, 1928; s. Leland Louis and Vera Marguerite (Carey) B.; m. Constance Margaret Lattin, Sept. 29, 1957; children: Craig, Eileen, Lynn. BSEE, U. Calif., Berkeley, 1950; postgrad., Stanford U., 1953-54. Jr. engr. Boeing Co., Seattle, 1950-52; design engr. Hewlett-Packard Co., Palo Alto, Calif., 1952-59; sr. staff engr. Ampex Computer Products, Culver City, Calif., 1959-60; dir. engring. Kauke & Co., Santa Monica, Calif., 1960-61; program mgr. Space Gen. Corp., El Monte, Calif., 1961-68, Aerojet Electronics Div., Azusa, Calif., 1968-89; prin. D.L. Broderick, Arcadia, Calif., 1989—. Contbr. articles to profl. jours. Mem. Jr. C. of C., Woodland Hills, Calif., 1963-64. With USN, 1945-46. Fellow Inst. for Advancement of Engring.; mem IEEE (chmn. profl. group on audio 1955-59, mem. exec. com. San Francisco sect. 1957-59, chmn. San Gabriel Valley sect. 1964-71, chmn. sects. com. L.A. coun. 1971-72, chmn. L.A. coun. 1972-76, chmn. bd. WESCON conv. 1976-80, bd. dirs. IEEE Electronics Conv. Inc. 1981-84, 1995-98, Centennial medal 1984), AIAA (sec. L.A. sect. 1986-88, sec. nat. tech. com. on command control comm. and intelligence, Washington, 1985-89, chmn. devel. com. L.A. coun. 1986-94). Achievements include 2 patents on high frequency communications technology; design of USAF 487-L low frequency communications system; first successful aircraft-ground station communications via satellite; design of first INTELSAT communications station in Africa; design and development of Ground Station computer software program for the USAF Satellite System, which achieved first successful detection and reporting of missile launches. Home: 519 E La Sierra Dr Arcadia CA 91006-4321

BRODERICK, HAROLD CHRISTIAN, interior designer; b. Oakland, Calif., Apr. 8, 1925; s. Harold Christian and Laura Jane (Lloyd) B. BA, U. Tex., 1947. A founder Arthur Elrod Assos., Inc., Palm Springs, Calif., 1954, now pres.; bd. dirs. The Living Desert. Mem. Planning Commn., City of Palm Springs, 1972-74; trust Palm Springs Desert Mus.; mem. devel. com. Barbara Sinatra Children's Ctr. Mem. Am. Soc. Interior Designers. Republican. Office: Arthur Elrod Assocs Inc PO Box 2890 Palm Springs CA 92263-2890

BRODERICK, MARSHA, interior designer, general contractor; b. Alameda, Calif., Oct. 15; d. Edwin and Lois Ione (Mockel) Mullin; m. Don Plehn, May 24, 1975; children: Tracy, Veronica. Student, San Diego City Coll., 1961-64, San Diego State Coll., 1961-64. Lic. gen. contractor, Calif. Sec., city mgr. San Diego, 1966-69; pres. Pink Ladies Design and Constrn., Calabasas, Calif., 1971—; lectr. to contractors and educators. Contbr. articles on constrn. and design to profl. jours.; appeared on numerous TV and cable shows. Mem. adv. commn. Equity Re-entry program L.A. Trade Tech. Coll., 1987-88; chair Women's Implementation Century Freeway Adv. Bd., L.A., 1990; state commr. Senator Roberti's Small Bus. Adv. Commn.; v.p. disabled access divsn. L.A. City Commn., Dept. Bldg. and Safety; mem. Senate Select Com. on Northridge Earthquake. Recipient People Who Make a Difference award USA Today, 1985, Golden Nike award Bus. and Profl. Women's Club, 1986, Woman of Achievement award YWCA/YMCA, 1987, Commendations L.A. City Coun., Mayor Tom Bradley, Cal Trans - Century Fwy., others. Mem. Internat. Soc. Interior Design (chair San Fernando Valley 1984-88, pres. 1988-90, 1st pl. comml. divsn. 1992, 1st pl. residential divsn. 1993), Am. Soc. Interior Designers (cert. profl. interior designer). Office: Pink Ladies Design & Constrn Co 23501 Park Sorrento Ste 218 Calabasas CA 91302-1381

BRODHEAD, CHARLES NELSON, III, lay worker; b. Phila., Nov. 1, 1963; s. Charles Lindberg Jr., and Doris Esther (Mink) B.; m. Leesa Ky Charlton, Mar. 28, 1987; children: Charles Douglas IV, Emylee Grace. BSBA, U. Redlands, 1986. [illegible] the Nazarene, Riverside, Calif., 1986—, youth dir., 1987—, dir. Puppeteer Express profl. puppet team, 1987—, pres. Nazarene Youth Internat., 1986-87; owner, pres. M.E. Embroidery, Riverside, 1988—. Coach, mgr. Pachappa Little League, Riverside, 1986-89; mem. Com. for Moral Concerns. Recipient Ch. Youth of Month, Kiwanis, 1986. Mem. Nazarene Multiple Staff Assn. Republican. Office: Arlington Ave Ch Nazarene 5475 Arlington Ave Riverside CA 92504-2504

BRODIE, HOWARD, artist; b. Oakland, Calif., Nov. 28, 1915; s. Edward and Anna (Zeller) B. Student, Art Inst. San Francisco, Art Student's League, N.Y.C., U. Ghana, Accra; LHD (hon.), Acad. Art Coll., San Francisco, 1984. Mem. staff Life mag., Yank: the Army Weekly, Collier's, AP, CBS News, 1969-89; freelance artist, journalist, 1990—. Author: (book) Howard Brodie War Drawings, 1963, Drawing Fire, A Combat Artist At War, 1996; art journalist: (major wars) World War II, Korea, French Indo-China, Vietnam, (trials) Jack Ruby, Ray, Sirhan, My Lai, Charles Manson, Chicago Seven, Watergate, John Hinckley, Klaus Barbie in France, (famous people) John Wayne, Pres. Kennedy, James Jones; art at White House, 1946, 48; work represented in permanent collections Calif. Palace of Legion of Honor, San Francisco, Soc. Illustrators, N.Y., Libr. Congress, Washington, Air Force Acad., Colo.; prints, books: U.S. Army Infantry Mus., Ft. Benning, Ga., U.S. Army Mus., Presidio, Monterey, Oreg. Nat. Mil. Mus., The Hoover Instn. on War, Revolution and Peace, Anne S.K. Brown Mil. Collection Brown U. Libr., The Mus. of Books, Lenin Libr., Moscow, Gorky Sci. Libr., Moscow, Admiral Nimitz State Hist. Park, Tex., Henry E. Huntington Libr. (award), San Marina, New Britain Mus. Am. Art, Conn., West Point Libr., N.Y., Brown U. Libr., R.I.; commd. to draw The Contemporary Soldier in Action, AUSA, 1999; guest on Merv Griffin Show, Charles Kuralt Sunday Morning program, Ted Koppel program, Night Line; featured Andy Rooney CBS Sunday Morning program, Nostagia Network, Dennis Wholey Am. Program. Sgt., U.S. Army. Decorated Bronze Star; recipient honor medals Freedom Found., 1957, 58, 60, 61. Office: PO Box 221940 Carmel CA 93922

BRODINE, VIRGINIA WARNER, writer; b. Seattle, Feb. 18, 1915; d. Hayward Dare and Grace Kendall (McKibben) Warner; m. Russell Victor Brodine, Oct. 19, 1941; children: Cynthia, Marc. Student, Reed Coll., Portland, Oreg., 1933-34, 36-38. Dir. pub. rels. ctrl. states region Internat. Ladies AFL-CIO, St. Louis, 1954-62; editor Environment mag., St. Louis, 1962-69; freelance writer St. Louis, 1969-78, Roslyn, Wash., 1978—. Author: (non-fiction) Air Pollution, 1973, Radioactive Contamination, 1975, (novel) Seed of the Fire, 1996; cons. editor Sci. Inst. Pub. Info., N.Y.C., 1987-75. Mem. exec. com. Ctrl. Wash. Peace and Environment, 1991-96; bd. dirs. RIDGE, Rosylyn, 1998. Mem. Orgn. Am. Historians, Nat. Writers Union, Authors Guild, Women's Internat. League for Peace and Freedom, Western Assn. Women Historians, Pacific NW Labor History Assn. Avocation: walking. Home and Office: PO Box 197 Roslyn WA 98941-0197

BRODY, DAVID, artist, educator; b. N.Y.C., Feb. 16, 1958; s. Jules and Roxane (Offner) B. BA, Bennington (Vt.) Coll., 1981; MFA, Yale U., 1983. Vis. prof. Carnegie Mellon U., Pitts., 1990-91; head grad. studies Studio Art Ctr. Internat., Florence, Italy, 1992-96; asst. prof. U. Wash., Seattle, 1996—. One-person shows include Gallery NAGA, Boston, 1989, 92, 94, 96, Hewlett Gallery, Carnegie Mellon U., Pitts., 1991, Galeria Gilde, Guimarães, Portugal, 1996, Esther Claypool Gallery, Seattle, 1999; exhibited in group shows Chgo. Ctr. for Print, 1985, FPAC Gallery, Boston, 1986, Bridgewater Gallery, N.Y., SixToSix Gallery, N.Y.C., 1987, Gallery NAGA, Boston, 1989, 95, Mills Gallery, Boston Ctr. for Arts, 1989, 90, 91, Hewlett Gallery, 1990, Fitchburg Art Mus., Mass., 1991, 93, Limner Gallery, N.Y.C., 1992, Tribeca Gallery 148, N.Y., Decordova Mus., Lincoln, Mass., 1994, RipArte Art Fair, Rome, Italy, 1995, FAC Art Fair, Lisbon, Portugal, 1995, Trevi Flash Art Mus., Italy, 1996, The Painting Center, N.Y.C., 1996, The Alternative Mus., N.Y.C., 1996, Mus. Fine Arts, Fla. State U., Tallahassee, 1997, ARCO Art Fair, Madrid, 1996, 97, 99, Ctr. on Contemporary Art, Seattle. Grantee Guggenheim Found., N.Y.C., 1991, Fulbright Found., Washington, 1992, Elizabeth Found. for Arts, N.Y.C., 1994, Basil H. Alkazz award, 1998. Office: U Wash Box 353440 Seattle WA 98195

BRODY, DEANNA MAUREEN, interior designer; b. L.A., Sept. 15, 1948; d. Patrick Daniel and Nadeane (Moore) B. BFA, Ariz. State U., 1970; MFA, Art Inst. Chgo., 1973. Cert. interior designer, Calif. V.p. Canterbury Interiors, Newport Beach, Calif., 1980-88; CEO Design Works, Newport Beach, 1988—; cons. Calif. Interior Design Inst., Newport Beach, 1990-97. Contbr. articles to Model Home Outline, O.C. Mag., Home & Garden Mag. Chmn. Jr. C. of C., Newport Beach, 1989; chmn. showcase house Philharm. Soc., Orange County, Calif., 1997. Mem. Am. Soc. Interior Design (chmn. 1994-97), Nat. Home Furnishings League (pres. 1994, Presdl. award), Internat. Furniture and Design Assn. (pres. 1996, mem. nat. adv. bd. 1995). Roman Catholic. Avocations: raising shetland sheepdogs, gardening, travel. Office: Design Works 177F Riverside Ave Newport Beach CA 92663

BRODY, FLORIAN TOBIAS, electronic publishing and new media consultant; b. Vienna, Austria, Oct. 31, 1953; came to U.S., 1991; s. Peter I. and Agnes (Bleier) B. MA, Vienna U., 1982. Sr. info. mgr. Austrian Nat. Libr., Vienna, 1978-90; multimedia evangelist Apple Computer Austria, Vienna, 1986-90; mng. dir. Brody/Newmedia, Vienna, 1986—; tech. dir. Voyager Co., Santa Monica, Calif., 1990-92; pres., CEO Brody Inc., L.A., 1997—; internat. media cons., 1984—; instr. new media Art Ctr. Coll. of Design, Pasadena, Calif., 1995—; instr. U. Vienna, 1990—; assoc. prof. multimedia Multimedia Art Sch., Salzburg, Austria, 1996; spkr. in field. Prodr.: (CD-ROM) Electronic Publishing, 1996; prodr.: (web project) Der Standard-Austrian Bus. Newspaper, 1995; co-inventor: (electronic book software) Expanded Books, 1991-92. Avocations: painting, sailing. E-mail: brody@brodynewsmedia.com. www.brodynewmedia.com. Office: Brody Inc 2243 Linnington Ave Los Angeles CA 90064-2339

BROGDEN, STEPHEN RICHARD, library administrator; b. Des Moines, Sept. 26, 1948; s. Paul M. and Marjorie (Kueck) B.; m. Melinda L. Raine, Jan. 1, 1983; 1 child, Nathan. BA, U. Iowa, 1970, MA, 1972. Caretaker Eya Fechin Branham Ranch, Taos, N.Mex., 1970-72; dir. Harwood Found. U. N.Mex., Taos, 1972-75; vis. lectr. U. Ariz., Tucson, 1975-76; rd. mgr. Bill and Bonnie Hearne, Austin, Tex., 1976-79; head fine arts Pub. Libr. Des Moines, 1980-90; dep. dir. Thousand Oaks (Calif.) Libr., 1990—. Author book revs., Annals of Iowa, 1980; columnist Taos News, 1973. Mem. Am. Libr. Assn., Calif. Libr. Assn., Films for Iowa Librs. (pres. 1983-86), Metro Des Moines Libr. Assn. (pres. 1980). Office: Thousand Oaks Libr 1401 E Janss Rd Thousand Oaks CA 91362-2199

BROGLIATTI, BARBARA SPENCER, television and motion picture executive; b. L.A., Jan. 8, 1946; d. Robert and Lottie Spencer; m. Raymond Haley Brogliatti, Sept. 19, 1970. BA in Social Scis. and English, UCLA, 1968. Asst. press. info. dept. CBS TV, L.A., 1968-69, sr. publicist, 1969-74; dir. publicity Tandem Prodns. and T.A.T. Comm. (Embassy Comm.), L.A., 1974-77, corp. v.p., 1977-82; sr. v.p. worldwide publicity, promotion and advt. Embassy Comm., L.A., 1982-85; sr. v.p. worldwide corp. comm. Lorimar Telepictures Corp., Culver City, Calif., 1985-89; pres., chmn. Brogliatti Co., Burbank, Calif., 1989-90; sr. v.p. worldwide TV publicity, promotion and advt. Lorimar TV, 1991-92; sr. v.p. worldwide TV publicity, promotion and pub. rels. Warner Bros., Burbank, 1992-97; sr. v.p. corp. comm. Warner Bros., Inc., 1997—. Mem. bd. govs. TV Acad., L.A., 1984-86; bd. dirs. KIDSNET, Washington, 1987—, Nat. Acad. Cable Programming, 1992-94; mem. Hollywood Women's Polit. Com., 1992-93; mem. steering com. L.A. Free Clinic, 1997-98. Recipient Gold medallion Broadcast Promotion and Mktg. Execs., 1984. Mem. Am. Diabetes Assn. (bd. dirs. L.A. chpt. 1992-93), Am. Cinema Found. (bd. dirs. 1994-98), Dirs. Guild Am., Publicists Guild, Acad. TV Arts and Scis. (vice chmn. awards com.). Office: Warner Bros Studios 4000 Warner Blvd Burbank CA 91522-0002

BROIDA, REBECCA ERIN, magazine editor; b. Silver Spring, Md., June 27, 1969; d. David Samuel and Susan Rose (Greenhood) B. BS, Syracuse U., 1991. Reporter Daily Camera, Boulder, Colo., 1991-94; editor Inline Retailer, Boulder, Colo., 1994-97, Inline Mag. Peterson Publishing, Boulder, [illegible] Place award Spot News Reporting Soc. Profl. Journalists, 1993, Colo. Associated Press, 1994, Second Place award Investigative Reporting Soc. Profl. Journalists, 1994. Democrat. Jewish. Avocations: inline skating, hiking, weight training, reading, cooking. Office: Peterson Publishing 33046 Calle Aviador San Juan Capistrano CA 92675-4704

BROKAW, NORMAN ROBERT, talent agency executive; b. N.Y.C., Apr. 21, 1927; s. Isadore David and Marie (Hyde) B.; children—David M., Sanford Jay, Joel S., Barbara M., Wendy E., Lauren Quincy. Student pvt. schs., Los Angeles. With William Morris Agy., Inc., Beverly Hills, Calif., 1943—, sr. agt. and co. exec., 1951-74, v.p. world-wide ops., 1974-80, exec. v.p., dir., 1980—, co-chmn. bd., 1986-91, pres., CEO, 1989-91, chmn. bd., CEO, 1991-97, chmn. bd. worldide, 1997—. Pres. Betty Ford Cancer Center, Cedars-Sinai Med. Center, Los Angeles, 1978—; bd. dirs. Cedars-Sinai Med. Center; industry chmn. United Jewish Welfare Fund, 1975. With U.S. Army, World War II. Mem. Acad. Motion Picture Arts and Scis. Clubs: Hillcrest Country (Los Angeles). Clients include former Pres. and Mrs. Gerald R. Ford, Bill Cosby, Gen. Alexander Haig Jr., Tony Randall, Donald Regan, C. Everett Koop, Priscilla Presley, Andy Griffith, Brooke Shields, Juliette Lewis, Marcia Clarke, Christopher Darden. Office: William Morris Agy 151 S El Camino Dr Beverly Hills CA 90212-2775 also: William Morris Agy Inc 1325 Avenue Of The Americas New York NY 10019-6026

BROM, LIBOR, journalist, educator; b. Ostrava, Czechoslovakia, Dec. 17, 1923; came to U.S., 1958, naturalized, 1964; s. Ladislav and Bozena (Bromova) B.; m. Gloria S. Mena, Aug. 31, 1961; 1 son, Rafael Brom. *Father Ladislav was a school director, an enterpreneur, an inventor, and a store and real estate owner. He was a Czechoslovak patriot imprisoned by the Nazis and the Communists. Wife Gloria, from Chicago, was educated in Nicaragua and the U.S. She is an oil medium artist. She is an executive senior director for Mary Kay Cosmetics, previously working for BOAC and Air France. Son Rafael, a Sarajevo Institue for Commercial Art graduate, is a graphic artist at Unocal Oil Company. He is president of Cosmotone Records, and a member of the American Society of Composers and Publishers; recording nine records.* Ing., Czech Inst. Tech., 1948; JUC, Charles U. Prague, 1951; postgrad., San Francisco State Coll.; MA, U. Colo., 1962, PhD, 1970. V.p. Brom, Inc., Ostrava, 1942-48; economist Slovak Magnesite Works, Prague, Czechoslovakia, 1948-49; economist, chief planner Vodostavba, Navika, Prague, 1951-56; tchr. Jefferson County Schs., Colo., 1958-67; prof., dir. Russian area studies program U. Denver, 1967-91, prof. emeritus, 1992—; journalist, mem. editorial staff Denni Hlasatel-Daily Herald, Chgo., 1978-96; editorial staff Jour. of Interdisciplinary Studies, 1988—; Pres. Colo. Nationalities Council, 1970-72; comptroller Exec. Bd. Nat. Heritage Groups Council, 1970-72; mem. adv. bd. Nat. Security Council, 1980-85; acad. bank participant Heritage Found; adv. bd. Independence Inst. *Over 40 years of intensive activities as a Czech journalist with articles appearing in three continents and selectively published in eight books by Comenius World Council (Munich-Harford-Melbourne) and Moravia Publishing Inc. (Toronto). In the United States, Libor Brom has appeared at public regional, national and international conferences, including those of the U.S. Department of State, Strategic Seminars, Inc., National Catholic Education Association, National Fraternal Congress of Lutheran Brotherhood, Shavano Institute of National Leadership, the National Federation of State High School Associations, and others.* Author: Ivan Bunin's Proteges, Leonid Zurov, 1973, Alexander Zinoviev's Concept of the Soviet Man, 1991; co-author: Has the Third World War Already Started, 1983, Christianity and Russian Culture in Soviet Society, 1990, The Search for Self-Definition in Russian Literature, 1991; translator: Problems of Geography, 1955; author: (in Czech) In the Windstorm of Anger, 1976, Time and Duty, 1981, Teacher of Nations and Our Times, 1982, The Way of Light, 1982, On the Attack, 1983, Between the Currents, 1985, Homeland After 50 Years Nazi & Communist Occupation, 1992. V.p. Colo. Citizenship Day, 1968-69; pres. Comenius World Coun., 1976-85, World Representation of Czechoslovak Exiles, 1976-84; pres. Czech World Union, 1985-94; gen. sec. Czechoslovak Rep. Movement, 1980-91. Recipient Americanism medal DAR, 1969, Disting. Service award Am. by Choice, 1968, Kynewisbov Pioneer award Denver U., 1989; named Tchr. with Superlative Performance MLA, 1961, Outstanding Faculty mem. Omicron Delta Kappa, 1972, The Order of M.R. Stefanik Provisional Czechoslovak Govt. in Exile. Mem. Econ. Inst. Rsch. and Edn., Am. Assn. Tchrs. Slavic and Ea. European Langs. (v.p. 1973-75), Intercollegiate Studies Inst., Rocky Mountain Assn. Slavic Studies (sec./treas. 1975-78, v.p. 1978-81, pres. 1982-83), Nat. Assn. Scholars, Czechoslovak Christian Dem. Movement in Exile (ctrl. com. 1970-79), Dobro Slovo (hon.), Slava (hon.), Aleksandr Solzhenitsyn Soc., Shavano Inst. Nat. Leadership, Nat. Rep. Nationalities Coun. (co-chmn. human rights com. 1979-81), Phi Beta Kappa (hon.). Republican. Roman Catholic. Home: 434 A Woodview Rd Barrington IL 60010-1770 Office: U Denver Denver CO 80208-0293

BROM, ROBERT H., bishop; b. Arcadia, Wis., Sept. 18, 1938. Ed., St. Mary's Coll., Winona, Minn., Gregorian U., Rome. Ordained priest Roman Catholic Ch., 1963, consecrated bishop, 1983. Bishop of Duluth Minn., 1983-89; coadjutor bishop Diocese of San Diego, 1989-90, bishop, 1990—. Office: Diocese of San Diego Pastoral Ctr PO Box 85728 San Diego CA 92186-5728*

BRONESKY, JOSEPH J., lawyer; b. Milw., Aug. 6, 1947; s. Joseph Francis and Rita Cornelia B.; m. Jacquelin A. Medina, Mar. 15, 1985; children: Jessica, Amanda, Antoinette. BA, Marquette U., 1969; JD, U. Chicago, 1972. Bar: Wis. 1972, U.S. Ct. Mil. Appeals 1974, U.S. Supreme Ct. 1975, Colo. 1977, U.S. Dist. Ct. Colo. 1977. Law clk. to judge Latham Castle U.S. Ct. Appeals 7th cir., Chgo., 1972-73; assoc. Sherman & Howard, Denver, 1976-80, ptnr., 1980—. Asst. editor U. Chgo. Law Review, 1971-72. Bd. dirs. Camp Fire Denver area coun. 1983-86, Montessori Sch. Denver, 1992-94, Mile Hi coun. Girl Scouts U.S., Denver, 1992—, fin. com. 1989—. Lt. JAGC USN, 1973-76. Mem. ABA, Colo. Bar Assn., Colo. Trial Lawyers Assn. Democrat. Roman Catholic. Avocations: skiing, bicycling, hiking. Office: Sherman & Howard 633 17th St Ste 3000 Denver CO 80202-3665*

BRONSTER, MARGERY S, state attorney general; b. N.Y., Dec. 12, 1957; married; 1 child. BA in Chinese Lang., Lit. and History, Brown U., 1979; JD, Columbia U., 1982. Assoc. Sherman & Sterling, N.Y., 1982-87; ptnr. Carlsmith, Ball, Wichman, Murray, Case & Ichiki, Honolulu, 1988-94; atty. gen. State of Hawaii, 1994—; co-chair planning com. Citizens Conf. Judicial Selection, 1993. Mem. Am. Judicature Soc. (bd. dirs.; chair gov. com. on crime, VAWA planning com.). Office: Office Attorney General 425 Queen St Honolulu HI 96813-2903

BROOK, WINSTON ROLLINS, retired audio-video design consultant; b. Cameron, Tex., Aug. 20, 1931; s. Winston Marshall and Maude Katherine (Woody) B. BA, U. Denver, 1955. Lic. radiotelephone operator, FCC. Engr. Sta. WKNO-TV, Memphis, 1965-67; instr. Memphis State U., 1967-69; audio-visual dir. So. Coll. Optometry, Memphis, 1968-73; sr. cons. Bolt Beranek and Newman, Chgo. and L.A., 1973-87; prin. RB Sys., L.A., 1987-97; ret., 1997; assoc. editor Theater Design & Tech. mag., N.Y.C., 1981-87; tech. cons. Sound & Video Contractor mag., Overland, Kans., 1987—; lectr. in field. Co-author: Handbook for Sound Engineers, 1987; contbr. articles to profl. jours. Mem. Audio Engring. Soc., Acoustical Soc. Am., U.S. Inst. for Theatre Tech. Democrat. Mormon. Home: 5715 Calvin Ave Tarzana CA 91356-1108

BROOKBANK, JOHN W(ARREN), retired microbiology educator; b. Seattle, Apr. 3, 1927; s. Earl Bruce and Louise Sophia (Stoecker) B.; m. Marcia Ireland, Sept. 16, 1950 (div. 1978); children: Ursula Ireland, John W. Jr., Phoebe Bruce; m. Sally Satterberg Cahill, Aug. 6, 1983. BA, U. Wash., 1950, MS, 1953; PhD, Calif. Inst. Tech., 1955. Asst. prof. biology U. Fla., Gainesville, 1955-58, assoc. prof., 1958-68, prof. microbiology and cell sci., 1968-85, prof. emeritus, 1985—; vis. assoc. prof. U. Fla. Coll. Medicine, Gainesville, 1961-63, U. Wash., Seattle, 1965; cons. in field, Friday Harbor, Wash. 1986—. Author: Developmental Biology, 1978, (with W. Cunningham) Gerontology, 1988; editor: Improving Quality of Health Care of the Elderly, 1977, Biology of Aging, 1990; contbr. articles to profl. jours. Pres. Griffin Bay Preservation Com., Friday Harbor, 1985—, Bridge Council on Narcotics Addiction, Gainesville, 1974, Marine Environ. Consortium, [illegible], San Juan Nature Inst., 1997-98, founding pres. Gainesville Regional Council on Alcoholism, 1976; mem devel. adv. bd. U. Wash. Friday Harbor Lab., 1995-98. Research grantee NIH, 1957-80, NSF, 1972-73. Mem. Gerontol. Soc. Am., Seattle Tennis Club. Republican. Episcopalian. Avocations: fishing, boating, tennis, skiing. Home: PO Box 2688 Friday Harbor WA 98250-2688

BROOKE, EDNA MAE, retired business educator; b. Las Vegas, Nev., Feb. 10, 1923; d. Alma Lyman and Leah Mae (Ketcham) Shurtliff; m. Bill T. Brooke, Dec. 22, 1949; 1 child, John C. BS in Acctg., Ariz. State U., 1965, MA in Edn., 1967, EdD, 1975. Grad. teaching asst. Ariz. State U., Tempe, 1968-69; prof. bus. Maricopa Tech. Coll., Phoenix, 1967-72, assoc. dean instl. services, 1972-74; prof. bus. and acctg. Scottsdale (Ariz.) Community Coll., 1974-93; ret., 1993; cons. in field. Author: The Effectiveness of Three Techniques Used in Teaching First Semester Accounting Principles to Tech. Jr. College Students, 1974. Home: 1330 E Calle De Caballos Tempe AZ 85284-2404

BROOKE, TAL (ROBERT TALIAFERRO), company executive, author; b. Washington, Jan. 21, 1945; s. Edgar Duffield and Frances (Lea) B. BA, U. Va., 1969; M in Theology/Philosophy, Princeton (N.J.) U., 1986. V.p. pub. rels. nat. office Telecom Inc., 1982-83; pres., chmn. Spiritual Counterfeits Project, Inc., Berkeley, 1989—; guest lectr. Cambridge U., Eng., 1977, 86, 97, Oxford and Cambridge U., 1979, 84. *Tal Brooke authored eight books including, When the World Will be as One, and autobiographical, Lord of the Air. Brooke's work was recognized in Marquis Who's Who in the World, Contemporary Authors, The International Who's Who of Authors. Brooke is president, chairman of SCP Inc. SCP Journal editor, Brooke received the EPA first place award, critical review category. Brooke was a speaker at Cambridge, Oxford, Princeton, Sorbonne, Berkeley, University of Virginia, University of Edinburgh. Brooke was a guest on ABC & NBC News, MSNBC, CNET, Fox Network News, Extra, BBC1&2 Radio. Brooke's interviews were in Newsweek, The Washington Post, The Chicago Tribune, San Francisco Chronicle, LA Times, USA Today.* Author: Lord of the Air, 1990, When the World Will Be As One, 1989 (bestseller 1989-90), Riders of the Cosmic Circuit, 1986, Avatar of Night, 1987 (bestseller in India 1981-84), The Other Side of Death, Lord of the Air: The International Edition, 1976, America's Warning Light, 1994, Virtual Gods, 1997. Mem. Internat. Platform Assn., Authors Guild, Soc. of The Cincinnati. Office: SCP Inc PO Box 4308 Berkeley CA 94704-0308

BROOKES, MONA E., author, lecturer, art educator; b. L.A., May 9, 1937; d. John Arthur Brookes and Mary Elizabeth Baker Boles; m. Charles Hall, Jan. 1966 (div. Aug. 1968); 1 child, Mark Evan. BA in Art and Psychology magna cum laude, George Pepperdine U., L.A., 1959. Founder Monart Drawings Schs. (30 locations), Ojai, Calif., 1981—; cons. in field; condr. seminars in field; lectr. in field. TV talk show guest Daybreak L.A., 1982, Disney Mag., 1983, Today Show, 1987, ABC Home Show, 1988. Author: Drawing with Children, 1986, Drawing for Older Children and Teens, 1991; contbr. articles to profl. jours. Adv. bd. Nat. Learning Ctr., Washington, 1989-91. Calif. Arts Coun. grantee, 1980-83. Home and Office: PO Box 1630 Ojai CA 93024-1630

BROOKES, VALENTINE, retired lawyer; b. Red Bluff, Calif., May 30, 1913; s. Langley and Ethel (Valentine) B.; m. Virginia Stovall Cunningham, Feb. 11, 1939; children: Langley Brookes Brandt, Lawrence Valentine, Alan Cunningham. A.B., U. Calif., Berkeley, 1934, J.D., 1937. Bar: Calif. 1937, U.S. Supreme Ct. 1942. Asst. franchise tax counsel State of Calif., 1937-40; dep. atty. gen. Calif., 1940-42; spl. asst. to U.S. atty. gen., asst. to solicitor gen. U.S., 1942-44; partner firm Kent & Brookes, San Francisco, 1944-70, Alvord & Alvord, Washington, 1944-50, Lee, Toomey & Kent, Washington, 1950-79; partner firm Brookes and Brookes, San Francisco, 1971-88, of counsel, 1988-90; legal cons. Orinda, Calif., 1990—; lectr. Hastings Coll. Law, U. Calif., 1941-48, U. Calif. Law Sch., Berkeley, 1948-70; cons. fed. taxation. Author: The Continuity of Interest Test in Reorganizations, 1946, The Partnership Under the Income Tax Laws, 1949, The Tax Consequences of Widows Elections in Community Property States, 1951, Corporate Trasactions Involving Its Own Stock, 1954, Litigation Expenses and the Income Tax, 1957. Bd. dirs. Children's Hosp. Med. Center of N. Calif., 1963-74, v.p., 1968-70; trustee Oakes Found., 1957-70; regent St. Mary's Coll., Calif., 1968-88, pres. bd., 1970-72, emeritus mem., 1988—. Fellow Am. Bar Found. (life); mem. Am. Law Inst. (life), ABA (chmn. com. on statute of limitations 1954-57, mem. coun., tax sect. 1960-63), Calif. Bar Assn. (chmn. com. on taxation 1950-52, 60-61), Soc. Calif. Pioneers (v.p. 1964, 75-86), Phi Kappa Sigma, Phi Delta Phi. Republican. Clubs: Pacific Union, Orinda Country, World Trade. Home and Office: 7 Sycamore Rd Orinda CA 94563-1418

BROOKINS, JACOB BODEN, artist; b. Princeton, Mo., Aug. 28, 1935; s. Eugene Clements and Alice Jeno (Young) B.; m. Delores Miller, June 15, 1954 (div. Mar. 1, 1970); children: Cynthia, Robert, Natalie, Andrea. BS in Design, U. Oreg., 1963, MFA in Design, 1967, MFA in Sculpture, 1969. Instr. Sch. Arch. & Allied Arts U. Oreg., Eugene, 1967-69; asst. prof. studio arts No. Ariz. U., Flagstaff, 1969-75; asst. to the dir. Mus. No. Ariz., Flagstaff, 1975-79; EMT Blue Ridge Hotshots U.S. Forest Svc., Conconino Nat. Forest, Ariz., 1979-80; battalion chief Doney Pk. Fire Dist., Flagstaff, 1980-86; designer Orbis Design, Auckland, New Zealand, 1987-89; health svc. adminstr. Bulpe Rural Health Zone, Kasai Occidental, Zaire, 1989-91; artist Flagstaff. With USN. Support grantee Ariz. Arts Commn., 1975; Project grantee NEA, 1977, 78. Avocations: sailing, hiking, wilderness treks. Home: 6355 N Cosnino Rd Flagstaff AZ 86004-9784

BROOKLER, HARRY AARON, retired physician; b. Winnipeg, Man., Can., Jan. 16, 1915; came to U.S., 1954; s. Samuel David and Rachel (Farbstein) B.; m. Gertrude Mandel, Jan. 1, 1941; children: Jerome, Rickey, Jackie, Resa, Maxwell. MD, Man. U., 1938. Diplomate Am. Bd. Anesthesiology; licentiate Med. Coun. Can. Resident in surgery Winnipeg Gen. Hosp., 1937-39; pvt. practice Lemberg, Sask., 1940-41, Weyburn, Sask., 1941-54, San Diego, 1954-59, 61-85; resident in anesthesia Harbor Gen. Hosp.-UCLA, Torrance, 1959-61; med. dir. skilled nursing facilities Casa Blanca Corp., San Diego, 1976—; surg. cons. Weyburn Mental Hosp., Sask., 1942-54; chief of staff Weyburn Gen. Hosp., Sask., 1945-50, Doctors (Sharp Cabrillo) Hosp., San Diego, 1964-66; coroner Sask. Govt., 1944-54; cons. Can. Pacific Railway, Weyburn, 1941-54. Bd. dirs. Beth Jacob Congregation, San Diego, 1958-60, Jewish Family Svc., San Diego, 1960-62; workshipful master Masons, Weyburn, 1952; chmn. bd. dirs. Jewish Family Svc., San Diego, 1961. Recipient Isbister scholarships Man. Govt., 1931, 32, 33. Fellow Am. Geriatrics Soc., Am. Coll. Anesthesia; mem. AMA, Calif. Med. Assn., San Diego County Med. Assn. (chmn. skilled nursing com. 1961-66, staff survey com. 1967—), Calif. Assn. Med. Dirs. (bd. dirs., founder 1980-85, treas. 1980-85). Avocations: family, photography, travel, reading. Home and Office: 5310 Prosperity Ln San Diego CA 92115-2145

BROOKMAN, ANTHONY RAYMOND, lawyer; b. Chgo., Mar. 23, 1922; s. Raymond Charles and Marie Clara (Alberg) B.; m. Marilyn Joyce Brookman, June 5, 1982; children: Meribeth Brookman Farmer, Anthony Raymond, Lindsay Logan Christensen. Student, Ripon Coll., 1940-41; BS, Northwestern U., 1947; JD, U. Calif., San Francisco, 1953. Bar: Calif. 1954. Law clk. to presiding justice Calif. Supreme Ct., 1953-54; ptnr. Nichols, Williams, Morgan, Digardi & Brookman, 1954-68; sr. ptnr. Brookman & Talbot, Inc. (formerly Brookman & Hoffman, Inc.), Walnut Creek, Calif., 1969-92, Brookman & Talbot Inc., Sacramento, 1992—. Pres. Young Reps. Calif., San Mateo County, 1953-54. 1st lt. USAF. Mem. ABA, Alameda County Bar Assn., State Bar Calif., Lawyers Club Alameda County, Alameda-Contra Costa County Trial Lawyers Assn., Assn. Trial Lawyers Am., Calif. Trial Lawyers Assn., Athenian Nile Club, Masons, Shriners. Republican. Office: 901 H St Ste 200 Sacramento CA 95814-1808 also: 1990 N California Blvd Walnut Creek CA 94596-3742 also: 1746 Grand Canal Blvd Ste 11 Stockton CA 95207-8111

BROOKS, DONALD LEE, civil engineering and scientific consulting firm executive; b. Boston, 1956; s. Douglas Lee and Elizabeth Brooks; m. Terry O'Sullivan, 1987 (div. 1989); m. Jill Blondin, 1991; children: Nathan Donald, Kylie Elizabeth. BA in Environ. Biology, Earlham Coll., Richmond, Ind., 1979; postgrad., U.Ariz., 1984. Registered profl. engr., Ariz.; diplomate Am. Coll. Forensic Examiners. Field biologist/vegetation mgr. Colo. River Projects Ariz. State U. Ctr. for Environ. Studies, 1980-81; rsch. asst. dept. watershed mgmt. U. Ariz., Tucson, 1982-84; subdivsn. engr., devel. divsn. mgr. Pima County Dept. Transp. & Flood Control Dist., Tucson, 1984-89; mgr. water resources Anderson-Passarelli, Tucson, 1989; v.p. URBAN Engring., Tucson, 1989-92; project mgr. Johnson-Brittain Assocs., Tucson, 1992; client mgr. David Evans & Assocs., Tucson, 1992-93; pres., prin. engr. ICON Cons. USA, Inc., Tucson, 1993—; prin. engr., environ. scientist Total Infrastructure Solutions LLC, Tucson, 1998—; hydraulic engr., cons. Devel. Alternatives Inc./U.S. Agy. Internat. Devel., Cochabamba, Bolivia, 1993. Contbr. articles to profl. jours. Bd. dirs. Saguaro Credit Union, 1998,. Mem. ASCE, Am. Inst. Hydrology (profl. hydrologist), Ariz. Floodplain Mgmt. Assn. (Outstanding Svc. award 1990-91), Assn. State Floodplain Mgrs., Am. Water Resources Assn., So. Ariz. Home Builders Assn., Adventure Club N.Am., Rocks & Ropes Tucson, Cliffhanger Soc. (v.p.). Mem. Soc. Friends. Avocations: rock climbing, skiing, electronic music, motorcycling. E-mail: dbrooks@iconusainc.com. Home: 1514 N Plaza De Lirios Tucson AZ 85745-1600 Office: ICON Cons USA Inc 1931 W Grant Rd Ste 350 Tucson AZ 85745-1104

BROOKS, EDWARD HOWARD, college administrator; b. Salt Lake City, Mar. 2, 1921; s. Charles Campbell and Margery (Howard) B.; m. Courtaney June Perren, May 18, 1946; children: Merrillee Brooks Runyan, Robin Anne (Mrs. R. Bruce Pollock). B.A., Stanford U., 1942, M.A., 1947, Ph.D., 1950. Mem. faculty, adminstrn. Stanford U., 1949-71; provost Claremont (Calif.) Colls., 1971-81; v.p. Claremont U. Center, 1979-81; sr. v.p. Claremont McKenna Coll., 1981-84; provost Scripps Coll., 1987-89, pres., 1989-90; ret., 1990. Trustee EDUCOM, 1978-80, Webb Sch. of Calif., 1979-90, Menlo Sch. and Coll., 1985-88; bd. overseers Hoover Instn., 1972-78; bd. dirs. Student Loan Mktg. Assn., 1973-77; mem. Calif. Student Aid Commn., 1984-88, chmn., 1986-88. Served with AUS, 1942-45. Mem. U. Club Pasadena. Home: 356 S Orange Grove Blvd Pasadena CA 91105-1746

BROOKS, JIMMY ALAN, editor, writer; b. Havre de Grace, Md., Feb. 1, 1949; s. Jimmy Maynard and Edna Lee Brooks; m. Jodie Ann Chatfield, June 20, 1987; children: Kyra Marie, Shane Michael. Cert., Nat. Outdoor Leadership Sch., 1970; BS, U. Del., 1971. Editor Natural Resource Ecology Lab., Fort Collins, Colo., 1974-76, Colo. State U., Fort Collins, Colo., 1976-85, Am. Tel. and Telegraph Co., Denver, 1985-94; owner Alan Brooks Comm., Denver, 1994-96; editor World of Wood Internat. Wood Soc., Albuquerque, 1995—; lectr. Colo. State U., 1977-83; cons. Around the World in 80 Ways, Riner, Va., 1980-81, Colo. Purchasing Assn., Denver, 1992-93; bd. trustee Internat. Wood Soc., Hiroshima, Japan, 1995—. Editor: Colorado Comments, 1976-83, Denver Views, 1985-94, Trail & Road Encounters, 1994-96. Recipient Cmty. Svc. award Colo. Environ. Action Exch., 1990. Mem. Intercollegiate Outing Club Assn. (exec. dir. 1969-71), Internat. Assn. Bus. Communicators, Greater Albuquerque C. of C. Avocations: natural sciences, western history, contra dancing, hiking, road trips. Home and Office: 13105 Candelaria Rd NE Apt B Albuquerque NM 87112-2167

BROOKS, JOHN LANIER, JR., county official; b. Lakeland, Fla., July 30, 1964; s. John L. Brooks and Sandra L. (Umbaugh) Chiselbrook; m. Julie M. Thomas, 1993; children: Rachel, Morgan. BA in econs., U. Colo., 1986. Gen. mgr. Henderson Tech., Boulder, Colo., 1987-92; ops. coord. AMR of Colo., Boulder, 1988-97; dir. ops., ambulance divsn. Summit County, Frisco, Colo., 1997-99; dir. ops. Pridemark Paramedics, Boulder County Divsn., 1999—; cons., mng. ptnr. HTM Graphics, Westminster, Colo., 1992—. Recipient USAF scholarship, 1982-84. Republican. Lutheran. Avocations: water sports, skiing, golf. Office: Summit County 227 CR 1003 Boulder CO 80301

BROOKS, JOHN SCOTT, county official; b. Ventura, Calif., June 9, 1964; s. John Wilburn and Carolyn Ruth (Hartley) B.; m. Maria Acela Nunez, May 8, 1990; children: Sierra Lynn, Shasta Lee, Jason Scott. AA, Ventura (Calif.) C.C., 1987; BS in Environ. Planning and Comms., Humboldt State U., Arcata, Calif., 1990; postgrad., U. So. Calif. Econ. devel. fin. profl. Waste mgmt. specialist Calif. Integrated Waste Mgmt. Bd., Sacramento, 1990-93, assoc. waste mgmt. specialist, 1993-96; program dir. Regional Coun. Rural Counties, Environ. Svcs. Joint Powers Authority, Sacramento, 1996—; pres., founder Ventura Coll. Biol. Assn., 1986; apptd. local govt. adv. task force by Gov. Wilson, 1997—. Co-author, editor: The Rural Cookbook-Recipes for Successful Waste Prevention, 1994. V.p., co-founder Ventura Indian Student Assn., 1985. Recipient Customer Svc. award Calif. EPA, Sacramento, 1995, Outstanding Achievement award Calif. Integrated Waste Mgmt. Bd., Sacramento, 1994, Rural County Assistance award Regional Coun. of Rural Counties, Sacramento, 1994. Mem. Solid Waste Assn. N.Am., Toastmasters (sgt. at arms 1994, edn. v.p. 1995, Toastmasters on TV 1995). Avocations: genealogy, golf, camping. Office: Regional Coun Rural Counties Environ Svcs Joint Powers 1020 12th St Ste 400 Sacramento CA 95814-3917

BROOKS, LILLIAN DRILLING ASHTON, adult education educator; b. Grand Rapids, Mich., May 27, 1921; d. Walter Brian and Lillian Church; m. Frederick Morris Drilling, 1942 (div. Apr. 1972); children: Frederick Walter, Stephen Charles, Lawrence Alan, Lynn Anne; m. Richard Moreton Ashton, Aug. 25, 1973 (dec.); m. Ralph J. Brooks, May 21, 1994. Student, Grand Rapids Jr. Coll., 1939-41, Wayne State U., 1941-42, Grand Rapids Art Inst., 1945-49, UCLA, 1964-69, Loyola Marymount Coll., Westchester, Calif., 1970-73. Life teaching credential, Calif. Decorator John Widdicomb Furniture Co., 1945-49; tchr. art Inglewood (Calif.) Sch. Dist., 1965-73; tchr. adult edn. art Downey (Calif.) Unified Sch. Dist., 1973-95; lectr. Downey Art League, 1990-92, Whittier (Calif.) Art Assn., 1991, h.s. and mid. sch. lectr., 1994-95; judge Children's Art Exhibit, Downey, 1992; participant Getty Found. at San Francisco, 1993, Getty Found. seminar at Cranbrook, 1994, Getty Conf. on Aesthetics, 1995, Cin. U., 1992, El SEgundo, 1994; mem. state accreditation com. Inglewood and Downey United Sch. Dists., 1966-70, 75-80, 85—; owner A & B Furniture Svc. Ctr., 1995—. One woman shows include El Segundo Mcpl. Libr., 1965, Pico Rivera Art Gallery, 1978, Downey Art Mus., 1999; exhibited in group shows at Fairlane Show, Dearborn, Mich., 1959, Jane Lessing Art Gallery, 1966, Westchester Mcpl. Libr., 1971, Inglewood City Hall, 1973, Aegina Sch., Greece, 1973, Downey Art Mus., 1992; represented in permanent collection at U. Mich. Pres. bd. dirs. Downey Art Mus., 1998-99, dir. Mus., 1998, vol. dir., 1999; former mem. Mich. Cultural Com.; art commr. City of Dearborn, Mich., 1954-59; former pres. Dearborn Art Inst., Pacific Art Guild; pres. bd. dirs. Downey Art Mus., 1997-98; pres. Downey Art League, 1991-92, 93-94, Exhbn. Ch., 1995, v.p. 1996-98; lectr. on art as a career local Downey high and mid. schs. Recipient Certs. of Appreciation for contbn. of leadership Coord. Coun. Downey, Downey Governing Bd., Downey Bd. Edn., 1997, Cmty. Svc. award for Outstanding Svc. Downey Rotary, 1994; named Tchr. of Yr., Masons, Downey, 1986. Mem. Calif. Coun. on Art Edn. (parliamentarian Downey 1990-92, Calco Excellence in Tchg. award 1991, various certs.). Avocations: reading, hiking, internat. travel, photography, painting. Home: 9318 Fostoria St Downey CA 90241-4020

BROOKS, SIDNEY B., bankruptcy judge; b. 1945; married; 2 children. BA in Polit. Sci., U. Colo.; JD, U. Denver Coll. Law. Assoc. atty. Nelson and Haridng, Denver, 1971-73; asst. atty. gen. Office of Atty. Gen., Denver, 1973-75; ptnr. Nelson & Harding, Denver, 1975-80, Smart DeFurio Brooks Eklund and McClure, Denver, 1980-84; pres. Brooks and Krieger P.C., 1984-87; judge U.S. Bankruptcy Ct. Colo., 1988—; guest spkr. Russian Law Conf., Russian Rsch. Ctr., Harvard U. Law Sch., 1994, Russian Bankruptcy Conf., Moscow, 1994; participant Conf. on Chinese Bankruptcy Law Reform, Internat. Rep. Inst., Beijing, 1995; cons. World Bank Legal Advisors, USAID, Orgn. Econ. Corp. and Devel., Internat. Jud. Rels. Com. of U.S. Jud. Conf.; advisor/cons. on jud. tng. and comml. ct. programs various countries; mem. and advisor Am. Law Inst.; spkr./lectr. for Fed. Jud. Ctr., Nat. Conf. of Bankruptcy Judges and Am. Bankruptcy Inst., 1997-98. Contbr. over 50 articles to profl. jours. Office: US Bankruptcy Ct Colo 721 19th St Rm 560 Denver CO 80202-2508

BROOKS, WILLIAM GEORGE, aeronautical engineer; b. Calgary, Alta., Can., June 6, 1940; came to U.S., 1965; s. William Henry Charles and Mary Robertson (Henderson) B.; m. Lynn Chung. BS in Aero. Engring., Wichita State U., 1963, BSME, 1965; MBA, Pepperdine U., 1978. Engr. Sun Oil Co., Estevan, Sask., Can., 1964; design engr. The Carlson Co., Wichita, Kans., 1965-66; engr. United Airlines, San Francisco, 1966-67, aero. engr. B, 1967-70, aero. engr. A, 1970-71, aircraft engr. A, 1971-84, staff engr., 1984-91, sr. staff rep. engring., 1991—. Mem. ASME, Soc. Automotive Engrs. Internat. Avocations: walking, hiking. Home: 1001 Sandhurst Dr Vallejo CA 94591-6881 Office: United Airlines San Francisco Int Airport San Francisco CA 94128-3800

BROPHY, DENNIS RICHARD, psychology and philosophy educator, administrator, clergyman; b. Milw., Aug. 6, 1945; s. Floyd Herbert and Phyllis Marie (Ingram) B.; BA, Washington U., St. Louis, 1967, MA, 1968; M.Div., Pacific Sch. Religion, 1971; PhD in Indstrl. and Orgnl. Psychology, Texas A & M U., 1995. Cert. coll. tchr., Calif. Edn. rschr. IBM Corp., White Plains, N.Y., 1968-71; edn. minister Cmty. Congl. Ch., Port Huron, Mich., 1971-72, Bethlehem United Ch. of Christ, Ann Arbor, Mich., 1972-73, Cmty. Congl. Ch., Chula Vista, Calif., 1974; philosophy instr. Southwestern Coll., Chula Vista, 1975; assoc. prof. psychology and philosophy Northwest Coll., Powell, Wyo., 1975-96, prof., 1996—, chmn. social sci. divsn., 1992-95; religious edn. cons. Mont.-No. Wyo. Conf. United Ch. of Christ. Mem. APA (Daniel Berlyne award 1996), Wyo. Coun. for Humanities, Soc. Indsl. Orgnl. Psychology, Yellowstone Assn. of United Ch. of Christ, Phi Kappa Phi, Phi Beta Kappa, Sigma Xi, Omicron Delta Kappa, Theta Xi, Golden Key Nat. Honor Soc. Home: 533 Avenue C Powell WY 82435-2401 Office: Northwest Coll 231 W 6th St Powell WY 82435-1898

BRORBY, WADE, federal judge; b. 1934. BS, U. Wyo., 1956, JD with honor, 1958. Bar: Wyo. County and prosecuting atty. Campbell County, Wyo., 1963-70; ptnr. Morgan Brorby Price and Arp, Gillette, Wyo., 1961-88; judge U.S. Ct. Appeals (10th cir.), Cheyenne, Wyo., 1988—. With USAF, 1958-61. Mem. ABA, Campbell County Bar Assn., Am. Judicature Soc., Def. Lawyers Wyo., Wyo Bar Assn. (commr. 1968-70). Office: US Ct Appeals 10th Cir O'Mahoney Fed Bldg Rm 2018 PO Box 1028 Cheyenne WY 82003-1028*

BROSNAN, PETER LAWRENCE, documentary filmmaker; b. Bklyn., July 6, 1952, s. John Joseph and Audrey Barbara (Holran) B. BFA, NYU, N.Y.C., 1974; MA, U. So. Calif., 1979, Pepperdine U., 1995. Documentary filmmaker, writer L.A., 1980—; dir. DeMille Project, Hollywood Heritage, L.A., 1988—. Author: (screenplays) Heart of Darkness, 1992, The Ark, 1994, Perfect Target, 1996; co-author: (book) PML Report, 1989; writer: (documentary film) Ghosts of Cape Horn, 1980 (World Ship Trust award); prodr., dir.: (TV documentary) The Lost City, 1992; writer, segment prodr.: (PBS series) Faces of Culture, 1983-84 (Emmy award 1984), Writer Marketing, 1984 (Emmy award 1985); dir.: (documentary) Sand Castles, 1995. Democrat.

BROTMAN, CAROL EILEEN, adult education educator, advocate; b. L.A., Feb. 17, 1955; d. Hyman and Beverly Joanne (Krause) B. AA, L.A. Pierce Coll., 1977; BA, U. So. Calif., L.A., 1984; postgrad., UCLA, 1990, cert. legal asst., 1991. Cert. adult edn. tchr., Calif. Tchr. divsn. adult and career edn. L.A. Unified Sch. Dist., 1986—; tchr. adult edn. and ESL North Hollywood (Calif.) Adult Sch., 1987-94, dept. chair, 1990-91; pre-employment trainer Refugee Employment Tng. Project, 1995—; tchr. ESL Met. Skills Ctr., L.A. Founder Families for Quality Care, San Fernando Valley, Calif., 1983-86; mem. com. L.A. Pub. Libr. Ctrl. Libr., internat. langs. dept. Langs. Expertese and Resources Network, 1991; vol. paralegal Harriet Buhai Ctr. for Family Law, 1992-94; organizer adult-student cmty. group Thanksgiving dinner for new immigrants St. Patrick's Ch., North Hollywood, 1987-90. Recipient Mayor's Commendation, 1984, Older Women's League, 1985, Cert. of Tribute, Harriet Buhai Ctr. for Family Law, 1992, 93, Cert. of Appreciation for Outstanding Vol. Work, Family Law Sect., L.A. County Bar Assn. and Superior Ct. of L.A., 1993. Mem. AAUW, NAFE, United Tchrs. of L.A., Rare Fruit Gardenrs Assn. Home: 10921 Reseda Blvd Northridge CA 91326-2803

BROTMAN, JEFFREY H., variety stores executive; b. 1942. JD, U. Wash., 1967. Ptnr. Lasher-Brotman & Sweet, 1967-74, with ENI Exploration Co., 1975-83; co-founder Costco Wholesale Corp., 1983, chmn. bd., chief exec. officer, 1983-88, chmn. bd., 1988—. Office: Costco Wholesale PO Box 34331 Issaquah WA 98027*

BROTMAN, RICHARD DENNIS, counselor; Detroit, Nov. 2, 1952; s. Alfred David and Dorothy G. (Mansfield) B.; m. Debra Louise Hobold, Sept. 9, 1979. AA, E. L.A. Jr. Coll., 1972; AB, U. So. Calif., 1974, MS, 1976. Instructional media coord. Audio-Visual Div., Pub. Library, City of Alhambra, Calif., 1971-78; clin. supr. Hollywood-Sunset Community Clinic, L.A., 1976—; client program coord. N. L.A. County Regional Ctr. for Developmentally Disabled, 1978-81; sr. counselor Eastern L.A. Regional Ctr. for Developmentally Disabled, 1981-85; dir. community svcs. Almansor Edn. Ctr., 1985-87; tng. and resource devel. Children's Home Soc. Calif., 1987-90; program supr. Pacific Clinics-East, 1990-94; dir. clin. svcs. Alma Family Svcs., 1994—; probable cause hearing officer Orange County (Calif.) Healthcare Agy., 1986—; intern student affairs div., U. So. Calif., 1976. Corp. dir. San Gabriel Mission Players, 1973-75. Lic. marriage, family and child counselor, Calif.; cert. counselor Calif. Community Coll. Bd. Mem. Am. Assn. For Marriage and Family Therapy (approved supr.), Calif. Personnel and Guidance Assn. (conv. participant, 1976, 77, 79), Calif. Rehab. Counselors Assn. (officer), San Fernando Valley Consortium of Agys. Serving Developmentally Disabled Citizens (chmn. recreation subcom.), L.A. Aquarium Soc. Democrat. E-mail: RdemsB@MSN.COM. Home: 3515 Brandon St Pasadena CA 91107-4542 Office: Alma Family Svcs 9140 Whittier Blvd Pico Rivera CA 90660

BROUGH, BRUCE ALVIN, public relations and communications executive; b. Wayland, N.Y., Nov. 22, 1937; s. Alvin Elroy and Marjorie Huberta (McDowell) B.; m. Jane Virginia Koethen, Aug. 9, 1958; children: John David, Pamela Marjorie, Robert Bruce. BS in Pub. Rels., U. Md., 1960; MS in Mass Comm., Am. U., Washington, 1967. Comm. mgr. IBM Corp., various locations, 1965-74; owner, pres. Bruce Brough Assocs., Inc., Boca Raton, Fla., 1974-75; worldwide press rels. rep. Tex. Instruments Inc., 1975-76; v.p. pub. rels. Regis McKenna Inc., 1976-77; pres., prin. Pease/Brough Assocs., Inc., Palo Alto, Calif., 1978-80, Franson/Brough Assocs., Inc., San Jose, Calif., 1980-81; sr. v.p., dir. Advanced Tech. Network Hill and Knowlton, Inc., San Jose, Calif., 1981-86; sr. v.p., gen. mgr. Hill and Knowlton, Inc., Santa Clara, Calif., 1989; mgr. corp. pub. rels. Signetics Corp., 1986-87; mktg. comm. mgr. Corp. Ctr. Philips Components divsn. Philips Internat., B.V., Eindhoven, The Netherlands, 1987-89; dir. corp. comm. Centigram Comm. Corp., San Jose, Calif., 1989-90; prin. Brough Comm., Santa Cruz, Calif., 1994—; dir. pub. rels. Acer Am. Corp., San Jose, 1998—; dir. Pub. Rels. Acer Am. Corp., San Jose, 1998—; lectr. San Jose State U., 1977-83, 91—; cons. comm. and pub. rels., 1986—. Author: Publicity and Public Relations Guide for Business, 1984, revised edit., 1986, The Same Yesterday, Today and Forever, 1986; contbg. editor Family Bible Ency., 1973. Recipient Sustained Superior Performance award NASA, 1964, award Freedom's Found., 1963. Mem. Pub. Rels. Soc. Am. (accredited), Soc. Tech. Comm., Nat. Press Club, Sigma Delta Chi. Republican. Roman Catholic. Avocations: writing, fishing, skiing, boating, travel. Fax: 408-922-2949. E-mail: bruceúbrough@acer.com. Home: 155 Rabbits Run Rd Santa Cruz CA 95060-1526 Office: Acer Am Corp 2641 Orchard Pkwy San Jose CA 95134

BROUGHTON, JAMES WALTER, real estate development executive, consultant; b. Atlantic City, Dec. 16, 1946; s. Walter Lennie and Janet Caroline (Mossman) B.; m. Sharon Carter, Mar. 10, 1980; children—Jennifer Christine, Matthew James. Student U. Colo.-Colorado Springs, 1967-68, U. Md., 1968-70, U. Colo.-Denver, 1972-73. Asst. regional sales dir. Del E. Webb Corp., Denver, 1972-76; dir. mktg. Interval Internat. Miami, Fla., 1981-82, exec. dir. Time Sharing Inst., Miami, 1981-82; pres. J. Broughton, Inc., Miami, 1976-83, Spectrum Mktg. Group, Denver, 1983-84, Ocean Resorts Devel. Co., Ventura, Calif., 1984-85; sr. v.p. Fairfield Communities, Inc., Atlanta, 1985; chmn., pres. CEO Lexes Leisure Group, Las Vegas, 1985—; bd. dirs. Resort Computer Corp., Denver, 1983-87, Spectrum Group, Denver, 1983-85, Internat. Found. Time Sharing, Washington, 1983-87, Internat. Resort Group, Inc., Las Vegas, 1992-94; pub. Time Sharing Ency., 1981, Time Sharing Ind. Rev., 1981. Contbr. articles to profl. jours. Served with USAF, 1964-71. Mem. Am. Resort Devel. Assn. (recruitment award 1983, NTC Svc. award 1987, Leader of Yr. 1991, Industry Visionary Leader of Yr. award 1993, bd. dirs. 1985—, exec. com. 1988—, meetings coun. chmn. 1991—, chmn. resort devel. forum 1993—, treas. 1993—), Nat. Time Sharing Council (chmn. 1984-86, bd. govs. 1984-92, recruitment award 1984), Interval Internat. (adv. bd. 1982-91), Urban Land Inst. (recreational devel. coun. 1993—). Republican. Office: Lexes Leisure Group 6550 S Pecos Rd Ste B-138 Las Vegas NV 89120-2828

BROUGHTON, RAY MONROE, economic consultant; b. Seattle, Mar. 2, 1922; s. Arthur Charles and Elizabeth C. (Young) B.; BA, U. Wash., 1947, MBA, 1960; m. Margret Ellen Ryno, July 10, 1944 (dec.); children: Linda Rae Broughton Silk, Mary Catherine Broughton Boutin; m. Carole Jean Packer, 1980. Mgr. communications and managerial devel. Gen. Electric Co., Hanford Atomic Products Ops., Richland, Wash., 1948-59; mktg. mgr., asst. to pres. Smyth Enterprises, Seattle, 1960-62; dir. rsch. Seattle Area Indsl. Council, 1962-65; v.p., economist (mgr. econ. rsch. dept.) First Interstate Bank of Oreg., N.A., Portland, 1965-87; ind. economic cons., 1987—; mem. econ. adv. com. to Am. Bankers Assn., 1980-83; mem. Gov.'s Econ. Adv. Council, 1981-88; dir. Oregonians for Cost Effective Govt., 1989-90; instr. bus. communications U. Wash., Richland, 1956-57. Treas., dir. Oreg. affiliate Am. Heart Assn., 1972-78, chmn., 1980-81, dir., 1980-84. Served to 1st lt. U.S. Army, 1943-46; ETO. Mem. Western Econ. Assn., Pacific N.W. Regional Econ. Conf. (dir. 1967-94), Nat. Assn. Bus. Economists (co-founder chpt. 1971), Am. Mktg. Assn. (pres. chpt. 1971-72), Alpha Delta Sigma. Author: Trends and Forces of Change in the Payments System and the Impact on Commercial Banking, 1972; contbg. editor Pacific Banker and Bus. mag., 1974-80. Home and Office: 10127 SW Lancaster Rd Portland OR 97219-6302

BROUSSARD, THOMAS ROLLINS, lawyer; b. Houston, May 30, 1943; s. Charles Hugh and Ethel (Rollins) B.; m. Mollie Brewster, Jan. 13, 1968. B.S. cum laude in Econs., U. Pa., 1964; J.D. cum laude, Harvard U., 1967. Bar: N.Y. 1968, Calif. 1973. Tax atty. Esso Standard Eastern, Inc., N.Y.C., 1967-70; gen. tax counsel Atlantic Richfield Co., N.Y.C., Los Angeles, 1970-74; v.p. corp. affairs, sec., gen. counsel Technicolor, Inc., Los Angeles, 1974-80; mem. firm Nelson & Broussard, Los Angeles, 1980-81; pres. Thomas R. Broussard, Ltd., P.C., Los Angeles, 1981—. Mem. ABA, Calif., Los Angeles County bar assns., Assn. of the Bar of the City of N.Y. Office: 5757 Wilshire Blvd Ste 648 Los Angeles CA 90036-3686

BROWER, DAVID ROSS, conservationist; b. Berkeley, Calif., July 1, 1912; s. Ross J. and Mary Grace (Barlow) B.; m. Anne Hus, May 1, 1943; children: Kenneth David, Robert Irish, Barbara Anne, John Stewart. Student, U. Calif., 1929-31; DSc (hon.), Hobart and William Smith Colls., 1967; DHL (hon.), Claremont Colls. Grad. Sch., 1971, Starr King Sch. for Ministry, 1971, U. Md., 1973; PhD in Ecology (hon.), U. San Francisco, 1973, Colo. Coll., 1977; other hon. degrees, New Sch. for Social Rsch., 1984, Sierra Nev. Coll., 1985, Unity Coll., Maine, 1989. Editor U. Calif. Press, 1941-52; exec. dir. Sierra Club, 1952-69, also bd. dirs., mem. editorial bd., 1935-69, hon. v.p., 1972—; dir. John Muir Inst. Environ. Studies, 1969-71, v.p., 1968-72; pres. Friends of the Earth, 1969-79; founder, chmn. Friends of the Earth Found., 1972-84, bd. dirs.; founder Environ. Liaison Ctr., Nairobi, 1974; founder, chmn. Earth Island Inst., San Francisco, 1982—; founder, pres. Earth Island Action Group, 1989; founder biennial Fate and Hope of the Earth Confs., N.Y.C., 1982, Washington, 1984, Ottawa, 1986, Managua, 1989; activist in conservation campaigns, Kings Canyon Nat. Pk., 1938-40, Dinosaur Nat. Monument, 1952-56, Alaska parks and forests, 1954—, North Cascades Nat. Pk., 1955-94, Cape Cod, Fire Island, Point Reyes nat. seashores, 1960-68, Redwood Nat. Pk., 1963-68, Great Basin Nat. Park, 1965, Galapagos Islands World Heritage, 1965-68, Grand Canyon 1952-68, Snowdonia Nat. Park, 1970, 71, population and growth control and nuclear proliferation issues, Nat. Wilderness Preservation System, 1951-64, James Bay defense, 1991-94, conservation lectr., U.S., 1939—, Finland, 1971, Sweden, 1972, Kenya, 1972, 74, Italy, 1972, 74, 79, 82, 91, 94, Australia and N.Z., 1974, Japan, 1976, 78, 90, 92, U.K., 1968, 70, 93, USSR, 1985, 88, 90, 91, 92, France, 1970, 90-91, Fed. Republic Germany, 1989, Berlin, 1990, Nicaragua, 1988, 89, Brazil, 1992, The Netherlands, 1993-94; founder Trustees for Conservation, 1954, sec., 1960-61, 64-65; founder Sierra Club Found., 1960; bd. dirs. Citizens Com. Natural Resources, 1955-78; chmn. Natural Resources Coun. Am., 1955-57; bd. dirs. North Cascades Conservation Coun., from 1957, Rachel Carson Trust for Living Environment, 1966-72, cons. expert, from 1973; founder, steering com. League Conservation Voters, 1969-80; founder Les Amis de la Terre, Paris, 1970; founder, guarantor Friends of the Earth U.K., 1970-88; chmn. Earth Island Ltd., London, 1971-74; active Restoring-the-Earth movement, from 1986, founder Global CPR Svc., 1990, leader del. to Lake Baikal, Siberia, 1988, 90, 91, 92, mem. various adv. bds. including Found. on Econ. Trends, Nat. Strategy, Coun. Econ. Priorities, Zero Population Growth, Yosemite Concessions Svc., Earth Day 1990, 94; mem. Com. on Nat. Security; adv. to pres. Interface, Inc., 1997—. Initiator, designer, gen. editor: Sierra Club Exhibit Format Series, 20 vols., 1960-68, Friends of the Earth series The Earth's Wild Places, 10 vols., 1970-77, Celebrating the Earth series, 3 vols., 1972-73; numerous other films and books, biographee in Encounters with the Archdruid (John McPhee), 1970; (autobiography) Vol. 1, For Earth's Sake: The Life and Times of David Brower, 1990, Vol. 2, Work in Progress, 1991; co-author: (Steve Chapple) Let the Mountains Talk, Let the Rivers Run, 1995; contbr. articles to nat. mags., profl. publs., others; subject video documentary produced for Sta. KCTS, Seattle, shown nationally on PBS; contbr. to U.S. Army mountain manuals, instruction, 1943-45. Participant in planning for 1992 UN Conf. on Environment, Rio de Janiero, 1989-92. Served as 1st lt. with 10th Mountain div. Inf. AUS, 1943-45; maj. Inf.-Res. ret. Decorated Bronze Star; recipient awards Calif. Conservation Coun., 1953, Nat. Parks Assn., 1956, Bklyn. Coll. Libr. Assn., 1970, also Carey-Thomas award, 1964, Paul Bartsch award Audubon Naturalist Soc. of Cen. Atlantic States, 1967, Golden Ark award the Prince of The Netherlands, 1979, Golden Gadfly award Media Alliance, San Francisco, 1984, Rose award World Environment Festival, Ottawa, Can., 1986, Strong Oak award New Renaissance Ctr., 1987, Lewis Mumford award Architects Designers Planners for Social Responsibility, 1991, Robert Marshall award, 1994, Blue Planet prize Asahi Glass Found., Japan, 1998; hon. fellow John Muir Coll., U. Calif., San Diego, 1986; nominated Nobel Peace Prize, 1978, 79, 98. Mem. Nat. Parks and Conservation Assn. (hon.), The Mountaineers (hon.), Appalachian Mountain Club (hon.), Sierra Club (1933—, John Muir award 1977), Am. Alpine Club (hon.). Many first ascents, 70 in Mountain Ranges in Sierra Nevada, 1934-41, 3 in Pinnacles, N.Mon., 1934-35, Shiprock, N. Mex., 1939. Office: Earth Island 300 Broadway St San Francisco CA 94133-4545

BROWER, MAITLAND DIRK, church administrator, writer; b. Emporia, Kans., Sept. 29, 1943; s. Grant Crapo and Doris Ellen (Bayly) B.; m. Cheryl Lynn Nelson, Dec. 30, 1948; Grant, Debbie, Beckie, Anna, David, Lydia. BA in History, Idaho State U., 1970. Specification group mgr. LDS Ch., Salt Lake City, 1976—. With U.S. Army, 1968-70. Mem. Constrn. Specifications Inst. (honorable mention in specification competition 1997). Republican. LDS. Avocation: genealogy. Office: Ch Jesus Christ LDS 50 E North Temple Fl 10 Salt Lake City UT 84150-0002

BROWN, ALAN H., marketing executive; b. Monroe, Mich., Oct. 12, 1938; s. Earl K. Brown and Florence I. (Beabor) Lawwill; m. Judith L. Lawwill, July 23, 1960; children: Marc, Jeff. BS, Miami U., Oxford, Ohio, 1959; MS, San Diego State U., 1963; DBA, Calif. Pacific U., 1992. Bus. instr. Allen Hancock Jr. Coll., Santa Maria, Calif., 1963-64; market rschr. San Diego Union Tribune, 1964-68; v.p. mktg. Hydronic Sys., San Diego, 1968-70; broker Percy Goodwin & Co., San Diego, 1968-70; v.p. real estate Western Home Loan Corp., San Diego, 1970-74; pres. Omega Mktg., Cour d'Alene, Idaho, 1978—. Author: Cannibal Gold, 1996, (screenplays) The Harani Trail, 1997, The Organ Peddler, 1998. Pres. Mission Beach Town Coun., San Diego, 1968-69, 73-74; mem. Mission Beach Task Force, San Diego, 1984. Lt. (j.g.) USNR, 1959-61. Recipient Testimonial award Mission Beach Town Coun., 1970, Writer's award CDA Libr., 1995. Mem. Idaho Writer's Guild. Republican. Avocations: swimming, skiing, hiking. Fax: (208) 667-4640. E-mail: abrown3832@aol.com. Office: Omega Mktg Group 501 Indiana Ave Coeur D Alene ID 83814

BROWN, ANTHONY B., aerospace executive; b. Mpls., Apr. 5, 1922; s. Wayland Hoyt and Adele (Birdsall) B.; m. Mary Alice Ann Anderson, July 28, 1956. BS, Rutgers U., 1949; postgrad. U. So. Calif., 1968-69; PhD, U. Beverly Hills, 1986. Cert. data processing systems profl. Sr. system analyst Thrifty Corp., L.A., 1957-69; system engr. Informatics Gen., Inc., L.A., 1969-73; contract instr. computer software York U., 1970, McGill U., U. [illegible] U., U. Guelph, 1972; sr. system engr. Jet Propulsion Lab., La Canada, Calif., 1974-76; sr. system engr. Informatics Gen., Inc., Anchorage, L.A., Washington, 1976-78; supr. project control Hughes Aircraft Co., L.A., 1978-81; contr. western ops. Space Comms. Co., Redondo Beach, Calif., 1981-88. Author: A Century of Blunders--America's China Policy 1844-1949. Rep. precinct capt., presdl. election, 1964, vol. Reason Found.; chmn. bd. govs. La Brea Vista Townhouses, 1967-68; active numerous animal welfare orgns. Served with Finance Corps, U.S. Army, 1951-57. Decorated Bronze Star. Fellow Brit. Interplanetary Soc.; mem. AAAS, The Planetary Soc., Nature Conservancy, Town Hall of Calif., Assn. Computer Machinery (chpt. sec. 1973-74), Assn. Systems Mgmt., Mensa, Intertel, Armed Forces Communications and Electronics Assn., Assn. Inst. Cert. Computer Profls., Am. Assn. Fin. Profls., Am. Def. Preparedness Assn., Washington Legal Found., Am. Security Council (mem. nat. adv. bd.), Calif. Soc. SAR, Mil. Order World Wars, Aircraft Owners and Pilots Assn., Internat. Platform Assn., Theodore Roosevelt Assn., Res. Officers Assn., Delta Phi Epsilon. Republican. Club: Calif. Yacht Club. Lodges: Masons, Shriners, Nat. Sojourners. Home: 4333 Redwood Ave Marina Del Rey CA 90292-7641

BROWN, ARTHUR CARL, JR., retired minister; b. Stockton, Calif., Dec. 16, 1915; s. Arthur Carl and Maud (Twitchings) B.; m. Inez Lundquist, May 10, 1940 (dec. Aug. 1982); 1 child, Arthur Carl III. BA, Coll. of the Pacific, 1937; MA, San Francisco Theol. Sem., 1939, BD with honors, 1940; postgrad., Stanford U.,, 1949-50. Ordained to ministry Presbyn. Ch., 1940. Pastor Presbyn. Ch., Sedro Woolley, Wash., 1940-44, Community Ch., Santa Clara, Calif., 1944-46; assoc. pastor First Presbyn. Ch., San. Jose, Calif., 1946-49; minister edn. First Presbyn. Ch., Palo Alto, Calif., 1949-51; organizing pastor Covenant Presbyn. Ch., Palo Alto, 1951-74; pastor Trinity Presbyn. Ch., Santa Cruz, Calif., 1974-78; outreach assoc. Los Gatos (Calif.) Presbyn. Ch., 1978-81; commr. to gen. assembly United Presbyn. Ch., 1947, 52, 59; moderator San Jose Presbytery, 1950, chmn. various coms., 1950-78; mem. Synod Golden Gate and Synod of Pacific coms. Synod of Calif., 1947-82; pastor emeritus Covenant Presbyn. Ch. Treas., chmn. fin. com., bd. dirs. Internat. House, Davis, Calif., 1984-90, chmn. nominating com., 1990-96, mem. devel. com., 1991097. Avocations: gardening, sports, study of Greek words in New Testament, writing, family history. Home: 4414 San Ramon Dr Davis CA 95616-5018

BROWN, BAILLIE RUSSELL, health services administrator; b. Olympia, Wash., Sept. 29, 1953; d. Montgomery and Patience (Baker) Russell; m. Harry Silsby Brown, Dec. 6, 1980. Student, St. Martin's Coll., 1970-75; cert. fin. planning for non-profits, U. Calif., Santa Barbara, 1992. Cert. charter optician Opticians Assn. Am., 1975; ophthalmic surg. technician Surg. Office Specialists, 1986. Lic. optician mgr. Cole Nat., Ann Arbor, Mich., 1973-74, Santa Barbara, 1975; lic. optician mgr. Geneau Optical, Santa Barbara, 1976, Robert Cibull, OD, Santa Barbara, 1977-81; med. pub. rels. program officer Direct Relief Internat., Santa Barbara, 1981-85; pub. rels. cons. Santa Barbara Bank & Trust, 1985-89; exec. dir., CFO S.E.E. Internat., Santa Barbara, 1985-97, pres., CEO, 1997—. Author: Doctor, My Eyes Are Running, 1984; contbr. articles to profl. jours. Vol. visual aids cons. Braille Inst., Santa Barbara, 1988-91; vol. health care provider Santa Barbara Sch. Dist., 1990—. Fellow Nat. Acad. Ophthalmology; mem. Optician Assn. Am., Calif. Assn. Ophthalmology, Internat. Assn. Vol. Effort (cert. appreciation 1979), Am. Women for Internat. Understanding (v.p., sec., trustee 1979, cert. appreciation 1981). Republican. Anglican. Avocations: running, scuba diving, piano. Office: SEE Internat 27 C-2 East De La Guerra St Santa Barbara CA 93101

BROWN, CAROL ELIZABETH, management educator; b. Boise, Idaho, Jan. 26, 1950; d. Mason Oliver Brown and Hazel (Metcalf) Henderson; m. Richard Bruce Wodtli, Aug. 16, 1989. BS in Art, U. Wis., 1972; MS in Acctg., U. Oreg., 1977; PhD in Computer Sci., Oreg. State U., 1989. CPA. Bookkeeper Stone Fence Inc., Madison, Wis., 1972-74; staff acct. Baillies, Denson, Erickson & Smith, Madison, 1974-75, Minihan, Kernutt, Stokes & Co., Eugene, 1977-78; instr. Oreg. State U., Corvallis, 1978-89, asst. prof., 1989-92, assoc. prof., 1992—. Assoc. editor Jour. Info. Sys., 1989-92; mem. editl. rev. bd. Internat. Jour. Intelligent Sys. in Acctg., Fin. and Mgmt., 1991—, Internat. Jour. Applied Expert Sys., 1994—; guest editor Expert Sys. With Applications, 1991, 95; contbr. articles to profl. jours. Bd. dirs. United Way of Benton County, Corvallis, 1989-96, sec.-treas., 1993-96; vol. acct., 1982-86. Recipient Outstanding Vol. Svc. award United Way of Benton County, 1986, 93; rsch. grant Oreg. State U., 1988, 90, Scholarship award, 1992, 93; rsch. grant TIAA-CREF, 1990, 91. Mem. IEEE Computer Soc., Am. Acctg. Assn. (program adv. com. 1990-91, artificial intelligence/expert sys. sect., vice chairperson 1991-92, chairperson-elect 1992-93, chairperson 1993-94, Pioneer Svc. award 1994), Am. Assn. Artificial Intelligence, Inst. Mgmt. Accts. (dir. manuscripts Salem, Oreg. area 1990—, bd. dirs. 1990—, Merit cert. 1990-91, Rsch. grantee 1993), Oreg. Soc. CPA (com. mem. 1989-94, vice chmn. computer svcs. com. 1990-91, Recognition cert. for Leadership Excellence 1989-90, Outstanding Svc. award 1990-91), Assn. Computer Machinery, others. Home: 1949 Ingalls Way Eugene OR 97405 Office: Oreg State U Coll Bus 200 Bexell Hall Corvallis OR 97331-8527

BROWN, CAROLYN SMITH, communications educator, consultant; b. Salt Lake City, Aug. 12, 1946; d. Andrew Delbert and Olive (Crane) Smith; m. David Scott Brown, Sept. 10, 1982. BA magna cum laude, U. Utah, 1968, MA, 1972, PhD, 1974. Instr. Salt Lake Ctr., Brigham Young U., Salt Lake City, 1976-78; vis. asst. prof. Brigham Young U., Provo, 1978; asst. prof. Am. Inst. Banking, Salt Lake City, 1977—; prof., chmn. English, communication and gen. edn. depts. Latter Day Saints Bus. Coll., Salt Lake City, 1973—, dean acad. affairs, 1986-96, v.p. for acad. affairs, 1996—; founder, pres. Career Devel. Tng., Salt Lake City, 1979—; cons. in-house seminars 1st Security Realty Svcs., USDA Natural Resource Conservation Svc., Utah Power & Light, Utah Soc. Svcs., Adminstrv. Office of Cts., HUD, Intermountain Health Care, Fidelity Investments, Am. Inst. Banking; mem. NW Assn. Schs. & Colls. Liaison, 1980—, Utah Bus. Coll. Dean's com., 1990—. Author: Writing Letters & Reports That Communicate, 8th edit., 1994; contbr. articles to profl. jours. Demi-soloist Utah Civic Ballet (now Ballet West), Salt Lake City, 1964-68; active Mormon Ch.; C. of C. Bus. Edn. com., 1991-92. Named Tchr. of Month, Salt Lake City Kiwanis, 1981; NDEA fellow, U. Utah, 1972. Mem. Am. Bus. Communications Assn. (lectr. West/N.W. regional chpt. 1987), Delta Kappa Gamma (2d v.p. 1977-79), Lambda Delta Sigma (Outstanding Woman of Yr. 1983), Kappa Kappa Gamma (Outstanding Alumnus in Lit. 1974). Republican. Clubs: Alice Louise Reynolds Literary (Salt Lake City) (v.p. 1978-79, sec. 1985-86). Avocations: swimming, hiking, slide lectures on Israel and literary topics. Office: LDS Bus Coll 411 E South Temple Salt Lake City UT 84111-1302

BROWN, CATHIE, city official; b. Seattle, Mar. 23, 1944; d. G. Warren and Dorothy (Patterson) Cryer; m. Tom Brown, July 1, 1967; children: Amy, James W. BA in Criminology, U. Calif., Berkeley, 1966; MPA, Calif. State U., Hayward, 1985. Juvenile probation officer Santa Clara (Calif.) County, 1967-72; founder, dir. Tri-Valley Haven for Women, Livermore, Calif., 1976-79; planning commr. City of Livermore, 1980-82, city coun. mem., 1982-89; exec. dir. Alameda County Project Intercept, Hayward, 1986-92; dir. Svcs. for Families of Inmates, Pleasanton, Calif., 1981-82; mayor City of Livermore, 1989—; active County Justice System Adv. Group, Oakland, Calif., 1990—; co-founder Tri-Valley Community Fund, Pleasanton. Active Alameda County Mayors' Conf., 1989—; del. Assn. Bay Area Govts., 1982-89; founder Youth For Action, Livermore, 1984-86, Youth Task Force, Livermore, 1989-90. Named Woman of Yr. Calif. State Legislature, 1990. Mem. League Calif. Cities (pres. East Bay div. 1982-89), MPA Alumni Assn. (pres. Calif. State U. chpt. 1989—). Democrat. Avocations: music, racquetball, reading. Home: 1098 Angelica Way Livermore CA 94550-5701*

BROWN, CHESTER D., artist, educator; b. Denver, June 1, 1965; s. Chester and Cecelia Rose (Begay) B. BA, Ft. Lewis Coll., 1989; M of Ednl. Leadership, No. Ariz. U., 1997. Counselor ednl. talent search Colo. State U., Durango, 1989-92; coord. Upward Bound program Pueblo C.C., Cortez, Calif., 1990-95; grad. asst. multicultural student ctr. No. Ariz. U., Flagstaff, 1995-96, grad. asst. Inst. Human Devel., 1996-97; instrnl. specialist Am. Indian Rehab. Rsch. and Tng. Ctr., Flagstaff, 1998—. Mem. parent adv. com. Montezuma County/Ute Mountain, Cortez, Colo., 1992-95. Mem. N.Am. Arnis Assn. (basic instr. 1993—), Internat. Modern Arnis Fedn., Red Mesa Art Coun. Mem. Native Am. Ch. Avocations: martial arts, reading, [illegible] Home: 400 W Maloney Ave [illegible] NM 87301-5216

BROWN, CHRISTOPHER PATRICK, health care administrator, educator; b. Phoenix, June 7, 1961; s. [illegible] B.; m. Tracey Ann Wallenberg, May 23, 1987; 1 child, Ryan Matthew. AA in Biol. Scis., Shasta Coll., Redding, Calif., 1976; AS in Liberal Arts, SUNY, Albany, 1977; grad. Primary Care Assoc. Program, Stanford U., 1978; BA in Community Svcs. Adminstrn., Calif. State U., Chico, 1982; M. in Health Svcs., U. Calif., Davis, 1984. Gen. mgr. Pacific Ambulance Svc., El Cajon, Calif., 1974; primary care assoc. Family Practice, Oregon-Calif., 1978-82; cons. Calif. Health Profls., Chico, 1982-84; bus. ops. mgr. Nature's Arts, Inc., Seattle, 1985-86; instr. North Seattle C.C., 1984-89, program dir., 1986-89; asst. dir. Pacific Med. Clinic North, Seattle, 1990-92; dir. Pacific Med. Clinic Renton (Wash.), Pacific Med. Ctr., 1992-95; dir. ops./physician svcs. St. Luke's Regional Med. Ctr., Boise, Idaho, 1995-97, adminstr. ambulatory care, 1997-98; adminstr. St. Luke's Meridian (Idaho) Med. Ctr., 1997-98; COO, sr. assoc. adminstr. Physician Ptnrs. Inc. and the Medford (Oreg.) Clinic, 1998—. Mem. Butte County Adult Day Care Health Coun., Chico, 1982-84; bd. dirs., pres. Innovative Health Care Svcs., Chico, 1982-84; bd. dirs. Highline W. Seattle Mental Health Ctr., 1985-90, v.p. 1988-90; tech. adv. com. North Seattle C.C., 1992-93; bd. dirs. ARC, 1997-98. Mem. Internat. Platform Assn., Soc. Ambulatory Care Profls., Med. Group Mgmt. Assn., Multispecialty Group Exec. Soc., Accreditation Assn. for Ambulatory Health Care (accreditation surveyor 1996-97). Avocations: gardening, woodworking, church activities. Home: 2687 Hayden Pl Medford OR 97504-5073 Office: Physician Ptnrs Inc Medford Clinic PC 555 Black Oak Dr Medford OR 97504-8311

BROWN, DAVID R., academic administrator. Pres., dir. Art Ctr. Coll. Design, Pasadena, Calif., 1985—. Office: Art Ctr Coll of Design Office of Pres 1700 Lida St Pasadena CA 91103-1924

BROWN, DAVID RICHARD, school system administrator, minister; b. Manhattan, Kans., Oct. 22, 1929; s. Marion Arthur and Dorothy (Bailey) B.; m. Jeanette Christine Phoenix, July 28, 1962; children: David M., Mark, Thomas. BA, U. So. Calif., 1951; MDiv, U. Chgo., 1955; postgrad., U. So. Calif., 1956, 57. Ordained minister, Presbyn. Ch. Assoc. pastor Federated Community Ch., Flagstaff, Ariz., 1957-59; minister of edn. Lakeside Presbyn. Ch., San Francisco, 1959-62; pastor of edn. 1st Presbyn. Ch., Medford, Oreg., 1962-69; pastor 1st Presbyn. Ch., Newark, Calif., 1969-75; founder, pastor Community Presbyn. Ch., Union City, Calif., 1975-89; founder, supt. Christian Heritage Acad., Fremont, Calif., 1984—; organizing pastor New Life Presbyn. Ch., Fremont, 1989—; asst. prof. Chabot Coll., Hayward, Calif., 1975-80; moderator Presbytery of No. Ariz., 1959. Dir. various Shakespearian theatrical prodns., 1982-84 (Thesbian award 1984). Pres. Boys Christian League, L.A., 1953-54, Coconino Assn. for Mental Health, Flagstaff, 1958-59; chaplain Mozumdar YMCA Camp, Crestline, Calif., 1952-56; chmn. Tri-City Citizens Action Com., 1986-90. Recipient plaque KC, 1989. Mem. Rotary (chpt. pres. 1988-89, Paul Harris fellow 1989). Avocations: skiing, stamps, choir, drama. Office: Christian Heritage Acad PO Box 7688 Fremont CA 94537-7688

BROWN, DAVID W., lawyer; b. Seattle, Jan. 29, 1955. Student, Albion Coll.; BS, U. Oreg., 1977, JD, 1980. Bar: Oreg. 1980. Ptnr. Miller, Nash, Wiener, Hager & Carlsen, Portland, Oreg. Mem. Oreg. State Bar. Office: Miller Nash Wiener Hager & Carlsen 111 SW 5th Ave Ste 3500 Portland OR 97204-3699*

BROWN, DON, museum director. Dir. Internat. Wildlife Mus., Tucson, Ariz. Office: Internat Wildlife Mus 4800 W Gates Pass Rd Tucson AZ 85745-9600

BROWN, DONALD MALCOLM, plastic surgeon; b. Nelson, N.Z., May 28, 1945; came to U.S., 1947; s. Donald Roland and Edna M. (McPherson) B.; m. Susan E. Boeing, Sept. 3, 1989. MD, U. B.C., 1970. Diplomate Am. Bd. Otolaryngology and Plastic Surgery. Resident in otolarngology Manhattan Eye and Ear Hosp., N.Y.C., 1976; resident in plastic surgery Columbia U., N.Y.C., 1980; pvt. practice San Francisco, 1981—; vis. prof. plastic surgery U. Liberia, Africa, 1980-81. Mem. AMA, Calif. Med. Assn., San Francisco Med. Assn., Am. Soc. Plastic and Reconstructive Surgery, Am. Soc. Aesthetic Surgery, Pacific Union Club, St. Francis Yacht Club. Avocations: flying helicopters, skiing, wind surfing. Office: 2100 Webster St Ste 429 San Francisco CA 94115-2380

BROWN, DONALD W., banker; b. Mich., Sept. 15, 1955; m. Jennifer H. Brown, Dec. 29, 1979; children: Alexander, Nathaniel. Student, Internat. Christian U., Mitaka, Japan, 1975-76; BA, U. Mich., 1977; M of Internat. Mgmt., Am. Grad. Sch. Inst. Mgmt., Glendale, Ariz., 1982. CFA, Va.; cert. cash mgr., Md. Asst. v.p. Indsl. Bank of Japan, L.A., 1983-88; v.p., 1st v.p. San Paolo Bank, L.A., 1988-94, 1st v.p., gen. mgr., 1994-96, 1st v.p., rep., 1996—; dir. OR Concepts Applied, Whittier, Calif., 1989—. Dir. Murphy Hill Homeowners Assn., Whittier, 1991—. Lt. USN, 1978-81. Mem. Assn. for Investment Mgmt. and Rsch., Treasury Mgmt. Assn. Office: San Paolo Bank 444 S Flower St Ste 4550 Los Angeles CA 90071-2945

BROWN, EDMUND GERALD, JR. (JERRY BROWN), mayor, former governor; b. San Francisco, Apr. 7, 1938; s. Edmund Gerald and Bernice (Layne) B. B.A., U. Calif.-Berkeley, 1961; J.D., Yale U., 1964. Bar: Calif. 1965. Research atty. Calif. Supreme Ct., 1964-65; atty. Tuttle & Taylor, Los Angeles, 1966-69; sec. state Calif., 1970-74; gov. State of Calif., 1975-83; chmn. Calif. Dem. Party, 1989-90; Dem. candidate for Pres. of United States, 1992; mayor Oakland, Calif., 1999—. Trustee Los Angeles Community Colls., 1969. Address: One Frank Ogawa Plaza 1 City Hall Plaza 3rd Flr Oakland CA 94612*

BROWN, GAY WEST, school psychologist; b. L.A., Nov. 20, 1953; d. James Dale and Ola Maye (Daniels) West; m. Lorenzo Hubbard, Nov. 26, 1977 (dec. Feb. 1990); 1 child, Loren Rochelle; m. Fred Lyndle Brown, Jr., Dec. 28, 1992. BA, Calif. State U., Dominguez Hills, 1975; MS, U. So. Calif., 1976; PhD, UCLA, 1991. Lic. ednl. psychologist; cert. sch. psychologist. Student counselor Dignity Ctr. for Drug Abuse, L.A., 1974-76; community health worker Am. Indian Free Clinic, Compton, Calif., 1974-76; student psychologist Martin Luther King Hosp., L.A., 1976-77; counselor aide Washington High Sch., L.A., 1974-77; vocat. counselor Skill Ctr., L.A., 1977-78; sch. psychologist L.A. Unified Sch. Dist., 1978—, tchr., advisor, 1988-90; psychol. asst. Verdugo Hills (Calif.) Mental Health, 1984-85; counselor, coord. Crenshaw High Sch., L.A., 1985-87; part-time instr. Calif. State U., Dominguez Hills, 1996—; asst. behavior sci. cons. Coalition Mental Profls., L.A., 1992-93; psychol. asst. Martin Luther King Hosp., L.A., 1992-93; part-time prof. Calif. State U., L.A., 1994-95. Mem. APA, Nat. Assn. Sch. Psychologists, Calif. Assn. Sch. Psychologists, L.A. Assn. Sch. Psychologists, Assn. Black Psychologists (sec. 1992-93, historian 1995-96), Pan African Scholars Assn., United Tchrs. L.A., Delta Sigma Theta (chair teen lift com. 1994—). Democrat. United Methodist. Avocations: walking, Christian counseling. Office: Sch Mental Health Clinic 439 W 97th St Los Angeles CA 90003-3968

BROWN, GEORGE EDWARD, JR., congressman; b. Holtville, Calif., Mar. 6, 1920; s. George Edward and Bird Alma (Kilgore) B.; m. Marta Macias. BA, UCLA, 1946; grad. fellow, Fund Adult Edn., 1954. Mgmt. cons. Calif., 1957-61; v.p. Monarch Savs. & Loan Assn., Los Angeles, 1960-68; mem. Calif. Assembly from 45th Dist., 1959-62; former mem. 88th-91st congresses from 29th Dist. Calif., 93d Congress from 38th Dist. Calif.; agrl. sci. com. 94th-105th Congresses from 36th (now 42nd) Dist. Calif.; mem. standing com. on agr., chmn. sci. space and tech. com. 94th-101st Congresses from 36th Dist. Calif., 1987; mem. agriculture com., ranking dem. mem. sci. com.; chmn. Office of Tech. Assessment; mem. 106th Congress 42d Dist. Calif.; coll. lectr., radio commentator, 1971. Mem. Calif. Gov.'s Adv. Com. on Housing Problems, 1961-62; mem. Mayor Los Angeles Labor-Mgmt. Com., 1961-62, Councilman, Monterey Park, Calif., 1954-58, mayor, 1955-56; candidate for U.S. Senate, 1970. Served to 2d lt., inf. AUS, World War II. Recipient Chmn.'s award Am. Assn. Engring. Socs., 1993, Ralph Coast [illegible] UCLA, Sci. Policy award MIT, Pub. Svc. award Am. Chem. Soc., others. Mem. Am. Legion, Colton C. of C., Urban League, Internat. Brotherhood Elec. Workers, AFL-CIO, Friends Com. Legislation, Ams. for Dem. Action. Democrat. Methodist. Lodge: Kiwanis. Office: US Ho of Reps 2300 [illegible]

BROWN, GEORGE STEPHEN, physics educator; b. Santa Monica, Calif., June 28, 1945; s. Paul Gordon and Frances Ruth (Moore) B.; m. Nohema Fernandez, Aug. 8, 1981 (div. 1992); 1 child, Sonya; m. Julie Claire Dryden, Mar. 22, 1997. BS, Calif. Inst. Tech., 1967; MS, Cornell U., 1968, PhD, 1973. Mem. tech. staff Bell Labs., Murray Hill, N.J., 1973-77; sr. research assoc. Stanford (Calif.) U., 1977-82, rsch. prof. applied physics, 1982-91; prof. physics U. Calif., Santa Cruz, 1991—, chair dept. physics, 1997—; assoc. dir. Stanford Synchrotron Radiation Lab., Stanford, 1980-91. Mem. editorial bd. Rev. Sci. Instruments, 1983-86; contbr. articles to profl. jours. Fellow Am. Phys. Soc. Avocation: music performance. Home: 404 Village Cir Santa Cruz CA 95060-2461 Office: U Calif Dept Physics Santa Cruz CA 95064

BROWN, GERRI ANN, physical therapist; b. N.Y.C., May 1, 1948; d. S. Stanley and Corinne (Carlin) Schkurman; m. Michael Edward Brown, Oct. 2, 1971. BS in Phys. Therapy, Ithaca Coll., 1969. Registered phys. therapist, Colo., N.Y. Lectr. U. Colo. Med. Sch., Denver, 1970-81; dir. phys. therapy and team facilitator Wheatridge (Colo.) Regional Ctr., 1969-81; phys. therapist Ptnrs. Home Health Care, Lakewood, Colo., 1982-83, Mt. Evans Home Health Care, Evergreen, Colo., 1983-88, Western Home Health, Arvada, Colo., 1988-93, ICON Home Care, Lakewood, 1993-97, Vis. Nurse Assn., Denver, 1995—, 1995—; lectr. U. Colo., Denver, 1970-81, U. No. Colo., Greeley, 1977-81; tchr., cons. ICON Home Care, Lakewood, 1993-97, Western Home Health Care, Arvada, 1988-93, Mt. Evans Health Care, 1983-88, Vis. Nurses Denver, 1996—; chairperson task force State of Colo., Denver, 1972-73. Mem. Citizens for Action, Idledale, Colo., 1975-76. Mem. Am. Phys. Therapy Assn. (sect. on geriatrics and home health care), Hiwan Golf Club. Avocations: golf, travel, music. Home: PO Box 88 Idledale CO 80453-0088

BROWN, H. WILLIAM, urban economist, private banker; b. L.A., Sept. 6, 1933; s. Homer William Brown and Carol Lee (Thompson) Weaver; m. Verlee Nelson, Aug. 1953 (div. 1955); 1 child, Shirlee Dawn; m. Shirley Rom, Jan. 18, 1955 (div. 1962). BA in Pub. Adminstrn., Calif. State U., 1956; MA in Bus. Adminstrn., Western States U., 1983, Phd in Urban Econs., 1984. Pres. Real Estate Econs., Sacramento, 1956-60; dir. spl. projects Resource Agy. Calif., Sacramento, 1960-65; program planning officer U.S. Dept. Housing and Urban Devel., Washington, 1965-66; asst. dir. regional planning U.S. Dept. Commerce, Washington, 1967-69; dir. internat. office Marshall and Stevens, Inc., L.A., 1970-72; vice chmn., CEO Investment Property Econ. Cons., 1972-97; chmn., CEO The Northpoint Investment Group, San Francisco, 1986-97; chmn. Global Adv. Resources, Palo Alto, Calif., 1997—; chmn. Trade and Devel. Ctr. For UN, N.Y. 1983-88, pres. Ctr. for Habitat and Human Settlements, Washington 1977-90. Author: The Changing World of the Real Estate Market Analyst-Appraiser, 1988. Mem. MAI Appraisal Inst., Le Groupe (charge d'affaires, pvt. bankers assn.). Avocation: worldwide people photography. Office: Global Adv Resources 236 Stanford Ctr 130 Palo Alto CA 94304

BROWN, HANK, former senator, university administrator; b. Denver, Feb. 12, 1940; s. Harry W. and Anna M. (Hanks) B.; m. Nana Morrison, Aug. 27, 1967; children: Harry, Christy, Lori. BS, U. Colo., 1961, JD, 1969; LLM, George Washington U., 1986, M in Tax Law, 1986. Bar: Colo. 1969; CPA, 1988. Tax acct. Arthur Andersen, 1967-68; asst. pres. Monfort of Colo., Inc., Greeley, 1969-70; corp. counsel Monfort of Colo., Inc., 1970-71; v.p. Monfort Food Distbg., 1971-72, v.p. corp. devel., 1973-75, v.p. internat. ops., 1975-78, v.p. lamb div., 1978-80; mem. 97th-101st Congresses from Colo. 4th dist., 1981-90; mem. Colo. State Senate, 1972-76, asst. majority leader, 1974-76; U.S. senator from Colo. Washington, 1991-96; co-dir. Ctr. for Pub. Policy and Contemporary Policies, U. Denver, 1997-98; pres. U. No. Colo., Greeley, 1998—; chmn. Fgn. Rel. subcom. Near Ea. and South Asian affairs, Judicorp subcom. on constl. law. With USN, 1962-66. Decorated Air medal, Vietnam Svc. medal, Nat. Defense medal, Naval Unit citation. Republican. Congregationalist. Office: Univ of Northern Colorado Office of the Pres Greeley CO 80639

BROWN, HORACE STUART, county surveyor; b. Derby, Vt., Apr. 6, 1933; s. Horace Stuart and Charlena Etta (Brooks) B.; m. Jaynet Mary Rand, June 20, 1964. Student, U. Vt., 1951-53; BS in Forestry, U. Maine, 1962. Registered profl. land surveyor, Vt., Mont. Forestry aide U.S. Dept. Interior-Bur. Indian Affairs, Glendale, Wash., 1953-55, 57-59; survey cons. Heath Cons., Wellesly Hills, Mass., 1962-64; pvt. practice cons. forester and surveyor Glover, Vt., 1964-73; survey tech. III Missoula County, Mont., 1974; chief of party Missoula County, 1974-86, county surveyor, 1987—; mem. transp. tech. adv. com. Missoula County, 1987—, mem. pk. bd., 1994—. Artwork appeared in mag. Bitterroot, 1980. Active Dem. Party, Missoula, 1986. Avocations: hunting, skiing, fishing, camping, painting. Home: 2000 Eaton St #3 Missoula MT 59801 Office: County Surveyors Office 200 W Broadway Missoula MT 59802

BROWN, JACK EDWARD, lawyer; b. Omaha, Mar. 15, 1927; B.S. with distinction, Northwestern U., 1949; LL.B., Harvard U., 1952. Bar: N.Y. 1954, Ariz. 1959. Law clk. to presiding justice Ariz. Supreme Ct., 1959, U.S. Dist. Ct., Mass., 1952-53; assoc. Cravath, Swaine & Moore, N.Y.C., 1953-59, Evans, Kitchel & Jenckes, Phoenix, 1959-60; sr. ptnr. Brown & Bain, P.A., Phoenix, 1960—; lectr. in field. Pres. Phoenix Jewish Community Ctr., 1963-64; Ariz. region NCCJ, 1969—, nat. del., 1971, vice chmn., 1976-82, chmn., 1983-84; adv. mem. Navajo Tribal Fair Commn., 1971; bd. dirs. Ariz. Acad., 1975—, Friends of KAET-TV, 1975—, Reading is Fundamental, 1976—; trustee Lawyers Com. Civil Rights Under Law, 1976—, Law and Tech. Inst., 1982—. Recipient Disting. Service award Ariz. State U. Sch. Law, 1983. Mem. ABA, Ariz. Bar Assn., Maricopa County Bar Assn., Am. Arbitration Assn. Contbr. articles on law to profl. jours. Office: Brown & Bain PO Box 400 Phoenix AZ 85001-0400*

BROWN, JAMES CARRINGTON, III (BING BROWN), public relations and communications executive; b. Wilmington, Del., May 17, 1939; s. James Carrington Jr. and Virginia Helen (Miller); m. Carol Osman, Nov. 3, 1961. Grad. security mgmt. group, Indsl. Coll. of the Armed Forces; BBS, Ariz. State U., 1984. Accredited, Pub. Rels. Soc. Am., 1988. Newsman, disc jockey, program dir. various radio stas., Ariz., 1955-60; morning news editor Sta. KOY, Phoenix, 1960-61; staff writer, photographer Prescott (Ariz.) Evening Courier, 1961; bus. editor, staff writer, photographer Phoenix Gazette, 1961-65; various communications positions Salt River Project, Phoenix, 1965-89; pres. Carrington Communications, Phoenix, 1989—; cons. comm., freelance writing, photography The Browns, Phoenix, 1965—; pub. info. officer Water Svcs. Dept., City of Phoenix, 1991—; instr. Rio Salado C.C., Phoenix, 1989-93; guest lectr. various colls. and univs., 1975—; prof. Walter Cronkite Sch. Journalism and Telecomm., Ariz. State U., 1990—; exec. prodr., prodr., asst. prodr. various ednl. videos. Bd. dirs. Grand Canyon coun. Boy Scouts Am., 1985-89, mem. adv. coun., 1990—; mem. exec. com. Cmty. Svc. Fund Drive, 1992—; mem. environment com. Phoenix Futures Forum, 1991-93; mem. project adv. com. for Am. Waterworks Assn. Rsch. Found. study of Pub. Involvement Strategies, 1994-95; deacon Meml. Presbyn. Ch., 1980-82, elder, 1985-87; mem. spl. gifts com. United Way, Phoenix, 1986-89. Recipient Golden Eagle award Boy Scouts Am., 1992. Mem. Western Systems Coord. Coun. (chmn. pub. info. com. 1969-89), Ariz. Newspapers Assn. (Billy Goat award, Allied Mem. of Yr. 1985), Ariz. Broadcasters Assn., Western Coalition Arid States (chmn. comm. subcom. 1991-93, chmn. com. and mem. com. 1993—, editor WESTCAS News 1991—, Disting. Performance award 1996), Western Energy Supply and Transmission Assocs. (mem. pub. info. com. 1967-89), Phoenix Press Club (pres. 1982-83), PRSA, Nat. Acad. TV Arts/Scis., Ariz. Zool. Soc., Heard Mus. Anthropology and Primitive Art, Nature Conservancy, Jazz in Ariz., World Affairs Coun., City, County Comms. and Mktg. Assn. (Savvy award for outstanding video 1995—). Republican. Avocations: fly fishing, golf, photography, reading, cooking. Home and Office: Carrington Comm 3734 E Campbell Ave Phoenix AZ 85018-3507 also: Phoenix Water Svcs Dept 200 W Washington St Phoenix AZ 85003-1611

BROWN, JAMES CHANDLER, college administrator; b. Garden City, N.Y., Aug. 5, 1947; s. Harry Chandler and Lillian Marie (Cutter) B. BA, Susquehanna U., Selinsgrove, Pa., 1970; License es Lettres, Geneva U., 1978; postgrad., Stanford U., 1984. Rsch. asst. Geneva (Switzerland) U., 1972-79; asst. Galerie Jan Krugier, Geneva, 1978-81; coord. pubs. So. Oreg. State Coll., Ashland, 1982-84; dir. pubs. So. Oreg. U., 1984—; cons. in field. Author: How to Sharpen Your Publications (brochure, Case award) 1985, College Viewbook (booklet), 1985. Sec. bd. dirs. Schneider Mus. Art, Ashland, 1985-94. Canton of Geneva grantee, 1974-79; awardee, Coun. for Advancement and Support of Edn., 1987-88, 95. Mem. Coun. for Advancement and Support of Edn., Omicron Delta Kappa Leadership Soc. Methodist. Avocations: reading, hiking, cross country skiing, computer programming in hypercard, jogging. Home: 385 Guthrie St Ashland OR 97520-3023 Office: So Oreg Univ 1250 Siskiyou Blvd Ashland OR 97520-5010

BROWN, J'AMY MARONEY, journalist, media relations consultant, investor; b. L.A., Oct. 30, 1945; d. Roland Francis and Jeanne (Wilbur) Maroney; m. James Raphael Brown, Jr., Nov. 5, 1967 (dec. July 1982); children: James Roland Francis, Jeanne Raphael. Attended U. So. Calif., 1963-67. Reporter L.A. Herald Examiner, 1966-67, Lewisville Leader, Dallas, 1980-81; editor First Person Mag., Dallas, 1981-82; journalism dir. Pacific Palisades Sch., L.A., 1983-84; free-lance writer, media cons., 1984-88; press liaison U.S. papal visit, L.A., 1987; media dir., chief media strategist Tellem Inc., 1990-92, comm. cons., issues mgr. 1992—; pres., CEO and owner PRformance Group Comm., 1995—; auction chmn. Assn. Pub. Broadcasting, Houston, 1974, 75; vice chmn. Dallas Arts Council, 1976-80; vice chmn. Met. March of Dimes, Dallas, 1980-82; del. Dallas Council PTAs, 1976-80; bd. dirs. Santa Barbara City Coll. Bus. and Industry Coun.; mem. core-coun. Santa Barbara Coun. on Self-Esteem; coord. specialist World Cup Soccer Organizing Com. Recipient UPI Editors award for investigative reporting, 1981. Mem. NAFE, Pub. Rels. Soc. Am. (accredited), Women Meeting Women, Women in Comm., Am. Bus. Women's Assn., Santa Barbara C. of C. (media com.). Republican. Roman Catholic. Home: 1143 High Rd Santa Barbara CA 93108-2430

BROWN, JANICE ANNE, political organization executive; b. Nov. 13, 1942; d. Rexford S. and Helen L. (Stickel) B.; divorced; 1 child, Kevin Scott Carey. Asst. mgr. front desk Stratosphere Hotel and Casino, Las Vegas. Mem. Carson City Dem. Ctrl. Com., Nev. Dem. State Ctrl. Com., 1986—; mem., treas. Clark County (Nev.) Dem. Ctrl. Com.; bd. dirs. Nev. Common Cause, 1988-94. Mem. Womens Polit. Caucus, Carson City Dem. Women's Club (pres. 1986-89), Clark County Women's Club. Roman Catholic. Office: 1785 E Sahara # 496 Las Vegas NV 89108-2357

BROWN, JANICE ROGERS, state supreme court justice. Assoc. justice Calif. Supreme Ct., San Francisco. Office: Calif Supreme Ct 350 McAllister St San Francisco CA 94102-3600

BROWN, JERRY See BROWN, EDMUND GERALD, JR.

BROWN, JOSEPH E., landscape architecture executive; b. 1947. BA, Cath. U., 1970; M in Landscape Architecture and Urban Design, Harvard U., 1972. With Edaw, Inc., San Francisco, 1973—, now pres. Office: Edaw Inc 753 Davis St San Francisco CA 94111*

BROWN, KATE, state legislator; b. Torrejon de Ardoth, Spain, 1960. BA, U. Colo.; JD, Lewis and Clark Northwestern. Mem. Oreg. Ho. of Reps., 1991-96, Oreg. Senate, 1996—; atty. Democrat. Address: PO Box 82699 Portland OR 97282-0699 Office: Oreg State Senate State Capitol 5323 State Capitol Salem OR 97310

BROWN, KATHAN, publisher of artists' etchings and woodcuts; b. N.Y.C., Apr. 23, 1935; d. Elwood Stanley and Clarissa Brown; m. Jeryl Louis Parker, 1960 (div. 1965); 1 child, Kevin Powis Parker; m. Thomas Robert Marioni, June 14, 1983. BA, Antioch Coll., 1958; MFA, Calif. Coll. Arts and Crafts, Oakland, 1962, DFA (hon.), 1985; DFA (hon.), San Francisco Art Inst., 1990. Founder, dir. Crown Point Press, San Francisco, 1962—. Author: Ink, Paper, Metal, Wood--Painters and Sculptors at Crown Point Press, 1996. Democrat. Office: Crown Point Press 20 Hawthorne St San Francisco CA 94105-3902

BROWN, KEITH LAPHAM, retired ambassador; b. Sterling, Ill., June 18, 1925; s. Lloyd Heman and Marguerite (Briggs) B.; m. Carol Louise Liebmann, Oct. 1, 1949; children: Susan, Briggs (dec.), Linda, Benjamin. Student, U. Ill., 1943-44, Northwestern U., 1946-47; LLB, U. Tex., 1949. Bar: Tex., Okla., Colo. Assoc. Lang, Byrd, Cross & Ladon, San Antonio, 1949-55; v.p., gen. counsel Caulkins Oil Co., Oklahoma City, 1955-70, Denver, 1955-70; founder, developer Vail Assocs., Colo., 1962; pres. Brown Investment Corp., Denver, 1970-87; developer Colo. State Bank Bldg., Denver, 1971; amb. to Lesotho Dept. State, 1982-84; amb. to Denmark Dept. State, Copenhagen, 1988-92; ret., 1992; chmn. Brown Investment Corp., Denver, 1993—. Chmn. Rep. Nat. Fin. Com., 1985-88; hon. trustee, past pres. bd. Colo. Acad. Served with USN, 1943-46. Mem. Denver Country Club, San Antonio Country Club, Univ. Club, Bohemian Club. Presbyterian. Address: PO Box 1172 Edwards CO 81632-1172 also: 11 Auburn Pl San Antonio TX 78209-4739 Office: 1490 Colo State Bank Bldg 1600 Broadway Denver CO 80202-4927

BROWN, LESTER B., social work educator; b. Whitmire, S.C., Jan. 11, 1943; s. William Barney and Minnie Eugenia (Vaughn) B. AB in Psychology, U. Chgo., 1969, AM in Social Work, 1971, PhD in Social Treatment, 1980. Sr. child care counselor, therapist Nicholas J. Pritzker Ctr. and Hosp., Chgo., 1964-68, 69; social worker I, Ill. Dept. Children and Family Services, Chgo., 1967-70, social worker II, 1971; group homes social worker Jewish Children's Bur., Chgo., 1971-73; social worker, field instr. Jackson Park Hosp., Chgo., 1973, clin. dir., 1973-74, cons., 1975-77; cons. SUNY-Albany, 1981, asst. prof. social work, chmn. under-grad. social welfare program, 1981-86; prof. social work Wayne State U., 1986-89; assoc. prof. social work Calif. State U., Long Beach, 1989-95, prof. social work and Am. Indian studies, dir. Am. Indian studies, 1995—; lectr. U. Wis.-Milw., 1977-78, instr., 1978-70; lectr. U. Chgo., 1977-78; guest lectr. Boston Coll., 1981; cons., presenter in field. Author: Two Spirit People: American Indian Lesbian Women and Gay Men, 1997, Aging Gay Men, 1997; contbr. articles to profl. jours., chpts. to books; mem. editl. bd. Health Care Mgmt. Rev., 1981-84. Condr. workshops on ethnic sensitive work Pittsfield Sch. Dist., Mass., 1984; participant workshops on mental health and child welfare; bd. dirs. Capital Dist. Travelers Aid Soc., 1983-86; mem. com. Urban League. Grantee Sch. Social Welfare, 1982, SUNY, 1981, U.S. Dept. HHS, 1981. Mem. NASW, Acad. Cert. Social Workers, Coun. Social Work Edn. Democrat. Avocation: baking/cooking. Office: Calif State Univ Long Beach Am Indian Studies and Social Work 1250 N Bellflower Blvd Long Beach CA 90840-0006

BROWN, LILLIAN ERIKSEN, retired nursing administrator, consultant; b. Seattle, Feb. 7, 1921; d. Peter Louis and Lena (Lien) Eriksen; m. Jan. 21, 1942 (div. Nov. 1963); children: Patricia Lee, Michael Gregory, Kevin William. Student, U. Calif., Berkeley, 1939-40; diploma, St. Luke's Hosp. Sch. Nursing, San Francisco, 1943; AB, Calif. State U., San Francisco, 1952; MPA, U. So. Calif., 1975. RN, Calif. Pub. health nurse San Francisco Dept. Health, 1946-50; asst. dir. nursing San Francisco Gen. Hosp., 1950-56; dir. nursing Weimar (Calif.) Med. Ctr., 1956-62, Orange County Med. Ctr., Orange, Calif., 1962-76; assoc. dir. hosp. and clins., dir. nursing, lectr. U. Calif. Med. Ctr., Irvine, 1976-82; assoc. hosp. adminstr. King Khalid Eye Specialist Hosp., Riyadh, Saudi Arabia, 1982-86; cons. AMI-Saudi Arabia Ltd., Jeddah, 1986-90; chmn. Western Teaching Hosp. Coun. Dirs. Nursing, 1972-75, 80-81; mem. planning project com. Calif. Dept. Rehab., 1967-69, mem. adv. com., 1970-73; mem. ad hoc president's com. on hosp. governance U. Calif., 1981-82; pres. dirs. nursing coun. Hosp. Coun. So. Calif., 1972-74, mem. pers. practices com., 1976-78, 80-83, area rep., 1975-82; mem. dept. nursing adv. com. to establish baccalaureate program U. So. Calif., 1980-82; mem. adv. bd. various coll. nursing programs. Contbr. articles to profl. jours. Sec. Olive (Calif.) Little League, 1967-72; mem. com. on emergency med. svcs. Orange County Health Planning Coun., 1977-78, mem. health promotion task force, 1978-79. 2d lt. Nurse Corps, U.S. Army, 1944-45. Recipient Lauds and Laurels award U. Calif., Irvine, 1981. Fellow Am. Acad. Nurses; mem. ANA (cert. nurse adminstr. advanced), Nat. League for Nursing, APHA, Am. Orgn. Nurse Execs., Nat. Critical Care Inst. Edn., Calif. Nurses Assn. (Lillian E. Brown award named in her honor 1989), Calif. Orgn. for Nurse Execs. (hon.), Calif. Soc. for Nursing Svc. Adminstr., NOW. Republican. Avocations: travel, stamp collecting. Home: 1806 N Nordic Pl Orange CA 92865-4637

BROWN, LILLIE MCFALL, elementary school principal; b. Feb. 29; d. Clayton and Septertee (Dewberry) McFall; m. Charles Brown, Oct. 4, 1958; 1 child, Eric McFall. BA in Home Econ., Sci., Langston Univ., 1956; MA in Spl. Edn., Chgo. Tchrs. Coll., 1964; MA in Adminstrn., Seattle Univ., 1976. Home econ. tchr. Altue (Okla.) Separate Pub. Schs., 1955-56, first grade tchr., 1956-57, fourth grade tchr., 1957-60; middle sch. tchr. Chgo. Pub. Sch.s, 1960-64; spl. edn. primary tchr. Seattle Pub. Schs., 1966-67, spl. edn. intermediate tchr., 1967-68, program coord., 1968-71, elem. asst. prin., 1971-76, elem. prin., 1976—; Mem. Project READ, Seattle, 1968. Contbr. articles to profl. jours. Treas. African Am. Alliance, 1980—; historian Wash. Alliance Black Sch. Educators, 1991—; vol. Olympic Games, Seattle, 1990; participant First African-African Am. Summit, Ibidijan, Cote d'Ivoire, 1991-92; mem. rsch. bd. advisors Am. Biog. Inst., 1995—. Sears Found. grantee, 1967; recipient Disting. Alumni award Nat. Assn. for Equal Opportunity in Higher Edn., 1997. Mem. NAACP, Nat. Assn. Elem. Sch. Prins., Assn. Wash. Sch. Prins., Elem. Prins. Assn. Seattle Pub. Schs., Prins. Assn. Wash. State, Prin. Assn. Seattle Pub. Schs., Ednl. Leadership, Phi Delta Kappa, Kappa Delta Pi, Delta Sigma Theta. Democrat. Baptist. Avocations: swimming, dance, bicycling, travel, reading. Home: 2736 34th Ave S Seattle WA 98144-5561

BROWN, LINDA JEAN, nursing administrator; b. Pana, Ill., Mar. 13, 1947; d. William H. and Meribah J. (Wardall) Laughlin; m. Robert W. Brown, Aug. 25, 1968; children: William H., Jeffrey A. RN, Decatur (Ill.) Meml. Hosp. Sch. Nursing, 1969; BS, Millikin U., 1969. RN, Colo.; cert. Profl. Healthcare Quality, Colo. Dir. quality assurance, utilization rev. St. Vincent Meml. Hosp., Taylorville, Ill., 1975-81, Cedar Springs Hosp., Colorado Springs, Colo., 1982-89; dir. quality assurance Ft. Morgan (Colo.) Community Hosp., 1989-90; dir. nursing Bethesda Care Ctr., Paonia, Colo., 1990-91; asst. adminstr. Mountain Crest Hosp., Ft. Collins, Colo., 1991-95; adminstr. First Am. Home Care, Denver, 1995—; PRN cons., Brim & Assocs., Portland, Oreg., 1989-90, conf. speaker, 1990; PRN cons. Horizon Mental Health Svcs., Denton, Tex., 1992; cons. Meritcare, Pitts., 1990. Author: (with others) Nurse Clinician Pocket Manual: Nursing Diagnosis, Care Planning and Documentation, 1989. Mem. Colo. Nurse Exec. Assn. Home: 12079 Forest St Denver CO 80241-3241

BROWN, LINDA M., elementary education educator; b. Alton, Ill., Oct. 13, 1951; d. James E. and Virginia A. (Holm) Meyers; m. Michael C. Brown, Dec. 28, 1974; 1 child, Emilie Lynne. BS in Edn., Ill. State U., Normal, 1974; MAT, Webster U., Kansas City, Mo., 1984. Cert. in gifted edn. Tchr. grades 1-8 Loretto Sch., Kansas City; tchr. 5th and 6th grades Pembroke-Hill, Kansas City; tchr. 5th and 6th grades Center Schs., Kansas City, tchr. gifted and talented; computer tchr. K-8 Montesorri Sch., Lake Forest, Calif. Recipient Bus. and Edn. Working Together award Joliet C. of C. Mem. Assn. for Supervision and Curriculum Devel.

BROWN, MARK STEVEN, medical physicist; b. Denver, July 12, 1955; s. Clarence William and Gail Margaret (Farthing) B.; m. Mary Linda Avery, Oct. 9, 1988 (div. July 1995). Student, Northwestern U., 1973-74; BS, Colo. State U., 1977; PhD in Phys. Chemistry, U. Utah, 1984. GE postdoctoral fellow Yale U. Sch. Medicine, New Haven, 1984-86, assoc. rsch. scientist, 1986-87; rsch. asst. prof. U. N.Mex. Sch. Medicine, Albuquerque, 1987-89; med. physicist Swedish Med. Ctr. Porter Meml. Hosp., Englewood, Colo., 1989-92; instr. C.C. Denver, Denver, 1990, 91; asst. clin. prof. radiology U. Colo. Sch. Medicine, Denver, 1991-92, asst. prof. radiology, 1992-96; clin. physicist Elscint MR Inc., Ft. Collins, Colo., 1997-98; faculty dept. chemistry Met. State Coll. Denver, 1998—; cons. InVivo Metrics, 1996-97, The Transinformics Group, 1996-97. Author: (with others) NMR Relaxation in Tissues, 1986; contbr. articles to profl. jours. Mem. Am. Chem. Soc., Internat. Soc. Magnetic Resonance In Medicine. Avocations: lead guitar and vocals for Otis T. & the Hammers and Ace Butler and the Aces, skiing, swimming. Home: 971 S Dahlia St #102 Denver CO 80246

BROWN, MARTA MACÍAS, legislative staff member, executive assistant; b. San Bernardino, Calif., Nov. 29, 1944; m. George E. Brown Jr., Mar. 27, 1989. BA, Calif. State U., San Bernardino, 1970; postgrad., U. Calif., Riverside, 1971. Publ., editor El Chicano Cmty. Newspaper, San Bernardino, 1968-75; cmty. edn. specialist human resources agy. County of San Bernardino, 1972-73, dir. of info. and referral svcs., 1973-75; student affirmative action officer U. Calif., Riverside, 1975-80; exec. asst., dist. press sec. to Congressman George Brown, Calif., 1980—; bd. dirs. Casa Ramona Inc., San Bernardino, Ramona Sr. Complex, San Bernardino. Mem. Senator Barbara Boxer's judicial appts. com., 1992—; adv. bd., sponsor, Peacebuilders, 1994—; mem. Calif. Dem. Party Ctrl. Com., 1994—, family preservation planning com. County of San Bernardino, 1995—. U. Calif. grad. fellow, 1970. Mem. LWV, Democratic Spouses, Kiwanis (bd. dirs. greater San Bernardino chpt. 1990—). Roman Catholic. Avocation: water gardens. Home: 873 Bernard Way San Bernardino CA 92404-2413 Office: c/o Congressman George E Brown Jr 2300 Rayburn HOB Washington DC 20515

BROWN, MARVIN LEE, minister; b. Birmingham, Ala., Nov. 11, 1933; s. Thomas Lee and Ruth (Myers) B.; m. Felisa Llanes Regner, Nov. 30, 1961 (div. 1987); 1 child, Viola Lee Brown Freeman. BA, Calif. Bapt. Coll., Riverside, 1980; M in Black Ch. Studies, Ecumenical Theology Ctr., L.A., 1983; MDiv, Am. Bapt. Sem., Berkeley, Calif., 1983; postgrad., Mt. Zion Bible Sem., Sacramento, 1990—. Ordained to ministry Bapt. Ch., 1983; Calif. (emergency) teaching credentials. Assoc. min. Temple Missionary Bapt. Ch., San Bernardino, Calif., 1976-79; asst. pastor New Hope Missionary Bapt. Ch., San Bernardino, 1980-84, pastor protem, 1984-85; sr. pastor First Bapt. Ch., Perris, Calif., 1987—; pub. rels. officer Interdenominational Mins. Alliance, Perris, 1988—; enlisted USAF, 1953, ret., 1975; pres. Interdenominational Mins. Alliance, San Bernardino, 1985-87; dist. missionary Tri County Dist. Assn., Calif., 1985-88; pres. Congress Christian Edn. Tri County, 1988—; founder, pres. Perris Valley Sch. Theology, 1988—; pres. Perris Valley Police Clergy, 1988—. Dir. edn. A. Philip Randolph Inst., San Bernardino, 1983-87; chmn. Westside Leadership Coalition, San Bernardino, 1985-87; pres. NAACP Br. #1145, Perris, 1989—. Named Pastor of Yr. Tri County Dist. Assn., So. Calif., 1990. Democrat. Home: P O Box 1381 210 E 5th St Perris CA 92570-2402 Office: 1st Bapt Ch PO Box 1399 277 E 5th St Perris CA 92570-2401

BROWN, MICHAEL A., computer hardware company executive; b. 1958. BA in Econs., Harvard U.; MBA, Stanford U. Rsch. assoc. Braxton Assocs., strategic planning cons., 1982-84; various mktg. positions Quantum Corp., Milpitas, Calif., 1984-89, dir. product mktg., 1989-90, v.p. mktg., 1990-92, exec. v.p. responsible for hard drive bus., 1992-93, COO, 1993, pres. desktop and portable storage group, 1993-95, CEO, 1995—, also chmn. Office: Quantum Corp 500 McCarthy Blvd Milpitas CA 95035*

BROWN, MICHAEL GORDON, design and real estate consultant, writer; b. Peoria, Ill., Dec. 6, 1943; s. M.A. and Helen Louise (Norris) B.; m. Jane Wiseman, Dec. 26, 1969 (div. June 1977); 1 child, Robert Anthony; m. Jane Kruizenga Schade, Oct. 12, 1986. BS, U. Ill., 1970; MBA, U. Pa., 1981; MS in Arch., U. London, 1982. Mgmt. cons. Phila., 1975-77; designer, office mgr. Skidmore Owings and Merrill, Chgo., 1978-80; project arch. Douglas Schroeder Assoc., Chgo., 1980-81; asst. prof. Sch. Arch., Ill. Inst. Tech., Chgo., 1983-84; assoc. prof. Sch. Arch., Ariz. State U., Tempe, 1984-87; assoc. dean Sch. Arch., U. Colo., Denver, 1987-88; prin. Space Analytics, LLC, Denver, 1988—; planner Planning Svcs., Inc., New Orleans, 1966-68; planning adv. Ill. Dept. Local Govt., Springfield, 1970-71; program planner Phila. Urban Coalition, Phila., 1971-72; assoc. Camil Assocs., Phila., 1972-73; Cass Gilbert vis. lectr. U. Minn. Coll. Arch., 1998. Columnist Arch. and Urban Design, Denver Bus. Jour., 1993—; contbr. articles to profl. jours. Program chair, bd. dirs. MIT Forum Colo., Denver, 1989-93; treas., sec., bd. dirs. City Club Denver, 1995-97; trustee Denver Found. for Agrl., 1998—. With USAFR, 1963-67. Mem. Am. Real Estate Soc. Avocations: Irish Wolfhounds, skiing, fencing. Office: Space Analytics LLC 1315 Milwaukee St Ste 100 Denver CO 80206

BROWN, PAMELA SUE, accountant; b. Inglewood, Calif., Sept. 25, 1959; d. Bruce Kellner and Joyce (Wixom) B.; m. Victor Stanford Frake, Aug. 30, 1986; children: Emily Anne, Katie Nicole. AA, El Camino Coll., 1979; BS, Calif. State U., Long Beach, 1981. CPA, Calif. Staff acct. Richard H. O'Hara & Co., CPA, City of Industry, Calif., 1982-87; tax mgr. Fagan, Stiles

& Co., CPA, Long Beach, Calif., 1987-88; pub. acct. Pamela Sue Brown, CPA, Long Beach, Calif., 1988—. Vol. Children's Miracle Network Telethon, Anaheim, Calif., 1988-89, Vol. Income Tax Assistance Program, Torrance, Calif., 1981. Mem. Am. Soc. Women Accts. (pres.-elect 1984-85, pres. 1985-87), Inst. Mgmt. Accts. (com. chairperson), Calif. Soc. CPAs, Long Beach Area C. of C. Avocations: bicycling, cooking, baking, skiing, tennis. Office: 263 Belmont Ave Long Beach CA 90803-1523

BROWN, PATRICIA DONNELLY, software industry executive; b. Plainfield, N.J., Sept. 6, 1954; d. Vincent Joseph and Rita Joan (Carroll) Donnelly; m. Douglas P. Brown, Oct. 17, 1986; children: Douglas, Christopher. BA in Liberal Arts, Rosemont Coll., 1978. Sales rep. Control Data Corp., Phila., 1978-81; dir. mktg. Columbia Software, Bryn Mawr, Pa., 1981-82; dir. tech. support Cullinet Software, Westwood, Mass., 1982-89; dir. engring. AT&T GIS/Teradata, San Diego, L.A., 1989-95; v.p. AT&T GIS, San Diego, 1995-96; v.p. strategic relationships HNC Software, San Diego, 1996-97, v.p. product mgmt. and software devel., 1998—. Vol. San Diego Urban League, 1994-95, Jackie Robinson YMCA, San Diego, 1994-95; exec. sponsor AT&T Alliance, 1994-96. Republican. Unitarian Universalist. Avocations: computers, skiing, hiking, reading.

BROWN, PAUL FREMONT, aerospace engineer, educator; b. Osage, Iowa, Mar. 10, 1921; s. Charles Fremont and Florence Alma (Olson) B.; m. Alice Marie Culver, Dec. 5, 1943; children—Diane, Darrell, Judith, Jana. BA in Edn. and Natural Sci., Dickinson State Coll., 1942; BS in Mech. Engring., U. Wash., 1948; MS in Cybernetic Systems, San Jose State U., 1971. Profl. quality engr., Calif., 1978; cert. reliability engr., Am. Soc. Quality Control, 1976. Test engr., supr. Boeing Aircraft Corp., Seattle, 1948-56; design specialist, propulsion systems, Lockheed Missiles and Space Co., Sunnyvale, Calif., 1956-59; supr. system effectiveness, 1959-66, staff engr., 1966-76, mgr. product assurance Hubble Space Telescope Program, 1976-83; v.p. research, devel. Gen. Agriponics Inc. of Hawaii, 1971-76; owner Diversatek Engring. and Product Assurance Conss., 1983—; coll. instr., lectr., San Jose State U. Active in United Presbyn. Ch., 1965—; scoutmaster, Boy Scouts Am., 1963-65. Served to 1st lt., USAF, 1943-46. Recipient awards for tech. papers, Lockheed Missiles and Space Co., 1973-75. Mem. Am. Soc. Quality Control, AIAA. Clubs: Toastmasters (Sunnyvale, Calif.), Calif. Writers' (pres. South Bay br. 1993-94). Author: From Here to Retirement, 1988; contbr. articles to profl. jours. Home and Office: 19608 Braemar Dr Saratoga CA 95070-5046

BROWN, RAYNER, composer, educator, performer; b. Des Moines, Feb. 23, 1912; s. Frank O. and Gayl (Hoskinson) B.; m. Barbara Patrick Smith; children: Zachary, Marthella. MusB, U. So. Calif, 1938, MusM, 1947. Prof. organ, composition Biola U., La Mirada, Calif., 1950-77, prof. emeritus, 1977—. Composer: Symphony No. 1, 1952, Symphony No. 2, 1957, Symphony No. 3, 1958, Symphony No. 4, 1980, Symphony No. 5, 1982, Concerto for Organ and Orch., 1959, Concerto for Flute and Orch., 1980, Concerto for Trombone and Orch., 1981, Concerto for Clarinet and Orch., 1984, Concerto for Violin, Harp and Orch., 1987, Concerto for Organ Duet and Orch., 1989, Cantata The Son of Zechariah, 1990, Sonata for Harpsichord and Organ, 1990, Sonata for Organ Duet and Brass Quintet, 1990, Sonata for Saxophone and Organ, 1991, Four Sonatas for Organ, 1991-93, Piano Sonata No. 4, 1991, Cantata True Simplicity for Chorus and Orchestra, 1992, Cantata Letania de Nuestro Señor Don Quijote for Chorus and Brass Choir, 1993, Concerto for Cello and Orch., 1995, 13 Preludes for Piano, 1995, Sonatina for Two Pianos, 1995, Zodilev for Piano, 1995, Sonata for Four Flutes and Organ, 1996, Six Bergen Pieces for Organ, 1996, Quing for Organ, 1996, Phantasie for Organ, 1997, Sonata for Viola and 2 Pianos, 1997, Sonata No. 3 for Two Pianos, 1997, Sketches 1998 for Organ, 1998, Children's Song for Organ and Children's Choir, 1998, numerous sonatas for organ, 1958-87, many chamber works; rec. artist 9 albums. Recipient numerous awards ASCAP; grantee Ford Found. Mem. Am. Guild Organists (dean, chmn.), Nat. Art Assn., Sigma Alpha Iota. Home: 2423 Panorama Ter Los Angeles CA 90039-2537

BROWN, ROBERT MUNRO, museum director; b. Riverside, N.J., Mar. 4, 1952; s. James Wendell and Janet Elizabeth (Munro) B.; m. Mary Ann Noel, June, 1973 (div. 1977); m. Claudia Leslie Haskell, Jan. 14, 1978. BA in Polit. Sci. cum laude, Ursinus Coll., 1973; MA in Social Scis., Rivier Coll., 1978; PhD in Early Am. History, U. N.H., 1983. Grad. asst. dept. history U. N.H., Durham, 1979-83, instr., 1983-84; site curator T.C. Steele State Hist. Site Ind. State Mus. System, Nashville, Ind., 1984-91; exec. dir. Hist. Mus. at Ft. Missoula, Mont., 1991—; hist. interpreter Strawberry Banke, Portsmouth, N.H., 1980-83; instr. Rivier Coll., Nashua, N.H., 1986-91, N.H. Coll., Nashua and Salem, 1986-91; supr. pub. programs Mus. Am. Textile History, North Andover, Mass., 1985-91; sec.-treas. Western Mont. Heritage Ctr./No. Rockies Heritage Ctr., 1992-93; mem. grad. com. U. Mont., 1993; mem. steering com. Ft. Missoula, 1993; reviewer Inst. Mus. Svcs., 1993, 94, 95, 97, 98; reviewer Am. Assn. Mus.-Mus. Asessment Programs, 1997—; mem. Mont. Com. of the Humanities Spkrs. Bur., 1995—; lectr., presenter, chair panels in field. Contbr. articles to profl. jours. Trustee Historic Harrisville, N.H., 1989-91; bd. dirs. United Peoples Found., 1991-93, v.p., 1993; mem. planning com. Western Mont. Heritage Ctr., 1991, U. Mont. Centennial Celebration, 1992, Leadership Missoula, 1992; active open space, parks and resource planning and mgmt. project team City of Missoula, 1993; mem. blue ribbon task force Five Valleys Luth. Retirement Community Planning Com., 1994. Scholar U. N.H., 1979-83, rsch. grantee, 1982; grantee Mass. Coun. on Arts and Humanities, 1986, 87, 88, Int. Mus. Svcs., 1988, 89, 90, 91, 93, 95, 97, AT&T, 1988, Am. Wool Coun., 1988, BayBank, 1989, Am. Yarn Assn., 1989, North Andover Arts Lottery Coun., 1989, 90, Mass. Cultural Coun., 1990, Greater Lawrence Cmty. Found., 1991, Mass. Arts Lottery Coun., 1991, Gallery Assn. for Greater Art, 1991, 92, 94, 95, 96, 97, 98, Mont. Com. for Humanities, 1991, 92, 93, 94, 95, 96, 97, 98, Sinclair Oil Co., 1991, Mont. Rail Link, 1992, 98, U. Mont. Found., 1992, Pepsi-Cola Co., 1992, 93, 94, 95, 96, 97, Coca-Cola Bottling Co., 1998, Cmty. Med. Ctr., 1999, St. Patrick Hosp., 1999, U.S. WEST Found., 1992, 95, The Missoulian, 1992, 95, Champion Internat., 1992, Mont. Cultural Trust, 1993, 95, 97, Missoula Rotary, 1993, Tex. Mus. Assn., 1993, Inst. Mus. Svcs., 1993, 95, Zip Beverage Co., 1994, Bitterroot Motors, 1994, 95, 96, 97, 98, Grizzly Hackle, 1994, University Motors, 1995, 96, Earl's Distributing, 1996, Norwest Bank, 1996, 97, 98; Kellogg Found. fellow, 1987. Mem. Am. Assn. Mus., Am. Assn. State and Local History (state membership rep. 1996-98), Am. Hist. Assn., Assn. Records Mgrs. and Adminstrs. (charter Big Sky chpt. 1992-94), Mont. Hist. Soc., Mus. Assn. Mont. (panelist 1994), Western Mont. Fundraisers Assn. (charter 1991, v.p. 1993-95, pres. 1995-97), Mtn. Plains Mus. Assn. (Mont. state rep. 1995-97, ann. meeting local arrangements chair 1997, chmn. scholarship com. 1998, 99, sec. 1998—), Greater Boston Mus. Educator's Roundtable (steering com. 1988-90), Masons (Missoula chpt.), Kiwanis (Sentinel chpt.), Phi Alpha Theta (Psi Pi chpt.). Democrat. Avocations: canoeing, cross-country skiing, snowshoeing. Home: 216 Woodworth Ave Missoula MT 59801-6050 Office: Hist Mus at Ft Missoula Ft Missoula Bldg 322 Missoula MT 59801

BROWN, RONALD LAMING, lawyer; b. Springfield, Mass., Aug. 26, 1944; s. Douglas Seaton and Elizabeth Ruth (Stover) B.; m. Barbara Jo Roesler Moher, June 13, 1967 (div. Mar., 1987); children: Kimberly Lynn, Kathryn Jo, Karen Elizabeth, Kristine Ann, John Paul; m. Susan Janet Toth, Jan. 2, 1988; 1 child, Megan Christina. Chapman Coll., 1968-70; JD, Creighton U., 1972. Bar: Neb. 1973, U.S. Dist. Ct. Neb. 1973, U.S. Ct. Appeals (8th cir.) 1974, U.S. Dist. Ct. Wyo. 1974, U.S. Ct. Appeals (10th cir.) 1976, Colo. 1987, U.S. Dist. Ct. Colo. 1987. 2d v.p., comml. loan counsel Omaha Nat. Bank, Omaha, 1973-74; prosecuting atty. Natrona County Atty., Casper, Wyo., 1974-75; partner Brown, Drew, Apostolos, Massey & Sullivan, Casper, Wyo., 1975-83; shareholder Burke & Brown, Casper, Wyo., 1983-86; pvt. practice Casper, Wyo., 1986-88, Ft. Collins, Colo., 1987—; bd. dirs. Tooke Internat., Inc.; trustee Brown Investment Trust, Ventura, Calif., 1996—; lectr. Casper (Wyo.) Col., 1980. Mem. sch. bd. St. Anthony's Sch., Casper, Wyo., 1979-82, Ft. Collins (Colo.) Connections, 1995—. Sgt. USMC, 1964-68. Mem. Neb. Bar Assn., Wyo. Bar Assn., Colo. Bar Assn. Republican. Avocations: golf, motor cycling, auto restoration, reading, home repair. Home: 1400 Wildwood Rd Fort Collins [illegible] Fort Collins CO 80521-2864

BROWN, RONALD MALCOLM, engineering corporation executive; b. Hot Springs, S.D., Feb. 21, 1938; s. George Malcolm and Cleo Lavonne (Plumb) B.; m. Sharon Ida Brown, Nov. 14, 1964 (div. Apr. 1974); children: Michael, Troy, George, Curtis, Lisa, Brittney. AA, Southwestern Coll., 1970; BA, Chapman Coll., 1978. Commd. USN, 1956, advanced through grades to master chief, 1973, ret., 1978; engring. mgr. Beckman Inst., Fullerton, Calif., 1978-82; mech. engring. br. mgr. Northrop Corp., Hawthorne, Calif., 1982-83; dir. of ops. Transco, Marina Del Rey, Calif., 1983-85; v.p. ops. Decor Concepts, Arcadia, Calif., 1985—; design dir. Lockheed Aircraft Corp., Ontario, Calif., 1987-97; v.p. engring., space programs Ducommon Inc., Carson, Calif., 1997—. Mem. Soc. Mfg. Engrs., Inst. Indsl. Engrs., Nat. Trust for Hist. Preservation, Fleet Res. Assn., Am. Film Inst., Nat. Mgmt. Assn. Avocations: golf, running, racquetball.

BROWN, (JERENE) ROXANNE, sales executive; b. L.A., July 5, 1947; d. John Phillip and Margaret Leona (Dalrymple) Ortiz; m. Terry Lee Wood, May 7, 1966 (div. Sept. 1969); 1 child, Tiffany Christine Wood Suraco; m. Christopher Corey Brown, July 17, 1984; children: Jason Michael and John Charles (twins); m. Richard L. Gibbs, Apr. 18, 1996. Student, Casper Coll., 1977. Info. operator Gen. Telephone, Baldwin Park, Calif., 1965-67; long distance operator Gen. Telephone, Santa Maria, Calif., 1967-69; office mgr. Monroe Calculator, Las Vegas, Nev., 1972-74; mgr. Exch. Club, Salt Lake City, 1977-81, Pouches Inc., Salt Lake City, 1981-82; asst. producer KSTU TV 20, Salt Lake City, 1982-84; sec. ADVO - Sys., Inc., Orange, Calif., 1984-85, terr. sales rep., 1985-88; major account exec. ADVO - Sys., Inc., Garden Grove, Calif., 1988-95; v.p. JRB & Assocs., Long Beach, Calif., 1995—; cons. Rice - Urmana Advt., Huntington Beach, Calif., 1989-91. Bd. dirs. ACLU, Salt Lake City, 1977; precinct worker Voter Registrar, Huntington Beach, 1988, Long Beach, Calif., 1990; bd. dirs., sec. Alamitos Bay Beach Peninsula Preservation Group, 1996—. Mem. ACLU, Platform Speakers Assn., Alamitos Bay Garden Club (v.p., ways and means com. 1996—). Avocations: sculpting, photography, sailing. Home: 6119 E Seaside Walk Long Beach CA 90803-5654

BROWN, SALLY (SARAH JANE ENGLAND), minister; b. Manila, Dec. 20, 1923; d. Frederick Ocean and Sarah Mathloma (Powell) England; m. David Randolph Brown, Dec. 17, 1944; children: Philip, Ellen, Polly, Ann. BA in English, U. Wash., 1945; MS in Recreation, San Jose (Calif.) State U., 1970; MDiv, Pacific Sch. of Religion, Berkeley, Calif., 1988. Bd. cert. hosp. chaplain. Staff chaplain VA Med. Ctr., Palo Alto, Calif., 1988-98; community chaplain Palo Alto, 1988—; co-chair United Ch. Christ com. on ministry No. Calif. Conf., 1991-94. Co-author: Our Children Are Alcoholics: Coping with Children Who Have Addictions, 1997. Fellow Coll. of Chaplains, Nat. Assn. of Vets. Affairs Chaplains, Am. Soc. Aging. Home: 1470 Sand Hill Rd Apt 309 Palo Alto CA 94304-2029

BROWN, SALLY ANN, research scientist; b. N.Y.C., Sept. 8, 1959; d. Richard Daniel and Joann Ellen (Detschel) B. BS in Biology, SUNY, Geneseo, 1981, MA in Biology, 1989; postgrad., Loyola Marymount U., L.A. Grad. tchg. asst. biology dept. SUNY, Geneseo, 1983; rsch. technician dept. neurology U. Rochester, N.Y., 1984-88; rsch. assoc. dept. neurogerontology U. So. Calif., L.A., 1989-95; presenter in field. Co-author: The Basal Ganglia II Structure and Function, 1987, Aging: The Universal Human Experience, 1987; contbr. articles to profl. jours.; mem. staff Internat. and Comparative Law Jour., 1996-97, sr. note and comment editor, 1997-98. Participant, tutor Literacy Vols./ESL, Rochester, 1978; active Big Bro.-Big Sister Program, Rochester, 1985-88. Leone-Haggerty Meml. scholar Miller Place (N.Y.) PTA, 1977, Regents scholar N.Y. State Bd. Regents, Albany, 1978, Am. Mensa Edn. and Rsch. Found. scholar, 1989; Sci. and Math. fellow N.Y. State Higher Edn., Albany, 1983; Mabel Wilson Richards scholar, 1997-98. Mem. ABA (student divsn., sci. and tech. divsn.), St. Thomas More Law Honor Soc., Phi Delta Phi. Home: 7230 Franklin Ave Apt 327 Los Angeles CA 90046

BROWN, SHIRLEY MARGARET KERN (PEGGY BROWN), interior designer; b. Ellensburg, Wash., Mar. 30, 1948; d. Philip Brooke and Shirley (Dickson) Kern; m. Ellery Kliess Brown, Jr., Aug. 7, 1970; children: Heather Nicole Coco, Rebecca Cherise, Andrea Shirley Serene, Ellery Philip. BA in Interior Design, Wash. State U., 1973. Apprentice, then interior designer L.S. Higgins & Assocs., Bellevue, Wash., 1969-72; interior designer ColorsPlus Interiors, Inc., Bellevue, 1972, Strawns Office Furniture & Interiors, Inc., Boise, Idaho, 1973-75, Empire Furniture Inc., Tulsa; owner Inside-Out Design Co. Ltd., Boise, 1973-82; interior designer Architekton, Inc., Tulsa, 1984-86; Johnson Brand Design Group, Inc., 1986-87; Ellery Brown & Assoc. Arch. AIA, 1987—; Seattle Design Ctr.-Visions & Studio Programs, 1994-98, Scottsdale, 1998—, Mehagian's Fine Furniture, Scottsdale; lectr. in field. Contbr. articles to profl. jours. Pres. PTA, co-chair capital bond prin. selection com., enrollment rev. com., 1989-95; bd. dirs. Paradise Valley Young Life. Mem. Am. Soc. Interior Designers (Wash. state presdl. citation 1995, 96, 97, presdl. citation Oreg. chpt. 1977, 95-96, dir. chpt. 1976-77, chmn. Boise subchpt. 1977-79, sec. 1980-81, Wash. chpt. 2 step workshop chmn., NCIDQ chmn. 1993-97), Nat. Soc. Interior Designers, Idaho Hist. Co., AAUW, Wash. State U. Alumni Assn., Jr. League Seattle, Jr. League Phoenix, Zonta, Alpha Gamma Delta. Republican. Presbyterian. Office: 16227 N 50th St Scottsdale AZ 85254-9652

BROWN, STEVEN BRIEN, radiologist; b. Ft. Collins, Colo., Jan. 18, 1952; s. Allen Jenkins and Shirley Irene (O'Brien) B.; m. Susan Jane DiTomaso, Sept. 10, 1983; children: Allison Grace, Laura Anne. BS, Colo. State U., 1974; MD, U. Calif., San Diego, 1978. Diplomate Am. Bd. Radiology, Am. Bd. Neuroradiology and Vascularand Interventional Radiology. Intern U. Wash., Seattle, 1978-79; resident in radiology Stanford (Calif.) U., 1979-82; fellow in interventional and neuro-radiology Wilford Hall, USAF Med Ctr., San Antonio, 1982-83; staff radiologist Wilford Hall, USAF Med Ctr., 1983-86; staff radiologist Luth. Med. Ctr., Wheat Ridge, Colo., 1986—, chief angiography and interventional radiology, 1987-94; chief dept. med. imaging Luth. Med. Ctr. Joint Venture, Wheat Ridge, Colo., 1994-96; pres. Luth. Med. Ctr. Joint Venture, 1992-95; mem. bd. mgrs. Primera HealthCare LLC, 1995-97; pres. HealthCare Select Inc., 1995—. Contbr. articles to profl. jours. Mem. Rep. Nat. Com., Washington, 1984—, Nat. Rep. Senatorial Com., 1985—, Rep. Presdl. Task Force, 1986—; bd. dirs. The Health Care Initiative. Maj. USAF, 1982-86. Fellow Radiol. Soc. N.Am.; mem. Colo. Radiol. Soc. (pres. 1995-96), Rocky Mt. Radiol. Soc. (pres. 1994-95), Am. Coll. Radiology (exec. com. intersoc. commn. 1996—), Soc. Cardiovasc. and Interventional Radiology, Western Neuroradiol. Soc., Am. Soc. Neuroradiology, Colo. Preferred Physicians Orgn. (bd. dirs. 1987—), World Wildlife Orgn., Colo. Angio Club. Republican. Presbyterian. Avocations: skiing, sailing, gardening. Office: Luth Med Center 8300 W 38th Ave Wheat Ridge CO 80033-6005

BROWN, TIMOTHY DONELL, professional football player; b. Dallas, July 22, 1966. BA, U. Notre Dame, 1988. Wide receiver L.A. Raiders, 1988—. Recipient Heisman trophy, 1987; named Wide Reciever on The Sporting News Coll. All-Am. team, 1986, 87; Coll. Football Player of the Yr. The Sporting News, 1987, Kick Returner The Sporting News NFL All-Pro Team, 1988. Played in Pro Bowl, 1988, 91, 93-96. Office: Oakland Raiders 1200 Harbor Bay Pkwy Alameda CA 94502-6501*

BROWN, TOD DAVID, bishop; b. San Francisco, Nov. 15, 1936; s. George Wilson and Edna Anne (Dunn) B. BA, St. John's Coll., 1958; STB, Gregorian U., Rome, 1960; MA in Theology, U. San Francisco, 1970, MAT in Edn., 1976. Dir. edn. Diocese of Monterey, Calif., 1970-80, vicar gen., clergy, 1980-82, chancellor, 1982-89, vicar gen., chancellor, 1983-89; pastor St. Francis Xavier, Seaside, Calif., 1977-82; bishop Roman Catholic Diocese of Boise, Idaho, 1989-98; appointed and installed bishop Roman Cath. Diocese of Orange, Calif., 1998; mem. subcom. on laity, mem. 3d millenium com. Nat. Conf. Cath. Bishops; mem. episcopal bd. govs. N.Am. Coll. Named Papal Chaplain Pope Paul VI, 1975. Mem. Cath. Theol. Soc. Am., Cath. Biblical Assn., Canon Law Soc. Am., Equestrian Order of the Holy Sepulchre in Jerusalem. Avocations: films, travel, reading, exercise. Office: Diocese of Orange Marywood Ctr 2811 E Villa Real Dr Orange CA 92867-1932

BROWN, WALTER CREIGHTON, biologist; b. Butte, Mont., Aug. 18, 1913; s. D. Frank and Isabella (Creighton) B.; m. Jeanette Snyder, Aug. 20, 1950; children: Pamela Hawley, James Creighton, Julia Elizabeth. AB, Coll. Puget Sound, 1935, MA, 1938; PhD, Stanford U., 1950. Chmn. dept. Clover Park High Sch., Tacoma, Wash., 1938-42; acting instr. Stanford U., Calif., 1949-50; instr. Northwestern U., Evanston, Ill., 1950-53; dean sci. Menlo Coll., Menlo Park, Calif., 1955-66, dean instrn., 1966-75; rsch. assoc., fellow Calif. Acad. Sci., San Francisco, 1978—; lectr. Sillman U., Philippines, 1954-55, dir. rsch. Program on Ecology and Systematics of Philippine Amphibians and Reptiles, 1958-74; rschr. rels. of amphibian faunas of Philippines & Indo-Australian Archipelago; vis. prof. biology Stanford U., 1962, 64, 66, 68, Harvard U., Cambridge, Mass., 1969, 72. Author: Philippine Lizards of the Family Gekkonidae, 1978, Philippine Lizards of the Family Scincidae, 1980, Lizards of the Genus Emoia (Scincidae) with Observations of Their Evolution and Biogeography, 1991, Philippine Amphibians: An Illustrated Field Guide ; contbr. over 80 articles to profl. jours. Served with U.S. Army, 1942-46. Fellow AAAS; mem. Am. Soc. Ichthyologists and Herpetologists, Am. Inst. Biol. Scis., Sigma Xi. Office: Calif Acad Scis Dept Herpetology Golden Gate Park San Francisco CA 94118

BROWN, WAYNE J., mayor; b. 1936. BS, Ariz. State U. Staff acct. Arthur Andersen & Co. CPA's, 1960-63; mng. ptnr. Wayne Brown & Co. CPA's, 1964-79; dir. acctg. Ariz. State Dept. Adminstrn., 1979-80; chmn. Brown Evans Distbg. Co., Mesa, Ariz., 1980—; mayor City of Mesa, 1996—. Office: Office of the Mayor PO Box 1466 Mesa AZ 85211-1466*

BROWN, WILLIE LEWIS, JR., mayor, former state legislator, lawyer; b. Mineola, Tex., Mar. 20, 1934; s. Willie Lewis and Minnie (Boyd) B.; children: Susan, Robin, Michael. B.A., San Francisco State Coll., 1955; LL.D., Hastings Coll. Law, 1958; postgrad. fellow, Crown Coll., 1970, U. Calif.-Santa Cruz, 1970. Bar: Calif. 1959. Mem. Calif. State Assembly, Sacramento, 1964-95; speaker Calif. State Assembly, 1980-95, chmn. Ways and Means Com., 1971-74; chmn. revenue and taxation com., 1976-79; Democratic Whip Calif. State Assembly, 1969-70, majority floor leader, 1979-80, chmn. legis. black caucus, 1980, chmn. govtl. efficiency and economy com., 1968-84; mayor San Francisco, 1995—. Mem. U. Calif. bd. regents, 1972, Dem. Nat. Com., 1989-90; co-chmn. Calif. del. to Nat. Black Polit. Conv., 1972, Calif. del. to Nat. Dem. Conv., 1980; nat. campaign chmn. Jesse Jackson for Pres., 1988. Mem. State Legis. Leaders Found. (dir.), Nat. Conf. State Legislatures, NAACP, Black Am. Polit. Assn. Calif. (co-founder, past chmn.), Calif. Bar Assn., Alpha Phi Alpha, Phi Alpha Delta. Democrat. Methodist. Office: Office of the Mayor 401 Van Ness Ave Rm 336 San Francisco CA 94102 also: 1388 Sutter St Ste 820 San Francisco CA 94109-5453*

BROWNE, JOSEPH PETER, retired librarian; b. Detroit, June 12, 1929; s. George and Mary Bridget (Fahy) B.; A.B., U. Notre Dame, 1951; S.T.L., Pontificium Athenaeum Angelicum, Rome, 1957, S.T.D., 1960; MS in L.S., Cath. U. Am., 1965. Joined Congregation of Holy Cross, Roman Cath. Ch., 1947, ordained priest, 1955; asst. pastor Holy Cross Ch., South Bend, Ind., 1955-56; libr., prof. moral theology Holy Cross Coll., Washington, 1959-64; mem. faculty U. Portland (Oreg.), 1964-73, 75—, dir. libr., 1966-70, 76-94, dean Coll. Arts and Scis., 1970-73, assoc. prof. libr. sci. 1967-95, prof. emeritus, 1995—, regent, 1969-70, 77-81, chmn. acad. senate, 1968-70, 1987-88; prof., head dept. libr. sci. Our Lady of Lake Coll., San Antonio, 1973-75; chmn. Interstate Libr. Planning Coun., 1977-79. Mem. Columbia River chpt. Huntington's Disease Soc. Am., 1975-90, pres., 1979-82; pastor St. Birgitta Ch., Portland, 1993—; chmn. Archdiocesan Presbyteral Coun., 1994-98; mem. coll. of cons. Archdiocese of Portland, 1995—. Recipient Culligan award U. Portland, 1979. Mem. Cath. Libr. Assn. (life, pres. 1971-73), ALA, Cath. Theol. Soc. Am., Pacific N.W. Libr. Assn. (pres. 1985-86), Oreg. Libr. Assn. (life, pres. 1967-68), Nat. Assn. Parliamentarians, Oreg. Assn. Parliamentarians (pres. 1985-87), Mensa Internat., All-Ireland Cultural Soc. Oreg. (pres. 1984-85). Democrat. Club: KC. Home: 11820 NW Saint Helens Rd Portland OR 97231-2319

BROWNE-MILLER, ANGELA CHRISTINE (ANGELA DEANGELIS), author, educator, social research association executive, metaphysician, political analyst; b. Whittier, Calif., June 26, 1952; d. Lee Winston and Louisa Francesca (de Angelis) Browne; m. Richard Louis Miller, Feb. 22, 1986; 1 child, Evacheska. BA in Biology and Lit. with honors, U. Calif., Santa Cruz, 1976; postgrad. in spl. edn., Sonoma State U., 1976-77; MSW, U. Calif., Berkeley, 1981, MPH, 1983, PhD in Social Welfare with distinction, 1983, PhD in Edn., 1992. Lic. clin. social worker, Calif. Child and family counselor Clearwater Ranch Children's Home, Mendocino County, Calif., 1976-77; conselor, spl. edn. tchr. Bachman Hill Sch., Mendocino County, Calif., 1977-78; substitute tchr. Marin County (Calif.) Sch. Dist., 1978-79; founder Metatech/Metasome Corp. Svcs., 1982—; also bd. dirs. Whole Care Inst.; rsch. dir. Cokenders Alcohol and Drug Inst., Emeryville, Calif., 1983-89; exec. cons. Parkside Med. Svcs., Chgo., 1989-90; policy and program analyst White House Conf. on Families, Washington, summer 1980 to spring 1981; rsch. analyst Office for Families, Adminstrn. for Children Youth and Families HHS, 1981, grant reader, 1982, 84, 85, 86; day care program evaluator, budget cons. San Francisco Bay area, 1980-83; lectr. Sch. Social Welfare, Haas Sch. Bus. U. Calif., Berkeley, 1984-95; program cons. Wilbur Hot Springs Health Sanctuary, 1984-95; pres. Cokenders Alcohol and Drug Inst., Emeryville, 1983-90; lectr. Sch. Pub. Policy U. Calif., Berkeley, 1986-88; guest White House Conf. for a Drug-Free Am., 1987-88; bd. dirs. Underground Rising; CEO Metaterra Inc., Publs. and Prodns.; lectr. in field. Author: The Daycare Dilemma, 1990, Working Dazed, 1991, Transcending Addiction, 1992, Gestalting Addiction, 1993, Learning to Learn, 1994, Intelligence Policy, 1995, Omega Point, 1995, Adventures in Death, 1995, Shameful Admissions, 1996, Embracing Death, 1996, How to Die and Survive, 1997, Flesh Trade, 1998; contbr. numerous articles to profl. jours.; panelist numerous nat. radio and TV appearances, Oprah Winfrey Show, Talk of the Nation. Pub. dir. Californians for Drug Free Youth Conf., 1986; mem. Nat. Task Force on Drug Abuse, 1984. Recipient Presdl. Mgmt. Internship award, 1982; grantee Adminstrn. for Children Youth and Family Welfare stipend, 1980; NIMH postdoctoral fellow, 1987-89. Mem. Am. Pub. Health Assn., Nat. Assn. Social Workers, Assn. Ednl. Rschrs. and Adminstrs., Am. Acad. Psychotherapists, Mensa. Avocations: spiritual healing, piano, guitar, painting. Office: 98 Main St # 315 Belvedere Tiburon CA 94920-2517

BROWNFIELD, FLORENCE ELIZABETH, periodical editor, genealogist; b. Ironwood, Mich., Oct. 14, 1920; d. Erick Emil and Fanny Elizabeth (Salmela) Konstenius; m. Gerald Winston Brownfield, Sept. 24, 1949; children; Faye Evelyn, Gene Winston, Janice Elizabeth, Timothy Mark. BA with honors, No. Mich. U., 1942; MA with honors, Wayne State U., 1962. Cert. tchr., Mich., cert. libr., Calif. Tchr. Rock River Twp. H.S., Eben Junction, Mich., 1942-46; tchr., libr. Cheboygan (Mich.) H.S., 1946-48; rsch. libr. Curtis Pub. Co., Detroit, 1948-50; tchr. Detroit Pub. Schs., 1957-64; sr. libr. clerk Orange Coast Coll., Costa Mesa, Calif., 1964-68; libr. Garden Grove U.S.D., Fountain Valley, Calif., 1968-85; editor, writer Brownfield Gleanings, Tustin, Calif., 1979—; pres. Garden Grove U.S.D. Librs., 1990. Author: (with others) Days and Ways in Old South Pabst, 1988, Men of the 931st, 1991, Ossi's Story, 1991, History of the 931st, 1992, Aurora, a Michigan Mining Location, 1994, A Catalog of Memories, 1995, Three Michagan Mining Locations, 1996; libr. columnist, Chebogan, 1947-48; newspaper columnist Township News, Detroit, 1956-58. Sec. Tustin (Calif.) Village II Home Owners Assn., 1994—; tchr., moderator, deaconess, Christian edn. bd., First Bapt. Ch., Tustin, 1964—; historian, editor, Brownfield Gleanings, 1979—. Republican. Baptist. Avocations: writing, bible teaching and research, crossword puzzles. Home: 16661 Townehouse Dr Tustin CA 92780-4132

BROWNING, JAMES ROBERT, federal judge; b. Great Falls, Mont., Oct. 1, 1918; s. Nicholas Henry and Minnie Sally (Foley) B.; m. Marie Rose Chapell. BA, Mont. State U., Missoula, 1938; LLB with honors, U. Mont., 1941, LLD (hon.), 1961; LLD (hon.), Santa Clara U., 1989. Bar: Mont. 1941, D.C. 1950, U.S. Supreme Ct. 1952. Spl. atty. antitrust div. Dept. Justice, 1941-43, spl. atty. gen. litigation sect. antitrust div., 1946-48, chief antitrust dept. N.W. regional office, 1948-49; asst. chief gen. litigation sect. antitrust div. Dept. Justice (N.W. regional office), 1949-51, 1st asst. civil div., 1951-52; exec. asst. to atty. gen. U.S., 1952-53; chief U.S. (Exec. Office for [illegible] Law, 1953, Georgetown U. Law Center, 1957-58; clk. Supreme Ct. U.S., 1958-61; judge U.S. Ct. Appeals 9th Circuit, 1961-76, chief judge, 1976-88, judge, 1988—; mem. Jud. Conf. of U.S., 1976-88, exec. com. of conf., 1978-87, com. on internat. conf. of appellate judges, 1987-90, com. on ct. adminstrn., 1969-71, chmn. subcom. on jud. stats., 1969-71, com. on the

budget, 1971-77, adminstrn. office, subom. on budget, 1974-76, com. to study U.S. jud. conf., 1986-88, com. to study the illustrative rules of jud. misconduct, 1985-87, com. on formulation of standard of conduct of fed. judges, 1969, Reed justice com. on cont. edn., tng. and adminstrn., 1967-68; David T. Lewis Disting. Judge-in-residence, U. Utah, 1987; Blankenbaker lectr. U. Mont., 1987, Sibley lectr. U. Ga., 1987, lectr. Human Rights Inst. Santa Clara U. Sch. Law, Strasbourg. Editor-in-chief, Mont. Law Rev. Dir. Western Justice Found.; chmn. 9th Cir. Hist. Soc. 1st lt. U.S. Army, 1943-46. Decorated Bronze Star; named to Order of the Grizzly, U. Mont., 1973; scholar in residence Santa Clara U., 1989, U. Mont., 1991; recipient Devitt Disting. Svc. to Justice award, 1990. Fellow ABA (judge adv. com. to standing com. on Ethics and Profl. Responsibility 1973-75); mem. D.C. Bar Assn., Mont. Bar Assn., Am. Law Inst., Fed. Bar Assn. (bd. dirs 1945-61, Nat. council 1958-62), Inst. Jud. Adminstrn., Am. Judicature Soc. (chmn. com. on fed. judiciary 1973-74, bd. dirs. 1972-75), Herbert Harley award 1984), Am. Soc. Legal History (adv. bd. jour.), Nat Lawyers Club (bd. govs. 1959-63). Office: US Ct Appeals 9th Cir PO Box 193939 San Francisco CA 94119-3939*

BROWNING, JESSE HARRISON, entrepreneur; b. Kingsville, Mo., July 27, 1935; s. Jesse Harrison and Anna Love (Swank) B.; m. Vicki Carol Thompson, Dec. 21, 1957; children: Caroline Kaye, Marcia Lynn, Nanci Ann, Susan Louise. MPA, U. So. Calif., 1988; PhD, U. Wash., 1995. Cert. mfg. engr. Field engr. The Boeing Co., Los Angeles, 1961-64; gen. mgr. SPI, Los Angeles, 1964-70; chmn. Browning Inc., Los Angeles, 1970-95; dir. global trade, transp. and logistic studies U. Wash., Seattle, 1995—; chmn. Vapor Engring., Los Angeles, 1979-87; U.S. del. Asia Pacific Econ. Cooperation; mem. transp. working group. Patentee in field. Mem. ASPA, World Coun. on Internat. Trade, World Affairs Coun., Am. Helicopter Soc., Am. Assn. Geographers, Soc. Mgr. Engrs., Propellor Club. Lutheran. Avocations: snow skiing, flying helicopters and airplanes, traveling, working out.

BROWNING, NORMA LEE (MRS. RUSSELL JOYNER OGG), journalist; b. Spickard, Mo., Nov. 24, 1914; d. Howard R. and Grace (Kennedy) B.; m. Russell Joyner Ogg, June 12, 1938. A.B., B.J., U. Mo., 1937; M.A. in English, Radcliffe Coll., 1938. Reporter Los Angeles Herald-Express, 1942-43; with Chgo. Tribune, from 1944, Hollywood columnist, 1966-75; Vis. lectr. creative writing, editorial cons., mem. nat. adv. bd. Interlochen Arts Acad., Northwood Inst. Author: City Girl in the Country, 1955, Joe Maddy of Interlochen, 1963, (with W. Clement Stone) The Other Side of the Mind, 1965, The Psychic World of Peter Hurkos, 1970, (with Louella Dirksen) The Honorable Mr. Marigold, 1972, (with Ann Miller) Miller's High Life, 1972, Peter Hurkos: I Have Many Lives, 1976, Omarr: Astrology and the Man, 1977, (with George Masters) The Masters Way to Beauty, 1977, (with Russell Ogg) He Saw A Hummingbird, 1978, (with Florence Lowell) Be A Guest At Your Own Party, 1980, Face-Lifts: Everything You Always Wanted to Know, 1981, Joe Maddy Of Interlochen: Portrait of A Legend, 1991; Contbr. articles to nat. mags. Recipient E.S. Beck award Chgo Tribune. Mem. Theta Sigma Phi, Kappa Tau Alpha. Address: 226 E Morongo Rd Palm Springs CA 92264-8402

BROWNING, WILLIAM DOCKER, federal judge; b. Tucson, May 19, 1931; s. Horace Benjamin and Mary Louise (Docker) B.; children: Christopher, Logan, Courtenay; m. Zerilda Sinclair, Dec. 17, 1974; 1 child, Benjamin. BBA, U. Ariz., 1954, LLB, 1960. Bar: Ariz. 1960, U.S. Dist. Ct. Ariz. 1960, U.S. Ct. Appeals (9th cir.) 1965, U.S. Supreme Ct. 1967. Pvt. practice Tucson, 1960-84; judge U.S. Dist. Ct., Tucson, 1984—; mem. jud. nominating com. appellate ct. appointments, 1975-79; mem. Commn. on Structural Alternatives, Fed. Ct. Appeals, 1997—; apptd. Commn. on Structural Alternatives for the Fed. Ctrs. of Appeals. Del. 9th Cir. Jud. Conf., 1968-77, 79-82; trustee Inst. for Ct. Mgmt., 1978-84; mem. Ctr. for Pub. Resources Legal Program. 1st lt. USAF, 1954-57, capt. USNG, 1958-61. Recipient Disting. Citizen award U. Ariz., 1995. Fellow Am. Coll. Trial Lawyers, Am. Bar Found.; mem. ABA (spl. com. housing and urban devel. law 1973-76, com. urban problems and human affairs 1978-80), Ariz. Bar Assn. (chmn. merit selection of judges com. 1973-76, bd. gove. 1968-74, pres. 1972-73, Outstanding Mem. 1980), Pima County Bar Assn. (exec. com. 1964-68, med. legal screening panel 1965-75, pres. 1967-68), Am. Bd. Trial Advocates, Am. Judicature Soc. (bd. dirs. 1975-77), Fed. Judges Assn. (bd. dirs.). Office: US Dist Ct US Courthouse Rm 301 55 E Broadway Blvd Tucson AZ 85701-1719

BROWNLEE, JUDITH MARILYN, priestess, psychotherapist, psychic; b. Beaumont, Tex., May 16, 1940; d. Alvin Maurice and Juanita M. (Whittington) B.; m. Theodore Blakey Peak, Apr. 12, 1974 (div. 1981); 1 child, Daniel David Brownlee Peak; m. Floyd S. Bond, Aug. 18, 1996. BA, Lamar U., Beaumont, Tex., 1962; postgrad., U. Denver, 1971, Avalon Inst., Boulder, Colo., 1989-92; student, Our Lady Perpetual Responsibility, The Silent Cir., 1975-79. Wiccan priestess. Tchr. Deer Trail (Colo.) H.S., 1963-64, Lutcher Stark H.S., Orange, Tex., 1967-69; libr. technician Denver Pub. Libr., 1970-73; bus. exec. Weight Watchers Rocky Mtn., Denver, 1974; mail order divsn. mgr. Mile High Comics and Books, Denver, 1975-81; religious tchr. The Silent Cir., Denver, 1979-83; gov. employee Colo. Atty. Gen. Office, Denver, 1983-92; minister Fortress Temple, Denver, 1984-96; psychotherapist, 1992—; pub. spkr. Spring Mysteries Festival, Seattle, 1988-92; counselor Profl. Psychic Counselors Network, 1993-96, Morningstar Inc., 1997, Psychic Choice, 1997—; pub. spkr. Denver, 1988—; workshop leader Spring Mysteries Festival, Seattle, 1988, 92, Dragonfest Pagan Festival, Denver, 1987-92; lectr. Isis Metaphys. Ctr., workshop leader, 1985—; lectr. Raven & Rose Bookstore, Ft. Collins Colo., 1992-93, Enchanted Chalice Bookstore, 1994—, Herbs & Arts Bookstore, 1996, Spirit Ways Bookstore, 1998; organizer Front Range Pagan Festival, 1985; guest spkr. Greeley (Colo.) Unitarian Fellowship, 1992; spkr. Rocky Montain Fiction Writers Conv., 1993; creator, dir. Edn. for Pagan Youth com. Pagan Sch., 1990-94, 96-97. Author: Pagan Parenting, 1987, The Wheel of the Year, 1988; contbr. articles to profl. jours. Interviewee KOA Radio, 1984, 92, 95, 96, KNUS and KYBG, 1992, KUSA Channel 9, 1987, 90, Rocky Mountain News, Denver, 1992, 96; cmty. prodr. Mile High Cablevision, 1987; tel. counselor Lifeline of Colo., Denver, 1988; field tng. supr. Iliff Sch. Theology, Denver, 1995-96. Recipient Hart and Crescent Disting. Youth Svc. award Covenant of the Goddess, 1995. Mem. Colo. Assn. Psychotherapists, Assn. Past Life Rsch. and Therapy, Women's Spiritual Leadership Alliance (bd. dirs. 1992—), Daus. of New Moon (founder, facilitator), Soc. for Creative Anachronism (Colo. founder, CEO 1970-73, treas. 1981-83), Denver Area Sci. Fiction Assn. (editor 1969-70, dir. 1974-75, conf. chmn. 1970-75), Denver Area Interfaith Clergy Conf., Covenant Unitarian Universalist Pagans. Avocations: reading, theatre, films, science fiction, internet. E-mail: judith1152@aol.com. Office: PO Box 172271 Denver CO 80217-2271

BROWNLEE, WILSON ELLIOT, JR., history educator; b. Lacrosse, Wis., May 10, 1941; s. Wilson Elliot Sr. and Pearl (Woodings) B.; m. Mary Margaret Cochran, June 25, 1966; children: Charlotte Louise, Martin Elliot. BA, Harvard U., 1963; MA, U. Wis., 1965, PhD, 1969. Asst. prof. U. Calif., Santa Barbara, 1967-74, assoc. prof., 1974-80, prof. history, 1980—, spl. advisor to systemwide provost, 1995, assoc. systemwide provost, 1996; vis. prof. Princeton (N.J.) U., 1980-81; chmn. dept. history U. Calif., Santa Barbara, 1984-87, acad. senate, 1983-84, 88-90, systemwide acad. senate, 1992-93; dir. U. Calif.-Santa Barbara Ctr., Washington, 1990-91; chmn. exec. com. dels. Am. Coun. Learned Socs., N.Y.C., 1988-90, bd. dirs.; bd. dirs. Nat. Coun. on Pub. History, Boston; bicentennial lectr. U.S. Dept. Treasury, 1989; faculty rep. U. Calif. Bd. Regents, 1991-93; adj. prof. history Calif. State U., Sacto., 1997-99; mem. bd. control, U. Claif. Press, 1996—. Author: Dynamics of Ascent, 1974, 2nd edit., 1979, Progressivism and Economic Growth, 1974, Federal Taxation in America: A Short History, 1996; coauthor: Essentials of American History, 1976, 4th edit., 1986, America's History, 1987, 3rd edit., 1997; editor: Women in the American Economy 1976, Funding the American State, 1996; contbr. numerous articles to profl. jours., chpts. to books. Chmn. schs. com. Harvard Club, Santa Barbara, 1971-80, 85, 86; pres. Assn. for Retarded Citizens, Santa Barbara, 1982-84; 1st v.p. Assn. for Retarded Citizens Calif., Sacramento, 1983-84; pres. Santa Barbara Trust for Hist. Preservation, 1986-87, 95-97; trustee Las Trampas Inc., 1994-97. Charles Warren fellow Harvard U., 1978-79, fellow Woodrow Wilson Ctr., Washington, 1987-88; recipient Spl. Commendation, Calif. Dept. Pks. and Recreation, 1988, Oliver Johnson award for Disting. Svc. U. Calif. Acad. Senate, 1998. Mem. Am. Hist. Assn., Orgn. Am. Historians, Econ. History Assn., Am. Tax Policy Inst. Office: U Calif Dept History Santa Barbara CA 93106

BROWNSON, JACQUES CALMON, architect; b. Aurora, Ill., Aug. 3, 1923; s. Clyde Arthur and Iva Kline (Felter) B.; m. Doris L. Curry, 1946; children—Joel C., Lorre J., Daniel J. BS in Architecture, Ill. Inst. Tech., 1948, MS, 1954. Instr., asst. prof. architecture Ill. Inst. Tech., 1949-59; prof. architecture, chmn. dept. U. Mich., 1966-68; chief design C.F. Murphy Assocs., Chgo., 1959-61; project architect, chief designer Chgo. Civic Ctr. Architects, 1961-68; dir. state bldg. div. State of Colo., Denver, 1986-88; pvt. practice Denver, 1988—; former mng. architect Chgo. Pub. Bldg. Commn.; past dir. planning and devel. Auraria Ctr. for Higher Edn., Denver; bd. dirs. Capital Constrn., Denver; guest lectr. architecture in U.S. and Europe. Prin. works include Chgo. Civic Ctr., Lake Denver, Colo., 1985, Chgo. Tribune/Cabrini Green Housing, 1993; author: History of Chicago Architects, 1996, Oral History of Jacuqes Calmon Brownson, 1996. Recipient award for Geneva House Archtl. Record mag., 1956; Design award for steel framed factory Progressive Architecture mag., 1957. Home and Office: 659 Josephine St Denver CO 80206-3722

BRUBAKER, WILLIAM ROGERS, sociology educator; b. Evanston, Ill., June 8, 1956; s. Charles William and Elizabeth (Rogers) B. BA summa cum laude, Harvard U., 1979; MA, Sussex U., Eng., 1980; PhD, Columbia U., 1990. Prof. UCLA, 1994—, assoc. prof. sociology, 1991-94. Author: The Limits of Rationality, 1984, Citizenship and Nationhood in France and Germany, 1992, Nationalism Reframed, 1996; editor: Immigration and Politics of Citizenship in Europe and North America, 1989. Jr. fellow Soc. Fellows Harvard U., 1988-91; MacArthur fellow, 1994—; NSF Young Investigator awardee. Office: U Calif Dept Sociology 264 Haines Hall 405 Hilgard Ave Los Angeles CA 90095-9000

BRUCE, JOHN ALLEN, foundation executive, educator; b. Kansas City, Mo., Sept. 17, 1934; BA, Wesleyan U., Middletown, Conn., 1956; MDiv, Gen. Theol. Sem., N.Y.C., 1959; PhD, U. Minn., 1972. Ordained to ministry Episcopal Ch., 1959. Clergyman, 1959-68; prof. U. Ala., Tuscaloosa, 1972-74; exec. dir. E.C. Brown Found., Portland, Oreg., 1974-98; cons. to philanthropies and corp. programs; clin. prof. community medicine Sch. Medicine, Oreg. Health Scis. U., Portland, 1976-98. Author various scholarly publs. Exec. producer various ednl. films on family life, health and values. Bd. dirs., officer various community orgns. Served to lt. USN, 1964-67. Recipient various awards and grants from med. orgns. and related groups. Mem. Nat. Coun. on Family Rels. (Disting. Service to Families award 1979), Oreg. Coun. on Family Rels. (pres. 1981), Cosmos Club. Republican.

BRUCE, JOHN ANTHONY, artist; b. L.A., Apr. 8, 1931; s. Merle VanDyke and Katherine Mary (Butler) B.; children: Marsha Lee, Margaret Lorren, James Cole, Glenn Allen, Mark Corwin, Leslie Ann. BA in Psychology and Art, Calif. State U., L.A., 1965. Design engr. N.Am. Aviation Corp., Downey, Calif., 1952-57; comml. artist Aerojet Gen. Corp., Sacramento, 1957-59; advt. mgr. Flow Equipment Co., Santa Fe Springs, Calif., 1959-63; art dir. Barnes-Champ Advt., Santa Ana, Calif., 1963-66, Long Beach (Calif.) Ind. Press Telegram News, 1970-73; freelance art cons. Epcot project Walt E. Disney Enterprises, Glendale, Calif., 1976-77. Permanent collections Smithsonian Inst., Washington, D.C.; one man shows Ghormley Gallery, L.A., 1966, Les Li Art Gallery, L.A., 1970, Upstairs Gallery, Long Beach, Calif., 1973, El Prado Gallery, Sedona, Ariz., 1987; group shows Newport Beach Invitational, Newport Beach, Calif., 1964, Laguna Beach Art Festival, Laguna Beach, Calif., 1962, 63, 64, 65, Butler Inst. Am. Art, Youngstown, Ohio, 1970, Allied Artists, N.Y.C., 1988; currently exhibiting with Bartfield Gallery, N.Y.C., Tex. Art Gallery, Dallas. With U.S. Army, 1949-52, Korea. Recipient John B. Grayback award Am. Profl. Artists League, 1988, Best of Show award Gene Autry Mus. AICA Show, 1996, San Dimas Festival of Western Art, 1996, numerous others. Mem. Knickerbocker Artists (Philip Isinberg award 1988), Am. Indian and Cowboy Artists (Eagle Feather award 1988, 89). Republican. Studio: 5394 Tip Top Rd Mariposa CA 95338-9609

BRUCE, THOMAS EDWARD, psychology educator, thanatologist; b. Vinton, Iowa, Dec. 3, 1937; s. George Robert and Lucille Etta (Aurner) B.; children: Scott Thomas and Suzanne Laura. BA, U. No. Iowa, 1961, MA, 1964; postgrad., U. Colo., 1968-71; MA, U. San Francisco, 1985. Lic. psychology educator, counselor, Calif. Tchr. various Iowa high schs., 1961-65; sociologist, counselor Office Econ. Opportunity, Denver, 1965-66; social sci. educator Arapahoe Coll., Littleton, Colo., 1966-69; lectr. U. Colo., Boulder, 1968-71; psychology educator Sacramento City Coll., Calif., 1972—; thanatology cons. for hospices, survivor support groups, No. Calif., 1984—. Author: Grief Management: The Pain and the Promise, 1986, Thanatology: Through the Veil, 1992; contbr. articles to profl. publs. Cofounder, bd. dirs. Bereavement Resources Network, Sacramento, 1983-87; profl. dir. Children's Respite Ctr., Sacramento, 1985-88; pres.-elect., bd. dirs. Hospice Care of Sacramento, 1979-85. With U.S. Army, 1955-58. Recipient Pres.'s award Nat. Hospice Orgn., 1985. Mem. Sacramento Mental Health Assn. (Vol. Svc. award 1985, 87), Assn. for Death Edn. and Counseling, Thanatology Found., Am. Fedn. Tchrs., Faculty Assn. Calif. C.C.'s, Pi Gamma Mu, Phi Delta Kappa. Presbyterian. Avocations: music, visual arts, travel, reading. Office: Sacramento City Coll 3835 Freeport Blvd Sacramento CA 95822-1318

BRUELAND, CLYDE EUGENE, advancement director; b. Somers, Iowa, May 31, 1931; s. Clyde Godfrey and Lavonne Mettie (Mack) B.; children: Gregory M., Joel A., Maren C., Brent. AA, Waldorf Coll., Forest City, Iowa, 1952; BS, Concordia Coll., 1954; grad. in theology, Luther Sem., St. Paul, 1958. Pastor in parish Luth. Ch., Iowa, N.D., Minn., 1958-77; devel. dir. Luth. Ch., Moorhead, Minn., 1977-86; devel. assoc. Wheatridge Found., Chgo., 1986-87; devel. dir. Healthcare, Morris, Minn., 1988-91; assoc. estate planning Am. Lung Assn., L.A., 1991-92; advancement dir. David and Margaret Home, La Verne, Calif., 1992—; bd. dirs. Nat. Soc. Fund Raising Execs./Greater L.A. chpt. Mem. Nat. Soc. Fund Raising Execs. (mem. and bd. dirs. greater L.A. chpt.), Assn. Luth. Devel. Execs., Planned Giving Roundtable. Lutheran. Avocations: building, design, construction, needlework. Office: David and Margaret Home Inc 1350 3d St La Verne CA 91750-5299

BRUGGEMAN, LEWIS LEROY, radiologist; b. N.Y.C., Sept. 9, 1941; s. Louis LeRoy and Edwina Jane (Mickel) B.; m. Ann Margaret Kayajan, May 28, 1966; children: Gretchen Ann, Kurt LeRoy. AB, Dartmouth Coll., 1963, B in Med. Sci., 1965; MD, Harvard U., 1968. Intern Los Angeles County Harbor Gen. Hosp., Torrence, Calif., 1968-69; resident in diagnostic radiology Columbia Presbyn. Med. Ctr., N.Y.C., 1969-72; chief dept. radiology Bremerton (Wash.) Naval Regional Med. Ctr., 1972-74; pvt. practice diagnostic radiology South Coast Med. Ctr., South Laguna, Calif., 1974-96, dir. dept. radiology, 1983-95, hosp. bd. trustees, 1985-87; pvt. practice diagnostic radiology Saddleback Community Hosp., Laguna Hills, Calif., 1974-95; pres., chmn. bd. dirs. South Coast Med. Group Inc., South Laguna, Calif., 1983-95; ret., 1996; pres. So. Coast Radiol. Med. Group Inc., South Laguna, 1986-95; vice-chmn. and bd. trustees South Coast Med. Ctr. Found., 1993—. Lt. comdr. Med. Corps USN, 1972-74. Mem. Am. Coll. Radiology, Dartmouth Club Orange County. Avocations: golf, investing, skiing.

BRUGGERE, THOMAS H., computer science company executive; b. Berkeley, Calif., 1946; m. Kelley Bruggere; 2 children. BA in Math., U. Calif., Santa Barbara; MS in Computer Sci., U. Wis.; MBA, Pepperdine U. Founder Mentor Graphics Corp.; venture capitalist Tektronix, Wilsonville, Oreg., 1977—; mem. Oreg. State Bd. Higher Edn.; bd. dirs. Will Vinton Studios, Reed Coll. Bd. dirs. Oreg. Symphony. Mem. Am. Electronics Assn. (bd. dirs.), Portland C. of C. (bd. dirs.). Office: 30000 SW 35th Dr Wilsonville OR 97070-6775

BRUMBAUGH, ROLAND JOHN, bankruptcy judge; b. Pueblo, Colo., Jan. 21, 1940; s. Leo Allen and Ethel Marie (Brummett) B.; m. Pamela Marie Hultman, Sept. 8, 1967; children—Kenneth Allen, Kimberly Marie. B.S. in Bus. with honors, U. Colo., 1968, J.D., 1971. Bar: Colo. 1971, U.S. Dist. Ct. Colo. 1972, U.S. Ct. Appeals (10th cir.) 1973, U.S. Supreme Ct. 1980. Legal intern HUD, Denver, 1971-72; sole practice, Denver, 1972-75; chief dep. city atty. City of Lakewood, Colo., 1975; dep. dir. Colo. Dept. of Revenue, Denver, 1975-78; asst. U.S. atty. Dist. of Colo., Denver, 1978-82; judge U.S. Bankruptcy Ct. Dist. of Colo., Denver, 1982—; lectr. in field. Author: Colorado Liquor and Beer Licensing-Law and Practice, 1970; Handbook for Municipal Clerks, 1972. Contbr. articles to profl. jours. Served with USAF, 1962-65. Recipient numerous awards for excellence in law. Mem. Colo. Bar Assn., Alpha Kappa Psi, Beta Gamma Sigma, Rho Epsilon, Sigma Iota. Home: 1845 Sherman St Ste 400 Denver CO 80203-1167 Office: US Custom House 721 19th St Denver CO 80202-2508*

BRUMFIELD, JACK, executive. Sr. exec. v.p. Stoorza Ziegaus & Metzer, San Diego. Office: Stoorza Ziegaus & Metzer 225 Broadway Ste 1800 San Diego CA 92101-5027

BRUMMER, STEVEN E., police chief. Chief of police Bakersfield, Calif. Office: PO Box 59 1601 Truxtun Ave Bakersfield CA 93302*

BRUMMETT, ROBERT EDDIE, pharmacology educator; b. Concordia, Kans., Feb. 11, 1934; s. Gordon Legonia and Gladys Leona (Anderson) B.; m. Naomi Deen Weaver, Dec. 19, 1954; children: Randall, Wendy, Robin, Philip. BS, Oreg. State U., 1959, MS, 1960; PhD, U. Oreg., 1964. Registered pharmacist, Oreg. Asst. prof. pharmacology Oreg. State U., Corvallis, 1961-62; asst. prof. otolaryngology Oreg. Health Scis. U., Portland, 1964-70, assoc. prof. otolaryngology and pharmacology, 1970-80, prof. otolaryngology and Pharmacology, 1981-97, prof. emeritus, 1997—; mem. Oreg. Coun. on Alcohol and Drug Problems, Salem, 1979-85; instr. Am. Acad. Otolaryngology, Washington, 1964—; mem. adv. panel otorhinolaryngology U.S. Pharmacopeia, 1985—, mem. drug info. adv. panel, 1988—, mem. coun. on naturopathic physicians formulary, 1990—. Contbr. more than 100 articles to profl. jours.; patentee in field. Comdr. U.S. Power Squadron, Portland, 1988-89, adminstrv. officer, 1987, dist. ednl. officer, 1991-94, dist. adminstrv. officer, 1994-95, dist. exec. officer, 1995-96, dist. comdr. 1996-97, nat. rear comdr., 1997—. Grantee NIH, 1969—, Deafness Research Found., 1970, Med. Research Found., 1979, 83. Mem. AAAS, Am. Acad. Otolaryngology (instr. 1964—), Head and Neck Surgery, Associated Rschrs. in Otolaryngology, Hayden Island Yacht Club, Elks, Sigma Xi. Republican. Avocations: sailing, celestial navigation, fishing, wood carving. Home: 2366 N Menzies Ct Portland OR 97217-8219 Office: Oreg Health Scis U 3181 SW Sam Jackson Park Rd Portland OR 97201-3011

BRUN, MARGARET ANN CHARLENE, semiconductor industry buyer, planner; b. Toledo, Ohio, June 19, 1945; d. John Joseph and Maude Elizabeth (Harrell) Bartos; m. Paul Joseph Brun, June 17, 1967. Student, Phoenix Coll., 1964-67, Glendale C.C., 1991-93; Assocs., Mesa C.C., 1996. Cert. purchasing mgr. Contr. material inventory Digital Equipment Corp., Phoenix, 1975-76, contr. prodn. inventory, 1976-77, prodn. control planner, 1977-79, inventory control planner, 1979, buyer, 1979-91; buyer, planner ASM Am., Inc., 1991-95, sr. buyer, 1996—. Named Buyer of Yr., Purchasing World mag., 1987. Mem. Purchasing Mgmt. Assn. Ariz. affiliate of Nat. Assn. Purchasing Mgmt. Democrat. Methodist. Avocations: softball, golfing.

BRUNACINI, ALAN VINCENT, fire chief; b. Jamestown, N.Y., Apr. 18, 1937; s. John N. and Mary T. Brunacini; B.S., Ariz. State U., 1970, M.P.A., 1975; m. Rita McDaugh, Feb. 14, 1959; children—Robert Nicholas, John Nicholas, Mary Candice. Mem. Phoenix Fire Dept., 1959—, bn. chief, then asst. fire chief, 1971-78, fire chief, 1978—; condr. nat. seminar on fire dept. mgmt., 1970—. Redford scholar, 1968. Mem. Am. Soc. Public Adminstrn. (Superior Service award 1980), Nat. Fire Protection Assn. (chmn. fire service sect. 1974-78, dir. 1978), Internat. Assn. Fire Chiefs, Soc. Fire Service Instrs. Author: Fireground Command; also articles in field. Office: Office of Fire Chief 455 N Fifth St Phoenix AZ 85004-2301*

BRUNELLO-MCCAY, ROSANNE, sales executive; b. Cleve., Aug. 26, 1960; d. Carl Carmello and Vivan Lucille (Caranna) B.; m. Walter B. McCay, Feb. 26, 1994 (div. 1998); 1 child, Angela Breanna. Student, U. Cin., 1978-81, Cleve. State U., 1981-82. Indsl. sales engr. Alta Machine Tool, Denver, 1982; mem. sales./purchases Ford Tool & Machine, Denver, 1982-84; sales/ptnr. Mountain Rep. Enterprises, Denver, 1984-86; pres., owner Mountain Rep. Ariz., Phoenix, 1986—; pres. Mountain Rep. Oreg., Portland, 1990—, Mountain Rep. Wash., 1991—; pres. Mountain Rep. Calif., Sunnyvale, 1997—, San Clemente, 1998—; sec. Computer & Automated Systems Assoc., 1987, vice chmn., 1988, chmn., 1989. Active mem. Rep. Party, 1985—; mem. Phoenix Art Mus., Grand Canyon Minority Coun., 1994; vol. Make-A-Wish Found. fund raiser, 1995-98. Named Mrs. Chandler Internat. by Mrs. Ariz. Internat. orgn., 1996, Mrs. East Valley U.S., 1997; finalist Mrs. Ariz. Internat., 1996. Mem. NAFE, Soc. Mfg. Engrs. (pres. award 1988), Computer Automated Assn. (sec. 1987, vice chmn. 1988 chmn. 1989), Nat. Hist. Soc., Italian Cultural Soc., Tempe C. of C., Vocat. Ednl. Club Am. (mem. exec. bd., pres. 1987—). Roman Catholic. Avocations: sports, aerobics, dancing, skiing, golfing, tennis. E-mail: rosanne@mtnrep.com. Office: Mountain Rep Ariz 410 S Jay St Chandler AZ 85224-7668

BRUNER, JAMES ERNEST, screenwriter, film production executive; b. Indpls., May 12, 1952; s. James Lyman and Anne Raymond (Hennen) B.; m. Nancy Elizabeth Hilgerman; 1 child, Jennifer. BA in History, U. Wis., 1974. Pres. SagaFilm, Inc., Encino, Calif., 1984—. Screenwriter: (films) An Eye for an Eye, 1981, Missing in Action, 1984, Invasion U.S.A., 1985, The Delta Force, 1986, Braddock, 1988. Mem. Writers Guild Am. Office: SagaFilm Inc PO Box 17360 Encino CA 91416-7360

BRUNER, NANCY J., publishing executive. Dir. new media Seattle Times. Office: Seattle Times PO Box 70 Seattle WA 98111-0070

BRUNER, RICHARD WALLACE, writer; b. Burlington, Iowa, June 26, 1926; s. Eugene Floyd and Dorothy Katherine (Gavin) B.; m. Rosemary Gertrude Holahan, June 14, 1947 (div. Nov. 1980); children: Sean H., Susan V., Richard E.; m. Erzsebet Maria Szeip, Aug. 24, 1991; 1 stepchild, Marko Molnar. BA, U. Minn., 1949. Editor, pub. Fridley (Minn.) Free Press, 1950-51; reporter Mankato (Minn.) Free Press, 1951-53; editor, program coord. United Packing House, Des Moines, 1953-57; news writer NBC Radio and TV, Chgo. and N.Y.C., 1957-66; freelance writer various locations, 1966—. Author: (books) Black Politicians, 1971, Whitney M. Young, Jr., The Story of a Pragmatic Humanst, 1972, (Off-Broadway plays) A Small Disturbance, Amistad; editor: (newspaper) Budapest Week, 1992-93; regular contbr. to periodicals including Electronic News, SKY Mag., Delta Airlines inflight mag.; contbr. numerous articles to profl. publs. and popular mags. With U.S. Army Air Corps, 1944-46. Democrat. Avocation: tennis. Home: 2608 W Aiden St Tucson AZ 85745-3341

BRUNETT, ALEXANDER J., bishop; b. Detroit, MI, Jan. 13, 1958. ordained priest July 13, 1958. Ordained bishop Diocese of Helena, 1994; archbishop Diocese of Seattle, 1997—. Office: Chancery Office 910 Marion St Seattle WA 98104-1274

BRUNETTI, MELVIN T., federal judge; b. 1933; m. Gail Dian Buchanan; children: Nancy, Bradley, Melvin Jr. Student, U. Nev.; JD, U. Calif., San Francisco, 1964. Mem. firm Vargas, Bartlett & Dixon, 1964-69, Laxalt, Bell, Allison & Lebaron, 1970-78, Allison, Brunetti, MacKenzie, Hartman, Soumbeniotis & Russell, 1978-85; judge U.S. Ct. Appeals (9th cir.), Reno, 1985—. Mem. Council of Legal Advisors, Rep. Nat. Com., 1982-85. Served with U.S. Army N.G., 1954-56. Mem. ABA, State Bar of Nev. (pres. 1984-85, bd. govs. 1975-84). Office: US Ct Appeals US Courthouse 400 S Virginia St Ste 506 Reno NV 89501-2194*

BRUNING, NANCY PAULINE, writer; b. N.Y.C., Nov. 7, 1948; d. Nicholas Cornelius Bruning and Anne Marie (Liebenberg) Jacelon. BA, Pratt Inst., 1969. Author: Breast Implants, 1995, Coping With Chemotherapy, 1995, Healing Homeopathic Remedies, 1996, Ayurveda: The A-Z Guide to Healing Techniques from Ancient India, 1997, The Real Vitamin & Mineral Book, 1997, The Mend Clinic Guide to Natural Medicines for Menopause and Beyond, 1997, Natural Medicines for Colds and Flu, 1998, Natural Relief for Your Child's Asthma, 1999, Effortless Beauty and Weight Control, 1999. Bd. dirs. Breast Cancer Action, 1990-91, Urban Ecology, Oakland, 1992-97. Office: 980 Bush St Apt 503 San Francisco CA 94109-6327

BRUNNER, HOWARD WILLIAM, professional land surveyor; b. Mobile, Ala., July 24, 1946; s. Joseph Edward and Beaulah (Howard) B.; m. Linda

Marie Parker, Dec. 20, 1963 (div. June 1978); children: Leah Marie, Anne Marie; m. Catherine Cecilia Byrnes, June 27, 1981; 1 child, Jordan Thomas Howard. Grad. high sch., Santa Rosa, Calif. Lic. profl. land surveyor, Calif., Wash., Nev. Survey technician Roemer & Estes, Mill Valley, Calif., 1964-65, Ken Frost & Assocs., Mill Valley, 1965-66; engring. aide County of Marin, San Rafael, Calif., 1966-75; pres. Engring. Field Svcs., San Rafael, 1975-77, Brunner, Phelps & Assocs., Inc., Cotati, Calif., 1977-80; v.p. Ray Carlson & Assocs., Inc., Santa Rosa, Calif., 1980-92; ptnr. Bedford Brunner, Santa Rosa, 1993-96; prin. Howard W. Brunner, Profl. Land Surveyor, Santa Rosa, 1996—; expert examiner, profl. land surveyor, cons., registrar, tech. adv. com. mem., expert witness, chmn. item writing com. Bd. Registration for Profl. Engrs. and Land Surveyors, Sacramento, 1985-96. Mem. Geysers Geothermal Assn. (bd. dirs. 1985-92), Calif. Land Surveyors Assn. (treas. 1987-88, sec. 1988-89, pres. 1990), Am. Consulting Engrs. Coun. (chmn. coun. profl. land surveyors 1995-96). Roman Catholic. Avocations: boating, skiing, skin diving, antique automobiles, Porsche's. Home: 1161 Valley View Dr Healdsburg CA 95448-4540 Office: 320 College Ave Ste 220 Santa Rosa CA 95401-5144

BRUNO, CATHY EILEEN, management consultant, former state official; b. Binghamton, N.Y. d. Martin Frank and Beverly Carolyn (Hamlin) Piza; m. Frank L. Delaney (div.); m. Paul R. Bruno, May 5, 1990. BA, SUNY, Binghamton; MSW, Syracuse U. Psychiat. social worker Willard (N.Y.) Psychiat. Ctr., 1968-73, Broome Devel. Ctr., Binghamton, 1973-74, 76; congl. legis. aide, 1975; asst. dir. Bur. Program and Fiscal audits N.Y. State Office Mental Retardation and Devel. Disabilities, Albany, 1976-80, statewide coord. Intermediate Care Facilities for Developmentally Disabled, 1980, cert. coord. Western County Svc. Group, 1980-83, Upstate unit dir. Bur. Cert. Control, 1983-85; dir. ICF/DD Survey and Rev., 1985-89; area dir. Bur. Program Cert., 1989-95; dir. Bur. Transitional Svcs., 1995-97; mgmt. cons., 1997—; adj. instr. SUNY Sch. Social Welfare, Albany, 1982-83. Grantee HEW, 1975-76. Mem. Am. Mgmt. Assn.

BRUNO, JUDYTH ANN, chiropractor; b. Eureka, Calif., Feb. 16, 1944; d. Harold Oscar and Shirley Alma (Farnsworth) Nelson; m. Thomas Glenn Bruno, June 1, 1968; 1 child, Christina Elizabeth. AS, Sierra Coll., 1982; D of Chiropractic, Palmer Coll. of Chiropractic West, Sunnyvale, Calif., 1986. Diplomate Nat. Bd. Chiropractic Examiners. Sec. Bank Am., San Jose, Calif., 1965-67; marketer Memorex, Santa Clara, Calif., 1967-74; order entry clk. John Deere, Milan, Ill., 1977; system analyst Four Phase, Cupertino, Calif., 1977-78; chiropractic asst. Dr. Thomas Bruno, Nevada City, Calif., 1978-81; chiropractor Chiropractic Health Care Ctr., Nevada City, 1987—; pvt. practice Cedar Ridge, Calif., 1991—. Area dir. Cultural Awareness Coun., Grass Valley, Calif., 1977—; vol. Nevada County Libr., Nevada City, 1987-88, Decide Team III, Nevada County, 1987-92, Active Parenting of Teen Facilitator Nev. Union H.S., 1989-93, judge sr. projects, 1992—. Recipient Bus. and Profl. Woman of Yr. award No. Mines, 1997. Mem. Women Health Practitioners of Nevada County (founder 1993—), Nevada County C. of C. (vol. task force health care 1993), Toastmasters (sec. 1988, pres. 1989, 98, edn. v.p. 1990). Republican. Avocations: spiritual growth, skiing, origami, ecology. Office: Chiropractor Health Care PO Box 1718 Cedar Ridge CA 95924-1718

BRUNO, PETER JACKSON, counselor, consultant, pastor; b. White Plains, N.Y., Dec. 27, 1945; s. Charles Fredrick and Barbara (Jackson) B.; m. Barbara Suesens; 1 child, Linda; 2d m. Corky Jean Brown, July 3, 1976; children: Benjamin, Elizabeth. BA in Psychology, Brown U., 1968; MEd in Counseling, Mont. State U., 1978. Ordained min. Evangelical Ch.; lic. profl. counselor, Mont.; nat. cert. counselor. Addictive disease counselor Mont. State Hosp., Galen, 1973-76; tchg. asst. Mont. State U., Bozeman, 1977-78; psychologist V Ea. Mont. Mental Health, Miles City, 1979-92; pvt. practice counselor Glendive, Mont., 1992-98; clin. cons. Dept. Family Svcs., Miles City, Home on the Range, Sentinel Butte, N.D., Pine Hills Sch., Miles City, all 1992-94; clin. dir. Big Sky Ranch, Glendive, 1992-97. Author: New Ways Workbook, 1992. Pres. Montanans for Children, Youth and Families, Inc. Named Mont.'s Outstanding Direct Svc. Provider, Mental Health Assn. Mont., 1982. Mem. Great Plains Counseling Assocs. (dir.), Toastmasters Internat. (Disting. Leadership award 1995), Nat. Spkrs. Assn., Internat. Platform Assn. Office: Complete Marriages PO Box 684 513 N Merrill Ave Glendive MT 59330-1829

BRUNTON, DANIEL WILLIAM, mechanical engineer; b. Ft. Wayne, Ind., Sept. 25, 1956; s. Paul Edward and Margaret Alice (Rice) B.; m. Carol Marie Pryor, Feb. 19, 1994; children: Edward Daniel, Ann Marie. BS, UCLA, 1978, MS in Engring., 1980, M of Engring., 1986. Mem. tech. staff Hughes Missiles Group, Canoga Park, Calif., 1978-89, dept. mgr., 1989-93; mech. engr. dept. mgr. Litton Itek, Lexington, Mass., 1993-94; sr. engr. Raytheon Missile Sys. Co., Tucson, 1994-97, prin. engr., 1997—. Mem. Soc. Photonic Instrumentation Engrs., Tau Beta Pi. Achievements include 4 patents filed on cryogenics, optical material testing, and mechanisms. Office: Raytheon Missile Sys Co PO Box 11337 Tucson AZ 85734-1337

BRUNTON, DONNA LEE, secretarial services manager; b. Denver, May 20, 1929; d. Harry Leroy and Myrtle Evelina McCarthy; m. James Ewing Brunton, Aug. 20, 1948 (div. 1979); children: Mark Lionel, Valerie Lee Stotts. Student, Pasadena City Coll., 1963-64; cert. paralegal, U. So. Calif., 1979. Sec. Gray, White & Burkitt, Pasadena, Calif., 1964-79; office mgr. Hill, Gould & Pearson, L.A., 1979-81; owner Quick Response Secretarial Svc., Glendale, Calif., 1981—. Editor: (weekly bull.) Sunrise Rotary, 1993-94. Mem. Rotary Internat., Order of Ea. Star. Republican. Presbyterian. Avocations: gourmet cooking, reading, gardening, walking dog. Office: Quick Response Sec Svc 700 N Brand Blvd Ste 1190 Glendale CA 91203-1238

BRUSASCHETTI, MARILEE MARSHALL, media executive; b. Albuquerque, Sept. 16, 1962; d. John Lawrence and Carol Kay (Turner) Marshall; m. James Douglas Brusaschetti, July 22, 1995; 1 child, Nicholas Rocco. BSBA, Ariz. State U., 1984. Asst. media planner DDB Needham, L.A., 1985-86; media planner Saatchi & Saatchi, DFS, Torrance, Calif., 1986-87; media planner, sr. Keye, Donna, Pearlstein, L.A., 1987-88; media dir. Owens & Assocs., Phoenix, 1988-90; assoc. media dir. Foote, Cone & Belding, Santa Ana, Calif., 1990-94; media supr. Goldberg, Moser, O'Neill, San Francisco, 1994-96; founder M2B Media Consulting, 1998—; lectr. mktg. dept. Ariz. State U., Tempe, 1988-89. Mem. Ariz. State U. Alumna Assn. (sec. 1993-94), Young Profls. Against Cancer, L.A. Ad Club, Delta Delta Delta. Republican. Methodist. Avocations: race car driving, writing, music.

BRUST, DAVID, physicist; b. Chgo., Aug. 24, 1935; s. Clifford and Ruth (Klapman) B.; BS, Calif. Inst. Tech., 1957; MS, U. Chgo., 1958, PhD, 1964. Rsch. assoc. Purdue U., Lafayette, Ind., 1963-64; rsch. assoc. Northwestern U., Evanston, Ill., 1964-65, asst. prof. physics, 1965-68; theoretical rsch. physicist U. Calif., Lawrence Radiation Lab., Livermore, Calif., 1968-73; cons. Bell Telephone Lab., Murray Hill, N.J., 1966. Campaign co-ordinator No. Calif. Scientists and Engrs. for McGovern, 1972. NSF travel grantee, 1964; NSF rsch. grantee, 1966-68. Mem. Am. Phys. Soc., Am. Assn. Coll. Profs., Internat. Solar Energy Soc., Astron. Soc. of Pacific, Nature Conservancy, Calif. Acad. Sci., Commonwealth Club of Calif., World Affairs Coun. No. Calif. Commonwealth Club Anza Borrego Desert, Natural History Assn., Planetary Soc., Sierra Club, Sigma Xi. Office: PO Box 13130 Oakland CA 94661-0130

BRYAN, A(LONZO) J(AY), service club official; b. Washington, N.J., Sept. 17, 1917; s. Alonzo J. and Anna Belle (Babcock) B.; student pub. schs.; m. Elizabeth Elfreida Koehler, June 25, 1941 (div. 1961); children: Donna Elizabeth, Alonzo Jay, Nadine; m. Janet Dorothy Onstad, Mar. 15, 1962 (div. 1977); children: Brenda Joyce, Marlowe Francis, Marilyn Janet. Engaged as retail florist, Washington, N.J., 1941-64. Fund drive chmn. ARC, 1952; bd. dirs. Washington YMCA, 1945-55, N.J. Taxpayers Assn., 1947-52; mem. Washington Bd. Edn., 1948-55. Mem. Washington Grange, Sons and Daus. of Liberty, Soc. Am. Florists, Nat. Fedn. Ind. Businessmen, Florists Telegraph Delivery Assn., C. of C. Methodist. Clubs: Masons, Tall Cedars of [illegible] (pres. Washington (N.J.) 1952, lt. gov. internat. 1953-54, gov. N.J. dist. 1955, sec. N.J. dist. 1957-64, sec. S.E. area Chgo. 1965-74; editor The Jersey Kiwanian 1958-64, internat. staff 1964-85); Breakfast (pres. 1981-82) (Chgo.); sec., treas. Rocky Mtn. Kiwanis Dist., 1989; pres. South Denver, 1990-91; editor Rocky Mountain Kiwanian, 1990-96. Home: 8115 S Poplar Way B 203 Englewood CO 80112-3174 Office: 8859 Fox Dr Ste 100 Denver CO 80221 6831

BRYAN, GORDON REDMAN, JR., retired career officer; b. Cleve., Dec. 1, 1928; s. Gordon Redman and Iola (Schecter) B.; m. Janet Louise McIntyre, Aug. 1, 1951 (div. Oct. 1985); children: Gordon L., Steven G.; m. Judith Hager, July 5, 1987. BA, Brown U., 1951; MS, George Washington U., 1970. Commd. ensign USN, 1951, advanced through grades to capt., 1971; comdg. officer 4 navy ships and 5 shore commands, 1965-78, submarine squadron, 1972-74; ret., 1978; marine design cons. various aerospace and engring. cos., Seattle, 1979-81; engring. cons. U.S. Nuc. Regulatory Commn. and U.S. Dept. Energy, Seattle, 1982-95. Decorated Legion of Merit. Mem. Am. Nuclear Soc., Am. Radio Relay League, N.Y. Acad. Scis., Rotary. Republican. Avocations: amateur radio, travel. Home and Office: SaddleBrooke Country Club 37810 S Rolling Hills Dr Tucson AZ 85739-1069

BRYAN, JOHN RODNEY, management consultant; b. Berkeley, Calif., Dec. 29, 1953; s. Robert Richard and Eloise (Anderson) Putz; m. Karen Nelson, Jan. 20, 1990. BA in Chemistry, U. Calif., San Diego, 1975; MBA, Rutgers U., 1985. Agt. Prudential, San Diego, 1975-79; sales mgr. Herman Schlorman Showrooms, L.A., 1980-83; pvt. practice mgmt. cons. Basking Ridge, N.J., 1983-85; mgmt. cons. The Brooks Group, Hollywood, Fla., 1985—; pvt. practice San Diego, 1988—; with Western Productivity Group, 1990-95. Elder La Jolla Presbyn. Ch., 1991—. Mem. Inst. Indsl. Engring., Rutgers Club So. Calif., Beta Gamma Sigma. Avocations: opera, classical music, literature, jazz, singing. E-mail: John Bryan@aol.com. Office: 6265 Hurd Ct San Diego CA 92122-2917

BRYAN, JUDITH HAGER, travel consultant, educator; b. Bklyn., May 9, 1938; d. Wesley Harold and Charlotte (Sweet) Hager; m. Ralph Edward Tuggle, June 20, 1959 (div. Oct. 1986); children: David William Tuggle, Rebecca Joanne Tuggle Friendly, Robert Scott Tuggle, Kevin Bradley Tuggle; m. Gordon Redman Bryan, Jr., July 7, 1987. BA, DePauw U., 1959; postgrad., Old Dominion U., 1968-69. Tchr. Ocean Air Elem. Sch., Norfolk, Va., 1959-60, Ohau (Hawaii) Pub. Schs., 1960, Groton (Conn.) Pub. Schs., 1960, San Diego Pub. Schs., 1960-63; travel agt., cons., 1967—. Pres. Submarine Officers Wives Club, Groton, Conn., 1960-62, chair art shows, 1970; pres. U.S. Naval PG Sch. Student Wives Club, Monterey, 1965-69, USNA '59 Wives Club, Norfolk, 1966-68, PTA, San Diego, 1981-83; gray lady ARC, 1961; mem. USN Relief Assn., San Diego, 1963-65, United Meth. Chs., 1959—, Navy Officers Wives Choral Assembly, Ohau, 1965-66, Mus. Arts and Scis., Norfolk, 1969, Keynote Music Club, Monterey, Calif., 1969; youth counselor San Diego Schs., 1963-65; trustee Congl. Ch., Suquamish, Wash., 1993; hostess Adobe House Tours, Monterey, 1966, Jamestown Exposition, Norfolk, 1969, Norfolk Week house tours, 1969; leader Cub Scouts, Norfolk, 1973-75, San Diego, 1977-84, Girl Scouts, San Diego, 1983-84, Brownies, San Diego, 1980-81. Named one of Outstanding Young Women Am., 1970; recipient commendation ARC, 1961, commendation USS Pargo, USN, 1973. Mem. Bay View Assn., Kappa Kappa Gamma Alumni, P.E.O. (treas. 1981-91, chaplain 1984-85, sec. 1988-89). Methodist. Avocations: golf, travel, photography, crafts, singing. Home: 37810 S Rolling Hills Dr Tucson AZ 85739-1069 Office: Copper Travel 16150 N Oracle Rd Tucson AZ 85739-8720

BRYAN, RICHARD H., senator; b. Washington, July 16, 1937; m. Bonnie Fairchild; 3 children. BA, U. Nev., 1959; LLB, U. Calif., San Francisco, 1963. Bar: Nev. 1963. Dep. dist. atty. Clark County, Nev., 1964-66; public defender Clark County, 1966-68; counsel Clark County Juvenile Ct., 1968-69; mem. Nev. Assembly, 1969-73, Nev. Senate, 1973-79; atty. gen. State Nev., 1979-83, gov., 1983-89; senator from Nevada U.S. Senate, 1989—; mem. U.S. Senate coms. on commerce, sci. and transp.; mem. Dem. Policy Com.; mem. Fin. Com.; mem. Banking, Housing and Urban Affairs Com.; mem. Sen. Nom. Steering and Coor. Com.; mem. select. Com. on Intelligence. Bd. dirs. March of Dimes; former v.p. Nev. Easter Seal Soc.; former pres. Clark County Legal Aid Soc. Served with U.S. Army, 1959-60. Recipient Disting. Svc. award Vegas Valley Jaycees. Mem. ABA, Clark County Bar Assn., Am. Judicature Soc., Council of State Govts. (past pres.), Phi Alpha Delta, Phi Alpha Theta. Democrat. Clubs: Masons, Lions, Elks. Office: US Senate 269 Russell Senate Office Bldg Washington DC 20510-2804*

BRYAN, ROBERT J., federal judge; b. Bremerton, Wash., Oct. 29, 1934; s. James W. and Vena Gladys (Jensen) B.; m. Cathy Ann Welander, June 14, 1958; children: Robert James, Ted Lorin, Ronald Terence. BA, U. Wash., 1956, JD, 1958. Bar: Wash. 1959, U.S. Dist. Ct. (we. dist.) Wash. 1959, U.S. Tax Ct. 1965, U.S. Ct. Appeals (9th cir.) 1985. Assoc., then ptnr. Bryan & Bryan, Bremerton, 1959-67; judge Superior Ct., Port Orchard, Wash., 1967-84; ptnr. Riddell, Williams, Bullitt & Walkinshaw, Seattle, 1984-86; judge U.S. Dist. Ct. (we. dist.) Wash., Tacoma, 1986—; mem. State Jail Comm., Olympia, Wash., 1974-76, Criminal Justice Tng. Com., Olympia, 1978-81, State Bd. on Continuing Legal Edn., Seattle, 1984-86; mem., sec. Jud. Qualifications Commn., Olympia, 1982-83; chair Wash. Fed.-State Jud. Coun., 1997-98. Author: (with others) Washington Pattern Jury Instructions (civil and criminal vols. and supplements), 1970-85, Manual of Model Criminal Jury Instructions for the Ninth Circuit, 1992, Manual of Model Civil Jury Instruction for the Ninth Circuit, 1993. Chmn. 9th Ct. Jury Com., 1991-92. Served to maj. USAR. Mem. 9th Cir. Dist. Judges Assn. (sec.-treas. 1997—). Office: US Dist Ct 1717 Pacific Ave Rm 4427 Tacoma WA 98402-3234

BRYAN, SUKEY, artist; b. Summit, N.J., Apr. 4, 1961; d. Barry Richard and Margaret Susannah (Elliot) Bryan; m. James Duane Brooks, July 8, 1989; children: Matthew Lyle Brooks, William Elliot Brooks. BA, Yale U., 1983; MFA, Md. Inst./Coll. of Art, Balt., 1990. Artist. Solo exhbns. include Essex (Md.) C.C., 1990, 91, Johns Hopkins U., Balt., 1992, H. Pelham Curtis Gallery, New Canaan, Conn., 1992, Galerie Francoise e.s.f., Balt., 1994, C. Grimaldis Gallery, Balt., 1995, 97; exhibited in group shows The BauHouse, Balt., 1991, Ctr. for Creative Arts, Yorklyn, Del., 1992, Edinboro U. Pa., 1992, Dundalk (Md.) Art Gallery, 1993, Addison Gallery Arm Art, Andover, Mass., 1993, Kristal Gallery, Warren, Vt., 1994, Fifth Column, Washington, 1995, St. Mary's Coll. Md., 1995, Balt. Festival for the Arts, 1992, 93, 95, C. Grimaldis Gallery, 1995, 96, 97, 98, Art Sites, Rockville (Md.) Art Place, 1996, Corcoran Gallery Art, Washington, 1996, Balt. Sch. for the Arts, 1997, Goya-Girl Press, Balt., 1997, U. Pacific, Stockton, Calif., 1998, Susan Cummins Gallery, Mill Valley, Calif., 1999, others; represented in collections at Balt. Mus. of Art, Cathedral of the Incarnation, Balt., Piper & Marbury, Balt.; author, artist: Tidal Grass, 1993. Recipient Individual Artist award Md. State Arts Coun., 1991; Visual Artist fellow Nat. Endowment for Arts, 1993-94. Democrat. Episcopalian.

BRYANS, RICHARD WALDRON, JR., musician, lawyer; b. Athens, Ga., Sept. 12, 1955. BS, Regis Coll., 1988; JD, U. Denver, 1990. Bar: Colo. 1991. Drummer, vocalist, bus. mgr. music group Dreams, Denver, 1973-77; drummer, vocalist, co-arranger Aviary, Los Angeles, 1977-80; drummer Badfinger, Los Angeles, 1980-81; free-lance producer Denver, 1981-86; ptnr. Bryans & Bryans P.C., Denver. Drummer, vocalist (album) Aviary, 1979; drummer (album) Say No More, 1981. Mem. Am. Fedn. Musicians, Broadcast Music, Inc. Avocations: photography, painting, swimming, cycling, golf. Home: 1675 S Birch St Apt 1104 Denver CO 80222-4152 Office: Bryans & Bryans PC 1700 Broadway Denver CO 80290-1700

BRYANT, CAROL LEE, public health educator, psychotherapist, consultant; b. L.A., Aug. 17, 1946; d. John Thomas and Janice Hathaway (Haislip) B.; m. Norman Alexander, June 4, 1966 (div. 1975); children: Ian Alexander, Colin Alexander; m. Reinhard Alexander Fritsch, June 14, 1983; 1 child, Briana Noelle Fritsch-Bryant. AA, Diablo Valley Jr. Coll., Pleasant Hill, Calif., 1975; BA, San Francisco State U., 1978; MA in Transpersonal Counseling, John F. Kennedy U., Orinda, Calif., 1982, MA in Clin. Psychology, 1982; PhD in Clin. Psychology, Sierra U., 1986. Lic. marriage, family, and child counselor, Calif. Instr., tchr. Community Recreation [illegible] Walnut Creek, Calif., [illegible], John F. Kennedy U., Orinda, Calif., 1980-81; adminstrv. dir. Touchstone Counseling Svc., Walnut Creek, 1981-83; tchr. Diablo Valley Jr. Coll., 1984; exec. dir. Battered Women's Alternatives, Concord, Calif., 1984-85, Child Abuse Prevention Coun., Walnut Creek, 1985-90; psychotherapist InVision Assocs., Lafayette, Calif., 1984-94; pub. health educator Mariposa (Calif.) Health Dept., 1990—; cons. Computer Using Educators, Menlo Park, Calif., 1988 90; lectr. in field; mem., chairperson Mariposa Mental Health Adv. Bd.; vice chairperson Mariposa Drug and Alcohol Adv. Bd., maternal child health adv. bd., mem. John C. Fremont Hosp. Found. Contbr. articles to profl. jours. and books. Chmn. No. Calif. Legis. Children and Family Coalition, Berkeley, 1987-90; adv. bd., chmn. Women's Recovery Ctr., Bass Lake, Calif., 1990-92; coord./mem. No. Calif. Child Death Review Coalition, San Francisco, 1988-90, Children and Family Trust Fund Com., Concord, 1989-90. Mem. Assn. Marriage Family Therapists. Avocations: writing, hiking, travel, community service. Home: PO Box 453 Joseph OR 97846-0453 Office: Mariposa Pub Health Dept PO Box 5 Mariposa CA 95338-0005

BRYANT, DARYL LESLIE, painter, educator; b. L.A., Feb. 11, 1940; d. Colin Willis and Virginia Rouseau (Graves) Timmons; m. Dennis Rourke Murphy, 1960 (div. 1972); children: John Ashley, Sarah; m. Daniel Walster Bryant, 1985. Student, U. So. Calif., Acad. Arts, Florence, Italy; AA, Valley Coll., Van Nuys, Calif. Asst. designer Koret Calif., San Francisco, 1959-60; freelance artist Studiowork, Studio City, Calif.; art dir. Brentwood (Calif.) Publs., 1978-87; painter, graphic designer South Pasadena, Calif., 1987—; tchr. Creative Arts Group, Sierra Madre, Calif., 1996—. Works published in books and mags. Mem. Mid Valley Arts League (bd. dirs. 1993—), Nat. Watercolor Soc. (signature), Watercolor West (signature), Calif. Art Club (signature). Avocations: swimming, hiking, travel, journal keeping. Home: 2940 Lorain Rd San Marino CA 91108-2733

BRYANT, DON ESTES, economist, scientist; b. Truman, Ark., May 18, 1917; s. James Monroe and Olivia (Mayfield) B.; m. Jess Ann Chailer, Jan. 27, 1956; children: Stephen Williamson (dec.), Patrice Ann. Student, Cass Tech. Trade Coll., 1938-41. Pres., founder Consol. Aircraft Products, El Segundo, Calif., 1949-57, Trilan Corp., El Segundo, 1957-62, The Am. Inventor, Palos Verdes Estates, Calif., 1962-68; chmn., founder Message Control Crop., Palos Verdes Estates, 1968-70; scientist Econ. Rsch., Palos Verdes Estates and Lake Arrowhead, Calif., 1970—; cons. Svc. Corps. Ret. Execs. Assn.-SBA, L.A., 1965-67; founder Bryant Inst. and Club U.S.A. (United to Save Am.), 1991, J. Ayn Bryant and Assocs., 1991. Inventor missle and satellite count-down systems for USAF, 1958; formulator sci. of human econs.; host TV talk show World Peace Through Free Enterprise, 1985; author: 10-book children's series The 1, 2, 3's of Freedom and Economics, 1988. Served with USN, 1935-37. Republican. Roman Catholic. Avocations: sailing, woodworking. Home: 329 Greenview Ln Fallbrook CA 92028-1864

BRYANT, GARY JONES, minister; b. Stockton, Mo., Aug. 20, 1942; s. John Franklin and Imogene Eunice (Jones) B.; m. Deborah A. Brewer, Aug. 20, 1965; children: Gary Jason, Gareth Joshua. BA in Bible, Cen. Bible Coll., Springfield, Mo., 1966; BS in Religious Studies, Bethany Bible Coll., Santa Cruz, Calif., 1968; MA in Religion, Crossroad Grad. Sch. Div., Muncie, Ind., 1973, PhD in Religion, 1975. Ordained to ministry Assemblies of God, 1969, Internat. Ch. of the Foursquare Gospel, 1994. Pastor Vista (Calif.) Assembly of God Ch., 1972-75, First Assembly of God Ch., Porterville, Calif., 1976-83, Christian Life Ch., Pitts., 1982-84; dir. Heart of Am. Counseling Ctr., Kansas City, Mo., 1984-85; pastor, dir. Peoples Ch.-Peoples Counseling Ctr., Las Cruces, N.Mex., 1986-99; pastor Stream in the Desert Foursquare Gospel Ch., 1999—; Christian edn. advisor So. Calif. Dist. Assemblies of God, Costa Mesa, 1978-80, youth leader, San Diego, 1976-78, presbyter, Costa Mesa, 1980-83. Author: Flight of the Dove - Cedar County, 1975. Bd. dirs. So. Calif. Coll., Costa Mesa, 1980-83; adv. bd. Tulare County Mental Health Hosp. and Clinics, 1979-82; adv. com. Cen. Bus. Dist. Coun., Las Cruces, 1991; pastor Lighthouse Ch., Vincennes, Ind., 1996—; divsn. supt. Great Lakes Divsn. Foursquare Chs., So. Ing., 1996—. Mem. Rotary. Republican. Home: 361 N Lovekin Blvd Blythe CA 92225

BRYANT, JAMES PATRICK, art educator, artist; b. Indpls., Nov. 18, 1967; s. Fred James Bryant and Bonnita Lee (Bobo) White. AA, Pensacola (Fla.) Jr. Coll., 1988; BFA, Herron Sch. of Art, Indpls., 1992; MFA, La. State U., 1995. Illustrator Indpls. Star, 1991; art dir. Printsly Creations, Indpls., 1988-92; instr. Southeastern La. U., Hammond, 1995-96; asst. prof. dept. art Ea. N.Mex. U., Portales, 1996—; Designer UN, 1996-98. Instrl. Devel. grantee Ea. N.Mex. U., 1998. Home: 400 S Ave B Portales NM 88130-6355 Office: ENMU Art Dept Portales NM 88130

BRYANT, KOBE, basketball player; b. Aug. 23, 1978. Student, Lower Merion (Pa.) High Sch. Player L.A. Lakers, 1996—. Named to NBA All-Rookie 2nd Team, 1996-97. Office: c/o LA Lakers PO Box 10 Inglewood CA 90306-0010*

BRYANT, PAMELA ANNE, career officer, retired, business owner; b. Detroit, July 15, 1950; d. Theodore Louis and Martha Marie (Nordstrom) Cogut; children: Tessa A. McGeaughay, Sean L. BS in Vocat. Indsl. Edn., U. Md., 1976; student, Mich. State U., East Lansing, 1969-71; MS, Troy (Ala.) State U., 1986. Commd. 2d lt. USAF, 1980, advanced through grades to maj., 1984; chief cargo ops., reports and systems div. 22d Air Force, Travis AFB, Calif., 1989-90; chief support div. directorate transp. Hdqrs USAF Res., Robins AFB, Ga., 1990-94; squadron commdr. 650th Transp. Squadron, Edwards AFB, Calif., 1994—; owner Bryant Enterprises, 1991—; lectr. Clifton-Morenci (Ariz.) Rotary Club, 1989. Soccer team coord. Am. Youth Assn., RAF Laken Heath, Eng., 1983; troop leader Girl Scouts U.S., RAF Laken Heath, 1982; membership chmn. Boy Scouts Am., RAF Laken Heath, 1983. U. Md. scholar, 1976. Mem. Nat. Def. Transp. Assn., NAFE, Air Force Assn. (life), Alpha Sigma Lambda.

BRYANT, THOMAS LEE, magazine editor; b. Daytona Beach, Fla., June 15, 1943; s. Stanley Elson and G. Bernice (Burgess) B.; m. Patricia Jean Bryant, June 30, 1979. BA in Polit. Sci., U. Calif., Santa Barbara, 1965, MA in Polit. Sci., 1966. Fgn. svc. officer U.S. Dept. State, Washington, Buenos Aires, 1967-69; radio broadcaster KDB Sta., Santa Barbara, Calif., 1969-72; magazine editor, now editor-in-chief Road & Track, Newport Beach, Calif., 1972—. Mem. Internat. Motor Press Assn., Motor Press Guild, Sports Car Club of Am. Avocations: golf, trap and skeet shooting. Office: c/o Hachette Filipacchi Mags Inc 1499 Monrovia Ave Newport Beach CA 92663-2752*

BRYANT, WOODROW WESLEY, architect; b. San Jose, Calif., June 5, 1949; s. Foy Eldean and Loraine (McKee) B.; m. Becky Ann Hoffmaster, June 27, 1981; 1 stepson: Jeremy Saul Martin. Student, Am. River Coll., Sacramento, Calif., 1968; BArch, Calif. State Polytechnic U., 1973. Registered architect, Calif., Nev., Utah, Idaho, Ariz. Designer, project mgr. Angello & Vitiello Assoc., Sacramento, 1971-75; draftsman Caywood, Nopp & Ward, Sacramento, 1975; architect W. Bryant Enterprises, Sacramento, 1975-76, Wright, Bryant & Johnson, Ketchum, Idaho, 1976—; bd. dirs. Elkhorn Archtl. Design Commn., Uniform Bldg. Code Bd. Appeals, Ketchum, Uniform Fire Code Bd. Appeals, Ketchum, Blaine County, Idaho. Recipient Best Archtl. Interior Detailing award, Custom Builder mag., 1993. Mem. AIA. Avocations: photography, watercolors, computer graphics, snow skiing, sailing. Office: Wright Bryant & Johnson PO Box 21 Sun Valley ID 83353-0021*

BRYCELEA, CLIFFORD, artist; b. Shiprock, N.M., Sept. 26, 1953; s. David B., Sr. and Flora Mae (Walter) Lee; m. Lucretia Ann Vigil, Dec. 1, 1979; children: Sonya Garnet Montoya, Daryl Anthony Brycelea. BA, Fort Lewis Coll., 1975. Artist-in-residence, Durango, Colo., 1976—; profl. artist, Dulce, N.Mex., 1977-84, Durango, Colo., 1985—. Graphic artist murals Kiva Room and Intercultural Ctr., Ft. Lewis Coll., Durango, 1974, logos Dulce High Sch. Gym, 1983; illustrator book Pieces of White Shell, 1984, airline mag. American Way, 1976, book cover Haunted Mesa, 1987. Recipient Meml. award, 1st Place Gallop Ceremonial Intertribal, 1986. Mem. Indian Arts And Crafts Assn. (3rd place 1983, Artist of Yr. 1987), Am. Indian and Cowboy Artists (gold medals 1981-82). Home: 1721 [illegible]

BRYCHEL, RUDOLPH MYRON, engineer, consultant; b. Milw., Dec. 4, 1934; s. Stanley Charles and Jean Ann (Weiland) B.; m. Rose Mary Simmons, Sept. 3, 1955; children: Denise, Rita, Rudolph Myron Jr., Patrick,

Bradford, Matthew. Student, U. Wis., Stevens Point, 1953, U.S. Naval Acad., 1954-55, U. Del., 1957, Colo. State U., 1969, North Park Coll., Chgo., 1973, Regis U., Denver, 1990-91. Lab. and quality tech. Thiokol Chem. Co., Elkton, Md., 1956; final test insp. Martin Aircraft Co., Middle River, Md., 1956-57; system final insp. Delco Electronics Co., Oak Creek, Wis., 1957-58; test equipment design engr. Martin Marietta Co., Littleton, Colo., 1958-64; prodn. supr. Gates Rubber Co., Denver, Colo., 1964-65; freelance mfr., quality and project engr. Denver and Boulder, Colo., Raton, N.Mex., 1965-67; quality engr. IBM, Gaithersburg (Md.), Boulder (Colo.), 1967-73; sr. quality engr. Abbott Labs., North Chicago, Ill., 1973-74; instrumentation and control engr. Stearns Roger Co., Glendale, Colo., 1974-81; staff quality engr. Storage Tech., Louisville, Colo., 1981-83; sr. quality engr. Johnson & Johnson Co., Englewood, Colo., 1983-84; quality engr., cons. Staodynamics Co., Longmont, Colo., 1984-85; sr. engr. for configuration and data mgmt. Martin Marietta Astronautics Group, Denver, 1985-91; freelance cons. Littleton, Colo., 1991—. With USN, 1953-56. Mem. Am. Soc. Quality Control (cert. quality engr.), Regulatory Affairs Profl. Soc., Soc. for Tech. Communications (regional chpt. chmn. 1970), KC. Democrat. Roman Catholic. Avocations: berry and fruit gardening. Home and Office: 203 W Rafferty Gardens Ave Littleton CO 80120-1710

BRYDON, HAROLD WESLEY, entomologist, writer; b. Hayward, Calif., Dec. 6, 1923; s. Thomas Wesley and Hermione (McHenry) B.; m. Ruth Bacon Vickery, Mar. 28, 1951 (div.); children: Carol Ruth, Marilyn Jeanette, Kenneth Wesley. AB, San Jose State Coll., 1948; MA, Stanford U., 1950. Insecticide sales Calif. Spray Chem. Corp., San Jose, 1951-52; entomologist, fieldman, buyer Beech-Nut Packing Co., 1952-53; mgr., entomologist Lake County Mosquito Abatement Dist., Lakeport, Calif., 1954-58; entomologist, adviser Malaria Eradication Programs AID, Kathmandu, Nepal, 1958-61, Washington, 1961-62, Port-au-Prince, Haiti, 1962-63; dir. fly control research Orange County Health Dept. Santa Ana, Calif., 1963-66; free-lance writer in field, 1966—; research entomologist U. N.D. Sch. Medicine, 1968; developer, owner Casierra Resort, Lake Almanor, Calif., 1975-79; owner Westwood (Calif.) Sport Shop, 1979-84; instr. Lassen Community Coll., Susanville, Calif., 1975—; bio control cons., 1980—. Mem. entomology and plant pathology del. People to People Citizen Ambassador Program, China, 1986; citizen ambassador 30th Anniversary Caravan to Soviet Union, 1991, Vietnam Initiative Del., 1992, Initiative for Edn., Sci. and Tech. to The Republic of South Africa, 1995; mem. Bus. Intelligence Bd., 1995. Contbr. profl. jours. and conducted research in field. Served with USNR, 1943-46. Recipient (with others) Samuel Crumbine award to Orange County Health Dept., Calif., 1964, Meritorious Honor award for work in Nepal, AID, U.S. Dept. State, 1972. Mem. Entomol. Soc. Am., Am. Mosquito Control Assn., Pacific Coast Entomol. Soc., Am. Legion. Republican. Methodist. Club: Commonwealth of California. Lodges: Masons, Rotary. Home: 7012 La Cuesta Ln Citrus Heights CA 95621-4207

BRYDON, RUTH VICKERY, history educator; b. San Jose, Calif., June 2, 1930; d. Robert Kingston and Ruth (Bacon) Vickery; m. Harold Wesley Brydon, Mar. 28, 1951 (div.); children: Carol Ruth Brydon Koford, Marilyn Brydon Belove, Kenneth Wesley. BA, Stanford U., 1952; student San Jose State Coll., 1964-65, MA, Calif. State Coll., Chico, 1987. Cert. tchr., Calif., cert. sch. adminstr. Tchr., Lincoln Sch., Kathmandu, Nepal, 1959-60; tchr. Am. Sch., Port-au-Prince, Haiti, 1962-63; tchr. social studies Norte Vista High Sch., Riverside, Calif., 1965-67, chmn. social studies dept., 1966-67; tchr. home econs., social studies Westwood (Calif.) H.S., 1967-90, mentor tchr., 1984-85; media specialist Lake Havasu H.S., 1990-91; history instr. Mohave C.C., Lake Havasu Campus, 1990—; instr. Elderhostel, 1992—; coord. extended day classes Lassen Coll., 1977-84. Author: Westwood, California: A Company Town in Comparative Perspective, 1900-1930, 1995. Co-chairperson Almanor Art Show, 1980-84. NDEA grantee, 1967. Mem. Archeol. Soc. Ariz. and Lake Havasu, Lake Havasu City Hist. Soc. (bd. dirs.). Episcopalian. Home: 2681 N Cisco Dr Lake Havasu City AZ 86403-5020

BRYNER, ALEXANDER O., state supreme court justice; b. Tientsin, China; came to U.S., 1969; m. Carol Crump; children: Paul, Mara. BA, Stanford U., JD. Law clk. to Chief Justice George Boney Ala. Supreme Ct., 1969-71; legal editor Bancroft Whitney Co., San Francisco, 1971; with Pub. Defender Agy., Anchorage, 1972-74; ptnr. Bookman, Bryner & Shortell, 1974—; mem. dist. ct. bench Anchorage, 1975-77; U.S. atty. Ala., 1977-80; chief judge U.S. Ct. Appeals, 1980-97; judge Alaskan Supreme Ct., Anchorage, 1997—. Office: Alaskan Supreme Ct 303 K St Anchorage AK 99501-2013*

BRYNGELSON, JIM, educational administrator; b. Billings, Mont., Mar. 8, 1941; s. Ivan Carl and Clarie (Ellingwood) B.; m. Judy Bryngelson, June 29, 1969; children: Joy, Nick. Home: 1144 Henry Rd Billings MT 59102-0811 Office: Youth Dynamics 2601 Uir Ln Billings MT 59102

BRYNIE, FAITH HICKMAN, writer, educator; b. Bluefield, W.Va., July 7, 1946; d. Cleland Henry and Helen Freda (Belcher) Mace; m. Lloyd Earl Brynie, July 28, 1989. BA, W.Va. U., 1967; MA, U. Colo., 1981, PhD, 1983. Project dir. biol. scis. curriculum study Boulder, Colo., 1969-82; asst. prof. U. Colo. Sch. Edn., 1982-86; tchr. Dept. Def. Dependents Schs., Eng., 1986-91; freelance writer, 1991—. Author: Genetics and Human Health: A Journey Within, 1995, Six-Minute Science Experiments, 1996, AIDS: Facts, Issues, Choices, 1997, Six-Minute Nature Experiments, 1998, Painless Science Projects, 1998, 101 Questions Your Brain Has Asked About Itself but Couldn't Answer...Until Now, 1998, 101 Questions About Skin that got Under Your Skin...Until Now, 1999; editor: Odyssey (tchrs. guide), 1997—; contbr. articles to profl. jours. Recipient Presl. Scholar award, Washington, 1964. Mem. NSTA, Nat. Assn. Biology Tchrs. (past v.p., treas.), Colo. Biology Tchrs. Assn. (life). Home: 170 Tall Pines Ct Bigfork MT 59911-3730

BRYSON, DOROTHY PRINTUP, retired Latin educator; b. Britton, S.D., Dec. 2, 1894; d. David Lawrence and Marion Harland (Gamsby) Printup; m. Archer Butler Hulbert, June 16, 1923 (dec. Dec. 1933); children: Joanne Woodward, Nancy Printup; m. Franklin Fearing Wing, Oct. 15, 1938 (dec. Mar. 1942); m. Arthur Earl Bryson, Feb. 15, 1964 (dec. Apr. 1979). AB, Oberlin Coll., 1915; AM, Radcliffe Coll., 1916; LHD (hon.), Colo. Coll., 1989. Instr. Latin, Tenn. Coll., Murfreesboro, 1916-18; tchr. Latin, prin. high sch., Britton, 1918-20; instr. classics Colo. Coll., Colorado Springs, 1921-22, 23-25, sec., instr., head resident, 1951-60; tchr. latin San Luis Prep. Sch., Colorado Springs, 1934-36, 41-42, Sandia Sch., Albuquerque, 1937-39, Westlake Sch., L.A., 1946-49; exec. dir. YWCA, Colorado Springs, 1942-46, 49-51; editor western history Stewart Commn., Colorado Springs, 1934-41; ret., 1960. Editor: Overland to the Pacific, 5 vols., 1934-41. Bd. dirs. Day Nursery, Colorado Springs 1933-37. Fellow Aelioian Lit. Soc., 1920-21; scholar U. Chgo., 1920-21. Mem. LWV (v.p., bd. dirs. Colorado Springs 1943-45), Women's Edn. Soc. Colo. Coll. (pres., bd. dirs. 1955—), Reviewers Club, Tuesday Discussion Club, Pikes Peak Posse Westerners, Women's Literary Club, Phi Beta Kappa, Gamma Phi Beta. Republican. Episcopalian. Avocations: reading, travel, needlepoint, sewing, hiking, bridge. Home: 30 E Pikes Peak Ave Colorado Springs CO 80903-1504

BRYSON, GARY SPATH, cable television and telephone company executive; b. Longview, Wash., Nov. 8, 1943; s. Roy Griffin and Marguerite Elizabeth (Spath) B.; m. Bobbi Bryson; children: Kelly Suzanne, Lisa Christine. AB, Dartmouth Coll., 1966; MBA, Tuck Sch., 1967. With Bell & Howell Co., Chgo., 1967-79; pres. consumer and audio-visual group Bell & Howell Co., 1977-79; chmn. bd., CEO Bell & Howell Mamiya Co., Chgo., 1979-81; exec. v.p. Am. TV & Communications Corp., subs. Time, Inc., Englewood, Colo., 1981-88; v.p. diversified group US West, Englewood, 1988-89, pres. cable communications div., 1989-92; pres., CEO TeleWest Internat., 1992-93; pres. SkyConnect, Boulder, 1994-96; comm. cons., 1996—. Mem. Phi Beta Kappa, Sigma Alpha Epsilon. Republican. Lutheran. Home: 2221 Carriage Hills Dr Boulder CO 80302-9481

BRYSON, JOHN E., utilities company executive; b. N.Y.C., July 24, 1943; m. Louise Henry. B.A. with great distinction, Stanford U., 1965; student, Freie U. Berlin, Federal Republic Germany, 1965-66; J.D., Yale U., 1969. Bar: Calif., Oreg., D.C. Asst. in instrn. Law Sch., Yale U., New Haven, Conn., 1968-69; law clk. U.S. Dist. Ct., San Francisco, 1969-70; co-founder, atty. Natural Resources Def. Council, 1970-74; vice chmn. Oreg. Energy Facility Siting Council, 1975-76; assoc. Davies, Biggs, Strayer, Stoel & Boley, Portland, Oreg., 1975-76; chmn. Calif. State Water Resources Control Bd., 1976-79; vis. faculty Stanford U. Law Sch., Calif., 1977-79; pres. Calif. Pub. Utilities Commn., 1979-82; ptnr. Morrison & Foerster, San Francisco, 1983-84; sr. v.p. law and fin. So. Calif. Edison Co., Rosemead, 1984; exec. v.p., chief fin. officer Edison Internat. and So. Calif. Edison Co., 1985-90; chmn. of bd., CEO Edison Internat. and So. Calif. Edison Co., Rosemead, 1990—; lectr. on pub. utility, energy, communications law.; former mem. exec. com. Nat. Assn. Regulatory Utility Commrs., Calif. Water Rights Law Rev. Commn., Calif. Pollution Control Financing Authority; former mem. adv. bd. Solar Energy Research Inst., Electric Power Research Inst., Stanford Law Sch.; bd. dirs. Pacific Am. Income Shares Inc. Mem. bd. editors, assoc. editor: Yale U. Law Jour. Bd. dirs. World Resources Inst., Washington, Calif. Environ. Trust, Claremont U. Ctr., Grad. Sch., Stanford U. Alumni Assn.; trustee Stanford U., 1991. Woodrow Wilson fellow. Mem. Calif. Bar Assn., Oreg. Bar Assn., D.C. Bar Assn., Nat. Assn. Regulatory Utility Commrs. (exec. com. 1980-82), Stanford U. Alumni Assn. (bd. dirs. 1983-86), Phi Beta Kappa. Office: Edison Internat 2244 Walnut Grove Ave Rosemead CA 91770-3714*

BRYSON, VERN ELRICK, nuclear engineer; b. Woodruff, Utah, May 28, 1920; s. David Hyrum and Luella May (Eastman) B.; m. Esther Sybil de St Jeor, Oct. 14, 1942; children: Britt William, Forrest Lee, Craig Lewis, Nadine, Elaine. Commd. 2d lt. USAAF, 1941; advanced through grades to lt. col. USAF, 1960, ret., 1961; pilot, safety engr., civil engr., electronic engr., nuclear engr., chief Aeronaut. Systems div., Aircraft Nuclear Propulsion Program, Wright-Patterson AFB, Ohio, 1960-61; chief Radiation Effects Lab., also chief Radiation Effects Group Boeing Airplane Co., Seattle, 1961-65; nuclear engr. Aerospace Corp., San Bernardino, Calif., 1965-68; service engr., also head instrumentation lab., Sacramento Air Logistic Ctr. USAF, McClellan AFB, Calif., 1968-77; owner, mgr. Sylvern Valley Ranch, Calif., 1977—; Mem. panel Transient Radiation Effects on Electronics, Weapon Effects Bd., 1959-61. Contbr. research articles on radiation problems to profl. pubs. Decorated D.F.C. with oak leaf cluster, Air medal with 12 oak leaf clusters. Mem. IEEE. Mem. Ch. Jesus Christ of Latter-day Saints. Home: 1426 Caperton Ct Penryn CA 95663-9515

BUBIEN, M. STANLEY, software engineer; b. L.A., Jan. 26, 1965; s. John F. Bubien. BA in Computer Sci., U. Calif., San Diego, 1989, MS in Computer Sci., 1991. Engr. Prepress, Inc., Carlsbad, Calif., 1992-93; software engr. Global Imaging, Solana Beach, Calif., 1993—. Author, editor: The Areopagus, 1991-96, Story Bytes, 1996—; author: Desert Wind, 1996. Avocations: surfing, reading, bicycling. Fax: (619) 481-5794. Home: PO Box 1227 Del Mar CA 92014-1227 Office: Global Imaging 201 Lomas Santa Fe Dr Ste 380 Solana Beach CA 92075-1286

BUBLITZ, DEBORAH KEIRSTEAD, pediatrician; b. Boston, Feb. 28, 1933; d. George and Dorothy (Kingsbury) Keirstead; m. Clark Bublitz, Mar. 1, 1958; children: Nancy B. Dyer, Susan B. Schooleman, Philip K. Bublitz, Caroline D. Bublitz, Elizabeth E. Bublitz. BS, Bates Coll., 1955; MD, Johns Hopkins U., 1959. Resident St. Louis Children's Hosp., 1959-60, U. Colo. Health Sci. Ctr. and Dept. Health and Hosps., Denver, 1968-74; pvt. practice Littleton, Colo., 1974—; asst. clin. prof. pediatrics U. Colo. Health Sci. Ctr. and Children's Hosp., 1975-87, assoc. clin. prof. pediatrics, 1987—; creditials com. Swedish/Porter Hosp., Englewood, Colo., 1985-87, chief dept. pediatrics, 1985-87; med. assoc., advisor LaLeche League, 1975—. Author: (with others) Clinical Pediatric Otolaryngology, 1986. Fellow Am. Acad. Pediatrics; mem. AMA, Colo. Med. Soc. (women's governing coun. 1990-96, asst. chair women's governing coun. 1993-94, chair, 1994-95), Arapahoe Med. Soc., Am. Women's Med. Assn. Episcopalian. Avocations: painting, gardening, bird watching, church choir, grandchildren. Home: 5621 Blue Sage Dr Littleton CO 80123-2713 Office: Littleton Pediatric Med Ctr 206 W County Line Rd Ste 110 Highlands Ranch CO 80126-2319

BUCCOLA, VICTOR ALLAN, physical education educator, sports association executive; b. L.A., June 20, 1933; s. Carl and Josephine (Canzoneri) B.; m. Sally Louise Ward, Jan. 17, 1959; children: David, Anna, Victoria. BS in Phys. Edn., Calif. Polytechnic State U., 1956, MS in Edn., Phys. Edn., 1957; EdD, Ariz. State U., 1972. Phys. edn. instr., football, boxing and track coach Coll. Idaho, Caldwell, 1958-61; health and sci. instr., asst. football and track coach Mark Keppel High Sch., Alhambra, Calif., 1961-62; phys. edn. instr., asst. football coach Calif. Polytechnic State U., San Luis Obispo, 1962-73, prof. phys. edn., 1981-86, athletics dir., 1973-81; commr. Western Football Conf., San Luis Obispo, 1982-93, Am. W. Conf., 1993-96; chair divsn. II Football Com. NCAA, 1980-83, mem. championship com. divsn. II, 1986-92. Contbr. articles to jours. in field. Mem. bd. dirs. SESLOC Fed. Credit Union, San Luis Obispo, 1980-90, v.p. 1984-90; mem. Youth Football Bd., San Luis Obispo, 1972; asst. coach Little League Baseball Team, San Luis Obispo, 1971-73. Capt. Artillary, 1957. Mem. AAHPERD, Calif. Assn. Health, Phys. Edn., Recreation and Dance. Avocations: computers, trains, sporting events. Office: Cal Poly San Luis Obispo CA 93407

BUCHANAN, DONALD EDWIN, nematologist; b. Atlanta, Apr. 21, 1954; s. Willard B. and Consuela A. (Munoz) B.; m. Janet E. Kofkin, Feb. 14, 1981; children: Sarah, Cara. BA, The Johns Hopkins U., 1976, MD, 1980. Diplomate Am. Bd. Pediats., Am. Bd. Neonatal Perinatal Med. Intern in pediatrics Harriet Lane Svc. Johns Hopkins Hosp., Balt., 1980-81, resident in pediatrics, 1982-84; instr. pediats. The U. Pitts., 1985-86; neonatologist Sunrise Children's Hosp., Las Vegas, Nev., 1986—. Fellow Am. Acad. Pediats. Office: Magella Medical Assocs 3196 S Maryland Pkwy Ste405 Las Vegas NV 89109

BUCHANAN, JERRY MAJOR, advertising executive; b. Seattle, Dec. 10, 1923; s. Herbert H. and Doris Kathryn (DeNully) B. Airplane mechanic Boeing Airplane Co., Seattle, 1946-50; salesman various cos., Seattle, 1950-74; prin. J.B. Advt. Agy., Vancouver, Wash., 1974—; prin., editor, pub. TOWERS Club USA, Inc., Vancouver, 1974—; prin., chief exec. officer Jerry Buchanan Advt. Agy., Vancouver, 1976—; mktg. cons., ad copywriter, direct response adv. agy. owner. Author: Writer's Utopia Formula Report, 1974, Profitable Self-Publishing, 1992, The Ego Trip, 1992, The Three Phases of Ease, 1993; editor, publisher TOWERS Club Info Marketing Report, 1992—. With USMC, 1943-46, PTO. Democrat. Avocations: travel, music, philosophy. Fax: 360-576-8969. Home: 9107 NW 11th Ave Vancouver WA 98665-8401 Office: Towers Club Press Inc PO Box 2038 Vancouver WA 98668-2038

BUCHANAN, JOHN E., JR., museum director; b. Nashville, July 24, 1953. Exec. dir. Portland (Oreg.) Art Mus., 1994—. Office: Portland Art Museum 1219 SW Park Ave Portland OR 97205-2486*

BUCHANAN, LEE ANN, public relations executive; b. Albuquerque, July 6, 1955; d. William Henry Buchanan and Juanita Irene (Pilgrim) Wood; m. Charles Stanton Wood, Jan. 17, 1987. BA, U. Calif., Irvine, 1977. Exec. asst. to Congressman William Thomas, U.S. Ho. of Reps., Washington, 1979-83; dep. chief staff Gov. George Deukmejian, Sacramento, 1983-84; sr. v.p., ptnr. Nelson Comm., Costa Mesa, Calif., 1985-95. Bd. govs. Rep. Assocs. of Orange County, 1985—; founding sec. Orange County Young Reps., 1985. Mem. Internat. Assn. Bus. Communicators, Am. Assn. Polit. Cons., Pub. Relations Soc. Am., U. Calif.-Irvine Alumni Assn. Avocations: skiing, hiking. Address: PO Box 1741 Mammoth Lakes CA 93546-1741

BUCHANAN, TERI BAILEY, communications executive; b. Long Beach, Calif., Feb. 24, 1946; d. Alton Hervey and Ruth Estelle (Thompson) Bailey; m. Robert Wayne Buchanan, Aug. 14, 1964 (div. May 1979). BA in English with highest honors, Ark. Poly. Coll., 1968. With employee communications AT&T, Kansas City, Mo., 1968-71; freelance writer Ottawa, Kans., 1971-73; publs. dir. Ottawa U., 1973-74; regional info. officer U.S. Dept. Labor, Kansas City, 1974; owner, operator PBT Communications, Kansas City, 1975-79; sr. pub. affairs rep., sr. editor, exhibit supr., communications specialist Standard Oil/Chevron, San Francisco, 1979-84; owner The Resource Group/Comms., Napa, Calif., 1984—; mem. faculty pub. rels. master's program Golden Gate U., San Francisco, 1987. Pub. rels. trainer Bus. Vols. for Arts, San Francisco, 1985-93; mem. Nat. trust for Hist. Preservation, Napa County Landmarks. Recipient Internat. Assn. Bus. Communicators Bay Area Gold and Silver awards, 1984. Mem. Yountville C. of C., North Bay Assn. Realtors. Democrat. Episcopalian. Avocations: piano, photography, travel. Office: The Resource Group 134 Golden Gate Cir Napa CA 94558-6186

BUCHANAN, WALTER WOOLWINE, electrical engineer, educator and administrator; b. Lebanon, Ind., Oct. 6, 1941; s. Eugene Neptune and Amy Malvina (Woolwine) B.; m. Carol Ann Saunders, Dec. 28, 1968 (div. 1978); children: William Saunders, John Douglas; m. Charlotte Jane Drake, 1985. BA, Ind. U., 1963, JD, 1973, PhD, 1993; BS in Engring., Purdue U., 1982, MS in Elec. Engring., 1984. Bar: Ind.; registered profl. engr., Ind., Fla., Tenn., Oreg. Aerospace engr. Martin Co., Denver, 1963-64, Boeing Co., New Orleans, 1964-65; audit coord. Ind. Tax Bd., Indpls., 1970-73; atty. VA, Indpls., 1973-79; electronics engr. Naval Avionics, Indpls., 1979-86; asst. prof. Ind. U.-Purdue U., Indpls., 1986-93, U. Ctrl. Fla., Orlando, 1993-95; assoc. prof., chair Mid. Tenn. State U., Murfreesboro, 1995-96; prof., dean Oreg. Inst. Tech., Klamath Falls, 1996—; cons. Benjamin/Cummings Pubs., Menlo Park, Calif., Holt, Rinehart & Winston, N.Y.C., Houghton Mifflin Co., Boston, MacMillan Pub. Co., Columbus, Delmar Pub. Co., Albany, Prentice Hall, Simon & Schuster, Columbus, Oxford U. Press, N.Y.C., Discovery Press, L.A., Inst. for Sci. Info., Phila.; evaluator Accreditation Bd. for Engring. and Tech., Balt.; mem. Tech. Accreditation Commn.; grants reviewer NSF, Washington. Contbr. over 60 articles to profl. publs. Com. chair theater adv. bd. Ind. U.-Purdue U., Indpls., 1985-91, mem. faculty coun., 1989-92, mem. exec. com., 1991-92; fundraiser Ind. U. Found., Indpls.; mem. tech. com. Ind. Bus. Modernization Corp., Indpls., 1990-93. Lt. comdr. USN, 1965-69, Vietnam. Recipient Glenn W. Irwin award, Peter Marbaugh award Ind. U.-Purdue U. Indpls., 1988; Wright scholar Ind. U., 1961; rsch. grantee Ctr. on Philanthropy, 1992, Fla. Engring. and Indsl. Experimentation Sta., 1993. Mem. NSPE (educator, exec. bd., past sec., Profl. Engr. in Edn. award 1993, 97), IEEE (sr., com. tech. accreditation activities, sec., press electronics tech. editl. bd.), Soc. Mfg. Engrs. (sr.), Am. Soc. for Engring. Edn. (exec. bd. ednl. rsch. and methods divsn. 1986-92, exec. com. engring. tech. divsn. 1994-98, chair 1999—, rsch. grantee, Centennial award 1993), Engring. Tech. Leadership Inst. (exec. coun., past chair), Ind. Soc. Profl. Engrs. (chair engring. edn. 1988-92), Fla. Engring. Soc. (chair engring. edn. 1993-95), Tenn. Soc. Profl. Engrs. (chair engring. edn. 1996), Oreg. Soc. Profl. Engrs. (chair engring. edn. 1997—), Indpls. Sci. and Engring. Found. (bd. dir. 1988-92), Scientech Club (bd. dirs. 1990-92), Univ. Faculty Club (bd. dirs. 1988-93), Engring. and Sci. Hall of Fame, Order of Engr., Tau Alpha Pi, Delta Phi Alpha. Republican. Episcopalian. Achievements include systems test evaluation on the Apollo booster rocket. Office: Oreg Inst Tech Sch Engring and Indsl Tech 3201 Campus Dr Klamath Falls OR 97601-8801

BUCHANAN, WILLIAM MICHAUX, JR., electrical distribution executive; b. Richmond, Va., Nov. 22, 1962; s. William Michaux and Ann Harck (Cockrell) B.; m. Carrie Flynn, June 20, 1998. BA, Va. Commonwealth U., 1986. Retail broker Merrill Lynch, Washington, 1986-89; v.p. CWL Inc., Richmond, Va., 1989-93; pres. CWL Inc., San Francisco, 1993—. Office: CWL Inc 180 Pennsylvania Ave San Francisco CA 94107-2525

BUCHTA, EDMUND, engineering executive; b. Wostitz, Nikolsburg, Czechoslovakia, May 11, 1928; came to U.S., 1979; Kaufmann, Deutsche Wirtschaftoberschule, Bruenn, Czechoslovakia, 1942-45. Shop foreman Messerklinger, Ernsting, Austria, 1949-51; constrn. foreman Hinteregger, U.S. Mil. Project, Salzburg, Siezenheim, Austria, 1951-52, Auserehl Constrn. Corp., N.Y.C., 1963; pres. Grout Concrete Constrn. Ltd., Edmonton, Alta., Can., 1966-73; pioneer & explorer Canol Project Parcel B and Land Ownership N.W. Can., 1968—; pres. Barbarosa Enterprises Ltd., Yellowknife, Can., 1971—; owner (with Barbarosa Enterprises Ltd.) Canol Project Parcel B, 1968—. Mem. Dem. Senatorial Campaign Com. With German Mil., 1943-45. Named Emperor of the North, McLean Mag., Can., 1976. Mem. Internat. Platform Assn., Dem. Senatorial Campaign Com. Home: PO Box 7000-713 Redondo Beach CA 90277

BUCHTEL, MICHAEL EUGENE, optical mechanical engineer; b. Denver, Jan. 29, 1939; s. William Paxton and Lorraine Edith (Hammond) B.; m. Gloria Jean Guerrero, Sept. 29, 1967. BS, West Coast U., Compton, Calif., 1972. Sr. engr. Ford Aerospace Corp., Newport Beach, Calif., 1972-92; pres. The Techtel Co., Costa Mesa, Calif., 1992—; cons. Internat. Orgn. for Standards, Pforzheim, Switzerland, 1993—. Patentee for optical scanner in U.S. and Japan. With U.S. Army, 1962-64. Mem. Internat. Soc. for Optical Engrs., Am. Soc. Design Engrs. Republican. Roman Catholic. Office: The Techtel Co 1666 Newport Blvd Costa Mesa CA 92627-3717

BUCK, LINDA DEE, recruiting company executive; b. San Francisco, Nov. 8, 1946; d. Sol and Shirley D. (Setterberg) Press; student Coll. San Mateo, Calif., 1969-70; divorced. Head hearing and appeals br. Dept. Navy Employee Rels. Svc., Philippines, 1974-75; dir. human resources Homestead Savs. & Loan Assn., Burlingame, Calif., 1976-77; mgr. VIP Agy., Inc., Palo Alto, Calif., 1977-78; exec. v.p., dir. Sequent Personnel Svcs., Inc., Mountain View, Calif., 1978-83; founder, pres. Buck & Co., San Mateo, 1983-91. Publicity mgr. for No. Calif., Osteogenesis Imperfecta Found. Inc., 1970-72; cons. Am. Brittle Bone Soc., 1979-88; mem. Florence (Oreg.) Area Humane Soc., 1994—, Friends of Libr., Florence, 1994—; bd. dirs. Florence Festival Arts, 1995; bd. dirs., dir. women Rhododendron Scholarship Program, Florence, Oreg., 1995. Jewish.

BUCK, WILLIAM FRASER, II, marketing executive; b. Salt Lake City, May 6, 1944; s. William Fraser and Ada (Dabling) B.; m. Lynette Riding, Jan. 27, 1967; children: Kimberly, Arienne, Tamara, Joshua Fraser, Zackary Erne, Gabriel Robert, Bethany, Emily, Cassandra. BS, Brigham Young U., 1977, MBA, 1988. Clk. Clark Drugs Inc., Hawthorne, Calif., 1962-63; gen. mdse. clk. Albertson's Inc., Orem, Utah, 1967-68, grocery mgr., Utah div., 1976-81; asst. mgr. Allen's Markets, Orem, 1968-72; mgr. Quality Market, Delta, Utah, 1972-76; gen. mdse. mgr. BYU Bookstore Brigham Young U., Provo, Utah, 1981-90, mktg. adminstr. student auxiliary svcs., 1990-96, mktg. adminstr. student life/student aux. svcs., 1996—. Troop leader Boy Scouts Am., Provo, 1969-85, dist. pub. chmn., Delta, 1973-76; mem. Delta Planning and Zoning Bd., 1974-76; sec.-treas. West Millard Golf Com., Delta, 1973-76; pres. Sunset ward elders quorum Ch. Jesus Christ of Latter-day Saints, Provo, 1971-72, ward exec. sec., 1976-77, pres. Orem (Utah) 25th ward elders quorum, 1988-92; exec. sec. Orem 2nd ward bishopric, 1993-97; asst. ward clk. Am. Fork Hillcrest 2nd ward, 1997—. Mem. Am. Mktg. Assn. (exec.), Nat. Assn. Coll. Stores (cert.), Western Coll. Bookstore Assn., Planetary Soc., Nat. Wildlife Fedn., Mountain States Coll. Stores Assn. (instr. seminars 1983-85), Nat. Youth Coaches Assn. (cert.), Provo C. of C. (com. chmn. 1981-83), Ch. of Jesus Christ Latter-day Saints. Avocations: hiking, camping, reading, astronomy, bicycling. Office: Brigham Young U Student Life Creative Mktg 283 SASB Provo UT 84602

BUCKHOLZ, MARK, language arts and theater educator, dramatist; b. Detroit, May 25, 1951; s. Chester Raymond and Helen (Jantosz) B.; m. Jane Elizabeth Ackling, May 15, 1993; 1 child, Abigail Rose. BA with high distinction and honors in English, Wayne State U., 1973; MFA, Yale U., 1976; Tchr. Cert., Tulane U., 1984. Instr. Wayne State U., Detroit, 1976-77; tchr. English Mt. Carmel Acad., New Orleans, La., 1982-84, Columbus H.S., Miami, Fla., 1984-92; lectr. U. Miami, Coral Gables, Fla., 1985-88; assoc. instr. Miami-Dade C.C., 1994-96; adj. prof. Coll. of S.W., Carlsbad, N.Mex., 1997—; asst. prof. N.Mex. State U., Carlsbad, 1996—; artistic dir. South Beach Writers Theater, Miami Beach, 1988-89; dramaturg Shakespeare on the Road, Miami Beach Conv. Authority, 1990; founding writer Writers Alliance, Theatre League South Fla., Coral Gables, 1992-96; organizer "Poetry in the Galleries", Ctr. for Fine Arts, Miami, 1994-95; artist-in-residence Fla. Artist Dir., 1995-97; v.p. faculty assn. N.Mex. State U., 1997—; presenter Two Year Coll. Assn. Conf. S.W. Region Nat. Conv. Tchrs. English, 1998; bd. mem. editl. adv. bd. Collegiate Press, San Diego, 1998—; rep. N.Mex. Commn. on Higher Edn., 1998—; presenter to N.Mex. Endowment for Humanities, 1999. Prodr./guest "The Poet's Word", WDNA Pub. Access Radio, Miami, 1987-95; dramatist Yale U. Sch. Drama, 1975, Fla. Internat. U., 1988, South Fla. Art Ctr., Miami Beach, 1989; presenting author "Write in Our Midst", Miami Book Fair Internat., 1991, 93, 95; stage dir. (play) Ft. Lauderdale Pub. Theater, 1990, 91, 92; author short stories and poetry; dramatist (play) "44/84", 1994, Effort and Study Habits, 1976, Burner, 1987, Margaret Zelle, 1988. Vol. Ctr. for Fine Arts, Miami, 1993-94, Miami Book Fair Internat., 1994. Recipient Leadership award Cultural Affairs Coun., Broward County, Fla., 1994, Ind. Artist

award Divsn. Cultural Affairs, Fla., 1994, Fiction prize Nat. Writers Assn., 1994, Poetry prize Nat. Writers Assn., 1994. Mem. Acad. Am. Poets, Dramatists Guild (assoc.), Friends of the Living Desert, Carlsbad Caverns/Guadalupe Mountains Assn., Two Yr. Coll. Assn.-SW Region, Yale Alumni Assn., Yale Drama Alumni Assn., Phi Beta Kappa, Kappa Delta Pi. Avocations: writing, reading, hiking, travelling. Home: 924 N Thomas Carlsbad NM 88220 Office: NMex State Univ 1500 University Dr Carlsbad NM 88220

BUCKINGHAM, MICHAEL JOHN, oceanography educator; b. Oxford, Eng., Oct. 9, 1943; s. Sidney George and Mary Agnes (Walsh) B.; m. Margaret Penelope Rose Barrowcliff, July 15, 1967. BSc with hons., U. Reading (Eng.), 1967, PhD, 1971. Postdoctoral rsch. fellow U. Reading, 1971-74; sr. sci. officer Royal Aircraft Establishment, Farnborough, Eng., 1974-76; prin. sci. officer Royal Aircraft Establishment, 1976-82; exchange scientist Naval Rsch. Lab., Washington, 1982-84; vis. prof. MIT, Cambridge, 1986-87; sr. prin. sci. officer Royal Aircraft Establishment, 1983-86, 1987-90; prof. oceanography Scripps Instn. of Oceanography, La Jolla, Calif., 1990—; vis. prof. Inst. Sound and Vibration rsch., Southampton, Eng., 1990—; UK nat. rep. Commn. of European Communities, Brussels, Belgium, 1989-92; dir. Arctic rsch. Royal Aerospace Establishment, Farnborough, 1990-94. Author: Noise in Electronic Devices and Systems, 1983; editor: Sea Surface Sound '94, Proceedings of the III Internat. Mtg. on Natural Phys. Processes Related to Sea Surface Sound; sr. editor Jour. Computational Acoustics; editor Phys. Acoustics; contbr. articles to profl. jours.; patentee in field. Recipient Clerk Maxwell Premium, Inst. Electronic and Radio Engrs. London, 1972, A.B. Wood Medal, Inst. Acoustics, Bath, Eng., 1982, Alan Burman Pub. award, Naval Rsch. Lab., 1988, Commendation for Disting. Contbns. to ocean acoustics Naval Rsch. Lab., 1986. Fellow Inst. Acoustics (U.K.), Inst. Elec. Engrs. (U.K.), Acoustical Soc. Am. (chmn. acoustical oceanography tech. com. 1991—, Sci. Writing award for profls. in acoustics 1997), Explorers Club; mem. Am. Geophys. Union, N.Y. Acad. Scis., Sigma Xi. Avocations: photography, squash, flying gliders. Home: 7921 Caminito Del Cid La Jolla CA 92037-3404 Office: Scripps Inst Oceanography Marine Phys Lab La Jolla CA 92093-0213

BUCKLEY, RICHARD GEORGE, architect, educator; b. Urbana, Ill., Feb. 25, 1953; s. George and Madeline (Murad) B.; m. Diane Joy Stone, Feb. 14, 1987. BArch magna cum laude, U. Wash., 1980; MArch, U. Pa., 1982. Registered architect, Idaho, Wash., Nev. Instr. Phila. Inst. Art, 1982-84, U. Pa., Phila., 1983-84; architect Venturi, Rauch and Scott Brown, Phila., 1981-84; design ptnr., architect NBBJ Architecture, Design and Planning, Seattle, 1984—; vis. prof. Coll. Arch. and Urban Planning U. Wash., Seattle, 1984—; bd. dirs. dept. arch. profl. adv. bd. U. Wash., 1995—. Prin. works include Sun Mountain Lodge (Interiors Mag. ann. internat. design awards best in hospitality award 1991), Market Pl. Tower (AIA Hon. Mention award 1988), Fluke Hall (AIA Honor award 1987). Chmn. Pioneer Sq. Hist. Preservation Bd., Seattle, 1992-95; bd. dirs. Mayor's Pine St. Task Force, Seattle, 1995; mem. Patrons of N.W. Civic, Charitable and Cultural Orgns., Seattle, 1995—; mem. Seattle Art Mus. Young Leaders Orgn., 1996. E. Lewis Dales traveling fellow, 1981; Narramore scholar, 1981-82, Aurhur Spayd Brooke Gold Medal in Design. Mem. AIA. Avocations: travel, collecting wine, history. E-mail: rbuckley@nbbj.com. Home: 915 37th Ave Seattle WA 98122-5226 Office: NBBJ Arch Design Planning 111 S Jackson St Seattle WA 98104-2820

BUCKLEY, VICTORIA, state official; b. Denver, 1947; 3 children. AA, Sieble Sch. Drafting; grad., U. Colo., Denver, Met. State Coll. Exec. dir. Opportunity Industrialization Ctr., Orlando, Fla., 1971-73; sec. of state State of Colo., 1995—. Office: Office of the Sec of State Civic Ctr Plz 1560 Broadway Ste 200 Denver CO 80203-6000*

BUCKLIN, LOUIS PIERRE, business educator, consultant; b. N.Y.C., Sept. 20, 1928; s. Louis Lapham and Elja (Barricklow) B.; m. Weylene Edwards, June 11, 1956; children: Randolph E., Rhonda W. Student, Dartmouth Coll., 1950; MBA, Harvard U., 1954; PhD, Northwestern U., 1960. Asst. prof. bus. U. Colo., Boulder, 1954-56; instr. in bus. Northwestern U., Evanston, 1958-59, assoc. dean Grad. Sch. Bus. Adminstrn., 1981-83; prof. bus. adminstrn. U. Calif., Berkeley, 1960-93, prof. emeritus, 1993—; vis. prof. Stockholm Sch. Econs., 1983, INSEAD, Fontainebleau, France, 1984, Erasmus U., Rotterdam, Netherlands, 1993-94, Cath. U. Leuven, Belgium, 1994; prin. Bucklin Assocs., Lafayette, Calif., 1975—;mem. adv. bd. Gemini Cons., San Francisco, 1987-94. Author: A Theory of Distribution Channel Structure, 1966, Competition Evolution in The Distributive Trades, 1972, Productivity in Marketing, 1979; editor: Vertical Marketing Systems, 1971, Channels and Channel Institutions, 1986, Jour. of Retailing, 1996—. Mem. City of Lafayette Planning Commn., 1990-93. Capt. USMC, 1951-53, Korea. Recipient Alpha Kappa Psi Found. award for best paper in Jour. Mktg., 1993. Mem. Inst. for Ops. Rsch. Mgmt. Scis., Am. Mktg. Assn. (Paul D. Converse award 1986), Lafayette-Langeac Soc. (bd. dirs. 1988-92). Democrat. Avocations: travel, microcomputers, photography. Office: U Calif Haas Sch Bus Berkeley CA 94720-1900

BUCKNER, PAUL EUGENE, sculptor, educator; b. Seattle, June 16, 1933; s. Martin Monroe and Edna Laurel (Olson) B.; B.A., U. Wash., 1959; M.F.A., Claremont Grad. Sch., 1961; postgrad Slade Sch., Univ. Coll. London, 1961-62; m. Kay Lamoreux, Aug. 15, 1959; children—Matthew, Nathan. Studio asst., sculptor Albert Stewart, Claremont, 1959-61; one man shows Oreg. Mus. Art, Eugene, 1964, 86; Gallery West, Portland, Oreg., 1977; Frye Art Mus., Seattle, 1979, Jadite Galleries, N.Y.C., 1988; exhibited in group shows Seattle Art Mus., 1964, 67; Oreg. Sculpture, Portland, 1968; Mainstreams Internat. Exhbns., Marietta, Ohio, 1971, 76, 77; Portland Art Mus., 1976, Clark Art Ctr. Rockford (Ill.) Coll., 1985; represented in permanent collections Salem (Oreg.) Civic Center, Olympic Coll., Bremerton, Wash., Oreg. Mus. Art, Mt. Angel Abbey, St. Benedict, Oreg., St. Paul's Cath. Ch., Silverton, Oreg., Ea. Oreg. Correctional Inst., Pendleton, Oreg., Leighton Pool, U. Oreg., Eugene, Sacred Heart Gen. Hosp., Eugene, Multnomah Athletic Club, Portland, United Ch. of Christ, Forest Grove, Oreg., Timberline Lodge, Oreg.; instr. sculpture U. Wash., Seattle, summer 1959, 62, San Bernardino Valley Coll., 1961; mem. faculty Oreg., 1962—, prof., 1972-95, prof. emeritus, 1995—. Served with USCG, 1953-57. Avery fellow, 1959-61; Fulbright grantee, 1961-62; Oreg. U. faculty grantee, 1965; recipient prize Nat. Sculpture Rev., N.Y.C., 1977, Thomas F. Herman Disting. Tchg. award U. Oreg., 1995. Home: 2332 Rockwood St Eugene OR 97405-1413 Office: U Oreg Sch Architecture & Allied Arts Eugene OR 97403

BUCKNER, PHILIP FRANKLIN, newspaper publisher; b. Worcester, Mass., Aug. 25, 1930; s. Orello Simmons and Emily Virginia (Siler) B.; m. Ann Haswell Smith, Dec. 21, 1956 (div. Nov. 1993); children: John C., Frederick S., Catherine A.; m. Mary Emily Aird, Dec. 15, 1995. AB, Harvard U., 1952; MA, Columbia U., 1954. With Bay State Abrasive Products Co., 1954-59; Reporter Lowell (Mass.) Sun, 1959-60; pub. East Providence (R.I.) Post, 1960-62; asst. to treas. Scripps League Newspapers, Seattle, 1964-66, divsn. mgr., 1966-71; pres. Buckner News Alliance, Seattle, 1971—; pub. daily newspaper group including Carlsbad (N.Mex.) Current-Argus, 1971-90, Pecos (Tex.) Enterprise, 1971—, Fontana (Calif.) Herald-News, 1971-89, Banning and Beaumont (Calif.) Gazette, 1971-74, Lewistown (Pa.) Sentinel, 1971-93, Tiffin (Ohio) Advertiser-Tribune, 1973-93, York (Pa.) Daily Record, 1978—, Winsted (Conn.) Citizen, 1978, Excelsior Springs (Mo.) Standard, 1978, Oroville (Calif.) Mercury-Register, 1983-89, Corona (Calif.) Independent, 1984-89, Minot (N.D.) News, 1989-93. Avocation: mountain climbing. Office: Buckner News Alliance 2101 4th Ave Ste 2300 Seattle WA 98121-2317*

BUCKSTEIN, CARYL SUE, writer; b. Denver, Aug. 10, 1954; d. Henry Martin and Hedvig (Neulander) B. BS in Journalism, U. Colo., 1976. Editor Rifle (Colo.) Telegram, 1976; corr. So. Colo. Pueblo (Colo.) Star-Jour. and Chieftain, 1977-84, corr. The Denver Post, 1985; staff editor Nat. Over-the-Counter Stock Jour., Denver, 1985-89; writer Rocky Mountain News, Denver, 1990-92; editor Urban Spectrum, Denver, 1993; contbg. writer Boulder (Colo.) County Bus. Report, 1992—. Bd. mem. Holiday Project, Denver, 1996; mem. exec. bd. Denver Newspaper Guild, 1998. Recipient 1st Place Gen. Assignment Bus. Articles, Colo. Press Women, Denver, 1985, 90, 91. Mem. Colo. Soc. Profl. Journalists (sec.-treas. 1988), Denver Newspaper Guild (bd. dirs. 1998). Avocations: inventing, writing.

BUDDE, JAMES ALFRED, art educator; b. Red Bud, Ill., June 9, 1958; s. Henry and Esther B.; m. Nancy Elizabeth Quinn, June 27, 1987. BA, So. Ill. U., 1981; MA, Calif. State U., Fullerton, 1984, MFA, 1987. Studio asst. Jerry Rothman, Laguna Beach, Calif., 1981-86; instr. ceramics Glen A. Wilson H.S., Hacienda Heights, Calif., 1988-94; asst. prof. Boise State U., 1994—. Quick Arts grantee Idaho Commn. on Arts, Boise, 1997. Avocations: shooting pool, reading, walking. Home: 608 Ranch Rd Boise ID 83702-1342

BUDNER, LAWRENCE JAY, psychiatrist; b. Long Branch, N.J., Aug. 13, 1957; m. Teri M. Wright, Aug. 16, 1989; 1 child, Jeffrey. BA, Brown U., 1979, MD, 1982. Diplomat Am. Bd. Psychiatry and Neurology. Intern U. Calif., Irvine, 1982-83, resident, 1983-86, fellowship, 1986-88; pvt. practice Orange, Calif., 1982—; chmn. psychiatry sect. Children's Hosp. of Orange County, Orange, 1990—. Fellow Am. Psychiat. Assn., Am. Acad. Child and Adolescent Psychiatry; mem. Orange County Psychiat. Soc. (councilor 1997—). Fax: (714) 997-3314. Office: 1330 W Stewart Dr Ste 302 Orange CA 92868-3842

BUDZINSKI, JAMES EDWARD, interior designer; b. Gary, Ind., Jan. 4, 1953; s. Edward Michael and Virginia (Caliman) B. Student U. Cin., 1971-76. Mem. design staff Perkins & Wills Architects, Inc., Chgo., 1973-75, Med. Architectonics, Inc., Chgo., 1975-76; v.p. interior design Interior Environs., Inc., Chgo., 1976-78; pres. Jim Budzinski Design, Inc., Chgo., 1978-80; dir. interior design Robinson, Mills & Williams, San Francisco, 1980-87, dir. design, interior architecture Whisler Patri, San Francisco, 1987-90; v.p. design sales and mkig. Deepa Textiles, 1990-95; dir. Workplace Studio, San Jose, Calif., 1997—; instr. design Harrington Inst. Design, Chgo.; cons. Chgo. Art Inst., Storwal Internat., Inc.; speaker at profl. confs. Designs include 1st Chgo. Corp. Pvt. Banking Ctr., 1st Nat. Bank Chgo. Monroe and Wabash Banking Ctr., 1978, IBM Corp., San Jose, Deutsch Bank, Frankfort, Crowley Maritime Corp., San Francisco, offices for Brobeck, Phleger and Harrison, offices for chmn. bd. Fireman's Fund Ins. Cos., Nob Hill Club, Fairmont Hotel, San Francisco, offices for Cooley, Godword, Castro, Huddleson, and Tatum, Palo Alto, Calif, offices for Pacific Bell Acctg. div., San Francisco, showroom for Knoll Internat., San Francisco, lobby, lounge TransAm. Corp. Hdqrts, San Fransisco, offices for EDAW, San Francisco, showroom for Steelcase Inc., Bally of Switzerland, N.Am. Flagship store, San Francisco; corp. Hqrs. Next Inc., Redwood City, Calif., Schafer Furniture Design, Lobby Renovation 601 California, San Francisco, Bennedetti Furniture Inc. Furniture Design. Pres. No. Calif. chpt. Design Industries Found. for AIDS.

BUECHLER, RALPH WOLFGANG, German language and literature educator; b. Winsen, Germany, July 21, 1948; came to U.S., 1958; s. William Emil and Hilde (Blümchen) B. BA in German, Washington U., St. Louis, 1971; MA in German, U. Ill., 1973, MAS in Acctg., 1976; PhD in German, U. Wis., 1988. Tchg. asst. U. Ill., Urbana, 1971-76; auditor Price Waterhouse & Co., St. Louis, 1977-79; tchg. asst. U. Wis., Madison, 1979-83, instr., 1983-88, lectr., 1988-89; assoc. prof. German lang. and lit. U. Nev., Las Vegas, 1989—, chair dept. fgn. langs., 1995—; libr. Goethe Haus Pub. Libr., Milw., summer 1981; bibliographer U. Wis., 1981-82, adminstrv. asst., 1983-85, vis. asst. prof., 1990, 92. Author: The Essays of Lichtenberg, 1990; contbr. articles to profl. publs. Mem. MLA, Soc. for Eighteenth-Century Studies, Soc. for Lit. and Sci. Democrat. Avocations: reading, classical music, cycling, hiking. Office: U Nev Dept Fgn Langs 4505 S Maryland Pkwy Las Vegas NV 89154-9900

BUECHNER, JOHN C., academic administrator. Dir. govtl. rels., then dir. pub. affairs U. Colo. System Office, Denver, until 1989; chancellor U. Colo., Denver, 1988-96, pres., 1996—. Office: U Colo-Denver Office of Pres Campus Box 35 Boulder CO 80309-0035*

BUEL, BOBBIE JO, editor. Mng. editor Tucson, 1991—. Office: Arizona Daily Star PO Box 26807-85726-6807 4850 S Park Ave Tucson AZ 85714-1637*

BUELL, EDWARD RICK, II, lawyer; b. Des Moines, Jan. 28, 1948; s. Edward Rick and Betty-Jo (Heffron) B.; B.S. with high honors, Mich. State U., 1969; J.D. magna cum laude, U. Mich., 1972; children—Erica Colleen, Edward Rick III. Bar: D.C. 1973, Calif. 1975; cert. specialist in taxation law, Calif. Assoc. firm Arent, Fox, Kintner, Plotkin & Kahn, Washington, 1972-74, Brobeck, Phlegher & Harrison, San Francisco, 1974-77; ptnr. Winokur, Schoenberg, Maier & Zang, San Francisco, 1977-81; ptnr. Buell & Berner, San Francisco, 1981—. Mem. ABA, San Francisco Bar Assn., Order of Coif. Contbr. articles to legal jours. Home: 50 Stewart Dr Belvedere Tiburon CA 94920

BUELL, EVANGELINE CANONIZADO, consumer cooperative official; b. San Pedro, Calif., Aug. 28, 1932; d. Estanislao C. and Felicia (Stokes) Canonizado; student San Jose State Coll., 1952-53; grad. U. San Francisco, 1978; m. Ralph D. Vilas, 1952 (dec.); m. Robert Alexander Elkins, July 1, 1961 (dec.); children: Nikki Vilas, Stacey Vilas, Danni Vilas Plump; m. William David Buell, Feb. 21, 1987. With Consumers Coop. of Berkeley (Calif.) Inc., 1958—, edn. asst. for community relations, 1964-73, supr. edn. dept., 1973-76, asst. to edn. dir., 1976-78, program coordinator edn. dept., 1980-81, personnel tng. coordinator, 1981-92; ret.; events coordinator Internat. House, U. Calif., Berkeley, 1984; also guitar tchr. Mem. Community Adv. Com., Bonita House, Berkeley, 1974; mem. steering com. for cultural and ethnic affairs Guild of Oakland Mus., 1973-74; dir. various activities YMCA, YWCA, Oakland City Recreation Dept., 1959-73; pres. Berkeley Community Chorus and Orch.; co-chair Berkeley Art Commn., 1992-94; bd. dirs. Philippine Ethnic Arts & Cultural Exch.; pres. Berkeley Art Ctr., 1998, bd. dirs. 1999, others. Recipient Honor award U. Calif. Student Coop., 1965, Outstanding Staff award U. Calif. Berkeley Chancellor, 1992, Nat. Philanthropy Disting. Vol. award, 1993, Outstanding Instrn. Program Support award Cole Sch. Visual & Performing Arts, Outstanding Berkeley Woman award Berkeley Commn. on the Status of Women, 1996, other awards. Mem. Filipino Am. Nat. Hist. Soc. (pres. East Bay chpt. 1996, Silver Arts & Music award 1994), Coop. Educators Network Calif. Democrat. Unitarian. Columnist Coop. News, 1964—. Home: 516 Santa Barbara Rd Berkeley CA 94707-1746

BUELOW, GRACE CARLSON, state agency surveyor, nurse; b. Mandan, N.D., Dec. 16, 1937; d. Ralph M. and Grace I. (Falkenstein) Carlson; m. Roger H. Buelow, Sept. 1, 1961; children: William Henry, Stephanie J. BSN, Jamestown (N.D.) Coll., 1960. RN, N.Mex., Utah, N.D. Staff nurse Jamestown Hosp., 1960-62; mem. staff Primary Children's Hosp., Salt Lake City, 1962-63, Pediatric Clinic, Jamestown, 1963-64, Thomas D. Meml. Hosp. and Ogden (Utah) Pub. Health, 1964; pub. health nurse Salt Lake County Health Dept., 1964-68; sch. nurse Granite Sch. Dist., Salt Lake City, 1964-68; staff nurse Dr. P. Harris, Santa Fe, 1969-71, Albuquerque Vis. Nurse Svcs., 1971-74; community health worker, educator Albuquerque Family Health Ctrs., 1974-75; dir. nursing svcs., and adminstr. Med. Personnel Pool, Albuquerque, 1982-86; program evaluator Medicare Blue Cross Blue Shield N.Mex., Albuquerque, 1987-91; health facility surveyor State N.Mex. Dept. of Health, Albuquerque, 1992—; part-time staff nurse St. Vincent Hosp., Santa Fe, 1969-71. Republican. Lutheran. Avocations: gardening, needle work, reading, music. Office: State of NMex Pub Health Divsn Bur Licensing & Cert 4111 Montgomery Blvd NE Albuquerque NM 87109-1102

BUENO, ANA, healthcare marketing and public relations executive, writer; b. N.Y.C., N.Y., Apr. 27, 1952; m. David M. Kreitzer, June, 1973 (div. Feb. 1979); 1 child, Anatol C. Kreitzer. Sr. writer healthcare Integral Sys., Inc., Walnut Creek, Calif., 1986-88; freelance writer L.A., 1989-92; cons. mktg. Health Net, L.A., 1992-96; pres. Bueno Healthcare Mktg., L.A., 1996-98; dir. mktg. and creative svcs. City of Hope Cancer Ctr., L.A., 1999—. Author: Special Olympics: The First 25 Years, 1994; contbr. articles to profl. jours. Sponsor, vol. Spl. Olympics, Calif., 1988-96. Recipient Disting. Vol. Svc. award Spl. Olympics, 1992. Mem. AAUW, Jewish Bus. and Profl. Women, The Jewish Fedn. Jewish. Avocation: art collector.

BUENO DE MESQUITA, BRUCE JAMES, political science educator; b. N.Y., Nov. 24, 1946; s. Abraham and Clara (Pieniek) B.; m. Arlene Carol Steiner, Aug. 11, 1968; children: Erin, Ethan, Gwen. BA, Queens Coll., 1967; MA, Univ. Mich., 1968, PhD, 1971; DHL, U. Groninger, 1999. Asst. prof. Mich. State Univ., East Lansing, 1971-73; from asst. prof. to prof. Univ. Rochester, Rochester, N.Y., 1973-86; sr. fellow, prof. Stanford Univ., Stanford, Calif., 1986—; dir. Policon, Washington, 1981-89, Decision Insight Inc., N.Y., 1989—. Author: The Wartrap, 1981, War and Reason, 1992, Red Flag Over Hong Kong, 1996, Forecasting Political Events, 1985. V.p. Internat. Studies Assn., 1998—; bd. advisors James Baker Inst. Rice Univ., 1997—; bd. dirs. Tex. A&M Political Rsch., 1994—. Recipient Guggenheim fellow, Guggenheim Found., 1978, Karl Deutsch award Internat. Studies Assn., 1985, Alumni star award Queens Coll., 1998. Mem. AAAS, Internat. Studies Assn., Am. Pol. Sci. Assn. (coun. mem. 1967—), Peace Sci. Soc. (counsellor 1990—). Avocations: squash, border war ballads. Office: Hoover Institution Stanford Univ Stanford CA 94305

BUFANO, RALPH A., museum director. Mem. Museum Museum of Flight, Seattle. Office: Museum of Flight 117 S Main St Seattle WA 98104-2540*

BUFFINGTON, LINDA BRICE, interior designer; b. Long Beach, Calif., June 21, 1936; d. Harry Bryce and Marguerite Leonora (Tuccirone) Van Bellehem; student El Camino Jr. Coll., 1955-58, U. Calif., Irvine, 1973-75; children: Lisa Ann, Phillip Lynn. Cert. interior designer and gen. contractor, Calif.; lic. gen. contractor, Calif. With Pub. Fin., Torrance, Calif., 1954-55, Beneficial Fin., Torrance and Hollywood, Calif., 1955-61; interior designer Vee Nisley Interiors, Newport Beach, Calif., 1964-65, Leon's Interiors, Newport Beach, 1965-69; ptnr. Marlind Interiors, Tustin, Calif., 1969-70; owner, designer Linda Buffington Interiors, Villa Park, Calif., 1970—, LBI, Contractors License, 1993—, cert. interior designer, Calif.; cons. builders, housing developments. Mem. Bldg. Industry Assn. (past pres. Orange County chpt. 1989, 90), Internat. Soc. Interior Designers, Nat. Assn. Home Builders. Republican. Office: 17853 Santiago Blvd Ste 107 Villa Park CA 92861-4113

BUFFORD, SAMUEL LAWRENCE, federal judge; b. Phoenix, Ariz., Nov. 19, 1943; s. John Samuel and Evelyn Amelia (Rude) B.; m. Julia Marie Metzger, May 13, 1978. BA in Philosophy, Wheaton Coll., 1964; PhD, U. Tex., 1969; JD magna cum laude, U. Mich., 1973. Bar: Calif., N.Y., Ohio. Instr. philosophy La. State U., Baton Rouge, 1967-68; asst. prof. Ea. Mich. U., Ypsilanti, 1968-74; asst. prof. law Ohio State U., Columbus, 1975-77; assoc. Gendel, Raskoff, Shapiro & Quittner, L.A., 1982-85; atty. Paul, Weiss, Rifkind, Wharton & Garrison, N.Y.C., 1974-75, Sullivan Jones & Archer, San Francisco, 1977-79, Musick, Peeler & Garrett, L.A., 1979-81, Rifkind & Sterling, Beverly Hills, Calif., 1981-82, Gendel, Raskoff, Shapiro & Quittner, L.A., 1982-85; U.S. bankruptcy judge Ctrl. Dist. Calif., 1985—; bd. dirs. Fin. Lawyers Conf., L.A., 1987-90, Bankruptcy Forum, L.A., 1986-88; lectr. U.S.-Romanian Jud. Delegation, 1991, Internat. Tng. Ctr. for Bankers, Budapest, 1993, Bankruptcy Technical Legal Assistance Workshop, Romania, 1994, Comml. Law Project for Ukraine, 1995-96, Ea. Europe Enterprise Restructuring and Privitization Project, U.S. AID, 1995-96; cons. Calif. State Bar Bd. Examiners, 1989-90; bd. trustees Endowment for Edn.; bd. dirs., exec. com. nat. Conf. Bankruptcy Judges, 1994—; mem. San Pedro Enterprise Community, 1997—. Editor-in-chief Am. Bankruptcy Law Jour., 1990-94; contbr. articles to profl. jours.; columnist Norton Bankruptcy Advisor, 1988-90. Younger Humanist fellowship NEH. Mem. ABA, L.A. County Bar Assn. (mem. profl. responsibility and ethics com. 1979—, chair profl. responsibility and ethics com. 1985-86, chair ethics 2000 liaison com. 1997—), Order of Coif. Office: US Bankruptcy Ct 255 E Temple St Ste 1582 Los Angeles CA 90012-3334

BUGBEE, PETER L., management consultant, institute administrator; b. Brattleboro, Vt., Oct. 14, 1946; s. Richard Harwood and Edith Dorothy (Jensen) B.; m. Sheila Ann Underwood, June 12, 1965 (div. Mar. 1976); m. Nancy Markham, Jan. 1, 1977; children: Megan, Kristin, Andrew. BS, Boston U., 1968, MS, 1973. Publ. editor Pacific Gas & Electric, San Francisco, 1969-70; mgr.orgn. comm. New Eng. Electric, Westborough, Mass., 1970-74; prin. to cons. Towers Perrin, Boston, 1974-86; prin., office mgr. Towers Perrin, Denver, 1986-96; mng. dir. Higher Ground Inst., Greenwood Village, Colo., 1997—; pres. Higher Ground Assocs., Greenwood Village, 1997—. Author: Downsizing for Japanese Companies, 1994; contbr. articles to profl. jours. Chmn. Webelos transition Denver Area coun. Boy Scouts Am., 1992-95. Mem. Internat. Assn. Bus. Comm. (accredited bus. communicator), Rocky Mountain Masters/USSA. Presbyterian. Avocations: alpine and cross-country skiing, sailing, ski racing. Office: Higher Ground Assocs 5671 S Elm St Littleton CO 80121-2170

BUGBEE-JACKSON, JOAN, sculptor; b. Oakland, Calif., Dec. 17, 1941; d. Henry Greenwood and Jeanie Lawler (Abbot) B.; m. John Michael Jackson, June 21, 1973; 1 child, Brook Bond. BA in Art, U. Calif., San Jose, 1964, MA in Art/Ceramics, 1966; student Nat. Acad. Sch. Fine Arts, N.Y.C., 1968-72, Art Students League, N.Y.C., 1968-70. Apprentice to Joseph Kiselewski, 1970-72; instr. art Foothill (Calif.) Jr. Coll., 1966-67; instr. design De Anza Jr. Coll., Cupertino, Calif., 1967-68; instr. pottery Greenwich House Pottery, N.Y.C., 1969-71, Craft Inst. Am., N.Y.C., 1970-72, Cordova (Alaska) Extension Center, U. Alaska, 1972-79, Prince William Sound Community Coll., 1979—; represented by B Street Artworks, Cordova, Ark.; one-woman exhbns. in Maine, N.Y.C., Alaska and Calif.; group exhbns. include Allied Artists Am., 1970-72, Nat. Acad. Design, 1971, 74, Nat. Sculpture Soc. Ann., 1971, 72, 73, Alaska Woman Art Show, 1987, 88, Cordova Visual Artists, 1991-96, Alaska Artists Guild Show, 1994, Am. Medallic Sculpture Nat. Travelling Exhbn., 1994-95; pres. Cordova Arts and Pageants Ltd., 1975-76; commns. include Merle K. Smith Commemorative plaque, 1973, Eyak Native Monument, 1978, Anchorage Pioneer's Home Ceramic Mural, 1979, Alaska Wildlife Series Bronze Medal, 1980, sculpture murals and portraits Alaska State Capitol, 1981, Pierre De Ville Portrait commn., 1983, Robert B. & Evangeline Atwood, 1985, Armin F. Koernig Hatchery Plaque, 1985, Cordova Fishermen's Meml. Sculpture, 1985, Alaska's Five Govs., bronze relief, Anchorage, 1986, Reluctant Fisherman's Mermaid, bronze, 1987, Charles E. Bunnell, bronze portrait statue, Fairbanks, 1988, Alexander Baranof Monument, Sitka, Alaska, 1989, Wally Noerenberg Hatchery Plaque, Prince William Sound, Alaska, 1989, Russian-Alaskan Friendship Plaque (edit. of 4), Kayak Island, Cordova, Alaska and Vladivostok & Petropavlovsk-Kamchatskiy, Russia, 1991, Sophie-Last Among Eyak Native People, 1992, Alaska Airlines Medal Commn. 1993, Hosp. Aux. plaque, 1995; also other portraits. Bd. dirs. Alaska State Coun. on the Arts, 1991-95. Scholarship student Nat. Acad. Sch. Fine Arts, 1969-72; recipient J.A. Suydam Bronze medal, 1969; Dr. Ralph Weiler prize, 1971; Helen Foster Barnet award, 1971; Daniel Chester French award, 1972; Frishmuth award, 1971; Allied Artists Am. award, 1972; C. Percival Dietsch prize, 1973; citation Alaska Legislature, 1981, 82, Alaskan Artist of the Yr., 1991. Fellow Nat. Sculpture Soc. Address: PO Box 374 Cordova AK 99574-0374

BUGLI, DAVID, conductor, arranger, composer; b. N.Y.C., Apr. 2, 1950. BMus, Ithaca Coll., 1972; MMus, U. Mass., 1978. Founder, musical dir., condr. Carson City Symphony (formerly Carson City Chamber Orch.), Nev., 1984—; pub. sch. music tchr., 1972-77; computer programmer/analyst, 1979—; 1st pres. Carson Access TV Found., 1991. Office: Carson City Symphony PO Box 2001 Carson City NV 89702-2001*

BUHLER, JILL LORIE, editor, writer; b. Seattle, Dec. 7, 1945; d. Oscar John and Marcella Jane (Hearing) Younce; 1 child, Lori Jill Moody; m. John Buhler, 1990; stepchildren: Christie, Cathie Zatarian, Mike. AA in Gen. Edn., Am. River Coll., 1969; BA in Journalism with honors, Sacramento State U., 1973. Reporter Carmichael (Calif.) Courier, 1968-70; mng. editor Quarter Horse of the Pacific Coast, Sacramento, 1970-75, editor, 1975-84; editor Golden State Program Jour., 1978, Nat. Reined Cow Horse Assn. News, Sacramento, 1983-88, Pacific Coast Jour., Sacramento, 1984-88, Nat. Snaffle Bit Assn. News, Sacramento, 1988; pres., chief exec. officer Communications Plus, Port Townsend, Wash., 1988—; mag. cons., 1975—. Interviewer Pres. Ronald Regan, Washington, 1983; mng. editor Wash. Thoroughbred, 1989-90. Mem. 1st profl. communicators mission to USSR, 1988; bd. dirs. Carmichael Winding Way, Pasadena Homeowners Assn., 1985-87; mem. scholarship com. Thoroughbred Horse Racing's United Scholarship Trust; Wash. State Hosp. Assn. gov. bds. com., 1996—, hosp. commr. Jefferson Gen. Hosp., 1995—, chair bd. dirs. 1997—; mem. Jefferson County Bd. Health, 1997, vice chair, 1998; vice-chair Jefferson County Bd.

Health, 1998—. Recipient 1st pl. feature award, 1970, 1st pl. editorial award Jour. Assn. Jr. Colls., 1971, 1st pl. design award WCHB Yuba-Sutter Counties, Marysville, Calif., 1985, Photography awards, 1994, 95, 96. Mem. Am. River Jaycees (Speaking award 1982), Am. Horse Publs. (1st Pl. Editl. award 1983, 86), Port Townsend C. of C. (trustee, v.p. 1993, pres. 1994, officer 1996, 97, 98), Mensa (bd. dirs., asst. local sec., activities dir. 1987-88, membership chair 1988-90), Kiwanis Internat. (chair maj. emphasis program com., treas. 1992—), 5th Wheel Touring Soc. (v.p. 1970). Republican. Roman Catholic. Avocations: sailing, photography. Home: 440 Adelma Beach Rd Port Townsend WA 98368-9605

BUHLER, RICHARD GERHARD, minister; b. Cottonwood, Ariz., July 18, 1946; s. Henry Richard and A. Genevieve (Woodward) B.; m. Linda M. Bates, Dec. 9, 1966; children: Karin, Kristin, Karise, Kenneth, Kevin, Kim, Keith. BA, Biola U., 1968, LLD, 1990; cert., Omega Ctr., Santa Ana, Calif., 1978. Announcer Sta. KBBI-FM, L.A., 1964-68; writer, editor, prodr. Sta. KFWB-AM, L.A., 1968-72, 74-76; writer, editor Sta. KNX-AM Radio, L.A., 1972-74; pres. Branches Comms., Orange, Calif., 1981—; host Tabletalk daily radio program, 1990-96, Talk From the Heart radio show, 1981-90; program dir. Sta. KBRT, L.A., 1984-90. Author: Love...No Strings Attached, 1986, Pain and Pretending, 1988, New Choices, New Boundaries, 1991, Be Good To Yourself, 1993. Recipient Angel award Religion in Media, L.A., 1986. Mem. Writer's Guild Am. Republican. Office: Branches Communications PO Box 6688 Orange CA 92863-6688

BUICHL, ANNA ELIZABETH, city official; b. Canonsburg, Pa., Aug. 9, 1940. AA, El Camino Jr. Coll., 1960; BA, Long Beach State Coll., 1963; MBA, Pepperdine U., 1985. Programmer analyst L.A. Dept. Airports, 1973-88, info. sys. mgr., 1988—; mem. adv. bd. Govt.-Bus. Tech. Expn., Sacramento, 1996; chmn. infotel com. Airports Coun. Internat. N.Am., Washington, 1996. Avocation: reading. Office: LA World Airports One World Way Los Angeles CA 90045

BUIDANG, GEORGE (HADA BUIDANG), educator, administrator, consultant, writer; b. Danang, Vietnam, Dec. 30, 1924; came to U.S., 1981; s. Bui Dang Do and Ha Thi Yen; m. Pham Thi Hong, Feb. 25, 1951; children: Bui Tu Long, Bui Nguyen Khanh, Bui Minh Hoang, Bui Thi Tuong Vi. Grad., Providence Inst., Vietnam, 1944. Head translator USMC, 1956-61; dep. employment officer Hdqrs. Support Activity Saigon USN, 1962-65; asst. dir. Ctrl. Tng. Inst. U.S. Army, Vietnam, 1966; pers. dir. Foremost Dairies Vietnam of Foremost-McKesson Internat., 1966-79; instr. of French Un Bateau Pour L'Asie Du Sud-Est, Brussels, Belgium, 1980; asst. dir. edn. Career Resources Devel. Ctr., Inc., San Francisco, 1981-93; ind. cons. San Francisco, 1993—. Author George Buidang's Microcomputing Series, including: Using WordPerfect 5.0, 1989, Using Lotus 1-2-3 Release 2.2., 1991, Using WordPerfect 5.1, 1991, Using Microsoft Windows 3.1, 1993, Using WordPerfect 6.0 for DOS, 1994, Using Lotus 1-2-3 for Windows, 1995, Using WordPerfect for Windows, 1996, Using Microsoft Word 97 for Windows 95, 1997, Using Microsoft Access 97 for Windows 95, 1998. Home: 565 Geary St Apt 411 San Francisco CA 94102-1660

BUIST, NEIL ROBERTSON MACKENZIE, medical educator, medical administrator; b. Karachi, India, July 11, 1932; m. Sonia Chapman; children: Catriona, Alison, Diana. Degree with commendation, U. St. Andrews, Scotland, MB, ChB, 1956; Diploma of Child Health, London U., England, 1960. Diplomate Am. Bd. Med. Genetics, Am. Bd. Clinical Genetics. House physician internal medicine Arbroath Infirmary, 1956-57; house physician externe cardiopulmonary dept. Hosp. Marie Lannelongue, Paris, 1957; house surgeon Royal Hosp. Sick Children, Edinburgh, Scotland, 1957; commd. far east med. officer Regimental Military Svc., 1957-60; house physician Royal Infirmary, Dundee, Scotland, 1960; registrar internal medicine Maryfield Hosp., Dundee, Scotland, 1960-62; lectr. child health U. St. Andrews, Dundee, Scotland, 1962-64; rsch. fellow pediatric microchemistry, Sch. Health Sci. U. Colo., Denver, 1964-66; asst. prof. pediatrics, Sch. Medicine U. Oreg., Portland, 1966-70; dir. Pediatrics Metabolic Lab, Oreg. Health Sci. U., Portland, 1966-93, Metabolic Birth Defects Ctr., Oreg. Health Sci. U., Portland, 1966—; assoc. prof. pediatrics and med. genetics Health Sci Ctr., U. Oreg., Portland, 1970-76; prof. pediatrics and med. genetics Oreg. Health Scis. U., 1976—; med. cons. Northwest Regional Newborn Screening Program, Portland, 1970—; vis. prof. WHO, China, 1988, U. Colo., 1990, Wesley Med. Ctr., Kans., 1991, Phoenix Children's Hosp., Ariz., 1991, Tucson Med. Ctr., Ariz., 1991, U. Ill., Chgo., 1991, Kapoiolani Med. Ctr., Hawaii, 1992, Shriners Hosp. for Crippled Children., Hawaii, 1992, Ark. Children's Hosp., 1993, Australasian Soc. for Human Genetics, New Zealand, 1994, LBJ Med. Ctr., Americas Samoa, 1994, Mahidol U., Bangkok, 1996, U. P.R., 1996, U. Auckland (New Zealand), 1997. Author: (with others) Textbook of Pediatrics, 1973, Inherited Disorders of Amino Acid Metabolism, 1974, 1985, Clinics in Endocrinolog and Metabolism: Aspects of Neonatal Metabolism, 1976, Textbook of Pediatrics, 1978, Practice of Pediatrics, 1980, Management of High-Risk Pregnancy, 1980, Current Occular Therapy, 1980, Practice of Pediatrics, 1981, Clinics in Endocrinology and Metabolism: Aspects of Neonatal Metabolism, 1981, Textbook of Pediatrics, 1984, Disorders of Fatty Acid Metabolism in the Pediatric Practice, 1990, Birth Defects Encyclopedia, 1990, 1991, Treatment of Genetic Disease, 1991, Pediatric Clinics of North Americs Medical Genetics II, 1992, Forfar & Arneil's Textbook of Paediatrics, 1992, 97, Galactosemia New Frontiers in Research, 1993, New Horizons in Neonatal Screening, 1994, New Trends in Neonatal Screening, 1994, Alpha-1-Antitrypsin Deficiency, 1994, Diseases of the Fetus and Newborn, 1995, Inborn Metabolic Diseases: Diagnosis and Treatment, 1995; cons. editor: Inborn Metabolic Disease Text, 1995; editorial bd. mem.: Jour. of Inherited Metabolic Diseases, 1977—, Kelley Practice of Pediatrics, 1980-87, Screening, 1991-96; jour. reviewer: Am. Jour. of Human Genetics, Jour. of Pediatrics, Pediatric Rsch., Screening. Adv. com. Tri County March of Dimes, Portland, 1977—; physician Diabetic Children's Camp, 1967—, Muscle Biopsy Clinic Shriners Hosp., 1989—; bd. dirs. Mize Info. Enterprises, Dallas, 1987—. Fellow Royal Coll. Physicians Edinburgh, Fogarty Internat. Vis. Scientist, Royal Coll. Physicians Edinburgh; mem. Brit. Med. Assn., Western Soc. Pediatric Rsch. (coun. mem. 1966—), Pacific North West Pediatric Soc., Am. Pediatric Soc., Soc. for the Study of Inborn Errors of Metabolism, Soc. for Inherited Metabolic Disorders (treas. 1977—), Oreg. Pediatric Soc., Oreg. Diabetes Assn., Portland Acad. Pediatrics, Internat. Newborn Screening Soc. Coun. (founding mem. 1988—). Avocations: fishing, gardening, travel. Office: Ore Health Scis Univ Metabolic Clinic CDRC-F PO Box 574 Portland OR 97207-0574

BUJOLD, DAVID ALEXIS, career officer; b. Albany, N.Y., Apr. 4, 1961; s. John Joseph and Mary Elizabeth (Hughes) B. BS in Mech. Engring., Rensselaer Poly. Inst., 1983; MS in Bus. Adminstrn., Boston U., 1990. Commd. 2d lt. USAF, 1983, advanced through grades to lt. col., 1998; RC-135 instr. 55th Wing, Offutt AFB, Nebr., 1984-88; C-130E chief tng. Frankfurt, Germany, 1989-90; flight test engr. Air Force Flight Test Ctr., Edwards AFB, Calif., 1990-93; staff officer Joint Staff Joint Chiefs of Staff, Pentagon/Washington, 1994-96; squadron comdr. Air Force Flight Test Ctr., Edwards AFB, Calif., 1996—; advisor Def. Intelligence Agy., Washington, 1994, Nat. Security Coun., Washington, 1995, Weapons Source Selection, Washington, 1998. Coach Little League, 1994. Mem. Assn. Old Crows, Air Force Assn. Roman Catholic. Avocations: skiing, flying, reading, jogging. Office: Air Force Flight Test Ctr Edwards AFB CA 93524

BUKOWIECKI, SISTER ANGELINE BERNADETTE, nun; b. Edmonton, Alta., Can., Aug. 24, 1937; came to U.S. 1960; d. Felix Peter and Stella Isabelle (Yagos) B. BA, Marillac Coll., St. Louis, 1969; MA in Dogmatic/Systematic Theology, St. Louis U., 1971. Joined Hosp. Sisters of the Third Order of St. Francis, 1962; co-foundress Franciscan Sisters of New Covenant, Roman Cath. Ch., 1979. Provincial Franciscan Sisters of New Covenant, Denver, 1979—; founder, dir. Cath. Evangelization Tng. Ctr., Denver, 1983-91; internat. dir. Assn. of Coords. of Cath. Schs. Evangelization/2000, Rome, 1991-92, Cath. Evangelizaton Tng. Ctr., Denver, 1991—; adminstrv. bd. Immaculate Heart of Mary Parish Coun., Northglenn, Colo., 1983-85. Author or co-author 16 books, 1983-91. Mem. Nat. Coun. Cath. Evangelization (bd. dirs. 1983-85). Home: 10620 Livingston Dr Denver CO 80234-3732

BULL, HENRIK HELKAND, architect; b. N.Y.C., July 13, 1929; s. Johan and Sonja (Geelmuyden) B.; m. Barbara Alpaugh, June 9, 1956; children: Peter, Nina. *Father Johan Bull, a native of Norway, was a noted illustrator who was on the New Yorker from the magazine's founding in 1925 till 1932. He drew the "Adventures of Eustace Tilley" series and was also known for horse and sports action drawings. Johan Bull served with the Norwegian Government in exile information services during World War II. Uncle Frederik Bull was an inventor who started Machines Bull, now the largest computer company in France. Great great uncle Ole Bull was a world renowned violinist and composer who founded the utopian community Oleanna in northern Pennsylvania in the mid 1850's.* B.Arch., Mass. Inst. Tech., 1952. With Mario Corbett, San Francisco, 1954-55; pvt. practice, 1956-68; ptnr. Bull, Field, Volkmann, Stockwell, Calif., 1968-82, Bull, Volkmann, Stockwell, Calif., 1982-90, Bull Stockwell and Allen, Calif., 1990-93, Bull, Stockwell, Allen & Ripley, San Francisco, 1993-96, BSA Architects, San Francisco, 1996—; Vis. lectr. Syracuse U., 1963; Mem. adv. com. San Francisco Urban Design Study, 1970-71. *Recipient of more than 40 major design awards. Best known for timeless designs which fit sensitively into their environments. Regular contributor to Snow Country and Ski Area Management magazines. A recognized authority on the design of buildings in harsh climates. Winner of an invited competition for the planning of the proposed Capital City of Alaska in 1978.* Works include Sunset mag. Discovery House, Tahoe Tavern Condominiums, Lake Tahoe, Calif., Snowmass Villas Condominiums, Aspen, Colo., Northstar Master Plan Village and Condominiums, Moraga Valley Presbyn. Ch., Calif., Spruce Saddle Restaurant and Poste-Montane Hotel, Beaver Creek, Colo., Bear Valley visitor ctr., Point Reyes, Calif., The Inn at Spanish Bay, Pebble Beach, Calif., Taluswood Cmty., Whistler, B.C. Served as 1st lt. USAF, 1952-54. Winner competition for master plan new Alaska capital city, Willow, 1978. Fellow AIA (pres. N. Calif. chpt. 1968, Firm award Calif. chpt. 1989). Democrat. Office: BSA Architects 350 Pacific Ave San Francisco CA 94111-1708

BULLOCK, DONALD WAYNE, elementary education educator, educational computing consultant; b. Tacoma Park, Md., Mar. 24, 1947; s. B.W. and Margaret (Harris) B.; m. Pamela Louise Hatch, Aug. 7, 1971. AA in Music, L.A. Pierce Coll., Woodland Hills, Calif., 1969; BA in Geography, San Fernando Valley State Coll., 1971; Cert. Computer Edn., Calif. Luth. U., 1985, MA in Curriculum-Instrn., 1987. Tchr. music Calvary Luth. Sch., Pacoima, Calif., 1970-71; elem. tchr. 1st Luth. Sch., Northridge, Calif., 1971-73; elem. tchr. Simi Valley (Calif.) Unified Sch. Dist., 1973—, computer insvc. instr., 1982-85, computer mentor tchr., 1985-87, mentor tchr. ednl. tech., 1992-95; lectr. Calif. Luth. U., Thousand Oaks, 1985-92; ednl. computer cons. DISC Ednl. Svcs., Simi Valley, 1985—; speaker profl. confs. Contbr. articles to profl. publs. Pres. Amen Choir, Van Nuys, Calif., 1981-83. Recipient Computer Learning Month grand prize Tom Snyder Prodns., 1988, Computer Learning Found., 1990, Spl. Commendation of Achievement, Learning mag. profl. best tchr. excellence awards, 1990, Impact II Disseminator award Ventura County Supt. of Schs. and Ventura County Econ. Devel. Assn., 1995; grantee Tandy-Radio Shack, Inc., 1985, Calif. Dep. Edn., 1985. Mem. NEA, ASCD, Internat. Soc. Tech. in Edn., Computer Using Educators Calif., Gold Coast Computer Using Educators (bd. dirs. 1988-89, 95-96), Basset Hound Club am., Basset Hound Club So. Calif. (bd. dirs. 1994-95, pres. 1995-98). Avocations: singing, travel, photography, writing, woodworking. Home: 2805 Wanda Ave Simi Valley CA 93065-1528 Office: Garden Grove Elem Sch 2250 Tracy Ave Simi Valley CA 93063-2753

BULLOCK, MOLLY, retired elementary education educator; d. Wiley and Annie M. Jordan; m. George Bullock; children: Myra A. Bauman, Dawn M. BS in Edn., No. Ariz. U., 1955, postgrad., 1958; postgrad., LaVerne U., 1962, Claremont Grad. Sch., 1963, Calif. State U. L.A., 1966. Tchr. Bur. Indian Affairs, Kaibeto, Ariz., 1955-56, Crystal, N.Mex., 1956-59; tchr. Covina (Calif.) Valley Unified Sch. Dist., 1961-95, supervising master tchr. for trainees of LaVerne U. and Calif. State U. - L.A., 1961-71, mem. curriculum devel. adv. bd., 1977-79; ret., 1995; mem. voting com. Excellence in Edn. awards Lawry's Foods. Poet: A Tree (Golden Poet 1991), What is Love (Golden medal of honor). Vol., visitor area convalescent hosps. Mini grantee Hughes/Rotary Club/Foothill Ind. Bank, Covina, 1986-90. Mem. Internat. Platform Assn., Internat. Soc. Poets (hon. charter), Covina Unified Edn. Assn. Avocations: poetry, collecting jewelry, dolls, paintings.

BULLOCK, WELDON KIMBALL, health facility administrator, pathologist, pathology educator; b. Vernal, Utah, Jan. 6, 1908; s. John Kimball and Adelaide (Arnold) B.; m. Dosia Opal Newton, Dec. 26, 1931; children: John, Jim. BA, U. Utah, 1930; MD, Northwestern U., 1934, MSc in Pathology, 1932. Diplomate Am. Bd. Pathology; lic. MD, Calif., Idaho, Utah. Intern Alameda County Hosp., 1933-34; resident in medicine Cook County Hosp., 1940-41; resident in pathology L.A. County-U. So. Calif. Med. Ctr., 1946-47; head surg. pathology LAC-U. So. Calif. Med. Ctr., 1949-69; instr. pathology Sch. Medicine U. So. Calif., 1947-48, asst. prof., 1955-62, clin. prof., 1963-74, clin. prof. emeritus, 1974—; exec. dir. Calif. Tumor Tissue Registry, various locations, 1955-95; dir. emeritus Calif. Tumor Tissue Registry, 1995—; chief pathology svc. Orthop. Hosp., 1956-63; assoc. pathologist St. Luke Hosp., 1963-70, chief pathologist, 1970-77, assoc. pathologist, 1977-81; clin. prof. pathology Sch. Medicine Loma Linda U., 1992—; James Ewing fellow in pathology Meml. Hosp. for Cancer and Allied Disease, 1948-49; cons. Calif. Assn. Cytotechnologists, 1962—, So. Calif. Acad. Oral Pathology, 1963—, Orthop. Hosp., 1963—; mem. Am. Joint Com. Cancer Staging and End Result Reporting, 1963-69, chmn. audio-visual task force, 1966-69, mem. exec. com., 1969; mem. rev. com. clin. cancer tng. grants Nat. Cancer Inst., 1965-68; mem. cancer planning com. Calif. Regional Med. Program, Area V, U. So. Calif., 1967-69; mem. pub. health svc. spl. project rev. com. HEW, State of Calif., 1967-69; meml. lectr. Arthur Purdy Stout Soc. Surg. Pathologists, 1979. Author: Oral Cancer & Tumors of the Jaws, 1956; contbr. articles to profl. jours. Lt. Col. U.S. Army Res., 1941-45, PTO. Decorated Bronze Star. Mem. AMA, Coll. Am. Pathologists (mem. com. cancer 1965-70), Am. Soc. Clin. Pathologists, Soc. Surg. Oncology, Calif. Med. Assn., Calif. Soc. Pathologists (mem. exec. com. 1960-62, sec.-treas. 1962-65, pres.-elect 1965-66, pres. 1966-67), L.A. County Med. Assn. (chmn. com. med. examiner 1968-72), L.A. Soc. Pathologists (past pres. exec. com. 1961-62), Soc. Grad. Pathologists-L.A. County-U. So. Calif. Med. Ctr., Soc. Grad. Surgeons-L.A. County-U. So. Calif. Med. Ctr. E-mail: CTTR@linkline.com. Home: 1460 Vandyke Rd San Marino CA 91108-2747 Office: Calif Tumor Tissue Registry 11021 Campus St # 335 Loma Linda CA 92354

BULTMANN, WILLIAM ARNOLD, historian; b. Monrovia, Calif., Apr. 10, 1922; s. Paul Gerhardt and Elsa (Johnson) B.; AB, UCLA, 1943, PhD, 1950; m. Phyllis Jane Wetherell, Dec. 28, 1949; 1 child, Janice Jane. Assoc. prof. history Central Ark. U., Conway, 1949-52, prof., 1954-57; assoc. prof. Ohio Wesleyan U., Delaware, 1957-61, prof., 1961-65; prof. Western Wash. U., Bellingham, 1965-87, chmn. dept., 1968-70, dean arts and scis., 1970-72, provost, 1971-73; vis. assoc. prof. U. Tex., Austin, 1952-53; vis. prof. U. N.H., summers 1965, 66; acad. cons. Wash. Commn. for Humanities, 1973-87, Nat. Endowment for Humanities, 1976-87; reader Ednl. Testing Service Princeton, 1973-85. Bd. dirs. Bellingham Maritime Heritage Found., 1980-85; mem. The Nature Conservancy, 1992—, Washington Arboretum Found., 1992-97; adminstrv. officer Bellingham Power Squadron, 1981-82, comdr., 1982-84. Fulbight sr. lectr. Dacca (Bangladesh) U., 1960-61; Ohio Wesleyan U. rsch. fellow, 1964; Fund for Advancement Edn. fellow for fgn. study, 1953-54; recipient rsch. award Social Sci. Rsch. Coun., 1957. Mem. AAUP. Am. Hist. Assn., Nat. Tropical Botanical Garden Soc., Nat. Boating Fedn., Ch. Hist. Soc., Conf. Brit. Studies, Pacific, Pacific N.W. confs. Brit. studies, Mystery Writers of Am., Interclub Boating Assn. Washington, Seattle Power Squadron, Phi Beta Kappa, Phi Delta Kappa, Pi Gamma Mu. Episcopalian. Clubs: Park Athletic Recreation, Bellingham Yacht (chmn. pub. rels. com. 1981-86), Squalicum Yacht (trustee 1979-82), Birch Bay Yacht; Wash. Athletic. Co-author: Border Boating, 1978; co-founder, mem. editorial bd. Albion, 1968-84; mng. editor Brit. Studies Intelligencer, 1973-80; co-editor Current Research in British Studies, 1975; editor Jib Sheet, 1981-86; feature writer, columnist Sea mag., 1974-93; feature writer Venture mag., 1981-85, Poole Publs., 1988-92. Home: 1600 43rd Ave E Apt 101 Seattle WA 98112-3245

BUMBAUGH, ROBERT WARREN, SR., oil industry executive; b. L.A., Sept. 8, 1937; s. Warren Herbert and Nina May (Browning) B.; m. Betty Jean Harkless, Apr. 14, 1956; children: Robert Warren Jr., Scott Arthur, Cheryllyn Jean. Student, Santa Ana (Calif.) Jr. Coll., 1960-62, Orange Coast Coll., 1965-66, Kenai Peninsula Coll., 1989-92. Cert. journeyman painter, CPR, internat. coating inspector. Painter Garden Grove (Calif.) Unified Sch. Dist., 1964-67, Kent (Ohio) U., 1968-69, Nicholas and Nicholas Painting, Orange, Calif., 1969-70, Stockwell Painting Contractors, 1970-71; owner, operator Bumbaugh's Painting, 1971-79; painter Sledge & Son Painting, 1979-81; painter, foreman Roger's Alaskan Painting, 1981-83; owner, operator Bumbaugh's Alaskan Enterprises, 1983-86; foreman Wade Oilfield Svc. Co., Inc., 1986-89; supr. Alaska Petroleum Contractors, Nikiski, 1989—. Bd. dirs. Ch. of Nazarene, Coeur d' Alene, Idaho, 1947-94. Avocations: pilot, hunting, fishing. Home: PO Box 748 Sterling AK 99672-0748 Office: Alaska Petroleum Contractor PO Box 8113 Nikiski AK 99635-8113

BUMGARDNER, LARRY G., foundation administrator, law and political science educator; b. Chattanooga, June 10, 1957; s. Walter G. and Kathryn (Hamrick) B. BA, David Lipscomb Coll., 1977; JD, Vanderbilt U., 1981. Bar: Tenn. 1981, U.S. Dist. Ct. (cen. dist.) Tenn. 1982, Calif. 1984, U.S. Dist. Ct. (cen. dist.) Calif. 1985. From reporter to copy editor Nashville (Tenn.) Banner, 1975-79; editor Tenn. Attorneys Memo, Tenn. Jour., Nashville, 1979-83; dir. founds. Pepperdine U., Malibu, Calif., 1983-85, asst. v.p. comm. and grants, 1985-92, assoc. vice chancellor for founds. and rsch., asst. prof. comms., 1992-94, adj. prof. law and polit. sci., 1994—; dep. dir. Ronald Reagan Presdl. Found., Simi Valley, Calif., 1994-95; exec. dir. Ronald Reagan Presdl. Found. and Reagan Ctr. Pub. Affairs, 1995—. Contbr. numerous articles to various publs. Mem. ABA, Calif. Bar Assn. Home: 2700 Westham Cir Thousand Oaks CA 91362-5379 Office: 40 Presidential Dr Simi Valley CA 93065-0600

BUNCHMAN, HERBERT HARRY, II, plastic surgeon; b. Washington, Feb. 23, 1942; s. Herbert H. and Mary (Halleran) B.; m. Marguerite Fransioli, Mar. 21, 1963 (div. Jan. 1987); children: Herbert H. III., Angela K., Christopher; m. Janet C. Quinlan, Oct. 4, 1998. BA, Vanderbilt U., 1964; MD, U. Tenn., 1967. Diplomate Am. Bd. Surgery, Am. bd. Plastic Surgery. Resident in surgery U. Tex., Galveston, 1967-72, resident in plastic surgery, 1972-75; practice medicine specializing in plastic surgery Mesa, Ariz., 1975—; chief surgery Desert Samaritan Hosp., 1978-80. Contbr. articles to profl. jours. Eaton Clin. fellow, 1975. Mem. AMA, Am. Soc. Plastic and Reconstructive Surgery, Am. Soc. Aesthetic Plastic Surgery, Singleton Surgical Soc., Tex. Med. Assn., So. Med. Assn. (grantee 1974), Ariz. Med. Assn. Office: Plastic Surgery Cons PC 1520 S Dobson Rd Ste 314 Mesa AZ 85202-4727

BUNDE, CON, state legislator, communication educator; b. Mankato, Minn., Aug. 4, 1938; s. Ralph Louis and Leona Dorothy (Lehman) B.; m. Angelene Hammer, Aug. 22, 1964; children: Joy, Kurt. BA, Ctrl. Wash. U., 1966, MS, 1970; AA, Anchorage C.C., 1970. Cert. speech pathologist. Speech therapist Gig Harbor (Wash.) Schs., 1967-68, Anchorage Sch. Dist., 1968-70; asst. prof. speech comm. Anchorage C.C., 1970-88; prof. U. Alaska, Anchorage, 1988-93; mem. Alaska Ho. of Reps., Juneau, Anchorage, 1993—; pilot Ketchum Air Svc., Anchorage, 1975—; seminar leader in field. Mem. citizens adv. coun. Dept. Fish and Game, Anchorage, 1991-92, instr. bowhunter edn. program; active Anchorage Community Theater; mem. citizen's adv. bd. U. Alaska Anchorage Aviation Airframe and Power Plant degree program. With U.S. Army, 1956-59. Mem. Alaska Sled Dog Racing Assn. (pres. 1970-78), Alaska Airmen's Assn., Alaska Bowhunter Assn. (bd. dirs. 1991-92), Alaska Sportfishing Assn., Alaska Outdoor Coun. Republican. Avocations: flying, fishing, hunting, sled dog racing, community theater. Office: Alaska State Legislature Ho of Reps 716 W 4th Ave Ste 410 Anchorage AK 99501-2133*

BUNDESEN, FAYE STIMERS, investment and management company owner, educator; b. Cedarville, Calif., Sept. 16, 1932; d. Floyd Walker and Ermina Elizabeth (Roberts) Stimers; m. Allen Eugene Bundesen, Dec. 27, 1972 (dec. 1991); children: William, David, Edward Silvius; Ted, Eric Bundesen. BA, Calif. State U.-Sacramento, 1955; MA, Calif. State U.-San Jose, 1972. Licensed real estate broker, Calif. Elem. sch. tchr. San Francisco Pub. Schs., 1955-60; elem. and jr. h.s. tchr., lang. arts specialist Sunnyvale (Calif.) Schs., 1978-83; cons. Santa Clara County Office of Edn. and Sunnyvale Sch. Dist., 1983-86; v.p. Bundesen Enterprises, Elk Grove, Calif., 1975-81, pres., 1981—. Bd. dirs. Sunnyvale Sch. Employees' Credit Union, 1983-86, v.p., 1984-86; co-chmn. Elk Grove Taxpayers Assn. for Incorporation, 1994; pres. Elk Grove/Laguna Civic League, 1994—; pers. chmn. Bethany Presbyn. Ch., 1992-95; mem. City of San Jose Tenant/Landlord Hearing Com., 1983-86, v.p., 1984-85. Mem. Assn. Supervision and Curriculum Devel., Calif. Scholarship Fedn. (life), AAUW, Calif. Apartment Assn., Nat. Apartment Assn., Calif. Assn. Realtors, Nat. Assn. Realtors, Sacramento Assn. Realtors, Sacramento Valley Apt. Assn., Soroptimist Internat. Rio Cosumnes, Elk Grove C. of C. Presbyterian. Office: PO Box 2006 Elk Grove CA 95759-2006

BUNDY, ROBERT CHARLES, prosecutor; b. Long Beach, Calif., June 26, 1946; s. James Kenneth and Kathleen Ilene (Klosterman) B.; m. Virginia Bonnie Lembo, Feb. 3, 1974; 2 children. BA cum laude, U. So. Calif., L.A., 1968; JD, U. Calif., Berkeley, 1971. Bar: Alaska 1972, Calif. 1972. Supervising atty. Alaska Legal Svcs. Corp., Nome, Alaska, 1972-75; dist. atty. Second Jud. Dist., Nome, 1975-78; asst. dist. atty. Alaska Dept. Law, 1978-80, asst. atty. gen. antitrust sect., 1980-82; chief asst. dist. atty. Alaskan Dept. Law, Anchorage, 1982-84; ptnr. Bogle & Gates, Anchorage, Alaska, 1984-94; now U.S. atty. for Alaska dist. U.S. Dept. Justice, Anchorage, 1994—. Mem. Trout Unlimited, Alaska Flyfishers. Office: Office US Atty for Alaska Rm C-253 222 W 7th Ave Unit 9 Anchorage AK 99513-7504*

BUNGE, RUSSELL KENNETH, writer, poet, editor; b. Long Beach, Calif., Apr. 28, 1947; s. Kenneth Duncan Bunge and Mona Irene (Deleree) Coker; ptnr. Mr. Kelly A. Quiros. BA in Creative Writing, Calif. State U., Long Beach, 1972; MA in Humanities, Calif. State U., Dominguez Hills, 1985. Cert. C.C. tchr., Calif. Spl. svcs. cons. AT&T Comms., San Luis Obispo, Calif., 1973-90; info. cons. Obispo Info. Group, San Luis Obispo, 1990-95; pub. deleree com, San Luis Obispo, Calif., 1996—; mem. adv. bd. Calif. Online Resources for Edn., Long Beach, 1993-94; edn. coord. SLONET Info. Network, 1993-95, dir., 1997-98. Author: Double Lives: Poems 1984-85, 1985; editor: Obispo Web Digest: on the World Wide Web, 1994-96; contbr. poems to profl. publs. Founding mem. AIDS Support Network, San Luis Obispo, 1984. Mem. MLA, Associated Writing Programs, Nat. Coun. Tchrs. English. Office: Deleree Com PO Box 771 San Luis Obispo CA 93406-0771

BUNKER, JOHN BIRKBECK, cattle rancher, retired sugar company executive; b. Yonkers, N.Y., Mar. 28, 1926; s. Ellsworth and Harriet (Butler) B.; m. Emma Cadwalader, Feb. 27, 1954; children: Emma, Jeanie, Harriet, John C., Lambert C. BA, Yale U., 1950. With Nat. Sugar Refining Co., 1953-62; pres. Gt. Western Sugar Co., Denver, 1966; pres., CEO Holly Sugar Co., Colorado Springs, Colo., 1967-81, chmn., CEO, 1971-81; pres., CEO Calif. and Hawaiian Sugar Co., San Francisco, 1981-88, vice chmn., 1988-89, ret., 1989; gen. ptnr. Bunker Ranch Co., 1989—; chmn. Wheatland Bankshares and First State Bank of Wheatland, 1992—. Trustee Colo. Coll., 1973-94, Asia Found., 1985-94. Mem. Wyo. Nature Conservancy, Wyo. Stockgrowers Assn., Wyo. Heritage Found., Wyo. Farm Bur., Colo.-Wyo. Nat. Farmers Union. Home: 1451 Cottonwood Ave Wheatland WY 82201-3412

BUNN, DOROTHY IRONS, court reporter; b. Trinidad, Colo., Apr. 30, 1948; d. Russell and Pauline Anna (Langowski) Irons; children: Kristy Lynn, Wade Allen, Russell Ahearn. Student No. Va. C.C., 1970-71, U. Va., Fairfax, 1971-72. Registered profl. reporter; cert. shorthand reporter. Pres., CEO Ahearn Ltd., Springfield, Va., 1970-81, Bunn & Assocs., Glenrock, Wyo., 1981—; cons. Bixby Hereford Co., Glenrock, 1981-89, co-mgr., 1989-97. Del., White House Conf. on Small Bus., Washington, 1986, 95, state chair, 1995; mem. Wyo. adv. coun. Small Bus. Adminstrn., 1994-96. Mem. NAFE, Am. Indian Soc., Nat. Ct. Reporters Assn., Nat. Fedn. Ind. Bus., Wyo. Shorthand Reporters Assn., Nat. Fedn. Ind. Businesses (guardian 1991-96), Nat. Fedn. Bus. and Profl. Women (1st v.p. Casper 1994-95, pres. 1995-96, pub. rels. chair, Choices chair), Assn. for Advancement of CAT Tech. Avocation: photography. Office: Bunn & Assocs 2036 Adobe Ave Douglas WY 82633-3016 also: PO Box 1618 Glenrock WY 82637-1618

BUNN, NADINE, store owner; b. Cleveland, Ohio; d. Avery John and Fortunetta (Dottore) B. BA, Univ. Calif., 1972. Supr. Dept. Pub. Social Svcs., E. Los Angeles, 1973-79; owner/mgr. Folk Mote Music, Santa

Barbara, Calif., 1980—; editor of folk harp jour. Internat. Soc. Folk Harpers & Craftsman, Anaheim, Calif., 1985—; bd. dirs. Internat. Soc. Folk Harpers & Craftsman, 1984-88. Adv. bd. dir. Santa Barbara Soc. Traditional Music, 1985-95, Calif. Traditional Music Soc., 1994—. Avocations: harpist, reading, computers. Office: Folk Harp Journal 1034 Santa Barbara St Santa Barbara CA 93101-2109

BUNN, PAUL A., JR., oncologist, educator; b. N.Y.C., Mar. 16, 1945; s. Paul A. Bunn; m. Camille Ruoff, Aug. 17, 1968; children: Rebecca, Kristen, Paul H. BA cum laude, Amherst Coll., 1967; MD, Cornell U., 1971. Diplomate Nat. Bd. Med. Examiners, Am. Bd. Internal Medicine, Am. Bd. Med. Oncology. Intern U. Calif., H.C. Moffitt Hosp., San Francisco, 1971-72, resident, 1972-73; clin. assoc. medicine br. Nat. Cancer Inst., NIH, Bethesda, Md., 1973-76; sr. investigator med. oncology br. Nat. Cancer Inst., Washington VA Hosp., 1976-81; asst. prof. medicine med. sch. Georgetown U., 1978-81; head cell kinetic sect., Navy med. oncology br. Nat. Cancer Inst., Bethesda, 1981-84; assoc. prof. medicine uniformed svcs. Univ. Health Scis., Bethesda, 1981-84; prof. medicine health scis. ctr. U. Colo., Denver, 1984—, head divsn. med. oncology, 1984-94, dir. cancer ctr., 1987—; mem. instl. rev. bd. NIH, Nat. Cancer Inst., 1982-84; mem. intramural support contract rev. com. Nat. Cancer Inst., 1982-84; cons. Coulter Immunology, 1984-89, Abbott Labs., 1992-94, Seragen, 1993—, others; mem. cancer com. U. Colo., 1984—, mem. faculty senate health scis. ctr., 1985-94, mem. exec. com. sch. medicine, 1987—; mem. fin. com. Univ. Physicians, Inc., 1986-91; mem. med. bd. Univ. Hosp., 1987—; external sci. advisor cancer ctr. U. Miami, 1988-92, U. Ark., 1989-94, U. Va., 1991-94, others; mem. oncology drug adv. com. FDA, 1992—; mem. sci. secretariat 7th World Conf. Lung Cancer, 1994; bd. dirs. Univ. Hosp. Resource Coun.; mem. oncology drug adv. com. FDA, 1993—. Author: Carboplatin (JM-8) Current Perspectives and Future Directions, 1990, Clinical Experiences With Platinum and Etoposide Therapy in Lung Cancer, 1992, (with M.E. Wood) Hematology/Oncology Secrets, 1994; assoc. editor Med. and Pediatric Oncology, 1984—, Jour. Clin. Oncology, 1991—, Cancer Rsch., 1992—, others; contbr. chpts. to books and articles to profl. jours. Bd. dirs. Colo. divsn. Am. Cancer Soc., 1989—, Leukemia Soc. Am., 1991—; bd. dirs. The Cancer Venture, 1993-94, Fair Share Colo., 1993-94; chmn. Solid Tumor Oncology Edn. Found., 1996—. With USPHS, 1973-84. Decorated Medal of Commendation; recipient Sci. of Yr. award Denver chpt. ARCS, 1992; named one of 400 Best Drs. in Am., Good Housekeeping Mag., 1991, 92; grantee Schering Plough, 1988-89, Burroughs Wellcome, 1991—, Bristol-Myers Squibb, 1993—, others. Fellow ACP; mem. AAAS, Am. Soc. Hematology (mem. sci. subcom. neoplasia 1989-92), Am. Assn. Cancer Rsch., Am. Soc. Clin. Oncology (chair program subcom. 1985-86, 90), Am. Fedn. Clin. Rsch., Am. Assn. Cancer Insts. (bd. dirs. 1992—), Internat. Assn. Study Lung Cancer (bd. dirs. 1988—, pres. 1994—), Wesstern Assn. Physicians, S.W. Oncology Group (mem. lung and leukemia com. 1986—, mem. biologic response modifier com. 1987—), Lung Cancer Study Group, Alpha Omega Alpha. Office: U Colo Cancer Ctr Box B188 4200 E 9th Ave Denver CO 80220-3706

BUNTING, KENNETH FREEMAN, newspaper editor; b. Houston, Dec. 9, 1948; s. Willie Freeman and Sarah Lee (Peterson) B.; m. Juliana Amy Jafvert, July 13, 1989; 1 child, Maxwell Freeman. Student, U. Mo., 1966-67; AA in Journalism, Lee Coll., 1968; BA in Journalism and History, Tex. Christian U., 1970; advanced exec. program, Northwestern U., 1996. Mgmt. trainee, reporter Harte-Hanks Newspapers Inc., Corpus Christi, Tex., 1970-71; reporter, then copy editor San Antonio Express-News, 1971-73; exec. asst. to Hon. G.J. Sutton Tex. Ho. of Reps., San Antonio, 1973-74; reporter Cin. Post, 1974-78, Sacramento Bee, 1978; reporter, asst. city editor, state capitol corr. L.A. Times, 1978-87; capitol bur. chief, city editor, dep. mng. editor, sr. editor Ft. Worth Star-Telegram, 1987-93; mng. editor Seattle Post-Intelligencer, 1993—; journalism instr. Orange Coast Coll., Costa Mesa, Calif., 1981-82; mem. adv. bd. Maynard Inst., Oakland, Calif., 1994—. Bd. dirs. Seattle Symphony, 1995—; mem. commn. Woodland Park Zoo, Seattle, 1995-96; mem. Leadership Ft. Worth; mem. journalism adv. bd. Tex. Christian U.; former mem. minorities task force Assn. for Edn. in Journalism and Mass Comms.; past pres. Press Club, Orange County, Calif.; past bd. dirs. Covington (Ky.) Cmty. Ctr.; past 1st v.p. Young Dems. of Tex.; past treas., mem. exec. bd. Freedom of Inro. Found. of Tex. Mem. Nat. Assn. Black Journalists, AP Mng. Editors Assn. (mem. ethics com. 1995-96), Am. Soc. Newspaper Editors (mem. minorities com.), APME (bd. dirs. 1996—), Soc. Profl. Journalists (bd. dirs. western Wash. chpt. 1995-96), Seattle C. of C. (mem. cmty. devel. roundtable 1994—), Tex. Christian U. Alumni Assn. (bd. dirs.), Freedom of Info. Found. Tex., Rainier Club, Washington Athletic Club. Unitarian. Avocations: tennis, bridge, reading. Office: Seattle-Post Intelligencer PO Box 1909 101 Elliott Ave W Seattle WA 98111*

BURAS, NATHAN, hydrology and water resources educator; b. Barlad, Romania, Aug. 23, 1921; came to U.S., 1947; s. Boris and Ethel (Weiser) B.; m. Netty Stivel, Apr. 13, 1951; 1 child, Nir H. BS with highest honors, U. Calif., Berkeley, 1949; MS, Technion, Haifa, Israel, 1957; PhD, UCLA, 1962. Registered profl. engr., Israel. Prof. hydrology and water resources Technion, 1962-80, dean, 1966-68; vis. prof. Stanford (Calif.) U., 1976-81; prof., head of dept. hydrology and water resources U. Ariz., Tucson, 1981-89, prof. hydrology and water resources, 1989—; vis. prof. Technical U. Valencia, Spain, 1998; cons. Tahal, Ltd., Tel Aviv, 1963-73, World Bank, Washington, 1972-76, 79-81, Regional Municipality of Waterloo, Ont., Can., 1991-93, U.S. AID, Washington, 1992-93, Great No. Paper Co., 1992—; apptd. mem. standing com. on terminology Internat. Glossary of Hydrology UNESCO, 1996. Author: Scientific Allocation of Water Resources, 1972; editor: Control of Water Resources Systems, 1976, Management of Water Resources in North America, 1995, Reflections on Hydrology, 1997. Mem. Israel-Mex. Mixed Commn. on Sci. Cooperation, 1976, So. Ariz. Water Resource Assn., 1982—; active Pugwash Workshops, 1991, 92, 93. Named Laureat du Congres, Internat. Assn. Agrl. Engring., 1964; recipient Cert. of Appreciation, USDA., 1970, award for Edn. and Pub. Svc. in Water Resources U. Coun. on Water Resources, 1994, award for Excellence Gov. of Ariz., 1995. Fellow ASCE (life), Ariz.-Nev. Acad. Sci., Internat. Water Resources Assn.; mem. Am. Geophys. Union, Am. Water Resources Assn. (charter). Jewish. Avocations: music, hiking. Home: 5541 E Circulo Terra Tucson AZ 85750-1003 Office: U Ariz Dept Hydrology and Water Resources Tucson AZ 85721

BURBIDGE, E. MARGARET, astronomer, educator; b. Davenport, Eng.; d. Stanley John and Marjorie (Stott) Peachey; m. Geoffrey Burbidge, Apr. 2, 1948; 1 child, Sarah. B.S., Ph.D., U. London; Sc.D. hon., Smith Coll., 1963, U. Sussex, 1970, U. Bristol, 1972, U. Leicester, 1972, City U., 1973, U. Mich., 1978, U. Mass., 1978, Williams Coll., 1979, SUNY, Stony Brook, 1985, Rensselaer Poly. Inst., 1986, U. Notre Dame, 1986, U. Chgo., 1991. Mem. staff U. London Obs., 1948-51; rsch. fellow Yerkes Obs. U. Chgo., 1951-53, Shirley Farr fellow Yerkes obs., 1957-59, assoc. prof. Yerkes Obs., 1959-62; rsch. fellow Calif. Inst. Tech., Pasadena, 1955-57; mem. Enrico Fermi Inst. for Nuclear Studies, 1957-62; prof. astronomy dept. physics U. Calif. San Diego, 1964—; dir. Royal Greenwich Obs. (Herstmonceux Castle), Hailsham, Eng., 1971-73; univ. prof. U. Calif., San Diego, 1984-91, prof. emeritus, 1991—, rsch. prof. dept. physics, 1990—; Lindsay Meml. lectr. Goddard Space Flight Ctr., NASA, 1985; Abby Rockefeller Mauze prof. MIT, 1968; David Elder lectr. U. Strathclyde, 1972; V. Gildersleeve lectr. Barnard Coll., 1974; Jansky lectr. Nat. Radio Astronomy Observatory, 1977; Brode lectr. Whitman Coll., 1986. Author: (with G. Burbidge) Quasi-Stellar Objects, 1967; editor: Observatory mag., 1948-51; mem. editorial bd.: Astronomy and Astrophysics, 1969—. Recipient (with husband) Warner prize in Astronomy, 1959, Bruce Gold medal Astronomy Soc. Pacific, 1982; hon. fellow Univ. Coll., London, Girton Coll., Lucy Cavendish Coll., Cambridge; U.S. Nat. medal of sci., 1984; Sesquicentennial medal Mt. Holyoke Coll., 1987, Einstein medal World Cultural Coun., 1988. Fellow Royal Soc., Nat. Acad. Scis. (chmn. sect. 12 astronomy 1986), Am. Acad. Arts and Scis., Royal Astron. Soc.; mem. Am. Astron. Soc. (v.p. 1972-74, pres. 1976-78; Henry Norris Russell lectr. 1984), Internat. Astron. Union (pres. commn. 28 1970-73), Grad. Women Sci. (nat. hon. mem.). Office: U Calif-San Diego Ctr Astrophysics Space Scis Mail Code # 0424 La Jolla CA 92093

BURCH, MARY LOU, organization consultant, housing advocate; b. Billings, Mont., Apr. 4, 1930; d. Forrest Scott Sr. and Mary Edna (Hinshaw) Chillicott; m. J. Sheldon Robinson, June 10, 1949 (div. 1950); m. C. Howard Burch, Nov. 27, 1957 (div. 1984); children: Julie Lynne Scully, Donna Eileen, Carol Marie Kimball, Alan Robert, Christine Philips Spruill Enomoto. AA, Grant Tech. Coll., Sacramento, 1949; AB, Sacramento State Coll., 1955; student, U. Alaska, 1976-78, Santa Rosa (Calif.) Jr. Coll., 1987. Diagnostic tchr. Calif. Youth Authority, Perkins, 1955-57; com. chmn. on pub. info. Sequoia Union High Sch. Dist., So. San Mateo County, Calif., 1970-72; exec. dir. Presbyn. Hospitality House, Fairbanks, Alaska, 1979-80; realtor Century 21 Smith/Ring, Renton, Wash., 1980-81; cons. Fairbanks, Alaska, 1981-84; exec. dir. Habitat for Humanity of Sonoma County, Santa Rosa, Calif., 1986-89, Affordable Housing Assoc., Santa Rosa, Calif., 1989-90; pvt. cons. in housing and orgn. Scottsdale, Ariz., 1991-92, Prescott and Dewey, Ariz., 1992—; bd. dirs. Hosp. Chaplainey Svcs, Santa Rosa, Villa Los Alamos Homeowners Assn.; cons. Access Alaska, Anchorage, 1983; contractor Alaka Siding, Fairbanks, 1982-83; founder Let's Get Organized!. Local coord. fgn. exch. student program Acad. Yr. in Am., 1993-94; acad. coord. fgn. exch. student program Cultural Homestay Internat., 1994-97; vol. coms. Habitat for Humanity, exec. asst. long term organizing project, 1997—. Named vol. of the year, Hosp. Chaplaincy Svcs., 1987. Democrat. United Ch. of Christ. Home and Office: 1288 Tapadero Dr #D-PCC Dewey AZ 86327-5823

BURCHARD, THOMAS KIRK, psychiatrist; b. Boston, Feb. 16, 1948; s. Charles Henry and Helen (Schwob) B.; m. Geri Diane Margolese. BS, Antioch Coll., 1970; MD, U. Va., 1973. Intern Cin. Children's Hosp., 1974-75; adult psychiatry resident Sepulveda VA Hosp., L.A., 1975-77; child psychiatry fellow UCLA, 1977-79; dir. Mental Health Ctr. child and family programs Community Hosp. of the Monterey Peninsula, Monterey, Calif., 1979-91, dir. child and adolescent outpatient programs, 1991—; chmn. Psychiatry Dept. Cmty. Hosp. Monterey Peninsula, 1985-87; asst. clin. prof. UCLA, 1979-80; instr. Antioch-West, Pacific Grove, Calif., 1982. Mem. AMA, Am. Acad. Child and Adolescent Psychiatry, Am. Psychiat. Assn., Calif. Med. Assn., No. Calif. Psychiat. Assn. Avocations: cinema, magic. Fax: 831-625-4610. Office: Community Hosp of Monterey Peninsula PO Box HH Monterey CA 93942-1085

BURCHELL, PAUL WILLIAM, petroleum engineer; b. Butte, Mont., Aug. 22, 1933; s. James Harrison and Ivana (Pluth) B.; m. Marilyn Joyce Dolan, June 11, 1955; children: Teresa Lynn, William James, Paula Rene, Pamela Joyce. BS, Mont. Coll. Min. Sci. & Tech., 1956. Registered profl. engr., Utah. Roughneck Kulberg Drilling Col, Cut Bank, Mont., 1953-54; roustabout Stanolind (Amoco) Oil & Gas Co., Midwest, Wyo., 1954-55; sr. geophysicist Texaco, various, 1956-62; chief petroleum engr. Utah Oil & Gas Conservation Commn., Salt Lake City, 1962-74; conservation engr. El Paso (Tex.) Natural Gas Co., 1974-92; petroleum engr., cons. Salt Lake City, 1992—. Author: Geologic Guidebook, 1964, 2d edit., 1969. Precinct chmn. Salt Lake County Rep. Party, 1997—. Mem. Soc. Petroleum Engrs., Utal Geol. Assn., El Paso Geol. Soc. (pres. 1982), Intermountain Assn. Geologists (pres. 1967, engring. com. Gov. Rampton rep. Interstate Oil & Gas Compact Commn. 1967), Utah Geophys. Soc. (pres. 1961). Republican. Roman Catholic. Home and Office: 2884 Willow Hills Dr Sandy UT 84093-1931

BURD, STEVE, food service executive; b. 1949. BS, Carroll Coll., 1971; MA in Econs., U. Wis., 1973. With fin. and mktg. So. Pacific Transp. Co., San Francisco; with Arthur D. Little, N.Y.C., 1982-87; mgmt. cons., 1986-91; cons. Stop & Shop Cos., Boston, 1988-89, Fred Meyer Inc., Portland, Oreg., 1989-90, Safeway Inc., Oakland, Calif., 1986-87, 91—; pres., CEO Safeway Inc., 1992—, chmn. bd. dirs. Office: Safeway Inc 5918 Stoneridge Mall Rd Pleasanton CA 94588-3229*

BURDGE, RICHARD JAMES, JR., lawyer; b. Long Beach, Calif., Dec. 4, 1949; children: Kristin Alexis, Lindsay Michelle, Margaret Lynn, Kelly Anne. BS, Yale U., 1972; JD, UCLA, 1979. Bar: Calif. 1979, U.S. Dist. Ct. (cen. dist.) Calif. 1979, U.S. Ct. Appeals (9th cir.) 1980, U.S. Dist. Ct. (no. dist.) Calif. 1984, U.S. Supreme Ct. 1984, U.S. Dist. Ct. (ea. dist.) Calif. 1987, U.S. Dist. Ct. (so. dist.) Calif. 1990. Assoc., then ptnr. Lillick, McHose & Charles, L.A., 1979-86; ptnr. Dewey Ballantine and predecessor firms, L.A., 1986—; del. L.A. County Bar Del. to Calif. State Bar Conf. of Dels., 1988—. Mng. editor UCLA Law Rev., 1978-79, mem. edit. staff, 1977-78. Chmn. UCLA Law Ann. Fund, 1989-91; co-chair UCLA Law Libr. Alumni Campaign, 1994-97. Lt. USN, 1972-76. Mem. Assn. Bus. Trial Lawyers (gov. 1989-91, 93-95, ann. seminar chair 1992, jud. coll. chair 1995, treas. 1995-96, sec. 1996-97, v.p. 1997-98, pres. 1998—), Chancery Club. Office: Dewey Ballantine LLP 333 S Hope St Ste 3000 Los Angeles CA 90071-3039

BURDICK, BRENDA LYNN, secondary education educator; b. Payson, Utah, Sept. 11, 1957; d. William Duane and Patsy Anne Curtis; m. Brad M. Burdick, Sept. 19, 1975; children: Monica Burdick Valerio, Angela. Student, Utah Valley State Coll., 1984-85; BA in Art Edn., Brigham Young Univ., 1985-89. Cert. K-12 tchr., Utah. Art tchr. Payson H.S., Utah, 1989—; cheerleading advisor, Payson H.S., Utah, 1889-93, art rep., 1990-98, yearbook advisor, 1996-97. Mem. Nat. Arts Educators Assn. Avocations: boating, waterskiing, biking, painting, drawing. Home: 153 N 100 W Payson UT 84651 Office: 1050 S Main St Payson UT 84651-3319

BURDICK, CLAUDE OWEN, pathologist; b. Oconomowoc, Wis.; s. Lawrence Theodore and Florence (Owens) B.; m. Margaret Huiskamp, June 18, 1955; children: Katherine, Roberta, Lawrence, Jack (dec.). BS in Med. Sci., U. Wis., 1955, MD, 1958. Diplomate Am. Bd. Pathology, Am. Bd. Dermatopathology. Intern Letterman Army Med. Ctr., San Francisco, 1958-59, resident, 1959-63; pathologist, chief hematology Berkshire Med. Ctr., Pittsfield, Mass., 1968-70; pathologist, dir. labs. Valley Care Health Sys., Livermore/Pleasanton, Calif., 1970-98; chmn., bd. dirs. Valley Care Health Sys., 1993-96; med. dir., cons. Spectra Labs., Inc., Fremont, Calif., 1994—; pres. Livermore Alameda Valley Med. Group, 1972-76. Lt. col. U.S. Army, 1957-68. Fellow Am. Soc. Clin. Pathology, Coll. Am. Pathologists; mem. AMA, Calif. Med. Assn., Calif. Soc. Pathologists (bd. dirs. 1983-86), Alameda Contra Costa Med. Soc., Am. Soc. Blood Banks, South Bay Pathology Soc. (pres. 1981). Democrat. Presbyterian. Avocation: choral music (Ohlone College Chamber Singers). Office: Western Labs Med Group 2945 Webster St Oakland CA 94609-3496

BURDICK, ROBERT W., newspaper editor; b. Feb. 11, 1948; m. Patty Burnett; 1 child, David. B in Polit. Sci., Fla. Atl. U., 1969. Reporter Miami Herald, Fla. Today; night city editor Palm Beach (Fla.) Post; mng. editor Palm Beach Daily News; asst. mng. editor Wichita (Kans.) Eagle; city editor/metro editor/asst. to exec. editor San Jose (Calif.) Mercury News, 1978-82; asst. mng. editor Denver Post, 1982-84; asst. mng. editor/mng. editor/editor L.A. Daily News, 1984-94; mng. editor, editor Rocky Mountain News, Denver, 1994-98, pres., 1998—. Mem. Am. Soc. Newspaper Editors, Soc. Profl. Journalists, AP News Execs. Coun. (past bd. mem., past pres. Calif., Nev. chpt., past editor AP Mng. Editors News). Avocations: skiing, hiking. Office: Rocky Mountain News 400 W Colfax Ave Denver CO 80204-2694*

BURG, JEFFREY HOWARD, technology company executive; b. Cherry Hill, N.J., Aug. 26, 1977; s. Jerome Stuart and Janis Elaine (Lyon) B. Student, Ariz. State U., 1996—. Sales rep. Shambis Corp., Scottsdale, Ariz., 1995-96; pvt. practice Phoenix, 1996-98; prin., owner Burg Worldwide Enterprises, Tempe, Ariz., 1998—; cons. U.S. Secret Svc., Phoenix, 1996-98. Vol. Scottsdale (Ariz.) Pub. Schs., 1994—. Recipient Family of Yr. award Phoenix Boy's Choir, 1997. Mem. Soc. Broadcast Engrs., Soc. Motion Picture and TV Engrs., Inst. Elec. Electronics Engrs. Republican. Jewish. Avocations: travel, skiing. E-mail: jeff@burg.net. Office: Burg Worldwide Enterprises PO Box 3291 Tempe AZ 85280-3291

BURG, JEROME STUART, financial planning consultant; b. N.Y.C., Aug. 2, 1935; s. Norman and Ruth (Schkurman) B.; m. Janis Elaine Lyon, May 26, 1974; children: Jeffrey Howard, David Matthew, Audree, Harriet, Robert, Stephanie. Student, Temple U., 1953-56; CLU, Am. Coll., 1973, chartered fin. cons., 1984; cert. fin. planner, Coll. Fin. Planning, 1983. Pres., CEO Jerome Burg Assoc., Inc., Cherry Hill, N.J., 1963-79, Contemporary Fin. Planning, Scottsdale, Ariz., 1979-89; sr. acct. mgr. Acacia Group, Phoenix, 1989—; instr. Glendale and Scottsdale C.C., 1983-92, Nat. Inst. Fin., N.J., 1984-90. Host (radio program) Money Talks Sta. KFNN, Phoenix, 1995-96. Pres. N.J. Assn. Life Underwriters, Trenton 1965-85; instr. Jr. Achievement, Scottsdale, 1985-89; bd. dirs. Phoenix Boys Choir, 1997—; 1st v.p. Pres. Cabinet-Acacia Group, Washington, 1991, 93, co-pres., 1992, mem. pres.' cabinet, 1989—. With U.S. Army, 1956-58. Mem. Internat. Assn. Fin. Planning (bd. dirs. Greater Phoenix chpt. 1982—), Inst. Cert. Fin. Planners. Avocations: golf, skiing. Office: Acacia Group 3200 E Camelback Rd Ste 245 Phoenix AZ 85018-2320

BURG, WALTER A., airport terminal executive. Gen. manager, ceo Tucson Airport Authority, Ariz., 1966-79, pres., CEO, 1979—. Office: Tucson Internat Airport 7005 S Plumer Ave Tucson AZ 85706-6926*

BURGARINO, ANTHONY EMANUEL, environmental engineer, consultant; b. Milw., July 20, 1948; s. Joseph Francis Burgarino and Mardelle (Hoeffler) T.; m. Gail Fay DiMatteo, Mar. 13, 1982; children: Paul Anthony, Joanna Lynn. BS, U. Wis., 1970; MS, Ill. Inst. Tech., 1974, PhD, 1980. Registered profl. engr., Ariz. Sales engr. Leeds & Northrup, Phila., 1970-72; rsch. asst. Ill. Inst. Tech., Chgo., 1972-75; chemist City of Chgo., 1975-79; instr. Joliet (Ill.) Jr. Coll., 1978-79; sr. project engr. Carollo Engrs., Walnut Creek, Calif., 1980—; cons. City of Clovis, Calif., 1981-83, City of Fresno, Calif., 1983-96, City of Phoenix, 1981-90, City of Yuma, Ariz., 1989—, City of Santa Maria, Calif., 1991-95, City of Vallejo, Calif., 1992—, City of Peoria, Ariz., 1996—. Contbr. articles to profl. jours. EPA grantee, 1970-72; NSF fellow, 1973, Ill. Inst. Tech. Rsch. Found. fellow, 1974. Mem. Am. Water Works Assn. Roman Catholic. Avocations: mechanical and electronics projects building, stock and real estate investments. Home: 2321 Lafayette Dr Antioch CA 94509-5871 Office: Carollo Engrs 2700 Ygnacio Valley Rd Ste 300 Walnut Creek CA 94598-3466

BURGE, WILLARD, JR., software company executive; b. Johnson City, N.Y., Oct. 2, 1938; s. Willard Sr. and Catherine Bernice (Matthews) B.; m. Carol Crockenberg, June 16, 1961; children: Willard III, Pennie Lynn. Registered profl. engr., Ohio. Indsl. engr. Harnischfeger Corp., Escanaba, Mich., 1966-67; sr. indsl. engr. Gen. Electric, Ladson, S.C., 1968-74; advanced mfg. engr. Gen. Electric, Mentor, Ohio, 1971-74; corp. staff engr. Eaton Corp., Willoughby Hills, Ohio, 1974-79, supr. N/C programming, 1979-80, supr. mfg. engring., 1980-82, mgr. mfg. systems engring., 1982-87; bus. unit mgr. MSC Products, Eaton Corp., Costa Mesa, Calif., 1987-91; pres., CEO CAM Software, Inc., Provo, Utah, 1991-93; chief exec. officer Key Svcs., Cypress, Calif., 1993—; bd. dirs. CAM Software, Inc.; presenter in field. With U.S. Army, 1957. Mem. Soc. Mfg. Engrs. Republican. Avocations: photography, computers, start-up businesses. Home and Office: Key Svcs 13280 Saint Andrews Dr Seal Beach CA 90740-3796

BURGER, EDMUND GANES, architect; b. Yerington, Nev., Mar. 28, 1930; s. Edmund Ganes and Rose Catherine (Kobe) B.; m. Shirley May Pratini, Jan. 21, 1968; 1 dau., Jane Lee. B.M.E., U. Santa Clara, 1951; B.Arch., U. Pa., 1959. Engr. Gen. Electric Co., 1951-52; design engr. U. Calif. Radiation Lab., 1952-57; John Stewardson fellow in architecture, 1959; architect Wurster, Bernardi & Emmons, San Francisco, 1960-63; founder Burger & Coplans, Inc. (Architects), San Francisco, 1964; pres. Burger & Coplans, Inc. (Architects), 1964-79; owner Edmund Burger (Architect), 1979—; guest lectr. U. Calif., Berkeley. important works include Acorn Housing Project, Oakland, Calif., Crescent Village Housing Project, Suisun City, Calif., Coplans residence, San Francisco, Betel Housing Project, San Francisco, Grand View Housing Project, San Francisco, Albany (Calif.) Oaks Housing, Grow Homes, San Pablo, Calif., Mariposa Housing, Dunleavy Plaza Housing, Potrero Ct. Housing, San Francisco, Lee residence, Kentfield, Calif., Burger residences, Lafayette, Calif., Oceanside, Oreg., and El Cerrito, Calif., Yamhill Valley Vineyards Winery, McMinneville, Oreg., Portico De Mar, shop and restaurant complex, Barcelona, Spain, Hendrickson residence, Newport Beach, Calif., Hamilton residence, Winters, Calif., Sanders residence, Yuba City, Calif.; author: Geomorphic Architecture, 1986. Recipient citation for excellence in community architecture AIA, 1969, award of merit AIA, award of merit Homes for Better Living, 1970, 79, 1st Honor award, 1973, 81, Holiday award for a beautiful Am., 1970, Honor award 4th Biennial HUD awards for design excellence, 1970, Bay Area awards for design excellence, 1969, 74, 78, Apts. of Year award Archtl. Record, 1972, Houses of Year award, 1973, Calif. Affordable Housing Competition award, 1981, HUD Building Value into Housing award, 1981, Community Design award Calif. Council AIA, 1986; design grant Nat. Endowment for Arts, 1980, HUD, 1980; constrn. grant HUD, 1981. Office: PO Box 10193 Berkeley CA 94709-5193

BURGER, PAULA, artist; b. Novogrudek, Poland, July 27, 1934; came to U.S., 1949; d. Wolf and Sarah (Ginenski) Koladicki; m. David Zapiler, Nov. 25, 1951 (div. 1978); children: Susan, Freda A., Steven M.; m. Samuel Burger, Apr. 5, 1981. Student, U. Denver, 1977-78, U. Colo., 1979, Art Students League, Denver, 1989-91. Lic. health care adminstr., real estate agt., Colo. Artist Denver, 1978—; Holocaust survivor lectr. One-woman and group shows include U. Denver Law Libr., 1992, 94, Town Hall Arts Ctr., Colo., 1993-94, Jewish Women & Art, Colo., 1994, Cross Currents Gallery, Ill., 1991, Creative Design Gallery, Colo., 1990, Art Zone, Colo., 1990-93; represented in permanent collections at U. Denver Law Sch. Libr., BMH Congregation, Colo., Landmark Edn., Colo., Zapiler & Ferris Attys. at Law, Colo. State Capitol. Mem. Denver Art Mus., Mus. Modern Art N.Y. Studio: 160 S Monaco Pky Denver CO 80224-1125

BURGESS, LARRY LEE, aerospace executive; b. Phoenix, May 13, 1942; s. Byron Howard and Betty Eileen (Schook) B.; m. Mary Jane Ruble, Mar. 9, 1985; children: Christopher, Patrick; children from previous marriage: Byron, Damian. BSEE, MSEE, Naval Postgrad. Sch. Officer USN, Washington, 1964-85; corp. exec. Lockheed-Martin, Denver, 1985—; pres. L & M Capital Investments, Denver, 1987-98; CEO L&M Property Mgmt. Co., 1988—; pub. 2 papers 4th Internat. Conf. on Tethers, 1995. V.p. Denargo Market Neighborhood Assn.; co-pres. Upper Larimer Neighborhood Assn.; coach Youth Activities, Corpus Christi, 1976-78; coach youth basketball Littleton (Colo.) YMCA, 1994-99, Columbine Competitive Basketball, 1996-99, Jefferson County Recreational Basketball, 1997-98; spkr. in local schs., Littleton, 1987-90. Inducted into the Kans. Basketball Hall of Fame, 1993. Mem. AIAA (dir.), SASA, Armed Forces Comm. Navy League and Electronic Agy. Republican. E-mail: lbur208057@aol.com. Home: 3 Red Fox Ln Littleton CO 80127-5710

BURGESS, SCOTT ALAN, computer scientist; b. Spokane, Wash., Apr. 14, 1964; s. Roy Walter and Betty Jane (Kapel) B. BS, So. Oreg. U., 1986; MS, Rutgers U., 1991; postgrad., Oreg. State U., 1998. Intern IBM, San Jose, Calif., 1993, 95; rschr. Oreg. State U., Corvallis, 1993—; cons. Hewlett-Packard, McMinnville, Oreg., 1993. Author: The Work of Dean Ing, 1990, The Work of Reginald Bretnov, 1989, Adventures of a Freelancer, 1993. Recipient Merit Scholar award Phi Kappa Phi, 1986, Merit award Data Processing Mgmt. Assn., 1986. Mem. Assn. for Computing Machinery, Am. Assn. for Artificial Intelligence. Avocations: photography, hiking, writing. Home: 2846 Newton Pl Philomath OR 97370

BURK, GARY MAURICE, architect; b. Dallas, Nov. 8, 1943; s. Houston Maurice and Evelyn (Howell) B. BArch, Tex. Tech U., 1968; MArch, U. Ill., 1970. Registered architect; NCARB cert. Asst. prof. Tex. Tech U., Lubbock, 1970-79; project designer Hellmuth, Obata & Kassabaum, Dallas, 1979-80; assoc. Richard Ferrara, Architect, Dallas, 1980-83; cons. designer Myrick, Newman, Dahlberg, Dallas, 1982-83; assoc. prof. Calif. State U., Pomona, Calif., 1983-85; sr. facility planner Am. Med. Internat., L.A., 1985-86; dir. facilities planning URS Cons., Cleve., 1986-88, URS Consultants, N.Y. and N.J., 1988-91; sr. med. planner Ellerbe Becket, Inc., L.A., 1991-95; v.p. Ellerbe Becket, Inc., San Francisco, 1995-96; prin. Ratcliff Architects, Berkeley, Calif., 1996—; owner Strategic & Facility Planning for Healthcare, San Francisco, 1996—; cons. City Hosp./St. Thomas Med. Ctr., Merger Task Force, Akron, 1988-89, L.A. County Pub. Health Programs and Svcs., 1992-94, Palo Alto (Calif.) Med. Found., 1992-96, U. Tex. med. br., Galveston, 1994-96; dir. Hosp. of the Future research studio, 1985. Mem. Dallas Civic Chorus, 1980-83, St. Alban's Parish Choir, Cleveland Heights, Ohio, 1987-88, All Saints Parish Choir, Hoboken, N.J., 1988-90, Cleve. Opera Assocs., 1987-88; mem. steering com. Judith Resnik Women's Health Ctr., Summa Health System, Akron, 1989-91, Friends of N.Y. Philharm, 1990-91. Research grantee Tex. Tech U., 1976. Mem. AIA (ednl. fellow 1968, Calif. coun.), AIA Acad. on Architecture for Health (steering com.), San Francisco AIA (health facilities program com.), Healthcare Strategies and Perspectives. Democrat. Episcopalian. Avocations: vocal music, current Am. fiction, medieval European history, archtl. antiquities. Home: 155 Jackson St Apt 2204 San Francisco CA 94111-1940 Office: Ratcliff Architects PO Box 1022 Berkeley CA 94701-1022

BURK, MAKSYMILIAN, retired sceintist, writer; b. Cracow, Poland, Mar. 9, 1919; came to U.S., 1959; s. Osias Necker and Zonia Kancruker; married; 2 children. MSChemE, Silesian Poly., Glivitz, Poland, 1947; PhD in Phys. Chemistry, Acad. Mining & Metallurgy, Cracow, 1957. Mem. ceramic faculty Acad. Mining & Metallurgy, Cracow, 1948-58; with Coors Porcelain Co., Golden, Colo., 1960-63; sr. scientist Allied Chem., Morristown, N.J., 1965-69; sr. staff scientist TRW, Manhattan Beach, Calif., 1969-86, ret., 1986. Author: (nonfiction) Gold, Silver and Uranium from Seas and Oceans. The Emerging Technology, 1989, rev. edit., 1991, The Essence and Meaning of Life, 1989, (fiction) The Smoke from Auschwitz Chimneys and Other Holocaust Verses, 1989, The Holocaust Verses, 1990, (collections) Heart and Wit, 1991, Sir Mistake and Mister Blunder as Two Politicians, 1989, The Human Menagerie, 1989, rev. edit., 1991, Politicos, Crooks, Dumbbelles and Quacks, 1992; contbr. numerous articles to sci. jours. Mem. Am. Chem. Soc., Am. Ceramic Soc. Home: 7804 Vicksburg Ave Los Angeles CA 90045-2927

BURK, YVONNE TURNER, artist, educator; b. Ames, Iowa, Jan. 11, 1928; d. Clarence George and Vida Selma (Zwiefel) Turner; m. Creighton A. Burk, June 3, 1949; children: Adrienne A., Laurie L., B. Diane. Student, Layton Sch. Art, 1946-48, U. Wyo., 1949-50, Arts Student League, 1960-62, Calif. Coll. Arts and Crafts, 1982-83. instr. The Visual Arts Sch. Princeton and Trenton, 1989; work has appeared at Tex. Fine Arts Citation Show, Austin, Hunterdon (N.J.) Art Ctr., N.J. City Mus., N.J. State Mus., Robinson Gallery, Houston, Laguna Gloria Art Mus.; commd. N.J. State Mus. One-woman shows include 1991 Retrospective R.G.K. Found., Austin. Recipient Art Chair award K.L.R.U. Auction, 1992. Home and Studio: 10 Glorieta Santa Fe NM 87505-2257

BURKE, ARTHUR THOMAS, engineering consultant; b. Pueblo, Colo., Nov. 26, 1919; s. Daniel Michael and Naomi Edith (Brashear) B.; BS, U.S. Naval Acad., 1941; postgrad. UCLA; m. Regina Ahlgren Malone, June 15, 1972 (dec. July 1996); children: Arthur Thomas, Craig Timothy, Laura Ahlgren, Scott Ahlgren. With USN Electronics Lab. Center, San Diego, 1947-72, sr. satellite communications cons., 1964-72, satellite communications engring. cons., 1974—. Sweepstakes judge, San Diego Sci. Fair, 1960—. With USN, 1938-46; comdr. Res., ret. Recipient Presdl. Unit citation, 1942, Superior Performance award USN Electronics Lab. Center, 1967. Mem. IEEE (mem. San Diego membership com. 1958-68), AAAS, San Diego Astronomy Assn., San Diego Computer Assn., Am. Radio Relay League. Patentee electronic bathythermograph. Home and Office: 4011 College Ave San Diego CA 92115-6704

BURKE, DONALD WARREN, anesthesiologist; b. Ridgecrest, CA, Aug. 1, 1960; s. Kenneth Wayne and Elsie Juanita (Pannell) B. BS in Biochemistry cum laude, U. Calif., Davis, 1981; MD, Baylor U., 1986. Diplomate Am. Bd. Anesthesiology. Resident in anesthesiology Cornell Med. Ctr., N.Y.C., 1986-90; staff anesthesiologist Long Beach (Calif.) Comty. Med. Ctr., 1991—; provider BLS, ACLS, and PALS, Am. Heart Assn., Long Beach, Calif., 1987—, instr. Pediatric Advanced Life Support, Am. Heart Assn., Long Beach, Calif., 1995—. Med. vol. Mission to Ensenada, Mex., 1000 Smiles Found., Carlsbad, Calif., 1995; sponsor Charity Golf Found., Comty Hosp. Found., Long Beach, Calif., 1996. Mem. AMA, Am. Soc. Anesthesiologists, Long Beach Surgical Soc., U. Calif. Davis Alumni Assn. (life), Sierra Club (life), MENSA (life), Sigma Xi (Rsch. award 1976). Republican. Avocations: marathon running (finished N.Y.C.), computers, modern art. Home and Office: 5318 E 2nd St Apt 504 Long Beach CA 90803-5354

BURKE, EDMOND WAYNE, retired judge, lawyer; b. Ukiah, Calif., Sept. 7, 1935; s. Wayne P. and Opal K. B.; children from previous marriage: Kathleen R., Jennifer E.; m. Anna M. Hubbard, Dec. 29, 1990. A.B., Humboldt State Coll., 1957, M.A., 1958; J.D., U. Calif., 1964. Bar: Calif., Alaska, Mont. Individual practice law Calif. and Alaska, 1965-67; asst. atty. gen. State of Alaska, 1967; asst. dist. atty. Anchorage, Alaska, 1968-69; judge Superior Ct., Alaska, 1970-75; justice Supreme Ct. State of Alaska, Anchorage, 1975-93, chief justice, 1981-84; of coun. Bogle & Gates, 1994-95; mem. Burke Bauermeister, Anchorage, 1996—. Republican. Presbyterian.

BURKE, MARIANNE KING, state agency administrator, financial executive; b. Douglasville, Ga., May 30, 1938; d. William Horace and Evora (Morris) King; divorced; 1 child, Kelly Page. Student, Ga. Inst. Tech., 1956-59, Anchorage C.C., 1964-66, Portland State U., 1968-69; BBA, U. Alaska, 1976. CPA, Alaska. Sr. audit mgr. Price Waterhouse, 1982-90; v.p. fin., asst. sec. NANA Regional Corp., Inc., Anchorage, 1990-95; v.p. fin. NANA Devel. Corp., Inc., Anchorage, 1990-95; sec.-treas. Vanguard Industries, J.V., Anchorage, 1990-95, Alaska United Drilling, Inc., Anchorage, 1990-95; treas. NANA/Marriott Joint Venture, Anchorage, 1990-95; v.p. fin. Arctic Utilities, Inc., Anchorage, 1990-95, Tour Arctic, Inc., Anchorage, 1990-95, Purcell Svcs., Ltd., Anchorage, 1990-95, Arctic Caribou Inn, Anchorage, 1990-95, NANA Oilfield Svcs., Inc., Anchorage, 1990-95, NANA Corp. Svcs., Inc., Anchorage, 1992-95; dir. divsn. ins. State of Alaska, 1995—; mem. State of Alaska Medicaid Rate Commn., 1985-88, State of Alaska Bd. Accountancy, 1984-87; bd. dirs. Nat. Assn. Ins. Commrs. Edn. and Rsch. Found. Bd. dirs. Alaska Treatment Ctr., Anchorage, 1978, Alaska Hwy. Cruises; treas. Alaska Feminist Credit Union, Anchorage, 1979-80; mem. fund raising com. Anchorage Symphony, 1981. Mem. AICPA, Internat. Assn. Ins. Suprs. (funded mem.), Alaska Soc. CPAs, Govtl. Fin. Officers U.S. and Can., Fin. Execs. Inst. (bd. dirs.), Nat. Assn. Ins. Commrs. (bd. dirs.). Avocations: travel, reading. Home: 3818 Helvetia Dr Anchorage AK 99508-5016 Office: State Office Bldg PO Box 110805 333 Willoughby Ave Juneau AK 99801 also: 3601 C St Ste 1324 Anchorage AK 99503-5948

BURKE, TAMARA LYNN, marketing professional; b. Appleton, Minn., July 4, 1960; d. Merlyn Eugene and Patricia Yvonne (Johnson) Munsterman; m. James Warren Burke, Jr., Mar. 26, 1983 (div. June 1993); 1 child, Madelyn Amanda. BA, U. Minn., 1982; MBA student, CLU, 1999. Asst. acct. exec. Sheggeby Advt., Mpls., 1982-83, BBDO, Inc., L.A., 1983-84; program mgr. Cable Music Channel, Hollywood, Calif., 1984-85; acct. exec. Ogilvy & Mather, L.A., 1985-88; mktg. mgr. Teleflora, L.A., 1988-93; asst. mgr. mktg. & merchandising Jafra Cosmetics Internat. Inc. (A Gillette Co.), Westlake Village, Calif., 1993-97, mgr. product mktg., 1997-98; mgr. mktg. Jafra Cosmetics Internat. Inc., Westlake Village, Calif., 1998-99; group mktg. mgr. Sebastian Internat., Inc., Woodland Hills, Calif., 1999—. Recipient Silver Clio award, 1986, N.Y. Internat. Film and TV Festival bronze award, 1986, Ogilvy & Mather Creative Excellence award, 1986, Disting. Scholar award Calif. Luth. U., 1998. Mem. Rho Lambda Hon. Soc. Office: Sebastian Internat Inc 6109 DeSoto Ave Woodland Hills CA 91367

BURKEE, IRVIN, artist; b. Kenosha, Wis., Feb. 6, 1918; s. Omar Lars and Emily (Quardokas) B.; diploma Sch. of Art Inst. Chgo., 1945; m. Bonnie May Ness, Apr. 12, 1945; children: Brynn, Jill, Peter (dec.), Ian (dec.). Owner, silversmith, goldsmith Burkee Jewelry, Blackhawk, Colo., 1950-57; painter, sculptor, Aspen, Colo., 1957-78, Cottonwood, Ariz., Pietrasanta, Italy, 1978—; instr. art U. Colo., 1946, 50-53, Stephens Coll., Columbia, Mo., 1947-49. John Quincy Adams travel fellow, Mex., 1945. Executed copper mural of human history of Colo. for First Nat. Bank, Englewood, Colo., 1970, copper mural of wild birds of Kans. for Ranchmart State Bank, Overland Park, Kans., 1974; exhibited Art Inst. Chgo., Smithsonian Instn. (award 1957), Milw. Art Inst., Krannert Mus., William Rockhill Nelson Gallery, St. Louis Art Mus., Denver Art Mus.; represented in southwestern galleries, also pvt. collections throughout U.S.; work illustrated in books Design and Creation of Jewelry, Design through Discovery, Walls. Mem. Nat. Sculpture Soc., Sedona Chamber Music Soc.; printer, pub. White Tanks Press. Address: PO Box 5361 Lake Montezuma AZ 86342-5361

BURKETT, WILLIAM ANDREW, banker; b. nr. Herman, Nebr., July 1, 1913; s. William H. and Mary (Dill) B.; m. Juliet Ruth Johnson, Oct. 5, 1940 (dec. Mar. 1976); children: Juliet Ann Burkett Hooker, Katherine C. Burkett Congdon, William Cleveland; m. Nancy Schallert Morrow, June 20, 1992. Student, U. Nebr., 1931-32, Creighton U. Law Sch., 1932-33; LL.B., U. Omaha, 1936. Exec. trainee Bank Am., 1937-38; Sr. spl. agt., intelligence unit Treasury Dept., 1945-50; exec. v.p. Calif. Employers Assn. Group, Sacramento, 1950-53; dir. Calif. Dept. Employment, 1953-55; chmn. Calif. Employment Stabilization Commn., 1953-55; supt. banks, chmn. Dept. Investments Calif., 1955-59; dir. Liquidation Yokohama Specie Bank; also Sumitomo Bank, San Francisco, 1955-59; cons. Western Bancorp, San Francisco, 1959-61; chmn. bd., pres. Security Nat. Bank Monterey County, Monterey-Carmel, Calif., 1961-66, Burkett Land Co., Monterey, 1966—; chmn. bd. Securities Properties Corp., Monterey; witness Calif. Crime Com., U.S. Senate Kefauver Crime Com., 1950-52, U.S. Congress Banking Com., 1991; nat. chmn., founder Bank Savs. & Loan Depositor's League, 1991. Author: Mount Rushmore National Memorial's History of America, 1776-1904, 1971. Elected nominee Nebr. Sec. State, 1936; witness Calif. Crime Commn. and U.S. Senate Kefauver Crime Commn., 1950-52, U.S. Congress Banking Com., 1991; dir. banking and investments, cabinet gov., Calif., 1953-59; dir. Calif. Emergency Manpower Commn., 1953-55; chmn. Gov. Calif. Com. Refugee Relief, 1953-55; mem. Calif. Securities Commn., 1955-59; mem. financial bd. Pine Manor Jr. Coll., Chestnut Hill, Mass., 1967—; mem. Monterey County Hist. Commn., Nat. Trust Found., Royal Oak Found.; bd. dirs. Monterey Symphony Assn.; chmn. bd. trustees Nat. Hist. Found.; trustee Monterey Mus. Art, Bishop Kip Sch., Carmel Valley, Calif.; co-chmn., trustee Mt. Rushmore Hall of Records Commn., 1987; mem. adv. bd. Robert Louis Stevenson Sch., Pebble Beach, Calif., 1971-74, candidate for gov. Calif., 1978 . Served as officer USCGR, 1943-45. Mem. Am., Calif., Ind. bankers assns., Nat. Assn. Supts. State Banks (pres. 1958-59), Monterey History and Art Assn., Mt. Rushmore Nat. Meml. Soc. (life mem., trustee), Amvets (dept. comdr. Calif. 1947, nat. vice comdr. 1948), Soc. Calif. Pioneers, Bank and Savs. and Loan Depositor's League (nat. chmn. 1991—), Monterey Peninsula Mus. Art, Mt. Rushmore Hall of Records Commn. Inc. (nat. co-chmn.1990—). Episcopalian. Clubs: Monterey Peninsula Golf and Country (Pebble Beach), Beach and Tennis (Pebble Beach), Stillwater Yacht (Pebble Beach); Carmel Valley Golf and Tennis; Commonwealth (San Francisco), Rotary (San Francisco); Sutter Lawn (Sacramento). Home: PO Box 726 Pebble Beach CA 93953-0726 Office: Viscaino Rd Pebble Beach CA 93953

BURKHALTER, SHELLEY, English language educator; b. Lubbock, Tex., Aug. 19, 1953; d. Harold and Ellie Glenn (Nettles) B. BA in English, Tex. Tech. U., 1975; Paralegal Cert., S.W. Tex. U., 1983; M in English, Tex. Tech. U., 1993. Paralegal Brown and Maroney, Austin, 1984-86, Tex. Legis. Coun., Austin, 1986-90; tchg. asst. Tex. Tech. U., Lubbock, 1990-92; computer lab. asst. South Plains Coll., Levelland, Tex., 1992-94; asst. prof. English N.Mex. State U., Carlsbad, 1994—. Mem. Mystery Writers Am., 2-Yr. Coll. Assn., S.W. MLA, Alpha Delta Zeta. Methodist. Avocations: writing, singing, swimming, collecting Beatle memorabilia. Office: NMex State Univ 1500 University Dr Carlsbad NM 88220-3509

BURKHART, DOROTHY P., art critic, catalog essayist; b. Newark, Oct. 16, 1924; d. James and Leena (Lemme) Pallante; m. William H. Burkhart; children: Douglas Kimball, Willow Rodriguez, Christopher William. Student, Boston U., 1946, 48; BA in Art, San Jose State U., 1976, MA, 1978; postgrad., Stanford U., 1977. Art critic San Jose (Calif.) Mercury News, 1980-92; ind. curator Triton Mus. Art, Santa Clara, Calif., 1992-94; mem. coun. for Soc. for Encouragement of Contemporary Art, San Francisco Mus. Modern Art, 1993—; past tchr. art history San Francisco Art Inst.; spkr. in field. Author, editor: (catalogs) Robert Cottingham's Modernist On the Move, 1994, Ann Hogle: The Refocused Frame, 1998; contbr. revs., features, column to San Jose Mercury News, ARTWEEK, ARTnews. Mem. Internat. Assn. Art Critics. Home: 225 N Avalon Dr Los Altos CA 94022-2320

BURKHEAD, VIRGINIA RUTH, rehabilitation nurse; b. Marlow, Okla., Apr. 11, 1937; d. Norvin Woodrow Whitehead and Harriet Louise (Pittman) Mayes; m. Marvin Vern Foster, Oct. 16, 1956 (div. 1964); children: Deborah, Marcia, Marva, Laurie, Sheila; m. Robert Burdett Burkhead, Apr. 11, 1987. ADN, Casper Coll., 1971; BSN, Wash. State U., 1994. RN, Wash. Staff nurse, house supr., enterostomal therapy nurse Meml. Hosp. Natrona County, Casper, Wyo., 1971-79; enterostomal therapy nurse, coord. ostomy program Holy Family Hosp., Spokane, 1979—, coord. neurol. rehab. program, 1985—. Deaconess 1st Christian Ch., Spokane, 1986—. Mem. Assn. Rehab. Nurses, Wound, Ostomy and Contence Nurses Soc., Jacks and Jennys Square Dance Club (coun. del. 1992), Sigma Theta Tau. Mem. Christian Ch. (Disciples of Christ). Avocations: square dancing, bird watching, reading, travel. Home: 2116 E Lincoln Rd Spokane WA 99217-7723 Office: Holy Family Hosp 5633 N Lidgerwood St Spokane WA 99207-1295

BURKHOLDER, GRACE ELEANOR, archeologist, educator; b. Sumas, Wash., Sept. 21, 1920; d. George Lewis and Leah (Benke) Welch; m. Warren Stanford Burkholder, June 4, 1938 (div. Apr. 1957); children: Warren Stanford, Carol Joyce Brackett. BEd cum laude, U. Miami, Fla., 1956; MEd, U. Okla., 1980. Tchr., Laurel Sch., Oceanside, Calif., 1956-58; elem. tchr. U.S. Navy, Kwajalein, M.I., 1958-59, Transport Co. Tex., Kwajalein, 1959-60, Arabian Am. Oil Co., Dhahran, Saudi Arabia, 1960-80. Author: An Arabian Collection: Artifacts from the Eastern Province, 1984, Perceptions of the Past: Solar Phenomena in Southern Nevada, 1995, author: (with others) Rock Art Papers, vol. 7, 1990, vol. 8, 1991, vol. 9, 1992, vol. 10, 1993, vol. 12, 1995, American Indian Rock Art, vol. 17, 1992; rsch., publs. on Ubaid sites and pottery in Saudi Arabia. Active San Diego Mus. Man, Mus. No. Ariz., Clark County Heritage Mus., Lost City Mus. Mem. Am. Rock Art Rsch. Assn., Nev. Archael. Assn. (Ting-Perkins Outstanding Contrbns. award 1995).

BURKS, ROCKY ALAN, social services executive, disability consultant; b. San Bernardino, Calif., June 12, 1952; s. Lloyd Jackson and Vivian Elnora B.; m. Nikki Ann Stone (div. 1974); 1 child, Gannon LeRoy; m. Lydia Ann Deatherage, Aug. 20, 1983. BA in Social Welfare, Calif. State U., Chico, 1979, BA in Sociology, 1979. Instrument flight instr. USAF, Del Rio, Tex., 1971-75; dir. outreach and recruitment, Office of Vets. Affairs Calif. State U., Chico, 1976-81; exec. dir. Easter Seal Soc. of Butte County, Chico, 1981-82, No. Calif. Ind. Living Program, Chico, 1982-85; soc. worker Butte County (Calif.) Welfare Dept., 1985-87; exec. dir. Ind. Living Svcs. of N. Calif., Inc., Chico, 1988—; social worker, adult protective svcs. Butte County Welfare Dept., Oroville, Calif., 1985-87; bd. dirs. Calif. Coalition of Ind. Living Ctrs., Sacramento, Calif., pres., 1991-94; bd. dirs. Pub. Interest Ctr. on Long-term Care, Sacramento, treas., 1994-98; mem. disability access adv. bd. Divsn. of the State Arch., Sacramento, 1995—, Disabled Access Bd. of Appeals, Butte County Building Divsn., Oroville, 1994—. Editor: (newsletter) Independent Life, 1988—, Voice, 1976-81. Mem. Transp. Adv. Commn., Butte County Assn. Govts., Oroville, 1992—; mem. Californians for Disability Rights. With USAF, 1971-75. Recipient Cert. of Congl. Recognition, Congressman Wally Herger, Chico, 1993, 96, Disability Advocate award Calif. Assn. Persons with Handicaps, 1994, Region IX Disability Advocate award Nat. Coun. Ind. Living, 1998, Master Instr. award Air Tng. Command, USAF, 1975; named citizen Chickasaw Indian Nation. Mem. Am. Legion, Vietnam Vets. Am., Masons, Shriners, Scottish Rite, Chico Breakfast Lions (pres. 1991-92, Lion of Yr. award 1990, Melvin Jones fellow), Lions Eye Found. Calif. and Nev. (life). Avocations: scuba diving, boating, reading, art. Home: 4135 Keefer Rd Chico CA 95973-8956 Office: Ind Living Svcs No Calif 555 Rio Lindo Ave Ste B Chico CA 95926-1847

BURNETT, ERIC STEPHEN, environmental consultant; b. Manchester, Eng., Apr. 5, 1924; s. William Louis and Edith Winifred (Gates) B.; came to U.S., 1963; naturalized, 1974; BSc in Physics (with honors), London U., 1954; MS in Environ. Studies, Calif. State, Dominguez Hills, 1976; PhD in Environ. Engring., Calif. Coast U., 1982. children: Diana, Ian, Brenda, Keith. Program mgr. Brit. Aircraft Corp., Stevenage, Eng., 1953-63; sr. systems engr. RCA, Princeton, N.J., 1963-66; project mgr. Gen. Electric Co., Valley Forge, Pa., 1966-67; dept. head TRW systems Group, Redondo Beach, Calif., 1967-72; dir. energy and pollution control ARATEX Svcs., Inc., Calif., 1974-81, dir. tech. devel., 1981-83, staff cons., 1983-91, retired, 1992; cons., lectr. in spacecraft sensor tech., energy conservation, environ. and contamination controls. With Royal Air Force, 1942-47. Assoc. fellow AIAA; mem. Inst. Environ. Scis. (sr.). Contbr. articles in field to profl. jours. Home and Office: 3423 Excalibar Rd Placerville CA 95667-5418

BURNETT, SANDRA JO, primary education educator; b. Blair, Nebr., May 13, 1946; d. Morris Edward and Cornelia D. (Pearson) Boyd; children: Alex Crowder, Joanna Crowder, Andy Burnett. BA, U. Iowa, 1968; MEd, U. Nev., 1971. Tchr. kindergarten Clark County Sch. Dist., Las Vegas, Nev., 1970-72, tchr. 1st grade, 1978—; supervising tchr. U. Nev., Las Vegas, 1978—. Mem. Ch. Coun., Cmty. Luth. Ch., Las Vegas, 1982; bd. dirs. PTA, 1991-92. Named One of Outstanding Nev. Educators, Nev. Dept. Edn., Carson City, 1997-98. Mem. U. Iowa Alumni Assn., Jr. Mesquite Club, Assistance League, Delta Delta Delta Alumni Assn. Republican. Lutheran. Avocations: music, reading, travel. Home: 1936 Coralino Dr Henderson NV 89014-1008 Office: Frank Lamping Elem Sch 2551 Summit Grove Dr Henderson NV 89012-4924

BURNEY, VICTORIA KALGAARD, business consultant, civic worker; b. Los Angeles, Apr. 12, 1943; d. Oscar Albert and Dorothy Elizabeth (Peterson) Kalgaard; children: Kim Elizabeth, J. Hewett. BA with honors, U. Mont., 1965; MA, U. No. Colo., 1980; postgrad. Webster U., St. Louis, 1983-84. Exec. dir. Hill County Community Action, Havre, Mont., 1966-67; community orgn. specialist ACCESS, Escondido, Calif., 1967-68; program devel. and community orgn. specialist Community Action Programs, Inc., Pensacola, Fla., 1968-69; cons. Escambia County Sch. Bd., Fla., 1969-71; pres. Kal Kreations, Kailua, Hawaii, 1974-77; instr., dir. office human resources devel. Palomar Coll., San Marcos, Calif., 1978-81; chief exec. officer IDET Corp., San Marcos, 1981-87; dir. United Syss. Inst., 1998—; cons. County of Riverside, Calif., 1983. Mem. San Diego County Com. on Handicapped, San Diego, 1979; cons. tribal resource devel., Escondido, Calif., 1979; mem. exec. com. Social Services Coordinating Council, San Diego, 1982-83; mem. pvt. sector com. and planning and rev. com. Calif. Employment and Tng. Adv. Council, Sacramento, 1982-83; bd. mgrs. Santa Margarita Family YMCA, Vista, Calif., 1984-86; bd. dirs. North County Community Action Program, Escondido, 1978, Casa de Amparo, San Luis Rey, Calif., 1980-83; mem. San Diego County Pub. Welfare Adv. Bd., 1979-83, chairperson, 1981; mem. Calif. Rep. Cen. Com., Sacramento, 1989—; ofcl. San Diego County Rep. Cen. Com., 1985-93, exec. com., 1987-92, 2nd vice-chmn. 1991-92; chmn. 74th Assembly Dist. Rep. Caucus, 1989-90; chmn. Working Ptnrs., 1987-90; trustee Rancho Santa Fe Community Ctr., 1991-92; active Nat. Assistance League, 1993—; bd. dirs. Assistance League North Coast, 1994—, mem. 1993—. Mem. Nat. Assn. County Employment and Tng. Adminstrs. (chairperson econ. resources com. 1982-85), Calif. Assn. Local Econ. Devel., San Diego Econ. Devel. Corp., Oceanside Econ. devel. Council (bd. dirs. 1983-87), Oceanside C. of C., San Marcos C. of C. (bd. dirs. 1982-85), Carlsbad C. of C. (indsl. council 1982-85), Escondido C. of C. (comml. and indsl. devel. council 1982-87), Vista C. of C. (vice chairperson econ. devel. com. 1982-83), Vista Econ. Devel. Assn., Nat. Job Tng. Partnership, San Diego County Golden Eagle Club. Home: 2010 Valley Rd Oceanside CA 92056-3111

BURNINGHAM, KIM RICHARD, former state legislator; b. Salt Lake City, Sept. 14, 1936; s. Rulon and Margie (Stringham) Burningham; m. Susan Ball Clarke, Dec. 19, 1968; children: Christian, Tyler David. BS, U. Utah, 1960; MA, U. Ariz., 1967; MFA, U. So. Calif., 1977. Cert. secondary tchr., Utah. Tchr. Bountiful (Utah) High Sch., 1960-88; mem. Utah Ho. of Reps., Salt Lake City, 1979-94; cons. Shipley Assocs., Bountiful, 1989-94, Franklin Covey, 1994—; gubernatorial appointee as exec. dir. Utah Statehood Centennial Commn., 1994-96, mem. Utah State Bd. Edn., 1999—. Author dramas for stage and film, also articles. Mem. state strategic planning com. Utah Tomorrow, 1989—. Mem. NEA, PTA (life), Utah Edn. Assn., Davis Edn. Assn., Nat. Forensic League. Republican. Mem. LDS Ch. Avocations: gardening, history. Home: 932 Canyon Crest Rd Bountiful UT 84010-2002

BURNS, BRENDA, state legislator; b. LaGrange, Ga., Nov. 22, 1950; m. Bruce Burns; 3 children. Sen. dist. 17 State of Ariz.; pres. Ariz. Senate, 1997; pres. Ariz. State Senate, 1997—; nat. dir. Am. Leg. Exch. Coun.; exec. bd. Am. Legis. Exch. Coun., chair com. state sovereignty. Republican. Home: 8220 W Orange Dr Glendale AZ 85303-6006 Office: State Capitol 1700 W Washington St Phoenix AZ 85007-2812*

BURNS, CONRAD RAY, senator; b. Gallatin, Mo., Jan. 25, 1935; s. Russell and Mary Frances (Knight) B.; m. Phyllis Jean Kuhlmann; children: Keely Lynn, Garrett Russell. Student, U. Mo., 1952-54. Field rep. Polled Hereford World Mag., Kansas City, Mo., 1963-69; pub. rels. Billings (Mont.) Livestock Com., 1969-73; farm dir. KULR TV, Billings, 1974; pres., founder No. Ag-Network, Billings, 1975-86; commissioner Yellowstone County, Billings, 1987-89; U.S. Senator from Montana, 1989 —; Mem. Aging Com., Small Bus. Com., Nat. Rep. Senatorial Com., chmn. Appropriations Subcom. of Military Constrn., Chmn. Com. Sci. and Transp. Subcom. of Sci. Tech. and Space, chmn. Energy and Nat. Rescs. Subcom. of Energy Rsch & Devel. With USMC, 1955-57. Mem. Nat. Assn. Farm Broadcasters, Am. Legion, Rotary, Masons, Shriners. Republican. Lutheran. Avocation: football officiating. Office: US Senate 187 Dirksen Senate Office Washington DC 20510*

BURNS, DAN W., manufacturing company executive; b. Auburn, Calif., Sept. 10, 1925; s. William and Edith Lynn (Johnston) B.; 1 child, Dan Jr. Dir. materials Menasco Mfg. Co., 1951-56; v.p., gen. mgr. Hufford Corp., 1956-58; pres. Hufford div. Siegler Corp., 1958-61; v.p. Siegler Corp., 1961-62, Lear Siegler, Inc., 1962-64; pres., dir. Electrada Corp., Culver City, Calif., 1964; pres., chief exec. officer Sargent Industries, Inc., L.A., 1964-85, chmn. bd. dirs., 1985-88; now chmn. bd. dirs., CEO Arlington Industries, Inc.; bd. dirs. Gen. Automotive Corp., Dover Tech. Internat., Inc., Kistler Aerospace Corp. Bd. dirs. San Diego Aerospace Mus., Smithsonian Inst., The Pres.'s Cir., Nat. Acad. Scis., Atlantic Coun. of U.S., George C. Marshall Found. Capt. U.S. Army, 1941-47; prisoner of war Japan; asst. mil. attache 1946, China; adc to Gen. George C. Marshall 1946-47. Mem. OAS Sports Com. (dir.), L.A. Country Club, St. Francis Yacht Club, Calif. Club, Conquistador del Cielo, Cosmos Club Washington. Home: 7400 Bryan Canyon Rd Carson City NV 89704-9588

BURNS, DENISE RUTH, artist; b. Bellville, N.J., Oct. 17, 1943; d. A. Richard and Ruth Jean (Landers) Culkin; m. Robert P. Burns Jr., Apr. 8, 1960; children: Michael R, David R. Studied, Sergei Bongart Sch. Art, 1971-73; studied with Dan McCaw, Scottsdale Sch. Art, 1980, 89, studied with, 1988; studied with, Harley Brown, 1994, Michael Lynch and, Ovanes Berberian, 1995. One-woman shows include Off White Gallery, 1984, 85, 86, 93; two-woman show May Gallery, Scottsdale, Ariz., 1993; group shows include May Gallery, 1987-92, 94-95, Roy Miles Gallery, London, 1993, Art du Monde, Japan, 1993, N.C. Mus. History, 1995, N.C. Mus. Hist. Spring Show, 1995, Oil Tips, London-Quarto Pub., 1995, How To Put Movement in Your Paintings, 1996, Plein Air Painters Show Oakland Mus. 1996, How to Put Movement in Your Paintings, 1996; featured in Swart Mag., 1992. Instr. Chambersburg (Pa.) Art Alliance, 1985-86, 87-89, Omaha Artist Group, 1988, Pocono Pines (Pa.), 1994, Catalina Art Assn., Avalon, Calif., 1990-91; dir. Plein Air Painters Show, Catalina Island, 1986-97; judge Big Bear Art Festival, 1986, Children's Show, L.A. County Libr., Avalon, 1990. Recipient 2nd Pl. award Scottsdale Art Sch., 1991; named Emerging Artist by Am. Artist Mag., 1984, Best of Show by Catalina Art Festival, 1984, 86, 87, 89-91, Oil Painters of Am. Regional Best of Show, 1994; Gold medal artist award May Galleries, 1994. Mem. Plein Air Painters Am. (dir., founder), Catalina Art Assn. (pres. 1985-86), Oil Painters of Am., Calif. Art Club, Western Acad. Women Artists (signature mem.), Palos Verde Art Ctr. Home: PO Box 611 Avalon CA 90704-0611

BURNS, DENVER P., forestry research administrator; b. Bryan, Ohio, Oct. 27, 1940; married; 1 child. BS, Ohio State U., 1962, MS, 1964, PhD in Entomology, 1967; MPA, Harvard U., 1981. Asst. entomologist So. Forest Experiment Sta., 1962-68, rsch. entomologist, 1968-72, asst. dir., 1972-74; staff asst. to dep. chief for rsch. U.S. Forest Svc., 1974-76; dep. dir. North Ctrl. Experiment Sta., 1976-81; dir. Northeastern Forest Experiment Sta., Radnor, Pa., 1981-92, Rocky Mountain Sta., 1992—. Mem. AAAS. Office: US Forest Service 240 W Prospect Rd Fort Collins CO 80526-2002

BURNS, FRANCIS RAYMOND, biofeedback instructor, researcher; b. Ogden, Utah, Oct. 13, 1935; s. Gerald Eugene and Lucy Marie (Sargent) B.; m. Marilyn McDonald, Feb. 15, 1959 (div. Sept. 1968); children: Lawrence R., John W.; m. Lucia Esperanza Gaitan, Sept. 19, 1993; 1 child, Francis Leonard. AA, San Francisco City Coll., 1961; BA, San Francisco State U., 1968, postgrad., 1968-72. Dir. Biofeedback Clinic Noogenesis Inc., San Francisco, 1968—, dir. clinic, head R&D, 1968—, dir., pres., 1968—. Inventor in field. Vol. coord. San Francisco Neighborhood Renovation Group, 1972-74. With USN, 1953-56. Avocations: gardening, camping,

travel, innovative research, reading. Office: Noogenesis Inc Ste 102 1301 Ignacio Valley Rd Walnut Creek CA 94598

BURNS, KITTY, playwright; b. Chgo., Feb. 1, 1951; d. Joseph Lewis and Evelyn Marian (Smith) B. CNA, Bay City Coll., San Francisco, 1971. Adminstrv. asst. Syntex, Palo Alto, Calif., 1984-94. Author: (plays) Terminal Terror, 1991 (Silver award San Mateo Playwriting Contest 1991), Psycho Night at the Paradise Lounge, 1994, If God Wanted Us to Fly He Would Have Given Us Wings!, 1996. Treas. Hillbarn Theatre, Foster City, 1986, social chmn., 1987-89, 96-98, bd. dirs. Mem. Dramatists Guild. Democrat. Avocations: writing children's books, poetry, short stories, acting, horseback riding.

BURNS, LOUIS FRANCIS, retired history educator; b. Elgin, Kans., Jan. 2, 1920; s. Lee Robert and Bessie Pearl (Tinker) B.; m. Ruth Blake, Apr. 24, 1945; chldren: Alice Bettie Burns Thomas, Keith Lee. BS in Edn., Kans. State U., 1949, MS, 1950. Cert. secondary educator, jr. coll. educator, Kans., Mo., Calif. Teaching fellowship Kans. State U., Emporia, 1950; instr. geography, U.S. history Shawnee-Mission (Kans.) Sr. High Sch., 1950-60; instr. U.S. history Santa Ana (Calif.) Coll., 1965-76; author, speaker self-employed Fallbrook, Calif., 1977-94; ret., 1994; presenter and speaker in field; advisor Osage Tribal Mus., Pawhuska, Okla., 1990-94. Author: (book) Osage Indian Customs & Myths, 1984, A History of the Osage People, 1989, Symbolic & Decorative Art of the Osage People, 1994 and related books; editor Osage News, 1982-84, Osage Hist. Feature Writer; contbr. related articles to profl. jours. Rep. Osage Indian Nation, Montauban, France, 1990, 92. Staff sgt. USMC, 1942-45. Recipient Chevalier de L'Hypocras du Foix, Companions of L'Hypocras, 1992; named in Mottled Eagle Clan, Osage Indian Tribe, 1988; admitted to I'n Lon Schka, Pawhuska Camp, Osage Tribe, 1988. Mem. NEA, Okla. Hist. Soc., Kans. State Hist. Soc., Western History Assn. Democrat. Roman Catholic. Avocations: craft work, genealogy, rock hound. Home: 654 Golden Rd Fallbrook CA 92028-3452

BURNS, MARY MITCHELL, educator; b. L.A., Oct. 22, 1928; d. William Henry Flynn and Fern Ruth Cummins; m. John David Mitchell, Aug. 2, 1962 (dec. Mar. 1972); 1 child, John William Thomas; m. Robert Berry Burns, June 19, 1982; children: Nancy Lynne Thomas, Tobias. MA, Calif. State U., Chico, 1978; EdD, Calif. State U., Santa Ana, 1980, PhD, 1995. Tchg. credentials. Tchr. Calif. pub. schs. Redding and Sacramento, 1972-87; substitute tchr. Calif. pub. schs. Redding, 1987—. Avocation: travel agent. Home: 3732 Harrow Ct Redding CA 96002-3233

BURNS, RICHARD GORDON, retired lawyer, writer, consultant; b. Stockton, Calif., May 15, 1925; s. Earl Gordon and Alberta Viola (Whale) B.; m. Eloise Estelle Beil, June 23, 1951 (div. May 25, 1985); children: Kenneth Charles, Donald Gordon. AA, U. Calif., Berkeley, 1948; AB, Stanford U., 1949, JD, 1951. Atty. Clausen & Burns, San Francisco, 1951-61; pvt. practice Corte Madera, Calif., 1961-86; cons. Wyo. Pacific Oil Co., L.A., 1986—; pub. Good Book Pub., Kihei, Hawaii, 1991—. Author (As Dick B.): New Light on Alcoholism: God, A.A. and Sam Shoemaker, 1999, The Akron Genesis of Alcoholics Anonymous, 1998, (with Bill Pittman) Courage To Change, 1998, Anne Smith's Journal, 1998, Dr. Bob and His Library, 1998, The Good Book and The Big Book: AA's Roots in the Bible, 1998, The Oxford Group and Alcoholics Anonymous, 1998, That Amazing Grace, 1996, The Books Early AAs Read for Spiritual Growth, 1998, Good Morning! Quiet Time, Morning Watch, Meditation, and Early A.A., 1998; Turning Point: A History of Early A.A.'s Spiritual Roots and Successes, 1997, Hope!: The Story of Geraldine D., 1998, Utilizing A.A.'s Spiritual Roots for Recovery Today, 1999, The Golden Text of A.A., 1999; case editor Stanford Law Rev., 1950. Dir. Almonte Sanitary Bd., Marin County, Calif., 1962-64; v.p./sec. Lions Club, Corte Madera, 1961-64; pres. Almonte Improvement Club, Mill Valley, Calif., 1960, Cmty. Ch., Mill Valley, 1971, C. of C., Corte Madera, 1972, Corte Madera Ctr. Merchant Co., 1975, Redwoods Retirement Ctr., Mill Valley, 1980. Sgt. U.S. Army, 1943-46. Mem. Am. Hist. Assn., Authors Guild, Maui Writers Guild, Christian Assn. for Psychol. Studies, Phi Beta Kappa. Avocations: travel, Bible study, swimming. Office: PO Box 837 Kihei HI 96753-0837

BURNS, RICHARD LELAND, marketing consultant, columnist; b. Oakland, Calif., Sept. 22, 1930; s. Leland S. and Rachel Hammond (Borncamp) B.; m. Apr. 2, 1955; children: Lisa Anne, Shelley Kristine, Richard Clark. BA in Econs., Stanford U., 1952. Account exec. Westinghouse Broadcasting Co., San Francisco, 1954-61; advt./mktg. dir. Phila. Reading Corp., Elizabeth, N.J., 1961-65; v.p. Edward S. Kellogg Co., San Francisco, 1965-68, Gross, Pera, Rockey Inc., San Francisco, 1968; pres., dir. Latham Found., Alameda, Calif., 1970-78; cons./supr. George S. May Co., San Francisco, 1979-83; pres. Mktg. Assocs., Alameda, Calif., 1980—. Bd. dirs., chmn. Stanford U. Ann. Fund Athletics, 1961—; exec. com. Boy Scouts Am., Piedmont, Calif., 1983-88. With U.S. Army, 1952-54. Recipient Am. Honor medal, U.S. Govt., 1952. Mem. Am. Mgmt. Assn., Coun. on Founds., Stanford Assocs., Medallion Soc., Commonwealth Club of Calif., Athenian-Nile Club, Buck/Cardinal Club, Rancho Canada Golf Club, Nat. Football Found. (bd. dir.), SPCA, Stanford. Republican. Presbyterian. Avocations: music, writing, gardening, sports, travel. Office: Marketing Associates PO Box 5701 Carmel CA 93921-5701

BURNS, WILLIAM DAVID, technical writer, technical consultant; b. Mountain Home AFB, Idaho, Dec. 18, 1964; s. John Barry and JoAnn (McDonough) B.; m. J. Dené Breakfield, June 8, 1991; children: Jaron K. Bass, Kellina J. Burns Breakfield. BA in English and Liberal Arts, Boise State U., 1990, MA in English, 1993. Tech. writer, supr. Micron Tech., Boise, 1994-97; tech. cons. Internat. Lang. Engring., Boise, 1997—; adj. instr. Boise State U., 1993-96. Contbr. articles to profl. jours. Mem. Soc. for Tech. Comms., Assn. for Computing Machinery, Phi Kappa Phi, Sigma Tau Delta. Avocations: Shotokan karate, music performance, reading literature.

BURNS-MCCOY, NANCIE E., English literature educator; b. Sacramento, Sept. 24, 1952; d. Barry Anthony Gorman and Beverly Ann (Burns) Christiansen; m. Michael John McCoy, Dec. 29, 1973; children: Carrie Ellen, Heather Jean. BA in Lit., Sacramento State U., 1990; MA in English, U. Idaho, 1992, PhD in Edn., 1998. Mentor, tutor Bur. Indian Affairs, Placerville, Calif., 1989-90; instr. U. Idaho, Mowcow, 1990-92; lectr. U. Idaho, 1992-98, prof., 1998—; textbook reviewer Broadview Press, Peterborough, Ont., 1995, Allen Bacon Press, N.Y., 1997; cons. bus. and comm. Gritman Meml. Hosp., Moscow, 1998. Contbr. articles to mags. Mem. Nat. Coun. Tchrs. English, Northern Rocky Mountain Edn. Rsch. Assn. Avocations: karatedo doshinkan, spinning wool, weaving. Office: Univ Idaho Dept English 200 Brink Hall Moscow ID 83844-1102

BURNWORTH, RANDY JAMES, video company executive; b. Portland, Oreg., Aug. 1, 1949; s. Arliegh Clifton and Virginia May (Bobbit) B.; m. Carolyn Ruth Bowers, Apr. 18, 1967; children—James Randy, Deanna Michelle, Darrin Daniel. A.A., Bates Coll., 1969; postgrad. Pierce Coll., 1974, San Jose State U. Chief exec. officer Video Ventures, Inc. and Showtime Video Ventures, Tillamook Oreg., 1978—; sr. sci. and tech. officer Rave Engring. Corp., San Diego; founder, tech. provider NuWave Techs. Corp.; designer show booths for 33 internat. trade shows, also featured spkr.; contbr articles to profl. jours. Elder Mormon Ch.; mem. Republican Presdl. Task Force. Recipient Merit medal Rep. Presdl. Task Force, 1982; named Man of Decade, Audio Video Digest, 1982; Entrepreneur of Yr., Video Entertainment, 1982; Best Products of Yr. awards, 1980, 81, 82, Video Rev., 1982; Internat. EIA Design and Engring. awards (11); 2 awards for innovative engring. and design video and audio products Omni mag., 17 internat. design and engring. awards for video, computer, audio and personal electronics; Acad. Award nominee for tech. achievement Motion Picture Acad. Arts and Scis. Clubs: U.S. Senatorial, Elks. Inventor 1st phone TV sys., auto phaser, picture phone, smart bd., hyper graphics video computer, also others, , contbr. tech. articles to profl. jours. Avocations: fishing, automobile racing, collecting fine art. Home: 13444 Turlock Ct San Diego CA 92129-2171 Office: Rave Engring Corp 12300 Stowe Dr Bldg A&B Poway CA 92064

BURRELL, CALVIN ARCHIE, minister; b. Fairview, Okla., June 22, 1943; s. Lawrence Lester and Lottie Edna (Davison) B.; m. Barbara Ann Mann, May 29, 1966; children: Debra, Darla, Donna. BS, Northwestern State U., 1965; MA, So. Nazarene U., Bethany, Okla., 1978. Ordained to ministry Ch. of God, 1966. Tchr., prin., dean boys Spring Vale Acad., Owosso, Mich., 1964-76; pastor Ch. of God (Seventh Day), Ft. Smith, Ark., 1970-73, Shawnee, Okla., 1976-78, Denver, 1978-88; pastor Ch. of God, Galena Park, Tex., 1996—; pres. gen. conf. Ch. of God, Denver, 1987-97; editor Bible Advocate mag., Denver, 1997—; instr. Summit Sch. Theology, Denver, 1978-95; officer Bible Sabath Assn., 1983-96. Editor: Bible Advocate, 1997—. Office: Ch of God 330 W 152d Ave PO Box 33677 Denver CO 80233-0677

BURRELL, GARLAND E., JR., federal judge; b. L.A., July 4, 1947. BA in Sociology, Calif. State U., 1972; MSW, Washington U., Mo., 1976; JD, Calif. Wes. Sch. Law, 1976. Bar: Calif. 1976, U.S. Dist. Ct. (ea. dist.) Calif. 1976, U.S. Ct. Appeals (9th cir.) 1981. Dep. dist. atty. Sacramento County, Calif., 1976-78; dep city atty. Sacramento, 1978-79; asst. U.S. atty., dep. chief civil divsn. Office of U.S. Atty. for Ea. Dist. Calif., 1979-85, asst. U.S. atty., chief civil divsn., 1990-92; litigation atty. Stockman Law Corp., Sacramento, Calif., 1985-86; sr. dep. city atty. Office of City Atty., Sacramento, 1986-90; judge U.S. Dist. Ct. (ea. dist.) Calif., Sacramento, 1992—. With USMC, 1966-68. Office: Dist Ct 501 I St Sacramento CA 95814-4708

BURRESS, CHARLES RICHARD, journalist; b. Clarksville, Tenn., Apr. 16, 1948; s. Charles Richard Jr. and Jimmie Helen (Williams) B.; m. Taeko Maeda, Mar. 17, 1992; children: Rentaro Samuel, Kentaro William. AB in Govt. with honors, Harvard U., 1970; M Journalism, U. Calif., Berkeley, 1995. Staff writer, editl. editor, arts editor Daily Californian, Berkeley, Calif., 1978-81; staff writer Contra Costa Ind., Richmond, Calif., 1981-82, San Francisco Examiner, 1982-83, San Francisco Chronicle, 1983—; freelance writer various newspapes and mags. U.S., Japan, Can., 1976—; spkr., panelist on Japan, Asia-Pacific issues U. Calif., Berkeley, East-West Ctr., Honolulu, U. Tokyo, Temple U., others, 1990-97. Co-author: Japan Made in U.S.A., 1998; contbr. articles and book revs. to profl. jours. Fulbright scholar Fulbright Fgn. Scholarship Bd., Tokyo, 1996-97, Jefferson fellow East-West Ctr., Honolulu, Japan, Hong Kong, China, 1994, Am. Journalists grantee Japan Newspaper Pubs. and Editors Assn., 1997; recipient numerous newspaper awards, various orgns., Calif., 1984—. Avocations: reading, bicycling. Office: San Francisco Chronicle 901 Mission St San Francisco CA 94103-2905

BURRI, BETTY JANE, research chemist; b. San Francisco, Jan. 23, 1955; d. Paul Gene and Carleen Georgette (Meyers) B.; m. Kurt Randall Annweiler, Dec. 1, 1984. BA, San Francisco State U., 1976; MS, Calif. State U., Long Beach, 1978; PhD, U. Calif. San Diego, La Jolla, 1982. Research asst. Scripps Clinic, La Jolla, 1982-83, research assoc., 1983-85; research chemist Western Human Nutrition Rsch. Ctr., USDA, San Francisco, 1985—; adj. prof. nutrition dept. U. Nev., 1993-98; mem. steering com. Carotenoid Rsch. Interaction Group, 1994-97. Co-editor Carotenoid News; contbr. articles to profl. jours. Grantee NIH, 1982, 85, USDA, 1986-98, Spinal Cord Rsch. Found., 1998; affiliate fellow Am. Heart Assn., 1983, 84. Mem. Assn. Women in Sci. (founding dir. San Diego chpt.), N.Y. Acad. Sci., Carotenoid Rsch. Interaction Group, Am. Soc. Nutrition Sci. Office: Western Human Nutrition Rsch Ctr PO Box 29997 San Francisco CA 94129-0997

BURROUGHS, FRANKLIN TROY, academic administrator; b. Wilmington, Calif., Nov. 12, 1936; s. Charles Jackson and Alberta (Robbins) B.; m. Mahin Molavi, Jan. 29, 1959; children: Ladan Christine, Rana Carolyn. BA, Pepperdine U., 1958; MS, U. So. Calif., 1961; EdD, UCLA, 1964; postdoctoral student, U. Tehran, 1966-68. Cons. UNESCO, Paris, 1970-71; dean Inst. Lang. and Orientation, Tehran, Iran, 1971-74; dir. for Iran AMIDEAST, Washington, 1974-77; exec. dir. U.S. C. of C. in Iran, Tehran, 1977-80; gen. mgr. Strategic Office Systems, Santa Rosa, Calif., 1980-81; cons., writer Burroughs and Assocs., San Francisco, 1981-82; dir., cons. Zolman Internat., San Francisco, 1982-86; dir. Am. English Ctr. Armstrong Coll., Berkeley, Calif., 1986-88; cons. under U.S. Presdl. appointment to U.S. Dept. Commerce Internat. Policy for small and minority-owned bus., 1984-88; pres. Armstrong Coll., Berkeley, Calif., 1988-90; prin. Burroughs Internat., 1990-92; pres. Nobel Group and Global Edn. Assn., 1996—; chair MBA dept. prof. bus. adminstrn. Coll. Notre Dame, Belmont, Calif., 1991—; adj. prof. univ. ext. U. Calif., Berkeley, 1991-93; cons. Fgn. Trade Coun., N.Y.C., 1980; mem. keynote spkr. Task Force, Export '89, Washington. Author: An Historical Outline of Education in Iran, 1972, Europe 1992 and U.S.-EC Trade Flow, 1989, The Global Approach to Management, 1995.

BURROWS, ELIZABETH MACDONALD, religious organization executive, educator; b. Portland, Oreg., Jan. 30, 1930; d. Leland R. and Ruth M. (Frew) MacDonald. Certificate, Chinmaya Trust Sandeepany, Bombay; PhD (hon.), Internat. U. Philosophy and Sci., 1975; ThD, Christian Coll. Universal Peace, 1992. Ordained to ministry First Christian Ch., 1976. Mgr. credit Home Utilities, Seattle, 1958, Montgomery Ward, Crescent City, Calif., 1963; supr. Oreg. Dist. Tng. West Coast Telephone, Beaverton, 1965; pres. Christian Ch. Universal Peace, Seattle, 1971—; prof. religion Christian Coll. Universal Peace, also bd. dirs.; pres. Archives Internat., Seattle, 1971—; v.p. James Tyler Kent Inst. Homeopathy, 1984-95; sec. Louis Braille Inst. for the Blind, 1995—. Author: Crystal Planet, 1979, Pathway of the Immortal, 1980, Odyssey of the Apocalypse, 1981, Maya Sangh, 1981, Harp of Destiny, 1984, Commentary for Gospel of Peace of Jesus Christ According to John, 1986, Seasons of the Soul, 1995, Voyagers of the Sand, 1996, The Song of God, 1998, Hold the Anchovies, 1996, Pilgrim of the Shadow, 1998, The Song of God, 1998; author of poetry (Publisher's Choice award Poets of the New Era, Disting. Poets of Am.). Recipient Pres. award for literary excellence CADER, 1994, 95, 97, Diamond Homer award Famous Poets Soc., 1998. Mem. Internat. Speakers Platform, Internat. New Thought Alliance, Cousteau Soc., Internat. Order of Chivalry, The Planetary Soc. Home: 10529 Ashworth Ave N Seattle WA 98133-8937

BURROWS, JAMES, television and motion picture director, producer; b. L.A., Dec. 30, 1940; s. Abe Burrows. BA, Oberlin Coll.; MFA, Yale U. Off-Broadway prodns.: dir. (motion picture) Partners, 1982, (TV film) More Than Friends, 1978, (TV series episodes) Mary Tyler Moore Show, Bob Newhart, Taxi, Lou Grant, Dear John, Night Court (pilot), Wings (pilot), Roc (pilot), Frasier (pilot), Friends (pilot), Newsradio (pilot), Third Rock from the Sun (pilot), Caroline in the City (pilot); co-creator, co-exec. producer, dir. (TV series) Cheers. Recipient Dirs. Guild Am. award for comedy direction, 1984, 91, 94, Emmy awards NATAS for dir. in comedy series Taxi, 1979-80, 81-82 seasons, Cheers, 1982-83, 90-91 seasons; Emmy award as co-producer Cheers, 1982-83, 83-84, 89-90, 90-91 seasons; Emmy award as director of a Comedy Series for Fraiser, 1994. Office: care Paramount TV Prodns 5555 Melrose Ave Los Angeles CA 90038-3112*

BURRY, KENNETH ARNOLD, physician, educator; b. Monterrey Park, Calif., Oct. 2, 1942; s. Frederick H. and Betty Jean (Bray) B.; m. Mary Lou Tweedy, June 4, 1964 (div. 1981); 1 child, Michael Curtis; m. Katherine A. Johnson, Apr. 3, 1982; 1 child, Lisa Bray. BA, Whittier Coll., 1964; MD, U. Calif.-Irvine, 1968. Diplomate Am. Bd. Ob-Gyn, Am. Bd. Reproendocrine. Intern, Orange County Med. Ctr., Calif.; resident U. Oreg. Med. Sch.; sr. rsch. fellow U. Wash., Seattle, 1974-76; asst. prof. Oreg. Health Sci. U., Portland, 1976-80, assoc. prof., 1980-89, prof., 1989—; dir. Oreg. Reproductive Rsch. and Fertility Program, Portland, 1982—; dir. Fellowship Program, Portland, 1984—, asst. chmn. Dept. Ob-Gyn, 1986—, dir. divsn. Reproendocrine, 1992—; sci. presentations to profl. assns. Author: In Vitro Fertilization and Embryo Transfer, Oregon Health Sciences University Patient Handbook, 1984 (with others). Contbr. abstracts, articles to profl. publs. Served to capt. U.S. Army, 1969-71. Decorated Bronze Star, Air medal, Army Commendation medal oak leaf cluster; recipient Combat Med. badge. Fellow Am. Coll. Ob-Gyn; mem. Endocrine Soc., Am. Soc. Reproductive Medicine, Am. Fedn. Clin. Rsch., Soc. Reproductive Endocrinologists, Soc. Reproductive Surgeons, Pacific Coast Obstet. and Gynecol. Soc. Republican, Pacific Coast Fertility Soc. (pres. 1996-97), Lutheran. Home: 8630 SW Pacer Dr Beaverton OR 97008-6980 Office: Oreg Health Scis U 3181 SW Sam Jackson Park Rd Portland OR 97201-3011

BURSTEIN, [illegible], elementary education educator; b. San Jose, Calif., Jan. 12, 1960; d. Carroll Jay and Olivia (Chang) Biggerstaff; m. Steven Michael Burstein, Mar. 26, 1988; children: Alexander, Cameron, Natalie. AA, West Valley Coll., 1980; BA, UCLA, 1984; MA with honors, U. Calif., Northridge, 1995. Tchr. elem. sch. L.A. Unified Sch. Dist., 1987-92; tchr. elem. sch., curriculum writer social studies Stephen S. Wise Elem. Sch., L.A., 1992-94; elem. tchr., portfolio specialist Burton St. Sch., Panorama City, Calif., 1994—; cons. in field. Recipient Bank of Am. Music award, San Jose, 1978. Mem. Nat. Coun. Tchrs. English, Nat. Coun. for Social Studies, UCLA Alumni Assn. Avocation: violin. Home: 18318 Erwin St Reseda CA 91335-7026

BURT, THOMAS WILLIAM, lawyer; b. Spokane, Wash., Jan. 24, 1955; s. Jack Wallace and Peggy (Windes) B.; m. Ann Darling, Apr. 2, 1989; children; Trevor D. Welling, Griffin D., Caroline D. AB in Human Biology, Stanford U., 1976; JD, U. Wash., 1979. Bar: Wash. 1979, U.S. Ct. Appeals (9th cir.) 1979, U.S. Dist. Ct. (we. dist.) Wash. 1980. Law clk. to judge Ozell Trask U.S. Ct. Appeals (9th cir.), Phoenix, 1979-80; ptnr., atty. Riddell, Williams, Bullitt & Walkinshaw, Seattle, 1980-95; sr. corp. atty. litigation Microsoft Corp., Redmond, Wash., 1995—, now assoc. gen. coun. litigation. Bd. dirs. Bainbridge Island (Wash.) Land Trust, 1990-91. Mem. ABA, Wash. Bar Assn., Seattle-King County Bar. Avocations: sports car racing, skiing, sailing. Office: Microsoft Corp One Microsoft Way Redmond WA 98052*

BURTON, EDWARD LEWIS, retired industrial procedures and training consultant, educator; b. Colfax, Iowa, Dec. 8, 1935; s. Lewis Harrison and Mary Burton; m. Janet Jean Allan, July 29, 1956; children: Mary, Cynthia, Katherine, Daniel. BA in Indsl. Edn., U. No. Iowa, 1958; MS in Indsl. Edn., U. Wis.-Stout, 1969; postgrad., Ariz. State U., 1971-76. Tchr. apprentice program S.E. Iowa Community Coll., Burlington, 1965-68; tchr. indsl. edn. Keokuk (Iowa) Sr. H.S., 1965-68, Oak Park (Ill.)-River Forest High Sch., 1968-70; tchr. Rio Salado Community Coll., Phoenix, 1972-82; tchr. indsl. edn. Buckeye (Ariz.) Union High Sch., 1970-72; cons. curriculum Westside Area Career Opportunities Program - Ariz. Dept. Edn.; instr. vocat. automotive Dysart High Sch., Peoria, Ariz., 1979-81; tng. adminstr. Ariz. Pub. Service Co., Phoenix, 1981-90; tng. devel. cons. NUS Corp., 1991-95; tchr. vocat. automobile Holbrook (Ariz.) H.S., 1995-96, Gila Bend (Ariz.) H.S., 1996—; mem. dispatcher tng. com. Western Systems Coord. Coun., Salt Lake City, 1986-90; owner Aptitude Analysis Co., 1987—; mem. IEEE Dispatcher Tng. Work Group, 1988-91. Editor: Bright Ideas for Career Education, 1974, More Bright Ideas for Career Education, 1975. Mem. Citizens Planning Com., Buckeye, 1987-90, Town Governing Coun., Buckeye, 1990-91. NDEA grantee, 1967. Mem. NEA (life), NRA (life, endowment), Ariz. Rifle and Pistol Assn., Ariz. Indsl. Edn. Assn. (life), Mensa (test proctor 1987—), Masons. Republican. Methodist. Avocations: shooting, photography, camping, boating, travel. Home and Office: 19845 W Van Buren St Buckeye AZ 85326-5676

BURTON, JOHN, state official; b. Ohio, Dec. 15, 1932; 1 child, Kimiko. Student, San Francisco State Coll., San Francisco Law Sch. Mem. Assembly State of Calif., 1964-74, 88-96; mem. U.S. Congress, 1974-82; Pres. pro tem Calif. State Senate, 1998—. Founder Point Reyes Wilderness Area, Farallon Marine Sanctuary. Named Legislator of Yr. Calif. Abortion Rights Action League, Animal Rights Legislator of Yr.; recipient Community United Against Violence award, Sean Mcbride award, award Ancient Order of Hibernians. Office: State Capitol Rm 205 Sacramento CA 95814 also: 601 Van Ness Ave Ste 2030 San Francisco CA 94102*

BURTON, JOHN PAUL (JACK BURTON), lawyer; b. New Orleans, Feb. 26, 1943; s. John Paul and Nancy (Key) B.; m. Anne Ward; children: Jennifer, Susanna, Derek, Catherine. BBA magna cum laude, La. Tech. U., 1965; LLB, Harvard U., 1968. Bar: N.Mex. 1968, U.S. Dist. Ct. N.Mex. 1968, U.S. Ct. Appeals (10th cir.) 1973, U.S. Supreme Ct. 1979. Assoc., Rodey, Dickason, Sloan, Akin & Robb, Albuquerque, 1968-74, dir., 1974—, chmn. comml. dept., 1980-81, mng. dir. Santa Fe, N.Mex., 1986-90. Co-author: (book) Boundary Disputes in New Mexico, 1992, Unofficial Update on the Uniform Ltd. Liab. Co. Act, 1994. Mem. Nat. Coun. Commrs. on Uniform State Laws, 1989—, drafting com. UCC Article 5, 1990-95, UCC Article 9, 1993-95, Uniform Ltd. Liability Co. Act, 1993-95, legis. coun., 1991—, divsn. chair, 1993-95, chair legis. com., 1995—, exec. com., 1995—; liaison for exec. com. to joint editorial bd. Unincorporated Bus. Orgns., 1994-95; pres. Brunn Sch., 1987-89. Fellow Am. Coll. Real Estate Lawyers, Lex Mundi Coll. of Mediators, State Bar Found.; mem. ABA, N.Mex. State Bar Assn. (chmn. comml. litigation and antitrust sect. 1985-86), Am. Law Inst. (rep. to UCC Article 5 drafting com. 1992-95), Am. Coll. Mortgage Attys., Am. Arbitration Assn. (panel arbitrators). Office: Rodey Dickason Sloan Akin & Robb PA PO Box 1357 Santa Fe NM 87504-1357

BURTON, MIKE, regional government administrator. Mem. Oregon Ho. Reps.; chmn. bus. mgmt. dept. Marylhurst Coll.; exec. officer Metro, Portland, Oreg., 1995—. Mem. N.W. Coun. of Pres. Clinton's Coun. on Sustainable Devel., Transatlantic Policy Coun. for Clean Air and Transp., Oregon Gov.'s Growth Task Force, Gov.'s Salmon Strategy Group. Office: Metro 600 NE Grand Ave Portland OR 97232-2799

BURTON, PAUL FLOYD, social worker; b. Seattle, May 24, 1939; s. Floyd James and Mary Teresa (Chovanak) B.; BA, U. Wash., 1961, MSW, 1967; m. Roxanne Maude Johnson, July 21, 1961; children: Russell Floyd, Joan Teresa. Juvenile parole counselor Div. Juvenile Rehab. State of Wash., 1961-66; social worker VA, Seattle, 1967-72, social worker, cons. Work Release program King County, Wash., 1967-72; supr., chief psychiatry sect. Social Work Svc. VA, Topeka, Kans., 1972-73; pvt. practice, Topeka and L.A., 1972—; chief social work svc. VA, Sepulveda, Calif., 1973—, EEO coord. Med. ctr., 1974-77. Mem. NASW (newsletter editor Puget Sound chpt. 1970-71), Acad. Cert. Social Workers, Ctr. for Studies in Social Functioning, Am. Hosp. Assn., Soc. Social Work Adminstrs. in Health Care, Assn. VA Social Work Chiefs (founder 1979, charter mem. and pres. 1980-81, newsletter editor 1982-83, 89-91, pres. elect 1993-95, pres. 1995-97). Home: 14063 Remington St Arleta CA 91331-5359 Office: 16111 Plummer St Sepulveda CA 91343-2036

BURTON, RANDALL JAMES, lawyer; b. Sacramento, Feb. 4, 1950; s. Edward Jay and Bernice Mae (Overton) B.; children: Kelly Jacquelyn, Andrew Jameson; m. Kimberly D. Rogers, Apr. 29, 1989. BA, Rutgers U., 1972; JD, Southwestern U., 1975. Bar: Calif. 1976, U.S. Dist. Ct. (ea. dist.) Calif. 1976, U.S. Dist. Ct. (no. dist.) Calif., 1990, U.S. Supreme Ct, 1991. Assoc. Brekke & Mathews, Citrus Heights, Calif., 1976; pvt. practice, Sacramento, 1976-93; ptnr. Burton & White, Sacramento, 1993—; judge pro tem Sacramento Small Claims Ct., 1982—. Bd. dirs. North Highlands Recreation and Park Dist., 1978-86, Family Svc. Agy. of Sacramento, 1991-96; active Local Bd. 22, Selective Svc., 1982—, Active 20-30 Club of Sacramento, 1979-90, pres., 1987. Recipient Disting. Citizen award, Golden Empire Council, Boy Scouts Am. Mem. Sacramento Bar Assn., Sacramento Young Lawyers Assn. Presbyterian. Lodge: Rotary (pres. Foothill-Highlands club 1980-81). Office: 1540 River Park Dr Ste 224 Sacramento CA 95815-4609

BURTON, ROBERT LYLE, accounting firm executive; m. Lee Sanders; 2 children. Diploma, Kinman Bus. U. CPA. With LeMaster & Daniels, Spokane, Wash., 1963-86; mng. ptnr. LeMaster & Daniels, 1986-97, sr. advisor, 1997—; mem. adv. bd. acctg. dept. U. Wash.; chmn. The Am. Group of CPA Firms. Trustee Econ. Devel. Coun.; past chmn. Samaritan Hosp. Found., Moses Lake, Wash. Mem. AICPA (agri-bus. com., adv. group B), Washington Soc. CPAs (former dir., v.p., com. chmn., legis. com.), Spokane Club, Inland Empire Fly Fishermen, Moses Lake Golf and Country Club, Rotary. Office: LeMaster & Daniels 8817 E Mission Spokane WA 99212*

BURY, DAVID ALFRED, fundraising executive; b. Mpls., June 19, 1933; s. Alfred Frank and Annie Viola (Howard) B.; m. Joyce Annette Steen, Aug. 6, 1955; children: Michael David, Diane Joyce, Steven George, Cheryl Jean. ThB, North Ctrl. U., 1955; postgrad., Seattle Pacific U., 1960-70. Ordained to ministry, 1959, certified fundraising exec. (CFRE). Youth pastor Peoples Ch., Mpls., 1955-57; youth pastor, music dir. Westminster Assembly, Seattle, 1958-60; club dir. Seattle Youth for Christ, 1960-63, exec. dir., 1963-71, exec. dir. Portland (Oreg.) Youth for Christ, 1975-84, San Gabriel-Pomona Valley Youth for Christ, Calif., 1984-91; fundraising cons., 1992-96; western region acct. exec. Master Software, 1996-97; COO Westminster Gardens, Duarte, Calif., 1997—; v.p. Pacific N.W. area Youth for Christ Internat., 1964-68; instr. music North Cen. U., Mpls., 1955-56.

Mem. adv. bd. Campus Life mag., 1966-69; producer religious radio and multi media presentations. Mem. Nat. Soc. Fundraising Execs., Christian Mgmt. Assn., C. of C., Rotary. Office: 1420 Santo Domingo Ave Duarte CA 91010

BUSCH, JOYCE IDA, small business owner; b. Madera, Calif., Jan. 24, 1934; d. Bruno Harry and Ella Fae (Absher) Toschi; m. Fred O. Busch, Dec. 14, 1956; children: Karen, Kathryn, Kurt. BA in Indsl. Arts & Interior Design, Calif. State U., Fresno, 1991. Cert. interior designer, Calif. Stewardess United Air Lines, San Francisco, 1955-57; prin. Art Coordinates, Fresno, 1982—, Busch Interior Design, Fresno, 1982—; art cons. Fresno Community Hosp., 1981-83; docent Fresno Met. Mus., 1981-84. Treas. Valley Children's Hosp. Guidance Clinic, 1975-79, Lone Star PTA, 1965-84,; mem. Mothers Guild San Joaquin Mem. H.S., 1984-88. Mem. Am. Soc. Interior Designers. Republican. Roman Catholic. Club: Sunnyside Garden (pres. 1987-88). Avocations: gardening, art history.

BUSH, JUNE LEE, real estate executive; b. Philippi, W.Va., Sept. 20, 1942; d. Leland C. and Dolly Mary (Costello) Robinson; m. Jerry Lee Coffman, June 15, 1963 (div. 1970); 1 child, Jason Lance; m. Richard Alfred Bush, May 20, 1972. Grad., Fairmont State Coll., 1962, Dale Carnegie, Anaheim, Calif., 1988. Exec. sec. McDonnell Douglas, Huntington Beach, Calif., 1965-72; adminstrv. asst. Mgmt. Resources, Inc., Fullerton, Calif., 1978-80; bldg. mgr. Alfred Gobar Assocs., Brea, Calif., 1980-95; treas. Craig Park East, Fullerton, 1982, bd. dirs., 1982-84. Author instrn. manual Quality Assurance Secretarial Manual, 1971. Sec. PTA, La Palma, 1974. Mem. Gamma Chi Chi. Avocations: golf, sailing, reading. Home: 12553 Crystal Ranch Rd Moorpark CA 93021-2913

BUSH, REX CURTIS, lawyer; b. Longview, Wash., Oct. 21, 1953; s. Rex Cole Bush and Arline (Quanstrom) Fitzgerald; m. Joy Ann Pallas, July 22, 1977 (div.); children: Alicia, Angela, Carrie; m. Janet Rae Hicks July 2, 1988; children: Jeni, Mykal. BA cum laude, Brigham Young U., 1980; JD, U. Utah, 1983. Bar: Utah 1983, U.S. Dist. Ct. (no. dist.) Utah 1983, U.S. Tax Ct. 1985. Tax atty. Arthur Andersen & Co., Houston, 1983-84; assoc. Mortensen & Neider, Midvale, Utah, 1984-85; in-house counsel Fin. Futures, Salt Lake City, 1985-87; registrar Hollander Cons., Portland, Oreg., 1987-88; in-house counsel Bennett Leasing, Salt Lake City, 1987-88; pres. Bush Law Firm, Sandy, Utah, 1988—; judge pro tempore 3d Cir. Ct., Salt Lake City, 1985-87. Author: (booklet) What To Do in Case of an Automobile Accident, 1994. Mayor University Village, U. Utah, 1981-82; Rep. candidate Utah state senate, 1992; Rep. voting dist. sec., treas., 1992. Recipient Meritorious Leadership award, Nat. Com. for Employer Support of Guard and Reserve, 1990. Mem. ATLA, Utah Trial Lawyers Assn., Utah State Bar (chmn. small firm and solo practitioners com. 1994-96, honored for outstanding svc. to legal profession 1996). Office: Bush Law Firm 9615 S 700 E Sandy UT 84070-3557

BUSH, SARAH LILLIAN, historian; b. Kansas City, Mo., Sept. 17, 1920; d. William Adam and Lettie Evelyn (Burrill) Lewis; m. Walter Nelson Bush, June 7, 1946 (dec.); children: William Read, Robert Nelson. AB, U. Kans., 1941; BS, U. Ill., 1943. Clk. circulation dept. Kansas City Pub. Library, 1941-42, asst. librarian Paseo br., 1943-44; librarian Kansas City Jr. Coll., 1944-46; substitute librarian San Mateo County Library, Woodside amd Portola Valley, Calif., 1975-77; various temporary positions, 1979-87; owner Metriguide, Palo Alto, Calif., 1975-78. Author: Atherton Lands, 1979, rev. edition 1987. Editor: Atherton Recollections, 1973. Pres., v.p. Jr. Librarians, Kansas City, 1944-46; courtesy, yearbook & historian AAUW, Menlo-Atherton branch (Calif.) Br.; asst. Sunday sch. tchr., vol. Holy Trinity Ch., Menlo Park, 1955-78, v.p., membership com., libr. chairperson, English reading program, parent edn. chairperson Menlo Atherton High Sch. PTA, 1964-73; founder, bd. dirs. Friends of Atherton Community Library, 1967—, oral historian, 1968—, chair Bicentennial event, 1976; bd. dirs. Menlo Park Hist. Assn., 1979-82, oral historian, 1973—; bd. dirs. Civic Interest League, Atherton, 1978-81; mem. hist. county commn. Town of Atherton, 1980-87; vol. Allied Arts Palo Alto Aux. to Children's Hosp. at Stanford, 1967—, oral historian, 1978—, historian, 1980—; vol. United Crusade, Garfield Sch., Redwood City, 1957-61, 74-88, Encinal Sch., Menlo Park, Calif., 1961-73, program dir., chmn. summer recreation, historian, sec.; vol. Stanford Mothers Club, 1977-81, others; historian, awards chairperson Cub Scouts Boy Scouts Am.; founder Atherton Heritage Assn. 1989, bd. dirs., 1989—, dir., 1989-94; mem. Guild Gourmet, 1971—, Mid Peninsula History Consortium, 1993-95. Recipient Good Neighbor award Civic Interest League, 1992. Mem. PTA (life). Episcopalian. Avocations: gourmet cooking, entertaining, reading.

BUSH, STANLEY GILTNER, secondary school educator; b. Kansas City, Mo., Nov. 4, 1928; s. Dean Thomas and Sallie Giltner (Hoagland) B.; m. Barbara Snow Adams, May 23, 1975 (dec. Mar. 1994); stepchildren: Deborah Gayle Duclon, Douglas Bruce Adams. BA, U. Colo., 1949, MA, 1959, postgrad., 1971; postgrad., U. Denver, 1980, 85, 90. Tchr. Gering (Nebr.) Pub. Schs., 1949-51, 54-57, Littleton (Colo.) Pub. Schs., 1957-91; emergency plan dir. City of Littleton, 1961—; safety officer Littleton Pub. Schs., 1968—; founder, chief Arapahoe Rescue Patrol, Inc., Littleton, 1957-92, search mission coord., 1975—; pres. Arapahoe Rescue Patrol, Inc., 1957—, Expedition, Inc., Littleton, 1973—; owner Emergency Rsch. Cons., 1990—. Contbr. chpts. to Boy Scout Field Book, 1984; co-author: Managing Search Function, 1987; contbr. articles to profl. jours. Safety advisor South Suburban Parks Dist., Littleton, 1985-96; advisor ARC, Littleton, 1987—, Emergency Planning Com., Arapahoe County, Colo., 1987—; coord. search and rescue Office of Gov., Colo., 1978-82; state judge Odyssey of the Mind, 1996-97. Sgt. U.S. Army, 1951-54. Shell Oil Co. fellow, 1964; recipient Silver Beaver award Boy Scouts Am., 1966, Vigil-Order of Arrow, 1966, Award of Excellence Masons, 1990. Mem. Nat. Assn. for Search and Rescue (life, Hall Foss award 1978), Colo. Search and Rescue Bd., NEA (life). Methodist. Avocations: mountaineering, wilderness emergency care, emergency services. Home: 2415 E Maplewood Ave Littleton CO 80121-2817 Office: Littleton Ctr 2255 W Berry Ave Littleton CO 80165

BUSH, WILLIAM GLENN, manufacturing company executive, engineer; b. Lakeland, Fla., Nov. 28, 1937; s. William Baker and Lois (Collins) B.; m. Ruby Joyce King, June 10, 1960; children: Wesley Glenn, William Stuart, Brian Lewis. B in Indsl. Engring., Ga. Inst. Tech., 1960. Registered profl. engr., Calif. Indsl. engr. Procter & Gamble, Perry, Fla., 1960-61; indsl. engr. FMC Corp., Lakeland, 1961-62, shop foreman, 1962-63, supr. mfg. engring., 1963-65, mgr. prodn. control, 1966-70, mgr. mfg., 1970-72; gen. mgr. ops. FMC Corp., Riverside, Calif., 1972-75; div. gen. mgr. FMC Corp., Fairmont, W.Va., 1975-79; corp. dir. bus. planning FMC Corp., Chgo., 1979-80, group exec., 1980-81, corp. v.p., 1981-89; chief engr. Durand Machinery, Woodbury, Ga., 1965-66; dir. engring. Mark Industries, Brea, Calif., 1990-92; dir. product engring. Indsl. Dynamics Inc., Torrance, Calif., 1992—; bd. govs. mfrs. div. Am. Mining Congress, 1976-78; chmn. bd. dirs. BS&B Engring., 1985-86. Mem. agrl. adv. com. U. Calif., Riverside, 1974-75; mem. adv. bd. Ga. Inst. Tech., 1988-91; bd. dirs. Riverside C. of C., 1973-75, United Way, Riverside, 1973-75, Fairmont C. of C., 1977-79. Mem. NSPE. Republican. Presbyterian. Home: 832 3rd St Apt 302 Santa Monica CA 90403-1155 Office: Indsl Dynamics Inc 3100 Fujita St Torrance CA 90505-4007 Address: 832 3rd St Apt 302 Santa Monica CA 90403-1155

BUSHMAN, EDWIN FRANCIS ARTHUR, engineer, plastics consultant, rancher; b. Aurora, Ill., Mar. 16, 1919; s. George J. and Emma (Gengler) B.; B.S., U. Ill., 1941, postgrad., 1941-42, Calif. Inst. Tech., 1941; m. Louise Kathryn Peterson, Jan. 3, 1946; children: Bruce Edwin, Gary Robert, Joan Louise, Karen Rose, Mary Elisabeth, Paul George. Jr. engr. Gulf Refining Co. Gulf Oil Corp., Mattoon, Ill., 1940-41; engr. radio and sound lab. war rsch. div. U. Calif. at Navy Electronics Lab., Pt. Loma, San Diego, 1942-45; project engr. Bell and Howell Co., Lincolnwood, Ill., 1945-46; research cons., Scholl Mfg. Co., Inc., Chgo., 1946-48; project engr. deepfreeze div. Motor Products Corp., North Chicago, Ill., 1948-50; research and product design engr. Bushman Co., Aurora, Ill. also Mundelein, Ill., 1946-55; with Plastics div. Gen. Am. Transp. Corp., Chgo., 1950-68, tech. dir., 1950-55, mgr. sales and sales engring. Western states, Compton, Calif., 1955-68, sales and sales engring. research and devel. div., 1962-64; with USS Chems., 1968-70; plastics cons. E.F. Bushman Co., 1970—, Tech. Conf. Assocs., 1974-80. Program mgr. Agriplastics Symposium Nat. Agrl. Plastics Conf., 1966; program mgr. Plastics in Hydrospace, 1967; originator Huisman Plastics awards, 1970, Un-Carbon Polymer prize and Polymer Pool Preserve Plan, 1975, Polymer Independence award, 1977, 78. Bd. dirs. Coastal Area Protective League, 1958-66, Lagunita Community Assn., 1959-66 (pres. 1964-65), Calif. Marine Parks and Harbors Assn., 1959-69. Sr. editor Plastic Trends mag., 1985-90. Recipient Western Plastics Man of Yr. award, 1972. Mem. Soc. Plastics Industry Inc. (chpt. pres. 1971-72), Soc. Plastic Engrs. (Lundberg award 1981), Western Plastics Pioneers, Western Plastics Mus. and Pioneers, Plastics Pioneers Assn., Sunkist Growers, Cal. Citrus Nurserymen's Soc., Calif. Farm Bur. Fedn. U. Ill. Alumni Assn., Soc. for Advancement Materials and Process Engring., Geopolymers Inst. Roman Catholic. Author various profl. and strategic resource papers. Patentee in field of plastics, carbon and colored glass fibers, process, and applications. Home: 19 Lagunita Ln Laguna Beach CA 92651-4237 Office: PO Box 581 Laguna Beach CA 92652-0581

BUSHMAN-CARLTON, MARILYN, poet; b. Lehi, Utah, Nov. 18, 1945; d. F. Wayne and Shirley Dodge (Tobler) Bushman; m. Blaine Lynn Carlton, June 12, 1969; children: Alisa, Jari Lyn, Christian, Jacob, Justin. BA in English, U. Utah, 1989. Author book of poems on keeping things small, 1995. Recipient $500 prize Utah Arts Coun., Salt Lake City, 1996, 2d pl. Utah Arts Coun., 1997. Mem. Utah State Poetry Soc. Democrat. Mem. LDS Ch. Avocations: reading, travel, jogging, gardening, classical music. Home: 3394 Aura Cir Salt Lake City UT 84124-2173

BUSHNELL, RODERICK PAUL, lawyer; b. Buffalo, Mar. 6, 1944; s. Paul Hazen and Martha Atlee B.; m. Suzann Yvonne Kaiser, Aug. 27, 1966; 1 child, Arlo Phillip. BA, Rutgers U., 1966; JD, Georgetown U., 1969. Bar: Calif. 1970, U.S. Supreme Ct. 1980; cert. civil trial specialist. Atty. dept. water resources Sacramento, 1969-71; ptnr. Bushnell, Caplan & Fielding, San Francisco, 1971—; adv. bd. dirs. Bread & Roses, Inc., Mill Valley, Calif. Bd. dirs. Calif. Lawyers for the Arts, Ft. Mason, San Francisco, 1985—. Mem. ATLA, San Francisco Bar Assn. (arbitrator), San Francisco Superior Ct. (arbitrator), Fed. Ct. Early Neutral Evaluator, Calif. Bar Assn., Consumer Attys. Calif., San Francisco Trial Lawyers Assn., No. Calif. Criminal Trial Lawyers Assn., Nat. Employment Lawyers Assn., Calif. Employment Lawyers Assn., Consumer Attys. L.A. Fax: 415-217-3820. Office: Bushnell Caplan & Fielding 221 Pine St Ste 600 San Francisco CA 94104-2715

BUSIG, RICK HAROLD, mining executive; b. Vancouver, Wash., June 21, 1952; s. Harold Wayne and Ramona (Riley) B. AA, Clark Coll., Vancouver, 1972; BA in Econs., U. Wash., 1974. CPA, Wash. Acct., Universal Svcs., Seattle, 1975-78; acct., acctg. mgr., controller Landura Corp., Woodburn, Oreg., 1978-80; asst. controller Pulte Home Corp., Laramie, Wyo., 1980-81; treas., controller Orcal Cable, Inc., Sparks, Nev., 1981-82; controller Saga Exploration Co., Reno, Nev., 1982—; acct. Sterling Mine Joint Venture, Beatty, Nev., 1982-95. Del. Nev. State Dem. Conv., Reno, 1984, 94, Las Vegas, 1988. Recipient Spaatz award CAP. Mem. AICPA, Wash. Soc. CPA's, Oreg. Soc. CPA's. Home: 2735 Lakeside Dr # A Reno NV 89509-4203 Office: Saga Exploration Co 2660 Tyner Way Reno NV 89503-4926

BUSS, JERRY HATTEN, real estate executive, sports team owner; Children: John, Jim, Jeanie, Jane. BS in Chemistry, U. Wyo.; MS, PhD in Chemistry, U. So. Calif., 1957. Chemist Bur. Mines; past mem. faculty dept. chemistry U. So. Calif.; mem. missile div. McDonnell Douglas, Los Angeles; partner Mariani-Buss Assos.; former owner Los Angeles Strings; chmn. bd., owner Los Angeles Lakers (Nat. Basketball Assn.), 1979—; until 1988 owner Los Angeles Kings (Nat. Hockey League), 1979—. Office: care LA Lakers PO Box 10 3900 W Manchester Blvd Inglewood CA 90306*

BUSSEY, GEORGE DAVIS, psychiatrist; b. Salta, Argentina, Apr. 14, 1949; s. William Harold and Helen (Wygant) B.; m. Moira Savage, July 26, 1975; children: Andrew Davis, Megan Elizabeth. BS, U. Denver, 1969; MD, Ea. Va. Med. Sch., 1977; JD, U. Hawaii, 1993. Diplomate in psychiatry, forensic psychiatry and addiction psychiatry Am. Bd. Psychiatry and Neurology. Intern Eastern Va. Grad. Sch. Medicine, 1977-78; resident Ea. Va. Grad. Sch. Medicine, 1978-79, Vanderbilt U. Hosp., Nashville, 1979-81; staff psychiatrist Hawaii State Hosp., Kaneohe, 1981-82; asst. prof. dept. psychiatry U. Hawaii, Honolulu, 1982-84; dir. adult svcs. Kahi Mohala Hosp., Ewa Beach, Hawaii, 1983-89; assoc. med. dir. Queens Healthcare Plan, Honolulu, 1988-94, v.p., 1997—; med. dir. Queen's Health Mgmt., Honolulu, 1994—; clin. assoc. prof. Dept. Psychiatry U. Hawaii, Honolulu, 1990—. Mem. U. Hawaii Law Rev., 1991-93; contbr. articles to profl. jours. Fellow Am. Psychiat. Assn., Hawaii Psychiat. Soc. (treas. 1982-83, pres. 1985-87).; mem. Am. Coll. Physician Execs. (cert.).

BUSTAMANTE, CRUZ M., state official; b. Dinuba, Calif., 1953; s. Cruz and Dominga Bustamante Jr.; m. Arcelia De La Pena; children: Leticia, Sonia, Marisa. Student, Fresno City Coll., Fresno State U. Past intern for Congressman B.F. Sisk Washington; formerly with Fresno employment and tng. commn. City of Fresno, past program dir. summer youth employment tng. program; past dist. rep. Congressman Rick Lehman and Assemblyman Bruce Bronzan State of Calif.; mem. Calif. State Assembly, 1993, spkr. of assembly, 1996-98; lt. gov. State of Calif., 1998—. Trustee Calif. State U. Named Legislator of Yr. Faculty Assn. Cmty. Colls., Assn. Mexican Am. Educators, U. Calif. Alumni Assn., True Am. Role Model Mexican Am. Polit. Assn.; recipient Lifetime award Golden State Mobilehome Owners League, Friend of Labor award Mexican Am. Polit. Assn. Office: State Capitol Rm 1114 Sacramento CA 95814*

BUTENHOFF, SUSAN, public relations executive; b. N.Y.C., Jan. 13, 1960. BA in Internat. Rels. with hons., Sussex U., Eng.; MPhil, Wolfson Coll., Cambridge U., Eng. Account exec. Ellen Farmer Prodns., 1984-85; account exec. Ketchum Pub. Rels., N.Y.C., 1988-90, v.p., account supr., 1990-91; prin., CEO Access Pub. Rels., San Francisco, 1991—. Mem. Pub. Rels. Soc. Am. Office: Access Pub Rels 101 Howard St San Francisco CA 94105-1629

BUTLER, BILLIE RAE, educational administrator; b. Waverly, Tenn., Aug. 2, 1941; d. Clifford Ronald and Pauline Elizabeth (Forsythe) Hunter; m. E.D. Longest (div.); children: Tamara Dianne, Teresa Denise, Tanya Darlene; m. William R. Butler, Dec. 16, 1979. AA, Hartnell Coll., Calif., 1973; BA, Chapman Coll., Calif., 1978. Cert. life permit Children's Ctr., Calif. Commn. for Tchr. Prep. and Licensing. Tchr. Monterey County Office of Edn., Salinas, Calif., 1973-78, coord., 1978-80, program dir., 1980—; mem. Monterey County Child Care Planning, 1992—; bd. dirs., officer Monterey Bay Parents as Tchrs., Monterey County, 1990-96. Mem., officer Salinas Valley Child Abuse Prevention Coun., Monterey County, 1980-84; mem. Family Self-Sufficiency Coord. Coun., Monterey Coun. Mem. AAUW, Calif. Head Start Assn. (bd. dirs. 1991-93), Cen. Coast Assn. for Edn. of Young Children (bd. dirs. 1984-90). Avocations: flower arranging, cooking/regional and ethnic cuisines, history, travel. Office: Monterey County Office Edn 901 Blanco Cir Salinas CA 93901-4401

BUTLER, BYRON CLINTON, obstetrician, gynecologist; b. Carroll, Iowa, Aug. 10, 1918; 1; s. Clinton John and Blance (Prall) B.; m. Jo Ann Nicolls; children: Marilyn, John Byron, Barbara, Denise; 1 stepdau., Marrianne. MD, Columbia Coll. Physicians and Surgeons, 1943; ScD, Columbia U., 1952; G.G. grad. gemologist, Gemol. Inst. Am., 1986. Diplomate Am. Bd. Ob/Gyn. Intern Columbia Presbyn. Med. Ctr.; resident Sloane Hosp. for Women; instr. Columbia Coll. Physicians and Surgeons, 1950-53; dir. Butler Rsch. Found., Phoenix, 1953-86, pres., 1970—; ret. as gyn. surgeon, 1989; pres. World Gems/G.S.G., Scottsdale, Ariz., 1979—, World Gems Software, 1988, World Gems Jewelry, 1990—; cosmologist, jewelry designer Extra-Terrestrial-Alien Jewelry & Powerful Personal Talismans, 1992—, 3rd Millineum Line of Tektite Jewelry, 1994—; cons. in diagnosis, treatment, prognosis of HIV, AIDS, sexually transmitted diseases, 1975. Patentee in field. Bd. dirs. Heard Mus., Phoenix, 1965-74; founder Dr. Byron C. Butler, G.G., Fund for Inclusion Research, Gemol. Inst. Am., Carlsbad, Calif., 1987. Served to capt. M.C. AUS, 1944-46. Grantee Am. Cancer Soc., 1946-50, NIH, 1946-50, 50-53. Fellow Mufon, Mutual UFO Networks. Featured in Life; patentee in field; discovery of cause of acute fibrinolysis in humans; research on use hypnosis for relief of pain in cancer patients, use of tPA (tissue plaminogen activator) in acute coronary occlusion treatment, research in indochinite tektite origins, chemical analysis, radioactive ingredients, psychic powers; designer jewelry using polished tektite, finder tplasminogen as cause of incoaguable blood during premature separation of placenta in pregnancy. Home and Office: 77 E Missouri Ave Unit 20 Phoenix AZ 85012-1380

BUTLER, DANIEL BLAKE, lawyer; b. Orange, Calif., June 4, 1960; s. Harry Allison and Mary Jane Butler; m. Caroline Cornell Penna, Sept. 3, 1988; children: Alessandra Noel, Daniel Armand, Kelly Claire. BA in Drama, U. Tex., 1982; JD, UCLA, 1992. Bar: Calif., 1992. Assoc. Hill Wynne Troop & Meisinger, L.A., 1992-94; sr. counsel legal affairs MGM/UA Music, Santa Monica, Calif., 1994-95; dir. bus. affairs MGM/UA Music, Santa Monica, 1995-96; v.p. bus. and legal affairs music Rysher Entertainment, Santa Monica, 1996-98; dir. bus. and legal affairs music Warner Bros., Burbank, 1998—. Mem. Assn. Ind. Music Pubs., Calif. Copyright Conf., State Bd. Calif., Beverly Hills Bar Assn. Office: Warner Bros 4000 Warner Blvd Burbank CA 91522-1705

BUTLER, DASCHEL E., protective services official. Chief of police Berkeley, Calif. Office: 2171 Mckinley Ave Berkeley CA 94703-1519*

BUTLER, EDWARD EUGENE, plant pathology educator; b. Wilmington, Del., Dec. 8, 1919; s. Edward Harry and Julia (Ennis) B.; m. Mildred Norene Godden, Dec. 20, 1947; children: David, Stephen, Susan, Thomas, James. BS, U. Del., Newark, 1943; MS, Mich. State U., 1948; PhD, U. Minn., 1954. Instr. plant pathology U. Minn., St. Paul, 1951-54; jr. plant pathologist U. Calif., Davis, 1955-56; asst. plant pathologist U. Calif., 1957-61, assoc. prof. plant pathology, 1961-68, prof. plant pathology, 1968-90, prof. emeritus, 1990—; vis. prof. U. P.R., 1966-67; vis. scientist Rancho Santa Ana Bot. Garden, Claremont, Calif., 1983-84. Assoc. editor Phytopathology, 1973 76; editorial bd. Mycologia, 1978-88, Mycopathologia, 1992—; contbr. to profl. jours. Capt. U.S. Army, 1943-46, PTO. Named to U. Del. Wall of Fame, 1996. Fellow AAAS; mem. Mycol. Soc. Am. (W.H. Weston award 1981), Am. Phytopathol. Soc. (Lifetime Achievement award Pacific divsn. 1996), Brit. Mycol. Soc. Democrat. Home: 402 12th St Davis CA 95616-2023 Office: U Calif Dept Plant Pathology Davis CA 95616

BUTLER, EUGENIA PERPETUA, artist; b. Washington; d. James Gerard and Eugenia B.; m. Isaac Malitz (div. Aug. 1991); 1 child, Corazon del Sol. BA, U. Calif., Berkeley, 1968. Lectr. UCLA Ext., 1987-90, Art Ctr. Sch., Pasadena, Calif., 1987, 99; assoc. prof. So. Calif. Inst. Arch., L.A., 1995—. One woman show includes Gallery Paradiso, 1998; artist: (book) The Book of Lies, vol. I 1996, vol. II 1997. Advisor Inglewood (Calif.) Cultural Master Plan, 1997; bd. dirs. L.A. Inst. Contemporary Art, 1986-87. Pub. Access Press grant So. Calif. Inst. Arch., 1996-97; recipient Recognition award Inglewood City Coun., 1997, Found. for Art Resources award, 1998. Office: Ariel Prods 672 S Ave 21 Ste 4 Los Angeles CA 90031-2892

BUTLER, JOHN LOWE, IV, psychiatrist, educator; b. Accquia, Idaho, Nov. 5, 1920; s. John Lowe III and Bertha Malvina (Thurber) B.; m. Marjorie Lu Call, Aug. 12, 1945; children: Kenneth Lee, Janet Sue Westwood, John Lowe V. BSE, U. Idaho, 1942; MD, Johns Hopkins U., 1946. Acting supt. Kooskia (Idaho) Pub. Schs., 1942-43; Carnegie postdoctoral fellow, Sch. of Indsl. & Labor Rels. Cornell U., Ithaca, N.Y., 1950-52; indsl. psychiatrist Mut. Security Agy., Paris, 1952-53, The Hague, The Netherlands, 1954-55; dir. mental health Idaho State Bd. of Health, Boise, 1956-58; prof. psychiatry Oreg. Health Scis. U., Portland, 1958—; pvt. practice Portland, 1959-92; cons., writer, 1958—; vis. prof. psychology U. Idaho, 1950—; staff mem. Guidance & Counseling Inst., Oreg. State Sys. of Higher Edn., Portland, 1960-68; co-dir. Pastoral Leadership & Counselor Tng. Inst., Portland, 1960-75; cons. tng. in human rels. improvement, 1952—. Contbr. articles to profl. jours. Mem. various coms. City Club of Portland, 1969—. Lt. (j.g.) USN, 1943-50. Recipient Career Tchr. grant U.S. Nat. Inst. Mental Health, 1959-61; named to Hall of Fame Alumni Assn. U. Idaho, 1997. Life fellow Am. Psychiat. Assn. (pres. Oreg. Dist. br. 1977-78), North Pacific Soc. of Neurology & Psychiatry (bd. dirs. 1976-78); mem. Johns Hopkins Med. and Surg. Soc. (pres. Oreg. chpt. 1970-71), Oreg. Med. Assn. (life), Phi Beta Kappa. Democrat. Unitarian/Universalist. Home: 2229 SW Kings Ct Portland OR 97205-1121

BUTLER, KATHLEEN LOIS, museum administrator, independent scholar; b. Berkeley, Calif., Sept. 22, 1963; d. William Philip and Mary Lois (Mulholland) B.; m. Michael Steven Shackley, June 24, 1995. BA, Mills Coll., 1985; MA, U. Calif., Berkeley, 1987, PhD, 1994. Coord. collectors forum San Francisco Mus. Modern Art, 1988-90; lectr. San Francisco State U., fall 1989; instr. U. Calif. Berkeley, summer 1992; registrar N.A.G.P.R.A. unit Phoebe Hearst Mus. Anthropology, Berkeley, 1993-96, adminstrv. coord., 1995-98, asst. dir., 1998—; presenter art dept. Mills Coll., 1994. Contbr.: (exhbn. catalog) Wayne Thiebaud, 1984, 97, (biog. entry) Am. Nat. Biography, 1996. Dissertation completion grantee U. Calif. Berkeley, 1992-93, humanities grad. rsch. grantee, 1990, 92. Mem. Am. Studies Assn. (presenter, organizer session 1994, 96), Assn. Historians of Am. Art, Coll. Art Assn., Am. Assn. Mus. Democrat. Avocations: mountain biking, fly fishing, home brewing.

BUTLER, KEITH ARNOLD, psychologist, software researcher; b. L.A., Dec. 22, 1945; s. John Harold and Phyllis Alder (Falke) B.; m. Janis Lynn Mowry, Dec. 23, 1972 (div. Jan. 1981); children: Iraj, Reza, Leila, John Keith. BA, Calif. State U., Long Beach, 1972; PhD in Exptl. Psychology, Tufts U., Medford, Mass., 1980. Lectr. Emmanual Coll., Boston, 1975-77; mem. tech. staff Bell Telephone Labs., Piscataway, N.J., 1978-81; sr. prin. scientist The Boeing Co., Bellevue, Wash., 1981—; tutorial lectr. SIGCHI Conf., 1989—, gen. co-chair, New Orleans, 1991; sr. prin. scientist Boeing Tech. Fellowship, Seattle, 1991. Contbr. articles to profl. jours. Founding bd. mem. Citizens for Better Schs., Snoqualmie, Wash., 1989-91. With U.S. Army, 1967-69. Mem. Assn. Computing Machinery. Congregationalist. Achievements include development of an engineering method for the design of usable human-computer interfaces; organized industry-wide initiative for usability criteria in software product selection; design of the experiment which revealed the role of beta-estradiol in male reproductive behavior. Avocations: endurance sports, operatic singing, coaching youth sports. Office: Boeing IS&S AR&T PO Box 3707 Seattle WA 98124-2207

BUTLER, LESLIE ANN, advertising agency owner, artist, writer, editor; b. Salem, Oreg., Nov. 19, 1945; d. Marlow Dole and Lala Ann (Erlandson) Butler. Student Lewis and Clark Coll., 1963-64; BS, U. Oreg., 1969; postgrad. Portland State U. 1972-73, Lewis & Clark Coll., 1991. Creative trainee Ketchum Advt., San Francisco, 1970-71; asst. advt. dir. Mktg. Systems, Inc., Portland, Oreg., 1971-74; prodn. mgr., art dir., copywriter Finzer-Smith, Portland, 1974-76; copywriter Gerber Advt., Portland, 1976-78; freelance copywriter, Portland, 1983-84, 83-85; copywriter McCann-Erickson, Portland, 1980-81; copy chief Brookstone Co., Peterborough, N.H., 1981-83; creative dir. Whitman Advt., Portland, 1984-87; prin. L.A. Advt., 1987—. Author: The Dream Road and Other Tales From Hidden Hills, 1997; arts and antiques editor Portland Living mag. Co-founder, v.p., newsletter editor Animal Rescue and Care Fund, 1972-81; mem. Friends of One Performing Arts Ctr., Portland Art Mus., Oreg. Humane Soc. Recipient Internat. Film and TV Festival N.Y. Finalist award, 1985, 86, 87, 88, Internat. Radio Festival of N.Y. award, 1984, 85, 88, Hollywood Radio and TV Soc. Internat. Broadcasting award, 1981, TV Comml. Festival Silver Telly award, 1985, TV Comml. Festival Bronze Telly, 1986, AVC Silver Cindy, 1986, Los Angeles Advt. Women LULU, 1986, 87, 88, 89 Ad Week What's New Portfolio, 1986, N.W. Addy award Seattle Advt. Fedn., 1984, Best of N.W. award, 1985, Nat. winner Silver Microphone award, 1987, 88, 89. Mem. ASPCA, Portland Advt. Fedn. (Rosey Finalist award 1986), People for Ethical Treatment of Animals. Home and Office: 7556 SE 29th Ave Portland OR 97202-8827

BUTLER, PETER, JR., retired secondary education educator; b. New Orleans, Dec. 28, 1929; s. Peter and Ada (Smith) B.; m. Annie Mae Darrington, Dec. 24, 1956; children: Simone Walton, Daryl R., Phyllis E. Young, Deidre M. Hudson, Myra A. Cuff. BA, So. U., Baton Rouge, 1954; MEd, La. State U., 1959; EdD, U. So. Calif., 1976. Cert. elem. tchr., secondary sch. tchr., gen. adminstrv. svcs., Calif. Tchr. English, New Orleans Pub. Schs., 1954-56, 59-63; tchr. English Archdiocese Schs., New Orleans, 1956-59; tech. writer The Boeing Co., New Orleans, 1963-64; tchr. English Inglewood (Calif.) Unified Sch. Dist., 1964-67, asst. prin., 1967-69, prin., dir. secondary edn., asst. supt. pers. svcs., 1969-89; adj. prof. Chapman U., Orange, Calif., 1994—. Contbr. articles to profl. jours. With U.S.

Army, 1947-50. Mem. ASCD, Kappa Alpha Psi. Methodist. Avocations: reading, walking, watching sporting events, travel, writing. Home: 19202 Hillford Ave Carson CA 90746-2656

BUTLER, REX LAMONT, lawyer; b. New Brunswick, N.J., Mar. 24, 1951; s. Ekker and Beatrice (Curry) B.; m. Stephanie Butler; children: Nijel Jaibrun, Vikteria Lamontra, Octavia Reneè Lamontra, Synclaire Lamontra. AA with honors, Fla. Jr. Coll., 1975; BA, U. North Fla., 1977; JD, Howard U., 1983. Bar: Alaska 1983, U.S. Dist. Ct. Alaska 1983, U.S. Ct. Appeals (9th cir.) 1984, U.S. Ct. Appeals (D.C. cir.) 1984, U.S. Supreme Ct. 1996. Assoc. M. Ashley Dickerson, Inc., Anchorage, 1983-84; profl. legis. asst. State of Alaska, Juneau, 1984; asst. atty. gen. State of Alaska, Anchorage, 1984-85; pvt. practice Anchorage, 1985—; adj. prof. law Anchorage C.C., 1985; adj. prof. U. Alaska, Anchorage, 1990—; mem. State Ct. Criminal Pattern Jury Instructions Com., 1997; chmn. lawyer rep. com. Alaska 9th Cir. Judicial Conf., 1997-98. Pres. Alaska Black Caucus, Anchorage, 1986, bd. dirs., 1987-88; gen. counsel NAACP, Anchorage, 1985-87, life mem.; commr. Anchorage Telephone Utility, 1985-87; trustee Anchorage Sr. Ctr., Inc., 1985-87, Shiloh Missionary Bapt. Ch., Anchorage, 1985—; bd. dirs. Ctr. Drug Problems, Anchorage, 1985-86, Alaska Civil Liberties Union, 1987-88; active fin. com. Dem. Cen. Com. Alaska. With USN, 1969-73. Named one of Outstanding Young Men Am., 1984; recipient Cert. Appreciation, African Relief Campaign, 1985. Mem. ABA, Nat. Bar Assn., Nat. Assn. Criminal Defense Lawyers, Alaska Bar Assn., Assn. Trial Lawyers Am., Anchorage Bar Assn., Alaska Trial Lawyers Assn., Lions Internat., Omega Psi Phi (dist. counselor 1995-96). Democrat. Fax: (907) 276-3306. E-mail: rexb@pobox.alaska.net. Home: PO Box 200025 Anchorage AK 99520-0025 Office: 745 W 4th Ave Ste 300 Anchorage AK 99501-2136

BUTMAN, HARRY RAYMOND, clergyman, author; b. Beverly, Mass., Mar. 20, 1904; s. John Choate and Elsie Louise (Raymond) B.; m. Jennette Alice Stott, Jan. 5, 1929; children: Beverly, Raymond, Jack, Jennette. BD, Bangor Sem., 1928; postgrad., U. Vt., 1933; DD (hon.), Piedmont Coll., 1955. Ordained to ministry Congregational Ch., 1932. Minister Federated Ch., Edgartown, Mass., 1932-37, Congl. Ch., Randolph, Mass., 1937-45, Allin Congl. Ch., Dedham, Mass., 1945-53, Ch. of the Messiah, L.A., 1953-78; interim minister First Congl. Ch., L.A., 1978-81, cons., 1982—; moderator Nat. Assn. Congl. Christian Chs., 1963, chmn. exec. com., 1958, 59, 74; editor, The Congregationalist, 1967-68; chmn. Internat. Congl. Fellowship, London, 1977-81. Author: History of Randolph, 1942, Far Islands, 1954, Preamble to Articles of Assn. for Nat. Assn. Congl. Christian Chs., 1956, The Measure of the Immeasurable, 1967, The Lord's Free People, 1968, Serve with Gladness, 1971, The Theology of Congregationalism, 1975, The Chislehurst Thanksgiving, 1976, The Argent Year, 1980, World Book Ency., Manuscript of Nat. Assn. Congl. Christian Chs., 1981, The Desert Face of God, 1985, Brown Boy, 1987, The Good Beasts, 1991, The Soul's Country, 1994, Symbols of Our Way, 1994, A Quiet and Durable Joy, 1996; contbr. articles to profl. jours. Named for Best Patriotic Sermon Freedoms Found., 1972; honoree of the Harry R. Butman Endowed Chair of Religion and Philosphy Piedmont Coll., Demorest, Ga., 1994; prelate The Soc. of Descendants of Knights of the Most Noble Order of the Garter, 1972—. Republican. Avocations: boating, desert driving. Home: 2451 Soledad Canyon Rd Acton CA 93510-2416

BUTTERFIELD, ANTHONY SWINDT, photographic oscillograph paper manufacturing company executive; b. Jackson, Mich., Apr. 20, 1931; s. William Swindt and Sally (Jackson) B.; m. Sarah Pennell, May 16, 1964; children: Sally Butterfield Klotz, Annie Pennell Dittmore, Anthony Swindt Jr. BA, Williams Coll., 1954. Sales engr. Macklin Co., Jackson, Mich., 1956-58; dispatcher Indsl. Asphalt Co., Los Angeles, 1958-60; salesman U.S. Motors, San Francisco, 1960-62; account exec. Xerox Corp., San Francisco, 1962-82; owner, mgr. Pacific Coast Photo Co., Santa Cruz, Calif., 1985—. Republican. Avocations: hunting, fishing, skiing. Home and Office: Pacific Coast Photo Co 280 Cress Rd Santa Cruz CA 95060-1036

BUTTERFIELD, BONNIE SUE, psychology educator, librarian, researcher; b. Covina, Calif., Dec. 31, 1942; d. Robert David and Marjorie Helen (Vosberg) Berry; m. David Charles Butterfield, Dec. 4, 1965; children: Stacie Ann Butterfield Cruz, Devin David. BA, Calif. State U., 1965; MA, Immaculate Heart Coll., 1968; MA in Neuroscience, Calif. State U.Calif. Coast U., 1997. Libr. Los Angeles County Pub. Libr., Baldwin Park, Calif., 1968-78; neurosci. rschr. U. Calif., Riverside, 1990-93; computer libr. Calif. State U., San Bernadino, 1993—, prof. psychology, 1993—. Contbr. articles to profl. jours. Rsch. grantee Calif. State U., 1996. Mem. Cherokees Calif. Democrat. Avocations: poetry, writing, oil paintings. Home: 11842 Beverly Ct Loma Linda CA 92354-3933 Office: Calif State U 5500 University Pkwy San Bernardino CA 92407-7500

BUTTERFIELD, DONALD GENE, physician, gastroenterologist; b. Bloomfield, Iowa, Dec. 20, 1937; s. James Delbert and Sada Larue (Beckly) B.; m. Beverly Bebe Butters, June 12, 1960 (dec. Oct. 1974); children: Bradley James, Andrew Edward, Matthew Willard; m. Cynthia Wentworth Strickland, June 28, 1975; stepchildren: Geoffry H. Manning, Meredith S. Manning. BA in Biology, Cornell Coll., Mt. Vernon, Iowa, 1960; MD, Iowa State U., 1963. Diplomate Am. Bd. Internal Medicine, Am. Bd. Gastroenterology. Intern Phila. Gen. Hosp., 1963-64; resident U. Colo. Med. Ctr., Denver, 1966-68, fellow in gastroenterology, 1968-70; practice medicine specializing in gastroenterology Denver and Aurora, Colo., 1970—; mem. staff, chmn. div. gastroenterology, dir. gastrointestinal lab. Presbyn. Med. Ctr., 1970—, chief of staff, 1981-84, chief of medicine, 1977-79; pres. consol. med. bd. Presbyn./St. Luke's Hosps., 1985, also bd. dirs.; mem. staff St. Joseph Hosp., 1970—, St. Luke's Hosp., 1970—, Mercy Hosp., 1970—; asst. clin. prof. internal medicine U. Colo. Health Scis. Ctr., Denver, 1978-86, assoc. clin. prof., 1986—; bd. fellows U. Denver, 1985—; bd. dirs. Denver Presbyn. Hosp., physician Nat. Advisory bd. Am. Med. Internat., Beverly Hills, Calif., 1986—, bd. dirs.; founding mem., sec. Colo. Trust, Denver, 1985—. Contbr. articles to profl. jours. Served to capt. USAF, 1964-66. Mem. ACP, Am. Soc. Internal Medicine, Colo. Soc. Internal Medicine, Denver Med. Soc., Colo. Med. Soc., AMA, Am. Soc. Gastrointestinal Endoscopy, Am. Gastroenterology Assn., Denver Symphony Orch. Assn., Denver Mus. Natural History, Denver Bot. Gardens, Denver Art Mus., Denver Mus. Western Art, Phi Beta Kappa, Alpha Omega Alpha. Republican. Congregationalist. Clubs: Racquet World (Denver), Snowmass Country (Colo.). Avocations: skiing, tennis, golf, gardening. Office: Denver/Aurora Gastroenterologist 1721 E 19th Ave Ste 520 Denver CO 80218-1243

BUTTERWORTH, ROBERT ROMAN, psychologist, researcher, media therapist; b. Pittsfield, Mass., June 24, 1946; s. John Leon and Martha Helen (Roman) B. BA, SUNY, 1972; MA, Marist Coll., 1975; PhD in Clin. Psychology, Calif. Grad. Inst., 1983. Asst. clin. psychologist N.Y. State Dept. Mental Hygiene, Wassaic, 1972-75; pres. Contemporary Psychology Assocs., Inc., L.A. and Downey, Calif., 1976—; cons. L.a. County Dept. Health Svc.; staff clinician San Bernardino County Dept. Mental Health, 1983-85; staff psychologist State of Calif. Dept. Mental Health, 1985—; media interviews include PA, L.A. Times, N.Y. Times, USA Today, Wall St Jour., Washington Post, Redbook mag., London Daily Mail and many others; TV and radio interviews include Larry King Live, CBA, NBA and ABC networks, Oprah Winfrey Show, CNN Newsnight, Can. Radio Network, Mut. Radio Network and many others. Served with USAF, 1965-69. Mem. Am. Psychol. Assn. for Media Psychology, Calif. Psychol. Assn., Nat. Accreditation Assn. Psychoanalysis. Office: PO Box 76477 Los Angeles CA 90076-0477

BUTTON, GLENN MARSHALL, aeronautical engineer; b. L.A., June 26, 1958; s. Albert Ronald Button and Laurel Lang (Bluske) B.; m. Mary Josephine Puetzer, May 16, 1981; children: Nichole Elisabeth, Jessica Sarah, Laura Marie. BS in Physics, Ariz. State U., 1980. Counselor Adventure Unlimited Ranches, Buena Vista, Colo., 1977; aerodynamics engr. aircraft divsn. Northrop Grumman Corp., Hawthorne, Calif., 1980-82, structures rsch. engr. aircraft divsn., 1982-85, engring. specialist aircraft divsn., 1986-91; database application software developer B-2 divsn. Northrop Grumman Corp., Pico Rivera, Calif., 1991-92, lead configuration specialist, design application software aircraft divsn.; prin. GMB Assocs. Mktg., Cypress, Calif., 1988—; electronic process devel. prin. engr., scientist Long Beach (Calif.) Divsn., The Boeing Co., Long Beach, Calif., 1996-98; supplier integration mgr. Long Beach (Calif.) Divsn., The Boeing Co., Long Beach, 1998—; aerodynamics cons. Kachina Racing, Tempe, Ariz., 1977-93; software cons. Aeromax, Cypress, 1989—. Contbr. articles to sci. jours. Pres. Villas Figueroa Homeowners Assn., Carson, Calif., 1983; tchr. Grace Ch., Cypress, Calif., 1990—. Mem. Soc. Automotive Engrs. Republican. Mem. Christian Ch. Avocations: cycling, teaching, skiing, reading, mountain climbing. Home: 10441 Santa Elise St Cypress CA 90630-4234 Office: The Boeing Co 3855 N Lakewood Blvd Long Beach CA 90846-0003

BUTTON, JERRY EDWARD, biologist; b. Coos Bay, Oreg., Dec. 8, 1946; s. George Deward and Gladys Wilhelmina (Lunden) B.; m. Dorothy P. Steele, June 17, 1977 (div. Aug. 1991). BS summa cum laude, Lewis & Clark Coll., 1969; MS with honors, U. Oreg., 1974; EdD, Portland State U., 1991. Grad. tchg. fellow dept. biology U. Oreg., Eugene, 1971-73; prof. biology Portland C.C., 1973—; cons. in field. Vol. numerous orgns. NSF grant, 1998; named Outstanding Instr., Heart Inst., 1994, Great Tchr., Great Tchrs. Assn. Mem. AAAS, Human Anatomy & Physiology Soc., Union of Concerned Scientists, N.W. Biology Assn., Oreg. Acad. Sci., N.Y. Acad. Sci. Democrat. Unitarian. Avocations: flower gardening, photography, physical fitness, travel, reading. Office: Portland CC 12000 SW 49th Ave Portland OR 97219-7132

BUTTS, EDWARD PERRY, civil engineer, environmental consultant; b. Ukiah, Calif., July 29, 1958; s. Edward Oren Butts and Orvilla June (Daily) Hutcheson; m. JoAnne Catherine Zellner, Aug. 14, 1978; children: Brooke C., Adam E. Cert. continuing studies in Irrigation Theory and Practices, U. Nebr., 1980. Registered profl. engr., Oreg., Wash.; cert. water rights examiner, Oreg.; registered control sys. engr., Oreg. Technician Ace Pump Sales, Salem, Oreg., 1976; technician Stettler Supply Co., Salem, 1976-78, assoc. engr., 1978-86, chief engr., 1986-90, v.p. engring., 1990-97, pres., 1997—; profl. engr. exam. question reviewer Nat. Coun. Engring. Examiners, Clemson, S.C., 1989—; profl. engr. exam. supr. Oreg. State Bd. Engring. Examiners, Salem, 1986—; lectr. various water works profl. groups; mem. Marion County Water Mgmt. Coun., 1993—. Contbr. articles to Jour. Pub. Works Mag., AWWA Opflow, Water Well Jour. Coach Little League Cascade Basketball Leage, Turner, Oreg., 1990-94; vol. Jr. Achievement. Recipient Merit award Am. City and County Mag., 1990, Cmty. Vol. citation City of Keizer, Oreg., 1993, Cert. of appreciation Oreg. State Bd. Engring. Examiners, 1996, Letter of Commendation for flood assistance City of Salem, 1996, Application Design award Spraying Systems Co., 1996. Mem. ASCE, NSPE, Am. Pub. Works Assn., Assn. Groundwater Scientists and Engrs., Profl. Engrs. Oreg. (mid-Willamette chpt. v.p. 1990-91, pres. 1992-93, state v.p. 1993-95, state pres.-elect 1995-96, state pres. 1996-97, nat. dir. 1999—, Young Engr. of Yr. award 1993-94), Am. Water Works Assn., Oreg. Assn. Water Utilities (bd. dirs. 1998—). Republican. Achievements include devel. of system used to install multiple pumps in water wells, cert. sprinkler irrigation designer. Office: 1810 Lana Ave NE Salem OR 97303-3116

BUTZ, OTTO WILLIAM, political science educator; b. Floesti, Romania, May 2, 1923; came to U.S., 1949, naturalized, 1959; s. Otto E. and Charlotte (Engelmann) B.; m. Velia DeAngelis, Sept. 13, 1961. B.A., Victoria Coll., U. Toronto, 1947; Ph.D., Princeton, 1953. Asst. prof. polit. sci. Swarthmore Coll., 1954-55; asst. prof. politics Princeton U., 1955-60; asso. editor Random House, N.Y.C., 1960-61; prof. social sci. San Francisco State Coll., 1961-67; academic v.p. Sacramento State Coll., 1967-69, acting pres., 1969-70; pres. Golden Gate U., 1970-92; pres. emeritus, 1992—. Author: German Political Theory, 1955, The Unsilent Generation, 1958, Of Man and Politics, 1960, To Make a Difference—A Student Look at America, 1967. Recipient Calif. State Colls. Outstanding Tchr. award, 1966. Mem. Am. Polit. Sci. Assn. Home: Wolfback Rdg Sausalito CA 94965 Office: 536 Mission St San Francisco CA 94105-2921

BUTZIGER, ROBERT ANTON, minister; b. Pawtucket, R.I., Jan. 17, 1937; s. Edwin Lewis and Edna (Myers) B.; m. Marianne Stahowski, Sept. 1, 1962; children: Caryl M., Peter, Laura. BA, U. R.I., 1958; postgrad., U. Conn., 1962; MDiv, Princeton Theol. Sem., 1969; D Ministry, San Francisco Theol. Sem., 1988. Ordained to ministry Presbyn. Ch., 1969. Pastor W.Va. Mountain Project, Dry Creek, 1969-71; supr. clin. pastoral edn. Appalachian Reg. Hosp., Middlesboro, Ky., 1971-72; dir. Morgan-Scott Project, Deer Lodge, Tenn., 1972-80; pastor Farragut (Tenn.) Presbyn. Ch., 1980-86, St. Andrew Presbyn. Ch., Albuquerque, 1986-95; dir. South Albuquerque Coop. Ministry, 1996—; sec. com. on ministry Presbytery of Santa Fe.; marriage and family therapist, 1980—. Author: Family Commitments, 1988. Bd. dirs. Contact Teleministry, Knox, Tenn. & Albuquerque, 1982-88; v.p. Assn. for Couples in Marriage Enrichment, Winston-Salem, N.C., 1979-84; chmn. bd. dirs. Re-Visioning N.Mex., 1996—. Lt. USN, 1960-64. Fellow Am. Assn. Pastoral Counselors; mem. N.Mex. Conf. of Churches (marriage and family chmn. 1988—). Home: 2200 Marie Park Dr NE Albuquerque NM 87112-3641

BUURSMA, WILLIAM F., architect. BArch, U. Mich., 1964; MArch, U. Pa., 1965. Lic. arch. With various archtl. design firms; joined John Graham Assocs/DLR Group, Seattle, 1976—, prin.; tchg. fellow U. Tenn., also assoc. prof. France program. Prin. works include Madigan Army Med. Ctr., Ft. Lewis, Wash., Clackamas Town Ctr., Portland, Oreg., Kauai Hilton Resort and Condominium Complex, Hawaii, high-rise office bldgs., retail shopping malls, and numerous other complexes. Mem. AIA. Office: John Graham Assoc 900 4th Ave Ste 700 Seattle WA 98164-1003*

BUYERS, JOHN WILLIAM AMERMAN, agribusiness and specialty foods company executive; b. Coatesville, Pa., July 17, 1928; s. William Buchanan and Rebecca (Watson) B.; m. Elsie Palmer Parkhurst, Apr. 11, 1953; children: Elsie Buyers Viehman, Rebecca Watson Buyers-Basso, Jane Palmer Buyers-Russo. B.A. cum laude in History, Princeton U., 1952; M.S. in Indsl. Mgmt., MIT, 1963. Div. ops. mgr. Bell Telephone Co. Pa., 1964-66; dir. ops. and personnel Gen. Waterworks Corp., Phila., 1966-68; pres., chief exec. officer Gen. Waterworks Corp., Phila, 1971-75; v.p. adminstrn. Internat. Utilities Corp., Phila., 1968-71; pres., chief exec. officer, dir. C. Brewer and Co., Ltd., Honolulu, 1975—, chmn. bd., 1982—; chmn. Calif. and Hawaiian Sugar Co., 1982-84, 86-90; pres. Buyco, Inc., 1986—; mem. Hawaii Joint Coun. Econ. Edn., Japan-Hawaii Econ. Coun.; bd. dirs. 1st Hawaiian Inc., John B. Sanfilippo & Sons, Inc., Outrigger Hotels and Restors; chmn. bd. C. Brewer Homes, Inc.; vice chmn. Pacific Internat. Ctr. for High Tech. Rsch., 1976—. Trustee U. Hawaii Found., Hawaii Prep. Acad., 1986—; chmn. bd. dirs. Hawaii Visitors Bur., 1990-91; mem. Gov.'s Blue Ribbon Panel on the Future of Healthcare in Hawaii; bd. dirs. Hawaii Sports Found., 1990—; mem. adv. group to U.S. Dist. Ctr. With USMC, 1946-48. Sloan fellow, 1963. Mem. Hawaiian Sugar Planters Assn. (chmn. bd. dirs. 1980-82, dir.), c. of C. Hawaii (chmn. bd. dirs. 1981-82), Nat. Alliance Bus. (chmn. Hawaii Pacific Metro chpt. 1978), Cap and Gown Club (Princeton), Hilo Yacht Club, Oahu Country Club, Pacific Club, Waialae county Club, Prouts Neck (Maine) County Club, U.S. C. of C. (mem. food and gr. com. 1991—), Beretania Tennis Club. Presbyterian. Clubs: Cap and Gown (Princeton); Hilo Yacht, Oahu Country, Pacific, Waialae Country; Prouts Neck (Maine) Country. Home: Grand Penthouse West 1080 S Beretania St Honolulu HI 96814-1400 Office: C Brewer & Co Ltd PO Box 1826 Honolulu HI 96805-1826 also: Buyco Inc 827 Fort Street Mall Honolulu HI 96813-4317

BUZUNIS, CONSTANTINE DINO, lawyer; b. Winnipeg, Man., Can., Feb. 3, 1958; came to U.S., 1982; s. Peter and Anastasia (Ginakes) B. BA, U. Man., 1980; JD, Thomas M. Cooley Law Sch., 1985. Bar: Mich. 1986, U.S. Dist. Ct. (ea. and we. dists.) Mich. 1986, Calif. 1986, U.S. Dist. Ct. (so. dist.) Calif. 1987, U.S. Supreme Ct. 1993. Assoc. Church, Kritselis, Wyble & Robinson, Lansing, Mich., 1986; assoc. Neil, Dymott, Perkins, Brown & Frank, San Diego, 1987-94, ptnr., 1994—; arbitrator San Diego County Mcpl. and Superior Cts.; judge pro tem San Diego Mcpl. Ct. Sec., treas. Sixty Plus Law Ctr., Lansing, 1985; active Vols. in Parole, San Diego, 1988—; bd. dirs. Hellenic Cultural Soc., 1993-98. Mem. ABA, FBA, ATLA, Mich. Bar Assn., Calif. Bar Assn., San Diego County Bar Assn., Desert Bar Assn., San Diego Trial Lawyers Assn., So. Calif. Def. Coun., State Bar Calif. (gov. 9th dist. young lawyers divsn. 1991-94, 1st v.p. 1993-94, pres. 1994-95, bd. govs. 1995-96) San Diego Barristers Soc. (bd. dirs. 1991-92), Pan Arcadian Fedn., Order of Ahepa (chpt. bd. dirs., v.p. 1995-98), Phi Alpha Delta. Home: 3419 Overpark Rd San Diego CA 92130-1865 Office: Neil Dymott Perkins Brown & Frank 1010 2nd Ave Ste 2500 San Diego CA 92101-4913

BUZZA, BONNIE WILSON, academic administrator; b. Mpls., Feb. 23, 1944; d. Henry Woodrow and Bonnie Laurette (Carlson) Wilson; m. David Thomas Buzza, Mar. 19, 1967. BA, Macalester Coll., St. Paul, 1966; MA, U. Denver, 1967, PhD, 1970. Prof. weekend and evening coll. Met. State Coll., Denver, 1970-73; lectr. Colo. Women's Coll., Denver, 1974; prof., dept. chmn. Ripon (Wis.) Coll., 1974-88; prof. communication, chmn. dept. Coll. of Wooster, Ohio, 1988-90; asst. dean Coll. Fine Arts and Humanities, St. Cloud (Minn.) State U., 1990-92; dean Coll. Liberal Arts Winona (Minn.) State U., 1992-96; provost, dean Albertson Coll., Caldwell, Idaho, 1996—; cons. Communication Mgmt. Assocs.; dir. London-Florence program Assoc. Colls. Midwest, London, 1983. Contbr. articles to profl. publs. Mem. exec. bd. Wayne County Women's Network, Wooster, 1990, Ctrl. Minn. AIDS Project, 1990-92, Forum Exec. Women, 1991-92; bd. dirs. YWCA, Winona, 1993-96, Women's Resource Ctr., Winona, 1992-96, Winona Women in Bus., 1996, Exec. Women Internat., Boise, 1996— (bd. mem., 1998—), Boise Beaux Arts Société, 1996 (bd. mem., 1998—). Recipient Outstanding Young Tchr. award Ctrl. States Speech Assn., 1977, Disting. Citizen award Macalester Coll. Alumni Assn., 1981, Severy award for teaching excellence Ripon Coll., 1988; fellow Am. Assn. State Colls. and Univs. Acad. Leadership Acad., 1991-93. Mem. AAUP, NAFE, Nat. Communication Assn., Assn. Communication Adminstrn., Ctrl. States Communication Assn. (Program of Excellence award small coll. com. 1990), Coun. Colls. Arts and Scis., Ripon Coll. Soc. Scholars (co-founder, life), Pi Kappa Delta, Alpha Psi Omega. Office: Albertson Coll Idaho 2112 Cleveland Blvd Caldwell ID 83605-4432

BYARS, HOWARD MARVIN, construction executive, civil engineer, educator; b. San Francisco, Nov. 6, 1930; s. Gilbert Theodore Thompson and Lois Fern (Davidson) Dula; m. Tosca Lee, Aug., 1952; children: Mark, Christine, Sheril. BSCE, U. Nev., 1952, MSCE, 1954. Lic. civil engr., Nev. Chief estimator Isbell Constrn. Co., Reno, Nev., 1952-62; gen. mgr. Helms Constrn. Co., Reno, 1962-65; CEO, owner Byars Constrn. Co., Reno, 1965—. Past bd. dirs., YMCA, Reno, Nev., Campfire Girls, Reno; chmn. Washoe Airport Authority, Reno, 1985, Reno Nat. Championship Air Race, 1985—. Mem. Nat. Soc. Profl. Engrs. (Engr. of Yr. 1983), Nev. Soc. Profl. Engrs. (Engr. of Yr. 1983), Assn. Gen. Contractors (nat. bd. dirs. 1972—), Hidden Valley Country Club (bd. dirs.). Republican. Avocations: golf, skiing, scuba diving, flying, water color painting. Home: 3377 Skyline Blvd Reno NV 89509-5672 Office: HM Byars Constrn Co 7770 Security Cir Reno NV 89506-1943

BYCZYNSKI, EDWARD FRANK, lawyer, financial executive; b. Chgo., Mar. 17, 1946; s. Edward James and Ann (Ruskey) B.; children—Stefan, Suzanne. B.A., U. Wis., 1968; J.D., U. Ill., 1972; Certificat de Droit, U. Caen, France, 1971. Bar: Ill. 1972, U.S. Dist. Ct. (no. dist.) Ill. 1972, U.S. Supreme Ct. 1976. Title officer Chgo. Title Ins. Co., 1972-73; asst. regional counsel SBA, Chgo., 1973-76; pres. Alderstreet Investments, Portland, Oreg., 1976-82; pres. Nat. Tenant Network, Portland, 1981—, Bay Venture Corp., Portland, 1984—; ptnr. Haley, Pirok, Byczynski. Chgo., 1973-76. Contbr. articles to profl. jours. Mem. ABA, Ill. Bar Assn. Democrat. Home: PO Box 2377 Lake Oswego OR 97035-0614 Office: 525 SW 1st Ste 105 Lake Oswego OR 97034

BYERS, CHARLES FREDERICK, public relations executive, marketing executive; b. Johnstown, Pa., Jan. 30, 1946; s. Walter Hayden and Mary Ann Elizabeth (Succop) B.; m. Vicki Louise Beard, June 3, 1967 (div. Apr. 1992); children: Natalie L., Tamara N., Valerie A.; m. Janette Lanora Buck, Apr. 23, 1993. BS in Journalism, Ohio U., 1968; MA in Mass Comm., U. Tex., 1969. Gen. reporter Springfield (Ohio) Daily News, 1967-68; promotion specialist GE, Chgo., 1969-71; account supr. Burson-Marsteller, Chgo., 1971-78; group v.p. Carl Byoir & Assocs., Chgo., 1978-82; gen. mgr. Carl Byoir & Assocs., Atlanta, 1982-85; pres. Camp-Byers Pub. Rels., Atlanta, 1985-91; client svc. dir. Kalman Comm., L.A., 1991-92; v.p., COO Hayes Pub. Rels., San Jose, Calif., 1992-95; mktg. comms. mgr. Actel Corp., Sunnyvale, Calif., 1995-98; dir. comm. TSMC, USA, San Jose, 1998—. Pres. Hoffman Estates (Ill.) Jaycees, 1976; dir., treas. Brookcliffe Home Owners Assn., 1988-89; comm. chair Ga. Heart Assn., Atlanta, 1990. Recipient Golden Trumpet, Chgo. Publicity Club, 1980. Mem. Pub. Rels. Soc. Am. (accredited pub. rels. practitioner, bd. dirs. Silicon Valley chpt. 1993, v.p. chpt. 1994, pres.-elect 1995, pres. 1996, del. nat. assembly 1997, 99, bd. dirs. L.A. chpt. 1992, Silver Anvil award 1978, Compass award Bay Area chpts. 1997). Avocations: lacrosse official, golf, photography, tennis, tropical fish. Office: TSMC USA 1740 Technology Dr San Jose CA 95110-1373

BYRD, MARC ROBERT, florist; b. Flint, Mich., May 14, 1954; s. Robert Lee and Cynthia Ann (Poland) B.; m. Bonnie Jill Berlin, Nov. 25, 1975 (div. June 1977). Student, Ea. Mich. U., 1972-75; grad., Am. Floral Sch., Chgo., 1978. Gen. mgr., dir. flowers shop; designer Olive Tree Florist, Palm Desert, Calif., 1978-79, Kayo's Flower Fashions, Palm Springs, 1979-80; owner, designer Village Florist, Inc., Palm Springs, 1980-85; pres. Mon Ami Florist, Inc., Beverly Hills, 1986-87; gen. mgr. Silverio's, Santa Monica, 1987; gen. mgr., hotel florist, creative dir. Four Seasons Hotel, Beverly Hills, 1988-90; pres. Marc Fredericks, Inc., Beverly Hills, 1990-97; event florist Marc Byrd of Floral Works, L.A., 1997—. Author: Celebrity Flowers, 1989. Del., Dem. County Conv., 1972, Dem. County Conv., 1972, Dem. State Conv., 1972, Dem. Nat. Conv., 1972. Mem. Soc. Am. Florists, So. Calif. Floral Assn., Desert Mus., Robinson's Gardens. Republican. Mem. Dutch Reformed Ch. Avocations: skiing, tennis, community service. Fax: (323) 962-9275. Home: 2415 Creston Dr Los Angeles CA 90068-2203 Office: Marc Fredericks Inc 2415 Creston Dr Los Angeles CA 90068-2203

BYRD, MILTON BRUCE, college president, former business executive; b. Boston, Jan. 29, 1922; s. Max Joseph and Rebecca (Malkiel) B.; m. Susanne J. Schwerin, Aug. 30, 1953; children: Deborah, Leslie, David. A.B. cum laude, Boston U., 1948, M.A., 1949; Ph.D., U. Wis., 1953; postgrad. (fellow), U. Mich., 1961-62. Teaching asst. English U. Wis., 1949-53; instr., asst. prof. English Ind. U., 1953-58; asst. prof., asso. prof. humanities So. Ill. U., 1958-62, head div. humanities, 1958-60, supr. acad. advisement, 1959-60, asso. dean, 1960- 62; v.p. acad. affairs No. Mich. U., 1962-66; pres. Chgo. State U., 1966-74; provost Fla. Internat. U., 1974-78; pres. Adams State Coll., Alamosa, Colo., 1978-81; v.p. corp. devel. Frontier Cos., Anchorage, 1981-85; pres. Charter Coll., 1985—; bd. dirs Chgo. Council for Urban Edn., Union for Experimenting Colls. and Univs., Am. Assn. State Colls. and Univs., Resource Devel. Council Alaska, Alaska Commn. Econ. Edn.; v.p. Common Sense for Alaska, Inc.; former pres. Alaska Support Industry Alliance. Author: (with Arnold L. Goldsmith) Publication Guide for Literary and Linguistic Scholars, 1958; contbr. to profl. jours. Commr. Alaska Commn. on Postsecondary Edn. Served with USAAF, 1943-46. Mem. MLA, Nat. Council Tchrs. English, Coll. English Assn., Am. Studies Assn., AAUP, Fla. Assn. Univ. Adminstrs. (former pres.), Rocky Mountain Athletic Conf. (former pres.), Assn. for Higher Edn., Pub. Relations Soc. Am., NEA, Alaska Press Club, Mich. Edn. Assn., Phi Beta Kappa, Phi Delta Kappa. Club: Rotary. Office: # 120 2221 E Northern Lights Blvd Anchorage AK 99508-4143

BYRD, RONALD DALLAS, civil engineer; b. Reno, Nov. 30, 1934; s. Eugene Richard and Helen Madelyn (Hursh) B.; m. Irene Josephine Phenix, Sept. 19, 1953; children: Kevin Gregory, Helen Christine, Stephanie Irene. BSCE, U. Nev., 1960. Registered profl. engr., Nev., Calif., Oreg., Wash., Idaho., Wyo. Staff engr. Sprout Engrs., Sparks, Nev., 1960-64, design engr., 1964-67; office mgr. Sprout Engrs., Seattle, 1967-70; exec. v.p. Sea, Inc., Seattle, 1970-72, Sparks, 1972-97; v.p. Stantech Cons. Inc. SW, 1997-98, Stantec Cons. Inc. SW, 1998—; bd. dirs. Am. Cons. Engrs. Coun. Nev., 1987-95, pres., 1993-94, nat. dir. 1994-95. Fellow ASCE (sec. 1966-67); mem. NSPE (bd. dirs. 1983-86), Am. Pub. Works Assn., U. Nev. Reno Engring. Alumni Assn. (sec. 1983-86), U. Nev. Reno Alumni Assn. (pres. 1989-90), Kiwanis (pres. Sparks club 1971-72), Rotary (pres. Federal Way, Wash. club 1971-72, bd. dirs. Reno Sunrise 1992-98, pres. 1996-97), Elks, Masons. Republican. Methodist. Home: 30 Ocelet Way Reno NV 89511-4751 Office: Stantec Cons Inc 950 Industrial Way Sparks NV 89431-6092

BYRD, THOMAS RUSSELL, health educator; b. Palo Alto, Calif., Mar. 9, 1942; s. Oliver Erasmus and Jennie Christine (Sonnichsen) B.; children:

Patrick, Kristina, Jaime Lynn, Jenna; m. Kathi Finrow, Mar. 29, 1988. AA, Menlo Coll., 1961; BS in Health Sci., Calif. State U., San Jose, 1963; MA in Health Edn., Stanford U., 1965. Cert. state c.c. tchg. credential, Calif. Tchr. Palo Alto (Calif.) Unified Sch. Dist., 1966-68; prof. De Anza Coll., Cupertino, Calif., 1968—; educator Calif. Assn. Alcohol and Drug Abuse Educators, Calif., 1983—; cons. numerous colls. and univs., 1978—. Author: Medical Readings on First Aid, 1971, Medical Readings on Counseling and Psychological Services, 1971, Medical Readings on Family Life, 1971, Medical Readings on Vision, 1971, Medical Readings on Heroin, 1972, Medical Readings on the Heart, 1973, Medical Readings in Health Sciences, 1974, Preventive Health Concepts, 1976, Health Sciences: Selected Medical Readings, 1979, Addictive Awareness, 1990, Lives Written in Sand, 1997. Mem. U.S. Masters Swimming (nat. champ long distance open water swim Capitola to Santa Cruz 6 mile, 1998). Democrat. Avocations: landscaping, gardening, open water swimming, writing. Home: 1533 Madrono Ave Palo Alto CA 94306-1016 Office: De Anza Coll 21250 Stevens Creek Blvd Cupertino CA 95014-5702

BYRNE, GEORGE MELVIN, physician; b. San Francisco, Aug. 1, 1933; s. Carlton and Esther (Smith) B.; BA, Occidental Coll., 1958; MD, U. So. Calif., 1962; m. Joan Stecher, July 14, 1956; children: Kathryne, Michael, David; m. Margaret C. Smith, Dec. 18, 1982. Diplomate Am. Bd. Family Practice, 1971-84. Intern, Huntington Meml. Hosp., Pasadena, Calif., 1962-63, resident, 1963-64; family practice So. Calif. Permanente Med. Group, 1964-81, physician-in-charge Pasadena med. office, 1966-81; asst. dir. Family Practice residency Kaiser Found. Hosp., L.A., 1971-73; clin. instr. emergency medicine Sch. Medicine, U. So. Calif., 1973-80; v.p. East Ridge Co., 1983-84, sec., 1984; dir. Alan Johnson Porsche Audi, Inc., 1974-82, sec., 1974-77, v.p., 1978-82. Bd. dirs. Kaiser-Permante Mgmt. Assn., 1976-77; mem. regional mgmt. com. So. Calif. Lung Assn., 1976-77; mem. pres.'s circle Occidental Coll., L.A. Drs. Symphony Orch, 1975-80; mem. profl. sect. Am. Diabetes Assn. Fellow Am. Acad. Family Physicians (charter); mem. Am., Calif., L.A. County Med. Assns., Calif. Acad. Family Physicians, Internat. Horn Soc., Quarter Century Wireless Assn., Am. Radio Relay League (Pub. Service award), Sierra (life), So. Calif. Dx Club. Home: 528 Meadowview Dr La Canada Flintridge CA 91011-2816

BYRNE, GERARD ANTHONY, publishing company executive, marketing consultant; b. N.Y.C., Apr. 27, 1944; s. Thomas Edward and Eileen (Reilly) B.; m. Elizabeth Julia Daly, Dec. 6, 1969; children: Megan, Gavin. BA in Econs., Fordham U., 1966. Advt. sales rep. N.Y. Daily News, N.Y.C., 1969-73, Advt. Age, N.Y.C., 1973-77; internat. sales dir. Advt. Age, 1977-80; ea. sales mgr. Advt. Age, N.Y.C., 1980-82; pub., v.p. Electronic Media, N.Y.C., 1982-84; v.p./pub. Crain's N.Y. Bus., N.Y.C., 1984-87; v.p., dir. corp. communications Crain Communications, N.Y.C., 1987-88; sr. v.p. corp. planning and internat. devel. Act III Pub., N.Y.C., 1988-89; pub. Variety, N.Y.C., 1990-92, v.p., dir. pub. ops., 1993-95; group v.p., pub. Daily Variety and Weekly Variety, N.Y.C., 1996-97; v.p., group pub. Variety, Inc., N.Y.C., 1997—. Bd. dirs. African Med. Relief Found., Environ. Media Assn., Operation Smile Internat., Cath. Youth Orgn., N.Y.C., Mus. Moving Image, The Intrepid Mus., The Westhampton Performing Arts Ctr. Capt. USMC, 1966-69, Vietnam. Recipient combat action ribbon, Navy achievement medal, Show East Salah Hassanein Humanitarian award, 1996; named Pub. of Yr., East Midtown C. of C., 1986. Mem. Internat. Radio and TV Soc., N.Y. Athletic Club, VFW, Friendly Sons of St. Patrick, Greater Miami C. of C. (co-chair long-range planning com. entertainment task force). Roman Catholic. Avocations: fishing, tennis, photography, skiing, golf. Home: 10 Wintergreen Way Quogue NY 11959 Office: Cahners Pub Co Divsn Reed Elsevier 5700 Wilshire Blvd Ste 120 Los Angeles CA 90036-3659

BYRNE, JOHN VINCENT, higher education consultant; b. Hempstead, N.Y., May 9, 1928; s. Frank E. and Kathleen (Barry) B.; m. Shirley O'Connor, Nov. 26, 1954; children: Donna, Lisa, Karen, Steven. AB, Hamilton Coll., 1951, JD (hon.), 1994; MA, Columbia U., 1953; PhD, U. So. Calif., 1957. Research geologist Humble Oil & Refinery Co., Houston, 1957-60; assoc. prof. Oreg. State U., Corvallis, 1960-66, prof. oceanography, 1966—, chmn. dept., 1968-72, dean Sch. Oceanography, 1972-76, acting dean research, 1976-77, dean research, 1977-80, v.p. for research and grad. studies, 1980-81, pres., 1984-95; adminstr. NOAA, Washington, 1981-84; pres. Oreg. State U., 1984-95; higher edn. cons. Corvallis, 1996—; program dir. oceanography NSF, 1966-67; exec. dir. Kellogg Commn. on Future of State and Land Grant Univs., 1996—; dir. Oreg. Coast Aquarium, Harbor Br. Ocean Inst. Recipient Carter teaching award Oreg. State U., 1964. Fellow AAAS, Geol. Soc. Am., Am. Meteorol. Soc.; mem. Am. Assn. Petroleum Geologists, Am. Geophys. Union, Sigma Xi, Chi Psi. Home: 3190 NW Deer Run St Corvallis OR 97330-3107 Office: Autzen House 811 SW Jefferson Ave Corvallis OR 97333-4506

BYRNE, NOEL THOMAS, sociologist, educator; b. San Francisco, May 11, 1943; s. Joseph Joshua and Naomi Pearl (Denison) B.; m. Dale W. Elrod, Aug. 6, 1989. BA in Sociology, Sonoma State Coll., 1971; MA in Sociology, Rutgers U., 1975, PhD in Sociology, 1987. Instr. sociology Douglass Coll., Rutgers U., New Brunswick, N.J., 1974-76, Hartnell Coll., Salinas, Calif., 1977-78; from lectr. to assoc. prof. dept. mgmt. Sonoma State U., Rohnert Park, Calif., 1978-94, chmn. dept. of mgmt., 1990-91, from. assoc. prof. to prof. sociology dept., 1994—, chmn. dept. sociology, 1997—; cons. prof. Emile Durkheim Inst. for Advanced Study, Grand Cayman, B.W.I., 1990-93. Contbr. articles and revs. to profl. lit. Recipient Del Pub. award Rutgers U. Grad. Sociology Program, 1976, Louis Bevier fellow, 1977-78. Mem. AAAS, Am. Sociol. Assn., Pacific Sociol. Assn., N.Y. Acad. Sci., Soc. for Study Symbolic Interaction (rev. editor Jour. 1980-83), Soc. for Study Social Problems, Commonwealth Club. Democrat. Home: PO Box 660 Cotati CA 94931-0660 Office: Sonoma State U Dept Sociology Rohnert Park CA 94928

BYRNE, THOMAS J., lawyer; b. Rochester, N.Y., June 17, 1944; m. Brenda C. Byrne, June 4, 1994; children: Thomas, David, Heather. AB, U. Rochester, 1967; JD, U. Denver, 1976. Bar: Colo. 1977, Calif. 1977, U.S. Ct. Appeals (10th cir.) 1977, U.S. Dist. Ct. Colo. 1977, U.S. Dist. Ct. (so. dist.) Tex. 1990, N.Y. 1990, U.S. Ct. Appeals (3d cir.) 1992, U.S. Dist. Ct. (ea. dist.) Pa. 1992, U.S. Dist. Ct. (ea. dist.) Va. 1992, U.S. Ct. Appeals (4th cir.) 1993, U.S. Dist. Ct. (no. dist.) Ill. 1993, U.S. Dist. Ct. Ariz. 1993, U.S. Dist. Ct. Utah 1996, U.S. Dist. Ct. (so. dist.) N.Y. 1997. Law clk. Dist. Ct. Colo., Denver, 1976-77; assoc. Ullstrom Law Offices, Denver, 1978-83; ptnr., Denver mgr. Conklin & Adler, Ltd., Denver and Chgo., 1983-86; mng. ptnr. Byrne, Kiely & White LLP, Denver, 1986—. Mem. fin. com. Citizens for Romer, Denver, 1990—. Capt. USAF, 1967-73. Mem. ABA (tort and ins. practice sect., vice chair aviation and space law com., litigation sect., forum on air and space law), Internat. Bar Assn., Colo. Bar Assn., Denver Bar Assn., State Bar Calif., N.Y. State Bar Assn., Def. Rsch. Inst., Colo. Def. Lawyers Assn., Nat. Bus. Aircraft Assn., Lawyer-Pilot Bar Assn., Aviation Ins. Assn. Avocations: flying, travel, sports. Office: Byrne Kiely & White LLP 1120 Lincoln St Ste 1300 Denver CO 80203-2140

BYRNE, WILLIAM MATTHEW, JR., federal judge; b. L.A., Sept. 3, 1930; s. William Matthew Sr. and Julia Ann (Lamb) B. BS, U. So. Calif., 1953, LLB, 1956; LLD, Loyola U., 1971. Bar: Calif. 1956. Ptnr. Dryden, Harrington & Schwartz, 1960-67; asst. atty U.S. Dist. Ct. (so. dist.) Calif., 1958-60; atty. U.S. Dist. Ct. (cen. dist.) Calif., Los Angeles, 1967-70, judge, 1971—; now sr. judge U.S. Dist. Ct. (cen. dist.) Calif.; exec. dir. Pres. Nixon's Commn. Campus Unrest, 1970; instr. Loyola Law Sch., Harvard U., Whittier Coll. Served with USAF, 1956-58. Mem. ABA, Fed. Bar Assn., Calif. Bar Assn., Los Angeles County Bar Assn. (vice chmn. human rights sect.), Am. Judicature Soc. Office: US Dist Ct 110 Dist Courthouse 312 N Spring St Ste 110 Los Angeles CA 90012-4703

BYRNE-DEMPSEY, CECELIA, journalist; b. L.A., Aug. 7, 1925; d. John Joseph and Margaret Agnes (Frakell) B.; m. John Dempsey, Mar. 25, 1951 (dec. June 1981); children: Margaret, Elizabeth, John, Cecelia, Catherine, Patricia, Bridget, Charles, Mary Teresa. *Cecelia's Great Grandmother Hannah Payne Loftus' father, Sea Captain Robert Payne witnessed and wrote about the Boston Tea Party. Three years prior, in 1770, her Uncle Edward Payne, Esq., observed the Boston Massacre from his shop doorway and was wounded. Also in Boston, 1770, her Grandfather, Sir Ralph Payne, later Baron, became the Royal Appointed Governor of the Leeward Islands in the Caribbean Sea. After 35 years of stewardship, he was instrumental in the English Parliamentary process of the Emancipation of Slavery in the Islands. John Adams granted her father a presidential pardon for his loyalist activities during the War of Independence.* Student, Immaculate Heart Coll., 1944; BA in Psychology, Calif. State U., Northridge, 1975, BA in Journalism, 1978, MA in Mass Communication, 1992. Staff Lockheed Aircraft Corp., Burbank, Calif., 1943—, Office Naval Rsch., San Francisco, 1947—; with Sisters of Mercy, Burlingame, Calif., 1945—, Sisters of Presentation, San Francisco, 1949—; mem. staff Calif. State U., Calif., 1976—; rschr., journalism historian early Am. newspapers, 1978—. Mentor 4-H Club; past mem. Urban Corp., L.A. Mem. Mensa, Kappa Gamma Delta. Republican. Jewish. Avocations: poetry, gardening, philosophical meditation.

BYRNES, EDWARD RICHARD, JR., sales and marketing executive; b. North Tonawanda, N.Y.; s. Edward Richard Byrnes Sr. and Julia Ann (Keleman) Herman; m. Joan Marie Ellison, Dec. 6, 1958; children: Kathleen Elizabeth Byrnes Reitman, Ann Marie Byrnes Peterson, Edward Richard III, Eleanor Frances Byrnes Kraynak, William Michael. BSChemE, BSMetE, U. Mich., 1960; MBA in Mktg., No. Ill. U., 1987. Chief metallurgist, engring. sci. divn. Am. Metal Products, Ann Arbor, Mich., 1959-64; mktg. mgr. Abar Ipsen Industries, Rockford, Ill., 1964-97; dir. key accounts GM Enterprises, Corona, Calif., 1997—. Author: Vacuum Heat Treating, edit. 4, vol. 4, 1984. Pack chmn. Boy Scouts Am., Rockford, 1968-74. Mem. Am. Soc. Materials (mem., chmn. coms. Rockford chpt. 1964-97, chmn. chpt. 1978-79, presenter 1972, 80, Pres.'s award 1997), KC. Roman Catholic. Avocations: reading, gardening, golf. Home: 765 Orange Hill Dr Corona CA 91719 Office: GM Enterprises 525 Klug Cir Corona CA 91720-5452

BYRNES, LAWRENCE WILLIAM, dean; b. Windsor, Ont., Can., June 17, 1940; s. Carl Wilfred and Alice Hendrie (Thomson) B.; m. Margaret Amelia Snavely, June 26, 1965; children: Andrew Carl, Mary Margaret. BA in Social Sci., Mich. State U., 1963, MA in History, 1967, PhD in Edn., 1970. Tchr. social studies Grosse Pointe (mich.) Schs., 1963-66; prof. Calif. State U., Northridge, 1969-78; dean edn. Southeastern La. U., Hammond, 1978-83, Moorhead (Minn.) State U., 1983-88, Edinboro (Pa.) U., 1988-91; dir. Ctr. for Teaching and Learning U. So. Colo., 1991-95; dean Coll. Edn. and Tech. Eastern N.Mex. U., Portales, 1995—; ptnr., cons. ML Byrnes and Assocs., Erie, Pa. Author: Religion and Republic Education, 1975; co-author: Total Quality Management in Higher Education, 1991, The Quality Teacher: Implementing TQM in the Classroom, 1992. Mem. Gov.'s Steering Com. on Strengthening Quality in Schs., N. Mex. Mem. Am. Assn. Colls. Tchr. Edn. (chmn. global and internat. tchrs. edn. com.), N. Mex. Assn. Colls. Tchr. Edn. (pres.), Phi Delta Kappa (pres. Moorhead chpt. 1987-88, historian Erie chpt. 1991—. hist. South Colo. chpt. 1994—). Democrat. Episcopalian. Avocations: running, drums, music. Home: 416 E 17th Ln Portales NM 88130-9266 Office: ENMU Coll Edn & Tech Portales NM 88130

BYRNES, PETER, lawyer; b. Albuquerque, Feb. 28, 1970; s. Joe and Anna (Hunter) B. BA, U. N.Mex., 1992, JD, 1993. Bar: N.Mex. 1993. Ptnr. Werik & Byrnes, Clovis, N.Mex., 1993—; adj. mem. faculty U. N.Mex. Contbr. articles to profl. jours. Active United Way. Mem. ABA, N.Mex. Lawyers Assn. Democrat. Roman Catholic. Avocations: reading, movies. Office: Werik & Byrnes 121 W 4th St Clovis NM 88101-7405

BYSSHE, FREDERICK HERBERT, JR., lawyer; b. Long Beach, Calif., Sept. 16, 1937; s. Frederick H. and Virginia (Sterzing) B.; m. Judith Reaves, Feb. 13, 1982; children: Michael Adams, Kelly Rains, Mark Rains, Christopher Ernest. BA, U. Redlands, 1959; JD, U. Calif., San Francisco, 1962. Bar: Calif. 1963, U.S. Ct. Appeals (9th cir.) 1963. Dep. dist. atty. Riverside (Calif.) County, 1963-66, chief trial dep., 1966-68, chief dep. dist. atty., 1968-70; pvt. practice Ventura, Calif., 1970—; lectr. U. Calif., 1968-69. Assoc. editor U. Calif. Hastings Law Rev., 1961-62. Pres. Riverside County Peace Officers Assn., 1968; mem. Ventura County Cancer Soc., 1978-80; trustee Ventura County Law Library, 1974-79, v.p.; bd. dirs. Boys & Girls Clubs Ventura County, Ventura County YMCA, 1972-75. With USAR, 1963-69. Named Ventura Citizen of the Yr., 1990. Mem. ABA, Ventura County Bar Assn. (exec. com. 1973-74, pres. 1982), Ventura County Criminal Bar Assn. (pres. 1973), Ventura County Trial Lawyers Assn. (pres. 1978-79), Consumer Attys. Calif. (state bd. govs. 1993—), Rotary (pres. Ventura County chpt. 1976). Republican. Office: 10 S California St Ventura CA 93001-2802

BYYNY, RICHARD LEE, academic administrator, physician; b. South Gate, Calif., Jan. 6, 1939; s. Oswald and Essa Burnetta (McGinnis) B.; m. Jo Ellen Garverick, Aug. 25, 1962; children: Kristen, Jan, Richard. BA in History, U. So. Calif., 1960, MD, 1964. Intern and resident in internal medicine Columbia Presbyn. Med. Ctr., N.Y.C., 1964-66, chief resident, 1968-69; fellow in endocrinology Vanderbilt U., Nashville, 1969-71; asst. prof. medicine U. Chgo., 1971-74, head div. internal medicine, 1972-77, assoc. prof., 1975-77; prof. internal medicine U. Colo., Denver, 1977—, head div. internal medicine, 1977-94; vice-chmn. dept. medicine U. Colo. Health Scis. Ctr., Denver, 1977-85; exec. vice chancellor U. Colo., Denver, 1994-95, v.p. acad. affairs, 1995-97; chancellor U. Colo., Boulder, 1997—; med. dir. ambulatory care, 1990-92; mem. Coun. on Econ. Devel., Boulder, Colo. Author: A Clinical Guide in the Care of Older Women, 1990, 95; contbr. numerous articles to profl. jours., chpts. to textbooks, monographs. Pres. Ill. Council Continuing Med. Edn., Ill., 1976-77; bd. dirs. Denver affiliate Am. Heart Assn., 1987— (pres. 1994-95), Boulder Com. Hosp., 1997—, U.S. Coun. on Competitiveness Big 12 Conf. Served to capt. USAF, 1966-68. Recipient Merck award U. So. Calif., 1964; Am. Coun. Edn. fellow, 1992-93. Fellow ACP; mem. AAAS, Soc. for Gen. Internal Medicine (pres. 1979-80), Am. Soc. Hypertension, Western Soc. Clin. Investigation, Endocrine Soc., Am. Fedn. for Clin. Rsch., Am. Coun. Edn. (commn. leadership instl. effectiveness), Alpha Omega Alpha (bd. dirs. 1996—). Clubs: U. Club Denver; Arapahoe Tennis (Englewood, Colo.), Boulder Country Club. Avocations: tennis, skiing, running, surfing, sailing. Fax: 303-492-8866. E-mail: richard.byyny@colorado.edu. Home: 2900 Park Lake Dr Boulder CO 80301-5139 Office: Office of Chancellor Regent Adminstrv Ctr Room 301 Campus Box 17 Boulder CO 80309-0017

CABADA, JOSE LUIS, publisher; b. Callao, Peru, Jan. 30, 1935; s. Luis S. Cabada and Felicia (Delgado) Nolasco; m. Patricia Seymour, Apr. 12, 1968 (div. Mar. 1973); children: Corali, Luis, Felicia, Anita; m. Eleanor Weis, mar. 3, 1983. AA, Columbia Coll., L.A., 1964; cert., Calif. State U., Fullerton, 1993, Colegio de Periodistas de Lima, Peru, 1988, 1996. Reporter Ultima Hora newspaper, Lima, Peru, 1955-59; disc jockey Sta. KOFY, San Francisco, 1970-72; news dir. Sta. KEMO-TV, San Francisco, 1973; fgn. corr. Expreso newspaper, Lima, 1970-85, numerous pubs., Lima, 1985—; pres. Mayta Multimedia Enterprises Inc., Dana Point, Calif., 1987. Author, editor: No Perdida de la nacionalidad peruana; publ., editor: Peru de los 90. Recipient Orden de la Paz award Instituto de Desarrollo y Accion Social, Lima, 1993, Medalla Civica Municipalidad de La Victoria, Lima, 1996. Mem. Colegio de Periodistas del Peru. Avocations: writing, photography, traveling. Home: 24042 Leeward Dr Dana Point CA 92629-4454 Office: Peru de los 90 PO Box 6152 Laguna Niguel CA 92607-6152

CABLE, MARY, writer; b. Cleve., Jan. 24, 1920; d. Robert Winthrop and Elizabeth (Southwick) Pratt; m. Arthur Goodrich Cable, May 25, 1949 (dec. Mar. 1997); 1 child, Cassandra. BA, Barnard Coll., 1941. Various editl. positions New Yorker, N.Y.C., 1944-49, Harper's Bazaar, N.Y.C., 1949-51; assoc. editor Am. Heritage and Horizon, N.Y.C., 1964-66. Author: Black Odyssey: The Case of the Slaveship Amistad, 1971, paperback edit., 1997, The Little Darlings: How Children Have Been Brought Up in America, 1975, Lost New Orleans, 1981 (La. Libr. Assn. award 1981), The Blizzard of '88, 1988, 7 others; contbr. many short stories and articles to lit. publs. Grantee, Nat. Endowment for Arts, 1977, NEH, 1978.

CABOT, ANTHONY NATHAN, lawyer, educator; b. Lakewood, Ohio, June 8, 1956; s. Nathan and Lucy (Costanzo) C.; m. Linda Marie Lewandowski, Nov. 24, 1982; children: Nicolas Trace, Dani Marie. BA in Social Svc., Cleve. State U., 1978; JD, Ariz. State U., 1981. Ptnr. Lionel Sawyer & Collins, Las Vegas, Nev., 1981—; adj. prof. Internat. Gaming Inst., Las Vegas, 1994—. Author: Casino Gaming: Policy Economics and Regulation, 1996, Internet Gambling, 1997, 3d edit. 1999; editor: International Casino Law, 1994, 3d edit. 1999, Nevada Gaming Law, 1995, 3d edit. 1999. Bd. advisors U. Nev. Internat. Gaming Inst., Las Vegas, 1994—, Las Vegas Art Mus., 1997; chmn. bd. dirs. Gaming Industry Ann. Rerts Awards, Las Vegas, 1997. Mem. Internat. Assn. Gaming Attys. (gen. counsel 1989-90, pres. 1992-94), Casino Mgmt. Assn. (bd. dirs. 1994-98). Avocations: baseball, computer technology. Home: 5450 Mantela Cir Las Vegas NV 89118 Office: Lionel Sawyer & Collins 300 S 4th St Ste 1700 Las Vegas NV 89101-6053

CABOT, HUGH, III, painter, sculptor; b. Boston, Mar. 22, 1930; s. Hugh and Louise (Melanson) C.; m. Olivia P. Taylor, Sept. 8, 1967; student Boston Museum, 1948, Ashmolean Mus., Oxford, Eng., 1960, Coll. Ams., Mexico City, 1956, San Carlos Acad., Mexico City. Portrait, landscape painter; sculptor in bronze; one-man shows: U.S. Navy Hist. and Recreation Dept., U.S. Navy Art Gallery, The Pentagon, Nat. War Mus., Washington, La Muse de la Marine, Paris; group shows include: Tex. Tri-state, 1969 (1st, 2d, 3d prizes), Starmont Vail Med. Ctr. Topeka, Kans., Tucson Med. Ctr. Ariz., Harwood Found. Taos, N.Mex., Washburn U. Topeka, Kans., U. Ariz. Tucson, Ariz. Served as ofcl. artist USN, Korean War. Named Artist of Yr., Scottsdale, Ariz., 1978, 30th ann. Clubs: Salmagundi (N.Y.C.). Author, illustrator: Korea I (Globe).

CABRALES, LUISITA KATIGBAK, nurse administrator, consultant, entrepreneur; b. Lipa City, Batangas, The Philippines, June 8, 1950; came to U.S., 1985; d. Luis Ramirez and Teofila Dimaano (Maoatañgay) Katigbak; m. Anastacio Japzon Cabrales, Jan. 9, 1974; children: Christopher Allan, Christian Albert, Chester Arvin, Ana Luisa. BS in Commerce, U. Santo Tomas, Manila, 1971; BSBA, U. of East, Manila, 1985. Lic. vocat. nurse, Calif. Merchant teller Tokai Bank, L.A., 1985-86; sr. credit analyst Tokai Credit Corp., Pasadena, Calif., 1986-89; office mgr. ARA Corp. San Gabriel Med. Ctr., Pasadena, Calif., 1989-91; charge nurse Heritage Manor, Monterey Park, Calif., 1992-95, San Gabriel (Calif.) Convalescent, 1992-93; office mgr., acct. Bethany Home Health, Pasadena, 1993; pres., CEO Healthcare Providers Calif., Walnut, 1995—; ptnr. Med. Billing Solutions, Walnut, 1995—. Mem. NAFE. Office: Healthcare Providers Calif PO Box 454 Walnut CA 91788-0454

CADE, JACK CARLTON, marketing professional; b. San Mateo, Calif., Mar. 9, 1948; s. Ross Dean and Florence Evelyn (Carlton) C. AA in Vacuum Tech., San Jose City Coll., 1968; BS in Bus., San Jose State U., 1972. Budget analyst Naval Elec. Lab. Ctr., San Diego, 1972-75, Dept. of the Air Force, Sunnyvale, Calif., 1975-78; contract negotiator Dept. of the Air Force, Sunnyvale, 1978-80, staff price analyst, 1980-81, sr. contract negotiator, 1981-82, contracting officer, 1982-86; sr. contract specialist Lockheed Martin Western Devel. Lab., San Jose, Calif.,, 1986-93; contract mgr. space programs Loral Aerospace Corp., Sunnyvale, 1993-95; dir. of contracts, 1995—. Mem. Air and Space Mus., active cen. com. Santa Clara (Calif.) County Rep. Party, 1969-72; team mgr., league pres. El Camino Little League, Santa Clara, 1982-83; pres. council San Jose State U.; bd. dirs. Santa Clara County Big Bros., 1972. Mem. Nat. Contract Mgmt. Assn., San Jose State U. Alumni Assn. (bd. dirs.), Smithsonian Assocs., Yosemite Fund Club. Avocations: football, outdoors. Home: 1756 Roll St Santa Clara CA 95050-4024 Office: Lockheed Martin Western Devel Labs 3200 Zanker Rd San Jose CA 95134-1949

CADIERO-KAPLAN, KAREN, education and English educator; b. Wilmington, Mass., May 29, 1958; d. Emmanuel James Cadiero and Theresa (Gagnon) English; m. Roger Mark Kaplan, June 9, 1985. BA in Psychology, U. San Diego, 1989; MA in Policy Studies in Lang., Cross-Cultural Edn., San Diego State U., 1994, postgrad., 1996—. Cert. learning handicapped specialist, multiple subject K-12 tchr. ESL, Culture, Lang. and Devel. and social/emotional disturbed, Calif. Spl. day class tchr., job coach coord. Inst. for Effective Edn., San Diego, 1989-92; spl. day class tchr. San Diego Unified Sch. Dist., 1992-93; ESL instr. San Diego Job Corps, Imperial Beach, 1993-94; spl. edn. instr. Grossmont Union H.S. Dist., El Cajon, Calif., 1995-96; ESL instr. Grossmont C.C., El Cajon, Calif., 1994—; tchr. edn. Am. Reads coord. San Diego State U., 1997—; test devel. coord. (ESL program) Grossmont Coll., 1996-99; tech. coord. Cesar Chavez Elem. Sch., San Diego, 1997; reading cons. CETYS Diplomado, Tijuano, Baja, Calif., Mex., 1998; presenter in field. Vol. Peace essay contest Peace Resource Ctr., San Diego, 1996-97. Recipient Ernest Boyer Grant Tech. Devel. grant Corp. Pub. Broadcasting, 1997-98. Mem. TESOL, Am. Edn. Rsch. Assn., Nat. Assn. Bilingual Edn., Calif. TESOL. Avocations: hiking, rock climbing, reading, camping. Office: San Diego State U Coll Edn 5500 Campanile Dr San Diego CA 92182

CAFFEY, BENJAMIN FRANKLIN, civil and mechanical engineer; b. Jacksonville, Fla., Nov. 18, 1927; s. Eugene Mead and Catherine (Howell) C.; m. Laura Marlowe, Oct. 2, 1949 (dec. Jan. 1991); children: Benjamin, John, Lochlin; m. Suzanne Morris, Aug. 10, 1991; stepchildren: Jay, Julie, Kelly. BCE, Ga. Inst. Tech., 1949; MSCE, U. So. Calif., L.A., 1964. Registered profl. engr., Calif.; cert. project mgmt. profl. Resident engr. Sch. Dist. of Glendale, Calif., 1950-51; constrn. engr. Fluor Corp., L.A., 1951-56; v.p. Petroleum Combustion & Engring. Co., L.A., 1956-58, Sesler & Caffey, Inc., Gardena, Calif., 1958-69, Fluor Corp., L.A., 1969-76; pres. Fluor Arabia, Ltd., Saudi Arabia, 1976-81; sr. v.p. Fluor Daniel, Inc., Irvine, Calif., 1981—; adv. bd. Ga. Tech. Sch. Civil Engring., Atlanta, 1992—. Lt. U.S. Army, 1946-48; lt. col. USAR (ret.). Fellow ASCE; mem. Project Mgmt. Inst. (trustee 1991), Soc. Am. Mil. Engrs., Chi Epsilon. Republican. Episcopalian. Office: Fluor Daniel Inc 3353 Michelson Dr Irvine CA 92698-0001

CAHAN, CHRISTOPHER SYKES, journalist; b. N.Y.C., July 21, 1953; s. William George and Mary Arnold (Sykes) C.; m. Vicki Bunch, Apr. 21, 1988; children: Joseph, Nicolas. BA, Sarah Lawrence, 1975. Assoc. producer NBC Network News, L.A., 1978-82; producer newswriter KNBC, KABC, KCOP, L.A., 1983-89; producer Financial News Network, L.A., 1989-91; producer assign editor ABC Network News, L.A., 1993-95; assignment mgr. Fox News Channel, L.A., 1998—. Recipient Communicator of Yr. Assn. of Visual Communicators, 1986, 1985, Nat. Emmy award Acad. TV Arts & Scis., 1981. Office: Fox News Channel 2044 Armacost Ave West Los Angeles CA 90025-6113

CAHILL, ANDRE G., video producer, editor; b. Montreal, Que., Can., Oct. 15, 1943; s. Walter Bernard and Jeanne (Pinsonneault) C.; m. Mary Sue Tate (div. 1980); 2 children; m. Ana Cristy Rosales; 2 children. BA, Notre Dame Coll., Montreal, 1964. Mgr. Wells Fargo Bank/Telecom., San Francisco; owner Video Images Prodn., Rohnert Park, Calif.; cons. North Bay Videographers, Rohnert Park, 1988—. Sgt. U.S. Army, 1964-67. Mem. Assn. Profl. Videographers, Profl. Video Assn. of North Bay, Wedding/Event Videographers Assn. Avocations: camping, tennis, 4-wheel driving. Office: Video Images Prodns 1088 Holly Ave Rohnert Park CA 94928-1508

CAHILL, MICHAEL EDWARD, general counsel, managing director; b. Montreal, Quebec, Can., Feb. 22, 1951; m. Tania de Jong, Aug. 23, 1985. BA, Bishop's U., 1972; LLB, Osgoode Hall, Toronto, 1975; LLM, Harvard U., 1978. Bar: Can. 1977, Calif. 1978, U.S. Dist. Ct. (so. dist.) Calif. 1978, U.S. Supreme Ct. 1983, Ont., Can. 1977. Prin. Shenas & Robbins, San Diego, 1978-83, O'Melveny & Myers, Los Angeles, 1983-89; sr. v.p., gen. counsel Act III Communications, L.A., 1989-91; mng. dir., gen. counsel Trust Co. of the West, L.A., 1991—. Barlow scholarship, 1976. Mem. ABA (com. on fed. regulation of securities), Calif. State Bar Assn. (com. for corp. counsel), Assn. of Corporate Counsel of Am. (bd. dirs.), Constitution Rights Found. (bd. dirs.). Office: Trust Co of the West 865 S Figueroa St Los Angeles CA 90017-2543

CAHILL, RICHARD FREDERICK, lawyer; b. Columbus, Nebr., June 18, 1953; s. Donald Francis and Hazel Fredeline (Garbers) C.; m. Helen Marie Girard, Dec. 4, 1982; children: Jacqueline Michelle, Catherine Elizabeth, Marc Alexander. Student, Worcester Coll., Oxford, 1973; BA with highest honors, UCLA, 1975; JD, U. Notre Dame, 1978. Bar: Calif. 1978, U.S. Dist. Ct. (ea. dist.) Calif. 1978, U.S. Dist. Ct. (cen. dist.) Calif. 1983, U.S. Dist. Ct. (so. dist.) Calif. 1992, U.S. Ct. Appeals (9th cir.) 1992. Dep. dist. atty. Tulare County Dist. Atty., Visalia, Calif., 1978-81; staff atty. Supreme Ct. of Nev., Carson City, 1981-83; assoc. Acret & Perochet, Brentwood, Calif., 1983-84, Thelen, Marrin, Johnson & Bridges, L.A., 1984-89; ptnr. Hammond Zuetel & Cahill, Pasadena, Calif., 1989-98, Pivo & Halbreich, Irvine, Calif., 1999—. Mem. Pasadena Bar Assn., Los Angeles County Bar Assn., Assn. So. Calif. Defense Counsel, Notre Dame Legal Aid and Defender Assn. (assoc. dir.), Phi Beta Kappa, Phi Alpha Delta (charter, v.p. 1977-78), Pi

Gamma Mu, Phi Alpha Theta (charter pres. 1973-74), Phi Eta Sigma, Sigma Chi. Republican. Roman Catholic. Avocation: tennis. Home: 201 Windwood Ln Sierra Madre CA 91024-2677 Office: Pivo & Halbreich 1920 Main St Ste 800 Irvine CA 92614-7227

CAI, TIAN TAO, artist; b. Guangzhou, China, July 21, 1941; s. Hong and Xiao Yun (Lee) C. Dean dept. art Guangming Sch., Guangzhou, 1978-86; pres. Guangzhou Oriental Art Rsch. Inst., 1980-86; dean Chinese painting dept. Guangzhou Fine Art U., 1984-86; vis. prof. Nat. Art Acad., Stuttgart, Germany, 1986, Oriental Rsch. Inst., Heidelburg (Germany) U., 1987; pres. Tiaotao Art Ctr., San Marino, Calif., 1990—. Exhibited in group shows at Chinese Fine Arts Show, The Philippines, 1978, 80, Guangzhou, 1980, Chinese Worls of Art Exhbn., Fukuoka, Japan, 1980, Chinese Famous Artists Calligraphy and Painting Exhbn., Hong Kong, 1981, Himeji, Japan, 1983, Kobe, Japan, 1984, Singapore, 1984, Famous Artists Calligraphy and Painting Exhbn., Macau, 1984, Contemporary Famous Artists Calligraphy and Painting Exhbn., Hong Kong, 1985, Five Province Show Ctrl. and So. China, Guangzhou, 1985 (Award of Excellence), Locarno, Switzerland, 1986, Stuttgart, Germany, 1986, Heilbronne, Germany, 1986, Kaufbeuren, Germany, 1986, Tubingen, Germany, 1987, 5th U.S. Joint Exhbn. Internat. Artists, San Francisco, 1988 (1st place award 1988), Monterey Park, Calif., 1988, L.A., 1989, Toronto, Can., 1989, Alhambra, Calif., 1990, Pasadena, Calif., 1991, San Marino, Calif., 1992, San Francisco, 1993; represented in numerous permanent collections; contbr. articles to profl. jours. Mem. Chinese Artists Assn., Profl. Painters Rsch. Inst. Arts and History, Chinese Liberal Arts Alliance Assn. Avocations: stone collecting, literature, travel. Office: Tian Tao Art Ctr 2326 Huntington Dr San Marino CA 91108-2641

CAIN, PATRICIA JEAN, accountant; b. Decatur, Ill., Sept. 28, 1931; d. Paul George and Jean Margaret (Horne) Jacka; m. Dan Louis Cain, July 12, 1952; children: Mary Ann, Timothy George, Paul Louis. Student, U. Mich., 1949-52, Pasadena (Calif.) City Coll., 1975-76; BS in Acctg., Calif. State U., L.A., 1977, MBA, 1978; M in Taxation, Golden Gate U., Los Angeles, 1988; Diploma in Pastry, Hotel Ritz, France, 1991. CPA, Calif.; cert. personal fin. planner; cert. advanced fin. planner. Tax supr. Stonefield & Josephson, L.A., 1979-87; CFO Loubella Extendables, Inc., L.A., 1987-96; pvt. practice Pasadena, Calif., 1996—; participant program in bus. ethics U. So. Calif., L.A., 1986; trainer for A-Plus in house tax Arthur Andersen & Co., 1989-90; instr. Becker CPA Rev. Course, 1989-93. Bd. dirs. Sierra Madre coun. Girl Scouts U.S.A., 1968-73, treas., 1973-75, nat. del., 1975; mem. Town Hall, L.A., 1987—, L.A. Bus. Forum, 1991—. Listed as one of top six tax experts in L.A. by Money mag., 1987. Mem. AICPA (chair nat. tax teleconf. 1988, taxation com./forms subcom. 1994—), Am. Women's Soc. CPAs (bd. dirs. 1986-87, v.p. 1987-90), Calif. Soc. CPAs (chair free tax assistance program 1983-85, high road com. 1985-86, chair pub. rels. com. 1985-89, microcomputer users discussion group taxation com., fin. com./speaker computer show and conf. 1987-93, planning com. and speaker San Francisco Tax and Microcomputer show 1988, state com. on taxation 1991—, speaker Tax Update 1992, dir. L.A. chpt. 1993-95, v.p. 1995-96), Internat. Arabian Horse Assn., Wrightwood Country Club, Beta Alpha Psi. Democrat. Episcopalian. Avocations: gourmet cooking, hiking, fishing, rug making, Arabian horses.

CAIN, ROBERT JOSEPH, elementary school educator; b. Floral Park, N.Y., June 18, 1947; s. Edwin Thomas and Cecilia Marie (Dunn) C. BA in English, Hofstra U., 1972; BA in Edn., Ariz. State U., 1978, MEd, 1988. Cert. elem. tchr. Auditor Williamsburgh Savs. Bank, Bklyn., 1973-74; skip tracer, adjuster Ariz. Bank, Phoenix, 1974-75; tchr. 1st & 2d grade Paradise Valley Unified Sch. Dist. #69, Phoenix, 1979—. Actor City of Phoenix Shakespeare, 1978, Janus Theatre, Phoenix, 1980-81; actor, dir. Glendale Little Theatre, 1974-80; cantor St. Joseph's Ch., 1974—; benefactor Ariz. Opera, 1989—; supporter Met. Opera, 1980—; mem. Titanic Hist. Soc., 1980—. With U.S. Army, 1968-69. Republican. Roman Catholic. Avocations: singing, acting, antique record players and 78 rpm records, Titanic memorabilia and history, Maria Callas bibliography and discography. Home: 11012 N 45th St Phoenix AZ 85028-3013 Office: Quail Run Elem Sch 3303 E Utopia Rd Phoenix AZ 85050-3900

CAINE, CAROLYN MOORE, activist, publishing executive, author, consultant; b. Oakland, Calif., June 10, 1922; d. Rollin Bascom and Mildred (Knox) M.; m. George Eccles Caine, Jan. 24, 1946 (dvi. July 1, 1972); children: Lynda, George Jr., Lisa. Student, Berkeley (Calif.) H.S., 1940. Asst. to dir. ARC, Oakland, Calif., 1943-44; social worker Children's Hosp., Oakland, Calif., 1944-45; asst. to treas. Markle Found., N.Y.C., 1947-49; rsch. dir. Data Rsch. Inst., Salt Lake City, 1970-71; cons., mem. panel NEA, Washington, 1974-78; bd. dirs., pres. Utah Environ. Ctr., Salt Lake City, 1973-79. Author: On Your Own in San Francisco, 1988, rev. edit., 1996. State chair ARTRAIN, Salt Lake City, 1972-73, Utah's Festival of Arts for Young, Salt Lake City, 1972-78; bd. dirs., chair Women's Coun. U. Utah, Salt Lake City, 1972-77; adv. Congressman Lloyd, Salt Lake City, 1975-77; mem., officer Sister City Com., Salt Lake City, 1974-79; cons. Sustainable San Francisco, 1995-96. Recipient Civic Beautification award Salt Lake City, 1971, award of Merit Met. Transp. Commn., San Francisco, 1996; named Most Admired Woman Phi Mu Sorority, 1977. Mem. Internat. Diplomacy Coun., Sr. Action Network, Jr. League, San Francisco Planning and Urban Rsch. Assn. Avocations: travel, reading, photography, research. Office: Blue Pearl Press PO Box 460548 San Francisco CA 94146-0548

CAINE, STEPHEN HOWARD, data processing executive; b. Washington, Feb. 11, 1941; s. Walter E. and Jeanette (Wenborne) C. Student Calif. Inst. Tech., 1958-62. Sr. programmer Calif. Inst. Tech., Pasadena, 1962-65, mgr. sys. programming, 1965-69, mgr. programming, 1969-70; pres. Caine, Farber & Gordon, Inc., Pasadena, 1970—; gen. mgr. Gatekeeper Systems, Pasadena, 1995—; lectr. applied sci. Calif. Inst. Tech., Pasadena, 1965-71, vis. assoc. elec. engring., 1976, vis. assoc. computer sci., 1976-84. Dir. San Gabriel Valley Learning Ctrs., 1992-95. Mem. Pasadena Tournament of Roses Assn., 1976—. Mem. AAAS, Nat. Assn. Corrosion Engrs., Am. Ordnance Assn., Assn. Computing Machinery, Athanaeum Club (Pasadena), Houston Club. Home: 77 Patrician Way Pasadena CA 91105-1039

CAIRNS, DIANE PATRICIA, motion picture executive; b. Fairbanks, Alaska, Mar. 2, 1957; d. Dion Melvin and Marsha Lala (Andrews) C. BBA, U. So. Calif., 1980. Literary agt. Sy Fischer Agy., L.A., 1980-85; sr. v.p. Internat. Creative Mgmt., L.A., 1985-96; sr. v.p. prodn. Universal Pictures, L.A., 1996-97. Mem. NOW, Acad. Motion Picture Arts and Scis., Women in Film, Amnesty Internat., L.A. County Mus. of Art, Mus. of Contemporary Art (L.A.).

CAKEBREAD, STEVEN ROBERT, minister, chef; b. Pittsburg, Calif., June 19, 1946; s. Robert Harold Cakebread and Mildred Irene (McQeen) Cowing; m. Margaret Anne Spandall, July 16, 1967; children: Robert, Scott, Andrew. ABS, Nazarene Bible Coll., Colorado Springs, Colo., 1977; BA, Mid. Am. Nazarene Coll., 1979; MDiv, Am. Bapt. Sem. of the West, Berkeley, Calif., 1983; grad., Calif. Culinary Acad., San Francisco, 1996. Ordained to ministry Ch. of the Nazarene, 1980, Am. Bapt. Ch., 1984. Pastor Ch. of the Nazarene, Brookfield, Md., 1978-80; hosp. chaplain VA Hosp., San Francisco, 1988—, Oakland (Calif.) Naval Hosp./Operation Desert Storm, 1990-91, Naval Res./Naval Base, San Francisco, 1985—; pastor 21st Ave Bapt. Ch., San Francisco, 1984-92, Yountville (Calif.) Cmty. Ch., 1992—; ret. Naval Res. Chaplain Corps, 1994; chef, 1994—; Coun. mem. Coun. of Chs., San Francisco, 1988. E-5 USN, 1966-70, Vietnam. Decorated Humanitarian Svc. medal USN, Navy Achievement medal (Desert Storm). Mem. Naval Res. Assn., ABA/USA Chaplains Coun., Am. Legion. Avocations: profl. chef, caterer, movies, walking a foggy beach. Office: Am Baptist Personnel Svc 35 E 19th St Antioch CA 94509-2643

CAL, CLARENCE ADAM, SR., aerospace engineer; b. Palmetto, La., Aug. 21, 1935; s. Sullivan Austin Cal and Mary Cecilia (Marshall) Green; m. Frances Ophelia Johnson, Mar. 7, 1956; children: Clarence Jr., Barry Wayne, Sherry Lynnette, Theron Kenneth, Daria Bernice, Anita Marie. BS in Chemistry and Zoology, So. U., 1959; MBA, Seattle U., 1970. Registered profl. engr., Calif. Quality [illegible] 1962-70; adminstrv. asst. Seattle Sch. Dist. #1, Seattle, 1970-72; dir. cmty. affairs Seattle City Light, Seattle, 1972-74; quality engr. Atlantic Richfield, Richland, Wash., 1974-75; quality profl. engr. Wash. Pub. Power Supply, Richland, 1975-79; corp. standards engr. Boeing, Seattle, 1979—. Mem. Mayor's Commn. on Edn., Seattle, 1970-74, New Careers, 1970-74. Capt. U.S. Army, 1960-67. Mem. Am. Def. Prep. Assn. (exec. bd. 1993—), Alpha Kappa Mu, Beta Beta Beta. Achievements include development of a thickness guage for silicone rubber, development of a process for forming parts on minuteman missile. Avocations: tennis, bowling, golf, softball. Home and Office: 3517 S Austin St Seattle WA 98118-4018

CALDER, ROBERT MAC, aerospace engineer; b. Vernal, Utah, Oct. 16, 1932; s. Edwin Harold and Sydney (Goodrich) C.; m. Yoshiko Iemura, Feb. 14, 1959; children: Suzanne, Alexis, Irene, John. BSChemE, U. Utah, 1956, M.S. in Math. and Geology (NSF grantee), 1967; postgrad., U. Wash., 1964, Utah State U., 1965, U. Iowa, 1966. Cert. secondary tchr., Utah. Tchr. Utah Pub. Schs., 1958-79. V.p. Sydney Corp., Bountiful, Utah, 1958-82; sr. engr. aero. div. Hercules Inc., Magna, Utah, 1979—; owner RMC Enterprises, Nations Imports; cons. in field, 1960—; cultural exchange participant to Israel, Egypt, 1983, 87. Active Boy Scouts Am., 1945-75, instr., Philmont Scout Ranch, 1972, asst. scoutmaster Nat. Jamboree Troop, 1973; instr. hunter safety and survival, Utah Dept. Fish and Game, 1964-74; state advisor U.S. Congl. Adv. Bd., 1982—; mem. Rep. Nat. Com. Capt. USAF, 1956-70. Mem. AIAA, NRA (life), Am. Quarter Horse Assn., Internat. Platform Assn., Oratorio Soc. Utah, The Planetary Soc., Hercules Toastmasters Club (treas. 1980, v.p. edn. 1981, pres. 1982), N.Am. Fishing Club (life). Mormon. Home and Office: 2258 Deer Run Dr South Weber UT 84405-9474

CALDERWOOD, NEIL MOODY, retired telephone traffic engineer, consultant; b. Vinalhaven, Maine, June 19, 1910; s. Austin Shirley and Eliza Louise (Carver) C.; m. Katherine Foster Mariani, Oct. 13, 1940; children: John Carver, James Foster, Bruce Glidden. BSCE, U. Maine, Orono, 1932, MS in Math., 1935. Sr. engr. Resettlement Adminstrn., Camden, Maine, 1935-37; sr. engr. Pacific Telephone, San Francisco, 1937-42, staff engr., dist. traffic engr., gen. traffic engr., staff dir. network ops., 1946-75; telecom. expert Internat. Telecom. Union, UN, Geneva, 1975-76; cons. telephone numbering plans Libyan Govt., Benghazi, Tripoli, 1976; traffic engring. cons. Las Vegas Telephone Co., 1952, Hawaiian Telephone Co., 1963; expert witness Public Utilities Commn. of Calif. hearings on all number calling cases, San Francisco and L.A., 1962-64. Lt. comdr. USNR, 1942-46. Mem. Am. Rose Soc., Pierce-Arrow Soc., Telephone Pioneers, Phi Gamma Delta. Republican. Avocations: piano, roses, antique clocks, Pierce-Arrow motor cars. Home: 49 Dolores Way Orinda CA 94563-4154

CALDERWOOD, WILLIAM ARTHUR, physician; b. Wichita, Kans., Feb. 3, 1941; s. Ralph Bailey and Janet Denise (Christ) C.; m. Nancy Jo Crawford, Mar. 31, 1979; children: Lisa Beth, William Arthur II. MD, U. Kans., 1968. Diplomate Am. Bd. Family Practice. Intern Wesley Med. Ctr., Wichita, 1968-69; gen. practice family medicine Salina, Kans., 1972-80, Peoria, Ariz., 1980—; med. dir. First Am. Home Care, 1994-96, First Am. Homecare, 1995—; pres. staff St. John's Hosp., Salina, 1976; 28th jud. dist. coroner State of Kans., Wichita, 1978-80; cons. in addiction medicine VA Hosp., 1989-94; bd. dirs. Pelms House; asst. prof. Midwestern U., Phoenix AZ, 1998—. Inventor, patentee lighter-than-air-furniture. Bd. dirs. Pelms House (For Chem. Dependence), 1995—, Gen. Health Medcare, 1995—. Fellow Am. Acad. Family Physicians; mem. AMA, Ariz. Med. Soc. (physicians med. health com., exec. com. 1988-92), Maricopa County Med. Soc., Ariz. Acad. Family Practice (med. dir. N.W. Orgn. Vol. alternatives 1988-91), Am. Med. Soc. on Alcoholism and Other Drug Dependencies (cert.), Shriners. Home: 7015 W Calavar Rd Peoria AZ 85381-4706 Office: 14300 W Granite Valley Dr Sun City West AZ 85375-5783

CALDWELL, ALLAN BLAIR, health services company executive; b. Independence, Iowa, June 13, 1929; s. Thomas James and Lola (Ensminger) C.; BA, Maryville Coll., 1952; BS, NYU, 1955; MS, Columbia U., 1957; MD, Stanford U., 1964; m. Elizabeth Jane Steinmetz, June 13, 1955; 1 child, Kim Allistair; m. Susan A. Koss, Feb. 12, 1984. Med. intern Henry Ford Hosp., Detroit, 1964-65; resident Jackson Meml. Hosp., Miami, Fla., 1956-57; admstr. Albert Schweitzer Hosp., Haiti, 1957-58; asst. admstr. Palo Alto-Stanford Hosp. Center, 1958-59; asso. dir. program in hosp. adminstrn. U. Calif. at Los Angeles, 1965-67; dir. bur. profl. service Am. Hosp. Assn., Chgo., 1967-69; v.p. Beverly Enterprises, Pasadena, Calif., 1969-71; exec. v.p., med. dir. Nat. Med. Enterprises, Beverly Hills, Calif., 1971-73; pres., chmn. bd. Emergency Physicians Internat., 1973—, Allan B. Caldwell, M.D., Inc., 1973—; dir. indsl. medicine Greater El Monte Cmty. Hosp., South El Monte, Calif., 1973-83; pres. Am. Indsl. Med. Svcs., 1978—; chmn. bd. dirs. Technicraft Internat., Inc., San Mateo, Calif., 1970-76; pres., med. dir. Shelton-Livingston Med. Group, 1984—; dir. Career Aids, Inc., Glendale, Calif., 1969-75; cons. TRW Corp., Redondo Beach, Calif., 1966-71; lectr. UCLA, 1965—, Calif. Inst. Tech., 1971—, Calif. State U., Northridge, 1980-85; examiner Civil Service Commn., L.A., 1966; adviser Western Center for Continuing Edn. in Hosps. and Related Health Facilities, 1965—; cons. L.A. Hosp. and Nursing and Pub. Health Dept., 1965—; adv. council Calif. Hosp. Commn., 1972-78; commr. Emergency Med. Services Commn. Bd. dirs. Comprehensive Health Planning Assn. Los Angeles County, 1972-76; vice chmn. Emergency Med. Care Commn., Los Angeles County, 1977-78, chmn., 1978-79. Recipient Geri award Los Angeles Nursing Home Assn., 1966, Outstanding Achievement award Health Care Educators, 1978; USPHS scholar, 1961-63. Diplomate Am. Bd. Med. Examiners. Mem. Am., United (pres. 1971-72) hosp. assns., Am. Coll. Hosp. Adminstrs., Am., Calif. med. assns., Los Angeles County Med. Assn., Am. Acad. Family Physicians, Am. Coll. Emergency Physicians (v.p. 1975-77 dir. continuing med. edn. for Western U.S., Hawaii, Australia, N.Z., 1976-84), Hosp. Fin. Mgmt. Assn., Am. Indsl. Hygiene Assn., Rolls Royce Owners' Club (dir. 1982—, vice chmn. 1982, chmn. 1983), Classic Car Club of Am. (life 1983), Antique Automobile Club Am., Model T Club Am. Home: 384 Saddlehorn Trl Palm Desert CA 92211-3295 Office: 1414 S Grand Ave Ste 123 Los Angeles CA 90015-3067

CALDWELL, COURTNEY LYNN, lawyer, real estate consultant; b. Washington, Mar. 5, 1948; d. Joseph Morton and Moselle (Smith) C. Student, Duke U., 1966-68, U. Calif., Berkeley, 1967, 1968-69; BA, U. Calif., Santa Barbara, 1970, MA, 1975; JD with highest honors, George Washington U., 1982. Bar: D.C. 1984, Wash. 1986, Calif. 1989. Jud. clk. U.S. Ct. Appeals for 9th Cir., Seattle, 1982-83; assoc. Arnold & Porter, Washington, 1983-85, Perkins Coie, Seattle, 1985-88; dir. western ops. Edn. Real Estate Svcs., Inc., Irvine, Calif., 1988-91, sr. v.p., 1991-98; ind. cons., Orange County, Calif., 1998—. Bd. dirs. Univ. Town Ctr. Assn., 1994; bd. dirs. Habitat for Humanity, Orange County, 1993-94, chair legal com., 1994. Named Nat. Law Ctr. Law Rev. Scholar, 1981-82. Mem. Calif. Bar Assn. Avocation: foreign languages. Home and Office: 140 Cabrillo St Apt 15 Costa Mesa CA 92627-3038

CALDWELL, HOWARD BRYANT, English language educator; b. London, Ky., Jan. 28, 1944; s. Stratton and Linda Emily (Bryant) C. BA, Berea (Ky.) Coll., 1966; MA, U. Calif., Berkeley, 1977. Cert. adult edn. tchr. Tchr. L.A. Unified Sch. Dist., 1977—. Mem. L.A. County Mus. Art, N.Y. Met. Mus. Art, L.A. World Affairs Coun. With USAF, 1966-70, The Philippines. Mem. United Tchrs. L.A., London Victory Club. Republican. Baptist. Avocations: international travel, languages, classical music.

CALDWELL, JO ANN KENNEDY, elementary educator; b. Franklin, Va., Oct. 31, 1937; d. Benjamin and Bertha (Cicacco) Kennedy; m. Charles Gary Caldwell, Dec. 23, 1962; 1 child, Richard Blair. BA, Baylor U., 1959; MS, No. Mich. U., 1969, MA, 1970. Cert. tchr., Tex., Mich., Calif. Tchr. Univ. Jr. High Sch./Waco (Tex.) Sch. Dist., Gwinn (Mich.) Middle Sch., No. Mich. Lab. Sch., Marquette, Fairfield (Calif.)-Suisun Unified Sch. Dist.; mentor tchr.; presenter workshops; cons. creative oral langs. activities, choral reading, storytelling Readers Theatre. Recipient Solano County's Celebrate Literacy award, 1994. Mem. NEA, ASCD, Internat. Reading Assn., Calif. Reading Assn., Calif. Tchrs. Assn., Delta Kappa Gamma, Phi Delta Kappa.

CALDWELL, JONI, psychology educator, small business owner; b. Chgo., Aug. 8, 1948; d. Bruce Wilber and Eloise Ethel (Ijams) C. BS in Home [illegible] 1978. Cert. high sch. and coll. tchr., Mich. Instr. Northwestern Mich. Coll., Traverse City, 1972-78, Mott Community Coll., Flint, Mich., 1974-78; tchr. Grand Blanc (Mich.) High Sch., 1970-73, Clio (Mich.) High Sch., 1974-78; parent educator, vol. coord. Family Resource Ctr., Monterey, Calif., 1981-82; owner, gen. mgr. Futons & Such, Monterey, 1982—; instr. psychology Hartnell Coll., Salinas, Calif., 1993-96; spl. project dir. YWCA, 1996-97; instr. women's studies Monterey Peninsula Coll., 1997. Bd. dirs., v.p., pres. Ch. Religious Sci., Monterey, 1984-87; mem. bd. stewards Pacific Coast Ch., Monterey, 1988-92, v.p.; bd. dirs. YWCA, Monterey, 1986-88, mem. nominating com., 1995-98, pers. comm., 1996—; vol., fund raiser Buddy Program, 1992—; membership com. Profl. Womens Network, 1989—. Mem. AAUW (state del., 1997, co-chair equity comm., 1998—), New Monterey Bus. Assn. (past pres., bd. dirs. 1984-95, v.p. 1993-97), Monterey C. of C. (cons. workshop com. 1985-87, Small Bus. Excellence award 1990), del. First Women's Conv., 1998. Avocations: skiing, sailing, skin diving, remodeling houses, travel. Home: 29 Portola Ave Monterey CA 93940-3731 Office: Futons & Such 475 Alvarado St Monterey CA 93940-2722

CALDWELL, STRATTON FRANKLIN, kinesiology educator; b. Mpls., Aug. 25, 1926; s. Kenneth Simms and Margaret Mathilda (Peterson) C.; m. Mary Lynn Shaffer, Aug. 28, 1955 (div. May 1977); children: Scott Raymond, Karole Elizabeth; m. Sharee' Deanna Ockerman, Aug. 6, 1981; 1 stepchild, Shannon Sharee' Calder. Student, San Diego State Coll., 1946-48; BS in Edn. cum laude, U. So. Calif., 1951, PhD in Phys. Edn., 1966; MS in Phys. Edn., U. Oreg., 1953. Teaching asst. dept. phys. edn. UCLA, 1953-54, assoc. in phys. edn., 1957-65, vis. asst. prof. phys. edn., 1967; dir. phys. edn. Regina (Sask., Can.) Young Men's Christian Assn., 1954-56; tchr. sec. grades, dir. athletic Queen Elizabeth Jr.-Sr. High Sch., Calgary, Alta., Can., 1956-57; asst. prof. phys. edn. San Fernando Valley State Coll., Northridge, Calif., 1965-68, assoc. prof., 1968-71; prof. phys. edn. dept. kinesiology Calif. State U., Northridge, 1971-90, prof. kinesiology, 1990-92, prof. kinesiology emeritus, 1992; vis. asst. prof. phys. edn. UCLA, 1967; vis. assoc. prof. phys. edn. U. Wash., Seattle, 1968, U. Calif., Santa Barbara, 1969. Author (with Cecil and Joan Martin Hollingsworth) Golf, 1959, (with Rosalind Cassidy) Humanizing Physical Education: Methods for the Secondary School Movement Program, 5th edit., 1975; also poetry, book chpts., articles in profl. jours., book revs. With USN, 1944-46. Recipient Meritorious Performance and Profl. Promise award Calif. state U., 1986, 87, 89, Disting. Teaching award, 1992; AAPHERD fellow, 1962, Am. Coll. Sports Medicine fellow, 1965, Can. Assn. for Health, Phys. Edn., and Recreation fellow, 1971. Fellow Am. Alliance for Health, Phys. Edn., Recreation and Dance (Centennial Commn. 1978-85, cert. appreciation 1985), Am. Coll. Sports Medicine; mem. Calif. Assn. for Health, Phys. Edn., Recreation and Dance (pres. L.A. coll. and univ. unit 1969-70, v.p. phys. edn. com. 1970-71, mem. editorial bd. CAHPER Jour. 1970-71, mem. forum 1970-71, Disting. Svc. award 1974, Honor award 1988, Verne Landreth award 1992), Nat. Assn. for Phys. Edn. in Higher Edn. (charter), Sport Art Acad., Nat. Assn. for Sport and Phys. Edn., N.Y. Acad. Scis., N.Am. Soc. for Sports History, Sport Lit. Assn., Acad. Am. Poets, Phi Epsilon Kappa (Svc. award 1980), Alpha Tau Omega (charter,Silver Circle award 1976), Phi Delta Kappa, Phi Kappa Phi, others. Republican. Mem. Christian Ch. Avocations: docent, reading, writing. Home: 80 Kanan Rd Oak Park CA 91377-1105

CALDWELL, WALTER EDWARD, editor, small business owner; b. L.A., Dec. 29, 1941; s. Harold Elmer and Esther Ann (Fuller) C.; m. Donna Edith Davis, June 27, 1964; 1 child, Arnie-Jo. AA, Riverside City Coll., 1968. Sales and stock professional Sears Roebuck & Co., Riverside, Calif., 1963-65; dispatcher Rohr Corp., Riverside, Calif., 1965-67; trainee Aetna Fin., Riverside, 1967-68; mgr. Aetna Fin., San Bruno, Cal., 1968-70, Amfac Thrift & Loan, Oakland, Calif., 1970-74; free lance writer San Jose, Calif., 1974-76; news dir. Sta. KAVA Radio, Burney, Cal., 1977-79; editor-pub. Mountain Echo, Fall River Mills, Calif., 1979—. Contbg. author Yearbook of Modern Poetry, 1976. Del. Farmers and Ranchers Congress, St. Louis, 1985; participant Am. Leadership Conf., San Diego, 1989; pres. United Way, Burney, 1979, co-chmn., 1977, chmn., 1979; disaster relief worker ARC, Redding, Calif., 1988-91, disaster action team leader, 1991-95; bd. dirs. Shasta County Women's Refuge, Redding, 1988-91, Shasta County Econ. Devel. Corp., 1986-90, Crossroads, 1985; bd. dirs. Shasta County Econ. Devel. Task Force, 1985-86, exec. bd. dirs., 1988; pres. Intermountain Devel. Corp., 1989; leader Girl Scouts U.S.A., San Jose, 1973-76; announcer various local parades; trustee Mosquito Abatement Dist., Burney, 1978-87, 89—, chmn., 1990—; commr. Burney Fire Protection Dist., 1987-91, v.p., 1990, pres., 1991; chmn. Burney Basin Days Com., 1984-95, Hay Days Com., 1995-96; candidate for Shasta County Bd. Supvrs., 1992; alt. commr. Local Agy. Formation Commn. Shasta County, 1995—. With USMC, 1959-63. Mem. Burney Basin C. of C. (advt. chmn. 1982, Cmty. Action award 1990, 93), Fall River Valley C. of C. (bd. dirs. 1991, pres. 1995), Am. Legion (citation of recognition 1987, Cmty. Action award 1989, 93), Calif. Newspaper Pubs. Assn., Rotary (pres. 1977-78, chmn. bike race 1981-85), Lions (student spkr. chmn. Fall River 1983—, 1st v.p. 1991, pres. 1992, co-chmn. disaster com., newsletter chmn. dist. 4-C1 1989-91), Moose, Masons (master 1995), Shriners (sec.-treas. 1992-94). Republican. Avocations: photography, painting, archeology. Office: Mountain Echo Main St Fall River Mills CA 96028 also: PO Box 224 Fall River Mills CA 96028-0224

CALDWELL, WILLIAM MACKAY, III, business executive; b. Los Angeles, Apr. 6, 1922; s. William Mackay II and Edith Ann (Richards) C.; BS, U. So. Calif., 1943; MBA, Harvard U., 1948; m. Mary Louise Edwards, Jan. 16, 1946 (dec. 1980); children: William Mackay IV, Craig Edwards, Candace Louise; m. Jean Bledsoe, Apr. 27, 1985. Sec.-treas., dir. Drewry Photocolor Corp., 1957-60, Adcolor Photo Corp., 1957-60; treas., dir. Drewry Bennetts Corp., 1959-60; sr. v.p., chief fin. officer Am. Cement Corp., 1960-67; sr. v.p. corp., 1966-70, pres. cement and concrete group, 1967-70; pres., chmn. bd., chief exec. officer Van Vorst Industries, 1969; pres. Van Vorst Corp., Washington, 1969-77; chmn. bd., pres. So. Cross Industries, U.S. Bedding Co., 1979-84, St. Croix Mfg. Co., 1979-81, Hawaiian Cement Corp.; pres. Englander Co., 1979-84; v.p., dir. Am. Cement Internat. Corp., Am. Cement Properties; chmn. Kyco Industries Inc., 1982—; pres. BHI Inc., 1984—; cons. prof. U. So. Calif. Mem. men's com. Los Angeles Med. Center; bd. dirs. Commerce Assocs., Calif. Mus. Sci. and Industry, U. So. Calif. Assocs., bd. dirs. Pres.'s Circle; bd. dirs. Am. Cement Found. Served to lt. USNR, 1943-46. Mem. Newcomen Soc., Friends Huntington Library, L.A. Country Club, Town Hall Club, Calif. Club (L.A.), Trojan Club, Annandale Golf Club, Eldorado Country Club, Chaparral Golf Club, Harvard Bus. Sch. of So. Calif. (dir. 1960-63), Kappa Alpha, Alpha Delta Sigma, Alpha Pi Omega. Presbyterian. Office: PO Box 1151 Pasadena CA 91102-1151

CALDWELL-PORTENIER, PATTY JEAN GROSSKOPF, advocate, educator; b. Davenport, Iowa, Sept. 28, 1937; d. Bernhard August and Leontine Virginia (Carver) Grosskopf; m. Donald Eugene Caldwell Mar. 29, 1956 (dec. Feb. 1985); children: John Alan, Jennifer Lynn Caldwell Lear; m. Walter J. Portenier, Oct. 3, 1992. BA, State U. Iowa, 1959. Hearing officer Ill. State Bd. Edn., Springfield, 1979-91, Appellate Court, 1986-91; pres., bd. dirs. Tri-County Assn. for Children With Learning Disabilities, Moline, Ill., 1972-79; adv. vol., Iowa and Ill., 1979-91; mem. adv. coun. Prairie State Legal Svcs., Inc., Rock Island, Ill., 1984-91; mem. profl. svcs. com. United Cerebral Palsy N.W. Ill., Rock Island, 1986-88; arbitrator Am. Arbitration Assn., Chgo., 1986-91, Better Bus. Bur., Davenport, 1986-91. Founder, pres. Quad Cities Diabetes Assn., Moline, 1969-72, bd. dirs., 1973—; mem. com. Moline Internat. Yr. Disabled, 1981; mem. Assn. for Retarded Citizens, Rock Island, 1987; mem. vol. Coun. on Children at Risk, Moline, 1988-91; reader for the blind Sta. WVIK, Rock Island, 1989-91; bd. dirs. First United Meth. Ch. Nursery Sch., Santa Monica, 1997—; docent Petersen Automotive Mus., L.A., 1997—. Mem. Ill. Assn. for Children with Learning Disabilities (bd. dirs., adv. 1980-83). Methodist. Avocations: travel, reading, crocheting. E-mail: p-jportenier@beachnet.com. Fax: 310-472-8327. Home and Office: 2443 La Condessa Dr Los Angeles CA 90049-1221

CALHOUN, ROSE TAYLOR, health services administrator; b. Kaufman, Tex., Aug. 24, 1950; d. Harvey Stokely Taylor and Theresa Marie (Dendy) Eubanks; m. William Benjamin Calhoun III, Aug. 21, 1982. BSN, Tex. Women's U., 1976; MEd, U. Houston, 1980. RN, Calif. Profl. svcs. cons. Hillhaven - Tacoma (Wash.) Region, 1983-85; area admissions, nursing adminstr. Hillhaven - So. Calif. Region, Ontario, 1985-88; dir. nursing Camarillo (Calif.) Convalescent Hosp., 1988-93; v.p. profl. Channel Islands [illegible] Calif., 1993—; CEO The Victorian, Ventura, 1994—; chair health scis. adv. bd. Oxnard (Calif.) Adult Sch., 1990—. Allocation com. Cmty. Svc. Funds, Westlake Village, Calif., 1992; vestry mem. Ch. of the Epiphany, Westlake Village, 1990-91. Mem. Am. Coll. Nursing Home Adminstrs., Nat. Ger-

ontol. Assn., Calif. Nurses Assn. Episcopalian. Avocations: golf, skiing, hiking. Home: 32116 Beach Lake Ln Westlake Village CA 91361

CALIC, LJUBOMIIZ NEBOJSA, art dealer; b. Belgrade, Yugoslavia, Apr. 14, 1946; s. Ljubomir Ilija and Zivka Petar (Zivkovic) C.; m. Mirjana Rosini, Mar. 4, 1972; children: Alexander, Petar. BA in Arch., U. Belgrade. Owner, designer Bele Arte, Paris, 1971-73, Calic's Art, San Francisco, 1973-82; owner, art dealer Calic Contemporary, San Francisco, 1982-87; art dealer Calic Internat., Alameda, Calif., 1987—, owner, 1990—. Republican. Office: Calic Internat 1699 Valleyo St San Francisco CA 94123

CALIENDO, THEODORE JOSEPH, pediatrician, neonatalogist; b. Bklyn., Nov. 9, 1941; s. Leo J. and Anna C.; m. Arlene Mann, Jan. 7, 1970 (div. Aug. 1984); children: Michael, Robert, Barbra, David. BS, St. John's U., Bklyn., 1962; MD, N.Y. Med. Coll., 1966. Intern, resident Cedars Sinai Med. Ctr., L.A., 1966-69; pediatrician, neonatalogist Kaiser-Permanente, Mission Viejo, Calif., 1973—; attending physician Cedars Sinai Med. Ctr., L.A., 1971-81, Kaiser Hosp., Anaheim, Calif., 1979—; asst. prof. pediatrics UCLA Med. Sch., 1971-82. Lt. comdr. USN, 1969-71. Fellow Am. Acad. Pediatrics; mem. L.A. Pediatric Soc., Ritz Bros., Monarch Bay Club, Rancho Niquel Club, Ferrari Club Am. Avocations: collecting contemporary art, collecting wine, fine dining, skiing, sports cars. Office: Kaiser Permanente 23781 Maquina Mission Viejo CA 92691-2765

CALLAHAN, GARY BRENT, lawyer; b. Ashland, Oreg., Apr. 24, 1942; s. Donald Burr and Joyce Valeri (Powers) C.; m. Nancy Kay King, Feb. 1967 (div. 1978); children: Shawn, Christopher; m. Sally Kornblight, Jan. 18, 1983; 1 child, Zachary. Student, Sacramento State U.; JD, U. of Pacific, 1970. Bar: Calif. 1971, U.S. Dist. Ct. (ea. dist.) Calif. 1971. Assoc. Rust & Mills, Sacramento, Calif., 1971-73, Barrett, Matheny & Newlon, Sacramento, 1973-77; ptnr. Westley & Callahan, Sacramento, 1977-80, Wilcoxen, Callahan, Montgomery & Harbison, Sacramento, 1980-94, Callahan & Deacon, Sacramento, 1994—; instr., lectr. Continuing Edn. Bar, Berkeley, Calif., 1978—; faculty mem. advocacy skills workshop Sch. Law Stanford U., 1994—, Sch. Law U. San Francisco, 1994—. Served with USN, 1960-63. Recipient Outstanding Alumnus award U. The Pacific McGeorge Sch. of Law, 1989. Mem. Calif. Bar Assn., Assn. Trial Lawyers Am. (sustaining), Consumer Attys. Calif., Capitol City Consumer Attys. (pres. 1984-85), Am. Bd. Profl. Liability Attys., Am. Bd. Trial Advs., Nat. Bd. Trial Advs. Democrat. Avocations: lecturing, instructing on trial advocacy, sailing, boating. Office: Callahan & Deacon 77 Cadillac Dr Ste 240 Sacramento CA 95825-8328

CALLAHAN, MARILYN JOY, social worker; b. Portland, Oreg., Oct. 11, 1934; d. Douglas Q. and Anona Helen Maynard; m. Lynn J. Callahan, Feb. 27, 1960 (dec.); children: Barbara Callahan Baer, Susan Callahan Sewell, Jeffrey Lynn. BA, Mills Coll., 1955; MSW, Portland State U., 1971, secondary teaching cert., 1963. Bd. cert. diplomate in clin. social work. Developer, adminstr. ednl. program Oreg. Women's Correctional Ctr., Oreg. State Prison, Salem, 1966-67; mental health counselor Benton County Mental Health, Corvallis, Oreg., 1970-71; inst. tchr. Hillcrest Sch., Salem, Oreg., 1975-81; social worker protective svcs. Mid Willamette Valley Sr. Svcs. Agy., Salem, 1981-88; psychiat. social worker dept. forensics Oreg. State Hosp., 1988-93; pvt. practice treatment of adult male and female sexual offenders Salem, 1987—; pvt. practice in care/mgmt. of elderly, 1987—; panel mem. Surgeon Gen.'s N.W. Regional Conf. on Interpersonal Violence, 1987; speaker in field; planner, organizer Seminar on Age Discrimination, 1985. Mem. NASW (past mem. bd. dirs. Oreg. chpt.), Nat. Org. Forensic Social Work, Am. Acad. Forensic Scis., Acad. Cert. Social Workers (lic. clin. social worker), Assn. for Treatment Sex Abusers, Oreg. Gerontol. Assn., Catalina 27 Nat. Sailing Assn. E-mail: marilynC@teleport.com. Office: Ste 304 780 Commercial St SE Salem OR 97301-3455

CALLAHAN, RONALD, federal investigator, historian; b. San Francisco, Jan. 8, 1947; s. Raymond Edward and Camille (Masucci) C.; m. Delores Leona Cody Callahan, Nov. 15, 1986; children: Randell James Stowe, Miranda Dawn Stowe, Christopher Ronald Callahan, Kimberly Ann Callahan. BS, Calif. State U., 1973, student, 1987-91. Cert. spl. agt. Air traffic controller USAF, Davis-Monthan AFB, Ariz., 1967-68; air trafic controller USAF, Kadena AB, Japan, 1968-70; clk. Franchise Tax Bd., Sacramento, 1973; acct. clk. Employment Devel. Dept., Sacramento, 1973-74; air cargo specialist 82d Aerial Port Squadron, Travis AFB, Calif., 1978-80; adjudicator VA, San Francisco, 1974-82; historian 349th Mil. Airlift Wing, Travis AFB, Calif., 1980-82, Fourth Air Force, McClellan AFB, Calif., 1986-90; sr. investigator Def. Security Svc., Sacramento, 1982—. Author: Annual Histories of McClellan and Travis Air Bases, 1980-82, 86-90, Airpower Journal, 1991-93. Vol. El Dorado County Juvenile Svc. Coun., Placerville, Calif., 1992, Calvary Refuge, Sacramento, Marysville, Calif., 1992-97, Calvary Chapel of Placerville, 1997—; mem. Grace Cmty. Ch., Pleasant Valley, Calif., 1993—; adult literacy tutor El Dorado County Literacy Action Coun., Placerville, 1994—; mem. bd. elders Calvary Refuge, 1996-97. Sgt. USAF, 1966-70. Named Dean's Honors list Calif. State U., Sacramento, 1971, 72; recipient Spl. Act award Def. Investigative Svc., Sacramento, 1983, Air Force Commendation medal USAF, McClellan AFB, Calif., 1989. Mem. Air Force Assn., Orgn. Am. Historians, Am. Christian History Inst., Friends of Libr., Grace Cmty. Ch., Calvary Refuge, Phi Alpha Theta. Republican. Avocations: writing, collecting rare books and memorabilia, tutoring, teaching history. Home: 1640 Glen Dr Placerville CA 95667-9302 Office: Def Security Svc 801 I St Rm 488 Sacramento CA 95814-2510

CALLAN, GWEN, interior designer; b. Denver, June 5, 1943; m. John Louis Callan, June 3, 1966; children: Elizabeth Lee Hoskins, Stephanie Lynn. BA, Mich. State U., 1965. Prin., ptnr. Design Concepts, Alamo, Calif., 1974-92; prin. Callan Studio of Interior Design, Danvilla, Calif., 1992—. Vol. Danville C. of C., 1979-97, San Francisco Symphony, Benefit Guild of the East Bay, Oakland, Calif., 1972-79. Mem. Am. Soc. Interior Designers (profl.), Calif. Cert. Interior Designers. Avocations: tennis, skiing, music. Office: Callan Studio 537 Sycamore Valley Rd W Danville CA 94526-3900

CALLAN, JOSI IRENE, museum director; b. Yorkshire, Eng., Jan. 30, 1946; came to U.S., 1953; d. Roger Bradshaw and Irene (Newbury) Winstanley; children: James, Heather, Brett Jack; m. Patrick Marc Callan, June 26, 1984. BA in Art History summa cum laude, Calif. State U., Domingues Hills, 1978, MA in Behavioral Scis., 1981. Dir. community rels./alumni affairs Calif. State U., Dominguez Hills; adminstrv. fellow office chancellor Calif. State U., Long Beach, assoc. dir. univ. svcs. office chancellor, 1979-85; dir. capital campaign, assoc. dir. devel. Sta. KVIE-TV, Sacramento, 1985-86; dir. project devel. Pacific Mountain Network, Denver, 1986-87; dir. mktg. and devel. Denver Symphony Orch., 1988-89; assoc. dir. San Jose (Calif.) Mus. Art, 1989-91, dir., 1991—; asst. prof. sch. social and behavioral scis. Calif. State U., Dominguez Hills, 1981—; mem. adv. com. Issues Facing Mus. in 1990s JKF U., 1990-91. Mem. com. arts policy Santa Clara Arts Coun., 1990-92; chair San Jose Arts Roundtable, 1992-93; active ArtTable, 1992—, Community Leadership San Jose, 1992-93, Am. Leadership Forum, 1994; mem. adv. bd. Bay Area Rsch. Project, 1992—; mem. Calif. Arts Coun., Visual Arts Panel, 1993-95, Santa Clara Arts Coun. Visual Arts Panel, 1993; bd. dirs. YWCA, 1993—. Recipient Leadership award Knight Found., 1995; Women of Vision honoree Career Action Ctr., 1998; fellow Calif. State U., 1982-83. Mem. AAUW, Am. Assn. Mus., Nat. Soc. Fund Raising Execs. (bd. dirs. 1991), Colo. Assn. Fund Raisers, Art Mus. Devel. Assn., Assn. Art Mus. Dirs., We. Mus. Assn., Calif. State U. Alumni Coun. (pres. 1981-83), Rotary Internat. Office: San Jose Mus Art 110 S Market St San Jose CA 95113-2383

CALLAS, JOHN PETER, director, producer; b. Jersey City, N.J., Feb. 3, 1950; s. Gus Callas and Pauline (Peterson) Alexander. B, Loretto Heights Coll., 1972; MA, Occidental Coll., 1975. Freelance asst. dir. L.A., 1975-80, 89-91, freelance prodr., 1980-84; pres., dir., prodr. The Prodn. House, L.A., 1982-89; cons. various producers, 1981-83; agency freelance producer Foote, Cone and Belding, 1985-86; lectr. various insts., 1985-87. Dir., prodr.: (featurette) Myrons Millions, 1979, (short) The White Gorilla Awards, (TV spot) Fuji Electrocelli Corp., 1987; dir.: (series) Potentials, 1982, (short film) Late for the Date, 1987, (feature film) Lone Wolf, 1988 (Best of the West award), Bobby's World (80 episodes), 1990 (Emmy nominee); prodr., co-dir. 1993 Tristar Logo; prodr.: (commls.) Sunkist, Sea World, Sizzler, Baskin Robbins, McDonalds, Ramada Inn, Volkswagen, Calvin Klein, Paul Masson and others, (home video) Infant and Child CPR Review, (music videos) Glenn Fry ("Smuggler's Blues" Best Concept award MTV 1984), Go Go's, Sammy Hagar, Neil Diamond, Flesh Tones, Rick Springfield, Jefferson Starship, Bill Wyman, Doobie Brothers, Red Hot Chili Peppers, LaToya Jackson and others, (feature film trailers) The Blob, Poltergeist III, Cocoon II, Betrayed, Spaceballs, The Golden Child, The Glass Menagerie, Date With an Angel, Bill and Ted's Excellent Adventure, Phantom of the Opera, The Two Jakes, My Girl, Body of Evidence, Glenngary Glen Ross, A Few Good Men. Recipient Clio awards, Belding award, Worldfest Internat. Film Festival award, Breckenridge Festival award, Cindy awards, Deauville (France) Film Festival award, others. Mem. Dirs. Guild of Am., Padi Scuba Club (L.A.). Avocations: sailing, scuba diving, snow skiing.

CALLEN, LON EDWARD, county official; b. Kingman, Kans., Mar. 31, 1929; s. Cleo Paul and Josephine Nell (Mease) C.; BA in Math. and Physics, U. Wichita (Kans.), 1951; m. Barbara Jean Sallee, Oct. 12, 1954; children: Lon Edward, Lynnette J. Commd. 2d lt. USAF, 1951, advanced through grades to lt. col., 1968; comdr. Tuslog Detachment 93, Erhac, Turkey, 1966-67; sr. scientist Def. Atomic Support Agy., Washington, 1967-71; ret., 1971; dir. emergency preparedness City-County of Boulder, Colo., 1976—; bd. dirs. Boulder County Emergency Med. Svcs. Coun., 1977, Boulder County Amateur Radio Emergency Svcs., 1978—. Mem. hon. awards com. Nat. Capital Area council Boy Scouts Am., 1971; chmn. Boulder County United Fund, 1976-82; mem. asst. staff Indian Princesses and Trailblazer programs Boulder YMCA, 1974-78. Decorated Joint Svc. Commendation medal; recipient cert. achievement Def. Atomic Support Agy., 1970. Mem. AAAS, Am. Ordnance Soc., Am. Soc. Cybernetics, Planetary Soc., Math. Assn. Am., N.Y. Acad. Scis., Fedn. Am. Scientists, Nat. Assn. Atomic Vets., Union Concerned Scientists, Boulder County Fire Fighters Assn., Colo. Emergency Mgmt. Assn., Ret. Officers Assn., Colo. Front Range Protective Assn., Mensa, Sigma Xi, Pi Alpha Pi. Clubs: Boulder Knife and Fork, Boulder Gunbarrel Optimists, Denver Matrix, U. Colo. Ski, U. Wichita. Author articles in field. Home: 4739 Berkshire Ct Boulder CO 80301-4055 Office: County Courthouse PO Box 471 Boulder CO 80306-0471

CALLENDER, LORNA OPHELIA, nurse administrator; b. Potsdam, Jamaica, Dec. 15, 1944; d. Banaldino Aciento and Gladys Felicita (Juleye) Robinson; m. Robert Fitzgerald Callender, June 25, 1966; children: Gavin Shaun St. Elmo, Robert Fitzgerald II. AAS, N.Y.C. C.C., 1975; BA, CUNY, 1978; MA, New Sch. for Social Rsch., N.Y.C., 1981. RN, Calif. Bank teller Mfrs. Hanover Trust, N.Y.C., 1968-70, proof clk., 1970-74; front office clk. Howard Johnson Hotel, Queens, N.Y., 1974-84; front office supr. Vista Internat. Hotel, N.Y.C., 1980-82; vocat. nurse Temporary Nursing Svc., East Orange, N.J., 1985-86, Calif. Psychiat. Placement Svc., Diamond Bar, 1986-90; team leader, nurse Casa Colina Hosp., Pomona, Calif., 1990-91; DON, United Care, Inc., Culver City, Calif., 1991-93; adminstr. Excelsior Home Health, Cucamonga, Calif., 1993-94, 95—, Calabar Home Health, Mira Loma, Calif., 1995-97, Flying High Companion Care, Las Vegas, Nev., 1996—, Wolmers Corp., Las Vegas, 1996—; dir. Inland AIDS Project, 1994—. Lobbyist Calif. Assn. Heath Svc. at Home, Sacramento, 1994, Home Care Assn. Am., Jacksonville, Fla., 1995. Mem. NAFE, AAUW. Democrat. Episcopalian. Home: 1012 Washington Oaks St Las Vegas NV 89128-2132

CALLINICOS, BRENT, assistant treasurer; b. Cape Town, South Africa, Dec. 17, 1965; s. Demetreos N. and Marleen (Frank) C.; m. Julie B. Beard, Dec. 20, 1987. BS in Bus., U. N.C., 1987, MBA, 1989. CPA, N.C. Internat. treasury analyst Procter & Gamble, Cin., 1989-90; cost/budget analyst, acctg. mgr. Procter & Gamble, Greensboro, N.C., 1990-91; profit forecaster Procter & Gamble, Cin., 1991-92; sr. fin. analyst Walt Disney Co., Burbank, Calif., 1992-93; product group fin. analyst Microsoft Corp., Redmond, Wash., 1993-94, mgr. corp. fin. and fgn. exch., 1994-96, dir. corp. fin. and fgn. exch., 1996-98, asst. treas., 1998—. Mem. AICPA, N.C. Assn. CPAs. Fax: (425) 936-7329. Home: 2512 261st Ct NE Redmond WA 98053 Office: Microsoft Corp 1 Microsoft Way Redmond WA 98052

CALLISON, NANCY FOWLER, nurse administrator; b. Milw., July 16, 1931; d. George Fenwick and Irma Esther (Wenzel) Fowler; m. B.G. Callison, Sept. 25, 1954 (dec. Feb. 1964); children: Robert, Leslie, Linda. Diploma, Evanston Hosp. Sch. Nursing, 1952; BS, Northwestern U., 1954. RN, Calif.; cert. case mgr. Staff nurse, psychiat. dept. Downey VA Hosp., 1954-55; staff nurse Camp Lejeune Naval Hosp., 1955, 59-61; obstet. supr. Tri-City Hosp., Oceanside, Calif., 1961-62; pub. health nurse San Diego County, 1962-66; sch. nurse Rich-Mar Union Sch. Dist., San Marcos, Calif., 1966-68; head nurse San Diego County Community Mental Health, 1968-73; dir. patient care services Southwood Mental Health Ctr., Chula Vista, Calif., 1973-75; program cons. Comprehensive Care Corp., Newport Beach, Calif., 1975-79; dir. Manpower Health Care, Culver City, Calif., 1979-80; dir. nursing services Peninsula Rehab. Ctr., Lomita, Calif., 1980-81; clinic supr., coordinator utilization and authorizations, acting dir. provider relations Hawthorne (Calif.) Community Med. Group, 1981-86; mgr. Health Care Delivery Physicians of Greater Long Beach, Calif., 1986-87; cons. Quality Rev. Assocs., West L.A., 1988-93; case mgr. Mercy Physicians Med. Group, 1992-93; med. mgmt. specialist The Zenith Ins., 1993—; mem. Rehab. Nurse Coord. Network, 1992-97, treas. 1997-98; clin. coord., translator Flying Samaritans, 1965—, mem. internat. bd. dirs., 1975-77, 79-86, 89—, dir. San Quentin project, 1991-93, dir. univ. program, 1996—, pres. South Bay chpt., 1975-81, v.p., 1982-85, bd. dirs. San Diego chpt., 1987-90, pres. San Diego chpt. 1991-92, adminstr. Clinica Esperanza de Infantil Rosarito Beach 1990-93. Mem. Rehab. Nurse Coord. Network (bd. dirs., treas. 1997-98), U.S.-Mex. Border Health Assn., Cruz Roja Mexicana (Delegacion Rosarito 1986-92).

CALLISTER, LOUIS HENRY, JR., lawyer; b. Salt Lake City, Aug. 11, 1935; s. Louis Henry and Isabel (Barton) C.; m. Ellen Gunnell, Nov. 27, 1957; children: Mark, Isabel, Jane, Edward, David, John Andrew, Ann. BS, U. Utah, 1958, JD, 1961. Bar: Utah 1961. Asst. atty. gen. Utah, 1961; sr. ptnr. Callister Nebeker & McCullough (formerly Callister, Duncan & Nebeker), Salt Lake City, 1961—; bd. dirs. Am. Stores Co., 1985-97, Quailbluff Devel. Co. Vice-chmn. Salt Lake City Zoning Bd. Adjustment, 1979-84; bd. govs. Salt Lake Valley Hosps., 1983-91; treas. exec. com. Utah Rep. Com., 1965-69; chmn. Utah chpt. Rockefeller for Pres. Com., 1964-68; sec., trustee Salt Lake Police/Sheriff Hon. Cols., 1982-97; trustee, mem. exec. com. Utah Econ. Devel. Corp., 1992—, chmn., 1998—; trustee U. Utah, 1987—, vice-chmn., 1989—, bd. dirs. U. Utah Hosp., 1993—. Mormon. Home: 22 Ironwood Dr North Salt Lake UT 84054-3318 Office: Callister Nebeker & McCullough Gateway Tower E Ste 900 Salt Lake City UT 84133-1102

CALMAN, CRAIG DAVID, writer, actor, director; b. Riverside, Calif., June 11, 1953. Student, Pacific U., Forest Grove, Oreg., 1971-72, U. de Querétaro, Mex., 1972-73; BA in Motion Picture/TV, UCLA, 1975. Sr. admitting worker UCLA Med. Ctr., 1974-76; actor/playwright Old Globe Theatre, San Diego, 1977-78, Off Broadway and regional, N.Y.C. and East Coast, 1979-86; exec. asst. various film/TV studios and law firms, L.A., 1986-89, Orion Pictures Corp., L.A., 1989-90; dir. staged readings L.A., 1991—; Actor with starring roles (TV and film) ADP Industrial, Teamwork, Macbeth, Flesteron in Amazonia, co-starring roles in Commercial Break, Sullivan's Travels; actor with co-starring/lead roles (theatre) in Book of the Dead, Dark Lady of the Sonnets, Hamlet, Rosencrantz and Guildenstern are Dead, Much Ado About Nothing, Too True to be Good, Henry V, The Counterfeit Rose, Richard III, The Rivals, Merchant of Venice, A Day for Surprises, The Tavern, Madame De..., and others; columnist World Wide Web mag. FilmZone, 1995-97. Author play/screenplays: The Turn of the Century, Strangled Nocturne, Skidoo Ruins; author novel: The Turn of the Century; author one-act plays, screenplays, full-length plays, poetry; writer asst. Hal Roach, Bel Air, Calif., 1987-88. Vol. book reader Recording for the Blind, L.A., 1991—. Recipient Old Globe Theatre Atlas award for best actor in a comedy role for Too True to be Good, 1977-78; Helene Wurlitzer Found. of N.Mex. Writers Residency grantee, 1988; finalist Walt Disney fellowship program, 1992, Chesterfield Film Writers Project, 1997. Mem. SAG, Actors Equity Assn. Office: 6632 Lexington Ave Ste 77 Los Angeles CA 90038-1306

CALVERT, JAMES DONALD, JR., civil engineer, researcher, consultant; b. Springfield, Ohio, June 10, 1924; s. James Donald and Mildred Florence (Henley) C.; m. Beverlee Barbara Barrett, Jan. 29, 1950; Rebecca, Sally, John, Thomas, Annabel. BS in Civil Engring, U. Mich., 1948. Registered profl. engr., Ill., Wis., Mich., N. Mex., N.D., S.D., Iowa. Resident engr. Fargo Engring. Co., Ladysmith, Wis., 1948-53; v.p. Fargo Engring. co., Jackson, Mich., 1957-62; sr. engr. Harza Engring. Co., Chgo., 1953-57; cons. engr. Jackson, Mich., 1962-87, 85-96; dir. environ. sys. divsn. Commonwealth Assocs., Jackson, 1967-75; v.p., gen. mgr. InterAm. Consultants, Rio de Janeiro, 1975-77; exec. cons. Gilbert Commonwealth, Jackson, Mich., 1977-85; rsch. assoc. Sch. Pub. Health, U. Mich., Ann Arbor, 1963-66. Contbr. articles to profl. jours. including Power Engring.; also presentations to engring. confs. Mem. troop com. Boy Scouts Am., Elk Grove, Calif., 1988-90. With U.S. Navy, 1943-46 ETO. Recipient cert. appreciation Am. Soc. Engrs., 1981. Fellow Am. Soc. Civil Engrs. (br. pres. 1948-96); mem. ASME, Nat. Soc. Profl. Engrs., (br. pres. 1959-66, Br. Engr. of Yr. 1974). Achievements include U.S. patent on hydroelectric barge, 1984. Home and Office: 2264 NW Thorncroft Dr Apt 414 Hillsboro OR 97124-9030

CALVERT, KEN, congressman; b. Corona, Calif., June 8, 1953. AA, Chaffey Coll., 1973; BA Econs., San Diego State U., 1975. Corona/ Norco youth chmn. for Nixon, 1968, 82; county youth chmn. rep. Vesey's Dist., 1970, 43d dist., 1972; congl. aide to rep. Vesey, Calif., 1975-79; gen. mgr. Jolly Fox Restaurant, Corona, Calif., 1975-79, Marcus W. Meairs Co., Corona, Calif., 1979-81; pres., gen. mgr. Ken Calvert Real Properties, Corona, Calif., 1981—; Reagan-Bush campaign worker, 1980; co chmn. Wilson for Senate Campaign, 1982, George Deukmejian election, 1978, 82, 86, George Bush election, 1988, Pete Wilson senate elections, 1982, 88, Pete Wilson for Gov. election, 1990; mem. 104th Congress (now 106th Congress) from 43rd Calif. dist., 1993—; mem. natural resources com., sci., space and tech. com., 1993—, also mem. ag. com.; former v.p. Corona/ Norco Rep. Assembly; chmn. Riverside Rep. Party, 1984-88, County Riverside Asset Leasing; bd. realtors Corono/ Norco. Exec. bd. Corona Community Hosp. Corp. 200 Club; mem. Corona Airport adv. commn.; adv. com. Temescal/ El Cerrito Community Plan. Mem. Riverside County Rep. Winners Circle (charter), Lincoln Club (co-chmn., charter, 1986-90), Corona Rotary Club (pres. 1991), Elks, Navy League Corona Norco, Corona C. of C. (pres. 1990), Noroco C. of C., Monday Morning Group, Corona Group (past chmn.), Econ. Devel. Ptnrship., Silver Eagles (March AFB support group, charter). Office: US Ho of Reps 1034 Longworth HOB Washington DC 20515-0543*

CALVIN, ALLEN DAVID, psychologist, educator; b. St. Paul, Feb. 17, 1928; s. Carl and Zelda (Engelson) C.; m. Dorothy VerStrate, Oct. 5, 1953; children—Jamie, Kris, David, Scott. B.A. in Psychology cum laude, U. Minn., 1950; M.A. in Psychology, U. Tex., 1951, Ph.D. in Exptl. Psychology, 1953. Instr. Mich. State U., East Lansing, 1953-55; asst. prof. Hollins Coll., 1955-59, assoc. prof., 1959-61; dir. Britannica Center for Studies in Learning and Motivation, Menlo Park, Calif., 1961; prin. investigator grant for automated teaching fgn. langs. Carnegie Found., 1960; USPHS grantee, 1960; pres. Behavioral Research Labs., 1962-74; prof., dean Sch. Edn., U. San Francisco, 1974-78; Henry Clay Hall prof. Orgn. and leadership, 1978—; pres. Pacific Grad. Sch. Psychology, 1984—. Author textbooks. Served with USNR, 1946-47. Mem. Am. Psychol. Assn., AAAS, Sigma Xi, Psi Chi. Home: 1645 15th Ave San Francisco CA 94122-3523 Office: Pacific Grad Sch Psychology 935 E Meadow Dr Palo Alto CA 94303-4233

CALVIN, DOROTHY VER STRATE, computer company executive; b. Grand Rapids, Mich., Dec. 22, 1929; d. Herman and Christina (Plakmyer) Ver Strate; m. Allen D. Calvin, Oct. 5, 1953; children: Jamie, Kris, Bufo, Scott. BS magna cum laude, Mich. State U., 1951; MA, U. San Francisco, 1988; EdD, U. San Francisco, 1991. Mgr. data processing. Behavioral Rsch. Labs., Menlo Park, Calif., 1972-75; dir. Mgmt. Info. Systems Inst. for Prof. Devel., San Jose, Calif. 1975-76; systems analyst, programmer Pacific Bell Info. Systems, San Francisco, 1976-81; staff mgr., 1981-84; mgr. applications devel. Data Architects Inc., San Francisco, 1984-86; pres. Ver Strate Press, San Francisco, 1986—. Instr., Downtown C.C., San Francisco, 1980-84, Cañada C.C., 1986-92, Skyline Coll., 1988-92, City Coll. of San Francisco, 1992—; mem. computer curriculum adv. coun. San Francisco City Coll., 1982-84. V.p. LWV, Roanoke, Va., 1956-58; pres. Bulliss Purissima Parents Group, Los Altos, Calif., 1962-64; bd. dirs. Vols. for Israel, 1986-87. Mem. NAFE, Assn. Computing Machinery, IEEE Computer Soc., Assn. Systems Mgmt., Assn. Women in Computing, Phi Delta Kappa. Democrat. Avocations: computing, gardening, jogging, reading. Office: Ver Strate Press 1645 15th Ave San Francisco CA 94122-3523

CAMARA, JORGE DE GUZMAN, ophthalmologist, educator; b. Ann Arbor, Mich., May 21, 1950; s. Augusto A. and Feliciana (de Guzman) C.; m. Virginia Valdes, June 23, 1977; 1 child, Augusto Carlos. BS in Pre-Medicine, U. Philippines, 1972, MD cum laude, 1976. Diplomate Am. Bd. Ophthalmology. Surg. intern U. Tex, Houston, 1977-78; resident in ophthalmology Baylor Coll. Medicine, Houston, 1978-81, fell in ophthalmic plastic and reconstructive surgery, 1981-82; ophthalmologist Straub Clinic and Hosp., Honolulu, 1982-88; pvt. practice Honolulu, 1988—; assoc. prof. U. Hawaii Sch. Medicine, Honolulu, 1982—; cons. Tripler Army Hosp., Honolulu, 1982—; chmn. dept. ophthalmology and otorhinolaryngology, bd. dirs. St. Francis Med. Ctr.; bd. dirs. Am. Savs. Bank, Hawaiian Electric Industries. Bd. dirs. Aloha Med. Mission, Honolulu, 1988—. Fellow Am. Acad. Ophthalmology, Am. Soc. Ophthalmic Plastic and Reconstructive Surgery; mem. AMA, Hawaii Ophthal. Soc. (pub. rels. officer 1984-85, pres. 1992, chmn. com. for indigent svcs. 1994—), Philippine Med. Assn. Hawaii (pres. 1988—). Roman Catholic. Avocations: tennis, piano. Office: 2228 Liliha St Ste 106 Honolulu HI 96817-1651

CAMBRE, ATHLEO LOUIS, JR., plastic surgeon; b. L.A., Feb. 21, 1954. MD, Case Western Res. U., 1981. Intern U. Colo. Sch. Medicine, Denver, 1981-82, gen. surgeon, 1982-86; burn surgery fellow Cornell-N.Y. Hosp., N.Y.C., 1986-87; plastic surgeon UCLA, 1987-89, Cedars-Sinai Med. Ctr., L.A., 1989—; asst. clin. prof. plastic surgery UCLA. Office: Plastic and Recostruction Surg 120 S Spalding Dr Ste 205 Beverly Hills CA 90212-1840

CAMERINO, JAY MEDINA, assistant principal; b. Tijuana, Mexico, July 13, 1970; came to U.S., 1973; s. Emmanuel Sapinoso and Eglay Olivia (Medina) C.; m. Nov. 21, 1997. BA, Calif. State U., Long Beach, 1994; MA, Calif. State U., Dominguez Hills, 1997. Tchr. Long Beach Unified Sch. Dist., 1994-97, asst. prin., 1997—. Vol. Nat. Assn. of Latino Elected Officials, L.A., 1990-94 (Outstanding Vol. award 1991). Recipient scholarship Tchr.'s Assn. of Long Beach, 1996. Mem. Assn. Calif. Sch. Adminstrs., Calif. Assn. BIL Educators, Assn. Mex.-Am. Educators, Computer Using Educators, Phi Kappa Phi. Avocations: basketball, tennis, biking.

CAMERON, CHARLES HENRY, petroleum engineer; b. Greeley, Colo., Oct. 21, 1947; s. Leo Leslie and Naomi Tryphena (Phillips) C.; m. Cheryl Christine Debelock, Aug. 30, 1969; 1 child, Ericka Dawn. AS, Mesa State Coll., 1968; BS in Geology, Mesa Coll., 1978; AS in Hazardous Materials Tech., Front Range C.C., Wesminister, Colo., 1990. Cert. info. resource mgmt. approving ofcl. (CIAO), 1998. Retardation technician Colo. State Home and Tng. Sch., Grand Junction, 1967-69; journeyman carpenter Brotherhood of Carpenters and Joiners, Grand Junction, 1969-76; hydrocompaction mgr. Colo. Dept. Hwys., Grand Junction, 1975-77; rsch. geologist Occidental Oil Shale, Inc., Grand Junction, 1977-78; geol. engr. Cleveland Cliffs Iron Co., Morgantown, W.Va., 1978-81; tech. advisor Ute Indian Tribe, Ft. Duchesne, Utah, 1981-86; ops. mgr. Charging Ute Corp., Golden, Colo., 1986-87; cons. Golden, 1987-90; petroleum engr. U.S. Dept. Interior/Bur. of Indian Affairs, Ft. Duchesne, 1990—, hazardous material mgr., freedom of info./privacy act coord., 1990—, natural resources officer, 1996—, ADP com. chmn., LAN adminstr., PL 93-638 com. chmn. grants/loan mgr., 1990—; minerals specialist Phoenix area Bur. Indian Affairs, pt. of contact for Fed. Govt. Y2K Project, 1998. Contbr. articles to profl. jours. Mem. Colo. Oil Field Investigators Assn., Vernal (Utah) C. of C., Internat. Platform Assn. Avocations: motorcycle touring, antiques, photography, hunting, fishing. Home: 255 East 200 North Vernal UT 84078-1713 Office: BIA Uintah Ouray Agy 988 S 7500 E PO Box 130 Fort Duchesne UT 84026-0130

CAMERON, JANICE CAROL, executive assistant; b. Pitcairn, N.Y., Feb. 16, 1940; d. Lawrence Baird and Alice Irene (Manchester) Morgan; m.

Albert A. Cameron, III, June 11, 1960 (div. Oct. 26, 1967); children: Albert A. IV, Richard D. AA, Jefferson C.C., Watertown, 1978; BA in Mgmt., St. Mary's Coll., Moraga, Calif., 1984. Nat. dir. Howard Ruff cmty. forums Target, Inc., 1982-86; sr. mktg. adminstr. IPF divsn. The Pacific Bank N.A./Providian Bancorp, San Francisco, 1989-96; with legal dept. Nat. IPF, Mesa, Ariz., 1996-97; exec. asst. to pres. and v.p. Smith-Southwestern, Inc., Mesa, Ariz., 1997—; notary public. Contbr. articles to profl. jours. Founder, chair First Support Group for Parents of Gay Mormons LDS, Social Svcs. Divsn., Fremont, Calif., 1986-94; Utah Gen. Authorities for Soc. Svcs. Program; 1st chpt. dir. Parents, Families and Friends of Lesbians and Gays, Danville-San Ramon chpt., Calif., 1993-94. Democrat. Home: 2400 E Baseline Ave Lot 147 Apache Junction AZ 85219-5712

CAMERON, JUDITH LYNNE, secondary education educator, hypnotherapist; b. Oakland, Calif., Apr. 29, 1945; d. Alfred Joseph and June Estelle (Faul) Neel; m. Richard Irwin Cameron, Dec. 17, 1967; 1 child, Kevin Dale. AA in Psychol., Sacramento City Coll., 1965; BA in Psychol., German, Calif. State U., 1967; MA in Reading Specialization, San Francisco State U., 1972; postgrad., Chapman Coll.; PhD, Am. Inst. Hypnotherapy, 1987. Cert. tchr., Calif. Tchr. St. Vincent's Cath. Sch., San Jose, Calif., 1969-70, Fremont (Calif.) Elem. Sch., 1970-72, LeRoy Boys Home, LaVerne, Calif., 1972-73; tchr. Grace Miller Elem. Sch., LaVerne, Calif., 1973-80, resource specialist, 1980-84; owner, mgr. Pioneer Take-out Franchises, Alhambra and San Gabriel, Calif., 1979-85; resource specialist, dept. chmn. Bonita H.S., LaVerne, Calif., 1984—; mentor tchr. in space sci. Bonita Unified Sch. Dist., 1988—, rep. LVTV; owner, therapist So. Calif. Clin. Hypnotherapy, Claremont, Calif., 1988—; bd. dirs., recommending tchr., asst. dir. Project Turnabout, Claremont, Calif.; Teacher-in-Space cons. Bonita Unified Sch. Dist., LaVerne, 1987—; advisor Peer Counseling Program, Bonita High Sch., 1987—; advisor Air Explorers/Edwards Test Pilot Sch., LaVerne, 1987—; mem. Civil Air Patrol, Squadron 68, Aerospace Office, 1988—; selected amb. U.S. Space Acad.-U.S. Space Camp Acad., Huntsville, Ala., 1990; named to national (now internat.) teaching faculty challenger ctr. for Space Edn., Alexandria, Va., 1990; regional coord. East San Gabiel Valley Future Scientists and Engrs. of Am.; amb. to U.S. Space Camp, 1990; mem. adj. faculty challenger learning ctr. Calif. State U., Dominguez Hills, 1994; rep. ceremony to honor astronauts Apollo 11, White House, 1994. Vol. advisor Children's Home Soc., Santa Ana, 1980-81; dist. rep. LVTV Channel 29, 1991; regional coord. East San Gabriel Valley chpt. Future Scientists and Engrs. of Am., 1992; mem. internat. investigation Commn. UFOs, 1991; field mem. Ctr. for Search for Extraterrestrial Intelligence, 1996. Recipient Tchr. of Yr., Bonita H.S., 1989, continuing svc. award, 1992; named Toyolaa Tchr. of Yr., 1994. Mem. NEA, AAUW, Internat. Investigations Com. on UFOs, Coun. Exceptional Children, Calif. Assn. Resource Specialists, Calif. Elem. Edn. Assn., Calif. Tchrs. Assn., Calif. Assn. Marriage and Family Therapists, Planetary Soc., Mutual UFO Network, Com. Sci. Investigation L5 Soc., Challenger Ctr. Space Edn., Calif. Challenger Ctr. Crew for Space Edn., Orange County Astronomers, Chinese Shar-Pei Am., Concord Club, Rare Breed Dog Club (L.A.). Republican. Avocations: skiing, surfing, guitar, flying, astrophotography. Home: 3257 La Travesia Dr Fullerton CA 92835-1455 Office: Bonita High Sch 115 W Allen Ave San Dimas CA 91773-1437

CAMERON, PAUL DRUMMOND, research facility administrator; b. Pitts., Nov. 9, 1939; s. Nelson Drummond and Veronica (Witco) C.; m. Virginia May Rusthoi. BA, L.A. Pacific Coll., 1961; MA, Calif. State U., L.A., 1962; PhD, U. Colo., 1966. Asst. prof. psychology Stout State U., Menomonie, Wis., 1966-67, Wayne State U., Detroit, 1967-69; assoc. prof. psychology U. Louisville, 1970-73, Fuller Grad. Sch. Psychology, Pasadena, Calif., 1976-79; assoc. prof. marriage and family U. Nebr., Lincoln, 1979-80; pvt. practice psychologist Lincoln, 1980-83; chmn. Family Rsch. Inst., Washington, 1982-95, Colo. Springs, 1995—; reviewer Am. Psychologist, Jour. Gerontology, Psychol. Reports; presenter, witness, cons. in field. Author: Exposing the AIDS Scandal, 1988, The Gay 90's, 1993; contbr. articles to profl. jours. Mem. Ea. Psychol. Assn., Nat. Assn. for Rsch. and Treatment of Homosexuality. Republican. Lutheran. Achievements include investigation of health effects of second-hand tobacco smoke; investigation of first comprehensive national random sample of sexuality; documented abbreviated lifespan of homosexuals. Office: Family Rsch Inst PO Box 62640 Colorado Springs CO 80962-2640

CAMERON, ROY EUGENE, scientist; b. Denver, July 16, 1929; s. Guy Francis and Ilda Annora (Horn) C.; m. Margot Elizabeth Hoagland, May 5, 1956 (div. July 1977); children: Susan Lynn, Catherine Ann; m 2d Carolyn Mary Light, Sept. 22, 1978. BS, Wash. State U., 1953, 54; MS, U. Ariz., 1958, PhD, 1961. Research scientist Hughes Aircraft Corp., Tucson, 1955-56; sr. scientist Jet Propulsion Lab., Pasadena, Calif., 1961-68, mem. tech. staff, 1969-74; dir. research Darwin Research Inst., Dana Point, Calif., 1974-75; dep. dir. Land Reclamation Lab. Argonne Ill. Nat. Lab., 1975-77, dir. energy resources tng. and devel., 1977-85; sr. staff scientist Lockheed Environ. Systems and Techs. Co., Las Vegas, Nev., 1986-95; quality assurance officer Lockheed Engring. and Scis. Co., Las Vegas, Nev., 1990-95; bioremediation lab. mgr. TAD Lockheed, 1991-95; environ. advisor Mashantucket (Conn.) Pequot Tribal Nation, 1995-96; cons. Lunar Receiving Lab. Baylor U., 1966-68, Ecology Ctr. Utah State U., Desert Biome, 1970-72, U. Alaska Tundra Biome, 1973-74, U. Maine, 1973-76, numerous others; mem. Nat. Agr. Rsch. and Extension Users Adv. Bd., 1986-92; tribal rep. stormwater phase 2 subcom. U.S. EPA, 1995-98, cons. sci. adv. bd., 1996—. Contrb. articles to sci. books; participated in 7 Antarctic expdns. Served with U.S. Army, 1950-52, Korea, Japan. Recipient 3 NASA awards for tech. briefs, EPA award of Excellence for global climate program, 1988; Paul Steere Burgess fellow U. Ariz., 1959; grantee NSF, 1970-74; Dept. Interior, 1978-80. Mem. AAAS, Soil Sci. Soc. Am., Am. Chem. Soc., Am. Soc. Microbiology, Am. Soc. Agronomy, Antarctican Soc., Soil and Water Conservation Soc. Am., World Future Soc., Internat. Soc. Soil Sci., Coun. Agrl. Sci. and Tech., Am. Inst. Biol. Sci., Am. Geophys. Union, Sigma Xi. Lutheran.

CAMERON, WINIFRED SAWTELL, astronomer; b. Oak Park, Ill., Dec. 3, 1918; d. Amos Alexander and Mildred Winifred (Shields) S.; m. Robert Curry Cameron, Oct. 17, 1953 (dec. Dec. 1972); children: Selene Jean Cameron Green, Sheri Carina Cameron Katz. BE, No. Ill. U., 1940; MA in Astronomy, Ind. U., 1952. Rsch. asst. Weather Forecasts, Inc., Chgo., 1943-46, 49-50; instr. astronomy Mount Holyoke Coll., South Hadley, Mass., 1950-51; solar researcher U.S. Naval Obs., Washington, 1951-58; researcher planetologist NASA-Goddard Space Flight Ctr., Greenbelt, Md., 1959-84, lectr., 1960-84; ind. lectr. and rsch. various civic and sci. orgns., schs., 1960—. Contbr. chpts. to books, encys., numerous articles to profl. jours. Recipient Disting. Alumnus award No. Ill. U., numerous other awards. Mem. Internat. Astron. Union, Internat. Assn. Planetology (v.p. 1985—), Am. Astron. Soc., Am. Geophys. Union, Assn. Lunar and Planetary Observers (Lunar Transiet Phenomena Lunar Recorder 1973-93), Brit. Astron. Assn. (hon.), Goddard Astronomy Club (v.p. Greenbelt chpt. 1972-74, pres. 1974-76). Home and Office: 200 Rojo Dr Sedona AZ 86351-9329

CAMMALLERI, JOSEPH ANTHONY, financial planner, retired air force officer; b. Bronx, N.Y., Feb. 2, 1935; s. Leo Anthony and Angela Marie (Mirandi) C.; BS, Manhattan Coll., 1956; M.S., Okla. State U., 1966; postgrad. Golden Gate U., 1974; children: Anthony R., Aaron L., Thomas K., Jeffrey A. Cert. life ins. instr., Calif. Commd. 2d lt. USAF, 1956, advanced through grades to lt. col., 1973; trainee flight crew, 1956-58; crew mem. B-52, 1958-64; behavioral scientist Aerospace Med. Rsch. Labs., Wright-Patterson AFB, Ohio, 1966-68; EB-66 crew mem. Tahkli AFB, Thailand, 1968-69; faculty mem. dept. life and behavioral sci. USAF Acad. (Colo.), 1969-74, assoc. prof., dir. operational psychology div., 1972-74, B-1 human factors engring. mgr. Air Force Flight Test Center, Edwards AFB, Calif., 1974-76, chief handbook devel., 1976-77; ret., 1977; account exec. Merrill Lynch, Pierce, Fenner & Smith, Sherman Oaks, Calif., 1977-80; acad. program rep. U. Redlands (Calif.), 1980-84, regional dir. admissions, 1984-86, mem. faculty Whitehead Coll., 1979—, assoc. dean admissions, 1986-89; faculty Golden Gate U., 1975-80; account exec. Humanomics Inc., 1989-90; corp. dir. tng. and edn. Fin. West Group, 1990-92, prin. CEO Spectrum Securities, Inc.; Westate Finance Grain 1952 sr. registered prin. annunadem United North Whitehead Coll. U. of Redlands, 1996—; registered gen. securities prin. Thomas F. White & Co., Inc., 1996—; CFO, registered prin. PLC Securities Corp., Ventura, Calif., 1996—; adj. faculty Calif. Luth. U., 1990—, Antioch U., 1992—; sec., 7th Ann. Narrow Gauge Conv. Com., Pasadena, Calif.,

1986. Contbr. articles to profl. jours. Sec. com. centennial celebration Rio Grande So. Ry., Dolores, Colo., 1991; USAF Acad. Liason Officer, North Los Angeles County, 1992—. Decorated D.F.C., Air medal (5), Meritorious Service medal. Mem. Nat. Ry. Hist. Soc., Ry. and Locomotive Hist. Soc., Rocky Mountain R.R. Club, L.A. Live Steamers, Nat. Model R.R. Assn., Colo. R.R. Hist. Found. (life), Santa Fe Ry. Hist. Soc., USAF Acad. Athletic Assn. (life), DAV, Psi Chi. Home: 601 Hampshire Rd Apt 550 Westlake Village CA 91361-2303 Office: PLC Securities Corp 1727 Mesa Verde Ave Ste 203 Ventura CA 93003-6540 also: Thomas F White & Co Inc 1727 Mesa Verde Ave Ste 203 Ventura CA 93003-6540

CAMP, ROGER ORTHO, fine arts educator, artist, photographer; b. Colfax, Wash., Feb. 19, 1945; s. Ortho O. and Helen E. (Minnassian) C.; m. Susan Margerison Lee-Warren, Dec. 22, 1982; children: Jason Hibbs, Ashley Hibbs. BA, U. Calif., Goleta, 1967; MA, U. Tex., 1968, U. Iowa, 1973; MFA, U. Iowa, 1974. Instr. Ea. Ill. U., Charleston, 1968-69; asst. prof. photography Cmty. Svcs., Huntington Beach, 1990—; contract photographer Black Star, N.Y.C., 1987—, Graphistock, N.Y.C., 1995—; artist Yancey Richardson Gallery, N.Y.C., 1990—. Photographer: Swimmers, 1988, Graphis Photo 94, 1994, Exploring Color Photography, 1995, At The Water's Edge, 1995, Shoreline: The Camera, 1996. Guest curator Huntington Beach Art Ctr., 1995; mem. Friends of South Coast Repertory, Costa Mesa, Calif., 1980—; assoc. Performing Arts Ctr., Costa Mesa, 1994. Named Artist of Yr., City of Huntington Beach, 1992; recipient Leica medal of Excellence, Leitz/New Sch., N.Y.C., 1989, Best Sports Photograph award Agfa/Graphis, 1995; Fulbright Hays fellow Fulbright Found., Brazil, 1988, Richard Florsheim fellow Fine Arts Work Ctr., Provincetown, 1982-83. Mem. Soc. Photographic Educators. Avocations: travel, gardening. Office: Golden West Coll 15744 Golden West St Huntington Beach CA 92647

CAMPBELL, ADDISON JAMES, JR., writer; b. Dilliner, Pa., Dec. 16, 1933; s. Addison James Campbell and Nora Lee (Marshall) Reynolds; m. Fumie Murashige, Oct. 13, 1962; 1 child, Gary Clark Campbell. *Wife Fumie Murashige Campbell was born in Hawaii and graduated from Maui High School in 1957. She attended the University of Houston where she attained a Masters Degree in Education in 1962. She has taught at all levels of public schools as well as an instructor at Prairie View A&M College. She is the inspiration and the beloved protagonist in her husband's first published fictional piece. In 1972 the family relocated to the "Aloha State" where she continues in her profession and a marriage of over thirty-five years.* Pres. Action Bolt Corp., Houston, 1965-72. Author: Nanci's World, Ukelele Lil of Lihue, The Object; co-author: Fumie Murashige Campbell, 1994; contbr. numerous articles and research papers to profl. jours. Sgt. USMC, 1952-55. Recipient recognition award for Adult Correction Officer for Island of Kauai, State of Hawaii, 1987, 88.

CAMPBELL, ANN MARIE, artist; b. Burbank, Calif., June 14, 1956; d. Stephen and Ann Marie (Luis) C.; children: Richard Arthur, Robert Campbell, Victoria Ann. BA in Painting, Sculpture, Graphic Arts, UCLA, 1980. spkr. Mural Art Seminar, ASID Student Career Forum, 1995. Artist (murals): The Pickle Barrel, 1992, Old World Sky with Angels, 1996, Cottage Garden, 1995, Two Street Window, 1996, Heather's Jazz Band, 1996, California Groaning Board, 1997, History of Virgin Records, 1997, numerous others throughout U.S. and Can., San Francisco, N.Y., L.A., Las Vegas, Orlando, Dallas, Phoenix, New Orleans, Denver, Chgo., Miami, and Vancouver, B.C. Mem. Nat. Soc. Mural Painters, Am. Soc. Portrait Artists, Alpha Lambda Delta. Roman Catholic. Office: PO Box 581 Folsom CA 95763-0581

CAMPBELL, ARLENE MARIE, photojournalist; b. Hefner, Oreg., Feb. 17, 1954; d. Martin Gerald and Sumiko Mary (Kanada) Whalen; m. Sidney Micheal Campbell, July 30, 1981 (div. July 1991); children: Julian Ray Whalen Campbell, Jenniffer Cheri Campbell, Sidney Martin Campbell, Martin Sidney Campbell. Data Processing Diploma, So. Nev. Vocat. Tech. Coll. With Temp Svc. Orgn., Denver, 1983-89, Monterey, Calif., 1993—. Prodr.: (documentaries) Village Voice, 1993-98, General Store, 1989-90. Home: 1130 Fremont Blvd # 165 Seaside CA 93955-5700 Office: Mountai View Cmty TV Ste A 950 N Rengstorf Ave Mountain View CA 94043

CAMPBELL, BEN NIGHTHORSE, senator; b. Auburn, Calif., Apr. 13, 1933; m. Linda Price; children: Colin, Shanan. BA, Calif. U., San Jose, 1957. Educator Sacramento Law Enforcement Agy.; mem. Colo. Gen. Assembly, 1983-86, U.S. Ho. Reps., 1987-93; U.S. Senator from Colorado, 1993—; rancher, jewelry designer, Ignacio, Colo. Chief No. Cheyenne Tribe. Named Outstanding Legislator Colo. Bankers Assn., 1984, Man of Yr. LaPlata Farm Bur., Durango, Colo., 1984; named one of Ten Best Legislators Denver Post/Channel 4, 1986. Mem. Am. Quarter Horse Assn., Am. Brangus Assn., Am. Indian Edn. Assn. Republican. Office: US Senate 380 Russell Senate Office Bldg Washington DC 20510-0605*

CAMPBELL, CAROLYN EVANS, adult education educator; b. Denver, June 3, 1935; d. George Thurston and Florence Genevieve (Cole) Evans; m. Russell Theodore Campbell, May 30, 1959; children: Russell Cole, Jordan Stuart. BA, U. Colo., 1957. Cert. tchr., Colo. Tchr. Colegio Franklin D. Roosevelt, Lima, Peru, 1957-58; history and English tchr. Sao Paulo and Caracas (Venezuela) schs., 1965-70; ESL tchr. San Jose (Calif.) Pub. Schs., 1985-88, poetry specialist, 1988-90; poetry specialist Jefferson County Adult Edn., Evergreen, Colo., 1991—; spkr. in field; performer poetry at women's groups, Denver, 1994—; judge Colo. Poetry Soc., Denver, 1995. Author: (poetry) Waiting for the Condor, 1990, Reflections of a White Bear, 1995, Soiled Doves of Colorado and the Old West, 1997, Tattooed Woman, 1998 (Colo. Ctr. for the Book award 1998); founding editor, pub. Buffalo Bones, 1993-98, Seasonings for A Colorado Afternoon, 1996 (Best Food for Thought award Westward), Her Day Begins Flamingo Pink, 1997. Grantee Sci. and Cultural Facilities Dist., 1993, Evergreen Area Coun. for Arts, 1994, Denver Woman's Press Club, 1994, 95; recipient Colo. Ctr. for the Book award, 1998. Mem. Colo. Author's League (Top Hand award 1995-98), Colo. Poetry Soc., Evergreen Poets and Writers (pres. 1994—). Avocations: drama, music, art, travel.

CAMPBELL, (CHARLES) ROBERT, architect. BS in Archtl. Engring., U. N.Mex., 1958. Registered architect, N.Mex., Tex., Ariz., Colo., Okla. With SMPC Architects, Albuquerque, 1955—, prin., 1969—, pres., CEO, 1991—; mem. State Bd. Examiners Architects, 1992-93, vice chmn., 1994, chmn., 1995-96; mem. adv. com. sch. architecture U. N.Mex.; vis. critic U. N.Mex. Profl. mem. Bernalillo County Bd. Appeals; bd. dirs. Presbyn. Healthcare Found. Mem. AIA (corp., pres., v.p.; sec. Albuquerque chpt., mem. joint practice com. 1981-82), Am. Arbitration Assn., Nat. Coun. Archtl. Registration Bd. (cert., juror/grader architecture registration exam, mem. architecture registration exam com. 1993-94, 94-95, 95-96), N.Mex. Soc. Architects (sec. 1974, pres. 1975-76). Office: 115 Amherst Dr SE Albuquerque NM 87106-1425*

CAMPBELL, COLIN HERALD, former mayor; b. Winnipeg, Man., Can., Jan. 18, 1911; s. Colin Charles and Aimee Florence (Herald) C.; m. Virginia Paris, July 20, 1935; children: Susanna Herald, Corinna Buford, Virginia Wallace. BA, Reed Coll., 1933. Exec. sec. City Club of Portland, 1934-39; alumni sec., dir. endowment adminstrn. Reed Coll., 1939-42, exec. sec. N.W. Inst. Internat. Rels. 1940-42, instr. photography, 1941-42; contract supr. engr. Kaiser Co., Inc. 1942-45; asst. pers. dir. Portland Gas & Coke Co., 1945-48; dir. indsl. rels. Pacific Power & Light Co., Portland, 1948-76. Mem. Oreg. Adv. Com. on Fair Employment Practices Act, 1949-55; trustee, chmn., pres. Portland Symphonic Choir, 1950-54; trustee Portland Civic Theater, 1951-54; bd. dirs. Portland Symphony Soc., 1957-60, Community Child Guidance Clinic, 1966-68; active United Way, 1945-75; bd. dirs. Contemporary Crafts Assn., 1972-76, treas., 1975-76; bd. dirs. Lake Oswego Corp., 1961-65, 71-73, 74-76, corp. sec., 1964, pres., 1973-74, treas., 1975-76; mem. Com. on Citizen Involvement, City of Lake Oswego, 1975-77; chmn. Bicentennial Com., Lake Oswego; sec. treas. Met. Area Communications Communic 1966-68 treas. Clackamas County Community Action (199-76, 1992—, 1982-85; mem. fin. adv. com. W. Clackamas County LWV, 1974-76, 78-80; councilman City of Lake Oswego, 1977-78, mayor, 1979-85, chmn. libr. growth task force, 1987-89, chmn. hist. rev. bd., 1990-92; chmn. energy adv. com. League Oreg. Cities, 1982-84; mem. adv. bd., chmn. fin. com. Lake

Oswego Adult Community Ctr. 1985-88; pres. Oswego Heritage Coun., 1992-95, sec., 1995-96, treas., 1997—; mem. County Blue Ribbon Com. on Law Enforcement, 1987-89; mem. fee arbitration panel Oreg. State Bar Assn., 1995—. Mem. Edison Electric Inst. (exec. com.), N.W. Electric Light and Power Assn., Lake Oswego C. of C. (v.p. 1986-87, chmn. Land Use com. 1990-91), Nat. Trust for Hist. Preservation, Hist. Preservation League Oreg., Portland Art Mus., Pacific N.W. Pers. Mgmt. Assn. (past regional v.p.), St. Andrews Soc., Oreg. Hist. Soc., Rotary (treas. Lake Oswego chpt. 1990-93). Republican. Presbyterian. Home: 398 Furnace St Lake Oswego OR 97034-3917

CAMPBELL, DAVID NEIL, physician, educator; b. Peoria, Ill., Dec. 1, 1944; s. William Neil and Ullian May (Hunter) C.; m. Charlyn Harris, Nov. 16, 1968; children: Scott, Chris, Brad. BA, Northwestern U., 1966; MD, Rush Med. Sch., 1974. Resident in gen. and cardiothoracic surgery U. Colo. Health Sci. Ctr., Denver, from asst. prof. to prof. surgery, 1988-95, prof. surgery, 1995—; cons., Denver, Colo., 1986—. Lt. U.S. Army, 1966-67, Korea. Office: U Colo Health Sci Ctr 4200 E 9th Ave # C310 Denver CO 80220-3706

CAMPBELL, DEMAREST LINDSAY, artist, designer, writer; b. N.Y.C., d. Peter Stephen III and Mary Elizabeth (Edwards) C.; m. Dale Gordon Haugo, 1978. BFA in Art History, MFA in S.E. Asian Art History, MFA in Theatre Design. Art dir., designer murals and residential interiors Campbell and Haugo Design Consultants, San Francisco, 1975—; chargeman scenic artist Am. Conservatory Theatre, 1976—. Designed, painted and sculpted over 200 prodns. for Broadway, internat. opera, motion pictures. Mem. NOW, Asian Art Mus. Soc., San Francisco. Mem. United Scenic Artists, Scenic & Title Artists and Theatrical Stage Designers, Sherlock Holmes Soc. London, Amnesty Internat., Nat. Trust for Hist. Preservation (Gt. Brit. and U.S.A. chpt.), Shavian Malthus Soc. (charter Gt. Brit. chpt.). Avocations: medical history, pre-Twentieth Century military history.

CAMPBELL, FREDERICK HOLLISTER, retired lawyer, historian; b. Somerville, Mass., June 14, 1923; s. George Murray and Irene Ivers (Smith) C.; A.B., Dartmouth, 1944; J.D., Northwestern U., 1949; postgrad. Indsl. Coll. Armed Forces, 1961-62; M.A. in History, U. Colo., 1984, PhD in History, 1993; m. Amy Holding Strohm, Apr. 14, 1951; 1 dau., Susan Hollister. Served with USMCR, 1943-46, 50-53; joined USMC, 1953, advanced through grades to lt. col., 1962; admitted to Ill. bar, 1950, U.S. Supreme Ct. bar, 1967, Colo. bar, 1968; judge adv. USMC, Camp Lejeune, N.C., Korea, Parris Island, S.C., El Toro, Calif., Vietnam, Washington, 1950-67; asso. editor Callaghan and Co., Chgo., 1949-50; practiced law, Colorado Springs, Colo., 1968-88; ptnr. firm Gibson, Gerdes and Campbell, 1969-79; pvt. practice law, 1980-88; gen. counsel 1st Fin. Mortgage Corp., 1988-96, vice chmn., corp. sec., 1993-96; hon. instr. history U. Colo., Colorado Springs, 1986—; vis. instr. U. Colo. Coll., 1993-95, asst. prof., 1996—. Mem. Estate Planning Coun., Colorado Springs, 1971-81, v.p., 1977-78. Rep. precinct committeeman, 1971-86; del. Colo. Rep. State Conv., 1972, 74, 76, 80, alt., 1978; trustee Frontier Village Found., 1971-77; bd. dirs. Rocky Mountain Nature Assn., 1975—, pres., 1979-92; dir. Rocky Mountain Nat. Park Assocs. 1986-, v.p. 1986-92, sec. 1992-95. Mem. Colo. Bar Assn., El Paso County Bar Assn., Am. Arbitration Assn. Marines Meml. Club, Phi Alpha Theta. Congregationalist. Author: John's American Notary and Commissioner of Deeds Manual, 1950. Contbr. articles to profl. jours. Home and Office: 2707 Holiday Ln Colorado Springs CO 80909-1217

CAMPBELL, HARRY WOODSON, geologist, mining engineer; b. Carthage, Mo., Jan. 14, 1946; s. William Hampton and Elizabeth Verle (LeGrand) C. BSEE, Kans. State U., 1969; MBA, U. Oreg., 1973, BS in Geology, 1975; MS in Geology, Brown U., 1978. Registered profl. engr., Wash.; cert. profl. geologist, Va. Geologist, mining engr. and phys. scientist U.S. Bur. Mines, Spokane, 1980-96; geologist U.S. Geol. Survey, Spokane, 1996—. Served with U.S. Army, 1969-71. Recipient Spl. Achievement award U.S. Bur. Mines, 1983, 86, 88. Mem. Geol. Soc. Am., Soc. Mining Engrs. Avocation: genealogy. Office: US Bur Mines 4257 E 26th Ave Spokane WA 99223-5623

CAMPBELL, HOLLY VICTORIA PINK, university administrator; b. Highland Park, Ill. BA in Studio Art, No. Ill. U., 1979; JD, U. Oreg., 1991. Assoc. dir. Oreg. Humanities Ctr, U. Oreg., Eugene, 1993-98; dir. Tanner Humanities Ctr., U. Utah, Salt Lake City, 1998—; cons. legal rsch., 1991—; rsch. asst., ct.-appointed lead counsel in Hanford Nuclear Reservation Litigatin, 1992-93. Vol. honor code com. Student Bar Assn., 1989-90, Redwood Nat. Park, Crescent City, Calif., 1984. Mem. Coun. for Advancement and Support of Edn. Avocations: art, writing, hiking, camping, fly fishing. Office: U Utah Tanner Humanities Ctr 201 Carlson Hall 380 S 1400 E Salt Lake City UT 84112

CAMPBELL, IAN DAVID, opera company director; b. Brisbane, Australia, Dec. 21, 1945; came to U.S., 1982; m. Ann Spira; children: Benjamin, David. BA, U. Sydney, Australia, 1967. Prin. tenor singer The Australian Opera, Sydney, 1967-74; sr. music officer The Australia Council, Sydney, 1974-76; gen. mgr., stage dir. The State Opera of South Australia, Adelaide, 1976-82; asst. artistic adminstr. Met. Opera, N.Y.C., 1982-83; gen. dir. San Diego Opera, 1983—; guest lectr. U. Adelaide, 1978; guest prof. San Diego State U., 1986—; cons. Lyric Opera Queensland, Australia, 1980-81; bd. dirs. Opera Am., Washington, 1986-95, 97—; chmn. judges Met. Opera Auditions, Sydney, 1989, Masterclasses, Music Acad. of the West, 1993-96. Producer, host San Diego Opera Radio Program, 1984—, At the Opera with Ian Campbell, 1984—; stage director La Boheme, 1981, The Tales of Hoffmann, 1982 (both in South Australia), Falstaff (San Diego Opera), 1999. Mem., bd. dirs. San Diego Conv. and Visitors Bur., 1997—. Recipient Peri award Opera Guild So. Calif., 1984; named Headliner of Yr., San Diego Press Club, 1991, Father of Yr., San Diego, 1997. Fellow Australian Inst. Mgmt.; mem. Kona Kai Club, Rotary, San Diego Pres Club (Headliner award 1991). Avocations: squash, golf, tennis. Office: San Diego Opera 1200 3rd Ave Fl 18 San Diego CA 92101

CAMPBELL, JEFF B., realtor; b. San Jose, Calif., June 4, 1961; s. Gerald Campbell and DeAnna Chavez; m. Nadia Campbell, Mar. 24, 1990; children: Rebecca, Ford. Grad. h.s., San Diego, 1979. Adult edn. and vocat. tchr. Grossmont Unified Sch. Dist., Alpine, Calif., 1997—.

CAMPBELL, JOHN D., religious organization administrator. Media contact, coord. ch. svc. mission Ch. God. Office: Ch God We Can Assembly, 4717 56th St, Camrose, AB Canada T4V 2C4

CAMPBELL, RAYMOND WILLIAM, surgical nurse; b. Orlando, Fla., Sept. 3, 1956; s. Frank Richard Sr. and Edythe Bertha (Voyles) C.; children: Rachael D., Raymond W. II. AD, Kellogg Coll., Battle Creek, Mich., 1989. Cert. ACLS, emergency med. tech., nurse-operating room. Indsl. emergency med. technician Ingalls Shipbldg., Pascagoula, Miss., 1976-79; chief urodynamics technician Lucerne Gen. Hosp., Orlando, 1978-79; psychiat. nursing asst. U.S. VA Med. Ctr., Battle Creek, 1980-87; scrub and circulating nurse Battle Creek Health Sys., 1989-94, oper. rm. charge nurse, 1994; scrub and circulating nurse, neurosurg. svcs. coord. Borgess Med. Ctr., 1994—, cln. preceptor, 1994—; mem. oper. rm. safety and infection control policy and procedure com. Battle Creek Health Systems, chmn. oper. rm. product edn. com.; operating rm. reprocessing com. Borgess Med. Ctr., 1996—, neurosurgery preceptor, 1994—. Trustee Village of Augusta, Mich., fire marshall and police commr.; ward mission leader Ch. Jesus Christ of LDS, Kalamazoo, 1994-95. With USN, 1974-76. Mem. Am. Assn. Neurosci. Nurses, Assn. Operating Rm. Nurses. Office: Am Mobile Nurses San Diego Corp Ctr 12730 High Bluff Dr Ste 400 San Diego CA 92130-2079

CAMPBELL, ROBERT CHARLES, minister, theology educator; b. Chandler, Ariz., Mar. 9, 1924; s. Alexander Joshua and Florence (Betzner) C.; m. Lotus Idamae Graham, July 12, 1945; children: Robin Carl, Cherry Colinni ThM, 1949, ThD, 1951, DD (hon.). 1974; MA, U. So. Calif., 1959; postgrad., Dropsie U., 1949-51, U. Pa., 1951-52, NYU, 1960-62, U. Cambridge, Eng., 1969; DLitt (hon.), Am. Bapt. Sem. of West, 1972; HHD (hon.), Alderson-Broaddus Coll., 1979; LHD (hon.), Linfield Coll., 1982; LLD

(hon.), Franklin Coll., 1986. Ordained to ministry Am. Bapt. Ch., 1947; pastor 34th St. Bapt. Ch., Phila., 1945-49; instr. Eastern Bapt. Theol. Sem., Phila., 1949-51; asst. prof. Eastern Coll., St. Davids, Pa., 1951-53; assoc. prof. N.T. Am. Bapt. Sem. of West, Covina, Cal., 1953-54, dean, prof., 1954-72; gen. sec. Am. Bapt. Chs. in U.S.A., Valley Forge, Pa., 1972-87; pres. Eastern Bapt. Theol. Sem., Phila., 1987-89, ret.; Vis. lectr. Sch. Theology at Claremont, Calif., 1961-63, U. Redlands, Calif., 1959-60, 66-67, Fuller Theology Seminary, Calif., 1992-97; Bd. mgrs. Am. Bapt. Bd. of Edn. and Publ., 1956-59, 65-69; v.p. So. Calif. Bapt. Conv., 1967-68; pres. Am. Bapt. Chs. of Pacific S.W., 1970-71; Pres. N.Am. Bapt. Fellowship, 1974-76; mem. exec. com. Bapt. World Alliance, 1972-90, v.p., 1975-80; mem. exec. com., gov. bd. Nat. Council Chs. of Christ in U.S.A., 1972-87; del. to World Council of Chs., 1975, 83, mem. central com., 1975-90. Author: Great Words of the Faith, 1965, The Gospel of Paul, 1973, Evangelistic Emphases in Ephesians, Jesus Still Has Something To Say, 1987. Home: 125 Via Alicia Santa Barbara CA 93108-1769

CAMPBELL, ROBERT HEDGCOCK, investment banker, lawyer; b. Ann Arbor, Mich., Jan. 16, 1948; s. Robert Miller and Ruth Adele (Hedgcock) C.; m. Katherine Kettering, June 17, 1972; children: Mollie DuPlan, Katherine Elizabeth, Anne Kettering. BA, U. Wash., 1970, JD, 1973. Bar: Wash. 1973, Wash. State Supreme Ct. 1973, Fed. 1973, U.S. Dist. Ct. (we. dist.) Wash. 1973, Ct. Appeals (9th cir.) 1981. Assoc. Roberts & Shefelman, Seattle, 1973-78, ptnr., 1978-85; sr. v.p. Lehman Bros., Inc., Seattle, 1985-87, mng. dir., 1987—; dir., treas. Nat. Assn. Bd. Lawyers, Hinsdale, Ill., 1982-85; pres., trustee Wash. State Soc. Hosp. Attys., Seattle, 1982-85; mem. econs. dept. vis. com. U. Wash., 1995-97; mem. econs. dept. vis. com. U. Wash., 1995-98, mem. Law Sch. dean's adv. bd., 1999—. Contbr. articles to profl. jours. Trustee Bellevue (Wash.) Schs. Found., 1988-91, pres., 1989-90; nation chief Bellevue Eastside YMCA Indian Princess Program, 1983-88; trustee Wash. Phikeia Found., 1983-91, Sandy Hook Yacht Club Estates, Inc., 1993-98; mem. Wash. Gov.'s Food Processing Coun., 1990-91. Republican. Avocations: skiing, wind surfing, bike riding, physical fitness, golf. Home: 8604 NE 10th St Medina WA 98039-3915 Office: Lehman Bros Columbia Seafirst Ctr 701 5th Ave Ste 7101 Seattle WA 98104-7016

CAMPBELL, SANDRA RUTH, English as second language educator; b. Tomahawk, Wis., Sept. 2, 1951; d. Donald James and Anna Cecilia (Tresness) C. BA, U. Alta., Edmonton, Can., 1972; tchr. cert., Simon Fraser U., Burnaby, B.C., Can., 1976; MEd, U. Wash., 1998. Cert. tchr., Wash. Tchr. Canboo-Chilcotin Sch. Dist., Williams Lake, B.C., 1977-80; tchr., coord. Vancouver (B.C.) C.C., 1980-81; instr. Camosun Coll., Victoria, B.C., 1989-93; cons. Adult Basic Literacy Network, Seattle, 1989-93; instr. Lake Washington Tech. Coll., Kirkland, Wash., 1993—. Reviewer software programs; writer curriculum in field. Mem. TESOL, Adult Basic Literacy Educators, Washington Assn. Second Lang. Educators. Avocations: horseback riding, skiing, biking, running. Office: Lake Washington Tech Coll 11605 132d Ave NE Kirkland WA 98034

CAMPBELL, SCOTT, newspaper publishing company executive; b. May 25, 1956. BS, U. Oreg., 1979. Pub. The Columbian, Vancouver, Wash., 1980-86, pres., COO, 1986-88, pub., 1988—. Chair adv. coun. Wash. State U.; chair S.W. Wash. Higher Edn. Consortium; mem. exec. bd. Columbia River Econ. Devel. Coun. Mem. Newspaper Assn. Am. (mem. bus. devel. com.), Pacific N.W. Newspaper Assn. (pres.), Allied Daily Newspapers Wash. Office: Columbian Pub Co PO Box 180 701 W 8th St Vancouver WA 98666*

CAMPBELL, STEWART CLAWSON, retired sales executive, artist; b. Salt Lake City, Aug. 18, 1903; s. Alexander Stewart and Alice Young (Clawson) C.; m. Mary M. McIntyre, June 27, 1942 (dec. July 1983); children: Stewart, Jeffrey, David (dec.), James, Scott, Judith. Student, U. Utah, 1928-31. Pres. Mormon Mission Conf., Dresden, Germany, 1924-28; surveyor Wasatch Gas Co., Salt Lake City, 1928-31, United Gas Sys., Houston, 1931-32; warehouse supr. Maceys Dept. Store, N.Y.C., 1932-35; overseer Alaska Rural Rehab. Corp., Palmer, 1935-39; regional adminstr. Nat. Youth Adminstrn., Cleve., 1939-41; spl. asst. Fed. Civil Def. Emergency Adminstrn., Washington, 1941-42; pres. Utah Wonderland Stages, Salt Lake City, 1946-51; regional adminstr. Fed. Civil Def. Adminstrn., 1952-56; gen. sales mgr. O.C. Tanner Co., Salt Lake City, 1956-75; ret., 1975. One-man shows include Wilma Wayne Gallery, London; maker Petrohlyphs replicas (ancient Indian images in stone), Galerie Royal, Paris, 1984; conceived (new art form) Tower-Mosaic for Human Rights Space Movement and Tower: Mosaic; proposed meml. to Am.'s ten pioneer astronaut heroes; originator of painting with fire art form. Lt. col. USAF, 1942-46. Named to Hon. Order of Ky. Colonels, 1953. Mem. LDS Ch. Avocations: reading, alpine skiing, ice skating, ballroom and contemporary dancing. Home: Apt 10 A 777 E South Temple Salt Lake City UT 84102-1274

CAMPBELL, TENA, judge; b. Wendell, Idaho, Dec. 11, 1944. BA, U. Idaho, 1967; MA in French Lit. with honors, Ariz. State U., 1970, JD, 1977. Bar: Utah 1977, U.S. Dist. Ct. Utah 1977, U.S. Ct. Appeals (10th cir.) 1982. Tchr. French Twin Falls (Idaho) Sch. Dist., 1967-69, Tempe (Ariz.) H.S., Phoenix Jr. Coll., 1972-73; assoc. atty. Johnson Durham and Moxley, Salt Lake City, 1977-79, Fabian and Clendenin, Salt Lake City, 1979-81; dep. county atty. Salt Lake County, Salt Lake City, 1981; asst. U.S. atty. criminal divsn. Office of U.S. Atty. Dist. Utah, 1981-95; judge U.S. Dist. Ct. Utah, 1995—. Mem. Utah Bar Assn., Ft. Douglas HIdden Valley Country Club. Office: US Dist Ct Utah Rm 110 US Ct House 350 S Main St Salt Lake City UT 84101-2106*

CAMPBELL, THOMAS J., congressman; b. Chgo., Aug. 14, 1952; s. William J. and Marie Campbell; m. Susanne Martin. BA, MA in Econs. with highest honors, U. Chgo., 1973, PhD in Econs. with highest dept. fellowship, 1980; JD magna cum laude, Harvard U., 1976. Law clk. to presiding justice U.S. Ct. Appeals (D.C. cir.), 1976-77; law clk. to Justice Byron R. White U.S. Supreme Ct., Washington, 1977-78; assoc. Winston & Strawn, Chgo., 1978-80; White Ho. fellow Office Chief of Staff and White Ho. of Counsel, Washington, 1980-81; exec. asst. to dep. atty. gen. Dept. Justice, Washington, 1981; dir. Bur Trade Competition FTC, Washington, 1981-83, head del. to OECD, Paris, com. experts on restictive bus. practices, 1982, 83; mem. 101st-105th Congresses from Calif. 12th Dist., 1989-92; mem. com. on sci., space and tech., com. on judiciary, banking, fin. and urban affairs 101st Congress from Calif. 12th Dist., 1989-92; mem. 104th - 105th Congress (now 106th Congress) from Calif. 15th Dist., 1995—; prof. Stanford Law Sch., 1983-89; mem. Congressional Com. on Banking and Fin. Svcs., 1997—, Internat. Rels., 1997—. Referee Jour. Polit. Economy, Internat. Rev. Law and Econs. Mem. San Francisco Com. on Fgn. Relations. Mem. ABA (antitrust sect., coun. 1985-88, program chmn. 1983-84). Office: US Ho of Reps 2442 Rayburn House Office Bldg Washington DC 20515-0515*

CAMPBELL, VIRGINIA KOLNICK, retired rehabilitation counselor; b. Smelterville, Idaho, Feb. 21, 1934; d. Dolph and Ruberta Rhoda (Hunt) Towles; m. Phillip Kolnick, Dec. 30, 1953 (div. Apr. 1963); children: Jo Ann, Phyllis Ann, Betty Sue; m. Robert Lloyd Campbell, Sept. 18, 1993. AA in Nursing, Phoenix Coll., 1961; BS in Sociology, Ariz. State U., 1966, MA in Edn., 1968, M of Counseling, 1971. RN Ariz.; cert. rehab. counselor. Coord. pvt. duty nursing Med. Personnel Pool, Phoenix, 1971-72; nurse health evaluation Ariz. Health Plan, Phoenix, 1973; instr. continuing edn. program Phoenix Coll., Maricopa County C.C. Dist., 1973-75; vocat. rehab. counselor III, cardio-pulmonary specialist State of Ariz., Phoenix, 1974-92, ret., 1992. Mem. Am. Assn. Cardiovascular Pulmonary Rehab. (fellow), Ariz. Cardiovascular Pulmonary Rehab. Assn. Avocations: bird watching, reading, pinochle, hiking, computers. Home: 9224 E Bighorn Dr Prescott Valley AZ 86314-7302

CAMPBELL, WILLIAM JOSEPH, academic director; b. Bklyn., N.Y., Nov. 26, 1944; s. William Joseph and Loretta Jane (Graessle) C. BA in Philosophy, U. Dayton, 1966; MS in Edn., Fordham U., 1972; MA in Theology, St. John's U., 1977; MA in Pvt. Sch. Adminstrn., U. San Francisco, 1986; EdD in Ednl. Mgmt., U. LaVerne, 1990. Cert. sch. adminstr., Calif.; cert. guidance counselor, N.Y. Tchr., dean students Most Holy Trinity H.S., Bklyn., 1966-68; tchr., coach Charlotte (N.C.) Cath. H.S., 1968-69; tchr., dir. freshman guidance Chaminade H.S., Mineola, N.Y., 1969-82; tchr., counselor Junipero Serra H.S., Gardena, Calif., 1982-84; academic asst. prin. Archbishop Riordan H.S., San Francisco, 1984-87; prin. Chaminade Coll. Prep., West Hills, Calif., 1987-90; dir. edn. Marianists, Cupertino, Calif., 1990-95; asst. supt. Archdiocese of Portland, Oreg., 1996—. Bd. dirs. Regis H.S., Staton, Oreg.; chmn. bd. regents Chaminade U., Honolulu. Mem. ASCD, Nat. Assn. Secondary Sch. Prins., Nat. Cath. Edn. Assn., World Future Soc., Assn. for Religious and Values Issues in Counseling, Phi Delta Kappa. Avocations: golfing, reading, cooking. Office: Archdiocese of Portland 2838 E Burnside St Portland OR 97214-1895

CAMPER, JOHN SAXTON, public relations and marketing executive; b. Trenton, N.J., Apr. 24, 1929; s. Thomas Emory and Mildred Ruth (Burke) C.; m. Ferne Arlene Clanton; children: Susan Jennifer, John Saxton III. BS in History and Econs., U. Nebr., 1968. Enlisted U.S. Army, 1948, commd. to 1st lt., advanced through ranks to maj., 1972, ret., 1972; regional mktg. officer First Bank System, Mont., 1978-83; lectr., instr. mktg. and advt. pub. rels.; pres. Camper Comm., Helena, 1983—; dir. Profl. Devel. Ctr., Mont., 1984-91. Decorated Legion of Merit. Mem. Helena Advt. Fedn. (1st pres., founder), Rotary Internat. (dist. gov. 1998-99). Republican. Methodist.

CAMPIONE, MARY ELLEN, software engineer, consultant, writer; b. Salinas, Calif., Aug. 30, 1963; d. David Arthur Sr. and Ellen Loraine (Loughran) McNabb; m. Richard James Campione, Oct. 2, 1993; 1 child, Sophia Ann. BS in Computer Sci., Calif. Poly., 1985. Programmer Ford Aerospace, Palo Alto, Calif., 1985-88; software engr. Sun Microsystems, Mountain View, Calif., 1988-89; developer support engr. Next Computer Inc., Redwood City, Calif., 1990-91; ind. software cons., writer San Francisco, 1991-96; tech. writer Sun Microsystems, Mountain View, Calif., 1996—. Author: Typesetting Tables on The Unix System, 1990, Postscript By Example, 1992, The Java Tutorial, 1996, 2d edit., 1998. Avocations: paper art, snowboarding, cycling, sewing.

CAMPOS, JOAQUIN PAUL, III, chemical physicist, regulatory affairs analyst; b. L.A., Feb. 16, 1962; s. Joaquin Reyna and Maria Luz (Chavez) C.; m. Barbara Ann Esquivel, Oct. 31, 1987; children: Courtney Luz, Nathaniel Alexander. Student, U. Calif., Santa Cruz, 1980-85, UCLA, 1985-86. Tutor U. Calif., Santa Cruz, 1980-82, admissions liaison, 1982-84; chem. teaching assoc. L.A. Unified Sch. Dist., 1985-87; pvt. tutor Santa Clara, L.A., 1987-89; tech. specialist Alpha Therapeutics Corp., L.A., 1989-95; regulatory affairs specialist III Gensia Labs., Ltd., Irvine, Calif., 1995-96; sr. assoc. Genentech, Inc., South San Francisco, 1996—; cons. L.A. Unified Sch. Dist., 1985-87. Docent in tng. L.A. Mus. of Sci. and Industry, 1989. Scholar, grantee So. Calif. Gas Co., L.A., 1980-84, Sloan Rsch. fellow, 1981-82. Mem. Am. Chem. Soc., N.Y. Acad. Sci., Am. Inst. Chemists, Am. Assn. Physics Tchrs., AAAS, Fed. Am. Scientists, Pharm. Rsch. Mfrs. Am., Internat. Union of Pure and Applied Chemistry, Drug Info. Assn., Math. Assn. Am., Soc. Hispanic Profl. Engrs., IEEE. Avocations: reading, playing chess, computer programming, family. Office: Genentech Inc 460 Point San Bruno Blvd South San Francisco CA 94080-4990

CAMPOS, SANTIAGO E., federal judge; b. Santa Rosa, N.Mex., Dec. 25, 1926; s. Ramon and Miquela Campos; m. Patsy Campos, Jan. 27, 1947; children: Theresa, Rebecca, Christina, Miquela Feliz. J.D., U. N.Mex., 1953. Bar: N.Mex. 1953. Asst., 1st asst. atty gen. State of N.Mex., 1955-57; judge 1st Jud. Dist. N.Mex., 1971-78; judge U.S. Dist. Ct. N.Mex., Santa Fe, 1978—, sr. judge, 1992—. Served as seaman USN, 1944-46. Mem. State Bar of N.Mex., First Jud. Dist. Bar Assn. (hon.), Hon. Order of Coif. Office: US Dist Ct PO Box 2244 Santa Fe NM 87504-2244*

CAMRON, ROXANNE, editor; b. Los Angeles; d. Irving John and Roslyn (Weinberger) Spiro; m. Robert Camron; children: Ashley Jennifer, Erin Jession. B.A. in Journalism, U. So. Calif. West Coast fashion and beauty editor, Teen mag., Los Angeles, 1969-70; sr. editor Teen mag., 1972-75, editor, 1976—; pub. relations rep. Max Factor Co., 1970; asst. to creative dir. Polly Bergen Co., 1970-71; lectr. teen groups; freelance writer. Active Homeowners Assn. Mem. Am. Soc. Exec. Women. Office: Teen Mag 6420 Wilshire Blvd Los Angeles CA 90048-5502

CAMY, ANN L., English language educator; b. Denver, Nov. 9, 1940; d. Everett L. and Margaret E. (Garrison) B.; 1 child, Dagny Ann. BA, U. No. Colo., 1963, MA, 1969. Cert. master English tchr., Colo. High sch. English tchr. Jefferson County Pub. Schs., Lakewood, Colo., 1963-68, 73-75; pub. Courage (Ea.) Ltd., Eastbourne, Eng., 1969-73; info. rschr. Coors Brewing Co., Golden, Colo., 1977-84; trainer mgmt. and comm. skills Speak/Write, Denver, 1984-90, Camy, Cady & Barnhardt, Denver, 1984-90; instr. comm. U. Phoenix, Englewood, Colo., 1989-93; instr. English, U. No. Colo., Greeley, 1968-69, Met. State Coll., Denver, 1991-92; part-time instr. English, Red Rocks C.C., Lakewood, Colo., 1986-93, instr. English, 1993—. Co-chair Citizens Adv. Coun. to Gilpin and Jefferson Counties Dist. Atty., Golden, 1986-87, co-chair steering com. Jefferson County Sch. Age Child Care Initiative, Golden, 1986-89; mem. steering com. Jefferson County Sch.-to-Career Initiative. Named Outstanding Bus. Woman, Eastbourne, 1972, Woman of Achievement Honoree, YWCA, Colo., 1984, Distance Educator of Yr., Telecoop-Colo., 1996. Mem. Nat. Coun. Tchrs. English. Avocation: writing poetry. Home: 13019 W Ohio Ave Lakewood CO 80228-3105 Office: Red Rocks CC Coord Eng and SPE & Com Program 13300 W 6th Ave Lakewood CO 80228-1213

CANADA, WILLIAM H., plastic surgeon; b. Huntington, W.Va., Sept. 5, 1930. MD, W.Va. U., 1956. Intern Meml. Hosp., Charleston, W.Va., 1956-57, gen. surgeon, 1957-59; plastic surgeon Baylor U. Med. Ctr., Houston, 1959-61; chief plastic surgeon Las Vegas Surgery Ctr., 1987—; attending surgeon Univ. Med. Ctr., Las Vegas; clin. instr. plastic surgery Baylor U., Houston. Fellow ACS. Office: 8068 W Sahara Ave Ste G Las Vegas NV 89117-1973

CANADAY, RICHARD A., lawyer; b. Alton, Ill., Aug. 26, 1947. AB, Stanford U., 1969; JD, U. Calif., 1973. Bar: Oreg. 1973, Wash. 1987. Ptnr. Miller, Nash, Wiener, Hager & Carlsen, Portland, Oreg. Mem. ABA, Oreg. State Bar, Wash. State Bar Assn. Office: Miller Nash Wiener Hager & Carlsen 111 SW 5th Ave Ste 3500 Portland OR 97204-3699

CANBY, WILLIAM CAMERON, JR., federal judge; b. St. Paul, May 22, 1931; s. William Cameron and Margaret Leah (Lewis) C.; m. Jane Adams, June 18, 1954; children—William Nathan, John Adams, Margaret Lewis. A.B., Yale U., 1953; LL.B., U. Minn., 1956. Bar: Minn. 1956, Ariz. 1972. Law clk. U.S. Supreme Ct. Justice Charles E. Whittaker, 1958-59; asso. firm Oppenheimer, Hodgson, Brown, Baer & Wolff, St. Paul, 1959-62; asso., then dep. dir. Peace Corps, Ethiopia, 1962-64; dir. Peace Corps, Uganda, 1964-66; asst. to U.S. Senator Walter Mondale, 1966; asst. to pres. SUNY, 1967; prof. law Ariz. State U., 1967-80; judge U.S. Ct. Appeals (9th cir.), Phoenix, 1980-96, sr. judge, 1996—; chief justice High Ct. of the Trust Ter. of the Pacific Islands, 1993-94; bd. dirs. Ariz. Center Law in Public Interest, 1974-80, Maricopa County Legal Aid Soc., 1972-78, D.N.A.-People's Legal Services, 1978-80; Fulbright prof. Makerere U. Faculty Law, Kampala, Uganda, 1970-71. Author: American Indian Law, 1998; also articles; note editor: Minn. Law Rev, 1955-56. Precinct and state committeeman Democratic Party Ariz., 1972-80; bd. dirs. Central Ariz. Coalition for Right to Choose, 1976-80. Served with USAF, 1956-58. Mem. State Bar Ariz., Minn. Bar Assn., Maricopa County Bar Assn., Phi Beta Kappa, Order of Coif. Office: US Ct Appeals 9th Cir US Courthouse Rm 6445 230 N 1st Ave Phoenix AZ 85025-0230

CANDELA, MICHAEL A., producer, director; b. Bklyn., Mar. 3, 1948; s. Harry and Christina (Candela) P.; m. Marsha Brooks, Aug. 18, 1996. BA, U. Calif. Santa Cruz, 1971-74. Mem. dir. 92nd St. YMHA, N.Y.C., 1982-84; casting dir. Skyline Casting, N.Y.C., 1983-87, L.A., 1988-91; casting dir. W.E.E., L.A., 1992-97; prodr. Candela Entertainment Corp., L.A., 1997—; artistic dir. Theatre Harmony Ensemble, L.A., 1971—, co artistic dir., Am. Theatre of Opera, L.A., 1975—, cons. Hollywood H.S., L.A., 1990—. Author: Santa Cruz Poets, 1971. Organizer, Hollywood Ctr. Religion Science, L.A., 1996-98. Office: Candela Entertainment Corp 6650 Santa Monica Blvd Los Angeles CA 90038-1312

CANE, WILLIAM EARL, nonprofit organization executive; b. San Francisco, Aug. 15, 1935; s. Joseph Earl and Mae M. (McDermott) C.; m. Patricia Ann Mathes (div. 1997). MDiv, St. Patrick's Sem., 1973; ThD, San Francisco Theol., 1976. Assoc. pastor St. Joseph Ch., Cupertino, Calif., 1960-65; dir. St. Benedict Ctr., San Francisco, 1966-72; prof. Grad. Theol., Berkeley, Calif., 1973-79; dir. IF, Santa Cruz, Calif., 1975—; editor Integrities, Santa Cruz, 1985—; pres. Assn. Priests Union, San Francisco, 1970-72; bd. dirs. Gaia Ctr., Santa Cruz, Friends of Cantera, Santa Cruz; lectr. in field. Author: Thru Crisis to Freedom, 1980, Circles of Hope, 1992; contbr. articles to profl. jours. Founder Friends of the Deaf, San Francisco, 1970; co-founder Santa Cruz (Calif.) Sanctuary, 1987. Grantee Rascob Found., San Francisco, 1970, Santa Cruz (Calif.) Cmty. Found., 1988, Mervyn's Found., 1988, Eschaton Found., Santa Cruz, 1994. Avocations: gardener, water diviner, tennis, chef. Home and Office: 3015 Freedom Blvd Watsonville CA 95076-0436

CANFIELD, GRANT WELLINGTON, JR., management consultant; b. L.A., Nov. 28, 1923; s. Grant Wellington and Phyllis Marie (Westland) C.; m. Virginia Louise Bellinger, June 17, 1945; 1 child, Julie Marie. BS, U. So. Calif., 1949, MBA, 1958. Personnel and indsl. relations exec., L.A., 1949-55; employee relations cons., regional mgr. Mchts. and Mfrs. Assn. L.A., 1955-60; v.p., orgnl. devel. cons. Hawaii Employers Council, Honolulu, 1960-75; pres., dir. Hawaiian Ednl. Council, 1969-92, chmn., CEO, 1989-92, chmn. emeritus, 1992; prin. cons. Grant W. Canfield CMC, 1993—; faculty assignments Calif. State U., L.A., 1957-59, U. So. Calif., 1958-59, U. Hawaii, 1963-72; exec. v.p. Hawaii Garment Mfrs. Assn., 1965-75, Assn. Hawaii Restaurant Employers, 1966-75; exec. dir. Hawaii League Savs. Assns., 1971-78; exec. dir. Pan-Pacific Surg. Assn., 1980-81, exec. v.p., 1982-83; exec. dir. Hawaii Bus. Roundtable, 1983-89; sec., treas. Econ. Devel. Corp. Honolulu, 1984-85; sec., treas. Hawaii Conv. Park Council, Inc., 1984-86, hon. dir., 1986-88. Co-author: Resource Manual for Public Collective Bargaining, 1973. Bd. dirs. Hawaii Restaurant Assn., 1974-76, bd. dirs. Hawaii chpt. Nat. Assn. Accts., 1963-67, nat. dir., 1965-66; bd. dirs. Vol. Service Bur. Honolulu, 1965-66, pres., 1966-68; bd. dirs. Vol. Info. and Referral Service Honolulu, 1972-75, Goodwill Vocat. Tng. Ctrs. of Hawaii, 1973-81, Girl Scout council Pacific, 1961-65, 71-72; bd. dirs. Hawaii Com. Alcoholism, 1962-71, co-chmn., 1964-68; pres., dir. Friends of Punahou Sch., 1972-75; mem. community adv. bd. Jr. League Honolulu, 1968-70; exec. bd. Aloha council Boys Scouts Am., 1962-65; bd. regents Chaminade U., 1983-85. Served to 1st lt. inf. AUS, 1943-46. Decorated Bronze Star, Purple Heart, Combat Inf. badge. Mem. ASTD, Am. Soc. Assn. Execs. (cert. assn. exec.), Inst. Mgmt. Cons. (cert.), Soc. for Human Resource Mgmt., Pacific Club, Healdsburg Mus. and Hist. Soc. (chmn. exec. com. 1993-95, dir. 1994—, pres. 1995-97), Santa Rosa Symphony Assn. (bd. dirs. 1993—, mem. exec. com. 1995-97), Rotary, Masons. Home: 1950 W Dry Creek Rd Healdsburg CA 95448-9747

CANFIELD, JACK, writer, speaker, trainer; b. Ft. Worth, Aug. 19, 1944; s. Elmer Elwyn and Ellen Waterhouse (Taylor) C.; m. Judy Ohlbaum, 1971 (div. Nov. 1976); children: Oran, Kyle; m. Georgia Lee Noble, Sept. 9, 1978; 1 child, Christopher. BA, Harvard U., 1966; MEd, U. Mass., 1973; PhD, U. Santa Monica, 1981. Educator Clinton (Iowa) Job Corps Ctr., 1968-69; dir. edn. W.C. Stone Found., Chgo., 1969-70; co-dir. New Eng. Ctr., Leverett, Mass., 1971-77; instr. U. Mass., Amherst, 1978-80; dir. ednl. svcs. Insight of Tng. Seminars, Santa Monica, Calif., 1981-83; pres. Self-Esteem Seminars, Culver City, Calif., 1983—, Santa Barbara, Calif., 1983—; pres. Inst. Holistic Edn., Amherst, 1975-81; mem. adv. bd. The Wyland Found., Laguna, Calif., 1997—. Author: Personalized Learning: Confluent Processes in the Classroom, 1976, Self-Esteem and Peak Performance: A Transcript, 1991, Los Angeles Dodgers Team Esteem Program: A Self-Esteem Curriculum Guide, 1992; co-author: (with H.C. Wells) About Me: A Curriculum for a Developing Self, 1971, Japanese edit., 1977, 100 Ways to Enhance Self-Concept in the Classroom: A Handbook for Teachers and Parents, 1976, rev. edit., 1993, (with others) Self-Esteem in the Classroom: A Curriculum Guide, 1986, (with A. Mecca, et al) Toward A State of Esteem: The Final Report of the California Task Force to Promote Self-Esteem and Personal and Social Responsibility, 1990, (with. F. Siccone) 101 Ways to Develop Student Self-Esteem and Responsibility in the Classroom, Vol. II: The Power to Succeed in School and Beyond, 1992, vol. I, 1994, (with M.V. Hansen) Chicken Soup for the Soul: 101 Stories to Open the Heart and Rekindle the Spirit, 1993, large print edit., 1996, various translations (Abby award Am. Booksellers Assn. 1995, other awards, #1 N.Y. Times Best Seller List over 2 years, #1 Pubs. Weekly Best Seller List over 2 years, others), Dare to Win, 1994, various translations, 1996—, (with K. Goldberg) Follow Your Dreams: A Goals Setting Workbook, 1994, (with M.V. Hansen) A 2nd Helping of Chicken Soup for the Soul: 101 More Stories to Open the Heart and Rekindle the Spirit, 1995, large print edit., 1996, various translations (various awards), The Aladdin Factor: How to Ask for and Get Everything You Want in Life, 1995, various translations, (with M.V. Hansen and D. Von Welanetz Wentworth) Chicken Soup for the Soul Cookbook: Stories and Recipes from the Heart, 1995, (with M.V. Hansen) A 3rd Serving of Chicken Soup for the Soul: 101 More Stories to Open the Heart and Rekindle the Spirit, 1996, (with J. Miller) Heart at Work: Stories and Strategies for Building Self-Esteem and Reawakening the Soul at Work, 1996, various translations, (with M.V. Hansen) The Chicken Soup for the Soul Journal, 1996, (with M.V. Hansen, P. Aubery, and N. Mitchell) Chicken Soup for the Surviving Soul: 101 Stories of Courage and Inspiration from Those Who Have Survived Cancer, 1996, various translations, (with M.V. Hansen and B. Spilchuk) A Cup of Chicken Soup for the Soul, 1996, (with M.V. Hansen and P. Hansen) Condensed Chicken Soup for the Soul, 1996, Chicken Soup for the Kid's Soul, 1998, (with M.V. Hansen, M. Shimoff, and J. Hawthorne) Chicken Soup for the Woman's Soul: 101 Stories to Open the Heart and Rekindle the Spirits of Women, 1996, various translations, Chicken Soup for the Mother's Soul: 101 Stories to Open the Hearts and Rekindle the Spirits of Women, 1997, (with M.V. Hansen, M. Rutte, M. Rogerson, and T. Clauss) Chicken Soup for the Soul at Work: 101 Stories of Courage Compassion and Creativity in the Workplace, 1996, (with M.V. Hansen, H. McCarty, and M. McCarty) A Fourth Course of Chicken Soup for the Soul: 101 Stories to Open the Heart and Rekindle the Spirit, 1997, (with M.V. Hansen and K. Kirberger) Chicken Soup for the Teenage Soul: 101 Stories About Life, Love and Learning, 1997, (with M.V. Hansen and P. Aubery) Chicken Soup for the Christian Soul: 101 Stories to Open the Hearts and Rekindle the Spirits of Christians, 1997, (with M.V. Hansen) A Little Sip of Chicken Soup for the Soul: Inspiring Stories of Self-Affirmation, 1997, Another Sip of Chicken Soup for the Soul: Heartwarming Stories of the Love Between Parents and Children, 1997, A Fifth Portion of Chicken Soup for the Soul: 101 Stories to Open the Heart and Rekindle the Spirit, 1998, (with M.V. Hansen, M. Becker, DVM, and C. Kline) Chicken Soup for the Pet Lover's Soul: 101 Stories to Open the Hearts and Rekindle the Spirits of Pet Lovers, 1998, (with M.V. Hansen and R. Camacho) Chicken Soup for the Country Soul: 101 Stories Served up Country Style and Straight from the Heart, 1998. Named Outstanding Young Man of Am., U.S. Jaycees, 1978; recipient So. Calif. Book Publicist of the Yr. award, L.A., 1995, Body Mind Spirit Book award Body Mind Spirit Mag., 1996. Mem. Nat. Coun. for Self-Esteem (founder, bd. dirs. 1986-98, adv. bd. 1986—, Nat. Leadership award 1993), Nat. Spkrs. Assn. (Cert. Speaking Profl. award 1989). Democrat. Avocations: tennis, travel, guitar. Office: Chicken Soup for the Soul Enterprises Inc 929 Via Fruteria Santa Barbara CA 93110

CANFIELD, JAMES, art director. Art dir. Oreg. Ballet, Portland, 1988—. Office: Oregon Ballet 1120 SW 10th Ave Portland OR 97205-2400*

CANFIELD, STELLA STOJANKA, artist, art gallery owner; b. Varna, Bulgaria, Jan. 17, 1950; emigrated to W. Germany, 1980, came to U.S., 1985; d. Stamat and Pepa-Despenna (Blisnacova) Bogdanov; m. Peter Petrov, Feb. 28, 1971 (div. Mar. 1988); children: Nicoletta, Peter; m. Michael Canfield, Mar. 27, 1988; adopted children: Jennifer, Paul. M, U. Phys. Edn. and Sports, Sofia, 1973. Lic. sport phys. therapy, Bulgaria. Phys. edn. and sports pedagogue H.S., Tolbuhin, Bulgaria, 1974-75, Med. U., Sofia, Bulgaria, 1975-76, middle and H.S., Sofia, 1976-80; owner Stella restaurant, Dusseldorf, Germany, 1982-83; with Oberheid Ceramic Studio, Dusseldorf, 1983-85; retail sales rep. The Ltd., Walnut Creek, Calif., 1989-90; savs. rep. Calif. Savs. & Loans, Montclair, 1990-92. Bd. dirs. Coupeville (Wash.) Arts Ctr., 1993—; treas., exhibitor Penn Cove Gallery, Coupeville, 1995—. Recipient 3 awards Tulip Festival, La Conner, Wash., 1994, 2 awards, 1995, 96, 2 awards, 1997, 1 award, 1998. Mem. Youth Coalition, Northwest Watercolor Soc. Avocations: languages, reading, travel, sports, gardening. Home: PO Box 1676 5 NW 8th St Coupeville WA 98239

CANIN, STUART VICTOR, violinist; b. N.Y.C., Apr. 5, 1926; s. Monroe H. and Mary (Becker) C.; m. Virginia Yarkin, June 8, 1952; children: Aram

Roy, Ethan Andrew. Student, Juilliard Sch. Music, 1946-49. Asst. prof. violin State U. Iowa, Iowa City, 1953-57; assoc. prof. State U. Iowa, 1957-61; prof. Oberlin Conservatory, 1961-66; concertmaster Chamber Symphony of Phila., 1966-68, San Francisco Symphony Orch., 1970-80, various Hollywood (Calif.) film and TV studio Orchs., 1980—; musical dir. New Century Chamber Orch., San Francisco; Fulbright prof. Staatliche Musikhochschule, Freiburg, Germany, 1956-57; sr. lectr. U. Calif., Santa Barbara, 1983-92. Chamber music artist Aspen (Colo.) Summer Music Festival, 1962, 63, 64, Santa Fe Chamber Music Festival, 1975, Spoleto Festival Two Worlds, Charleston, S.C., and Spoleto Italy, 1980, Music Acad. of West, Summer Music Festival, Santa Barbara, 1983-91, Waterloo Festival and Sch. Music, Waterloo Village, N.J., 1987, 88; concert master Casals Festival Orch., San Juan, P.R., 1977, 78, Mostly Mozart Summer Festival, Lincoln Ctr., 1980; condr. master classes Shanghai (China) Conservatory Music, 1989. Served with U.S. Army, 1944-46. Recipient 1st prize Paganini Internat. Violin Competition, Genoa, Italy, 1959; Handel medal N.Y.C., 1960. *

CANNADY, WALTER JACK, lawyer; b. Alameda, Calif., July 9, 1942; s. Jack Stephen and Marie E. (Schmalenberger) C.; m. Shirley Padovan, June 26, 1966 (div. June 1980); 1 child, Amber L. BS in Polit. Sci., Calif. State U., Hayward, 1964; JD, Lincoln U., San Francisco, 1969. Bar: Calif. 1970, U.S. Dist. Ct. (no. dist.) Calif. 1970. Pvt. practice Oakland, Calif., 1970-79; ptnr. Cannady & Whitehorn, Oakland, 1979-82; of counsel Moore Clifford Wolfe et al, Oakland, 1982-85; pvt. practice San Leandro, Calif., 1985-96, Emeryville, Calif., 1996—. Office: 2200 Powell St Ste 680 Emeryville CA 94608-1876

CANNIZZARO, GERRY NORTH, music producer; b. Buffalo, Nov. 17, 1959; d. Philip Andrew and Maryanne (Miranda) Cannizzaro. BA in Comms., Canisius Coll., 1981. Prodn. asst. All Saints Ch., Buffalo, 1973-77; mgr., agt., musician The Parousia Group, Buffalo and L.A., 1978-92; claims adjuster Crawford & Co., L.A., 1987—; prodr., musician Saturn Studios, L.A., 1992-98; prodn. coord. Rock Dog Records, L.A., 1987-98. Musician/prodr. (audio CD) Turnaround, 1985, A Separate Reality, 1995, Variations on a Dream, 1997, Abduction, 1998, The Technology of Art, 1999. Avocation: helping underprivledged children. Home: PO Box 3687 Hollywood CA 90078

CANNON, CHRISTOPHER B., congressman; b. Salt Lake City, Oct. 20, 1950; m. Claudia Fox, 1978; 7 children. BS, Brigham Young U., 1974, JD, 1980; postgrad., Harvard U., 1974-75. Bar: Utah 1980. Atty., 1979-83; dep. assoc. solicitor U.S. Dept. Interior, 1983, assoc. solicitor, 1984-86; owner Cannon Industries, 1987—; mem. 105th Congress (now 106th Congress) from 3d Utah dist., 1996—; mem. Resources, Judiciary, and Sci. coms. Republican. Office: US House of Reps 118 Cannon Bldg Washington DC 20515-4403*

CANNON, ELIZABETH ANNE, special education educator; b. Chgo., May 22, 1946; d. Peter Francis and Mary Patricia (Tangney) Foley; m. Martin Francis Cannon, July 10, 1982. BSEd, Chgo. Tchrs. Coll., 1969; MS in Spl. Edn. Learning Disabilities, Chgo. State U., 1982, MA in Edn. Adminstrn. and Supervision, 1988; postgrad., Northeastern Ill. U., 1988, Colo. State U., 1992-94, U. Denver, 1992-94. Cert. elem. and secondary tchr., adminstr., spl. edn., EMH, TMH, ED, BD, LD, gifted, supervision and adminstrn. spl. edn., Ill., Colo. Sch. clk. Chgo. Pub. Schs., summer 1965-69, tchr. spl. edn. mentally handicapped, 1969-90, tchr. regular and spl. summer schs., 1970-76; tchr. adult edn. City Colls. Chgo., 1971-81; tchr. spl. edn. Lake Mid. Sch. Denver Pub. Schs., 1992—; cooperating tchr. trainer Chgo. State U., Roosevelt U., U. Ill., Denver Metro Coll., U. Colo.; mem. local sch. coun., 1974-90, prin.'s adv. coun., 1974-90, mem. PTA Chgo. Bd. Edn., 1969-90. Leader Girl Scouts Chgo. St. Barnabus Sch., 1968-72; mem. Archbishop's Guild (Denver) Mother of Perpetual Help Circle. Recipient Gov.'s Master Tchr. award State of Ill., Springfield, 1983, Tchr. of Merit award Chgo. Bd. Edn., Dists. 16, 19, 1974-88, PTA, Chgo., 1974-88. Mem. ASCD, AAUW, Coun. Exceptional Children (Ill. chpt.), Am. Fedn. Sch. Adminstrs., Colo. Assn. Sch. Execs., Coun. Learning Disabilites, Kappa Delta Pi, Delta Kappa Gamma Internat. (Denver chpt.). Democrat. Roman Catholic. Avocations: swimming, hiking mountain trails, camping, bike riding, arts and crafts. Home: 2041 S Wolff St Denver CO 80219-5044

CANNON, GARY CURTIS, lawyer, publishing executive; b. Ft. Worth, May 28, 1951; s. Curtis Warfield and Lucile (Curran) C. BA, U.S. Internat. U., 1974; MBA, Nat. U., 1984, JD, 1987. Bar: Calif. 1987, U.S. Dist. Ct. (so. dist.) Calif. 1987, U.S. Dist. Ct. (ctrl. dist.) Calif. 1993, U.S. Ct. Appeals (9th cir.) 1993, U.S. Ct. Internat. Trade 1993, U.S. Supreme Ct. 1993. Pvt. practice San Diego, 1987-89; v.p. Am. Pub., San Diego, 1988-89; pres. Emerald Bay Pub. Inc., San Diego, 1989—; sr. ptnr. Cannon, Potter & Scott, 1989-93, Cannon, Potter & Day, 1993-94; pvt. practice, 1994-95; gen. and corp. counsel Builders Staff Corp., 1995-97, F.Y. Partnership Inc., 1995-97, MUG Corp., 1995-97, Lexo Ins. Brokers Inc., 1995-97; chmn. bd. Fin. Svcs. and Investments Corp., 1994-96; v.p., gen. and corp. counsel Alpha Omega Corp., 1997—; gen. and corp. counsel F-Y Partnership, Inc., Loxo Ins. Brokers, Inc., Mug Corp., 1995-97; adj. prof. bus. law Nat. Univ., 1990—. Mem. ABA, Calif. Bar Assn., San Diego County Bar Assn., San Diego Trial Lawyers Assn. Republican. Presbyterian. Office: 9868 Erma Rd Apt 17 San Diego CA 92131-2416

CANNON, KEVIN FRANCIS, sculptor; b. N.Y.C., Nov. 27, 1948; s. Connell and Maud (Brogan) C. AA, CCNY, 1971. One-man shows include Willard Gallery, N.Y.C., 1982, James Corcoran Gallery, L.A., 1984, Charles Cowles Gallery, N.Y.C., 1985-86, Rena Bransten Gallery, San Francisco, 1987, New Gallery, Houston, 1987, and others; exhibited in group shows Ft. Worth Gallery, 1984, Am. Crafts Mus., N.Y.C., 1986, Charles Cowles Gallery, N.Y.C., 1987, Modern Objects Gallery, L.A., 1987 and others; represented in permanent collections Lannan Found., Cin. Mus., Bklyn. Mus., Am. Crafts Mus., JB Speed Art Mus., Albuquerque Mus. Nat. Endowment for the Arts grantee, 1986.

CANNON, THOMAS R., architect; b. Wailuku, Hawaii. BA in Psychology, Claremont McKenna Coll., 1971, BA in Philosophy, 1971; BArch, U. Hawaii, 1982. Registered architect, Hawaii. Journeyman carpenter Carpenters Union Local 756, Kanulul, Maui, Hawaii, 1972-78; project mgr. Wimberly, Allison, Tong & Goo, Honolulu, 1983-85; assoc. Territorial Architects, Wailuku, Maui, Hawaii, 1985-87; prin. Architects Maui, Haiku, Maui, Hawaii, 1989—. Mem. AIA. Avocations: Hawaiian plants, surfing. Office: Architects Maui 720 Awalau Rd Haiku HI 96708

CANNON-WILSON, MARGARET ELIZABETH, art educator, artist; b. Marquette, Mich., May 26, 1923; d. Carl Arthur and Elizabeth Justina (Jacobson) Erickson; m. John Pershing Cannon, Sept. 4, 1947 (dec. Aug. 1983); children: Miguel, Colleen Nicholson, Ericka Kramer; m. Robert Carlton Wilson, Aug. 16, 1992. BA in Art Edn., U. Ams., Mexico City, 1953, MFA, 1954; MA in Drawing and Painting, Calif. State U., Fullerton, 1967; studies with Aniela Jaffe, C.J. Jung Inst., Zürich, Switzerland; studied with Diego Rivera, studied with Jose Guitierrez. Lecturer U. of the Americas, Mexico City, 1954; art lecturer Adult School, Fullerton, Calif., Cerritos, Cypress and Fullerton Jr. Colls., Calif. (Fullerton) State U., 1967, Chapman U., San Diego, Calif., 1982-92. Author: Patriots-Female Version, 1961, The Great Painting Escape, 1996; one-woman shows include Paideia Gallery, La Cienega, L.A. and others; exhibited in group shows at Laguna Museum of Art, Cerritos Coll. Gallery, Calif. U. at Fullerton, U. Americas, Mexico, La Mirada Festival of Arts, Orange County Art Assn., L.A. Art Assn., Fine Arts Assn. Invitational, Warsaw, Poland, U. Calif., Irvine, San Diego Art Inst., 1996 others. With USNR, 1944-52. Mem. U.S. Former Mems. of Congress Wives, Aerospace Mus., San Diego Mus. of Art, San Diego Art Inst., San Diego Watercolor Soc. Avocations: swimming, painting, writing. Home: 1640 Maple Dr Chula Vista CA 91911-5942

CANO, KRISTIN MARIA, lawyer; b. McKeesport, Pa., Oct. 27, 1951; d. John S. and Sally (Kavic) C. BS in Biochemistry, Pa. State U., 1973; MS in Forensic Sci., George Washington U., 1975; JD, Southwestern U., 1978; LLM in Securities Regulation, Georgetown U., 1984. Bar: Calif. 1979, U.S. Dist. Ct. (cen., no. and so. dists.) Calif. 1984, U.S. Dist. Ct. Ariz., 1988, U.S. Supreme Ct. 1988, U.S. Ct. Appeals (9th cir.) 1992. Assoc. Yusim, Cassidy, Stein & Hanger, Beverly Hills, Calif., 1979-81, Walker and Hartley, Newport Beach, Calif., 1981-82, Milberg, Weiss, Bershad, Spethrie & Lerach, San Diego, 1984; pvt. practice Newport Beach, 1984—. Bd. dirs., v.p. Sandcastle Community Assn., Corona del Mar, Calif., 1987-97; active Leadership Tomorrow Class of 1994. Mem. Orange County Bar Assn., Balboa Bay Club. Democrat. Roman Catholic. Avocations: ballet, ice skating, bicycling, photography, golf. Office: 1 Corporate Plaza Dr Ste 110 Newport Beach CA 92660-7924

CANOVA-DAVIS, ELEANOR, biochemist, researcher; b. San Francisco, Jan. 18, 1938; d. Gaudenzio Enzio and Catherine (Bordisso) Canova; m. Kenneth Roy Davis, Feb. 10, 1957; children: Kenneth Roy Jr., Jeffrey Stephen. BA, San Francisco State U., 1968, MS, 1971; PhD, U. Calif., San Francisco, 1977. Lab. asst. Frederick Burk Found. for Edn., San Francisco, 1969-71; rsch., tchg. asst. U. Calif., San Francisco, 1972-77, asst. rsch. biochemist, 1980-84; NIH postdoctoral fellow U. Calif., Berkeley, 1977-80; sr. scientist Liposome Tech., Menlo Park, Calif., 1984-85, Genentech, Inc., South San Francisco, 1985—. Contbr. articles to profl. jours. Recipient Nat. Rsch. Svc. award NIH, 1977-80, Honors Convocation award San Francisco State U., 1966; grantee Chancellor's Patent Fund, U. Calif., San Francisco, 1976, Earl C. Anthony Trust; grad. div. fellow U. Calif., San Francisco, 1972-73. Mem. Am. Chem. Soc., Calif. Scholarship Fedn., Sequoia Woods Country Club, Protein Soc., Am. Soc. Mass Spectrometry. Roman Catholic. Avocations: reading, sewing, bridge. Home: 1203 Edgewood Rd Redwood City CA 94062-2728 Office: Genentech Inc 1 DNA Way South San Francisco CA 94080-4990

CANSLER, PHILIP TRENT, music educator; b. Kansas City, Mo., Nov. 3, 1953; s. Loman Doyle and Laura June (McElwain) C.; m. Jeannine Ann Zielke, May 24, 1975. MusB in Edn., Washburn U., 1976; MusM, U. Oreg., 1977, D in Mus. Arts, 1984. Asst. dir. marching band U. Oreg., Eugene, 1977-78; asst. prof. music Buena Vista Coll., Storm Lake, Iowa, 1978, 80; assoc. prof. U. Portland, Oreg., 1980—; condr. trumpet workshops; adjudicator mus. ensembles, N.W. U.S. Author: Twentieth-Century Music for Trumpet and Organ, 1984, Cansler's Proven Routine for Trumpet, 1986; trumpet performances on tours to Europe, Japan, Sri Lanka, Africa; performer CDs Thine is the Glory, 1997, Bravo! Baroque!, 1998. Min. of music 1st Bapt. Ch., 1995—. Recipient Cmty. Svc. award Music Dept., Topeka, 1976, Contbn. to Arts award City of Gresham, Oreg., 1991; grantee Portland Musicians Union, 1992, Albert J. Dennis Fund, Portland, 1993. Mem. Coll. Band Dirs. Assn., Internat. Trumpet Guild (news corr. 1991—), Toastmsters Internat. (pres. 1996—, numerous Disting. awards). Avocations: carving, hiking, bird watching. Fax: (503) 943-7399. E-mail: cansler@up.edu. Home: 18147 NW St Helens Rd Portland OR 97231 Office: Univ Portland Dept Performing & Fine Arts 5000 N Willamette Blvd Portland OR 97203-5798

CANTO, DIANA CATHERINE, nurse practitioner; b. Antioch, Calif., Mar. 20, 1939; d. William Light and Emma Catherine (Disher) Clark; children: Paul Petroni, Peter Petroni, Patrick Canto, Alexander Canto. AS with honors, Contra Costa Coll., San Pablo, Calif., 1982; BSN summa cum laude, Holy Name Coll., Oakland, Calif., 1984; MS, U. Calif., San Francisco, 1987. RN, Calif.; cert. PNP, FNP, CPR. RN Children's Hosp. Oakland, Calif., 1984-86, Merrithew Meml. Hosp., Martinez, Calif., 1986-87; family nurse practitioner Contra Costa County Detention Facility, Martinez, Calif., 1987, Berkeley (Calif.) City Pub. Health Dept., West Berkeley (Calif.) Health Clin., 1987-88, Maxicare Health Svcs., Calif., 1988-90, Homeless Program Alameda, San Leandro, Calif., 1989-90; nurse practitioner, founder student health svcs. U. San Francisco, 1989-90; with San Francisco Pub. Health Dept., 1989-91; ind. nurse practitioner family, pediatrics, family planning, women's health care, 1991—; researcher Contra Costa County P.H.D., Pitts., 1984, Ctr. for New Americans, Concord, Calif., 1985, UCSF, 1986-87, edn. program developer, Children's Hosp. Oakland, 1984-85, other ctrs. Mem. Walnut Creek Com. on Aging. Mem. AAUW, LWV, NOWA, ANA, APHA, Calif. Nurses Assn., Calif. Coalition Nurse Practitioners, Wash. State Nurses Assn., Nat. Assn. Pediatric Nurse Practitioner Assn., Coun. Nursing and Anthropology, Intercultural Interest Group of the Bay Area, Kappa Gamma Pi, Sigma Theta Tau. Avocations: gardening, reading, piano, gourmet cooking, opera. Home: 1915 Abernathy Creek Rd Longview WA 98632-9791 Office: Sky River Health Ctr 615 Stevens Ave Ste D Sultan WA 98294-9458

CAO, DAC-BUU, software engineer; b. Ninh Hoa, Khanh Hoa, Vietnam, Feb. 21, 1949; came to U.S., 1980; s. Thuan and Tiep Thi (Le) C.; m. Amy My-Hao Luong, Nov. 11, 1967; children: Valerie Phuong-Bao, Jesse Chau, Mike Minh-Chau. B of Law, U. Saigon, Vietnam, 1972; BS in Computer Sci., U. Calif., Irvine, 1985; MS in Computer Sci., West Coast U., L.A., 1991. Spl. corr. Progress Daily News, Saigon, 1965-69, mng. editor, 1969-72; asst. editor Dem. Daily News, Saigon, 1973-74; programmer, analyst Eaton Corp., Costa Mesa, Calif., 1981-85; system design engr. EPC Internat., Newport Beach, Calif., 1985-89; sr. application specialist McDonnell Douglas System Integration, Cypress, Calif., 1989-91; sr. systems engr. Unigraphics div. EDS Corp., 1991—. Author: (Vietnamese) Tien Don Yeu Dau, 1969, Ngon Doi Tuyet Vong, 1970. Recipient Vietnamese Journalism award Nat. Press Coun., U.S. Govt., 1966, Systems Integration MVP award McDonnell Douglas Corp., 1990. Mem. Assn. for Computing Machinery, N.Y. Acad. Scis. Republican. Buddhist. Achievements include invention of protector for motor vehicles; design of cellular air time tracking system, pager tracking system. Avocations: gardening, photography. Office: Electronic Data Systems Corp 10824 Hope St Cypress CA 90630-5214

CAO, JIE-YUAN, electronics engineer, researcher; b. Shanghai, July 24, 1944; s. Zong-Quan and Pei-Li (Zheng) C.; m. Ai-Yu Lu, Dec. 8, 1973; 1 child, Wei-Wei. BS, Beijing Poly. Inst., 1966; MSc, Shanghai Jiao Tong U., 1981. Engr. Microwave Tech. Rsch. Inst., Du Yuan, 1966-78; lectr. Shanghai Jiao Tong U., 1981-87, rsch. fellow, 1990-95; vis. scientist Internat. Ctr. Theoretical Physics, Trieste, Italy, 1988-89; sr. scientist EXB Tech. Inc., Sunnyvale, Calif., 1995-97, Kaifa Tech, Inc., Sunnyvale, 1998—. Co-author: Optical Fiber Transmission Technology, 1988; patentee in field. Mem. IEEE, Chinese Comm. Soc., Internat. Soc. Optical Engring., Optical Soc. Am. Achievements include work on a novel manufacturing method for plastic optical fiber star couplers. Avocations: photography, stamp collecting. Home: 3076 San Juan Ave Santa Clara CA 95051-1640 Office: Kaifa Tech Inc 388 Oakmead Park Way Sunnyvale CA 94086

CAO, THAI-HAI, industrial engineer; b. Saigon, Republic of Vietnam, July 8, 1954; came to U.S., 1975; s. Pho Thai and Anh Ngoc (Nguyen) C.; m. Hue Thi Tran, June 29, 1979; children: Quoc-Viet Thai, Quoc-Nam Thai, Huyen-Tran Thai, Uyen-Phuong Thai. BS in Indsl. Engring., U. Wash., 1980; grad., Gen. Electric Mfg. Mgmt. Prgm., 1982. Mfg. engr. GE, San Jose, Calif., 1980-82; mgr. mfg. engring. and quality assurance Broadcast Microwave div. Harris Corp., Mountain View, Calif., 1982-85; mgr. mfg. engring. John Fluke Mfg. Co., Everett, Wash., 1986-90; mgr. quality engring. Advanced Tech. Labs., Bothell, Wash., 1990—; sr. prin. electronic process engr. Primex Aerospace Co., 1990—; cons. total quality mgmt. Vinatek. Mem. Am. Soc. Quality Control (chmn. membership com. 1987-88), Soc. Vietnamese Profls. (pres. 1988), Soc. Mfg. Engrs., Inst. Indsl. Engrs., Am. Prodn. and Inventory Control. Avocations: reading, travel. Home: 23502 22nd Ave SE Bothell WA 98021-9553

CAPELLE, MADELENE CAROLE, opera singer, educator, music therapist; b. Las Vegas, Nev., July 29, 1950; d. Curtis and Madelene Glenna (Healy) C. BA, Mills Coll., 1971; MusM, U. Tex., 1976; postgrad., Ind. U., 1976-77; diploma cert., U. Vienna, Austria, 1978; postgrad. in creative arts, Union Coll. Cert. K-12 music specialist, Nev.; cert. hypnotherapist, hypnoanaesthesiologist. Prof. voice U. Nev., C.C. So. Nev., Nev. Sch. for the Arts, Las Vegas, 1986—; music therapist Charter Hosp., Las Vegas, 1987—; pvt. practice music therapy, Las Vegas, 1989—; music specialist Clark County Sch. Dist., Las Vegas, 1989—; contract music therapist Nev. Assn. for Handicapped, Las Vegas, 1990; guest voice coach U. Basel, Switzerland, 1992; presenter concerts in Kenya, self-esteem workshops for children and adult women; artist-in-residence, Nev., Wyo., S.D., Oreg., Idaho, N.D., Utah, 1988—; mem. cons. roster Wyo. Arts Cou., 1988—; cons. U.S. rep. [illegible] workshops in music therapy and humor therapy Germany, Austria, Switzerland; workshop day treatment program dir. Harmony Health Care; judge Leontyne Price Nat. Voice Competition; creative arts cons. Utah Festival Opera; artistic cons. Utah Fest Opera. Opera singer, Europe, Asia, S.Am., U.S., Can., Australia, 1978—; roles include Cio Cio San in Madama Butterly, Tosca, Turandot and Fidelio, Salome Electra; community concerts artist; featured PBS artist Guess Who's Playing the Classics; featured guest All Things Considered PBS radio, 1985; co-writer (one-woman show) The Fat Lady Sings, 1991 (Women's Awareness award), The Undone Divas: Hysterical/Historical Perspective (Nev. Humanities grant 1996); concerts Africa, Kenya, Somalia; concerts for Jugaslavian Relief throughout Europe; guest soloist national anthem San Francisco 49ers. Pres., founder, cons. Children's Opera Outreach, Las Vegas, 1985—; artist Musicians Emergency Found., N.Y.C., 1978-82; vol. Zoo Assn., Allied Arts, Ziegfeld Club (first Junior Ziegfeld Young Woman of Yr.), Las Vegas, 1979—; clown Very Spl. Arts, Nev., Oreg., S.D., 1989-90; goodwill and cultural amb. City of Las Vegas, 1983; panelist Kennedy Ctr., Washington, 1982; artist Benefit Concerts for Children with AIDS; mem. Nev. Arts Alliance, Make a Wish Found., Lyric Opera of Las Vegas; CEO Outreach for Creative Arts, Opera Piccolo; ednl. outreach cons. Utah Fest Opera. Named Musician of Yr. Swiss Music Alliance, 1993; recipient Congl. Cert. of Merit for work in the arts, 1993, 96; Nev. Humanities Torr grantee. Mem. Internat. Platform Assn., Nat. Assn. Tchrs. Singing (featured guest spkr.), Performing Arts Soc. Nev., Cultural Arts Soc. (co-founder 1995), Brown Bag Concert Assn. (bd. dirs.), Make a Wish Found., Las Vegas Lyric Opera (bd. dirs.). Democrat. Features on Women's Cable Network. Avocations: gardening, refinishing antique furniture, gourmet cooking, puppetry magic, pet therapy. Home: 3266 Brentwood St Las Vegas NV 89121-3316

CAPENER, REGNER ALVIN, electronics engineer, minister, author, inventor; b. Astoria, Oreg., Apr. 18, 1942; s. Alvin Earnest and Lillian Lorraine (Lehtosaari) C.; divorced; children: Deborah, Christian, Melodie, Ariella; m. Della Denise Melson, May 17, 1983; children: Shelley, Danielle, Rebekah, Joshua. Student, U. Nebr., 1957-58, 59-60, Southwestern Coll., Waxahachie, Tex., 1958-59, Bethany Bible Coll., 1963-64. Ordained minister Full Gospel Assembly Ch., 1971. Rsch. engr. Lockheed Missiles & Space Corp., Palo Alto, Calif., 1962-64; engr., talk show host Sta. KHOF-FM, Glendale, Calif., 1966-67; youth min. Bethel Union Ch., Duarte, Calif., 1966-67; pres. Intermountain Electronics, Salt Lake City, 1967-72; assoc. pastor Full Gospel Assembly, Salt Lake City, 1968-72, Long Beach (Calif.) Christian Ctr., 1972-76; v.p. Refuge Ministries, Inc., Long Beach, 1972-76; pres. Christian Broadcasting Network-Alaska, Inc., Fairbanks, 1977-83; gen. mgr. Action Sch. of Broadcasting, Anchorage, 1983-85; pres., pastor House of Praise, Anchorage, 1984-93; chief engr. KTBY-TV, Inc., Anchorage, 1988-93; pres. R & DC Engring., Anchorage, 1993—; area dir. Christian Broadcasting Network, Virginia Beach, 1977-83; cons., dir. Union Bond and Trust Co., Anchorage, 1985-86; author, editor univ. courses, 1984-85; dep. gov. Am. Biog. Inst. Rsch. Assn., 1990—. Author: Spiritual Maturity, 1975, Spiritual Warfare, 1976, The Doctrine of Submission, 1988, A Vision for Praise, 1988, Ekklesia, 1993, For the Marriage of the Lamb Has Come, 1996, Open Letters to the Ekklesia, 1997; author, composer numerous gospel songs; creator numerous broadcasting and electronic instrument inventions. Sec., Christian Businessmen's Com., Salt Lake City, 1968-72; area advisor Women's Aglow Internat., Fairbanks, 1981-83; local co-chmn. campaign Boucher for Gov. Com., Fairbanks, 1982; campaigner for Boucher, Anchorage, 1984, Clark Gruening for Senate Com., Barrow, Alaska, 1980; TV producer Stevens for U.S. Senate, Barrow, 1978; fundraiser City of Refuge, Mex., 1973-75; statewide rep. Sudden Infant Death Syndrome, Barrow, 1978-82; founder Operation Blessing/Alaska, 1981; mem. resch. bd. advisors Am. Biog. Inst., 1990—; advisor Anchorage chpt. Women's Aglow Internat., 1990-91. Mem. Soc. Broadcast Engrs., Internat. Soc. Classical Guitarists (sec. 1967-69), Alaska Broadcaster's Assn., Nat. Assn. Broadcasters, Anchorage C. of C. Republican. Avocations: musician, ancient history, ancient langs. Office: R & DC Engring 709 S 7th St Sunnyside WA 98944-2218

CAPOZZI, ANGELO, surgeon; b. Solvay, N.Y., Apr. 20, 1933; s. Angelo and Daminana (Pirro) C.; m. Louise Armanetti, June 18, 1960; children: Angelo III, Leonard, Jeanne. BS, U. Notre Dame, 1956; MD, Loyola U., Chgo., 1960. Diplomate Am. Bd. Plastic Surgery. Intern St. Francis Hosp., Evanston, Ill., 1960-61, resident in gen. surgery, 1962-64; resident in plastic surgery U. Wis., Madison, 1964-66; chief plastic surgery USAF, Travis AFB, Calif., 1966-68; chief dept. plastic surgery St. Marys Hosp., San Francisco, 1974-77; assoc. clin. prof. dept. surgery U. Calif., San Francisco; chmn. dept. plastic and reconstructive surgery St. Francis Meml. Hosp., San Francisco, 1987-98, dir. plastic surgery residency program, 1987-98; mem. tchg. staff St. Francis Meml. Hosp., Bothin Burn Ctr., San Francisco, 1968-98; attending staff Shriners Hosp., San Francisco, 1999—, pres. Calif. Soc. of Plastic Surgeons, 1998-99. Author: Change of Face, 1984; contbr. articles to profl. jours. Mem. parks and recreation com. City of Tiburon, Calif., 1973. Capt. USAF, 1966-68. Recipient Alumni citation Loyola U., 1983, Bru Brunnier fellow award San Francisco Rotary Found., 1996; named Man of Yr., U. Notre Dame Alumni, 1983. Mem. San Francisco Olympic Club, San Francisco Rotary (Outstanding Svc. award 1993, Svc. Above Self award 1995), Rotoplast, Inc. (founding mem.). Avocations: running, biking. Office: 1199 Bush St Ste 640 San Francisco CA 94109-5977

CAPPS, LOIS RAGNHILD GRIMSRUD, congresswoman, school nurse; b. Ladysmith, Wis., Jan. 10, 1938; d. Jurgen Milton and Solveig Magdalene (Gullixson) Grimsrud; m. Walter Holden Capps, Aug. 21, 1960 (dec.); children: Lisa Margaret, Todd Holden, Laura Karolina. BSN with honors, Pacific Luth. U., 1959; MA in Religion, Yale U., 1964; MA in Edn., U. Calif., Santa Barbara, 1990. RN, Calif.; cert. sch. nurse, Calif.; jr. coll. instr., Calif. Asst. instr. Emanuel Hosp. Sch. Nursing, Portland, Oreg., 1959-60; surgey flr. nurse Yale/New Haven Hosp., 1960-62, head nurse, out patient, 1962-63; staff nurse Vis. Nurse Assn., Hamden, Ct., 1963-64; sch. nurse Santa Barbara (Calif.) Sch. Dists., 1968-70, 77-98; dir. teenage pregnancy and parenting project Santa Barbara, 1985-86; mem. 105th Congress (now 106th Congress) from 22d Calif. dist., Washington, 1998—; mem. sci. com., internat. rels. com. U.S. Congress, campaign finance reform task force, budget task force, Calif. ISTEA task force, congl. caucus women's issues, congl. task force tobacco and health, diabetes caucus, congl. caucus on the arts; instr. Santa Barbara City Coll., 1990—. Bd. dirs. Am. Heart Assn., Santa Barbara, 1989—, The Adoption Ctr., Santa Barbara, 1986-90, Family Svc. Agy., Santa Barbara, 1994—, Stop AIDS Now, Santa Barbara, 1994—, Santa Barbara Women's Polit. Com., 1991—; instr. CPR, first aid, ARC, Santa Barbara, 1985—; bd. dirs. Pacific Luth. Theol. Sem. Democrat. Lutheran. Fax: (202) 225-5632. E-mail: lois.capps@mail.house.gov. Home: 1724 Santa Barbara St Santa Barbara CA 93101-1025 Office: US House of Reps 1118 Longworth HOB Washington DC 20515-0522*

CAPPUCCI, DARIO TED, JR., veterinarian, scientist; b. Plains, Pa., Aug. 19, 1941; s. Dario and Julie Aurelia (Bizzicotti) C. BS, U. Calif.-Davis, 1963, DVM, 1965, MS, 1966; PhD, U. Calif.-San Francisco, 1976; MPH, Loma Linda U., 1977; AS, SUNY-Albany, 1977. Diplomate Am. Coll. Vet. Preventive Medicine, Am. Coll. Epidemiology. Registered Am. Registry Cert. Animal Scientists. Commd. officer USPHS, 1966, advanced through grades to lt. (s.g.), 1968, resigned, 1968; vet. officer Calif. Dept. Food and Agr., Petaluma, 1969-70; pub. health veterinarian, Calif. Dept. Health Services, Berkeley, 1970-76; pvt. practice vet. medicine, No. Calif., 1970-76, 77-78; vet. officer U.S. Govt., 1978-92, prof. epidemiology and pub. health, Tuskegee U., 1992-97; epidemiology preceptor USPHS/HHS, Rockville, Md., 1980-87; mem. adv. group HEW, Washington, 1979-81; mem. task force Dept. Def., U.S. Dept. Agr., Lancaster, Pa., 1983-84; guest lectr. U. Calif., Davis, 1970-73. Contbr. articles to jours., chpts. to books. Vol. various groups for protection domestic and wild animal life, 1970—. Served to lt. col. USAR, 1983—, Persian Gulf. Decorated Bronze Star, 1991, Combat Med. Badge, 1991; recipient Merit award State of Calif., 1972; Combined Fed. Service award U.S. Govt., 1980; Equal Opportunity award FDA, 1983. Fellow Am. Coll. Epidemiology; mem. AVMA, Am. Pub. Health Assn., AAAS, Am. Inst. Biol. Scis., Wildlife Disease Assn., Am. Soc. Animal Sci., Res. Officers Assn. U.S., Assn. Mil. Surgeons U.S., Assn. U.S. Army, World Assn. for History of Vet. Medicine, Soc. for Epidemiologic Research, Conf. Pub. Health Veterinarians, Assn. Tchrs. Vet. Pub. Health and Preventive Medicine, Vietnam Vets. Am., Sigma Xi, Alpha Zeta, Phi Zeta, Phi Kappa Phi, Delta Omega. Adventist. Home and Office: 1077 Sanchez St San Francisco CA 94114-3360

CAPRARIO, KATHLEEN MARIA, artist, art educator; b. Elizabeth, N.J., Dec. 18, 1951; d. Louis George and Mina Bedford (Galatian) C.; m. James E. Ulrich, June 18, 1982; 1 son. Cert. completion, Newark Sch. Fine & Indsl. Arts, 1973; student, Art Students League, 1973-76, N.Y. Studio Sch.,

Paris, 1974. Textile designer various design studios, N.Y.C., 1973-76; adj. instr. U. Oreg., Eugene, 1983, 87-89, 95; instr. Lane C.C., Eugene, 1995—. Artist; exhbns. include: Portland (Oreg.) Art Mus., 1978, 89, U. Oreg. Mus. of Art, (solo), 1986, Henry Gallery, U. Wash., Seattle, 1993, Mus. of Arts, L.A., 1998; collections include: Saks Fifth Ave., Microsoft, Wash. State Arts Commn., Larson Drawing Collection, Austin Peay State U., Clarksville, Tenn., Oreg. State Percent for Art Projects; pub. New American Paintings, 1998. Recipient artists' residency Ucross (Wyo.) Found., 1985, fellowship Oreg. Arts Commn., 1989, Art in Gov.'s Office, Oreg. Arts Commn., Salem, 1992, President's award, Nat. Works on Paper Exhbn., U. Tex., Tyler, 1998. Avocations: travel, reading, hiking. Home: 384 W D St Springfield OR 97477-3862 Office: Lane CC Art Dept 4000 E 30th Ave Eugene OR 97405-0640

CAPUTO, GARY RICHARD, radiology educator; b. Newark, Nov. 26, 1951. AB in Chemistry, Coll. of the Holy Cross, 1973; MD, Mt. Sinai Sch. Medicine, 1977. Diplomate Am. Bd. Internal Medicine, Am. Bd. Nuclear Medicine. Intern in internal medicine Mt. Sinai Hosp., 1977-78, resident in internal medicine, 1978-79; fellow in cardiology U. Wash., Seattle, 1979-81, 82-83; resident in internal medicine St. Vincent's Hosp. & Med. Ctr., Portland, Ore., 1981-82; resident in nuclear medicine U. Wash., 1983-85; fellow in cardiovascular imaging U. Calif., San Francisco, 1985-86; asst. prof. internal medicine, adj. prof. med. informatics U. Utah Sch. Medicine, Salt Lake City, 1986-89; asst. prof. U. Calif., San Francisco, 1989-92; assoc. prof. U. Calif., 1992—; clin. instr. U. Wash., 1982-83; dir. advanced cardiac imaging svc. LDS Hosp., Salt Lake City, 1986-89; supr. clin. cardiovascular magnetic resonance rsch. program and vis. fgn. scholars, 1989—; adminstr. NIH tng. grant, 1989-92; coord. in-svc. tng. program, 1990-91; mem. com. on human rsch., 1991-93; lectr. Fla. Radiol. Soc., 1988—; cons. GE Med. Sys., Milw., 1991—; dir. nuclear cardiology fellowship tng. program U. Utah Sch. of Medicine, 1987-89, mem. PhD candidate com. dept. med. informatics, 1987-91; apptd. bioengring. grad. group U. Calif., Berkeley, San Francisco, 1992—, staff scientist Lawrence Berkeley Nat. Lab., 1992—, U. Calif. San Francisco Lab. for Radiolog. Informatics, 1993—, U. Calif. San Francisco Magnetic Resonance Sci. Ctr., 1993-95, assoc. dir., staff scientist, 1993-95, U. Calif. San Francisco Position Emission Tomography Ctr., 1993—, assoc. dir., staff scientist 1993—. Grantee Deseret Found., 1987, Am. Heart Assn., 1988, Richards Meml. Med. Found., 1988, Merritt-Peralta Rsch. Found., 1990, NIH, 1986—, numerous others. Fellow Am. Heart Assn. Coun. Cardiovascular Radiology; mem. Radiol. Soc. N.Am., N.Am. Soc. Cardiac Imaging, Soc. Nuclear Medicine, San Francisco Radiol. Soc. Office: U Calif Dept Radiology Box 0628 San Francisco CA 94143-0628

CARADINE, LINDA HILDEGARD, contract analyst; b. San Pedro, Calif., Dec. 14, 1954; d. Cecil Lyn and Hildegard Marianne (Hessler) Climer; (div.); 1 child, Lisa Denise. Student, U. Mo., 1979-80, Drake U., 1984-86. Tech. writer Ozark Airlines, St. Louis, 1978-82; acad. asst. Drake U., Des Moines, 1984-86; computer operator Std. Ins., Portland, Oreg., 1986-89; project analyst Std. Ins., Portland, 1989-95, contract analyst, 1995—. Author: The Hard Way, 1998; columnist (book revs.) This Week mag., 1992-95; contbr. articles to profl. jours. Mem., contbr. Urban League, Portland, 1997, Portland Art Mus., 1997. Recipient Poetry award Midwest Poetry Forum, Des Moines, 1985, 1st place short fiction N.W. Writers Conf., Edmund, Wash., 1993. Mem. Life Office Mgmt. Assn. (assoc. 1989—), Willamette Writers Assn., Toastmasters Internat. Democrat. Avocations: travel, birding, the arts. Home: 7700 SW Garden Home Rd Apt 16 Portland OR 97223-7470 Office: Std Ins Co 900 SW 5th Ave # C5A Portland OR 97204-1235

CARATAN, ANTON G., food products executive; b. 1955. With Anton Caratan & Son, Delano, Calif., 1976—, ptnr., 1984—. Office: Anton Caratan & Son 1625 Road 160 Delano CA 93215-9436*

CARATAN, GEORGE, food products executive; b. 1929. With Anton Caratan & Son, Delano, Calif., 1952—. Office: Anton Caratan & Son 1625 Road 160 Delano CA 93215-9436*

CARD, DEBORAH FRANCES, orchestra administrator; b. Pottstown, Pa., Sept. 30, 1956; d. Marshall Anthony and Winifred (Hitz) R. BA, Stanford U., 1978; MBA, U. So. Calif., 1985. Orch. mgr. L.A. Philharm., 1978-86; exec. dir. L.A. Chamber Orch., 1986-92, Seattle Symphony, 1992—. Bd. dirs. AIDS project L.A., 1985-92; active Jr. League L.A., 1982-92. Mem. Am. Symphony Orch. League, Assn. Calif. Symphony Orchs. (pres. 1988-91), Assn. N.W. Symphony Orchs. (bd. dirs. 1993—), Chamber Music Soc. L.A. (bd. dirs. 1987-92), Ojai Festival (pres.'s coun.). Democrat. Episcopalian. Avocations: skiing, tennis, gardening, reading. Office: Seattle Symphony Ctr House PO Box 21906 Seattle WA 98111-3906*

CARD, ELIZABETH STROBEL, import company executive, journalist; b. N.Y.C., Apr. 12, 1932; d. Josef Alois and Bertje (Slieker) Strobel; m. J.S. Schoenfeld, June 5, 1952 (div. Nov. 21, 1989); children: Jamie Elizabeth Schoenfeld Naylor, Marilee Elizabeth Schoenfeld Nickelson; m. William C. Card, Mar. 1, 1991. BS in Journalism, U. Utah, 1953, postgrad. Reporter Deseret News, Salt Lake City, 1971-85; freelance journalist Netherlands, Czechoslavakia, U.S.A., Wales, 1985-91; v.p. Archtl. Specialities, Salt Lake City, 1992—; lectr. numerous orgns. in field of glass cutting and genealogy. Author 7 books for LDS readers; author: Blood of My Blood-The Czech Glassmakers, 1994, New York, Birthplace of Utah (History of Mormon Church 1830-1950), 1994 (Utah Arts Coun. award). Chmn. Class of '53, U. Utah, 1993-94; vol. Czech Mormon Ch., Czech Republic, 1980—. Recipient award Utah Bicentennial Commn., 1976, award Utah Heritage Found., 1980, Utah Hist. Soc., 1981, Czech Freedom Revolution Moravian and Bohemian Univs., 1990. Avocations: genealogy, history.

CARD, ROYDEN, artist; b. Cardston, Alta., Can., Aug. 2, 1952; came to U.S., 1954; s. Eldon Joseph and Jean (Low) C.; m. Judith Rose Martinson, Aug. 9, 1974 (div. Feb. 1993); children: Demian, Jeramy, Joshua, Suri, Jesse, Leah. BFA in Painting, Brigham Young U., 1976, MFA in Painting and Sculpture, 1979. Printmaking instr. Brigham Young U., Provo, 1980-96; artist Salt Lake City, 1974—; artist-in-resident Utah Arts Coun., various cities and schs., Utah, 1981-84, Entrada Inst., Torrey, Utah, 1998. Illustrator, printer: Dale Morgan's Utah, 1987 (Purchase award 1987), The Alphabet, 1982 (award 1982); author, illustrator: Utah Drawings, 1996. Recipient Purchase award Utah Arts Coun., 1978, 87, cash award Mus. Fine Arts, 1984, Dir.'s award Springville Mus. Art, 1997. Mem. Nat. Soc. Painters in Casein and Acrylic, Solar Cookers Internat. (vol. trainer demonstrator 1987-96). Avocations: hiking, camping, writing poetry, advocate of solar energy. Home: Apt 4 130 E Second Ave Salt Lake City UT 84103-4729

CARDEN, THOM(AS) RAY, psychologist; b. Indpls.; s. Howard Ray Carden and Mary Ola Eacret; m. Shirley A. Towles, 1953 (div. 1968); m. Anita Van Natter, May 26, 1973; children: Thom H., Kevin L., Shawn D., Dennis P., Suzanne M., Marlene, Cindy, Lorrie, Linda, Alayne. AA in Psychology, Cerritos Coll., 1973; BA in Psychology, Calif. State U., Northridge, 1975; MS in Psychology, U. So. Calif., 1976; PhD in Psychology, Walden U., 1980. Tchr. spl. edn. L.A. Unified Schs., 1976-81; spl. cons. Torrance (Calif.) Unified Sch. Dist., 1977-78; pvt. practice Northridge, Calif., 1977-92, Durango, Colo., 1993—. Author: Birth Control for Disabled, 1977, V.D. is Very Dangerous, 1977, Sexuality Tutoring for Developmentally Disabled Persons, 1976, (computer program) Personality Index Spectral Analysis, 1987; contbr. articles to profl. jours. With USN, 1950-51. Republican. Mormon. Avocations: computers, genealogy, vocalist.

CARDENAS-CLAGUE, ADELINE, dean; b. San Antonio, Aug. 27, 1951; d. Felix P. and Dora M. Cardenas; m. W. Donald Clague, Jr., Aug. 30, 1975; children: Jessica, Alexander. BA, Whittier Coll., 1974; MA, U. La Verne, 1984. Admissions staff Whittier (Calif.) Coll., 1974-75; dean acad. svcs. U. La Verne, Calif., 1975—. Office: Univ La Verne 1950 3rd St La Verne CA 91750-4443

CARET, ROBERT LAURENT, university president; b. Biddeford, Maine, Oct. 7, 1947; s. Laurent J. and Anne (Santorsola) C.; m. Elizabeth Zoltan; children: Colin Ready, Katherine Ready, Katalyn Ford, Kellen Ford. BA, Suffolk U., 1969; PhD, U. N.H., 1974; DSc (hon.), Suffolk U., 1996; DHL (hon.), Nat. Hispanic U., 1997. Dean Coll. Natural and Math. Scis. Towson (Md.) State U., 1981-87, prof. chemistry, 1994—, assoc. v.p., 1985-86, exec. asst. to pres., 1986-87, provost, exec. v.p., 1987-95; pres. San Jose (Calif.) State U., 1995—. Author: (with A.S. Wingrove) Quimca Organica, 1984, Study Guide and Answer Book to Organic Chemistry, 1981, Organic Chemistry, 1981, (with P. Plante) Myths and Realities in Higher Education Administration, 1990, (with K. Denniston and J.J. Topping) Principles and Applications of Organic and Biological Chemistry, 1995, 2d edit., 1997, Principles and Applications of Inorganic, Organic and Biological Chemistry, 1992, 2d edit., 1997, Foundations of Inorganic, Organic and Biological Chemistry, 1995; contbr. articles to profl. jours. Chmn. Baltimore County Higher Edn. Adv. Bd., Towson, 1989—; co-chmn. Balt. Sci. Fair/Kiwanis, Towson, 1983-88; bd. dirs. San Jose Repertory Theater, San Jose Opera, Calif. State U. Inst. Recipient Employee Incentive award State of Md., 1987, Outstanding Chemistry Tchr. award Md. Inst. Chemists, 1971, Award for Excellence Suffolk U. Gen. Alumni Assn., 1986; Lester A. Pratt fellow U. N.H., 1972, Albert W. Diniak fellow, U. N.H., 1972. Mem. AAUP (Towson State U. chpt., mem. exec. com. 1978-81, v.p. 1975-80, divsn. and dept. rep. 1975-80), Am. Assn. Higher Edn., Am. Assn. Univ. Adminstrs. (Md. membership rep. 1986—), Am. Coun. on Edn., EDUCOM (instl. rep. 1986-87), Am. Chem. Soc. (Chesapeake sect. alt. counselor 1979-87, mem. exec. com. 1978-87, mem.-at-large 1978-79, various coms. 1978-87), Am. Assn. State Colls. and Univs. (adv. bd. 1986—, Kellogg Leadership bd. 1989—, state rep. 1989—, joint venture Silicon Valley bd. dirs. 1997, co-chair econ. devel. team 1996—, co-chair econ. property coun. 1998—), Silicon Valley Mfg. Group (bd. dirs.), San Jose C. of C. (bd. dirs.), Sigma Xi (Towson State U. chpt. pres. 1975-76), Sigma Zeta, Phi Beta Chi, Omicron Delta Kappa. Avocations: jogging, tae kwan do, cross country skiing, golf. Office: San Jose State U One Washington Sq San Jose CA 95192-0002

CAREY, AUDREY LANE, interior designer, motivational speaker, educator; b. Spokane, Wash., Sept. 26, 1936; d. Glen Howard and Beatrice M. (Olsen) L.; m. Willard Keith Carey, July 4, 1959; children—Natalie Kay, Robert Lane, Willard Arthur. B.S. with honors in Home Econs., Wash. State U., 1958; postgrad. U. Wash., 1958, Eastern Oreg. State Coll., 1960—. High sch. home econs. tchr. Coulee City, Wash., 1958, Reardan, Wash., 1958-59; substitute tchr. LaGrande pub. schs. (Oreg.), 1960-65; nutrition instr. Eastern Oreg. State Coll., 1968-71; owner, mgr. Audrey Lane Carey Studio of Interior Design, LaGrande, 1973-85; vol. mgmt. tng. U. Colo., 1988, Nat. Vol. Conf., 1987, 88; family task force rep. 13 western states and Guam N.G. Assn. U.S., 1986-89; speaker in field. Active local Episcopal Ch., 1960—; youth activities dir. City of LaGrande, 1959-60; v.p., bd. dirs. Grande Ronde Symphony, 1960-64; den mother Blue Mountain council Boy Scouts Am., 1970; leader 4-H Clubs, 1971-73; pres. DeMolay Mothers Club, 1983; advisor EOSC Canterbury Club, 1961-65; campaign chmn. Union County, Sec. State, 1976, 80; pres. Union County Rep. Women, 1968; advisor Rainbow Girls, 1974-78; sponsor S.E. Asian Family, 1980-84; mem. Gov.'s Higher Edn. Mission, 1985; Eastern Oreg. chmn. Employer Support of Guard and Res. Family Readiness Program, 1985; mem. bd. trustees Oreg. State Library, 1986-94, chair, 1993-94. Viola Coulter scholar, 1957; recipient Patrick Henry citation Nat. Guard Assn. U.S., 1994. Mem. Am. Soc. Interior Designers, Kappa Alpha Theta (rush bd. chmn. 1960-84), Phi Kappa Phi, Pi Lambda Theta, Omicron Nu. Republican. Episcopalian. Club: PEO (past pres., charter mem. 1962—) (La Grande).

CAREY, GREGORY D., writer, videographer, producer; b. Mitchell, S.D., Jan. 26, 1950; s. Dale D. and Doris M. Carey; life ptnr., Rahn Mark Anderson. Grad. in Elec. Engring., S.D. Sch. Mines and Tech., 1972. Sta. mgr. KTE2 FM, Rapid City, S.D., 1970-71; video dir. Cable II TV, Rapid City, S.D., 1971-72; writer, video prodr. Sencoe Inc., Sioux Falls, S.D., 1972-91; sr. sales counselor The Good Guys, San Francisco, 1991-95; gen. mgr. Peerless Video, San Francisco, 1995—; pres. Sioux Empire Gay Coalition, Sioux Falls, 1978-91; founder Ea. Dakota AIDS Network, Sioux Falls, 1985-91; onwer Carey Systems, San Francisco, 1994—. Writer, prodr. (video movie) South Dakota Has AIDS, 1991; prodr. (video documentary) Reclaiming the Cross, 1997 (Telly award 1998); contbr. articles to profl. jours. Pres., treas. SEGLC, Sioux Falls, 1978-91; AIDS educator EDAN, Sioux Falls, 1985-91; ch. documentary prodr. MCC San Francisco, 1997—. Recipient Achievement award Soc. Tech. Comm., 1984, Gay Activist of Yr., SEGLC, 1985. Office: Carey Systems 4104 24th St # 374 San Francisco CA 94114-3615

CAREY, JAMES C., JR., plastic surgeon; b. Chgo., 1932. MD, Northwestern U., 1957. Intern Cook County Hosp., Chgo., 1957-58, resident in gen. surgery, 1958-63; plastic surgeon U. Mo., Kansas City, 1980-82; now plastic surgeon Twin Cities Cmty. Hosp., Templeton, Calif. Office: 959 Las Tablas Rd Ste B3 Templeton CA 93465-9703

CAREY, KATHRYN ANN, advertising and public relations executive, editor, consultant; b. Los Angeles, Oct. 18, 1949; d. Frank Randall and Evelyn Mae (Walmsley) C.; m. Richard Kenneth Sundt, Dec. 28, 1980. BA in Am. Studies with honors, Calif. State U., L.A., 1971; postgrad. Georgetown U., Boston Coll. Cert. commercial pilot instrument rated, advanced cert. in corporate cmty. rels. Tutor Calif. Dept. Vocat. Rehab., L.A., 1970; teaching asst. U. So. Calif., 1974-75, UCLA, 1974-75; claims adjuster Auto Club So. Calif., San Gabriel, 1971-73; corp. pub. rels. cons. Carnation Co., L.A., 1973-78; cons., adminstr. Carnation Community Svc. Award Program, 1973-78; pub. rels. cons. Vivitar Corp., 1978; sr. advt. asst. Am. Honda Motor Co., Torrance, Calif., 1978-84; exec. dir. Am. Honda Found., 1984—, Honda Philanthropy, Office of the Ams., 1996—; adminstr. Honda Matching Gift and Vol. Program, Honda Involvement Program; mgr. Honda Dealer Advt. Assns., 1978-84; cons. advt., pub. rels., promotions. Editor: Vivitar Voice, Santa Monica, Calif., 1978, Rod Machado's Instrument Pilots' Survival Manual, c. 1991; editor Honda Views, 1978-84, Found. Focus, 1984—; asst. editor Friskies Research Digest, 1973-78; contbg. editor Newsbriefs and Momentum, 1978—, Am. Honda Motor Co., Inc. employees publs. Calif. Life Scholarship Found. scholar, 1967; recipient Silver award, Wilmer Shields Rich award Coun. Founds. Excellence in Comm., 1995, Gold award, 1997, award of Excellence, Soc. Tech. Comm., 1995, Merit award, 1996, 97, Apex award Excellence in Comms., 1997. Mem. Advt. Club L.A., Pub. Rels. Soc. Am., So. Calif. Assn. Philanthropy, Coun. on Founds., Affinity Group on Japanese Philanthropy (pres.), Ninety-Nines, Am. Quarter Horse Assn., Aircraft Owners and Pilots Assn., Los Angeles Soc. for Prevention Cruelty to Animals, Greenpeace, Ocicats Internat., Am. Humane Assn., Humane Soc. U.S., Elsa Wild Animal Appeal, Calif. Advocates Nursing Home Reform (bd. dirs. 1997—). Office: Am Honda Found 1919 Torrance Blvd Torrance CA 90501-2722

CAREY, PETER KEVIN, reporter; b. San Francisco, Apr. 2, 1940; s. Paul Twohig and Stanleigh M. (White) C.; m. Joanne Dayl Barker, Jan. 7, 1978; children: Brendan Patrick, Nadia Marguerite. BS in Econs., U. Calif., Berkeley, 1964. Reporter San Francisco Examiner, 1964; reporter Livermore (Calif.) Ind., 1965-67, editor, 1967; aerospace writer, spl. projects and investigative reporter San Jose (Calif.) Mercury, 1967—. Recipient Pulitzer prize for internat. reporting Columbia U., 1986, George Polk award L.I. U., 1986, Investigative Reporters and Editors award, 1986, Jessie Meriton White Svc. award Friends World Coll., 1986, Mark Twain award Calif.-Nev. AP, 1983, staff team Pulitzer prize for gen. reporting, Columbia U., 1990, Thomas L. Stokes award Washington Journalism Ctr., 1991, Malcolm Forbes award Overseas Press Club of Am., 1993, Gerald Loeb award UCLA Grad. Sch. Mgmt., 1993, Best of the West, First Amendment Funding Inc., 1993, 95, Pub. Svc. award Calif. Newspapers Pub. Assn., 1996, Fairbanks award for pub. svc. AP, 1996; NEH profl. journalism fellow, Stanford U., 1983-84. Mem. Soc. Profl. Journalists, Investigative Reporters and Editors. Avocation: classical piano. Office: San Jose Mercury-News 750 Ridder Park Dr San Jose CA 95131-2432

CAREY, PRESTON BRADLEY, minister; b. Castro Valley, Calif., May 12, 1958; s. Willard Russell and Loretta Nevada (Smith) C. PhD in Pastoral Counseling, Am. Internat. U., 1996; D Christian Edn., Spirit of Truth Inst., 1998; JD, Bernadean U., 1999. Registered counselor, Wash.; ordained minister Ind. Bapt. Chs. Am., 1985, Full gospel of Christ Fellowship, 1997. Specialist, cons. HTA Enterprises, Tweed Heads, NSW, Australia, 1995—; v.p. PEP Co., LLC, Anacortes, Wash., 1995—; theology rsch. specialist, pastoral counselor, advisor United Faith Ministry, Wellborn, Fla., 1996—; pres. Christian Works, Burlington, Wash., 1996—, Inst. for Christian Works, Burlington, 1997—; Wash. state rep. Full Gospel of Christ Fellowsip, Richmond, Va., 1998—; v.p. Angelic Ministries, Sacramento, 1998—; bd. dirs. Internat. Overcoming Sch. Religion, Columbia, S.C., 1998—; bishop Pentecostal Overcoming Ch., Inc., Columbia, S.C. Author: The Darkness in The Light, 1996, The Quickening Begins, 1996, the Mayflower Priest, 1998, SpellBinder: The New Dark Age, 1998. Ex-officio bd. trustees Am. Police Hall of Fame. Recipient Pres.' Nat. medal of Patriotism, Am. Police Hall of Fame, 1996, Christian Teamwork award United Faith Ministry, 1996. Mem. Assn. Ind. Clergies. Litertarian. Fax: (360) 299-3203. E-mail: DrBCarey@cryogen.com. Office: Inst Christian Works 504 E Fairhaven Ave Ste 210-44 Burlington WA 98233-1846 Office: Inst Christian Works Burlington WA 98233-1846

CAREY, THERESA WILKINSON, small business owner, writer, editor; b. Santa Monica, Calif., July 9, 1955; d. Robert Raymond and Margaret Ann (Norris) Wilkinson; m. Kent W. Carey, June 25, 1977; children: Colleen Robin, Katharine Suzanne. BA in Econs., U. Calif., 1977; MS in Econometrics, U. Santa Clara, 1981. Sr. bus. analyst United Vintners, Heublein Wines, San Francisco, 1981-83; mgr, bus. analyst ISC Wines Calif., San Francisco, 1983-84; owner Alta Bus. Solutions, Palo Alto, Calif., 1984—. Contbg. editor: Barron's mag., 1995—, Microsoft Interactive Developer, 1996—; contbr. over 500 articles to computer, fin. mags. Task Force mem. Palo Alto Child Care, 1987-89; mgr., coach Palo Alto Bobby Sox, 1995-97 (v.p. 1996-97). Avocations: piloting, softball and volleyball coaching, travelling. Home: 1-9-18 Seta Setagaya-Ku, Tokyo 158-0095, Japan Office: Alta Business Solutions PO Box 1630 Palo Alto CA 94302-1630

CARL, JUDITH LEE, psychologist; b. L.A., Aug. 26, 1944; d. Herbert Frank and June Pauline (Culler) Malone; m. Richard Allen Carl, Aug. 15, 1969 (div. Jan. 1989). BA, Calif. State U., L.A., 1968, MS, 1975; PhD, U. So. Calif., L.A., 1983. Lic. psychologist, Calif. Tchr. Hawaii Bd. of Edn., Honolulu, 1969-70; tchr. Torrance (Calif.) Unified Sch. Dist., 1970-75, counselor, 1975-82; pvt. practice marriage, family and child counselor Torrance, 1978-88; psychol. asst. dr. Melvyn Lewin, Palos Verdes Estate, Calif., 1980-88; pvt. practice Palos Verdes Estate, 1988—; clin. dir. Pev Mar Recovery, Torrance, 1984-85, Place in the Valley, Grants Pass, Oreg., 1989—; corp. cons. Internat. Law Ctr., Torrance, 1990—. Named Woman of the Yr., YWCA, 1981. Mem. APA, Calif. State Psychol. Assn., CAP-PAC, L.A. County Psychol. Assn. Avocations: authentic Argentine Tango, S.Am. travel, Tango performances. Office: 716 Yarmouth Rd Palos Verdes Peninsula CA 90274-2675

CARLANDER, JOHN ROBERT, art educator; b. Moorhead, Minn., Mar. 22, 1943; s. Roy Arthur and Agnes Ingeborg (Erickson) C.; m. Marilyn Lee Strange, Dec. 29, 1965; children: Jay Robert, Lee Allan. BA, Concordia Coll., 1965; MFA, Bowling Green (Ohio) State U., 1968. Instr. Ashland (Ohio) Coll., 1967-69; asst. prof. Concordia Coll., Moorhead, 1969-72; assoc. prof. Augustana Coll., Sioux Falls, S.D., 1972-80; prof. Westmont Coll., Santa Barbara, Calif., 1980—. Dir. Red River ARt Ctr., Moorhead, 1970-72. Mem. Coll. Art Assn., Phi Kappa Phi (pres. 1991). Democrat. Lutheran. Home: 743 Palermo Dr Santa Barbara CA 93105-4449 Office: Westmont Coll 955 La Paz Rd Santa Barbara CA 93108-1023

CARLE, HARRY LLOYD, retired social worker, career development specialist; b. Chgo., Oct. 26, 1927; s. Lloyd Benjamin and Clara Bell (Lee) C.; BSS, Seattle U., 1952; MSW, U. Wash., 1966; m. Elva Diana Ulrich, Dec. 29, 1951 (div. 1966); adopted children: Joseph Francis, Catherine Marie; m. Karlen Elizabeth Howe, Oct. 14, 1967 (dec. Feb. 1991); children: Kristen Elizabeth and Sylvia Ann (twins), Eric Lloyd; m. Diane Wyland Gambs, May 23, 1993. Indsl. placement and employer rels. rep. State of Wash., Seattle, 1955-57, parole and probation officer, Seattle and Tacoma, 1957-61, parole employment specialist, 1961-63, vocat. rehab. officer, 1963-64; clin. social worker Western State Hosp., Ft. Steilacoom, Washington and U.S. Penitentiary, McNeil Island, Wash., 1964-66; exec. dir. Shohomish County Community Action Council/Social Planning Council, Everett, Wash., 1966-77; employment and edn. counselor Pierce County Jail Social Services, Tacoma, 1979-81; dir. employment devel. clinic, coord. vocat. program North Rehab. Facility, King County Div. Alcoholism & Substance Abuse, Seattle, 1981-90; counselor Northgate Outpatient Ctr. Lakeside Recovery , Inc., Seattle, 1991; staff devel. cons. Counseling for Ind. Living, Newport, R.I., 1992; community orgn./agy. problems mgmt. cons., 1968-92; vol. Vis. Nurse Svc. of Washington Hospice and Home Care, Montlake Terrace, Wash., 1996-98; mem. social service project staff Pacific Luth. U., Tacoma, 1979-81. Cons. to pres. Geneal. Inst., Salt Lake City, 1974-78, ret., Oct., 1998. Served with USN, 1944-46. U.S. Office Vocat. Rehab. scholar, 1965-66, named First Honoree Hall of Success Iowa Tng. Sch. for Boys, 1969. Mem. NASW, Seattle Geneal. Soc. (pres. 1974-76), Soc. Advancement Mgmt. (chpt. exec. v.p. 1970-71), Acad. Cert. Social Workers, Henckel Family Nat. Assn., various hist. and geneal. socs. in Cumberland, Perry and Lancaster counties, Pa., Peoria and Fulton Counties, Ill., Seattle Japanese Garden Soc. (v.p. 1993-96). Roman Catholic. Home: Poem Rising Garden 258 Two Crane Ln NW Poulsbo WA 98370-9700

CARLEONE, JOSEPH, aerospace executive; b. Phila., Jan. 30, 1946; s. Frank Anthony and Amelia (Ciaccia) C.; m. Shirley Elizabeth Atwell, June 29, 1968; children: Gia Maria, Joan Marie. BS, Drexel U., 1968, MS, 1970, PhD, 1972. Civilian engring. trainee, mech. engr. Phila. Naval Shipyard, 1963-68; grad. asst. in applied mechanics Drexel U., Phila., 1968-72, postdoctoral rsch. assoc., 1972-73, NDEA fellow, 1968-71, adj. prof. mechanics, 1974-75, 77-82; chief rsch. engr. Dyna East Corp., Phila., 1973-82; chief scientist warhead tech. Aerojet Ordnance Co., Tustin, Calif., 1982-88. v.p., gen. mgr. warhead systems div. GenCorp. Aerojet Precision Weapons, Tustin, 1988-89; v.p., dir. armament systems, Aerojet Electronics Systems Divsn., Azusa, Calif., 1989-94, v.p. tactial def. and armament products., Aerojet, Calif. 1994-97, v.p. ops., 1997—. Editor: Tactical Missile Warheads, 1993. Mem. ASME,, AIAA, NDIA. Sigma Xi, Tau Beta Pi, Pi Tau Sigma, Phi Kappa Phi. Contbr. articles to profl. jours.; rschr. explosive and metal interaction, ballistics, projectile penetration, impact of plates. Home: 2112 Campton Cir Gold River CA 95670-8302 Office: Aerojet PO Box 13222 Sacramento CA 95813-6000

CARLESIMO, P. J. (PETER J. CARLESIMO), former college basketball coach, professional basketball coach; b. Scranton, Pa., May 30, 1949. Grad., Fordham U., 1971. Asst. basketball coach Fordham U., Bronx, N.Y., N.H. Coll., Manchester; mem. staff Wagner Coll., Staten Island, N.Y.; head coach Seton Hall U., South Orange, N.J., 1982-94, Portland Trailblazers, 1994-97, Golden State Warriors, Oakland, Calif., 1997—. Office: Golden State Warriors 1011 Broadway Oakland CA 94607-4027*

CARLESON, ROBERT BAZIL, public policy consultant, corporation executive; b. Long Beach, Calif., Feb. 21, 1931; s. Bazil Upton and Grace Reynolds (Wilhite) C.; m. Betty Jane Nichols, Jan. 31, 1954 (div.); children: Eric Robert, Mark Andrew, Susan Lynn; m. Susan A. Dower, Feb. 11, 1984. Student, U. Utah, 1949-51; B.S., U. So. Calif., 1953, postgrad., 1956-58. Adminstrv. asst. City of Beverly Hills, Calif., 1956-57; asst. to city mgr. City of Claremont, Calif., 1957-58; sr. adminstrv. asst. to city mgr. City of Torrance, Calif., 1958-60; city mgr. City of San Dimas, Calif., 1960-64, Pico Rivera, Calif., 1964-68; chief dep. dir. Calif. Dept. Public Works, 1968-71; dir. Calif. Dept. Social Welfare, 1971-73; U.S. commr. welfare Washington, 1973-75; pres. Robert B. Carleson & Assocs., Sacramento, Calif. and Washington, 1975-81; chmn. Robert B. Carleson & Assocs., Washington, 1987-93, San Diego, 1993—; pres. Innovative Environ. Svcs. Ltd., Vancouver, B.C., Can., 1992; spl. asst. to U.S. pres. for policy devel. Washington, 1981-84; prin., dir. govt. rels. KMG Main Hurdman, Washington, 1984-87; dir. transition team Dept. HHS, Office of Pres.-Elect, 1980-81; spl. adviser Office of Policy Coordination; sr. policy advisor, chmn. welfare task force Reagan Campaign, 1980; bd. dirs. Fed. Home Loan Bank of Atlanta, 1987-90, I.E.S., Ltd., Can., Transenviro Co., USA, Churchill Co., USA; adv. com. Fed. Home Loan Mortgage Corp., 1985-87; mem. strengthening family policy coun. Nat. Policy Forum, Washington, 1994. *Robert Carleson is considered Ronald Reagan's voice in welfare policy matters. He achieved this right initially through service on Governor Reagan's welfare reform task force of 1970 and then as the chief architect and implementor of the successful welfare reform program of 1971-72. Later, as U.S. Commissioner of Welfare, his assignment was to carry Reagan style welfare reforms to the other States and to oppose efforts to enact a guaranteed income. He authored the*

successful 1981 Reagan national welfare reforms. As a private citizen he warned against the welfare reform of 1988 which added over 3 million persons to welfare, but this was rectified by the welfare reform of 1996 which contained his long held proposal to replace the 1935 family welfare program with finite appropriations to the States and requiring work for benefits. Adv. coun. gen. govt. Rep. Nat. Com., Washington, 1980-81; sr. fellow Free Congress Found., 1994—; chmn. Am. Civil Rights Union, 1998—. Officer USN, 1953-56. Clubs: Masons, Rotary (pres. 1964), Army & Navy (Washington), Capitol Hill, Fairfax Hunt. Home and Office: 1911 Willow St San Diego CA 92106-1823

CARLETON, DAVID, consumer products executive; b. Silver Spring, Md., Feb. 24, 1955; s. Henry and Barbara C.; m. Barbara Carleton, June 9, 1985. BS in Mktg., Ind. U., 1977; MBA in Mktg., Adelphi U., 1981. Dist. sales asst. Michelin Tire Corp., Lake Success, N.Y., 1977-79; sales merchandiser Duracell Battery co., Bethel, Conn., 1979, mgr. territory, 1979-80, regional sales trainer, 1980, mgr. area sales, 1981, mgr. dist. sales, 1982-84, mgr. regional sales, 1984-87; mgr. nat. sales automotive products Black & Decker, Hunt Valley, Md., 1987-88, mgr. nat. sales, mktg.-buck knives, 1988-92; natl. sales & mktg. mgr. Inter Metro Industries, 1992-96; v.p. sales, mktg. Am. Tech. Corp., Poway, Calif., 1996—. Mem. Am. Mktg. Assn., Poway C. of C. (bd. dirs.), San Diego Mktg. Assn. (bd. dirs.). Avocations: snow skiing, scuba diving, toastmasters. Office: Am Tech Corp 13114 Evening Creek Dr S San Diego CA 92128-4108

CARLETON, THOMAS J., architect; b. Ann Arbor, Mich., Nov. 9, 1944; m. Valerie Steuck, Dec. 27, 1969; children: James, Johanna. BArch, Boston Archtl. Ctr., 1986. Registered architect, Calif. Architect pvt. practice, Salinas, Calif., 1992—. Mem. AIA (pres. Monterey Bay chpt. 1997, citation for Excellence in Archtl. Design 1998). Avocations: writing, illustration, sailing. Office: 264 Maryal Dr Salinas CA 93906-3342

CARLIN, BETTY, educator; b. N.Y.C.; d. Samuel and Rose Sara (Bernstein) Grossberg; m. Arthur S. Carlin, July 18, 1953 (dec.); children: Lisa Anne Skinner, James Howard. BA, UCLA, 1952; MA, U. Calif., Berkeley, 1955. Educator L.A. Sch. Dist., 1952-55; owner Carlin's Shoes, L.A., 1952-68; educator Berkeley (Calif.) Sch. Dist., 1957-58; master tchr. spl. programs Calif. State Coll., Hayward, 1967-84; educator U. Calif., Berkeley, 1984-86; tchr. demonstrator C.V.U. Sch. Dist.; student tchr. supr. Calif. State U., Hayward; co-owner Art-Car Corp., 1978-88. Creator ednl. videos for children Study in Characteristics of an Effective and Loving Mother, Children's Play as Related to Intelligence, An Eclectic Approach to Teaching Reading. Mem. Nat. Tchrs. Assn., Calif. Tchrs. Assn., Commonwealth Club, San Francisco Opera Guild. Avocations: swimming, opera, theater, gardening, vocal study.

CARLIN, JOY, actress, director; b. Boston, Apr. 1, 1932; d. Jacob Morris and Esther (Fisher) Grodzins; m. Jerome Edward Carlin, Oct. 10, 1954; children: Nicholas Aaron, Alexander Paul, Nancy Jennifer. BA, U. Chgo., 1951; postgrad., Yale U., 1951-53. Interim artistic dir. Berkeley (Calif.) Repertory Theatre, 1983-84; assoc. artistic dir. Am. Conservatory Theater, San Francisco, 1987-92. Dir. House of Bernarda Alba, The Lady's Not for Burning, The Doctor's Dilemna, Golden Boy, Marco Millions, Hapgood, Food and Shelter; appeared in numerous theatrical prodns., including The House of Blue Leaves, The Little Foxes, The Cherry Orchard, The Belle of Amherst, The Glass Menagerie, The Floating Lightbulb, The Way of the World, Cat on a Hot Tin Roof, Missing Persons; dir. theatrical prodns. Passion Play, The Country Girl, Death of a Salesman, The Sisters Rosenwieg, You Can't Take it With You, others. Recipient 18 Bay Area Critics' Cir. awards for acting and directing, Barbara Bladen Porter award for continued excellence in acting and directing, 1997. Home: 981 Creston Rd Berkeley CA 94708-1501

CARLSEN, JOHN RICHARD, engineer; b. Palo Alto, Calif., June 16, 1970. Attended, San Jose State U., 1988-91, De Anza Coll., 1992-93, 97—, Austin C.C., 1995. Engrng. contractor Nolan K. Bushnell, Mountain View, Calif., 1988-89; engrng. contractor Iguana Entertainment, Inc., Sunnyvale, 1991-93, sr. hardware engr., 1993-96; engrng. contractor AAPPS Corp., Sunnyvale, Calif., 1989, Media Vision, Inc., Fremont, Calif., 1991-92; advanced layout engr. Altera Corp., San Jose, 1996—; pres. Carlsen Electronic Rsch., Sunnyvale, 1988-93. Mem. IEEE. Achievements include design of interfaces and software tools for development of video games on Sony Playstation, Sega Saturn, Super Nintendo and Atari Jaguar; contributing designs for PC and Macintosh multimedia cards; creation of fully-custom CMOS integrated circuits, layout training program for college graduates. Home: 1592 Heatherdale Ave San Jose CA 95126-1308 Office: Altera Corp 101 Innovation Dr San Jose CA 95134-1941

CARLSON, BRUCE WILLIAM, production company executive; b. Seattle, Dec. 17, 1959; s. Jack and Osobel C.; m. Maria Barge, June 24, 1989. BA in Comm., U. Wash., 1982. Editor KOMO Television, Seattle, 1985-86, assoc. producer, 1986-88, producer, 1989-91; ptnr. One Bounce Prodns., Seattle, 1989-94, pres., 1994—; mem. adv. bd. U. Wash. Film & Video Program, 1996—. Producer, dir. (films) Clear Water, Clear Choices, 1995, The Future Starts Now, 1996. Mem. Nat. Acad. Television Arts & Scis. (gov. 1990-94, com. chair 1994—), Swedish-Am. C. of C. Avocations: tennis, guitar, bicycling. Office: One Bounce Prodns 12002 38th Ave NE Seattle WA 98125-5710

CARLSON, CARL, waste water operator; b. Yakima, Wash., May 4, 1949; s. Herbert Phillip and Ester (Kittlesen) C.; married, Apr. 6, 1976; 1 stepchild, Kimberly Stevens. Waste water operator VVWRA, Victorville, Calif., 1989—. With USAF, 1969-89. Avocation: Nascar racing. Home: 14341 Princeton Ct Adelanto CA 92301-3746

CARLSON, CURTIS EUGENE, orthodontist, periodontist; b. Mar. 30, 1942; m. Dona M. Seely; children: Jennifer Ann, Gina Christine, Erik Alan. BA in Divisional Scis., Augustana Coll., 1965; BDS, DDS, U. Ill., 1969; cert. in periodontics, U. Wash., 1974, cert. in orthodontics, 1976. Dental intern Oak Knoll Navy Hosp., Oakland, Calif., 1969-70; dental officer USN, 1970-72; part-time dentist VA Hosp., Seattle, 1972-73; part-time periodontist Group Health Dental Coop., Seattle, 1973-76, part-time orthodontist, 1976-78; clin. instr. U. Wash., 1976; prin. Bellevue (Wash.) Orthodontic and Periodontic Clinic, 1976—; clin. instr., trainer Luxar Laser Corp., Bothell, Wash., 1992—; presenter in field. Master of ceremonies Auctioneer Friendship Fair, Augustana Coll., 1965, orientation group leader, 1965, mem. field svcs. com. for high sch. recruitment, 1965. Fellow Am. Coll. Dentists; mem. ADA, Am. Acad. Periodontology, Am. Assn. Orthodontics, Western Soc. Periodontology (bd. dirs. 1984-85, 86, program chmn. 1986, v.p. 1988, pres. elect 1989, pres. 1990), Seattle King County Dental Soc. (grievance, ethics and pub. info. coms.), Wash. State Dental Assn., Wash. State Soc. Periodontists (program chmn., pres. elect 1987, pres. 1988, 89), Wash. Assn. Dental Specialists (com. rep. 1987, 88, 89), Omicron Kappa Upsilon (dental hon. fraternity), Pi Upsilon Gamma (social chmn. 1964, pres. 1965). Home: 16730 Shore Dr NW Seattle WA 98155-5634 Office: Bellevue Orthodontic and Periodontic Clinic 1248 112th Ave NE Bellevue WA 98004-3712

CARLSON, CURTIS R., electronics research industry executive. PhD, Rutgers U. Founder, leader high definition TV program Sarnoff Corp. subs. SRI Internat., Princton, N.J., past exec. v.p., past head ventures and licensing; pres., CEO SRI Internat., Menlo Park, Calif., 1998—; co-founder, exec. dir. Nat. Info. Display Lab., 1990; past mem. adv. bd. USAF; past mem. rsch. lab. tech. assessment bd. U.S. Army; active Joint. Civilian Ops. Conf., 1996; served on several govt. task forces; cons. and presenter in field. Author 15 U.S. patents in the fields of image quality, image coding and computer vision. Mem. IEEE, Soc. Motion Picture and TV Engrs., Highlands Group (charter mem.), Sigma Xi, Tau Beta Pi. Address: 333 Ravenswood Ave Menlo Park CA 94025*

[illegible] Yakima, Wash., Oct. 15, 1954; s. Glenn Elmer and Helen Mary (McLean) Carlson. AA, Yakima Community Coll., 1975; BA in Communications, U. Wash., 1977. Dir. pub. affairs Sta. KCMU, Seattle, 1976-77; dir. programming and promotions Sta. KAPP-TV, Yakima, 1978-80; dir. promotions Sta. WBZ-TV, Boston, 1980-84; producer Sta. KCBS-TV, Los Angeles, 1985; dir. creative services Metromedia Producers, Los Angeles, 1985-86; dir. promo tion publicity 20th Century Fox, Los Angeles, 1986—. Writer: (TV animation program) Bruno, the Kid, 1996; writer, co-prodr. (TV movie) Coaching a Murder, 1994; prodr., dir. M*A*S*H* 15th Ann. Campaign, 1987 (Internat. Film and TV Festival N.Y. award), The Fox Tradition, 1988 (Internat. Film and TV Festival N.Y. award, Clio finalist award 1988, Telly award 1988, B.P.M.E. award 1988); prodr., writer, dir. Consumer Reports, 1983 (Internat. Film and TV Festival N.Y. award, Houston Internat. Film and TV award). Mem. Broadcast Promotion and Mktg. Execs., Nat. Assn. TV Program Execs., Beta Theta Pi. Avocations: photography, scuba diving, history, traveling. Home: 1510 Rock Glen Ave Glendale CA 91205-2063 Office: 20th Century Fox Film Corp PO Box 900 Beverly Hills CA 90213-0900

CARLSON, LAURIE MARIE WINN, educator, writer; b. Sonora, Calif., Jan. 27, 1952; d. Edwin E. and Juanita M. (Davey) Winn; m. Terrance Carlson, May 19, 1973; children: Ed, John. BS, U. Idaho, 1975; MEd, Ariz. State U., 1991; MA in History, Ea. Wash. U., 1998. Tchr. Whitepine Sch. Dist., Idaho, 1975-80, U. Idaho, 1980, Mesa (Ariz.) Pub. Schs., 1988-92. Author: Home Study Opportunities, 1989, Kids Create, 1990, Eco Art!, 1992, More Than Bows and Arrows, 1993, Colonial Kids, 1997, On Sidesaddles to Heaven, 1998, Boss of the plains, 1998, Classical Kids, 1998, Fits & Fevers: Salem's Witches and the Forgetten Epidemic, 1999. Mem. Western Writers Am., Women in Writing the West, Authors Guild, Nat. Alliance for Mentally Ill. Democrat. Roman Catholic. Avocations: sculpture, fishing. Home and Office: 16502 W Stoughton Rd Cheney WA 99004-8633

CARLSON, LAWRENCE ARVID, English language educator, real estate agent; b. San Diego, Dec. 29, 1935; s. Arvid Fritiof and Ruth Mathilda (Hedman) C.; m. Patricia Catherine Barlow, Sept. 8, 1963; children: Lawrence Stephen, Janine Catherine. BA in History, Roanoke Coll., 1957; MS in Edn., S.D. State U., 1962; MA in English, Calif. State U., Fullerton, 1966. Tchr. Edison Jr. High Sch., L.A., 1962-63, Anaheim (Calif.) High Sch., 1963-66; prof. English Orange Coast Coll., Costa Mesa, Calif., 1966—; instr. karate Orange Coast Coll., Costa Mesa, 1984-95; sales assoc. Real Estate Offices, San Juan Capistrano, Calif., 1993—. Host, writer (ednl. TV show) Creative Writers Viewpoint, 1975. Horseback riding tour leader Rock Creek Pack Sta., Bishop, Calif., 1990-95; leader 4-H, Orange County, Calif., 1993; vol. Liberty Walk, Dana Point, Calif., 1997. Maj. USMCR, 1957-67. Recipient Excellence award Nat. Inst. Staff Orgnl. Devel., 1993. Mem. Nat. Assn. Realtors, Calif. Assn. Realtors, Faculty Assn. C.C., Orange County Realtors Multple Listing Svc. Democrat. Lutheran. Avocations: horseback riding, karate, surfing. Home: PO Box 1266 Rancho Carrillo 10871 Verdugo Rd San Juan Capistrano CA 92693 Office: Orange Coast Cmty Coll 2701 Fairview Rd Costa Mesa CA 92626

CARLSON, NANCY LEE, English language educator; b. Spokane, Wash., June 1, 1950; d. Catherine Esther Paight. BS, Wash. State U., 1973; MEd, curriculum specialist, Ea. Wash. U., 1987. Tchr. Stevenson-Carson Sch. Dist., Wash., 1973-74, Spokane Sch. Dist., 1974—; vis. faculty Ea. Wash. U., 1989-91, 93-95; active steering com. Spokane County Children's Alliance, 1992—. Spokane County co-chmn. Sen. Slade Gorton campaign, 1988, mem. adv. bd., 1989—; Rep. precinct committeeperson, 1988-90, 92-94; bd. dirs. West Ctrl. Cmty. Ctr., Spokane Civic Theater, sec., 1992-94; mem. affordable housing com. Spokane County, 1990-91; treas. Inland Empire for Africa, Spokane, 1985-86; vice chmn. Ea. Wash. phone bank for Sen. Dan Evans, Spokane, 1984; mem. Mayor's Task Force on the Homeless, 1987-88; mem. Spokane County adv. bd. City of Spokane Cmty. Ctr., 1990-92; lay min. First Presbyn. Ch., deacon, 1994—, sec. bd. deacons, 1994-96, vice moderator bd. deacons, 1996-97, moderator, 1997—, chair bd. deacons, 1997—; mem. Rep. George Nethercutt's Ednl. Adv. Bd., 1997—; bldg. rep. United Way, 1994—. Mem. NEA, ASCD, Nat. Coun. Tchrs. English, Wash. Coun. Tchrs. English, Wash. Edn. Assn., Spokane Edn. Assn., Wash. State U. Alumni Assn. (area rep. 1987-90). Republican. Presbyterian. Avocations: golfing, reading, stamp collecting, politics. Office: Rogers High Sch Sch Dist # 81 1622 E Wellesley Ave Spokane WA 99207-4299

CARLSON, PAUL WESTLIE, accountant; b. Minot, N.D., July 23, 1972; s. Westlie Arthur and Martha Faith (Hansen) C. BS in Accounting, Minot State U., 1993; MBA, U. N.D., 1994; student, Ariz. State U., 1996—. Sr. acct. Hydro-Search, Goldent, Colo., 1994-96. E-mail: PaulCarlson@asu.edu. Home: 2524 S El Paradiso Unit 69 Mesa AZ 85202-7474 Office: Arizona State U PO Box 873606 Tempe AZ 85287-3606

CARLSON, ROBERT ERNEST, freelance writer, architect, lecturer; b. Denver, Dec. 6, 1924; s. Milton and Augustine Barbara (Walter) C.; m. Jane Frances Waters, June 14, 1952 (div. June 1971); children: Cristina, Bob, Douglas, Glenn, James. BS in Archtl. Engrng., U. Colo., 1951. Registered architect, Colo. Architect H.D. Wagener & Assocs., Boulder, Colo., 1953-75; pvt. practice architect Denver, 1975-82; health and promotion cons. Alive & Well Cons., Denver, 1982-85; freelance writer Denver, 1985—; mem. Colo. Gov.'s Coun. for Fitness, Denver, 1975—; state race walking chmn. U.S. Track & Field, Denver, 1983—; bd. dirs. Colo. Found. for Phys. Fitness, Denver, 1987—; lectr. in field. Author: Health Walk, 1988, Walking for Health, Fitness and Sport, 1996. Vol. Colo. Heart Assn., 1985—, Better Air Campaign, 1986-87, Cystic Fibrosis, 1989-91, Multiple Sclerosis Soc., 1988-91, Qualife, 1989—, March of Dimes, 1989, United Negro Coll. Fund, 1989, bd. trustees, 1990. With U.S. Army, 1943-46, ETO. Decorated Bronze Star; named One of Ten Most Prominent Walking Leaders in U.S.A., Rockport Walking Inst., 1989. Mem. Colo. Author's League, Phidippides Track Club (walking chmn. 1981-85), Rocky Mountain Rd. Runners (v.p. 1983-84), Front Range Walkers Club (founder, pres. Denver chpt. 1985—), Lions (bd. dirs. 1965-72). Episcopalian. Avocations: racewalking, skiing, cross-country skiing, orienteering. Home and Office: 2261 Glencoe St Denver CO 80207-3834

CARLSON, THOMAS E., bankruptcy judge; b. 1947; m. Cynthia Hustad. BA, Beloit Coll., 1969; JD, Harvard U., 1975; LLM, NYU, 1985. Bar: Calif. 1976; U.S. Dist. Ct. (no. dist.) Calif. 1977, U.S. Dist. Ct. (cen. dist.) Calif. 1984, U.S. Ct. Appeals (9th cir.) 1978. Law clk. to Hon. Thomas Roberts U.S. Supreme Ct., R.I., 1976-77; law clk. to Hon. Donald Wright Supreme Ct. Calif., 1977-78; assoc. atty. Cooper, White & Cooper, San Francisco, 1978-84; dep. staff dir. Ninth Cir. Ct. Appeals, San Francisco, 1984; judge U.S. Bankruptcy Ct. No. Dist. Calif., San Francisco, 1997—. Mem. Nat. Conf. Bankruptcy Judges. Office: US Bankruptcy Ct Calif PO Box 7341 235 Pine St San Francisco CA 94104-7341*

CARLSTROM, R. WILLIAM, retired special education educator; b. Seattle, Oct. 22, 1944; s. Roy Albert Carlstrom and Dorothy (Anderson) Hart; m. Ann Scheffer, July 29, 1967; children: Trina Anderson Carlstrom, Paul Scheffer. BA, Lewis & Clark Coll., 1967; MA, U. Wash., 1970. Tchr. Shoreline Pub. Schs., Seattle, 1968-71; program coordinator fo adult handicapped City of Seattle, 1971-72; spl. edn. tchr. South Shore Middle Sch., Seattle, 1972-75, Sharples Jr. High, Seattle, 1975-78, Ryther Child Ctr., Seattle, 1978-89; edn. specialist Therapy Clinic of Whidbey Island, Oak Harbor, Wash., 1995-98; sec., treas., bd. dirs. Glaser Found., Inc., Edmonds, Wash., 1974-86, exec. dir., 1983-91, bd. pres. 1997—, trustee, 1983—; dir. adminstrn. First Place Sch. for Homeless Children, 1994-95; adv. com. mem. U. Wash. Dentistry for Handicapped, Seattle, 1979-94, pres., cons. Funding Resources Group, Inc., Edmonds, 1984-94; pres. NP Mktg., 1994-98; co-founder, bd. trustee Snohomish County Youth Cmty. Found., 1992-93; pres. Current Health Techniques, Inc. 1992-93; edn. specialist Edmonds Cybersch., 1996—; pres., bd. dirs. Whidbey Clinic Inc., 1995-98. Coun. mem. U. Wash. Grad. Sch. for Dentistry, 1979-94; trustee Edmonds Unitarian Ch., 1980-81, Pub. Edn. Fund, Dist. 15, Edmonds, 1986-88, Home Care Wash.; pres. Madrona Mid. Sch. PTA, Edmonds, 1983-84; v.p., bd. dirs. South Whidbey Schs. Found., 1995-98, pacific NW regional rep. Nat. Network for Early Language Learning, 1997—. Grantee Seattle Masonic Temple, 1974-75, Fed. Govt., 1970-71. Mem. NEA, Island Athletic Club. [illegible] Edmonds Cybersch 7821 224th St SW Edmonds WA 98026-8336

CARLTON-ADAMS, DANA GEORGIA MARIE ANNE, psychotherapist; b. Kansas City, Mo.; d. George Randolph Carlton and Harriett Marie (Smith) Carlton-Witt; m. John Adams; 1 child, J.J. II. Student, Kansas City (Mo.) Jr. Coll., Rockhill Coll., Trinity Coll., Dublin, Ireland, 1973, City U. of London (Eng.), 1978. Owner Pure White Electric Light and Magic, Lakewood, Calif., 1985—; dir., owner Trauma Buddy's, Lakewood, 1988—; clin. hypotherapist Inner Group Mgmt., Cerritos, Calif., 1989—; cons. Rockwell, McDonnell Douglas, Long Beach, Calif., 1987-90; assoc. staff, instr. Talbert Med. Group; owner In Print mag., 1990—; staff counselor FHP. Author: Who Calls on Pandora, 1969, Jupiter in Scorpio, 1974, Burma Route, 1989, Counterstrike: Dimitri Manulski, 1990, Kitty-Morphis, 1982, Mouse Tails, 1991, Bookish Miss Emma, 1993, A Little Trip Through the Universe, 1993, Handbook for the Living, 1990. Adv. Greater Attention Victims Violent Crimes; active Animal Rights Pet Protection Soc., Calif. Preventive Child Abuse Orgn., Sierra Club, Women's Abuse Shelters. Mem. Calif. Astronomy Assn., Acoustic Brain Rsch., Inner Group Mgmt., NLP Integration Soc. (pres. 1988-89), British Psychol. Assn., C. of C., Willmore Heritage Ctr. for Neighborhood Downtown Preservation. Avocations: writer, photoreader, firewalker, painter. Developed virtual reality program for cellular reconstruction and to restore organs and health through vivid 3-D visualization, 1995-96. Address: PO Box 16304 Long Beach CA 90806-0804

CARMACK, MILDRED JEAN, retired lawyer; b. Folsom, Calif., Sept. 3, 1938; d. Kermit Leroy Brown and Elsie Imogene (Johnston) Walker; m. Allan W. Carmack, 1957 (div. 1979); 1 child, Kerry Jean Carmack Garrett. Student, Linfield Coll., 1955-58; BA, U. Oreg., 1967, JD, 1969. Bar: Oreg. 1969, U.S. Dist. Ct. Oreg. 1980, U.S. Ct. Appeals (9th and fed. cirs.) 1980, U. S. Claims Ct. 1987. Law clk. to Hon. William McAllister Oreg. Supreme Ct., Salem, 1969-73, asst. to ct., 1976-80; asst. prof. U. Oreg. Law Sch., Eugene, 1973-76; assoc. Schwabe, Williamson & Wyatt, Portland, Oreg., 1980-83, ptnr., 1984-96, ret., 1996; writer, lectr., legal educator, Oreg., 1969—; mem. exec. bd. Appellate sect. Oreg. State Bar, 1993-95. Contbr. articles to Oreg. Law Rev., 1967-70. Mem. citizen adv. com. State Coastal Planning Commn., Oreg., 1974-76, State Senate Judiciary Com., Oreg., 1984; mem. bd. visitors Law Sch. U. Oreg., 1992-95. Mem. Oreg. State Bar Assn., Multnomah County Bar Assn., Order of Coif.

CARMI, AVIRAM, technology executive; b. Jerusalem, Israel, Nov. 1, 1964; came to U.S., 1981; s. Meir and Rheim Carmi; m. Aura Lowama, Aug. 13, 1995; 1 child, Meital Oshrit. BS in Computer Sci. and Math., Calif. State U., 1987, MS in Computer Sci., 1994. Engr. Jet Prop Lab, Pasadena, Calif., 1987-91, Hughes Aircraft, Canoga Park, Calif., 1991-95; exec. v.p. tech. Over the Net, Camarillo, Calif., 1995—. Author: Advances in Genetic Programming, 1994. Office: Over the Net PO Box 1499 Camarillo CA 93011-1499

CARMICHAEL, PAUL LOUIS, ophthalmic surgeon; b. Phila., July 8, 1927; s. Louis and Christina Ciamaichela; B.S. in Biology, Villanova U., 1945; M.D., St. Louis U., 1949; M.S. in Medicine, U. Pa., 1954; m. Pauline Cecilia Lipsmire, Oct. 28, 1950; children—Paul Louis, Mary Catherine, John Michael, Kevin Anthony, Joseph William, Patricia Ann, Robert, Christopher. Rotating intern St. Joseph's Hosp., Phila., 1949-50; resident in ophthalmology Phila. Gen. Hosp., 1952-54; certified isotope methodology Hahnemann Med. Coll., Phila., 1960, asst. prof. ophthalmology, 1960-66, clin. assoc. prof. nuclear medicine, 1974-90; radioactive isotope dept. Wills Eye Hosp., Phila., 1956-61, sr. asst. surgeon, 1961-65, assoc. surgeon, 1966-72, assoc. surgeon retinal svc., 1972-90; attending ophthalmologist Holy Redeemer Hosp., Meadowbrook, Pa., 1963-65; assoc. ophthalmologist Grand View Hosp., Sellersville, Pa., 1958-75; instr. ophthalmology Grad. Sch. Medicine, U. Pa., Phila., 1956-63; clin. assoc. prof. ophthalmology Temple U., Phila., 1967-72; clin. assoc. prof. ophthalmology Thomas Jefferson U. Sch. Medicine, Phila., 1971-90; chief ophthalmology North Penn Hosp., Lansdale, 1959-90, pres. staff, 1959; pres. Ophthalmic Assocs., Lansdale, 1969-90. Pres. bd. dirs. N. Pa. Symphony, 1976-78. Capt., M.C., U.S. Army, 1950-51. Named Outstanding Young Man of Yr., Lansdale Jaycees, 1959, Outstanding Young Man State of Pa. Jaycees, 1960. Diplomate Am. Bd. Ophthalmology. Fellow A.C.S., Internat. Coll. Surgeons, Coll. Physicians Phila.; mem. AMA, Montgomery County Med. Soc., Pa. State Med. Soc., Am. Acad. Ophthalmology, Pa. Acad. Ophthalmology, Assn. Rsch. in Ophthalmology, Inter-County Ophthalmol. Soc. (co-founder, pres. 1975-78), Ophthalmic Club Phila. (pres. 1964), Delaware Valley Ophthalmol. Soc. (pres. 1985-89). Roman Catholic. Co-author: Nuclear Ophthalmology, 1976; contbr. chpts. to books, papers to profl. confs., articles to publs. in field. Home: Box 680308 2567 Columbine Ct Park City UT 84068

CARMICHAEL, SHARON ESTELLE, commercial real estate broker; b. Paterson, N.J., June 20, 1957; d. Harold Everitt and Anna Estelle (Lewis) Knorr; m. Bruce Allan Carmichael, Oct. 12, 1991. Student, E. Tex. State U., 1977-78, Richland Jr. Coll., Dallas, 1978-80. Lic. real estate agt. Tex., Calif. V.p. real estate Henry S. Miller/ Grubb & Ellis, Dallas, 1984-88; v.p. real estate Grubb & Ellis, San Jose, Calif., 1988-90, Oakland, Calif., 1990; v.p. real estate Fox & Carskadon, San Jose, 1990-91; sr. retail assoc. Meacham Oppenheimer, Santa Clara, 1992-93; sr. retail specialist Terranomics Retail Svcs., San Jose, 1993—. Mem. Internat. Coun. Shopping Ctrs., Women's Golf Assn. NCA, Silver Creek Women's Club, Silver Creek Valley Country Club (bd. govs. 1996-99). Republican. Presbyterian. Avocations: golf, sailing. Home: 5827 Killarney Cir San Jose CA 95138-2345 Office: Terranomics Retail Svcs 455 N Point St San Francisco CA 94133-1451

CARMONY, KEVIN BRACKETT, recording company executive; b. Ogden, Utah, Sept. 26, 1959; s. Clifford Conrad and Marion Janette (Fletcher) C.; BA in Bus. and Econs., Weber State U., 1983. Dist. mgr. Consol. Theatres, Salt Lake City, 1980-82; founder, chief exec. officer Streamlined Info. Systems, Inc., Ogden, 1982-91; pres. New Quest Technologies, Inc., Salt Lake City, 1991-92; v.p. tech. Franklin Quest Co., Salt Lake City, 1992-93; with I.N.V.U., Inc., Bountiful, Utah, 1993-95; pres. Cinemark Records, Bountiful, 1995—; bd. dirs. Pro Image, Inc., Salt Lake City. Trustee Weber State U., 1992-93; exec. v.p., COO I.N.V.U., Inc., 1993-95; elder's pres. LDS Ch., Ogden, 1987-89, Stake Mission pres., 1989-92. Named Ouststanging Bus. Grad., Weber State U., 1983. Mem. Internat. Platform Assn. Republican. Home: 3940 Laurel Canyon Blvd # 634 North Hollywood CA 91604-3709

CARNESALE, ALBERT, university administrator; b. Bronx, N.Y., July 2, 1936; two children: Keith, Kimberly. BME, Cooper Union, 1957; MS, Drexel U., 1961, LLD (hon.), 1993; PhD, N.C. State U., 1966, LLD (hon.), 1997; MA (hon.), Harvard U., 1979; DSc (hon.), N.J. Inst. Technology, 1984. Chief Def. Weapons System U.S. Arms Control and Disarmament Agy., Washington, 1969-72; prof. N.C. State U., Raleigh, 1972-74; prof. and acad. dean John F. Kennedy Sch. of Govt. Harvard U., Cambridge, Mass., 1981-91; dean John F. Kennedy Sch. of Govt., 1991-95; provost Harvard U., Cambridge, 1994-97; chancellor UCLA, 1997—. Author: (books) New Nuclear Nations: Consequences for US Policy, Fateful Visions: Avoiding Nuclear Catastrophy, Superpower Arms Control: Setting the Record Straight.. Gano Dunn award for Outstanding Achievement, Cooper Union, N.Y.C. Mem. Am. Nuclear Soc. (exec. com. 1968-71), Am. Soc. Engrng. Edn. (chmn. 1969-70), Assn. for Pub. Policy Analysis and Mgmt., Coun. on Fgn. Rels., Inst. for Strategic Studies. Office: U of California Office of the Chancellor 405 Hilgard Ave Los Angeles CA 90095-1405

CARNEY, JOHN OTIS, JR., architect; b. St. Paul, Aug. 20, 1949; m. Nancy Murdock, Sept. 4, 1977; children: Nora, Hannah, Ella, Will. BA, Stanford U., 1972; MArch, Harvard U., 1977. Lic. archiect, Wyo., Colo. Apprentice Metz Train & Youngren, Chgo., 1977-81; assoc. Metz Train & Youngren, Denver, 1981-83; prin. John Carney & Assocs., Denver, 1983-90, Urban Design Group, Denver, 1990-92, Carney Architects, Jackson, Wyo., 1992—. Bd. mem. Denver Bot. Garden, 1989-92; bd. mem., pres.. Urban Design Forum, Denver, 1984-85; planning commr. Teton County Planning Commn., Jackson, Wyo., 1994-98. Mem. AIA (honor award 1996, award of citation Western Mountain region 1998), AIA Colo. (bd. mem. 1984-85). Office: Carney Architects PO Box 9218 Jackson WY 83002-9218

CARNEY, KEVIN HUGHES, animator; b. Redwood City, Calif., Jan. 3, 1974; s. Francis John and Margaret Rose (Hughes) C. BA in Visual Arts, U. Calif., San Diego, 1996. Prodn. asst. Propaganda Films, L.A., 1996; 3D character animator OCS/Pixel Magic, Toluca Lake, Calif., 1997, Saban

Entertainment, Westwood, Calif., 1997—. Mem. SIGGRAPH. Avocations: sailing, skiing, backpacking.

CARNEY, T. J, lawyer; b. Denver, July 18, 1952; s. Thomas Joseph Carney and Patricia (Amack) Carney Calkins; m. Deborah Leah Turner, Mar. 20, 1976; children: Amber Blythe, Sonia Briana, Ross Dillon. BA in Econs., U. Notre Dame, Ind., 1974; JD, U. Denver, 1976. Bar: Colo. 1977, Kans. 1977, U.S. Dist. Ct. Colo. 1977, U.S. Dist. Ct. Kans. 1977, U.S. Dist. Ct. Ariz. 1995, U.S. Ct. Appeals (10th cir.) 1983. Legal asst. Turner & Hensley, Chartered, Great Bend, Kans., 1977; atty.-shareholder Turner and Boisseau, Chartered, Great Bend, 1977-84; atty., shareholder Bradley, Campbell, Carney & Madsen, Golden, Colo., 1984-92, 95-97; atty.-shareholder Deborah & T.J. Carney, P.C., Lakewood and Golden, 1992-95; atty. officer Carney Law Office, 1997—; CLE instr. Nat. Inst. Trial Advocacy, 1st Jud. Bar Assn.; cons. Vocat. Econs., Inc., 1998, others. Precinct com. Rep. Party, Jefferson County, Colo., 1988-94, area capt., 1994-96. Mem. ABA, Colo. Bar Assn., Colo. Trial Lawyers Assn., Kansas Bar Assn., Kans. Trial Lawyers Assn., 1st Jud. Dist. Bar Assn. (trustee 1990-94), Phi Delta Phi (Province Grad. of Yr. 1977). Avocations: flying, martial arts, skiing. Fax: 303-526-9843. E-mail: tjc@carneylaw.net. Office: Carney Law Office 21789 Cabrini Blvd Golden CO 80401

CARNOCHAN, WALTER BLISS, retired humanities educator; b. N.Y.C., Dec. 20, 1930; s. Gouverneur Morris and Sibyll Baldwin (Bliss) C.; m. Nancy Powers Carter, June 25, 1955 (div. 1978); children—Lisa Powers, Sarah Bliss, Gouverneur Morris, Sibyll Carter; m. Brigitte Hoy Fields, Sept. 16, 1979. A.B., Harvard, 1953, A.M., 1957, Ph.D., 1960. Asst. dean freshmen Harvard U., 1954-56; successively instr., asst. prof., assoc. prof., prof. English, Stanford (Calif.) U., 1960-94, prof. emeritus, 1994—, chmn. dept. English, 1971-73, dean grad. studies, 1975-80, vice provost, 1976-80, dir. Stanford Humanities Ctr., 1985-91, Anthony P. Meier Family prof. humanities, 1988-91, Richard W. Lyman prof. humanities, 1993-94, Richard W. Lyman prof. emeritus, 1994—, acting dir. Stanford Humanities Ctr., 1999—; mem. overseers com. to visit Harvard Coll, 1979-85. Author: Lemuel Gulliver's Mirror for Man, 1968, Confinement and Flight: An Essay on English Literature of the 18th Century, 1977, Gibbon's Solitude: The Inward World of the Historian, 1987, The Battleground of the Curriculum: Liberal Education and American Experience, 1993, Momentary Bliss: An American Memoir, 1999. Trustee Mills Coll., 1978-85, Athenian Sch., 1975-88, Univ. Art Mus., Berkeley, Calif., 1983-96, 98—. Home: 138 Cervantes Rd Portola Valley CA 94028-7725 Office: Stanford U Dept English Stanford CA 94305-2087

CARO, MIKE, writer, editor, publisher; b. Joplin, Mo., May 16, 1944; s. Peter Klaus and Marguerite (Zuercher) C.; m. Bonita Marie Polniak, June 6, 1965 (div. June 1972); m. Phyllis Marsha Goldberg. Gen. mgr. Huntington Park (Calif.) Casino, 1985; chief strategist Bicycle Club, Bell Gardens, Calif., 1984-85; editor, pub. Mike Caro's Pro Poker monthly, 1993; gaming author, cons., 1993—; founder Mad Genius Brain Trust; actor, instr. video tape Play to Win Poker, 1988. Author: Caro on Gambling, 1984, Mike Caro's Book of Tells-The Body Language of Poker, 1985, Poker for Women-A Course in Destroying Male Opponents at Poker and Beyond, 1985, New Poker Games, Gambling Times Quiz Book, Bobby Baldwin's Winning Poker Secrets, Caro's Fundamental Secrets of Poker, 1991; editor-in-chief Poker Player; poker editor Gambling Times; mng. editor B&G Pub.; contbr. articles to gambling mags.; programmer ORAC: Artificially Intelligent Poker Player, 1983; developer programming tools Mike Caro's Poker Engine, audio tapes Real Life Strategy, Positive Poker, Pro Poker Secrets, Pro Hold 'em Secrets, 1992, four-color deck, 1992; video Caro's Power Poker Seminar, 1995, Caro's Pro Poker Tells, 1995, Caro's Guide to Super/System, 1997. Avocations: computers, poker, strategic games, sports handicapping. Known professionally as America's Mad Genius or The Mad Genius of Poker. Address: 4535 W Sahara Ave Ste 105 Las Vegas NV 89102-3733

CAROLLO, BERT ROSS, radiologist; b. Denver, Apr. 16, 1954; s. Bert A. and Alice C. C.; m. Mary L. Krueger, June 19, 1977. BS, U. Colo., 1976; MD, Baylor U., 1979; cert. additional qualification, 1997. Diplomate Am. Bd. Radiology. Resident U. Okla., Oklahoma City, 1980-84; MRI fellow Tufts New Eng. Med. Ctr., Boston, 1988-89; diagnostic radiologist Meml. Hosp., Colorado Springs, Colo., 1990—. Contbr. chpts. to books, articles to profl. jours. Mem. Radiology Soc. N.Am., Am. Roentgen Ray Soc., Am. Coll. Radiology, Internat. Soc. Magnetic Resonance in Medicine. Avocations: running, bicycle riding, photography. Office: Meml Hosp 1400 E Boulder St Colorado Springs CO 80909-5599

CARON, JAMES EDWARD, artist, musician; b. Columbus, Ohio, May 17, 1953; s. James Joseph and Ethel Caron. AA, Golden West Coll., 1974. Drummer Disneyland, Anaheim, Calif., 1969-70; owner, mgr. nightclub Wildman Sam's, Garden Grove, Calif., 1974-76; prodn. mgr. King Johnson Films, Westminster, Calif., 1976-78, Merlin Inc., Garden Grove, 1978-82; artist, musician Garden Grove, 1982—; instr. Shotokan Karate of Am., Inc., Garden Grove, 1989—. Author, artist: (book) The Brimsley Tiger, 1985; drummer: (record albums) The Best in the World (Kickfire!), 1979, Dancing in the Sun (Kickfire!), 1987; exhibitions: The Caged Chamelion, Santa Ana, CA, 1995, Kelly Havens Gallery, Santa Ana, 1996, Irvine Fine Arts Ctr., Irvine, CA, 1996, Z-Gallery/Restaurant, Irvine, 1996; contr. artist Coagula Fine Art Jour, 1997-98. Recipient 7th pl. award Irvine (Calif.) Fine Arts Ctr., 1995, 3d pl. award, 1996. Avocation: playing drums at local nightclubs and coffeehouses. Home: 9102 Imperial Ave Garden Grove CA 92844-2148

CARP, CAROLE M., writer, law firm support services professional; b. Bronx, N.Y., Apr. 25, 1937; d. Charles and Yetta (Alewitz) Mishkin; m. Jerome D. Carp, June 16, 1956 (div. 1971); children: Randi Sue, Wendy May, Edward Yale. BA, CCNY, 1957; postgrad., Babson Coll., 1970-72. Sales specialist Digital Equipment Corp. of Am., Maynard, Mass., 1972-76; mktg. specialist Container Corp. of Am., N.Y.C., 1976-82; writer, advt. and pub. rels. specialist N.Y.C. and Parsippany, N.J., 1982-89; writer L.A., 1990—. Editor (newsletter) Fit Parade, 1983-90. Coord. George McGovern for Pres., Middlesex County, Mass., 1972; fund raising coord. Congressman Robert F. Drinan, Wayland, Mass., 1972-74; county coord. Robert F. Kennedy Presdl. Campaign, Santa Clara County, Calif., 1968; pres. Morris County (N.J.) Fedn. Dem. Women, 1974-89; chair Morris County Women's Polit. Caucus; vice chair issues N.J. Women's Polit. Caucus; Morris County coord. Frank Askin for Congress, 1982, pub. rels. coord., 1986; Dem. Committeewoman; candidate N.J. State Assembly Dist. 26., 1982. Mem. Am. Film Inst., Nat. Fedn. Press Women, Women's Nat. Book Assn. (L.A. chpt.), Women at Work, Writers Workshop, Calif. Press Women. Avocations: theater, film. Office: 10061 Riverside Dr # 313 Toluca Lake CA 91602

CARPENTER, FRANK CHARLES, JR., retired electronics engineer; b. L.A., June 1, 1917; s. Frank Charles and Isobel (Crump) C.; A.A., Pasadena City Coll., 1961; B.S. in Elec. Engring. cum laude, Calif. State U.-Long Beach, 1975, M.S. in Elec. Engring., 1981; m. Beatrice Josephine Jolly, Nov. 3, 1951; children—Robert Douglas, Gail Susan, Carol Ann. Self-employed design and mfgr. aircraft test equipment, Los Angeles, 1946-51; engr. Hoffman Electronics Corp., Los Angeles, 1951-56, sr. engr., 1956-59, project mgr., 1959-63; engr.-scientist McDonnell-Douglas Astronautics Corp., Huntington Beach, Calif., 1963-69, spacecraft telemetry, 1963-67, biomed. electronics, 1967-69, flight test instrumentation, 1969-76; lab. test engr. Northrop Corp., Hawthorne, Calif., 1976-82, spl. engr., 1982-83; mgr. transducer calibration lab. Northrop Corp., Pico-Rivera, Calif., 1983-86. Served with USNR, 1941-47. Mem. IEEE (life), Amateur Radio Relay League. Contbr. articles to profl. jours. Patentee transistor squelch circuit; helicaland whip antenna. Home: 2037 Balearic Dr Costa Mesa CA 92626-3514

CARPENTER, FRANK ROBERT, minister; b. Southampton, England, Apr. 13, 1946; came to U.S., 1946; s. Frank Ralph and Margaret Joan (Trezise) C.; m. Merrilee Yvonne Quiring, Mar. 16, 1974; children: Karen Johanna, Lisa Marie, Brittany Brooke. BS in Sociology/Polit. Sci., U. Oreg., 1968; MDiv, Western Conservative Bapt., 1977. Ordained to ministry Bapt. Ch., 1982. Assoc. pastor Palo Verde Bapt. Ch., Tucson, 1977-79, Hillsboro (Oreg.) First Bapt. Ch., 1980-98, Capitol Ministries, Hillsboro, 1998—. Chaplain Oreg. Legislature, Salem, 1985—; del. Rep. Nat. Conv., New Orleans, 1988; chmn. Hillsboro Mayors Prayer Breakfast Com., 1986-88; vol. police chaplain City of Hillsboro, 1982—; long range planning com. mem. Hillsboro C. of C., 1990—; del. Rep. Nat. Conv., Houston, 1992, chaplain to Oreg. delegation, 1996; field dir. Bill Witt for Congress campaign, 1994; chmn. Greater Hillsboro Ministerial Assn., 1995-98; founder, trustee Heritage Christian Sch., 1996—; co-chair Greater Hillsboro Luis Palau Crusade, 1997; trustee House of Ruth, 1997—. Recipient Sr. Achievement award Western Conservative Bapt. Sem., 1977, Am. Legion Citizenship award, 1964. Mem. Oreg. Assn. Evangs. (exec. com. 1983-87, v.p. 1992-93), Lower Columbia Assn. (chmn. camping com. 1982-87). Republican. Home: 385 SE 71st Pl Hillsboro OR 97123-3698 Office: First Bapt Ch PO Box 186 Hillsboro OR 97123-0186

CARPENTER, JOHN EVERETT, retired principal, educational consultant; b. Tarrytown, N.Y., Nov. 27, 1923; s. Everett Birch and Mary (Avery) C.; student Union Coll., 1943; B.A., Iona Coll., 1946; M.A., Columbia, 1949, profl. diploma, 1961; m. Marie F. McCarthy, Nov. 14, 1944; 1 son, Dennis Everett. Tchr., Blessed Sacrament High Sch., New Rochelle, N.Y., 1946-50; tchr., adminstr. Armonk (N.Y.) pub. schs., 1950-62; dir. guidance Ridge Street Sch., Port Chester, N.Y., 1962-64; counselor Rye (N.Y.) High Sch., 1964-66, prin., 1966-78, ret.; guest lectr. Served to lt. USNR; now lt. comdr. ret. Res. Decorated Bronze Star medal. Mem. Middle States Assn. Colls. and Schs. (commn. on secondary schs.), Am. (life), Westchester-Putnam-Rockland (past pres.) personnel and guidance assns., NEA, Am. Legion (past comdr.), Phi Delta Kappa, Kappa Delta Pi. Rotarian (past pres., Paul Harris fellow). Clubs: Tarrytown Boat (past commodore). Home: 321 N Paseo De Los Conquista Green Valley AZ 85614-3137

CARPENTER, PETER ROCKEFELLER, bank executive; b. Sunbury, Pa., Apr. 18, 1939; s. Alvin Witmer and Katharine (Rockefeller) C.; m. Janet Ross Buck, Aug. 24, 1963; children: Karen Louise Althaus, Jean Ellen Chronis, Peter Alvin. BA, Pa. State U., 1962. Mgr. dept. J.C. Penney Co., Menlo Park, N.J., 1964-67; ops. mgr. Allstate Ins. Co., Summit, N.J., 1967-73; adminstrv. mgr. Prudential Property & Casualty, Scottsdale, Ariz., 1973-75; v.p. Fortune Properties, Scottsdale, 1975-76; life underwriter Conn. Mutual Life, Phoenix, 1976-81; v.p. and dir. sales and mktg. No. Trust Bank, Phoenix, 1981-89; v.p. M&I Marshall & Ilsley Trust Co., 1989-94; dir. planned giving Luth. Social Svcs. of the S.W., 1994-95; v.p. trust dept. Founders Bank of Ariz., Scottsdale, 1995-96; v.p. dir sales & mktg. Southwest Region Wells Fargo Pvt. Client Svcs., 1996—; mem. adv. bd. No. Ariz. U. Coll. Edn., 1997—. Sec. exec. bd. Samuel Gompers Rehab. Ctr., 1981-84, chmn. bd., 1984-91, bd. dirs. emeritus, 1998; div. chmn. Phoenix United Way, 1981, 82, 86, 90; Rep. committeeman, Phoenix, 1978-86; bd. dirs. Scottsdale Boys and Girls Club, bd. govs., 1997—, sec.; bd. dirs. Scottsdale Cultural Coun. Adv., Herberger Theatre Ctr.; mem. adv. bd. Devereaux Ariz., 1998—; mem. support campaign Maricopa County C.C., 1997—. With USN, 1962-64. Mem. Nat. Assn. Planned Giving Roundtable, Pa. State U. Alumni Assn. (southwest region dir. 1979-86), SAR, Ariz. Club (bd. dirs., pres. 1999), U.S. Navy League, Kiwanis (Disting. pres., Disting. lt. gov.), Sigma Alpha Epsilon. Lutheran. Home: 13076 N 101st St Scottsdale AZ 85260-7281 Office: Wells Fargo PCS 7501 E Mccormick Pkwy # 105 Scottsdale AZ 85258-3495

CARPENTER, SUSAN ANN, financial planner; b. Huntington Park, Calif., Nov. 10, 1944; d. Clarence William and Lillian Mary (Reed) M.; m. Robert Ray Carpenter, Jan. 9, 1993; children: Lorrie King, Letitia Martin, Tania Radecki, Lance Brooks, Landry Carpenter, India Brooks, Shelli Carpenter. Degree, Coll. of Fin. Planning, 1991. CFP. Co-owner Jhirmack of Ctrl. L.A., 1974-82, Recur-L Systems Inc., L.A., 1979-90; fin. advisor IDS/Am. Express Fin. Advisors, Riverside, Calif., 1985—. Mem. Internat. Assn. of Fin. Planners, Soroptimist Internat. of Running Springs, Soroptimist Internat. of the Foothills, Inc. (pres., v.p., rec. sec., treas., Soroptimist of Yr. 1990). Avocations: hiking, puzzels. Home: PO Box 2285 Running Springs CA 92382-2285 Office: Am Express Fin Advisors 5055 Canyon Crest Dr Riverside CA 92507-6015

CARR, BETTY LEE, artist, educator; b. Santa Cruz, Calif., Aug. 21, 1946; d. Carl Ceasar and Barbara Jean (Penoyar) Kratzenstein; m. Michael Paul Rypka, Feb. 1966 (div.); 1 child, Tammy Lee; m. Howard Lewis Carr, Jan. 12, 1980. AA, Cabrillo Jr. Coll., Aptos, Calif., 1966; BA in Art, U. Calif., Santa Cruz, 1973, MFA in Art, 1978, tchg. credential, 1984. Cert. tchr., Colo., Calif. Arts instr. Santa Cruz Adult Edn., 1973-86, City of Ft. Collins, Colo., 1985-86; arts and phys. edn. instr. Pajaro Valley Unified Sch. Dist., Aptos, 1981-83; arts dir. Sign Graphics, Boulder, Colo., 1983-85; arts dir., instr. City of Boulder, 1983-85; arts dir., instr., coord. Boulder Art Sch., 1983-85; arts instr. K-12 Poudre Sch., Ft. Collins, 1986-88; artist workshop instr., 1988—; artist demonstrator at colls., chs. and schs., 1973—; lectr. in field; represented by El Presidio Gallery, Tucson, Taos Gallery, Scottsdale, Ariz., Lee Youngman Galleries, Calistoga, Calif., Mountain Trails Gallery, Sedona, Ariz., Michael Atkinson Gallery, Santa Fe, Huntsman Gallery, Apsen, Colo. One woman shows include Gallery 304-U. Calif., Santa Cruz, 1972, Sierka Gallery, Smith River, Calif., 1970-77, Cooperhouse Gallery, Santa Cruz, 1976-79, Group 21 Gallery, Los Gatos, Calif., 1976, St. Francis Hotel, San Francisco, 1976, Gallery Artvarks, San Jose, Calif., 1979, Qume Corp., San Jose, 1980, Baskin House, Santa Cruz, 1981, Gallery of Art-U. Calif., Santa Cruz, 1981, Boulder (Colo.) Reservoir, 1985; exhibited in group shows at Ann. Woman's Invitational Art Expo, Capitola, Calif., 1974, Cabrillo Music Festival, Aptos, 1973-76, Libr. Gallery-U.S. Santa Cruz, 1972, Sesnon Gallery, 1972, Castle Art Gallery, Santa Cruz, 1969-71, Soc. Houston Arts, 1992, Southwestern Art Festival, Calistoga, Calif., 1992-96, Ariz. Watercolor Assn., 1994, 95, 96 (award of excellence), Phoenix Art Mus., 1994, N.Mex.-Diabetes Found., 1992, 93, 95, Vanier Roberts Gallery, 1995-96, Santa Fe (N.Mex.) Artists for Children 1991, Prescott's Mus., 1995, Prescott Fine Arts, 1995, Mountain Oyster Club, Tucson, 1996, 97, 98, Mayo Clinic Women Artists Invitational, Scottsdale, 1997, Western Fedn., 1998; contbr. art to various publs. Fellow No. Ariz. Watercolor Soc. (Jurors award 1998), Ariz. Watercolor Assn. (Purchase award 1996), Knickerbocker Soc. Artists (Signature status). Home: 1270 Kelli Ln Cottonwood AZ 86326-5682

CARR, PETER EMILE, publisher; b. La Habana, Cuba, Oct. 16, 1950; came to U.S., 1962; s. Pedro Emilio Carr and Carmen Emelina Luaces; m. Sheryl A. Strayer, Nov. 18, 1995. BA in Anthropology, Calif. State U., Long Beach, 1986. Asst. mgr. Hides & Skins Unltd., L.A., 1976-85; archaeol. cons. Archaeol. Enterprises, L.A., 1985-91; pres. The Cuban Index, San Luis Obispo, Calif., 1991—; cons. Soc. for Hispanic Hist. and Ancestral Rsch., Westminster, Calif., 1992—, Calif. Geneal. Alliance, San Francisco, 1992—. Author: Guide to Cuban Genealogical Research, 1991 (reference book series) San Francisco Passenger Departure Lists, Vols. I-V, 1992, 93, 94, Censos, Padrones y Matriculas de la Poblacion de Cuba, 1993, Genealogical Resources of Hispanic Central and South America, 1996; author, editor jours. Caribbean Hist. and Geneal. Jour., 1993-94. Recipient Spl. Honor award Anthropology Students Assn., 1985, Gold Poet award Internat. Poetry, 1988. Mem. Nat. Geneal. Soc., Coun. for Genealogy Columnists, Inc. (co-editor newsletter 1992-95), Manchester and Lancashire Family History Soc., Cercle Genealoguique de la Brie, Mortar Bd. Honor Soc. Mem. Humanist Party. Roman Catholic. Avocations: swimming, golf, hiking, fishing, old books. Office: TCI Genealogical Resources PO Box 15839 San Luis Obispo CA 93406-5839

CARR, RUTH MARGARET, plastic surgeon; b. Waco, Tex., July 2, 1951. MD, U. Okla., 1977. Intern U. Okla. Med. Sch., Oklahoma City, 1977-78; resident U. Okla. Health Sci. Ctr., Oklahoma City, 1978-81, UCLA, 1981-83; plastic surgeon St. John's Hosp., 1989—, Santa Monica (Calif.) Hosp., 1989—; clin. asst. prof. UCLA, 1983—. Office: 1301 20th St Ste 470 Santa Monica CA 90404-2082

CARRAHER, MARY LOU CARTER, art educator; b. Cin., Mar. 9, 1927; d. John Paul and Martha Leona (Williams) Carter; m. Emmett Carraher, Nov. 6, 1943 (div. July 1970); children: Candace Lou Holsenbeck-Smith, Michael Emmett, Cathleen C. Kruska. Student, U. Cin., 1946-48, Calif. State U., 1973-74. Lifetime credential in adult edn.: art, ceramics, crafts. Substitute tchr. Cobb County Schs., Smyrna, Ga., 1961-63; art tchr. pvt. lessons Canyon Country, Calif., 1968-72; adult edn. art tchr. Wm. S. Hart H.S. Dist., Santa Clarita, Calif., 1973-97; children's art and calligraphy cmty. svcs. Coll. of the Canyons, Santa Clarita, Calif., 1976-96; art dir. Santa Clarita Sr. Ctr., 1998; founder, bd. dirs. Santa Clarita Art Guild, 1972-80; art dir. European tours Continental Club, Canyon Country, 1977-81; art tour guide and travel cons. Northridge (Calif.) Travel, 1981-91; vol. art tchr. stroke patients Henry Newhall Meml. Hosp., Valencia, Calif., 1993-96; craft tchr. for respite care program, Newhall, Calif., 1995-96, Respite Care Ctr., Santa Clarita Valley Sr. Ctr., 1995-96. Artist, author: History of Moreland School District, San Jose, California, 1965; artist: Paintings for each season of Church Year, 1970's, Baptismal painting, 1988, Sr. Ctr. Watercolors Center Scenes, 1993, Watercolors of Christmas Charity Home Tour, 1993, Henry Mayo Newhall Meml. Hosp., 1997. Tchr., mem. Santa Clarita United Meth. Ch., 1966-96; judge for art contests and exhibits, Santa Clarita, 1973-96; mem. Santa Clarita Valley Hist. Soc., 1989-96; mem. Alumni Assn., Norwood (Ohio) City Schs., 1993-96. Recipient Bravo award nomination for Outstanding Achievement in Art, 1995, Sr. of Yr. Santa Clarita Valley Sr. Ctr., 1995, Christian Svc. award Santa Clarita United Meth. Ch., 1988; vited by Citizen Amb. Program of People to People Internat. to join U.S. del. to assess bus. and trade opportunities of the craft industry in China. Mem. Santa Clarita Valley Arts Coun., Hosp. Home Tour League, Nat. Women in the Arts (charter, Washington). Republican. Methodist. Avocations: travel, art related crafts, reading.

CARREKEA, JAMES, electronics company executive. CEO, chmn. Aspect Telecomm., San Jose, Calif. Office: Aspect Telecomm 1730 Fox Dr San Jose CA 95131-2311*

CARREL, ANNETTE FELDER, writer; b. San Francisco, Dec. 11, 1929; m. Robert E. Carrel (dec. 1989); 3 children. AA, Notre Dame Coll.; BA, Lone Mountain Coll.; MA in Spl. Edn., U. Calif., San Francisco. Home: 2010 Garden St Santa Barbara CA 93101

CARREY, NEIL, lawyer, educator; b. Bronx, N.Y., Nov. 19, 1942; s. David L. and Betty (Kurtzburg) C.; m. Karen Krysher, Apr. 9, 1980; children: Jana, Christopher; children by previous marriage: Scott, Douglas, Dana. BS in Econs., U. Pa., 1964; JD, Stanford U., 1967. Bar: Calif. 1968. Mem. firm, v.p. corp. DeCastro, West, Chodorow, Inc., L.A., 1967-97; of counsel Jenkens & Gilchrist, L.A., 1998—; instr. program for legal paraprofls. U. So. Calif., 1977-89; lectr. U. So. Calif. Dental Sch., 1987—, Employee Benefits Inst., Kansas City, Mo., 1996. Author: Nonqualified Defered Compensation Plans-The Wave of the Future, 1985. Officer, Vista Del Mar Child Care Center, L.A., 1968-84; treas. Nat. Little League of Santa Monica, 1984-85, pres., 1985-86, coach, 1990-95, coach Bobby Sox Softball Team, Santa Monica, 1986-88, bd. dirs. 1988, umpire in chief, 1988; referee, coach Am. Soccer Youth Orgn., 1989-95; curriculum com. Santa Monica-Malibu Sch. Dist., 1983-84, comm. health adv. com., 1988-95, chmn., 1989-95, sports and phys. edn. adv. com., chmn., 1993—, dist. com. for sch. based health ctr., 1991-94, title/gender equity com., chmn., 1992—, athletic study com., chmn., 1989-91, fin. adv. com., 1994, ad hoc com. dist. facilities chmn., 1998; dir. The Santa Monica Youth Athletic Found., 1995— (exec. comm. 1997-98, v.p. 1998—); dir. The Small Bus. Coun. of Am., 1995—, dir. Santa Monica H.S. Booster Club, 1995-97, dir. Santa Monica Bay Rep. Club, 1995-96; dir. Santa Monica Police Activities League, 1995-97, v.p. fin., 1997-98, pres.-elect, 1998—; pres. Gail Dorin Music Found., 1994—; v.p. Sneaker Sisters, 1996—; pres. Santa Monica Bay Jr. Rowing, 1997—; legal cons. 33rd Dist. Calif. PTA, 1997—; dir. Santa Monica League Women Voters. Mem. LWV (dir. 1997—), U. Pa. Alumni Soc., So. Calif. (pres. 1971-79, dir. 1979-87), Alpha Kappa Psi (life), Mountaingate Tennis Club. Independent. Jewish. Home: 616 23rd St Santa Monica CA 90402-3130 Office: 12100 Wilshire Blvd Fl 15 Los Angeles CA 90025-7120

CARRICO, DONALD JEFFERSON, public transit system manager; b Dallas, June 15, 1944; s. Ivan and Helen Mae (Jefferson) C.; m. Prudence Louise Cornish, Aug. 17, 1968; children: Bryan Jefferson, Alan Jefferson. BSBA, Ohio State U., 1967; MA in Bus. Mgmt., Cen. Mich. U., 1977. Commd. 2d lt. USAF, 1967, advanced through grades to maj., 1979; various supervisory positions USAF Air Freight Terminals, 1967-72; mgr. passenger travel and cargo br. USAF Transp. Div., Rickenbacker AFB, Ohio, 1972-74; transp. and air terminal insp. USAF Insp. Gen. Team, Hawaii, 1974-76; liaison officer US Naval Supply Ctr., Pearl Harbor, Hawaii, 1976-78; transp. staff officer USAF Hdqrs. Tactical Air Command, Langley AFB, Va., 1978-83; chief transp. USAF Transp. Div., Incirlik AB, Turkey, 1983-85, Williams AFB, Ariz., 1986-88; vehicle fleet mgr. V&B Svcs., Phoenix, 1989-91; asst. mgr. dispatch svcs. Phoenix Transit System, 1991-92, ops. mgr., 1993-95, logistics mgr., 1996-98, ops. dir., 1998—. Logistics chief Gilbert Food Bank Cmty. Food Dr., Gilbert, Ariz., 1987, chmn., 1988; asst. cubmaster Pack 282 Boy Scouts Am., Gilbert, 1987; mem. Town of Gilbert Gen. Plan Rev. Task Force, 1992-93, total quality mgmt. rsch. panel Transp. Rsch. Bd., Washington, 1992-95; transp. coord. Super Bowl XXX, Tempe, 1995-96. Decorated Bronze Star. Avocations: community planning, videotaping, automotive restoration. Home: 683 E Washington Ave Gilbert AZ 85234-6401

CARRIGAN, JIM R., arbitrator, mediator, retired federal judge; b. Mobridge, S.D., Aug. 24, 1929; s. Leo Michael and Mildred Ione (Jaycox) C.; m. Beverly Jean Halpin, June 2, 1956. Ph.B., J.D., U. N.D., 1953; LL.M. in Taxation, NYU, 1956; LLD (hon.), U. Colo., 1989, Suffolk U., 1991, U. N.D., 1997. Bar: N.D. 1953, Colo. 1956. Asst. prof. law U. Denver, 1956-59; vis. assoc. prof. NYU Law Sch., 1958, U. Wash. Law Sch., 1959-60; Colo. jud. adminstr., 1960-61; prof. law U. Colo., 1961-67; partner firm Carrigan & Bragg (and predecessors), 1967-76; justice Colo. Supreme Ct., 1976-79; judge U.S. Dist. Ct. Colo., 1979-95; mem. Colo. Bd. Bar Examiners, 1969-71; lectr. Nat. Coll. State Judiciary, 1964-77, 95; bd. dirs. Nat. Inst. Trial Advocacy, 1971-73, 78—, chmn. bd. 1986-88, also mem. faculty, 1972—; adj. prof. law U. Colo, 1984, 1991—; bd. dirs. Denver Broncos Stadium Dist., 1996—. Editor-in-chief: N.D. Law Rev., 1952-53, Internat. Soc. Barristers Quar., 1972-79; editor: DICTA, 1957-59; contbr. articles to profl. jours. Bd. regents U. Colo., 1975-76; bd. visitors U. N.D. Coll. Law, 1983-85. Recipient Disting. Svc. award Nat. Coll. State Judiciary, 1969, Outstanding Alumnus award U. N.D., 1973, Regent Emeritus award U. Colo., 1977, B'nai Brith Civil Rights award, 1986, Thomas More Outstanding Lawyer award Cath. Lawyers Guild, 1988, Oliphant Disting. Svc. award Nat. Inst. Trial Advocacy, 1993, Constl. Rights award Nat. Assn. Blacks in Criminal Justice (Colo. chpt.), 1992, Disting. Svc. award Colo. Bar Assn., 1994, Amicus Curiae award ATLA, 1995. Fellow Colo. Bar Found., Boulder County Bar Found.; mem. ABA (action com. on tort system improvement 1985-87, TIPS sect. long range planning com., 1986-97; coun. 1987-91, task force on initiatives and referenda 1990-92, size of civil juries task force 1988-90, class actions task force 1995-97), Colo. Bar Assn., Boulder County Bar Assn., Denver Bar Assn., Cath. Lawyers Guild, Inns. of Ct., Internat. Soc. Barristers, Internat. Acad. Trial Lawyers (bd. dirs. 1995—), Fed. Judges Assn. (bd. dirs. 1985-89), Am. Judicature Soc. (bd. dirs. 1985-89), Tenth Circuit Dist. Judges Assn. (sec. 1991-92, v.p. 1992-93, pres. 1994-95), Order of Coif, Phi Beta Kappa. Roman Catholic. Office: Judicial Arbiter Group 1601 Blake St Ste 400 Denver CO 80202-1328

CARRINGTON, JAMES DONALD, minister; b. Pitts., Sept. 25, 1933; s. Edward and Susie Mae (Jones) C.; m. Doris Jones, Apr. 9, 1960; children: Darlene Denise Carrington Haynes, Roderick. BTh, Reed Coll. of Religion, 1964; DD, Reed Christian Coll. and Sem., 1981. Ordained to ministry Bapt. Ch., 1958. Pastor Friendship Bapt. Ch., Yorba Linda, Calif., 1964—; v.p. Am. Bapt. Chs. of Pacific S.W., 1984, pres., 1985, bd. mgrs., 1991—; bd. dirs. Am. Bapt. Chs. U.S.A., 1986—, Am. Bapt. Credit Union, 1991—, Bapt. World Alliance, 1991—, Mins. and Missionaries Bd., 1991—. V.p. Orange County Br. NAACP; advisor Calif. State U., Fullerton Martin Luther King, Jr. Com.; mem. Fullerton Police Community Coun., North Orange County Fair Housing Adv. Bd., Youth Devel. Coun., Minority Adv. Bd.; pres. Am. Bapt. Black Caucus of Pacific S.W., 1984. Named Man of Yr. Ford Motor Co. of Orange County, 1971. Office: Friendship Bapt Ch 17145 Bastanchury Rd Yorba Linda CA 92886-1703

CARROLL, BONNIE, publisher, editor; b. Salt Lake City, Nov. 20, 1941. Grad. high sch., Ogden, Utah. Owner The Peer Group, San Francisco, 1976-78; pub., editor The Reel Directory, Cotati, Calif., 1978—. Pub., editor The Reel Thing newsletter, San Francisco, 1977-78. Mem. Assn. Visual Communicators (bd. dirs. 1987-90), No. Calif. Women in Film, San Francisco Film Tape Council (exec. dir. 1979-81). Office: The Reel Directory PO Box 866 Cotati CA 94931-0866

CARROLL, DAVID TODD, computer engineer; b. West Palm Beach, Fla., Apr. 8, 1959; s. David Irwin and Lois Ellen (Spriggs) C. Student, U. Houston, 1978-81. Lab. technician Inst. for Lipid Rsch., Baylor Coll. Medicine, Houston, 1978-81; software specialist Digital Equipment Corp., Colorado Springs, Colo., 1982-86, systems engr., 1986-91, systems support cons., 1991-94; systems cons. Mentec, Inc., Colorado Springs, 1994—. Mem. AAAS, Digital Equipment Corp. Users Soc. Home: 7332 Aspen Glen Ln Colorado Springs CO 80919-3024 Office: Mentec Inc 305 S Rockrimmon Blvd Colorado Springs CO 80919-2303

CARROLL, EARL HAMBLIN, federal judge; b. Tucson, Mar. 26, 1925; s. John Vernon and Ruby (Wood) C.; m. Louise Rowlands, Nov. 1, 1952; children—Katherine Carroll Pearson, Margaret Anne. BSBA, U. Ariz., 1948, LLB, 1951. Bar: Ariz., U.S. Ct. Appeals (9th and 10th cirs.), U.S. Ct. of Claims, U.S. Supreme Ct. Law clk. Ariz. Supreme Ct., Phoenix, 1951-52; assoc. Evans, Kitchel & Jenckes, Phoenix, 1952-56, ptnr., 1956-80; judge U.S. Dist. Ct. Ariz., Phoenix, 1980—; spl. counsel City of Tombstone, Ariz., 1962-65, Maricopa County, Phoenix, 1955, City of Tucson, 1974, City of Phoenix, 1979; designated mem. U.S. Fgn. Intelligence Surveillance Court by Chief Justice U.S. Supreme Ct., 1993-99; chief judge Alien Terrorist Removal Ct., 1996—. Mem. City of Phoenix Bd. of Adjustment, 1955-58; trustee Phoenix Elem. Sch. Bd., 1961-72; mem. Gov.'s Council on Intergovtl. Relations, Phoenix, 1970-73; mem. Ariz. Bd. Regents, 1978-80. Served with USNR, 1943-46; PTO. Recipient Nat. Service awards Campfire, 1973, 75, Alumni Service award U. Ariz., 1980, Disting. Citizen award No. Ariz. U., Flagstaff, 1983, Bicentenial award Georgetown U., 1988, Disting. Citizen award U. Ariz., 1990. Fellow Am. Coll. Trial Lawyers, Am. Bar Found.; mem. ABA, Ariz. Bar Assn., U. Ariz. Law Coll. Assn. (pres. 1975), Phoenix Country Club, Sigma Chi (Significant Sig award 1991), Phi Delta Phi. Democrat. Office: US Dist Ct US Courthouse & Fed Bldg 230 N 1st Ave Ste 6000 Phoenix AZ 85025-0005

CARROLL, JON, newspaper columnist. Columnist San Francisco Chronicle. Office: Chronicle Pub Co 901 Mission St San Francisco CA 94103-2988*

CARROLL, PHILIP JOSEPH, engineering company executive; b. New Orleans, Sept. 24, 1937; s. Philip Joseph and Rosemary Agnes (McEntee) C.; m. Charlene Marie Phillips, Jan. 3, 1959; children: Philip III, Kenneth, Bruce. BS in Physics, Loyola U., New Orleans, 1958; MS in Physics, Tulane U., 1961. Petroleum engr. Shell Oil Co., New Orleans, La., N.Y.C. and Midland, Tex., 1961-73; dir. energy conservation div. U.S. Dept. Commerce, Washington, 1973-74; exec. dir. Nat. Energy Conservation Coun., Washington, 1974; regional engr., mgr. so. exploration and prodn. Shell Oil Co., New Orleans, 1974-75; div. mgr. prodn., western exploration and prodn. Shell Oil Co., Houston, 1975-78, gen. mgr. prodn., western ops., 1978-79, gen. mgr. plans and integration, 1979, v.p. pub. affairs, 1979-85; mng. dir. Shell Internat. Gas, Shell Internat. Petroleum Co., London, 1985-86; sr. v.p. adminstrn. Shell Oil Co., Houston, 1986-88, exec. v.p. adminstrn., 1988-93, pres., CEO, 1993-98, mem. bd. dirs., 1990; chmn., CEO Fluor Corp, Irvine, 1998—; bd. dirs. Boise Cascade Corp. Bd. dirs. Am. Petroleum Inst., Cen. Houston, Tex. Med. Ctr., Am. Air Mus.; trustee Com. for Econ. Devel., 1991—, Baylor Coll. Medicine, Boys & Girls Clubs of Am.; mem. Gov.'s Bus. Coun. (Tex.), Nat. Petroleum Coun., Conf. Bd., 1991—, Nat. Action Coun. for Minorities in Engring., 1993—; bd. dirs.; adv. bd. mem. Salvation Army; bd. adminstrs. adv. bd. mem. Ctr. Bioenviron. Rsch., Tulane U. Mem. 25 Yr. Club Petroleum Industry, Tchefuncta Country Club (Covington, La.), River Oaks Country Club, Champions Golf Club. Avocation: golf. *

CARROLL, SIBYL, writer; b. Cuervo, N.Mex., Aug. 5, 1918; d. Joe Abbot and Lela Eugenia (Bell) Callaway; m. Jack Richard Carroll, Oct. 11, 1942 (wid. Jan. 1965); children: Robert Wayne, Jesse Richard, Clifford G., Tamara E. Diploma/Montessori Primary Edn., St. Nicholas Sch., London, 1975. Operator Sunshine Montessory Sch., Yuma, Ariz., 1951-89; advisor in child devel. Ariz. Western Coll., Yuma, 1965-80, Ariz. Welfare Dept., Phoenix, 1963-66. Author: (books) Lela and joe, 1996, Complete Montessori for Home and School, 1997, From theMouth of Babes, 1997. Mem. Yuma Writers Club, Phi Theta Kappa. Avocations: drawing, painting. Home: 1901 S 7th Ave Yuma AZ 85364-5550

CARSCH, RUTH ELIZABETH, consulting librarian; b. London, May 3, 1945; came to U.S., 1949; d. Harry and Ellen Margot (Adler) C.; 1 child, Zachariah Robert. BA, CUNY, 1967; MS, Columbia U., 1968. Cert. libr. N.Y., Calif. Reference libr. N.Y. Pub. Libr., 1968-70; tech. info. specialist Bechtel, Inc., San Francisco, 1972-75; rsch. assoc. Erick & Lavidge Mkt. Rsch. Assocs., San Francisco, 1980; instrnl. reference libr. San Mateo County C.C. Dist., 1987—; cons. Port Authority N.Y. and N.J., 1982-84, Camp, Dresser, McKee Engrs., Boston, 1988, Met. Mus. Art, 1992, Calif. Conservation Corps., 1992, Haas Fund, 1995, Oregon Shakespeare, 1995, Oak Grove Sch. Dist., San Jose, Calif., 1998; libr. adv. bd. Acad. Art Coll., 1995—. Mem. Art Libris. Soc., No. Calif. Architecture-Engring. Libris. Roundtable, U. Calif. Berkeley Libr. Futures Inst., 1997. Office: 1453 Rhode Island St San Francisco CA 94107-3248

CARSON, ELIZABETH LORRAINE NEAL, small business owner, civilian military employee; b. Glendale, Calif., Oct. 2, 1958; d. Harold Dean and Viola Gertrude (Neal) Donaldson; m. Robert Lawrence Chally, Aug. 7, 1981 (div. Sept. 1985); m. Richard Wayne Carson, Oct. 5, 1992. BS, Spring Arbor Coll., 1979; MS, Air Force Inst. Tech., 1988. Loan sec. Sacramento (Calif.) Savs. and Loan, 1979, acctg. clk., 1979-81; equipment specialist trainee Civil Svc. USAF, McClellan AFB, 1981-84, equipment specialist, 1984-86; logistics specialist Civil Svc. USAF, L.A. AFB, 1986-88; dep. systems program mgr. Civil Svc. USAF, Sacramento, 1988-89, chief, resource and plans, 1989-90, program mgr., 1990-93, integrated weapon system mgr., program mgmt. process action team rep., 1991-92; asst. chef Hermit Basin Conf. Ctr. and Resort, Westcliffe, Colo., 1997, dir. food svc. mgmt., head chef, mktg. mgr., 1997—; adj. prof. Colo. Tech. Coll., Colorado Springs, 1989-91; advisor Logistics Adv. Bd., Colorado Springs, 1988-92; integrated weapon sys. mgmt. program mgr., process action team mem. Air Force Material Command, 1991-93; co-owner Colors of Nature Gallery, Westcliffe, In Home, Westcliffe. Organist/pianist Orangevale Free Meth. Ch., 1971-76, fin. com. 1981-82, music com., 1971-76, 80-85, chmn. music com., 1984. Mem. Soc. Reliability Engrs., Soc. Logistics Engrs., Sigma Iota Epsilon. Republican. Avocations: stained glass, restoration of old homes, photography, tennis, cooking. Office: Hermit Basin Conf Ctr and Resort PO Box 25 Westcliffe CO 81252-0025

CARSON, G(ARY) B(ENSON), art appraiser; b. Helena, Mont., Feb. 28, 1950; m. Karen Schein, Oct. 27, 1989; 1 child, Miranda. BA, U. Calif., Berkeley, 1977. Prin. G.B. Carson Art Consultation & Appraisals, Berkeley, 1983—. Office: G B Carson PO Box 8502 Berkeley CA 94707-8502

CARSON, GREGORY DONALD, information scientist; b. Chgo., June 29, 1963; s. George Ivan and JoAnn Ruth (Platt) C.; m. Marian Angel, June 27, 1988; children: Annie, Christy, Brandon. BS in Engring., U. Iowa, 1986, MS in Engring., 1992. Capt. USAF, 1986-96; clin. sys. engr. WHMC, San Antonio, 1986-88, 13th Med. Ctr., Angeles City, Philippines, 1988-91; chief tech. officer 3rd Med. Ctr., Anchorage, Alaska, 1993—; cons. Info. Tech. Adv. Coun., N.Y.C., 1994—; Pacific Air Forces, Honolulu, 1994, 96; pres., dir. Angel Works, Anchorage, 1995—. Author: General Purpose Medical Imaging Program, 1992, (software) Fishman, 1996; contbr. articles to profl. jours. Mem. Alaska High Tech. Bus. Coun., 1995—. Recipient Commendation medal USAF, 1988, 91, Achievement medal, 1989. Mem. Nat. Info. Infrastructure Alaska (founding), Health Info. Mgmt. Sys. Soc. Home: 7420A I St Elmendorf AFB AK 99506-1232 Office: 3MDG/SGC 24800 Hospital Dr Elmendorf AFB AK 99506-3701

CARSON, MEREDITH SHELTON, poetess, homemaker; b. Bklyn., Oct. 27, 1913; d. Allen Wellington and Marion (Brown) Shelton; m. Hampton [text obscured] Sarah Lawrence Coll., 1937. Author: Book of Poetry, Infinite Morning, 1997, (Hollis Summers prize Ohio U. 1997). Mem. AAUW (active vol.). Avocations: modern dance, art, sci. philosophy, eco-travel. Home: 2001 Ualakaa St Honolulu HI 96822-2081

CARSON, WALLACE PRESTON, JR., state supreme court justice; b. Salem, Oreg., June 10, 1934; s. Wallace Preston and Edith (Bragg) C.; m. Gloria Stolk, June 24, 1956; children: Scott, Carol, Steven (dec. 1981). BA in Politics, Stanford U., 1956; JD, Willamette U., 1962. Bar: Oreg. 1962, U.S. Dist. Ct. Oreg. 1963, U.S. Ct. Appeals (9th cir.) 1968, U.S. Supreme Ct. 1971, U.S. Ct. Mil. Appeals 1977; lic. comml. pilot FAA. Pvt. practice law Salem, Oreg., 1962-77; judge Marion County Cir. Ct., Salem, 1977-82; assoc. justice Oreg. Supreme Ct., Salem, 1982-92, chief justice, 1992—. Mem. Oreg. Ho. of Reps., 1967-71, maj. leader, 1969-71; mem. Oreg. State Senate, 1971-77, minority floor leader, 1971-77; dir. Salem Area Community Council, 1967-70, pres., 1969-70; mem. Salem Planning Commn., 1966-72, pres., 1970-71; co-chmn. Marion County Mental Health Planning Com., 1965-69; mem. Salem Community Goals Com., 1965; Republican precinct commiteeman, 1963-66; mem. Marion County Rep. Central Exec. Com., 1963-66; com. predinct edn. Oreg. Rep. Central Com., 1965; vestryman, acolyte, Sunday Sch. tchr., youth coach St. Paul's Episcopal Ch., 1935—; task force on cts. Oreg. Council Crime and Delinquency, 1968-69; trustee Willamette U., 1970—; adv. bd. Cath. Ctr. Community Services, 1976-77; mem. comprehensive planning com. Mid-Willamette Valley Council of Govts., 1970-71; adv. com. Oreg. Coll. Edn. Tchr. Edn., 1971-75; pres. Willamette regional Oreg. Lung Assn., 1973-74, state dir., exec. com., 1975-77; pub. relations com. Williamette council Campfire Girls, 1976-77; criminal justice adv. bd. Chemekata Community Coll., 1977-79; mem. Oreg. Mental Health Com., 1979-80; mem. subcom. Gov.'s Task Force Mental Health, 1980; you and govt. adv. com. Oreg. YMCA, 1981—. Served to col. USAFR, 1956-59. Recipient Salem Disting. Svc. award, 1968; recipient Good Fellow award Marion County Fire Svc., 1974, Minuteman award Oreg. N.G. Assn., 1980; fellow Eagleton Inst. Politics, Rutgers U., 1971. Mem. Marion County Bar Assn. (sec.-treas. 1965-67, dir. 1968-70), Oreg. Bar Assn., ABA, Willamette U. Coll. Law Alumni Assn. (v.p. 1968-70), Salem Art Assn., Oreg. Hist. Soc., Marion County Hist. Soc., Stanford U. Club (pres. Salem chpt. 1963-64), Delta Theta Phi. Office: Oregon Supreme Ct Supreme Ct Bldg 1163 State St Salem OR 97310-1331*

CARTER, BONNIE MARIE, publisher, advertising sales; b. Colfax, Wash.; d. Seabert James and Albina Agnes (Buckley) C.; 1 child, Darin Wayne Flisram. Student Journalism, Mt. Hood C.C., Gresham, Oreg., 1975-76. Publisher, editor Crooked Arrow Publs., Portland, Oreg., 1977—. Mem. adv. bd. Portland (Oreg.) C.C., 1996-97. Mem. Cascade Blues Assn. Roman Catholic. Avocations: music, dancing. E-mail: positive@teleport.com. Office: Crooked Arrow Pub Co PO Box 92154 Portland OR 97292

CARTER, HENRIETTA MCKEE, educator; b. Boston, Aug. 13, 1936; d. Horace Adolphus and Thelma Henrietta McKee; m. William Grandvil Carter, June 9, 1980 (dec. Dec. 1993); children: Darius Grandvil, Grandvil Elliott, Jonathan Grandvil. BS in biology, Northeastern Univ., 1959; MM in voice, New Eng. Conservatory, 1964; MS in edn., National Univ., 1988. Dir. music Walnut Hill Sch., Natick, Mass., 1964-68; instr. voice and theory Inner City Inst., L.A., 1972-74; instr. voice Univ. So. Calif. Preparatory Sch. of Arts, L.A., 1970-74; rsch. fellow Univ. Ghana, Legion, Accra, Ghana, 1974-75; prof. voice music Golden West Coll., Huntington Beach, Calif., 1976—, chair music and dance, 1993-98, chair performing arts, 1998—; pvt. voice studio, Huntington Beach, Calif., 1976—, voice cons., Southern Calif., 1976—, pvt. voice studio, Legon Accra, Ghana, 1974-75, voice cons., 1974-75; prof. soprano soloist for recitals, TV, radio and others. Bd. dirs. Scout Trail Homeowners Assn., 1992. Recipient Woman of Yr. award Northeastern Univ., 1959; recipient numerous rsch. fellowships. Mem. Music Assn. of Calif. Cmty. Colls. (v.p. 1980-81), Coll. Music Soc., Soc. for Ethnomusicology, Delta Sigma Theta. Democrat. Avocations: photography, swimming, theatre and concerts, reading. Office: Golden West Coll 15744 Golden West St Huntington Beach CA 92647

CARTER, HUGH DAVID, architect, graphic artist; b. Melbourne, Australia, Dec. 8, 1952 (parents Am. citizens); s. John Daniel and Janet Louise (Graham) C. BArch. with honors, Calif. State Poly. U., 1976. Registered architect, Calif. from draftsman to project architect Fisher-Friedman Assocs., San Francisco, 1976-82; owner Hugh David Carter Architects, AIA, Santa Cruz, Calif., 1982-99; sr. ptnr. Carter and Salazar Architects, Santa Cruz, 1999—; designer Diablo Writing Project, Santa Cruz, 1982-85. Author articles. Active Solidardity Affinity Group, Santa Cruz, 1983-85. Mem. Architects Assn. Santa Cruz County (pres. 1987-89), commr. hist. preservation commn., vice-chmn. 1999). Democrat. Office: 522 S Branciforte Ave Santa Cruz CA 95062-3327

CARTER, JANE FOSTER, agriculture industry executive; b. Stockton, Calif., Jan. 14, 1927; d. Chester William and Bertha Emily Foster; m. Robert Buffington Carter, Feb. 25, 1952 (dec. Dec. 1994); children: Ann Claire Carter Palmer, Benjamin Foster; m. Frank Anthony Ballman, Aug. 15, 1998. BA, Stanford U., 1948; MS, NYU, 1949. Pres. Colusa (Calif.) Properties, Inc., 1953—; owner Carter Land and Livestock, Colusa, 1965—; sec.-treas. Carter Farms, Inc., Colusa, 1975-94, pres., 1994—. Author: If the Walls Could Talk, Colusa's Architectural Heritage, 1988; author, editor: Colusa County Survey and Plan for the Arts, 1981, 82, 83, Implementing the Colusa County Arts Plan, 1984, 85, 86. Mem. Calif. Gov.'s Commn. on Agr., Sacramento, 1979-82, Calif. Rep. Cntl. Com., 1976-94; del. Rep. Nat. Conv., Kansas City, Mo., 1976, Detroit, 1980, Dallas, 1984; trustee Calif. Hist. Soc., 1979-89, regional v.p., 1984-89; mem. Calif. Reclamation Bd., 1982-96, sec., 1986-96; mem. Calif. Hist. Resources Commn., 1994—, vice chair, 1996-97, chair person, 1997-99; mem. Colusa Heritage Preservation Com., 1976—, chmn., 1977-83, vice chmn., 1983-91; bd. dirs. Colusa Cmty. Theatre Found., 1980—; bd. dirs. English-Speaking Union, San Francisco, 1992—, pres., 1993-95, v.p., 1995—; bd. dirs. The English-Speaking Union of the U.S., N.Y.C., 1995—; bd. dirs. Leland Stanford Mansion Found., Sacramento, 1992—; trustee Calif. Preservation Found., 1989-95. Recipient award of Merit for Historic Preservation Calif. Hist. Soc., 1989, Design award Calif. Preservation Found., 1990. Mem. Sacramento River Water Contractors Assn. (sec. 1992—, exec. com. 1974—), Francisca Club, Kappa Alpha Theta. Episcopalian. Avocations: travel, the arts, hist. preservation. Home and Office: 4746 River Rd Colusa CA 95932-4200

CARTER, JANICE JOENE, telecommunications executive; b. Portland, Oreg., Apr. 17, 1948; d. William George and Charline Betty (Gilbert) P. Student, U. Calif., Berkeley, 1964, U. Portland, 1966-67, U. Colo., Boulder, 1967-68; BA in Math, U. Guam, 1970; MBA, Golden Gate U., 1998. Computer programmer Ga.-Pacific Co., Portland, 1972-74; systems analyst ProData, Seattle, 1974-79; systems analyst, mgr. Pacific Northwest Bell, Seattle, 1979-80; data ctr. mgr. Austin Co., Renton, Wash. 1980-83; developer shared tenent svcs. Wright-Runstad, Seattle, 1983-84; system adminstr. Hewlett-Packard, Bellevue, Wash., 1984; global telecom. mgr. Nordstrom, Inc., Seattle, 1984-96; global telecom. mgr. Hewlett-Packard Co., Palo Alto, Calif., 1996-98, 20th Century Fox, L.A., 1998—. Ski instr. Alpental, Snoqualmie Pass, Wash., 1984-87; bd. dirs. Educationally Gifted Children, Mercer Island, Wash., 1978-80; mem. curriculum com. Mercer Island Sch. Bd., 1992-95. Avocations: skiing, reading, German, French, traveling. Office: 20th Century Fox 2121 Ave of the Stars Los Angeles CA 90067

CARTER, JOY EATON, electrical engineer, consultant; b. Comanche, Tex., Feb. 8, 1923; d. Robert Lee and Carrie (Knudson) Eaton; m. Clarence J. Carter, Aug. 22, 1959; 1 child, Kathy Jean. Student, John Tarleton Agrl. Coll., 1939-40; B Music cum laude, N. Tex. State Tchrs. Coll., 1943, postgrad., 1944-45; postgrad., U. Tex., 1945; MSEE, Ohio State U., 1949, PhDEE and Radio Astronomy, 1957. Engr. aide Civil Service Wright Field, Dayton, Ohio, 1945-46; instr. math. Ohio State U., Columbus, 1946-48, asst., then assoc. Rsch. Found., 1947-49, from instr. to asst. prof. elec. engring., 1949-58; rsch. engr. N.Am. Aviation, Columbus, 1955-56; mem. tech. staff Space Tech. Labs. (later TRW Inc.), Redondo Beach, Calif., 1958-68; sect. head, staff engr. electronics tech. labs. The Aerospace Corp., El Segundo, 1968-72, staff engr. and mgr. system and terminals, USAF Satellite Communications System Program Office, 1972-77, mgr. communications sub- [text continues] cons. Mayhill, N.Mex., 1977—. Active Mayhill Vol. Fire Dept., 1986—; bd. dirs. Mayhill Cmty. Assn., 1988—, sec. bd. dirs., 1988—; co-chair music com. Mayhill Bapt. Ch., 1988—, trustee, 1988-92, 94-97; bd. dirs. Otero County Farm Bur., 1987—. Named Cow Belle of Yr., Otero CowBelles,

1988. Mem. IEEE (sr., life), Nat. Assn. Family and Cmty. Edn., Am. Astron. Soc., Am. Nat. Cattlewomen (sec. Otero CowBelles chpt. 1986-87, 1st v.p. 1988, historian 1989), Calif. Rare Fruit Growers, Native Plant Soc. N.Mex., Sacramento Mountains Hist. Soc. (bd. dirs. 1986—, treas. 1997—), High Country Horseman's Assn., Sigma Xi (life), Eta Kappa Nu (life), Sigma Alpha Iota (life), Alpha Chi, Kappa Delta Pi, Pi Mu Epsilon, Sigma Delta Epsilon. Avocations: breeding Tenn. Walking Horses, photography, sculpture, local history, gardening with unusual plants. Home and Office: PO Box 23 Mayhill NM 88339-0023

CARTER, KATHRYN ANN, mental health nurse; b. Milw., June 10, 1953; d. Adrian H. and Eleanor R. (Kurth); m. G.R. Lewellyn, Oct. 14, 1972 (div.); children: Anna, Cynthia; m. David Lee Carter, June 15, 1985; children: Ryan, Rebekah; stepchildren: Dana, Derek, Angel. Med. asst., Sch. Nursing, San Diego, 1973; AS, Madison Area Tech. Coll., 1979; BS, Coll. St. Francis, 1989; MS, U. Wis., Whitewater, 1994. RN, Wis., N.Mex.; lic. profl. counselor, N.Mex. RN Mendota Mental Health, Madison, 1983-89, U. Wis. Hosps., Madison, 1989-94, Presbyn. Home Health, Springer, N.Mex., 1995-97; pvt. practice counselor Raton, N.Mex., 1995-97; cons. Citizens for the Developmentally Disabled, Raton, 1995-97. Leader Girl Scouts, Columbus, Wis., 1992-94. Mem. AAUW (membership v.p. 1994-95), ACA, NRA, Internat. Inst. Wis., Internat. Tae Kwon Do Assn. Avocations: linguistics, ecology, art, outdoor sports, travel. Home: 1045 W 550 S Payson UT 84651-2605 Office: Mental Health Counseling PO Box 854 Raton NM 87740-0854

CARTER, MELVIN WHITSETT (MEL CARTER), artist, educator; b. Ill., Nov. 19, 1941; s. Mallory and Claudia (Whitsett) C. BFA, U. Ill., 1963; MFA, U. Gunajuato, Mex., 1968. Tchr. art Denver Pub. Schs., 1963-68; instr. Fine Arts Community Coll., Denver, 1968-71; coord. Fine Arts Community Auraria, Denver, 1971-89; artist, instr. Art Students League Denver, 1987—; guest prof. art Western N.Mex. U., summer 1994; artist cons., bd. dirs. Cherry Creek Arts Festival, Denver, 1991-92. Numerous one-man shows and group exhbns., 1964-96, including residence U.S. amb. to Austria, Vienna; illustrator: Occupational Communications, 1969; artist (withothers) Figure Drawing Workshop, 1985; featured artist New Choices mag., 1995, How to Sell Your Art (Carole Katchen), 1996; solo exhibn. (AIDS rsch. benefit) Celebration of Life, Denver, 1989. Commr. art Mayors Commr. Art, Culture, Film, 1992; artist advisor, bd. dirs. Cherry Creek Arts Festival, Denver, 1991. Sgt. USAF, 1959-61. Named Prof. Art, Colo. Community Colls. Abroad, Rome, Paris, London, 1970, Outstanding Educator Am., Bd. Dirs., Washington, 1974, State of Colo., 1987; recipient medal Excellence in Higher Edn., U. Tex., Austin, 1989; Fulbright scholar USIA, Netherland Am. Agy., 1987. Avocations: travel, art, antiques. Home: 511 16th St Ste 600 Denver CO 80202-4248 Office: Art Students League Denver 200 Grant St Denver CO 80203-4020

CARTER, MICHAEL DWAYNE, sales and marketing executive; b. Dallas, Mar. 28, 1959; s. Dwayne Marvin and Helen Mae (Davis) C.; m. Sandra Fay Williams, July 11, 1981; children: Christopher Michael, Danielle Suzanne, Bryan Kimball, Melissa Deborah. Student, Brigham Young U., 1978, 1980, U. Texas, San Antonio, 1981-82. Co-owner PIP Printing Franchise, San Antonio, 1981-84; co-owner, pres. Color Quick, L.A. and Irvine, 1987-89; co-owner, v.p. Chroma Copy Internat., L.A., 1989-90; co-owner, v.p., cons. RNR Consulting, L.A., 1990-93; owner, pres. Money Mailer of Utah (Utah) County, 1993-96; dir. sales mktg. Vitality Alliance Consulting, Utah County, Utah, 1996—; mentor and counselor S.C.O.R.E. Small Bus. Adminstrn., Utah County, 1995-97, Svc. Corps Ret. Execs.-S.B.A., 1995-97; conv. spkr. Money Mailer Inc. Franchises, Utah County, 1993. Contbr. articles to profl. jours. Elder LDS Ch., 1977-97; active Boy Scouts Am., 1981-97; planning commr. Woodland Hills (Utah) Planning Commn., 1995-97. Recipient Platinum 30's Top Franchise award, 1993, cert. of merit Utah Nat. Parks Coun. Boy Scouts Am., 1996. Republican. Avocations: mentoring, youth volunteer work, fishing, photography, most sports. Home: 800 S Oak Dr Woodland Hls UT 84653-2049 Office: Vitality Alliance Consulting 55 N University Ave Ste 225 Provo UT 84601-4429

CARTER, PAUL DENNIS, pastor; b. St. Joseph, Mo., May 9, 1950; s. Frank Clem and Nancy (Operman) C.; m. Linda Lee Wennihan, Sept. 12, 1971; children: Erica Nancy, Alan Lowell. Degree in law enforcement, Colby Community Coll., 1974; BA cum laude, Criswell Coll., 1985; MA in Counseling, Liberty U., 1988. Ordained minister So. Bapt. Ch. Emergency med. technician Thomas County Ambulance Svc., Colby, Kans., 1972-74; police officer Colby Police Dept., 1972-74, Olathe (Kans.) Police Dept., 1974-76, Green River (Wyo.) Police Dept., 1976-79; pastor Wamsutter (Wyo.) Bapt. Ch., 1979-81; adminstrv. asst. Criswell Coll., Dallas, 1981-86; sr. pastor Del Ray Bapt. Ch., Alexandria, Va., 1986-89; pastor Hillcrest Bapt. Ch., Riverton, Wyo., 1989—. Contbr. articles to profl. publs. Bd. dirs. Good News Jail and Prison Ministry, Arlington, Va., 1988-89; chaplain Alexandria Hosp., 1986-89, Fremont County Sheriff's Office, 1989—, Riverton Police Dept., 1989—. Mem. Am. Assn. Counseling Devel., Energy Basin Bapt. Assn. (chmn. evangelism 1978-79), Mt. Vernon Bapt. Assn. (bd. dirs., ethnic commn. 1987-88, evangelism commn. 1988—), Kiwanis. Republican. Avocations: computers, telecommunications.

CARTER, RICHARD BERT, retired church official, retired government official; b. Spokane, Wash., Dec. 2, 1916; s. Richard B. and Lula Selena (Jones) C.; BA in Polit. Sci., Wash. State U., 1939; postgrad. Georgetown U. Law Sch., 1941, Brown U., 1944, Brigham Young U. Extension, 1975-76; m. Mildred Brown, Sept. 6, 1952; children: Paul, Mark, Janis, David. *Immigrant surname ancestor: William Carter, blacksmith, glass blower, born February 12, 1821, Ledbury, Herefordshire, England; joined Church of Jesus Christ of Latter-day Saints, 1840; migrated to Nauvoo, Illinois 1841; married Ellen Benbow 1843 and posterity includes Church Apostle Jeffrey Roy Holland; served as scout in first Brigham Young pioneer company to Utah 1847; entered valley with advance party and plowed first half-acre ground July 23, 1847 before Brigham arrived; married second wife Harriet Temperance Utley, 1853, whose ancestor is Congregational Church minister Littlejohn Utley from whom also descends Apostle David Bruce Haight* Advt. credit mgr. Elec. Products Consol., Omaha, 1939-40; pub. affairs ofcl., investigator FBI, Washington, 1940-41, Huntington, W.Va., 1941, Houston, 1942, Boston, 1943, S. Am., 1943, Providence, 1944-45, N.Y.C., 1945, Salt Lake City, 1945, P.R., 1946-48, Phoenix, 1948-50, Washington, 1950-51, Cleve., 1952-55, Seattle, 1955-75, ret., 1975; assoc. dir. stake and mission pub. affairs dept. Ch. Hdqrs., Ch. of Jesus Christ of Latter-day Saints, Salt Lake City, 1975-77. Dist. chmn. Chief Seattle coun. Boy Scouts Am., 1967-68, coun. v.p., 1971-72, coun. commr., 1973-74, nat. coun. rep., 1962-64, 72-74; life mem., area II Nat. Eagle Scout Assn., 1984—. Mem. Freedoms Found. Valley Forge, Utah chpt., 1988—; bd. dirs. Salvation Army, 1963, United Way, 1962-63, mem. allocations com., 1962, 1987-88, JayCees, Omaha, Neb., 1939-40; organizer First Family History Lib., Seattle, 1971. Served to lt., Intelligence Corps, U.S. Army, 1954. Recipient Silver Beaver award Boy Scouts Am., 1964, Vigil Honor, 1971, Alumni Achievement award for Disting. Svc. Wash. State U., 1997; named Nat. Media Man-of-Month Morality in Media, Inc., N.Y.C., 1976. Mem. Profl. Photographers Am., Internat. Assn. Bus. Communicators, Am. Security Council (nat. adv. bd.), Internat. Platform Assn., Sons Utah Pioneers (nat. adv. bd. 1982, Disting. Svc. award 1985), SAR (pres. Salt Lake City chpt. 1987-88, Law Enforcement Commendation medal 1987, Meritorious Svc. award 1987, Gen.'s Program Excellence award, Oliver R. Smith medal 1990, Grahame T. Smallwood award 1990, Liberty medal 1991, Patriot medal 1992), Utah State Soc. (pres. 1989-90), Amicus Club of Deseret Found., chmn. membership com. 1988—), Gold Caduceus award, 1993, Wall of Honor), World Sr. Games (adv. com, 1987—), William Carter Family Orgn. (nat. pres.), Nat. Assn. Chiefs of Police (Am. Police Hall of Fame, John Edgar Hoover Distin. Pub. Svc. medal 1991, Nat. Patriotism medal, 1993), Scabbard and Blade, Crimson Circle, Am. Media Network (nat. adv. bd.), Utah Sheriffs' Assn., Assn. Former Intelligence Officers, Soc. Profl. Journalists, Alpha Phi Omega, Pi Sigma Alpha, Phi Delta Theta, Mem. LDS Ch. (coord. pub. affars council Seattle area 1973-75, br. pres. 1944-45, seventies quorum pres. 1952, dist. pres. 1954-55, high priest 1958—, stake pres. counselor 1959-64, stake Sunday Sch. pres. 1980-81, temple staff 1987—). Clubs: Bonneville Knife and Fork (bd. dirs. 1963-69), Rotary Intl. (editor The Rotary Bkc, 1982-83, Paul Harris fellow 1982, Richard L. Evans fellow 1987, Best Club History in Utah award 1988, Best Dist. Newsletter award 1983, Rotarian of Month 1988, membership com. 1995—, club 24 found. bd. 1995—). Author: The Sunbeam Years-An Autobiography, 1986; assoc. editor FBI Investigator,

1965-75; contbg. author, editor: Biographies of Sons of Utah Pioneers, 1982; contbr. articles to mags. Home: 2180 Elaine Dr Bountiful UT 84010-3120

CARTER, ROBERTA ECCLESTON, therapist, counselor; b. Pitts.; d. Robert E. and Emily B. (Bucar) Carter; divorced; children: David Michael Kiewlich, Daniel Michael Kiewlich. Student Edinboro State U., 1962-63; BS, California State U. of Pa., 1966; MEd, U. Pitts., 1969; MA, Rosebridge Grad. Sch., Walnut Creek, Calif., 1987. Tchr., Bethel Park Sch. Dist., Pa., 1966-69; writer, media asst. Field Ednl. Pub., San Francisco, 1969-70; educator, counselor, specialist Alameda Unified Sch. Dist., Calif., 1970—; master trainer Calif. State Dept. Edn., Sacramento, 1984—; personal growth cons., Alameda, 1983—. Author: People, Places and Products, 1970, Teaching/Learning Units, 1969; co-author: Teacher's Manual Let's Read, 1968. Mem. AAUW, NEA, Calif. Fedn. Bus. and Profl. Women (legis. chair Alameda br. 1984-85, membership chair 1985), Calif. Edn. Assn., Alameda Edn. Assn., Charter Planetary Soc., Oakland Mus., Exploratorium, Big Bros. of East Bay, Alameda C. of C. (svc. award 1985). Avocations: aerobics, gardening, travel. Home: 1516 Eastshore Dr Alameda CA 94501-3118

CARTER, STEVEN ANDREW, writer, consultant; b. N.Y.C., Oct. 23, 1956; s. Alfred M. and Sydelle C.; m. Jill Augustine, Oct. 26, 1996. BS, Cornell U., 1978; postgrad. studies, U. Mass., 1988-89, Antioch U., 1990. Tennis dir. Little Dix Bay Hotel, Virgin Gorda, V.I., 1979; head tennis profl. Dorado Beach (P.R.) Hotel, 1980-81, vis. tennis profl., 1982-86; author, 1984—. Author: Men Who Can't Love, 1987 (N.Y. Times bestseller), What Really Happens in Bed, 1989, What Smart Women Know, 1990, Lives Without Balance, 1992, He's Scared, She's Scared, 1993, Men Like Women Who Like Themselves, 1996, Getting to Commitment, 1998. Mem. Quill and Dagger. Avocations: drawing, travelling, photography.

CARTER, WILLIAM GEORGE, III, career officer; b. Buffalo, June 18, 1944; s. William George Jr. and Elaine Ruth (Weber) C.; m. Linda Fay Yener, Oct. 2, 1965; children: Kris Ann, William George. BS, U. Tampa, 1972; MA, U. Shippensberg, 1982; MPE, U. Pitts., 1984. Commd. 2d. lt. U.S. Army, 1965, advanced through grades to lt. gen., 1995; various command and staff positions, 1964-77; exec. officer 3d Brigade, 1st Armored Div., Bamberg, Fed. Republic Germany, 1977-79; comdr. 1st Bn., 52d Inf., Bamberg, 1979-81, G3 1st Armored Div., VII U.S. Corps, Ansbach, Fed. Republic Germany, 1981-83; chief Plans and Integration Office, Hdqrs. U.S. Army, Washington, 1983-86; comdr. 1st Brigade, 4th Inf. Div., Ft. Carson, Colo., 1986-88; exec. asst. Office Chief of Staff Army, Washington, 1988-89; asst. div. comdr. 1st Inf. Div., Ft. Riley, Kans., 1989-91; comdr. Nat. Tng. Ctr., Ft. Irwin, Calif., 1991-93, 1st Armored Divsn., 1993-95; chief of staff Allied Forces So. Europe, 1995-97. Decorated DDSM with oak leaf cluster, DSM with oak leaf cluster, Legion of Merit with six oak leaf clusters, Bronze Star with V device and two oak leaf clusters, Purple Heart with oak leaf cluster. Mem. Soc. of the Big Red One, Alpha Chi. Avocations: golf, hunting. *

CARTIER, MARIE ANNE, writer; b. Exeter, N.H., Feb. 27, 1956; d. Jacques Francois and Joanne marie (Curtin) C.; m. Connie Smith, Mar. 1984 (div. Sept. 1992). BA, U. N.H., 1974; MA, Colo. State U., 1984; MFA, UCLA, 1990; postgrad., Claremont Grad. U., 1998—. Film lectr. U. Calif., Irvine, 1992—; lectr. Calif. State U., Northridge, 1998—. Author: (poetry books) I am Your Daughter, Not Your Lover, 1994 (plays) Freeze Count, 1995, Come Out, Come Out Wherever You Are, 1995, Stumbling Into Light, 1995, Closer to Home, 1995, Leave a Light on When You Go Out, 1995. Recipient Govl's award Cultural Affairs, Colo., 1984, grantee, 1992; grantee Calif. Artists Residence, Calif., 1990. Mem. Dramatists' Guild, Poets and Writers Amnesty Internat. Democrat. Roman Catholic. Avocation: karate/brown belt. Office: U Calif Irvine 235 Humanities Instrn Bldg Irvine CA 92697-2435

CARTWRIGHT, CHAS, historic site administrator; married. BA in Anthropology, Mich. State U., 1972. Seasonal fire fighter, fire lookout, river ranger U.S. Forestry Svc., Calif. and Idaho, 1972-75; seasonal archaeologist B.L.M., Idaho, Ariz. and Utah, 1979-87; archaeologist B.L.M., Great Basin and Colorado Plateau, Utah, 1979-87; archaeologist Arches and Canyonlands Nat. Parks, Natural Bridges Nat. Monument Nat. Pk. Svc., 1987-89; supt. Hovenweep Nat. Monument Nat. Pk. Svc., Utah and Colo., 1989-98; supt. Knife River Indian Villages Nat. Hist. Site Nat. Pk. Svc., N.D., 1989-98; supt., dir. Devils Tower (Wy.) Nat. Monument Nat. Pk. Svc., 1998—. Office: care Devils Tower Monument PO Box 10 Devils Tower WY 82714

CARTWRIGHT, PETER, electronics company executive. Pres., CEO Calpine, San Jose, Calif. Office: Calpine 50 W San Fernando St Ste 550 San Jose CA 95113-2424*

CARVAJAL, JORGE ARMANDO, endocrinologist, internist; b. Chiscas, Boyaca, Colombia, Dec. 20, 1935; came to U.S., 1963; s. Julio and Natividad (Caicedo) C.; m. Carlota Mellonunes Ribeiro, Sept. 5, 1965; children: Jorge Jr., Fernando, Eduardo. MD, U. Nacional Fac. Medicine, Bogota, Colombia, 1963. Diplomate Am. Bd. Internal Medicine, Am. Bd. Endocrinology. Resident Hosp. San Jose, Bogota, 1962-63; intern Meth. Hosp., Peoria, Ill., 1963-64; resident in medicine Meml. Hosp., Detroit, 1964-65, Mt. Sinai Hosp., Mpls., 1965-66, VA Med. Ctr., Long Beach, Calif., 1966-67; fellow in endocrinology VA Med. Ctr., L.A., 1967-69; asst. prof. U. Rosario, Bogota, 1969-72; fellow in metabolism U. Calif.-Davis, Sacramento, 1972-73; staff endocrinologist Kaiser-Permanente Hosp., Sacramento, 1973-75; staff physician VA Med. Ctr., Long Beach, Calif., 1975-76; pvt. practice Anaheim, Calif., 1976—; staff Anaheim Meml. Hosp., 1976—. Democrat. Roman Catholic. Avocations: jogging, reading. Home: 16562 Grimaud Ln Huntington Beach CA 92649-1828 Office: 1211 W La Palma Ave Ste 702 Anaheim CA 92801-2814

CARVALHO, WAYNE G., protective services official. Chief of police Hilo, Hawaii. Office: City of Hilo Police Dept 349 Kapiolani St Hilo HI 96720-3912*

CARVER, DOROTHY LEE ESKEW (MRS. JOHN JAMES CARVER), retired secondary education educator; b. Brady, Tex., July 10, 1926; d. Clyde Albert and A. Maurine (Meadows) Eskew; student So. Ore. Coll., 1942-43, Coll. Eastern Utah, 1965-67; BA, U. Utah, 1968; MA, Cal. State Coll. at Hayward, 1970; postgrad. Mills Coll., 1971; m. John James Carver, Feb. 26, 1944; children: John James, Sheila Carver Bentley, Chuck, David. Instr., Rutherford Bus. Coll., Dallas, 1944-45; sec. Adolph Coors Co., Golden, Colo., 1945-47; instr. English, Coll. Eastern Utah, Price, 1968-69; instr. speech Modesto (Calif.) Jr. Coll., 1970-71; instr. personal devel. men and women Heald Bus. Colls., Oakland, Calif., 1972-74, dean curricula, Walnut Creek, Calif., 1974-86; instr. Diablo Valley Coll., Pleasant Hill, Calif., 1986-87, Contra Costa Christian H.S.; ret., 1992; communications cons. Oakland Army Base, Crocker Bank, U.S. Steel, I. Magnin, Artec Internat.; presenter in field. Author: Developing Listening Skills. Mem. Gov.'s. Conf. on Higher Edn. in Utah, 1968; mem. finance com. Coll. Eastern Utah, 1967-69; active various cmty. drives. Bd. dirs. Opportunity Ctr., Symphony of the Mountain. Mem. AAUW, Bus. and Profl. Womens Club, Nat. Assn. Deans and Women Adminstrs., Delta Kappa Gamma. Episcopalian (supt. Sunday Sch. 1967-69). Clubs: Soroptimist Internat. (pres. Walnut Creek 1979-80 sec., founder region 1978-80); Order Eastern Star. Home: 20 Coronado Ct Walnut Creek CA 94596-5801

CARVER, JUANITA ASH, plastic company executive; b. Indpls., Apr. 8, 1929; d. Willard H. and Golda M. Ashe; children: Daniel Charles, Robin Lewis, Scott Alan. Student Ariz. State U., 1948, 72, Mira Mar Coll., 1994. Cons. MOBIUS, 1983—; pres. Carver Corp., Phoenix, 1977—. Bd. dirs. Scottsdale Meml. Hosp. Aux., 1964-65, now assoc. Republican. Methodist. Patentee latch hook rug Yarner, Pressure Lift.

CARY, FREDERICK ALBERT, lawyer; b. Trieste, Italy, Apr. 6, 1950; came to U.S., 1966; s. Frederick W. and Lydia (Tozzini) C.; 1 child, Amelia Rose. JD, Thomas Jefferson U., 1984. Bar: Calif., D.C., U.S. Ct. Appeals (2nd, 4th, 6th, 9th, and 11th). Pvt. practice Ft. Lauderdale, San Diego. Office: The Cary Law Firm PO Box 273 Rancho Santa Fe CA 92067-0273

CARYL, NAOMI, artist; b. N.Y.C., June 27, 1931; d. Joseph Herman and Jennie (Berman) Hirshhorn. Student, Feagin Sch. Drama & Radio, 1951-52. Artist, composer, actor, producer L.A., 1962—. One-woman shows include Ankeum Gallery, L.A., 1962, 69, 71, 72, 75, 83, 87, Zara Gallery, San Francisco, 1973, Lighthouse Gallery, Fla., 1989, Foster Harmon Gallery, Sarasota, Fla., 1991, Jerry Soloman Gallery, L.A., 1997; composer Spoon River Anthology, 1963 (Emmy nomination 1969), Mirror Image, 1995, others; author (plays) Nobody Safe Here (new play award L.A. Weekly 1981), 1981, The Start of The Blues, 1987, The Dressing Room, 1988, others. Co-chair, producer The S.T.A.G.E. Benefit, L.A., 1986—. Recipient L.A. Beautiful award Cactus Garden, 1989, Crystal Apple award AIDS Project, L.A., 1991. Mem. ASCAP, SAG, Equity, Dramatists Guild, Theatre West. Avocations: gardening, reverand, personalized weddings. Home and Office: 2071 Castilian Dr Los Angeles CA 90068-2608

CASALE, FRANCIS JOSEPH, minister; b. Hartford, Conn., Jan. 14, 1947; s. Joseph Lawrence and Elizabeth Frances (Torza) C.; m. Kimie Hiasa, Apr. 25, 1982; children: Naomi Ruth, Grace Megumi. BA, Gallaudet U., 1970; MA, Calif. State U., Northridge, 1974, BA, 1988; AA in Practical Theology, Christ for all Nations Inst., Dallas, 1984; ThD, Internat. Sem., 1989, PhD, 1990. Ordained to ministry Internat. Ministerial Assn., 1989. Evangelist, tchr. Christ for Nations Inst., Dallas, 1983-84; ind. missionary-tchr. various orgns., world-wide, 1984-87; evangelist, tchr. Christian Deaf Fellowship Mission, Downey, Calif., 1987-90; spiritual counselor Immanuel Deaf Bible Coll. and Immanuel Ch. Deaf, Downey, 1987-90; tchr. Bible, spiritual counselor Ind.-Internat. Ministerial Assn., Downey, 1990—; tchr. Calif. State U., Northridge, 1976-79; jr. bd. dirs. Immanuel Church of the Deaf., Downey, 1985—; asst. dir. Immanuel Deaf Bible Coll., Downey, 1986-89; adv. coun. bd. Christian Deaf Fellowship (Mission Orgn.), Downey, 1986—; counselor various locations, Calif. and Conn., 1980—. Illustrator: (sign lang.) L. A. Pierce Coll., Woodland Hills, Calif., 1975-78; editor: (mag.) Silent Evangel, 1988—, (newsletter) The Casales' Times/Teaching the Gospel, 1989—. Active in deaf ministry. Mem. Nat. Christian Counselors Assn. (assoc.), Internat. Ministerial Assn., Deaf Evang. Assn. N.Am. (treas. 1988—). Home and Office: 504 E Covina Blvd Covina CA 91722-2953

CASALS, ROSEMARY, professional tennis player; b. San Francisco, Sept. 16, 1948. Profl. tennis player, 1968—; nat. championships and major tournaments include U.S. Open singles (finalist), 1970, 71, U.S. Open doubles, 1967, 71, 74, 82, U.S. Open mixed doubles, 1975, Wimbledon doubles, 1967, 68, 70, 71, 73; nat. championships and major tournaments include Wimbledon mixed doubles, 1971, 73, finalist with Dick Stockton, 1976; finalist with Dick Stockton Italian doubles, 1967, 70; finalist with Dick Stockton Family Circle Cup (winner), 1973, Wightman Cup, 1967, 76-81; Wightman Cup Bridgeston doubles championships (finalist), 1975, Spalding mixed doubles, 1976, 77, U.S. Tennis Assn. Atlanta doubles, 1976, Fedn. Cup, 1967, 76-81; winner 1st Virginia Slims tournament, 1970; 3d place Virginia Slims Championships, 1976, 4th place, 1977, 78; winner Murjani-WTA championship, 1980; Fla. Fed. Open doubles, 1980; pres. sports promotion co. Sportswoman, Inc., Sausalito, Calif., 1981—; Virginia Slims Legends Tour, 1995—; Mem. Los Angeles Strings team, World Team Tennis, 1975-77. Virginia Slims Event tennis winner, 1986, doubles winner (with Martina Navratilova), 1988, 89; inducted in to Internat. Tennis Hall of Fame, Newport, R.I., 1996. Mem. Women's Internat. Tennis Assn. (bd. dirs.). Office: Sportswoman Inc PO Box 537 Sausalito CA 94966-0537

CASE, CHARLES G., II, federal bankruptcy judge; b. Phoenix, Ariz., Jan. 17, 1948. BA cum laude, Harvard U., 1969; JD magna cum laude, Ariz. State U., 1975. Bar: Ariz. 1975. With Lewis and Roca, Phoenix, 1975-88, Meyer, Hendricks, Victor, Osborn & Maledon P.C., Phoenix, 1988-93; judge U.S. Bankruptcy Ct., Phoenix, 1994—; judge pro tempore Ariz. Ct. Appeals; adj. prof. law Ariz. State U., 1988-91, 97—. Contbg. author Comml. Law and Practice Guides, 1991. Mem. ABA. Home: PO Box 34151 Phoenix AZ 85067-4151 Office: Ninth Floor 2929 North Central Ave Phoenix AZ 85012*

CASE, LEE OWEN, JR., retired academic administrator; b. Ann Arbor, Mich., Nov. 5, 1925; s. Lee Owen and Ava (Comin) C.; m. Dolores Anne DeLoof, July 1950 (div. Feb. 1958); children: Lee Douglas, John Bradford; m. Maria Theresia Breninger, Feb. 27, 1960; 1 adopted dau., Ingrid Case Dunlap. AB, U. Mich., 1949. Editor Washtenaw Post-Trib, Ann Arbor, 1949; dir. pub. rels. Edison Inst., Dearborn, Mich., 1951-54; field rep. Kersting, Brown, N.Y.C., 1954-58; campaign dir. Cumerford Corp., Kansas City, Mo., 1958-59; v.p. devel., pub. rels. U. Santa Clara, 1959-69; v.p. planning, devel., Occidental Coll., L.A., 1969-90, ret., 1990; interim v.p. Inst. Advance Calif. State U., L.A., 1994.Mem. Sr. Cons. Network. Chmn. Santa Clara City Proposition A, 1966; mem. Santa Clara County Planning Com. on Taxation and Legis., Santa Clara, 1968. Served to 1st lt. USAAF, 1943-46. Mem. Am. Coll. Pub. Relations Assn. (bd. dirs. 1968-74), Council for Advancement and Support Edn. (founding bd. dirs. 1974-75), 1st Tribute for Distinction in Advancement, Dist. VII, 1985), Santa Clara C. of C. (pres. 1967), Santa Clara County C. of C. (founding bd. dirs. 1968), Aviation Pioneers Assn. Republican. Lodge: Rotary. Home and Office: 2633 Risa Dr Glendale CA 91208-2355

CASEY, ANN LOUISE, college administrator; b. Warwick, R.I., May 25, 1951; d. Robert F. and Louise F. (Leprу) C. BS, U. R.I., 1973; MA in Tchg., Lewis and Clark Coll., 1975. Tchr., coach Sunset H.S., Beaverton, Oreg., 1973-83; athletic dir. Gladstone (Oreg.) H.S., 1983-85; tchr., coach San Diego State U., 1985-88, City Coll. of San Francisco, 1988-89; dir. sports ctr. Reed Coll., Portland, 1989—; mediation cons. Parish coun. mem. St. Francis Ch., Portland, 1997—. Recipient Meritorious Svc. award USA Volleyball, 1997. Mem. No. Oreg. Volleyball Offcls. (commr.), Women's Sports Found. (adv. bd.), AAHPERD. Avocations: sailing, skiing, kayaking. Office: Reed Coll 3203 SE Woodstock Blvd Portland OR 97202-8138

CASEY, DARLA DIANN, elementary school educator; b. West Linn, Oreg., Mar. 21, 1940; d. Karl F. and Lucille Iona (Wilson) Lettenmaier; m. Charles Emerson Casey, July 30, 1965; children: John, Michael, Kim. BSEd, U. Wis., Milw., 1965; MEd, Oreg. State U., postgrad.; postgrad., U. Oreg., West State, Port State. Cert. tchr. grades K-9, basic art grades 1-12. Tchr., grade 3, swimming instr., grades 4-6 Lakeside (Oreg.) Elem.; tchr., readiness rm. K-1 Siuslaw Elem., Florence, Oreg.; tchr., grades K-1, spl. reading, art Washington Elem., Canon City, Colo.; tchr., grade 1 Sam Case Elem. Sch., Lincoln County Sch. Dist., Newport, Oreg.; mentor tchr. N.W. Sci. Survey Com.; speaker in field. Contbr. articles to profl. jours. Named Oreg. Elem. Sci. Tchr. of Yr. Am. Electronics Assn. and Dept. Edn., 1989; NASA scholar, 1992, 95, Oreg. Cadre for All tchrs. of Sci. scholar, 1993, NASA Flight Opportunities for Sci. Tchr. Enrichment Project scholar, 1995, Am. Astron. Soc. Tchr. Resource Agt., 1996, ASTRA scholar U. Tex. and McDonald Observatory, 1996. Mem. Oreg. Sci. Tchrs. Assn., Oreg. Reading Assn., Oreg. Seacoast Reading Coun. (past pres.), Oreg. Math. Tchrs. Assn., Phi Delta Kappa. Home: PO Box 514 Siletz OR 97380-0514

CASEY, PATRICIA LEE, film producer; b. N.Y.C.; d. Joseph and Johanna Lina (Tanner) C.; m. Judd Bernard, Feb. 18, 1972; 1 child, Alicia; stepchildren: Adrianna, Michael. Student, L.A. City Coll. Ballet dancer Radio City Music Hall, N.Y.C.; ballerina L.A. Ballet Co., 1959-64; producer Kettledrums Films, Valley Village, Calif. Dancer, choreographer (film) Double Trouble, 1965; assoc. prodr. Blue, 1967, Man Who Had Power Over Women, 1969, Glad All Over, 1970, Inside Out, 1973, Marseilles Contract, 1975, The Class of Miss MacMichaels, 1979; asst. prodr. Point Blank, 1966; co-star Fade In, 1967; prodr. Monty Python's And Now For Something Completely Different, 1971, The Playboy Guide to Amsterdam, 1980, Blood Red, 1989. Avocations: art, traveling, reading, films. Office: Kettledrum Films 4961 Agnes Ave Valley Village CA 91607

CASEY, PATRICK ANTHONY, lawyer; b. Santa Fe, Apr. 20, 1944; s. Ivanhoe and Eutimia (Casados) C.; m. Gail Marie Johns, Aug. 1, 1970; children: Christopher Gaelen, Matthew Colin. BA, N.Mex. State U., 1970; JD, U. Ariz., 1973. Bar: N.Mex. 1973, U.S. Dist. Ct. N.Mex. 1973, Ariz. 1973, U.S. Ct. Appeals (10th cir.) 1979, U.S. Supreme Ct. 1980. Assoc. firm Bachicha & Corlett, Bachicha & Casey, Santa Fe, 1973-76; pvt. practice law, Santa Fe, 1976—. Bd. dirs. Santa Fe Sch. Arts and Crafts, 1974, Santa Fe Animal Shelter, 1975-81, Cath. Charities of Santa Fe, 1979-82, Old Santa Fe Assn., 1979-88, Santa Fe Fiesta Coun., 1982—; bd. dirs. United Way, 1986-89, N.Mex. State U. Found., 1985-93. With USN, 1961-67. Mem. ATLA (state del. 1988-89, bd. govs. 1990-91, 93-95), ABA, Western Trial Lawyers Assn. (bd. dirs. 1988-91, parlimentarian 1990-91, gov. 1987-90, treas. 1991-95, sec. 1991-92, pres. elect 1995-96, pres. 1996-97), N.Mex. Trial Lawyers Assn. (dir. 1977-79, 85—, treas. 1979-83, pres. 1983-84), Bar Assn. 1st Jud. Dist. (pres. 1980), Hispanic Bar Assn., Am. Legion, Vietnam Vets. of Am., VFW, Elks. Office: 1421 Luisa St Ste P Santa Fe NM 87505-4073

CASEY, SHANNON GLORIA, visual effects producer; b. Edmonton, Alta., Can., Apr. 2, 1957; came to U.S., 1988; d. Dennis and Gloria June (Brooks) C.; m. John Howard Copeland, Nov. 20, 1987. Attended, U. Alta., 1975-77; Diploma in Dance, Grant McEwan Coll., Alta., 1980. Visual effects prodr., prin. Air Age Found. Imaging, Calif., 1992-96; visual effects prodr. Rhythm & Hues Studios, L.A., 1996—. Mem. ACLU, Acad. TV Arts and Scis. (Emmy award 1993). Avocations: cooking, horseback riding and dressage training, reading, travel, photography.

CASEY, WILLIAM CARLETON, physician, urologist, pschiatrist; b. Borton, Ill., Feb. 1, 1924; s. Albert O'Neil and Pauline Marjorie (Monroe) C.; m. Regina Rummel, Nov. 3, 1957 (div. Jan. 1963); children: Giselle Susan, David William; m. Susan Maureen Fowler, Oct. 2, 1965; 1 child, Patrick Sean McGahey. BSc, U. Ill., Champaign-Urbana, 1944; MD, U. Ill., Chgo., 1946. Diplomate Am. Bd. Urology; lic. physician, Calif., Ill. Rotating intern Cook County Hosp., Chgo., 1946-47, resident in urology, 1947, 52-53; resident in urology Michael Reese Hosp., Chgo., 1953, UCLA, L.A. County Harbor Gen. Hosp., Torrance, Calif., 1953-54; clin. isntr. UCLA Sch. Medicine, 1955-67; resident in psychiatry Callan Park Psychiat. Hosp., Sydney, Australia, 1967-71; clin. dir. Lakehead Psychiat. Hosp., Thunder Bay, Ont., Can., 1972-74; dir. children's and adolescents' svc. Dr. McKinnon Phillips Hosp., Owen Sound, Ont., 1974-76; clin. asst. prof. urology UCLA Sch. Medicine, 1977—. Capt. U.S. Army, 1948-50. Fellow Ryal Australian and New Zealand Coll. Psychiatrists; mem. Am. Urol. Assn. (1st prize sci. exhibit 1954, others), Am. Urol. Assn. Western Sect., L.A. County Med. Assn., L.A. County Urol. Soc., Royal Coll. Physicians (London), Royal Coll. Surgeons (Eng.), Royal Coll. Physicians and Surgeons Can., Brit. Royal Coll. Psychiatrists (found. mem.). Roman Catholic. Avocations: violin, saxophone and clarinet, golf, surfing, squash, bridge, photography. Address: Burbank Hotel 2721 Willow St #317 Burbank CA 91506

CASH, DEANNA GAIL, nursing educator, retired; b. Coatesville, Pa., Nov. 28, 1940. Diploma, Jackson Meml. Hosp., 1961; BS, Fla. State U., 1964; MN, UCLA, 1968; EdD, Nova U., Ft. Lauderdale, Fla., 1983. Staff and relief charge nurse Naples (Fla.) Community Hosp., 1961-62; staff nurse Glendale (Calif.) Community Hosp., 1964-65; instr. Knapp Coll. Nursing, Santa Barbara, Calif., 1965-66; staff nurse, team leader Kaiser Found. Hosp., Bellflower, Calif., 1968-69; prof. nursing El Camino Coll., Torrance, Calif., 1969-96, ret., 1996; coord., instr. Internat. RN Rev. course, L.A., 1974-76; mentor statewide nursing program, Long Beach, Calif., 1981-88; clin. performance in nursing exam. evaluator Western Performance Assessment Ctr., Long Beach, 1981-96. Mem. ANA.

CASHATT, CHARLES ALVIN, retired hydro-electric power generation company executive; b. Jamestown, N.C., Nov. 14, 1929; s. Charles Austin and Ethel Buren (Brady) C.; m. Wilma Jean O'Hagan, July 10, 1954; children: Jerry Dale, Nancy Jean. Grad. high sch., Jamestown. Bldg. contractor, Jamestown, 1949-50; 1954-58; powerhouse foreman Tri-Dam Project, Strawberry, Calif., 1958-66; power project mgr. Merced Irrigation Dist., Calif., 1966-92; ret. 1992; mem. U.S. com. large dams, 1988-92. Contbr. articles to ASCE pub. and books. Pres. Merced County Credit Union, 1981-82. Served with USAF, 1950-54. Mem. Am. Legion. Republican. Lodge: Elks, Odd Fellows.

CASHEN, SUSAN, executive. BA in Russian Studies, Hamilton Coll. V.p. Blanc & Otus, Mountain View, Calif. Office: 444 Castro St Ste 1020 Mountain View CA 94041-2062*

CASHMAN, MICHAEL RICHARD, small business owner; b. Owatonna, Minn., Sept. 26, 1926; s. Michael Richard and Mary (Quinn) C.; m. Antje Katrin Paulus, Jan. 22, 1972 (div. 1983); children: Janice Katrin, Joshua Paulus, Nina Carolin. BS, U.S. Mcht. Marine Acad., 1947; BA, U. Minn., 1951; MBA, Harvard U., 1953. Regional mgr. Air Products & Chems., Inc., Allentown, Pa., 1959-64; then pres. so. div. Air Products & Chems., Inc., Washington, 1964-68; mng. dir. Air Products & Chems., Inc. Europe, Brussels, 1968-72; internat. v.p. Airco Indsl. Gasses, Brussels, 1972-79; pres. Continental Elevator Co., Denver, 1979-81; assoc. Moore & Co., Denver, 1981-84; prin. Cashman & Co., Denver, 1984—. Committeeman Denver Rep. Com., 1986—, congl. candidate, 1988; chmn. "Two Forks or Dust" Ad Hoc Citizens Com.. Lt. (j.g.) USN, 1953-55. Mem. Bldg. Owners and Mgrs. Assn., Colo. Harvard Bus. Sch. Club, Am. Rights Union, Royal Golf de Belgique, Belgian Shooting Club, Rotary, Soc. St. George, Phi Beta Kappa. Avocations: skiing, golf, sailing, guitar, opera. Home: 2512 S University Blvd Apt 802 Denver CO 80210-6152

CASHMAN, THOMAS JOSEPH, marketing executive; b. Mpls., July 26, 1935; s. Bernard J. and Ann Anges (Slatoski) C.; m. Barbara A Gilbertsen, Jul. 5, 1958 (div. Feb. 1993); children: Ann, Robin, Mark; m. Lin Houston, May 31, 1997. Student, Univ. Minn., 1953-57; BS in applied behavioral sci., City Univ., 1994. Regional mktg. mgr. Sharp Electronics Corp., Mahwah, N.J., 1986-95; mentor, cons. Proline/Intellisys, Bellevue, Wash., 1995—; trustee bd. chmn. Anamchairde, Cin., 1997—, trustee bd. dirs. Earth Ministry, Seattle, 1995—; speaker, workshop and retreat leader. Contbr. numerous articles to profl. jours. With USMC, 1957-66. Mem. Orgn. Devel. Network, The Albin Inst. Episcopalian. Avocations: fly-fishing, music, cooking. Home: 30303 22nd Court S Federal Way WA 98003 Office: Proline/Intellisys 1233 120th Ave NE Bellevue WA 98005

CASIDA, KATI, artist; b. Viroqua, Wis., Mar. 28, 1931; d. Gerhard Aniel and Eloise Margaret (Nedland) Monson; m. John Edward Casida, Jne 16, 1956; children: Mark Earl, Eric Gerhard. BS in Art Edn., U. Wis., 1953. Tchr. art Beaver Dam (Wis.) Schs., 1954-55, Upsala Coll., East Orange, N.J., 1955-56, Spring Harbor Sch., Madison, Wis., 1960, Adult Vocat. Sch., Madison, 1961; freelance artist, sculptor Berkeley, Calif., 1963—; founder Nordic 5 Arts, San Francisco Bay area, 1993—. Contbr. articles to Hellenic Jour., 1974-98. Recipient Pub. Art Sculpture award Divsn. Cultural Arts, City of Oakland, Calif., 1992. Mem. Internat. Sculpture, Pacific Rim Sculpture Group, Calif. Soc. Printmakers, Headlands for Arts, Nat. Mus. Women in Arts, Kala-Printmakers, Greek Cypriots No. Calif. Avocations: Greek folk dancing, travel, photography. Home: 1570 La Vereda Rd Berkeley CA 94708-2036

CASPER, GERHARD, academic administrator, law educator; b. Hamburg, Germany, Dec. 25, 1937; s. Heinrich and Hertha C.; m. Regina Koschel, Dec. 26, 1964; 1 child, Hanna. Legal state exam., U. Freiburg, U. Hamburg, 1961; LL.M., Yale U., 1962; Dr.iur., U. Freiburg, Germany, 1964. Asst. prof. polit. sci. U. Calif., Berkeley, 1964-66; assoc. prof. law and polit. sci. U. Chgo., 1966-69, prof., 1969-76, Max Pam prof. law, 1976-80, William B. Graham prof. law, 1980-87, William B. Graham Disting. Svc. prof. law, 1987-92, dean law sch., 1979-87, provost, 1989-92; prof. law Stanford (Calif.) U., 1992—, pres., 1992—; vis. prof. law Cath. U., Louvain, Belgium, 1970, U. Munich, 1988, 91; bd. dirs. Ency. Britannica. Author: Realism and Political Theory in American Legal Thought, 1967, (with Richard A. Posner) The Workload of the Supreme Court, 1976; co-editor: The Supreme Ct. Rev., 1977-91, Separating Power, 1997. Fellow Am. Acad. Arts and Scis.; mem. Internat. Acad. Comparative Law, Am. Bar Found. (bd. dirs. 1979-87), Coun. Fgn. Rels., Am. Law Inst. (coun. 1980—), Oliver Wendell Holmes Devise (permanent com. 1985—), Am. Philos. Soc. *

CASPER, SCOTT E., historian; b. Bellefont, Pa., Nov. 20, 1964. AB, Princeton U., 1986; MA, Yale U., 1990, MPhil, 1990, PhD, 1992. Asst. prof. History U. Nev., Reno, 1992-97, assoc. prof., 1997—. Author: Constructing American Lives: Biography and Culture in 19th Century America, 1999; contbr. articles to profl. jours. Recipient Field Dissertation prize Yale U., 1992; Mellon fellow in the humanities Woodrow Wilson Found., 1986-92, Peterson fellow Am. Antiquarian Soc., 1990-91, 98-99, Kahrl fellow Houghton Library Harvard U., 1993-94, NEH fellow Winterthur Mus. and

Libr., 1998—. Mem. Am. Studies Assn., Am. Historical Assn., Orgn. Am. Historians. Office: Dept History U Nevada Reno NV 89557

CASS, LEE H., fashion industry consultant; b. Little Rock, Nov. 10; d. William Frederick and Ora Lee (Baldridge) Meyer; m. Alonzo B. Cass, June 1952; 1 child, Christopher; stepchildren: Timothy, Linda, Nicholas, Julie, Liza. AA, U. Ark.; student, So. Meth. U. Producer, writer,host NBC affiliate sta., Hollywood, Calif., 1949-52; fashion dir. Bullock's, L.A. 1952-60; fashion dir., advt. mgr. Catalina Inc. L.A., 1960-63; sales promotions dir. Bullock's, L.A., 1964-66; v.p. Carter Hawley Hale, L.A., 1966-89; nat. fashion mdse. dir. Sears Roebuck & Co., Chgo., 1989-93; cons. Australian Govt. Fashion panel, 1989; advisor, speaker Fashion Industries of Australia, 1979. Mem. AFTRA (bd. dirs. 1949-53), Fashion Group Internat. (bd. dirs. N.Y. 1960-66, L.A. 1993-97), L.A. County Museum Art and Costume Coun. (bd. dirs. 1963-68), Com. of Profl. Women, Muses (bd. dirs. 1997—), Hollywood Womens Press Club. Democrat. Avocations: travel, reading, swimming, photography, philanthropy.

CASSENS, NICHOLAS, JR., ceramics engineer; b. Sigourney, Iowa, Sept. 8, 1948; s. Nicholas and Wanda Fern (Lancaster) C.; B.S. in Ceramic Engring., Iowa State U., 1971, B.S. in Chem. Engring., 1971; M.S. in Material Sci. and Engring., U. Calif., Berkeley, 1979; m. Linda Joyce Morrow, Aug. 30, 1969; 1 son, Randall Scott, Jr. research engr. Nat. Refractories and Minerals Corp., Livermore, Calif., 1971-72, research engr., 1972-74, sr. research engr., 1974-77, staff research engr., 1977-84, sr. staff research engr., 1984—. Mem. Am. Ceramic Soc. Democrat. Patentee in field, U.S., Australia, S.Am., Japan, Europe. Home: 4082 Suffolk Way Pleasanton CA 94588-4117 Office: 1852 Rutan Dr Livermore CA 94550-7635

CASSERLY, JOHN JOSEPH, author, journalist; b. Chgo., Jan. 4, 1927; s. William J. and Hannah (Kane) C.; m. Joy Ruth Price, Sept. 17, 1955; children—Kevin, Terence, Jeffrey, Lawrence. BA, Marquette U., 1951. Reporter Milw. Sentinel, 1951; bur. reporter Internat. News Service, Chgo., 1952; assigned Tokyo bur. Internat. News Service, 1952, war corr. Korea, 1952-53, assigned Paris bur., 1954, assigned N.Y.C., 1954-55; bur. mgr. Internat. News Service, Rome, Italy, 1957-58; with CBS Network News, 1955-56; Rome bur. chief Hearst Headline service, 1958-61; chief Rome bur. ABC News, 1961-64; assigned Washington bur. ABC News, 1964-68; part-time fgn. reporting; overseas pub. info. mgr. Ford Motor Co., Dearborn, Mich., 1968-70; dir. pub. affairs pub. info. Bur. Census, U.S. Dept. Commerce, Suitland, Md., 1970-74; speechwriter White House staff Exec. Office Pres., Washington, 1974-76; free-lance writer, 1976-80; editorial writer Ariz. Republic, Phoenix, 1980-86; editorial asst. to Editor-in-Chief Hearst Newspapers, N.Y.C., 1988-91. Author: Goldwater, 1988, We, The Americans, 1973, The Ford White House...Diary of a Speechwriter, 1977, The Hearsts: Father and Son, 1991, Scripps: The Divided Dynasty, 1993, The Dancing Angel, Iowa, 1994, Once Upon a Time in Italy, 1994; contbr. articles to profl. jours., mags. Disting. Alumnus, Quigley Prep, Chgo., 1996; recipient Byline award for disting. reporting Marquette U. Sch. Journalism, 1982; fellow Inst. Politics, John F. Kennedy Sch. Govt., Harvard U., 1985. Mem. The Authors Guild, Overseas Press Club, Soc. of Profl. Journalists. Home: 39530 Country Mill Rd Murrieta CA 92562-3106

CASSIDY, DONALD LAWRENCE, former aerospace company executive; b. Stamford, Conn., May 26, 1933; s. John Dingee and Ursula Agnes (Lynch) C. BS, MIT, 1954; grad. mgmt. policy inst., U. Southern Calif., L.A., 1973. Sr. exec. Johns-Manville Corp., N.Y.C., 1954-55; contracting officer U.S. Army Signal Corps Electric Lab., Ft. Monmouth, N.J., 1955-57; with contract dept. field svc. and support div. Hughes Aircraft Co., L.A., 1957-69, mgr. contracts support systems, 1969-78; dir. contracts Hughes Aircraft Co., Long Beach, Calif., 1978-87; group v.p. bus. ops., 1987, v.p., chief contracts officer, 1987-92. 1st lt. U.S. Army, 1955-57. Mem. Am. Def. Preparedness Assn. (L.A. chpt. bd. dirs.), Nat. Contract Mgmt. Assn., Nat. Security Indsl. Assn., Aerospace Industries Assn. (procurement finance coun. exec. group). Republican. Avocation: skiing.

CASSIDY, RICHARD ARTHUR, environmental engineer, governmental water resources specialist; b. Manchester, N.H., Nov. 15, 1944; s. Arthur Joseph and Alice Ethuliette (Gregoire) C.; m. Judith Diane Maine, Aug. 14, 1971; children: Matthew, Amanda, Michael. BA, St. Anselm Coll., 1966; MS, U. N.H., 1969, Tufts U., 1972. Field biologist Pub. Service Co. of N.H., Manchester, 1968; jr. san. engr. Mass. Div. Water Pollution Control, Boston, 1968-69; aquatic biologist Normandeau Assocs., Bedford, N.H., 1969-70; hydraulic engr. New Eng. div. U.S. Army C.E., Waltham, Mass., 1972-77, environ. engr., Portland Dist., Oreg., 1977-81, supr., environ. engr., 1981—. Contbr. articles to books and profl. jours. Den leader Pack 164 and 598 Columbia Pacific council Cub Scouts Am., Beaverton, Oreg., 1982-83, Webelos leader, 1984-85, 90-91, troop 764 committeeman, 1985-87, asst. scoutmaster, 1992, scoutmaster, 1993-94 troop 598 scoutmaster, 1995—, Cascade Pacific council troop 598 Boy Scouts Am., 1985-87; mem. Planning Commn. Hudson, N.H., 1976-77. Recipient commendation for exemplary performance Mo.-Miss. flood, 1973, commendation for litigation defense, 1986, commendation for mgmt. activities, 1987, 91, Comdr.'s award for civilian svc., 1997. Mem. Am. Inst. Hydrology (cert., profl. ethics com. 1986, v.p. Oreg. sect. 1987-89, pres. Oreg. sect. 1990-92, nat. treas. 1995—), Internat. Tng in Communication (pres. West Way Club 1989-90), N.Am. Lake Mgmt. Soc. Democrat. Roman Catholic. Home: 7655 SW Belmont Dr Beaverton OR 97008-6335 Office: Portland Dist CE Chief Reservoir Reg & Water Quality PO Box 2946 Portland OR 97208-2946

CASSIDY, SAMUEL H., lawyer, lieutenant governor, state legislator; m. Jillian Jacobellis; children: Rachael Kathryn, Sarah Woyneve, Alexandra, Samuel H. IV. BA, U. Okla., 1972; JD, U. Tulsa, 1975; postgrad., Harvard U., 1991. Bar: Okla., 1975, U.S. Supreme Ct. 1977, U.S. Ct. Appeals (10th cir.), 1977, Colo. 1982. Ptnr. Cassidy, Corely & Ganem, Tulsa, 1975-77, Seigel, Cassidy & Oakley, Tulsa, 1977-79, Beustring, Cassidy, Faulkner & Assocs., Tulsa, 1979-82; pvt. practice Pagosa Springs, Colo., 1982-94; mem. Colo. State Senate, 1991-94; lt. gov. State of Colo., 1994-95; pres. Jefferson Econ. Coun., 1995-97; pres., CEO Colo. Assn. Commerce and Industry, 1997—; bd. dirs. Capital Reporter; instr. U. Tulsa, 1978-81, Tulsa Jr. Coll., 1979; owner High Country Title Co.; developer Townhome Property, Mountain Vista; ptnr. Hondo's Inc.; pres. Sam Cassidy, Inc., mem. agriculture and natural resources com. 1991-92, state, mil. and vet. affairs com., 1991-92, local govt. com. 1991, legal svcs. com. 1991-92, hwy. legis. review com. 1991-93, nat. hazards mitigation coun., 1992-93, appropriations com., 1993, judiciary com., 1993; pres. Econ. Devel. Coun. of Colo., 1997—; exec. com. legis. coun., 1993-94, senate svcs. com. 1993; elected Senate Minority Leader, 1993-94, exec. com. Colo. Gen. Assembly. Mem. State Dem. Ctr. Com., 1987-95; bd. dirs. Colo. DLC, 1993-95, Leadership Jefferson County, Rocky Flats Local Impacts Initiative, dir.; chmn. bd. Arts Comm., Inc. Named Outstanding Legislator for 1991 Colo. Bankers Assn., ACLU Outstanding Legis. 1994; recipient Outsatnding Legis. Efforts award Colo. Counties, Guardian of Small Bus. award, NFIB, 1992, 94; fellow Gates Found., 1991, U. Denver sr. fellow. Mem. Colo. Bar Assn. (bd. govs. 1993-94), S.W. Colo. Bar Assn., Nat. Conf. State Legis. (Colo. rep., task force on state-tribe rels.), Rotary Internat. (member, sustaining Paul Harris fellow), Club 20 (bd. dirs.), San Juan Forum (chmn., bd. dirs.). Avocations: statuary painting, skiing, hiking, camping, fishing. Home: 1390 Ash St Denver CO 80220-2409 Office: 1776 Lincoln St Ste 1200 Denver CO 80203-1029

CASTBERG, EILEEN SUE, construction company owner; b. Santa Monica, Calif., Mar. 12, 1946; d. George Leonard and Irma (Loretta) Conroy; m. David Christopher Castberg, Oct. 27, 1967; children: Eric, Christopher. Grad. high sch., U. High Sch., L.A., 1964; certificate, Anthony Schs., 1990. Lic. real estate agt., Calif. Exec., co-founder Advanced Connector Telesis, Inc., Santa Ana, Calif., 1987-89; exec. Western Energy Engrs., Inc., Costa Mesa, Calif., 1987-89; owner Dave Castberg and Assoc., Inc., Ramona, Calif., 1989—; sales assoc. Ramona and Country Estates Realty, Keller Williams Realty, 1999—; cons. Watt Asset Mgmt., Santa Monica, 1990-91. Mem. choir Ramona Luth. Ch.; 3d v.p. Holy Cross Luth. Ch. Women's League, Cypress, Calif., 1983; bd. dirs., sec. San Diego Country Estates Timeshare Coop. Internatinoal Republican Women's Club San Diego Bd. Realtors, Ramona Real Estate Assn. (bd. dirs.), Intermountain Rep. Women's Fedn. (past pres.), Ramona Christian Women's Club, San Vicente Valley Club. Republican. Avocations: statuary painting, singing, gardening, decorating, reading.

CASTELLANO, MICHAEL ANGELO, research forester; b. Bklyn., June 26, 1956; s. Biagio and Mildred Anne (Cucco) C.; m. Elizabeth Marie Phillips, July 14, 1979; children: Nicholas Aaron, Daniel Robert Feller, Kelly Marie, Katlyn Morgan. AAS, Paul Smiths Coll., 1978; BS, Oreg. State U., 1982, MS, 1984, PhD, 1988. Forest technician Weyerhaeuser Co., Columbus, Miss., 1979; forester trainee USDA Forest Svc., Corvallis, Oreg., 1980-84, forester, 1984-87, rsch. forester, 1987—; cons. CSIRO, Div. of Forestry, Australia, 1988-95, Spanish-Am. Binational Prog., Barcelona, 1987, 91. Author: Key to Hypogeous Fungi, 1989, (agr. handbook) Mycorrhizae, 1989; contbr. articles to profl. jours. Bishop LSD Ch. Named one of Outstanding Young Men, Am. JayCees, 1984. Mem. Soc. Am. Foresters, N.Am. Truffling Soc. (advisor), Soil Ecology Soc., Mycol. Soc. of Am. (nomenclature 1986), Sigma Xi. Avocations: genealogy, baseball, computers, stamps, literature. Home: 1835 NW Garfield Ave Corvallis OR 97330-2535 Office: USDA Forest Svc 3200 SW Jefferson Way Corvallis OR 97331-4401

CASTELLANOS, RICHARD HENRY, lawyer; b. San Ysidro, Calif., Oct. 8, 1965; s. Roberto and Rachel (Garcia) C. BA in Polit. Sci./Sociology, U. Calif., San Diego, 1987; JD, U. Calif., Berkeley, 1990. Bar: Calif. 1990, U.S. Dist. Ct. (ctrl. dist.) Calif. 1990. Assoc. atty. Wyman Bautzer Kuchel & Silbert, Century City, Calif., 1990-91, Nossaman Guthner Knox & Elliott, L.A., 1991-93; legal advisor, of counsel Gangs for Peace, 1993-94; discrimination atty. AIDS Project L.A., 1993-94; atty. San Diego County Pub. Defender's Office, 1994—; instr. role model program L.A. County Sch. Dist., L.A., 1990—. Active Rebuild L.A. Task Force, L.A., Ptnrs. for Success, Legal Los Padrinos Program, Vols. in Parole, 1997—. Alba 80 Soc. scholar ALBA 80 Soc., 1987-90. Mem. ABA, Mex.-Am. Bar Assn., Hispanic Profl. Roundtable, Calif. Pub. Defenders Assn. La Kaza Lawyers Assn., San Diego County Bar Assn., L.A. County Bar Assn., Beverly Hills Bar Assn., Juvenile Justice Com., Nat. Moot Ct. Com., Children's Rights Com. Home: 129 Olive Dr San Diego CA 92173 Office: Office of Pub Defender 233 A St Ste 300 San Diego CA 92101-4008

CASTILLO, DIANA MAY, religious organization administrator; b. Pontiac, Mich., July 22, 1945; d. John Robert and Ellen May (Steele) Burkhart. AA in Humanities magna cum laude, U. Cin., 1992, BA in English magna cum laude, 1994; postgrad. in Rescue Ministry, Rescue Coll., 1994—. Lic. real estate sales agt., W. Va.; notary pub., Ariz. Delayed birth cert. clk. State of W. Va. Dept. Health, Charleston, 1979-86; proofreader Anderson Publ. Co., Cin., 1987-88, Press Cmty. Papers, Cin., 1987-88; word processing specialist U. Cin., 1990-94; supr. Hope Cottages Women's Gospel Mission, Flagstaff, Ariz., 1996-98; intern Tucson Rescue Mission, 1996, Denver Rescue Mission, 1998—; writer, editor St. John Social Svc. Ctr., Cin., 1989; proofreader, desktop publisher Dept. English, U. Cin., 1994, Florence (Ky.) Bapt. Temple, 1994-95, desktop publ., Beechgrove (Ky.) Boosters, 1995; juror Goodwin, Raup PC, Phoenix, 1998; spkr. in field of homelessness. Mem. editl. bd. Daily Sun, 1997; newsletter reporter Mountain Friends, 1998. Poll vol. Coconino County Bd. Elections, Flagstaff, Ariz., 1996-98; CPR instr. Am. Heart Assn., Charleston, W. Va., 1983; vol. respite care provider, United Home Care, Cin. 1987; vol. worship leader Women's Gospel Mission, Flagstaff, 1995-96; crisis response team Nat. Orgn. for Victim Assistance, Flagstaff, 1997-98; Bible study facilitator Coconino County Jail, Flagstaff, 1997-98; libr. asst. Flagstaff Christian Fellowship, 1997-98; pastoral counselor, Overcomers facilitator; victim witness vol., 1998; instr. English as 2d Lang. Sunnyside Bapt. Ch., Flagstaff, 1997; participant Quick Ct. Tng., Coconino County Law Libr., Flagstaff, 1997; facilitator Prison Fellowship, Flagstaff, 1998; grad. Citizen's Police Acad., Flagstaff, 1998. Presidential scholarship W. Va. State Coll., Institute, W. Va., 1985. Mem. Internat. Platform Assn., Internat. Union Gospel Missions, Women in Comm., Inc., Freelance Edtl. Assn., Golden Key, Alpha Sigma Kappa, Phi Kappa Epsilon. Republican. Baptist. Avocations: travel, singing, reading, photography, fine arts. Home: 4 S San Francisco St # 330 Flagstaff AZ 86001-5737

CASTILLO, EDWARD DANIEL, humanities educator; b. Riverside, Calif., Aug. 25, 1947; s. Edward Rudolph and Elizabeth Louise (Haymes) C.; divorced; children: Cassandra K., Andrew K. BA, Univ. Calif., 1969, MA, 1976, D in philosophy, 1978. Lectr. dept. Native Am. studies Univ. Calif., L.A., 1969-70, Berkeley, Calif., 1971-76; asst. prof., dept. chair dept. Native Am. studies Univ. Calif., Santa Cruz, Calif., 1978-81; program dir., tchr. Laytonville (Calif.) Unified Sch. Dist., 1981-87; scholar in residence Calif. State Dept. Edn., Sacramento, 1987-88; prof., chmn. Native Am. studies Somoma State Univ., Rohnert Park, Calif., 1989—; cons. Smithsonian Inst. Mus. Am. Indians, Washington, 1991-92; training Native Am. Faculty Stanford Univ., 1993; editorial asst. Houghton Mifflin/McMillan Co., N.Y., 1995-98; chmn. Native Am. studies com. Calif. State Univ., 1994—. Co-author: Indians Franciscans and Spanish Colonization, 1995; author: Native American Perspectives on the Hispanic Colonization of Alla Calif., 1989, Living Traditions A Museum Guide for Indian People, 1992; contbr. articles to profl. jours. Bd. dirs. Ya-Ka AMA Edn. Ctr., Forestville, Calif., 1994-96, presentor of documentation for United Nations Hearing on Discrimination Against Indigeanos Populations, Geneva, Switzerland, 1977; tribal rep. Assembly for Econ. Justice, Washington, 1998. Recipient Outstanding Faculty award Univ. Calif., 1975, Faculty Meritorious Performance award Sonoma State Univ., 1990, Faculty award for Scholarly Excellence Friends of the Library, 1998. Mem. Nat. Am. & Alaskan Native Faculty Assn., Native Am. Heritage Comm. (commissioner 1977-83), Calif. Coun. Humanities Sesquintennial (adv. mem. 1992—). Avocations: snow skiing, jet skiing, camping, hunting, fishing. Office: Native American Studies Dept Sonoma State Univ 1801 E Cotati Ave Cotati CA 94928-3613

CASTLE, EMERY NEAL, agricultural and resource economist, educator; b. Eureka, Kans., Apr. 13, 1923; s. Sidney James and Josie May (Tucker) C.; m. Merab Eunice Weber, Jan. 20, 1946; 1 child, Cheryl Diana Delozier. BS, Kans. State U., 1948, MS, 1950; PhD, Iowa State U., 1952, LHD (hon.), 1997. Agrl. economist Fed. Res. Bank of Kansas City, 1952-54; from asst. prof. to prof. dept. agrl. econs. Oreg. State U., Corvallis, 1954-65; dean faculty Oreg. State U., 1965-66, prof., head dept. agrl. econs., 1966-72, dean Grad. Sch., 1972-76, Alumni disting. prof., 1970, prof. univ. grad. faculty econs., 1986—; v.p., sr. fellow Resources for the Future, Washington, 1976-79; pres. Resources for the Future, 1979-86; vice-chmn. Environ. Quality Commn. Oreg., 1988-95. Editor: The Changing American Countryside: Rural People and Places, 1995; mem. editl. bd. Land Econs., 1969—. Recipient Alumni Disting. Service award Kans. State U., 1976; Disting. Service award Oreg. State U., 1984. Fellow AAAS, Am. Assn. Agrl. Economists (pres. 1972-73), Am. Acad. Arts and Scis. Home: 1112 NW Solar Pl Corvallis OR 97330-3640 Office: Oreg State U 227 Ballard Extension Hall Corvallis OR 97331-8538

CASTLE, NANCY MARGARET TIMMA, accountant, banker; b. Seattle, June 16, 1945; d. Guy Church and Nancy L. (Fraser) B.; m. George L. Wittenburg (div. May 1972); 1 child, Guy Charles; m. Geoffrey Baird Castle, Dec. 12, 1992. Student, Stephens Coll., 1963-64. Legal adminstr. Mullen, McCaughey & Henzell, Santa Barbara, Calif., 1965-67; trust adminstr. First Interstate Bank of Calif., Santa Barbara, 1974-84; pres., owner, acct. N.T.B. Profl. Bus. Svc., Santa Barbara, 1984—; owner Castle Enterprises, Ltd., Castle Catering Co., 1992—; mem. Continuing Edn. Bar. Mem. Am. Inst. Banking, Nat. Assn. Female Execs, Nat. Fedn. Ind. Bus. Republican. Episcopalian. Mem. Santa Barbara Assocs., University (Santa Barbara), Santa Barbara Yacht Club, Cottage Assocs., Santa Barbara Cottage Hosp. Avocation: tennis.

CASTLEBERRY, ARLINE ALRICK, architect; b. Mpls., Sept. 19, 1919; d. Bannona Gerhardt and Meta Emily (Veit) Alrick; m. Donald Montgomery Castleberry, Dec. 25, 1941; children: Karen, Marvin. B in Interior Architecture, U. Minn., 1941; postgrad., U. Tex., 1947-48. Designer, draftsman Elizabeth & Winston Close, Architects, Mpls., 1940-41, Northwest Airlines, Mpls., 1942-43, Cerny & Assocs., Mpls., 1944-46; archtl. draftsman Dominick and Van Benscotten, Washington, 1946-47; ptnr. ... Burlingame, 1965-90. Recipient Smith Coll. scholarship. Mem. AIA, Am. Inst. Bldg. Designers (chpt. pres. 1971-72), Commaisini, Alpha Alpha Gamma, Chi Omega. Democrat. Lutheran. Home and Office: 1311 Parrott Dr San Mateo CA 94402-3630

CASTLEMAN, BREAUX BALLARD, health management company executive; b. Louisville, Aug. 19, 1940; s. John Pryor and Mary Jane (Ballard) C.; m. Sue Ann Foreman (div. 1995); children: Matthew B., Shea B. BA in Econs., Yale U., 1962; postgrad., NYU, 1963. Mgmt. trainee Bankers Trust Co., N.Y.C., 1963-65; mng. dir. Castleman and Co., Houston, 1965-71; dir. program planning, econ. U.S. Dept. HUD, Ft. Worth, Dallas, 1971-73; v.p., office mgr. Booz Allen and Hamilton, Dallas, Houston, 1973-85; mng. dir. Castleman Group, Houston, 1985-87; CEO Kelsey-Seybold Clinic, P.A., Houston, 1987-95; pres. physician resources divsn. Caremark Internat., Inc., 1994-96; pres. Scripps Clinic, La Jolla, Calif., 1996—. Contbr. articles to profl. jours. Candidate state legislature, Houston, 1968. Mem. Am. Med. Group Assn. (bd. dirs. 1996—), Planning Forum (chmn. 1985-86), Univ. Club San Diego. Office: Scripps Clinic 10666 N Torrey Pines Rd La Jolla CA 92037-1092

CASTOR, JON STUART, electronics company executive; b. Lynchburg, Va., Dec. 15, 1951; s. William Stuart and Marilyn (Hughes) C.; m. Stephanie Lum, Jan. 7, 1989; 1 child, David Jon. BA, Northwestern U., 1973; MBA, Stanford U., 1975. Mgmt. cons. Menlo Park, Calif., 1981-96; pres. TeraLogic, Inc., 1996—. Dir. Midwest Consumer Adv. Bd. to FTC, 1971-73; v.p., bd. dirs. San Mateo coun. Boy Scouts Am., 1991-93; bd. dirs. Pacific Skyline Coun. Boy Scouts Am., 1994—; trustee Coyote Point Mus. Environ. Edn., San Mateo, 1992-95. Office: TeraLogic Inc 1240 Villa St Mountain View CA 94041-1124

CASTOR, WILBUR WRIGHT, futurist, writer, consultant; b. Harrison Twp., Pa., Feb. 3, 1932; s. Wilbur Wright and Margaret (Grubbs) C.; m. Donna Ruth Schwartz, Feb. 9, 1963; children: Amy, Julia, Marnie. BA, St. Vincent Studies, 1959; PhD, Calif. U. Advanced Studies, 1990. Sales rep. IBM, Pitts. and Cleve., 1959-62; v.p. data processing ops. Honeywell, Waltham, Mass. 1962-80; pres., chief exec. officer Aviation Simulation Tech., Lexington, Mass., 1980-82; sr. v.p. Xerox Corp., El Segundo, Calif., 1982-89; freelance cons., 1989—. Author: (play) Un Certaine Soirire, 1958, (mus. comedy) Breaking Up, 1960, (stage play) This is Your Wife, 1997, (book) The Information Age and the New Productivity, 1990, (play) This is Your Wife, 1997; contbr. articles to profl. jours. Mem. Presdl. Rep. Task Force; pres., bd. dirs. Internat. Acad., Santa Barbara; active Town Hall Calif. Served to capt. USN, 1953-58, with USAFR, 1958-76. Recipient Disting. Alumnus of Yr. award St. Vincent Coll., 1990. Mem. World Bus. Acad., The Strategy Bd., U. Denver "Netthink", World Future Soc., Aircraft Owners and Pilots Assn., Caballeros Country Club, Rolling Hills (Calif.) Club, Tennis Club, U.S. Senator's Club. Avocations: flying, scuba diving, music, reading, writing. Home: 19 Georgeff Rd Rolling Hills CA 90274-5272

CASTREJON, ELIZABETH BLACKWELL, artist; b. East Orange, N.J., Feb. 10, 1935; d. William Thomas and Helen Williams (Hardy) Blackwell; m. Jose Castrejon Rodriguez, Oct. 20, 1957 (div. July 1984); children: Jose, Pedro. BFA, Syracuse U., 1956. U. Ams., 1957. Asst. mgr. Monte de Tacxo, Mexico, 1970-74; corp. interior designer Posados de Mexico, Mexico City, 1974-80, Krystal Hotels, Mexico City, 1980-85; interior designer Wesloh Designs, Costa Mesa, Calif., 1985-87, Barbara Swartz Interiors, Westlake Village, Calif., 1987, Interior Form & Function, Camarillo, Calif., 1987-92; owner Castrejon Originals, Westlake Village, 1992—. Mem. Am. Soc. Interior Design, Calif. Coun. Interior Design, Conejo Assn. Interior Designs. Republican. Home: 1111 Via Colinas Westlake Village CA 91362-5056

CASTRO, DAVID ALEXANDER, construction executive; b. L.A., Dec. 30, 1950; s. Victor A. and Guadalupe (Valadez) C.; m. Katherine Winfield Taylor, Sept. 30, 1990; children: Sarah Taylor, Kyle Christian, Andrew Joseph. A Liberal Arts, U. Md., 1976, BS in Bus. and Mgmt., 1978; A Engring. Asst., C.C. USAF, 1986; MS in Systems Mgmt., Golden Gate U., 1991. Enlisted USAF, 1970, advanced through grades to Chief Master Sgt., 1989; quality control mgr. 6950 security wing USAF, Royal AFB Chicksands, U.K., 1976-79; supr. engring. support 2851 civil engring. squadron USAF, McClellan AFB, Calif., 1979-82, inspector major projects 2851 civil engring. squadron, 1982-85, supt. engring. svcs. 2851 civil engring. squadron, 1985-87; dep. dir. pub. works tech. assistance team USAF, Beni Seuf, Egypt, 1987-88; contract mgr., then program mgr. 60 civil engring squadron USAF, Travis AFB, Calif., 1988-91; ret. USAF, 1991; acct. rep. Melt. Life Ins. Co., Fairfield, Calif., 1991-92; construction mgr. Pacifica Svcs. Inc., Travis AFB, Calif., 1992-96; constrn. program mgr. CAL Inc., Vacaville, Calif., 1996-97, chief construction divsn., 1997—; mem. USAF Enlisted Coun., Washington, 1984-86. Group leader Neighborhood Watch, North Highlands, Calif., 1983-86; vol. Loaves and Fishes, Sacramento, 1984-86, Christman Promise, Sacramento, 1983-85; coach Little League Baseball, U.K. and Sacramento, 1976-81. Mem. Air Force Assn. (named Outstanding Airman 1985), Air Force Sgts. Assn., Travis Chiefs Group (treas. 1990-92), Am. Legion. Republican. Roman Catholic. Avocations: volleyball, golf, jogging, gardening. Home: 514 Crownpointe Cir Vacaville CA 95687-5556

CASTRO, DONALD STEVEN, history educator; b. Bakersfield, Calif., June 27, 1940; s. Emilio Castro-Galvez and Lilia (Mayer) Castro; m. Constance Lee Picella, June 12, 1970; children: Antonia Carolina, Daniela Emilia. AB, UCLA, 1962, MA, 1964, PhD, 1970. Asst. prof. history Calif. State Poly. U., Pomona, 1967-69, assoc. prof., 1969-72, 1978-87, dir. Ctr. Chicano and Am. Indian Studies, 1969-72, dean undergrad. studies, 1978-80, dean instrn. Office grad. undergrad. studies, 1980-87; assoc. dir. office internat. programs Chancellor's office, Calif. State U. Hdqrs., Long Beach, 1972-78; prof. history, dean sch. humanities - social scis. Calif. State U., Fullerton, 1993—; presenter numerous confs. on Latin Am. studies; mem. gen. edn. rev. com. Calif. State U. system, 1980—; steering com. Calif. State U. NEXA consortium, 1982—, outside evaluator Univ. Honors Program, Chico, 1985-86; cons. Office Internat. Edn. Am. Assn. State Colls. and Univs., 1972-76, on minority edn., Calif. sch. dists., 1969—; mem. social sci. adv. com. Ryan Commn. Calif. Dept. Edn., 1972-74; faculty senate rep. Sch. of Arts on Campus, 1969-72; guest lectr. Instituto Ricardo Levene, Facultad de Filosofia y Letras, U. Nacional de Buenos Aires, 1965-66; assoc. v.p. grad. student Researchand Internat. Program, Calif. State U., Northridge, 1987-88; mem. Acad. Senate on Campus, 1987-88; program rev. Internationalizing Curriculum Calif. State U. Office of Chancellor; invited participant Intenat. Conf. Rome, 1982, 86, Amsterdam, 1988. Contbr. articles to profl. jours. Community rep. Bilingual Edn. Com. Pomona Unified Sch. Dist., 1980-83; commnr. City of Claremont (Calif.) Environ. Quality Commn., 1982—; bd. govs. Fund for Pub. Edn., Claremont, 1981—; mem. Claremont Unified Sch. Dist. adv. council, 1983—, chmn., 1985—. Fulbright fellow, 1965-67; grantee Kellogg Found., 1971. Mem. Pacific Coast Council Latin Am. Studies (bd. govs. 1976-80, 1983-85, 88—, mem. exec. bd. 1989—), Council on Latin Am. Studies (founding pres. 1979-82, bd. dirs. 1982—), So. Calif. Consortium on Internat. Studies (bd. govs. 1980-88, com. Latin Am. Studies 1972—, chmn. 1984—, chmn. subcom. Latin Am. Studies Coop. program 1972-79, chmn. subcom. Latin Am. Studies Outreach 1979—), Am. Hist. Assn. (conf. Latin Am. History Rio de la Plata Area studies com. 1970—), Latin Am. Studies Assn. (membership com. 1977-79), Nat. Assn. Fgn. Student Advisors, Calif. State U. Assn. Deans of Undergrad. Studies, Acad. Planning, Calif. State U. Assn. Deans of Grad. Studies (chmn. com. improving grad. studies), Calif. State U. Assn. undergrad. advisors (founding mem.), Calif. State U. Consortium on Overseas Studies (bd. govs. 1979-88, chmn. 1983-88, interim dir. 1983-84), Golden Key, Phi Alpha Theta, Pi Gamma Mu. Email: dscastre@fullerton.edu. Office: Calif State Fullerton HSS MH115 PO Box 6850 Fullerton CA 92834-6850

CASTRO, JOSEPH ARMAND, music director, pianist, composer, orchestrator; b. Miami, Ariz., Aug. 15, 1927; s. John Loya and Lucy (Sanchez) C.; m. Loretta Faith Haddad, Oct. 21, 1966; children: John Joseph, James Ernest. Student, San Jose State Coll., 1944-47. Mus. dir. Herb Jeffries, Hollywood, Calif., 1952, June Christy, Hollywood, 1953-62, Anita O'Day, Hollywood, 1963-65, Tony Martin, Hollywood, 1962-64, Tropicana Hotel, Las Vegas, Nev., 1980—, Desert Inn, Las Vegas, 1992-93; orch. leader Mocambo Night Club, Hollywood, 1952-54; soloist Joe Castro Trio, L.A., N.Y.C. Honolulu, 1951-61 Sands Hotel Desert Inn Las Vegas 1975-80; mus. dir. Folies Bergere, 1980-89. Recs. include Cool School with June Christy, 1960, Anita O'Day Sings Rodgers and Hart, 1961, Lush Life, 1966, Groove-Funk-Soul, Mood Jazz, Atlantic Records, also albums with Teddy Edwards, Stan Kenton, Jimmy Borges with Joe Castro Trio, 1990, Loretta

Castro with Joe Castro Trio, 1990, Honolulu Symphony concerts; command performance, Queen Elizabeth II, London Palladium, 1989, Concerts with Jimmy Borges and Honolulu Symphony Pops Concerts, 1991; jazz concert (with Nigel Kennedy) Honolulu Symphony, 1990; jazz-fest, Kailua-Kona, Hawaii, 1990; leader orch. Tropicana Hotel, 1989-94. With U.S. Army, 1946-47. Roman Catholic. Home: 2812 Colanthe Ave Las Vegas NV 89102-2026

CASTRO, LEONARD EDWARD, lawyer; b. L.A., Mar. 18, 1934; s. Emil Galvez and Lily (Meyers) C.; 1 son, Stephen Paul. A.B., UCLA, 1959, J.D., 1962. Bar: Calif. 1963, U.S. Supreme Ct. 1970. Assoc. Musick, Peeler & Garrett, Los Angeles, 1962-68, ptnr., 1968—. Mem. ABA, Internat. Bar Assn., Los Angeles County Bar Assn. Office: Musick Peeler & Garrett 1 Wilshire Blvd Ste 2000 Los Angeles CA 90017-3876

CASTRUITA, RUDY, school system administrator. BA in Social Sci., Utah State U., 1966, MS in Sch. Adminstrn., 1967; EdD, U. So. Calif., 1983. Cert. adminstrv. svcs., std. secondary, pupil svcs. Dir. econ. opportunity program City of El Monte, Calif., 1966-67; secondary tchr., counselor, program coord. El Monte Union High Sch. Dist., 1967-75, asst. prin. Mountain View High Sch., 1975-80; prin. Los Alamitos (Calif.) High Sch. Los Alamitos Unified Sch. Dist., 1980-85; asst. supt. secondary divsn. Santa Ana (Calif.) Unified Sch. Dist., 1985-87, assoc. supt. secondary divsn., 1987-88, supt., 1988-94; supt. schs. San Diego County, 1994—; adj. prof. Calif. State U., Long Beach, 1981-88, mem. adv. com. dept. ednl. adminstrn., 1983-86; adj. prof. U. San Francisco, 1984-88; mem. State Tchr. of Yr. Selection Com., 1988, Student Tchr. Edn. Project Coun., SB 620 Healthy Start Com., SB 1274 Restructuring Com., Joint Task Force Articulation, State High Sch. Task Force; mem. Latino eligibility study U. Calif., mem. ednl. leadership inst.; mem. state adv. coun. Supt. Pub. Instrn.; Delta Epsilon lectr. U. So. Calif.; rep. Edn. Summit; mem. selection com. Calif. Ednl. Initiatives Fund; co-chair subcom. at risk youth Calif. Edn. Com., 1989; mentor supt. Harvard Urban Supt.'s Program, 1993—. Chair Orange County Hist. Adv. Coun., South El Monte Coordinating Coun.; mem. exec. coun. Santa Ana 2000; mem. articulation coun. Rancho Santiago C.C. Dist.; active Hacienda Heights Recreation and Pks. Commn., Santa Ana City Coun. Stadium Blue Ribbon Com.; exec. dir. Orange County coun. Boy Scouts Am.; mem. adv. com. Bowers Mus.; mem. exec. bd. El Monte Boys Club; hon. lifetime mem. Calif. PTA; bd. dirs. Santa Ana Boys and Girls Club, Orange County Philharm. Soc., Santa Ana Pvt. Industry Coun., El Monte-South El Monte Consortium, Drug Use is Life Abuse, EDUCARE sch. edn. U. So. Calif. Named Supt. of Yr. League United Latin Am. Citizens, 1989; state finalist Nat. Supt. Yr. award, 1992. Mem. ASCD, Assn. Calif. Sch. Adminstrs. (rep. region XVII secondary prins. com. 1981-85, presenter region XVII 1984, Calif. Supt. of Year award 1991, Marcus Foster award 1991), Calif. Sch. Bds. Assn. (mem. policy and analysis com.), Assn. Calif. Urban Sch. Dists. (pres. 1992—), Orange County Supts. (pres.), Santa Ana C. of C. (bd. dirs.), Delta Epsilon (pres. 1990-91), Phi Delta Kappa. Office: San Diego County Supt Office 6401 Linda Vista Rd San Diego CA 92111*

CATANO, LUCY BACA, gallery manager; b. Roswell, N.Mex., Aug. 1, 1946; d. Mike Y. and Sostena (Sambrano) Baca; children: Teresa, Cuki, John, Robert. Asst. libr. Artesia (N.Mex.) Pub. Libr., 1966-72; arts and crafts tchr. WASA, Willcox, Ariz., 1990—; demonstrator Demos, Ltd., Tucson, 1989—; part-time mgr. Wildwood Gallery & Book Bank, Willcox, 1990—. Author children's stories; poet. Voter registrar Youth-Willcox Schs., 1992-94. Recipient award for Outstanding Dedication to Youth, City of Willcox, 1992, 1st place poetry award Willcox C. of C., 1996, 98; named Citizen of Yr., 1998, Outstanding Poet, 1998. Mem. Willcox Against Substance Abuse, Writer's Bloc, Friends of the Libr., Poet's Soc. Democrat. Roman Catholic. Home: 408 N Arizona Ave Willcox AZ 85643-1526

CATE, FLOYD MILLS, electronic components executive; b. Norfolk, Va., Aug. 2, 1917; s. Floyd Mills and Ellen (Lewis) C.; m. Ann Willis, Jan. 31, 1943; 1 child Carol Cate Webster. B.A. U. Tenn., 1940; student exec. program UCLA, 1958; B.A. (hon.) Calif. Inst. Tech., 1947. With special sales dept. Cannon Electric Co., Los Angeles, 1940-46, western sales mgr., 1946-50, with internat. sales dept., 1950-57, v.p. sales, mktg., 1957-62, pres. internat. sales, 1958-62, v.p. sales and mktg. electronics, 1962-69; v.p. sales, mktg. divsn. Japan Aviation Electronics Zemco, Irvine, Calif., 1977-80, cons., 1977-80; pres., owner F.E.S. Cons., San Clemente, Calif., 1968-94; 2R engring. cons. dir., San Marcos, Calif., 1987-94; consulting agent LHC Shorecliff Golf Club; U.S.A. agent Ocean Resources Engr. Co-chmn. Ron Packard for Congress, San Clemente, 1984; chmn. ad hoc com. Sea Sade Village, 1986-94; pres. Assn. Shorecliffs Residence, San Clemente, 1986-94; dir. La Christianitos pagents Samaritan Hosp. Guild. Mem. IEEE, Internat. Electric Electronic Engrs., San Clemente C. of C., San Clemente Hist. Soc. Democrat. Roman Catholic. Club: Shorecliff Golf (bd. dirs. San Clemente). Office: 205 Via Montego San Clemente CA 92672-3625

CATRAMBONE, EUGENE DOMINIC, magazine editor; b. Chgo., June 5, 1926; s. Nicola and Maria Theresa (Catrambone) C.; m. Mary Gloria Gaimari, Mar. 26, 1951; children: Mary, Eugene Jr., Jane, David, Jill. BA, St. Benedict Coll., 1950; postgrad., Kans. State U., 1952-54; MA, DePaul U., 1960; postgrad., UCLA, 1962-63. Cert. secondary tchr., coll. instr., Calif. Tchr. high schs. Chgo., 1950-62, L.A., 1963-88; cons. pub. rels. Westlake Village, Calif., 1986—; mng. editor Internat. Film Festival Mag.; tech. writer U. Chgo., 1956-59, Douglas Missile div. USN, L.A. and Ventura, Calif., 1962-75; reporter, editor Las Virgenes Enterprise, Calabasas, Calif., 1968-75; evening instr. L.A. City Coll., 1965-68. Author: Requiem for a Nobody, 1993, The Golden Touch: Frankie Carle, 1981; poems "Exit dust", 1982, "Tender Moments", 1996, "The Portrait", 1997; contbr. articles on edn. to profl. publs., 1959-60, feature stories to local newspapers, 1968-75. Sgt. U.S. Army, 1944-46. Recipient Fostering Excellence award L.A. Unified Sch. Dist., 1986-87, nominee Apple award, 1986. Mem. NEA (life), VFW, Calif. Tchrs. Assn., Book Publicists So. Calif., United Tchrs. L.A., Am. Legion, Westlake Village Men's Golf Club (pub. rels. editor 1986—, bd. dirs., pres. 1989—). Democrat. Roman Catholic. Avocations: coins, World War II history, golf, poetry. Home: 31802 Tynebourne Ct Westlake Village CA 91361 Office: Golden Touch Assocs 31802 Tynebourne Ct Westlake Village CA 91361

CATTANEO, JACQUELYN ANNETTE KAMMERER, artist, educator; b. Gallup, N.Mex., June 1, 1944; d. Ralph John and Gladys Agnes (O'Sullivan) Kammer; m. John Leo Cattaneo, Apr. 25, 1964; children: John Auro, Paul Anthony. Student Tex. Woman's U., 1962-64. Portrait artist, tchr. Gallup, N. Mex., 1972; coord. Works Progress Adminstrn. art project renovation McKinley County, Gallup, Octavia Fellin Performing Arts wing dedication, Gallup Pub. Library; formation com. mem. Multi-modal/Multi-Cultural Ctr. for Gallup, N.Mex.; exch. with Soviet Women's Com., USSR Women Artists del., Moscow, Kiev, Leningrad, 1990; Women Artists del. and exch. Jerusalem, Tel Aviv, Cairo, Israel; mem. Artists Del. to Prague, Vienna and Budapest.; mem. Women Artists Del. to Egypt, Israel and Italy, 1992, Artist Del. Brazil, 1994, Greece, Crete and Turkey, 1996, Spain, 1996. One-woman shows include Gallup Pub. Libr., 1963, 66, 77, 78, 81, 87, Gallup Lovelace Med. Clinic, Santa Fe Station Open House, 1981, Gallery 20, Farmington, N.Mex., 1985—, Red Mesa Art Gallery, 1989, Soviet Restrospect Carol's Art & Antiques Gallery, Liverpool, N.Y., 1992, 97, N.Mex. State Capitol Bldg., Santa Fe, 1992, Lt. Govt. Casey Luna-Office Complex, Women Artists N.Mex. Mus. Fine Arts, Carlsbad, 1992, Rio Rancho Country Club, N.Mex., 1995, Carol's Art & Antiques, Liverpool NY, 1997; group shows include: Navajo Nation Library Invitational, 1978, Santa Fe Festival of the Arts Invitational, 1979, N.Mex. State Fair, 1978, 79, 80, Catharine Lorillard Wolfe, N.Y.C., 1980, 81, 84, 85, 86, 87, 88, 89, 91, 92, 4th ann. exhbn. Salmagundi Club, 1984, 90, 98, 3d ann. Palm Beach Internat., New Orleans, 1984, Fine Arts Ctr. Taos, 1984, The Best and the Brightest O'Brien's Art Emporium, Scottsdale, Ariz., 1986, Gov.'s Gallery, 1989, N.Mex. State Capitol, Santa Fe, 1987, Pastel Soc. West Coast Ann. Exhbn. Sacramento Ctr. for Arts, Calif., 1986-90, gov.'s invitational Magnifico Fest. of the Arts, Albuquerque, 1991, Assn. Pour La Promotion Du Patrimone Artistique Français, Paris, Nat. Mus. of the Arts for Women, Washington, 1991, Artists of N.Mex., Internat. Nexus '92 Fine Art Exhbn., Trammell Crow Pavilion, Dallas, Carlsbad (N.Mex.) Mus. Fine Art; represented in permanent collections: Zuni Arts and Crafts Ednl. Bldg., U. N.Mex., C.J. Wiemar Collection, McKinley Manor, Gov.'s Office, State Capitol Bldg., Santa Fe, Historic El Rancho Hotel, Gallup, N.Mex., Sunwest Bank. Fine Arts Ctr., En Taos, N.Mex., Armand Hammer Pvt. Collection, Wilcox Canyon Collections, Sadona, Ariz., Galaria Impi, Netherlands, Woods Art and Antiques, Liverpool, N.Y., Stewarts Fine Art, Taos, N.Mex., Rohoboth McKinley Christian Hosp. & Sacred Heart Cathedral, Gallup, NM. Mem. Dora Cox del. to Soviet Union-U.S. Exchange, 1990. Recipient Cert. of Recognition for Contbn. and Participation Assn. Pour La Patrinome Du Artistique Français, 1991, N.Mex. State Senate 14th Legislature Session Meml. # 101 for Artistic Achievements award, 1992, Award of Merit, Pastel Soc. West Coast Ann. Membership Exhbn., 1998, Holbein Award Excellence in painting, Pastel Soc. West Coast Internat. Juried Exhibition. Mem. Internat. Fine Arts Guild, Am. Portrait Soc. (cert.), Oil Painters of Am., Pastel Soc. of W. Coast (cert., Hobein award), Mus. N.Mex. Found., N.Mex. Archtl. Found., Mus. Women in the Arts, Fechin Inst., Artists' Co-op. (co-chair), Gallup C. of C., Gallup Area Arts and Crafts Council (nat. and internat. artist of distinction award 1997), Am. Portrait Soc. Am., Pastel Soc. N.Mex., Catharine Lorillard Wolfe Art Club of N.Y.C. (oil and pastel juried membership), Chautaugua Art Club, Oil Painters of Am., Soroptimists (internat. woman of distinction 1990), Salmagundi Art Club. Address: 210 E Green St Gallup NM 87301-6130

CATTERALL, JAMES, education educator, researcher; b. Feb. 20, 1948; m. Rebecca S. Epps, Sept. 25, 1983; children: Hannah, Grady. BA in Econs. with honors, Princeton U., 1970; MA in Pub. Policy Adminstrn., Hubert Humphry Inst. Pub., 1973; PhD in Edn. Adminstrn. and Policy, Stanford U., 1982. Program officer budget and fiscal planning N.J. State Dept. Higher Edn., 1970-71; researcher, writer tax study commn. Minn. Ho. of Reps., St. Paul, 1972-73; prin., asst. dir. summer programs Shattuck Sch., Faribault, Minn., 1973-76; instr. maths. Oreg. Episcopal Sch., Portland, 1976-77; rsch. tchg. asst. Sch. Edn. Stanford U., Palo Alto, Calif., 1977-80; asst. prof. edn. UCLA, 1981—, assoc. prof. edn., 1988-95, prof. edn., 1995—, dir. Imagination Project,; dir. Ctr. for Study of Edn. Policy, Palo Alto, Calif., 1978-80; cons. The Rand Corp., Sant Monica, Calif.; cons. writer Calif. State Sch. of Supts. Wilson Riles and Bil Honic, U.S. Sec. of Edn. Lauro Cavasos. Editor: School Choice Forum; assoc. editor: Economic Evaluation of Public Programs, 1985, Educational Evaluation and Policy Analysis, 1995-97. Bd. trustees The Keys Sch., Palo Alto, 1979-81, Wildwood Sch., Santa Monica, 1987-90; demonstrator, performer Music in the Schs. Fellow Ford Found., 1977-81; recipient Civic Achievement award L.A. Times, 1988. Mem. Am. Ednl. Rsch. Assn., Am. Ednl. Fin. Assn., Policy Analysis Spl. Interest Group, Politics of Edn. Spl. Interest Group, The Topanga (Calif.) Symphony (charter), The Topanga Brass. Avocations: tennis, sailing, music, cooking, cartooning. Office: UCLA Grad Sch Edn and Info 405 Hilgard Ave Los Angeles CA 90095-9000

CATTERTON, MARIANNE ROSE, occupational therapist; b. St. Paul, Feb. 3, 1922; d. Melvin Joseph and Katherine Marion (Bole) Maas; m. Elmer John Wood, Jan. 16, 1943 (dec.); m. Robert Lee Catterton, Nov. 20, 1951 (div. 1981); children: Jenifer Ann Dawson, Cynthia Lea Uthus. Student, Carleton Coll., 1939-41, U. Md., 1941-42; BA in English, U. Wis., 1944; MA in Counseling Psychology, Bowie State Coll., 1980; postgrad., No. Ariz. U., 1987-91. Registered occupational therapist, Occupational Therapy Cert. Bd. Occupational therapist VA, N.Y.C., 1946-50; cons. occupational therapist Fondo del Seguro del Estado, Puerto Rico, 1950-51; dir. rehab. therapies Spring Grove State Hosp., Catonsville, Md., 1953-56; occupational therapist Anne Arundel County Health Dept., Annapolis, Md., 1967-78; dir. occupational therapy Eastern Shore Hosp. Ctr., Cambridge, Md., 1979-85; cons. occupational therapist Kachina Point Health Ctr., Sedona, Ariz., 1986; regional chmn. Conf. on revising Psychiat. Occupational Therapy Edn., 1958-59; instr. report writing Anne Arundel Community Coll., Annapolis, 1974-78. Editor Am. Jour. Occupational Therapy, 1962-67. Active Md. Heart Assn., 1959-60; mem. task force on occupational therapy edn. Md. Dept. of Health, 1971-72; chmn. Anne Arundel Gov. Com. on Employment of Handicapped, 1959-63; gov.'s com. to study vocat. rehab., Md., 1960; com. mem. Annapolis Youth Ctr., 1976-78; ministerial search com. Unitarian Ch. Anne Arundel County, 1962; curator Dorchester County Heritage Mus., Cambridge, 1982-83; v.p., officer Unitarian-Universalist Fellowship Flagstaff, 1988-93, v.p., 1993-97; co-moderator, founder Unitarian-Universalist Fellowship Sedona, 1994—, pres., 1997-98; citizen interviewer Sedona Acad. Forum, 1993, 94; vol. Respite Care, 1994—, VerdeValley Caregivers, 1996—. Mem. P.R. Occupl. Therapy Assn. (co-founder 1950), Am. Occupl. Therapy Assn. (chmn. history com. 1958-61), Md. Occupl. Therapy Assn. (del. 1953-59), Ariz. Occupl. Therapy Assn., Pathfinder Internat., Dorchester County Mental Health Assn. (pres. 1981-84), Internat. Platform Assn., Ret. Officers Assn., Air Force Assn. (Barry Goldwater chpt., sec. 1991-92, 94-98), Severn Town Club (treas. 1965, sec. 1971-72, 94-95), Internat. Club (Annapolis, publicity chmn. 1966), Toastmasters, Newcomers (Sedona, pres. 1986), Pathfinder, Zero Population Growth, Nature Conservancy, Delta Delta Delta. Republican. Home: 415 Windsong Dr Sedona AZ 86336-3745

CATZ, BORIS, endocrinologist, educator; b. Troyanov, Russia, Feb. 15, 1923; s. Jacobo and Esther (Galbmilion) C.; came to U.S., 1950, naturalized, 1955; m. Rebecca Schechter; children: Judith, Dinah, Sarah Lea, Robert. BS, Nat. U. Mexico, 1941, MD, 1947; MS in Medicine, U. So. Calif., 1951. Intern, Gen. Hosp., Mexico City, 1945-46; prof. adj., sch. medicine U. Mexico, 1947-48; research fellow medicine U. So. Calif., 1949-51, instr. medicine, 1952-54, asst. clin. prof., 1954-59, assoc. clin. prof., 1959-83, clin. prof., 1983—; pvt. practice, Los Angeles, 1951-55, Beverly Hills, Calif., 1957—; chief Thyroid Clinic Los Angeles County Gen. Hosp., 1955-70; sr. cons. thyroid clin. U. So. Calif.-Los Angeles Med. Center, 1970—; clin. chief endocrinology Cedars-Sinai Med. Ctr., 1983-87. Served to capt. U.S. Army, 1955-57. Boris Catz lectureship named in his honor Thyroid Research Endowment Fund, Cedars Sinai Med. Ctr., 1985. Fellow ACP, Am. Coll. Nuclear Medicine (pres. elect 1982), Royal Soc. Medicine; mem. AMA, AAAS, Cedars Sinai Med. Ctr. Soc. for History of Medicine (chmn.), L.A. County Med. Assn., Calif. Med. Assn., Endocrine Soc., Am. Thyroid Assn., Soc. Exptl. Biology and Medicine, Western Soc. Clin. Research, Am. Fedn. Clin. Research, Soc. Nuclear Medicine, So. Calif. Soc. Nuclear Medicine, N.Y. Acad. Scis., L.A. Soc. Internal Medicine, Collegium Salerni, Cedar Sinai Soc. of History of Medicine, Beverly Hills C. of C., Phi Lambda Kappa. Jewish. Mem. B'nai B'rith. Club: The Profl. Man's (past pres.). Author: Thyroid Case Studies, 1975, 2d edit., 1981. Contbr. numerous articles on thyroidology to med. jours. Home: 300 S El Camino Dr Beverly Hills CA 90212-4212 Office: 435 N Roxbury Dr Beverly Hills CA 90210-5027

CAUDILL, MAUREEN, author and computer consultant; b. Portsmouth, Ohio, July 14, 1951; d. Elmon C. and Harriet L. (Sisler) C. BA, U. Conn., 1973; MA in Teaching, Cornell U., 1974. Customer engr. Raytheon Data Systems, Wellesley, Mass., 1975-78; mem. tech. sales support staff Hewlett-Packard Co., Wallingford, Conn., 1978-81; project programmer Gould Ocean Systems div., Cleve., 1982-83; sr. software engr. Data Systems div. Gen. Dynamics Co., San Diego, 1983-85; computer cons. Rockwell Internat., Hughes Aircraft Corp., Honeywell Corp., other corps., 1985-89; founder, computer cons. Adaptics, San Diego, 1987-89; engring. specialist space systems div. Gen. Dynamics, San Diego, 1989-90; mgr. tech. and applications support Sci. Applications Internat. Corp., 1990-91; owner, cons., writer NeuWorld Svcs., San Diego, 1991-93; co-founder, dir. rsch. NeuWorld Fin., San Diego, 1993-96; organizer ann. meetings on neural networks, San Diego, Boston, Washington, Seattle, 1987-90; instr. San Diego Extension in Intelligent Systems Technologies U. Calif., 1990—; presenter on neural networks, U.S., Japan, Mex., also others, 1987—. Author: Neural Network Primer, 1989, Naturally Intelligent Systems, 1990, Understanding Neural Networks: Computer Exploration, 1992, In Our Own Image, 1992, Using Neural Networks, 1994, Daddy Candidate, 1996, Never Say Goodbye, 1998; contbg. editor Finance mag., 1994-96. Mem. IEEE.

CAUDRON, JOHN ARMAND, accident reconstructionist, technical forensic investigator; b. Compton, Calif., Sept. 26, 1944; s. Armand Robert and Evelyn Emma (Hoyt) C.; m. Marilyn Edith Fairfield, Mar. 16, 1968; children: Melita, Rochelle. AA, Ventura Coll., 1965; BA, Calif. State U., Fullerton, 1967; postgrad., U. Nev., 1975-78; MS, U. So. Calif., 1980. Dist. rep. GM, Reno, 1969-75; mgr. Snyder Rsch. Lab., Reno, 1976-78, v.p., El Monte, Calif., 1978-82, pres., 1982—; prin. Fire and Accident Reconstruction, Rowland Heights, Calif., 1985—. Pub. accident reconstrn. newsletter. With U.S. Army, 1967-69. Mem. ASCE; fellow Am. Bd. Forensic Examiners (bd. cert.); mem. Inst. Forensic Examiners, Am. Soc. Safety Engrs., Nat. Fire Protection Assn., Geol. Soc. Am., Firearms Rsch. and Identification Assn. (pres. 1978—), Am. Soc. Metals, Nat. Safety Coun., Nat. Soc. Profl. Engrs., Nat. Assn. Profl. Accident Redonstruction Specialists, Ft. Tejon Hist. Assn. (info. adviser 1983—). Republican. Baptist. Avocations: hiking, traveling, photography. Office: Fire & Accident Reconstruction 21465 E Fort Bowie Dr Walnut CA 91789-5106

CAUFIELD, MARIE CELINE, religious organization administrator; b. Chgo., Aug. 11, 1929; d. John Patrick and Anna Marie (Clear) C. MA in Religious Edn., Fordham U., 1975; DMin in Creative Ministry, Grad. Theol. Found., Bristol, Ind., 1989. Elem. prin. St. Martin's Sch., Kankakee, Ill., 1952-64; missionary Congregation de Notre Dame, Guatemala, Ctrl. Am., 1964-71; dir. religious edn. St. Colomba, N.Y.C., 1971-75, St. Bernard, Pirtleville, Ariz., 1975-76; dir. Hispanic ministry Diocese of Providence (R.I.), Central Falls, 1976-81; dir. of the Office of Hispanic ministry Roman Cath. Diocese of Boise, 1981-96; nat. exec. dir. The Cath. Migrant Farmworker Network, 1996—. Author numerous poems; contbr. articles to profl. jours. Bd. dirs. Cath. Migrant Farmworkers' Network, Toledo, 1992—; founder Idaho's Cath. Golden Age Chpt., Boise, 1983-87. Grantee Am. Bd. Cath. Missions, 1991. Mem. Nat. Writers Assn., Fedn. of Returned Overseas Missioners (N.W. contact person 1990-94). Roman Catholic. Avocations: networking, writing, photography, walking, music. Home: 1111 N 17th St Boise ID 83702-3306 Office: Catholic Migrant Farmworker Network 1915 University Dr Boise ID 83706-3022

CAUGHLIN, STEPHENIE JANE, organic farmer; b. McAllen, Tex., July 23, 1948; d. James Daniel and Betty Jane (Warnock) C. BA in Family Econs., San Diego State U., 1972, MEd, 1973; M. in Psychology, U.S. Internat. U., San Diego, 1979. Cert. secondary life tchr., Calif. Owner, mgr. Minute Maid Svc., San Diego, 1970-75; prin. Rainbow Fin. Svcs., San Diego, 1975-78; tchr. San Diego Unified Sch. Dist., 1973-80; mortgage broker Santa Fe Mortgage Co., San Diego, 1980-81; commodity broker Premex Commodities, San Diego, 1981-84; pres., owner Nationwide Futures Corp., San Diego, 1984-88; owner, sec. Nationwide Metals Corp.; owner, gen. mgr. Seabreeze Organic Farm, 1984—. Sec. Arroyo Sorrento Assn., Del Mar, Calif., 1978—. Mem. Greenpeace Nature Conservancy, DAR, Sierra Club, Jobs Daus. Republican. Avocations: horseback riding, swimming, skiing, gardening. Home and Office: 3909 Arroyo Sorrento Rd San Diego CA 92130-2610

CAULFIELD, W. HARRY, health care industry executive, physician; b. Waverly, N.Y., Aug. 22, 1936; m. Mary Sisk; children: Mary, Harry, James, Michael. AB, Harvard U., 1957, postgrad., 1976; MD, U. Pa., 1961. Diplomate Am. Bd. Internal. Medicine, Am. Bd. Cardiology. Rotating intern Hosp. U. Pa., 1961-62; resident Pa. Hosp., 1962-64; fellow in cardiology Georgetown U. Hosp., 1964-66; dir. ICU Kaiser Found. Hosp., San Francisco, 1969-75, asst. chief of staff, 1971-75, chief of staff, 1975-80; physician-in-chief, mem. exec. com. Permanente Med. Group, San Francisco, 1975-80, mem. internal medicine staff cardiology, 1968—, from exec. dir.-elect to exec. dir., 1990—; assoc. clin. prof. medicine U. Calif., San Francisco, 1971-96. Capt. U.S. Army Med. Corps, 1966-68. Fellow Am. Coll. Cardiology, Am. Heart Assn.; mem. AMA (adv. com. on group practice physicians 1994—, fedn. study consortium 1994—), San Francisco Med. Soc. (alt. del. to Calif. Med. Assn. 1992, del. 1993-94, managed care task force, leadership devel. com.), Calif. Med. Assn., Calif. Hosp. Assn. (membership com. 1987), Am. Hosp. Assn., Calif. Acad. Medicine, Am. Med. Group Assn. (trustee 1994—, vice chmn. bylaws com. 994, fin. com. 1996—), Soc. Med. Adminstrs., Am. Assn. Health Plans (bd. dirs. 1994—). Office: Permanente Med Group Inc 1950 Franklin St Oakland CA 94612-5103

CAUSEY, GILL TERRY, recreation company executive; b. L.A., May 22, 1950; s. Gill B. and June Celeste (Hillman) C. BA, Whittier Coll., 1972. With Causey & Rhodes Devel. Co., Newport Beach, Calif., 1972-75, Causey Investment Co., Laguna Beach, Calif., 1973-80, B&C Wines Importers, Kamuela, Hawaii, 1980-86; pres. Charter Locker, Inc., Kailua-Kona, Hawaii, 1986—, Big Island Yacht Sales, Inc., Kailua-Kona, Hawaii, 1986-93, Paradise Rafting Adventures, Inc., Agana, Guam, 1991—; v.p. Atoll Express, Inc., Kailua-Kona, 1988—; dir. Pelorus Maritime Ltd., Rarotonga, Cook Islands, Causey Trust Investments, newport Beach. Vice pres. Nancy Griffith, Inc., Kailua-Kona, 1987—. Mem. Pacific Ocean Rsch. Found., nat. Assn. Charterboat Operators, Kona Sailing Club, Hawaii Yacht Club. Presbyterian. Avocations: sailing, cooking, navigation. Office: Charter Locker Inc 74-425 Kealakehe Pkwy Kailua Kona HI 96740-2708

CAUSIN, JANIS EISENHOWER, artist; b. Tacoma, Wash., Apr. 5, 1922; d. Edgar and Louise (Alexander) Eisenhower; m. William Oliver Causin, Aug. 31, 1947; children: William E., Jean Causin Ramey. M in Fine Arts, U. Puget Sound, 1971. Owner, pres. Lakehouse Studio, Lakewood, Wash., 1975-95; CEO Special Additions, Inc., Silverdale, Wash., 1995—. Ceramist; creates large ceramic murals, 1975—. Mem. Philanthropic Ednl. Orgn., Tacoma Arts and Crafts Assn. (juried awards 1970—), Garden Club Am. (bd. dirs. local chpt.). Avocation: golf. Home: 2027 Narrows View Cir NW Gig Harbor WA 98335-6806

CAVANAUGH, JAN CATHLEEN, art historian; b. Fullerton, Calif., Jan. 8, 1946; d. Wallace Joseph Cavanaugh and Shirley Mae (Johnson) Shaver. BA in English Lit., U. Calif., Berkeley, 1967, MA in Art, 1972; PhD in Art History, U. Tex., Austin, 1989. Asst. prof. Middle Tenn. State U., Murfreesboro, Tenn., 1985-86; curator of art Reed Coll. Douglas F. Cooley Art Gallery, Portland, Oreg., 1989-91; asst. prof. U. Hawaii, Manoa, 1991-92, U. Mo., Columbia, 1995-96; rschr., 1996—. Author: Selections from the Reed Coll. Art Collection, 1989, Out Looking In: Early Modern Polish Art, 1890-1918, 1999; editor The Modernist Aesthetic In Polish Art, 1987. Recipient Stanford U., U. Warsaw exchange program, 1974-76, Fulbright Hays/IREX grant, 1981-82, U. Tex. fellowship, 1983-84, numerous grants. Mem. College Art Assn. of Am., Soc. Historians of East European and Russian Art and Architecture, Russian and East European Ctr., U. Ill. Avocation: painting. Home: 19852 Maritime Ln Huntington Beach CA 92648

CAVARRA, ROBERT N, music educator, musician; b. Denver, Colo., Feb. 23, 1934; s. Alfonso and Mary M. (Bianco) C.; m. Barbara Sedlmayr, Aug. 9, 1941; children: Karla Marie Cavarra Britton, R. Christopher, Stephan Gian, Matthew Nicholas. BA, St. Thomas Sem., Denver, 1956; MusB summa cum laude, U. Colo., 1961, MusM cum laude, 1963. Organist St. Joseph Ch., Denver, 1946-52, St. Thomas Sem., Denver, 1952-57, Pontifcal N. Am. Coll., Rome, 1957-58, First U. Meth. Ch., Ft. Collins, 1986-97; prof. music Colo. State U., Ft. Collins, 1961—; organist, producer Mus. Heritage Soc., 1968—; co-founder Pro Organo Pleno XXI Found., Ft. Collins, Colo., 1994—. Composer: Suite for Organ, 1974, Two Pieces for Organ and Trumpet, 1983; organist, producer: recordings for Musical Heritage Soc., 1968—. Fellow Danforth Found., 1979. Mem. Am. Guild Organists (dean), Iota Kappa Lambda. Avocations: photography, salt-water aquaria, model railroading. Home: 1717 Hillside Dr Fort Collins CO 80524-1966 Office: Colo State U Dept Music Theater Dance Fort Collins CO 80523

CAVNAR, SAMUEL MELMON, author, publisher, activist; b. Denver, Nov. 10, 1925; s. Samuel Edward and Helen Anita (Johnston) C.; m. Peggy Nightengale, Aug. 14, 1977; children by previous marriage: Dona Cavnar Hambly, Judy Cavnar Bentrim; children: Heather Anne Hicks, Heide Lynn MacLeod. Student pub. schs., Denver. Dist. mgr. U.S. C. of C., various locations, 1953-58; owner Cavnar & Assocs., mgmt. cons., Washington, Las Vegas, Nev., Denver and Reseda, Calif., 1958—; v.p. Lenz Assoc. Advt., Inc., Van Nuys, Calif., 1960—; dist. mgr. Western States Nu-Orm Plans, Inc., Los Angeles, 1947-52; cons. to architect and contractor 1st U.S. Missile Site, Wyo., 1957-58; prin. organizer Westway Corp. and subsidiaries, So. Calif. Devel. Co., 1958—; chmn. bd. Boy Sponsors, Inc., Denver, 1957-59; pres. Continental Am. Video Network Assn. Registry, Inc., Hollywood, Calif., 1967—; pres. United Sales Am., Las Vegas and Denver, 1969—; sr. mgmt. cons. Broadcast Mgmt. Cons. Service, Hollywood, Las Vegas, Denver, Washington, 1970—; pres., dir., exec. com. Am. Ctr. for Edn., 1968—; pub. Nat. Ind., Washington, 1970—, Nat. Rep. Statesman, Washington, 1969—, Nat. Labor Reform Leader, 1970—, Nat. Conservative Statesman, 1975—; owner Ran Vac Pub., Las Vegas and Los Angeles, 1976—; ptnr. P.S. Computer Services, Las Vegas, 1978—, C & A Mgmt., Las Vegas, 1978—, Westway Internat., 1983—, Internet Cons., 1997—, Af-

filiate Internet Presentations, Inc., 1997—; lectr. in field; spl. cons. various U.S. senators, congressmen, 1952—. Author: Run, Big Sam, Run, 1976, The Girls on Top, 1978, Big Brother Bureaucracy, The Cause and Cure, 1977, Kiddieland West, 1980, Games Politicians Play: How to Clean Up Their Act, 1981, A Very C.H.I.C. President, 1981, How to Clean Up Our Act, 1982, Assassination By Suicide, 1984, How to Get Limited Government, Limited Taxes, 1985, Tax Reform or Bust, 1985, At Last: Real Tax Reform, 1986, On the Road to a Real Balanced Budget, 1989, It's Time for Term Limitation, 1990, Clinton's "Investments": Just More Taxes, 1993, Hillary-Billary's New Road to Socialism, 1993, The Cause and the New Cure, 1995, Messin' With My Mind and Body, 1995, Reaction to Messin With My Mind, 1996, Millenium 5000 Chronicles, 1998. Nat. gen. chmn. Operation Houseclean, 1966-81; nat. candidate chmn. Citizens Com. To Elect Rep. Legislators, 1966, 68, 70, 72-74, 85—; mem. Calif. and Los Angeles County Rep. Cen. Coms., 1964-70; nat. gen. chmn. Project Prayer, 1962—; exec. dir. Project Alert, 1961—; nat. chmn. Nat. Labor Reform Com., 1969—; sustaining mem. Rep. Nat. Com., 1964—; Western states chmn. and nat. co-chmn. Am. Taxpayers Army, 1959—; area II chmn. Calif. Gov.'s Welfare Reform Com., 1970; chmn. Com. Law and Order in Am., 1975; mem. Nev. State Rep. Com., 1972—; mem. Clark County Rep. Com., 1972—; bd. dirs. Conservative Caucus, Las Vegas, 1974, 76, 82, 92; Rep. candidate for U.S. Senate from Nev., 1976, 82, 92, U.S. Congress from 1st dist. Nev., 1998; Rep. nominee for U.S. Congress from 30th dist. Calif., 1968, 70; nat. chmn. Return Pueblo Crew, 1968, Citizens League for Labor Reform, 1984—; nat. co-chmn. U.S. Taxpayers Forces, 1985—; pres., trustee Community Youth Activities Found., 1977—; nat. chmn. Operation Bus Stop, 1970—, P.R.I.D.E. Com., 1981—, Positivics Program, 1982—; co-chmn. Question 8 Com., 1980-82, S.H.A.F.T.E.D. Tax Repeal Com., 1982 C.H.I.C. Polit. Edn. Com., 1977—, People Against Tax Hikes Com., 1983—; bd. dirs., Nev. co-chmn. Pres. Reagan's Citizen's Com. for Tax Reform, 1985-86; nat. chmn. Term Limitation Com., 1988—; nat. chmn. Combined Coms. for Republican's Contract With Am., 1994—; chmn. Citizen's To Return Barloon and Daliberti, 1995—. Served with USN, 1942-45, USAF, 1950-53, Korea; comdr. USCG Aux., 1959-60. Recipient Silver medal SAR. Mem. Am. Legion (comdr. 1947-48, mem. nat. conv. disting. guest com. 1947-52), DAV, VFW, Am. Security Council (nat. adviser 1966—), U. S. C. of C. (sr. mem. rep. 1986—). Home: 301 Misty Isle Ln Apt A Las Vegas NV 89107-1135 Office: 1615 H St NW Washington DC 20062-0001

CAWLEY, LEO PATRICK, pathologist, immunologist; b. Oklahoma City, Aug. 11, 1922; s. Pat Bernard and Mary Elizabeth (Forbes) C.; m. Joan Mae Wood, June 20, 1948; children: Kevin Patrick, Karin Patricia, Kary Forbes. BS in Chemistry, Okla. State U., 1948; MD, Okla. Sch. Medicine, 1952. Diplomate Am. Bd. Pathology, Am. Bd. Nuclear Medicine, Am. Bd. Allergy and Immunology, Am. Bd. Med. Lab. Immunology, Am. Bd. Pathology in immunopathology. Intern Wesley Med. Ctr., Wichita, 1952-53, resident in pathology, 1953-54; resident in pathology Wayne County Gen. Hosp., Eloise, Mich., 1954-56, chief resident in pathology, 1956-57; clin. pathologist, asst. dir. lab. Wesley Med. Ctr., Wichita, Kans., 1957-69, dir. sci., 1965-86, dir. labs., 1969-77, dir. clin. immunology, 1979-86; med. dir. Roche Biomed. Lab., Wichita, Kans., 1979-86; dir. clin. labs. Iatric Corp., Tempe, Ariz., 1988—; pres. Kilcawley Enterprises, 1986—. Author: Electrophoresis/Immunoelectric Phoresis, 1969; editor series Lab Med Little Brown, 1965-81; contbr. 210 articles to profl. jours. Pfc. USM, 1942-45. Fellow Am. Soc. Clin. pathologist (bd. dirs. 1968, Disting. Svc. award 1980, Dist. Pathology edn. award, 1998), Coll. Am. Pathologist; mem. AAAS, ACS, Am. Assn. Clin. Chemists, Alpha Pi Mu, Phi Lambda Upsilon, Alpha Omega Alpha. Avocations: reading, history. Office: KilCawley Enterprises 7135 E Main St Scottsdale AZ 85251-4315

CAYETANO, BENJAMIN JEROME, governor, former state senator and representative; b. Honolulu, Nov. 14, 1939; s. Bonifacio Marcos and Eleanor (Infante) C.; m. Vicky Tiu, 1997; children: Brandon, Janeen, Samantha. BA, UCLA, 1968; JD, Loyola U., 1971; D in Pub. Svc. (hon.), Loyola Marymount U., 1998. Bar: Hawaii 1971. Practiced in Honolulu, 1971-86; mem. Hawaii Ho. of Reps., 1975-78, Hawaii Senate, 1979-86; lt. gov. State of Hawaii, 1986-95, gov., 1994—; bar examiner Hawaii Supreme Ct., 1976-78, disciplinary bd., 1982-86; arbitration panel 1st Cir. Ct. State of Hawaii, 1986; adv. U. Hawaii Law Rev., 1982-84. Mem. bd. regents Chaminade U., 1980-83; mem. adv. council U. Hawaii Coll. Bus. Adminstrn., 1982-83. Recipient Excellence in Leadership Medallion Asia-Pacific Acad. Consortium for Pub. Health, 1991, UCLA Alumni award for excellence in pub. svc., 1993, Leadership award Harvard Found., 1996, Edward A. Dickson Alumnus of Yr. award UCLA, 1998. Democrat. Office: Office of Gov State Capitol 415 S Beretenia St 5th Fl Honolulu HI 96813*

CAZEAU, CHARLES JAY, geologist; b. Rochester, N.Y., June 25, 1931; s. Floyd Alfred and Nan Marie (Barbehenn) Carroll; m. Janet Grace Donovan, Aug. 11, 1960 (dec. Nov. 1971); children: Sharon, Suzanne. BS, Notre Dame Univ., 1954; MS, Fla. State Univ., 1955; PhD, North Carolina Univ., 1962. Geologist Exxon, Houston, 1955-58; asst. prof. Clemson Univ., Clemson, S.C., 1960-63; assoc. prof. SUNY, Buffalo, 1963-86; cons., writer CPF Assocs., Mesa, Ariz., 1986-91, Deary, Idaho, 1991—; cons. CPF Assocs., 1975-86; tech. cons. Codesh, Buffalo, N.Y., 1976—; dir. summer session Park Sch., Buffalo, N.Y., newspaper cons. Gannett News Svc., Rochester, N.Y. Author: Science Trivia, 1986, Exploring The Unknown, 1979, Physical Geology, 1976, Earthquakes, 1975. Hon. mayor Town of Avon, Avon, Idaho, 1993-98. Mem. Coun. for Secour Humanism. Avocations: stamp collecting, essayist, computers, birding. Home: 1084 Rue Loop Deary ID 83823-9659

CAZIER, BARRY JAMES, electrical engineer, software developer; b. Phoenix, May 10, 1943; s. James Henry and Dorothy Marie (Lynton) C.; m. Susan Arline Shewey, June 13, 1964 (dec. July 1979); children: Suzanne, Bryan; m. Illene D. Miller, Dec. 19, 1994. Student, Colo. Sch. Mines, 1961-62; BSEE, U. Colo., 1965; student advanced bus. adminstrn., Ariz. State U., 1974-77. Mfg. mgmt. Gen. Electric, Richland, Wash., 1965-66, Warren, Ohio, 1966-67; system engr. Gen. Electric, Schenectady, N.Y., 1967-69; project mgr. Honeywell, Phoenix, 1970-80, dir. field ops., 1980-85, program mgr., 1985—; prin. Cazier Software Designs, Scottsdale, Ariz., 1985—. adv. Jr. Achievement, Phoenix, 1972. Club: IBM PC Users (Phoenix). Avocations: music, jogging, camping, fishing, reading. Home: 8508 E Via Montoya Scottsdale AZ 85255-4936 Office: Honeywell 16404 N Black Canyon Hwy Phoenix AZ 85053-3095

CAZORT, BARNEY DOUGLAS, college counselor; b. El Dorado, Ark., Dec. 21, 1943; s. John Harold and Carolyn (McMullan) C.; m. Constance Layman, May 20, 1978; 1 child, Max Barney. BA, Vanderbilt U., 1966; MA in English, San Diego State U., 1980; MS in Counseling Psychology, U. So. Calif., 1987, MPW in Profl. Writing, 1988. Rotary Found. fellow U. Basel, Switzerland, 1966-67; freelance writer Del Mar, Calif., 1971-75; owner North Coast Cabinets, Del Mar, 1975-81; grad. tchg. fellow U. So. Calif., L.A., 1982-86; mem. faculty Pepperdine U., Malibu, Calif., 1987-93, Linn-Benton C.C., Albany, 1994—. Author: (reference) Under the Grammar Hammer, 1992, rev. edit., 1997, (how-to) Chairman Cazort's Little Red Book of Writing, 1993. Capt. inf., USMC, 1968-71, Vietnam. Decorated Bronze Star, Purple Heart; Cross of Gallantry (Vietnam). Mem. Oreg. Developmental Studies Orgn. (treas. 1997-98, pres. 1998-99), Oreg. Counseling Assn., Phi Kappa Phi (writing award 1982). Avocations: grammar, swimming, hiking. Home: 4445 N Shasta Loop Eugene OR 97405 Office: Linn-Benton CC 6500 Pacific Blvd SW Albany OR 97321

CECH, THOMAS ROBERT, chemistry and biochemistry educator; b. Chgo., Dec. 8, 1947; m. Carol Lynn Martinson; children: Allison E., Jennifer N. BA in Chemistry, Grinnell Coll., 1970, DSc (hon.), 1987; PhD in Chem., U. Calif., Berkeley, 1975; DSc (hon.), U. Chgo., 1991; Drury Coll., 1994. Postdoctoral fellow dept. biology MIT, Cambridge, Mass., 1975-77; from asst. prof. to assoc. prof. chemistry U. Colo., Boulder, 1978-83, prof. chemistry and biochemistry also molecular cellular and devel. biology, 1983—, disting. prof., 1990—; rsch. prof. Am. Cancer Soc., 1987—; investigator Howard Hughes Med. Inst., 1988—; co-chmn. Nucleic Acids Gordon Conf., 1984; Phillips disting. visitor Haverford Coll., 1984; Vivian Ernst meml. lectr. Brandeis U., 1984, Cynthia Chan meml. lectr. U. Calif., Berkeley; mem. Welch Found. Symposium, 1985; Danforth lectr. Grinnell Coll. 1986; Pfizer lectr. Harvard U., 1986, Hastings lectr., 1992; Verna and Marrs McLean lectr. Baylor Coll. Medicine, 1987; Harvey lectr., 1987; Mayer lectr. MIT, 1987, HHMI lectr., 1989, T.Y. Shen lectr., 1994; Martin D. Kamen disting. lectureship, U. Calif., San Diego, 1988; Alfred Burger lectr. U. Va., 1988; Berzelius lectr. Karolinska Inst., 1988; Osamu Hayaishi lectr. Internat. Union Biochemistry, Prague, 1988; Beckman lectr. U. Utah, 1989; Max Tishler lectr. Merck, 1989; Abbott vis. scholar U. Chgo., 1989; Herriott lectr. Johns Hopkins U., 1990; J.T. Baker lectr., 1990; G.N. Lewis lectr. U. Calif., Berkeley, 1990; Sonneborn lectr. Ind. U., 1991; Sternbach lectr. Yale U., 1991; W. Pauli lectr., Zürich, 1992; Carter-Wallace lectr. Princeton U., 1992; Stetten lectr. NIH, 1992; Dauben lectr. U. Wash., 1992; Marker lectr. U. Md., 1993; Hirschmann lectr. Oberlin Coll., 1993; Beach lectr. Purdue U., 1993; Abe White lectr. Syntex, 1993; Robbins lectr. Pomona Coll., 1994; Bren lectr. U. Calif., Irvine, 1994; Wawzonek lectr. U. Iowa, 1994; Sumner lectr. Cornell U., 1994; Steenbock lectr. U. Wis., 1995; Murachi lectr. FAOB Congress, Sydney, 1995; Streck award lectr. U. Nebr., 1996; Gardner-Davern lectr. U. Utah, 1996, Priestley lectr. Pa. State U., 1996; Beckman lectr. Calif. Inst. Tech., 1996, Lemieux lectr. U. Alta., Can., 1997, Hogg Award lectr. MD Anderson Cancer Ctr., 1997, DeCoursey Nobel Lectr. Trinity U., 1998, Tschirgi lectr. U. Calif. San Diego, 1998. Assoc. editor Cell, 1986-87, RNA Jour.; mem. editl. bd. Genes and Development; dep. editor Sci. mag. Non-resident fellow Salk Inst.; trustee Grinnell Coll. NSF fellow, 1970-75, Pub. Health Svc. rsch. fellow Nat. Cancer Inst. 1975-77, Guggenheim fellow, 1985-86; recipient medal Am. Inst. Chemists, 1970, Rsch. Career Devel. award Nat. Cancer Inst., 1980-85, Young Sci. award Passano Found., 1984, Harrison Howe award, 1984, Pfizer award, 1985, U.S. Steel award, 1987, V.D. Mattia award, 1987, Louisa Gross Horowitz prize, 1988, Newcombe-Cleveland award AAAS, 1988, Heineken prize Royal Netherlands Acad. Arts and Scis., 1988, Gairdner Found. Internat. award, 1988, Lasker Basic Med. Rsch. award, 1988, Rosenstiel award, 1989, Warren Triennial prize, 1989, Nobel prize in Chemistry, 1989, Hopkins medal Brit. Biochem. Soc., 1992, Feodor Lynen medal, 1995, Nat. Sci. medal, 1995, Mike Hogg award, 1997, Wright prize, 1998; named to Esquire Mag. Register, 1985, Westerner of Yr. Denver Post, 1986. Mem. AAAS, Am. Soc. Biochem. Molecular Biology, NAS, Am. Acad. Arts and Scis., European Molecular Biology Orgn., RNA Soc. (v.p. 1993-96). Office: U Colo Dept Chem & Biochemistry PO Box 215 Boulder CO 80309-0215

CECI, JESSE ARTHUR, violinist; b. Phila., Feb. 2, 1924; s. Luigi Concezio and Catherine Marie (Marotta) C.; m. Catherine Annette Stevens, Aug. 5, 1979. BS, Juilliard Sch. Music, 1951; license de concert, L'Ecole Normale de Musique, Paris, 1954; MusM, Manhattan Sch. Music, 1971. Assoc. concertmaster New Orleans Philharm. Orch., 1953-54; violinist Boston Symphony Orch., 1954-59, N.Y. Philharm. Orch., N.Y., 1959-62, Esterhazy Orch., N.Y.C., 1962-68; concertmaster Denver Symphony Orch., 1974-89, Colo. Symphony Orch., 1989-95; over 50 performances of 22 major works; mem. Zimbler Sinfonietta, Boston, 1957-59; participant Marlboro Festival Chamber Orch. Vt., summmers 1960-62, 65, Marlboro Festival Chamber Orch. European-Israeli tour, 1965, Grand Teton Festival, Wyo., 1972, with Denver Duo, 1975—, N.Mex. Festival, Taos, 1980, Carmel (Calif.) Bach Festival, 1987—, Whistler (B.C., Can.) Mozart Festival, 1989-90, Bear Valley (Calif.) Festival, 1995—, Mendocino (Calif.) Festival, 1996—; mem. faculty Congress of Strings, Dallas, 1985, N.Y. Coll. Music, 1961-71, NYU, 1971-74, U. Colo., 1975-79; guest mem. faculty Univ. Denver, 1986; mem., assoc. concertmaster Casals Festival Orch., San Juan, P.R., 1963-77; violinist Cleve. Orch. fgn. tours, 1967, 73, 78, Cin. Symphony Orch. world tour, 1966; 1st violinist N.Y. String Quartet in-residence at U. Maine, Orono, summer 1969; guest violinist Fla. West Coast Symphony, Sarasota, 1993—; concertmaster Minn. Orch., summers 1970-71, Denver Chamber Orch., 1985-90; guest concertmaster Pitts. Symphony Orch., Pitts., L.A., 1988, mem. N.Y. Philharmonia Chamber Ensemble in-residence at Hopkins Ctr., Dartmouth U., summer 1973; recitalist, Paris, 1963, Amsterdam, 1963, recitalist Carnegie Recital Hall, N.Y.C., 1963, Town Hall, N.Y.C., 1968, 70, Alice Tully Hall, N.Y.C., 1972; fgn. tour Pitts. Symphony Orch., 1989; soloist Royal Chamber Orch. Japan, 1997-98. Cpl. U.S. Army, 1943-46, PTO. Fulbright fellow Paris, 1951-52. Democrat. Roman Catholic. Office: Colo Symphony Orch 1031 13th St Denver CO 80204-2156

CECIL, PAULA BERNICE, writer, management consultant, educator, publisher; b. Renwick, Iowa, July 14, 1927; d. Samuel Henry Klassie and Oneida Badgely; m. William J. Cecil, Mar. 27, 1954 (div. 1965); 1 child, Michelle E. BA, State U. Iowa, 1949; MA, U. Redlands, 1979. Systems support rep. IBM Corp., San Jose, Calif., 1965-71; customer support mgr. Trendata Corp., Sunnyvale, Calif., 1971-72; sales tng. analyst Xerox Corp., Rochester, N.Y., 1972-73; writer, cons. Automated Office Resources, Aptos, Calif., 1973—; tchr. San Mateo (Calif.) Sch. Dist., 1975-76; instr. West Valley Coll., Saratoga, Calif. 1975-79, Hartnell C.C., Salinas, Calif., 1975-88; instr. Cabrillo C.C., Aptos, 1975—, mem. bus. office skills and med. asst. adv. coms., 1975—; guest spkr. office automation confs.; mem. bus. office skills adv. com. Foothill Coll., Evergreen Coll. Author: (textbooks) Word Processing in the Modern Office, 1976, 2d ed., 1980, Management of Word Processing, 1980, Office Automation--Careers, Concepts & Customer Service, 1984; publisher, editor: The Observer, 1979—. Asst. campaign mgr. Candidate for Superior Judge, Los Gatos, Calif., 1980. Mem. Aptos C. of C., Santa Cruz Symphony Orgn., Friends of Shakespeare Santa Cruz, Seascape Seagals (capt. 1992), Calif. Writers Club, Spring Hills Ladies Golf Club. Republican. Methodist. Avocations: golf, swimming, bridge, running, vol. student advisor. Home: 812 Via Tornasol Aptos CA 95003-5624 Office: Cabrillo Coll Bus Office Tech Lab Aptos CA 95003

CECIL, ROBERT SALISBURY, telecommunications company executive; b. Manila, Philippines, May 28, 1935; came to U.S., 1941; s. Robert Edgar and Susan Elizabeth (Jurika) C.; m. Louise Nuttal Millholland, Nov. 30, 1963; children: Scott Douglass, James Hilliard. BSEE, U.S. Naval Acad., 1956; MBA, Harvard U., 1962. Commd. 2d lt. USAF, 1956, advanced through grades to 1st lt., 1958, ret., 1960; dir. govt. programs IBM, Washington, 1976-77; corp. v.p. mktg. Motorola Inc., Schaumburg, Ill., 1977-84; pres. Cellular Group Lin Broadcasting, N.Y.C., 1984-91; chmn. Plantronics, Inc., Santa Cruz, Calif., 1992—; bd. dirs. GT Group Telecom. Mem. Lyford Cay Club, Vancouver Lawn Tennis and Badminton Club, Rotary Internat. Republican. Episcopalian. Office: Plantronics Inc, Plantronics Inc, 1703-560 Cardero St, Vancouver, BC Canada V6G 3E9

CEDOLINI, ANTHONY JOHN, psychologist; b. Rochester, N.Y., Sept. 19, 1942; s. Peter Ross and Mary J. (Anthony) C.; m. Clare Marie De Rose, Aug. 16, 1964; children: Maria A., Antonia C., Peter E. Student, U. San Francisco, 1960-62; BA, San Jose State U., 1965, MS, 1968; PhD in Ednl. Pscyhology, Columbia Pacific U., 1983. Lic. ednl. psychologist, sch. adminstr., marriage, family, child counselor, sch psychologist, sch. counselor, social worker, Calif.; Lic. real estate broker, Calif. Mng. ptnr. Cienega Valley Vineyards and Winery (formerly Almaden Vineyards) and Comml. Shopping Ctrs., 1968—; coord. psychol. svcs. Oak Grove Sch. Dist., San Jose, Calif., 1968-81, asst. dir. pupil svcs., 1977-81; dir. pupil svcs. Oak Grove Sch. Dist., San Jose, 1981-83; pvt. practice, ednl. psychologist Ednl. Assocs., San Jose, 1983—; co-dir. Biofeedback Inst. of Santa Clara County, San Jose, 1976-83; ptnr. in Cypress Ctr.-Ednl. Psychologists and Consultancy, 1978-84; cons., program auditor for Calif. State Dept. Edn.; instr. U. Calif., Santa Cruz and LaVerne Coll. Ext. courses; guest spkr. San Jose State U.; lectr., workshop presenter in field. Author: Occupational Stress and Job Burnout, 1982, A Parents Guide to School Readiness, 1971, The Effect of Affect, 1975; contbr. articles to profl. jours. and newspapers. Founder, bd. dirs. Lyceum of Santa Clara County, 1971—. Mem. NEA, Calif. Tchrs. Assn., Calif. Assn. Sch. Psychologists, Nat. Assn. Sch. Psychologists, Coun. for Exceptional Children, Calif. Assn. for Gifted, Assn. Calif. Sch. Adminstrs., Calif. Personnel & Guidance Assn., Biofeedback Soc. Am., Nat. Assn., Tau Delta Phi. Avocations: collecting antique furniture and coins, stained glass, wine making, classic cars. Home and Office: 1183 Nikulina Ct San Jose CA 95120-5441

CELLA, JOHN J., freight company executive; b. 1940; married. BBA, Temple U., 1965. Regional mgr. Japan ops. Airborne Freight Corp., Seattle, 1965-71, v.p. Far Ea. ops., 1971-72, sr. v.p. internat. div., from 1982, now exec. v.p. internat. div. Office: Airborne Freight Corp 3101 Western Ave Seattle WA 98121-1043*

CENARRUSA, PETE T., secretary of state; b. Carey, Idaho, Dec. 16, 1917; s. Joseph and Ramona (Gardoqui) C.; m. Freda B. Coates, Oct. 25, 1947; 1 son, Joe Earl. B.S. in Agr., U. Idaho, 1940. Tchr. high sch. Cambridge, Idaho, 1940-41, Carey and Glenns Ferry, Idaho, 1946; tchr. vocat. agr. VA, Blaine County, Idaho, 1946-51; farmer, woolgrower, nr. Carey, 1946-95; mem. Idaho Ho. of Reps., 1951-67, speaker, 1963-67; sec. state Idaho, 1967-90, 91—; mem. Idaho Bd. Land Commrs., Idaho Bd. Examiners; pres. Idaho Flying Legislators, 1953-63; chmn. Idaho Legis. Council, 1964—, Idaho Govt. Reorgn. Com.; Idaho del. Council State Govts., 1963—. Elected ofcl., mem. BLM Adv. Coun., Boise Dist.; Rep. adminstr. Hall of Fame, 1978; sr. mem. State Bd. Land Commrs., 1967-96. Maj. USMCR, 1942-46, 52-58. Named Hon. Farmer Future Farmers Am., 1955; named to Agrl. Hall of Fame, 1973; Idaho Athletic Hall of Fame, 1976, Basque Hall of Fame, 1983. Mem. Blaine County Livestock Mktg. Assn., Idaho Wool Growers Assn. (chmn. 1954), Carey C. of C. (pres. 1952), U. Idaho Alumni Assn., Gamma Sigma Delta, Tau Kappa Epsilon. Republican. Office: Office of Sec State PO Box 83720 Boise ID 83720-3720*

CENTERWALL, WILLARD RAYMOND, physician; b. Missoula, Mont., Jan. 16, 1924; s. Willard Raymond Centerwall, Sr. and Charlotte Amanda (Brandon) Wood; m. Siegried Louise Achorn Centerwall, Sept. 2 , 1949 (dec. July 1992); children: Theodore, Brandon, Krista, Alison, Jennifer, Rebecca. BS in Zoology, Yale U., 1949, MD, 1952; MPH in Maternal & Child Health, U. Mich., 1967, MS in Human Genetics, 1968; D in Cultural Anthropology (hon.), World U., 1983. Diplomate Am. Bd. Pediatrics, Am. Bd. Preventive Medicine, Am. Bd. Med. Genetics. Rotating internship White Meml. Hosp., L.A., 1952-53; first yr. pediatric residency White Meml. Hosp., L.A. County Gen. Hosp., 1953-54; sr. yr. pediatric residency L.A. Children's Hosp., 1954-55; instr., asst. clin. prof., asst. prof. pediatrics Coll. Med. Evangelists Sch. of Medicine, L.A., 1955-61; lectr., reader, assoc. prof. pediatrics Christian Med. Coll., Vellore, South India, 1961-66; organizer, first head of dept. pediatrics Miraj Med. Sch., Maharashtra State, India, 1965; assoc. prof. pediatrics Loma Linda U. Sch. Medicine, 1968, prof. pediatrics, 1970-78; assoc. prof. pub. health Loma Linda U. Sch. Health, Calif., 1968, prof. maternal & child health, 1970-78, gen. cons., 1982—; prof. anthropology Loma Linda U. Grad. Sch., Calif., 1976-78; prof. emeritus of pediatrics and genetics Loma Linda U. Sch. Medicine, 1986; prof. pediatrics and genetics U. Calif. Sch. Medicine, Davis, 1978-85; prof. in residence dept. reproduction U. Calif. Sch. Veterinary Medicine, Davis, 1981-85; prof. emeritus of pediatrics and genetics U. Calif., Davis, 1986; clin. prof. depts. med. genetics & pediatrics Oreg. Health Scis. U. & Sch. Medicine, Portland, 1986—; ret.; dir. Satellite Genetic Diagnostic and Counseling Clinic, Reno, 1983-85, State Newborn Metabolic Screening Program at U. Calif., Davis, 1980-85, Chico-Oroville (Calif.) Satellite Genetic Diagnostic and Counseling Clinic, 1980-85, Satellite Genetic Diagnostic & Counseling Clinic, Redding, Calif., 1980-83, Genetic Disorders and Birth Defects Clinic Alta Regional Ctr., Sacramento, Calif., 1978-83; civilian med. specialist cons. in pediatrics David Grant USAF Med. Ctr., Travis AFB, 1982-85; organizer, 1st med. dir. Birth Defects and Genetics Clinic, Lakeport, Calif., 1978-84, Birth Defects and Genetics Diagnostic and Counseling Svc. Riverside County Health Dept., Calif., 1978, Birth Defects and Genetics Diagnostic and Counseling Svc. Loma Linda U. Med. Ctr., Calif., 1969-78, Birth Defects and Genetics Svc. Clarke County Dept. Pub. Health, Las Vegas, 1972, Birth Defects and Chromosome Lab. Svcs. Loma Linda U. Med. Ctr., Calif., 1969-78; organizer, 1st dir. Birth Defects and Genetics Clinic at Regional Ctr. for Devel. Disabilities, San Bernardino, Calif., 1976-78; spl. cons. to genetic disease section maternal & child health branch State Calif. Dept. Health, 1977-85, mem. adv. com. on inherited disorders, 1976; med. dir. Orthopedically Handicapped Clinic, Redlands, Calif., 1971-78; med. cons. Calif. Sch. for the Deaf, Riverside, Calif., 1969-78; pediatric cons. Pacific State Hosp. for Mentally Retarded, Pomona, Calif., 1955-60, 69-78, Sch. for Cerebral Palsied Children of Southern Calif., Altadena, 1956-60, and numerous others; vol. clin./acad. positions in Oreg., 1985—. Med. editor: Introduction series of booklets, 1958—; speaker in field. 1st lt. U.S. Army Corps of Engrs., 1943-47. Recipient of rsch. grants NIH, U.S. Pub. Health Svc., Meda Johnson & Co., Alumni Assn. of the Coll. of Med. Evangelists, Nat. Assn. for Retarded Children, Walter E. MacPherson Soc., The Nat. Found. March of Dimes, The Nat. Cancer Inst. and HEM Rsch., Inc., Calif. State Dept. Health; recipient Outstanding Svc. award for Excellence in the Provision of Med. Svcs. to Mentally Retarded Sacramento Assn. for the Retarded, Inc., 1982, 1st J.B.S. Haldane Oration medal Soc. Bionaturalists, 1985, Children's Bur. fellowship in Pub. Health and Human Genetics U. Mich., Ann Arbor, 1966-68. Avocations: travel, lecturing, birds and animals. Home: 101 Silverwood Ln Silverton OR 97381-9739

CEPPOS, JEROME MERLE, newspaper editor; b. Washington, Oct. 14, 1946; s. Harry and Florence (Epstein) C.; m. Karen E. Feingold, Mar. 7, 1982; children: Matthew, Robin. B.S. in Journalism, U. Md., 1969; postgrad., Knight-Ridder Exec. Leadership Program, 1989-90. Reporter, asst. city editor, night city editor Rochester (N.Y.) Democrat & Chronicle, 1969-72; from asst. city editor, to nat. editor, to asst. mng. editor The Miami (Fla.) Herald, 1972-81; assoc. editor San Jose (Calif.) Mercury News, 1981, mng. editor, 1983-94, exec. editor, sr. v.p., 1995—; mem. nat. adv. bd. Knight Ctr. Specialized Reporting, U. Md.; mem. Accrediting Coun. on Edn. in Journalism and Mass Comm. Mem. AP Mng. Editors (bd. dirs.), Am. Soc. Newspaper Editors, Calif. Soc. Newspaper Editors (former mem. bd. dirs., past pres.), Soc. Profl. Journalists, Assn. for Edn. in Journalism and Mass Comm., Silicon Valley Capital Club. Home: 14550 Pike Rd Saratoga CA 95070-5359 Office: San Jose Mercury News 750 Ridder Park Dr San Jose CA 95131-2432*

CERNAK, KEITH PATRICK, health care and financial consultant; b. Northampton, Mass., Mar. 17, 1954; s. Samuel and Geraldine (Dykstra) C.; m. Kristin Freedman, Sept. 10, 1983; children: Emily Samantha, Melanie Kristin. BA magna cum laude, U. Mass., 1976; MPH, U. Hawaii, 1980; MBA, UCLA, 1984. Healthcare researcher U. Hawaii, Honolulu, 1978; health planning cons. Guam Health Planning Agy., Agana, 1979; rsch. dir. Hawaii Dept. Health, Honolulu, 1980-81; mgmt. cons. Am. Med. Internat., Beverly Hills, Calif., 1982; v.p. Crocker Bank, L.A., 1984-86; v.p. fin. Weyerhaeuser, San Francisco, 1986-91; dir. health status consortium Group Health Cooperative Evergreen Med. Ctr. Providence Health System, Seattle, 1992—; health care cons.; nat. presenter in field. Author papers in field. Health Svc. scholar U. Hawaii, 1978; Award Nat. NOVA. Mem. UCLA Sch. Mgmt., Beta Gamma Sigma. Home: 24503 SE 43rd Pl Issaquah WA 98029-7542

CERNY, CHARLENE ANN, museum director; b. Jamaica, N.Y., Jan. 12, 1947; d. Albert Joseph and Charlotte Ann (Novy) Cerny; children: Elizabeth Brett Cerny-Chipman, Kathryn Rose Cerny-Chipman. BA, SUNY, Binghamton, 1969. Curator Latin-Am. folk art Mus. Internat. Folk Art, Santa Fe, 1972-84, mus. dir., 1984—; adv. bd. C.G. Jung Inst., Santa Fe, 1990—. Mem. Mayor's Commn. on Children and Youth, Santa Fe, 1990-93, adv. bd. Recipient Exemplary Performance award State of N.Mex., 1982, Internat. Ptnr. Among Mus. award; Smithsonian Instn. travel grantee, 1976; Florence Dibell Bartlett Meml. scholar, 1979, 91; Kellogg fellow, 1983. Mem. Am. Assn. Mus. Internat. Coun. Mus. (bd. dirs. 1991—, exec. bd. 1991-95), Am. Folklore Soc., Mountain-Plains Mus. Assn., N.Mex. Assn. Mus. (chair membership com. 1975-77). Office: Mus Internat Folk Art PO Box 2087 Santa Fe NM 87504-2087*

CERVANTEZ, GIL LAWRENCE, venture capital company executive; b. Concord, Calif., July 14, 1944; s. Val J. and Laura E. (Verdugua) C.; m. Pamela A. Richmond, Feb. 14, 1965; children: Jeffrey, Thomas. BS, U. Oreg., 1965; MBA, U. Calif., Berkeley, 1972. V.p. Gt. Western Nat. Bank, Portland, Oreg., 1971-74, Heller Internat., San Francisco, 1975-76; dir. Control Data, San Francisco, 1976-79; sr. v.p. Century Bank, San Francisco, 1979-85; dir. syndications Pacificorp Ventures, Portland, 1988-90; pres. Latipac Fin., San Francisco, 1985-90; pres. A, G & T Investments, Inc., Walnut Creek, Calif., 1990—, also bd. dirs.; CEO Terameth Industries, Inc., Walnut Creek, 1990—, also bd. dirs.; bd. dirs. Tyratech Industries. Lt. comdr. USN, 1965-71, Vietnam. Mem. Robert G. Sproul Assocs., U. Calif. Alumni Assn., Libr. Assocs., Smithsonian Assocs., Bear Backers, Commonwealth Club Calif. Republican. Roman Catholic. Avocations: skiing, fly fishing, flying. Home: 177 Ardith Ct Orinda CA 94563-4344 Office: A G & T Investments Inc PO Box 4689 Walnut Creek CA 94596-0689

CERVERA, DAVID RAY, television producer; b. Fullerton, Calif., Jan. 31, 1975; s. Freddy Ray and Josefina Dasinger. Student, U. Nev. Master controller U. Nev., Las Vegas, 1996—; rep. Time Warner Entertainment

Assoc., Glendale, Calif., 1996; engr. Kaleidoscope TV, Las Vegas, 1997; video editor HL Films, Las Vegas, 1998—; rep. Telex Comms., Mpls., 1998; assoc. prodr. City of Lakewood, Calif., 1991-94. Assoc. editor: MovieSoundPage.com., 1998—; prodr.: (music video) The Daniel Ray Band, 1993, (Woody award 1994); audio mixer: (program series) Academic Cafe, 1998; dir. (program series) You Oughta Know!, 1998; videographer: (program series) Fly on the Wall, 1998. Avocations: sound mixing, authoring web pages, arcade games, martial arts. Home: PO Box 35375 Las Vegas NV 89133-5375

CESEÑA, CARMEN, education educator, education administrator; b. Ensenada, Calif., July 16, 1947; d. Teodoro L. Ceseña and Guadalupe (Miranda) Carrillo; m. Rogelio A. Cardenas, Feb. 16, 1978; children: Maya-Ixel Ceseña-Cardenas. BA, San Jose State, 1969, standard elem. credential, 1972, MA, 1975; postgrad., Claremont Grad. Sch., 1986—. Cert. community coll. life credential. Lectr. U. Calif., Berkeley, 1975-86; lectr., supr. Sonoma State U., Rhonert Park, Calif., 1978-79; instr. Stanislaus State U., Turlock, Calif., 1982-84, Victor Valley Coll., Victorville, Calif., 1990—; mem. acad. senate Victor Valley Coll., Victorville, 1991—; dist. advisory mem. Victor Elem. Sch. Dist., Victorville, 1990—; chairperson dept. Victor Valley Coll. Gain Program, Victorville, 1991-93; site coun. chair Del Rey Elem. Sch., Victorville, 1990—. Founding mem. Calif. Assn. Bilingual Edn., San Jose, 1970, High Desert Latino Coalition, 1993; mem. Victor Valley Little League, 1988—; Kaleidoscope Leadership trainer Nat. Inst. for Leadership Devel., 1994; bd. dirs. A Better Way Shelter for Domestic Abuse, Victor Valley Coll., 1994-95. Recipient WHOO (We Honor Our Own) award; Kellogg fellow Univ. Austin, 1993-94. Mem. AAUW, Assn. for Study of Higher Edn., Nat. Assn. Pers. Adminstrs., Am. Assn. Women in Community and Jr. Colls., Pi Lambda Theta. Avocations: reading, gardening, traveling, antique collecting. Home: 15852 Inyo Ct Victorville CA 92392-3479 Office: Victor Valley Coll 18422 Bear Valley Rd Victorville CA 92392-5850

CESMAT, BRANDON, writer, educator; b. Escondido, Calif., Nov. 1, 1960; s. Wesley Davis and Donna Sheryl Cesmat; m. Andrea Susana Rodriguez, May 28, 1983; children: Jesse Dylan, Keaton Taylor, Rafael Benjamin. BA, San Diego State U., 1987, MFA, 1991. Columnist Times Advocate, Escondido, Calif., 1992-95; lectr. Calif. State U., San Marcos, 1995—; adj. instr. Palomar C.C., San Marcos, 1992—; poet tchr., bd. dirs. fair com. Border Voices, San Diego, 1993—; mem. spkr.'s bur. Calif. State U., 1996—. Football coach YMCA, Escondido, 1997. Career-path grantee Inter-Tech, Palomar Coll., 1997; recipient Tech. Utilization in Learning and Instrn. Platforms (TULIP) award Calif. State U., San Marcos, 1998. Mem. Calif. Poets in the Schs. Avocations: horseback riding, guitar, running. Office: Coll Arts and Scis Calif State U San Marcos CA 92096

CHABOT, GERRI LOUISE, counselor, nurse; b. Detroit, Oct. 2, 1949; d. Henry L. and Betty J. (Hale) Busuttil; m. Robert J. Chabot, Aug. 8, 1970 (div. Aug. 1975); 1 child, Michelle. AS in Arts and Nursing, L.A. Pierce Coll., 1980; B in Psychology cum laude, Calif. State U., Northridge, 1984; M in Counseling Psychology, Pepperdine U., 1986. RN, Calif. Chemotherapy cert., 1984, ONS cert., 1986, PICC cert., 1993, Medtronics Pain Mgmt. cert., 1995. Nurse Valley Presbyn. Hosp./Nursery, Van Nuys, Calif., 1978-80; staff nurse Med. Ctr. of Tarzana, Calif., 1980-82; staff nurse renal and surg. units Holy Cross Hosp., Mission Hills, Calif., 1982-84, staff nurse chem. dependency unit, 1984-85, nurse clin. level III oncology dept., 1986-91; clinician/case mgr. AIDS specific home healthcare. Critical Care Am., Van Nuys, 1991-94; owner, dir. Santa Clarita (Calif.) Counseling Ctr., 1989-96; infusion nurse Apria Healthcare, Chatsworth, Calif., 1995; infusion specialist Ctr. Infusions Homecare, Van Nuys, 1995—; cons. Holy Cross Med. Ctr., 1988; lectr. in field. Henry Mayo Hosp. Community Health Edn. Com. fellow, 1989—. Fellow Calif. Assn. Marriage and Family Therapists, Oncology Nursing Soc., Intravenous Nursing Soc. Roman Catholic. Avocations: swimming, travel. Home and Office: 27480 Country Glen Rd Agoura Hills CA 91301-3533

CHACON, MICHAEL ERNEST, computer networking specialist; b. L.A., Feb. 14, 1954; s. Ernest Richard and Teresa Marie (Venegas) C.; m. Virginia Marie; children: Mylan Graham, Aubrie Sarah, Christina Nabseth, Caitlyn Nabseth, Julia Anna. Student, Pierce Coll., 1972-74, Boise State U., 1980-82; BSBA, U. Phoenix, 1997. Sys. cons. MEC & Assocs., Riverside, Calif., 1986-91; regional mgr. Inacom Corp., Garden Grove, Calif., 1991-97; chief tech. officer Ascolta Tng. Co., Irvine, Calif., 1997—; cons. in field; lectr. Microsoft Corp., Bellvue, Wash., 1990-92; chief tng. officer Ascolta Tng. Co., Irvine, Calif.; bd. dirs. Info. Tech. Tng. Assn. Author: Understanding Networks, 1991; columnist Microsoft Cert. Profl. Mag.; contbr. articles to profl. jours. Named to Dean's List, Pierce Coll., 1973, 74. Mem. Lake Elsinore Sportsman Assn., L.A. World Affairs Coun., 3Com Adv. Coun. (pres. tech. adv. bd. 1986-92). Avocations: songwriting/composing, rocketry, shooting, photography. Office: Ascota Tng Co 2351 Mcgaw Ave Irvine CA 92614-5831

CHAE, YOON KWON, minister, educator; b. Seoul, Korea, Feb. 13, 1932; came to U.S., 1973; s. Sang H. and Bong Soo (Cho) Chae (Choi); m. Geon Min, Mar. 3, 1981 (dec.); m. Kook Ja Park, Dec. 4, 1982; 1 child, John Wooshik. BA, San Jose Bible Coll., 1960; MA, Lincoln Christian Sem., 1961; DD, Am. Bible Inst., 1968; ThD, Immanuel Bapt. Sem., 1976. Ordained to ministry Christian Ch., 1960. Pastor numerous Christian Chs., Korea and U.S., 1962—; pres., chancellor Korea Christian Coll., Seoul, 1965—; prof. San Jose Christian Coll., 1985—; bd. dirs. Geon Christian Children's Home, Seoul, 1966—, Korea Gospel Mission, San Jose, 1974—. Author: My Dear American Friends I, 1973, II, 1982, III, 1989, The Shattered Cross I, 1972, II, 1978, III, 1985, Yoon Kwon Chae Column, 1988, Sermons for 52 Weeks, 1987. 1st lt. Korean Army, 1953-56. Mem. Kiwanis (pres. Seoul 1983-84, gov. 1987-88). Republican. Home: 1043 Forest Knolls Dr San Jose CA 95129-3015 Office: San Jose Christian Coll 12th And Virginia San Jose CA 95112

CHAFFEE, JAMES ALBERT, protective services official; b. Balt., Aug. 14, 1952; s. John Dempster and Elizabeth May (Holden) C.; m. Virginia Rose Braun, Oct. 4, 1980; children: Andrew James, Thomas John, Elizabeth Mary. AA, Alan Hancock Coll., 1973; BA, Chapman Coll., 1980; MBA, St. Thomas Coll., 1986. Lic. EMT, L.A. County; lic. police officer, Minn. Police officer Minnetonka (Minn.) Police Dept., 1976-87, police supr., 1982-87; pub. safety dir. City of Chanhassen, Minn., 1987-90; dir. security Walt Disney Co., Burbank, Calif., 1990—; dir. S.W. Metro Drug Task Force, Chanhassen, 1988-90; adv. com. 1991 U.S. Open, Chaska, Minn., 1989-90. Founding mem. Chanhassen Rotary Club, 1987, v.p., 1990; pres. Emblem Sch. Site Coun., Saugus, Calif., 1992. With USAF, 1972-76. Mem. Chief Spl. Agts. Assn. (dir. 1991—), Am. Soc. for Indsl. Security, Community Police and Security Team. Republican. Roman Catholic. Avocations: golf, softball, skiing, fishing. Office: Walt Disney Co 500 S Buena Vista St Burbank CA 91521-0004

CHAFFEE, MAURICE AHLBORN, geologist; b. Wilkes-Barre, Pa., Jan. 10, 1937; s. William Galbraith and Sarah Hollenback (Ahlborn) C.; m. Annette Fern Eckdahl, Aug. 8, 1959; children: Bradley Alan, Kim Chaffee Reweti. Degree in geol. engring., Colo. Sch. Mines, 1959; MS, U. Ariz., 1964, PhD, 1967. Geologist N.J. Zinc Co., Austinville, Va., 1960-62; grad. student U. Ariz., Tucson, 1962-67; geologist U.S. Geol. Survey, Denver, 1967—. Editl. bd. Jour. Geochem. Exploration, 1975-94; contbr. articles to profl. jours. Capt. U.S. Army, 1959-64. Fellow Soc. Econ. Geologists (membership sec. 1982-87), Assn. Exploration Geochemists (v.p. 1986-88, pres. 1988-89). Presbyterian. Office: US Geol Survey Federal Ctr MS 973 Denver CO 80225-0046

CHAGALL, DAVID, journalist, author; b. Phila., Nov. 22, 1930; s. Harry and Ida (Coopersmith) C.; m. Juneau Joan Alsin, Nov. 15, 1957. Student, Swarthmore Center Coll., 1948-49; B.A., Pa. State U., 1952; postgrad., Sorbonne, U. Paris, 1953-54. Social caseworker State of Pa., Phila., 1955-57; sci. editor Jour. I.E.E., 1959-61; pub. relations staff A.E.I.-Hotpoint Ltd., London, 1961-62; mktg. research assoc. Chilton Co., Phila., 1962-63; mktg. research project dir. Haug Assos., Inc. (Roper Orgn.), Los Angeles, 1964-74; research cons. Haug Assos., 1976-79; investigative reporter for nat. mags., 1975—; host TV series The Last Hour, 1994—. Author: Diary of a Deaf Mute, 1960, The Century God Slept, 1963, The Spieler for the Holy Spirit, 1972, The New Kingmakers, 1981, The Sunshine Road, 1988, Surviving the Media Jungle, 1996; contbr.: Television Today, 1981, The Media and Morality, 1999; pub.: Inside Campaigning, 1983; contbr. Television Today, 1981, The Media and Morality, 1999, syndicated column, articles, revs., stories and poetry to mags., jours., newspapers; contbg. editor: TV Guide, L.A. Mag. Apptd. to Selective Svc. Bd., 1991; bd. dirs. Chosen Prophetic Ministries, 1991. Recipient U. Wis. Poetry prize, 1971; nominee Nat. Book award in fiction, 1972, Pulitzer prize in letters, 1973, Disting. Health Journalism award, 1978; Presdl. Achievement award, 1982; Carnegie Trust grantee, 1964. Home: PO Box 85 Agoura Hills CA 91376-0085

CHAI, WINBERG, political science educator; b. Shanghai, China, Oct. 16, 1932; came to U.S., 1951, naturalized, 1973; s. Ch'u and Mei-en (Tsao) C.; m. Carolyn Everett, Mar. 17, 1966 (dec. 1996); children: Maria May-lee, Jeffrey Tien-yu. Student, Hartwick Coll., 1951-53; BA, Wittenberg U., 1955, DHL, 1997; MA, New Sch. Social Rsch., 1958; PhD, NYU, 1968; DHL, Wittenberg U., 1987. Lectr. New Sch. Social Rsch., 1957-61; vis. asst. prof. Drew U., 1961-62; asst. prof. Fairleigh Dickinson U., 1962-65; asst. prof. U. Redlands, 1965-68, assoc. prof., 1969-73, chmn. dept., 1970-73; prof., chmn. Asian studies CCNY, 1973-79; disting. prof. polit. sci., v.p. acad. affairs, spl. asst. to pres. U. S.D., Vermillion, 1979-82; prof. polit. sci., dir. internat. programs U. Wyo., Laramie, 1988—; chmn. Third World Conf. Found., Inc., Chgo., 1982—; pres. Wang Yu-fa Found., Taiwan, 1989—. Author: (with Ch'u Chai) The Story of Chinese Philosophy, 1961, The Changing Society of China, 1962, rev. edit., 1969, The New Politics of Communist China, 1972, The Search for a New China, 1975; editor: Essential Works of Chinese Communism, 1969, (with James C. Hsiung) Asia in the U.S. Foreign Policy, 1981, (with James C. Hsiung) U.S. Asian Relations: The National Security Paradox, 1983, (with Carolyn Chai) Beyond China's Crisis, 1989, In Search of Peace in the Middle East, 1991, (with Cal Clark) Political Stability and Economic Growth, 1994, China Mainland and Taiwan, 1994, revised edit. 1996, Hong Kong Under China, 1998; co-translator: (with Ch'u Chai) A Treasury of Chinese Literature, 1965. Haynes Found. fellow, 1967, 68; Ford Found. humanities grantee, 1968, 69, Pacific Cultural Found. grantee, 1978, 86, NSF grantee, 1970, Hubert Eaton Meml. Fund grantee, 1972-73, Field Found. grantee, 1973, 75, Henry Luce Found. grantee, 1978, 80, S.D. Humanities Com. grantee, 1980, Pacific Culture Fund grantee, 1987, 90-91. Mem. Am. Assn. Chinese Studies (pres. 1978-80), AAAS, AAUP, Am. Polit. Sci. Assn., N.Y. Acad. Scis., Internat. Studies Assn., NAACP. Democrat. Home: 1071 Granito Dr Laramie WY 82072-5045 Office: PO Box 4098 Laramie WY 82071-4098

CHAIET, MARGARET SZEGO, artist, writer; b. N.Y.C., Dec. 6, 1916; d. Oscar and Rose (Gelbstein) Szego; m. Richard Vogt, Nov. 21, 1940 (dec. June 1951); 1 child, Douglas Bradley Vogt; m. Harold Chaiet, Mar. 29, 1959. Student, Sch. Indsl. Art, 1935-40, Pierce Coll., 1968. Author, pub. reference book: Register of U.S. Artists, 1968; exhibited in group show at Art of Today Gallery, N.Y.C. Mem., vol. Jewish Cmty. Ctrs. L.A. Recipient award for photographic excellence Dynachrome Nat. Color Transparency Competition, 1980's, Commendation, Mayor of City of L.A., 1991.

CHAKRABORTY, ARUP K., chemical engineering educator; b. Calcutta, India, Nov. 26, 1961; s. Ajit K. and Meena C.; m. Shanmila Chatterjee; 1 child, Meenakshi. BTech in Chem. Engring., Indian Inst. Tech., Kanpur, 1983; PhD in Chem. Engring., U. Del., 1988. Rsch. assoc. dept. chem. engring. and material sci. U. Minn., 1987-88; from asst. to assoc. prof. dept. chem. engring. U. Calif., Berkeley, 1988-97, prof. chem. engring., chemistry, 1997—; vis. prof. dept. chem. engring. MIT, 1996; Allan P. Colburn Meml. lectr. U. Del., 1993. Contbr. over 25 articles to sci. publs. Shell Young Faculty fellow, 1989-92, ICI fellow Royal Acad. Engring. (U.K.)., 1993-98. Mem. AIChE (Allan P. Colburn award 1996), Am. Chem. Soc., Am. Phys. Soc., Alpha Chi Sigma. Avocations: history of science, squash, professional sports. Office: U Calif Berkeley 201 Gilman Hall Berkeley CA 94720-1400

CHALK, EARL MILTON, retired art director; b. Deerlodge, Mont., Sept. 14, 1927; s. Forrest A. and Jeanette Curtis (Robinson) C.; m. Carole Estelle, Feb. 9, 1963 (div. 1974); children: Teri, Kevin, Quinn. BFA, U. Wash., 1953. Artist Facilities Boeing, Seattle, 1954-57; writer, artist Facilities Boeing, Renton, Wash., 1957-60; supr. mfg. Facilities Boeing, Seattle, 1960-56; sr. supr. planning Facilities Boeing, Auburn, Wash., 1965-71, art dir. mfg. engring., 1971-87; painter in oils, 1987—; co-mgr., owner Art Galary, 1967-74. Artist Puget Sound Group of North West Painters, Seattle, 1968-78, artist Puyallup, Wash., 1987—. 1st class petty officer USN, 1945-49. Recipient Rotary scholarship U. Wash., 1953. Mem. Grapha Techna. Avocations: bicycling, hiking, fishing, gardening, computers. Home and Office: 1803 7th Ave SE Puyallup WA 98372-4010

CHALLEM, JACK JOSEPH, health, advertising/public relations writer; b. Montreal, Quebec, Can., May 29, 1950; came to U.S., 1954; s. Alex and Sara Bella (Novack) C.; m. Renate Lewin, Sept. 30, 1977; 1 child, Evan G. BA, Northeastern Ill. U., 1972. Advt. mgr. J.R. Carlson Labs., Arlington Heights, Ill., 1973-78; editor-in-chief Physician's Life Mag., Evanston, Ill., 1978; graphics mgr. Eberline Instrument Corp., Santa Fe, 1979-81; sci. writer, media rels. specialist Los Alamos (N.Mex.) Nat. Lab., 1981-88; contbg. editor Let's Live Mag., L.A., 1978—; writer KVO Advt. & Pub. Rels., Portland, Oreg., 1988-94. Author: What Herbs Are All About, 1979, Vitamin C Updated, 1983, Getting the Most out of Your Vitamins and Minerals, 1993, Homocysteine: The "New" Cholestorol, 1996, The Health Benefits of Soy, 1996, The Natural Health Guide to Beating the Supergerms, 1997, All About Vitamins, 1998, All About Vitamin E, 1999, All About Carotenoids, 1999; contbr. Natural Health Mag., 1992—; editor: Avery FAQ book series, 1998—; editor, pub.: The Nutrition Reporter Newsletter, 1992—; contbr. articles to profl. jours. Home: 6782 SW 167th Pl Beaverton OR 97007-6310

CHALUPA, LEO M., neurobiologist, educator, science administrator; b. Possneck, Germany, Mar. 28, 1945; came to U.S., 1949; s. Michael J. and Stephania (Hnatiw) C.; m. Tanya Keis, July 30, 1966; children: Alexandra, Andrea. BA, Queens Coll., N.Y.C., 1966; PhD, CUNY, 1970. Postdoct. fellow Brain Rsch. Inst. UCLA, 1970-75; asst. prof. U. Calif., Davis, 1975-78, assoc. prof., 1979-82, prof., 1982—, dir. ctr. neurosci., 1996-98, chmn. neurobiology, physiology and behavior, 1998—; cons. NSF, Washington, 1987-89; grant reviewer NIH, Washington, 1988—; vis. scholar Cambridge (Eng.) U., 1978-79. Editor: Organization and Development of Retina, 1998, Jour. Cell and Developmental Biology, 1998; mem. editl. bd. Visual Neurosci., 1990-93, Acta Neurobiologiae, 1994—; contbr. over 150 articles to profl. jours. Guggenheim fellow Guggenheim Found., 1978, Internat. fellow NIH Fogarty Ctr., 1992, Japan Sci. fellow Japan Soc. Sci. Promotion, 1993; named exch. scientist Nat. Acad. Sci., 1973. Fellow AAAS; mem. Internat. Brain Rsch. Orgn., Soc. Neurosci., U. Club San Francisco, Sigma Xi. Office: U Calif Sect of Neurobiology Physiology and Behavior Davis CA 95616

CHAMBERLAIN, ISABEL CARMEN (ISA CHAMBERLAIN), environmental chemist; b. Buenos Aires; came to U.S., 1974; Degree in biochemistry, Tucuman (Argentina) U., 1974; MS in Analytical Chemistry, U. Wash., 1987. Biochemist Olympic Med. Labs., Bremerton, Wash., 1974-81; microbiologist Saudi Med. Svcs., Saudi Arabia, 1982-84; analytical chemist Puget Sound Naval Shipyard, Bremerton, 1987-88, EPA, Manchester, Wash., 1988—; instr. Pierce Coll., Tacoma, 1988; spkr. USA-Mex. Environ. Symposium, 1995; drinking water labs. cert. officer. Vol. speaker career day to schs. and colls., 1987—. Recipient regional exch. award EPA, Washington, 1995. Mem. Assn. Analytic Chemists Internat. (chmn. 1994, past chmn. 1995, edtl. bd. 1995). Avocations: travel, sailing, skiing, camping, aerobics. Office: EPA Region 10 7411 Beach Dr E Port Orchard WA 98366-8204

CHAMBERLAIN, OWEN, nuclear physicist; b. San Francisco, July 10, 1920; divorced 1978; 4 children; m. June Steingart, 1980 (dec.). AB (Cramer fellow), Dartmouth Coll., 1941; PhD, U. Chgo., 1949. Instr. physics U. Calif., Berkeley, 1948-50, asst. prof., 1950-54, assoc. prof., 1954-58, prof., 1958-89, prof. emeritus, 1989—; civilian physicist Manhattan Dist., Berkeley, Los Alamos, 1942-46. Recipient Nobel prize (with Emilio Segrè) for physics, for discovery anti-proton, 1959, The Berkeley citation U. Calif., 1989; Guggenheim fellow, 1957-58; Loeb lectr. at Harvard U., 1959. Fellow Am. Phys. Soc., Am. Acad. Arts and Scis.; mem. Nat. Acad. Scis., Berkeley Fellows. Office: U Calif Physics Dept 367 LeCont Hall Berkeley CA 94720*

CHAMBERLAIN, WILLIAM EDWIN, JR., management consultant; b. St. Louis, June 8, 1951; s. William Edwin Sr. and Grace (Salisbury) C. AA in Bus. Mgmt., Mesa (Ariz.) Community Coll., 1983; BBA, U. Phoenix, 1988. Tng. and human resources devel. specialist Motorola, Inc., Phoenix, 1979-87; pres., seminar speaker Chamberlain Cons. Svcs., Chino Valley, Ariz., 1987—. Curator, dir. ops. U.S. Wolf Refuge and Adoption Ctr. Mem. ASTD, Network for Profl. Devel. Avocations: wildlife preservation and management, hiking, backpacking, tennis, basketball, racquetball.

CHAMBERLIN, EUGENE KEITH, historian, educator; b. Gustine, Calif., Feb. 15, 1916; s. Charles Eugene and Anina Marguerite (Williams) C.; B.A. in History, U. Calif. at Berkeley, 1939, M.A., 1940, Ph.D., 1949; m. Margaret Rae Jackson, Sept. 1, 1940; children—Linda, Thomas, Rebecca, Adrienne (dec.), Eric. Tchr. Spanish, Latin, Lassen Union High Sch. and Jr. Coll., Susanville, Calif., 1941-43; tchr. history Elk Grove (Calif.) Joint Union High Sch., 1943-45; teaching asst. history U. Calif., Berkeley, 1946-48; instr. history Mont. State U., Missoula, 1948-51, asst. prof., 1951-54; asst. prof. to prof. San Diego City Coll., 1954-78; part time cab driver San Diego Yellow Cab Co., 1955-74, 79, 86; vis. prof. history Mont. State Coll., Bozeman, summer 1953, U. Calif. Extension, 1964-68, San Diego State Coll., 1965-68, others; instr., coordinator history lectures San Diego Community Colls.-TV, 1969-77; prof. history San Diego Miramar Coll., 1978-83, San Diego Mesa Coll., 1983-86, MiraCosta Coll., 1998; mem. adv. com. Quechan Crossing Master Plan Project, 1989-90; historian San Diego First Ch. Of The Brethren, 1954-98. Huntington Library-Rockefeller Found. grantee, 1952; Fulbright-Hays grantee, Peru, 1982; recipient merit award Congress of History San Diego County, 1978, Outstanding Educator award, San Diego City Coll., 1970, award for dedicated svc. to local history San Diego Hist. Soc., 1991, Ben Dixon award Congress History, San Diego and Imperial Counties, 1997. Mem. AAUP (various coms., nat. council 1967-70, pres. Calif. conf. 1968-70, acting exec. sec. 1970-72), San Diego County Congress of History (pres. 1976-77, newsletter editor 1977-78), Am. Hist. Assn. (life, Beveridge-Dunning com. 1982-84, chmn. 1984), Pacific Coast Council on Latin-Am. Studies, Cultural Assn. of the Californias, The Westerners (Calafia, S.D. chpts.), E Clampus Vitus Squibob Chpt. (historian 1970-96, emeritus historian and archivist 1996—, chpt. pres. 1972-73, ECV dir. proctor 1983-89, grand council mem. 1972-93, dir. T.R.A.S.H 1979-93, pres. 1983-84), Phi Alpha Theta (sec. U. Calif. Berkeley chpt. 1947-48, organizer and faculty adv., Mont. State U. chpt. 1948-54). Democrat. Mem. Ch. of the Brethren (del. 200th Annual Conf. 1986). Author numerous booklets on SW Am. history and numerous articles on Mexican NW to profl. jours. Home: 3033 Dale St San Diego CA 92104-4929

CHAMBERS, CAROLYN SILVA, communications company executive; b. Portland, Oreg., Sept. 15, 1931; d. Julio and Elizabeth (McDonnell) Silva; widowed; children: William, Scott, Elizabeth, Silva, Clark. BBA, U. Oreg. V.p., treas. Liberty Comm., Inc., Eugene, Oreg., 1960-83; pres. Chambers Comm. Corp., Eugene, 1983-95, chmn., 1996—; chmn., CEO, bd. dirs. Chambers Constrn. Co., 1986—; bd. dirs., dep. chair bd. Fed. Res. Bank, San Francisco, 1982-92; bd. dirs. Portland Gen. Corp.; bd. dirs. U.S. Bancorp. Mem. Sacred Heart Med. Found., 1980—, Sacred Heart Gov. Bd., 1987-92, Sacred Heart Health Svcs. Bd., 1993-95, PeaceHealth Bd., 1995—; mem. U. Oreg. Found., 1980—, pres., 1992-93; chair U. Oreg. Found., The Campaign for Oreg., 1988-89; pres., bd. dirs. Eugene Arts Found.; bd. dirs., treas., dir. search com. Eugene Symphony; mem. adv. bd. Eugene Hearing and Speech Ctr., Alton Baker Park Commn., Pleasant Hill Sch. Bd.; chmn., pres., treas. Civic Theatre, Very Little Theatre; negotiator, treas., bd. dirs., mem. thrift shop Jr. League of Oreg. Recipient Webfoot award U. Oreg., 1986, U. Oreg. Pres.'s medal, 1991, Disting. Svc. award, 1992, Pioneer award, 1983, Woman Who Made a Difference award Internat. Women's Forum, 1989, U. Oreg. Found. Disting. Alumni award, 1995, Tom McCall awrd Oreg. Assn. Broadcasters, 1995, Disting. Alumni award U. Oreg., 1995, Outstanding Philanthropist award Oreg. chpt. Nat. Soc. Fund Raising Execs., 1994. Mem. Nat. Cable TV Assn. (mem. fin. com., chmn. election and by-laws com., chmn. awards com., bd. dirs. 1987-89, Vanguard award for Leadership 1982), Pacific Northwest Cable Comm. Assn. (conv. chmn., pres.), Oreg. Cable TV Assn. (v.p., pres., chmn. edn. com., conv. chmn., Pres.'s award 1986), Calif. Cable TV Assn. (bd. dirs., conv. chmn., conv. panelist), Women in Cable (charter mem., treas., v.p., pres., recipient star of cable recognition), Wash. State Cable Comm. Assn., Idaho Cable TV Assn., Community Antenna TV Assn., Cable TV Pioneers, Eugene C. of C. (first citizen award, 1985). Home: PO Box 640 Pleasant Hill OR 97455-0640 Office: Chambers Comm Corp PO Box 7009 Eugene OR 97401-0009

CHAMBERS, CLYTIA MONTLLOR, public relations consultant; b. Rochester, N.Y., Oct. 23, 1922; d. Anthony and Marie (Bambace) Capraro; m. Joseph John Montllor, July 2, 1941 (div. 1958); children: Michele, Thomas, Clytia; m. Robert Chambers, May 28, 1965. BA, Barnard Coll., N.Y.C., 1942; Licence en droit, Faculte de Droit, U. Lyon, France, 1948; MA, Howard U., Washington, 1958. Assoc. dir. dept. rsch. Coun. for Fin. Aid to Edn., N.Y.C., 1958-60; asst. to v.p. indsl. rels. Sinclair Oil Corp., N.Y.C., 1961-65; writer pub. rels. dept. Am. Oil Co., Chgo., 1965-67; dir. editorial svcs., v.p. Hill & Knowlton Inc., N.Y.C., 1967-77; sr. v.p., dir. spl. svcs. Hill & Knowlton Inc., L.A., 1977-90, sr. cons., 1990—; cons. and trustee Childen's Inst. Internat., L.A., 1988-93. Co-author: The News Twisters, 1971; editor: Critical Issues in Public Relations, 1975. Mem. Calif. Rare Fruit Growers (editor Fruit Gardener 1979—). E-mail: clytia@112358.com. Home: 11439 Laurelcrest Dr Studio City CA 91604-3872

CHAMBERS, HENRY GEORGE, orthopedic surgeon; b. Portsmouth, Va., June 22, 1956; s. Walter Charles and Teresa Frances (Fernandez) C.; m. Jill Annette Swanson, June 10, 1978; children: Sean Michael, Reid Christopher. BA summa cum laude in Biochemistry, U. Colo., 1978; MD, Tulane U. Sch. Medicine, 1982. Diplomate Am. Bd. Orthopaedic Surgery. Commd. 2d lt. U.S. Army, 1978, advanced through grades to maj., 1988; intern Fitzsimmons Army Med. Ctr., Aurora, Colo., 1982-83; orthopaedic surgery resident Brooke Army Med. Ctr., Ft. Sam Houston, Tex., 1983-87, chief resident, 1986-87, staff orthopaedic surgeon to asst. residency program dir., 1987-89, asst. chief surgeon orthopaedic surgery svc., 1990-92; staff orthopaedic surgeon DeWitt Army Hosp., Ft. Belvoir, Va., 1987; pediatric orthopaedic fellow San Diego Children's Hosp., 1989-90; asst. prof. surgery Uniformed Svcs. U. Health Scis., Bethesda, Md., 1987—; asst. program dir. Brooke Army Med. Ctr. Orthopaedic Surgery, 1987-92; asst. prof. U. Calif.-San Diego Med. Ctr., 1989—; pvt. practice San Diego, 1992—; chmn. dept. orthopedic surgery San Diego Children's Hosp., 1997—; adj. prof. natural scis. Incarnate Word Coll., San Antonio, 1986—. Co-author: Long Distance Runner's Guide to Training, 1983; contbr. various articles to profl. jours. Physician St. Vincent de Paul Clinic for Homeless, San Diego, 1989—; v.p. United Cerebral Palsy. Recipient Comdrs. award for oustanding rsch. Brooke Army Med. Ctr., 1987. Fellow Acad. Cerebral Palsy Devel. Medicine (bd. dirs.), Pediatric Orthopedic Soc. N.Am., Am. Acad. Pediatrics, Acad. Orthopedic Soc., Orthopedic Rsch. Soc., Am. Acad. Orthopedic Surgeons, Physicians for Social Responsibility, Physicians Coun. for Responsible Medicine, We. Orthopedic Soc., World Wildlife Fedn., Wilderness Soc., Union Concerned Scientists, Friends of Earth, Handgun Control, Phi Beta Kappa. Democrat. Unitarian. Avocations: bicycling, weight lifting, golf, tennis. Home: 5458 Sandburg Ave San Diego CA 92122-4128

CHAMBERS, JOHN T., computer company executive; m. Elaine Chambers; 2 children. BS, BA, W.Va. U., JD; MBA, Ind. U. Sr. v.p. worldwide ops. Cisco Sys., Inc., San Jose, Calif., 1991-94, exec. v.p., 1994-95, pres., CEO, 1995—; bd. dirs. Clarify, Inc., San Jose, Arbor Software, Sunnyvale, Calif. Office: Cisco Sys Inc 170 W Tasman Dr San Jose CA 95134*

CHAMBERS, LOIS IRENE, insurance automation consultant; b. Omaha, Nov. 24, 1935; d. Edward J. and Evelyn B. (Davidson) Morrison; m. Peter A. Mscichowski, Aug. 16, 1952 (div. 1980); 1 child, Peter Edward; m. Frederick G. Chambers, Apr. 17, 1981. Clk. Gross-Wilson Ins. Agy., Portland, Oreg., 1955-57; sec., bookkeeper Reed-Paulsen Ins. Agy., Portland, 1957-58; office mgr., asst. sec., agt. Don Biggs & Assocs., Vancouver, Wash., 1958-88, v.p. ops., 1988-89, automation mgr., 1989-91, mktg. mgr., 1991-94; automation cons. Chambers & Assocs., Tualatin, Oreg., 1985—; system mgr. Contractors Ins. Svcs., Inc., 1997—; chmn. adv. com. Clark Community

Coll., Vancouver, 1985-93, adv. com., 1993-94. Mem. citizens com. task force City of Vancouver, 1976 78, mem. Block Grant rev. task force, 1978—. Mem. Ins. Women of S.W. Wash. (pres. 1978, Ins. Woman of Yr. 1979), Nat. Assn. Ins. Women, Nat. Users Agena Systems (charter; pres. 1987-89), Soroptimist Internat. (Vancouver)(pres. 1978-79, Soroptimist of the Year 1979-80). Democrat. Roman Catholic. Office: Chambers & Assocs 8770 SW Umatilla St Tualatin OR 97062-6340

CHAMBERS, MILTON WARREN, architect; b. L.A., Aug. 5, 1928; s. Joe S. and Barbara N. (Harris) C.; m. Elizabeth M. Smith, Nov. 27, 1949; children: Mark, Michael, Daniel, Matthew. Student, Coll. of Sequoias, 1948-49, Harvard U., 1990. Lic. architect, Calif., Nev., Colo., Hawaii, Mont.; cert. Nat. Coun. Archtl. Registration Bds. Apprentice architect Kastner & Kastner Architects, Visalia, Calif., 1950-57; project architect Wurster, Bernardi & Emmons, Architects, San Francisco, 1958-63, Claude Oakland, Architect, San Francisco, 1964-65; chief architect Bank of Am., San Francisco, 1965-68; pres., owner Milton W. Chambers, Architect, San Rafael, Calif., 1969-82, The Chambers Group, Architects, Rancho Mirage, Calif., 1983—. Architect, designer St. Margaret's Episcopal Church, 1988. Foreman Marin County Grand Jury, San Rafael, 1976; mem. Archtl. Design Rev. Bd., Rancho Mirage, 1986—; trustee Marywood Sch., Rancho Mirage, 1990—. Cpl. U.S. Army, 1946-48, PTO, 50-51. Mem. AIA (pres. Calif. Desert chpt. 1986-87, 96&, dir. Calif. coun. 1989-90, 96—), Rotary Internat., Terra Linda Rotary Club (pres. 1975-76, dist. gov. 1993-94), Rancho Mirage Rotary Club (pres. 1986-87). Republican. Episcopalian. Avocations: playing the banjo and guitar. Office: The Chambers Group 44267 Monterey Ave Ste B Palm Desert CA 92260-2710

CHAMBERS, THOMAS FRANCIS, classical vocalist, financial consultant; b. Dearborn, Mich., July 1, 1958; s. Gene Chambers and Frances Rose (Krall) Fielden; m. Dawn JoAnn Chaney Kalavity, July 31, 1982 (div. 1990); m. Sheila Dean Wormer, Jan. 4, 1992; 1 child, Natalie Anne Chambers. Grad. high sch., Snohomish, Wash., 1976; ChFC, Am. Coll., 1988. Internat. opera singer, 1978—; pres. Chambers & Assocs., Edmonds, Wash., 1985—, La Stella, Inc., Edmonds, Wash., 1989—; mng. dir. La Stella Found., Edmonds, Wash., 1990—; prodr. Can Bel to Singers, Snohomish, 1976-82; gen mgr. World Stage, Seattle, 1978-80; exec. prodr. La Stella Prodns., Seattle, 1990—; assoc. prodr. La Stella Duo, N.Y.C., 1992—. Author: (screenplays) And She Sings Good, Too, 1990, Be My Love, 1997; prodr. (opera recording) Impresario, Bastien & Bastienne, 1990, (stage prodn.) Salute to Mario Lanza, 1994 (Pillin award 1997). Cmty. Outreach performer Seattle Opera Guild, 1976—; music dir. St. Thomas Moore Ch., Lynnwood, Wash., 1984—, St. Mary's Ch., Monroe, Wash., 1992-95; entertainer for Muscular Distrophy, Seattle, 1995; prodr., dir. Viva Roma fundraiser, 1995-96. Recipient Everett (Wash.) Opera sholar, 1976, Key to the City award, Fondi Music Festival, Italy, 1990; named Best Male Vocalist, Hollywood (Calif.) Pillin Awards, 1997. Mem. KC (adv. 1987—), Seattle Jaycees (cmty. svc. 1986, v.p. 1986-87), Feed the Children (chmn. 1986, cmty. svc. 1986), Episcopal Actor's Guild. Avocations: fishing, travelling, sailing, collecting hist. opera recordings, karate.

CHAMPAGNE, DUANE WILLARD, sociology educator; b. Belcourt, N.D., May 18, 1951; children: Talya, Gabe, Demelza. BA in Math., N.D. State U., 1973, MA in Sociology, 1975; PhD in Sociology, Harvard U., 1982. Teaching fellow Harvard U., Cambridge, Mass., 1981-82, rsch. fellow, 1982-83; asst. prof. U. Wis., Milw., 1983-84; asst. prof. UCLA, 1984-91, assoc. prof., 1991-97, prof., 1997—; publs. dir. Am. Indian Studies Ctr., UCLA, 1986-87, assoc. dir., 1990, acting dir., 1991, dir., 1991—; adminstrv. co-head interdepartmental program for Am. Indian studies UCLA, 1992-93; mem. grad. rsch. fellowship panel NSF, 1990-92, minority fellowship com. ASA; cons. Energy Resources Co., 1982, No. Cheyenne Tribe, 1983, Realis Pictures, Inc., 1989-90, Sta. KCET-TV, L.A., 1990, 92, Salem Press, 1992, Book Prodns. Systems, 1993, Readers Digest, 1993, Rattlesnake Prodns., 1993. Author: American Indian Societies, 1989, Social Order and Political Change, 1992; editor: Native North American Almanac, 1994, Chronology of Native North American, 1994, Native American of the peoples Portrait, 1994; co-author: A Second Century of Dishonor: Federal Inequities and California Tribes, 1996, Service Delivery for Native American Children in Los Angeles County, 1996; editor: Native Am. Studies Assn. Newsletter, 1991-92; co-editor: Native American Activism: Alcatraz to the Longest Walk, 1997, Contemporary Native American Cultural Issues, 1999; book rev. editor Am. Indian Culture and Rsch. Jour., 1984-86, editor, 1986—; contbr. numerous articles to profl. jours. Mem. city of L.A. Cmty. Action Bd., 1993, L.A. County/City Am. Indian Commn., 1992—, chair, 1993, 95-97, v. chair, 1997—; mem. subcom. for cultural and econ. devel. L.A. City/County Native Am. Commn., 1992-93; bd. dirs. Ctr. for Improvement of Child Caring, 1993—, Greater L.A. Am. Indian Culture Ctr., Inc., 1993, Incorporator, 1993; bd. trustees Southwest Mus., 1994-97, Nat. Mus. Am. Indian, 1998—; Master of Coll. of Humanities and Social Sci., N.D. State U., 1996. Recipient L.A. Sr. Health Peer Counseling Cmty. Vol. Cert. of Recognition, 1996; grantee Rockefeller Found., 1982-83, U. Wis. Grad Sch. Rsch. Com., 1984-85, Wis. Dept. Edn., 1984-85, 87-88, 88-89, NSF, 1985-88, 88-89), Nat. Endowment for Arts, 1987-88, 91-92, NRC, 1988-89, Nat. Sci. Coun., 1989-90, John D. and Catherine T. MacArthur Found., 1990-91, Hayes Found., 1990-91, 92-93, Calif. Coun. for Humanities, 1991-92, Ford Found., 1990-92, Gale Rsch. Inc., 1991-93, 93-95, Rockwell Corp., 1991-93, GTE, 1992-93, Kellog Found., 1997—, Pequot Mus. and Rsch. Ctr., 1997-98, So. Calif. Indian Ctr., 1998; Fund for the Improvement of Post Secondary Edn., 1998—; Am. Indian scholar, 1973-75, 80-82, Minority fellow Am. Sociol. Assn., 1975-78, RIAS Seminar fellow, 1976-77; Rockefeller Postdoctoral fellow, 1982-83, NSF fellow, 1985-88, Postdoctoral fellow Ford Found., 1988-89. Avocations: chess, basketball. Home: 28012 Ridgecove Ct N Rancho Palos CA 90275-3377 Office: UCLA Am Indian Studies Ctr PO Box 951548 Los Angeles CA 90095-1548

CHAMPLIN, CHARLES DAVENPORT, television host, book critic, writer; b. Hammondsport, N.Y., Mar. 23, 1926; s. Francis Malburn and Katherine Marietta (Masson) C.; m. Margaret Frances Derby, Sept. 11, 1948; children: Charles Jr., Katherine, John, Judith, Susan, Nancy. AB cum laude, Harvard U., 1947. Reporter Life mag., N.Y.C., 1948-49; corr. Life mag., Chgo., 1949-52, asst. editor, 1954-59; corr. Denver, 1952-54, Time mag., L.A., 1959-62, London, 1962-65; arts editor, columnist L.A. Times, 1965-91, prin. film critic, 1967-80, book critic, 1981-96; host-commentator Ste. KCET-TV, L.A., ETV Network, Z Channel Cable TV, Bravo Channel, 1969-96; adj. prof. Loyola-Marymount U., 1969-86; adj. prof. U. So. Calif., 1986-96. Author: (with C. Sava) How to Swim Well, 1960, The Flicks, 1977, The Movies Grow Up, 1981, Back There Where the Past Was, 1989, George Lucas: The Creative Impulse, 1992, enlarged, 1997, John Frankenheimer: A Conversation, 1995, Woody Allen at Work, 1995, Hollywood's Revolutionary Decade, 1998; contbr. numerous articles to mags. and publs. Bd. dirs. Am. Cinemateque; trustee L.A. Film Tchrs. Assn. With U.S. Army, 1944-46, ETO. Decorated Purple Heart; recipient Order Arts and Letters, France, 1977. Mem. PEN, Nat. Book Critics Cir., L.A. Film Critics Assn., Authors Guild, Overseas Press Club. Democrat. Home: 2169 Linda Flora Dr Los Angeles CA 90077-1408

CHAN, DANNY K.W., construction inspector; b. South Vietnam, May 27, 1952; came to U.S., 1984; s. Fung and Thi Tan (Lam) C.; m. Lua Chuen Wang; 1 child, Virginia. BSCE, Chu Hai Coll., Hong Kong. Lic. gen. bldg. and engring. contractor, Calif. Constrn. insp. Acon Builders Constrn. Co., Campbell, Calif. Mem. U.S. C. of C. Office: Acon Builders Constrn Co 1506 Dell Ave Ste D Campbell CA 95008-6911

CHAN, FRED S.L., executive. Chmn., pres., CEO ESS Tech, Fremont, Calif. Office: ESS Tech 48401 Fremont Blvd Fremont CA 94538-6581*

CHAN, MICHAEL CHIU-HON, chiropractor; b. Hong Kong, Aug. 31, 1961; came to U.S., 1979; s. Fuk Yum and Chun Wai (Ma) C. D of Chiropractic, Western States Chiropractic Coll., 1985; fellow, Internat. Acad. Clin. Acupuncture, 1986. Assoc. doctor Widoff Chiropractic Clinic, [illegible] North Ranch Chiropractic Assoc., Scottsdale, Ariz., 1988-91; pvt. practice Phoenix, 1991—; founder Horizon Info. Group, 1996; dir. Neighborhood Chiropractic, Phoenix, 1988-89. Contbr. articles to profl. jours. Mem. Am. Chiropractic Assoc., Internat. Platform Assn., Coun. on Diagnostic Imaging, Paradise Valley Toastmaster Club. Avocations: golf, reading, traveling, computer. Office: 3302 W Thomas Rd # 3 Phoenix AZ 85017-5601

CHAN, PAUL D., executive editor; b. Kailua, Hawaii, Oct. 26, 1964; s. Herman S. and Corinne (Louie) C.; m. Camille Marie de Tonnancour, Oct. 7, 1995; 1 child, Winston Paul. BS, Champman U., 1986; MD, Chgo. Med. Sch., 1990. Exec. editor Current Clin. Strategies Publ., Laguna Hills, Calif., 1989—. Author: Practice Parameters in Medicine, 1996, Current Clinical Strategies, Medicine, 1997, Current Clinical Strategies, Pediatrics, 1997; editor Jour. of Primary Care On-line, 1997. Office: Current Clin Strategies Pub 27071 Cabot Rd Ste 126 Laguna Hills CA 92653-7011

CHAN, PETER WING KWONG, pharmacist; b. L.A., Feb. 3, 1949; s. Sherwin T.S. and Shirley W. (Lee) C.; children: Kristina Dionne, Kelly Alison, David Shoichi. BS, U. So. Calif., 1970, D in Pharmacy, 1974. Lic. pharmacist, Calif. Clin. instr. U. So. Calif., 1974-76; staff clin. pharmacist Cedars-Sinai Med. Ctr., L.A., 1974-76; 1st clin. pharmacist in ophthalmology Alcon Labs., Inc., Ft. Worth, 1977—, formerly in Phila. monitoring patient drug therapy, teaching residents, nurses, pharmacy students, then assigned to Tumu Tumu Hosp., Karatina, Kenya, also lectr. clin. ocular pharmacology tng. course, Nairobi, Cairo, Athens, formerly dist. sales mgr. Alcon/BP, ophthal. products div. Alcon Labs., Inc., Denver; v.p., gen. mgr. Optikem Internat., Sereine Products Div., Optacryl, Inc., Denver, 1980-91; product mgr. hosp. pharmacy products Am. McGaw div. Am. Hosp. Supply Corp., 1981-83; internat. market mgr. IOLAB subs. Johnson & Johnson, 1983-86, dir. new bus. devel. Iolab Pharms., 1986-87, dir. Internat. Mktg., 1987-89, dir. new products mktg., 1989; bus. and mktg. strategies cons. to pharm. and med. device cos. Chan & Assocs., Northridge, Calif., 1989-98; regional mng. dir. Pacific Rim, Leiner Health Products, Inc., Carson, Calif., 1998—; ptnr., chmn., CEO PreFree Techs., Inc., 1992-96; med. dir., Clin Profl. Affairs, Nexstar Pharms., Inc., Boulder, 1996-97; ptnr. Vitamin Specialties Corp., 1993-95, JSP Ptnrs., Ltd., 1992—; med. dir., clin. and profl. affairs, Nexstar Pharm. Inc., Boulder, Colo.; regional Mang Dir. Pacific Aim Leiner Health Products, 1998—; bd, dirs. SUDCO Internat., L.A. Del. Am. Pharm. Assn. House of Dels., 1976-78, Calif. Youth Theatre at Paramount Studios, Hollywood 1986-87, 91—; bd. councillors U. So. Calif. Sch. Pharmacy, 1995—. Recipient Hollywood-Wilshire Pharm. Assn. spl. award for outstanding svc., 1974. Mem. Chinese Am. Pharm. Assn., Am. Pharm. Assn., Calif. Pharm. Assn., Hollywood-Wilshire Pharm. Assn. (bd. dirs. 1972-76), Am. Soc. Hosp. Pharmacists, Am. Pharm. Assn. Acad. of Pharmacy Practice, U. So. Calif. Assocs. (life), U. So. Calif. Gen. Alumni Assn., U. So. Calif. (steering com. lifescis. info. networking coun.), Granada Hills H.S. Highlanders Booster Club (bd. dirs. 1991, 92, 93, chmn.-Project 2000), QSAD Centurions, U. So. Calif. Lifetime Assocs., Gamma Epsilon Omega Alumni Assn. (bd. dirs.), Phi Delta Chi, NRA (life), Golden Eagle, Calif. Rifle and Pistol Assn. (life mem.). Republican. Home: 49 Bridgeport St Dana Point CA 92629-3242 Office: Leiner Health Products Inc 901 E 233rd St Carson CA 90745-6204

CHAN, THOMAS TAK-WAH, lawyer; b. Kowloon, Hong Kong, June 5, 1950. BA magna cum laude, U. Wis., Whitewater, 1973; JD, U. Wis., 1979. Bar: Wis. 1979, U.S. Dist. Ct. (ea. dist.) Wis. 1979, Minn. 1983, Calif. 1987. Judicial intern Wis. Supreme Ct., 1978; atty. Wausau (Wis.) Ins., 1979-82; staff atty. CPT Corp., Eden Prairie, Minn., 1982-84; gen. counsel Lee Data Corp., Eden Prairie, 1984-85; dep. gen. counsel Ashton-Tate Corp., Torrance, Calif., 1985-87; pres. Chan Law Group LC, L.A., 1989—; mem. adv. bd. SBA Export Devel. Ctr., 1992—; founder Bus. Software Alliance, Washington, 1987; U.S. trade rep., mem. adv. com. industry sector U.S. Dept. Commerce, 1988-91; founder Asian Pacific Am. Coord. Com., 1996. Mem. Asian Pacific Am. Bar Assn. (founder, dir. 1998—), Minn. Bar Assn. (lectr. computer law com. 1985), Wis. Bar Assn., Calif. Bar Assn. (lectr. 1988) Computer Law Assn., So. Calif. Chinese Lawyers Assn. (gov. 1990-92) Export Mgrs. Assn. So. Calif. (dir. 1990-92), Cause (dir. 1994-97, chmn. 1995-96), Phi Kappa Phi. Avocations: skiing, hiking. Office: Chan Law Group 911 Wilshire Blvd Ste 2288 Los Angeles CA 90017-3451

CHANCE, KENNETH DONALD, engineer; b. Denver, July 27, 1948; s. John Jefferson and Evelyn Pauline (Jacobs) C. AA, Red Rocks Coll., Golden, Colo., 1982. Stationery operating engr. EG&G Rocky Flats, Golden, 1980—.

CHANDLER, ALLEN, food products executive; b. 1942. With Northwest Wholesale, Wenatchee, Wash., 1964-68; with No. Fruit Co., Wenatchee, Wash., 1968—, now v.p. Office: Northern Fruit Co PO Box 1986 Wenatchee WA 98807*

CHANDLER, BRUCE FREDERICK, internist; b. Bohemia, Pa., Mar. 26, 1926; s. Frederick Arthur and Minnie Flora (Burkhardt) C.; m. Janice Evelyn Piper, Aug. 14, 1954; children: Barbara, Betty, Karen, Paul, June. Student, Pa. State U., 1942-44; MD, Temple U., 1948. Diplomate Am. Bd. Internal Medicine, Am. Bd. Pulmonary Disease. Commd. med. officer U.S. Army, 1948, advanced through grades to col., 1967; intern Temple U. Hosp., Phila., 1948-49; chief psychiatry 7th Field Hosp., Trieste, Italy, 1950; resident Walter Reed Gen. Hosp., Washington, 1949-53; battalion surgeon 2d Div. Artillery, Korea, 1953-54; chief renal dialysis unit 45th Evacuation Hosp. and Tokyo Army Hosp., Korea, Japan, 1954-55; various assignments Walter Reed Gen. Hosp., Fitzsimons Gen. Hosp., Letterman Gen. Hosp., 1955-70; comdg. officer 45th Field Hosp., Vicenza, Italy, 1958-62; pvt. practice internist Ridgecrest (Calif.) Med. Clinic, 1970-76; chief med. svc. and out-patients VA Hosps., Walla Walla, Spokane, Wash., 1976-82; med. cons. Social Security Adminstrn., Spokane, Wash., 1983-87; ret., 1987; lectr. in field. Panel mem. TV shows, 1964-70; contbr. articles to profl. jours. Decorated Legion of Merit. Fellow ACP, Am. Coll. Chest Physicians; mem. AMA, Am. Thoracic Soc., N.Y. Acad. Scis., So. European Task Force U.S. Army Med. Dental Soc. (pres., founder 1958-62). Republican. Methodist. Avocations: photography, travel, fishing, collecting books (especially by Jules Verne and Agatha Christie). Home: 6496 N Callisch Ave Fresno CA 93710-3902

CHANDLER, KAREN REGINA, career guidance specialist; b. Billings, Mont., Nov. 10, 1937; d. James Daniel Romine and Regina (Graham) Middleton; m. Dave Chandler, June 28, 1959; children: Dan, Lance, Trina. BS in Social Sci., Mont. State U., 1959; cert. summa cum laude, Seattle U., 1982. Employment specialist Magna & Assocs. Vocat. Rehab., Federal Way, Wash., 1983-84; instr., employment specialist Pvt. Industry Coun., Auburn, Wash., 1985; career guidance specialist Kent (Wash.) Pub. Schs., 1986—. Chmn. LWV, Kent, 1978. Mem. Wash. Career specialist Assn. (legis. chmn. 1986—, founder), Wash. Vocat. Assn. (sec. 1993-94, Occupational Info. Specialist award 1993), Wash. State Guidance Task Force, Wash. Vocat. Assn. Guidance (sec. 1993-94, pres.-elect 1994-95, pres. 1995—), Wash. Guidance & Counseling Plan (mem. writing team), W.Va. Guidance Assn. (pres. 1995-96). Democrat. Presbyterian. Avocations: reading, horseback riding, gourmet cooking, collecting antiques. Home: 13306 12th Ave E Tacoma WA 98445-3559 Office: Kent Pub Schs 12430 SE 208th St Kent WA 98031-2231

CHANDLER, KRIS, computer consultant, educator; b. Cleveland Heights, Ohio, June 26, 1948; d. Gerhard A. and Hanna R. (Rittmeyer) Hoffmann; children: Karen, Heidi. BSBA with honors and spl. distinction U. So. Colo., 1984, postgrad., 1984-85; MBA, U. Ark., 1987; PhD in C.C. Adminstrn. Colo. State U, 1993. Owner, mgr. V&W Fgn. Car Svc., Canon City, Colo., 1970-80; prin. The Chandlers, Computer Cons., Pueblo, Colo., 1982-88; ptnr. Jak Rabbit Software, 1989—; faculty Pikes Peak Community Coll., chair computer info. systems dept., U. So. Colo., also mgr. Sch. Bus. microcomputer lab. Bd. dirs. Canon City Community Svc. Ctr., 1978-80, Canon City chpt. ARC, 1978-81. Mem. Assn. for Computing Machinery, Data Processing Mgmt. Assn. (advisor student chpt. Pikes Peak Community Coll. 1989—), U. So. Colo. Honors Soc. (pres.), U. So. Colo. Grad. Assn. (founder), Alpha Chi, Sigma Iota Epsilon. Home and Office: 401 S Neilson Ave Pueblo CO 81001-4238

CHANDLER, LOIS JEANNE, religious studies educator; b. Detroit, Mar. 15, 1919; d. Forrest Arlo and Mable Cicelia (Alexander) Aseltine; m. Ward B. Chandler, Aug. 20, 1954; children: Ward Daniel, Timothy Franklin. Grad., Moody Bible Inst., Chgo., 1943. Assoc. editor Shepherd's Staff Mag., Witness Press, Pasadena, Canyon Country, Calif., 1960-81; regional dir. Women's Aglow Orgn., Lynnwood, Wash., 1977-78, v.p. fin., nat. bd., 1978-80; pastor's wife, Bible tchr., spkr. women's groups Little Brown Ch., Canyon Country, 1973—. Author: Treasures to Teach and Pearls to Preach, 1996; contbr. monthly column to Shepherd's Staff, 1964-80. Republican. Office: Witness Press Inc PO Box 1277 Canyon Country CA 91386-1277

CHANDLER, MARSHA, academic administrator, professor. BA, CCNY, 1965; PhD, UNC Chapel Hill, 1972. Prof. political econ. Univ. Toronto, 1977—, Dean Arts and Sci., 1990-97; vis. scholar Harvard Univ., Boston, MA, 1995-96. Co-author: Trade and Transmissions, 1990, The Political Economy of Business Bailouts, 2 vols., 1986, The Politics of Canadian Public Policy, 1983, Public Policy and Provincial Politics, 1979, Adjusting to Trade: A Comparative Perspective, 1988; contbr. articles to profl. jours. Fellow, Royal Soc. of Canada, mem., Dept. of Political Sci., Faculty of Law, bd. dirs. San Diego Opera, Mingei Mus. of Internatl. Folk Art, UCSD Found. Bd. and the Charter 100, adv. com. on Fed. Judicial Appts., bd. of Canadian Inst. for Adv. Rsch.; trustee, Art Gall. of Ontario, Mt. SInai Hosp., Huntsman Marine Sci. Ctr., Ontario Lightwave, Laser Rsch. Ctr. Office: U Calif 9500 Gilman Dr La Jolla CA 92093-5003

CHANDLER, VANESSA ALISON YELVINGTON, lawyer; b. Daytona Beach, Fla., Mar. 6, 1966; d. Ralph Oscar Jr. and Marilyn Joanne (Van Blaricom) Yelvington; m. Mark Joseph Chandler, Sept. 26, 1981 (div. Sept. 1985); children: Mari Antoinette, Parker Shane. AA in Comms. with high honors, Daytona Beach C.C., 1986; BS in Maths., Stetson U., 1988; JD, U. Va., 1997. Bar: Va. 1997. Tchr. Flagler Palm Coast H.S., Bunnell, Fla., 1990-92, Deland (Fla.) H.S., 1992-94; atty. Vinson & Elkins, Washington, 1997—. Mem. Va. State Bar Assn., Va. Women Attys. Assn., Va. Trial Lawyers Assn. Avocations: powerlifting, racquetball, reading. Fax: (202) 639-6604. E-mail: shedvl1@aol.com; vchandler@velaw.com. Home: 7121 Old Dominion Dr Mc Lean VA 22101-2703 Office: Vinson & Elkins 1455 Pennsylvania Ave NW Fl 7 Washington DC 20004-1013

CHANDRAMOULI, RAMAMURTI, electrical engineer; b. Sholinghur, Madras, India, Oct. 2, 1947; s. Ramamurti and Rajalakshmi (Ramamurti) Krishnamurti; m. Ranjani, Dec. 4, 1980; children: Suhasini, Akila. BSc, Mysore U., 1965, BE, 1970, MEE, Pratt Inst., 1972; PhD, Oreg. State U., 1978. Instr., Oreg. State U., Corvallis, 1978; sr. engr. R & D group, tech. staff spacecraft datasystems sect. Jet Propulsion Lab., Pasadena, Calif., 1978-81; staff engr., design automation group Am. Microsystems Inc., Santa Clara, Calif., 1982-83; staff software engr. corp. computer-aided design Intel, Santa Clara, 1983-86; project leader computer-aided design Sun Microsystems, Mountain View, Calif., 1986-93; tech. mktg. engr. Mentor Graphics, San Jose, Calif., 1993-95; dir. Bist Products Logicvision, San Jose, 1995-98; product line mgr. test products Synopsys, Mountain View, Calif., 1998—; adj. lectr. Calif. State U., Fullerton, 1987—. Sec., South India Cultural Assn., L.A., 1980-81; bd. dirs. Am. Assn. East Indians. Mem. IEEE, IEEE Computer Soc., Sigma Xi, Eta Kappa Nu. Home: 678 Tiffany Ct Sunnyvale CA 94087-2439 Office: LV Software Inc 1735 N 1st St San Jose CA 95112-4529

CHANDRAMOULI, SRINIVASAN (CHANDRA CHANDRAMOULI), management and systems consultant; b. Kumbakonam, Tamil Nadu, India, Nov. 14, 1952; came to U.S., 1978; s. Veda and Padmavathi Srinivasan; m. Janaki Chandramouli. BS in Math. and Physics, Ferguson Coll., Pune, India, 1973; postgrad., Indian Inst. Tech., New Delhi, 1973-74; MBA in Mktg. and Gen. Mgmt., Indian Inst. Tech., Ahmedabad, 1976; MBA in Fin. and Acctg., U. Chgo., 1980. CPA, Ill. Cons. Hindustan Petroleum Corp. Ltd., Bombay, India, 1975; fin. mgr. prodn. Associated Cement Cos., Bombay, 1976-77; cons., researcher The World Bank, Washington, 1979-80; v.p. Am. Mgmt. Systems Inc., Chgo., 1980—; vis. faculty mem. K.C. Coll. Mgmt. U. Bombay, 1976-77. Editor newsletter India Assn. Pitts., 1977-78. Gen. sec. Jawahar Mitra Mandal, Pune, 1970-74. Fellow Inst. Profl. Acctg. U. Chgo., 1979-80; Open Merit and Nat. Merit scholar Govt. of India U. Poona, 1969-73. Mem. Am. Inst. CPA's, Ill. CPA Soc., Beta Gamma Sigma. Republican. Hindu. Avocation: bridge, chess. Home: 16118 E Prentice Pl Aurora CO 80015-4172 Office: Am Mgmt Systems Inc 14033 Denver West Pkwy Golden CO 80401-3107

CHANDRASHEKARAN, VINOD, financial economist, educator. BTech in Electronics Engring., Indian Inst. Tech., Madras, 1984; postgrad. diploma in mgmt., Indian Inst. Tech., Calcutta, 1986; PhD in Fin., U. Calif., Berkeley, 1994. Sys. exec. Nat. Inst. Info. Tech., Bangalore, India, 1986-87; sys. analyst Karnataka State Coun. for Sci. and Tech., Bangalore, 1987-88; cons. BARRA Inc., Berkeley, Calif., 1994-96, sr. cons., 1996—. Contbr. articles to profl. jours. Citibank fellow Indian Inst. Mgmt., 1985, Coleman fellow, U. Calif., 1989, Richard D. Irwin Found. fellow, U. Calif., 1993. Mem. Fin. Mgmt. Assn. (program com. 1998), Am. Fin. Assn., Acad. Fin. Svcs. (program com. 1998), Midwest Fin. Assn. (program com. 1997-98). Avocation: movies, reading, current events. E-mail: vinodc@barra.com. Fax: 510-548-1709. Office: BARRA Inc 2100 Milvia St Berkeley CA 94704-1113

CHANEN, STEVEN ROBERT, lawyer; b. Phoenix, May 15, 1953; s. Herman and Lois Marion (Boshes) C. Student, UCLA, 1971-73; BS in Mass Communications, Ariz. State U., 1975, JD, 1979. Bar: Ariz. 1980, U.S. Dist. Ct. Ariz. 1980, U.S. Ct. Appeals (9th cir.) 1980, Calif. 1981, U.S. Dist. Ct. (no. dist.) Calif. 1982. Ptnr. Wentworth & Lundin, Phoenix, 1980-86, of counsel, 1986-87; pres. Chanen Constrn. Co., Inc., 1987—; appointed bd. dirs. Ariz. Gov.'s Commn. on Motion Pictures and TV, 1986, chmn., 1990; appointed bd. dirs., exec. v.p. Chanen Corp.; fin. intermediary, chmn. bd. dirs. S.R. Chanen and Co, Inc.; pres. Chanen Constrn. Co., Inc. Bd. dirs. Anytown, Am., Phoenix, 1986—, COMPAS, Inc., Phoenix, 1986—, Ariz. Mus. Sci. and Tech., Phoenix, 1987—, Mus. Theater Ariz., Phoenix, 1988-89, Temple Beth Isreal, Ariz. Politically Interested Citizens, Jewish Fedn.; v.p. bd. dirs. Community Forum, Phoenix, Phoenix Children's Hosp., Nat. Conf. (dir.) Maricopa County C.C. Dist. Found. (pres.). Recipient J. Leonard Amdur Man of the Year award; Leader of Distinction award Anti-Defamation League. Mem. ABA (forum com. entertainment and sports industries 1981—), Ariz. Bar Assn., Calif. Bar Assn., Maricopa County Bar Assn., Assn. Trial Lawyers Am. Republican. Jewish. Office: 3300 N 3rd Ave Phoenix AZ 85013-4304

CHANEY, ROBERT GALEN, religious organization executive; b. LaPorte, Ind., Oct. 27, 1913; s. Clyde Galen and Maree (Francis) C.; student Miami U., Ohio, 1931-33; D.D., Coll. Universal Truth, 1954; m. Earlyne Cantrell, Oct. 4, 1947; 1 dau., Sita. Ordained to non-denominational ministry, 1939; pastor various parishes, Eaton Rapids and Lansing Mich., 1938-50; founder, pres. Astara, Los Angeles, 1956-76, Upland, Calif., 1976—. Republican. Lodges: Mason, Kiwanis. Author: The Inner Way, 1962; Adventures in ESP, 1975; Mysticism: The Journey Within, 1979, The Power of Your Own Medicine, 1995. Office: Astara 792 W Arrow Hwy W Upland CA 91786

CHANG, HOWARD FENGHAU, law educator, economist; b. Lafayette, Ind., June 30, 1960; s. Joseph Juifu and Mary Hsueh-mei C. AB in Govt. cum laude, Harvard Coll., 1982; M in Pub. Affairs, Princeton (N.J.) U., 1985; JD magna cum laude, Harvard U., 1987; SM in Econs., MIT, 1988, PhD in Econs., 1992. Bar: N.Y. 1989, D.C. 1989. Law clk. to hon. Ruth Bader Ginsburg U.S. Ct. of Appeals, Washington, 1988-89; asst. prof. law U. So. Calif. Law Sch., L.A., 1992-94, assoc. prof. law, 1994-97, prof., 1997—; vis. assoc. prof. law Georgetown U. Law Ctr., Washington, 1996-97; vis. prof. law Stanford Law Sch., 1998; vis. scholar U. Pa. Law Sch., Phila., 1999. Supervising editor Harvard Law Rev., Cambridge, 1986-87. John M. Olin fellowship Dept. Econs. MIT, 1987, 90, 91; nat. merit scholar IBM, 1978. Mem. Am. Econ. Assn., Am. Law and Econs. Assn. Office: U So Calif Law Sch University Park Los Angeles CA 90089-0071

CHANG, I-SHIH, aerospace engineer; b. Taipei, Taiwan, Dec. 2, 1945; came to U.S., 1966; s. I.H. and T.C. Chang; m. O.J. Chang, May 25, 1974; children: Anna, Brandon. Degree in mech. engring., Taipei Inst. of Tech., 1965; MS, U. Kans., 1969; PhD, U. Ill., 1973. Scientist assoc.-rsch. Lockheed Missiles & Space, Huntsville, Ala., 1973-76; mem. tech. staff Rockwell Internat., Anaheim, Calif., 1976-77, mem. tech. staff The Aerospace Corp., El Segundo, Calif., 1977-80, engring. specialist, 1980-90, sr. engring. specialist, 1990-91, disting. engr., 1991—. Contbr. articles to profl. jours. Fellow AIAA (assoc.); mem. Phi Kappa phi. Democrat. Home: 890

S Calle Venado Anaheim CA 92807-5004 Office: The Aerospace Corp M4/967 2350 E El Segundo Blvd El Segundo CA 90245-4691

CHANG, KUANG-YEH, microelectronics technologist; b. Nanjing, China, Sept. 1, 1948; came to U.S., 1971; s. Yi and Wen-Teh (Tang) C.; m. Huey-Lian Ding, June 30, 1975; children: Fen, Wendy, Sherry, Sean. BSEE, Nat. Taiwan U., 1970; MSEE, U. Tenn., 1973; PhD, U. Pitts., 1978. Mem. tech. staff Hughes Aircraft Co., Newport Beach, Calif., 1978-83; mem. tech. staff Advanced Micro Devices, Sunnyvale, Calif., 1983-85, tech. integration mgr., 1994-96; device mgr. Motorola, Austin, Tex., 1985-89; engring. mgr. VLSI Tech., San Jose, Calif., 1989-91; fellow Compass Design Automation, San Jose, 1991-94; dir. ops. United Microelectronics Corp. Science Park, Hsinchu, Taiwan, 1996—; com. mem. ASIC Conf., Rochester, 1993-94. Patentee in field. 2d lt. Chinese Army, 1970-71. Mem. IEEE, Phi Kappa Phi. Avocations: swimming, skiing, classical guitar, saxaphone, camping. Home: PO Box 2922 Saratoga CA 95070-0922 Office: UMC Science Park, 10 Innovation Rd 1, Hsinchu Taiwan

CHANG, MARIA HSIA, political science educator; b. Hong Kong, Mar. 17, 1950; d. Pao-en and Lu (Huang) C.; m. A. James Gregor, Dec. 22, 1987; children: Charles Elmo, Gabriel Raphael. BA in Polit. Sci., U. Calif., Berkeley, 1973, MA in Polit. Sci., 1975, PhD in Polit. Sci., 1983. Asst. prof. politics and govt. U. Puget Sound, Tacoma, Wash., 1983-89; assoc. prof. polit. sci. U. Nev., Reno, 1989-98, prof., 1998—; vis. asst. prof. Wash. State U., Pullman, 1980-82; lectr. U.S. Office of Personnel mgmt., Denver, 1992—; cons. on Chinese immigration for U.S. immigration attys., 1990—; book rev. editor: Am. Jour. of Chinese Studies, 1992-95. Author: (books) The Labors of Sisyphus, 1998 (Mousel-Feltner award 1998), The Chinese Blue Shirt Society, 1985; co-author: (book) Human Rights in the P.R. of China, 1988; co-editor: (book) Aftermath of 1989 Tiananmen Crisis, 1992. Bd. advisors Carrying Capacity Network, Washington, 1997—, nat. adv. bd. Diversity Coalition for an Immigration Moratorium, 1995-97; adv. bd. Diversity Alliance for a Sustainable Am., 1998—; mem. standing com. Chinese Alliance for Democracy, N.Y., 1985-88. Recipient Individual Rsch. fellowship Chiang Ching-kuo Found., Washington, 1995; finalist White House fellowship, 1985; nat. fellow Hoover Instn., Stanford, Calif., 1984. Mem. Am. Assn. for Chinese Studies (bd. dirs. 1988-92, 96-99), Assn. of Chinese Social Scientists in N.Am. Avocations: aerobics, arts and crafts, gardening. Office: Univ of Nev Political Sci/302 Reno NV 89557

CHANG, RODNEY EIU JOON, artist, dentist; b. Honolulu, Nov. 26, 1945; s. Alfred Koon Bo and Mary Yet Moi (Char) C.; m. Erlinda C. Feliciano, Dec. 4, 1987; children: Bronson York, Houston Travis, Rochelle Jessica. BA in Zoology, U. Hawaii, 1968; AA in Art, Triton Coll., 1972; DDS, Loyola U., 1972; MS in Edn., U. So. Calif., 1974; MA in Painting and Drawing, U. No. Ill., 1975; MA in Community Leadership, Cen. Mich. U., 1976; BA in Psychology, Hawaii Pacific U., 1977; MA in Psychology of Counseling, U. No. Colo., 1980; PhD in Art Psychology, The Union Inst., 1980; MA in Computer Art, Columbia Pacific U., 1989. Pvt. practice dentist Honolulu, 1975—; dir. SOHO too Gallery and Loft, Honolulu, 1985-89; freelance artist Honolulu, 1982—; curator Webfelt Mus. of Early Cyberart, Honolulu, 1996—; founder Pygoya Internat. Art Group, 1990—; founder Art Cap Group, Slap Caps Co., Honolulu, 1993; columnist Milk Cap News; dir. ann. Honolulu City Hall Hawaiian Computer Art Exhbn., 1990-92; speaker on art psychology and computer art, also numerous TV and radio interviews. Author: Mental Evolution and Art, 1980, Rodney Chang: Computer Artist, 1988, Commentaries on the Psychology of Art, 1980; host (radio show) Disco Doc Hour, Sta. KISA; one-man shows include Honolulu Acad. Arts, 1986, Shanghai State Art Mus., People's Republic of China, 1988, Retrospective Exhbn. 1967-87, Ramsay Gallery, Honolulu, 1987, Visual Encounters Gallery, Denver, 1987, The Bronx Mus. of the Arts, N.Y.C., 1987, Nishi Noho Gallery, N.Y.C., 1987, Eastern Wash. U. Gallery of Art, 1988, Salon de la Jeune Peinture, Paris, 1989, Holter Art Mus., Mont., 1989, Las Vegas Art Mus., 1990, Forum Art Sch. Gütershoh, Fed. Republic of Germany, 1990, Siggraph-Dallas, 1990, Tartu State Art Mus., Estonia/USSR, 1990, U. Oregon Continuation Ctr., Portland, 1991—, Kauai Art Mus., Hawaii, 1993, RC Gallery of Computer Art, Honolulu, 1994, Archtl. Design of the Pygoya Home Mus., 1994; conceived, produced 1st milk cap art exhbn., Arts of Paradise Gallery, Waikiki Beach, 1993. Judge Jr. Miss Contest, Honolulu, 1981. Served to capt., U.S. Army, 1973-74. Mem. ADA, Hawaii Dental Assn., Assn. of Honolulu Artists (pres. 1989), Nat. Computer Graphics, Acad. Gen. Dentistry, Hawaii Space Soc., Bernice Bishop Mus. Honolulu. Roman Catholic. Achievements include publication and issue of world's first pre-paid long distance telephone cards as signed and numbered, limited edition fine art prints, Pygoya Webmuseum of Cyberart on Internet, 1997; dir. Internet Programs, Las Vegas Art Mus. Office: 2119 N King St Ste 206 Honolulu HI 96819-4550

CHANG, RONALD CHIU MUN, greeting cards company executive; b. Honolulu, June 6, 1965; s. Lemuel Chong Wing and Janice Siu Quon (Young) C. BBA, U. Wash., 1988. Owner, mgr. Orchids Unltd., Honolulu, 1979-83; greeting cards exec. Alpha Centauri Design, Honolulu, 1983—; credit systems officer Security Pacific Bancorp. NW, Seattle, 1989-92; examiner Bank of Hawaii, Honolulu, 1992—; plant buyer Ono Plant and Flower Shop, Honolulu, 1985; data processor, operator copyctr. U. Wash., Seattle, 1987-88. Mem. Golden Key. Home: 1026 Awawamalu St Apt A Honolulu HI 96825-2626

CHANG, SHENG-TAI, English language educator; b. Shanghai, Dec. 12, 1951; came to the U.S., 1986; s. Shucheng and Miaoxin (Xu) C. BA in English, East China Normal U., 1982; MA, U. Calgary, 1986; PhD in Comparative Lit., U. So. Calif., 1993, MA in East Asian Langs. and Cultures, 1994. English tchr. East China Normal U., Shanghai, 1982-84; instr. Chinese L.A. Trade-Tech. Coll., 1991; asst. lectr. in Chinese U. So. Calif., L.A., 1991; adj. asst. prof. Occidental Coll., L.A., 1993; lectr. U. So. Calif., L.A., 1994; instr., prof. South Puget Sound C.C., Olympia, Wash., 1994—. Editor, translator: The Tears of Chinese Immigrants, 1990; contbr. articles to profl. jours. Grantee Can. Ministry Multiculturalism, 1986. Mem. MLA, Philological Assn. Pacific Coast, Am. Assn. for Asian Studies, Am. Comparative Lit. Assn., Internat. Soc. for Comparative Study Civilizations, Phi Kappa Phi. Office: South Puget Sound CC 2011 Mottman Rd SW Olympia WA 98512-6218

CHANG, SYLVIA TAN, health facility administrator, educator; b. Bandung, Indonesia, Dec. 18, 1940; came to U.S., 1963.; d. Philip Harry and Lydia Shui-Yu (Ou) Tan; m. Belden Shiu-Wah Chang, Aug. 30, 1964 (dec. Aug. 1997); children: Donald Steven, Janice May. Diploma in nursing, Rumah Sakit Advent, Indonesia, 1960; BS, Philippine Union Coll., 1962; MS, Loma Linda (Calif.) U., 1967; PhD, Columbia Pacific U., 1987. Cert. RN, PHN, ACLS, BLS instr., cmty. first aid instr., IV, TPN, blood withdrawal. Head nurse Rumah Sakit Advent, Bandung, Indonesia, 1960-61; critical care, spl. duty and medicine nurse, team leader White Meml. Med. Ctr., L.A., 1963-64; nursing coord. Loma Linda U. Med. Ctr., 1964-66; team leader, critical care nurse, relief head nurse Pomona (Calif.) Valley Hosp. Med. Ctr., 1966-67; evening supr. Loma Linda U. Med. Ctr., 1967-69, night supr., 1969-79, adminstrv. supr., 1979-94; sr. faculty Columbia Pacific U., San Rafael, Calif., 1986-94; dir. health svc. La Sierra U., Riverside, Calif., 1988—; site coord. Health Fair Expo La Sierra U., 1988-89; adv. coun. Family Planning Clinic, Riverside, 1988-94; blood and bone marrow drive coord. La Sierra U., 1988—. Counselor Pathfinder Club Campus Hill Ch., Loma Linda, 1979-85, crafts instr., 1979-85, music dir., 1979-85; asst. organist U. Ch., 1982-88. Named one of Women of Achievement YWCA, Greater Riverside C. of C., The Press Enterprise, 1991, Safety Coord. of Yr. La Sierra U., 1995. Mem. Am. Coll. Health Assn., Assn. Seventh-day Adventist Nurses, Pacific Coast Coll. Health Assn., Adventist Student Pers. Assn., Loma Linda U. Sch. Nursing Alumni Assn. (bd. dirs.), Sigma Theta Tau. Republican. Seventh-day Adventist. Avocations: music, travel, collecting coins, shells and jade carvings. Home: 11466 Richmont Rd Loma Linda CA 92354-3523 Office: La Sierra U Health Svc 4700 Pierce St Riverside CA 92505-3332

CHANG, TAIPING, marketing executive, magazine publisher; b. Tainan, Taiwan, Apr. 20, 1949; came to U.S., 1975; d. Lanfeng Chang and Shuchun Liu; m. David R. Knechtges, June 7, 1976; 1 child, Jeanne Y. BA, Tunghai U., 1971, MA, 1974; PhD, U. Wash., 1981. Lectr. Tunghai U., Taichung, Taiwan, 1974-75; asst. prof. Pacific Luth. U., Tacoma, 1986-88; pub. Asia Pacific Bus. Jour., Seattle, 1988-94; pres. Asia Media Group, Inc., Seattle, 1989-94; asst. prof. Asian studies program U. Puget Sound, Tacoma, Wash., 1994-95; asst. prof. Asian langs. and lit. dept. U. Wash., Seattle, 1996—; bd. dirs. Chong-Wa Benevolent Assn., Seattle, No. Seattle (Wash.) C.C.; chmn. World Trade Club-Taiwan Forum, Seattle, 1991—. Editor: Editor-in-Chief, 1988. Named Woman of Yr., Asia Am. Soc., Seattle, 1990. Mem. Rotary Club. Office: Univ Wash Asian Lang Lit Dept Seattle WA 98195

CHANG, TSU-SHUAN, electrical engineering educator; b. Taiwan, Republic of China, Feb. 10, 1950; came to U.S., 1976; s. Tao-Ming and Erh-Chun (Teng) C.; m. Fen-Liang Pan; children: Alexander, Ernest, Lemuel. BS, Nat. Chiao Tung U., Taiwan, Republic of China, 1971, MS, 1973; SM, PhD, Harvard U., 1981. Instr. Chinese Navy Communication and Electronic Sch., Taiwan, 1974-75, Nat. Chiao Tung U., Hsinchu, Taiwan, 1975-76; research asst. IBM T.J. Watson Research Ctr., Yorktown Heights, N.Y., 1977; asst. prof. elec. engring. SUNY, Stony Brook, 1981-84; asst. prof. elec. engring. U. Calif., Davis, 1984-88, assoc. prof., 1988-97, prof., 1997—; cons. Harvard U., Cambridge, 1981, 82; vis. researcher U. Ill., Urbana and Champaign, 1988. Contbr. articles to profl. jours. Served to 2d lt. Chinese Navy, 1973-75. Fellow Harvard U., 1977, NSF, 1984, 85, 88, U. Calif. and FJM Corp., 1985-90. Mem. Control Systems Soc. of IEEE (robotics and automation, pub. chair in IEEE conf. on Decision and Control, assoc. editor transaction on automatic control 1992-94), Phi Tau Phi. Office: U Calif Elec & Computer Engring One Shields Ave Davis CA 95616

CHANG, WALTER TUCK, SR., drafting and autoCAD educator, real estate agent; b. Honolulu, Feb. 16, 1920; s. Awai Abner and Clara Pa'a'auau (Fairman) C.; m. Rita AnaMarie Yee Chang, Aug. 16, 1950 (div. June 1959); children: Walter Tuck Jr., Nani; m. Mercedes Arroyo Chang, June 15, 1961 (div. June 1973); m. Evelyn Show Chiao Huang, Aug. 25, 1973. *Great-grandfather, Chang Atong, arrived Lahaina, Maui, from China, 1865, became Hawaiian citizen March 1, 1870. Married Kalei Hoopio Kellett, established himself as import-export merchant. Grandfather, Chan Amona Chang, born Lahaina, 1873, raised and educated Macao, China, married Chong Shee by family agreement, had 14 children. Father, Abner Awai, born 1896 married Clara Pauau'au Fairman, had 6 children. Son, Walter Tuck Jr., attended Cornell University, Ithaca, University of California, Hayward. Built computers, IBM, San Jose, hired by AT&T, San Francisco, Computer Engineer. Daughter, Nani BA English, French, Mills College, California, MBA San Diego State University executive manager quality assurance analysis Augsburg Fortress Publishing House, has one daughter.* BA, San Jose State U., 1945; MA, San Francisco State U., 1959. Gen. secondary credential, Calif., spl. subject supervision vocat. class A, spl. subject supervision vocat. class C1, spl. secondary life diploma in indsl. arts, secondary sch. adminstrn., Calif.; profl. secondary cert. in indsl. arts, Hawaii. Nat. defense instr., lead machinist Joshua Henry Iron Works, Sunnyvale, Calif., 1942-45; machinist San Jose Food Machinery, 1946, Ames Aero. Lab., Sunnyvale, Calif., 1946-51; vocat. instr. San Jose State U., 1942-45; boring machine operator Johnston Machine Shop, San Jose, 1946; adult evening vocat. instr. Leland Evening H.S., San Jose, 1951; vocat. inst. John Swett Union H.S., Crockett, Calif., 1951-59, vocat. dir., night prin., 1952-59; indsl. arts, English, Soc. Studies instr. McKinley H.S., Honolulu, 1959-62; indsl. arts metal works instr. Kailua (Hawaii) H.S., 1962; indsl. arts tchr. edn. instr. U. Hawaii Coll. Edn. Manoa Campus, Honolulu, 1962-64; drafting instr. archtl. engring. Kamehameha Schs., Honolulu, 1964-90; automotive machinist Garden City Scales and Svc., San Jose, 1945-46. *Mr. Chang graduated from Kamehameha School for Boys as Cadet 1st Lieutenant withhonors. He attended San Jose State Teachers College, graduated 1945, BA Industrial Arts. He worked for Ames Aeronautical Laboratory (NASA), Moffett Field, California, 1946-51. He matriculated at 5 colleges. Received his State Credentials in Trade and Industry, University of California, Berkeley. Received MA Education Administration, San Francisco State University, 1959. Continued graduate studies University of Hawaii, Manoa, and attended University of Maryland for his doctorate dissertation. He became an Assistant Professor, University of Hawaii, and taught at Kamehameha Schools, Honolulu from 1964 until his retirement in 1990.* Author: Getting Started With the Calipro, 1965. Hawaiian musician entertainer ARC, San Francisco Bay Area, 1942-49; Sunday Sch. tchr. Hayward (Calif.) Missionary Bapt. Ch., 1958-59, Missionary Bapt. Chs. on Oahu, Hawaii, 1960—. Recipient Best Auto-CAD Architecture in Hawaii award Sausilito Software, 1985; named Most Outstanding Educator, Kamahameha Alumni Assn., Honolulu, 1984. Avocations: photography, raising gold fish, travel, reading books, sports. Home: 98-410 Koauka Loop Apt 11D Aiea HI 96701-4513

CHANG, WILLIAM ZHI-MING, physicist, researcher; b. Shanghai, China, June 6, 1955; s. Yinfang Chang and Shanlin Chen; m. Sandra Schlachter, Aug., 1987; 1 child, Caroline Dagmar. BS, U. So. Calif., 1984, MS, 1985, PhD, 1992. Rsch. assoc. U. So. Calif., L.A., 1992-93; rsch. scientist Max Planck Soc. x-ray optics group Friedrich-Schiller U., Jena, Germany, 1993-96; sr. scientist advanced rsch. and applications corp. Aracor, Sunnyvale, Calif., 1996—. Contbr. articles to profl. jours. Disting. scholar Microbeam Analysis Soc., San Jose, Calif., 1991, Boston, 1992. Mem. N.Y. Acad. Scis. Avocations: opera, calligraphy. Home: 8592 Peachtree Ave Newark CA 94560-3342 Office: Aracor 425 Lakeside Dr Sunnyvale CA 94086-4716

CHANG, ZHAO HUA, biomedical engineer; b. Zibo, Shandong, China, July 3, 1963; s. Xuzhong and Sumai (Wang) C.; m. Xiaojing Yang, Aug. 5, 1987; 1 child, Brian Yale. MS, Shanghai Inst. Mech. Engring., 1985; PhD, SUNY, Binghamton, 1992. Rsch. assoc. SUNY, Binghamton, N.Y., 1987-90; cons. Cryomedical Sci., Inc., Rockville, Md., 1990, sr. engr., 1991, dir. rsch. & devel., v.p. cryosurg. engring., 1995-96; v.p. R & D, Endocare, Inc., Irvine, Calif., 1996—; cons. Life Cell Inc., Houston, 1988-89. Author: Cryobiological Engineering, 1985; contbr. articles to profl. jours. Mem. Cryobiology Soc. Achievements include invention of and patent for new cryosurgical systems that have simplified many surgeries; provision of the first calometric evidence of nuclei formation below the glass transition temperature. Home: 28422 Via Pasito San Juan Capistrano CA 92675-6306

CHAO, FRANK W., computer consultant; b. Oakland, Calif., May 21, 1951; s. Fu-Chuan and Lydia Lai-Yuk (Chui) C. AA, El Camino Coll., 1981; BA, U. Calif., L.A., 1973; MBA, U. So. Calif., L.A., 1975. Sales rsch. analyst Mattel Inc., Hawthorne, Calif., 1976-77; alarm tech. Morse Signal Devices of Calif., L.A., 1977-79; network engr. specialist Northrop Grumman Corp., Hawthorne, Calif., 1979—. Active L.A. Free-Net, 1994—. Mem. L.A. Computer Soc., Greater South Bay PC Users Group, L.A. NT Users Group. E-mail: ac602@lafn.org. Fax: (310) 332-0111. Office: Northrop Grumman Corp PO Box 6930 Torrance CA 90504-6930

CHAO, JAMES MIN-TZU, architect; b. Dairen, China, Feb. 27, 1940; came to U.S., 1949; naturalized, 1962; m. Kirsti Helena Lehtonen, May 15, 1968. BArch, U. Calif., Berkeley, 1965. Registered arch., Calif., Ariz., Colo., Ill., N.Mex.; cert. instr. real estate, Calif. Intermediate draftsman Spencer, Lee & Busse, Archs., San Francisco, 1966-67; asst. to pres. Import Plus Inc., Santa Clara, Calif., 1967-69; job capt. Hammaberg and Herman, Archs., Oakland, Calif., 1969-71; project mgr. B A Premises Corp., San Francisco, 1971-79; constrn. mgr. The Straw Hat Restaurant Corp., San Francisco, 1979-81, mem. sr. mgmt., dir. real estate and constrn., 1981-87; mem. mktg. com. Straw Hat Coop. Corp., San Francisco, 1988-91; pvt. practice Berkeley, 1987—; dir. real estate Papillon Devel. Inc., 1998—; pres. Food Svc. Cons. Inc., 1987-89; pres., CEO Stratsac, Inc., 1987-92; prin. arch. Alpha Cons. Group Inc., 1991-98; v.p. Intersyn Industries Calif., 1993—; nat. tng. dir. Excel Telecom., Inc., 1995—; CEO Nuts and Bolts Books, 1997—; lectr. comml. real estate site analysis and selection for profl. real estate seminars; coord. minority vending program, solar application program Bank of Am.; guest faculty mem. N.W. Ctr. for Profl. Edn. Author: The Street-Smart Restaurant Development Handbook, 1996; patentee tidal electric generating system; author 1st comprehensive consumer orientated performance specification for remote banking transaction. Mem. AIA, Encinal Yacht Club (bd. dirs. 1977-78). Republican.

CHAPLIN, GEORGE, newspaper editor; b. Columbia, S.C., Apr. 28, 1914; s. Morris and Netty (Brown) C.; m. Esta Lillian Solomon, Jan. 26, 1937; children: Stephen Michael, Jerry Gay. BS, Clemson Coll., 1935; Nieman fellow, Harvard U., 1940-41; HHD (hon.), Clemson U., 1989; LHD (hon.), Hawaii Loa Coll., 1990. Reporter, later city editor Greenville (S.C.) Piedmont, 1935-42; mng. editor Camden (N.J.) Courier-Post, 1946-47, San Diego Jour., 1948-49; mng. editor, then editor New Orleans Item, 1949-58; asso. editor Honolulu Advertiser, 1958-59, editor in chief, 1959-86, editor at large, 1986—; mem. selection com. Jefferson fellowships East-West Ctr.; chmn. Gov.'s Conf. on Year 2000, 1970; chmn. Hawaii Commn. on Year 2000, 1971-74; co-chmn. Conf. on Alt. Econ. Futures for Hawaii, 1973-75; charter mem. Goals for Hawaii, 1979-81; alt. U.S. rep. South Pacific Commn., 1978-81; chmn. search com. for pres. U. Hawaii, 1983; chmn. Hawaii Gov.'s Adv. Coun. on Fgn. Lang. and Internat. Studies, 1983-94; rep. of World Press Freedom Com. on missions to Sri Lanka, Hong Kong, Singapore, 1987. Editor, officer-in-charge: Mid-Pacific edit. Stars and Stripes World War II; editor: (with Glenn Paige) Hawaii 2000, 1973, Presstime in Paradise: The Life and Times of the Honolulu Advertiser 1856-1995, 1998. Bd. dirs. U. Hawaii Rsch. Corp., 1970-72, Inst. for Religion and Social Change, Hawaii Jewish Welfare Fund, Charleston Christian-Jewish Coun.; mem. bd. govs. East-West Ctr., Honolulu, 1980-89, chmn., 1983-89; mem. bd. govs. Pacific Health Rsch. Inst., 1984-90, 93-97, pres., 1995-96; bd. govs. Straub Med. Found., 1989-98, Hawaii Pub. Schs. Found., 1986-87; trustee Clarence T. C. Ching Found., 1986-95; Am. media chmn. U.S.-Japan Conf. on Cultural and Ednl. Interchange, 1978-86; co-founder, v.p. Coalition for Drug-Free Hawaii, 1987-90; panelist ABA Conf., 1989; mem. Civilian Adv. Group, U.S. Army, Hawaii, 1985-95; co-chair Hawaii State Commn. on Judicial Salaries, 1995-98. Capt. AUS, 1942-46. Decorated Star Solidarity (Italy), Order Rising Sun (Japan), Prime Minister's medal (Israel); recipient citations Overseas Press Club, 1961, 72, Headliners award, 1962, John Hancock award, 1972, 74, Distinguished Alumni award Clemson U., 1974, E.W. Scripps award Scripps-Howard Found., 1976, Champion Media award for Econ. Understanding, 1981, Judah Magnes Gold medal Hebrew U. Jerusalem, 1987, Herbert Harley award Am. Judicature Soc., 1991, Regents medal of distinction U. Hawaii, 1998; inductee Honolulu Press Club Hall of Fame, 1987. Mem. Honolulu Symphony Soc., Pacific and Asian Affairs Council (dir.), Internat. Press Inst., Am. Soc. Newspaper Editors (dir., treas. 1973, sec. 1974, v.p. 1975, pres. 1976), Friends of East-West Ctr. Home: Ashley House 7AB 14 Lockwood Dr Charleston SC 29401-1126

CHAPLIN, WILLIAM RATCLIFFE, cleaning service executive; b. Ft. Bragg, Calif., Feb. 18, 1959; s. Charles Ray and Elizibeth Waldo (Hayes) C.; m. Susan Williams, Mar. 19, 1979 (div. Aug. 1983); 1 child, Nicole Michelle Chaplin-Bogue. AA in engring., U. Calif., San Diego. Supr. ServiceMaster Co., Eldridge, Calif.; owner/operator Wine Country Cleaners, Sonoma, Calif.; design cons. Teledyne-Ryan Co., San Diego. Contbr. poems, thoughts Billeakage, 1997. Mem. NOW (bd. dirs., v.p. 1996—), Amnesty Internat. (v.p. 1994—). Avocations: aviation, electronics, medicine. Home: 700 Verano Ave Sonoma CA 95476-5530 Office: Wine Country Cleaners PO Box 962 Eldridge CA 95431-0962

CHAPMAN, GEORGE J., agricultural products executive; b. 1936. With Magi Inc., Brewster, Wash., 1966—, now pres. Office: Magi Inc PO 157 Brewster WA 98812*

CHAPMAN, LORING, psychology, physiology educator, neuroscientist; b. L.A., Oct. 4, 1929; s. Lee E. and Elinore E. (Gundry) Scott; m. Toy Farrar, June 14, 1954 (dec.); children: Robert, Antony, Pandora (dec.). BS, U. Nev., 1950; PhD, U. Chgo., 1955. Lic. psychologist, Oreg., N.Y., Calif. Rsch. fellow U. Chgo., 1952-54; rsch. assoc., asst. prof. Cornell U. Med. Coll., N.Y.C., 1957-61; rsch. dir. Music Rsch. Found., N.Y.C., 1958-61; assoc. prof. in residence Neuropsychiat. Inst., UCLA, 1961-65; rsch. prof. U. Oreg., Portland, 1965; br. chief NIH, Bethesda, Md., 1966-67; prof., chmn. dept. behavioral biology, joint prof. human physiology Sch. Medicine U. Calif., Davis, 1967-81, prof. psychiatry and head Divsn. of Clin. Psychology, 1981-91; prof. emeritus Sch. Medicine U. Calif., 1991—, prof. neurology, 1977-81, prof. human physiology, 1977-81; asst. dean, rsch. affairs Sch. Medicine U. Calif., Davis, 1972-74; vice chmn. div. of sci. basic to medicine, 1976-79; Lic. psychologist, Calif. Author: Pain and Suffering, 3 vols, 1967, Head and Brain 3 vols, 1971, (with E.A. Dunlap) The Eye, 1981; assoc. editor courtroom medicine series updates, 1965-91; contbr. sci. articles to publs. Fogarty Sr. Internat. fellow, 1980; grantee NASA, 1969-80; grantee NIH, 1956-91; grantee Nat. Inst. Drug Abuse, 1971-80; recipient Thorton Wilson prize, 1958, Career award USPHS, 1964, Commonwealth Fund award, 1970. Mem. Am. Acad. Neurology, Am. Physiol. Soc., Am. Psychol. Assn., Royal Soc. Medicine (London)., Am. Neurol. Assn., Am. Assn. Mental Deficiency, Aerospace Med. Assn., Soc. for Neurosci. Home: 7610 Rush River Dr Apt 121 Sacramento CA 95831-5517 Office: U Calif Med Ctr Dept Psychiatry 2315 Stockton Blvd Sacramento CA 95817-2201

CHAPMAN, RICHARD GRADY, engineer; b. Greer, S.C., Oct. 25, 1937; s. Richard Grady Sr. and Mary Idell (Davis) C.; m. Eleanor Raye Kernells, Oct. 13, 1956 (div. Apr. 1978); children: Abby Leigh, Pamela Kathryn, Robert Pope; m. Georgia Ann Burke, Apr. 7, 1978. BS in Engring., U. Nebr., 1974, MS in Geoenviron. Engring., Shippensburg U., 1984. Registered profl. engr., Terr. of Guam. Commd. 2d lt. U.S. Army, 1959, advanced through grades to col., 1984; aviation officer U.S. Army, U.S. and Vietnam, 1966-71; engr. officer U.S. Army, U.S., Europe and Asia, 1971-89; ret. U.S. Army, 1989; designer Coleman & Townes Architects and Engrs., Greenwood, S.C., 1960-66; rsch. engr. U. N.Mex., Albuquerque, 1990-97; cons. engr. Colorado Springs, Colo., 1997—; co-chair U.S.-Japan environ. com. U.S. Forces Japan, Tokyo, 1980-83; chief of facilities U.S. Army, Europe, Heidelberg, Germany, 1984-86; comdr. Kwajalein Missile Range, Marshall Islands, 1986-88; CINCPAC rep. to pres. Marshall Islands, U.S. Army, Kwajalein Atoll, 1986-88. Author: (tng. program) Hazardous Waste Management Course for BLM, 1990, (books) Energy Master Plan, 1994, NORAD's Cheyenne Mountain, 1996; co-author manual: Combat Air Base Planning Principles, 1991. Dir. Regional Water Dist., El Paso County, Colo., 1994-98, Regional Fire Dist., el Paso County, 1994-98; vice chmn. County-Wide Policy Plan, El Paso County, 1994-98; guide, v.p. Visually Impaired and Blind Skiers of Colorado Springs, 1998—. Recipient Resolution award Parliament, Republic of Marshall Islands, 1988, Bd. Commrs. El Paso County, 1998, plaque Visually Impaired and Blind Skiers of Colorado Springs, 1998. Fellow Am. Soc. Mil. Engrs. (pres. 1977-78, cert. 1985), Ret. Officers Assn. bapt. Avocations: skiing, scuba diving, art, travel. Home and Office: 4455 Spiceglen Dr Colorado Springs CO 80906-7691

CHAPMAN, RICHARD LEROY, public policy researcher; b. Yankton, S.D., Feb. 4, 1932; s. Raymond Young and Vera Everette (Trimble) C.; m. Marilyn Jean Nicholson, Aug. 14, 1955; children: Catherine Ruth Hoff, Robert Matthew, Michael David, Stephen Raymond, Amy Jean. BS, S.D. State U., 1954; postgrad., Cambridge (Eng.) U., 1954-55; MPA, Syracuse U., 1958, PhD, 1967. With Office of Sec. of Def., 1958-59, 61-63; dep. dir. rsch. S.D. Legis. Rsch. Coun., 1959-60; mem. staff Bur. of the Budget, Exec. Office of Pres., Washington, 1960-61; profl. staff mem. com. govt. ops. U.S. Ho. of Reps., Washington, 1966; program dir. NIH, Bethesda, Md., 1967-68; sr. rsch. assoc. Nat. Acad. Pub. Adminstrn., Washington, 1968-72, dep. exec. dir., 1973-76, v.p., dir. rsch., 1976-82; sr. rsch. scientist Denver Rsch. Inst., 1982-86; mem. adv. com. Denver Rsch. Inst. U. Denver, 1984-86; ptnr. Milliken Chapman Rsch. Group Inc., Denver, 1986-88; v.p. Chapman Rsch. Group, Inc., Littleton, 1988-98; cons. U.S. Office Pers. Mgmt., Washington, 1977-81, Denver, 1986-98; cons. CIA, Washington, 1979, 80, 81, Arthur S. Fleming Awards, Washington, 1977-81; exec. staff dir., cons. U.S. Congressman Frank Denholm; lectr. on sci., tech., govt. and pub. mgmt. Author: (with Fred Grissom) Mining the Nation's Braintrust, 1992; contbr. over 70 articles and revs. to profl. jours. and congl. staff reports. Mem. aerospace com. Colo. Commn. Higher Edn., Denver, 1982-83; chmn. rules com. U. Denver Senate, 1984-85; bd. dirs. S.E. Englewood Water Dist., Littleton, 1984-88, pres. 1986-88; mem. strategic planning com. Mission Hills Bapt. Ch., 1986; bd. dirs. Lay Action Ministry Program, 1988-96, chmn. 1992-96; established Vera and Raymond Chapman Scholarship Fund, S.D. State U.; mem. Fairfax County Rep. Ctrl. Com., Va., 1969-71, Fairfax County Com. of 100, 1979-82. With U.S. Army, 1955-57, Korea, capt. Res. Syracuse U. Maxwell Sch. fellow, 1957-58, 63-64, Brookings Inst. fellow, 1964-65. Mem. Tech. Transfer Soc. (bd. dirs. 1987-95, Pres.'s award 1991, founder Colo. chpt., Thomas Jefferson award 1996), Fed. Lab. Consortium (nat. adv. com. 1989-98), S.D. State U. Found. (bd. dirs. 1992-98, vice chmn. 1994-96, chmn. bd. 1996-98), Southglen Country Club, Masons, KT, Order of DeMolay (Cross of Honor 1982), Rotary (fellow Internat. Found. 1954-55, Paul Harris fellow 1989). Republican. Avocations: hunting, fishing, golf, reading, gardening.

CHAPMAN, RICHARD W. K., electronics company executive. Pres., CEO ThermoQuest Corp., San Jose, Calif. Office: ThermoQuest Corp 355 River Oaks Pkwy San Jose CA 95134-1908*

CHAPMAN, ROBERT GALBRAITH, retired hematologist, administrator; b. Colorado Springs, Colo., Sept. 29, 1926; s. Edward Northrop and Janet Galbraith (Johnson) c.; m. Virginia Irene Potts, July 6, 1956; childen: Lucia Tully Chapman Chatzky, Sarah Northrop Chapman Bohrer, Robert Bostwick. Student, Westminster Coll., 1944-45; BA, Yale U., 1947; MD, Harvard U., 1951; MS, U. Colo., 1958. Diplomate Am. Bd. Internal Medicine and Pathology; lic. physician, Colo., Calif. Intern Hartford (Conn.) Hosp., 1951-52; resident in medicine U. Colo. Med. Ctr., Denver, 1955-58; fellow in hematology U. Wash., Seattle, 1958-60; chief resident in medicine U. Colo., Denver, 1957-58, instr. medicine, 1960-62, asst. prof. medicine, 1962-68, assoc. prof., 1968-91; chief staff VA Hosp., Denver, 1968-70; dir. Belle Bonfils Meml. Blood Ctr., Denver, 1977-91; mem. regionalization com. Am. Blood Commn., Washington, 1985-87, Colo.sickle cell com., Denver, 1978-91, gov.'s AIDS Coun., 1987-88; trustee Coun. Community Blood Ctrs., v.p., 1979-81, pres., 1989-91, mem. rsch. inst. bd. Palo Alto Med. Found., 1991-97. Contbr. articles to profl. jours. Served as capt. USAF, 1953-55. USPHS fellow, 1958-60. Fellow ACP; mem. Am. Assn. Blood Banks, Mayflower Soc., Denver Med. Soc., Colo. Med. Soc., Western Soc. Clin. Rsch., Am. Radio Relay League. Mem. United Ch. Christ. Avocations: amateur radio, computers, investments, genealogy. Home: 47 La Rancheria Carmel Valley CA 93924-9424

CHAPPELL, DAVID WELLINGTON, religious studies educator; b. St. John, N.B., Can., Feb. 3, 1940; came to U.S., 1966; s. Hayward Lynsin and Mary Elvira (Mosher) C.; m. Bertha Vera Bidulock, Aug. 23, 1960 (div. Jan. 1976); children: Cynthia Joan, Mark Lynsin David; m. Stella Quemada, July 11, 1981. BA, Mt. Allison U., Sackville, N.B., 1961; BD, McGill U., Montreal, Que., Can., 1965; PhD, Yale U., 1976. Min. United Ch. Can., Elma, Ont., Can., 1964-66; prof. U. Hawaii, Honolulu, 1971—; asst. prof. U. Toronto, Toronto, Ont., 1977-78; vis. prof. U. Pitts., 1982; vis. lectr. Taisho U., Tokyo, 1986-88; dir. East West Religions Project, Honolulu, 1980—, Buddhist Studies Program, U. Hawaii, 1987-92. Editor: T'ien-t'ai Buddhism, 1983, Buddhist and Taoist Practice, 1987; editor Buddhist-Christian Studies jour., 1980-95. Mem. Am. Acad. Religion, Assn. Asian Studies, Internat. Assn. Buddhist Studies, Soc. Buddhist-Christian Studies (past pres.). Democrat. Avocations: interreligious dialogue, tennis. Home: 47-696 Hui Kelu St Apt 1 Kaneohe HI 96744-4636

CHAPPELL, PAUL GALE, religious studies educator, minister; b. Norfolk, Va., July 2, 1947; s. Carlton William and Anne Bell (Hollowell) C.; m. Marilyn Joyce Fisk, Sept. 10, 1971; 1 child, Bradley Paul. BA, Oral Roberts U., Tulsa, 1968; MDiv, Asbury Theol. Sem., Wilmore, Ky., 1971; ThM, Princeton (N.J.) Theol. Sem., 1972; MPhil, Drew U., 1979, PhD, 1982. Assoc. pastor Capital Assembly of God, Trenton, N.J., 1971-75; prof. theol./hist. studies Sch. of Theology-Oral Roberts U., 1975-96, acad. dean, 1978-89, dean, CEO, 1989-96; exec. v.p., chief acad. officer The King's Coll. and Sem., L.A., 1996—; also bd. dirs.; exec. dir. The Jack W. Hayford Sch. of Pastoral Nurture, L.A., 1997—. Author: Great Things He Hath Done, 1981; contbr. to books: Twentieth Century Shapers of American Religion, 1988, Evangelical Theological Dictionary, 1984, Healing in the Christian Church, 1986, The Concise Evangelical Dictionary of Theology, 1992, others. Assoc. pastor The Ch. on the Way, Van Nuys, Calif., 1996—; bd. dirs. So. Calif. Urban Theol. Edn. Partnership, L.A., 1997—. Mem. Internat. Christian Accrediting Assn., N.J. Dist. Assemblies of God. Republican. Avocations: chess, billards. Office: The Kings Sem 14800 Sherman Way Van Nuys CA 91405-2233

CHAPUT, EUGENE MICHAEL, advertising executive; b. San Francisco, July 5, 1941; s. Eugene Rene and Lucille Marie (Longuy) C.; m. Susan Mary Oliphant, Dec. 18, 1965; children: J. Michael, E. John, Thomas Patrick. BS, U. So. Calif., 1963, MBA, 1965. Sr. media planner Young & Rubicam, San Francisco, 1965-69; v.p., dir. mktg. svcs. Grey Advertising, San Francisco, 1969-78; v.p., mgmt. supr. Hoefer, Dieterich & Brown, San Francisco, 1978-79; v.p. Young & Rubicam, San Francisco, 1979—. Patentee: inflatable portable sofa, 1996, electronic self defense weapon disguised as personal accessory, 1997; copyright holder parent-child bonding exercise program; contbr. to numerous creative advertising concepts. Coach Little League Baseball, Youth Soccer, Portola Valley, Calif., 1973-86; chmn. Portola Valley Parks and Recreation, 1978-83. Recipient numerous advtg. awards (especially in radio) 1985—; named first honoree Top of the Dial award, No. Calif. Broadcasters Assn., 1995. Mem. San Francisco Olympic Club (physical fitness commr. 1982-87, Weight Lifting record 1998). Avocations: physical fitness, skiing, tennis, motorcycling. Office: Young & Rubicam Inc 100 First St San Francisco CA 94105

CHARCZENKO, PETER, Internet development company executive; b. Hampton, Va., Aug. 5, 1962; s. Nickolai and Swetlana (Ramensky) C.; m. April Charczenko; 1 child, Alexander Coltrane. BA, U. Denver, 1983. Pres. Alpha Interactive Group, Inc., Denver, 1986—. Mem. Bus. Mktg. Assn. Avocations: mountain climbing, sailing. Office: Alpha Interactive Group Inc 1140 Delaware St Denver CO 80204-3608

CHARION, CRAIG ALBERT, computer programmer; b. Longmont, Colo., Feb. 2, 1964; s. Robert Philbrook and Nadene Ellen (Decker) C.; m. Lisa Renee Tomlinson, Dec. 18, 1993; children: Robert Craig, Carolyn Nadene. BS in Aviation Mgmt. summa cum laude, Met. State Coll., Denver, 1987; postgrad., U. Colo., Denver, 1994—. Cert. paralegal, Colo. Paralegal Ciancio, Tasker, Dupree P.C., Westminster, Colo., 1989-98; programmer United Airlines, Englewood, Colo., 1998—. Deacon Abundant Harvest Bible Ch., Federal Heights, Colo., 1997-98, Broomfield (Colo.) Assembly God, 1994-95; ministry team leader Calvary Temple, Denver, 1991-92. Mem. Assn. for Computing Machinery. Avocations: aviation, theomatics. Home: 12172 Bannock Cir Apt E Westminster CO 80234 Office: United Airlines 5347 S Valentia Way Englewood CO 80111

CHARLES, BLANCHE, retired elementary education educator; b. Spartanburg, S.C., Aug. 7, 1912; d. Franklin Grady and Alice Florida (Hatchette) C. BA, Humboldt State U., 1934; adminstrv. cert., U. So. Calif., 1940. Tchr. Calexico (Calif) Unified Sch. Dist., 1958-94; libr. Calexico Pub. Libr., El Centro Pub. Libr. Elem. sch. named in her honor, 1987. Mem. NEA, ACT, Calif. Tchrs. Assn., Nat. Soc. DAR, Nat. Soc. Daus. of Confederacy, Delta Kappa Gamma. Avocations: gardening, reading. Home: 37133 Highway 94 Boulevard CA 91905-9524

CHARLES, CHERYL, non-profit business executive; b. Seattle, Nov. 4, 1947; d. Tom E. Charles and Irene D. (Brown) Shelver; m. Robert E. Samples, Sept. 15, 1973; 1 child, Stician M. BA, U. Ariz., 1969; MA, Ariz. State U., 1971; PhD, U. Wash., 1982. Lic. secondary edn. Tchr. Phoenix Union H.S., 1969-71; staff assoc. Social Sci. Edn. Consortium, Boulder, Colo., 1971-72; social studies dept. chmn. Trevor Browne H.S., Phoenix, 1972-73; asst. dir. Essentia: Environ. Studies for Urban Youth, Olympia, Wash., 1973-75; nat. dir. Project Learning Tree, Tiburon, Calif. & Boulder, Colo., 1976-84; exec. dir. Project Wild, Boulder, 1981-93; with Sol y Sombra Found., Santa Fe, N.Mex., 1991—; exec. dir. Ctr. for Study of Cmty., Santa Fe, 1993—; chief operating officer The Santa Fe Group; owner Hawksong Assocs.; COO Santa Fe Group; chief operating officer The Santa Fe Group; prin. investigator MacArthur Found., Chgo., 1993-94, Bradley Found., Milw., 1995—, Ednl. Found. Am., Westport, Conn., 1995—; project dir. McCune Found., Santa Fe, N.Mex., 1995—. Co-author: The Whole School Book, 1977; editor: Project Wild Elementary and Secondary Guide, 1983-92, Project Wild Aquatic Guide, 1987-92; co-editor, designer Windstar Jour., 1987-90. Mem. nat. adv. com. U. Mich. Coll. Engring., East Lansing, Mich., 1990-93; nat. judge Seiko Youth Challenge, 1994; bd. advisors Aspen (Colo.) Global Change Inst., 1990—; bd. trustees Hispanic Culture Found., Albuquerque, 1995-98; pres. bd. trustees Windstar Land Conservancy, 1996—; chair bd trustees Windstar Found., 1995—. Recipient Leadership award U.S. Forest Svc., internat. region, 1985, L.B. Sharp award excellence in outdoor/environ. edn., 1993, Gold medal Pres. Environ. and Conservation Challenge award, Washington, 1991; named Profl. of Yr. Western Assn. Fish/Wildlife Agys., 1991. Mem. N.Am. Assn. Environ. Edn., Nat. Coun. Social Studies, N.Mex. First Town Hall, No. N.Mex. Grant Makers. Avocations: writing, horseback riding, dancing, cooking, reading. Office: The Santa Fe Group 3 N Chamisa Dr Ste 2 Santa Fe NM 87505-9463

CHARLES, MARY LOUISE, newspaper columnist, photographer, editor; b. L.A., Jan. 24, 1922; d. Louis Edward and Mabel Inez (Lyon) Kusel; m. Henry Loewy Charles, June 19, 1946; children: Susan, Henry, Robert, Carol. AA, L.A. City Coll., 1941; BA, San Jose (Calif.) State U., 1964. Salesperson Bullock's, L.A., 1940-42, Roos Bros., Berkeley, Calif., 1945-46; ptnr. Charles-Martin Motors, Marysville, Calif., 1950-54; farm editor Indep. Herald, Yuba City, Calif., 1954-55; social worker Sutter County, Yuba City, 1955-57; social worker Santa Clara County, San Jose, 1957-61, manual coordinator, 1961-73, community planning specialist, 1973-81; columnist Sr. Grapevine various weekly newspapers, Santa Clara County, 1981-86; editor Bay area Sr. Spectrum Newspapers, Santa Clara, 1986-90; columnist, 1990-94; columnist Santa Clara Valley edit. Senior Mag., 1994-95; columnist San Jose Mercury News, 1994-97, Prime Times Monthly Mag. (now Get Up and Go), 1994—; founder, pres. Triple-A Coun. Calif., 1978-80. Vice chmn. Santa Clara County Sr. Care Commn., 1987-89, chmn., 1989-91, mem. social svcs. com., 1993—; mem. adv. coun. Coun. on Aging of Santa Clara County, 1995—; mem. aging and disabled adv. com. Met. Transp. Commn., 1995—. With WAVES, USNR, 1942-45. Recipient Social Welfare award Daniel E. Koshland Found., 1973, Friends of Santa Clara County Human Rels. Commn. award, 1992, first ann. Angelina Aguilar Yates Humanitarian award, 1995; named 24th State Assembly Dist. Woman of Yr., 1990. Mem. NASW, APHA, LWV (bd. dirs. San Jose/Santa Clara chpt. 1993-96, Bay Area bd. transp. chmn. 1996), Nat. Coun. Sr. Citizens (bd. dirs. 1988—), Svc. Employees Internat. Union (mem. local 535, state exec. bd. dirs. 1973—, pres. sr. mems. and retiree chpt. 1982—), Congress of Calif. Srs. (bd. dirs. 1987—, region IV pres. 1992-98, trustee 1993-97, no. v.p. 1997—), Older Women's League (bd. dirs. 1980-84), Older Women's League of Calif. (edn./resource coord. 1987-89, pres. 1990-91, Golden Owl award 1995), Am. Soc. on Aging (co-chair women's concerns com. 1985-86, awards com. 1990-93), Nat. Coun. on the Aging, Calif. Specialists on Aging (treas. 1985-93), Calif. Srs. Coalition (chmn. 1986, treas. 1993—), Calif. Writers Club (cen. bd. dels. 1995—). Home and Office: 2527 Forbes Ave Santa Clara CA 95050-5547

CHARLOT, MARTIN DAY, painter, muralist, writer, filmmaker, educator; b. Athens, Ga., Mar. 6, 1944; s. Jean and Zohmah Dorothy (Day) C.; m. Susanne Lee Obermiller, Aug. 22, 1966 (annulled 1980); children: Kawena O Keanu Kea, Jean Kekoa Pakoa, Martin Kamalu O Ka Aina, Kipano Keone A Ke Kai Ko'o; m. Phyllis Susanne Coffey, Dec. 20, 1980 (div. Dec. 1985). Grad. St. Louis High Sch., 1962; studies with Ansel Adams, 1958. News cameraman Martin Rhody Co., Honolulu, 1962; doorman Royal Theaters, Honolulu, 1964-65; illustrator Collins Assn. N.Y., N.Y.C., 1968; art dir. Bravura Films, Mountain View, Calif., 1970; self-employed artist, Honolulu, 1970—; lectr. St. John's U., Collegeville, Minn., 1969, Fresno U., Calif., 1981, U. Hawaii; tchr. Honolulu Acad. Arts, 1970; founding bd. mem. Hawaii Film Bd., Honolulu, 1971-73; founding bd. mem., art dir. 1st Hawaiian Internat. Film Festival, 1971. Executed murals, Konawaena High Sch., Kealakekua, Hawaii, 1976, Waiahole Poi Factory, Oahu, Hawaii, 1977, Kaneohe Dist. Park Gymnasium, Oahu, 1978, Hawaii State Sr. Ctr., Kalihi, Oahu, 1978, Kauai Intake Ctr., Hawaii, 1980, Waipahu High Sch., Oahu, 1980, King Intermediate, Kaneohe, Hawaii, 1981, Ala Moana Ctr., Ctr. Art Gallery, 1983, Waiahole Intermediate Sch., 1983, Barbers Point Elem. Sch., 1984, McDonalds Restaurant, Kaheohe, 1985, Waikiki, 1987, Kalaheo High Sch., Kailua, 1986, Aiea High Sch., Aiea, 1986, Consolidated Theater, Kahala, 1986, Show People Hawaii, 1985; one man shows include De Mena Gallery, N.Y., 1967, Gima Art Gallery, 1964, 69, Hawaii State Library, Honolulu, 1972, Kaimuki Regional Library, Volcano Arts Ctr., 1976, Contemporary Arts Ctr., Hawaii, 1979, Fed. Bldg., 1980, Kauai Library, 1980, Hawaii Loa Coll., 1984; exhibited in group shows at Showhouse 80, 1980, Artists of Honolulu, 1980, Great Hawaiian Open, Honolulu, 1980, Kirin Beer, 1981, Fed. Bldg., 1980, Hale Kaua III, Fed. Bldg., 1981, A Vision of America at Peace, The Concourse, San Francisco, 1984, Have You Got A Minute? Contermporary Arts Ctr., 1985, Wearable Art, East West Ctr., 1986; author/illustrator: Once Upon a Fishhook, 1972, Sunnyside Up, 1972; illustrator: Mystery on the Rancho Grande: 1969, Illustrated Atlas of Hawaii, 1970, On Hawaiian Music, 1971, Felisa, 1973, Hawaii Insight Guides, 1980, Mira, 1979, The Hula, 1982; Hawaiian Voices, 1983, Chanting the Universe, 1983, Celebration, 1984, The Hawaiian Poetry of Religion and Politics, 1985; illustrator Hawaii Film Festival, 1971, Kamehameha Day for Bank of Hawaii, 1972, Dillingham Corp. Tide Chart, 1974, opening poster Leeward Community Coll. Theater, 1974, Hawaiian Telephone cover, 1982, Honolulu Advertiser Progress Edit., 1982, calendar Mental Health Assn., 1982, Islands, 1983, Mokuleia Polo Club, 1987, record cover Hui Ohana, 1987; filmmaker (features) Memento Mei, 1962, Apocolypse 3:16, 1963, Kalapana, 1964, (shorts) Baby Dinosaur, 1957, An Artist Commits Suicide, 1967; screenwriter (shorts) Snow Crystals, 1969, Canoe, 1970, On Hawaiian Music, 1970, (features) Blinds, 1972, Two Horses, Apples, and Wood, 1974; contbr. articles to profl. jours. Mem. steering com. Waiahole, Waikane Community Assn., 1973-77. Served with U.S. Army, 1965-67. Recipient The Akamai Bus. award Kaneohe Bus. Group, 1983; named Fellow in Perpetuity Met. Mus. Art, N.Y.C., 1980. Mem. Screen Actors Guild, Hawaii Painters and Sculptors League. Democrat. Studio: 1510 Abbot Kinney Blvd Venice CA 90291-3743

CHARLSON, DAVID HARVEY, executive search company professional; b. Pitts., May 26, 1947; s. Raymond Milton and Helen Joan (Wesley) C.; m. Michal Brooke Riley, Aug. 22, 1969; 1 child, Adam David. BS, U. Ariz., 1969. Personnel dir. internat. div. Bank of Am., San Francisco, 1969-73; mgr. employment Gen. Foods Corp., White Plains, N.Y., 1973-74; staff v.p. Staub-Warmbold Assocs., San Francisco, 1974-76; mng. dir., sr. ptnr. Korn-Ferry Internat., Chgo., 1976-84; exec. v.p., mng. dir. Richards Cons., Chgo., 1984-89; pres., CEO Chestnut Hill Internat., Chgo., 1989—; cons. Walgreens Health Care Plus, 1978-84, Blue Cross-Blue Shield Ill., Chgo., 1978—, Health Care Svc. Corp., Chgo., 1993, Sherring-Plough Corp., 1989—, Marrin-Merrill Daw, 1986—; bd. dirs. Rush-Presbyn. St. Lukes Hosp., Dental Network Am., Kemper Ins. Co., I.V.T. Corp., Bertellsman, USA, Sonopress, Gensen-Sicor Entertainment, Warner Music Universal Music Corp., Allergan, Amgen, Peroit Sys., Gen Probe. Contbr. articles to profl. publs. Mem. Oak Park (Ill.) Sch. Dist. Bd. Edn., 1978-80; bd. dirs. U. Chgo. Grad. Sch. Bus., 1982-84, mem. bd. advisors; bd. dirs. Better Boys Found., Chgo., 1982-84; treas. Chgo. Dist. Tennis Assn., 1984-86; chmn. Ill. Citizens for Perot, 1992; sr. advisor Clinton-Gore Presdl. Campaign, 1992, Ill. Dem. Com., 1992—; mem. adv. bd. Little City Found.; mem. bd. advisors Highland Park Hosp.; mem., advisor to White House pers. Dem. Nat. Com. Recipient NFL Players Assn. award Better Boys Found., 1984; named One of Am.'s Top 100 Exec. Recruiters, Harper & Row Publs., One of 150 Top Exec. Recruiters in Am., 1992, One of 200 Top Exec. Recruiters in N.Am., 1994. Mem. Internat. Motor Sports Assn., Pharm. Mfrs. Assn., Assn. Exec. Recruitment Cos., Univ. Club Chgo., Pres.' Club U. Ariz., Sports Car Club Am., Execs. Club Chgo. Avocations: automobile racing, golf, tennis, Tae Kwon Do. Home: 2040B N Cleveland Ave # B Chicago IL 60614-4517 Office: Chestnut Hill Internat 4275 Executive Sq La Jolla CA 92037-9123

CHARLTON, JOHN KIPP, pediatrician; b. Omaha, Jan. 26, 1937; s. George Paul and Mildred (Kipp) C. A.B., Amherst Coll., 1958; M.D., Cornell U., 1962; m. Susan S. Young, Aug. 15, 1959; children: Paul, Cynthia, Daphne, Gregory. Intern, Ohio State U. Hosp., Columbus, 1962-63; resident in pediatrics Children's Hosp., Dallas, 1966-68, chief pediatric resident, 1968-69; nephrology fellow U. Tex. Southwestern Med. Sch., Dallas, 1969-70; pvt. practice medicine specializing in pediatrics, Phoenix, 1970; chmn. dept. pediatrics Maricopa Med. Ctr., Phoenix, 1971-78, 84-93, assoc. chmn. dept. pediatrics, 1979-84, med. staff pres., 1991; med. dir., bd. dirs. Crisis Nursery, Inc., 1977—; dir. Phoenix Pediatric Residency, 1983-85, Phoenix Hosps. affiliated pediatric program, 1985-88; clin. assoc. prof. pediatrics U. Ariz. Coll Medicine. Pres. Maricopa County Child Abuse Coun., 1977-81; bd. dirs. Florence Critenton Svcs., 1980-83, Ariz. Children's Found., 1987-91; mem. Gov.'s Coun. on Children, Youth and Families, 1984-86. Officer M.C., USAF, 1963-65. Recipient Hon Kachina award for volunteerism, 1980, Jefferson award for volunteerism, 1980, Horace Steel Child Advocacy award, 1993; named Clin. Sci. Educator of Yr. U. Ariz., 1997. Mem. Am. Acad. Pediatrics, Ariz. Pediatric Soc., Maricopa County Pediatric Soc. (past pres.). Author articles, book rev. in field. Home: 6230 E Exeter Blvd Scottsdale AZ 85251-3060 Office: Maricopa Med Ctr 2601 E Roosevelt St Phoenix AZ 85008-4973

CHARLTON, RANDOLPH SEVILLE, psychiatrist, educator; b. Salt Lake City, Nov. 16, 1944; s. Randolph Seville and Patricia Joy (Jensen) C.; m. Louise Bryden Buck, Feb. 14, 1975; children: Genevieve, Blake. BA, Wesleyan U., 1966; MD, Cornell U., 1970. Diplomate Am. Acad. Psychoanalysis. Intern U. Calif., San Francisco, 1970-71; resident psychiatry Stanford U., 1971-74; clin. faculty Standford Med. Sch., Palo Alto, Calif., 1974—; prof. clin. psychiatry Stanford (Calif.) U. Med. Ctr., 1990—; pvt. practice psychiatrist Palo Alto, 1974—. Editor: Treating Sexual Disorders, 1996; contbr. chpt. to book, articles to profl. jours. Bd. trustees Castilleja Sch., Palo Alto, 1992-96; bioethics com. Recovery Inn, Menlo Park, Calif., 1994—. Fellow Am. Acad. Psychoanalysis; mem. C.G. Jung Inst. (tng. analyst 1978—). Democrat. Avocations: running, skiing. Office: 690 Waverley St Palo Alto CA 94301-2549

CHARTIER, VERNON LEE, electrical engineer; b. Ft. Morgan, Colo., Feb. 14, 1939; s. Raymond Earl and Margaret Clara (Winegar) C.; m. Lois Marie Schwartz, May 20, 1967; 1 child, Neal Raymond. BSEE, BS in Bus., U. Colo., 1963. Registered profl. engr., Pa.; cert. electromagnetic compatibility engr. Rsch. engr., cons. Westinghouse Electric Co., East Pittsburgh, Pa., 1963-75; principal engr. high voltage phenomena Bonneville Power Adminstrn., Vancouver, Wash., 1975-95; power sys. EMC cons., Portland, 1995—. Contbr. articles to profl. jours. Fellow IEEE (past mem. fellow com. 1993-96, Herman Halperin Transmission and Distribution award 1995); mem. IEEE Power Engring. Soc. (chmn. transmission and distribution com. 1987-88, chmn. fellows com. 1990-92), Internat. Conf. Large High Voltage Electric Systems, W.G. 36.01 EMC Aspects of Corona and Magnetic Fields, Bioelectromagnetics Soc., Internat. Electrotech. Commn. (U.S. rep. to sub-com. on High Voltage Lines & Traction Systems), Chartier Family Assn. Baptist. Home and Office: 13095 SW Glenn Ct Beaverton OR 97008-5664

CHATARD, PETER RALPH NOEL, JR., aesthetic plastic surgeon; b. New Orleans, June 25, 1936; s. Peter Ralph Sr. and Alberta Chatard; m. Patricia Myrl White, Jan. 31, 1963; children: Andrea Michelle, Faedra Noelle, Tahra Deonne. BS in Biology, Morehouse Coll., 1956; MD, U. Rochester, 1960. Diplomate Am. Bd. Plastic Surgery, Am. Bd. Otolaryngology. Intern Colo. Gen. Hosp., 1960-61; asst. resident in gen. surgery Highland Gen. Hosp., Rochester, N.Y., 1963-64; resident in otolaryngology Strong Meml. Hosp., Rochester, 1964-67; resident in plastic and reconstructive surgery U. Fla., 1980-82; staff otolaryngologist Group Health Corp. of Puget Sound, Seattle, 1967-68; practice medicine specializing in otolaryngology Seattle, 1968-80, practice medicine specializing in plastic surgery, 1982—; clin. asst. prof. otolaryngology, head and neck surgery U. Wash., Seattle, 1975—; plastic surgery cons. western sec. Maxillofacial Rev. Bd. State of Wash., 1982-90, cons. Conservation of Hearing Program, 1968-80; trustee Physicians and Dentist Credit Bur., 1974-80, 84-87, pres. 1976-77, 84-85; active staff mem. Northwest Hosp., Seattle; courtesy staff Swedish Hosp., Children's Hosp. Med. Ctr., Seattle, Providence Hosp., Seattle, Stevens Meml. Hosp., Edmond, Wash., Seattle, others. Capt. USAF, 1961-63. Fellow ACS, Am. Rhinologic Soc., Seattle Surg. Soc., Am. Acad. Facial Plastic and Reconstructive Surgery, Am. Acad. Otolaryngology-Head and Neck Surgery, Northwest Acad. Otolaryngology and Head and Neck Surgery, Soc. for Ear, Nose and Throat Advances in Children, Pacific Oto-Ophthalmological Soc.; mem. Am. Soc. Plastic and Reconstructive Surgeons, Am. Soc. for Aesthetic Plastic Surgery, Inc., Lipoplasty Soc. N. Am., Wash. Soc. Plastic Surgeons, Nat. Med. Assn., King County Med. Soc., Wash. Med. Assn., N.W. Soc. of Plastic Surgeons. Avocations: photography, cynology, microcomputing, architecture and design. Home: 13211 Frazier Pl NW Seattle WA 98177-4132 Office: Chatard Plas Surg Ctr 1200 N Northgate Way Seattle WA 98133-8916

CHATHAM, RUSSELL, landscape artist; b. San Francisco, Oct. 27, 1939; m. Mary Fanning (div.); m. Doris Meyer (div.); m. Suzanne Porter; children: Georgina, Lea, Rebecca, Paul. Ed., San Francisco. Painter, writer, Calif.; landscape artist, lithographer, Mont., 1972—. Address: PO Box 659 Livingston MT 59047-0659 Also: c/o Angler Art & Gifts Cherry Creek North 201 Fillmore St Ste D Denver CO 80206*

CHATROO, ARTHUR JAY, lawyer; b. N.Y.C., July 1, 1946; s. George and Lillian (Leibowitz) C.; m. Christina Daly, Aug. 6, 1994; 1 child, Alexander. *Wife Christina Daly Chatroo practices anesthesia at the VAMC San Diego, is an ACLS instructor, Sigma Theta Tau Honor Society member, enjoys yoga, playing bridge, growing orchids, and genealogy. She has been a student at the College of New Rochelle, American College in Paris, France, New York Medical College Graduate School, and Case Western Reserve University. Her parents are Dr. Charles and June Daly. She has two brothers, Owen Grant and Douglas Patrick, and a sister, Deborah June.* BChemE, CCNY, 1968; JD cum laude, New York Law Sch., 1979; MBA with distinction, NYU, 1982. Bar: N.Y. 1980, Ohio 1992, Calif. 1993, U.S. Patent Office 1998. Process engr. Std. Oil Co. of Ohio, various locations, 1968-73; process specialist BP Oil, Inc., Marcus Hook, Pa., 1974-75; sr. process engr. Sci. Design Co., Inc., N.Y.C., 1975-78; mgr. spl. projects The Halcon SD Group, N.Y.C., 1978-82; corp. counsel, tax and fin. The Lubrizol Corp., Wickliffe, Ohio, 1982-85; sr. counsel spl. investment projects The Lubrizol Corp., Wickliffe, 1989-90; gen. counsel Lubrizol Enterprises, Inc., Wickliffe, 1985-89; chmn. Correlation Genetics Corp., San Jose, Calif., 1990-91; gen. counsel Agrigenetics Co., Eastlake, Ohio, 1990-92; gen. counsel, dir. comml. contracting Agrigenetics, L.P., San Diego, 1992-93; counsel Agrigenetics, Inc. dba Mycogen Seeds, Mycogen Corp., San Diego, 1994-97; dir. legal affairs Mycogen Corp., San Diego, 1997-98; exec. v.p. bus. devel., legal and regulatory affairs Global Agro, Inc., Encinitas, Calif., 1998—. Mem. Met. Parks Adv. com., Allen County, Ohio, 1973. Mem. ABA, AIChE, Am. Chem. Soc., N.Y. State Bar Assn., San Diego County Bar Assn., Am. Corp. Counsel Assn., Jaycees (personnel dir. Lima, Ohio chpt. 1972-73), Licensing Execs. Soc., Toastmasters, Omega Chi Epsilon, Beta Gamma Sigma. Club: Toastmasters. Avocations: sailing, photography, skiing. Home: 3525 Del Mar Hts Rd # 285 San Diego CA 92130-2122 Office: Global Agro Inc 12626 High Bluff Dr Ste 250 San Diego CA 92130

CHATTERJI, ANGANA P., anthropologist; b. Calcutta, India, Nov. 17, 1966; d. Bhola and Anubha (Sengupta) C.; m. Richard Murray Shapiro, May 10, 1998. MA, U. Delhi, 1989; PhD, Calif. Inst. Integral Studies, San Francisco, 1999. Cons. Planning Com. India, New Delhi, 1990-92; assoc. Asia forest network program Ctr. South Asia Studies U. Calif., Berkeley, 1992—; asst. adj. prof. Calif. Inst. Integral Studies, 1997—; cons. Swed Forest Internat., Stockholm, 1997—; cons. in field. Author: In Search of Reality, 1984. Ford Found. grantee, 1993. Mem. Am. Anthropol. Assn. Avocations: gliding, reading, computers, travel, symphony.

CHAU, HUNG, engineer, educator; b. Kontum, Vietnam, Aug. 28, 1948; came to U.S., 1978; s. Chuong Van and Tuy Thi (Nguyen) C.; m. Bach-Tuyet Nguyen, Jan. 20, 1979; children: Johann, Johnny, Jeffrey, Jerald. Diploma-engring., U. Hannover, Germany, 1978; MS, Ill. Inst. of Tech., 1983; EdD, U. So. Calif., L.A., 1993. Indsl. engr. Fort Howard Paper Co., Chgo., 1979-84; sr. mgmt. engr. Ind. U. Med. Ctr., Indpls., 1984-86, Straub Clinic and Hosp., Inc., Honolulu, Hawaii, 1986-90; indsl. engr. Dept. of the Army, Honolulu, 1990-97; prof. edn. Troy State U., Pacific Region, Hawaii, 1994—; ltd. ptnr. Neozyme Internat., Inc., Aliso Viejo, Calif., 1996—. Contbr. articles to profl. jours. Pres. Vietnamese Students Assn., Germany, 1974, Inst. of Indsl. Engrs., Honolulu, 1986. Mem. Am. Ednl. Rsch. Assn., U. So. Calif. Gen. Alumni Assn. (life), Phi Delta Kappa. Roman Catholic. Avocations: travel, golf, swimming. Home: 507 Iolani Ave Honolulu HI 96813-1835 Office: Systems Engr Bldg 104 Wright Ave Dir of Pub Works Schofield Barracks HI 96857

CHAVEZ, ALBERT BLAS, financial executive; b. L.A., Jan. 1, 1952; s. Albert Blas and Yolanda (Garcia) C.; m. Irma Laura Cavazos, Dec. 21, 1996. BA, U. Tex., El Paso, 1979; MBA, Stanford U., 1985. CPA, Calif. Mem. profl. staff Deloitte Haskins and Sells, L.A., 1980-83; planning analyst corp. fin. planning Boise (Idaho) Cascade Co., 1984; treasury analyst corp. treasury RCA Corp., N.Y.C., 1985; asst. contr. RCA/Ariola Records, Mexico City, 1986; fin. analyst corp. exec. office GE Co., Fairfield, Conn., 1987-90; fin. cons. Entertainment Industry and Litigation Support Svcs., L.A., 1990-91; co-founder, sr. v.p., CFO El Dorado Comm., Inc., L.A., 1991-98; fin. cons. entertainment industry pvt. practice, 1998—. Bd. dirs., treas. L.A. Conservation Corps, 1990—. Mem. AICPA, Calif. Soc. CPAs. Democrat. Home: 18744 Strathern St Reseda CA 91335-1221

CHÁVEZ, DENISE ELIA, drama educator, writer, actress; b. Las Cruces, N.Mex., Aug. 15, 1948; d. Ernesto E. and Delfina (Rede) C.; m. Daniel Zolinsky, Dec. 29, 1984. BA in Theatre, N.Mex. State U., 1971; MFA in Theatre, Trinity U., 1974; MA in Creative Writing, U. N.Mex., 1984. Prof. English and theatre Northern N.Mex. C.C., Española, 1977-80; artist-in-the-schs. N.Mex. Arts Divn., Santa Fe, 1977-83; prof. theatre U. Houston, 1988-91; asst. prof. creative writing, playwriting, and Chicano lit. N.Mex. State U., Las Cruces, 1996—; prof. creative writing Munson Sr. Ctr., Las Cruces; tchr. theatre and creative writing N.Mex. Sch. Visually Handicapped; vis. prof. creative writing N.Mex. State U., 1992-93, 95-96; artistic dir. Border Book Festival, 1994—; del. forum U.S.-Soviet Dialogue, Moscow and Russia; mem. N.Mex. Street Theatre; presenter reading workshops; lectr. in field. Author: The Last of Menu Girls, 1986 (Puerto del Sol Fiction award 1986), Face of an Angel, 1994 (Am. Book award 1995, Premio Aztlán award 1995, Mesilla Valley Author of Yr. 1995), (plays) Plaza, 1989, The Flying Torhila Man, 1987, The Woman Who Knew the Language of the Animals, 1993; one woman shows include Women in the State of Grace, U.S. Recipient Human Svcs. award citizen advocacy Doña Ana County, Creative Artist award Cultural Arts Coun., Houston, 1990, Rockefeller Playwriting award Rockefeller Found., N.Mex., 1984, Writers of Pass award El Paso Herald Post, 1995, Gov.'s award achievement in arts in lit., 1995, Luminaria award N.Mex. Cmty. Found., 1996, Woman Distinction award edn. Soroptimist Internat. Ams. Club, 1996, Papen Family Arts award, 1998; Nat. Endowment Arts grantee, 1982, U. Houston rsch. grantee, 1989; vis. scholar U. Houston, 1988; Rockefeller Found. fellow, 1984. Democrat. Roman Catholic. Avocations: swimming, bowling, movies. Office: NMex State U Dept 3 E Box 30001 Las Cruces NM 88003

CHAVEZ, EDWARD, police chief; b. Stockton, Calif., Mar. 22, 1943; m. Nancy Ruhr; children: Eric, Jill. AA, San Joaquin Delta Coll., 1971; BA, Calif. State U., 1972; MS, Calif. Polytechnic Pomona, 1990; grad., POST Command Coll., Delinquency Control Inst., Leadership Stockton Program, FBI Nat. Acad. With USAF, 1962-70; officer Stockton Police Dept., 1973, sgt., 1980, lt., 1986, capt., 1990, dep. chief of police, 1990, acting chief of police, 1993, chief of police, 1993—. Bd. dirs. St. Joseph's Med. Ctr., San Joaquin United Way, Lilliput Childrens Svcs., Greater Stockton C. of C.; active Hispanics for Polit. Action; adv. com. Leadership, Stockton. With USAF, 1962-70. Mem. Calif. Peace Officers Assn., Hispanic Am. Police Command Officer's Assn., Mexican Am. C. of C., Stockton E. Rotary, Coun. for Spanish Speaking (past bd. dirs.), Leadership Stockton Alumni Assn. Office: Stockton Police Dept 22 E Market St Stockton CA 95202-2802*

CHAVEZ, GILBERT ESPINOZA, bishop; b. Ontario, Calif., Mar. 19, 1932; ed. St. Francis Sem., El Cajon, Calif., Immaculate Heart Sem., San Diego, U. Calif., San Diego. Ordained priest Roman Cath. Ch., 1960; titular bishop of Magarmel and aux. bishop Diocese of San Diego, 1974—. Office: St Joseph Cathedral 1535 3rd Ave San Diego CA 92101-3101

CHAVEZ, MANNY, film company executive; b. L.A., Oct. 14, 1958; s. Manuel and Lupe C.; m. Pamela; 2 children. BS, Calif. State U., L.A., 1987; M of Pub. Rels., Calif. State U., Northridge, 1993. Deputy state fire marshal Calif. Stae Fire Marshal, Hollywood, 1986-95; v.p. motion picture & TV prodn. AON Ins./Disney Studio, Burbank, Calif., 1995—. Author: Filming in California, A Fire Protection Handbook, 1993, Set on Safety, 1995. With USN, 1976-80. Mem. Nat. Fire Protection Assn., Am. Soc. Safety Engrs., Alliance Motion Picture & TV Prodicers (safety com.). Republican. Office: Walt Disney Studios 500 S Buena Vista St Burbank CA 91521-0004

CHAYKIN, ROBERT LEROY, manufacturing and marketing executive; b. Miami, Fla., May 2, 1944; s. Allan Leroy and Ruth (Levine) C.; m. Patty Jean Patton, Feb. 1971 (div. May 1975); m. Evalyn Marcy Slodzina, Sept. 3, 1989; children: Stephanie Lee, Michelle Alee, Catrina Celia, Ally Sue. BA in Polit. Sci., U. Miami, Fla., 1965, LLB, 1969. Owner, operator Serrating Svcs. Miami, 1969-71, Serrating Svcs. Las Vegas, Nev., 1971-84; pres. Ser-Sharp Mfg., Inc., Las Vegas, 1984 ; nat. mktg. dir. Coscrco Corp., Las Vegas, 1987—. Patentee in mfg. field. With U.S. Army, 1962. Recipient 2d degree black belt Tae Kwon Do, Profl. Karate Assn., 1954-61. Avocations: travel, camping.

CHAZEN, MELVIN LEONARD, retired chemical engineer; b. St. Louis, Sept. 26, 1933; s. Saul and Tillie (Kramer) C.; m. Dorothea Glazer, June 29, 1958; children: Jamie Lynn, Avery Glazer. BS in Chem. Engring., Washington U., St. Louis, 1955. Registered profl. engr., Mo. Thermodynamics engr. Bell Aerospace Textron, Buffalo, 1958-59; devel. engr. Bell Aerospace Textron, 1959-62, project engr., 1962-65, chief sec. rocket engines, 1965-72, prog. mgr., tech. dir., 1972-74, project engr., 1974-84, chief engr. rocket devel., 1984-87; sr. staff engr. Space and Tech. div. TRW, Redondo Beach, Calif., 1987-99; ret.; bd. dirs. Unimed Corp., Rochester. Contbr. articles to profl. jours.; patentee in field. Recipient Innovation award Enterprise Devel. Inc., 1994, Recognition Cert. NASA, 1994, TRW Chmn.'s award, 1995. Mem. AIAA, Alpha Chi Sigma. Avocations: photography, travel, sports. Home: 12522 Inglenook Ln Cerritos CA 90703-7837

CHEAH, KEONG-CHYE, psychiatrist; b. Georgetown, Penang, West Malaysia, Mar. 15, 1939; came to U.S., 1959; s. Thean Hoe and Hun Kin (Keong) C.; m. Sandra Massey, June 10, 1968; children: Chylynn, Maylynn. BA in Psychology, U. Ark., 1962; MD, U. Ark., Little Rock, 1967, MS in Microbiology, 1968. Diplomate Am. Bd. Psychiatry and Neurology (examiner 1982, 85); cert. Ark. State Sci. Bd., Ark. State Med. Bd. Intern U. Ark. Med. Ctr., 1967-68; resident VA Med. Ctr. and U. Ark. Med. Ctr., Little Rock, 1968-72; chief addiction sect. Little Rock (Ark.) VA Med. Ctr., 1972-73, staff psychiatrist, 1975-80; chief psychiatry Am. Lake VA Med. Ctr., Tacoma, Wash., 1981-86; chief consultation, liason Am. Lake VA Med. Ctr., Tacoma, 1986-94; asst. prof. medicine, psychiatry U. Ark., Little Rock, 1975-81; asst. prof. psychiatry and behavioral scis. U. Wash., Seattle, 1981-86, clin. assoc. prof., 1987—; mem. dist. br. com. The CHAMPUS, 1977-91; site visitor AMA Continuing Med. Edn., 1979-83; book reviewer Jour. Am. Geriatrics Soc., 1984-85; mem. task force alcohol abuse VA Med. Dist. 27, 1984, survey mem. Sytematic External Rev. Process, 1985; mem. mental health plan adv. com. State of Ark., 1976-81, chmn. 1979-81, chmn. steering com., 1979; mem. Vietnamese Resettlement Program, 1979; many coms. Am. Lake VA Med. Ctr. including chmn. mental health coun. 1981-84, utilization rev. com., 1981-86. Contbr. articles and abstracts to profl. jours.; presenter to confs. and meetings of profl. socs. Mem. Parents Adv. Com., Lakes H.S., Wash., 1987-91; mem. Mayor's Budget and Fin. Foresight Com., 1992—, chmn. 1990-92; sch. cons. Child Study Ctr. U. Ark., 1972-74; bd. dirs. Crisis Ctr. Ark., 1974-79, chmn. pub. rels. com., 1975-79, mem. pers. com. 1974, vice chmn. bd. 1977; pres. Chinese Assn. Ctrl. Ark., 1977; mem. gifted edn. adv. coun. Clover Park Sch. Dist. 400, Wash., 1983-85, Parent Tchr. Student Orgn. Recipient U.S. Govt. scholarship 1959, cert. merit State of Ark., 1973, Leadership award, Mental Health Svcs. Divsn., State of Ark., 1980. Fellow Am. Psychiat. Assn. (sec. treas. Asian Am. caucus 1985-87, pres. 1987-94); mem. Assn. Mil. Surgeons U.S., Wash. State Psychiat. Assn. (mem. peer rev. com. 1982-92, chmn. pub. psychiatry com. 1985-93, exec. coun. 1985-93), N. Pacific Soc. Neurology and Psychiatry Assn. (sec.-treas. 1986—, pres. 1993), S. Puget Sound Psychiat. Assn., Assn. Chinese-Am. Psychiatrists, Ark. Caduceus Club, Alpha Epsilon Delta, Psi Chi, Phi Beta Kappa. Avocations: reading, target shooting. Office: Am Lake Divsn VA Puget Sound Health Care System Tacoma WA 98493

CHEATHAM, DAVID TODD, software company executive; b. L.A., June 2, 1956; s. Robert Tracy and Jane C.; m. Sharon Bond, Sept. 9, 1979; children: Michael, Alyssa, Victoria. BA in Bus. Adminstrn., Principia Coll., 1979; MBA in Mgmt., Pepperdine U., 1984. Ops. mgr. Microcheck, Inc., Long Beach, Calif., 1979-81; chief fin. officer Data Trek, Inc., Carlsbad, Calif., 1981-84; pres. EOS Data Trek, Inc., Encinitas, Calif., 1984—. Developer mgr. series and profl. series libr. automation software. Recipient Outstanding Tech. award Assn. Info. Mgrs., 1985. Mem. ALA, Spl. Libr. Assn., Assn. Law Librs., Med. Libr. Assn., Internat. Interactive Communications Soc. Achievements include development of medical information network - database of all U.S. doctors including bioraphical, educational and disciplinary data; development of Information Quest web-based software to access scientific, technical and medical journals. Avocations: music, antique car restoration, basketball, skiing, tennis. Office: Data Trek Inc 5838 Edison Pl Carlsbad CA 92008-6519

CHEDID, JOHN G., bishop; b. Eddid, Lebanon, July 4, 1923. Educated, Sems. in Lebanon and Pontifical Urban Coll., Rome. Ordained priest Roman Cath. Ch., 1951. Titular bishop of Callinico and aux bishop St. Maron of Bklyn., 1981. Office: Our Lady of Lebanon Ch 333 S San Vicente Blvd Los Angeles CA 90048-3313*

CHEE, LAMBERT HU-KEE, physician; b. Kwangtung, China, July 1, 1949; came to U.S., 1959; s. Won and Poon Shee Chee; m. Sandra Yat-Ngo Jim, Aug. 31, 1972; children: Allison, Ken. Emilyn. BA, Columbia U., 1971; MD, U. Calif., San Francisco, 1975. Diplomate Am. Bd. Internal Medicine. Intern San Francisco Gen. Hosp., 1975-76; resident VA Med. Ctr., Martinez, Calif., 1976-78, fellowship in cardiovascular diseases, 1978-80; cons. cardiologist Diable Cardiology Med. Group, Walnut Creek, Calif., 1980—. Mem. AMA, Am. Coll. Cardiology, Alameda-Contra Costa-Med. Assn. Avocations: reading, gardening, traveling. Office: Diablo Cardiology Med Group Inc 1399 Ygnacio Valley Rd Ste 11 Walnut Creek CA 94598-2816

CHEE, PERCIVAL HON YIN, ophthalmologist; b. Honolulu, Aug. 29, 1936; s. Young Sing and Den Kyau (Ching) C.; m. Carolyn Tong, Jan. 27, 1966; children: Lara Wai Lung, Shera Wai Sum. BA, U. Hawaii, 1958; MD, U. Rochester, 1962. Intern Travis AFB Hosp., Fairfield, Calif., 1962-63; resident Bascom Palmer Eye Inst., Miami, Fla., 1965-68, Jackson Meml. Hosp., Miami, 1965-68; partner Straub Clinic, Inc., Honolulu, 1968-71; practice medicine specializing in ophthalmology, Honolulu, 1972—; mem. staffs Queen's Med. Center, St. Francis Hosp., Kapiolani Children's Med. Center, Honolulu; clin. assoc. prof. surgery U. Hawaii Sch. Medicine, 1971—; cons. Tripler Army Med. Center. Mem. adv. bd. Services to Blind; bd. dirs. Lions Eye Bank and Makana Found. (organ bank), Multiple Sclerosis Soc. Served to capt. USAF, 1962-65. Fellow Am. Acad. Ophthalmology, ACS; mem. AMA, Pan Am. Med. Assn., Pan Pacific Surg. Assn., Am. Assn. Ophthalmology, Soc. Eye Surgeons, Hawaii Ophthal. Soc. Pacific Coast Ophthal. Soc., Am. Assn. for Study Headache, Pan Am. Ophthal. Found. Contbr. articles to profl. pubs. Home: 3755 Poka Pl Honolulu HI 96816-4409 Office: Kukui Pla 50 S Beretania St Ste C116 Honolulu HI 96813-2225

CHEE, URIEL HIRAM, biomedical engineer; b. Ensenada, Mexico, Aug. 6, 1959; came to the U.S., 1975; s. Gregorio and Guadalupe (Gutierrez) C.; m. Akemi Tome Philbrick, Sept. 16, 1989. BSChemE, U. Calif., San Diego, 1983; cert. in bioengring., U. Calif., Irvine, 1984. Engr. in tng., Calif. Assoc. engr. Baxter Edwards, Irvine, 1983-84, engr., 1984-85, staff engr., 1985-86, sr. staff engr., 1986-87; sr. engr. Target Therapeutics, San Jose, Calif., 1987-88, mgr., 1988-90, dir., 1990—; v.p., 1992-97; entrepreneur in residence U.S. Venture Ptners., Menlo Park, Calif., 1998; v.p. Microheart, Sunnyvale, Calif., 1998—. Mem. Am. Inst. Chem. Engrs., Soc. Plastic Engrs., Soc. for Biomaterials. Roman Catholic. Achievements include U.S. patents in medical devices for the treatment of stroke, cancer and other diseases. Home: 127 Dolton Ave San Carlos CA 94070-1629 Office: Microheart 1049 Kiel Ct Sunnyvale CA 94089

CHEESEMAN, DOUGLAS TAYLOR, JR., wildlife tour executive, photographer, educator; b. Honolulu, July 16, 1937; s. Douglas Taylor Cheeseman and Myra Bettencourt; m. Gail Macomber, Apr. 7, 1963; children: Rosie M., Ted F. BA, San Jose (Calif.) State U., 1959, MA, 1964. Cert. secondary tchr., Calif. Naturalist Crater Lake (Oreg.) Nat. Park, summers 1959-60; tchr. biology Woodside High Sch., Redwood City, Calif., 1961-65; teaching asst. U. Colo., Boulder, 1966-67; prof. biology De Anza Coll., Cupertino, Calif., 1967—, dir. environ. study area, 1970—, dir. Student Ecology Rsch. Lab., 1990—; pres. Cheeseman's Ecology Safaris, Saratoga, Calif., 1981—; instr. wildlife and natural history photography, Saratoga, 1984—; rsch. cooperator Fish and Wilflife Svc., 1972—, guest lectr. numerous conservation groups, No. Calif., 1978—; spkr. on rainforest destruction, zone depletion, global warming; participant, spkr. to save planet; spkr. Calif. Acad. Antarctic Ecology, Am. Acad. African Birds, 1996; expdn. leader Sengey Vavilov, Antarctic, 1994; active in saving flora and fauna in third world; expdn. leader, Antarctica, 1996, ship Alla Tarasova, 1996; expdn. leader in Antarctic. Photographs represented in books and on calendars. Recipient Outstanding Svc. and Tchr. award, Pres.'s award De Anza Coll., 1988, Nat. Leadership award U. Tex., Austin, 1989; NSF fellow, 1969, 71; NEDA Title III grantee, 1970. Mem. Ecol. Soc. Am., Am. Ornithologists Union, Am. Soc. Mammalogists, Brit. Trust Ornitology, Brit. Ornithologists Union, AfricanWildlife Soc., Marine Mammal Soc. (founding), Calif. Native Plants Soc., Bay Area Bird Photographers (co-founder), Santa Clara Valley Audubon Soc. (bd. dirs., v.p., program chmn. 1983—), Cooper Soc. Avocations: wildlife rsch. and photography, lecturing on rainforest conservation, studying natural ecosystems, birding. Home: 20800 Kittridge Rd Saratoga CA 95070-6322 Office: De Anza Coll Dept Biology Cupertino CA 95014

CHEIFETZ, LORNA GALE, psychologist; b. Phoenix, Mar. 22, 1953; d. Walter and Ruth Cheifetz. BS, Chapman Coll., Orange, Calif., 1975; D of Psychology, Ill. Sch. Profl. Psychology, 1981. Psychology intern Cook County Hosp., Chgo., 1979-80; clin. psychologist City of Chgo., 1980-84, Phoenix Inst. for Psychotherapy, 1984-87; pvt. practice Phoenix, 1987—; cons. to judges, attys., cts., 1984—; adj. faculty Met. U., Phoenix, 1984-88, Ill. Sch. Profl. Psychology, 1982-86. Contbr. chpt. to book Listening and Interpreting, 1984; contbg. editor Internat. Jour. Communicative Psychoanalysis and Psychotherapy, 1991-93. Cons., vol. Ariz. Bar Assn. Vol. Lawyer Program, 1985—; co-coord. Psychology Info. Referral Svc., Maricopa County, Ariz., 1984-96. Named Psychologist of Yr. Ariz. Bar Assn., 1987, 95. Mem. APA (activist 1989—), Nat. Register Health Svc. Providers in Psychology. Avocations: parenting. Office: 3930 E Camelback Rd Ste 207 Phoenix AZ 85018-2634

CHEN, CARLSON S., SR., mechanical engineer; b. Orange, N.J., Mar. 17, 1960; s. Kao and May Chen; m. Lynn Duong, Dec. 5, 1992; 1 child, Christopher D. BSME, Brown U., 1982; MBA, U. Pitts., 1987. Engr. Westinghouse Corp., Pitts., 1982-89; sr. engr. Gen. Dynamics, San Diego, 1989-91, GPS Techs., San Diego, 1991-93; sr. mech. engr. Nat. Steel & Shipbuilding, San Diego, 1993—, Nat. Steel & Shipbuilding (A Gen. Dynamics Divsn.), San Diego, 1998—. Contbg. author Standard Handbook of Powerplant Engineering, 1997. Active Brown Cmty. Outreach, 1979-80. Mem. ASME, Soc. Naval Architects & Marine Engrs. (publicity and meetings chmn. San Diego chpt.), Brown Club of San Diego. Office: Nat Steel & Shipbuilding Co Harbor Dr & 28th St San Diego CA 92186

CHEN, EDNA LAU, art educator, artist; b. Lanai City, Hawaii, Apr. 20, 1932; d. George S.H. and Amy Lau; m. Francis F. Chen, Mar. 31, 1956; children: Sheryl Frances, Patricia Ann, Robert Francis. BA, U. No. Colo., 1954; MA, Columbia U., 1955. Cert. tchr., Calif. Tchr. Somerville (N.J.) H.S., 1955-56, Littlebrook Sch., Princeton, N.J., 1956-57, L.A. County Mus., 1978-81, Beverly Hills (Calif.) Adult Sch., 1976—; vol., founder, dir. Garret 21, Warner Sch., L.A., 1971-77; artist-in-residence Volcano (Hawaii) Art Ctr., 1978, 80. Solo shows include Gallery 100, Princeton, N.J., 1964, 68, 72, 73, Jacqueline Anhalt Gallery, L.A., 1975, Elaine Starkman Gallery, N.Y.C., 1983, Art Loft, Honolulu, 1983, 85, 87. Named Tchr. of Yr., Beverly Hills Kiwanis Club, 1979. Democrat. Unitarian. Avocations: tennis, triathlon, backpacking, gardening. Home: 638 Westholme Ave Los Angeles CA 90024-3248

CHEN, GEORGE CHI-MING, energy company executive; b. Shanghai, China, Sept. 21, 1923; s. Harvey Kun-Fan and Margaret Wen-Yao (Sang) C.; m. Nora Tzu-Ling Pan, Oct. 15, 1953; children: Priscilla Hsu-Lu, Peter Hsu-Ling. BS, Harvard U., 1946. Mgr. Kian Gwan Co., Shanghai, 1947-49, Hong Kong, 1949-50; mng. dir. Kian Gwan Co., Taipei, 1950-51; chmn. George Chen & Co., Taipei, 1951-87, Lien Chen Ltd., Taipei, 1951-87; mng. dir. Shing Nung Group, Tai Chung, 1961-87; chmn. Shell Pacific Devel., Singapore, 1970-87. Trustee Northfield Mt. Hermon Sch., Mass., 1988-98, Libr. Found. of San Francisco, 1996—; mem. bd. overseers Harvard U., 1998—. Lt. Col. Chinese Army. Mem. China Petroleum Soc. (life). Republican. Roman Catholic.

CHEN, JOHN CALVIN, child and adolescent psychiatrist; b. Augusta, Ga., Apr. 30, 1949; s. Calvin Henry Chen and Lora (Lee) Liu. BA in History, Pacific Union Coll., 1971; MD, Loma Linda U., 1974; PhD in Philosophy, Claremont Grad. U., 1984; JD, UCLA, 1987. Bar: Calif. 1987, U.S. Dist. Ct. (ctrl. dist.) Calif. 1988; diplomate Am. Bd. Psychiatry and Neurology, Child and Adolescent Psychiatry. Resident in psychiatry Loma Linda U. Med. Ctr., 1975-77; fellow in child and family psychiatry Cedars-Sinai Med. Ctr., L.A., 1977-78; psychiat. cons. San Bernardino (Calif.) County Mental Health Dept., 1979-83; pvt. practice Claremont, Calif., 1980-84; fellow in child and adolescent psychiatry U. So. Calif., L.A., 1983-84; law clk. to Hon. William P. Gray U.S. Dist. Ct., L.A., 1987-88; mental health psychiatrist Los Angeles County Dept. Mental Health, L.A., 1988-94, Alameda County Health Care Svcs. Agy., Fremont, Calif., 1994-97; psychiat. cons. Edgewood Ctr. for Children and Families, San Francisco, 1996-97; physician specialist L.A. County Health Care Svcs. Agy., L.A., 1997—; attending physician Martin Luther King Jr. Hosp., L.A., 1997—; child and adolescent psychiatrist Augustus F. Hawkins Mental Health Ctr., L.A., 1997—, chief psychiatrist, child and adolescent clinic, 1998—; adj. instr. philosophy Fullerton (Calif.) Coll., 1989-90; adj. asst. prof. psychiatry Charles Drew U., 1998—; asst. clin. prof. psychiatry UCLA Sch. of Medicine, 1998—. Recipient Cert. Recognition L.A. County Mental Health Dept., 1993; univ. fellow Claremont Grad. Sch., 1980-81. Mem. ABA, Am. Philos. Assn., Chinese for Affirmative Action, Soc. for Exploration of Psychotherapy Integration, Chinese Hist. Soc. Am., Calif. Hist. Soc., Chinese Hist. Soc. So. Calif., So. Calif. Chinese Lawyers Assn. Office: 745 E Valley Blvd # 120 San Gabriel CA 91776-3549

CHEN, KAO, consulting electrical engineer; b. Shanghai, China, Mar. 21, 1919; came to U.S., 1947; s. Chi-son and Wei C. (Hsu) C.; m. May Yee Yoh, Nov. 14, 1948; children: Jennifer H., Arthur B., Carlson s. BSEE, Jiao Tong U., Shanghai, 1942; postgrad., Brit. Industries scholar, Rugby, Eng., 1945-47; MSEE, Harvard U., 1948; postgrad. degree in Elec. Engring., Poly. U., 1953. Registered profl. engr., N.J., N.Y. Relay specialist Am. Gas & Electric Co., N.Y.C., 1950-52; project supr. Ebasco Internat., N.Y.C., 1953-55; sr. project engr. Westinghouse Electric Corp., Bloomfield, N.J., 1956-67, fellow engr., 1968-83; fellow engr., cons. N.Am. Philips Lighting Corp., Bloomfield, N.J., 1983-86; pres. Carlsons Cons. Engrs., San Diego, Calif., 1987—; vis. prof. Fudan U., 1982; cons. in field. Author: Industrial Power Distribution and Illuminating Systems, 1990, Energy Effective Industrial Illuminating Systems, 1994; editor-in-chief Std. Handbook Powerplant Engring., 1997, Energy Management in Illuminating Systems, 1999; contbr. chpts. to 3 engring. handbooks, 6 IEEE stds., over 95 articles and papers to profl. jours.; patentee in field. Exec. PTA, Cedar Grove, N.J., 1960-62; exec. Essex coun. Boy Scouts Am., West Orange, 1966-70; mem. Repub. Presdl. Task Force, 1989—. Recipient Rep. Presdl. award, 1994. Fellow IEEE (life fellow, del. to visit China 1982, vice chmn. indsl. utilization sys. dept. 1981-84, chmn. 1985-87, chmn. prodn. and application of light com. 1983-84, mem. new stds. com. 1985-86, IEEE rep. to IEC TC34 lamps and related equipment 1997—, Soc. best paper awards 1981, 83, Centennial medal 1984, IEEE-IAS award of merit 1985, Richard Harold Kaufmann award 1992, IEEE-IAS Disting. Lectr. 1996-97, IAS Recognition award to disting. lect. 1997, RAB Larry K. Wilson transnational award 1998), Power Engring. Soc. (energy engring. seminar leader 1991), Industry Applications Soc. (mem. transactions adv. bd. 1981-84); mem. NSPE (life), Assn. Energy Engrs., Illuminating Engring. Soc. (emeritus), U.S. Nat. Com. of the Internat. Commn. on Illumination, Am. Biog. Inst. (rsch. bd. advisors, Commemorative Medal of Honor 1987), Energy Svcs. Mktg. Soc. (charter), Jiao Tong Alumni Assn. (v.p. 1962-63), Harvard Club (N.J., sch. com. 1975-83), Harvard Club (San Diego). Achievements include research and development in energy management of industrial power and illuminating systems. Home: 11816 Caminito Corriente San Diego CA 92128-4550

CHEN, LI, computer scientist, software engineer; b. Lishui, Jian Su, China, Apr. 23, 1961; came to U.S., 1991; s. Zhengxi and Suqin (Wang) C.; m. Lan Zhang, Apr. 18, 1987; 1 child, Boxi. BS, Wahan (China) U., 1982; MS, Utah State U., 1995. Asst. engr. Rsch. Inst. of Geophys. Prospecting, Nanjing, China, 1982-85; lectr. Nanjing Inst. Tech., 1985-89, Wuhan U., 1989-91; sr. software engr. Spiricon, Inc., Logan, Utah, 1994—; prin. rsch. scientist Sci. and Practical Computing Lab., North Logan, 1997—; adj. assoc. prof. Wuhan U., China, 1997—. Contbr. articles to profl. jours. and internat. confs. Recipient Award Rsch. Fund of Chinese Acad. Sci. for Young Scientists, 1987, 2d Class award Chinese Min. Geology, 1991; named Outstanding Scientist of Wuhan U., 1991. Achievements include definition of gradually varied surfaces and interpolation algorithms; the definition of general discrete manifolds and the classification of digital surface points; optimal algorithm for optimal minimum odd-weigh-column SEC-DED code's check matrix; inventor fuzzy sub-fiber, possibility-based neural networks. Avocation: Chinese flute. Office: Scientific & Practical Computing Lab PO Box 6081 North Logan UT 84341

CHEN, LYNN CHIA-LING, librarian; b. Peking, China, Dec. 3, 1932; came to U.S., 1955; d. Shu-Peng Wang; m. Di Chen, June 14, 1958; children: Andrew A., Daniel T. BA, Nat. Taiwan U., 1955; MLS, U. Minn., 1957. Cataloger Hennepin County Libr., Edina, Minn., 1972-80; libr./programmer Prorodeo Hall of Champions, Colorado Springs, Colo., 1981-83; ref. libr. Meml. Hosp., Colorado Springs, 1983-85; asst. libr. Am. Numismatic Assn., Colorado Springs, 1985-90, head libr., 1991—. Mem. Colo. Libr. Assn., Spl. Libr. Assn. Home: 2127 Centerview Ln Mound MN 55364-1616 Office: American Numismatic Assn 818 N Cascade Ave Colorado Springs CO 80903-3279

CHEN, PETER WEI-TEH, mental health services administrator; b. Fuchow, Fukien, Republic of China, July 20, 1942; came to U.S., 1966; s. Mao-Chuang and Sheu-Lin (Wang) C.; m. Lai-Wah Mui, Nov. 8, 1969; children: Ophelia Mei-Chuang, Audrey Mei-Hui. BA, Nat. Chung Hsing U., Taipei, Taiwan, Republic of China, 1964; MSW, Calif. State U., Fresno, 1968; D of Social Work, U. So. Calif., 1976. Case worker Cath. Welfare Bur., L.A., 1968-69; psychiat. social worker L.A. County Mental Health Svcs., 1969-78, mental health svcs. coordinator, 1978; sr. rsch. analyst Jud. and Legis. Bur. L.A. County Dept. Mental Health, 1978-79; Forensic In-Patient Program dir. L.A. County Dept. Mental Health, 1979-86, chief Jail Mental Health Svcs., 1986-89, asst. dep. dir. Adult Svc. Bur., 1989, dir. cmty. care programs, 1989—; clin. prof. dept. psychiatry Harbor/UCLA Med. Ctr., 1997—; pres. Orient Social and Health Soc., Los Angeles, 1973-75; bd. dirs. Am. Correctional Health Assn., 1986-87. Author: Chinese-Americans View Their Mental Health, 1976. Bd. dirs. San Marino (Calif.) Cmty. Chest, 1986-87; trustee San Marino Schs. Found., 1987-90; advisor San Marino United Way, 1989-92, AIDS Commn. L.A. County, 1993; founder, chmn. Chinese Sch. of San Marino, 1998—. 2d lt. Chinese Marine Corps, Taiwan, Republic of China, 1964-65. Recipient several cmty. svc. awards, 3 spl. awards Nat. Assn. County Orgn. Mem. Nat. Assn. Social Workers (bd. dirs. Calif. chpt. 1979-80), Nat. Correctional Health Assn., Forensic Mental Health Assn. Calif., L.A. World Affairs Coun., Chinese Am. Profl. Soc. (pres. 1997-98, chmn. bd. dirs. 1998—). Clubs: Chinese of San Marino (pres. 1987-88), San Marino City. Avocations: sports, fishing, bridge. Home: 2161 E California Blvd San Marino CA 91108-1348 Office: LA County Dept Mental Health 155 N Occidental Blvd Los Angeles CA 90026-4641

CHEN, SHERRY XIAOHONG, artist, educator; b. Chendu, Sichuan, China, Jan. 1, 1966; came to U.S., 1987; d. Li-Li Chen and Da Xiu Jiang. BFA, Ctrl. Inst. Art and Craft, Beijing; MA, U. S.C., 1989. Adj. faculty mem. San Diego Marimar Coll., 1997; artist Combined Orgn. for Visual Art, San Diego, 1995—. Contbr. paintings to various publs.; exhibited at Yokohama Citizen's Gallery, Japan, 1992, Artexpo, N.Y., 1998, Artexpo, L.A., 1998. Mem. San Diego Chinese Art Soc.

CHEN, STEPHEN SHAU-TSI, retired psychiatrist, physiologist; b. Tou-Nan, Yun-Lin, Taiwan, Aug. 18, 1934; s. R-Yue and Pi-Yu (Huang) C.; m. Clara Chin-Chin Liu, Sept. 7, 1936; children: David, Timothy, Hubert. MD, Nat. Taiwan U., Taipei, 1959; PhD, U. Wis., 1968. Diplomate Am. Bd. Psychiatry and Neurology, also sub. bd. Geriatric Psychiatry. Intern Nat. Taiwan U. Hosp., 1959; instr. dept. physiology U. Wis., Madison, 1968-71, asst. prof., 1971-75; resident in psychiatry SUNY, Stony Brook, 1975-78; asst. prof. psychiatry dept. psychiatry U. Pitts., 1978-80; asst. prof. psychiatry dept. psychiatry and behavioral sci. U. Wash., Seattle, 1981-86, clin. asst. prof. psychiatry, 1986-97; chief mental health clinic VA Med. Ctr., Tacoma, 1981-85. Contbr. articles to Am. Jour. Physiol., Jour. Physiology, Can. Jour. Physiology and Pharmacology, Acta Physiol. Fellow Wis. Heart

Assn., 1966-68. Mem. APA, North Pacific Soc. Neurology and Psychiatry. Presbyterian. Avocations: tennis, gardening.

CHENG, HENG-DA, computer scientist; b. Shenyang, Liaoning, China, May 1, 1944; came to U.S., 1980; s. Ji Cheng and Yu-Zhi Pan; m. Xiaohong Hao (Haybina Hao); children: Yang-Yang, Yue-Yue, Lydia. BS, Harbin (China) Inst. Tech., 1967; MS, Wayne State U., 1981; PhD, Purdue U., 1985. Instr. Harbin Shipbuilding Inst., 1971-76; rschr., technician Harbin Railway Sci. and Tech. Rsch. Inst., Harbin, 1976-78, Computing Tech. Inst., 1978-80; vis. asst. prof. U. Calif., Davis, 1985-86; asst. prof. Concordia U., Montreal, Que., Can., 1987-88; assoc. prof. Tech. U. N.S., Halifax, Can., 1988-91; assoc. prof. Utah State U., Logan, 1991-93, adj. assoc. prof., 1993—; co-chmn. Vision Interface '90, 4th Can. Conf., Halifax, 1990; com. mem. Vision Interface '92, 1992, Vision Interface '96, 1996; panelist 2d Internat. Conf. Fuzzy Theory and Tech., 1993; mem. best paper award evaluation com., session chmn. Internat. Joint Conf. on Info. Scis., 1994, 95; com. mem. Internat. Conf. on Tools with Artificial Intelligence, 1995, 17th Internat. Conf. on Computer Processing of Oriental Langs., 1997; chmn. 1st Internat. Workshop on Computer Vision, Pattern Recognition & Image Processing, 1998; lectr. in field. Co-editor Pattern Recognition: Architectures Algorithms and Applications, 1991; assoc. editor: Pattern Recognition and Info. Scis.; contbr. articles to profl. jours. and confs.; reviewer sci. jours. and cons. Recipient grants Nat. Scis. and Engring. Rsch. Coun. Can., NSF, 1987—, NSERC, 1989-93, Utah State U., 1992-93, Utah Dept. Transp., 1996—, others. Mem. IEEE (sr.), Computer Soc. of IEEE, Cirs. and Sys. Soc. of IEEE, Geosci. and Remote Sensing Soc. of IEEE, Robotics and Automation Soc. of IEEE, Sys., Man and Cybernetics Soc. of IEEE, Signal Processing Soc. of IEEE, Engring. in Medicine and Biology Soc. of IEEE, Assn. for Computing Machinery. Avocations: swimming, biking, table tennis, reading. Office: Utah State Univ Dept Computer Sci Logan UT 84322-4205

CHENG, WEN-HAO, process engineer; b. Taipei, Taiwan, July 8, 1962; came to U.S., 1990; s. Wei-Han and Kuei-Mei (Hsu) C.; m. Li-ling Ko, May 25, 1991; 1 child, Weber. PhD, U. Md., 1995. Rsch. assoc. U. Calif., Berkeley, 1995-97; sr. process engr. Intel Co., Santa Clara, Calif., 1997—. Contbr. articles to profl. jours. 2d lt. Taiwan Army, 1987-89. Recipient Twin Creek Lit. award Soochow U., Taipei, 1984. Mem. Am. Phys. Soc. Avocations: music, reading, movie, swimming.

CHENOWETH, HELEN P., congresswoman; b. Topeka, Kans., Jan. 27, 1938; 2 children. Attended, Whitworth Coll., 1975-79; cert. in law office mgmt., U. Minn., 1974; student, Rep. Nat. Com. Mgmt. Coll., 1977. Bus. mgr. Northside Med. Ctr., 1964-75; state exec. dir. Idaho Rep. Party, 1975-77; chief of staff Congressman Steve Symms, 1977-78; campaign mgr. Symms for Congress Campaign, 1978, Leroy for Gov., 1985-86; v.p. Consulting Assocs., Inc., 1978—; mem. House of Reps., Washington, mem. agriculture com., resources com., vet. affairs com.; mem. agriculture, resources, vets. affairs coms.; bd. dirs. Ctr. Study of Market Alternatives. Deacon Capitol Christian Ctr., Boise. Office: US Ho of Reps 1727 Longworth Bldg Washington DC 20515-1201*

CHERIS, ELAINE GAYLE INGRAM, business owner; b. Ashford, Ala., Jan. 8, 1946; m. Samuel David Cheris, June 8, 1980; 1 child, Zachariah Adam Abraham. BS, Troy State U., 1971. Aquatics dir. Yale U., New Haven, 1976-79; owner, mgr. Cheyenne Fencing Soc., Denver, 1980—; chmn. organizing com. World Fencing Championships, 1989, World Jr./Cadet Fencing Championships, 1993; nat. devel. coord. Modern Pentathlon, 1998. Author: Handbook for Parents - Fencing, 1988, 2d edit., 1992; editor Yofen Mag., 1988-90, 1992—. Mem. Gov.'s Coun. on Sports and Fitness, Colo., 1990—; commr. Colo. State Games-Fencing, 1989—; nat. devel. chmn., nat. chmn. youth and cadet, club coord. Modern Pentathlon, 1998. Mem. U.S. Olympic Foil Team, 1980, 88 (6th place fencing), U.S. Olympic Epee Team, 96 (8th place), 98 (1st place), mem. U.S. Pan-Am. Games Team, 1987 (Gold medal women's foil team), 1991 (Gold medal women's epee team); named Sportswoman of Yr. Fencing, YWCA, 1980, 81, 82, to Sportswoman Hall of Fame, 1982; mem. U.S. World Championship Fencing Team, 1982, 85, 87, 90, 91, 92, 93, U.S. Maccabiah Fencing Team, 1981 (1 gold, 1 silver medal); recipient Gold Medal of Honor from Fedn. Internat. d'Escrime, 1993. Mem. AAPHERD, U.S. Fencing Assn. (youth chmn. 1988-90, editor Youth mag., 1988-90, 92—, chmn. Colo. divsn., 1992-94), Fedn. Internat. d'Escrime (chmn. Atlanta fencing project '96, chmn. World Fencing Day 1994). Jewish. Office: Cheyenne Fencing Soc 5818 E Colfax Ave Denver CO 80220-1507

CHERKIN, ADINA, interpreter, translator; b. Geneva, Nov. 22, 1921; came to U.S., 1940; d. Herz N. and Genia (Kodriansky) Mantchik; m. Arthur Cherkin, Mar. 14, 1943 (div. Sept. 1980); children: Della Peretti, Daniel Craig. BA in Premed. Studies, UCLA, 1942, MA in Russian Linguistics, 1977. Pvt. practice med. interpreter in 5 langs. L.A., 1942-80; translator UCLA Med. Sch., 1970-79; pres. acad. forum Jewish studies Herz Mantchik Amity Cir., L.A., 1973—. Author: Terse Verse and Oodles of Doodles, 1999; author numerous poems. Active L.A. Internat. Vis. Coun., 1991—; pub. rels. Judge Stanley Mosk's Campaign, L.A., 1960; vol. Senator Cranston's Campaign, 1960. Recipient Community Svc. award L.A. City Coun., 1992. Mem. Am. Soc. for Technion Israel Inst. Tech. (bd. regents). Avocations: dance improvisation, figure skating. Home and Office: 2369 N Vermont Ave Los Angeles CA 90027-1253

CHERRY, DEANNA DUELUND, social services center administrator; b. Palo Alto, Calif., Aug. 17, 1969; d. Eugene Cline and Karen Deanna (Søe) C.; 1 child, Mahalia Oni Wallace. BA in Devel. Studies, UCLA, 1993, BA in Intergroup Rels. & Discrimination, 1993. Asst. policy analyst Nat. Urban League, Washington, 1990; asst. project mgr. Rebuild L.A., 1992; acad. coord. men's basketball athletic dept. UCLA, 1994-95, fundraising cons. student media, 1996-97; devel. dir. MarVista Family Ctr., Culver City, Calif., 1993—; postgrad. fellow Covo So. Calif., L.A., 1993; chmn. UCLA Comms. Bd., L.A., 1995-96. Foster parent Westside Children's Ctr., Culver City, 1997-98; bd. dirs. Hollywood (Calif.) Boys & Girls Club, 1996-98, ADAMMA Found., L.A., 1998. Avocation: photography. Office: Mar Vista Family Ctr 5075 S Slauson Ave Culver City CA 90230-5663

CHERRY, RICHARD DUANE, architect; b. Brokenbow, Nebr., Jan. 23, 1943; s. Joe Thompson and Doris C.; m. Joan Kathleen; 1 child, John. BA in Arch., Tex. A&M, 1970. Assoc. project architect C.T. Choi & Assocs., Colorado Springs, Colo., 1979-81; ptnr., architect Nelson-Cherry & Assocs., Colorado Springs, Colo., 1981-86; architect pvt. practice, Pueblo, Colo., 1986-91, 95—; architect, facility mgr. Qualmed Plans for Health, Pueblo, Colo., 1991-95. Bd. dirs. Rosemount Mus., Pueblo, 1994—; com. mem. Harp Bus. Com., Pueblo, 1996-97; pres. Pueblo Choral, 1992-94. Mem. AIA (bd. dirs. Colo. south chpt. 1984-86). Avocation: music. Office: 110 E D St Pueblo CO 81003-3410

CHESEMORE, DAVID LEE, adult education educator, biologist; b. Janesville, Wis., Nov. 3, 1939; s. Kenneth and Hazel (Rodawalt) C.; m. Janice Ann Smith, June 10, 1961 (dec. 1979); m. Marion Teresa Wren McOsker, Nov. 23, 1979; children: Sandra, John Donald, Daniel, Kathleen. Student, U. Wis., 1957-58; BS, U. Wisc. (Stevens Point), 1961; MS, U. Alaska, 1967; PhD in Wildlife Ecology, Okla. State U., 1975; student, Am. Inst Taxidermy, 1995. Rsch. biologist Alska Coop. Wildlife Rsch. Unit, U. Alaska, Fairbanks, 1967-68; rsch. asst. Okla. Coop. Wildlife Rsch. Unit, Okla. State U., Stillwater, 1968-72; prof. Calif. State U., Fresno, 1972—; cons. Ms. Donna Knapp, Kern County, Calif, 1974-77, Calif. Dept. Fish and Game, 1975, 77, 79, 82, 84-86, 87, U.S. Forest Svc., 1974-77, Kings River Conservation Dist., 1977-78, U.S. Fish and Wildlife Svc., Can. Wildlife Svc., Smithsonian Instn., Calif. Waterfowl Assn., 1978, U.S. Bur. Land Mgmt., 1979-80, Sport Fishing Inst., 1980, McGlasson and Assocs., Fresno, 1980, Nat. Geographic Soc. mag. World, 1980, 87, Nature Conservacy, Kern County, 1982, Am. Forest Products, Inc., 1983, Oak Ridge (Tenn.) Nat. Lab., 1984, Merced County, Calif., 1986, J.H. Kleinfelder and Assocs., 1986, Sunflower Valley Energy, Kern County, 1986, Calif. Dept. Pks. Recreation, 1986, 87, USN, 1987, Calif. Dept. Food and Agr., 1987-90, Environ. Sci. Assocs., San Francisco, 1989, Siemer and Assocs., Modesto, Calif., 1989, M. Skenfield Consulting, 1990, Farm and Home Adminstrn., Merced, Calif., 1991, Ctrl. Valley Sci. Ctr., 1994, Am. Inst. Taxidermy, 1995, Sch. Natural Scis., 1996, 97, others; lectr. Tenn. Tech. U., 1981; adv. Roosevelt H.S., 1993; rschr. Wildlife Techs., 1996; spkr. in field. Contbr. over 150 articles to wildlife conservation, scientific, and ecology mags., 1968—. Pres. Future Farmers Am., 1956-57; gen. chmn. first winter carnival U. Wis., 1960-61; bd. dirs. Outting Club, U. Wis., 1960-61; student union bd. social com., U. Wis., 1960-61; vol. Peace Corps, Nepal, 1964-65; Calif. State U. Bilogy Dept. rsch. and grad. com. (mem. 1974-75, 78-79, 86-88, 94-98, chmn. 1975-78, 85-86); budget com. (mem. 1973-74, 76-78, 89, chmn. 198081, 90-92); staffing and scheduling com. (mem. 1992-94, chmn. 1977-78, 80-83); colloquium com. mem. 1973-74; curriculum com. chmn. 1983-85; Ad Hoc coms. chmn. 1973-74, mem. 1984-85; Sch. Natural Scis. rsch. com. mem. 1975-76, chmn. 1976-78; rsch. planning group mem. 1978; senator 1984-87; advancement, retention, promotion, and tenure review com. 1991-94, 97—; Ad Hoc com. Assoc. Dean Ziegler review 1995-96; field biology com. chmn. 1995-96; animal welfare com. 1983-96; co-chair Ad Hoc awards com. 1985; Univ. rsch. com. mem. 1984-87, chmn. 1985-87; organizing com. Ctrl. Calif. Rsch. Symposium mem. 1984-94; Liaison, Dept. Biology Coop. Edn. Program grad. com. mem. 1987-88, 92-94, chmn. 1993-94; human resources com. mem. 1987-88; Ad Hoc com. to form a coll. liberal arts 1992—; mem. Bioregion Task Force, Sierra Club 1992-93; com. mem. review of Calif. State U. undergraduate and grad. acad. programs 1994; Performance Salary Step Appeals panel, 1996; mem. Task Force D, Vision for the 21st century, 1997. Recipient Oustanding Wildlife Biologist award San Joaquin Chpt. Wildlife Soc., 1981, Superior award for photography, Fresno County Fair, 1983, Beyond War award, Peace Corps, 1987; Fox River Assn. Wis. Garden Clubs scholar, 1960-61. Mem. NRA, Nat. Wildlife Fedn., Nat. Geographic Soc., Am. Fisheries Soc., Am. Soc. Mammalogists, Audobon Soc., Quail Unlimited, San Joaquin Chpt. Wildlife Soc. (v.p. 1973-74, pres. 1974-76, chpt. rep. western sect. 1976-77), Western Sect. Wildlife Soc. (sec., treas. 1975-76, chmn. local arrangements com. ann. meeting, Fresno, 1976), Sigma Xi. Avocations: hunting, fishing, wilderness trekking, camping, photography. E-mail: davidüchesemore@csufresno.edu. Fax #: (209) 278-3963. Office: California State University Dept of Biology Fresno CA 93740-0073

CHESHIRE, WILLIAM POLK, retired newspaper columnist; b. Durham, N.C., Feb. 2, 1931; s. James Webb and Anne Ludlow (McGehee) C.; m. Lucile Geoghegan, Aug. 1, 1959; children—William Polk, Helen Wood Cheshire Elder, James Webb. A.B., U. N.C., Chapel Hill, 1958. Reporter Richmond News Leader, Va., 1958-61; assoc. editor Canton (N.C.) Enterprise, 1961-62, Charleston Evening Post, S.C., 1963-68, The State, Columbia, S.C., 1968-72; editorial dir. Capital Broadcasting Co., Raleigh, N.C., 1972-75; editorial page editor Greensboro Record, N.C., 1975-78; editor-in-chief Charleston Daily Mail, W.Va., 1978-84; editor, editorial pages Washington Times, 1984-87; editor, editorial pages The Ariz. Republic, Phoenix, 1987-93, sr. editorial columnist, 1993-96, ret., 1996; prof. journalism U. Charleston, 1979-83; commentator Voice of Am., 1986-87. Dir. comm. N.C. Senate Campaign, 1972; bd. dirs. Sunrise Mus., Charleston United Way, 1978-84. With USCG, 1952-56. Recipient Council for the Def. of Freedom award, 1980, George Washington Honor medal Freedoms Found., 1975; named Disting. Fellow in Journalism, Heritage Found., 1987; Media fellow Hoover Instn., 1991. Mem. N.C. Soc. Cin. (pres. 1988-91), Phila. Soc., Nat. Press Club, Phoenix Country Club, Washington Yacht and Country Club, Sigma Delta Chi (pres. Piedmont chpt. 1978). Episcopalian.

CHESNEY, MAXINE M., judge; b. 1942. BA, U. Calif., Berkeley, 1964, JD, 1967. Trial atty. Office Dist. Atty., San Francisco, 1968-69, sr. trial atty., 1969-71, prin. trial atty., 1971-76, head atty., 1976, asst. chief dep., 1976-79; judge San Francisco Mcpl. Ct., 1979-83, San Francisco Superior Ct., 1983-95, U.S. Dist. Ct. (no. dist.) Calif., San Francisco, 1995—. Bd. dirs. San Francisco Child Abuse Coun., 1976-79, Hosp. Audiences, 1978-81. Mem. Fed. Judges Assn., Nat. Assn. Women Judges, Edward J. McFetridge Am. Inn of Ct., U.S. Assn. Constl. Law, Queen's Bench, Ninth Jud. Cir. Hist. Soc. Office: US Dist Ct No Dist Calif PO Box 36060 450 Golden Gate Ave San Francisco CA 94102-3661

CHESNUT, CAROL FITTING, lawyer; b. Pecos, Tex., June 17, 1937; d. Ralph Ulf and Carol (Lowe) Fitting; m Dwayne A. Chesnut, Dec. 27, 1955; children: Carol Marie, Stephanie Michelle, Mark Steven. BA magna cum laude, U. Colo., 1971; JD, U. Calif., San Francisco, 1994. Rsch. asst. U. Colo., 1972; head quality controller Mathematica, Inc., Denver, 1973-74; cons. Mincome Man., Winnipeg, Can., 1974; cons. economist Energy Cons. Assocs. Inc., Denver, 1974-79; exec. v.p. tng. ECA Intercomp, 1980-81; gen. ptnr. Chestnut Consortium, S.F., 1981—; sec., bd. dirs. Critical Resources, Inc., 1981-83. Rep. Lakehurst Civic Assn., 1968; staff aide Senator Gary Hart, 1978; Dem. precinct capt., 1982-88. Mem. ABA, ACLU, AAUW (1st v.p. 1989-90), Am. Mgmt. Assn., Soc. Petroleum Engrs., Am. Nuclear Soc. (chmn. conv. space activities for 1989, chair of spouse activities 1989), Am. Geophys. Union, Assn. Women Geoscientists (treas. Denver 1983-85), Associated Students of Hastings (rep. 1994), Calif. State Bar, Nev. State Bar, Nev. Trial Lawyers Assn., Nat. Acad. Elder Law Attys., Canyon Ranch Homeowners Assn. (sec. bd. dirs. 1994-97), Phi Beta Kappa, Phi Chi Theta, Phi Delta Phi. Unitarian. Office: 2921 N Tenaya Way Ste 201 Las Vegas NV 89128-0454

CHESTER, LYNNE, foundation executive, artist; b. Fargo, N.D., May 29, 1942. BA in Music, Hillsdale Coll., 1964; MA in Guidance Counseling, Mich. State U., 1965; PhD in Psychology, U. Mich., 1971. Tchr. Warren (Mich.) Consol. Schs., 1965-70; curriculum advisor Royal Oak (Mich.) Pub. Schs., 1974-75; co-founder, exec. dir. Peace Rsch. Found., Carmel, Calif., 1993-98; assoc. Hillsdale Coll., 1989—; guest lectr. ceramics James Milliken U., Decatur, Ill., 1991; guest lectr. creative covergence Carl Cherry Ctr. for Art, Carmel, 1991, Compton lectr., Monterey, Calif., 1996—; co-founder, bd. dirs. Monterey Peninsula Coll. Art Gallery, 1991—; guest juror Monterey County Essay Contest, 1997; cons. Monterey Mus. of Art; guest lectr. Hillsdale (Mich.) Coll., 1997; juror Monterey County Poetry Contest, 1993—; juror photographic show Beauty at the Heart of Things, Carl Cherry Ctr. for Arts, Carmel, 1999. Artist of multiple commd. sculptures for pvt. collections; also ceramics, sculpture and photographs in pvt. and corp. collections; represented in permanent collection at Krammert Art Mus., Champaign, Ill., Fresno (Calif.) Mus. Art; juried show Ctr. for Photographic Art, Carmel, Calif., 1996; art represented at Who's Who in Art, Monterey, 1989—, Christmas Miniatures/Invitational Ctr. for Photographic Art, Carmel, 1996, Holiday Print Show Ctr. for Photographic Art, Carmel, 1996 (Dir.'s Choice 1996); author of poetry; juror essay contest Personal Heroes Monterey County K-12, 1997; juror poetry contest Monterey County 9-12 grades, Carl Cherry Ctr. for the Arts, 1993—; exhibited in photography show at Asilomer Conf. Ctr., Monterey Peninsula Airport, Pacific Grove Art Ctr., Carl Chevry Ctr., Seaside City Hall, Pacific Grove Mus. Natural History, 1995-98, Hillsdale Coll., 1997, Monterey Peninsula Airport, 1998, Calif. State U., Monterey Bay, 1998, Pacific Grove (Calif.) Art Ctr., 1998, Carl Cherry Ctr. for Arts, Carmel, Calif., 1998, Pacific Grove Mus. Nat. History, 1998, Salinas (Calif.) Courthouse, 1998, Asilomar Conf. Ctr., Pacific Grove, 1998, Prints Charming Gallery, Carmel, 1998; represented by Prints Charming Gallery and Carmel Express Internat. Co-founder Southfield (Mich.) Symphony, 1972, World Rhythms Festival, Carmel, 1996—; co-founder, bd. dirs. Monterey Bay Artists Day, Sta. KAZU-FM, 1987-89; pres., bd. dirs. Carl Cherry Ctr. for Arts, Carmel, 1988-94, 95—; bd. dirs. Monterey Peninsula Mus. Art, 1991-93, Carmel Pub. Libr. Found., 1991-93, Monterey Inst. for Rsch. in Astronomy, 1985-95, Cultural Coun. for Monterey County, 1993-98; fundraiser Student Art Gallery, Monterey Peninsula Coll., 1990-97, mem. mentors program Women Helping Women, 1998—. Recipient Citizens Adv. Coun. award City of Royal Oak, 1978-83, Best of Show award for monoprint Monterey Peninsula Coll., 1990, Poetry prizes Carl Cherry Ctr. for Arts, 1990-94, Benefactor of Arts award Monterey County Cultural Coun., 1992, 93, 94, Soccer Mgr./Coach of Yr. 1976-81, 1st pl. award photography contest Monterey Regional Park Dist. Celebration of Open Space, 1998; artist-in-residence Naubinway, Mich., 1997. Mem. AAUW, Internat. Platform Assn., Internat. Sculpture Ctr., Nat. Soc. Fund Raising Execs., Nat. Mus. Women in Art (charter mem.), Am. Crafts Coun., Sigma Alpha Iota (Ruby Sword of Honor 1963). Avocations: reading, playing piano, composing, hiking, photography. Home: 9645 Sandbur Pl Salinas CA 93907-1031

CHESTER, MARVIN, physics educator; b. N.Y.C., Dec. 29, 1930; s. Herman and Sadye C.; m. Ruth Chester (div. 1960); 1 child, Karen; m. Sandra Chester (div. 1963); 1 child, Lisa; m. Elfi Bollert, July 30, 1977; children: Chaim Peter, Sadye Vera. BS, CCNY, 1952; PhD, Calif. Inst. Tech., 1961. Prof. physics U. Calif., L.A., 1961-92, prof. emeritus, 1992—; sr. rsch. fellow U. Sussex, Eng., 1973. Author: Primer of Quantum Mechanics, 1987; contbr. articles to profl. jours. Recipient Alexander von Humboldt award, Von Humboldt Stifftung, 1974-75. Mem. Am. Phys. Soc. Office: UCLA Dept Physics Los Angeles CA 90024

CHESTER, SHARON ROSE, photographer, natural history educator; b. Chgo., July 12, 1942; d. Joseph Thomas and Lucia Barbara (Urban) C. BA, U. Wis., 1964; grad., Coll. San Mateo, 1974, U. Calif., Berkeley, 1977, San Francisco State U., 1989. Flight attendant Pan Am. World Airways Inc., San Francisco, 1965; free lance photographer San Mateo, Calif., 1983—; stock photographer Comstock, N.Y.C., 1987—; lectr. Soc. Expdns., Seattle, 1985-91, Abercrombie & Kent, Chgo., 1992-94, Seven Seas Cruise Line, San Francisco, 1994-95; owner Wandering Albatross, 1993. Author (checklist) Birds of the Antarctic and Sub-Antarctic, 1986, revised, 1994, Antarctic birds and Seals: A Pocket Guide, 1993, South to Antarctica, 1994, The Northwest Passage, 1994; author and illustrator, Birds of Chile, Aves de Chile, 1995; co-author: The Birds of Chile: A Field Guide, 1993, The Arctic Guide, 1996, The Marquesas Islands: Mave Mai, 1997, Ia Orana Tahiti, 1998; photos featured in Sierra club Book: Mother Earth Through the Eyes of Women Photographers and Writers, 1992; photographer mag. cover King Penguin and Chick for Internat. Wildlife Mag., 1985, Sierra Club Calendar, 1986; exhibited photos at Royal Geographic Soc. London. Mem. Calif. Acad. Sci. Avocations: writing, ice dancing, birdwatching. Home: 724 Laurel Ave Apt 211 San Mateo CA 94401-4131

CHESTON, MICHAEL GALLOWAY, airport executive; m. Laurie; children: Kenny, Geoffrey. AA in Gen. Edn., Catonsville (Md.) C.C., 1975; BA in English, St. Mary's Coll. of Md., 1977; MBA in Real Estate Devel., George Washington U., 1994. Cert. air traffic control specialist. Corporate recruiting supr., computer resource acquisition specialist Electronic Data Sys., Inc., Bethesda, Md., 1984-86; dir. European ops. Corporate Devel. Sys., Inc., Wellesley, Mass., 1986-87; acting mgr., ops. officer, bus. analyst Met. Washington Airports Authority, Alexandria, Va., 1987-93; airport mgr. Portland (Oreg.) Internat. Airport, 1993—, gen. mgr. ops., maintenance and aviation. Comdr. USMC, 1977-84; maj., USMCR. Mem. Am. Assn. Airports Execs., Airports Coun. Internat., Portland Highland Games Assn. (pub. safety mgr.), Marine Corps Assn., Marine Corps Res. Officers Assn. (chpt. pres.). Office: Portland Internat Airport PO Box 3529 Portland OR 97208-3529*

CHETWYND, LIONEL, screenwriter, producer, director; b. London, Jan. 29; s. Peter and Betty (Dion) C.; m. Gloria Carlin, June 2; children: Michael Anthony, Joshua Stephen. BA with honors, Sir George Williams U., Montreal, Que., 1963; B in Civil Law, McGill U., Montreal, Que., 1967; post-grad., Trinity Coll. of Oxford (Eng.) U., 1968. Bar: PQ 1967. With acquisition/distbn. dept. Columbia Pictures, London, 1968-72; screenwriter, 1971—; mem. faculty Grad. Film Sch., NYU; lectr. screenwriting Frederick Douglass Ctr., Harlem; appointed pres.. Am. Cinema Found. Writer: (stage prodns.) Maybe That's Your Problem, 1971, Bleeding Great Orchids, 1971, (feature films) The Apprenticeship of Duddy Kravatz, 1974 (also adaptor, Acad. award nomination 1974), Morning Comes, 1975 (also dir.), Two Solitudes, 1978 (also prodr., dir., Grand award Salonika 1979), Quintet, 1978, Hot Touch, 1981 (Genie nomination), The Hanoi Hilton, 1987 (also dir.), (TV films) Johnny, We Hardly Knew Ye, 1976 (also prodr., George Washington Honor medal Freedom Found. 1976), It Happened One Christmas, 1977 (citation Am. Women in Film and TV 1979), Goldenrod, 1977 (also prodr.), A Whale for the Killing, 1980, Miracle on Ice, 1981 (Christopher award 1981), Escape From Iran: The Canadian Caper, 1981, Sadat, 1983 (NAACP Image award 1983), Children in the Crossfire, 1984 (Prix D'Association Mondiale des Amis de L'Enfants 1985, award Monte Carlo Internat. TV Festival 1985), To Heal a Nation, 1988 (also prodr., Vietnam Vets. Meml. Fund Patriots award, George Washington Honor medal Freedom Found. 1989), The American 1776 (ofcl. U.S. bicentennial film); co-writer, co-prodr. (stage prodn.) We The People...200, 1987; exec. prodr. Evil in Clear River, 1988 (Spl. award Am. Jewish Com., Christopher award); writer, dir., exec. prodr. So Proudly We Hail (Bnai Zion Creative Achievement award 1990), Heroes of the Desert Storm, 1991; exec. prodr., writer, creator (PBS documentary series) Reverse Angle, 1993, The Bible-Jacob, The Bible-Joseph (Emmy award), The Bible-Moses, (cable films) The Doom's Day Gun, Kissinger and Nixon, 1996, The Man Who Captured Eichmann, 1996. Co-chair Arts and Entertainment Commn. for Reagan/Bush, L.A., 1978-80; exec. bd. dirs. Can. Ctr. for Advanced Cinema Studies, Toronto, 1986—; mem. exec. bd. L.A. chpt. Am. Jew Com.; named to panel on sexuality and social policy Am. Enterprise Inst.; bd. dirs. Profl. Friends of Dept. Film and Theatre UCLA; mem. nat. com. Vietnam Vets. Meml. Fund. Mem. Acad. Motion Picture Arts and Scis., Acad. TV Arts and Scis., Am. Cinema Found. (pres.), Writers Guild Am. (exec. bd. 1972-76, nat. exec. 1975, Writers Guild award 1974), Writers Guild Britain, Can. Bar Assn., Dirs. Guild Am., Broadcast Music, Inc., Assn. Can. TV and Radio Artists, UCLA Film TV and Edn. Assn. (bd. dirs.), Am. Cinema Found. (pres. 1996-97), Caucus of Writers, Prodrs. and Dirs. (steering com.). Jewish. Avocations: ice hockey, youth baseball. Fax: (310) 275-9372. Office: care Gang Tyre Raymer & Brown 6400 W Sunset Blvd Los Angeles CA 90028-7307

CHEUNG, HING ALAN, artist, writer; b. Shanghai, Dec. 12, 1954; came to U.S., 1980; s. T.M. and K.L. (Chen) C. MFA, Otis Art Inst., 1982. Author: Art Appreciation, 4 vols., 1991-94, Western Art History Series, 4 vols., 1994-97; exhibited in solo and group exhbns., N.Y., San Francisco, L.A., Asia, 1982—. Recipient L.A. Artist grant L.A. Cultural Dept., 1993, Art Writing grant Dimension Found. for Arts, Taipei, 1995, Nat. Book award Taiwan Cultural Dept., 1996. Mem. No. Am. Chinese Artist Assn. (co-founder 1992—). Avocations: movies, hiking, canoeing, reading. Home: 4430 20th St San Francisco CA 94114-2740

CHEUNG, JOHN B., research and development executive; b. 1943. COO Quest Integrated, Inc., Kent, Wash.; pres. Flow Dril Corp., Kent. Office: Flow Dril Corp 21414 68th Ave S Kent WA 98032-2416*

CHEUNG, VINCENT HUA-SHENG, television writer, producer; b. Washington, Oct. 16, 1956; s. Keung Tsi and Elaine Ho-Yee (Lee) C.; m. Laura Lynn Lawrence, May 3, 1998. BA, UCLA, 1979. Page NBC, Burbank, Calif., 1979-80; asst. story dept. NBC Entertainment, Burbank, 1980, story assoc., 1980-86; film, T.V. dir. of devel. ITC Prodns., Studio City, Calif., 1986-89; T.V sitcom writer Warner Bros. Studios, 1989-92; sitcom writer, prodr. various studios, 1992—. Sitcoms include Growing Pains, Night Court, Empty Nest, Roc, Married With Children, The Steve Harvey Show. Mem. Acad. T.V. Arts and Scis.

CHEVALIER, BARBARA LANSBURGH, interior designer; b. San Francisco, Aug. 19, 1907; d. S. Laz and Ethel (Newman) Lansburgh; children: Suzanne Chevalier-Skolnikoff, Haakon L. Chevalier. Student, Mills Coll., 1926, Stanford U., 1927; BA, U. Calif., Berkeley, 1931. Social worker U.S. Govt. (Alameda County), Calif., 1936-37; apprentice interior designer San Francisco, 1938-43; personal sec. to Elizabeth Arden, 1944; owner, mgr. Barbara Chevalier Interiors, San Francisco, 1947—; pres. Chevalier-Rogers, Inc., San Francisco, 1962-70. Designer Stinson Beach Wedding Gardens and many residencies. Bd. dirs. San Francisco Boys Chorus, Shakespeare by the Beach, Stinson Beach, Calif. Mem. Am. Soc. Interior Designers, Phi Beta Kappa. Fax: (415) 346-5434. Home and Office: Barbara Chevalier Interiors 2298 Pacific Ave # 3 San Francisco CA 94115-1452

CHEVERS, WILDA ANITA YARDE, probation officer; b. N.Y.C.; d. Wilsey Ivan and HerbertLee (Perry) Yarde; m. Kenneth Chevers, May 14, 1950; 1 child, Pamela Anita. BA, CUNY, 1947; MSW, Columbia, 1959; PhD, NYU, 1981. Probation officer, 1947-55; supr. probation officer, 1955-65; br. chief Office Probation for Cts. N.Y.C., 1965-72, asst. dir. probation, 1972-77, dep. commr. dept. probation, 1978-86; prof. pub. adminstrn. John Jay Coll. Criminal Justice CUNY, 1986-91; conf. faculty mem. Nat. Council Juvenile and Family Ct. Judges; mem. faculty N.Y.C. Tech. Coll., Nat. Coll. Juvenile Justice; mem. adv. com. Family Ct., First Dept. Sec. Susan E. Wagner Adv. Bd., 1966-70. Sec., bd. dirs. Allen Community Day Care Ctr., 1971-75; bd. dirs. Allen Sr. Citizens Housing, Queensboro Soc. for Prevention Cruelty to Children; chairperson, bd. dir. Allen Christian Sch., 1987-91; mem. Las Vegas EMA Ryan White Title I planning coun., 1998—. Named to Hunter Coll. Hall of Fame, 1983. Mem. ABA (assoc.), N.Y. Acad. Pub. Edn., Nat. Council on Crime and Delinquency, Nat. Assn. Social Workers,

Acad. Cert. Social Workers. Middle Atlantic States Conf. Correction, Alumni Assn. Columbia Sch. Social Work, N.Y.U. Alumni Assn., NAACP, Am. Soc. Pub. Adminstrn. (mem. council), Counseliers, Hansel and Gretel Club (pres. 1967-69, Queens, N.Y.). Delta Sigma Theta. Home: 9012 Covered Wagon Ave Las Vegas NV 89117-7010

CHEVERTON, RICHARD E., newspaper editor. BSJ, Northwestern U., 1964, MSJ, 1965. Reporter Chgo. Today, 1970; editor Sunday Mag. Detroit Free Press, 1970-71; asst. editor Sunday Mag., editor review & opinion sect. Phila. Inquirer, 1972-75; mng. editor The New Paper, Phila., 1975; freelance Phila., 1975-76; features editor Phila. Daily News, 1976-79; newsfeatures editor Seattle Times, 1979-81; asst. mng. editor, features Orange County Reporter, Santa Ana, Calif., 1982-90, asst. mng. editor strategy and adminstrn., 1990-91, dep. editor strategy and adminstrn., 1991—; pub. Way Point Book, La Palma, Calif.; guest lectr. Poynter Inst., Am. Press Inst. Media mgr. Gray for Cong. campaign; speechwriter Friedman for Mayor campaign, Chgo., 1970. With US Army, 1967-69, Vietnam. Decorated Bronze Star; edited series that won Pulitzer Prize for Spl. Local Reporting, 1982. Mem. Am. Assn. Sunday and Feature Editors. Avocations: painting, sculpture, writing screenplays and short stories, travel. Home: 7211 Monterey Ln La Palma CA 90623-1143 Office: PO Box 11626 Santa Ana CA 92711-1626

CHEW, LINDA LEE, fundraising management executive; b. Riverside, Calif., Mar. 3, 1941; d. LeRoy S. and Grace (Ham) Olson; m. Dennis W. Chew, July 23, 1965; children—Stephanie, Erica. B.Mus., U. Redlands, 1962. Cert. fund raising exec. Dir. pub. events U. Redlands (Calif.), 1962-69; dir. fin. and communications San Gorgonio council Girl Scouts U.S.A., Colton, Calif., 1969-71; exec. dir. United Cerebral Palsy Assn. Sacramento-Yolo Counties, 1972-73; fin. devel. dir. San Francisco Bay coun. Girl Scouts U.S.A., 1973-76; chief devel. and pub. info. East Bay Regional Park Dist., Oakland, Calif., 1976-86; cons. Chew & Assocs., Alamo, Calif., 1986-96; pres. Providence Hosp. Found., Oakland, 1991-92; dir. major gifts Alta Bates Found., Berkeley, Calif., 1996—. Bd. dirs. San Ramon Valley Edn. Found., 1984-88; Calif. Conservation Corps Bay Area Ctr. Adv. Bd., 1988-89; Mem. AAUW (pres. Redlands br. 1968-69), Nat. Soc. Fund Raising Execs. (nat. bd. dirs. 1981-90, nat. vice chmn. 1982-84, pres. Golden Gate chpt. 1979-80, bd. dirs. 1987-90, Abel Hanson Meml. award 1977, Outstanding Fund Raising Exec. 1988), Assn. Healthcare Philanthropy (Region 11 cabinet mem. 1991-94), Am. Guild Organists (dean Riverside-San Bernardino chpt. 1969-71), Pub. Rels. Soc. Am., Alamo Rotary, Oakland Rotary, Lamorinda Volleyball Club (pres. 1994-95). Office: 2450 Ashby Ave Berkeley CA 94705-2067

CHIANG, ALBERT CHIN-LIANG, electrical engineer; b. Putai, Taiwan, Jan. 25, 1937; s. San Chi and Chiu (Hsu) C.; BS in Elec. Engring., Nat. Taiwan U., 1959; MS in Elec. Engring., Chiaotung U., Taiwan, 1963; PhD, U. So. Calif., 1968; m. Steffie F.L. Huang, Dec. 24, 1966; children: Margaret, Stacy, Kathy, George. Came to U.S., 1963, naturalized, 1973. Research asst. U. So. Calif., Los Angeles, 1963-68; engr. specialist Litton Industries, Woodland Hills, Calif., 1968-70; dir. internat. sales Macrodata Co., Woodland Hills, Calif., 1970-77; pres. Tritek Internat. Co., Woodland Hills, Calif., 1977—. Mem. IEEE, Sigma Xi, Eta Kappa Nu. Home: 24132 Lupin Hill Rd Hidden Hills CA 91302-2430 Office: Tritek Internat Co 5000 Parkway Calabasas Calabasas CA 91302-1400

CHIANG, KUANG-TSAN KENNETH, metallurgical and materials engineer; b. Taichung, China, Sept. 19, 1950; arrived in U.S., 1974; s. Chun-Lin and Mien-Che (Hu) C.; m. Katy Ho Chiang, Nov. 19, 1979; children: Christina, Jamie. BS, Tsing Hua U., 1972; MS, U. Pitts., 1975, PhD, 1980. Rsch. assoc. U. Pitts., 1980-81; mem. tech. staff RCA, Lancaster, Pa., 1981-86; rsch. scientist Lockheed, Missile & Space, Palo Alto, Calif., 1986-88; engring. specialist Rockwell, Rocketdyne, Canoga Park, Calif., 1988-96, Boeing North American, Inc., Canoga Park, 1996—; panel mem. Rockwell Material Sci. and Engring. Panel on Corrosion, Canoga Park, 1990-92; chmn. NASP Workshop on Coatings, Canoga Park, 1990. Mem. AIAA, Am. Soc. for Metals, So. Calif. Tsing Hua Alumni Assn. (pres. 1995-96), Sigma Xi. Achievements include patent on vacuum electron tube having an oxide cathode comprising chromium reducing agent and blanching resistant coating for copper alloy rocket engine main chamber lining. Office: Boeing North Am Inc Rocketdyne 6633 Canoga Ave Canoga Park CA 91303-2703

CHIANG, YUET-SIM D., English educator; b. Singapore, Oct. 30, 1953; came to U.S., 1984; BS, S.E. Asia Union Coll., 1974; MS in English Studies, U. Nebr., 1988, PhD, 1992. Tchr. San Yu H.S., Singapore, 1975-79; lectr. English dept. U. Nebr., Lincoln, 1988-92; lectr. U. Calif., Berkeley, 1993—; vis. lectr. Nanyang Tech. U., Singapore, 1993-94; tchr., rschr., cons. Bay Area Writing Project, Berkeley, 1995—. Contbr: Situated Stories: Valuing Diversity, 1998. Grantee Nat. Coun. Tchrs. English, 1995, U. Calif. Office of the Pres., 1996; NEH fellow, 1998. Mem. MLA, Nat. Coun. Tchrs. English, Tchrs. of English to Spkrs. of Other Lang. Office: U Calif Coll Writing Programs 216 Dwinelle Annex Berkeley CA 94720

CHIAPPELLI, JOHN ARTHUR, controller, accountant; b. Sonora, Calif., Dec. 17, 1949; s. Louis Joseph and Lois Evelyn (Gandolfo) C.; m. Helen Sue Patriquin, Feb. 3, 1973; children: Mark Jason, Teresa Lyn. BS in Commerce, U. Santa Clara, 1972. Staff acct. Nattinger, Lowery & Co., CPA, Modesto, Calif., 1972-73, John Lane, P.A., Modesto, 1973-74; acct., controller W.E. Mason, Inc., Los Gatos, Calif., 1974-85; controller Jonce Thomas Constrn. Co., Inc., Fremont, Calif., 1985—, D & J Constrn., Inc., Fremont, 1985—; acct. Jon-Don Throughbred Farms, Livermore, Calif., 1985—. Dir. Gilroy (Calif.) Little League, 1990-91. Avocations: golf, gardening, swimming.

CHIATE, KENNETH REED, lawyer; b. Phoenix, June 24, 1941; s. Mac Arthur and Lillian (Lavin) C.; m. Jeannette Jensen, Aug. 21, 1965; children: Gregory Jensen, Carley McKay. B.A. with honors, Claremont Men's Coll., 1963; J.D., Columbia U., 1966; postgrad. U. So. Calif. Law Sch., 1967. Bar: Calif. 1967, U.S. Dist. Ct. (cen. dist.) Calif. 1967, Ariz. 1971, U.S. Dist. Ct. Ariz. 1971, U.S. dist. (no. dist.) Calif. 1982. Law clk. presiding justice U.S. Dist. Ariz., 1971; ptnr. Lillick McHose & Charles, L.A., 1966-91, Pillsbury Madison & Sutro, L.A., 1991—; arbitrator Los Angeles Superior Ct. Arbitration Panel, 1979-82; mcpl. ct. judge protem Los Angeles, 1979-81; mem. Jury Instrn. Com. Los Angeles County, 1991—. Vice chmn. Los Angeles Open Com., 1969-71. Mem. ABA, Los Angeles County Bar Assn., Calif. State Bar Assn., Ariz. State Bar Assn., Maricopa County Bar Assn., So. Calif. Def. Assn., Am. Trial Lawyers Assn., Maritime Law Assn. of U.S.A., Los Angeles Port Propeller Club, mem. L.A. B.A.J.I. com., 1993-95. Office: Pillsbury Madison 725 S Figueroa St Ste 1200 Los Angeles CA 90017-5443

CHIAVARIO, NANCY ANNE, business and community relations executive; b. Centralia, Ill., Aug. 17, 1947; d. Victor Jr. and Alma Maria (Arsenault) C. Asst. mgr. rent supplement B.C. Housing Mgmt. Commn., Vancouver, 1975-81, adminstrv. asst., 1981-84, mgr. tenants and ops. svc., 1985-86, adminstrv. asst., 1986-87; commr., vice chmn. Vancouver Park Bd., 1986-90, chair, 1991-93; trustee Vancouver Pub. Libr., 1987-93; city councillor Vancouver, 1993—; dir. Greater Vancouver Regional Dist., 1996—; v.p. Greater Vancouver Housing Corp., 1997—; bd. dirs. GVHC, 1993—. Bd. dirs. B.C. Recreation and Parks Assn., 1986-91, pres. 1989-90; exec. dir. B.C. Sport and Fitness Coun. for the Disabled, 1989-90; dir. B.C. Wheelchair Sports Assn., 1991-92, Tree Can. Found., 1995—; mem. Non-Partisan Assn., 1986—; vice chair Lower Mainland (Aboriginal) Treaty Adv. Com., 1994-96, chair, 1997—; bd. mem. Oceans Blue Found., 1987-97. Mem. Inst. Housing Mgmt. (cert. adminstr. 1983, cert. finance 1985), West End Commn. Ctr. Assn. (pres. 1985-86), Mt. Pleasant Commn. Ctr. Assn. (pres. 1981-83). Democrat. Avocations: journalism. Home: 90 E 11th Ave, Vancouver, BC Canada V5T 2B8 Office: Vancouver City Coun, 453 W 12th Ave, Vancouver, BC Canada V5Y 1V4

CHIEN, KUEI-RU, chemical physicist; b. Nantung, Kiangsu, China, Dec. 14, 1945; came to U.S. 1969; s. Hun-Wen and Jang-Jen (Tsao) C.; m. Ming-Hsia Lee, July 25, 1983. BS, Nat. Taiwan Normal U., 1968; PhD, MIT, 1973. Research assoc. MIT, Cambridge, Mass., 1973-74, Cornell U., Ithaca, N.Y., 1974-76; with TRW, Redondo Beach, Calif., 1976-83; sr. staff engr. Hughes Aircraft, El Segundo, Calif., 1983-85; sect. head Hughes Aircraft, 1985-87, sr. scientist, 1987-88, dept. mgr., 1988-92, sr. scientist, 1992-93; engring. dir. Hughes Power Products, Hughes Electronics, 1993—. Contbr. articles to profl. jours.; inventor in laser field. Recipient Outstanding Publ. of Yr. award Hughes Electro-optical Data System Group. Mem. Illuminating Engring. Soc. N.Am., Optical Soc. Am., Sigma Xi. Home: 17310 Evening Star Ave Cerritos CA 90703-8318 Office: Hughes Power Products 1925 E Maple Ave El Segundo CA 90245-3412

CHIERIGHINO, BRIANNE SIDDALL, voice-over, actress, assistant location manager; b. Encino, Calif., Aug. 25, 1963; d. Earl Richard and Loretta Jeanette Siddall; m. D. Deven Chierighino, Apr. 4, 1987. AA in Art cum laude, L.A. Valley Coll., Van Nuys, Calif., 1985; student, Glendale (Calif.) C.C., 1990-94; BA in Art magna cum laude, Calif. State U., Northridge, 1995; postgrad., Loyola Marymount U., L.A., 1995—. Freelance asst. sound editor L.A., 1985-89, illustrator, 1985—; voice over artist, actor Tisherman Agy., L.A., 1990—; location asst., 1996—. Art exhibited at San Bernardino (Calif.) County Mus., 1995. Civic vol. fundraiser AIDS Meml. Quilt, Northridge, 1995. Recipient Outstanding Citizen award Coun. City L.A., 1987, L.A. Police Dept., 1987. Mem. SAG, AFTRA, Golden Kay Nat. Honor Soc., Phi Kappa Phi, Psi Chi. Avocations: ice skating, in-line skating, bicycling, softball, tennis. Office: 2219 W Olive Ave Ste 110 Burbank CA 91506-2625

CHIKALLA, THOMAS DAVID, retired science facility administrator; b. Milw., Sept. 9, 1935; s. Paul Joseph and Margaret Ann (Dittrich) C.; m. Ruth Janet Laun, June 20, 1960; children: Paul, Mark, Karyn. BS in Metallurgy, U. Wis., 1957, PhD in Metallurgy, 1966; MS in Metallurgy, U. Idaho, 1960. Research scientist Gen. Electric Co., Richland, Wash., 1957-62; sr. research scientist Battelle Pacific N.W. Labs., Richland, 1964-72, sect. mgr., 1972-80, programs mgr., 1980-83, dept. mgr., 1983-86, assoc. dir., 1986-95; ret., 1995; tchr. U. Wis., Madison, 1962-64. Contbr. articles to profl. jours. Fellow AEC. Fellow Am. Ceramic Soc. (counselor 1974-80); mem. AAAS, Am. Nuclear Soc., Sigma Xi. Republican. Roman Catholic. Clubs: Desert Ski (pres. 1958-59), Alpine. Avocations: skiing, golfing, woodworking, mountain climbing. Home: 2108 Harris Ave Richland WA 99352-2021

CHILD, JOSEPH ALAN, minister; b. Gary, Ind., Jan. 6, 1959; s. Larry Gene and Dorothy Marcella (Walton) C.; m. Teri Lynn Geil, Nov. 10, 1979; children: Michael, Madison, Mackenzie, Morgan. Diploma, Rhema Bible Tng. Ctr., 1982; BA summa cum laude, Bethel Christian Ctr., 1988, MRE magna cum laude, 1990. Ordained to ministry Rhema Ministerial Assn. Internat., 1989. Assoc. pastor Victory Christian Ctr., Palm Springs, Calif., 1986-93; sr. pastor Impact Christian Ctr., Colorado Springs, Colo., 1996—; prof. grad. sch. theology, Bethel Christian Coll., Riverside, Calif., 1989—. Mem. Western States Ministerial Assn., Rhema Alumni Assn., Rhema Ministerial Assn. Internat. Republican. Home: 5705 Altitude Dr Colorado Springs CO 80918-5247 Office: Impact Christian Ctr 4440 Barnes Rd Ste 100 Colorado Springs CO 80917

CHILDS, DONALD SAMUEL, truck driver; b. Wichita, Kans., Apr. 22, 1941; s. Donald and Dora Viola (Miner) C.; m. Jeannette Louise MacMillan, Apr. 11, 1969; 1 child, Jennifer Louise. BBA, Wichita State U., 1967. Petroleum landman Denver, 1968-89; truck driver various, Denver, 1989—. With USN, 1961-63. Methodist. Home: PO Box 1665 Arvada CO 80001-1665

CHILDS, JOHN DAVID, computer hardware and services company executive; b. Washington, Apr. 26, 1939; s. Edwin Carlton and Catherine Dorothea (Angerman) C.; m. Margaret Rae Olsen, Mar. 4, 1966 (div.); 1 child, John-David. Student Principia Coll., 1957-58, 59-60; BA, Am. U., 1963. Jr. adminstr. Page Communications, Washington, 1962-65; account rep. Friden Inc., Washington, 1965-67; Western sales dir. Data Inc., Arlington, Va., 1967-70; v.p. mktg. Rayda, Inc., Los Angeles, 1970-73, pres., 1973-76, chmn. bd., 1976-84; v.p. sales Exec. Bus. Systems, Encino, Calif., 1981-87, sr. v.p. sales and mktg., 1987—; sr. assoc. World Trade Assocs., Inc., 1976—. Pres. Coll. Youth for Nixon-Lodge, 1959-60, dir. state fedn.; mem. OHSHA policy formulation com. Dept. Labor, 1967. Served with USAFR, 1960-66. Mem. Assn. Data Ctr. Owners and Mgrs. (chmn. privacy com. 1975, sec. 1972-74, v.p. 1974). Democrat. Christian Scientist. Office: 3089 Clairemont Dr Ste 213 San Diego CA 92117-6887

CHILOW, BARBARA GAIL, social worker; b. Grand Forks, N.D., June 7, 1936; d. Alfred Thomas and Florence (Micken) Seeley; m. Steven Chilow, Aug. 15, 1987; children: John Mark Doss, Timothy Stephen Doss, Elizabeth De La Cruz, David Chilow. BS, UCLA, 1957; MSW, U. So. Calif., 1970; MPA, Calif. State U., Long Beach, 1985. Lic. social worker, Calif., Utah, marriage, family and child counselor, Calif. Social worker Dept. Pub. Welfare, San Diego, 1957, Dep. Pub. Assistance, Whitman, Mass., 1966-68; psychiat. social worker State of Calif., Pomona, 1971-73; clin. social worker Orange County Dept. Mental Health, Santa Ana, Calif., 1973-74, sr. clin. social worker, 1974-79; dep. dir. mental health Orange County Human Svcs. Agy., Santa Ana, 1979-80, dep. regional mgr., 1980-82, adminstrv. mgr. II, 1982-93; clin. coord. Brightway at St. George, Utah, 1993—; pvt. practice clin. social worker Newport Beach, Calif., 1977-93; chmn. So. Calif. Case Mgmt. Coun., 1987-89, Orange County Bd. and Care Quality Com., Santa Ana, 1984-89; owner, mgr. Desert Hills Therapeutic Svcs., Inc., St. George, 1998—. Pres. Winchester Hills Homeowners Assn., St. George, 1995-97; bd. dirs. Southwestern Spl. Svc. Dist., 1997—, Leadership Dixie, 1998—; trustee Music Hall Found. Mem. NASW, AAUW, DAR (Boston Tea Party chpt.), Alliance for Mentally Ill (pres. Orange County chpt. 1994-95), Phi Alpha Alpha, Gamma Phi Beta. Democrat. Presbyterian. Avocations: hiking, piano, reading, travel. Home: 1110 W 5830 N Saint George UT 84770-5944 Office: Brightway at St George 115 W 1470 S Saint George UT 84770-6763 also: Desert Hills Therapeutic Svcs Troon Park Plz 1240 E 100 S Ste 18B Saint George UT 84790

CHILTON, CLAUDE LYSIAS, minister, former career officer; b. N.Y.C., Feb. 19, 1917; s. Claude Lysias and Clara Caroline (Weidman) C.; m. Juanita Christine Eastis, Aug. 17, 1939; children: Robert Hamilton, Claudia Jeanne Britt, Linda Christine Morgan. BTh, Bethany Nazarene Coll. (now So. Nazarene U.), 1939, BA, 1940; MA, Calif. Grad. Sch. Theology, Glendale, 1974, PhD, 1975. Ordained to ministry Ch. of the Nazarene, 1939. Pastor Ch. of the Nazarene, Ala., Okla, Ohio, 1936-43, Calif., Ala., 1946-51, Phoenix, 1971-79; ret. Ch. of the Nazarene, 1982; commd. 1st lt. U.S. Army, 1943-46; recalled to active duty as capt. USAF, 1951, advanced through grades to lt. col., 1962, chaplain various Air Force bases, 1951-71, ret., 1971. Author: The Nazarene Serviceman, 1953, Chaplains in Mission: Fifty Years of Ministry, 1992; co-author: Chaplains See World Missions, 1946; contbr. articles to profl. jours. Trustee Trevecca Nazarene Coll., Nashville, 1949-52; pres. Mobile Ministerial Assn., Ala., 1950-51; active ministerial assns., Phoenix, 1976—. Recipient various mil. decorations and awards. Mem. Air Force Assn., Ret. Officers Assn., Christian Holiness Assn., Nat. Assn. Evangels., Wesleyan Theol. Soc., Mil. Chaplains Assn. Republican. Avocation: collecting more than 14,000 different religious periodicals. Home: 13215 N 56th Ave Glendale AZ 85304-1221

CHIMERA, DONNA MAE, marketing professional, writer; b. Dubuque, Iowa, Feb. 7, 1958; d. Donald Michael and Joyce Beth (Ludwig) Ahmann; 1 child, Betsy. BA, Loras Coll., 1980. Regional mktg. dir. Convalescent Svcs., Inc., Houston, 1983-89; mktg. dir. River Oaks Imaging & Diagnostic, Houston, 1989-92, Center for Indsl. Rehab., Houston, 1992-95, Boulder (Colo.) Ctr. Accelerative Learning, 1995-96; pres. Wolfstar Prodns., Boulder, 1996—. Author: Wolfstar, 1997 (finalist Benjamin Franklin Book awards 1998). Recipient Author Series award Colo. Libr. Assn., Berthead (Colo.) Cmty. Found., 1998. Mem. Full Circle Entrepreneur Cmty. Avocations: writing, gardening, hiking, camping. Office: Wolfstar Productions PO Box 11168 Boulder CO 80301-0002

CHIMOSKEY, JOHN EDWARD, physiologist, medical educator; b. Traverse City, Mich., Apr. 15, 1937; s. Edward John and Jane Marie (Langworthy) C.; m. Dianne Marie Dailey, June 1962 (div. 1973); children: Stefan John, David Clifford. Student, U. N.Mex., 1955-56, Cen. Mich. U., 1956-58; MD, U. Mich., 1963. Rsch. fellow in physiology U. Mich., Ann Arbor, 1959-63; intern dept. medicine U. Calif., San Francisco, 1963-64; rsch. fellow in physiology Harvard Med. Sch., Boston, 1964-66; rsch. fellow in muscle rsch. Retina Found., Boston, 1966-67; assoc. prof. in physiology Hahnemann U., Phila., 1969-70; resident, rsch. fellow in dermatology Stanford U., Palo Alto, Calif., 1970-71; asst. prof. in bioengring. U. Wash., Seattle, 1971-74; assoc. prof. in physiology and surgery Baylor Med. Coll., Houston, 1974-78; prof. Mich. State U., East Lansing, 1978-99, chmn. dept. physiology, 1989-93, prof. emeritus, 1999—; guest scientist U.S. Naval Air Devel. Ctr., Johnsville, Pa., 1969-70; adj. assoc. prof. in bioengring. Rice U., Houston, 1974-78; dir. Taub Labs. for Mech. Circulatory Support, 1974-78; physiology cons. Stedman's Med. Dictionary, 1990-97; dir. grad. program Mich. State U., East Lansing, 1986-90, dir. cardiovascular tng. program, 1982-94; del. U.S.-USSR cooperation in artificial heart devel., 1976-77. Contbr. articles to profl. jours. Lt. comdr. USNR, 1967-69. Fulbright fellow, Brazil, 1990. Mem. Am. Physiol. Soc., Kauai (Hawaii) Hist. Soc., Victor Vaughn Soc., Alpha Omega Alpha. Home: PO Box 480 Kapaa HI 96746-0480

CHIN, MING, state supreme court justice; b. Klamath Falls, Oreg., Aug. 31, 1942; m. Carol Lynn Joe, Dec. 19, 1971; children: Jennifer, Jason. BA in Polit. Sci., U. San Francisco, 1964, JD, 1967. Bar: Calif., 1970, U.S. Fed. Ct., U.S. Tax Ct. Assoc., head trial dept. Aiken, Kramer & Cummings, Oakland, Calif., 1973-76, prin., 1976-88; dep. dist. atty. Alameda County, Calif., 1970-72; judge Alameda County Superior Ct., 1988-90; assoc. justice divsn. 3 Ct. Appeal 1st Dist., 1990-94; presiding justice 1st Dist. Ct. Appeal Divsn. 3, San Francisco, 1994-96; assoc. justice Calif. Supreme Ct., San Francisco, 1996—. Capt. U.S. Army, 1967-69, Vietnam, USAR, 1969-71. Mem. ABA, Calif. Judges Assn., State Bar Calif., Alameda County Bar Assn., San Francisco Dist. Atty.'s Commn. Hate Crimes, Commonwealth Club of Calif. (pres. 1998), Asian Am. Bar Assn., Alpha Sigma Nu. Office: Supreme Court Calif 350 McAllister St San Francisco CA 94102-3600

CHIN, SUE SOONE MARIAN (SUCHIN CHIN), conceptual artist, portraitist, photographer, community affairs activist; b. San Francisco; d. William W. and Soo-Up (Swebe) C. Grad. Calif. Coll. Art, Mpls. Art Inst., (scholar) Schaeffer Design Ctr.; student, Yasuo Kuniyoshi, Louis Hamon, Rico LeBrun. Photojournalist, All Together Now show, 1973, East-West News, Third World Newscasting, 1975-78, Sta. KNBC Sunday Show, L.A., 1975, 76, Live on 4, 1981, Bay Area Scene, 1981; graphics printer, exhbns. include Kaiser Ctr., Zellerbach Pla., Chinese Culture Ctr. Galleries, Capricorn Asunder Art Commn. Gallery (all San Francisco), Newspace Galleries, New Coll. of Calif., L.A. County Mus. Art, Peace Pla. Japan Ctr., Congress Arts Communication, Washington, 1989; SFWA Galleries, Inner Focus Show, 1989—, Calif. Mus. Sci. and Industry, Lucien Labaudt Gallery, Salon de Medici, Madrid, Salon Renacimento, Madrid, 1995, Life Is a Circus, SFWA Gallery, 1991, 94, UN/50 Exhibit, Bayfront Galleries, 1995, Somar Galleries, 1997, Sacramento State Fair, AFL-CIO Labor Studies Ctr., Washington, Asian Women Artists (1st prize for conceptual painting, 1st prize photography), 1978, Yerba Buena Arts Ctr. for the Arts Festival, 1994; represented in permanent collections L.A. County Fedn. Labor, Calif. Mus. Sci. and Industry, AFL-CIO Labor Studies Ctr., Australian Trades Coun., Hazeland and Co., also pvt. collections; author (poetry) Yuri and Malcolm, The Desert Sun. 1994 (Editors Choice award 1993-94). Del. nat., state convs. Nat. Women's Polit. Caucus, 1977-83, San Francisco chpt. affirmative action chairperson, 1978-82, nat. conv. del., 1978-81, Calif. del., 1976-81. Recipient Honorarium AFL-CIO Labor Studies Ctr., Washington, 1975-76; award Centro Studi Ricerche delle Nazioni, Italy, 1985; bd. advisors Psycho Neurology Found. Bicentennial award L.A. County Mus. Art, 1976, 77, 78. Mem. Asian Women Artists (founding v.p., award 1978-79, 1st award in photography of Orient 1978-79), Calif. Chinese Artists (sec.-treas. 1978-81), Japanese Am. Art Coun. (chairperson 1978-84, dir.), San Francisco Women Artists, San Francisco Graphics Guild, Pacific/Asian Women Coalition Bay Area, Chinatown Coun. Performing and Visual Arts. Chmn., Full Moon Products; pres., bd. dir. Aumni Oracle Inc. Address: PO Box 421415 San Francisco CA 94142-1415

CHINCHINIAN, HARRY, pathologist, educator; b. Troy, N.Y., Mar. 7, 1926; s. Ohaness and Armen (Der Arakelian) C.; m. Mary Corcoran, Aug. 22, 1952; children: Armen, Marjorie, Matthew. BA, U. Colo., 1952; MS, Marquette U., 1956, MD, 1959. Cert. anatomic and clin. pathologist. Co-dir. Pathologists Regional Labs., Lewiston, Idaho, 1964-96; chief of staff Tri-State Hosp., Clarkston, Wash., 1967, St. Joseph's Hosp., Lewiston, 1971; assoc. prof. pathology Wash. State U., Pullman, 1972—. Author: Antigens to Melanoma, 1957, Parasitism and Natural Resistance, 1958, Pathologist in Peril, 1996, Immigrant Son, 1996, Murder in the Mountains, 1997, Princess and the Beggar, 1998, Holly and the Dragon Dingle, 1998, Beware of the Drifters, 1998; co-author: Malakoplakia, 1957, Pneumocystis, 1965, Immigrant Son Book Two, 1997. Pres. Am. Cancer Soc., Asotin County, Wash., 1968, Lewiston Roundup, 1972-73, N.W. Soc. Blood Banks, 1973-74. Sgt. U.S. Army, 1944-46. Fellow Am. Coll. Pathologists (cert., lab. inspector 1970—), Am. Soc. Clin. Pathologists; mem. Idaho Soc. Pathologists (pres. 1970). Avocations: writing, drawing, horses. Home: 531 Silcott Rd Clarkston WA 99403-9784

CHING, ANDY KWOK-YEE, minister; b. Shanghai, People's Republic of China, Apr. 12, 1956; arrived in Hong Kong, 1961; arrived in Can., 1973; came to U.S., 1989.; s. Jan Wai and Hon Wah (Kwan) C.; m. Rosita Wai-Mui Tsoi, June 4, 1989; children: Abigail, Aaron. B of Applied Sci., U. Toronto, 1981; M of Theol. Studies, Ontario Theol. Sem., 1982; DD, Internat. Sem., 1988; postgrad., Fuller Theol. Sem., 1996—. Ordained to ministry Christian and Missionary Alliance, 1989. Asst. pastor North York Chinese Bapt. Ch., Willowdale, Ont., Can., 1982-83; interim pastor Montreal Chinese Bapt. Ch., Quebec, Can., 1984; lit. coord. Christian Reformed Ch., Toronto, Ont., 1988; gen. sec. Harvester Evangelical Press, Willowdale, 1985-89; pastor Chinese Christian Alliance Ch., Northridge, Calif., 1989-95, The Lord's Grace Christian Ch., Palo Alto, Calif., 1996—; guest lectr., Christ Internat. Theol. Sem., Alhambra, Calif., 1990-95; reporter, mem., Evangelical Press. Assn., Canoga Park, 1990—; tchr. trainer, Evangelical Tchr. Tng. Assn., Wheaton, Ill., 1989—; interpreter, Toronto Bd. Edn., 1986-88, instr,m 1986-87. Editor: Onward Christian Soldiers, Toronto, 1982, Three Episodes of Life, 1982; translator (books) Reasons to Believe, 1988, Called to Ministry, 1989; contbr. articles to profl. jours. Vol. Scott Missions to Native People, Toronto, 1983-84; bd. dirs. China Grad. Sch. Theology Bay Area Coun., 1997—. Mem. Internat. Missions Inc., Cultural Regeneration Rsch. Soc., USA (bd. dirs. 1996—). Office: The Lord's Grace Christian Ch 555 College Ave Palo Alto CA 94306-1433

CHING, ERIC SAN HING, health care and insurance administrator; b. Honolulu, Aug. 13, 1951; s. Anthony D.K. and Amy K.C. (Chong) C. BS, Stanford U., 1973, MS, MBA, 1977. Fin. analyst Mid Peninsula Health Service, Palo Alto, Calif., 1977; acting dep. exec. dir. Santa Clara County Health Systems Agy., San Jose, Calif., 1977-78; program officer Henry J. Kaiser Family Found., Menlo Park, Calif., 1978-84; dir. strategic planning Lifeguard Health Maintenance Orgn., Milpitas, Calif., 1984-90; v.p. strategic planning and dir. ops. Found. Life Ins. Co., Milpitas, 1986-90; sr. planning analyst Kaiser Found. Health Plan, Oakland, Calif., 1990-94, coord. product and competition analysis, 1994-95, mgr. ins. ops. and competitive intelligence cons., 1995-97; nat. product leader Kaiser Found. Health Plan, Oakland, 1997—; adj. faculty Am. Pistol Inst., 1991-94. Mem. vol. staff Los Angeles Olympic Organizing Com., 1984; mem. panel United Way of Santa Clara County, 1985, panel chmn., 1986-87, mem. com. priorities and community problem solving, 1987-90, Project Blueprint, 1988-90. Mem. NRA, ACLU, Am. Soc. Law Enforcement Trainers, Internat. Assn. Law Enforcement Firearms Instrs., Internat. Wound Ballistics Assn., Stanford Alumni Assn., Stanford Bus. Sch. Alumni Assn., Stanford Swordmasters (pres. 1980-89). Avocations: firearms instrn., shoot, photography, travel. Office: Kaiser Found Health Plan Inc One Kaiser Pla 25th Fl Oakland CA 94612

CHINN, DOUGLAS OWEN, urologist, cryosurgeon; b. L.A., Sept. 4, 1950; s. James and Helen (Lee) C.; m. Eva Jew, May 1975; children: Cynthia, Jonathan, Michael, Krystal. BS, U. So. Calif., 1972, MD, 1976. Diplomate Am. Bd. Urology. Resident L.A County-U. So. Calif. Med. Ctr., L.A., 1979-83; intern L.A. County So. Calif. Med. Ctr., L.A., 1976-77; mem. staff Chinn Urology Med. Group, Arcadia, Calif., 1983—; cons. Boston Sci., Natick, Mass., 1997—, Endocare, Inc., Irvine, Calif., 1996—. Author: (jour.) Cancer, 1997; method patentee medical. Mem. Am. Urologic Assn., Western Sect. Am. Urologic Assn., Calif. Urologic Assn., L.A. County Med. Assn. (bd. dirs. 1993—). Achievements include method patent which com-

bines imaging and temperature monitoring in prostate cryosurgery. Avocation: computers. Office: 65 N 1st Ave Ste 101 Arcadia CA 91006-3251

CHIOLIS, MARK JOSEPH, television executive; b. Walnut Creek, Calif., Dec. 29, 1959; s. Richard Spiro and Muriel Marie (Kottinger) C. Student aeronautics, Sacramento Community Coll., 1980-82; student, American River Coll., 1982. With on-air ops. Sta. KRBK-TV, Sacramento, 1979-81; on-air ops. trainer, crew chief Sta. KVIE-TV, Sacramento, 1981-85; trainer on air ops., ops. crew chief Sta. KRBK-TV, Sacramento, 1981-84; producer, dir., ops. crew chief Sta. KVIE-TV, Sacramento, 1985-87, Sta. KRBK-TV, Sacramento, 1984-87; prodn. mgr., producer, dir. Sta. KVIE-TV, Sacramento, 1987—; production mgr., producer, dir. spl. programs, comml. productions Sta. KRBK-TV, Sacramento, 1987—; with on-air ops. Sta. KVIE-TV, Sacramento, 1980-82; regional sales mgr. BTS-Broadcast T.V. Systems, Inc., 1992—; promotion chmn. Capital Concour d'Elegance, Sacramento, 1984—, gen. chmn., 1987-89. Producer (music videos) Running Wild, Running Fee, 1984, Rocket Hot-/The Image, 1984 (Joey award 1985); producer, dir. (music video) Haunting Melodies, 1991; dir. (documentary) Behind Closed Doors, 1984; producer, dir. FLIGHTLOG, The Jerry Reynolds Show, CountryMile country music show, 1991; dir. (video camera) Reno Nat. Championship Air Races, 1992, 93, 94, 95, 96, 97, dir. photography, 1998; Money Insights, 1993; tech. video dir. for state franchise bd. Tax Talk, 1992, 93, 94, 96, Teleconf. uplinks; segment prodr. Daylight Run 97 Camrac Studios. Video producer Calif. N.G., 1980-82; video trainer Am. Cancer Soc., Sacramento, 1983-85; cons. Sacramento Sheriff's Dept., Sacramento, 1984—, United Way-WEAVE, Sacramento, 1984-85; bd. dirs. Woodside Homeowners Assn., 1989—. Recipient Gold Addy award, 1986, 87, Addy award, 1989. Mem. Calif. Broadcasters Assn. (bd. dirs. 1996—), Am. Advt. Fedn., Sacramento Advt. Club (awards video producer 1984—, chmn. judging 1988-89, bd. dirs. 1989—, co-chair awards banquet 1989-90), Aircraft Owners and Pilots Assn., Computer Users Group. Republican. Avocations: flying, helicopters, writing, tennis, racquetball. Office: Philips Broadcast TV Sys 111 N 1st St Ste 100 Burbank CA 91502-1851

CHIPMAN, JACK, artist; b. L.A., Oct. 31, 1943; s. George Geotz and June Naomi (Hanson) C. BFA, Calif. Inst. Arts, 1966. Dealer Calif. pottery Calif. Spectrum, Redondo Beach, 1980-90; cons. Schroeder Pub., Paducah, Ky., 1982—. Author: Complete Collectors Guide Bauer Pottery, 1982, Collector's Encyclopedia California Pottery, 1992, 2d edit., 1998, Collector's Encyclopedia Bauer Pottery, 1997, (periodicals) Antique Trader Weekly, 1981-83, Am. Clay Exch., 1982-88; one-person shows include Oakland Mus. Calif., Long Beach Mus. Art, U. Santa Clara Art Mus.; represented in permanent collections at Oakland (Calif.) Art Mus., Long Beach (Calif.) Mus. Art, U. Santa Clara (Calif.) Art Mus. Bd. dirs. Angels Gate Cultural Ctr., San Pedro, Calif., jour. editor, 1990-93. Avocation: collecting Calif. pottery. Office: PO Box 1079 Venice CA 90294-1079

CHIRAPRAVATI, PATTARATORN, art historian, educator; b. Bangkok, Apr. 10, 1958; came to U.S., 1982; d. M. R. Vadhanatorn and Rojana (Rice) C.; m. Richard Earl Breedon, Jan. 11, 1992; children: Earl Chira Breedon, Franz Chira Breedon. Bachelor's degree, Silpakorn U., Bangkok, 1987; Master's degree, Ohio State U., 1984; PhD, Cornell U., 1994. Headmistress Mahanark Art Sch., Bangkok, 1989-90; instr. Silpakorn U., 1989-90, U. Tsukuba, Japan, 1993-94, Sonoma State U., Rohnert Park, Calif., 1997—; asst. curator S.E. Asian art Asian Art Mus. of San Francisco, 1997—; peer reviewer Sacramento Met. Art Coun., 1997. Author: (book) Votive Tablets in Thailand: Origin, Styles, and Uses, 1997; editor: (book) Letters of King Chulalongkorn to H.R.H. Nakhonchaisri, 1998. Mellon fellow, 1987. Mem. Am. Coun. for So. Asian Art, Assn. for Asian Studies, Coll. Art Assn., Archaeol. Inst. Thailand, Alpha Epsilon chpt. Phi Beta Delta (founding mem.). Avocation: yoga. Office: Asian Art Mus San Francisco Golden Gate Park San Francisco CA 94118

CHIROT, DANIEL, sociology and international studies educator; b. Bélâbre, Indre, France, Nov. 27, 1942; came to U.S., 1949; s. Michel and Hélène C.; m. Cynthia Kenyon, July 19, 1974; children: Claire, Laura. BA in Social Studies, Harvard U., 1964; PhD in Sociology, Columbia U., 1973. Asst. prof. sociology U. N.C. Chapel Hill, 1971-74; asst. prof. to prof. internat. studies and sociology Henry M. Jackson sch. U. Wash., 1975—. Author: Social Change in a Peripheral Society, 1976, Social Change in the Twentieth Century, 1977, translations: Korean, 1984, Italian, 1985, Social Change inthe Modern Era, 1986, translations: Korean, 1984, Chinese, 1991, Modern Tyrants: The Power and Prevalence of Evil in Our Age, 1994, rev. edit., 1996, Polish translation, 1997, How Societies Change, 1994, Romanian translation, 1996; translator: (with Holley Coulter Chirot) Traditional Romanian Villages (Henri H. Stahl), 1980; editor: The Origins of Backwardness in Eastern Europe, 1989, The Crisis of Leninism and the Decline of the Left, 1991, (with Anthony Reid) Essential Outsiders, 1997; founder and editor Ea. European Politics and Socs., 1986-89. John Simon Guggenheim fellow 1991-92. Avocations: skiing, hiking. Office: U Washington Jackson Sch Intl Studies 503 Thompson Hall Seattle WA 98195

CHISHOLM, TOM SHEPHERD, environmental engineer; b. Morristown, N.J., Nov. 28, 1941; s. Charles Fillmore and Eileen Mary (Fenderson) C.; m. Mary Virginia Carrillo, Nov. 7, 1964; children: Mark Fillmore, Elaine Chisholm. Student, Northeastern U., Boston, 1959-61; BS in Agrl. Engring., N.Mex. State U., 1964; MS in Agrl. Engring., S.D. State U., 1967; PhD in Agrl. Engring., Okla. State U., 1970. Registered profl. engr., Ariz., La.; cert. Class A indsl. wastewater operator. Agrl. engr. U.S. Bur. Land Mgmt., St. George, Utah, 1964-65; asst. prof. U. P.R., Mayaguez, 1970-74, La. State U., 1974-77; assoc. prof. S.D. State U., 1977-81; environ. engr. Atlantic Richfield Subsidiary, Sahuarita, Ariz., 1981-86, Ariz. Dept. Environ. Quality, Phoenix, 1986-88; environ. mgr. Galactic Resources, Del Norte, Colo., 1988-91; v.p. M&E Cons., Inc., Phoenix, 1991-94; pres. Chisholm & Assocs., Phoenix, 1991—; v.p. 3R Resources, Tucson, 1994—; cons. various mfrs., Calif., Tex., Ill., Mex., 1980-91. Contbr. articles to profl. jours. NSF fellow, 1965-66, 68-69. Mem. Am. Soc. Agrl. Engrs. (faculty advisor student chpt. 1978-79), Phi Kappa Phi, Sigma Xi, Alpha Epsilon, Beta Gamma Epsilon. Avocations: hiking, running, investing, solar energy. Office: Chisholm & Assocs PO Box 47554 Phoenix AZ 85068-7554

CHISM, JENNY CAROL, nurse, sculptor; b. Medford, Oreg., Sept. 6, 1955; d. Hadley Austin and Margaret Sue (Snead) Yow; m. Glen Anthony Miller, Nov. 13, 1982 (div. 1990); children: Joshua, Jesse, Erik, Leah Mae; m. Bradley Dean Chism, Sept. 4, 1993. AS, Umpqua C.C., Roseburg, Oreg., 1983, AS in Nursing, 1984. RN, Oreg. Emergency med. technician Sutherlin (Oreg.) Ambulance, 1977-78, Glide (Oreg.) Paramed. Ambulance, Comty. One Ambulance, Roseburg, Oreg., 1979-82; nurse part time Douglas County Corrections, Roseburg, Oreg., 1984-87; proprietor, artist Chism's Gallery and Mercantile Store, Canyonville, Oreg., 1995-97; nurse part time VA Med. Ctr., Roseburg, Oreg., 1987—; sculptor, painter Home Studio, Dillard, Oreg., 1987—. Artist: pencil and oil portraits, 1973— (awards); sculptor western history and wildlife, 1994— (awards). Airborne med. specialist U.S. Army XIII Airborne Corps, 7th spl. forces group, 1974-76, med. specialist Oreg. Nat. Guard, Roseburg, 1977, 81-85. Mem. Oreg. Nurses Assn. Republican. Avocations: fishing, photography, gardening. Home: PO Box 516 Dillard OR 97432-0516

CHITTICK, ARDEN BOONE, steamship agency executive; b. Sunnyside, Wash., Aug. 5, 1936; s. Herbert Boone and Maude Ellen (George) C.; m. Nina Sorensen, Apr. 16, 1960; children: Kyle, Kirsten. BS, Wash. State U., 1964. Ops. mgr. Kerr Steamship Co. Inc., Seattle, 1979-81, marine mgr. PNW, 1981-84; dist. ops. mgr. Merit Steamship Agy. Inc., Seattle, 1984-86, Pacific N.W. ops. mgr., 1986-87; ops. mgr. Internat. Shipping Co. Inc., Seattle, 1987-89, v.p. ops., 1989-91, regional v.p. ops., 1991-96; v.p. Internat. Shipping Co. Inc., Portland, Oreg., 1991-96, bd. dirs., dir., 1996—; v.p. Marine Exch. of Puget Sound, Seattle, 1982-88; pres. Puget Sound Steamship Operators Assn., Seattle, 1987, v.p., 1983, 86, 95. Troop com. mem. Boy Scouts Am., Bainbridge Island, Wash., 1984. Capt. USMCR, 1957-64; comdr. USCG, 1964-70. Mem. Puget Sound Coast Guard Officers Assn. (pres. 1978), Propeller Club of U.S. (gov. Seattle chpt. 1984-87, 89-94). Republican. Methodist. Avocations: fishing, sports, landscape gardening, history. Home: RR 1 Box 57B Porter Hill Rd Bear Lake PA 16402-9622 Office: Internat Shipping Co Inc 1111 3rd Ave Ste 1825 Seattle WA 98101-3207

CHIU, JOHN TANG, physician; b. Macao, Jan. 8, 1938; s. Lan Cheong and Yau Hoon C.; m. Bonnie Doolan, Aug. 28, 1965 (div. Apr. 1986); children: Lisa, Mark, Heather. Student, U. Vt., 1959, BA, 1960, MD, 1964. Diplomate Am. Bd. Allergy & Immunology. Pres. Allergy Med. Group, Inc., Newport Beach, Calif., 1969-72, 1972—; clin. prof. medicine U. Calif., Irvine, 1975—. Contbr. articles to profl. jours. Active Santa Ana Heights Adv. Commn., 1982-83; life mem. Orange County Sheriff's Adv. council, 1987—. Recipient Freshman Chem. Achievement award, Am. Chem. Soc., 1958. Fellow Am. Acad. Allergy Asthma and Immunology, Am. Coll. Allergy and Immunology, Am. Coll. Chest Physicians (sec. steering com. allergy 1977-81), Orange County Med. Assn. (chmn. communications com. 1985-88, communications com., mem. bulletin edit. bd. 1995—). Avocations: snow skiing, swimming, aerobics, travels, windsurfing. Office: Allergy Med Group Inc 400 Newport Center Dr Newport Beach CA 92660-7601

CHIU, MARGARET CHI YUAN LIU, real estate broker; b. Quangzhou, Quangdong, China, Nov. 3, 1926; d. Chien Shan and Wen Bing Liu; m. Wan-Cheng Chiu, Feb. 6, 1954; children: Linda, Ellen, Elaine Amy. BA, Nat. Taiwan U., 1950; MBA, N.Y.U., 1956. Clk. Taiwan Supply Bur., Taipei, Taiwan, 1950-53; realtor assoc. Tropic Shore Realty, Honolulu, 1973-79; realtor broker Urner & Assocs., Inc., Honolulu, 1979-93; realtor/broker Savio Realty, Ltd./Better Homes and Gardens, Honolulu, 1993—. Chinese paintings shown in various exhibitions, 1990—. Joint U.S. and Republic of China fellow, 1951-52. Mem. Nat. Assn. Realtors, Hawaii Assn. Realtors, Honolulu Bd. Realtors, Chinese Women's Benevolent Assn. Hawaii (pres. 1987-91), Hawaii Chinese Assn. (v.p. 1985), Lung Kong Kung Shaw Soc. (sec. 1990-92). Avocations: Chinese painting, singing, dancing. Home: 216 Kalalau St Honolulu HI 96825-2012

CHIU, PETER YEE-CHEW, physician; b. China, May 12, 1948; came to U.S., 1965; naturalized, 1973; s. Man Chee and Yiu Ying Chiu. BS, U. Calif., Berkeley, 1969, MPH, 1970, DrPH, 1975; MD, Stanford U., 1983. Diplomate Am. Bd. Family Practice; registered profl. engr., Calif.; registered environ. health specialist, Calif. Asst. civil engr. City of Oakland, Calif., 1970-72; assoc. water quality engr. Bay Area Sewage Services Agy., Berkeley, 1974-76; prin. environ. engr. Assn. Bay Area Govts., Berkeley, 1976-79; intern San Jose (Calif.) Hosp., 1983-84, resident physician, 1984-86; ptnr. Chiu and Crawford, San Jose, 1986-89, Good Samaritan Med. Group, San Jose, 1989-90, The Permanente Med. Group, 1991—; adj. prof. U. San Francisco, 1979-83; clin. asst. prof. Stanford U. Med. Sch., 1987—. Contbr. articles to profl. publs.; co-authored one of the first comprehensive regional environ. mgmt. plans in U.S.; composer, pub. various popular songs Southeast Asia, U.S. mem. Chinese for Affirmative Action, San Francisco, 1975—; bd. dirs. Calif. Regional Water Quality Control Bd.,Oakland, 1979-84, Bay Area Comprehensive Health Planning Coun., San Francisco, 1972-76; mem. Santa Clara County Ctrl. Dem. Com., 1987—; mem. exec. bd. Calif. State Dem. Ctrl. Com.; commr. U.S. Presdl. Commn. on Risk Assessment and Risk Mgmt., Washington, 1993-97. Recipient Resident Tchr. award Soc. Tchrs. Family Medicine, 1986, Resolution of Appreciation award Calif. Regional Water Quality Control Bd., 1985. Fellow Am. Acad. Family Physicians; mem. Am. Pub. Health Assn., Chi Epsilon, Tau Beta Pi. Democrat. Avocations: songwriting, recording. Office: The Permanente Med Group 770 E Calaveras Blvd Milpitas CA 95035-5491

CHLIWNIAK, LUBA, higher education consultant, educator; b. Bois du Lac, Belgium, Apr. 22, 1950; came to U.S., 1972; d. Walter Chliwniak and Anna (Nizolek) Syrik; m. John F. Redavid, Jan. 3, 1981 (div. Oct. 1982). BA, U. Ariz., 1975, MEd, 1976, PhD, 1996. Counselor, employment specialist Pima County Adult Edn., Tucson, Ariz., 1977-79; refugee program coord. Pima County Adult Edn., Tucson, 1979-80; coord. women's correctional program Tucson Women's Commn., 1980-81; state coord. Ariz. Dept. Econ. Security, Phoenix, 1981-85; campus dir. Apollo Coll., Tucson, 1985-93; dir. edn. and compliance Apollo Coll., Phoenix, 1993-95; prof., cons. Consulting and Contract Svcs., Tucson, 1995—. Author: Analyzing the Gender Gap in Higher Education, 1997. Treas. Am. Ukrainian Soc., 1995-97. Recipient Travel award Coll. Edn., U. Ariz., 1995, 96, Ctr. Study Higher Edn., U. Ariz., 1996; rsch. grantee Nat. Assn. Student Personnel Adminstrs., 1998. Avocation: gardening. Home: 3301 N Stewart Ave Tucson AZ 85716-1221

CHMELIR, LYNN KAY, academic librarian; b. Berwyn, Ill., Jan. 11, 1946; d. John Joseph and Dolores Margaret (Svehla) C.; m. John Philip Webb, June 12, 1976; 1 child, Lauren Jane Webb. AB, U. Ill., 1967, AM, 1970, MS in Libr. Sci., 1976. Catalog libr. Lewis and Clark Coll., Portland, 1976-78; tech. svcs. libr. Linfield Coll., McMinnville, Oreg., 1978-81, coll. libr., 1981—. Chair Portals Coun. of Librs., Portland, 1995-96, Orbis Consortium, Eugene, 1997-98. Mem. ALA, Assn. of Coll. and Rsch. Librs. (com. chair, pres. Oreg. chpt. 1983-84), Oreg. Libr. Assn. (pres. 1988-89), Alpha Lambda Delta, Beta Phi Mu. E-mail: lchmelir@linfield.edu. Home: 3540 16th Ct S Salem OR 97302-4001 Office: Linfield Coll 900 SE Baker Mcminnville OR 97128

CHO, LEE-JAY, social scientist, demographer; b. Kyoto, Japan, July 5, 1936; came to U.S., 1959; s. Sam-Soo and Kyung-Doo (Park) C.; m. Eun-Ja Chun, May 20, 1973; children: Yun-Kyong Nuy, Sang-Mun Ray, Han-Jae Jeremy. BA, Kookmin Coll., Seoul, Korea, 1959; MA in Govt., George Washington U., 1962; MA in Sociology (Population Council fellow), U. Chgo., 1964, PhD in Sociology, 1965; D in Econs. (hon.), Dong-A U., 1982; DSc in Demography, Tokyo U., 1983; D in Econs., Keio U., Tokyo, 1989. Statistician Korean Census Council, 1958-61; research assoc., asst. prof. sociology Population Research and Tng. Center, U. Chgo., 1965-66; asso. dir. Community and Family Study Center, 1969-70; sr. demographic adv. to Malaysian Govt., 1967-69; assoc. prof. U. Hawaii, 1969-73, prof., 1973-78; asst. dir. East-West Population Inst., East-West Center, Honolulu, 1971-74; dir. East-West Population Inst., East-West Center, 1974-92; pres. pro tem East-West Center, 1980-81, v.p., 1987-98, sr. advisor, 1998—; cons. in field; mem. Nat. Acad. Scis. Com. on Population and Demography; mem. U.S. 1980 Census Adv. Com., Dept. Commerce. Author: (with others) Differential Current Fertility in the United States, 1970; editor: (with others) Introduction to Censuses of Asia and the Pacific: 1970-74, 1976, (with Kazumasa Kobayashi) Fertility Transition in East Asian Populations, 1979, (with Suharto, McNicoll and Mamas) Population Growth of Indonesia, 1980, The OWN Children of Fertility Estimation, 1986, (with Y.H. Kim) Economic Development of Republic of Korea: A Policy Perspective, 1989, (with Kim) Korea's Political Economy: An Institutional Perspective, 1994, (with Yada) Tradition and Change in the Asian Family, 1994, (with Y.H. Kim) Hedging Bets on Groth in a Globalizing Industrial Order, 1997, (with Y.H. Kim) Korea's Choices in Emerging Global Competition and Cooperation, 1998, (with Kim) Ten Paradigms of Market Economies and Land Systems, 1998; contbr. numerous articles on population and econ. devel. to profl. jours. Bd. dirs. Planned Parenthood Assn., Hawaii, 1976-77. Ford Found. grantee, 1977-79; Population Council grantee, 1973-75; Dept. Commerce grantee, 1974-78; recipient Award of Mugunghwa-Jang, govt. Republic of Korea, 1992, 4th N.E. Asia Niigata prize, 1996. Mem. Internat. Statis. Inst. (tech. adv. com. World Fertility Survey), Internat. Union Sci. Study Population, Population Assn. Am., Am. Statis. Assn., Am. Sociol. Assn., N.E. Asia Econ. Forum (founding chmn.). Home: 1718 Halekoa Dr Honolulu HI 96821-1027 Office: 1601 E West Rd Honolulu HI 96848-1601

CHO, ZANG HEE, physics educator; b. Seoul, Korea, July 15, 1936; came to U.S., 1972; m. Jung Sook. BSc, Seoul Nat. U., 1960, MSc, 1962; PhD, Uppsala (Sweden) U., 1966. Assoc. prof. Stockholm U., 1971-76, UCLA, 1972-78; prof. Columbia U., N.Y.C., 1979-85, U. Calif., Irvine, 1985—; hon. chair prof. Korea Acad. Indsl. Tech., 1990—; assoc. dir. Imaging Rsch. Ctr., Columbia U., 1979-84; dir. Nuclear Magnetic Resonance rsch. U. Calif., Irvine, 1985—; organizer tech. programs, symposia and workshops. Author: Foundations of Medical Imaging, 1993; editor-in-chief Internat. Jour. Imaging Sys. and Tech., 1991—; guest editor IEEE Nuclear Sci., 1974, Computers Medicine and Biology, 1976, Image Sci. and Tech., 1989; mem. editorial bd. Physics in Medicine and Biology, Inst. Physics, U.K., 1993, Magnetic Resonance in Medicine, 1984, Computerized Med. Imaging and Graphics, 1989; author/co-author more than 200 original sci. papers in internat. tech. and sci. jours. Named Disting. Scientist, Asilomar, 1982; recipient Grand Sci. prize Seoul, 1984, Jacob Javits Neurosci. award, NIH, 1984, Sylvia Sorkin Greenfield award Am. Assn. Med. Physicists, 1989, Nat. Applied Sci. prize (presdl. award) Korea Sci. Found., 1995, Nat. Acad. Sci. prize Nat. Acad. Scis., Republic of Korea, 1997. Fellow IEEE, Instn. Elec. Engrs. (U.K.), Third World Acad. Sci., Korea Acad. Sci. and Tech. (life); mem. Korea Nat. Acad. of Scis., Inst. Medicine of NAS, Nat. Acad. Scis. Korea. Home: 29 Harbor Pointe Dr Corona Del Mar CA 92625-1333 Office: Univ Calif Dept Radiological Sci Irvine CA 92697

CHOCK, ALVIN KEALI'I, retired botanist; b. Honolulu, June 18, 1931; s. Hon and Eleanor Kam Hoon (Au) C.; AA, Hannibal-LaGrange Coll. (Mo.), 1949; BA, U. Hawaii at Manoa, 1951, MS in Botany, 1953; postgrad. U. Mich., 1953-55, U.S. Dept. Agr. Grad. Sch., 1959, Pacific Asian Mgmt. Inst., 1988, 90, U. Hawaii at Manoa, 1988, 90; m. Yona Nahenahe Bielefeldt, June 18, 1962; children: T. Makana, D. 'Alana, D. Malama. Tech. adminstrv. asst. European Exchange Svc., Katterbach bei Ansbach/Mfr., Fed. Republic Ger., 1958-59; plant quarantine insp. Agrl. Rsch. Svc., U.S. Dept. Agr., N.Y.C., 1959-60, Honolulu, 1961-67, supervisory insp., Balt., 1967-70; program specialist Office of Pesticide Programs, EPA, Washington, 1970-71, supervisory program specialist, 1971-74, supervisory biologist, 1975; agrl. officer (plant quarantine) FAO, Rome, 1975-78, also tech. sec. Near East Plant Protection Commn. and Caribbean Plant Protection Commn., 1976; supervisory biologist, registration div. Office of Pesticide Programs, EPA, Washington, 1978-81; acting coord. internat. programs Plant Protection and Quarantine, Animal and Plant Health Inspection Svc. Dept. Agr., Hyattsville, Md., 1981-82, dir. Region II (Europe, Near East and Africa), 1981-82, The Hague, Netherlands, 1982-88; dir. region III (Asia and Pacific), Hyattsville, Md., 1988-92; lectr. botany U. Hawaii, Manoa, 1961-67, 69, 72, 79, 84, 86, 88, 90, 93, 95, 96, 97, 98; adj. instr. botany U. Hawaii, Manoa, 1993-95, adj. colleague, 95—; asst. botanist B.P. Bishop Mus., Honolulu, 1961-65; botanist Kokee Natural History Mus., Hawaii, 1953-55; bot. cons. Nat. Park Svc., 1962-63; mem. work panels European and Mediterranean Plant Protection Orgn., Paris, 1976-78; plant quarantine cons. Coun. Agr. Rep. China, Taiwan, 1993—. Mem. governing bd. Nat. Conf. State Socs., Washington, 1972-75, dep. dir. gen., 1973-74, 2d v.p., 1974-75; governing bd. Asian Pacific Am. Heritage Coun., Inc., 1979-81, 88-92; sec. PTA, Overseas Sch. Rome, 1976-77; USDA rep., 1988, observer, 1990-91, governing bd. Am. Fgn. Svc. Assn. Served with inf. U.S. Army, 1955-57. Plant species Cyanea chockii named in his honor; recipient other awards in field. Mem. Hawaiian Acad. Sci. (dir. jr. acad. 1963-64), Lloyd Shaw Found., Assn. Tropical Biology (charter), Hawaiian Bot. Soc. (sec. 1962, dir. 1963, 65, 94-95, pres. 1964), Internat. Assn. Plant Taxonomists, Pacific Sci. Assn., Soc. Econ. Botany, FAO Assn. Profl. Staff (appeals and procedures com. 1976-77, standing com. career devel. 1976-78), Nat. Capital Area Square Dance Leaders Assn. (editor newsletter 1980-81), Mediterranean Area Callers and Tchrs. Assn. (founder; publicity dir. 1977-78), European Callers and Tchrs. Assn., Contralab, Hawaii State Soc. of D.C. (dir. 1968-69, 88-91, 1st v.p. 1969-71, pres. 1971-72, adv. 1978-79, 2d v.p. 1979-80, Hawaii rep. 1995—), Hawaii Fedn. Square & Round Dance Clubs (treas. 1996-98), Hawaii State Dance Coun. (bd. dirs. 1996—, sec. 97—), Consumers Union, Bishop Mus. Assn., Pacific Sci. Assn., Sigma Xi. Club: Ramblin' Romans Sq. Dance (founder), Ewa Gentry Cmty. Assn. (v.p. 1993-95, pres. 1995-96, v.p. 1997—, newsletter editor 1993-94), Arbors Assn. Apt. Owners, (bd. dirs. 1994—, newsletter editor 1994—), Roosevelt H.S. Alumni Assn. (bd. dirs. 1993—), Roosevelt Alumni Found (v.p. 1994-96, pres. 1996—). Founding editor Hawaii Bot. Soc. newsletter, 1962-63, 66; editor Fed. Plant Quarantine Insps. Nat. Assn. newsletter, 1963-65, Ka Nupepa, 1968-71; chmn. editorial com. FAO Plant Protection Bull., 1976-78; contbg. author books; editor: (with G. L. Addicott) Favorite Songs of the Hawaii State Society, 1973; contbr. articles to profl. jours. Home: 91-1064 Laaulu St Apt E Ewa Beach HI 96706-3866

CHOCK, CLIFFORD YET-CHONG, family practice physician; b. Chgo., Oct. 15, 1951; s. Wah Tim and Leatrice (Wong) C. *Foster son Ryan Makoto Sato born 10/10/84 became an accomplished snow skier by the age of 5 (while living in Hawaii) and began earning National Standard Race Ranking. Before the age of 13 he had earned (at Iolandi Elementary School in Honolulu) 5 awards: citizenship, sportsmanship, School Service and twice for Headmaster's Certificate. He first demonstrated these qualities at the age of 6 when he recognized his great-grandfather's need for an escort to the elementary school's lavatory. So he asked his teacher for permission to do so without any adult instructing him to volunteer.* BS in Biology, Purdue U., 1973; MD, U. Hawaii, 1978. Intern in internal medicine Loma Linda (Calif.) Med. Ctr., 1978-79, resident in internal medicine, 1979; resident in internal medicine U. So. Calif.-L.A. County Med. Ctr., L.A., 1980; physician Pettis VA Clinic, Loma Linda, Calif., 1980; pvt. practice Honolulu, 1981—; chmn. Dept. of Family Practice, 1990-98, chmn. utilization rev. com. 1991, 95; physician reviewer St. Francis Med. Ctr., Liliha, Hawaii,, 1985—, chmn. Quality Care for Family Practice, 1990-93, 95-98; chmn. credentials Family Practice, 1990-93, 95-96, acting chmn. credentials com., 1992; physician reviewer Peer Rev. Orgn. Hawaii, Honolulu, 1987-93. Fellow Am. Acad. Family Physicians, Internat. Platform Assn. Avocations: model construction, swimming, Christian ministry, King James Bible study, toy collection. Office: 321 N Kuakini St Ste 513 Honolulu HI 96817-2361

CHOMKO, STEPHEN ALEXANDER, archaeologist; b. Bklyn., Nov. 18, 1948; s. Paul and Lucy Isabella (Bisaccio) C.; m. Leslie M. Howard, Aug. 1972 (div. 1980). BA in Anthropology cum laude, Beloit Coll., 1970; MA in Anthropology, U. Mo., 1976. Mem. rsch. staff Nassau County Mus. Natural History, Glen Cove, N.Y., 1969-71; grad. rsch. asst. U. Mo., Columbia, 1972-74, 75-78; rsch. asst. Ill. State Mus., Springfield, 1974-75; dist. archaeologist Bur. Land Mgmt., Rawlins, Wyo., 1978-80; archaeologist Office of Fed. Inspector, Denver, 1980-82; dir. Paleo Environ. Cons., Wheat Ridge, Colo., 1980-86; archaeologist Interagy. Archaeol. Svcs., Denver, 1982-92; chief rsch. and resource mgmt. Mesa Verde (Colo.) Nat. Park, 1992; chief tng. mgmt. Fort Carson, 1994—. Writer, dir. (video program) Our Past Our Future, 1992; contbr. articles to profl. jours. Grantee Cave Rsch. Found., Yellow Springs, Ohio, 1976; Anthropology scholar U. Mo., Columbia, 1978; recipient Quality Performance award Nat. Park Svc., Denver, 1992, 93, Environ. Quality award Dept. of Army, 1996, Environ. Stewardship award Dept. of Def., 1997. Mem. Soc. Am. Archaeology, Am. Anthropol. Assn., Am. Quaternary Assn., Wyo. Assn. Profl. Archaeologists (exec. com. 1979-82), Mont. Archaeol. Soc., Plains Anthropol. Soc. (v.p. 1988-89, bd. dirs. 1986-89). Home: 1144 Rock Creek Canyon Rd Colorado Springs CO 80926-8710 Office: Decam 801 Tevis St Fort Carson CO 80913-4000

CHOOK, EDWARD KONGYEN, university official, disaster medicine educator; b. Shanghai, Apr. 15, 1937; s. Shiu-heng and Shuiking (Shek) C.; m. Ping Ping Chew, Oct. 30, 1973; children by previous marriage: Miranda, Bradman. MD, Nat. Def. Med. Ctr., Taiwan, 1959; MPH, U. Calif., Berkeley, 1964, PhD, 1969; ScD, Phila. Coll. Pharmacy & Sci., 1971; JD, La Salle U., 1994. Assoc. prof. U. Calif., Berkeley, 1966-68; dir. higher edn. Bay Area Bilingual Edn. League, Berkeley, 1970-75; prof., chancellor United U. Am., Oakland and Berkeley, Calif., 1975-84; regional adminstr. U. So. Calif., L.A., 1984-90; pres. Pacific Internat. U., Berkeley and Pomona, Calif., and Guam, 1996—, Shanghai Internat. Coll., 1997—; chancellor Bi-Lingual Coll. Zhuhai (China)-Pacific Internat. Joint U., Hong Kong, 1998—; vis. prof. Nat. Def. Med. Ctr., Taiwan Armed Forces U., 1982—, Tongji U., Shanghai, 1992, Foshan U., China, 1992—; cons. specialist Beijing Hosp., 1988—; founder, pres. United Svc. Coun., Inc., 1971—; pres. Pan Internat. Acad., Changchun, China and San Francisco, 1979—, China Gen. Devel. Corp., U.S., 1992—; pub. Unity Jour./Power News, San Francisco, 1979—; mem. NAS-NRC, Washington, 1968-71; spl. cons. cultural sensitivity seminars; spl. lectr. KPMG/Peat Warwick Accts., 1996; advisor Ka Wa Bank, Hong Kong, 1986-96. Assoc. editor U.S.-Chinese Times, 1996-98; pub. US-China Times, 1996—, Unity Jour., N.Am. edit., 1996—; contbr. articles to profl. jours. Trustee Rep. Presdl. Task Force, Washington, 1978—; advisor on mainland China affairs Ctrl. Com. Chinese Nationalist party, Taiwan, 1994-97; deacon Am. Bapt. Ch.; sr. advisor U.S. Congl. Adv. Bd.; mem. Presdl. Adv. Commn., 1991—; hon. dep. sec. of state State of Calif., 1990-93; spl. advisor to sec. of state, 1991—; pres. Yuen Kong Found. for Internat. Understanding (aka March Fong EU Found.), 1994-96, 96—; mem. Nat. Heart Coun., 1994—; senatorial commn. Rep. Senatorial Inner Cir., 1996. August 9, 1997 proclaimed Ed Chook Day by City of Oakland. Mem. World Affairs Coun. San Francisco, Rotary (com. chmn. 1971—). Achievements include rsch. on hearing conservation program in U.S. Army, criteria for return to work, principles and practices of nuclear, biol. and chem. weapons. Office: PIU Adminstrn Office 555 Pierce Ste B-2 Albany CA 94706-1044

CHOPP, FRANK, state official; m. Nancy Long; 2 children. BA magna cum laude, U. Wash., 1975. Exec. dir. Fremont Pub. Assn., 1983—; part-time lectr. U. Wash. Grad. Sch. Pub. Affairs, 1992-95; co-speaker of house State of Wash. 43d Dist., Olympia. Dir. Cascade Cmty. Ctr., 1975-76; mgr. No. Cmty. Svc. Ctr. Seattle Dept. Human Resources, 1976-79, 81-83; administrv. dir. Pike Market Senior Ctr., 1980-81. Office: 3d Fl Legislative Bldg Olympia WA 98504-0600 also: 4209 Sunnyside Ave N Seattle WA 98103*

CHOUDHURY, RAJ DEO, economist; b. N.Y.C., Feb. 3, 1969; s. Deo Chand and Annette P. Choudhury. BA, Princeton U., 1990; MA, Stanford U., 1993. Evaluation analyst Arco Ak. Inc., Anchorage, 1993-96; sr. planning analyst Atlantic Richfield Co., L.A., 1996-98; cons. Global Alternative Propulson Ctr., GM, Mainz, Germany, 1998—; bd. mem. Internat. Assn. Energy Econs., Anchorage Chpt., 1992-93. Mem. Soc. Automotive Engrs., Nat. Assn. Bus. Economists, Internat. Assn. Energy Econs. (bd. dirs. Anchorage chpt. 1992-93), Asia Soc., L.A. World Affairs Coun. Avocations: photography, amateur radio, mountaineering. E-mail: panamint@hotmail.com. Home: Luxemburgstr 9, 65185 Wiesbaden Germany

CHOW, WINSTON, engineering research executive; b. San Francisco, Dec. 21, 1946; s. Raymond and Pearl C.; m. Lilly Fah, Aug. 15, 1971; children: Stephen, Kathryn. BSChemE, U. Calif. Berkeley, 1968; MSChemE, Calif. State U., San Jose, 1972; MBA cum laude, Calif. State U., San Francisco, 1985. Registered profl. chem. and mech. engr.; instr.'s credential Calif. Community Coll. Chem. engr. Sondell Sci. Instruments, Inc., Mountain View, Calif., 1971; mem. R & D staff Raychem Corp., Menlo Park, Calif., 1971-72; supervising engr. Bechtel Power Corp., San Francisco, 1972-79; sr. project mgr. water quality and toxic substances control program Electric Power Rsch. Inst., Palo Alto, Calif., 1979-89, program mgr., 1990-97, product line mgr. land and water issues, 1997—. Editor: Hazardous Air Pollutants: State-of-the-Art, 1993; co-editor: Clean Water: Factors that Influence Its Availability, Quality and Its Use, 1996; co-author: Water Chlorination, vols. 4, 6; co-editor 1997 Internat. Clean Water Conf.-Today's Sci. for Tomorrows Policies, The Environ. Profl., 1997; contbr. articles to profl. jours. Pres., CEO Directions, Inc., San Francisco, 1985-86, bd. dirs., 1984-87, chmn. strategic planning com., 1984-85; industry com. Am. Power Conf., 1988—; with strategic long-range planning and restructuring com. Sequoia Union H.S. Dist., 1990-93, chmn. dist. ctrl. com., 1992-94. Recipient Grad. Disting. Achievement award, 1985; Calif. Gov.'s Exec. fellow, 1982-83. Mem. ASME, AIChE (profl. devel. recognition award), NSPE, Calif. Soc. Profl. Engrs. (pres. Golden Gate chpt. 1983-84, v.p. 1982-83, state dir.), Water Environ. Fedn., Air and Waste Mgmt. Assn. (mem. electric utility com. 1990—), Calif. State U. Alumni Assn. (bd. dirs., treas. 1989-91), U. Calif. Alumni Assn., Beta Gamma Sigma. Democrat. Presbyterian. Office: Electric Power Rsch Inst 3412 Hillview Ave Palo Alto CA 94304-1344

CHOWNING, ORR-LYDA BROWN, dietitian; b. Cottage Grove, Oreg., Nov. 30, 1920; d. Fred Harrison and Mary Ann (Bartels) Brown; m. Kenneth Bassett Williams, Oct. 23, 1944 (dec. Mar. 1945); m. Eldon Wayne Chowning, Dec. 31, 1959. *Husband and partner, Eldon Wayne Chowning, earned a Bachelors of Architecture from the University of Oregon in 1974. One of his design options was creating environments for older Americans. In 1975 they joined Dr. Walter McKain, social gerontologist, from the University of Connecticut on a tour of the Caucasus area in the Soviet Union, to study why people age differently in different societies. Eldon's mother was born in New Denhof, Saratov, in 1908. In 1984, the home they designed and built in 1959 became the Chownings Adult Foster Home, Inc. Their residents enjoy the experience of living longer in an environment that promotes their varied interests.* BS, Oreg. State Coll., 1943; MA, Columbia U., 1950. Dietetic intern Scripps Metabolic Clinic, LaJolla, Calif., 1944; sr. asst. dietitian Providence Hosp., Portland, Oreg., 1945-49; contact dietitian St. Lukes Hosp., N.Y.C., summer 1949; cafeteria food svc. supr. Met. Life Ins. Co., N.Y.C., 1950-52; set up food svc. and head dietitian McKenzie-Willamette Meml. Hosp., Springfield, Oreg., 1955-59; foods dir. Erb Meml. Student Union, Eugene, Oreg., 1960-63; set up food svc. and head dietitian Cascade Manor Retirement Home, Eugene, 1967-68; owner, operator Veranda Kafe, Inc., Albany, Oreg., 1971-80; owner, operator, sec.-treas. Chownings Adult Foster Home, Albany, 1984—. Contbr. articles to profl. jours. Lin County Women's chmn. Hatfield for Senator Spaghetti Rally, Albany H.S., 1966; food preparation chmn. Yi for You, Mae Yih for State Senate, Albany Lebanon, Sweet Home, 1982; Silver Clover Club sponsor Oreg. 4-H Found., Oreg. State U., Corvallis, 1994, 95, 96. Recipient coll. scholarship Nat. 4-H Food Preparation Contest, Chgo., 1939. Mem. Am. Dietetic Assn. (registered dietitian, gerontol. nutritionist dietetic practice group 1988—), Oreg. Dietetic Assn. (diet therapy chairperson, newsletter editor 1963-64), Willamette Dietetic Assn., Kappa Delta Pi (Kappa chpt.), Mu Beta Beta. Republican. Mem. Disciples of Christ. Avocations: gardening, genealogy, swimming, traveling, pet therapy. Home and Office: Chownings Adult Foster Home 4440 Woods Rd NE Albany OR 97321-7353

CHOY, HERBERT YOUNG CHO, federal judge; b. Makaweli, Hawaii, Jan. 6, 1916; s. Doo Wook and Helen (Nahm) C.; m. Dorothy Helen Shular, June 16, 1945. BA, U. Hawaii, 1938; JD, Harvard U., 1941. Bar: Hawaii 1941. Law clk. City and County of Honolulu, 1941; assoc. Fong & Miho, 1947-48; ptnr. Fong, Miho and Choy, 1948-57; atty. gen. Territory of Hawaii, 1957-58; ptnr. Fong, Miho, Choy & Robinson, Honolulu, 1958-71; sr. judge U.S. Ct. Appeals (9th cir.), Honolulu, 1971—; adv. com. on constrn. judiciary bldgs. Chief Justice Hawaii, 1970-71; compilation commn. to compile Revised Laws of Hawaii, 1955, 1953-57; com. to draft Hawaii rules of criminal procedure Supreme Ct., 1958-59; com. on pacific ocean territories Jud. Conf. the U.S., 1976-79. Dir. Legal Aid Soc. Hawaii, 1959-61; trustee Hawaii Loa Coll., 1963-79. Capt. U.S. Army, 1941-46, lt. col. Res. Recipient Order of Civil Merit award Republic of Korea, 1973. Fellow Am. Bar Found.; mem. ABA, Hawaii Bar Assn. (exec. com. 1953, 57, 61, legal ethics and unauthorized practices com. 1953, com. on legis. 1959). Office: US Ct Appeals 300 Ala Moana Blvd Rm C305 Honolulu HI 96850-0305

CHOYKE, GEORGE RAYMOND, educator, consultant; b. Ferndale, Mich., July 2, 1929; s. George Francis Choyke and Blanche Marie (Archambeau) Gordon; m. Ruth Marion Whaley, Jan. 8, 1982; children: Kip Noble Hayes, Falene Darby. Student, U. Mich., 1951-54, San Diego State U., 1967-70, U. Calif., La Jolla, 1961-63, 64-65; BS in Liberal Arts, Regents Coll., U. State N.Y., 1994. Spanish interpreter County of San Diego, 1959-67; bus. mgr. Gemstar Co., LaJolla, Calif., 1967-76, bus. owner, 1976-86; educator Nat. Safety Coun., San Diego, 1986-92, Robinsons May Sch., San Diego, 1986—; cons. Automobile Assn. of So. Calif., 1990-94; acad. advisor La Salle U.; instr. Coll. Extended Studies, San Diego State U.; bd. dirs. San Diego State U. Coll. Extended Studies Ednl. Growth Opportunities Program. Contbr. articles to profl. jours. Mem. Rep. Ctrl. Com., San Diego, 1964. With U.S. Army, 1951-54. Bus. scholarship AIESEC, 1968; grantee U. Mich., 1953; recipient Achievement award Nat. Safety Coun., San Diego, 1988. Mem. Am. Numismatic Assn., Regents Coll.Alumni Assn., Heartland Numismatic Assn., Spinal Cord Soc. (asst. dir. regional 1988—), Mt. Helix Improvement Assn., Numismatic Soc. Mex., S.D. Numismatic Soc.; fellow Clements Libr. of Am. History, U. Mich. Republican. Roman Catholic. Avocations: numismatics, woodworking, hiking, amateur theatre. Home: 4410 Shade Rd La Mesa CA 91941-6953 Office: Robinson's May Sch 111 W Pomona Blvd Monterey Park CA 91754-7208

CHRIST, CAROL TECLA, academic administrator, English educator; b. N.Y.C., May 21, 1944; d. John George and Tecla (Bobrick) Christ; m. Larry Sklute, Aug. 15, 1975 (div. Dec. 1983); children—Jonathan, Elizabeth. B.A., Douglas Coll., 1966; M.Ph., Yale U., 1969, Ph.D., 1970. Asst. prof. English U. Calif., Berkeley, 1970-76, assoc. prof. English, 1976-83, prof. English, 1983—, dean dept. English, 1985-88, dean dept. humanities, 1988, acting provost, dean, 1989-90, provost, dean Coll. Letters and Sci., 1990-94, vice chancellor, provost, 1994—; former dir. summer seminars for secondary and coll. tchrs. NEH; former tchr. Bread Loaf Sch. of English; invited lectr. Am. Assn. Univs., Am. Coun. Edn. Author: The Finer Optic: The Aesthetic of Particularity in Victorian Poetry, 1975, Victorian and Modern Poetics, 1984; mem. editl. bd. Victorian Literature, The Victorian Visual Imagination, The Norton Anthology of English Literature; contbr. articles to profl. jours. Mem. MLA. Office: Univ Calif Office Exec VP & Provost 200 California Hall # 1500 Berkeley CA 94720-1500*

CHRIST, RONALD, writer, translator, publisher, editor; b. Teaneck, N.J., Oct. 25, 1936; s. Thomas Alfred and Evelyn May (Wareham) Patrick. BA, Columbia Coll., 1958; MA, Columbia U., 1960; PhD, NYU, 1968. Asst. prof. Manhattan Coll., Riverdale, N.Y., 1961-69; prof. Rutgers U., New Brunswick, N.J., 1969-95, emeritus, 1996—; dir. lit. program Ctr. for Inter-american Rels., N.Y.C., 1973-78; chmn. Lumen, Inc., Santa Fe, 1978—. Author: The Narrow Act, 1969; co-author: New York: Nomadic Design (Primavera 1993); editor: Review, 1970-75, Woody Vasulka: The Brotherhood, 1998; mng. editor Sites, 1978-84; translator: E. Luminata, 1997 (Kayden prize 1997); writer, dir. (video): Text/Tiles, Tujol/Gaudi, Bench/Park Güell, 1987, The Barcelona Pavilion, 1990. Grantee NEH, 1966, NEA, 1987, Witter Bynner, 1980, 91, Fulbright, 1976, 77. Mem. Toastmasters (treas. 1998—), Pen Am. Ctr. (exec. bd. 1977-83), Pen N.Mex. Avocation: papermaking. Home: 40 Camino Cielo Santa Fe NM 87501

CHRISTENSEN, CAROLINE, vocational educator; b. Lehi, Utah, Oct. 5, 1936; d. Byam Heber and Ruth (Gardner) Curtis; m. Marvin Christensen, June 16, 1961; children: Ronald, Roger, Robert, Corlyn, Richard, Chad. BS, Brigham Young U., 1958, MS, 1964. Sec. Brigham Young U., Provo, Utah, 1954-58; instr. bus. Richfield (Utah) H.S., 1958-61, Sevier Valley Applied Tech. Ctr., Richfield, 1970-92, dept. chairperson, 1988-92. Historian, Sevier Sch. Dist. PTA, 1968, 69; chmn. Heart Fund Dist., 1983, Voting Dist., 1988-90; dist. chmn. Am. Cancer Drive, 1994-95, 98; guide Hist. Cove Fort, Utah, 1996-98, election judge, 1998. Mem. Utah Edn. Assn., Am. Vocat. Assn., Utah Vocat. Assn., Nat. Bus. Edn. Utah Bus. Edn. Assn. (sec. 1986-87), NEA, Western Bus. Edn. Assn., Sevier Valley Tech. Tchrs. Assn. (sec. 1971-92, pres. 1986-87, adv. com. chair 1997—), Delta Pi Epsilon (historian), Delta Kappa Gamma (treas. 1975-90, pres. 1990-92, state nominating com. 1993-97, chmn. 95-97, state treas. 1993-95, state conv. chair 1997-98), Profl. Bus. Leaders (advisor 1988-92).

CHRISTENSEN, DONALD J., architectural design executive, planning consultant; b. Eureka, Calif., Nov. 1, 1934; s. Sophus and Catherine DeWolf (Dickson) C.; m. Mary Frances McGrew, Sept. 27, 1960; children: Karen R., Mara M. BArch, U. Calif., Berkeley, 1958; M in City Planning, Yale U., 1969. Registered arch., Calif. Arch. John Bolles & Ernest Born, San Francisco, 1960, George Matsumoto, San Francisco, 1963-65, DeMars & Reay, Berkeley, Calif., 1965; arch., urban designer Hoberman & Wasserman, N.Y.C., 1968; city and regional planner Grunwald & Crawford, Hanford, Calif., 1969-72; prin. Donald Christensen, AIA, Hanford, 1972-91; sr. ptnr. Christensen & Rhoads, Archs., Hanford, 1991—. Commr. Hist. Resources Commn., Hanford, 1980-88 (chmn. 1985-86); bd. dirs. Calif. Roadside Coun., San Francisco, 1972-74. Recipient Design Excellence award City of Vacaville, Calif., 1986; fellow HUD, 1967-69. Mem. AIA (pres. Sequoia sect. 1980-81, award of honor for design 1989), Soc. Am. Registered Archs., Hanford Improvement Assn. (bd. dirs. 1995—, pres. 1995-96, Svc. award 1996, beautification award 1974), Rotary (treas. 1997-98),. Avocations: drawing, painting, photography, traveling, research. Office: Christensen and Rhoads Archs 310 N Irwin St Hanford CA 93230-4479

CHRISTENSEN, DONN WAYNE, insurance executive; b. Atlantic City, Apr. 9, 1941; s. Donald Frazier and Dorothy (Ewing) C.; BS, U. Santa Clara, 1964; m. Marshella Abraham, Jan. 26, 1963 (div.); children: Donn Wayne, Lisa Shawn; m. Mei Ling Fill, June 18, 1976 (div.); m. Susan Kim, Feb. 14, 1987; stepchildren: Don Kim, Stella Kim. West Coast div. mgr. Ford Motor Co., 1964-65; agt. Conn. Mut. Life Ins. Co., 1965-68; pres. Christensen & Jones, Inc., L.A., 1968—; v.p. Rsch. Devel. Systems Inc. Pres. Duarte Community Drug Abuse Coun., 1972-75; pres. Woodlyn Property Owners Assn., 1972-73; mem. L'Ermitage Found., 1985-90, Instl. Rev. Bd. White Meml. Hosp., L.A., 1975—, Friend's Med. Rsch., 1992—. Recipient Man of Yr. award L.A. Gen. Agts. and Mgrs. Assn., numerous. Mem. Nat. Life Underwriters Assn., Calif. State Life Underwriters Assn., Investment Co. Inst. (assoc.), Soc. Pension Actuaries, Foothill Community Concert Assn. (pres. 1970-73). Registered Investment Advisor, SEC, 1984. Office: 22 Woodlyn Ln Bradbury CA 91010

CHRISTENSEN, LEE NORSE, architect; b. Passaic, N.J., Apr. 29, 1940; s. Olaf and Elsie Johanna (Reese) C.; m. Mary Ellen Lewis, Nov. 1967 (div. Aug. 1972); m. Elizabeth Pusch, Nov. 25, 1974 (div. May 1978); children: Kate, Susan, Emily; m. Doree Adele Seronde, Nov. 25, 1987; 1 child, Ceridwen Adele. BArch, U. Ariz., 1966. Registered architect, Ariz. Draftsman John L. Mascarelia & Assocs., Tucson, 1963-65; architect in tng. Louis L. Coon & Assocs., Tucson, 1965-72; architect Schoneberger Straub Florence & Assocs., Phoenix, 1973-75; v.p. Sjuart Corp., Phoenix, 1975-76; architect pvt. practice, Sedona, Ariz., 1976—; Jerome Design Review Bd. (former chair), Jerome Planning and Zoning Com. (former chair). Keep Sedona Beautiful, 1979-86,; mem. Nat. Trust Hist. Preservation, Washington, 1976—. Recipient City of Tempe (Ariz.) Merit award, 1976, Jerome Hist. Soc. Hist. Preservation award, 1988. Mem. AIA, Nat. Coun. Archtl Registration Bds.(N.C.A.R.B.); former chair, former1st v.p. Verde Valley Concert Assn. Avocation: classical music. Fax: 520-282-8470. E-mail: lchristensen@sedona.net. Office: 450 Jordan Rd Ste C Sedona AZ 86336-4100

CHRISTENSEN, MARILYN D., writer; b. Frederick, Okla., Mar. 31, 1944; d. Robert C. and Ethel L. (Kallberg) Franzen; m. Kent T. Christensen, Aug. 27, 1988; children: Erik Holm, Kathryn Layon, John Holm. BA in English, Augsburg Coll., 1966; MA in Psychology, U. Minn., 1970. Tchr. of English Alex Ramsey H.S., St. Paul, Minn., 1966-68; vocat. rehab. counselor State of Wyo., 1973-77; family social worker Wyo. Child Welfare, 1978-88; freelance writer, 1988—. Author: (books) Tell Me Why, 1985, Shall the Circle Be Unbroken, 1986. Named Wyo. Rehab. Counselor of Yr., State of Wyo., 1977, Jaycee Outstanding Young Person, Worland, Wyo., 1975. Mem. Am. Humane Soc., Nat. Assn. Counsel for Children, Rocky Mountain Fiction Writers. Lutheran.

CHRISTENSEN, ROBERT WAYNE, oral maxillofacial surgeon, minister; b. N.Y.C., Apr. 6, 1925; s. Charles Joseph Brophy and Eva Sutherland (Hart) Christensen; m. Ann Forsyth (div.); children: Robert, Joan, Elizabeth, Peter, Mary, Colleen, Patricia, Michelle; m. Lynne Blindbury; children: Andrew, Matthew. DDS, NYU, 1948. Oral surgery tng. L.A. County Gen. Hosp., 1950; oral maxillofacial surgeon, 1950-88; pres. TMJ Implants, Inc., Golden, Colo., 1988—; minister, founder Covenant Marriages Ministry, Golden, 1988—; pres. Design Dynamics Internat., Golden, 1994—; R&D med. adv. bd. mem. Sch. Medicine LLU, Loma Linda, Calif.; pres.'s cabinet mem. Jerry Savelle Ministry, Ft. Worth, 1994—; adj. prof. bioengring. Sch. Engring., Clemson U.; pres. Med. Modeling Corp., 1997. Inventor of 5 U.S. patents. Lt. USNR. Robert W. Christensen fellow TM Joint Surgery, U. Tenn. Sch. Med., 1997. Republican. Avocations: skiing, gardening, photography. Office: TMJ Implants Inc 17301 W Colfax Ave Ste 135 Golden CO 80401-4800

CHRISTENSEN, ROBERT WAYNE, JR., financial and leasing company executive; b. Chester, Calif., Nov. 11, 1948; s. Robert Wayne and Ann (Forsyth) C.; m. Debra Schumann, Dec. 6, 1988; children: Heather, Megan. BA with honors, Coll. Gt. Falls, 1976; MBA, U. Puget Sound, 1978. Cert. flight instr. Corp. pilot Buttrey Food Stores, Gt. Falls, Mont., 1972-74; asst. to pres. Pacific Hide & Fur, Gt. Falls, 1974-76; fin. analyst Olympia Brewing Co., Olympia, Wash., 1977; chmn., CEO Westar Fin. Svcs. Inc., Olympia, 1978—; pres. PacWest Fin. Corp., Olympia, 1984—; bd. dirs. Westar Fin. Svcs., Inc., Olympia, Wash. Independent Bancshares, Olympia, 1982—, PacWest Fin. Corp., Olympia. Trustee CASR Trust, 1993—. Served to sgt. USAF, 1969-72. Mem. Nat. Vehicle Leasing Assn. (bd. dirs. 1978-88, 2d. v.p. 1984, pres. 1986), Western Assn. Equipment Lessors, Western Leasing Conf., Mensa, Rotary (bd. dirs. 1982-89, v.p. 1986-88, pres. 1988-89). Office: Westar Fin Svcs Inc The Republic Bldg PO Box 919 Olympia WA 98507-0919

CHRISTENSEN, STEPHEN D., academic administrator, educational fund raiser; b. Bklyn., Sept. 29, 1959. BS in Political Sci., Calif. State U., Fullerton, 1990; MPA, Calif. State U., San Bernardino, 1996. Cert. fund raising exec. Dir. special gifts Boy Scouts of Am., N.Y.C., 1977-83; dir. special projects Meml. Sloan Kettering Cancer Ctr., N.Y.C., 1981-83; dir. major gifts U. Calif., Irvine, 1983-89; v.p. Robert B. Sharp Co., Santa Ana, Calif., 1989-95; exec. dir. devel. Calif. State U.;, San Bernardino, 1995; v.p. Chapman U., Orange, Calif., 1995—. Republican. Lutheran.

CHRISTENSON, ANDREW LEWIS, archaeologist; b. Seattle, Feb. 15, 1950; s. Carl James and Geraldine (Beleu) C. BA in Anthropology, UCLA, 1973, MA in Anthropology, 1976, PhD in Anthropology, 1981. Curator, archaeology Mus. of Cultural History, UCLA, L.A., 1980-83; assoc. scientist So. Ill. Univ., Carbondale, Ill., 1983-87; adj. faculty Prescott (Ariz.) Coll., 1988—; archaeologist CSWTA, Inc., Tuba City, Ariz., 1990-93; adj. faculty Yavapai Coll., 1995—; archaeology cons. U.S. Army, Washington, 1980, Zuni (N.Mex.) Archaeology Program, 1989-90, Nat. Park Svcs., 1990-93; assoc. editor Bull. of History of Archaeology, 1990—. Co-editor: (book) Modeling Change in Prehistoric Subsistence Economies, 1980; Co-author: (book) Prehistoric Stone Technology on Northern Black Mesa Arizona, 1987; editor: (book) Tracing Archaeology's Past, 1989. Bd. trustees Smoki Mus., 1996—. Grantee Am. Philosophical Soc., 1985, NEH, 1985, S.W. Pks. and Monuments Assn., 1987. Mem. Soc. for Am. Archaeology (com. on the history of archaeology), Ariz. Archaeological Coun. (sec. 1998-99). Achievements include the use of mathematical and economic models to study prehistoric societies. Home and Office: 746 Redondo Rd Prescott AZ 86303-3724

CHRISTENSON, CHARLES ELROY, art educator; b. Gary, Ind., Jan. 2, 1942; s. Christian Monroe and Violet May (Kirkland) C.; m. Coral Yvette Demar, Feb. 26, 1966 (div. May 1990); children: Michael Eric, Tessa Diahann, Leah Renee; m. cheryl Lane Grubb, Mar. 27, 1999. Student, U. Tex., 1960-63; BFA, San Francisco Art Inst., 1966; MFA, U. Wash., Seattle, 1970. Staff artist Taylor Press, Dallas, 1962-63; freelance artist San Francisco, 1963-64, 65-66; comml. artist The Emporium, San Francisco, 1964-65; art educator U. Wash., 1970-71; art instr. Shoreline C.C., Seattle, 1971-75, North Seattle C.C., Seattle, 1971—; acting chmn. humanities div. North Seattle Community Coll., Seattle, 1978-79, gallery dir., 1977—; advisor art group North Seattle C.C., 1978—; juror Equinox Arts Festival, Everett, Wash., 1981; curator exhbns. Wash. C.C. Humanities Conv., Bellevue, 1986, 87; bd. advisors Noon Star Prodns., Seattle, 1992—; co-owner, tour leader Sketching and Touring Through France, Seattle, 1992—. Writer, illustrator: Simple Crafts for the Village, 1968; author poems. Vol. Am. Peace Corps, Andra Pradesh, India, 1966-68; beef leader Riverview Champs-4-H Club, Everett, 1980-81; coach Snohomish (Wash.) Youth Soccer, 1982-88; mem. Seattle Art Mus. Recipient Beyond War Found. award, 1987, Gov.'s Faculty Recognition award, 1987; Seattle C.C. Dist. grantee, 1988, Fulbright grantee India, 1990—, Indonesia, 1994; named to Humanities Exemplary Status, Wash. C.C. Humanities Assn., 1987. Mem. Wash. C.C. Humanities Assn., Smithsonian Inst., Artist's Trust, Seattle C.C. Fedn. Tchrs. (human div. rep. 1977-78), Nat. Coun. for Social Studies, Nat. Campaign for Freedom Expression, Amnesty Internat. Avocations: travel, soccer, skiing, sailing. Office: North Seattle CC 9600 College Way N Seattle WA 98103-3514

CHRISTIAENS, CHRIS (BERNARD FRANCIS CHRISTIAENS), financial analyst, state senator; b. Conrad, Mont., Mar. 7, 1940; s. Marcel Jules and Virgie Jeanette (Van Spyk) C. BA in Chemistry, Coll. Gt. Falls, 1962, M in human svcs., 1994. Fin. and ins. mgr. Rice Motors, Gt. Falls, Mont., 1978-84; senator State of Mont., 1983-87, 1991—, majority whip 49th legis., 1985-86; fin. planner Jack Stevens CPA, Gt. Falls, 1984-85; adminstr., fin. analyst Gt. Falls Pre-Release, 1986-92; owner Oak Inn-Bed and Breakfast, 1989-95; mem. faculty U. Gt. Falls, part-time 1995—; bd. dirs. World Wide Press Inc., svc. rep., 1994—. Chmn. Balance of State Pvt. Industry Coun., Mont., 1984—; mem. Mont. Human Rights Commn., 1981-84; bd. dirs. St. Thomas Child and Family Ctr., Gt. Falls, 1983—, Coll. of Gt. Falls, 1984—, Cascade County Mental Health Assn., 1986—, Salvation Army, Habitat for Humanity, 1992-95; mem. adv. bd. State Drug and Alcohol Coun., State Mental Health Coun.; bd. dirs. treas. Gt. Falls Cmty. Food Bank, 1984-86; Dem. committeeman Cascade County, 1976-82; Mont. del. to Nat. Rules Conv., 1980; pub. chmn. Cascade County chpt. ARC, 1986; mem. adv. bd. Cambridge Court Sr. Citizen Apt. Complex, 1986; treas. Cascade County Mental Health Ctr.; vice chmn. Gov.'s Task Force on Prison Overcrowding, mem. regional jail com.; mem. Re-Leaf Gt. Falls Com., 1989—, mem. steering com.; mem. Gt. Falls and Cascade County Housing Task Force, 1995—. Recipient Outstanding Young Alumni award Coll. of Gt. Falls, 1979, Hon. Alumni Achievement award, 1994; Disting. Svc. award Rocky Mountain Coun. Mental Health Ctrs., 1995. Roman Catholic. Clubs: Gt. Falls Ski, Toastmasters. Lodge: Optimists. Avocations: skiing, tennis, fishing, reading, hiking. Address: 600 36th St S Great Falls MT 59405-3508

CHRISTIAN, ROLAND CARL (BUD CHRISTIAN), retired English language and speech communications educator; b. LaSalle, Colo., June 7, 1938; s. Roland Clyde and Ethel Mae (Lattimer) C.; m. Joyce Ann Kincel, Feb. 15, 1959; children: Kathleen Marie Christian Dunham, Kristine May Christian Sweet. BA in English and Speech, U. No. Colo., 1962, MA, 1966. Cert. tchr., N.Y., Colo. Tchr. Southside Jr. High Sch., Rockville Ctr., N.Y., 1962-63, Plateau Valley High Sch., Collbran, Colo., 1963-67; prof. English Northeastern Jr. Coll., Sterling, Colo., 1967-93, prof. emeritus, 1993—; presenter seminars, workshops, Sterling, 1967—; emcee/host Town Meeting of Am., Sterling, 1976. Author: Be Bright! Be Brief! Be Gone! A Speaker's Guide, 1983, Potpourrivia, A Digest of Curious Words, Phrases and Trivial Information, 1986, Nicknames in Sports: A Quiz book, 1986; lit. adv. New Voices mag., 1983-93; contbr. Ways We Write, 1964, The Family Treasury of Great Poems, 1982, Our Twentieth Century's Greatest Poems, 1982, Anti-War Poems; vol. II, 1985, Impressions, 1986, World Poetry Anthology, 1986, American Poetry Anthology, 1986, Chasing Rainbows, 1988, The Poetry of Life, 1988, Hearts on Fire, 1988, Wide Open Magazine, 1986, 87, 88; columnist South Platte Sentinel, 1988—. Served with U.S. Army, 1956-59. Recipient Colo. Recognition of Merit scholarship, 1956, Merit cert. Poets Anonymous, 1983, Award of Merit (9), 1985, 86, Golden Poet of Yr. award World of Poetry Press, 1985, 86, 87, 88, Joel Mack Tchr. of Yr. award Northeastern Jr. Coll., 1986; Jr. Coll. Found. grantee, 1986, 87. Avocations: fishing, hunting, sports, trivia, music. Home: 603 Park St Apt 105 Sterling CO 80751-3855

CHRISTIAN, SUZANNE HALL, financial planner; b. Hollywood, Calif., Apr. 28, 1935; d. Peirson M. and Gertrude (Engel) Hall; children: Colleen, Carolyn, Claudia, Cynthia. BA, UCLA, 1956; MA, Redlands U., 1979; cert. in fin. planning, U. So. Calif., 1986. CFP. Instr. L.A. City Schs., 1958-59; instr. Claremont (Calif.) Unified Schs., 1972-84, dept. chair, 1981-84; fin. planner Waddell & Reed, Upland, Calif., 1982-96, sr. account exec., 1986; br. mgr. Hornor, Townsend & Kent, Claremont, 1996—; corp. mem. Pilgrim Place Found., Claremont; lectr. on fin., estate and tax planning for civic and profl. groups. Author: Strands in Composition, 1979; host Money Talks with Suzanne Christian on local TV cable, 1993—. Mem. legal and estate planning com. Am. Cancer Soc., 1988—; profl. adv. com. YWCA-Inland Empire, 1987; treas. Fine Arts Scripps Coll., 1993-94; bd. dirs. Casa Colina Hosp., Galelio Soc. Harvey Mudd Coll. Recipient Athena Internat. Businesswoman of Yr. award, 1997. Mem. Inst. CFPs, Internat. Assn. Fin. Planners, Planned Giving Roundtable, Estate Planning Coun. Pomona Valley, Claremont C. of C. (pres., bd. dirs. 1994-95), Curtain Raisers Club Garrison (pres. 1972-75), Circle of Champions (pres.'s coun. 1994-95, Silver Crest award 1985-87, 94, 95), Rotary (bd. dirs.), Harvey Mudd Coll. Galelio Soc. (bd. dirs. 1997-98), Kappa Kappa Gamma (pres. 1970-74). Avocations: tennis, gardening, archaeology. Home: PO Box 1237 Claremont CA 91711-1237 Office: Hornor Townsend & Kent 419 Yale Ave Claremont CA 91711-4340

CHRISTIANSEN, ERIC ALAN, software development executive; b. Salt Lake City, May 14, 1958; s. Don Parley and Lilian Patricia (Clegg) C.; m. April Gay Willes, Jan. 9, 1988; children: Amber, Carly. BS in Computer Sci., West Coast U., L.A., 1981. Software engr. Lear Siegler Astronics, Santa Monica, Calif., 1980-82; sr. software specialist Digital Equipment Corp., Culver City, Calif., 1982-83; software cons. L.A., 1983-84; v.p. Mindcode Devel. Corp., Salt Lake City, 1984-85; software cons. Van Nuys, Calif., 1985-89; sr. software engr. ITT Gilfillan, Van Nuys, 1989-90; prin. Wells Fargo Nikko Investment Advisors, San Francisco, 1990—, Barclays Global Investors, San Francisco, 1996—; strategic advisor Tri-Pacific Cons. Corp., Alameda, Calif., 1991-93; guest lectr. George Mason U. and Joint Tactical Command, Control, and Comm. Agy., 1991; mem. rsch. team devel.

quantitive stock market investment model. Developer (comml. software program) Structurer preprocessor enhancing command interface and language for VAX/VMS, 1989; contbr. articles to profl. jours. Mem. IEEE, Assn. for Computing Machinery, Digital Equipment Computer Users Soc. (local user group bd. 1988-90). Republican. Avocations: basketball, reading. Office: BZW Barclays Global Investors 45 Fremont St Ste 1500 San Francisco CA 94105-2263

CHRISTIANSON, ROGER GORDON, biology educator; b. Santa Monica, Calif., Oct. 31, 1947; s. Kyle C. and Ruby K. (Parker) C.; m. Angela Diane Rey, Mar. 3, 1967; children: Lisa Marie, David Scott, Stephen Peter. BA in Cell and Organismal Biology, U. Calif., Santa Barbara, 1969, MA in Biology, 1971, PhD in Biology, 1976. Faculty assoc. U. Calif., Santa Barbara, 1973-79, staff rsch. assoc., 1979-80; asst. prof. So. Oreg. U., Ashland, 1980-85, assoc. prof., 1985-93, prof., 1993—, coord. gen. biology program, 1980—, chmn. biology dept., 1996, 97—; instr. U. Calif., Santa Barbara, summers 1976, 78, 80. Contbr. articles to profl. jours. Active Oreg. Shakespeare Festival Assn., Ashland, 1983-87; mem. bikeway com. Ashland City Coun., 1986-88; coord. youth program 1st Bapt. Ch., Ashland, 1981-85, mem. ch. life commn., 1982-88, bd. deacons, 1993-95, mem. outreach com., 1994, 95; organizer Bike Oreg., 1982-92, Frontline h.s. staff, 1985—, Mex. Orphanage short-term mission work, 1986—; ofcl. photographer Ashland H.S. Booster Club, 1987-92; youth leader jr. and sr. H.S. students Grace Ch., Santa Barbara, Calif., 1973-80. Mem. AAAS (chair Pacific divsn. edn. sect. 1985—, coun. Pacific divsn. 1985—, chair Pacific divsn. student awards com. 1997—, exec. com. Pacific divsn. 1998—), Am. Mus. Natural History, Oreg. Sci. Tchrs. Assn., Assn. for Biology Lab. Edn., Sigma Xi, Beta Beta Beta. Republican. Avocations: youth work, sports, photography, multimedia presentations, amateur radio operator. Home: 430 Reiten Dr Ashland OR 97520-8762 Office: Southern Oregon U Dept Biology 1250 Siskiyou Blvd Ashland OR 97520-5010

CHRISTIE, GEORGE BRIAN, lawyer, minister; b. Durban, South Africa, Nov. 9, 1946; came to the U.S., 1969; s. George Alexander and Roma Amy Sophia C.; m. Tina Sue Bangle, May 31, 1969; children: Paul, Michael, Steven. BA, Calvary Bible Coll., 1971; ThM, Dallas Theological Seminary, 1975; JD, U. Tex., 1979. Bar: Tex. 1979, Calif 1990. Lawyer Brown-Maroney, Austin, Tex., 1978-80; pvt. practice Georgetown, Tex., 1980-90; lawyer Goode-Wildman, Newport Beach, Calif., 1991-94; in house counsel ARV Housing, Costa Mesa, Calif., 1994-96; pvt. practice Newport Beach, Calif., 1997—. Pastor Eastfield Bible Ch., Dallas, Tex., 1973-75, Grace Bible Fellowship, Georgetown, Tex., 1980-84; Walk Through Bible Tchr., Georgetown, Newport Beach, 1985-98. Mem. Newport Beach C. of C. Mem. of Bible Ch. Avocations: tennis, golf, running, preaching. E-mail: tschristie@mindspring.com. Fax: 949-955-2456. Home: 332 Evening Canyon Rd Corona Del Mar CA 92625-2638 Office: The Christie Law Firm 20101 SW Birch St Newport Beach CA 92660-1748

CHRISTMAN, ALBERT BERNARD, historian; b. Colorado Springs, Colo., May 18, 1923; s. James S. and Olga Emelia (Nelson) C.; m. Kate Gresham, July 1945 (div. July 1952); 1 child, Lloyd James; m. Jean Stewart, Apr. 4, 1954 (dec. Sept. 1984); children: Neil Stewart, Laura Elizabeth. BA, U. Mo., 1949, BJ, 1950; MA, Calif. State U., Dominguez Hills, 1982. Reporter Comml. Leader, North Little Rock, 1950-51; tech. editor, writer Naval Ordnance Test Sta., China Lake, Calif., 1951-55, head presentation divsn., 1956-63; historian, info. specialist Naval Weapons Ctr., China Lake, Calif., 1963-72, head pubs., 1973-79; historian Navy Labs., San Diego, 1979-82; freelance historian, writer San Marcos, Calif., 1982—. Author: Sailors, Scientists and Rockets, 1971, Naval Innovators, 1776-1900, 1989, Target Hiroshima, Deak Parsons and the Creation of the Atomic Bomb, 1998; co-author: Grand Experiment at Inyokern, 1979; contbr. articles to profl. jours. Founding mem. Red Rock Canyon State Park Adv. Com., Tehachapi, Calif., 1969-74. Pvt. U.S. Army, 1942-45; maj. USAFR, ret. Recipient Robert H. Goddard Meml. award Nat. Space, 1972, Superior Civilian Svc. award Dept. of The Navy, 1982, Helen Hawkins Meml. Rsch. grant, 1994. Mem. Maturango Mus. (trustee-sec. 1973-76), Naval Hist. Found., USN Inst., OX-5 Aviation Pioneers, Smithsonian Inst. (assoc.), Libr. of Congress Assn. (founding mem.). Democrat. Unitarian. Avocations: photography, golfing, tennis, hiking. Home and Office: 1711 Birchwood Dr San Marcos CA 92069-9609

CHRISTMAN, HELEN DOROTHY NELSON, resort executive; b. Denver, Nov. 25, 1922; d. Hector C. and Dorothy C. (Hansen) Russell; m. James Ray Christman, Aug. 7, 1942 (dec. June 1986); children: J. Randol, Linda Rae. Student, Colo. U., 1940-42. Producer Sta. KRMA-TV, Denver, 1960-62; resident mgr. Mana Kai Maui, Maui, Hawaii, 1974-76, exec. coord., 1976-78; pres. Resort Apts., Inc., 1986—; bd. dirs. Kihei Cmty. Assn. Pres. Stephen Knight PTA, Denver, 1957; radio and TV chmn. Colo. PTA, 1958-59; producer ednl. TV programs for PTA, Denver County, 1960-61; bd. dirs. Maui United Way, 1983—, Am. Lung Assn., chmn. Maui sect., 1995—, Hawaii State bd., 1995—; precinct pres. Maui Reps.; chmn. Maui County Rep. Com., 1989-91; mem. adv. bd. State of Hawaii Reapportionment Com., Maui, 1991—; bd. dirs. Hale Makua Found., 1994—, Hui No Eau, 1996—. Mem. Delta Delta Delta, Women's Golf Club (chmn. Silverswood chpt.), Maui Country Club (chmn. women's golf assn. 1987), Waiehu Women's Golf Assn. (pres. 1992-93), Maui Liquor Commn. Address: 3448 Hookipa Pl Kihei HI 96753-9216

CHRISTOFFERSEN, SUSAN GRAY, small business owner; b. Oakland, Calif., Aug. 11, 1942; d. Edward Kiley Gray and Mabel Genevieve (Griffiths) Lee; m. Timothy Robert Christoffersen, July 24, 1965; children: Jenny, Shannon. BA, Stanford U., 1964, MA, 1965. U.S. history tchr. Leonia High Sch., N.J., 1965-67; frontier intern Nat. and World Coun. Chs., Brazil, India, Switzerland, 1967-68; U.S. history tchr. Pacifica High Sch., West Pittsburg, Calif., 1969-70; advt. chairwoman Kennedy-King Found.; bus. officer Pacific Sch. Religion, Berkeley, Calif., 1977-78; tax preparer Expatriate Tax Dept. Chevron Corp., San Francisco, 1983; from engring. dept. to quality cons. AT&T, San Francisco, Pleasanton, Calif., 1983-88; pres. Quality Efficiency, Alamo, Calif., 1988—; substitute tchr., counselor Juvenile Hall, Martinez, Calif., 1969-75; mgr. rental properties, 1977—. Chairwoman land use subcom. East Bay Regional Parks Adv. Com., 1978-80; co-founder Las Trampas Ridgelands Assn., 1980-82; singer Gospel Choir, Community Presbyn. Ch., Danville, 1989-92. Mem. AAUW (bd. dirs. Danville, Calif. br. 1992-93), Stanford Women of East Bay. Democrat. Episcopal. Avocations: swimming. Home: 234 Via Bonita Alamo CA 94507-1840

CHRISTOPHER, RENNY TERESA, liberal studies educator; b. Newport Beach, Calif., Mar. 4, 1957; d. Richard T. and Bebi (Ruhland) C. BA, Mills Coll., 1982; MA, San Jose (Calif.) State U., 1986; PhD, U. Calif., Santa Cruz, 1992. Features editor Horse Lover's Nat. Mag., Burlingame, Calif., 1976-79; prodn. editor Lit. of Liberty, Menlo Park, Calif., 1982; graphic artist Gilroy (Calif.) Dispatch, 1983-84; substitute tchr. Morgan Hill (Calif.) Unified Sch. Dist., 1984-85; lectr. San Jose State U., 1986-87; instr. Cabrillo Community Coll., Aptos, Calif., 1988—; asst. prof. Calif. State U., 1995-98, assoc. prof., 1998—; film reviewer Matrix Women's Newspaper, Santa Cruz, 1990—; fiction editor Quarry West, U. Calif., 1990-91, advisor Giao Diem/Crosspoint Student Pub., 1991-95. Author: The Viet Nam War/The American War, 1995, Viet Nam and California, 1998; author poems and short story; contbr. articles to profl. jours. Yanklee Meml. fellow San Jose State U., 1985, U. Calif. fellow, 1991. Mem. Modern Lang. Assn., Am. Studies Assn., Popular Culture Assn., Nat. Coun. Tchrs. of English. Avocations: running, bicycling. Office: Calif State U English Dept 801 W Monte Vista Ave Turlock CA 95382-0256

CHRISTOPHER, STEVEN LEE, religious studies educator; b. Long Beach, Calif., May 29, 1956; s. Lehland James and Harriet Ann (Werner) C.; m. Doris Dianne Deterding, Aug. 19, 1978; children: LeAnna Helen, Brett Steven. BS in Edn., Concordia Coll., Seward, Nebr., 1979; MA, U. San Diego, 1989. Ordained to ministry Luth. Ch.-Mo. Synod, 1979; tchr.'s diploma, cert. dir. Christian edn. Min. youth and edn. Bethany Luth. Ch., Long Beach, 1979-85; coord. youth ministries Christ Luth. Ch., La Mesa, [illegible] program Concordia U. Calif., 1988—; chmn. youth com. Pacific SW dist. Luth. Ch.-Mo. Synod, Irvine, 1983-88, mem. extended staff bd. for youth svcs., St. Louis, 1988-91, com. mem. nat. youth gathering, 1986, 89; chmn. 1991 Nat. Dirs. Christian Edn. Conf., River Forest, Ill., 1989-91; mem. youth bd. Abiding Savior Luth. Ch., El Toro, Calif., 1989-94; spkr. various workshops and youth gatherings. Author young adult Bible study and youth Bible study, 1983, 3 devotions for children, 1988, chapel talks for children, 1989; contbr. articles to profl. jours. Mem. Theol. Educators in Assoc. Ministries (pres.-elect 1988-90, pres. 1990-92), Profl. Assn. Christian Educators, Religious Edn. Assn. Office: Concordia U 1530 Concordia Irvine CA 92612-3203

CHRISTOPHERSON, BURTON G., JR., equal opportunity officer; b. Omaha, Nebr., Oct. 7, 1947; s. Burton Glen and Pear Monrieve (Rhoades) C.; Sandra Renee Christopherson, Aug. 28, 1977; children: Jessica Nel, Zachary Ross. BS, Creighton Univ., 1971; postgrad., Georgetown Univ., 1971-76; masters legal sci. program, Antioch Law Sch., 1980-82. Ptnr. B.J. Christophersons SOns., Omaha, 1977-80; civil rights investigator City Omaha, Omaha, 1980-84; asst. dir. AA/EO Univ. Nebr. Medical Ctr., Omaha, 1984-88; dir. AA/EO Oregon Health Sci. Univ., Portland, 1988—; reg. dir. Am. Assn. for Aff. Actions, Indpls., 1993-97; pres., bd. dirs. Greater Omaha Assn. for Retarded Citizens, 1986-88. Nat. gynmastic official U.S.A. Gymnastics, Indpls., 1977—; little league mgr. S.W. Portland, 1990—, pop warner football coach P.I.L./P.A.L., Portland, 1995—, hunter safety instr. Oreg. Dept. Fish & Wildlife, 1997—; pres., philosophy soc. Creighton Univ., 1971. Mem. AM. Assn. for Aff. Action, U.S.A. Gymnastics, Nat. Rifle Assn. Avocations: hunting, fishing. Home: 2532 SW Hamilton Ct Portland OR 97201-1214 Office: Oregon Health Scis Univ 3181 SW Sam Jackson Park Rd Portland OR 97201-3011

CHRISTY, THOMAS PATRICK, human resources executive, educator; b. Urbana, Ill., May 18, 1943; s. Edward Michael and Iona Theresa (Rogers) C.; m. Marjorie Anne McIntyre, June 1966 (div. May 1973); children: Thomas Patrick Jr., Derek Edward; m. Sandra Allen Stern, May 19, 1984 (div. Aug. 1996); children: Patrick Edward, Margaret Allen. BA in Psychology, Adams State Coll., 1965; MBA, Chapman U., 1997. Tchr. Colorado Springs Pub. Sch., 1965-69; regional personnel dir. Forest Service USDA, Washington, 1969-81; sr. account exec. Mgmt. Recruiters Inc., Costa Mesa, Calif., 1981-84; v.p. Coleman & Assoc. Inc., Santa Monica, Calif., 1984; asst. v.p. Union Bank, Los Angeles, 1984-88; v.p., human resources dir. TOPA Savs. Bank, Los Angeles, 1988-89, Cenfed Bank, Pasadena, Calif., 1989-91; v.p., regional human resources mgr., nat. dir. tng. Tokio Marine Mgmt., Inc., Pasadena, 1991-94, UCLA, 1991—; adj. prof. Coll. Bus. Mgmt., Northrop U., L.A., 1985-91, Coll. Bus. Mgmt., UCLA, 1991-98; bd. dirs. Human Resources Mgmt. Inst., L.A., pres., 1993-95; bd. dirs. The Employers Group; mem. editorial rev. bd. Calif. Labor Letter, L.A. Arbitrator/Bus. and Consumer Arbitrator program Better Bus. Bur., Los Angeles and Orange County; New IOB Dist. Dir. 27th Dist. U.S. Congress, Pasadena, Calif., 1998—; mem. Calif. Lincoln Clubs. Mem. Amer. Assn. Univ. Prof./Calif. Faculty Assn., Pers. and Indsl. Rels. Assn. (pres. 1993), Soc. Human Resources Mgmt. (Calif. state legis. affairs dir.), bd.dirs. Pasadena C. of C. and Civil Assn., Employment Mgmt. Assn., Soc. Profls. in Dispute Resolution, Am. Compensation Assn., Vestry St. Edmund's Episc. Ch., San Marino. Calif., Japanese Am. Soc. So. Calif., Adams State Coll. Alumni Assn. (Calif. state pres.), Town Hall Calif., Valley Hunt Club, L.A. Athletic Club, Beach Club, Sigma Pi Alumni Assn. Episcopalian. Avocations: fly fishing, golf, skiing, collecting antiques, bridge, trapshooting.

CHRITTON, GEORGE A., film producer; b. Chgo., Feb. 25, 1933; s. George A. and Dorothea C.; m. Martha Gilman, Aug. 26, 1956 (div. May 26, 1978); children: Stewart, Andrew, Douglas, Laura, Neil, Lyle. BA, Occidental Coll., 1955; postgrad., Princeton U., 1955-57. With CIA & various U.S. govt. agys., 1960-89; gen. ptnr. Margeo Investment Co., L.A., 1963-76; pres. Wildacre Prodns., Inc., L.A., 1990—; pres., CEO Fin. Svcs. Bancorp, Reno, 1990—; pres. Sycamore Prodns. Ltd., Nev. and Calif., 1994—. Mem. Am. Fgn. Svc. Assn., Washington, 1960—; chmn. bd. Neighborhood Learning Ctr., Capitol Hill, Washington, 1985-87; vol. Options House, Hollywood, Calif.; vol. coord. Rebuild L.A. Maj. USAF, 1957-60. Named Princeton Nat. Fellow, 1955-56, Vis. Fellow & Lectr. U. Calif., 1987-88. Mem. AFTRA, Am. Film Inst., Nat. Assn. Ind. Film & T.V. Prodrs., Phi Beta Kappa, Phi Gamma Delta, Alpha Mu Gamma, Alpha Phi Gamma, Princeton Club (So. Calif.). Office: Wildacre Prodns Inc PO Box 719 Beverly Hills CA 90213-0719

CHRYSIKOPOULOS, CONSTANTINOS VASSILIOS, environmental engineering educator; b. Corfu, Greece, Mar. 4, 1960; s. Vassilios and Stavroula Chrysikopoulos. BS in Chem. Engring., U. Calif., San Diego, 1982; MS in Chem. Engring., Stanford U., 1984, Engr. degree in Civil Engring., 1986, PhD in Civil Engring., 1990. Postdoctoral fellow Stanford U., 1990-91; asst. prof. U. Calif., Irvine, 1991-96, assoc. prof., 1996—. Contbr. articles to profl. jours. Grantee NSF, EPA. Home: 80 Whitman Ct Irvine CA 92612-4063 Office: Univ of California Civil and Environmental Engineering Dept ET844C Irvine CA 92697

CHRYSTAL, WILLIAM GEORGE, minister; b. Seattle, May 22, 1947; s. Francis Homer and Marjorie Isabell (Daubert) C.; m. Mary Frances King, Aug. 24, 1970; children: Shelley, Sarah, John, Philip. BA, U. Wash., 1969, MEd, 1970; MDiv, Eden Theol. Sem., 1978; MA, Johns Hopkins U., 1984. Ordained to ministry, United Ch. of Christ, 1977. Learning resources specialist Seattle C.C. Dist., 1970-71; dir. learning resources ctr. Whatcom C.C., Ferndale, Wash., 1971-73; minister St. Peter's United Ch. of Christ, Granite City, Ill., 1978-79; sr. minister 1st Congl. Ch., Stockton, Calif., 1979-83; minister Trinity United Ch. of Christ, Adamstown, Md., 1983-85; sr. minister Edwards Congl. Ch., Northampton, Mass., 1985-86, 1st Congl. Ch., Reno, Nev., 1991—; hosp. chaplain Washoe Med. Ctr., Reno, 1993—; host Thomas Jefferson Hour, on nat. pub. radio stas. Author: Young Reinhold Niebuhr: His Early Writings, 1911-1931, 1977, 2d edit., 1982, A Father's Mantle: The Legacy of Gustav Niebuhr, 1982, The Fellowship of Prayer, 1987; author monographs; contbr. articles to profl. jours. V.p. Reno-Sparks Met. Ministry, Reno, 1994-97; Chautauqua scholar Great Basin Chautauqua, Reno, 1993, 94, 98. Lt. comdr. USN, 1986-91, maj. Nev. Army N.G., 1992-96. Decorated (2) Meritorious Svc. medal. Mem. Am. Soc. Ch. History, Nev. Soc. Mayflower Descs. (gov.), Am. Legion, Disabled Vets. (life), VFW (life), Rotary Club (Paul Harris fellow 1997). Home: 3820 Bluebird Cir Reno NV 89509-5601 Office: 1st Congl Ch 627 Sunnyside Dr Reno NV 89503-3515

CHU, ALLEN YUM-CHING, automation company executive, systems consultant; b. Hong Kong, June 19, 1951; arrived in Can., 1972; s. Luke King-Sang and Kim Kam (Lee) C.; m. Janny Chu-Jen Tu, Feb. 27, 1993. BSc in Computer Sci., U. B.C., Vancouver, Can., 1977; BA in Econs., U. Alta., Edmonton, Can., 1986. Rsch. asst. dept. neuropsychology and rsch. Alta. Hosp., Edmonton, 1977-78; systems analyst dept. agr. Govt. of Alta., Edmonton, 1978-81; systems analyst for computing resources City of Edmonton, 1981-86; pres. ANO Automation Inc., Vancouver, 1986-92; v.p., bd. dirs. ANNOVA Bus. Group, Inc., Can., 1993—; mem. Vancouver Bd. Trade. Mem. IEEE Computer Soc., N.Y. Acad. Sci. Office: ANO Automation Inc, 380 W 2d Ave 2d Flr, Vancouver, BC Canada V5Y 1C8

CHU, SHIH-FAN (GEORGE CHU), economics educator; b. Hubei, China, Dec. 6, 1933; came to U.S., 1959; s. Teh-Chuan and Kuang-Hsin (Chou) C.; m. Li-Ming Kuo, Aug. 18, 1963; children: David Soo-lin, Diana Soo-Yin. BA, Nat. Taiwan U., 1955; MS, U. Ill., 1965, PhD, 1968. Asst. prof. econs. U. Nev., Reno, 1967-70, assoc. prof., 1970-77, prof., 1977—, chmn. dept. econs., 1992—; vis. prof. econs. Huazhong U. Sci. and Tech., Wuhan, China, 1981, Wuhan U., 1984, Nat. Taiwan U., Taipei, 1989. Contbr. numerous articles to econs. jours. Fulbright Travel grantee; Ford Found. Dissertation fellow; Inst. Internat. Edn. grad. scholar. Mem. numerous profl. orgns. in econs. Home: 4490 Gibraltar Dr Reno NV 89509-5620 Office: U Nev Dept Econs Reno NV 89557

CHU, VALENTIN YUAN-LING, author; b. Shanghai, Republic of China, Feb. 14, 1919; came to U.S., 1956, naturalized, 1961; s. Thomas V.D. and Rowena S.N. (Zee) Tsu; m. Victoria Chao-yu Tsao, Sept. 25, 1954; 1 child, Douglas Chi-hua. BA, St. John's U, Shanghai, 1940. Asst. Shanghai Mcpl. Coun., 1940-42; asst. mgr., pub., printer Thomas Chu & Sons, Shanghai, 1943-45; chief reporter China Press, Shanghai, 1945-49; pub. rels. officer Cen. Air Transport Corp., Hong Kong, 1949; Hong Kong corr. Time & Life mags., Hong Kong, 1949-56; with Time, Inc., N.Y.C., 1956-76; writer, asst. editor Time-Life Books, N.Y.C., 1968-76; assoc. editor Reader's Digest Gen. Books, N.Y.C., 1978-83; lectr. on China. Author: Ta Ta, Tan Tan: Fight, Talk Talk, 1963, Thailand Today, 1968, (with others) U.S.A., A Visitor's Handbook, 1969, The Yin-Yang Butterfly---Ancient Chinese Sexual Secrets for Western Lovers, 1993; contbr. articles to popular mags. Recipient spl. award UN Internat. Essay Contest, 1948. Mem. Authors League Am., Authors Guild, China Inst. in Am., Inst. Noetic Scis. Presbyterian. Home: 4520 Wildcat Cir Antioch CA 94509-7149

CHUA, CONSTANTINO PINA, electrical and instrument engineer, consultant; b. Cebu, The Philippines, Mar. 11, 1937; came to U.S., 1961; s. Francisco and Rosalia (Sy) C.; m. Monina M. Sanchez, Jan. 23, 1965; children: Margaret, Marie. BSEE, Cebu Inst. Tech., 1960, Heald's Coll., 1962. Elec. engr. Spreckels Sugar Co., Pleasanton, Calif., 1963-91; engring. cons. Pacific Gas Transmission, San Francisco, 1992-95, Bayer Corp., Berkeley, Calif., 1995—; with pharm. divsn. Bayer Corp., Berkeley, 1995—. Author: Beet Sugar Technology, 1982. Republican. Roman Catholic. Avocations: woodworking, auto mechanic, computer programming, investing. Office: CPC Engring 1817 School St Moraga CA 94556-1728

CHUCK, WALTER G(OONSUN), lawyer; b. Wailuku, Maui, Hawaii, Sept. 10, 1920; s. Hong Yee and Aoe (Ting) C.; m. Marian Chun, Sept. 11, 1943; children: Jamie Allison, Walter Gregory, Meredith Jayne. Ed.B., U. Hawaii, 1941; J.D., Harvard U., 1948. Bar: Hawaii 1948. Navy auditor Pearl Harbor, 1941; field agt. Social Security Bd., 1942; labor law insp. Terr. Dept. Labor, 1943; law clk. firm Ropes, Gray, Best, Coolidge & Rugg, 1948; asst. pub. prosecutor City and County of Honolulu, 1949; with Fong, Miho & Choy, 1950-53; ptnr. Fong, Miho, Choy & Chuck, 1953-58; pvt. practice law Honolulu, 1958-65, 78-80; ptnr. Chuck & Fujiyama, Honolulu, 1965-74; ptnr. firm Chuck, Wong & Tonaki, Honolulu, 1974-76, Chuck & Pai, Honolulu, 1976-78; pres. Walter G. Chuck Law Corp., Honolulu, 1980-94; pvt. practice Honolulu, 1994—; dist. magistrate Dist. Ct. Honolulu, 1956-63; gen. ptnr. M & W Assocs., Kapalama Investment Co.; bd. dirs. Aloha Airlines, Inc., Honolulu Painting Co., Ltd. Chmn. Hawaii Employment Rels. Bd., 1955-59; bd. dirs. Nat. Assn. State Labor Rels. Bds., 1957-58, Honolulu Theatre for Youth, 1977-80; chief clk. Hawaii Ho. of Reps., 1951, 53, Hawaii Senate, 1959-61; govt. appeal agt. SSS, 1953-72; former mem. jud. coun. State of Hawaii; mem. exec. com. Hawaiian Open; former dir. Friends of Judiciary History Ctr. Inc., 1983-94; former mem. bd. dirs. YMCA. Capt. inf. Hawaii Terr. Guard. Recipient Ha'Aheo award for cmty. svc. Hawaii chpt. Am. Bd. Trial Advocates, 1995. Fellow Internat. Acad. Trial Lawyers (founder, dean, bd. dirs., state rep.), Am. Coll. Trial Lawyers; mem. ABA (former chmn. Hawaii sr. lawyers divsn., former mem. ho. of dels.), Hawaii Bar Assn. (pres. 1963), ATLA (former editor), U. Hawaii Alumni Assn. (Disting. Svc. award 1967, former dir., bd. govs.), Law Sci. Inst., Assoc. Students U. Hawaii (pres.), Am. Judicature Soc., Internat. Soc. Barristers, Am. Inst. Banking, Chinese C. of C., U. Hawaii Founders Alumni Assn. (v.p., bd. dirs., Lifetime Achievement award 1994), Harvard Club of Hawaii, Waialae Country Club (pres. 1975), Pacific Club, Oahu Country Club. Republican. Home: 2691 Aaliamanu Pl Honolulu HI 96813-1216 Office: Pacific Tower 1001 Bishop St Ste 2750 Honolulu HI 96813-3410

CHUNDURI, NARENDRA R., engineer, computer consultant; b. Kakinada, South Andhra, India; came to U.S., 1978; s. Lakshminarayana and Anjamma C.; m. Pongprapa Kasemsant, June 8, 1985. BS, Andhra (India) State U., Eluru, 1972; MS, Andhra (India) State U., Waltair, 1975; MBA, Calif. State U., Long Beach, 1981, MSE in Environ. Engring., 1994. Inventory controller Savin Corp., Cerritos, Calif., 1979-81; programmer-analyst Starkist, Long Beach, 1981-84; mem. computing staff Hughes Aircraft Co., El Segundo, Calif., 1984-87; mem. tech. support The Aerosapce Corp, El Segundo, 1987-89; mem. tech. staff Aerospace Corp., El Segundo, 1989-91, project mgr., engring. specialist, 1992-94; mgmt. info. systems, faculty Calif. State U., Fullerton, 1994-96; mgmt. cons. Douglas Aircraft Co., Long Beach, Calif., 1995-96, sr. mgr. automation and process improvements, 1997—; v.p. ops. Ragaswara, Huntington Beach, 1996—, KC Internat., Costa Mesa, Calif., 1995—; cons. Dr. C. V. Chelapati & Assocs., Huntington Beach, Calif., 1981—. Mem. Soc. Cost Estimation and Analysis, Assoc. MBA Execs. Avocation: model airplanes. Office: Douglas Aircraft Co 3855 N Lakewood Blvd Long Beach CA 90846-0003

CHUNG, AMY TERESA, lawyer, property manager; b. San Francisco, Sept. 1, 1953; d. Burk Him and Mary Angeline (Lin) C.; m. Andrew Nathan Chang, May 5, 1979; children: Adrian Thomas, Alison Nicole. AB in Psychology, U. Calif., Berkeley, 1975; JD, U. Calif., San Francisco, 1978. Bar: Calif. Legal counsel M & B Assocs., San Francisco, 1978—; v.p. Anza Parking Corp., Burlingame, Calif., 1993—. Mem. adv. com. U. Calif., San Francisco, 1992—; v.p. Castle Peak Homeowners Assn., West Hills, Calif., 1987-89; v.p. Chinatown Stockton St. Mchts. Assn., San Francisco, 1981—; chair Chinese Cmty. Housing Corp., San Francisco, 1991—; project area com. Mid-Market, San Francisco, 1996—. Mem. Calif. Bar Assn. Avocations: piano, singing, ballet, swimming. Office: M & B Assocs 835 Washington St San Francisco CA 94108-1211

CHUNG, JIN SOO, ocean mining and offshore engineer; b. Seoul, Korea, Jan. 27, 1937; s. Hyun Mo and Soon Mo (Yoo) C.; B.S.E. in Naval Architecture, Seoul Nat. U., 1961; M.S., U. Calif., Berkeley, 1964; Ph.D. in Engring. Mechanics, U. Mich., 1969; m. Yang Ja Park, Aug. 11, 1967; children—Claude H., Christine M. Sr. research engr. Exxon Prodn. Research Co., Houston, 1969-73; staff engr. Lockheed Missiles & Space Co., Sunnyvale, Calif., 1973-80; prof. Colo. Sch. Mines, Golden, 1980—; cons. in hydrodynamics to Inter-Govtl. Maritime Consultative Orgn., UN, 1981; chmn., editor Proceedings of 1st Offshore Mechanics/Arctic Engring. Symposium, New Orleans, 1982, chmn., editor 2d Internat. Symposium, Houston, 1983, 3d Internat. Symposium, New Orleans, 1984, 4th Internat. Symposium, Dallas, 1985, 5th Internat. Symposium and Exhibit, Tokyo, 1986, 7th Internat. Conf., Houston, 1988, 8th Internat. Conf., Hague, The Netherlands, 1989. Recipient Eugene W. Jacobson award Energy Tech. Conf., Houston, 1978. Mem. ASME (Ralph James award 1980, policy bd. communication 1981-85, chmn. offshore mechanics com., 1982-84, paper revs. chmn. Petroleum Div. 1980-84, 1st chmn. offshore mechanics and arctic engring. div. 1984-86, Outstanding Achievement award 1987, editor various publications 1981—), Internat. Council on Offshore Mechanics and Arctic Engring. (founder, chmn. 1986-95), Soc. Petroleum Engrs., Internat. Journal Offshore and Polar Engring. (editor 1990—), Internat. Soc. Offshore and Polar Engrs. (exec. dir., Neptune award), Soc. Naval Architects Japan, Sigma Xi, Tau Beta Pi. Sr. editor Transactions Jour. of Energy Resources Tech., 1980-85; assoc. editor Applied Mechanics Rev., 1985-91; pioneer in advanced tech. devel. and position control simulation of deep ocean mining system. Fax: (303) 420-3760. Home: 12757 W 57th Dr Arvada CO 80002-1301 Office: Internat Soc Offshore & Polar Engrs PO Box 1107 Golden CO 80402-1107

CHURCH, BRYAN P., business owner, educator; b. Toledo, Oreg., Nov. 1, 1960; s. Harry P. and Nadine I. (Peace) Ch.; m. Rana B. Heller, Aug. 23, 1991; children: Schyler B., Matthew A. BS, Sacramento State U., 1982, MBA, 1983. Cert. cmty. coll. tchr., Calif.; lic. real estate broker, Calif. Terr. sales mgr. Coca-Cola USA, Atlanta, 1983-87; sales mgr. Macmillan/McGraw Hill Pub., Columbus, Ohio, 1987-93; western regional sales mgr. Dearborn Fin. Pub., Chgo., 1993-95; owner Accredited Real Estate Schs., Fair Oaks, Calif., 1995—; adj. assoc. prof. mktg. Sch. Mgmt. Golden Gate U., San Francisco, 1998—; mem. bus. adv. bd. San Joaquin Delta Coll., Stockton, Calif., 1985, Hawaii Bus. Educators Assn., Honolulu, 1992, Sierra Coll., Rocklin, Calif., 1992, Saddleback Coll., Mission Viejo, Calif., 1994; guest speaker Inst. Mgmt. Accts., Sacramento, 1993, Svc. Corps of Ret. Execs., Sacramento, 1995; coord. tng. project Golden Gate U., San Francisco, 1994. Author: Playing the Corporate Game, 1994, Real Estate Principles, 1995, Real Estate Contracts, 1996, California Real Estate Practice, 1997. Vol. baseball coach Mills Jr. H.S., Sacramento, 1994. Recipient various awards. Mem. Hawaii Bus. Educators Assn., Calif. Assn. Realtors (affiliate). Avocations: bicycling, fly fishing, flying. Office: Accredited Real Estate Schs 6716 Madison Ave Ste 4 Fair Oaks CA 95628-3151

CHURCH, PETER DAWSON, publishing executive; b. Cape Town, South Africa, Nov. 15, 1956; s. Peter and Ada Helen (Amm) C.; m. Brenda Lynn Plowman; children: Lionel, Angela. BA in Mass Comm., Baylor U., 1979. Owner, operator Dawson Design, N.Y.C., 1979-87; pub. Asian Publishing, Boulder Creek, Calif., 1987-91; CEO Atrium Publishers Group, Santa Rosa, Calif., 1991-96; publisher Celebrity Press, Santa Rosa, Calif., 1997 [illegible]

Apple Computer, Cupertino, Calif., 1990, Whole Life Expo, San Francisco, 1989. Author: The Heart of the Healer, 1987, Communing With the Spirit of Your Unborn Child, 1989, Facing Death, Finding Love, 1994; editor approximately 50 books; contbr. numerous articles incl. Los Angels Times. Mem. Publishers Mktg. Assn. (4 Ben Franklin awards 1988-94). Office: 4444 Wood Rd Guerneville CA 95446

CHURCH-GAULTIER, LORENE KEMMERER, retired government official; b. Jordan, Mont., Oct. 18, 1929; d. Harry F. and Laura (Stoller) Kemmerer; m. Scott Johnston, Sept. 8, 1948 (div. 1953); children: Linda M., Theodore O.; m. Fred C. Church, May 9, 1956 (dec. 1967); children: Ned B., Nia J.; m. Charles F. Gaultier, Oct. 1996. Student, Portland Community Coll., 1973-76, Portland State U., 1978-79. Sec. intelligence div. IRS, Portland, Oreg., 1973-75; trade asst. Internat. Trade Adminstrn., U.S. Dept. Commerce, Portland, 1975-84, internat. trade specialist, 1984-94; ret., 1995. Mem. NAFE, World Affairs Coun., N.W. China Coun., Portland C. of C. (Europe 1992 com. 1988-89, internat. trade adv. bd. 1988-89, treas. dist. export coun. 1996—), Western Internat. Trade Coun. Democrat. Roman Catholic. Avocations: music, growing roses. Home: 19725 SW Pike St Beaverton OR 97007-1446 Office: US Dept Commerce US&FCS 121 SW Salmon St Portland OR 97204-2901

CHURCHILL, SHARAL TOMIKO, motion picture company executive; b. Honolulu, Jan. 31, 1963; d. Harry Teraoka and Virginia (Saito) Valdez. Student, UCLA, 1980-82. Graphic artist Joy Printers, Monrovia, Calif., 1979-80; ind. concert promoter Duarte, Calif., 1981-83; concert promoter Nederlander, Hollywood, Calif., 1985-86; asst. Herbie Hancock, Hollywood, 1986; mgr. Herbie Hancock AGM, Hollywood, 1986-89; music coord. Soundtrack Co., Pacific Palisades, 1989; music supr. The Music Cons., L.A., 1989—; film prodr. Premiere Picture Arts, L.A.; music supr. tchr. UCLA, L.A., 1997—; mentor, L.A., 1997—. Avocations: film, music, bicycling, food. Office: The Music Cons LLC PO Box 69857 Los Angeles CA 90069-4519

CHURCHILL, WARD L., social sciences educator, writer; b. Urbana, Ill., Oct. 2, 1947; s. Jack Churchill and Maralyn L. (Allen) Debo; m. Leah R. Kelly, Aug. 8, 1995; 1 child, Jasmine Ann. AA, Ill. Ctrl. Coll., 1972; BA, Sangamon State U., 1974, MA, 1975; LHD (hon.), Alfred U., 1992. Program dir. Boulder Valley Sch. Dist., Boulder, 1977-78; program dir. U. Colo., Boulder, 1978-90, assoc. prof., 1991-97, full prof., 1997—; vis. prof. Alfred U., N.Y., 1990-91. Author: Struggle for the Land, 1993, Indians Are Us?, 1994, Since Predator Came, 1995, From a Native Son, 1996, A Little Matter of Genocide, 1997; editor: New Studies on the Left, 1987-94; contbg. editor: Z Magazine, 1987—, Issues in Radical Therapy, 1982-87, Dark Night Field Notes, 1992—. Mem. governing coun. Colo. AIM, Denver, 1993—, co-dir., 1982-93; comms. dir. Am. Indian Anti-Defamation Coun., Denver, 1992-94; mem. steering com. Yellow Thunder Camp, Rapid City, S.D., 1981-85. Recipient Gustavus Myers award in writing Gustavus Myers Ctr., 1984. Avocation: films. Office: U Colo Dept Ethnic Studies CB 339 Boulder CO 80309-0339

CHURCHILL, WILLIAM DELEE, retired education educator, psychologist; b. Buffalo, Nov. 4, 1919; s. Glenn Luman and Ethel (Smith) C.; AB, Colgate U., 1941; MEd, Alfred U., 1951; EdD, U. Rochester, 1969; m. Beulah Coleman, Apr. 5, 1943; children: Cherylee, Christie. Tchr. secondary sci., Canaseraga, N.Y., 1947-56; dir. guidance Alfred-Almond Sch., Almond, N.Y., 1956-63; grad. asst. U. Rochester, 1963-65; asst. prof. psychology Alfred (N.Y.) U., 1965-66; assoc. prof. edn. Ariz. State U., Tempe, 1966-86. Lt. col. USAAF, 1942-79, PTO. Mem. Ariz. Psychol. Assn. Author: Career Survey of Graduates, 1973. Home: 11454 N 85th St Scottsdale AZ 85260-5727

CHURCHMAN, DAVID ALAN, conflict management educator; b. N.Y.C., July 20, 1938; s. Stanley and Elizabeth (Lawson) C. BA, U. Mich., 1960, MA, 1964; PhD, UCLA, 1972. Social worker Dept. Pub. Social Svcs., Bakersfield, Calif., 1964-65; tchr. Am. Internat. Sch., Tangier, Morocco, 1965-66, Newtown (Pa.) High Sch., 1966-68; rsch. assoc. UCLA, 1972-76; prof. negotiations and conflict mgmt. Calif. State U., Dominguez Hills, 1976—; bd. dirs. Wildlife on Wheels, L.A., 1985—, Orangutan Found., L.A., 1986-92; Calif. coord. Nat. Coun. U.S.-Arab Rels., 1993-94; cons. Nat. Inst. Drug Abuse, State of Hawaii, Minn., N. Mex., Tribal Am. Corp., UCLA Harbor Gen. Hosp., others; mem. adv. bd. Bur. Land Mgmt., Calif., 1984-87. Author: Negotiation Tactics, 1988, 1993, 95, (with others) Evaluation Workshop, 1971, American Indian Life Environments, 1975; contbr. numerous articles to profl. jours. Mem. ctrl. com. Calif. Rep. Party; mem. pres.'s club Nat. Rep. Com. 1st lt. U.S. Army, 1960-62. Grantee NSF, Calif. Dept. Fish and Game, Calif. Comty. Found., Chevron, Arco, Nestle U.S.A. and others; Malone fellow Nat. Coun. on U.S.- Arab Rels., 1993. Mem. Aquarium & Zoo Assn., Internat. Assn. Zoo Educators, Internat. Assn. Conflict Mgmt., Wednesday Morning Club, L.A. World Affairs Coun., Rotary Internat., So. Calif. Rep. Women and Men. Republican. Avocations: rifle marksmanship, chess, cooking, travel, photography. Office: Calif State U Dominguez Hills 1000 E Victoria St Carson CA 90747-0001

CIA, MANUEL LOPEZ, artist; b. Las Cruces, N.Mex., Jan. 4, 1937; s. Anastacio Cea Lopez and Mercedes Rivera. Student, Am. Acad. Art, Chgo., 1958-61, Art Inst. San Francisco, 1962, L.A. Trade Tech., 1963-64, U. N.Mex., 1990. Author: Color Quest, 1991, Theory of Sophisticism, 1993; Exhibited in group shows at The Fundacion Teleton de Honduras, Teguicigalpa, 1989, France-USA, Paris, 1991, Arts and the Quincentennial, Albuquerque, 1992, U.S. Artists, Phila., 1993, State of the Art, Boston, 1993, Miniatures 1993, Albuquerque, 1993, Montserrat Gallery, N.Y.C., 1995; one man shows include El Prado Galleries, Sedonia, Ariz. and Santa Fe, N.Mex., 1989, 90, 95. With USAF, 1954-57. Recipient Outstanding Individual award Youth Devel., Albuquerque, 1991. Mem. Internat. Assn. Contemporary Art, Soc. Am. Impressionists. Avocations: study and writing of aesthetics. Home: PO Box 7332 Albuquerque NM 87194-7332

CICCIARELLI, JAMES CARL, immunology educator; b. Toluca, Ill., May 26, 1947; s. Maurice Cicciarelli and Helen Ippolito; 1 daughter: Nicola. BS, Tulane U., 1969; PhD, So. Ill. U., 1977. Lic. clin. lab. dir., Calif. Fellow dept. surgery UCLA, 1977-79, asst. prof. immunology, 1980-87, assoc. prof., 1987-91; prof. urology and microbiology U. So. Calif., L.A., 1992—; lab. dir. Metic Transplant Lab., Inc., L.A., 1984—; bd. dirs.. So. Calif. Organ Procurement Agy.; clin. lab. dir. Am. Bd. Bioanalysis, 1991—; mem. histocompatibility com. United Network Organ Sharing, 1991-94; mem. scientific adv. com. United Network for Organ Sharing, 1997—; lab. dir. Sharp Hosp. and Clinic, San Diego. Contbr. articles to profl. jours., chpts. to books. Rsch. grant NIH, 1985-88. Mem. Am. Soc. Histocompatibility and Immunogenetics, Internat. Transplant Soc., Am. Soc. Transplant Physicians, Internat. Soc. Heart Lung Transplantation. Libertarian. Roman Catholic. Avocations: boating, biking, skiing, tennis, running. Home: 5 W Ringbit Rd Rolling Hills CA 90274 Office: USC Dept Urology Metic Transplant Lab 2100 W 3rd St Ste 280 Los Angeles CA 90057-1922

CICERONE, RALPH JOHN, geophysicist; b. New Castle, Pa., May 2, 1943; married; 1 child. SB, MIT, 1965; MS, U. Ill., 1967, PhD in Elec. Engrng. and Physics, 1970. Physicist U.S. Dept. Commerce, 1967; rsch. asst. aeronomy U. Ill., 1967-70; assoc. rsch. scientist aeronomy space physics rsch. lab. U. Mich., Ann Arbor, 1970-78; assoc. rsch. chemist ocean rsch. divsn. U. Calif., San Diego, 1978-80, rsch. chemist Scripps inst. oceanography, 1980-81; Daniel G. Aldrich prof., chair geosci. dept. U. Calif., Irvine, 1989—; dean Sch. Phys. Scis., 1994—; sr. scientist, dir. atmospheric chemistry divsn. Nat. Ctr. Atmospheric Rsch., Boulder, Colo., 1980-89; chancellor U. Calif., Irvine, 1998—; lectr., asst. prof. elec. engrng. U. Mich., Ann Arbor, 1973-75. Assoc. editor Jour. Geophysics Rsch., 1977-79, editor, 1979-83. Recipient Bower award for Achievement in Sci., Franklin Inst., 1999. Fellow AAAS, Am. Chem. Soc., Am. Meteorol. Soc., Am. Geophysical Union (Macelwane award 1979); mem. NAS (elected, mem. com. atmospheric sci. 1980-82, mem. bd. atmospheric sci. and climate 1987-89, mem. commn. geosci., environment and resources). Office: U Calif Irvine Chancellors Office 509 Administration Bldg Irvine CA 92697*

CIFFONE, DONALD, electronics company executive. Pres., CEO EXAR, Freemont, Calif. Office: EXAR 48720 Kato Rd Fremont CA 94538*

CIMBOLO See **GIMBOLO, ALEKSEI FRANK CHARLES**

CINNAMON, WILLIAM, III, elementary and special education educator; b. Kansas City, Mo., Aug. 19, 1953; s. William and Joan C. (Davidson) C. BA in Education, U. N.Mex., 1975; MA in Spl. Edn., Loyola Marymount U., 1990. Cert. Adult Multiple Subject, Calif., Single Subject, N.Mex. History, English tchr. Order of Friars Minor St. Elizabeth's High Sch., Oakland, Calif., 1975-83; elem. tchr. Archdiocese of L.A. Christ the King Sch., Hollywood, Calif., 1983-89, L.A. Unified Sch. Dist. Fernangeles Art St., Sun Valley, Calif., 1989-94; tchr. Richard E. Byrd Mid. Sch., 1994-98, mentor tchr., 1992-95, dept. chairperson, 1994-98; mem. Sch. Decision-Making Coun., Sun Valley, Calif., 1991-98; cons. Spl. Edn. in Cath. Schs., L.A., 1985-89; participant, math. edn. leader FATHOM: Spl. Math. Edn. Leadership Tng., 1993-96. Contbr. articles to profl. jours. Mem. Christopher St. West, West Holywood, Calif., 1990, Mcpl. Elections Com., L.A.; vol. L.A. Olympic Orgn. Com., L.A., 1984, Stonewall Club. Recipient personal invitation to meet Pope John Paul II, Archdiocese of L.A., St. Vibiana's Cathedral. 1988. Mem. Gay and Lesbian Issues Com., Gay Lesbian Straight Educators Network, L.A. City Math. Tchrs., United Tchrs. L.A., English Coun. L.A., Disneyland Alumni Club, Phi Delta Kappa. Roman Catholic. Avocations: travel, photography, computers, sailing, modeling, cats. Home: 11601 Burbank Blvd Apt 3 North Hollywood CA 91601-2321 Office: Byrd Mid Sch 9171 Telfair Ave Sun Valley CA 91352-1844

CIPRIANO, PATRICIA ANN, secondary education educator, consultant; b. San Francisco, Apr. 24, 1946; d. Ernest Peter and Claire Patricia (Croak) C. BA in English, Holy Names Coll., Oakland, Calif., 1967; MA in Edn. of Gifted, Calif. State U.-L.A., 1980. Cert. tchr., tchr. gifted, adminstrv. svc., lang. devel. specialist, Calif. Tchr. English, math. Bancroft Jr. High Sch., San Leandro, Calif., 1968-79, 83-85, coord. gifted edn., 1971-79; tchr. English, math., computers San Leandro High Sch., 1979-83, 85-96, mentor tchr., 1991-94, chmn. English dept., 1992-96, coord. gifted and talented edn., 1981-83; tchr. English, social studies, ELD, math. Los Cerritos Mid. Sch., Thousand Oaks, Calif., 1996—, chmn. English dept., 1996—; cons. Calif. State Dept. Edn., various Calif. sch. dists.; dir. Calif. Reading and Lit. Project Policy Bd. Recipient Hon. Svc. award Tchr. of Yr., Bancroft Jr. High Sch. PTA, 1973; bd. dirs. Calif. Curriculum Correlating Coun. Mem. NEA, ASCD, Calif. Assn. for Gifted, World Coun. Gifted and Talented, Cen. Calif. Coun. Tchrs. English (past pres.), Southland Coun. Tchrs. English, Calif. Assn. Tchrs. English (bd. dirs., past pres., disting. svc. award 1996), Nat. Coun. Tchrs. English (bd. dirs.), Unified Assn. Conejo Tchrs., Calif. Tchrs. Assn., Computer Using Educators, Curriculum Study Commn. (bd. dirs.), Delta Kappa Gamma (past pres.). Roman Catholic. Avocations: reading, piano, calligraphy, tennis, photography. Contbr. articles to profl. jours. Office: Los Cerritos Mid Sch 2100 E Avenida De Las Flores Thousand Oaks CA 91362-1530

CIRINO, LEONARD JOHN, poet, editor; b. L.A., Sept. 11, 1943; s. Herbert and Marjorie (Burtle) C. BA in English, Sonoma State U., 1977. Instr. Coll. of Redwoods, Ft. Bragg, Calif., 1980-89; editor Pygmy Forest Press, Eureka, Calif., 1989—. Author: (poetry) The Source of Precious Life, 1988, Rocking Over Dawn, 1992, Waiting for the Sun to Fill with Courage, 1994, The Terrible Wilderness of Self, 1998, 96 Sonnets Facing Conviction, 1999. Avocations: painting, blues harmonica player, beach walking, camping, hiking. Office: Pygmy Forest Press Box 7097 Eureka CA 95502

CLABAUGH, ELMER EUGENE, JR., lawyer; b. Anaheim, Calif., Sept. 18, 1927; s. Elmer Eugene and Eleanor Margaret (Heitshusen) C.; m. Donna Marie Organ, Dec. 19, 1960 (div.); children: Christopher C., Matthew M. BBA cum laude, Woodbury U.; BA summa cum laude, Claremont McKenna Coll., 1958; JD, Stanford U., 1961. Bar: Calif. 1961, U.S. Dist. Ct. (cen. dist.) Calif., U.S. Ct. Appeals (9th cir.) 1961, U.S. Supreme Ct. 1971. With fgn. svc. U.S. Dept. State, Jerusalem and Tel Aviv, 1951-53, Pub. Adminstrn. Svc., El Salvador, Ethiopia, U.S., 1953-57; dep. dist. atty. Ventura County, Calif., 1961-62; pvt. practice, Ventura, Calif., 1962-97; mem. Hathaway, Clabaugh, Perrett and Webster and predecessors, 1962-79, Clabaugh & Perloff, Ventura, 1979-97; state inheritance tax referee, 1968-78, ret. Bd. dirs. San Antonio Water Conservation Dist., Ventura Community Meml. Hosp., 1964-80; trustee Ojai Unified Sch. Dist., 1974-79; bd. dirs. Ventura County Found. for Parks and Harbors, 1982-96, Ventura County Maritime Mus., 1982-94. With USCGR, 1944-46, USMCR, 1946-48. Mem. NRA, Calif. Bar Assn., Safari Club Internat., Mason, Shriners, Phi Alpha Delta. Republican.

CLABAUGH, MATTHEW MARTINSEN, venture capitalist, real estate investor; b. Redwood City, Calif., May 6, 1959; s. Elmer Eugene C. and Elizabeth Ellen Chapman Bowman. BA, U. Redlands, 1981; MBA, Chapman U., 1984. Asst. mgr. Bank of Am., Newport Beach, Calif., 1984-88; v.p. Nat. Bank So. Calif., Lake Forest, 1988-91; cfo Valencia Group, Inc., Irvine, Calif., 1991—; sr. advisor Sch. Bus. Chapman U., Orange, Calif., 1986-94; del. Moscow Conf. on Law, Moscow, 1992, Beijing Conf. on Econ. Coop., 1995; mem. econ. coop. Nat. Writers Congress, 1994-98. With USMC, 1979-81. Mem. NRA, Urban Land Inst., Rotary Internat. Avocations: golf, tennis, scuba, trap/skeet shooting, travel. Office: Valencia Group Inc 19762 Macarthur Blvd Irvine CA 92612-2410

CLAES, DANIEL JOHN, physician; b. Glendale, Calif., Dec. 3, 1931; s. John Vernon and Claribel (Fleming) C.; AB magna cum laude, Harvard U., 1953, MD cum laude, 1957; m. Gayla Christine Blasdel, Jan. 19, 1974. Intern, UCLA, 1957-58; Bowyer Found. fellow for rsch. in medicine, L.A., 1958-61; pvt. practice specializing in diabetes, L.A., 1962—; biotech. cons. SIRA Techs., 1995—; v.p. Am. Eye Bank Found., 1978-83, pres., 1983—, dir. rsch., 1980—, chmn., CEO 1995—; pres. Heuristic Corp., 1981—. Mem. L.A. Mus. Art, 1960—. Mem. AMA, AAAS, Calif. Med. Assn., L.A. County Med. Assn., Am. Diabetes Assn. (profl. coun. on immunology, immunogenetics and transplantation), Internat. Diabetes Fedn., Internat. Pancreas & Islet Transplant Assn. Clubs: Harvard and Harvard Med. Sch. of So. Calif.; Royal Commonwealth (London). Contbr. papers on diabetes mellitus, computers in medicine to profl. lit. Office: Am Eyebank Found 15237 W Sunset Blvd Ste 108 Pacific Palisades CA 90272-3690

CLAES, GAYLA CHRISTINE, writer, editorial consultant; b. L.A., Oct. 17, 1946; d. Henry George and Glorya Desiree (Curran) Blasdel; m. Daniel John Claes, Jan. 19, 1974. AB magna cum laude, Harvard U., 1968; postgrad., Oxford (Eng.) U., 1971; MA, McGill U., Montreal, 1975. Adminstrv. asst. U. So. Calif., L.A., 1968-70; teaching asst. English lit. McGill U., Montreal, 1970-71; editorial dir. Internat. Cons. Group, L.A., 1972-78; v.p. Gaylee Corp., L.A., 1978-81, CEO, 1981-88; writer, cons. L.A. and Paris, 1988—; dir. pub. rels. Centre Internat. for the Performing Arts, Paris and L.A., 1991—. Author: (play) Berta of Hungary, 1972, (novel) Christopher Derring, 1990; contbr. articles to lit. and sci. jours. Mem. Harvard-Radcliffe Club of So. Calif., Royal Commonwealth Soc. (London).

CLAIR, THEODORE NAT, educational psychologist; b. Stockton, Calif., Apr. 19, 1929; s. Peter David and Sara Renee (Silverman) C.; A.A., U. Calif. at Berkeley, 1949, A.B., 1950; M.S., U. So. Calif., 1953, M.Ed., 1963, Ed.D., 1969; m. Laura Gold, June 19, 1961; children: Shari, Judith. Tchr., counselor Los Angeles City Schs., 1957-63; psychologist Alamitos Sch. Dist., Garden Grove, Calif., 1963-64, Arcadia (Calif.) Unified Sch. Dist., 1964-65; head psychologist Wiseburn Sch. Dist., Hawthorne, Calif., 1966-69; asst. prof. spl. edn., coordinator sch. psychology program U. Iowa, Iowa City, 1969-72; dir. pupil personnel services Orcutt (Calif.) Union Sch. Dist., 1972-73; adminstr. Mt. Diablo Unified Sch. Dist., 1973-77; program dir., psychologist San Mateo County Office of Edn., Redwood City, 1977-91; assoc. prof. John F. Kennedy U. Sch. Mgmt., 1975-77; pvt. practice as ednl. psychologist and marriage and family counselor, Menlo Park, Calif., 1978—, Menlo Park, Calif., 1977-93, dir. Peninsula Vocat. Rehab. Inst., 1978—; psychologist Coll. Counseling Svc., Menlo Pk., 1992—, Calif. Pacific Hosp., San Francisco, 1993—. Served with USNR, 1952-54. Mem. APA, Nat. Assn. Sch. Psychologists, Calif. Assn. Marriage and Family Counselors, Nat. Rehab. Assn, Palo Alto B'nai B'rith Club (pres.). Author: Phenylketonuria and Some Other Inborn Errors of Amino Acid Metabolism, 1971; editor Jour. Calif. Ednl. Psychologists, 1992-94; contbr. articles to profl. jours. Home and Office: 56 Willow Rd Menlo Park CA 94025-3654

CLAIRE, FRED, professional baseball team executive. AA, Mt. San Antonio Coll.; BA in Journalism, San Jose State Coll., 1957. Formerly sports writer and columnist Long Beach Ind. Press Telegram and Whittier News; sports editor Pomo Progress-Bull, Calif., until 1969; dir. publicity Los Angeles Dodgers, Nat. League, 1969-75, v.p. pub. relations and promotions, 1975-82, exec. v.p., from 1982, now exec. v.p. player personnel, 1987—; bd. dirs. Major League Baseball Promotion Corp. Bd. dirs. Greater Los Angeles Vistors and Conv. Bur. Named The Sporting News Major League Exec. of Yr., 1988. Mem. Echo Park C. of C. Lodge: Los Angeles Rotary. Office: LA Dodgers Dodgers Stadium 1000 Elysian Park Ave Los Angeles CA 90012-1112

CLAPP, CARL ROGER, physical education educator; b. Santa Barbara, Calif., Nov. 2, 1958. BA in Phys. Edn., U. Calif., Santa Barbara, 1981, BA in Psychology, 1981; MS in Athletic Adminstrn., U. Ariz., 1984. Asst. football coach Santa Barbara City Coll., 1979-81, U. Ariz., Tucson, 1981, Ariz. State U., Tempe, 1982-84, Wichita (Kans.) State U., 1984-86; asst. dir. athletics Emporia (Kans.) State U., 1988-92; dir. athletics Avila Coll., Kansas City, Mo., 1992-95; dir. athletics/phys. edn. U. Redlands, Calif., 1995—; presenter in field. Contbr. articles to profl. jours. E-mail: clapp@uor.edu. Home: 1152 Jasmine St Redlands CA 92374-4923 Office: U Redlands 1200 E Colton Ave PO Box 3080 Redlands CA 92373-0999

CLARK, AARON LEE, environmental consulting executive; b. Fondulac, Wis., Sept. 24, 1955; s. Darrel R. and Geraldine M. (Vander Galien) C.; m. Gretchen L. Harrison. Sr. scientist Woodward-Clyde Consultants, San Diego, 1979-81; coord. regulatory affairs Amoco Prodn. Co., Denver, 1981-87; pres. PIC Techs., Inc., Denver, 1987—. Trustee Black-Footed Ferret Recovery Found., Denver, 1996—. Office: PIC Techs Inc 1133 Pennsylvania St Denver CO 80203-2502

CLARK, ARTHUR JOSEPH, JR., mechanical and electrical engineer; b. West Orange, N.J., June 10, 1921; s. Arthur Joseph and Marjorie May (Courter) C.; BS in Mech. Engrng., Cornell U., 1943; MS, Poly. Inst. Bklyn., 1948; MS in Elec. Engrng., U. N.Mex., 1955; m. Caroline Katherine Badgley, June 12, 1943; children: Arthur Joseph, III, Durward S., David P. Design engr. Ranger Aircraft Engines Co., Farmingdale, N.Y., 1943-46; sr. structures engr. propeller div. Curtis Wright Co., Caldwell, N.J., 1946-51; mgr. space isotope power dept., also aerospace nuclear safety dept. Sandia Labs., Albuquerque, 1951-71, mgr. environ. systems test lab., 1971-79, mgr. mil. liaison dept., 1979-86; pres. Engring. Svcs. Cons. Firm, 1987; mem. faculty U. N.Mex., 1971-75; invited lectr. Am. Mgmt. Assn. Pres. Sandia Base Sch. PTA, 1960-61; chmn. finance com. Albuquerque chpt. Am. Field Svc., 1964-66; chmn. Sandia Labs. div. U.S. Savs. Bond drive, 1972-74, chmn. employee contbn. drive, 1973-75; active local Boy Scouts Am., 1958-66. Recipient Order Arrow, Boy Scouts Am., 1961, Order St. Andrew, 1962, Scouters Key award, 1964; cert. outstanding service Sandia Base, 1964. Fellow ASME (nat. v.p. 1975-79, past chmn. N.Mex. sect.); mem. IEEE (sr.), Cornell Engrng. Soc., Theta Xi. Clubs: Kirtland Officers, Four Hills Country. Home: 905 Warm Sands Trl SE Albuquerque NM 87123-4332

CLARK, BRIAN THOMAS, mathematical statistician, operations research analyst; b. Rockford, Ill., Apr. 7, 1951; s. Paul Herbert and Martha Lou (Schlensker) C.; m. Suzanne Drake, Nov. 21, 1992; 1 child, Branden Ward. BS cum laude, No. Ariz. U., 1973; postgrad. Ariz. State U., 1980-82. Math. aide Center for Disease Control, Phoenix, 1973-74, math. statistician, 1979-83; math. Statistician Ctrs. for Disease Control, Atlanta, 1983-84 ops. research analyst U.S. Army Info. Systems Command, Ft. Huachuca, Ariz., 1984—; math. statistician U.S. Navy Metrology Engring. Center, Pomona, Calif., 1974-79. Republican. Mormon. Office: US Army Signal Command Dep Chief Staff Resource Mgmt G8 Managerial Acctg Pricing Fort Huachuca AZ 85613

CLARK, BRUCE WOODRUFF, graphic designer; b. Camden, N.J., Sept. 18, 1951. BFA, U. Colo., 1973. Graphic artist Mountain Bell Telephone, Denver, 1973-76; free-lance tech. illustrator Denver, 1976-77, Hospal Med., Littleton, Colo., 1977-78; art dir. Gen. Graphics, Denver, 1978-88; sr. designer Cobe Labs., Lakewood, Colo., 1988-96; graphic designer Denver Instrument, Arvada, Colo., 1996—; guest tchr. Loretto Heights Coll., Denver, 1979; cons. in field. Avocation: sculpture. Home and office: Bruce Clark Design 7347 Robb St Arvada CO 80005-3540

CLARK, CHARLENE ELIZABETH, nursing educator; b. Spokane, Wash., Jan. 8, 1941; d. Carl G. and Anna E. (Miller) Miller; m. Robert S. Clark, Apr. 14, 1962; children: Robert S. Jr., Jeffrey C. Diploma in nursing, Sacred Heart Sch. Nursing, Spokane, 1962; BS, Whitworth Coll., 1965, MEd, 1974. RN, Wash. Instr Sacred Heart Sch. Nursing, Spokane, 1962-66; instr. RN refresher course Spokane Community Coll., 1968; from instr. to prof. Intercollegiate Ctr. for Nursing Edn. Wash. State U., Spokane, 1969—, dir. learning resource Intercollegiate Ctr. for Nursing Edn., 1981-95, asst. dean for instrnl. resources, 1995-98, assoc. dean for instrnl. resources and extended coll. activities, 1998—; cons. in field. Contbr. articles to profl. jours. Recipient Nurse Excellence award Delta Chi chpt. Sigma Theta Tau. Mem. ANA, Assn. Ednl. Comm./Tech. (continuing edn. com.), Am. Acad. Nursing, Sigma Theta Tau. Office: Wash State U 2917 W Fort George Wright Dr Spokane WA 99224-5202

CLARK, CHARLES SUTTER, interior designer; b. Venice, Calif., Dec. 21, 1927; s. William Sutter and Lodema Ersell (Fleeman) C. Student Chouinard Art Inst., Los Angeles, 1950-51. Interior designer LM.H. Co., Gt. Falls, Mont., 1956-62, Andreason's Interiors, Oakland, Calif., 1962-66, Western Contact Furnishers Internat., Oakland, 1966-70, Design Five Assocs., Lafayette, Calif., 1972-73; owner, interior designer Charles Sutter Clark Interiors, Greenbrae, Calif., 1973-91, San Rafael, Calif., 1991—. Served with USAF, 1951-55. Recipient prizes Mont. State Fair, 1953-55. Mem. Am. Soc. Interior Designers. Home: 429 El Faisan Dr San Rafael CA 94903-4517

CLARK, EDGAR SANDERFORD, insurance broker, consultant; b. N.Y.C., Nov. 17, 1933; s. Edgar Edmund, Jr., and Katharine Lee (Jarman) C.; student U. Pa., 1952-54; BS, Georgetown U., 1956, JD, 1958; postgrad. INSEAD, Fountainbleau, France, 1969, Golden Gate Coll., 1973, U. Calif., Berkeley, 1974; m. Nancy E. Hill, Sept. 13, 1975; 1 child, Schuyler; children by previous marriage: Colin, Alexandra, Pamela. Staff asst. U.S. Senate select com. to investigate improper activities in labor and mgmt. field, Washington, 1958-59; underwriter Ocean Marine Dept., Fireman's Fund Ins. Co., San Francisco, 1959-62; mgr. Am. Fgn. Ins. Assn., San Francisco, 1962-66; with Marsh & McLennan, 1966-72, mgr. for Europe, resident dir. Brussels, Belgium, 1966-70, asst. v.p., mgr. captive and internat. div., San Francisco, 1970-72; v.p., dir. Risk Planning Group, Inc., San Francisco, 1972-75; v.p., dir. global constrn. group Alexander & Alexander Inc., San Francisco, 1975-94; exec. dir. The Surplus Line Assn. of Calif., 1995-97; CEO Risk Solutions Corp., 1997—; lectr. in field; guest lectr. U. Calif., Berkeley, 1973, Am. Grad. Sch. Internat. Mgmt., 1981-82, Golden Gate U., annually 1985-91; dir. Soc. Ins. Brokers, 1991-94; del. Calif. Agts. and Brokers Legis. Coun., 1992-95; pres. Ins. Forums San Francisco. With USAF, 1956-58. Mem. Am. Mgmt. Assn., Am. Risk and Ins. Assn., Internat. Insurance Soc., Chartered Ins. Inst., Am. Soc. Internat. Law, Soc. Calif. Pioneers San Francisco, Meadow Club, Fairfax, Calif., World Trade San Francisco. Republican. Episcopalian. Mem. editl. bd. Risk Mgmt. Reports, 1973-76. Office: Risk Solutions Corp c/o 72 Millay Pl Mill Valley CA 94941-1501

CLARK, GLEN EDWARD, judge; b. Cedar Rapids, Iowa, Nov. 23, 1943; s. Robert M. and Georgia L. (Welch) C.; m. Deanna D. Thomas, July 16, 1966; children: Andrew Curtis, Carissa Jane. BA, U. Iowa, 1966; JD, U. Utah, 1971. Bar: Utah 1971, U.S. Dist. Ct. Utah 1971, U.S. Ct. Appeals (10th cir.) 1972. Assoc. Fabian & Clendenin, 1971-74, ptnr., 1975-81, dir., chmn. banking and comml. law sect., 1981-82; judge U.S. Bankruptcy Ct. Dist. Utah, Salt Lake City, 1982-86, chief judge, 1986—; bd. govs. nat. Conf. Bankruptcy Judges, 1988-94; mem. com. on bankruptcy edn. Fed. Jud. Ctr., 1989-92; vis. prof. U. Utah, Salt Lake City, 1977-79, 83; pres. Nat. Conf. Bankruptcy Judges, 1992-93; chair bd. trustees Nat. Conf. Bankruptcy Judges Endowment for Edn., 1990-92. vis. assoc. prof. law Univ. Utah; instr. adv. bus. law Univ. Utah. Articles editor: Utah Law Review. With U.S. Army, 1966-68. Finkbine fellow U. Iowa. Fellow Am. Coll. Bankruptcy (charter, mem. bd. regents 1995—); mem. Jud. Conf. U.S. (mem. com. jud. br. 1992—, 10th cir. bankruptcy appellate panel 1996—), Utah Bar Assn.,

Order of Coif. Presbyterian. Office: 365 US Courthouse 350 S Main St Rm 365 Salt Lake City UT 84101-2106*

CLARK, JANET, retired health services executive; b. Detroit, Oct. 3, 1941; d. John Francis Bullock and Martha Barbara (Bauer) Clark; m. Donald Bruce Tyson, Feb. 29, 1964; children: William John, Barbara June; m. Herman John Husmann, Nov. 11, 1988. AAS in Dental Hygiene, Broome C.C., 1961; BS in Health Edn., SUNY, Cortland, 1963; MPA in Mgmt., SUNY, Albany, 1993. Dental hygiene tchr. West Genessee Ctrl. Schs., Camillus, N.Y., 1964-65; health educator N.Y. State Dept. of Health, Syracuse, 1965-70; sr. sanitarian N.Y. State Dept. of Health, Monticello, 1977-80; prin. sanitarian N.Y. State Dept. of Health, N.Y.C., 1980-86; field ops. rep. N.Y. State Dept. of Health, Albany, 1986-89, mgr. Indian health, 1990-95, ret., 1995; sanitarian, health educator Onondaga County Health Dept., Syracuse, 1970-77; chmn., CEO Ha'awi Found. for Econ. Deve. in Indigenous Nations, 1994—; office mgr. Latham Area C. of C., 1995-97; CEO, CFO Workplace Safety Svcs. LLC, 1998—, Alpha Strike Computers, 1998—. Mem. AAUW, NAFE, Am. Legion Aux., Nat. Environ. Health Assn., N.Y. Soc. Profl. Sanitarians (sec. 1970-84), N.Y. State Registry of Sanitarians (treas. 1987-90, pres. 1990-95, Meritorious Svc. award 1986), Hawaii C. of C., Elks. Avocations: reading, real estate, music, snorkeling, cards. Office: PO Box 6190 Hilo HI 96720

CLARK, JEFFREY RAPHIEL, research and development company executive; b. Provo, Utah, Sept. 29, 1953; s. Bruce Budge and Ouida (Raphiel) C.; m. Anne Margaret Eberhardt, Mar. 15, 1985; children: Jeffrey Raphiel, Mary Anne Elizabeth, Edward William Eberhardt. BS, Brigham Young U., 1977, MBA, 1979. CPA, Tex. Fin. analyst Exxon Coal USA, Inc., Houston, 1979-83; constrn. mgr. Gen. Homes, Inc., Houston, 1983-84; controller Liberty Data Products, Houston, 1984-86; v.p. Tech. Rsch. Assocs., Inc., Salt Lake City, 1987—; also dir. Tech. Rsch. Assocs., Inc. Scoutmaster Boy Scouts Am., Salt Lake City, 1989-91. Mem. AICPA, Utah Inst. CPAs, Salt Lake C. of C. (legis. action com.), Salt Lake Country Club. Republican. Mormon. Avocations: snow skiing, golf, mountain climbing. Home: 1428 Michigan Ave Salt Lake City UT 84105-1609 Office: Technical Rsch Assocs 2257 S 1100 E Salt Lake City UT 84106-2379

CLARK, JOHN MUNRO, superintendent of schools; b. Grand Canyon, Ariz., Sept. 16, 1951; s. James K. and Marica Clark; m. Margery Harrision, Aug. 6, 1976; children: Jaime, Preston, Kyndal, Spenser. BA, No. Ariz. U., 1977, MA, 1981. Tchr. Whiteriver (Ariz.) Pub. Schs., 1977-81; asst. prin. Crane Sch. Dist., Yuma, Ariz., 1981-83; prin. Douglas (Ariz.) Pub. Schs., 1983-89; asst. supt. Holbrook (Ariz.) Pub. Schs., 1989-93; supt. Whiteriver (Ariz.) Pub. Schs., 1993—; presenter in field. With U.S. Army, 1971-73, Viet Nam. Decorated Air medal, Bronze star U.S. Army, Viet Nam, 1971; named Outstanding Young Men of Am., U.S. Army, 1984. Mem. Am. Assn. Sch. Administrators., Ariz. Sch. Adminstrs., Ariz. Sch. Svcs. Through Ednl. Tech. (pres. 1994—), Am. Legion, Elks, Masons, Rotary Club. Democrat. Episcopalian. Avocation: collecting old watches and fishing reels. Office: Whiteriver Pub Schs PO Box 190 Whiteriver AZ 85941-0190

CLARK, JONATHAN L., photographer, printer, publisher; b. Ottawa, Ill., Mar. 24, 1952; s. Keith S. and Harriet S. Clark. BA in Photography, U. Calif., Santa Cruz, 1974. Self employed artist, 1975—; founder, propr. The Artichoke Press, Mountain View, Calif., 1975—. Editor The Hedgehog arts rev., San Francisco, 1997—; exhibited 16 one-man shows in U.S., Japan and Europe; exhibited in more than 60 group shows. Mem. visual arts com. City of Mountain View, Calif. Photography fellow Arts Coun. Santa Clara County, 1997, Book Club of Calif. grantee, 1997; USIS travel grantee, Poland, 1994; travel grantee, Barcelona, 1994. Avocation: bicycling. Home: 550 Mountain View Ave Mountain View CA 94041-1941

CLARK, KAREN SUE, editor, communication educator; b. Spokane, Wash., Aug. 15, 1952; d. Clifford French and Patty Ann (Ellis) C. BS in Wildlife Biology, Wash. State U., Pullman, 1974; MS in Comm., Ea. Wash. U., Cheney, 1993. Lab. technician molecular genetics dept., plant pathology dept. Wash. State U., Pullman, 1972-75; accounts payable supr. Gen. Store, Spokane, 1975-77; purchasing bookkeeper B.J. Carney & Co., 1977-81; supr. accounts payable Romac Corp., Spokane, 1981-82; bookkeeper lodge #228 Elks, Spokane, 1982-84; copy editor Internat. Amb. Programs, Spokane, 1984-86, sr. sci. editor, 1986-88, dir. publs. dept., 1988-89; grad. asst. comm. program Ea. Wash. U., Cheney, 1991-92; instr. intercultural and interperson comm., pub. speaking Gonzaga U., Spokane C.C. Editor: Aerospace Education, 1988, Wildlife Management, 1988, Automatic Control Technology, 1988, Shellfish Production, 1987. Sch. bd. dir. Dist. 325/179, 9 Mile Falls, Wash., 1988-95, chair; acad. coach, Wash. State Nat. 4-H Horse Bowl Team, Washington, Denver, 1981, 83, 85; Spokane County alt. del. Rep. Convention, 1986, 88, 90; monitor water quality Assn. for Protection of Lake Spokane; founding sponsor Challenger Ctr. for Space Sci. Edn.; mem. comm. subject adv. com. Wash. State Commn. on Student Learning. Mem. Wash. State Sch. Dirs. Assn. (rep. 5th legis. dist. network 1989, 90, 91), Spokane Astron. Soc. Avocation: saddlemaking.

CLARK, LLOYD, historian, educator; b. Belton, Tex., Aug. 4, 1923; s. Lloyd C. and Hattie May (Taylor) C.; m. Jean Reeves, June 17, 1950; children: Roger, Cynthia, Candyce. BSJ, So. Meth. U., 1948; B in Fgn. Trade, Am. Grad. Sch. Internat. Mgmt., 1949; MPA, Ariz. State U., 1972. String corr. A.P., Dallas, 1941-42; reporter Dallas Morning News, 1947; editor, pub. Ex-Press, Arlington, Tex., 1945-48; publicity mgr. Advt. Counselors Ariz., Phoenix, 1949; reporter Phoenix Gazette, 1949-65; asst. pub. Ariz. Weekly Gazette, 1965-66; founder Council on Abandoned Mil. Posts-U.S.A., 1966; project cons. City of Prescott, Ariz., 1971-72; dep. dir. adminstrv. svcs. No. Ariz. Coun. Govts., Flagstaff, 1972-73; regional adminstr. South Eastern Ariz. Govts. Orgn., Bisbee, 1973-75; local govt. assistance coordinator Ariz. Dept. Transp., Phoenix, 1975-80, program adminstr., 1980-83; history instr. Rio Salado Community Coll., Phoenix, 1983-89, Ariz. State U.-West, Sun City, 1995-98; proprietor LC Enterprises, 1993—; editor and pub. Clark Biog. Reference, 1956-62; mem. spkrs. bur. Ariz. Humanities Coun., 1998—. Bd. dirs. Friends of Channel 8, 1984-86; mem. transit planning com. Regional Pub. Transit Authority, 1988; bd. dirs. Friends of Ariz. Highways Mag., 1989-92; mem. Ariz. State Geographic and Historic Names Bd., 1994—. Served to lt. AUS, 1942-46; maj., 1966-70; col. Res. Recipient Ariz. Press Clubs exemplary gen. news coverage award, 1960, outstanding news reporting, 1961; Lloyd Clark Journalism scholarship named in honor U. Tex. at Arlington Alumni Assn., 1992. Mem. Am. Grad. Sch. Internat. Mgmt. Alumni Assn. (pres. Phoenix chpt. 1965), Ariz. Hist. Soc. (bd. dirs. cen. Ariz. chpt. 1992-93, state bd. dirs. 1993-95), Sharlot Hall Hist. Soc. (life), Res. Officers Assn. (life), Ex-Students Assn. No. Tex. Agrl. Coll. Arlington (pres. 1946-48), U. Tex. Arlington Alumni Assn. (life, bd. dir. 1994—, Disting. Alumni Svc. award 1997, Mil. Sci. Dept. Hall of Honor 1998), The Westerners (sheriff Phoenix Corral 1986-88), Sigma Delta Chi (pres. Valley of Sun chpt. 1964). Club: University (Phoenix). Author: Lloyd Clark's Scrapbook, Vol. 1, 1958, Vol. 2, 1960, Here's Looking at You, 1997, The Usual Suspects, 1998, You Must Remember This, 1999. Address: PO Box 1537 Surprise AZ 85378-1537

CLARK, LOYAL FRANCES, public affairs specialist; b. Salt Lake City, July 16, 1958; d. Lloyd Grant and Zina (Okelberry) C. Student, Utah State U., 1976-78. Human resource coord. U.S. Forest Svc., Provo, Utah, 1984—, fire info. officer, 1987—, pub. affairs officer, interpretive svcs. coord., edn. coord., 1988—; mem. Take Pride in Utah Task Force, Salt Lake City, 1989—; chairperson Utah Wildlife Ethics Com., Provo, 1989—. Instr. Emergency Svcs., Orem, Utah, 1990—. Recipient Presdl. award for outstanding leadership in youth conservation programs Pres. Ronald Reagan, 1985, Superior Svc. award USDA, 1987, Exemplary Svc. award U.S. Forest Svc., 1992, Nat. Eyes on Wildlife Achievement award USDA Forest Svc., 1993. Mem. Nat. Wildlife Fedn., Nat. Assn. Interpretation, Utah Soc. Environ. Educators, Utah Wildlife Fedn. (bd. dirs. 1981-85, v.p. 1985-87, Achievement award 1982, 86, 87), Utah Wilderness Assn., Am. Forestry Assn., Nature Conservancy, Women in Mgmt. Coun., Nat. Assn. Female Execs. Avocations: hiking, photography, gardening, antiques. Office: Uinta [illegible]

CLARK, MARY ELEANOR, retired biology educator; b. San Francisco, Apr. 28, 1927; d. Walter and Eleanor (Crafton) Lawrence; m. Robert B. Clark, July 19, 1957 (div. Dec. 1970). BA in Biochemistry, U. Calif., Berkeley, 1949, MA in Biology, 1951, PhD, 1960. Prof. zoology San Diego State U., 1969-89; Drucie French Cumbie chair conflict resolution Inst. Conflict Analysis and Resolution, George Mason U., Fairfax, Va., 1990-92; vis. prof. zoology Lund (Sweden) U., spring 1967; Laura C. Harris vis. prof. Denison U., Granville, Ohio, spring 1993; Vacca vis. prof. U. Montevallo, Ala., spring 1994. Author: (textbook introductory) Contemporary Biology, 1973, 2d edit., 1979, (book) Ariadne's Thread: Search..., 1989; author, editor: (book) Rethinking Curriculim, 1990. Mem. adv. com. Port of San Diego, 1970-72; mem. quality of life bd. City of San Diego, 1972-80. Named Nat. Prof. of Yr., Coun. Advancement and Support Edn., 1981, San Diego Woman of Yr., S.D. Pres.'s Coun., 1982; recipient Living Ethics award Campus YMCA, San Diego State U., 1986; fellow Inst. Human Ecology, 1994. Fellow AAAS (mem. nominating com. chair sect. G 1973-77, mem. biology and health sci. panel Project 2061 1985-89); mem. Am. Assn. State Colls. and Univs. (mem. nat. com. role of state colls. and univs. 1985-86), N.Y. Acad. Scis., Sigma Xi (San Diego chpt.), Phi Kappa Phi (San Diego chpt.), Phi Beta Kappa (San Diego chpt.). Avocations: writing books, community activism, piano, family. Home: 780 Girard Ct Cottage Grove OR 97424

CLARK, R. BRADBURY, lawyer; b. Des Moines, May 11, 1924; s. Rufus Bradbury and Gertrude Martha (Burns) C.; m. Polly Ann King, Sept. 6, 1949; children: Cynthia Clark Maxwell, Rufus Bradbury, John Atherton. BA, Harvard U., 1948, JD, 1951; diploma in law, Oxford U., Eng., 1952; D.H.L., Ch. Div. Sch. Pacific, San Francisco, 1983. Bar: Calif. 1952. Assoc. O'Melveny & Myers, L.A., 1952-62, sr. ptnr., 1961-93; mem. mgmt. com., 1983-90; of counsel O'Melveny & Myers LLP, L.A., 1993—; bd. dirs. Golden State Water Co., Econ. Resources Corp., Brown Internat. Corp., Automatic Machinery & Electronics Corp., John Tracy Clinic, also pres. 1982-88, Tracy Family Hearing Ctrs. Editor: California Corporation Laws, 6 vols, 1976—. Chancellor Prot. Episcopal Ch. in the Diocese of L.A., 1967—, hon. canon, 1983—. Capt. U.S. Army, 1943-46. Decorated Bronze Star with oak leaf cluster, Purple Heart with oak leaf cluster; Fulbright grantee, 1952. Mem. ABA, State Bar Calif. (chmn. drafting com. on gen. corp. law 1973-81, drafting com. on nonprofit corp. law 1980-84, mem. exec. com. bus. law sect. 1977-78, 84-87, sec. 1986-87, mem. com. nonprofit orgns. 1991—), L.A. County Bar Assn., Harvard Club, Chancery Club, Alamitos Bay Yacht Club (Long Beach, Calif.). Republican. Office: O'Melveny & Myers LLP 400 S Hope St Los Angeles CA 90071-2899

CLARK, RAYMOND OAKES, banker; b. Ft. Bragg, N.C., Nov. 9, 1944; s. Raymond Shelton and Nancy Lee (McCormick) C.; m. Patricia Taylor Slaughter; children: Matthew Patrick, Geoffry Charles. BBA, U. Ariz., 1966; postgrad., U. Wash., 1984-86. Mgmt. trainee First Interstate Bank, Phoenix, 1966, credit analyst, 1968-69, asst. br. mgr., Scottsdale, Ariz., 1969-72, asst. v.p., br. mgr., Tempe, Ariz., 1972-90, v.p. br. mgr. Scottsdale, 1990-92, v.p. mgr. main office Phoenix, 1992—. Pres., bd. dirs. Sun Devil Club, Tempe, 1975-98; bd. dirs. Valley Big Brothers/Big Sisters, 1994-98; pres. Tempe Diplomats, 1979-89; pres. Tempe Diablos, 1975—; major chmn. Fiesta Bowl, Tempe, 1975-79, mem. com., 1996—; bd. dirs. Maricopa County Bd. Mgrs., Phoenix, 1973, YMCA, Tempe, 1974, Tempe Design Rev. Bd., 1983-87. Named one of Outstanding Young Men of Am., 1978. Bd. dirs., treas. East Valley divsn. Am. Heart Assn., 1989-92. Served with U.S. Army, 1966-68. Mem. Tempe C. of C. (pres. 1979-80), Kiwanis (dist. lt. gov. 1972-87). Republican. Episcopalian.

CLARK, RICHARD WARD, trust company executive, consultant; b. N.Y.C., Oct. 23, 1938; s. Richard Leal and Dorothy Jane (Whittaker) C. BA with distinction, U. Rochester, N.Y., 1960; MBA in Fin., U. Pa., 1962. Corp. planning analyst Campbell Soup Co., Camden, N.J., 1965-67; asst. product mgr. Gen. Mills, Inc., Mpls., 1967-70; sr. fin. analyst McKesson Corp., San Francisco, 1970-71, asst. div. controller, 1971-72, div. controller, 1972-78, gen. mgr. grocery products devel., 1978-79; v.p., controller McKesson Foods Group/McKesson Corp., 1979-85, dir. strategic planning, 1985-87; v.p. fin., CFO, Provigo Corp., San Rafael, Calif., 1987-90; cons. on hotel devel., Napa Valley Assocs., S.A., San Francisco, 1990-92, health care cons., 1993-97; exec. trust dir. Park Trust, Ltd., San Francisco, 1998—; bd. dirs. Taylor Cuisine, Inc., San Francisco. Author: Some Factors Affecting Dividend Payout Ratios, 1962; musician (albums) Dick Clark at the Keyboard, I Love a Piano, 1990, I Play the Songs, 1993, On My Way to You, 1997. Adv. bd. Salvation Army, San Francisco, 1984—, chmn., 1993—; bd. dirs. Svcs. for Srs., San Francisco, 1990-93. Lt. (j.g.) USNR, 1962-64, PTO. Sherman fellow U. Rochester, 1960. Mem. Bohemian Club, Beta Gamma Sigma. Republican. Presbyterian. Avocations: piano, skiing, tennis, singing, jogging. Home: 2201 Sacramento St Apt 401 San Francisco CA 94115-2314

CLARK, ROGER WILLIAM, museum director, history educator; b. Phoenix, May 3, 1951; s. Lloyd Clayton and Ethyl Jean (Reeves) C.; m. Joëlle Genviève Noe, July 22, 1988; children: Jean-Philippe William, Janine Genvieve. BS, No. Ariz. U., 1973; M of Forestry, Yale U., 1976, PhD, 1978. Asst. prof. U. Calif., Berkeley, 1979-82; river guide ECHO: The Wilderness Co., Oakland, Calif., 1981-85; educator Resource Ctr. for Environ. Edn., Flagstaff, Ariz., 1983-89; sci. coord. Flagstaff Pub. Schs., 1989; v.p. Grand Canyon Trust, Flagstaff, 1990-94; dir. edn. Mus. No. Ariz., Flagstaff, 1994—; bd. dirs. Flagstaff Festival of Sci.; bd. dirs., v.p. Flagstaff Arts and Leadership Acad. Contbr. articles to profl. jours. Mem. Gov.'s Commn. on Environ. Edn., Phoenix, 1990-91; mem. pub. adv. commn. Grand Canyon Visibility Transport Commn., 1991-95. Recipient Ben C. Avery award Ariz. Clean and Green, 1995, Centennial Educator award No. Ariz. U., 1997. Mem. Mus. Assn. Ariz. Avocations: hiking, river rafting, gardening, reading. Office: Mus No Ariz 3101 N Fort Valley Rd Flagstaff AZ 86001-8348

CLARK, SCOTT H., lawyer; b. Logan, Utah, Jan. 7, 1946. BA with honors, U. Utah, 1970; JD, U. Chgo., 1973. Bar: Utah 1973. Ptnr. Ray, Quinney & Nebeker P.C., Salt Lake City, 1980—. Mem. ABA, Utah State Bar, Salt Lake County Bar Assn., Phi Beta Kappa, Phi Kappa Phi, Pi Sigma Alpha. Office: Ray Quinney & Nebek PC PO Box 45385 Salt Lake City UT 84145-0385*

CLARK, THOMAS P., JR., lawyer; b. N.Y.C., Sept. 16, 1943. AB, U. Notre Dame, 1965; JD, U. Mo., Kansas City, 1973. Bar: Calif. 1973. Ptnr. Stradling, Yocca, Carlson & Rauth P.C., Newport Beach, Calif., 1978—. Editor-in-chief The Urban Lawyer, 1972-73; contbr. articles to profl. jours. Capt. USMC, 1966-70. Mem. State Bar Calif., Orange County Bar Assn., Phi Kappa Phi, Bench and Robe. Office: Stradling Yocca Carlson & Rauth PC 660 Newport Center Dr Newport Beach CA 92660-6401*

CLARK, THOMAS RYAN, retired federal agency executive, business and technical consultant; b. Aberdeen, Wash., Sept. 16, 1925; s. George O. and Gladys (Ryan) C.; m. Barbara Ann Thiele, June 14, 1948; children: Thomas R. III, Kathleen Clark Sandberg, Christopher J.T. Student, U. Kans., 1943-44; BS, U.S. Mil. Acad., 1948; MSEE, Purdue U., 1955; cert., U.S. Army Command and Gen. Staff Coll., 1960, Harvard U., 1979. Commd. C.E., U.S. Army, 1948, advanced through grades to col., 1968; ret. U.S. Army, 1968; program mgr. U.S. AEC, Washington, 1968-75; dep. mgr. Dept. of Energy, Albuquerque, 1976-83; sr. exec. svc., 1977; mgr. Nev. ops. Dept. of Energy, Las Vegas, 1983-87, ret., 1987; cons. in field Las Vegas and Albuquerque, 1987—; mem. adv. bd. Dept. Chem. and Nuclear Engring., U. N.Mex., 1984—; mem. statewide adv. bd. Desert Research Inst., U. Nev., 1985-88. Editor, co-author: Nuclear Fuel Cycle, 1975. Trustee Nev. Devel. Authority, Las Vegas, 1984-88, Nat. Atomic Mus. Found., 1993—, pres., 1997—. Decorated Legion of Merit, Bronze Star; named Disting. Exec., Pres. of U.S., 1982. Mem. Las Vegas C. of C. (bd. dirs. 1983-87), Sigma Xi, Tau Beta Pi, Eta Kappa Nu, Rotary Club of Albuquerque (pres. 1993-94). Episcopalian. Lodge: Rotary.

CLARK, VIOLET CATHRINE, retired school administrator, volunteer; b. Mpls., Oct. 16, 1915; d. John Albert and Ellen Charlotte (Carlson) Lundgren; m. Robert Edward Clark, May 6, 1944 (div. June, 1954); children: Linda Cathrine [illegible] Cert. tchr., adminstr., Calif. Rsch. asst. horticulture U. Minn., Mpls., Duluth, 1942-44; elem. sch. tchr. Elsinore, Calif., 1945-48; elementary sch. tchr. Riverside (Calif.) Pub. Schs., 1953-58, prin., 1958-81; rschr. raspberries, MMMs Sponsor U. Minn., Duluth, 1942-44. Contbr. articles to newspapers and Hortculture jours., 1942-46. Vol. Ecumenical Ctr. Homeless Shelter and Meals, Oceanside, 1982—, Country Friends, Rancho Santa Fe, 1982—. Reading, Carlsbad, 1991-94, vote solicitor, Carlsbad, 1985-86. Recipient plaque Ecumenical Ctr., 1989, cert., 1995. Mem. Altrusa (com. chair 1943-83), Eastern Star, Alpha Delta Kappa (pres. 1947). Lutheran. Avocations: gardening, golf, volunteering, travel, photography. Home: 4740 Birchwood Cir Carlsbad CA 92008-3706

CLARK, WILLIAM ARTHUR V., geographer, demographer; b. Christchurch, N.Z., Mar. 21, 1938; came to U.S., 1961; s. Edward Arthur and Gertrude Rita (MacDonald) C.; m. Valmai Ruth Kirklam, July 1, 1961 (div. Oct. 1971); m. Irene Stephanee Borah, Mar. 25, 1978; children: Elisa, Louisa, Clifton, Justin. BA, U. N.Z., 1960; MA, U. Canterbury, N.Z., 1961; PhD, U. Ill., 1964; Doctorem Honoris Causa, U. Utrecht, The Netherlands, 1992; DSc, U. Auckland, N.Z., 1994. Lectr. U. Canterbury, 1964-66; asst./assoc. prof. U. Wis., Madison, 1966-70; prof. geography UCLA, 1970—, chmn. dept. geography, 1987-92, 95-97, assoc. dir. Inst. Social Sci. Rsch., 1984-87; vis. prof. U. Amsterdam, 1981; Belle Van Zuylen prof. U. Utrecht, 1989; cons. state atty. gens. Mo., Calif., Wis., Minn. Author: Human Migration, 1986, Households and Housing, 1996, The California Cauldron: Immigration and the Fortunes of Local Communities, 1998; author/editor: Residential Mobility and Public Policy, 1980, Rediscovering Geography: New Relevance for Science and Society, 1997. Fellow-in-residence Netherlands Inst. Advanced Studies, The Hague, 1993, Guggenheim fellow, 1994-95. Fellow Royal Soc. New Zealand (elected hon.); mem. Assn. Am. Geographers (Honors award 1986), Population Assn. Am. Anglican Ch. Achievements include research in district and appellate court rulings on demographic change and school desegregation. Avocations: skiing, scuba diving, sailing, music. Office: UCLA Dept Geography 405 Hilgard Ave Los Angeles CA 90095-9000

CLARKE, BENJAMIN KING, retired anethesiologist, state representative; b. Columbus, Ohio, Apr. 23, 1928; s. Benjamin King Clarke and Harriett Lucinda (Russ) Wilson; m. Mavis Moreen Hooper, July 7, 1956; 1 child, Benjamin Clarke III; 1 stepchild, Edgar Dumas. BS in Chemistry, U. Denver, 1950; MD, U. Colo., 1959. Diplomate Am. Bd. Anesthesiologists. Mem. staff Maimonides Hosp., Brooklyn, N.Y., 1962-64; chief Whitestone Queens, N.Y., 1964-66; mem. staff Harlem Hosp., N.Y.C., 1966-68, Roosevelt Hosp., N.Y.C., 1968-69, General Rose & Mercy Hosp., Denver, 1969-70; mem. staff Porter & Swedish Hosp., Denver, 1971-80, chief anesthesiologist, 1980-93, retired, 1993. Bd. dirs. Hue Man Experience Books, Denver, 1983-92, Youth Soc. Devel. Ctr., Denver; mem. Englewood (N.J.) Bd. Edn., 1968-69. With U.S. Army, 1950-52. Recipient Best Politician 1997 award Westword News, Denver. Mem. AMA, Am. Soc. Anesthesiologists, Colo. Medical Soc., Mile Hi Medical Soc. (pres. 1978-79). Democrat. Episcopalian. Avocations: tennis, travel.

CLARKE, GORDON, clergyman; b. Charleston, W.Va., Mar. 3, 1931; s. Leonard Gordon and Marguerite (Lyons) C.; m. Martha Thompson, Nov. 3, 1950; children: Daniel Gordon, David Allen. AB in Religion, Marion (Ind.) Coll., ThM; DD (hon.), C.T.S. Ordained to ministry Friends Ch. Dir. Creative Ministries, Indpls., 1959-69; regional exec. sec. Am. Bible Soc., Chgo., 1959-77; pastor Forsyth Friends Ch. Winston-Salem, N.C., 1977-79; sr. pastor Garden Grove (Calif.) Friends Ch., 1979—; chaplain Garden Grove Police Dept.; chmn. Bd. Spiritual Life Friends United Meeting, chmn. program meeting 1987, mem. meeting ministries commn.; mem. exec. com. bd. adminstrn. S.W. Yearly Meeting, chmn. spiritual life com.; pres. bd. trustees Calif. Friends Homes; founder Chaplain-on-Call. Mem. Spl. Task Force of Religious Well Being for White House Conf. on Aging; mem. Gov.'s Commn. on Aging, Gov.'s Commn. on Tourism, Gov.'s Com. on Migrant Labor. Sgt. USAF. Mem. Coll. Chaplains Am. Protestant Hosp. Assn., Correctional Chaplains Assn., Internat. Platform Assn., Nat. Assn. Religious Broadcasters, Leisure Fellowship Ministry. Home: 102 Woods Mill Rd Goldsboro NC 27534-9122 Office: Garden Grove Friends Ch 12211 Magnolia St Garden Grove CA 92841-3318

CLARKE, LEO CREUSOT, retired meteorologist; b. Concordia, Kans., Jan. 9, 1920; s. Charles Clarke and Gabrielle (Creusot) Prime; m. Vivian, May 11, 1946 (dec. Aug. 1995); children: Julie, Anne, Jacqueline, Elizabeth, Leo, Vivian, Patricia. BS, U. Miami, 1941; MS, USN Postgrad. Sch., Monterey, Calif., 1962. Comdr. USN, 1942-62; meteorologist, head models dept. Fleet Numerical METOC Ctr., Monterey, 1962-97, cons., 1997—. Fellow Am. Meteorol. Soc. (Charles L. Mitchell award 1987). Home: 26548 Fisher Dr Carmel CA 93923-9017

CLARKE, RICHARD ALAN, electric and gas utility company executive, lawyer; b. San Francisco, May 18, 1930; s. Chauncey Frederick and Carolyn (Shannon) C.; m. Mary Dell Fisher, Feb. 5, 1955; children: Suzanne, Nancy C. Stephen, Douglas Alan. AB Polit. Sci. cum laude, U. Calif., Berkeley, 1952, JD, 1955. Bar: Calif. 1955. V.p., asst. to chmn. Pacific Gas and Electric Co., San Francisco, 1979-82, exec. v.p., gen. mgr. utility ops., 1982-85, pres., 1985-86, chmn. bd., CEO, 1986-94, chmn. bd., 1994-95; ptnr. Rockwell, Fulkerson and Clarke, San Rafael, Calif., 1960-69; bd. dirs. Pacific Gas & Electric Co., Potlach Corp., CNF TransInc.; mem. Bus. Coun. Pres.' Coun. on Sustainable Devel. Bd. dirs., past chmn. Bay Area Coun.; trustee Boalt Hall Trust, Sch. Law U. Calif., Berkeley; mem. adv. bd. Walter A. Haas Sch. Bus., U. Calif., Berkeley; chmn. adv. bd. Ctr. for Orgnl. and Human Resource Effectiveness, U. Calif., Berkeley;bd. dirs. Nature Conservancy of Calif.; co-chair U. Calif. Regents Outreach Task Force. Mem. Calif. C. of C. (past dir.), San Francisco C. of C. (past dir., v.p. econ. devel.), Edison Elect. Inst. Office: Pacific Gas & Electric Co H17F 123 Mission St San Francisco CA 94105-1551

CLARKE, ROBERT F., utilities company executive; b. Oakland, Calif.. BA, U. Calif., Berkeley, 1965, MBA, 1966. Pres., CEO Hawaiian Electric, 1991—. Office: Hawaiian Electric Industries Inc 900 Richards St Honolulu HI 96813-2919*

CLARKE, ROBERT FRANCIS, nuclear physicist, consultant; b. Mpls., Mar. 20, 1915; s. Charles Patrick and Maurine Elizabeth (Clark) C.; m. Charlotte Adele Radwill, July 24, 1966; children: Robert, Carol, David. BS with honors, U. Fla., 1948; MS, U. Ariz., 1971. Merchant marine, 1938-40; meteorologist, U.S. Weather Bur., 1940-42, 48-50, 52-55; supervisory electronics engr., chief navigation br. aviation dept. U.S. Army Electronics Proving Ground, 1956-58, nuclear physicist, chief scientist nuclear surveillance div., 1958-62; aerospace engr. NASA, Lewis Rsch. Ctr., 1962-66; physicist Hughes Aircraft Co., 1966-68; instr. Math. Pima Community Coll., 1969-74, and San Juan campus N.Mex. State U., 1974-75; instr. math. Am. Internat. Sch., Kabul, Afghanistan, 1976-78; dep. sheriff Cochise County, Ariz., 1960-61; Radiol. def. officer Fed. Emergency Mgmt. Agy.; dir. aerospace edn. CAP, Ariz., 1972-76. Trustee Rep. Presdl. Task Force; del. Pres. Kennedy's Inauguration, 1961; mem. Republican Presdl. Adv. Coun., at-large del. planning com.; mem. mayor's com. Celebration of Bicentennial of Constn., 1987; mem. Gov.'s Alliance Against Drug Abuse, Ariz., 1989—; life mem. Rep. Nat. Com., Rep. Presidential Task Force; rep. Retiree Activities Office, Davis-Monthan AFB, to Tucson Mayor and City Coun., 1994—. Served with U.S. Army, 1942-46, USAF, 1950-52; col. Res. ret. Recipient nat. award for best articles in Officer Rev.; honor cert. for excellence in published works Freedoms Found. of Valley Forge, Presdl. Medal of Merit.; nat. Sci. Found. Grad. scholar. Mem. AAUP, IEEE (sr. mem. emeritus plasma physics and computer sects.), AIAA; mem. Am. Nuclear Soc. (emeritus, fusion power and reactor physics sect.), Space Studies Inst., Fusion Power Assocs., Soc. Photo-Optical Instrumentation Engrs., Am. Merchant Marine Vets., Am. Meteorol. Soc., Am. Optical Soc., Soc. Unmanned Vehicle Systems, Arctic Inst. N.Am., Assn. Former Intelligence Officer, Am. Def. Preparedness Assn., Scientists and Engrs. for Secure Energy, N.Y. Acad. Scis., Ariz.-Nev. Acad. Scis., Navy League, Am. Legion, VFW (Dept. Ariz. POW-MIA officer and state patriotic instr. 1984-85, pres. 1986, honor degree), AMVETS, Ret. Officers Assn. (pres. Tucson chpt. [illegible] Assn., Mil. Order World Wars (chpt. commdr. 1987-88), Korean War Vets. Assn., U.S. Navy Meml. (charter, nat. adv. coun.), Nat. Security Com., Am. Security Council, City of Tucson's Vets. Affairs (com. chmn. 1986), Inst. Polit. Sci., Republican Presdl. Legion of Merit. Club: Army and Navy. Lodges: Odd Fellows, Elks. Contbr. articles in aerospace and nat. def. to

mags., jours. Avocation: mountain climbing. Home: 5846 E South Wilshire Dr Tucson AZ 85711-4540

CLARKE, URANA, writer, musician, educator; b. Wickliffe-on-the-Lake, Ohio, Sept. 8, 1902; d. Graham Warren and Grace Urana (Olsaver) C.; artists and tchrs. diploma Mannes Music Sch., N.Y.C., 1925; cert. Dalcroze Sch. Music, N.Y.C., 1950; student Pembroke Coll., Brown U.; BS, Mont. State U., 1967, M of Applied Sci., 1970. Mem. faculty Mannes Music Sch., 1922-49, Dalcroze Sch. Music, 1949-54; adv. editor in music The Book of Knowledge, 1949-65; v.p., dir. Saugatuck Circle Housing Devel.; guest lectr. Hayden Planetarium, 1945; guest lectr., bd. dirs. Roger Williams Park Planetarium, Providence; radio show New Eng. Skies, Providence, 1961-64, Skies Over the Big Sky Country, Livingston, Mont., 1964-79, Birds of the Big Sky Country, 1972-79, Great Music of Religion, 1974-79; mem. adv. com. Nat. Rivers and Harbors Congress, 1947-58; instr. continuing edn. Mont. State U. Chmn. Park County chpt. ARC, 1967-92, chmn. emeritus 1992—, co-chmn. county blood program, first aid instr. trainer, 1941-93; instr. ARC cardio-pulmonary resuscitation, 1976-84; mem. Mont. Commn. Nursing and Nursing Edn., 1974-76; mem. Park County Local Govt. Study Com., 1974-76, chmn., 1984-86, vice-chair, 94-96. Mem. Am. Acad. Polit. Sci., Am. Musicol. Soc., Royal Astron. Soc. Can., Inst. Nav., Maria Mitchell Soc. Nantucket, N.Am. Yacht Racing Union, AAAS, Meteoritical Soc., Internat. Soc. Mus. Research, Skyscrapers (sec.-treas. 1960-63), Am. Guild Organists, Park County Wilderness Assn. (treas.), Trout Unlimited, Nature Conservancy, Big Sky Astron. Soc. (dir. 1965—), Sierra Club. Lutheran. Club: Cedar Point Yacht. Author: The Heavens are Telling (astronomy), 1951; Skies Over the Big Sky Country, 1965; also astron. news-letter, View It Yourself, weekly column Big Skies, 1981-98; contbr. to mags. on music, nav. and astronomy. Pub. Five Chorale Preludes for Organ, 1975; also elem. two-piano pieces. Inventor, builder of Clarke Adjustable Piano Stool. Address: Log-A-Rhythm 9th St Island Livingston MT 59047

CLARK-JOHNSON, SUSAN, publishing executive. Pres., pub. Reno Gazette-Jour., 1985—; sr. group pres. Pacific Newspaper Group, Gannett, 1985—; bd. dirs. Harrah's Entertainment, Inc.; bd. visitors John S. Knight Fellowships for Profl. Journalists, Stanford U. Office: Gannett Co Inc Box 22000 955 Kuenzli St Reno NV 89502-1160*

CLARKSON, LAWRENCE WILLIAM, airplane company executive; b. Grove City, Pa., Apr. 29, 1938; s. Harold William and Jean Henrietta (Jaxtheimer) C.; m. Barbara Louise Stevenson, Aug. 20, 1960; children: Michael, Elizabeth, Jennifer. BA, DePauw U., 1960; JD, U. Fla., 1962. Counsel Pratt & Whitney, West Palm Beach, Fla., 1967-72, program dep. dir., 1972-75, program mgr., 1974-75; v.p., mng. dir. Pratt & Whitney, Brussels, Belgium, 1975-78; v.p. mktg. Pratt & Whitney, West Palm Beach, 1978-80; v.p. contracts Pratt & Whitney, Hartford, Conn., 1980-82, pres. comml. products div., 1982-87; sr. v.p. Boeing Comml. Airplanes Group, Seattle, 1988-91; corp. v.p. planning and internat. devel. Boeing Co., Seattle, 1992-93, sr. v.p., 1994-97; pres. Boeing Enterprises, Seattle, 1997—; dir. Partnership for Improved Air Travel, Washington, 1988-91. Trustee DePauw U., Greencastle, Ind., 1987—; overseer Tuck Sch. Dartmouth, Hanover, N.H., 1993—; corp. coun. Interlochen (Mich.) Ctr. for Arts, 1987, trustee, 1988—, chmn., 1996—; trustee Seattle Opera, 1990—, chmn., 1991—; pres. Japan-Am. Soc., Wash., 1993, pres. Wash. State China Rels. com., 1992-93; chmn. Nat. Bur. of Asia Rsch., Coun. Fgn. Rels.; chmn. U.S. Pacific Econ. Corp. Coun., 1993—. Mem. Nat. Assn. Mfrs. (bd. dirs.), N.Y. Yacht Club, Seattle Yacht Club, Met. Opera Club, Wings Club (bd. govs. 1987-91, Order of St. John (commdr. 1994—), Met. Club D.C., Am. Inst. Contemporary German Studies (bd. dirs.). Episcopalian. Home: 13912 NE 31st Pl Bellevue WA 98005-1881 Office: The Boeing Co MS 7R-81 PO Box 3707 Seattle WA 98124-2207

CLARKSON, RICHARD CLAIR, publisher, editor, photographer; b. Aug. 11, 1932; s. Maurice Wolford and Mary Meta (Murphy) C. BS in Journalism, U. Kansas, 1956. Dir. photography Topeka (Kans.) Capital-Jour., 1958-79; asst. mng. editor/graphics The Denver Post, 1980-84; dir. photography, sr. asst. editor Nat. Geographic Soc., Washington, 1985-87; prin. Rich Clarkson and Assocs., LLC, Denver, 1987—; organizer, producer ann. workshops in sports photography with U.S. Olympic Com., and editorial and wildlife photography in Jackson Hole, Wyo; past lectr. adj. faculty U. Kansas Sch. of Journalism; lectr. at Mo. and Maine photographic workshops and at the Internat. Ctr. of Photography, N.Y.C.; juror Pulitzer prize in photography, 1986-87; judge and advisor Sasakawa Sports Found. and Competition, Tokyo. Co-author: (books) (with Cordner Nelson) The Jim Ryun Story, 1967, (with Bill Bruns), Sooner, 1972, Montreal 76, 1976, (with Bob Hammel) Knight with the Hoosiers, 1975, Silver Knight, 1996, (with Billy Reed) The Final Four, 1988; compiling editor The Kansas Century: 100 Years of Jayhawk Basketball, 1997; dir. of photography (book) A Day in the Life of America, 1986; producer-coord. (Brian Lanker project) I Dream a World: Portraits of Black Women Who Changed America, 1989; compiling editor World Champion Broncos, 1998. Trustee William Allen White Found., U. Kans; mem. hon. adv. coun. Nat. Mus. Wildlife Art, Jackson, Wyo., exec. com. W. Eugene Smith Meml. Fund, chmn. grant jury, 1995; founding officer Nat. Press Photographers Found. Named 1 of 50 most influential individuals in Am. photography, Am. Photo Mag., 1988. Mem. Nat. Press Photographers' Assn. (pres. 1975-76, past chmn. edn. com., twice chmn. Picture of Yr. jury). Office: Rich Clarkson & Assocs Denver Place Plaza Tower 1099 18th St Ste 1840 Denver CO 80202-1918

CLARREN, STERLING KEITH, pediatrician; b. Mpls., Mar. 12, 1947; s. David Bernard and Lila (Reifel) C.; m. Sandra Gayle Bernstein, June 8, 1970; children: Rebecca Pia, Jonathan Seth. BA, Yale U., 1969; MD, U. Minn., 1973. Pediatric intern U. Wash. Sch. Medicine, Seattle, 1973-74, resident in pediatrics, 1974-77, asst. prof. dept. pediatrics, 1979-83, assoc. prof., 1983-88, prof., 1988, Robert A. Aldrich chair in pediatrics, 1989—; head divsn. congenital defects U. Wash. Sch. Medicine, 1987-95; dir. dept. congenital defects Children's Hosp. and Med. Ctr., Seattle, 1987-96, dir. fetal alcohol syndrome clinic Child Devel. and Mental Retardation Ctr. U. Wash., 1992—, dir. Fetal Alcohol Syndrome Network, 1995—; dir. infant inpatient svcs. Children's Hosp. & Med. Ctr., Seattle, 1996—. Contbr. articles to profl. jours.; patentee for orthosis to alter cranial shape. Cons. pediatrician Maxillofacial Rev. Bd., State of Wash., Seattle, 1984—, chmn. Health-Birth Defects Adv. Com., Olympia, 1980—; mem. gov.'s task force on FAS State of Wash., 1994-95; mem. fetal alcohol adv. com. Children's Trust Found., Seattle, 1988—; mem. adv. bd. Nat. Orgn. on Fetal Alcohol Syndrome; mem. fetal alcohol com. Inst. Medicine, NAS, 1994-95. Rsch. grantee Nat. Inst. Alcohol Abuse & Alcoholism, 1982—, Ctrs. for Disease Control, 1992—. Fellow AAAS; mem. Am. Acad. Pediatrics, Soc. for Pediatric Rsch., Teratology Soc., Rsch. Soc. on Alcoholism (pres. fetal alcohol study group 1993), Am. Cleft Palate Assn., N.Y. Acad. Scis. Avocations: cross-country skiing, fishing, hiking, sailing. Home: 8515 Paisley Dr NE Seattle WA 98115-3944 Office: Children's Hosp and Med Ctr Divsn Congenital Defects PO Box C-5371 Seattle WA 98105

CLARY, WILLIAM VICTOR, minister; b. Baraboo, Wis., May 27, 1946; s. Harry Theone and Ruth Margaret (Harris) C.; m. F. Marie Bush, Aug. 12, 1966; children: Donna, Vicki, William. AA, Rochester Coll., 1966; BA, Okla. Christian U., 1968; postgrad., Abilene Christian U., 1972, No. Ill. U., 1973. Ordained to ministry Ch. of Christ, 1966. Min. Clinton, Ill., 1974-78, Lincoln, Ill., 1978-84, Anchorage, 1984—. v.p. Ill. Christian Camp, Decatur, 1978-84, dir., 1976-84; dir. Ill. Ch. of Christ Exhibit, Springfield, Ill., 1977-84; chaplain Abraham Lincoln Hosp., Lincoln, 1978-84, Logan County Jail, Lincoln, 1983-84; host-parent Am. Field Svcs., 1988-90, 92-94, chpt. pres., 1988-92. Republican. Avocations: reading, athletics, fishing, photography, traveling. Home: 1031 W 73rd Ave Anchorage AK 99518-2139 Office: 7800 Stanley Dr Anchorage AK 99518-2645

CLAUSEL, NANCY KAREN, minister; b. Jackson, Tenn., Jan. 1, 1948; s. Clinton Prentice and Martha Juanita (Felker) C.; children: Richard D. Harwood Jr., Kara Harwood Fricke. Student Lambuth Coll., 1966-67, George Peabody Coll. for Tchrs.; BSE, Memphis State U., 1971; MDiv summa cum laude, Memphis Theol. Sem., 1980. Ordained to ministry United Meth.; cert. counselor Tenn. Ch. Dir. Christian edn. Grimes United Meth. Ch., Memphis, 1977-79, Wesleyan Hills United Meth. Ch., Memphis, 1979-80; assoc. minister St. James United Meth. Ch., Memphis, 1981-82; dir. Wesley Pastoral Counseling Ctr., Memphis, 1982-85; co-dir. Connection: Holistic Counseling Ctr., Memphis, 1985-87; co-founder, co-min. The Connection Ch., 1986-87; founder, min., Ch. in the Round; chaplain Addiction Recovery Sys., 1993-95; pastor Stevenson United Meth. Ch., 1995-98; pastor Montesano (Wash.) United Meth. Ch., 1998—; bd. dirs. Wesley Found.-Memphis State, 1979-80, 82-84; vice chmn. commn. on status and role of women Memphis Ann. Conf., 1980-86; mem. work area on worship McKendree Dist. Memphis Ann. Conf., 1980-84; mem. Bd. Pensions Memphis Ann. Conf., 1983-84; supervising pastor Candidacy for Min. program Memphis Ann. Conf., 1984-86. Vol. Johnson Aux. City of Memphis Hosp., 1975; sec. Peacemakers Memphis, 1979; clergy rep. adv. bd. Memphis chpt. Parents Without Ptnrs., 1984-85; mem. Network, Memphis, 1984-87; chmn. Pacific N.W. ann. conf. UMC Episcopal Task Force on Children and Poverty; chmn. bd. discipleship sect. on worship and spirituality PNWAC; bd. dirs. Greater Columbia Regional Adv. Network. Mem. Internat. Transactional Analysis Assn. (clin. mem. 1981—, provisional teaching mem. 1982—), Assn. for Specialists in Group Work, Memphis Mins. Assn. (treas. 1985-86), Altrusa Internat., Skamania County Ministers Assn. (pres.), Pacific N.W. Conf. Coun. Ministry, Phi Kappa Phi. Columnist: The Light (newspaper). Avocations: hiking, music. Home: 415 Spruce Ave East Montesano WA 98563

CLAUSEN, BARBARA ANN, coatings company executive; b. Portland, Oreg., Mar. 20, 1945; d. John Wesley and Marion Josephine (Hill) Clausen; children: Shamaz, Hukam, Mardana. BA, Lindenwood Coll. for Women, 1968; MA, Portland State U., 1972. Owner Shamaz Trading Co., Ukiah, Calif., 1974-77; mgr. small bus. dept. Ernst & Ernst, Portland, 1977-78; CFO All Heart Lumber Co., Ukiah, 1978-83; CFO, CEO Performance Coatings Inc., Ukiah, 1983—, chmn. bd. dirs., 1992—; chmn. bd. dirs. Rural Visions; treas. chmn. fin. com. Mendocino County Health Clinic; CEO, chmn. bd. dirs. Dusky Rose & Assoc., Botanics of Calif. Founder, chair Penofin Jazz Festival; chmn. bd. dirs. Mendocine Ballet Co. Mem. Nat. Paint and Coatings Assn., Golden State Paint and Coatings Assn., Ukiah C. of C. (mem. econ. devel. com. 1993-94), Women in Coatings (Leadership award 1994), Leadership Mendocino. Avocations: horseback riding, reading, children, bass guitar, dancing. E-mail: ceo@penofin.com. Office: Performance Coatings Inc PO Box 1569 Ukiah CA 95482-1569

CLAUSEN, BRET MARK, industrial hygienist, safety professional; b. Hayward, Calif., Aug. 1, 1958; s. Norman E. and Barbara Ann (Wagner) C.; m. Cheryl Elaine Carlson, May 24, 1980; children: Kathrine, Eric, Emily. BS, Colo. State U., 1980, MS, 1983. Cert. indsl. hygienist, safety profl., hazard control mgr., hazardous materials mgr.; cert. in comprehensive practice Am. Bd. Inds. Hygiene; cert. in comprehensive practice and mgmt. aspects Bd. Cert. Safety Profls. Assoc. risk mgmt., indsl. hygienist, safety rep. Samsonite Corp., Denver, 1980-83, mgr. loss prevention, 1984-88; health, safety and environment rep. Storage Tech., Longmont, Colo., 1984; sr. project cons. Occusafe Inc., Denver, 1988; numerous indsl. hygiene and safety mgmt./tech. assignments Rocky Flats Environ. Tech. Site, Golden, Colo., 1988—; mem. radiol. assistance program team U.S. Dept. Energy, Region VI, 1994—. Local emergency planning com. Weld County, Colo., 1996—. Mem. Am. Indsl. Hygiene Assn. (pres. Rocky Mountain sect. 1988-89), Am. Soc. Safety Engrs. (prof., acad. acreditation com. site evaluator 1998—, profl. and ednl. stds. com. 1998—), Inst. Hazardous Materials Mgmt. (cert. sr. level), Ins. Inst. Am. (assoc. in risk mgmt.), Am. Nat. Stds. Inst. (com. on confined spaces 1993—), Am. Acad. Indsl. Hygiene (diplomate, acad. accreditation com. site evaluator 1994—). Republican. Lutheran. Avocations: hunting, backpacking, snowshoeing. Home: 16794 Weld County Rd # 44 La Salle CO 80645 Office: Safe Sites of Colo PO Box 464 Mail Stop T452A Golden CO 80402-0464

CLAUSON, GARY LEWIS, chemist; b. Peoria, Ill., Feb. 25, 1952; s. Cecil Lewis and Virgie Grace (Shryock) C. AAS, Ill. Cen. Coll., East Peoria, 1974; BA in Chemistry, U. Calif., San Diego, 1977; MS in Chem., Bradley U., Peoria, 1981; PhD in Organic Chemistry, U. Ill., 1987. Engring. technician U.S. Naval Sta., San Diego, 1974-75; lab. analyst Lehn & Fink Products Co., Lincoln, Ill., 1978-79; part-time faculty Bradley U., Peoria, 1980-81; sci. asst. Ill. State Geol. Survey, Urbana, 1986-87; sr. chemist Ciba-Geigy Corp., McIntosh, Ala., 1987-92; rsch. scientist Gensia, Inc., San Diego, 1992-95, cons., 1995-96; prin. scientist Alliance Pharm. Corp., San Diego, 1996—. Mem. Am. Chem. Soc., Assn. Ofcl. Analytical Chemists. Avocations: paleontology, tennis, basketball, softball, bicycling. Home: 3277 Berger Ave Apt 20 San Diego CA 92123-1933

CLAUSSEN, BONNIE ADDISON, II, aerospace company executive; b. Pueblo, Colo., Jan. 11, 1942; s. Bonnie A. I and Gertrude A. (Poe) C.; m. Charlotte J. Dipert, July 11, 1961; children: Christopher Addison, Raymond Dale. BS in Math., U. So. Colo., 1967; postgrad., Pa. State U., King of Prussia, 1968-69. Programmer Gen. Electric Corp., King of Prussia, 1967-69, sr. programmer, 1969-71; project mgr. Martin Marietta Aerospace Co., Denver, 1971-79; co-founder, exec. v.p. CTA, Inc., Englewood, Colo., 1979-97, co-founder, pres. SymSystems, LLC, Englewood, Colo., 1995-98. Designer: (software) Real-Time Flight, 1967-78, Viking Mars Lander Flight, 1975; contbr: Real-Time Simulation Publs., 1975-78. With USAF, 1962-65. Recipient Pub. Service medal Nat. Aeronautics and Space Adminstrn., 1976. Republican. Fax: (303) 858-4004. E-mail: ba@symsystems.com. Office: SymSystems LLC 12508 E Briarwood Ave Englewood CO 80112-6764

CLAY, SEAN COCHRANE, software development company executive; b. Oklahoma City, May 4, 1956; s. Robert Almonton and Maxine (Jackson) C.; m. Sharon Barlow, Jul. 14, 1984; children: Colby, Erin. AA, Saddleback C.C., 1977; student, Calif. State U., Fullerton, 1978, Riverside C.C., 1991. Programmer, software engr. Mai/Basic Four, Tustin, Calif., 1979-88; owner Clayco, Yucca Valley, Calif., 1988—; ptnr. Desert Gold, Yucca Valley, Calif.; cons. Priority Computer Sys., Irvine, Calif., 1988—, Venus Raches, Indio, Calif., 1991—. Author (software) Custom Password Utility, 1990, Bookstore Management Sys., 1994; inventor dynamic wheel balancer. Recipient Cert. of Appreciation Toastmasters Internat., 1983, Area Contest Highest Honors, 1982. Mem. Hi Desert Aero Barons, Yucca Mesa Improvement Assn., Channel Bandits, Yucca Mesa Adv. Coun., Masonic Lodge. Avocations: aircraft, hiking, fishing, classic cars. Office: Clayco 2572 Yucca Mesa Rd Yucca Valley CA 92284-9272

CLAYTON, WAYNE CHARLES, protective services official, educator; b. Topeka, Kansas, Dec. 16, 1932; s. Alford Henry and Anna Ellen (Lynch) C.; m. Donna Marie Corrigan, March 3, 1962; Mark Wayne, Leslie Marie. AA in Liberal Arts, Mt. San Antonio Coll., 1959; BS, Calif. State U., L.A., 1968, cert. tchr., Calif. From reserve police officer to dep. chief El Monte Police Dept., 1957-1978, chief, 1978—; mem. session FBINA, 1980. With U.S. Navy, 1952-56. Recipient Golden Apple award West San Gabriel Valley Adminstrs. Assn., 1982, Spl. Medallion award Boys Club Am., 1982, Disting. Svc. award Dept. Youth Authority, 1983, Outstanding Svc. award C. of C. 1983, Spl. Appreciation award El Monte Police Officers Assn., 1985, Calif. Police Chief Officer of the Yr. award Internat. Union Police Assns. AFL-CIO, 1986, Exec. of Yr. award Exec. Mag., 1986, Dr. Byron E. Thompson Disting. Scouter award El Monte Explorer Post # 522, 1988, Appreciation award, 1992, Outstanding Svc. award Internat. Footprint Assn., 1991, award for continuing concern and dedication to the well being of Officers of El Monte Police Dept. Calif. Orgn. of Police and Sheriffs, 1991, Police Chief of the Yr. Perpetual award First Annual Shriners Club, 1994, C. of C. Citizen of Yr., 1994, Coord. Coun. Lifetime Achievement award, 1995. Mem. FBI Nat. Acad. Assocs., L.A. County Police Chiefs Assn., San Gabriel Valley Police Chiefs Assn., San Gabriel Valley Peace Officers Assn. (past pres.), Boys and Girls Club of San Gabriel Valley (v.p.), Civitan of El Monte (internat., charter pres. 1973). Democrat. Roman Catholic. Avocations: fishing, water skiing, reading. Office: Police Dept Box 6008 11333 Valley Blvd El Monte CA 91731-3210*

CLEARY, SHIRLEY JEAN, artist, illustrator; b. St. Louis, Nov. 14, 1942; d. Frank and Crystal (Maret) C.; m. (Leo) Frank Cooper, June 18, 1982; stepchildren: Clay Cooper, Alicia Cooper, Curt Cooper. BFA, Wash. U., St. Louis, 1964; MFA, Temple U., Phila., Rome, 1968; postgrad., The Corcoran, Washington, 1967-71. adv. coun. Mont. Trout Unlimited. Prin. works include illustrations in mags. Flyfishing Quar., Fly Fishers Mag., Flyfishing News, Mont. Outdoors, Flyfisherman, Flyfishing Heritage; contbr. articles to profl. jours.; exhibited in group shows at Mo. Hist. Soc., St. Louis, 1987, Wild Wings, Mpls., 1985-98, Settlers West Galleries, Tucson, 1984, 96-99, Tucson Mus. Art, 1995-96; one-woman shows include Am. Mus. Fly Fishing, Manchester, Vt., 1997; artist 1990 Oreg. Trout Stamp (Artist of Yr. award 1992, Assn. N.W. Steelheaders print winner 1992). Bd. dirs. Mont. State Arts Coun., Mont., 1973-81, Helena Civic Ctr., Mont., 1983-89; active leadership Helena, 1985. Apprenticeship grantee Western Starts Art Found., Artist in Residence, River Meadow, Jackson, Wyo, 1989-94, 97, Herning Hojskole, Herning, Denmark, 1981, Wyo. Artist in the Schools, Sheridan, Wyo., 1977; named Arts for Parks Top 100 Artist, 1989, 94, 97, 98, 99, Jackson One Fly Artist of Yr., 1990-92. Mem. Miniature Art Soc. of N.J., Mont. Assn. Female Execs., Trout Unlimited (adv. bd. Mont. chpt.), Coll. Art Assn. Democrat. Avocations: flyfishing, travel. Home: 1804 Beltview Dr Helena MT 59601-5801

CLEARY, WILLIAM JOSEPH, JR., lawyer; b. Wilmington, N.C., Aug. 14, 1942; s. William Joseph and Eileen Ada (Gannon) C.; AB in History, St. Joseph's U., 1964; JD, Villanova U., 1967. Bar: N.J. 1967, U.S. Ct. Appeals (3d cir.) 1969, Calif. 1982, U.S. Ct. Appeals (9th cir.) 1983, U.S. Dist. Ct. (ctrl. dist.) Calif. 1983, U.S. Supreme Ct., 1992. Law sec. to judge N.J. Superior Ct. Jersey City, 1967-68; assoc. Lamb, Blake, H&D, Jersey City, 1968-72; dep. pub. defender State of N.J., Newark, 1972-73; 1st asst. city corp. counsel, Jersey City, 1973-76; assoc. Robert Wasserwald, Inc., Hollywood, Calif., 1984-86, 88-89, Gould & Burke, L.A., 1986-87; pvt. practice, 1989—. Mem. ABA, FBA, N.J. State Bar, Calif. Bar Assn., L.A. County Bar, Alpha Sigma Nu, Nat. Jesuit Honor Soc. Democrat. Roman Catholic. Office: 1853 1/2 Canyon Dr Los Angeles CA 90028-5607

CLECAK, DVERA VIVIAN BOZMAN, psychotherapist; b. Denver, Jan. 15, 1944; d. Joseph Shalom and Annette Rose (Dveirin) Bozman; m. Pete Emmett Clecak, Feb. 26, 1966 (div. 1993); children: Aimée, Lisa; m. John Pricz, Sept. 12, 1998. BA, Stanford U., 1965; postgrad., U. Chgo., 1965; MSW, UCLA, 1969. Lic. clin. social worker, Calif.; lic. marriage, family and child counselor, Calif. Social work supr. Harbor City (Calif.) Parent Child Ctr., 1969-71; therapist Orange County Mental Health Dept., Laguna Beach, Calif., 1971-75, area coordinator, 1975-79; pvt. practice psychotherapy Mission Viejo, Calif., 1979—; founder, exec. dir. Human Options, Laguna Beach, 1981—; mem, co-chmn. domestic violence com. Orange County Commn. on Status of Women, 1979-81; mem. mental health adv. com. extension U. Calif., Irvine, 1983, counseling psychologist, 1980, lectr., 1984-85; lectr. Saddleback Community Coll., Mission Viejo, 1981-82, Chapman Coll., Orange, 1979; field instr. UCLA, 1970-71, 77-78. Co-chair Nat. Philanthropy Day, Orange County, 1996. Recipient Women Helping Women award Saddleback C.C., 1987, Cert. for child abuse prevention Commendation State of Calif. Dept. Social Svcs., 1988, Comty. Svc. award Irvine Valley Coll. Found., 1989, Disting. Svc. award in field of domestic violence Nicole Brown Simpson Found., 1996, Amelia Earhart award for svc. to women Women's Opportunity Ctr., U. Calif.-Irvine, 1997, Lee Steelman award South Orange County Cmty. Svcs., 1998; named Orange County Non-profit Exec. of Yr., 1994, Humanitarian of Yr., Alexis de Tocqueville Soc., 1997, Woman of Distinction, Laguna Beach Soroptimists, 1998, Desert Dist. Soroptimists, 1998. Mem. NASW, Calif. Marriage Family and Child Counselors' Assn., Phi Beta Kappa.

CLEMENS, CHARLES JOSEPH, insurance agent; b. Phila., Mar. 1, 1942; s. Charles Wesley and Jane Elizabeth (Nesselhauf) C.; m. Keiko Kobayashi, Aug. 12, 1965 (div. 1994); 1 child, Charles S. BA, Calif. State U., Fullerton, 1970; MBA, U. So. Calif., 1972. CLU. Asst. mgr. ins. N.Y. Life Ins. Co., Anaheim, Calif., 1971-74; ins. agt. Santa Ana, Calif., 1974-77; brokerage mgr. Alliance Ins. Co., Santa Ana, 1977-79; regional mgr. CIGNA, Orange, Calif., 1979-87; ins. agt. Garden Grove, Calif., 1987-93; ins. agt., broker Anaheim, 1993—. Major USAF-ANG, 1961—. Mem. NALU (pres. 1976, 80, Nat. Quality award). Republican. Avocations: jogging, biking, auto restoration.

CLEMENT, BETTY WAIDLICH, literacy educator, consultant; b. Honolulu, Aug. 1, 1937; d. William G. Waidlich and Audrey Antoinette (Roberson) Malone; m. Tom Morris, Jan. 16, 1982; 1 child, Karen A. Bratesani. BA in Elem. Edn., Sacramento State U., 1960; MA in Elem. Reading, U. No. Colo., 1973, MA in Adminstrn., EdD in Edn. & Reading, 1980. Elem. sch. tchr. pub schs., Colo., Calif., 1960-66; reading specialist, title I European area U.S. Dependent Schs., various locations, 1966-75; grad. practicum supr. U. No. Colo. Reading Clinic, Greeley, 1976-77; grant cons. Colo. Dept. Edn., Denver, 1978-81; adult edn. tutor, cons. various orgns., Boulder, Colo., 1983-87; student tchr. supr. U. San Diego, 1989-90; adult literacy trainer for vols. San Diego Coun. on Literacy, 1988—; adj. prof. U. Colo., Denver, 1981-82, U. San Diego, 1994—; adj. prof. comm. arts Southwestern Coll., Chula Vista, Calif., 1990—; presenter various confs. Co-author, editor: Adult Literacy Tutor Training Handbook, 1990, rev. edit., 1998. Grantee Fed. Right-to-Read Office Colo. Dept. Edn., 1979, curriculum writing Southwestern Coll., 1992. Fellow San Diego Coun. on Literacy (chair coop. tutor tng. com. 1991-93); mem. Whole Lang. Coun. San Diego, Calif. Reading Assn. Avocation: psychology. Office: U San Diego Olin Hall Alcala Park San Diego CA 92110

CLEMENT, MARGARITA NORMA, psychologist; b. Oranjestadt, Aruba, Jan. 14, 1949; came to U.S., 1970; d. Miguel and Maria (Orman) C. BS, Calif. State U., 1981; MA, Marymount Loyola U., 1985; PhD in Psychology, Calif. Grad. Inst., 1993. RN, Calif. Renewal unit head nurse Century City (Calif.) Hosp., 1981-82; program charge nurse Cmty. Hosp., Pasadena, Calif., 1982-84; dir. patient care svc. Mountain Lodge Hosp., Glendale, Calif., 1985-88; psychiat. nurse Dept. Vet. Affairs, L.A., 1988-98, psychiat. rschr., 1998—; counselor suicide hotline L.A. County Human Svc. Dept., 1992-97; bd. dirs. TeenAge Grief, Inc., L.A.; vis. lectr. Loyola Marymount U., L.A., 1996—; cons. in field. Inventor Decubex body support. Mem. Asian Bus. Assn., Latino Bus. Assn., Women in Health & Adminstrn., Nat. Network Hispanic Women, Calif. Multi-Cultural Assn. Avocations: writing, gardening, travel. Home: 17537 Blythe St Northridge CA 91325-4331 Office: USVA Med Ctr Mental Health Clinic Wilshire & Sawtelle Los Angeles CA 90073

CLEMENT, WALTER HOUGH, retired railroad executive; b. Council Bluffs, Iowa, Dec. 21, 1931; s. Daniel Shell and Helen Grace (Hough) C.; AA, San Jose (Calif.) City Coll., 1958; PhD, World U., 1983; m. Shirley Ann Brown, May 1, 1953; children: Steven, Robert, Richard. Designer, J.K. Konerle & Assocs., Salt Lake City, 1959-62; with U.P. R.R. Co., 1962—, class B draftsman, Salt Lake City, 1971-75, sr. right of way engr. real estate dept., 1975-80, asst. dist. real estate mgr., 1980-83, asst. engr. surveyor, 1983-87; owner, pres. Clement Sales and Svc. Co., Bountiful, Utah, 1987—. Mem. Republican Nat. Com., Rep. Congl. Com. With USN, 1950-54, Korea. Lic. realtor, Utah. Mem. Am. Ry. Engring. Assn., Execs. Info. Guild (assoc.), Bur. Bus. Practice. Methodist. Home: 290 W 1200 N Bountiful UT 84010-6826

CLEMENTE, PATROCINIO ABLOLA, psychology educator; b. Manila, Philippines, Apr. 23, 1941; s. Elpidio San Jose and Amparo (Ablola) C.; came to U.S., 1965; BSE, U. Philippines, 1960; postgrad. Nat. U., Manila, 1961-64; MA, Ball State U., 1966, EdD, 1969; postgrad. U. Calif., Riverside, 1970, Calif. State Coll., Fullerton, 1971-72. High sch. tchr. gen. sci. and biology, div. city schs., Quezon City, Philippines, 1960-65; doctoral fellow dept. psychology Ball State U., Muncie, Ind., 1966-67, dept. spl. edn., 1967-68, grad. asst. dept. gen. and exptl. psychology, 1968-69; tchr. educable mentally retarded high sch. level Fontana (Calif.) Unified Sch. Dist., 1969-70, intermediate level, 1970-73, dist. sch. psychologist, 1973-79, bilingual edn. counselor, 1979-81; resource specialist Morongo (Calif.) Unified Sch. Dist., 1981-83, spl. day class tchr., 1983-90, tchr. math, sci., Spanish, English, 1990—; adj. assoc. prof. Chapman Coll., Orange, Calif., 1982-91. Adult leader Girl Scouts of Philippines, 1963-65; mem. sch. bd. Blessed Sacrament Sch., Twentynine Palms, Calif. State bd. scholar Ball State U., 1965-66. Fellow Am. Biographical Inst. (hon. mem. research bd. advisors, life); mem. ASCD, NEA, Coun. for Exceptional Children, Am. Assn. on Mental Deficiency, Nat. Assn. of Sch. Psychologists, Found. Exceptional Children, Assn. for Children with Learning Disabilities, Nat. Geographic Soc., Calif. Tchrs. Assn., Morongo Tchrs. Assn., Smithsonian Inst. Roman Catholic. Home: PO Box 637 Twentynine Palms CA 92277-0637

CLEMENTS, JOHN ROBERT, real estate professional; b. Richmond, Ind., Nov. 2, 1950; s. George Howard and Mary Amanda (McKown) C. Grad.

high sch., Phoenix. Sales assoc. Clements Realty, Inc., Phoenix, 1973-75; office mgr. Clements Realty, Inc., Mesa, Ariz., 1975-78, v.p., co-owner Clements Realty, Inc., Phoenix, 1978-80; broker, assoc. Ben Brooks & Assocs., Phoenix, 1980-88; pres. John R. Clements, P.C., 1984—; broker Keller Williams Realty, Phoenix and Mesa, Ariz., 1994-96; facilities dir. Outdoor Sys., Phoenix, 1996—. Real estate dir. Circle K Corp., Western Region, 1989-92; bd. dirs., v.p. Big Sisters Ariz., Phoenix, 1974-80; trustee Ariz. Realtors Polit. Action Com., 1975-85, Realtors Polit. Action Com., Ill., 1985-88; appointee Govtl. Mall Co., Ariz., 1986—, commr. chair, 1991-95. Mem. Ariz. Assn. Realtors (bd. dirs., pres. 1981), Mesa-Chandler-Tempe Bd. Realtors (past bd. dirs., pres., 1978), Nat. Assn. Realtors (past bd. dirs., exec. com.), Residential Sales Coun. Realtors, Nat. Mktg. Inst. (bd. govs. 1986—, v.p. 1990, pres. 1991), Ariz. Country Club. Republican. Presbyterian. Home: 3618 N 60th St Phoenix AZ 85018-6708 Office: Outdoor Sys 2502 N Black Canyon Hwy Phoenix AZ 85009-1800

CLEMENTS, RUTH LORETTA, humanities educator, writer, editor; b. Bourne, Mass.. M in Writing and Am. Studies, U. So. Calif., 1982, PhD in English, 1994. Lectr. UCLA, 1981-84; writer, journalist Globe and Mail and Toronto Star, Toronto, 1984-87; instr. U. Iowa, Iowa City, 1987-88; lectr. U. So. Calif., 1988-94; prof. U. S.C., Lancaster, 1994-97; lectr. UCLA, 1997—; dir. honors program, U. S.C., Lancaster, 1994-97, dir. writing ctr., 1994-97. Author: (dissertation) Pursuing Happiness, The Shaping of State and Soul in the American Enlightenment, 1994. Finalist Disting. Tchr. award, U. S.C., Lancaster. 1997. Mem. Am. Lit. Assn., Cath. Bible Inst., Loyola Marymount U. Avocation: religious edn. Office: UCLA Writing Programs 271 Kinsey Hall 405 Hillard Ave Los Angeles CA 90095

CLEMENTS, WILLIAM LEWIS, JR. (BILL), minister; b. Sacramento, Nov. 5, 1952; s. William L. C. Sr. AA, Am. River, 1973; BA, Southern Calif., 1976; MS, Calif. State U., Fresno, 1980; MBA, Nat. U., 1986. Assoc. Assembly of God, Orange, Calif., 1975-79, Cerritos, Calif., 1979-80; pastor Assembly of God, Folsom, Calif., 1980-83; bus. adminstr. Trinity Ch., Sacramento, 1983—. Mem. Nat. Assn. Ch. Bus. Adminstrn. (pres. 1989-90), Christian Mgmt. Assn. (pres. 1990-91), CMMA. Office: Trinity Ch 5225 Hillsdale Blvd Sacramento CA 95842-3596

CLEMO, RONALD CARL (REV.), priest; b. San Francisco, May 17, 1934; s. Carl Eugene and Edith May Clemo. BA with honors, Gonzaga U., 1961; MA, Santa Clara U., 1968; MALS, Dartmouth U., 1985. Joined S.J., 1954; ordained priest Roman Cath. Ch., 1967. Tchr. U.S. history St. Ignatius Coll. Prep., San Francisco, 1969-70; asst. prin. Bellarmine Coll. Prep., San Jose, Calif., 1970-74, coll. guidance counselor, 1975-87, tchr. U.S. history, 1988—. Mem. Am. Hist. Assn. Avocations: music, sports, drama. Office: Bellarmine Coll Prep 850 Elm St San Jose CA 95126-1813

CLEVELAND, WILLIAM CHARLES, aerospace executive; b. Chgo., Dec. 13, 1926; s. William Charles and Janice Meredith (Rash) C.; m. Dorothy Louise Jones, June 21, 1947; children: Susan, Nancy, Judith. BEE, Purdue U., 1949, MEE, 1950; MS, UCLA, 1965; PhD, Calif. Coast U., 1976. Cert. fin. planner. Mgr. Gen. Dynamics Co., San Diego, 1952-58, Martin Marietta Corp., Denver, 1958-61, Ford Aerospace & Communication Corp., Newport Beach, Calif., 1961-88; pres. Cleve. Enterprises, Putney, Vt., 1974—; pres. Cleve. Consulting Co., Putney, 1986—. Contbr. tech. papers to profl. jours.; author fiction prose; inventor, patentee in field. With USN, 1944-46. Mem. Inst. Cert. Fin. Planners, Assn. Registered Fin. Planners, Assn. Old Crows. Republican. Avocations: writing, reading, hiking. Home and Office: 812 Ronda Mendoza # 0 Laguna Hills CA 92653-5915

CLEVENGER, JEFFREY GRISWOLD, mining company executive; b. Boston, Sept. 1, 1949; s. Galen William and Cynthia (Jones) C. BS in Mining Engring., N.Mex. Inst. Mining and Tech., Socorro, 1973; grad. advanced mgmt. program, Harvard U., 1996. Engr. Phelps Dodge, Tyrone, N.Mex., 1973-78, gen. mine foreman, 1979-81, mine supt., 1981-86; mine supt. Phelps Dodge, Morenci, Ariz., 1986, gen. supt., 1987; asst. gen. mgr. Chino Mines Co., Hurley, N.Mex., 1987-88; asst. gen. mgr. Phelps Dodge, Morenci, 1988-89, gen. mgr., 1989-92; pres. Phelps Dodge Morenci, Inc., 1989-92, Morenci Water & Electric Co., 1989-92; sr. v.p. Cyprus Copper Co., Tempe, 1992-93; pres. Cyprus Climax Metals Co., Tempe, 1993—; sr. v.p. Cyprus Amax Minerals Co., Littleton, Colo., 1993-97, exec. v.p., 1998—. Contbr. articles to profl. jours. Bd. dirs. Valley of the Sun YMCA, Mining Hall of Fame; chmn. Copper Devel. Assn. Recipient Disting. Achievement award N.Mex. Inst. Mining & Tech., 1988. Mem. AIME (chmn. S.W. N.Mex. chpt. 1982), Soc. Mining Engrs. (Robert Peele award 1984), Mining and Metall. Soc. Am., Coppr Devel. Assn. (chmn.), Elks. Home: 4575 N Launfal Ave Phoenix AZ 85018-2961 Office: Cyprus Climax Metals Co PO Box 22015 1501 W Fountainhead Pkwy Tempe AZ 85282-1868

CLEWETT, RAYMOND WINFRED, mechanical design engineer; b. Upland, Calif., Nov. 7, 1917; s. Howard Jasper and Pansy Gertrude (Macy) C.; m. Hazel Royer, June 11, 1938; children: Alan Eugene, Patricia Gail, Charles Raymond, Richard Howard, Beverly Lynn. Student, Chaffey Jr. Coll., 1937. Exptl. mechanic Douglas Aircraft Co., Santa Monica, Calif., 1937-51; shop foreman, exptl. designer Lear, Inc., Los Angeles, 1945-51; design engr., shop mgr. The RAND Corp., Santa Monica, Calif., 1951-83, also design cons.; owner, mgr. HY-TECH Engring. and Devel. Lab., Malibu, Calif., 1983—; design cons. Pacific-Sierra Research Corp. Works include mech. design of JOHNNIAC early model electronic computer on permanent display Comp. Mus., Boston; designer variouscomputer input/output devices, 1953-70; developer low vision reading aids for the blind, 1970-75; design and constrn. spl. equipment for sci. and research, 1983—, stone sculptor, 1994—; patentee in field. Mem. AAAS, Soc. Mfg. Engrs., Am. Soc. Metals. Republican. Office: HY-TECH Engring & Devel Lab 7069 Fernhill Dr Malibu CA 90265-4240

CLIFFORD, STEVEN FRANCIS, science research director; b. Boston, Jan. 4, 1943; s. Joseph Nelson and Margaret Dorothy (Savage) C.; children from previous marriage: Cheryl Ann, Michelle Lynn, David Arthur; m. Theresa Kavanagh, Aug. 1996. BSEE, Northeastern U., Boston, 1965; PhD, Dartmouth Coll., 1969. Postdoctoral fellow NRC, Boulder, Colo., 1969-70; physicist Wave Propagation Lab., NOAA, Boulder, 1970-82, program chief, 1982-87, dir. environ. tech. lab., 1987—; mem. electromagnetic propagation panel, NATO, 1989-93; vis. sci. closed acad. city Tomsk, Siberia, USSR. Author: (with others) Remote Sensing of the Troposphere, 1978; contbr. 125 articles to profl. jours.; patentee in acoustic scintillation liquid flow measurement, single-ended optical spatial filter. Recipient 5 Outstanding publs. awards Dept. Commerce, 1972, 75, 89, 96. Fellow Optical Soc. Am. (editor atmospheric optics 1978-84, advisor atmospheric optics 1982-84), Acoustical Soc. Am.; mem. IEEE (sr.), Nat. Acad. Engring., Internat. Radio Sci. Union, Am. Geophys. Union; inducted NAE. Avocations: running, cross country skiing. Office: NOAA Environ Tech Lab 325 Broadway St Boulder CO 80303-3337

CLIFFORD, WALTER JESS, microbiologist, immunologist; b. Safford, Ariz., July 18, 1944; s. Walter Elijah, Jr. and Helen (Taylor) C.; m. Laura Bigler Clifford, Dec. 15, 1967; children: Jess. A., Terri L., Vera L., Jerald G., Joseph L. Rachel D., Jason C., Eva R. Student, Eastern Ariz. Coll., Thatcher, 1963, 65; BS, U. Ariz., Tucson, 1968, MS, 1975. Registered Microbiologist (Am. Acad. of Microbiology). Officer U.S. Army, 1968-72; staff microbiologist Tucson Med. Ctr., Tucson, 1972-73; tech. dir. Cochise Pathology Cons., Sierra Vista, Ariz., 1973-75; lab supr./dir. S.E. Svcs., Inc., Sierra Vista, Ariz., 1975-77, Benson Health Svc., Benson, Ariz., 1977-78; dir. of tech. svc. AID Lab., Richardson, Tex., 1978-80; v.p., tech. Bio Med Labs., N. Hollywood, Calif., 1980-83; dir. of rsch. Toxic Element Rsch. Found., Colorado Springs, Colo/, 1986-88; pres. and dir. Clifford Consulting and Rsch., Colorado Springs, Colo., 1982—; instr. Cochise Coll., Douglas, Ariz., 1977-78; UT Tech. Coll., Provo, UT, 1985-86. Author: Biomaterials Microbiology, 1980, 86, 90. Sch. Bd. Mem. Westside Union Sch. Dist., Rotary Club Mem. Rotary, Internat., Ad hoc steering com. Nat. Registry for Microbiologists. Recipient Phillip Hoekstra Memorial Lecture, Great Lakes Assn. for Alternative Medicine, Provisional Approval Materials Reactivity Testing Protocol, Internat. Acad. of Oral Medicine and Toxicology. Fellow Internat. Acad. Oral Medicine and Toxicology; mem. Am. Soc. for Microbiology, Am. Assn. for the Advancement of Sci., Am. Chemical Soc., N.Y. Acad. of Sci., Nat. Registry for Microbiologists, Am. Assn. for Clin. Chemistry. Republican. Mem LDS Ch. Avocations: aviation, gardening, music, photography. Office: Clifford Consulting & Rsch 2275 Waynoka Rd Ste J Colorado Springs CO 80915-1635

CLIFT, WILLIAM BROOKS, III, photographer; b. Boston, Jan. 5, 1944; s. William Brooks C. and Anne (Pearmain) Thomson; m. Vida Regina Chesnulis, Aug. 8, 1970; children: Charis, Carola, William. Free lance comml. photographer in partnership with Steve Gersh under name Helios, 1963-71; pres. William Clift Ltd., Santa Fe, 1980-85; cons. Polaroid Corp., 1965-67. Photographer one-man shows, Carl Siembab Gallery, Boston, 1969, Mus. Art, U. Oreg., Eugene, 1969, New Boston City Hall Gallery, 1970, U. Mass., Berkshire Mus., Pittsfield, Mass., William Coll., Addison Gallery of Am. Art, Wheaton Coll., Mass., Worcester Art Mus., 1971, Creative Photography Gallery, MIT, 1972, St. John's Coll. Art Gallery, Santa Fe, 1973, Wiggin Gallery, Boston Pub. Library, 1974, Australian Ctr. for Photography, Sydney, 1978, Susan Spiritus Gallery, Newport Beach, Calif., 1979, MIT Creative Photography Gallery, 1980, William Lyons Gallery, Coconut Grove, Fla., 1980, Eclipse Gallery, Boulder, Colo., 1980, Atlanta Gallery of Photography, 1980, Phoenix Art Mus., 1981, Jeb Gallery, Providence, 1981, Portfolio Gallery, 1981, Images Gallery, Cin., 1982, Boston Atheneum, 1983, Bank of Santa Fe, 1984, Susan Harder Gallery, N.Y.C., 1984, Cleve. Art Mus., 1985, Art Inst. Chgo., 1987, Amon Carter Mus., Ft. Worth, 1987, Clarence Kennedy Gallery, Cambridge, Mass., 1988, Equitable Gallery, N.Y.C., 1993, Vassar Coll. Art Mus., N.Y., 1994, Vassar Coll. Art Gallery, N.Y., 1995; exhibited in group shows Gallery 216, N.Y., N.Y. Grover Cronin Gallery, Waltham, Mass., 1964, Carl Seimbab Gallery, Boston, 1966, Lassall Jr. Coll., 1967, Hill's Gallery, Santa Fe, Tyler Mus. Art, Austin, Tex., Dupree Gallery, Dallas, 1974, Quindacqua Gallery, Washington, 1978, Zabriskie Gallery, Paris, 1978, Am. Cultural Ctr., Paris, 1978; photographer AT&T Project-Am. Images, 1978, Seagram's Bicentennial Project, Courthouse, 1975-77, Readers Digest Assn. Project, 1984, Hudson River Project, 1985-92; author: Photography Portfolios, Old Boston City Hall, 1971, Photography Portfolios, Courthouse, 1979, Photography Portfolios, New Mexico, 1975, Certain Places, Photographs, 1987, A Hudson Landscape, Photographs, 1993. Nat. Endowment for Arts photography fellow, 1972, 79; Guggenheim fellow, 1974, 80, N.Mex. Gov.'s Excellence in The Arts award, 1987. Home and Office: PO Box 6035 Santa Fe NM 87502-6035

CLIFTON, MARK STEPHEN, administrator; b. San Diego, May 25, 1955; s. Paul Clifford and Dorothy Jean (Gross) C.; m. Margaret Eileen Hower, July 20, 1985; 1 child, Casey Mariah. Student, Grossmont Coll., 1973-74, San Diego City Coll., 1981. Oper. supr. San Diego Unified Sch. Dist., 1979—; owner A Home Touch Housecleaning, San Diego, 1985—; speaker in field. Author: There Goes the Neighborhood, 1993; contbr. articles to profl. jours. Mem. Ocean Beach Town Coun., San Diego, 1993—. Recipient Hon. Svc. award PTA, Point Loma High Sch., 1989. Mem. San Diego Writers and Editor's Guild, Christian Writers Guild, Adminstrs. Assn., Maranatha Surfing Assn. (founder, pres. 1983-86), Christian Surfing Assn. (co-founder 1982-83). Republican. Avocations: surfing, golf, walking, exercise, Aikido-martial arts. Office: San Diego Unified Sch Dist 8460 Ruffner St San Diego CA 92111

CLIFTON, MAURICE S., III, real estate broker, real estate educator; b. Raleigh, N.C., May 3, 1938; s. Maurice S. Jr. and Anna Boyd (Wilson) C.; m. Mary Helen Morgan, Dec. 29, 1961 (div. Jan. 1990); children: Maurice S. IV, Mary Ann Markovetz. BA, Whittier Coll., 1960; Grad., Real Estate Inst. Credit man Richfield Oil, L.A., 1960-63; asst. v.p. Bank of Am., L.A., 1963-71; v.p. real estate loan mgr. Bank of Idaho, Boise, 1971-76; assoc. broker Westmark & Co., Boise, 1976-81, ERA City Realty, Boise, 1982-92; broker ERA West Wind, Boise, 1992—. Author: Practical Solutions with the HP-12C, 1984, 90, 96, Working with the T.I. BA-35, 1990, 94; editor: Fund of Real Estate Finance, 7th edit., 1996. Vol. Boise Family YMCA, 1977-78, Red Cross, Boise, 1990-94. Sgt. Calif. Air Guard, 1961-67. Mem. Nat. Assn. Realtors (dir. 1996-97), Real Estate Educators Assn. (pres. 1984, Disting. Real Estate Instr. 1985), Idaho Real Estate Edn. Coun. (chmn. 1988-97), ADA County Assn. Realtors (dir. 1976-97), Idaho Assn. Realtors (pres. 1996-97). Episcopalian. Avocations: woodworking, fishing, hiking. Home: 3200 Summerset Way Boise ID 83709-3821 Office: ERA West Wind 950 N Cole Rd Boise ID 83704-8640

CLIFTON, MICHAEL EDWARD, English language educator; b. Reedley, Calif., Jan. 6, 1949; s. Edward Eugene and Helen May (Peters) C.; m. Anita May Bernardi, June 22, 1973. BA, Calif. State U., Fresno, 1971, MA with distinction, 1977; PhD, Ind. U., 1984. Tchr. English Hoover High Sch., Fresno, 1971-74; assoc. instr. Ind. U., Bloomington, 1978-80; lectr. Calif. State U., Fresno, 1982—; reader, presenter Internat. Assn. Fantastic in Arts, Ft. Lauderdale, Fla., 1988, 93, Houston, Tex., 1987, Am. Imagery Assn., San Francisco, 1986, Eaton Conf., U. Calif. Riverside, 1985. Contbr. articles to popular mags. and profl. jours. Chair Tower Dist. Design Rev. Com. Mem. MLA, AAUP. Democrat. Avocations: reading, birding, computers, historical preservation. Home: 921 N San Pablo Ave Fresno CA 93728-3627 Office: Calif State U Dept English Peters Bldg Fresno CA 93740

CLINCH, NICHOLAS BAYARD, III, business executive; b. Evanston, Ill., Nov. 9, 1930; s. Nicholas Bayard Jr. and Virginia Lee (Campbell) C.; m. Elizabeth Wallace Campbell, July 11, 1964; children: Virginia Lee, Alison Campbell. Student, N.Mex. Mil. Inst., Roswell, 1948-49; AB, Stanford U., 1952, LLB, 1955. Bar: Calif. 1959. Expedition leader First Ascent, Gasherbrum I (26,470 ft.), Pakistan, 1958, First Ascent, Masherbrum (25, 660 ft.), Pakistan, 1959-60; assoc. Voegelin, Barton, Harris & Callister, L.A., 1961-68; pvt. practice Washington, 1968-70; v.p., counsel Lincoln Savs. & Loan Assn., L.A., 1970-74; exec. dir. Sierra Club Found., San Francisco, 1975-81; environ. cons. Fluor Corp., Grass Valley, Calif., 1981-84; v.p., sec. CCA, Inc., Denver, 1984—; bd. dirs. Growth Stock Outlook Inc., Potomac, Md., Recreational Equipment Inc., Seattle. Author: A Walk in the Sky, 1982. Leader Am. Antarctic Mountaineering Expdn., Sentinel Range, 1966-67; co-leader Chinese Am. Ulugh Muztagh Expdn., Kun Lun Range, Xinjiang, 1985, Am. Expdns. to Kang Karpo Range, Yunnan-Tibet border, 1988, 89, 92, 93; co-founder, trustee Calif. League Conservation Voters, San Francisco, 1972-97. 1st lt. USAF, 1956-57. Recipient John Oliver La Gorce medal Nat. Geog. Soc., Washington, 1967. Fellow Royal Geog. Soc., Explorers Club; mem. ABA, Am. Alpine Club (hon., pres. 1967-70), Appalachian Mountain Club (hon.), State Bar Calif., Alpine Club (hon. London), Chinese Assn. Sci. Expdns. (hon.). Republican. Episcopalian. Avocations: mountaineering, skiing, book collecting. Home: 2001 Bryant St Palo Alto CA 94301-3714 Office: CCA Inc 4100 E Mississippi Ave Ste 1750 Denver CO 80246-3067

CLINE, CAROLYN JOAN, plastic and reconstructive surgeon; b. Boston; d. Paul S. and Elizabeth (Flom) Cline. BA, Wellesley Coll., 1962; MA, U. Cin., 1966; PhD, Washington U., 1970; diploma Washington Sch. Psychiatry, 1972; MD, U. Miami (Fla.) 1975. Diplomate Am. Bd. Plastic and Reconstructive Surgery. Rsch. asst. Harvard Dental Sch., Boston, 1962-64; rsch. asst. physiology Laser Lab., Children's Hosp. Research Found., Cin., 1964, psychology dept. U. Cin., 1964-65; intern in clin. psychology St. Elizabeth's Hosp., Washington, 1966-67; psychologist Alexandria (Va.) Community Mental Health Ctr., 1967-68; research fellow NIH, Washington, 1968-69; chief psychologist Kingsbury Ctr. for Children, Washington, 1969-73; sole practice clin. psychology, Washington, 1970-73; intern internal medicine U. Wis. Hosps., Ctr. for Health Sci., Madison, 1975-76; resident in surgery Stanford U. Med. Ctr., 1976-78; fellow microvascular surgery dept. surgery U. Calif.-San Francisco, 1978-79; resident in plastic surgery St. Francis Hosp., San Francisco, 1979-82; practice medicine, specializing in plastic and reconstructive surgery, San Francisco, 1982—. Contbr. chpt. to plastic surgery textbook, articles to profl. jours. Mem. Am. Soc. Plastic and Reconstructive Surgeons, Royal Soc. Medicine, Calif. Medicine Assn., Calif. Soc. Plastic and Reconstructive Surgeons, San Francisco Med. Soc.

CLINE, DARRELL EUGENE, dentist; b. Auburn, Wash., Apr. 28, 1962; s. Melvin Robert Cline and Rose Marie (MacKenzie) Reed; m. Debbie Ann Monize, Apr. 19, 1997. BS, Union Coll., 1984; DDS, Loma Linda U., 1988. Gen. dentist Craig, Alaska, 1988-93, North Seattle, Wash., 1993—. Recipient award for orthodontics Am. Assn. of Orthodontists, Loma Linda, 1988, operative dentistry award Acad. of Operative Dentistry, Loma Linda, 1988, Acad. All-Am. Honors Nat. Collegiate Med. Professions award, 1988. Mem. ADA, Acad. Gen. Dentistry. Republican. Seventh Day Adventist. Avocations: waterskiing, backpacking, bird watching, snow skiing, sport fishing.

CLINE, FRED ALBERT, JR., retired librarian, conservationist; b. Santa Barbara, Calif., Oct. 23, 1929; s. Fred Albert and Anna Cecelia (Haberl) C. AB in Asian Studies, U. Calif., Berkeley, 1952, MLS, 1962. Resident Internat. House, Berkeley, 1950-51; trainee, officer Bank of Am., San Francisco, Düsseldorf, Fed. Republic Germany, Kuala Lumpur, 1954-60; adminstrv. reference libr. Calif. State Libr., Sacramento, 1962-67; head libr. Asian Art Mus. San Francisco, 1967-93; ret., 1993. Contbg. author: Chinese, Korean and Japanese Sculpture in the Avery Brundage Collection, 1974; author, editor: Ruth Hill Cooke, 1985; contbr. articles and book revs. on AIDS to various publs. Bd. dirs. Tamalpais Conservation Club, 1990-94, 98—, chmn. Found., The Desert Protective Coun.; AIDS activist. Sgt. M.C., U.S. Army, 1952-54. Mem. Metaphys. Alliance (sec., bd. dirs. San Francisco chpt. 1988-91), Sierra Club. Democrat. Avocations: hiking, music, reading. Home: 825 Lincoln Way San Francisco CA 94122-2369

CLINE, PLATT HERRICK, author; b. Mancos, Colo., Feb. 7, 1911; s. Gilbert T. and Jessie (Baker) C.; m. Barbara Decker, Sept. 11, 1934. Grad., N.Mex. Mil. Inst., 1930; student, Colo. U., 1930-31; LittD, No. Ariz. U., 1966, BS, 1982. Advt. solicitor Denver Post, 1931; with Civilian Conservation Corps., 1934-36; Nat. Monument ranger, 1936; pub. Norwood (Colo.) Post, 1937-38; advt. mgr. Coconino Sun, Flagstaff, Ariz., 1938-41; mng. editor Holbrook Tribune-News, 1941-45; editor Coconino Sun, 1945-46; mng. editor Ariz. Daily Sun, 1946-53, pub., 1953-69, pres., 1969-76, v.p., 1976-96; rsch. assoc. Mus. No. Ariz., 1976—; adj. prof. history No. Ariz. U., 1983—. Author: They Came to the Mountain, 1976, Mountain Campus, 1983, The View From Mountain Campus, 1990, Mountain Town, Flagstaff in the 20th Century, 1994. Mountain Campus Centennial, 1999. Mem. Ariz. Commn. Indian Affairs, 1952-55, Norwood (Colo) Town Coun., 1937-38; chmn. Flagstaff Citizen of Yr. Com., 1976-96; bd. dirs., past pres. Raymond Edn. Found., No. Ariz. U. Found.; bd. dirs. Transition Found; trustee Flagstaff Community Hosp., 1954-58. Recipient Ariz. Master Editor-Pub. award, 1969, El-Merito award Ariz. Hist. Soc., 1976; named Flagstaff Citizen of Yr., 1976, Disting. Citizen, No. Ariz. U. Alumni, 1983, Outstanding Flagstaff Citizen of Century award, 1994; dedicatee No. Ariz. U. Libr., 1988. Mem. Ariz. Newspapers Assn. (past pres., Golden Svc. award 1989), No. Ariz. Pioneers Hist. Soc. (trustee 1972-75), Odd Fellows, Sigma Delta Chi, Phi Alpha Theta, Phi Kappa Phi, Masons. Home: PO Box 578 Flagstaff AZ 86002-0578

CLINE, ROBERT STANLEY, air freight company executive; b. Urbana, Ill., July 17, 1937; s. Lyle Stanley and Mary Elizabeth (Prettyman) C.; m. Judith Lee Stucker, July 7, 1979; children: Lisa Andre, Nicole Lesley, Christina Elaine, Leslie Jane. BA, Dartmouth Coll., 1959. Asst. treas. Chase Manhattan Bank, N.Y.C., 1960-65; v.p. fin. Pacific Air Freight Co., Seattle, 1965-68; exec. v.p. fin. Airborne Express (formerly Airborne Freight Corp.), Seattle, 1968-78, vice chmn., CFO, dir., 1978-84, chmn., CEO, dir., 1984—; bd. dirs. Seattle-First Nat. Bank, Metricom Corp., Safeco Corp. Trustee Seattle Repertory Theatre, 1974-90, chmn. bd., 1979-83; trustee Children's Hosp. Found., 1983-91, 96—, Corp. Coun. of Arts, 1983—; bd. dirs. Washington Roundtable, 1985—, chmn. 1995-96; chmn. bd. dirs. Children's Hosp. Found., 1987-89; trustee United Way of King County, 1991-93. With U.S. Army, 1959-60. Home: 1209 39th Ave E Seattle WA 98112-4403 Office: Airborne Express PO Box 662 Seattle WA 98111-0662

CLINE, WILSON ETTASON, retired judge; b. Newkirk, Okla., Aug. 26, 1914; s. William Sherman and Etta Blanche (Roach) C.; m. G. Barbara Verne Pentecost, Nov. 1, 1939 (div. Nov. 1960); children: William, Catherine Cline MacDonald, Thomas; m. Gina Lana Ludwig, Oct. 5, 1969; children: David Ludwig, Kenneth Ludwig. Student, U. Ill., 1932-33; A.B., U. Okla., 1935, B.S. in Bus. Adminstrn., 1936; J.D., U. Calif., Berkeley, 1939; LL.M., Harvard U., 1941. Bar: Calif. 1940, U.S. Ct. Appeals (9th cir.) 1941, U.S. Dist. Ct. (no. dist.) Calif. 1943, U.S. Supreme Ct. 1953. Atty. Kaiser Richmond Shipyards, 1941-44; pvt. practice Oakland, 1945-49; prof., asst. dean, dean Eastbay Div. Lincoln U. Law Sch., Oakland, 1946-50; atty., hearing officer, asst. chief adminstrv. law judge, acting chief adminstrv. law judge Calif. Pub. Utilities Commn., San Francisco, 1949-80, ret. administrative law judge, 1981, dir. gen. welfare Calif. State Employees Assn., 1966-67, chmn. retirement com., 1965-66, mem. member benefit com., 1980-81, mem. ret. employees div. council dist., 1981-82; executor estate of Warren A. Cline. Past trustee Cline Ranch Trust, various family trusts. Mem. ABA, State Bar Calif., Conf. Calif. Pub. Utility Counsel (steering com. 1967-71), Am. Judicature Soc., Boalt Hall Alumni Assn., Harvard Club of San Francisco, Commonwealth Club San Francisco, Sleepy Hollow Swim and Tennis Club (Orinda, Calif.), Masons (Orinda lodge # 494 sec. 1951-55, past Master 1949), Sirs (Peralta chpt. 12), Phi Beta Kappa (pres. No. Calif. assn. 1969-70), Beta Gamma Sigma, Delta Sigma Pi (Key award 1936), Phi Kappa Psi, Phi Delta Phi, Pi Sigma Alpha. Democrat. Mem. United Ch. Christ. Home: 110 Saint Albans Rd Kensington CA 94708-1035 Office: 3750 Harrison St Unit 304 PO Box 11120 Oakland CA 94611-0120

CLINKINGBEARD, CYNTHIA LOU, endocrinologist, educator, researcher; b. Boise, Idaho, Apr. 2, 1953; d. William Edley and Elsie Jean (Todd) C.; children: Taylor, Tess. AB in Human Biology with distinction, Stanford U., 1975; MD, U. Wash., 1979. Diplomate Am. Bd. Internal Medicine, Am. Bd. Geriatrics, Am. Bd. Endocrinology and Metabolism; cert. DEA. Intern Univ. Hosp., Seattle, 1979-80; resident in internal medicine Presbyn. Hosp., San Francisco, 1980-81, chief resident, 1981-82; fellow in psychiatry William S. Middleton VA Hosp., Madison, Wis., 1987-88, rsch. fellow in geriatric medicine, 1989-90; fellow in endocrinology and metabolism U. Wis., Madison, 1987-89; physician various hosps. and med. ctrs., Calif. and Wis., 1982-93; asst. prof. medicine Stanford U. Sch. Medicine, 1990-93; cons. physician VA Hosp., Boise, 1993—; med. dir. Humphreys Diabetes Ctr., Boise, 1993—; pvt. practice endocrinologist Boise, 1993—; staff physician Northview Hosp., Boise, 1997—; med. advisor Pacific Coast Clin. Coordinators, Inc., Boise, 1997—; clin. asst. prof. medicine U. Wash. Sch. Medicine, Seattle, 1993-97, clin. assoc. prof., 1997—; mem. adv. bd. Idaho Diabetes Control Program, Ctrs. for Disease Control, 1994—; mem. Healthwise Med. Review Bd., 1995—; mem. pharmacy and therapeutics com. Regence Blue Shield of Idaho, 1997—; mem. med. staff planning com. St. Alphonsus Regional Med. Ctr., 1994—. Contbr. over 20 articles and abstracts to med. publs. Stetler Rsch. Fellow for Women Physicians, 1989; Pitney-Bowes Acad. Scholar, 1971-75; rsch. grantee Bristol Meyer Squibb, 1995, 97. Mem. The Endocrine Soc., Am. Diabetes Assn. (mem. exec. com. Idaho affiliate 1995—), Am. Assn. Diabetes Educators, Women's Rsch. Collective, Idaho Med. Soc., Diabetes Alliance of Idaho, Bay Area Soc. Women Endocrinologists, Ada County Med. Soc. Avocations: hiking, fishing, reading. Fax: 208-322-2490. Office: 1000 N Curtis Rd Ste 102 Boise ID 83706-1345

CLORE, FRANK CALDIN, pastor, chaplain; b. Bremerton, Wash., Feb. 3, 1942; s. Frank H. Clore and Audrey F. (Garinger) Wrestling; m. Teresa Mae Scofield, May 19, 1984; 1 child, Frank Anthony. Student, Oreg. Coll. Edn., 1960-64, Warner Pacific Coll., Portland, Oreg., 1984-87. Ordained to ministry Ch. of God (Anderson, Ind.), 1990. Pastor Milwaukie (Oreg.) Congl. Ch., 1984-85; interim pastor Olney (Oreg.) Community Ch., 1985; sr. pastor 1st Ch. of God, Grants Pass, Oreg., 1986-91, Oregon City, Oreg., 1991—; sr. chaplain Josephine County Sheriff's Office, Grants Pass, 1987-91; chaplain Hull & Hull Funeral Home, Grants Pass, 1987-91; state dir. primary camp Chs. of God, Oreg., 1987-91; mem. Social Concerns Commn., Oreg. Ch. of God, 1988—. State dir. Josephine County Juvenile Svcs. Commn., 1989; mem. Josephine County Mental Health Adv. Bd., 1988-91, Josephine County Juvenile Adv. Coun., 1991—; mem. nat. steering com. Nat. Sheriff's Chaplaincy Program; past bd. dirs. Lovejoy Hospice; mem. Josephine County Dist. Atty.'s Adv. Coun., 1989. Mem. Grants Pass Ministerial Assn. (v.p. 1987, pres. 1988-90), Internat. Conf. Police Chaplains. Address: 1st Ch of God Oregon City OR 97045

CLOSE, JACK DEAN, SR., physical therapist; b. Provo, Utah, Apr. 21, 1943; s. Melvin D. Sr. and Hope (Coleman) C.; m. Gaylee King, Dec. 7, 1962; children: Jack Dean Jr., Tiffany Lee, Kristina Louise, Stephen William. BS in Zoology, Brigham Young U., 1967; MA in Phys. Therapy, U. So. Calif., 1970; postgrad., U. Nev. Las Vegas, 1978-87. Registered phys. therapist, Calif. and Nev. Staff phys. therapist Glendale (Calif.) Meml.

Hosp., 1969-70; phys. and respiratory therapist So. Nev. Meml. Hosp., Las Vegas, 1970-71; pres. Phys. Therapy Svcs., Las Vegas, 1971-74, Close and Kleven, Ltd., Las Vegas, 1974-96; pres./CEO Jack D. Close and Assocs., Phys. Therapy & Rehab. Ctr., Las Vegas, 1996—; clin. instr. 14 major univs.; adv. com. respiratory therapy Clark County Community Coll., 1980; adv. bd. phys. therapy U. Nev. Las Vegas, 1988—, instr. U. Nev., mem adv. bd. Phys. Therapy Asst. Program C.C. of So. Nev., 1982—; presenter various confs., profl. meetings. Contbr. articles to profl. jours. Chmn. reunions Las Vegas High Sch. Class 1961; numerous leadership positions LDS Ch.; mem. exec. com. Nev. Friendship Force; past mgr., coach Little League Baseball; past mem. profl. adv. staff Easter Seal, cons. staff Muscular Dystrophy, med. adv. bd. Multiple Sclerosis, adv. coun. and gov. bd. Health Systems Agy. adv. com. Clark County Community Devel., 1981-83; mem. Nev. State Assemblyman Dist. 15 (Las Vegas), mem. ways & means, election/procedures and ethics, and commerce coms., 1995, 1997—. Allied Health Profession scholar; named one of Outstanding Young Men of Am. Brigham Young U. Alumni Assn., 1979; recipient Bachelor Commr. Sci. award Boulder Dam area coun. Boy Scouts Am., 1989, Master Commr. Sci. award, 1990, Merit award, 1991, Silver Beaver award. Fellow Am. Phys. Therapy Assn. (v.p., chmn. joint task force, trustee and exec. com. Found. Phys. Therapy 1990, pres. APT Svcs. Corp. 1989, Lucy Blair Svc. award); mem. AACD, Nat. Athletic Trainers Assn. (assoc.), Am. Running and Fitness Assn., Nat. Strength and Conditioning Assn., Nat. Wellness Assn., Aquatic Exercise Assn., Nev. Athletic Trainers Assn. Avocations: politics, sports, antique auto restoration, coin collecting, travel. Office: Jack D Close and Assocs Phys Therapy & Rehab Ctr 4560 S Eastern Ave Ste B-18 Las Vegas NV 89119-6182

CLOSE, SANDY, journalist; b. N.Y.C., Jan. 25, 1943. BA, U. Calif., Berkeley, 1964. Exec. dir., editor Pacific News Svc., San Francisco. MacArthur fellow, 1995. Office: Pacific News Service 660 Market St Ste 210 San Francisco CA 94104*

CLOUD, JAMES MERLE, university and hospital administrator, learning specialist; b. Winston-Salem, N.C., Feb. 16, 1947; s. Merle Vail and Jane Crawford (Moore) C.; BA, U. N.C., 1970; PhD, Columbia Pacific U., 1979. Co-founder Wholistic Health and Nutrition Inst., Mill Valley, Calif., 1974, dir. edn., 1974-76, dir. health resource consultation, 1976-78; dir., v.p. No. Calif. Internat. Coop. Coun., 1975-77; admissions dir. Columbia Pacific U., 1978-84, sec.-treas., dir., 1978-84; v.p. Calif. U. for Advanced Studies, Novato, 1984-85; dir. Wholistic Health and Nutrition Inst., 1974-85; adminstr. Autumn Care Convalescent Hosp., 1989-90; founder Memorobics Seminars of Memory Skills for Fgn. Lang. Study, 1992, Speed Learning Systems, 1992, Learning Made Easy Study Skills Seminars. Author: The Healthscription, 1979, Directory of Active Senior Organizations and Communications Resources, 1989, The Foreign Language Memory Book, 1995, The Bible Memory Book, 1995, The Memory Game: Learning Made Easy!, 1996; (poetry) Aeolus, 1971, No One Loves with Solitude, 1970. Sec., dir. Citizens of Marin Against Crime, 1983. Columnist Ukiah Penny Pincher, 1990. Mem. Assn. Holistic Health (v.p. 1976, dir.), Airplane Owners and Pilots Assn., Am. Assn. Active Srs. (v.p. 1988-89), Internat. Friends of the Iron Horse (founder, pres. 1990—), Internat. Assn. of Body Mechanics (pres. 1991—), Mendocino County Railway Soc. (dir. 1991), Nat. Assn. of Railway Passengers, Train Riders Assn. of Calif., Pacific Internat. Trapshooters Assn. Home: 4286 Redwood Hwy San Rafael CA 94903-2610

CLOUGH, SARALYN LOUISE, speech and language pathologist; b. Fontana, Calif., Nov. 8, 1971; d. Robert Lee Clough and Pamela Melindagale (Warren) Salazar. BA, Chico State U., 1993; MA, San Jose State U., 1995. Lic. speech-lang. pathologist. Speech-lang. pathologist aide West Valley Jr. Coll., Saratoga, Calif., 1993-95; speech-lang. pathologist Ortho-Neurol. Rehab., Los Gatos, Calif., 1996—. Educator Chico Women's Ctr., Napa (Calif.) State Hosp., 1990-93; bd. dirs. Gay Lesbian Bisexual Alliance, Chico, 1992-93, Chico Hate Crimes Com., 1992-93; emotional supporter AIDS Resources and Info. Svcs., Santa Clara, Calif., 1994-95. Mem. Am. Speech and Hearing Assn., Lesbian and Gay Audiologists and Speech Pathologists, NOW (v.p., Outstanding Feminist Activity award 1992). Democrat. Buddhist. Avocations: reading, animals, activism in support of women's equality. Office: Sierra Sunrise Health Ctr 2850 Sierra Sunrise Ter Chico CA 95928-8401

CLOUSE, VICKIE RAE, biology and paleontology educator; b. Havre, Mont., Mar. 28, 1956; d. Olaf Raymond and Betty Lou (Reed) Nelson; m. Gregory Scott Clouse, Mar. 22, 1980; 1 child, Kristopher Nelson. BS in Secondary Sci. Edn., Mont. State U. No., Havre, 1989; postgrad., Mont. State U., Bozeman, 1991-94. Teaching asst. biology and paleontology Mont. State U.-No., Havre, 1986-90; rsch. asst. dinosaur eggs and embryos Mus. of the Rockies, Bozeman, 1992-95; instr. biology and paleontology Mont. State U.-No., Havre, 1990—; dir. dinosaur rsch. expdns. Bd. trustees H.E. Clack Mus., Havre, 1991-97, H.E. Clack Mus. Found., Havre, 1991-97, Mont. Bd. Regents of Higher Edn., Helena, 1989-90, Mont. Higher Edn. Student Fin. Assistance Corp., Helena, 1989-90; mem. Ea. Mont. Hist. Soc., 1993—. Named Young Career Woman of Yr., Bus. and Profl. Woman's Club, 1986. Mem. AAAS, Soc. Vertebrate Paleontologists, Mont. Geol. Soc. Avocations: collecting vertebrate fossils, dir. dinosaur excavations for laypersons, boating. E-mail: ClouseV@yahoo.com. Office: Mont State U-No Hagener Sci Ctr Havre MT 59501

CLOWES, ALEXANDER WHITEHILL, surgeon, educator; b. Boston, Oct. 9, 1946; s. George H.A. Jr. and Margaret Gracey (Jackson) C.; m. Monika Meyer (dec.). AB, Harvard U., 1968, MD, 1972. Resident in surgery Case Western Reserve, Cleve., 1972-74, 76-79; rsch. fellow in pathology Harvard Med. Sch., Boston, 1974-76; fellow in vascular surgery Brigham and Womens Hosp. Harvard Med. Sch., 1979-80; asst. prof. surgery U. Wash., Seattle, 1980-85, assoc. prof., 1985-90, prof., 1990—, assoc. chmn. dept., 1989-91, acting chmn. dept., 1992-93, adj. prof. pathology, 1992, chief divsn. vascular surgery, 1995—, dept. vice chmn., 1995—. Contbr. chpts. to books; author numerous sci. papers. Trustee Marine Biol. Labs., Woods Hole, Mass., 1989—, Seattle Symphony, 1994— (v.p. 1998—); bd. dirs. Seattle Chamber Music Festival, 1990. Recipient NIH Rsch. Career Devel. award, 1982-87; NIH Tng. fellow, 1974-77; Loyal Davis Traveling Surg. scholar ACS, 1987. Mem. Am. Surg. Assn., Am. Assn. Pathologists, Am. Heart Assn. (coun. on arteriosclerosis), Am. Soc. Cell Biology, Internat. Soc. Applied Cardiovasc. Biology, Seattle Surg. Soc., Soc. Vascular Surgery, Cruising Club Am., Quisset Yacht Club, Sigma Xi. Episcopalian. Home: 702 Fullerton Ave Seattle WA 98122-6432 Office: U Wash Dept Surgery PO Box 356410 Seattle WA 98195-6410

COAD, DENNIS LAWRENCE, real estate broker; b. St. Louis, Mar. 16, 1959; s. Stanley Meredith and Olga Martha (Salarano) C.; m. Linda Marie Kasmarzik, June 20, 1980 (div. May, 1982): 1 child, Jason Christopher. AA, Jefferson Coll., Pevely, Mo., 1979; BS, S.W. Mo. State U., 1988, MBA, 1990. Systems engr. Computer Task Group, St. Louis, 1981-84; owner, mng. dir. Sci. Resources Cons. Group, La Mirada, Calif., 1990-97; dir. bus. devel. AGCT Inc., Irvine, Calif., 1993-97; real estate broker, owner Home Town Realty, Hemet, Calif., 1997—. Author: Nature, 1994—, Genetic Engring News, 1993—, Biotechniques, 1996. Active United We Stand, Calif., 1992. With U.S. Army, 1984-87. Boatmen's Bank scholar, 1977. Mem. AAAS, Am. Mgmt. Assn., Smithsonian Inst., Regulatory Profl. Soc. Roman Catholic. Avocations: computer programming, camping, hiking, cycling, boating. Home: 2070 Rosemary Ct Hemet CA 92545-5614 Office: Home Town Realty PO Box 4471 Hemet CA 92546-4471

COATES, E. JOYCE, retired English educator; b. Rocksprings, Tex., May 17, 1934; d. Charles Elmer and Eula Mae (Casey) Talley; m. Arthur John Coates, Nov. 24, 1952; children: Phyllis Rae Gaylord, Perri Fern Benemelis, Charles Elmer Coates. AA, Glendale C.C., 1969; BA in Secondary Edn., English, Grand Canyon U., 1973. Cert. secondary english tchr., Ariz. Sec., bus driver Hayward Ave. Day Sch., Phoenix, 1964-67; audiovisual coord. Phoenix Coll., 1973-76, computer courseware author, 1976-79; writer, reporter Foothills Sentinel, Cave Creek, Ariz., 1983-84, Apache Peak News, New River, Ariz., 1984-85; dir. New River (Ariz.) Sr. Ctr., 1992-94. Contbr. articles to newspapers, mags., and profl. jours. Precinct committeeman Maricopa County, Ariz., 1983-96; COMCARE rep. Maricopa County, Ariz., 1992-96; pres. Phoenix Coll. employee rels. council, 1974-79. Recipient Outstanding Cmty. Vol. award Maricopa County Bd., Ariz., 1997. Mem. Willow Hills First Southern Baptist Ch. (publicity dir.). Avocations: painting, playing Spanish guitar, writing.

COATES, WAYNE EVAN, agricultural engineer; b. Edmonton, Alta., Can., Nov. 28, 1947; came to U.S., 1981; s. Orval Bruce Wright and Leora (Raesler) C.; m. Patricia Louise Williams, Aug. 28, 1970. BS in Agr., U. Alta., 1969, MS in Agrl. Engring., 1970; PhD in Agrl. Engring., Okla. State U., 1973. Registered profl. engr., Ariz., Sask. Forage systems engr. Agr. Can., Melfort, Sask., 1973-75; project engr., tech. advisor, asst. sta. mgr. Prairie Agrl. Machinery Inst., Humboldt, Sask., 1975-81; cattle, grain farmer pvt. practice, Humboldt, 1975-81; assoc. prof. U. Ariz., Tucson, 1981-91, prof., 1991—; prof. titular ad honorem U. Nat. de Catamarca, Argentina, 1993—; cons. Vols. in Coop. Assts. and Ptnrs. of Ams., 1991—, Paraguayan Govt. UN Devel. Program, 1987-90, Argentine Govt., univs. and pvt. industry, 1991—, govt., univ. and agrl. orgns., Mid East agrl. projects, 1986-89, 98—; spkr. at internat. confs., Australia, Paraguay, Argentina, Peru, Chile, U.S.; expert witness in field. Designer farm equipment primarily for alternative crops and tillage; patentee in field; contbr. articles to profl. jours. Pres. Sunrise Ter. Village Townhomes Homeowners Assn., Tucson, 1990-92, 98—. Grantee USDA, Washington, 1981—, Ariz. Dept. Environ. Quality, Phoenix, 1989—, U.S. Dept. of Energy, Washington, 1991-98, agrl. industries western U.S., 1982—. Mem. AAAS, NSPE, Am. Soc. Agrl. Engrs. (chmn. Ariz. sect. 1984-85, vice-chmn. Pacific region 1988-89, dir. dist. 4 1991-93, rep. to AAAS Consortium of Affiliates for Internat. Programs 1992-97, internat. dir. 1994-96), Assn. for Advancement of Indsl. Crops (pres. 1994-95, Outstanding Rschr. award 1997), Soc. Automotive Engrs., Air and Waste Mgmt. Assn., Coun. for Agrl. Sci. and Tech., Can. Soc. Agrl. Engring., Australian Soc. for Agrl. Engring., Asian Assn. for Agrl. Engring., Asociacion Latinoamericana de Ingenieria Agricola, Sigma Xi. Avocations: jogging, hiking. Office: U Ariz Office Arid Lands Studies 250 E Valencia Rd Tucson AZ 85706-6800

COBB, ROY LAMPKIN, JR., retired computer sciences corporation executive; b. Oklahoma City, Sept. 23, 1934; s. Roy Lampkin and Alice Maxine Cobb; B.A., U. Okla., 1972; postgrad. U. Calif., Northridge, 1976-77; m. Shirley Ann Dodson, June 21, 1958; children—Kendra Leigh, Cary William, Paul Alan. Naval aviation cadet U.S. Navy, 1955, advanced through grades to comdr., 1970; ret., 1978; mktg./project staff engr. Gen. Dynamics, Pomona, Calif., 1978-80; mgr. dept. support svcs. Computer Scis. Corp., Point Mugu, Calif., 1980-97. Decorated Navy Commendation medal, Air medal (13). Mem. Assn. Naval Aviators, Soc. Logistic Engrs. (editor Launchings 1990-98). Republican. Christian. Club: Las Posas Country, Spanish Hills Country Club. Home: 2481 Brookhill Dr Camarillo CA 93010-2112 Office: Computer Scis Corp PO Box 42273 Port Hueneme CA 93044-4573

COBB, SHIRLEY ANN, public relations specialist, journalist; b. Oklahoma City, Jan. 1, 1936; d. William Ray and Irene Dodson; m. Roy Lampkin Cobb, Jr., June 21, 1958; children: Kendra Leigh, Cary William, Paul Alan. BA in Journalism with distinction, U. Okla., 1958, postgrad., 1972; postgrad., Jacksonville U., 1962. Info. specialist Pacific Missle Test Ctr., Point Mugu, Calif., 1975-76; corr. Religious News Svc., N.Y.C., 1979-81; splty. editor fashion and religion Thousand Oaks (Calif.) News Chronicle, 1977-81; pub. rels. cons., Camarillo, Calif., 1977—; media mgr. pub. info City of Thousand Oaks, 1983—. Contbr. articles to profl. jours. Trustee Ocean View Sch. Bd., 1976-79; pres. Point Mugu Officers' Wives Club, 1975-76; bd. dirs. Camarillo Hospice, 1983-85; sec. Conejo Valley Hist. Soc., 1993-96; sec. Ednl. TV for Conejo, 1997-98, pres., 1998, 99. Recipient Spot News award San Fernando Valley Press Club, 1979. Mem. Pub. Rels. Soc. Am. (L.A. chpt. liaison 1991), Calif. Assn. Pub. Info. Ofcls. (pres. 1989-90, Paul Clark Lifetime Achievement award 1993), Sigma Delta Chi, Phi Beta Kappa, Chi Omega. Republican. Clubs: Las Posas Country, Spanish Hills Country, Town Hall of Calif. Home: 2481 Brookhill Dr Camarillo CA 93010-2112 Office: 2100 E Thousand Oaks Blvd Thousand Oaks CA 91362-7610

COBIANCHI, THOMAS THEODORE, engineering and marketing executive, educator; b. Paterson, N.J., July 7, 1941; s. Thomas and Violet Emily (Bazzar) C.; m. Phyllis Linda Asch, Feb. 6, 1964; 1 child, Michael. Student, Clemson U., 1963; BS, Monmouth Coll., 1968, MBA, 1972; postgrad., U. Pa., 1987; D Bus. Adminstrn., U.S. Internat. U., 1994. Sales mgr. Westinghouse Electric Corp., Balt., 1968-74; sr. internat. sales engr. Westinghouse Electric Corp., Lima, Ohio, 1975-77; program mgr. Westinghouse Electric Corp., Pitts., 1977-78, mgr. bus. devel., 1978-82; dir. mktg. Westinghouse Electric Corp., Arlington, Va., 1982-86; acting dir., engring. mgr. General Dynamics Corp., San Diego, 1986-89; dir. bus. devel. RPV Programs Teledyne Ryan Aero., San Diego, 1989-90; pres. Cobianchi & Assocs., San Diego, 1990; v.p. strategic planning and program devel. S-Cubed div. Maxwell Labs., Inc., San Diego, 1991; v.p. corp. devel. Orincon Corp., 1995—; instr., lectr. various ednl. instns. Active various polit. and ednl. orgns.; mem. bus. adv. coun. U.S. Internat. U.; bd. dirs. Cath. Charities San Diego; vol. exec., sect. chmn. United Way San Diego. Mem. Armed Forces Communications and Electronics Assn. (acting chmn. 1988), Princeton Club of Washington, Nat. Aviation Club, General Dynamics Health Club, Delta Sigma Pi. Home: PO Box 500027 San Diego CA 92150-0027

COBLE, HUGH KENNETH, engineering and construction company executive; b. Rochester, Pa., Sept. 26; s. John L. and Victoria (Neilson) C.; m. Constance Stratton, June 2, 1956; children: Keith Allen, Kimberly Ann, Jon Arthur, Scott Arnold, Neal Stewart. BSChemE, Carnegie Mellon U., 1956; postgrad., UCLA, 1966, U. Houston, 1963-65, Stanford U., 1981. Engr. Standard Oil Calif., El Segundo, 1956-61; sales mgr. Turco Products, Houston, 1961-63; sales dir. W.R. Grace, Houston, 1963-65; vice chmn. emeritus Fluor Corp., Irvine, Calif., 1966-97, 1997—; bd. dirs. Beckman Instruments, Inc., Flowserve Corp., ICO Global Comm. Bd. dirs. John Henry Found., Orange, Calif., 1992-96, Sedona Cultural Park, Sedona Med. Ctr.; trustee Scripps U., Claremont, Calif., 1991-93, Fluor Found.; mem. adv. bd. Thunderbird U., Phoenix, 1992—; exec. engring. adv. com. U. Calif.-Irvine. Mem. Am. Petroleum Inst., Am. Inst. Chem. Engrs. (bd. dirs. 1983-88). Presbyterian. Avocation: golf, piano, organ.

COBLER, CHRISTOPHER CRAIG, editor; b. Topeka, Kans., Aug. 4, 1960; s. Walter Laverne and Nancy (Boley) C.; m. Paula Lynn Cobler, Jan. 19, 1991; children: Nicole, Paul. BA, U. Kans., 1982. Reporter Topeka Capital-Jour., 1982-83, Colorado Springs (Colo.) Gazette, 1983-85; asst. city editor Sioux Falls (S.D.) Argus Leader, 1985-87; asst.mng. editor Ft. Collins Coloradoan, 1987-93; editor Denton (Tex.) Record-Chronicle, 1993-95, Greeley (Colo.) Tribune, 1995—. Recipient 1st place, editl. writing Soc. Profl. Journalists, Colo., 1997. Office: Greeley Tribune 501 8th Ave Greeley CO 80631-3913

COBURN, MARJORIE FOSTER, psychologist, educator; b. Salt Lake City, Feb. 28, 1939; d. Harlan A. and Alma (Ballinger) Polk; m. Robert Byron Coburn, July 2, 1977; children: Polly Klea Foster, Matthew Ryan Foster, Robert Scott Coburn, Kelly Anne Coburn. B.A. in Sociology, UCLA, 1960; Montessori Internat. Diploma honor grad. Washington Montessori Inst., 1968; M.A. in Psychology, U. No. Colo., 1979; Ph.D. in Counseling Psychology, U. Denver, 1983. Licensed clin. psychologist. Probation officer Alameda County (Calif.), Oakland, 1960-62, Contra Costa County (Calif.), El Cerrito, 1966, Fairfax County (Va.), Fairfax, 1967; dir. Friendship Club, Orlando, Fla., 1963-65; tchr. Va. Montessori Sch., Fairfax, 1968-70; spl. edn. tchr. Leary Sch., Falls Church, Va., 1970-72, sch. adminstr., 1973-76; tchr. Aseltine Sch., San Diego, 1976-77, Coburn Montessori Sch., Colorado Springs, Colo., 1977-79; pvt. practice psychotherapy, Colorado Springs, 1979-82, San Diego, 1982—; cons. spl. edn., agoraphobia, women in transition. Mem. Am. Psychol. Assn., Am. Orthopsychiat. Assn., Phobia Soc., Council Exceptional Children, Calif. Psychol. Assn., San Diego Psychological Assn., The Charter 100, Mensa. Episcopalian. Lodge: Rotary. Contbr. articles to profl. jours.; author: (with R.C. Orem) Montessori: Prescription for Children with Learning Disabilities, 1977. Office: 826 Prospect St Ste 101 La Jolla CA 92037-4206

COCHRAN, JACQUELINE LOUISE, management executive; b. Franklin, Ind., Mar. 12, 1953; d. Charles Morris and Marjorie Elizabeth (Rohrbaugh) C. BA, DePauw U., 1975; MBA, U. Chgo., 1977. Fin. analyst Pan Am World Airways, N.Y.C., 1977-79, Gen. Bus. Group W. R. Grace & Co., N.Y.C., 1979-80; sr. fin. analyst Gen. Bus. Group div. W. R. Grace & Co., N.Y.C., 1980-81, mgr. fin. analysis, 1981-82; dir. fin. planning and analysis Gen. Bus. Group div. W. R. Grace & Co., N.Y.C., 1982-85; v.p. fin. Am. Breeders Svc. div. W. R. Grace & Co., DeForest, Wis., 1985-87, v.p. feed ops. Grace Animal Svc. div., 1987-89; gen. mgr., chief ops. officer SoftKat div. W. R. Grace & Co., Chatsworth, Calif., 1990; pres. SoftKat div. W.R. Grace & Co., Chatsworth, Calif., 1990-92; vice-chmn., chief adminstrv. officer Baker & Taylor, Inc., Chatsworth, Calif., 1992, pres. SoftKat div., 1992; exec. cons. Jacqueline Cochran Cons., Westlake Village, Calif., 1993; gen. mgr. Attica Cybernetics, Inc., Chatsworth, Calif., 1995; pres., owner CorporateLinks, Westlake Village, Calif., 1996—. Bd. visitors DePauw U., 1993-96. Recipient Women of Distinction award Madison (Wis.) YWCA, 1987; named to Acad. Women Achievers YWCA N.Y., 1984. Mem. Nat. Assn. Corp. Dirs., ABCD, The Microcomputer Industry Assn. (adv. coun. 1992), AAUW, Phi Beta Kappa, Alpha Lambda Delta, Delta Delta Delta (advisor scholarship com. Madison chpt. 1985-89, treas. 1986-89, ho. corp. bd. dirs. 1986-89, fin. advisor 1986-89). Republican. Methodist. Avocations: reading, golf.

COCHRAN, JERI LYNN, entrepreneur; b. Bethesda, Md., Jan. 3, 1961; d. Carl R. and Mildred (Tanaka) C. BA in Edn., U. Guam, 1985; resource specialist credential, Calif. Luth. U., 1996. Cert. tchr., Guam. Substitute tchr. Dept. Edn., Guam, 1979, tchr., 1985-89; disc jockey Sta. KGUM 567, Guam, 1989; office mgr. PSI Guam, 1989; tchr. L.A. Unified Sch. Dist., 1990-93; distr. Amway, L.A., 1993—; Belmont Colloquim leader L.A. Unified Sch. Dist., 1995-96; chief of staff Motivational Seminar, Guam, 1989, mentor Teamworks team, 1993, 94, 95, 96; fashion cons. Designs on You, L.A., 1992; leadership coun. Berendo Middle Sch., L.A., 1992-93. L.A. Tchrs. Union rep. for Belmont Cluster # 12 Instrnl. Cabinet. Regent scholar U. Guam, 1985, Tchr. Tng. scholar, 1985. Mem. NAFE, Berendo Family Orgn., Sierra Club. Avocations: dirt biking, singing, scuba diving, sailing, outdoors. Home: 6233 Roy St Los Angeles CA 90042-2013

COCHRAN, JOHN HOWARD, plastic and reconstructive surgeon; b. Muncie, Ind., Sept. 6, 1946; s. John H. and Lois M. (Woolridge) C.; m. Elizabeth M. Cochran; 1 child, Ryan K. BS cum laude, Colo. State U., 1968; MD, U. Colo. Sch. Medicine, 1973. Intern surgery U. Calif., San Diego, 1973-74; resident head and neck surgery Stanford U., Palo Alto, Calif., 1974-77; resident plastic surgery U. Wis., Madison, 1979-81; pvt. practice plastic surgery Denver, 1981-90; chief plastic surgery St. Joseph Hosp., Denver, 1987-93, Colo. Med. Group, Denver, 1990-95; chmn. dept. surgery St. Joseph Hosp., 1993—. Pres. bd. trustees Kilimanjaro Children's Hosp., Tanzania, E. Africa, 1989—. Fellow Am. Soc. Plastic and Reconstructive Surgery, Am. Coll. SUrgeons, Acad. Otolaryngology, Head and Neck Surgery; mem. Am. Assn. Plastic Surgeons. Avocations: fly fishing, skiing. Office: 2045 Franklin St Denver CO 80205-5437

COCHRAN, WENDELL, science editor; b. Carthage, Mo., Nov. 29, 1929; s. Wendell Albert and Lillian Gladys (Largent) C.; m. Agnes Elizabeth Groves, Nov. 9, 1963; remarried Corinne Des Jardins, Aug. 25, 1980. A.B., U. Mo., Columbia, 1953, A.M. in Geology, 1956, B.J., 1960. Geologist ground-water br. U.S. Geol. Survey, 1956-58; reporter, copyeditor Kansas City (Mo.) Star, 1960-63; editor Geotimes and Earth Sci. mags., Geospectrum newsletter, Alexandria, Va., 1963-84; v.p. Geol. Survey Inc., Bethesda, Md., 1984-86. Co-author: Into Print: A Practical Guide to Writing, Illustrating, and Publishing, 1977; sr. editor: Geowriting: A Guide to Writing, Editing and Printing in Earth Science, 1973; contbr. articles to profl. jours. and encys. Mem. geol. socs. Washington, London, Assn. Earth Sci. Editors (award Outstanding Contbns. 1982), Dog in the Night-time. Home: 4351 SW Willow St Seattle WA 98136-1769

COCKHILL, BRIAN EDWARD, historical society executive; b. Aug. 13, 1942; s. Linda Ann Moudree Cockhill, Sept. 10, 1966; 1 child, William Frederick Cockhill. Student, Mont. Sch. Mines, Butte, 1960-63; BA in History (hon.), U. Mont., Missoula, 1964, MA in Western Am. History, 1970. Metallurgical rsch. tech. Anaconda (Mont.) Co., 1964-66; teaching asst., rsch. fellow U. Mont., 1967-70; asst. archivist, 1969-70, acting archivist, 1970-71; asst. archivist Mont. Historical Soc., 1971-73; state archivist, 1973-84; program mgr. Ctrl. Svcs. Mont. Historical Soc., 1984-91; deputy dir., 1991-92, dir., 1992—; coord. Mont. Historic Records Adv. Coun., 1976-84; records adv. com. Mont. State, 1977-84; served on Mont. State Records Adv. Com., 1977-84. editor/compiler: (with Dale Johnson) Guide to Manuscripts in Montana Repositories, 1973, Not in Precious Metals Alone: A Manuscript History of Montana, 1976. Recipient Larry Dobell scholarship, 1961-62, Outstanding Am. History Student in a Montana Coll., 1962, U. Mont. Teaching Assistantships, 1967-70. Mem. Soc. Am. Archivists, Am. Hist. Assn., Phi Alpha Theta, Phi Kappa Phi. Office: Montana Historical Soc PO Box 201201 Helena MT 59620-1201

COCKRELL, FRANK BOYD, II, film production company executive; b. Redding, Calif., May 3, 1948; s. Alfred Marion Sr. and Blanch Delma (Webb) C.; children: Catherine, Francis Marion V, Ross, Brooke, Amanda, Richard Sears III. AA, Shasta Jr. Coll., 1968; BS, Sacramento (Calif.) State U., 1970; postgrad., U. Pacific, 1970-72. Pres., chmn. Als Towing & Storage Co., Sacramento, 1976-78, Compacts Only Rental Cars, Sacramento, 1976-78; film producer, actor, comedian Sacramento, L.A. and Las Vegas, Nev., 1976—; fin. cons., 1974—; pres., chmn. Cockrell Prodns., Inc., L.A., 1984—, Palm Spring Employment Agy., Inc., Palm Desert, Calif., 1986; chmn. Contractor's Surety and Fidelity Co., Ltd., U.S. Mining Corp., 21st Century Ins. Group, Inc.-Nev., Hollywood, Calif., 1992—, 21st Century Travel, Inc., Camarillo, Calif., 1992—; CEO, 1st Am. Contractors Bonding Assn., Inc. Author: Vietnam History, 1970. Candidate Assembly 6th Dist. Rep. Party, Sacramento, 1974; mem. Sacramento Rep. Cen. Com., 1975-76, Calif. State Cen. Rep. Com., 1974-76. Bank of Am. scholar, 1966, Shasta Coll. scholar, 1967. Lodge: Optimists (pres. Sacramento chpt. 1975-76, lt. gov. 1976-77). Avocations: karate, scuba diving, movies, swimming, boating. Office: Cockrell Prodns Inc PO Box 1731 Studio City CA 91614-0731

COCKRUM, WILLIAM MONROE, III, investment banker, consultant, educator; b. Indpls., July 18, 1937; s. William Monroe C. II and Katherine J. (Jaqua) Moore; m. Andrea Lee Deering, Mar. 8, 1975; children: Catherine Anne, William Monroe IV. AB with distinction, DePauw U., 1959; MBA with distinction, Harvard U., 1961. With A.G. Becker Paribas Inc., L.A., 1961-84, mgr. nat. corp. fin. div., 1968-71, mgr. pvt. investments, 1971-74, fin. and adminstrv. officer, 1974-80, sr. v.p., 1975-78, vice chmn., 1978-84, also bd. dirs.; prin. William M. Cockrum & Assocs., L.A., 1984—; mem. faculty Northwestern U., 1961-63; vis. lectr. grad. sch. mgmt. UCLA, 1984-88, adj. prof., 1988—. Mem. Monterey Club (Palm Desert, Calif.), Deke Club (N.Y.C.), UCLA Faculty Club, Alisal Golf Club (Solvang, Calif.), Bel-Air Country Club (L.A.), Delta Kappa Epsilon.

COE, MARGARET LOUISE SHAW, community service volunteer; b. Cody, Wyo., Dec. 25, 1917; d. Ernest Francis and Effie Victoria (Abrahamson) Shaw; m. Henry Huttleston Rogers Coe, Oct. 8, 1943 (dec. Aug. 1966); children: Anne Rogers Hayes, Henry H.R., Jr., Robert Douglas II. AA, Stephens Coll., 1937; BA, U. Wyo., 1939. Asst. to editor The Cody Enterprise, 1939-42; mem. Australian Procurement, 1942-43, War Labor Bd., 1943-44; editor The Cody Enterprise, 1968-71. Chmn. bd. trustees Buffalo Bill Hist. Ctr., Cody, 1966—, Cody Med. Found., 1964—; commr. Wyo. Centenniel Commn., Cheyenne, 1986-91. Recipient The Westerner award Old West Trails Found., 1980, Gold Medallion award Nat. Assn. Sec. of State, 1982, disting alumni award U. Wyo., 1984, exemplary alumni award, 1994, Gov.'s award for arts, 1988; inducted Nat. Cowgirl Hall of Fame, 1983. Mem. P.E.O., Delta Delta Delta. Republican. Episcopalian. Avocation: duplicate bridge. Home: 1400 11th St Cody WY 82414-4206

COE, WILLIAM CHARLES, psychology educator; b. Hanford, Calif., Oct. 22, 1930; s. Bernard and Bertha (Vaughan) C.; m. Charlene L. Brown; children: Karen Ann, William Vaughan. B.S., U. Calif., Davis, 1958; postgrad., Fresno State Coll., 1960-61; Ph.D. (NSF fellow), U. Calif., Berkeley, 1964. Rsch. helper Fresno State Coll., 1960-61; rsch. asst. U. Calif., Berkeley, 1961-62, 63-64; NSF rsch. fellow U. Calif., 1963-64; clin. psychology trainee VA Hosp., San Francisco, 1962-63; staff psychologist Langley Porter Neuropsychiat. Inst., San Francisco, 1964-66; asst. clin. prof. med. psychology U. Calif. Sch. Medicine, San Francisco, 1965-66; instr. corr. div. U. Calif., Berkeley, 1967-76; asst. prof. psychology Fresno State Coll.,

1966-68; assoc. prof. psychology Calif. State U., Fresno, 1968-72; prof. Calif. State U., 1972—, chmn. dept. psychology, 1979-84; instr. Calif. Sch. Profl. Psychology, Fresno, 1973, Northeastern U., Boston, 1974; research assoc. U. Calif., Santa Cruz, 1975; cons. Tulare and Kings County Mental Health Clinics, Kingsview Corp., 1966-68, Visalia Unified Sch. Dist., 1967-68; Head Start Program, Fresno, 1970-71, Fig Garden Hosp., Fresno, 1972-73, Concentrated Employment Program, Fresno, 1973-74, VA Hosp., Fresno, 1974; vis. prof.U. Queensland, Australia, 1982. Author: (with T.R. Sarbin) The Student Psychologists Handbook: A Guide to Source, 1969, Hypnosis: A Social Psychological Analysis of Influence Communication, 1972, Challenges of Personal Adjustment, 1972, (with L. Gagnon and D. Swiercinsky) instructors Manual for Challenges of Personal Adjustment, 1972, Psychology X118: Psychological Adjustment, 1973, (with T.R. Sarbin) Mastering Psychology, 1984; Contbr.: chpts. to Behavior Modification in Rehabiliation Settings, 1975, Helping People Change, 1975, 80, Encyclopedia of Clinical Assessment, 1980, Hypnosis: The Cognitive-Behavioral Perspective, 1989, Hypnosis: Current Theory, Research and Practice, 1990, Theories of Hypnosis: Current Models and Perspectives, 1991, Contemporary Hypnosis Research, 1992; contbr. articles to profl. jours. Served with USAF, 1951-55. Decorated D.F.C., Air medal with oak leaf cluster.; NSF grantee, 1967, 71. Fellow Am. Psychol. Assn. (pres. div. 30 psychol. hypnosis 1986-87), Soc. for Clin. and Exptl. Hypnosis; mem. Western Psychol Assn., Calif. Psychol Assn., San Francisco Psychol Assn. (editor San Francisco Psychologist 1966), Central Calif. Psychol. Assn. (pres. 1969, dir. 1972-73), Assn. for Advancement Behavior Therapy, Phi Beta Kappa, Sigma Xi, Phi Kappa Phi, Psi Chi. Office: Calif State U Dept Psychology 5241 M Maple Ave Fresno CA 93740-0011*

COEL, MARGARET SPEAS, writer; b. Denver, Oct. 11, 1937; d. Samuel Francis and Margaret Mary (McCloskey) Speas; m. George William Coel, July 22, 1961; children: William (dec.), Kristin, Lisa Coel Harrison. BA, Marquette U., 1960. Newspaper reporter Westminister (Colo.) Jour., 1960-61; freelance journalist Boulder, Colo., 1972-90; writing tchr. cmty. colls., Denver, 1985-90, U. Colo, Boulder, 1985-90. Author: (biography) Chief Left Hand, 1981 (Best Non-Fiction Book award 1981), Goin' Railroading, 1986 (Colo. Authors award 1986), The Eagle Catcher, 1995, The Ghost Walker, 1996, The Dream Stalker, 1997; contbr. articles to profl. jours. Assoc. fellow Ctr. for Studies of Great Plains, U. Nebr. Mem. Colo. Authors League (pres. 1990-91, Best Non-Fiction Articles award 1991, Best Novel award 1996, 97), Western Writers Am., Mystery Writers Am., Denver Women's Press Club. Democrat. Roman Catholic. Avocations: competitive tennis, skiing. Home: 3155 Lafayette Dr Boulder CO 80303-7112

COFER, BERDETTE HENRY, public management consulting company executive; b. Las Flores, Calif.; s. William Walter and Violet Ellen (Elam) C.; m. Ann McGarva, June 27, 1954 (dec. Feb. 20, 1990); children: Sandra Lea Cofer-Oberle, Ronald William; m. Sally Ann Shepherd, June 12, 1993. AB, Calif. State U., Chico, 1950; MA, U. Calif., Berkeley, 1960. Tchr. Westwood (Calif.) Jr.-Sr. High Sch., 1953-54, Alhambra High Sch., Martinez, Calif., 1954-59; prin. adult and summer sch. Hanford (Calif.) High Sch., 1959-60, asst. supt. bus., 1960-67; dean bus. svcs. West Hills Coll., Coalinga, 1967-76; vice chancellor Yosemite Community Coll. Dist., Modesto, 1976-88; pres. BHC Assocs., Inc., Modesto, 1988—; chmn. Valley Ins. Program Joint Powers Agy., Modesto, 1986-88. Contbr. articles to profl. publs. Pres. Coalinga Indsl. Devel. Corp., 1972-74, Assn. for Retarded Citizens, Modesto, 1985; mayor City of Coalinga, 1974-76; foreman Stanislaus County Grand Jury, Modesto, 1987-88. 1st lt. USAF, 1951-53. Recipient Outstanding Citizen award Coalinga C. of C., 1976, Walter Starr Robie Outstanding Bus. Officer award Assn. Chief Bus. Officers Calif. Community Colls., 1988. Mem. Assn. Calif. C.C. Adminstrs. (life), Lions (dist. gov. 1965-66), Phi Delta Kappa (pres. Kings-Tulare chpt. 1962-63), Am. Legion, 40 and 8, Sons in Retirement. Democrat. Avocation: bowling. Home and Office: 291 Leveland Ln # D Modesto CA 95350-6806

COFER, DEBORAH END, artist; b. Norfolk, Va., Feb. 27, 1954; d. Marion Albert End and Mary Virginia (Haga) Harbert; m. Richard Saunders Cofer III, May 26, 1973; children: Lee Victoria, Mark Thomas. BFA cum laude, East Carolina U., 1977; postgrad., N.Mex. State U., 1978. Ordained min. Kingsway Fellowship Internat. asst. dir. Inst. of the Arts, El Paso, Tex., 1978-80. One-woman and group shows include Ghent Gallery, Norfolk, Va., R.J. Reynolds Industries, N.C. Artists Collection, Winston-Salem, Kate Lewis Gallery, Greenville, N.C., Mendenhall Gallery, Greenville, East Carolina U., Greenville, Old House Gallery, Nags Head, N.C., Petersburg (Va.) Area Art Ctr., U. Tex., El Paso, N.Mex. State U., Las Cruces, Griffith Gallery, Miami, Fla., Chrysler Mus. Art, Norfolk, Nev. West Gallery, Reno, Aesthete Gallery, El Paso, N.C. Mus. Art, Raleigh, Va. Mus. Art, Richmond, El Paso Mus. Art, U. Nev., Reno, Sierra Nev. Mus. Art, Reno, Nat. Gallery Modern Art, Lisbon, Portugal, others; represented in permanent collections Chrysler Mus. Art, Norfolk, El Paso Mus. Art, R.J. Reynolds Industries World Hdqrs., Winston-Salem, East Carolina U., Greenville, Norfolk Pub. Libr., Appalachian State U., Boone, N.C., N.C. Mus. Art, Raleigh, Sierra Nev. Mus. Art, Reno, others. Spkr. Streams in the Desert Internat., Reno, 1995—. Mem. Aglow Internat. (area bd. 1985-96), Phi Kappa Phi, Delta Phi Delta (scholar). Republican. Avocations: writing, reading, raquetball, travel.

COFFILL, MARJORIE LOUISE, civic leader; b. Sonora, Calif., June 11, 1917; d. Eric J. and Pearl (Needham) Segerstrom; A.B. with distinction in Social Sci., Stanford U., 1938, M.A. in Edn., 1941; m. William Charles Coffill, Jan. 25, 1948, (dec.); children: William James, Eric John. Asst. mgr. Sonora Abstract & Title Co. (Calif.), 1938-39; mem. dean of women's staff Stanford, 1939-41; social dir. women's campus Pomona Coll., 1941-43, instr. psychology, 1941-43; asst. to field dir. ARC, Lee Moore AFB, Calif., 1944-46; partner Riverbank Water Co., Riverbank and Hughson, Calif., 1950-68. Mem. Tuolumne County Mental Health Adv. Com., 1963-70; mem. central advisory coun. Supplementary Edn. Ctr., Stockton, Calif., 1966-70; mem. advisory com. Columbia Jr. Coll., 1972-89, pres., 1980—; pres. Columbia Found., 1972-74, bd. dirs., 1974-77; mem. Tuolumne County Bicentennial Com., 1974—; active PTA, ARC. Pres., Tuolumne County Rep. Women, 1952—, assoc. mem. Calif. Rep. Central Com., 1950. Trustee Sonora Union High Sch., 1969-73, Salvation Army Tuolumne County, 1973—; bd. dirs. Lung Assn. Valley Lode Counties, 1974—, life 1986—. Recipient Pi Lambda Theta award, 1940, Outstanding Citizen award C. of C., 1974, Citizen of Yr. award, 1987, Woman of Distinction award Soroptimist Internat., 1993; named to Columbia Coll. Hall of Fame, 1990; named Alumnus of Yr., Sonora Union High Sch., 1994. Mem. AAUW (charter mem. Tuolumne County br., pres. Sonora br. 1965-66). Episcopalian (mem. vestry 1968, 75). Home: 376 Summit Ave Sonora CA 95370-5728

COFFIN, THOMAS M., federal magistrate judge; b. St. Louis, May 30, 1945; s. Kenneth C. and Agnes M. (Ryan) C.; m. Penelope Teaff, Aug. 25, 1973; children: Kimberly, Laura, Colleen, Corey, Mary, Brendan, T.J. BA, St. Benedict's Coll., 1967; JD, Harvard, 1970. Bar: Mo. 1970, Calif. 1972, Oreg. 1982, U.S. Dist. Ct. (so. dist.) Calif. 1971, U.S. Dist. Ct. Oreg. 1980, U.S. Ct. Appeals (9th cir.) 1971. Asst. U.S. atty., chief criminal divsn. U.S. Attys. Office, San Diego, 1971-80; asst. U.S. atty., supr. asst. U.S. atty. U.S. Attys. Office, Eugene, Oreg., 1980-92; U.S. Magistrate judge U.S. Dist. Ct., Eugene, Oreg., 1992—; sr. litigation counsel U.S. Dept. Justice, 1984. Mem. Oreg. Bar Assn. Avocations: soccer, jogging. Office: US Dist Ct 211 E 7th Ave Eugene OR 97401-2774*

COFFINGER, MARALIN KATHARYNE, retired career officer, consultant; b. Ogden, Iowa, July 5, 1935; d. Cleo Russell and Katharyne Frances (McGovern) Morse. BA, Ariz. State U., 1957, MA, 1961; diploma, Armed Forces Staff Coll., 1972, Nat. War Coll., 1977; postgrad., Inst. for Higher Def. Studies, 1985. Commd. 2nd lt. USAF, 1963, advanced through grades to brig. gen., 1985; base comdr., dep. base comdr. Elmendorf AFB, Anchorage, Alaska, 1977-79; base comdr. Norton AFB, San Bernardino, Calif., 1979-82; chmn. spl. and incentive pays Office of Sec. Def., Pentagon, Washington, 1982-83; dep. dir. pers. programs USAF Hdqrs., Pentagon, Washington, 1983-85; command dir. NORAD [illegible] Mountain Complex, Colo., 1985-86; dir. pers. plans USAF Hdqrs., Pentagon, Washington, 1986-89; ret. USAF, 1989; dir. software products ops. Walsh America, 1992-94. Keynote speaker, mem. dedication ceremonies Vietnam Meml. Com., Phoenix, 1990; mem. Phoenix Symphony Orch., 1954-63; prin. flutist Scottsdale Cmty. Orch., Scottsdale Concert Band, Sonoran Wind Quintet. Decorated Air Force D.S.M., Def. Superior Svc. medal, Legion of Merit, Bronze Star, recipient Nat. Medal of Merit. Mem. NAFE, Air Force Assn. (vet./retiree coun., pres. Sky Harbor chpt. 1990), Nat. Officers Assn., Ret. Officers Assn., Maricopa County Sheriff's Exec. Posse, Ariz. State U. Alumni Assn. (Profl. Excellence award 1981), Nat. Assn. Uniformed Svcs. Roman Catholic. Home: 8059 E Maria Dr Scottsdale AZ 85255-5418

COFFMAN, VIRGINIA E(DITH), writer; b. San Francisco, July 30, 1914; d. William Milo and Edythe Louise (DeuVaul) C. AB, U. Calif., Berkeley, 1938. from sec. to script writer and rewriter, various film studios, Hollywood, Calif., 1944-56. Novelist: published 109 novels, 1959—, 90 hardcover. Recipient trophy for Romantic Times Historical and Gothic novels (hardcovers), 1983; elected to Nevada Writers Hall of Fame at U. Nev., 1990. Democrat. Avocations: reading history and biography. Home: 100 N Arlington Ave Apt 20C Reno NV 89501-1252

COFIELD, PHILIP THOMAS, educational association administrator; b. Monmouth, Ill., July 3, 1951; s. Earl Crescant and Vera (Shunick) C.; divorced; children: Calla, Megan. BA in English, St. Ambrose U., 1973. Dir. Jr. Achievment of Quad Cities, Davenport, Moline, Iowa, Ill., 1980-83; account exec. Jr. Achievment Inc., 1983-85; pres., CEO Jr. Achievment of Utah, Salt Lake City, 1985—. Established Utah Bus. Hall of Fame, 1991; bd. dirs. Utah Partnership for Ednl. and Econ. Devel. Mem. Utah Coun. on Economic Edn. (bd. dirs.), Salt Lake area C. of C., Rotary Club, (com. co-chmn. Salt Lake City). Office: Jr Achievement of Utah 182 S 600 E Salt Lake City UT 84102-1909

COGGIN, CHARLOTTE JOAN, cardiologist, educator; b. Takoma Park, Md., Aug. 6, 1928; d. Charles Benjamin and Nanette (McDonald) Coggin; BA, Columbia Union Coll., 1948; MD, Loma Linda U., 1952, MPH, 1987; DSc (hon.), Andrews U., 1994. Intern, L.A. County Gen. Hosp., L.A., 1952-53, resident in medicine, 1953-55; fellow in cardiology Children's Hosp., L.A., 1955-56, White Meml. Hosp., L.A., 1955-56; rsch. assoc. in cardiology, house physician Hammersmith Hosp., London, 1956-57; resident in pediatrics and pediatric cardiology Hosp. for Sick Children, Toronto, Ont., Can., 1965-67; cardiologist, co-dir. heart surgery team Loma Linda (Calif.) U., asst. prof. medicine , 1961-73, assoc. prof., 1973-91, prof. medicine, 1991—, asst. dean Sch. Medicine Internat. Programs, 1973-75, assoc. dean, 1975—, spl. asst. to univ. pres. for internat. affairs, 1991, co-dir., cardiologist heart surgery team missions to Pakistan and Asia, 1963, Greece, 67, 69, Saigon, Vietnam, 1974, 75, to Saudi Arabia, 1976-87, People's Republic China, 1984, 89-91, Hong Kong, 1985, Zimbabwe, 1988, Kenya, 1988, Nepal, 1992, 93, China, 1992, Zimbabwe, 1993, Myanmar, 1995, North Korea, 1996, Penang, Malaysia, 1999; mem. Pres's. Advisory Panel on Heart Disease, 1972—; hon. prof. U. Manchuria, Harbin, People's Republic China, 1989, hon. dir. 1st People's Hosp. of Mundanjiang, Heilongjiang Province, 1989. Apptd. mem. Med. Quality Rev. Com.-Dist. 12, 1976-80. Recipient award for service to people of Pakistan City of Karachi, 1963, Medallion award Evangelismos Hosp., Athens, Greece, 1967, Gold medal of health South Vietnam Ministry of Health, 1974, Charles Elliott Weinger award for excellence, 1976, Wall Street Jour. Achievement award, 1987, Disting. Univ. Svc. award Loma Linda U., 1990; named Honored Alumnus Loma Linda U. Sch. Medicine, 1973, Outstanding Women in Gen. Conf. Seventh-day Adventists, 1975, Alumnus of Yr., Columbia Union Coll., 1984, Outstanding Achievement in Edn., Adventist Alumni Achievement award, 1999. Diplomate Am. Bd. Pediatrics. Mem. Am. Coll. Cardiology, AMA (physicians adv. com. 1969—) Calif. Med. Assn. (com. on med. schs., com. on member services), San Bernardino County Med. Soc. (chmn. communications com. 1975-77, mem. communications com. 1987-88, editor bull. 1975-76, William L. Cover, M.D. Outstanding Contbn. to Medicine award 1995), Am. Heart Assn., AAUP, Med. Research Assn. Calif., Calif. Heart Assn., AAUW, Am. Acad. Pediatrics, World Affairs Council, Internat. Platform Assn., Calif. Museum Sci. and Industry MUSES (Outstanding Woman of Year in Sci. 1969), Am. Med. Women's Assn., Loma Linda Sch. Medicine Alumni Assn. (pres. 1978), Alpha Omega Alpha, Delta Omega. Author: Atrial Septal Defects, motion picture (Golden Eagle Cine award and 1st prize Venice Film Festival 1964); contbr. articles to med. jours. Democrat. Home: 11495 Benton St Loma Linda CA 92354-3682 Office: Loma Linda U Magan Hall Rm 105 11060 Anderson St Loma Linda CA 92350

COGHILL, DAVIS GAROLD, chiropractic physician, counselor, psychotherapist; b. Gallup, N.M., Mar. 25, 1948; s. Donald Garold and June Elizabeth (Davis) C.; m. Dianna H. Glick, Jan. 26, 1991; children: Matthew Donald, Anna Janell. BA in Psychology, Calif. State U., L.A., 1973, MA in Spl. Edn., 1975, MA in Psychology, 1981; PhD in Counseling Psychology, U. Santa Barbara, 1985; D in Chiropractic cum laude, Life Chiropractic Coll. West, 1990; PsyD, Am. Behavioral Studies Inst., 1998. Lic. marriage, family and child counselor; lic. doctor of chiropractic. Instr., counselor L.A. County Office Edn., 1976—; acad. counselor, drug/alcohol abuse prevention coord. Life Chiropractic Coll. West, San Lorenzo, Calif., 1987-90; pvt. practice So. and No. Calif., 1982—; oral commr. Bd. Behavioral Sci. Examiners, Calif., 1987—; counselor Montebello Unified Sch. Dist., 1993—; mem. med. team Humanitarian Med. Mission, Trinidad and Tobago, 1996, 97; lectr. in field. Patentee in field. Fellow Nat. Grief Counselors Assn., Nat. Poetry Therapy Assn., Soc. Traumatic Stress Studies, Intergenerational Psychotherapy Soc. (founding mem.). Avocations: martial arts, dance, woodworking, guitar and vocal performances. Office: 100 N Hill Ave Ste 205 Pasadena CA 91106-1943

COHAN, CHRISTOPHER, professional sports team executive; b. Salinas, Calif., 1951; s. Helen C.; m. Angela; three children. BA, Ariz. State U., 1973. With Feather River Cable TV Corp., Orinda, Calif., 1973-77; owner Sonic Comms., Alaska, 1977; owner, CEO Golden State Warriors, Calif.; bd. dirs. Calif. TV Assn. Office: c/o Golden State Warriers 1011 Broadway Oakland CA 94607-4019 also: Golden State Warriors 1221 Broadway Fl 20 Oakland CA 94612-1822*

COHEN, BARBARA ANN, artist; b. Milw., Feb. 18, 1953; d. Joseph and Irene Marion (Brown) C. BS in Art, U. Wis., 1975. One-woman shows include 1st Wis. Nat. Bank, 1981; exhibited in group shows at San Francisco State, 1975-76, Comprehensive Employment Tng. Act, Milw., 1979, San Dieguito Art Guild, 1981, Imperial Valley Art Show, 1982, La Jolla Light Photo Contest, 1986, Clairemont Art Guild, 1989-95. Recipient 1st place award for oil painting Imperial Valley Art Show. Democrat. Jewish. Home: 8627 Via Mallorca Apt D La Jolla CA 92037-9021

COHEN, BRENT ROSS, lawyer; b. Cheyenne, Wyo., Apr. 17, 1956; s. Laurence Joseph and Arline (Pasternack) C.; m. Dana Lynn Klapper, Sept. 7, 1997. BS, U. Colo., 1978, JD, 1981. Bar: Colo. 1981, Wyo. 1982. Law clk. Hon. C.A. Brimmer-U.S. Dist. Ct., Cheyenne, 1981-82; atty. Rothgerber, Johnson & Lyons LLP, Denver, 1982—. State counsel Dem. Nat. Com., Washington, 1991—. Avocations: skiing, running, guitar. Office: Rothgerber Johnson & Lyons 1200 17th St Ste 3000 Denver CO 80202

COHEN, CYNTHIA MARYLYN, lawyer; b. Bklyn., Sept. 5, 1945. AB, Cornell U., 1967; JD cum laude, NYU, 1970. Bar: N.Y. 1971, U.S. Ct. Appeals (2nd cir.) 1972, U.S. Dist. Ct. (so. and ea. dists.) N.Y. 1972, U.S. Supreme Ct. 1975, U.S. Dist. Ct. (cen. and no. dists.) Calif. 1980, U.S. Ct. Appeals (9th cir.) 1980, U.S. Dist. Ct. (so. dist.) Calif. 1981, U.S. Dist. Ct. (ea. dist.) Calif. 1986. Assoc. Simpson Thacher & Bartlett, N.Y.C., 1970-76, Kaye, Scholer, Fierman, Hayes & Handler, N.Y.C., 1976-80; assoc. Stutman, Treister & Glatt, P.C., L.A., 1980-81, ptnr., 1981-87; ptnr. Hughes Hubbard & Reed, N.Y.C. and L.A., 1987-93, Morgan, Lewis & Bockius, LLP, L.A., Phila., N.Y.C., 1993-98, Jeffer, Mangels, Butler & Marmaro LLP, L.A. and San Francisco, 1998—. Bd. dirs. N.Y. chpt. Am. Cancer Soc., 1977-80. Recipient Am. Jurisprudence award for evidence, torts and legal instns., 1968-69; John Norton Pomeroy scholar NYU, 1968-70, Founders Day Cert., [illegible] Bar City N.Y. (trade regulation com. 1976-79), Assn. Bus Trial Lawyers, Fin. Lawyers Conf., N.Y. State Bar Assn. (chmn. class-action com. 1979), State Bar Calif., Los Angeles County Bar Assn., Order of Coif, Delta Gamma. Avocations: tennis, bridge, rare books, wines. Home: 4531 Dundee Dr Los Angeles CA 90027-1213 Office: Jeffer Mangels Butler Marmaro LLP 2121 Ave Of Stars Fl 10 Los Angeles CA 90067-5010

COHEN, D. ASHLEY, clinical neuropsychologist; b. Omaha, Oct. 2, 1952; d. Cenek and Dorothy A. (Bilek) Hrabik; m. Donald I. Cohen, 1968 (div. 1976); m. Lyn J. Mangiameli, June 12, 1985. BA in Psychology, U. Nebr., Omaha, 1975, MA in Psychology, 1979; PhD in Clin. Psychology, Calif. Coast U., 1988. Lic. psychologist, Calif.; lic. marriage and family therapist, Nev. Family specialist Ea. Nebr. Human Svcs. Agy. Consultation & Edn., 1979-80; psychotherapist Washoe Tribe, Gardnerville, Nev., 1980; therapist Family Counseling Svc., Carson City, Nev., 1980-93; psychotherapist Alpine County Mental Health, Markleeville, Calif., 1981-89, dir., 1990-93; psychologist Golden Gate Med. Examiners, San Francisco, San Jose, Calif., 1993-97; pvt. practice assessment and neuropsychology CogniMetrix, San Jose, 1997—; conf. presenter and spkr. in field; presenter rsch. findings 7th European Conf. Personality, Madrid, 1994, Oxford (Eng.) U. ISSID Conf., 1991; site coord. nat. standardization Kaufmann brief intelligence test A.G.S., 1988-90. Vol. EMT, Alpine County, 1983-93. Recipient Svc. to Youth award Office Edn., 1991. Mem. APA, Internat. Neuropsychol. Soc., Internat. Soc. Study Individual Differences, Am. Psychol. Soc., Nat. Acad. Neuropsychology. Avocation: astronomy, adventure travel, dog training. Office: 320 S 3d St # 201 San Jose CA 95112

COHEN, DANIEL MORRIS, museum administrator, marine biology researcher; b. Chgo., July 6, 1930; s. Leonard U. and Myrtle (Gertz) C.; m. Anne Carolyn Constant, Nov. 4, 1955; children—Carolyn A., Cynthia S. BA, Stanford U., 1952, MA, 1953, PhD, 1958. Asst. prof., curator fishes U. Fla., Gainesville, 1957-58; systematic zoologist Bur. Comml. Fisheries, Washington, 1958-60; dir. systematics lab. Nat. Marine Fisheries Service, Washington, 1960-81; sr. scientist Nat. Marine Fisheries Service, Seattle, 1981-82; chief curator life scis. Los Angeles County Mus. of Natural History, 1982-93, dep. dir. rsch. and collections, 1993-95; emeritus, 1995—; adj. prof. biology U. So. Calif., 1982-98. Contbr. numerous articles to profl. jours. Fellow AAAS, Calif. Acad. Sci.; mem. Am. Soc. Ichthyologists and Herpetologists (v.p. 1969, 70, pres. 1985, Gibbs award 1997), Biol. Soc. Washington (pres. 1971-72), Soc. Systematic Biology (mem. coun. 1976-78). Avocation: gardening, cooking, reading. E-mail: acohen@neteze.com. Home: PO Box 192 Bodega Bay CA 94923-0192

COHEN, ELLIS AVRUM, producer, writer, investigative journalist; b. Balt., Sept. 15, 1945; s. Leonard Howard and Selma Jean (Lattin) C. AA in Comm., C.C. of Balt., 1965. Dir. pub. rels. The Camera Mart, Inc., N.Y.C., 1971-72; editor-in-chief TV/New York mag., N.Y.C., 1972-74; dir. worldwide pub. rels., advt. and mktg. William Morris Agy., N.Y.C., 1974-77; sr. publicist Solters, Roskin & Friedman, L.A., 1977-78; sr. v.p. creative affairs Don King Prodns., N.Y.C., 1978; TV-movie prodr. (staff) CBS Entertainment Prodns., Studio City, Calif., 1979-88; CEO/pres. Hennessey Entertainment, Ltd., L.A., 1983—; film cons. Assn. Film Commrs., 1987—. Author: Dangerous Evidence, 1995, Avenue of the Stars, 1991; prodr. (CBS-TV) Love, Mary, 1985 (Luminas award 1986), (Lifetime Cable Network movie) Dangerous Evidence: The Lori Jackson Story, 1999, (network TV movies) First Steps, 1985 (Film Adv. Bd. award 1985), Aunt Mary, 1979 (Grand prize winner MIFED film festival, Milan, Italy 1980); on-camera spokesperson for Web TV and Sony Infomercials; movie and book cons. Polit. cons. Mayor Tom Bradley re-election campaign, L.A., 1977; mayoral appointee Com. in the Pub. Interest, N.Y.C., 1973-77; prodr., dir., cons. Dem. Nat. Conv., N.Y.C., 1975-76. With U.S. Army, 1965-67. Recipient Gov.'s award for employment of the handicapped, L.A., 1980, Christopher award, 1980, Humanities cert. Human Family Cultural & Ednl. Inst., L.A., 1986, Key-to-City mayor of Balt., 1979. Mem. AARP, NATAS, Prodrs. Guild of Am., Writers Guild of Am., West (nominated Outstanding TV Movie Story 1979), Investigative Reporters and Editors, The Reporters Networks, Nat. Writers Union, Internat. Fedn. Journalists, HTML Writers Guild. Democrat. Jewish. Avocations: photography, hat collecting, exploring islands of the world, trail riding, volunteering. Office: Hennessey Entertainment Ltd PO Box 481164 Los Angeles CA 90048-9319

COHEN, JERRY SANFORD, music editor; b. Scranton, Pa.; s. Joseph and Irene Cohen. AA, Keystone Coll.; BA, NYU; MA, U. So. Calif., L.A.; JD, San Fernando Valley Coll. Law. Pvt. practice film editor N.Y.C.; film editor, music editor Army Pictorial Ctr., L.I.; pvt. practice film and music editor Hollywood, Calif.a; comml. film editor Columbia Pictures, Hollywood; music editor Universal Studios, Hollywood, 1968—. Recipient Emmy award for music editing on Miami Vice, TV Acad. Arts and Scis., 1985. Mem. TV Acad. Arts and Sci., Film Editors Union. Home: PO Box 8881 Universal City CA 91618

COHEN, MARSHALL, philosophy and law educator; b. N.Y.C., Sept. 27, 1929; s. Harry and Fanny (Marshall) Cohen; m. Margaret Dennes, Feb. 15, 1964; children: Matthew, Megan. BA, Dartmouth Coll., 1951; MA, Harvard U., 1953; postgrad., Magdalen Coll., Oxford, Eng., 1953-54; MA, Oxford U., 1977. Asst. prof. philosophy and gen. edn. Harvard U., Cambridge, Mass., 1958-62; asst. prof. philosophy U. Chgo., 1962-64, assoc. prof. philosophy, 1964-67, acting chair Coll. Philosophy, 1965-66; assoc. prof. philosophy Rockefeller U., 1967-70; prof. philosophy Richmond Coll. (now Coll. of S.I.), 1970-83; prof. grad. sch. CUNY, 1970-83, exec. officer program in philosophy, 1975-83; dean divsn. humanities U. So. Calif., L.A., 1983-94, prof. philsophy and law, 1983-98, dean emeritus Coll. Letters, Arts and Scis., 1983—, prof. emeritus philosophy and law, 1998—, prof. emeritus phil. of law, 1998—; vis. prof. U. Calif., Berkeley, 1971, Harvard U., 1972, New Sch. for Social Rsch., 1973-74, Cornell U., 1974, Yale U., 1975, Barnard Coll., Columbia U., 1979-81, U.S. Mil. Acad., West Point, N.Y., 1982; prin. investigator Andrew W. Mellon Found., 1981-83, 91-95; N.Y. Coun. for Humanities lectr., 1982-83. Author: Film Theory and Criticism, 1974, 5th edit., 1998, others; editor: Philosophy and Public Affairs, 1971—; contbr. numerous articles, essays and revs. to profl. jours. Fellow ACLS, 1951-52, Yale Law Sch., 1964-65, Trumbull Coll. Yale U., 1968-73, Sheldon traveling fellow Harvard U., 1953-54, Guggenheim fellow, 1976-77, Rockefeller Found. humanities fellow, 1977; vis. fellow All Souls Coll., Oxford, Eng.; NEH grantee, 1975; Phi Beta Kappa vis. scholar, 1975-76. Mem. Am. Philos. Assn., Soc. for Philosophy and Pub. Affairs, Amintaphil. Office: U So Calif Law Sch Los Angeles CA 90089-0071

COHEN, PAUL MARTIN, magazine editor, writer; b. Balt., June 4, 1951; s. Sidney and Sylvia (Resnick) C.; m. Carol Ellen Vieth, Apr. 5, 1991; children: Samuel J., Emily D. BA, San Francisco State U., 1978. Asst. editor New West/Calif. Mag., San Francisco, 1978-83; mng. editor Atari, Sunnyvale, Calif., 1984-86; mgr. publs. The Peabody Group, San Francisco, 1986; editor Tom Peters Group, Palo Alto, Calif., 1989-95; mng. editor Leader to Leader quar., San Francisco, 1995—. Co-author: Working Wisdom, 1995; co-editor: Leader to Leader: Enduring Insights on Leadership from the Drucker Foundation's Award-winning Journal, 1999; contbr. articles to profl. jours. and mags. Recipient Maggie award for best trade quar. Western Publs. Assn., 1998. Office: Jossey Bass Pubs 350 Sansome St San Francisco CA 94104

COHEN, RONALD JAY, lawyer; b. Des Moines, Mar. 2, 1948; s. Maurice Marvin and Edith (Levitt) C.; m. Ruthie Eisenberg, Dec. 19, 1984; children: Daniel, Brad. BA, U. Wis., 1970; JD, U. Minn., 1972. Bar: Ariz. 1972. Assoc. Streich Lang, Phoenix, 1972-76; ptnr. Streich, Lang, Weeks & Cardon, Phoenix, 1977-91; dir., ptnr. Cohen & Cotton, P.C., Phoenix, 1991—; vis. prof. Ind. U., 1976; adj. prof. Ariz. State U., 1980; appointed judge pro tempore Maricopa County Superior Ct., 1983-91. Contbr. articles to profl. jours. Mem. ABA (program chair litigation sect., 1992, chair nat. inst., 1992-93), Maricopa County Bar Assn. (Robert E. Mills Mem. of Yr. award 1986). Office: Cohen & Cotton PC 400 E Van Buren St Ste 440 Phoenix AZ 85004-2223

COHEN, SANFORD BARRY, radio executive, consultant; b. Detroit, June 17, 19[illegible]; s. Edward Cohen and Arlene (Rosenberg) Hirsch; m. Terry Susan Pollack, Aug. 30, 1981. BA in Econs., Mich. State U., 1979. V.p. Nat. Phonecasting Co. div. Gannett Broadcasting, Atlanta, 1982-84; owner, pres. Prescott Valley (Ariz.) Broadcasting Co., Inc., 1983—; pres. Broadcast Careers, Inc., Atlanta, 1980-82; ind. cons., Ariz., Ga., Ala., N.Y., 1982—. Inventor U.S.'s first solar powered FM radio sta., 1986 (Energy Innovation award 1987, named S.B.A. Innovative Advocate of Yr. 1987). Mem. Nat. Assn. Broadcasters. Avocations: music, sports, art, theater. Office: Sta KPPV-FM/KQNA-AM PO Box 26523 Prescott Valley AZ 86312-6523

COHEN, SHARLEEN COOPER, interior designer, writer; b. L.A., June 11, 1940; d. Sam and Claretta (Ellis) White; m. R. Gary Cooper, Dec. 18, 1960 (dec. Feb., 1971); m. Martin L. Cohen, M.D., Aug. 27, 1972; children: Cami Gordon, Dalisa Cooper Cohen. Student, U. Calif., Berkeley, 1957-58, UCLA, 1958-60, L.A. Valley Film Sch., 1976-78. Owner, mgr. Designs on You, L.A., 1965-77; writer L.A., 1977—; prodr. Jewish Repertory Theatre, N.Y.C., 1996. Author: (books) The Day After Tomorrow, 1979, Regina's Song, 1980, The Ladies of Beverly Hills, 1983, Marital Affairs, 1985, Love, Sex and Money, 1988, Lives of Value, 1991, Innocent Gestures, 1994; (play) Solomon and Sheba, 1990; (musical) Sheba, 1996; assoc. prodr. Broadway show Street Corner Symphony; prodr. Cookin' At The Cookery, The Best of Times; assoc. prodr. Duet. Mem. exec. com. Women of Distinction United Jewish Appeal, 1990-95; chair L.A. chpt. Nat. Gaucher Found., 1991-95; bd. dirs., mem. com. chair Calif. Coun. for the Humanities, San Francisco, 1992-98. Recipient Hon. Mention, Santa Barbara Writers Conf., 1978. Mem. PEN, Writers Guild of Am.

COHEN, SHIRLEY MASON, educator, writer, civic worker; b. Jersey City, June 24, 1924; d. Herman and Esther (Vinik) Mason; m. Herbert Leonard Cohen, June 24, 1951; children: Bruce Mason, Annette Pauline, Carol Elyse, Debra Tamara. BA, Rutgers U., 1945; MA, Columbia U., 1946; postgrad., U. Calif., Berkeley, 1946-51. Instr. U. Calif., Berkeley, 1946-51, Am. River Coll., Sacramento, 1962; tchr. various H.S., Sacramento, 1975-92; mentor tchr. Sacramento City Unified Sch. Dist., 1987-88. Author: Yearning to Breathe Free: The Story of the Vinik, Mason, and Gatkin Families, 1997. Bd. dirs. Sacramento Cmty. Concerts, 1965—. Mem. Phi Beta Kappa. Avocations: theatre, music, tennis, writing, literature.

COHEN, WILLIAM, construction executive; b. 1962. Graduate, Loyola U., 1974. Assoc. Monteleone & McCrory, L.A., 1974-80; v.p. Valley Crest Landscape, Inc., Calabasas, Calif., 1980—. Office: Valley Crest Landscape Inc 24121 Ventura Blvd Calabasas CA 91302-1449*

COHN, BRUCE, film and television company executive; b. San Francisco, Apr. 8, 1931; s. Theodore and Rosebud Enid (Schmulian) C.; m. Jeanette Pacheco, July 16, 1966 (div. 1988); 1 child, Mitchell Barry. M of Journalism, U. Calif., Berkeley, 1954. Writer, producer Clete Roberts News Sta. KTLA-TV, Hollywood, Calif., 1957-62; west coast producer Huntley-Brinkley and Today Show NBC, Burbank, Calif., 1962-63; news dir. Sta. KNBC-TV, Burbank, 1963-66; Washington producer ABC Evening News, 1966-68; west coast producer Los Angeles, 1968-71; exec. producer Nat. Pub. Affairs Ctr. for TV Pub. Broadcasting System, Washington, 1971-73; ind. producer, writer various film studios, Burbank, 1973-75, 1973—; pres. Bruce Cohn Prodns., Inc., Mill Valley, Calif., 1975—. Screenwriter ((film) Good Guys Wear Black, 1979; writer, producer (TV documentary) 1968-A Crack in Time, 1978, Secret Files of J. Edgar Hoover, 1990; producer (documentary series) Time Was, 1980; producer, dir. (documentary series) Rember When, 1981; writer, producer, dir. (documentary) Kisses with Lauren Bacall, 1991; writer, producer (documentary) Tom Clancy Presents John Ehrlichman In the Eye of the Storm, 1998. Recipient Cable Ace award, 1979, 81, 2 Gold medals N.Y. Internat. Film Festival, 1981, Gold plaque Chgo. Internat. Film Festival, 1982, Emmy award Acad. TV Arts and Scis., 1984, 97. Mem. Writers Guild Am., Am. Film Inst. Home and Office: 1 Weatherly Dr Ste 101 Mill Valley CA 94941-3231

COHN, DANIEL HOWARD, laboratory director; b. Santa Monica, Calif., Aug. 24, 1955; s. Sidney Lorber and Mynda Ellen (Zimmerman) C.; m. Ludmila Bojman, May 16, 1982; children: Zachary, Marissa, Rachel. BA, U. Calif., Santa Barbara, 1977; PhD, Scripps Inst. Oceanography, 1983. Postdoctoral fellow U. Wash., Seattle, 1983-88; 0sch. scientist, asst. prof. Cedars-Sinai Med. Ctr./UCLA, 1988-93, assoc. prof., 1993-97, prof., 1997—; mem. genetics tng. program UCLA, 1988—; reviewer various jours. and granting agys. Editorial bd. various jours.; contbr. articles to profl. jours. and books. Grants com. chair, bd. dirs. Concern Found. for Cancer Rsch., L.A., 1988—. Recipient Martin Kamen award U. Calif., San Diego, 1983, Eckhart prize Scripps Inst. Oceanography, 1983; postdoctoral award NIH, 1985-88, grantee, 1988—. Mem. AAAS, Phi Beta Kappa. Democrat. Jewish. Avocations: gardening, golf, volleyball, waterskiing, snow skiing. Office: Cedars-Sinai Med Ctr 8700 Beverly Blvd Los Angeles CA 90048-1865*

COHN, LAWRENCE STEVEN, physician, educator; b. Chgo., Dec. 21, 1945; s. Jerome M. and Francis C.; BS, U. Ill., 1967, MD, 1971; m. Harriett G. Rubin, Sept. 1, 1968; children: Allyson and Jennifer (twins). Intern, Mt. Zion Hosp., San Francisco, 1971-72, resident, 1972-73; resident U. Chgo., 1973-74; practice medicine specializing in internal medicine, Paramount, Calif.; pres. med. staff Charter Suburban Hosp., 1981-83; mem. staff Long Beach Meml. Hosp., Harbor Gen. Hosp; clin. prof. medicine UCLA. Maj. USAF, 1974-76. Recipient Disting. Teaching award Harbor-UCLA Med. Ctr., 1980, 90; diplomate Am. Bd. Internal Medicine. Fellow Am. Coll. Physicians; mem. A.C.P., AMA, Calif. Med. Assn., L.A. County Med. Assn., Am. Heart Assn., Soc. Air Force Physicians, Phi Beta Kappa, Phi Kappa Phi, Phi Lambda Upsilon, Phi Eta Sigma, Alpha Omega Alpha. Home: 6608 Via La Paloma Palos Verdes Peninsula CA 90275-6449 Office: 16415 Colorado Ave Ste 202 Paramount CA 90723-5054

COHN, MICHAEL JAY, psychologist, consultant, educator; b. Chgo., Apr. 22, 1951; s. Myron and Jacqueline P. (Gollob) C.; m. Linda Dock, Mar. 22, 1986. BA, Ariz. State U., 1973, M of Counseling, 1975; EdD, Ball State U., 1979. Lic. psychologist; diplomate Am. Bd. Forensic Examiners, Am. Bs. Med. Psychotherapists. Doctoral fellow Ball State U., Muncie, Ind., 1977-79; prevention cons. Ind. Dept. Edn., Indpls., 1980-83; staff therapist Tri-County Mental Health Ctr., Carmel, Ind., 1983; asst. adminstr. Fairbanks Hosp., Indpls., 1983-86; CEO Treatment Ctrs. of Am., Scottsdale, Ariz., 1986; pres. Michael Jay Cohn, P.C., Scottsdale, Ariz., 1986—; mem. faculty U. Phoenix, 1988—; faculty assoc. Ariz. State U., Tempe, 1988—; lectr. Internat. Conf. on Drugs, Atlanta, 1984-86. Author: Technoshock: Combatting Stress in the 90's and Beyond, Al K. Hall Talks About Alcohol and Your Safety, 1986, (chpt.) Psychological Maltreatment of Children and Youth, 1987. Mem. community adv. com. U. Phoenix Counseling Dept., 1990—; pres. Ind. Juvenile Justice Task Force, Indpls., 1985; prevention com. chair Ind. Mental Health Assn., Indpls., 1985. Recipient Key to City, City of Indpls., 1986, Placque of Appreciation, Fairbanks Hosp., 1986, Placque of Appreciation, Ind. Juvenile Justice Task Force, 1986; named Hon. Lt. Col., Ind. State Police, 1986. Mem. APA, Ariz. Psychol. Assn. (conv. co-chair 1985—), Am. Soc. Clin. Hypnosis, Am. Bd. Forensic Examiners. Office: Michael J Cohn PC 7330 E Earll Dr Scottsdale AZ 85251-7221

COHRS, MARLIN E., academic facility administrator; b. Denver, Jan. 20, 1947; s. Raymond William and Margaret C.; m. Pauline Ann Hicks, Dec. 27, 1969. BA, U. Colo., 1972, MBA, 1989. Tchr., chair sci. dept. St. Andrews H.S., Glendale, Colo., 1969-72; from program specialist to network mgr. U. Colo. Health Sci. Ctr., Denver, 1972—. Home: 330 S Emerson St Denver CO 80209-2214

COIT, R. KEN, financial planner; b. L.A., Aug. 26, 1943; s. Roger L. and Thelma D. C.; BS, U. Ariz., 1967; MBA, Pepperdine U., 1981; m. Donna M. Schemanske, Oct. 8, 1977; children: Kristin M., Shannon, Darren, Lauryn. Prin. Coit Fin. Group, 1981; mem. adj. faculty Coll. Fin. Planning, Denver, 1978-79; pres. Walnut Creek adv. bd. Summit Bank, 1987-95, Sequoia Equities Securities Corp., Walnut Creek, Calif.; bd. dirs. R.H. Phillips Winery; mem. adv. bd. Mt. Diablo Nat. Bank, 1996—. Mem. dean's adv. bd. Pepperdine U., 1988-91; nat. bd. advisor Coll. Pharmacy U. Ariz.; bd. dirs., chmn. investment com. East Cmty. Found., 1994—. Recipient Outstanding Alumnus award Pepperdine U. Sch. Bus. and Mgmt., 1986. Mem. Internat. Assn. Fin. Planners (chpt. pres. 1978-79), Inst. Cert. Fin. Planners, East Bay Gourmet Club, Blackhawk Country Club. Office: 1655 N Main St Ste 270 Walnut Creek CA 94596-4642

COKER, MATTHEW TOD, newspaper editor, magazine editor; b. San Bernardino, Calif., Dec. 2, 1960; s. Kenneth James and Patricia Ruth (Cooper) C.; m. Jodi Lynn Vr Meer, Oct. 30, 1982; children: Dustin Matthew, Adam James, Emily Patricia. BA, U. LaVerne, 1982. Lot boy Nat. Car Rental, Kona, Hawaii, 1980; attractions host Disneyland, Anaheim, Calif., 1980-82; staff writer Daily Report, Ontario, Calif., 1982-86; asst. city editor Daily Report now Inland Valley Daily Bull., Ontario, 1986-89; entertainment editor Daily Pilot, Costa Mesa, Calif., 1989-95; assoc. editor Orange County Golf Mag., Santa Ana, Calif., 1995—; calender editor OC Weekly, Costa Mesa, 1995-96, mng. editor, 1996—; contest judge journalism dept. U. La Verne. Editor (various awards Orange County Press Club and Assn. Alternative Newspapers 1996, 97, 98); author (weekly newspaper columns) Off the Fringe-Orange County Golf Mag., 1995—, A Clockwork Orange-OC Weekly, 1996—. Vol. Rep. Party Orange County, Mission Viejo, Calif., 1996. Recipient various writing and editing award Orange County Fair Assn., Costa Mesa, 1990-96, Best Entertainment Section award Calif. Newspaper Pubs. Assn., Sacramento, 1993-94, Best Features award Religious Newswriters Assn., 1994. Mem. Orange County Press Club (various awards). Avocations: golf, snow skiing, softball. E-mail: mattcoker@aol.com. and mcoker@ocweekly.com. Fax: (714) 708-8410. Office: OC Weekly Ste H-10 151 Kalmus Costa Mesa CA 92626

COLANGELO, JERRY JOHN, professional basketball team executive; b. Chicago Heights, Ill., Nov. 20, 1939; s. Larry and Sue (Drancek) C.; m. Joan E. Helmich, Jan. 20, 1961; children: Kathy, Kristen, Bryan. B.A., U. Ill., 1962. Partner House of Charles, Inc., 1962-63; assoc. D.O. Klein & Assocs., 1964-65; dir. merchandising Chgo. Bulls basketball club, 1966-68; gen. mgr. Phoenix Suns basketball club, 1968-87, now also exec. v.p., until 1987, pres., chief exec. officer, 1987—; mng. gen. ptnr. Arizona Diamondbacks, Phoenix, AZ, 1998—. Mem. Basketball Congress Am. (exec. v.p., dir.), Phi Kappa Psi. Republican. Baptist. Clubs: University, Phoenix Execs. Office: Phoenix Suns 201 E Jefferson St Phoenix AZ 85004-2412*

COLBERT, MARGARET MATTHEW, artist; b. N.Y.C., Apr. 18, 1911; d. William Diller and Kate (Lee) Matthew; m. Edwin Harris Colbert, July 8, 1933; children: George, David, Philip, Daniel, Charles. BFA, Calif. Coll. Arts and Crafts, 1931. Sci. illustrator Am. Mus. Natural History, N.Y.C., 1931-33. Contbr. numerous illustrations to books; executed murals of extinct life for Mus. No. Ariz., Big Bend Nat. Pk., Petrified Forest Nat. Pk., Albuquerque Natural History Mus. Recipient engraved crystal award Soc. Vertebrate Paleontology, plaque Dinosaur Soc. Avocations: watercolor and oil portraits, ceramics, various crafts.

COLBURN, RICHARD DUNTON, business executive; b. Carpentersville, Ill., June 24, 1911; s. Cary R. and Daisy (Dunton) C.; children: Richard Whiting, Carol Dunton, Keith Whiting, Christine Isabel, David Dunton, McKee Dunton, Daisy Dunton. Student, Antioch Coll., 1929-33. Pres. Consol. Foundries Mfg. Corp. (and predecessors), 1944-64; chmn. U.S. Rentals Inc., Decco Ltd., U.K. Engrng., London, Marlowe Holdings, Edmundson Elec. Ltd., London; dir. Consol. Elec. Distbrs., Inc., Hajoca Corp., Rolled Alloys, Inc.; underwriting mem. Lloyds of London. Home and Office: 1120 La Collina Dr Beverly Hills CA 90210-2616 also: 30 Chester Sq, London SW1W 9HT, England

COLBY, JENNIFER LOUISE, artist; b. Oxnard, Calif., Mar. 9, 1957; d. John III and Janet Gay (Fiske) C.; m. Mark Eric Newman, Sept. 17, 1983; children: Sarah Jean Colby Newman, Rebekah Lynn Colby Newman. BA in Biology/Art, U. Calif., Santa Cruz, 1980; MA in Art, Calif. State U., Fresno, 1985; MA in Theology, Grad. Theol. Union, Berkeley, Calif., 1987. Instr. Gavilan Coll. Comm. Edn., Gilroy, Calif., 1989-95; faculty Hartnell Coll., Salinas, Calif., 1992-94, Chapman U., Monterey, Calif., 1989-96, Santa Catalina Sch., Monterey, 1995-96; dir./owner Galeria Tonantzin, San Juan Bautista, Calif., 1992-97; art. coord. Bade Mus./Pacific Sch. Religion, Berkeley, 1991—; adj. faculty Pacific Sch. of Religion, Berkeley, 1994-97; curator Women's Caucus for Art, Monterey, 1992-94. Exhbns. include Face to Face, 1987, Border Crossings, 1985; curator: (exhibit) Flyways: Women and Ecology, 1992; contbr. articles to profl. jours. Pres. Monterey Bay Women's Caucus for Art, 1990-93. Recipient Ina Gregg Meml. award Calif. State U., Fresno, 1984, Best of Show award IFRA, 1987; artist-in-residence, Calif. Arts Commn., Sacramento, 1991-92. Mem. Monterey Bay Women's Caucas for Art (pres. 1990-93). Avocations: swimming, hiking, music, sewing. Home: PO Box 264 Aromas CA 95004-0264 Office: Galeria Tonantzin PO Box 606 San Juan Bautista CA 95045-0606

COLBY, JOHN KINGSBURY, III, physician assistant; b. Boston, Sept. 8, 1964; s. John Kingsbury Colby II and Drusilla (Flather) Farley; m. Ann Marie Smith Colby, Aug. 26, 1989; children: Maarten Krigbaum, Drusilla Ashley. BA in Mgmt., Marietta Coll., 1987; M in Health, Duke U., 1993. Cert. physician asst. Transplant physician asst. Baylor U. Med. Ctr., Dallas, 1994-95, Dr. Koep, Phonix, 1995-96, U. Med. Ctr., Tuscon, 1996—. Recipient Michael Sheridan award for the most valuable surg. intern Montifore Med. Ctr., 1994. Mem. Am. Assn. Physician Assts., Ariz. Assn. Physician Assts. Republican. Avocations: Hiking, running, biog. reading, dogs. Home: 6884 W Hermitage Pl Tucson AZ 85743

COLE, BARRY ELIOT, health science association administrator; b. L.A., May 26, 1953; s. Harvey Melvin and Norma Jane (Snyderman) C.; m. Deborah Taverniti, Mar. 21, 1982; children: Candala Autumn, Joshua Alan, Elliot Daniel. AB, U. Calif., Berkeley, 1975; MD, Wake Forest U., 1980; MPA, U. Nev., Las Vegas, 1997. Diplomate Am. Acad. Pain Mgmt.; cert. Am. Bd. Psychiatry and Neurology. Chief resident Bowman Gray Sch. Medicine, Winston Salem, N.C., 1985; med. dir. Hospice No. Nev., Reno, 1988-90; med. dir. sr. care Harris Hosp., Newport, Ark., 1992-93, Randolph County Med. Ctr., Pocahontas, Ark., 1992-93; med. dir. So. Nev. Adult Mental Health, Las Vegas, 1993-96, adminstrv. officer, 1994-96; statewide med. program dir. Nev. Divsn. Mental Hygiene, Carson City, Nev., 1995-96; interim exec. dir. Am. Acad. Pain Mgmt., Sonora, Calif., 1996—; vice chmn. dept. psychiatry U. Nev., Las Vegas, 1994-97. Author: (chpt.) Hospice Cancer Pain Management and Symptom Control, 1998, Types of Pain and Classification Systems, 1998; mem. editl. rev. bd.: Pain Management: A Practical Guide for Clinicians, 1998. Den leader Boy Scouts Am., Newport, 1991-93, asst. scoutmaster, 1993, Las Vegas, 1994—. Mem. AMA, Nev. State Med. Assn., Am. Psychiat. Assn., Am. Pain Soc., Internat. Assn. Study Pain, Am. Acad. Pain Mgmt. (pres. 1994-95), Nev. Assn. Psychiat. Physicians (pres. 1989-91), N.C. Psychiat. Assn. (co-chmn. mem.-in-tng. com. 1982-83). Avocations: flying, camping. Home: 9123 Fawn Grove Dr Las Vegas NV 89147-6810 Office: Am Acad Pain Mgmt 13947 Mono Way # A Sonora CA 95370-2807

COLE, CHARLES EDWARD, lawyer, former state attorney general; b. Yakima, Wash., Oct. 10, 1927; married; 3 children. BA, Stanford U., 1950, LLB, 1953. Law clk. Vets. Affairs Commn. Territory of Alaska, Juneau, 1954, Territorial Atty. Gen.'s Office, Fairbanks, Alaska, 1955-56, U.S. Dist. Ct. Alaska, Fairbanks, 1955-56; city magistrate City of Fairbanks, 1957-58; pvt. practice law, 1957-90; atty. gen. State of Alaska, 1990-94; pvt. law comml. litigation, 1995—; profl. baseball player, Stockton, Calif. and Twin Falls, Idaho, summers of 1950, 51, 53. With U.S. Army, 1946-47. Mem. Calif. State Bar, Washington State Bar Assn., Alaska Bar Assn. Office: Law Dept State of AK Office of Atty Gen PO Box 110300 Juneau AK 99811-0300 also: Law Offices of Charles E Cole 406 Cushman St Fairbanks AK 99701-4632

COLE, DAVID MACAULAY, journalist, consultant; b. Richmond, Calif., Feb. 17, 1954; s. Frederick George and Norma Ann (Caudle) C. Student, San Francisco State U., 1972-77. Mng. editor Feed/Back Mag., San Francisco, 1974-78, exec. editor, 1978-83; asst. music editor Rolling Stone Mag., San Francisco, 1976-77; from copy editor to asst. mng. editor The San Francisco Examiner, 1979-87, asst. mng. editor, 1987-89; prin., owner The Cole Group, Daly City, Calif., 1989—. Editor, publisher The Cole Papers, 1989—, NewsInc., 1997—; author: Cole's Notes--Profiles in Pagination, 1996, Cole's Guide to Publishing Systems, 1994, 95, 96, 97; contbg. editor Presstime Magazine, 1994—. Trustee Jr. Statesman Found, San Mateo, Calif., 1997—. Mem. Nat. Press Photographers Assn., Soc. News Design, Soc. Profl. Journalists (v.p. local chpt. 1979). Avocations: steam train preservation. E-mail: dmc@colegroup.com. Fax: 650-994-2108. Office: The Cole Group PO Box 3426 Daly City CA 94015-0426

COLE, DIANA L., lawyer; b. Tacoma, Jan. 13, 1946; d. James Donald and Lillian Julia (Runyan) C. AA, Tacoma C.C., 1966; BA, U. Puget Sound, 1968; MA, Calif. State U., Long Beach, 1971; postgrad., Southwestern Sch. Law, 1976. Bar: Calif. 1977. Spl. edn. tchr. Tacoma Sch. Dist., 1968-69; home econs. and consumer edn. tchr. L.A. Unified Sch. Dist., 1969-76; pvt. practice law L.A., 1976—; br. mgr. Commodity Trading Advisor, L.A., 1996—. Sec. Homeowners Bd., Park Oakhurst. Mem. Consumer Attys. Assn. L.A., Phi Alpha Delta. Office: 3960 Wilshire Blvd Ste 507 Los Angeles CA 90010-3324

COLE, GEORGE WILLIAM, foundation administrator; b. Denver, Oct. 1, 1950; s. Herbert Merril and Frances Jane (Buchanan) C. Grad. high sch., Denver. Cert. real estate investment counselor. Owner Jayhawker Investment Co., Inc., 1965--95; pres. Herb Cole Real Estate, Inc., Denver, 1969-95; bd. dirs. Cos. West Group, Inc., Denver, Jayhawker Investment Co., Denver; cons. Bus. Concepts Corp., Denver, 1981-84, Centennial Growth Equities Corp., 1981-82; pres. Co. West Group, 1982-93; exec. dir. Cole Found., 1993—. Author: Real Estate Investing for the Future, 1981, Mom: A Study in Grieving Grace, 1990; pub.: (newlsetter) Encouraging Words, 1986-92. Deacon Baptist Ch., 1987; bd. dirs. World Wide Leadership coun., Compa Food Mins., others. Grace Lay Min. Sch. fellow. Republican. Avocations: history, photography, fishing, travel. Home and Office: 3270 E Virginia Ave Denver CO 80209-3523

COLE, GLEN DAVID, minister; b. Tacoma, Dec. 21, 1933; s. Ray Milton and Ruth Evelyn (Ranton) C.; m. Mary Ann Von Moos, June 6, 1953; children: Randall Ray, Ricky Jay. BA in Theology, Cen. Bible Coll., 1956; DD, Pacific Coast Bible Coll., 1983. Pastor Assembly of God, Marion, Ohio, 1957-60, Maple Valley, Wash., 1960-65; assoc. pastor Calvary Temple, Seattle, 1965-67; sr. pastor Evergreen Christian Ctr., Olympia, Wash., 1967-78; sr. pastor Capital Christian Ctr., Sacramento, 1978-95, pastor emeritus, 1995—; dist. supr. Assemblies of God, Sacramento, 1997—; exec. presbyter Assemblies of God, Springfield, 1985—; trustee Bethany Bible Coll., Santa Cruz, Calif., 1979—; bd. dirs. Cen. Bible Coll., Springfield, Mo., 1988—; bd. dirs. Calif. Theol. Sem., Fresno, 1985-90. Mem. Rotary (pres. Olympia chpt. 1977-78). Republican. Office: Assemblies of God 6051 S Watt Ave Sacramento CA 95829 Address: 525 Washoe Ct Roseville CA 95747-8259*

COLE, JULIE PARSONS, social worker; b. Pasadena, Calif., Jan. 10, 1946; d. Winchell Monroe and Elisabeth Loreen (Moss) Parsons; m. Carter Lee Cole, May 10, 1975; children: Katherine E., Craig A. Smith. BA with honors, U. of the Pacific, 1967; MSW, UCLA, 1970. Lic. clin. social worker; bd. cert. diplomate; cert. Acad. Cert. Social Workers. Case worker II San Joaquin County Bur. Pub. Assistance, Stockton, Calif., 1967-68; caseworker I and II L.A. County Dept. Pub. Social Svcs., Pasadena, Calif., 1968, L.A. Dept. Adoptions, Compton, Calif., 1970-74; caseworker III Family Svcs. of L.A., Calif., 1974-80; pvt. practice lic. clin. social worker, 1981—; chairperson San Fernando Valley Child Abuse Resource Com., 1978-80; cons., lic. clin. social worker Villa Esperanga, Apoura, Calif., 1987-94. Chairperson, editor: San Fernando Valley Child Abuse Resource Directory, 1979. Founder The Elisabeth M. and Winchell M. Parsons Scholarship, ASME Aux., N.Y.C., 1985; bd. mem. ASME Aux., L.A., 1989-98, chairperson, 1994-98, Distinguised Svc. award L.A. section, 1994. Recipient Vol. of the Yr. award Family Svcs. L.A., 1980, United Way Vol. award United Way San Fernando Valley, 1980; fellow HEW, Washington, 1968-70. Mem. NASW, Soc. for Clin. Social Workers, Acad. Cert. Social Workers, Am. Bd. Examiners in Clin. Social Workers, C.G. Jung Inst. (life), Elisabeth K. Ross Ctr. (life), UCLA Sch. Social Welfare Alumni, Phi Kappa Phi. Mem. Self Realization Fellowship. Avocations: travel, collecting swans, interior decorating, attending the theater, antiquing. Home: 1736 Upper Ranch Rd Westlake Vlg CA 91362-4260

COLE, LECIL, agricultural products company executive. With Puna (Hi.) Sugar; pres. Hawaiian Sweet, Inc., Keaau, Hi., 1991—. Office: Hawaiian Sweet Inc PO 210 Keaau HI 96749*

COLE, MALVIN, neurologist, educator; b. N.Y.C., Mar. 21, 1933; s. Harry and Sylvia (Firman) C.; A.B. cum laude, Amherst Coll., 1953; M.D. cum laude, Georgetown U. Med. Sch., 1957; m. Susan Kugel, June 20, 1954; children: Andrew James, Douglas Gowers. Intern, Seton Hall Coll. Medicine, Jersey City Med. Ctr., 1957-58; resident Boston City Hosps., 1958-60; practice medicine specializing in neurology, Montclair and Glen Ridge, N.J., Montville, N.J., 1963-72, Casper, Wyo., 1972—; teaching fellow Harvard Med. Sch., 1958-60; Research fellow Nat. Hosp. for Nervous Diseases, St. Thomas Hosp., London, Eng., 1960-61; instr. Georgetown U. Med. Sch., 1961-63; clin. assoc. prof. neurology N.J. Coll. Medicine, Newark, 1963-72, acting dir. neurology, 1965-72; assoc. prof. clin. neurology U. Colo. Med. Sch., 1973-88, clin. prof., 1988—; mem. staff Wyo. Med. Ctr., Casper, U. Hosp., Denver. Served to capt. M.C., AUS, 1961-63. Licensed physician, Mass., N.Y., Calif., N.J., Colo., Wyo.; diplomate Am. Bd. Psychiatry and Neurology, Nat. Bd. Med. Examiners. Fellow ACP, Am. Acad. Neurology, Royal Soc. Medicine; mem. Assn. Research Nervous and Mental Disease, Acad. Aphasia, Am. Soc. Neuroimaging, Internat. Soc. Neuropsychology, Harveian Soc. London, Epilepsy Found. Am., Am. Epilepsy Soc., Am. EEG Soc., N.Y. Acad. Sci., Osler Soc. London, Alpha Omega Alpha. Contbr. articles to profl. jours. Office: 246 S Washington St Casper WY 82601-2921

COLE, RICHARD GEORGE, public administrator; b. Irvington, N.J., Mar. 11, 1948; s. Warner W. and Laurel M. (Wilson) C. AS in Computer Sci., Control Data Inst., Anaheim, Calif., 1972; BA in Sociology with high honor, Calif. State U., Los Angeles, 1974; MA in Social Ecology, U. Calif., Irvine, 1976; postgrad., So. Oreg. State Coll., 1979. Computer operator Zee Internat., Gardena, Calif., 1971; teaching asst. U. Calif., Irvine, 1974-75; planner Herman Kimmel & Assocs., Newport Beach, Calif., 1976-78; program analyst The Job Council, Medford, Oreg., 1980-81, compliance officer, 1981-82, bus. mgr., 1982—; instr. credential Calif. C.C.; chmn. bd. trustees Job Coun. Pension Trust, Medford, 1982-97; mem. curriculum adv. com. Rogue C.C., Grants Pass, Oreg., 1986; mgr. computer project State of Oreg., Salem, 1983-84; mem. Oreg. Occupational Info. Coordinating Com., Salem, 1982-84. Pres. bd. trustees Vector Control Dist., Jackson County, Oreg., 1985, treas., 1986, bd. dirs., 1984-87, mem. budget com., 1988—, sec., 1988-89; cand. bd. dirs. Area Edn. Dist., Jackson County, 1981; treas. Job Svc. Employer Com., Jackson County, 1987— (Spl. Svc. award 1991); dir. fin. joint pub. venture System Devel. Project, Salem, Oreg., 1986-89; mem. adv. bd. New Jobs Planning, Medford, Oreg., 1987-88, Fin. Audit and Risk Mgmt. Task Force, 1987-91, chm., 1989-90. Fellow LaVerne Noyes, U. Calif., Irvine, 1974; Dr. Paul Doehring Found. scholar, Glendale, Calif., 1973; Computer Demonstration grantee State of Oreg., Salem, 1983; recipient Award of Fin. Reporting Achievement Govt. Fin. Officers Assn. of U.S. and Can., 1989-90, Fin. Ops. recognition Vector Control Dist., Jackson County, Oreg., 1990, Nat. 2d Pl. Chpt. award Jackson County Job Svc. Employer Com., 1989, Oreg. Job Svc. Employer Com. Stat award, 1991, Oreg. Individual Citation award Internat. Assn. Profls. in Employment Security, 1993. Mem. Soc. for Human Resources Mgmt., Assn. So. Oreg. Pub. Adminstrs., Oreg. Employment and Tng. Assn., Pacific N.W. Personnel Mgmt. Assn. (chpt. treas. 1985-87, orgnl. liaison dir. 1988-89, Appreciation award 1985), Govt. Fin. Officers Assn., Oreg. Mcpl. Fin. Officers assn., The Nature Conservancy. Home: 575 Morey Rd Talent OR 97540-9725 Office: The Job Council 673 Market St Medford OR 97504-6125

COLE, TERRI LYNN, organization administrator; b. Tucson, Dec. 28, 1951; m. James R. Cole II. Student, U. N.Mex., 1975-80; cert., Inst. Orgn. Mgmt., 1985. Cert. chamber exec. With SunWest Bank, Albuquerque, 1971-74, employment adminstr., 1974-76, communications dir., 1976-78; pub. info. dir. Albuquerque C. of C., 1978-81, gen. mgr., 1981-83, pres., 1983—; pres. N.Mex. C. of C. Execs. Assn., 1986-87, bd. dirs., 1980—; bd. regents Inst. for Orgn. Mgmt., Stanford U., 1988—, vice chmn., 1990-91, chmn., 1991; bd. dirs. Hosp. Home Health, Inc. Recipient Bus. Devel. award Expn. Mgmt. Inc., 1985, Women on Move award YWCA, 1986; named one of Outstanding Women of Am., 1984. Mem. Am. C. of C. Execs. Assn. (chmn. elect bd. 1992—). Republican. Avocations: skiing, cycling, gardening. Office: Greater Albuquerque C of C PO Box 25100 Albuquerque NM 87125-0100

COLE, WILLIAM L., lawyer; b. L.A., May 13, 1952. AB magna cum laude, U. Calif., Irvine, 1974; JD, Stanford U., 1977. Bar: Calif. 1977. Atty. Mitchell, Silberberg & Knupp, L.A., mng. ptnr., 1991—. Mem. ABA, State Bar Calif., Los Angeles County Bar Assn. (mem. exec. com. labor law sect. 1989-90), Phi Beta Kappa, Order of Coif. Office: Mitchell Silberberg & Knupp 11377 W Olympic Blvd Los Angeles CA 90064-1625*

COLEMAN, ARLENE FLORENCE, nurse practitioner; b. Braham, Minn., Apr. 8, 1926; d. William and Christine (Judin) C.; m. John Dunkerken, May

30, 1987. Diploma in nursing, U. Minn., 1947, BS, 1953; MPH, Loma Linda U., 1974. RN, Calif. Operating room scrub nurse Calif. Luth. Hosp., L.A., 1947-48; indsl. staff nurse Good Samaritan Hosp., L.A., 1948-49; staff nurse Passavant Hosp., Chgo., 1950-51; student health nurse Moody Bible Inst., Chgo., 1950-51; staff nurse St. Andrews Hosp., Mpls., 1951-53; pub. health nurse Bapt. Gen. Conf. Bd. of World Missions, Ethiopia, Africa, 1954-66; staff pub. health nurse County of San Bernadino, Calif., 1966-68, sr. pub. health nurse, 1968-73, pediatric nurse practitioner, 1973—. Contbr. articles to profl. jours. Mem. bd. dist. missions Bapt. Gen. Conf., Calif., 1978-84; mem. adv. coun. Kaiser Hosp., Fontana, Calif., 1969-85, Bethel Sem. West, San Diego, 1987—; bd. dirs. Casa Verdugo Retirement Home, Hemet, Calif., 1985—; active Calvary Bapt. Ch., Redlands, Calif., 1974—; mem. S.W. Bapt. Conf. Social Ministries, 1993—. With Cadet Nurse Corps USPHS, 1944-47. Calif. State Dept. Health grantee, 1973. Fellow Nat. Assn. Pediatric Nurse Assocs. and Practitioners; mem. Calif. Nurses Assn. (state nursing coun. 1974-76). Democrat. Avocations: gardening, travel, reading. Home: 622 Esther Way Redlands CA 92373-5822

COLEMAN, BARBARA MCREYNOLDS, artist; b. Omaha, May 5, 1956; d. Zachariah Aycock and Mary Barbara (McCulloh) McR.; m. Stephen Dale Dent, Mar. 12, 1983 (div. Dec. 20, 1992); children: Madeleine Barbara, Matthew Stephen; m. Ross Coleman, Oct. 16, 1993; 1 child, Marie Jeanne Coleman. Student, U. N.Mex., 1979, MA in Community and Regional Planning, 1984. Artist, 1986-92; lectr. U. N.Mex. Sch. of Architecture, Albuquerque, 1979-82, 91—; assoc. planner, urban designer City of Albuquerque Planning Div., 1982-84; city planner, urban designer City of Albuquerque, N.Mex. Redevel. Div., 1984-88; cons. City of Albuquerque Redevel. Dept., 1987-88; urban design cons. Southwest Land Rsch., Albuquerque, 1991. Columnist for "Kids and Art", 1990-92; author: Coors Corridor Plan (The Albuquerque Conservation Assn. urban design award 1984), Electric Facilities Plan, Downtown Core Revitalization Strategy and Sector Development Plan; contbg. author: Anasazi Architecture and American Design, 1994; contbr. articles to profl. publs.; exhibited in shows at Dartmouth St. Gallery, Albuquerque, Chimayo (N.Mex.) Trade and Mercantile, JoAnne Chappel Gallery, San Francisco, Southwest Arts Festival, Albuquerque, Act I Gallery, Taos, N.Mex. Vol. art tchr. Chaparral Elem. Sch., Roosevelt Mid. Sch., Albuquerque, 1989-97. Recipient First Pl. for Pastels, 20th Ann. Nat. Small Painting Exhibition, N.Mex. Art League, 1991, Best of Show awards Pastel Soc. of N.Mex., 1990, Award of Merit, Pastel Soc. of S.W., 1989, TACA award for Urban Design, 1984. Mem. Pastel Soc. of Am., Pastel Soc. N.Mex. (pres. 1991-92). Democrat. Episcopalian. Avocations: hiking, skiing, running. Works featured in books. Office: U NMex Sch Architecture Albuquerque NM 87131

COLEMAN, DAVID HOWARD, web design company owner; b. Tupelo, Miss., Jan. 8, 1964; s. Howard Clark and Virginia (Sorrels) C.; m. Laura Wilson, Sept. 20, 1991. BFA in Filmic Writing, U. So. Calif., 1986. Story analyst Delaurentis Entertainment Group, Beverly Hills, Calif., 1987-90, screenwriter, 1991; asst. story editor TV series Twilight Zone, L.A., 1992; screenwriter Universal Pictures, Universal City, Calif., 1993, Columbia Pictures, L.A., 1994; co-owner Kudzu New Media, Van Nuys, Calif., 1995—. Editor mag. Remote Jockey Digest, 1996. Recipient Web Site Excellence award Seattle Film & Video Consortium, 1998, Web Site Innovation award PConnections, 1998, Cool Reality award Artistic Reality, 1998. Mem. HTML Writer's Guild, Writers Guild Am. Office: Kudzu New Media 5632 Van Nuys Blvd # 186 Van Nuys CA 91401-4602

COLEMAN, GARTH JOHN, painter, investor; b. Brigham, Utah, Apr. 16, 1945; s. Ray Willian and Lucille Emma (Harris) C.; m. Rosemarie Bansil Lazaro, Dec. 21, 1985; children: Cora Leigh, James Ray. BFA in Painting, San Francisco Art Inst., 1971. Hydraulic specialist Food Machines, Chem., San Jose, Calif., 1974-79; technician Nat. Semiconductor, West Jordan, Utah, 1979-81; artist Sandy, Utah, 1981—; ins. agt. Jackson Nat. Time, Sandy, 1993-97. Exhibited in group shows at Art Barn, Salt Lake City, 1981, Diego Rivera Gallery, San Francisco, 1971. With USN, 1962-65. Recipient Ellis award, 1969. Mem. San Francisco Art Inst. Alumni Assn. Avocations: music, literature, finance. Home: 9428 S David St Sandy UT 84070-3432

COLEMAN, HENRY JAMES, JR., management educator, consultant; b. Cleve., Nov. 28, 1947; s. Henry James and Kathryn Adele (Ketchum) C.; m. Sharon Ann Boothe, Sept. 12, 1971 (div. Jan. 1975). AB, Dartmouth Coll., 1969, MBA, 1970; PhD, U. Calif., Berkeley, 1978. Employment mgr. Lima (Ohio) Meml. Hosp., 1977-78; strategic planner NCR Corp., Dayton, Ohio, 1980-81; vis. asst. prof. Calif. Poly. State U., San Luis Obispo, 1983-85; dean Sch. Mgmt., Columbia Pacific U., San Rafael, Calif., 1985-92; assoc. prof. mgmt. St. Mary's Coll. Calif., Moraga, 1992—; adj. prof. Holy Names Coll., Oakland, Calif., 1987, 90-92; mgmt. cons. Orgn. Dynamics, Berkeley, 1970, Comm. Workers Am., San Francisco, 1971, Exide Corp., Reading, Pa., 1988-89, Retirement Fin. Ctrs. Am., Las Vegas, Nev., 1996. Contbr. articles to profl. jours. Nat. Def. Grad. fellow, 1971. Mem. Western Acad. Mgmt., Phi Beta Kappa. Episcopalian. Avocations: color photography, music appreciation. Office: Saint Marys Coll Calif 1928 Saint Marys Rd Moraga CA 94556-2715

COLEMAN, LEWIS WALDO, bank executive; b. San Francisco, Jan. 2, 1942; s. Lewis V. and Virginia Coleman; m. Susan G.; children: Michelle, Gregory, Nancy, Peter. BA, Stanford U., 1965. With Bank Calif., San Francisco, 1965-73; With Wells Fargo Bank, San Francisco, 1973-86, exec. v.p., chmn. credit policy com., until 1986; vice chmn., CFO, treas. Bank Am., San Francisco, 1986-95; sr. mng. dir. Montgomery Securities, San Francisco, 1995-98; CEO Nations Bank Mongomery Securities, San Francisco, 1998—. *

COLEMAN, PAUL JEROME, JR., physicist, educator; b. Evanston, Ill., Mar. 7, 1932; s. Paul Jerome and Eunice Cecile (Weissenberg) C.; m. Doris Ann Fields, Oct. 3, 1964; children: Derrick, Craig. BS in Engring. Math., U. Mich., 1954, BS in Engring. Physics, 1954, MS in Physics, 1958; PhD in Space Physics, UCLA, 1966. Rsch. scientist Ramo-Wooldridge Corp. (name now TRW Systems), El Segundo, Calif., 1958-61; instr. math. U. So. Calif., L.A., 1958-61; mgr. interplanetary scis. program NASA, Washington, 1961-62; rsch. scientist UCLA, 1962-66, prof. geophysics, space physics, 1966—; asst. lab. dir., mgr. Earth and Space Scis. divsn., chmn. Inst. Geophysics and Planetary Physics Nat. Lab., Los Alamos, N.Mex., 1981-86; dir. Inst. Geophysics and Planetary Physics UCLA, 1989-92; dir. Nat. Inst. for Global Environ. Change, 1994-96; pres. Univs. Space Rsch. Assn., Columbia, Md., 1981—; bd. dirs. Lasertechnics Inc., Albuquerque, Southeast Interactive Tech., Durham, N.C., Sandia Imaging Sys., Dallas, others; mem. adv. bd. San Diego Supercomputer Ctr., 1986—, chmn., 1987-88, others; trustee Univs. Space Rsch. Assn., Columbia, Md., 1981—, Am. Tech. Initiative, 1990—, Internat. Small Satellite Orgn., 1992-96; vis. scholar U. Paris, 1975-76; vis. scientist Lab. for Aeronomy Ctr. Nat. Rsch. Sci., Verrieres le Buisson, France, 1975-76; com. mem. numerous sci. and ednl. orgns., cons. numerous fin. and indsl. cos. Co-editor: Solar Wind, 1972; co-author: Pioneering the Space Frontier, 1986; mem. editorial bd. Geophysics and Astrophysics Monographs, 1970—; assoc. editor Cosmic Electrodynamics, 1968-72; contbr. revs. to numerous profl. jours. Apptd. to Nat. Commn. on Space, Pres. of U.S., 1985, apptd. to Space Policy Adv. Bd., Nat. Space Coun., v.p. of U.S., 1991; bd. dirs. St. Matthew's Sch., Pacific Palisades, Calif., 1979-82, v.p., 1981-82. 1st lt. USAF, 1954-56, Korea. Recipient Exceptional Sci. Achievement Medal NASA, 1970, 1972, spl. recognition for contributions to the Apollo Program, 1979; Guggenheim fellow 1975-76, Fulbright scholar, 1975-76, Rsch. grantee NASA, NSF, Office Naval Research, Calif. Space Inst., Air Force Office Sci. Research, U.S. Geol. Survey. Mem. AAAS, AIAA, Am. Geophys. Union, Am. Phys. Soc., Internat. Acad. Astronautics, Bel Air Bay Club (L.A.), Birnam Wood Golf Club (Monteceito, Calif.), Cosmos Club (Washington), Explorers Club (N.Y.C.), Eldorado Country Club (Indian Wells, Calif.), Tau Beta Pi, Phi Eta Sigma. Avocations: flying, skiing, racquetball, tennis, golf. Home: 1323 Monaco Dr Pacific Palisades CA 90272-4007 Office: UCLA Inst Geophysics & Planetary Physics 405 Hilgard Ave Los Angeles CA 90095-9000

COLEMAN, REXFORD LEE, lawyer, educator; b. Hollywood, Calif., June 2, 1930; s. Henry Eugene and Antoinette Christine (Dobry) C.; m. Aiko Takahashi, Aug. 28, 1953 (dec.); children: Christine Eugenie, Douglass Craig; m. Sucha Park, June 15, 1978. Student, Claremont McKenna Coll., 1947-49; A.B., Stanford U., 1951, J.D., 1955; M. in Jurisprudence, Tokyo U., 1960. Bar: Calif. 1955, Mass. 1969. Mem. faculty Harvard U., 1959-69; mem. firm Baker & McKenzie, 1969-83, income ptnr., 1971-73, capital ptnr., 1973-83, mng. ptnr. Tokyo office, 1971-78; sr. ptnr. The Pacific Law Group, L.A., 1983—; adj. prof. McGeorge Sch. Law, U. Pacific, 1989—; lectr. Gray's Inn, The Inns of Ct. Sch. Law, London, 1989; cons. U.S. Treasury Dept., 1961-70; counselor Japanese-Am. Soc. for Legal Studies, 1964—; guest lectr. Ford Seminar on Comparative History, MIT, 1968; lectr. Legal Tng. and Research Inst., Supreme Ct., Japan, 1970-73; guest lectr. Colloquium Scholars, Calif. Luth. U., 1989; chmn. fgn. bus. customs consultative comm. Bur. Customs, Ministry of Fin., Govt. of Japan, 1971-72; chmn. fgn. bus. consulatative commn. Japanese Ministry of Internat. Trade and Industry, 1973-76; mem. U.S. Del., U.S.-Japan Income Tax Treaty Negotiations, 1961, internat. bd. advisors, McGeorge Sch. Law, U. Pacific, 1989—. Author: Am. Index to Japanese Law, 1961, Standard Citation of Japanese Legal Materials, 1963, The Legal Aspects Under Japanese Law of an Accident Involving a Nuclear Installation in Japan, 1963, An Index to Japanese Law, 1975; editor: Taxation in Japan, World Tax Series, 1959-70; founding chmn. bd. editors: Law in Japan: An Ann., 1964-67; mem. bd. editors Stanford Law Rev., 1954-55, Japan Ann. Internat. Law, 1970-92; mem. Internat. Adv. Bd., The Transnational Lawyer, 1988—. Participant in Japanese-Am. Program for Cooperation in Legal Studies, 1956-60; co-chmn. Conf. on Internat. Legal Protection Computer Software, Stanford Law Sch., 1986, Tokyo, Japan, 1987. Served to 1st lt., Inf. AUS, 1951-53; lt. col. Ret. Ford Found. grantee, 1956-60. Mem. ABA, State Bar Calif., Mass. Bar Assn., Japanese-Am. Soc. for Legal Studies, Assn. Asian Studies, Am. Polit. Sci. Assn., Internat. Studies Assn., Internat. Fiscal Assn. (U.S. and Japan), Acad. Polit. Sci., Am. Acad. Polit. and Social Sci., Am. Soc. Internat. Law, Am. Fgn. Law Assn., Mil. Govt. Assn., Res. Officers Assn. (v.p. army dept. Far East 1974-75), U.S. Army Judge Adv. Gen.'s Sch. Alumni Assn., Internat. House Japan (Tokyo), Stanford U. Alumni Assn., Gakushi Kai., Internat. Law Assn. Japan, Japan-Western Assn., Pacific Basin Econ. Council, (U.S. exec. com. 1985-87), Nihon Shihō Gakkai, Nihon Kok usai Hō Gakkai, Nihon Kokusai Shihō Gakkai, Sozei Hō Gakkai, Phi Alpha Delta. Episcopalian (vestryman 1966-69, del. Conv. Episcopal Diocese Mass. 1968, Conv. Episcopal Diocese L.A., 1989-91, Bishop's com. 1983-87, 91-93). Clubs: Tokyo Am; Harvard (N.Y.C.), North Ranch Country. Home: 32314 Blue Rock Rdg Westlake Village CA 91361-3912 Office: The Pacific Law Group 12121 Wilshire Blvd Ste 205 Los Angeles CA 90025-1164

COLEMAN, ROGER DIXON, bacteriologist; b. Rockwell, Iowa, Jan. 18, 1915; s. Major C. and Hazel Ruth Coleman; A.B., UCLA, 1937; postgrad. Balliol Coll., Oxford (Eng.) U., 1944; MS, U. So. Calif., 1952, PhD, 1957; m. Lee Aden Skov, Jan. 1, 1978. Sr. laboratorian Napa (Calif.) State Hosp., 1937-42; dir. Long Beach (Calif.) Clin. Lab., 1946-86, pres., 1980-86; mem. Calif. State Clin. Lab. Commn., 1953-57. Served as officer AUS, 1942-46. Diplomate Am. Bd. Bioanalysts. Mem. Am. Assn. Bioanalysts, Am. Assn. Clin. Chemists, Am. Soc. Microbiologists, Am. Chem. Soc., Am. Venereal Disease Assn., AAAS (life), Calif. Assn. Bioanalysts (past officer), Med. Research Assn. Calif., Bacteriology Club So. Calif., Sigma Xi, Phi Sigma (past chpt. pres.). Author papers in field. Home: 31086 Montesa Laguna Niguel CA 92677-2721 Office: PO Box 7073 Laguna Niguel CA 92607-7073

COLEMAN, RONNY JACK, fire chief; b. Tulsa, May 17, 1940; s. Clifford Harold and Elizabeth Ann (Teter) C.; m. Susan René Calvert, July 18, 1963 (div. Jan. 1971); children: Lisa René, Christopher Alan; m. Marie Katherine McCarthy, Nov. 18, 1972. AS in Fire Sci., Rancho Santiago Coll., 1971; BS in Polit. Sci., Calif. State U., Fullerton, 1974; MS in vocat. edn., Calif. State U., Long Beach, 1993. Tanker, foreman U.S. Forest Svc., Trabuco, Calif., 1960-62; ops. chief Costa Mesa (Calif.) Fire Dept., 1962-73; fire chief San Clemente (Calif.) Fire Dept., 1973-85, Fullerton (Calif.) Fire Dept., 1985-92; chief dep. dir. and state fire marshal Dept of Forestry & Fire Protection, Sacramento, CA; pres. Phenix Tech., Inc., San Clemente, 1971—. Author: Management of Fire Service Operations, 1975, Fire Truck Toys for Men and Boys, Vols. I and II, 1978, Alpha to Omega: History of Fire Sprinklers, 1983; patentee firefighter helmets. Chmn. Pete Wilson's Fire Brigade, San Clemente, 1990, United Fund Dr., Costa Mesa, 1968. Cpl. USMC, 1957-60. Rayford-Worsted scholar, 1968, Moore scholar, 1961; named Polyurethane Man of Yr. Polyurethane Assn., 1988, Richard Parmalee award Am. Fire Sprinkler Assn., 1989. Mem. Internat. Assn. Fire Chiefs (pres. 1988-89, chmn. Nat. Fire Svcs. Accreditation Commn. 1988—, v.p. Comite Technique Internat. De Prevention et D'Extinction Du Feu (CTIF)), Nat. Fire Protection Assn., League of Calif. Cities (pres. fire chiefs dept. 1988-89), Orange County Fire Chief's Assn. (pres. 1983-84), Orange County Burn Assn. (bd. dirs. 1990). Republican. Avocations: photography, creative writing, antiques. Home: 8866 Saint Anthony Ct Elk Grove CA 95624-9443 Office: Dept Forestry & Fire Protection PO Box 944246 Sacramento CA 94244-2460

COLE-MCCULLOUGH, DANIEL, music educator, conductor, clinician; b. Portland, Oreg., May 22, 1946; s. John Virgle and Barbara Jean (Johnson) Cole; 1 child, Erika Kristine. BA in Music, Marylhurst Coll., 1984; MMus in Conducting, U. Portland, 1987; MAT, Lewis and Clark Coll., 1996; PhD in Music Edn., 1999. Cert. music tchr., Oreg., Wash. Music instr., orch. condr. Clark Coll., Vancouver, Wash., 1975-89; music instr. Marylhurst (Oreg.) Coll., 1985-94; prof. music edn., dir. bands Warner Pacific Coll., Portland, Oreg., 1993-97; condr., music dir. Pacific Crest Wind Ensemble, Marylhurst, 1988-97; prof. music U. Ala., Fairbanks, 1997-98; guest condr. Pres.'s USCG Band, 1994, Mercer U. Band, 1996. Author: Mardsan Guitar Method, 1979; editor Oreg. Music Educators Assn. mag., 1994-97. With USAR, 1966-73. Recipient Clark County Theater Art award, 1988, Disting. Svc. to Music Edn. award Oreg. Music Educators, 1994. Mem. Music Educators Nat. Conf., Conductors Guild, World Assn. Symphonic Bands and Ensembles, Coll. Music. Soc., Coll. Band Dirs. Nat. Assn., Nat. Band Assn., Quarter Horse Assn., Alaska Band Dirs. Assn. (pres.-elect), Phi Mu, Tau Kappa Epsilon. Avocations: horseback trail riding, golf. E-mail: professor.dan@excite.com. Fax: 360-693-0503. Home: 4115 NE 60th St Vancouver WA 98661 Office: U Alaska Dept Music Fairbanks AK 99775

COLER, MYRON A(BRAHAM), chemical engineer, educator; b. N.Y.C., Mar. 30, 1913; s. Marcus and Bertha (Bebarfald) C.; m. Viola Ethel Buchbinder, Nov. 15, 1942 (dec. Jan. 1993); children: Mark D., Sandra Coler Carson; m. Lena Amark, Feb. 16, 1996 (div. Mar. 1998). AB, Columbia U., 1933, BS, 1934, ChE, 1935, PhD, 1937; postgrad., NYU, Bklyn. Poly. Inst. With NYU, N.Y.C., 1941-75, prof., dir. surface tech. program dir. creative sci. program; supr., rsch. scientist Manhattan Project, 1943-45; founder, pres., dir. chmn. bd. Markite Co., Markite Corp., Markite Engring. Co., 1948-67, Coler Engring. Co., 1967—, The Vulcan Press Divsn., Valmath, 1988—; sponsor-in-residence Franklin Inst. Rsch. Labs., 1975-81; cons. numerous cos. and govt. agys. Author: Aircraft Engine Finishes, 1941; editor, contbg. author: Essays on Creativity in the Sciences, 1963, Essays on Invention and Education, 1977; numerous articles to profl. jours.; patentee in field. Bd. dirs. Woodward Envicon, Marcus and Bertha Coler Found.; mem. adv. com. dept. phys. and engring. metallurgy Polytechnic Inst. N.Y.; mem. pres.'s com. for Sch. Continuing Edn., NYU; appointee Nat. Inventors Coun., 1966-74; mem. state tech. svc. com. Dept. Commerce; with divsn. cultural studies UNESCO-Dept. State, 1982. Named hon. prof. Polytechnic Inst. N.Y.; Weston fellow Electrochem. Mem. AAAS, Am. Math. Soc., Materials Rsch. Soc., Am. Nuclear Soc., N.Y. Acad. Sci., Electrochem. Soc., Am. Ceramic Soc., Am. Chem. Soc., Am. Soc. for Metals, Am. Def. Preparedness Assn., Internat. Precious Metals Inst., Sigma Xi, Phi Beta Kappa, Phi Lambda Upsilon, Tau Beta Pi, Epsilon Chi, Kona Kai Club. Address: Empress Hotel 7766 Fay Ave La Jolla CA 92037-4309

COLFACK, ANDREA HECKELMAN, elementary education educator; b. Yreka, Calif., July 17, 1945; d. Robert A. Davis and June (Reynolds) Butler; m. David Lee Heckelman, Sept. 5, 1965 (div. Nov. 1982); children: Barbara, Julie; m. Neal Cleve, Jan. 1, 1984; 1 stepchild, Karl. AB, Calif. State U., L.A., 1966; MA, Calif. State U., Fresno, 1969. Life std. elem. credential, Calif. cert. competence: Spanish, Calif.; ordained to ministry Faith Christian Fellowship Internat., 1987; Calif. preliminary administrv. credential, 1995. Tchr. Tulare (Calif.) City Schs., 1966-67, Palo Verde Union Sch. Dist., 1967-70, Cutler-Orosi (Calif.) Union Sch. Dist., 1979-82, Hornbrook (Calif.) [illegible] bilingual tchr. West Contra Costa (Calif.) Unified Sch. Dist., 1984-95; prin. Bayview Elem. Sch. West Contra Costa (Calif.) Unified Sch. Dist., San Pablo, Calif., 1995—; site mentor Bayview Elem. Sch., Richmond, 1990-92; ELD mentor, Richmond, 1992-94, mentor selection com., 1994-95; summer sch. prin. Grant Elem. Sch., Richmond, 1995. Co-author: Project Mind Expansion, 1974. Recipient Calif. Dist. Sch. award, 1998; East Bay C.U.E. Tech. grantee, 1995. Mem. Calif. Assn. Bilingual Educators (sec. Richmond 1990-91), AAUW (pres. Tulare br. 1967-68), Calif. Assn. Sch. Adminstrs., Richmond Assn. Sch. Adminstrs. Democrat. Pentecostal. Avocations: leading music and home bible studies. Home: 5461 Hackney Ln Richmond CA 94803-3830 Office: Bayview Elem Sch 3001 16th St San Pablo CA 94806-2352

COLGIN, KEVIN JON, poet; b. Northridge, Calif., May 22, 1957; s. Russel W. Colgin and Anne (Anderson) Forthoffer. Poet: Two People, 1995 (Editor's Choice 1995), Life Is, 1996 (Editor's Choice 1996), I Have Rainbows Inside Me, 1996 (Editor's Choice 1996), Peace Is, 1996 (Editor's Choice 1996). Mem. Internat. Soc. Poets. Avocation: collecting baseball autographs.

COLLAMER, SONJA MAE SOREIDE, retired veterinary facility administrator; b. Rapid City, S.D., Sept. 3, 1937; d. Louis Severin and Mae Marie (Barber) Soreide; m. John Harry Collamer, Dec. 30, 1959; children: Debra, Michael, Kenneth, Kerry. BS in Bacteriology, Colo. State U., 1959. Practice mgr. Saratoga (Wyo.) Vet. Clinic, 1966-94, ret., 1994; sec., v.p. Wyo. Bd. Medicine, 1995—. Pres., mem. Wyo. Jaycettes, 1962-70; mem. deacon, elder, clk. session First Presbyn. Ch., Saratoga, 1966—, chair pastor nominating com., 1998; neighborhood chmn., leader Girl Scouts Am., Saratoga, 1967-77; sec., mem. Snowy Range Cattlewomen, Carbon County, Wyo., 1967—; active bd. of edn. Sch. Dist. #9, Saratoga, 1968-72; chmn., treas. bd. edn. Sch. Dist. #2, Carbon County, 1972-81; mem. Platte Vallley Rep. Women, 1972—, Carbon County Rep. Ctrl. Com., 1980—, Wyo. state com. woman, 1982-86; vice chair, mem. Saratoga Sr. Ctr. Bd., 1982-86; pres., mem. Snowy Range Ambs., Saratoga, 1984-97; chair Region VIII Child Devel. Program, Carbon County, 1985-90; mem., fundraiser Saratoga Cmty. Choir, 1988—; mediator Wyo. Agrl. Mediation Bd., 1988-97; co-chair Thomas for Congress Com., Carbon County, 1990; chair Saratoga Hist. and Cultural Assn. Bd., 1988-97; active Planning & Devel. Commn., Carbon County, 1994—. Mem. Am. Vet. Med. Assn. Auxiliary, Wyo. Vet. Med. Assn. Auxiliary (pres.), Kappa Delta. Republican. Presbyterian. Home: PO Box 485-806 Rangeview Saratoga WY 82331

COLLAS-DEAN, ANGELA G., state commissioner, small business owner; b. Manila, The Philippines, Oct. 20, 1933; came to the U.S., 1960; d. Juan Damocles and Soledad Garduño (Martinez) Collas; m. Bruce Goring Dean, Aug. 8, 1961; children: Heather Frances, Jennifer Ashton. BA in English Lit. and Humanities, U. of the Philippines, Diliman, Quezon City, 1955; MA in Drama, Baylor U., 1962. Owner Philippine Party Foods, Eugene, Oreg., 1984-96; dir., pres. Philippine Am. C. of C., 1996-97; instr. U. of the Philippines, Diliman, Quezon City, 1963-65, Baylor U., Waco, Tex., 1965-68. Com. mem. Affirmative Action Adv. Com., Lane County, Oreg., 1972-76; bd. mem. Sign Code Bd. Appeals, Eugene, 1985-87; city commr. Human Rights Commn., Eugene, 1985-87, Cultural Arts Commn., Eugene, 1989-93; com. mem. Joint Soc. Svc. Fund, Lane County, Eugene and Springfield, 1986-88; bd. advisors U. Oreg. Ctr. for Asian Pacific Studies. Fulbright/Smith-Mundt grantee U.S. Dept. Edn., Manila, 1959, Fulbright grantee U.S. Dept. Edn., Manila, 1960. Mem. Philippine Am. Assn. (founding mem., officer Eugene 1983—), Asian Coun. (founding mem., officer Eugene and Springfield 1985—), Asian Am. Found. (founding mem., officer Eugene 1993—). Office: Philippine Trading Co Inc 2092 Roland Way Eugene OR 97401-2061

COLLEN, MORRIS FRANK, physician; b. St. Paul, Nov. 12, 1913; s. Frank Morris and Rose (Finkelstein) C.; m. Frances B. Diner, Sept. 24, 1937; children: Arnold Roy, Barry Joel, Roberta Joy, Randal Harry. BEE, U. Minn., 1934, MB with distinction, 1938, MD, 1939. Diplomate Am. Bd. Internal Medicine. Intern Michael Reese Hosp., Chgo., 1939-40; resident Los Angeles County Hosp., 1940-42; chief med. service Kaiser Found. Hosp., Oakland, Calif., 1942-52; chief of staff Kaiser Found. Hosp., Oakland, 1952-53; med. dir. Permanente Med. Group, West Bay Div., 1953-79, dir. med. methods research, 1962-79, dir. tech. assessment, 1979-83, cons. div. research, 1983—; chmn. exec. com. Permanente Med. Group, Oakland, 1953-73; dir. Permanente Services, Inc., Oakland, 1958-73; lectr. Sch. Pub. Health, U. Calif., Berkeley, 1966-78; lectr. info. sci. U. Calif., San Francisco, 1970-85; lectr. U. London, 1972, Stanford U. Med. Ctr., 1973, 75, 84-86, Harvard U., 1974, Johns Hopkins U., 1976, also others; cons. Bur. Health Services, USPHS, 1965-68, chmn. health care systems study sect., 1968-72, mem. adv. com. demonstration grants, 1967; advisor VA, 1968; cons. European region WHO, 1968-72; cons. med. fitness program U.S. Air Force, 1968; cons. Pres.'s Biomed. Research Panel, 1975; mem. adv. com. automated Multiphasic Health Testing, 1971; discussant Nat. Conf. Preventive Medicine, Bethesda, Md., 1975; mem. com. on tech. in health care NAS, 1976; mem. adv. group Nat. Commn. on Digestive Diseases, U.S. Congress, 1978; mem. adv. panel to U.S. Congress Office of Tech. Assessment, 1980-85; mem. peer rev. adv. group TRIMIS program Dept. Def., 1978-90; program chmn. 3d Internat. Conf. Med. Informatics, Tokyo, 1980; chmn. bd. sci. counselors Nat. Library Medicine, 1985-87; mem. lit. selection tech. rev. com. Nat. Libr. of Medicine, 1997—. Author: Treatment of Pneumococcic Pneumonia, 1948, Hospital Computer Systems, 1974, Multiphasic Health Testing Services, 1978, Medical Informatics: A Historical Review, 1995; editor: Permanente Med. Bull., 1943-53; mem. editl. bd. Preventive Medicine, 1970-80, Jour. Med. Sys., Methods Info. Medicine, 1980-97, Diagnostic Medicine, 1980-84, Computers in Biomed. Rsch., 1987-94; contbr. articles to med. jours., chpts. to books. Recipient Computers in Health Care Pioneer award, 1992; Johns Hopkins Centennial scholar, 1976; fellow Ctr. Advanced Studies in Behavioral Scis., Stanford U., 1985-86; scholar-in-residence Nat. Libr. Medicine, 1987—. Fellow ACP, Am. Coll. Cardiology, Am. Coll. Chest Physicians, Am. Inst. Med. and Biol. Engring.; mem. AMA, Inst. Medicine of NAS (chmn. tech. subcom. for improving patient records 1990, chmn. workshop on informatics in clin. preventive medicine 1991), Am. Fedn. Clin. Rsch., Am. Coll. Med. Informatics (pres. 1987-88, Morris F. Collen medal named in his honor 1993), Salutis Unitas (v.p. 1972), Soc. Adv. Med. Sys. (pres. 1973), Nat. Acad. Practice in Medicine (chmn. 1982-88, co-chmn. 1989-91), Am. Med. Informatics Assn. (bd. dirs. 1985-96), Internat. Health Evaluation Assn. (pres. 1995-96, Lifetime Achievement award 1992, David E. Morgan award for achievement in health care info. 1998), Internat. Med. Informatics Assn. Sr. Officers Club, Alpha Omega Alpha, Tau Beta Pi. Home: 4155 Walnut Blvd Walnut Creek CA 94596-5834 Office: 3505 Broadway Oakland CA 94611-5714

COLLETT, MERRILL JUDSON, management consultant; b. Winona Lake, Ind., Feb. 20, 1914; s. Charles Alfred and Dora (Jenkins) C. BA, Stanford (Calif.) U., 1934; MPA, Syracuse (N.Y.) U., 1938. With Pub. Adminstrn. Svs., Chgo., 1940-43; U.S. Bur. of Budget, 1945-46; pers. dir. Bonneville Power Adminstrn., Portland, Oreg., 1946-50; dir. pers. and mgmt. prodn., mktg. adminstrn. USDA, Washington, 1950-52; dir. wartime organizational planning Office Def. Mobilization, Washington, 1954-58; co-owner Collett and Clapp, P.R., 1958-65; founder, pres. Exec. Mgmt. Svc., Arlington, Va., 1967-82; editor-at-large The Bureaucrat, Washingt, 1981—; cons. for mgmt. Tucson Met. Ministry, 1985-88. Contbr. articles to profl. jours. Moderator Calvary Bapt. Ch., Washington, 1981-83; bd. dirs. Efforts from Ex-Convicts, Washington, 1967-83, Bacone Coll., Muskogee, Okla., 1980-86, 91—, Tucson Met. Ministry, 1989-91. Lt. USNR, 1943-46. Mem. Internat. Pers. Mgmt. Assn. (hon. life, Stockberger award), Ariz. Pers. Mgmt. Assn. (hon. life).

COLLETT, ROBERT LEE, financial company executive; b. Ardmore, Okla., July 1, 1940; s. Pat (Dowell) Conway; m. Sue Walker Healy; 1 child, Catherine April. BA in Math., Rice U., 1962; MA in Econs., Duke U., 1963. Chief actuarial asst. Am. Nat. Ins. Co., Galveston, Tex., 1963-66; actuary Milliman & Robertson, Inc., Phila., 1966-70; prin. Milliman & Robertson, Inc., Houston, 1970-89, pres., 1990; pres., CEO Milliman & Robertson, Inc., Houston and Seattle, 1991-92, Seattle, 1992—. Bd. dirs. Seattle Symphony, 1992—. Fellow Soc. Actuaries (chmn. internat. sect. 1992—); mem. Rainier Club. Episcopalian. Avocations: tennis, traveling, music, reading. Office: Milliman & Robertson Inc 1301 5th Ave Ste 3800 Seattle WA 98101-2646*

COLLEY, JANET SCRITSMIER, investment consultant; b. Pomona, Calif., May 21, 1960; d. Jerome Lorenzo and Mildred Joan (Lloyd) Scrit-

smier; children: Justin Michael, Corey Gray, Cody James; m. Glenn Turner Colley, Dec. 27, 1996. Student Calif. State Poly. U., 1978-79. Vice pres. sales E.L.A. Co., Industry, Calif., 1979-84; investment cons. Cameron Properties Inc., Covina, Calif., 1980—. Asst. instr. Dale Carnegie Sales Course, 1981-82, Human Relations, 1983. Republican. Mormon. Home: 1440 E Puente St Covina CA 91724-3214

COLLIER, ALAN M., management company executive; b. Salt Lake City, Apr. 30, 1953; s. James Alan and Myrne (Moss) C.; m. Mindy Jo Dance, June 22, 1984; children: Heather, Melissa, Ashley, James, Michael. Student, U. Utah, 1971-72; BBA, Western States U., 1989. Cert. shopping ctr. mgr. ICSC. Mktg. dir., asst. mgr. Buena Park Mall, Riverside, Calif., 1975-76; mgr. Parker Mgmt. & Devel., Albuquerque, 1976-78; regional mgr. CHA Mgmt. & Devel., Roanoke, Va., 1978-79; dir. of prop., ptnr. Collier Heinz & Assocs., Salt Lake City, 1979-83; pres. Collier Mgmt. & Devel., Bountiful, Utah, 1983—; mem. faculty U. Shopping Ctrs., San Francisco, 1988, ICSC Mgmt. II Inst., Ariz., Calif., 1989, 90, 91; spkr. Mountain States Idea Exch., Salt Lake City, 1989. Contbr. articles to profl. jours. Found. bd. mem. Westminster Coll., Salt Lake City, 1987; pres. Amicus Club, Salt Lake City, 1991-92; chmn. Deseret Found., Salt Lake City, 1995; state del. Rep. Party, Davis County, Utah, 1997-98. Recipient Gold Caduceus, Deseret Found., Salt Lake City, 1996. Mem. Rotary Club, Am. Mensa, Ltd., Elephant Club, Hon. Col. Avocations: golf, guitar, snowmobiling. Office: Collier Mgmt & Devel 880 S Main St Bountiful UT 84010-6345

COLLIER, NEAL HOWARD, sales professional; b. L.A., May 28, 1969; s. Gerald Collier and Meryl (Simon) Rizzotti; m. Tracy Elizabeth Leal, Sept. 27, 1997. BA, UCLA, 1991; MBA, U. So. Calif., 1997. New accounts rep. Wells Fargo Bank, Beverly Hills, Calif., 1988-91; buyer May Dept. Stores, North Hollywood, Calif., 1991-95; assoc. product mgr. Hunt Wesson, Fullerton, Calif., 1997-98; asst. mktg. mgr. Buena Vista Home Entertainment, Burbank, Calif., 1998—. Avocations: enology, hiking, writing. Home: 1871 Greenfield Ave Apt 101 Los Angeles CA 90025-4478 Office: Buena Vista Home Entertainment 3900 W Alameda Ave Burbank CA 91505-4316

COLLIER, PETER ANTHONY, writer; b. Hollywood, Calif., June 2, 1939; s. Donnovan L. and Doris Y. (Cohen) C.; m. Mary Josephine Giachino, Sept. 27, 1967; children: Andrew, Caitlin, Nicholas. BA in English, U. Calif., Berkeley, 1961, MA in English, 1963. Editor Ramparts Mag., San Francisco, 1967-73; cons. editor Calif. mag., L.A., 1984-87; editor Heterodoxy mag., L.A., 1992—; co-founder Ctr. for Study Popular Culture, L.A., 1992—; pub. Encounter Books, San Francisco, 1998—. Author: The Roosevelts: An American Saga, 1994, The Fords: An American Epic, 1989, Destructive Gneration, 1987, The Kennedys: An American Dream, 1984, Downriver: A Novel, 1978, The Rockefellers: An American Dynasty, 1976. Roman Catholic. Office: Encounter Books 116 New Montgomery St San Francisco CA 94105-3607

COLLIER, RICHARD BANGS, philosopher, foundation executive; b. Hastings, Nebr., Aug. 12, 1918; s. Nelson Martin and Stella (Butler) C. BA, U. Wash., 1951. Fgn. aid officer GS14, air traffic control supr. engr. & airway comms. engr., civil aviation Am. embassy, Bangkok, Thailand, 1958-63; founder, dir. Pleneurethics Society, Tacoma, 1985—; founder Inst. Ethics & Sci., Tacoma, 1988—, Pleneurethics Inst., 1995—. Carnegie fellow Inst. Pub. Affairs, Grad. Sch., U. Wash., 1950-51. Nat. adv. bd. Am. Security Council. Capt. USAF, 1965-66. Recipient Rep. Presdl. Legion of merit, Medal of Freedom, Rep. Senatorial, 1964. Mem. Assn. Supervision & Curriculum Devel., Soc. Health & Human Values, Senatorial Trust (U.S. Senatorial Medal of Freedom), Royal Inst. Philosophy (Eng.), Nat. Rep. Senatorial Inner Circle (Presdl. commn.), Rep. Nat. Com. (life, Eisenhower commn., charter mem. chmn's. adv. bd.). Author: Pleneurethic, 20 vols., 1964-93, Pleneurethics: A Philosophical System Uniting Body, Brain and Mind, 2d edit. 1990, contrb. to Journal of Pleneurethics. Home: 319 Tacoma Ave N Apt 1607 Tacoma WA 98403-2722

COLLIER, WILLIAM THAYER, bandleader, musician, educator; b. Phoenix, Feb. 25, 1928; S. Stanford Fitzgerald and Irene (Biehn) C.; 1 child, Catherine Jean. Student, Los Angeles City Coll., 1946-48. Band leader, musician various nightclubs, U.S. and Japan, 1948—; pvt. voice tchr., 1950—; voice cons. Capitol Records, A&M Records, S&R Pub. Co., 1950-55; voice tchr. Cerritos Coll., Norwalk, Calif., 1986—, Downey (Calif.) Adult Sch., 1986—. Author: How to Sing a Little or a Lot, 1981; contbr. articles to profl. jours. Mem. Am. Fedn. Musicians (life), NEA, Calif. Tchrs. Assn. Avocations: sculpture, painting, woodwork, carpentry, writing. Home and Office: 9128 Brock Ave Downey CA 90240-2737

COLLINGS, CELESTE LOUISE (SHORTY VASSALLI), marketing executive, professional artist; b. Highland Park, Ill., Dec. 9, 1948; d. Robert Zane Jr. and Laura (Vasaly) C.; m. John Austin Darden III, July 17, 1971 (div. July 1975); 1 child, Desiree Anne; m. John Cochran Barber, Dec. 13, 1984 (div. Aug. 1998). BA, U. Ariz., 1970; postgrad., N.Mex. State U., 1975; completed mktg. mgr. seminar, U. Calif., Irvine, 1978; cert. of achievement, Wilson Learning Course, 1983. Art tchr. Devargas Jr. High Sch., Santa Fe, 1971; artist, pvt. tchr. Las Cruces, N.Mex., 1971-75; sales rep. Helpmates Temp. Services, Santa Ana, Calif., 1975-76; sales account mgr. Bristol-Myers Products, N.Y.C., 1976-82; sales mgr. Profl. Med. Products, Greenwood, S.C., 1982-85; mktg. mgr. med. products Paper-Pak Products, La Verne, Calif., 1985-88; owner Multi-Media West, Newport Beach, Calif., 1988—; mgmt. trainee Bristol-Myers, Kansas City, Mo., 1978; sales trainee Profl. Med. Products, Greenwood, 1983, product strategy, 1984, chmn. nat. adv. com., 1983-84; owner and pres. Accent Shoji Screens, Newport Beach, Calif., 1981—. Exhibited in one-woman shows at Nancy Dunn Studio and Gallery, San Clemente, Calif., 1980, The Collectables, San Francisco, 1980, Breeden Gallery, Orange Calif., 1992, Orange County Cen. for Contemporary Art, Santa Ana, Calif., Laguna Beach (Calif.) Festival of the Arts Art-A-Fair, 1981, Ariz. Inter-Scholastic Hon. Exhibit, 1st place award, 1962-66, Glendale Fed. Savs. Art Exhitibition, 1982; numerous others; represented by Patricia Corriea Art Gallery, Santa Monica, Calif., Breeden Gallery, Orange, Calif., L.A. Artcore. Mem. Orange County Performing Arts Ctr., Colona Del Mar, Calif., 1981, Orange County Visual Artists, 1990, Orange County Ctr. for Contemporary Art, 1993; asst. dir. Orange County Satelittle, Womens Caucus for Art, organizer, 1993. Recipient 10 sales awards Bristol-Meyers, 1976-82, Western Zone Sales Rep. award Profl. Med. Products, 1984, Gainers Club award, 1984; named Nat. Sales Rep. of Yr. Profl. Med. Products, 1984. Mem. Humanities Assocs., U. Ariz. Alumni Assn., Kappa Alpha Theta Alumni.

COLLINGS, CHARLES LEROY, supermarket executive; b. Wewoka, Okla., July 11, 1925; s. Roy B. and Dessie L. Collings; m. Frances Jane Flake, June 28, 1947; children—Sandra Jean, Dianna Lynn. Student, So. Methodist U., 1943-44, U. Tex., 1945. Sec., contr., dir. Noble Meat Co., Madera, Calif., 1947-54; chief acct. Montgomery Ward & Co., Oakland, Calif., 1954-56; with Raleys, Sacramento, 1956—; sec. Raleys, 1958—, pres., 1970-96, CEO, 1993-98, CEO emeritus, bd. dirs., 1998—. Bd. dirs. Pro Athlete Outreach, Kevin Johnson's St. Hope Acad. With USNR, 1943-46. Mem. Calif Retailers Assn. (past mem. bd. dirs.). Republican. Baptist. Home: 6790 Arabella Way Sacramento CA 95831-2325 Office: Raley's PO Box 13778 Sacramento CA 95853-3778

COLLINS, DANE H., marketing executive; b. Champaign, Ill., Feb. 2, 1961; s. Ronald Milton Collins and Beverly Carolyn (Brown) Patnaude; m. Leigh Ann Paulsen, Oct. 4, 1989. Student, Iowa State U., 1979-82. Acct. exec. Phoenix Pub., Inc., 1982-83, advt. mgt., 1983-85; comml. artist Jackie Awerman Assocs., Phoenix, 1983-88; acct. svcs. supr. The Lutzker Group, Phoenix, 1985-86; advt. dir. Intersouth Communications, Scottsdale, Ariz., 1986-87; mktg. dir. Ariz. Bus. & Devel., Phoenix, 1988-89; v.p. S.W. Communications, Phoenix, 1988-90, Balloon Buddies, Inc., Mesa, Ariz., 1988-90; mktg. dir. Orange-Sol, Inc., Gilbert, Ariz., 1989-91, 1993—; ptnr. Interactive Techs., Inc., 1996-97; cons. Continental Am. Corp., Wichita, Kans., 1990-92, Ariz. Bus. & Devel., Phoenix, 1990-91. Illustrator: (books) Power, Influence, Sabotage: The Corporate Survivor's Coloring Book & Primer, 1986, Good Morning Mr. President, 1988; patentee decorative message display. Vol. DeNovo, Phoenix, 1984, Cystic Fibrosis Found., Scottsdale, 1985, Aid to Women's Ctr., Phoenix, 1987, Dayspring U.M.C. Missions for Homeless, Tempe, Ariz., 1990-93. Mem. Phoenix Soc. Communicating Arts. Republican. Methodist. Avocations: sports, fine arts, family, church, travel. Home: 2650 E South Fork Dr Phoenix AZ 85048-8976

COLLINS, DENNIS ARTHUR, foundation executive; b. Yakima, Wash., June 9, 1940; s. Martin Douglas and Louise Constance (Caccia) C.; m. Mary Veronica Paul, June 11, 1966; children: Jenifer Ann, Lindsey Kathleen. BA, Stanford U., 1962, MA, 1963; LHD, Mills Coll., 1994. Assoc. dean admissions Occidental Coll., Los Angeles, 1964-66, dean admissions, 1966-68, dean of students, 1968-70; headmaster Emma Willard Sch., Troy, N.Y., 1970-74; founding headmaster San Francisco U. High Sch., 1974-86; pres. James Irvine Found., San Francisco, 1986—; trustee Coll. Bd., N.Y.C., 1981-85, Ind. Ednl. Svcs., Princeton, N.J., 1981-85, Calif. Assn. Ind. Schs., L.A., 1982-86, Branson Sch., 1987-89, Aspen Inst. Nonprofit Sector rsch. Fund, 1992—; chmn. bd. So. Calif. Assn. Philanthropy, L.A., 1989-91, No. Calif. Grantmakers, 1987-90; dir. Rebuild L.A., 1992-93. Trustee Cathedral Sch. for Boys, San Francisco, 1976-82, Marin Country Day Sch., Corte Madera, Calif., 1978-84, San Francisco Exploratorium, 1984-86, Ind. Sector, Washington, 1987-95, Am. Farmland Trust, Washington, 1992—; bd. dirs., vice chmn. Children's Hosp. Found., San Francisco, 1984-86; chmn. bd. dirs. Coun. for Cmty. Based Devel., Washington, 1989-92. Mem. Council on Founds. Democrat. Episcopalian. Clubs: World Trade, University; California (L.A.). Home: 432 Golden Gate Ave Belvedere Tiburon CA 94920-2447 Office: The James Irvine Found Steurt Tower 1 Market St Ste 2500 San Francisco CA 94105*

COLLINS, FUJI, mental health professional; b. Tokyo, Nov. 3, 1954; s. Boyd Leslie and Kimiko (Terayama) C.; 1 child, Lacey Nichole. BS, Ariz. State U., 1977; MS, Ea. Wash. U., 1989; MA, The Fielding Inst., 1993, PhD, 1994. Registered clin. therapist. Commd. 2d lt. U.S. Army, 1978, advanced through grades to maj., 1989, lt. platoon leader, adminstrv. officer, 1978-79; lt. bat. adjutant 509th Airborne Bat. Combat Team, 1977-80; capt., air def. fire coordination officer U.S. Army, 1981-83, capt. battery comdr., 1983-85, capt., 1985-86; clin. therapist Wash. State Patrol, 1985-95; dir. of adminstrn., Japanese Counseling Program Richmond Area Multi-Svcs., Inc., San Francisco, 1995-97, dir. children and youth svcs., 1995-97; prof. psychology Ctrl. Wash. U., Ellensburg, 1997—; adj. prof. John F. Kennedy U.; coord. Wash. State Patrol Critical Incident/Peer Support Team, Wash. State Hostage Negotiator; mem. Thurston/Mason County Critical Incident Stress Debriefing Team; dir. Richmond Counseling Ctr., 1995—; vis. lectr. Georgetown U., 1996—; faculty Nat. Asian Am. Psychology Tng. Ctr., San Francisco, 1996—. Vol. Thurston/Mason County Crisis Clinic; mem. steering com. Thurston/Mason County Critical Incident Team. Mem. ACA, APA, Wash. State Psychol. Assn., Asian Am. Psychol. Assn., Soc. for Psychol. Study of Ethnic Minority Issues, Am. Critical Incident Stress Found., Wash. State Hostage Negotiation Assn., Assn. Police Planning and Rsch. Officers. Home: 400 S Walnut St Ellensburg WA 98926-3823 Office: Dept Psychology Ctrl Washington U Ellensburg WA 98926-7575

COLLINS, GEORGE TIMOTHY, computer software consultant; b. Connersville, Ind., Aug. 21, 1943; s. Robert Emerson and Oma (Richie) C.; m. Martha Elizabeth Holt, Apr. 30, 1966; children: Kirsten Stephanie, Eowyn Erika. BA in Math., Ind. U., 1966; MS in Computer Sci., Rensselaer Poly. Inst., 1971. Engr. program analyst Sikorsky Aircraft, Stratford, Conn., 1966-70; research mathematician Peter Eckrich, Ft. Wayne, Ind., 1970-75; sr. systems analyst Pyrotek Data Service, Ft. Walton Beach, Fla., 1975-77; sr. aerosystems engr. Gen. Dynamics, Ft. Worth, 1977-79; sr. specialist Electronic Data Systems, Las Vegas, Nev., 1979-81; sr. assoc. CACI Fed., San Diego, 1981-82; prin., gen. mgr. Structured Software Systems, Escondido, Calif., 1982-88; sr. software engr. Sci. Applications Internat. Corp., San Diego, 1988-94; pvt. practice cons. Escondido, 1994-96; prin. engr. Orbital Scis. Corp., 1996—; cons. Hi-Shear Corp., Los Angeles, 1973-75. Developer (computer model and data base) Aircraft Stores Interface, 1975, (computer model) TAC Disrupter, 1981; co-developer (computer model) Tactical Air Def., Battle Model, 1978, Tactical Air and Land Ops., 1980; prime contbr. (computer data collection and analysis sys.) Mobile Sea Range, 1988-90; contbr. (computer comm. sys.) Lightweight Deployable Comm., 1990, Joint Advanced Spl. Ops. Radio Sys., 1992, Orbital Scis. Corp.'s Maj. Constituent Analyzer Environ. Control/Life Scis. Sys. for Internat. Space Station (team received NASA Manned Flight Awareness award 1994), Orbital Scis. Corp. Software Lead Meterology Sensor Module, 1996, Point of Contact Support MCA Integration in Internat. Space Station, 1998, Software Engr. MCA EDP bd. self-test debug, 1998. Bd. dirs. Family and Children's Service, Ft. Wayne, 1974. Mem. N.Y. Acad. Scis., North County Chess Club. Unitarian. Avocations: chess, tennis, astronomy. Home: 121 W 8th Ave Escondido CA 92025-5001 also: Orbital Scis Corp 2771 N Garey Ave Pomona CA 91767-1809

COLLINS, GORDON DENT, recording company executive; b. Berkeley, Calif., Mar. 27, 1924; s. Edward Everett and Dorothy Janet (Doyle) C.; m. Louise Norma Krivicich, July 23, 1960; children: Daniel Edward, Patrick Doyle, Christine Anne, Gordon Jr. Student, U. Maine, 1943-44; BSEE, U. Wash., 1948; postgrad., Stanford U., 1960-63. Registered profl. engr., N.Y. Founder, chief executive officer Collins Rec. Co., Los Altos, Calif., 1968—. Served to lt. U.S. Army Signal Corps, 1943-52. Named Man of Yr. Elfun Soc., San Jose, Calif., 1980. Mem. Soc. Engrs. and Scientists of France. Club: No. Calif. Golf Assn. (San Jose). Pioneer in rec. on location in divers venues, 13 states, 19 countries, 5 continents; first co. to record ann. awards ceremony of Nat. Acad. Rec. Arts and Scis. Patentee in field. Avocations: playing golf, travel, photography. Office: PO Box 934 Los Altos CA 94023-0934

COLLINS, MICHAEL K., lawyer; b. Sikeston, Mo., Feb. 13, 1943. AB, Washington U., St. Louis, 1965, JD, 1969. Bar: Calif. 1970, U.S. Dist. Ct. (cen., so. and no. dists.) Calif. 1970, U.S. Ct. Appeals (9th cir.) 1970. With Greenberg, Glusker, Fields, Claman & Machtinger, L.A., 1969—. Editor-in-Chief Washington U. Law Quar., 1968-69. Mem. Assn. Bus. Trial Lawyers, State Bar Calif., L.A. County Bar Assn. (exec. com. real property sect. 1981-83), Century City Bar Assn., Order of Coif, Wilshire Hunting Club. Office: Greenberg Glusker Fields Claman & Machtinger Ste 421 1900 Avenue Of The Stars Los Angeles CA 90067-4301

COLLINS, MICHAEL PAUL, secondary school educator, earth science educator, consultant; b. Chula Vista, Calif., Jan. 2, 1959; s. William Henry and Linda Lee (Capron) C.; children: Christopher M., Matthew R., Kyle P., Colby W. A in Gen. Studies, Clatsop Community Coll., Astoria, Oreg., 1983; BS in Sci. Edn., Oreg. State U., 1987, BS in Geology, 1987; postgrad., U. Alaska, Anchorage. Cert. tchr., Wash., Alaska. Emergency med. technician II, fireman Sitka (Alaska) Fire Dept., 1978-80; paramedic Medix Ambulance, Astoria, 1980-83; cartographer technician U.S. Geol. Survey, Grants Pass, Oreg., 1985; earth sci. tchr. Lake Oswego (Oreg.) Sch. Dist., 1987-88; sci. tchr. Gladstone (Oreg.) Sch. Dist., 1988-90; radon technician Radon Detection Systems, Portland, Oreg., 1988-90; sales and mktg. dir. Evergreen Helicopters of Alaska, Inc., Anchorage, 1990-91; sci./math tchr. Anchorage Sch. Dist., 1991—; instr. geology Alaska Jr. Coll., Anchorage, 1992-93; cons. earth sci. edn. Project ESTEEM, ctr. astrophysics Harvard U., Cambridge, Mass., 1992—; field technician Water Quality Divsn., City of Anchorage, 1993; cons. Am. Meteorol. Assn., atmospheric ednl. resource agt. Project Atmosphere, 1994—; cons. Ala. State H.S. Scis. Olympics, coord., 1994; cons. Project MicroObservatory Ctr. for Astrophysics, Harvard U., 1995—; coord. Instr. Project DataStreme Am. Meteorol. Soc., 1996—; cons. geologist Unocal Alaska, 1997-98; geologist Shannon & Wilson, Inc., 1998. Co-author: Merrill Earth Science Lab Activities, 1989. With USCG, 1977-81. Mem. NEA, Am. Assn. Petroleum Geologists, Geol. Soc. Am., Nat. Sci. Tchrs. Assn., Am. Geol. Inst., Am. Meteorol. Soc., Alaska Geol. Soc. Inc., Nat. Assn. Geosci. Tchrs. (pres. N.W. sect. 1995—). Avocations: weight training, fishing, hiking, camping. Home: 2240 Sentry Dr Apt 404 Anchorage AK 99507-4604 Office: West Anchorage HS 1700 Hillcrest Dr Anchorage AK 99517-1347

COLLINS, MICHAEL SEAN, obstetrician and gynecologist, educator; b. Yankton, S.D., Sept. 8, 1951; s. Edward Daniel and Joyce (Slatky) C.; m. Judy Furman, Sept. 20, 1975; children: Lauren, Sean, Carolyn. BS, Davidson Coll., 1973; MD, Med. U. S.C., 1977. Diplomate Am. Bd. Ob-Gyn. Chief resident in ob-gyn Med. U. S.C., Charleston, 1980-81; instr. ob-gyn U. Oreg. Health Scis. Ctr., Portland, 1981—; chmn. dept. ob-gyn Good Samaritan Hosp., Portland, 1983-85; cons. Prepared Childbirth Assn., Portland, 1981—, Triplet Connection, L.A., 1985—. Fellow ACOG (adv. coun. 1991—, chmn. Oreg. sect.); mem. AMA, Oreg. Med. Assn., Oreg. Ob-Gyn. Soc., Pacific Coast Ob-Gyn. Soc., Pacific N.W. Ob-Gyn. Soc., Am. Fertility Soc., Porsche Club Am., Oreg. Ob-Gyn. Soc. (vice-chmn. 1991-94, chmn. 1995—), Am. Assn. Gynecologic Laparoscopists, Internat. Soc. Advancement Humanistic Studies Medicine, Alpha Omega Alpha. Republican. Roman Catholic. Avocations: photography, jogging, travel, skiing, hiking. Home: 716 NW Rapidan Ter Portland OR 97210-3129 Office: Portland Ob-Gyn Assocs 1130 NW 22nd Ave Ste 120 Portland OR 97210-2934

COLLINS, RICHARD AUGUSTINE, mechanical engineer; b. Plain City, Ohio, Oct. 13, 1933; s. John Bernard and Mildred Leona (Klein) C.; m. Rieta June Peterson, Aug. 3, 1963; children: Daphne Lynn, Andrew Douglas. BS in Mech. Engring., Ohio State U., 1956; MS in Mech. Engring., Ga. Inst. Tech., Atlanta, 1961. Chief engr. Solar Industries, Inc., Tempe, Ariz., 1967-68; sr. devel. engr. A. Rsch. Mfg. Co., Phoenix, 1968-79; asst. project engr. Garrett Engine Divsn., Phoenix, 1979-85; project engr. Allied Signal, Phoenix, 1985-91, mgr. II, 1991-93, prin. engr., 1993-98; cons. Solar Designs & Sales, Tempe, 1976-98. Contbr. articles to profl. jours.; patentee in field. Founding pres. N. Tempe Homeowners Assn., 1975; mem., chmn. City Tempe Design Rev. Bd., 1975-81; nation chief Indian Guides, Tempe, 1981. With Corp. Engrs., U.S. Army, 1957. Mem. ASME (dir. 1977-81, 93-97, Lifetime Svc. award 1996). Avocations: backpacking, golfing, fishing. Home: 1736 N Mcallister Ave Tempe AZ 85281-1406

COLLINS, SARAH HELEN BOLI, landscape architect; b. Warren, Pa., July 18, 1958; d. Hugh C. and Elizabeth (Harper) Wood; m. Robert McPherson Boli Collins, Dec. 22, 1982; 1 child, Jonathan William. AA in Liberal Arts, Jamestown Community coll., N.Y., 1978; BA in Environ. Science, Alfred U., N.Y., 1980; B in Landscape Architecture, U. Wash., 1991. Lab. asst. Jamestown Community Coll., Jamestown, N.Y., 1976-78; dir. commercial ops. Tech and Turf Inc., Madison, N.J., 1980-81; mgr. King's Motel Pacific Land Assoc., Enumclaw, Wash., 1985-90; intern landscape architect Harvard and Assocs., Seattle, 1991; landscape designer Tecton Landscape, Seattle, 1992; owner Plan'dscape, 1985-92, Collins Farm, 1992—; mem. design rev. bd. City of Enumclaw. Author: Jamestown Community College Preserve, 1978. Tourism com. C. of C., Enumclaw, Wash., 1985; mem. North Harmony Planning Bd.; mem. Chautauqua Area Girl Scout Coun. Property Mgmt. Bd. Mem. Assn. U.S. Army, Am. Soc. Landscape Architects (Student Merit awards Washington chpt. 1988), Bus. and Profl. Women (Young Career Woman award Wash. state dist. 4 1986), Sigma Lambda Alpha, Tau Sigma Delta (pres. Iota chpt. 1989). Republican. Methodist. Avocations: skiing, golfing, painting, skydiving. Home and Office: 4205 Auburn Way S Trlr 111 Auburn WA 98092-7286

COLLINS, SCOTT EDGAR, magazine editor; b. Evanston, Ill., July 9, 1964; s. Edgar F. and Esther Marie (Dalby) C.; m. Elena Lisa Maganini, June 18, 1994. BA, Northwestern U., 1986. Staff reporter Daily Southtown, Chgo., 1989-93; staff reporter, contbr. L.A. Times, 1994-97; mng. editor Hollywood Reporter Weekly, L.A., 1997—. Mem. Soc. Profl. Journalists (Peter Lisagor award 1990, 91), Authors Guild, Phi Beta Kappa. Office: Hollywood Reporter 5055 Wilshire Blvd Ste 600 Los Angeles CA 90036-4396

COLLINS, STEVEN THOMAS, archaeologist, educator; b. Santa Monica, Calif., Sept. 11, 1950; s. Thomas Van and Evelyn (Lee) Collins; m. Danette Rae Mosher. BS, U. N.Mex., 1972; MDiv., S.W. Bapt. Theol. Sem., 1975; D in Ministry, Luther Rice Sem., 1978; PhD, Trinity Theol. Sem., 1983. Assoc. pastor Highland Bapt. Ch., Albuquerque, 1975-78, Gracemont Bapt. Ch., Tulsa, Okla., 1978-80; prof. Luther Rice Extension Campus, Tulsa, Okla., 1980-85; pres. S.W. Bibl. Sem., Tulsa, 1985-89; prvt. practice Albuquerque, 1989-91; exec. dir., dean, prof. bibl. studies, arch., apologetics Trinity Coll. and Sem., Albuquerque, 1991—; field archaeologist Bethsaida Excavation, Israel, 1995, 96, 98, Khirbet el-Maqatir Excavation, Israel, 1995—; curator Mus. Archaeology and Bibl. History, Albuquerque, 1998—; lectr. in archaeology and ceramic typology; adj. prof. of Archaedogy and Bib. history Jerusalem Ctr. for Bib. Studies, Israel. Author: Christian Discipleship, 1988, Championing the Faith, 1991, Mastering New Testament Greek, 1996. Mem. Near East Archaeol. Soc., Evangelical Theol. Soc., Am. Schs. or Oriental Rsch. Republican. Avocations: cooking, hiking, 4-wheel driving. Office: Trinity Coll and Sem SW Campus 10110 Constitution Ave NE Albuquerque NM 87112-5208

COLLINS, TERRY, professional baseball manager. Mgr. Houston Astros, 1994-96, Anaheim Angels, 1996—. Office: Anaheim Angels 2000 E Gene Autry Way Anaheim CA 92806-6100*

COLLINS, WILLIAM LEROY, telecommunications engineer; b. Laurel, Miss., June 17, 1942; s. Henry L. and Christene E. (Finnegan) C. Student, La Salle U., 1969; BS in Computer Sci., U. Beverly Hills, 1984. Sr. computer operator Dept. Pub. Safety, Phoenix, 1975-78, data communications specialist, 1978-79, supr. computer ops., 1981-82; mgr. network control Valley Nat. Bank, Phoenix, 1979-81; mgr. data communications Ariz. Lottery, Phoenix, 1982-85; mgr. telecommunications Calif. Lottery, Sacramento, 1985—; Mem. Telecomm. Study Mission to Russia, Oct. 1991. Contbr. to profl. publs. Served as sgt. USAF, 1964-68. Mem. IEEE, Nat. Sys. Programmers Assn., Centrex Users Group, DMS Centrex User Group, Accunet Digital Svcs. User Group, Telecomms. Assn. (v.p. edn. Sacramento Valley chpt. 1990-94, pres. 1995, chpt. assn. dir. 1996-97, chpt. past pres. 1996, Prestigious Svc. award 1997), Telecom. Assn. (chmn. corp. edn. com. 1994-95, conf. com. 1994-95, co-chair conf. program com. 1996, program dir. edn. 1996, corp. dir. edn. 1996-97, pres.-elect 1998, pres. and ceo, 1999), SynOptics User Group, Timeplex User Group, Assn. Data Comm. Users, Soc. Mfg. Engrs., Data Processing Mgmt. Assn., Am. Mgmt. Assn., Assn. Computing Machinery, Am. Soc. for Quality Control, Bldg. Industry Cons. Svc. Internat., Assn. for Quality and Participation, KC, Calif. Integrated Svcs. Digital Network User Group, Computer Security Inst., Assn. Pub. Comms. Officials, Armed Forces Comms. and Electronics Assn., Assn. Info. Tech. Profls., H.P. Open View Forum. Roman Catholic. Home: 116 Valley Oak Dr Roseville CA 95678-4378 Office: Calif State Lottery 600 N 10th St Sacramento CA 95814-0393

COLLMER, RUSSELL CRAVENER, data processing executive, educator; b. Guatemala, Jan. 2, 1924; s. G. Russell and Constance (Cravener) C.; m. Ruth Hannah Adams, Mar. 4, 1950; 1 child, Reed Alan. BS in Math., U. N.Mex., 1951; MS in Meteorology, Calif. Inst. Tech., 1954; MS in Math., State U. Iowa, 1955. Staff mem. Lincoln Lab., MIT, Lexington, 1955-57; mgr. systems modeling, computer dept. GE, Phoenix, 1957-59; mgr. ARCAS Thompson Ramo Wooldridge, Inc., Canoga Park, Calif., 1959-62; assoc. mgr., tech. dir. CCIS-70 Bunker-Ramo Corp., L.A., 1962-64; sr. assoc. Planning Rsch. Corp., L.A., 1964-65; pres. R. Collmer Assocs., Benson, Ariz., 1965—; pres. Benson Econ. Enterprises Corp., 1968-69; lectr. computer scis. Pima C.C., Tucson, 1970—. With USAAC, 1942-46, capt. USAF, 1951-53. Mem. IEEE, Am. Meteorol. Soc., Assn. for Computing Machinery, Assn. Instnl. Rsch., Phi Delta Theta. Office: R Collmer Assocs PO Box 864 Benson AZ 85602-0864

COLMAN, RONALD WILLIAM, computer science educator; b. L.A., Sept. 13, 1930; s. William Maynard Colman and Edna Eliza (Halford) Smith. BA in Math., UCLA, 1957; PhD in Computer Sci., U. Calif., Irvine, 1976. Electronics tech. Lockheed Aircraft Corp., Burbank, Calif., 1952-53; staff specialist Western Electric Co., N.Y.C., 1957-58; assoc. math. Burroughs Corp., Pasadena, Calif., 1958-60; sr. computer analyst Beckman Instruments, Inc., Fullerton, Calif., 1960-62; mgr. L.A. dist. Digital Equipment Corp., L.A., 1962-64; chmn. computer sci. Calif. State U., Fullerton, 1964-80; prof. computer sci. Calif. State U., Northridge, 1980-89; ptnr. Windward Ventures, Venice, Calif.; chmn. session on heuristic search Internat. Joint Conf. on Artificial Intelligence, Stanford, 1973; chmn. nat. symposium on computer sci. edn. Assn. Computing Machinery, Anaheim, Calif., 1976; chmn. registration Nat. Computer Conf., Anaheim, 1978, 80. With USN, 1948-52. Avocations: skiing, opera, scuba diving. Home: 2800 Baywater Ave Apt 8 San Pedro CA 90731-6695

COLMANO, MARINO GIOVANNI AUGUSTO, director, cinematographer, producer, media executive; b. Bologna, Italy, Oct. 21, 1948; came to U.S., 1951; s. Germille and Miranda C. BFA in Film, Photography,

San Francisco Art Inst., 1972. Freelance photojournalist, 1972-76; owner, founder IMAGENATION, San Francisco, 1976-79; founder, pres., producer BRAVO Entertainment, Inc., L.A., 1980—. Dir. TV spls. including Jazz House, The Rating Game, Straight Time: He Wrote it for Criminals (starring Dustin Hoffman); producer, dir., cinemtographer numerous commls. including work for Honda, Disney Home Video, San Diego Transit (Telly award); dir., cinematographer comml. campaign People Helping People (Telly award Metromedia 11 1985); dir. of photography short dramatic films Happy Ending (six Internat. Film Festival awards); producer, co-dir. of photography (comml. campaign) End of the Rainbow (six 1st place awards including Silver Hugo award Chgo. Internat. Film Festival, Mannhein, Portugal), (promo packages) original TV series Batman Small Wonder (Telly award, BPME cert. merit), San Diego Transit No Fuss Bus (Telly award), Last Call, The Gordon Elliott Show, The CChevy Chase Show, M*A*S*H, The Simpsons, Studs, The Beatrice Berry Show, Mr. Baseball; co-producer, dir. A Golden Opportunity, 1986; dir., cinematographer & editor Reservoirs of Strength (Gold Cindy award, Gold Apple award, Silver award Houston Internat. Film Festival, finalist Media Access Awards), 1990; dir. photography The Fantasy Worlds of Irwin allen, A&E Biography. San Francisco Art Inst. scholar.

COLN, WILLIAM ALEXANDER, III, pilot; b. Los Angeles, Mar. 20, 1942; s. William Alexander and Aileen Henrietta (Shimfessel) C.; m. Lora Louise Getchel, Nov. 15, 1969 (div. July 1979); 1 child, Caryn Louise. BA in Geography, UCLA, 1966. Cert. airline transport pilot, flight engr. Commd. USN, Pensacola, Fla., 1966; pilot, officer USN, Fighter Squadron 102, 1969-71, Port Mugu, Calif., 1975-77; pilot, officer USNR, Port Mugu, Calif., 1971-75, advanced through grades to lt. comdr., 1978; ret. USNR, 1984; capt. Delta Airlines, Inc. (formerly Western Airlines Inc.), Los Angeles, 1972—. Recipient Nat. Def. medal USN, 1966. Mem. Nat. Aero. Assn., Airline Pilots Assn., Aircraft Owners and Pilots Assn., UCLA Alumni Assn., Am. Bonanza Soc., Internat. Platform Assn., Santa Barbara Yacht Club. Democrat. Club: Santa Barbara (Calif.) Athletic, Santa Barbara Yacht. Avocations: sailing, scuba diving, flying, computers, electronics. Home: 486 Cota Ln Montecito CA 93108 Office: Delta Air Lines Inc LA Internat Airport Los Angeles CA 90009

COLON, RICHARD WALTER, retired stockbroker; b. Coalinga, Calif., Oct. 26, 1924; s. Walter E. and Edith C. (Roseetti) C.; m. Lavonne H. Colon, Oct. 18, 1947; children: Robert, Gary, Christine. BS/BA, U. Nev., 1949. Stockbroker Watson Johnson & Higgins, Reno, Nev., 1949-50; gen. mgr. KOLO Radio & TV, Reno, 1953-58; sr. v.p. Morgan Stanly Dean Witter, Reno, 1958-92. Ensign USN, 1943-46, WWII, lt. USN, Korea, 1950-53. dir., pres. Utility Shareholders of Nev., Inc., Reno, 1988-98. Avocations: golf, skiing, boating, reading, automobiles.

COLOPY, CHERYL GENE, reporter; b. Houston, July 4, 1944; d. C. Eugene and Ernestyne (White) C. BA, Mills Coll., 1966; PhD, U. Calif., 1980. Asst. prof. U. Hawaii, Honolulu, 1980-82, Calif. State U., Chico, 1982-87; reporter Sta. KQED FM, San Francisco, 1995—. Recipient John Swett award Calif. Tchrs. Assn., 1994. Mem. Assn. of Inds. in Radio, Media Alliance. Avocations: tennis, swimming, hiking, camping. Home: 835 58th St Oakland CA 94608-1403 Office: KQED FM 2601 Mariposa St San Francisco CA 94110

COLTON, ROY CHARLES, management consultant; b. Phila., Feb. 26, 1941; s. Nathan Hale and Ruth Janis (Baylinson) C.; B.A., Knox Coll., 1962; M.Ed., Temple U., 1963. With Sch. Dist. of Phila., 1963-64; systems analyst Wilmington Trust Co., 1967-69; exec. recruiter Atwood Consultants Inc., Phila., 1969-71; pres. Colton Bernard Inc., San Francisco, 1971—; occasional lectr. Fashion Inst. Tech., Phila. Coll. Textiles and Scis. Served with AUS, 1964-66. Mem. San Francisco Fashion Industries, San Francisco C. of C., Calif. Exec. Recruiter Assn., Nat. Assn. Exec. Recruiters, Am. Apparel Mfrs. Assn., Am. Arbitration Assn. (panel arbitrators). Office: Colton Bernard Inc 870 Market St Ste 822 San Francisco CA 94102-2903

COLVIN, CLARK SHERMAN, educator, management consultant; b. Seattle, Oct. 26, 1958; s. Henry Alfred and Dorothy Angie (Tigner) C.; m. Patricia Ann Stanford, Mar. 12, 1989. BA, U. Wash., 1984; MPA, Seattle U., 1986; postgrad., Golden Gate U., 1986—, U.S. Naval War Coll., 1987—, Oxford U., 1989. Owner, mgr. COMCAR Computerized Auto Network, Bellevue, Wash., 1981-82; spl. asst. Wash. State Senate, Olympia, 1983-84; state chmn., pres. Wash. State Pub. Lands Assn., Seattle, 1984-86; master tchr. Independent Learning High Sch., Berkeley, Calif., 1986-87; gen. ptnr. Armand E.R. Mulden & Assoc., Livermore, Calif., 1987—; adj. prof. Chapman Coll., Vallejo, Calif., 1987-88; legis. liaison Ken Selander, Atty., Burien, Wash., 1984; faculty assoc. Intercollegiate Studies Inst., Bryn Mawr, Pa., 1988; lectr. Am. U., Washington, 1989-90. Author: Where Jurisdictions Meet, 1984, (with others) Conflict Analysis and Resolution, 1988. Mgr. Danville (Calif.) City Coun. campaign, 1987. Lt. USNR, 1977-81, 86—; mem. Rep. Nat. Com., Washington; mem. Woodrow Wilson Internat. Ctr. for Scholars. Mem. Soc. for U.S. Constitution, Assn. Mil. Surgeons U.S. (medal), Nav. Res. Assn., Ctr. for Study of Presidency, As. Soc. Pub. Adminstrn., Oxford Ctr. Mgmt. Studies Assn. Methodist. Avocations: archaeology, philosophy, sailing. Office: 3040 Comml St SE Ste 200 Salem OR 97302

COLVIN, GRETA WILMOTH, entrepreneur; b. Odessa, Tex., Mar. 24, 1962; d. Charles Hayden and Sherry Beth (Browning) Wilmoth; m. Michael Anthony Colvin, Aug. 16, 1986; 1 child, Michael Anthony Jr. AA in Radio-TV-Film, San Antonio Coll.; BS, U. Tex.; grad., Dale Carnegie, 1993; post-grad., St. Mary's U., San Antonio, 1997—. Lic. broadcaster, paralegal, pvt. investigator. Various media positions W.M. Entertainment, San Antonio, 1978-86; co-owner Image Nightclubs, San Antonio, 1986-88; owner W.C. Advt., San Antonio, 1980-88; retail mgr. Hastings, San Antonio, 1989-94; pres. Paradigm Enterprises, Flagstaff, Ariz., 1994—. Democrat. Avocations: motorcycle racing, skiing, reading, rock scaleing, going to drag races. Address: 2800 Cerrillos Rd Santa Fe NM 87505-2313 also: 11623 Whisper Valley St San Antonio TX 78230-3737

COLVIS, JOHN PARIS, aerospace engineer, mathematician, scientist; b. St. Louis, June 30, 1946; s. Louis Jack and Jacqueline Betty (Beers) C.; m. Nancy Ellen Fritz, Mar. 15, 1969 (div. Sept. 16, 1974); 1 child, Michael Scott; m. Barbara Carol Davis, Sept. 3, 1976; 1 child, Rebecca Jo; stepchildren: Bruce William John Zimmerly, Belinda Jo Zimmerly Little. Student, Meramec Community Coll., St. Louis, 1964-65, U. Mo., 1966, 72-75, Palomar Coll., San Marcos, Calif., 1968, U. Mo., Rolla, 1968-69; BS in Math., Washington U., 1977. Assoc. system safety engr. McDonnell Douglas Astronautics Co., St. Louis, 1978-81; sr. system safety engr. Martin Marietta Astronautics Group-Strategic Systems Co., Denver, 1981-87; sr. engr. Martin Marietta Astronautics Group-Space Launch Systems Co., Denver, 1987-95, Lockheed Martin Astronautics Co.-Space Launch Sys., Denver, 1995—; researcher in field. Precinct del., precinct committeeman, congl. dist. del., state del. Rep. Party. Lance cpl. USMC, 1966-68, Vietnam. Mem. VFW (post 4171), Colo. Home Educators' Assn. (pres. 1989), Khe Sanh Vet Incorp. Evangelical. Achievements include the quantum postulate and the quantum philosophy of science and mathematics; identification and correction of empirical flaw in foundations of science and mathematics; resolution of several ancient and contemporary conjectures in science and mathematics through application of revolutionary new, complete and verifiable logic-quantum synthesis; correction of fundamental misconception concerning integral and differential limits of calculus; identification of principles and dynamics of nature responsible for such things as relativity, consistency, wave/particle duality, quantum events, black holes, chaos, and irreversibility; clarification and expansion of the Second Law of Thermodynamics allowing for more comprehensive, diverse, and pervasive applications; development of mathematical algorithm which greatly enhanced accuracy and efficiency in which engineering component failure analysis of large complex systems is performed. Avocations: camping, hiking, swimming. Home: 4970 S Hoyt St Littleton CO 80123-1988 Office: Lockheed Martin Astronautics Group-SLS PO Box 179 Denver CO 80201-0179

COMBS, W(ILLIAM) HENRY, III, lawyer; b. Casper, Wyo., Mar. 18, 1949; s. William Henry and Ruth M. (Wooster) C.; divorced; 1 child, J. Bradley. Student, Northwestern U., 1967-70, BS, U. Wyo., 1972, JD, 1973. Bar: Wyo. 1975, U.S. Dist. Ct. Wyo. 1975, U.S. Ct. Appeals (10th cir.) 1990, U.S. Supreme Ct. 1990. Assoc. Murane & Bostwick, Casper, 1975-77, ptnr., 1978—. Mem. com. on resolution of fee disputes, 1988-92. Mem. ABA (tort and ins. practice, law office mgmt. sects.), NRA, Natrona County Bar Assn., Def. Rsch. Inst., Am. Judicature Soc., Wyo. Trial Def. Counsel, Assn. Ski Def. Attys., Nat. Bd. Trial Advocacy (cert.), U.S. Handball Assn., Am. Water Ski Assn., Casper Boat Club, Casper Petroleum Club, Porsche Club Am., BMW Club Am., Nat. Riflemans Assn. Republican. Episcopalian. Avocations: handball, waterskiing, snow skiing, climbing, driving. Office: Murane & Bostwick 201 N Wolcott St Casper WY 82601-1922

COMER, LORI ANN, secondary educator; b. Canton, Ohio, Nov. 25, 1958; d. Robert Gene and Letha Ann (Barton) C.; m. Daniel Orin Quinton, Aug. 16, 1981; 1 child, Michael David. BA in English summa cum laude, Met. State Colll., Denver, 1981; MA in Ednl. Adminstrn., U. Colo., Denver, 1989. Lic. tchr., Colo., profl. prin., Colo. Substitute tchr. Jefferson County Schs., Lakewood, Colo., 1981; tchr. Denver Pub. Schs., 1982—, com. mem. S.W. extended campus, mem. sch. to work com., 1996-97. Mem. NEA, ASCD, Nat. Coun. Tchrs. English, Denver Classroom Tchrs. Assn. Democrat. Roman Catholic. Avocations: computer, gourmet cooking, jewelry making, music. Home: 4375 W Rutgers Pl Denver CO 80236-3470 Office: Denver Pub Schs John F Kennedy HS 2855 S Lamar St Denver CO 80227-3809

COMERFORD, SUSAN MARIE, artist; b. Drain, Oreg., Mar. 6, 1933; d. Samuel Roy and Eleanor Ruth (Crandall) Ball; m. William Brown Comerford, Dec. 31, 1964 (dec. Jan. 1989); children: Anita, Kim Blodgett, Kelly Wadsworth; m. Frank Rusch, 1994. AA, Umpqua C.C., Roseburg, Oreg., 1974; BA, U. Oreg., 1979, MFA, 1983. Artist Best Sign Co., Las Vegas, Nev., 1962-64, Comerford Sign Co., Las Vegas, 1964-70; artist, owner Comerford Studio & Gallery, Roseburg, 1988—; tchg. fellow U. Oreg., Eugene, 1982-83; mem. adv. bd. Umpqua C.C., 1976-78; mem. N.W. Print Coun., Portland, 1982—, Roseburg Mural Com., 1997—. Exhibited works in various galleries in the Northwest. Initiator, artist mural program City of Roseburg, 1988-97. Recipient Disting. Svc. award City of Roseburg, 1994. Mem. Roseburg Area C. of C. (bd. dirs. 1989—, Beautification award 1995), Exec. Club (pres. 1998). Democrat. Mem. LDS Ch. Avocations: gardening, travel, outdoor activities, music. Office: Comerford Studio & Gallery 717 SE Cass Ave Roseburg OR 97470-4908

COMES, ROBERT GEORGE, research scientist; b. Bangor, Pa., July 7, 1931; s. Victor Francis and Mabel Elizabeth (Mack) C.; student U. Detroit, 1957-58, Oreg. State Coll., 1959-60, U. Nev., 1960, Regis Coll., 1961-62; m. Carol Lee Turinetti, Nov. 28, 1952; children: Pamela Jo, Robert G. II, Shawni Lee, Sheryl Lynn, Michelle Ann. Tech. liaison engr. Burroughs Corp., Detroit, 1955-60, mgr. reliability and maintainability engring., Paoli, Pa., 1962-63, Colorado Springs, Colo., 1963-67; sr. engr. Martin Marietta Corp., Denver, 1960-62; program mgr., rsch. scientist Kaman Scis. Corp., Colorado Springs, 1967-75; dir. engring. Sci. Applications, Inc., Colorado Springs, 1975-80; mgr. space def. programs Burroughs Corp., Colorado Springs, 1980-82; tech. staff Mitre Corp., Colorado Springs, 1982-85; dir. Colorado Springs opn. Beers Assoc., Inc., 1985; dir. space programs Electro Magnetic Applications, Inc., Colorado Springs, 1985-87; dir. Space Systems, Profl. Mgmt. Assocs., Inc., 1987-88; mgr. Computer Svcs., Inc., Colorado Springs, 1989—; dir. mktg. Proactive Techs., Inc., Colorado Springs, 1990—; chmn. Reliability and Maintainability Data Bank Improvement Program, Govt.-Industry Data Exch. Program, 1978-80—; cons. in field. Youth dir. Indian Guides program YMCA, 1963-64; scoutmaster Boy Scouts Am., 1972-73; chmn. bd. dirs. Pikes Peak Regional Sci. Fair, 1972-84. Served with USAF, 1951-55. Mem. AAAS, IEEE, Inst. Environ. Scis., Soc. Logistics Engrs., Am. Soc. Quality Control. Lutheran. Club: Colorado Springs Racquet. Author: Maintainability Engineering Principles and Standards, 1962. Inventor Phase Shifting aircraft power supply, 1957. Home and Office: Proactive Tech Inc 4309 Tipton Ct Colorado Springs CO 80915-1034

COMFORT, JOSEPH ROBERT, physics educator; b. Fayetteville, Ark., July 18, 1940; s. Edwin G.H. and Roberta M. (Robinson) C.; m. Patricia H. Kennedy, Jan. 7, 1983; children: Neal Brian, Ryan William, Alison Elizabeth. AB, Ripon Coll., 1962; MS, Yale Univ., 1963, PHD, 1968. Rsch. assoc. Argonne (Ill.) Nat. Lab., 1968-70; instr. Princeton U., 1970-72; asst. prof. Ohio U., 1972-74; vis. scientist U. Groningen, The Netherlands, 1974-75, Ind. U., 1976; rsch. assoc. prof. U. Pitts., 1976-81; assoc. prof. Ariz. State U., 1981-84, prof., 1984—; mem. nuclear energy rsch. adv. com. Dept. Energy. Office: Ariz State Univ Physics Dept Tempe AZ 85287

COMINGS, DAVID EDWARD, physician, medical genetics scientist; b. Beacon, N.Y., Mar. 8, 1935; s. Edward Walter and Jean (Rice) C.; m. Shirley Nelson, Aug. 9, 1958; children: Mark David, Scott Edward, Karen Jean.; m. Brenda Gursey, Mar. 20, 1982. Student, U. Ill., 1951-54; BS, Northwestern U., 1955, MD, 1958. Intern Cook County Hosp., Chgo., 1958-59; resident in internal medicine Cook County Hosp., 1959-62; fellow in med. genetics U. Wash., Seattle, 1964-66; dir. dept. med. genetics City of Hope Med. Ctr., Duarte, Calif., 1966—; mem. genetics study sect. NIH, 1974-78; mem. sci. adv. bd. Hereditary Disease Found., 1975—, Nat. Found. March of Dimes, 1978-92. Author: Tourette Syndrome and Human Behavior, 1990, Search for the Tourette Syndrome and Human Behavior Genes, 1996, The Gene Bomb, 1996; editor: (with others) Molecular Human Cytogenetics, 1977; mem. editorial bd.: (with others) Cytogenetics and Cell genetics, 1979—; editor in chief Am. Jour. Human Genetics, 1978-86. Served with U.S. Army, 1962-64. NIH grantee, 1967—. Mem. Assn. Am. Physicians, Am. Soc. Clin. Investigation, AAAS, Am. Soc. Human Genetics (dir. 1974-78, pres. 1988), Am. Soc. Cell Biology, Am. Fedn. Clin. Research, Western Soc. Clin. Research, Council Biology Editors. Office: City of Hope Med Ctr 1500 Duarte Rd Duarte CA 91010-3000

COMMANDER, EUGENE R., lawyer; b. Sioux City, Iowa, Jan. 10, 1953. BA in Architecture, Iowa State U., 1975; JD with distinction, U. Iowa, 1977. Bar: Iowa 1977, Colo. 1981. Mem. Hall & Evans, LLC, Denver, 1981—. Mem. ABA (forum com. on constrn. industry, subcoms. on bonds, liens, ins. and contract documents, tort and ins. practice sect. coms. on fidelity, surety law, property ins.), AIA (profl. affiliate, Colo. chpt.), Am. Arbitration Assn. (panel constrn. industry arbitrators 1983—), Am. Law Firm Assn. (constrn. industry practice group), Def. Rsch. Inst. (constrn. law and fidelity and surety law coms.), Profl. Liability Underwriting Soc. Office: Hall & Evans LLC 1200 17th St Ste 1700 Denver CO 80202-5817*

COMPTON, ALLEN T., state supreme court justice; b. Kansas City, Mo., Feb. 25, 1938; m. Sue Ellen Tatter; 3 children. B.A., U. Kans., 1960; LL.B., U. Colo., 1963. Pvt. practice Colorado Springs, 1963-68; staff atty. Legal Svcs. Office, Colorado Springs, 1968-69, dir., 1969-71; supervising atty. Alaska Legal Svcs., Juneau, Alaska, 1971-73; pvt. practice Juneau, 1973-76; judge Superior Ct., Alaska, 1976-80; justice Alaska Supreme Ct., Anchorage, 1980-98, chief justice, 1995-97. Mem. 4 bar assns. including Juneau Bar Assn. (past pres.). Office: Alaska Supreme Ct 303 K St Anchorage AK 99501-2013

COMSTOCK, MARGOT MARY, editor, writer, graphic designer, consultant, artist; b. Paterson, N.J., Oct. 11, 1940; d. Kenneth Franklin and Phyllis Abigail (Taylor) C.; m. Allan Richard Tommervik, Oct. 14, 1972; children: Roberta Ann, Kirin Lee. BA, Heidelberg Coll., Tiffin, Ohio. Crossword puzzle constructor Daily Variety, L.A., 1987-91, editorial desk, 1989-92; co-founder, pres., editor Softalk Pub. Inc., North Hollywood, Calif., 1980-84; mgr. creativity ctr. Broderbund Software, Novato, Calif., 1992-93; founder, owner MC ART Comm., Fairfax, Calif., 1994—; co-founder Digital Sports Network, Fairfax, Calif., 1994-96; cons. Origin Systems, Austin Tex., 1981-88, Sirtech Software, 1986-87; cons., reviewer San Luis Revue, San Luis Obispo, Calif., 1986-88; cons. columnist II Computing, San Francisco, 1985-86; assoc. designer computer adventure for Sierra software "Rama"; developer, tchr. Creative Publ. Design and Editing, Coll. of Marin, Kentfield, Calif., 1997—. Founder, editor periodical Softalk, 1980-84. Tchr. of literacy Laubach Literacy Action, Arroyo Grande, Calif., 1986-89; foster parent Childreach Plan Internat., 1985—. Named Microcomputer Pioneer, Smithsonian Instn., 1987. Mem. NOW (newsletter editor Marin chpt. 1993-95, bd. dirs.), Marin Arts Coun., Women's Caucus for Art, Nat. Writers Union, Assn. for Software Design, Hackers Conf./Think Found. Avocations: oil painting, sculpture, drawing, writing fiction, community theater. Office: MC ART 61 Tamalpais Rd Fairfax CA 94930-1655

COMUS, LOUIS FRANCIS, JR., lawyer; b. St. Marys, Ohio, Feb. 26, 1942. BA, Antioch Coll., 1965; JD, Vanderbilt U., 1968. Bar: N.Y. 1969, Ariz. 1973. Dir. Fennemore Craig P.C., Phoenix, 1975—. Notes editor Vanderbilt Law Rev., 1967-68. Fellow Am. Coll. Trust and Estate Counsel; mem. ABA, State Bar Ariz., Maricopa County Bar Assn., Order of Coif. Office: Fennemore Craig PC 3003 N Central Ave Ste 2600 Phoenix AZ 85012-2913

CONANT, KIM UNTIEDT, elementary education educator; b. Del Norte, Colo., July 26, 1944; d. Warren Malvern and Annine (Gredig) Untiedt; m. Spicer Van Allen Conant, July 9, 1966 (div. Mar. 1983); children: Spicer V., Reid F., Lee G. BA in Am. Studies, Scripps Coll., 1966; MA in Secondary Reading, San Diego State U., 1996. Cert. elem. tchr., Calif. Tchr. asst. Greenwich (Conn.) Country Day Sch., 1966-67; tchr. Katherine Delmar Burke Sch., San Francisco, 1969-70, Cupertino (Calif.) Schs., 1968-69, Kachina Country Day Sch., Phoenix, 1980-83, Paterson (N.J.) Schs., 1985, Black Mountain Mid. Sch., San Diego, 1985-89, Bernardo Heights Mid. Sch., San Diego, 1989—; tchr. trainer Poway (Calif.) Unified Schs., 1996—. Fulbright Exch. tchr. Exeter, Eng., 1998-99. Avocations: swimming, scuba diving, reading, gardening. Home: 14735 Poway Mesa Dr Poway CA 92064 Office: Bernardo Heights Mid Sch 12990 Paseo Lucido San Diego CA 92128

CONANT, RALPH WENDELL, educator, consultant, author; b. South Hope, Maine, Sept. 7, 1926; s. Earle Raymond Conant and Margaret Verrill (Long) Young; m. Audrey Florence Karl, Aug. 27, 1950; children: Beverlie Elaine, Lisa Audrey, Jonathan Arnold. BA, U. Vermont, 1949; MA, U. Chgo., 1954, PhD, 1959. Asst. prof. Mich. State U., E. Lansing, Mich., 1955-57; rsch. assoc. Nat. Mcpl. League, N.Y.C., 1957-59; asst. prof. U. Denver, 1960-62; asst. dir. Joint Ctr. for Urban Studies, Harvard U. and MIT, Cambridge, Mass., 1962-67; assoc. dir. Ctr. for Study of Violence, Brandeis U., Waltham, Mass., 1967-69; pres. S.W. Ctr. for Urban Rsch., Houston, 1969-75, Shimer Coll., Mt. Carroll, Ill., 1975-78, Unity (Maine) Coll., 1978-80, Conant Assocs., Winslow, Maine, 1980-87; dean Mercy Coll., Dobbs Ferry, N.Y., 1987-89; sr. fellow Phelps Stokes Fund, N.Y.C., 1989—. Author 15 books, including The Prospects for Revolution, 1971, The Conant Report, A Study of the Education of Librarians, 1980, Public Ends, Private Means, 1987; contbr. articles to profl. jours. Exec. dir. Citizens for Mich., 1959-60; trustee Shimer Coll., 1978—; chmn. Shimer Coll. Found., 1982—; candidate U.S. Congress, 1st Dist., Maine, 1982, 86; mem. Dem. State Com., 1984-92, Maine State Bd. Edn., 1985-90. Named Disting. Alumnus, U. Vt., Burlington, 1978. Home: RR 2 Box 2200 Winslow ME 04901-9601 Office: Asgard Found 1326 Stagecoach Rd Trinidad CA 95570-9705

CONCANNON, GEORGE ROBERT, business educator; b. Berkeley, Calif., June 2, 1919; s. Robert Lawrence and Hilda (Morgan) C. AB, Stanford U.; MBA, Harvard U.; postgrad., Stanford U., U. Calif., Berkeley, Hudson Inst., U.S. Fgn. Svc. Inst., U.S. Nat. War Coll., U.S. Indsl. Coll. Armed Forces. Sales exec. Marchant Calculators, Inc.; U.S. govt. v.p. Holiday Airlines; corp. v.p. Kaiser Industries; pres., CEO Concannon Wine Co., Concannon Co.; prof. bus. U. Calif., Berkeley; mem. Dun's Rev. Indsl. Roundtable; vis. prof. Webster U., Austria, Ecole Superieure Commerce de Tours, France, U. Wollongong, Australia, Urals Electromech. Inst., Russia, Estonian Bus. Sch., Estonia, Concordia Internat. U., Estonia. Contbr. articles to profl. jours. Tech. advisor State of Calif. Econ. Devel. Agy.; bd. dirs. Stanford Camp Assn.; mem. Am. Indsl. Devel. Coun., World Affairs Coun. Recipient Service to Country award Internat. Exec. S.C. Mem. Urban Land Inst. Home: 2995 Woodside Rd Ste 400 Woodside CA 94062-2446

CONDIE, CAROL JOY, anthropologist, research facility administrator; b. Provo, Utah, Dec. 28, 1931; d. LeRoy and Thelma (Graff) C.; m. M. Kent Stout, June 18, 1954; children: Carla Ann, Erik Roy, Paula Jane. BA in Anthropology, U. Utah, 1953; MEd in Elem. Edn., Cornell U., 1954; PhD in Anthropology, U. N.Mex., 1973; Quivira Rsch. Ctr. Edn. coordinator Maxwell Mus. Anthropology, U. N.Mex., Albuquerque, 1973, interpretation dir., 1974-77; asst. prof. anthropology U. N.Mex., 1975-77; cons. anthropologist, 1977-78; pres. Quivira Research Ctr., Albuquerque, 1978—; cons. anthropologist U.S. Congl. Office Tech. Assessment, chair Archeol. Resources Planning Adv. Com., Albuquerque, 1985-86; leader field seminars Crow Canyon Archeol. Ctr., 1986—; appointee Albuquerque dist. adv. coun., bur. land mgmt. U.S. Dept. Interior, 1989; study leader Smithsonian Instn. Tours, 1991; mem. Albuquerque Heritage Conservation Adv. Com., 1992. Author: The Nighthawk Site: A Pithouse Site on Sandia Pueblo Land, Bernalillo County, New Mexico, 1982, Five Sites on the Pecos River Road, 1985, Data Recovery at Eight Archeological Sites on the Rio Nutritas, 1992, Data Recovery at Eight Archeological Sites on Cabresto Road Near Questa, 1992, Archeological Survey in the Rough and Ready Hills/Picacho Mountain Area, Dona Ana County, New Mexico, 1993, Archeological Survey on the Canadian River, Quay County, New Mexico, 1994, Archeological Testing at LA 103387, Nizhoni Extension, Gallup, McKinley County, New Mexico, 1995, Two Archeological Sites on San Felipe Pueblo Land, New Mexico, 1996, Four Archeological Sites at La Cienega, Santa Fe County, New Mexico, 1996, A Brief History of Berino, Berino Siding, and Early Mesilla Valley Agriculture, Dona Ana County, New Mexico, 1997, (with M. Kent Stout) Historical and Architectural Study of the Old Peralta Elementary School, Valencia County, New Mexico, 1997, Archeological Survey of 720 Acres on Ball Ranch, Sandoval County, New Mexico, 1998; co-editor: Anthropology in the Desert West, 1986. Mem. Downtown Core Area Schs. Com., Albuquerque, 1982. Ford Found. fellow, 1953-54; recipient Am. Planning Assn. award, 1985-86, Gov.'s award, 1986, Archaeol. Achievement award Archaeol. Soc. N.Mex., 1998. Fellow Am. Anthrop. Assn.; mem. Soc. Am. Archeology (chmn. native Am. rels. com. 1983-85), N.Mex. Archeol. Coun. (pres. 1982-83, hist. preservation award 1988), Albuquerque Archeol. Soc. (pres. 1992), Maxwell Mus. Assn. (bd. dirs. 1980-83), Las Arañas Spinners and Weavers Guild (pres. 1972), N.Mex. Heritage Preservation Alliance. Democrat. Avocations: spinning, weaving, gardening. Home and Office: Quivira Research Ctr 1809 Notre Dame Dr NE Albuquerque NM 87106-1011

CONDIT, GARY ADRIAN, congressman; b. Salina, Okla., Apr. 21, 1948. AA, Modesto Jr. Coll., 1970; BA, Calif. State Coll., 1972. Councilman City of Ceres, Calif., 1972-74, mayor, 1974-76; supr. Stanislaus County, Calif., 1976-82; assemblyman State of Calif., 1982-89; mem. 101st-105th Congresses (now 106th Congress) from 15th (now 18th) Calif. Dist., 1989—; ranking minority mem. Ag. subcom. on nutrition & fgn. ag., mem. govt. reform & oversight, agriculture coms. Democrat. Office: US Ho of Reps 2245 Rayburn Washington DC 20515-0518*

CONDIT, PHILIP MURRAY, aerospace executive, engineer; b. Berkeley, Calif., Aug. 2, 1941; s. Daniel Harrison and Bernice (Kemp) C.; m. Madeleine K. Bryant, Jan. 25, 1963 (div. June 1982); children: Nicole Lynn, Megan Anne; m. Janice Condit, Apr. 6, 1991. BS MechE, U. Calif., Berkeley, 1963; MS in Aero. Engring., Princeton U., 1965; MS in Mgmt., MIT, 1975. Engr. The Boeing Co., Seattle, 1965-72, mgr. engring., 1973-83, v.p., gen. mgr., 1983-84, v.p. sales and mktg., 1984-86, exec. v.p., 1986-89, exec. v.p., gen. mgr. 777 div., 1989-92, pres., 1992-96, chmn., CEO, 1996—; mem. adv. coun. Dept. Mech. and Aerospace Engring., Princeton (N.J.) U., 1984—; chmn. aero. adv. com. NASA Adv. Coun., 1988-92; bd. dirs. The Fluke Corp., 1987—, Nordstom, Inc., 1993—. Co-inventor Design of a Flexible Wing, 1965. Mem. Mercer Island (Wash.) Utilities Bd., 1975-78; bd. dirs. Camp Fire, Inc., 1987-92; mem. exec bd. chief Seattle coun. Boy Scouts Am., 1988-90; trustee Mus. of Flight, Seattle, 1990—. Co-recipient Laurels award Aviation Week & Space Tech. magazine, 1990; Sloan fellow MIT, Boston, 1974. Fellow AIAA (aircraft design award 1984, Edward C. Wells tech. mgmt award 1982, Wright Brothers Lectureship Aeronautics 1996), Royal Aero. Soc.; mem. NAE, Soc. Sloan Fellows (bd. govs. 1985-89), Soc. Automotive Engrs. Clubs: Rainier, Columbia Tower (Seattle). Office: The Boeing Co PO Box 3707 7755 E Marginal Way S Seattle WA 98108-4000

CONDO, JAMES ROBERT, lawyer; b. Somerville, N.J., Mar. 2, 1952; s. Ralph Vincent and Betty Louise (MacQuaide) C.; m. Rhonda H. King, June 7, 1997. BS in Bus. and Econs., Lehigh U., 1974; JD, Boston Coll., 1979. Bar: Ariz. 1979, U.S. Dist. Ct. Ariz. 1979, U.S. Ct. Appeals (9th cir.) 1982, U.S. Ct. Appeals (D.C. cir.) 1989, U.S. Ct. Appeals (10th cir.) 1989, U.S. Supreme Ct. 1983, U.S. Ct. Appeals (6th cir.) 1991, U.S. Ct. Appeals (4th cir.) 1994. Assoc. Snell & Wilmer, Phoenix, 1979-84, ptnr., 1985—; judge

pro tem Ariz. Ct. Appeals. Fellow Ariz. Bar Found.; mem. ABA, State Bar Ariz., Maricopa County Bar Found. Office: Snell & Wilmer One Arizona Ctr Phoenix AZ 85004

CONDON, STANLEY CHARLES, gastroenterologist; b. Glendale, Calif., Feb. 1, 1931; s. Charles Max and Alma Mae (Chinn) C.; m. Vaneta Marilyn Mabley, May 19, 1963; children: Lori, Brian, David. BA, La Sierra Coll., 1952; MD, Loma Linda U., 1956. Diplomate Nat. Bd. Med. Examiners, Am. Bd. Internal Medicine, Am. Bd. Gastroenterology; cert. nutrition support physician. Intern L.A. County Gen. Hosp., 1956-57, resident gen. pathology, 1959-61; resident internal medicine White Meml. Med. Ctr., L.A., 1961-63, attending staff out-patient clinic, 1963-64; active jr. attending staff L.A. County Gen. Hosp., 1964-65; dir. intern-resident tng. program Manila Sanitarium and Hosp., 1966-71, med. dir., 1971-72; chief resident internal medicine out-patient clinic Loma Linda U. Med. Ctr., 1972-74; fellow in gastroenterology Barnes Hosp./Wash. U., 1974-76; attending staff, asst. prof. medicine Loma Linda U. Med. Ctr., 1976-91, assoc. prof. medicine, 1991—, med. dir. nutritional support team, 1984—. Contbr. articles to profl. jours. Capt. U.S. Army, 1957-59. Fellow ACP; mem. AMA, Am. Soc. for Parenteral and Enteral Nutrition, Am. Gastroent. Assn., Calif. Med. Assn., So. Calif. Soc. Gastroenterology, Inland Soc. Internal Medicine, San Bernardino County Med. Soc. Republican. Seventh-day Adventist. Avocations: trombone, choral singing, camping, hiking, gardening. Home: 11524 Ray Ct Loma Linda CA 92354-3630 Office: Loma Linda U Med Ctr 11370 Anderson St Loma Linda CA 92354-3450

CONDRY, ROBERT STEWART, retired hospital administrator; b. Charleston, W.Va., Aug. 16, 1941; s. John Charles and Mary Louise (Jester) C.; m. Mary Purcell Heinzer, May 21, 1966; children: Mary-Lynch, John Stewart. BA, U. Charleston, 1963; MBA, George Washington U., 1970. Asst. hosp. dir. Med. Coll. of Va., Richmond, 1970-73, assoc. adminstr., 1973-75; assoc. hosp. dir. McGaw Hosp., Loyola U., Maywood, Ill., 1975-84, hosp. dir., 1984-93, ret., 1993; pres. Inter-Hosp. Planning Assn. of Western Suburbs, Maywood, 1983-93; bd. dirs. PentaMed, Inc., San Antonio. Bd. dirs. Met. Chgo. Healthcare Coun., 1985-93, mem. exec. com., 1989-93; bd. dirs. Cath. Hosp. Alliance, 1992, chmn. bd. dirs., 1992, mem. exec. com. 1988-94; mem. Ill. Gov.'s Adv. Bd. on Infant Mortality Reduction, 1988-93, Rev. Bd. on Emergency Medicine Svcs., 1989-93. With U.S. Army, 1964-66. Recipient preceptorship George Washington U., 1985, U. Chgo., 1984, St. Louis U., 1984, Tulane U., 1984, Yale U., 1991. Fellow Am. Coll. Healthcare Execs., Am. Acad. Med. Adminstrs.; mem. Am. Hosp. Assn., Cath. Hosp. Assn., Am. Mgmt. Assn. Republican. Roman Catholic. Avocations: golf, tennis, camping, travel.

CONE, LAWRENCE ARTHUR, research medicine educator; b. N.Y.C., Mar. 23, 1928; s. Max N. and Ruth (Weber) C.; m. Julia Haldy, June 6, 1947 (dec. 1956); m. Mary Elisabeth Osborne, Aug. 20, 1960; children: Lionel Alfred. AB, NYU, 1948; MD, U. Berne, Switzerland, 1954; DSc (hon.), Rocky Mountain Coll., 1993. Diplomate Am. Bd. Internal Medicine, Am. Bd. Infectious Diseases, Am. Bd. Allergy and Immunology, Am. Bd. Med. Oncology. Intern Dallas Meth. Hosp., 1954-55, resident internal medicine, 1955; resident Flower 5th Hosp., N.Y.C., 1957-59, Met. Hosp., N.Y.C., 1959-60; rsch. fellow infectious diseases and immunology NYU Med. Sch., N.Y.C., 1960-62; from asst. prof. to assoc. prof. N.Y. Med. Coll., N.Y.C., 1962-72, chief sect immunology and infectious diseases, 1962-72; assoc. clin. prof. medicine Harbor UCLA Med. Sch., 1984—; clin. prof. internal medicine U. Calif., Riverside, 1997—; career scientist Health Rsch. Coun. N.Y.C., 1962-68; chief sect. immunology and infectious diseases Eisenhower Med. Ctr., Rancho Mirage, Calif., 1973—, chmn. dept. medicine, 1976-78, pres. elect, pres., past pres. med. staff, 1984-90; cons. infectious disease Desert Hosp., Palm Springs, Calif., 1980-85; lectr. basic sci. U. Calif., Riverside Biomed. Scis.; mem. mycosis study group NIAID, 1993—, co-cardiodonycocis study group, 1993—, eastern coop. oncology group affil. Stanford U., 1994. Contbr. articles to profl. jours. Bd. dirs. Desert Bighorn Rsch. Inst., Palm Desert, Calif., pres., bd. dirs., 1995-99; nat. adv. coun., mem., bd. trustees Rocky Mountain Coll., Billings, Mont.; mem. med. adv. staff Coll. of Desert, Palm Desert; Pres. Cir. Desert Mus., Palm Springs, Calif., Idaho Conservation League, Gilcrease Mus., Tulsa, Sun Valley Ctr. for Arts and Humanities. L.A. County Mus., Smithsonian Inst., Buffalo Bill Historic Mus., Cody, Wyo.; mem. Nat. Mus. Wildlife Art; life mem. The Living Desert, Palm Desert, L.A. County Mus.; mem. cmty. adv. coun. Jr. League. Recipient Outstanding Contbn. to Medicine award Riverside County Med. Assn., 1998, Disting. Achievement award AMC Cancer Rsch. Ctr., 1998. Fellow ACP, Royal Soc. Medicine, Interam. Soc. Chemotherapy, Am. Coll. Allergy, Am. Acad. Allergy and Immunology, Am. Soc. Infectious Diseases, Am. Geriatric Soc. (founding fellow we. divsn.); mem. AAAS, Internat. AIDS Soc., Am. Soc. Microbiology, Reticulocudothelial Soc., Am. Fedn. for Clin. Rsch., Faculty Soc. UCLA, Surg. Soc. N.Y. Med. Coll. (hon.), Woodstock Artists Assn., Harvey Soc., N.Y. Acad. Scis., NYU Alumni Assn., Berne Alumni Assn., Lotos Club, Tamarisk Country Club, Coachella Valley Gun and Wildlife Club, Faculty Soc. UCLA Harbor Med. Ctr., O'Donnell Golf Club, Sigma Xi. Republican. Avocations: golfing, fishing, hunting, skiing. Home: 765 Via Vadera Palm Springs CA 92262-4170 Office: Probst Profl Bldg # 308 39000 Bob Hope Dr Rancho Mirage CA 92270-3221 also: Larkspur Condominiums PO Box 1503 Sun Valley ID 83353-1503

CONE, STEPHANIE J., producer; b. Roanoke, Va., Nov. 26, 1969; d. Phyllis Jane (Carpenter) Cone. Prodn. coord. freelance, L.A., 1993-95; psot prodn. supr. various, including Bastard Out of Carolina, L.A., 1995-96; assoc. prodr. comedy variety series Tracey Takes On, L.A., 1995-97, coprodr., 1997-98, prodr., 1998—; prodr. various ind. projects, L.A. Recipient Emmy award, 1997, Emmy nominee, 1998. Mem. Acad. TV Arts and Scis.

CONG, JASON JINGSHENG, computer scientist, educator, consultant, researcher; b. Beijing, Feb. 20, 1963; came to U.S., 1986; m. Jing Chang, Jan. 28, 1995. BS, Peking U., China, 1985; MS, U. Ill., 1987, PhD, 1990. Intern Xerox Palo Alto (Calif.) Rsch. Ctr., summer 1987, Nat. Semiconductor Co., Santa Clara, Calif., summer 1988; rsch. asst. U. Ill., 1986-90; asst. prof. UCLA, 1990-94, assoc. prof., 1994-98, prof., 1998—; cons. Intel Corp., Santa Clara, 1994—; mem. tech. adv. bd. Mentor Graphics, San Jose, Calif., 1994-96, Magma Design Automation, Palo Alto, 1997—. Author: Yield Enhancement of Reconfigurable VISI Systems, 1992; contbr. over 100 articles to profl. jours. Recipient Young Investigator award NSF, 1993. Sr. mem. IEEE (Best Paper award 1995), Assn. Computing Machinery (adv. bd. 1993—, assoc. editor 1995—, meritorius svc. award 1998). Office: UCLA 4711 Boelter Hall Los Angeles CA 90095

CONGDON, ROGER DOUGLASS, theology educator, minister; b. Ft. Collins, Colo., Apr. 6, 1918; s. John Solon and Ellen Avery (Kellogg) C.; m. Rhoda Gwendolyn Britt, Jan. 2, 1948; children: Rachel Congdon Lidbeck, James R., R. Steven, Jon B., Philip F., Robert N., Bradford B., Ruth A. Mahner, Rebecca York Skones, Rhoda J. Miller, Marianne C. Potter, Mark Alexander. BA, Wheaton Coll., 1940; postgrad, Eastern Bapt. Sem., 1940-41; ThM, Dallas Theol. Sem., 1945; ThD, Dallas Theology Sem., 1949. Ordained to ministry Bapt. Ch., 1945. Exec. sec., dean Altanta Bible Inst., 1945-49; prof. theology Carver Bible Inst., Atlanta, 1945-49; prof. Multnomah Bible Coll., Portland, Oreg., 1950-87; pastor Emmanuel Bapt. Ch., Vancouver, Wash., 1985—; past dean of faculty, dean of edn., v.p., chmn. libr. com., chmn. achievement-award com., chmn. lectureship com., advisor grad. div. and mem. pres.'s cabinet Multnomah Bible Co.; chmn. Chil Evang. Fellowship of Greater Portland, 1978—; founder, pres. Preaching Print Inc., Portland, 1953—. Founder, speaker semi-weekly radio broadcast Bible Truth Forum, KPDQ, Portland, Oreg., 1989-98, KPAM 1999—, DZAM, Manila, Philippines, 1996—, Radio Africa 2, 1998—; author: The Doctrine of Conscience, 1945. Chmn. Citizen's Com. Info. on Communism, Portland, 1968-75. Recipient Outstanding Educators of Am. award, 1972, Loraine Chafer award in Systematic Theology, Dallas Theol. Sem. Mem. Am. Assn. Bible Colls. (chmn. testing com. 1953-78), N.Am. Assn. Bible Colls. (N.W. rep. 1960-63), Near East Archaeol. Soc., Evang. Theol. Soc. Republican. Home: 16539 NE Halsey St Portland OR 97230-5607 Office: Emmanuel Bapt Ch 14810 NE 28th St Vancouver WA 98682-8357

CONKLIN, HAL (HAROLD CONKLIN), mayor; b. Oakland, Calif., Dec. 11, 1945; s. Ralph Harold and Stella (Garabedian) C.; m. Barbara Elaine Lang, Mar. 25, 1972; children: Nathaniel, Joseph Lucas, Zachary. Student, Calif. State U., Hayward, 1967-71. Editor New Focus Mag., Santa Barbara, Calif., 1969-72; co-dir. Community Environ. Coun., Santa Barbara, 1972-82; pres. Santa Barbara Renaissance Fund, 1983—; mayor City of Santa Barbara, 1993—; dir. pub. affairs So. Calif., Edison, Calif. Councilman City of Santa Barbara, 1977-93; bd. dirs. Santa Barbara Redevel. Agy., 1978—, Calif. Local Govt. Commn., Sacramento, 1979—, Nat. League of Cities, 1987-89, Santa Barbara Civic Light Opera; pres. Calif. Ctr. Civic Renewal, La Casa do Maria Retreat Ctr.; v.p. Santa Barbara Romantic Design Co.; v.p. Nat. League of Cities, 1994. Mem. League of Calif. Cities (bd. dirs. 1986—, pres. 1991-92), Calif. Resource Recovery Assn. (pres. 1978-82). Methodist. Avocation: photography. Home: 214 El Monte Dr Santa Barbara CA 93109-2006

CONLAN, IRENE ESTELLE, health care administrator; b. Emmett, Idaho, Sept. 25, 1935; d. Carl O. Danielson and Mona A. Cardwell; m. John B. conlan, Sept. 13, 1968 (div. 1993); children: Christopher, Kevin. BS in Nursing, The Cath. U. Am., 1964, MS in Nursing, 1965; RHT, Nat. Hypnotherapy Tng. Ctr., 1996. Dir. St. Anthony Sch. Nursing, Oklahoma City, 1965-66; mem. faculty Coll. Nursing Ariz. State U., Tempe, 1966-67, Sch. Nursing No. Ariz. U., Flagstaff, 1966; dir. nursing adminstrn. St. Luke's Hosp Med. Ctr., Phoenix, 1967-72; asst. dir. div. emergency med. services and health care facilities Ariz. State Health Dept., Phoenix, 1987-89; founder, CEO Cartridge Care, Inc., Scottsdale, Ariz., 1989-95; founder, pres. The Power Zone, Scottsdale, 1995—; cons. grant rev. office child and family services HHS, Washington, 1985, office adolescent pregnancy, 1986—. Author: Women We Can Do It, 1976; co-author: 1984 and Beyond, 1984. Pres. Scottsdale Rep. Women, 1978; bd. dirs. The Enterprise Network, Ariz. Women's Employment and Edn.; mem. St. Luke's Svc. League, Phoenix, 1970—, Scottsdale Leadership Class IX, 1995. Mem. Nat. Assn. Women Bus. Owners, Nat. Spkrs. Assn., Sigma Theta Tau. Home: 11349 E Poinsettia Dr Scottsdale AZ 85259-3143

CONLEY, JAMES CORT, writer, literature director, publisher; b. Oakland, Calif., May 19, 1944; s. Robert William and Mary Lee (McClain) C.; 1 child, Keats Raptosh Conley. UD, U. Calif., 1969. Mgr. Wilderness Encounters, Cambridge, Idaho, 1973-80; dir. U. Idaho Press, Moscow, 1986-88; lit. dir. Idaho Commn. Arts, Boise, 1991—; bd. mem. Idaho Geographic Place Names, Boise, 1988—, Idaho Ctr. for the Book, Boise. Author: (nonfiction) The Middle Fork, 1976, Hell's Canyon of Snake River, 1978, River of No Return, 1980, Idaho, 1986, Idaho for the Curious, 1986, Idaho Loners, 1995; co-author, editor: (anthology) Modern American Memoirs, 1996. Recipient Orchid award Idaho Hist. Preservation Coun., Boise, 1984. Mem. Idaho Outfitters and Guides Assn., Authors Guild. Roman Catholic. Avocations: natural history, river guiding. Home: 2208 Sunset Boise ID 83702-0336 Office: Idaho Commn on the Arts 304 W State St Boise ID 83720

CONLEY, ZEB BRISTOL, art gallery director; b. Andrews, N.C., Feb. 12, 1936; s. Zeb Bristol and A. Elizabeth (Faircloth) C.; student N.C. State Coll., 1954-55, Mars Hill Coll., 1955-57, Coll. William and Mary, 1957-61; m. Betty Ann Wiswall, May 25, 1974; stepchildren—Peter Wiswall Betts, Stephen Wood Betts, Frederick Beale Betts, III. Designer, Seymour Robins, Inc., N.Y.C., 1961, First Nat. Bank, Las Vegas (N.Mex.), 1964-65, Swanson's Inc., Las Vegas, 1965-73, v.p., 1969-86; dir. Jamison Galleries, Santa Fe, 1973—, guest curator Alfred Morang: A Retrospective at Mus. of S.W. Midland, Tex., 1985; sec. Marbasconi, Inc., d.b.a. Jamison Galleries, 1974-80, pres., 1980—. Republican. Office: care The Jamison Galleries 560 Montezuma Ave Ste 103 Santa Fe NM 87501-2590

CONLIN, CATHERINE, writer, studio owner, designer; b. Hammond, Ind., Jan. 12, 1960; d. Adolph Lawrence Cherechinsky and Nancy Mary (Dubravich) Cherechinsky Balzer; m. Mark Conlin, Sept. 22, 1984 (div. Jan. 1990). BS, Ind. U., 1995. Sales assoc. Marshall Fields, River Oaks, Ill., 1976; asst. buyer in tng. Styx, Baer & Fuller, St. Louis, 1981; sales mgr. L.S. Ayres, Bloomington, Ind., 1982-83; asst. buyer L.S. Ayres, Indpls., 1983-84; store mgr., buyer Benetton, Bloomington, 1985-90; group sales mgr. Macy's, San Francisco, 1990-91; owner, designer Wiggy Flowers, Bodega, Calif., 1991—. Contbr. short story, poetry, to lit. publs. such as The Dickens, Convolvulus, Paragraph, Tiny Lights.. Recipient Merit award Sebastopol (Calif.) Ctr. for Arts, 1997, 98, English dept. award Santa Rosa (Calif.) Jr. Coll., 1997. Avocations: yoga, running (1st place divisional winner Marine Corp. 5K run, 1998), gardening.

CONNELLY, BETTY FEES, lay ministries consultant; b. L.A., Apr. 13, 1924; d. Ferdinand R. and Margaret (Lewis) Fees; m. Daniel Snyder Connelly, Apr. 20, 1946; children: Richard, Kathleen, Patrick. BA, Pomona Coll., Claremont, Calif., 1945; BS in Edn., U. Minn., 1947; postgrad., Claremont Grad. Sch., 1962-63. Pres. officer Women of Episcopal Ch. Triennial, Denver, 1977-80; lay min. cons. St. James Episcopal Ch., Newport Beach., Calif., 1981-83, dir. lay ministries and evang. svc. and outreach, 1988-93; mem. exec. coun. Episcopal Ch., 1982-88; mem. Coun. for Devel. Ministry, 1988-94; mem. exec. com. Anglican Fellowship of Prayer, dep. gen. conv. Episcopal Ch., 1982, 85, 88, 94, 97; vice chair bd. trustees Pension Group Episcopal Ch. With USN, 1944-46. Republican. Home: 3706 S Sea Breeze Santa Ana CA 92704-7141

CONNELLY, JAMES P., prosecutor; b. Hartford, Conn., Apr. 15, 1947. BA, Marquette U., 1969; JD, Georgetown U., 1972. Bar: Wis. 1972. Spl. asst. to Sec. of Treasury, 1975-76; ptnr. Foley & Lardner, Milw.; U.S. atty. U.S. Dist. Ct. (ea. dist.) Wash., Spokane, 1994—. Editor-in-chief Georgetown Law Jour., 1971-72. Mem. State Bar Wis., Phi Alpha Delta. Office: U S Atty Office U S Courthouse PO Box 1494 920 W Riverside Ave Spokane WA 99210-1494*

CONNELLY, THEODORE SAMPLE, communications executive; b. Middletown, Conn., Oct. 15, 1925; s. Herbert Lee and Mabel Gertrude (Wells) C.; B.A., Wesleyan U., 1948, postgrad., 1951, U. Paris, 1950. Sec. Nat. Com. Edn., Am. Trucking Assn., Inc., Washington, 1952-54; dir. pub. affairs Nat. Automobile club, San Francisco, 1955-62; pres., chmn. Connelly Corp., San Francisco, 1963—; treas. Ednl. Access Cable TV Corp.; dir. Mission Neighborhood Ctrs., Inc., Neighborhood Devel. Corp.; mem. adv. com. Calif. motor vehicle legis., 1955-62, Calif. State C. of C. com. hwys., 1958-62. Trustee, sec., v.p. Lincoln U.; sec. Lincoln U. Found., 1968-82; bd. dirs. San Francisco Program for Aging; founder, dir. Comm. Libr., 1963—, Comm. Inst., 1978—; founding mem. Calif. Coun. UN U., 1976; organizer Internat. Child Art Collection; co-founder African Rsch. Commn., 1970; established Connelly Fund, 1981; mem. founding regents Am. Pan-Pacific U., 1991; co-established awds. for excellence in writing about comm., 1981—; mem. steering com. Mesopotamian Exhibit, 1993—; co-founder Computer Learning Ctr. for Srs., St. Francis Meml. Hosp., 1988. With USNR, 1943-54. Recipient cert. of merit San Francisco Jaycees, 1959, award of merit USPHS, 1980, citation U.S. Dept. H&HS, 1981, commendations U.S. Coun. World Comm., 1983. Mem. AAAS, AAUP, NAACP, SAR, Pub. Rels. Round Table San Francisco, Atlanta Hist. Soc., Asian Mass Comm. and Info. Ctr. (Singapore), UN Assn. USA. Club: Dolphin Swimming and Boating (San Francisco), Golden Gate Swimmer. Author/compiler: BCTV Bibliography on Cabletelevision, 1975—, 13,000 Refereces on Cable-TV: 1975—, Electromagnetic Radiation, 1976; editor: An Analysis of Joint Ventures in China, 1982; contbr. articles to profl. jours.; prodr., writer, dir. numerous TV programs. Office: Lock Box 472139 Marina Sta San Francisco CA 94147-2139

CONNER, LINDSAY ANDREW, screenwriter, producer; b. N.Y.C., Feb. 19, 1956; s. Michael and Miriam (Mintzer) C. BA summa cum laude, UCLA, 1976; MA, Occidental Coll., 1977; JD magna cum laude, Harvard U., 1980. Bar: Calif. 1980, U.S. Dist. Ct. (cen. dist.) Calif. 1983. Assoc. Kaplan, Livingston, Goodwin, Berkowitz & Selvin, Beverly Hills, Calif., 1980-81, Fulop & Hardee, Beverly Hills, 1982-83, Wyman, Bautzer, Kuchel & Silbert, L.A., 1983-86; ptnr., entertainment dept. head Hill Wynne Troop & Meisinger, L.A., 1986-93. Author: (with others) The Courts and Education, 1977; editor: Harvard Law Rev., 1978-80. Trustee L.A. Community Coll., 1981-97, bd. pres., 1989-90; pres. Calif. Community Coll. Trustees, 1992-93. Mem. ABA, UCLA Alumni Assn. (life), Harvard-Radcliffe Club, Phi Beta Kappa. Office: 54th St Prodns 10880 Wilshire Bld Ste 1840 Los Angeles CA 90024-4101

CONNER, TOM M., real estate broker; b. Carthage, Mo., Oct. 10, 1937; s. Harold B. and Twyla E. (Wilkenson) C.; m. Susan E. Pottle, Nov. 7, 1959; children: Scott, David, Kevin. BSBA, U. Kans., 1960. From merchandise mgr. to mgr. J.C. Penney, Co., Inc., Colo., 1960-84; pres. Frostline USA, 1985-88; assoc. broker Telluride (Colo.) Real Estate Corp., 1989—; bd. dirs. Inland Oil Co., Colo.. V.p. United Way, Mesa County, Colo., 1982-87. Named boss of the yr. Bus. & Profl. Women, Colo., 1983. Mem. Assn. Realtors (pres. 1991-98), Colo. Assn. Realtors (dist. v.p. 1997-98), Rotary. Avocations: skiing, fishing, biking, camping. Home: 687 Fox Farm Rd PO Box 1895 Telluride CO 81435

CONNER, WILLIAM ANGUS, II, writer; b. New London, Conn., May 31, 1974; s. William Angus and Nola Jean (Grimes) C. Editor, publisher Carpe Diem Publishing, The Dalles, OR, 1994—; cons. The Dalles Oregonian, 1996—, Grass Valley (Oregon) Station, 1997. Author: THIRST, 1994, THIRST: Balance of the Electric Haze, 1998, Concert Production, 1998, Skool Daze-Party of the Year, 1998, New Year's Resolution, 1999; editor: The Nine Inch Nails Sourcebook, 1995; editor THIRST, 1996—. Active The Dalles/Wasco (Oregon) County Libr. Friends of the Libr., 1994—. Mem. Publishers Mktg. Assn. Avocations: law, basketball, reading, travel. E-mail: waconner@aol.com. Office: Carpe Diem Publishing 1705 E 17th St Ste 400 The Dalles OR 97058-3314

CONNERLY, DIANNA JEAN, business official; b. Urbana, Ill., June 7, 1947; d. Ellsworth Wayne and Imogene (Sundermeyer) Connerly. Student Ill. Comml. Coll., 1967. Bookkeeper, Jerry Earl Pontiac, 1968-72; officer mgr. Jack Nicklaus Pontiac, 1972-76; office mgr. Simon Motors Inc., Palm Springs, Calif., 1977-83, bus. mgr., 1983—. Vol. counselor How Found., 1992. Mem. Am. Bus. Women's Assn. (pub. rels. dir. Trendsetter chpt. 1983-85). Office: 78-611 Highway 111 La Quinta CA 92253

CONNOLLY, JOHN EARLE, surgeon, educator; b. Omaha, May 21, 1923; s. Earl A. and Gertrude (Eckerman) C.; m. Virginia Hartman, Aug. 12, 1967; children: Peter Hart. John Earle, Sarah. AB, Harvard U., 1945, MD, 1948. Diplomate: Am. Bd. Surgery (bd. dirs. 1976-82), Am. Bd. Thoracic and Cardiovascular Surgery, Am. Bd. Vascular Surgery. Intern. in surgery Stanford U. Hosps., San Francisco, 1948-49, surg. research fellow, 1949-50, asst. resident surgeon, 1950-52, chief resident surgeon, 1953-54, surg. pathology fellow, 1954-55, 1957-60, John and Mary Markle Scholar in med. scis., 1957-62; surg. registrar professional unit St. Bartholomew's Hosp., London, 1952-53; resident in thoracic surgery Bellevue Hosp., N.Y.C., 1955; resident in thoracic and cardiovascular surgery Columbia-Presbyn. Med. Ctr., N.Y.C., 1956; from instr. to assoc. prof. surgery Stanford U., 1957-65; prof. U. Calif., Irvine, 1965—, chmn. dept. surgery, 1965-78; attending surgeon Stanford Med. Ctr., Palo Alto, Calif., 1959-65; chmn. cardiovascular and thoracic surgery Irvine Med. Ctr. U. Calif., 1968—; attending surgeon Children's Hosp., Orange, Calif., 1968—, Anaheim (Calif.) Meml. Hosp., 1970—; vis. prof. Beijing Heart, Lung, Blood Vessel Inst., 1990, A.H. Duncan vis. prof. U. Edinburgh, 1984; Hunterian prof. Royal Coll. Surgeons Eng., 1985-86; Kinmonth lectr. Royal Coll. Surgeons, Eng., 1987, Hume Lectr. Soc. for Clin. Vascular Surgery, 1998, Dist. Prof. Lectr. Unified Svcs. Med. Ctr., 1998; mem. adv. coun. Nat. Heart, Lung, and Blood Inst.-NIH, 1981-85; cons. Long Beach VA Hosp., Calif., 1965—. Contbr. articles to profl. jours.; editorial bd.: Jour. Cardiovascular Surgery, 1974—, chief editor, 1985—; editorial bd. Western Jour. Medicine, 1975—, Jour. Stroke, 1979—, Jour. Vascular Surgery, 1983—. Bd. dirs. Audio-Digest Found., 1974—; bd. dirs. Franklin Martin Found., 1975-80; regent Uniformed Svcs. U. of Health Scis., Bethesda, 1992—. Served with AUS, 1943-44. Recipient Cert. of Merit, Japanese Surg. Soc., 1979, 90. Fellow ACS (gov. 1964-70, regent 1973-82, vice chmn. bd. regents 1980-82, v.p. 1984-85), Royal Coll. Surgeons Eng. (hon.), Royal Coll. Surgeons Ireland (hon.), Royal Coll. Surgeons Edinburgh (hon.); mem. Am. Surg. Assn., Soc. U. Surgeons, Am. Assn. Thoracic Surgery (coun. 1974-78), Pacific Coast Surg. Assn. (pres. 1985-86), San Francisco Surg. Soc., L.A. Surg. Soc., Soc. Vascular Surgery, Western Surg. Assn., Internat. Cardiovascular Soc. (pres. 1977), Soc. Internat. Chirurgie, Soc. Thoracic Surgeons, Western Thoracic Surg. Soc. (pres. 1978), Orange County Surg. Soc. (pres. 1984-85), James IV Assn. Surgeons (councillor 1983—), San Francisco Golf Club, Pacific Union Club, Bohemian Club (San Francisco), Harvard Club (N.Y.C.), Big Canyon Club (Newport Beach, Calif.). Home: 7 Deerwood Ln Newport Beach CA 92660-5108 Office: U Calif Dept Surgery Irvine CA 92717

CONNOLLY, K. THOMAS, lawyer; b. Spokane, Wash., Jan. 23, 1940; s. Lawrence Francis and Kathleen Dorothea (Hallahan) C.; m. Laurie Samuel, June 24, 1967; children: Kevin, Megan, Amy, Matthew. BBA, Gonzaga U., Spokane, Wash., 1962; JD, Gonzaga U., 1966; LLM in Taxation, NYU, 1972. Bar: Wash. 1966, U.S. Ct. Mil. Appeals 1967, U.S. Tax Ct. 1983. Assoc. Witherspoon, Kelley, Davenport & Toole, Spokane, 1972-77; ptnr./prin. Witherspoon, Kelley, Davenport & Toole, 1977—; assoc. prof. law Gonzaga Sch. Law, 1973-77. Bd. overseers Gonzaga Prep. Sch., Spokane, 1988-89; bd. trustees Spokane Guild Sch. for the Handicapped, 1975-78, Wash. State U. Found. Bd., 1992-97, Whitman Coll. Planned Giving Coun., 1994—. Capt. U.S. Army, 1966-70. Recipient Wall St. Jur. award, 1962; decorated Bronze Star medal. Mem. Wash. State Bar Assn. (founder, chmn. health law sect. 1989-92, health law coun. 1989-94, pres. tax sect. 1987-88, mem. tax coun. 1984—), ABA (chmn. health care subcom. 1990-94). Republican. Avocations: tennis, astronomy. Office: Witherspoon Kelley Davenport & Toole 1100 Old National Bldg Spokane WA 99201

CONNOLLY, THOMAS JOSEPH, bishop; b. Tonopah, Nev., July 18, 1922; s. John and Katherine (Hammel) C. Student, St. Joseph Coll. and St. Patrick Sem., Menlo Park, Calif., 1936-47, Catholic U. Am., 1949-51; JCD, Lateran Pontifical U., Rome, 1952; DHL (hon.), U. Portland, 1972. Ordained priest Roman Cath. Ch., 1947. Asst. St. Thomas Cathedral, Reno, 1947, asst., rector, 1953-55; asst. Little Flower Parish, Reno, 1947-48; sec. to bishop, 1949; asst. St. Albert the Gt., Reno, 1952-53; pastor St. Albert the Gt., 1960-68, St. Joseph Ch., Elko, 1955-60, St. Theresa's Ch., Carson City, Nev., 1968-71; bishop Baker, Oreg., 1971—; Tchr. Manogue High Sch., Reno, 1948-49; chaplain Serra Club, 1948-49; officialis Diocese of Reno; chmn. bldg. com., dir. Cursillo Movement; moderator Italian Cath. Fedn.; dean, mem. personnel bd. Senate of Priests; mem. Nat. Bishops Liturgy Com., 1973-76; region XII rep. to adminstrv. bd. Nat. Conf. Cath. Bishops, 1973-76, 86-89, mem. adv. com., 1974-76; bd. dirs. Cath. Communications Northwest, 1977-82. Club: K.C. (state chaplain Nev. 1970-71). Office: Bishop of Baker PO Box 5999 911 SE Armour Dr Bend OR 97702-1489

CONNOR, DAVID JOHN, health care executive, accountant; b. Indpls., Oct. 26, 1953; s. David J. Jr. and Amy (Thomas) C.; m. Beatrice U. Maier, Apr. 24, 1982; children: David C., Brian A. BBA, U. Notre Dame, 1975; MBA, Capital U., 1988. CPA, Ohio. Various positions Coopers & Lybrand, Cin., 1975-84; sr. v.p., chief fin. officer Mount Carmel Health, Columbus, Ohio, 1984-91, St. Anges Med. Ctr., Fresno, Calif., 1991—; chmn. bd. dirs. Health Response, Columbus, 1990-91; bd. dirs., treas. Cen. Valley Health Plan, 1991—; bd. dirs. Health Matrix Corp., Columbus, Hosp. Choice Health Plan; bd. dirs., mem. fin. com. Holy Cross Health Systems, South Bend, Ind., 1987-91. Bd. dirs. Gladden Community House, Columbus, 1987-88; corp. fund raiser United Appeal, Cin., 1981; active Up Down Towners, Cin., 1980-82, Columbus Zoo Capital Campaign task force; mem. Leadership Fresno, 1992-93. Recipient Community Svc. award, Ohio Ho. of Reps., Columbus, 1988. Mem. Ohio Soc. CPAs, Calif. Soc. CPAs, Healthcare Fin. Mgrs. Assn., Ohio Hosp. Assn. (fin. com. 1989-91), Calif. Assn. Hosps. and Health Systems and Hosp. Coun. (fin. com. 1992—), Columbus C. of C., Notre Dame Club, Monogram Club. Office: St Anges Med Ctr 1303 E Herndon Ave Fresno CA 93720-3309

CONNOR, GARY EDWARD, manufacturing company marketing executive; b. S.I., N.Y., Nov. 13, 1948; s. Everett M. and Josephine (Amato) C.; B.S. in Elec. Engring., U. Md., 1973; M.B.A., U. Santa Clara (Calif.), 1979. Quality assurance engr. Frankford Arsenal, 1973; quality assurance engr., field service engr. Lockheed Electronics Co., 1973-74; group leader memory test engring. sect. head bipolar product engring. Nat. Semicondr. Corp., 1975-79; internat. mktg. mgr. Am. Microsystems Inc., 1979-80; mktg. mgr. GenRad-STI, Santa Clara, 1980-82; prodn. mktg. exec. AMD, Sunnyvale, Calif., 1982-86; dept. mgr. IDT, Santa Clara, Calif., 1986—. Mem. IEEE, Electronics Internat. Adv. Panel, Am. Security Council (nat. adv. bd.), Franklin

Mint Collectors Soc. Republican. Home: 5121 Kozo Ct San Jose CA 95124-5527 Office: 2670 Seely Ave San Jose CA 95134 1929

CONOVER, FREDERIC KING, lawyer; b. Portchester, N.Y., June 4, 1933; s. Julian D. and Josephine T. Conover; m. Kathryn B. Conover, Dec. 21, 1955; children: Frederic, Elizabeth, Pamela, Margaret; m. 2d, Jacquelyn Wonder, Aug. 24, 1979. B.A., Amherst Coll., 1955; J.D., U. Mich., 1961. Bar: Colo. 1962, U.S. Dist. Ct. Colo. 1962, U.S. Ct. Appeals (10th cir.) 1962. Ptnr. Conover, McClearn & Heppenstall, P.C., Denver, 1972-88, Faegre & Benson, Devner, 1988—, ptnr. in charge dispute resolution svcs. The Faegre Group, 1993—. Trustee Mt. Airy Psychiat. Ctr.; dir. Legal Aid Soc.; chmn. citizens adv. com. Denver Regional Council Govts., bd. govs., trustee, Nat. Ctr. for Preventive Law, pannel of disting. neutrals, Ctr. for Pub. Resources; bd. dirs., Lawyers Alliance for World Security. Served to lt. USN, 1955-59. Fellow Am. Coll. Trial Lawyers, Am. Bar Found., Colo. Bar Found.; mem. ABA, Denver Bar Assn. (pres. 1983-84), Colo. Bar Assn. (pres. 1990-91), Law Club (v.p.), City Club of Denver (dir.), Denver Tennis Club. Democrat. Office: The Faegre Group 2500 Republic Plz 370 17th St Denver CO 80202-1370*

CONQUEST, (GEORGE) ROBERT (ACWORTH), writer, historian, poet, critic, journalist; b. Malvern, Worcestershire, Eng., July 15, 1917; s. Robert Folger Westcott and Rosamund Alys (Acworth) C.; m. Joan Watkins, 1942 (div. 1948); children: John, Richard; m. Elizabeth Neece, Dec. 1, 1979. Student, Winchester Coll., Eng., 1931-35, U. Grenoble, France, 1935-36, U. Oxford, 1936-39; MA, U. Oxford, Eng., 1972; DLitt, U. Oxford, 1975. First sec. H.M. Fgn. Svc., Sofia, Bulgaria, U.N., London, 1946-56; rsch. fellow London Sch. Econs., 1956-58; vis. poet U. Buffalo, N.Y., 1959-60; lit. editor The Spectator, London, 1962-63; sr. fellow Russian Inst. Columbia U., N.Y.C., 1964-65; fellow Woodrow Wilson Internat. Ctr., Washington, 1976-77; sr. rsch. fellow Hoover Inst., Stanford (Calif.) U., 1977-79, 81—; disting. vis. scholar Heritage Found., Washington, 1980-81; adv. bd. Freedom House, N.Y.C., 1980—; rsch. assoc. Ukrainian Rsch. Inst. Harvard U., Cambridge, Mass., 1983—; adj. fellow Washington Ctr. Strategic Studies, 1984—. Author: Poems, 1955, A World of Difference, 1955, Common Sense About Russia, 1960, Power and Policy in the USSR, 1961, The Pasternak Affair, 1962, Between Mars and Venus, 1962, (with Kingsley Amis) The Egyptologists, 1965, Russia after Khrushchev, 1965, The Great Terror, 1968, Arias from a Love Opera, 1969, The Nation Killers, 1970, Where Marx Went Wrong, 1970, V I Lenin, 1972, Kolyma: The Arctic Death Camps, 1978, Coming Across, 1978, The Abomination of Moab, 1979, Forays, 1979, Present Danger: Towards a Foreign Policy, 1979, We and They: Civic and Despotic Cultures, 1980, (with Jon. M. White) What to do When the Russians Come, 1984, Inside Stalin's Secret Police: NKVD Politics 1936-39, 1985, The Harvest of Sorrow: Soviet Collectivization and the Terror-Famine, 1986, New and Collected Poems, 1988, Stalin and the Kirov Murder, 1988, Tyrants and Typewriters, 1989, The Great Terror: A Reassessment, 1990, Stalin: Breaker of Nations, 1991, Demons Don't, 1999, Reflections on a Ravaged Century, 1999. Capt. inf. Brit. Army, 1939-46, ETO. Decorated Officer Order of the Brit. Empire, London, 1955, Companion Order St. Michael and St. George, London, 1996; recipient Alexis de Tocqueville award, 1992Light Verse award Acad. Arts and Letters, 1997; Jefferson lectr. in the humanities, Washington, 1993; Royal Soc. Lit. fellow, 1972. Fellow Brit. Acad., Brit. Interplanetary Soc.; mem. Soc. for Promotion of Roman Studies. Club: Travellers (London). Home: 52 Peter Coutts Cir Stanford CA 94305-2506 Office: Stanford U Hoover Inst Stanford CA 94305-6010

CONRAD, BONNIE LYNN, artist; b. Murray, Utah, Feb. 23, 1947; d. Wayne E. and Lorraine (Childress) Johnson; m. D. Roger Conrad, Sept. 10, 1968; children: Tamra, Bret, Kari, Kelly, Kristen, Tiffany. BA, Brigham Young U., 1968. Freelance artist, 1988-98. One-woman shows include Dakota Artist's Guild, Rapid City, S.D., 1996; exhibited in group shows Old West Mus., Cheyenne, Wyo., 1994, Kans. Indian Market, Kansas City, 1994, Visions West Gallery, Livingston, Mont., 1994, Old Trail Town, Cody, Wyo., 1994, Western Heritage Artists, Great Falls, Mont., 1996, Orlando (Fla.) Wildlife Western Art Expo., 1997, C.M. Russell Show, Great Falls, Mont., 1997, 98, Custer County Art Mus., Miles City, Mont., 1997, Clymer Mus., Ellensburg, Wash., 1997, Desert Caballeros Mus., Wickenburg, Ariz., 1997, Joan Cawley Gallery, Scottsdale, Ariz., 1998, others; contbr. articles to mags. Mem. Am. Acad. Women Artists (sec. 1997—). Home and Studio: 675 S Woodland Hills Dr Woodland Hills UT 84653-2009

CONRAD, CHARLES THOMAS, lawyer; b. Milw., Aug. 8, 1949; s. Robert Joseph and Monica Mary (Farrell) C.; m. Georgeana Jane Shoemaker, Feb. 24, 1973; children: Charles, Michael. BA cum laude, Gonzaga U., 1972, JD, 1977. Bar: U.S. Dist. Ct. (ea. dist.) Wash. 1977, U.S. Ct. Appeals (9th cir.) 1980. Atty. Schimanski, Leeds & Conrad, Spokane, Wash., 1977-93; sole practice law Spokane, 1993—; arbitrator NASD, San Francisco, 1989—, Nat. Futures Assn., Chgo., 1996—. Mem. Wash. State Bar assn., Wash. State Trial Lawyers Assn., Spokane County Bar Assn. Avocations: skiing, scuba diving. Home: 6605 S Westchester Dr Spokane WA 99223-6221 Office: 9011 E Valleyway Ave Spokane WA 99212-2835

CONRAD, DIANE, psychiatric nurse practitioner; b. N.Y.C.. MA, SUNY, Stony Brook, 1971; MS, Adelphi U., 1978. RN; cert. psychiat./mental health practitioner. Instr. Pilgrim State Hosp., Brentwood, N.Y., 1968-71; staff nurse VA, N.Y. and Calif., 1972-79, 83-85; therapist pvt. practitioner, Northport, N.Y., 1979-83; therapist, educator Conrad Co., Reno, Nev., 1986-89; therpist pvt. practitioner, Boise, Idaho, 1989-90; unit coord. CPC Intermountain Hosp., Boise, 1989-90; unit asst. dir. Providence Hosp., Seattle, 1991-92; therapist pvt. practitioner, Brookings, Oreg., 1993-98, Albany & Corvallis, Oreg., 1998—; mem. adv. bds. hospice, pub. health, mental health Curry County, Oreg., 1994-98; pub. Health Press, Brookings, 1992-98. Author: Nurse Person: Handbook for Conceptualizing Nursing, 1993; also articles. Mem. ANA, Sigma Theta Tau.

CONRAD, JANE KATHRYN, writer; b. Phila., Mar. 12, 1916; d. Charles and Alice Leah (Hachenburg) Goodman; m. R. Conrad, 1942 (dec. Jan. 1952); children: Ruthie, Kathy. BA in Polit. Sci., Met. State U., 1974. Mem. staff Office of Commandant, USMC and Secret Svc., Washington, 1939-43; liaison to state agys. State of Del., Dover; columnist Mobile Home Life, Denver, 1971-79. Author: Pillars of Religion, 1978, Skeptics, Scoffers and Deists, 1983, Mad Madalyn, 1982, rev. edit., 1996, Child Abuse Hysteria, 1989, rev. edit., 1990; contbr. articles to profl. publs.; editor newsletter Quest for Truth, 1976—. Leader Girl Scouts U.S., 1936-52; lobbyist Mobile Home Owners, Denver, 1974; mayor Town of Lochbuie, Colo., 1985; mem. Colo. Mobile Home Licensing Bd., Denver, 1975-78; consumer rep. Nat. Fire Protection Assn., Boston, 1973-75; mem. HUD Mobile Home Commn., 1977. Mem. ACLU, Ams. United for Separation of Ch. and State, Rocky Mountain Skeptics, Anti-Defamation League. Avocations: gardening, travel, politics, study of psychology.

CONRAN, JAMES MICHAEL, consumer advocate, public policy consultant; b. N.Y.C., Mar. 15, 1952; s. James Adrian and Mary Ellen (McGarry) C.; m. Phyllis Jean Thompson, Aug. 1, 1984; children: Michael O., Thomas O. BA, Calif. State U., Northridge, 1975; M in Urban Studies, Occidental Coll., 1978. Mgr. regulatory rels. Pacific Bell, San Francisco, 1985-88, mgr. pub. affairs & pub. issues, 1988-91; dir. State of Calif. Dept. Consumer Affairs, Sacramento, 1991-94; founder, pres. Consumers First, 1994—; bd. dirs. Consumer Interest Rsch. Inst., Nat. Consumers League, Elec. Consumers Alliance, TRW Consumer Adv. Coun., Great Western Fin. Corp., Consumer Adv. Panel, Electric Inst. Consumer Adv. Panel; mem. Coun. Licensing Enforcement and Regulation; nat. bd. certification occupl. therapy World Inst. on Disabilities. Contbr. articles to profl. jours. Bd. dirs. Fight Back! Found., L.A., 1991—, Disabled Children's Computer Group, Orinda, Calif., Telecomm. Edn. Trust Fund-Calif. Pub. Utilities Commn., San Francisco, 1990-91; chair adminstrv. sect. United Calif. State Employees Campaign, Sacramento; mem. Stream Preservation Commn., Orinda, 1988-91, Calif. Rep. Party Cen. Com., Orinda, 1992; del. Rep. Nat. Conv., Houston, 1992; regional chair Bush-Quayle campaign, Orinda, 1992. Fellow Coro Found., 1977, Levere Meml. Found., 1976. Mem. Coro Assn., Calif. Agenda for Consumer Edn., Sigma Alpha Epsilon. Roman Catholic. Avocations: politics, golf, camping, skiing, wine collecting.

CONSIDINE, KEVIN CHARLES, family physician; b. San Diego, Aug. 21, 1963; s. Timothy Malcolm and Sharon Elaine (Culver) C.; m. Sally Anne Grant, July 23, 1988; children: Krystina Lynne, Lisa Marie, Brian Timothy. BS in Biology, San Diego State U., 1987; DO, U. Health Scis./Coll. Osteo., 1991. Diplomate Am. Bd. Family Practice, Am. Osteo. Bd. Family Physicians. Resident in family practice resident Warren Hosp., Phillipsburg, N.J., 1991-94; family practice physician Scripps Clinic Med. Group, San Diego, 1994-96; pvt. practice Coronado, Calif., 1997—; mem. adv. bd. for manual medicine Scripps Clinic Med. Group, San Diego, 1995-96; mem. utilization rev. com. Scripps Clinic, Rancho Bernardo, 1995-96. Mem. 717 Club, Coronado, 1995—. Mem. Am. Acad. Osteopathy, Am. Osteo. Assn., Am. Acad. Family Physicians, Osteo. Physicians and Surgeons Calif., Am. Coll. Osteo. Family Physicians, Calif. Acad. Family Physicians, San Diego Osteo. Med. Assn., San Diego County Med. Soc. Republican. Roman Catholic. Avocations: computers, cooking, wine tasting, traveling, bicycling. Office: 171 C Ave Coronado CA 92118-1423

CONSTANT, CLINTON, chemical engineer, consultant; b. Nelson, B.C., Can., Mar. 20, 1912; came to U.S., 1936, naturalized, 1942; s. Vasile and Annie (Hunt) C.; m. Margie Robbel, Dec. 5, 1965. BSc with honors, U. Alta., 1935, postgrad., 1935-36; PhD, Western Res. U., 1939. Registered profl. engr., Calif., Wis. Devel. engr. Harshaw Chem. Co., Cleve., 1936-38, mfg. foreman, 1938-43, sr. engr. semi-works dept., 1948-50; supt. hydrofluoric acid dept. Nyotex Chems., Inc., Houston, 1943-47, chief devel. engr., 1947-48; mgr. engring. Ferro Chem. Co., Bedford, Ohio, 1950-52; tech. asst. mfg. dept. Armour Agrl. Chem. Co. (name formerly Armour Fertilizer Works), Bartow, Fla., 1952-61, mfg. research and devel. div., 1961-63; mgr. spl. projects Research div. (co. name changed to USS Agri-Chems 1968), Bartow, Fla., 1963-65, project mgr., 1965-70; chem. adviser Robert & Co. Assocs., Atlanta, 1970-79; chief engr. Almon & Assocs., Inc., Atlanta, 1979-80; project mgr. Engring. Service Assocs., Atlanta, 1980-81; v.p. engring. ACI Inc., Hesperia, Calif., 1981-83; sr. v.p., chief engr. MTI (acquisition of ACI), Hesperia, 1983-86; engring. cons. San Bernardino County APCD, Victorville, Calif., 1986-90; instr. environ. chemistry Victor Valley C.C., 1990; pvt. cons. Victorville, Calif., 1991—; cons. in engring., 1992—. Author tech. reports, sci. fiction; patentee in field. Fellow AAAS, Am. Inst. Chemists, Am. Inst. Chem. Engrs., N.Y. Acad. Scis., AIAA (assoc.); mem. Am. Chem. Soc., Am. Astron. Soc., Astron. Soc. Pacific, Royal Astron. Soc. Can., NSPE, Am. Water Works Assn., Calif. Water and Pollution Control Assn., Air Pollution Control Assn., Soc. Mfg. Engrs., Calif. Soc. Profl. Engrs.

CONSTANTINEAU, CONSTANCE JULIETTE, retired banker; b. Lowell, Mass., Feb. 18, 1937; d. Henry Goulet and Germaine (Turner) Goulet-Lamarre; m. Edward Joseph Constantineau; children: Glen Edward, Alan Henry. Student, Bank Adminstrn. Inst. and Am. Inst. Banking, 1975-87. Mortgage sec. The Cen. Savs. Bank, Lowell, 1955-57; head teller First Fed. Savs. & Loan, Lowell, 1957-59, Lowell Bank & Trust Co., Lowell, 1973-74; br. mgr. Century Bank & Trust Co., Malden, Mass., 1975-78; v.p. purchasing, mgr. support svcs. First Security Bank of N.Mex. (formerly First Nat. Bank Albuquerque), 1983-96; ret., 1996; mem. planning purchasing mgr.'s conf. Bank Adminstrn. Inst., San Antonio, Orlando, Fla., New Orleans; treas. polit. action com. First Nat. Bank, 1986. Bd. dirs., historian Indian Pueblo Cultural Ctr., Albuquerque, 1986-89. Home: 13015 Deer Dancer Trl NE Albuquerque NM 87112-4831

CONTI, ISABELLA, psychologist, consultant; b. Torino, Italy, Jan. 1, 1942; came to U.S., 1964; d. Giuseppe and Zaira (Melis) Ferro; m. Ugo Conti, Sept. 5, 1964; 1 child, Maurice. J.D., U. Rome, 1966; Ph.D. in Psychology, U. Calif.-Berkeley, 1975. Lic. psychologist. Sr. analyst Rsch. Inst. for Study of Man, Berkeley, Calif., 1967-68; postgrad. rsch. psychologist Personality Assessment and Rsch. Inst., U. Calif.-Berkeley, 1968-71; intern U. Calif.-Berkeley and VA Hosp., San Francisco, 1969-75; asst. prof. St. Mary's Coll., Moraga, Calif., 1978-84; cons. psychologist Conti Resources, Berkeley, Calif., 1977-85; v.p. Barnes & Conti Assocs., Inc., Berkeley, 1985-90; pres. Lisardco, El Cerrito, Calif., 1989—; bd. dirs. ElectroMagnetic Instruments, Inc., El Cerrito, Calif., 1985—. Trustee Monterey Inst. Internat. Studies, 1996-98. Author: (with Alfonso Montuori) From Power to Partnership, 1993; contbr. articles on creativity and mgmt. cons. to profl. jours. Regents fellow U. Calif.-Berkeley, 1972; NIMH predoctoral rsch. fellow, 1972-73. Mem. APA. Office: Lisardco 1318 Brewster Dr El Cerrito CA 94530-2526

CONTO, ARISTIDES, advertising agency executive; b. N.Y.C., Feb. 10, 1931; s. Gus Dimitrios and Osee (Kenney) C.; BA, Champlain Coll., 1953; MS in Journalism, UCLA, 1958, certificate in indsl. rels., 1965; m. Phyllis Helen Wiley, June 22, 1957; 1 son, Jason Wiley. Reporter, City News Svc., L.A., 1958; dir. pub. rels. Galaxy Advt. Co., Los Angeles, 1959-60; news media chief Los Angeles County Heart Assn., 1960-61; pub. rels. assoc. Prudential Ins. Co., L.A., 1961-64; advt. mgr. Aerospace Controls Co., L.A., 1964-65; comml. sales promotion coord. Lockheed-Calif. Co., Burbank, 1965-73; pres. Jason Wiley Advt. Agy., L.A., 1973-92; dir. Tower Master, Inc., L.A. With U.S. Army, 1955-56. Recipient advt. awards. Mem. Nat. Soc. Published Poets, L.A. Press Club, Bus.-Profl. Advt. Assn. L.A.s, Pub. Rels. Soc. Author: The Spy Who Loved Me, 1962; The Diamond Twins, 1963, Edit Me Dead, 1992, I Marcus, 1994, A Short Life, 1995, (screenplays) Lannigan, 1973, Haunted Host, 1976, Captain Noah, 1977, Government Surplus, 1983.

CONTOS, PAUL ANTHONY, engineer, investment consultant; b. Chgo., Mar. 18, 1926; s. Anthony Dimitrios and Panagiota (Kostopoulos) C.; m. Lilian Katie Kalkines, June 19, 1955 (dec. Apr. 1985); children: Leslie, Claudia, Paula, Anthony. Student, Am. TV Inst., Chgo., 1946-48, U. Ill., 1949-52, 53-56, Ill. Inst. Tech., 1952-53, U. So. Calif., 1956-57. Engr. J.C. Deagan Co., Inc., Chgo., 1951-53, Lockheed Missile and Space Co., Inc., Sunnyvale, Calif., 1956-62; engring. supr. Lockheed Missile and Space Co., Inc., Sunnyvale, 1962-65, staff engr., 1965-88; pres. PAC Investments, Saratoga, Calif., 1984-88; pres. PAC Investments, San Jose, Calif., 1988—, also advisor, 1984—. Mem. Pres. Coun. U. Ill., 1994—. With U.S. Army, 1944-46, ETO. Decorated Purple Heart. Mem. DAV (life, commdr. Chgo. unit 1948-51), VFW (life), Pi Sigma Phi (pres. 1951-53). Republican. Greek Orthodox. Home and Office: 1009 Blossom River Way Apt 105 San Jose CA 95123-6305

CONVIS, CHARLES LESTER, publisher; b. Lansford, N.D., Apr. 21, 1926; s. Lester Campbell and Ada Margaret (McHaney) C.; m. Mary Anne Crawley, July 30, 1949; children: Charles Jr., Mary M. Kadoyama, James, William, David. BSCE, U. Tex., 1951; JD, Harvard Law Sch., 1956; PhD, U. Tex., 1980. Bar: Calif. Lawyer Standard Oil Co. of Calif., San Francisco, 1957-60; deputy dist. atty. Marin County, San Rafael, Calif., 1960-64; ptnr. Convis, Kennedy & Shaw, San Rafael, 1964-76; coll. prof. S.W. Tex. State U., San Marcos, 1976-82; law prof. Duquesne U., Pitts., 1982-85; deputy dist. atty. San Joaquin County, Stockton, Calif., 1985-95; owner, CEO Pioneer Press, Carson City, Nev., 1995—. Author: (biography) The Honor of Arms, 1990, (9-vol. series) True Tales of the Old West, 1995—. Coun. commr. Boy Scouts of Am., San Rafael, Redding, Calif., 1964-76; dir. Marin Coun. ARC, Boy Scouts of Am., Marin Coun., Econ. Opportunity Coun., Marin County. With USMC, 1943-46. Recipient W. St. John Garwood award U. Houston, 1953, Wall Street Journal Student award, Cambridge, Mass., 1956. Mem. Coun. on America's Mil. Past, Order of the Indian Wars, Oreg.-Calif. Trail Assn., Santa Fe Trail Assn., 4th Marine Divsn. Assn. Democrat. Presbyterian. Avocations: travel, skiing, pub. speaking. Home: 2185 Court Side Ct Carson City NV 89703-7364 Office: Pioneer Press PO Box 216 Carson City NV 89702-0216

CONWAY, JAMES VALENTINE PATRICK, forensic document examiner, former postal service executive; b. Scottdale, Pa., July 16, 1917; s. James Aloysius and Mary Margaret (Yahner) C.; m. Mildred E. Garypie, Aug. 6, 1936; children: James W., Ruth A. Conway Masonek, Colleen L. Conway Weyland, Judith Conway Henderson. Student, St. Vincent Coll., Latrobe, Pa., 1931-34, Cambria-Rowe Bus. Coll., Greensburg, Pa., 1935-36. Diplomate Am. Bd. Forensic Document Examiners. With U.S. Postal Svc., 1939-80; regional chief insp. U.S. Postal Svc., San Francisco, 1971-73; exec. asst. to Postmaster Gen., Washington, 1973-75; sr. asst. postmaster gen. for employee and labor rels., 1975-76; dep. Postmaster Gen., 1976-80; bd. govs., 1978-80; forensic document examiner Alameda, Calif., 1980—. Author: Evidential Documents, 1959; contbr. articles to profl. jours. Bd. dirs. Regional Civil Def. Bd., Santa Rosa, Calif., 1964-69. Recipient Benjamin Franklin award Postmaster Gen.'s, 1980; named Staff Man of Yr. Fed. Bus. Assn., San Francisco, 1957. Fellow Am. Acad. Forensic Scis. (chmn. document sect. 1960-61, chmn. adv. council 1960-61); mem. Internat. Assn. Chiefs Police (life), Internat. Assn. Identification (chmn. subcom. questioned document 1953-56), Am. Soc. Questioned Document Examiners (pres. 1988-90). Democrat. Roman Catholic. Lodge: Elks. Avocations: cantoring, tennis.

CONWAY, JOHN E., federal judge; b. 1934. BS, U.S. Naval Acad., 1956; LLB magna cum laude, Washburn U., 1963. Assoc. Matias A Zamora, Santa Fe, 1963-64; ptnr. Wilkinson, Durrett & Conway, Alamogordo, N.Mex., 1964-67, Durrett, Conway & Jordon, Alamogordo, 1967-80, Montgomery & Andrews, P.A., Albuquerque, 1980-86; city atty. Alamogordo, 1966-72; mem. N.Mex. State Senate, 1970-80, minority leader, 1972-80; chief fed. judge U.S. Dist. Ct. N.Mex., Albuquerque, 1986—. 1st lt. USAF, 1956-60. Mem. Nat. Commrs. on Uniform State Laws, Fed. Judges' Assn. (bd. dirs.), 10th Cir. Dist. Judges' Assn. (pres.), N.Mex. Bar Assn., N.Mex. Jud. Coun. (vice chmn. 1973, chmn. 1973-75, disciplinary bd. of Supreme Ct. of N.Mex. vice chmn. 1980, chmn. 1981-84), Albuquerque Lawyers Club. Office: US Dist Ct 333 Lomas Blvd NW #770 Albuquerque NM 87102

CONWAY, LOIS LORRAINE, piano teacher; b. Caldwell, Idaho, Oct. 20, 1913; d. William Henry and Auttie Arrola (Bierd) Crawford; m. Edward Owen Conway, June 23, 1934; children: Michael David, Judith Ann, Steven Edward, Kathleen Jean. *Son Michael David Conway is a Captain at United Airlines. Daughter Judith A. Conway Matrin owns and operates Judith Conway Fine Jewelry Designs. Son Dr. Steven Edward Conway is a Washington State Legislator from 1992 to present. Daughter Kathleen Jean Conway was named Most Valuable Employee from 1996-98 at Good Will Industry's.* Degree, Albertson Coll. of Idaho, 1960's; student, Shorwood Music Sch., Chgo., Coll. of Notre Dame, San Francisco. Pvt. piano tchr. Ontario, Oreg., 1940-74, Pendleton, Oreg., 19774-92; ret., 1992; Nat. Guild Piano Tchrs. adjudicator spring auditions Am. Coll. Musicians, Austin, Tex., 1972-96. Author: (poetry) Pacifica-The Voice Within (Semi-finalist 1995). Chmn. Nat. Guild Auditions, Ontario, Oreg., 1959-72, Pendleton, Oreg., 1972-80; v.p., publicity Community Concerts Assn., Ontario, 1960-72, membership work, 1972-75. Democrat. Avocations: gardening, playing piano, bridge, duplicate bridge, motor home travel. Home: 114 Shamrock Cir Santa Rosa CA 95403-1156

CONWAY, NANCY ANN, editor; b. Foxboro, Mass., Oct. 15, 1941; d. Leo T. and Alma (Goodwin) C.; children: Ana Lucia DaSilva, Kara Ann Martin. Cert. in med. tech., Carnegie Inst., 1962; BA in English, U. Mass., 1976, cert. in secondary edn., 1978. Tchr. Brazil-Am. Inst., Rio de Janeiro, 1963-68; freelance writer, editor Amherst, Mass., 1972-76; staff writer Daily Hampshire Gazette, North Hampton, Mass., 1976-77; editor Amherst Bull., 1977-80, Amherst Record, 1980-83; features editor Holyoke (Mass.) Transcript/Telegram, 1983-84; gen. mgr. Monday-Thursday Newspapers, Boca Raton, Fla., 1984-87; dir. editorial South Fla. Newspaper Network, Deerfield Beach, 1987-90; pub., editor York (Pa.) Newspapers, Inc., 1990-95; exec. editor, v.p. Alameda Newspaper Group, Pleasanton, Calif., 1996—. Bd. dirs. Math.: Opportunities in Engring., Sci. and Tech.-Pa. State, York, 1991-95. Recipient writing awards, state newspaper assns. Mem. Am. Soc. Newspaper Editors, Soc. Profl. Journalists. Avocations: literature, photography, communication gardening. Office: 66 Jack London Sq Oakland CA 94607-3726*

CONWAY, WALLACE XAVIER, SR., retired curator; b. Washington, June 11, 1920; m. Jessie Dedeaux, June 1, 1943. B.A., Miner Tchrs. Coll., 1941; postgrad. Cath. U., Washington, 1957, 58, 61, Trenton State Coll., 1977-78, U. Paris, Sorbonne, 1977, NYU, 1987, 88, Mercer County Coll., 1975-76, MA. 1988; postgrad Venice, Italy, 1989, Art Inst. Chgo., 1990, NYU. Owner, dir. Co-Art Studios, Washington, 1950-64; graphic artist Dept. Commerce, U.S. Weather Bur., Washington, 1964-65; graphic supr. Smithsonian Inst., Washington, 1965-69; curator, chmn. exhibits bur. N.J. State Mus., Trenton, 1969-88; ret.; tech. cons. mural The Life of Martin Luther King at Martin Luther King Libr., Washington, 1984-86; cons. Pa. Council on the Arts/Minority Arts; museum cons. Mother Bethel A.M.E. Ch., nat. hist. landmark, Phila.; mem. art com. Mercer Med. Ctr.; cons. Afro-Am. Hist. Soc. Mus., Jersey City. Mem. adv. bd. Minority Arts Council, Phila.; past mem. Art Students League (Colo. chpt., Best of Show award, two honorable mentions, First Place print category). Mem. Colo. Springs Pioneer Mus. (adv. bd.), Kappa Alpha Psi, Beta Kappa (charter). Home: 2119 Olympic Dr Colorado Springs CO 80910-1262

COOK, ALBERT THOMAS THORNTON, JR., financial advisor; b. Cleve., Apr. 24, 1940; s. Albert Thomas Thornton and Tyra Esther (Morehouse) C.; m. Mary Jane Blackburn, June 1, 1963; children: Lara Keller, Thomas, Timothy. BA, Dartmouth Coll., 1962; MA, U. Chgo., 1966. Asst. sec. Dartmouth Coll., Hanover, N.H., 1972-77; exec. dir. Big Brothers, Inc., N.Y.C., 1977-78; underwriter Boettcher & Co., Denver, 1978-81; asst. v.p. Dain Bosworth Inc., Denver, 1981-82, Colo. Nat. Bank, Denver, 1982-84; pres. The Albert T.T. Cook Co., Denver, 1984—; arbitrator Nat. Assn. Securities Dealers, N.Y.C., 1985—, Mcpl. Securities Rulemaking Bd., Washington, 1987-98. Pres. Etna-Hanover Ctr. Community Assn., Hanover, N.H., 1974-76; mem. Mayor's Task Force, Denver, 1984; bd. dirs. Rude Park Community Nursery, Denver, 1985-87, Willows Water Dist., Colo., 1990—, pres., 1998—; trustee The Iliff Sch. Theol., Denver, 1986-92; mem. Dartmouth Coll. Com. on Trustees, 1990-93. Mem. Dartmouth Alumni Coun. (exec. com., chmn. nominating and trustee search coms. 1987-89), University Club (chmn. admissions com. 1997-98), Cactus Club (Denver), Dartmouth Club of N.Y.C., Yale Club, Lions (bd. dirs. Denver chpt. 1983-85, treas. 1986-87, pres. Denver Found. 1987-88), Delta Upsilon. Congregationalist. Avocations: fly fishing, furniture making, running, skiing, backpacking. Home: 7099 E Hinsdale Pl Englewood CO 80112-1610 Office: One Tabor Ctr 1200 17th St Ste 960 Denver CO 80202-5835

COOK, DIERDRE RUTH GOORMAN, school administrator, secondary education educator; b. Denver, Nov. 4, 1956; d. George Edward and Avis M. (Wilson) Goorman; m. Donald Robert Cook, Apr. 4, 1981; 1 child, Christen. BA in Theatre Arts, Colo. State U., 1980, MA in Adminstrn., MEd, 1995. Cert. secondary tchr. Tchr. Centennial High Sch., Ft. Collins, Colo., 1983-87; tchr., also dir. student activities Poudre H.S., Ft. Collins, 1987-95; asst. prin. Lesher Jr. H.S., Ft. Collins, 1995—; mem. curriculum devel. com. Poudre R-1 Sch. Dist., Ft. Collins, 1984, mem. instrnl. improvement com., 1985-94, trainer positive power leadership, 1986-87, mem. profl. devel. com. 1992-94; comm. cons. Woodward Gov. Com., Ft. Collins, 1991, 92, 95; mem. evaluation visitation team North Ctrl. Evaluation, Greeley, Colo., 1991. Campaign worker Rep. Party, Littleton, Colo., 1980, Ft. Collins, 1984, 88; mem. Colo. Juvenile Coun., Ft. Collins United Way, 1986, 88, loaned exec., 1987; bd. dirs. Youth Unltd., 1994-95; mem. Leadership Ft. Collins, 1992-93; troop leader Girl Scouts U.S., 1991-94. NEH scholar, 1992; named Disting. Tchr. 1993 Colo. Awards Coun.; recipient Tchr. Excellence award Poudre High Sch., 1992. Mem. NEA, ASCD, Colo. Edn. Assn., Poudre Edn. Assn. (rep. 1989-91), Nat. Speech Comm. Assn., Nat. Forensics League (degree for outstanding distinction 1992), Nat. Platform Soc., Kappa Kappa Gamma (pres. Epsilon Beta chpt. 1985-90, mem. corp. house bd., alumni pres. Ft. Collins 1996-97), Evangelica Free Ch. Avocations: water skiing, snow skiing, gardening, golf. Home: 2809 Lake Dr Loveland CO 80538-3130 Office: Poudre R-1 Sch Dist 1400 Stover St Fort Collins CO 80524-4249

COOK, DONALD E., pediatrician; b. Pitts., Mar. 24, 1928; s. Merriam E. and Bertha (Gwin) C.; BS, Colo. Coll., 1951; MD, U. Colo., 1955; m. Elsie Walden, Sept. 2, 1951; children: Catherine, Christopher, Brian, Jeffrey. Intern, Fresno County Gen. Hosp., Calif., 1955-56; resident in gen. practice Tulare (Calif.) County Gen. Hosp., 1956-57; resident in pediatrics U. Colo., 1957-59; practice medicine specializing in pediatrics, Aurora, Colo., 1959-64, Greeley (Colo.) Med. Clin., Greeley Sports Medicine Clin., 1964-93; med. adv. Centennial Develop. Svcs., Inc., 1993-95, clin. faculty U. Colo., clin. prof., 1977—; organizer, dir. Sports Medicine Px Exam Clinic for indigent Weld Co. athletes, 1990-96, mem. adv. bd. Nat. Center Health Edn., San Francisco, 1978-80; mem. adv. com. on maternal and child health programs Colo. State Health Dept., 1981-84, chmn., 1981-84; preceptor Sch. Nurse Practitioner Program U. Colo., 1978-88. Mem. Weld County Dist. 6 Sch. Bd., 1973-83, pres., 1973-74, 76-77, chmn. dist. 6 accountability com., 1972-

73; mem. adv. com. dist. 6 teen pregnancy program, 1983-85; mem. Weld County Task Force on teen-aged pregnancy, 1986-89, Dream Team Weld County Task Force on sch. dropouts, 1986-92, Weld County Interagy. Screening Bd., Weld County Cmty. Ctr. Found., 1984-89, Weld County Task Force Speakers Bur. on AIDS, 1987-94; mem. Weld County Task Force Adolescent Health Clinic; mem. Task Force Child Abuse, C. of C.; bd. dirs. No. Colo. Med. Ctr., 1993-98, No. Colo. Med. Ctr. Found., 1994—; med. advisor Weld County Sch. Dist. VI-Nurses, 1987—; mem. Sch. Dist. 6 Health Coalition, Task Force on access to health care; group leader neonatal group Colo. Action for Healthy People Colo. Dept. Pub. Health, 1985-86; co-founder Colorodoans for seatbelts on sch. buses, 1985-90; co-founder, v.p. Coalition of primary care physicians, Colo., 1986; mem. adv. com. Greeley Cen. Drug and Alcohol Abuse, 1984-86, Rocky Mtn. Ctr. for Health Promotion and Edn., bd. dirs., 1984—, v.p., 1992-93, pres. 1994-95; rep. coun. on med. specialty soc., AAP, 1988-89, mem. coun. pediatric rsch., 1988-89, oversight com. fin., oversight com. communications, rep. to nat. PTA, 1990-94, mem. coun. on govt. affairs, 1989-90, rep. to coun. sects. mgmt. com., mem. search com. for new exec. dir.; med. cons. Sch. Dist. 6, 1989—; adv. com. bd. comm., adv. com. bd. membership comm., adv. com. bd. finance, adv. com. bd. dirs. AAP 1990-95, AAP com. govt. affairs, 1990; United Way Weld County, 1993-98; founder, med. dir. Monfort Children's Clinic, 1994-98; affiliate prof. nursing U. No. Colo., 1996. With USN, 1946-48. Recipient Disting. Svc. award Jr. C. of C., 1962, Disting. Citizenship award Elks, 1975-76, Svc. to Mankind award Sertoma Club, 1972, Spark Plug award U. No. Colo., 1981, Eta Sigma Gamma Svc. award, 1996; Mildred Doster award Colo. Sch. Health Coun. for sch. health contbns., 1992, Citizen of Yr. award No. Colo. Med. Ctr. Found., 1996, Humanitarian of Yr. award Weld County United Way, 1996, Alfred Winchester Humanitarian award Greeley/Weld Sr. Found., Inc., 1996, Silver and Gold award U. Colo. Med. Alumni Assn., 1997, Franklin Geggenbach award Denver Children's Hosp. Pediatric Alumni award, 1997. Diplomate Am. Bd. Pediatrics., 1961. Mem. Colo. Med. Soc. Sch. Health Com. (chmn. 1967-78), Am. Acad. Pediatrics (alt. dist. chmn. 1987-93, dist. chmn. dist. VIII 1993-98, chmn. alt. dist. chmn. com. 1991-93, chmn. sch. health com. 1975-80, chmn. Colo. chpt. 1982-87, mem. task force on new age of pediatrics 1982-85, Ross edn. and award com. 1985-86, media spokesperson Speak Up for Children 1983—, mem. coun. sects. mgmt. 1991-92, mem. search com., exec. dir., candidate for pres., 1998, pres. elect 1998-99, v.p., AAP, 1998-99), AMA (chmn. sch. and coll. health com. 1980-82, James E. Strain Community Svc. award 1987, 94, coun. pediatric practice), Adams Aurora Med. Soc. (pres. 1964-65), Weld County Med. Soc. (pres. 1968-69), Colo. Med. Soc. (com. on sports medicine, 1980-90, com. chmn. 1986-90, chmn. com. sch. health 1988-91, A.H. Robbins Community Svc. award 1974), Centennial Pediatric Soc. (pres. 1982-86), Rotary (bd. dirs. Greely chpt. 1988-91, mem. immunization com. 1994—, chmn. immunization campaign Weld county, 1994). Republican. Methodist. Home: 1710 21st Ave Greeley CO 80631-5143 Office: Greeley Sports Medicine Clinic 1900 16th St Greeley CO 80631-5114

COOK, DONALD RAY, pastor; b. L.A., May 24, 1943; s. Burnie and Ardie Mae (Dewitt) C.; m. Debra Rue Cotton, Nov. 1981; children: Chisha Christine, Donald R. II, Barrington Jason. BA, Pepperdine U., 1976; MA, Eula Wesley U., 1984; DD (hon.), L.A. Bible Coll. and Sem., 1986; PhD, Eula Wesley U., 1990. Lic. to ministry Chs. of God in Christ, 1966; ordained, 1972; cert. mental health counselor. Chaplain L.A. County Jail Sheriffs Dept., 1973-76; sr. pastor, organizer Calif. Harvest Tabernacle Ch., L.A., 1976—; police clergy coun. L.A. Police Dept., 1970—; exec. bd. Southwest Ecclesiastic Jurisdiction of Calif., 1988—, supt. of 4th dist., 1988—; commr. edn. Chs. of God in Christ, Santa Monica, Calif., 1988—; reserve L.A. Police Dept., 1990—; bd. dirs. Pentecostal Heritage Found., L.A., 1989—; rsch. cons. in field; acad. tutor, dublin Magnet Sch., L.A., 1991; lectr., West Coast Coll. Assn., Calif., 1974-79; pub. rels., L.A. Police Dept., 1991. With U.S. Army, 1966-68. Mem. Martinist Soc., Ancient Mystic Order Rosicrucian, Internat. Soc. Athletes (life). Office: Calif Harvest Tabernacle Ch 1744 E 55th St Los Angeles CA 90058-3835

COOK, DOUGLAS NEILSON, theater educator, producer, artistic director; b. Phoenix, Sept. 22, 1929; s. Neil Estes and Louise Y. (Wood) C.; m. Joan Stafford Buechner, Aug. 11, 1956; children: John Richard, Peter Neilson, Stephen Barton. Student, Phoenix Coll., 1948-49, U. Chgo., 1949-50, UCLA, 1950-51, Los Angeles Art Inst., 1948; B.F.A., U. Ariz., 1953; M.A., Stanford U., 1955; postgrad., Lester Polakov Studio Stage Design, 1966-67. Instr. San Mateo (Calif.) Coll., 1955-57, Nat. Music Camp, Interlochen, Mich., 1961; asst. prof. drama U. Calif., Riverside, 1957-66; assoc. prof., chair theatre dept. U. Calif., 1967-70; head dept. Pa. State U., University Park, 1970-88, sr. prof. theatre arts, 1988-92; prof. emeritus Pa. State U., 1992—; prodr., artistic dir. Utah Shakespearean Festival, Cedar City. Actor Corral Theatre, Tucson, 1952-53, Orleans (Mass.) Arena Theatre, 1953; dir., designer Palo Alto (Calif.) Community Theatre, 1954, Peninsula Children's Theatre, 1956-57; assoc. producer Utah Shakespearean Festival, Cedar City, 1964-90, producing artistic dir., 1990—; producer Pa. State Festival Theatre, State College, 1970-85, The Nat. Wagon Train Show, 1975-76. Instl. rep. Juniata Valley council Boy Scouts Am., 1973-77; bd. dirs. Central Pa. Festival Arts, 1970-75, 84-87, v.p., 1984-86; bd. dirs. Nat. theatre Conf., 1980-90, v.p. 1983-85, pres. 1987-88. Recipient disting. alumni award U. Ariz., 1990; named to Coll. of Fellows of the Am. Theatre, 1994. Mem. AAUP, Shakespeare Theatre Assn. Am. (v.p. 1990-92, pres. 1993-94), Nat. Assn. Schs. Theatre, Am. Theatre Assn. (bd. dirs. 1977-86, exec. com. 1979-80, pres. 1984-85), U.S. Inst. Theatre Tech., Am. Soc. Theatre Rsch., Univ. Resident Theatre Assn. (bd. dirs. 1970-88, v.p. 1975-79, pres. 1979-83), Theatre Assn. Pa. (bd. dirs. 1972-76). Home: PO Box 10194 Phoenix AZ 85064-0194 Office: Utah Shakespearean Festival 351 W Center St Cedar City UT 84720-2470*

COOK, GARY MORRIS, energy corporation executive; b. Lincoln, Nebr., Apr. 11, 1942; s. Eugene E. and Mary Margaret (Morris) C.; m. Diane Grafe, Sept. 3, 1966 (div. 1989); children: Christian M., Lauren S. BA in Econs. with honors, Wesleyan U., 1964; JD (hon.), Harvard U., 1967. Mgmt. cons. McKinsey & Co. Inc., N.Y.C., 1967-70; spl. asst. to sec., dep. asst. sec. HEW, Washington, 1970-72; dep. asst. sec., acting dir. Bur. Domestic Commerce, Dept. Commerce, Washington, 1972-74; sr. v.p. Agrico Chem. Co., Tulsa, 1974-78; chmn. Trend Constrn. Corp., Tulsa and Oklahoma City, 1978-82; pres., chief operating officer Barringer Resources Inc., Golden, Colo., 1983-84; mng. dir. Gary M. Cook Interests., Denver, 1980—; mng. ptnr. Kimbrel & Cook Inc., Tulsa and Denver, 1985—; pres. chief exec. officer, dir. Kimce Energy Corp., Dallas, Denver, 1987—; vice-chmn. OECD Industry Com., Paris 1973-74. Contbr. articles to profl. jours. Mem. Coun. on Fgn. Rels. Clubs: Sankaty Golf (bd. dirs 1982), Sankaty Casino (Nantucket); Harvard (N.Y.); Univ. (Washington), Denver. Avocations: skiing, windsurfing, golf. Office: Cook & Co 170 Marion St Ste 200 Denver CO 80218-3926

COOK, GLEN ANDRÉ, lawyer; b. Oakland, Calif., Dec. 31, 1954; s. Curtis Clifton and Mary Lynn (Bostick) C.; m. Melody Waters, Apr. 19, 1980; children: Glen Jr., Sarah, Benjamin, Mary Katherine. BA, U. Okla., 1978; JD, Brigham Young U., 1982; diploma, Nat. Inst. Trial Advocacy, 1991. Bar: Utah 1982, U.S. Dist. Ct. Utah 1982, U.S. Ct. Claims 1991, Ct. Appeals for the Armed Forces 1998. Staff atty. Social Security Adminstrn., Phoenix, 1985-87; trial counsel Salt Lake Legal Def. Assn., Salt Lake City, 1987-88; asst. city prosecutor Salt Lake City, 1988-90, pvt. practice, 1990—; mem. Cook Skeen & Robinson LLC, Salt Lake City, 1997—; pro-tem judge 3rd dist. ct. Small Claims Divsn., Salt Lake City, 1988—; examiner Utah State Bar, 1992—; mem. bd. editors Utah Bar Jour., 1990—. Author: (with others) Summary of Utah Corporate Law, 1983; editor Jour. Legal Studies, 1981-82; contbr.: Utah Women and the Law, 1991, Navy Legal Assistance Handbook, 1991. Bd. dirs. Salt Lake City chpt. NAACP, 1991-96 (Atty. of Yr. 1996). With JAGC USN, 1982-85, comdr. JAGC USNR; dist. counsel USCG Aux., 1995-96. Cortez Ewing fellow, 1976; Internat. Rotary scholar, 1977. Mem. ABA, FBA, ATLA, NACDL, Naval Res. Assn. (life), Utah State Bar (chair mil. law sect. 1993), Res. Officers Assn. (life), Navy League (life), U.S. Naval Inst. (life), Masonic Youth Found. Utah (bd. dirs. 1995—), Am. Legion (life), Masons, Ind. Order of Foresters, Noble Soc. of Celts, Philatethes Soc. (life), Niadh Nask, Heraldry Soc., Venerable Order of St. John, Sons of Confederate Vets., Mil. Order of World Wars, Continental Soc. Sons of Indian Wars, Order of First World War, Utah Scottish Soc. (life), St. Andrews Soc. Utah. Mem. LDS Ch.

COOK, JENIK ESTERM, artist, educator; b. Rezaieh, Iran, July 7, 1940; came to U.S., 1964; d. Sameual Amijon and Nanajan (Amreh Sarkissian) Simonian; m. Carrol Ross Cook, Sept. 28, 1961; children: Fiona Gitana Cook Anderson, Herold H. Studied with Hossein Delrish, Iran, 1968-70; studied with Barbara Lae, Scotland, 1970-78; studied with Chalita Robinson, 1981-87, studied with Jake Lee, 1987-90, studied with Dr. Alex Vilumsons, 1988-94. Tchr. art. One-woman shows include Pacific Design Ctr., L.A., 1996, Orlando Gallery, 1997, 98; exhibited in groups shows at Orlando Gallery, 1998, L.A. Conv. Ctr., 1998. Rheinfelden (Germany) Town Hall, 1998, Gallery Merkel, Grenzack, Germany, 1998, L.A. Art Expo, 1998. Office: Everywoman's Village 5650 Sepulveda Blvd Van Nuys CA 91411

COOK, KAY ELLEN, remedial programs coordinator; b. Wenatchee, Wash., Sept. 13, 1942; d. Leonard Melius and Ardys Darlene (McMillan) Erickson; m. Terry Joseph Cook, June 15, 1963; children: Paul Erickson, Joseph Douglas. BA in Edn. and Social Studies, Wash. State U., 1964; MA in Reading, Ctrl. Wash. U., 1975, prin. cert., 1985. Tchr. Selah (Wash.) Schs., 1960-62, West Valley Schs., Yakima, Wash., 1970-79; remedial programs coord. West Valley Schs., Yakima, 1979—. Mem. ASCD, Wash. Orgn. Reading Devel., Internat. Reading Assn., Alpha Delta Kappa. Avocations: golf, gardening, handicrafts. Office: West Valley Schs Wide Hollow Elem 1000 S 72nd Ave Yakima WA 98908-1857

COOK, LYLE EDWARDS, retired fund raising executive, consultant; b. Astoria, Oreg., Aug. 19, 1918; s. Courtney Carson and Fanchon (Edwards) C.; m. Olive Freeman, Dec. 28, 1940; children: James Michael (dec.), Ellen Anita Cook Otto, Mary Lucinda Cook Vaage, Jane Victoria. A.B. in History, Stanford U., 1940, postgrad., 1940-41. Instr. history Yuba Jr. Coll., Marysville, Calif., 1941-42; methods analyst Lockheed Aircraft Corp., 1942-45; investment broker Quincy Cass Assocs., Los Angeles, 1945-49; mem. staff Stanford U., 1949-66, asso. dean Sch. Medicine, 1958-65; sr. staff mem. Lester Gorsline Assos., Belvedere, Calif., 1966-72, v.p., 1967-70, exec. v.p., 1970-72; v.p. univ. relations U. San Francisco, 1973-75; fund-raising and planning cons., 1975; dir. fund devel. Children's Home Soc. Calif., 1976-78; exec. dir. That Man May See, Inc., San Francisco, 1978-87; co-founder, trustee, chmn. bd. The Fund Raising Sch., 1977-86; spl. cons. NIH, 1960-62. Mem. Marin County Grand Jury, 1987-88. Mem. Nat. Soc. Fund Raising Execs. (bd. dirs. 1976-88, chmn. certification bd. 1988-90, recipient first Nat. Chmn.'s award 1981, named Outstanding Fund Raising Exec. 1987), Stanford Assocs., Stanford Founding Grant Soc. (dir. 1994—), Belvedere Tennis Club, Theta Delta Chi. Democrat. Episcopalian. Home: 25 Greenwood Bay Dr Tiburon CA 94920-2252

COOK, MERRILL A., congressman, explosives industry executive; b. Phila., May 6, 1946; s. Melvin A. and Wanda (Garfield) C.; m. Camille Sanders, Oct. 24, 1969; children: Brian, Alison, Barbara Ann, David, Michelle. BA magna cum laude, U. Utah, 1969; MBA, Harvard U., 1971. Profl. staff cons. Arthur D. Little, Inc., Cambridge, Mass., 1971-73; mng. dir. Cook Assocs., Inc., Salt Lake City, 1973-78; pres. Cook Slurry Co., Salt Lake City, 1978-97; mem. com. on banking and fin., sci. and transp. and infrastructure 105th Congress (now 106th Congress) from 2d Utah dist., 1997—. Patentee in field. Del. Rep. Nat. Conv., Kansas City, Mo., 1976, San Diego, 1996. Mem. Salt Lake City C. of C., Phi Kappa Phi. Mormon. Home: 631 16th Ave Salt Lake City UT 84103-3704 Office: US House of Reps 1431 Longworth HOB Washington DC 20515-4402 also: 125 S State St Ste 2311 Salt Lake City UT 84138-1131*

COOK, PAUL MAXWELL, technology company executive; b. Ridgewood, N.J., BSChemE, MIT, 1947. With Stanford Rsch. Inst., Menlo Park, Calif., 1948-53, Sequoia Process Corp., 1953-56; with Raychem Corp., Menlo Park, Calif., 1957-95, founder, former pres., CEO, until 1990, chmn., bd. dirs., until 1995; chmn., CEO CellNet Data Sys., San Carlos, Calif., 1990-94, also bd. dirs.; chmn., bd. dirs. SRI Internat., 1993-98; chmn., CEO DIVA Sys. Corp., Menlo Park, Calif., 1995—. Mem. exec. com. San Francisco Bay Area Coun., 1988-94, chmn., 1990-91. Recipient Nat. Medal Tech., 1988. Mem. NAE, Am. Acad. Sci., Environ. Careers Orgn. (past chmn., bd. trustees), MIT Corp. (life). Office: Diva Sys Corp Bldg 205 333 Ravenswood Ave Menlo Park CA 94025-3453

COOK, ROBERT DONALD, financial service executive; b. Chicago Heights, Ill., Nov. 1, 1929; s. Webster Warren and Gladys (Miner) C.; m. Maxine Jensen, Nov. 11, 1950; children: Carolyn Jean, Robert Donald II. BS in Bus., U. Md., 1956; grad. advanced mgmt. program, Harvard U., 1973. CPA, Md. Audit mgr. Arthur Andersen & Co. (CPAs), Washington, 1956-63; comptroller Peoples Drug Stores, Washington, 1963-68; v.p., controller Booz, Allen & Hamilton, Inc., Chgo., 1968-72; pres. Cookemper Rentals, Inc., Barrington, Ill., 1971-73; controller Esmark, Inc., Chgo., 1973-77; pres., chief operating officer Castle & Cooke, Inc., San Francisco, 1977-86; chmn. R.D. Cook Mgmt. Corp., 1986—; chmn. bd., dir. Yorkshire Foods Inc., 1997—; chmn. bd. dirs. Am. Nursery Products, Inc.; bd. dirs. Redwood Empire Bancorp, PAFCO, Inc.; CEO Tri Valley Growers. Served with USNR, 1948-52. Mem. Inst. CPAs, Fin. Execs. Inst., Beta Alpha Psi. Clubs: Masons (32 deg.), Shriners. Home and Office: RD Cook Mgmt Corp 75 Rolling Hills Rd Belvedere Tiburon CA 94920-1501

COOK, STANLEY JOSEPH, English language educator, poet; b. Spicer, Minn., June 9, 1935; s. William Joseph and Lillie Esther (Feeland) C.; m. Janet Lucille Terry, Oct. 9, 1964 (div. June 1988); children: John Hildon, Laurel Erin; m. Michaela Dianne Higuera, Dec. 18, 1989; 1 step-child, Richard Scott. BA, U. Minn., 1957; MA, U. Utah, 1966, PhD (NDEA fellow), 1969. Project specialist in English, U. Wis., Madison, 1967; instr. English, U. Utah, Salt Lake City, 1968-69; prof. English and fgn. langs. Calif. State Poly. U., Pomona, 1969—; cons. communications. Served with USMCR, 1958-64. NSF grantee, 1966; Calif. State U. and Colls. grantee, 1973-74. Mem. SUBUD, AAUP, NEA, Phi Beta Kappa. Democrat. Roman Catholic. Editor: Language and Human Behavior, 1973, Man Unwept: Visions from the Inner Eye, 1974; author: (with others) The Scope of Grammar: A Study of Modern English, 1980, Cal Poly through 2001: A Continuing Commitment to Excellence, 1987; fieldworker Dictionary of Am. Regional English, 1986—. Home: 1744 N Corona Ave Ontario CA 91764-1236 Office: Calif State Poly U 3801 W Temple Ave Pomona CA 91768-2557

COOK, STEPHEN CHAMPLIN, retired shipping company executive; b. Portland, Oreg., Sept. 20, 1915; s. Frederick Stephen and Mary Louise (Boardman) C.; m. Dorothy White, Oct. 27, 1945 (dec. Sept. 1998); children: Mary H. Cook Goodson, John B., Samuel D., Robert B. (dec.). Student, U. Oreg., 1935-36. Surveyor U.S. Engrs. Corp., Portland, Oreg., 1934-35; dispatcher Pacific Motor Trucking Co., Oakland, Calif., 1937-38; manifest clk. Pacific Truck Express, Portland, 1939; exec. asst. Coastwise Line, San Francisco, 1940-41, mgr. K-Line svc., 1945-56; chartering mgr. Ocean Svc. Inc. subs. Marcona Corp., San Francisco, 1956-75, ret., 1975; cons., San Francisco, 1976-78. Author 1 charter party, 1957. Mem. steering com. Dogwood Festival, Lewiston, Idaho, 1985-92; sec. Asotin County Reps., Clarkston, Wash., 1986-88; adv. bd. Clarkston Pt. Commrs., 1989-92. Lt. USN, 1941-45, PTO. Recipient Pres.'s award Marin (Calif.) coun. Boy Scouts Am., 1977, Order of Merit, 1971, 84, Skillern award Lewis Clark coun., 1982, Silver Beaver award 1987; Lewis-Clark Valley Vol. award, 1987, Youth Corps award Nat. Assn. Svc. and Conservation Corps, 1990, Pres.'s Spl. award Clarkston C. of C., 1983. Mem. VFW, Asotin County Hist. Soc. (hon. life pres. 1982-83, bd. dirs.), Asotin C. of C. (v.p. 1994-95). Republican. Mem. Stand for United Ch. of Christ. Avocations: hiking, camping, stamp collecting.

COOKE, CHRISTOPHER ROBERT, state judge; b. Springfield, Ohio, Dec. 23, 1943; s. Warren and Margaret Louise (Martin) C.; m. Margaret (Nick), July 1, 1970; children—Karen, Anastasia, Nicholas. B.A., Yale U., 1965; J.D., U. Mich., 1968. Bar: Ohio 1968, Alaska 1970, U.S. Dist. Ct. Alaska 1970. Atty., Alaska Legal Services Corp., Anchorage, 1968-71, supervising atty., Bethel, 1971-73; mem. firm Rice, Hoppner & Hedland, Bethel, 1973-76; superior ct. judge State of Alaska, Bethel, 1976-86; ptnr. Hedland, Fleischer, Friedman, Brennan & Cooke, Bethel and Anchorage, 1986—. Composer, singer Chris Cooke's Tundra Music, 1981. Bd. regents U. Alaska-Fairbanks, 1975-77; mem. com. Alaska Humanities Forum, Anchorage, 1979-86; adv. bd. Bethel Sch. Bd., 1982-83. Mem. ABA, Alaska Bar Assn. Home and Office: PO Box 555 Bethel AK 99559-0555*

COOKE, JOHN BYRNE, writer, musician; b. N.Y.C., Oct. 5, 1940; s. Alistair and Ruth (Emerson) C. BA, Harvard U., 1963. Singer, guitarist Charles River Valley Boys, Cambridge, Mass., 1961-67; rd. mgr. Janis Joplin, San Francisco, 1967-70; ind. writer various locales, 1971—; singer, guitarist The Stagecoach Band, Jackson, Wyo., 1982-92. Author: The Snowblind Moon, 1985 (Spur award and Medicine Pipe Bearer's award Western Writers Am. 1986), South of the Border, 1989, The Committee of Vigilance, 1994; contbr. book revs. to Washington Post, N.Y. Times, L.A. Times, Acad. Jours., 1985—; creator, writer (TV series) Outlaws and Lawmen, 1996. Mem. The Authors Guild, Writers Guild Am. West, Western Writers Am. Avocations: skiing, bicycling, swimming. Home: PO Box 7415 Jackson WY 83002-7415 Office: Candace Lake Agy 9200 W Sunset Blvd Los Angeles CA 90069-3502

COOLEY, WES, former congressman; b. L.A., Calif., Mar. 28, 1932; married; 4 children. AA, El Camino C. C.; BS in Bus., U. So. Calif., 1958. Asst. to pres. Hyland Labs. divsn. Baxter Labs. Allergan Pharmaceuticals; asst. to chmn. bd. ICN, divsn. mgr., dir. drug regulatory affairs; v.p. Virateck divsn.; founder, co-owner Rose Labs., Inc., 1981—; mem. Oregon State Senate, 1992-94; congressman 104 Congress from 2nd Oreg. dist., 1994-96; mem. House Com. Agriculture, House Com. Resources, House Com. Veteran Affairs, Subcommittee Gen. Farm Commodities, Subcommittee on Livestock, Dairy and Poultry, Subcommittee on Nat. Pks., Forests and Lands, Subcom. Water and Power Resources. With U.S. Army Spl. Forces, 1952-54. Address: 25550 Walker Rd Bend OR 97701-9323

COOMBE, GEORGE WILLIAM, JR., lawyer, retired banker; b. Kearny, N.J., Oct. 1, 1925; s. George William and Laura (Montgomery) C.; A.B., Rutgers U., 1946; LL.B., Harvard, 1949; m. Marilyn V. Ross, June 4, 1949; children—Susan, Donald William, Nancy. Bar: N.Y. 1950, Mich. 1953, Calif. 1976, U.S. Supr. Ct. Practice in N.Y.C., 1949-53, Detroit, 1953-69; atty., mem. legal-staff Gen. Motors Corp., Detroit, 1953-69, asst. gen. counsel, sec., 1969-75; exec. v.p., gen. counsel Bank of Am., San Francisco, 1975-90; ptnr. Graham and James, San Francisco, 1991-95; sr. fellow Stanford Law Sch., 1995—. Served to lt. USNR, 1942-46. Mem. Am., Mich., Calif., San Francisco, Los Angeles, N.Y.C. bar assns., Phi Beta Kappa, Phi Gamma Delta. Presbyterian. Home: 2190 Broadway St Apt 2E San Francisco CA 94115-1311 Office: Am Arbitration Assn Asia Pacific Ctr 225 Bush St San Francisco CA 94104

COONERTY, NEAL PATRICK, small business owner; b. Santa Maria, Calif., Mar. 17, 1946; s. Kevin and Ann Sophia (McGinley) C.; m. Candy Debra Issenman, July 1, 1971; children: Ryan Emmett, Casey Ann. BA, U. Calif., Berkeley, 1969. Pres. Bookshop Santa Cruz, Calif., 1973—. Mayor City of Santa Cruz, 1992-93, council mem., 1990-94. Mem. Am. Booksellers assn. 9v.p., sec. treas. 1987-94, v.p. 1998—), No. Calif. Booksellers Assn. (pres.). Democrat. Office: Bookshop Santa Cruz 1520 Pacific Ave Santa Cruz CA 95060-3903

COONEY, MIKE, state official; b. Washington, Sept. 3, 1954; s. Gage Rodman and Ruth (Brodie) C.; m. Dee Ann Marie Gribble; children: Ryan Patrick, Adan Cecelia, Colin Thomas. BA in Polit. Sci., U. Mont., 1979. State rep. Mont. Legislature, Helena, 1976-80; exec. asst. U.S. Sen. Max Baucus, Butte, Mont., 1979-82, Washington, 1982-85, Helena, Mont., 1985-89; sec. of state State of Mont., Helena, 1988—. Bd. dirs. YMCA; mem. adv. panel Fed. Clearinghouse. Mem. Nat. Secs. of State (pres.), Nat. Assns. Secs. of State (pres. 1997). Home: PO Box 754 Helena MT 59624-0754 Office: Office Sec of State PO Box 20281 225 E 6th Ave Helena MT 59620-4026*

COOPER, AUSTIN MORRIS, chemist, chemical engineer, consultant, researcher; b. Long Beach, Calif., Feb. 1, 1959; s. Merril Morris and Charlotte Madeline (Wittmer) C. BS in Chemistry with honors, Baylor U., 1981; BSChemE with honors, Tex. Tech U., 1983, MSChemE with honors, 1985. Solar energy researcher U.S. Dept. Energy, Lubbock, Tex., 1983-85; advanced mfg. and process engring. mgr. McDonnell Douglas Space Systems Co., Huntington Beach, Calif., 1986-87, chem.-process line mgr., 1987-89, sr. material and process engr., 1989—. Contbr. articles to profl. jours. Mem. Am. Inst. Chem. Engrs., Am. Chem. Soc., Soc. Advancement of Materials and Process Engrs., Sigma Xi, Omega Chi Epsilon, Kappa Mu Epsilon, Beta Beta Beta.

COOPER, BOBBIE (MINNA LOUISE MORGAN COOPER), volunteer; b. Pierce County, Wash., Nov. 21, 1913; d. William Clarence and Eda (Krause) Morgan; m. Vincent Leon Cooper, Feb. 14, 1936 (div. Oct. 1979); children: Marjorie Suzanne, Nancy Jane, O. Leon. Student, Ariz. State U., Tempe, 1954-57, Grand Canyon U., 1962-63, Phoenix Coll., 1984-87. Supr. Hallmark Cards, Kansas City, Mo., 1930-41; with Iron Lung-Polio Meml. Hosp., Phoenix, 1951-52; ch. and civic vol. Telephone Rsch. & Svcs. Vol., Phoenix, 1952-60, 60-94; music rschr. KOY, 1970-80. Officer Oasis Women's Club, Gen. Fedn. Women's Clubs, Phoenix, 1943-88; chmn. bd. dirs. 21st Century Charter Schs. of Ariz., 1995—. Mem. Valley Innkeepers Assn. Republican. Baptist. Avocations: travel, meditating, cross word puzzles, family.

COOPER, DANIEL S., securities trader, financial services executive; b. N.Y.C., Apr. 9, 1953; s. Bertram Joseph and Jean Rosyleyn C.; m. Graziela Mello Silveira. Student, Naropa Inst., 1978-80, Vajradhatu Seminary, 1979, 84; BFA, U. Colo., 1980, MBA, 1985. Fin. mgr. Vajradhatu, Boulder, Colo., 1977-84; securities dealer Govt. Securities Dealers, N.Y.C., 1985-88, Lik Securities, Denver, 1988-90, TDI, Inc., Denver, 1990-96; pres. The Great Sky, Inc., Boulder, Colo., 1997—; assoc. Maxim Fin. Corp., Boulder, 1997—. Artist: (photography) exhbns. include one man show, 1995, various group shows in western U.S., 1973— and in Denver Art Mus., 1975—. Dir. Namdroling Buddhist Meditation Ctr., Boulder, 1996—. Mem. Shambhala Lodge, (color of the great east 1985), Vajradhatu-Kama Dzong (meditation instr. 1976—). Home and Office: 1605 Pine St Boulder CO 80302-4371

COOPER, GENE ALFRED, finance company executive; b. Bryan, Ohio, Sept. 26, 1936; s. George Wayne and Agnes Anibel (Fisher) C.; B.S., Bowling Green State U., 1958; M.B.A., U. Toledo, 1960; m. Carolyn Marie Bearss, Apr. 14, 1962; children—Steven William, Jeffrey Wayne. Auditor, Arthur Young & Co., Toledo, 1960-64; asst. to controller Princeton (N.J.) U., 1964-67; controller Kenyon Coll., Gambier, Ohio, 1967-69; sr. internal auditor, staff asst. policies and procedures, mgr. corp. reporting, div. controller Westinghouse Electric Corp., 1969-79; v.p., controller Westinghouse Beverage Group, Vernon, Calif., 1979—; grad. asst. U. Toledo, 1959-60; acctg. instr. Bowling Green State U., 1963-64, Rider Coll., 1965-67. Bd. dirs., treas. Wesley Found., Princeton. C.P.A., Ohio, N.J., Pa. Mem. Am. Inst. C.P.A.s, Am. Mgmt. Assn., Nat. Assn. Accts., Am. Acctg. Assn., Ohio Soc. C.P.A.s, Nat. Soft Drink Assn., Sigma Phi Epsilon. Methodist. Home: 3474 Storm Cloud Thousand Oaks CA 91360 Office: 3220 E 26th St Los Angeles CA 90023-4208

COOPER, GINNIE, library director; b. Worthington, Minn., 1945; d. Lawrence D. and Ione C.; m. Richard Bauman, Dec. 1995; 1 child, Daniel Jay. Student, Coll. St. Thomas, U. Wis., Parkside; BA, S.D. State U.; MA in Libr. Sci., U. Minn. Tchr. Flandreau (S.D.) Indian Sch., 1967-68, St. Paul Pub. Schs., 1968-69; br. libr. Wash. County Libr., Lake Elmo, Minn., 1970-71, asst. dir., 1971-75; assoc. adminstr., libr. U. Minn. Med. Sch., Mpls., 1975-77; dir. Kenosha (Wis.) Pub. Libr., 1977-81; county libr. Alameda County (Calif.) Libr., 1981-90; dir. librs. Multnomah County Libr., Portland, Oreg., 1990—. Chair County Mgr. Assn.; county adminstr. Mayor's Exec. Roundtable. Mem. ALA (mem. LAMA, PLA and RASD coms., elected to coun. 1987, 91, mem. legislation com. 1986-90, mem. orgn. com. 1990—), Calif. Libr. Assn. (pres. CIL, 1985, elected to coun. 1986, pres. Calif. County Librs. 1986), Oreg. Libr. Assn., Pub. Libr. Assn. (pres. 1997-98). Office: Multnomah County Libr 205 NE Russell St Portland OR 97212-3708

COOPER, GREGORY M., protective services official. Chief of police Provo, Utah. Office: 48 S 300 W Provo UT 84601-4362*

COOPER, JAMES MELVIN, healthcare executive, consultant; b. Prescott, Ariz., Oct. 29, 1940; s. Audrey Louise Cooper; m. Marlene Kitay, Oct. 29, 1960; children: Jamie Lynn Hill, David Paul. BS in Adminstrn., George

Washington U., 1976, MBA, 1979. Cert. healthcare exec. Enlisted USN, 1959, advanced through grades to capt.; officer-in-charge pers. support detachment Naval Hosp., San Diego, 1979-81; dir. for ambulatory care Naval Hosp., Camp Pendleton, Calif., 1981-83; manpower analyst The Pentagon, Washington, 1983-85; dir. for adminstrn. Naval Med. Clinics, San Diego, 1985-88; exec. officer Naval Hosp., Long Beach, Calif., 1988-91; comdg. officer U.S. Naval Hosp., Naples, Italy, 1991-93; ret. USN, 1993; v.p. Capital Health Svcs., San Diego, 1994-97; treas. Ramona/Julian Health Care Adv. Coun., 1996—. Bd. dirs., chmn. Ramona (Calif.) Food and Clothes Closet, 1995—. Decorated Legion of Merit, Meritorious Svc. medal (3). Fellow Am. Acad. Med. Adminstrs.; mem. Am. Coll. Healthcare Execs. (diplomate), Am. Coll. Managed Care Execs., San Diego Women in Health Adminstrn., Fed. Health Care Execs. Inst. (life), DAV (life), Assn. Med. Svc. Corps Officers (chmn. mentoring com. 1996—), Kiwanis of Ramona (pres. 1996-97), VFW (life). Avocations: jogging, horseback riding, leather tooling. Home: 2148 Cook Pl Ramona CA 92065-3214 Office: Ambulatory Care Cons PO Box 1912 Ramona CA 92065-0925

COOPER, JON HUGH, public television executive; b. Wynnewood, Okla., Aug. 6, 1940; s. John Hughes and Sarah Edna (Ray) C.; m. L. Ilene Batty, Dec. 16, 1961 (div. Jan. 1984); children: Jon Shelton, Geoffrey Harold; m. Patricia Carol Kyle, Jan. 28, 1989; children: Cynthia Lynne Elliott, Jennifer Jon Kyle. BA, Okla. State U., 1962; postgrad., U. Ariz., U. Denver, U. Colo., Denver. Mgmt. positions with Evening Star Broadcasting, Washington and Lynchburg, Va., 1962-67; producer, program mgr., dir. prodn. Sta. KUAT-AM-TV, Tucson, 1967-73; exec. dir. Rocky Mountain Network, Denver, 1973-77; exec. dir. Pacific Mountain Network, Denver, 1977-79, also bd. dirs.; gen. mgr. Sta. KNME-TV, Albuquerque, 1979—; lectr. speech and journalism U. Ariz., 1967-73; mem. interconnection com. PBS, 1983-92, bd. dirs., 1986-92, mem. exec. com., 1988-90, 91-92; bd. dirs. PBS Enterprises and Nat. Datacast, 1990-94; bd. dirs. Pacific Mountain Network Japan Survey Team. Bd. dirs., v.p., pres. Pueblo Los Cerros Homeowners Assn., 1987-88; bd. dirs. Samaritan Counseling Ctr., Albuquerque, 1987, N.Mex. Better Bus. Bur., 1991—; bd. advisors Pub. TV Outreach Alliance, 1992—; mem. N.Mex. Edn. Tech. Coun., 1992-94; chmn. N.Mex. Commn. Pub. Broadcasting, 1992—; mem. steering com. Western Coop. on Ednl. Telecommunications. Named Govt. Bus. Adv. of Year U.S. Hispanic C. of C. Region II, 1990. Mem. Albuquerque Rotary Club.

COOPER, LARRY S., carpet industry consultant; b. Bklyn., June 14, 1957; s. Jack and Evelyn (Weinfeld) C.; m. Tryna Lee Giordano, Dec. 31, 1975; children: Jonathan, Jennifer, Jillian. Student, U. Colo., 1975-78. Cert. master cleaner, sr. level carpet insp. Inst. of Inspection, Cleaning and Restoration. Owner Cooper's Carpet Cleaners, Boulder, Colo., 1975-79; pres. Profl. Cleaning Network, Denver, 1979-97; owner Textiles Cons., Denver, 1986—. Chmn. Broomfield (Colo.) Connection, 1988-90; mayor pro-tem City of Broomfield, 1995-96, mem. city coun., 1996—. Named Cleanfax Man of Yr., Clean Fax Mag., 1990. Mem. Profl. Carpet and Upholstery Cleaners Assn. (pres. 1980-81, 84-86), Internat. Inst. of Carpet and Upholstery Cert. (v.p. 1984-85, pres. 1985-87, chmn. bd. dirs. 1988, chmn. cert. bd. 1990—, hon. dir.). Avocations: snow mobiling, fishing. Office: Textile Cons Inc PO Box 21373 Denver CO 80221-0373

COOPER, ROBERTA, mayor; b. Mar. 18, 1937; m. Jerrel Cooper. BA, MA. Ret. secondary sch. tchr.; mem. Hayward (Calif.) City Coun., 1988-92; elected mayor City of Hayward, 1994—; former mem. Gen. Plan Revision Task Force, dir. League of Calif. Cities. Active Eden (Calif.) Youth Ctr., Literacy Plus, Hayward Edn. Assn. Democrat. Avocations: needlepoint, reading mysteries. Office: Office of Mayor 777 B St Hayward CA 94541-5007

COOPER, SHIRLEY RUTH, artist, illustrator; b. Kansas City, Mo., June 6, 1945; d. Omer and Thelma Ruth (Gunn) Henderson; m. Melvin C. Monk, Aug. 30, 1986; children: Geoffrey Donovan Cooper, Jules Mason Cooper. AA in Comml. Art, Everett (Wash.) C.C., 1973; BA in Human Svcs., Western Wash. U., 1976; BFA in Design and Illustration, Cornish Coll. of the Arts, 1994. Counseling intern Children's Resource Ctr., Snohomish County Mental Health, Everett, 1975-76; tchrs. aide Everett Sch. Dist., 1976-79; home base educator Head Start, Everett, 1983-84; family adv. Snohomish County Head Start, Edmonds, Wash., 1984-86; south dist. dir. Pilchuck Area Coun. Campfire, Everett, 1986-87; family life instr. Everett C.C., 1988-91; pvt. practice artist and illustrator Everett, 1994—. Works exhibited in shows at Gallery North, Edmonds, Everett Ctr. for the Arts, Greater Marysville Artists Guild, 1995, Artsplash '95, 1995, Evergreen State Fair, 1995, Spring Into Monroe, 1996, 97, Greater Marysville Artists Guild, 1996, N.W. Pastel Soc., 1996, Burien Gallery, 1997, Edmonds Arts Festival, 1997, Arts Coun. Snohomish County, 1997, Arts of the Terrace, 1997, others. Vol., gallery com. Snohomish County Arts Coun., Everett, 1994—. Mem. Soc. for Childrens Book Writers and Illustrators, N.W. Pastel Soc., Seattle Women's Caucus for the Arts, Seattle Co-Arts, Sky Valley Art Guild, Gallery North. Avocations: plein air painting, teaching, gardening, reading, writing. Home: 6209 Commercial Ave Everett WA 98203-4053

COOPER, STEVEN JON, health care management consultant, educator; b. Oct. 19, 1941; B.A., U. Calif., Los Angeles, 1966; M.Ed., Loyola U., 1973; PhD Union Sch., 1979; m. Sharon M. Lepack; children: Robin E., Erik S. Ednl. coordinator dept. radiology Mt. Sinai Hosp. Med. Ctr., Chgo., 1969-72; chmn. dept. radiol. scis. U. Health Scis., Chgo. Med. Sch., VA Hosp., North Chicago, 1972-79; v.p. C&S Inc., Denver, 1980-81; pres. Healthcare Mktg. Corp., Denver, 1981-84; corp. officer, exec. v.p. Sharon Cooper Assocs. Ltd., Englewood, Colo., 1984—; cons. HEW; lectr. in field. Pres. bd. dirs. Hospice of St. John. Served with USAF, 1960-64, USAFR, 1964-66. Mem. W.K. Kellogg Found. grantee. Mem. Am. (mem. edn., curriculum review coms., task force), Ill. (chmn. annual meeting 1976, program Midwest conf., 1977) socs. radiol. tech., Coll. Radiol. Scis., Am. Hosp. Radiology Adminstrs. (mem. edn. com., treas. Midwest region, nat. v.p.), AMA (com. on allied health edn. and accreditation), Kiwanis Club of Inverness (charter, pres., lt. gov. divsn. 15 1997-98), Sovereign Order of St. John of Jerusalem, Knights of Malta, Inverness Club (bd. dirs.), Sigma Xi. Author numerous publs. in field. Home: 8522 E Dry Creek Pl Englewood CO 80112-2701 Office: 10 Inverness Dr E Ste 210 Englewood CO 80112-5612

COOPER, WILLIAM CLARK, physician; b. Manila, P.I., June 22, 1912 (father Am. citizen); s. Wibb Earl and Pearl (Herron) C.; MD, U. Va., 1934; MPH magna cum laude, Harvard U., 1958; m. Ethel Katherine Sicha, May 1, 1937; children: Jane Willoughby, William Clark, David Jeremy, Robert Lawrence. Intern, asst. resident U. Hosps., Cleve., 1934-37; commd. asst. surgeon USPHS, 1940, advanced through grades to med. dir., 1952; chief occupational health Field Hqrs., Cin., 1952-57; mem. staff div. occupational health USPHS, Washington, 1957-62, chief div. occupational health, 1962-63; ret., 1963; rsch. physician, prof. occupational health in residence Sch. Pub. Health, U. Calif.-Berkeley, 1963-72; med. cons. AEC, 1964-73; sec.-treas. Tabershaw-Cooper Asso., Inc., 1972-73, v.p., sci. dir., 1973-74; v.p. Equitable Environ. Health Inc., 1974-77; cons. occupational medicine, 1977-94. Served to 1st lt. M.C., U.S. Army, 1937-40. Diplomate Am. Bd. Internal Medicine, Am. Bd. Preventive Medicine, Am. Bd. Indsl. Hygiene. Fellow AAAS, Am. Pub. Health Assn., Am. Coll. Chest Physicians, Am. Coll. Occupational Medicine, Royal Soc. Medicine (London); mem. Internat. Commn. on Occupational Health, Western Occupational Med. Assn., Am. Indsl. Hygiene Assn., Cosmos Club. Contbr. articles to profl. jours. Home: 8315 Terrace Dr El Cerrito CA 94530-3060

COOPER, WILLIAM PATRICK, library assistant; b. Key West, Fla., Mar. 21, 1970; s. George Thomas and Yit Wan (Soon) C. BA, U. Ariz., 1993; postgrad. studies in Libr. Sci., San Jose State U., 1997—. Student tutor Napa (Calif.) Coll., 1994-96; asst. Napa Libr., 1993—; editor Rooknet, Napa, 1997—; advisor Rooknet.com, Napa, 1996—; participant Napa Writer's Conf., 1994. Contbr. poetry and short story to lit. publs. Mem. ALA, Calif. Libr. Assn., U. Ariz. Alumni Assn. Office: Napa Libr 580 Coombs St Napa CA 94559-3396

COOPERSMITH, FREDRIC [illegible] Phillip and Ruth L. (Brown) C.; divorced; children: Lisa, Jeffrey, Steven. BS, NYU, MBA. Cert. life underwriter; cert. fin. planner; chartered fin. cons. Cons. fin. planning Englewood, N.J., 1961—; adj. prof. fin. NYU, Rutgers U.; vis. lectr. in fin. planning Wharton Sch. U. Pa. Contbr. articles to profl. jours. Lt. U.S. Army. Named Man of Yr., Nat. C. of C.; recipient Man in Fin. award Finance Club (N.Y.C.). Mem. Internat. Assn. Fin. Planners, Nat. Council Fin. Planners, Nat. Assn. Estate and Fin. Planners, Duke U. Met. Alumni Club, Princeton Club. Club: NYU (N.Y.C.). Lodge: Masons. Avocations: tennis, music, theater.

COOR, LATTIE FINCH, university president; b. Phoenix, Sept. 26, 1936; s. Lattie F. and Elnora (Witten) C.; m. Ina Fitzhenry, Jan. 18, 1964 (div. 1988); children: William Kendall, Colin Fitzhenry, Farryl MacKenna Witten; m. Elva Wingfield, Dec. 27, 1994. AB with high honors (Phelps Dodge scholar), No. Ariz. U., 1958; MA with honors (Univ. scholar, Universal Match Found. fellow, Carnegie Corp. fellow), Washington U., St. Louis, 1960, PhD, 1964; LLD (hon.), Marlboro Coll., 1977, Am. Coll. Greece, 1982, U. Vt., 1991. Adminstrv. asst. to Gov. Mich., 1961-62; asst. to chancellor Washington U., St. Louis, 1963-67, asst. dean Grad. Sch. Arts and Scis., 1967-69, dir. internat. studies, 1967-69, asst. prof. polit. sci., 1967-76, vice chancellor, 1969-74, univ. vice chancellor, 1974-76; pres. U. Vt., Burlington, 1976-89; prof. public affairs, and pres. Ariz. State U., Tempe, 1990—; cons. HEW; spl. cons. to commr. U.S. Commn. on Edn., 1971-74; chmn. Commn. on Govtl. Rels., Am. Coun. on Edn., 1976-80; dir. New Eng. Bd. Higher Edn., 1976-89; co-chmn. joint com. on health policy Assn. Am. Univs. and Nat. Assn. State Univs. and Land Grant Colls., 1976-89; mem. pres. commn. NCAA, 1984-90, chmn. div. I, 1989; mem. Ariz. State Bd. Edn., 1993-98. Trustee emeritus Am. Coll. Greece. Mem. Nat. Assn. Stae Univs. and Land Grant Colls. (chmn. bd. dirs. 1991-92), New Eng. Assn. Schs. and Colls. (pres. 1981-82), Am. Coun. on Edn. (bd. dirs. 1991-93, chmn. Pacific 10 Conf. 1995-96), Kellogg Commn. on Future of State and Land-Grant Univs. Office: Ariz State U Office of Pres Tempe AZ 85287

COORS, WILLIAM K., brewery executive; b. Golden, Colo., Aug. 11, 1916. BSChemE, Princeton U., 1938, grad. degree in chem. engring., 1939. Pres. Adolph Coors Co., Golden, Colo., from 1956, Chmn. bd., 1970—, also corp. pres. Office: Adolph Coors Co 16000 Table Mountain Pkwy Golden CO 80403-1640

COOVER, DORIS DIMOCK, artist; b. Beaverdam, Wis., Aug. 8, 1917; d. Almon Crowe and Alma Josephine (Johnson) Dimock; m. Francis Merle Coover, Apr. 11, 1945; children: Cheryl, Danelle. Student in Fashion and Design, Woodbury U., 1937. One-woman shows include Chappqua (N.Y.) Pub. Libr., 1964-79, Katonah (N.Y.) Gallery, 1967-72, Briarcliff (N.Y.) Coll., 1969, Silvermine (Conn.) Guild of Artists, 1965-81, Am. Can Corp., Greenwich, Conn., 1971—, Village Gallery at Gallmofry, Croton, N.Y., 1974-81, Manhattan Savs. Bank N.Y.C.-White Plains, 1963-68; gallery artist Virginia Barrett, Chappqua, 1964-98; exhibited in groups shows at Okla. Art Ctr., Oklahoma City, 1959, Tex. Oil Industry, Dallas, 1958, Delgado Mus., New Orleans, 1958, Dallas Mus. art, 1958-59, Westchester Art Soc., White Plaine, N.Y., 1962-74, Silvermine Guild Artists, 1970-81, Crocker Art Mus. Art Auction, 1981-98, Neuberger Mus., Purchase, N.Y., 1985, Sacramento Fine Arts, 1985 and many others; cover artist Sci. and Tech. Mag., 1966; work included in Am. Refs., 1978, Who's Who in Am. Art, 1996-97, Rockport Pubs.-Painting Color, 1997, 98, Sketching and Drawing, 1998. Mem., historian Officers Club, L.A., 1940-45; artist judge No. Westchester chpt. Cancreare, Bedford Village, N.J., 1958. Recipient numerous awards for art. Mem. Nat. Watercolor Soc. (assoc.), Am. Watercolor Soc. (assoc.), Nat. Mus. Woman in Arts (charter), Crocker Art Mem. Republican. Avocations: visiting galleries with friends, reading mysteries, experimenting with art.

COPELAND, ANN (VIRGINIA W. FURTWANGLER), writer, educator; b. Hartford, Conn., Dec. 16, 1932; d. William Michael and Agnes (Bresnahan) Walsh; m. Albert J. Furtwangler, Aug. 17, 1968; children: Thomas Gavin, Andrew Edward. BA, Coll. New Rochelle, 1954; MA, Cath. U. Am., 1959; PhD, Cornell U., 1970; D of Letters (hon.), U. New Brunswick, Canada, 1997. Asst. prof. Mt. Allison U., Sackville, N.B., Can., 1976-77; vis. prof. Linfield Coll., McMinnville, Oreg., 1980-81; vis. fiction writer U. Idaho, Moscow, Idaho, 1986-87, Bemidgi (Idaho) State U., 1987, Wichita (Kans.) State U., 1988; writer in residence Mt. Allison U., Sackville, Canada, 1990-91; prof. english, vis. fiction writer Willamette U., Salem, Oreg., 1996—; workshop conductor Haystack, Portland State, Linfield Coll., New Brunswick, Nova Scotia, Oreg., Idaho. Author: At Peace, 1978, The Back Room, 1979, Earthen Vessels, 1984, The Golden Thread, 1989, Strange Bodies on Strange Shore, 1994, The ABC's of Writing Fiction, 1996, Season of Apples, 1996; contbr. articles to newspapers. Recipient Ingram Merrill award Ingram Merrill Found., N.Y.C., 1990; grantee Canadian Council, 1977, 80, 82, 88; writing fellow Nat. Endowment for the Arts, 1978, 94. Mem. Internat. Women's Writing Guild, Associated Writing Programs, Author's Guild, New Brunswick Writer's Fedn. Avocations: piano. Home: 235 Oak Way NE Salem OR 97301 Office: Willamette Univ 900 State St Salem OR 97301

COPELAND, JOHN HOWARD, communications executive, television producer; b. San Diego, Oct. 13, 1950; s. Glenn H. and Luella Louise (Schmid) C.; m. Shannon Gloria Casey, Nov. 20, 1987. BA, Chapman U., 1973. Asst. to exec. prodr. Evan Lloyd Prodns., London, 1974-76; mem. TV and audio visual staff Chapman U., Orange, Calif., 1977-78; asst. to prodr. Media Prodns., Inc., L.A., 1978-79; post prodn. supr. Rattlesnake Prodns., Inc., L.A., 1979-81, assoc. prodr., 1986-88, prodr., 1988-95; post prodn. supr. Walt Disney Pictures, Burbank, Calif., 1981-82; assoc. prodr. Walt Disney Pictures/Rattlesnake Prodns., Burbank, 1983-85; prodr., exec. v.p. Netter Digital Entertainment Inc., L.A., 1995—, also sec. bd. dirs. prodr. (TV documentary) The Wild West, 1993 (Emmy nomination 1994), (TV show) Babylon 5, 1993-98, (TV movie) Siringo, 1994; co-prodr. (TV pilot) Babylon 5 - The Gathering, 1993; supervising prodr. (TV show) Hypernauts, 1995-96; prodr. (TV movies) Babylon 5: In the Beginning, 1997, Babylon 5: Third Space, Babylon 5: The River og Souls, 1998, Babylon 5: A Call to Arms, Crusade, 1998. Named Alumni of the Yr. Chapman U., Orange, 1996; Recipient Hugo award World Sci. Fiction Soc., 1996, E. Pluribus Unum award Am. Cinema Found., 1997; recipient Hugo award World Sci. Fiction Soc., 1997. Mem. NATAS (Emmy 1994, 95), Dir.'s Guild of Am. Office: Netter Digital Entertainment Inc 5200 Lankershim Blvd Ste 290 North Hollywood CA 91601-3100

COPELAND, LAWRENCE R., construction company executive; b. 1947. Graduate, U. Notre Dame. With Fluor Corp., Irvine, Calif., 1969-93; now pres. Fluor Constructors Internat., Irvine, Calif., 1993—. Office: Fluor Constructors Intl 3353 Michelson Dr Irvine CA 92698-0010*

COPELAND, PHILLIPS JEROME, former academic administrator, former air force officer; b. Oxnard, Calif., Mar. 22, 1921; s. John Charles and Marion Moffatt) C.; student U. So. Calif., 1947-49; BA, U. Denver, 1956, MA, 1958; grad. Air Command and Staff Coll., 1959, Indsl. Coll. Armed Forces, 1964; m. Alice Janette Lusby, Apr. 26, 1942; children: Janette Ann Copeland Bosserman, Nancy Jo Copeland Briner. Commd. 2d lt. USAAF, 1943, advanced through grades to col. USAF, 1964, pilot 8th Air Force, Eng., 1944-45; various flying and staff assignments, 1945-51; chief joint tng. sect. Hdqrs. Airsouth (NATO), Italy, 1952-54; asst. dir. plans and programs USAF Acad., 1955-58; assigned to joint intelligence, Washington, 1959-61; plans officer Cincpac Joint Staff, Hawaii, 1961-63; staff officer, ops. directorate, then team chief Nat. Mil. Command Center, Joint Chiefs Staff, Washington, 1964-67; dir. plans and programs USAF Adv. Group, also adviser to Vietnamese Air Force, Vietnam, 1967-68; prof. aerospace studies U. So. Calif., L.A., 1968-72, exec. asst. to pres., 1972-73, assoc. dir. office internat. programs, 1973-75, dir. adminstrv. services Coll. Continuing Edn., 1975-82, dir. employee relations, 1982-84. Decorated D.F.C., Bronze Star, Air medal with 3 clusters; Medal of Honor (Vietnam). Mem. Air Force Assn., Order of Daedalians. Home: 81 Cypress Way Palos Verdes Peninsula CA 90274-3416

COPELAND, SUZANNE JOHNSON, real estate executive; b. Chgo., Aug. 1; d. John Berger and Eleanor (Dreger) Johnson; m. John Robert Copeland, Aug. 1, 1971 (div. June 1976). Assoc. French Lang. and Culture, Richland [illegible] Dallas, 1971; [illegible] U., Bloomington, 1965. Commercial artist Barney Donley Studio, Inc., Chgo., 1966-69; art dir. Levines Dept. Store, Dallas, 1970-74; creative dir. Titche-Goettinger, Inc., Dallas, 1974-78; catering mgr. Dunfey Hotel, Dallas, 1978-82; regional dir. corp. sales Rayburn Country Resort, Austin, Tex., 1982-84; real estate sales assoc. Henry S. Miller, Dallas, 1984-86; v.p. Exclusive Properties Internat., Inc., Dallas, 1986—; cons. North Tex. Commn., Dallas, 1988. Acquisitions editor: Unser, An American Family Portrait, 1988. Mem. The Rep. Forum, Dallas, 1983-94; vol. Stars for Children, Dallas, 1988, Soc. for Prevention of Cruelty to Animals, Dallas, 1973-92, Preservation of Animal World Soc., 1986-92, Sedona Acad., 1996—, Sedona Humane Soc., 1996—; charter mem. P.M. League Dallas Mus. Art. Mem. Nat. Assn. Realtors, Tex. Assn. Realtors, Greater Dallas Assn. Realtors (com. chmn., Summit award 1984, 85), North Tex. Arabian Horse Club (bd. dirs. 1975-76, Pres.'s award 1978), Dallas Zool. Soc., Humane Soc. Dallas County (v.p. 1973-74), Humane Soc. U.S./Gulf States Humane Edn. Assn. (bd. dirs. 1990-91), Am. Montessori Soc., Delta Phi Delta, Phi Theta Kappa. Lutheran. Avocations: Arabian and thoroughbred horses, scuba diving, equitation instr. Office: Exclusive Properties 325 Wilson Rd Sedona AZ 86336-4814

COPLEY, ED, artist; b. Little Rock, July 4, 1944; s. Hayes and Margie (Wisemore) C.; m. Sally, Aug. 27, 1993; children: Greg, Karen. BA, Cols Coll. Art/Design, 1962; BFA, Famous Artist, Westport, Ohio, 1966. Layout artist Bayer & Co., Columbus, Ohio, 1964-66; illustrator Shaw Barton Advt. Co., Coshocton, Ohio, 1966-70; art dir. Varsity House Inc., Columbus, 1970-72, Rhino Graphics Inc., Columbus, 1972-79, Repo-Graphics Inc., Columbus, 1979-82; art dir., illustrator BAD Mag. Inc., Chandler, Ariz., 1982-86; owner Copley Artworks, Mesa, Ariz., 1986—. Represented in permanent collection Museo Cusarare, Chihuahua, Mex. With U.S. Marine Corps., 1962-64. mem. Am. Soc. Classical Realism, Oil Painters Am., Nat. Sculpture Soc. (colleague). Home: 236 S Noble Mesa AZ 85208-8711 Office: Copley Artworks 435 E Stapley Dr Ste 13 Mesa AZ 85204-2651

COPLEY, HELEN KINNEY, newspaper publisher; b. Cedar Rapids, Iowa, Nov. 28, 1922; d. Fred Everett and Margaret (Casey) Kinney; m. James S. Copley, Aug. 16, 1965 (dec.); 1 child, David Casey. Attended, Hunter Coll., N.Y.C., 1945. Assoc. The Copley Press, Inc., 1952—, chmn. exec. com., chmn. corp., dir., 1973—, chief exec. officer, sr. mgmt. bd., 1974—; chmn. bd. Copley News Svc., San Diego, 1973—; chmn. editorial bd. Union-Tribune Pub. Co., 1976—; pub. The San Diego Union-Tribune, 1973—; bd. dirs. Fox Valley Press., Inc. Chmn. bd., trustee James S. Copley Found., 1973—; life mem. Friends of Internat. Ctr., La. Jolla, Mus. Contemporary Art, San Diego, San Diego Hall of Sci., Scripps Meml. Hosp. Aux., San Diego Opera Assn., Star of India Aux., Zool. Soc. San Diego; mem. La Jolla Town Coun. Inc., San Diego Soc. Natural History, YWCA, San Diego Symphony Assn.; life patroness Makua Aux.; hon. chmn., bd. dirs. Washington Crossing Found.; hon. chmn. San Diego Coun. Literacy. Mem. Inter-Am. Press Assn., Newspaper Assn. Am., Calif. Press Assn., Am. Press Inst., Calif. Newspaper Pubs. Assn., Calif. Press Inst., San Francisco Press Club, L.A. Press Club. Republican. Roman Catholic. Clubs: Aurora (Ill.) Country, Army and Navy (D.C.), Univ. Club San Diego, La Jolla Beach and Tennis, La Jolla Country. Office: Copley Press Inc 7776 Ivanhoe Ave La Jolla CA 92037-4574*

COPMAN, LOUIS, radiologist; b. Phila., Jan. 17, 1934; s. Jacob and Eve (Snyder) C.; m. Avera Schuster, June 8, 1958; children: Mark, Linda. BA, U. Pa., 1955, MD, 1959. Diplomate Am. Bd. Radiology; Nat. Bd. Med. Examiners. Commd. ensign Med. Corps USN, 1958; advanced through grades to capt. M.C. USN, 1975; ret.; asst. chief radiology dept. Naval Hosp., Pensacola, Fla., 1966-69; chief radiology dept. Doctors Hosp., Phila., 1969-73; radiologist Mercer Hosp. Ctr., Trenton, N.J., 1973-75; chmn. radiology dept. Naval Hosp., Phila., 1975-84; chief. radiology dept. Naval Med. Clinic, Pearl Harbor, Hawaii, 1984-89; pvt. practice radiologist Honolulu, 1989-92; cons. Radiology Services, Wilmington, Del., 1978-84, Yardley (Pa.) Radiology, 1979-84. Author: The Cuckold, 1974. Recipient Albert Einstein award in Medicine, U. Pa., 1959. Mem. AMA, Assn. Mil. Surgeons of the U.S., Royal Soc. Medicine, Radiol. Soc. N.Am., Am. Coll. Radiology, Photographic Soc. Am., Sherlock Holmes Soc., Phi Beta Kappa, Alpha Omega Alpha. Avocations: photography, hang-gliding, scuba diving. Home: PO Box 384767 Waikoloa HI 96738-4767 Office: 68-1771 Makanahele Pl Waikoloa HI 96738-5128

COPPERMAN, WILLIAM H., value engineer, consultant; b. Cleve., Dec. 4, 1932; s. Jack Jason and Ruth (Rollnick) C.; m. Rena June Dorn, Dec. 26, 1954; children: Randy Lee, David Marc. BS, Duquesne U., 1954; MBA, U. So. Calif., L.A., 1962; JD, U. San Fernando, 1977. Cert. value specialist. Corp. mgr., value engr. Hughes Aircraft Co., L.A., 1957-89; pres. Copperman Assocs. in Value Engring., Inc., L.A., 1983—; bd. dirs. Miles Value Found., Washington; cert. bd. SAVE, Chgo., 1986-88. Author books, video tape series in value engring.; contbr. articles to profl. jours. Recipient Outstanding Achievement award U.S. Army, 1986, Value Engring. award Purchasing Mag., Washington, 1987, Achievement in Value Engring. U.S. Army, 1977, 78, 79, 80, 82. Mem. SAVE Internat., the Value Soc. (exec. v.p. 1975—). Avocations: computer programming, tennis, golf. Home and Office: Copperman Assocs Value Eng 32 Lincoln Pl Rancho Mirage CA 92270-1970

COPPERSMITH, JO ELLEN, English language educator; b. Carmel, Calif., Aug. 26, 1941; d. Joseph Harold and Helen Marie (Brown) Stangle; m. Jay Don Coppersmith, Jan. 4, 1975; children: Clifford, Leslie, Catherine, Brian, Laura, Dale, Kurt. BA, St. Bonaventure U., 1975, MEd, 1981. Cert. secondary English, N.Y. Adj. prof., English dept. St. Bonaventure U., Allegany, N.Y., 1980-82; adj. prof. Utah Tech. Coll., Orem, 1985-89; asst. prof. Utah Valley C.C., Orem, 1989-93; assoc. prof. Utah Valley C.C., 1994-96, Utah Valley State Coll., Orem, 1996—; writing program coord. Utah Valley State Coll., 1997-99; ednl. cons. Prentice Hall Pubs., Englewood Cliffs, N.J., 1995. Contbr. articles to profl. jours. Citizen activist Utah State Legis., 1998; ch. worker LDS Ch., Orem, 1990—. Mem. NCTE (exec. bd. 1995-96), 2-Yr. Coll. English Tchrs. (exec. office 1995-97), 2-Yr. Coll. English Tchrs. West (nat. rep. 1995-97, membership chmn. 1997—), Utah chpt. Internat. Emily Dickinson Soc. (program chair 1995-96). Avocations: piano, organ, genealogy, rose gardening. Office: Utah Valley State Coll English Dept 1200 S 800 W Orem UT 84058-5900

COPPERSMITH, SAM, lawyer; b. Johnstown, Pa., May 22, 1955; m. Beth Schermer, Aug. 28, 1983; children: Sarah, Benjamin, Louis. AB in Econs. magna cum laude, Harvard U., 1976; JD, Yale Law Sch., 1982. Fgn. svc. officer U.S. Dept. State, Port of Spain, Trinidad, 1977-79; law clk. to Judge William C. Canby Jr. U.S. Ct. Appeals (9th cir.), Phoenix, 1982-83; atty. Sacks, Tierney & Kasen, P.A., Phoenix, 1983-86; asst. to Mayor Terry Goddard City of Phoenix, 1984; atty. Jones, Jury, Short & Mast P.C., Phoenix, 1986-88, Bonnett, Fairbourn & Friedman P.C., Phoenix, 1988-92; mem. 103d Congress from 1st Ariz. Dist., 1993-95; atty. Coppersmith Gordon Schermer Owens & Nelson PLC, 1995—. Former dir., pres. Planned Parenthood Ctrl. and No. Ariz.; former chair City of Phoenix Bd. of Adjustment; former dir. Ariz. Cmty. Svc. Legal Assistance Found., 1986-89; chair Ariz. Dem. Party, 1995-97; trustee Devereux Found., 1997—. Mem. ABA, State Bar of Ariz., State Bar of Calif., Maricopa County Bar Assn. Democrat. Office: Coppersmith Gordon Schermer Owens & Nelson PLC Ste 300 2633 E Indian School Rd Phoenix AZ 85016-6759

COPPOCK, RICHARD MILES, nonprofit association administrator; b. Salem, Ohio, Mar. 17, 1938; s. Guy Lamar and Helen Angeline (Johnston) C.; m. Rita Mae McArtor, June 20, 1961 (div. 1973); 1 child, Carole; m. Trelma Anne Kubacak Hafer, Nov. 21, 1973; children: James, Lori. BS, USAF Acad., 1961; MSME, U. Colo., 1969. Commd. 2d lt. USAF, 1961, advanced through grades to lt. col., 1983, ret., 1983; pres., CEO, Assn. Grads. USAF Acad., Colo., 1983—; also bd. dirs.; bd. dirs. Air Acad. Nat. Bank, Colo.; v.p. Nat. Assns. in Colorado Springs. Decorated DFC (4), Air medal (29); named Outstanding Alumnus Salem H.S., 1980. Mem. Colorado Springs C. of C. (mil. affairs coun. 1985-90), VFW (life), Am. Legion, Air Force Assn., Ret. Officers Assn., Elks. Republican. Methodist. Avocations: music, history. Home: 2513 Mirror Lake Ct Colorado Springs CO 80919-3515 Office: USAF Acad Assn Grads 3116 Academy Dr U S A F Academy CO 80840-4499

[illegible], DAVID DANIEL, marketing professional; b. San Diego, Oct. 1[illegible], 1962; s. Thomas Harry and Joan Catherine (Reuter) C.; m. Irma Elizabeth Aquino, Jan. 14, 1989 (dec. July 1991); children: Catherine May, Corinna Briann, Carston James, Caitlin Kay; m. Corinna Kay Ward, May 6, 1995. AS with honors, Miramar Coll., 1989; honor grad. sheriff acad. basic

tng., Southwestern Coll., 1986. Computer oper. Cubic Data Systems, San Diego, 1981-83, Electronic Data Systems, San Diego, 1983-84; ct. svc. officer San Diego County Marshal, 1985-86, dep. marshal, 1986—; pres. Coram Cons. Group, 1994—; owner franchise Fantastic Sams Hair Salon, 1998. Mediator San Diego Community Mediation Ctr., 1990—; soccer coach Temecula Valley Soccer Assn., dir. referees; mem. nominating com. Outstanding Young Women Am. Awarded Gold medal soccer Ariz. Police Olympics, 1990, 91, Silver medal, 1993, Marksmanship award San Diego Marshal, Outstanding Young Men Am. award, 1989; 2d pl. Mid. Weight San Diego Gold's Gym Classic, 1993, Bronze medal Bodybuilding Calif. Police Olympics, 1994. Mem. Calif. State Marshal's Assn. (dir. on state bd. 1994), San Diego County Marshal's Assn. (parliamentarian 1988, dir. 1989-91, 93-94), San Diego County Marshal's Athletic Fedn. (dir. 1993-95), Nat. Physique Com. (contest judge). Republican. Avocations: golf, baseball, camping, computers, weight lifting. Office: Coram Cons Group 45620 Corte Montril Temecula CA 92592-1206

CORAY, JEFFREY WARREN, assistant principal, instructor; b. Chgo., July 16, 1958; s. Warren George and Rose (Paul) C. Student, U. Calif., Berkeley, 1976-77; BA, Occidental Coll., 1980; MA, Calif. State U., San Bernardino, 1996. Instr. Damien High Sch., La Verne, Calif., 1982-98, dir. student activities, 1983-87, chair social sci. dept., 1986-88, asst. prin. student activities, 1987-88, asst. prin. acad. affairs, instr. social sci., 1988-98; mgr. tech. support and tng., project mgr. Netel Ednl. Systems, Inc., Claremont, Calif., 1998—; cons. advanced placement program N.J. Coll. Bd., 1987-98, exam reader, 1988-98. Mem. Omicron Delta Epsilon, Phi Kappa Phi. Republican. Roman Catholic. Avocations: music, theatre, opera. Home: PO Box 116 La Verne CA 91750-0116 Office: Netel Ednl Systems Inc 250 W 1st St Ste # 346 Claremont CA 91711

CORBETT, GORDON LEROY, minister; b. Melrose, Mass., Dec. 11, 1920; s. Winfield Leroy and Lalia Estey (Fiske) C.; m. Winifred Pickett, Sept. 7, 1946; children: Douglas Leroy, Christine, Patricia, Carolyn. AB, Bates Coll., 1943; MDiv, Yale U., 1948. Ordained to ministry Bapt. Ch., 1948. Pastor Montowese Bapt. Ch., North Haven, Conn., 1948-52; assoc. pastor First Presbyn. Ch., Glen Falls, N.Y., 1952-59; synod exec. Synod of Ky., Lexington, 1959-71; assoc. synod exec. for Alaska, 1971-84; interim synod exec. Synod of Lincoln Trails, Indpls., 1987-88; interim Presbyn. exec. Santa Barbara (Calif.) Presbytery, 1991-92; trustee Appalachian Regional Hosps., Lexington, 1969-72, Sheldon Jackson Coll., Sitka, Alaska, 1972-84; chmn. chaplaincy com. Alaska Christian Conf., 1975-78, Alaska Pipeline Chaplaincy. Author: Thirteen Generations of Descendants of Robert Corbett, who died in Woodstock, Conn., 1695, 1995. Mem. Santa Barbara Presbytery; chmn., bd. dirs. Encina Royale, Inc., 1997-98. Dist. chmn. Rep. Party, Anchorage, 1974-78. 1st lt. USAAF, 1944-45, China. Recipient Christian Citizenship award Sheldon Jackson Coll., 1984. Home: 5940 Encina Rd Apt 1 Goleta CA 93117-2242

CORBETT, JUDITH A., municipal administrator; b. San Francisco, Nov. 26, 1938; d. Ralph Allen and Serena Azalda (Winn) Springer; m. Michael Norman Corbett, Sept. 2, 1961; children: Lisa Michele, Christopher Michael. AB in Microbiology, U. Calif., Davis, 1960, MS in Ecology, 1974. Med. technologist Sierra Vista Hosp., San Luis Obispo, Calif., 1962-64, Marin Med. Labs., San Rafael, Calif., 1964-69, U. Calif., Davis, 1971-79; developer Village Homes, Davis, 1973-78; dir. Solar Cal Local Govt. Commn., Sacramento, 1979-83; exec. dir. Local Govt. Commn., Sacramento, 1983—; cons. Calif. State Legislature, Sacramento, 1983-88. Co-author: Village Homes: Solar House Designs 1979, A Better Place to Live, 1981, Land Use Strategies For More Livable Places, 1991. Mem. adv. bd. Clean Air Ptnrship, Washington, 1995—; bd. dirs. Ctr. for Civic Renewal, Santa Barbara, 1996—, Davis Cable Coop., 1983-85. Recipient Nat. award for edn. Am. Planning Assn., 1997, Award for Planning, Renew Am., 1996; named a Hero for the Planet, Time Mag., 1999. Mem. Congress for the New Urbanism (bd. dirs. 1996—). Avocations: biking, swimming, sailing, skiing. Office: Local Govt Commn 1414 K St Ste 250 Sacramento CA 95814-3929

CORBIN, KRESTINE MARGARET, manufacturing company executive, fashion designer, columnist; b. Reno, Apr. 24, 1937; d. Lawrence Albert and Judie Ellen (Johnston) Dickinson; m. Lee D. Corbin, May 16, 1959 (div. 1982); children: Michelle Marie, Sheri Karin. BS, U. Calif., Davis, 1958. Asst. prof. Bauder Coll., Sacramento, 1974—; columnist Sacramento Bee, 1976-81; owner Creative Sewing Co., Sacramento, 1976—; pres., chief exec. officer Sierra Machinery Inc., Sparks, Nev., 1984, also bd. dirs.; nat. sales and promotion mgr. Westwood Retail Fabrics, N.Y.C., 1985—; bd. dirs. Sierra Pacific Resources, Sierra Pacific Power Co., NEWTRAC; cons. in field. Author: Suede Fabric Sewing Guide, 1973, Creative Sewing Book, 1978, (audio-visual) Fashions in the Making, 1974; producer: (nat. buyers show) Cream of the Cream Collections, 1978—, Style is What You Make It!, 1978-83. Named Exporter of Yr. State of Nev., 1989. Mem. Crocker Art Gallery Assn., 1960-78, Rep. Election Com., Sacramento, 1964, 68; apptd. by Gov. of Nev. to Internat. Program Adv. Com.; elected head Bd. Federal Reserve Bank 12th Dist., 1995—. Mem. Home Economists in Bus., Am. Home Econs. Assn., Internat. Fashion Group, Women's Fashion Fabrics Assn., Nat. Machine Tool Builders Assn. (mem. internat. export com.), Nat. Fluid Power Assn., Nev. World Trade Coun. (bd. dir.), Omicron Nu. Office: Sierra Machinery Inc 1651 Glendale Ave Sparks NV 89431-5912 also: PO Box 435 Reno NV 89504-0435

CORBIN, ROSEMARY MACGOWAN, mayor; b. Santa Cruz, Calif., Apr. 3, 1940; d. Frederick Patrick and Lorena Maude (Parr) MacGowan; m. Douglas Tenny Corbin, Apr. 6, 1968; children: Jeffrey, Diana. BA, San Francisco State U., 1961; MLS, U. Calif., Berkeley, 1966. Libr. Stanford (Calif.) U., 1966-68, Richmond (Calif.) Pub. Libr., 1968-69, Kaiser Found. Health Plan, Oakland, Calif., 1976-81, San Francisco Pub. Libr., 1981-82, U. Calif., Berkeley, 1982-83; mem. coun. City of Richmond, 1985-93, vice mayor, 1986-87, mayor, 1993—; mem. Solid Waste Mgmt. Authority, 1985—, Contra Costa Hazardous Materials Commn., Martinez, Calif., 1987—, San Francisco Bay Conservation and Devel. Commn., 1987—; mem. League of Calif. Cities Environ. Affairs Com., 1994—; mem. energy and environ. com. U.S. Conf. Mayors and Nat. League of Cities, 1993—. Contbr. articles to profl. publs. Mem. LWV, NOW, Nat. League Cities, Nat. Women's Polit. Caucus, U.S. Conf. Mayors, Calif. Libr. Assn., Local Govt. Commn., League Calif. Cities. Democrat. Avocations: reading, hiking, golf, quilting. Home: 114 Crest Ave Richmond CA 94801-4031 Office: Richmond City Hall 2600 Barrett Ave Richmond CA 94804-1654

CORBOY, JAMES MCNALLY, investment banker; b. Erie, Pa., Nov. 3, 1940; s. James Thomas and Dorothy Jane (Schluraff) C.; m. Suzanne Shaver, July 23, 1965; children: Shannon, James McNally. BA, Allegheny Coll., 1962; MBA, U. Colo., 1986. Sales staff Boettcher & Co., Denver, 1964-70; sales staff Blyth Eastman Dillon, Denver and Chgo., 1970-74, William Blair & Co., Chgo., 1974-77; mgr. corp. bond dept. Boettcher & Co., Denver, 1977-79; ptnr. in charge William Blair & Co., Denver, 1979-86; first v.p. Stifel, Nicolaus & Co., Denver, 1986-88; pres., CEO SKB Corboy Inc., Denver, 1988-97, Century Capital Group Inc., 1997—. With USMC, 1962-67. Mem. Nat. Assn. Securities Dealers (bd. arbitrators), Country Club at Castle Pines, Met. Club. Republican. Presbyterian. Home: Castle Pines Village 870 Homestake Ct Castle Rock CO 80104-9081 Office: 6530 S Yosemite St Englewood CO 80111-4906

CORDELL, R. LEWIS, English educator, writer; b. Pasadena, Calif., Nov. 3, 1966; s. Jerry D. and Carolyn E. Cordell. BA, Pt. Loma Nazarene U., 1990, MA, 1994. Tchr. Cajon Valley Union, El Cajon, Calif., 1989-92; English tchr. River Delta Unified, Rio Vista, Calif., 1992-95, Carlsbad (Calif.) Unified, 1995—; advisor associated student body and creative writing club mem. Carlsbad H.S. Author: In Pursuit of a Roadrunner, 1996, The Light and The Crush, 1997, (screenplay) Prodigus, 1997. Mem. NEA, Assn. Calif. Adminstr. Avocations: surfing, walking, writing, reading, traveling.

CORDNER, TOM, advertising executive. Co-chmn. bd., creative dir. Team One Advertising, El Segundo, Calif. Office: Team One Advertising 1960 E Grand Ave El Segundo CA 90245*

CORDOVA, ALEXANDER M., city clerk; b. Phoenix, June 22, 1943; s. Alexander A. and Violet (Moreno) C.; m. Joyce Hendricks, June 12, 1982. Student, Ariz. State U., 1962, Phoenix Coll., 1965. Cert. mcpl. clk. Right of way aid City of Phoenix, 1965-67, right of way agt. I, 1967-70, oper. analyst, 1970-72, election supr., 1974-80, elections and gen. svcs. adminstr., 1980-86; chief dep. city clk. City of Phoenix Mcpl. Employees Assn., 1986—. Mem. Internat. Right of Way Assn., 1975-85, Statewide Election Reform, 1987-88. With USN, 1962-64. Mem. Ariz. Mcpl. Clks., Internat. Inst. Mcpl. Clks., Am. Mgrs. Assn., Internat. Assn. County Recorders, Election Ofcls. and Treas., Ariz. Assn. Election Ofcls. and County Records, Am. Legion. Roman Catholic. Avocations: golf, exercise. Office: City of Phoenix 200 W Washington St Ste 1500 Phoenix AZ 85003-1611

COREY, JO ANN, senior management analyst; b. Methuen, Mass., Jan. 26, 1965; d. Joseph Augustine and Marie Ellen (Dowe) C. BA, Calif. State U., Fullerton, 1987, MPA, 1989. Adminstrv. intern City of Brea, Calif., 1987-90; mgmt. analyst City of Mission Viejo, Calif., 1990-92, sr. mgmt. analyst, 1992—. Mem. Mcpl. Mgmt. Assts. So. Calif. (programming com. 1987—, sec. 1997), Calif. Parks and Recreation Soc., Calif. League of Cities, Phi Alpha Theta. Democrat. Roman Catholic. Avocations: music, concerts, trivia, sports. Office: City of Mission Viejo 25909 Pala Mission Viejo CA 92691-2778

COREY, STUART MERTON, minister; b. Tacoma, Wash., Apr. 20, 1933; s. Harold Marvin and Vera Lydia (Wonderly) C.; m. Laraine Kathryn Ober, May 1, 1956; children: Nathan, Rebecca, MaryBeth. BS, U.S. Naval Postgrad. Sch., 1961, MS, 1965. Ordained to ministry, 1984. Commd. USN, 1955, advanced through ranks to capt., 1977; served in Korea, Vietnam, ret., 1978, Bible tchr., conf. speaker, 1961—; pres., founder Island Ministries, Oak Harbor, Wash., 1979—; owner Corey Oil Co., Oak Harbor, Wash., 1978—. Adv. coun. Coupeville (Wash.) Pub. Sch., 1982-83; mem. Econ. Devel. Coun., Island County, Wash., 1984-85. With USNR, 1950-53. Mem. North Whibey Ministerial Assn., Petroleum Marketers Assn., Aircraft Pilots & Owners Assn. Home: 431 S Race Rd Coupeville WA 98239-9536 Office: Island Ministries 3124 300th Ave E Oak Harbor WA 98277-3020

CORIDEN, MICHAEL WARNER, lawyer, consultant; b. Sioux City, Iowa, June 3, 1948; s. Thomas Lou and Patricia (Warner) C.; m. Karen Baldrige, Oct. 12, 1974; children: Courtney Anne, Torrey Erin, Shannon Marielle. B of Gen. Studies, U. Iowa, 1971; postgrad., Inst. Internat. & Compar. Law, Paris, 1973; JD, Creighton U., 1974; MBA, U. Denver, 1983. Bar: Iowa 1974, Nebr. 1974, U.S. Tax Ct. 1974, U.S. Ct. Claims 1976, U.S. Internat. Trade 1976, Colo. 1980, U.S. Supreme Ct. 1980. Atty. Land of Lincoln Legal Assistance Found., Champaign, Ill., 1974-75; asst. atty. gen. State of Iowa, Des Moines, 1975-77; atty. Peter Kiewit Sons' Inc., Omaha, 1977-79; counsel La. Land and Exploration Co., Lakewood, Colo., 1979-83; gen. counsel Tenneco Minerals Co., Lakewood, 1983-85; pvt. practice law Denver, 1985-88; gen. counsel, sec. CF&I Steel Corp., Pueblo, Colo., 1988-93; gen. counsel CF&I Steel, L.P., Pueblo, 1993—; of counsel LeBouef, Lamb, Greene & MacRae, Denver, 1993-95; atty. pvt. practice, Denver, 1995—; bd. dirs. Pueblo Diversified Industries, Inc., Aspen Lane Ltd., Ctr. Hearing, Speech & Lang.; instsr. Denver Paralegal Inst., 1988. Mem. ABA, Colo. Bar Assn., Am. Corp. Counsel Assn., Colo. Assn. Corp. Counsel, Am. Soc. Corp. Secs. Office: 2289 S Hiwan Dr Evergreen CO 80439-8927

CORKERN, ROBERT J., agricultural products company executive; b. 1944. Graduate, U. Nev., 1966. With Klein Bros., Stockton, Calif., 1971-92; pres. Klein-BergerCo., Stockton, Calif., 1992—. With U.S. Army, 1967-70. Office: Klein-Berger Co PO Box 609 Stockton CA 95201-2625*

CORKUM, BETTY JEAN, foundation administrator, former nurse, author; b. Leominster, Mass., Apr. 8, 1946; d. Stewart William Corkum and Evelyn Claire (Rivard) Mallorey; m. Joseph Guy Alonzo Le Blanc, July 1, 1967 (dec. Jan. 1980); children: Julie Elizabeth, Michelle Denise. BS, Boston Coll., 1971. Nurse, 1971-84, author, poet, 1985-94; humanitarian Corkum Found., Lancaster, Calif., 1990—. Author: Aura of Rain, 1987; poet included in Am. Anthology of Poets, 1990, 93. Co-authored brochure So. Ariz. Spina Bifida Assn., assisted charter, 1987. Recipient for meritorious work for students of Inglewood, Calif. Project Invest award Inglewood Sch. Dist., 1982. Democrat. Jewish. Avocations: reading, collecting seashells, crocheting. Home: 44303 Hardwood Ave Lancaster CA 93534-4334 Address: 13617 Judd St Pacoima CA 91331-2929

CORLESS, DOROTHY ALICE, nurse educator; b. Reno, Nev., May 28, 1943; d. John Ludwig and Vera Leach (Wilson) Adams; children: James Lawrence Jr., Dorothy Adele Carroll. RN, St. Luke's Sch. Nursing, 1964. Clinician, cons., educator, grant author, adminstr. Fresno County Mental Health Dept., 1970-94; pvt. practice mental health nurse Fresno, 1991-94; instr. police sci. State Ctr. Tng. Facility, 1991-94; pvt. practice, mental health con., educator Florence, Oreg., 1994—. Res. asst. officer ARC, Disaster Mental Health Svcs., 1993—. Maj. USAFR, 1972-94. Mem. NAFE, Forensic Mental Health Assn. Calif., Calif. Peace Officer's Assn., Critical Incident Stress Found. Office: 2006 Highway 101 Florence OR 97439-9723

CORLISS, BRYAN CHARLES, journalist; b. Belfair, Wash., Apr. 29, 1964; s. Donald Blaine and Elizabeth Ann (Root) C.; m. Donna Marie Kemp, Nov. 28, 1998. BA in Comm., Wash. State U., 1986. Reporter, news editor, editor Hagadone North Idaho Comm., Priest River/Post Falls, 1986-88; editor Colusa (Calif.) City Sun-Herald, 1988; reporter, news editor The Idahonian, Moscow, 1989-91; reporter Walla Walla (Wash.) Union-Bull., 1992—. Lead reporter (newspaper series) Fear in the Fields, 1989 (Blethen award 1990), This Land is My Land, 1995 (Sigma Delta Chi award 1995). Mem. Soc. Profl. Journalists (William O. Douglas chpt. dir. 1996—). Office: Walla Walla Union Bull PO Box 1358 Walla Walla WA 99362-0306

CORMAN, EUGENE HAROLD, motion picture producer; b. Detroit, Sept. 24, 1927; s. William and Anne (High) C.; m. Nan Chandler Morris, Sept. 4, 1955; children: Todd William, Craig Allan. B.A., Stanford U., 1948. Vice-pres. Music Corp. Am., Beverly Hills, Calif., 1950-57; owner, operator Corman Co., Beverly Hills, 1957—; pres. Penelope Prodn. Inc., Los Angeles, 1965—, Chateau Prodn. Inc., Los Angeles, 1972—; v.p. 20th Century Fox TV, Beverly Hills; exec. v.p. 21st Century Film Corp. of Worldwide Prodn. Producer: The Big Red One, 1978-79, F.I.S.T. 1977-78. Recipient Emmy award for A Woman Called Golda, Cath. Christopher award for A Woman Called Golda. Mem. Acad. Motion Picture Arts and Scis., TV Acad. Arts and Scis., Los Angeles County Mus. Art (patron), Beverly Hills Tennis Club, Theta Delta Chi. Roman Catholic. Office: 20th Century Fox TV PO Box 900 Beverly Hills CA 90213-0900

CORNABY, KAY STERLING, lawyer, former state senator; b. Spanish Fork, Utah, Jan. 14, 1936; s. Sterling A. and Hilda G. C.; m. Linda Rasmussen, July 23, 1965; children: Alyse, Derek, Tara, Heather, Brandon. AB, Brigham Young U., 1960; postgrad. law Heidelberg (Ger.), 1961-63; JD, Harvard U., 1966. Bar: N.Y. 1967, Utah 1969, U.S. Patent and Trademark Office 1967. Assoc. Brumbaugh, Graves, Donahue & Raymond, N.Y.C., 1966-69; ptnr. Mallinckrodt & Cornaby, Salt Lake City, 1969-72; sole practice, Salt Lake City, 1972-85; mem. Utah State Senate, 1977-91, majority leader, 1983-84; shareholder Jones, Waldo, Holbrook & McDonough, Salt Lake City, 1985—; mem. adv. coun. Salt Lake Dist. SBA, 1984-91. Mem. Nat. Commn. on Uniform State Laws, 1988-93; mem. adv. bd. U. Mich. Ctr. For Study Youth Policy, 1990-93, Utah State Jud. Conduct Commn., 1983-91, chmn. 1984-85; bd. dirs. KUED-KUER Pub. TV and Radio, 1982-88, adv. bd. KUED, 1982—; bd. dirs. Salt Lake Conv. and Visitors Bur., 1985—. Mem. New York Bar, Utah Bar, Utah Harvard Alumni Assn. (pres. 1977-79), Harvard U. Law Sch. Alumni Assn. (pres. 1995—). Office: Jones Waldo Holbrook & McDonough 1500 1st Interstate Plz 170 S Main St Salt Lake City UT 84101-1605

CORNELL, ANNIE AIKO, nurse, administrator, retired army officer; b. L.A., Sept. 23, 1954; d. George and Fumiko (Iwai) Okubo; m. Max A. Cornell, Dec. 10, 1990. BSN, U. Md., 1976. RN, Calif. Enlisted U.S. Army, 1972, advanced through grades to maj.; clin. staff nurse surg. ICU U.S. Army, Presidio of San Francisco; clin. head nurse ICU U.S. Army, Seoul, Korea; clin. head nurse gen. medicine ward U.S. Army, Ft. Ord, Calif., chief nursing adminstrn.; ret. U.S. Army, 1992; nursing supr. Home Health Plus; dir. patient svcs. Hollister Vis. Nurses Assn., Calif.; asst. dir. patient svcs. Monterey Vis. Nurses Assn., Calif.; case mgr. supr. Cmty. Hosp. Home Health Svcs., Monterey. Recipient Walter Reed Army Inst. nursing scholarship. Mem. Sigma Theta Tau. Home: 199 Linde Cir Marina CA 93933-2206

CORNIA, IVAN EDWARD, art educator, curriculum supervisor; b. South Weber, Utah, Mar. 12, 1929; s. William Edward and Ada Viola (Harbertson) C.; m. Donna Vee Kendell, Nov. 21, 1950; children: Donette, Ray, Deanne, Janette. BS, Utah State U., 1955, MS in Fine Arts, 1958. Cert. secondary tchr., Utah, cert. gen. adminstr., Utah. Art tchr. Davis H.S., Kaysville, Utah, 1955-60, Clearfield (Utah) H.S., 1960-68; art supr. Davis County Sch. Dist., Farmington, Utah, 168-94; dir. arts and crafts, Davis County, Farmington, Utah, 1958-61; mem. adv. com. Davis dist. gifted/talented program. Co-author: (text book) Art is Elementary, 1976; (text book, student and tchr.'s manuals) Drawing Insight, 1994, Performance Assessment Charts, 1994, Art History Time Line, 1994, Drawing Diagnostic Charts, 1994. With U.S. Army, 1950-52. Recipient Cardon Art award Utah State U., 1955, Official Citation Utah State Senate, 1994. Mem. Nat. Art. Edn. Assn. (life mem., chmn. visual comm. divsn. nat. conv. 1968, coord. innovative programs nat. conv. 1977, Art Educator of Yr. Pacific Region 1982), Utah Art Edn. Assn. (life mem., Art Educator of Yr. 1968). Avocations: painting, gardening, travel. Home: 5608 S 5500 W Hooper UT 84315-9585

CORNISH, LINDA SOWA YOUNG, children's books author and illustrator, educator; b. Woodburn, Oreg., May 14, 1943; d. Cecil Edward and Marian Regina (Nibler) Sowa; m. Edmund Y.W. Young, June 11, 1966 (div. July 1988); children: Laura Young Engelmann, Amy L.H. Young, Kimberly Young Brummund; m. H.T. Cornish, Oct. 6, 1991. BA, U. Portland, 1966; EdM, Temple U., 1968. Tchr. spl. edn. Phila. Sch. System, 1966-69; tchr. elem. and spl. edn. North Clackamas Dist. 12, Milwaukie, Oreg., 1974-92; author, illustrator Dahlia Pub. Co., Hillsboro, Oreg., 1994—. Author, illustrator: Pong and the Birthday Journey, 1984, Pong's Visit, 1994, Pong's Ways, 1995, Bobby's Story: A Family's Struggle with Mental Illness, 1997. Adv. for homeless mentally ill women. Mem. AAUW, ASCD, Assn. for Childhood Edn. Internt., Oreg. Coun. Tchrs. English, Northwest Assn. Book Publishers. Democrat. Methodist. Avocations: watercolor painting, country gospel music, volunteer work with elderly and mentally ill. Home: 1295 SW Brookwood Ave Hillsboro OR 97123-7593 Office: Dahila Pub Co PO Box 1123 Hillsboro OR 97123-1123

CORNWALL, DORA JANE, artist, painter, poet, songwriter; b. Jacksonville, Fla., Aug. 29, 1940; d. Robert Emmet and Evelyn Baltzell (Werner) C.; m. Joel Herbert Kramer, 1963 (div. 1974); children: Lesa Zoe Kramer, Surya Ru Kramer. Student, U. Fla., 1957-59, Jacksonville Mus. Art, 1960. Illustrator: The Passionate Mind, 1974; author: (poetry) A Break in the Clouds, 1993 (Editor's Choice award 1993). Mem. Marin Arts Coun.; mem. Bolinas Mus. Avocations: walking, gardening, yoga, dance, mime (mask movement). Home: PO Box 393 Bolinas CA 94924-0393

CORNWALL, MARIE, sociology educator; b. Salt Lake City, Sept. 21, 1949; d. Stephen LeRoy and Jaclyn (McAllister) C. BA in English, U. Utah, 1971; MS in Sociology, Brigham Young U., 1976; PhD in Sociology, U. Minn., 1985. Rsch. supr. Ch. of Jesus Christ of Latter-Day Saints, Salt Lake City, 1977-79, 82-85; asst. prof. sociology Brigham Young U., Provo, Utah, 1985-90, assoc. prof., 1990-95, prof., 1995—; Belle Spafford vis. prof. Grad. Sch. Social Work U. Utah, Salt Lake City, 1993-94. Mem. editl. bd. Social Forces, 1993-97; contbr. numerous articles to profl. jours. Founding mem. Women for the 21st Century, Salt Lake City, 1996—; active Utah Centennial Celebration Video Prodn., KUED, Salt Lake City, 1995. Recipient Merit award Utah Humanities Coun., 1996, Commendation award Am. Women in Radio and TV, 1996. Mem. Am. Sociol. Assn., Assn. for Study of Religion, Soc. for Sci. Study of Religion (treas. 1995-96, exec. officer 1997—). Mormon/. Office: Brigham Young U Provo UT 84602

CORNYN, JOHN EUGENE, III, management consultant; b. Evanston, Ill., May 5, 1945; s. John Eugene and Virginia Ryder (Shannahan) C.; 1 child, Kelly. B.S. in Hotel and Restaurant Adminstrn., Okla. State U., 1968. Mgr. Indian Trail Restaurant, Winnetka, Ill., 1970-71; employee services mgr. Zenith Corp., Chgo., 1971-72; mgr. Red Lion Corp., Portland, Oreg., 1973; cons. Pannell, Kerr, Forster, Chgo., 1973-75; prin., ptnr. The Cornyn Fasano Group, Portland, 1976—; v.p. Seven Seas, Inc., Winnetka, Ill., 1978—, All Seas, Inc., Winneka, 1980—. Co-author: Noncommercial Foodservice-An Administrator's Handbook, 1994. Served to 1st lt. U.S. Army, 1968-70. Mem. Foodservice Cons. Soc. Internat. (chmn. mgmt. cons. com. 1983—), Inst. Mgmt. Cons. Republican. Club: Portland City. Home: 3350 NE Holladay St Portland OR 97232-2533 Office: The Cornyn Fasano Group 1618 SW 1st Ave Ste 315 Portland OR 97201-5708

CORONA, LUIS, interior designer, floral designer; b. Carapoato, Mex., June 12, 1951; s. Augustine and Dolores (Licea) C. Designer Brady's Interiors, Scottsdale, Ariz., 1982-85; owner, prin. designer Casa Del Encanto Inc., Scottsdale, 1985—. Named Master of the West, Phoenix Home and Garden, 1996. Mem. Am. Soc. Interior Designers (1st pl. design awards 1992, 94, 96, 97). Avocations: gardening, music. Office: Casa Del Encanto 6939 E 1st Ave Scottsdale AZ 85251

COROVIC, MICHAEL M., engineering educator, consultant; b. Valjevo, Yugoslavia, June 19, 1944; came to U.S., 1958; s. Milar and Smilja (Tosic) C.; m. Carole Moore, Nov. 2, 1968 (dec. May 1983); children: Marc, Dana, Christine; m. Maria Mihalak, Mar. 16, 1991; 1 child, Michael. BSEE, NYU, 1965, MSEE, 1968. Engr. Gen. Cable Corp., N.Y.C., 1965-66; asst. prof. Acad. Aeronautics, N.Y.C., 1966-68; prof. Calif. Poly. State U., San Luis Obisbo, 1968—; dir. adv. devel. Sirius Sys. Tech., Scotts Valley, Calif., 1981-82, dir. R&D, Victor Technologies, Scotts Valley, 1982-83; pres. CK Assocs., San Luis Obispo, 1991—. Author 6 textbooks, 8 software products. Named Most Inspirational Prof. student br. IEEE, 1970, 76, 88, 93, 95. Avocation: tennis. Office: Calif Poly State U Dept Elec Engring San Luis Obispo CA 93407

CORPUZ, SHEILA MAE, nurse; b. Honolulu, June 8, 1968; d. Antonio Abunan and Aida (Chan) C. BSN, Loma Linda U., 1990. RN, Calif; cert. neonatal intensive care nurse Nat. Cert. Corp. for Ob.-Gyn. and Neonatal Nursing Spltys. Nursing asst. Loma Linda (Calif.) U. Med. Ctr., 1988, unit sec., 1988-89, RN, 1989—; neonatal transport asst. Loma Linda U. Med. Ctr., 1993—. Mem. Nat. Assn. Neonatal Nurses. Avocations: playing piano, rubber stamping, step aerobics. Home: 1487 Sycamore Ln San Bernardino CA 92408-3698

CORRADINI, DEEDEE, mayor. Student, Drew U., 1961-63; BS, U. Utah, 1965, MS, 1967. Adminstrv. asst. for public info. Utah State Office Rehab. Svcs., 1967-69; cons. Utah State Dept. Community Affairs, 1971-72; media dir., press sec. Wayne Owens for Congress Campaign, 1972; press sec. Rep. Wayne Owens, 1973-74; spl. asst. to N.Y. Congl. Rep. Richard Ottinger, 1975; asst. to pres., dir. community rels. Snowbird Corp., 1975-77; exec. v.p. Bonneville Assocs., Inc., Salt Lake City, 1977-80; pres. Bonneville Assocs., Inc., 1980-89, chmn., CEO, 1989-91; mayor Salt Lake City, 1992—; pres. U.S. Conf. of Mayors, 1998—, mem. unfunded fed. mandates task force, mem. crime and violence task force; chair Mayor's Gang Task Force; mem. interngovtl. policy adv. com. U.S. Trade Rep., 1993-94; mem. transp. and comm. com. Nat. League of Cities, 1993-94. Bd. trustees Intermountain Health Care, 1980-92; bd. dirs., exec. com. Utah Symphony, 1983-92, vice chmn., 1985-88, chmn., 1988-92; dir. Utah chpt. Nat. Conf. Christians and Jews, Inc., 1988; bd. dirs. Salt Lake Olympic Bid Com., 1989—; chmn. image com. Utah Partnership for Edn. and Econ. Devel., 1989-92; co-chair United Way Success by 6 Program; pres. Shelter of the Homeless Com.; active Sundance Inst. Utah Com., 1990-92; disting. bd. fellow So. Utah U., 1991; active numerous other civic orgns. and coms. Mem. Salt Lake Area C. of C. (bd. govs. 1979-81, chmn. City/County/Govt. com. 1976-86). Office: Office of Mayor City Hall 451 S State St Rm 306 Salt Lake City UT 84111-3104

CORREA, E. SHAN, author, editor; b. Spokane, Wash., May 14, 1941; d. Everett Eugene and Ava Pearl (Nolt) Eggers; m. Leslie Herbert Correa, Aug. 31, 1968; children: Leslie Evan, Brandon Paul. Student, Eastern Wash. State Coll., Cheney, 1959-61; BA, U. Wash., 1962; MA, U. Hawaii, 1968. Banker Seattle First Nat. Bank, 1962-66; instr. English and journalism Honolulu C.C., 1967-88; instr. English Hawaii Pacific U., Honolulu, 1988-92; English

lang. editor Media Horizon, Jakarta, Indonesia, 1990—; editor Japan-Am. Jour., Honolulu, 1989—; owner, writing/editing bus.. Correa Creative Enterprises, Honolulu, 1984—; presenter workshops Honolulu Writers Conf., Nat. League Am. Pen Women, Soc. Children's Book Writers and Illustrators, Honolulu, 1978—; judge Hawaii Edn. Assn., PTA Reflections Competitions, Lorrin Tar Gill Competition, 1974—; vol. writer, newsletter editor Hahaione Sch., Honolulu, 1992-95. Author, editor: The Official Proceedings of the First International Symposium of Japan-American Societies, 1996, Temple (1st pl. Nat. League Am. Pen Women biennial lit. competition 1996, 98), The Guitar Man (1st pl. Lorin Tarr Gill Lit. Competition 1994); contbr. to various publs. including Cicada, Japanophile, The Pen Woman, American Poets & Poetry, Honolulu Mag. Legis. aide, writer Hawaii State Rep., 1969-81. Recipient Writer of Yr. award Windward Cmty. Arts Coun., Kaneohe, Hawaii, 1994. Mem. Nat. League Am. Pen Women (state pres. 1986-88, chmn. Writers Conf. 1988, 98, disting. svc. award 1994), Nat. Soc. Arts and Letters, Soc. Children's Book Writers and Illustrators, Hawaii Lit. Arts Coun., Japan-Am. Soc. Hawaii (outstanding lit. achievements award 1993). Avocations: music, reading, cooking, travel. Home and Office: Correa Creative Enterprises 6633 Kii Pl Honolulu HI 96825-1001

CORRICK, DAVID LAWRENCE, radio producer, editor, journalist; b. Redondo Beach, Calif., May 31, 1964; s. Lawrence Rexford Corrick and Eleanora Pizzoruss. BA in History, San Diego State U., 1986. Cert. in transp. of hazardous materials. Pub. affairs officer USAFR, Van Nuys, Calif., 1987-90; logistics officer USAF, Dover and worldwide, Del., 1990-91; traffic mgr. Applied Graphics Tech., Glendale, Calif., 1992-93; co-host cooking show Sta. KIEV, Glendale, Calif., 1994-95; prodr. radio show Paul Wallach Inc., L.A., 1995; art dir. Golden Mean Prodns., L.A., 1995-96; art dir. dept. film and TV, UCLA, 1997—; mem. adv. bd. bd. Heroic Employees of Restaurants Awards, L.A., 1995—. Editor: Paul Wallach Restaurant Guide, 1995—, Dining Out with Style, 1996; food editor Hot Lava Mag., 1994-95; editor, pub.: (book) Lounge Los Angeles, 1993-96 (Magellan award); actor (comedy video short) Night Flight TV, 1991; constrn. coord. (feature film) Isle of Lesbos, 1996, (tv series) Push; contbr. articles to mags. Campaign dir. Nick Pacheco for Sch. Bd., L.A., 1995; activist 50's Coffeeshop Preservation Group, L.A., 1991. Capt. USAFR, 1987-94. Decorated Nat. Def. Svc. medal, 1991. Mem. IATSE, VFW, Air Force Assn. (life), Nat. Hist. Trust for Archtl. Preservation, L.A. Conservancy, St. Jude Hunt and Fish Club (founder), Eagle Rock C. of C. Roman Catholic. Avocations: auto mechanics, cigar smoking, gardening. Office: Guide Publs PO Box 1000 Los Angeles CA 90041

CORRIGAN, MARY KATHRYN, theater educator; b. Mpls., July 11, 1930; d. Arthur Joseph Kolling and Hazel (Pierce) Colp; children: Michael Edward, Timothy Patrick. BA, U. Minn., Mpls., 1965, MA, 1967. Advisor, counselor Coll. Liberal Arts U. Minn., Mpls., 1964-65, instr. dept. theatre, 1966-69, asst. prof. dept. theatre, 1969-73; assoc. prof. dept. theatre Fla. State U., Tallahassee, 1973-75; assoc. prof. dept. theatre U. Calif., San Diego, 1975-89, 92-96, prof. emeritus, 1996—; assoc. dir. U. Calif. Study Ctr. U.K., Ireland, 1989-91; faculty dir. ednl. bd. U.C., San Diego, 97—; faculty dir. Brit. Am. Drama Acad. Balliol Coll., Oxford, England, 87-98; master tchr. Brit. Am. Drama Acad., Balliol Coll., Oxford U., Eng., summers, 1987—, chair undergrad. & intermediate programs midsummer, 1992-97. Actress nat. pub. radio Chopin, 1984, video film Ultrasonography, 1986; author: (with others) The Vocal Vision, 1997. Mem. adv. com. United Ministeries, Mpls., 1968-73, Mpls. Sch. Bd., 1968-72; vol. KPBS Reading Svc.; vol. dir. for Actors Alliance; mediator work with juvenile offenders. Recipient Tozier Found. award, Eng., 1967, Best Actress award Globe Theatre, San Diego, 1979, NEH award Folger Shakespeare Theatre, 1992-93; grantee Rockefeller Found., 1968, McMillan grantee U. Minn., Eng., 1968, U. Calif.-San Diego, 1982-87, NEH grantee Folger Inst., Washington, 1993-94, Stanford U., summer 1994, Creativity LaJolla Conf., 1995, Am. U., Cairo, Egypt, 1996, U. Richmond, Va., 1997, Edn. Abroad Program U. Calif., 1997—. Mem. Am. Theatre Assn. (exec. com., v.p. performance tng. 1984-86), Voice and Speech Theater Assn. (bd. dirs. 1986-89). Democrat. Avocations: hiking, theatre, reading, art. Home: 2645 Gobat Ave San Diego CA 92122-3127 Office: U Calif San Diego Theatre Dept La Jolla CA 92093-0344

CORRIGAN, ROBERT ANTHONY, academic administrator; b. New London, Conn., Apr. 21, 1935; s. Anthony John and Rose Mary (Jengo) C.; m. Joyce D. Mobley, Jan. 12, 1975; children by previous marriage: Kathleen Marie, Anthony John, Robert Anthony; 1 stepdau., Erika Mobley. A.B., Brown U., 1957; M.A., U. Pa., 1959, Ph.D., 1967; LHD (hon.), 1995. Researcher Phila. Hist. Commn., 1957-59; lectr. Am. civilization U. Gothenburg, Sweden, 1959-62, Bryn Mawr Coll., 1962-63, U. Pa., 1963-64; prof. U. Iowa, 1964-73, 75; dean U. Mo., Kansas City, 1973-74; provost U. Md., 1974-79; chancellor U. Mass., Boston, 1979-88; pres. San Francisco State U., 1988—. Author: American Fiction and Verse, 1962, 2d edit., 1970, also articles, revs.; editor: Uncle Tom's Cabin, 1968. Vice chmn. Iowa City Human Rels. Commn., 1970-72, Gov.'s Commn. on Water Quality, 1983-84; mem. Iowa City Charter Commn., 1972-73; chmn. Md. Com. Humanities, 1976-78, Assn. Urban Univs., 1988-92; mem. Howard County Commn. Arts, Md., 1976-79; bd. dirs. John F. Kennedy Libr.; trustee San Francisco Econ. Devel. Corp., 1989-92, Modern Greek Studies Found., Found. of Spain and U.S., Adv. Coun. of Calif. Acad. Scis., Bishop Desmond Tutu South African Refugee Scholarship Fund, Calif. Historical Soc., 1989-92; co-chmn., bd. dirs. Calif. Compact, 1990-93; mem. exec. com. Campus Compact, 1991—, chmn., 1995—; Mayor's Blue Ribbon Commn. on Fiscal Stability, 1994-95; chmn. Pres. Clinton's Steering Com. of Coll. Pres. for Am. Reads and Am. Counts, 1996-97. Smith-Mundt prof., 1959-60; Fulbright lectr., 1960-62; grantee Standard Oil Co. Found., 1968, NEH, 1969-74, Ford Found., 1969, Rockefeller Found., 72-75, Dept. State, 1977; recipient Clarkson Able Collins Jr. Maritime History award, 1956, Pa. Colonial Soc. Essay award, 1958, 59, William Lloyd Garrison award Mass. Ednl. Opportunity Assn., 1987; Disting. Urban Fellow Assn. Urban U., 1992. Mem. San Francisco C. of C. (bd. dirs.), San Francisco World Affairs Coun. (bd. dirs.), Pvt. Industry Coun. (bd. dirs.), Boston World Affairs Coun. (1983-88), Greater Boston C. of C. (v.p. 1987-89), Fulbright Alumni Assn. (bd. dirs. 1978-80), Univ. Club, City Club, World Trade Club, Commonwealth Club (bd. dirs. 1995—), Phi Beta Kappa. Democrat. Office: San Francisco State U 1600 Holloway Ave San Francisco CA 94132-1722

CORRIGAN, WILFRED J., data processing and computer company executive; b. 1938. Divsn. dir. Motorola, Phoenix, 1962-68; pres. Fairchild Camera & Instrument, Sunnyvale, Calif., 1968-80; chmn. bd., CEO LSI Logic Corp., Milpitas, Calif., 1980—, also dir. Office: LSI Logic Corp 1551 Mccarthy Blvd Milpitas CA 95035-7451*

CORRY, CHARLES ELMO, geophysicist, consultant; b. Salt Lake City, May 15, 1938; s. Elmo Leigh Corry and Sylvia Birch; children: Christopher Charles, Matthew Lee. BS in Geology, Utah State U., 1970; MS in Geophysics, U. Utah, 1972; PhD in Geophysics, Tex. A&M U., 1976. Electronic missile checkout GD Convair-Astronautics, San Diego, 1960-64; rsch. assoc. Scripps Inst. Oceanography, La Jolla, Calif., 1965-68, Woods Hole (Mass.) Oceanographic Inst., 1968; mgr. geophys. rsch. AMAX, Golden, Colo., 1977-82; v.p. Nonlinear Analysis, Inc., Bryan, Tex., 1982-84; vis., adj., assoc. prof. geophysics Tex. A&M U., College Station, 1983-87; assoc. prof. geophysics U. Mo., Rolla, 1984-89; coord. world ocean circulation experiment Woods Hole Oceanographic Inst., 1990-95; cons. Golden, Denver, 1995—. Author: Laccoliths, Mechanics of Emplacement and Growth, 1988, Geology of the Solitario, Trans-Pecos Texas, 1990 (award); contbr. articles to profl. jours. and conf. procs., including Trans. Am. Geophys. Union, Jour. Applied Geophysics, others. Cpl., USMC, 1956-59, Calif. Mem. Am. Geophys. Union, Geol. Soc. Am., Soc. Exploration Geophysicists. Buddhist. Achievements include overturning of paradigm that had existed for over 150 years, regarding galvanic current flow in ore bodies; discovery that ore minerals are commonly ferroelectrics and that ore bodies behave as a polarized dielectric medium, or solid plasma, in electrical surveys; development of the controlled source audiomagnetotelluric method for electrical exploration; field and theoretical studies of magmatic intrusions; terrestrial heat flow studies in the North Pacific; coordination of hydrographic program of World Ocean Circulation Experiment. E-mail: ccorry@earthnet.net. Home: 36 S Holman Way Apt 2D Golden CO 80401-5140

CORSINI, RAYMOND JOSEPH, psychologist; b. Rutland, Vt., June 1, 1914; s. Joseph August and Evelyn Carolyn (Lavaggi) C.; m. Kleona Rigney, Oct. 10, 1965; 1 dau., Evelyn Anne. BS, CCNY, 1939, MS in Edn, 1941; PhD, U. Chgo., 1955. Prison psychologist Auburn (N.Y.) Prison, 1941-45, San Quentin Prison, 1945-47, Wis. Prison System, 1947-50; research assoc. U. Chgo., 1955-57; pvt. practice indsl. psychology Alfred Adler Inst., Chgo., 1957-63; assoc. prof. Ill. Inst. Tech., 1964-65, U. Calif. at Berkeley, 1965-66; pvt. practice psychology Honolulu, 1965-89; faculty research affiliate Sch. Pub. Health, U. Hawaii, 1970—; affiliate grad. faculty dept. psychology, U. Hawaii, 1988—; founder, sr. counselor Family Edn. Centers Hawaii, 1966—. Author: Methods of Group Psychotherapy, 1957, Roleplaying in Business and Industry, 1961, Roleplaying in Psychotherapy, 1966, The Family Council, 1974, The Practical Parent, 1975, Role Playing, 1980, Give In or Give Up, 1981, Individual Psychology: Theory and Practice, 1982, Effective Discipline in the Home and the School, 1989, Five Therapists and One Client, 1990, Coping with Your Teenager, 1990; editor: Critical Incidents in Psychotherapy, 1959, Adlerian Family Counseling, 1959, Critical Incidents in Teaching, 1965, Critical Incidents in School Counseling, 1972, Critical Incidents in Nursing, 1973, Current Psychotherapies, 1973, 77, 83, 89, 95, Current Personality Theories, 1978, Great Cases in Psychotherapy, 1979, Alternative Educational System, 1979, Theories of Learning, 1980, Comparative Educational Systems, 1981, Handbook of Innovative Psychotherapies, 1981, Adolescence: The Challenge, Encyclopedia of Psychology, 1984, 2d edit., 1994, Concise Encyclopedia of Psychology, 1987, 2d rev. edit. 1996, Encyclopedia of Aging, 1987, Corsini Dictionary of Psychology. Bd. dirs. Hawaii chpt. John Howard Assn., 1966-68. Recipient James McKeen Cattell award psychology Psychol. Corp., 1944; Sertoma award, 1980. Mem. Am. Psychol. Assn. (Significant Profl. Contbn. award Hawaii chpt. 1985), N.Am. Soc. Adlerian Psychology. Club: Waikiki Yacht (Honolulu). Address: 140 Niuiki Cir Honolulu HI 96821-2349

CORSON, KIMBALL JAY, lawyer; b. Mexico City, Sept. 17, 1941; came to U.S., 1942; s. Harland Jerry and Arleen Elizabeth (Jones) C.; m. Ann Dudley Wood, May 25, 1963 (div. Apr. 1978); 1 child, Claudia Ring; m. Joy Lorann Sligh, June 16, 1979; children: Bryce Manning, Jody Darlene. BA, Wayne State U., 1966; MA, U. Chgo., 1968, JD, 1971. Bar: Ariz. 1972, U.S. Dist. Ct. 1971, U.S. Supreme Ct. 1991. Assoc. Lewis & Roca, Phoenix, 1971-74, ptnr., 1974-90; ptnr. Horne Kaplan & Bistrow, Phoenix, 1990—. Co-author: Document Control: Organization, Management and Production, 1988; co-author: Litigation Support Using Personal Computers, 1989. Co-founder Desert Hills Improvement Assn., Phoenix, 1988—. With U.S. Army, 1961-64. Fellow Woodrow Wilson Found., 1966-67. Mem. ABA (civil practice and procedures com. antitrust sect. 1988—), Ariz. Bar Assn. (spkr. 1991—), Maricipa County Bar Assn., Internat. Trademark Assn. (editl. bd. The Trademark Reporter 1993-94, mem. publs. com. 1995-96, INTA Speaker, Am. Sailing Assn., Phi Beta Kappa. Avocations: music, computers, sailing, photography, first century history. Home: Summit Ranch 35808 N 15th Ave Phoenix AZ 85027-7228 Office: Horne Kaplan & Bistrow 40 N Central Ave Ste 2800 Phoenix AZ 85004-4497

CORTESE, CHARLES FRANKLIN, sociologist, educator, planning consultant; b. Pueblo, Colo., Aug. 31, 1940; s. Charles and Frances (Sichile) C.; m. Marian Jane Archer, Aug. 10, 1963 (div. Mar. 1981); children: Jennifer Cortese Hallam, Elisabeth Archer Cortese; m. Judith Baxter, Oct. 12, 1985. BA, U. Denver, 1962, MA, 1966; PhD, Brown U., 1974. Asst. in sociology Brown U., Providence, R.I., 1968-70; instr. U. Denver, 1971-73, asst. prof., 1973-77, assoc. prof., internship dir., 1977—, dean coll., 1984-89, chmn. dept. sociology, 1993-96; cons. NAS, Washington, 1976, mem. subcom., 1978-79; mem. def. svc. bd. U.S. Dept. Defense, Washington, 1980-81; sr. sociologist Louis Berger and Assocs., Anchorage, 1979-82; mem. def. sci. bd. U.S. Dept. Def., Washington, 1980-81; rsch. sociologist Nat. Park Svc., Washington, 1981-92. Editor: Social Impacts of Energy Development in the West, 1981; assoc. editor Soc. & Nat. Resources, 1992-95; contbr. articles to profl. jours. Founder, officer Washington Park Neighborhood Assn., Denver, 1973-78; cons., vol. Found. Urban & Neighborhood Devel., Denver, 1977-80, So. Ute Indian Tribe, Ignacio, Colo., 1981; mem. natural resources com. Rocky Mt. Arsenal Wildlife Refuge, Denver, 1989-92. Recipient Nat. Inst. Advising/ADA/ Ass. for Coll. Tchg. award, 1989. Fellow Am. Sociol. Assn., Western Social Sci. Assn. (v.p. 1977-78, 82-83), Am. Assn. for Advancement of Core Curriculum (nat. dir. 1990-93); mem. Am. Water Resources Assn., Internat. Assn. Impact Assn., Front Range Fly Fishers (pres. 1990-92). Democrat. Roman Catholic. Avocations: fly fishing, hiking, woodcarving. E-mail: ccortese@du.edu. Fax: 303-871-2020. Home: 3234 S Gregg Ct Denver CO 80210-6943 Office: U Denver 2040 S Race St Denver CO 80210-4308

CORTEZ, XAVIER CÁZARES, artist; b. Yuma, Ariz., Aug. 20, 1966; s. Francisco Noriega and Emma Cazares C. Instr. Amory Ctr. Arts, Pasadena, Calif., 1992; artist, educator Palm Springs Desert Mus., 1994—; guest lectr. Carmalite H.S., L.A., 1991, Hamilton H.S., L.A., 1991, Calif. State U. San Bernadino, U. Calif. Riverside, Coll. of the Desert, Palm Desert, Calif.; vis. artist Santa Monica Mus. Art, Shennondoah Elem. Sch., Santa Monica, Calif., 1992. One-man shows include Java, L.A., 1991, Gorky's, L.A., 1991, Casa Libre, L.A., 1991, Kaos Network, L.A., 1991, Out Gallery, Hollywood, Calif., 1992, Topic Gallery, U.S.C., L.A., 1992, Pik Me Up, L.A., 1992, S. Benay Fine Art, Palm Desert, Calif., 1995, Valerie Miller Fine Art, Palm Desert, Calif., 1995, J. Behman The Gallery, Palm Springs, 1997, Learsi Gallery, Palm Desert, Calif., 1998; group shows include: La Ventana Gallery, L.A., 1992, Park Plz. Hotel, L.A., 1992, Art Gallery, L.A., 1992, Plaza de la Raza, L.A., 1992, Barnsdall Mcpl. Art Park, Hollywood, 1992, Galeria Otravez, L.A., 1992, L.A.C.E., L.A., 1992, Arc Gallery, L.A., 1992, Santa Monica Mus. Art, L.A., 1992, Grove Gallery, La Jolla, Calif., 1993, Galeria Otra Vez, L.A., 1993, Phoenix Art Mus., 1994, Valerie Miller Fine Art, Palm Desert, Calif., 1994, Breeden Gallery, Orange, Calif., 1994, S. Benay Fine Art, Palm Desert, 1995, Riverside Art Mus., Calif., 1995, Laguna Art Mus., Laguna Beach, Calif., 1995, Mex. Fine Arts Ctr., Chgo., 1995, Watts Towers Art Ctr., L.A., 1995, U. Ariz., Tucson, 1995, Amory Ctr. for arts, Pasadena, Calif., 1996, CHCG, Pasadena, 1996, Whiskey Pete's, Stateline, Nev., 1996, Huntington Beach (Calif.) Art Ctr., 1996, Riverside Art Mus., 1997, J. Behman, The Gallery, Palm Springs, 1997, Edward Dean Mus., Cherry Valley, Calif., 1997, Trizec Hahn Commn., Palm Desert, Calif., 1997, City of Palm Springs Art Commn., 1997, Palm Springs Desert Mus., 1997, 98, Cerritos Coll. Art Gallery, Norwalk, Calif., 1997, others. Democrat. Buddhist. Home: 3521 N Conejo Cr San Bernardino CA 92404 Office: Palm Springs Desert Mus 101 N Museum Dr Palm Springs CA 92262-5659

CORTINEZ, VERONICA, literature educator; b. Santiago, Chile, Aug. 27, 1958; came to U.S. 1979; d. Carlos Cortinez and Matilde Romo. Licenciatura en Letras, U. Chile, 1979; MA, U. Ill., Champaign, Ill., 1981, Harvard U., 1983; PhD, Harvard U., 1990. Teaching asst. U. Chile, Santiago, 1977-79, U. Ill., Champaign, 1979-80; teaching fellow Harvard U., 1982-86, instr., 1986-89; assoc. prof. colonial and contemporary Latin Am. lit. UCLA, 1989—; fgn. corres. Caras, Santiago, 1987—. Editorial bd. Mester/Dept. Spanish and Portuguese of UCLA, 1989—; editor Plaza mag., 1981-89, Harvard Rev., 1983-89; contbr. articles to profl. jours. Recipient award for Tchg. Excellence Derek Bok Ctr., Harvard U., 1982, 83, 84, 85, 86, Tchg. prize Romance Lang. Dept., Harvard U., 1986, Disting. Tchg. award UCLA, 1998; Whiting fellow. Mem. Cabot House, Phi Beta Phi. Avocations: reading, classical films, writing. Office: UCLA Dept Spanish and Portuguese 5310 Rolfe Hall Los Angeles CA 90095

CORTRIGHT, INGA ANN, accountant; b. Silver City, N.Mex., Sept. 30, 1949; d. Lester Richard and Claudia Marcella (Huckaby) Lee; m. Russell Joseph Cortright, June 25, 1987. BS in Acctg., Ariz. State U., 1976, MBA, 1978; postgrad., Walden U., 1991—. CPA, Ariz., Tex. Sole practice cert. pub. acctg. Ariz., 1981—; cons. in field. Mem. AICPA, Beta Alpha Psi. Republican. Episcopalian. Avocation: travel. Office: 12630 N 103d Ave Ste 241-O Sun City AZ 85351-3423

CORY, ANGELICA JO, author, spiritual consultant; b. Marshalltown, Iowa, Feb. 28, 1950; d. Douglas Alan and Mary Lou (Brewster) Beckwith; m. Phillip Charles Cory, Feb. 24, 1971 (div. Feb. 1985); children: Shane Douglas, Sean Phillip. BS in BA, U. N.Mex., 1971. Lic. real estate broker, Ariz.; lic. pilot, Ariz. Bookkeeper Goodyear Tires, Inc., Albuquerque, 1968-71; instr., model Barbizon Sch. Modeling, Phoenix, 1972-75; cons., pilot Cory's Gasoline Sta., Inc., Mesa, Ariz., 1975-80; dir., cons. Sunshine Fuels, Mesa, 1980-83; dir. mgmt. and real estate Cimmarron Devel., Phoenix, 1984-86; owner, broker KCB Brokerage, Mesa, 1986-91; owner, dir. Ultimate Practices, Mesa, 1989-91; spiritual cons. Mesa, 1991—. *After her divorce, Angelica raised her two surviving sons while creating a Commercial Real Estate Company, in addition to a Medical Consulting firm both personally owned. In 1991, she withdrew from the corporate world to follow her heart's dream of inspirational writing and consulting those ones whom were choosing to become self-empowered to their hearts' dreams. Angelica, then founded the TARA-ANGELICA FOUNDATION committed to the Enlightenment of Humanity, preserving spiritual integrity through the development of supportive programs for the peace and serenity of mind, body and soul. She continues to write and consult spreading hope and inspiration into the world.* Author: Reflections of Perfections, 1995, Reflections of the Mind, 1995, Reflections of the Heart, 1996, Thoughts to Ponder, A Treasure Chest of Golden Rays of Light, 1998; contbg. composer: (cassette-CD) Light of the World, 1996, (5 cassette-CDs) Sound of Poetry, 1996-98; contbg. author: (poetry) Morning Song, 1996, Best Poems of 1997, 1996-97, Best Poems of 1998, Prisms of Thought, 1997, The Scenic Route, 1997, Sketches of the Soul, 1997; contbr. articles, poetry to profl. jours. Founder Tara-Angelica Found., 1997. Recipient Poet's Choice award, 1997, Nat. Libr. of Poets Internat. Poet of Merit, 1997. Mem. Internat. Soc. Poets (Disting. Mem. 1996—). Avocations: writing, international travel, fixed wing and hot air balloon pilot.

CORY, ROLLAND WAYNE, business administrator; b. Camp Zama, Sagamihira, Japan, Feb. 7, 1957; s. Claude Charles Cory and Kyoko (Narasaki) Reibel; m. Victoria Athena Dale Plasting, Nov. 8, 1980. AS in Transp. and Bus. Adminstrn., Chaffey Coll., 1992. With PR Photography, Fontana, Calif.; safety chmn. United Steelworkers of Am., 1983-88, rec. sec., 1985-88, legis. educator, 1985—, sec., treas., 1995-97. Mem. Nat. Geog. Soc. (cert. 1982), Calif. Turtle and Tortoise Club (treas. Inland Empire chpt. 1990-96, Plaque 1991). Democrat. Avocations: reading, geography, photography, scuba and other water sports, history and anthropology. Office: PR Photography PO Box 976 Fontana CA 92334-0976

CORY, WALLACE NEWELL, state official, civil engineer; b. Olympia, Wash., Mar. 10, 1937; s. Henry Newell and Gladys Evelyn (Nixon) C.; m. Roberta Ruth Matthews, July 4, 1959; children: Steven Newell, Susan Evelyn Cory Carbon. BS in Forestry, Oreg. State U., 1958, BSCE, 1964; MSCE, Stanford U., 1965. Registered profl. engr., Idaho, Oreg. Asst. projects mgr. CH2 M/Hill, Boise, Idaho, 1965-70; environ. mgr. Boise Cascade Corp., 1970-78, dir. state govt. affairs, 1978-82; dir. indsl. group JUB Engrs., Boise, 1982-84; chief engr. Anchorage Water & Wastewater, 1984-90; dir. pub. works City of Caldwell, Idaho, 1990-92; prin. engr. Montgomery Watson, Pasadena, Calif., 1992-95; adminstr. Idaho Divsn. Environ. Quality, Boise, 1995—. Precinct committeeman Idaho Rep. Com., Boise, 1968-72, region chmn., 1973-77. Capt. USAF, 1958-62. Mem. ASCE, NSPE, Idaho Soc. Profl. Engrs. (pres. 1976-77, Young Engr. of Yr. award 1971), Air Pollution Control Assn. (chmn. Pacific N.W. sect. 1977-78), Idaho Assn. Commerce and Industry (chmn. environ. com. 1974-75). Avocations: hunting, fishing, shooting. Home: 7174 Cascade Dr Boise ID 83704-8632

COSGROVE, CAMERON, insurance executive; b. Arcadia, Calif., July 25, 1957; s. Joseph Patrick Jr. and Marion (Barrons) C.; (div.); children: Christopher Farley, Steven Patrick. BS in Mgmt., Calif. State U., Long Beach, 1980. Asst. v.p. Pacific Life Ins. Co., Newport Beach, 1982—. Co-author city ordnance Regulation of Ozone, Depleting Compounds, 1989-90; contbr. articles to newspaper. Fin. commr. City of Irvine, Calif., 1983-87, planning commr. 1987-88, city councilman, 1988-90; bd. dirs. Irvine Transp. Authority, 1988-90.; founding advisor Irvine Conservancy, advisor, 1986-88, Irvine Infrastructure Authority, 1988-90; founder San Joaquin Marsh Adv. Com., chair 1988-90. Recipient Sea and Sage Audubon Conservation award, 1990. Mem. Life Office Mgmt. Assn. (tech. and mgmt. com. 1990-96). Republican. Avocation: environmentalist. Office: Pacific Life Ins 700 Newport Center Dr Newport Beach CA 92660-6307

COSTA, MICHAEL F., multimedia communications executive; b. N.Y.C., May 10, 1968; s. Nicholas and Sandra (McClure) C. BSBA, U. So. Calif., 1991. Account exec. Bear Stearns & Co., L.A., 1991-93; CEO Vision Digital Comms., Irvine, Calif., 1993-98; v.p. Genesis Intermadia, Costa Mesa, Calif., 1999—; mem. adv. bd. Speedway, Newport Beach, Calif., 1997—. Multiple patents in field. Avocations: sports, scuba diving, auto racing.

COSTA, THOMAS PETER, clergyman, writer, lecturer; b. Mt. Pleasant, Pa., June 21, 1922; s. Louis A. and Carmela (Rega) C. BA in Psychology and Sociology, UCLA, 1955; Doctorate, Religious Sci. Internat., Spokane, Wash., 1984. Ordained to ministry Ch. of Relieioug Sci., 1974. Founder Ch. of Religious Sci., Palm Desert, Calif., 1973, min., 1973—. Author: Excuse Me While I Call God, 1984, Life, Wanna Make Something of It, 1988. Mem. adv. bd. Desert AIDS Project, Palm Springs, 1995—; bd. dirs. Religious Sci. Int., Spokane, 1982-94. Avocations: theatre, golf, walking, piano. Home: 73-040 Shadow Mountain Dr Palm Desert CA 92260 Office: Religious Sci Ch of Desert 45630 Portola Ave Palm Desert CA 92260-4834

COSTA, WALTER HENRY, architect; b. Oakland, Calif., July 2, 1924; s. Walter H.F. and Mamie R. (Dunkle) C.; m. Jane Elisabeth Ledwich, Aug. 28, 1948; 1 dau., Laura. B.A., U. Calif., Berkeley, 1948, M.A., 1949. Designer Mario Corbett (architect), San Francisco, 1947-48, Ernst Born (architect), San Francisco, 1949; draftsman Milton Pflueger, San Francisco, 1950-51; designer Skidmore, Owings & Merrill, San Francisco, 1951-57, participating assoc., then assoc. prtnr., 1957-69, gen. prtnr., 1969-89, ret., 1990. Bd. dirs. East Bay Regional Park Dist., 1977-87, pres., 1984-85; mem. city council, Lafayette, Calif., 1972-76, mayor, 1973. Served with USSNR, 1943-46. Fellow AIA. Clubs: Olympic (San Francisco), Univ. (San Francisco), Lakeview (Oakland, Calif.). Home: 1264 Redwood Ln Lafayette CA 94549-2416 Office: Skidmore Owings & Merrill 333 Bush St Ste 2020 San Francisco CA 94104-2894*

COSTANZO, PATRICK M., construction executive. Sr. v.p., asst. sec. Granite Constrn. Inc., Watsonville, Calif. Office: Granite Construction Inc PO Box 50024 Watsonville CA 95077-5024

COSTEA, ILEANA, manufacturing and automation engineer, educator, consultant, researcher; b. Bucuresti, Romania, May 20, 1947; came to U.S., 1973.; d. Paul and Ana (Ciumetti) Paunescu; m. Nicolas Vincent Costea, Apr. 20, 1973. MArch, Ion Mincu Inst., Bucuresti, 1972; MA in Indsl. Design, UCLA, 1974, PhD in Engring., 1982. Clif teaching asst. UCLA, 1981; scientist ground systems analysis sect. Hughes Aircraft Co., Fullerton, Calif., 1982; lectr. dept. mgmt. sci. Sch. Bus. Adminstrn. Calif. State U., Northridge, 1982-83; cons. CAE Office vehicle engrng. div. Aerospace Corp., El Segundo, Calif., 1984; sr. scientist, cons. Perceptronics, Inc., Woodland Hills, Calif., 1985; asst. prof. dept. civil and indsl. engring. Calif. State U., Northridge, 1983-86; cons. Jet Propulsion Lab. Calif. Inst. Tech., Pasadena, 1986-87, assoc. prof. dept. civil and indsl. engring. and mechanics, 1986-89, prof. dept. civil and indsl. engring. and applied mech., 1989—; vis. prof. U. Calif., Davis, 1980, U. Metz, France, 1989-93, U. Claude Bernard, Lyon, France, U. Metz, U. Catholique de l'Ouest, Angers. France, Inst. Français du Petrole, France, Rueil Malmaison, France, 1989-93, Ecole Centrale de Lille, France, U. Milan, Italy, 1990-91; vis. rschr. Social Sci. Rsch. Inst., U. So. Calif., 1982. Author: Artificial Intelligence/Expert Systems/CAD/CAM and Computer Graphics; contbr. articles to profl. jours.; reviewer for NSF and IEEE Computer jours. Recipient Merit award San Fernando Valley Engrs.' Coun., 1986. Mem. AAAS, IEEE (sec. Systems, Man and Cybernetics), AAUP, AIAA (chair interactive computer graphics tech. com., 1996—), Computer Soc. of IEEE, Nat. Computer Graphics Assn., Assn. for Computing Machinery, Inst. Mgmt. Sci., Ops. Rsch. Soc. Am., Calif. Faculty Assn., Am. Inst. for Decision Scis., Women in Sci. and Engring., Am. Assn. Artificial Intelligence, European Assn. for Computer Graphics, Am. Inst. Indsl. Engrs., Computer and Automated Systems Assn., Soc. Women Engrs., MICAD (internat. org. com., 1985—). Avocations: travel, tennis, swimming, photography. Home: 3651 Terrace View Dr Encino CA 91436-4019 Office: Calif State U 18111 Nordhoff St Northridge CA 91330-0001

COSTELLO, MARCELLE WELLING, marketing consultant; b. Dallas, July 20, 1964; d. Brent Carlson and Vikilee (Norrish) Welling; m. Keith

Conan Costello, Nov. 5, 1994. BA in English with honors, U. Calif., Berkeley, 1986, BA in Mass. Comm. with honors, 1986. Account exec. Murdoch Mags., N.Y.C., 1987-88; sr. account exec., launch team Calif. Mags. Inc., San Francisco, 1988-90; mktg. mgr., launch team Licensing Group Internat., San Francisco, 1990-92; mktg. dir. Barcelino Continental Corp., San Francisco, 1992-94; spl. asst. to dir. Art in Embassies program U.S. Dept. State, San Francisco/Washington, 1994-97; mktg. cons. San Francisco, 1998—. Bd. dirs., pub. rels. mgr. San Francisco Children's Zoo's "Zoo II," San Francisco, 1994-96; pub. rels. mgr. Grace Cathedral, San Francisco, 1993-96; mem., bd. nominee San Francisco Opera's "Bravo" Club, 1995; mem. San Francisco Ballet's "Encore" Club, 1994-97, Women Make a Difference, San Francisco, 1993-94. Mem. Internat. Assn. Bus. Communicators (mgr. membership directory 1994-96, v.p. nominee 1995), Women in Comms., San Francisco Young Collectors. Republican. Episcopalian. Avocations: marketing for non-profit organizations, skiing, reading, family.

COSTERTON, JOHN WILLIAM FISHER, microbiologist; b. Vernon, B.C., Can., July 21, 1934; married, 1955; 4 children. BA, U. B.C., 1955, MA, 1956; PhD in Microbiology, U. Western Ont., Can., 1960. Prof. biology Baring Union Christian Coll., Punjab, India, 1960-62, dean sci., 1963-64; fellow bot. Cambridge (Eng.) U., 1965; prof. assoc. microbiology McGill U., 1966-67, asst. prof., 1968-70; assoc. prof. U. Calgary, Alta., Can., 1970-75, prof. microbiology, 1975-93, indsl. rsch. chair biofilm microbiology, 1985-93; dir. Ctr. Biofilm Engring. Mont. State U., Bozeman, 1993—. Author 2 books on biofilms; contbr. more than 750 articles to profl. jours. Recipient Sir Frederick Haultain prize, 1985, Isaac Walton Killam prize, 1990. Mem. Can. Soc. Microbiology, Am. Soc. Microbiology. Achievements include research in architecture of bacterial cell walls and including extracellular carbohydrate coats; originator of universal biofilm theory in microbiology; thought of as leader in the biofilm concept in engring., medicine, dentistry, and environ. sci. Office: Montana State Univ-Bozeman Ctr Biofilm Engineering 366 ETS Bldg Bozeman MT 59717*

COSTILOW, VIRGINIA KATHERINE, artist, sculptor, poet; b. Soddy, Tenn., Mar. 28, 1942; d. Youldon Chauncy and Frances (Schuman) Howell; children: Christopher, Timothy, Mathew. Student, Pasadena City Coll., UCLA, Mesa Jr. Coll. Graphic designer San Diego. Exhibited in group shows at Bullock's Pasadena Students Exhibit, Escondido Municipal Gallery, Church of the Resurrection, Murrieta Calif. Murals, J.Rod Lowell and Assocs., Annette Reinker, Calloway Winery. Home: Apt R 427 W 4th Ave Apt R Escondido CA 92025-5048

COTCHETT, JOSEPH WINTERS, lawyer, author; b. Chgo., Jan. 6, 1939; s. Joseph Winters and Jean (Renaud) C.; children—Leslie F., Charles P., Rachael E., Quinn Carlyle, Camilla E. B.S. in Engring., Calif. Poly. Coll., 1960; LL.B., U. Calif. Hastings Coll. Law, 1964. Bar: Calif. 1965, D.C. 1980. Ptnr. Cotchett, Pitre & Simon, Burlingame, Calif., 1965—; mem. Calif. Jud. Coun., 1975-77, Calif. Commn. on Jud. Performance, 1985-89, Commn. 2020 Jud. Coun., 1991-94; select com. on jud. retirement, 1992—. Author: (with R. Cartwright) California Products Liability Actions, 1970, (with F. Haight) California Courtroom Evidence, 1972, (with A. Elkind) Federal Courtroom Evidence, 1976, (with Frank Rothman) Persuasive Opening Statements and Closing Arguments, 1988, (with Stephen Pizzo) The Ethics Gap, 1991, (with Gerald Uelmen) California Courtroom Evidence Foundations, 1993; contbr. articles to profl. jours. Chmn. San Mateo County Heart Assn., 1967; pres. San Mateo Boys and Girls Club, 1971; bd. dirs. U. Calif. Hastings Law Sch., 1981-93. With Intelligence Corps, U.S. Army, 1960-61; col. JAGC, USAR, ret. Fellow Am. Bar Found., Am. Bd. Trial Advs., Am. Coll. Trial Lawyers, Internat. Acad. Trial Lawyers, Internat. Soc. of Barristers, Nat. Bd. Trial Advs. (diplomate civil trial adv.), State Bar Calif. (gov. 1972-75). Clubs: Commonwealth, Press (San Francisco). Office: 840 Malcolm Rd Burlingame CA 94010-1401 also: 12100 Wilshire Blvd Ste 1100 Los Angeles CA 90025-7124

COTÉ, RALPH WARREN, JR., mining engineer, nuclear engineer; b. Berkeley, Calif., Oct. 5, 1927; s. Ralph Warren and Clara Maria (Neves) C.; m. Lois Lydia Maddox, Aug. 8, 1950; children: Ralph Warren III, Michele Marie. BSME, N.Mex. Inst. Mining and Tech., 1952. Registered profl. nuclear engr., Calif.; grad. Realtor Inst. Resident engr. Am. Smelting and Refining Co., Page, Idaho, 1952-54; shift boss Bunker Hill Co., Kellogg, Idaho, 1954-57, gen. mine foreman, 1958-60; project engr. Union Carbide Nuclear Co., Grand Junction, Colo., 1957-58; shift supr. GE, Richland, Wash., 1960-63; shift supr. GE, Vallecitos, Calif., 1963-66, maintenance mgr., 1966-67; start-up shift supr. GE, San Jose, Calif., 1967-71; project start-up mgr. Bechtel Power Corp., San Francisco, 1971-89; realtor retirement real estate Prudential Preferred Properties, Sun City West, Ariz. Served to 2d lt. U.S. Army and U.S. N.G., 1946-50. Mem. VFW. Republican. Home: 14610 W Sky Hawk Dr Sun City West AZ 85375-5925 Office: Prudential Perferred Properties 13576 W Camino Del Sol Ste 20 Sun City West AZ 85375-4428

COTE, RICHARD JAMES, pathologist, researcher; b. L.A., May 10, 1954; s. Richard Patrick and Kathrine (Bisbas) C.; m. Anne Louise Foxen, Feb. 8, 1992; children: Nicholas Foxen, Juliet Anne, Grace Elizabeth. BS in Biology, U. Calif., Irvine, 1976, BA in Chemistry, 1976; MD, U. Chgo., 1980. Diplomate Am. Coll. Pathologists. Intern in surgery U. Mich. Hosp., Ann Arbor, 1980-81; rsch. fellow, immunology Meml. Sloan-Kettering Cancer Ctr., N.Y.C., 1981-83; rsch. assoc., immunology Meml. Sloan-Kettering Hosp., N.Y.C., 1983-85, fellow, pathology, 1987-88, chief fellow, pathology, 1988-90; resident, pathology Cornell U. Med. Ctr., N.Y.C., 1985-87; asst. prof., pathology U. So. Calif., L.A., 1990-95, assoc. prof., 1995-99, prof., 1999—; attending pathologist Kenneth Norris Cancer Ctr., L.A., 1990—; dir. genitourinary program U. So. Calif./Norris Cancer Ctr., 1997—; founder, dir. Impath, Inc., N.Y.C., 1987—; scientific dir. Neoprobe Corp., Columbus, Ohio, 1992-97; sci. dir. ChromaVision Med. Sys., Inc., San Juan Capistrano, Calif., 1997—; sci. dir. John Wayne Cancer and Rsch. Inst., Santa Monica, Calif.; mem. numerous nat. and internat. adv. bds. in field. Author: Immunomicroscopy, 1994; editor Modern Surg. Pathology; assoc. editor Applied Immunohistochemistry; contbr. scientific papers to profl. jours., book chpts. Patentee in field. Am. Cancer Soc. fellow, 1988; recipient rsch. grants, awards NIH, ACS, others, 1981—. Mem. Soc. for Basic Urologic Rsch., Internat. Soc. for Hematotherapy, Phi Beta Kappa. Avocations: golf, photography, skiing, writing. Office: U So Calif 1441 Eastlake Ave Los Angeles CA 90033-1048

COTSAKOS, CHRISTOS MICHAEL, internet financial services company executive; b. Paterson, N.J., July 29, 1948; s. Michael John and Lillian (Scoulikas) C.; m. Hannah Batami Fogel, July 1, 1973; 1 child, Suzanne Renee. BA in Communications and Polit. Sci., William Paterson Coll., 1972; MBA, Pepperdine U., 1984. Tour guide Universal Studios, Burbank, Calif., 1973; courier Fed. Express Corp., Burbank, 1973-74; sales rep. Fed. Express Corp., Long Beach, Calif., 1974; sta. mgr. Fed. Express Corp., San Jose, Calif., 1974; we. dist. mgr. Fed. Express Corp., 1974; region engring. mgr. Fed. Express Corp., Denver, 1975; mng. dir. Fed. Express Corp., Chgo., 1975-80; v.p. Fed. Express Corp., Sacramento, Calif., 1980-92; pres., chief operating officer Nielsen, Europe, Middle East, Africa, 1992-93; pres., chief exec. officer Nielsen Internat., 1993-95; pres., co-chief exec. officer, chief operating officer, dir. A.C. Nielsen, Inc., 1995-96; pres., chief exec. officer E*TRADE Group, Inc., Palo Alto, Calif., 1996—; instr. Consumers River Coll., Placerville, Calif., 1985-86; bd. dirs. Airlifeline, Sacramento, Nat. Processing, Inc., Louisville, Forté Software, Inc., Oakland, 4th Comms. Network, San Jose, Datacard, Mpls. Served as sgt. U.S. Army, 1967-70, Vietnam. Decorated Bronze Star, 1967, Purple Heart, 1967. Mem. World Econ Forum (Davos, Switzerland), Sutter Club, Comstock Club. Office: E*TRADE Group Inc 2400 Geng Rd Palo Alto CA 94030*

COTTAM, CALVIN, retired chiropractor, author; b. Salt Lake City, Mar. 28, 1925; s. Nephi Livesay and Edwardena (Parry) C. Grad., Cal Arts (formerly Chouinard Art Inst.), L.A., 1949; MA in Psychology, David Seabury Sch. Psychology, L.A., 1953; D of Chiropractic, Cleve. Coll., L.A., 1965. Co-founder, instr. Found. for Living, Problems Anonymous, 1953-64; radio program co-host Living Today, L.A., 1954-55; practice Calif., New Zealand, 1965-1995; ret., 1995; dir. Inst. for Study of Human Resources, 1984—, security dir. One Inst. U. So. Calif., L.A., 1995—, lectr. in field. Author: Head First for Health, 1952, Fun, How To Take a Vacation Every Day, Living Without Strain, Don't Be Afraid of your Mind, Magic of Meditation; (with Bert M. Anderson) How To Write True To Yourself, 1960; (with Reid Rasmussen) Craniopathy for You and Others, 1975, Cranial/Facial Adjusting Step-by-step, 1985, Illustrated Seminars, 1986, Technique in Pictures, 1987, Secret Sacred Story "Rosetta Stone", 1996, Headaches? Eyesight? Hearing? Breahing? TMJ?, 1997, How to Get Positive in Spite of Negative People and Events, 1997. Tech. sgt. U.S. Army, WWII, Korea. Mem. Nat. Writers League (nat. pres. 1958), David Seabury Sch. Psychology Alumni Assn. (pres. 1955-56), Internat. New Thought Alliance (chair govt. affairs 1957), C. of C., Civil Def. Nat. Vocat. Guidance Assn., Wilshire Ctr., Country Club Park Neighborhood Assn. (dir. info. coun. 1989-95), Prime Timers Sr. Men's Club (founder L.A. chpt.). Avocations: art, philosophy. Office: CORACO 1017 Arlington Ave Los Angeles CA 90019-3513

COTTER, JOHN JOSEPH, management consultant, writer, educator; came to U.S., 1963; Student, Univ. Coll., Dublin, Ireland, 1956-59, Chelsea Coll. Sci. and Tech., 1960-62, UCLA, 1972-75. Rsch. physicist Mullard Ctrl. Rsch. Labs., Sussex, Eng., 1959-63; product design mgr. Huggins Labs., Sunnyvale, Calif., 1963-65; v.p. ops. E & M Labs., Westlake Village, Calif., 1969-72; v.p., gen. mgr. microwave components and sys. divsn. Sterling Electronics Corp., Houston, 1972-75; founding mem. Ctr. for Quality of Working Life, Inst. of Indsl. Rels., UCLA,1975-80; instr. orgn. design Claremont Grad. U.; mem. faculty leadership and mgmt. program and exec. program for scientists and engrs. U. Calif., San Diego; bd. dirs. Ismeca, Sinjinc; presenter univ. seminars at U. Ariz., U. Calif., various campuses, U. Chgo., MIT, Harvard U., U. Mich., Stanford U., others; conf. spkr., workshop presenter, orgns. including AT&T, Boise Cascade, Hewlett-Packard, Nabisco, Sony, U.S. Steel, other cos., profl. assns. including ASTD, Orgn. Devel. Network, IEEE, Indsl. Rels. Rsch. Assn., Soc. Mfg. Engrs., many others; cons. in field. Author: The 20% Solution: Using Rapid Redesign to Create Tomorrow's Organizations Today, 1995; contbr. articles to profl. publs.; guest radio and TV programs; patentee high-speed microwave switching devices. Bd. dirs. Inst. for Advancement of Leadership, U. San Diego; mem. exec. com. H.R. Round Table for Sr. Execs., UCLA. Fax: 619-456-9540. E-mail: cotterassoc@earthlink.net. Home and Office: 7839 Prospect Pl La Jolla CA 92037-3720

COTTER, LAWRENCE RAFFETY, management consultant; b. Albany, Calif., Aug. 13, 1933; s. Malcolm Thompson Cotter and Una Elyse Raffety. AA, U. Calif., Berkeley, 1953, BA in Astronomy, 1956; MS in Bus. Adminstrn., The George Washington U., 1967; PhD in Mgmt. Theory, UCLA, 1977. Commd. 2nd lt. USAF, 1956, advanced through grades to col., 1975, ret., 1982; orbital analyst, network controller Project Space Track USAF, Bedford, Mass., 1958-61; staff scientist Hdqs. N.Am. Air Def. Command, Colorado Springs, Colo., 1962-66, Hdqrs. USAF, Washington, 1967-70; dir. test and deployment DEF. Support program USAF, Los Angeles, 1975-76; commdr. detachment 1 Electronic Systems Div. USAF, Tehran, Iran, 1976-78; system program dir. Electronic Systems div. USAF, Bedford, Mass., 1978-79; dep. commdr. network plans and devel. AF Satellite Control Facility USAF, Sunnyvale, Calif., 1979-82; mgmt. cons. Berkeley, 1982—; adminstrv. asst. Arnold Air Soc., Washington, 1959-72. Co-author: The Arnold Air Soc. Manual, 1956; (computer program) SPACE, 1970; editor: The Arnold Air Soc. Manual 1964-72. Recipient Departmental Citation U. Calif. Berkeley, 1955, Citation of Honor, Arnold Air Soc., 1967. Mem. AF Assn., The Royal AF Club, Beta Gamma Sigma.

COTTRELL-ADKINS, LEONE, opera company director. Artistic dir. Kitsap Opera, Bremerton, Wash.; founder Kitsap Peninsula Opera, 1992. Office: Kitsap Opera PO Box 1071 Bremerton WA 98337*

COUCH, JOHN CHARLES, diversified company executive; b. Bremerton, Wash., May 10, 1939; s. Richard Bailey and Frances Harriet (Gilmore) C. BS in Engring., U. Mich., 1963, MS, 1964; MBA, Stanford U., 1976. With Ingalls Shipbldg. div. Litton Industries, 1967-74; asst. to sr. v.p. engring. and marine ops. Matson Navigation Co. subs. Alexander and Baldwin., San Francisco, 1976-78, v.p., 1978-84, exec. v.p., chief operating officer, 1984, pres., chief operating officer, 1985; pres., chief operating officer Alexander and Baldwin Inc., Honolulu, 1991—; pres., chief exec. officer Alexander and Baldwin, Inc., Honolulu, 1992-95, chmn., pres., CEO, 1995—; bd. dirs. A&B Devel. Co., Calif., A&B Properties, Inc., McBryde Sugar Co., Ltd., Kauai Coffee Co., Inc., WDCI Inc., Calif. and Hawaiian Sugar Co., First Hawaiian Bank, First Hawaiian Inc., Hawaiian Sugar Transp. Co., Inc., A&B Hawaii, Inc., Alexander & Baldwin, Inc., Kukuiula Devel. Co., Inc., Matson Navigation Co., Inc. Mem. Maui Econ. Devel. Bd., 1986—; mem. exec. bd. Aloha coun. Boy Scouts Am., 1986—; bd. dirs. Aloha United Way, 1988, campaign chmn., 1988, chmn. bd. dirs.; bd. dirs. Alexander & Baldwin Found., The Std. Steamship Owners' Protection and Indemnity Assn. (Bermuda) Ltd.; chmn. bd. trustees Bishop Mus., 1997—. Mem. Hawaii Maritime Ctr. (vice-chmn. 1988-89, 97—, chmn. 1990-97), Honolulu Club, Oahu Country Club, Plaza Club, Pacific Club, The Pacific-Union Club. Office: Alexander & Baldwin Inc PO Box 3440 822 Bishop St Honolulu HI 96813-3925

COUCH, ROBERT G., civil engineer; b. Leavenworth, Wash., May 23, 1951; s. Andrew C. and Hazel L. C.; m. Jennifer, Aug. 28, 1971; children: Lawrence, Stephanie. BSCE, Wash. State U., Pullman, 1973. Lic. profl. engr., Wash. Civil engr. U.S. Naval Surface Weapons Lab, Dahlgren, Wash., 1973-75; base civil engr. USAF, Andrews AFB, Md., 1975-79; office engr. U.S. Army Corps of Engrs., Chief Joseph Dam, Wash., 1979-80; project engr. U.S. Army Corps of Engrs., Dworshak Dam, Idaho, 1980-89; chief contract adminstr. U.S. Army Corps of Engrs., Walla Walla, Wash., 1989-97; chief constrn. U.S. Army Corps of Engrs., Portland, Wash., 1997—. Mem. bdlg. com. Christ Luth. Ch., Walla Walla, Wash., 1996. Mem. NRA, Waitsburg Gun Club, Rocky Mountain Elk Found. Lutheran. Avocations: fishing, hunting, hiking. Home: 4412 Gifford Pl Washougal WA 98671-9150 Office: US Army Corps of Engrs 333 SW 1st Ave Portland OR 97204-3440

COUGHENOUR, JOHN CLARE, federal judge; b. Pittsburg, Kans., July 27, 1941; s. Owren M. and Margaret E. (Widner) C.; m. Gwendolyn A. Kieffaber, June 1, 1963; children: Jeffrey, Douglas, Marta. B.S., Kans. State Coll., 1963; J.D., U. Iowa, 1966. Bar: Iowa 1963, D.C. 1963, U.S. Dist. Ct. (we. dist.) Wash. 1966. Ptnr. Bogle & Gates, Seattle, 1966-81; vis. asst. prof. law U. Washington, Seattle, 1970-73; judge U.S. Dist. Ct. (we. dist.) Wash., Seattle, 1981-97, chief judge, 1997—. Mem. Iowa State Bar Assn., Wash. State Bar Assn. Office: US Dist Ct US Courthouse 1010 5th Ave Ste 609 Seattle WA 98104-1189*

COUNELIS, JAMES STEVE, education educator; b. Streator, Ill., June 26, 1927; s. Steve and Mary (Drivas) C.; m. Anna Catherine Marakas, Nov. 25, 1962; children: Steven George, George James. AA, Chgo. City Jr. Coll., 1948; AM, U. Chgo., 1951, PhD, 1961. Cert. high sch., jr. coll. tchr., pub. sch. principal, Ill. High sch. tchr. Chgo. Pub. Schs., 1951-55; asst. prof. history and social scis. Chgo. City Jr. Coll., Woodrow Wilson br., 1955-62, dir. evening program, 1962-64; asst. prof. edn. Chgo Tchrs. Coll., 1964-66; assoc. prof. edn. Pa. State U., University Park, 1966-67; sr. adminstrv. analyst U. Calif., Berkeley, 1968-70; prof. edn. U. San Francisco, 1970—, dir. instl. studies and mgmt. info. systems, 1971-75, coord. evaluation Sch. Edn., 1986-90, chmn. orgn. and leadership program, 1989-91. Author, editor: To Be A Phoenix: The Education Professoriate, 1969; author: Higher Learning and Orthodox Christianity, 1990, Inheritance and Change in Orthodox Christianity, 1995; contbr. articles, revs. and papers to profl. publs. pres., trustee Greek Orthodox Cathedral of the Ascension, Oakland, Calif., 1973; pres. Hellenic Am. Profl. Soc., San Francisco, 1974, 75; trustee tenure Hellenic Coll./Holy Cross, 1951-53, trustee, 1982-86; mem. Calif. Council on Criminal Justice, 1987; bd. dirs. Paul Wattson Lecture series, 1989. Served with Signal Corps, U.S. Army, 1946-47. Recipient Archon Chartoularius (honoris causa) award Ecumenical Patriarchate Constantinople and New Rome, 1976, Norbert Wiener award The World Orgn. Gen. Systems and Cybernetics, 1978, Scholar U. Chgo., 1951-52, 60-61, Pacific Sch. Religion, 1958; U. Calif. grantee, Berkeley, 1962; Coolidge Rsch. fellow Andover-Newton Theol. Sch., 1985, Wayne J. Doyle Rsch. award, 1986, Hellenic Coun. on Edn. award for scholarship and univ. teaching, 1991. Mem. AAAS, Am. Assn. Artificial Intelligence, Am. Assn. Higher Edn., Am. Assn. Instnl. Rsch., Am. Ednl. Rsch. Assn., Am. Ednl. Studies Assn., Internat. Soc. System Scis., Hellenic Am. Profl. Soc. (Axion award 1982), Hellenic Coun. on Edn. (award for Scholarship and University Teaching 1991), Orthodox Theol. Soc. Am., U. San Francisco Faculty Assn., Mensa, Gold Key, Phi Delta Kappa (U. San Francisco chpt. v.p. for programs 1990-91, pres. 1991-92). Avocations: travel, photography, reading, music. Office: U San Francisco Sch Edn San Francisco CA 94117-1080

COUNSIL, WILLIAM GLENN, electric utility executive; b. Detroit, Dec. 13, 1937; s. Glenn Dempsey and Jean Beverly (Rzepecki) C.; m. Donna Elizabeth Robinson, Sept. 10, 1960; children: Glenn, Craig. Student, U. Mich., 1955-56; BS, U.S. Naval Acad., 1960; Advanced Mgmt. Program, Harvard U., 1991. Ops. supr., asst. plant supt.. sta. supt. N.E. Nuclear Energy Co., Waterford, Conn., 1967-76; project mgr., v.p. nuclear engring. and ops. N.E. Utilities, Hartford, Conn., 1976-80, sr. v.p. nuclear engring. and ops., 1980-85; exec. v.p. nuclear engring. and ops., electric-generating div. Tex. Utilities Generating Co., 1985-88; vice chmn. Tex. Utilities Electric Co., 1989-93; mng. dir. Wash. Pub. Power Supply System, Richland, 1993-96. With USN, 1956-67. Recipient Outstanding Leadership award ASME, 1986. Republican. Presbyterian.

COURNOYER, PETER JOSEPH, sales professional; b. San Jose, Calif., Aug. 31, 1969; s. Richard Joseph Cournoyer and Barbara (Williams) Schneider. Grad. h.s., San Jose. Traffic mgr. Masstor Sys. Corp., Santa Clara, Calif., 1991-94; contractor sales Pacific Packaging, Milpitas, Calif., 1994—; contractor packaging industry, Milpitas, 1994—. Cpl. USMC, 1987-91. Avocation: softball. Home: 182 N 9th St San Jose CA 95112-3451 Office: Pacific Packaging 970 S Milpitas Blvd Milpitas CA 95035-6323

COURT, ARNOLD, climatologist; b. Seattle, June 20, 1914; s. Nathan Altshiller and Sophie (Ravitch) C.; m. Corinne H. Feibelman, May 27, 1941 (dec. Feb. 1984); children: David, Lois, Ellen; m. Mildred Futor Berry, Apr. 6, 1988. BA, U. Okla., 1934; postgrad., U. Wash., 1938, MS, 1949; PhD, U. Calif., Berkeley, 1956. Reporter and city editor Duncan (Okla.) Banner, 1935-38; observer, meteorologist U.S. Weather Bur., Albuquerque, Washington, Little Am., Los Angeles, 1938-43; chief meteorologist U.S. Antarctic Service, 1939-41; climatologist office Q.M. Gen. U.S. Army, Washington, 1946-51; research meteorologist U. Calif., Berkeley, 1951-56; meteorologist U.S. Forest Service, Berkeley, 1956-60; chief applied climatology, Cambridge Research Labs. USAF, Bedford, Mass., 1960-62; sr. scientist Lockheed-Calif. Co., Burbank, 1962-65; prof. climatology San Fernando Valley State Coll. (now Calif. State U.), Northridge, 1962-85, chmn. dept. geography, 1970-72, prof. emeritus, 1985—; part-time prof. Calif. State U., Northridge, 1986-87, UCLA, 1987-90. Editor: Eclectic Climatology, 1968; assoc. editor Jour. Applied Meteorology, 1978-88; chmn. editorial bd. Jour. Weather Modification, 1978-86; contbr. articles and revs. to profl. jours. Served to 1st lt. USAAF, 1943-46. Recipient Spl. Congl. medal, 1944. Fellow AAAS, Am. Meteorol. Soc., Royal Meteorol. Soc.; mem. Am. Geophys. Union (life), Am. Statis. Assn., Assn. Am. Geographers, Assn. Pacific Coast Geographers (pres. 1978-79), Calif. Geog. Soc., Weather Modification Assn. (trustee 1973-76), Western Snow Conf., Sigma Xi, Phi Beta Kappa. Home: 17168 Septo St Northridge CA 91325-1672 Office: Calif State U Dept Geography Northridge CA 91330-8249

COURTNEY, ANGELA, veterinarian, researcher; b. L.A., Jan. 25, 1963; d. Walter James and Betty Jean (Stout) C. AS, AS Pierce Coll., 1980; DVM, Miss. State U., 1992. Med. lic. Calif., Fla. Extern Johns Hopkins Sch. of Medicine, 1992; animal health tech. rsch. asst. Letterman Army Inst. of Rsch., San Francisco, 1983-85; emergency animal tech. Calif. Animal Hosp., L.A., 1986; sr. clinician Cen. Orange County Emergency Animal Clinic, Newport Beach, Calif., 1992—; veterinary cons. Healthy PetsInc., La Habra, Calif., 1993—. With U.S. Army, 1983-85. Mem. Am. Veterinary Med. Assn., Am. Acad. Scis., N.Y. Acad. Scis. Avocations: snorkeling, outdoor and water activities. Home: 24 Balise Ln Foothill Ranch CA 92610

COURY, MARYANNE, advertising-marketing consultant; b. Valley Forge, Pa., Aug. 15, 1946; d. Paul Marshall and Dorothy Marie (Basca) Cole; m. Chandler Jeffory Coury, Mar. 1, 1969 (div. 1983). BA in Psychiatry, UCLA, Westwood, Calif., 1968; BA in Psychology, UCLA, 1970. V.p. 20th Century Fox Studios, 1975-82; with mktg. svcs. Playboy Enterprises, Inc., 1982-83; media dir., v.p. media and coop. advt. MGM/United Artists Sudios, 1983-88; mktg. cons. D'Arcy, Masius, Benton & Bowles Advt., 1988; account mgr. spl. mktg. Foote, Cone & Belding/Impact Advt., 1988-89; v.p. time and SPACE Media, L.A., 1996—; tchr. classes in movie and music advt. Steven Spielberg Film Sch., U. S.C. Vol. Dem. League, Beverly Hills, Calif.; active Project Angle Food for Terminally Ill People with AIDS, Hollywood, Calif. Recipient RIAA award, 1982. Roman Catholic. Avocations: skiing, snorkeling, watching & keeping library of old films, flying. Home: 133 S Spalding Dr Beverly Hills CA 90212-1806

COUSINEAU, PHILIP ROBERT, writer, filmmaker; b. Columbia, S.C., Nov. 26, 1952; s. Stanley Horace and Rosemary Marie (La Chance) C.; 1 child, Jack Philip Blue Beaton-Cousineau. BA cum laude, U. Detroit, 1974. Writer-in residence Shakespeare and Co. Bookstore, Paris, 1987; script judge Bay Guardian Scriptwriting Contest, 1987-89; judge Nat. Ednl. Film and Video Festival, 1990; mem. adv. bd. Joseph Campbell Archives and Libr., 1991—; documentary film judge Emmy Awards, 1992; dir. mythological tours Joseph Campbell Found., 1993-96; documentary judge San Francisco Film Festival, 1993-95. Author: The Hero's Journey: Joseph Campbell on His Life and Work, 1990, Portuguese edit., 1995, Deadlines, 1991, UFOs: Manual for the Millenium, 1995, German edit., 1997, Portugese edit., 1998, Soul Moments: Marvelous Stories from the World of Synchronicity, 1997, Spanish edit., 1998, The Book of Roads, 1998, The Art of Pilgrimage, 1998 (Quality Paperback Book Club selection 1993); editor: The Soul of the World, 1993 (Quality Paperback Book Club selection 1993, Book of Yr. award Contemporary Photography 1994), Soul: An Archaeology, 1994, Chinese edit., 1997, Prayers at 3 A.M., 1995, Design Outlaws, 1997, Riddle Me This: A World Treasury of Folk Riddles, 1998; co-dir., screenwriter documentary films The Peyote Road, 1993 (best documentary award Gt. Plains Film Festival, Cine Golden Eagle award, Bronze Telly award, silver award Chgo. Film Festival, award Mill Valley Film Festival), The Red Road to Sobriety, 1995 (Cine Golden Eagle award 1995, Gold award Red River Film Festival 1998), Ecological Design, 1994 (Golden Gate award, Cine Golden Eagle award, Sundance Film Festival), Your Humble Serpent: The Legacy of Reuben Snake, 1996 (Silver Apple award Nat. Ednl. Film Festival, Gold award Red Earth Film Festival); co-writer The 1932 Ford V888, Silverado Prodns., 1986, The Presence of the Goddess, Balcorman Films, 1987, (film) Eritrea: A Portrait of the Eritrean People, 1989; co-writer video Wiping the Tears of Seven Generations, 1991 (Best Video award Am. Indian Film Festival, Silver Telly award, Gold Apple award Nat. Ednl. Film Festival; co-writer, assoc. prodr. The Hero's Journey: The World of Joseph Campbell, 1987 (Silver Apple award Ednl. Film and Video Festival); co-writer film Forever Activists: Stories from the Veterans of the Abraham Lincoln Brigade, 1990 (Acad. Award nomination, jury prize San Francisco Film Festival), also others. Trustee Native Land Found., 1993-96. Recipient award Nat. Assn. Ind. Pubs., 1991; fellow Calif. Inst. Integral Studies, 1991-95. Avocation: travel. Office: Harper San Francisco Pubs 353 Sacramento St San Francisco CA 94111-3620

COUSINS, WILLIAM THOMAS, mechanical engineer; b. Orange, N.J., Oct. 14, 1954; s. Thomas Joseph and Joan Catherine (Blum) C.; m. Nina Ruth Davis, Sept. 2, 1979; children: Katherine, Jonathan. BS, Va. Poly. Inst. and State U., 1978, MS, 1979, PhD, 1997. Faculty mech. engring. Va. Poly. Inst. and State U., 1979-85; from engring. specialist to prin. engr. AlliedSignal Aerospace, Phoenix, 1985—. Mem. AIAA, ASME (membership devel. chmn. Ariz. sect. 1985-86, treas. 1986-87, sec. 1987-88, vice chmn. 1988-89, chmn. 1989-90, region XII operating bd. regional program 1990-91, asst. to v.p. region XII 1991-92, v.p. elect region XII 1992-93, v.p. Region XII 1993-95, adv. to coun. on member affairs 1995-96, v.p. profl. devel. 1996—). Home: 2864 E Fountain St Mesa AZ 85213-5445

COUZENS, JULIA, artist; b. Auburn, Calif., July 9, 1949; d. John Richard and Jean (Little) C.; m. Jay-Allen Eisen, Mar. 22, 1975. BA, Calif. State U., Chico, 1970; MA, Calif. State U., Sacramento, 1987; MFA, U. Calif., Davis, 1990. vis. lectr. Scripps Coll., Claremont, Calif., 1990-91, U. Calif., Davis, 1993, 95, 98, U. Calif., Santa Cruz, 1995; guest artist Coll. Creative Studies, U. Calif., Santa Barbara, 1995, Claremont Grad. Sch., 1995; vis. artist San Francisco Art Inst., 1997-98; guest curator Armory Ctr. for Arts, Pasadena, 1995-96; artist-in-residence U. Nev., Las Vegas, 1997. One-person shows include Christopher Grimes Gallery, Santa Monica, Calif., 1991, 93, 95, 96,

97, Calif. State U., Sacramento, 1997, Donna Beam Fine Art Gallery, U. Nev., Las Vegas, 1993; exhibited in group shows Am. Cultural Ctr., Brussels, 1992, Crocker Art Mus., Sacramento, 1995, 97, L.A. Mcpl. Gallery, 1995, San Francisco Art Inst., 1995, P.P.O.W., N.Y.C., 1995, Ten in One Gallery, Chgo., 1996, Weatherspoon Art Gallery, U. N.C., Greensboro, 1996, Armand Hammer Mus., L.A., 1997, Nev. Inst. Contemporary Art, Las Vegas, 1997, Palace of the Legion of Honor, San Francisco, 1997, Orange County Mus. of Art, Newport Beach, Calif., 1997; represented in pub. collections M.H. de Young Mus., San Francisco, Oakland Mus. Calif., Univ. Art Mus., Berkeley, Yale U., New Haven. Art-in-pub. places project grantee Sacramento Met. Arts Commn., 1986, artist-in-residence grantee Roswell Mus. and Art Ctr., 1994-95, grantee Louis Comfort Tiffany Found., 1995; grad. rsch. fellow U. Calif., Davis, 1989, fellow Art Matters, Inc., 1995. Mem. Coll. Art Assn. Home and Studio: PO Box 450 Clarksburg CA 95612-0450

COVELL, RUTH MARIE, medical educator, medical school administrator; b. San Francisco, Aug. 12, 1936; d. John Joseph and Mary Carolyn (Coles) Collins; m. James Wachob Covell, 1963 (div. 1972); 1 child, Stephen; m. Harold Joachim Simon, Jan. 4, 1973; 1 child, David. Student, U. Vienna, Austria, 1955-56; BA, Stanford U., 1958; MD, U. Chgo., 1962. Clin. prof. and assoc. dean sch. medicine U. Calif. San Diego, La Jolla, 1969—; dir. Acad. Geriatric Resource Ctr.; bd. dirs. Calif. Coun. Geriatrics and Gerontology, Beverly Found., Pasadena, Alzheimer's Family Ctr., San Diego, San Diego Epilepsy Soc., Devel. Svcs. Inc., San y Sidro Health Ctr., NIH SBIR Stude Sect. Geriatrics; cons. Agy. Health Care Policy and Rsch. Contbr. articles on health planning and quality of med. care to profl. jours. Mem. AMA, Am. Health Svcs. Rsch., Assn. Tchrs. Preventive Medicine, Am. Pub. Health Assn., Assn. Am. Med. Colls. Group on Instl. Planning (chair 1973-74, sec. 1983-84), Phi Beta Kappa, Alpha Omega Alpha. Home: 1604 El Camino Del Teatro La Jolla CA 92037-6338 Office: U Calif San Diego Sch Medicine M-002 La Jolla CA 92093

COWAN, GEORGE ARTHUR, chemist, bank executive, director; b. Worcester, Mass., Feb. 15, 1920; s. Louis Abraham and Anna (Listic) C.; m. Helen Dunham, Sept. 9, 1946. BS, Worcester Poly. Inst., 1941; DSc, Carnegie-Mellon U., 1950. Research asst. Princeton U., 1941-42, U. Chgo., 1942-45; mem. staff Columbia U., N.Y.C., 1945; mem. staff, dir. rsch., sr. fellow Los Alamos (N.Mex.) Sci. Lab., 1945-46, 49-88, sr. fellow emeritus, 1988—; teaching fellow Carnegie Mellon U., Pitts., 1946-49; chmn. bd. dirs. Trinity Capital Corp., Los Alamos, 1974-95; pres. Santa Fe Inst., 1984-91; mem. The White House Sci. Coun., Washington, 1982-85, cons., 1985-90, Air Force Tech. Applications Ctr., 1952-88; chmn. Los Alamos Nat. Bank, 1965-94; bd. dirs. Title Guaranty, Inc., Universal Properties, inc. Contbr. sci. articles to profl. jours. Bd. dirs. Santa Fe Opera, 1964-79; treas. N.Mex. Opera Found., Santa Fe, 1970-79; regent N.Mex. Inst. Tech. Socorro, 1972-75; bd. dirs. N.Am. Inst., Santa Fe Inst., Coalition for Quality TV. Recipient E.O. Lawrence award, 1965, Disting. Scientist award N.Mex. Acad. Sci., 1975, Robert H. Goddard award Worcester Poly. Inst., 1984, Enrico Fermi award, Presdl. Citation, Dept. Energy, 1990. Fellow AAAS, Am. Phys. Soc.; mem. Am. Chem. Soc., Am. Acad. Arts and Scis., N.Mex. Acad. Sci., Sigma Xi. Avocations: skiing, fly-fishing. Home: 721 42nd St Los Alamos NM 87544-1804 Office: Santa Fe Inst 1399 Hyde Park Rd Santa Fe NM 87501-8943

COWAN, JAMES CORNELIUS, security firm executive; b. Little Rock, June 28, 1929; s. George Thomas and Willie Francis (Thomas) C.; m. Elnora Aileen Mattison, Aug. 9, 1950; children: John Frederick, Evelyn Dianne, Kathryn Dianne. MS in Adminstrn., Calif. State U., Carson, 1979; PhD in Mgmt., Calif. Coast U., 1996. Cert. pvt. patrol operator, Calif. Bur. Consumer Affairs; life designated tchg. credential in security and law enforcement, Calif. Sr. materials and process engrng. analyst Douglas Missile & Materials and Process Engrng. Dept., Torrance, Calif., 1955-61; staff mgr. Universal Life Ins. Co., L.A., 1956-57; sr. engrng. checker and parts complier Butler's Engrng., Hawthorne, Calif., 1957-59; sr. engrng. rsch. asst., mech. rsch. engrng. lab. supr. Hughes Aerospace Divsn., Culver City, Calif., 1961-74; founder, pres. L.A. Inst. for Security Officers, 1971-73, Cowan's Security, Patrol and Investigatives Svcs., Moreno Valley, Calif., 1973—. Author: Mechanical Engineering Testing of Metallic and Non-Metallic Materials for Satellites and Space Vehicles from -315 deg F to 2800 deg F, 1964, Juvenile Justice and the Juvenile, 1979, Saga of a Security Guard, 1995, Comparative Study of Two State Mandated Security Guard Training Prograrms and a New Proposed Enhanced Security Training Program, 1996, Management in the Christian Church, 1998; contbr. articles to profl. jours. Platoon sgt., L.A. res. dep. sheriff L.A. County Sheriff Acad., 1970; L.A. spl. police officer L.A. Bd. Police Commr., 1973-75; pilot instr., curriculum developer for security and law enforcement L.A. S.W. Coll., 1973-78, founding bd. dirs. adminstrn. of justice adv. bd., 1973; mem. examining bd. for L.A. Internat. Airport, Ontario (Calif.) Internat. Airport, Palm Dale Internat. Airport, Port of Long Beach, City of L.A., 1975-78; mgr. pers., payroll, EEO/AAO, ins., comm. Ark. Dept. Corrections, Pine Bluff, Ark., 1978-79; acad. asst. to pres., provisional pres. Ark. Bapt. Coll., Little Rock, 1980-81, interim pres., chair North Ctrl. Assn. of Accrediation; adj. instr. Bus. and Econs. Philander Smith Coll., Little Rock, 1981; adj. prof. mktg. Adminstrn. Justice and Forensic Sci., Nat. U., Riverside, Orange and L.A. Campuses, Calif., 1996—; bd. mem. Sunnymead Ranch Homeowners Assn., Moreno Valley, 1989-90; adv. bd. mem. Calif. State U. Dominguez Hills Alumni Bd. Dirs., Carson, 1991-92; mem. alumni coun. Calif. State U. Sys., 1992; chancellor appointee Triennial Rev. of Campus Pres., Calif. State U. Sys., Long Beach, 1992; founding bd. dirs. Calif. Bur. Consumer Affairs Bur. of Security and Investigative Svcs., 1973, Pres.'s Adv. Bd. of Greater Little Rock, Ark. Consortium of Historically Black Colls. Ctr. of Higher Edn.; founding adminstr. Justice Bd. L.A. S.W. Coll., 1973; City of L.A. appointee for L.A. Internat. Airport, Ont. Internat. Airport, Palm Dale Internat. Airport, Port of Long Beach Internal Review Bds., 1975. Mem. Am. Optometric Assn. (coun. optometric edn. 1998—). Democrat. Methodist. Achievements include engineering material research and experimental testing for National/International Am. Soc. Testing Materials Standards; cryogenic testing of O'rings to -315 degrees F to determine elastomeric failure for satellites, planetary, lunar and manned space missions; mechanical testing retrieved TV camera from the Moon by Astronaut Neil Armstrong to determine affects of lunar temperature to its componments; rocket nose cone mechanical properties determination to 2800 degrees F in 7 seconds to simulate nose cone entry/re-entry into the Ionosphere.Avocations: golfing, fishing. Home: 22500 Country Gate Rd Moreno Valley CA 92557-2661 Office: Cowans Mgmt and Cons PO Box 1418 Moreno Valley CA 92556-1418

COWAN, STUART MARSHALL, lawyer; b. Irvington, N.J., Mar. 20, 1932; s. Bernard Howard and Blanche (Hertz) C.; m. Marilyn R.C. Toepfer, Apr., 1961 (div. 1968); m. Eleanor Schmerel, June, 1953 (dec.); m. Jane Alison Averill, Feb. 24, 1974 (div. 1989); children: Fran Lori, Catherine R.L., Erika R.L., Bronwen P.; m. Victoria Yi, Nov. 11, 1989. BS in Econ., U. Pa., 1952; LLB, Rutgers U., 1955. Bar: N.J. 1957, Hawaii 1962, U.S. Supreme Ct., 1966. Atty., Greenstein & Cowan, Honolulu, 1961-70, Cowan & Frey, Honolulu, 1970-89, pvt. practice, 1989—; of counsel Price Okomoto Himeno & Lum, 1993—; arbitrator Fed. Mediation & Conciliation Svc., Honolulu, 1972—, Am. Arbitation Assn., Honolulu, 1968—, Hawaii Pub. Employee Rels. Bd., 1972—. Bd. dirs. Honolulu Symphony; pres. Hawaii Epilepsy Soc., 1984-86; acquisition chair Hawaii Family Support Ctr., 1995-97. Lt. USN, 1955-61. Jewish. Mem. ABA, Hawaii Bar Assn., Am. Judicature Soc., Assn. Trial Lawyers Am. (state committeeman for Hawaii 1965-69, bd. govs. 1972-75), Consumer Lawyers Hawaii, Hawaii Trial Lawyers Assn. (v.p. 1972-78), Japan-Hawaii Lawyers Assn., Soc. Profls. in Dispute Resolution, Inter Pacific Bar Assn., Honolulu Symphony Soc. (bd. dirs. 1989—), Hawaii Epilepsy Soc. (pres. 1984-86), Royal Order of Kamehomehai, Order of St. Stanislas, Waikiki Yacht Club, St. Francis Yacht Club, Hawaii Yacht Club, Plaza Club, Honolulu Club, Hawaii Scottish Assn. (chieftain 1983-88), St. Andrews Soc., Caledonian Soc. (vice chieftain 1983-85),Honolulu Pipes and Drums (sec.-treas. 1985-90), New Zealand Police Pipe Band, Masons (York Rite, Scottish Rite, Grand Lodge Hawaii, grand orator 1992, sr. grand steward 1993, jr. grand warden 1994, sr. grand warden 1995, grand master 1997), Red Cross of Constantine, Royal Order Scotland, Pearl Harbor (master 1971, chaplain 1992-96), Masada (#51 N.J.), Hawaiian Koolau, Elks, Chinese Acacia Club, Waikiki Yacht Club. Home: 47-339 Mapumapu Rd Kaneohe HI 96744-4922 Office: 707 Richards St Honolulu HI 96813-4616 also: 47-653 Kamehameha Hwy # 202 Kaneohe HI 96744-4965

COWELL, ERNEST SAUL, lighting designer, consultant; b. Hollywood, Calif., Jan. 27, 1927; s. Ernest S. and Bernice Michael (Waterman) C.; m. Beverly Sue Bloom, Apr. 15, 1950 (div. May 1960); children: Steven Richard, Craig Wesley, Marilyn Tobiann. BA, UCLA, 1950; student, Moorpark Coll., 1971, Cerritos Jr. Coll., 1979; MS Illuminating Engrng., Penn State U. Regional mgr. Prentice Hall Inc., San Francisco, 1954-59; pvt. practice indsl. and govtl. sales L.A., 1959-70; area mgr. Philips Lighting, L.A., 1970-79; v.p. Coons & Cowell Lighting Unltd., Thousand Oaks, Calif., 1979-83; pres. Lighting Designs, L.A., 1983—; cons. City of Thousand Oaks, 1970-90; crime prevention specialist L.A. Police Dept., 1991—, adv. bd., 1994—. Mem. Rep. Presdl. Task Force, 1978—, Rep. Nat. Com., 1992—; mem. gen. plan com. City of Thousand Oaks, 1967, gen. plan rev. com., 1984, 86, 88; commdg. officer Betsy Ross divsn. U.S. Naval Sea Cadet Corps, 1994-95, dep. dir. for aviation tng., 1995—. Founding Officer Ronald Reagan Divsn., 1995, com. chair, 1996—, Sgt. U.S. Army, 1943-46, PTO; with USNR, 1950-58, 70-90. Recipient Edison award Excellence in Lighting, Gen. Electric Corp., 1985, 86. Fellow Inst. Advancement Engrng.; mem. Illuminating Engrng. Soc. (bd. dirs. So. Calif. sect. 1977-85, nat. chmn. schs. and colls. lighting stds. com., residential lighting stds. com., Internat. Illumination Design award 1983, 84, 85, 87, Disting. Svc. award), Internat. Assn. Lighting Designers, U.S. Nat. Com. to Internat. Commn. Illumination, Libr. Lighting Stds. (nat. chmn. 1988-90), Designers Lighting Forum (bd. dirs. 1988-95), Internat. Soc. Interior Designers (design affiliate), Navy League (pres. Hollywood/L.A. coun. 1993-94, bd. dirs. Beverly Hills coun. 1994—), Roadway Lighting Forum (bd. dirs. 1988-90), Kiwanis (pres. Westlake Village club 1977-79), Am. Legion. Avocations: sailing, photography, travel.

COWELL, FULLER A., publisher; m. Christmas Cowell; 1 child, Alexis. BBA, U. Alaska Fairbanks. With McClatchy Newspapers, 1981—; pub. Gavilan Newspapers, Calif., 1987-91, Anchorage Daily News, 1993—; former pub. Cordova Times. Office: Anchorage Daily News PO Box 149001 Anchorage AK 99514-9001

COWEN, DONALD EUGENE, retired physician; b. Ft. Morgan, Colo., Oct. 8, 1918; adopted s. Franklin and Mary Edith (Dalton) C.; BA, U. Denver, 1940; MD, U. Colo., 1943; m. Hulda Marie Helling, Dec. 24, 1942; children: David L., Marilyn Marie Cowen Dean, Theresa Kathleen Cowen Cunningham Byrd, Margaret Ann Cowen Koenigs. Intern, U.S. Naval Hosp., Oakland, Calif., 1944; gen. practice medicine, Ft. Morgan, 1947-52; resident internal medicine U. Colo. Med. Ctr., Denver, 1952-54; practice medicine specializing in allergy, Denver, 1954-90, ret., 1990; mem. staff Presbyn. Med. Ctr., Denver, Porter, Swedish hosps., Englewood, Colo.; clin. asst. prof. medicine U. Colo. Med. Center, 1964-91, ret., 1991; postgrad. faculty U. Tenn. Coll. Medicine, Memphis, 1962-82; cons. Queen of Thailand, 1973, 75, 77. Pres. Community Arts Symphony Found., 1980-82. Served to lt. M.C., USN, 1943-47. Fellow ACP, Am. Coll. Chest Physicians (vice chmn. com. on allergy 1968-72, 75-87, sec.-treas. Colo. chpt. 1971-77, pres. 1978-80), Am. Coll. Allergy and Immunology, Acad. Internat. Medicine, West Coast Allergy Soc., Southwest Allergy Forum, Am. Acad. Otolaryngic Allergy, Colo. socs. internal medicine, Colo. Allergy Soc. (past pres.), Ill. Soc. Opthalmology and Otolaryngology (hon.), Denver Med. Soc. (chmn. library and bldg. com. 1963-73), Arapahoe Med. Soc. (life emeritus mem.). Presbyterian (ruling elder 1956—). Club: Lions. Contbr. numerous articles to profl. jours. Home: 18560 Polvera Dr San Diego CA 92128-1120

COWHEY, PETER FRANCIS, international relations educator, consultant; b. Chgo., Sept. 28, 1948; s. Eugene F. and Vivien (High) C.; m. Mary Pat Williams, July 1973 (div. June 1978); m. M. Margaret McKeown, June 29, 1985; 1 child, Megan. BS in Fgn. Svc., Georgetown U., 1970; MA, PhD, U. Calif., Berkeley, 1976. Lectr. U. Calif., Berkeley, 1975-76; from asst. to assoc. prof. polit. sci. U. Calif. San Diego, La Jolla, 1976-88, prof. polit. sci. & internat. rels., 1989—; sr. counselor internat. econ. and competition policy FCC, Washington, 1994-97, chief internat. bur., 1997; market planner AT&T Internat., Basking Ridge, N.J., 1985-86; advisor Telemation Assocs., Washington, 1987-88; mem. telecom. adv. bd. A.T. Kearney, Chgo., 1988-91; co-dir. project on internat. and security affairs U. Calif., San Diego, 1990-94; rsch. scholar Berkeley Roundtable on the Internat. Economy, 1992-94; vis. prof. Juan March Inst., Madrid, 1992; rsch. prof. Inst. of Oriental Culture, U. Tokyo, 1993; U.S. del. G-7 Ministerial, 1995, U.S. del. Asian Pacific Econ. Cmty. Ministerial, 1995; mem. sec. gen. ITU Expert Group on Acctg. Rates, 1997-98; policy advisor Harris Wiltshire and Grannis, 1998—. Author: Problems of Plenty, 1985; co-author: Profit and the Pursuit of Energy, 1983, When Countries Talk, 1988, Managing the World's Economy, 1993; co-editor: Structure and Policy in Japan and the United States, 1994; mem. editl. bd. Internat. Orgn., 1989-94. Mem. adv. bd. Project Promothee, Paris, 1985-94, Ctr. on Telecom. Mgmt., Lincoln, Nebr., 1988-92; com. mem. NRC, 1992-93. Rockefeller Found. internat. affairs fellow, 1984-87. Mem. Am. Polit. Sci. Assn., Coun. Fgn. Rels. (internat. affairs fellow 1985-86), Internat. Studies Assn. Democrat. Home: 1522 40th Ave Seattle WA 98122-3510 also: Internat Bur FCC 2000 M St NW Fl 8 Washington DC 20036-3307

COWLES, WILLIAM STACEY, publisher; b. Spokane, Wash., Aug. 31, 1960; s. William Hutchinson 3rd and Allison Stacey C.; m. Anne Cannon, June 24, 1989. BA in Econs., Yale Coll., 1982; MBA in Fin., Columbia U., 1986. V.p., pub. The Spokesman Rev., Spokane, Wash. Office: Cowles Publishing Co PO Box 2160 Spokane WA 99210-2160

COX, (CHARLES) CHRISTOPHER, congressman; b. St. Paul, Oct. 16, 1952; s. Charles C. and Marilyn A. (Miller) C.; m. Rebecca Gernhardt; children: Charles, Kathryn. BA, U. So. Calif., 1973; MBA, JD, Harvard U., 1977. Bar: Calif. 1978, D.C. 1980. Law clk. to judge U.S. Ct. Appeals (9th cir.), 1977-78; assoc. Latham & Watkins, Newport Beach, Calif., 1978-82; lectr. bus. adminstrn. Harvard U., 1982-83; ptnr. Latham & Watkins, Newport Beach, Calif., 1984-86; sr. assoc. counsel to the Pres. The White House, Washington, 1986-88; mem. 101st-104th Congresses (now 106th Congress) from 40th (now 47th) dist. Calif., Washington, 1986-87; mem. U.S. Ho. of Reps., Washington, mem. budget com., joint econ. com., govt. ops. com., ranking mem. subcom. on commerce, consumer & monetary affairs, mem. commerce com., govt. reform and oversight com., Ho. Rep. steering com.; mem. Bipartisan Commn. on Entitlement and Tax Reform, Washington, 1994—; chmn. Rep. policy com., mem. commerce com., 1995—; prin., founder Context Corp., St. Paul, 1984-88. Editor Harvard Law Rev., 1975-77. Roman Catholic. Office: 1 Newport Place Dr Ste 420 Newport Beach CA 92660-2412 Office: US Ho of Reps 2402 Rayburn HOB Washington DC 20515-0547*

COX, CINDY ANNICE, composer, educator; b. Houston, Sept. 12, 1961; d. Percy Terrel and Anne Miller (Watkins) C.; m. Charles Piriwal Hurst, May 14, 1988 (div. July 1998). MusB, Tex. Christian U., 1985; MusM, Ind. U., 1988, DMA, 1992. Adj. faculty DePauw U., Green Castle, Ind., 1990-91; assoc. prof. music U. Calif., Berkeley, 1991—. Composer Cathedral Spires for orch., 1993, Columba Aspexit for string quartet, 1995, Primary Colors for trio, 1996, Geode for quintet, 1997. Recipient Acad. award AAAL, 1998, 1st Nat. Commissioning award Woman's Philharmonic, San Francisco, 1992; composer fellow Fromm Found., Harvard U., 1994, NEA, Washington, 1993. Mem Am. Music Ctr., Soc. of Composers. Office: UC Berkeley Dept Music No 1200 Berkeley CA 94720

COX, CLARICE R., writer; b. Helena, Mont., May 11, 1914; d. William Mont and Adelia Anne (Geier) Robinson; m. Gene H. Cox, June 11, 1938 (dec. June 1996); children: William Edward, James Laurence, Willa Margaret. BA in English, Intermountain Union, 1935; MEd in Comms., U. Hawaii, 1968. H.S. tchr. Mont., Oreg. and Hawaii schs., 1936-60; asst. base edn. adviser 408th Fighter Group USAF, Klamath Falls, Oreg., 1960-61; writer, demonstrator Maui Project NIMH, Wailuku, Hawaii, 1965-67; instr. Honolulu C.C., 1967-73, 75-79; freelance writer Roseburg, Oreg., 1995—; cons., lectr. Mont. Pers. Devel. Ctr., Helena, 1979-88; cons., lectr. Queen's Med. Ctr., Honolulu, 1980-89, Am. Soc. Ind. Security, Honolulu, 1981, Honolulu Police Dept., 1980-88; presenter in field. Author: Criminal Justice: Improving Police Report Writing, 1977, Instant Teaching Skills, 1995; (with Jerrold G. Brown) Report Writing for Criminal Justice Professionals, 1991, 2d edit., 1998; contbr. articles, poems, short stories to profl. jours. and popular mags. Mem. Oreg. Com. on Aging, 1996-98, Hawaii Com. on Aging, 1973-78; mem. panel John Jay Coll. Criminal Justice, N.Y.C., 1996, Acad. Criminal Justice Scis., Albuquerque, 1998; vol. Mercy Hosp., Roseburg, Oreg., 1995—. Recipient Lifetime Achievement award Police Writers Club, 1997. Mem. ACJS, Am. Soc. Criminology, Am. Soc. Indsl. Security, Internat. Assn. Women Police (assoc.), Police Writers Club (panelist). Home: 16925 Hierba Dr Apt 242 San Diego CA 92128-2662

COX, DONALD CLYDE, electrical engineering educator; b. Lincoln, Nebr., Nov. 22, 1937; s. Elvin Clyde and C. Gertrude (Thomas) C.; m. Mary Dale Alexander, Aug. 27, 1961; children: Bruce Dale, Earl Clyde. BS, U. Nebr., 1959, MS, 1960, DSc (hon.), 1983; PhD, Stanford U., 1968. Registered profl. engr., Ohio, Nebr. With Bell Tel. Labs., Holmdel, N.J., 1968-84, head radio and satellite systems rsch. dept., 1983-84; mgr. radio and satellite systems rsch. divsn. Bell Comm. Rsch., Red Bank, N.J., 1984-91, exec. dir. radio rsch. dept., 1991-93; prof. elec. engrng. Stanford (Calif.) U., 1993—, Harald Trap Friis Prof. Engrng., 1994—, dir. telecomms., 1993—; em. commns. U.S. nat. com. Internat. Union of Radio Sci.; participant enbanc hearing on Personal Comm. Sys., FCC, 1991. Contbr. articles to profl. jours.; patentee in field. 1st lt. USAF, 1960-63. Johnson fellow, 1959-60; recipient Guglielmo Marconi prize in Electromagnetic Waves Propagation, Inst. Internat. Comm., 1983. Fellow IEEE (Morris E. Leeds award 1985, Alexander Graham Bell medal 1993), AAAS, Bellcore 1991, Radio Club Am.; mem. NAE, Comm. Soc. of IEEE (Leonard G. Abraham Prize Paper award 1992, Comms. Mag. Prize Paper award 1990), Vehicular Tech. Soc. of IEEE (Paper of Yr. award 1983), Antennas and Propagation Soc. of IEEE (elected mem. adminstrn. com. 1986-88), Sigma Xi. Achievements include rsch. in low-power wireless personal portable communication systems, cellular radio systems, radio propagation. Home: 924 Mears Ct Stanford CA 94305-1029 Office: Stanford U Dept Elec Engrng Durand 305 Stanford CA 94305-9515

COX, JONATHAN CHRISTOPHER STONINGTON, lawyer; b. Ipswich, Mass., Oct. 25, 1944; s. Stanley Cullen and Nancy Virginia (Stonington) C.; m. Christina Gillian Higgins, Mar. 23, 1968 (div. Jan. 1975); children: Fiona Carolan Cox Millar, Nigh Song; m. Constance Chalberg, May 23, 1975; children: Stonington Christopher, Kathrine Constance. BA, Stanford U., 1967; MA, U. Denver, 1970, JD, 1971. Bar: Colo., Tex., Calif., N.Y., U.S. Dist. Ct. Colo., U.S. Dist. Ct. Tex., U.S. Dist. N.Y., U.S. Dist. Ct. Calif., U.S. Ct. Appeals (5th cir.), U.S. Ct. Appeals (9th cir.), U.S. Ct. Appeals (10th cir.), U.S. Tax Ct., U.S. Supreme Ct. Lawyer Horigan & Boss, U.K., 1971, Law Offices of John Cogswell, 1971-73; ptnr. Cogswell & Cox, 1973-74; pvt. practice Jonathan C.S. Cox, 1974-77; ptnr. Cox, Buchanan, Padmore & Shakarchy, Palo Alto, Calif., 1997—; mem. Profl. Liability Ins. Com.; mem. jud. panel Multi-Dist. Litigation; arbitrator mining claims case; arbitrator U.S. Dist. Ct., 1984; expert on legal fees.. Contbr. articles to profl. jours. Mem. ABA, Calif. Bar Assn., Colo. Bar Assn., Colo. Trial Lawyers Assn., Denver Bar Assn., San Mateo County Bar Assn., Univ. Club Denver, Univ. Club San Francisco. Avocations: soccer, tennis, squash, golf, skiing. Office: Cox Buchanan Padmore and Shakarchy 755 Page Mill Rd # A-280 Palo Alto CA 94304-1018

COX, JOSEPH WILLIAM, academic administrator; b. Hagerstown, Md., May 26, 1937; s. Joseph F. and Ruth E. C.; m. Regina M. Bollinger, Aug. 17, 1963; children—Andrew, Matthew, Abigail. B.A., U. Md., 1959, Ph.D., 1967; Doctor (hon.), Towson State U., 1990. Successively instr., asst. prof., assoc. prof., prof. history Towson (Md.) State U., 1964-81, dean evening and summer programs, 1972-75, acting pres., 1978-79, v.p. acad. affairs and dean of univ., 1979-81; prof. history, v.p. acad. affairs. No. Ariz. U.,, Flagstaff, 1981-87; pres. So. Oregon Coll., Ashland, 1987-94; chancellor Oreg. Univ. Sys., Eugene, 1994—. Author: Champion of Southern Federalism: Robert Goodloe Harper of South Carolina, 1972, The Early National Experience: The Army Corps of Engineers, 1783-1812, 1979; mem. bd. editors Md. Hist. Mag., 1979-89; columnist So. Oreg. Hist. Mag., 1989-94; contbr. articles to profl. jours. Bd. dirs. Oreg. Hist. Soc., Oreg. Shakespearean Festival, 1989-95, So. Oreg. Econ. Deve. Bd., 1988-94, Jackson/Josephine Co. Mem. AAUP, Am. Assn. Higher Edn., Am. Assn. State Colls. and Univs., Phi Kappa Phi, Omicron Delta Kappa. Episcopalian. Home: 2237 Spring Blvd Eugene OR 97403-1897 Office: Oreg Univ Sys Office of Chancellor PO Box 3175 Eugene OR 97403-0175

COX, PAT, artist; b. Pasadena, Calif., Mar. 6, 1921; d. Walter Melville and Mary Elizabeth (Frost) Boadway; m. Dale William Cox Jr., Feb. 19, 1946; children: Brian Philip, Dale William III, Gary Walter. BA, Mills Coll., 1943, MA, 1944. Graphic artist Pacific Manifolding Book Co., Emeryville, Calif., 1944-45; tchr. art to adults China Lake, Calif., 1957-63; tchr. art to children Peninsula Enrichment Program, Rancho Palos Verdes, Calif., 1965-67; graphic artist Western Magnum Corp., Hermosa Beach, Calif., 1970-80; tchr. art workshop Art at Your Fingertips, Rancho Palos Verdes, 1994-95. One-woman shows include Palos Verdes Art Ctr., Rancho Palos Verdes, Calif., 1977, 79, 83, 92, Thinking Eye Gallery, L.A., 1988, Ventura (Calif.) Coll. Art Galleries, 1994, Mendenhall Gallery, Whittier (Calif.) Coll., 1995, The Gallery at Stevenson Union, So. Oreg. Coll., Ashland, 1996; two person exhibits Laguna Art Mus., Laguna Beach, Calif., 1971, Creative Arts Gallery, Burbank, Calif., 1993; group exhibits include Long Beach Mus. Art, Art Rental Gallery, 1979, L.A. County Mus. Art, Art Rental Gallery, 1979, Palm Springs Mus. Art, 1980, Laguna Art Mus., 1981, N.Mex. Fine Arts Gallery, 1981, Pacific Grove Art Ctr., 1983, Phoenix Art Mus., 1983, Riverside Art Mus., 1985, Laguna Art Mus., 1986, Zanesville Art Ctr., Ohio, 1987, The Thinking Eye Gallery, L.A., 1987, 89, Hippodrome Gallery, Long Beach, 1988, N.Mex. State Fine Arts Gallery, 1988, Long Beach City Coll., 1989, Newport Harbor Art Mus., 1988, Downey Mus. Art, 1990, 92, Rachele Lozzi Fine Art Gallery, L.A., 1991, Internat. Contemporary Art Fair L.A., 1986, 87, 88, 92, U. Tex. Health Sci. Ctr., 1992, Long Beach Arts, 1991, 92, 93, Young Aggressive Art Mus., Santa Ana, 1993, U. Ark. Fine Arts Gallery, Fayetteville, 1994, Laura Knott Art Gallery, Bradford Coll., Mass., 1994, Bridge Street Gallery, Big Fork, Mont., 1994, St. John's Coll. Art Gallery, Santa Fe, 1995, L.A. Harbor Coll., Calif., 1995, Walker Art Collection, Garnett, Kans., 1995, San Francisco State U., 1996, Coleman Gallery, Albuquerque, 1996, Loyola Law Sch., L.A., 1996, San Bernardino County Mus., 1996, Prieto Gallery, Mills Coll., Oakland, Calif., 1996, U. So. Calif. Hillel Gallery, L.A., 1997, Fresno Art Mus., 1998. Trustee L.A. Art Assn., 1972-79; bd. dirs. Palos Verdes Art Ctr., 1966-70, 87-89, chair exhbn. com., 1982-85, co-chair Art for Fun(d)s Sake, 1966; judge Tournament of Roses Assn., Pasadena, 1975; mem. strategic planning Palos Verdes Art Ctr., 1988; mem. Pacific Pl. Planning Commn. Percent for Art, San Pedro, Calif., 1989; juror Pasadena Soc. Artists, 1973, 81, Women Painters West, 1984-85. Recipient Silver Pin award Palos Verdes Art Ctr., 1988, Calif. Gold Discovery award V.I.P. Jury Panel, L.A., 1994. Mem. Nat. Watercolor Soc. (juror 1981, 1st v.p. 1980, 4th v.p. 1984), Nat. Mus. Women in the Arts, Oakland Mus. Art, Mus. Contemporary Art, L.A. County Mus. Art, Palos Verdes Cmty. Art Assn. (cert. appreciation 1981). Avocations: gardening, reading.

COX, PATRICIA JEAN, artist, researcher; b. Lusk, Wyo., Aug. 16, 1922; d. Kenneth Gregory and Helen Esther (Mott) Miller; children: Christine Louise Kaitlyn, Kelly Dennis. BA, Evergreen State Coll., 1982. Artist, illustrator Dept. Transp., Olympia, Wash., 1968-73; graphic artist Dept. Natural Resources, Olympia, Wash., 1973-78; freelance iconographer Olympia, 1990—; tchr. life drawing State Capitol Mus., Olympia, Wash., 1980-84, Benefits to Feed the Poor, Olympia, 1996-99; dir. art gallery Earth Magic Giftshop, Olympia, 1984-85; spkr. Olympia Art League, 1993; founder Olympia Iconographers, 1994—. Author, artist, printer: 24 Haiku, 1976, Potpourri, 1978; contbr. poems to Madamorphosis, 1976; exhibits include Wash. State U., Pullman, 1977, Daniel Evans Libr. Evergreen State Coll., Olympia, 1976, 78, Wash. Writers Rm.-State Libr., Olympia, 1976, 78, Biannual Artwalks, Olympia, 1991-98, KTCS TV, Olympia, 1997. Facilitator Holistic Health Workshops, 1985-90. Mem. Nat. Mus. Women in Arts, Arts Olympia, Art Deco Soc. Northwest, Assn. Rsch. and Enlightment Virginia Beach. E-mail: patrician@scsmall.com. Home: 1821 Bigelow Ave NE Olympia WA 98506-4603

COX, PAUL ALAN, biologist, educator; b. Salt Lake City, Oct. 10, 1953; s. Leo A. and Rae (Gabbitas) C.; m. Barbara Ann Wilson, May 21, 1975; children: Emily Ann, Paul Matthew, Mary Elisabeth, Hillary Christine, Jane Margaret. BS, Brigham Young U., 1976; MSc, U. Wales, 1978; AM, Harvard U., 1978, PhD, 1981. Teaching fellow Harvard U., Cambridge, Mass., 1977-81; Miller research fellow Miller Inst. Basic Research in Sci., Berkeley, Calif., 1981-83; asst. prof. Brigham Young U., Provo, Utah, 1983-

86, assoc. prof., 1986-91, prof., 1991-93, dean gen. edn. and honors, 1993-97; King Gustav XVI prof. environ. sci. Swedish Agrl. U., 1997-98; dir. Nat. Tropical Botanical Garden, Lawai, Hawaii, 1998—; ecologist Utah Environ. Coun., Salt Lake City, 1976; project ecologist Utah MX Coordination Office, Salt Lake City, 1981. Mem. editorial bd. Pacific Studies. Recipient Bowdoin prize, The Goldman Environ. prize, 1997;; Danforth Found. fellow, 1976-81, Fulbright fellow, 1976-77, NSF fellow, 1977-81, Linnaen Soc. fellow, Melbourne Univ. fellow, 1985-86, named NSF Presdl. Young Investigator, 1985-90. Mem. AAAS, Brit. Ecol. Soc., Internat. Soc. Ethnopharmacology (pres.), Am. Soc. Naturalists, Assn. Tropical Biology, Soc. Econ. Botany (pres.), New Eng. Bot. Club. Mormon. Office: Dir Nat Tropical Botanical Gardens PO Box 340 Lawai HI 96765-0340

COYLE, ROBERT EVERETT, federal judge; b. Fresno, Calif., May 6, 1930; s. Everett LaJoya and Virginia Chandler C.; m. Faye Turnbaugh, June 11, 1953; children—Robert Allen, Richard Lee, Barbara Jean. BA, Fresno State Coll., 1953; JD, U. Calif., 1956. Bar: Calif. Ptnr. McCormick, Barstow, Sheppard, Coyle & Wayte, 1958-82; chief judge U.S. Dist. Ct. (ea. dist.) Calif., 1990-96, sr. judge, 1996—; former chair 9th Cir. Conf. of Chief Dist. Judges, chair 9th Cir. space and security com., mem. com. on state and fed. cts. Mem. Calif. Bar Assn. (exec. com. 1974-79, bd. govs. 1979-82, v.p. 1981), Fresno County Bar Assn. (pres. 1972). Office: US Dist Ct 5116 US Courthouse 1130 O St Fresno CA 93721-2201*

COYNE, BRIAN JOSEPH, lawyer; b. Yonkers, N.Y., Apr. 8, 1940; s. John Henry and Della (O'Brien) C.; m. Fumiko Hoshida; Mar. 26, 1965; children: Cheryl Lee, Moira Julliette. BA, Cornell U., 1963; PhD, U. Chgo., 1968; JD, Boston U., 1976. Bar: Wash. 1976, U.S. Patent Office 1980. Asst. atty. gen. State of Wash., Olympia, 1976-81; assoc. J. Leggett, Tacoma, 1981-83; pvt. practice Olympia, 1983-85; ptnr. Miles, Way, Coyne & Humphrey (now Miles Way Coyne, PLLC), Olympia, 1985—. Sec., treas. Thurston Community TV Assn., Olympia, 1985-88, v.p., 1988—, pres. 1989-91. Mem. Wash. State Bar Assn. Home: 2918 Orange St SE Olympia WA 98501-3655

COZAD, LYMAN HOWARD, city manager; b. Painesville, Ohio, May 22, 1914; s. William Howard and Ethyl (Phelps) C.; children: Bradford, Roberta, Kimberly. BSBA, Ohio State U., 1935, MS in Pub. Adminstrn., 1936; postgrad., Yale U., 1936-37, USC, 1948-57. Dir. exam City of L.A., 1939-42; personnel officer Nat. Housing Agy., Washington, 1942-43; personnel dir. UNRRA, Washington, 1944-47; So. Calif. mgr. Louis J. Kroeger & Assocs., L.A., 1947-56; city mgr. City of Colton, 1957-64; adminstrv. officer City of Beverly Hills, Calif., 1964-66; city mgr. City of Arcadia, Calif., 1966-77; So. Calif. mgr. League of Calif. Cities, 1977-84; ranger rider, 1985-98; v.p., So. Calif. rep. Pub. Svc. Skills Inc., Sacramento, 1986-98; instr. U. So. Calif., 1941-42, 48-58, U. Calif., Riverside, 1961-63, Calif. State U., Long Beach, 1974-77. Contbr. articles to profl. jours. With U.S. Army, 1943-44. Mem. ASPA, Internat. City Mgrs. Assn., City Mgrs. Dept. League of Calif. Cities (Sacramento pres. 1972, life), So. Calif. Pub. Pers. Assn. L.A. (pres. 1942), Rotary (Colton chpt. dir. 1961-62, Arcadia chpt. 1970-77). Avocation: gardening. Home: 952 Canyon View Dr La Verne CA 91750-1811

COZEN, LEWIS, orthopedic surgeon; b. Montreal, Aug. 14, 1911; came to U.S. 1922; AB, U. Calif., San Francisco, 1929, MD, 1934. Diplomate Am. Bd. Orthopedic Surgery. Intern San Francisco Hosp., 1933-34; resident orthopedic surgeron U. Iowa, 1934-35; resident and fellow orthopedic surgery San Francisco County Hosp., 1935-36, Children's Hosp. and Mass. Gen. Hosp., Boston, 1936-39; pvt. practice orthopedic surgery L.A., 1939-40, 45—; clin. prof. orthopedic surgery UCLA, 1965-93; assoc. clin. prof. emeritus Loma Linda Med. Sch., 1963—; attending orthopedic surgeon, emeritus Cedars Sinai Med. Ctr., 1939—, Orthopaedic Hosp., 1939—; chief orthopedic surgery City of Hope, 1948-67; sr. attending orthopedic surgeons, emeritus Unit One L.A. County Hosp., 1950-63; vis. lectr. U. Santo Tomas, Manila, U. Madrid, Spain; Far East Sch. of Medicine, Manila, 1994, Hadassah Med. Ctr., Jerusalem, 1994, U. Brussels; lectr. in field; vis. lectr. Brussels, U. London, Stammore, Eng., U. Guadalajara, Mexico, others. Author: Office Orthopedics, 1955, 4th edit. 1973, Operative Orthopedic Clinics (with Dr. Avia Brockway), 1960, Atlas of Orthopedic Surgery, 1966, Difficult Orthopedic Diagnosis, 1972, Plannings and Pitfalls in Orthopedic Surgery, Natural History of Orthopedic Disease, 1993, Supplement Book, 1996; mem. editl. bd. Resident & Staff Physician; contbr. numerous articles to profl. jours. Vol. physician Internat. Children's Program, Orthopedic Hosp., Mexicali, Mexico. Lt. col. U.S. Army, 1940-45. Fellow ACS, Internat. Coll. Surgeons, Am. Coll. Rheumatology, Royal Soc. Medicine; mem. Am. Rheumatism Assn., Internat. Orthopedic Assn., Am. Orthopaedic Assn. (sr.), Am. Acad. Orthopaedic Surgeons, So. Calif. Rheumatism Assn. (pres. 1979), Western Orthopaedic Assn., Phi Beta Kappa, Alpha Omega Alpha. Avocations: swimming, golf, dancing, travel.

CRABBS, ROGER ALAN, publisher, consultant, small business owner, educator; b. Cedar Rapids, Iowa, May 9, 1928; s. Winfred Wesley and Faye (Woodard) C.; m. Marilyn Lee Westcott, June 30, 1951; children: William Douglas, Janet Lee Crabbs Turner, Ann Lee Crabbs Menke. B.A. in Sci., State U. Iowa, 1954; M.B.A., George Washington U., 1965, D.B.A., 1973, M.Christian Leadership, 1978. Commd. 2nd lt. USAF, 1950, advanced through grades to lt. col., 1968, Ret., 1972; prof. mgmt. U. Portland, Oreg., 1972-79; prof. bus. George Fox Coll., Newberg, Oreg., 1979-83; pres. Judson Bapt. Coll., The Dalles, Oreg., 1983-85; pres. Host Pubs. Inc., pres., chmn. various corps., 1974-86; past chmn. nat. adv. bd. TRAVELHOST, Inc.; cons. to small bus. for Oreg. Econ. Devel., cons. to various orgns., corps. and agys. Author: The Infallible Foundation for Management-The Bible, 1978, The Secret of Success in Small Business Management-Is in the Short Range, 1983; co-author: The Storybook Primer on Managing, 1976. Past pres. English Speaking Union, 1994-96, bd. dirs., 1994-97; bd. dirs. Christ Cmty. Ch., Washington County Visitors Assn., Oakhills Townhouse Assn., v.p., 1991-95; mem. Minority Conv. Tourism Adv. Coun., Oreg. Decorated Air Force Commendation medal with oak leaf cluster, Meritorious Service medal Dept. Def.; rated Command Air Force Missileman; recipient regional, dist. and nat. awards SBA. Mem. Acad. Mgmt., Am. Arbitration Assn., Svc. Corps Ret. Execs., Air Force Assn., Portland Officers Club, Rotary (past pres.), Masons, Kiwanis, Lang Syne Soc. of Portland, Alpha Kappa Psi, Delta Epsilon Sigma, Phi Mu Alpha. Republican. Office: Host Publs Inc 822 NW Murray Blvd Ste 173 Portland OR 97229-5868

CRAFT, ROBBIE WRIGHT, artist; b. St. Louis, Feb. 22, 1951; d. Robert Edward and Irene (Tosch) Wright; m. Joseph Walter Epply III (div. 1978); 1 child, Joseph Walter IV; m. Raymond Wood Craft II, Feb. 14, 1987. Student, Casper Jr. Coll., 1969-71. Mgr. restaurant and bar Widow Browns, Crofton, Md., 1978-84; adminstrv. asst. U.S. Dept. Def., Andrews AFB, Md., 1974-75; illustrator, supr. U.S. Dept. Def., Cheyenne, Wyo., 1985-88, EEO counselor, 1987—, chief visual info., 1988—, chief, support flt., 1996—; ind. artist Maryland, Wyo., 1974—; ind. interior designer Wyo., 1985—. Mem. visual info. bd. USAF. Lutheran. Avocations: snow and water skiing, swimming, needlework, reading, writing. Home: 7223 Tumbleweed Dr Cheyenne WY 82009-1014 Office: Visual Info Bldg 242 Cheyenne WY 82005

CRAGUN, CALVIN, business owner; b. Salt Lake City, Nov. 14, 1940; s. Robert Wallace and Vivian (Parker) C.; m. Celestia Van Tussenbroek, Dec. 20, 1967; children: Marlayn, Caroline, David, Robert. BS, U. Utah, 1963, MS, 1966. Cert. tchr. profound/severely disabled. Tchr. Utah Sch. for the Deaf, Ogden, 1966-72; from salesperson to mgmt. dept. Home Life of N.Y., Salt Lake City, 1972-82; with ins. sales dept. Standard of Oreg., Salt Lake City, 1982-84; owner Custom Benefits, Salt Lake City, 1984—, Rocky Mt. Brokerage, Salt Lake City, 1985-88, Ins. Designers, Salt Lake City, 1988—; mem. Gov.'s com. for managed healthcare for the disabled, 1996. Mem. Nat. Conf. for Autism, Salt Lake City, 1983; regional coord. Internat. Winter Spl. Olympics, Salt Lake City, 1985; mem. Utah Gov.'s Com. for Handicapped, Salt Lake City, 1983-84, Family Support Adv. Coun., 1995; vol. Jr. Achievement, 1991; tchr. Life Underwriter Tng. Coun., 1992; chmn. steering com. Adult Handicap Social Club, 1993—. Mem. Utah Coun. for Handicapped (v.p. 1982-83), After Hours (chairperson 1993—). Home and Office: 2686 Towne Dr Salt Lake City UT 84121-5146

CRAIG, CAROL MILLS, marriage, family and child counselor; b. Berkeley, Calif.. BA in Psychology with honors, U. Calif., Santa Cruz, 1974; MA in Counseling Psychology, John F. Kennedy U., 1980; doctoral student, Calif. Sch. Profl. Psychology, Berkeley, 1980-87, Columbia Pacific U., San Rafael, Calif., 1987—. Psychology intern Fed. Correction Inst., Pleasanton, Calif., 1979-81, Letterman Army Med. Ctr., San Francisco, 1980-82; psychology intern VA Mental Hygiene Clinic, Oakland, Calif., 1981-82, Martinez, Calif., 1982-83; instr. Martinez Adult Sch., 1983, Piedmont Adult Edn., Oakland, 1986; biofeedback and stress mgmt. cons. Oakland, 1986—; child counselor Buddies-A Nonprofit, Counseling Svc. for Persons in the Arts, Lafayette, Calif., 1993—; founder Chesley Sch., 1994, Healing with Music for People and All Animals, 1996, Music Therapy for animals, 1998—; rsch. asst. Irvington Pubs., N.Y.C., 1979, Little, Brown and Co., Boston, 1983; music therapist for people and animals, 1998—. Mem. Calif. Assn. Marriage and Family Therapists (clin.), Calif. Scholarship Fedn. (life). Avocations: music-guitar, violin, folk and opera singing, song writing, art.

CRAIG, LARRY EDWIN, senator; b. Council, Idaho, July 20, 1945; s. Elvin and Dorothy Craig. B.A., U. Idaho; postgrad, George Washington U. Farmer, rancher Midvale area, Idaho; mem. Idaho Senate, 1974-80, 97th-101st Congresses from 1st Dist. Idaho, 1981-90; senator 102nd Congress from Idaho, 1990-97, mem. com. agr., nutrition and forestry, com. energy and natural resources, spl. com. on aging, chmn. com. Rep. policy, vets. affairs, appropriations, chmn. subcom. on forests and pub. land mgmt., chmn. subcom. energy rsch., devel., prodn. and regulation, subcom. water and power; senator 105th Congress from Idaho (now 106th Congress), 1996—; chmn. Idaho Rep. State Senate Races, 1976-78, chmn. senate steering com.; mem. joint econ. com., com. veterans' affairs, subcom. energy R & D. Pres. Young Rep. League Idaho, 1976-77; mem. Idaho Rep. Exec. Com., 1976-78; chmn. Rep. Central Com. Washington County, 1971-72; advisor vocat. edn. in public schs. HEW, 1971-73; mem. Idaho Farm Bur., 1965-79. Served with U.S. Army N.G., 1970-74. Mem. NRA (bd. dirs. 1983—), Future Farmers of Am. (v.p. 1965). Methodist. Office: US Senate 313 Hart Senate Office Bldg Washington DC 20510-1203*

CRAIG, STEPHEN WRIGHT, lawyer; b. N.Y.C., Aug. 28, 1932; s. Herbert Stanley and Dorothy (Simmons) C.; m. Margaret M. Baker, June 10, 1958 (div. 1984); children: Amelia Audrey, Janet Elizabeth, Peter Baker; m. Bette Piller, 1984. AB, Harvard U., 1954, JD, 1959. Bar: Maine 1959, Calif. 1960, Ariz. 1963. Reporter Daily Kennebec Jour., Augusta, Maine, 1956; with pub. rels. staff Am. Savoyards, 1957; atty. IRS, San Francisco, 1959-61; atty.-adviser U.S. Tax Ct., 1961-63; ptnr. Snell & Wilmer, Phoenix, 1963-78, Winston & Strawn (formerly Craig, Greenfield & Irwin), Phoenix, 1978-87; investment banker Myers, Craig, Vallone, Francois, 1987-89; ptnr. Brown & Bain, Phoenix and Palo Alto, Calif., 1989-97; guest lectr. Amos Tuck Sch. Bus., Dartmouth U., 1962; lectr. Ariz. and N.Mex. Tax Insts., 1966-67; guest lectr. sch. law Ariz. State U., 1984, adj. prof. law, 1985-87. Chmn. Jane Wayland Child Guidance Ctr., 1968-70; mem. Maricopa County Health Planning Coun., chmn. mental health task force; bd. dirs. Combined Met. Phoenix Arts, 1968, adv. bd., 1968-69; adv. bd. Ariz. State U. Tax Insts., 1968-70; bd. dirs. Phoenix Cmty. Coun., Phoenix Cmty. Alliance, Arizona Acad.

CRAIN, RAY, statistician, consultant; b. St. Louis, Apr. 17, 1944; s. Chester Raymond and Mary Louise (Landers) C.; m. Barbara Hope Fagnan, Sept. 2, 1967; 1 child, Michelle Wigmore. AB, Knox Coll., 1965; MA, U. Calif., Riverside, 1967; PhD, U. N.Mex., 1974. Rsch. statistician Knoll Pharm. Co., Whippany, N.J., 1980; mgr. stats. McNeil Pharm., Spring House, Pa., 1980-81; sr. biostatistician Miles Pharms., West Haven, Conn., 1981-83; dir. statis. svcs. Boots Pharms., Shreveport, La., 1983-84; mgr. biometrics Du-Pont Co., Wilmington, Del., 1984-85, cons. dept. cen. R & D, 1985-90; dept. coord. Corp. Electronic Info. Security Com., 1987-90; sr. statistician Baxter Hyland Div., Glendale, Calif., 1990-91, Advanced Micro Devices, Sunnyvale, Calif., 1991-93; ind. cons., 1993—. Author: Scientific Computing Division's Enhanced Statistical Products Product Plan; contbr. articles to profl. jours. Mem. ASTD, Am. Soc. Quality (chmn-elect local sect. 1995), Am. Statis. Assn., Soc. Clin. Trials, Orgn. Devel. Network, Phi Beta Kappa, Sigma Xi. Democrat. Unitarian. Home: 1038 Sandalwood Ln Milpitas CA 95035-3232

CRALLEY, LESTER VINCENT, retired industrial hygienist, editor; b. Carmi, Ill., Mar. 27, 1911; s. John W. Cralley and Martha Jones; m. Gertrude E. Wilson, Aug. 24, 1940; 1 child, Agnes D. BS, McKendree Coll., 1933; PhD, U. Iowa, 1942. Res. officer USPHS, Bethesda, Md., 1941-45; chief indsl. hygienist Aluminum Co. of Am., Pitts., 1945-67, mgr. environ. health svcs., 1968-74; mem. Sec. of Labor's Nat. Safety Adv. Com., Washington, 1969-70. Co-editor: Theory and Rationale of Industrial Hygiene Practice, 1985, new edit., 1994, In Plant Practices for Job Related Health Hazards Control, 1989, Health and Safety Beyond the Workplace, 1990. Mem. Am. Indsl. Hygiene Assn. (hon., treas. 1953-56, pres. 1956-57, Cummings Meml. award 1971), Am. Acad. Indsl. Hygiene, Internat. Commn. on Occupational Health, Planetary Soc. Home: 1453 Banyan Dr Fallbrook CA 92028-1105

CRAM, DONALD JAMES, chemistry educator; b. Chester, Vt., Apr. 22, 1919; s. William Moffet and Joanna (Shelley) C.; m. Jane Maxwell, Nov. 25, 1969. BS, Rollins Coll., 1941; MS, U. Nebr., 1942; PhD, Harvard U., 1947; PhD (hon.), U. Uppsala, 1977; DSc (hon.), U. So. Calif., 1983, Rollins Coll., 1988, U. Nebr., 1989, U. Western Ontario, 1990, U. Sheffield, 1991. Rsch. chemist Merck & Co., 1942-45; asst. prof. chemistry UCLA, 1947-50, assoc. prof., 1950-56, prof., 1956-90, S. Winstein prof., 1985-95, univ. prof., 1988-90, univ. prof. emeritus, 1990—; chem. con. Upjohn Co., 1952-88, Union Carbide Co., 1960-81, Eastman Kodak Co., 1981-91, Technicon Co., 1984-92, Inst. Guido Donegani, Milan, 1988-91; State Dept. exch. fellow to Inst. de Quimica, Nat. U. Mex., 1956; guest prof. U. Heidelberg, Fed. Republic Germany, 1958; guest lectr. S. Africa, 1967; Centenary lectr. Chem. Soc. London, 1976. Author: From Design to Discovery, 1990, (with Pine, Hendrickson and Hammond) Organic Chemistry, 1960, 4th edit., 1980, Fundamentals of Carbanion Chemistry, 1965, (with Richards and Hammond) Elements of Organic Chemistry, 1967, (with Cram) Essence of Organic Chemistry, 1977, (with Cram) Container Molecules and Their Guests, 1994; contbr. chpts. to textbooks, articles in field of host-guest complexation chemistry, carbanions, stereochemistry, mold metabolites, large ring chemistry. Named Young Man of Yr. Calif. Jr. C. of C., 1954, Calif. Scientist of Yr., 1974, Nobel Laureate in Chemistry, 1987, UCLA medal, 1993; recipient award for creative work in synthetic organic chemistry Am. Chem. Soc., 1965, Arthur C. Cope award, 1974, Richard Tolman medal, 1985, Willard Gibbs award, 1985, Roger Adams award, 1985, Herbert Newby McCoy award, 1965, 75, Glenn Seaborg award, 1989, Nat. Medal of Science, Nat. Sci. Found., 1993; award for creative rsch. organic chemistry Synthetic Organic Chem. Mfrs. Assn., 1965; Nat. Rsch. fellow Harvard U., 1947, Am. Chem. Soc. fellow, 1947-48, Guggenheim fellow, 1954-55. Fellow Royal Soc. (hon. 1989); mem. NAS (award in chem. scis. 1992), Am. Acad. Arts and Scis., Am. Chem. Soc., Royal Soc. Chemistry, Surfers Med. Assn., San Onofre Surfing Club, Sigma Xi, Lambda Chi Alpha. Office: UCLA Dept Chemistry Los Angeles CA 90095-1569*

CRAMER, ESTHER RIDGWAY, author, historian, retired supermarket executive; b. La Habra, Calif., Jan. 17, 1927; d. Claude Arthur and Ida Alma (Leutwiler) Ridgway; m. Stanley Edward Cramer, June 17, 1948; children: Cynthia Ann Cramer Freeman, Melinda Cramer Ching, Janet Cramer Esguerra Brooks. BA, Pomona Coll., Claremont, Calif., 1948; postgrad., U. So. Calif., 1949, Calif. State U., Fullerton, 1960-67. Cert. secondary sch. tchr., Calif. Supr. phys. edn. Fullerton Schs., 1948-51; city historian City of La Habra, Calif., 1965—; v.p. cmty. rels. Alpha Beta Co., La Habra, 1979-86, dir. consumer affairs, 1973-79; author, historian Orange County, Calif., 1965—; mem. Orange County Hist. Commn., Santa Ana, Calif., 1973—; commr. USDA Meat and Poultry Inspection Bd., Washington, 1982-84; v.p. Orange County Centennial, Santa Ana, 1987-89. Author: La Habra, The Pass Through the Hills, 1970, The Alpha Beta Story, 1973, Brea, The City of Oil, Oranges and Opportunity, 1992, A Bell in the Barranca, 1996; editor: A Hundred Years of Yesterdays, 1989, Early Business History of Orange County, 1992, others; numerous oral histories in collection at Calif. State U., Fullerton. Mem. adv. bd. Orange County coun. Boys and Girls Club, 1978—, past pres.; mem. adv. bd. La Habra Boys and Girls Clubs, 1987, past pres.; mem. adv. bd. La Habra Children's Mus., 1980—. Recipient Donald Pfleuger award for local history Hist. Soc. So. Calif., 1992, Outstanding Author award U. Calif., Irvine, 1970; named to Hall of Fame, So. Calif. Grocers, 1985, Hall of Fame, Fullerton Union H.S., 1994. Mem. Orange County Hist. Soc. (pres. 1971-72), Orange County Pioneer Coun. (pres. 1993-94), La Habra Old Settlers Hist. Soc. (historian 1973—), Mortar Board, Phi Beta Kappa. Republican. Methodist. Avocations: writing, travel. Home: 600 Linden Ln La Habra CA 90631-3124

CRAMER, EUGENE NORMAN, nuclear power engineer, computer educator; b. Arkansas City, Kans., Apr. 26, 1932; s. Norman Charles and Hulda Margaret (Maier) C.; m. Donna Marie Gagliardi, May 18, 1957 (dec. 1984); children: Lorene, Kristine, Eileen, Carla; m. Marlene McLean, Dec. 29, 1985. BS in Physics, Kans. State Coll., 1955, BS in Math., 1955; grad. Oak Ridge Sch. Reactor Tech., 1959; MA in Mgmt., Claremont Grad. Sch., 1976, MBA, 1985. Registered profl. engr., Calif. Jr. engr. Westinghouse Bettis, Pitts., 1955-57; devel. engr. Oak Ridge Nat. Lab., 1959-69; cons. examiner AEC, 1961-73; engr. advanced energy system So. Calif. Edison, Los Angeles, 1969-88, mgr. nuclear comm., 1988-95, pres., asst. to edn. 1995—; sec. task force on nuclear safety research Electric Research Council, 1969-74; chmn. Pub. Edn. Utility Nuclear Waste Mgmt. Group, 1978-81, Pub. Edn. Calif. Radioactive Waste Mgmt. Forum, 1982-97. Sect. editor Nuclear Safety jour., 1964-69. Contbr. articles to profl. jours. Mem. Capistrano Unified Sch. Dist. Edn. Found., 1994-96. Served as 1st lt. Signal Corps, U.S. Army, 1957-59. Fellow Inst. for Advancement Engrng.; mem. Am. Nuclear Soc. (bd. dirs. 1978-81, Meritorious Service award 1981, pub. info. com. 1983—), Health Physics Soc., Soc. for Risk Analysis. Republican. Roman Catholic. Club: Sierra. Home and Office: 2176 Via Teca San Clemente CA 92673-5648

CRAMER, FRANK BROWN, engineering executive, combustion engineer, systems consultant; b. Long Beach, Calif., Aug. 29, 1921; s. Frank Brown and Clara Bell (Ritzenthaler) C.; m. Hendrika Van der Hulst, 1948 (div. 1962); children: Frieda Hendrika, Eric Gustav, Lisa Monica, Christina Elena; m. Paula Gil, Aug. 3, 1973; children: Alfred Alexander, Consuelo F., Peter M. BA, U. So. Calif., 1942, postgrad., 1942-43, 46-51. Rsch. fellow U. So. Calif., L.A., 1946-51; supr. engring. Rocketdyne, Canoga Park, Calif., 1953-63; pres. Multi-Tech, Inc., San Fernando, Calif., 1960-69; systems cons. Electro-Optical Systems, Pasadena, Calif., 1969-70, McDonnell-Douglas Astronautic, Huntington Beach, Calif., 1971-72; pres. Ergs Unltd. Inc., Mission Hills, Calif., 1973-89, Acquisition, Mission Hills, 1988—; instr. engring. stats. U. So. Calif., L.A., 1955-57; sys. cons. dept. medicine, 1959-68; sys. cons. Jet Propulsion Lab., Pasadena, 1964-68; mem. coun. Realtors Coun. Comml. and Investment Brokers. Author: Statistics for Medical Students, 1951, Combustion Processes/Liquid Rocket Engring., 1968; contbr. articles to profl. jours.; patentee in field. Committeeman Libertarian Party, San Fernando Valley, Calif., 1966, Rep. Party, Mission Hills, 1967-68; dir. realtor's com. on the air quality mgmt. plan So. Calif. Air Quality Control Dist., treas. realtor com. for air quality, 1994-95, vice chmn., 1996; pres. San Fernando Rep. Club, 1967-68; dir., mem. exec. com. Los Angeles County Bd. Realtors. Office: Acquisition 14800 Alexander St Mission Hills CA 91345-1210

CRAMER, JAMES DALE, physicist, scientific company executive; b. Canton, Ohio, Aug. 4, 1937; s. Dale and Vera Arlene (Lindower) C.; B.S., Calif. State U. at Fresno, 1960; M.S., U. Oreg., 1962; Ph.D., U. N.Mex., 1969; m. Geraldine M. Bendoski, July 20, 1957; children—Karen Lynn, Eric James. Mem. tech. staff U. Calif., Los Alamos, 1962-70; v.p., Davis-Smith Corp., San Diego, 1970-73; mem. tech. staff Sci. Applications Inc., LaJolla, Calif., 1970-73, group v.p., Albuquerque, 1973-80, dir., 1974-80; pres. Sci. & Engring. Assocs., Inc., Albuquerque, 1980—; cons. in field. Pres. Albuquerque Mus. Found., 1981-83. Mem. Am. Phys. Soc., IEEE. Contbr. articles to profl. publs. nuclear physics. Home: PO Box 30691 Albuquerque NM 87190-0691 Office: 6100 Uptown Blvd NE Ste 700 Albuquerque NM 87110-4143*

CRAMPTON, ESTHER LARSON, sociology and political science educator; b. Plainview, Nebr., Apr. 14, 1915; d. Charles W. and Anna Margrethe (Staugaard) Larson; m. Francis Asbury Crampton, Jan. 19, 1949 (dec.); children: Jacqueline, Edith. AB, Colo. Coll. of Edn., 1935; MA, U. Wis., 1937; PhD, Am. U., 1972. Observer, writer U.S. Weather Bur., Washington, 1942-48; interpreter Portuguese RFC Rubber Devel. Corp., Manaos, Brasil, 1943; tchr. Latin Glenn County High Sch., Willows, Calif., 1954-57; tchr. Latin/German Scottsdale (Ariz.) High Sch., 1957-62; tchr. Latin Natrona County High Sch., Casper, Wyo., 1962-64; tchr. social studies Bourgade High Sch., Phoenix, 1964-65; substitute tchr. Phoenix High Sch., 1965-66; instr. supr. We. N.Mex. U. Lab. Sch., Silver City, 1966-67; prof. sociology and polit. sci. Cochise C.C., Douglas, Ariz., 1967-77. Editor: Lily, Chinese Notes of the Late Frank Crampton, 1888-1961, 1990; copyright owner Deep Enough by Frank Crampton. Sec., v.p., bd. dirs. Easter Seal Soc. of Santa Cruz, 1979-81; active Nat. Women's Polit. Caucus Br., Santa Cruz, 1979; tutor reading Literacy Coun., San Luis Obispo, 1988. Grantee Amazonia Rsch. Orgn. of Am. States, 1970, Am. Coun. of Learned Socs., 1941. Mem. AAUW (chair 1977-81, internat. rels. group Santa Cruz br. mem.-at-large 1981—), Am. Assn. Women in Cmty. and Jr. Colls. (charter mem.). Avocations: Amazonia, geneaological research.

CRANCH, HAROLD COVERT, minister; b. Bryn Athyn, Pa., Oct. 10, 1911; s. Walter Appleton and Clara (Covert) C.; m. Jean Seville Smith, June 20, 1936; children—Virginia, Walter, Jonathan, Suzanne, Nora, Claudia, Margaret, Gabrielle. AA, Coll. Acad. of the New Ch., 1933, BTh, 1941, MDiv, 1990. Ordained to ministry Swedenborgian Ch., 1941. Pastor Sharon Ch., Chgo., 1941-52, Gabriel Ch., Glendale, Calif., 1952-66, Olivet Ch., Toronto, Ont., Can., 1966-76; assoc. pastor Immanuel Ch., Glenview, Ill., 1976-80; pastor Boston Soc., 1980-82; assoc. pastor Gabriel Ch., LaCrescenta, Calif., 1982—; dir. religion lesson, 1941-45, evangelization, 1952-66, religious programming Sta. WMWA-FM, Glenview, Ill, 1978-80; mem. Bishop's Consistory, 1955-70; exec. v.p. Gen. Ch. of New Jerusalem in Can., 1972-74; lectr. Edn. Coun. Archaeology, Acad. of New Ch., 1990. Recipient Glencairn Found. award, 1986. Author: Building Succesful Sunday Schools, 1954, Leader of His People, 1957, Principles of Evangelization, 1958, Ten Commandments, 1968, Teach Us to Pray, 1977, Monotheism and the Gods, 1989; contbr. articles to profl. jours. Mem. Coun. Clergy, Swedenborg Sci. Assn., Swedenborg Found. (life), Swedenborg Soc. (London, life), Bibl. Archaeology Soc. Republican. Home: 501 Porter St Glendale CA 91205-1911

CRANE, CHARLES ARTHUR, college president; b. Sweet Home, Oreg., July 4, 1938; s. Claude Carl Crane and Jessie LaVelle (Waters) Blevins; m. Margaret Lucile Ross, Nov. 28, 1957; children: Douglas Gordon, Steven Alan, Carol Elizabeth Hawn. B.Sacred Lit., Northwest Coll. of the Bible, 1962; MA, Lincoln Christian Sem., 1975, MDiv, 1977; D.Ministry, Luther-Rice Sem., 1978. Sr. min. Your Neighborhood Ch. of Christ, Sutherlin, Oreg., 1962-66, Southeast Christian Ch., Salt Lake City, 1966-73; sr. min. First Christian Ch., Moweaqua, Ill., 1973-76, Caldwell, Idaho, 1976-83; sr. min. Santa Clara Ch. of Christ, Eugene, Oreg., 1983-90; pres. Boise (Idaho) Bible Coll., 1990—; trustee Intermountain Bible Coll., Grand Junction, Colo., 1967-73; trustee, pres. Navajo Christian Mission, Tecnos Pos, N.Mex., 1967-73; committeeman N.Am. Christian Conv., Cin.; pres. Western Area Christian conv., Denver, 1973. Author: Do You Know What the Mormon Church Teaches?, 1972, Mormon Missionaries in Flight, 1973, The Bible and Mormon Scriptures Compared, 1975, A Practical Guide to Soulwinning, 1989, Ashamed of Joseph-Mormon Foundations Crumble, 1994, Effective Witnessing to Mormons, 1994; contbr. articles to profl. jours. Scoutmaster Boy Scouts Am., Sutherlin, 1965-66. Mem. Kiwanis Internat. (spiritual life chmn. Caldwell chpt. 1980-83). Republican. Avocations: photography, old car restoration, flying, travel, art. Office: Bible Coll 8695 Marigold St Boise ID 83714-1220

CRANE, FRANK MELVIN, agricultural company executive; b. Mankato, Minn., June 10, 1923; s. Lucas Melvin and Marie Regina (Lindquist) C.; m. Audrey Mae Kraus, June 26, 1948 (dec. 1985); children: Carolyn, Keith, Suzanne; m. Hildegarde S. Streufert, July 11, 1987. BS, U. Minn., 1948, MS, 1949, PhD, 1954. Instr. U. Minn., St. Paul, 1948-51; rsch. dir. Land O' Lakes, Inc., Arden Hills, Minn., 1951-70; v.p. mktg. Land O' Lakes, Inc., Ft. Dodge, Iowa, 1970-74; v.p rsch. Land O' Lakes, Inc., Ft. Dodge, 1974-82; chmn. bd. dirs. Frank M. Crane & Assocs., Ft. Dodge and Tempe, Ariz., 1982—; chmn. bd. Am. Feed Industry Assn., Washington, 1980-82; cons., advisor Pres. Carter, Pres. Ford, Pres. Reagan, 1974-88, numerous secs. of agrl., 1952-90, Am. Soybean Assn., U.S. Feed Grains Coun., 1960-91; lectr. in field; participant in numerous seminars in confs. Contbr. numerous articles to internat. profl. jours.; inventor Land O' Lakes calf milk replacer,

1951. Chmn. United Way, Ft. Dodge, 1974-77; dir. Friendship Haven Retirement Home, Ft. Dodge, 1976-87; chmn. fin. com. Ft. Dodge Meth. Ch., 1976-80; sec. ch. coun. Mountain View Lutheran Ch., Phoenix, 1989—. Mem. Am. Soc. Animal Sci., Am. Dairy Sci. Assn., Poultry Sci. Assn., World's Poultry Assn., Am. Registry of Profl. Animal Scientists (cert.), Ft. Dodge C. of C. (bd. dirs., fin. com. 1976-80), Rotary (pres. 1984-85), Alpha Zeta, Alpha Gamma Rho (pres. 1960-70, Man of the Year 1989), Gamma Alpha. Avocation: photography. Home and Office: 11239 S Tomah St Phoenix AZ 85044-1915

CRANE, PETER, financial consultant; b. Jersey City, Dec. 15, 1945; s. Robert D. and Anna Marie (Little) C.; m. Paula T. Cain, June 22, 1968; children: Hillary, Magan. BS in Polit. Sci., Xavier U., 1967; MA in Pub. Adminstrn., George Wash. U., 1972. Mgmt. interpreter U.S. Dept. Health, Washington, 1969-72; mgmt. analyst U.S. Dept. Health, Seattle, 1972-76; trident coord. Kitsap County, Port Orchard, Wash., 1976-80; pres. Ctr. for Govt. Rels., Rolling Bay, Wash., 1980-83; 1st v.p., fin. cons. Salomon Smiith Barney, Silverdale, Wash., 1983—. Pres., bd. dirs. Kitsap United Way, Bremerton, Wash., 1980—; pres., libr. trustee Kitsap Regional Libr., Bremerton, 1995—; founding mem. Kitsap Cares Partnership, Bremerton, 1995—; state del. Washington Dem. Party, Seattle, 1981-83; founding mem., bd. dirs. Kitsap Econ. Devel. Coun., 1980—, Dispute Resolution Ctr., 1991-93; bd. dirs. Kitsap Mental Health Svcs., 1980-82. Mem. Kitsap Housing and Transp. Assn., (founding mem., pres. 1980-82), Rotary (bd. dirs. 1983—), Silverdale C. of C. (v.p. 1980—). Democrat. Officee: Salomon Smith Barney 9633 Levin Rd NW Silverdale WA 98383-8131

CRANE, STEVEN, financial company executive; b. Los Angeles, Jan. 21, 1959; s. Roger D. and Violet (Heard) C.; m. Susan Jean Perea June 27, 1998; 1 child Allison Nicole. Grad. high sch. With Mobar Inc., Torrance, Calif., 1976-78; v.p. internat. Fluid Control Internat., Marina del Rey, Calif., 1978-79; pres. Energy Devel. Internat., Torrance, 1979-85; pres., chief exec. officer Kaempen USA, Inc., Anaheim, Calif., 1985-91; founding ptnr., chmn. Western Fin. Group, Inc., Redondo Beach, Calif., 1991-95; CEO, Artist Network, Huntington Beach, Calif., 1993-95; chmn., bd. dirs. CorpHQ Inc., Long Beach, 1995—; bd. dirs. Artist Network; chmn. bd. dirs. We. Finance Group, Inc. Mem. Avocations: kickboxing, photography, basketball, bird hunting. Office: CorpHQ Inc 110 W Ocean Blvd #604 Long Beach CA 90802-4430

CRANSTON, HOWARD STEPHEN, lawyer, management consultant; b. Hartford, Conn., Oct. 20, 1937; s. Howard Samuel and Agnes (Corvo) C.; m. Karen Youngman, June 16, 1962; children: Margaret, Susan. BA cum laude, Pomona Coll., 1959; LLB, Harvard U., 1962. Bar: Calif. 1963. Assoc. MacDonald & Halsted, L.A., 1964-68; ptnr. MacDonald, Halsted & Laybourne, L.A., 1968-82, of counsel, 1982-86; pres. Knapp Comm., L.A., 1982-87; pres. S.C. Cons. Corp., 1987—; bd. dirs. Boys Republic, Mental Health Assn. L.A. 1st lt. U.S. Army, 1962-64. Mem. San Gabriel Country Club, Harvard Club (N.Y.). Republican. Episcopalian. Author Handbook for Creative Managers, 1987, Management Decision Mag., 1988—. Office: 1613 Chelsea Rd # 252 Pasadena CA 91108-2419

CRAPO, MICHAEL DEAN, senator, former congressman, lawyer; b. Idaho Falls, Idaho, May 20, 1951; s. George Lavelle and Melba (Olsen) C.; m. Susan Diane Hasleton, June 22, 1974; children: Michelle, Brian, Stephanie, Lara, Paul. BA Polit. Sci. summa cum laude, Brigham Young U., 1973; postgrad., U. Utah, 1973-74; JD cum laude, Harvard U., 1977. Bar: Calif. 1977, Idaho 1979. Law clk. to Hon. James M. Carter U.S. Ct. Appeals (9th cir.), San Diego, 1977-78; assoc. atty. Gibson, Dunn & Crutcher, L.A., 1978-79; atty. Holden, Kidwell, Hahn & Crapo, Idaho Falls, 1979-92, ptnr., 1983-92; mem. Idaho State Senate from 32A Dist., 1984-93, asst. majority leader, 1987-88; pres. Pro Tempore, 1989-92; congressman U.S. House of Reps., 2d Idaho dist., Washington, 1992-98; mem. commerce com., new mem. leader 103rd Congress, sophomore class leader 104th Congress, co-chair Congl. Beef Caucus, dep. whip western region U.S. House of Reps., Washington, vice chair energy and power subcom., strategic planning leader House Leadership 105th Congress, mem. house resources com., mem. commerce com., mem. resources com.; senator U.S. Senate, 1999—; precinct committeeman Dist. 29, 1980-85; vice chmn. Legislative Dist. 29, 1984-85; Mem. Health and Welfare Com., 1985-89, Resources and Environ. Com., 1985-90, State Affairs Com., 1987-92; Rep. Pres. Task Force, 1989. Leader Boy Scouts Am., Calif., Idaho, 1977-92; mem. Bar Exam Preparation, Bar Exam Grading; chmn. Law Day; Bonneville County chmn. Phil Batt gubernatorial campaign, 1982. Named one of Outstanding Young Men of Am., 1985; recipient Cert. of Merit Rep. Nat. Com., 1990, Guardian of Small Bus. award Nat. Fedn. of Ind. Bus., 1990, 94, Cert. of Recognition Am. Cancer Soc., 1990, Idaho Housing Agy., 1990, Idaho Lung Assn., 1985, 86, 89, Friend of Agr. award Idaho Farm Bur., 1989-90, medal of merit Rep. Presdl. Task Force, 1989, Nat. Legislator of Yr. award Nat. Rep. Legislators Assn., 1991, Golden Bulldog award Watchdogs of the Treas., 1996, Thomas Jefferson award Nat. Am. Wholesale Grocers Assn.-Ind. Food Distbrs. Assn., 1996, Spirit of Enterprise award U.S. C. of C., 1993, 94, 95, 96. Mem. ABA (antitrust law sect.), Idaho Bar Assn., Rotary. Mormon. Avocations: sports, backpacking, hunting, skiing. Office: US Senate G50 Dirksen Senate Office Bldg Washington DC 20510*

CRAPO, SHEILA ANNE, telecommunications company professional, artist; b. Elko, Nev., June 11, 1951; d. John Lewis and June Florene (Lani) C. BA, U. Nev., 1974. Various svc. positions Citizens Comm. (formerly Alltel-Nevada Inc.), Elko, 1974-78, svc. rep., 1978-84, bus. office supr., 1984-87, bus. supr. Nev. office, 1987-94, bus. supr., state pub. rels. coord., 1994-97; results coord., project mgmt. support person Citizens Comm. (formerly Alltel-Nevada Inc.), Elk Grove, Calif., 1997, supr. customer ops. escalations and exec. complaints, 1998—; active Citizens Ambassador program People to People Internat., 1995-98; writer, artist, 1974—; speaker in field. Contbg. author: Fence Post to Fiber, 1998. Officer, organizer Freedom Com., Elko, 1984; mem., treas. Elk Grove Cmty. Action Team, 1997-98. Mem. AAUW (editor newsletter Elko 1980-82, v.p. programs 1991-93, sec. 1995-96), Northeastern Nev. Hist. Soc., Soroptimists Internat. (treas. 1992-93, sec. 1993-94, v.p. 1995-96, pres. 1996-97). Office: Citizens Comm PO Box 340 Elk Grove CA 95759-0340

CRATER, BONNIE LOCKHART, computer software company executive; b. Glen Ridge, N.J., July 27, 1962; d. David Hopkins Crater and Nancy Edmondson Jandl; m. Christpher Alan Buja, June 1, 1985; 1 child, Spencer Buja. BA in Biology, Princeton U., 1984. Mgr. Oracle Corp., Redwood Shores, Calif., 1988-93, dir., 1994-95, v.p., 1996-97; v.p. Network Computer, Inc., Redwood Shores, 1997-98, Netscape Comms., Mountain View, Calif., 1998—. Mem. Horsepark Polo Club (bd. dirs. 1997-98), Sigma Xi. Avocations: skating, riding. Home: 172 Wayside Rd Portola Valley CA 94028-7224

CRAVEN, JAMES MICHAEL, economist, educator; b. Seattle, Mar. 10, 1946; s. Homer Henry and Mary Kathleen Craven; 1 child, Christina Kathleen Florindo-Craven. Student, U. Minn., 1966-68; BA in Sociology, U. Manitoba, Winnipeg, Can., 1971, BA in Econs., 1971, MA in Econs., 1974. Lic. pilot; cert. ground instr. Instr. econ. and bus. Red River C.C., Winnipeg, 1974-76; lectr. rsch. methods of stats. U. Manitoba, Winnipeg, 1977-78; instr. econ. and bus. Big Bend C.C., Moses Lake, Wash., 1980-81; planning analyst Govt. P.R., San Juan, 1984; prof. econs. and bus. Interam. U. P.R., Bayamon, 1984-85; instr. econs., lectr. history Green River C.C., Auburn, Wash., 1988-92; prof. dept. chair econs. Clark Coll., Vancouver, Wash., 1992—; vis. prof. St. Berchman's U., Kerala, India, 1981, 83, 86, 91; instr. econs. Bellevue (Wash.) C.C., 1988-92; cons. Bellevue, 1988—, Irwin Pubs., 1995—. Inventor in field; contbr, articles to profl. jours. Platform com. mem. Wash. State Dem., Seattle, 1992; cons. Lowry for Gov. Campaign, Seattle, 1992; mem. (assoc.) Dem. Party Nat. Com., 1994—; mem. Nat. Steering Com. for Re-election of Pres. Clinton, 1995-96; mem. Pres.'s Second Term Com., 1996—; tribunal judge Inter-Tribal Tribunal on Residential Schs. in Can., Vancouver, 1998; mem. Blackfoot Confederacy. With U.S. Army, 1963-66. Recipient pilot wings FAA, 1988-92; Govt. Can. fellow, 1973-74. Mem. Internat. Platform Assn., Assn. Northwest Econ. Educators, Wash. Edn. Assn., Assn. Nat. Security Alumni, Blackfoot Confederacy. Syrian Orthodox. Avocations: flying, languages, tennis, hiking. Home: 904 NE Minnehaha St Apt C9 Vancouver WA 98665-8732 Office: Clark Coll Dept Econs 1800 E Mcloughlin Blvd Vancouver WA 98663-3598

CRAW, NICHOLAS WESSON, motor sports association executive; b. Governor's Island, N.Y., Nov. 14, 1936; s. Demas Thurlow Craw and Mary Victoria Wesson. BA cum laude, Princeton U., 1959; MBA, Harvard U., 1982. Dir. ops. Project Hope, Washington, 1960-68; pres., CEO Scorpio Racing, Washington, 1968-80, Sports Car Club Am., Englewood, Colo., 1983—; pres. Sports Car Club Am. Found, Englewood, 1986—; chmn. Nat. Motorsports Coun., 1992—; bd. dirs. SCCA Pro Racing Ltd., SCCA Enterprises, Inc., USRRC, Rsch. Sys., Inc. Dir. Manpower divsn. VISTA, Washington, 1970-72; assoc. dir. ACTION, Washington, 1972-73; dir. U.S. Peace Corps, Washington, 1973-74. Office: Sports Car Club Am 9033 E Easter Pl Englewood CO 80112-2122

CRAWFORD, CURTIS J., computer and electronics company executive. CEO Zilog, Campbell, Calif. Office: Zilog 910 E Hamilton Ave Ste 110 Campbell CA 95008-0612*

CRAWFORD, MIA LOUISA, television network operations coordinator; b. L.A., Aug. 27, 1964; d. Donald Paul and Ethel Lee (Gilliam) C. BA in Radio and TV Broadcasting, Calif. State U., Northridge, 1987; continuing edn. student in cinema and TV, U. So. Calif., 1992-95. Program mgr. Western World/The Video Tape Co., North Hollywood, Calif., 1987-91; fin. aid counselor U. So. Calif., L.A., 1991-95; video engr. RJM Inc., L.A., 1987—; network ops. coord. Fox Digital (Divsn. Fox Broadcasting), L.A., 1995—; camera person RJM Inc., 1987—, tech. dir., 1990—. Co-prodr. (cable TV show) Women and Health, 1987. Youth instr. RJM, Inc., 1988—. Mem. Calif. State U. Northridge Alumni Assn. Avocations: cinematography, editing, antiques, viewing documentaries, guitar.

CRAWFORD, MICHAEL, city council; married. BS in Computer Sci., Wright State U., 1988; law degree, U. Ariz., 1991. Clk. Ariz. Ct. Appeals; computer software cons.; vice chmn. Ariz. Common Cause; criminal def. atty. Pima County Pub. Defenders Office, 1994-98; with O'Connor, Cavanaugh, Malloy, Jones, Tucson, AZ, 1998—. Office: O'Connor Cavanaugh Malloy Jones 32 N Stone Ave Ste 2100 Tucson AZ 85702-1403*

CRAWFORD, NATALIE WILSON, applied mathematician; b. Evansville, Ind., June 24, 1939; d. John Moore and Edna Dorothea (Huthsteiner) Wilson; BA in Math., U. Calif., L.A., 1961, postgrad., 1964-67; m. Robert Charles Crawford, Mar. 1, 1969. Programmer analyst N.Am. Aviation Corp., El Segundo, Calif., 1961-64; mem. tech. staff RAND Corp., Santa Monica, Calif., 1964—, project leader, engring. tech., theater conflict and force employment programs, 1975—; dir. Theater Forces Program, 1988-90, Theater Force Employment Program, 1990-92, Force Structure and Force Modernization Program, 1992-93, Force Modernization and Employment Program, 1993-95, assoc. dir. Project Air Force, 1995-97, v.p. rand, dir. project, 1997—; mem. Air Force Sci. Adv. Bd., 1988—, vice-chair, 1990-91, co-chair, 1996—; cons., joint tech. coordinating group munition effectiveness. Named YWCA Woman of Yr., 1983. Mem. Am. Def. Preparedness Assn., USAF Assn. Republican. Home: 20940 Big Rock Dr Malibu CA 90265-5316

CRAWFORD, PHILIP STANLEY, bank executive; b. Wichita, Kans., Nov. 30, 1944; s. Carson Eugene and Elizabeth Ellen (Childs) C.; m. Carolyn Louise Stephenson, June 10, 1989. BA, Sterling Coll., 1967; MBA, Baruch Coll., 1973. Programmer, analyst City of N.Y., 1968-72; planning analyst Fed. Reserve Bank, Boston, 1972-74; cons. Index Systems, Cambridge, Mass., 1974-79; sr. cons. Ernst & Whinney, Los Angeles, 1979; v.p. Union Bank, Los Angeles, 1979—. Mem. Pres.'s Coun. Sterling Coll. Mem. Mgmt. Info. Continuing Seminar (pres. 1985), Assn. Computing Machinery. Republican. Avocations: photography, genealogy. Home: 3815 Olive Ave Long Beach CA 90807-3519 Office: Union Bank 1980 Saturn St Monterey Park CA 91755-7417

CRAWFORD, R. GEORGE, investment manager, educator; b. Mpls., Oct. 30, 1943; s. Robert John and Agnes C.; m. M. Holly Shissler, May, 17, 1980; 1 child, Katherine Barnes. BA, Harvard U., 1965, JD, 1968. Bar N.Y. 1974, DC 1970, Calif. 1972, Ohio, 1969. Law clk. to Hon. Byron R. White U.S. Supreme Ct., Washington, 1968-69; staff asst. to President Washington, 1970-72; v.p. Archon, Inc., L.A., 1972-74; chair pvt. capital sect. Jones Day Reavis & Pogue, L.A., 1974-93; prof. Stanford U., Calif., 1993—; pres. AII, Palo Alto, Calif., 1997—; rsch. fellow Hoover Instn., Stanford, Calif., 1994-97. Author: Derivatives for Decision Makers, 1996; contbr. articles to profl. jours. Dir. Fiduciary Found., Incline Village, Nev., 1992—. Mem. Internat. Corp. Governance Network, London (mem. com. on governance stds. 1997—), Supervisory Coun. Internat. Ctr. Not-for-Profit Law, Washington, 1998. Fax: (702) 832-9772. E-mail: geo@leland.stanford.edu. Home: 930 Tahoe Blvd # 802-269 Incline Village NV 89451-9451 Office: All 236 Stanford Ctr # 243 Palo Alto CA 94304

CREAR, MILDRED CLEAREATHA, nursing administrator; b. Lorman, Miss., June 8, 1939; d. Luther James and Julia (Gordan) Green; m. Jeff Archie Crear, June 16, 1962; 1 child, Julia Ann. BS in Nursing, U. Calif., San Francisco, 1962; MA in Edn., San Francisco State U., 1970; MPH in Adminstrn., U. Calif., Berkeley, 1978. Cert. pub. health nurse, Calif. Psychol. nurse Langle Porter, San Francisco, 1962-63; pub. health nurse San Francisco Health Dept., 1963-71, pub. health nursing supr., 1971-82, dep. dir. children's med. svcs., 1982-94, maternal, children, adolescent health dir., 1994—. Co-prodr. (video) Parenting-African American Perspective, 1996. Chmn. Maternal, Child Health adv. bd., 1992-94, mem., 1982—; bd. dirs. Support for Parents, San Francisco, 1992—, Bridge (residential drug rehab.), Berkeley, 1980—. Recipient Svc. certification Mayor San Francisco, 1990; grantee Bay Area March Dimes, 1995. Mem. APHA, ANA, Nat. Black Nurses Assn., Bay Area Black Nurses Assn (pres. 1978-82, chair nursing and cmty. edn. com. 1984—). Democrat. Baptist. Avocations: knitting, sewing, reading. Home: 5845 Mendocino Ave Oakland CA 94618-1808 Office: San Francisco Health Dept-MCAH 680 8th St Ste 200 San Francisco CA 94103-4942

CRECELIUS, DANIEL NEIL, history educator; b. St. Louis, Jan. 15, 1937; s. Wilson John and (Imhof) R.; m. Anahid Tashjian, July 21, 1963; 1 child, Gia Maria. BA, Colo. Coll., 1959; MA, Princeton U., 1962, PhD, 1967. Asst. prof. Calif. State U., L.A., 1964-68, assoc. prof., 1968-73, prof. Mid. East history, 1974—, chairperson, 1980-83, 98—; vis. lectr. UCLA, 1966-67, Colo. Coll., 1990, Cairo U., 1992. Contbr. numerous articles to profl. jours. Trustees' scholar Colo. Coll., 1955-59; Woodrow Wilson Nat. fellow, 1959-60, Princeton U. Near East fellow, 1961-62; grantee U. Mich., 1960, Princeton U., 1961, Fulbright Found., 1962-63, 91-92, 92, 95-96, 96, Nat. Def. Fgn. Lang. grantee, 1963-64, Am. Rsch. Ctr., 1972, 79, 96, Am. Philos. Soc., 1975, 80, 89, Social Sci. Rsch. Coun., 1973, Dept. HEW Office Edn., 1973, Calif. State U., L.A., 1975, NEH, 1980-82, 83-84, 87, 91-92, 92, Calif. State U. L.A. Found., 1979, 81, others; Joseph P. Malone fellow, 1998. Mem. Mid. East Studies Assn., Turkish Studies Assn., Phi Beta Kappa, Pi Gamma Mu. Lutheran. Avocations: travel, hiking, bird watching. Office: Calif State U LA 5151 State University Dr Los Angeles CA 90032

CREECH, WILBUR LYMAN, retired career officer; b. Argyle, Mo., Mar. 30, 1927; s. Paul and Marie (Maloney) C.; m. Carol Ann DiDomenico, Nov. 20, 1969; 1 son, William L. Student, U. Mo., 1946-48; B.S., U. Md., 1960; M.S., George Washington U., 1966; postgrad., Nat. War Coll., 1966. Commd. 2d lt. U.S. Air Force, 1949; advanced through grades to gen.; fighter pilot 103 combat missions USAF, North Korea, 1950-51; pilot USAF Thunderbirds, 1953-56; comdr., leader Skyblazers, Europe aerial demo team USAF, 1956-60; dir. Fighter Weapons Sch., Nellis AFB, Nev., 1960-61; advisor to comdr. Argentine Air Force, 1962; exec., aide to comdr. Tactical Air Command, 1962-65; dep. comdr. fighter wing, 177 combat missions in F-100 fighters and asst. dep. chief staff for ops. 7th Air Force, Vietnam, 1968-69; comdr. fighter wings USAF in Europe, Spain and W.Ger., 1969-71; dep. for ops. and intelligence Air Forces Europe, 1971-74; comdr. Electronic Systems Div., Hanscom AFB, Mass., 1974-77; asst. vice chief of staff HQS Air Force, Washington, 1977-78; comdr. Tactical Air Command, Langley AFB, Va., 1978-85; lectr., internat. mgmt. expert; cons. in field. Author: The Five Pillars of TQM, 1994. Decorated D.S.M. with three oak leaf clusters, Silver Star medal, Legion of Merit with two oak leaf clusters, D.F.C. with three oak leaf clusters, Air medal with 14 oak leaf clusters, Air Force Commendation medal with two oak leaf clusters, Army Commendation medal; Spanish Grand Cross. Home and Office: 20 Quail Run Rd Henderson NV 89014-2147

CREER, JAMES READ, financial officer; b. Ogden, Utah, Oct. 26, 1942; s. Harold and Geraldine (Jacobson) C.; m. Ann L. Curran, Aug. 7, 1964 (div. Aug. 1974); children: Wendy, Kellie, Mark, Jennifer; m. Carolyn Rudd, Jan. 11, 1985. BS in Acctg., U. Utah, 1968. CPA. Staff acct. PMM & Co., L.A., 1968-71; sr. acct. PMM & Co., Salt Lake City, 1971-72, Haynie, Tebbs & Smith, Salt Lake City, 1972-73; ptnr. Roberts & Creer, Salt Lake City, 1973-74; pvt. practice Salt Lake City, 1974-81; pres., CEO Johnstone Supply, Salt Lake City, 1995—; v.p., CFO ACW Enterprises Inc., Salt Lake City, 1989—; pres. Creer Corp., 1995—; acctg. instr. Utah Tech. Coll., Stevens-Henegar Coll. Bus., 1973-76. With USMC, 1960-63. Mem. Children's Justice Ctr. (adv. bd.), Rotary (pres. so. Salt Lake City chpt. 1989-90, Paul Harris fellow 1988). Republican. Mem. LDS Ch. Avocations: hunting, fishing, boating, golf, travel. Office: Johnstone Supply 2940 S 300 W Salt Lake City UT 84115-3482

CREIGHTON, JOHN W., JR., retired forest products company executive; b. Pitts., Sept. 1, 1932; married; 3 children. BS, Ohio State U., 1954, JD, 1957; MBA, U. Miami, 1965. With Arthur Andersen and Co., 1957-59, Arvida Corp., 1959-66; exec. v.p. Mortgage Cons. Inc., 1966-70; gen. mgr. Shelter Group Weyerhaeuser Co., 1970, corp. v.p., 1970-85, exec. v.p., 1985-88, pres., dir., 1988—, pres., CEO, ret., 1997; bd. dirs. United Airlines, Unocal Corp., Totem Resources, Local Initiatives Support Corp., NHP, Inc.; mem. press devel. adv. bd. U. Wash.; co-chair 2020 Commn. on post secondary edn. Wash. Trustee U. Puget Sound; pres. Boy Scouts Am. With U.S. Army, 1954-56. Office: Weyerhaeuser Co 33663 Weyerhaeuser Way S Federal Way WA 98001-9629

CREIGHTON, JOHN WALLIS, JR., consultant, author, former management educator; b. Yeung Kong, China, Apr. 7, 1916; s. John Wallis and Lois (Jameson) C.; m. Harriet Harrington, June 30, 1940; childrn: Carol (Mrs. Brian LeNeve), Joan (Mrs. Robert Nielsen). Student, Wooster Coll., 1933-36; BS in Forestry, U. Mich., 1938; AB, Hastings Coll., 1939; PhD in Wood Tech. and Indsl. Engring., U. Mich., 1954. Operator, sawmill Cayahoga Falls, Ohio, 1939-41; mem. staff U.S. Bd. Econ. Warfare, Ecuador, 1941-43; asst. gen. mgr. R.S. Bacon Veneer Co., Chgo., 1943-44; gen. mgr., v.p. Bacon Lumber Co., Sunman, Ind., 1943-45; mem. faculty Mich. State U., Lansing, 1945-54; prof. wood tech. Mich. State U., 1945-54; asst. to gen. mgr., v.p. Baker Furniture Inc., Grand Rapids, Mich., 1954-58; pres. Creighton Bldg. Co., Santa Barbara, Calif., 1958-65; prof. mgmt. Colo. State U., Fort Collins, 1965-67, U.S. Naval Postgrad. Sch., Monterey, Calif., 1967-86; emeritus prof. U.S. Naval Postgrad. Sch., 1986—, chmn. dept., 1967-71, dir. fed. exec. mgmt. program, 1974-82; cons. to govt. Assoc editor and co-founder Jour. Tech. Transfer, 1975-88; contbr. papers to field. Former mem. Forestry Commn., Carmel, Calif., 1986-95. Recipient various research grants in lumber mfg., research and orgn. studies for U.S. Navy and U.S. Forest Service. Mem. Tech. Transfer Soc., Writer's Internat. Network, Calif. Writer's Club. Presbyterian. Home: 8065 Lake Pl Carmel CA 93923-9514

CREMER, RICHARD ANTHONY, lawyer; b. Portland, Oreg., Aug. 3, 1950; s. Cornelius Vincent and Madeleine Josephine (Avena) C.; m. Teresa Ann Headrick, Oct. 1, 1988. BS, Portland State U., 1972; JD cum laude, Lewis & Clark Coll., 1975. Bar: Oreg. 1975, U.S. Dist. Ct. Oreg. 1979. Law clk. Judge Phillip Roth, Portland, Oreg., 1976; staff Pub. Defender's Office, Roseburg, Oreg., 1976-94; pvt. practice Roseburg, 1995—; bd. dirs. Dist. 6 Manpower, Roseburg, 1975. Commr., pres. City of Roseburg Planning Commn., 1977-87; mem. Eagle Scout Bd. of Rev., Roseburg, 1980—; referee Douglas County Football Officials, Roseburg, 1990—. Mem. Nat. Assn. Criminal Defense Lawyers (bd. dirs.), Oregon Criminal Defense Lawyers (pres. 1988-89). Avocations: skiing, bicycling, mountain climbing, hiking. Office: 727 SE Cass St Ste 306 Roseburg OR 97470-4954

CRESWELL, DONALD CRESTON, management consultant; b. Balt.; s. Carroll Creston and Verna Moore (Taylor) C.; student Johns Hopkins U.; MBA, U. Dayton; postgrad. bus. Stanford U.; m. Terri Sue Tidwell; 1 child, Creston Lee. Cons. engr. A.D. Ring & Assocs., Washington; sales and mktg. mgr. Ampex Corp., Redwood City, Calif.; dir. mktg., magnetic products div. RCA Corp., N.Y.C.; staff v.p. sales and advt. Pan Am. World Airways, N.Y.C.; prin. mgmt. cons., dir. mktg. svcs. Stanford Rsch. Inst., Menlo Park, Calif.; v.p. and gen. mgr. Decisions Systems; dir. R & D Strategy Practice; gen. mgr. R & D Decision Quality Assoc.; with Strategic Decisions Group, Menlo Park, Calif., 1987—; bd. dirs. Rogerson Aircraft Controls, 1981-85; bd. dirs., mgmt. com. Jets Cybernetics, 1987-94; lectr. planning and mktg. mgmt. Am. Mgmt. Assn., 1968-69; program chmn. Grad. Bus. Assn., 1965; rep. to Electronics Industries Assn., 1968-71, to Internat. Air Transport Assn., 1971-74. Bd. dirs. Peninsula Youth Soccer Club, 1981-82; nat. dir. referee assessment, mem. referee com. U.S. Soccer Fedn., 1986-88; regional chief referee San Carlos Am. Youth Soccer Orgn., 1981-85; State dir. assessment Calif. Soccer Assn., 1982-85; mem. L.A. Olympics Organizing Com., 1983-84, nat. referee assessor, 1987—; ofcl. N. Am. Soccer League, 1983-84, World Cup, 1994; sponsor Silicon Valley Roundtable. Mem. Am. Mktg. Assn. (exec. mem.), Am. Theatre Organ Assn. (bd. dirs. 1978-79), Nat. Intercollegiate Soccer Ofcls. Assn. (World cup video inspector, 1994), Charles Lindbergh Fund, U.S. Soccer Fedn. (cert. nat. assessor, USSF referee inspector), Silicon Valley Roundtable, The Churchill Club, Stanford Jazz Com. Republican. Home: 8 Pyrola Ln San Carlos CA 94070-1532 Office: Strategic Decisions Group 2440 Sand Hill Rd Menlo Park CA 94025-6900

CREWS, WILLIAM ODELL, JR., seminary administrator; b. Houston, Feb. 8, 1936; s. William O. Sr. and Juanita (Pearson) C.; m. Wanda Jo Ann Cunningham; children: Ronald Wayne, Rhonda Ann Crews Bolei. BA, Hardin Simmons U., 1957, HHD, 1987; BDiv, Southwestern Bapt. Theol. Sem., 1964; DD, Calif. Bapt. Coll., 1987. Ordained to ministry Bapt. Ch., 1953. Pastor Grape Creek Bapt. Ch., San Angelo, Tex., 1952-54, Plainview Bapt. Ch., Stamford, Tex., 1955-57, 1st Bapt. Ch., Sterling City, Tex., 1957-60, 7th St. Bapt. Ch., Ballinger, Tex., 1960-65, Woodland Heights Bapt. Ch., Brownwood, Tex., 1965-67, Victory Bapt. Ch., Seattle, 1967-72, Met. Bapt. Ch., Portland, Oreg., 1972-77; dir. comm. N.W. Bapt. Conv., Portland, 1977-78; pastor Magnolia Ave Bapt. Ch., Riverside, Calif., 1978-86; pres. Golden Gate Bapt. Theol. Sem., Mill Valley, Calif., 1986—; pres. N.W. Bapt. Conv., Portland, 1974-76, So. Bapt. Gen. Conv. Calif., Fresno, 1982-84. Trustee Fgn. Mission Bd., Richmond, Va., 1973-78, Golden Gate Bapt. Theol. Sem., 1980-85, Marin Cmty. Hosp. Found., 1992-95; bd. dirs. Midway Seatac Boys Club, Des Moines, 1969-72. Mem. Marin County C. of C. (bd. dirs. 1987-95), Midway C. of C. (bd. dirs. 1968-72), Rotary (bd. dirs. San Rafael chpt. 1992—, pres. Portland club 1975-76, pres.-elect Riverside club 1984-85). Home: 157 Chapel Dr Mill Valley CA 94941-3168 Office: Golden Gate Bapt Theol Sem 201 Seminary Dr Mill Valley CA 94941-3197

CRICK, FRANCIS HARRY COMPTON, science educator, researcher; b. June 8, 1916; s. Harry and Anne Elizabeth (Wilkins) C.; m. Ruth Doreen Dodd, 1940 (div. 1947); 1 son; m. Odile Speed, 1949; 2 daus. B.Sc., Univ. Coll., London; PhD, Cambridge U., Eng. Scientist Brit. Admiralty, 1940-47, Strangeways Lab., Cambridge, Eng., 1947-49; with Med. Rsch. Coun. Lab. of Molecular Biology, Cambridge, 1949-77; Kieckhefer Disting. prof. Salk Inst. Biol. Studies, San Diego, 1977—, non-resident fellow, 1962-73, pres., 1994-95; adj. prof. psychology U. Calif., San Diego; vis. lectr. Rockefeller Inst., N.Y.C., 1959; vis. prof. chemistry dept. Harvard U., 1959, vis. prof. biophysics, 1962; fellow Churchill Coll., Cambridge, 1960-61; Korkes Meml. lectr. Duke U., 1960; Henry Sidgewick Meml. lectr. Cambridge U., 1963; Graham Young lectr., Glasgow, 1963; Robert Boyle lectr. Oxford U., 1963; Vanuxem lectr. Princeton U., 1964; William T. Sedgwick Meml. lectr. MIT, 1965; Cherwell-Simon Meml. lectr. Oxford U., 1966; Shell lectr. Stanford U., 1969; Paul Lund lectr. Northwestern U., 1977; Dupont lectr. Harvard U., 1979, numerous other invited meml. lectrs. Author: Of Molecules and Men, 1966, Life Itself, 1981, What Mad Pursuit, 1988, The Astonishing Hypothesis: The Scientific Search for the Soul, 1994; contbr. papers and articles on molecular, cell biology and neurobiology to sci. jours. Recipient Prix Charles Leopold Mayer French Academies des Scis., 1961, (with J.D. Watson) Rsch. Corp. award, 1961, Warren Triennial prize, 1959, (with J.D. Watson & Maurice Wilkins) Lasker award, 1960, Nobel Prize for medicine, 1962; Gairdner Found. award, 1962, Royal Medal Royal Soc., 1972, Copley medal, 1975, Michelson-Morley award, 1981, Benjamin P. Cheney medal, 1986, Golden Plate award, 1987, Albert medal Royal Soc. Arts, London, 1987, Wright Prize VIII Harvey Mudd Coll., 1988, Joseph Priestly award Dickinson Coll., 1988, Order of Merit, 1991, Disting. Achievement award Oreg State U. Friends of Libr., 1995. Fellow AAAS, Univ. Coll. London,

Royal Soc., Indian Nat. Sci. Acad., Rochester Mus., Indian Acad. Scis. (hon.), Churchill Coll. Cambridge (hon.), Royal Soc. Edinburgh (hon.), Caius Coll. Cambridge (hon.), John Muir Coll. U. Calif., San Diego (hon.), Tata Inst. Fundamental Rsch., Bombay (hon.), Inst. Biology London (hon.); mem. Acad. Arts Scis. (fgn. hon.), Am. Soc. Biol. Chemists (hon.), U.S. Nat. Acad. Scis. (fgn. assoc.), German Acad. Sci., Am. Philos. Soc. (fgn. mem.), French Acad. Scis. (assoc. fgn. mem.), Royal Irish Acad. (hon.), Hellenic Biochemical and Biophysical Soc. (hon.), Academia Europaea. Office: Salk Inst Biol Studies PO Box 85800 San Diego CA 92186-5800

CRILLY, EUGENE RICHARD, engineering consultant; b. Phila., Oct. 30, 1923; s. Eugene John and Mary Virginia (Harvey) C.; m. Alice Royal Roth, Feb. 16, 1952. ME, Stevens Inst. Tech., 1944, MS, 1949; MS, U. Penn., 1951; postgrad., UCLA, 1955-58. Sr. rsch. engr. N.Am. Aviation, L.A., 1954-57, Canoga Park and Downey, Calif., 1962-66; process engr. Northrop Aircraft Corp., Hawthorne, Calif., 1957-59; project engr., quality assurance mgr. HITCO, Gardena, Calif., 1959-62; sr. rsch. splst. Lockheed-Calif. Co., Burbank, Calif., 1966-74; engring. splst. N.Am. aircraft ops. Rockwell Internat., El Segundo, Calif., 1974-89. Author tech. papers. Mem. nat. com. 125th Anniversary Founding of Stevens Inst. Tech. in 1870. Served with USNR, 1943-46; comdr. Res. ret. Mem. Soc. for Advancement Material and Process Engring. (chmn. L.A. chpt. 1978-79, gen. chmn. 1981 symposium exhbn., nat. dir. 1979-86, treas. 1982-85, Award of Merit 1986), Naval Inst., ASM Internat., Naval Res. Assn., VFW, Mil. Order World Wars (adj. San Fernando Valley chpt. 1985, 2d vice comdr. 1986, commdr. 1987-89, vice comdr. West, Dept. Cen. Calif., 1988-89, comdr. Cajon Valley San Diego chpt. 1990-92, adj./ROTC chmn. region XIV 1990-91, comdr. Dept. So. Calif. 1991-93, vice comdr. regionXIV, 1992-93, dept. comdr. Gen. Staff Officer region XIV 1993-94, comdr. region XIV, 1994-95, Disting. Chpt. Comdr. Region XIV 1990-91), Former Intelligence Officers Assn. (treas. San Diego chpt. one 1990-94), Ret. Officers Assn. (treas. Silver Strand chpt. 1992—, asst. treas. Convention 2000), Navy League U.S. (treas. Coronado coun. 1997—), Naval Order U.S., Naval Intelligence Profls. Assn., Brit. United Svc. Club L.A., Marines Meml. Club (San Francisco), Coronado Round Table, Hammer Club of San Diego, Sigma Xi, Sigma Nu. Republican. Roman Catholic. Home and Office: 276 J Ave Coronado CA 92118-1138

CRIMINALE, WILLIAM OLIVER, JR., applied mathematics educator; b. Mobile, Ala., Nov. 29, 1933; s. William Oliver and Vivian Gertrude (Sketoe) C.; m. Ulrike Irmgard Wegner, June 7, 1962; children: Martin Oliver, Lucca. B.S., U. Ala., 1955; Ph.D., Johns Hopkins U., 1960. Asst. prof. Princeton (N.J.) U., 1962-68; asso. prof. U. Wash., Seattle, 1968-73; prof. oceanography, geophysics, applied math. U. Wash., 1973—, chmn. dept. applied math., 1976-84; cons. Aerospace Corp., 1963-65, Boeing Corp., 1968-72, AGARD, 1967-68, Lenox Hill Hosp., 1967-68, ICASE, NASA Langley, 1990—; guest prof., Can., 1965, France, 1967-68, Germany, 1973-74, Sweden, 1973-74, Scotland, 1985, 89, 91, Eng., 1990, 91, Stanford, 1990, Brazil, 1992, Italy, 1999; Nat. Acad. exch. scientist, USSR, 1969, 72. Author: Stability of Parallel Flows, 1967; Contbr. articles to profl. jours. Served with U.S. Army, 1961-62. Boris A. Bakmeteff Meml. fellow, 1957-58, NATO postdoctoral fellow, 1960-61, Alexander von Humboldt Sr. fellow, 1973-74, Royal Soc. fellow, 1990-91. Fellow Am. Phys. Soc.; mem. AAAS, Am. Geophys. Union, Fedn. Am. Scientists. Home: 1635 Peach Ct E Seattle WA 98112-3428 Office: U Wash Dept Applied Math Box 352420 Seattle WA 98195-2420

CRIPPEN, BRUCE D., senator, real estate manager; b. Billings, Mont., June 13, 1932; m. Mary Crippen; 4 children. BS, U. Mont., 1956, grad. Sch. Law; grad. Sch. Law, NYU. Mem. Mont. Ho. of Reps., Billings, 1981—, minority whip, 1985-86, minority leader, 1991-92, 93-94, pres. pro tempore, 1997-98, pres. senate, 1999—, mem. ethics com., jud. com., legis. administrn. com., rules com. Served USN, 1952-54. Lutheran. Office: PO Box 80747 Billings MT 59108-0747 also: Capitol Station Helena MT 59620-1702

CRIPPENS, DAVID LEE, broadcast executive; b. Nashville, Sept. 23, 1942; s. Nathaniel and Dorothy (Sharp) C.; m. Eloise Brown, Aug. 3, 1968; 1 child, Gerald Chinua. BA in Polit. Sci., Antioch Coll., 1964; MSW, San Diego State U., 1968. Vol. Peace Corps, Nigeria, 1964-66; assoc. dir. ednl. opportunities program San Diego State U., 1968-69; producer KPBS-TV, San Diego, 1969-71; staff producer, writer, newsperson WQED-TV, Pitts., 1971-73; dir. ednl. svc. KCET, L.A., 1973-77, v.p. ednl. svc., 1977-80, v.p., sta. mgr., 1980-83, v.p. nat. prodns., 1983-85, sr. v.p. ednl. enterprises, 1985—; Rufus Putnam vis. prof. Ohio U. Sch. Telecommunications, Athens, fall 1995. Exec. producer Count On Me, New American Work Force, Not the Way to Go/Get a Life, Begingin the Journey, Giving Care Taking Care, Community Under Siege, Mindworks; contbr. articles to profl. publs. Bd. dirs. Unite-LA, Inroads L.A.; mem. Editl. Projects in Edn. Bd. Recipient Excellence in Edn. Commendation award Calif Poly Black Faculty and Staff Assn., 1991, Prin.'s Orgn. award Sr. High Sch. Prins., 1991, honor Assn. Adminstrs. L.A., 1988, Calif. Coalition for Pub. Edn., 1987, Nat. Assn. Media Women, 1986, Calif. Assembly Legis. Com., 1971, San Diego State Black Student Coun., 1971, named One of Pitts.' Most Influential Blacks, Pitts. Post Gazette, 1973, Outstanding Ednl. Leadership award Phi Delta Kappa, 1992, Nat. Citation award, 1993, Positive Image award Frank D. Parent PTA, 1992, John Senett award for outstanding coverage of educational concerns Calif. Tchrs. Assn., 1993, Martin award INROADS, L.A., Inc., 1996, award for outstanding coverage of pub. edn. Calif. Assn. Calif. Sch. Adminstrs., 1998. Home: 5252 W 64th St Inglewood CA 90302-1016 Office: KCET 4401 W Sunset Blvd Los Angeles CA 90027-6090

CRISCUOLO, WENDY LAURA, lawyer, interior design consultant; b. N.Y.C., Dec. 17, 1949; d. Joseph Andrew and Betty Jane (Jackson) C.; m. John Howard Price, Jr., Sept. 5, 1970 (div. Apr. 1981); m. Ross J. Turner, July 23, 1988. BA with honors in Design, U. Calif., Berkeley, 1973; JD, U. San Francisco, 1982. Space planner GSA, San Francisco, 1973-79; sr. interior designer E. Lew & Assocs., San Francisco, 1979-80; design dir. Beier & Gunderson, Inc., Oakland, Calif., 1980-81; sr. interior designer Environ. Planning and Rsch., San Francisco, 1981-82; interior design cons. Rancho Santa Fe, Calif., 1982—; law clk. to Judge Spencer Williams U.S. Dist. Ct., San Francisco, 1983-84; atty. Ciros Investments, Rancho Santa Fe, Calif., 1984—. Author: (with others) Guide to the Laws of Charitable Giving, 3d rev. edit., 1983; staff mem. U. San Francisco Law Rev., 1983. Bd. dirs., v.p. and treas. Marin Citizens for Energy Planning, 1986-89; bd. dirs., pres. Calif. Ctr. for Wildlife, 1987-90; trustee Cayote Point Mus. for Environ. Edn., 1990-93. Mem. State Bar Calif. Episcopalian. Avocation: creative writing.

CRISMAN, MARY FRANCES BORDEN, librarian; b. Tacoma, Nov. 23, 1919; d. Lindon A. and Mary Cecelia (Donnelly) Borden; m. Fredric Lee Crisman, Apr. 12, 1975 (dec. Dec. 1975). BA in History, U. Wash., 1943, BA in Librarianship, 1944. Asst. br. librarian in charge work with children Mottet br. Tacoma Pub. Libr., 1944-45, br. librarian, 1945-49, br. librarian Moore br., 1950-55, asst. dir., 1955-70, dir., 1970-74, dir. emeritus, 1975—; mgr. corp. libr. Frank Russell Co., 1985-96, ret., 1997; chmn. Wash. Community Library Council, 1970-72. Hostess program Your Library and You, Sta. KTPS-TV, 1969-71. Mem. Highland Homeowners League, Tacoma, 1980—, incorporating dir. 1980, sec. and registered agt., 1980-82. Mem. ALA (chmn. mem. com. Wash. 1957-60, mem. nat. library week com. 1965, chmn. library adminstrn. div. nominating com. 1971, mem. ins. for libraries com. 1970-74, vice chmn. library adminstrn. div. personnel adminstrn. sect. 1972-73, chmn. 1973-74, mem. com. policy implementation 1973-74, mem. library orgn. and mgmt. sect. budgeting acctg. and costs com. 1974-75), Am. Library Trustee Assn. (legis. com. 1975-78, conf. program com. 1978-80, action devel. com. 1978-80), Pacific N.W. (trustee div. nominating com 1976-77), Wash. Library Assn. (exec. bd. 1957-59, state exec., dir. Nat. Library Week 1965, treas., exec. bd. 1969-71, 71-73), Urban Libraries Council (editorial sec. Newsletter 1972-73, exec. com. 1974-75), Ladies Aux. to United Transp. Union (past pres. Tacoma), Friends Tacoma Pub. Library (registered agt. 1975-83, sec. 1975-78, pres. 1978-80, bd. dirs. 1980-83), Smithsonian Assocs., Nat. Railway Hist. Soc., U. Wash. Alumni Assn., U. Wash. Sch. Librarianship Alumni Assn. Roman Catholic. Club: Quota Internat. (sec. 1957-58, 1st v.p. 1960-61, pres. 1961-62, treas. 1975-76, pres. 1979-80) (Tacoma). Home: 6501 N Burning Tree Ln Tacoma WA 98406-2108 also: 9054 N 109th Ave Sun City AZ 85351-4676

CRISPIN, JAMES HEWES, engineering and construction company executive; b. Rochester, Minn., July 23, 1915; s. Egerton Lafayette and Angela (Shipman) C.; m. Marjorie Holmes, Aug. 5, 1966. AB in Mech. Engring., Stanford U., 1938; MBA, Harvard U., 1941; grad., Army Command & Gen. Staff Sch., 1943. Registered profl. mech. engr., Calif. With C.F. Braun & Co. Alhambra, Calif., 1946-62; treas. Bechtel Corp., San Francisco, 1962-73, v.p., mem. fin. com., 1967-75, mgr. investment dept., 1973-75; retired, 1976; investment cons., Santa Barbara, Calif., 1978—. Trustee Santa Barbara Mus. Art, 1979-91, 97—, pres., 1986-88, life. hon. trustee, 1992—. Lt. col. Ordnance Corps, AUS., 1941-46. Decorated Army Commendation medal with oak leaf cluster. Mem. Mil. Order World Wars, S.R., Soc. Colonial Wars, Colonial Wars Calif., Baronial Order Magna Carta, Mil. Order Crusades, Am. Def. Preparedness Assn., World Affairs Coun. No. Calif. (trustee 1968-75), Santa Barbara Mus. Art (trustee 1979-91, 97—, pres. 1986-88, life hon. trustee 1992), Calif. Hist. Soc. (trustee 1979-86), Valley Club of Montecito (pres. 1987-90, bd. dirs. 1981-91), Calif. Club L.A., World Trade Club San Francisco (pres. 1977-78, bd. dirs. 1971-78), Santa Barbara Club (pres. 1995-96, bd. dirs. 1991-96), Pacific Union Club, San Francisco, Beta Theta Pi. Republican. Home Fax: 805-565-9077, Office fax: 805-966-2081. Home: 470 Eastgate Ln Santa Barbara CA 93108-2248 Office: La Arcada Bldg 1114 State St Ste 220 Santa Barbara CA 93101-6712

CRISTIANO, MARILYN JEAN, speech communication educator; b. New Haven, Jan. 10, 1954; d. Michael William and Mary Rose (Porto) C. BA, Marquette U., 1975, MA, 1977; postgrad., Ariz. State U., 1977; EdD, Nova Southeastern U., 1991. Speech comm. instr. Phoenix Coll., 1977-87, Paradise Valley C.C., Phoenix, 1987—; presenter at profl. confs., workshops and seminars. Author tng. manual on pub. speaking, 1991, 92, 95, 97; contbr. articles to profl. publs. Mem. ASTD, Speech Comm. Assn., Western Speech Comm. Assn., Ariz. Comm. Assn. Avocation: tennis. Office: Paradise Valley CC 18401 N 32nd St Phoenix AZ 85032-1210

CRISWELL, KIMBERLY ANN, public relations executive, dancer; b. L.A., Dec. 6, 1957; d. Robert Burton and Carolyn Joyce (Semko) C. BA with honors, U. Calif.-Santa Cruz, 1980; postgrad. Stanford U., 1993—. Instr., English Lang. Services, Oakland, Calif., 1980-81; freelance writer Verbum mag., San Diego, Gambit mag., New Orleans, 1981; instr. Tulane U., New Orleans, 1981; instr., editor Haitian-English Lang. Program, New Orleans, 1981-82; instr. Delgado Coll., New Orleans, 1982-83; instr., program coord. Vietnamese Youth Ctr., San Francisco, 1984; dancer Khadra Internat. Folk Ballet, San Francisco, 1984-89; dir. mktg. comm. Centram Systems West, Inc., Berkeley, Calif., 1984-87; comm. coord. Safeway Stores, Inc., Oakland, 1985; dir. corp. comm. TOPS, div. Sun Microsystems, Inc, 1987-88; pres. Criswell Comm., 1988—; dir. corp. comm. CyberGold, Inc., Berkeley, Calif., 1996—. Vol. coord. Friends of Haitians, 1981, editor, writer newsletter, 1981; dancer Komenka Ethnic Dance Ensemble, New Orleans, 1983; mem. Contemp. Art Ctr.'s Krewe of Clones, New Orleans, 1983, Americans for Nonsmokers Rights, Berkeley, 1985; active San Francisco Multimedia Developers Group, Artspan. Mem. Sci. Meets the Arts Soc. (founding), Oakland Mus. Assn., Mus. Soc. Democrat. Avocations: visual arts, travel, creative writing.

CRISWELL, STEPHEN, astronomer. Program mgr. Fred Lawrence Whipple Obs., Amada, Ariz. Office: Fred Lawrence Whipple Obs PO Box 97 Amado AZ 85645-0097

CRITCHETT, HUGH ADAMS, minister; b. Holister, Mich., Jan. 4, 1914; s. Carl and Anna Eliza (Coffin) C.; m. Edith Elizabeth Hoppner, Nov. 10, 1935; children: Herbert Adams, Elizabeth Critchett DeBerry. AB, Nebr. Wesleyan U., 1937; ThM, Iliff Sch. Theology, Denver. Ordained deacon, 1940, ordained elder, 1942, The Meth. Ch. Pastor Meth. Epis. Ch., Nemaha, Nebr., 1935-36, Palmyra, Nebr., 1936-37; pastor Kowa County Parish/The Meth. Ch., Eads, Colo., 1938-42; pastor The Meth. Ch., Yuma, Colo., 1942-45, Monte Vista, Colo., 1946-52, Montclair, Denver, 1952-61; dist. supt. The Meth. Ch., Pueblo, Colo., 1961-67; pastor The Meth. Ch., Westminster, Colo., 1967-71, First United Meth. Ch., Pueblo, 1971-76, Brighton (Colo.) United Meth. Ch., 1976-79, Beulah (Colo.) United Meth. Ch., 1981-92; Author: (book) His Final Days, 1995. Mem. Masons, Scottish Rite, Kiwanis. Home: 1525 W 31st St Pueblo CO 81008-1265

CROCKER, J. A. FRAZER, JR., minister, social worker; b. Detroit, Oct. 4, 1935; s. J. A. Frazer, Sr. and Marjorie Olievia (May) C.; m. Jaqueline Fairchild Arnold, Apr. 15, 1961 (div. Aug. 1972); children: John A. F. III, Matthew M.; m. Diana Worden, June 4, 1977; 1 stepchild, Colin E. Brayton. AB, Kenyon Coll., Gambier, Ohio, 1957; MDiv, Ch. Div. Sch. of the Pacific, Berkeley, Calif., 1960; MSW, U. Utah, 1974; DMin, Grad. Theol. Found., 1992. Lic. clin. social worker; ordained to ministry Episcopal Ch. as deacon then priest, 1960. Asst. min. Trinity Cathedral, Davenport, Iowa, 1960-61; priest in charge St. Paul's Ch., Sioux City, Iowa, 1961-64; assoc. rector Grace Ch., Jamaica, N.Y., 1964-67; rector St. Mary's Ch., Provo, Utah, 1967-72; program dir. Utah State Prison Alcohol Treatment Program, Draper, 1974-81; pvt. practice Salt Lake City, 1981-83; dir. mental health Family Health Plan, Salt Lake City, 1983-88; bishop's canon Episcopal Diocese Utah, Salt Lake City, 1988-95; protestant chaplain Utah State Prison, 1968-74; asst. chaplain St. Mark's Hosp., Salt Lake City, 1983; exec. dir. Episcopal Social and Pastoral Ministries, 1990-95, ret. 1995. Pres. Utah Mental Health Assn., Salt Lake City, 1970-72; flotilla comdr. USCG Aux., Salt Lake City, 1980; bd. dirs. Ctr. for Family Devel., Salt Lake City, 1989-94, pres., 1991-93; bd. dirs. Olympus View Hosp., Salt Lake City, 1992-94, United Episcopal Charities, 1993-96, treas., 1994-96; mem. coun. Our Lady of the Mountains Retreat House, 1992-95. Mem. Great Salt Lake Yacht Club (bd. dirs. 1980-82). Avocations: sailing, reading, back-packing, fishing.

CROCKER, JOY LAKSMI, concert pianist and organist, composer; b. San Antonio, June 12, 1928; d. Hugo Peoples and Anna Kathryn (Ball) Rush; m. Richard Lincoln Crocker, July 24, 1948 (div. July 1977); children: Nathaniel Homer, Martha Wells, David Laramie. MusB, Yale U., 1950; MS, Yale U., Berkeley, Calif., 1956; postgrad., Grad. Theol. Sem., 1978-81. Min. music First Congl. Ch., Branford, Conn., 1949-62; dir. music therapy West Haven (Conn.) VA Hosp.; min. music St. Stephen's Episcopal Ch./Sch., Orinda, Calif., 1963, First Bapt. Ch., Oakland, Calif., 1964-66, Greek Orthodox Cathedral, Oakland, 1969, San Quentin (Calif.) Protestant Chapel, 1976-78, Plymouth United Ch. of Christ, Oakland, 1977-84; pianist, assoc. dir. First Bapt. Ch., Managua, Nicaragua, 1984-94; organist, pianist Mills Grove Christian Ch., 1995; organist St. Andrews Presbyn. Ch., Pleasant Hill, Calif., 1996; prof. organ San Francisco Conservatory Music, 1962-69; chmn. piano dept. Nicaraguan Nat. Conservatory Music, 1984-93; founder-dir., prof. Bapt. Conservatory of Music, Managua, 1989—; instr. Yogalayam Yoga Ashram; creator, dir. diverse low-budget innovative music edn. programs, 1969—; mem. adjudicator Nat. Guild Piano Tchrs., Music Tchrs. Assn. Calif. civic and legislation coord. Ch. Women United, Oakland unit and state unit, 1996—; pianist, organist Ch. Women United State Unit. Named Woman of Yr., Bus. and Profl. Women's Club,, Inc., 1995; recipient prizes for compositions San Francisco Concerto Orch., 1997, Music Tchrs. Assn. Calif., 1998. Mem. Am. Guild Organists, Am. Coll. Musicians, Music Tchrs. Assn. Democrat. Mem. United Ch. of Christ. Avocation: traveling. Home: 3065 Monterey Blvd Oakland CA 94602-3559

CROCKER, KENNETH FRANKLIN, data processing consultant; b. Centralia, Wash., July 29, 1950; s. Earl Thomas and Mary Jane (Hamil) C.; m. Mary Louise Underwood, June 15, 1974 (div. Dec. 1987); children: Matthew A., Benjamin F., Jonathan C.; m. Sally Marlene Gammelgard, Dec. 21, 1987 (div. 1992). AS in Computer Programming and System Design, Control Data Inst., Long Beach, Calif., 1972. Programmer City of Greenville, S.C., 1973; computer operator Winn Dixie Stores, Greer, S.C., 1973-75; programmer Piedmont Industries, Greenville, S.C., 1975-78; systems engr. Micro-Systems, Greenville, 1978; sr. programmer Reeves Bros., Lyman, S.C., 1978-80; systems analyst Cryovac div. W.R. Grace Co., Duncan, S.C., 1980-84; sr. cons. Cap Gemini Am., San Francisco, 1984-85; prin. mem. tech. staff Citibank-FSB Calif., Oakland, 1985-91; sr. software engr. Lucky Stores Inc., Dublin, Calif., 1991-94; tech. cons. Lawrence Berkeley Labs., Berkeley, Calif., 1994-95, Delta-Net, San Francisco, 1995; plan architect, DBA technician Safeway, Walnut Creek, Calif., 1995—. Umpire Contra Costa Ofcls. Assn., 1990-96. Libertarian. Baptist. Avocation: children's sports activities. Home and Office: 1590 Thornwood Dr Concord CA 94521-1918

CROFTS, RICHARD A., academic administrator. PhD in Info., Duke U. Mem. faculty U. Toledo; assoc. v.p. rsch., dean Grad. Sch. E. Tenn. State U.; dep. commr. acad. affairs Mo. Univ. Sys., Helena, 1994-96; interim commr. higher edn. Mo. Univ. Sys., Helena, Mont., 1996-97, commr. higher edn., 1997—. Office: Mont Univ Sys PO Box 203101 2500 E Broadway St Helena MT 59620-3101*

CRONAN, JOSEPH E. See KELLY, KURT

CRONE, RICHARD ALLAN, cardiologist, educator; b. Tacoma, Nov. 26, 1947; s. Richard Irving and Alla Marguerite (Ernst) C.; m. Becky Jo Zimmerlund, Dec. 11, 1993. BA in Chemistry, U. Wash., 1969, MD, 1973. Intern Madigan Army Med. Ctr., Tacoma, 1973-74, resident in medicine, 1974-76, fellow in cardiology, 1977-79; commd. med. officer U.S. Army, Tacoma, Denver, San Francisco, 1972; advanced through grades to lt. col. U.S. Army, 1981; dir. coronary care unit Fitzsimons Army Med. Ctr., Denver, 1979-81; practice medicine specializing in cardiology Stevens Cardiology Group, Edmonds, Wash., 1981—, also dir. coronary care unit, cardiac catheter lab, 1982—; clin. assoc. prof. medicine U. Wash., Seattle, 1983—. Fellow Am. Coll. Angiology; mem. AMA, Am. Coll. Cardiology, Am. Heart Assn., Seattle Acad. Internal Medicine, Wash. State Soc. Internal Medicine, Wash. State Med. Assn. Republican. Roman Catholic. Avocations: skiing, wine collecting. Home: 10325 66th Pl W Mukilteo WA 98275-4559 Office: 21701 76th Ave W Ste 100 Edmonds WA 98026-7536

CROOK, SEAN PAUL, aerospace systems program manager; b. Pawtucket, R.I., July 6, 1953; s. Ralph Frederick and Rosemary Rita (Dolan) C.; m. Mary Wickman, June 10, 1978; children: Kimberly Anne, Kelly Dolan, Erin Webster, Mary Katherine. BSME, U.S. Naval Acad., 1975; MBA, U. So. Calif., 1991. Commd. ensign USN, 1975, advanced through grades to lt., 1979, resigned, 1981; sr. systems engr. space div. Gen. Electric Co., Springfield, Va., 1982-84; sr. aerospace systems engr. Martin Marietta Aero. Def. Systems, Long Beach, Calif., 1984-87; sr. aerospace system engring. mgr. Martin Marietta Aero Def. Systems, Long Beach, Calif., 1987-93; chief engr. GDE Sys. Inc., A Tracer Co., San Diego, 1993-96, program mgr., 1996-99; program mgr. Marconi Integrated Systems, San Diego, 1999—; sec., bd. dirs. Guardian Minerals Inc. Commdr. USNR, 1992—. Mem. Am. Mgmt. Assn., U. So. Calif. Exec. MBA Alumni Assn. (bd. dirs.), U.S. Naval Acad. Alumni Assn. Avocation: fin. planning. Home: 23565 Via Calzada Mission Viejo CA 92691-3625 Office: Marconi Integrated Systems PO Box 509008 San Diego CA 92150-9008

CROOKE, STANLEY THOMAS, pharmaceutical company executive; b. Indpls., Mar. 28, 1945; m. Nancy Alder (dec.); 1 child, Evan; m. Rosanne M. Snyder. BS in Pharmacy, Butler U., 1966; PhD, Baylor Coll., 1971, MD, 1974. Asst. dir. med. rsch. Bristol Labs., N.Y.C., 1975-76, assoc. dir. med. rsch., 1976-77, assoc. dir. R&D, 1977-79, v.p. R&D, 1979-80; v.p. R&D Smith Kline & French Labs., Phila., 1980-82; pres. R&D Smith Kline French, Phila., 1982-88; chmn. bd., chief exec. officer ISIS Pharms., Inc., Carlsbad, Calif., 1989; chmn. bd. dirs. GES Pharms., Inc., Houston, 1989-91; adj. prof. Baylor Coll. Medicine, Houston, 1982, U. Pa., Phila., 1982-98; chmn. bd. dirs. GeneMedicine, Houston, 1996—; bd. dirs. Calif. Healthcare Inst., Indsl. Biotech. Assn., Washington, Idun Pharms., San Diego, Epix Med., Cambridge, Mass., BIO, Washington; mem. sci. adv. bd. SIBIA, La Jolla, Calif.; adj. prof. pharmacology UCLA, 1991, U. Calif. San Diego, 1994. Mem. editl. adv. bd. Molecular Pharmacology, 1986-91, Jour. Drug Targeting, 1992; editl. bd. Antisense Rsch. and Devel., 1994; sect. editl. bd. for biologicals and immunologicals Expert Opinion on Investigational Drugs, 1995. Trustee Franklin Inst., Phila., 1987-89; bd. dirs. Mann Music Ctr., Phila., 1987-89; children's com. Children's Svcs., Inc., Phila., 1983-84; adv. com. World Affairs Coun., Phila. Recipient Disting. Prof. award U. Ky., 1986, Julius Stermer award Phila. Coll. Pharmacy and Sci., 1981, Outstanding Lectr. award Baylor Coll. Medicine, 1984. Mem. AAAS, Am. Assn. for Cancer Rsch. (state legis. com.), Am. Soc. for Microbiology, Am. Soc. Pharmacology and Exptl. Therapeutics, Am. Soc. Clin. Pharmacology and Therapeutics, Am. Soc. Clin. Oncology, Indsl. Biotech. Assn. (bd. dirs. 1992-93). Achievements include numerous patents in field. Office: ISIS Pharms Inc 2292 Faraday Ave Carlsbad CA 92008-7208

CROOKER, CONSTANCE HELEN EMERSON, lawyer; b. Portland, Maine, July 23, 1946; d. Charles Wescott and Elizabeth (Bates) C. BA, Reed Coll., 1969; JD, Lewis & Clark Coll., Portland, Oreg., 1977. Bar: Oreg. 1977, U.S. Dist. Ct. Oreg. 1977, U.S. Ct. Appeals (9th cir.) 1979, U.S. Dist. Ct. (no. dist.) Calif. 1988, U.S. Supreme Ct. 1994. Pvt. practice Portland, Oreg., 1977-83, 88—; dir., chief felony atty. Tillamook (Oreg.) Pub. Defender, 1983-87. Author: Paint My Mailbox Blue, 1977, Sing and Don't Cry, 1994, The Art of Legal Interpretation; A Guide for Court Interpreters, 1995, (with others) Criminal Law Vol. II, 1986. Bd. dirs. ASAP Treatment Svcs., Inc., Portland, 1990-95, Multnomah Defenders, Inc., Portland, 1994—. Mem. Nat. Assn. Criminal Def. Lawyers (forefeiture abuse task force com. 1994), Oreg. Criminal Def. Lawyers Assn., Oreg. Bar Assn. (indigent def. com. 1987, ethcis com. 1991-94), Oreg. Criminal Def. Lawyers Assn. (race, gender and ethnicity com. 1994), Multnomah Bar Assn., Tillamook County Bar Assn. (pres. 1985), Hispanic Met. C. of C. Avocations: skiing, hiking, guitar, photography, writing. Office: 815 SW 2nd Ave Ste 500 Portland OR 97204-3026

CROSBY, JOHN O'HEA, conductor, opera manager; b. N.Y.C., July 12, 1926; s. Laurence Alden and Aileen Mary (O'Hea) C. Grad., Hotchkiss Sch., 1944; BA, Yale U., 1950, DFA (hon.), 1991; LittD (hon.), U. N.Mex., 1967; MusD (hon.), Coll. of Santa Fe, 1968, Cleve. Inst. Music, 1974; LHD (hon.), U. Denver, 1977. pres. Manhattan Sch. Music, 1976-86. Accompanist, opera coach, condr., N.Y.C., 1951-56, gen. dir., mem. conducting staff Santa Fe Opera, 1957—; guest condr. various opera cos. in U.S. and Can. and Europe, 1967—; condr. U.S. stage premiere Daphne, 1964; U.S. profl. premier Friedenstag, 1988; world premiere Wuthering Heights, 1958. With inf. AUS, 1944-46, ETO. Recipient Nat. Medal of Arts, 1991, Verdienstkreuz 1st klasse Bundesrepublik, Deutschland, 1992. Roman Catholic. Clubs: Metropolitan Opera (N.Y.C.), Century Assn. (N.Y.C.), University (N.Y.C.). Office: Santa Fe Opera PO Box 2408 Santa Fe NM 87504-2408

CROSS, BRUCE MICHAEL, lawyer; b. Washington, Jan. 30, 1942. AB magna cum laude, Dartmouth Coll., 1964; JD magna cum laude, Harvard U., 1967. Bar: Wash. 1967. Law clk. to Hon. Frank P. Weaver Supreme Ct. Wash., 1967-68; mem. Perkins Coie, Seattle. E-mail: crosb@perkinscoie.com. Office: Perkins Coie 1201 3rd Ave Fl 40 Seattle WA 98101-3099

CROSS, BRYAN ROBERT KEVIN, software engineer; b. Pensacola, Fla., Sept. 29, 1969; s. Robert Clinton and Susan Frances Cross. BA in Anthropology, U. Calif., Santa Cruz, 1990. Archeologist Paul H. Rosenthal Inc., Hilo, Hawaii, Agana, Guam, 1990-92, Greenwood & Assocs., Hemet, Calif., 1992-96; software engr. Precision Resource, Chico, Calif., 1996-97; software cons. in pvt. practice, 1996-98; software engr. Innovative Solutions, Sacramento, 1998—; cons. Harrah's Entertainment, Stateline, Nev., 1997-98, Bank of Am., San Francisco, 1998. Avocations: shooting sports, sailing, golf, cycling. E-mail: bcross@isinc.com. Office: Innovative Solutions Inc 1300 National Dr Sacramento CA 95834-1908

CROSS, CHARLEY BRADFORD, software consultant; b. San Diego, Apr. 13, 1957; s. Richard Francis III and Nancy Eleanor (Spicer) C.; m. Karen Kay Gremmels, Aug. 6, 1978; children: Julia Marie, Alexander Bradford. BS in Math., Calif. Poly. State U., 1978. Dir. tech. svcs. R.F. Cross Assoc., Ltd., Alexandria, Va., 1979; software engr. Wang Labs., Lowell, Mass., 1979-97; cons. Eastman Software, Kodak, Folsom, Calif., 1997—. Patentee multitask subscription data retrieval sys. Vol. New England Aquarium, Boston, 1985-87; v.p. Parkway Owners Assn., Folsom, 1996—. Avocations: running, bicycling, reading, family activities, travel. Office: Eastman Software 1269 Humbug Creek Ct Folsom CA 95630-7643

CROSS, GLENN LABAN, engineering company executive, development planner; b. Mt. Vernon, Ill., Dec. 28, 1941; s. Kenneth Edward and Mildred Irene (Glenn) C.; m. Kim Lien Duong, Aug. 30, 1968 (div. Oct. 1975); m. Tran Tu Thach, Dec. 26, 1975; children: Cindy Sue, Cristy Luu, Crystal Tu, Cassandra Caitlynn; BA, Calif. Western U., 1981, MBA, 1982. Hosp.

adminstr. pub. health div. USAID, Dept. State, Washington, 1966-68; pers. mgr. Pacific Architects and Engrs., Inc., L.A., 1968-70, contract adminstr., 1970-73, mgr. mgmt. svcs., 1973-75; contracts adminstr. Internat. Svcs. div., AVCO, Cin., 1975-77; sr. contract adminstr. Bechtel Group, Inc., San Francisco, 1977-80, Arabian Bechtel Co. Ltd.; contract adminstrv. supr. Bechtel Civil, Inc., Jubail Industrial City, Saudi Arabia, 1980-85; cons. Bechtel Western Power Corp., Jakarta, Indonesia, Pacific Engrs. and Constructors, 1985-90, prin. contract adminstr. Ralph M. Parsons Co., Pasadena, Calif., 1990-93, contract adminstr. Parsons-Brinckerhoff, Costa Mesa, Calif., 1993; project mgr. Pacific Architects and Engrs., Inc., 1993-96, contracts mgr., Bechtel Internat. Inc., Bandung, Indonesia, 1997-98, prin. contract administr., Parsons Corp., Pasadena CA, 1998—. Author: Living With a Matrix: A Conceptual Guide to Organizational Variation, 1983. Served as sgt. 1st spl. forces group, airborne, AUS, 1962-65; Okinawa, Vietnam. Decorated Combat Infantryman's Badge. Mem. Nat. Contract Mgmt. Assn., Construction Mgmt. Assn. Am., Internat. Pers. Mgmt. Assn., Assn. Human Resource Systems Profls., Human Resource Planning Soc., Assn. MBA Execs., Am. Mgmt. Assn., Am. Arbitration Assn., Internat. Records Mgmt. Coun., Adminstrv. Mgmt. Soc. Republican. Avocations: swimming, reading. Fax: 949-859-0405. E-mail: glennúcross@email.msn.com. Home: 25935 Faircourt Ln Laguna Hills CA 92653-7517 Office: Al Jubail Petrochem Co, PO Box 10084, Jubail 31961, Saudi Arabia

CROSS, NANCY KAY, educator; b. Corvallis, Oreg., Mar. 16, 1944; d. Roger Conrad and Aileen Grace (Lindquist) Devitt; m. Carlton Edward Cross, June 11, 1967; children: Jeffrey, Tara. BA, Walla Walla Coll., 1966; MA, U. Oreg., 1970. Tchr. Sch. Dist. 509J, Corvallis, 1967-72, Walla Walla Coll., College Place, Wash., 1982—. Mem. sch. bd. Walla Walla Valley Acad., 1990-97. Mem. Nat. Coun. Tchrs. English. Office: Walla Walla Coll 204 S College Ave College Place WA 99324-1139

CROSS, ROBERT LOUIS, realtor, land use planner, writer; b. Alton, Ill., Aug. 9, 1937; s. Louis William and Marion (Hanna) C.; m. Paula Sutton, June 8, 1958 (div. June 1970); children: Britomart, Christopher, Amoret; m. Carolee Sharko, May 5, 1990. BA, U. Kans., 1959, MA, 1961; grad., UCLA, 1969, Realtors Inst., L.A., 1980. Lectr. English lang. U. Kans., Lawrence, 1959-60, Washburn U., Topeka, Kans., 1960-61; editorial-mktg. rep. Prentice-Hall, Inc., Englewood Cliffs, N.J., 1962-64; dir. pub. info. Forest Lawn Meml. Pk., Glendale, Calif., 1964-68; account exec. pub. rels. J. Walter Thompson, L.A., 1968-70; sr. account exec. pub. rels. Botsford Ketchum, L.A., 1970-71, Harsh, Rotman & Druck, L.A., 1971-72; pres. Crossroads Combined Communications, L.A., 1973-80; real estate agt. Carmel (Calif.) Bd. Realtors, 1979—; gen. ptnr. Crossroads Design Ltd., Big Sur, Calif., 1990—; co-owner Big Sur Properties; cons. Watts Mfg. Corp., L.A., 1970-73, U.S. Office Edn., Washington, 1971, U.S. Dept. Interior, Washington, 1972, Calif. State Coastal Commn., San Francisco, 1980-85. Author: Henry Miller: The Paris Years, 1991; assoc. editor Calif. Life Mag., 1976; contbr. IN Monterey Mag., 1977; real estate editor Monterey Life Mag., 1978. Pres., dir. Big Sur Hist. Soc., 1980-90, Coastlands Mut. Water Co., Big Sur, 1984—; co-founder Dialogue for Big Sur, 1984; dir. Big Sur Natural History Assn., 1984-86; founding docent Dept. Pks. and Recreation, Pt. Sur Historic State Park, Big Sur, 1987; With U.S. Army, 1961-63. Mem. Archeol. Inst. Am., Nat. Assn. Realtors, Am. Soc. Landscape Architects, Nat. Assn. Real Estate Appraisers (cert.), Calif. Assn. Realtors, Monterey County Assn. Realtors (Multiple Listing Svc. Sales award 1980), Carmel Multiple Listing Svc., Big Sur Grange, Coast Property Owners Assn., Environ. Assesment Assn. (cert.). Avocations: art, travel, music, reading. Office: Big Sur Properties & Crossroads Design Ltd PO Box 244 Big Sur CA 93920-0244

CROSSON, JOHN ALBERT, advertising executive; b. L.A., Oct. 5, 1961; s. Albert J. and Virginia (Kienzle) C.; m. Carolyn Stevens, Oct. 3, 1992. BA, Loyola Marymount U., 1983; MBA, U. So. Calif., 1984. Exec. v.p. Dailey & Assocs. Advt., L.A., 1984-98; exec. v.p., mng. dir. L.A., Grey Advt., 1998—; lectr. Loyola Marymount U., L.A., 1986-89. Avocations: tennis, golf.

CROW, MARY, poet, educator; divorced; children: David Woerner, Robert Woerner. BA, Coll. Wooster; MA, Ind. U.; postgrad., U. Iowa. Prof. English Colo. State U., Ft. Collins, 1964—; poet laureate State of Ohio, 1996—. Author: (poems) Borders, 1989, I Have Tasted the Apple, 1996; translator: (poems) Country of Nevermore: Woman Who Has Sprouted Wings: Poems by Contemporary Latin American Women Poets, 2d edit., 1987, Jorge Teillier, 1989, Vertical Poetry: Roberto Juarroz, 1992 (Colo. Book award 1992). Recipient Poetry fellowship Nat. Endowment Arts, 1985, Creative Writing award Fulbright Found., Yugoslavia, 1988, Rsch. awards Fulbright Found., Peru, Chile, Argentina and Venezuela, 1982, 91. Mem. Associated Writing Programs, Am. Lit. Translators Assn., PEN, Acad. Am. Poets, Poetry Soc. Am. Office: Colo State Univ Dept English Fort Collins CO 80523

CROWDER, RICHARD MORGAN, pilot; b. Wurzburg, Bavaria, Germany, July 22, 1963; (parents Am. citizens); s. Richard Thomas and Margaret Taylor (Rainey) C. BS, U. Minn., 1986; postgrad., U. Colo., 1995—. Pilot Classic Aviation, Mpls., 1985-87, Air South, Homestead, Fla., 1987, AVAir, Raleigh, N.C., 1987-88, Am. Eagle, Dallas, 1988-89, USAir, Arlington, Va., 1989-92, United Airlines, Chgo., 1992—. Republican. Methodist. Avocations: reading, running, hunting, trap shooting.

CROWE, JOHN T., lawyer; b. Cabin Cove, Calif., Aug. 14, 1938; s. J. Thomas and Wanda (Walston) C.; m. Marina Protopapa, Dec. 28, 1968; 1 child, Erin Aleka. BA, U. Santa Clara, 1960, JD, 1962. Bar: Calif. 1962, U.S. Dist. Ct. (ea. dist.) Calif. 1967. Lawyer Visalia, Calif., 1964—; ptnr. Crowe, Mitchell & Crowe, 1971-85; bd. dirs. World Parts Industries, Willson Ranch Co., pres. 1997—; referee State Bar Ct., 1976-82; gen. counsel Sierra Wine, 1986—. Bd. dirs. Mt. Whitney Area Coun. Boys Scouts Am., 1966-85, pres., 1971, 72; bd. dirs. Visalia Associated In-Group Donors (AID), 1973-81, pres., 1978-79, Tulane County Libr. Found.; mem. Visalia Airport Commn., 1982-90. 1st lt. U.S. Army, 1962-64; mem. policy com. Army Res. Forces, 1995—, chmn., 1997, 98. Decorated D.S.M., Legion of Merit with oak leaf cluster, Meritorious Svc. Medal with 3 oak leaf clusters, Army Commendation Medal; named Young Man of Yr., Visalia, 1973; Senator Jr. Chamber Internat., 1970; recipient Silver Beaver awrd Boy Scouts Am., 1983. Mem. ABA, Tulare County Bar Assn., Nat. Assn. R.R. Trial Counsel, State Bar Calif., Visalia C. of C. (pres. 1979-80), Rotary (pres. 1980-81). Republican. Roman Catholic. Home: 3939 W School Ave Visalia CA 93291-5514

CROWHURST LENNARD, SUZANNE HEATHER, organization executive; b. Leicester, Eng., July 11, 1944; came to the U.S., 1969; d. James Glanville and Margret Hewson (Stanley) Crowhurst; m. Henry L. Lennard, Jan. 25, 1976. Diploma, Royal West Eng. Sch. Arch., Bristol, 1968; BArch with honors, Bristol U., 1968; MArch, U. Calif., Berkeley, 1970, PhD in Arch., 1974. Lectr. U. Calif., Berkeley, 1970-76; asst. prof. SUNY, Buffalo, 1976-77; lectr. SUNY, New Paltz, 1977-80; rsch. assoc. Project for Pub. Spaces, N.Y.C., 1980-81; lectr. Oxford (Eng.) Poly., 1981-82; vis. prof. New Sch. for Social Rsch., N.Y.C., 1983-85; exec. dir. Internat. Making Cities Livable Coun., Carmel, Calif., 1985—; cons. Family Study Sta., San Francisco, 1972-76, City of Charleston, S.C., 1988-91, City of Freiburg, Germany, 1994-96; presenter in field. Author: Explorations in the Meaning of Architecture, 1980, Public Life in Urban Places, 1984, Livable Cities Observed, 1995, The Forgotten Child, 1999; editor: Making Cities Livable, 1997; editor Verkehr und Umwelt, 1985-88, Making Cities Livable newsletter, 1985—. Mem. 2016 Com., Carmel, 1994-96. Profl. fellow Nat. Endowment for the Arts, 1979; rsch. grants Graham Found., 1985, Lyndhurst Found., 1986, 89. Mem. Assn. Collegiate Schs. Arch. Avocations: collecting piazzas, photography, classical music, theater and opera. Office: Internat Making Cities Livable Coun PO Box 7586 Carmel CA 93921-7586

CROWLEY, JOHN CRANE, real estate developer; b. Detroit, June 29, 1919 [illegible] Gilfillan, Jan. 12, 1945; children: F. Alexander, Leonard, Philip, Eliot, Louise, Sylvia. BA, Swarthmore Coll., 1941; MS, U. Denver, 1943. Asst. dir. Mcpl. Finance Officers Assn., Chgo., 1946-48; So. Calif. mgr. League Calif. Cities, Los Angeles, 1948-53; mgr. City of Monterey Park, Calif., 1953-56; founder, exec. v.p. Nat. Med. Enterprises, L.A., 1968; pres. Ventura Towne House (Calif.), 1963-96; mem. faculty U. So. Calif. Sch. Pub. Adminstrn., 1950-53; bd. dirs. Regional Inst. of So. Calif., The L.A. Partnership 2000, Burbank-Glendale-Pasadena Airport Authority. Trustee Pacific Oaks Friends Sch. and Coll., Pasadena, 1954-57, 92-98, Swarthmore Coll., 1987—; bd. dirs. Pasadena Area Liberal Arts Ctr., 1962-72, pres., 1965-68; bd. dirs. Pacificulture Found. and Asia Mus., 1971-76, pres., 1972-74; bd. dirs. Nat. Mcpl. League, 1986-92, AAF Rose Bowl Aquatics Ctr., 1997—; chmn. Pasadena Cultural Heritage Commn., 1975-78; city dir. Pasadena, 1979-91; mayor City of Pasadena, 1986-88; bd. dirs. Western Justice Ctr., 1992—, v.p., 1995—, LA County Commn. on Efficiency and Economy, 1994—. Sloan Found. fellow, 1941-43; recipient Arthur Nobel award City of Pasadena. Mem. Am. Soc. Pub. Adminstrn. (local chpt., Winston Crouch award 1990), Internat. City Mgmt. Assn., Nat. Mcpl. League (nat. bd. 1980-92, Disting. Citizen award, 1984), Inst. Pub. Adminstrn. (sr. assoc.), Phi Delta Theta. Democrat. Unitarian. Home: 615 Linda Vista Ave Pasadena CA 91105-1122

CROWLEY, JOSEPH NEIL, university president, political science educator; b. Oelwein, Iowa, July 9, 1933; . James Bernard and Nina Mary (Neil) C.; m. Johanna Lois Reitz, Sept. 9, 1961; children: Theresa, Neil, Margaret, Timothy. BA, U. Iowa, 1959; MA, Calif. State U., Fresno, 1963; PhD (Univ. fellow), U. Wash., 1967. Reporter Fresno Bee, 1961-62; asst. prof. polit. sci. U. Nev., Reno, 1966-71, asso. prof., 1971-79, prof., 1979—, chmn. dept. polit. sci., 1976-78, pres., 1978—; bd. dirs. Citibank Nev.; policy formulation officer EPA, Washington, 1973-74; dir. instl. studies Nat. Commn. on Water Quality, Washington, 1974-75. Author: Democrats, Delegates and Politics in Nevada: A Grassroots Chronicle of 1972, 1976, Notes From the President's Chair, 1988, No Equal in the World; An Interpretation of the Academic Presidency, 1994; editor: (with R. Roelofs and D. Hardesty) Environment and Society, 1973. Mem. Commn. on Colls., 1980-87; mem. adv. comn. on mining and minerals rsch. U.S. Dept. Interior, 1985-91; mem. coun. NCAA, 1987-92, mem. pres.' commn., 1991-92, pres., 1993-95; bd. dirs. Nat. Consortium for Acads. and Sports, 1992—; mem. Honda Awards Program Adv. Bd., 1994—; bd. dirs., campaign chmn. No. Nev. United Way, 1985, 97—. Recipient Thornton Peace Prize U. Nev., 1971, Humanitarian of Yr. award NCCJ, 1986, Alumnus of Yr. award Calif. State U., 1989, ADL Champion of Liberty award, 1993, Disting. Alumni award U. Iowa, 1994, Giant Step award Ctr. for Study of Sport in Soc., 1994, William Anderson award AAHPERD, 1998; Nat. Assn. Schs. Pub. Affairs and Adminstrn. fellow, 1973-74. Mem. Nat. Assn. State Univs. and Land Grant Colls. (bd. dirs. 1998—). Roman Catholic. Home: 1265 Muir Dr Reno NV 89503-2629 Office: U Nev Office of Pres Reno NV 89557-0095

CROWLEY, KIM WILLIAM, sculptor; b. Jackson, Mich., July 2, 1950; s. William Earl and Beatrice Elizabeth (Savage) C.; m. Jann Hollis Huizenga, Feb. 6, 1950. BA, U. Mich., 1972, BFA, 1977; MFA, Carnegie-Mellon U., 1979. Pres. Sculpture Basis, Santa Fe, N.Mex., 1984—. Prin. works include Yorktown Victory Ctr., Ariz. Hist. Soc., Nat. Coll. Football Hall of Fame, Mus. African-Am. History, Detroit. Home: 313Z Rosario Blvd Santa Fe NM 87501-1343

CROWTHER, RICHARD LAYTON, architect, consultant, researcher, author, lecturer; b. Newark, Dec. 16, 1910; s. William George and Grace (Layton) C.; m. Emma Jane Hubbard, 1935 (div. 1949); children: Bethe Crowther Allison, Warren Winfield, Vivian Layton; m. 2d Pearl Marie Tesch, Sept. 16, 1950. Student, Newark Sch. Fine and Indsl. Arts, 1928-31, San Diego State Coll., 1933, U. Colo., 1956. Registered architect, Colo. Prin. Crowther & Marshall, San Diego, 1946-50, Richard L. Crowther, Denver, 1951-66, Crowther, Kruse, Landin, Denver, 1966-70, Crowther, Kruse, McWilliams, Denver, 1970-75, Crowther Solar Group, Denver, 1975-82, Richard L. Crowther FAIA, Denver, 1982—; vis. critic, lectr. U. Nebr., 1981; holistic energy design process methodology energy cons. Holistic Health Ctr., 1982-83; adv. cons. interior and archtl. design class U. Colo., 1982-83, Cherry Creek, Denver redevel., 1984-88, Colo. smoking control legislation, 1985, interior solar concepts Colo. Inst. Art, 1986, Bio-Electro-Magnetics Inst., 1987-88; mentor U. Colo. Sch. Architecture, 1987-88. Author Sun/Earth, 1975 (Progressive Architecture award, 1975), rev. edit., 1983, reprint, 1995, Affordable Passive Solar Homes, 1983, reprint, 1996, Paradox of Smoking, 1983, Women/Nature/Destiny: Female/Male Equity for Global Survival, 1987, (monographs) Context in Art and Design, 1985, Existence, Design and Risk, 1986, Indoor Air: Risks and Remedies, 1986, Human Migration in Solar Homes for Seasonal Comfort and Energy Conservation, 1986, 88, Ecologic Architecture, 1992, Ecologic Digest, 1993, Ecologic Connections, 1996, Colorado Architect Monographs on Environmental Themes, 1998, others. NSF grantee, 1974-75. Fellow AIA (commr. research, edn. and environ. Colo. Central chpt. 1972-75, bd. dirs. chpt. 1973-74 AIA Research Corp. Solar Monitoring Program contract award, spkr. and pub. Colo. Ecologic Connections open forum 1996). Achievements include bio-toxic and bio-electromagnetic research.

CROXTON, DOROTHY AUDREY SIMPSON, speech educator; b. Las Vegas, N.Mex., Feb. 29, 1944; d. Clyde Joseph and Audrey Shirley (Clements) Simpson; m. Gary Alan Beimer, May 13, 1972 (div. Apr. 1986); children: Laura Lea Beimer Nelson, Rose Anne Colleen Beimer; m. Ian B. Croxton, Dec. 27, 1992 (div. Oct. 1993). BA, N.Mex. Highlands U., 1965; MS, U. Utah, 1968; EdD, U. N.Mex., 1989. Cert. secondary edn., N.Mex. Tchr. West Las Vegas (N.Mex.) H.S., 1966-67, Santa Rosa (N.Mex.) H.S., 1968-71, Questa (N.Mex.) Consol. Schs., 1972-73; prof. speech comm. N.Mex. Highlands U., Las Vegas, 1975—. Author: Hovels, Haciendas, and House Calls: The Life of Carl H. Gellenthien, M.D., 1986, Speaking for Life: A Speech Communication Guide for Adults, 1990, Wreck of the Destiny Train, 1993. Active Calvary Bapt. Ch., Las Vegas, 1959—. Recipient Educator of Yr. award Pub. Svc. Co. of N.Mex., Albuquerque, 1990. Mem. P.E.O. Republican. Avocation: writing. Home: PO Box 778 Las Vegas NM 87701-0778 Office: NMex Highlands Univ Communication Arts Dept Las Vegas NM 87701

CROYLE, DOUGLAS EUGENE, career officer; b. Tripoli, Lioya, Africa, Feb. 6, 1956; s. James Armin and Rose Travis (Bradley) C.; m. Susan Bernice Blomeley, Dec. 27, 1974; children: Alexa Virginia, Bethany Rose, abigail Lynn. A. in Telecom. Sci., USN TechTraCen, San Diego, 1991. Commd. USCG, 1974—, advanced through grades; watchstander COMMSTA USCG, Kodiak, Alaska, 1982-86; watchstander Group Grand Haven USCG, Grand Haven, Mich., 1986-89; watch supr. USCG, Guam, 1989-91; radioman in chg. Yocona (WMEC 168) USCG, Kodiak, 1994-96, commSysTech/watch supr., 1991—; with BNGI, Miami, Fla., 1979-82; loadmaster Emery Airfreight, Miami, 1980-82; fin. cons. Gen. Fin. corp., Miami, 1978-79. Author poetry in jours. Sec. Kodaik Rodeo and State Fairgrounds, 1992-93, Kodiak Rodeo and State Fair, 1995-96. Mem. Acad. Am. Poets (assoc.), Chief Petty Officers assn., N.Am. Hunting Club. Republican. Avocations: gemology, military miniatures, rare coins, writing, painting. Home: 1217A Selief Ln Kodiak AK 99615-6222

CRUE, BENJAMIN LANE, JR., retired neurosurgeon; b. Rahway, N.J., May 22, 1925; s. Benjamin Lane and Grace J. (Cornish) C.; m. Beverly Marie Malyon, Sept. 22, 1943 (dec. June 1997); children: Catherine, Benjamin III, Elizabeth, Jane. BS, MD, U. Chgo., 1948. Intern, gen. surgery resident USN, 1948-60; neurosurgeon City of Hope Nat. Med. Ctr., Duarte, Calif., 1960-80, Pasadena (Calif.) Hosp., 1980-85, Mercy Med. Ctr., Durango, Colo., 1985-93; chmn. neurology, neurosurgery City of Hope Pain Ctr., 1960-80; emeritus clin. prof. neurosurgery U. So. Calif. Sch. Medicine, L.A., 1980—. Author: Medullo Blastoma, 1958, Pain and Suffering, 1970, Pain—Research and Treatment, 1975, Chronic Pain—Further Observations from City of Hope, 1979; contbr. over 170 articles to profl. jours. Pres. Am. Pain Soc., Am. Acad. Pain Medication. Recipient Gold Medal award Law Sci. Acad., Crested Butte, Colo., 1965, Gold Medal award City of Hope Hosp., 1978. Fellow ACS, AMA. Republican. Mem. LDS Ch. Avocation: hunting. Home: 580 Oakcrest Dr Durango CO 81301-6905

CRUES, JOHN VERNON, III, radiologist, educator; b. Lubbock, Tex., [illegible] Jayne Ausanka, Aug. 7, 1976; children: Drew, Ry, Melissa. AB, Harvard U., 1972; postgrad., U. Salzburg, Austria, 1972; MS, U. Ill., 1975; MD, Harvard U., 1979. Diplomate Am. Bd. Internal Medicine, Am. Bd. Radiology, Nat. Bd. Med. Examiners; lic. physician, Calif.; cert. drug enforcement adminstrn., basic life support in cardiopulmonary resuscitation; lic. amateur radio operator, sr. parachute rigger, single engine pvt. pilot. Intern L.A. County-U. So. Calif. Med. Ctr., L.A., 1979-80; resident in internal medicine Cedars-Sinai Med. Ctr., L.A., 1980-82, resident in diagnostic radiology, 1982-85; rsch. engr. dept. elec. and computer engring. U. Calif., Santa Barbara; asst. clin. prof. radiology UCLA, 1987—; dir. magnetic resonance, musculoskeletal and emergency radiology Cedars-Sinai Med. Ctr., L.A., 1993-96; co-med. dir. RadNet Mgmt., Inc., 1996—; mem. rsch. bd. F. I. Internat.; mem. adv. bd. Teleradiology Svcs. Inc., Boston. Assoc. editor: Jour. Magnetic Resonance Imaging, 1993-96; column editor: Applied Radiology; mem. editl. bd.: Magnetic Resonance Quar., 1990-95; manuscript reviewer; contbr. articles to med. jours.; editor book chpts. Recipient Crues and Kressel award for outstanding contbns. to edn. of magnetic resonance technologists Sect. for Magnetic Resonance Technologists, 1991; Schlumberger scholar Harvard U., 1968-72. Mem. Soc. Magnetic Resonance (pres.), Radiol. Soc. N.Am., Am. Coll. Radiology (commn. on neurology and magnetic resonance; com. stds. and accreditation 1991—, com. mktg. and pub. rels. 1991—, com. human resources 1991—, com. magnetic resonance biol. effects 1993—, com. rsch. and tech. assessment 1993—), Internat. Soc. for Magnetic Resonance in Medicine (pres. 1994-95), Am. Soc. Emergency Radiology (charter), Internat. Skeletal Soc. Avocations: sailing, camping.

CRUICKSHANK, JOHN DOUGLAS, newspaper editor; b. Toronto, Ont., Can., Apr. 7, 1953; s. Norman and Jean (McPherson) C.; m. Jennifer Hunter; children: Simone, Noah. BA with honors, U. Toronto, 1975. Reporter The Kingston (Ont., Can.) Whig-Standard, 1977-79, The Montreal Gazette, 1979-81; edn. writer The Globe & Mail, Toronto, 1981-82, Queen's Park writer, 1982-85; bur. chief The Globe & Mail, Vancouver, 1985-88; editorial writer The Globe & Mail, Toronto, 1988-90, assoc. editor, 1990-92, mng. editor, 1992-95; editor-in-chief The Vancouver Sun, 1995—. Office: 200 Granville St Ste 1, Vancouver, BC Canada V6C 3N3*

CRUMLISH, CHRISTIAN THOMAS SPITZNAS, writer, editor, literary agent; b. N.Y.C., Oct. 30, 1964; s. Arthur Edward, Sr. and Gabrielle (Spitznas) C. AB, Princeton U., 1986. Editor: (lit. Webzine) Enterzone, 1994—; co-editor: (book) Coffeehouse, 1997. Office: Open Pub 1440 Broadway Ste 920 Oakland CA 94612

CRUMP, GLORIA JEAN, elementary and adult educator; b. L.A., Nov. 7, 1951; d. Robert and Florence (Spencer) C.; 1 child, Lavelle Gabrielle Alexander. BS, U. So. Calif., 1974. Tchr. Inglewood Unified Sch. Dist., L.A., 1975—, L.A. Unified Sch. Dist., 1980—. Poet: (anthology) Darkside of the Moon, 1995 (Best Poems of 1995, Internat. Poet of Merit award 1995). Mem. Internat. Soc. Poets, Delta Sigma Theta. Democrat. Presbyterian. Avocations: singing, reading, tennis, sewing, cooking. Home: PO Box 470446 Los Angeles CA 90047-0246 Office: 401 S Inglewood Ave Inglewood CA 90301-2501

CRUSE, ALLAN BAIRD, mathematician, computer scientist, educator; b. Birmingham, Ala., Aug. 28, 1941; s. J. Clyde and Irma R. Cruse. AB, Emory U., 1962, PhD, 1974; postgrad. (Woodrow Wilson fellow) U. Calif., Berkeley, 1962-63, MA, 1965; tchg. fellow Dartmouth Coll., 1963-64. Instr., U. San Francisco, 1966-73, asst. prof. math., 1973-76, assoc. prof., 1976-79, prof., 1979—, chmn. math. dept. 1988-91; vis. instr. Stillman Coll., summer 1967; vis. assoc. prof. Emory U., spring 1978; prof. computer sci. Sonoma State U., 1983-85; cons. math edn. NSF fellow, 1972-73. Mem. Am. Math. Soc., Math. Am. Math. Soc., Math. Assn. Am. (chmn. No. Calif. sect. 1995-96), Assn. Computing Machinery, U. San Francisco Faculty Assn., Sigma Xi (Dissertation award 1974). Author: (with Millianne Granberg) Lectures on Freshman Calculus, 1971; research, publs. in field. Office: U San Francisco Harney Sci Ctr San Francisco CA 94117

CRUSE, DENTON W., marketing and advertising executive, consultant; b. Washington, May 21, 1944; s. Denton W. Sr. and Frances Rankin (Moore) C.; m. Susan Costello, June 11, 1988; 1 child, Thomas Moore. BS, Va. Commonwealth U., 1966; MBA, So. Ill. U., 1977. Media supr. Procter & Gamble Co., Cin., 1967-73; assoc. media dir. Ralston Purina Co., St. Louis, 1973-78; dir. advt. Armour-Dial Co., Phoenix, 1978-81; mktg. dir. Valentine Greeting Inc., Phoenix, 1981-82; dir. mktg. svcs. J. Walter Thompson/USA, L.A., 1982-83; cons. L.A., 1983-86; dir. advt. svcs. Mattel Inc., L.A., 1986-88; cons. C and O Assocs., L.A., 1988—; instr. UCLA, 1986—; spkr. internat. mktg. seminar Tech. Tng. Corp., 1993—. Editor-in-chief: Cobblestone, 1965. Marathon monitor L.A. Olympic Organizing Com., 1984; bd. dirs. Old Hometown Fair. Mem. Mktg. Club L.A., Beta Gamma Sigma, Pi Sigma Epsilon. Republican. Presbyterian.

CRUTHERS, MARK CARROLL HAROLD, social studies educator, religous instructor; b. Richland, Wash., Oct. 21, 1967; s. Evan Douglas and Anita (Wilcomb) C. BA, U. Hawaii, 1989; MA, Fuller Theol. Seminary, 1992. Lit., phys. edn. tchr. Southwestern Acad., Pasadena, Calif., 1991-93; social studies tchr. Star of the Sea Sch., Honolulu, 1994—; religion instr. Chminade U., Honolulu, 1998—. Cand. Bd. Edn., Hawaii, 1996. With USNG, 1990-92, U.S. Army Res., 1988-89. Republican. Avocations: basketball, running, weight training, reading. Home: PO Box 161006 Honolulu HI 96816-0922 Office: Star of the Sea School 4469 Malia St Honolulu HI 96821-1195

CSENDES, ERNEST, chemist, corporate and financial executive; b. Satu-Mare, Szatmár-Németi, Romania, Mar. 2, 1926; came to U.S., 1951, naturalized, 1955; s. Edward O. and Sidonia (Littman) C.; m. Catharine Vera Tolnai, Feb. 7, 1953; children: Audrey Carol, Robert Alexander Edward. BA, Protestant Coll., Hungary, 1944; BS, U. Heidelberg (Ger.), 1948, MSc, 1950, PhD summa cum laude, 1951. Rsch. asst. chemistry U. Heidelberg, 1950-51; rsch. assoc. biochemistry Tulane U., New Orleans, 1952; rsch. fellow chemistry Harvard U., 1952-53; rsch. chemist organic chems. dept. E. I. Du Pont de Nemours and Co., Wilmington, Del., 1953-56, elastomer chems. dept., 1956-61; dir. rsch. and devel. agrl. chems. div. Armour & Co., Atlanta, 1961-63; v.p. corp. devel. Occidental Petroleum Corp., L.A., 1963-64, exec. v.p. rsch., engring. and devel., mem. exec. com., 1964-68; COO, exec. v.p., dir. Occidental Rsch. and Engring. Corp., L.A., London, Moscow, 1963-68; mng. dir. Occidental Rsch. and Engring. (U.K.) Ltd., London, 1964-68; pres., CEO TRI Group, London, Amsterdam, Rome and Bermuda, 1968-84; chmn., CEO Micronic Techs., Inc., L.A., 1981-85; mng. ptnr. Inter-Consult Ltd., Pacific Palisades, Calif.; internat. cons. on tech., econ. feasibility and mgmt., 1984—; pres., CEO, chief tech. officer Gen. Grinding Corp., L.A., 1991—; chmn., CEO Eden Mgmt. Ltd., L.A. and London, 1993—. Contbr. 250 articles to profl. and trade jours., studies and books; achievements include 34 patents; rsch. in area of elastomers, rubber chemicals, adhesives, dyes and intermediates, organometallics, organic and biochemistry, high polymers, antioxidants, superphosphoric acid and ammonium polyphosphates, plant nutrients, pesticides, process engineering, design of fertilizer plants, sulfur, potash, phosphate and iron ore mining and metallurgy, coal burning and acid rain, coal utilization, methods for aerodynamic grinding of solids, particles technology, advanced building materials, petrochemicals, biomed. engring., consumer products; also acquisitions, mergers, internat. fin. related to leasing investments and loans, trusts and ins., new Eurodollar instruments; regional indsl. devel. related to agr. and energy resources; projects in western Europe, no. Africa, Russia, Japan, Saudi Arabia, India, China and the Philippines. Recipient Pro Mundi Beneficio gold medal Brazilian Acad. Humanities, 1975; Harvard U. fellow, 1953. Fellow AAAS, Am. Inst. Chemists, Royal Soc. Chemistry (London); mem. AIAA, IEEE, SMME, AIChE, Am. Chem. Soc., German Chem. Soc., N.Y. Acad. Sci., Am. Concrete Inst., Am. Water Works Assn., AMS Internat., Acad. Polit. Sci., Nat. Def. and Indsl. Assn., Sigma Xi. Home: 514 N Marquette St Pacific Palisades CA 90272-3314

CUBILLOS, ROBERT HERNAN, church administrator, philosophy educator; b. Long Beach, Calif., Sept. 16, 1957; s. Roberto Hernan and Jacqueline Lee (Smith) C.; m. Deborah Sue Forbes, June 21, 1986; children: Robby, Kelli. BS, Calif. State U., Carson, 1983; cert. in human rights, Internat. [illegible] Greenleaf Sch. of Law, Orange, Calif., 1985; MA in Theology, Fuller Theol. Sem., Pasadena, Calif., 1986; postgrad. studies, Claremont (Calif.) Grad. Sch., 1987.; MA in Social Ethics and Religion, U. So. Calif., 1996. Ch. bus. adminstr. The Harbor Ch., Lomita, Calif., 1983-87, Rolling Hills Covenant

Ch., Rolling Hills Estates, Calif., 1987—; asst. prof., co-editor Law Review Simon Greenleaf Sch. of Law, Orange, Calif., 1987—; thesis sec., dean of students Simon Greenleaf Sch. of Law, Orange, 1988—. Contbr. articles to religious and philos. jours. Mem. Am. Acad. Religion, Christian Mgmt. Assn., Evangel. Theol. Soc., Soc. Bibl. Lit., Pi Delta Phi. Office: Rolling Hills Covenant Ch 2222 Palos Verdes Dr N Palos Verdes Peninsula CA 90274-4220

CUBIN, BARBARA LYNN, congresswoman, former state legislator; b. Salinas, Calif., Nov. 30; d. Russell G. and Barbara Lee (Howard) Sage; m. Frederick William Cubin, Aug. 1; children: William Russell, Frederick William III. BS in Chemistry, Creighton U., 1969. Chemist Wyo. Machinery Co., Casper, Wyo., 1973-75; social worker State of Wyo.; office mgr. Casper, Wyo.; mem. Wyo. Ho. Reps., 1987-92, Wyo. Senate, 1993-94; pres. Spectrum Promotions and Mgmt., Casper, 1993-94; congresswoman, Wyo., at large U.S. House Reps., Washington, 1995—; mem. fin. & Hazardous materials, health & environment, commerce com., resources com., chmn., energy and mineral subcom., mem. com. Nat. Coun. State Legislators, San Francisco, 1987—, Lexington, Ky., 1990—. Mem. steering com. Exptl. Program to Stimulate Competitive Rsch. (EPSCOR); mem. Coun. of State Govts.; active Gov.'s Com. on Preventive Medicine, 1992; vice chmn. Cleer Bd. Energy Coun., Irving, Tex., 1993—; chmn. Wyo. Senate Rep. Conf., Casper, 1993—; mem. Wyo. Rep. Party Exec. Com., 1993; pres. Southridge Elem. Sch. PTO, Casper, Wyo. Toll fellow Coun. State Govts., 1990, Wyo. Legislator of Yr. award for energy and environ. issues Edison Electric Inst., 1994. Mem. Am. Legis. Exch. Coun., Rep. Women. Avocations: duplicate bridge, golfing, singing, reading, hunting. Office: US House Reps Office House Mem 1114 Longworth HOB Washington DC 20515

CUCCHIARI, TONY, photographer, cinematographer; b. N.Y.C., June 23, 1951; m. Linda Kay Rendina. BFA, NYU, 1978. Dir. photography, cinematographer L.A. Dir. photography (film) Managua, 1997, Suicide, The Comedy, 1998. Mem. IASTE. Avocation: music. Home: 3271 Mountain View Ave Los Angeles CA 90066-1042

CUCINA, VINCENT ROBERT, retired financial executive; b. Balt., Mar. 31, 1936; s. Anthony James and Josephine (Lazzaro) C.; m. Rosemary Warrington, Apr. 24, 1965; children: Victor, Gregory, Russell. BS in Acctg. magna cum laude, Loyola Coll., Balt., 1958; MS in Fin. Mgmt., George Washington U., 1967. CPA, Calif. Auditor Haskins & Sells, CPAs, Balt., 1958, 61-63; acctg. mgr. books and reports Chesapeake & Potomac Telephone Co. (AT&T), Cockeysville, Md., 1964-68; mgr. fin. controls ITT, N.Y.C., 1968; contr. ITT World Directories, N.Y.C., 1969-70; v.p. fin. analysis and planning Dart Industries, Inc., L.A., 1970-82; v.p. fin., chief fin. officer Epson Am., Inc., Torrance, Calif., 1984-87; cons. Westlake Village, Calif., 1988-95; lectr. planning and fin. Calif. Luth. U., 1991-95. Capt. U.S. Army, 1959-60, USAR, 61-64. Mem. AICPA, Fin. Execs. Inst. Roman Catholic. Avocations: travel, reading, target shooting. Home: 32305 Blue Rock Rdg Westlake Village CA 91361-3912

CUGGINO, CHARLES, information systems specialist; b. Bronx, Jan. 2, 1960; s. Charles Arthur Cuggino and Barbara Jean (McCann) DiCarlo. BA, Boston Coll., 1982. Sys. designer Rolm, N.Y.C., 1983-84; sr. cons. Natel & Co., Tustin, Calif., 1984-86; sales Telex Computer Prodns., L.A., 1986-87; mktg. mgr. Fujitsu Bus. Comm., Anaheim, Calif., 1987-88; sr. cons. Robin & Dackerman, L.A., 1988-89; regional mgr. Centigram Comm. Corp., San Jose, 1989-91; prin./founder Tech. for Bus., Manhattan Beach, Calif., 1991—. Home: 4240 Park Newport Apt 203 Newport Beach CA 92660-6041 Office: Technology for Business 1112 Ocean Dr Ste 202 Manhattan Beach CA 90266-5435

CULBERT, MICHAEL LEON, communications executive; b. Wichita, Kans., May 9, 1937; s. Otto Leon and Gylah Bess (Buckingham) C. BS, Wichita State U., 1960; DSc (hon.), Sri Lanka Indigenous Health Min., 1985. Journalist various orgns., 1959-65; editor Berkeley Daily Gazette and Richmond Ind., Calif., 1966-75; pres., chmn., editor Com. for Freedom Choice in Medicine Inc., Calif., 1975—; info. dir. AB-Mex. Hosp., Tijuana, Mex., 1979—; v.p. Am. Biologics, Chula Vista, Calif., 1979—; founder, pres. C & C Comm., San Diego, 1992—; mem. ad hoc com. non-traditional medicine NIH, Bethesda, Md., 1992. Author or co-author 15 books. Formerly with Berkeley Boy Scouts, Berkeley-Sakai Sister City Com., Berkeley-Albany Red Cross, Commn. of Californias. Recipient Man of Yr. award United Reps. Calif., 1969, Editl. award Freedoms Found., 1971, Editl. award Calif. Newspaper Pubs. Assn., 1972. Mem. Commonwealth Club Calif. Avocations: philosophy, religion, astronomy, paranormal phenomena, herbology. Office: Am Biologics 1180 Walnut Ave Chula Vista CA 91911-2622

CULBERT, PETER V., lawyer; b. San Antonio, July 27, 1944; s. Robert William and Dorothy Fairfax (Kift) C.; m. Elizabeth Tamara Spagnola, July 12, 1980; children: Michael, Daniel, Robert, David, William. BA, Cornell U., 1966; MA, SUNY, Buffalo, 1969; JD, U. N.Mex., 1977. Bar: N.Mex. 1977, U.S. Dist. Ct. N.Mex. 1977, U.S. Ct. Appeals (10th cir.) 1977. Law clk. to Hon. Mack Easley N.Mex. Supreme Ct., Santa Fe, 1977-78; sr. ptnr. Jones, Snead, Wertheim, Wentworth & Jaramillo, Santa Fe, 1978-98; pvt. practice Santa Fe, 1999—. Mem. adv. bd., legal counsel Desert Chorale, Santa Fe, 1991—, bd. dirs., 1986-91. Recipient hon. cert. Strathmore Registry Bus. Leaders, 1995-97. Mem. ABA, ATLA, N.Mex. Trial Lawyers Assn., Canyon Assn., Alpha Delta Phi. Avocations: flamenco guitarist, bicycling, horticulture, camping. Office: 911 Old Pecos Trail Santa Fe NM 87501

CULL, CHRIS ALAN, operations executive; b. Las Cruces, N.Mex., Jan. 3, 1947; s. William Roy Cull and Doris Jean (Compton) Morgan; m. DuAnne Elizabeth Diers King, July 26, 1967 (div. 1979); children: Joey Lynn, Jamie Ayn, Brandon Alan. BS, N.Mex. State U., 1976. Lab./field technician N.Mex. State U., Las Cruces, 1973-76; research soil scientist Mont. State U., Bozeman, 1976-77; reclamation supr. Western Energy Co., Colstrip, Mont., 1977-80; mgr. ops. permitting Western Energy Co., Billings, Mont., 1980-85; asst. project mgr. En Tech Inc., Butte, Mont., 1985-86; mgr. ops. Spl. Resource Mgmt. Inc., Billings, 1986-87; owner EnviroChek Inc., Billings, 1987-88; dir. environ. svcs. Western Tech. Inc., Tucson, 1988-90; dir. regulatory affairs Western Tech. Inc., Golden, Colo., 1990-91; mgr. regulatory affairs Sergent, Hauskins & Beckwith, Lakewood, Colo., 1991-92; mgr. regulatory svcs. Morrison-Maierle Environ., Billings, Mont., 1992; mgr. regulatory svcs. Morrison-Maierle Environ. Corp., Billings, 1992—, v.p. regulatory svcs., 1994-98; prin. EHS Svcs., Billings, 1998—. Contbr. articles to profl. jours. Mem. Nat. Assn. Environ. Profls., Soil Conservation Soc. Am. (chmn. surface mine reclamation com. 1978-80, mem. univ. and coll. rels. com. 1977-78, spl. task force surface mine reclamation divsn. 1977-79, pres. Mont. chpt. 1980-82), Mont. Coal Coun. (co-chmn. environ./tech. com. 1983-85), Mining and Reclamation Coun. Am. (tech. com. 1983-85), Am. Coun on Sci. and Health. Avocations: fishing, camping, golf. Home: 3295 Granger Ave E Apt 18 Billings MT 59102-6064 Office: EHS Svcs 2020 Grand Ave Billings MT 59102-2679

CULLEN, JACK JOSEPH, lawyer; b. Sept. 20, 1951; s. Ray Brandes (stepfather) and Helen Cullen; m. Deborah L. Vick, Oct. 28, 1978; children: Cameron, Katherine. BA, Western Wash. State Coll., 1973; JD, U. Puget Sound, 1976. Bar: Wash. 1977, U.S. Dist. Ct. (we. dist.) Wash. 1977, U.S. Dist. Ct. (ea. dist.) Wash. 1977, U.S. Tax Ct. 1984, U.S. Ct. Appeals (9th cir.) 1980. Staff atty. Wash. State Bar Assn., Seattle, 1977-79; assoc. Hatch & Leslie, Seattle, 1979-85, mng. ptnr., 1985-91; ptnr. Foster Pepper & Shefelman, Seattle, 1991-96, mng. ptnr., 1996—, mng. chair, 1991—; spkr. in field. Co-author: Prejudgment Attachment, 1986. Active Frank Lloyd Wright Bldg. Conservancy, 1989—. Mem. ABA (bus. law sect.), Am. Bankruptcy Inst., Wash. State Bar Assn. (creditor-debtor sect., chair exec. 1982-90, spl. dist. counsel 1988—, hearing officer 1990), Seattle-King County Bar Assn. (bankruptcy rules subcom. 1988-90), Vancouver-Seattle Involvency Group (charter mem. 1990—), U.S. Sport Parachuting Team (nat. and world champions 1976, instrument rated pilot), Wash. Athletic Club. Avocations: skiing, bicycling. Office: Foster Pepper & Shefelman PLLC 1111 3rd Ave Ste 3400 Seattle WA 98101-3299*

CULLEN, ROBERT JOHN, publishing executive, financial consultant; b. York, Pa., Feb. 14, 1949; s. John Joseph and Florence Susanne (Staab) C.; m. Elizabeth Maule, Oct. 20, 1984; 1 child, Michael Joseph. BA, Winona (Minn.) State U., 1972. CFP; registered investment advisor. Editor-in-chief Overseas Life, Leimen, Fed. Republic of Germany, 1978-80; feature editor L.A. Daily Commerce, 1980-83; pres. HighTech Editorial, L.A., 1983—; fin. planner Cullen Fin. Svcs., Rancho Cucamonga, Calif., 1989—; computer editor Plaza Communications, Irvine, Calif., 1984-91. With U.S. Army, 1974-78, ETO. Mem. Inst. of Cert. Fin. Planners, Calif. Advs. Nursing Home Reform. Avocations: golf, chess, creative writing, public speaking.

CULPEPPER, MABEL CLAIRE, artist; b. St. Louis, Mo., June 20, 1936; d. John Raymond and Mabel Lorene (Hardy) Bondurant; m. James William Culpepper, Dec. 24, 1957; children: Julie Ann, James Jeffrey, John William. AA, Columbia Coll., 1956; BS in Edn., Mo. U., 1958, MEd, 1965. Represented by Artel Gallery, Emmitsburg, Md., 1987-88, Nob Hill Artisans, Albuquerque, 1993-94, Amapola Gallery, Albuquerque, 1995-98; art tchr. Twinbrook BApt., Rockville, Md., 1972-75. One woman exhbn. Artel Gallery, 1987; group exhbns. Rockville (Md.) Art League, 1987, N. Mex. Watercolor Soc., 1989-96. Host parent, officer Am. Field Svc., Damascus, Md., 1978-80; program chmn. Albuquerque Newcomers, 1989-91; docent Albuquerque Mus., 1990-94. Recipient First Prize Rockville Art League, 1987. Mem. Nat. Mus. Women in the Arts, Nat. League Am. Penwomen (pres. Yucca Br. 1998), N. Mex. Watercolor Soc. (pres. 1992-93, First Prize 1990, 1998, Best of Show 1993), Frederick County Art Assn. (pres. 1988), Delta Gamma, Mortar Bd. Avocations: hiking, singing in church choir, crafts, Bible study, travel. Home: 3208 Casa Bonita Dr NE Albuquerque NM 87111-5610

CULTON, PAUL MELVIN, retired counselor, educator, interpreter; b. Council Bluffs, Iowa, Feb. 12, 1932; s. Paul Roland and Hallie Ethel Emma (Paschal) C. BA, Minn. Bible Coll., 1955; BS, U. Nebr., 1965; MA, Calif. State U., Northridge, 1970; EdD, Brigham Young U., 1981. Cert. tchr., Iowa. Tchr. Iowa Sch. for Deaf, Council Bluffs, 1956-70; ednl. specialist Golden West Coll., Huntington Beach, Calif., 1970-71, dir. disabled students, 1971-82, instr., 1982-88; counselor El Camino Coll., Via Torrance, Calif., 1990-93, acting assoc. dean, 1993-94; counselor El Camino Coll., Via Torrance, Calif., 1994-97; interpreter various state and fed. cts., Iowa, Calif., 1960-90; asst. prof. Calif. State U., Northridge, Fresno & Dominguez Hills, 1973, 76, 80, 87-91; vis. prof. U. Guam, Agana, 1977; mem. allocations task force, task force on deafness, trainer handicapped students Calif. C.C.s, 1971-81. Editor: Region IX Conf. for Coordinating Rehab. and Edn. Svcs. for Deaf proceedings, 1970, Toward Rehab. Involvement by Parents of Deaf conf. proceedings, 1971; composer Carry the Light, 1986. Bd. dirs. Iowa NAACP, 1966-68, Gay and Lesbian Cmty. Svcs. Ctr., Orange County, Calif., 1975-77; founding sec. Dayle McIntosh Ctr. for Disabled, Anaheim and Garden Grove, Calif., 1974-80; active Dem. Cent. Com. Pottawattamie County, Council Bluffs, 1960-70; del. People to People N.Am. Educators Deaf Vis. Russian Schs. & Programs for Deaf, 1993. League for Innovation in Community Coll. fellow, 1974. Mem. Registry of Interpreters for Deaf, Congress Am. Instrs. Deaf, Am. Deafness and Rehab. Assn., Calif. Assn. Postsecondary Educators Disabled, Am. Fedn. Tchrs., Nat. Assn. Deaf. Mem. Am. Humanist Assn. Avocations: vocal music, languages, community activism, travel, politics. Home: 2567 Plaza Del Amo Apt 203 Torrance CA 90503-8962

CUMMINGS, BARTON, musician; b. Newport, N.H., July 10, 1946; s. C. Barton and Ruth (Ricard) C.; m. Florecita L. Lim, July 23, 1983;. BS in Music Edn., U. N.H., 1968; MusM, Ball State U., Muncie, Ind., 1973. Dir. music Alton (N.H.) Pub. Sch., 1971-72; lectr. San Diego State U., 1974-79; instr. music Point Loma Coll., San Diego, 1976-79; instr. San Diego Community Coll. Dist., 1977-79, Delta State U., Cleveland, Miss., 1979-82, supr. Clarksdale Separate Sch. Dist., 1982-84; dir. music Walnut (Calif.) Creek Concert Band, 1985--, Richmond Unified Sch. Dist., 1988—, Golden Hills Concert Band, 1990—; condr. Devil Mountain Symphony, 1991—; tuba player Vallejo Symphony Orch., 1988—, Concord Pavilion Pops Orch., 1985—, Brassworks of San Francisco, 1985—, Solano Dixie Jubilee. Author: The Contemporary Tuba, 1984, The Tuba Guide, 1989, Teaching Techniques for Brass Instruments, 1989; composer over 6 dozen pub. compositions; recorded on Capra, Coronet and Crystal, Channel Classics, Mark labels. Mem. ASCAP, NACUSA, T.U.B.A., Am. Fedn. of Musicians, Conductor's Guild, Phi Mu Alpha Sinfonia. Avocations: traveling, cooking, writing, composing, reading. Home: 550 Cambridge Dr Benicia CA 94510-1316

CUMMINGS, DAROLD BERNARD, aircraft engineer; b. Batavia, N.Y., June 27, 1944; s. Bernard Laverne and Doris Helen (Klotzbach) C.; children from a previous marrage: Carla, Bret; m. Karen Jean Cacciola, Dec. 19, 1992; children: Kyle, Scott. BS in Indsl. Design, Calif. State U., Long Beach, 1967. Engr. aircraft design Rockwell Internat., L.A., 1967-82; chief engr. Boeing N.Am., Long Beach, Calif., 1988—; chief designer advanced design Northrop Corp., Hawthorne, Calif., 1982-88; lectr. Calif. State U., Long Beach, 1969-73; pres. Matrix Design, Hawthorne, 1967—; tech. fellow Boeing, 1997. Author: What Not to Name Your Baby, 1982; cons., actor (movie) Search for Solutions, 1979; multiple patents in field. Mem. AIAA, Air Force Assn. Republican. Avocations: prospecting, hunting. Home: 5320 W 124th Pl Hawthorne CA 90250-4154 Office: Rockwell Internat Long Beach CA 90807

CUMMINGS, JOHN PATRICK, lawyer; b. Westfield, Mass., June 28, 1933; s. Daniel Thoams and Nora (Brick) C.; m. Dorothy June D'Ingianni, Dec. 27, 1957 (div. May 1978); children: John Patrick, Mary Catherine, Michael Brick, Kevin Andrew, Colleen Elise, Erin Christine, Christopher Gerald; m. Marilyn Ann Welch, May 23, 1980. BS, St. Michael's Coll., 1955; PhD, U. Tex., 1969; JD, U. Toledo, 1973, MCE, 1977. Bar: Ohio 1973, U.S. Mil. Appeals 1974, U.S. Dist. Ct. (no. dist.) Ohio 1979. Mgr. Hamilton Mgmt., Inc., Austin, Tex., 1962-68; scientist Owens Ill., Toledo, 1968-73, risk mgr., 1974-76, staff atty., 1977-80, mgr. legis. affairs, 1981-84; pres. Hansa World Cargo Svc., Inc., Oakland, Calif., 1984-86; in-house counsel Brown Vence & Assocs., San Francisco, 1987-88; gen. counsel Pacific Mgmt. Co., Sacramento, 1986-88; pres. John P. Cummings & Assoc., Fremont, Calif., 1988—; cons. Glass Packaging Inst., Washington, 1970-83, EPA, Washington, 1970-74. Contbr. articles to profl. jours.; patentee in field. With USAF, 1955-62, 68-69, 75-76, 84-85, col. Res. ret. 1986. USPHS fellow, 1963-66. Fellow Royal Chem. Soc.; mem. ABA, VFW, Am. Chem. Soc., ASTM (chmn. 1979), Am. Ceramic Soc. (chpt. chmn. 1973), Res. Officers Assn. (legis. chmn. 1979-85), Am. Legion, KC (4th degree). Roman Catholic. Avocations: reading, travel, coin and stamp collecting. Home: 843 Barcelona Dr Fremont CA 94536-2607 Office: PO Box 2847 Fremont CA 94536-0847

CUMMINGS, LESLIE EDWARDS, hospitality management educator; b. Modesto, Calif., Feb. 17, 1951; d. George Robert and Mary Lou (Bomberger) Edwards; m. William Theodore Cummings Jr., Mar. 12, 1977. BS in Home Econs., Ariz. State U., 1974, MS in Agriculture, 1977, D in Pub. Adminstrn., 1990. Intern General Mills, Inc., Golden Valley, Minn., summer 1968; diet technician Mesa (Ariz.) Luth. Hosp., 1972-73; salesperson Romney Products, Inc., 1974; pharm. ins. auditor Pharm. Card Sys., Inc., 1974-76; mem. chain hdqrs. staff Fry's Supermarkets, Inc., 1977; adj. instr. foodsvc. Auburn (Ala.) U., 1978-79, from asst. mgr. to mgr. Campus Ctr. Foodsvcs., 1979-80; customer support analyst WANG Labs., Inc., 1981-83; asst. prof. U. Nev., Coll. Hotel Adminstrn., Las Vegas, 1983-87, assoc. prof., 1987-93, prof., 1993—; presenter Hotel-Motel Expo, 1985, So. Nev. Dietetics Assn. and So. Nev. Home Econs. Assn., Las Vegas, 1986, Inst. Food Technologists, Las Vegas, 1987, Universidad Madre y Maestra System, Santo Domingo, Dominican Republic, 1987, Internat. Assn. Hospitality Accts., Las Vegas, 1986, Foodsvc. and the Environment, Scottsdale, Ariz., 1990, State of Ariz. Dietetics Assn., Scottsdale, 1991, Assn. for the Study of Food and Soc., Tucson, 1991, ASPA, Las Vegas, 1991, Foodsvcs. Sys. Beyond 2000 Conf., Israel, 1992, Gaming Educator's Conf., Las Vegas, Hospitality Info. Tech. Assn., New Orleans, 1995, Environments for Tourism Conf., Las Vegas, 1996, Internat. Hospitality Tech. Conf., Nashville, 1996; panelist, spkr. in field of applied tech. and gaming trends. Author: (textbook) (with Lendal Kotschevar) Nutrition Management for Foodservices, 1989, Instructor's Manual for Nutrition Management for Foodservices, 1989; contbr. numerous articles on hospitality applications of tech. and distance edn. to acad. jours. Vol. Women's Resource Network Career Event, Annual Nev. Gov.'s Conf. for Women. Recipient Nat. Assn. Schs. Pub. Adminstrn. dissertation award, 1990, Boyd Rsch. award, 1991, Ace Denken Disting. Rsch. award, 1996-98; fellow Rotary Internat., 1978. Mem. ASPA, Am. Dietetic Assn. (treas. environ. nutrition dietetic practice group 1992-95, registered dietitian), Inst. Internal Auditors (cert.), Coun. on Hotel, Restaurant and Instnl. Edn., Phi Beta Kappa, Phi Kappa Phi, Pi Alpha Alpha. Avocations: horse training, learning about plants and animals, listening. Office: WF Harrah Coll Hotel Adminstrn Food & Beverage Mgmt Dept 4505 S Maryland Pkwy Las Vegas NV 89154-9900

CUMMINGS, NICHOLAS ANDREW, psychologist; b. Salinas, Calif., July 25, 1924; s. Andrew and Urania (Sims) C.; m. Dorothy Mills, Feb. 5, 1948; children: Janet Lynn, Andrew Mark. AB, U. Calif., Berkeley, 1948; MA, Claremont Grad. Sch., 1954; PhD, Adelphi U., 1958. Chief psychologist Kaiser Permanente No. Calif., San Francisco, 1959-76; pres. Found Behavioral Health, San Francisco, 1976—; chmn., CEO Am. Biodyne, Inc., San Francisco, 1985-93, Kendron Internat., Ltd., Reno, Nev., 1992-95; chmn. Nicholas & Dorothy Cummings Found., Reno, 1994—; chmn., pres. U.K. Behavioural Health, Ltd., London, 1996-98; Disting. prof. U. Nev., 1997—; chmn., CEO DynaMed Integrated Care, Inc., 1998—; co-dir. South San Francisco Health Ctr., 1959-75; pres. Calif. Sch. Profl. Psychology, L.A., San Francisco, San Diego, Fresno campuses, 1969-76; chmn. bd. Calif. Cmty. Mental Health Ctrs., Inc., L.A., San Diego, San Francisco, 1975-77; pres. Blue Psi, Inc., San Francisco, 1972-80, Inst. for Psychosocial Interaction, 1980-84; mem. mental health adv. bd. City and County San Francisco, 1968-75; bd. dirs. San Francisco Assn. Mental Health, 1965-75; pres., chmn. bd. Psycho-Social Inst., 1972-80; dir. Mental Rsch. Inst., Palo Alto, Calif., 1979-80; pres. Nat. Acads. of Practice, 1981-93. Served with U.S. Army, 1944-46. Fellow Am. Psychol. Assn. (dir. 1975-81, pres. 1979); mem. Calif. Psychol. Assn. (pres. 1968). Office: Nicholas & Dorothy Cummings Found 561 Keystone Ave Ste 212 Reno NV 89503-4331

CUMMINGS, RUSSELL MARK, aerospace engineer, educator; b. Santa Cruz, Calif., Oct. 3, 1955; s. Gilbert Warren and Anna Mae (Phillips) C. BS, Calif. Poly. State U., 1977, MS, 1985; Engr. Aerospace Engring., 1982; PhD, U. So. Calif., 1988. Tech. staff Hughes Aircraft Co., Canoga Park, Calif., 1979-86; rsch. assoc. Nat. Rsch. Coun. at NASA Ames Rsch. Ctr., Moffett Field, Calif., 1988-90; prof. aerospace engring. Calif. Poly. State U., San Luis Obispo, Calif., 1986—; dept. chmn. aero. engring. dept. Calif. Poly. State U., 1992-96; vis. acad. computing lab. Oxford U., 1995-97; presenter in field. Contbr. chpt. to book Numerical and Physical Aspects of Aerodynamic Flows, 1990; assoc. editor Jour. Spacecraft and Rockets, 1994-99; contbr. 20 articles to profl. jours. Eagle Scout, Boy Scouts of Am. Hughes Engring. fellow 1980-84, Howard Hughes Doctoral fellow 1984-86; NASA grant, 1986-99; recipient Group Achievement awards NASA, 1989-90, AIAA Nat. Faculty Advisor award, 1994, Northrop Grumman Excellence in Teaching and Applied Rsch. award, 1995, Undergraduate Faculty Advisor award BF Goodrich Nat. Collegiate Inventors Program, 1998. Fellow AIAA (assoc., student activities com. 1991-99, missile sys. tech. com. 1988-91); mem. Am. Soc. Engring. Educators, Royal Aero. Soc., Aircract Owners and Pilots Assn., Sigma Xi, Sigma Gamma Tau. Republican. Mem. Evangelical Christian Ch. Avocations: piano, tennis, pvt. pilot, skiing, volleyball, baseball. Office: Calif Poly State U Dept Aero Engring San Luis Obispo CA 93407

CUMMINS, ERIK HOWCROFT, newspaper editor; b. Neubroke, Germany, Aug. 29, 1968; s. Robert Warren and Cheryl C. (Carlisle) C.; m. Angela Nicole Ramirez, Mar. 20, 1993. BA, cert. in journalism, Sonoma State U., 1993. Sports editor, columnist Santa Rosan, Santa Rosa, Calif., 1984-86; entertainment editor, columnist Oakleaf, Santa Rosa, 1987-88; reporter Sonoma State Star, Rohnert Park, Calif., 1992-93; editor, reporter, photographer Sonoma County Herald Recorder, Santa Rosa, 1988—. Monthly columnist On the Docket, 1996—. Mem. Sonoma County Press Club (pres. 1995-96), E Clampus Vitus. Avocations: local historical research, softball, reading, hiking, travel. Office: Sonoma County Herald-Recorder 1818 4th St Santa Rosa CA 95405

CUMMINS, JOHN STEPHEN, bishop; b. Oakland, Calif., Mar. 3, 1928; s. Michael and Mary (Connolly) C. A.B., St. Patrick's Coll., 1949. Ordained priest Roman Catholic Ch., 1953; asst. pastor Mission Dolores Ch., San Francisco, 1953-57; mem. faculty Bishop O'Dowd High Sch., Oakland, 1957-62; chancellor Diocese of Oakland, 1962-71; rev. monsignor, 1962, domestic prelate, 1967; exec. dir. Calif. Cath. Conf., Sacramento, 1971-77; consecrated bishop, 1974; aux. bishop of Sacramento, 1974-77; bishop of Oakland, 1977—; Campus minister San Francisco State Coll., 1953-57, Mills Coll., Oakland, 1957-71; Trustee St. Mary's Coll., 1968-79. Home: 634 21st St Oakland CA 94612-1608 Office: Oakland Diocese 2900 Lakeshore Ave Oakland CA 94610-3614

CUMMINS, NANCYELLEN HECKEROTH, electronics engineer; b. Long Beach, Calif., May 22, 1948; d. George and Ruth May (Anderson) Heckeroth; m. Weldon Jay Cummins, Sept. 15, 1987; children: Tracy Lynn, John Scott, Darren Elliott. Student, USMC, Memphis, 1966-67. From tech. publ. engr. to engring. instr. Missile and Space divsn. Lockheed Corp., Sunnyvale, Calif., 1973-77; test engr. Gen. Dynamics, Pomona, Calif., 1980-83; quality assurance test engr. Interstate Electronics Co., Anaheim, Calif., 1983-84; quality engr., certification engr. Rockwell Internat., Anaheim, 1985-86; sr. quality assurance programmer Point 4 Data, Tustin, Calif., 1986-87; software quality assurance specialist Lawrence Livermore Nat. Lab., Yucca Mountain Project, Livermore, Calif., 1987-89, software quality mgr., 1989-90; from sr. constrn. insp. to sr. quality assurance engr. EG&G Rocky Flats, Inc., Golden, Colo., 1990-91, engr. IV software quality assurance, 1991-92, instr., developer environ. law and compliance, 1992-93; software, computer cons. CRI, Dabois, Wyo., 1993-97; contractor Dept. of Energy, Golden, Colo., 1997-98; test mgr. Keane Inc., Lakewood, Colo., 1998; project officer Keane Inc., Lakewood, 1998—; customer engr. IBM Gen. Sys., Orange, Calif., 1979; electronics engr. Exhibits divsn. LDS Ch., Salt Lake City, 1978; electronics repair specialist Weber State Coll., 1977-78. Author: Package Area Test Set, 6 vols., 1975, Software Quality Assurance Plan, 1989. Vol., instr. San Fernando (Calif.) Search and Rescue Team, 1967-70; instr. emergency preparedness and survival, Claremont, Calif., 1982-84, Modesto, Calif., 1989; mem. Lawrence Livermore nat. Lab. Employees Emergency Vols., 1987-90, EG&G Rocky Flats Bldg. Emergency Support Team, 1990-93, Dubois Search and Rescue, 1995-97. Mem. NAFE, NRA, Nat. Muzzle Loading Rifle Assn., Am. Soc. Quality, Job's Daus. (majority mem.). Republican. Avocations: living history, survival, weapons, camping, native Am. crafts.

CUNNANE, PATRICIA S., medical facility administrator; b. Clinton, Iowa, Sept. 7, 1946; d. Cyril J. and Corinne Spain; m. Edward J. Cunnane, June 19, 1971. AA, Mt. St. Clare Coll., Clinton, Iowa, 1966. Mgr. Eye Med. Clinic of Santa Clara Valley, San Jose, Calif. Mem. Med. Adminstrs. Calif. Polit. Action Com., San Francisco, 1987. Mem. Med. Group Mgmt. Assn., Am. Coll. Med. Group Adminstrs. (nominee), Nat. Notary Assn., NAFE, Exec. Women Internat. (v.p. 1986-87, pres. 1987—), Profl. Secs. Internat. (sec. 1979-80), Am. Soc. Ophthalmic Adminstrs., Women Health Care Execs., Healthcare Human Resource Mgmt. Assn. Calif. Roman Catholic. Avocations: calligraphy, golf. Home: 232 Tolin Ct San Jose CA 95139-1445 Office: Eye Med Clinic of Santa Clara Valley 220 Meridian Ave San Jose CA 95126-2903

CUNNING, TONIA, newspaper managing editor. BS in Journalism, U. Nev. Soc. editor/feature writer-editor/asst. mng. editor Reno (Nev.) Gazette-Jour., 1971-92, mng. editor, 1992—. Office: Reno Gazette-Journal PO Box 22000 Reno NV 89520-2000*

CUNNINGHAM, ANDY, executive; m. Rand Siegfried; 2 children. Pres., CEO Cunningham Comm., Inc., Palo Alto, Calif. Office: Cunningham Comm Inc 1510 Page Mill Rd Palo Alto CA 94304-1125*

CUNNINGHAM, BRIDGET EUGENIA, medical records administrator; b. Detroit, June 28, 1952; d. Eugene B. and Consuella V. (McSmith) C. AS, East Los Angeles Coll., 1979; BA, Coll. St. Scholastica, 1990. Med. records coder Los Angeles County.-U. So. Calif. Med. Ctr., 1979-81; cancer case abstractor Los Angeles County-U. So. Calif. Med. Ctr., 1981-84; tumor registry supr. Los Angeles Coll.-U. So. Calif. Med. Ctr., 1984-86; dir. med. records CPC Alhambra Hosp., Rosemead, Calif., 1986—. Vol. worker health fair Am. Cancer Soc., Pasadena, 1984-86. With USAF, 1973-77.

Mem. NAFE, Am. Med. Records Assn., Nat. Assn. Med. Staff Services, So. Calif. Med. Library Assn., So. Calif. Tumor Registry Assn. (treas. 1986), Greater L.A. Coding Network (treas. 1989). Democrat. Roman Catholic. Club: Sierra (Los Angeles). Avocations: aerobics, dancing, skiing, reading, theater.

CUNNINGHAM, DAVID FRATT, lawyer; b. N.Y.C., May 23, 1944; s. David Fratt (dec.) and Burnley (Chenery) Wadsworth; m. Tracy Griswold, June 1966 (div. 1973); 1 child, David Fratt Jr.; m. Helen C. Sturm, Feb. 1979 (div. July 1988); children: Meghan Cunningham, Cory Cunningham; m. Janet E. Clow, Jan. 27, 1989. BA, Stanford U., 1966; JD, U. Calif., Hastings, 1969. Bar: N.Y. 1970, N.Mex. 1983. Asst. dist. atty. Manhattan Dist. Attys. Office, N.Y.C., 1969-72; chief asst. and acting spl. prosecutor Office of Spl. Narcotics Prosecutor, N.Y.C., 1972-80; chief investigative divsn. Manhattan Dist. Attys. Office, N.Y.C., 1980-83; ptnr., chief litigation sect. White, Koch, Kelly & McCarthy, PA, Santa Fe, 1983—; Commr. N.Mex. Organized Crime Commn., 1983-87; gen. counsel Zuni Tribe, 1987—. Co-author: Trial of a Criminal Case, 1980. Mem. ABA, Inn of the Ct. (Oliver Seth br. counsel 1994—). Democrat. Avocations: fly fishing, running. Office: White Koch Kelly & McCarthy PA PO Box 787 433 Paseo De Peralta Santa Fe NM 87501-1958

CUNNINGHAM, DONNA RAE, writer, astrologer; b. Onawa, Iowa, July 5, 1942; d. Walter Woodrow Wilson and Zelma (Hedges) C. BS in Psychology, Grinnell Coll., 1964; MSW, Columbia U., 1967. Cert. social worker, N.Y.; cert. profl. astrologer, Am. Fedn. Astrologers; cert. profl. astrologer, Profl. Astrologers Inc.; lic. cert. social worker, Calif. Pvt. practice Portland, Oreg.; dir. social svc. St. Mary's Hosp., Bklyn.; spkr. in field. Author: An Astrological Guide to Self-Awareness, 1979, Healing Pluto Problems, 1986, (with Andrew Ramer) Further Dimensions of Healing Addictions, 1988, (with Andrew Ramer) Spiritual Dimensions of Healing Addictions, 1988, Astrology and Vibrational Healing, 1988, Moon Signs: The Key to Your Inner Life, 1988, Astrology and Spiritual Development, 1989, The Flower Remedies Handbook, 1992, The Consulting Astrologer's Guidebook, 1994, The Moon in Your Life, 1996 and others; editor NCGR-NY Newsletter, 1979, CASE Reports, 1993-95, (on-line mag.) Vibration mag., 1998—; editor, pub. (astrology jour.) Shooting Star, 1988-89; advice columnist Dell Horoscope Mag., 1994—; contbr. over 1000 articles to profl. jours. Recipient Lifetime Achievement award Profl. Astrologers Inc., 1986, Regulus award for theory and understanding United Astrology Congress, 1998. Mem. Nat. Coun. Geocosmic Rsch., Assn. for Astrol. Networking, Org. Astrol. Assn., Quimper Astrology Guild (program chair 1993-96), Phi Beta Kappa. Avocations: mysteries, figure skating fan, surfing the net. Home and Office: PO Box 25331 Portland OR 97298-0331

CUNNINGHAM, ELDON LLOYD, artist, educator; b. Colby, Kans., Mar. 2, 1956; s. Gordon Keith and Annie (Gardner) C.; m. Allison Mary Cunningham, May 29, 1982; 1 child, Kevin Lloyd. BFA, Wichita State U., 1979; MFA, U. Colo., 1982. Grad. instr. U. Colo., Boulder, 1980-81; master printer Master Editions Ltd., Englewood, Colo., 1982-84; instr. Univ. Without Walls-Laretto Hts. Coll., Denver, 1984; prof. art Met. State Coll., Denver, 1983—, chmn. dept. art. Author: Printmaking: A Primary Form of Expression, 1992; dir., publ. (video) Nat. Printmaking Slide Video Exch., 1990; one-man shows include Wichita State U., 1995, U. Wyo., 1997. Mem. Coll. Art Assn., Mid.-Am. Print Coun. (pres. 1994-96, bd. dirs. 1996—), So. Graphics Coun. Mem. Ch. of Brethren. Avocations: water gardening, beer brewing. Office: Met State Coll CB 59 PO Box 173362 Denver CO 80217-3362

CUNNINGHAM, GEORGE, senator; m. Marjorie Fisher; children: Paul, Eve, Molly. B of Pub. Adminstrn., U. Ariz., M of Pub. Adminstrn. Spl. asst. to pres. Ariz. State Senate, Tucson, 1956; v.p. adminstrv. svcs. U. Ariz., Tucson, 1985-88; chief of staff Gov. Rose Mofford, 1988-90; with U. Ariz., Tucson, 1990-93; rep. State of Ariz., 1993-96, senator, 1996—; co-chmn. Pima County Com. on Property Tax and State Revenue Reform, 1996. *

CUNNINGHAM, JOEL DEAN, lawyer; b. Seattle, Feb. 19, 1948; s. Edgar Norwood and Florence (Burgunder) C.; m. Amy Jean Radewan, Oct. 1, 1970; children: Erin Jane, Rad Norwood. BA in Econs., U. Wash., 1971, JD with high honors, 1974. Lawyer, ptnr. Williams, Kastner & Gibbs, Seattle, 1974-95; ptnr. Luvera, Barnett, Brindley, Beninger & Cunningham, Seattle, 1995—. Fellow Am. Coll. Trial Lawyers, Am. Bd. Profl. Liability Attys.; mem. Am. Bd. Trial Attys. (pres. Washington chpt. 1994), Order of Coif. Avocations: fishing, cycling, boating. Office: Luvera Barnett Brindley Beninger & Cunningham 6700 Columbia Ctr 701 Fifth Ave Seattle WA 98104-7016

CUNNINGHAM, RANDY, congressman; b. L.A., Dec. 8, 1941; m. Nancy Jones; 3 children. BA, U. Mo., MA; MBA, Nat. U. Mem. 102nd-105th Congresses from Calif. dist. 44 (now 51), 1991—, mem. nat. security com., mem. appopriations com. Republican. Christian. Office: US Ho of Reps 2238 Rayburn HOB Washington DC 20515

CUNNINGHAM, RON, choreographer, artistic director; b. Chgo., Sept. 15, 1939; m. Carrine Binda, June 12, 1982; children: Christopher, Alexandra. Student, Allegro Ballet, 1961-65, Am. Ballet Theatre, 1968-70; studies with Merce Cunningham, N.Y.C., 1968-70; BS in Mktg., Roosevelt U., 1966. Dancer Allegro Am. Ballet Co., Chgo., 1962-66; artistic dir. Ron Cunningham Contemporary Dance Co., Chgo., 1966-68; dancer Lucas Hoving Dance Co., 1968-72, Lotte Goslar Pantomime Circus, 1968-72, Daniel Nagrin Dance Co., 1968-72; prin. dancer, resident choreographer Boston Ballet, 1972-85; artistic dir. Balt. Ballet, 1985-86; artistic assoc. Washington Ballet, 1986-87; ind. choreographer, 1987-88; artistic dir. Sacramento Ballet, 1988—; panelist various regional and state art councils, 1979—; dir. Craft of Choreography, 1985; adjudicator, master tchr. Nat. Assn. Regional Ballet, 1985—, Am. Coll. Dance Assn., 1986. Dancer, choreographer 40 original internat. ballets, 1972—, 4 ballets Nat. Choreography Plan, 1978—, Cinderella, Peoples Republic of China, 1980. Nat. Endowment Arts fellow, 1977, 86, Mass. Art Council fellow, 1984, Md. Arts Council fellow, 1988. Mem. Nat. Assn. Regional Ballet, Dance/U.S.A. Avocation: archeology--bronze age cultures. *

CURCIO, CHRISTOPHER FRANK, city official; b. Oakland, Calif., Feb. 3, 1950; s. Frank William and Virginie Theresa (Le Gris) C. BA in Speech/Drama, Calif. State U., Hayward, 1971; MBA in Arts Adminstrn., UCLA, 1974; MPA in Pub. Policy, Ariz. State U., 1982. Intern John F. Kennedy Ctr. for Arts, Washington, 1973; gen. mgr. Old Eagle Theatre, Sacramento, 1974-75; cultural arts supr. Fresno (Calif.) Parks and Recreation Dept., 1975-79; supr. cultural and spl. events Phoenix Parks, Recreation and Libr. Dept., 1979-87, budget analyst, 1987, mgmt. svcs. adminstr., 1987-97, dep. dir., 1997—; mgmt. and budget analyst City of Phoenix, 1985; grants panelist Phoenix Arts Commn., 1987, Ariz. Commn. on Arts, 1987-88; voter Zony Theatre Awards, 1991-92; freelance theater critic, 1987-89; theater critic Ariz. Republic, 1990—, PHX Downtown, 1997—, CityAZ, 1997—. Active Valley Leadership Program, Phoenix, 1987—, Valley Big Bros./Big Sisters, 1980-94; chair allocation panel United Way, 1990-92; sec. Los Olivos Townhome Assn., Phoenix, 1986-92. Mem. Am. Soc. Pub. Adminstrn., Nat. Recreation and Park Assn., Am. Theatre Critics Assn., Internat. Theater Critics Assn., Ariz. Park and Recreation Assn. Republican. Avocations: theater history, writing, reading, cooking, gardening. Office: Phoenix Parks Recreation Libr Dept 200 W Washington St Fl 16 Phoenix AZ 85003-1611

CURD, JOHN GARY, physician, scientist; b. Grand Junction, Colo., July 2, 1945; s. H. Ronald and Edna (Hegested) C.; m. Karen Wendel, June 12, 1971; children: Alison, Jonathan, Edward, Bethany. BA, Princeton U., 1967; MD, Harvard U., 1971. Diplomate Am. Bd. Internal Medicine, Am. Bd. Rheumatology, Am. Bd. Allergy and Immunology. Rsch. assoc. NIH, Bethesda, Md., 1973-75; fellow in rheumatology U. Calif., San Diego, 1975-77; fellow in allergy-immunology Scripps Clinic, La Jolla, Calif., 1977-78, asst. mem. rsch. inst., 1978-81, mem. div. rheumatology, 1981-91, head div. rheumatology, vice chmn. dept. medicine, 1989-91; pres. med. staff Green Hosp., La Jolla, 1988-90; clin. dir. Genentech Inc., South San Francisco, Calif., 1991-96; sr. dir., head clin. sci. Genentech Inc., South San Francisco, 1996-97, v.p. clin. devel., 1997—. Author numerous. sci. papers in field. Med. dir. San Diego Scleroderma Found., 1983-91, sec. San Diego Arthritis Found., 1986-87. Lt. comdr. USPHS, 1973-75. Mem. Princeton Club No. Calif. Republican. Home: 128 Reservoir Rd Hillsborough CA 94010-6957 Office: Genentech Inc 1 Dana Ct South San Francisco CA 94080-5713

CUREAU, FRANK RAYMOND, furniture company executive; b. Tours, France, Aug. 29, 1955; came to U.S., 1981; s. Jean-Marie and Jacqueline (Marquenet) C.; m. Armelle Therese Deakin, Apr. 6, 1987; 1 child, Xavier. BA, Descartes U., Tours. Export mgr. Guinard Pumps, Paris, 1979-81; gen. mgr. Guinard Pumps, Chgo., 1981-84, T.F.G., London, 1984-85, Grosfillex, Inc., Oxnard, Calif., 1986—; physics of fluids tchr., Guinard Pumps, Paris, 1980-82. Coord. Rassemblement Pour La Republique, Paris, L.A., 1987, 88. Lt., French mil., 1976-77.

CURLEY, ELMER FRANK, librarian; b. Florence, Pa., Jan. 13, 1929; s. Augustus Wolfe and Bessie (Andrews) C. BA, U. Pitts., 1961; MLS, Carnegie Mellon U., Pitts., 1962; Adv. Cert., U. Pitts., 1964. Ref. librarian U. Pitts., 1962-64; head ref. dept. SUNY-Stony Brook, 1964-67; head pub. svcs. U. Nev.-Las Vegas, 1967-76, asst. dir. libr. svcs., 1976-81, ref. bibliographer, 1981-94, ret., 1994.

CURLEY, MICHAEL JOSEPH, English language educator; b. N.Y.C., Dec. 23, 1942; s. William Paul and Theresa Helen Curley; m. Sandra Jean Plann; children: Austin, Brendan. BA, Fairfield U., 1964; MA in Teaching, Harvard U., 1965; PhD, U. Chgo., 1973. Prof. English U. Puget Sound, Tacoma, 1971—, dir. honors program, 1984—; vis. prof. U. Wash., Seattle, 1988. Author: Physiologus, 1979, Marie de France: Purgator of Saint Patrick, 1993, Geoffrey of Monmouth, 1994. Recipient Graves award Graves Found., 1982-83; NEH fellow, 1977-78, Am. Coun. Learned Soc. fellow, 1979-80; NEH grantee, 1974, 87. Mem. Medieval Acad. Am., Celtic Soc. N.Am., Internat. Arthurian Soc., Medieval Assn. The Pacific. Office: U Puget Sound N Lawrence St Tacoma WA 98416

CURNUTT, BRIAN JOE, religious studies educator; b. Montebello, Calif., Jan. 26, 1962; s. Gerald Ray and Barbara Jean (Cichirillo) C.; m. Heidi Elizabeth Notter, June 28, 1986. AA in Bibl. Lit., Cascade Bible Coll., 1986, M Ministry, 1990; BA in Bibl. Lit., Northwest Coll., 1988. Cert. cons. Youth pastor Kirkland (Wash.) 1st Bapt. Ch., 1984-86; assoc. pastor Calvary Chapel, Seattle, 1988; prof. Cascade Bible Coll., Bellevue, Wash., 1988—; spl. rep. of pres. Cascade Bible Coll., 1989—. Author/programmer: (software database) Kyrios Church Manager and Accounting, 1990-91, Counseling Reference Database, 1991. Office: PC Answers Inc 18700 33rd Ave W Ste B245 Lynnwood WA 98037-4743

CUROTTO, RICKY JOSEPH, lawyer, corporate executive; b. Lomita Park, Calif., Dec. 22, 1931; s. Enrico and Nora M. (Giusso) C.; m. Lynne Therese Ingram, Dec. 31, 1983; children: Dina L., John F., Alexis J. BS cum laude, U. San Francisco, 1953, JD, 1958. Bar: Calif. 1959. Assoc. Peart, Baraty & Hassard, San Francisco, 1958-60; sr. counsel, asst. sec. BHP Minerals Internat. Inc.(formerly BHP-Utah Internat. Inc.), San Francisco, 1960—; of counsel Curotto Law Offices, Oakland and Sacramento, Calif., 1984—; sec. AOFR, Inc., BHP Engineering Inc., BHP Instruments Inc., Austgen-Biojet Inc., EcoScience Inc.; bd. dirs. Fathom Mgmt. Corp., Newco Trading Corp., Inc., Broken Hill Proprietary (U.S.A.) Inc., BHP Securities Inc., BHP Transport USA Inc., BHP Internat. Marine Transport Inc., Garden Hotels Investment Co., Family Housing and Adult Resources Inc. Contbr. articles to law revs. Trustee emeritus U. San Francisco; dir. and v.p. Shorebird Homeowners Assn. 1st lt. U.S. Army, 1954-56. Named to U. San Francisco Athletic Hall of Fame, 1985, Alumnus of Yr. U. San Francisco, 1989; recipient Bur. Nat. Affairs award, 1958, Disting. Svc. award U. San Francisco, 1981. Mem. ABA, State Bar Calif., San Francisco Bar Assn., Am. Arbitration Assn. (nat. panel arbitrators), Am. Corp. Counsel Assn., Commonwealth Club of Calif. Republican. Roman Catholic. Office: BHP Minerals Internat Inc 550 California St Ste 500 San Francisco CA 94104-1006

CURRAN, WILLIAM P., lawyer; b. Mpls., Feb. 27, 1946; s. William P. and Margaret L. (Killoren) C.; m. Jean L. Stabenow, Jan. 1, 1978; children: Patrick, Lisa, John. BA, U. Minn., 1969; JD, U. Calif., Berkeley, 1972. Law clk. Nev. Supreme Ct., Carson City, 1973-74, state ct. adminstr., 1973-74; assoc. Wiener, Goldwater & Galatz, Las Vegas, Nev., 1974-75; chief dept. dist. atty. Clark County Dist. Atty.'s Office, Las Vegas, 1975-79; county counsel Clark County, Las Vegas, 1979-89; pvt. practice Las Vegas, 1989-94; ptnr. Curran & Parry, Las Vegas, 1994—. Co-author: Nevada Judicial Orientation Manual, 1974. Mem. Nev. Gaming Commn., Carson City, 1989—, chmn., 1991—. Recipient Educator Yr. award UNLV Internat. Gaming Inst., 1998. Mem. ABA (state del. 1994—), Internat. Assn. Gaming Regulators (chmn. 1992-94), Nat. Assn. County Civil Attys. (pres. 1984-85), State Bar Nev. (pres. 1988-89). Democrat. Roman Catholic. Office: Curran & Parry 601 S Rancho Dr Ste C-23 Las Vegas NV 89106-4825

CURRIER, ALFRED PATRICK, artist; b. Allentown, N.J., May 5, 1943; m. Phoebe Currier, June 17, 1964 (div. Feb. 1979); children: Patrick, Chris; m. Regina (Daubenmire), Oct. 17, 1982. BFA, Am. Acad. Art, Chgo.; postgrad., Columbus Coll. Art & Design, Columbus, Ohio. bd. dirs. Palette & Chisel Acad. Fine Arts, Chgo., 1987-88. Artist: (children's book) How Far to Heaven, 1993, (impasto painting on cover) Am. Artist Mag., 1997, (Best of the West) Southwest Art, 1997. Avocations: sailing, travel. Home and Office: PO Box 1374 Anacortes WA 98221-6374

CURRIER, ROBERT STEPHEN, theater company artistic director; b. San Gabriel, Calif., Nov. 3, 1947; s. Velda Ursula (Berfelz) Miller; m. Lesley Jane Schisgall, June 25, 1988; children: Sara Abigail, Jackson Cole, Nathaniel Richard. BA in Drama, U. Calif., Irvine, 1969, MFA in Directing, 1972. Actor, dir. Woodstock (Ill.) Opera House, 1972-77; artistic dir. Ukiah (Calif.) Players Theatre, 1977-89, Marin Shakespeare Co., San Rafael, Calif., 1989—; assoc. artistic dir. Ukiah Players, 1989—. Dir. (play) Midsummer Night's Dream, 1994. Mem. Shakespeare Theatre Assn. Am. Avocations: tennis, carpentry, gardening, music. Home: 144 Garden Ave San Rafael CA 94903-4220 Office: Marin Shakespeare Co PO Box 4053 San Rafael CA 94913-4053

CURRIVAN, BRUCE JOSEPH, electronics engineer; b. Nicosia, Cyprus, Nov. 14, 1950; father Am. citizen; s. Eugene Ambrose and Rachel (Marash) C.; m. Annamaria Panunzio, Nov. 12, 1978; children: Joseph, Jean Anne, Peter. BS in Elec. Engring., Cornell U., 1972; MS in Engring., Princeton U., 1976. Assoc. engr., Astro-Electronics Div. RCA, Princeton, NJ, 1972-76; comms. sys. design engr. Stanford Telecom., Sunnyvale, Calif., 1977-81, tech. dir., 1984-97; ingénieur d'études Thomson-CSF, Gennevilliers, France, 1982-83; tech. dir. modern devel. WaveSpan Corp., Mountain View, Calif., 1997-98; dir. modem hardware engring. Broadcom Corp., Irvine, Calif., 1998—. Presenter in field; contr. articles to profl. jours; patentee in field. Natural Law candidate for U.S. Ho. of Reps., 1996; chmn. Natural Law Party Central Com., Santa Clara County, Calif., 1996-98. Mem. IEEE (sr., chmn. 802.14 cable modem phys. layer subcom. 1995-97). Office: Broadcom Corp 16215 Alton Pkwy Irvine CA 92618-3616

CURRY, ROGER, trucking industry executive; married; two children. Grad., Morningside Coll.; MS, U. Nebr., 1964. Sys. analyst Consolidated Freightways, Portland, Oreg., 1969-72; dir. terminal properties Consolidated Freightways, Menlo Park, Calif., 1972-75; pres. AirFreight divsn. Consolidated Freightways, Menlo Park, 1975-85, sr. v.p. mktg., 1986-91; pres., CEO Emergy Worldwide, 1991-94, Consolidated Freightways, Menlo Park, 1994—; also with Canadian Freightways Ltd., Milne and Craighead, U.S. and Can. Office: Consolidated Trucks 175 Linfield Dr Menlo Park CA 94025-3750

CURRY, WILLIAM SIMS, county government administrator; b. Mt. Vernon, Washington, Feb. 6, 1930; s. Eli Herbert Curry and Winona Geraldine (Davis) Mickelson; m. Kirsten Ingeborg Arms, May 20, 1971; children: William II, Kevin, Randal, Kim Cannova, Derek. BS in Bus. Mgmt., Fla. State U., 1967; MBA, Ohio State U., 1968. Cert. profl. contracts mgr. Asst. purchasing officer Stanford (Calif.) Linear Accelerator Ctr., 1977-80; subcontract adminstr. Lockheed Missiles & Space Co., Sunnyvale, Calif., 1980-81; materials mgr. Altus Corp., San Jose, Calif., 1981-86; purchasing mgr. Litton Electron Devices, San Carlos, Calif., 1986-95, Comms. & Power Industries, Palo Alto, Calif., 1995-97; contracts manager Landacorp, Chico, Calif., 1998; purchasing svcs. mgr. Butte County, Oroville, Calif., 1998—; bd. dirs. Industry Coun. for Small Bus. Devel., Sunnyvale, 1992-97, v.p. programs, 1992-93, exec. v.p., 1994-95, pres., 1995-97. Contbr. articles to profl. jours. Capt. USAF, 1955-77. Decorated Meritorious Svc. medal with one oak leaf cluster, USAF, 1977. Fellow Nat. Contract Mgmt. Assn.; mem. Am. Mensa, Ltd., Beta Gamma Sigma. Republican. Avocations: chess, writing, cycling. Home: 17 Northwood Commons Pl Chico CA 95973-7213 Office: Butte County 25 County Ctr Dr Oroville CA 95965-3388

CURT, BRIGITTE, artist, educator; b. Paris, Feb. 9, 1949; came to U.S., 1987; d. Andre and Liliane (Curt) Baquiast. M in Ethno Sociology, U. Abidjan, Ivory Coast, 1975. Workshop instr. color theory, landscape ann. Calif. Acad. Painters, Palo Alto, 1992-98, plein air landscape instr., 1992—, instr., tour leader workshops in France, 1994—, curator ann. show, 1996-98; art instr. Pacific Art League, Palo Alto, 1996-97; painting demonstrator Channel 6, Palo Alto, 1998; studio asst. Ovanes Berberian Workshops, 1995-98; founder, education dir. Calif. Acad. Politics, San Jose, 1994. One-woman shows include Maturango Mus., Ridgecrest, Calif., 1994, Rosicrucian Mus., San Jose, Calif., 1994, Robson Gallery, Sharon Park Gallery, Menlo Park, Calif., Waterhouse Gallery, Santa Barbara, Dassin Gallery, Hollywood, San Jose, Calif., 1994; represented at Robson Gallery, San Diego, Sharon Park, among others. Muralist Tropical Rainforest Coalition, San Jose, Calif., 1993. E-mail: bcurt@classant.org. Office: Calif Acad Painters 3790 El Camino Real Ste 195 Palo Alto CA 94306-3314

CURTIN, DAVID STEPHEN, newswriter; b. Kansas City, Mo., Dec. 18, 1955; s. Gerald and Nadine (Pemberton) C. BS in Journalism, U. Colo., 1978. Newswriter Littleton (Colo.) Independent, 1976-77, Boulder (Colo.) Daily Camera, 1978-79, Greeley (Colo.) Daily Tribune, 1979-84, Durango (Colo.) Herald, 1984-87, Colorado Springs (Colo.) Gazette Telegraph, 1987-97, Denver Post, 1997—; Pulitzer Prize juror, 1991-92. Recipient Pulitzer Prize for feature writing, 1990. Democrat. Methodist. Avocations: skiing, hiking, mountain climbing.

CURTIN, THOMAS LEE, ophthalmologist; b. Columbus, Ohio, Sept. 9, 1932; s. Leo Anthony and Mary Elizabeth (Burns) C.; m. Constance L. Sallman; children: Michael, Gregory, Thomas, Christopher. BS, Loyola U., L.A., 1954; MD, U. So. Calif., 1957; cert. navy flight surgeon U.S. Naval Sch. Aerospace Medicine, 1959. Intern, Ohio State U. Hosp., 1957-58; resident in ophthalmology U.S. Naval Hosp., San Diego, 1961-64; practice medicine specializing in ophthalmology, Oceanside, Calif., 1967—; mem. staff Tri City, Scripps Meml. Mercy hosps.; sci. adv. bd. So. Calif. Soc. Prevention Blindness, 1973-76; bd. dirs. North Coast Surgery Ctr., Oceanside, 1987-96; cons. in field. Trustee, Carlsbad (Calif.) Unified Sch. Dist., 1975-83, pres., 1979, 82, 83; trustee Carlsbad Libr., 1990-99, pres, 1993, 98. Served as officer M.C., USN, 1958-67. Diplomate Am. Bd. Ophthalmology. Mem. Am., Calif. Med. Assns., San Diego County Med. Soc., Am. Acad. Ophthalmology, Aerospace Med. Assn., San Diego Acad. Ophthalmology (pres. 1979), Calif. Assn. Ophthalmology (bd. dirs.), Carlsbad Rotary, El Camino Country Club. Republican. Roman Catholic. Office: 3231 Waring Ct Ste S Oceanside CA 92056-4510

CURTIS, JOHN BARRY, archbishop; b. June 19, 1933; s. Harold Boyd and Eva B. (Saunders) C.; m. Patricia Emily Simpson, 1959; four children. BA, U. Toronto, 1955, LTh, 1958; student, Theol. Coll., Chichester, Sussex, Eng.; DD (hon.), Trinity Coll., 1985, U. Toronto, 1985. Ordained to deacon The Anglican Ch. of Can., 1958, priest, 1959. Asst. curate Holy Trinity, Pembroke, Ont., 1958-61; rector Parish of March, Kanata, Ont., 1961-65, St. Stephen's Ch., Buckingham, Que., 1965-69, All Saints (Westboro), Ottawa, Ont., 1969-78; program dir. Diocese of Ottawa, 1978-80; rector Christ Ch., Elbow Park, Calgary, Alta., 1980-83; bishop Diocese of Calgary, 1983-94; archbishop Calgary-Met. of Rupert's Land, 1994—. Mem. Ranchmen's Club (Calgary). Office: Diocese Calgary, 3015 Glencoe Rd SW, Calgary, AB Canada T2S 2L9

CURTIS, LEGRAND R., JR., lawyer; b. Ogden, Utah, Aug. 1, 1952. BA summa cum laude, Brigham Young U., 1975; JD cum laude, U. Mich., 1978. Bar: Utah 1978, U.S. Ct. Appeals (10th cir.) 1985, U.S. Ct. Claims 1986, U.S. Supreme Ct. 1987. Ptnr. Manning, Curtis Bradshaw & Bednar, LLC, Salt Lake City, 1997—. Mem. Utah State Bar, Salt Lake County Bar Assn. Office: Manning Curtis Bradshaw & Bednar LLC 370 E South Temple Ste 200 Salt Lake City UT 84111-1259*

CURTIS, MICHAEL, food products executive; b. 1922; s. Glen C. Real estate broker Yuma, Ariz., 1950-72; with Glen Curtis, Inc., Yuma, Ariz., 1971-72, now v.p. Office: Glen Curtis Inc 4400 E Us Highway 80 Yuma AZ 85365-7518*

CURTIS, STEVE, political organization administrator. Chmn. Rep. State Ctrl. Com. Colo., Denver. Fax: (303) 629-0459. Office: Rep State Ctrl Com Colo 1275 Tremont Pl Denver CO 80204*

CURTIS, TERENCE, graphic designer; b. Redlands, Calif., Aug. 14, 1968; s. Donald and Martha C. BA in Graphic Design, San Jose State U., 1995. Graphic designer San Jose State U., 1992-95, Holmes Typography, San Jose, 1995-97, Gist & Erdmann, Inc., San Jose, 1995-96; art dir. Orloff/Williams & Co., San Jose, 1996-97; graphic designer 7th World, San Jose, 1996-97. Mem. Works/San Jose. Roman Catholic. Avocations: fine art, music, soccer. Home: 7198 Rosencrans Way San Jose CA 95139-1343

CUSUMANO, JAMES ANTHONY, pharmaceutical company executive; b. Elizabeth, N.J., Apr. 14, 1942; s. Charles Anthony and Carmella Madeline (Catalano) C.; m. Jane LaVerne Melvin, June 15, 1985; children: Doreen Ann, Polly Jean. *James Cusumano's paternal grandparents emigrated from Sicily in the early 1900's and built a road construction and insurance sales business. His maternal grandparents also emigrated from Sicily about the same time and established a tailoring business. James Anthony is the oldest of ten children (six girls and four boys) born to Charles Anthony and Carmella Madeline Cusumano. James is an avid mountain climber, having recently successfully summited 19,340 foot Mount Kilimanjaro in Tanzania and 14,162 foot Mount Shasta in California.* BA, Rutgers U., 1964, PhD, 1967; grad. Exec. Mktg. Program, Stanford U., 1981, Harvard U., 1988. Mgr. catalyst rsch. Exxon Rsch. and Engring. Co., Linden, N.J., 1967-74; pres., chief exec. officer, founder Catalytica Inc., Mountain View, Calif., 1974-85, chmn., 1985—, also bd. dirs.; pres., CEO, bd. dirs. Catalytica Fine Chems., Inc., Mountain View, Calif., 1993-97; chmn., CEO, bd. dirs. Catalytica Pharms., Inc., 1997—; lectr. chem. engring. Stanford U., 1978, Rutgers U., 1966-67, Charles D. Hurd lectr. Northwestern U., 1989-90, Jean Day hon. lectr. Rutgers U.; advisor Fulbright scholar progam Inst. Internat. Edn.; mem. dean's adv. bd. Rutgers U., 1997—; speaker in field; mem. com. on catalysts and environ. NSF; exec. briefings with Pres. George Bush and Cabinet mems., 1990, 92, plenary lectr. in field; bd. dirs. Catalytica Advanced Techs., Inc. *Reach for a distant shining star. Celebrate life each day. Falter not your basic values. And you will find a way. James Cusumano's recent accomplishments include assisting in the growth of Catalytica Pharmaceuticals, Inc. from annual revenues of about $20 million to more than $350 million by acquisition of Glaxo Wellcome's pharmaceutical plant in Greenville, North Carolina. In 1997, Catalytica's stock posted the highest annual percentage growth (200%) in price of all companies in Silicon Valley.* Author: Catalysis in Coal Conversion, 1978, (with others) Critical Materials Problems in Energy Production, 1976, Advanced Materials in Catalysis, 1977, Liquid Fuels from Coal, 1977, Kirk-Othmer Encyclopedia of Chemical Technology, 1979, Chemistry for the 21st Century, Perspectives in Catalysis, 1992, Science and Technology in Catalysis 1994, 1995; contbr. articles to profl. jours., chpts. to books; founding editor Jour. of Applied Catalysis, 1980; rec. artist with Royal Teens and Dino Take Five for ABC Paramount, Capitol and Jubilee Records, 1957-67; single records include Short Shorts, Short Shorts Twist, My Way, Hey Jude, Rosemarie, Please Say You Want Me, Lovers Never Say Goodbye; albums include The Best of the Royal Teens, Newies But Oldies; appeared in PBS TV prodn. on molecular engring., Little by Little, 1989. Recipient Surface Chemistry award Continental Oil Co., 1964; Henry Rutgers scholar, 1963, Lever Bros. fellow, 1965, Churchill Coll. fellow Cambridge Univ., 1992. Mem. AIChE, Am. Chem. Soc. (plenary lectr. to chem. educators nat. meeting 1994), Am. Phys. Soc., N.Y. Acad. Scis., Soc. Organic Chems. Mfrs. (bd. dirs. 1996), Am. Mus.

Natural History, Pres.'s Assn., Smithsonian Assocs., Sigma Psi, Phi Lambda Upsilon. Republican. Roman Catholic. Achievements include 20 patents in catalysis and surface science; avocations: mountain climbing, skiing, hiking, sailing, swimming, travel. Home: 1450 Oak Creek Dr Apt 408 Palo Alto CA 94304-2027 Office: Catalytica Inc 430 Ferguson Dr Ste 3 Mountain View CA 94043-5272

CUTIETTA, ROBERT ALAN, music school administrator, educator; b. Cleve., June 28, 1953; s. Vincent Allen and Julia (Delte) C.; m. Marybeth Svoboda, Dec. 27, 1994; children: Nathan, Madeline, Melanie. MusB, Cleve. State U., 1975, MusM, 1978; PhD, Pa. State U., 1982. Prof. music Mont. State U., Bozeman, 1981-85, Kent (Ohio) State U., 1985-94; prof. music U. Ariz., Tucson, 1994-97, assoc. dir. Sch. Music and Dance, 1997—. Author: Encountering Music, 1989, Spin-offs, 1994; contbr. articles to profl. jours. Scout master Boy Scouts Am. Office: Univ Ariz Sch Music and Dance Tucson AZ 85721

CUTINO, BERT PAUL, restaurant owner, chef; b. Carmel, Calif., Aug. 7, 1939; m. Bella Manigiapane; children: Marc, Bart. AA in Bus., Monterey Peninsula Coll., 1964; D of Culinary Arts (hon.), Johnson and Wales Coll., 1988; D of Food Svc. (hon.), N.Am. Assn. Edn. Equipment Found. Cert. exec. chef. Various restaurant positions Monterey, Calif.; co-founder Sardine Factory, Monterey, 1968—, Cannery Row Co., Monterey, 1976—; with Pacific Hospitality, Inc., 1983—; protocol chmn. 1992 USA Nat. Culinary Team (recipient gold medals in culinary competitions, 1966, 67); formation of Western Region Culinary Team to 1988 Culinary Olympics, Frankfurt; founder Culinary Arts Program at local community coll., 1981; hospitality amb. internat. teams to Am. Culinary Classic, 1991; bd. trustees Antonin Careme Soc., 1997; bd. dirs. Calif. Culinary Acad., San Francisco; nat. chmn. Am. acad. of Chefs 1996-99; chmn. Disting. Restaurants of N. Am., DiRona, 1997; spkr. and lectr. in field. Contbr. articles for hospitality industry publs. and profl. jours.; featured in TV commls. for Am. Express; Chef and Host Chef TV show Celebrated Chefs; guest on TV shows including Good Morning Am., others. V.p. Monterey Peninsula C. of C., 1984-88; mem. Sheriff's Adv. Com., Monterey County; hon. judge March of Dimes Gourmet Gala, 1985-92; dir. Found. to Support Monterey Peninsula Schs., 1984-86. With USNR, 1959-67. Recipient numerous awards including Disting. Restaurants N.Am., Mobil Guide, Nat. Restaurant News Hall of Fame, Calif. Top 10 Restaurants, Town and Country, local Cal. State and Nat. Chef of Yr. awards, Lobo Hall of Fame Alumni award Monterey Peninsula Coll., Chef Hermann G. Rusch Humanitarian award; one of 50 restaurants in Am. selected to serve at Pres. Reagan's Inauguration, 1981, 85; recipient Alumni award Calif. C.C., 1982, Antonin Careme Soc. medal Chefs Assn. of Pacific Coast, 1987, Medal of Honor, Escoffier Soc., 1986, Presdl. Medallion, Les Toques Blanches Internat., 1989, 1st Soviet-Am. Culinary Exchange Medallion, 1988, Medallion of World Trade Ctr., Moscow, 1988; named Chef of Yr., Monterey Peninsula Chefs Assn., 1983, Humanitarian of Yr., Boy Scouts Am., 1996; named to Les Toques Blanches Internat. Hall of Fame, 1993, named 1st nat. pres. U.S.A., 1994, Nations Restaurant News top 50 hospitality preferred in U.S.; inducted into Calif. Tourism Hall of Fame, Calif. Trade and Commerce Agy., 1997; recognized by local, state, U.S. Congress by Hon. Leon Panetta; asst. to Calif. Assemblyman Sam Farr for Culinary Art Bill 1850-51. Mem. Am. Culinary Fedn. (life, cert. exec. chef, western region v.p. 1985-89, bd. dirs. The Chef and the Child Found. 1989, accreditation team 1987, Pres.'s medal 1982, 89, Pres. Recognition award 1994), Am. Acad. Chefs (nat. chmn. 1995—), Am. Acad. of Restaurant Scis., Am. Inst. of Wine and Food (founding), Knights of Vine (master knight), Wine Inst., Soc. for Am. Cuisine (founding), bd. mem. Calif. Culnary Acad., San Francisco, Calif. Restaurant Assn. (Chef of Yr., 1984), Nat. Restaurant Assn., Guild of Sommeliers Eng., Am. Inst. Food and Wine, Les Amis d'Escoffier Soc. N.Y. (amb.-at-large), Internat. Assn. Cooking Profls., Soc. Advancement of Food Svc. Rsch., Italian Restaurant Soc., Calif. Culinary Acad. (adv. bd. 1990—), L'Ordre Mondial Des Gourmets Degustateurs (spl. medal of honor, 1991), Confrerie de la Chaine Des Rotisseurs (bailli 1995, Bronze medal, 1990), Assn. Des Maitres Conseils en Gastronomie Francaise (comdr.), Les Toques Blanches Internat. Club (France, founder Monterey chpt., mem. internat. bd., 1st nat. pres., Presdl. Medallion). Travel Industry Assn. (F. Norman Clark Entrepreneur award 1992), Monterey Peninsula C. of C. (v.p.), Disting. Restaurants of N.Am. (nat. chmn. 1996-97), Euro Toque European Cooks in U.S. Office: Restaurants Central 765 Wave St Monterey CA 93940-1016

CUTLER, DAVID HORTON, editor, publisher; b. Boston, May 26, 1934; s. Fred Abbott and Elizabeth Horton (Carnahan) C.; m. Martha Marie Emery, Dec. 6, 1959; children: Geoffrey, Gregory. BA in Journalism, U. Nev., 1959. Editor, publ. The Merchant mag., Newport Beach, Calif., 1962—; publ., founder Bldg. Products Digest, Newport Beach, 1982—. With U.S. Army, 1953-55. Mem. Masonic Lodge, Scottish Rite, Shriners. Office: The Merchant Mag 4500 Campus Dr Ste 480 Newport Beach CA 92660

CUTLER, JEFFRY DOUGLAS, lawyer, consultant; b. Ross, Calif., May 17, 1964; s. John Harvey and Marjorie Gay (Ellman) C.; m. Carina Anita Pastor, June 21, 1997. BA with honors, U. Calif., Santa Barbara, 1986; JD, U. Oreg., 1995. Bar: Calif. 1995. Mem. profl. ski patrol Squaw Valley U.S.A., Olympic Valley, Calif., 1987-91; assoc. Law Offices of Louis Basile, Tahoe City, Calif., 1985-86; asst. exec. dir. League to Save Lake Tahoe, South Lake Tahoe, Calif., 1996-98; cons. Kings Beach, Calif., 1998—. Mem. Calif. Bar Assn. Avocations: mountaineering, mountain biking, skiing, ultimate frisbee. Home: PO Box 488 Kings Beach CA 96143-0488

CUTRIGHT, FRANCES LARSON, marriage and family therapist; b. Visalia, Calif., July 11, 1935; d. Francis Oscar and Faye (Sawyer) Larson; m. Forest F. Cutright, June 30, 1962 (div. 1982); children: Melinda, Forest F. BA, U. Calif., Berkeley, 1958, MA, 1982; PhD, Profl. Sch. Psychol. Studies, San Diego, 1986. Lic. marriage and family therapist, Calif. Group therapist in alcohol and drug dependence program VA Hosp., La Jolla, Calif., 1982-85; mem. staff Psychotherapy Inst. of San Diego, 1982-87; co-founder, v.p. Ctr. for Healing Group, San Diego, 1987-92; women's group therapist San Diego, 1991—, psychotherapist in pvt. practice, 1992—; instr. drugs and alcohol U. Calif., San Diego, 1988—; adj. faculty The Union Inst., San Diego, 1984—. Contbr. articles to mags. Educator, trainer San Diego AIDS Project, 1989-91, Oasis, Serenity House Counselling Staffs, Escondido, Calif., 1987-89; developer, trainer adolescent and family groups Fellowship House, 1987-89. Mem. Am. Assn. Marriage and Family Therapists (clin. mem.), Calif. Assn. Marriage and Therapy Therapists (clin. mem.), San Diego Assn. Marriage and Family Therapists (clin. mem.), Nat. Assn. for Children of Alcoholics, Am. Orthopsychiatric Assn. (clin. mem.), Am. Group Psychotherapy (clin. mem.). Avocations: volunteerism, travel, gardening. Office: 5230 Carroll Canyon Rd Ste 220 San Diego CA 92121-1780

CWIK, MICHAEL JOSEPH, natural resource statistician; b. Grand Rapids, Mich., June 3, 1944; s. William Stanley and Felicia (Sutula) C.; m. Patricia Anne Crawford, Feb. 22, 1968; children: Erin, Kevin, Patrick, Mary, Christopher, Joseph. BS, Colo. State U., 1970; MS, Tex. A&M U., 1973. Staff ecologist Dames & Moore, Cin., 1973-75; project mgr. Dames & Moore, Phoenix, 1975-79; founder, prin., environ. rschr. Enrett Ltd., Post Falls, Idaho, 1979—; pres. Sci-Med, Inc., 1998. Editor Environ. Discovery Jour., 1993. Mem. Am. Statis. Assn. Roman Catholic. Achievements include designing reclamation plan for successfully reclaiming largest open pit uranium mine in world using native geologic materials; designed method to accurately estimate annual CO stack emissions to reduce inaccuracies in conventional approach; designed and developed numerous innovative, cost-effective and workable solutions to address environmental difficulties encountered by private-sector natural resource industries. Office: Sci-Med Inc 509 E Seltice Way Post Falls ID 83854-7655

DABIRI, ALI, mechanical engineer, researcher; b. Tehran, Iran, Oct. 15, 1944; came to U.S., 1979; s. Mahmoud and Rezvan (Montasser) D.; m. Suzy Modjtahedi, June 10, 1974 (div. Dec. 1981); 1 child, Synthia. BSME, Tehran Poly., 1966; MSME, MIT, 1968, PhD, 1970. Lectr. dept. mech. engring. MIT, Cambridge, Mass., 1970-71; prof. mech. engring. Sharif U., Tehran, 1971-78, chmn. dept. mech. engring., 1976-78; sr. scientist Sci. Application Internat. Corp., San Diego, 1979-88, dir. engring., 1988—, mem. exec. coun. sci. and tech., 1990—. Author: Classical Thermodynamics, 1978; contbr. 75 articles to profl. jours. Recipient Medal of Ednl. Honor, Shah of Iran, 1966. Achievements include patents on radioisotope production facility for use with positron emission tomography; methods and apparatus for detecting vehicle occupants under the influence of alcohol; hyperspectral imaging methods and apparatus for non-invasive diagnosis of tissue for cancer; automatic sequencer/genotyper having extended spectral response; patent pending integrated pumping and/or energy recoevery system. Office: Sci Applications Internat Co 4161 Campus Point Ct San Diego CA 92121-1513

DACH, JOHN RICHARD, manufacturing executive, farmer; b. Long Beach, Calif., Dec. 18, 1945; s. Richard John and Lilas Elizabeth (Retzlaff) D.; divorced, 1987; 1 child, Elise Christine; m. Cynthia Thomas, Dec. 22, 1996. AA, Long Beach City Coll., 1966; BS in Mktg., Long Beach State Coll., 1972. Tour dir. and office mgr. Novitiate Winery, Los Gatos, Calif., 1970-72; ptnr., corp. vineyard mgr. Dach Vineyards, Philo, Calif., 1972-83; ptnr., operator Bearcreek Winery, Los Gatos, 1971-74; mgr. Dach Ranch, Philo, 1976-94; corp. officer Anderson Valley Beverage Corp./Grapple, Philo, 1985-94; owner, operator Maiden Metals, 1992—; cons. Philo; ptnr. Anderson Valley Agrl. Services, Philo, 1974-78. Served with USCG, 1967-73. Recipient Quartermaster award Explorer Scout div. Boy Scouts Am. Mem. Calif. Farm Bur., Calif. Cert. Organic Farmers (statewide rep. and cons. 1978-94). Republican. Lodge: Lions. Avocations: diving, fishing, boating, swimming, handball.

DACKOW, OREST TARAS, insurance company executive; b. Wynyard, Sask., Can., Sept. 17, 1936; s. Luke Dackow and Irene Stacheruk; m. Florence Dorothy Waples, Sept. 20, 1958; children: Trevor Wade, Heather Lynn, Donna Louise. B.Commerce with honors, U. Man., Winnipeg, Can., 1958; Grad. Advanced Mgmt. Program, Harvard U., 1976. Enrolled actuary. V.p. individual ops. Great-West Life Ins. Co., Winnipeg, Man., Can., 1976-78, sr. v.p. individual ops., 1978-79, sr. v.p. U.S., 1979-83; exec. v.p., chief operating officer U.S. Great-West Life Assurance Co., Denver, 1983-88; exec. v.p. corp. fin. and control Great-West Life Assurance Co., Winnipeg, 1988-90, pres., 1990-94, dir., 1992—; pres., CEO, dir. Great-West Lifeco Inc., 1992—; bd. dirs. London Life, 1997—. Bd. dirs. Met. YMCA, Winnipeg, 1971-80, pres., 1979-80; bd. dirs. Met. YMCA, Denver, 1981-84, Colo. Alliance of Bus., 1986-87, Nat. Jewish Ctr. for Immunology and Respiratory Medicine, 1985—, Health Scis. Centre Rsch. Found., 1990-94, Instrumental Diagnostics Devel. Office, 1992-94. Fellow Soc. Actuaries, Can. Inst. Actuaries; mem. Am. Acad. Actuaries. Avocation: sailing.

DACLES-MARIANI, JENNIFER SAMSON, engineering educator; b. Quezon City, Philippines, June 28, 1959; came to U.S., 1972; d. Simplicio and Anita (Samson) Dacles; m. Peter William Mariani, Aug. 18, 1990. BS in Engring., Calif. State U., Northridge, 1982; MSChemE, U. Mich., 1984, MSME, 1985; PhD, U. Calif., Davis, 1990. Jr. engr. Rockwell Internat., Santa Susana (Calif.) Lab., 1981; mem. tech. staff Rocketdyne divsn. Rockwell Internat., Canoga Park, Calif., 1984; rsch. engr. KMS Fusion, Ann Arbor, Mich., 1985; rsch. assoc. Nat. Rsch. Coun., NASA Ames Rsch. Ctr., Moffett Field, Calif., 1991-94; asst. rsch. prof. U. Calif., Davis, 1994—; rsch. assoc. U. Calif. Davis, 1986-91; rsch. asst. U. Mich., 1983-85. Contbr. articles to profl. jours. Patricia Harris fellowship award U. Calif., 1987-90; Getty Oil scholarship Calif. State U., 1982. Mem. AIAA, Soc. of the Divine Savior. Democrat. Roman Catholic. Acheivements include research on assesment of a accurate computational simulation of a wingtip vortex flowfield; co-investigator on project which uses a computational fluid dynamics as a tool to study and numerically simulate the interaction of cosmic dust, gases and turbulence in the solar nebula. Office: NASA Ames Rsch Ctr MS T27B-1 Moffett Field CA 94035

DAEHLING, WILLIAM A., retired academic administrator. Chancellor Mont. State U. No., Havre. Office: Mont State U No Office of Chancellor PO Box 7751 Havre MT 59501-7751

DAGGETT, BARBARA DALICANDRO, secondary education director; b. Chgo., Aug. 10, 1949; d. Robert Patrick and Mary Camille (Moreschi) Dalicandro; m. Michael Thomas Daggett, July 21, 1984; children: Samantha, Anthony. BA, U. No. Colo., 1971; MEd, Nat. Lewis U., Evanston, Ill., 1974, CAS, 1980. Cert. tchr. English, reading, psychology; cert. in supervision, adminstrn., superintendency; cert. prin. Instr. lang. arts Mannheim Jr. H.S., Melrose Park, Ill., 1971-81, dept. coord., 1978-81; summer sch. dir. Deer Valley Sch. Dist., Phoenix, 1983-86, tchr. English/reading, 1981-86, asst. prin., 1986-87; prin. Vocat. Tech. Ctr., Phoenix, 1987-89; dir. Deer Valley Sch. Dist., Phoenix, 1989—. Bd. dirs. Jobs for Am. Grad.'s, Phoenix, 1992-94, The Ariz. Partnership, Phoenix, 1992. Named Outstanding Prin., Chase Bank, 1991; recipient Pride award Deer Valley Sch. Dist., 1990, Adminstr. award Health Occupations, 1989. Mem. ASCD, Deer Valley Adminstrs. Assn. (pres. 1991-93), Ariz. Coun. Occupational Vocat. Adminstrs. (pres. 1991-92, Outstanding Contbn. award 1992, 93), Am. Vocat. Assn., Ariz. Vocat. Assn. (bd. dirs. 1991-92), Mannheim Tchrs. Assn. (v.p. 1978-79), Ariz. Sch. Adminstrs., Nat. Assn. Secondary Sch. Prins., Phi Delta Kappa. Avocations: travel, theater. Home: 13630 N Coral Gables Dr Phoenix AZ 85023-6270 Office: Deer Valley Sch Dist 97 20402 N 15th Ave Phoenix AZ 85027-3636

DAGGETT, ROBERT SHERMAN, lawyer; b. La Crosse, Wis., Sept. 16, 1930; s. Willard Manning and Vida Naomi (Sherman) D.; children: Ann Daggett McCluskey, John Sullivan; m. Helen Hosler Ackerman, July 20, 1976. AB in Polit. Sci./Journalism with honors, U. Calif., Berkeley, 1952, JD, 1955. Bar: Calif. 1955, U.S. Supreme Ct. 1967. Assoc. firm Brobeck, Phleger & Harrison, San Francisco, 1958-66, ptnr., 1966-95, of counsel, 1996—; counsel Calif. Senate, 1972-73; adj. prof. evidence and advocacy Hastings Coll. Law, 1982-84; instr. No. Dist. Fed. Practice Program, 1982-83; demonstrator-instr. Nat. Inst. for Trial Advocacy, 1981—, Stanford and U. San Francisco Law Schs., Hastings Ctr. for Trial and Appellate Advocacy, 1981-88, mem. adv. bd., 1983-88; vol. pro tem judge San Francisco Mcpl. Ct., 1981-88, San Francisco Superior Ct., 1990—, chmn. com. ind. judiciary, 1995-96; arbitrator and pvt. comml. arbitrator, 1984—; co-host Face to Face, Sta. KQED-TV; commentaries Sta. KQED-FM. Bd. editors Calif. Law Rev., 1953-55; author: Daggett's Dicta (www.brobeck.com), 1997—; narrator and writer, Music in the Mountains; contbr. articles and lectures to profl. jours. Bd. dirs San Francisco Legal Aid Soc.; bd. visitors U. Calif., Santa Cruz. 1st lt. JAGC, U.S. Army, 1958-62. Walter Perry Johnson scholar, 1953. Fellow Am. Bar Found.; mem. ABA, FBA (pres. no. dist. Calif. chpt. 1992-95), AFTRA, State Bar Calif., San Francisco Bar Assn. (past bd. dirs.), Am. Judicature Soc., Am. Law Inst., Federalist Soc. (mem. San Francisco Adv. Bd.), Bohemian Club, Commonwealth Club, Comml. Club (bd. dirs. 1989—, pres. 1993), Order of Golden Bear, Phi Delta Phi, Theta Xi. Republican. Office: Brobeck Phleger & Harrison Tower 1 Market Plz Spear St San Francisco CA 94105-1019

DAGORT, AIDA MULIERI, musician; b. L.A., May 11, 1918; d. John and Aida (Massanova) M.; m. Vincent Dagort, June 25, 1945; 1 child, Philip. B in edn. of music, Univ. Calif., 1940. Sch. music. tchr. Sierra Madre, Calif., 1941; harpist Warner Bros. Studio, Burbank, Calif., 1942-48, Paramount Studio, Hollywood, Calif., 1949-68; asst. tchr. Fernald Sch., West L.A., 1972-75. Author: Harps Are Not for Angels, 1996. Recipient scholarship Allied Art Assn., 1931. Avocations: golf, artist, writer.

DAHL, DONALD DOUGLAS, newswriter; b. Savage, Mont., Mar. 25, 1920; s. Alfred Kristian and Elsie (McDonell) D.; m. Helen Copeland, Oct. 6, 1946 (div. 1978); children: Christine Dahl, Karen McKenzie. BA, U. N.D., 1941; MS, Columbia U., 1950. Supr. Fed. Writers Project, Bismarck, N.D., 1941; extension editor U. N.H., Durham, 1946-49; reporter Journal Bulletin, Providence, 1950; correspondent United Press, Manila, The Philippines, 1951-53; copy editor, wire editor, news editor The Albuquerque Tribune, 1954-82. Lt. USNR, 1942-46, PTO. Mem. Beta Theta Pi. Presbyterian. Home: 1305 Girard Blvd SE Albuquerque NM 87106-2905

DAHLGREN, DOROTHY, museum director; b. Coeur d'Alene, Idaho; m. Robert Eagan, 1985; 1 child, Ivan. BS in Museology and History, U. Idaho, 1982; postgrad., Gonzaga U., 1997—. Dir. Mus. N. Idaho, Coeur d'Alene, 1982—; grant reviewer gen. operating support grants Inst. Mus. and Libr. Svcs., 1993—; mem. Kootenai County Historic Preservation Commn. Author: (with Simone Carbonneau Kincaid) In All the West No Place Like This; A Pictorial HIstory of the Coeur d'Alene Region, 1996. mem. Idaho Heritage Trust com. N. region. Office: Mus N Idaho PO Box 812 Coeur D Alene ID 83816-0812

DAHLIN, DENNIS JOHN, landscape architect, environmental consultant; b. Ft. Dodge, Iowa, June 12, 1947; s. Fred E. and Arlene (Olson) D.; m. Jeanne M. Larson, Mar. 2, 1969 (div. 1990); 1 child, Lisa. BA, Iowa State U., 1970; M in Landscape Architecture, U. Calif., Berkeley, 1975. Lic. landscape arch., Calif. Assoc. planner San Luis Obispo County, Calif., 1971-73; prin. Dennis Dahlin Assocs., Modesto, Calif., 1975-90; pres. WPM Planning Team, Inc., Sacramento, 1991—; bd. dirs. El Porvenir Found., Sacramento, 1991—. Contbg. author: The Energy Primer, 1976, Restoring Our River, 1997. Bd. dirs. Ecology Action Ednl. Inst., Modesto, 1984-85, Econ. Conversion Coun., San Diego, 1988-89; pres. San Joaquin Habitat for Humanity, Stockton, Calif., 1986-87. Ferrand fellow U. Calif., 1974, Kearney fellow Harvard U., 1975. Mem. Am. Planning Assn., Am. Soc. Landscape Architects (bd. dirs. Sierra chpt. 1993-95). Methodist. Avocations: canoeing, travel, folk music. Office: PO Box 261 Sacramento CA 95812-0261

DAHLIN, ELSIE, architect; b. Portadown, No. Ireland, Mar. 1, 1936; came to U.S., 1946; m. Gene L. Dahlin, 1955; children: Leah, Kevin. Cons., 1960-68; sec., treas. Best Fluorescent Maintenance Co., Inc., 1968-75; pres., CEO Ladd Fabrication, Inc., 1976-82; pres. Fundidora Cal, Tijuana, Mex., 1991—; pres., CEO Environ. Lighting for Architecture, Calif., 1983—. Bd. dirs. Ind. Nat. Bank, 1984-86, Linder Caster & Truck Co., Inc., El Monte & San Diego, 1980-81; mem. Industry Mfrs. Coun., 1984—; nat. founding pres. Netowrk Exec. Women in Hospitality, Inc., 1990-94, pres. L.A. founding chpt., 1990-91, 91-92, bd. dirs., 1987. Mem. Nat. Assn. Women Bus. Owners. Avocations: cooking, gardening, football, golf. Office: ELA Co 17891 Arenth Ave City Of Industry CA 91748

DAHLQUIST, PAUL A., museum director; b. Honolulu, Hawaii, Dec. 24, 1940; s. Harold P. and Helen Kina'u (Wilder) D.; m. Charlene F. Pfalzgraf, June 14, 1965; children: Andrew Judd, Kristine Kindu. BA, Yale Univ., 1963; MA, Ohio State Univ., 1968, PhD, 1972. Prof. Ohio Wesleyan Univ., Delaware, Ohio, 1968-88; curator Lyman Mus., Hilo, Hawaii, 1988-96, dir., 1996—. Author: Kohdo Museum Food Change in Pohnjei, 1972, (book chpt.) Political Development in Micronesia, 1974. Bd. dirs. Hawaii Visitors Bureau, 1997—, bd. dirs., pres. Destination Hilo, 1996—; county central com. Dem. Party, 1986-88. Fellow Am. Anthropological Assn., Assn. for Social Anthropology Oceania (newsletter editor 1972—); mem. Am. Assn. Mus., Hawaii Mus. Assn., Hilo Rotary Club. Avocations: golf, farming, photography, travel. Home: 68-1902 Koiula Pl Waikoloa HI 96738-5322 Office: Lyman Mus 276 Haili St Hilo HI 96720-2927

DAHLSTEN, SHIRLEY ANNETTE, artist, educator; b. Salina, Kans., Jan. 11, 1940; d. William Woodrow and Clara Lenora (Kunau) Hudson; m. John Wendell Dahlsten, Dec. 28, 1959; 1 child, James Michael. Student, Kans. State U., 1962, Cloud County C.C., Concordia, Kans., 1966, Clatsop C.C., Astoria, Oreg., 1970; BA in Painting, Portland State U., 1984. Artist. asst. to Stan Wanlass, Astoria, 1977-78; ct. room artist Sta. KATU, Portland, Oreg., 1978; tchr. art Cannon (Oreg.) Beach Artist Group, 1988-89; instr. art Tillamoon Bay C.C., Manzanita, Oreg., 1987, Clatsop C.C., 1975—; owner Dahlsten Studio Gallery, Astoria, 1990—; chmn., developer Art Reigns Gallery, Astoria, 1990—. One-woman shows include The Edge Gallery, Astoria, 1987, On The Edge Gallery, Salem, Oreg., 1988, Michael's Gallery, Astoria, 1989; group exhbns. include Ariel Gallery, N.Y.C., 1989-90, Hilton Gallery, Portland, 1988-89, Victoria Mann Gallery, Sun River, Oreg., 1989, Bill Dodge Gallery, Carmel, Calif., 1989, Attic Gallery, Portland, 1990; represented in permanent collections Health Link Corp, Portland, Hudson Concrete Corp., Livermore, Calif., Bruno Rubeo Collection, Hollywood, Calif.; works represented in Ency. Living Am. Artists, 3d edit., 1988, Internat. Catalog Contemporary Artists, 1989, Manhattan Arts mag., 1990. Chmn. Astoria Arts Celebration, 1990-91, co-chmn., 1991-92, Astoria Downtown Arts Project, 1990—; pres. coun. 1st Luth. Ch., Astoria, 1991-92. Mem. P.E.O. (sec. chpt. DL 1991-92). Democrat. Avocations: Victorian house restoration, promotion all arts. Home and Studio: PO Box 1123 1280 Cypress St Cannon Beach OR 97110-1123

DAHN, RICHARD F., artist, designer; b. Toledo, Sept. 20, 1932; s. Frederick Z.and Lucile (Carter) D.; m. Barbara Elizabeth Dahn, July 9, 1955; children: Mark F., Denise E. BFA, Miami U., 1954; MFA, Yale U., 1959. Designer Bert Ray Studio, Chgo., 1959-63, Toledo Mus. Art, 1963-65; prof. graphic design U. Wash., Seattle, 1965-97; designer, owner Dahn Design, Seattle, 1986—. Exhibited in groups shows at Corcoran Gallery, Washington, 1967. With U.S. Army, 1954-56. Recipient Katherine B. Baker Meml. award Seattle Art Mus., 1966, Gold award in poster design Univ. and Coll. Designers Assn., 1978, Enos Mill Guide award Nat. Assn. Interpretation, 1989, 1st place award in poster design Nat. Assn. Interpretation, 1991. Episcopalian.

DAILEY, DAWN ELAINE, public health service official; b. Berkeley, Calif., Feb. 2, 1965; d. Stanley Wilfred Sr. and Mercedes Anderson; m. Kenneth Lamar Dailey, Apr. 19, 1986; 1 child, Mariana. BSN, U. San Francisco, 1988; MSN, Samuel Merritt Coll., 1997. RN, CNS, Calif.; bd. cert. Clinical Specialist in Cmty. Health Nursing. Nurse Alta Bates Hosp., Berkeley, 1988-91; home health nurse Kaiser Permanente, Martinez, Calif., 1992-94; coord. Contra Costa SIDS Program, Martinez, 1995—; coord. fetal infant mortality rev. program Kaiser Permanente, Martinez, 1998—; pub. health nurse Contra Costa County, Martinez, 1989—; cons. Calif. SIDS Program, Fair Oaks, 1994-98; mem. Calif. SIDS Adv. Coun., Sacramento, 1996—, pres. No. Calif. Regional SIDS Adv. Coun., Berkeley, 1993-88; mem. Contra Costa Immunization Coalition, Martinez, 1996-97, Childhood Injury Prevention Coalition, Contra Costa County, 1993—; bd. mem. Fetal and Infant Mortality Rev. Bd., Berkeley; coord. fetal infant mortality review program, 1996-88; v.p. Assn. of SIDS and Infant Mortality Program. Bd. dirs. Child Abuse Prevention Coun. Contra Costa County. Shirley C. Titus scholarship Calif. Nurses Assn., 1995, Nursing Edn. scholarship, 1996; recipient Contra Costa County award of Excellence, 1998. Mem. APHA, AMA, Assn. SIDS and Infant Mortality Programs (v.p.), Assn. SIDS Program Profls., Calif. Pub. Health Nursing Assn., Sigma Theta Tau, Chi Eta Phi (Basileus 1997, Omicron Phi chpt.). Avocations: boating, quilting. Home: 898 Sage Dr Vacaville CA 95687-7391

DAILEY, DIANNE K., lawyer; b. Great Falls, Mont., Oct. 10, 1950; d. Gilmore and Patricia Marie (Linnane) Halverson. BS, Portland State U., 1977; JD, Lewis & Clark Coll., 1982. Assoc. Bullivant, Houser, Bailey, et. al., Portland, Oreg., 1982-88, ptnr., 1988—. Contbr. articles to profl. jours. Mem. ABA (vice chair tort and ins. practice sect. 1995-96, chair-elect tort and ins. practice sect. 1996-97, chair tort and ins. practice sect. 1997-98, governing coun. 1992—, property ins. law com., ins. coverage litigation com., comm. com., chair task force on involvement of women 1990-93, liaison to commn. on women 1993-97, chair task force CERCLA reauthorization, litigation sect., sect. natural resources energy and environment, chair officers conf. sect. 1998—), Wash. Bar Assn., Oreg. State Bar, Oreg. Assn. Def. Counsel, Multnomah Bar Assn. (bd. dirs. 1994-95), Internat. Assn. Def. Counsel, Def. Rsch. Inst., Fedn. Ins. and Corp. Counsel. Office: Bullivant Houser Bailey 300 Pioneer Tower 888 SW 5th Ave Ste 300 Portland OR 97204-2089

DAILY, JOHN G., protective services official; b. Lafayette, Ind., June 27, 1950; s. Jewell T. and Barbara (Gunnels) D.; m. Carolyn Jean Schorr, May 31, 1975; children: Jeremy Scott, Jennifer Lynn. BSME, Purdue U., 1972; postgrad., U. Wyo., 1973, 75. Owner Jackson (Wyo.) Hole Engring., 1977-93, Jackson Hole Sci. Investigations, 1993—; dep. sheriff Teton County Sheriff's Office, Jackson, 1977-89, sgt., 1989—; mem. adj. teaching faculty U. North Fla., Jacksonville, 1982—, course devel. cons., 1982—; cons. traffic accident reconstruction Jackson Hole Sci. Investigations. Inventor new type of discarding sabot; author: Fundamentals of Traffic Accident Reconstruction, 1988; co-author: Fundamentals of Applied Physics for Traffic Accident Investigators, 1996. Chmn. J.H. chpt. ARC, Jackson, 1976—. Named Peace Officer of Yr., Teton County Peace Officer Assn., 1981. Mem. SAE, ASME, Ill. Assn. Tech. Accident Investigators, Soc. Accident Reconstructionists, J.H. Rotary Club, Elks, 4-H (ch. coun. 1980-94). Republican. Lutheran. Avocations: hiking, fishing, hunting, back-packing, golf. Home: PO Box 2206 Jackson WY 83001-2206

DAILY, JOHN SCOTT, SR., small business owner, consumer products executive; b. Everett, Wash., Feb. 21, 1948; s. John Hiram and Lucina (Manual) D.; m. Ellen Wilmoth Matthews Daily, Mar. 21, 1970; children: John Scott Jr., Kristen Michelle. BBA in Pers. Mgmt./Acctg., U. Tex., El Paso, 1971. Branch ops. mgr. Graybar Electric Co., Jackson, Miss., 1971-79; support svcs. mgr. Xerox Corp., Leesburg, Va., 1979-82; distbn. ctr. mgr. Computercraft, Inc., Dallas, 1983-84; owner, gen. mgr. J & M Answering Svc., Dallas, 1983-84; facilty mgr. Mervyn's, Plano, Tex., 1984-86; dir. facility svcs. FoxMeyer Drug Co., Carrollton, 1986-93; sr. project mgr. Corp. Express, Inc., Broomfield, Colo., 1994—; co-owner Triple D Enterprises, Carrollton, Texas, 1993—. Presbyterian. Avocations: private pilot, golf, bowling, reading. Home: 3701 Grasmere Dr Carrollton TX 75007

DAJEE, HIMMET, cardiothoracic surgeon; b. Capetown, South Africa, May 22, 1942; m. Debra Lynn Haag; children: Olivia, Isabelle. BSc, U. Capetown, 1968; MD, Royal Coll. Surgeons, Dublin, Ireland, 1974; MBBS, U. London, 1976. Anatomy dissection instr. Royal Coll. Surgeons, Dublin, 1971, intern, 1974-75; intern, resident in gen. surgery Dalhousi U., Halifax, Can., 1975-80; resident in thoracic surgery U. Calif., Davis, 1980-81; CVT fellow Pacific Med. Ctr. Presbyn. Hosp., San Francisco, 1981-82; cardiothoracic fellow UCLA, 1982-83, clin. asst. prof. cardio-thoracic surgery, 1983—; staff cardiothoracic surgeon Kaiser Med. Ctr., 1984-87; chmn. dept. cardiovasc. and thoracic Fountain Valley Hosp., 1987—; lectr. in field. Contbr. articles to profl. jours. Fellow Am. Coll. Surgeons, Am. Coll. Chest Physicians; mem. Soc. Thoracic Surgeons, Am. Heart Assn. (life), Internat. Soc. Heart Transp. Avocations: classical music, art, antiques, political history. Home: 5 Narbonne Newport Beach CA 92660-6823 Office: 11100 Warner Ave Ste 350 Fountain Valley CA 92708-7513

DAL BELLO, PETER THOMAS, writer; b. Santa Barbara, Calif., Dec. 10, 1971; s. Joseph Jordano and Irene Bernice (Zandona). AA, Santa Barbara City Coll., 1993; postgrad., Calif. State Northridge. Corrs. Santa Barbara News-Press, 1996; staff writer Daily Sundial, Northridge, 1996; corr. L.A. Times, 1996-99; sports editor Daily Sundial, Northridge, 1996-97; sr. corrs. La Canada Valley Sun, La Canada Flintridge, Calif., 1997; contbg. writer San Fernando (Calif.) Valley Sun, 1997-98; sports reporter Our Times, West Ventura County, Calif., 1998-99. Mem. Soc. for Am. Baseball Rsch., Soc. Profl. Journalists. Republican. Roman Catholic. Avocations: reading, golf.

DALE, DEBRA EILEEN, elementary school educator; b. Schurz, Nev., Dec. 1, 1953; d. William Winston and Marlene Coffey; m. Kee Dale Jr., Oct. 11, 1970; 1 child, Eileen Frances. AA, Truckee Meadows C.C., 1980; BS in Elem. Edn., U. Nev., 1982; M in Curriculum Instrn., Lesley Coll., Cambridge, Mass., 1992. Cert. tchr. K-8, Nev. Tchr. aide Reno/Sparks Headstart Program, Reno, 1972-73; tchr. aide summer sch. Washoe County Sch. Dist., Reno, 1972-81; community rels. tchr. aide Libby Booth Elem. Sch., Reno, 1973-78; tutor Reno/Sparks Colony, Reno, 1979-82; tchr. summer sch. Washoe County Sch. Dist., 1982; community rels. counselor Wooster/Reed High Schs., Reno, 1982-83; tchr. Roger Corbett Elem. Sch., Reno, 1983—; mem. multi-cultural com. Washoe County Sch. Dist., 1992-93; tchr. rep. Title V Indian Edn. Program, 1991—. Co-author: Celebrating Nevada Indians, 1992. Res. police officer Reno/Sparks Indian Colony Tribal Police, Reno, 1989-94. Recipient Outstanding Student Tchr. award U. Nev., 1982. Mem. NEA, Nev. State Edn. Assn., Nev. Native Am. Edn. Assn., Nev. Indian Rodeo Assn., Washoe County Tchrs. Assn., Delta Kappa Gamma (nat. and internat.). Avocations: sewing, arts and crafts, drawing and painting. Office: Washoe County Sch Dist 425 E 9th St Reno NV 89512-2800

DALE, VIRGINIA MARIPOSA, author, educator; b. Washington; d. Robert Grant and Doris (Davis) Bywater; m. Hans Bannmeyer, Dec. 27, 1966 (div. July 1972). BA in Psychology, U. Calif., Berkeley, 1964; MA in Reading, U. Calif., Santa Barbara, 1977. Tchr. Santa Barbara Adult Edn., 1979—. Author: Nevery Marry in Morocco, 1996, (poetry) Womb-men, 1998.

DALESIO, WESLEY CHARLES, former aerospace educator; b. Paterson, N.J., Mar. 26, 1930; s. William James and Sarah (Sheets) Delison; m. Dorothy May Zellers, Nov. 17, 1951; children: Michael Kerry, Debra Kaye Dalesio Weber. Student, Tex. Christian U., 1950, U. Tex., Arlington, 1957. Enlisted USAF, 1948, advanced through grades to sr. master sgt., 1968; aircraft engine mech., mgmt. analyst USAF, worldwide, 1948-70; ins. agt. John Hancock Ins., Denver, 1970-71; office mgr. Comml. Builder, Denver, 1972-73; aerospace educator Sch. Dist. 50, Westminster, Colo., 1973-93; dir. aerospace edn. CAP, Denver, 1982-86, 94—. Mem. Crimestoppers, Westminster, 1988-91, Police and Citizens Teamed Against Crime, Westminster, 1992-93. Lt. col. CAP, 1981—. Mem. Nat. Assn. Ret. Mil. Instrs. (charter mem.), Westminster Edn. Assn., 7th Bomb Wing B-36 Assn., Internat. Platform Assn., Nat. Aeronautic Assn., Acad. Model Aeronautics, Arvada Associated Modelers (life). Episcopalian. Avocations: antique collecting, leatherwork, flying miniature aircraft, model car collecting. Home: 2537 W 104th Cir Westminster CO 80234-3507

DALESSIO, DONALD JOHN, physician, neurologist, educator; b. Jersey City, Mar. 2, 1931; s. John Andrea and Susan Dorothy (Minotta) D.; m. Jane Catherine Schneider, Sept. 4, 1954 (dec. Mar. 1998); children: Catherine Leah, James John, Susan Jane. BA, Wesleyan U., 1952; MD, Yale U., 1956. Diplomate Am. Bd. Internal Medicine. Intern in medicine N.Y.C. Hosp., 1956-57, asst. resident in medicine and neurology, 1959-61; resident in medicine Yale Med. Ctr., 1961-62; pres. med. staff Scripps Clinic, La Jolla, Calif., 1974-78; chmn. dept. medicine Scripps Clin., La Jolla, Calif., 1974-89, chmn. emeritus, 1989—, cons., 1982—, pres. med. group, 1980-81; clin. prof. neurology U. Calif., San Diego, 1973—; physician in chief Green Hosp., La Jolla, 1974-89; Musser-Burch lectr. Tulane U., 1979, Kash lectr. U. Ky., 1979; pres. Am. Assn. Study Headache, Chgo., 1974-76, Nat. Migraine Found., Chgo., 1977-79; chmn. Fedn. Western Soc. Neurology, Santa Barbara, Calif., 1976-77. Author: Wolff's Headache, 6th edit., 1993, Approach to Headache, 1973, 5th edit., 1992; editor: Headache jour., 1965-75, 79-84, Scripps Clinic Personal Health Letter; mem. editorial bd.: Jour. AMA, 1977-87; columnist San Diego Tribune. Capt. U.S. Army, 1957-59. Recipient Disting. Alumnus award Wesleyan U., Middletown, Conn., 1982. Fellow ACP; mem. Am. Acad. Neurology (assoc.), World Fedn. Neurology (Am. sec. 1980-90, rsch. group on migraine), La Jolla Country Club, La Jolla Beach/Tennis Club. Republican. Roman Catholic. Avocations: tennis, squash, piano. Home: 8891 Nottingham Pl La Jolla CA 92037-2131 Office: Scripps Clinic & Rsch Found 10666 N Torrey Pines Rd La Jolla CA 92037-1092

DALFOLLO-DALEY, STEPHEN CHARLES ANTHONY, web developer; b. Niskayana, N.Y., Feb. 10, 1967; s. Louis Eugene and Marcia Ann (Ford) Daley; m. Paola MariaRosa Dall'Ora, Sept. 16, 1995. Grad., high sch., 1985. Supt. DCP Inc., Glen Rose, Tex., 1986-90; tech. writer, tchr. Berlitz Internat., Tokyo, 1990-95, Oxford Lang. Schs., Vicenza, Italy, 1995-97; web developer, tech. writer MCI Worldcom, Colorado Springs, Colo., 1997—. Sr. mem. CAP, Colorado Springs, 1997—. Mem. Aircraft Owners and Pilots Assn., Colo. Pilots Assn., Exptl. Aircraft Assn. Roman Catholic. Avocations: flying, woodworking, ice and rock climbing, computers, investing. Home: 1318 Iowa Ave Colorado Springs CO 80909

DALIS, IRENE, mezzo-soprano, opera company administrator, music educator; b. San Jose, Calif., Oct. 8, 1925; d. Peter Nicholas and Mamie Rose (Boitano) D.; m. George Loinaz, July 16, 1957; 1 child, Alida Mercedes. AB, San Jose State Coll., 1946; MA in Teaching, Columbia U., 1947; MMus (hon.), San Jose State U., 1957; studied voice with, Edyth Walker, N.Y.C., 1947-50, Paul Althouse, 1950-51, Dr. Otto Mueller, Milan, Italy, 1952-72; MusD (hon.), Santa Clara U., 1987. Prin. artist Berlin Opera, 1955-65, Met. Opera, N.Y.C., 1957-77, San Francisco Opera, 1958-73, Hamburg (Fed. Republic Germany) Staatsoper, 1966-71; prof. music San Jose State U., Calif., 1977—; founder, gen. dir. Opera San Jose, 1984—; dir. Met. Opera Nat. Auditions, San Jose dist., 1980-88. Operatic debut as dramatic mezzo-soprano Oldenburgisches Staatstheater, 1953, Berlin Staedtische Opera, 1955; debut Met. Opera, N.Y.C., 1957, 1st Am.-born singer, [illegible] commemorative Wagner 150th Birth Anniversary; opened 1963 Met. Opera Season in Aida; premiered: Dello Joio's Blood Moon, 1961, Henderson's Medea, 1972; rec. artist Parsifal, 1964 (Grand Prix du Disque award); contbg. editor Opera Quarterly, 1983. Recipient Fulbright award for study in Italy, 1951, Woman of Achievement award Commn. on Status of Women, 1983, Pres.'s award Nat. Italian Am. Found., 1985, award of merit People of San Francisco, 1985, San Jose Renaissance award for sustained and outstanding artistic contbn., 1987, Medal of Achievement Acad. Vocal Arts, 1988; named Honored Citizen City of San Jose, 1986; inducted into Calif. Pub. Edn. Hall of Fame, 1985, others. Mem. Beethoven Soc. (mem. adv. bd. 1985—), San Jose Arts Round Table, San Jose Opera Guild, Am. Soc. Univ. Women, Arts Edn. Week Consortium, Phi Kappa Phi, Mu Phi Epsilon. Office: Opera San Jose 2049 Paragon Dr San Jose CA 95131

DALLAS, SANDRA, correspondent, writer; b. Washington, June 11, 1939; d. Forrest Everett and Harriett (Mavity) Dallas; m. Robert Thomas Atchison, Apr. 20, 1963; chidlren: Dana Dallas, Povy Kendal Dallas. BA, U. Denver, 1960. Asst. editor U. Denver Mag., 1965-66; editorial asst. Bus. Week, Denver, 1961-63, 67-69, bur. chief, 1969-85, 90-91, sr. corr., 1985-90; freelance editor, 1990—; book reviewer Denver Post, 1961—, regional book columnist, 1980—. Author: Gaslights and Gingerbread, 1965, rev. edit., 1984, Gold and Gothic, 1967, No More Than 5 in a Bed, 1967, Vail, 1969, Cherry Creek Gothic, 1971, Yesterday's Denver, 1974, Sacred Paint, 1980, Colorado Ghost Towns and Mining Camps, 1985, Colorado Homes, 1986, Buster Midnight's Cafe, 1990, reissued 1998, The Persian Pickle Club, 1995, The Diary of Mattie Spenser, 1997; editor: The Colorado Book, 1993; contbr. articles to various mags. Bd. dirs. Vis. Nurse Assn., Denver, 1983-85, Hist. Denver, Inc., 1979-82, 84-87. recipient Wrangler award Nat. Cowboy Hall of Fame, 1980, Lifetime Achievement award Denver Posse of Westerners, 1996, disting. svc. award U. Colo., 1997; named Colo. Exceptional Chronicler of Western History by Women's Library Assn. and Denver Pub. Library Friends Found., 1986; finalist Spur award We. Writers of Am., 1998. Mem. Women's Forum Colo., Denver Woman's Press Club, Western Writers Am., Women Writing the West. Democrat. Presbyterian. Home and Office: 750 Marion St Denver CO 80218-3434

DALLDORF, THOMAS E., publisher; b. St. Paul, June 16, 1942; s. Thomas E. Dalldorf and Kathleen (Jackson) McBrayer; m. Arlene L. Besemer, Feb. 9, 1963; children: Thomas E. Jr., Cathy. AA, Coll. San Mateo, Calif.; BA, Calif. State U., Hayward, postgrad. Owner Vintage Cellar Wine, Hayward, 1979-89; owner, pub. Celebrator Beer News, Hayward, 1990—. With USAF, 1960-63. Mem. Inst. for Breing Studies. Avocations: music, wine appreciation, travel. Office: Celebrator Beer News 20958 Corsair Blvd Hayward CA 94545-1002

DAL POGGETTO, SANDRA HOPE, artist, writer; b. Sonoma, Calif., Nov. 2, 1951; d. Newton Francis and Helene Irene (Watts) Dal P.; m. Brian Jackson Kahn, Oct. 3, 1982; 1 child, Dylan Pembroke Kahn. BA in Art Studio with honors, U. Calif., Davis, 1975; MA in Painting and Drawing, San Francisco State U., 1982. lectr. Holter Mus. Art, Helena, 1992, 97, Missoula (Mont.) Mus. of Arts, 1991, Augusta State U., 1996; instr. life drawing Archie Bray Found. for Ceramic Arts, Helena, 1994, 95; drawing instr. continuing edn. Mont. State U., 1996; artist-in-residence Helena Nat. Forest, Holter Mus. Art, 1996; vis. artist Augusta State U., Augusta, Ga., 1996. One-person shows include Dana Reich Gallery, San Francisco, 1985, Meml. Union Art Gallery, U. Calif., Davis, 1989, J. Noblett Gallery, Sonoma, 1992, Beall Park Art Ctr., Bozeman, Mont., 1996; exhibited in group shows Davis Art Ctr., 1975, San Francisco State U., 1982, Napa Valley Coll., Napa, Calif., 1985, San Jose (Calif.) Inst. Contemporary Art, 1987, San Jose Inst. Contemporary Art, 1990, U. Alaska, Anchorage, 1992, J. Noblett Gallery, Sonoma, 1993, Holter Mus. Art, Helena, 1995, 97, Museo ItaloAmericano, San Francisco, 1986, 96; represented in collections South Bay Contemporary Mus. Art, Torrance; contbr. essays to Gray's Sporting Jour., The Structurist; works featured in publs. including No. Lights, Cutbank, Am. Artists, Art Rev. Helene Wurlitzer fellow in painting, Taos, N.Mex., 1996. Avocation: hunting.

DALTCHEV, ANA RANGUEL, sculptor; b. Sofia, Bulgaria, Jan. 25, 1926; came to U.S., 1979; d. Ranguel and Struma Popov; m. Lubomir Daltchev, Jan. 23, 1949; 1 child, Lubomir. MA, Higher Inst. Visual Arts, Sofia, Bulgaria, 1952. Registered sculptor Europe, 1953-79; free-lance sculptor U.S.A., 1979—. Exhibited in group shows in U.S., Germany, Bulgaria, France, Yugoslavia, India, Greece, Rumania; prin. works include Motherhood, Fount, Weaver, Joy, Sophia, Youth, California Women, Dance; participation with sculptures in XIV World Biennial of Sculpture, Milan, European Biennial of Small Sculpture, Budapest, Hungary; rresented in pvt. collections. Mem. San Francisco Mus. Modern Arts, Women in Arts. East Orthodox. Achievements include: half a century dedicated to research and creation of new feminine forms in sculpture. Office: PO Box 70054 Sunnyvale CA 94086-0054

DALTON, JAMES EDWARD, aerospace executive, retired air force officer; b. N.Y.C., Oct. 17, 1930; s. Edward A. and Marion (Conway) D.; m. Betty Jane Irwin, Nov. 28, 1958; children: Christopher, Stephanie, Todd. B.S., U.S. Mil. Acad., 1954; M.S.E. in Instrumentation Engring, U. Mich., 1960, M.S.E. in Aero./Astronautical Engring, 1960; grad. with distinction, Air Command and Staff Coll., 1965, Indsl. Coll. Armed Forces, 1970. Commd. 2d lt. U.S. Air Force, 1954, advanced through grades to gen., 1983; served in numerous operational and research assignments, 1954-73; comdr. 39th Aerospace Rescue and Recovery Wing, Eglin AFB, Fla., 1973-75, Air Res. Personnel Center, Denver, 1975-76; dep. dir. concepts Hdqrs. USAF, Washington, 1976-77; dep. dir. Force Devel. and Strategic Plans, Plans and Policy Directorate, Office Joint Chiefs of Staff, Washington, 1977-78; vice dir. Joint Staff, 1978-80; commandant Indsl. Coll. of Armed Forces, Washington, 1980-81; dir. Joint Staff, 1981-83; chief of staff SHAPE, 1983-85; pres. Logicon RDA, corp. v.p.; bd. dirs. The Presley Cos. Decorated Def. Disting. Service medal with two oak leaf clusters, Legion of Merit with 1 oak leaf cluster, D.F.C., Bronze Star, Air medal with 5 oak leaf clusters, Meritorious Service medal with 2 oak leaf clusters, Air Force Commendation medal. Mem. Air Force Assn., Assn. Grads. U.S. Mil. Acad., Council Fgn. Relations. Roman Catholic. Home: 61 Misty Acres Rd Palos Verdes Peninsula CA 90274-5749 Office: Logicon R & D Assocs PO Box 92500 Los Angeles CA 90009-2500

DALTON, PHYLLIS IRENE, library consultant; b. Marietta, Kans., Sept. 25, 1909; d. Benjamin Reuben and Pearl (Travelute) Bull; m. Jack Mason Dalton, Feb. 13, 1950. BS, U. Nebr., 1931, MA, 1941; MA, U. Denver, 1942. Tchr. city schs., Marysville, Kans., 1931-40; reference libr. Lincoln Pub. Libr., Nebr.; libr. U. Nebr., Lincoln, 1941-48; libr. Calif. State Libr., Sacramento, 1948-57, asst. state libr., 1957-72; pvt. libr. cons., Scottsdale, Ariz., 1972—. Author: Library Services to the Deaf and Hearing Impaired Individuals, 1985, 91 (Pres.' Com. Employment of Handicapped award 1985), also poems; contbr. chpt., articles, reports to books and publs. in field. Mem. exec. bd. So. Nev. Hist. Soc., Las Vegas, 1983-84; mem. So. Nev. Com. on Employment of Handicapped, 1980-89, chairperson, 1988-89; mem. adv. com. Nat. Orgn. on Disability, 1982-94; mem., sec. resident coun. Forum Pueblo Norte Retirement Village, 1990-91, pres. resident coun., 1991-94; bd. dirs. Friends of So. Nev. Libraries; trustee Univ. Library Soc., U. Nev.-Las Vegas; mem. Allied Arts Council, Pres.' Com. on Employment of People with Disabilities, mem. emeritus 1989—, Ariz. Gov's. Com. on Employment of People with Disabilities, 1990—, Scottsdale Mayor's Com. on Employment of People with Disabilities, 1990—, chmn. 1996—; mem.Scottsdale Pub. Libr. Ams. With Disabilities Com., 1994—. Recipient Libraria Sodalitas, U. So. Calif., 1972, Alumni Achievement award U. Denver, 1977, Alumni Achievement award U. Nebr., Lincoln, 1983, Disting. Svc. award Internat. United Laureate Poets in Eng., 1997, Outstanding Sr. Citizen Vol. award City of Scottsdale, 1997; named Mover and Shaker Scottsdale Mag., 1994. Mem. LWV, ALA (councilor 1963-64, exceptional svc. award 1981, award com. O.C.L.C. Humphreys Forest Press award 1994), Am. Assn. U. Women, Assn. State Librs. (pres. 1964-65), Calif. Libr. Assn. (pres. 1969), Nev. Libr. Assn. (hon.), Internat. Fedn. Libr. Assns. and Instns. (chair working group on libr. svc. to prisons, mem. standing com. Sect. Librs. Serving Disadvantaged Persons 1981-95), Nat. League Am. Pen Women (Las Vegas chpt. 1988-94, mem. com. on qualifications for Letters membership [illegible] state chpt. 1996-98, sec. 1998—), Am. Correctional Assn. (libr. svcs. instns. com. 1994—), Internat. Soc. Poets (disting.), Pilot Internat. (mem.-at-large). Republican. Presbyterian. Home: 7090 E Mescal St Apt 261 Scottsdale AZ 85254-6125

DALTON, THOMAS GEORGE, paralegal, social worker, legal consultant; b. Hoonah, Alaska, Mar. 13, 1940; s. George and Jessie K. (Starr) D.; m. Hazel Hope, Nov. 1960 (div. Sept. 1965); children: Roderick O., Rhoeda J. Garcia, Pamela Y. Masterman; m. Kathy Pelan, Sept. 1972 (div. Feb. 1980); children: Deirdra J. (dec.), Thomas L., Michael G. AAS, Shoreline Community Coll., Seattle, 1981; BA, Seattle Pacific U., 1984. Paralegal, social worker Pub. Defender's Assn., Seattle, 1983—; client advocate in criminal justice system Seattle, 1984—; legal cons., Seattle; tchr. Tlingit Culture and Lang., Northwest Indian Coll., Bellingham, Wash. Elder United Presbyn. Ch., Hoonah, 1973—; pres. Alaska Native Brotherhood, Seattle, 1984—, Nat. Am. Community Coun., Seattle, 1990—; pres. Seattle chpt. Tlinget and Haida Indians Alaska; bd. dirs. LANCE (Leading Am. Native for Excellence), 1996—. Recipient Founder's award Alaska Native Brotherhood, 1989. Democrat. Home: 7009 10th Ave NW Seattle WA 98117-5242 Office: Ctrl Bldg 8th fl 810 3rd Ave Seattle WA 98104-1655

DALY, JOHN MICHAEL, rancher, lawyer; b. Gillette, Wyo.; s. James R. and H. Elizabeth (Kerns) D.; m. Sandra Lynn Barney, Jan. 27, 1966; children: Jamie Ann Lyn, H. Brent, T. Tad. BS, U. Wyo., 1969, JD, 1972. Bar: Wyo. 1972, U.S. Dist. Ct. 1972, U.S. Ct. Appeals (10th cir.) 1972, U.S. Tax Ct. 1987, U.S. Supreme Ct. 1976. Sec. Daly Livestock, Gillette, Wyo., 1972—; pres. Daly Law Assocs., Gillette, Wyo., 1972—; mng. ptnr. Rawhide Resources, Gillette, Wyo., 1978—, West 4th St Assoc., Gillette, 5, 1978—, 20 Mile Land Co., Gillette, 5, 1980—, Justice Oil, Gillette, 5, 1996—. Chmn. bd. First Presbyn. Ch., 1980-81. Recipient fellow Wyo. LEAD, 1981-88. Mem. Wyo. State Bar (pres. 1988-89), Wyo. Stock Growers (2d v.p. 1998), Wyo. State Trapshooters (pres. 1998—), Gillette Rotary (pres. 1997-98), Campbell County Chamber (bd. dirs. 1994-97, GALI fellow 1988). Republican. Office: Daly Law Assocs 510 S Gillette Ave Gillette WY 82716-4204

DALY, PAUL SYLVESTER, mayor, retired academic administrator; b. Belmont, Mass., Jan. 8, 1934; s. Matthew Joseph and Alice Mary (Hall) D.; m. Maureen Teresa Kenny, May 25, 1957; children: Judith Mary, Paul S. Jr., Susan Marie, John Joseph, Maureen H. BS in Engring. Sci., Naval Postgrad. Sch., 1968; MBA, U. W. Fla., 1971. Commd. ensign USN, 1955; coll. dean Embry-Riddle Aero. U., Daytona Beach, Fla., 1979-81; advanced through grades to capt. Embry-Riddle Aero. U., 1979, chancellor, 1981-95; mayor City of Prescott, Ariz., 1996—; lectr. seminars, 1977-85; cons. British Aerospace, 1979-84, McDonnell Douglas, 1979-84, IBM, 1983-84; sr. faculty U. Phoenix, 1983-86. Bd. dirs. Yavapai Regional Med. Ctr., Prescott, Ariz., 1983-86, Ariz. Hosp. Fedn., Prescott C. of C., 1982-84; chmn. Ariz. State Bd. Pvt. Postsecondary Edn., Phoenix, 1982—, Interactive Health Corp.; pres. Ind. Coll. and Univs. of Ariz., Phoenix, 1982—; pres., founder West Yavapai County Am. Heart Assn. Chpt., chmn. affiliate of Am. Heart Assn./Ariz. Decorated Legion of Merit. Mem. Ariz. Airport Assn., Ret. Officers Assn., Ariz. Town Hall. Republican. Roman Catholic. Avocation: sports. Office: City of Prescott PO Box 2059 Prescott AZ 86302-2059

DALY, TOM, mayor; m. Debra Daly; children: Anna, Ryan. BA, Harvard U., 1976. Elected mem. City Council of Anaheim, 1988, elected mayor, 1992-94, 94—. mem. bd. trustees Anaheim Union Hish Sch. Dist., 1985—; active Anaheim Library Bd., 1985—; mem. adv. bd. Anaheim Boys and Girls Club; mem. bd. dirs. cmty. support group Anaheim Meml. Hosp.; mem. bd. dirs. Orange County Transp. Authority, Urban Water Inst.; mem. El Toro Citizens Adv. Commn.; chair regional adv. planning coun. Orange County, 1992—. Office: Office of the Mayor/City Council City Hall 200 S Anaheim Blvd Ste 733 Anaheim CA 92805-3820

DALZELL, GEORGE EDWARD, social worker, author; b. Pitts., Jan. 26, 1961; s. Robert Duff and Ruth Elizabeth (Speidel) D.; widowed. BS, Northwestern, 1983; M in social work, Barry Univ., 1994. Lic. clinical social worker. Therapist Family Svc. Agy., Ft. Lauderdale, Fla., 1993, The Village, Miami, Fla., 1994-95, Inst. for Human Potential, Miami, Fla., 1996-97, Dept. Mental Health County of L.A., L.A., 1997—. Author: The Blue Angel, 1998. Mem. Nat. Assn. Social Workers, Screen Actor's Guild. Avocation: television commercial actor. Home: 1935 N Vermont Ave Los Angeles CA 90027-1874 Office: Downtown Mental Health 515 E 6th St Los Angeles CA 90021-1009

DAMASCHINO, ANN TOOTHMAN, development consultant; b. Oakland, Calif., Dec. 14, 1938; d. James Wesley and Aileen Elizabeth (Cox) Toothman; m. Douglas Alan Damaschino, Aug. 12, 1961; children: Lori Damaschino Berry, Ellen Damaschino Mellies, Gerald, Anthony. BA in English Lit. with honors, Holy Names Coll., 1962; MA in Philanthropy and Devel., St. Mary's U., Minn., 1994. Reader in English/social studies Acalanes Union H.S. Dist., Lafayette, Calif., 1964-77; interior designer, ptnr. Damaschino/Thurling, Lafayette, Calif., 1973-81; tech. writer, editor Shell Oil Co., Martinez, Calif., 1981-85; dir. devel. St. Mary's Coll. H.S., Berkeley, Calif., 1985-96; cons. devel. fund-raising, Lafayette. Pres., sec., treas. Walnut Creek (Calif.) Gallery Guild, 1968-76; mem. Contra Costa County Bd. "Project Second Chance" Adult Literacy Program, 1986-88. Mem. AAUW, Coun. for Advancement and Support of Edn., East Bay Devel. Dirs., Diocese of Oakland Devel. Dirs. Democrat. Roman Catholic. Avocations: gardening, writing fiction, travel, tennis, oil painting.

D'AMICO, MICHAEL, architect, urban planner; b. Bklyn., Sept. 11, 1936; s. Michael and Rosalie (Vinciguerra) D.; BArch, U. Okla., 1961; postgrad. So. Meth. U. Sch. Law, 1962-63, Coll. Marin, 1988-89;, San Francisco Law Sch., 1994—; m. Joan Hand, Nov. 26, 1955; children: Michael III, Dion Charles. Supr. advanced planning sect. Dallas Dept. City Planning, 1961-63; designer, planner in charge Leo A. Daly Co., San Francisco, 1963-66; project planner Whisler, Patri Assos., San Francisco, 1966-67; architect, urban planner D'Amico & Assocs., San Francisco, N.Y., Guam, 1967-73, pres. D'Amico & Assocs., Inc., Mill Valley and San Francisco, Calif., and Guam, 1973—; pres. Jericho Alpha Inc., 1979-82, pres. Alpha Internet Syss., Inc., 1996—; cons. architect, planner City of Seaside (Calif.), 1967-72, 79-81, 89—; cons. urban redevel. Eureka (Calif.), 1967-82; cons. planner, Lakewood, Calif.; redevel. cons. to Daly City (Calif.), 1975-77; redevel. adviser to Tamalpais Valley Bus. Assn., 1975-77; archtl. and hist. analyst to Calif. Dept. Transp., 1975-77; agt. for Eureka, Calif. Coastal Commn., 1977-79; devel. cons. City of Scotts Valley, 1988-95, City of Suisun, 1988-89, City of Union City, 1989-91. Mem. steering com. San Francisco Joint Com. Urban Design, 1967-72. Recipient Community Design award AIA, 1970; First prize award Port Aransas (Tex.) Master Plan Competition, 1964; Design award Karachi Mcpl. Authority, 1987, Merit award St. Vincent's/Silveira. Mem. AIA (inactive), Am. Inst. Cons. Planners, Am. Planning Assn., Calif. Assn. Planning Cons. (sec., treas. 1970-72), World Future Soc., Solar Energy Soc. Am. Office: 525 Midvale Way Mill Valley CA 94941-3705

DAMSBO, ANN MARIE, psychologist; b. Cortland, N.Y., July 7, 1931; d. Jorgen Einer and Agatha Irene (Schenck) D. B.S., San Diego State Coll., 1952; M.A., U.S. Internat. U., 1974, Ph.D., 1975. Diplomate Am. Acad. Pain Mgmt., Am. Coll. Forensic Examiners, Am. Bd. Psychol. Spltys. Commd. 2d lt. U.S. Army, 1952, advanced through grades to capt., 1957; staff therapist Letterman Army Hosp., San Francisco, 1953-54, 56-58, 61-62, Ft. Devers, Ft. Devens, Mass., 1955-56, Walter Reed Army Hosp., Washington, 1958-59, Tripler Army Hosp., Hawaii, 1959-61, Ft. Benning, Ga., 1962-64; chief therapist U.S. Army Hosp., Ft. McPherson, Ga., 1964-67; ret. U.S. Army, 1967; med. missionary So. Presbyterian Ch., Taiwan, 1968-70; psychology intern So. Naval Hosp., San Diego, 1975; pre-doctoral intern Naval Regional Med. Ctr., San Diego, 1975-76, postdoctoral intern, 1975-76, chief, founder pain clinic, 1977-86; chief pain clinic, 1977-86; adj. tchr. U. Calif. Med. Sch., San Diego; lectr., U.S., Can., Eng., France, Australia; cons. forensic hypnosis to law enforcement agys.; approved cons. in hypnosis. Contbr. articles to profl. publs., chpt. to book. Tchr. Sunday sch. United Meth. Ch., 1945—; Rep. Nat. Candidate Trust Presdl. adv. com., platform planning commn. at-large-del. Fellow Am. Soc. Clin. Hypnosis (psychology mem.-at-large, exec. bd. 1989-90), San Diego Soc. Clin. Hypnosis (pres. 1980); mem. AAUW, Am. Phys. Therapy Assn., Calif. Soc. Clin. and [illegible] 1992-94), Internat. Platform Assn., Am. Soc. Clin. Hypnosis (exec. bd.), Ret. Officers Am., Ret. Officers Assn. (rep. presdl. task force, pres. adv. com.), Toastmasters (local pres.), Job's Daus. Republican. Home and Office: 1062 W Fifth Ave Escondido CA 92025-3802

DAMSKY, ROBERT PHILIP, communications executive; b. Boston, May 19, 1921; s. Mark and Ann (Wisser) D.; m. Rose Hollender, Jan. 18, 1955 (div. 1985); children: Marla Markley, Lori Diana. Cert., MIT, 1939, Tex. A&M U., 1944; diploma, Spartan Sch. Aero., Tulsa, 1946. Indsl. editor Spartan Aircraft Co., Tulsa, 1946-47; with Transocean Airlines, Hartford, Conn., 1947; chief pilot MIT, Beverly, Mass., 1947-48; sr. check pilot Civil Air Patrol, Beverly, 1948; airport mgr. Hartport, Inc., Bellfontaine, Ohio, 1948-49; airline pilot Slick Airlines and U.S. Overseas Airlines, Burbank, Calif. and Wildwood, N.J., 1949-55; founder Flight Edn. Assn., Santa Ana, Calif., 1955-80; pub., editor, pres. Aeromedia Nat. Syndicate, L.A., 1980—. Aviation editor: Beverly News, Mass., Gen. Aviation News. With U.S. Army Air Corps, 1940-45. Decorated Purple Heart, 1941. Mem. Airline Pilots Assn., Aircraft Owners and Pilots Assn., Silver Wings, VFW, Am. Legion, Pearl Harbor Survivors Assn. Avocations: flying, hiking, reading. Home: PO Box 2704 Costa Mesa CA 92628-2704

DANA, LAUREN ELIZABETH, lawyer; b. Hollywood, Calif., Sept. 30, 1950; d. Franklin Eugene and Margaret Elizabeth (Nixon) D.; m. Andrew Russell Willing, May 25, 1986; 1 child, Matthew Barkan Willing. BA cum laude, Calif. State U., Northridge, 1973; JD cum laude, Southwestern U., 1982. Bar: Calif. 1982, U.S. Dist. Ct. (cen. dist.) Calif. 1983, U.S. Ct. Appeals (9th cir.) 1983, U.S. Supreme Ct. 1987. Assoc. Law Office Andrew R. Willing, Los Angeles, 1982-84; dep. atty. gen. Calif. Dept. Justice-Atty. Gen., Los Angeles, 1984—. Assoc. editor legal update Police Officer Law Report, 1986-87. Recipient Am. Jurisprudence Book award Lawyers Coop. Pub. Co., 1980, Am. Jurisprudence Book award in Evidence, 1980. Mem. ABA, Fed. Bar Assn., Am. Judicature Soc., Constitutional Rights Found., Selden Soc., U.S. Supreme Ct. Hist. Soc., Los Angeles County Bar Assn.(conf. of delegates 1998, 99), Women Lawyers Assn. L.A., Am. Judicature Soc., Constitutional Rights Found., L.A. World Affairs Coun., Alliance for Children's Rights, Town Hall, Phi Alpha Delta, The Da Camera Soc. Republican. Avocations: music, collecting books on English history, reading, traveling. Office: Calif Dept Justice 300 S Spring St Los Angeles CA 90013-1230

DANA-DAVIDSON, LAOMA COOK, English language educator; b. Herndon, W.Va., Nov. 23, 1925; d. Virgil A. and Latha (Shrewsbury) Cook; m. William J. Davidson, Apr. 1946 (div. 1971); 1 child, Deborah Davidson Bollom. BE, Marshall U., 1946; MA in Adminstrn., Azusa U., 1981. Cert. tchr., Calif. Tchr. Cajon Valley Union Sch. Dist., El Cajon, Calif., 1958—, San Diego Diocese; master tchr. to 50 student tchrs. Author: Reading series used in dist., 1968. Former pres. El Cajon Rep. Women Federated; chaplin San Diego County Rep. Women; mem. El Cajon Hist. Assn.; v.p. Cajon Valley Union Sch. Bd.; active literacy program Rolling Readers; mem. Spa-Wars Edn. Com. for Navy Relocation; mem. Alcohol and Drug Prevention Task Force. Recipient sabbatical to study British Schs. Cajon Valley Union Sch. Dist., 1977-78. Mem. AAUW (pres. 1964-66, edn. com. 1993-94, policy com., women's issuees com., Chris Lynn Downey rsch. and projects award 1996), League of Women Voters, Grossmont Concert Assn., La Mesa C. of C. (edn. rep. Cajon Valley Sch. Dist.), Delta Kappa Gamma, Phi Delta Kappa. Avocations: travel, writing, reading, tennis, theatre. Fax: (619) 447-4512. Office: 609 Ecken Rd El Cajon CA 92020-7312

DANAO, DANILO GREGORIO, business owner; b. Seattle, May 20, 1960; s. Gregorio and Flordeliza (Maynigo) D.; m. Delia Montemayor, Jul. 3, 1990 (dec. Jul. 1994); 1 child, Davis M. BS in fin., San Francisco State Univ., 1983; MBA, Golden Gate Univ., 1988. Benefit authorizer trainee SOcial Security Adminstrn., Richmond, Calif., 1984-85; tax examiner IRS, Oakland, Calif., 1987-88; acct. assoc. Pacific Life Ins. Co., Honolulu, 1989-92; bus. owner Dan Danao Cons., Las Vegas, 1995— Avocations: golf, foreign languages, swimming, travel, computers. Office: Dan Danao Cons 3375 Glen Ave Ste 5-288 Las Vegas NV 89121-1596

DANCE, FRANCIS ESBURN XAVIER, communication educator; b. Bklyn., Nov. 9, 1929; s. Clifton Louis and Catherine (Tester) D.; m. Nora Alice Rush, May 1, 1954 (div. 1974); children: Clifton Louis III, Charles Daniel, Alison Catherine, Andrea Frances, Frances Sue, Brendan Rush; m. Carol Camille Zak, July 4, 1974; children: Zachary Esburn, Gabriel Joseph, Caleb Michael, Catherine Emily. BS, Fordham U., 1951; MS, Northwestern U., 1953, PhD, 1959. Instr. speech Bklyn. Adult Labor Schs., 1951; instr. humanities, coordinator radio and TV U. Ill. at Chgo., 1953-54; instr. Univ. Coll., U. Chgo., 1958; asst. prof. St. Joseph's (Ind.) Coll., 1958-60; asst. prof., then assoc. prof. U. Kans., 1960-63; mem. faculty U. Wis., Milw., 1963-71, prof. communication, 1965-71, dir. Speech Communication Center, 1963-70; prof. U. Denver, 1971—, John Evans prof., 1995—; content expert and mem. faculty adv. bd. to Internat. U. on Knowledge Channel, 1993-95; cons. in field. Author: The Citizen Speaks, 1962, (with Harold P. Zelko) Business and Professional Speech Communication, 1965, 2d edit., 1978, Human Communication Theory, 1967, (with Carl E. Larson) Perspectives on Communication, 1970, Speech Communication: Concepts and Behavior, 1972, The Functions of Speech Communication: A Theoretical Approach, 1976, Human Communication Theory, 1982, (with Carol C. Zak-Dance) Public Speaking, 1986, Speaking Your Mind, 1994, 2d edit., 1996; editor Jour. Comm., 1962-64, Speech Tchr., 1970-72; adv. bd. Jour. Black Studies; editl. bd. Jour. Psycholinguistic Rsch; contbr. articles to profl. jours. Bd. dirs. Milw. Mental Health Assn., 1966-67. 2d lt. AUS, 1954-56. Knapp Univ. scholar in communication, 1967-68; recipient Outstanding Prof. award Standard Oil Found., 1967; Master Tchr. award U. Denver, 1985, University Lectr. award U. Denver, 1986. Fellow Internat. Communication Assn. (pres. 1967); mem. Nat. Communication Assn. (pres. 1982), Psi Upsilon. Office: U Denver Dept Human Comm Studies Denver CO 80208

DANDO, HOWARD CHARLES, theatre and television producer; b. Phila., Aug. 22, 1943; s. Howard C. Sr. and Ann (Durkin) D.; m. Hilda Morales, Aug. 24, 1971 (div. Jan. 1979). BA, LaSalle U., 1966; MA, Temple U., 1969; postgrad., So. Ill. U. Dir. Phila. Arts Festival, 1970-71; producer Am. Dance Festival, Phila., 1973; dir. Stars of Am. Ballet, N.Y.C., 1974-80; arts dir. New World Festival of the Arts, Miami, 1980-83; producer, dir. Cintel TV, L.A., N.Y.C., 1983—; prof. Moore Coll. of Art, Phila., 1970-71, Lab. Inst. of Merchandising Coll., N.Y.C., 1976-80, West L.A. Coll.; adj. prof. CUNY, 1972-77, West L.A. Coll., 1989—. Producer (broadway plays) Tommy, 1971-73, Sargent Pepper's Lonely Hearts Club Band, 1972-74, dir. Elvis, 1975; writer (CD-Rom) Things We Do, The phantom Poet, 1998; (video) The Milky Way; prodr. (TV shows) A Time to Dance (PBS), Stars of American Ballet (A&E). Bd. dirs. Miami Coun. on Arts and Edn., 1980-82; mem. Miami Performing Arts Bldg. Com., 1980-82. Grantee NEA, 1974; named Best Dir. Pa. State Theatre Festival, 1973. Fellow Nat. Assn. of Profl. TV Execs., Nat. Tchr. Assn. Home and Office: 8180 Manitoba St Playa Del Rey CA 90293-8644

DANG, MARVIN S. C., lawyer; b. Honolulu, Feb. 11, 1954; s. Brian K.T. and Flora (Yuen) D. BA with distinction, U. Hawaii, 1974; JD, George Washington U., 1978. Bar: Hawaii 1978, U.S. Dist. Ct. Hawaii 1978, U.S. Ct. Appeals (9th cir.) 1979. Atty. Gerson, Steiner & Anderson and predecessor firms, Honolulu, 1978-81; owner, atty. Law Offices of Marvin S.C. Dang, Honolulu, 1981—; sr. v.p., bd. dirs. Rainbow Fin. Corp., Honolulu, 1984-95; bd. dirs. Foster Equipment Co. Ltd., Honolulu, Hawaii Cmty. Reinvestment Corp.; bd. dirs. Hawaii Fin. Svcs. Assn., sec., 1991, treas., 1992, v.p., 1993, pres. 1994; vice chmn. Hawaii Consumer Fin. Polit. Action Com., 1988-95; hearings officer (per diem) Adminstrv. Drivers License Revocation Office, Honolulu, 1991-95. State rep., asst. minority floor leader Hawaii State Legislature, Honolulu, 1982-84; chmn., vice chmn., mem. Manoa Neighborhood Bd., Honolulu, 1979-82, 84-87; pres., v.p., mem. Hawaii Coun. on Legal Edn. for Youth, Honolulu, 1979-86; mem. Hawaii Bicentennial Commn. of U.S. Constn., Honolulu, 1986-88. Recipient Cert. of Appreciation award Hawaii Speech-Lang.-Hearing Assn., Honolulu, 1984; named one of Ten Outstanding Young Persons of Hawaii, Hawaii State Jaycees, 1983. Mem. ABA (coun. of fund for justice and edn. 1993—, standing com. on law and electoral process 1985-89, spl. com. on youth edn. for citizenship 1979-85, 89-92, Hawaii membership chmn. 1981-93, exec. coun. young lawyers divsn. 1986-88), Hawaii State Bar Assn. (bd. dirs. young lawyers divsn. 1990). Avocations: family, law, politics. Office: PO Box 4109 Honolulu HI 96812-4109

DANI, ASHAY ARVIND, materials engineer; b. Bombay, Feb. 7, 1967; came to U.S., 1988; s. Arvind Shantaram and Vasudha Arvind (Dube) D.; m. Manisha Ashay (Babladi), June 14, 1993; 1 child, Advika Ashay. BS, U. Dept. Chem. Tech., Bombay, 1988; MS, Clemson U., 1990, PhD, 1995. Assoc. engr. BPCL, Bombay, 1987-88; from rsch. assoc. to instr. Clemson (S.C.) U., 1988-95; materials engr. Key Tronic Corp., Spokane, Wash., 1995-96, sr. materials scientist, 1996—, program mgr., 1998—; indsl. adv. Gonzaga U., Spokane, 1996—, liason engr., 1996-97; cons. in field. Contbr. articles to profl. jours. Sec. India Club, Clemson, 1992-93. Mem. AIChE, Soc. Plastics Engrs., Soc. for Advancement Materials & Processing, Am. Chem. Soc., South Asia Cultural Assn. (treas. 1997—). Avocations: hiking, tennis, painting, drama, reading.

DANIEL, GARY WAYNE, motivation and performance consultant; b. Wendall, Idaho, June 22, 1948; s. Milan Chauncey Daniel and Ila Fay (Cox) Harkins. AA, Boise Bus. Coll., 1969; PhD in Psychology, Westbrook U., 1994. Cert. master practitioner Neuro Linguistic Programming. Pres., chief exec. officer Victory Media Group, Santa Rosa, Calif., 1985—; gen. mgr. Victory Record Label, 1986—; also bd. dirs.; bd. dirs. Bay City Records, San Francisco; pres. Lightforce Music Pub., Santa Rosa, 1987—; mktg. cons. Fienze Records, San Francisco, 1987—, Capital Bus. Sys., Napa, Calif., 1986-91. Author: Concert Operations Manual, 1987; devel. of the Neuro Achievement System. Named Top Radio Personality Idaho State Broadcasters Assn., 1971. Mem. ASCAP, NARAS, Ind. Record Mfrs. and Distbrs., Am. Coun. Hypnotist Examiners, Hypnotist Examiners Coun. Calif., Am. Assn. Behavioral Therapists, Internat. Assn. Neuro Linguistic Programming. Office: Neuro Achievement Ctr 55 Maria Dr Ste 844 Petaluma CA 94954-3563

DANIEL, WILEY Y., lawyer; b. Louisville, Sept. 10, 1946; m. Ida S. Daniel; children: Jennifer, Stephanie, Nicole. BA in History, Howard U., JD. Atty. Gorsuch, Kirgis, Campbell, Walker & Grover, Denver, 1995; shareholder Popham, Haik, Schnobrich & Kaufman Ltd., Denver, 1995; judge U.S. Dist. Ct. Colo., Denver, 1995—. Trustee Iliff Sch. Theology, Denver. Mem. Colo. Bar Assn. (pres. 1992-93), Denver Bar Assn., State Bd. Architecture. Democrat. Office: US District Court of Colorado Byron White US Courthouse 1929 Stout St C 218 Denver CO 80294-0001*

DANIELS, FRANK EMMETT, mathematician; b. Miami, Fla., Sept. 28, 1963; s. Dan and Jewell Rae (Morgan) D. BS, U. Fla., Gainesville, 1985, MS, 1987. Grad. teaching asst. math. dept. U. Fla., Gainesville, 1985-92; teaching asst. math. dept. Santa Fe Community Coll., 1992-94; instr., sys. adminstr. Great Basin Coll., Ely, Nev., 1995—. Mem. Am. Math. Soc., Campus Advance (pres. 1988-91), Campus Christian Fellowship (pres. 1991-92), Phi Beta Kappa. Republican. Avocations: collecting comic books and Beatles items, Bibl. studies, role-playing games. Office: Great Basin Coll 2115 Bobcat Dr Ely NV 89301-3107

DANIELS, GANNON, artist, educator; b. Ann Arbor, Mich., Oct. 18, 1962; d. Edward and Virginia Harriette (Gannon) D.; m. Bjorn Johnson, Apr. 21, 1989 (div. 1992). BA, Ea. Mich. U., 1984; cert., Circle in the Square, 1986; postgrad., U. So. Calif., 1998—. Actress Va. Stage Co., Norfolk, Va., 1988, New Voice Theatre Co., N.Y.C., Vt., 1990-95; writer, actress, prodr. The Writers Wing, N.Y.C., 1993-94; actress Shakespeare Orange County, Calif., 1995; acting tchr. South Coast Repertory, Costa Mesa, Calif., 1995-98; dir. South Coast Reperatory, 1998; poetry tchr. Learning Tree U., Chatsworth, Calif., 1997-99; creator WRITE ON!, Hollywood. Scholarship Ea. Mich. U., 1984, Circle in the Square, 1986. Mem. L.A. Women's Shakespeare, Women Artist Group of L.A. (prodr., writer), Cottage Grove Prodn. Avocations: hiking, yoga.

DANIELS, LYDIA M., health care administrator; b. Louisville, Dec. 21, 1932; d. Effort and Gladys T. (Turner) Williams; student Calif. State U., Hayward, 1967, 69-72; BA, Golden Gate U., 1992, MS, 1993; cert. Samuel Merritt Hosp. Sch. Med. Record Adminstrs., 1959; student Cen. State Coll., Ohio, 1950-52; children by previous marriage: Danny Winston, Jeffrey Bruce, Anthony Wayne. Sec. chemistry dept. Cen. State Coll., Wilberforce, Ohio, 1950-52; co-dir. Indian Workcamp, Pala Indian Reservation, Pala, Calif., 1956-58; clk.-typist Camarillo (Calif.) State Hosp., 1956-58; student med. record adminstr. Samuel Merritt Hosp., Oakland, Calif., 1958-59, asst. med. record adminstr., 1962-63, asst. chief med. record adminstr., 1965, chief med. record adminstr., 1965-72; med. record adminstr. Albany (Calif.) Hosp., 1964-65; asst. med. record adminstr. Children's Hosp., San Francisco, 1960; co-dir. interns in community svc. Am. Friends Svc. Com., San Francisco, 1960-61; med. record adminstr. Pacific Hosp., Oakland, Calif., 1963-64; med. record cons. Tahoe Forest Hosp., Truckee, Calif., 1969-73; chief med. record adminstr. Highland Gen. Hosp., Oakland, 1972-74; dir. med. record svcs. U. Calif. San Francisco Hosps. and Clinics, 1975-82; mgr. patient appointments, reception and registration Kaiser-Permanente Med. Ctr., 1982-88; dir. ambulatory adminstrv. svcs., 1988-94, asst. dir. human resources, 1994-96, dir. human resources Brookside Hosp., San Pablo, Calif., 1996-97, Alameda County Med. Ctr., Oakland, Calif., 1998—; mgmt. tng. human resources cons. Daniels Consultation Svcs., Albany, 1997—; adj. prof. mgmt., labor mgmt. rels. Golden Gate U., 1978—; pres. Daniels Consultation Svcs., 1988—. Leader Girl Scouts Am. Oakland area council, 1960-62; sunday sch. tchr. Soc. of Friends, Berkeley, Calif., 1961-63, mem. edn. com., 1965-68; mem. policy and adv. bd. Far West Lab. Demonstration Sch., Oakland, 1973-75; bd. dirs. The Californians, Oakland, 1993—, Patrons of the Arts and Humanities, Oakland, 1994—, YWCA, Berkeley, 1995—. Recipient Mgmt. Fellowship award U. Calif., San Francisco, 1979-80. Mem. Am. Med. Record Assn., Calif. Med. Record Assn. (editorial bd. 1976-77, pres. 1974-75), East Bay Med. Record Assn. (chmn. edn. com. 1971-72, pres. 1969-70), Assn. Systems Mgmt., Am. Mgmt. Assn., San Francisco Med. Records Assn. (pres.-elect 1982-83, pres. 1983-84), Am. Assn. Tng. and Devel. (Golden Gate chpt., v.p. prof. devel. 1994-96). Author: Health Record Documentation: A Look at Cost, 1981; Inservice Training as a Tool in Managing the Changing Environment in the Medical Record Department, 1983; the Budget as a Management Tool, 1983. Issues editor Topics in Health Record Management, Parts I and II, 1983. Home: 545 Pierce St Apt 1105 Albany CA 94706-1048 Office: Fairmont Hosp 15400 Foothill Blvd San Leandro CA 94578-1015

DANIELS, RICHARD MARTIN, public relations executive; b. Delano, Calif., Feb. 24, 1942; s. Edward Martin and Philida Rose (Peterson) D.; m. Kathryn Ellen Knight, Feb. 28, 1976; children: Robert Martin, Michael Edward. A.A., Foothill Coll., 1965; B.A., San Jose State U., 1967; M.A., U. Mo., 1971. News reporter Imperial Valley Press, El Centro, Calif., summers 1963-66, San Diego (Calif.) Evening Tribune, 1967-68, Columbia Daily Tribune (Mo.), 1969-70; nat. news copy editor Los Angeles Times, 1966-67; staff writer San Diego Union, 1971-74, real estate editor, 1974-77; v.p. pub. relations Hubbert Advt. & Pub. Relations, Costa Mesa, Calif., 1977-78; ptnr. Berkman & Daniels, San Diego, 1979-91; prin. Nuffer, Smith, Tucker, Inc., 1991-94; prin. RMD Comms., 1994-97; exec. dir. comms. San Diego City Schs., 1997—; lectr. various bus. groups and colls., Chmn. bd. dirs. March of Dimes San Diego County, 1984-87; bd. dirs. Nat. Coun. Vols., 1983-91. Served with USN, 1959-62. Mem. Pub. Rels. Soc. Am., Counselors Acad. (accredited). Republican. Office: 2261 Ritter Pl Escondido CA 92029-5608

DANIELS, RONALD DALE, conductor; b. San Mateo, Calif., Aug. 19, 1943; s. Worth W. and Margurite Pearl (Chandler) D.; m. Judith Monson, July 24, 1993; 1 child, Ryan Stark. BMus, San Francisco Conservatory, 1968. Conductor, music dir. Musical Arts of Contra Costa (Calif.) County, 1968-75, U. Calif., Berkeley, 1973-75, Contra Costa Symphony, 1976-79; conductor, music dir. Reno (Nev.) Philharm., 1979-98, conductor Laureate, 1998—; guest conductor various orchs.; grants rev. cons. in field. With USMC, 1966. Recipient Lucien Wulsin award Baldwin Piano Co., Tanglewood Festival, 1968, Gov.'s Art award State of Nev., 1981. Avocations: ice skating, skiing, sailing, hiking. Office: Reno Philharm Assn 300 S Wells Ave Ste 5 Reno NV 89502-1670*

DANIELSON, CRAIG, wholesale grocery corporation executive. Chmn. United Grocers Inc., Portland, Oreg. Office: United Grocers Inc PO Box 5490 Oregon City OR 97045-8490*

DANIELSON, DEREK ARTHUR, lawyer, barrister; b. London, Eng., Nov. 9, 1950; came to U.S., 1996; s. John and Kitty (Friend) D.; 1 child, Tanis. B in Law, U. We. Ontario, London, Ontario, Can., 1974. Bar: Law Soc. Upper Can., 1976, Calif. 1994, U.S. Dist. Ct. (ctrl. dist.) Calif., 1996; cert trademark agt., Can., 1981. Ptnr. Solomon & Assocs., Toronto, Ontario, Can., 1976-79, Winton Altschuler, Toronto, 1979-81; sr. ptnr. Danielson & Assocs., Toronto, 1981-88, Danielson & Fox, Toronto, 1988-96; of counsel Law Offices Myles L. Berman, L.A., 1996—; area dir., com. mem. Ontario Legal Aid, Toronto, Can., 1985-96. Co-author: (book) Calif. DUI Trial Notebook, 1997; contbr. articles to profl. jours. instr., coord., Can. Red Cross Instr.'s Sch., Toronto, 1968-78, Royal Life Saving Soc. Instr.'s Sch., 1968-78; bd. dirs. Toronto Can. Red Cross, 1973-78. Mem. Century City Bar Assn. (chmn. entertainment sect.), Beverly Hills Bar Assn., Calif. Deuce Defenders, Criminal Cts. Bar Assn., Nat. Assn. Criminal Defense Lawyers (U.S.), Criminal Lawyers Assn. Can., The Canadian Acad. of Recording Arts and Scis., Can. Ind. Record and Producers Assn. Avocations: squash, swimming, skiing. Office: Law Offices Myles L. Berman 9255 W Sunset Blvd Ste 720 Los Angeles CA 90069-3304

DANIELSON, GORDON DOUGLAS, dentist; b. Everett, Wash., Nov. 11, 1942; s. Marvin and Elanor (Weers) D.; m. Jamie Lynn Waters, Jan. 9, 1977. BS with honors, U. Oreg., 1968; postgrad., MIT, 1968-69; MA in Molecular Biology, U. Calif., 1974, BS in Med. Sci., DDS, 1975. DDS. Pvt. practice Larkspur, Calif., 1975—; exec. v.p. Atmospheric Rsch. Tech., Sacramento, Calif., 1984-85; cons. Freeport Fin. Svcs., Denver, 1985-87; pres. Lynmar Enterprises Inc., Rno, 1987—; bd. dirs. Freeport Venture Fund. MIT fellow, 1968-69; U. Calif., Berkeley fellow, 1969-71; U. Calif., San Francisco fellow, 1973-75, pres. fellow, 1973-75. Mem. U. Calif. Dental Alumni Assn., U. Oreg. Alumni Assn., Marin County Dental Soc. (chmn. emergency care 1975-81), St. Francis Yacht Club (mem. com. 1973—), Aircraft Owners and Pilots Assn., Omicron Kappa Upsilon. Republican. Avocations: flying, yacht racing, scuba diving, golf. Office: 5 Bon Air Rd Ste 114 Larkspur CA 94939-1143

DANIHER, JOHN M., retired engineer; b. LaJunta, Colo., Aug. 2, 1926; s. Gerald and Mary Isabelle (Manly) D.; m. Edna Erle Hoshall, Sept. 4, 1948; children: Lyn Mari, Suzanne Laurie, Patricia Gail, Jerome Matthew, Michael Kevin. AB, Western State Coll., Gunnison, Colo., 1948; postgrad. Idaho State U., 1957-74, U. Idaho, 1974-76. High sch. tchr., Grand Junction, Colo., 1948-52; salesman Century Metalcraft, Denver, 1952-53; chem. plant supr. U.S. Chem. Corps., Denver, 1953-56; sr. engr. instrument and controls Phillips Petroleum Co., Idaho Falls, 1956-76; project engr. E G & G Idaho, Idaho Falls, 1976-85, engring. specialist, 1985-91; adv. Eastern Idaho Vocat. Tech. Sch., 1975-80. Cubmaster, Boy Scouts Am., 1970-75, asst. scoutmaster, 1975-80; v.p. Bonneville Unit Am. Cancer Soc., 1994, pres., v.p., 1995—. Recipient Cub Man of Yr., Boy Scouts Am., 1973. Mem. Am. Nuclear Soc. Roman Catholic. Club: K.C. (state dep. 1979-81, Supreme council 1979-84, 94) Home: 250 12th St Idaho Falls ID 83404-5370

DANILOV, VICTOR JOSEPH, museum management program director, consultant, writer, educator; b. Farrell, Pa., Dec. 30, 1924; s. Joseph M. and Ella (Tominovich) D.; m. Toni Dewey, Sept. 6, 1980; children: Thomas J., Duane P., Denise S. BA in Journalism, Pa. State U., 1945; MS in Journalism, Northwestern U., 1946; EdD in Higher Edn., U. Colo., 1964. With Sharon Herald, Pa., 1942, Youngstown Vindicator, 1945, Pitts. Sun-Telegraph, 1946-47, Chgo. Daily News, 1947-50; instr. journalism U. Colo., 1950-51; asst. prof. journalism U. Kans., 1951-53; with Kansas City Star, 1953; mgr. pub. relations Ill. Inst. Tech. and IIT Research Inst., 1953-57; dir. univ. relations and pub. info. U. Colo., 1957-60; pres. Profile Co., Boulder, Colo., 1960-62; exec. editor, exec. v.p. Indsl. Research Inc., Beverly Shores, Ind., 1962-69; pub., exec. v.p. Indsl. Research Inc., 1969-71; dir., v.p. Mus. Sci. and Industry, Chgo., 1971-77; pres., dir. Mus. Sci. and Industry, 1978-87, pres. emeritus, 1987—; dir. mus. mgmt. program, adj. prof. U. Colo., 1987—; mem. rural industrialization adv. group Dept. Agr., 1967; mem. panel internat. transfer tech. Dept. Commerce, 1968; mem. sci. info. coun. NSF, 1969-72; chmn. Conf. on Implications Metric Change, 1972, Nat. Conf. Indsl. Rsch., 1966-70; chmn. observance Nat. Indsl. Rsch. Week, 1967-70; chmn. Midwest White House Conf. on Indsl. World Ahead, 1972, Internat. Conf. Sci. and Tech. Museums, 1976, 82; mem. task force on fin. acctg. and reporting by non bus. orgns., others. Author: Public Affairs Reporting, 1955, Starting a Science Center, 1977, Science and Technology Centers, 1982, Science Center Planning Guide, 1985, Chicago's Museums, 1987, rev. edit., 1991, America's Science Museums, 1990, Corporate Museums, Galleries, and Visitor Centers: A Directory, 1991, A Planning Guide for Corporate Museums, Galleries, and Visitors Centers, 1992, Museum Careers and Training: A Professional Guide, 1994, University and College Museums, Galleries, and Related Facilities, 1996, Hall of Fame Museums: A Reference Guide, 1997; also articles; editor: Crucial Issues in Public Relations, 1960, Corporate Research and Profitability, 1966, Innovation and Profitability, 1967, Research Decision-Making in New Product Development, 1968, New Products--and Profits, 1969, Applying Emerging Technologies, 1970, Nuclear Power in the South, 1970, The Future of Science and Technology, 1975, Museum Accounting Guidelines, 1976, Traveling Exhibitions, 1978, Towards the Year 2000, 1981; editor profl. procs. V.p., trustee Women of the West Mus., 1991—; trustee La Rabida Childrens Hosp. and Rsch. Ctr., 1973-83; mem. U. Chgo. Citizens Bd., 1978-87. Mem. Am. Assn. Mus. (exec. com. 1976-77, bd. dirs. 1985-88, chmn. mus. studies task force 1988-89), AAAS, Assn. Sci.-Tech. Ctrs. (bd. dirs. 1973-84, sec.-treas. 1973-74, pres. 1975-76), Internat. Coun. Mus. (com. on sci. and tech. mus. 1972—, vice chmn. 1977-87, chmn. 1982-83, bd. dirs. 1985-88), Chgo. Coun. on Fine Arts (chmn. 1976-84), Ill. Arts Alliance (bd. dirs. 1983-86), Sci. Mus. Exhibit Collaborative (pres. 1983-86), Mus. Film Network (pres. 1984-86). Home: 250 Bristlecone Way Boulder CO 80304-0413 Office: Univ Colo Mus Mus Mgmt Program Campus Box 218 Boulder CO 80309-0218

DANNENBAUM, ROBERT MARCUS, publisher, editor; b. Houston, Jan. 14, 1933; s. Henry Joseph and Adele (Blissard) D.; m. Sandra Dannenbaum (div. 1979); children: Gary, Lisa, Rebecca; m. Rosalie Irene Ray, Aug. 21, 1982. BA in Liberal Arts, Tex. A&M U., 1955. Account mgr. Goodwin-Dannenbaum Advt., Houston, 1958-64; advt. mgr. Savage labs., Bellaire, Tex., 1964-66; v.p. mktg. G.D. Littman & Wingfield, Houston, 1966-68, Internat. Dairy Queen, Mpls., 1968-72; account mgr. Campbell-Mithun, Inc., Mpls., 1972-74; pres. Meyenberg Milk, L.A., 1975-79; acct. supr. George C. May, San Francisco, 1980-82; pub. West Coast Peddler, Whittier, Calif., 1982—. Chair policy adv. com. Minn. Farmer-Labor Dem. Party, Mpls., 1972; chmn. bd. dirs. Julia C. Hester House, United Fund, Houston, 1966. 1st lt. U.S. Army, 1956-58. Recipient Silver Anvil awrd Pub. Rels. Soc. Am., 1961, Grand Prix radio Houston Ad Club, 1967. Democrat. Avocations: philosophy, art and antiques collecting, bird watching. Office: West Coast Peddler 7007 Washington Ave Ste 311 Whittier CA 90602-3606

DANNENBERG, JAMES HARRY, lawyer, retired judge; b. Mpls., Nov. 14, 1944; s. Lester Dannenberg and Marcella (Austin) Harband; m. Catherine Jones, June 3, 1967; 1 child, Lester Alex. BS, U. Wis., 1965, MS, 1967, JD, 1969. Bar: Wis. 1969, U.S. Dist. Ct. (ea. and we. dists.) Wis. 1969, Calif. 1972, U.S. Ct. Appeals (9th cir.) 1972, U.S. Dist. Ct. (so. and no. dist.) Calif. 1972, U.S. Ct. Appeals (7th cir.) 1973, Hawaii 1980, U.S. Dist. Ct. Hawaii 1980. Pvt. practice, Milw., 1969-70, San Francisco, 1972-78; asst. prof. sociology San Francisco State U., 1970-74; legal counsel Youth Policy & Law Ctr., Madison, Wis., 1977; pres. Nosh Corp., Honolulu, 1978-80; dep. atty. gen. State of Hawaii, 1981-85, first dep. atty. gen., 1985-86, judge dist. ct., 1986-98; atty. Alston Hunt Floyd & Ing, Honolulu, 1998—; adj. prof. sociology U. Hawaii, Honolulu, 1981—, Richardson Sch. of Law, 1983—. Mem. Hawaii State Bar Assn., Calif. Bar Assn., Wis. Bar Assn. Office: Dist Ct 1111 Alakea St Honolulu HI 96813-2897

DANNER, PAUL KRUGER, III, telecommunications executive; b. Cin., Aug. 20, 1957; s. Paul Kruger Jr. and Phyllis Jean (Speak) D.; m. Cynthia Lee Hurst, May 5, 1984; children: Catherine Hurst, Elizabeth Speak, Caroline Tyree. BS, Colo. State U., 1979; MBA, Old Dominion U., 1986. Mktg. rep. Control Data Corp., Denver, 1985-86; dist. mgr. NEC Home Electronics (U.S.A.), Inc., Denver, 1987-88; regional mgr. NEC Home Electronics, Inc. subs. NEC Corp. (Tokyo), L.A., 1988-89, v.p. NEC Techs., Inc. subs., 1989-91; v.p. sales and mktg. Command Communications, Aurora, Colo., 1991-97; pres. Tech. Ventures, Inc., Denver, 1997—. Lt. USN, 1979-85; comdr. USNR, 1985—. Mem. Navy League of U.S., U.S. Naval Inst., NRA, Ducks Unltd. Republican. Avocations: skiing, scuba diving, fly fishing, hunting, golf.

DANOFF, DUDLEY SETH, surgeon, urologist; b. N.Y.C., June 10, 1937; s. Alfred and Ruth (Kauffman) D.; m. Hevda Amrani, July 1, 1971; children: Aurele Alfie, Doran. BA summa cum laude, Princeton U., 1959; MD, Yale U., 1963. Diplomate Am. Bd. Urology. Surg. intern Columbia-Presbyn. Med. Ctr., N.Y.C., 1963-64; resident in surgery Yale New Haven Med. Ctr., 1964-65; resident in urologic surgery Squier Urologic Clinic, Columbia-Presbyn. Med. Ctr., 1965-69; NIH trainee Francis Delafield Hosp., N.Y.C., 1969; asst. in urology Columbia U..Columbia-Presbyn. Hosp., N.Y.C., 1969; cons., surgeon New Orleans VA Hosp., 1970; asst. surgeon Tulane U., New Orleans, 1970; pvt. practice urologic surgery L.A., 1971—; attending urologic surgeon Cedars-Sinai Med. Ctr., L.A., Midway Hosp., L.A., Century City Hosp., L.A. VA Hosp., L.A.; attending urologic surgeon, clin. faculty UCLA. Author: Superpotency, 1993, Research: Laparoscopic Urologic Procedures; contbr. articles to profl. jours. Bd. dirs. Tel-Hashomer Hosp., Israel, Christian Children's Fund, Beverly Hills Edn. Found.; trustee Anti-Defamation League; mem. profl. adv. bd. The Wellness Comty.; mem. nat. exec. bd. Gesher Found.; mem. adv. com., past pres. Med. divsn. L.A. Jewish Fedn. Coun.; mem. nat. leadership cabinet United Jewish Appeal; chmn. Am. Friends of Assaf Harofeh Med. Ctr., Israel; pres. western states region and internat. bd. govs. Am. Friends Hebrew U. Jerusalem; pres. western region Am. Commn. for Shaare Zedek Med. Ctr. Jerusalem. Recipient Excellence in Medicine award Israel Cancer Rsch. Found., 1998. Fellow ACS; mem. AMA, Internat. Coll. Surgeons, Israeli Med. Assn., Am. Fertility Soc., Soc. Air Force Clin. Surgeons, Am. Urologic Assn., Societe International d'Urologie, Transplant Soc. So. Calif., Los Angeles County Med. Assn., Soc. for Minimally Invasive Surgery, Am. Technion Soc., Profl. Men's Club of L.A. (past pres.), Princeton Club So. Calif., Yale Club So. Calif., Hillcrest Country Club, Phi Beta Kappa, Sigma Xi, Alpha Omega Alpha, Phi Delta Epsilon (past pres., mem. exec. com.). Jewish. Avocations: golf, swimming, reading, writing. Fax: (310) 854-0267. Office: Cedars-Sinai Med Ctr Towers 8631 W 3d St Ste 915E Los Angeles CA 90048-5912

D'ANTONI, MIKE, professional basketball coach; b. Mullens, W.Va., May 8, 1951; m. Laurel D'Antoni; 1 child, Michael. Basketball player Kings NBA, 1973-1975, basketball player San Antonio Spurs, 1975-76; past basketball player Milan Italian League, winner 2 European Cups, 2 InterContinental Cups Milan, coach Milan, 1990-93, head coach Milan, 1996-97, winner Italian Cup, 1997; dir. player pers. Denver Nuggets NBA, 1997-98, profl. basketball coach Denver Nuggets, 1998—. Named to Marshall U. Hall of Fame, 1997. Office: care Denver Nuggets 1635 Clay St Denver CO 80204*

DANTSUKA, TRACY GAIL, police officer; b. Honolulu, Sept. 27, 1959; d. George Y. and Mildred (Dolfo) D. Chef Halekulani Hotel, Honolulu, 1978-81; met. police officer Honolulu Police Dept., 1982—. Author: (poetry books) Young Poets of America, 1977, America Sings, 1977; composer/lyricist: Keala, 1977. Mem. Police Activities League (first female field dir. 1993—). Avocations: golf, playing guitar, woodwork/crafts, singing, Hawaiiana. Home: 1506 Bernice St Honolulu HI 96817-2703

DANZIGER, LOUIS, graphic designer, educator; b. N.Y.C., 1923; m. Dorothy Patricia Smith, 1954. Student, Art Ctr. Sch., Los Angeles, 1946-47, New Sch., N.Y.C., 1947-48. Asst. art dir. War Assets Adminstrn., Los Angeles, 1946-47; designer Esquire mag., N.Y.C., 1948; freelance designer, cons. Los Angeles, 1949—; instr. graphic design Art Ctr. Coll. Design, Los Angeles, 1952-60, 86—, Chouinard Art Inst., Los Angeles, 1960-72; instr. Calif. Inst. Arts, 1972-88, head graphic design program, 1972-82; vis. prof. Harvard U., Cambridge, Mass., summers 1978-80, 83, 84, 86-88; instr. Art Ctr. Coll. Design; mem. graphic evaluation panel Fed. Design Program, Nat. Endowment Arts, 1975—; design cons. Los Angeles County Mus. Art, 1957—. Served with cav. U.S. Army, 1943-45; PTO. Recipient Disting. Achievement award Contemporary Art Coun., L.A. County Mus. Art, 1982, Disting. Designer award NEA, 1985, "Stars of Design" Lifetime Achievement award Pacific Design Ctr., 1997, numerous awards and medals in art design. Mem. Alliance Graphique Internationale, Am. Inst. Graphic Arts (medal 1998), Am. Ctr. for Design (hon.). Home: PO Box 660189 Arcadia CA 91066-0189

DARBY, JOANNE TYNDALE (JAYE DARBY), arts and humanities educator; b. Tucson, Sept. 22, 1948; d. Robert Porter Smith and Joanne Inloes Snow-Smith; stepchildren: Margaret Loutrel, David Michael. BA, U. Ariz., 1972; MEd, U. Calif., L.A., 1986, PhD, 1996. Cert. secondary tchr., gifted and talented tchr., Calif. Tchr. English, chmn. dept. Las Virgenes Unified Sch. Dist., Calabasas, Calif., 1979-82; tchr. English and gifted and talented edn. Las Virgenes Unified Sch.Dist., Calabasas, Calif., 1983-84; sch. improvement coord./lang. arts/social studies/drama tchr Las Virgenes Unified Sch. Dist., Calabasas, Calif., 1991-92; tchr. English and gifted and talented edn. Beverly Hills (Calif.) Unified Sch. Dist., 1982-83, 84-89, English and drama tchr., 1994; tchr., cons. Calif. Lit. Project, San Diego, 1985-87; cons., free lance editor L.A., 1977—; dir. Shakespeare edn. and festivals project Folger Libr., Washington, 1990-91; field work supr. tchr. edn. program Ctr. X, Grad. Sch. Edn. and Info. Studies, UCLA, 1992-96, Ctr. X postdoctoral scholar, tchr. edn. program, 1996-97; asst. researcher, co-dir. Project HOOP, Am. Indian Studies Ctr., UCLA, 1997—; cons. arts and edn., L.A., 1991—. Contbr. articles to profl. publs. Mem. Am. Alliance for Theatre and Edn., Am. Ednl. Rsch. Assn., Nat. Coun. Tchrs. English, Assn. for Theatre in Higher Edn., Phi Beta Kappa, Phi Beta Phi, Alpha Lambda Delta. Home: 972 Hilgard Ave Apt 310 Los Angeles CA 90024-3066

DARBY, WESLEY ANDREW, minister, educator; b. Glendale, Ariz., Sept. 19, 1928; s. Albert Leslie and Beulah E. (Lamb) D.; student Bible Inst. L.A., 1946, No. Ariz. U., 1946-47, Rockmont Coll., Denver, 1948-50, Ariz. State U., 1965, St. Anne's Coll., Oxford (Eng.) U., 1978; m. Donna Maye Bice, May 29, 1947; children: Carolyn Darby Eymann, Lorna Dale, Elizabeth Darby Larimer, Andrea Darby Perdue. Ordained to ministry Bapt. Ch., 1950; pastor Sunnyside Bapt. Ch., Flagstaff, Ariz., 1947-48, First Bapt. Ch. of Clifton, Ariz., 1950-55, West High Bapt. Ch., Phoenix, 1955-90; pastor emeritus, 1990—; dep. assessor Greenlee County, 1951-55; instr. English lit. and pastoral subjects Southwestern Conservative Bapt. Bible Coll., Phoenix, 1961-87. Chmn. bd. Conservative Bapt. Found. Ariz., 1974-83, Gospel Wings, 1960-88; v.p. Ariz. Bapt. Conf., 1976-83; pres. Ariz. Alcohol-Narcotic Edn. Assn., 1968-90. Dep. Maricopa County (Ariz.) Sheriff's Exec. Posse, 1993-97; chaplain Civil Air Patrol, 1951-55. Recipient God, Family and Country award Freeman Inst., 1981, Ronald Reagan Cert. of Excellence Maricopa County Rep. Com., 1996. Mem. Evang. Philos. Soc., Greater Phoenix Assn. Evangelicals (pres. 1960-63, 91-96), Ariz. Breakfast Club, (chaplain 1969-96, pres. 1996—), Ariz. Militia (chaplain 1994—). Contbr. articles to profl. jours. Republican. Home: 5628 N 11th Dr Phoenix AZ 85013-1714 Office: 3301 N 19th Ave Phoenix AZ 85015-5761

DARDICK, GEETA, writer, psychotherapist; b. St. Louis, July 15, 1942; d. Charles Kalman and Carol Jane (Kalish) Berger; m. Samuel Ian Dardick, Jan. 26, 1964; children: Caleb, Joshua, Samantha. Student, Wellesley Coll., 1960-62; BA, Wash. U., 1964; MA, U. San Francisco, 1993. Cert. marriage, family, and child counselor, Calif. Profl. writer North San Juan, Calif., 1982—, psychotherapist, 1993—. Contbr. more than 100 articles to profl. publs. Co-founder FREED Ind. Living Ctr., Nevada City, Calif., 1985, bd. dirs., 1986-92. Recipent Commendation for Volunteerism Bd. Suprs., 1987. Mem. Am. Soc. Journalists and Authors, U.S. Tennis Assn. (capt. 1992-98), Nat. Depression Assn. (co-dir. depression screening day 1997), Toastmasters Internat. Avocations: tennis, the Internet, skiing, journalism.

DARGIS, JEAN ANTHONY, retired voluntary health agency executive; b. Mpls., Mar. 9, 1931; s. Henry Joseph and Josephine Marie (Violette) D.; m. Mary Ruth Buschman, July 2, 1956; 1 child, Melissa Jeanne Dargis Herzog. BA, St. Paul (Minn.) Sem., 1952; MusB, Universite Laval, Quebec, Can., 1954. Tchr. St. Anthony Acad., Mpls., 1954-59, Holy Childhood Sch., St. Paul, 1955-57; various positions March of Dimes Birth Defects Found., White Plains, N.Y., 1959-92; v.p., dir. nat. office of vols. March of Dimes Birth Defects Found., White Plains, 1989-92. Author: (handbook) Manual for Chapters, 1990; editor: (handbook) Volunteer Development Guide, 1991, [illegible] Commn./Devel., San Jose, Calif., 1983-90; dir. Diocesan Choir, San Jose, 1983-90, St. Victor's Parish Choir, San Jose, 1971—. Mem. Mensa, Latin Liturgy Assn. Republican. Roman Catholic. Avocations: music, reading, walking, cooking. Home: 3479 Grossmont Dr San Jose CA 95132-3120

DARLING, RUSSELL EVERETT, software engineer; b. Springerville, Ariz., Feb. 23, 1970; s. Robert E. Darling and Andrea Jean (Isaacson) Nelson. BS in Computer Sci., Embry-Riddle Aeronautical U., 1994. Software engr. Sales Ptnr. Systems, Ormond Beach, Fla., 1991-95, Charles Schwab & Co., San Francisco, 1996; sr. systems programmer Indsl. Light and Magic, San Rafael, Calif., 1996—; spkr. Embry-Riddle Alumni Assn., Daytona Beach, Fla., 1997-98. Vol. Big Bros. of Marin County, San Rafael, 1998—. Mem. Film Arts Found. Republican. Mem. Ch. of LDS. Avocations: screenwriting, independent filmmaking. Home: 2500 Deer Valley Rd #823 San Rafael CA 94903 Office: Indsl Light and Magic PO Box 2459 San Rafael CA 94912

DARLING, SCOTT EDWARD, lawyer; b. Los Angeles, Dec. 31, 1949; s. Dick R. and Marjorie Helen (Otto) D.; m. Cynthia Diane Harrah, June 1970 (div.); 1 child, Smokie; m. Deborah Lee Cochran, Aug. 22, 1981; children: Ryan, Jacob. BA, U. Redlands, 1972; JD, U.S.C., 1975. Bar: Calif. 1976, U.S. Dist. Ct. (cen. dist.) Calif. 1976. Assoc. atty. Elver, Falsetti, Boone & Crafts, Riverside, 1976-78; ptnr. Falsetti, Crafts, Pritchard & Darling, Riverside, 1978-84; pres. Scott Edward Darling, A Profl. Corp., Riverside, 1984—; grant reviewer HHS, Washington, 1982-88; judge pro tem Riverside County Mcpl. Ct., 1980, Riverside County Superior Ct., 1987-88; bd. dirs. Tel Law Nat. Legal Pub. Info. System, Riverside, 1978-80. Author, editor: Small Law Office Computer Legal System, 1984. Bd. dirs. Youth Adv. Com. to Selective Svc., 1968-70, Am. Heart Assn. Riverside County, 1978-82, Survival Ministries, 1986-89; atty. panel Calif. Assn. Realtors, L.A., 1980—; pres. Calif. Young Reps., 1978-80; mem. GI Forum, Riverside, 1970-88; presdl. del. Nat. Rep. Party, 1980-84; asst. treas. Calif. Rep. Party, 1981-83; Rep. Congl. candidate, Riverside, 1982; treas. Riverside Sickle Cell Found., 1980-82, recipient Eddie D. Smith award; pres. Calif. Rep. Youth Caucus, 1980-82; v.p. Riverside County Red Cross, 1982-84; mem. Citizen's Univ. Com., Riverside, 1978-84, World Affairs Council, 1978-82, Urban League, Riverside, 1980-82. Calif. Scholarship Fedn. (life). Named one of Outstanding Young Men in Am., U.S. Jaycees, 1979-86. Mem. ABA, Riverside County Bar Assn., Speaker's Bur. Riverside County Bar Assn., Riverside Jaycees, Riverside C. of C. Lodge: Native Sons of Golden West. Avocations: skiing, swimming, reading. Office: 3697 Arlington Ave Riverside CA 92506-3938

DARMSTAETTER, JAY EUGENE, secondary education educator; b. Altadena, Calif., Nov. 30, 1937; s. Eugene Jamison and Virginia (Fagans) D. AA, L.A. City Coll., 1958; BA, L.A. State Coll., 1960, MA, 1962; postgrad., U. So. Calif., 1962-65. Cert. secondary edn. tchr., secondary adminstr. Tchr. L.A. Unified Schs., 1960-98, athletic dir., 1965-83; tng. tchr. UCLA, Calif. State U., Whittier Coll., L.A., 1966—; master tchr. L.A. Unified Schs., 1983-84; announcer L.A. Unified Schs., 1970—, CIF/So. Section, Artesia, Calif., 1964-85, State CIF, Fullerton, Calif., 1970-85. Soloist Christian Sci. Chs., L.A., 1958—; mem. Citizens Community Planning Coun., L.A. County, 1989-96. Recipient Nat. Def. Edn. Assn. award Dept. of Edn., L.A., 1968. Mem. NEA, Calif. Tchrs. Assn., United Tchrs. L.A., Phi Mu Alpha Sinfonia. Republican. Avocations: music, reading. Office: Wilson High/LA Schools 4500 Multnomah St Los Angeles CA 90032-3703

DARNALL, ROBERTA MORROW, academic administrator; b. Kemmerer, Wyo., May 18, 1949; d. C. Dale and Eugenia Stayner (Christmas) Morrow; m. Leslie A. Darnall, Sept. 3, 1977; children: Kimberly Gene, Leslie Nicole. BS, U. Wyo., Laramie, 1972. Tariff sec., ins. adminstr. Wyo. Trucking Assn., Casper, 1973-75; asst. clerical supr. Wyo. Legislature, Cheyenne, 1972-77; congl. campaign press aide, 1974; pub. relations dir. in Casper, Wyo. Republican Central Com., 1976-77; asst. dir. alumni relations U. Wyo., 1977-81, dir. of alumni, 1981—; bd. dir. Ivinson Meml. Hosp. Found. Mem. St. Matthews Altar Guild, Lector and Acolyte (coord.), Higher Edn. Assn. Rockies, Am. Soc. Assn. Execs., Laramie C. of C. (past edn. com.), U. Wyo. Alumni Assn., Cowboy Joe Club, PEO (former courtesy com., officer), Zonta Internat. Republican. Episcopalian. Home: 15 Snowy View Ct Laramie WY 82070-5358 Office: PO Box 3137 Laramie WY 82071-3137

DARNELL, CATHERINE MARGARET, anatomy and physiology educator; b. Oak Park, Ill., Aug. 29, 1957; d. Jon Nicholas and Violet Henderson (Low) Rougas; m. Gene Edwin Darnell, June 18, 1983; children: John Charles, Justin Lee, Ryan James. BS in Biology, Sioux Falls (S.D.) Coll., 1980; BS in Secondary Edn., MS in Zool. and Physiology, U. Wyo., 1988. Adj. prof. Laramie County Community Coll., Cheyenne, Wyo., 1989-94. Author booklet series: Your Body Intuitive; contbr. articles to profl. jours. Home: 7110 Lupine Trl Cheyenne WY 82009-5716 Office: Laramie County CC 1400 E College Dr Cheyenne WY 82007-3204

DARNELL, LEONARD ROBERT, information technology consultant; b. Beirut, Lebanon, Dec. 12, 1957; (parents Am. citizens); s. Robert Carter and Mary Lucy (Tunison) D.; m. Denise Michelle Cates, July 15, 1979; 1 child, Adriane Nicole. BS in Math., Loma Linda U., 1978. Programmer, analyst Loma Linda (Calif.) Med. Ctr., 1979-81; sr. programmer, analyst TRW, Orange, Calif., 1981-82; sr. mgr. Price Waterhouse, L.A., 1983—; frequent speaker on info. tech.; chmn. bus. trade show Bus. Net '85. Contbr. articles to profl. jours. Trustee L.A. Open Profl. Golfers Assn. tournament, 1987-92, v.p. 1987-89, pres. 1989-90; adv. bd. mem. L.A. Sports Coun., 1989-91, Magic Johnson Charity Golf Tournament, 1990-91; mem. adv. bd. Angel's Flight Shelter for Runaway Youth, 1992. Mem. Assn. for Cert. Computer Profls. L.A. Jr. C. of C. (chmn. bus. affairs 1985-86, bd. dirs. 1986-90, v.p., treas. 1987, 1st v.p, pres. elect 1987-88, pres. 1989-90, chmn. bd. 1990-91, pres. Century of the Pacific Conf., 1989-90, del. Conf. U.S. and Japanese Mayors and C. of C. Pres.), L.A. Area C. of C. (bd. dirs. 1990-91). Republican. Seventh-Day Adventist. Office: Price Waterhouse 400 S Hope St Ste 2300 Los Angeles CA 90071-2889

DARNELL, RAY D., zoo director. Dir. Rio Grande Zool. Park, Albuquerque. Office: Rio Grande Zool Park 903 10th St SW Albuquerque NM 87102-4029*

DA ROZA, VICTORIA CECILIA, human resources administrator; b. East Orange, N.J., Aug. 30, 1945; d. Victor and Cynthia Helen (Krupa) Hawkins; m. Thomas Howard Kaminski, Aug. 28, 1971 (div. 1977); 1 child, Sarah Hawkins; m. Robert Anthony da Roza, Nov. 25, 1983. BA, U. Mich., 1967; MA, U. Mo., 1968. Contract compliance mgr. City of San Diego, 1972-75; v.p. personnel Bank of Calif., San Francisco, 1975-77; with human resources Lawrence Livermore (Calif.) Nat. Lab., 1978-86; pvt. cons. Victoria Kaminski-da Roza & Assocs., 1986—; lectr. in field; videotape workshop program on mid-career planning used by IEEE. Contbr. numerous articles to profl. jours. Mem. social policy com. City of Livermore, 1982. Mem. Am. Soc. Tng. and Devel., Western Gerontol. Soc. (planning com. Older Worker Track 1983), Gerontol. Soc. Am. Home and Office: 385 Borica Dr Danville CA 94526-5457

DARPINO, FRED J., sculptor; b. Pueblo, Colo., Aug. 21, 1945; s. Manuel Fred and Ann (Giarratano) D.; m. Victoria Ann Gnojek; children: Nancy, Corrina, Julian, Nicholas, Joseph. BA, U. So. Colo., Pueblo, Colo.; MA, Adams St. Coll., Alamoso, Colo. Cert. tchr., Colo. Bd. dir. Capps Cappazolo Ctr. of Perf. Arts, 1995—. Numerous commissioned bronze sculptures. Pres. Alliance of Prof. Artists Assoc, Manitou Springs, Colo., 1990-97; artist rep. Bus. of Art Ctr., Manitou Springs, Colo., 1993-95. Studio: Darpino APA 513 Manitou Ave Manitou Springs CO 80829-1806

DARR, DAVID CARL, computer systems manager; b. Boulder, Colo., May 5, 1943; s. David James and Barbara Jean (Pinkstaff) D.; m. Linda Lois Blakely, May 5, 1977; children: Jeffrey Bryan, Robert Blakely, Monica Louise, Dawn Michelle, Shannon Marie, Jasonn Zachariah. AA, L.A. Mission Coll., 1990, BS, Univ. La Verne, 1993, MBA, 1997. Tech. writer Info. Handling Svcs., Hawthorne, Calif., 1966-79; owner Artistic Lawn & Landscape, Lawndale, Calif., 1979-83; mgr. Boeing Co. (Rockwell Internat.), Palmdale, Calif., 1983-98; adj. prof. Antelope Valley Coll., Lancaster, Calif., 1998—. Mem. Nat. Mgmt. Assn. Republican. Baptist. Avocations: camping, fishing, kung-fu, internet, bird watching. Home: 43919 Silver Bow Rd Lancaster CA 93535-4424 Office: Antelope Valley Coll 3041 W Avenue K Lancaster CA 93536-5402

DARROW, GEORGE F., natural resources company owner, consultant; b. Osage, Wyo., Aug. 13, 1924; s. George Washington and Marjorie (Ord) D.; m. Elna Tannehill, Oct. 23, 1976; children by previous marriage: Roy Stuart, Karen Josanne, Reed Crandall, John Robin. AB in Econs., U. Mich., 1945, BS in Geology, 1949. Geologist Amerada Petroleum Corp., Billings, Mont., 1949-50; v.p. Northwest Petroleum Co., 1951-58; prin. Resource Consultants, Billings, 1959-76; pres., CEO Crossbow Corp., Billings, 1962—; v.p. Kootenai Galleries, Bigfork, Mont., 1976—; sr. ptnr. Crossbow Assocs., resource mgrs., Bigfork, 1976—; chmn. Mont. Environ. Quality Coun., Helena, 1971-73; bd. dirs. Ord Ranch Corp., Lusk, Wyo.; apptd. faculty affil. U. Mont., 1995—. Contbr. articles on resource mgmt. and econs. to various publs. Elected mem. Mont. Ho. of Reps., 1967-69, 71-73, Mont. Senate, 1973-75; bd. dirs. Bigfork Ctr. Performing Arts, 1980—; apptd. mem. Mont. Ambs., 1994—. Lt. (j.g.) USNR, 1943-46, PTO. Fellow AAAS; mem. Internat. Soc. Ecol. Econs., Am. Assn. Petroleum Geologists (past pres. Rocky Mountain sect.), Am. Inst. Profl. Geologists (charter), Mont. Geol. Soc. (founder, charter), Billings Petroleum Club. Home and Office: Crossbow Corp 2014 Beverly Hill Blvd Billings MT 59102-2314 also: Paladin Farms 924 Chapman Hill Dr Bigfork MT 59911-6215

DART, JOHN SEWARD, religious material writer; b. Peekskill, N.Y., Aug. 1, 1936; s. Seward Homer and Vella Marion (Haverstock) D.; m. Gloria Joan Walker, Aug. 31, 1957; children—Kim, John W., Randall, Christopher. BA, U. Colo., 1958. Staff writer UPI, Indpls. and L.A., 1961-65; sci. writer Calif. Inst. Tech., Pasadena, 1966-67; religion writer L.A. Times, 1967-98. Author: The Laughing Savior, 1976, The Jesus of Heresy and History, rev., expanded edit., 1988; co-author: Unearthing the Lost Words of Jesus, 1998; contbr. reports for Freedom Forum First Amendment Ctr., Vanderbilt U. Served with U.S. Army, 1958-61. Recipient Supple Meml. award Religion Newswriters Assn., 1980, Merrell Meml. award Jim Merrell Religion Liberty Found., 1980, William F. Leidt award Episcopal Ch., 1980, Angel award Religion in Media, 1985; NEH fellow Stanford U., 1973-74, First Amendment Ctr. fellow Vanderbilt U., 1992-93. Mem. Soc. Profl. Journalists (chpt. pres. 1976), Religion Newswriters Assn. (pres. 1990-92), Soc. Bibl. Lit. (mem.-at-large exec. com. Pacific Coast region 1990-95). Democrat. Home: 12122 Bowmore Ave Northridge CA 91326-1002 Office: LA Times 20000 Prairie St Chatsworth CA 91311-6507

DARVAS, ENDRE PETER, artist; b. Kisvadra, Sz-Szatmar, Hungary, July 18, 1946; came to U.S., in 1957; s. Bela and Maria (Filtczer) Darvas. BFA, U. Tex., 1969. Pres. Studio Arts and Frames, Inc., South Lake Tahoe, Calif., 1974-78; owner Darvas Studio, South Lake Tahoe, 1969—. One-man shows include Dallas, 1963, Taos, N.Mex., 1971, Carmel, Calif., 1975, San Carlos, Mex., 1987, Galerias del Pacifico, Sonora, Mex., 1989, Studio Retrospective, Lake Tahoe, 1990, Sierra Galleries, Lake Tahoe, 1991-94; represented in permanent collections Sierra Galleries, Rosequist Gallery, Tucson. Recipient numerous awards from art exhibits. Mem. Soc. Am. Impressionists, Southwestern Watercolor Soc. Avocations: sailing, tennis. Office: Darvas Studio PO Box 711 South Lake Tahoe CA 96156-0711

DASHIELL, G. RONALD, marshal. U.S. marshal U.S. Dist. Ct. (ea. dist.) Wash., Spokane. Office: US Courthouse 920 W Riverside Ave Rm 888 Spokane WA 99201-1010*

DASTAGIR, ZARMINA, English as a second language educator; b. Kabul, Afghanistan, Apr. 27, 1949; came to U.S., 1978; d. Ghulam and Shreen Gul D.; m. Steven Scott Vogt, June 15, 1980; children: Crystal, Alexander, Sophia. BA, Kabul (Afghanistan) U., 1972; MA, U. No. Iowa, 1976. ESL instr. USAID, Kabul, 1973-74; prof. English Kabul U., 1976-78; instr. ESL St. Marys Coll., Moraga, Calif., 1978-80; ESL instr. Cabrillo Coll., Aptos, Calif., 1984—; ESL program dir. Cabrillo Coll., Aptos, 1993-95; ESL instr. USIS, Kabul, 1977-78; adv. bd. U. Calif., Santa Cruz, 1993. Fulbright scholar, 1974-76. Office: Cabrillo Coll English Dept 6500 Soquel Dr Aptos CA 95003-3119

DATLOWE, DAYTON WOOD, space scientist, physicist; b. N.Y.C., Mar. 16, 1942; s. Samuel A. and Marghretta (Wood) D. m. Karen Janine Mc Caffrey, Aug. 3, 1974; children: Nicholas, Elizabeth, Peter. SB in Physics, MIT, 1964; PhD in Physics, U. Chgo., 1970. Scientist U. Calif., San Diego, 1970-76, Lockheed Martin Advanced Tech. Ctr., Palo Alto, Calif., 1976—. Contbr. articles to Jour. Geophys. Rsch., Astrophys. Jour., Solar Physics, Nuclear Instruments and Methods, Geophys. Rsch. Letters. Mem. IEEE, Am. Geophys. Union, Am. Astron. Soc. Achievements include research on X-rays and relativistic electrons from solar flares, electrons in the near-earth space environment, and X-rays from the earth's auroral zone. Office: Lockheed ATC DH111 B252 3251 Hanover St Palo Alto CA 94304-1121

DATTA, PURNA CHANDRA, clinical psychologist, educator; b. Barisal, India, Jan. 1, 1943; came to U.S., 1980; s. Jogendra Kumar and Kanak (Ghosh) D.; m. Anita Rani, Feb. 7, 1969; children: Partha Michael, Aparna Kara. BA in Philosophy with honors, Dacca (Bangladesh) U., 1963, MA in Philosophy, 1964, MA in Psychology, 1967; PhD in Clin. Psychology, Newcastle U., NSW, Australia, 1979, M in Clin. Psychology, 1982. Lic. psychologist, Ga., Calif.; cert. eye movement desensitization reprocessing; diplomate Am. Bd. Forensic Examiners, Am. Bd. Forensic Medicine; diplomate-fellow Prescribing Psychol. Register. Psychologist Morisset (NSW) Hosp., 1974-80, clin. psychologist, 1983-84; psychologist Fairview State Hosp., Costa Mesa, Calif., 1980-83; psychologist Ctrl. State Hosp., Milledgeville, Ga., 1985-86, sr. psychologist, 1989-90; program dir. Gladesville (NSW) Hosp., 1984-85, So. Met. Devel. Disabilities Svc., Gladesville, 1986-88; staff psychologist Stockton (Calif.) Devel. Ctr., 1990-94, O.H. Close Sch. (Calif. Youth Authority), Stockton, 1994—; lectr. psychology Dacca Coll., 1968-69, Dacca U., 1969-73; tutor, demonstrator Newcastle U., 1973-74; lectr. psychiat. nursing Newcastle Tech. Coll., 1974-80; clin. instr. psychiatry U. Calif., Irvine, 1981-83; adj. prof. psychology U. Pacific, Stockton, 1992—; clin. psychologist mental health svcs. Perry Street Cmty. Ctr., Newcastle, 1976-77, 77; clin. psychologist pediatric unit Royal Newcastle Hosp., 1977-78; psychol. asst. Dr. F.M. Crinella, Costa Mesa. 1982-83; presenter in field. Contbr. articles to profl. jours. Talent scholar Commonwealth U. Dacca, 1960-64. Mem. APA, Calif. Psychol. Assn., Am. Assn. Clin. Hypnosis (cert. in hypnotherapy), Am. Coll. Forensic Psychology, Am. Coll. Forensic Examiners, Am. Coll. Forensic Counselors (master addiction counselor). Avocation: moving to different countries and visiting universities. Home: 7221 Shoreham Pl Stockton CA 95207-1224 Office: Behavior Therapy and Counseling Assocs 1652 W Texas St Ste 204 Fairfield CA 94533-5952

DAUGHERTY, KENNETH EARL, research company executive, educator; b. Pitts., Dec. 27, 1938; s. Thomas Hill and Laura Elizabeth (Schuda) D.; B.S. in Chemistry, Carnegie-Mellon U., 1960; Ph.D. in Analytical Chemistry (DuPont, Shell Oil, Standard Oil, NSF fellow), U. Wash., 1964; M. Bus. Econs., Claremont Grad. Sch., 1971; m. Joan Kay Ogrosky, Dec. 22, 1961; children—Brian Earl, Kirsten Kay. Chemist, Marbon Chem.-Borg Warner, Washington, W.Va., 1960; research chemist Rohm and Haas Corp., Bristol, Pa., 1964; group leader, sr. staff Amcord, Riverside, Calif., 1966-71; assoc. prof. chemistry U. Pitts., 1971-73; dir. research and devel. Gen. Portland Inc., Dallas, 1973-77; dir. energy and materials sci. Inst. Applied Scis., North Tex. State U., Denton, 1977-79, prof. chemistry, 1979—, chmn. analytical div., 1980—, pres. KEDS Inc., KD Cons., 1977—; owner TRAC Labs., Denton, 1981—; adj. prof. chemistry U. Pitts., 1973—, N. Tex. State U., Denton, 1974—; adj. faculty Army Command and Gen. Staff Coll., 1983—; cons. in field. Served to col. AUS, 1964-66, Res., 1966—. Decorated Army Commendation medal, Army Achievement medal. Fellow Am. Inst. Chemists; mem. Research Soc. Am., ASTM, Rilem, Nat. (transp. research bd.), N.Y. acads. scis., Am. Ceramic Soc. (program chmn. 1986), Am. Chem. Soc. (chpt. pres. 1960, chmn. Dallas-Ft. Worth 1986), Applied Spectroscopy Soc., Soc. Petroleum Engrs., Soc. Plastics Engrs., Sr. Army Comdrs. Assn., Sigma Xi, Pi Kappa Alpha, Omicron Delta Epsilon, Phi Lambda Upsilon, Alpha Chi Sigma. Republican. Methodist. Clubs: Masons (32 deg.), Shriners, Rotary. Author numerous publs. in field. Patentee in field. Home: 1912 Hunskor Rd Oak Harbor WA 98277-8666

DAVENPORT, ALFRED LARUE, JR., manufacturing company executive, b. Upland, Calif., May 6, 1921; s. Alfred Larue and Nettie (Blocker) D.; m. Darrow Ormsbee Beazlie, May 16, 1950 (div. 1953); m. Jean Ann Given, June 21, 1957 (wid. Apr. 1990); children: Lawrence, Terisa, Lisa, Nancy; m.

Inez Bothwell, Aug. 8, 1993. Student, Chaffey Jr. Coll., Ontario, Calif., 1940; BE in Indsl. Engring., U. So. Calif., 1943. Weight engring. Lockheed Aircraft, Burbank, Calif., 1940-41; ptnr. Pacific Traders, L.A., 1946-48; founder, pres. Pactra Industries, Inc., L.A., 1947-79; owner Davenport Internat., Ltd., Encino, Calif., 1979—; pres., founder Trans Container, Inc., Upland, Calif., 1970-79; pres., owner Pactra Hobby, Inc., Encino, Calif., 1983—, Davenport Export-Import, Inc., Encino, Calif., 1982-93; cons. Plasti-Kote, Inc., Medina, Ohio, 1985-87; pres. Pactra Coatings Inc., Hobby Div., Upland, 1985-89; mgr. craft div. Plasti-Kote Inc., Medina, Ohio, 1989-92; bd. dirs. R.C. Dudek, Inc., Oxnard, Calif.; stockholder, v.p., mktg. dir. Enviroman Inc., 1994-97; dir. mktg. Therap Ease Products, 1996—. Lt. USN, 1943-46. Recipient Blue Key, U. So. Calif., L.A., 1942. Mem. So. Calif. Hobby Industry Assn. (sec. 1959-62), Hobby Industry Assn. Am. (dir. 1961-64), Young Pres. Orgn. (L.A. chpt.), World Bus. Coun. (bd. dirs. 1980-84), Woodland Hills Country Club (treas. 1981-83), Balboa Basin Yacht Club, Travelers Century Club, Sigma Phi Epsilon (v.p. 1954-81, alumni bd. dirs. 1955-75, alumni house bd. dirs. 1997—, Alumni of Yr. award 1975, Disting. Bro. award 1979, Alumni Hall of Fame 1997). Republican. Congregationalist. Avocations: tennis, golf, power yachting. Home: 5330 Dubois Ave Woodland Hills CA 91367-6017 Office: Davenport Internat-Pactra Hobby Prod Inc Therap-Ease Prod 18075 Ventura Blvd Encino CA 91316-3517

DAVENPORT, BRIAN LYNN, lawyer; b. Spokane, Wash., June 11, 1947; s. Frank Joseph Davenport and Tolosa Ann (Wilson) Cartinella; m. Betty Jean Callahan, June 18, 1978; children: David, Bradley, Scott. BA, U. Nev., Reno, 1970; JD, Gonzaga U., 1976. Bar: Nev. 1976, U.S. Dist. Ct. Nev., 1977. Assoc. Echeverria & Osborne, Reno, Nev., 1976-78; lawyer pvt. practice, Reno, 1978-81; counsel First Interstate Bank, Reno, 1981-84; lawyer pvt. practice, Reno, 1984—; adj. prof. Old Coll. Sch. of Law, Reno, 1985-87; outside legal advisor to associated students U. Nev., Reno, 1987—. Mem. Phi Alpha Theta, Phi Kappa Phi, Pi Sigma Alpha. Avocations: camping, boating, reading, skiing, travel. Office: 458 Court St Reno NV 89501-1709

DAVENPORT, JANET LEE, real estate saleswomen, small business owner; b. Napa, Calif., Dec. 10, 1938; d. George Perry and Stella Dolores (Ramalho) Gomez; m. Bingo George Wesner, Aug. 4, 1957 (July 1978); children: Bing George, Diane Estelle; m. Marvin Eugene Davenport, Jan. 13, 1979. Student, U. Calif., Davis, 1956-57, Nat. Jud. Coll., 1975-79. Co-owner, operator Bar JB Ranch, Benicia, Calif., 1960-71, Lovelock, Nev., 1971-78; owner, mgr. Wesner Bookkeeping Svc., Lovelock, 1973-78; chief tribal judge Ct. Indian Offenses, Lovelock, 1975-79; justice of peace, coroner County of Pershing, Lovelock, 1975-79; paralegal, legal sec. Samuel S. Wardle, Carson City, Nev., 1979; dep. ct. adminstr. Reno Mcpl. Ct., Reno, 1979-81; co-owner horse farm Reno, 1979—, freelance real estate investor, 1979—; real estate saleswoman Merrill Lynch Realtors, Sparks, Nev., 1981-82; realtor, farm and ranch div. mgr. Copple and Assocs., Realtors, Sparks, 1982-91; real estate saleswoman Vail and Assocs. Realty, Reno, Nev., 1991—; co-owner, operator Lovelock (Nev.) Merc. Co., 1988—; sec. Nev. Judges Assn., 1977-78. Dir. Pershing County Drug and Alcohol Abuse Council, Lovelock, 1976-78. Mem. Reno/Sparks Bd. Realtors, Nat. Assn. Realtors, Nev. Assn. Realtors, Am. Quarter Horse Assn. Republican. Roman Catholic. Home: 4805 Sinelio Dr Reno NV 89502-9510 Office: Vail and Assocs Realty 1700 S Virginia St Reno NV 89502-2811

DAVENPORT, ROGER LEE, research engineer; b. Sacramento, Calif., Oct. 27, 1955; s. Lee Edwin and Ada Fern (Henderson) D.; m. Cynthia Ann Carle, June 20, 1998. AB Physics, U. Calif., Berkeley, 1977; MSME, U. Ariz., 1979. Assoc. engr. Solar Energy Rsch. Inst., Golden, Colo., 1979-82, cons. Darmstadt, Fed. Republic Germany, 1982-84; missionary Eastern European Sem., Vienna, Austria, 1984-87; staff researcher Sci. Applications Internat. Corp., San Diego, 1987—. Mem. Am. Solar Energy Soc., Denver Electric Vehicle Coun., Sierra Club, Colo. Mountain Club, Phi Beta Kappa. Home: 19076 W 59th Dr Golden CO 80403-1057 Office: SAIC 15874 W 6th Ave Golden CO 80401-5047

DAVEY, GERARD PAUL, lawyer; b. Alton, Ill., May 31, 1949; s. Paul D. and Mary G. (O'Neill) D.; m. Martha Ann Florus, Aug. 13, 1977; children: Brian, Matthew, Kelly, Laura. BS, U. Ill., 1971; JD, U. Houston, 1974, MBA, Golden Gate U., 1982. Bar: Tex. 1974, Calif. 1977, U.S. Supreme Ct. 1978, U.S. Ct. Appeals (5th cir.) 1975, (9th cir.) 1978, U.S. Dist. Ct. (so. dist.) Tex. 1975, U.S. Dist. Ct. (cen. dist.) Calif. 1978, U.S. Dist. Ct. (so. dist.) Calif. 1988. Sec., counsel SW Group Fin., Houston, 1974-77; sole practice, Newport Beach, Calif., 1977-78; v.p., corp. counsel Century 21 Real Estate, Irvine, Calif., 1978-81, also sec., dir. all subsidiaries, 1980-81; prin. Davey Law Corp., Newport Beach, 1981-87; ptnr. Hatter & Davey, Attys., 1987—; lectr. Calif. Continuing Edn. of Bar. Author: Texas Law Institute of Coastal and Marine Resources, 1974; Contbr. articles to profl. jours. Bd. dirs. South Coast Symphony, Costa Mesa, Calif., 1984. Ill. Gen. Assembly scholar U. Ill., 1967-71. Mem. ABA (forum com. on franchising 1980—), Calif. Bar Assn. (franchising legis. com. 1983-86), Tex. Bar Assn., U. Houston Legal Hon. Soc., Kiwanis (Irvine).

DAVI, MARIA S.C., artist, educator; b. El Paso, Tex., Sept. 3, 1947; d. Horace D. and Ana C. Davi. Cert., Contra Costa Coll.; BS in Chemistry, IDSC; cert., N. Inst. Am., N.Y.C.; MA in Interior Design, IDV. Art tchr. City of Hercules, Calif.; co-owner D.L.E. Assocs., Pinole, Calif.; art tchr. City of San Pablo, Calif., C.C. County, Montara Bay Comty. Ctr.; art tchr. Concord (Calif.) Unified Sch. Dist.; juror Richmond Sch. Dist. Art Exhbns., Richmond Mus. Exhibited in group shows Agora Gallery, ART EXPO, Jacob Javitz Ctr., Graham Horstman Galleries, U. Tex., Capitol, Fed. Savs. Bank, Calif.; works featured in publs. including Manhattan Arts Internat., Ency. of Living Artists of Am., Art of Calif. Mag. Recipient Bronze award Discovery Award, Art of Calif. Mag., Cert. of Excellence, Soho Internat. Art Competition, Cert. of Achievement Art of Calif. Mag., Congratulations letter City of Hercules, Congratulations letter Mt. Diablo Unified Sch. Dist. Democrat. Roman Catholic. Avocations: astronomy, geology, photography, china painting, watercolor. Home: 2695 Moraga Dr Pinole CA 94564-1238 Office: Davi Labs Environ 701B Belmont Way Pinole CA 94564-2661

DAVID, SHIRLEY HART, law librarian; b. Camp Lejeune, N.C., Oct. 21, 1949; d. Allen Lewis Hart and Florence Marie (Novak) Rainey; m. Donald John David, June 18, 1971. BA in LS and Polit. Sci., Coll. of St. Catherine, St. Paul, 1971. Librarian Minn. State Law Library, St. Paul, 1971-83; dir. Sacramento County Law Library, Sacramento, 1983—, sec. found., 1986—; del. White Ho. Conf. on Librs. and Info. Svcs., 1990. Recipient Liberty Bell award Sacramento County Bar Assn., 1985. Mem. Am. Assn. Law Librs. (sec.-treas. state ct. and county spl. interest sect. 1988-89, v.p., pres.elect 1998-99, exec. bd. 1990-93), Coun. Calif. County Law Librs. (v.p. 1984-86, pres. 1986-88), No. Calif. Assn. Law Librs. (v.p. 1987-88, pres. 1988-89, bd. dirs. 1989-90), Calif. Fedn. Bus. and Profl. Women, Downtown Capitol Local Orgn. (legis. chair 1985-92). Avocations: sailing, traveling, reading. Office: Sacramento County Law Libr 720 9th St Rm L6 Sacramento CA 95814-1311

DAVIDOW, JENNY JEAN, counselor, writer; b. Santa Monica, Calif., Mar. 25, 1953; d. Ray M. Davidow and Caroline D. (Kos) Lackmann; m. Bret S. Lyon, June 10, 1988. BA, UCLA, 1974; MA, Internat. Coll., Santa Monica, 1981; D Clin. Hypnotherapy, Am. Inst. Hypnotherapy, Irvine, Calif., 1994. Cert. clin. hypnotherapist. Pvt. practice L.A., 1981-92, Santa Cruz, Calif., 1992—; seminar leader, L.A., 1981-92, Santa Cruz, 1992—; bd. dirs. Tidal Wave Press, Santa Cruz; featured guest various TV and radio shows, L.A., 1983-88; spkr. Whole Life Expo, L.A., 1983-87; mem. Am. Bd. Hypnotherapy, 1989—. Author: Dream Therapy Workbook, 1983, Embracing Your Subconscious, 1996, Corners of the Soul, 1998; contbr. articles to various publs.; creator, presenter audiotape collection Comfortable and Capable, 1994. Mem. Assn. for Humanistic Psychology, Found. for Shamanic Studies, Focusing Inst., World Wildlife Fund (ptnr. in conservation 1995), Sierra Club (life). Democrat. Avocations: photography, gardening.

DAVIDSON, BILL (WILLIAM JOHN DAVIDSON), entertainment journalist, author; b. Jersey City, Mar. 4, 1918; s. Louis J. and Gertrude (Platt) D.; m. Muriel Roberts, May 21, 1960 (dec. Sept. 1983); 1 child, Carol; m. Maralynne Beth Nitz, July 27, 1986. BA, NYU, 1939. Assoc. editor Collier's mag., N.Y.C., 1946-56; contbg. editor Look mag., N.Y.C., 1956-61; editor-at-large Saturday Evening Post, N.Y.C., 1961-69; radio commentator NBC, N.Y.C., 1968-71; TV writer Universal Studios, Universal City, Calif., 1971-76; contbg. editor TV Guide, Radnor, Pa., 1971-90, L.A. Mag., 1992-95; chmn. alumni communications com. NYU, 1959-64; freelance writer, 1992—. Author: The Real and the Unreal, Six Brave Presidents, 1962, Indict and Convict, 1971, (with Sid Caesar) Where Have I Been?, 1982, Spencer Tracy: Tragic Idol, 1988, Jane Fonda: An Intimate Biography, 1990, (with Danny Thomas) Make Room for Daddy, 1991. Mem. N.Y. County Dem. com., N.Y.C., 1948-50. Served as sgt. U.S. Army, 1941-45, ETO. Recipient Disting. Reporting award Sigma Delta Chi, 1951, 53, Albert Lasker Med. Journalism award, 1953, Disting. Journalism award Family Service Assn. Am., 1963. Mem. Writers Guild Am. West. Democrat. Home: 13225 Morrison St Sherman Oaks CA 91423-2156

DAVIDSON, GORDON, theatrical producer, director; b. Bklyn., May 7, 1933; s. Joseph H. and Alice (Gordon) D.; m. Judith Swiller, Sept. 21, 1958; children: Adam, Rachel. B.A., Cornell U.; M.A., Case Western Res. U.; L.H.D. (hon.), Bklyn. Coll.; D. Performing Arts (hon.), Calif. Inst. Arts; D.F.A. (hon.), Claremont U. Ctr. Stage mgr. Phoenix Theatre Co., 1958-60, Am. Shakespeare Festival Theatre, 1958-60, Dallas Civic Opera, 1960-61, Martha Graham Dance Co., 1962; mng. dir. Theatre Group at UCLA, 1965-67; artistic dir., producer Center Theatre Group Mark Taper Forum, 1967—; co-founder New Theatre For Now, Mark Taper Forum, 1970; Past mem. theatre panel Nat. Endowment for Arts; past pres. Theatre Communications Group; mem. adv. council Internat. Theatre Inst.; mem. adv. com. Cornell Ctr. for Performing Arts; cons. Denver Center for the Performing Arts; bd. dirs. several arts orgns. including Am. Arts Alliance. Producer, dir. over 150 major theatrical prodns. including The Deputy, 1965, Candide, 1966, The Devils, 1967, Who's Happy Now, 1967, In the Matter of J. Robert Oppenheimer, 1968 (N.Y. Drama Desk award), Sew, Murderous Angels, 1970, Rosebloom, 1970, The Trial of the Catonsville Nine, 1971 (Obie award, Tony award nomination), Henry IV, Part I, 1972, Mass, 1973, Hamlet, 1974, Savages, 1974 (Obie award), Too Much Johnson, 1975, The Shadow Box, 1975 (Tony award, Outer Critics Circle Best Dir. award), And Where She Stops Nobody Knows, 1976, Getting Out, 1977, Black Angel, 1978, Terra Nova, 1979, Children of a Lesser God, 1979, The Lady and the Clarinet, 1980, Chekhov in Yalta, 1981, Tales from Hollywood, 1982, The American Clock, 1984, The Hands of Its Enemy, 1984, Traveler in the Dark, 1985, The Real Thing, 1986, Ghetto, 1986, A Lie of the Mind, 1988; dir. operas including Cosi Fan Tutte, Otello, Beatrice and Benedick, Carmen, La Boheme, Il Trovatore, Harriet, A Woman Called Moses, A Midsummer Night's Dream, 1988; TV film The Trial of the Catonsville Nine, 1971; exec. producer Zoot Suit, 1981; producer for TV It's the Willingness, PBS Visions Series, 1979, Who's Happy Now?, NET Theatre in Am. Series; dir. A Little Night Music, 1990. Trustee Ctr. for Music, Drama and Art; past pres. League Resident Theatres; past v.p. Am. Nat. Theatre Acad; advisor Fund for New Am. Plays. Recipient N.Y. Drama Desk award for direction, 1969; recipient Los Angeles Drama Critics Circle awards for direction, 1971, 74, 75, Margo Jones award New Theatre for Now, 1970, 76, Obie award, 1971, 77, Outer Critics Circle award, 1977, Tony award for direction, 1977, award John Harvard, award Nat. Acad. TV Arts and Scis., award Nosotros Golden Eagle, award N.Y. League for Hard of Hearing, award N.Y. Speech and Hearing Assn., award Am. Theatre Assn., award Los Angeles Human Relations Commn.; Guggenheim fellow, 1983. Mem. League Resident Theatres (past pres.), ANTA (v.p. 1975). Office: Ctr Theatre Group Mark Taper Forum 135 N Grand Ave Los Angeles CA 90012-3013*

DAVIDSON, HELEN GEORGETTE, author; b. Boylis Mill or Warsaw, Mo., Nov. 19, 1924; d. John Henry and Arette Alice (Bauchaud) Bishop; m. 1945 (div. 1954); 1 child, Suzanne Helene Crowell; m. Carl Davidson, Mar. 7, 1956 (div. Nov., 1983). Grad. h.s., Warsaw, Mo. Sec. Paramount Movers, Dallas, Tex., 1970-85. Author, publisher: (book) The Man in a Country Boy, 1996. Democrat. Avocations: gourmet cooking, dressmaking, golf, home decorating, gardening. Home: 606 Shenandoah Ave San Marcos CA 92069-7918

DAVIDSON, JOHN KEAY, IV, writer; b. Columbus, Ga., May 11, 1953; s. John Keay III and Bebe (Coney) D. BA in History, Emory U., 1975. Reporter Orlando (Fla.) Sentinel-Star, 1976-78, sci. writer, 1979-81, sci. writer L.A. Times/San Diego Bur., 1981-85, San Francisco Examiner, 1986—. Author: Twister, 1996; co-author: Wrinkles in Time, 1993. Recipient Westinghouse award AAAS, 1987, Responsibility in Journalism award Com. for Sci. Investigation of Claims of Paranormal, 1991, Sci.-in-Soc. award Nat. Assn. Sci. Writers, 1994. Office: San Francisco Examiner 110 5th St San Francisco CA 94103-2918

DAVIDSON, JOHN ROBERT (JAY), banking executive; b. L.A., Mar. 30, 1950; s. John Robert Davidson and Carolyn Rose Monson; m. Kristina Maria Jonson, Dec. 29, 1978; children: Joshua Kingsley, Michelle Maria. BSME, U. N.D., 1972; postgrad., AMP Corp. Leadership Coll., 1990. Engr. Dow Chem. Co., Pauls Valley, Okla., 1972-74; investor Mpls., 1974-77; account exec. AMP Inc., Boulder, Colo., 1977-83; mkt. mgr. AMP Inc., Harrisburg, Pa., 1983-86; dist. mgr. AMP Inc., Denver, 1986-90, nat. mgr., 1990-95; chmn. of bd., CEO 1st Am. State Bank of Denver, 1995—; dir./cons. Am. State Bank, Williston, N.D., 1988—, dir. funds mgmt. com., 1994—, dir. exec. com., 1996—; mem. exec. com., chmn. bd. dirs. First Am. State Bank, Denver, 1995—. Supporter Am. Heart Assn., Colo., Kempe Children's Found., Arapahoe Home, Colo. Easter Seals, F.A.C.E.S., Colo. Symphony Orch., Vols. of Am., Boy Scouts Am., Children's Hosp., Arthritis Found.; bd. dirs. Kempe Children's Found., mem. fin. com. and funds mgmt. com.; mem. Rep. Nat. Com.; mem. devel. bd. Am. Heart Assn., bd. devel. com.; event co-chairperson Arapahoe House, Easter Seals Colo., bd. dirs. Recipient Presdl. Legion of Merit, Colo. Rep. Party. Mem. Masons, Presdl. Legion of Merit. Avocations: snow skiing, mountain biking, photography, computers, music. Home: 5780 S Goldsmith Pl Englewood CO 80111 Office: 1st Am State Bank 8390 E Crescent Pkwy Greenwood Village CO 80111

DAVIDSON, JULI, creativity consultant; b. Houston, Aug. 23, 1960; d. Martin J. Davidson and Ruth Marder. Diploma, Park Sch., Brooklandville, Md., 1978; Cert., Richmond Coll., Surrey, Eng., 1978; student, Austin Coll., U. N.Mex, others, 1978-84, Hollywood Film Inst., 1996. Cert. med. terminology and transcription, 1981. Pres. mail order co. Surrenderings, Inc., Albuquerque, 1989-93; owner, artist Juli Davidson Studio Gallery, Albuquerque, 1987-89; freelance writer, editor, photographer Albuquerque, 1985-86; pres., paper artist, writer SI: A Paperworks Gallery, Sante Fe, 1993; exec. adminstr. Albuquerque Art Bus. Assn., 1989; bd. sec. Albuquerque United Artists, 1988; media, entertainment, and multimedia creativity cons. Author: Organic Plant Care: Root Division, 1998; editor, pub. 2C3P ZN, 1995; contbr. to various publs. and subject of various art revs.; writer, pub. mail-order publs., 1995; pub. creativity products for The Creative Process; screenplay and teleplay contest critic Southwest Writers Workshop, 1996; mkt. rsch. theatrical film reviewer, Audience Response, 1995; sitcom bible and pilot writer Think Tank Ink Prods, 1995; author screenplay Rockinghorse (shown at N.Y. Internat. Ind. Film and Video Festival 1998). Recipient 2d and 3d place photography awards Churches in New Mexico Exhibit, 1985, 4th place Colorfest Human Interest Category, Colo., 1986; recipient writing award Garden Writers Assn. of Am., 1993, for publishing handmade booklet on dividing and multiplying potted plants. Studio: PO Box 21669-WW Albuquerque NM 87154-1669

DAVIDSON, LEROY, musician; b. Oceanside, Calif., Oct. 29; s. David and Alice Louise (Story) D. AA, Mira Costa Coll., 1960-62; M, Mildred Alexander Method of Organ Mastery, Oceanside, 1964. Dir. edn. Mildred Alexander Methods, Inc., Oceanside, 1964—; staff musician Sea World, San Diego, 1966-68; staff writer Hurdy Gurdy mag., Mpls., 1973—; arranger Columbia Pictures Publs., Hialeah, Fla., 1975-80; concert organist Hammond Organ Co., Chgo., 1976-78; performing artist, workshop clinician Technics Mus. Instruments.

DAVIDSON, MARK, writer, educator; b. N.Y.C., Sept. 25, 1938; m. Elizabeth Browne, May 29, 1989. BA in Polit. Sci., UCLA, 1958; MS in Journalism, Columbia U., 1960. Sci. writer U. So. Calif., L.A., 1980-90; prof. comm. Calif. State U., Dominguez Hills, Carson, 1985-99; freelance writer; faculty adviser Soc. Profl. Journalists, 1993-96; lectr. in field; writer for Steve Allen Show, 1964, Dinah Shore Show, 1978, CBS Mag. Show with Connie Chung, 1980. Author: Uncommon Sense, 1984, Invisible Chains of Thought Control, 1999 (Nat. Emmy for writing NATAS), Watchwords: A Dictionary of American English Usage, 1999. Sackett scholar Columbia U. Mem. PEN, Am. Soc. Journalists and Authors, Nat. Assn. Sci. Writers, Am. Med. Writers Assn., Authors Guild, Writers Guild Am., Calif. Faculty Assn. (v.p. Dominguez Hills chpt. 1992-96), Soc. Advancement Edn. (assoc. mass media editor 1997—).

DAVIDSON, MELODY KAY, critical care nurse, educator; b. Carson City, Mich., Nov. 8, 1952; d. Donald Jay and Joan Estelle (Schweitzer) D. Vocat. nurse, Vocat. Nursing Sch. of So. Calif., L.A., 1971; ADN, U. State N.Y., Albany, 1981; BSN, Calif. Lutheran U., 1986; M in Nursing, U. Calif., L.A., 1988. CCRN. Staff nurse St Joseph Hosp., Orange, Calif., 1971-81, U. Calif. Med. Ctr., L.A., 1981, Valley Presbyterian Hosp., Van Nuys, Calif., 1981-88; clin. nurse specialist St. Joseph Med. Ctr., Burbank, Calif., 1988-89; clin. instr. Northridge (Calif.) Hosp. Med. Ctr., 1989-92; assoc. clin. prof. U. Calif., L.A., 1989—; clin. edn. specialist Hosp. of the Good Samaritan, L.A., 1992-93; clin. nurse specialist Doctors Med. Ctr., Modesto, Calif., 1993-95; program devel. specialist Am. Assn. Critical Care Nurses, Aliso Viejo, Calif., 1996—. Mem. AACN San Fernando Valley Chpt. (v.p. elect 1988-89, v.p. 1989-90, pres. elect 1992-93), Calif. Nurses Assn. Region 3 (treas. 1985-86, mem.-at-large 1984-85). Avocations: needlework, reading, travel, plays. Home: 28 Pappagallo Pt Aliso Viejo CA 92656-1376

DAVIDSON, PETER ROBERTSON, JR., art director, illustrator; b. San Rafael, Calif., Mar. 30, 1958; s. Peter R. Sr. and Helen Audrey (Alexander) D. BFA, Antioch U., 1982; MFA, NYU, 1991. Mus. exhibit asst. Nat. Park Svc., Interpretive Design Ctr., Harper's Ferry, W.Va., 1977; design intern The Architects Collaborative, Inc., Cambridge, Mass., 1980-81; principle Peter Davidson Design, Boston, 1982-91; asst. art dir. P.C. Comm. Spot, Manchester, N.H., 1992; art dir. Reunion Prodns., Watertown, Mass., 1993, Brown Prodns., Boston, 1993; set designer Witt Thomas Prodns., Hollywood, Calif., 1995; set designer Mrs. Santa Claus Hallmark Entertainment, Universal City, Calif., 1996; set designer Star Trek Voyager Paramount Pictures, L.A., 1996; set design cons. Disney Imagineering, Glendale, Calif., 1996; co-instr., lectr. Hollywood Hands on Union-Digital Tng. Ctr., North Hollywood, 1995-96; guest designer, panelist Calif. Art Coun. Annual Govs. Conf., L.A., 1996; seminar motivator digital techniques for film/TV art dept. Am. Film Inst., L.A., 1997, 98. set designer: The Silicon Wars HBO TV, L.A., 1997; digital set designer: The Pretender NBC TV, Burbank, Calif., 1977. Recipient Best Expression of the Medium of Set Design in Advt. award Worksource Pub., Cambridge, Mass., 1989. Mem. Internat. Alliance Theatrical and Stage Employees (Hollywood and New Eng. locals), L.A. MacIntosh Fine Art (artist), Digirati Digital Guild (designer). Home: 2525 Main St Ste 108 Santa Monica CA 90405-3538 Office: Peter Davidson Prodn Design 2525 Main St Ste 108 Santa Monica CA 90405-3538

DAVIES, HARRIETT MARIE (LOLLY DAVIES), secondary education educator; b. Chgo., July 2, 1942; d. Howard Jack and Mamie Marie (Harriett) Cox; m. Ronald Lee Davies, Mar. 22, 1975. BS in Home Econs., So. Ill. U., 1965, MS in Edn., 1973. Tchg. cert. in home econs., bus., mktg., Coop. Office Edn., Ariz. Home econs. tchr. Hanover (Ill.) H.S., 1965; home econs., health tchr., home econ. dept. head Sholes Jr. H.S., Milw., 1965-67; vocat. home econs., consumer edn. tchr. Roxana (Ill.) H.S., 1967-78; bus. instr. Lamson Bus. Coll., Tucson, Ariz., 1981-83; legal secretarial instr. Tucson Coll. Bus., 1983-84; instr. Portable Practical Edn. Preparation, Casa Grande, Ariz., 1984-85; tchr. bus. and hotel/restaurant mgmt., travel and tourism Casa Grande Union High Sch., 1985—; conv. coord. Ill. Consumer Edn. Assn., Springfield, Ill., 1973-75, v.p., 1975; spl. consumer cons. Ill. Office Edn., Springfield, 1975-78; mem. family fin. regional coun. Ind. State U., Terre Haute, Ind., 1973-75; coord. Sch.-Within-a-Sch., 1989-90. Food coord. C. of C. Golf Tourney, Casa Grande, 1993. Mem. NEA (life), Ariz. Edn. Assn., Ariz. Vocat. Assn., Casa Grande Edn. Assn. Avocations: reading, hunting, golf, travel. Home: 339 E Orange Dr Casa Grande AZ 85222-4043 Office: Casa Grande Union HS 2370 N Trekell Rd Casa Grande AZ 85222

DAVIES, KENT RICHARD, writer; b. Burns, Oreg., May 12, 1947; s. Richard Griffith and Dorothy Agnes (Buor) D.; m. D. Sharon Hill, Nov. 30, 1974. BA in Bus. Adminstrn., Seattle U., 1970; MBA, Pacific Luth. U., 1980. Econ. devel. specialist Cayuga County Action Program, Auburn, N.Y., 1971-73; vol. program mgr. King County Youth Svcs., Seattle, 1974-79; writer Anacortes, Wash.; adj. prof. U. Puget Sound, Seattle, 1980-84, Ctrl. Wash. U., Lynnwood, 1984-89. Contbr. articles to publs. VISTA vol. Office of Econ. Opportunity, N.Y.C.' mem. Leadership Tomorrow, Seattle, 1970-71; bd. dirs. Wash. Coalition of Citizens Disabilities, Seattle, 1983-84; appointee Gov.'s Com. on Disability, Olympia, Wash., 1982-88. Home: PO Box 458 La Conner WA 98257

DAVIES, MERTON EDWARD, planetary scientist; b. St. Paul, Sept. 13, 1917; s. Albert Daniel and Lucile (McCabe) D.; AB, Stanford, 1938, postgrad., 1938-39; m. Margaret Louise Darling, Feb. 10, 1946; children: Deidra Louise Stauff, Albert Karl, Merton Randel. Instr. math. U. Nev., 1939-40; group leader Math. Lofting, Douglas Aircraft Co., El Segundo, Calif., 1940-48; sr. staff Rand Corp., Santa Monica, Calif., 1948-59, 62—, liaison USAF, Washington, 1959-62. U.S. observer inspected stas. under terms Antarctic Treaty, 1967; TV co-investigator Mariner Mars, 1969, 71, Mariner Venus/Mercury 1973 Mission, Voyager Mission, Galileo Mission, Magellan Mission, Mars Observer Mission, Clementine Mission, Mars Global Surveyor Mission. Fellow AIAA (assoc.); mem. AAAS, Am. Soc. Photogrammetry. Author: (with Bruce Murray) The View from Space, 1971; (with others) Atlas of Mercury, 1978. Patentee in field. Home: 1414 San Remo Dr Pacific Palisades CA 90272-2737 Office: Rand Corp 1700 Main St Santa Monica CA 90401-3297

DAVIES, PAUL LEWIS, JR., retired lawyer; b. San Jose, Calif., July 21, 1930; s. Paul Lewis and Faith (Crummey) D.; m. Barbara Bechtel, Dec. 22, 1955; children: Laura (Mrs. Segundo Mateo), Paul Lewis III. AB, Stanford U., 1952; JD, Harvard U., 1957. Bar: Calif. 1957. Assoc. Pillsbury, Madison & Sutro, San Francisco, 1957-63, ptnr., 1963-89; gen. counsel Chevron Corp., 1984-89; bd. dirs. FMC Corp. Hon. trustee Calif. Acad. Scis., trustee, 1970-83, chmn., 1973-80; pres. Herbert Hoover Found.; bd. overseers Hoover Instn., chmn., 1976-82, 91-93; hon. regent U. of Pacific, regent, 1959-90. Lt. U.S. Army, 1952-54. Mem. Bohemian Club, Pacific-Union Club, Villa Taverna, World Trade Club (San Francisco), Claremont Country Club, Lakeview (Oakland, Calif.), Cypress Point (Pebble Beach, Calif.), Sainte Claire (San Jose, Calif.), Collectors, Explorers, Links (N.Y.C.), Met. Club, Chgo. Club, Phi Beta Kappa, Pi Sigma Alpha. Republican. Office: 50 Fremont St Ste 3520 San Francisco CA 94105-2239

DAVIES, THOMAS MOCKETT, JR., history educator; b. Lincoln, Nebr., May 25, 1940; s. Thomas Mockett and Faith Elizabeth (Arnold) D.; m. Eloisa Carmela Monzón Abate, June 10, 1968 (dec. Jan. 1994); 1 dau., Jennifer Elena; m. Rosemarie Adele Lindsay, Jan. 7, 1995. BA, U. Nebr., 1962, MA, 1964; student, Universidad Nacional Autonóma de México, 1961; PhD, U. N.Mex., 1970; postdoctoral fellow, U. Tex., Austin, 1969-70. Lectr. U. N.Mex. Peace Corps Tng. Center, 1964-66; asst. prof. Latin Am. history San Diego State U., 1968-72, asso. prof., 1972-75, prof., 1975—, chmn. Latin Am. studies, 1979—; dir. Center Latin Am. Studies, Henry L. and Grace Doherty Charitable Found. fellow, 1966-68. Author: (with others) Historia, problema y promesa. Homenaje a Jorge Basadre, 1978, Research Guide to Andean History: Bolivia, Chile, Ecuador and Peru, 1981, The Spanish Civil War: American Hemisphere Perspectives, 1982, EL APRA de la Ideología a la Praxis, 1989, Latin American Military History: An Annotated Bibliography, 1992; author: Indian Integration in Peru: A Half Century of Experience, 1900-48, 1974 (co-winner Hubert Herring Meml. award Pacific Coast Coun. on Latin Am. Studies 1973), (with Victor Villaneuva) 300 Documentos Para la Historia del APRA; Conspiraciones Apristas de 1935 a 1939, 1979, Secretos Electorales del APRA: Correspondencia y Documentos de 1939, 1982; (with Brian Loveman) The Politics of Anti-Politics: The Military in Latin America, 1978, 3d rev. edit., 1997, Che Guevara: Guerrilla Warfare, 1985 (Hubert Herring Meml. award 1985, 3d rev. edit., 1997); mem. editorial bd. Hispanic Am. Hist. Rev., 1985-1990; Contbr. (with Brian Loveman) articles to profl. jours. Recipient Outstanding Faculty award San

Diego State U. Alumni Assn., 1981-97, 1st ann. Internat. Scholar award Phi Beta Delta, 1992, Wiley W. Manuel award Calif. State Bar Assn., 1995, 98; grantee Dept. Edn. for Nat. Resource Ctr. for L.Am. Studies, 1979—; summer rsch. grantee San Diego State U. Found., 1971-73, 75, 76, 79, 80, faculty rsch. devel. grantee San Diego State U., 1988, 89, 90. Mem. Latin Am. Studies Assn., Conf. Latin Am. History (exec. sec. 1979-84), Pacific Coast Council Latin Am. (bd. govs. 1989-91, pres. 1996-97), Rocky Mountain Council on Latin Am. Studies (exec. com. 1980—, pres. 1996-97), Am. Hist. Assn., Consortium L.Am. Studies Programs (exec. sec.-treas. 1994—). Home: 4617 Edenvale Ave La Mesa CA 91941-5508 Office: San Diego State U Dept History San Diego CA 92182

DAVIES, WILLIAM RALPH, service executive; b. Santa Barbara, Calif., Aug. 17, 1955; s. Ralph Emmett and Georgann Marie (Cordingly) D.; m. Karen L. Blake, May 12, 1984 (div. 1999). AA in Real Estate, Am. River Coll., 1978; BS in Fin., Ins. and Real Estate, Calif. State U., Sacramento, 1980; postgrad. in Internat. Bus., Golden Gate U., 1982-84. Real estate assoc. Kiernan Realtors, Sacramento, 1975-77; co-owner real estate firm Sacramento, 1977, pvt. practice real estate cons., property mgr., 1978-80; broker assoc. MBA Bus. Brokers, Sacramento, 1980-85, pres., 1985—; pres. WRD Cons. Group, Sacramento, 1984—; bd. dirs. WRD, Inc., Sacramento. Mem. Assisted Living Fedn., Calif. Assisted Living Facilities Assn. (bd. dirs.). Republican. Avocations: history, bridge, golf. Office: 895 Embarcadero Dr Ste 203 El Dorado Hills CA 95762

DAVILA, WILLIAM, music educator. BA, Calif. State Polytechnic U., 1976; MMus in Guitar/Lute Performance, Calif. State U., L.A., 1981. Master class prof., performer Inst. Nat. de Bellas Artes: Escuela Superior De Musica, Mexico, 1983; freelance performer worldwide concerts at univs. and music ctrs., 1972—; prodr., host, engr. KPFK-FM Radio, L.A., 1981—; music cons. and rschrs. Pantechnicon, L.A., 1985-86; lectr. L.A. Harbor Coll., Wilmington, Calif., 1981-93, Calif. State U., L.A., 1983-85, Coll. of the Desert, Palm Desert, Calif., 1983-89, Rio Hondo Coll., Whittier, Calif., 1980—, Calif. State U., Dominquez Hills, 1983—, Palo Verde Coll., Blythe, Calif., 1993—. Concert guitarist: Davila in Concert, Spirit Windows. Recipient award Ingolf Dahl Competition. Office: PO Box 3359 Idyllwild CA 92549-3359

DAVIS, ALAN MARK, software engineering educator; b. Bklyn., Jan. 6, 1949; s. Barney and Hannah (Slobodow) D.; m. Virginia Susan Zachary, Nov. 1876; children: Marsha Sydney, Michael Zachary. BS in Math., SUNY, Albany, 1970; MS in Computer Sci., U. Ill., 1973, PhD, 1975. Asst. prof. computer sci. U. Tenn., Knoxville, 1975-77; mem. tech. staff GTE Labs., Waltham, Mass., 1977-78; mgr. software engring. dept. GTE Labs., Waltham, 1978-87, dir. software tech. ctr., 1981-83; dir. R&D GTE Comm. Systems, Phoenix, 1983-84; v.p. BTG, Inc., Vienna, Va., 1984-88; acting chair computer sci. dept. George Mason U., Fairfax, Va., 1990-91, prof. info. and software engring., 1990-91; El Pomar prof. software engring. U. Colo., Colorado Springs, 1991—; sole propr. Davis Co., Colorado Springs, 1991-95; bd. dirs. Requisite, Inc., Boulder. Author: Software Requirements, 1993, 201 Principles of Software Development, 1995; assoc. editor Jour. Systems and Software, 1987—. Bd. dirs. Colorado Springs Symphony Orch., 1992—. Fellow IEEE (editor-in-chief IEEE Software, 1991—, cert. appreciation Computer Soc., 1984); mem. Assn. Computing Machinery (recognition svc. award 1990, 92, assoc. editor Comm. ACM, 1981-91), Armed Forces Comm. and Elect. Assn., Sigma Xi. Office: U Colo 1867 Austin Bluffs Pkwy Colorado Springs CO 80918-7864

DAVIS, ALBERT RAYMOND, English language educator; b. Kansas City, Aug. 30, 1943; s. John Henry and Marsoleat E. (Minuette) D.; m. Rachel E., Feb. 14, 1971; children: Angelique Marie, Aaron Lee. BA in English/German, U. Mo., 1970; MA in Edn., Pacific Luth. U., 1972. Tchr. Tacoma Pub. Schs., 1970—; tchr. curriculum devel. Evergreen Coll., Tacoma, 1994-98; tchr., mentor Mesa, Tacoma, 1982-83; television instr. Tacoma Pub. Schs., 1984-91. Co-author: (test accreditation manual) Helping Students Achieve, 1986. With U.S. Army, 1962-65. Recipient Mesa Instr. award, 1984. Avocations: gardening, exercising, reading, volunteering. Office: Wilson HS 1202 N Orchard St Tacoma WA 98406-3299

DAVIS, ALLEN, professional football team executive; b. Brockton, Mass., July 4, 1929; s. Louis and Rose (Kirschenbaum) D.; m. Carol Segall, July 11, 1954; 1 son, Mark. Student, Wittenberg Coll., 1947; A.B., Syracuse U., 1950. Asst. football coach Adelphi Coll., 1950-51; head football coach Ft. Belvoir, Va., 1952-53; player-personnel scout Baltimore Colts, 1954; line coach The Citadel, 1955-56, U. So. Calif., 1957-59; asst. coach San Diego Chargers, 1960-62; gen. mgr., head coach Oakland Raiders (now Los Angeles Raiders), 1963-66, owner, mng. gen. ptnr., 1966—, now pres., gen. ptnr.; former mem. mgmt. council and competition com. Nat. Football League. Served with AUS, 1952-53. Named Profl. Coach of Year A.P., Profl. Coach of Year U.P.I., Profl. Coach of Year Sporting News, Profl. Coach of Year Pro-Football Illustrated, 1963; Young Man of Yr. Oakland, 1963; only individual in history to be an asst. coach, head coach, gen. mgr., league commr. and owner. Mem. Am. Football Coaches Assn. Office: Oakland Raiders 1220 Harbor Bay Pkwy Alameda CA 94502-6570*

DAVIS, ARTHUR DAVID, psychology educator, musician; m. Gladys Lesley Joyce, Dec. 29, 1965; children: Kimaili, Mureithi, Taisha. Student, Manhattan Sch. Music, 1953-56, Juilliard Sch. Music, 1953-56; BA suma cum laude, CUNY, 1973; MA, City Coll., N.Y.C., 1976, NYU, 1976; PhD with distinction, NYU, 1982. Lic. sch. psychologist. Musician various worldwide tours, 1962—, NBC-TV Staff Orch., N.Y.C., 1962-63, Westinghouse TV Staff Orch., N.Y.C., 1964-68, CBS-TV Staff Orch., N.Y.C., 1969-71; prof. Manhattan Community Coll., N.Y.C., 1971-86, U. Bridgeport, Conn., 1978-82; psychologist Lincoln Med. and Mental Health Ctr., Bronx, 1982-85; sch. psychologist, cons. Lakeside Union Free Sch. Dist., Spring Valley, N.Y., 1985-86; psychologist, tchr. N.Y. Med. Coll., Valhalla, 1982-87; prof. Orange Coast Coll., Costa Mesa, Calif., 1987—, Calif. State U., Fullerton, 1988-90, U. Calif.-Irvine, 1993-94; psychologist Cross Cultural Ctr., San Diego, 1986-91; cons. Head Start, Bklyn., 1981-82, Orange County Minority AIDS, Santa Ana, Calif., 1987-88, Orange County Fair Housing, Costa Mesa, 1988, Sickle Cell Anemia Assn., Santa Ana, Calif., 1987-88, Human Rels. Orange County City, Costa Mesa, 1988-89, William Grant Still Mus., L.A., 1988—; musician various symphonies Radio City Music Hall Orch. Nat. Symphony, Symphony of the Air N.Y. Philharmonic, Met. Opera Orch., L.A. Philharmonic, 1995; John Coltrane, others, 1960—. Author: The Arthur Davis System for Double Bass, 1976, A Brief History of Jazz, 1995; record composer Interplay, 1980, Art Davis Reemeryance, ARKIMU, 1985, Dr. Art Davis, Live, Soulnote, 1987, Art Davis, Live, A Time Remembered, 1995. Composer, condr., mem. coun. Diaglogue, Costa Mesa, 1988; mgr. Little League of Cortlandt, N.Y., 1979-82; pack master Cub Scouts Am., Cortlandt and Croton, N.Y., 1979-80, dist. chmn., 1980-81; bd. dirs. Local 47 Musicians' Union, Hollywood, Calif., 1993—, Orange County Urban League, Inc., 1992-95; chmn. Better Advantages for Students and Soc., Corona del Mar, Calif., 1993; adv. bd. dirs. John W. Cultrane Cultural Soc., Inc. NIMH grantee, 1976-77; named World's Foremost Double Bassist IBA, 1969—; recipient Lion award Black MBA Assn., 1985, Chancellor's Disting. Lectr.'s award U. Calif., Irvine, 1991-92, Exemplary Standards in Music Edn. award Orange County Urban League, 1993; Ann. Dr. Art Davis Scholarships established in his honor Dr. Art Davis Fan Club. Mem. APA, ASCAP, Am. Soc. Music Arrangers & Composers, Chamber Music Am., N.Y. Acad. Scis., Astron. Soc. of the Pacific (charter), Orange County Psychol. Assn., Assn. of Black Psychologists, Planetary Soc. (charter), Am. Hort. Soc., Nat Trust for Hist. Preservation Soc., Rec. Musicians Assn., Stanford U. Alumni Assn., NYU Alumni Assn., CCNY Alumni Assn., Sierra Club. Avocations: astronomy, gourmet cooking, gardening, photography, DXing. Office: ARKIMU 3535 E Coast Hwy Ste 50 Corona Del Mar CA 92625-2404*

DAVIS, BETTY JEAN BOURBONIA, real estate investment executive; b. Ft. Bayard, N.Mex., Mar. 12, 1931; d. John Alexander and Ora M. (Caudill) Bourbonia; BS in Elem. Edn., U. N.Mex., 1954; children: Janice Cox [illegible] 1977—. Bd. dirs. Albuquerque Opera Guild, 1977-79, 81-83, 85-86, 86-87, membership co-chmn., 1977-79; mem. Friends of Art, 1978-85, Friends of Little Theatre, 1973-85, Mus. N.Mex. Found.; mem. grand exec. com. N.Mex. Internat. Order of Rainbow for Girls; mem. Hodgin Hall Preservation com. U. N.Mex. Recipient Matrix award for journalism Jr. League. Mem. Albuquerque Mus. Assn., N.M. Hist. Soc., N.Mex. Symphony Guild, Jr. League Albuquerque, Alumni Assn. U. N.Mex. (dir. 1973-76), Mus. N.Mex. Found., Albuquerque Petroleum Club, Albuquerque Knife and Fork Club, Alpha Chi Omega (Beta Gamma Beta chpt., adv., bldg. corp. 1962-77), Tanoan Country Club, Order Eastern Star, Order Rainbow for Girls (past grand worthy adv. N.Mex., past mother adv. Friendship Assembly 50, state exec. com. N.Mex. Order 1989, chair pub. rels. com., co-chair gen. arrangements com. 1990-97), Albuquerque Knife and Fork Club. Republican. Methodist. Home: 9505 Augusta Ave NE Albuquerque NM 87111-5820

DAVIS, BOB, music educator, composer; b. Phila., July 17, 1947; s. Jordan Robert and Florence Ruth (Sorkin) D.; life ptnr. Carol A. Kleinmaier. BA, Franklin and Marshall Coll., Lancaster, Pa., 1969; MusB, San Francisco Conservatory Music, 1975; MFA, Mills Coll. Ctr. Contemporary Music, Oakland, Calif., 1977. Cert. cmty. coll. instr., Calif. Instr. dept. music San Francisco City Coll., 1976—, Solano C.C., Suisun Valley, Calif., 1998—; instr. dept. theater arts San Francisco State U., 1989—; composer, prodr., sound designer Audible Difference, San Francisco, 1995-97. Office: San Francisco State U Dept Theater Arts 1600 Holloway Ave San Francisco CA 94132-1722

DAVIS, BRIAN ADAM, physician; b. Chgo., Jan. 21, 1966; s. Paul Michael and Arlene Carol (Feinman) D.; m. Edith Carpio Bautista, May 23, 1992. BS magna cum laude, No. Ill. U., 1986; MD, Meharry Med. Coll., 1992. Intern Hosp. of U. Pa./Presbyn. Med. Ctr., Phila., 1992-93; resident U. Medicine and Dentistry N.J., Newark, 1993-96; assoc. attending Runnells Specialized Hosp., Berkeley Heights, N.J., 1994-97; clin. asst. prof. dept. phys. medicine and rehab. U. Utah, Salt Lake City, 1997—; staff physiatrist dept. phys. medicine and rehab. Salt Lake Regional Med. Ctr., Salt Lake City, 1997—; cons. dept. phys. medicine and rehab. Primary Children's Med. Ctr., Salt Lake City, 1997—; fellow Kessler Sports Inst., West Orange, N.J., 1996-97; cons. dept. phys. medicine and rehab. svcs. Vets. Affairs/N.J. Health System, Lyons, 1996-97; instr. dept. phys. medicine and rehab. U. Medicine and Dentistry N.J., Newark, 1997; med. advisor Utah State Boxing Commn., 1998—; mem. Salt Lake organizing com. Paralympics Med. Svcs. Com., 1998—. Contbr. articles to profl. jours. Student asst. I Have a Future, Nashville, 1991; med. dir. Paralympic Polyclinic U. Utah 2002 Paralympics, med. adv. paralympic br. Salt Lake Orgn. Com. Mem. AMA (AMA/Glaxo Leadership award), Am. Coll. Sports Medicine, Am. Acad. Phys. Med. & Rehab., Assn. Acad. Physiatrists, Utah Med. Assn., Salt Lake County Med. Assn., U.S. Amateur Boxing Assn., KC (participant, fundraiser 1985-86), Phi Kappa Delta (participant health screening 1990-92), Sigma Alpha Mu (participant, fundraiser 1985-86), Alpha Omega Alpha. Independent. Avocations: singing, collecting rare record albums, martial arts. Home: 2625 Stringham Ave Apt 119B Salt Lake City UT 84109-3912 Office: U Utah Hosp Dept Phys Med and Rehab 50 N Medical Dr # Ir15 Salt Lake City UT 84132-0001

DAVIS, CHARLES LEE, fire marshal; b. Anchorage, July 24, 1940; s. Edward V. and De Ette C. (Scholberg) D.; m. Mary Margaret Walker, Aug. 24, 1963; 1 child, Edward Charles. LLB, U. Idaho, 1966; grad. 28th Recruit Acad., Alaska Dept. Pub. Safety, 1977. Bar: Alaska 1967; cert. firefighter, Alaska, fire svc. instr., Alaska; uniform fire code cert., cert. mech. inspector, cert. plans examiner Internat. Conf. Bldg. Ofcls.; Nat. Fire Acad. fire/arson investigation, fire prevention specialist II; World Safety Orgn. cert. safety specialist, safety mgr., safety and security dir., level II fire extinguisher permit, Alaska. Law clk., atty. Hughes, Thorsness, Lowe, Gantz & Clark, Anchorage, 1966-68; adjustor, appraiser Gen. Adjustment Bur., Alaska, 1968-73; adjuster, damage appraiser Alaska Adjusting Co., Fairbanks, 1974-75; dep. fire marshal State of Alaska, Fairbanks, 1975-99. Contbr. posters, cards and photographs to numerous publs. Mem., past vestry mem., jr. warden St. Matthew's Episcopal Ch., Fairbanks, chmn. endowment bd., 1991—. Recipient prize Joint Pubs. of Am. Jurisprudence-Bancroft Whitney Co., 1966; scholar Rocky Mountain Mineral Law Inst., 1966. Mem. NRA, Alaska Bar Assn., Pioneers of Alaska (life, igloo #4), Moose (life lodge 1392), Alaska No.Ch. ICBO (founder, dir., v.p., pres.). Episcopalian. Avocations: photography, farming, bowling, skiing, home construction, physical fitness. Home: 1359 Great View Ln Fairbanks AK 99712-2136 Office: Alaska Dept Pub Safety Divsn Fire Prevention 1979 Peger Rd Fairbanks AK 99709-5257

DAVIS, CLIFTON D., actor, composer; b. Chgo., Oct. 4, 1945; s. Toussaint L'Overture Davis and Thelma (Van Putten) Davis-Goring; m. Ann L. DeShae, Nov. 24, 1981 (div. May 1994); children: Christian Noel, Holly Danielle. BA in Theology, Oakwood Coll., 1984; MDiv, Andrews U., 1987; LLD (hon.), Lincoln U., 1989. Composer Motown, L.A., 1971-76; co-star "Amen" NBC-TV, L.A., 1986-91; star of "Two Gentlemen of Verona" N.Y. Shakespeare Festival, N.Y.C., 1971-73; star of "That's My Mama" ABC-TV, N.Y.C., 1974-76; actor, singer, composer, lectr., 1971—; v.p. internat. bus. devel. Oasis Nuclear, 1993-94; interim vice chancellor devel. and planning Elizabeth City (N.C.) State U., 1995-96; pres., CEO Clifton Davis Enterprises, Inc., 1986-92, Clifton Davis Internat., Inc., 1996—; hon. membership chmn. Nat. PTA, 1989-91; mem. adv. coun. The Children's Def. Fund; host, presenter numerous award shows and TV spls.; cons., spkr. in field. Author (short story) A Mason Dixon Memory, 1993; starred in The Melba Moore, Clifton Davis Show; guest appearances on (TV) The Jamie Foxx Show, Living Single, Sparks, Malcolm & Eddie, Grace Under Fire, Party of Five, The Sentinel, The Gregory Hines Show, The John Larroquette Show, The Love Boat, Police Story, (made-for-TV movies) Dream Date, Little Ladies of the Night, Cindy, Murder at the Superdome, Scott Joplin, Don't Look Back, The Night the City Screamed, (talk shows) The Tonight Show, Live! With Regis and Kathie Lee, Oprah, The Arsenio Hall Show; appeared on Broadway in Hello Dolly!, Jimmy Shine, The Engagement Baby, Hapgood, (Off-Broadway) How to Steal an Election, To Be Young, Gifted, and Black, No Place to be Somebody and others; toured with Guys and Dolls, Daddy Goodness; co-star (with Lena Horne) Pal Joey, And Still I Rise; composer Never Can Say Goodbye. Recipient Tony award nomination (best actor in a mus.), 1972, Grammy award nomination (best R&B composition), 1972, Theater World award, 1971, Disting. Svc. citation UnCF, 1981, Oakwood Coll. Disting. Svc. citation UNCF, 1984, Disting. Leadership award UNDF, 1987, Disting. Svc. award UNCF, 1990, Svc. award UNDF, 1991, 92, Legacy of the Dreamer award SCLC, 1989, Heart and Torch award Am. Heart Assn., 1975, Dedicated Svc. award Nat. Black Child Devel. Inst., 1987 and others. Avocations: golf, pilot (lic.), scuba diver (cert.). Office: Clifton Davis Internat 4790 Irvine Blvd # 401 Irvine CA 92620-1973

DAVIS, CLISS JOHNSON, musician; b. Richmond, Utah, Dec. 3, 1921; d. Osbourn and Edna (Hendricks) Johnson; m. Edwin Reese Davis Sr., Feb. 4, 1942; children: Klair, Edwin Reese Jr. Cert. music tchr., Brigham Young U., 1944; affiliated tchr. piano, Sherwood Music Sch. Ext., Chgo., 1947-56. Tchr. Downey (Idaho) H.S., 1948-51, Box Elder Jr. H.S., Brigham City, Utah, 1953-56; bank teller Bank of L.A., 1956-57; pianist Santa Monica (Calif.) Jr. H.S. and Coll., 1966-74; organist LDS Jordan River Temple, South Jordan, Utah, 1987—; bank teller Box Elder County Bank, Brigham City, 1951-52; sec. City Nat. Bank, Santa Monica, 1958-65; assoc. accompanist So. Calif. Mormon Choir, L.A., 1956-74; pianist Joseph Smith Bldg., Salt Lake City, 1993—; organist LDS Glenmore 4th Ward, South Glenmore Stake, South Jordan, 1987-96; fin. chmn. Santa Cruz (Calif.) Symphony Guild, 1974-87; dir. Drum and Bugle Corp, Brigham City, 1951-56; pianist, accompanist Ind. Bankers Assn. No. Calif., 1975-87. Author story and music road show Atnas Zurk, 1974; oil paintings, 1974-87. Mem. Am. West Symphony and Choir (accompanist). Republican. Avocations: oil painting, sewing, swimming, gardening, walking. Home: 4418 Skye Dr South Jordan UT 84095-9712

DAVIS, CYNTHIA ALMARINEZ, nursing educator; b. Manila, Philippines, Dec. 25, 1949; d. Rosauro and Virginia (Alconcher) Almarinez; children: Christopher, Christina, Dean, Robert. Student, Troy State U., 1984-85, Auburn U., 1987-88, Coll. Sequoias, Visalia, Calif., 1988-89; BSN, Fresno State U., 1993. RN, Calif. Staff clk. Pacific Telephone Co., San [illegible] Cola/7-Up Bottling Co., Montgomery, Ala., 1982-85; staff clk. Montgomery Police Dept., 1986-88; nurse apprentice II St. Agnes Med. Ctr., Fresno, 1991-93; student nurse trainer Valley med. Ctr., Fresno, 1991—; grad. nurse VA Med. Ctr., Fresno, 1993-94, pub. health nurse, 1994—. Author/editor Newsbeat, 1991-92. Attendee Leadership Conf., seattle, 1992, Intercollegiate Leadership Conf., Fresno, 1992. Recipient Univ. and Comty. award Kings County Health Dept. Spirit of Nursing, 1993; pre-RN Rev. Course scholar, 1992. Mem. Calif. Nursing Students Assn. (pres. 1991-92), Sigma Theta Tau. Roman Catholic. Avocations: playing piano, crocheting, reading, movies/mysterie stories. Home: 1463 Belinda Dr Lemoore CA 93245-3975

DAVIS, DEBORAH JOHANNA, newspaper editor; b. White Salmon, Wash., June 16, 1948; d. Gardar Godfrey Lionel and Margaret Jean (North) Dahl; m. Stewart Kent Davis, July 15, 1966 (div. Apr. 1972); children: David Michael, Darcy Mariha Davis Boyd. BA in Journalism with honors, U. Mont., 1982. Outreach worker HeadStart/Planned Parenthood, Mineral County, Mont.; publicity coord. Literacy Coun. of Greater Missoula, Mont.; staff mem. Missoula Crisis Ctr., Mont.; hist. rschr. Superior (Mont.) Ranger Dist.; reporter Mullan Trail News, Missoula; justice of the peace Mineral County, Superior; editor, reporter, photography Mineral Ind. Newspaper, Superior; editor/writer mus. news Mineral County Pioneer, Superior, 1984-89, judge's assn. Mont. Magistrates newsletter, Superior, 1990-93; hist. cons. U.S. Forest Svc. Projects, Superior, 1994-98; sec. Mineral Co. Econ. Devel., Superior, 1995-96. Author: (book) Gumboot Gamblers, 1987. Curator Mineral County Mus., Superior, 1986-98; sec. Mineral County Fair Bd., 1983-94; tutor refugees, Missoula, Mont., 1980-81. Recipient scholarships U. Mont., 1982, Mont. Press Women Assn., 1980; recipient Sadie Erickson award U. Mont. Journalism Sch., 1982. Mem. Soc. Profl. Journalists, Mont. Newspaper Assn., Superior Area C. of C., Mineral County Hist. Soc. Methodist. Avocations: reading, outdoor recreation, gardening, sewing, puzzles. Home: 106 West Second Superior MT 59872 Office: Mineral Ind Newspaper 106 W Second Superior MT 59872

DAVIS, DONALD ALAN, author, news correspondent, lecturer; b. Savannah, Ga., Oct. 5, 1939; s. Oden Harry and Irma Artice (Gay) D.; m. Robin Murphy, Mar. 17, 1983; children by previous marriage—Russell Glenn, Randall Scott. B.A. in Journalism, U. Ga., 1962. Reporter Athens (Ga.) Banner-Herald, 1961-62, Savannah Morning News, 1962; with UPI, 1963-65; reporter, editor St. Petersburg (Fla.) Times, 1965-66; with UPI, 1967-83, Vietnam corr., 1971-73, New Eng. editor, 1977-80, White House corr., 1981-83; polit. reporter, columnist San Diego Union, 1983-91; pub. Pacific Rim Report newsletter, 1985-88; instr. journalism Boston U., 1979; instr. writing U. Colo., 1998—; lectr. U.S. Naval War Coll., 1983, Queen Elizabeth 2, 1991, Vistafjord, 1992; bd. dirs. Fgn. Corr. Club, Hong Kong, 1974. Author: The Milwaukee Murders, 1991, The Nanny Murder Trial, 1992, Bad Blood, 1994, Death of An Angel, 1994, Fallen Hero, 1994, Appointment with the Squire, 1995, Death Cruise, 1996, A Father's Rage, 1996, The Gris-Gris Man, 1997, Hush, Little Babies, 1997, The Last Man on the Moon, 1999. Fellow Keizai Koho Ctr., Tokyo, 1985. Presbyterian. Office: 6350 Modena Ln Longmont CO 80503-8770

DAVIS, DONALD ROMAIN, composer; b. Bellflower, Calif., Feb. 4, 1957; s. Donald Reuben and Agnes Anne (Romain) D.; m. Megan Jeanne MacDonald, May 25, 1986; 1 child, Kamyla Michele. BA in Music Composition, UCLA, 1979; studies with, Albert Harris, Henri Lazarof. Composer (films) Blackout, Hyperspace, (TV movies) Honor Bright, Lies Before Kisses (Emmy nomination), Home Fires Burning, Running Against Time, Quiet Victory, A Stoning in Fulham County, Bluegrass, (TV series) Beauty and The Beast (Emmy award), My Life and Times (Emmy nomination), Matlock, Tiny Toon Adventures, Sledge Hammer, Kay O'Brien, Hart to Hart, (orchestral and chamber music) Chamber Symphony, Chronym I-II-III, Symphony, Bleeding Particles, Chamber Variations, Harsh, Bleak, Going On; orchestrator (films) Robin Hood: Prince of Thieves, Hudson Hawk, If Looks Could Kill, Die Hard II, Police Acad. II-III-IV, Stewardess School, (TV films) The Saint in Manhattan, Double Agent, Down The Long Hills, Murder By the Book, Stranded, Lily, V, Senior Trip, A Hobo's Christmas, Kids Like These, The Winter of Our Discontent, Something About Amelia, Paper Dolls, (TV series) Moonlighting, Falcon Crest, Crazy Like A Fox, Lime Street, Cover Up, Detective In The House, Call To Glory, Lottery, Santa Barbar, T.J. Hooker, Matt Houston, Glitter, Hotel, Fall Guy, Voyagers, Fantasy Island, The Incredible Hulk. Recipient ASCAP award to Young Composers 1982, 83, Gaudeamus Found. Internat. Music Week Selection, 1983, 2nd Place Valention Bucchi Internat. String Quartet Composition Competition, 1983, Emmy award Beauty and The Beast A Time To Heal, Emmy nomination My Life and Times, Lies Before Kisses, Beauty and The Beast To Reign In Hell. Mem. NARAS, Broadcast Music Inc. (awards to student composers 1980, 81, 83), Am. Fedn. Musicians, Am. Music Ctr., Ind. Composers Assn., Soc. Composers & Lyricists, Acad. TV Arts & Scis. Office: Donavis Music Inc 16650 Schoenborn St Sepulveda CA 91343-6106

DAVIS, GAY RUTH, psychotherapist, social welfare educator, author, researcher, consultant; b. Bellingham, Wash., Sept. 19, 1935; d. Lee Laverne Wickersham and Altha (Lund) Wickersham Knight; m. Paul Cushing Davis, Dec. 20, 1956; children: Jeffrey Richards, Jennifer Lynn. Student, Brigham Young U., 1953-55; BA summa cum laude, Western Wash. U., 1976; MSW, U. Wash., 1978, PhD, 1985. Diplomate in clin. social work. Dir. Social Svcs. Sound Health Assn., Tacoma, 1977-78; social work profl. Harborview Med. Ctr., Seattle, 1979-81; instr. Sch. Social Work U. Wash., Seattle, 1984-85; pvt. practice cons. social work and psychotherapy Seattle, 1985-98; prin. investigator NINCDS Rsch., 1980-81; coord. Adult Svcs. Tng. Project, U. Wash., 1983-84. Contbr. articles to profl. jours. Mem. adv. bd. LDS Social Svcs., 1990-91. Grantee Wash. Dept. Health and Human Services, 1981-82. Mem. NASW (diplomate, qualified clin. social worker), Nat. Registry Clin. Social Work, Wash. Assn. Social Workers (cert.), Assn. Mormon Counselors and Psychotherapists. Democrat. Mormon. Avocations: genealogy, writing.

DAVIS, GRAY, governor; b. N.Y.C., Dec. 26, 1942; m. Sharon Ryer, Feb. 20, 1983. BA cum laude, Stanford U., 1964; JD, Columbia U., 1967. Chief of staff to Gov. Jerry Brown State of Calif., Sacramento, 1974-81, mem. Calif. State Assembly, 1982-86, state contr., 1986-94, lt. gov., 1995-99, gov., 1999—; chmn. Housing and Community Devel. Com., Calif. Coun. on Criminal Justice, Franchise Tax Bd., State Lands Commn.; mem. Bd. Equalization, State Tchrs. Retirement System, Pub. Employees Retirement System, Nat. Coun. Institutional Investors. Founder Calif. Found. for the Protection of Children. Office: Office of Governor State Capitol Sacramento CA 95814-4906*

DAVIS, GREG, football player; b. Rome, Ga., Oct. 29, 1965. Kicker San Diego Chargers. Office: San Diego Chargers PO Box 609609 San Diego CA 92160-9609

DAVIS, GREG WILLIAM, television producer; b. Denver, Oct. 24, 1960; s. William H. and Nancy Jeanne (Service) D.; m. Polly Brown, Feb. 15, 1992; children: Jennifer, Jarrod. BA, U. No. Colo., 1983. Asst. mgr. Morgan's Pharmacy, Denver, 1984-86; prodr., dir. U. Colo., Denver, 1986—; freelance prodr. Jade Prodns., Denver, 1994—. Author: The Deep and the Dark, 1997. Recipient silver peak award Internat. TV Assn., 1996, bronze peak award, 1996. Avocations: softball, camping, weight training. Office: U Colo Denver 1100 Stout St Ste 300 Denver CO 80204-2065

DAVIS, J. ALAN, lawyer, producer, writer; b. N.Y.C., Nov. 7, 1961. Student, Marlborough Coll., Eng., 1979; BA with distinction, So. Meth. U., 1983; JD with honors, U. Tex., 1987. Bar: Calif. 1988. Assoc. O'Melveny & Myers, L.A., 1987-89, Rosenfeld, Meyer & Susman, Beverly Hills, Calif., 1989-90; pvt. practice L.A., 1990-94; ptnr. Davis & Benjamin, L.A., 1995-97, Garvin, Davis & Benjamin, LLP, 1997—. Mem. Calif. Bar Assn., Beverly Hills Bar Assn. (entertainment law sect. exec. com.), Brit. Acad. Film and TV Arts, L.A. (mng. dir., bd. dirs.), British Film Office (exec. com.). Avocations: skiing, scuba diving, tennis. Office: Garvin Davis & Benjamin LLP 9200 W Sunset Blvd Ph 25 Los Angeles CA 90069-3502

DAVIS, JAMES LUTHER, retired utilities executive, lawyer; b. Memphis, May 8, 1924; s. Luther and Sarah (Carter) D.; m. Natalie Young, Jan. 26, 1947; children: James Luther, Fred C., Peggy E. BBA, U. Ariz., 1946, LLB, 1949. Bar: Ariz. 1949. Sole practice Tucson, 1949-52, asst. city atty., 1952-[illegible] Power Co.), 1955-96, exec. v.p., 1958-59, pres., 1959-76, also bd. dirs., 1961-89, emeritus, 1989-96, chmn. bd., 1967-88; bd. dirs. El Paso br. Fed. Res. Bd., Dallas, 1974-77, chmn. 1976-77. Mem. charter rev. com. City of Tucson, 1965-71; bd. dirs. Tucson Airport Authority, 1957-62, 64-70, pres.,

1965; bd. dirs. Tucson Med. Ctr., 1955-58, 59-65, pres., 1957-58; mem. Tucson Indsl. Devel. Bd., 1959-64; bd. dirs. Ariz. Town Hall, 1962-74, 78-82, Health Planning Coun. Tucson, 1964-71, Tucson Regional Plan, 1966-89, United Way, 1985-88; bd. dirs. Green Fields Sch., 1964-69, chmn. bd., 1964-66; bd. dirs. U. Ariz. Found., 1985-92, dir. emeritus, 1992-96. Mem. Nat. Assn. Mfrs. (bd. dirs. 1960-62), Pacific Coast Gas Assn. (bd. dirs. 1958-60), Pacific Coast Elec. Assn. (bd. dirs. 1972-86, pres. 1978-79), Western Energy and Supply Assn. (bd. dirs. 1964-76), Tucson C. of C. (bd. dirs. 1958-60, 64-66, 80-90, chmn. 1987-88), So. Ariz. Water Resources Assn. (bd. dirs. 1982-88, pres. 1987), Blue Key, Tucson Country Club, Phi Gamma Delta, Alpha Kappa Psi, Phi Delta Phi. Home: 6781 N Altos Primero Tucson AZ 85718-2054

DAVIS, JANE ANNE, preschool educator, writer, poet; b. Chanute, Kans., Aug. 21, 1948; d. Loren Wilson and Ethel G. Lawrence. Student, Santa Fe C.C., 1998—, U. Calif. San Diego, UCLA. Lead pre-sch. tchr. nonprofit pvt. sch. Garcia St. Club, Santa Fe. Avocations: writing, art, cooking, making jewelry, travel.

DAVIS, JEREMY MATTHEW, chemist; b. Bakersfield, Calif., Aug. 5, 1953; s. Joseph Hyman and Mary (Pavetto) D.; m. Bernadette Sobkiewicz, Aug. 28, 1976 (div.); children: Andrew Jeremy, Christopher Peter. BS in Biol. Scis., U. Calif., Irvine, 1974; M in Pub. Adminstrn., Calif. State U., Long Beach, 1983. Chemist I, II, Orange County Water Dist., Fountain Valley, Calif., 1977-84, chemist supr., 1984—. Papers in field. Lay reader St. Margaret of Scotland Episcopal Ch., San Juan Capistrano, Calif. Named Lab. Person of Yr., Calif. Water Environment Assn., Santa Ana River Basin, 1984. Mem. Am. Water Works Assn., Toastmasters Internat. (pres. Watermeisters club). Office: Orange County Water Dist PO Box 8300 Fountain Valley CA 92728-8300

DAVIS, JOHN WARREN, program integrator; b. York, Pa., Feb. 14, 1946; s. Frank Asbury Jr. and Lillian Margaret (Billings) D. BA in Polit. Sci., Drake U., 1968; AA in Real Estate, San Diego City Coll., 1976; MS in Acquisition and Contract Mgmt., West Coast U., 1987; postgrad., Walden U., 1992—. Real estate sales staff, 1972-79; clk. GS 3 Naval Ocean Sys. Ctr., 1979-80; contract intern, contract adminstr. Office of Naval Rsch., 1980-84; contract specialist, warranted ordering officer Gen. Svc. 1102-11 Naval Weapons Sta., 1984-86; contract specialist Gen Svc 1102-12 Navy Space Sys. Activity, 1986-88; procurement analyst Gen Svc. 102-12 COMNAVAIRPAC, 1988-98; with Def. Contract Mgmt. Command, 1998—; del. San Diego State U. to the Nat. Acad. Conf. for Contract Mgmt. Educators, 1991, 92, 93; profl. cons. Computer Applications, Inc., 1992; mem. tech. program com., chairperson for electronic data interchange Soc. of Logistics Engrs., 1995; mem. Golden Hill planning com. City of San Diego; adj. instr. San Diego State U., chmn. curriculum rev. com. for acquisition. Author, Paperless Contracting, The EDI Revolution, 1995, contbr. articles to profl. pubis. With U.S. Army, Vietnam, 1968-72. Fellow Nat. Contract Mgmt. Assn. (cert. profl. contract mgr.); mem. ABA (mem. sub-com. pub. law sector, sub-com. on intellectual property), SAR (nat., Calif. and San Diego chpts.), Am. Arbitration Assn. (nat. panel mem.), Soc. Govt. Meeting Planners (v.p. San Diego chpt.), Soc. Logistics Engrs., San Diego Athletic Club, San Diego Writers and Editors Guild, Author's Guild (past pres.). Episcopalian. Avocations: swimming, traveling. Home: PO Box 620657 San Diego CA 92162-0657 Office: DCMC (GSOC) 7675 Dagget St Ste 200 San Diego CA 92111-2256

DAVIS, JULIE LYNDA, adult and secondary education educator; b. Fresno, Calif., Nov. 5, 1964; d. Richard Arthur and Judith Karen (Haertling) Lang; children: Colton Trevor, Weston Anthony. AA, Modesto (Calif.) Jr. Coll., 1984; BS in Bus., Fresno State Coll., 1986; cert. in teaching, Chapman Coll., 1989, MAwith honors, 1992. Cert. secondary edn. tchr., Calif. Cons. J.C. Penney Co., Modesto, 1986-89; tchr. bus. Modesto High Sch., 1989; tchr. bus. Elliott Edn. Ctr., Modesto, 1989-91, tchr. adult edn., 1990—; tchr. bus. Grace M. Davis High Sch., Modesto, 1991—; bus. tech. and profl. devel. instr. Valley Comml. Coll., 1995—; site facilitator coop. learning Modesto City Schs., 1990—; advisor Future Bus. Leaders of Am., Modesto, 1991—; tech. prep. consortium Curriculum Improvement and Approval Com., 1993; fellow, contbg. author Great Valley Writing Project at Stanislaus State U., 1994. Author: Modesto City Schools Freshman Core Computer Literacy Curriculum, 1994. Campaign worker Wilson for Gov., Modesto, 1990, Lang for Assembly, Modesto, 1990; mem. Rep. Women, 1983—, LWV, Modesto, 1989. Mem. NEA, Calif. Tchrs. Assn., Modesto Tchrs. Assn., Alpha Kappa Psi, Phi Mu. Methodist. Avocations: writing, interior design, family, hunting. Office: Modesto City Schs 426 Locust St Modesto CA 95351-2631

DAVIS, LEO RUSSELL, safety engineer; b. Long Beach, Calif.; s. William Russell and Leota Ann (Fisher) D.; m. Mary Ann Lazo, Dec. 30, 1970; 1 child, Eric Patrick. AA, Fresno (Calif.) C.C., 1972; BA, Calif. State U., Fresno, 1974. Cert. safety profl. Bd. Cert. Safety Profls. Loss control rep. Royal Ins., Phoenix, 1974-76; sr. loss control rep. Royal Ins., Dallas, 1976-78, CNA Ins., Dallas, 1978-81, TIG/Transamerica Ins., Phoenix, 1981-94; loss control cons. Acordia of Ariz., Phoenix, 1995—. Staff sgt. USAF, 1965-69. Mem. Am. Soc. Safety Engrs. (pres. 1991-92). Republican. Avocations: fishing, hiking, woodworking. Office: Acordia of Ariz 3020 E Camelback Rd Ste 200 Phoenix AZ 85016-4423

DAVIS, LESLIE BERYL, curator archaeology, educator in anthropology; b. Shelby, Montana, Dec. 7, 1935. BA in Cultural Anthropology, Montana State U., 1959; MA in Cultural Anthropology, U. Montana, 1965; PhD in Archaeology N. Am., U. Calgary, Alberta, Can., 1972. Prof. anthropology Montana State U., Bozeman, 1978—; curator archaeology, ethnology Mus. of the Rockies, Montana State U., Bozeman, 1990—. Author, editor: (books) From Microcosm to Macrocosm: Advances in Tipi Ring Investigation and Interpretation, 1983, Avonlea Yesterday and Today: Archaeology and Prehistory, 1988; author, co-editor: (book) Hunters of the Recent Past, 1990. Recipient award Montana Hist. Soc., 1981, Chief of Forest Svcs.' Nat. award for excellence USDA Forest Svc., 1993, Charles and Nora Wiley Faculty award for meritorious research Montana State Univ. Found., Bozeman, 1995. Office: Mus The Rockies Montana State U Bozeman MT 59717-2730

DAVIS, LINDA JACOBS, municipal official; b. Miami, July 10, 1955; d. Martin Jacque and Doris Harriet (Stucker) Jacobs; m. John Joseph Mantos, Jan. 1, 1984 (dec. 1988); m. Perry Davis, June 4, 1989; children: Aaron, Jacob. Student, U. South Fla., 1977. Mgr. Werner Erhard & Assocs., San Francisco, 1978-82, program leader, 1979-90; asst. exec. dir. The Breakthrough Found., San Francisco, 1982-88; owner Mantagaris Galleries, San Francisco, 1988-92; dir. mktg. devel. Marin Child Care Coun., San Rafael, Calif., 1992-94; dir. devel. and pub. affairs Planned Parenthood of Marin, Sonoma and Menodcino, Calif., 1994-96; ptnr. Women's Initiative for Leadership Devel., 1994-96; pres., CEO Mill Valley C. of C., 1996—; profl. fund-raiser. Vol. The Hunger Project, Fla., 1977-78; bd. dirs. Marin Child Care Coun.; appointed commr. Marin Commn. on Women, 1994-97. Recipient Outstanding Young Women Am. Mem. NOW (pres. local chpt.), Marin Women's Coalition. Democrat. Jewish. Avocations: exercise, gardening, writing, public speaking, politics. Home: 419 Karla Ct Novato CA 94949-5478 Office: Mill Valley C of C 85 Throckmorton Mill Valley CA 94941

DAVIS, LOWELL LIVINGSTON, cardiovascular surgeon; b. Urbanna, Va.. BS in Biology, Morehouse Coll., 1949; MS in Biology, Atlanta U., 1950; MD, Howard U., 1955; postgrad., U. Pa., 1959-60. Diplomate Am. Bd. Surgery, Am. Bd. Thoracic Surgery. Intern Jersey City (N.J.) Med. Ctr., 1955-56; resident Margaret Hague Maternity Hosp., Jersey City, 1956-57; resident ob-gyn. Elmhurst (N.Y.) Gen. Hosp., 1957-58, chief resident ob-gyn., 1958-59; resident in gen. surgery U.S. VA Hosp., Tuskegee, Ala., 1960-61; resident to chief resident in gen. surgery Nassau County Med. Ctr., Hempstead, N.Y., 1961-64; resident in cardiothoracic surgery Cook County Hosp., Chgo., 1967-68, sr. resident, 1968-69; pvt. practice N.Y.C., 1964-65, pvt. practice thoracic and cardiovascular surgery, 1975—; clin. assoc. prof. surgery L.A. County Gen. Hosp., U. So. Calif. Med. Sch., 1988—; fellow U. Oreg., Portland, 1972, St. Vincent Hosp., Portland, 1972, Med. Coll. Wis., Milw., 1973, Pacific Med. Ctr. Inst. of Med. Scis., San Francisco, 1974, Allen-Bradley Med. Scis. Rsch. Lab. Med. Coll. Wis., 1975, Hosp. for Sick Children, London, 1977-78, Tex. Heart Inst., Houston, 1983, Cardiac Surgery Rsch. Lab., Hadassah Med. Sch. and U. Hosp., Jerusalem, 1987; vis. surgeon NYU Med. Sch., 1991, Mayo Clinic, Rochester, Minn., 1991, U. Dusseldorf, Germany, 1991, Deutsches Herzzentrum, Berlin, 1991, Deutsches Herzzentrum, Munich, 1991, Klinik für Thorat-Herz-Und Gefab Chirurgie, Hanover, Germany, 1991, U. Vienna, Austria, 1992. Contbr. articles to profl. jours. With USN, 1943-46, USNR, 1965-71, comdr., 1965-67, capt. USNR, 1970. Recipient Asiatic Pacific Campaign medal with one Gold Star, Presdl. Unit citation. Fellow ACS, Internat. Coll. Angiology, Am. Coll. Angiology, Internat. Coll. Surgeons, N.Y. Acad. Medicine, Am. Coll. Chest Physicians, Am. Coll. Cardiology; mem. AAAS, Assn. Mil. Surgeons U.S., Am. Assn. for Thoracic Surgery, Soc. Thoracic Surgeons, Albert Starr Cardiac Surg. Soc. (founding), Am. Coll. Emergency Physicians, Lyman Brewer III Internat. Surg. Soc., Royal Soc. Medicine, Denton A. Cooley Cardiovasc. Surgery Soc., L.A. Surg. Soc. Office: Ste 316 4518 186th St # 202 Redondo Beach CA 90278 Address: 1254 W 6th St Los Angeles CA 90014-1831

DAVIS, MARVIN, petroleum company executive, entrepreneur; b. Newark, Aug. 28, 1925; s. Jack Davis; m. Barbara Davis; 5 children. BSCE, NYU, 1947. Gen. ptnr., owner Davis Oil Co., Denver; co-owner 20th Century-Fox, 1981-85. Office: Davis Cos 2121 Ave Of Stars Ste 2800 Los Angeles CA 90067-5010*

DAVIS, MICHAEL RICO, county official; b. Charlotte, N.C.; s. Lawrence Kenneth and Myrtle Elizabeth (Antrum) D. BA, U. N.C., 1979; MPA, Calif. State U., 1994, MA, 1996. Intern, adminstrv. asst. to majorit floor leader Calif. Assembly, L.A., 1980-81, field rep. assemblywoman Maxine Waters, 1983-86; adminstrv. asst. Calif. Assembly, 1986-89; adminstrv. asst., dist. dir Congresswoman Maxine Waters, L.A., 1990-92; sr. counselor Optimist Homes & Ranch, Inc., L.A., 1981-83; sr. dep. 2nd dist. to Yvonne Burke L.A. County Bd. Suprs., L.A., 1993—. Author: Minorities in Business, 1997. Spl. asst. Jesse Jackson for President, L.A., 1984; dir. GOTV Tom Bradley for Mayor, L.A., 1989; del. Dem. Nat. Convention, L.A., 1992; regional dir. Bill Clinton for President, L.A., 1991-92; bd. dirs. Tng. Rsch./Head Start, L.A., 1984—; mem. black adv. com. L.A. Police Commn., 1984-87; mem. presdl. selection com. Charles Drew Med. U., L.A., 1997. Named to Outstanding Young Men of Am., 1981, 96, Young Leader, Am. Swiss Found., 1998. Mem. Am. Soc. Pub. Adminstrn., So. Calif. Mediation Assn., Kappa Alpha Psi (historian 1977-78, Outstanding Achievement 1978, regional dir. 1978-79, Man of Yr. 1979, chmn. social action 1997, bd. dirs. we. province 1982-84, contbr. to jour.), Phi Alpha Delta. Democrat. Home: PO Box 19672 Los Angeles CA 90019-0672 Office: LA County Bd Suprs 500 W Temple St Los Angeles CA 90012-2713

DAVIS, MURDOCH, editor-in-chief. BAA in Jounralism, Ryerson Polytech. Inst., 1975. Reporter, feature writer Toronto Star, Can., 1976-78; reporter, then asst. city editor, news editor, city editor Ottawa Citizen, Can., 1979-89; mng. editor Edmonton Jour., Can., 1989-92, editor, 1992—. Office: 10006 101 St, PO Box 2421, Edmonton, AB Canada T5J 2S6

DAVIS, OTIS JAY, chaplain; b. Chgo., Sept. 7, 1937; s. Wendell D. and Phyllis Mae (Rockefeller) D.; children: Cindy Davis Houghton, Buffy Davis Bruskas. BA, Hardin-Simmons U., 1964; M in Religious Edn., SWBTS, 1973; D. Min with honors, Internat. Sem., 1981, DD (hon.), 1982, PhD in Thanatology summa cum laude, 1991. Ordained min., 1964. Child placement specialist Dept. Human Svcs., Dallas, child protective svc. specialist, adult protective svc. specialist; chaplain Lovelace Med. Ctr., Albuquerque. With U.S. Army, 1955-58. Mem. Nat. Coun. Social Welfare, Albuquerque Com. for Social Action, Child Abuse Rsch. Ctr. (Father of Yr. 1982). Home: 4510 Joe Dan Pl NE Albuquerque NM 87110-5043

DAVIS, PATTI LYNN, news anchor; b. Pitts., Oct. 9, 1959; d. Walter James and Patricia Dawn (Anderson) D.; m. Tony Nunes Toste, Oct. 7, 1995; children: Cameron, Samantha. BA cum laude, U. Pitts., 1981. Intern KDKA-TV, Pitts., 1980-81; reporter WTOV-TV, Steubenville, Ohio, 1982-83; consumer reporter WGAL-TV, Lancaster, Pa., 1983-84; gen. assignment reporter WLPX-TV, Orlando, Fla., 1984-86, KXTV-TV, Sacramento, 1986-90; anchor morning show & noon news KOVR-TV, Sacramento, 1992—; producer, dir. Pvt. Prodns., 1990-94; spkr. in field. Bd. dirs. Emergency Food Bank, Stockton, 1992; facilitator cancer support group. Avocations: skiing, water skiing, gardening, cross-stitching, horseback riding. Office: KOVR-TV 2713 Kovr Dr West Sacramento CA 95605-1600

DAVIS, PAUL MILTON, communications administrator; b. Effingham, Ill., Dec. 21, 1938; s. Plaford Milton and Zona Matilda (Buchholz) D.; m. Marilynne Bohne, Aug. 26, 1961; children: Paul Mark, Glenn Stokes, Marinell Kathryn. Student, Georgetown (Ky.) Coll., 1956-58, Baylor U., 1958-60; BA, U. Ill., 1963. Anchor-reporter news dept. WCIA-TV, Champaign, Ill., 1960-67, news dir., 1967-80; news dir. WGN-AM and TV, Chgo., 1980-83, WGN-TV, Chgo., 1983-93; pres. Tribune Broadcasting News Network, Inc., Chgo., 1990-91, cons., 1993—; news dir. WLVI-TV, Boston, 1994-96; pres. The Paul Davis Co., 1994-98; sr. v.p. Found. for Am. Comms., L.A., 1998—; v.p. First Amendment Congress, 1979-87; mem. World Press Freedom Com.; chmn. UPI Broadcast Adv. Bd., 1983-88, mem. editorial rev. com., 1987; mem. nat. adv. com. Ctr. for Info. Law, John Marshall Law Sch.; mem. nat. adv. bd. Wharton Sch. Broadcast Mgmt. Programs, U. Pa., 1978-81; underwriter RTND Found. Directory of Minority Resources, 1996. Co-author Jane Pauley Task Force Report on State of Broadcast Journalism Edn., 1996; contbr. articles to profl. jours. Founding bd. mem., pres. Boys Club, Champaign/Urbana, 1968-71; pres. bd. Family Svc. Champaign County, 1969-72; nat. treas. Family Svc. Assn. Am., N.Y.C., 1975-77; chmn. Ill. Dept. Pub. Aid Title XX Adv. Coun., Springfield, Ill., 1977-79; v.p., founder United Way Ill., 1975-79; mem. adv. bd. Ill. Dept. Children and Family Svcs., 1968-70. Named Citizen of Yr., NASW, Champaign County, 1969; recipient award Nat. Ctr. Freedom of Info. Studies, Loyola U., Columbia-Dupont Citation, numerous reporting awards from wire svc. and profl. assns. Mem. NATAS (bd. govs., Gov.'s award Chgo. chpt. TV Acad. 1993), Radio-TV News Dirs. Assn. (pres. 1979, chmn. EEO com., disting. svc. award), Soc. Profl. Journalists (pres. 1989), Ill. News Broadcasters Assn. (pres. 1966, Illinoisan of Yr. 1993), Ill. State Bar Assn. (past chmn. media law com., mem. subcom. on cameras in the ct.), ABA (mem. media-law com. 1992—), Headline Club Chgo. (mem. bd. 1982-87, mem. long range planning com.), Ill. Freedom of Info. Coun. Avocations: fgn. travel, journalist assessment. Home: 17241 Boswell Pl Granada Hills CA 91344-1021 Office: Found Am Comms 3800 Barham Blvd Ste 409 Los Angeles CA 90068-1042

DAVIS, PETE BENTON, vocational school educator, retired; b. Sheridan, Wyo., Jan. 22, 1934; s. John Benton and Dorothy Mae (Adsit) D.; m. Cindy Jean Olheiser, Oct. 15, 1977; children: Diana, Dan, Krista. Assoc. BS, Sheridan Coll., 1970; BS, U. Wyo., 1972. Butcher, livestock buyer Columbus (Mont.) Market, 1952-54; butcher Icebox Grocery, Sheridan, Wyo., 1954-59; sch. maintenance engr. Dist. # 1, Big Horn, Wyo., 1959-70; vocat. educator Sheridan H.S., 1972-74, Riverton (Wyo.) H.S., 1974-94; ret., 1994; cowboy poet. Instr. first aid ARC, Sheridan, 1957-68; adv., scoutmaster Boy Scouts Am., Big Horn, 1959-68; vol. fireman Big Horn Fire Dept., 1960-65; chmn. bd. dirs. Riverton Educators Fed. Credit Union, 1987-94. Recipient Cowboy Poet award Pride Wyo. Com., 1992, 96. Mem. K of C (Man of Yr. 1991), Internat. Soc. Poets (disting., Hall of Fame 1996), Phi Beta Kappa, Phi Kappa Phi. Roman Catholic. Avocations: hunting, fishing, woodworking, writing. Home: 1411 E Park Ave Riverton WY 82501-3853

DAVIS, PETER (PETER PATHFINDER DAVIS), priest; b. Jersey City, Mar. 22, 1937; s. Joseph Anthony and Adele Elizabeth (Claveloux) D.; m. Catharine Buenz, 1958 (div. 1979); children: Richard, Robert; m. Wende Elizabeth Young, Dec. 31, 1994. Student, Rutgers U., 1973, U. Okla., 1979, Pacific Luth. U., 1980. Founder, archpriest Aquarian Tabernacle Ch. (Wicca), Seattle, 1979—; pub. info. officer Covenant of the Goddess, Berkeley, Calif., 1985-86; founding bd. dirs. Wiccan Info. Network, Vancouver, Can.; mem. religious adv. commn. Wash. Dept. Corrections; organizer Pagan Ch. Conf., 1990, other ann. confs. Contbg. author: Witchcraft Today, 1991; editor Panegyria, 1984-97. Councilman, then mayor Andover Twp., N.J., 1960-76; mem. Selective Svc. Bd., Newton, 1971-76; commr. Sussex County Election Commn., 1973-74; trustee Ctr. for Non-Traditional Religion, Seattle, 1980—, past pres. With N.J.A.R.N.G., 1956-62. Mem. Interfaith Coun. Wash. (sr. del. 1990—, pres. 1995-97), Am. Soc. for Indsl. Security (cert. protection profl.), Fellowship of Isis. Democrat. Office: Aquarian Tabernacle Ch PO Box 409 Index WA 98256-0409

DAVIS, RANDY L., soil scientist; b. L.A., Nov. 23, 1950; s. Willie Vernon and Joyce Christine (Manes) D. AA, Yuba Community Coll., 1972; BS in Soils and Plant Nutrition, U. Calif., Berkeley, 1976. Vol. soil scientist U.S. Peace Corps, Maseru, Lesotho, 1976-79; soil scientist Hiawatha Nat. Forest, Sault Saint Marie, Mich., 1979-86; project soil scientist Bridger-Teton Nat. Forest, Jackson, Wyo., 1986-91, forest soil scientist, 1991-97, soil and water program leader, 1997—; detailed soil scientist Boise (Idaho) Nat. Forest, 1989, 92, Mendocino (Calif.) Nat. Forest, 1996. Editor Soil Classifiers newsletter; contbr. articles to profl. jours. Pres. Sault Community Theater, Sault Saint Marie, 1984-86. Mem. Am. Chem. Soc., Soil Sci. Soc. Am., Soil and Water Conservation Soc. (bd. dirs. 1991-92, chpt. pres. 1993-97), Am. Water Resources Assn., Internat. Soc. Soil Sci., Soc. for Range Mgmt. Methodist. Home: PO Box 7795 Jackson WY 83002-7795 Office: Bridger-Teton Nat Forest PO Box 1888 Jackson WY 83001-1888

DAVIS, RICHARD CALHOUN, dentist; b. Manhattan, Kans., Jan. 4, 1945; s. William Calhoun and Alison Rae (Wyland) D.; Danna Ruth Ritchel, June 13, 1968; 1 child, Darin Calhoun. Student, Ariz. State U., 1963-65, BA, 1978; BA, U. Ariz., 1966; DDS, U. of Pacific, 1981. Retail dept. head Walgreens, Tucson, 1965-66; mgmt. trainee Walgreens, Tucson, San Antonio, 1967-70; asst. store mgr. Walgreens, Baton Rouge, 1970-72; field rep. Am. Cancer Soc., Phoenix, 1972-74; dept. head Lucky Stores, Inc., Tempe, Ariz., 1976-78; practice dentistry specializing in gen. dentistry Tucson, 1981—; bd. dirs. Home Again, Inc. Chmn. bd. Capilla Del Sol Christian Ch., Tucson, 1984. Fellow Internat. Congress Oral Implantologists, Am. Coll. Oral Implantology, Am. Soc. Osseointegration; mem. ADA, Acad. Gen. Dentists, Am. Straight Wire Orthodontic Assn., Am. Assn. Functional Orthodontics, Sleep Disorders Dental Soc., So. Ariz. Bus. Assn. (treas. 1998), N.W. Dental Study Club, Optimists (past pres. N.W. club, preceptorship in dental implantology), Elks. Republican. Mem. Disciples of Christ Ch. Avocation: golf, skiing, watersports, fishing, camping. Office: 2777 N Campbell Ave Tucson AZ 85719-3101

DAVIS, RICHARD ERNEST, engineer; b. San Francisco, Nov. 20, 1936; 1 child, Richard Jr.; m. Sharon L. Buss, Aug. 26, 1961; children: Dawn, Michelle. BS in Engring., Calif. State Poly. U., San Luis Obispo, 1967. Facilities engr., energy conservation engr. Naval Weapons Ctr., China Lake, Calif., 1967-77; solar program coordinator U.S. Dept. Energy, Oakland, Calif., 1977-78; program mgr. Solar Energy Research Inst., Golden, Colo., 1978-80; engring. specialist Holmes & Narver, Mercury, Nev., 1980-90; engring. specialist nuclear waste Nev./Yucca Mountain Project Raytheon Svcs., Mercury, 1990-93; constrn. engr. mgr. Fluor Daniel, Inc., 1993-96; city constrn. mgr. Fluor Daniel Telecom, 1996—. Contbr. articles to profl. jours. Served with USAF, 1954-62. Avocations: hiking, camping. Home: HC 69 Box 495 Amargosa Valley NV 89020-9740 Office: Fluor Daniel Inc 3333 Michelson Dr Irvine CA 92612-0625

DAVIS, ROBERT H., financial executive, arbitrator, mediator, educator; b. Phila., Mar. 26, 1943; student Los Angeles Valley Coll., 1965-67, Alexander Hamilton Inst., 1965-68, Grad. Sch. of Credit and Fin. Mgmt., Stanford U., 1977-80, Pepperdine U., 1981; 1 dau., Michelle R. Cert. arbitrator, mediator, counselor Am. Arbitration Assn., Singapore Arbitration Ctr. and Inst. Internat. Negotiation and Conflict Mgmt. Asst., sr. internat. arbitrator, Korean Commercial Arbitration Commission, 1996, controller, credit mgr. Wyo. Machinery Co., Casper, 1978-83; controller/sec.-treas., dir. John E. Burns Drilling Co., Casper, 1979-82; comptroller, v.p. Philip Crosby Assocs., Inc., Winter Park, Fla., 1982-84, 84—; v.p., treas. Crosby Assocs. Internat., Inc., Winter Park, Fla.; pres., CEO Davis, Keller & Davis, New Orleans, Oreg. and Wash., 1989-98; dir. credit, arbitration and legal affairs JBS, Inc., Stafford, Tex., 1998—; mgmt./cons. and internat. arbitrator/mediator, author, lectr. Am. Arbitration Assn., Singapore Arbitration Ctr., fin. cons. Western Energy Co., Huey's Smoked Meats, Nashville, Trans-Equip., Casper, Three Percent, Inc., Riverton, Wyo., 1979-80; mem. subcom. USA/NAFTA, Washington; arbitrator, mediator BBB of Oreg. Adv. bd. dirs. Highland Park Community Ch., 1980—. Served with USNR, 1961-63. Mem. Nat. Assn. Credit Mgmt. (state rep. 1979-82, founder, chmn. Casper Credit Group), Soc. Profls. in Dispute Resolution, Am. Soc. Internat. Law, Credit Mgrs. Assn. So. Calif. (dir. bus. re-orgn. and bankruptcy 1973-74), Credit Research Found., Am. Mgmt. Assn., Practicing Law Inst. (assoc.), Wash. Export Coun. (apptd. mem. by the sec. of commerce & U.S. Trade Rep.), La. Export Coun., U.S. Dept. Commerce Industry Consultation Program (customs com.), Stanford U. Alumni Assn., Internat. Platform Assn., Internat. Inst. Negotiation and Conflict Mgmt. (Australia); cons. U.S.A./NAFTA nat. com. mem. Alliance for GATT Pres's. Export Coun. Club: Order of Demolay (sr. award 1960). Author: Charting Your Businesses Practices-U.S. Small Business Adminstrn., Transnational Arbitration as a Means of Managing Corporate Risks, International Risk Management for U.S. Small Businesses, Leasing as a Secondary Source of Financing in the Heavy Equiptment Industry.

DAVIS, ROGER LEWIS, lawyer; b. New Orleans, Jan. 27, 1946; s. Leon and Anada A. (Russ) D.; m. Annette Vucinich; 1 child, Alexandra. BA, Tulane U., 1967; MA, UCLA, 1969; PhD, UCLA, 1971; JD, Harvard U., 1974. Bar: Calif. 1974. Assoc. Orrick, Herrington & Sutcliffe, L.L.P., San Francisco, 1974-79, ptnr., 1980—, chmn. pub. fin. dept., 1981—. Mem. Bay Area Coun., San Francisco, 1988-90. Fellow Am. Coll. of Bond Counsel; mem. ABA (tax sect., mem. com. tax exempt financing), Nat. Assn. Bond Lawyers (mem. com. profl. responsibility and gen. tax matters), Calif. Pub. Securities Assn. (dir. 1998—). Office: Orrick Herrington & Sutcliffe LLP 400 Sansome St San Francisco CA 94111-3143

DAVIS, RON LEE, clergyman, author; b. Carroll, Iowa, Oct. 17, 1947; s. David Clarence and Elizabeth Regina (Thompson) D.; m. Shirley Louise O'Connor, Aug. 31, 1973; children: Rachael LeeAnn, Nathan Paul. BA cum laude, Tarkio (Mo.) Coll., 1969; MDiv cum laude, Dubuque (Iowa) Theol. Sem., 1971; DDiv, Bethel Theol. Sem., St. Paul, 1977. Ordained to ministry Presbyn. Ch., 1971. Chaplain Minn. Vikings, Mpls., 1975-80; assoc. pastor Hope Presbyn. Ch., Mpls., 1971-80; sr. pastor First Presbyn. Ch., Fresno, Calif., 1981-86, Community Presbyn. Ch., Danville, Calif., 1986-91; tchr. Bible Oakland (Calif.) A's, 1990-91; writer, 1983—; sr. pastor Bear Creek Cmty. Ch., Stockton, Calif., 1997—; invited speaker at gen. sessions and confs. and on TV. Author: Gold in the Making, 1983, A Forgiving God in an Unforgiving World, 1984, Healing Life's Hurts, 1986, A Time for Compassion, 1986, Courage to Begin Again, 1988, Mistreated, 1989, Becoming a Whole Person in a Broken World, 1990, Mentoring, 1990. Mem. pres.'s adv. coun. Fellowship of Christian Athletes; bd. dirs. Youth for Christ, cen. Calif., 1982-85, Fresno Pacific Coll., 1983-84. Recipient award for outstanding leadership State Bar; named to Outstanding Young Men of Am. Avocation: running. Home: 3902 Stoneridge Dr Apt 3 Pleasanton CA 94588-8342

DAVIS, ROSWITA BEATE, architectural engineer; b. Ranzau, Germany, Sept. 27, 1945; came to U.S., 1966; d. Heinz Otto and Erika (Waht) Neander; 1 child, Erika Neander. Archtl. Draftsperson, Trade and Tech. Coll., Unna, Whestphalen, 1963. Lic. engr., Germany. Chmn. bd. Interior Design Assoc., 1978-81; sr. facilities engr. Ford Aerospace and Comm. Corp., 1981-85. Author: (poetry) Assorted Lives, 1996; (poetry anthologies) Seasons to Come, 1995 (award 1995), Beyond the Stars, 1996 (award 1996), A Tapestry of Thoughts (award 1996), Best Poems of 1996 (award 1996); (novel) Stones That Lie, 1996. Avocations: reading, writing, dining out. Office: 8992 E Calle Diego Tucson AZ 85710-7324

DAVIS, SCOTT CAMPBELL, writer; b. Seattle, Jan. 28, 1948; s. Donald Campbell and Marilyn (Hudson) D.; m. Mary Alice McConnel, June 30, 1979. BA, Stanford U., 1970. Social worker The Bethlehem Ctr., Richmond, Va., 1971-73; housing planner Skid Rd. Cmty. Council, Seattle, 1973-74; prin., owner Scott Davis Co., Seattle, 1976—, Cune Press, Seattle, 1994—. Author: The World of Patience Gromes, 1988 (gov.'s award 1989), Lost Arrow, 1995; editor, publisher: An Ear to the Ground, 1997; publisher Cune Mag., Seattle, 1996—. V.p. Northwest Review of Books, Seattle, 1986; Eagle Scout Boy Scouts of Am., Bellevue, Wash., 1962. Avocations: mountaineering, rock climbing. Home: 911 N 67th St Seattle WA 98103-5315

DAVIS, STANFORD MELVIN, engineering executive, publishing consultant; b. Camden, N.J., June 12, 1941; s. Winford and Rose Marie (Rich) D.; m. Pamela Davis, Nov. 25, 1967 (div. 1980); children: Peter, Shawna; m. Laura A. Rudolph, Feb. 21, 1987. AB, BSEE, Rutgers U., 1964; postgrad., UCLA, 1967; MBA, U. Portland, 1974. Elec. engr. RCA, Van Nuys, Calif., 1966-68; project engr. Tek, Wilsonville, Oreg., 1968-79; S/W mgr. Tektronix, Wilsonville, 1979-81, mgr. mktg., 1981-83; founder, v.p. engring. Concept Technologies, Portland, 1983-86; mgr. engring. program INTEL, Hillsboro, Oreg., 1986-87; product line mgr. INTEL, Hillsboro, 1987-88; engring. mgr. Graphic Printing div. Textronix, Wilsonville, Oreg., 1989-95; pres. Straight-on Industries, Beaverton, Oreg., 1995—; with worldwide Web, Internet design firm; pres. Internet Profls. Northwest; v.p. sales, mktg. PDX Web. Patentee in field. Served to capt. U.S. Army, 1964-66. Recipient Outstanding Product award Datapro, Delran, N.J., 1985. Mem. Internet Profls. N.W., Software Assn. Oreg., Portland City Club (Pres.'s award 1996). Avocations: skiing, gardening, camping, tennis, fishing. Home and Office: 7320 SW 103rd Ave Beaverton OR 97008-6048

DAVIS, T. RONALD, marketing professional; b. Memphis, Mar. 23, 1949; s. T.H. and Mary Lou (Stroud) D.; m. Jan Allison, Jan. 16, 1970; children: Jeremy, Benjamin, Allison. Student, La. State U., 1969-70, Phoenix Coll., 1978-80, Ariz. State U., 1982-83. Cert. tchr., Ariz. C.C.'s. Comms. tech. Am. Express, Memphis, 1970-73, sys. analyst, 1973-78; cons. Digital Equipment Corp., Phoenix, 1978-86, strategic acct. mgr., 1986-88; dir. corp. acct. mktg. Microsoft, Redmond, Wash., 1988-91, dir. worldwide sales tng., 1991-93; pres., ceo Intellect Mktg. Group, Inc., Redmond, 1993—; bd. dirs. Key Computer Corp., Seattle; acting chief info. officer QPoint Internat., Bellevue, Wash. Designer, devel. operating sys. for Am. Express, 1973. Polit. strategist to Mayor of Redmond, 1992; bd. dirs. Kindred Spirits Animal Sanctuary, 1995—; advisor Kirkland Boys and Girls Club, 1998—. Mem. N.W. Practical Pistol Assn. (club sec. 1996—), Sammamish Rowing Assn. (chmn. membership 1996—), Queen City Yacht Club. Avocations: sailing, rowing, shooting, music. Fax: 425-898-9726. E-mail: rond@intel-lect.com. Home and Office: Intellect Mktg Group Inc 25424 NE 39th Way Redmond WA 98053-3037

DAVIS, TERRELL, football player; b. San Diego, Dec. 28, 1972. Running back Denver Broncos. Office: Denver Broncos 13655 Broncos Pkwy Englewood CO 80112-4150

DAVIS, THERAN, photojournalist; b. Boulder, Colo., Apr. 1, 1968; s. Chade D. and Laury W. (Palma) D. BS, Colo. State U., 1991. Editor Sta. KUTV, Salt Lake City, 1992-94; photographer Sta. KTUX, Salt Lake City, 1994—; freelance editor, 1992-96. Emmy spot news, 1996. Home and Office: 1760 Fremont Dr Salt Lake City UT 84104-4215

DAVIS, VIRGINIA WHITEFORD, artist; b. Kansas City, Mo., Aug. 20, 1929; d. James Young and Virginia (Bowers) Palmer; m. Martin David Davis, Sept. 21, 1951; children: Harold Leon, Nathan Joseph. BA, Smith Coll., 1950; MA, U. Ill., 1953. Instr. Craft Student's League, N.Y.C., 1972-78, Riverside Sch. Arts and Crafts, N.Y.C., 1972-78, Santa Barbara (Calif.) City Coll., 1978-79, Kean Coll., Elizabeth, N.J., 1979-80; adj. prof. Montclair (N.J.) State Coll., 1980-91; ind. artist Berkeley, N.Y.C., Calif., 1975—. One-woman exhibits include Mus. for Textiles, Toronto, Textile Art Ctr., Chgo., NEA. Visual Arts fellow, 1982, 92, N.Y. State Found. Arts fellow, 1988, 95, fellow Indo-Am. Fulbright, 1990-91, NEA, Paris, 1994, Mexico City, 1995. Mem. Textile Study Group, Surface Design Assn., Textile Soc. Am., Costume Soc. Am., Coll. Art Assn. Home and Studio: 3360 Dwight Way Berkeley CA 94704-2523

DAVIS, WANDA ROSE, lawyer; b. Lampasas, Tex., Oct. 4, 1937; d. Ellis DeWitt and Julia Doris (Rose) Cockrell; m. Richard Andrew Fulcher, May 9, 1959 (div. 1969); 1 child, Greg Ellis; m. Edwin Leon Davis, Jan. 14, 1973 (div. 1985). BBA, U. Tex., 1959, JD, 1971. Bar: Tex. 1971, Colo. 1981, U.S. Dist. Ct. (no. dist.) Tex. 1972, U.S. Dist. Ct. Colo. 1981, U.S. Ct. Appeals (10th cir. 1981, U.S. Supreme Ct. 1976. Atty. Atlantic Richfield Co., Dallas, 1971; assoc. firm Crocker & Murphy, Dallas, 1971-72; prin. Wanda Davis, Atty. at Law, Dallas, 1972-73; ptnr. firm Davis & Davis Inc., Dallas, 1973-75; atty. adviser HUD, Dallas, 1974-75, Air Force Acctg. and Fin. Ctr., Denver, 1976-92; co-chmn. regional Profl. Devel. Inst., Am. Soc. Mil. Comptrollers, Colorado Springs, Colo., 1982; chmn. Lowry AFB Noontime Edn. Program, Exercise Program, Denver, 1977-83; mem. speakers bur. Colo. Women's Bar, 1995—, Lowry AFB, 1981-83; mem. fed. ct. liaison com. U.S. Dist. Ct. Colo., 1983; mem. Leaders of the Fed. Bar Assn. People to People Del. to China, USSR and Finland, 1986. Contbr. numerous articles to profl. jours. Bd. dirs. Pres.'s Coun. Met. Denver, 1981-83; mem. Lowry AFB Alcohol Abuse Exec. Com., 1981-84. Recipient Spl. Achievement award USAF, 1978; Upward Mobility award Fed. Profl. and Adminstrv. Women, Denver, 1979, Internat. Humanitarian award CARE, 1994. Mem. Fed. Bar Assn. (pres. Colo. 1982-83, mem. nat. coun. 1984—, Earl W. Kintner Disting. Svc. award 1983, 1st v.p. 10th cir. 1986-97, Internat. Humanitarian award CARE, 1994), Zach Found. for Burned Children (award 1995), Colo. Trial Lawyers Assn., Bus. and Profl. Women's Club (dist. IV East dir. 1983-84, Colo. pres. 1988-89), Am. Soc. Mil. Comptrollers (pres. 1984-85), Denver South Met. Bus. and Profl. Women's Club (pres. 1982-83), Denver Silver Spruce Am. Bus. Women's Assn. (pres. 1981-82; Woman of Yr. award 1982), Colo. Jud. Inst., Colo. Concerned Lawyers, Profl. Mgrs. Assn., Fed. Women's Program (v.p. Denver 1980), Colo. Woman News Community adv. bd., 1988—, Dallas Bar Assn., Tex. Bar Assn., Denver Bar Assn., Altrusa, Zonta, Denver Nancy Langhorn Federally Employed Women. (pres. 1979-80). Christian.

DAVIS, WILLIAM ALBERT, minister, educator; b. Portland, Oreg., Feb. 26, 1934; s. Earl A. and Mary Ruth (Pratt) D., children: David Albert, MD, Daniel Alyn, MD; B.A. in History, Wash. State U., 1961, B.A. in Philosophy, 1962, M.A. in History, 1962; Th.M., So. Meth. U., 1967; postgrad. U. Denver, 1967-73, 79-80, U. No. Colo., 1982-83, Colo. State U., 1983-84, 87, U. Colo., Denver, 1988-89; m. Vineta Alice Rensink, July 2, 1960; children—David Albert, Daniel Alyn, Derek Andrew. Tchr. social sci. Wenat High Sch., Wenatchee, Wash., 1962-63; chmn. social scis., asst. to pres. Wenatchee Valley Coll., 1963-64; ordained to ministry United Meth. Ch., 1965, elder, 1967, commd. missionary, 1994; pastor United Meth. Ch., Celeste, Tex., 1964-67; pastor Burns Meml. United Meth. Ch., Aurora, Colo., 1967-70, 74-75; youth and edn. minister Montclair United Meth. Ch., Denver, 1970-71; polit. scientist, philosophy faculty Community Coll. Denver (now Front Range Community Coll.), 1969-81, dir. div. arts and humanities, 1981-87, exec. dir. spl. projects, 1987; asst. dir. vocal edn. Aurora (Colo.) Pub. Schs., 1987-88; pvt. practice cons., 1988-91; supt. McCurdy Sch., Espanola, N.Mex., 1991-96; prin./headmaster Accelerated Sch., Denver, 1996-97; pastor First United Ch., Las Animas, Co., 1997—; cons. Denver Urban Observatory, 1970-71; faculty rep. Colo. Bd. Community Colls. and Occupational Edn., 1972-74; treas. Bd. Edn. Adams-Arapahoe Dist. 28J, 1973-75, sec., 1975-77, pres., 1977-79, sec., 1979-81, v.p., 1981-83, bd. dirs., 1983-85, pres., 1985-87; precinct committeeman Arapahoe County Democratic Party, 1969-71, 1980-82, dist. capt., 1972-73; bd. dirs. Aurora Community Mental Health Center, 1976-85, 89-91, pres., 1981-83; trustee Aurora Community Mental Health Found., 1976-78, Aurora Community Living Resources, Inc., 1981—, pres., 1987—; trustee Aurora Mental Health Research Inst., Inc., 1981—, pres., 1985, sec., 1988—; trustee Aurora Community Hosp., 1977-80, moderator, 1978-80; mem. Aurora Citizens Adv. Utilities Budget Com., 1983-91, vice chair, 1988-91. Served with AUS, 1954-57, USAR, 1957-62, USNR, 1968-75. Mem. United Ministries in Higher Edn. (chmn. Colo. commn. 1974-75, treas. 1982-88), Colo. Assn. Community Jr. Colls. (pres. faculty unit 1972-74, parliamentarian 1974-75), Am. Legion. Clubs: K.T., Masons (32 deg., hon. past master 1991), Kiwanis (pres. 1990-91, 1993-94), Shriners, Lions (pres. 1965), Optimists (pres. 1980-81), Las Animas Ministerial Assoc (v.p. 1997-98). Home: 13257 E Nevada Ave Aurora CO 80012-2432 Office: First United Meth Ch PO Box 127 Las Animas CO 81054-0127

DAWDY, FAYE MARIE CATANIA, photographer, lecturer; b. San Mateo, [illegible] m. John Thomas Dawdy, May 5, 1974; children: Tracy Marie, John Franco. AA, Coll. of San Mateo, 1979; student, San Francisco State U., 1979—. With Proctor & Gamble Distbg. Co., San Mateo, 1973-78; ptnr. Dawdy Photography, Millbrae, Calif., 1978—; dir., sec.-treas. Millbrae Stamp Co., 1980—; instr. Winona Sch. Profl. Photography, Mt. Prospect, Ill.; lectr. in field. Contbr. articles to profl. jours. Area chmn. Millbrae Am. Heart Assn. Ann. Fund Dr., 1977-82; mem. fund raising and nutrition coms. San Mateo County chpt. Am. Heart Assn., 1980-88; co-chmn. Miss Millbrae Pageant, 1981, Queen Isabella Columbus Day Festival, 1981; judge arts and crafts exhbns. Millbrae Art and Wine Festival; judge photography competition Marin County Fair Photography Exhibit; vol. photographer Rotoplast, La Serena, Chile, 1994; mem. sister city com. City of Millbrae; trustee Golden Gate Sch. Profl. Photographers, 1985-90; active exchange student program, La Serena, San Mateo County Visitors and Convention Bur. Recipient awards No. Calif. Coun. Camera Clubs, 1979, 81, Mktg. contest award Mktg. Today mag., 1988; photograph accepted for Profl. Photographers Am. loan collection and on exhibit at Epcot Ctr., Fla., 1995. Mem. Profl. Photographers Am. (photog. craftsman degree), Profl. Photographers Greater Bay Area, Profl. Photographers No. Calif., Profl. Photographers Calif., Wedding Photographers Assn., NAFE, Millbrae C. of C. (sec. women's divsn. 1979, bd. dirs. 1991), South San Francisco C. of C., Millbrae Art Assn. (pres. 1979-80), Portola Camera Club (nature chmn. 1978—), Millbrae Hist. Assn., Friends Millbrae Libr., Italian Cath. Fedn., Calif. Women in Profl. Photography, Fedn. Ind. Bus., St. Dunstan Women's Club, Soroptimist (sec. 1981-82). Democrat. Roman Catholic. E-mail: dawdy@aol.com. Office: 449 Broadway Millbrae CA 94030-1905

DAWES, DOUGLAS CHARLES, retired career officer; b. Detroit, Nov. 24, 1952; s. Carl Joseph and Margaret Elisabeth D.; m. Theresa Neel, June 9, 1990. BBA in Mgmt., Loyola U., New Orleans, 1974; grad. with honors, Command and Gen. Staff Coll., 1987; MA in Procurement and Acquisition Mgmt., Webster U., St. Louis, 1990. Field artillery officer U.S. Army, various locations, 1974-80; asst. fin. officer U.S. Army, Ft. Sill, Okla., 1980-82; deputy fin. and acctg. officer U.S. Army, Fed. Republic of Germany, 1982-86, Ft. Carson, Colo., 1986-87; comdr. and fin. officer U.S. Army, Ft. Carson, 1987-88, budget officer, asst. div. comptr., 1988-90, div. comptr., 1990-91; chief joint pay operation Joint Svc. Software, Def. Fin. and Acctg. Svc., Denver, 1991-94; ret., 1994; payroll mgr. Neodata Svcs., Inc., Louisville, Colo., 1995-98; corp. payroll mgr. Corp. Express, Inc., Broomfield, Colo., 1998—. Vol., water safety instr. trainer ARC. Mem. Disabled Am. Vets. (life), Delta Sigma Pi (life, chancellor Delta Nu chpt. 1973, 1st v.p. 1974), Am. Legion, Am. Payroll Assn. Republican. Avocations: skiing, scuba, softball, volleyball, antique car restoration. Home: 17523 E Caspian Pl Aurora CO 80013-4172

DAWSON, DEREK, investment company executive; b. 1942. With Hendale Group, London, 1965-82; officer Southbrook and City Holdings, London, 1982-87; chmn. Southbrook Corp., Beverley Hills, Calif., 1987—. Office: Southbrook Corp 150 El Camino Dr Ste 106 Beverly Hills CA 90212*

DAWSON, FRANCES EMILY, poet, nurse; b. Augsburg, Germany, Dec. 7, 1952; d. Emmett C. Jr. and B. Louise (Boddie) D. BS in Nursing, Pa. State U., 1974. RN, D.C. Staff nurse Howard U. Med. Ctr., Washington, 1974-75, charge nurse, 1975-77. Author: Live for Today, 1986, With You in Mind, 1987, Reflections, 1988, (poetry cassette rec.) Soul Connection, 1992. Active Disabled Resource Ctr., Lupus Found. Am., Calif. Assn. Physically Handicapped; model Operation Confidence Program for the Disabled, 1985-86, head cheerleader drill team, 1985-86; mem. Long Beach Task Force for the Ams. with Disabilities Act, 1994—; active Christ 2d Baptist Ch., 1985—. Recipient Golden Poetry award, 1985-92, excellence in lit. award Pinewood Poetry, 1987-89. Mem. BMI, Walt Whitman Guild, Internat. Soc. Poets (hon. charter), Pa. State U. Alumni Assn., Detroit Black Poets Guild. Democrat. Baptist. Avocations: needlepoint, sewing. Home: 250 Pacific Ave Long Beach CA 90802-3000

DAWSON, JOHN JOSEPH, lawyer; b. Binghamton, N.Y., Mar. 9, 1947; s. Joseph John and Cecilia (O'Neill) D. BA, Siena Coll., 1968; JD, U. Notre Dame, 1971. Bar: Ariz. 1971, Nev. 1991, Calif. 1993, D.C. 1994, N.Y. 1996. Sr. bankruptcy dir. Streich Lang, P.A., Phoenix, 1971—; reporter local rules ct. U.S. Bankruptcy Ct. for Dist. Ariz.; atty. rep. U.S. Ct. Appeals (9th cir.), 1992-95. Co-author: Advanced Chapter 11 Bankruptcy, 1991. Cpl. U.S. Army, USAR, 1964-70. Fellow Ariz. Bar Found.; mem. State Bar Ariz. (chmn. bankruptcy sect. 1976-77, 80-81), Am. Bankruptcy Inst., Comml. Law League Am. Republican. Roman Catholic. Avocations: sports, reading, movies, travel, writing. Office: Streich Lang PA Renaissance One Two North Central Ave Phoenix AZ 85004-2391

DAWSON, MARTHA MORGAN, minister, writer; b. Anderson, Ind., Aug. 30, 1908; d. Earl R. and Elena (Hill) Morgan. Student, Colo. U.; D. in Div. Sci. (hon.), Brooks Divinity Coll., 1986. Ordained to ministry, 1982. Sales profl., owner Denver, 1959-68; copywriter Maginot Advt. Co., Denver, 1968-71; travel host Middle East, 1971-84; instr. Brooks Divine Sci. Coll., 1979-91, Divine Sci. Sch., Washington, 1994—. Columnist: Aspire, 1978-81; contbr. articles, stories, poems to religious and gen. publs. Mem. Colo. Poetry Soc. (pres. 1977-79), Altrusa, Denver Woman's Press Club (pres. 1973-74).

DAY, ANTHONY, newspaper writer; b. Miami, Fla., May 12, 1933; s. Price and Alice (Alexander) D.; m. Lynn Ward, June 25, 1960; children—John, Julia (dec.). A.B. cum laude, Harvard U., 1955, postgrad. (Nieman fellow), 1966-67; L.H.D. (hon.), Pepperdine U., 1974. Reporter Phila. Bull., 1957-60, Washington, 1960-69; chief Washington bur. Phila. Bull., 1969; chief editorial writer L.A. Times, 1969-71, editor editorial pages, 1971-89, sr. corr., 1989-95; contbg. writer L.A. Times Book Review, 1995—. Mem. Signet Soc. Harvard, Asia Soc., Coun. Fgn. Rels., Pacific Coun. on Internat. Policy, Inst. Current World Affairs.

DAY, CAROLINE WOLFE, interior designer, entrepreneur; b. N.Y.C., Sept. 18, 1959; d. Lincoln Hubert and Caroline Alice (Taylor) D. BS, La Roche Coll., Pitts., 1988; BA, Bennington Coll., 1983. Designer The Phillips Janson Group, N.Y.C., 1988-91; artistic dir. Jack Travis Architect, N.Y.C., 1991-93; cons. N.Y.C., 1993; sr. designer Keogh Design, Inc., N.Y.C., 1993-94; entrepreneur Caroline Day Design, Washington, 1995-97, San Francisco, 1998—; guest critic Parsons Sch. Design, N.Y.C., 1992-94, Fashion Inst. Tech., N.Y.C., 1992-94. Work published in Home Office Design, Interiors, Facilities Design and Mgmt. Vol. Christmas in April, Washington, 1997. Mem. Am. Soc. Interior Designers (1st place award 1986). Democrat. Avocations: theatre, travel; jazz, modern and tango dancing. Office: Caroline Day Design 4003 24th St Apt 2 San Francisco CA 94114-3739

DAY, GERALD W., wholesale grocery company executive. With Albertson's, Heber City, Utah, 1945-72; CEO Days Markets; chmn., bd. dirs. Associated Food Stores Inc. Office: Day's Market 890 S Main St Heber City UT 84032-2463*

DAY, JOHN DENTON, retired company executive, cattle and horse rancher, trainer, wrangler, actor, educator; b. Salt Lake City, Jan. 20, 1942; s. George W. and Grace (Denton) Jenkins; m. Susan Hansen, June 20, 1971; children: Tammy Denton Wadsworth, Jeanett B. Lloyd. Student, U. Utah, 1964-65; BA in Econs. and Bus. Adminstrn. with high honors, Westminster Coll., 1971. Riding instr., wrangler Uinta wilderness area U-Ranch, Neola, Utah, 1955-58; stock handler, driver, ruffstock rider Earl Hutchinson Rodeo Contractor, Idaho, 1959; wrangler, riding instr. YMCA Camp Rodger, Kamas, Utah; with Mil. Data Cons., Inc., L.A., 1961-62, Carlseon Credit Corp., Salt Lake City, 1962-65; sales mgr. sporting goods Western Enterprises, Salt Lake City, 1965-69; founder Rockin d Ranch, Millcreek, Utah, 1969; ski instr. Brighton (Utah) Ski Sch., 1969-71; Western rep. PBR Co., Cleve., 1969-71; dist. sales rep. Crown Zellerbach Corp., Seattle and L.A., 1971-73; pres., founder Dapco paper, chem., instl. food and janitorial supplies, Salt Lake City, 1973-79, John D Day Greeting Cards, 1990—; owner, founder, pres. John D. Day, mfrs. reps., 1972—; dist. sales mgr. Surfonics Engrs., Inc., Woods Cross, Utah, 1976-78, Garland Co., Cleve., 1978-81; rancher Heber, Utah, 1976-90, horse tng. facility, horsemanship sch. and ranch, Temecula, Calif., 1984-90, St. George, Utah, 1989—; sec. bd. Acquadyne, 1974, 75. Actor, dir., prodr. (movies) The Big Sky, 1952, Rebel [illegible] Someday Soon, 1993, A Tour of Snows Canyon, 1993, All For the Love of Horse, 1982-83, Stallion Management, 1985, others; tv commls., Chev., Palmer, others; contbr. articles to jours., including Western Artist. Group chmn. Tele-Dex fund raising project Westminster Coll.; founder, supr. vol. group Day's Rangers, 1990—; vol. Dixie Nat. Forest, 1989-94, USDA Forest Svc.; 1st U.S. wilderness ranger USDA, US Forest Svc., Dixie Nat. Forest, Pine Valley Ranger Dist., Pine Valley Mountain Wilderness, So. Utah, 1994—. With AUS, 1963-64. Recipient grand nat. award Internat. Customer Car Show, San Diego, 1962, Key to City, Louisville, 1964, Champion Bareback Riding award, 1957, Vol. award USDA Forest Svc., 1991, 92, 93, nominated U.S. Vol. award, Safety award Dixie Nat. Forest, P.V.B.D., 1992-98; recipient Outstanding Performance award USDA, 1995, 98, Cert. Appreciation, 1997, DNF Outstanding Svc. award, 1997, Pine Valley Mountain Wilderness; Dally team roping heading and heeling champion, 1982. Mem. Internat. Show Car Assn. (co-chmn. 1978-79), Am. Quarter Horse Assn. (life, high point reining champion 1981, qualified for world championship, Dodge, Toyota Fall Futurite Circuit Champion Working Cowhorse 1994-95, World Championship Show qualifier and participant Oklahoma City Sr. Cutting 1994), Intermountain Quarter Horse Assn. (sr. reining champion 1981, champion AMAT reining 1979-81), Utah Quarter Horse Assn. (state champion AMAT reining 1979, 80, AMAT barrel racing 1980, working cowhorse champion 1982, trained working cowhorse and rider champion 1992, 98, trained amateur reining horse and rider champion 1996, open cutting res. champion 1993-95, 97, open cutting champion 1994, Menlove Dodge Toyota Fall Futurity circuit champion working cowhorse, 1994-95, open working cowhorse champion & broadmare halter champion 1995, Rose cir. working cowhorse champion 1995, 98, Rose cir. open cutting champion 1996, 97, bd. dirs. 1992-94, trained amateur barrel racing and amateur pole bending horse and rider 1998), Profl. Horseman's Assn., Nat. Cutting Horse Assn. (affiliate), Profl. Cowhorseman's Assn. (world champion team roping, heeling 1986, 88, high point rider 1985, world champion stock horse rider 1985-86, 88, world champion working cowhorse 1985, PCA finals open cutting champion, 1985-88, PCA finals 1500 novice champion 1987, PCA finals all-around champion 1985-88, inducted into Hall of Fame 1988, first on record registered Tex. longhorn cutting contest, open champion, PCA founder, editor newsletter 1985-89, pres. 1984-88), World Rodeo Assn. Profls. (v.p. Western territory 1989-98, judge nat. high sch. rodeo, cutting horse and rodeo queen contest, 1990—, hon. v.p. Western Terr. U.S. 1998—). Home and Office: PO Box 55 Saint George UT 84771-0055 also: 2323 S 1800 E Saint George UT 84790-6206

DAY, L. B., management consultant; b. Walla Walla, Wash., Sept. 16, 1944; s. Frank Edmond and Geraldine Eloise (Binning) D. BS, Portland State Coll., 1966; MBA, George Washington U., 1971. Design mktg. cons. Leadership Resources Inc., Washington, 1970-71; faculty mem. USDA Grad. Sch. of Spl. Programs, Washington, 1971-74; dir. Office of Employee Devel. Oreg. Dept. Transp., Salem, 1972-75; prin. Day-Henry Assoc. Inc., Portland, Oreg., 1975-78, Day-Floren Assocs. Inc., Portland, Oreg., 1978-95, LB Day & Co., Portland, Oreg., 1996—; cons. Allergan, Arthur Andersen & Co., AMD, Egghead.com, Intel Corp., Fujitsu, Peek, Exabyte, Sequent Computer Sys., VLSI Tech., Inc., also others; mem. faculty Am. Bankers Assn., Bank trainers Sch., 1981-84; adj. prof. Willamette U. Grad. Sch. Adminstrn., Salem, 1978, Oreg. Grad. Inst., 1994; bd. dirs. Microchip Tech., Inc. Author: The Supervisory Training Program, 1977, Performance Management, 1981, Team-Oriented Management, 1989; contbr. articles to profl. jours. With U.S. Army, 1967-70. Scottish Rite fellow George Washington U., 1970. Mem. ASTD. Avocations: marathon runner, horseback riding. Office: L B Day & Co Inc 806 SW Broadway Fl 11 Portland OR 97205-3333

DAY, LUCILLE LANG, health facility administrator, educator, author; b. Oakland, Calif., Dec. 5, 1947; d. Richard Allen and Evelyn Marietta (Hazard) Lang; m. Frank Lawrence Day, Nov. 6, 1965 (div. 1970); 1 child, Liana Sherrine; m. 2nd, Theodore Herman Fleischman, June 23, 1974 (div. 1985); 1 child, Tamarind Channah. AB, U. Calif., Berkeley, 1971, MA, 1973, PhD, 1979. Teaching asst. U. Calif., Berkeley, 1971-72, 75-76, research asst., 1975, 77-78; tchr. sci. Magic Mountain Sch., Berkeley, 1977; specialist math. and sci. Novato (Calif.) Unified Sch. Dist., 1979-81; instr. sci. Project Bridge, Laney Coll., Oakland, Calif., 1984-86; sci. writer and mgr. precollege edn. programs, Lawrence Berkeley (Calif.) Nat. Lab., 1986-90, life scis. staff coord., 1990-92; mgr. Hall of Health, Berkeley, Calif., 1992—; lectr. St. Mary's Coll. of Calif., Moraga, 1997—. Author numerous poems, articles and book reviews; author: (with Joan Skolnick and Carol Langbort) How to Encourage Girls in Math and Science: Strategies for Parents and Educators, 1982, Self-Portrait with Hand Microscope (poetry collection), 1982, Fire in the Garden (poetry collection), 1997. NSF Grad. fellow, 1972-75; recipient Joseph Henry Jackson award in lit. San Francisco Found., 1982. Mem. No. Calif. Sci. Writers Assn., Nat. Assn. Sci. Writers, Math/Sci. Network, Soc. for Pub. Health Edn. (No. Calif. chpt.), Phi Beta Kappa, Iota Sigma Pi. Home: 1057 Walker Ave Oakland CA 94610-1511 Office: Hall of Health 2230 Shattuck Ave Berkeley CA 94704-1416

DAY, RICHARD SOMERS, author, editorial consultant; b. Chgo., June 14, 1928; s. Milo Frank and Ethel Mae (Somers) D.; m. Lois Patricia Beggs, July 8, 1950; children: Russell Frank, Douglas Matthew, Gail Leslie. Student, Ill. Inst. Tech., 1946, U. Miami, 1947. Promotion writer, editor Portland Cement Assn., Chgo., 1958-62, promotion writer, 1963-66; editor Am. Inst. Laundering, Joliet, Ill., 1962-63; freelance writer, Monee, Ill., 1966-69, Palomar Mountain, Calif., 1969-87; cons. editor home and shop Popular Sci. mag., N.Y.C., 1966-89; editorial cons. St. Remy Multimedia, Montreal, Que., Can., 1987—; pres., exec. producer Vi-Day-O Prodns., Inc., Palomar Mountain, Calif., 1991-98. Author numerous home improvement & repair books including: Patios and Decks, 1976, Automechanics, 1982, Do-It-Yourself Plumbing--It's Easy with Genova, 1987, Building Decks, Patios, and Fences, 1992 (Nat. Assn. Home and Workshop Writers Stanley Tools Do-It-Yourself Writing award 1992); editor: (newspaper) Powderlines, 1958; (mag.) Concrete Hwys. and Pub. Improvements, 1958-62; (mag.) Soil-Cement News, 1960-62; (mag.) Fabric Care, 1962-63; prodr. videos: How to Cure Toilet Troubles, 1994, Mountain Man Horse Packing, 1994; contbr. chpts. to books. Bd. dirs. Palomar Mountain Planning Orgn., 1984-91. Mem. Nat. Assn. Home and Workshop Writers (mng. editor newsletter 1982-96, bd. dirs. 1974—, pres. 1984-85). Home: PO Box 10 Palomar Mountain CA 92060-0010

DAY, ROBERT WINSOR, cancer researcher; b. Framingham, Mass., Oct. 22, 1930; s. Raymond Albert and Mildred (Doty) D.; m. Jane Alice Boynton, Sept. 6, 1957 (div. Sept. 1977); m. Cynthia Taylor, Dec. 16, 1977; children: Christopher, Nathalia, Natalia, Julia. Student, Harvard U., 1949-51; MD, U. Chgo., 1956; MPH, U. Calif., Berkeley, 1958, PhD, 1962. Intern USPHS, Balt., 1956-57; resident U. Calif., Berkeley, 1958-60; research specialist Calif. Dept. Mental Hygiene, 1960-64; asst. prof. sch. medicine UCLA, 1962-64; dep. dir. Calif. Dept. Pub. Health, Berkeley, 1965-67; prof., chmn. dept. health services Sch. Pub. Health and Community Medicine, U. Wash., Seattle, 1968-72, dean, 1972-82, prof., 1982—; pres., dir. Fred Hutchinson Cancer Rsch. Ctr., Seattle, 1981-97, pres., dir. emeritus, 1997—, mem. pub. health scis., 1997—; mem. Nat. Cancer Adv. Bd., 1992-98, Nat. Cancer Policy Bd., 1996—; cons. in field. Served with USPHS, 1956-57. Fellow AAAS, Am. Pub. Health Assn., Am. Coll. Preventive Medicine; mem. Am. Soc. Clin. Oncology, Soc. Preventive Oncology, Am. Assn. Cancer Rsch., Assn. Schs. Pub. Health (pres. 1981-82), Am. Assn. Cancer Insts. (bd. dirs. 1983-88, v.p. 1984-85, pres. 1985-86, chmn. bd. dirs., 1986-87). Office: Fred Hutchinson Cancer Rsch Ctr PO Box 19024 LM-120 Seattle WA 98109-1024

DAY, VAUN CHARLES, accounting educator; b. Guthrie, Okla., Sept. 24, 1955; s. Charles M. and Wilma G. (Canning) D.; m. Linda J. Kimbley, June 30, 1989; 1 child, Sarah J. BBA, U. Okla., 1979; MEd, U. Ctrl. Okla., 1988; PhD, U. Wyo., 1998. CPA, Okla. Acct. Kerr-McGee Corp., Oklahoma City, 1979-81; corp. acct. Anta Corp., Oklahoma City, 1981-85; acctg. instr. Okla. Jr. Coll., Oklahoma City, 1986-88, Laramie County C.C., Cheyenne, Wyo., 1988—. Mem. Phi Kappa Phi. Office: Laramie County C C 1400 E College Dr Cheyenne WY 82007-3204

DAY-GOWDER, PATRICIA JOAN, retired association executive, consultant; b. Lansing, Mich., Apr. 9, 1936; d. Louis A. and Johanna (Feringa) Whipple; m. Duane Lee Day, Jan. 7, 1961 (div.); children: Kevin Duane, [illegible] U., 1958; MA, Lindenwood (Mo.) Coll., 1979; postgrad. U. So. Calif., 1982-83. Cert. secondary tchr., Calif. Health edn. asst. YWCA, Rochester, N.Y., 1958-59; tchr. jr. high schs., Flint, Mich., 1959-61; tchr. Brookside Acad., Montclair, N.J., 1963-68; adult program dir. YMCA, Long Beach, Calif.,

1968-73; community edn. dir. Paramount (Calif) Unified Sch. Dist., 1973-78; exec. dir. counseling ctr., Arcadia, Calif., 1978-80; sr. citizens program dir. City of Burbank (Calif.), 1981-83; div. dir. Am. Heart Assn., L.A., 1983-87; exec. dir. Campfire Orgn., Pasadena, 1987-89; exec. dir. greater L.A. chpt. Nat. Found. of Ileitis and Colitis, 1989-90; mgr. sr. citizens mktg. dept. Meth. Hosp. So. Calif., 1989-98, cons. 50 Mktg and event Planning, 1998—; cons. community edn. State Dept. Edn., Fed. Office Community Edn., L.A. County Office Edn. Bd. dirs., v.p. Children's Creative Ctr., Long Beach, Calif., 1969-73, Traveler's Aid Soc., 1969-72; vice-chmn. Cerritos YMCA, 1968-73. Mott Found. fellow, 1977-78. Mem. AAUW, Western Gerontology Assn., Nat. Assn. Female Execs., Calif. Community Edn. Assn. (sec.-treas., 1974-77), LWV. Democrat. Congregationalist. Avocations: tennis, hiking, bicycling, painting, reading. Home: 170 Oak Forest Cir Glendora CA 91741-3718 Office: Meth Hosp So Calif 300 W Huntington Dr Arcadia CA 91007-3402

DAYLEY, JON PHILIP, linguistics educator; b. Salt Lake City, Oct. 8, 1944; s. Mac and Shirely (Boyer) D. MA in Anthropology, Idaho State U., 1970; MA in Linguistics, U. Calif., Berkeley, 1973, PhD in Linguistics, 1981. Tchg. asst., lang. rschr. Idaho State U., Pocatello, 1968-70; tech. assessor Proyecto Linguistico Francisco Marroquin, Antigua, Guatemala, 1973-77; tchg./rsch. asst. U. Calif., 1970-73, 80-81, vis. lectr., 1982; asst. prof. linguistics Boise (Idaho) State U., 1982-87, assoc. prof., 1987-92, prof., 1992—; cons. Shoshoni Lang. Course, Owyhie, Nev., 1990—. Author: Tzutujil Grammar, 1985, Tümpisa (Panamint) Grammar and Dictionary, 1989; co-author: Western Shoshoni Grammar, 1993, Shoshoni Texts, 1997; editor: Diccionario Tz'utujil, 1996. Mem. Linguistic Soc. Am., Soc. for Study of Indigenous Langs. of the Ams., Assn. Lingüistas de Lenguas Mayas. Buddhist. Home: 5953 Eastweed Pl Boise ID 83702 Office: Boise State Univ Dept English 1910 University Dr Boise ID 83725

DEADMARSH, ADAM, hockey player; b. Trail, B.C., Can., May 10, 1975. Right wing Colo. Avalanche, Denver. Office: Colo Avalanche 1635 Clay St Denver CO 80204-1743

DEAHL, WAYNE GEORGE, English language educator, communications and theater educator; b. Torrington, Wyo., Oct. 18, 1951; s. Leonard Jesse and Pauline Mae (Smith) D.; m. Teresa Lee Hunt, Aug. 12, 1972 (div. June 1981); m. Catherine Rose Large, Feb. 28, 1986; children: Michael Edmond Bostick, Jessica Brook. AA, Ea. Wyo. Coll., 1974; BA, U. Wyo., 1982, MA in English Lit., 1985. Host Morning Edit. KUWR Radio, Laramie, Wyo., 1981-83; tchg. asst. U. Wyo., Laramie, 1983-85, lectr., 1985, part-time lectr., 1985; tchr. English and theater Campbell County Sch. Dist. # 1, Gillette, Wyo., 1985-89; instr. English, comm. and theater Ea. Wyo. Coll., Torrington, 1989—; summer theater instr., tchr. dir. Chadron (Nebr.) State Coll./Post Playhouse, 1985; part-time instr. Sheridan Coll., Gillette, 1985-89; humanities scholar Wyo. Humanities Coun., Laramie. Co-editor lit. jour. Westering, 1989-92; contbr. short stories to profl. publs. Vol. VJ Day 50th Anniversary Com., Torrington, 1996; mem. Goshen County Sheriff's Posse, Torrington, 1989-90; vol. instr. Torrington Police Dept.; coach Little League, Trail Elem. Sch. Girls' Softball, Torrington, 1991—; v.p. exec. bd. Torrington Little League, 1992. Recipient Speak Up, Movin' On award Wyo. State Jaycees, 1977. Mem. Nat. Coun. Tchrs. English, Wyo. Writers Inc. (parliamentarian 1997—), Jaycees. (treas., sec., internal v.p., bd. dirs. 1975-78, Outstanding Jaycee Laramie chpt., various state awards 1976, 77). Democrat. Baptist. Avocations: fishing, hunting, gardening, woodworking. E-mail: wdeahl@ewc1.ewc.whecn.edu. Home: RR 2 Box 173 Torrington WY 82240-8913 Office: Ea Wyo Coll 3200 W C St Torrington WY 82240-1603

DEAKINS, ROGER ALEXANDER, photographer; b. Torquay, Devon, Eng., May 24, 1949; citizen of Britain and Can.; s. William Albert and Josephine (Messum) D.; m. Isabella James Purefoy Ellis, Dec. 11, 1991. BA in Art and Design, Bath Acad. of Art, U.K., 1971; Fil Degree, Nat. film Sch., Beaconsfield, Bucks, U.K., 1975. adv. Am. Film Inst., L.A., 1997. Dir. of photography for numerous feature films, including: Kundun, Courage Under Fire, Dead Man Walking, Fargo, The Shawshank Redemption, Secret Garden, The Innocent, 1984, Another Time, Another Place, Barton Fink, Sid and Nancy, Hudsucker Proxy, others; (TV documentaries) Around the World with Ridgeway, Zimbabwe, Eritrea - Behind the Lines, Raj Gonds - India, S.E. Nuba - Sudan, When the World changed, Welcome to Britain, Van Morrison in Ireland. Nominated for Acad. award Acad. of Motion Picture Arts and Scis. for: Shawshank, 1995, Fargo, 1997, Kundun, 1998; recipient ASC Outstanding Feature Photographer, Am. Soc. Cinematographers, L.A. for Shawshank, 1995, Outstanding Cinematography awards N.Y. Film Critics, L.A. Film Critics, Chgo. Film Critics, Nat. Film Bord., CamerImage, others. Mem. Am. Soc. cinematographers, Acad. Motion Picture Arts and Scis., Brit. Soc. Cinematographers. Avocations: still photography, fishing, writing.

DEAL, BARBARA NEIGHBORS, literary agent; b. San Pedro, Calif., Oct. 25, 1948; d. Clarance Edwin and Neilya Marsh (Sharon) Neighbors; m. Robert Lewis Deal, Oct. 16, 1976. BA magna cum laude, Calif. Western U., 1970; MA, U.S. Internat. U., 1971; PhD, Columbia Pacific U., 1981. Pres., sr. agt. Barbara Neighbors Deal Literary Assocs., Ojai, Calif., 1978—; founder, pres. AmaDeus Group Publs. and Found., Walla Walla, Wash., 1985—; admnstr. Nat. Disaster Search Dog Found., Ojai, 1995—; tng. cons., writer Deal Cons. Svcs., Walla Walla, 1976-80. Advisor Common Ground Mediation, Walla Walla, 1978-83. Named living treasure Calif. State Senate, 1997. Avocations: rose gardening, philosophy, spirituality. Office: PO Box 1174 Ojai CA 93024-1174

DEAL, DAVID ALLEN, illustrator, cartoonist; b. Fargo, N.D., June 19, 1938; s. John Ernest and Clarice (Dibdahl) D.; m. Velia Vasquez, Mar. 21, 1960; 1 chil, Travis A. Degree in architecture, El Camino Jr. Coll., L.A., 1960. Owner Big Deal Design, Vista, Calif., 1968—. Author: Discovery of Ancient America, 1984, The Nexus, 1993; creator Deal's Wheels Model Series, 1965, Armor-All Graphic Design, 1972, MG Mitten, Ad Series, 1965-78; creator Hot Rod, Cartoons, Private Pilot, Super VW (France), Mattel Toys, AAFES, Car & Driver, Automobile Mags. With USMC, 1955-57. Achievements include the recent discovery of the city of Naxuan, the first post-flood city built by Noah and his Descendants, 1997; holder of world speed record Tijuana to La Paz, Mexico, 1973. Avocations: pilot, photography, linguistics.

DEAL, LUISA, management consultant, trainer, former educator; b. Naples, Italy, July 15, 1943; came to U.S., 1948; d. Elaine (DeMarino) Bonomo; children: Pamela, Mark, Paula. AA, Muskegon C.C., Mich., 1967; BA, Saginaw Valley State U., 1969; MA, Cen. Mich. U., 1973; Ednl. Specialist, Mich. State U., 1982. Tchr. Saginaw (Mich.) Twp. Cmty. Schs., 1969-72, reading cons., 1972-77, reading specialist, 1977-86; mgmt. devel. trainer Automobile Club of Mich., Dearborn, 1986; assoc. mgr. ops. Gen. Physics Corp., Troy, Mich., 1987; tng. analyst Ball Systems Engrng., San Diego, 1988; pres. Tng. Support Network, La Jolla, Calif., 1989—; spkr. in field. Active Nine-Nines Internat., Detroit and San Diego, 1988—. Mem. ASTD (Detroit chpt. bd. dirs. 1987-88, San Diego chpt. EFO 1989-90, sec. 1990-91), Am. Soc. for Quality (chmn. 1996-97, chair San Diego sect.), Nat. Speakers Assn., Deming User Group, Rotary. Avocations: flying (lic. pvt. pilot), tennis, skiing, golf, biking. Office: Tng Support Network PO Box 207 La Jolla CA 92038-0207

DEAL, LYNN HOFFMANN, interior designer; b. Atlantic City, N.J., Nov. 7, 1953; d. Ralph Eaton and Helen Hoffmann; d. Michael Stanton Hegner and Mary Clyde Brown; m. James A. Deal, Sept. 19, 1981; 1 child, Katherine M. Diploma in environ. and interior design, U. Calif., Irvine, 1989. Prin. Lynn Deal and Assocs., Newport Beach, Calif., 1982—; mem. adv. bd. U. Calif., Irvine, 1984-93. Chmn. Philharm. Showcase House, 1991, 92; mem. Philharm. Soc. Orange County, Jr. League Orange County, 1989-91; annual fund chmn. Lido Isle Philhormanic Soc. Orange County, 1998-99. Mem. Am. Soc. Interior Designers (prodr. video Orange County chpt., Chpt. award 1991, Pres.'s award 1992), Internat. Furnishings and Design Assn., Interior Educators Coun., Lido Isle Women's Club. Republican. Episcopalian. Avocations: sailing, skiing, world travel, arts.

DEAN, NAT, artist, educator; b. Redwood City, Calif., Jan. 13, 1956; d. Richard William and Marianne Ridley (Smith) D.; m. Paul Singdahlsen, May 24, 1987. Student, Calif. Inst. of Arts, 1972-76, Cooper Union Coll., 1975; BFA, San Francisco Art Inst., 1977. Freelance artist, educator Fla./Calif, 1978-95; annual workshop leader, lectr. Calif. Inst. of Arts, Valencia, 1985—; dir. career planning Calif. Inst. Arts, Valencia, 1986-89; dir. of career ctr. Ringling Sch. of Art and Design, Sarasota, Fla., 1989-92; conf. co-organizer Arts Placment Profls. Groups, 1989, 91, 92, 93; pres., owner Ruta Zinc Fine Arts Agy., San Francisco and L.A., 1980-89; freelance artist, educator N.Mex./Calif., 1995—; guest lectr. Iowa State U., Ames, 1992; adj. faculty Md. Inst., Balt.; lectr. L.A. Internat. Art Fair, 1988-94; organizer annual Dialogue Among Peers, Santa Fe, 1997—, numerous others. One-person shows and group exhbns. include Valencia C.C., Orlando, Fla., 1995, Durango (Colo.) Art Ctr., 1995, Manatee C.C., Bradenton, Fla., 1994, Ormond Beach (Fla.) Meml. Art Mus., 1994, Oreg. Sch. of Arts & Crafts, Portland, 1993, The Edn. Ctr. Gallery, Longboat Key, Fla., 1993, Nutaalite, Buena Park, Calif., 1993, Sarasota County (Fla.) Arts Coun., 1993, ARTarget, Sarasota, Fla., 1993, Selby Gallery, Sarasota, Fla., 1992, Ctr. Gallaery, Miami-Dade C.C., 1991, NCCA Gallery/New Ctr. for Creative Awareness, Sarasota, 1990, Scottsdale (Ariz.) Ctr. for Arts, 1992, 95, Boca Raton (Fla.) Mus. Art, 1991, Coll. Creative Studies, U. Calif., Santa Barbara, 1990, San Francisco Mus. Modern Art Rental Gallery, 1986, 89, Galerie Anton Meir, Geneva, 1988, Orange County Ctr. Contemporary Art, Santa Ana, Calif., 1990, The Fukuoka Mcpl. Mus., Japan, 1987, others; co-author: The Visual Artist's Business and Legal Guide, 1995. Chmn. visual artists task force Sarasota County Arts Coun., 1991-92; AIDS subcom. Planned Approach to Community Health, Sarasota, 1991-92; visual aids com., Visual Aids: Day Without Art, 1989—; program adv. Regional Occupational Program, Contra Costa Bd. Edn., 1986, numerous others. Recipient Residency award The Bemis Project, Omaha, 1986, Profl. Devel. grant Ringling Sch. of Art and Design, Sarasota, 1990, Merit award Calif. Inst. of Arts, Valencia, 1976, others. Mem. Coll. Art Assn. (speaker 1992, 93), Nat. Artists Equity (speaker 1992), Women's Caucus for Art (speaker 1993), Nat. Soc. Exptl. Learning (speaker 1988, 89, 92, 93), Nat. Art Edn. Assn. (speaker 1992), Nat. Assn. Artists Orgns., Coll. Placement Coun., others. Studio and Office: 110 Sierra Azul Santa Fe NM 87501-0188

DE ANDA, ALICIA, artist; b. L.A., Mar. 8, 1965; d. Simon and Alicia (Saenz) De A. AA, Brooks Coll., 1985. Sales assoc. The Broadway, Orange, Calif., 1985-86, Nordstrom, Cerritos, Calif., 1986-89; sec. The Reef Funds, Cerritos, 1989-90; model L.A., 1990-92; bus. mgr. Estee Lauder/Robinsons May, Canoga Park, 1992-95; make-up artist Lancome/Saks Fifth Ave., Beverly Hills, 1995—; bus. mgr. Estee Lauder, 1996—. Actress in theatrical prodns. in Woodland Hills and Calabasas, Calif. Mem. NAFE, L.A. County Mus. of Art, Nat. Mus. of Women in the Arts, Mus. Contemporary Art (L.A.), Armand Hammer Mus. Art. Democrat. Avocations: drawing, painting, ceramics, photography, acting. Office: Saks Fifth Ave 9600 Wilshire Blvd Beverly Hills CA 90212-2397

DEANE, DEBBE, psychologist, journalist, editor, consultant; b. Coatesville, Pa., July 30, 1950; d. George Edward and Dorothea Alice (Martin) Mays; widowed; children: Theo, Vonisha, Lorise, Voniece. AA in Psychology, Mesa Coll., 1989; BA Psychology, San Diego State U., 1993; MA in Psychology, Nat. U., 1995; postgrad., U.S. Internat. U., 1995—. News dir. Sta. KLDR, Denver, 1976-78; host, reporter Sta. KMGH-TV, Denver, 1978-81; news anchor, editor Sta. KHOW, Denver, 1978-79; news & pub. affairs dir. Sta. KLZ, Denver, 1979-80, Sta. KCBQ, San Diego, 1980-82; news anchor Sta. KOGO, San Diego, 1983-84; news anchor, reporter Sta. KCST-TV, San Diego, 1984-87; dir. comm. Omni Corp., San Diego, 1987—; news anchor Sta. KFI, L.A., 1990-91; sr. psychiat. therapist Behavioral Health Group, San Diego, 1993—; media liaison United Negro Coll. Fund, San Diego, 1990-92; dir. comm. United Chs. of Christ, San Diego, 1989-92; cons. San Diego Assn. Black Journalists, 1985-92, San Diego Coalition Black Journalists, 1985-92; family svc. ctr. cons. and program coord. San Diego Health Start, Inc., 1997—; cons. Home Start, Inc., 1996—; broadcast media cons., 1995—. Campaign fin. analyst San Diego County Registrar of Voters, San Diego, 1990; cons. San Diego County Office Disaster Preparedness, 1990-91, Nu Way Youth Ctr. & Neighborhood House, Inc., San Diego, 1991-92; counselor Project STARRT, San Diego, 1991-92; cons. United Way Home Start, Inc. Family Self-Sufficiency Program, 1996—; cons. and program coord. San Diego Healthy Start, Inc., 1997—, Samuel L. Gompers Secondary Inst. Math., Sci. & computer Tech., 1997—. Recipient San Diego Black Achievement award Urban League, 1989, Best News Show & Spot News award San Diego Press Club, 1985, Golden Mike award So. Calif. Broadcast Assn., L.A., 1986; named one of Top 25 Businesswomen Essence Mag., 1978, Outstanding Humanitarian Worldvision, 1993, Outstanding Humanities Alumna Mesa Coll., 1993, Woman of the Year, 1996 American Biographical Inst. Mem. AFTRA, APA, Am. Women in Radio & TV, Women in Comm., Black Students Sci. Orgn. (sec. 1989-91), Africana Psychol. Soc. (media coord. 1990-92), Psi Chi. Democrat. Avocations: photography, fashion design, travel, volunteering, skiing. Home: 3545 Valley Rd Bonita CA 91902-4163

DEANGELIS, ANGELA See BROWNE-MILLER, ANGELA CHRISTINE

DEANGELIS, DAN, transportation executive; b. Stockton, Calif., July 23, 1947; m. Shari Thornton, 1973; children: Ryan, Jamie. BA in Adminstrn. Justice, Delta Coll., 1967. Lic. comml. pilot; cert. airline transport pilot. Chief pilot, flight instr. Werner's Aero Svc. Stockton Metropolitan Airport; with City of Manteca, 1974-76; airport ops. dep. Dept. Aviation County of San Joaquin, 1976-85, asst. airport ops. mgr., 1985-87, dep. airport mgr. ops., 1987-90; airport mgr. Stockton Metropolitan Airport, 1990—. Office: Stockton Met Airport 5000 S Airport Way Ste 202 Stockton CA 95206-3911*

DEAR, RONALD BRUCE, social work educator; b. Phila., Sept. 23, 1933; s. John David and Margaret (McDade) D.; 1 child, Bruce. BA, Bucknell U., 1955; honors cert., U. Aberdeen, Scotland, 1955; MSW, U. Pitts., 1957; PhD in Social Work, Columbia U., 1972. Cert. social worker, N.Y., Wash. Chief social worker Mental Hygiene Cons. Svc., Aberdeen Proving Ground, Md., 1958-60; chief Neuropsychiat. Clinic, 7th Inf. Divsn., Korea, 1960-61; residence dir. Horizon House, Inc., Phila., 1961-64; prof. U. Wash., Seattle, 1970—; vis. prof. U. Bergen, Norway, 1984, U. Trondheim, Norway, 1996; faculty lobbyist U. Wash., 1983-85, 88-91, faculty pres., 1993-95; master tchr. Coun. on Social Work Edn., 1991, 93, 94, 97; mem. adv. bd. Internat. Population and Family Assocs., 1994—; bd. dirs. Wash. Future, 1994—. Editor: Poverty in Perspective, 1973; contbr. articles to profl. jours. and encys. Apptd. by gov. to income assistance adv. com., 1987-93, to adv. com. for Dept. S ocial and Health Svcs., 1980-83, Human Svcs. Policy Ctr., 1996—, adv. com. Wash. State Econ. Svcs., 1996—; mem. nat. adv. bd. Educating Students to Influence State Policy and Legislation, 1997—; appeared in centennial program of Columbia U. Sch. of Social Work, 1998. 1st lt. U.S. Army, 1957-61. Mem. NASW (Social Worker of Yr. Wash. chpt. 1981, mem. staff legis. N.Y.C. chpt. 1968-69), Acad. Cert. Social Workers, Coun. on Social Work Edn. Avocations: travel in over 45 countries, photography, hiking. Home: 7328 16th Ave NE Seattle WA 98115-5737 Office: U Wash Sch Social Work 4101 15th Ave NE Seattle WA 98105-6250

DEATS, RICHARD WARREN (DICKY DEATS), key grip; b. Los Angeles, Feb. 27, 1945; s. Rufus and Ruth (Baxter) D.; m. Emmy A. Zucca (div. 1980); children: Danielle, Jerry; m. Jessie Anne Harring, Sept. 23, 1980; 1 child, James Richard. Student high sch., Calif. Key grip operator films No Small Affair, Blow Out, The River, Heaven's Gate, Going South, Two Jakes, Maverick, Dante's Peak, Assassins, Hope Floats; rigging key grip operator films including Close Encounters of the Third Kind, Flesh and Blood, Jinxed; owner Day for Night, Inc., Calif., Dicky Deats, Inc., Calif., Glacier Film Equipment Co., Inc., Mont. Recipient Tech. Achievement award The Little Big Crane Acad. Motion Picture Arts and Scis., 1983.

DEAVER, PHILLIP LESTER, lawyer; b. Long Beach, Calif., July 21, 1952; s. Albert Lester and Eva Lucille (Welton) D. Student, USCG Acad., 1970-72; BA, UCLA, 1974; JD, U. So. Calif., 1977. Bar: Hawaii 1977, U.S. Dist. Ct. Hawaii 1977, U.S. Ct. Appeals (9th cir.) 1978, U.S. Supreme Ct. 1981. Assoc. Carlsmith, Wichman, Case, Mukai & Ichiki, Honolulu, 1977-83, ptnr., 1983-86; ptnr. Bays, Deaver, Hiatt, Lung & Rose, Honolulu, 1986, mng. ptnr., 1986-95. Contbr. articles to profl. jours. Dir. Parents and Children Together. Mem. ABA (forum com. on the Constrn. Industry), AIA (affiliate Hawaii chpt.), Am. Arbitration Assn. (arbitrator). Home: 2471 Pacific Heights Rd Honolulu HI 96813-1029 Office: Bays Deaver Hiatt Lung & Rose PO Box 1760 Honolulu HI 96806-1760

DE BARCZA, GLADYS MARY, art educator; b. Englewood, N.J., Sept. 4, 1939; d. Stephen Bela and Alice (Mayerberg) de Bence; m. George De Barcza, July 1959; 1 child, Monica. BA, CUNY, 1962, MS, 1966; PhD, U. Ga., 1988. Chair dept. art Am. Sch. Kuwait, 1983-86; instr. U. Ga., Athens, 1986-87; dir. art edn. Modern Mus. Art, Santa Ana, Calif., 1990-91; instr. Coastline C.C., Fountain Valley, Calif., 1991-93, Pasadena (Calif.) City Coll., 1993-95; art rschr., cons. Expedition Oceania, Fiji, 1995-97; bd. dirs. Internat. Surfing Mus., Huntington Beach, Calif.; founder, pres. Beauty at Your Doorstep, 1991-99. One-woman shows include Fili's Fancy, Vuda Point, Fifi, 1997; exhibited in group shows at Hist. Lyndon House, Athens, Ga., 1987, San Diego Convention Ctr., 1991, Sheraton Fiji Resort Art Gallery, 1996, Dado Art Gallery, Nadi, Fiji, 1996-97; represented in permenant collections Chevron Shipping Corp., Arabian Am. Oil Co.; author: Colour Me Fiji: An Educational Art Gallery, 1989, Color Me Old Town San Diego, 1991, Huntington Beach Educational Coloring Book, 1998; contbr. articles to profl. jours. Curatorial com. Pasadena Hist. Soc., 1991-92. Recipient Fulbright award, 1986. Mem. Western Arts & Crafts Soc., Coll. Art Assn., Internat. Soc. for Edn. Through Art, Pacific Arts Assn., Royal Suva Club, Musket Cove Yacht Club. Roman Catholic. Avocations: drawing, painting, theatre, tennis, sailing. Office: Beauty at Your Doorstep 20971 Coastview Ln Huntington Beach CA 92648-5271

DEBARD, ROGER, investment executive; b. Cleve., Nov. 10, 1941; d. Victor and Margaret Ann (Henderson) DeB.; m. Janet Marie Schulz, July 3, 1965; children: Eila Burns, Ryan Alexander. BS, Bowling Green State U., 1963; MBA, Case Western Res. U., 1968; MA, Claremont Grad. Sch., 1978, PhD, 1981. Asst. v.p. A.G. Becker & Co., L.A., 1972-76; sr. portfolio mgr. Scudder Stevens & Clark, L.A., 1976-81; v.p. Crocker Investment Mgmt., L.A., 1981-85; exec. v.p. Hotchkis and Wiley Funds, L.A., 1985—; prin., 1992-94; gen. ptnr. Hotchkis and Wiley, L.A., 1994-95; mng. dir., mem., 1995—; mng. dir. Merrill Lynch Mercury, London, 1997—; adj. prof. fin. Pepperdine U., L.A., 1981-85. Mem. The Founders-Music Ctr. L.A., L.A. World Affairs Coun., 1988—, L.A. Libr. Assn., 1976—, pres. 1980-81. Recipient First Pl. Pub. award Investment Dealers Digest, 1971, Outstanding Svc. award City of L.A., 1980; grad. fellow Rand Grad. Inst., 1974-76. Mem. L.A. Bd. Bond Club (sec./dir. 1986-89), L.A. Soc. Fin. Analysts, Newcomer Soc., Yosemite Assoc., Calif. Club, Bel-Air Bay Club, L.A. Country Club, Sigma Chi. Republican. Episcopalian. Avocations: rare books, golf, tennis. Home: 48 Haldeman Dr Santa Monica CA 90402-1004 also: PO Box 6926 230 Gaduate Ln Ketchum ID 83353 Office: Hotchkis and Wiley 725 S Figueroa St Ste 4000 Los Angeles CA 90017-5400

DEBARTOLO, EDWARD JOHN, JR., professional football team owner, real estate developer; b. Youngstown, Ohio, Nov. 6, 1946; s. Edward J. and Marie Patricia (Montani) DeB.; m. Cynthia Ruth Papalia, Nov. 27, 1968; children: Lisa Marie, Tiffanie Lynne, Nicole Anne. Student, U. Notre Dame, 1964-68. With Edward J. DeBartolo Corp., Youngstown, Ohio, 1960—, v.p., 1971-76, exec. v.p., 1976-79, chief adminstrv. officer, 1979-94; pres., CEO, 1995—; owner San Francisco 49ers, 1977-97; chmn. bd. DeBartolo Realty Corp., 1994—; chmn., CEO DeBartolo Entertainment, Inc. Trustee Youngstown State U., 1974-77; nat. adv. coun. St. Jude Children's Rsch. Hosp., 1978—, local chmn., 1979-80; chmn. local fund drive Am. Cancer Soc., 1975—; mem. Nat. Cambodia Crisis Com., 1980—; chmn. 19th Ann. Victor Warner award, 1985, City of Hope's Spirit of Life Banquet, 1986; apptd. adv. coun. Coll. Bus. Adminstrn. U. Notre Dame, 1988; adv. coun. Nat. Assn. People with AIDS, 1992; bd. dirs. Cleve. Clinic Found., 1991; lifetime mem. Italian Scholarship League. With U.S. Army, 1969. Recipient Man of Yr. award St. Jude Children's Hosp., 1979, Boy's Town of Italy in San Francisco, 1985, Sportsman of Yr. award Nat. Italian Am. Sports Hall of Fame, 1991, Cert. of Merit, Salvation Army, 1982, Warner award, 1986, Silver Cable Car award San Francisco Conv. and Visitors Bur., 1988, Nat. Football League Man of Yr. award Football News, 1989, Svc. to Youth award Cath. Youth Orgn., 1990, Hall of Fame award Cardinal Mooney High Sch., 1993. Mem. Internat. Coun. Shopping Ctrs., Italian Scholarship League (life), Tippecanoe Country Club, Fonderlac Country Club, Dapper Dan Club (dir. 1980—). Office: Edward J DeBartolo Corp PO Box 9128 Youngstown OH 44513-0128 also: care San Francisco 49ers 4949 Centennial Blvd Santa Clara CA 95054-1229*

DEBAS, HAILE T., gastrointestinal surgeon, physiologist, educator; b. Asmara, Eritrea, Feb. 25, 1937; came to U.S., 1981; s. Tesfaye and Keddes (Gabre) D.; m. Ignacia Kim Assing, May 23, 1969. BS in Biology, U. Coll., Addis Ababa, Ethiopia, 1958; MD, CM, McGill U., Montreal, Que., Can., 1963. Intern Ottawa (Ont.) Civic Hosp., Can., 1963-64; resident in surgery U. B.C., Vancouver, Can., 1964-69, asst. prof. surgery, 1971-75, assoc. prof., 1976-80; fellow in gastrointestinal physiology UCLA, 1972-74, prof. of surgery, 1981-85; chief gastrointestinal surgery U. Wash., Seattle, 1985-87; prof., chmn. dept. surgery U. Calif., San Francisco, 1987-93; dean U. Calif. Sch. Medicine, San Francisco, 1993—, chancellor, 1997-98, vice chancellor med. affairs, 1998—; key investigator Ctr. for Ulcer Rsch. and Edn., UCLA, 1980-90; cons. Bd. Med. Quality Assurance, Calif., 1981—; bd. dirs. Am. Bd. Surgery, 1990. Mem. editorial bd. Am. Jour. Physiology, Am. Jour. Surgery, Jour. Surg. Rsch., Western Jour. Medicine, Gastroenterology; contbr. articles to profl. jours. and chpts. to books. Fellow Med. Rsch. Coun. of Can., 1972-74; rsch. grantee NIH, 1976—. Fellow ACS, Royal Coll. Physicians and Surgeons Can.; mem. Am. Surg. Assn., Am. Gastroent. Assn. (bd. govs. 1995—), Am. Assn. Endocrine Surgeons, Collequium Internat. Chirugiae Digestivae, Soc. Univ. Surgeons, Soc. Surgeons Alimentary Tract (trustee 1984-89), Soc. Black Aced. Surgeons (pres. 1998—), Inst. Medicine, Am. Acad. Arts and Scis., Internat. Hepato-Biliary Pancreatic Assn. (pres. 1991-92), Assn. Minority Acad. Physicians (pres. 1992-93). Office: U Calif Sch Medicine Office of the Dean 513 Parnassus Ave # San Francisco CA 94122-2722

DEBENHAM, RAY GENE, electric supply company executive; b. Salt Lake City, Oct. 1, 1935; s. Shirley R. and Lillian (Greguhn) D.; m. Rita J. Peterson, Aug. 14, 1959; children: Debra, Julie, Michael, Shaun. BS, Alaska Pacific U., 1972; OPM, Harvard U., 1987. CEO Debenham Alaska Investments, Anchorage, 1960—; pres. Kiana Investments, Anchorage, 1968-91; CEO Taku Enterprises, Anchorage, 1988—; pres., CEO Kiana Investments, Anchorage, 1996-97; chmn. bd. dirs. Profl. Botanicals, Ogden, Utah, 1979-80; bd. advisers SBA, Washington, 1983-88, Philips Lighting, 1990-92, Cuttler Hammer, 1989-90. Mem. bd. trustees Alaska Pacific U., 1992—, chmn. bd. dirs. univ. facilities. Mem. Nat. Assn. Elec. Distbrs. (chmn. utility com. 1981-85), Nat. Assn. Disbtrs., Am. Legion. Mormon.

DEBOER, (STEWART) BRETT, graphic design educator; b. Rapid City, S.D., Jan. 5, 1954; s. William Leroy and Ruth Elaine (Allen) DeB.; m. Teresa Ann Brooks, Feb. 27, 1981 (div. 1989); m. Kathy Terese McKenzie, Aug. 12, 1994. BFA, U. North Colo., 1977; MS in Art Edn., Bank St. Coll. of Edn., 1985; MFA in Graphic Design, Rochester Inst. Tech., 1989. Cert. tchr. K-12, Colo. Graphic artist 6th Dist. Coun. of Govt., Rapid City, 1978-79; art instr. Abbey H.S., Cañon City, Colo., 1979-81; sculptor Art Castings of Colo., Loveland, 1981; art instr. Graland Country Day Sch., Denver, 1982-87; art dir., designer Rosanne Werner Design Assoc., Rochester, N.Y., 1989-91; instr. graphic design, computer graphics Greece (N.Y.) Oly. H.S., 1991; instr. graphic design, computer graphics N.W. Coll., Powell, Wyo., 1991—, coord. art dept., 1995—, designer coll. publs., 1992-95; cons., instr. computer graphics U. Wyo., Laramie, 1993-95. Designer: The Book of Wyoming, 1995. Faculty advisor for student designer Downtown Improvement Project, Powell, 1993, Big Horn Nat. Recreation Area, Lovell, Wyo., 1994—. Recipient Step by Step Mag. Package Design award, 1997. Mem. Am. Inst. for Graphic Arts. Avocations: biking, hiking, softball, piano, art. Home: 645 N Absaroka St Powell WY 82435-1828 Office: N W Coll 231 W 6th St Powell WY 82435-1898

DEBOER, DAVID BRIAN, engineer; b. Norwalk, Calif., Oct. 10, 1960; s. David and Rita (Hoekstra) DeB.; m. Beth Ann Shepherd, May 5, 1990; children: Emily Ann, Joshua Douwe. BA, Calif. State U., Fullerton, 1992, MS, 1997. Engrng. field technician E-Squared Engrng., Huntington Beach, Calif., 1981-84; engrng. estimator Kiewit Pacific Co., Santa Fe Springs, Calif., 1985; lab. technician Structural Composites Industries, Pomona,

Calif., 1986; air quality specialist South Coast Air Quality Mgmt. Dist., Diamond Bar, Calif., 1986—; environ. justice cmty. response team mem. South Coast Air Quality Mgmt. Dist., Diamond Bar, 1998—; statewide portable equipment workgroup compliance subgroup mem. Calif. Air Resources Bd., 1998—. Avocations: wilderness backpacking, mountain biking, skiing. Office: South Coast Air Quality Mgmt Dist 21865 Copley Dr Diamond Bar CA 91765-4178

DEBREU, GERARD, economics and mathematics educator; b. Calais, France, July 4, 1921; came to U.S., 1950, naturalized, 1975; s. Camille and Fernande (Decharne) D.; m. Françoise Bled, June 14, 1945; children: Chantal, Florence. Student, Ecole Normale Supérieure, Paris, 1941-44, Agrégé de l'Université, France, 1946; DSc, U. Paris, 1956; Dr. Rerum Politicarum honoris causa, U. Bonn, 1977; D. Scis. Economiques (hon.), U. Lausanne, 1980; DSc (hon.), Northwestern U., 1981; Dr. honoris causa, U. des Scis. Sociales de Toulouse, 1983, Yale U., 1987, U. Bordeaux I, 1988. Rsch. assoc. Centre Nat. De La Recherche Sci., Paris, 1946-48; Rockefeller fellow U.S., Sweden and Norway, 1948-50; rsch. assoc. Cowles Commn., U. Chgo., 1950-55; assoc. prof. econs. Cowles Found., Yale, 1955-61; fellow Ctr. Advanced Study Behavioral Scis., Stanford U., 1960-61; vis. prof. econs. Yale U., fall 1961; prof. emeritus U. Calif., Berkeley, 1962—, prof. Miller Inst. Basic Rsch. in Sci., 1973-74, prof. math., 1975—, univ. prof., 1985—; Guggenheim fellow, vis. prof. Ctr. Ops. Rsch. and Econometrics, U. Louvain, 1968-69, vis. prof., 1971, 72, 88; Erskine fellow U. Canterbury, Christchurch, New Zealand, 1969, 87, vis. prof., 1973; Overseas fellow Churchill Coll., Cambridge, Eng., 1972; Plenary address Internat. Congress Mathematicians, Vancouver, 1974; vis. prof. Cowles Found. for Rsch. in Econs., Yale U., 1976; vis. prof. U. Bonn, 1977; rsch. assoc. Cepremap, Paris, 1980; faculty rsch. lectr. U. Calif., Berkeley, 1984-85, univ. prof., 1985—, Class of 1958 Chair, 1986—; vis. prof. U. Sydney, Australia, 1987; lectr. in field. Author: Theory of Value, 1959, Mathematical Economics: Twenty Papers of Gerard Debreu, 1983; assoc. editor Internat. Econ. Rev., 1959-69; mem. editorial bd. Jours. Econ. Theory, 1972—, SIAM Jours. on Applied Math., 1976-79, Jours. of Complexity, 1985—, Games and Econ. Behavior, 1989—, Econ. Theory, 1991; mem. adv. bd. Jours. Math. Econs., 1974—; correspondent Math. Intelligencer, 1983-84. Served with French Army, 1944-45. Decorated Chevalier de la Légion d'Honneur, Commandeur de l'Ordre National du Mérite, Officier Le Légion d'Honneur; recipient Nobel Prize in Econ. Scis., 1983, Berkeley Citation, 1991; sr. U.S. Sci. awardee Alexander von Humboldt Found., 1977. Fellow AAAS, Econometric Soc. (mem. coun. 1964-72, 78-85, Fisher-Schultz lectr. 1969, exec. com. 1969-72, 80-82, pres. 1971), Am. Econ. Assn. (disting. fellow 1982, pres.-elect 1989, pres. 1990); mem. NAS (chmn. sect. econ. scis. 1982-85, com. human rights 1984-90, chair class V behavioral and social scis. 1989-92, mem. Coun. of NAS of USA 1993—), Am. Philos. Soc., French Acad. Scis. (fgn. assoc.), Berkeley Fellows.

DE BRUYCKER, LLOYD HENRY, rancher, feedlot operator; b. Great Falls, Mont., Dec. 1, 1933; s. Achiel Henry and Rose Presperine (Emperor) De B.; m. Jane Crystal, July 2, 1954; 7 children. Grad. high sch., Dutton, Mont. Grain elevator laborer, 1954-59, rancher, 1959—. Avocation: thoroughbred horses. Home: Box 7700 Dutton MT 59433 Office: North Mt Feeders Inc PO Box 218 Choteau MT 59422-0218

DEBUS, ELEANOR VIOLA, retired business management company executive; b. Buffalo, May 19, 1920; d. Arthur Adam and Viola Charlotte (Pohl) D.; student Chown Bus. Sch., 1939. Sec., Buffalo Wire Works, 1939-45; home talent producer Empire Producing Co., Kansas City, Mo., sec. Owens Corning Fiberglass, Buffalo; pub. rels. and publicity Niagara Falls Theatre, Ont., Can.; pub. rels. dir. Woman's Internat. Bowling Congress, Columbus, Ohio, 1957-59; publicist, sec. Ice Capades, Hollywood, Calif., 1961-63; sec. to contr. Rexall Drug Co., L.A., 1963-67; bus. mgmt. acct. Samuel Berke & Co., Beverly Hills, Calif., 1967-75; Gadbois Mgmt. Co., Beverly Hills, 1975-76; sec., treas. Sasha Corp., L.A., 1976-92; former bus. mgr. Dean Martin, Debbie Reynolds, Shirley MacLaine. Mem. Am. Film Inst. Republican. Contbr. articles to various mags.

DECARLO, ANGELA ROCCO, writer, journalist; b. Chgo., Sept. 11, 1949; d. Peter J. And Della (Serritella) Rocco; m. Daniel G. DeCarlo; children: Mark, Michael, Daniel. BA in Communications and Edn., Benedictine U., 1975. Cert. K-12 tchr., Ill. Disney writer Chgo. Tribune; columnist The Bus. Traveler Las Vegas (Nev.) Rev. Jour., 1985; pres. DeCarlo Comm., Orange, Calif., 1975—. Co-chair prologues, docent Opera Pacific. Mem. Profl. Writers Orange County (bd. dirs.). Avocations: reading, tennis, golf, opera. Office: DeCarlo Comm 2718 N Vista Knoll Rd Orange CA 92867-1750

DECARO, PAT ELIZABETH, artist, educator; b. Phila., June 30, 1951; d. Ralph and Dora Marie (Natali) DeC.; m. Cris Alan Bruch, July 28, 1991. BA, Temple U., 1973; MFA, U. Wash., 1982. Asst. prof. Seattle U., 1985-89; instr. in art Bellevue (Wash.) C.C., 1990—; spkr. in field. Exhbns. include Undercurrents, PCVA, 1987, Bellevue Mus., 1992, 94, Neddy Artist Fellowship Exhibit, 1997, Archer Gallery, Clark Coll., 1997. Ford Found. scholar, 1981; Fulbright-Hays fellow in painting, Italy, 1983-84, vis. artist fellow Brandywine Workshop, Phila., 1993; artist residency MacDowell Colony, 1982, 94. Mem. Lambda Rho Art Scholarship Assn. Office: Francine Seders Gallery 6701 Greenwood Ave N Seattle WA 98103-5225

DECATUR, RAYLENE, museum official. Pres. Denver Mus. of Natural History, 1995—. Office: Denver Mus of Natural History 2001 Colorado Blvd Denver CO 80205*

DE CHAMPEAUX DE LABOULAYE, DENNIS, computer scientist. BS in Math., U. Amsterdam, The Netherlands; PhD in Math., U. Leiden, The Netherlands. Rschr. U. Amsterdam, 1970-82; assoc. prof. Tulane U., New Orleans, 1982-84; staff engr. ADAC Labs., San Jose, Calif., 1984-86; engr., scientist Hewlett-Packard, Palo Alto, Calif., 1986-93; sr. SW cons. Rational, Santa Clara, Calif., 1993-94; cons. Scopus, Emeryville, 1994, Libr. U. Calif., Berkeley, 1994, NET, Redwood City, Calif., 1994, McKesson, San Francisco, 1995, Nat. Semiconductor, Santa Clara, 1995-96, KLA, San Jose, 1996, AllTell, San Jose, 1996, Kaiser Permanente, Oakland, Calif., 1996, KLA, San Jose, 1997, Sabre Decision Systems, Ft. Worth, 1997-98; lectr. in field. Mem. AAAI, Wiskundig Genootschap, Assn. Computing Machinery, Sigart.

DECHANCE, YVONNE RENÉ, music educator; b. Mather AFB, Calif., Apr. 6, 1966; d. Richard P. and Gladys A. (Claypool) D.; m. Gary E. Blackburn, June 22, 1996. BA, Whitworth Coll., Spokane, Wash., 1988; MusM, U. Tex., 1991, D of Musical Arts, 1994. Pvt. practice voice instr. YD Studio, Austin, 1989-96; voice instr. U. Tex. Informal Classes, Austin, 1994-96; pvt. instr. Dechance Studios, Redwood City, Calif., 1996—, ednl. web designer, 1997—; lectr. East Carolina U., Greenville, 1998. Mem. Nat. Assn. Tchrs. of Singing, U. Tex. Exes, Mu Phi Epsilon. Avocations: costume design, miniatures. Office: Dechance Studios 920 7th Ave Redwood City CA 94063-4227

DECHERT, PETER, photographer, writer, foundation administrator; b. Phila., Dec. 17, 1924; s. Robert and Helen Hope (Wilson) D.; m. Phoebe Jane Booth; children: Sandra, Robin Booth, Caroline. BA, U. Pa., 1948, MA, 1950, PhD, 1955. Owner, Peter Dechert Assocs., Bryn Mawr, Pa., 1956-68; asst. dir. Sch. of Am. Rsch., Santa Fe, 1968-71; pres. Indian Arts Fund, Santa Fe, 1971-72; pres. S.W. Found. for Audio-Visual Resources, Santa Fe, 1973-77; self-employed writer, photographer, Santa Fe; tchr., cons. photog. comm., 1964—. Author: Canon Rangefinder Cameras, 1933-68, 1985, The Contax Connection, 1990, Olympus Pen SLR Cameras, 1989, Canon SLR Cameras, 1959-91, 1992, The Contax S Camera Family, 1991, Los Alamos Ranch Book of Rosters, 1991; former contbg. editor Shutterbug mag., other photographic periodicals; contbr. articles on history and design of miniature cameras and other photog. topics to profl. publs. Bd. dirs. St. Vincent Hosp. Found. (pres. 1981-83, v.p. 1983-84); vestry Ch. of the Holy Faith, 1994-97; mem. St. Anthony Hall. With AUS, 1943-46. Mem. N.Mex. Poetry Soc. (pres. 1969-74), Am. Soc. Media Photographers, S.W. Assn. Indian Arts, Pa. Soc. SAR, N.Mex. Jazz Workshop, Don Quixotes of Santa Fe, Phi Beta Kappa. Address: PO Box 636 Santa Fe NM 87504-0636

DECIL, STELLA WALTERS (DEL DECIL), artist; b. Indpls., Apr. 26, 1921; d. William Calvin and Hazel Jean (Konkle) Smith; m. John W. Walters, June 19, 1940 (div. Sept. 1945); m. Casimir R. Decil, Feb. 6, 1965. Grad., Indpls. Acad. Comml. Art, 1939, John Heron Art Inst., Indpls., 1941. Staff artist William H. Block Co., Indpls., 1945-50, art dir., 1952-62; art dir. Frank R. Jelleff Co., Washington, 1950-51, Diamonds Dept. Stores, Phoenix, 1962-67; freelance artist Phoenix, Chgo., others, 1967-70; curator Mature Eye bi-ann. Prescott (Ariz.) Fine Arts Assn., 1996-98; instr., lectr. Mountain Artists Guild, Prescott, 1995-97; mem. visual arts bd. Prescott Fine Arts Assn., 1990—; painting instr. Art Groups in Ariz.-N.Mex., 1970—, Phoenix Art Mus., 1975-77. Exhibited work in galleries in Phoenix, Scottsdale, Ariz., Las Cruces, N.Mex.; 1-woman exhibits include Hoosier Salon, Indpls., Cave Creek and Carefree, Ariz.; represented in pvt. collections in more than 20 states; in corp. collections including Continental Bank, Humana Hosp., Pueblo Grande Mus., VA Med. Ctr., Prescott, Mayo Ctr. for Women's Health, Scottsdale. Mem. Scottsdale (Ariz.) Art League (past pres.). Recipient Maxine Cherrington Meml. award Hoosier Salon, 1973; named Ad Woman of Yr., Indpls. Ad Club, 1958. Mem. No. Ariz. Watercolor Assn., Ariz. Artists Guild, Ariz. Watercolor Assn. (past pres.), Mountain Artists Guild.

DECK, RICHARD ALLEN, political scientist, consultant, writer, human rights activist; b. Concord, N.H., May 6, 1953; s. Herbert Heller Jr. and Eleanor DuVall (Deyo) D.; m. Jo Ann Marie Passariello, Nov. 15, 1986. Student, Ripon Coll., 1972-73, Waseda U., Japan, 1974-75; BA in Polit. Sci. and East Asian Studies summa cum laude with honors, Macalester Coll., 1977; cert. Urban and Regional Planning and Design, Harvard U., 1978; Grad. Cert. in Brit. Fgn. Policy, Oxford (Eng.) U., 1980; MA in Econs. in Pub. Policy & Adminstrn., U. Manchester (Eng.), 1982; M in City Planning, U. Calif., Berkeley, 1982; AM in Polit. Sci., Stanford U., 1985; MALS, Dartmouth Coll., 1994; PhD in Polit. Sci., Stanford U., 1997. Internat./intercultural rels. seminar leader Assn. of Current English Keio U., Japan, 1975; mag writer and interviewer The English Jour., Japan, 1975; rschr. writer Dem. Farmer Labor Party, Minneapolis, 1976; survey rchr. and analyst Project on Volunteerism Adelphi U., L.I., 1978; legis. analyst rschr. Assembly Edn. Com. New York St. Assembly, Albany, 1979; co-chair external affairs Grad. Assembly U. Calif., Berkeley, 1981-82; fellow internat. peace and security studies Social Sci. Rsch. Coun. and John D. and Catherine T. MacArthur Found., Southeast Asia, 1986-88; vis. joint fellow nat. and internat. security U. So. Calif. and UCLA, 1989; rsch. fellow and project coord. Asian Regionalization Asia/Pacific Rsch. Ctr., Stanford U. and The Asia Found. San Francisco, Calif., 1991-92; v.p. Catalyst Concepts, Berkeley, 1992—; founding dir. Asia/Pacific Reg. Policy Rsch. Inst., Berkeley, 1998—; social sys. dir. and bd. dirs. U. Calif. Space Working Group, U. Calif., Berkeley, 1979-80, 81-82; grad. rep. from Berkeley campus for the student body pres. coun. U. Calif. (systemwide), 1981-82; tchg. asst. Stanford (Calif.) U., 1983, 86, mem. grad. studies com., 1983-84, head tchg. asst., 1984, observer Project Peace and Coop. Asia-Pacific Region, 1984, mem. internat. rels. sr. faculty search com., 1985-86, co-instr., 1991; seminar group discussion leader, M.A.L.S. Colloquium on Ctrl. Amer., Darmouth Coll., 1984; lectr. and participant World Affairs Coun. No. Calif., study group on the Assn. of So. East Asian Nat., San Francisco, 1985; participant Project Soviet Internat. Behavior, U. Calif., Berkeley and Stanford U., 1985-86; lectr. Inst. S.E. Asian Studies, 1988; conf. participant and delegate 40th Anniv. Commemoration of the Signing of the United Nat. Charter in San Francisco, 1985; ofcl. observer U.S. del. Pacific Econ. Cooperation Coun., PECC Gen. Meeting/Conf., San Francisco, 1992; global media dir. U.S.-S.E. Asian Alliance for a Dem. Asia, Cambridge, Mass., 1998—. Author: U.S. official delegation "Dialogue Partners" session, First ASEAN Economic Congress, ASEAN Chambers of Commerce and Industry, and the Institute of Strategic and International Studies, 1987, Fourth ASEAN Institutes Conference on the Association of Southeast Asian Nations and the United States, 1988; (with others) Peace, Conflict, and Strategic Culture in the Asia-Pacific Region, 1998; Contbr. to profl. articles; mem. edtl. bd., edtl. writer, polit. corr., and polit. feature writer The Stanford Daily, 1982-83; rschr. and writing cons. The Concept of Relationship in International Politics, 1989-90; contbr. papers to various organizations; interview subject (TV) Friday Background, Current Affairs Unit, Singapore Broadcasting Corp., 1987, Berita (Evening news), RTM (Malaysian govt. network), 1987, Official Questionner of Malaysian Prime Minister Mahathir bin Mohamad, Iseas Singapore Lecture, Inst. of Southeast Asian Studies, 1988; (film) co-narrator and co-interviewer The Pennsylvania Underground: The Sanctuary Movement and Illegal Ctrl. Am. Refugees in Philadelphia, 1986; (newspaper) Internat. Herald Tribune, Republic of Singapore, 1987, (radio) The Michael Fay Caning Affair, The World Tonight with Phil Till Show, Radio Can., Vancouver, 1994; spl. contbr. Asiaweek newsmag., Hong Kong, 1998. Del. candidate N.H. Pres. Preferences Primary, Dem. Nat. Conv., Keene, 1972, Calif. Pres. Primary, Stanford, 1984, Berkeley, 1992; candidate N.H. Constl. Conv., Keene, 1974; city and campus chairperson Calif. Dem. Pres. Primary Campaign, Stanford U. and Palo Alto, Calif., 1984, 92; chmn. N.H. Govs.' Youth Hwy. Safety Adv. Com., 1972; staff intern Minn. Dem. Farmer Labor Party Hdqs., 1976; bd. dirs. U. of Manchester Postgrad. Soc. (UK), 1980-81; conf. participant and del. 40th Anniversary Commemoration of the Signing of the UN Charter in San Francisco: Conf. Assessing the UN After 40 Years, UN Assn. San Francisco and World Affairs Coun. No. Calif., 1985; spl. fellowship coord. Open Soc. Inst., N.Y.C., 1997-98. Airman 3d class, USAF Aux., 1966. Recipient World Affairs Coun. Staff award, 1985; Nat. Forensics League scholar Ripon Coll., 1972-73; Harry Sherman scholar Macalester Coll., 1976-77; John W. Searle Meml. scholar Macalester Coll., 1976-77, Outstanding Sr. award, Minnesota Jaycees, College Court of Honor, 1977; N.Y. State Assembly Grad. Scholar fellow, 1979; Roothbert Fund fellow U. Calif., Berkeley, 1979-80, 81-82; Inst. Internat. Edn. scholar Oxford U., 1980; Rotary Internat. Grad. fellow U. Manchester, 1980-81; Lasker scholar U. Calif., Berkeley, 1981-82; Newhouse fellow U. Calif., Berkeley, 1981-82; Eisenhower Meml. Grad. scholar Stanford U., 1982-83; AMVETS scholar Stanford U., 1982-86; Stanford U. Grad. fellow 1982-86; MALS Grad. fellow Dartmouth Coll., 1984, 86; UN Assn. and World Affairs Coun. scholar, 1985; Fgn. Lang. and Area Studies grantee U.S. Dept. Edn., 1985; SSRC/MacArthur found. fellow in Internat. Peace and Security, N.Y.C., N.Y., and Chicago, 1986-88; USC-UCLA Visiting Joint fellowship in Nat. and Internat. Security, L.A., 1989; rsch. fellow Asia/Pacific Rsch. Ctr. Stanford U. and the Asia Found., San Francisco, 1991-92. Mem. Internat. Studies Assn. (presenter 1998), Asian Media Info. and Comm. Ctr., Assn. Asian Studies, Acad. Polit. Sci., Am. Polit. Sci. Assn., Pi Kappa Delta, Phi Alpha Theta, Pi Sigma Alpha, Phi Beta Kappa. United Ch. of Christ. Avocations: reading novels and screenplays, viewing films. Office: Catalyst Concepts PO Box 8393 Berkeley CA 94707-8393

DECKER, JAMES THOMAS, psychotherapist; b. Dayton, Ky., Jan. 16, 1944; s. Frank and Edith (Mountain) D.; m. Jane Campbell Fisher, May 6, 1972; children: Peter Campbell, James Mountain, Christina Campbell. AA, Los Angeles Pierce Coll., 1970; BA, Calif. State U., Northridge, 1972; MSW, SUNY, Stony Brook, 1974; PhD, U. Minn., 1976, Pacifica Grad. Inst. Research asst. U. Minn., Mpls., 1974-76; asst. prof. San Diego State U., 1976-78; dir., assoc. prof. U. Tex., El Paso, 1978-80; dir. cons. Kern View Hosp., Bakersfield, Calif., 1980-82; exec. dir. J.T. Decker Profl. Group, Bakersfield, Calif., 1982—; adj. prof. Calif. State Coll., Bakersfield, 1981—; sch. psychotherapist Friends Sch., Bakersfield, 1983—; nursing mgmt. cons. Meml. Hosp., Bakersfield, 1983—; out placement cons. Tosco Inc., Bakersfield, 1983—; employee asst. coordinator various orgns., Bakersfield, 1982—. Contbr. articles to profl. jours. Bd. dirs. Consumer Credit Counselors, Bakersfield, 1982—; chmn. Human Resources Com., Bakersfield, 1980-85; bd. dirs. Health Care Mgmt. Adv. Council, Bakersfield, 1982—; bd. dirs. United Way., San Diego and El Paso, Tex., 1977-80. Served with U.S. Army, 1960-64. Recipient Outstanding Alumni award Sch. Social Work, SUNY. Mem. Assn. Labor Mgmt. Adminstrs. and Cons. on Alcoholism, Nat. Assn. Social Workers (cert.). Avocation: golf. Home: 231 Oleander Ave Bakersfield CA 93304-2751

DECKER, MARY DURYEA, retired educator, community volunteer; b. Portland, Oreg., Mar. 17, 1928; d. Oliver Martin and Lois Marguerite (Mangus) Nisbet; m. Richard Adrian Duryea, Aug. 23, 1950 (dec. Apr.1958); 1 child, Maria Duryea; m. Edward Albert Decker, Jan. 28, 1967. BS in Speech and Sociology, Northwestern U., 1950; MA in Speech and Edn., Stanford U., 1961. Cert. adminstr., counselor, instr., Calif. cmty. colls. Social worker, supr. City of Austin, Tex., 1950-54; med. social worker Monterey (Calif.) County Hosp., 1955-57; instr. speech, counseling San Jose (Calif.) City Coll., 1961-62; residence hall dir. Stanford (Calif.) U., 1962-65; dean students Scripps Coll., Claremont, Calif., 1965-69; asst. vice chancellor U. Calif., San Diego, 1969-75; chief student svcs. officer 3 campuses San Diego C.C. Dist., 1976-88; project mgr. Combined Case Mgmt., Lincoln County, Oreg., 1991-93; mem., chair chief student svcs. offices Region X, Calif. C.C. Chancellor's Office, 1976-88; mem. Gov.'s Coun. on Nutrition and Volunteerism, 1978-80. Mem., pres. Vol. Bur. San Diego, 1970-72; mem., v.p. United Way, San Diego, 1971-78; bd. dirs., v.p. Girl Scouts San Diego, 1976-88; trustee North Lincoln Health Dist., Lincoln City, Oreg., 1990—, chair bd., 1995-97; vice chair Gov.'s Coun. Alcohol and Drug Programs, Salem, Oreg., 1994—; bd. dirs. Oreg. Pacific Area Health Edn. Ctr., Newport, 1992—. Recipient grant Ford Found., 1985-88. Mem. Univ. Club Portland. Republican. Presbyterian. Home: Box 721 Lincoln City OR 97367

DECKER, RICHARD JEFFREY, lawyer; b. Manhasset, N.Y., Aug. 26, 1959; s. Alan B. and Shelley T. (Belkin) D.; m. Carrie Ann Gordon, Aug. 13, 1989. BA, Union Coll., Schenectady, N.Y., 1981; JD, Boston U., 1984. Bar: N.Y. 1985, Calif. 1985, Mass. 1985, U.S. Dist. Ct. (cen. dist.) Calif. 1985. Assoc. Turner, Gesterfeld, Wilk & Tigerman, Beverly Hills, Calif., 1985-86, Shapiro, Posell & Close, L.A., 1986-90, Katten, Muchin, Zavis & Weitzman, L.A., 1990-93; of counsel Ginsburg, Stephan, Oringher & Richman, L.A., 1993—. Mem. Los Angeles County Bar Assn., Beverly Hills Bar Assn., Century City Bar Assn. Avocations: sports, guitar playing, travel, reading. Office: 10100 Santa Monica Blvd Ste 800 Los Angeles CA 90067-4100

DECKER, RICHARD KELSEY, equipment distribution company executive; b. Monrovia, Calif., Dec. 31, 1927; s. Raymond Grant and Dorothy Irene (Heady) D.; m. Barbara Carolyn Carlson, 1956; children—Richard Brian, Carolyn Ann Decker Johnson. B.S., U. So. Calif., 1952. Cost. acct. S.W. Products Co., Monrovia, 1953-55; controller Scotsman Refrigeration Inc., Monterey Park, Calif., 1955-64; with Scotsman Distbrs. of Los Angeles, Inc., La Verne, Calif., 1964—, retired, 1991; pres., chief exec. officer, 1976—. Served with USN, 1945-47. Mem. Alpha Kappa Psi (pres.), Beta Gamma Sigma.

DECKER, SHARYN LYNN, newspaper reporter; b. Santa Rosa, Calif., Nov. 6, 1960; d. Richard Lee and Vicki Catherine (Whearty) D. AA with honors, Shoreline C.C., Seattle, 1989; BA in Bus. Adminstrn. and Comm. magna cum laude, U. Wash., 1994. Groundskeeper Evergreen Washelli, Seattle, 1980-98; reporter news svcs. U. Wash., Seattle, 1994; freelance writer, 1994—; intern reporter The Herald, Everett, Wash., 1995-96; bus. reporter Valley Daily News, Kent, Wash., 1996, The Herald, Everett, Wash., 1998. Mem. Nat. Soc. Profl. Journalists (sec. Western Wash. profl. chpt. 1995-98, honorable mention Pacific Northwest Excellence Journalism comp. 1995), U. Wash. Comm. Alumni Assn., Golden Key Nat. Honor Soc., Beta Gamma Sigma, Phi Beta Kappa. Avocations: photography, travel. E-mail: sharyn1000@aol.com. Home: 9626 234th St SW Edmonds WA 98020-5036

DECKERT, FRANK, park administrator; m. Gloria Quick; children: Christopher, Jason, Alisa. BS in Forest Mgmt., Humboldt State Coll. With U.S. Forest Svc., Calif., 1963-66; ranger, dist. naturalist Shenandoah Nat. Park Nat. Park Svc., Va., 1967-71; dist. ranger Isle Royale Nat. Park Nat. Park Svc., Mich., 1971-73; interpretive specialist Lake Mead Nat. Recreation Area Nat. Park Svc., Ariz., Nev., 1973-75; chief park naturalist Big Bend Nat. Park Nat. Park Svc., Tex., 1975-80; regional chief of interpretation Alaska Regional Office Nat. Park Svc., Anchorage, 1980-86; supt. Petersburg Nat. Battlefield Nat. Park Svc., 1986-92, supt. Carlsbad (N.Mex.) Caverns Nat. Park, 1992—. Trustee San Vicente Common Sch. Dist. Recipient Silver Beaver award Boy Scouts of Am., 1992. Mem. Carlsbad Rotary Club (v.p./pres. elect 1997—). Office: 3225 National Parks Hwy Carlsbad NM 88220-5354*

DECKERT, HARLAN KENNEDY, JR., manufacturing company official; b. Evanston, Ill., May 22, 1923; s. Harlan Kennedy Sr. and Lady Otey (Hutton) D.; BS, U. Calif., Berkeley, 1949; MBA, U. So. Calif., 1962; m. Mary Emma Eldredge, Nov. 27, 1971; children: Mary Adrienne, Christine Ann, Daniel Gregory, Deborah Alice. Systems analyst Northrop Corp., Hawthorne, Calif., 1949-53, supr. engrng. adminstrv. svcs., 1953-57, adminstrv. systems engr., 1957-59; with AiResearch Indsl. div. Garrett Corp., Torrance, Calif., 1959-88, systems svc. adminstr., 1962-72, mgr. adminstrv. svcs., 1972-75, adminstr. internat. ops., 1975-80, sr. staff advisor Garrett Automotive Group Allied-Signal, Inc., 1980-88, ret., 1988. Active mem. L.A. County Mus. Art, Wild Beast Soc., docent; Greater L.A. Zoo Assn.; mem. L.A. County Mus. Natural History, San Luis Obispo Zool. Soc., Exotic Feline Breeding Compound, African Wildlife Found., Friends Cabrillo Marine Aquarium, Assn. Zoo & Aquarium Docents; supporting mem. Living Desert. With USAAF, 1943-46, CBI, capt. USAFR, 1946-57. Mem. Am. Assn. Zoo Keepers, Am. Zoo and Aquarium Assn., Nat. Wildlife Fedn., San Diego Zool. Soc. (Keeper's Club), World Wildlife Fund, Nature Conservancy, Wildlife Waystation, Sierra Club, Jane Goodall Inst., Santa Monica Mus. Flying. Home: 2433 33rd St Santa Monica CA 90405-2103

DE CLEMENTS, BARTHE FAITH, writer; b. Seattle, Wash., Oct. 8, 1920; d. Ralph Clinton and Doris Louise (Hutton) De C.; m. Don Macri (dec. 1940); m. Gordon Greimes, Oct. 24, 1947 (div. 1983); children: NIcole Southard, Mari, Christopher Greimes, Roger. BA, U. Wash., 1942, MEd, 1970. Psychologist Med.-Dental Psychiat., Seattle, 1946-47, Seattle Sch. Dist., 1950-55; tchr. Kirkland/Edmonds (Wash.) Schs., 1960-67; counselor Edmonds Sch. Dist., 1977-83; writer Snohomish, Wash., 1979—. Author: Nothing's Fair in Fifth Grade, 1981 (Alabama Young Reader's Choice award, Calif. Young Reader's medal, Hawaii Nene award, Iowa Children's Choice award, Kans. Golden Archer award, Mass. Children's Choice award, Minn. Maud Hart Lovelace award, Nebr. Golden Sower award, N.Mex. Land of Enchantment Children's Box award, Ohio Buckeye award, Tex. Bluebonnet award, Wis. Golden Archer award), How Do You Lose Those Ninth Grade Blues?, 1983 (IRA-CBC Children's Choice Book), Seventeen and In-Between, 1984, Sixth Grade Can Really Kill You, 1985 (IRA-CBC Children's Choice Book, Pacific Northwest Young Reader's Choice award, Fla. Sunshine State Young Reader's award, Land of Enchantment Children's Book award, Nebr. Golden Sower award, Nev. Young Reader's award, Ohio Buckeye award), I Never Asked You To Understand Me, 1986 (IRA Young Adult's Choice Book), No Place for Me, 1987, The Fourth Grade Wizards, 1988 (IRA-CBC Children's Choice Book), Five-Finger Discount, 1989 (Lit. award PEN Ctr. USA West 1989), Monkey See, Monkey Do, 1990, Breaking Out, 1991, Wake Me At Midnight, 1991, The Bite of the Gold Bug, 1992, The Pickle Song, 1993, The Red Chow, The Doctor, and Me, 1994, Tough Loser, 1994, Spoiled Rotten, 1996, Liar, Liar, 1998; co-author: Double Trouble, 1987. Mem. PEN, Authors Guild, Soc. Children's Book Writers Illustrators. Home: 1511 Russell Rd Snohomish WA 98290-5624

DE CONCINI, DENNIS, lawyer, former United States senator, consultant; b. Tucson, May 8, 1937; s. Evo and Ora (Webster) DeC.; children: Denise, Christina, Patrick Evo. BA, U. Ariz., 1959, LLB, 1963. Bar: Ariz. 1963, D.C. 1963. Mem. firm Evo DeConcini; ptnr. DeConcini & McDonald, Tucson, 1968-73; dep. Pima County atty. Sch. Dist. 1, 1971-72, county atty., 1972-76; U.S. Senator from Ariz., 1977-95; atty. Perry-Romani Assocs., Washington, 1995—, De Concini, McDonald, Yetwin & Lacy, Tucson, 1995—; mem. appropriations com., U.S. Senate, chmn. subcom. on Treasury, Postal Svc. and Gen. Govt.; mem. subcom. on Def., subcom. on Energy and Water Devel., subcom. on Fgn. Ops., subcom. on Interior Related Agys.; mem. Jud. com.; chmn. subcom. on Patents, Copyrights and Trademarks; mem. subcom. on Antitrust, Monopolies and Bus. Rights, subcom. on the Constitution, com. on Rules and Adminstrn., com. on Vets. Affairs; chmn. select com. on Intelligence; chmn. Commn. on Security and Cooperation in Europe; select com. Indian Affairs; mem. Internat. Narcotics Control Caucus, West Coalition of Senators, former pres., bd. dirs. Shopping Ctrs., Inc.; bd. dirs. Fed. Home Mortgage Corp., Schuff Steel. Chmn. legis. com. Tucson Dem. Cmty. Coun., 1966-67; mem. major gifts com., devel. fund drive St. Joseph's Hosp., 1970, mem. devel. coun., 1971-73; bd. dirs. Nat. Ctr. for Missing and Exploited Children, 1995—; mem. major gifts com. Tucson Mus. and Art Ctr. Bldg. Fund, 1971; adminstr. Ariz. Drug Control Dist., 1975-76; precinct committeeman Ariz. Dem. Ctrl. Com., 1958—; mem. Pima County Dem. Ctrl. Com., 1958-67, Dem. State Exec. Com., 1958-68; state vice chmn. Ariz. Dem. Com., 1964-66, 70-72; vice chmn. Pima County

Dem. Com., 1970-73. Served to 2d lt. JAG U.S. Army, 1959-60. Named Outstanding Ariz. County Atty., 1975. Mem. ABA, NAACP, Nat. Dist. Attys. Assn., Am. Judicature Soc., Ariz. Bar Assn., D.C. Bar Assn., Ariz. Sheriffs and County Attys. Assn., Ariz. Pioneer Hist. Soc., Pima County Bar Assn., U. Ariz. Alumni Assn., Pres.'s Club, Tucson Fraternal Order Police, Phi Delta Theta, Delta Sigma Rho, Phi Alpha Delta. Roman Catholic.

DE COTEAU, DENIS, music director, conductor; b. N.Y.C.. BA, MA in Music, NYU; studied, Mozarteum, Salzburg, Austria; MusD, Stanford U. Asst. condr. San Francisco Ballet, 1970-74, music dir., condr., 1974—; artistic advisor Stockton Symphony, 1994—; condr. Oakland Symphony Youth Orch., 1970-79, Aichii U. Orch., Nagoya, Japan, 1982—, Tokyo City Philarm. Orch., 1989, San Francisco Conservatory of Music; prin. guest condr. Deutches Jugendorchester, 1976, 78, 80; guest condr. Nat. Music Camp Assn. Australian Youth Orch., 1980—, Oreg. Mozart Players, 1989; assoc. condr. San Francisco Symphony, 1986; music dir., condr. Flagstaff (Ariz.) Festival of Arts, 1977-83. Guest appearances with numerous dance cos. including Kansas City Ballet, State of Ala. Ballet, San Diego Ballet, Ballet West, Honolulu Ballet, and Oakland Ballet; guest condr. BBC Scottish Symphony, St. Louis Symphony, New Orleans Philharm., Tokyo City Philharm, Radio Frei Orch. (Berlin), San Francisco Symphony, Seattle Symphony, Oakland Symphony, San Francisco Chamber Orch. and others; appeared with Yomiuri Orch., Tokyo; invited condr. (recs.) Nat. Philharm. London, (concerts) Australia's Bicentennial, World Expo, Brisbane; condr. opera premiere Song of Pegasus (Marin Theatre Playhouse). Recipient Pierre Monteux Conducting Prize, 1969, Adventuresome Programming award ASCAP, 1976. Office: Conservatory of Music Orch 1201 Ortega St San Francisco CA 94122-4411 also: San Francisco Ballet 455 Franklin St San Francisco CA 94102-4438*

DECRISTOFORO, MARY A., writer; b. N.Y., Dec. 5; d. David and Sarah (Pugliese) Ferrari; m. R. J. De Cristoforo, June 7, 1942; children: Daniel, David, Ronald John. Contributor Peninsula Living, Palo Alto, Calif., 1965-90; reporter Palo Alto Times, Palo Alto, Calif., 1958-85; reporter Los Altos Town Crier, Los Altos, Calif., 1951-98, columnist, 1986—. Contbr. articles to profl. jours. Active PTA St. Francis Sch., Los Altos, 1960, mem. women's auxiliary St. Alouyisius Ch., Palo Alto, 1951-54, com. City of Los Altos Hills, 1957; mem. Soc. Western Artists, Pacific Art League, 1976-93, Sunnyvale Art Club, 1974-85. Recipient Best Painting award Sunnyvale Art Club, 1976, Nat. Magazine Writing award Nat. Writers Club, 1982. Mem. Los Altos Hills Historical Soc., Nat. Writers Club, Los Altos Hiking Club. Avocations: hiking, reading, nutrition, history, drama. Fax: 650-948-2502.

DECTER, BETTY EVA, artist; b. Birmingham, Ala., Apr. 22, 1927; d. Kara Miracle; m. William Fenske, May 14, 1943 (div.); children: William Jr., Karalee; m. Gerald A. Decter, July 9, 1961; 1 stepchild, Tom. Freelance fashion model, 1950s; designer, stylist Decter Mannikin Co., Inc., 1962-92; v.p. Bellagio Arabians, 1985—. One-woman shows at Roger Morrison Gallery, L.A., 1985, Brand Libr. Art Gallery, Glendale, Calif., 1988, Riverside County Mus./Edward-Dean Mus., 1989, Sam Francis Gallery, Crossroads Sch. for Arts and Scis., Santa Monica, Calif., 1992, Thinking Eye Gallery, L.A., 1986, 87, Absolute Gallery, L.A., 1986, Warner Ctr. Gallery, 1987, Otis Art Inst. of Parsons Sch. Design, 1988, J.C. Cooper Gallery, 1988, Mus. Without Walls, Bemus Point, N.Y., 1992, Craig Cary Art Gallery, Brentwood, Calif., 1996, Regal Gallery, Carmel, Calif., 1996, Gallery 826, 1997, Finegood Art Gallery, 1998; group show at Laguna Mus. Art, 1997; contbr. articles to profl. jours. and encys. Founding mem., co-chair Save the Santa Monica Mountains Com., 1970; founding mem., chair No on Nowell Com., 1973-74; mem. L.A. City Atty.'s Com. on Polit. Reform, 1973-74; founding mem., chair Com. for Enforcement of Campaign Laws, 1974-78; founding mem. bd. William O. Douglas Outdoor Classroom, 1980-90; helped establish Nat. Urban Park in Santa Monica Mountains, 1976-80; active local politics, 1969—; mem. The Group, 1984-93; mem. adv. bd. Woman's Bldg., L.A., 1988. Recipient award Assocs. of Brand Libr., 1991, Bronze award Calif. Discovery Awards, 1994. Studio: 5412 W Washington Blvd Los Angeles CA 90016-1113

DEDEAUX, PAUL J., orthodontist; b. Pass Christian, Miss., Feb. 22, 1937; s. Mack and Harriet D.; m. Janet Louise Harter, June 29, 1971; children: Michele, Kristen, Kelly. BA, Dillard U., 1959; DDS, Howard U., 1963; MS, Fairleigh Dickinson U., 1975. Pvt. practice, Washington, 1976-93, Santa Ana, Calif., 1976-93; instr. Howard U., Washington, 1967-69; dental dir. Dr. Martin Luther King Health Ctr., Bronx, N.Y., 1969-70, dentist, 1970-76; chief dentist Calipatria State Prison, Calif., 1993-96, Calif. Med. Facility, Vacaville, 1996—; instr. Howard U., Washington, 1967-69; cons. Hostos C.C., Bronx, 1971-76; mem. adv. panel Dental Econs. mag., 1976; adj. assoc. prof. Columbia U., N.Y.C., 1970-72. Contbr. articles to profl. jours. Capt. U.S. Army, 1963-67, USAR, 1975—, col., 1985—, comdr., 1994—. Mem. Am. Assn. Orthodontists, Pacific Coast Soc. Orthodontists, ADA, Calif. Dental Assn., Assn. Mil. Surgeons of U.S. Democrat. Methodist. Avocations: photography, fishing. Home: 940 Celestine Cir Vacaville CA 95687-7853 Office: Calif Med Facility PO Box 2000 1600 California Dr Vacaville CA 95687

DEDERA, NANCY KOVEL, communications executive; b. New Britain, Conn., Sept. 26, 1931; d. Walter Henry and Margaret Ellen (Sullivan) Kovel; m. Fredric C. Joy, Sept. 16, 1966 (div. Aug. 1976); m. Donald E. Dedera, Aug. 16, 1981. BS, U. Conn., 1953; postgrad., Case Western Res. U., 1956. Registered dietition, Ariz. Womens editor, food editor Boston Herald Newspaper, 1956-66; food dir. The Houston Club, 1966-78; owner, operator The PanJoy Gourmetware Cooking Sch., Oceanside, Calif., 1978-83; pub. rels. mgr. Armour Food Co., Phoenix, 1983-85; dir. pub. rels. The Dial Corp., Phoenix, 1985-86; exec. dir. comms. ViadCorp., Phoenix, 1986—. Contbr. articles to profl. jours. Bd. dirs. Friends of Libr., Phoenix, 1992-93; founder, Friends of Ariz. Hwys., Phoenix, 1983-84. Mem. Internat. Assn. Bus. Communicators, Am. Dietetic Assn. (registered dietitian), Soap and Detergent Assn. (bd. dirs. 1987-96), Cosmetology, Toiletries and Fragrance Assn. (bd. dirs. 1991-96), Les Dames d'Escoffier (charter). Republican. Roman Catholic. Avocations: sailing, gardening, needlepoint, hiking. Home: 6001 E Le Marche Ave Scottsdale AZ 85254-6511

DE DONCKER, THOMAS DAVID, art dealer; b. Rock Island, Ill., Oct. 22, 1966; s. David and Carol Ann (Poole) De D. BA, U. Wis., 1988; MA, U. Kans., 1991, Sothebys Am. Arts Course, N.Y.C., 1992; postgrad., CCNY Grad. Ctr., 1992-94; appraisal cert., NYU, 1993. Curatorial intern, prints and drawings dept. Mpls. Inst. Arts, 1988, fine arts technician, 1988-89; cataloger, Am. paintings Sothebys, N.Y.C., 1992; fine art conservator Thomas Yost Conservation, N.Y.C., 1993-94; dir. Am. paintings Gerald Peters Galleries, Santa Fe, N.Mex., 1994-96; pres. De Doncker Fine Arts, L.A., 1997—; pres. De Doncker Fine Arts Svcs., N.Y.C., 1993-94. Selected author: (mus. collection catalog) American Paintings at the Nelson-Atkins Mus. Art, 1991. Big brother Big Brothers Little Sisters, Santa Fe, 1995. Recipient Am. Legion award, East Moline, Ill., 1984. Mem. Coll. Art Assn., Beverly Hills C.C. Office: Thomas de Doncker Fine Arts PO Box 691487 Los Angeles CA 90069-9487

DEEDER, JOHN DEAN, school system administrator; b. Kellogg, Idaho, Apr. 8, 1947; s. Clyde C. and Margaret E. (Collins) D.; m. Janet E. Olsen, Aug. 7, 1976; children: Jennifer, Jeff. BS in Edn., U. Idaho, 1969; MA in Tchg., Lewis and Clark Coll., 1973, supt. cert., 1983; prin. cert., Portland State U., 1979. continuing edn. tchr. Portland (Oreg.) State U., 1983-90; cons. N.W. Regional Edn. Lab, Portland, 1985—. Mem. ASCD, Am. Assn. Sch. Adminstrs., Oreg. Assn. Sch. Execs., Confedn. Oreg. Sch. Adminstrs. Democrat. Lutheran. Avocations: golf, reading, spectator sports, travel. Office: Reynolds Sch Dist 1204 NE 201st Ave Fairview OR 97024-2499

DEENEN, CHARLES PAULUS, audio director; b. Holthees, Brabant, The Netherlands, Jan. 15, 1970; came to U.S., 1991; s. Petrus Maria and Martini Petronella (Smits) D.; m. Ana Maria Iniguez, Dec. 12, 1993. Mng. dir. Maniacs of Noise, Holthees, 1985-91; audio dir. Interplay Entertainment, Irvine, Calif., 1991—. Mem. Interactive Acad. Office: Interplay 16815 Von Karman Ave Irvine CA 92606-4920

DEERNOSE, KITTY, museum curator; b. Crow Agency, Mont., Apr. 14, 1956. AA in Mus. Studies, Inst. Am. Indian Arts, Santa Fe, 1985. Mus. intern Heard Mus. Anthropology and Primitive Art, Phoenix, 1984; interpreter Little Bighorn Battlefield Nat. Monument, Crow Agency, Mont., 1985-90, mus. curator, 1990-99; mus. intern in Crow studies Smithsonian Instn., Washington, 1988. Recipient White Glove award Nat. Park Svc., 1995. Mem. Am. Assn. Muss., Am. Assn. State and Local History, Mountain Plains Mus. Assn. Office: Little Bighorn Battlefield Nat Monument PO Box 39 Crow Agency MT 59022-0039

DEFAZIO, LYNETTE STEVENS, dancer, choreographer, educator, chiropractor, author, actress, musician; b. Berkeley, Calif., Sept. 29; d. Honore and Mabel J. (Estavan) Stevens; children: J.H. Panganiban, Joanna Pang. student U. Calif., Berkeley, 1950-55, San Francisco State Coll., 1950-51; studied classical dance teaching techniques and vocab. with Gisella Caccialanza and Harold and Lew Christensen, San Francisco Ballet, 1952-56; D. Chiropractic, Life-West Chiropractic Coll., San Lorenzo, Calif., 1983, cert. Techniques of Teaching U. Calif., 1985, BA in Humanities, New Coll. Calif., 1986; Lic. Chiropracter, Mich. Diplomate Nat. Sci. Bd.; eminence in dance edn., Calif. Community Colls. dance specialist, standard services, childrens ctrs. credentials Calif. Dept. Edn., 1986. Contract child dancer Monogram Movie Studio, Hollywood, Calif., 1938-40; dance instr. San Francisco Ballet, 1953-65; performer San Francisco Opera Ring, 1960-67; performer, choreographer Oakland (Calif.) Civic Light Opera, 1963-70; dir. Ballet Arts Studio, Oakland, Calif., 1960; teaching specialist Oakland Unified Sch. Dist., 1965-80; fgn. exchange dance dir. Academie de Danses-Salle Pleyel, Paris, France, 1966; instr. Peralta Community Coll. Dist., Oakland, 1971—, chmn. dance dept., 1985—; cons., instr. extension courses UCLA, Dirs. and Suprs. Assn., Pittsburg Unified Sch. Dist., 1971-73, Tulare (Calif.) Sch. Dist., 1971-73; researcher Ednl. Testing Services, HEW, Berkeley, 1974; resident choreographer San Francisco Childrens Opera, 1970—, Oakland Civic Theater; ballet mistress Dimensions Dance Theater, Oakland, 1977-80; cons. Gianchetta Sch. Dance, San Francisco, Robicheau Boston Ballet, TV series Patchwork Family, CBS, N.Y.C.; choreographer Ravel's Valses Nobles et Sentimentales, 1976. Recipient Foremost Women of 20th Century, 1985, Merit award San Francisco Children's Opera, 1985, 90. Author: Basic Music Outlines for Dance Classes, 1960, rev., 1968, Teaching Techniques and Choreography for Advanced Dancers, 1965, Basic Music Outlines for Dance Classes, 1965, Goals and Objectives in Improving Physical Capabilities, 1970, A Teacher's Guide for Ballet Techniques, 1970, Principle Procedures in Basic Curriculum, 1974, Objectives and Standards of Performance for Physical Development, 1975, Techniques of the Ballet School, 1970, rev., 1974, The Opera Ballets: A Choreographic Manual Vols. I-V, 1986. Assoc. music arranger Le Ballet du Cirque, 1964; assoc. composer, lyricist The Ballet of Mother Goose, 1968; choreographer: Valses Nobles Et Sentimentales (Ravel), Transitions (Kashevaroff), 1991, The New Wizard of Oz, 1991, San Francisco Children's Opera (Gingold); Canon in D for Strings and Continuo (Pachelbel), 1979; appeared in Flower Drum Song, 1993, Gigi, 1994, Fiddler on the Roof, 1996, The Music Man, 1996, Sayonara, 1997, Sayonara, 1997; violinist Oakland Cmty. Concert Orch., 1995—. Mem. Calif. State Teacher Assn., Bay Area Chiropractic Research Soc., Profl. Dance Teacher Assn. Home and Office: 4923 Harbord Dr Oakland CA 94618-2506

DEFAZIO, PETER A., congressman; b. Needham, Mass., May 27, 1947; m. Myrnie Daut. BA in Econs. and Polit. Sci., Tufts U., 1969; postgrad., U. Oreg., 1969-71, MS in Pub. Adminstrn./Gerontology, 1977. Aide to U.S. Rep. Jim Weaver, 1977-82; sr. issues specialist, caseworker, dist. field office U.S. rep. Jim Weaver, 1977-78, legis. asst. Washington office, 1978-80, dir. constituent services, 1980-82; mem. commn. representing Springfield Lane County (Oreg.) Commn., 1982-86; mem. 100-103rd Congresses (now 106th Congress) from 4th Oreg. dist., Washington, D.C., 1987—; ranking minority mem. resources com., mem. transp. and infrastructure com. Mem. Lane County Econ. Devel. com., Ingergovtl. Relations com.; bd. dirs. Eugene-Springfield Met. Partnership; Lane County Dem. precinct person, 1982—. Served with USAFR. Mem. Assn. of Oreg. Counties (legis. com.), Nat. Assn. of Counties (tax and fin. com.). Office: US Ho of Reps 2134 Rayburn Bldg Washington DC 20515-3704*

DE FONVILLE, PAUL BLISS, historic organization administrator; b. Oakland, Calif., Mar. 3, 1923; s. Marion Yancey and Charlotte (Bliss) de F.; m. Virginia Harpell, June 17, 1967. Student, Calif. Poly. U., 1942-44, Michael Chekhov Group, 1947-52. Founder, pres. Cowboy Meml. and Libr., Caliente, Calif., 1969—; tchr. outdoor edn. Calif. State U., Bakersfield, 1980. Life mem. Presdl. Task Force, Washington, 1984—, Rep. Senatorial inner circle, Washington, 1989—, Nat. Rep. Congl. Com., Washington, 1990—, Rep. Nat. Com., 1987—, U.S. Senatorial Club, 1988—, Rep. Senatorial Commn., 1991, Presdl. Election Registry, 1992; del. Presdl. Trust, 1992; mem. Presdl. Commn. Am. Agenda; affiliate Lake Isabella Bd. Realtors, 1993; hon. marshall Lake Isabella, Kern County Christmas Parade, 1993. Recipient Slim Pickens award Calif. State Horsemen, 1980, Marshall-Working Western award Rose Parade, Pasadena, 1980, recognition Kern County, 1984, proclamations Mayor of Bakersfield, 1984, 85, Govt. of Calif., 1984, resolution Calif. Senate, 1988, Calif. Assembly, 1990, Presdl. Order of Merit, 1991, Congl. Cert. of Merit, 1992, Rep. Presdl. Legion of Merit award, 1992, Rep. Presdl. Legion of Merit award, 1992, document Gov. of Calif., 1993, Rep. Nat. Com. Cert. Recognition, 1992, Rep. Presdl. adv. Commn. Cert. award, 1993, Congl. Cert. Appreciation, 1993, Cert. Commendation Washington Legal Found., 1993, Rep. Presdl. award, 1994, Rep. Congl. Order of Liberty, 1993, Internat. Order of Merit medal, 1993, 20th Century award for achievement, 1993, Rep. Senatorial Medal of Freedom, 1994, Ronald Reagan Eternal Flame of Freedom medal and cert., 1995, Cmty. Svc. and Profl. Achievement medal, 1995, World Lifetime achievement award ABI-USA, 1996. Mem. SAG, NRA, Calif. State Horsemen (life), Equestrian Trails (life), Forty Niners (life), Calif. Rep. Assembly, Heritage Found., Cowboy Turtles Assn. (life), Rodeo Cowboys Assn. (life), Pro Rodeo Cowboys Assn. (life), Internat. Platform Assn., Lake Isabella C. of C., Kern County C. of C. Baptist. Avocations: heritage, horses, cowboys, mountain men, Indians. Home: 40371 Cowboy Ln Caliente CA 93518-1405

DE FORD, DOUGLAS ATMETLLA, biochemical, biomechanical and industrial engineer; b. San Jose, Costa Rica, Nov. 26, 1945; s. Douglas N. and Enriqueta (Atmetlla) De F.; m. Maria Felicia Zamorade, July 9, 1972 (div.); children: Fabiola de Prada, Dougie, Christopher, Steve. Degree in mech. engring., Monterrey Inst. Tech., 1970; MS in Biotechnology, Teesside U., England, 1985, PhD in Biochem. Engring., 1988; postgrad., Nat. U., 1990. Chief engr. CCSS Health Svcs., San Jose, Costa Rica, 1975-78; prodn. mgr. Blue Ribbon Meat Processing, Alajuela, Costa Rica, 1978-80; indsl. cons. CCSS Health Svcs., 1980-83; biotech. rschr. North East Biotech. Ctr., Middlesbrough, England, 1983-88; internat. cons. UNIDO, Vienna, Austria, 1988-96; gen. mgr. Pharma Ancla Labs., San Jose, 1988-90; chmn., founder British C. of C., San Jose, 1991-93; dir. rsch. & devel. CCSS Health Svcs., 1990-94; pres. BioBellessa Tropical Biotech., San Jose, 1988—. Author: Industrial Park for Health, 1982, The Concept of Bioreactor Number Applied to Fermentation Scale-Up, ACHEMA, 1985, Frankfurt am Main, Germany, Scale-up of Bioreactors: Physiological Effects on Microorganisms, BIOTECH Asia, Singapore, 1985, Scale-up-down Biotech Operations and Processes, 1988. British Coun. grantee, 1983-88, CCSS Health Svcs. grantee, 1983-87. Mem. Inst. Chem. Engring., Coll. Engrs. and Architects, CIEME, Biotech. Nat. Coun. Achievements include auto-sledge vehicle for bamboo transportation in bamboo farms; tropical biopharmaceutical active principles from Costa Rica BioDiversity; Anti-Colitis: Juanilamine; Anti-Hypertension and Anti-Hyperglycaemia Agent: Courarine, 1990-95; cibernetic simulation for bioreactor full scale-up-down; novel design multipurpose continuous high retention time algal pond for effluents degradation; novel design/development of a photolysis pretreatment reactor for agricultural and industrial wastewater affluents, 1993. Avocations: nature photography, country hicking, camping, soccer. Home: PO Box 5097 Oakland CA 94605-0097

DE FOREST, EDGAR LESTER, actor, poet, educator; b. Hull, Mass.; s. Edgar Leonard and Ellen Marian (Huntington) De F.; m. Beulah Mary Ingalls, Nov. 21, 1940; children: Peter, Stephen, David, Richard. Diploma, Leland Powers Sch. of Theatre, Boston, 1937; BS, Boston U., 1940; MA, U. So. Calif., 1941; EdD, Columbia U., 1954. Cert. elem. tchr., Calif. (life); cert. secondary tchr., Calif. (life); cert. sch. adminstr., Calif. Dir. reading Mich. State U. (formerly Mich. State Coll.), East Lansing, 1945-48, asst. dir. summer program, 1954-57; dir. students Suffolk U., Boston, 1948-52; assoc. survey research Columbia U., N.Y.C., 1952-53; acting dean instruction Ventura (Calif.) Coll., 1957-60; prof. Coll. Desert, Palm Desert, Calif., 1962-78, prof. emeritus, 1979—; dean of ship U. Seven Seas, Whittier, Calif., 1964-65. Author various poems; appeared in plays Man of La Mancha, 1982, Death of a Salesman, 1983, Homage to Dali, 1988, Becket, The Fantastiks, Booth Majority of One, The King and I. Mem. Mayor's cultural planning 2000 com., Palm Desert, 1985-86; pres. Friends of the Library Coll. of the Desert, Palm Desert, 1983-85. Named Ideal Citizen of the Age of Enlightenment, World Govt. for the Age of Enlightenment, 1971. Mem. Mich. Reading Assn. (founder 1956), Lambda Chi Alpha. Democrat. Avocations: hiking, cats. Home: 220 Pinyon Crest Mountain Center CA 92561-9756

DEFORGE, MICHELE, foundation executive. Pres. Nat. Found. for Fibromyalgia, San Diego, 1993—, San Diego Nat. Orgn. for Women Outreach Fund. Mem. Calif. Women's Health Leadership Program. Office: Nat Found for Fibromyalgia PO Box 3429 San Diego CA 92163-1429

DEGEL, JOHN WILLIAM, journalist, photographer; b. Glendive, Mont., June 27, 1950; s. Anthony and Vivian Dorene (Rathbun) D. Student, Mont. State U., 1978-81, 83-84, Western Mont. Coll., Dillon, Mont., 1984-85, Mount Angel Sem., St. Benedict, Oreg., 1986-87. Mil. journalist U.S. Army, 1972-77; reporter Sidney (Mont.) Herald, 1978; reporter/photographer Laurel (Mont.) Outlook, 1980; editor Red Lodge (Mont.) Weekly, 1981, Wescolite-WMC, Dillon, 1984-85; pub. affairs officer Civil Air Patrol, Great Falls, Mont., 1995-96; county reporter Whitefish (Mont.) Pilot/Hungry Horse News, 1996; reporter, photographer, interim mng. editor Sidney Herald-Leader, 1996-97; speechwriter Lt. Gov. Mont., Helena, 1989-92. Sgt., U.S. Army, 1968-77; 2d lt. Civil Air Patrol, 1995—. Recipient Gen. Excellence award Mont. Newspaper Assn., 1984. Mem. Soc. Profl. Journalists. Avocation: painting. Office: Sidney Herald-Leader 310 2nd Ave NE Sidney MT 59270-4404

DE GETTE, DIANA LOUISE, lawyer, congresswoman; b. Tachikawa, Japan, July 29, 1957; came to U.S., 1957; d. Richard Louis and Patricia Anne (Rose) De G.; m. Lino Sigismondo Lipinsky de Orlov, Sept. 15, 1984; children: Raphaela Anne, Francesca Louise. BA magna cum laude, The Colo. Coll., 1979; JD, NYU, 1982. Bar: Colo. 1982, U.S. Dist. Ct. Colo. 1982, U.S. Ct. Appeals (10th cir.) 1984, U.S. Supreme Ct. 1989. Dep. state pub. defender Colo. State Pub. Defender, Denver, 1982-84; assoc. Coghill & Goodspeed, P.C., Denver, 1984-86; sole practice Denver, 1986-93; of counsel McDermott & Hansen, Denver, 1993-96; mem. Colo. Ho. of Reps., 1992-96, asst. minority leader, 1995-96; mem. U.S. Ho. of Reps. (Colo.), 1997—. Editor: (mag.) Trial Talk, 1989-92. Mem. Mayor's Mgmt. Rev. Com., Denver, 1983-84; resolutions chair Denver Dem. Party, 1986; bd. dirs. Root-Tilden Program, NYU Sch. Law, N.Y.C., 1986-92; bd. trustees, alumni trustee Colo. Coll., Colorado Springs, 1988-94. Recipient Root-Tilden scholar NYU Sch. Law, N.Y.C., 1979, Vanderbilt medal, 1982. Mem. Colo. Bar Assn. (bd. govs. 1989-91), Colo. Trial Lawyers Assn. (bd. dirs., exec. com. 1986-92), Colo. Women's Bar Assn., Denver Bar Assn., Phi Beta Kappa, Pi Gamma Mu. Avocations: reading, backpacking, gardening. Office: McDermott & Hansen 1890 Gaylord St Denver CO 80206-1211

DE GEUS, AART J., executive. MSEE, Swiss Fedn. Polytech Inst.; PhD, So. Meth. U. Chmn., CEO Synopsys, Mountain View, Calif. Office: Synopsys 700 E Middlefield Rd Mountain View CA 94043-4033*

DEGUIRE, MARGARET ANN, nurse; b. Detroit, June 7, 1950; d. Gerard John and Althea Wenona (Orrill) DeG. AA, Riverside City Coll., 1973; AS, SUNY, Albany, 1981; postgrad., 1991—. RN, Calif.; CCRN; lic. vocat. nurse; cert. ACLS. Nurse Dr. Stamper, Riverside, Calif., 1973-75; team leader Knollwood Community Hosp., Riverside, Calif., 1975-77; nurse, critical care Riverside Community Hosp., 1977-78; staff nurse Kaiser Hosp., Fontana, Calif., 1978-81, 81-82, nurse, critical care, relief unit leader, 1982-86, treadmill nurse, 1986—. Mem. AACN, Am. Coll. Sport Medicine(exercise technologist), Internat. Dance Excercise Assn. (cert. fitness instr.), Am. Coun. Exercise (cert. aerobics instr.), Loma Linda Lopers. Completed 1988 Long Beach Marathon. Avocations: making porcelain dolls, race walking, boating, water sports. Home: 8809 Bennett Ave Fontana CA 92335-8648 Office: SCPMG 9961 Sierra Ave Fontana CA 92335-6720

DEHAAS, JOHN NEFF, JR., retired architecture educator; b. Phila., July 4, 1926; s. John Neff and Sadie Lavinia (Hagel) DeH.; m. C. Bernice Wallace, Dec. 27, 1950; children: Kenneth Eric, Jocelyn Hilda. BArch, Tex. A&M U., 1948, MEd, 1950. Registered architect, Mont. Instr. Tex. A&M U., College Station, 1948-50, U. Tex., Austin, 1950-51; successively instr. to prof. Mont. State U., Bozeman, 1951-80; supervisory architect Historic Am. Bldgs. Survey, summers San Francisco, 1962, Bozeman, 1963, 65, Milw., 1969; cons. Mont. Historic Preservation Office, Helena, 1977-78, mem. rev. bd., 1968-79. Author: Montana's Historic Structures, Vol. 1, 1864, Vol. 2, 1969, Historic Uptown Butte, 1977; editor quar. newsletter Mont. Ghost Town Preservation Soc., 1972—. Bd. dirs. Mont. Assn. for Blind, Butte, 1984-95. Recipient Centennial Preservation award Mont. Historic Preservation Office, 1989, Dorothy Bridgman award for Outstanding Svc. to the Blind Montana Assn. for the Blind, 1990. Fellow AIA (com. on historic resources 1974—); mem. Mont. Hist. Soc. (trustee's award 1989). Republican. Methodist. Home: 1021 S Tracy Ave Bozeman MT 59715-5329

DEHAVEN, KENNETH LE MOYNE, retired physician; b. The Dalles, Oreg., Mar. 28, 1913; s. Luther John and Dora (Beeks) DeH.; m. Ledith Mary Ewing, Jan. 11, 1937; children: Marya LeMoyne DeHaven Keeth, Lisa Marguerite DeHaven Jordan, Camille Suzanne DeHaven. BS in Pharmacy, North Pacific Coll. Oreg., 1935; MD, U. Mich., 1946. Intern USPHS Hosp., St. Louis, 1947; intern Franklin Hosp., San Francisco, 1947-48, resident, 1949; clinician Dept. Pub. Health, City San Francisco, Dept. V.D., 1949-51; practice family medicine, Sunnyvale, Calif., 1955-87; mem. staff El Camino Hosp., Mt. View, Calif., San Jose (Calif.) Hosp. Pres. Los Altos Hills Assn. Served to capt., USAF, 1952-55. Fellow Am. Acad. Family Practice; mem. AMA, Ariz. Med. Assn., Calif. Med. Assn., N.Y. Acad. Scis., Santa Clara County Med. Soc., Astron. Soc. Pacific, Sunnyvale C. of C. (bd. dirs. 1955-56), Book Club (San Francisco), Masons, Alpha Kappa Kappa. Republican. Home: 9348 E Casitas Del Rio Dr Scottsdale AZ 85255-4313

DEHERRERA, JUAN LEO, lawyer; b. Costilla, N.Mex., Sept. 25, 1939; s. Gilbert and Maria (Arellano) DeH.; m. Dora O. Garcia, Dec. 31, 1964; children: Kelly, Michelle, Amy, Karen. BA, U. Wyo., 1968, JD, 1971. Bar: Wyo. 1971, U.S. Dist. Ct. Wyo. 1971, U.S. Ct. Appeals (10th cir.) 1973, U.S. Supreme Ct. 1975. Atty. gen. State of Wyo., Cheyenne, 1971-74; atty. pvt. practice, Cheyenne, 1974-78, Legal Aid Southeast Wyo, Cheyenne, 1978-79, pvt. practice, Rawlins, Wyo., 1979—; bd. dirs. Equality State Bank, Cheyenne, 1977—, Equality Bankshares, Multi-Bank Holding Co., 1993—. With U.S. Army, 1960-66. Mem. Wyo. State Bar Assn., Wyo. Trial Lawyers Assn., Carbon County Bar Assn., VFW, Disabled Am. Vets., Am. Legion, U. Wyo. Alumni. Home: 1715 Inverness Blvd Rawlins WY 82301-4205 Office: PO Box 71 Rawlins WY 82301-0071

DEHGHANI, MOHAMMAD M., engineering educator, research scientist; b. Tehran, Iran, Aug. 22, 1955; came to U.S., 1977; s. Ali M. Dehghani and Khadijeh M. Askarian. BS in Mech. Engring., La. State U., 1980, MS in Mech. Engring., 1982, PhD, 1987. Registered profl. engr. Ohio, Calif. Prof. Ohio U., Athens, 1987-96; scientist Lawrence Livermore (Calif.) Nat. Lab., 1996—; Senator Ohio U., 1992-95; mem. review panel NSF, Washington, 1993—. Contbr. articles to profl. jours. Recipient numerous rsch. awards. Mem. ASME. Moslem. Avocation: pilot. Office: Lawrence Livermore Nat Lab 7000 East Ave Livermore CA 94550-9516

DEHM, SCOTT M., personnel specialist, consultant; b. Oswego, N.Y., Mar. 3, 1967; s. Kevin V. LeRoy and Donna M. (Bressler) D. BSBA, U. San Francisco. Acct. exec. AIG, San Francisco, 1994-95; sr. acct. exec. Mellon Bank, N.A., San Francisco, 1995-97; prin., owner Park Dehm Internat., Inc., San Francisco, 1997—. Republican. Roman Catholic. Office: Park Dehm International Inc 500 Sutter St Ste 212 San Francisco CA 94102-1111

DEHMELT, HANS GEORG, physicist; b. Germany, Sept. 9, 1922; came to U.S., 1952, naturalized, 1962; s. Georg Karl and Asta Ella (Klemmt) D.; 1 child from previous marriage, Gerd; m. Diana Elaine Dundore, Nov. 18, 1989. Grad., Graues Kloster, Berlin, Abitur, 1940; D Rerum Naturalium, U. Goettingen, 1950; D Rerum Naturalium (hon.), Ruprecht Karl-Universitat, Heidelberg, 1986; DSc (hon.), U. Chgo., 1987. Postdoctoral fellow U. Goettingen, Germany, 1950-52, Duke U., Durham, N.C., 1952-55; vis. asst.

prof. U. Wash., Seattle, 1955; asst. prof. physics U. Wash., 1956, asso. prof., 1957-61, prof., rsch. physicist, 1961—; cons. Varian Assocs., Palo Alto, Calif., 1956-76. Contbr. articles to profl. jours. Recipient Humboldt prize, 1974, award in basic research Internat. Soc. Magnetic Resonance, 1980, Rumford prize Am. Acad. Arts and Scis., 1985, Nobel prize in Physics, 1989, Nat. Medal of Science, 1995; NSF grantee, 1958—. Fellow Am. Phys. Soc. (Davisson-Germer prize 1970); mem. Am. Acad. Arts and Scis., Am. Optical Soc., Nat. Acad. Scis., Sigma Xi. Co-discoverer (with Hubert Krüger) nuclear quadrupole resonance, 1949; inventor schemes using single trapped atomic particles as million-fold quantum amplifier, employed them as a leader of groups in for the first time permanently isolating and identifying at rest in vacuum an individual electron, a subatomic particle, a charged atom, ion Astrid, an antimatter particle, positron Priscilla, and in demonstrating spontaneous quantum jumps and measuring magnetism and size on single electron and positron with precisions 1,000 times higher than previously attained on millions of them. Home: 1600 43rd Ave E Seattle WA 98112-3205 Office: U Wash Physics Dept Box 35-1560 Seattle WA 98195-1560*

DEICKEN, RAYMOND FRIEDRICH, psychiatric physician, clinical neuroscientist; b. Honolulu, June 28, 1957; s. Raymond T. and Miriam (Ogata) D. AB, Stanford U., 1980, MS, 1980; MD, U. Calif., San Francisco, 1984. Diplomate Nat. Bd. Med. Examiners, Am. Bd. Psychiatry and Neurology. Resident physician U. Calif., San Francisco, 1984-88, rsch. fellow, 1988-91, asst. prof. psychiatry, 1991-97, assoc. prof., 1997—; staff physician VA Med. Ctr., San Francisco, 1991—; invited lectr. World Congress of Biol. Psychiatry Symposium on Brain Imaging, Nice, France, 1997, Soc. Biol. Psychiatry Symposium on Magnetic Resonance Spectroscopy, San Francisco, 1993, Internat. Symposium on Schizophrenia, Sao Paulo, Brazil, 1998. Reviewer manuscripts Biol. Psychiatry, 1987—, Psychiatry Rsch., 1992—; contbr. articles to profl. jours. Alumni mentor Stanford U. Student Alumni Mentor Program, 1993—. Recipient Young Investigator award Nat. Alliance for Rsch. on Schizophrenia and Depression, 1992, 94, Stanley Found. rsch. award Nat. Alliance for Mentally Ill, 1997, 98, VA Physician Rsch. Assoc. Career Devel. award, 1991-95; Dista fellow Soc. Biol. Psychiatry, 1991. Mem. AMA, Soc. Biol. Psychiatry, Internat. Soc. Magnetic Resonance in Medicine, Am. Psychiat. Assn., Internat. Soc. Neuroimaging in Psychiatry, N.Y. Acad. Scis. Episcopalian. Home: 197 Carnelian Way San Francisco CA 94131-1780 Office: Dept Veterans Affairs Med Ctr 4150 Clement St San Francisco CA 94121-1545

DEIOTTE, CHARLES EDWARD, computer software company executive; b. Gary, Ind., Jan. 31, 1946; s. Raymond Louis and Dorothy Jane (Paulson) D.; A.A., Skagit Valley Jr. Coll., 1966; student Wash. State U.; children—Raymond, Karl, Ronald. Programmer, Wash. State U., Pullman, 1969-70; project dir. AGT Mgmt. Systems, Renton, Wash., sr. tech. cons., sect. mgr. McDonnell-Douglas Automation, Bellevue, Wash., 1972-73; sr. engr. Boeing Computer Services, Seattle, 1973-75, computer based instrn. specialist, Tng. div., 1975-79; mgr. microprocessor design support center Boeing Aerospace Co., Kent, Wash., 1979-80; mgr. concept research Federal Express Corp., Colorado Springs, Colo., 1980-81, mgr. microprocessor support group, 1981-82; pres. Deitron Systems, Inc., Auburn, Wash., 1976-81; pres., chmn. bd. Logical Systems Inc., Colorado Springs, 1981-87; chmn., CEO Cedsys Inc., 1987-91, sr. software engr., cons. LinCom Corp., 1992-93; software systems specialist, MCI Corp., 1993—; chmn. bd. Summit Med. Systems, Inc., 1985-86 . Neighborhood commr. Chief Seattle council Boy Scouts Am., 1971-72; v.p. REACT alert, Seattle, 1974; advisor Jr. Achievement, Colorado Springs, 1980; coach Odyssey of the Mind, 1991-92. Recipient Boeing Aerospace Co. Cert. of Achievement, 1979. Mem. Assn. Computing Machinery, IEEE, AAAS, Data Processing Mgmt. Assn., Am. Mgmt. Assn., Gamma Sigma Epsilon. Home: 285 W Frostad Rd Oak Harbor WA 98277-9564 Office: 4678 Alpine Meadows Ln Colorado Springs CO 80919-3159

DEISENROTH, CLINTON WILBUR, electrical engineer; b. Louisville, Aug. 9, 1941; s. Clifton Earl and Nell (Pierce) D.; m. Lisbeth D. Isaacs, May 10, 1974; 1 dau., Susan Michelle. BEE, Ga. Inst. Tech., 1965. With Raytheon Co., 1966-81, div. mgr. Addington Labs., Inc., solid state products div., Santa Clara, Calif., 1975-77, program mgr. electromagnetic systems div., Goleta, Calif., 1977-79, dir. surface navy electronic warfare systems, 1979-81; sr. v.p. systems div. Teledyne-MEC, 1981-84; pres. Teledyne CME, 1984-90; exec. v.p., gen. mgr. Aerospace Products div. G&H Tech., Inc., 1990-92; v.p. bus. devel. Whittaker Electronic Systems, 1992-94, v.p., gen. mgr., 1994-96, pres., 1996; pres. CWD and Assocs. Mem. IEEE. Home: 2052 Hartwick Circle Thousand Oaks CA 91360-1905

DEITER, NEWTON ELLIOTT, clinical psychologist; b. N.Y.C., Dec. 12, 1931; s. Benjamin and Anna (Leibowitz) D. BS, UCLA, 1957; MS, Leland Stanford, 1960; PhD in Clin. Psychology, U. Chgo., 1965. Cert. in clin. psychology. Pvt. practice clin. psychology L.A., 1965-90; exec. dir. Nat. Family Planning Coun., L.A., 1965-76, Gay Media Task Force, L.A., 1976-86; staff cons. Aaron Spelling Prodns., L.A., 1980-90, spl. cons. NBC, L.A., 1970-79, cons. broadcast stds. dept. CBS, L.A., 1968-82, cons. City Coun., City of L.A., 1975-85. Columnist Bottomline Mag., 1992—, Palm Springs Presents Mag., 1996—. Mem. Dem. Ctrl. Com., L.A., 1972-76; bd. dirs. Gay Cmty. Svcs. Ctr., L.A., 1970-75, Am. Cancer Soc., L.A., 1972-77, Palm Springs Gay Tourism Coun., 1993-95, Desert Gay Tourism Guild, 1996-99; commr. L.A. Probation Comm., 1977-85; mem. bd. advisors San Francisco Sheriffs Dept., 1969-79; vice chmn. recreation and pks. commr. City of Rancho Mirage, 1997—. Lt. col. USAFR, 1950-75. Inductee, Internat. Gay Travel Assn. Hall of Fame, 1994. Mem. NATAS, Press Club L.A., Internat. Gay Travel Assn. (bd. dirs. 1986-93, pres. 1991-92), Desert Bus. Assn. (v.p. 1993, bd. dirs. 1992), Internat. Food, Wine and Travel Writers Assn. (bd. dirs., v.p./treas. 1995-97, pres. 1997—), Air Force Assn., Am. Mensa, Masons. Avocations: photography, wine making, travel writing. Home: 71426 Estellita Dr Rancho Mirage CA 92270-4215 Office: Rancho Mirage Travel 71-428 US Highway 111 Rancho Mirage CA 92270-4130

DE JONG, CONSTANCE A., artist, educator; b. San Diego, Dec. 21, 1950; d. Rolland and Rita De Jong. BS in Edn., Bowling Green State U., 1972; MA, U. N.Mex., 1975, MFA, 1981. Asst. prof. art U. N.Mex., Albuquerque, 1989-95, assoc. prof., 1995—; lectr. Bezalel Acad. Art, Jerusalem, Israel, 1994. Exhibited in shows at Littlejohn/Sternau, N.Y.C., 1995, Linda Durham Gallery, Galisteo, N. Mex., 1996, SITE Santa Fe, 1996, Sheldon Meml. Art Galley/U. Nebr., Lincoln, 1997, Cedar Rapids (Iowa) Mus. Art, 1998; sculptures in collections at Albuquerque Fine Arts Mus., Mulvane Art Mus., Kans., Mus. N.Mex., Fisher-Landau Ctr., N.Y.C. Vol. Animal Humane Soc., Albuquerque, 1998. Named Outstanding Tchr. of Yr., U. N.Mex., 1994; Nat. Endowment for Arts fellow, 1982, U. N.Mex. rsch. grantee, 1980, N.Mex. Arts Commn. grantee, 1979. Mem. Albuquerque Zen Ctr. Avocation: scuba diving. Office: U NMex Dept Art And Art Hist Albuquerque NM 87131

DE JONG, ROBERT See DURIS, ROBERT

DEJOURNETT, WILLIAM N., music educator; b. Tallahassee, Fla., Nov. 19, 1967. BSE, Jacksonville State U., 1991; MM, No. Ill. U., 1993. Dir. bands Jacksonville (Ala.) High Sch., 1991-92; grad. asst. No. Ill. U., DeKalb, 1992-93; dir. bands Chetsnut Log Mid. Sch., Douglasville, Ga., 1994-95; grad. asst. U. Miss., Oxford, 1995-97; dir. athletic bands Colo. State U., Fort Collins, 1997—; cons. Blockbuster Music Corp., Marietta, Ga., 1994. Author: Brass Secrets of the Drum and Bugle Corps, 1997. Avocations: history, studying life and works of William Faulkner. E-mail: bdejournett@vines.colostate.edu. Office: Colo State U # 100 Music Fort Collins CO 80523

DEKEN, JEAN MARIE, librarian, archivist; b. St. Louis, Apr. 5, 1953; d. Cornelius John and Loretta Frances (McGuire) D.; m. James Roger Reed, Jan. 2, 1981. BA in English summa cum laude, Washington U., 1974, MA in English, 1976. Cert. archivist Acad. Cert. Archivists. Archivist Mo. Botanical Garden, St. Louis, 1975-78; mgmt. analyst Nat. Archives and [illegible] instr. of English St. Louis Community Coll., St. Louis, 1982-83; curator John W. Barriger III collections St. Louis Merc. Libr., 1983-85; libr. Ralston Purina, St. Louis, 1985-86; mgr. libr. svcs. Mantz, Inc., St. Louis, 1986-87; supervisory archivist Nat. Archives and Records Adminstrn., St. Louis, 1987-96; archivist Stanford U. Stanford Linear Accelerator Ctr., 1996—. Author: Henry Shaw: His Life and Legacy, 1977; contbr. articles to profl. jours. Mem. Spl. Librs. Assn., Midwest Archives Conf., Soc. Am. Archivists, Soc. Calif. Archivists (bd. mem.), Western Archives Inst. Avocation: swimming. Office: Stanford U Stanford Linear Accelerator Ctr PO Box 4349 Stanford CA 94309-4349

DE LACKNER, BARBARA ELIZABETH, author, educator; b. N.Y.C., Dec. 18, 1930; d. Donald Plass and Anna Fredenika (Schmucker) de Lackner; m. Alan Greiner, Jan. 28, 1956 (div. 1984); children: Michael Gene Greiner, Susan Jeanette Andrews, David Christopher Greiner. BA, Pomona Coll., 1953; MA, Portland (Oreg) State U., 1979. Acting tchr. Girls Collegiate Sch., Claremont, Calif., 1956-69; camp dir. Sherwood Forest, Nahcotta, Wash., 1960-84; acting tchr. Helen Bush Sch., Seattle, 1966-69, Catlin Gabel Sch., Portland, Oreg., 1972-77, Metropolitan Learning Ctr., Portland, Oreg., 1985—, Marylhurst Coll., Lake Oswego, Oreg., 1986—. Author 3 act plays, 1970-79, The Magic, 1983, 84; contbr. over 75 poems to jours. Pres. Mereview (Wash.) PTA; sec. Citizens Advisory Council to Sch. Bd., Mercer Island, Wash. Mem. Oreg. State Poetry Assn. (sec., treas., newsletter editor 1987-97), Oreg. Writers Colony (sec. 1987-95, pres. 1995-97, anthology editor), Willamette Writers (bd. sec. 1987-89). Office: Attn Elizabeth Bolton 17935 NW Skyline Blvd Portland OR 97231-1804

DELACOTE, GOERY, museum director. Exec. dir. The Exploratorium, San Francisco. Office: The Exploratorium 3601 Lyon St San Francisco CA 94123-1099

DELA CRUZ, JOSE SANTOS, retired state supreme court chief justice; b. Saipan, Commonwealth No. Mariana Islands, July 18, 1948; s. Thomas Castro and Remedio Sablan (Santos) Dela C.; m. Rita Tenorio Sablan, Nov. 12, 1977; children: Roxanne, Renee, Rica Ann. BA, U. Guam, 1971; JD, U. Calif., Berkeley, 1974; cert., Nat. Jud. Coll., Reno, 1985. Bar: No. Mariana Islands, 1974, U.S. Dist. Ct. No. Mariana Islands 1978. Staff atty. Micro. Legal Svcs. Corp., Saipan, 1974-79; gen. counsel Marianas Pub. Land Corp., Saipan, 1979-81; liaison atty. CNMI Fed. Laws Commn., Saipan, 1981-83; ptnr. Borja & Dela Cruz, Saipan, 1983-85; assoc. judge Commonwealth Trial Ct., Saipan, 1985-89; chief justice Supreme Ct. No. Mariana Islands, 1989-95; retired, 1995; mem. Conf. of Chief Justices, 1989-95, Adv. Commn. on Judiciary, Saipan, 1980-82; chmn. Criminal Justice Planning Agy., Saipan, 1985-95. Mem. Coun. for Arts, Saipan, 1982-83; chmn. Bd. of Elections, Saipan, 1977-82; pres. Cath. Social Svcs., Saipan, 1982-85. Mem. No. Marianas Bar Assn. (pres. 1984-85). Roman Catholic. Avocations: golf, reading, walking. Office: Commonwealth Supreme Ct Civic Ctr Saipan MP 96950

DE LA FUENTE, LAWRENCE EDWARD, artist; b. Chgo., Sept. 29, 1947. Student, Kansas City Art Inst., 1966-68. Exhbns. include San Francisco Art Commn., 1971, 72, Berkeley (Calif.) Art Ctr., 1973, San Jose (Calif.) State U., 1973, Gallery West, Mendocino, Calif., 1973, San Francisco Mus. Art, 1973, 74, 75, 76, 78, Mendocino Art Ctr., 1977, 80, 83, 93, Wilkinson-Cobb Gallery, Mendocino, 1977, Tucson (Ariz.) Mus. Art, 1977, Nat. Coll. Fine Art, Smithsonian, Washington, 1977, 80, mus. Mill Valley, Calif., 1978, Albuquerque Mus. Art, 1978, El Paso (Tex.) Mus.. Art, 1978, Blaffer Gallery, U. Houston, 1978, Taylor Mus. Art, Colorado Springs, 1978, Everson Mus., Syracuse, N.Y., 1979, Witte Mus., San Antonio, 1979, Contemporary Arts Mus., Chgo., 1979, U. Ga., Athens, 1979, Tyler U., Phila., 1979, Palacio de Mineria, Mexico City, 1980, Internat. Sculpture Conf., Washington, 1980, Western States Fair, Pomona, Calif., 1980, Macintosh-Drysdale Gallery, Washington, 1981, Fondo del Sol Gallery, Wahsington, 1981, Alternative Mus., N.Y.C., 1982, P.S.1 Clocktower, N.Y.C., 1982, Ronald Feldman Gallery, N.Y.C., 1982, Knot Art Gallery, Mendocino, 1983, U. Houston, 1984, Cultural Arts Ctr. Santa Barbara, 1985, Pulsations, Phila., 1986, Retreti Art Ctr., Helsinki, 1987, Living Art Show, Mendocino, 1987, Philbrook Mus. Art, Tulsa, Okla., 1987, Chgo. Pub. Libr., 1988, Kohler Mus. Art, Sheboygan, Wis., 1989, Va. Mus. Fine Art, Richmond, 1989, Orlando (Fla.) Mus. Art, 1989, Tokyo Mus. Modern Art, 1990, Kyoto (Japan) Mus. Modern Art, 1990, Smithsonian Instn. Renwick Gallery, 1990, Calif. State U. Chico, 1993, Natural History Mus., L.A., 1994, Smithsonian Traveling Exhbn., 1994, others. NEA fellow 1980, 88, 95. Home: PO Box 954 Mendocino CA 95460-0954 also: 41401 Comptche Ukiah Rd Mendocino CA 95460-9786

DELANCY, MICHAEL ROBINSON, minister; b. Abilene, Tex., Nov. 1, 1948; s. Leslie Jack Delancy and Gloria Eileen (Baker) Barnes; m. Fairy Marguerite Johnston, Nov. 23, 1966 (div. Aug. 1974); children: Lisa Marie, Michael Gary, Joseph Lamont; m. Patricia Robinson, Dec. 17, 1976; children: Patrick Sean, Mary Elizabeth. AA, St. John's Jr. Coll., 1975; BA, Concordia Sr. Coll., Ft. Wayne, Ind., 1977; MDiv, Concordia Theol. Sem., Ft. Wayne, Ind., 1981. Ordained to ministry Luth. Ch., 1981. Vicar Mt. Olive Luth. Ch., Billings, Mont., 1979-80; head min. Zion Evangelical Luth. Ch., Vassar, Kans., 1981-90; min. Outreach Calvary Luth. Ch., Topeka, 1990—; workshop leader Dist. Evangelism, Wichita, Kans., 1981, Dist. Singles, Wichita, 1983, Luth. Women's Missionary League Wksp., Vassar, 1983, Cir. 14 Sunday Sch., Salina, Kans., 1984; constitution ad hoc Kans. dist. Luth. Ch., Topeka, 1982-83, mgr. dist. conv., 1991, mgr. continuing edn. seminar, 1991; cir. youth rep. Cir. 4, Vassar, 1983—, youth pastoral advisor, 1983—, singles pastoral advisor, 1991—. Scoutmaster Boy Scouts Am., Oklahoma City, 1970-73, chaplain local troop, 1991—; organizer, chmn. Cub Pack, Ft. Wayne, 1977-79, treas., 1991—; organizer Young Reps. Fundraiser, Ft. Wayne, 1978; mem. Vet. Counseling Ctr., Ft. Wayne, 1979; bereavement coord. Osage County Hospice, 1987-88. Named Vol. of Yr., Boy Scouts Am., Ft. Wayne, 1979, Best New Poet, Am. Poetry Soc., 1988. Avocations: poetry, mechanics, woodworking, water skiing, nature. Office: Calvary Luth Ch 186 Pine Hollow Rd Stevensville MT 59870-6621

DELANEY, MARION PATRICIA, bank executive; b. Hartford, Conn., May 20, 1952; d. William Pride Delaney Jr. and Marian Patricia (Utley) Murphy. BA, Union Coll., Schenectady, N.Y., 1973. Adminstrv. asst. N.Y. State Assembly, Albany, 1973-74; account exec. Foote, Cone & Belding, N.Y.C., 1974-78; sr. account exec. Dailey & Assocs., L.A., 1978-81; pub. rels. cons. NOW, Washington, 1981-83; account supr. BBDO/West, L.A., 1983-85; v.p. Grey Advt., L.A., 1985-87, San Francisco, 1987-89; sr. v.p. McCann-Erickson, San Francisco, 1989-95; sr. v.p., dir. advt./mktg. comms. Bank of Am., San Francisco, 1995—. Del. Dem. Nat. Conv., San Francisco, 1984; bd. dirs. JED Found., Hartford, Conn., 1989—, Easter Seals Soc., Bay Area, 1995-97. Mem. NOW (v.p. L.A. chpt. 1980-83, pres. 1984, advisor 1985-87). Congregationalist. Home: 11 Gary Way Fairfax CA 94930-1002

DELANEY, MATTHEW SYLVESTER, mathematics educator, academic administrator; b. Ireland, Nov. 26, 1927; s. Joseph C. and Elizabeth M. (Bergin) D.; came to U.S., 1947, naturalized, 1952; student St. John's Coll., 1947-51; BA, Immaculate Heart Coll., L.A., 1958; MS, Notre Dame U., 1960; PhD, Ohio State U., 1971. Ordained priest Roman Cath. Ch., 1951; assoc. pastor L.A. Cath. Diocese, 1951-55; instr. math., physics Pius X High Sch., Downey, Calif., 1955-58, vice prin., 1960-62; instr. math. Immaculate Heart Coll., L.A., 1962-65, asst. prof., 1965-72, assoc. prof., 1972-76, prof., 1976—; asst. acad. dean, 1973-78; dean acad. devel. Mt. St. Mary's Coll., L.A., 1978-82, acad. dean, 1978-91; prof. math., 1991—, prof. emeritus, 1996—. NSF grantee, 1959-60, 61. Achievements include: Formal recognition of the eponyms, "Delaney Sets" and "The Delaney Symbol" in the disciplines of discrete geometry and math. crystallography, 1985. Mem. Internat. Union Crystallography, Am. Math. Soc., Math. Assn. Am., N.Y. Acad. Scis.. Democrat. Contbr. articles to math. publs., profl. jours. Home: Apt 32C 13700 El Dorado Dr Seal Beach CA 90740-3843 Office: Mount Saint Mary's Coll 12001 Chalon Rd Los Angeles CA 90049-1526

DELANEY, SHARON EILEEN, nurse educator, consultant, family and child nurse; b. Portsmouth, Va., Feb. 19, 1958; d. Thomas J. and Patricia M. (McSweeney) D.; divorced; children: Carolyn Marie, Jeffrey Thomas. BSN cum laude, Duke U., 1979; MPH, U. N.C., 1983. Cert. neonatal resuscitation provider, pediatric advanced life support. Staff and charge nurse Duke U. Hosp., Durham, N.C., 1979-84; asst. prof. N.C. Cen. U., Durham, 1983-[illegible] Employee Managed Care Corp., Missoula, 1990-91, Aeta Ins. Co., 1994—; mem. Missoula AIDS Coun.; mem. Mont. Lead Edn., Assessment and Detection Adv. Bd., 1993—. Mem. Assn. Women's Health, Obstetric and Neonatal Nurses, Sigma Theta Tau. Home: 1639 Mansfield Ave Missoula MT 59801-5856 Office: Mont State U Coll Nursing Missoula Upper Divsn Campus Missoula MT 59812

DE LA PIEDRA, XAVIER, III, computer and business systems analyst, programmer; b. L.A., Dec. 11, 1969; s. Francisco Xavier and Flora (Amador) de la P.; m. Michele Felix Gonzales; children: Xavier IV, Alicia. BS, U. Calif. Poly., Pomona, 1997. Owner CISC, Hacienda Heights, Calif., 1988—; v.p. Info. Products, Sherman Oaks, Calif., 1993-97; exec. v.p., part owner Realnet, Santa Ana, Calif., 1997—; programmer, sys. analyst Hot Line to Hot Properties, San Clemente, Calif., 1996—; sys. analyst, cons. 1st Team Realty, Yorba Linda, Calif., 1994—. Author: Using Software ASA Realtor, 1997; head programmer: Instant Impact, 1996 (Program of Yr. 1997). Pres. Student Against Drunk Drivers, Pomona, 1986-93, Safe-Ride, LaVerne, Calif., 1987-94. Republican. Roman Catholic. Office: CISC 417 S Associated Rd Ste A449 Brea CA 92821-5802

DE LAPPE, PELE PHYLLIS, retired journalist, artist; b. San Francisco, May 4, 1916; d. Wesley Raymond and Dorothy (Sheldon) de L.; m. Bertram Edises, 1935 (div. 1949); Steve Murdock, 1953 (div. 1969); children: Nina Sheldon Edises, Peter Edises. Student, Calif. Sch. Fine Arts., San Francisco, 1929-31, Art Students League, N.Y.C., 1931-33. Cartoonist New Masses, Daily Worker, N.Y.C., 1934-40; cartoonist, illustrator San Francisco Chronicle, Peoples World, 1934-75, Marine Workers Voice, San Francisco Mag., San Francisco, 1934-50; feature editor People's World, San Francico, 1940-53, 73-91; layout artist Moore Bus. Forms, Emeryville, Calif., 1953-72; caricaturist of authors San Francisco Chronicle Book section, 1940's. Artist, lithographer: one-person shows include: Art Center Gallery, Montgomery St., San Francisco, 1935, Book Shop Coop. Gallery, Washington, 1939; prints exhibited Annex Galleries, Santa Rosa, Calif., Ron Quericia, Duncan's Mills, Calif., Claudia Chapline Gallery, Stinson Beach, Calif., Dore Gallery, San Francisco, Bolinas Mus., Susan Teller Gallery, N.Y.C.; included in collections of Achenbach Found. for Graphic Art, Calif. Palace of Legion of Honor, San Francisco, Woodstock Artists Assn. permanent collection, Cameron Woo, Berkeley, Hazel and Aubrey Grossman, San Francisco, Marc Clavland, Marshall, Calif., Charles and Raquel Rasor, Santa Rosa, Calif, Lynn Cooper, Berkeley, Trudy O'Brien, San Francico, Ben and Bea Goldstein, N.Y.C. Home: 41 Acorn Cir Petaluma CA 94952-6310

DE LA TORRE, DAVID JOSEPH, art museum director; b. Santa Barbara, Calif., June 14, 1948; s. Joseph Raymond and Jacqueline (Ator) de la T.; m. Georgianna M. Lagoria, May 15, 1982. BA in Polit. Sci., U. San Francisco, 1970; MA in Museology, John F. Kennedy U., 1982. Intern, Mexican Mus., San Francisco, 1976-77; curatorial asst. Fine Arts Mus. San Francisco, 1977-79; dir. devel. Triton Mus. Art, Santa Clara, Calif., 1979-84; exec. dir. Mexican Mus., San Francisco, 1984-89; chief planning cons. The Latino Mus., 1989-91; assoc. dir. Honolulu Acad. of the Arts, 1991—; panelist NEA, 1984-94, Calif. Arts Coun., 1985-87, Met. Life Found., 1986-89, Hawaii State Found. Culture and Arts 1993—. Bd. dirs., regional v.p. Calif. Confedn. Arts, 1983-89; bd. dirs. Cultural Coun. Santa Clara County, 1981-84; chmn. Cultural Arts Alliance Santa Clara County, 1981-84, pres. Hawaii Consortium for the Arts. Democrat. Roman Catholic. Office: Honolulu Acad Arts 900 S Beretania St Honolulu HI 96814-1495

DELAYO, LEONARD J., JR., lawyer; b. New Rochelle, N.Y., Aug. 17, 1949; s. Leonard J. Sr. and Helen (Griffith) DeL.; m. Jean Ann Jourdan; children: Francesca Marie, David Joseph. BA, U. N.Mex., 1971, JD, 1974. Bar: N.Mex. 1974, U.S. Dist. Ct. 1974, U.S. Ct. Appeals (10th cir.) 1974, U.S. Supreme Ct. 1978. Atty. Toulouse, Krehbeil & DeLayo, Albuquerque, 1974-79, DeLayo, Olson & Blueher, Albuquerque, 1979-86, Leonard J. DeLayo, Jr., PC, Albuquerque, 1986—; bd. dirs. First State Bancorp., Albuquerque. Mem. bd. edn. Albuquerque Pub. Schs., 1987—, pres., 1992-93, 96—. Mem. ABA, U.S. Supreme Ct. Bar Assn., State Bar Assn. N.Mex. Office: 817 Gold Ave SW Albuquerque NM 87102-3014

DEL CAMPO, MARTIN BERNARDELLI, architect; b. Guadalajara, Mexico, Nov. 27, 1922; came to U.S., 1949; s. Salvador and Margarita (Bernardelli) Del C.; BA, Colegio Frances Morelos, Mexico City, 1941; Archtl. degree Escuela Nacional de Arquitectura, Mexico City, 1948; m. Laura Zaikowska, May 25, 1945; children: Felicia (dec.), Margarita, Mario. Ptnr., Del Campo & Fruiht, architects, Santa Rosa, Cal., 1955-56, Del Campo & Clark, San Francisco, 1957-63; mgr. Hotel Victoria, Oaxaca, Mexico, 1964-67; pres. Gulli-Del Campo, architects, San Francisco, 1968-70; ptnr. Del Campo Assocs., San Francisco, 1977-81. Lectr. archtl. design Coll. Environmental Design, U. Calif., Berkeley, 1973-74. Mem. AIA. Archtl. works include: Calif. Med. Facility South, Vacaville, Phillip Burton Fed. Bldg. remodeling, San Francisco, Hall of Justice, San Francisco, San Francisco Airport Internat. Terminal, Mex. Heritage Gardens, San Jose, Four Seasons Tower, San Francisco. Address: Del Campo & Maru Architects Inc 45 Lansing St San Francisco CA 94105-2611

DELEAR, RICHARD HENRY, personnel consultant; b. Wichita, Kans., Dec. 19, 1927; s. Ernest C. Delear and Clara M. Boberg; m. Helen J. Clark, Jan. 8, 1950 (dec. Mar. 1994); children: Cherie, Cindy, Kimberly, Kirkland, Dianne, Michelle. Student, Hiedleburg U., Germany, 1946-47, San Jose St. U., 1959-60. Cert. hypnotherapist. Enlisted U.S. Army, 1944, advanced through grades to m/sgt., 1952, ret., 1959; entrepreneur Calif., 1960-74; human resources cons. Success Thru Humaneering, Scotts Valley, Calif., 1974—. Author: Leadership Strategies, 1988. Pres. Exchange club, Scotts Valley, 1978-79. Decorated two Bronze Stars, two Purple Hearts, Silver Star. Republican. Roman Catholic. Office: Success Thru Humaneering 202 Burlwood Dr Scotts Valley CA 95066-3704

DE LEON, DANIEL BENITZ, minister; b. Uvalde, Tex., Mar. 15, 1941; s. Gilbert de Leon and Rosa Benitez; m. Ruth Ibarra, Aug. 6, 1966; children: Daniel B. Jr., Joseph Lee, Stephen Peter. BA, So. Calif. Coll., Costa Mesa, 1967; MA, Chapman Coll., Orange, Calif., 1969; MDiv, Melodyland Sch. Theology, Anaheim, Calif., 1977; DD (hon.), Gran Convencion, L.A., 1984. Ordained to ministry Assembly of God Ch., 1969. Youth coord. Western region Pacific Dist. Assembly of God, various locations, 1967-73; nat. youth coord. Latin Am. Assembly of God, 1969-71; chaplain Race Track Chaplain of Am., So. Calif., 1973-76; sr. pastor Templo Calvario, Santa Ana, Calif., 1976—; gen. presbyter Assembly of God, Springfield, Mo., 1982—, nat. coord. lang. groups, 1989—; v.p. L.A. '88, Santa Ana, Calif., 1985—; bd. dirs. Open Doors Internat., Santa Ana, 1989—. Mem. bd. Mayor's Prayer Breakfast, Santa Ana, 1983-87, Mayor's Study Com., Santa Ana, 1987-88, Orange County coun. Boy Scouts Am., 1989—. Named Fastest Growing Ch. in Calif., Nat. Assn. Sunday Schs., 1983, Largest Hispanic Ch. Am., 500 Largest Chs. in Am., 1983—. Mem. Nat. Assn. Evangelicals, Nat. Religious Broadcasters, Pacific Latin Am. Dist. (exec. presbyter 1980—), Hispanic Assn. for Bilingual Bicultural Ministries (founder, pres. 1985—). Republican. Office: Templo Calvario 2617 W 5th St Santa Ana CA 92703-1818

DELISI, DONALD PAUL, fluid mechanic, geophysicist; b. Pitts., Nov. 15, 1944; s. Samuel P. and Jennie (Moffie) D.; m. Adele Pedicord Orr, Aug. 7, 1971; 1 child, Bergen Orr Delisi. B.S.E. magna cum laude, Princeton U., 1966; MS, U. Calif., Berkeley, 1967, PhD, 1972. Resident rsch. assoc. Geophys. Fluid Dynamics Lab./NOAA, Princeton, N.J., 1972-74; sr. rsch. scientist Flow Rsch., Inc., Kent, Wash., 1974-77; staff scientist Phys. Dynamics Inc., Bellevue, Wash., 1977-86; v.p., treas., sr. rsch. scientist N.W. Rsch. Assocs., Inc., Bellevue, 1986—. Contbr. articles to Jour. Geophys. Rsch., Jour. of the Atmospheric Scis., Pure and Applied Geophysics, AIAA Jour., Jour. of Aircraft. Mem. Am. Meteorol. Soc., Am. Geophys. Union, AIAA, Am. Inst. Physics. Achievements include research on stratified shear and vortex flows; on observational studies of atmospheric dynamics. Office: NW Rsch Assocs Inc 14508 NE 20th St Bellevue WA 98007-3713

DELL, MARIA MARGARITA, anatomist; b. Chgo., Dec. 9, 1956; d. Nestor and Rafaela (Rivera) Dones; m. Louis Patrick Dell, Aug. 1, 1993; children: Brent, John-Louis. BSc, U. Puerto Rico, 1978; PhD in Anatomy, U. Okla., 1986. Tchr. asst. U. Puerto Rico, San Juan, 1979-82, U. Okla., Okla. City, 1983-86; instr. Okla. State U., Okla. City, 1989; asst. prof. Okla. [illegible] Coll., L.A., 1994—. Contbr. articles to profl. jours. Bd. dirs. Okla. Literacy Council, Okla. City, 1990-93, Okla. Literacy Commn., Okla. City, 1992-93. Recipient Gordon Rsch. award, Gainesville, Fla., 1988. Mem. Soc. Study Reproduction, Sigma Xi. Republican. Roman Catholic. Avocations: sew-

ing. E-mail: md.phd.@worldnet.att.net. Office: Cleveland Chiropractic Coll 590 N Vermont Ave Los Angeles CA 90004-2196

DELLAS, ROBERT DENNIS, investment banker; b. Detroit, July 4, 1944; s. Eugene D. and Maxine (Rudell) D.; m. Shila L. Clement, Mar. 27, 1976; children—Emily Allison, Lindsay Michelle. B.A. in Econs., U. Mich., Ann Arbor, 1966; M.B.A., Harvard U., Cambridge, 1970. Analyst Burroughs Corp., Detroit, 1966-67, Pasadena, Calif., 1967-68; mgr. U.S. Leasing, San Francisco, 1970-76; pres., dir. Energetics Mktg. & Mgmt. Assn., San Francisco, 1978-80; sr. v.p. E.F. Hutton & Co., San Francisco, 1981-85; prin. founder Capital Exchange Internat., San Francisco, 1976—; gen. ptnr. Kanland Assocs., Tex., 1982, Claremont Assocs., Calif., 1983, Lakeland Assocs., Ga., 1983, Americal Assocs., Calif., 1983, Chatsworth Assocs., Calif., 1983, Walnut Grove Assocs., Calif., 1983, Somerset Assocs., N.J., 1983, One San Diego Assocs., Calif., 1984, Big Top Prodns., L.P., Calif., 1994. Bd. dirs., treas. Found. San Francisco's Archtl. Heritage. Mem. U.S. Trotting Assn., Calif. Harness Horse Breeders Assn. (Breeders award for Filly of Yr. 1986, Aged Pacing Mare, 1987, 88, Colt of Yr. 1990), Calif. Golf Club San Francisco. Office: Capital Exch Internat 1911 Sacramento St San Francisco CA 94109-3419

DELNIK, ALEXANDER, engineering executive, business consultant; b. Zhitomir, Ukraine, Nov. 10, 1961; came to U.S., 1991; s. Yefim and Bera (Nevelskaya) D. MS, Civil Engring. Inst., Kiev, Ukraine, 1983, PhD, 1987; MBA, UCLA, 1997. Registered profl. engr., Calif. Engr. Civil Engring. Inst., Kiev, 1987-88, sr. rschr./lectr., 1988-91; engr./lab. supr. Soil Tech, Inc., Temecula, Calif., 1991-93; project mgr. Dames & Moore, Inc., L.A., 1993—. Editor: English-Russian-Ukrainian Geotechnical Dictionary, 1992; contbr. articles to profl. jours.; editl. bd. Ukrainian Jour. of Found. Engring., 1990-92. Mem. Townhall, L.A., 1994—. Recipient Diploma of Sr. Rschr., Coun. Ministers of USSR, 1990; Ministry of Higher Edn. Lenin's scholar, 1982-83, grantee, 1989-91. Mem. ASCE, Earthquake Engring. Rsch. Inst. Achievements include research and development of numerical techniques to simulate soil-structure interaction; design of foundations for nuclear power plants in Russia, Ukraine, Hungary; major design and construction projects worldwide. Home: 11786 Moorpark St Apt D Studio City CA 91604-2125 Office: Dames and Moore 911 Wilshire Blvd Ste 700 Los Angeles CA 90017-3499

DELOACH, ROBERT EDGAR, corporate executive; b. Daytona Beach, Fla., Jan. 6, 1939; s. Ollie Newman and Sally Gertrude (Schrowder) DeL. Student U. Alaska-Anchorage, 1967-69, Alaska Meth. U., 1970, Pacific Luth. U., 1972. Lic. elec. engr. and adminstr., Alaska, 1979; lic. pvt. pilot, real estate broker, ins. agt. Former chmn. bd. Alaska Stagecraft, Inc., Anchorage; pres. BG Systems Co., BG Tax & Acctg., Inc., The Electric Doctor, Inc., Apollo Travel, Inc.; former pres. Coastal Electronics, Inc.; former owner-mgr. Bargain Towne, Anchorage. Active Anchorage Community Theatre, Anchorage Theater Guild. Mem. Assn. Ind. Accts., Internat. Assn. Theatrical Stage Employees and Moving Picture Machine Operators U.S. (past pres. local 770), Ind. Elec. Contractors Assn., Internat. Assn. Elec. Insps. Home: 1207 W 47th Ave Anchorage AK 99503-6917

DEL OLMO, FRANK, newspaper editor; b. L.A., May 18, 1948; s. Francisco and Margaret Rosalie (Mosqueda) D.; m. Karen Margaret King, Feb. 6, 1970 (div. Sept. 1982); 1 child, Valentina Marisol; m. Magdalena Beltran-Hernandez, Nov. 10, 1991; 1 child, Francisco Manuel. Student, UCLA, 1966-68; BS magna cum laude in Journalism, Calif. State U., Northridge, 1970. Reporter-intern L.A. Times, 1970-71, gen. assignment reporter, 1971-80, columnist, editorial bd., 1980-90, deputy editor, 1990-98, assoc. editor, 1998—; instr. Chicano Studies, Calif. State U., 1970-71; contbg. editor Race Relations Reporter, Nashville, 1973-75; on-air host, writer "Ahora" Sta. KCET-TV, L.A., 1974; chief writer, rschr. KNBC, 1975; bd. contbrs., freelance reporter Nuestro Mag., 1976-81; program co-dir. Summer Program Minority Journalists, 1990, faculty mem. 1979, vis. faculty mem. 1978, 80-83, 85, 89; vis. profl. Dow-Jones Newspaper Fund U. So. Calif. Sch. Journalism, 1975, bd. dirs. Numerous lectrs., presentations at colls., univs. Named Senior Faculty of Summer Program Minority Journalists Inst. Journalism Edn.; recipient Emmy award, 1976, Sigma Delta Chi Achievement award, 1982, Profl. Achievement award UCLA Alumni, 1990, Pulitzer Prize, 1984; Neiman fellowship Harvard U., 1987-88. Office: Los Angeles Times 202 W 1st St Los Angeles CA 90012-4105

DE LONG, GEORGE MAHLON, clinical psychologist, developer; b. San Diego, May 12, 1947; s. Edward Mahlon and Theresa Margaret (Thayer) De L.; m. Elizabeth Keith McElfresh, Dec. 28, 1971. BA, San Diego State U., 1969; MA, Ariz. State U., 1971, PhD, 1977. Diplomate Am. Bd. Profl. Disability Consultants; lic. psychologist, Ariz. Pvt. practice Phoenix; pres., gen. mgr. Behavioral Health Systems Inc., Phoenix; cons. Hay Caneen Consultants, N.Y.C., 1988-93, Rudolf Dew and Assoc., Torrance, Calif., 1993-98. Author: Human Services Technology, 1975. Sec./treas. Mountain Park Homeowners Assn., Phoenix, 1989-93; mem. longrange planning com. South Mountain Preserve, Phoenix, 1993-95. Recipient Rehabilitator of Yr. award Mayor's Commn. on Employment of Handicapped, Phoenix, 1979. Mem. APA, Ariz. Psychol. Assn. Avocation: endurance sports. Office: PO Box 90295 202 E McDowell Rd # 135-8 Phoenix AZ 85066-0295

DE LORCA, LUIS E., educational administrator, educator, speaker; b. L.A., Oct. 18, 1959; s. Patricia Jean Clougher Harvey. AA, Rio Hondo Jr. Coll., Whittier, Calif., 1983; BA, Calif. State Poly. U., 1989; MA in Humanities, Calif. State U., Dominguez Hills, 1997; tchg. credential, Nat. U., 1997; adminstrv. credential, U. So. Calif., 1998. Football coach various high schs., So. Calif., 1980; pub. rels. dir. Calif. Poly Pomona Music Dept., 1987-89; pres. Exclusive Concerts, L.A., 1987-89; lifeguard L.A. City Recreation Dept., 1980-87; tchr. English Cathedral H.S., L.A., 1989-90; tchr., rsch. specialist Whittier (Calif.) Union H.S., 1990; founder, dir. The Learning Advantage Ctr., Whittier, 1991—; elem. tchr. St. Paul of the Cross Sch., La Mirada, Calif., 1993-95; CEO New Ednl. Wave Inc., Whittier, 1994—; tchr. L.A. County Office Edn., 1995-98; asst. prin. Bassett Unified Sch. Dist., 1998—. Active Big Bros. of Am., Fair Housing, Greenpeace. Mem. Whittier C. of C., Cousteau Soc. Democrat. Avocations: scuba, martial arts, swimming, handball, skiing. Home: # 102 16040 Leffingwell Rd Apt 102 Whittier CA 90603-3139

DELORENZO, DAVID A., food products executive; b. 1947. Colgate U.; MBA, U. Pa. With Dole Food Co., Inc., Thousand Oaks, Calif., 1970—, exec. v.p., 1990-91, 93—, pres., 1991-93; pres. Dole Food Co., Internat., 1993—. Office: Dole Food Co Inc 31365 Oak Crest Dr Westlake Village CA 91361-4633*

DE LOS SANTOS, ALFREDO GUADALUPE, JR., education administrator, consultant; b. Laredo, Tex., Feb. 20, 1936; s. Alfredo Garza and Hipolita (Hernandez) de los S.; m. Carmen Elizalde, Nov. 18, 1961; children: Patricio, Federico, Gerardo. AA, Laredo C.C., 1955, El Paso C.C., 1995; BA, U. Tex., 1957, MLS, 1959, PhD, 1963; Assoc. Gen. Studies, Mesa (Ariz.) C.C., 1989. Instr. English, Laredo C.C., 1960-63; dean R&D, Fla. Keys Jr. Coll., Key West, 1965-67; dean instrn. Northampton County Area C.C., Bethlehem, Pa., 1967-71; pres. El Paso C.C., 1971-76; dir. bilingual edn. S.W. Devel. Lab., Austin, 1976-78; vice-chancellor student and ednl. devel. Maricopa Cmty. Colls., Tempe, Ariz., 1978—; mem. adv. com. ERIC Clearinghouse for Jr. Colls., L.A., 1970—; bd. dirs. Coun. Higher Edn. Accreditation, Washington, 1996—, mem. exec. com., 1996—; chair outstanding dissertations competition Nat. Assn. Bilingual Edn., Washington, 1985—; mem. Nat. Adv. Com. on Instnl. Quality and Integrity, U.S. Dept. Edn., Washington, 1994—; hon. prof. U. Autonoma de Guadalajara, Mex., 1997. Contbr. chpts. to books, also articles to profl. pubs. Mem. bd. trustees The Tomas Rivera Policy Inst., Claremont, Calif., 1984—, Am. Coll. Testing, Iowa City, 1992—, Carnegie Found. for Advancement of Tchg., 1993—; bd. dirs. Partnership for Svcs.-Learing, N.Y.C., 1988-94. Recipient Howard McGraw, Jr. Edn. prize McGraw-Hill Cos., N.Y.C., 1998, Outstanding Adminstrv. Support to Devel. Edn. award Nat. Assn. Devel. Edn., Chgo., 1995, Ednl. Leadership award Ariz. Assn. Chicanos in Higher Edn., Washington, 1993, Educator Achievement award NSF, Washington, 1993, others. Democrat. Roman Catholic. Avocations: tennis, hiking, camping, travel, reading. Home: 2068 E Libra Dr Tempe AZ 85283-3322 Office: Maricopa Cmty Colls 2411 W 14th St Tempe AZ 85281-6941

DEL PAPA, FRANKIE SUE, state attorney general; b. 1949. BA, U. Nev.; JD, George Washington U., 1974. Bar: Nev. 1974. Staff asst. U.S. Senator Alan Bible, Washington, 1971-74; assoc. Law Office of Leslie B. Grey, Reno, Nev., 1975-78; legis. asst. to U.S. Senator Howard Cannon, Washington, 1978-79; ptnr. Thornton & Del Papa, 1979-84; pvt. practice Reno, 1984-87; sec. of state State of Nev., Carson City, 1987-91; atty. gen. State of Nev., 1991—. Mem. Sierra Arts Found. (bd. dirs.), Trust for Pub. Land (adv. com.), Nev. Women's Fund. Democrat. Office: Office of Atty Gen Capitol Complex 100 N Carson St Carson City NV 89701-4717*

DELU, HELENA O., director social welfare organization; b. Los Angeles, Calif.. BA in Psychology, UCLA, 1991; M in Real Estate Devel., U. So. Calif., 1993. Notary Pub., Calif. Counselor various hospitals in L.A. area, 1987-95; mng. proprietor African Roots, L.A., 1987-95; loan officer Household Fin., Burbank, Calif., 1990-92, Funding Plus, Reseda, Calif., 1993-94; exec. dir. Habitat for Humanity San Fernando, Santa Clarita Valleys, N. Hollywood, Calif., 1994—. Mem. Reserve Officer Assn., Urban Land Inst., commr. Assemblymember Hertzberg's Com. on Women and Families, mem. Valley Devel. Forum, Valley Industry and Commerce Assn. Home: PO BOx 92812 Pasadena CA 91109 Office: Habitat for Humanity 5525 Cakisnga Blvd North Hollywood CA 91601

DE LUCA, RODNEY JOHN, JR., secondary educator; b. Fresno, Calif., Dec. 3, 1963; s. Rodney John and Marcella De Luca. BA in English, Calif. State U, Sacramento, 1988, MA in English, 1996. Tchr. St. Francis H.S., Sacramento, Calif., 1990-96, dept. chair, 1994-96; tchr. Laguna Creek H.S., Elk Grove, Calif., 1996—. Bd. dirs. Village South Homeowners Assn., Sacramento, 1994—. Office: Laguna Creek HS 9050 Vicino Dr Elk Grove CA 95758-5859

DELUCA, THOMAS HENRY, soil scientist, researcher; b. Madison, Wis., Jan. 14, 1962; s. Hector Floyd and Emily (Swan) DeL.; m. Denise Kelley; children: Vincent Francesco, Emile Ettore, Henry James. BS in Natural Sci., U. Wis., 1984; MS in Soils, Mont. State U., 1987; PhD in Soil Sci., Iowa State U., 1993. Rsch. asst. N.C. State U., Raleigh, 1987-88; environ. specialist dept. agriculture Environ. Mgmt. divsn. State of Mont., Helena, 1988-90; rsch. assoc. Leopold Ctr. for Sustainable Agriculture, Iowa State U., Ames, 1990-93; asst. prof. agroecology Slippery Rock (Pa.) U., 1993-94; asst. prof. soil sci. Sch. Forestry U. Mont., Missoula, 1994-98, assoc. prof. soil sci., 1998—; mem. EQC-Groundwater Data Task Force, Helena, 1990; del. U. Mont. Coun. Water Resources; mem. Missoula Water Quality Coun. Mem. Big Bros. and Sisters of Helena, 1989; pres. Helena Competitive Cycling Club, 1990. Mem. AAAS, Am. Soc. Agronomy, Soil Sci. Soc. Am., Soil and Water Conservation Soc., Soc. Am. Foresters, Sigma Xi, Gamma Sigma Delta.

DELUCCHI, GEORGE PAUL, accountant; b. Richmond, Calif., Apr. 20, 1938; s. George Carl and Rose Caroline (Golino) D. BA, San Jose State U., 1959. CPA, Calif. Ptnr. Delucchi, Swanson & Co., Santa Clara, Calif., 1968-74, Delucchi, Swanson & Sandival, Santa Clara, 1974-76, Delucchi, Sandoval & Co., Santa Clara, 1976-77, Wolf & Co., San Jose, Calif., 1977-78; v.p. Lautze & Lautze, San Jose, 1978-82, also bd. dirs.; sr. ptnr. G.P. Delucchi & Assocs. (name changed to Delucchi, Robinson, Streit & Co., San Jose, 1982-95, Delucci, Hawn & Co., LLP, San Jose, 1996—. Treas. Crippled Children's Soc., San Jose, 1967-71, San Jose Catholic Charities, 1984-96, F. Schmidt Found. for Youth; bd. dirs. Serra Med. Found., Mission City Cmty. Fund, Bill Wilson Marriage and Family Counseling Ctr.; pres. Santa Clara Police Activity League, 1977-78; mem. bd. fellows Santa Clara U., 1975-94; chmn. pioneer dist. Santa Clara coun. Boy Scouts Am., 1992-94. Lt. U.S. Army, 1959-62. Mem. AICPA, Calif. Soc. CPAs (bd. dirs. 1993-93, treas. 1995-96, sec. 1996-97, pres., 1998—), Silicon Valley Capital Club, Serra Club, Elks (Santa Clara exalted ruler 1969-70), Rotary (pres. 1993-94, bd. dirs. 1986-89), Knights of Malta (invested, Knight of Magistral Grace). Republican. Roman Catholic. Avocations: model railroad, scuba diving, sailing, woodworking. Home: 774 Circle Dr Santa Clara CA 95050-5927 Office: 1871 The Alameda Ste 400 San Jose CA 95126-1753

DELUGACH, ALBERT LAWRENCE, journalist; b. Memphis, Oct. 27, 1925; s. Gilbert and Edna (Short) D.; m. Bernice Goldstein, June 11, 1950; children: Joy, David, Daniel, Sharon. B.J., U. Mo., 1951. Reporter Kansas City (Mo.) Star, 1951-60, St. Louis Globe Democrat, 1960-69, St. Louis Post Dispatch, 1969-70; investigative reporter Los Angeles Times, 1970-89. Served with USNR, 1943-46. Recipient Pultizer prize for spl. local reporting, 1969, Gerald Loeb award for disting. bus. and fin. journalism, 1984. Home: 4313 Price St Los Angeles CA 90027-2815

DEL VECCHIO, DAWN MARIE, theater manager; b. Phila., Mar. 16, 1957; d. Alfred Frederick and Edna Florence (McCoy) Del V. BS in Bus. Adminstrn., U. La Verne, Calif., 1994. Theatre mgr. Cinamerica Theatres, L.P., Encino, Calif., 1978—. Office: 650 W Huntington Dr Monrovia CA 91016-3261

DEMARCHI, ERNEST NICHOLAS, aerospace engineering administrator; b. Lafferty, Ohio, May 31, 1939; s. Ernest Costante and Lena Marie (Cireddu) D.; m. Sharon Titherley; B.M.E., Ohio State U., 1962; M.S. in Engring., UCLA, 1969; children—Daniel Ernest, John David, Deborah Marie. Registered profl. cert. mgr. With Space div. Rockwell Internat., Downey, Calif., 1962—, mem. Apollo, Skylab and Apollo-Soyuz missions design team in electronic and elec. systems, mem. mission support team for all Apollo and Skylab manned missions, 1962-74, mem. Space Shuttle design team charge elec. systems equipment, 1974-77, in charge Orbiter Data Processing System, 1977-81, in charge Orbiter Ku Band Communication and Radar System, 1981-85, in charge orbiter elec. power distbr., displays, controls, data processing, 1984-87, in charge space based interceptor flt. exper., 1987-88, kinetic energy systems, 1988-90, ground based interceptor program, 1990-97, dep. program mgr. Nat. Missile Def. Program, 1997—. Recipient Apollo Achievement award NASA, 1969, Apollo 13 Sustained Excellent Performance award, 1970, Astronaut Personal Achievement Snoopy award, 1971; Exceptional Service award Rockwell Internat., 1972, Outstanding Contbn. award, 1976; NASA ALT award, 1979; Shuttle Astronaut Snoopy award, 1982; Pub. Service Group Achievement award NASA, 1982; Rockwell Pres.'s award, 1983, 87; registered profl. engr., Ohio. Mem. AIAA, ASME, Nat. Mgmt. Assn., Varsity O Alumni Assn. Home: 8227 E Hillsdale Dr Orange CA 92869-2440 Office: 12214 Lakewood Blvd Downey CA 90242-2655

DEMARCO, RALPH JOHN, real estate developer; b. N.Y.C., Mar. 22, 1924; s. Frank and Mary (Castriota) DeM.; m. Arlene Gilbert, July 1, 1945; children: Sheryl DeMarco Grahn, Stephen, Laura DeMarco Wilson. BA, Claremont Men's Coll., 1956. Assoc. John B. Kilroy Co., Riverside, Calif., 1960-64, also mgr. ops. Riverside, San Bernardino counties, 1960-64; v.p. Marcus W. Meairs Co., 1964-67; pres. Diversified Properties, Inc., Riverside, 1967-72; v.p. Downey Savs. & Loan Assn., Calif., 1972-75; exec. v.p. DSL Svc. Co., 1972-75; pres. Interstate Shopping Ctrs., Inc., Santa Ana, Calif., 1975-87; exec. dir. comml. devel. Lewis Homes Mgmt. Corp., Upland, Calif., 1987-89; pvt. practice, San Diego, Calif., 1989—. Mem. City of Riverside Planning Commn., 1955-59, Airport Commn., 1960-70; mem. Urban Land Inst. 1st lt. USAF, 1942-45. Mem. Internat. Coun. Shopping Ctrs. Home: 44-489 Town Center Way # D 273 Palm Desert CA 92260-2723 Office: 16236 San Dieguito Rd #1-23 Rancho Santa Fe CA 92067

DE MASSA, JESSIE G., media specialist. BJ, Temple U.; MLS, San Jose State U., 1967; postgrad., U. Okla., U. So. Calif. Tchr. Palo Alto (Calif.) Unified Sch. Dist., 1966; librarian Antelope Valley Joint Union High Sch. Dist., Lancaster, Calif., 1966-68, ABC Unified Sch. Dist., Artesia, Calif., 1968-72; dist. librarian Tehachapi (Calif.) Unified Sch. Dist., 1972-81; media specialist, free lance writer, 1981—; assoc. Chris DeMassa & Assocs., 1988—. Contbr. articles to profl. jours. Mem. Statue of Liberty Ellis Island Found., Inc.; charter supporter U.S. Holocaust Meml. Mus., Washington; supporting mem. U.S. Holocaust Meml. Coun., Washington. Named to Nat. Women's Hall of Fame, 1995. Fellow Internat. Biog. Assn.; mem. Calif. Media and Libr. Educators Assn., Calif. Assn. Sch. Librs. (exec. coun.), AAUW (bull. editor chpt., assoc. editor state bull., chmn. publicity, 1955-68), Nat. Mus. Women in Arts (charter), Hon Fellows John F. Kennedy Libr. (founding mem.), Women's Roundtable of Orange County, Nat. Writer's Assn. (so. Calif. chpt.), Calif. Retired Tchrs. Assn. (Harbor Beach divsn. 77), The Heritage Found., Claremont Inst., Libr. of Congress (nat. charter mem.), Cato Inst. Home: 9951 Garrett Cir Huntington Beach CA 92646-3604

DEMELLO, AUSTIN EASTWOOD, astrophysicist, concert artist, poet, writer; b. New Bedford, Mass., Oct. 15, 1939; s. Manuel and Dora (Eastwood) De M; children: Adragon Eastwood De Mello, Brad Steven. BA in English, UCLA, 1974; MSc in Physics and Astronomy, Met. Coll. Inst., London, 1977, DSc in Theoretical Astrophysics, 1981. Engring. writer Raytheon Co., Santa Barbara, Calif., 1982; dir. research and sci. publs. Cosmosci. Research Inst., Sunnyvale, Calif., 1983—; sr. engring. writer, cons. Lockheed Martin, Sunnyvale, 1997. Author: Black Night Poetry, 1960, Tengu, 1962, (record) El Duende Flamenco, 1965, The Metagalactic System, 1969, The Four States of Man, 1971, Early Development of the Scientific Mind, 1981, Theory of Cosmodynamics, 1983, The Cosmotorsion Effect, 1984, James Bay Missionaries, 1986, The Origin and Influence of Flamenco Music on the Classics, 1992, Offenbach and the Can-Can Dance, 1993, Adragon: The Youngest Scholar, 1993, Legacy of Poetry and Philosophy, 1993, The Magic Formula, 1993, Views of Chaos, 1993, Haiku of the Sea Poet, 1997, Beware the Dragon of the Id, 1997, Evolution of an Assassin, 1997, The Scholar and the University, 1997, The Violent Life, 1997, (staged screen play) Petenera, 1997, The Ollave, 1998, Count Quentin, 1998. Acad. Merit scholar UCLA, 1972-74. Mem. AIAA, AAAS, N.Y. Acad. Sci., Am. Astronautical Soc., Mensa Internat. Home: PO Box 461 Moss Landing CA 95039-0461 Office: CSR Inst 663 S Bernardo Ave Sunnyvale CA 94087-1020

DEMEREE, GLORIA See LENNOX, GLORIA

DEMERS, MARY ADELAIDE, psychotherapist, educator; b. San Mateo, Calif., Sept. 9, 1955; d. Joseph Edward and Patricia Marie (Coughlin) Stanton; m. Paul Jordan, Feb. 15, 1992 (dec. July 1994); children: Jennifer, Philip, Katherine. BS, Santa Clara U., 1983, MA, 1989. Lic. marriage, family and child therapist, Bd. Behavioral Scis. Clin. staff therapist Santa Clara County Children Shelter, San Jose, Calif., 1989-95; clin. dir. Unity Care Group, Inc., San Jose, 1990-96; pvt. cons. Adolescent Clin. Svcs., San Jose, 1992—; instr. grad. divsn. Santa Clara U., 1995—; clin. dir. Gray's Adolescent Group Home, San Jose, 1995—; exec. dir. Adolescent Clin. Svcs., San Jose, 1995—. Featured in books Working Women Today, 1986, Women and Work, 1994. Vol. Kids Vote, San Jose, 1994—. Mem. NAFE, Am. Group Psychotherapy Assn., Calif. Assn. Marriage and Family Therapists. Democrat. Roman Catholic. Avocations: golf, bridge, acoustical guitar, book reviews. Office: Adolescent Clin Svcs 2130 The Alameda Ste 220 San Jose CA 95126-1125

DEMERY, DOROTHY JEAN, secondary school educator; b. Houston, Sept. 5, 1941; d. Floyd Hicks and Irene Elaine Burns Clay; m. Leroy W. Demery, Jan. 16, 1979; children: Steven Bradley, Rodney Bradley, Craig Bradley, Kimberly Bradley. AA, West L.A. Coll., Culver City, Calif., 1976; AS, Harbor Coll., Wilmington, Calif., 1983; BS in Pub. Adminstrn., Calif. State U., Carson, 1985; MS in Instructional Leadership, Nat. U., San Diego, 1991. Cert. real estate broker, tchr. math. and bus. edn., bilingual tchr., crosscultural lang. and acad. devel.; lang. devel. specialist. Eligibility social worker Dept. Pub. Social Svcs., L.A., 1967-74; real estate broker Dee Bradley & Assocs., Riverside, Calif., 1976—; tchr. math L.A. Unified Sch. Dist., 1985-91; math/computer sci. tchr. Pomona (Calif.) Unified Sch. Dist., 1991—; adj. lectr. Riverside C.C., 1992-93; mem. Dist. Curriculum Coun./Report Card Task Force, Pomona, 1994—; bd. dirs. Associated Pomona Tchrs. Chairperson Human Rights Com., Pomona, 1992—, sec. steering com., 1993—, adv. bd., 1993—; mem. polit. action com. Assoc. Pomona Tchrs., 1993-94. Recipient Outstanding Svc. award Baldwin Hills Little League Assn., L.A., 1972. Mem. Nat. Bus. Assn., Nat. Coun. Tchrs. Math., Aux. Nat. Med. Assn., Alpha Kappa Alpha. Avocations: hiking, tennis, walking. Home: PO Box 2796 Riverside CA 92516-2796 Office: Simons Middle School 900 E Franklin Ave Pomona CA 91766-5362

DEMETRESCU, MIHAI CONSTANTIN, research scientist, educator, computer company executive; b. Bucharest, Romania, May 23, 1929; s. Dan and Alina (Dragosescu) D.; M.E.E., Poly. Inst. of U. Bucharest, 1954; Ph.D., Romanian Acad. Sci., 1957; m. Agnes Halas, May 25, 1969; 1 child, Stefan. Came to U.S., 1966. Prin. investigator Research Inst. Endocrinology Romanian Acad. Sci., Bucharest, 1958-66; research fellow dept. anatomy UCLA, 1966-67; faculty U. Calif.-Irvine, 1967-83, asst. prof. dept. physiology, 1971-78, assoc. researcher, 1978-79, assoc. clin. prof., 1979-83; v.p. Resonance Motors, Inc., Monrovia, Calif., 1972-85; pres. Neurometrics, Inc., Irvine, Calif., 1978-82; pres. Lasergraphics Inc., Irvine, 1982-84, chmn., chief exec. officer, 1984—. Mem. com. on hon. degrees U. Calif.-Irvine, 1970-72. Postdoctoral fellow UCLA, 1966. Mem. Internat. Platform Assn., Am. Physiol. Soc., IEEE (sr.). Republican. Contbr. articles to profl. jours. Patentee in field. Home: 8 Sunset Hbr Newport Coast CA 92657-1706 Office: 20 Ada Irvine CA 92618-2303

DEMOFF, MARVIN ALAN, lawyer; b. L.A., Oct. 28, 1942; s. Max and Mildred (Tweer) D.; m. Patricia Caryn Abelov, June 16, 1968; children: Allison Leigh, Kevin Andrew. BA, UCLA, 1964; JD, Loyola U., L.A., 1967. Bar: Calif. 1969. Asst. pub. defender Los Angeles County, 1968-72; ptnr. Steinberg & Demoff, L.A., 1973-83, Craighill, Fentress & Demoff, L.A. and Washington, 1983-86; of counsel Mitchell, Silberberg & Knupp, L.A., 1987—. Mem. citizens adv. bd. Olympic Organizing Com., L.A., 1982-84; bd. trustees Curtis Sch., L.A., 1985-94, chmn. bd. trustees, 1988-93; sports adv. bd. Constitution Rights Found., L.A., 1986—; bd. dirs. 4A Found., 1988—. Mem. ABA (mem. forum com. on entertainment and sports), Calif. Bar Assn., UCLA Alumni Assn., Phi Delta Phi. Avocations: sports, music, art. Office: Mitchell Silberberg Knupp Los Angeles CA 90064

DEMOTT, MARGARET ANN, secondary educator; b. Lynwood, Calif., June 5, 1953; d. Stephen William and Dolores Ann (McCarthy) DeM. BA in Spanish, Immaculate Heart Coll., L.A., 1980; MA in TESOL (Teaching English to Speakers of Other Languages), Monterey Inst. Internat. Studies, 1983. Cert. English and ESL tchr., Calif. Tchr. English and ESL Laloma Jr. High Sch. Modesto (Calif.) City Schs., 1983-85, 86-93, Gonzales (Calif.) Union High Sch. Dist., 1985-86; part-time tchr. ESL Modesto Jr. Coll., 1989-94; tchr. English and ESL, group leader ESL program Peter Johansen H.S., Modesto, Calif., 1993—; essay corrector Ednl. Testing Svc., Berkeley, Calif., summers 1987, 88; Calif. Lit. participant, summer, 1993. Curriculum writer ESL, Modesto City Schs., spring 1989. Vol. Stanislaus Wildlife Care Ctr., Ceres, Calif., 1987—. Nominated to participate in Calif. Tchr. of Yr. program, La Loma Jr. High, 1993, 94. Mem. Calif. Assn. Tchrs. of English to Speakers of Other Langs. Avocations: watercolor, printmaking, swimming, writing. Office: Peter Johansen H S 641 Norseman Dr Modesto CA 95357-0405

DEMPSEY, BARBARA MATTHEA, medical, surgical and critical care nurse; b. The Netherlands, July 27, 1943; d. Petrus Antonius and Hendrika Petronella (Kemp) Petersen; m. James D. Dempsey, June 13, 1981; children: Jennifer, Daniel. AA, Santa Monica (Calif.) Coll., 1970; cert. lactation educator, UCLA, 1982; student, Senoma State U., 1997—. Staff nurse med./surg. Santa Monica Hosp., 1967-72; surg. intensive care nurse VA Wadsworth Hosp., L.A., 1973-77; staff nurse med./surg. Community Hosp., Santa Rosa, Calif., 1988-90; staff nurse Redwood Nurses Registry, Santa Rosa, 1990-93, Norrell Healthcare, Santa Rosa, Calif., 1990-93; charge nurse Creekside Convalescent Hosp., 1994, Friends House, Santa Rosa, 1997—. Office: Friends House 686 Benicia Dr Santa Rosa CA 95409-3007

DEMPSEY, HOWARD STANLEY, lawyer, mining executive, investment banker; b. LaPorte, Ind., Aug. 12, 1939; s. Howard Taft and Katheryn Alice (Prichard) D.; m. Judith Rose Enyart, Aug. 20, 1960; children: Howard Stanley, Whitney Owen, Bradford Evan, Matthew Charles. Student, Colo. Sch. Mines, 1956-57; BA, U. Colo., 1960, JD, 1964; cert., Harvard Sch. Bus., 1969. Bar: Colo. 1964. Ind. mine operator Colo. and Wyo., 1958-60; indsl. engr. Climax Molybdenum Co., Golden, Colo., 1960-61, asst. resident atty., 1964-65, resident atty., 1965-68, div. atty. western ops., 1968-72; gen. atty. law dept. western area, dir. environ. affairs AMAX Inc., Denver, 1972-76, v.p., 1977-83; ptnr. Arnold & Porter, Denver, 1983-87; pres. Denver Mining Fin. Co., 1987—; chmn., chief exec. officer Royal Gold, Inc., Denver, 1987—, also bd. dirs.; pres. Environ. Strategies, Inc., 1991—; chmn. AMAX Australia Ltd., 1980-83; chmn., exec. com. AMAX Iron Ore, 1980-83; bd.

dirs., dep. chmn. Australian Consol. Mines Ltd., 1980-83; bd. dirs. Hazen Rsch., Inc., Golden, Colo., Dakota Mining Corp., Denver, Behre Dolbear, Denver. Author: Mining the Summit, 1978; contbr. articles to profl. jours. Trustee Rocky Mountain Mineral Law Found., pres., 1980-81. Mem. Nat. Mining Assn. (mem. public lands com. 1967—, chmn. 1994—),Mining History Hall of Fame Mus. (bd. govs. 1998—, Am. Bar Assn. (chmn. hard minerals com. 1975-76), Colo. Bar Assn. (council mem. mineral law sect. 1971-73), Colo. Natural Resources Law Ctr. (bd. dirs. 1998—), Colo. Mining Assn. (pres. 1980-81), Continental Divide Bar Assn. (sec.-treas. 1969-73), Colo. Hist. Soc. (bd. dirs., chmn. 1991-93), Soc. Mining Law Antiquarians (pres. 1979-81), Mining and Metall. Soc. Am., Mining History Assn. (pres. 1992-94), Mountain States Employers Coun. (bd. dirs. 1990—), Masons, Rotary. Presbyterian. Clubs: Rollings Hills Country (Golden); Am. Alpine, Univ., Colo. Mountain (Denver); Harvard (N.Y.C.), Am. Nat. (Sydney, Australia). Lodges: Masons, Rotary. Office: Royal Gold Inc 1660 Wynkoop St Ste 1000 Denver CO 80202-1132

DEMPSTER, WILLIAM FRED, technical systems consultant; b. Berkeley, Calif., Dec. 10, 1940; s. John Ross and Anna Julia (Ramsperger) D.; 1 child from a previous marriage, Eden A. Harding; m. Sue Abigail Wight, May 29, 1959 (div. Oct. 1966); children: David Allen, Carolyn Sue. BA, U. Calif., Berkeley, 1963. Head computer users cons. office Lawrence Berkeley Lab., Berkeley, Calif., 1966-69; dir. energy and infrastructure syss. Synergia Ranch, Santa Fe, N.Mex., 1969-79; pres. Feedback Syss., Inc., Santa Fe, 1977-79; chief Amazon River expedition Inst. Ecotechnics, Brazil, Colombia, Peru, 1980-82; dir. quality control, engring. design Caravan of Dreams, Ft. Worth, 1982-85; dir. sys. engring., chief engr. Biosphere 2 Space Biospheres Ventures, Oracle, Ariz., 1985-94; pred. Biospheric Design Inc., Santa Fe, 1994—; bd. dirs. Ecofrontiers Co., Santa Fe, 1994—. Contbr. 7 articles to profl. jours.; patents for pressure balancing system, low leakage glazing system. Mem. Assn. Energy Engrs. Avocations: go, tennis. Home: 26 Synergia Rd Santa Fe NM 87505-0900 Office: Biospheric Design Inc 26 Synergia Rd Santa Fe NM 87505-0900

DEMUTH, ALAN CORNELIUS, lawyer; b. Boulder, Colo., Apr. 29, 1935; s. Laurence Wheeler and Eugenia Augusta (Roach) DeM.; m. Susan McDermott; children: Scott Lewis, Evan Dale, Joel Millard. BA in Econs. and Gen. Studies magna cum laude, U. Colo., 1958, LLB, 1961. Bar: Colo. 1961, U.S. Dist. Ct. Colo. 1961, U.S. Ct. Appeals (10th cir.) 1962. Assoc. Akolt, Turnquist, Shepherd & Dick, Denver, 1961-68; ptnr. DeMuth & DeMuth, 1968—. Conf. atty. Rocky Mountain Conf. United Ch. of Christ, 1970-95; bd. dirs. Friends of U. Colo. Library, 1978-86; bd. dirs., sponsor Denver Boys Inc., 1987-93, sec., 1988-89, v.p., 1989-90, pres. 1992-93; bd. dirs. Denver Kids, Inc., 1993—, Children's Ctr. for Arts and Learning, 1995—; mem. bd. advisors Lambuth Family Ctr. of Salvation Army, 1994—, chmn., 1994—; bd. advisors Metro Denver Salvation Army, 1988—, vice chmn. 1994-96. Mem. ABA, Colo. Bar Assn., Denver Bar Assn., Rotary (bd. dirs. 1996-98), Phi Beta Kappa, Sigma Alpha Epsilon, Phi Delta Phi. Republican. Mem. United Ch. of Christ. Office: DeMuth & DeMuth 990 S High St Denver CO 80209-4551

DENBROCK, KRISTIE ANN, state official; b. Coldwater, Mich., Aug. 10, 1963; d. John David and Wilma Ruth (Anderson) D.; 1 child, Katie Virginia Lopez. BS in Mass Comm., U. South Colo., 1990. Editl. asst. Denver Post, 1984-87, Pueblo (Colo.) Chieftain, 1991-93; host, announcer, news dir. Sta. KTSC-FM, Pueblo, 1989; exec. prodr., host Capitol Jour., Sta. KTSC-TV, Pueblo, 1989-93; dir. media rels. Colo. Senate, Denver, 1993—. Vol., writer state Rep. campaigns, 1993—; vol. St. Frances De Sales Sch., Denver, 1995—, Daisy Troop Girl Scouts U.S.A., Denver, 1995—. Mem. Am. Legion, Lincoln Club Denver. Republican. Avocations: reading, outdoor activities, crafts.

DENDAHL, JOHN, political organization administrator. Chmn. Rep. Party N.Mex., Albuquerque. Fax: (505) 292-0755. Office: Rep Party NMex 2901 Juan Tabo St NE Ste 116 Albuquerque NM 87112*

DENE, LINDA JO, financial executive; b. L.A., Apr. 26, 1948; d. Hyman Chaim and Ruth (Goldstein) Bergman; m. Richard Eugene Dene, Feb. 16, 1967; children: Ronald, Anthony, Angela. Cost control specialist South Bend (Ind.) Range Co., 1972-75; accounts payable specialist Thrifty Drug Co., West Los Angeles, Calif., 1975-76; cost acct. Sun Litho, Inc., Sepulveda, Calif., 1976-77; lead cost acct. Products Rsch. & Chem., Glendale, Calif., 1977-84; contr. PhotoSonics, Inc., Burbank, Calif., 1984—; CFO Instrumentation Mktg. Corp., Burbank, 1988—. Mem. NAFE. Republican. Jewish. Avocation: reading. Office: Instrumentation Mktg Corp 820 S Mariposa St Burbank CA 91506-3108

DE NEUFVILLE, ROBERT EUSTACE, political scientist, writer; b. Boston, Nov. 19, 1970; s. Richard Lawrence De Neufville and Judith Eleanor Innes. AB, Harvard U., 1992; MA, U. Calif., Berkeley, 1996, student, 1996—. Intern U.S. Dept. State, Seoul, Republic of Korea, 1991; site dir., course designer Test Takers, Roslyn Heights, N.Y., 1992-93; lead cons. Booz-Allen & Hamilton, N.Y.C., 1993-95; rsch. assoc. Berkeley (Calif.) Roundtable on the Internat. Economy, 1995-97; instr. U. Calif., Berkeley, 1997—. Nat. Merit scholar 1988, John Harvard scholar Harvard U., Boston, 1991. Avocations: theater, go. Home: 2821 Hillegass Ave Apt 8 Berkeley CA 94705-2129

DENGERINK, DON D., media production specialist; b. Beloit, Kans., July 11, 1946; s. E.G. and Betty (Forster) D.; m. Mary Elizabeth, June 21, 1969; children: David, Doug. BA in Social Sci., Azusa Pacific U., 1968; MA in Edn., Denver Seminary, 1976. Sales cons. Ark Book Store, Denver, 1980-86; media prodn. specialist Cherry Creek Schs., Englewood, Colo., 1990—. Illustrator (book) 501 Ways to Use the Overhead, 1982. Mem. Internat. Television Assn. Home: 2146 S Flora Ct Lakewood CO 80228-5907

DENHART, JEFFREY DONALD, elementary education educator; b. Emmetsburg, Iowa, Mar. 7, 1950; s. Donald Wilson and Lucille Caroline (Smith) D.; m. Susana Garcia Lopez, July, 1969 (div. 1976); 1 child, Wendy Sue; m. Peggy Ruth Thomas, June 25, 1983; 1 child, Denita. BA in English, Calif. State U., Fullerton, 1974, MS in reading, 1979. Cert. elem. tchr., C.C. tchr., reading specialist, Calif. Tchr. Brea Olinda Unified Sch. Dist., Brea, Calif., 1974-75; instr. Calif. State U., Fullerton, 1975-76, Compton (Calif.) C.C., 1975-91; tchr. Lynwood (Calif.) Unified Sch. Dist., 1976—. Author: (mystery novel) Just Bones, 1996. Mem. Nat. Writers Assn., Mystery Writers of Am., Contemporary Hist. Vehicle Assn. (bd. dirs. 1989—), Internat. Mercury Assn., Strictly Fifties Car Club, Cadillac-LaSalle Assn. Avocation: restoring old cars. Home: 6801 Beechley Ave Long Beach CA 90805-1332 Office: Hosler Jr H S 11300 Spruce St Lynwood CA 90262-3629

DENIOUS, JON PARKS, publishing executive; b. Buffalo, Apr. 5, 1939; s. Wilbur Franklin Jr. and Nancy (Parks) D.; m. Sharon Marie Fee, June 17, 1963; children: Timothy, Elizabeth. Owner Durango (Colo.) Printing and Graphics, 1985-90; publ. Silverton Standard and The Miner, Colo., 1990—. Mem. Nat. Newspaper Assn., Colo. Press Assn. Avocations: walking, reading. Office: The Silverton Standard The Miner 1257 Greene St Silverton CO 81433

DENIOUS, SHARON MARIE, publisher; b. Rulo, Nebr., Jan. 27, 1941; d. Thomas Wayne and Alma (Murphy) Fee; m. Jon Parks Denious, June 17, 1963; children: Timothy Scot, Elizabeth Denious Cessna. Grad. high sch. Operator N.W. Pipeline co., Ignacio, Colo., 1975-90; pub. The Silverton Standard & The Miner, Colo., 1990—. Mem. Colo. Press Assn., Nat. Newspaper Assn. Avocations: reading, hiking. Office: The Silverton Standard The Miner 1257 Greene St Silverton CO 81433

DENIS, RENÉE ROOSEVELT, writer; b. Montclair, N.J.; d. Armand Georges and Leila (Roosevelt) D.; m. Gustav Dalla Valle, May 1952 (div. Dec. 1961); 1 child, Marisa; m. Tane Aroita-Hopu, Feb. 1962; children: [illegible] French Polynesia, [illegible] with pub. rels. Maeva Beach Hotel, Tahiti, French Polynesia, 1970-73; conductor world tours Travelworld, L.A., 1975-80; owner, mgr. Rupe Rupe Ranch, French Polynesia, 1990-97. *Renée Roosevelt Denis is the daughter of explorers and cinemaphotographers Armand Denis and Leila Roosevelt, best remembered for the outstanding documentary of primitive Africa, "Dark Rapture" (1938). They first started filming with Renée's grandfather, André Roosevelt, in Bali in 1929 - and that was when Renée's adventures began, the first year of her life, in Bali. Her autobiography, "To Live in Paradise" (recommended by the National Geographic Traveler) tells all, up to the realization of her dream ranch, located in Tahiti, where she has lived for 37 years. She is now working on another book tentatively titled "Anglais, Vite et Facile".* Author: To Live in Paradise, 1996. Home: 801 W Covina Blvd San Dimas CA 91773

DENKE, PAUL HERMAN, aircraft engineer; b. San Francisco, Feb. 7, 1916; s. Edmund Herman and Ella Hermine (Riehl) D.; m. Beryl Ann Lincoln, Feb. 10, 1940; children: Karen Denke Mottaz, Claudia Denke Tesche, Marilyn Denke Oliver. BCE, U. Calif.-Berkeley, 1937, MCE, 1939. Registered profl. engr., Calif. Stress engr. Douglas Aircraft Co., Santa Monica, Calif., 1940-62, mgr. structural mechanics Long Beach, Calif., 1962-65, chief sci. computing, 1965-71, chief structures engr. methods and devel., 1972-78, chief scientist structural mechanics, 1979-84, staff mgr. Boeing fellow, 1985—; mem. faculty dept. engring. UCLA, 1941-50. Assoc. fellow AIAA; mem. Soc. Automotive Engrs. (Arch T. Colwell Merit award 1966, IAE Outstanding Engr. Merit award 1985), Sigma Xi, Chi Epsilon, Tau Beta Pi. Democrat. Pioneered and developed finite element method of structural analysis; author numerous technical papers. Home: 1800 Via Estudillo Palos Verdes Peninsula CA 90274-1908

DENNEY, DORIS ELAINE, pharmacist; b. Norwalk, Conn., Sept. 5, 1940; d. Harry Taylor and Mary Matilda (Lobeda) D. BS in Pharmacy, U. Conn., 1962; MBA, Boise State U., 1990. Registered pharmacist, Conn., Idaho, Mass. Retail pharmacist Gilbert Pharmacy, Noroton Heights, Conn., 1963-64; sr. pharmacist Children's Hosp. Med. Ctr., Boston, 1964-68; pharmacist Project Hope, Colombia, 1968-70; adminstrv. intern Denver Gen. Hosp., 1972; dir. pharmacy svcs. Terry Reilly Health Svcs., Nampa, Idaho, 1973—; cons. (Bolivia) Mgmt. Scis. for Health, Cambridge, Mass., 1976. Bd. dirs. Payada drug abuse orgn., Boise, 1983-88, Arts for Idaho, 1995—, v.p., 1996-97; mem. health adv. com. Idaho State U., Boise, 1988-89; bd. dirs., mem. Boise Master Chorale, pres., 1992-94; mem. Boise City Arts Commn., 1994—, First Night Boise, 1997—. Named Preceptor of Yr. Syntex Labs., 1987; recipient McKesson Leadership award McKesson-Robbins, 1987, Pharmacy Leadership award Nat. Assn. Retail Druggists, 1987, Bowl of Hygeia, 1997. Mem. Idaho State Pharm. Assn. (pres. 1987-88), Am. Pharm. Assn., Am. Pub. Health Assn. (cons. 1978), Am. Soc. of Hosp. Pharmacists, Boise City Arts Commn. (exec. com. 1994—), Lambda Kappa Sigma. Democrat. Lutheran. Avocations: sailing, skiing, singing. Home: 1519 N 19th St Boise ID 83702-0702 Office: Terry Reilly Health Svcs 223 16th Ave N Nampa ID 83687-4058

DENNING, MICHAEL MARION, entrepreneur, computer company executive; b. Durant, Okla., Dec. 22, 1943; s. Samuel M. and Lula Mae (Waitman) D.; m. Suzette Karin Wallance, Aug. 10, 1968 (div. 1979); children: Lila Monique, Tanya Kerstin, Charlton Derek; m. Donna Jean Hamel, Sept. 28, 1985; children: Caitlin Shannon, Meghan O'Donnell. Student, USAF Acad., 1963; BS, U. Tex., 1966, Fairleigh Dickinson U., 1971; MS, Columbia U., 1973. Mgr. systems IBM, White Plains, N.Y., 1978-79; mgr. svc. and mktg. IBM, San Jose, Calif., 1979-81; nat. market support mgr. Memorex Corp., Santa Clara, Calif., 1979-81, v.p. mktg., 1981-82; v.p. mktg. and sales Icot Corp., Mountain View, Calif., 1982-83; exec. v.p. Phase Info. Machines Corp., Scottsdale, Ariz., 1983-84, Tricom Automotive Dealer Systems Inc., Hayward, Calif., 1985-87; pres. ADS Computer Svcs., Inc., Toronto, Ont., Can., 1985-87, Denning Investments, Inc., Palo Alto, Calif., 1987, Pers. Solutions Group, Inc., Menlo Park, Calif., 1990-96, Crystal Rsch. Corp., Scottsdale, Ariz., 1997-98; pres., CEO Landtech Environmental Inc., Scottsdale, Ariz., 1998—; adj. prof. Ariz. State U., Coll. of Bus., 1997—. With USAF, 1962-66; Vietnam. Mem. Rotary, English Speaking Union, Phi Beta Kappa, Lambda Chi Alpha (pres. 1965-66). Republican. Methodist. Home: 9144 N 69th St Paradise Valley AZ 85253 Office: Crystal Rsch Corp 9144 N 69th St Paradise Valley AZ 85253-1930

DENNIS, CLINTON JOEL, property manager, small business owner; b. Detroit, Jan. 26, 1946; s. Chester and Pauline Dennis; m. Suzy Hart, Mar. 26, 1978 (div. May 1998); m. Jeannie Dennis, June 27, 1998; children: Travis, Bart, Angie. Student, U. Tenn., Chatanooga, 1969-71; degree, McKenzie Bus. Coll., 1968, Real Estate Coll., 1970; EDI, Real Estate Coll., 1978. Owner, mgr. Dennis' Glenwood Texaco, Chattanooga, 1967-76, Red Rock Amusements, Las Vegas, Nev., 1981-95, JD Prodns., Las Vegas, Nev., 1987-97, Game Zone Arcade, Las Vegas, Nev., 1988-90; landlord Room Rentals, Las Vegas, Nev., 1978—; pres., owner Beanies Galore, Las Vegas, Nev. Author: It's a Full House, 1996. Mem. 24 Karat Club, Horseshoe Club, Caesars Emporers Club, Treasure Island Club, Mirage Club. Avocations: boating, fishing, playing golf, video poker. Home: 109 N Minnesota St Las Vegas NV 89107-1819

DENNIS, JOHN DAVISON, minister; b. Pitts., Sept. 18, 1937; s. John Wellington and Helen Isabella (Davison) D.; m. Nancy Schumacher, Jan. 7, 1967; children: Michael, Andrew. *Wife Nancy Dennis served as chairperson of the Board of Directors of the Oregon Coast Aquarium (the home of Keiko, the whale in the movie Free Willy), 1996-97. Son Michael Dennis is a graduate student at the Haas School of Business at the University of California in Berkeley. Son Andrew Dennis is the assistant project director for The World Monuments Fund at the Angkor Wat temple complex in Cambodia.* AB, Wesleyan U., 1959; BD, Princeton Theol. Sem., 1962, ThM, 1965. Ordained to ministry United Presbyn. Ch. (USA), 1962. Asst. pastor First Presbyn. Ch., Germantown, Pa., 1962-69; sr. pastor First Presbyn. Ch., Corvallis, Oreg., 1969—; exch. min. St. Columbia's Presbyn. Ch., Johannesburg, Republic of South Africa, 1978. Chaplain Germantown Hosp., 1965-69; west coast dean Presbyn. Young Pastors Seminars, 1983-85; pres. Madison Ave. Task Force, 1975-77, pres. Corvallis Community Improvement, Inc., pres. USSR Sister City Assn., 1989-90; founder Corvallis Summer Music Festival, 1979, v.p., 1979-83; trustee, charter mem. Good Samaritan Hosp. Found., chmn., 1972-76; founder Corvallis Fish Emergency Aid Svc., 1969-76; trustee Ecumenical Ministries of Oreg., 1989—, chmn. bd. dirs. 1996-98; bd. dirs. United Way of Benton County, 1986-90; candidate U.S. Congress from Oreg. 5th dist., 1988; asst. squash coach Princeton Univ., 1959-62. Fellow Aspen Inst., 1987. Pacific coast doubles squash champions, 1972-73. Mem. Rotary (charter mem., dir. local club, Rotarian of Yr. 1998). Home: 2760 NW Skyline Dr Corvallis OR 97330-3168 Office: 114 SW 8th St Corvallis OR 97333-4546

DENNIS, KAREN MARIE, plastic surgeon; b. Cleve., Dec. 23, 1948; d. Chester and Adele (Wesley) D.; m. Miles Auslander, June 21, 1974; 1 child, Kristin. BS, Ohio State U., 1971, MD, 1974. Diplomate Am. Bd. Plastic Surgery, Am. Bd. Otolaryngology. Intern Kaiser Permanente, L.A., 1974-75; resident in otolaryngology Roosevelt Hosp., N.Y.C., 1976-79; resident in plastic surgery Ohio State Univ. Hosps., Columbus, 1979-81; pvt. practice Beverly Hills, Calif., 1981—. Mem. Am. Soc. Reconstructive and Plastic Surgeons, Calif. County Med. Assn., L.A. County med. Assn., L.A. Soc. Plastic Srugeons (sec. 1993-94), Phi Beta Kappa. Avocations: tennis, golfing, traveling, reading. Office: 433 N Camden Dr Beverly Hills CA 90210-4426

DENNISON, DANIEL WAYNE, television news executive; b. Gunnison, Colo., Mar. 12, 1957; s. Milton Ira and Mary Ruth (Butler) D. BA, Colo. State U., 1979. News dir. Sta. KGUC-AM, Gunnison, 1971-75, Sta. KSTR Radio, et al, Grand Junction, Colo., 1975-79; reporter Sta. KMGH-TV, Denver, 1979-82; reporter, bur. chief KUSA-TV, Denver, 1982-95; news dir. Sta. KRDO-TV, Colorado Springs, 1995-96, Sta. KOAA-TV, Colorado Springs, 1996—. Bd. dirs., treas. Western State Coll. Found., Gunnison, 1987-93; participant newsroom mgmt. Poynter Inst., St. Petersburg, Fla., 1996, participant power reporting, 1994. Named Nat. Communicator of Yr., Easter Seals Soc., 1983, 85, Broadcaster of Yr., Internat. Spl. Olympics, 1985; recipient Lowell Thomas award Colo. Ski Country USA, 1994, Regional Emmy award nominations, 1989, 94, 95. Mem. Radio TV News Dirs. [illegible] (pres. 1987-89), N.Am. Ski Journalists, Colo. Mountain Club (bd. dirs. 1988), Colorado Springs Press Assn. (bd. dirs. 1999). Lutheran. Avocations: climbing, skiing, hiking. Home: 5730 Dalton Dr Colorado Springs CO 80919-2487 Office: Sta KOAA-TV 530 Communication Cir Colorado Springs CO 80905-1744

DENNISON, GEORGE MARSHEL, academic administrator; b. Buffalo, Ill., Aug. 11, 1935; s. Earl Fredrick and Irene Gladys (McWhorter) D.; m. Jane Irene Schroeder, Dec. 26, 1954; children: Robert Gene, Rick Steven. AA, Custer County (Mont.) Jr. Coll., 1960; BA, U. Mont., 1962, MA, 1963; PhD, U. Wash., 1967. Asst. prof. U. Ark., Fayetteville, 1967-68; vis. asst. prof. U. Wash., Seattle, 1968-69; asst. prof. Colo. State U., Fort Collins, 1969-73, assoc. prof., 1973-77, assoc. dean Coll. Arts, Humanities and Social Sci., 1976-80, prof., 1977-87, acting acad. v.p., 1980-82, acting assoc. acad. v.p., 1982-86, assoc. acad. v.p., 1987; provost, v.p. acad. affairs Western Mich. U., Kalamazoo, 1987-90; pres. U. Mont., Missoula, 1990—; cons. U.S. Dept. Justice, 1976-84; bd. Community Med. Ctr, Missoula, 1st Bank, Missoula, Inst. Medicine and Humanities, Missoula. Author: The Dorr War, 1976; contbr. articles to jours. in field. Bd. dirs. Kalamazoo Ctr. for Med. Studies, 1989-90. With USN, 1953-57. ABA grantee, 1969-70; Colo. State U. grantee, 1970-75, Nat. Trust for Hist. Preservation grantee, 1976-78; U.S. Agy. for Internat. Devel. grantee, 1979—; Colo. Commn. on Higher Edn. devel. grantee, 1985. Mem. Am. Hist. Assn., Orgn. Am. Historians, Am. Assn. Higher Edn., Am. Soc. for Legal History. Avocations: handball, cross-country skiing. Office: U Montana Office of The Pres Univ Hall Rm 109 Missoula MT 59812*

DENNISON, RONALD WALTON, engineer; b. San Francisco, Oct. 23, 1944; s. S. Mason and Elizabeth Louise (Hatcher) D.; m. Deborah Ann Rutter, Aug. 10, 1991; children: Ronald, Frederick. BS in Physics and Math., San Jose State U., 1970, MS in Physics, 1972. Physicist, Memorex, Santa Clara, Calif., 1970-71; sr. engr. AVCO, San Jose, Calif., 1972-73; advanced devel. engr. Perkin Elmer, Palo Alto, Calif., 1973-75; staff engr. Hewlett-Packard, Santa Rosa, Calif., 1975-79; program gen. mgr. Burroughs, Westlake Village, Calif., 1979-82; dir. engring., founder EIKON, Simi Valley, Calif., 1982-85; sr. staff technologist Maxtor Corp., San Jose, 1987-90; dir. engring. Toshiba Am. Info. Systems, 1990-93, cons. engr., 1994—; materials. Author tech. publs. Served to sgt. USAF, 1963-67. Mem. IEEE, Am. Vacuum Soc., Internat. Soc. Hybrid Microelectronics, Internat. Disk Drive Equipment and Materials Assn. Republican. Methodist. Mem. Aircraft Owners and Pilots Assn., Internat. Comanche Soc. Home: 4050 Soelro Ct San Jose CA 95127-2711

DENNISTON, MARTHA KENT, business owner, author; b. Phila., Feb. 8, 1920; d. Samuel Leonard and Elizabeth (Cryer) Kent; m. Edward Shippen Willing, May 14, 1942 (div. 1972); children: Peter, Matthew, Thomas, Stephen; m. George C. Denniston, July 5, 1974. BA, Bryn Mawr (Pa.) Coll., 1941; MA, U. Wash., Seattle, 1965. Clinic dir. Population Dynamics, Seattle, 1973-84; pvt. practice investor, 1950—; resort owner Ecologic Pl., Port Townsend, Wash., 1972—; sec. bd. dirs. Ctr. for Population Communications, N.Y.C., 1983-86. Author: Beyond Conception, Our Children's Children, 1971, (poems) The Bladed Quiet, 1994. Bd. dirs. Population Action Coun., Washington, 1977-80. Mem. Nat. Soc. Colonial Dames Am., Am. Farmlands Trust, Sigma Xi. Avocations: genealogy, environmental concerns. Home: 13030 12th Ave NW Seattle WA 98177-4109

DENNY, CAROL LEE, financial officer; b. Billing, Mont., June 5, 1957; d. William John and Georgia Mae (Dorr) Foster; m. Choyla Thiel, Apr. 30, 1977 (div. Mar. 1990); children: Christopher, Katie; m. Lee Ray Denny, Sept. 28, 1991. Asst. v.p. Kay Bank Wyo., Worland; exec. dir. Niobrara County C. of C., Lusk, Wyo.; acct. Mueller & Assocs., Lusk; CFO, Niobrara County Hosp., Lusk, 1996—. Chmn. Niobrara County Libr., 1992-93, Niobrara County Hosp. Dist. Found., 1998—. Republican. Avocations: gardening, gourmet cooking, golf. Office: Niobrara County Hosp PO Box 780 Lusk WY 82225-0780

DENT, ERNEST DUBOSE, JR., pathologist; b. Columbia, S.C., May 3, 1927; s. E. Dubose and Grace (Lee) D.; m. Dorothy McCalman, June 16, 1949; children: Christopher, Pamela; m. 2d, Karin Frehse, Sept. 6, 1970. Student, Presbyn. Coll., 1944-45; M.D., Med. Coll. S.C., 1949. Diplomate clin. pathology and pathology anatomy Am. Bd. Pathology. Intern U.S. Naval Hosp., Phila., 1949-50; resident pathology USPHS Hosp., Balt., 1950-54; chief pathology USPHS Hosp., Norfolk, Va., 1954-56; assoc. pathology Columbia (S.C.) Hosp., 1956-59; pathologist, dir. labs. Columbia Hosp., S.C. Baptist Hosp., 1958-69; with Straus Clin. Labs., L.A., 1969-72; staff pathologist Hollywood (Calif.) Community Hosp., St. Joseph Hosp., Burbank, Calif., 1969-72; dir. labs. Glendale Meml. Hosp. and Health Ctr., 1972-94; ret.; bd. dirs. Glendale Meml. Hosp. and Health Ctr. Author papers nat. med. jours. Mem. Am. Cancer Soc., AMA, L.A. County Med. Assn. (pres. Glendale dist. 1980-81), Calif. Med. Assn. (councillor 1984-90), Am. Soc. Clin. Pathology, Coll. Am. Pathologists (assemblyman S.C. 1965-67; mem. publs. com. bull. 1968-70), L.A. Soc. Pathologists (trustee 1984-87), L.A. Acad. Medicine, S.C. Soc. Pathologists (pres. 1967-69). Lutheran. Home: 1605 La Plaza Dr San Marcos CA 92069-4841 Office: 1420 S Central Ave Glendale CA 91204-2508

DENTITH, HENRY, artist; b. Virmingham, Eng., June 5, 1931; came to U.S., 1988; s. Reginald and Daisy May (Ranford) D.; m. Adrienne, Nov. 27, 1983; children: James, Sharon, Lee. Student, Sir John Cass Art Coll., London. Overseas mgr. De la Rue. Represented in permanent collection Tate Gallery, London; represented in pvt. collections. With Israeli Army Res., 1973-83. E-mail: dhenry.com.

DENTON, RENA WILSON, religion educator; b. Atlanta, Jan. 20, 1943; d. Warren Russell and Mildred (Carr) Wilson; children: Anna Holland Denton, Kimball Clark Denton, Robyn Carr Denton. BA in History, Emory U., 1965; postgrad., U. Ga., 1967; MA in Theology, Fuller Theol. Sem., 1989, postgrad., 1990—. Cert. tchr., Calif. Tchr. adult edn. La Jolla (Calif.) Presbyn. Ch., 1978—; tchr. Bible Village Ch., Rancho Santa Fe, Calif., 1988—; speaker in field; elder La Jolla Presbyn. Ch., 1978—, mem. long range planning and adult edn. coms., 1978—, chmn. Circle, 1976-77. Member Community Concert Bd., Rancho Santa Fe, 1981; v.p. Rancho Santa Fe Elem. Sch. PTO, 1982, 83; advisor Nat. Charity League, San Diego, 1987—. Mem. DAR, Alpha Alpha Tau, Omicron Alpha Upsilon. Home: PO Box 1748 Rancho Santa Fe CA 92067-1748

DENVER, THOMAS H R, lawyer; b. N.Y.C., Oct. 29, 1944; s. Thomas H. Rorke and Eileen Ann Boland; m. Barbara Ann Denver, Dec. 19, 1987; children: Rorke, Nate. BS, Syracruse U., 1966; MS, U. Wash., 1967; J.D., U. Calif., San Francisco, 1973. Bar: Calif. 1973, U.S. Dist. Ct. (no. dist.) Calif. 1973. From assoc. to mng. ptnr. Hoge, Fenton, Jones & Apple, Inc., San Jose, Calif., 1973—; judge pro tem Santa Clara County Superior Ct., San Jose, 1980—; instr. Stanford U. Law Sch. Advocacy Program; mem. faculty Hastings Coll. of Advocacy; mediator, arbitrator. Contbr. articles to profl. jours. Fellow Am. Coll. Trial Lawyers; mem. Am. Bd. Trial Advocates, Santa Clara County Civil Litigation Com., Santa Clara County Bar Assn. (chmn. fast track com.). Avocations: running, fishing, reading. Office: Hoge Fenton Jones & Appel 60 S Market St San Jose CA 95113-2351

DEPAOLI, ALEXANDER MARK, endocrinologist; b. N.Y.C., Aug. 22, 1962; s. Alexander and Geraldine Mary (Budny) DeP.; m. Laura Bertoni, June 14, 1986; children: Alexander, Daniel, Julia. BS, U. Calif., Davis, 1984; MD, Hahnemann U., 1988. Diplomate Am. Bd. Internal Medicine. Resident in internal medicine U. Chgo., 1988-91, fellow in endocrinology, 1991-94; endocrinologist Sansum Med. Clinic, Santa Barbara, Calif., 1994-98; sr. scientist Sansum Med. Rsch. Found., Santa Barbara, Calif., 1998—; assoc. med. dir. Amgen Inc., 1998—; dir. Cottage Hosp. Diabetes and Metabolic Wellness Ctr., Santa Barbara, Calif., 1997—; guest investigator, bd. dirs. Sansum Med. Rsch. Found., Santa Barbara, 1994-97; bd. dirs. Am. Diabetes Assn., Santa Barbara, pres., 1997—. Avocations: art, writing, family, traveling. Office: Sansum Med Rsch Found 2219 Bath St Santa Barbara CA 93105-4321

DEPAOLIS, POTITO UMBERTO, food company executive; b. Mignano, Italy, Aug. 28, 1925; s. Giuseppe A. and Filomena (Macchiaverna) deP.; Vet. Dr., U. Naples, 1948; [illegible] naturalized, 1970. Prof. food service Vet. Sch., U. Naples, Italy, 1948-66; retired, 1966; asst. prof. A titre Benevole Ecole Veterinaire Alfort, Paris, France, 1956; vet. inspector U.S. Dept. Agr., Omaha, 1966-67; sr. research chemist Grain Processing Corp., Muscatine, Iowa, 1967-68; v.p., dir. product devel. Reddi Wip, Inc., Los Angeles, 1968-72; with Kubro Foods, Los

Angeles, 1972-73, Shade Foods, Inc., 1975—; pres. Vegetable Protein Co., Riverside, Calif., 1973—, Tima Brand Food Co., 1975—, Dr. Tima Natural Foods, 1977—. Fulbright scholar Cornell U., Ithaca, N.Y., 1954; British Council scholar, U. Reading, Eng., 1959-60; postdoctoral research fellow NIH, Cornell U., 1963-64. Mem. Inst. Food Technologists, Italian Assn. Advancement Sci., AAAS, Vet. Med. Assn., Biol. Sci. Assn. Italy, Italian Press Assn., Greater Los Angeles Press Club. Contbr. articles in field to prol. jours. Patentee in field. Home: Bel Air 131 Groverton Pl Los Angeles CA 90077-3732 Office: 19428 Londelius St Northridge CA 91324-3511 also: 6878 Beck Ave North Hollywood CA 91605-6205

DEPASQUALE, DONALD L., mathematics educator; b. Placerville, Calif., Aug. 31, 1944; s. Don and Frances M. (Daykin) D.; m. Carmelle Clark Knudsen, Apr. 8, 1982 (div. Dec. 1989). BA in Physics & Math., U. Calif., Berkeley, 1967, MA in Physics, 1968. Cert. secondary edn. physics, math. Geol. engr. U. Calif., 1965-68, tchg. asst., 1967-68; tchr. math., physics Albany (Calif.) Unified Sch. Dist., 1968—, sci. dept. chair, 1975-81, math. dept. chair, 1996—. Author: High School Math Textbook, 1992. Fellow Am. Phys. Soc.; mem. Albany Tchrs. Assn. (pres. 1994-96, negotiator 1995-97), Calif. Math. Coun. Democrat. Avocations: films, backpacking, jazz. Office: Albany HS 603 Key Route Blvd Albany CA 94706-1422

DE PASSE, DERREL BLAUVELT, electronics industry executive; b. Bronxville, N.Y., Jan. 17, 1950; d. Alfred Bernard and Josephine Martha (Weyland) De P. BA, U. Tex., 1971, MPA, 1973. Mgr. pub. affairs Container Corp. Am., Chgo., 1974-75; regional mgr. pub. affairs Container Corp. Am., Phila., 1976-78; dir. fed. pub. affairs Container Corp. Am., Washington, 1979-83; spl. asst. to dir. U.S. Peace Corps, Washington, 1984-85; dir. govt. affairs Varian, Palo Alto, Calif., 1985-90, v.p. govt. rels., 1990-92; v.p. worldwide govt. rels. Varian, Palo Alto, 1992—; chmn. industry sector adv. com. on electronics and instrumentation U.S. Dept. Commerce, Washington, 1987—; commr. Calif. state World Trade Com., 1992—. Pres. San Jose/Cleve. Ballet. Mem. Pub. Affairs Coun. (exec. com. bd. dirs. 1990—), Calif. Coun. for Internat. Trade (exec. com., bd. dirs. 1989—), Lincoln Club No. Calif. (exec. com.). Office: Varian 3050 Hansen Way Palo Alto CA 94304-1036

DEPAULO, ADYGENE GARRETT, art gallery owner; b. Spur, Tex., July 6, 1925; d. Walter and Teresa (Kearney) Garrett; m. John Joseph DePaulo, Oct. 7, 1943 (dec. June 1993); children: Francine, Joseph, James, John, Frank, Dana. Co-owner Double H Motel, Kettle Falls, Wash., 1969-92; owner Ctr. for Therapeutic Arts & Art Gallery, Marcus, Wash., 1993—; mayor Town of Marcus, 1995—. Home: 1310 N Highway 25 Marcus WA 99151-9997

DE PETRA, DEREK GUIDO, securities trader; b. N.Y.C., June 12, 1970; s. Peter Michael and margaret Durbrow de P.; m. Laura Miller, Sept. 15, 1996. BA in History, UCLA, 1993; postgrad., U. Calif., Berkeley. Trader Mellon Capital Mgmt., San Francisco, 1993-97, Montgomery Asset Mgmt., San Francisco, 1997—. Republican. Roman Catholic. Home: 3670 Fillmore St Apt 5 San Francisco CA 94123-1607

DEPEW, MARIE KATHRYN, retired secondary school educator; b. Sterling, Colo., Dec. 1, 1928; d. Amos Carl and Dorothy Emelyn (Whiteley) Mehl; m. Emil Carlton DePew, Aug. 30, 1952 (dec. 1973). BA, U. Colo., 1950, MA, 1953. Post grad. Harvard U., Cambridge, Mass., 1962; tchr. Jefferson County Pub. Schs., Arvada, 1953-73; mgr. Colo. Accountability Program, Denver, 1973-83; sr. cons. Colo. Dept. Edn., Denver, 1973-85, ret., 1985. Author: (pamphlet) History of Hammil, Georgetown, Colorado, 1967; contbr. articles to profl. jours. Chmn. Colo. State Accountability Com., Denver, 1971-75. Fellow IDEA Programs, 1976-77, 79-81. Mem. Colo. Hist. Assn., Jefferson County Edn. Assn. (pres. 1963-64), Colo. Edn. Assn. (bd. dirs. 1965-70), Ky. Colonels (hon. mem.), Phi Beta Kappa. Republican. Methodist. Avocations: historical research, writing, travel, collecting antiques. Home: 920 Pennsylvania St Denver CO 80203-3157

DEPLOIS, MOLLY, library director; b. Coos Bay, Oreg., July 12, 1956; d. John A. and Violette E. (Carrillo) Barrett; m. Jacques Philippe DePlois, Aug. 2, 1992; children: Emmeline Cosette Adele, Madeline Marie Violette. Libr. asst. Coquille (Oreg.) Pub. Libr., 1976-85, asst. llbr., 1985-86, llbr. dir., 1986—. Adv. coun. Southwestern Oreg. Cmty. Coll., Coos Bay, 1990-94; bd. dirs. Sawdust Theatre, Coquille, 1987-92, pres., 1991-92. Mem. ALA, LWV, Oreb. Libr. Assn. Democrat. Roman Catholic. Avocations: reading, hiking, walking, travel, amateur theater. Home: 1175 Lakewood Ln Coos Bay OR 97420-3468

DEPPISCH, PAUL VINCENT, data communications executive; b. Madison, Wis., Dec. 15, 1950; s. Vincent Francis and Evelyn Catherine (Eichmeier) D. Cable splicing foreman GTE Calif., Santa Monica, 1968-73; gen. foreman DataCom Inc., Santa Monica, 1973-78; sr. project mgr. A.I.D.C.O., North Hollywood, Calif., 1978-84; cons. Systex Group Ltd., Phoenix, 1984-90; pres. Ambient Data Tech. Inc., Upland, Calif., 1990—; founder, dir. Boogere Prodns. Internat., Santa Monica, 1973—; bd. dirs. Systex Group Ltd. Min. Universal Life Ch., Modesto, Calif. Mem. Bldg. Industry Cons. Svc., Inc., C. of C. Avocations: hunting, fishing, community service. Home: PO Box 1712 Santa Monica CA 90406-1712 Office: Ambient Data Tech Inc 517 N Mountain Ave # 101 Upland CA 91786-5016

DEPREIST, JAMES ANDERSON, conductor; b. Phila., Nov. 21, 1936; s. James Henry and Ethel (Anderson) De P.; m. Betty Louise Childress, Aug. 10, 1963; children: Tracy Elisabeth, Jennifer Anne; m. Ginette Grenier, July 19, 1980. Student, Phila. Conservatory Music, 1959-61; BS, U. Pa., 1958, MA, 1961, LHD (hon.), 1976; LHD (hon.), Reed Coll., 1990, Portland State U., 1993; MusD (hon.), Laval U., Quebec City, Can., 1980, Linfield Coll., 1986, Juilliard, 1993; DFA (hon.), U. Portland, 1983, Pacific U., 1985, Willamette U., 1987, Drexel U., 1989, Oreg. State U., 1990; Doctor of Arts and Letters (hon.), St. Mary's Coll., Moraga, Calif., 1985; HHD (hon.), Lewis and Clark U., 1986. Am. specialist music for State Dept., 1962-63; condr.-in-residence Bangkok, 1963-64; condr. various symphonies and orchs., 1964—. Condr.: Am. debut with N.Y. Philharm., 1964, asst. condr. to Leonard Bernstein, N.Y. Philharm. Orch., 1965-66, prin. guest condr. Symphony of New World, 1968-70, European debut with Rotterdam Philharm., 1969; Helsinki Philharm., 1993; assoc. condr. Nat. Symphony Orch., Washington, 1971-75, prin. guest condr. Nat. Symphony Orch., 1975-76; music dir. L'Orchestre Symphonique de Que., 1976-83, Oreg. Symphony, 1980—, prin. guest condr. Helsinki Philharmonic, 1993, Mus. Dir. Monte Carlo Philharm., 1994; appeared with Phila. Orch., 1972, 76, 84, 85, 87, 90, 92, 93, 94, Chgo. Symphony, 1973, 90, 92, 94, Boston Symphony, 1973, Cleve. Orch., 1974; condr.: Am. premiere of Dvorak's First Symphony, N.Y. Philharm., 1972; chief condr. Malmö Symphony, 1991-94; author: (poems) This Precipice Garden, 1987, The Distant Siren, 1989. Trustee Lewis and Clark Coll., 1983—. Recipient 1st prize gold medal Dimitri Mitropoulos Internat. Music Competition for Condrs., 1964, Merit citation City of Phila., 1969, medal of City of Que., 1983; grantee Martha Baird Rockefeller Fund for Music, 1969, Insignia of Comdr. of Order of Lion of Finland, 1992. Fellow Am. Acad. Arts and Scis.; mem. Royal Swedish Acad. Music. Office: Oreg Symphony Orch 921 SW Washington Ste 200 Portland OR 97205*

DERDENGER, PATRICK, lawyer; b. L.A., June 29, 1946; s. Charles Patrick and Drucilla Marguerite (Lange) D.; m. Jo Lynn Dickins, Aug. 24, 1968; children: Kristin Lynn, Bryan Patrick, Timothy Patrick. BA, Loyola U., L.A., 1968; MBA, U. So. Calif., 1971, JD, 1974; LLM in Taxation, George Washington U., 1977. Bar: Calif. 1974, U.S. Ct. Claims 1975, Ariz. 1979, U.S. Ct. Appeals (9th cir.) 1979, U.S. Dist. Ct. Ariz. 1979, U.S. Tax Ct. 1979, U.S. Supreme Ct. 1979; cert. specialist in tax law. Trial atty. honors program U.S. Dept. Justice, Washington, 1974-78; ptnr. Lewis and Roca, Phoenix, 1978—; adj. prof. taxation Golden Gate U., Phoenix, 1983-87; mem. Ariz. State Tax Ct. Legis. Study Commn., Tax Law Specialist Commn., Ariz. Property Tax Oversight Commn.; appt. Ariz. Property Tax Oversight Commn., 1997—. Author: Arizona State and Local Taxation, Cases and Materials, 1983, Arizona Sales and Use Tax Guide, 1990, Advanced Arizona Sales and Use Tax, 1987-96, Arizona State and Local Taxation, 1989, 93, 96, Arizona Sales and Use Tax, 1988-96. Arizona Property Taxation, 1993-96, ABA Sales and Use Tax Deskbook, Property Tax Deskbook. Past pres., bd. dirs. North Scottsdale Little League; apptd. Ariz. Property Tax Oversight Commn. Served to capt. USAF, 1968-71. Recipient U.S. Law Week award Bur. Nat. Affairs, 1974. Mem. ABA (taxation sect., various coms.), Ariz. Bar Assn. (taxation sect., former chair sect. taxation, former treas., chmn. state and local tax com., chmn. continuing legal edn. com., tax adv. com., others, mem. tax law specialist commn.), Maricopa County Bar Assn., Inst. Sales Taxation, Nat. Tax Assn., Inst. Property Taxation Met. C. of C., Ariz. C. of C. (chair tax com.), U. So. Calif. Alumni Club (past pres., bd. dirs.), Phi Delta Phi. Home: 10040 E Happy Valley Rd Scottsdale AZ 85255-2395 Office: Lewis and Roca 2 Renaissance Plz 40 N Central Ave Ste 1900 Phoenix AZ 85004-4429

DERGARABEDIAN, PAUL, JR., film analyst, box office tracker; b. L.A., Sept. 16, 1961; s. Paul and Mary Anna (Jansouzian) D. BA, Calif. State U., Long Beach, 1986; MA, U. So. Calif., 1988. Tech. writer The Aerospace Corp., El Segundo, Calif., 1988-89; comm. cons. Desktoppers, Torrance, Calif., 1989-90; video prodr./mktg. rep. HDR Archs., Irvine, Calif., 1990-93; exec. v.p. Exhibitor Rels. Co., Inc., L.A., 1993-99, pres., 1999—. Office: Exhibitor Rels Co Inc 116 N Robertson Blvd Ste 606 Los Angeles CA 90048-3109

DE ROO, REMI JOSEPH, bishop; b. Swan Lake, Man., Can., Feb. 24, 1924; s. Raymond and Josephine (De Pape) De R. Student, St. Boniface (Man.) Coll.; STD, Angelicum U., Rome, Italy.; LLD (hon.), U. Antigonish, N.S., 1983, U. Brandon, Man., 1987; DD (hon.), U. Winnipeg, Man., 1990; LLD (hon.), U. Victoria, B.C., 1991. Ordained priest Roman Cath. Ch., 1950. Curate Holy Cross Parish, St. Boniface, 1952-53; sec. to archbishop of St. Boniface, 1954-56; diocesan dir. Cath. action Archdiocese St. Boniface, 1953-54; exec. sec. Man. Cath. Con., 1958; pastor Holy Cross Parish, 1960-62; bishop of Victoria, B.C., Can., 1962—; Can. Episcopal rep. Internat. Secretariat Apostleship See, 1964-78, Pontifical Commn. Culture, 1984-87; chairperson Human Rights Commn. B.C., 1974-77; mem. social affairs commn. Can. Conf. Cath. Bishops, 1973-87, 91-95, mem. theology commn., 1987-91; pres. Western Cath. Conf. Bishops, 1984-88; hon. pres. World Conf. for Religion and Peace for Can., 1994—. Hon. fellow Ryerson Poly. Inst., 1987. Address: 4044 Nelthorpe St # 1, Victoria, BC Canada V8X 2A1

DEROSA, FRANCIS DOMINIC, chemical company executive; b. Seneca Falls, N.Y., Feb. 26, 1936; s. Frank and Frances (Bruno) DeR.; m. Vivian DeRosa, Oct. 24, 1959; children: Kevin, Marc, Terri. Student, Rochester Inst. Tech., 1959-61; BS, Chadwick U., MBA; PhD, City U. L.A. Cert. med. photographer. CEO Advance Paper & Equipment Supply Inc., Mesa, Ariz., 1974—, Pottery Plus Ltd., Mesa, 1984—, Advance Tool Supply Inc., Mesa, 1989-94. Vice chmn. bd. adjustments City of Mesa, 1983-89, bd. dirs. dept. parks and recreation, 1983-86; pres. Christ the King Mens Club, 1983-84; bd. dirs. Mesa C. of C., 1983-88. Mem. Ariz. Sanitary Supply Assn. (pres. 1983-84), Internat. Sanitary Supply Assn. (coord. Ariz. chpt. 1994-96, sec. bd. 1994-96), Gilbert, Ariz. C. of C. (bd. dirs., v.p. 1992-96, pres. 1996-97, sec. internat. bd. 1994-96), Gilbert Heights Owners Assn. (pres. 1992-93), Mesa Country Club, Calif. Yacht Club, Santa Monica (Calif.) Yacht Club, Rotary (pres. Mesa Sunrise chpt. 1987-88, Paul Harris fellow 1988), Masons (32 degree, pres. 1973), Sons of Italy (pres. 1983-84), Shriners. Avocations: music, physical fitness, sailing, golf. Home: 513 E Horseshoe Ave Gilbert AZ 85296-1705 Office: Advance Paper & Maintenance Supply Inc 33 W Broadway Mesa AZ 85210-1505

DEROUIN, JAMES G., lawyer; b. Eau Claire, Wis., July 11, 1944. BA cum laude, U. Wis., 1967, JD, 1968. Bar: Wis. 1968, Ariz. 1986. Ptnr. Steptoe & Johnson LLC, Phoenix, Ariz.; atty. Meyer, Hendricks, Victor, Osbonn & Maledon, Phoenix, Ariz.; ptnr. Dewitt, Ross & Stevens, Madison, Wis. PCB chair Wis. Dept. Natural Resources, 1976-78; mem. spl. com. on solid waste mgmt. Wis. Legis. Coun., 1976-79, ad hoc com. on hazardous waste mgmt., 1980-82, spl. com. on groundwater mgmt.; mem. Wis. Dept. Nat. Resources Metallic Mining Coun., 1978-85; chair Phoenix Environ. Quality Commn., 1986, Phoenix Environ. Quality Com., 1989-92; mem. Ariz. Govs. Regulatory Review Coun. 1986—; co-chair ADEQ/ADWR Groundwater Task Force, 1996-97. Chair. State Bar Ariz. (environ. and nat. resources law sect. 1989-90). Office: 40 N Central Ave Ste 2400 Phoenix AZ 85004-4453*

DEROULHAC, JOSEPH HAROLD, JR., minister; b. Albuquerque, Jan. 5, 1953; s. Joseph Harold and Bettie Leah (Wilson) DeR.; m. Lucinda Paglinawan Custodio, Mar. 29, 1980; 1 child, Christina. BA in Sociology, U. Ark., 1975; MDiv., So. Bapt. Theol. Sem., 1979; PhD in Religion and Social Ethics, U. So. Calif., L.A., 1983. Ordained to ministry Am. Bapt. Ch., 1983. Field staff Young Life in Ark., Little Rock, 1975-76; assoc. pastor Fourth Ave. Bapt. Ch., Louisville, 1978-79; coord. young adult ministries First Bapt. Ch., L.A., 1982-83; pastor North Hills Community Bapt. Ch., Pitts., 1984-89; sr. min. The First Bapt. Ch. of Redlands, Calif., 1989—; pres. Am. Bapt. Mins. Coun. of Pitts., 1986-88; bd. dirs. Am. Bapt. Theol. Ctr., Pasadena, Calif., 1990-96, 98—, pres., 1998—; trustee Am. Bapt. Homes of the West, Oakland, Calif., 1990—. Bd. dirs. Pitts. Bapt. Assn., 1986-88, North Hills Youth Ministry, Pitts., 1985-88; mem. bio-ethics com. Redlands (Calif.) Community Hosp., 1990—; bd. mgrs. Plymouth Village, Redlands, 1990—, chair, 1998; environ. scan com. United Way, Redlands, 1991; bd. dirs. Christian Counseling Svc., Redlands, 1997—. Oakley fellow Univ. So. Calif., L.A., 1979-82; recipient Eagle award Boy Scouts Am., North Little Rock, 1968. Mem. Mins. Coun. of the Am. Bapt. Chs. USA (senator 1986-88, nat. sec.-treas. 1990—), Bapt. Peace Fellowship N.Am., Phi Kappa Phi. Office: The First Bapt Ch Redlands 51 W Olive Ave Redlands CA 92373-5243

DERR, JEANNIE COMBS, bilingual educator, anthropology educator; b. L.A., May 17, 1954; d. Jack Vincent and Evelyn Mary (Weiss) Combs; m. Dennis Eugene Derr, Aug. 6, 1983; children: Natalie Winona, Jeremy Lloyd. AA in Anthropology, Pasadena City Coll., 1975; BA in Anthropology, Calif. State U., L.A., 1978, MA in Anthropology, 1979. Calif. C.C. credential anthropology; Calif. multiple subjects credential. Textbook adoptions western region corr. Bowmar Noble Pubs., Inc., Glendale, Calif., 1979-80; bilingual tchr. Pasadena (Calif.) Unified Sch. Dist., 1981-82; exch. tchr. bilingual L'ecole Aujourd'hui, Paris, 1982-83; migrant edn., bilingual tchr. Oxnard (Calif.) Sch. Dist., 1983—; instr. anthropology Oxnard Coll., 1989—; instr. humanities St. John's Seminary Coll., Camarillo, Calif., 1990—; instr. ethnic rels. U. LaVerne, Pt. Mugu, Calif., 1995—. Editor (resource booklet) Oxnard Migrant Education, 1987. Violinist Jr. Philharm. Orch. Calif., L.A., 1967—, Opus 1 Chamber Orch., L.A., 1976-79; soprano, officer San Marino (Calif.) Cmty. Ch., 1974-83. Mem. AAUW, Am. Mexican Am. Educators, Am. Soc. Anthropology, Soc. Am. Archeology, Soc. for the Study Evolution. Republican. Presbyterian. Avocations: music, travel, archeology, hiking, bicycling. Home: 1650 Shoreline Dr Camarillo CA 93010-6016

DERR, KENNETH T., oil company executive; b. 1936; m. Donna Mettler, Sept. 12, 1959; 3 children. BME, Cornell U., 1959, MBA, 1960. With Chevron Corp. (formerly Standard Oil Co. of Calif.), San Francisco, 1960—, v.p., 1972-85; pres. Chevron U.S.A., Inc. subs. Chevron Corp., San Francisco, 1978-84; head merger program Chevron Corp. and Gulf Oil Corp., San Francisco, 1984-85; vice-chmn. Chevron Corp., San Francisco, 1985-88, chmn., CEO, 1989—; bd. dirs. AT&T, Am. Productivity & Quality Ctr., Citicorp, Potlatch Corp. Trustee emeritus Cornell U. Mem. The Bus. Coun., Calif. Bus. Roundtable, Am. Petroleum Inst. (bd. dirs.), Nat. Petroleum Coun., Bus. Roundtable, San Francisco Golf Club, Orinda Country Club, Pacific Union Club. Office: Chevron Corp PO Box 7643 575 Market St San Francisco CA 94105-2856

DERR, LOUISE E., software engineer, educator; b. Balt., July 1, 1953; d. Vernon Ellsworth and Mary Louise (Van Atta) D. BA, BS, U. Colo., 1977, MS, 1986. Tchr. Houston Indep. Sch. District, 1979-82; programmer AIS Inc., Provo, Utah, 1987-88; sr. sys. designer Concept Sys., Phila., 1989-91; sr. software engr. American Libr. Svcs., Provo, Utah, 1991—; tchr. U. Phoenix, Salt Lake City, 1995—. Musician playing baroque-renaissance performances, 1993—. Avocations: archaeology, genealogy.

D'ERRICO, DIDI, executive. BA in Mass Comm., Ball State U, MA in Pub. Rels. V.p. Blanc & Otus, San Francisco. Office: 135 Main St Fl 12 San Francisco CA 94105-1812

DER TOROSSIAN, PAPKEN, executive. Chmn., CEO Silicon Valley Group, San Jose, Calif. Office: 101 Metro Dr Ste 400 San Jose CA 95110-1343*

DE SÁ E SILVA, ELIZABETH ANNE, secondary school educator; b. Edmonds, Wash., Mar. 17, 1931; d. Sven Yngve and Anna Laura Elizabeth (Dahlin) Erlandson; m. Claudio de Sá e Silva, Sept. 12, 1955 (div. July 1977); children: Lydia, Marco, Nelson. BA, U. Oreg., 1953; postgrad., Columbia U., 1954-56, Calif. State U., Fresno, 1990, U. No. Iowa, 1993; MEd, Mont. State U., 1978. Cert. tchr., Oreg., Mont. Med. sec., 1947-49; sec. Merced (Calif.) Sch. Dist., 1950-51; sec., asst. Simon and Schuster, Inc., N.Y.C., 1954-56; tchr. Casa Roosevelt-União Cultural, São Paulo, Brazil, 1957-59, Coquille (Oreg.) Sch. Dist., 1978-96; music tchr. Cartwheels Presch., North Bend, Oreg., 1997—; tchr. piano, 1967-78; instr. Spanish, Southwestern Oreg. C.C., Coos Bay, 1991-94; pianist/organist Faith Luth. Ch., North Bend, Oreg., 1995—, vocal soloist, 1996—, voice tchr., 1997—. Chmn. publicity Music in Our Schs. Month, Oreg. Dist. VII, 1980-85; sec. Newcomer's Club, Bozeman, Mont., 1971. Quincentennial fellow U. Minn. and Found. José Ortega y Gasset, Madrid, 1991. Mem. AAUW (sec., scholarship chmn., co-pres., pres., treas., editor newsletter), Nat. Trust Hist. Preservation, Am. Coun. on Tchg. Fgn. Langs., Am. Assn. Tchrs. Spanish and Portuguese, Nat. Coun. Tchrs. English, Music Educators Nat. Conf., Oreg. Music Educators Assn., Oreg. Coun. Tchrs. English, Confedn. Oreg. Fgn. Lang. Tchrs., VoiceCare Network. Republican. Avocations: swimming, walking, travel, drama. Home: 3486 Spruce St North Bend OR 97459-1130

DESANTIS, GREGORY JOSEPH, motion picture executive; b. L.A., July 12, 1954. Student, Durham U., Eng., 1970, Canaan Coll., 1970, Franklin Pierce Coll., 1974, U. So. Calif. Pres., CEO, Beverly Hills Prodns., L.A., 1974-88; pres., CEO Millennium OmniMedia, 1988—. Dir., prodr. features, documentary and sports films, including California Day, 1974, Volleyball: A Sport Come of Age; prodr. Car Trouble, 1985, The Companion, 1987, A Surfer's Journal, 1997, Our Musical; prodr., dir. Pass the Buck; exec. prodr. U.S. National Lifeguard Champions, 1997—; creator, exec. prodr. American Junior Lifeguard Championships, 1997—, Internat. Big Wave Championships, 1999, Internat. Bodyboard Championships, 1999, Internat. Tube Ride Championships, 1999. Prodr. U.S. Nat. Lifeguard Champions, Am. Lifeguard.

DE SHAY, WILLIAM LESLIE, minister; b. Columbus, Ohio, Sept. 23, 1930; s. William Henry Dewey and Aleatha Delilah (Brantley) De S.; m. Corinne Fauntleroy, Oct. 25, 1959; children: William Leslie, Mark Antoine. BA in Theology, Oakwood Coll., 1952; MS in Counseling Psychology, A&M U., Normal, Ala., 1971; PhD in Counseling, Ohio State U., 1975. Ordained to ministry Seventh-day Adventist Ch., 1959. Pastor Allegheny Conf. Seventh-day Adventists, 1954-64, Dupont Park Ch., Washington, 1965-69; chaplain, counselor adminstr. Oakwood Coll., Huntsville, Ala., 1969-72; adminstr., dir. black affairs, mem. exec. com. So. Calif. conf. Seventh-day Adventists, Glendale, 1976-87; pastor Altadena (Calif.) Seventh-day Adventists Ch., 1987-88, Del. Ave. Seventh-day Adventists Ch., Santa Monica, Calif., 1989—; trustee So. Calif. Conf. Assn., Glendale, 1976-91; mem. minority groups com. Pacific Union Conf., 1976—; del. youth congress Columbia Union Conf., Paris, 1951. Named Hon. Citizen State of Tenn., 1977; recipient Century Soul award So. Cen. Conf., 1972. Democrat. Home: 4612 Maybank Ave Lakewood CA 90712-3616 Office: So Calif Conf Seventh-day Adventists 1535 E Chevy Chase Dr Glendale CA 91206-4107

DESHAZER, RUTH SHOMLER, health information management professional; b. Glendale, Calif., July 17, 1954; d. Russell Paul and Pauline April (Lathrop) Shomler; 1 child, Michael Jr. BA magna cum laude, San Diego State U., 1982; AS, San Diego Mesa Coll., 1993. Accredited records technician; cert. profl. of healthcare quality. Med. records technician, coder Scripps Healthcare, La Jolla, Calif., 1993-94; cont. quality improvement coord. Adventist Health Systems, National City, Calif., 1994-96; applications specialist MED Data Systems Inc., San Diego, 1996-97; health info. mgmt. cons. Pyramid Healthcare Cons., L.A., 1997; health info. mgmt. sr. cons. Elacor Resources Group, L.A., 1997-98; health info. mgmt. dir. Brea (Calif.) Cmty. Hosp., Pacifica Hosp. of the Valley, Burbank, Calif., 1998—. Contbr. articles to profl. jours. Mem. Calif. Assn. Quality Profls., San Dieto Health Info. Assn. (various offices 1994-97), Greater Orange Counth Health Info. Assn. (pres.-elect 1998-99, pres. 1999—), Calif. Health Info. Assn. (nominating com. 1995-96, legis. com. 1996-97, convention com. 1997-98, chair convention com. 1998—, membership com. 1998—), Am. Health Info. Assn., Phi Beta Kappa, Phi Kappa Phi. Avocations: landscaping, floral design, swimming, travel. E-mail: cooknruth@aol.com.

DE SHAZO, BILLY W., physician, plastic surgeon; b. Ashford, Ala., Jan. 10, 1931; s. Neal C. and Woodie Lee (Harrison) De S.; m. Charlotte Jean McKay, Aug. 21, 1954; children: Jean, William, Edwin, John, Thomas. BS, So. Meth. U., 1952; MD, Southwestern Med. Sch., 1956. Diplomate Am. Bd. Plastic Surgery. Resident gen. surgery Calif. Hosp., L.A., 1959-62; resident plastic surgery U. Wis., Madison, 1962-64; chief plastic surgery Good Samaritan Hosp., St. Vincent's Hosp. Office: 1245 Wilshire Blvd Los Angeles CA 90017-4810

DESIMONE, RICHARD LOUIS, school assistant principal; b. Gilroy, Calif., May 6, 1952; s. Alfred Richard and Robbie Fay (Couch) D.; m. Ida Lee Arellano, July 5, 1975; children: Michael, Basilisa, Carlotta, Raquel. BA in Social Sci., San Jose State U., 1978, MA in Counselor Edn., 1991, adminstrv. credential, 1996. Cert. tchr., lang. devel. specialist, pupil pers. svcs. specialist, Calif. Retreat coord. Mission Trails Search Program, Gilroy, Calif., 1968-88; tchr. Morgan Hill (Calif.) Unified Sch. Dist., 1986-94, counselor, 1994—; English instr. KRATOS, Mexico City, 1991; mem. faculty counselor edn. San Jose State U., 1994—; family counselor Discover Alternatives, Gilroy, 1992-93; exec. dir. Internat. Edn. Specialists, San Jose, 1991-93; mem. Cultural Diversity Task Force, Morgan Hill, 1993—; mem. Calif. Sch. Leadership Team, Morgan Hill, 1993-94. Author: Cross-Cultural Issues in Counseling and Education, 1992; co-author: Child Abuse Reporting Procedures, 1990. Mem. St. Mary Parish Coun., Gilroy, 1984-88; mem. Conflict Resolution Team, Morgan Hill, 1993—; mem. Bilingual Parent Com., Morgan Hill, 1993—. Recipient Mayor's Cmty. Conf. award City of San Jose, 1992, Pope Paul VI Svc. award Archdiocese of San Jose, 1984. Mem. ASCD, Internat. Playback Theater Network, Calif. Continuation Edn. Assn. Avocations: guitar, camping, family. E-mail: desi@gilroy.com. Office: Britton Mid Sch 80 W Central Ave Morgan Hill CA 95037-4302

DESROCHES, DIANE BLANCHE, English language educator, writer, director, actor, editor; b. Webster, Mass., Nov. 17, 1947; d. Victor Joseph and Rose Blanche Blouin; m. Roger John DesRoches, Aug. 27, 1966 (div. Apr. 16, 1974); 1 child, Bill. AA with high honors in French, Mesa Coll., 1976; BA in English magna cum laude, San Diego State U., 1979, MA, 1981. Cert. lang. arts, lit. and ABE:ESL instr., Calif. community colls. ESL instr. Coll. of English Lang., San Diego, 1982—; ESL instr. North City Ctr., Kearny Mesa campus San Diego Community Coll. Dist., 1982—; presenter in field. Author: (short story) Something Special, 1979, Cinderella of the 80s, 1980; (software) Basic Map Reading Skills, 1981; writer (video) The College of English Language, 1989, numerous recipes, word search puzzles, variety puzzles and ednl. puzzles., 1980—; writer, dir. (video) The Challenge Is Ours, 1989; co-writer (multimedia show) Holiday Sky Show, 1988, (screen adaptation) The Wind From the Sun, 1989; contbr. articles to mags.; contbr. (reading comprehension series) Comprehension Plus, 1982, (student assessment system) CASAS, 1982; editl. cons. (multimedia shows) Dimensions, 1987, Cycles, 1987, Star Tracks, 1988, Thundering Water, 1988, Flying Blue Marble, 1988, Night on Dream Mountain, 1988, Mars, 1988, From Here to Infinity, 1989, To Worlds Beyond, 1989, Stars Over China, 1989, Eclipse!, 1991; translator: ABC of Ecology, 1982; actor (photoplay) And the Winner Is...?, 1982, (film) Killer Tomatoes Eat France, 1991, Tainted Blood, 1993; writer, dir., co-prodr. (TV comml.) Mount Laguna Observatory. Recipient Gregg award Gregg Inst., 1965; fellow State of Calif., 1979; DB Williams scholar San Diego State U., 1979. Mem. TESOL, Calif. TESOL, Am. Fedn. Tchrs., Am. Fedn. Tchrs./San Diego Adult Educators (union site rep. 1998—), Am. Film Inst., Phi Kappa Phi, Psi Chi, Pi Delta Phi. Democrat. Roman Catholic. Avocations: movies, racquetball, ice skating, swimming, reading.

DES SAGETTES, CHRISTIANE GUILLERMIN, pharmacist, biologist; b. Rodez, France, Dec. 17, 1932; came to the U.S., 1985; d. Charles Christian Loretz and Madeleine Causse; m. Ishan Dodan, Sept. 2, 1955 (dec. 1980); children: Inci, Ayben, Nihal; m. Baron Jean Claude Guillermin des Sagettes, Nov. 20, 1981. Diploma of pharmacist, Pharmacy Sch., Paris, 1961; serology cert., Faculty Medicine Paris, 1961; microbiology cert., Inst. Pasteur, 1962. Pharmacist in charge Hosp. Melun, France, 1969-75; owner dir., Med Ctr Arpajon, France, 1976-85; intern pharmacist Midwest Pharmacy, L.A.; owner French low calorie restaurant Baroness & Daughters, Santa Monica, Calif., 1986-87; intern pharmacist Pharmacare, Inglewood, Calif., 1989, Santa Maria Hosp., L.A., 1990; pharmacist in charge Million Dollars Pharmacy, L.A., 1991-95. Author: Femmes Sans Frontieres-Women Without Borders, 1981, Book of Nutrition: Dietetics, He Is An Homeless I'll Love You Forever, 1989. Roman Catholic. Home: 6310 Green Valley Cir Apt 309 Culver City CA 90230-7003

DESTAFFANY, SANDRA RUSSELL, childbirth educator, author; b. Billings, Mont., Mar. 15, 1957; d. Alexander Emmett and Cleora Jean (Saunders) Russell; m. Joe Lee DeStaffany, Oct. 13, 1979; children: Naomi Jo, Andrea Renee, James Russell. BS, Mont. State U., 1979. cert. childbirth educator. Childbirth educator Conrad (Mont.) Childbirth Edn. Assn., 1983—; U.S. western dir. Inter Childbirth Edn. Assn., Mpls., 1990-92, pres. elect 1992-94, pres. 1994-95. Contbr. numerous articles to profl. jours. Avocations: skiing, reading, writing, needlework, quilting.

DETATA, JUAN CARLOS, forensic psychiatrist; b. Buenos Aires, Sept. 6, 1932; came to U.S., 1957; s. Juan Carlos and Carmen Rosa (Feola) D.; divorced; children: Carmen, M. Karla. MD, U. Buenos Aires, 1956. Lic. MD, Calif., Wash., Hawaii. Intern French Hosp., San Francisco, 1956-57; Resident psychiatry Phila. Gen. Hosp., 1957-61; consulting psychiatrist Dept. Health, Honolulu, 1961-76; chief dept. in-patient psychiatry 97th Gen. Hosp., U.S. Army, Frankfurt, Fed. Republic of Germany, 1976-80; geriatric psychiatrist Western State Hosp., Tacoma, 1980-84; chief dept. neuropsychiatry 50th Gen. Hosp., U.S. Army Reserve Command, Seattle, 1980-95; forensic psychiatrist San Quentin State Prison, San Quentin, Calif., 1985—. Contbr. articles to profl. jours. Recipient Gov. Burns' award Gov. State Hawaii, 1970. Mem. Am. Psychiat. Assn., Calif. Psychiat. Assn., Nat. Railway Hist. Soc. Roman Catholic. Avocations: opera, langs., travel, trains, subways. Office: San Quentin State Prison Dept Psychiatry San Quentin CA 94964

DETERT, MIRIAM ANNE, chemical analyst; b. San Diego, Calif., Sept. 16, 1925; d. George Bernard and Margaret Theresa Zita (Lohre) D. BS, Dominican Coll., San Rafael, Calif., 1947. Chem. analyst Shell Devel. Co., Emeryville, Calif., 1947-72, Houston, 1972-86. Photo participant Wax Rsch.: Quest, 1981; contbr. poetry to books including The National Library of Poetry - Best Poems of the 90's, Spirit of the Age, The Nightfall of Diamonds. Vol. Falkirk Cultural Ctr., San Rafael, 1987-91, M.D. Anderson Tumor Inst., Houston, 1978-86, Rep. Party, San Rafael, 1990, 94; mem. Jewish Comm. Ctr. Recipient Disting. Alumni award Dominican Coll., 1994. Mem. Marin Geneal. Soc. Republican. Roman Catholic. Avocations: etching, oil painting, geneal. rsch. on Detert name, swimming (Sr. Olympic Swimming award 1991).

DE TOMASO, ERNEST PAT, general building contractor, developer; b. Pescara, Italy, July 27, 1915; s. Anthony and Frances Mary (Tarsa) DeT.; m. Lida Janet Sherlock, June 30, 1940; children: Ernest Patrick, John Anthony. Student, San Bernardino Valley Coll., 1961, Shabbarazzi Sch. Music, Rochester, N.Y., 1932. Musician Pat Thomas and His Orch., Rochester, 1931-37; baker Thrifty Drug Stores, L.A., 1938-46; ptnr. Anthony and Ernest P. DeTomaso Bldg. Contractors, Fontana, Calif., 1946-50; bldg. contractor Ernest P. DeTomaso Bldg. Contractor-Developer, Fontana, 1950-79; owner, lessor Towne Plaza Shopping Ctr., Fontana, 1987—; bd. dirs., v.p. Marygold Mut. Water Co., Bloomington, Calif. Mem. Greater Fontana United Fund, 1966-73, pres., 1973; mem. Planning Commn., Fontana, 1968-80, pres., 1970-71; founder, bd. dirs. Fontana Polit. Action Coalition, 1993—; trustee Eastern Star Homes of Calif., 1989-92. Recipient Devoted and Invaluable Svcs. award C. of C., Fontana, 1980, Outstanding Achievment award Greater Fontana United Fund, 1980, Svcs. Rendered award City of Fontana, 1981. Mem. Masons (Hiram award), Rotary, Order Eastern Star (worthy patron, grand officer, Exceptional Svc. award 1985). Republican. Avocations: music, fishing, travel. Home: 17155 Manzanita Dr Fontana CA 92335-5850

DETRICK, DONALD HOWARD, minister; b. Newberg, Oreg., Dec. 13, 1954; s. Howard Raymond and Madeline F. (Roth) D.; m. Jodi Lanette Dunlap, June 8, 1974; children: Kristina Lynne, Mark Andrew, Jana Kathleen. Student, Eugene Bible Coll., 1974-77; BA, Bapt. Christian Coll., 1985; MA in Counseling, Luther Rice Sem., 1990. Ordained to ministry Assemblies of God, 1980. Sr. pastor Dayton (Oreg.) Assembly of God, 1977-78; assoc. pastor First Assembly of God, Newberg, 1979-83; sr. pastor Abundant Life Ctr., Toledo, Oreg., 1983-91, Bethel Ch., Chehalis, Wash., 1991—; presbyter Oreg. Coun. Assemblies of God, Salem, 1986-91, exec. prebyter, 1987-91; presbyter NW Dist. Assemblies of God, 1994-96, exec. presbyter, 1996—. Contbr. articles to religious publs. Mem. Am. Assn. Christian Counselors. Republican. Office: Bethel Ch 132 Kirkland Rd Chehalis WA 98532-8724

DETTERMAN, ROBERT LINWOOD, financial planner; b. Norfolk, Va., May 1, 1931; s. George William and Jeanneille (Watson) D.; m. Virginia Armstrong; children: Janine, Patricia, William Arthur. BS in Engring., Va. Poly. Inst., 1953; PhD in Nuclear Engring., Oak Ridge Sch. Reactor Tech., 1954, postgrad., 1954; cert. in fin. planning, Coll. Fin. Planning, Denver, 1986. Registered investment advisor, Calif. Engring. test dir. Foster Wheeler Co., N.Y.C., 1954-59; sr. research engr. Atomics Internat. Co., Canoga Park, Calif., 1959-62; chief project engr. Rockwell Internat. Co., Canoga Park, Calif., 1962-68, dir. bus. devel., 1968-84, mgr. internat. program, 1984-87; pres. Bo-Gin Fin., Inc., Thousand Oaks, Calif., 1987—; owner Bo-Gin Arabians, Thousand Oaks, 1963—; nuclear cons. Danish Govt., 1960, Lawrence Livermore Lab., Calif., 1959. Trustee, mem. exec. com. Morris Animal Found., Denver, 1984—, chmn., 1984-88, now trustee emeritus; mem. pres.' adv. com. Kellog Arabian Ranch, U. Calif. Poly., Pomona; treas., trustee Arabian Horse Trust, Denver, 1979-94, now trustee emeritus; pres. Rolling Oaks Homes Assn., Thousand Oaks, Calif., 1980-82; chmn. Cal Bred Futurity. Named to Tent of Honor, Arabian Horse Trust, 1997. Mem. Nat. Assn. Personal Fin. Advisers, Internat. Assn. Fin. Planners, Inst. Cert. Fin. Planners, Am. Nuclear Soc., Acad. Magical Arts, Am. Horse Shows Assn., Am. Horse Coun., Magic Castle Club, Internat. Arabian Horse Assn. Club, Tau Beta Phi, Eta Kappa Nu, Phi Kappa Phi. Republican. Avocations: collecting stamps, growing orchids. Office: Bo-Gin Fin Inc Ste 220 3609 E Thousand Oaks Blvd Westlake Village CA 91362-6941

DETTON, DAVID K., lawyer; b. Rupert, Idaho, Sept. 20, 1949. BA cum laude, Brigham Young U., 1973, JD magna cum laude, 1976. Bar: Utah, 1976. Law clk. to Hon. David T. Lewis U.S. Ct. Appeals (10th cir.), 1976-77; ptnr. Dorsey & Whitney, Salt Lake City, 1997—; part time faculty Oil and Gas Law Brigham Young U., 1979—. Comment and Case Note editor Brigham Young U. Law Review, 1975-76. J. Clark Reuben scholar. Mem. Utah State Bar, Phi Kappa Phi. Office: Dorsey & Whitney LLP 170 S Main St Ste 925 Salt Lake City UT 84101-1605*

DETWILER, PETER MURRAY, legislative consultant, educator; b. Visalia, Calif., Nov. 5, 1949; s. Donald M. and Mary Alice (Murray) D.; m. Caroline Margaret Cain, Sept. 2, 1972; children: Stephen C., Eric J. BA in Govt., St. Mary's Coll. Calif., 1971; MA in Pub. Policy and Adminstrn., U. Wis., 1972. Asst. exec. officer Local Agy. Formation Commn., San Diego, 1972-75; dir. local govt. unit Gov.'s Office Planning and Rsch., Sacramento, 1975-81; staff dir. Senate Local Govt. Com., Sacramento, 1982-95; dir. staff Senate Housing and Land Use Com., Sacramento, 1995—; instr. Calif. State U., Sacramento, 1991—. Author: (chpt.) Calif. Environ. Law, 1989, State & Regional Initiatives for Managing Development, [illegible] editors, contbr. articles Land Use & Environment Forum, 1991-96. Leader Boy Scouts Am., Sacramento, 1984—. Democrat. Roman Catholic. Avocations: sailing, cross-country skiing. Office: Senate Housing and Land Use State Capitol Rm 407 Sacramento CA 95814-4906

DEUBLE, JOHN L., JR., environmental science and engineering services consultant; b. N.Y.C., Oct. 2, 1932; s. John Lewis and Lucille (Klotzbach) D.; m. Thelma C. Honeychurch, Aug. 28, 1955; children: Deborah, Steven. AA, AS in Phys. Sci., Stockton Coll., 1957; BA, BS in Chemistry, U. Pacific, 1959. Cert. profl. chemist, profl. engr., environ. inspector; registered environ. profl., registered environ. assessor. Sr. chemist Aero-Gen Corp., Sacramento, Calif., 1959-67; asst. dir. rsch. Lockheed Propulsion Co., Redlands, Calif., 1968-73; asst. div. mgr. Systems, Sci. and Software, La Jolla, Calif., 1974-79; gen. mgr. Wright Energy Nev. Corp., Reno, Nev., 1980-81; v.p. Energy Resources Co., La Jolla, 1982-83; dir. hazardous waste Aerovironment Inc., Monrovia, Calif., 1984-85; sr. program mgr. Ogden Environ. and Energy Svcs., San Diego, 1989-96; environ. cons. Encinitas, Calif., 1986-88, 97—. Contbr. articles profl. jours. With USAF, 1951-54. Recipient Tech. award Am. Ordnance Assn., 1969, Cert. of Achievement Am. Men and Women of Sci., 1986, Envrion. Registry, 1992. Fellow Am. Inst. Chemists; mem. ASTM, Am. Chem. Soc., Am. Inst. Chem. Engrs., Am. Meteorol. Soc., Am. Def. Inds. Assn., Air and Waste Mgmt. Assn., Calif. Inst. Chemists, Hazardous Materials Control Rsch. Inst., N.Y. Acad. Scis., Environ. Assessors Assn. Republican. Lutheran. Achievements include development and pioneering use of chemical (non-radioactive) tracers--gaseous, aqueous, and particulate in environmental and energy applications. Home and Office: Planning Asssocs 369 Cerro St Encinitas CA 92024-4805

DEUPREE, ROBERT MARSHALL, physician, minister, author; b. Elizabeth, Colo., Dec. 26, 1912; s. Elmer Burton and Mary Ayer (Griffin) DeuP.; m. Harriett Ann Janetos, Oct. 11, 1963; children: Carol J., R. Scott. Student, Santa Ana Coll., 1930-33, L.A. City Coll., 1937-38; DO, Coll. Osteo. Physicians and Surgeons, 1942; MD, Met. U., 1948; postgrad., UCLA, 1952-53; AB, Calif. State U., Fullerton, 1962; MA, Calif. State U., Long Beach, 1963; PhD, Purdue U., 1963-64; DD, Am. Fellowship Ch., 1988. Diplomate in aerospace medicine and occupational medicine. Editor-pub. San Juan Capistrano Coastline Dispatch, 1930-33; intern Wilshire Hosp., L.A., 1942-43, resident in neurology, 1943-44; pvt. practice medicine L.A., 1944-57, El Monte, Calif., 1957-58, Newport Beach, Calif., 1958-59; dir. Rush-Merced Clinic, 1957-58; assoc. med. dir. Aerojet Gen. Corp., Azusa, Calif., 1967-69, Am. Airlines, L.A., 1969; ships surgeon U. Calif. Scripps Inst. Oceanography, 1969; assoc. prof. U. Calif., San Diego, 1969; area med. officer Divsn. Fed. Employee Health USPHS, L.A., 1970-85; head dept. internal medicine and radiology Hiss Orthopedic Clinic, L.A., 1953-57; instr. differential diagnosis Coll. Osteo. Physicians and Surgeons, L.A., 1945-49; instr. med. terminology N. Orange Community Coll. Dist., 1966-78; pres., Deustar Internat. Corp.; rsch. fellow VA Hosp., Long Beach State Coll. UCLA Inst. Laryngol. Rsch., 1962-6; guest lectr. abnormal psychology Fuller Theol. Seminar, 1978-81. Author: The Cross and the Caduseus Deustar, 1996; author, editor: DeuPree International Emergency Medical Translations, 1972; co-author: Travis' Handbook of Speech Pathology and Audiology, 1972; editor Jour. Pro-Re-Nata, 1947-50; author, prodr. med. motion pictures, USN, 1950-51; cons. med. TV, films, 1952—. Nat. Inst. Dental Health fellow Purdue U., 1963-64. Fellow Royal Soc. Health, N.Y. Acad. Scis., Am. Aerospace Med. Assn. (assoc.), Am. Coll. Occupational Medicine, Royal Soc. Medicine, Internat. Clergy Soc.; mem. Aviation Hall of Fame (charter), Asclepiad. Home: 2625 Huckleberry Rd Santa Ana CA 92706-2106

DE URIOSTE, GEORGE ADOLFO, IV, software company executive; b. San Francisco, June 25, 1955; s. George Adolfo Sr. and Janet Germaine (Bruzzone) de U. BS, U. So. Calif., L.A., 1978; MBA, U. Calif., Berkeley, 1980. CPA, Calif. Auditor, cons. Deloitte Haskins & Sells, San Francisco, 1980-83; sr. fin. analyst Genstar Corp., San Francisco, 1983-85, Rolm Mil-Spec Computers, Inc., San Jose, Calif., 1986-88; mgr. fin. planning and analysis Ask Computer Systems, Inc., Mountain View, Calif., 1988-90; CFO TeamOne Systems, Inc., Sunnyvale, Calif., 1990-92; v.p. fin. and ops. Remedy Corp., Mountain View, Calif., 1992-98. Pres. U. So. Calif. Commerce Assocs., San Francisco, 1988-89. Mem. AICPA, Calif. Soc. CPAs, Churchill Club (bd. dirs., vice chmn. Palo Alto, Calif. 1989-94). Avocations: tennis, hunting, skiing, mountain bike riding, antique auto restoration. Home: 282 Walker Dr Mountain View CA 94043-2108 Office: Remedy Corp 1505 Salado Dr Mountain View CA 94043-1110

DEUSSEN, NANCY BLOOMER, composer, music educator, arts organizer; b. N.Y.C., Feb. 1, 1931; d. Horace Stanley and Julia (Thomas) Van Norman; m. Charles Joseph Webster, Aug. 2, 1952 (div.); 1 child, Christopher John; m. John Hayes Bloomer, Sept. 8, 1962 (div.); children: Jennifer Ann, Elizabeth Marie; m. Gary Ronald Deussen, Mar. 1, 1982. MusB in Composition, Manhattan Sch. Music, 1953; MusB in Music Edn., U. So. Calif., 1959; postgrad., Long Beach State U., 1961-62, UCLA, 1962-63, San Jose State U., 1963-64. Cert. secondary tchr., Calif. Assoc. faculty music Mission Coll., Santa Clara, Calif., 1993-99, Santa Clara U., 1997-98. Composer (solo works) Piano Prelude, 1988, Cascades, 1989, East Coast Triptych (A Suite for Piano), 1993, Musings: Circa 1940 (A Recollection, Youthful Frolics), 1995, Amber Waves (for solo piano), 1967, (solo instrumental with piano), Suite for Clarinet and Piano, 1959, Capriccio for Flute and Piano, 1986, Two Pieces for Violin and Piano, 1993, (chamber ensemble) Woodwind Quintet, 1965 (1st prize Mu Phi Epsilon 1987), Fanfare and Andante for Winds, 1988, Trio for Violin, Clarinet and Piano, 1989 (1st prize Britten-on-the-Bay 1996), San Andreas Suite, 1989, Pacific City (piano quintet), 1990, Trio for Violin, Cello and Piano, 1992, One of Nature's Majesties, 1994, The Baylands, 1994, Woodwind Quintet # 2, 1996, Canticles for Brass, 1997, Parisian Caper, 1997, Tribute to the Ancients for brass quintet, 1998, (orchestral) Rustic Sketches, 1987, Reflections on the Hudson, 1955 (Composer's Symposium award Bay Area 1994), Peninsula Suite, 1994, Concerto for Clarinet and Small Orchestra, 1995, Carmel by-the-Sea, 1987, Ascent to Victory, 1997, (concert band) City Festival Overture, 1991, The Voyage of Christopher Columbus, 1992, Aurora, 1997, (choral) Missa de Angelis, 1954, The Serpent, 1964, Easter Hymn, 1954, Canticles of Our Land, 1991, Sing Nowell, 1994, Flowers by the Sea, 1994, Sacred Places of the Earth, 1994, (solo voice with piano) Loveliest of Trees, 1953, The River, 1991, The Long Voyage, 1992, Christe Eleison, 1954, (recorder ensemble) Harvest Suite, 1955, Impressions around G, 1964, Little Fugue, 1956, The Long Voyage, 1992, Suite Breve, 1993. Peninsula Cmty. Found. grantee, 1987, 92, 93, 96, Arts Coun. Silicon Valley grantee, 1998. Mem. Nat. Assn. Composers (pres., founder San Francisco Bay Area chpt. 1991—), Am. Composer's Forum (grant 1997), Broadcast Music, Inc., Am. Music Ctr., Internat. Alliance Women in Music (coord. search for new music 1995-97), 20th Century Forum, Pi Kappa Lambda, Mu Phi Epsilon. Avocations: jewelry making, gemology, ice skating. E-mail: deussen@ix.netcom.com. Home: 3065 Greer Rd Palo Alto CA 94303-4008

DEUTSCH, BARRY JOSEPH, management development company executive; b. Gary, Ind., Aug. 10, 1941; s. Jack Elias and Helen Louise (La Rue) D. BS, U. So. Calif., 1969, MBA magna cum laude, 1970. Lectr. mgmt. U. So. Calif., L.A., 1967-70; pres., founder The Deutsch Group, Inc., L.A., 1970—; founder, CEO, chmn. bd. Investment Planning Network, Inc., 1988—. Author: Leadership Techniques, 1969, Recruiting Techniques, 1970, The Art of Selling, 1973, Professional Real Estate Management, 1975, Strategic Planning, 1976, Employer/Employee: Making the Transition, 1979, Managing by Objectives, 1980, Conducting Effective Performance Appraisal, 1982, Advanced Supervisory Development, 1984, Managing a Successful Financial Planning Business, 1988, How to Franchise Your Business, 1991. Chmn. bd. govs. Am. Hist. Ctr., 1980—. Mem. ASTD, Am. Mgmt. Assn., Am. Soc. Bus. and Mgmt. Cons., Internat. Mgmt. by Objectives Inst., Organization Devel. Network. Office: 1140 Highland Ave Ste 200 Manhattan Beach CA 90266

DEVALL, ESTHER LYNN, family and consumer sciences educator; b. Dade City, Fla., Sept. 27, 1956; d. Preston Eugene and Linnie Bell (Green) D.; m. Earl Reid Lance, Mar. 24, 1984; 1 child, Eric Reid Lance. BS, Fla. State U., 1978; MS, U. Ga., 1983, PhD, 1990. Cert. family life educator. Elem. tchr. Clayton County Schs., Lake City, Ga., 1978-81; prof. Ball State U., Muncie, Ind., 1989-91, N.Mex. State U., Las Cruces, 1991—; mem. adv. bd. Cmty. Action Agy.-Teen Parent Residence, Las Cruces, 1995—, Jardin De Los Niños, Las Cruces, 1996—, gerontology program Doña Ana Coll., [illegible] County Maternal Child Health Coun., Las Cruces, 1995—. Mem. Nat. Coun. Family Rels., Ind. Home Econs. Assn. (New Achiever award 1991), Soroptimist Internat. Las Cruces (pres. 1996-98), Gamma Sigma Delta. Democrat. Presbyterian. Home: 1920 Fairfax Ave Las Cruces NM 88001-1513 Office: NMex State Univ Family and Consumer Scis Gerald Thomas Hall Rm 308 Las Cruces NM 88003

DEVAN, DAVID, opera company director. Gen. mgr. Pacific Opera of Victoria, B.C., Can. Office: Pacific Opera Victoria, 1316 B Government St, Victoria, BC Canada V8W 1Y8*

DEVANEY, DONALD EVERETT, law enforcement official; b. Providence, Nov. 21, 1936; s. William Francis and Elizabeth Florence (Hill) D.; m. Tokiko Yoshida, May 19, 1960; 1 child, George Y. AA in Edn., El Paso Community Coll., 1973; BA, SUNY, Albany, 1979. Cert. healthcare protection adminstr. Internat. Healthcare Safety and Security Found. Sgt. maj. U.S. Army, 1954-83; customs inspector U.S. Customs Svc., Honolulu, 1983-84; provost marshal Tripler Army Med. Ctr., Honolulu, 1984—, regional chair Europe and Asia, 1989-93, 97—; past dir. Kalihi-Palama Immigrant Svc. Ctr.; extraordinary min. of the eucharist Tripler Catholic Cmty. Bd. dirs. USO, 1996, Coalition for a Drug Free Hawaii, 1996. Decorated Legion of Merit; recipient Disting Svc. award Hawaii Joint Police, 1977, 86, George Washington Honor medal Freedom's Found., 1973, Order Mil. Med. Merit, 1996, Elwood J. McGuire award Hawaii, 1997; elec. to Hawaii Jt. Police Assn. Hall of Fame, 1998, Nelson W. Aldrich Hall of Honor, 1998, Order of Military Medical Merit, 1997. Mem. USO (sec., bd. dirs. Hawaii chpt.), Hawaii Joint Police Assn. (pres. 1985, 98), U.S. Army CID Command (assoc.), Nat. Assn. for Uniformed Svcs. (v.p. Hawaii chpt., nat. bd. dirs. 1996—), U.S. Army Retiree Coun. (U.S. Army Hawaii vice chmn.), Hawaii Law Enforcement and Pvt. Security (chmn. awards com.), Hawaii Joint Police Assn. (pres. 1998), Internat. Assn. for Healthcare Security and Safety (region 17 chairperson), Hawaii Coun. Police and Pvt. Security (bd. dirs. 1996—), Noncommd. Officer Assn. (life), Ret. Enlisted Assn. (life), DAV (life chpt. 3), Friend Med. Regt., Rotary (pres. Pearl Harbor chpt. 1991-92, dir. cmty. svc. dist. 5000, 1992-93), KC. Roman Catholic. Avocation: coin and stamp collecting. Fax: (808) 433-4465. Home: 98-911 Ainanui Loop Aiea HI 96701-2766 Office: Office Provost Marshal Tripler Army Med Ctr Honolulu HI 96859-5000

DEVENOT, DAVID CHARLES, human resource executive; b. Indpls., May 27, 1939; s. Charles Joseph and Pearl (Geodfry) D.; children: Daniel, Mark. BBA, U. Hawaii, 1962. Dir. indsl. rels. USP Corp subs. Consol. Foods, Sara Lee, San Jose, Calif., 1964-70; sr. human resource cons. Hawaii Employers Coun., Honolulu, 1970—. Bd. dirs. Hawn Humane Soc., Honolulu, 1975—, Lanikila Rehab. Ctr., Honolulu, 1985—, Am. Cancer Soc., 1989, pres. Pacific divsn. Mem. Santa Clara Valley Pers. Assn. (pres. 1968-69), Soc. Human Resource Mgmt., Indsl. Rels. Rsch. Assn. Avocations: travel, skiing, photography, camping, bicycling. Home: 2803 Puuhonua St Honolulu HI 96822-1765 Office: Hawaii Employers Coun 2682 Waiwai Loop Honolulu HI 96819-1938

DEVENS, JOHN SEARLE, natural resources administrator; b. Shickshinny, Pa., Mar. 31, 1940; s. John Ezra and Laura (Bulkley) D.; m. Sharon I. Snyder (div. 1979); children: John, Jerilyn, James, Janis. BS, Belmont Coll., 1964; MEd, Emory U., 1966; PhD, Wichita State U., 1975. Dir. speech and hearing Columbia (S.C.) Coll., 1967-70; head dept. audiology Inst. Logopedics, Wichita, Kans., 1970-71; supr. audiology State of Alaska, Fairbanks, 1971-73; asst. prof. U. Houston, Victoria, 1975-77; pres. Prince William Sound C.C., Valdez, Alaska, 1977-92, Sterling Coll., Craftsbury Common, Vt., 1993-96; dir. Valdez Hearing and Speech Ctr.; exec. dir. Prince William Sound Regional Citizens' Adv. Coun., 1997—; owner, operator Valdez Hearing and Speech Ctr., 1977—. Prodr. films on hearing problems; contbr. articles to profl. jours. Mayor City of Valdez, 1985-89, mem. city coun., 1980-89; nat. chmn. adv. com. Horsemanship for Handicapped, 1964-67; mem. Alaska Gov.'s Coun. for Handicapped, 1980-82; pres. Valdez chpt. Alaska Visitors Assn., 1980; mem. small cities adv. coun. Nat. League Cities, 1983-87, mem. internat. econ. devel. task force; mem. Nat. Export Coun.; bd. dirs. Resource Devel. Coun.; Dem. nominee U.S. Ho. Reps., 1990, 92; hosted internat. conf. on oil spills for mayors; exec. dir. Prince William Sound Regional Citizens Adv. Coun., 1997—. Mem. Am. Speech-Lang. Hearing Assn. (cert. clin. competence in audiology and speech and lang. pathology), Am. C. of C. in Korea, Valdez C. of C., Alaska Mcpl. League (bd. dirs. 1984-89), Elks, Eagles. Methodist. Avocation: charter boat operator. Home: 1241 W 27th Ave #865 Anchorage AK 99503-2318 Office: 750 W 2nd Ave Ste 100 Anchorage AK 99501-2167

DEVER, THOMAS L., pastor; b. Louisville, Ky., Apr. 27, 1946; s. James Duddly and Lucille Talmage (Jackson) D.; m. Diane Lynn Dever, Sept. 23, 1978; children: Michelle Lucille, Christina Lynn. BA, U. Redland, Calif., 1987, MBA, 1991. Plant protection GM, South Gate, Calif., 1977-81; dir. children's ministry Calvary Bapt., Gardena, Calif., 1981-90; adminstr. Western Fed. Credit Union, L.A., 1990-95; pastor Cmty. Bapt. Ch., Torrance, Calif., 1995—. Office: Cmty Bapt Ch 1243 Artesia Blvd Manhattan Beach CA 90266-6997

DEVEREUX, BARBARA L., elementary school educator; b. Portland, Oreg., Oct. 4, 1940; d. Kenneth Bernard and Cecilia Elinor (Zorich) Carlson; m. Emmett L. Devereux, Dec. 26, 1958; children: Michael, Jill, Karen, Brian. BS, U. Oreg., 1973, MEd, 1980. Cert. in curriculum and instrn., reading K-12, Oreg. 1st grade tchr. Laurel Elem. Sch., Junction City, Oreg., 1974-77; 6th grade tchr. Siuslaw Mid. Sch., Florence, Oreg., 1977-81, kindergarten tchr., 1981-84; title I tchr. Rhododendron Primary Sch., Florence, 1984—; mentor tchr. Florence Sch. Dist., 1987-88. Recipient scholarship to internat. dyslexia conf. Oreg. Dyslexia Soc., 1987. Mem. ASCD, Internat. REading Assn. Avocations: reading, bicycling, computer applications. Office: Rhododendron Primary Sch 2221 Oak St Florence OR 97439-9529

DEVEUVE, SUZANNE, artist; b. Palo Alto, Calif., Mar. 10, 1954; d. Clarence Sims and Mary (Gilbert) deV.; m. Tom Kelly, May 18, 1984; children: Timothy Sean, Christopher Quinn, Anna Marie. BA, Acad. of Arts, 1982. Artist (bookcover) Grandmother of Time, 1990, Grandmother of Moon, 1994, Alchemist Almanac, 1991, Return of Pahana, 1992, (mag. cover) Sojourn, 1998. E-mail: sdeveuve@mcn.org. Fax: 707-847-3902.

DEVINCINTIS, LANI, adult education educator. Dean Glendale C.C., Glendale, Calif. Recipient Regional Person of Yr. award, 1993, State Cmty. Educator of Yr. award, 1996. Office: Glendale Community Coll 1500 N Verdugo Rd Glendale CA 91208-2809*

DEVINE, WALTER BERNARD, naval architect, marine engineer; b. Detroit, July 7, 1927; s. John Francis and Ethel Florence (Peoples) D.; m. Annemarie Jaggi, Dec. 29, 1956; children: Walter, Michael, Peter, David, Louise, Jessica, Andrew. BS in Marine Transp., U.S. Merchant Marine Acad., Kingspoint, N.Y., 1949; BS in Naval Arch., Marine Engring., U. Mich., 1953. 2nd mate Am. Presidents Lines, San Francisco, 1949-51; naval arch Md. Shipbldg., Balt., 1952-62, M. Mack Earle, Balt., 1962-65; v.p. Surface Separator Sys., Balt., 1963-65; naval arch. Exxon Corp., Houston, 1965-86; prin. Walter Devine & Sons, Escondido, Calif., 1986—; project mgr. Exxon, 1968-70, 1976-81, staff mgr., 1981-86. With USNR, 1945-51. Mem. Soc. Naval. Architecture and Marine Engring. (chmn. L.A. sect. 1992-93, chmn. Houstonsect. 1969-70). Roman Catholic. Achievements include patents for design of oil skimmer, design of large ice breaking vessel, design of oil tanker for extreme cold, design of access to pump room from engine room; research in conversion of tanker for oil processing, computer application in underwater inspection. Home & Office: Walter Devine & Sons 3621 Monte Real Escondido CA 92029-7911

DEVITT-GRASSO, PAULINE VIRGINIA, civic volunteer, nurse; b. Salem, Mass., May 13, 1930; d. John M. and Mary Elizabeth (Cologey) Devitt; m. Frank Anthony Grasso, Oct. 26, 1968; 1 stepson, Christopher Anthony. BSN, Boston Coll., 1952; student, Boston U., 1954-55, Boston State Tchrs. Coll., 1953-54. RN. Staff nurse J.P. Kennedy Jr. Meml. Hosp., Brighton, Mass., 1952-53; head nurse, day supr. J.P. Kennedy Jr. Meml. Hosp., Brighton, 1953-54, day supr., 1955, clin. instr., 1955-58, adminstrv. asst., 1968, dir. nursing edn., 1958-68; vis. instr. Boston Coll., Mass. State Coll., Meml. Hosp. Sch. Nursing, Newton, Mass. Meml. Hosp. Sch. Nursing, 1955-68, CUA S of N, 1990; bd. dirs. Behavioral Health Svcs. Inc., treas., 1996. Pres. Project H.O.P.E., Manhattan Beach, Calif., 1982; pres.

adv. coun. Meals on Wheels, Salvation Army, 1989, 90, 91, bd. dirs. Redondo Beach, 1992—, sec. bd. dirs., 1994; cons. Manhattan Beach Housing Found., 1986—, Manhattan Beach Case Mgr., 1982—; mem. adv. coun. South Bay Sr. Svcs., Torrance, Calif., 1986—, pres., 1995—, pres. adv. bd. 1995—; sr. advocate City of Manhattan Beach, 1982; bd. dirs. Ret. Sr. Vol. Program, Torrance, 1986-90; bd. dirs. Behavioral Health Svcs., 1992—, treas. 1996—, hosp. com., fin. com., exec. com.; neighborhood chair Girl Scouts U.S.; mem. Beach City Coun. on Aging, 1983-91; mem. Salvation Army Ladies Aux.; mem. adv. bd. Salvation Army Corps, Redondo Beach. Recipient Cert. of Appreciation, County of L.A., 1988, Vol. of the Yr. award City of Manhattan Beach, 1988, Award of Honor County of L.A., 1989, State of Calif. Senate Rules Com. Resolution Commendation, 1988; named Outstanding Vol. Cath. Daus. of Am., 1986, Vol. of Yr. City Manhattan Beach, 1986-87; Rose and Scroll award Manhattan Beach C. of C., 1989, Art Michel Meml. Community Svc. award Manhattan Beach Rotary Club, 1989, Cert. of Appreciation KC's Queen of Martyrs Coun., 1989, Redondo Beach Lila Bell award Salvation Army, 1989, others, Manhattan Beach Vol. Appreciation award, 1982, 83, 84, 85, 86, 88, 90, 91, 92, 93, cert. South Bay Centinela Credit Union, 1990; nominated for Pres's. Vol. Action award Project H.O.P.E., 1987. Mem. AARP, South Bay Geneal. Soc., New Eng. Hist. and Geneal. Soc., Polish Genal. Soc. So. Calif., Am. Martyrs Altar Soc. (pres. 1983, coun. mem.-at-large 1992), Cath. U. Am. Nat. Alumni Assn. (hon.), Cath. U. Am. Sch. Nursing Alumni Assn. (hon.), Boston Coll. Alumni Assn., Manhattan Beach Sr. Citizens Club (pres. 1985-86, 88-89), Lions (Citizen of Yr. award Manhattan Beach club 1986), DAV (comdr.'s club 1990, 91, 92), Lady in Equestrian Order of Holy Sepulchre of Jerusalem. Democrat. Roman Catholic. Avocations: gardening, needlecraft, genealogy, volunteerism. Home: 329 3rd St Manhattan Beach CA 90266-6410

DEVLIN, CHRISTOPHER MATTHEW, actor, writer, director, producer; b. Pitts., Mar. 1, 1968; s. Robert Raymond Devlin and Nancy Lea (Lenart) Lambert. BS in Mass Comm. magna cum laude, Towson State U., 1990. Appeared in TV shows including The Nanny, 1997, Pensacola, 1998; dir.: (film) Little Red, 1991; playwright: A Cup of Joe, 1997. Mem. SAG, AFTRA, Independent Feature Project, The Theater Group, The Beverly Hills Playhouse. Democrat. Roman Catholic. Avocations: rock climbing, painting, basketball. Home: 2270 Beachwood Dr #11 Hollywood CA 90068

DEVLIN, JAMIE L., interior designer; b. Lebanon, Oreg., Feb. 9, 1952; d. Edward L. and Paula Y. Devlin; m. Thomas A. Sherwood. Grad., South Eugene (Oreg.) H.S., 1970. Staff designer, class instr. Ethan Allen, Portland, Oreg., 1980-85; owner Devlin Designed Interiors, Tigard, Oreg., 1985—. Recipient Golden Home award for best master suite Portland Home Bldrs. Assn., 1995, for best kitchen, 1995. Mem. Am. Soc. Interior Designers (co-chair Symphony Show House 1995). Office: Devlin Designed Interiors 12402 SW Chandler Dr Tigard OR 97224-2827

DEVLIN, MIKE, software company executive. Pres. Rational Software, Cupertino, Calif. Office: Rational Software 18880 Homestead Rd Cupertino CA 95014-0721*

DEVLIN, PATRICIA, lawyer; b. Vallejo, Calif., July 25, 1945. BA magna cum laude, U. Wash., 1968; JD, U. Calif., 1977. Bar: Calif. 1977, Hawaii 1978, U.S. Dist. Ct. Hawaii 1978. With Carlsmith Ball, Honolulu. Mem. ABA, State Bar Calif., Hawaii Soc. Corp. Planners (pres. 1992-93), Phi Beta Kappa. Office: Carlsmith Ball Pacific Tower # 2200 1001 Bishop St Honolulu HI 96813-3429

DEVOE, KENNETH NICKOLAS, food service executive; b. Mineola, N.Y., Sept. 13, 1944; s. Kenneth Pettit and Wykiena (Bos) D.; m. Linda Faye Mizer, May 7, 1965; children: Andrea W., Christina L., Kenneth C., Paula A. Student, Merced Coll., 1970-75. Police sgt. Merced (Calif.) Police Dept., 1966-75; sheriff sgt. Mariposa (Calif.) County Sheriff, 1975-81; pk. mgr. Am. Campgrounds Inc., Bellevue, Wash., 1981-83; owner DeVoe Enterprises, Atwater, Calif., 1983—. Chmn. Merced County Assn. Govts., 1990-98, Atwater 4th of July Com., 1983—; asst. mayor City of Atwater, 1987-94, mayor, 1994-98. With USAF, 1962-66. Mem. Atwater C. of C. (dir. 1991, dir.-at-large 1983-86, Citizen of Yr. 1987), Merced Trade Club (dir. 1991—), Castle Air Force Base Cols. Club., Kiwanis, Masons. Republican. Avocations: coin collecting, community activities. Home: 3302 Sextant Dr Atwater CA 95301-4725 Office: Devoe Enterprises 1898 Bellevue Rd Atwater CA 95301-2668

DEVOE, RICK DANIEL, agent; b. Canoga Park, Calif., Nov. 21, 1968; s. Ron and Wendy Della (Ross) D.; m. Julie Ann Bakken, Sept. 30, 1995; 1 child, Ryder Keegan. AA, Pierce Coll., 1990; BA, San Diego State U., 1995. Shop mgr. Glen Kennedy Surf Shop, Woodland Hills, Calif., 1988-90; concert event coord. Big Dummy Prodns., San Diego, 1991-94; concert promoter, artist mgr. Bill Silva Presents, San Diego, 1994-96; artist mgr. Rick Devoe Mgmt., Cardiff by the Sea, Calif., 1996—; team mgr. Arnette Sunglasses, San Clemente, Calif., 1996-97, Reef Brazil, San Diego, 1997-98. Avocations: surfing, boating, fishing, snowboarding, wake boarding. Office: Rick DeVoe Mgmt 1534 Lake Dr Cardiff By The Sea CA 92007

DE VRIES, KENNETH LAWRENCE, mechanical engineer, educator; b. Ogden, Utah, Oct. 27, 1933; s. Sam and Fern (Slater) DeV.; m. Kay M. McGee, Mar. 1, 1959; children: Kenneth, Susan. AS in Civil Engring., Weber State Coll., 1953; BSME, U. Utah, 1959, PhD in Physics, Mech. Engring., 1962. Registered profl. engr., Utah. Rsch. engr. hydraulic group Convair Aircraft Corp., Fort Worth, 1957-58; prof. dept. mech. engring. U. Utah, Salt Lake City, 1969-75, 1976-91, disting. prof., 1991—, chmn. dept., 1970-81; sr. assoc. dean U. Utah Coll. Engring., Salt Lake City, 1983-97, acting dean, 1997-98; program dir. div. materials rsch. NSF, Washington, 1975-76; materials cons. Browning, Morgan, Utah, 1972—; cons. 3M Co., Mpls., 1985—; tech. adv. bd. Emerson Electric, St. Louis, 1978—; mem. Utah Coun. Sci. and Tech., 1973-77; trustee Gordon Rsch. Conf., 1989-97, chair, 1992-93. Co-author: Analysis and Testing of Adhesive Bonds, 1978; contbr. chpts. to numerous books, articles and abstracts to profl. publs. Fellow ASME, Am. Phys. Soc.; mem. Am. Chem. Soc. (polymer div.), Soc. Engring. Scis. (nat. officer), Adhesion Soc. (nat. officer). Mem. LDS Ch. Office: U Utah Coll Engring 2220 Merrill Engring Bldg Salt Lake City UT 84112

DE VRIES, MARY A., writer; b. Pella, Iowa, Sept. 16, 1937; d. John G. and Anna (Kool) De V. AA, George Washington U., 1957, BA, 1959; postgrad., U. Colo., 1959-60. Editl. asst. Nat. Geog. Mag., Washington, 1957-58; grad. tchg. asst. U. Colo., 1959-60; freelance editor N.J., N.H., Ariz., 1960-85; editor N.C. Jour. and N.C. Scene, 1965-75; writer Sedona, Ariz., 1960—; owner Editl. Svcs., Sedona, 1960—, cons., 1960—. Author: Secretary's Standard Reference Manual and Guide, 1978, Prentice Hall Complete Secretarial Letter Book, 1978, New Century Vest-Pocket Secretary's Handbook, 1980, Guide to Better Business Writing, 1981, Legal Secretary's Encyclopedic Dictionary, 3d edit., 1982, Secretary's Almanac and Fact Book, 1985, Practical Writer's Guide, 1986, Complete Office Handbook, 1987, New American Handbook of Letter Writing, 1988, Office Sourcebook, 1989, New Robert's Rules of Order, 1989, 2d edit., 1998, New American Dictionary of Abbreviations, 1991, Complete Word Book, 1991, Prentice Hall Style Manual, 1992, Prentice Hall Complete Book of Model Letters, Memos and Forms, 1992, Legal Secretary's Complete Handbook, 4th edit., 1992, Complete Secretary's Handbook, 7th edit., 1993, Complete Office Handbook, 1993, Professional Secretary's Encyclopedic Dictionary, 5th edit., 1994, Internationally Yours: Writing and Communicating Successfully in Today's Global Marketplace, 1994, How to Run a Meeting, 1994, Elements of Correspondence, 1995, Professional Secretary's Book of Lists & Tips, 1996, Business Thesaurus, 1996, Encyclopedic Dictionary of Business Terms, 1997, New American Three-Step Vocabulary Builder, 1998, Business Writer's Book if Lists, 1998, Encyclopedic Dictionary of Style and Usage, 1999; editor: The Practical Impact of Numerical Control, 1966, NC—A Vehicle for Progress, 1967, Tomorrow's Technology Today, 1968, From Tape to Time Sharing, 1969, Management's Key to the Seventies, 1970, Management Guide to NC, 1971, The Opening Door to Productivity and Profit, 1971, The Expanding World of NC, 1972, NC/CAM-Profits for the 70s, 1973, The International Future of NC/CAM, 1974. Mem. AARP, PETA, Nat. Human Soc. of U.S., Author's League Am., Alpha Phi. Avocations: painting, hiking, arts and crafts.

DEW, WILLIAM WALDO, JR., bishop; b. Newport, Ky., Dec. 14, 1935; s. William Waldo and Thelma (Dittus) D.; m. Mae Marie Eggers, Jan. 5, 1958; children: Linda Dew-Hiersoux, William, Marilyn. BA, Union Coll., Barbourville, Ky., 1957; MDiv, Drew Theol. Sch., 1961; PhD (hon.), Rust Coll., 1991, Union Coll., 1992. Ordained to ministry United Meth. Ch. as deacon, 1958, as elder, 1963. Pastor Springville (Calif.) United Meth. Ch., 1961-64, Lindsay (Calif.) United Meth. Ch., 1964-67, Meml. United Meth. Ch., Clovis, Calif., 1967-72, Epworth United Meth. Ch., Berkeley, Calif., 1972-79; dist. supt. Cen. Dist. Calif.-Nev. Annual Conf., Modesto, Calif., 1979-84; pastor San Ramon Valley United Meth. Ch., Alamo, Calif., 1984-88; bishop United Meth. Ch., Portland, Oreg., 1988-96, United Meth. Ch. Desert S.W. Conf., Phoenix, 1996—; lectr. Pacific Sch. Religion, Berkeley, 1976-79. Trustee Willamette U., Salem, Oreg., 1988-96, Alaska Pacific U., Anchorage, 1988-96, Claremont Sch. Theology, 1996—. Paul Harris fellow Rotary Internat., 1988. Democrat. Avocations: fishing, golf, reading, travel. Office: United Meth Desert Southwest Conf 1550 E Meadowbrook Ave # 200 Phoenix AZ 85014-4040*

DEWALL-OWENS, KAREN MARIE, marketing consultant; b. Phoenix, May 31, 1943; d. Merle C. and Agnes M. (Larson) Feller; m. Charles E. DeWall, Sept. 3, 1963 (div. Feb. 1988); 1 child, Leslie Karen; m. John Dailor Owens, Apr. 16, 1995. AA, Phoenix Coll., 1969. Media buyer Wade Advt., Sacramento, 1964-66; media dir., Harwood Advt., Phoenix, 1967-71; co-owner, account exec. DeWall & Assocs. Advt. Co., 1971-87; dir. advt. Auto Media, Inc./Automotive Investment Group, Phoenix, 1987-93; owner Karen & Co. Advt., Phoenix, 1993—. Sustaining mem. Jr. League of Phoenix; mem. adv. bd. Heritage Sq., City of Phoenix. Named Ad-2 Advt. Person of Yr., Phoenix, 1984. Mem. Am. Women in Radio and TV (achievement award 1986), Phoenix Union Alumni Assn. (pres. 1997—). Republican. Home: 10847 N 11th St Phoenix AZ 85020-5836 Office: Karen & Co Advt 10847 N 11th St Phoenix AZ 85020-5836

DEWEY, DONALD WILLIAM, magazine publisher, editor, writer; b. Honolulu, Sept. 30, 1933; s. Donald William and Theckla Jean (Engeborg) D.; m. Sally Rae Ryan, Aug. 7, 1961; children: Michael Kevin, Wendy Ann. Student, Pomona Coll., 1953-55. With Pascoe Steel Corp., Pomona, Calif., 1955-56, div. Reynolds Aluminum Co., Los Angeles, 1956-58, Switzer Panel Corp., Pasadena, Calif., 1958-60; sales and gen. mgr. Western Pre-Cast Concrete Corp., Ontario, Calif., 1960-62; editor, pub. R/C Modeler Mag., Sierra Madre, Calif., 1963—, Freshwater and Marine Aquarium Mag., Sierra Madre, 1978—; pres., chmn. bd. R/C Modeler Corp., Sierra Madre, 1963—. Author: Radio Control From the Ground Up, 1970, Flight Training Course, 1973, For What It's Worth, Vol. 1, 1973, Vol. 2, 1975; contbr. articles to profl. jours. Sustaining mem. Rep. Nat. Com., 1981—; charter mem. Nat. Congl. Club, 1981—; mem. Rep. Presdl. Task Force, 1981—, U.S. Senatorial Club, 1983—, 1984 Presdl. Trust, Conservative Caucus, Nat. Tax Limitation Com., Nat. Conservative Polit. Action Com., Ronald Reagan Presdl. Libr. Served with Hosp. Corps, USN, 1951-55. Mem. Acad. Model Aeronautics, Nat. Aeronautic Assn.,. Republican. Lutheran. Home: 410 W Montecito Ave Sierra Madre CA 91024-1716 Office: 144 W Sierra Madre Blvd Sierra Madre CA 91024-2435

DEWHURST, WILLIAM GEORGE, psychiatrist, educator, research director; b. Frosterley, Durham, Eng., Nov. 21, 1926; came to Can., 1969; s. William and Elspeth Leslie (Begg) D.; m. Margaret Dransfield, Sept. 17, 1960; children—Timothy Andrew, Susan Jane. B.A., Oxford U., Eng., 1947, B.M., B.Ch., 1950; MA, Oxford U., 1961; D.P.M. with distinction, London U., 1961. House physician, surgeon London Hosp., 1950-52, jr. registrar, registrar, 1954-58; registrar, sr. registrar Maudsley Hosp., London, 1958-62, cons. physician, 1965-69; lectr. Inst. Psychiatry, London, 1962-64, sr. lectr., 1965-69; assoc. prof. psychiatry U. Alta., Edmonton, Can., 1969-72, prof., 1972-92, prof. emeritus, 1992—, Hon. prof. pharmacy and pharm. scis., 1979-97, chmn. dept. psychiatry, 1975-90, dir. emeritus neurochem. rsch. unit, 1990—, hon. prof. oncology, 1983-97, chmn. med. staff adv. bd., 1988-90; mem. Atty. Gen. Alta. Bd. Rev., 1991, N.W.T. Bd. Rev., 1992-98, 95 Yukon Bd. Rev., 1994-98; pres.'s coun. U. Alta. Hosps., 1988-90, quality improvement coun., 1988-90, ethics consultative com., 1984-88, planning com. Vision 2000, 1985-87, hos ps.' planning com. and joint conf. com., 1971, 80, 87-90; cons. psychiatrist Royal Alexandra Hosp., Edmonton, Edmonton Gen. Hosp., Alberta Hosp., Ponoka, Ponoka Gen. Hosp.; chmn. med. coun. Can. Test Com., 1977-79, Royal Coll. Text Com. in Psychiatry, 1971-80, examiner, 1975-83. Co-editor: Neurobiology of Trace Amines, 1984, Pharmacotherapy of Affective Disorders, 1985; also conf. procs. Referee Nature, Can. Psychiat. Assn. Jour., Brit. Jour. Psychiatry; mem. editorial bd. Neuropsychobiology, Psychiat. Jour. U. Ottawa. Contbr. over 100 articles to profl. jours. Chmn. Edmonton Psychiat. Svcs. Steering Com., 1977-80; chmn. Edmonton Psychiat. Svcs. Planning Com., 1985-90; mem. Provincial Mental Health Adv. Coun., 1973-79, Mental Health Rsch. Com., 1973, Edmonton Bd. Health, 1974-76; Can. Psychiat. Rsch. Found., 1985— (also bd. dirs.); bd. dirs. Friends of Schizophrenics, 1980—, Alta., 1988; grant referee Health & Welfare Can., Med. Rsch. Coun. Can., Ont. Mental Health Found., Man. Health Rsch. Coun., B.C. Health Rsch. Found. Capt. Royal Army M.C., 1952-54. Fellow Can. Coll. Neuropsychopharmacology (pres. 1982-84, Coll. medal 1993), Am. Psychopathol. Assn., Am. Coll. Psychiatrists, Am. Psychiat. Assn., Royal Coll. Psychiatrist; mem. AAAS, Alta. Psychiat. Assn. (pres. 1973-74), Can. Psychiat. Assn. (pres. 1983-84), Alta Coll. Physicians and Surgeons, Alta. Med. Assn. (nominating coun. 1992-93, health issues coun. 1994-98, co-chmn. task force on drug info., 1996-98), Child and Adolescent Assn. (bd. dirs., v.p. 1992, pres. 1994-98), Assn. for Acad. Psychiatry, Brit. Med. Assn., Faculty Club. Anglican. Avocations: music, hockey, football, chess, athletics.

DEWITT, BARBARA JANE, journalist; b. Glendale, Calif., Aug. 5, 1947; d. Clarence James and Irene Brezina; m. Don DeWitt, Apr. 21, 1974; children: Lisa, Scarlett. BA in Journalism, Calif. State U., Northridge, 1971. Features editor The Daily Ind. Newspaper, Ridgecrest, Calif., 1971-84; fashion editor The Daily Breeze, Torrance, Calif., 1984-89; freelance fashion reporter The Seattle Times, 1990; fashion editor, columnist The Los Angeles Daily News, L.A., 1990—; instr. fashion writing UCLA, 1988, Am. Inter-Continental U., L.A., 1996—. Dir. Miss Indian Wells Valley Scholarship Pageant, 1980-84. Recipient 1st Pl. Best Youth Page, Calif. Newspaper Pubs. Assn., 1980, 1st Pl. Best Fashion, Wash. Press Assn., 1989, The Internat. Aldo award for fashion journalism, 1995, 96. Republican. Lutheran. Avocations: antiques, reading, swimming. Office: The Daily News 21221 Oxnard St Woodland Hills CA 91367-5081

DEWITT, LONNIE FAUSTINO, writer; b. El Centro, Calif., Jan. 4, 1947; s. James DeWitt and Alice Lee (Harris) Combs; m. Ruthie Louise Thorn, Apr. 13, 1968; children: Kenslo, Lonnie Jr., Shanei. AS, Victor Valley Coll., 1983; AA, U. Md., 1986, BS, 1986. Commd. USAF, 1965, advanced through grades to first sgt., ret., 1988; hotel mgr. Sequoia Hotel, Sacramento, 1988-89; officer Calif. Dept. Corrections-Folsom State Prison, 1989-92; parole agt. Calif. Dept. Corrections, San Jose, 1992-94; pvt. practice RLD Enerprise, Sacramento, 1994—; exec. sec., reports technician Fed. Emergency Mgmt. Agy., Rancho Cordova, Calif., 1997; area svc. rep. Gov.'s Office Emergency Svcs., Rancho Cordova, 1997-98. Author: iN tHE cAR, 1998. Mentor Ct. Apptd. Spl. Adv., Sacramento, 1996, People Reaching Out, Sacramento, 1998. Mem. Sacramento Pubs. Assn. Democrat. Baptist. Avocations: writing, mentoring. E-mail: lonnie@inthecar.com. Fax: (916) 422-4246. Home: 7513 Monte Brazil Dr Sacramento CA 95831-4649 Office: RLD Enterprise PO Box 22765 Sacramento CA 95822-0765

DEWITT-ROGERS, JOHARI MARILYN, community college administrator; b. Montgomery, Ala., Jan. 28, 1950; d. Rufus Birchard and Mary Lease (Borders) DeWitt; m. Paul Sabu Rogers, Dec. 21, 1976; children: Malachi Omari, Kofi Ayinde. BS, Howard U., Washington, 1971, MEd, 1973; postgrad., U. So. Calif., 1980-83. Abstractor APA, Washington, 1971-72; media technician San Diego Unified Schs., 1974-75; media coord. L.A. Regional Family Planning, 1975-79; asst. producer KABC TV News, 1979-80; dir. audio visual svcs. U. So. Calif. Dental Sch., 1979-81; dir. media Pasadena (Calif.) City Coll., 1987—; cons. City of Pasadena, 1991-92. Author: (play) All That Glitters, 1989. Sec. Linda Vista PTA, 1991, v.p., 1992; pres. Sch. Site Coun., 1992, 93, 94. Recipient Paragon award Nat. Coun. Mktg. and Pub. Rels., New Orleans, 1990, Pro award Calif. Assn. C.C., 1990. Mem. Am. Assn. Women in Colls. and Jr. Colls. (chpt. pres. 1992-93), Assn. Calif. Community Coll. Adminstrs. (mentor program 1992), Dirs. Ednl. Tech. in Calif. Higher Edn., Delta Sigma Theta. African Methodist Episcopal. Avocations: reading, theatre, travel, crafts, crossword puzzles. Office: Pasadena City Coll 1570 E Colorado Blvd Pasadena CA 91106-2003

DE WREEDE, CLARICE EVANS, retired special education educator; b. East St. Louis, Ill., July 12, 1928; d. Cecil Field and Clara Helen (Kindsvater) Evans; m. Harry Richard Schoen, June 21, 1947 (div. 1964); children: Richard Evans, Sara Diane, William Francis; m. John De Wreede, Mar. 29, 1967 (dec. 1986). BA cum laude, Mich. State U., 1964; postgrad., U. Mich., 1966-67, Santa Clara U., 1973. Tchr. Grand Rapids (Mich.) Sch. Dist., 1963-67; tchr. counselor for physically handicapped Kent County Edn. Dist., Grand Rapids, 1967-71; tchr. of deaf Union Sch. Dist., San Jose, Calif., 1971-88; home-tchr. of deaf East Side Union High Sch. Dist., San Jose, 1991. Mem. DAR (John Mitchell chpt. Anchorage), Daus. of Am. Colonists (Ala. chpt.), Am. Hist. Soc. of Germans from Russia (Golden Gate chpt. sec. 1990—), Calif. Assn for Tchrs. of Hearing-Impaired, Internat. Assn. Cancer Victors and Friends (nat. bd. govs. 1990—), South Bay Scottish Soc. Genealogy (chmn. 1991—), Santa Clara County Hist. and Geneal. Soc. (cons. in libr. genealogy room, chmn. family newsletter 1980—), Daus. of 1812 (David Farragut chpt. Santa Clara County, Calif.). Democrat. Lutheran. Avocations: aerobic dancing, tennis, Scottish country dancing. Address: 2296 Whitaker Dr Kearns UT 84118-1683

DEY, CAROL RUTH, secondary education educator; b. N.Y., Mar. 9, 1943; d. Robert Lewis Adelson and Anne Millman; m. John Peter Dey, Feb. 9, 1968 (div. Feb. 1978). AA, San Bernardino Valley Coll., 1965; BA, Calif. State U., Sacramento, 1969; MBA, Calif. State U., San Bernardino, 1983, postgrad., 1994-95. Sec. U.S. Dept of Interior, USAF, Retail Industry, San Bernardino, Sacramento, Calif., 1960-80; logistics mgr. USAF, San Bernardino, 1980-94; substitute tchr. San Bernardino Unified Sch. Dist., 1994—, Inland Empire Job Corp. Ctr., 1997—. Dancer Coppélia, San Bernardino, Calif., 1984; mem. St. Anne's Ch., San Bernardino, 1978—. Mem. Am. Bus. Women's Assn. (Calif. State Coll. scholar), Smithsonian Inst., AF Assn., Alumni Assn. Calif. State U. San Bernardino. Republican. Roman Catholic. Avocations: ballet, piano, sewing, cooking, singing.

DIAMA, BENJAMIN, retired educator, artist, composer, writer; b. Hilo, Hawaii, Sept. 23, 1933; s. Agapito and Catalina (Buscas) D. *Benjamin Diama's parents were early immigrants from Cebu in The Philippines. In 1922, they sailed on the Tenya Maru to Hawaii seeking a better livelihood and employment in the Sugar Plantation of Hawaii. In addition to the strong faith instilled in them by their Catholic-Christian heritage and education, their American freedom and opportunities also played a significant role in their ability to establish and operate several successful businesses on Mamo Street in downtown Hilo, Hawaii. However, the 1960 Tidal Wave destroyed businesses; but fortunately, they could operate another Billiard Business before they retired, on Mamo Street.* BFA, Sch. Art Inst. Chgo., 1956. Cert. tchr., Hawaii. Tchr. art, basketball coach Waimea (Kauai, Hawaii) High Sch., 1963-67; tchr. music and art Campbell High Sch., Honolulu, 1967-68; tchr. math. and art Waipahu High Sch., Honolulu, 1968-69; tchr. art and music Palisades Elem. Sch., Honolulu, 1969-70; tchr. typing, history, art and music Honokaa (Hawaii) High Sch., 1970-73; tchr. music Kealakehe Sch., Kailua, 1973-74; ret., 1974. Author, writer, composer: Hawaii, 1983; author: Poems of Faith, 1983-88, School One vs. School Two On The Same School Campus, 1983, The Calendar-Clock Theory of the Universe with Faith Above and Beyond, 1984-90, Phonetic Sound—Musical Theory, 1990; contbr. author to book: Benjamin Diama -- The Calendar Clock Theory of the Universe, 1991, 92; producer, composer (Cassette) Hawaii I Love You, 1986; inventor universal clock, 1984, double floater boat, 1985. Recipient Achievement award Waimea Dept. Edn., 1964-67, Purchase award State Found. Arts on Culture and the Arts, 1984, State Found. Arts and Culture Acquisition Painting Art award State of Hawaii Govt. Art Collection. Mem. NEA, Hawaii Tchrs. Assn., Hawaii Edn. Assn., AAAS, Nat. Geog. Soc., Smithsonian Assocs., ASCAP, N.Y. Acad. Scis., Nat. Libr. Poetry (assoc.), Internat. Soc. Poets, Am. Geophysical Union. Mem. Salvation Army. Avocations: singing, writing science, coaching basketball. Home: PO Box 2997 Kailua Kona HI 96745-2997

DIAMOND, RICHARD, secondary education educator; b. N.Y.C., June 23, 1936; s. Oscar and Frieda (Rosenfeld) D.; m. Donna Jean Berkshire Wilson, June 14, 1961 (div. June 1974); m. Betty Ruth Jane Foster, Nov. 17, 1975; children: Thomas, Laura, Rick, Jeff. BA, U. Calif., Berkeley, 1958. Cert. tchr., Calif. Tchr. Riverside (Calif.) Unified Schs., 1959-67, 73—, coord. social studies, 1967-69, program dir. compensatory edn., 1969-72, attendance officer, 1972-73; author curriculum programs Afro-Am. history and Chicano studies, 1968; developer law and youth H.S. course, 1978, track coach, 1975-88. Contbr. articles and photographs to profl. jours. Co-creator nationally recognized h.s. vol. program, h.s. svc. learning coord., 1995—; mem. Riverside County Hist. Commn., 1997—; Dem. Party worker, 1964-72; Rep. Party worker, 1992—; historic commn. liaison Riverside County Archives Commn., 1998—. Named Social Studies Tchr. of Yr., Inland Empire Social Studies Assn., 1980, Tchr. of Yr., Arlington H.S., Riverside, 1992; recipient hon. svc. award Dist. Coun. PTA, Riverside, 1993, Johnny Harris Youth Action award City of Riverside,, 1998. Mem. NEA, Calif. Tchrs. Assn., Riverside County Tchrs. Assn. Presbyterian. Avocations: gardening, travel, reading, woodworking. E-mail: ddiamond@ix.metcom.com. Office: Arlington HS 2951 Jackson St Riverside CA 92503-5732

DIAMOND, ROBERT FRANCIS, federal agency administrator; b. N.Y.C., Oct. 1, 1951; s. Francis Gerard and Evelyn Marie (Metz) D.; m. Evelyn Conty, Oct. 3, 1982; children: Kevin Richard, Angela Renee, Diane Conty. BS, SUNY, Stony Brook, 1973; MBA, So. Ill. U., 1977. Pers. mgmt. specialist U.S. Army Tng. Ctr., Ft. Dix, N.J., 1974-78; position classification specialist Chief Naval Ops., Washington, 1978-82; pers. mgmt. specialist European region Office Civilian Pers. Mgmt., London, 1982-86; supr. pers. mgmt. specialist Naval Aviation Depot, Alameda, Calif., 1986-88; position classification specialist Gen. Svcs. Adminstrn., San Francisco, 1988-89; supr. pers. mgmt. specialist chief ops. div. Consolidated Civilian Pers. Office, Yokosuka, Japan, 1989-92; pers. mgr. Def. Contract Mgmt. Dist. West, El Segundo, Calif., 1992-97, mgmt. analyst, 1997—. Mem. Beta Gamma Sigma. Roman Catholic. Avocations: skiing, travel, politics, reading.

DIAMOND, STANLEY JAY, lawyer; b. Los Angeles, Nov. 27, 1927; s. Philip Alfred and Florence (Fadem) D.; m. Lois Jane Broida, June 22, 1969; children: Caryn Elaine, Diana Beth. B.A., UCLA, 1949; J.D., U. So. Calif., 1952. Bar: Calif. 1953. Practiced law Los Angeles, 1953—; dep. Office of Calif. Atty. Gen., Los Angeles, 1953; ptnr. Diamond & Tilem, Los Angeles, 1957-60, Diamond, Tilem & Colden, Los Angeles, 1960-79, Diamond & Wilson, Los Angeles, 1979—; lectr. music and entertainment law UCLA; Mem. nat. panel arbitrators Am. Arbitration Assn. Bd. dirs. Los Angeles Suicide Prevention Center, 1971-76. Served with 349th Engr. Constrn. Bn. AUS, 1945-47. Mem. ABA, Calif. Bar Assn., Los Angeles County Bar Assn., Beverly Hills Bar Assn., Am. Judicature Soc., Calif. Copyright Conf., Nat. Acad. Rec. Arts and Scis., Zeta Beta Tau, Nu Beta Epsilon. Office: 12304 Santa Monica Blvd 3d Fl Los Angeles CA 90025-2551

DIAMOND, STEPHEN EARLE MICHAEL, investor, consultant, inventor; b. San Francisco, Dec. 2, 1944; s. Earl Conrad and Sally (Gonzales) D. Pvt. study music and drama, 1956-65; grad., Ft. Sam Houston Army Med. Sch., 1964; Cert. computer sci. programmer, Elkins Coll. Nat. Career Inst., 1969; PhD, World Acad. Assn., 1994; DMS, London Inst. Applied Rsch., 1994, LLD (hon.), 1995. Exec. dir. Gondia Corp., San Francisco, 1973-76, exec. chmn., 1976-78; chief exec. officer G.C.I. C'ies, San Francisco, 1978-80, chief adminstrv. officer, 1980-85; owner S.E. Diamond Founds., San Francisco, 1985-86, S.E. Diamond Assn., San Francisco, 1986—, The Dover Rd. Inn Group, 1990—; prof. neurophysics, life fellow Australian Inst. Coordinated Rsch., 1994. Discoverer in field, inventor; patentee in field; contbr articles to profl. jours.; assoc. prodr. Nat. Empowerment TV, 1992; author: Architeture Engineering, 1976—, Treatise on Cures and Treatments, 70 vols., 1971—; creator/designer monetary invention, others; originator, orator, writer The Actual 2,000,000 Words Vocabulary 1970-96; co-prodr., prin. narrator (TV mini-series) The Royal Genealogy, 1997—. Leader 5th

Congl. dist. Strategic Def. Initiative, chmn. high frontier def. com. 5th-8th Congl. dists. west region, 1989; active Am. Inst. Cancer Rsch., 1981—; charter founder Ronald Reagan Rep. Ctr., Washington, 1987; state advisor U.S. Congl. adv. bd., Washington and San Francisco, 1983-86; hon. charter mem. St. Mary's Hosp., San Francisco, 1988; friend San Francisco Symphony Orch., 1980—; founding mem. Am. Space Frontier Com., Falls Church, 1984-86, Challenger Space Ctr., 1987—, Am. Air Mus., Duxbury, Eng., 1994—; sponsor, prodr. Concerned Women for Am., 1984—; mem. world planning coun. WWII Victory 50th Anniversary Events, 1992—; charter mem. Citizens Against Govt. Waste, 1991—; charter mem. Rep. Nat. Commn. on Am. Agenda; founding charter mem. Normandy D-Day Mus., Caen, France, 1990—; charter founding mem. USN Meml. U.S.A. Washington Dist., 1989; charter founder mem. Nat. Com. to Preserve Social Security; mem. nat. gov. bd. U.S. Olympic Com. Shooting Team, 1994. Recipient merit award Rep. Nat. Com., 1984, merit award Rep. Party, 1985, Achievement award United Inventors and Scientists, L.A., 1975, Editor's Choice award Nat. Poetry Contest, 1995, 96; decorated Knight Comdr. Lofsensic Ursinius Orden, Knight Grand Cross Order of Saints Peter & Paul, 1996, Knight Templar, 1996; titled Count San Ciriaco, Italy, Lord Camster Burn Estate, Argylshire, Scotland, Baron Royal Order of Boheme, Duke Hay-on-Wye Castle Herefordshire, Eng., Lord Royal forest of the Peak Gotham Gate Estate, Derbyshire, Eng.; Capt. Legion de le Aisle de le Mer, The Netherlands, 1995. Mem. Nat. Small Bus. Assn., Nat. Taxpayers Union, Statue of Liberty and Ellis Island Found. (charter), Presdl. Task Force (charter), Clan Morrison Soc. (life active), North Shore Animal League, Internat. Affairs Inst. Paris, Internat. Cult. Corr. Inst. India, Academie Francoise, Maison Internat., Des Intellectuelles, M.I.D.I., A.M.U., Munich, Germany, 1994. Republican. Avocations: direct pedigree genealogy, ambidextrous athletics. Office: PO Box 246 South Lake Tahoe CA 96156-0246

DIAMONDS, BLANCA MARIA, mental health counselor; b. Havana, Cuba, Apr. 1, 1944; came to U.S., 1962; d. Mario Vicente and Josefa Basilisa (Suardiaz) Perés; 1 child, Neil Armstrong. BSN, U. Mo., 1968. Lic. realtor. Student nurse asst. med. surgical U. Mo., Columbia, 1963-67; student nurse, psychiat. nursing, head nurse Mid Mo. Mental Health Ctr., Columbia, 1966-68; med. surgical nurse Kuakini Hosp., St. Francis Hosp., Honolulu, 1969—; front office nurse Clay Barton & Thomas Smith, Gardena, Calif., 1971-72; nursing dir. Del Amo Hosp., Torrance, Calif., 1972-74; v.p., sec. Dewhurst Med. Corp., Torrance, 1975-91; mental health counselor Los Angeles County, L.A., 1991; realtor Amber Realty, 1995-96, Bankers Realty, Redondo Beach, Calif., 1996—, Moore & Assocs. Realtors, Torrance, Hermosa Beach; founder Cassiopeia Enterprises, Rollings Hills Estates, Calif.; nurse cons. to various profls., 1975—. Mental Health Student Nurse award U. Mo., 1966. Mem. L.A. World Affairs Coun., Wilson Ctr. Assocs., Nat. Trust for Historic Preservation, Nat. History Mus., Smithsonian Inst., Humane Soc. U.S. Democrat. Avocations: music, theater, target shooting, studying and maintaining exotic reptiles. Home: PO Box 1692 Redondo Beach CA 90278-0792

DIAZ, RAMON VALERO, retired judge; b. Manila, Oct. 13, 1918; came to Guam, 1951; s. Vicente and Bibiana (Valero) D.; m. Josefina Dela Concepcion, July 3, 1945; children: Marilu, Mariles, Maribel, Marilen, Maryann, Anthony, Vincent, Ramon, Maricar. PhB, U. St. Tomas, Manila, 1940, LLB, 1941; grad. U.S. Army J.A.G. Sch., 1945; Diploma Jud. Skills, Am. Acad. Jud. Edn., 1984. Bar: Philippines 1941, Guam 1956, U.S. Ct. Appeals (9th cir.) 1966, High Ct. of Trust Territories 1977, No. Marianas 1985. Assoc. Diokno Law Office, Manila, 1943-44; pvt. practice, Guam, 1960-80; judge Superior Ct. of Guam, Agana, 1980-94; ret. 1994; mem. U.S. Selective Service Bd. Appeals, Guam, 1950-62. Permanent deacon Roman Catholic Ch. Judge Adv. Gen.'s Svc., Philippine Army, 1941-51. Mem. Am. Judges Assn., Nat. Council Juvenile and Family Ct. Judges, VFW II and POW. Survivor Bataan Death March, 1942. Home: PO Box 22978 Barrigada GU 96921-2978

DIAZ-ZUBIETA, AGUSTIN, nuclear engineer, executive; b. Madrid, Spain, Mar. 24, 1936; came to U.S., 1953; s. Emilio Diaz Cabeza and Maria Teresa Zubieta Atucha; m. Beth Lee Fortune, Sept. 6, 1958; children: Walter Agustin, Michael Joel, Anthony John. B, U. Madrid, 1953; BSc in Physics, U. Tenn., 1958; MSc in Mech. Engring., Duke U., 1960; PhD in Nuclear Engring., U. Md., 1981. Nuclear engr. Combustion Engring., Tenn., 1954-58; instr. engring. Duke U., Durham, N.C., 1958-60; nuclear physicist Allis Chalmers Co., Washington, 1960-64; country mgr. South Africa Allis Chalmers Co., 1964-66; mgr. internat. power generation projects GE, N.Y.C., 1966-69, mgr. Europe and Middle East strategic planning, 1969-71; dir. internat. constrn. planning GE, Westport, Conn., 1971-75, dir. constrn., 1975-83; chief exec. officer GE Affiliate, Westport, 1983-87; v.p. internat. sales, devel. Internat. Tech. Corp., L.A., 1987-94; mng. dir. IT Italia S.P.A., IT Spain, S.A. Author: Measurement of Subcriticality of Nuclear Reactors by Stocastic Processes, 1981. Pres. Fairfield (Conn.) Assn. Condo Owners, 1983-87. Named Astronomer of Yr. Barnard Astronomical Soc., Chattanooga, 1957; fgn. exchange scholar U.S. Govt., 1953-58; grantee, NSF, 1958-60, U.S. Office of Ordinance Rsch. U.S. Army, 1958-60. Mem. Am. Nuclear Soc., Am. Soc. Mech. Engrs., Am. Soc. Profl. Engrs., Sigma Xi. Republican. Roman Catholic. Avocations: golf, tennis, swimming, sailing, music. Home: 47 Country Meadow Rd Rolling Hills Estates CA 90274

DIBBLE, SUZANNE LOUISE, nurse, researcher; b. Pittsburg, Calif., June 3, 1947; d. Charles Stanley and Evelyn Virginia (Hansen) D.; m. Myron Bottsford Palmer III, June 12, 1971 (div. July 1974); life ptnr. Jeanne Flyntz DeJoseph, 1984. BSN, U. Del., 1969; MSN, U. Calif., San Francisco, 1971, D Nursing Sci., 1986. RN, Del., Calif. Staff nurse emergency room Stanford (Calif.) U. Hosp., 1969-71, rschr. dept. nursing rsch., 1986-88; instr. med. and surg. nursing Stanford U., 1971-72, renal transplant nurse coord., 1972-73, nurse rschr. dept. diagnostic radiology, 1987-88; staff, charge, head nurse, then supr. Children's Hosp.-Stanford U., 1973-86; mem. faculty stats. dept. U. Phoenix, San Jose, Calif., 1985-92; pres. Data Mgmt. Assocs., San Carlos, Calif., 1985—; investigator, project dir. U. Calif., 1988—; rsch. grant cons. NIH, Oakland, Calif., 1992-94, Loma Linda (Calif.) U., 1995—; manuscript reviewer Oncology Nursing Forum, Pitts., 1993-96, Med.-Surg. Nursing, Pittmn, N.J., 1994—. Editor: Culture and Nursing Care, 1996; contbr. articles to nursing jours. Chmn. task force, mem. NOW, Palo Alto, Calif., 1978—; mem., chmn. Maternal, Child and Adolescent Health Bd., San Mateo County, Calif., 1987-90; mem. strategic planning com. San Mateo County Health Bd., 1989-90. Rsch. grantee Nat. Cancer Inst., 1992-97, Nat. Inst. for Nursing Rsch., 1994-99. Mem. ANA, Assn. for Care Children's Health (numerous offices), Oncology Nursing Soc. (numerous offices), Am. Statis. Assn., Sigma Theta Tau (pres. Alpha Eta chpt.). Democrat. Office: U Calif Box 0646 Inst Health & Aging San Francisco CA 94143-0646

DIBIETZ, ERICA MARGRETHE, cultural psychologist, educator; b. N.Y.C., Nov. 2, 1935; d. August and Elizabeth (Hutka) DiBietz; B.A., Columbia U., 1955; M.S.W. (John F. Kennedy fellow), U. Md., 1976, PhD in Human Devel., 1993; children: Regina Antunes Dufresne, Lisette Antunes Serra, Alexander Antunes. Asst. to sec. for trust and estate law Trust div. N.Y. State Bankers Assn., N.Y.C., 1956-59; tchr. child life and pediatrics Johns Hopkins Hosp., Balt., 1973-74; med. social worker John F. Kennedy Inst. Habilitation of Children, Balt., 1974-75; dir. spl. programs Md. Dept. Health and Mental Hygiene, Springfield Hosp. Center, Sykesville, Md., 1977-85, co-founder, first Family support group in state psychiatric hosp. AMI, 1979-82, dir. spl. population programs, developed and implemented first inpatient psychiatric program for deaf and hearing impaired, chmn. staff devel. com., 1978-79, spl. asst. to asst. secretariat, 1985-87, mem. patient adv. coms. Md. Atty. Gen.'s Office, 1979-83; mem. continuing edn. com. U. Md., 1978-80; coordinator human rights adv. com. Springfield Hosp., chmn. unit for deaf psychiat. patients steering com., Health and Mental Hygiene, 1983-92; spl. asst. to the secretariat Mental Health, Devel. Disabilities, Drug and Alcohol Prevention Adminstrn.; chief divsn. for dual diagnosis Mental Hygiene Adminstrn., 1987-93; cert. trainer addiction severity index V.A. Ctr. for Addiction Studies U. Pa., 1990—; dir. South Kachemak, Inc. Alcoholism Program, Seldovia, Alaska, 1994; pvt. practice Alaska; resource tech. & rsch. libr. Susan B. English Sch., 1997—; cons. dual diagnoses; cons. Regional Ctr. for Alcoholism and Other Addictions, Fairbanks, Alaska, 1996; Balt. Am. Indian Ctr., Inc., 1990-93, Family Svcs. for Deaf, Balt., 1992-93; biopsychosocial trainer N.E. Tex. Ctrs., Phila. and Del., 1993; adj. faculty mem. Md. State Office Edn. and Tng. for Addiction Svcs., 1989-92, Carroll County C.C., Westminster, Md., 1993; mem. curriculum com., field instr. Sch. S.W. U. Md., 1979-83. Mem. women's com. Balt. Symphony Orch., 1965-69; founder Dulaney Symphony Soc., 1968; del. public edn. nominating conv. Baltimore County Bd. Edn., 1977-78. HEW grantee, 1974. Mem. Am. Psychol. Assn. Episcopalian. Author works in field. Home: PO Box 263 Seldovia AK 99663-0263

DIBLE, ROSE HARPE MCFEE, special education educator; b. Phoenix, Apr. 28, 1927; d. Ambrose Jefferson and Laurel Mabel (Harpe) McFee; m. James Henry Dible, June 23, 1951 (div. Jan. 1965); 1 child, Michael James. BA in Speech Edn., Ariz. State U., Tempe, 1949; MA in Speech and Drama, U. So. Calif., L.A., 1950; fellow, Calif. State U., Fullerton, 1967. Cert. secondary tchr., spl. edn. tchr. English and drama tchr. Lynwood (Calif.) Sr. High Sch., 1950-51, Montebello (Calif.) Sr. High Sch., 1952-58; tchr. English and Social Studies Pioneer High Sch., Whittier, Calif., 1964-65; spl. edn. tchr. Bell Gardens (Calif.) High Sch., 1967-85, spl. edn. cons., 1985-90. Mem. DAR, Daus. Am. Colonists, Whittier Christian Woman Assn., La Habra Womans Club, Eastern Star Lodge, Kappa Delts, Phi Delta Gamma. Republican. Presbyterian. Avocations: church choir, tap dancing, doll collecting, travel. Home: 1201 Russell St La Habra CA 90631-2530 Office: Montebello Unified Sch Dist 123 Montebello Blvd Montebello CA 90640

DIBOS, DIANNE LOUISE, financial analyst; b. Elyria, Ohio, May 17, 1968; d. Ronald Eugene and Jan Melody (Gorbach) Leshinski; m. George Merwin Dibos, Mar. 26, 1994. BS, U. Dayton, 1990, MBA, 1993. Cert. mgmt. acct. Fin. analyst Lexis/Nexis, Dayton, Ohio, 1990-95; cost analyst Miller Brewing Co., Trenton, Ohio, 1995-96; mgr. fin. reporting JewelWay Internat., Tucson, 1996-97; fin. analyst Iridium North Am., Phoenix, 1997—. Presdl. scholar U. Dayton, 1986. Mem. Inst. Mgmt. Accts. Avocations: cycling, cooking, music, art.

DICK, ANITA See HAR, LI

DICK, HENRY HENRY, minister; b. Russia, June 1, 1922; s. Henry Henry and Mary (Unger) D.; m. Erica Penner, May 25, 1946; children—Janet (Mrs. Arthur Enns), Judith (Mrs. Ron Brown), James, Henry. Th.B., Mennonite Brethren Bible Coll., 1950. Ordained to ministry Mennonite Brethren Ch., 1950; pastor in Orillia, Ont., Can., 1950-54, Lodi, Calif., 1954-57, Shafter, Calif., 1958-69; faculty Tabor Coll., 1954-55; gen. sec. Mennonite Brethren Conf. of U.S.A., 1969-72; pres. Mennonite Brethren Bibl. Sem., Fresno, Calif., 1972-76; vice moderator Gen Conf. Mennonite Brethren Ch., 1975-78, moderator, 1979-84; pastor Reedley Mennonite Brethren Ch., 1976-88; ret., 1989; dir. ch. and constituency relations Mennonite Brethren Biblical Sem., 1987-89; moderator Pacific Dist. Conf., 1959-60, 61-63, 75-77; mem. exec. com. Mennonite Central Com. Internat., 1967-75, mem. bd. reference and counsel, 1966-69, 72-75, mem. bd. missions and services, 1969-72; exec. sec. Bd. Edn. Mennonite Brethren, 1969-72; chmn. Bd. Missions and Services, 1985-91; pastor emeritus Reedley Mennonite Brethren Ch., 1987. Columnist bi-weekly publ. Christian Leader, 1969-75. Bd. dirs. Bob Wilson Meml. Hosp., Ulysses, Kans., 1969-72; dist. minister Pacific Dist. Conf. Mennonite Brethren, 1989—. Recipient Humanitarian award Shafter C. of C., 1969, Citation bd. dirs. Bibl. Sem. Clubs: Kiwanis, Reedley Rotary. Home: 783 W Carpenter Ave Reedley CA 93654-3903 Office: 1632 L St Reedley CA 93654-3340

DICKAU, KEITH MICHAEL (MIKE DICKAU), artist, secondary school educator; b. Monterey Park, Calif., Apr. 20, 1944; s. Keith Robert and Beaula May (Chamness) D.; m. Ramona Sue Wilson, May 6, 1967; children: Robert Michael, Ian Christopher; m. Carolyn Gloria Isaak, Dec. 22, 1973. BA in Zoology, U. Calif., Davis, 1966. Cert. secondary tchr., Calif. Tchr. math. L.A. City Sch. Dist., 1967-70; tchr. sci. and math. Grant Joint Union H.S. Dist., Sacramento and Rio Linda, Calif., 1970—. Exhibited in numerous shows including Candy Store Gallery, Folsom, Calif., Artists' Collaborative Gallery, Sacramento, Fla. State U., Tallahassee, Crocker Art Mus. Sculpture Park, Sacramento, Whittier (Calif.) Mus., Gallery 25, Fresno, Calif., L.A. Artist Equity Assn., Sacramento Fine Arts Ctr., Mercer Gallery, Rochester, N.Y., The Artery, Davis, Archivio Artistico, Ravenna, Italy, Antic Ajuntament, Terragona, Spain, Santa Barbara (Calif.) Mus., SFAC Gallery, Carmichael, Calif., 1996, Ecole de Nuces, Valady, France, M.J.C., Saint-Cere, France, 1996, Seulement pour les Fous, Troyes, France, 1996, New Artworks Fine Arts Gallery, Fair Oaks, Calif., 1996, Bur. de Poste, Joigny, France, 1996, The Ink People Ctr. for the Arts, Eureka, Calif., 1996, Mercer Gallery, Monroe C.C., Rochester, N.Y., 1996, L'Inst. Superieur des Arts Appliques, Rennes, France, The Living Room, Santa Monica, Calif., 1997, Kawaguchi-Shi, Japan, 1997, Solomon Dubnick Gallery, Sacramento, 1998, Mercer Gallery, East Sacramento Art Garage, 1999, others; contbr. poetry and art to mags. Recipient Hon. Sci. award Bausch and Lomb, 1962, Sculpture award Calif. Art League, 1987, Artist of Month award No. Calif. Artists, numerous other awards; NSF grantee, 1972. Mem. NEA, Calif. Tchrs. Assn., Grant Dist. Edn. Assn., No. Calif. Artists, Inc. Democrat. Methodist. Avocations: music, travel.

DICKENS, THOMAS PAUL, security executive; b. Iowa City, Feb. 20, 1954. BA, U. Iowa, 1978. With Spyrus, San Jose, Calif., also bd. dirs.; global operating officer Spyrus, San Jose, 1998. Avocations: basketball, tennis, skiing, investments. Office: Spyrus 5303 Betsy Ross Dr Santa Clara CA 95054

DICKERMAN, ROBERT N., energy company executive; b. Boston, Sept. 29, 1955; s. Kenneth Lawrence and Lola (Glazerman) D.; m. Maira Esther Gutierrez, Jan. 1, 1959; children: David, Andres, Samuel, Sarah. BA in math., Union Coll., 1978; MBA, Univ. Chgo., 1980. Oil products trader Arco Products, L.A., 1980-84; wholesale mkt. mgr. Apex Oil Co., Balt., 1984-91; sales mgr. Louis Dreyfus Energy, Atlanta, 1991-92; pres. Dickerman Energy Cons., Atlanta, 1992-95; dir. commodity risk mgmt. Price Waterhouse, Houston, 1995-97; prin. Metzler & Assocs., Chgo., 1997; sr. v.p. Edison Source, L.A., 1997—. Recipient scholar award British-Am. Ednl. Found., London, 1973. Mem. Western Power Trading Forum, Western Systems Coord. Coun. Republican. Home: 101 Sutter Creek Monrovia CA 91016 Office: Edison Source 13191 Crossroads Pkwy N Ste 405 La Puente CA 91746-3443

DICKERSON, COLLEEN BERNICE PATTON, artist, educator; b. Cleburne, Tex., Sept. 17, 1922; d. Jennings Bryan and Alma Bernice (Clark) Patton; m. Arthur F. Dickerson; children: Sherry M., Chrystal Charmine. BA, Calif. State U., Northridge, 1980; studied with John Pike. presenter demonstrations Cayucos Art Assn., Morro Bay Art Assn., El Camino Real Art Assn. One-woman shows include Morro Bay Cmty. Bldg., Amandas Interiors, Arroyo Grande, Calif., 1996, Gt. Western Savs., San Luis Obispo, Calif.; exhibited in group shows; represented in permanent collections, including Polk Ins. Co., San Luis Obispo, Med. Ctr. MDM Ins. Co., L.A. Mem. Ctrl. Coast Watercolor Soc. (pres. 1986-87), Art Ctr., Oil Acrylic Pastel Group (chmn., co-chmn. 1989-98), Morro Bay Art Assn., San Luis Obispo Art Ctr. Avocations: Egyptology, Chinese painting, art history. Home and Studio: 245 Hacienda Ave San Luis Obispo CA 93401-7967

DICKERSON, CYNTHIA ROWE, marketing firm executive, consultant; b. Cin., Apr. 14, 1956; d. Richard Emmett and Frances Jeanette (Ellwanger) Rowe; m. Mark Alan Dickerson, Oct. 24, 1981; children: Shannon Gayle, Meredith Lynne. BSBA, U. So. Calif., 1979. Mgmt. asst. Computer Scis. Corp., Pasadena, Calif., 1974-78; rsch. asst. Dailey & Assocs., L.A., 1978-79; account exec. Young & Rubicam, L.A., 1979-81, Rowley & Linder Advt., Wichita, Kans., 1981-82, Chiat/Day Inc. Advt., San Francisco, 1983-85; product mgr. Sun-Diamond Growers of Calif., Pleasanton, 1985-88; mktg. cons. San Francisco, 1988-90; sr. bus. mgr. Del Monte Foods, San Francisco, 1990-93; dir. mktg. Yorkshire Dried Fruit & Nuts, Inc., San Francisco, 1993-94, Potlatch Corp., 1995-98; catagory dir. fruit mktg. Tri Valley Growers, 1999—. Named Outstanding Youth Women of Am., Jr. C. of C., 1985. Mem. Am. Mktg. Assn., Soc. Consumer Affairs Profls., Am. Rose Soc., Heritage Rose Group. Republican. Avocations: gardening, youth sports, playing piano, gourmet cooking.

DICKERSON, WILLIAM ROY, lawyer; b. Uniontown, Ky., Feb. 15, 1928; s. Banjamin Franklin and Honor Mae (Staples) D. BA in Acctg., Calif. State U., 1952; JD, UCLA, 1958. Bar. Calif. 1959. Dep. atty., ex-officio city prosecutor City of Glendale, Calif., 1959-62; assoc. James Brewer, Los Angeles, 1962-68, LaFollette, Johnson, Schroeter & DeHaas, Los Angeles, 1968-73; sole practice, Los Angeles, 1973—; arbitrator Los Angeles Superior Ct.; judge pro tem Los Angeles Mcpl. Ct., judge pro tem Los Angeles Superior Ct., Small Claims Ct., Traffic Ct.; lectr. and speaker in field. Bd. dirs. LosFeliz Improvement Assn., 1986-88, Zoning Commn.; co-chmn. Streets and Hwys. Commn. Mem. ABA, Calif. Bar Assn., Los Angeles County Bar Assn., Soc. Calif. Accts., Fed. Bar Assn., Am. Film Inst., Internat. Platform Assn. Home and Office: 813 N Doheny Dr Beverly Hills CA 90210-3528

DICKEY, DANIEL H., elementary education educator; b. San Jose, Calif., Dec. 13, 1952; s. Lester H. and Josephine Dickey; m. Sandy J. Edelen, Aug. 26, 1973; children: Julie, Shireen, Dayna, Erica. BA in Biology, Calif. State U., Turlock, 1983. Owner, operator Office Furnishing Network, Stevinson, Calif., 1985-87; tchr. Atwater (Calif.) Elem. Sch. Dist., 1988-94, mentor, tchr., 1990-94, tech. coord., 1994-97; trainer Nat. Edn. Networking Alliance, 1996—. Exec. bd. MGF, Turlock, 1994-97, bd. mem., NLCC, 1997. Mem. Am. Emu Assn. (region 4 pres. 1995-96). Avocation: oil painting. Office: Atwater Sch Dist 1491 Grove Ave Atwater CA 95301-3531

DICKEY, GARY ALAN, minister; b. Santa Monica, Calif., Jan. 25, 1946; s. Charles Harry and Audrey W. (White) D.; m. Tamara Jean Kimble, Jan. 11, 1976. BA, UCLA, 1968; MDiv, Fuller Theol. Sem., Pasadena, 1972; DMin, Sch. Theology, Claremont, Calif., 1974; PhD, Trinity Theol. Seminary, 1996. Assoc. pastor Magnolia Pk. United Meth. Ch., Burbank, Calif., 1974-78; sr. pastor St. James United Meth. Ch., Pasadena, 1978-90, First United Meth. Ch. of Canoga Park, 1990—; exec. com. mem. Calif.-Pacific Ann. Conf. Bd. of Ordained Ministry, 1980-88; chmn. Pasadena Dist. Com. on Ordained Ministry, 1978-90; supervising pastor Bd. Higher Edn., Nashville, 1978—. Recipient Polonia Restituta, 1990. Mem. Calif. State Gov. Soc. Colonial Wars, Soc. War of 1812 (chaplain 1989—, Calif. state pres. 1997-98, v.p. gen. Calif. 1999), Soc. of Sons of Am. Revolution (chaplain 1988—, pres. 1994, 95, Outstanding Citizenship award 1990, Meritorious Svc. award 1995, Silver Good Citizenship award 1996, Patriot medal 1997), Soc. of Sons of the Revolution, Descendants of Soldiers of Valley Forge, Soc. Sons Am. Colonists, Soc. Sons. Vets. Civil War, Vet. Corps Artillery State N.Y., United Empire Loyalists Assn. (Can.), Royal Soc. St. George (Eng.), Rotary (pres. 1989-90, Paul Harris fellow 1986), Am. Coll. Genealogists (accredited genealogist). Republican. Methodist. Avocations: photography, travel, genealogical research. Home: 22167 Bryant St Canoga Park CA 91304-2306 Office: First United Meth Ch 22700 Sherman Way Canoga Park CA 91307-2332

DICKEY, ROBERT MARVIN (RICK DICKEY), property manager; b. Charleston, S.C., Dec. 3, 1950; s. John Lincoln II and Ruth (Marvin) D.; m. Teresa Ann Curry, Dec. 19, 1969 (div. 1979); 1 child, Gena Lynette. A of Computer Sci., USMC Degree Program, Washington, 1975. Cert. apt. property supr. Nat. Apt. Assn., Wash., occupancy specialist Nat. Ctr.for Housing Mgmt., Wash. Enlisted USMC, 1968, advanced through grades to staff sgt., 1968-78; shop mgr., bookkeeper Amalgamated Plant Co., Las Vegas, Nev., 1978-79; supr. constrn. Joseph Yousem Co., Las Vegas, 1979-80; apt. mgr. Robert A. McNeil Corp., Las Vegas, 1980, comml. bldg. mgr., leasing agt., 1980-82; asst. v.p., regional property mgr. Westminster Co., Las Vegas, 1982-87, Weyerhaeuser Mortgage Co., Las Vegas, 1988-89; pres., ptnr. Equinox Devel., Inc., Las Vegas, 1989-91; dir. residental properties R.W. Robideaux & Co., Spokane, Wash., 1992-97; mgr. residential divsn. G&B Real Estate Svcs., Spokane, 1997—. Contbr. articles to profl. jours. Mem. Nat. Assn. Realtors, Wash. Assn. Realtors, Spokane Assn. Realtors, Inst. Real Estate Mgmt. (accredited residential mgr., legis. chmn. 1987-88, Accredited Residential Mgr. award 1985, 86, 90), Nev. Apt. Assn. (v.p. 1985, pres. 1988—, bd. dirs.), So. Nev. Homebuilders Assn., Las Vegas Bd. Realtors (mgmt. legis. com. 1988).

DICKEY, ROBERT PRESTON, author, educator, poet; b. Flat River, Mo., Sept. 24, 1936; s. Delno Miren D. and Naomi Valentine (Jackson) D.; children: Georgia Rae, Shannon Ezra, Rain Dancer. BA, U. Mo., 1968, MA, 1969; PhD, Walden U., 1975. Instr. U. Mo., 1967-69; asst. prof. English and creative writing U. So. Colo., 1969-73; assoc. mem. faculty Pima Coll., Tucson, 1975-78. Author: (with Donald Justice, Thomas McAfee, Donald Drummond) poetry Four Poets, 1967, Running Lucky, 1969, Acting Immortal, 1970; Concise Dictionary of Lead River, Mo., 1972, The Basic Stuff of Poetry, 1972, Life Cycle of Seven Songs, 1972, McCabe Wants Chimes, 1973, Admitting Complicity, 1973; opera librettos Minnequa, 1976, The Witch of Tucson, 1976; Jimmie Cotton!, 1979, Way Out West, 1979, The Poetica Erotica of R.P. Dickey, 1989, The Little Book on Racism and Politics, 1990, The Way of Eternal Recurrence, 1994, Ode on Liberty, 1996, The Lee Poems, 1998, Self-Liberation, 1998, Exercise Anytime, 1998, Collected Poems, 1999; contbr. poetry to popular mags., Poetry, Saturday Rev., Commonwealth, Prairie Schooner; founder, editor: The Poetry Bag quar., 1966-71; poetry editor: So. Colo. Std., 1973-74. With USAF, 1955-57. Recipient Mahan award for poetry U. Mo., 1965-66. Home: PO Box 87 Ranchos De Taos NM 87557-0087

DICKEY, TINA ANNE, artist, consultant; b. Stamford, Conn., Sept. 21, 1954; d. Thomas Atherton and Anne (Tredick) D. MA, Vt. Coll., 1989; student, N.Y. Studio Sch., 1984, Sch. Mus. Fine Art, Boston, 1981, U. Mass., 1976-77. Cons. Estate of Hans Hofmann, 1996—; editor Hans Hofmann Catalogue Raisonné, Seattle, 1997—; rschr. Hans Hofmann Oral History Project, Seattle, 1998—. Group show USA on Paper, Copenhagen, 1993; solo exhibits NIH, 1990, MIT, 1995; author: (with H. Friedel) Hans Hofmann, 1998. Grantee Ludwig Vogelstein Found., 1987; resident Vt. Studio Colony, Johnson, Vt., 1984, 86, Cummington (Mass.) Cmty. of Arts, 1983, 92, 93. Mem. Coll. Art Assn., Catalogue Raisonné Scholars Assn., Nat. Writer's Union. Office: PO Box 31234 Seattle WA 98103

DICKINSON, JACOB JOHN LOUIS, computer consultant; b. Honolulu, Dec. 17, 1957; s. Jacob Alan and Ruth (Curd) D.; m. Janis Miyeko Kibe, Feb. 25, 1983; children: Jacob Carl Toshiro, Ellen Tamiko, Alexander Seiji. Student, Deep Springs Coll., 1976-78, Washburn U., 1979; BSME, U. Wash., 1982; cert. advanced program in Artificial Intelligence, UCLA, 1988. Cert. knowledge engr. Sr. engr. Douglas Aircraft, Long Beach, Calif., 1983-87; engr., scientist specialist McDonnell Douglas Astronautics, Huntington Beach, Calif., 1987-89; lead engr. avionics software artificial intelligence group McDonnell Douglas Space Systems Co., Huntington Beach, Calif., 1989-93; founder Specialty Coffee and Food Co., 1993-95; owner Sprezza Cons., 1995—; sr. cons. IT Solutions, Gardena, Calif., 1998—. Chmn. decade fundraising Deep Springs Coll. Mem. AAAS, Am. Assn. for Artificial Intelligence. Avocations: bicycling, cooking, reading history, writing. E-mail: jacob@sprezza.com.

DICKINSON, JAMES GORDON, editor; b. Melbourne, Australia, Nov. 13, 1940; came to U.S., 1974, naturalized, 1983; s. David Rushbrook and Lorna Aida (Anderson) D.; m. Carol Rosslyn McBurnie, Sept. 7, 1963; children: Craig, Peter (dec.), Samantha; m. Sheila Laraine Ferguson McManus, Aug. 20, 1982. Student Melbourne U., 1960-63. Cadet reporter Hobart Mercury, 1957-59, Melbourne Age, 1959-63; reporter Melbourne Herald, 1963-64, TV Channel O, Melbourne, 1964-66; cons. Internat. Public Relations Pty. Ltd., 1966-68; editor, pub. Australian Jour. Pharmacy, 1968-74; asst. exec. dir. Am. Pharm. Assn., Washington, 1975; sr. editor FDC Reports Inc., Washington, 1975-78; founder, editor Washington Drugwire, 1978-79; Washington bur. chief Drug Topics, Med. Econs. Co., 1978-83; Washington corr. Scrip, Clinica World Med. Device News, Animal Pharm World Vet. News (U.K.), 1978-85, Pharm. Tech., Pharm. Exec., 1977-89, N.Z. Pharmacy, Brit. Pharm. Jour., Drug News & Perspectives mag. (Spain), Med. Device and Diagnostic Industry mag., Med. Mktg. & Media, 1990—; pres., chief exec. officer Ferdic Inc., 1982—; editor, pub. Dickinson's FDA and Dickinson's PSAO industry newsletters, 1985-93, VixeNews, 1989-90, Dickinson's Pharmacy newsletter, 1989-96, Dickinson's FDA Inspection newsletter, 1992-93, Dickinson's FDA Review, 1994—, Dickinson's FDA Update by Fax Weekly; columnist syndicated all state pharm. jours., 1986-94; cons. to drug industry; pres. Australian Monthly Newspapers and Periodicals Assn., 1972-74; founding sec. Melbourne Press Club, 1971-74. Editor: Weekly Pharmacy Reports, 1975-78. Mem. Australian Liberal Party, 1971-74; pres. Lee Forest Civic Assn., 1977-79. Mem. Periodical Corrs. Assn., Am. Pub. Health Assn. Club: Nat. Press (Washington). Office: 190 N Tegner St # 113 Wickenburg AZ 85390-1455

DICKINSON, JANET MAE WEBSTER, relocation consulting executive; b. Cleve., Oct. 2, 1929; d. Richard and Gizella (Keplinger) Fisher; m. Rodney Earl Dickinson, June 18, 1965 (div. 1976); 1 child, Kimberly Cae. Grad., Larson Coll. for Women, New Haven; student, Portland State Coll. Lic. broker, Oreg. Pub. rels./promotion dir. KPTV-Channel 27, Portland, Oreg., 1951-54; exec. dir. Exposition-Recreation Commn., Portland, 1954-58; v.p. Art Lutz & Co., Realtors, Portland, 1975-79, Lutz Relocation Mgmt., Portland, 1977-79; corp. relocation mgr. Ga. Pacific Corp., Portland, 1979-82; pres., broker Ga. Pacific Fin. Co., Portland, 1980-82; pres., chief exec. officer The Dickinson Cons. Group, Portland, 1982—; pres. Wheatherstone Press, Lake Oswego, Oreg., 1983—, The Relocation Ctr., Portland, 1984—; cons. in field; lectr. in field; conductor workshops/seminars in field. Author: The Complete Guide to Family Relocation, The International Move, Building Your Dream House, Obtaining the Highest Price for Your Home, Have a Successful Garage Sale, Moving with Children, My Moving Coloring Book, The Group Move, Counseling the Transferee, Games to Play in the Car, Portland (Oreg.) Facts Book, Welcome to the United States, many others; contbr. articles to profl. jours. Mem. Pres.'s Com. to Employ Physically Handicapped, Oreg. Prison Assn.; established Women's Aux. for Waverly Baby Home; bd. dirs. Columbia River coun. Girl Scouts U.S.A., Salvation Army; active various polit. orgns.; chmn. ways and means com. Oreg. Symphony Soc., Portland Art Mus., Assistance League, Portland Jr. Symphony, March of Dimes, others. Mem. Employee Relocation Coun., City Club, Multnomah Athletic Club, Tualatin Valley Econ. Devel. Assn. (dir. 1988—). Republican. Episcopalian. Home: 20 Wheatherstone Lake Oswego OR 97035 Office: The Dickinson Cons Group Lincoln Ctr 10250 SW Greenburg Rd Ste 125 Portland OR 97223-5470

DICKINSON, SUSAN JOAN, deaf studies educator, consultant; b. Marysville, Ohio, Dec. 25, 1953; d. Joseph Williams and Joan Louise (Grimm) Rupp; m. John Charles Dickinson, Mar. 31, 1990 (div. Dec. 1992); children: Miles, Kelsey. Student in English and sociology, U. Calif., Berkeley, 1971-73; BA in Audiology and Speech Pathology, U. Colo., 1975; MA in Deaf Edn., Gallaudet U., Washington, 1977; MA in Ednl. Adminstrn. and Supervision, Calif. State U., Northridge, 1981. Profl. tchr., Colo. Tchr. for the deaf Baker Jr. H.S.-Denver Pub. Schs., 1977-82, South H.S.-Denver Pub. Schs., 1983-88, Schenck Elem. Sch.-Denver Pub. Schs., 1989-94, Rock Ridge Elem. Sch.-Douglas County Schs., Castle Rock, Colo., 1994—, Buffalo Ridge Elem. Sch.-Douglas County Schs., Castle Rock, Colo., 1997—; deaf edn. cons. Star Schs. Grant Project, U.S. Dept. Edn., Washington, 1997—; mem. adv. bd. Colo. Sch. Deaf and Blind, Colorado Springs, 1988—; family facilitator Colo. Home Intervention Program, Denver, 1996—. Author, illustrator: Relay Colorado Handbook, 1993. Statewide interpreter evaluator Colo. Dept. Edn., Denver, 1992—, founder, presenter Deaf Adult Outreach Program, 1989-95; t. Edn., 1989-95; mem. bd. trustees Gallaudet U., 1994—; mem. curricular priorities com. captioning ednl. films U.S. Dept. Edn.-Nat. Assn. Deaf, Washington, 1994—. Recipient Sabbatical award US West Comm., 1988-89, Svc. to Mankind award Sertoma Clubs, 1990, 97, Edn. award Colo. Assn. Deaf, 1989 ; named Deaf Woman of Yr., Quota Internat., Washington, 1994, Tchrs. Who Make a Difference, Channel 4 T.V., Denver, 1987. Mem. Nat. Assn. Deaf, Assn. Coll. Educators of Deaf and Hard of Hearing, Coun. Am. Instructors of Deaf, Telecomm. for the Deaf, Gallaudet U. Alumni Assn. Avocations: paper making, skiing. Home: 7687 Halleys Dr Littleton CO 80125-8921 Office: Douglas County Schs 620 Wilcox St Castle Rock CO 80104-1730

DICKS, NORMAN DE VALOIS, congressman; b. Bremerton, Wash., Dec. 16, 1940; s. Horace D. and Eileen Cora D.; m. Suzanne Callison, Aug. 25, 1967; children: David, Ryan. BA, U. Wash., 1963, JD, 1968; LLD (hon.), Gonzaga U., 1987. Bars: Wash. 1968, D.C., 1978. Salesman, Boise Cascade Corp., Seattle, 1963; labor negotiator Kaiser Gypsum Co., Seattle, 1964; legis. asst. to Senator Warren Magnuson of Wash., 1968-73, adminstrv. asst., 1973-76; mem. 95th-106th Congress from 6th Wash. Dist., Washington, 1977—; mem. appropriations com., intelligence com. 95th-104th Congress from 6th Wash. Dist., Washington. Mem. U. Wash. Alumni Assn., Sigma Nu. Democrat. Lutheran. Office: US Ho Reps 2467 Rayburn Bldg Ofc Bldg Washington DC 20515-4706*

DICKSON, STEWART PRICE, graphics programmer; b. Cooperstown, N.Y., July 16, 1956; s. Frederick Stoever III and Jean Stewart (Price) D.; m. Rebecka DeAnn Yaeger, Oct. 2, 1981; children: Price Alexandra, Nathaniel Stewart, Maura Grace. BEE, U. Del., 1981. Janitor Rollins Broadcasting Sta. WAMS, Wilmington, Del., 1973-77; rsch. asst. Dept. Elec. Engring. and Physics, U. Del., Newark, 1978-79; devel. engr. Western Electric Co., Lisle, Ill., 1980-84, AT&T Technologies, Inc., Naperville, Ill., 1980-84; dir. computer-generated imagery Goldsholl Design and Film, Inc., Northfield, Ill., 1984-87; 3D graphics programmer The Post Group, Inc., Hollywood, Calif., 1988-93; with Rez-n-8 Prodns., Hollywood, Calif., 1993-95, Walt Disney Feature Animation, Burbank, Calif., 1996—; cons., lectr. Calif. Inst. of the Arts, Valencia, 1989—; cons., artist Wolfram Rsch., Inc., Champaign, Ill., 1990—. Contbr./illustrator articles to profl. jours.; profl. sculptor, 1981—; patentee in field. Commr. comm. & tech. adv. commn. Calagasas City Coun., 1998—. Mem. Am. Mensa, Ltd., Assn. for Computing Machinery (spl. project grant 1990 graphics spl. interest group), Internat. Sculpture Ctrs., Artists Using Sci. and Tech., Internat. Soc. for the Arts, Scis. and Tech. Avocations: off-road motoring, equestrian, skiing, snorkling, music. Home: 23115 Blue Bird Dr Calabasas CA 91302-1836 Office: Walt Disney Co 500 S Buena Vista St Burbank CA 91521-0004

DICOCCO, MARC, career officer, flight test engineer; b. Lackland AFB, Tex., Aug. 17, 1962; s. Severino and Anne Marie (Bopp) DiC. BS in Aerospace Engring., Va. Poly. Inst., 1985; MS in Aerospace Engring., U. Dayton, 1990. Cert. acquisition officer in program mgmt., test and evaluation and systems engring. Commd. 2d lt. USAF, 1985; advanced through ranks to maj., 1997; technician Prophet 21 Systems Inc., Yardley, Pa., 1984-85; advance concepts design engr. USAF Aeronautical Systems Divsn., Wright-Patterson AFB, Ohio, 1985-88, acquisition officer in tng., 1985-88, test project mgr., 1988-90; F-15E flight test engr. USAF Weapons and Tactics Ctr., Nellis AFB, Nev., 1990-94; chief upper stages divsn. Titan 4 Launch Vehicle Program, Space and Missile Ctr., L.A. AFB, 1994—; pres. aeronautic systems divsn. company grade officers adv. coun. Wright-Patterson AFB, 1989-90. Min. to youth club Our Lady of Peace Cath. Ch., Wright-Patterson AFB, 1987-90; altar server trainer Lady of the Skies Cath. Ch., Nellis AFB, 1993-94. Decorated Air Force Commendation medal (2), Air Force Achievement medal (2). Mem. AIAA, Aircraft Owners & Pilots Assn., Air Force Assn. (life). Avocations: flying, physical fitness, fine arts, travel, writing.

DIDOMIZIO, ROBERT ANTHONY, health facility administrator; b. Waterbury, Conn., Feb. 6, 1967; s. Vincent James and Alexandria Lee (Ramanauskas) D.; m. Wendy Darlene Emerson, April 4, 1998. BA in Psychology, U. Ariz., 1990; MBA, U. Phoenix, 1995. Tchr. Formento De Svcs. Linguisticos, Madrid, Spain, 1989; residential counselor Ariz. Children's Home Assn., Tucson, 1989-90; program mgr. Devereux Found., Scottsdale, Ariz., 1990-92; labor mkt. cons. Associated Rehab. Profls., Phoenix, 1992-95; mktg. asst. Desert Vista Hosp., Mesa, Ariz., 1995-96, dir. mktg., 1996-98; producer Studio 43 Film and Video Prodns., Phoenix, 1994—; bus. planner Sun Health Corp., 1998—. Mem. Ariz. Prodn. Assn., Adventure Club North Am., Greenpeace. Democrat. Avocations: mountain biking, hiking, camping, weight lifting. E-mail: robertdaz@aol.com. Fax: (602) 827-0412. Home: 5995 N 78th St Apt 2096 Scottsdale AZ 85250-6151 Office: Sun Health Corp 10401 W Thunderbird Rd Sun City AZ 85351

DIEDERICH, J(OHN) WILLIAM, internet publisher; b. Ladysmith, Wis., Aug. 30, 1929; s. Joseph Charles and Alice Florence (Yost) D.; m. Mary Theresa Klein, Nov. 25, 1950; children: Mary Theresa Diederich Evans, Robert Douglas, Charles Stuart, Michael Mark, Patricia Anne Diederich Irelan, Donna Maureen (dec.), Denise Brendan, Carol Lynn Diederich Weaver, Barbara Gail, Brian Donald, Tracy Maureen Diederich Jorgensen, Theodora Bernadette Diederich Davidson, Tamara Alice Diederich Williams, Lorraine Angela. PhB, Marquette U., Milw., 1951; MBA with high distinction, Harvard U., 1955. With Landmark Comm., Inc., Norfolk, Va., 1955-90, v.p., treas., 1965-73, exec. v.p. fin., 1973-78, exec. v.p. community newspapers, 1978-82, exec. v.p., CFO, 1982-90, fin. cons., 1990—; internet pub., 1996—; chmn. bd. dirs. Landmark Cmty. Newspapers, Inc., 1977-88; pres. Exec. Productivity Sys., Inc., 1982-88, LCI Credit Corp., 1991-93, Landmark TV Inc., 1991—, LTM Investments, Inc., 1991—; v.p., treas., KLAS, Inc., 1994-95; v.p. Internet Express, Inc., 1994—; pres., bd. dirs. Wide World Web Internat., 1995—, TWC Holdings, Inc., 1996—; instr. Boston U., 1954, Old Dominion U., 1955-59. Lt. col. USMC, 1951-53, USMCR, 1953-71. Baker scholar Harvard U., 1955. Mem. SAR, Nat. Assn. Accts., Am. Numismatic Assn., Nat. Geneal. Soc., Wis. Geneal. Soc., Pa. Geneal. Soc., Sigma Delta Chi. Roman Catholic. Home and Office: PO Box 7677 1466 Glarus Ct Incline Village NV 89451-7900

DIEDRICK, GERALDINE ROSE, retired nurse; b. Chgo.; d. Milton Edward and Rose Agnes (Michalski) Goodman; R.N., Mt. San Antonio Coll., Walnut, Calif., 1963; BS, Calif. State U., L.A., 1966; MS, UCLA, 1968; divorced; 1 son, Scott Wesley (dec.). Nurse, State of Calif., 1960-83, dir. nursing Met. State Hosp., Norwalk, 1977-83; cons. in mental health, devel. disabilities. Recipient Letter of Commendation, State of Calif., 1974-77. Mem. Am. Nurses Assn., Nat. League Nursing, Am. Assn. Devel. Disabilities, Calif. Nurses Assn. (svc. awards), Am. Hosp. Assn., World Future Soc., Town Hall Calif. Lutheran. Contbr. to profl. jours.

DIEFFENBACH, ALICEJEAN, artist; b. Nashville, Dec. 18, 1931; d. Bailey Everette and Elizabeth R. (Vinson) Thompson; m. Otto Weaver Dieffenbach, June 14, 1952; children: Otto W. III, Linda Madeleine Harrison, Susanne Elizabeth Hume. AB in Art History, Duke U., 1952; MS in Edn. Adminstrn., Johns Hopkins U., 1974. Soprano Balt. Opera Co., 1956-58; starring roles Met. Mus. Theatre, Actors Theatre, Balt., 1958-75; head art dept., tchr. Cockeysville (Md.) H.S., 1965-79; owner, designer Design Plus, Balt., 1972-80; real estate salesperson Merrill-Lynch/Cousins, Miami, Fla., 1980-82, Dieffenbach Real Estate, Rancho Santa Fe, Calif., 1982-89; artist, painter Solana Beach, Calif., 1992—. Soprano soloist Towson (Md.) Presbyn. Ch., 1955-80, Plymouth Congl. Ch., Coconut Grove, Fla., 1980-82, The Village Ch. Presby., Rancho Santa Fe, 1982—, The Handel Choir Balt., The Bach Soc. Balt.; soloist, performer San Diego Chamber Orch., 1985, 86, 89, 90, 91; soloist Balt. Symphony Orch.; solo show Rancho Santa Fe Libr., 1996. Mem. Rancho Santa Fe Libr. Guild, 1982—, Rep. Women, Rancho Santa Fe. Recipient 1st, 2d, and 3d Hon. Mention awards various juried art exhbns., 1993—. Mem. Artists Equity Assn. (treas. 1994-96), San Diego Art Inst. (numerous ribbons), San Dieguito Art Guild (numerous ribbons), San Diego Mus. Art Guild, San Diego Mus. Contemporary Art, Rancho Santa Fe Garden Club, Oil Painters Am., Rancho Santa Fe Art Guild. Presbyterian. Avocations: writing, needlepoint, dancing, traveling. Home: PO Box 261 Rancho Santa Fe CA 92067-0261 Studio: 130 S Cedros Ave Solana Beach CA 92075-1915

DIEHL, DOLORES, communication arts director; b. Salina, Kans., Dec. 28, 1927; d. William Augustus and Martha (Frank) D. Student pub. schs., Kans., 1941-45. Bus. rep. Southwestern Bell Telephone Co., St. Louis and Kansas City, Mo., 1948-49, Mountain States Telephone Co., Denver, 1949-50; edn. coord. pub. rels. Pacific Telephone/AT&T, L.A. and San Diego, 1950-83; cons. Bus. Magnet High Sch., L.A. Unified Sch. Dist., 1977-79; pres. First Calif. Acad. Decathlon, 1979; owner Community Connection, L.A., 1983—; mgr., dir. DelMar Media Arts, Burbank, Calif., 1985-89; mgr. Susan Blu workshops Blupka Prodns., L.A., 1989—; dir. animation and commls. voiceover workshops Elaine Craig Voicecasting, Hollywood, Calif., 1989—; freelance performer, voiceover L.A., 1990—; mgr. Sounds Great Film Looping Workshops, L.A., 1992—; owner Voiceover Connection, L.A., 1994-95; pres. Voiceover Connection, Inc., L.A., 1995—; v.p. pub. rels. San Diego Inst. Creativity, 1965-67; mem. exec. com. San Diego's 200th Anniversary Celebration, 1967. Recipient Dedication to Edn. award Industry Edn. Coun., Calif., 1964. Mem. L.A. Area C. of C. (bd. dirs. women's coun.), Calif. Magnet Sch. Consortium of Cities (chairperson), Industry Edn. Coun. Calif., L.A. and San Diego (past pres.), Bus. and Profl. Women's Club, Delta Kappa Gamma (hon.). Republican. Methodist. Home and Office: 691 Irolo St Apt 212 Los Angeles CA 90005-4110

DIENER, ROYCE, corporate director, retired healthcare services company executive; b. Balt., Mar. 27, 1918; s. Louis and Lillian (Goodman) D.; m. Jennifer S. Flinton; children: Robert, Joan, Michael, Dianne. BA, Harvard U.; LLD, Pepperdine U. Comml. lending officer, investment banker various locations to 1972; pres. Am. Med. Internat., Inc., Beverly Hills, Calif., 1972-75, pres., chief exec. officer, 1975-78, chmn., chief exec. officer, 1978-85, chmn. bd., 1986-88, chmn. exec. com., 1986-89; bd. dirs. Calif. Econ. Devel. Corp., Acuson, Inc., Advanced Tech. Venture Funds, Am. Health Properties, AMI Health Svcs., plc., Consortium 2000. Author: Financing a Growing Business, 1966, 4th edit., 1995. Bd. visitors Grad. Sch. Mgmt., UCLA; mem. governing bd. UCLA Med. Ctr.; mem. vis. com. Med. Sch. and Sch. Dental Medicine, Harvard U.; bd. dirs. L.A. Philharm. Assn., L.A. chpt. ARC, Heritage Sq. Mus., Santa Monica. Served to capt. USAF, 1942-46, PTO. Decorated D.F.C. with oak leaf cluster. Mem. L.A. C. of C. (bd. dirs.), Calif. C. of C. (bd. dirs.), Calif. Bus. Round Table (bd. dirs.), Harvard Club, Regency Club, Calif. Yacht Club, Riviera Country Club (L.A.), Marks Club (London), Outrigger Canoe Club (Oahu).

DIEPHOLZ, DANIEL RAY, real estate consultant, accountant; b. Calif., Aug. 25, 1964; s. Eugene L. and Ruby J. (Forsch) D. BSBA in Acctg., Valparaiso U., 1985; MS in Real Estate with acad. honors, NYU, 1990. CPA, Calif.; lic. real estate broker, Calif. Auditor Blue Cross Calif., Woodland Hills, 1986-87; corp. fin. assoc., v.p. Bateman Eichler, Hill Richards Inc., L.A., N.Y.C., 1987-89; real estate cons. Price Waterhouse, L.A., 1990-96; founder Diepholz & Co., Indian Wells, Calif., 1996—; chmn. bd. Taos Palms Inc., L.A., 1990—. Mem. Nat. Assn. Accts. (bd. dirs. 1990-95). Republican. Mem. LDS Ch. Avocations: tennis, golf, sailing. Home: 270 N Canon Dr # 1140 Beverly Hills CA 90210-5323 Office: Diepholz & Co 270 N Canon Dr # 1140 Beverly Hills CA 90210-5323

DIERICH, DARREN ROGER, controller; b. Soldotna, Alaska, June 3, 1968; s. Ernest R. and Betty Jean (Gjosund) D. BA, Wash. U., 1995. Asst. contr. Queen Fisheries, Seattle, 1994-96; contr. Passage Holdings, Inc., Seattle, 1996—. E-mail: darrend@mediapassage.com. Fax: (206) 281-4132. Home: 20906 NE 19th Pl Redmond WA 98053-4207 Office: Passage Holdings Inc 401 2nd Ave Seattle WA 98104-2880

DIETERICH A., CLAUDE, graphic designer; b. Colmar, France, Apr. 18, 1930; came to U.S., 1986; s. Paul and Renee (Ambrosini) D. BFA, Cath. U., Lima, Peru, 1974. Prin. graphic designer Claude Dieterick A., Paris, 1954-61, Lima, Peru, 1961-86; designer L. Martinez Assocs., Miami, Fla., 1986-89; prin. graphic designer Claude Dieterich A., San Francisco, 1992—. Mem. Type Dirs. Club, Friends of Caligraphy (coun. mem. 1983-97). Avocations: Karate, cooking, dancing. Home and office: 1417 Cabrillo St San Francisco CA 94118-3522

DIETRICH, WILLIAM ALAN, author, journalist; b. Tacoma, Sept. 29, 1951; s. William Richard and Janice Lenore (Pooler) D.; m. Holly Susan Roberts, Dec. 19, 1970; children: Lisa, Heidi. BA, Western Wash. U., 1973. Reporter Bellingham (Wash.) Herald, 1973-76, Gannett News Svc., Washington, 1976-78, Vancouver (Wash.) Columbian, 1978-82, Seattle Times, 1982-97; freelance writer, 1998—. Author: The Final Forest, 1992, Northwest Passage, 1995, Ice Reich, 1998. Recipient Paul Tobenkin award Columbia U., 1986, Pulitzer prize for nat. reporting, 1990; Nieman fellow Harvard U., 1987-88.

DIETZ, PATRICIA ANN, engineering administrator; b. L.A., Nov. 30, 1958; d. Joseph and Mary Jane (Gallegos) Duran; m. Frank Raymond Dietz, July 1, 1978; children: Lindy K., Frank R. Jr. BA in Polit. Sci., U. Colo., 1983; MA in Psychology, Pepperdine U., 1993; Paralegal Cert., U. San Diego, 1988. Investment broker 1st Investors Corp., Colorado Springs, Colo., 1986-88; paralegal Law Offices of Ben Williams, Santa Monica, Calif., 1988-89; mgmt. analyst Bur. of Engring., City of L.A., 1989—; camp commandant Operation Safe Harbor-Haitian Humanitarian Relief Effort, 1992. Mem. Parent Tchr. Student Assn., Rosamond, Calif., 1992. With U.S. Army, 1983-86, capt. USAR, 1986-98, Retired Reserve Status, 1998—. Nat. Urban fellow, 1991. Mem. Civil Affairs Assn., Res. Officers Assn., Engrs. and Architects Assn. Republican.

DIETZ, RUSSELL SCOTT, communications company executive; b. Freeport, N.Y., Mar. 1, 1963; s. Russell N. and Mary E. (Sattler) D.; m. Carla R. Cadwell, June 4, 1983. BS in Computer Sci., SUNY, Stony Brook, 1985. Computer system mgr. Shoreham Wading River Schs., Shoreham, N.Y., 1979-81; sr. computer programming RMS Data Svcs., Hicksville, N.Y., 1981-83; bd. dirs. Technically Elite Concepts Inc., Hermosa Beach, Calif.; sr. systems programmer/analyst Bendix Field Engring. Corp., St. Inigoes, Md., 1983-84; system implementation specialist Magnavox Electronic Systems Co., Ashburn, Va., 1984-87; prin. software specialist Digital Equipment Corp., Landover, Md., 1987-88; v.p. systems devel. Technically Elite Concepts Inc., Hermosa Beach, Calif., 1988-95; v.p. engring., chief tech. officer Technically Elite, Inc., Campbell, Calif., 1995—, chief tech. officer, 1995—; cons. Cedars-Sinai Med. Ctr., L.A., 1988-90. Contbr. articles to profl. jours. Mem. ch. coun. St. Timothy's Luth. Ch., 1997—, pres., 1998—. Mem. Digital Equipment Corp. User Soc., DC VAX Local Users Group (chmn. 1985-87). Republican. Lutheran. Avocation: yacht racing. Office: Technically Elite Inc 6330 San Ignacio Ave San Jose CA 95119-1209

DIETZEN, EDITH JANE, school counselor, educator; b. Portland, Oreg., May 17, 1945; d. Alfred Edward and Margaret Josephine (Jensen) Simantel; m. Gerald John Dietzen, July 25, 1970; children: David, Jonathan, Benjamin. BS, Concordia U., 1968; MA in Libr. Sci., Valparaiso U., 1971; postgrad., Seattle Pacific U., 1994—. Life lic. in tchg., Wash.; cert. std. elem. Ill.; cert. gen. elem., Ind. Intern tchr. St. Paul's Luth. Sch., Hammond, Ind., 1966-67, elem. tchr., 1968-70; elem. tchr. Nathan Hale Sch., Lansing, Ill., 1970-74; tchr. 5th and 6th grade Pilgrim Luth. Sch., Bellevue, Wash., 1979-85; tchr. 6th grade Heritage Christian Sch., Bothell, Wash., 1988-89, sch. counselor, 1989—; mem. sch. bd. Pilgrim Luth. Sch., pres. Womens Guild, 1985-86; treas. Valparaiso Guild Univ. Women, Redmond, Wash. Choir dir. All Sts. Luth., Bellevue, 1988-92. Mem. AAUW, Am. Assn. Marriage and Family Therapists (student mem.). Republican. Lutheran. Avocations: reading English literature, playing piano, gardening. Home: 14514 NE 76th St Redmond WA 98052-4132 Office: Heritage Christian Sch 10310 NE 195th St Bothell WA 98011-2930

DIGGS, BRADLEY C., lawyer; b. Missoula, Mont., Sept. 18, 1948. BA magna cum laude, Amherst Coll., 1970; JD cum laude, Harvard U., 1973. Bar: Wash. 1973. Mng. ptnr. Davis Wright Tremaine, Seattle. Mem. ABA, Phi Beta Kappa. Office: Davis Wright Tremaine 2600 Century Sq 1501 4th Ave Ste 2600 Seattle WA 98101-1688

DIGRAZIA, PETER MICHAEL, dentist; b. Battle Mountain, Nev., Aug. 30, 1939; s. Eugene John and Julia Maria (Nannini) DiG.; m. Susan Lee Cavitt, June 21, 1965; children: Michaelle, Jill, John, Susan. BA, U. Nev., 1964; DMD, U. Oreg., 1966. Gen. dentist Reno, Nev., 1968—; pres. Am. Assn. Dental Examiners, Chgo., 1984, Western Conf. Deans and Dental Examiners, 1978; chmn. Joint Com. on Nat. Dental Tests, 1985;. Pres. Nev. State Bd. Health, 1983-84, Mountain Rose Lions Club, 1985, Reno Sunrise Exch. Club, 1986, Nev. State Bd. Dentistry, 1980-81. Capt. U.S. Army, 1966-68. Fellow Acad. Gen. Dentistry, Acad. Dentistry Internat. (state chmn.), Internat. Coll. Dentists (editor Nev. 1986), Am. Coll. Dentists; m. ADA, Pierre Fauchard Acad. (state chmn., Dentist of Yr.). Roman Catholic. Avocations: hunting, fishing, boats. Office: 1625 Lakeside Dr Reno NV 89509-3408

DIJKSTRA, SANDRA, literary agent; b. N.Y., Feb. 11, 1942; m. Abraham Dijkstra. BA, Adelphi U., 1963; MA, U. Calif., Berkeley, 1964; PhD, U. Calif., San Diego, 1976. Asst. prof. San Diego State U., 1971-74, U. Va., Charlottesville, 1975-76; asst. prof. U. Calif., San Diego, 1976-77, Irvine, 1978-79, L.A., 1979-80, San Diego, 1980-83; lit. agt. Sandra Dykstra Lit. Agy., Del Mar, Calif., 1979—. Author: Feminism in the Age of George Sand, 1992. Avocations: reading, swimming, hiking. Office: Sandra Dijkstra Lit Agy 1155 Camino Del Mar # 515 Del Mar CA 92014-2605

DILBECK, CHARLES STEVENS, JR., real estate company executive; b. Dallas, Dec. 2, 1944; s. Charles Stevens Sr. and Betty Doris (Owens) D.; 1 child, Stephen Douglas; m. Carolyn Jane DeBoer, Sept. 4, 1994. BS, Wichita State U., 1968; MS, Stanford U., 1969, postgrad., 1970-71. Engr. United Tech. Ctr., Sunnyvale, Calif., 1971-72; cons. Diversicom, Inc., Santa Clara, Calif., 1972-73; engr. Anamet Labs., San Carlos, Calif., 1973-75; cons. real estate investment Cert. Capital Corp., San Jose, Calif., 1975-82; pvt. practice in real estate, San Jose, 1981—; prin. Am. Equity Investments, San Jose, 1982—; mem. Los Gatos (Calif.) Rent Adv. Com., 1988. Mem. Nat. Apt. Assn., San Jose Real Estate Bd., Tri-County Apt. Assn., Gold Key Club, Tau Beta Pi (pres. 1968), Sigma Gamma Tau. Republican. Avocation: ocean yacht racing. Home: 301 Alta Loma Ln Santa Cruz CA 95062-4620 Office: Am Equity Investments 301 Alta Loma Ln Santa Cruz CA 95062-4620

DILENSCHNEIDER, ANNE MARIE, clergywoman; b. Ft. Meade, Md., Dec. 8, 1955; d. John Joseph and Rose Marie (Oppenheim) D.; children: James, Sophia, Clara, Thomas. BA cum laude, U. Notre Dame, Ind., 1977; MDiv, Pacific Sch. Religion, Berkeley, Calif., 1987; postgrad., Ashland Theol. Sem., 1998—. Ordained elder United Meth. Ch., 1992. Asst. buyer Venture Stores, St. Louis, 1977-78; asst. mgr. Waldenbooks, Chesterfield, Mo., 1978-79; intern Concord (Calif.) United Meth. Ch., 1985-87; assoc. pastor Trinity United Meth. Ch., Chico, Calif., 1987-88, Paradise (Calif.) United Meth. Ch., 1988-92; instr. religious studies Calif. State U., Chico, 1992; pastor Ukiah (Calif.) United Meth. Ch., 1992-94, Crystal Springs United Meth. Ch., San Mateo, Calif., 1994—; co-leader 1st Yr. Great Books Seminar, U. Notre Dame, Ind., 1977; tutor Calif. Sch. for Deaf, Fremont, Calif., 1983; convenor feminist ethics Ctr. for Women and Religion, Pacific Sch. Religion, Grad. Theol. Union, Berkeley, Calif., 1987; leader weekly classroom music sessions with elem. sch. children, 1992-98; workshop leader Ctr. for Action and Contemplation, Albuquerque, 1990, 91, 93, 96, seminar leader U. Notre Dame's Reunion Seminars, 1996, 97; leader groups on spirituality and creativity, 1998; adminstrv. asst. HealthAm. Rockridge, Oakland, Calif., 1984-85; sec. Lawrence Berkeley Lab., 1985; mem. staff Grad. Theol. Union Libr., Berkeley, 1985-87; supervising pastor United Meth. ministerial candidates, 1994-96; bd. dirs. Coop. Ministries in Higher Edn., 1988-93; vice chair U. Meth. Bd. Higher Edn. and Campus Ministry, 1987-93; vol. chaplain VNA Hospice, 1994-96; cons. Fault Line Cons., 1998—. Editor Meditations, 1987-93, Voices and Silencies, 1989-91; contbr. articles to profl. jours.; author numerous poems. Vol. coord. Parent Info. Network, Fremont, Calif., 1981-83; bd. dirs. Art Has Heart, 1996—; pres. Ukiah Interfaith Network, 1992-94; bd. dirs. Witness for Peace, Ctrl. Pacific Region, 1986-92; bd. dirs. Ctr. for Women and Religion, 1985-87. Recipient women's award of achievement U. Notre Dame Alumni Assn., 1996; grantee Philanthropic Ventures Found., 1998. Mem. Peninsula United Meth. Assn., San Mateo Ministerial Assn., Paradise Ministerial Assn. (pres. 1991-92). Office: Crystal Springs United Meth. Ch. 2145 Bunker Hill Dr San Mateo CA 94402-3858

DILL, LADDIE JOHN, artist; b. Long Beach, Calif., Sept. 14, 1943; s. James Melvin and Virginia (Crane) D.; children: Ariel, Jackson Caldwell. BFA, Chouinard Art Inst., 1968. Chmn. of visual arts The Studio Sch., Santa Monica, Calif.; lectr. painting and drawing UCLA, 1975-88. Exhbns. include: San Francisco Mus. Modern Art, 1977-78, Albright Knox Mus., Buffalo, 1978-79, Charles Cowles Gallery, N.Y.C., 1983-85, The First Show, Los Angeles; represented in permanent collections: Mus. Modern Art, N.Y.C., Laguna Mus. Art, Los Angeles County Mus., Mus. Contemporary Art, Los Angeles, Santa Barbara Mus., San Francisco Mus. Modern Art, Seattle Mus., Newport Harbor Art Mus., Oakland Mus., Smithsonian Instn., IBM, Nat. Mus., Seoul, Republic of Korea, San Diego Mus. Art, La. Mus., Denmark, Am. Embassy, Helsinki, Finland, Corcoran Gallery Art, Washington, Chgo Art Inst., Greenville County (S.C.) Mus., Palm Springs Desert Mus., Phoenix Art Mus., William Rockhill Nelsen Mus., Kansas City, Phillips Collection. Nat. Endowment Arts grantee, 1975, 82; Guggenheim Found. fellow, 1979-80; Calif. Arts Council Commn. grantee, 1983-84.

DILL, YARON, computer programmer; b. Jerusalem, Israel, Feb. 22, 1970; came to U.S., 1997; s. Yossi and Levana (Ben-Eliezer) D. Technician, Ort Coll., Israel, 1989; sys. analyst, Israeli Def. Force, 1994. Project mgr. Israeli Def. Force, 1989-96; dept. mgr. Crystal, Costa Mesa, Calif., 1997—. With Israeli Mil., 1988-96. Jewish. Avocations: reading, diving, skiing, traveling.

DILLARD, JOHN MARTIN, lawyer, pilot; b. Long Beach, Calif., Dec. 25, 1945; s. John Warren and Clara Leora (Livermore) D.; student U. Calif., Berkeley, 1963-67; BA, UCLA, 1968; JD, Pepperdine U., 1976; m. Patricia Anne Yeager, Aug. 10, 1968; children: Jason Robert, Jennifer Lee. Instr. pilot Norton AFB, Calif., 1973-77. Bar: Calif., 1976. Assoc. Magana, Cathcart & McCarthy, L.A., 1977-80, Lord, Bissell & Brook, L.A., 1980-85; of counsel Finley, Kumble, Wagner, 1985-86, Schell & Delamer, 1986-94, Law Offices of John M. Dillard, 1986—, v.p., gen. counsel, dir. Resort Aviation Svcs, Inc., Calif., 1988-93; mng. ptnr. Natkin & Weisbach, So. Calif., 1988-89; arbitrator Orange County Superior Ct.; atty. settlement officer U.S. Dist. Ct. Ctrl. Dist. Calif. Active Am. Cancer Soc.; bd. dirs. Placentia-Yorba Linda Ednl. Found., Inc. Capt. USAF, 1968-73, Vietnam. Mem. ATLA (aviation litigation com.), Am. Bar Assn. (aviation com.), Orange County Bar Assn., Fed. Bar Assn., L.A. County Bar Assn. (aviation com.), Century City Bar Assn., Internat. Platform Assn., Res. Officers Assn., Orange County Com. of 100, Sigma Nu. Home: 19621 Verona Ln Yorba Linda CA 92886-2858 Office: 313 N Birch St Santa Ana CA 92701-5263

DILLARD, MARILYN DIANNE, property manager; b. Norfolk, Va., July 7, 1940; d. Thomas Ortman and Sally Ruth (Wallerich) D.; m. James Conner Coons, Nov. 6, 1965 (div. June 1988); 1 child, Adrienne Alexandra Dillard Coons (dec.). Studied with Russian prima ballerina, Alexandra Danilova, 1940's; student with honors at entrance, UCLA, 1958-59; BA in Bus. Adminstrn. with honors, U. Wash., 1962. Modeling-print work Harry Conover, N.Y.C., 1945; ballet instr. Ivan Novikoff Sch. Russian Ballet, 1955; model Elizabeth Leonard Agy., Seattle, 1955-68; mem. fashion bd., retail worker Frederick & Nelson, Seattle, 1962; retail worker I. Magnin & Co., Seattle, 1963-64; property mgr. Seattle, 1961—; antique and interior designer John J. Cunningham Antiques, Seattle, 1968-73; owner, interior designer Marilyn Dianne Dillard Interiors, 1973—; rsch. bd. advisors Am. Biog. Inst., Inc., 1990—. Author: (poetry) Flutterby, 1951, Spring Flowers, 1951; contbr., asst. chmn. (with Jr. League of Seattle) Seattle Classic Cookbook, 1980-83. Charter mem., pres. Children's Med. Ctr., Maude Fox Guild, Seattle, 1965—, Jr. Women's Symphony Assn., 1967-73, Va. Mason Med. Ctr. Soc., 1990—, Nat. Mus. of Am. Indian, Smithsonian Instn., 1992; mem. Seattle Jr. Club, 1962-65, 97—; bd. dirs. Patrons N.W. Civic, Cultural and Charitable Orgns., chmn. various coms., Seattle, 1976—, prodn. chmn., 1977-78, 84-85, auction party chmn., 1983-84, exec. com., 1984-85, chmn. bd. vols., 1990-91, adv. coun., 1991—; mem. U. Wash. Arboretum Found. Unit, 1966-73, pres., 1969; bd. dirs. Coun. for Prevention Child Abuse-Neglect, Seattle, 1974-75; bd. dirs., v.p., com. mem. Seattle Children's Theatre, 1984-90, asst. in lighting main stage plays, 1987-93, adv. coun., 1993—; asst. in lighting main stage plays Bathhouse Theatre, 1987-90; adv. bd. N.W. Asian Am. Theatre, 1987—, Co-Motion Dance Co., 1991—; organizer teen groups Episcopal Ch. of Epiphany, 1965-67; provisional class pres. Jr. League Seattle, 1971-72, next to new shop asst. chmn., 1972-73, bd. dirs. admissions chmn., 1976-77, exec. v.p., exec. com., bd. dirs., 1978-79, sustaining mem., 1984—; charter mem. Jr. Women's Symphony Assn., 1967-73; mem. Seattle Art Mus., 1975-90, Landmark, 1990—, Corp. Coun. for Arts, 1991—; founding dir. Adrienne Coons Meml. Fund, 1985, v.p., 1985-92, 95—, pres. 1992-95; mem. steering com. Heart Ball Am. Heart Assn., 1986, 87, auction chmn., 1986; mem. steering com. Bellevue Sch. Dist. Children's Theatre, 1983-85, pub. rels. chair, 1984, asst. stage mgr., 1985; mem. Hist. Seattle Preservation and Devel. Authority, 1997—; mem. Eastlake Cmty. Coun., 1997—. Named Miss Greater Seattle, 1964. Mem. U. Wash. Alumnae Assn. (life), Pacific N.W. Ballet Assn. (charter), Progressive Animal Welfare Soc., Associated Women (student coun. U. Wash. 1962), Profl. Rodeo Cowboys Assn. (assoc.), Seattle Tennis Club. Republican. Episcopalian. Avocations: needlepoint, horseback riding, theatre, travel, antique restoration. Home and Office: 2053 Minor Ave E Seattle WA 98102-3513

DILLARD, MICHAEL L., food products company executive; b. 1942. BS in Acctg., Miss. Coll., 1964. Various acctg. positions Chrysler Corp., Cape Canaveral, Fla., 1964-66; divsn. acct. Blue Goose Growers, Vero Beach, Fla., 1966-76; CFO Pure Gold, Redlands, Calif., 1976-85, Saticoy Lemon Assocs., Inc., Santa Paula, Calif., 1985—. Office: Saticoy Lemon Assoc Inc PO Box 46 Santa Paula CA 93061-0046*

DILLARD, SUZANNE, interior designer; d. Jerome Wallace and Mary Mae (Price) Sorenson; m. Warren Marcus Dillard; 1 child, Jeremy Blake. Student, Tex. A&M U., 1961-64; BS, U. Tex., 1965; student, Pepperdine U., 1974, UCLA, 1977-78. Interior designer Pepperdine U., Malibu, Calif., 1982-95, exec. bd. dirs. Ctr. Arts, 1993-97; cons., interior design Neptune and Thomas, Architects, Pasadena, Calif., 1979-80; pres. Suzanne Dillard Interiors, Pacific Palisades, Calif., 1974—; prin. on camera designer TV pilot, Dream House, Forecast Group Prodns., 1983; speaker in field. Treas. Nat. Arts Assn., L.A., 1982-83, benefit chair, 1992; pres. Fine Arts aux., Assistance League So. Calif., L.A., 1984; patron, sponsor, prodn. chmn. The Footlighters, L.A., 1985-86, pres., 1992-93; pres. League for Children, 1991-93, Achievement Awards Coll. Scientists, 1994-96; benefit chair Freedoms Found., 1995, 1st v.p., 1997-98, pres., 1998—; bd. dirs. Ctr. for Arts Pepperdine U. Mem. SAG, AFTRA, NATAS, Acad. TV Arts and Scis., Internat. Platform Assn. (pres. 1997—, adv. bd.), Internat. Found. for Ednl. and Performing Arts (adv. bd.), Delta Delta Delta (pres. L.A. chpt. 1970-72, pres. sleighbell 1993-94). Republican. Mem. Ch. of Christ. Avocations: piano, voice, oil painting, reading, skiing. Home and Office: Suzanne Dillard Interiors PO Box 491883 Los Angeles CA 99049

DILLARD, TERESA MARY, school counselor; b. Columbus, Ga., May 12, 1956; d. Francis Joseph and Sadayo (Takabayashi) Luther; m. David Howard Dillard, July 22, 1978; children: Christine Marie, Justin David. BA, U. Md., 1977, MEd, 1981. Cert. guidance counselor, social studies tchr., modern fgn. lang. tchr., Mass., N.C. Asst. to supr. Bur. Govtl. Rsch., U. Md., College Park, 1977-78; tchr. high sch. Montgomery County Pub. Schs., Rockville, Md., 1978-80; substitute tchr. Anne Arundel Pub. Schs., Annapolis, Md., 1981, Bourne County Pub. Schs., Cape Cod, Mass., 1982-84; guidance counselor Camden County Pub. Schs., Camden, N.C., 1989-95; counselor, advisor U. Md. Relief Ctr., College Park, 1977, tutor Japanese lang., 1977, vol. substitute instr. Japanese lang. dept., 1977; cons. UCNC Radio Talk Show, Elizabeth City, N.C., 1991; program developer Grandy Primary Sch., Camden, N.C., 1989-95. Designer, creator children's clothing. Religious edn. tchr. Ft. Meade (Md.) Chapel Ctr., 1978, St. Bernadette Ch., Severn, Md., 1979-80; religious edn. tchr. Otis Chapel, Otis Air Nat. Guard Base, Mass., 1982-83, coord., dir. religious edn. program, 1983-84; bd. dirs., tchr. Holy Family Religious Edn. Program, Elizabeth City, N.C., 1989-91; asst. music ministry Holy Family Ch., Elizabeth City, 1991-95. Mem. ACA, Am. Sch. Counselors Assn., U. Md. Alumni Assn., Phi Beta Kappa, Phi Kappa Phi, Alpha Kappa Delta. Roman Catholic. Avocations: sewing, needlework, writing, woodburning, tae kwon do martial arts.

DILLON, FRANCIS PATRICK, human resources executive, management and personnel sales consultant; b. Long Beach, Calif., Mar. 15, 1937; s. Wallace Myron and Mary Elizabeth (Land) D.; B.A., U. Va., 1959; M.S., Def. Fgn. Affairs Sch., 1962; M.B.A., Pepperdine U., 1976; m. Vicki Lee Dillon, Oct. 1980; children: Cary Randolph, Francis Patrick Jr., Randee, Rick. Traffic mgr., mgr. pers. svcs. Pacific Telephone Co., Sacramento and Lakeport, Calif., 1966-69; asst. mgr. manpower planning and devel. Pan-Am. World Airways, N.Y.C., 1969-71; mgr. pers. and orgn. devel. Continental Airlines, L.A., 1971-74; dir. human resources Bourns, Inc., Riverside, Calif., 1974-80; v.p. employee and cmty. relations MSI Data Corp., 1980-83; pres. Pavi Enterprises, 1983—; cons. mgmt. Pers. Outplacement Counseling/Sales/Mgmt., fin. svcs. and estate planning, 1983—; pres., CEO Pers. Products & Svcs., Inc., 1984-91; v.p. Exec. Horizons, Inc., 1988-94; sr. profl. svcs. cons. Right Assocs., 1994-97; pres. Meditrans Inc., 1977-80. Bd. dirs. Health Svcs. Maintenance Orgn., Inc., Youth Svcs. Ctr., Inc.; vol. precinct worker. Served to lt. comdr. USN, 1959-66; asst. naval attaché, Brazil, 1963-65. Recipient Disting. Svc. award Jaycees, 1969; Jack Cates Meml. Vol. of Year award Youth Svc. Ctr., 1977. Mem. Assn. Internal Mgmt. Cons.'s, Am. Soc. Personnel Adminstrn., Personnel Indsl. Rels. Assn., Am. Soc. Tng. and Devel., Am. Electronics Assn. (human resources com., chmn. human resources symposium), Lake Mission Viejo Assn. (sec., bd. dirs. 1990-94). Republican. Episcopalian. Clubs: Mission Viejo Sailing, YMCA Bike, Mission Viejo Ski, Caving, Toastmasters (pres. 1966-67), Have Dirt Will Travel, Capo Valley 4 Wheelers. Office: Pavi Enterprises 27331 Via Amistoso Mission Viejo CA 92692-2410

DILLON, JOSEPH NEIL, pastor; b. Fresno, Calif., July 31, 1945; s. Howard Arthur and Blanch Marie (Nichols) D.; m. Paula Ann Gunovich, June 17, 1973; children: Chandra M., Ryan A. 0BA, Pacific Luth. U., 1970; MDiv, Northwestern Luth. Theol. Sem., 1976. Ordained to ministry, Luth. Ch., 1976. Pastor 1st Luth. Ch., Anconda, Mont., 1976-82, Messiah Luth. Ch., Billings, Mont., 1982-85; assoc. pastor Messiah Luth. Ch., Auburn, Wash., 1985-88; sr. pastor Messiah Luth. Ch., 1988—; dean, Evergreen Conf., South King Coun., Wash., 1990—; regional coun. Region I ELCA Southwest Wash., 1987-90, pres., 1988-90; pres., Auburn Ministrial Assn., 1988-90. Mem. Gov. Coun. Employment Planning, Anaconda, 1980-83; pres., bd. dirs., Anaconda Devel. Disabled, 1978-82; bd. dirs., Auburn Youth Resources, 1987—; mem. Human Resources Commn., City Auburn, 1987—. Sgt. U.S. Army, 1963-66. Mem. Lions. Home: 6307 37th Pl SE Auburn WA 98092-7391 Office: Messiah Luth Ch 805 4th St NE Auburn WA 98002-5088

DILLY, MARIAN JEANETTE, humanities educator; b. Vining, Minn., Nov. 7, 1921; d. John Fredolph and Mabel Josephine (Haagenson) Linder; m. Robert Lee Dily, June 22, 1946 (dec. Oct. 1987); children: Ronald Lee, Patricia Jeanette Dilly Vero. Studetn, U. Minn., 1944-45; grad., John R. Powers Finishing Sch., N.Y.C., 1957, Zell McC. Fashion Career Sch., Mpls., 1957, Estelle Compton Models Inst., Mpls., 1966, Nancy Taylor Charm Sch., N.Y.C., 1967, Patricia Stevens Career Sch., Mpls., 1968; BS in English cum laude, Black Hills State U., Spearfish, S.D., 1975. Instr. Nat. Coll., Rapid City, S.D., 1966-68; instr., dir. Nancy Taylor Charm Sch., 1966-68; hostess TV shows, 1966-74; lectr. in personality devel., dir., prodr. beauty and talent pageants, freelance coord. in fashion shows, judge beauty and talent pageants of local, state and nat. levels, 1966—. Actress bit parts Nauman Films Inc., 1970. Active ARC; dir., 1st v.p. Black Hills Girl Scout Coun., 1967-72; chmn. bd. dirs., pres. Luth. Social Svc. Aux., Western S.D. and Eastern Wyo., 1960-65; chmn. women's events Dakota Days and Nat. Premiere, 1968; bd. dirs. YMCA, 1976-81; mem. Dallas Symphony Orch. League, 1987-90, Dallas Mus. of Art League, 1987-90, Women's Club. Dallas County, Tex., Inc., 1987-90. Recipient award Rapid City C. of C., 1968, Fashion awards March of Dimes, 1967-72, Svc. award Black Hills Girl Scout Coun., award of appreciation Yellowstone Internat. Toastmistress Club. Mem. AAUW (sec., mem. exec.b d. 1988-90), Nu Tau Sigma (past advisor), Delta Tau Kappa, Singing Tribe of Wahoo. Avocations: golf, bridge, music, skiing. Home: 330 Agate St Broomfield CO 80020-1924

DILORENZO, FRANCIS X., bishop; b. Philadelphia, PA, Apr. 15, 1942. ordained priest May 18, 1968. Titular bishop of Tigia, 1988; aux. bishop Diocese of Scranton, 1988; apostolic admin. Diocese of Honolulu, 1993-94, bishop, 1994—. Office: Chancery Office 1184 Bishop St Ste B Honolulu HI 96813-2858

DI MASSA, ERNANI VINCENZO, JR., broadcast executive, television producer, writer; b. Phila., Sept. 12, 1947; s. Ernani Vincenzo and Rita C. (Iacovoni) Di M.; m. Karen Sue Bryant, July 10, 1976; 1 child, Michael Colin. BS, La Salle Coll., 1970; MS, Temple U., 1972. Producer, writer Mike Douglas Show, Phila. and L.A., 1969-81, Regis Philbin Show, L.A., 1981, Fantasy NBC-TV, L.A., 1981-83; exec. producer, writer Thicke of the Night, L.A., 1983-84, Tony Orlando Show, L.A., 1985-86; supervising producer Hollywood Squares, L.A., 1987-89; sr. v.p. programming and devel. King World Prodns., L.A., 1989—. Supervising producer Candid Camera; exec. in charge prodn. Rolonda. Recipient Emmy award NATAS, 1982. Mem. Producers Guild Am., Writers Guild Am. Roman Catholic. Avocations: car collecting and restoring, photography. Office: Di Massa Prod Inc 15233 Ventura Blvd Fl 9 Sherman Oaks CA 91403-2250

DIMICHELE, DAVID JOHN, artist; b. Long Beach, Calif., Apr. 15, 1954; s. Guy Anthony and Joyce Carol (McVeedy) DiM.; m. Gayle Darlene Gaines, July 13, 1997. Student, U. Calif., Berkeley, 1972-74; BA in Fine Art, U Calif., Santa Cruz, 1976; MFA, Calif. State U., Long Beach, 1980. artist-in residence City of Long Beach, 1979; mem. edn. dept. Mus. Contemporary Art, L.A., 1996-98. One-man shows include Art Gallery, Calif. State U., Long Beach, 1980, Simard/Halm Gallery, L.A., 1985, Mira Costa Coll. Art Gallery, Oceanside, Calif., 1986, L.A. Art Core Gallery, 1990, William Turner Gallery, Venice, Calif, 1995, Pierce Coll. Art Gallery, Woodland Hills, Calif., 1996, Claremont (Calif.) Grad. Sch. Art Gallery, 1997, Mendenhall Art Gallery Whittier Coll., 1999; exhibited in group shows at Rutgers U. Art Gallery, Camden, N.J., 1983, Laguna Art Mus., Laguna Beach, Calif., 1987, Palos Verdes Art Ctr., Rancho Palos Verdes, Calid., 1989, Security Pacific Gallery, Costa Mesa, Calif., 1990, L.A. Contemporary Exhbns., L.A., 1991, L.A. Mcpl. Art Gallery, 1993, Andrew Shire Gallery, L.A., 1996, Haggerty Art Mus., Milw., 1997, Ubermain Gallery, L.A., 1998, Strange Air, L.A., 1998; represented in permanent collections at Laguna Art Mus., Laguna Beach, Calif., Bank of Am. Collection, L.A., Disney Corp., Burbank, Calif., Rebock Corp., Irvine, Calif., Trammel Crow Co., Irvine, Calif.; contbg. editor Artweek Mag., San Jose, Calif., 1992-97; contbr. articles to profl. jours. Recipient 2nd pl. award L.A. Art Core, 1997. Mem. L.A. River Artist and Bus. Assn., Downtown Artists Devel. Assn., Seeking It Through Exhbns. Democrat. Avocations: adventure travel, hiking, rock climbing. Home: 912 E 3rd St Ste 306 Los Angeles CA 90013-1852

DIMITRIADIS, ANDRE C., health care executive; b. Istanbul, Turkey, Sept. 29, 1940; s. Constantine N. and Terry D. BS, Robert Coll., Istanbul, 1964; MS, Princeton U., 1965; MBA, NYU, 1967, PhD, 1970. Analyst Mobil Oil Internat., N.Y.C., 1965-67; mgr. TWA, N.Y.C., 1967-73; dir. Pan Am. Airways, N.Y.C., 1973-76; asst. treas. Pan Am. Airways, 1976-79; v.p., chief fin. officer Air Calif., Newport Beach, 1979-82; exec. v.p. fin. and adminstrn., chief fin. officer Western Airlines, Los Angeles, 1982-85; dir. Western Airlines; sr. v.p. (fin) Am. Med. Internat., from 1985, chief fin. officer, 1985-89, exec. v.p., 1988-89; dir., exec. v.p. fin., chief fin. officer Beverly Enterprises Inc., Ft. Smith, Ark., 1989-92; chmn., CEO LTC Properties, Inc., 1992—; bd. dirs. Magellan Health Svc. Democrat. Greek Orthodox. Home: 4470 Vista Del Preseas Malibu CA 90265-2540 Office: Ltc Properties Inc 300 E Esplanade Dr Ste 1860 Oxnard CA 93030-1286

DIMITRIĆ, RADOSLAV MILAN, mathematician, translator; b. Loznica, Serbia, Yugoslavia, May 4, 1955; came to U.S., 1980; s. Milan Dobrivoje and Nadežda Blagojevic Jovan. BSc, U. Belgrade, Serbia, 1978, MSc, 1980; PhD, Tulane U., 1983. Tchg. asst. Tulane U., New Orleans, 1980-83; lectr. Dublin Inst. Tech., Ireland, 1985-87, U. Exeter, Eng., 1987-89; vis. prof. U. Calif., Davis, 1989-90; vis. scholar Stanford U., Calif., 1990-92; vis. prof. Pa. State U., Fayette, 1992-93; vis. prof., rsch. assoc. U. Calif., Berkeley, 1993-99; judge Calif. Fair of Sci. and Tech., L.A., 1990-94; panelist Am. Invitational Math. Examination, Am. H.S. Math. Examination, Am. Jr. H.S. Math. Examination, U.S. Math. Olympiad, 1995—. Contbr. articles, papers to profl. jours. With Signal Corps, Yugoslav Army, 1979-80. Recipient first award Union of Balkan Mathematicians, Sofia, Bulgaria, 1984; rsch. grantee British Royal Soc., London, 1989, congress grantee Internat. Mathematical Union, Helsinki, 1990. Mem. Am. Mathematical Soc., London Mathematical Soc. Serbian Orthodox. Achievements include classification of slender modules; examples in homological dimension of modules over valuation domains; interpretations of Kurepa's trees in algebra. Avocations: swimming, fishing, painting, music, singing. Office: Univ Calif Dept Math Berkeley CA 94720

DIMMICK, CAROLYN REABER, federal judge; b. Seattle, Oct. 24, 1929; d. Maurice C. and Margaret T. (Taylor) Reaber; m. Cyrus Allen Dimmick, Sept. 10, 1955; children: Taylor, Dana. BA, U. Wash., 1951, JD, 1963; LLD, Gonzaga U., 1982, CUNY, 1987. Bar: Wash. Asst. atty. gen. State of Wash., Seattle, 1953-55; pros. atty. King County, Wash., 1955-59, 60-62; sole practice Seattle, 1959-60, 62-65; judge N.E. Dist. Ct. Wash., 1965-75, King County Superior Ct., 1976-80; justice Wash. Supreme Ct., 1981-85; judge U.S. Dist. Ct. (we. dist.) Wash., Seattle, 1985-94, chief judge, 1994-97, sr. judge, 1997—, chmn. Jud. Resources Com., 1991-94, active, 1987-94. Recipient Matrix Table award, 1981, World Plan Execs. Council award, 1981, Vanguard Honor award King County of Washington Women Lawyers, 1996, Honorable mention U. Wash. Law Rev., 1997, Disting. Alumni award U. Wash. Law Sch., 1997. Mem. ABA, Am. Judges Assn. (gov.), Nat. Assn. Women Judges, World Assn. Judges, Wash. Bar Assn., Am. Judicature Soc., Order of Coif (Wash. chpt.). Office: US Dist Ct 713 US Courthouse 1010 5th Ave Ste 215 Seattle WA 98104-1189

DIMMICK, LAURETTA, art historian, educator; b. Pierre, S.D., Jan. 17, 1953; d. Ray and LInda (Busey) D.; 1 child, James Douglas Dimmick Bragg. BA, U. Denver, 1976; MA, U. Pitts., 1984, PhD, 1986. Chester Dale fellow Met. Mus. Art, N.Y.C., 1985-86, Andrew Mellon fellow, 1986-87; asst. curator Mus. Fine Arts, Boston, Mass., 1987-90; Gates Found. curator painting and sculptures Denver Art Mus., 1990-97. Contbg. author: America Paradise, The World of the Hudson River School, 1987, Dictionary of Art, 1996, Denver Art Museum: The First 100 Years. Democrat. Episcopalian. Home: 25 Fairfax St Denver CO 80220-6329

DIMOND, MICHAEL LEN, broadcast executive, director; b. Colorado Springs, Colo., July 30, 1959; s. Marvin Laverne and Geneva May (Ewer) D.; m. Janice Lynn Craze. BA, Colo. State U., 1981. Prodn. asst. Sta. KYCU-TV, Cheyenne, Wyo., 1981-82, Sta. KRDO-TV, Colorado Springs, 1982-83; videotape operator Telemation Prodns., Denver, 1983-84; producer, dir. United Cable TV, Englewood, Colo., 1984-88; sr. producer Prime Sports Network Rocky Mountain, Denver, Colo., 1988-93; exec. producer STARTV Prime Sports, Hong Kong, 1993-95; dir. programming & prodn. Fox Sports Rocky Mountain, Denver, 1995—. Home: 7332 Woodglen Pl Castle Rock CO 80104-8285 Office: Fox Sports Rocky Mountain 44 Cook St Ste 600 Denver CO 80206-5825

DINEL, RICHARD HENRY, lawyer; b. L.A., Sept. 16, 1942; s. Edward Price and Edith Elizabeth (Rheinstein) D.; m. Joyce Ann Korsmeyer, Dec. 26, 1970; children: Edward, Alison. BA, Pomona Coll., 1964; JD, Stanford U., 1967. Bar: Calif. Owner Richard H. Dinel, Profl. Law Corp., L.A., 1971-79; ptnr. Richards, Watson & Gershon, L.A., 1979-92, of counsel, 1992-93; pres. R.H. Dinel Investment Counsel, Inc., L.A., 1992—. Chmn. bd. Pomona Coll. Assocs., 1987-89; ex-officio trustee Pomona Coll., 1987-89; arbitrator Chgo. Bd. Options Exch., 1978—, Pacific Stock Exch., 1979—; bd. govs. Western Los Angeles County coun. Boys Scouts Am., 1993—. Mem. Securities Ind. Assn. (speaker compliance and legal div. 1978-92), Pomona Coll. Alumni Assn. (chmn. alumni fund and continuing edn. com. 1972-73), Nat. Assn. Securities Dealers (mem. nat. bd. arbitrators 1978-90), City Club on Bunker Hill, Bond Club L.A. Office: Ste 400 11661 San Vicente Blvd Los Angeles CA 90049-5112

DINI, JOSEPH EDWARD, JR., state legislator; b. Yerington, Nev., Mar. 28, 1929; s. Giuseppe and Elvira (Castellani) D.; m. Mouryne Landing; children: Joseph, George, David, Michael. BSBA, U. Nev., Reno, 1951. Mem. Nev. State Assembly, Carson City, 1967—; majority leader Nev. State Assembly, 1975; speaker Nev. State Assembly, Carson City, 1977, 87, 89, 91, 93, 97, 99; minority leader Nev. State Assembly, 1985; interim fin. com. mem., 1985-99, speaker pro tem, 1973; co-spkr. Nev. State Assembly, Carson City, 1995; chmn. water policy com. Western Legis. Conf., 1993-94, 96-97; pres. Dini's Lucky Club Casino, Yerington, Nev., 1972—; mem. legis. com. Nev. State Assembly, 1971-77, 91, 93, 95, 97, vice chmn., 1981-82, 96-97, chmn., 1982-83, 93-94. Mem. Yeringion Vol. Fire Dept.; mem. Lyon County Dem. Ctrl. Com., Nev. Am. Revolution Bicentennial Commn.; past dist. gov., active mem. 20-30 Club. Recipient Outstanding Citizen award Nev. Edn. Assn., 1973, Friend of Edn. award Nev. State Edn. Assn., 1986, Citizen of Yr. award Nev. Judges Assn., 1987, Dedicated and Valued Leadership award Nat. Conf. State Legislatures, 1989, Excellence in Pub. Svc. award Nev. Trial Lawyers Assn., 1990, Silver Plow award Nev. Farm Bur., 1991, Skill, Integrith, Responsibility award Assoc. Gen. Contractors, 1994, Guardian of Small Bus. award Nat. Fedn. Ind. Bus., 1996, Spl. Recognition award Nev. State Firefighters Assn., 1998; named Conservation Legislator of Yr. Nev. Wildlife Fedn., 1991, Alumnus of Yr., U. Nev., 1997, Alumni of Yr., U. Nev. Alumni Assn., 1997. Mem. Mason Valley C. of C. (pres.), Rotary (pres. Yerington 1989), Lions (pres. Yerington chpt. 1975), Masons, Shriners, York Rite, Scottish Rite, Order Ea. Star, Gamma Sigma Delta, Phi Sigma Kappa (Disting. Alumna award 1993). Home: 104 N Mountain View St Yerington NV 89447-2239 Office: Dini's Lucky Club Inc 45 N Main St Yerington NV 89447-2230

DINKELSPIEL, PAUL GAINES, investment banking and public financial consultant; b. San Francisco, Feb. 12, 1935; s. Edward Gaines and Pauline (Watson) D. A.B., U. Calif., Berkeley, 1959. Gen. ptnr. Stone & Youngberg, San Francisco, 1961-71; 1st v.p. Shearson Lehman Hutton and predecessor firms, San Francisco, 1971-79; pres., chmn. bd. dirs. Dinkelspiel, Belmont & Co., Inc., San Francisco; investment banking and pub. fin. cons., 1979—; bd. dirs. Gemstone Investors Assurance Corp., N.Y.C. With AUS, 1959-60. Mem. Govt. Fin. Officers Assn., Am. Water Works Assn., San Francisco Mcpl. Forum, Calif. Pub. Securities Assn. (public fin. com.), San Francisco Comml. Club, Commonwealth Club of Calif., Mcpl. Bond Club, N.Y. World Trade Club, Calif. Waterfowl Assn., Ducks Unltd., Sigma Chi. Home: PO Box 727 Stinson Beach CA 94970-0727 Office: 101 California St Fl 37 San Francisco CA 94111-5802

DINSMORE, CRAIG, zoo director. Exec. dir. Utah's Hoyte Zoo. Office: Utah's Hoyte Zoo PO Box 58475 Salt Lake City UT 84158-0475*

DINSMORE, PHILIP WADE, architect; b. Gilroy, Calif., Nov. 4, 1942; s. Wilbur Allen and Elizabeth Eleanor (Hill) D.; m. Mary Kathryn Mead; children: Robert Allen, Kerry Philip. B.Arch., U. Ariz., 1965. Registered arch., Ariz., Calif., Nev., N.C., Wyo. Nat. Coun. Archtl. Registration Bds. Designer, William L. Pereira & Assocs., L.A., 1965-67; assoc. CNWC Archs., Tucson, 1967-69; prin., ptnr. Architecture One Ltd., Tucson, 1970-90; pres. Durrant Architects Ariz., Phoenix and Tucson, 1995, bd. dir. Durrant Group, 1992—. Mem., chmn. Archtl. Approval Bd., City of Tucson, 1974-75, 77; bd. dir. Tucson Met. YMCA, 1993—, U. Az. Coll. Architecture, environ. design coun.; trustee AIA Benefit Ins. Trust, 1997—. Fellow AIA (nat. bd. dirs. 1981-84, nat. sec. 1984-88, Ariz. Archs. medal 1985, Western Mountain Region Citation award 1973, 76, 78, Award of Honor 1983, Silver medal 1992); mem. Am. Archtl. Found. (bd. regents 1988-92), Constrn. Specifications Inst., Ariz Soc. Archs. (citation 1977-80, 89). Recipient Tucker award Bldg. Stone Inst., 1986. Fellow AIA (regional fellows rep. 1990-96, trustee benefit ins. trust 1997—). Republican. Presbyterian. Office: Durrant Ariz 2980 N Campbell S-130 Tucson AZ 85719-2897

DION, SUSAN M., education director, educator; b. L.A., Sept. 15, 1947; d. Alfred H. and Marian B. (Fremont) Johnson; m. Raymond R. Dion, Jr., Feb. 6, 1971 (div. Nov. 1985); children: Scott R., Stacey S., Marian E. BS in Social Sci., Calif. Polytech. Inst., 1971; MA in Edn., U. San Francisco, 1982. Tchr., coach San Gabriel Mission Grammar Schs., 1968-77; prin. St. Dorothy's Sch., 1977-80; study ctr. dir. Walnut H.S., 1980-82; area coord., ctr. dir. Am. Learning Corp./The Reading Game, 1982-84; edn. coord. U. Hosp. Adolescent Unit, Denver, 1986-88; prin. Good Shepherd Sch., Denver, 1987-88; dir. edn. Charter Hosp., Aurora, Colo., 1988-90; tchr. Aurora Pub. Sch., 1990-92, Cherry Creek Sch. Dist., Aurora, 1992-93; transition svcs. dir. Excelsior Youth Ctr., Aurora, 1993-96; dir. edn. Jefferson Hills, Inc., Lakewood, Colo., 1996—. Author: Transition Skills Curriculum, 1994. Mem. adv. bd. for gifted and talented edn. Rowland Sch. Dist., Walnut, Calif., 1981-83. Mem. ASCD. Roman Catholic. Avocations: singing, guitar, choir director. Home: 2991 S Zeno Way Aurora CO 80013 Office: Jefferson Hills Inc 421 S Zang Lakewood CO 80228-4524

DI PALMA, JOSEPH ALPHONSE, airline company executive, lawyer; b. N.Y.C., Jan. 17, 1931; s. Gaetano and Michela May (Ambrosio) Di P.; m. Joycelyn Ann Engle, Apr. 18, 1970; children: Joycelyn Joan, Julianne Michelle. BA, Columbia U., 1952; JD, Fordham U., 1958; LLM in Taxation, NYU, 1959. Bar: N.Y. 1959. Tax atty. CBS, N.Y.C., 1960-64; v.p. tax dept. TWA, N.Y.C., 1964-74; pvt. practice law N.Y.C., 1974-87; investor, exec. dir. Di Palma Family Holdings, Las Vegas and N.Y.C., 1987—; cons. in field; head study group Comprehensive Gaming Study, N.Y.C. and Washington, 1990—; think tank exec. dir. Di Palma Position Papers; founder Di Palma Forum, U. Nev., Las Vegas; established The Di Palma Ctr. for Study of Jewelry and Precious Metals at Cooper-Hewitt, Nat. Design Mus., Smithsonian Instn., N.Y.C. Contbr. articles to profl. jours.; author: Di Palma Postion Papers. Bd. dirs. Friends of the Henry St. Settlement, N.Y.C., 1961-63, Outdoor Cleanliness Assn., N.Y.C., 1961-65; chmn. Air Transport Assn. Taxation Com., 1974. With U.S. Army, 1953-54. Recipient Disting. Svc. and Valuable Counsel commendation award Air Transport Assn., 1974, spl. commendation from N.Y.C. mayor Rudolph Giuliani, 1997. Mem. Internat. Platform Assn., N.Y. State Bar Assn., N.Y. Athletic Club. Roman Catholic.

Home: 3111 Bel Air Dr Apt 21B Las Vegas NV 89109-1506 Office: PO Box 72158 Las Vegas NV 89170-2158 also: 930 5th Ave # 4 J&H New York NY 10021-2651

DIPIETRO, ANTHONY MICHAEL, director, writer; b. La Jolla, Calif., Aug. 6, 1960; s. Virgilo Michael and Alice (Jones) DiP.; m. Abby Gibson, Feb. 28, 1983 (div. Feb. 1988). Grad., Am. Acad. Dramatic Arts-West, Pasadena, Calif., 1982; studetn, Hunter Coll./CCNY, 1990-92. Artistic dir. Art & Work Ensemble, N.Y.C., 1982-90, The Kraine Arts Ctr., N.Y.C., 1990-94; dir. Creative Concepts, N.Y.C., 1990-92, The Momemtum Project, L.A., 1995-97; co-founder Paloma Films, L.A., 1998—; dir., tchr. The Lambs Theatre, N.Y.C., Laughing Horse Theatre, Wash., Kutztown (Pa.) U., The New Sch., N.Y.C. Author: (screenplays) The Sweet Spot, 1997, Fair Hope, USA, 1998, Children to the Sun, 1998. Recipient New Plays of 1985 award Samuel French, Inc., 1985, New Play Festival award Third Step Theatre Co., 1986, Dramatic Writing Festival award NYU, 1989. Democrat. Avocations: baseball, surfing, running, reading.

DIPOTO, JERRY, baseball player; b. Jersey CIty, N.J., May 24, 1968. Pitcher Colo. Rockies, Denver. Office: Colo Rockies 2001 Blake St Denver CO 80205-2000

DIROLL, PATRICIA CORRIGAN, newspaper columnist, community volunteer; b. Glendale, Calif.; d. Robert Joseph and Cecile (Englande) Corrigan; m. Richard Albert Diroll, Aug. 31, 1961; children: Courtney Catherine, Robert Damien, Richard Blaise. Student, So Methodist U., 1952-54; BA, U. Calif., Berkeley, 1956. Society editor, newswriter San Gabriel Valley Newspaper Group, Pasadena, Calif., 1991—. Founding mem. Achievement Rewards for Coll. Scientists, L.A., 1958—; pres. Footlighters, Inc., L.A., 1962—. Recipient Eve award, Assistance League So. Calif., 1974. Mem. AFTRA, SAG, Greater L.A. Press Club, Soc. Profl. Journalists., Pi Beta Phi, U. Calif. Alumnae. Republican. Roman Catholic. Office: Pasadena Star-News 911 E Colorado Blvd Pasadena CA 91106-1700

DI ROMA, TOM, graphic technician, writer; b. Bronx, N.Y., Aug. 19, 1947; s. Angelo and Marie Di Roma. Grad. h.s., Norwalk High Sch., Norwalk, Conn., 1966. Mailroom clerk Lonestar Industries, Greenwich, Conn., 1971-74, Penn Central, Greenwich, Conn., 1974-87, Leisure Tech., Carlsbad, Calif., 1988-90; graphic tech. Try J Advertising, Carlsbad, Calif., 1990—. Author numerous short stories. With U.S. Air Force, 1967-71. Mem. Soc. Children's Books. Roman Catholic. Avocations: writing, movies. Home: 3566 Lookout Ct Apt 496 Oceanside CA 92056-5262 Office: Try J Advertising 5124 Paseo Del Norte Carlsbad CA 92008

DIRUSCIO, LAWRENCE WILLIAM, advertising executive; b. Buffalo, Jan. 2, 1941; s. Guido Carmen and Mabel Ella (Bach) DiR.; m. Gloria J. Edney, Aug. 19, 1972; children: Lawrence M., Lorie P., Darryl C., Teresa M., Jack D. With various broadcast stas. and instr., adminstr. Bill Wade Sch. Radio and TV, San Diego, San Francisco, Los Angeles, 1961-69; account exec. Sta. KGB Radio, San Diego, 1969, gen. sales mgr., 1970-72; pres. Free Apple Advt., San Diego, 1972-94, Fin. Mgmt. Assocs., Inc., San Diego, 1979-84, Self-Pub. Ptnrs., San Diego, 1981—, Media Mix Assocs. Enterprises, Inc., 1984-86; pres. Press-Courier Pub. Co., Inc., 1985-86; pres. Media Mix Advt. and Pub. Relations, 1985—, Taking Care of Bus. Pub. Co., 1990—; pres. Formula Mktg. Co., 1993. Chmn. bd. Quicksilver Enterprises, Inc., A Public Corp., 1992-93; lectr., writer on problems of small bus. survival. Served with USN, 1958-60. Five Emmy nominations for T.V. commercial writing and prodn. Mem. Nat. Acad. TV Arts and Scis. Democrat. Roman Catholic. Office: Media Mix Advt and Pub Rels 726 W Kalmia St San Diego CA 92101-1311

DISAIA, JOHN PHILIP, plastic surgeon, online author; b. New Haven, Conn., Mar. 10, 1964; s. Philip John and Ann Marie Margaret (DiJeser) DiS.; m. Penelope Stacy Jurmain, May 6, 1995. BA in Neurobiology, U. Calif., Berkeley, 1986; MD, U. Calif., Irvine, 1990. Staff writer Rock City News, Hollywood, Calif., 1990-92; writer, dir. Electric Shorts Online, Costa Mesa, Calif., 1992-; gen. surgery resident U. Calif., Irvine, Calif., 1990-95, plastic surgery resident, 1995-97; freelance writer Irvine, 1990-; mem. bd. dirs. info. svcs. U. Calif., Irvine, 1993-97; editl. bd. mem. Hosp. Physician, Wayne, Pa., 1996; asst. clin. prof., divsn. plastic surgery, U. Calif., Irvine, 1997-98. Author: (web site) Electric Shorts Online, 1995, Plastic Surgery Interactive Resource Page, 1996—, (RIMEnet column) Electric Shorts Online, 1992, (tutorial software) Medquiz, 1993, A Plastic Surgery Primer, 1997. Mem. Am. Soc. Plastic and Reconstructive Surgeons (affiliate). Roman Catholic. Avocations: scuba, weight lifting, computer design. Office: 3801 Katella Ave Ste 310 Los Alamitos CA 90720-3366

DISAIA, PHILIP JOHN, gynecologist, obstetrician, radiology educator; b. Providence, Aug. 14, 1937; s. George and Antoinette (Vastano) DiS.; divorced; children: John P., Steven D.; m. Patricia June; children: Dominic J., Vincent J. BS cum laude, Brown U., 1959; MD cum laude, Tufts U., 1963. Diplomate Am. Bd. Ob-Gyn. (examiner 1975—, bd. dirs. 1994, v.p. bd. dirs. 1997—), Am. Bd. Gynecologic Oncology (bd. dirs. 1987—). Intern Yale U. Sch. Medicine, New Haven Hosp., 1963-64, resident in ob-gyn., 1964-67, instr. ob-gyn., 1966-67; fellow in gynecologic oncology U. Tex. M.D. Anderson Hosp. and Tumor Inst., Houston, 1969-70, NIH sr. fellow, 1969-70, instr. ob-gyn., 1969-71; asst. prof. ob-gyn. and radiology U. So. Calif. Sch. Medicine, L.A., 1971-74, assoc. prof., 1974-77; prof., chmn. dept. ob-gyn. U. Calif., Irvine Med. Ctr. Calif. Coll. Medicine, 1977-88, prof., 1977—, prof. radiology, radiation therapy div., 1978—, assoc. vice chancellor for health scis. Irvine Coll. Medicine, 1987-89, Dorothy Marsh chair of reproductive biology, 1989—, dep. dir. cancer ctr., 1989—, pres. med. staff, 1993-97; pres. UCI Clin. Practice Group, 1994—; dir. div. gynecol. oncology Am. Bd. Obstetrics & Gynecology, 1995—, bd. dirs., 1994—; bd. dirs. U. Calif. Irvine Med. Ctr., 1995; clin. enterprise adv. coun. to pres. U. Calif., 1995; academic planning task force U. Calif. Irvine, 1994, continuing med. edn. com., 1991-94; cancer liaison commn. on cancer Am. Coll. Surgeons, 1981-94; bd. dirs., dir. at large Am. Cancer Soc., 1985—; clin. prof. dept. ob-gyn. U. Nev. Sch. Medicine, Reno, 1985—; chmn. site visit team for surgery br. Nat. Cancer Inst. NIH, 1983, subcom. surg. oncology rsch. devel., 1982-83, mem. sci. counselors div. cancer treatment, 1979-83; mem. gov.'s adv. coun. on cancer State of Calif., 1980-85; vis. prof., lectr., speaker various sci. meetings, confs., courses. Author: (with E.J. Quilligan) Ovarian Tumors, Current Diagnosis, 1974, (with others) Synopsis of Gynecologic Oncology, 1975, (with W.T. Creasman) Clinical Gynecologic Oncology, 1980, 4th edit. 1993, 5th edit. 1997; contbr. numerous articles to profl. jours., book chpts.; assoc. editor Gynecologic Oncology, Endocurietherapy/Hyperthermia Oncology, Danforth's Textbook of Obstetrics & Gynecology; mem. editorial adv. bd. Am. Jour. Reproductive Immunology, Cancer Clinical Trials, The Female Patient, New Trends in Gynecology and Obstetrics (Italian publ.); reviewer Am. Jour. Ob-Gyn., Med. and Pediatric Oncology, New Eng. Jour. Medicine, Ob-Gyn. jour., Cancer; physician cons. Patient Care Standards jour.; sci. adv. bd. The Clin. Cancer Letter. Recipient Disting. Alumnus award M.D. Anderson Hosp. and Tumor Inst. U. Tex., 1980, Silver Apple award U. Calif. Med. Students, 1983, Lauds and Laurels Profl. Achievement award U. Calif. Alumni Assn., 1983, Hubert Haussel's award Long Beach Meml. Hosp., 1983, Dist. Faculty Lectureship award for Teaching, U. Calif. Irvine Acad. Senate, 1993-94, also various rsch. awards. Fellow Am. Coll. Obstetricians and Gynecologists (com. on human rsch. for cancer 1979—, chmn. 1984—, chmn. subcom. on gynecologic oncology 1984-85, prolog editorial and adv. com. 1986—, various others), ACS (bd. govs. 1997—), Commn. on Cancer Liaison, Western Assn. Gynecologic Oncologists (founder 1971, pres. 1978-79), Am. Gynecol. and Obstet. Soc. (exec. coun. 1986—), Am. Gynecologic Soc., Pacific Coast Ob/Gyn Soc., South Atlantic Assn. Obstetricians and Gynecologists (hon.); mem. AMA, Am. Cancer Soc. (bd. dirs. L.A. County unit 1975-77, Orange County 1979, unit pres. 1993—; bd. dirs. Calif. div. 1985—, chmn. med. scientific com. 1993-94), Nat. Am. Cancer Soc. (dir.-at-large, bd. dirs. 1985—, chmn. program com. for nat. conf. 1986, vice-chmn. detection and treatment adv. group gynecol. cancer 1993-94, active in others), Am. Coll. Radiology (commn. on cancer 1984-85), Am. Soc. Clin. Oncologists, Soc. Gynecologic Oncologists (exec. coun. 1975-80, pres. 1982-83), Internat. Gynecologic Oncology Cancer Soc., Italian Soc. Ob-Gyn. (Camillo Golgi prof. U. Brescia 1991), Calif. Med. Assn., other profl. orgns., Alpha Omega Alpha. Office: U Calif Irvine Med Ctr 101 The City Dr S Rm 403 Orange CA 92868-3201

DI SALVO, ARTHUR FRANCIS, physician, public health official; b. N.Y.C., May 16, 1932; m. Shirley Sayre, 1958; 1 child. AAS, SUNY, Cobbleskill, 1951; BS, U. Ariz., 1954, MS, 1958; MD, Med. Coll. of Ga., 1965. Diplomate Am. Bd. Med. Microbiology. Rsch. asst. dept. med. microbiology Med. Coll. of Ga., 1959-63; bacteriologist Milledgeville (Ga.) State Hosp., 1958-59; intern Eugene Talmadge Meml. Hosp., Augusta, Ga., 1965-66; fellow med. microbiology Nat. Communicable Disease Ctr., Atlanta, 1966-68; pvt. practice in med. microbiology, 1968—; chief Bur. of Labs. S.C. Dept. Health and Environ. Control, Columbia, 1968-90; dir. Nev. State Health Lab., Reno, 1990-97; clin. asst. prof. lab. medicine Med. U. of S.C., Charleston, 1971-78, clin. assoc. prof., 1978-86, clin. prof. pathology and lab. medicine, 1986-97; clin. assoc. prof. med. microbiology U. S.C. Sch. Medicine, Columbia, 1976-80, adj. prof. med. microbiology, 1980—; prof. pathology and lab. medicine U. Nev. Sch. Medicine, Reno, 1991-93; cons. microbiology device classification panel FDA, 1977-81; bd. dirs. Water Co. of Edisto Beach (S.C.), 1974-78. Editor-in-chief Mycopathologia, 1989—; mem. editl. bd. JSC Med. Assn., 1981-90, Diagnostic Microbiology and Infectious Disease, 1982-95; contbr. articles on med. microbiology to profl. jours. With USAF, 1954. Fellow Am. Acad. Microbiology; mem. Am. Soc. Microbiology (sec., treas. S.C. bd. 1969-78), Am. Pub. Health Assn. (mem. governing coun. 1975-78, 81-85), Assn. State and Territorial Pub. Health Lab. Dirs. (pres. 1978-79), S.C. Pub. Health Assn., Med. Mycological Soc. Ams. (coun. 1975-76, sec.-treas. 1979-82, pres. 1984), Nev. Pub. Health Assn., John Henry Newman Soc., Columbia Med. Soc., Internat. Soc. for Human and Animal Mycology, AMA (Physicians Recognition award), S.C. Med. Assn., Nev. State Med. Assn. E-mail: afdisalvo@juno.com. Fax: (775) 852-9046.

DI SANTA CRISTINA, LEONARDO DE GRASSI, art historian, educator; b. East Orange, N.J., Mar. 2, 1928; s. Romulus-William and Anna Sophia (Sannicolo) DeG.; m. Dolores Marie Welgoss, June 24, 1961; children: Maria Christina, Paul. BA, U. So. Calif., 1950, BFA, 1951, MA, 1956; postgrad., Harvard U., 1953, Istituto Centrale del Restauro di Roma, 1959-60, U. Rome, 1959-60, UCLA, 1970-73. Tchr. art Redlands (Calif.) Jr. High Sch., 1951-53, Toll Jr. High Sch., Glendale, Calif., 1953-61, Wilson Jr. High Sch., Glendale, 1961; mem. faculty Glendale Coll., 1962—, prof. art history, 1974-92, chmn. dept., 1972, 89, prof. emeritus, 1992—. Prin. works include: (paintings) high altar at Ch. St. Mary, Cook, Minn., altar screen at Ch. St. Andrew, El Segundo, Calif., 1965-71, 14 Stas. of the Cross Ch. St. Mary, Cook, Minn., altar screen at Ch. of the Descent of the Holy Spirit, Glendale, 14 Stas. of the Cross at Ch. of St. Benedict, Duluth, Minn; also research, artwork and dramatic work for Spaceship Earth exhbn. at Disney World, Orlando, Fla., 1980. Decorated Knight Grand Cross Holy Sepluchre, 1974, knight St. John of Jerusalem, 1976, knight Order of Merit of Republic of Italy, 1973 Cross of Merit, 1984, 89; named First Disting. Faculty, 1987, Outstanding Educator of Am., 1971. Mem. Art Educators Assn., Am. Rsch. Ct. Egypt, Tau Kappa Alpha, Kappa Pi, Delta Sigma Rho. Office: 1500 N Verdugo Rd Glendale CA 91208-2809

DISHELL, WALTER DAVID, writer, medical adviser, physician; b. Detroit, July 16, 1939; s. Robert Allen and Ida (Kaufman) D.; m. Marilyn Persky; children: Adam Steven, Shana Leigh, Melissa Beth. BS, U. Mich., 1960, MD, 1964. Diplomate Am. Bd. of Otolaryngology, Head and Neck Surgery, diplomate Am. Bd. Facial Plastic and Reconstructive Surgery. Resident in head and neck surgery UCLA Med. Ctr., 1964-69; med. adviser Med. Ctr. CBS-TV, Los Angeles, 1969-76, med. adviser M*A*S*H*, 1971-83, med. adviser Trapper John, 1977-86, med. adviser House Calls, 1980-82; creator, co-writer Venice Med. pilot, Los Angeles, 1982; med. adviser After M*A*S*H CBS-TV, Los Angeles, 1984; co-creator, co-writer TV series Family Med. Ctr., Los Angeles, 1988; Producer med. segments (TV show) Women's Page, 1981; med. reporter, producer Sta. KNBC News TV, L.A., 1982-84; med. reporter Sta. KABC-TV, L.A., 1987; med. advisor motion picture For the Boys, 1991. Writer: Mash episode, Housecalls episodes, Emergency, TV pilot; med. adviser: Westside Medical, Rafferty, Lazurus Syndrome, Return of Ben Casey, Gunsmoke, Chicago Story, Maude, 9 to 5, Lou Grant, Knot's Landing, Charlie's Angels. Served as maj. USAF, 1969-71. Mem. AMA, ACS, AFTRA, Writers Guild Am. West, Calif. Med. Assn., Am. Acad. Facial Plastic Surgeons, Los Angeles County Med. Assn. Office: 16311 Ventura Blvd Ste 550 Encino CA 91436-4314

DISNEY, MICHAEL GEORGE, financial services executive; b. Harvey, Ill., Nov. 30, 1955. Grad. h.s., Harvey; grad., Life Underwriters Tng. Coun. Sales mgr. Met. Life Ins. Co., Naperville, Ill., 1979-84; regional dir. Firemens Fund Ins. Co., San Diego, 1984-85; owner, mgr. Disney Fin., Inc., San Diego, 1985—; pres., founding mem. Grossmont Letip, 1992—. Founding mem., pres. Grossmont Letip, 1993-94. Mem. Nat. Assn. Life Underwriters, Life Underwriters Tng. Coun. (moderator-cons. 1986-87), Million Dollar Round Table (coord., chmn. San Diego chpt. 1987-89), La Mesa (Calif.) C. of C., San Diego C. of C., El Cajon C. of C., Toastmasters. Grossmont Letip (founder, pres. 1994-96). Avocations: photography, camping, fishing. Home: 3910 Dorsie Ln La Mesa CA 91941-7335 Office: 2615 Camino Del Rio S Ste 308 San Diego CA 92108-3713

DISNEY, ROY EDWARD, broadcasting company executive; b. Los Angeles, Jan. 10, 1930; s. Roy Oliver and Edna (Francis) D.; m. Patricia Ann Dailey, Sept. 17, 1955; children: Roy Patrick, Susan Margaret, Abigail Edna, Timothy John. B.A., Pomona Coll., 1951. Guest relations exec. NBC, Hollywood, Calif., 1952; apprentice film editor Mark VII Prodns., Hollywood, 1942; asst. film editor, cameraman prodn. asst., writer, producer Walt Disney Prodns., Burbank, Calif., 1954-77, dir., 1967—; pres. Roy E. Disney Prodns. Inc., Burbank, 1978—; chmn. bd. dir. Shamrock Broadcasting Co., Hollywood, 1979—; chmn. bd. dir., founder Shamrock Holdings Inc., Burbank, 1980—; trustee Calif. Inst. Arts, Valencia, 1967—; vice chmn. Walt Disney Co., Burbank. Author: novelized adaptation of Perri; producer (film) Pacific High, Mysteries of the Deep (TV show) Walt Disney's Wonderful World of Color, others; exec. producer Cheetah; writer, dir., producer numerous TV prodns. Bd. dirs. Big Bros. of Greater Los Angeles; mem. adv. bd. dirs. St. Joseph Med. Ctr., Burbank; mem. U.S. Naval Acad. Sailing Squadron, Annapolis, Md.; fellow U. Ky. Recipient Acad. award nomination for Mysteries of the Deep. Mem. Dirs. Guild Am. West, Writers Guild Am. Republican. Clubs: 100, Confrerie des Chevaliers du Tastevin, St. Francis Yacht, Calif. Yacht, San Diego Yacht, Transpacific Yacht, Los Angeles Yacht. Office: Walt Disney Co 500 S Buena Vista St Burbank CA 91521-1890*

DISTECHE, CHRISTINE M., geneticist; b. Liege, Belgium, July 22, 1949. PhD, U. Liege, Belgium, 1976. Genetics fellow Harvard U., Boston, 1977-80; now med. geneticist U. Wash. Hosp., Seattle; prof. pathology U. Wash., Seattle. Office: U Wash Hosp Dept Pathology PO Box 357470 Seattle WA 98195-7470*

DISTEFANO, PETER ANDREW, insurance executive, entertainment photographer; b. N.Y.C., Nov. 26, 1939; s. Peter Julian Distefano; children: Diane Distefano-Ridgley, Daniel, Donald. AA, Orange Coast Coll., 1970. Cert. profl. ins. agent. Pres. Calif. Occupl. Safety Svcs., Concord, Calif., 1980-98, Distefano Enterprises, Concord, 1980-98; v.p. Brennan & Assocs., Emeryville, Calif., 1996-98; rock editor Bass Frontiers Mag., Rio Linda, Calif., 1996—; staff photographer Concord Pavilion, 1997—. Pres., bd. dirs. Chilpancingo Vista, Inc., Pleasant Hill, Calif., 1996—; adv. bd. mem. Sonoma Devel. Ctr., Eldridge, Calif., 1990—. Petty officer II USN, 1958-62. Home and Office: PO Box 973 Clayton CA 94517-0973

DISTLER, CHARLES, minister, administrator; b. N.Y.C., June 21, 1915; s. William and Anna Elizabeth (Weiscuff) D.; m. Daisy Laura Smith, March 21, 1936; children: Charles Jr., Daisy-Anna Powell, Ruth Naomi Gabel. D Bible Philosophy, Lighthouse Bible Coll., Rockford, Ill., 1945; BA, Shelton Coll., Cape May, N.Y., 1948; postgrad., East Bapt. Theol. Sem., Overbrook, Pa., 1949-54. Ordained to the ministry Conference of Fundamental Chs., 1945, Am. Bapt. Conv., 1949. Pastor various chs., N.Y. Ohio, 1948-70, Ill. Mich., 1970-87; adminstr. dir. Victory Mission, Salinas, Calif., 1988—; pres. Ohio Regional IFCA, Akron, 1965-68; bd. mem. Akron Christian Schs., 1965-68; chaplain Carthage Mem. Hosp., Ill., 1972-75; radio preacher WCAZ, Carthage, Ill., 1971-76. Chaplain N.Y.C. Post Office Dept., 1950-55; tank comdr. World War II, China-Burma, India, 1944-45; with U.S. Army 1944-46. Mem. Am. Numismatic Assn., Am. Legion. Home: 1216 Dickens Dr Salinas CA 93901-1704 Office: Victory Mission 43 Soledad St Salinas CA 93901-2837

DI TONNIO, ANTHONY MICHAEL PHILIP, recording company executive, minister,; b. Bklyn., N.Y., Jan. 26, 1954; s. Anthony Luther and Marie (Battilord) Di T; m. Rochelle Marie Thornburg; children: Joey Raymond, Aaron Paul, Brittany Marie. Student in Computer Sci., Kingston U., 1968-70; student in Bus. Adminstrn., Middletown (N.Y.) U., 1969-71; student criminal, civil investigation, UDETD, Universal City, Calif., 1972-74; DTh, World Christianship Ministries, Fresno, Calif., 1995. Producer Wild Country Records, Roundup, Montana, 1978—; pvt. detective Worldwide Intelligence Network, Canoga Park, Calif., 1988-95; minister World Christianship Ministries, Fresno, Calif., 1995—; studio engr. Hidden Studios, Roundup, Montana, 1989—; owner, mgr. Best Inn Motel, Roundup, 1995—. Pastoral counselor Youth of Am. Ministries, Roundup Mt., 1998; music minister Shining Mt. Ministry, 1998—. Recipient Gold Record award Hurt, 1980, Golden Eagle award Airplay Internat., 1997; hon. mention Investigator of Yr., 1985. Mem. Internat. Assn. Clergy. Avocations: martial arts, nature walks, horseback riding. Office: Wild Country Records 49 Buck Rub Rd Roundup MT 59072-6719

DITTMAN, DEBORAH RUTH, real estate broker; b. Sacramento, Apr. 15, 1932; d. Charles Harwood and Ruth (Potter) Kinsley; m. John Alvin Cardoza, Sept. 1950 (div. 1964); children: Harold Cardoza, Nancy Jongeward, John Allan Cardoza, Gregory Cardoza, Janice Boswell; m. Edgar Marshall Dittman, Jan. 22, 1967 (dec. Jan. 6 1982); m. Philip George Vrieling, July 7, 1990. Student Humprey's Coll., Stockton, Calif., 1966; grad. real estate sales Anthony Schs., 1978; cert. in real estate San Joaquin Delta Coll., 1977. Lic. real estate broker, Calif., 1978, real estate sales assoc., 1974-78; cert. residential specialist. Sec. Calif. Dept. Water Resources, Patterson and Tracy, 1966-72; hostess Welcome Wagon, Tracy, 1973-74; assoc. realtor Reeve Assocs., Tracy, 1975-80; broker Allied Brokers, Tracy, 1980-83; ptnr. real estate Putt, Fallavena, Willbanks & Dittman, Tracy, 1983-98; mem. adv. bd. Tracy Fed. Bank(formerly Tracy Savings & Loan), 1989-97, Women's Coun. Realtors, 1990—. Mem. Residential Sales Coun., 1989, Women's Coun. Realtors, 1990. Mem. Tracy Bd. Realtors (pres. 1981, 85, dir. 1976, 77, 80-83, 85-86), Calif. Assn. Realtors (dir. 1980-81, 85), Cert. Real Estate Specialists (v.p. no. Calif. chpt. 1990, pres. 1991), Nat. Assn. Realtors, Cen. Valley Assn. Realtors, So. Alameda Assn. Realtors, Tracy C. of C. (bd. dirs. 1988-90). Home: 12134 Midway Dr Tracy CA 95376-9113 Office: 1045 Tracy Blvd Tracy CA 95376

DIVINE, THEODORE EMRY, electrical engineer; b. Hailey, Idaho, May 27, 1943; s. Theodore Clyde and Muriel Juanita (Kirtley) D.; BSEE, U. Wash., Seattle, 1966, MBA, 1970; m. Roberta Louise Erickson, Mar. 19, 1966; children: Timothy Shannon, Brianna Kristine, Rachel Melissa. Engr., Gen. Telephone Co. of N.W., 1968-69; mem. tech. staff NW ops. Computer Scis. Corp., 1970-72; research engr. Battelle Pacific N.W. Labs., Richland, Wash., 1973—, research sect. mgr., 1978, staff engr., def. programs, 1980-89; program mgr., special programs Idaho Nat. Engr. Lab., Idaho Falls, 1989—, mgr. Nat. Security Programs Office, 1992-93, spl. programs mgr., 1993-96; staff scientist Battelle Pacific N.W. Nat. Labs., Richland, Wash., 1996-97, product line mgr. spl. programs, 1997, spl. programs sector dep., (Batelle Meml. Inst.) 1997—. Pres. Mid-Columbia

DIWU, ZHENJUN, chemist; b. Xunyi, China, June 29, 1962; came to U.S., 1993; s. Junxue Diwu and Qiaoyun Zhang; m. Cailan Zhang, Dec. 18, 1962; children: Y. Allan, X. Brooks. PhD, Chinese Acad. Scis., Beijing, 1988. Patent examiner The Chinese Patent Office, Beijing, 1989-90; postdoctoral fellow U. Alta., Edmonton, Can., 1990-93; prin. scientist Molecular Probes, Inc., Eugene, Oreg., 1993—; grant reviewer The Israel Sci. Found., 1993—; mem. drug rev. panel The Current Drugs, 1996—. Contbr. articles to profl. jours.; article reviewer Jour. Photochemistry and Photobiology, 1992—, Tetrahedron, 1993—. Mem. Am. Chem. Soc., Am. Photobiology Soc., Am. Oxygen Soc. Achievements include exploration of the therapeutic and diagnostic applications of hypocrellins and hypericin, development of a number of fluorescent probes for biomedical application. Office: Molecular Probes Inc 4849 Pitchford Ave Eugene OR 97402-9165

DIX, GARY ERROL, engineering executive; b. Bieber, Calif., Jan. 10, 1942; s. Errol Alvin and Evelyn Nadine (Miller) D.; m. Lanaya Diane Easley, Jan. 4, 1964. BS in Mech. Engring., U. Calif., Berkeley, 1963, MS in Mech. Engring., 1965, PhD in Mech. Engring., 1971. Engr. Gen. Electric Nuclear, San Jose, Calif., 1965-71; mgr. thermal devel. Gen. Electric Nuclear, San Jose, 1971-75, mgr. safety and hydraulics, 1975-82, mgr. core methods, 1982-85, mgr. automation sys., 1985-89, mgr. quality assurance and automation, 1989-94, mgr. devel. programs, 1994-97; code rev. group cons. Nuclear Regulatory Commn., Washington, 1976-85; cons. in field, 1997—. Contbr. articles to profl. jours.; patentee in field. Fellow Am. Nuclear Soc. (exec. com. Thermal Hydraulics divsn. 1981-91, chmn. 1986-87); mem. ASME. Avocations: computers, wine, motorcycles, basketball, movies. Office: PO Box 2394 Saratoga CA 95070-0394

DIXIT, VIVEK, biomedical scientist, medical educator; b. Mumbai, India, Nov. 7, 1954; came to U.S., 1988; s. Mahesh Chandra and Kaushal (Tiwari) Dikshit; m. Neeta Awasthi, Dec. 27, 1987; children: Vineet Aditya, Ram Anand. BSc in Biology magna cum laude, Concordia U., Montreal, Que., Can., 1978; MSc in Physiology, McGill U., Montreal, 1980, PhD in Physiology, 1986. Postdoctoral fellow Sunnybrook Med. Ctr./U. Toronto, Can., 1986-88; vis. asst. rschr. UCLA, 1988-91, asst. rschr., 1991-93, assoc. prof. medicine, 1993—; dir. rsch., liver bio-support, hepatitis rsch. lab., 1990—, co-dir. basic sci. tng. program divsn. digestive diseases, 1993-95; liver disease program steering com. mem. Sunnybrook Med. Ctr., Toronto, 1986-87; mem. sci. program com. 3rd Internet World Congress on Biomed. Scis., Symposium on Tissue Engring. and Bioartificial Organs, 1996; lectr. and presenter in field. Manuscript reviewer Artificial Organs, ASAIO Jour., Cell Transplantation, Digestive Disease and Sci., Jour. Infectious Diseases, Gastroenterology, Hepatology, Jour. of Artificial Cells, Blood Substitutes and Immobilization Biotech., Jour. Hepatology, and Liver Transplantation and Surgery. Sunnybrook Fund fellow U. Toronto, 1987, McGill U. fellow, 1981, 85, Ministry Edn. Que. fellow, 1981-83, 86-87; grantee UCLA, 1994, 96, Oppenheimer Found., 1995, 98, United Liver Assn., 1988, 90-92, 95, Physicians Svcs. Inc. Found., 1987-89. Mem. Internat. Soc. Artificial Organs, Internat. Soc. for Artificial Cells, Blood Substitutes and Immobilization Biotech. (mem. internat. program com., editl. bd. jour.), Internat. Assn. Study of Liver, Am. Soc. for Artificial Internal Organs (mem. sci. program com., editl. bd. jour.), Cell Transplant Soc. (editl. bd. jours.), Gastroenterology Rsch. Group, Am. Gastroenterol. Assn., Am. Assn. for Study Liver Diseases. Hindu. Achievements include pioneer investigator in hybrid bioartificial liver support systems, cell microencapsulation and transplantation, tissue engineering. Avocations: cartography, photography, swimming, wilderness hiking. Home: 5522 Babcock Ave North Hollywood CA 91607-1531 Office: UCLA Sch Medicine 675 Circle Dr S # 1240 Los Angeles CA 90095-8348

DIXON, BARRY PERCY, religion educator; b. Bklyn., June 3, 1950; m. Maria Theresa Ambos, June 14, 1974; children: Rahim, Yasmeen. BA, Calif. Bapt. Coll., 1972. Instr. Noohra Found., Irvine, Calif., 1983—; health facilities evaluator San Bernardino, Calif. Contbr. articles to profl. publs. Mem. Soc. Biblical Lit., Am. Acad. Religion, Ancient and Mystical Order Rosae Crucis (master 1983-84). Home: 3191 Kilkenny Dr Riverside CA 92503-5354 Office: Licensing and Cert 625 Carnegie Dr San Bernardino CA 92408-3510

DIXON, CHRISTOPHER JOBIE, editor, publisher; b. Cin., Dec. 20, 1966; s. Richard Jobie Dixon and Gloria Jean Ricks. B of Journalism, U. Ga., 1989, M of Journalism, 1992. Writer Surger Mag., Dana Point, Calif., 1989-98, online editor, surf report editor, 1995-99; writer Esquire Mag. U.K., London, 1992-96, Velo News Mag., Boulder, Colo., 1993-95, Bike Mag., Dana Point, 1993-98, Sports Afield Mag., N.Y.C., 1994-95; writer, reporter N.Y. Times, N.Y.C., 1994-95; internat. coord. Esquire Mag., N.Y.C., 1993, writer, editl. coord., 1992. Vol., media advisor Surfrider Found., San Clemente, Calif., 1997-98. Avocations: surfing, snowboarding, mountain bikes, Macintosh computers, antique Cadillacs. E-mail: dixoncj@aol.com. Home: 219 A Avenida Lobeiro San Clemente CA 92672

DIXON, FRED SOMERS, cattle rancher; b. Crisfield, Md., Jan. 12, 1960; s. Cullen William and Pauline Anne (Somers) D.; 1 child, Lauren Elizabeth. Student, Allegany C.C. Ranch mgr. Magness Land & Cattle, Pine, Colo., 1984—; owner Anvil Enterprises, Inc., Pine, 1994—; lectr. in field. Contbr. articles to profl. jours. Avocations: silversmithing, saddlemaking, music, historical programs, movie prop-making. Home: Hidden Valley Ranch Pine CO

DIXON, JULIAN CAREY, congressman; b. Washington, Aug. 8, 1934; m. Bettye Lee; 1 child, Cary Gordon. BS, Calif. State U., L.A., 1962; LLB, Southwestern U., L.A., 1967. Mem. Calif. State Assembly, 1972-78; mem. 96th-106th Congresses from Calif. 28th (now 32nd) Dist.; mem. House Appropriations Com. 96th-106th Congresses from Calif. 32d Dist.; mem. subcom. on D.C.; mem. subcom. Commerce, Justice, State and Judiciary; ranking mem. select com. on intelligence, mem. subcom. on nat. security, mem. appropriations subcom. on D.C.; bd. dirs. CBC Found., Inc., pres., 1986-90. With U.S. Army, 1957-60. Mem. NAACP, Urban League, Calif. Arts Commn. Democrat. Office: House of Representatives 2252 Rayburn Bldg Washington DC 20515-0532

DIXON, NEIL EDWARD, elementary school educator, paleoanthropologist; b. Inglewood, Calif.; s. Thomas Francis and Margaret (Donovan) D. BA, Pepperdine U., 1968, teaching credential, 1969; cert. sci. lang., U. So. Calif., 1987. Engr. trainee N.Am. Aviation Inc., Miami, Fla., 1964; elem. educator Woodcrest Sch., L.A. Unified Sch. Dist., 1969-88; curriculum developer L.A. Zoo, 1987-90; tchr. inservice leader L.A. Dept. Water and Power; curriculum developer L.A. County Museum Natural History, 1991; mem. rsch. expdn. to Amazon (Peru), 1981, 87, 98-99, to Sudan, 1982-83, rsch. expdn. to Amazon/Andes, 1987, 98. Author: (books) Chinese Golden Monkey, 1987, Stones and Bones Elementary Pathways, 1989. Named Tchr. of Yr., L.A. County, 1994, Tchr. of Yr., NAACP, 1990, participant Tchr. in Space, 1985-86; grantee Urban Quail Farm Project, 1986, L.A. Ednl. Partnership, 1989, computer tech. grantee Calif. A.B. 803, 1988, Louis B. Leakey Rsch. grantee, 1985-87; Advances in Biol. Sci. Program fellow NSF, 1987, 88, Smithsonian Inst./Nat. Acad. of Scis. Nat. Sci. Resources Ctr./ Elem. Sci. Inst., 1992; recipient Toberman award Black-Foxe Mil. Inst., 1965. Mem. NSTA, World Aerospace Educators Orgn., Mentor Sci. Tchr. Home: 1105 Van Buren Ave Venice CA 90291-5028

DIXON, PATRICIA LYNN, software consultant, graphic designer; b. Hayward, Calif., Apr. 16, 1967; d. Herman Richard and Mary Jo (COffey) Drennan; m. William Wesley Dixon Jr., June 4, 1988; children: Blake Allen, Aimee Jo. Grad. high sch., Sonora, Calif., 1985; cert. computer proficiency I and II, Folsom-Cordova Sch., Calif. Nursing asst. PRN Nursing Svc., Modesto, Calif., 1985-86; desk mgr. Hayward Hot Springs, 1987-88; call supr. Care Pt. Nursing Svc., Sacramento, 1988-89; sports medicine therapist Sunriver Chiropractic, Rancho Cordova, Calif., 1990-91; owner, graphic designer Dixon Graphic Design, Sonora, 1995—; software cons. WiredRed Software, San Diego, 1998—. Contbr. poetry to anthologies (Editor's Choice award 1997). Office mgr. ARC, Sonora, 1985; med. vol. Health Van I-Sonora Cmty. Hosp., 1985; vol. Kaiser Permanente Hosp., Sacramento, 1988-89. Recipient Medal of Merit in History DAR-Am. Legion Aux., Hayward, 1983. Republican. Office: Dixon Graphic Design 19229 Beauchamp Dr No 19 Sonora CA 95370

DJAWAD, SAID TAYEB See JAWAD, SAID TAYEB

DMYTRYSHYN, BASIL, historian, educator; b. Poland, Jan. 14, 1925; came to U.S., 1947, naturalized, 1951; s. Frank and Euphrosinia (Senchak) Dmytryshyn; m. Virginia Roehl, July 16, 1949; children: Sonia, Tania. BA, U. Ark., 1950; MA, U. Ark, 1951; PhD, U. Calif.-Berkeley, 1955; hon. diploma, U. Kiev-Mohyla Acad., 1993. Asst. prof. history Portland State U., Oreg., 1956-59; assoc. prof. Portland State U., 1959-64, prof., 1964-89, prof. emeritus, 1989—, assoc. dir. Internat. Trade and Commerce Inst., 1984-89; vis. prof. U. Ill., 1964-65, Harvard U., 1971, U. Hawaii, 1976, Hokkaido U., Sapporo, Japan, 1978-79; adviser U. Kiev-Mohyla Acad., 1993. Author books including: Moscow and the Ukraine, 1918-1953, 1956, Medieval Russia, 900-1700, 3d edit., 1990, Imperial Russia, 1700-1917, 3d edit., 1990, Modernization of Russia Under Peter I and Catherine II, 1974, Colonial Russian America 1817-1832, 1976, A History of Russia, 1977, U.S.S.R.: A Concise History, 4th edit., 1984, The End of Russian America, 1979, Civil and Savage Encounters, 1983, Russian Statecraft, 1985, Russian Conquest of Siberia 1558-1700, 1985, Russian Penetration of the North Pacific Archipelago, 1700-1799, 1987, The Soviet Union and the Middle East, 1917-1985, 1987, Russia's Colonies in North America, 1799-1867, 1988, The Soviet Union and the Arab World of the Fertile Crescent, 1918-1985, 1994; contbr. articles to profl. jours. U.S., Can., Yugoslavia, Italy, South Korea, Fed. Republic Germany, France, Eng., Japan, Russia, Ukraine. State bd. dirs. PTA, Oreg., 1963-64; mem. World Affairs Council, 1965-92. Named Hon. Rsch. Prof. Emeritus, Kyungnam U., 1989—; Fulbright-Hays fellow W. Germany, 1967-68; fellow Kennan Inst. Advanced Russian Studies, Washington, 1978; recipient John Mosser award Oreg. State Bd. Higher Edn., 1966, 67; Branford P. Millar award for faculty excellence Portland State U., 1985, Outstanding Retired Faculty award, 1994; Hillard scholar in the humanities U. Nev., Reno, 1992. Mem. Am. Assn. Advancement Slavic Studies (dir. 1972-75), Am. Hist. Assn., Western Slavic Assn. (pres. 1990-92), Can. Assn. Slavists, Oreg. Hist. Soc., Nat. Geog. Soc., Conf. Slavic and East European History (nat. sec. 1972-75), Am. Assn. for Ukrainian Studies (pres. 1991-93), Ctr. Study of Russian Am. (hon.), Assn. Study Nationalities (bd. mem.-at-large USSR & Ea. Europe 1993—), Czechoslovak Soc. Arts and Scis., Soc. Jewish-Ukraine Contacts, Assn. Home: 2745 S Via Del Bac Green Valley AZ 85614-1071

DO, TAI HUU, mechanical engineer; b. Quang Binh, Vietnam, May 31, 1942; came to U.S., 1975; s. Mau Do and Thi Hai Nguyen; 1 child, Frederick Quan. BSME, U. Paris, 1970, MS, 1971. Rsch. engr. Soc. Automobile Engrs., Paris, 1970-71; test engr. Yanmar Diesel Co., Ltd., Osaka, Japan, 1971-72; prodn. mgr. Vietnam Products Co., Ltd., Saigon, Vietnam, 1972-75; chief engr. European Parts Exchange, Irvine, Calif., 1975-77; project mgr. Fairchild Aerospace Div., Santa Ana, Calif., 1977—. Co-author: Literary Dissident Movement in Vietnam; editor: Khai Phong Mag.; patentee in field; contbr. articles to profl. jours. Mem. Soc. Automotive Engrs., Soc. Mfg. Engrs. Buddhist. Office: Fairchild Aerospace Div 3130 W Harvard St Santa Ana CA 92704-3937

DOAN, LARRY EMERY, real estate executive; b. L.A., Dec. 23, 1929; s. Larry Emery and Marie (Cochran) D.; m. Dudley Harbison, Jan. 27, 1951; children: Mary, Terry, Howard, Larry. BA, U. Calif., Berkeley, 1953. Lic. real estate broker. V.p. Harbison Henderson, L.A., 1956-62, McDonnell & Co., L.A., 1962-69; v.p., mgr. DuPont Glore Forgan Co., L.A., 1969-72; v.p. W.E. Hutton Co., L.A., 1972-74; sales assoc. Bliss Keeler Co., San Marino, Calif., 1974-79; pres. Doan Harbison Realty, San Marino, Calif., 1979-88; v.p., ptnr. Podley Caughey & Doan, Pasadena, Calif., 1988—. Lt. (j.g.) USN, 1953-56. Recipient Realtor of Yr. award San Marino/South Pasadena Bd. Realtors, 1985. Mem. San Gabriel Country Club (dir. 1997—). Republican. Avocations: golf, travel. Office: Podley Caughey and Doan 2124 Huntington Dr San Marino CA 91108-2024

DOBAY, SUSAN VILMA, artist; b. Budapest, Hungary, May 12, 1937; came to U.S., 1957; d. Otto and Lenke Stiasny Heltai; m. Endre Imre Dobay, Oct. 16, 1954; children: Vivian, Andrew. Diploma, Famous Artists Sch., Westport, Conn., 1963. Featured artist in exhbns. at Vasarely Mus., Budapest, 1993, Joslyn Arts Ctr., Torrance, Calif., 1994, Allied Arts Ctr., Richland, Wash., 1995; exhibited in group shows at Calif. Mus. Sci. and Industry, L.A., 1967, 75, UN Woman Conf., Nairobi, Kenya, 1985, Jillian Coldiron Fine Art, South Pasadena, Calif., 1993—, Hungarian Consulate, N.Y.C., 1996, Kortars Galleria, Budapest, 1996, Mus. Downtown L.A., 1998; illustrator Lloyd's Advt., L.A., 1963-64; fashion illustrator Pasadena Star News, 1963. Mem. World Fedn. Hungarian Artists, N.Y. Artists Equity, L.A. Artists Equity. Avocations: reading, travel, theater, movies, classical music. Home: 125 W Scenic Dr Monrovia CA 91016-1610

DOBBEL, RODGER FRANCIS, interior designer; b. Hayward, Calif., Mar. 11, 1934; s. John Leo and Edna Frances (Young) D.; m. Joyce Elaine Schnoor, Aug. 1, 1959; 1 child, Carrie Lynn. Student, San Jose State U., 1952-55, Chouinard Art Inst., L.A., 1955-57. Asst. designer Monroe Interiors, Oakland, Calif., 1957-66; owner, designer Rodger Dobbel Interiors, Piedmont, Calif., 1966 . Pub. in Showcase of Interior Design, Pacific edit., 1992, 100 Designers' Favorite Rooms, 1993, 2d edit., 1994; contbr. articles to mags. and newspapers. Decorations chmn. Trans Pacific Ctr. Bldg. Opening, benefit Oakland Ballet, various other benefits and openings, 1982—; chmn. Symphonic Magic, Lake Marritt Plaza, Opening of Oakland Symphony Orch. Season and various others, 1985—; cons. An Evening of Magic, Oakland Hilton Hotel, benefit Providence Hosp. Found., bd. dirs., 1991; auction chmn. County Meals on Wheels, 1994, 95; prodn. chmn. Nutcracker Ball, benefit Oakland Ballet, 1995; mem. bd. regents Holy Names Coll., 1997—. Recipient Cert. of Svc., Nat. Soc. Interior Designers, 1972, 74; recipient Outstanding Contbn. award, Oakland Symphony, 1986, Nat. Philanthropy Day Disting. Vol. award, 1991. Mem. Nat. Soc. Interior Designers (profl. mem. 1960-75, v.p. Calif. chpt. 1965, edn. found. mem. 1966—, nat. conf. chmn. 1966), Am. Soc. Interior Designers , Claremont Country, Diabetic Youth Found. Democrat. Roman Catholic. Avocations: travel, gardening.

DOBBINS, MAGGIE SONNE, real estate investment company executive; b. Pasadena, Calif., July 14, 1958; d. Roscoe Newbold Jr. and Ann Miriam (Vierhus) S.; m. Donald Alan Blackburn, Sept. 8, 1979 (div. 1983); m. Paul Dobbins, June 7, 1997. AS, Oreg. Inst. Tech., 1981, BS, 1983. Sales trainee NCR Corp., Dayton, Ohio, 1983-84; sales rep. NCR Corp., Portland, Oreg., 1984-86; account mgr. NCR Corp., Seattle, 1986-87; sr. account mgr. NCR Corp., Portland, 1987-88; sr. account rep. Wang Labs., Portland, 1988-91; account exec. Tandem Computers, Portland, 1991-94; sr. acct. exec. Fin. Svcs., L.A., 1994-96; pres. Trofast Investments, Altadena, Calif., 1998—. Active Emily's List, Project Vote Smart, Ams. for Change. Mem. Soc. Advancement Mgmt., Costeau Soc., Alpha Chi. Avocations: sailing, diving, skiing, biking, golf. Home: 1242 E Altadena Dr Altadena CA 91001-2004

DOBBROW, CHRIS, publishing executive. V.p. PC Computing, San Francisco. Office: PC Computing 50 Beale St Ste 13 San Francisco CA 94105-1819*

DOBBS, GREGORY ALLAN, journalist; b. San Francisco, Oct. 9, 1946; s. Harold Stanley and Annette Rae (Lehrer) D.; m. Carol Lynn Walker, Nov. 25, 1973; children: Jason Walker, Alexander Adair. B.A., U. Calif., Berkeley, 1968; M.S.J., Northwestern U., 1969. Assignment editor, reporter Sta. KGO-TV, San Francisco, 1966-68; news dir. San Francisco Tourist Info. Program Service, 1968; editor ABC Radio, Chgo., 1969-71; producer ABC News, Chgo., 1971-73; corr. ABC News, 1973-77, London, 1977-82, Paris, 1982-86, Denver, 1986-92; host The Greg Dobbs Show/Sta. KOA Radio, 1992—; lectr. Northwestern U. Sch. Journalism, 1975, 76; prof. U. Colo. Sch. Journalism, 1996—. Recipient Sigma Delta Chi Disting. Svc. award for TV reporting Soc. Profl. Journalists, 1980, Emmy award for outstanding documentary, 1989, award of excellence Colo. Broadcasters Assn., 1993, 94, award for best talk show Colo. Soc. Profl. Journalists, 1994; Lippmann fellow Ford Found., 1975. Office: 1153 Bergen Pkwy Ste M150 Evergreen CO 80439-9525

DOBELIS, GEORGE, manufacturing company executive; b. July 31, 1940; s. John and Dorothy Dobelis; m. Dolores Ann Nagle, Dec. 2, 1972; children: Sally Ann Berg, Christian Eric Berg, Kurt Conrad Berg. AA in Engring., Santa Monica Coll., 1963; student, Control Data Inst., 1970. Engring. Masterite Ind., Torrance, Calif., 1969-70; engring. mgr. Elco Corp., El Segundo, Calif., 1964-76, mgr. new products, 1976-77; pres. Connector Tech. Inc., Anaheim, Calif., 1977—. Patentee in field; contbr. articles to profl. jours. Served as sgt. N.G., 1963-69. Mem. IEEE. Republican. Avocations: golf, skiing, camping, hiking.

DOBRONSKI, MARK WILLIAM, judge, justice of the peace; b. Detroit, Oct. 8, 1957; s. Clarence Robert and Jean (Shotey) D.; m. Susan Kay Roach, Sept. 12, 1980; children: Clarence Robert III, Juli E. AS, crery Ford C.C., 1980. Cert. engr. Nat. Assn. Radio and Telecomm. Engrs. V.p. Mobilfone, Inc., Dearborn, Mich., 1977-79; asst. v.p. RAM Broadcasting Corp., N.Y.C., 1979-86; adminstr. State of Ariz., Phoenix, 1986-88, 89-97; divsn. comdr. City of Peoria (Ariz.) Police Dept., 1991; cons., expert witness Teletech, Inc., Dearborn, 1980-98. Mem., bd. dirs. Congl. Ch. of the Valley, United Ch. of Christ, Scottsdale, Ariz., 1994-98; mem. Maricopa County Sheriff's Exec. Posse, Phoenix, 1996-98. Mem. Am. Pvt. Radio Assn. (dir. 1989-98). Republican. Office: Scottsdale Justice Ct 3700 N 75th St Scottsdale AZ 85251

DOBROTKA, DAVID A., protective services official; m.; 2 children. BS, MPA. With Minn. Police Dept., Mpls., 1976-94; chief Glendale (Ariz.) Police Dept., 1994—. Office: Glendale Police Dept 6835 N 57th Dr Glendale AZ 85301-3218*

DOBY, KAREN ELAINE, data processing company executive; b. Amarillo, Tex., Nov. 1, 1955; d. Laurance Lee and Helen Marie (Davis) D. AS, Belleville (Ill.) Area Coll., 1976; BS, So. Ill. U., Edwardsville, Ill., 1977; MS, Georgetown U., 1978; MBA, Loyola U., New Orleans, 1984. Ops. researcher Dept. of Energy, Washington, 1977-78; geophysicist Naval Oceanographic Office, Bay St. Louis, Miss., 1978-82; engring. analyst Middle S. Utilities System, New Orleans, 1982; sr. systems analyst, mgr. Exploration and Devel. Systems CNG Producing Co., New Orleans, 1982-88; mgr. network security Sun Micro Systems, Inc., Mountain View, Calif., 1992-96; dir. enterprise network svcs. Sun Microsystems, Inc., Palos Altos, Ca., 1996—; cons. Macrobiotic Inst., New Orleans, 1987—. Mem. Nat. Computer Graphics Assn., IEEE Computer Soc., Am. Assn. Petroleum Geologists. Democrat. Avocations: macrobiotics, scuba gardening, biking, travel. Home: 4546 B-10 El Camino Real # 321 Los Altos CA 94022-1041

DOCKSTADER, JACK LEE, retired electronics executive; b. L.A., Dec. 14, 1936; s. George Earl and Grace Orine (Travers) D.; m. Kerry Jo King, Oct. 24, 1987; children: Travis Adam Mayer, Bridget Olivia Mayer. student UCLA, 1960-70. Rate analyst Rate Bur., So. Pacific Co., L.A., 1954-57; traffic analyst traffic dept. Hughes Aircraft Co., Fullerton, Calif., 1957-58, Culver City, Calif., 1958-59, traffic mgr. Hughes Rsch. Labs., Malibu, Calif., 1959-70, material mgr., 1970-75; material mgr. Hughes Aircraft Co., Culver City, 1975-80, prodn. material mgr. Electro-Optical and Data Systems Group, El Segundo, Calif., 1980-84, mgr. material total quality 1984-85, mgr. cen. material ops. and property mgmt. 1987-88, mgr. group property mgmt., 1988-93, mgr. electro optical systems, property mgmt., aerospace and def. sector, 1993; ret., 1993. Mem. adv. council transp. mgmt. profl. designation program UCLA, 1966-80, mem. Design for Sharing Com., 1977-82; adv. com. transp. program L.A. Trade Tech. Coll., 1970-80; vol. USN Ret. Activities Office, Seal Beach, Calif., 1995—; mem. Friends of Phineas Banning Mus., Wilmington, Calif., 1996—. Served with USNR, 1954-96, ret. 1996. Mem. Nat. Property Mgmt. Assn. (pres. L.A. chpt. 1992, 93), UCLA Alumni Assn., Nat. Contracts Mgmt. Assn., Naval Enlisted Res. Assn., Hughes Aircraft Co. Mgmt. Club, Hughes Aircraft Retirees Assn., Delta Nu Alpha (pres. San Fernando Valley chpt. 1965-66, v.p. Pacific S.W. region 1969-71, region man of year 1971). Presbyterian. Home: PO Box 3156 Redondo Beach CA 90277-1156

DOCTOR, KENNETH JAY, editor; b. L.A., Jan. 5, 1950; s. Joseph and Ruth (Kazdoy) D.; m. Katherine Conant Francis, June 14, 1971; children: Jenika, Joseph, Katy. BA in Sociology, U. Calif., Santa Cruz, 1971; MS in Journalism, U. Oreg., 1979. Editor, pub. Willamette Valley Observer, Eugene, Oreg., 1975-82; mng. editor Oreg. Mag., Portland, 1982-84; mng. editor, features Boulder (Colo.) Daily Camera, 1984-86; assoc. editor, features St. Paul Pioneer Press, 1986-90, mng. editor, features, 1990-94, mng. editor, 1994-97; v.p. editl. Knight Ridder New Media, San Jose, Calif., 1997—; chair Knight-Ridder Task Force on Family Readers, Miami, Fla., 1991. Recipient Achievement award Oreg. Civil Liberties Union, Eugene, 1982. Mem. Soc. Newspaper Design, Am. Soc. Newspaper Editors. Avocations: baseball, travel. E-mail: kdoctor@realcities.com. Office: Knight Ridder New Media 50 W San Fernando St Ste 700 San Jose CA 95113-2413

DOCTORS, SAMUEL ISAAC, management educator, researcher director; b. Phila., July 1, 1936; s. Abraham and Celia (Lakoff) D.; m. Meredith Cahn, 1988; 1 child, Olga; children from previous marriage: Eric, Rachel, Rebecca. BS, U. Miami, 1956; JD, Harvard U., 1967, DBA, 1969. Bar: Mass. 1967. Assoc. engr. Westinghouse Electric Corp., Balt., 1956-58; sr. math. analyst AC Sparkplug div. Gen. Motors, El Segundo, Calif., 1958-59; sr. devel. engr., work dir. aero. div. Honeywell, St. Petersburg, Fla., 1961-64; cons. tech., mgmt., econs. various orgns., 1968-81; project mgr. N. Lawndale Econ. Devel. Corp. & NUGSM, 1971-73; assoc. prof. Northwestern U., Evanston, Ill., 1969-73; faculty advisor, dir. Mgmt. Asst. Clinic, Northwestern U., Chgo., 1969-73; prof. U. Pitts., 1974-84, co-prin. investigator, project monitor, 1977-79; project mgr. Allegheny County Energy Study, 1977; prin. investigator Urban Tech. System Evaluation, NSF, 1978-81, Small Bus. Adminstrn. and Dept. Energy, Washington, 1979-80; prof. adminstrn. Calif. State U., Hayward, 1982—, founder, dir. Ctr. for Bus. & Environ. Studies, 1991—; founder, dir. Calif. Urban Environ. Rsch. and Edn. Ctr., Region IX EPA Environ. Fin. Ctr.; CEO Alameda Ctr. for Environ. Technologies, 1995; lectr. Harvard U. Bus. Sch., 1968-69; chmn. R & D workshop task force on minority bus. edn. and tng. U.S. Office Edn., 1972-73; bus. advisor David Community Devel. Corp., Ky., 1973-76; bd. dirs. Energy Policy Inst., U. Pitts., 1979-81; vis. prof. U. Calif. Sch. Bus., Berkeley, 1980-82; tech. advisor Western Gerontol. Soc., 1984—; prof. bus. adminstrn. Calif. State U. Hayward, 1983—; mem. steering com. Harvard Bus. Sch. Community Ptnrs dir. Ctr. Bus. & Environ. Studies, Calif. State U., Hayward, 1991—, Urban Environ. Rsch. & Edn. Ctr., 1993. Author books (9) and over 40 articles on management. V.p., bd. dirs. Sr. Citizens Service Corp., Pitts.; chairperson Energy Outlook '78, Allegheny County Air Pollution Control Bd. Sponsoring Agy., San Francisco Community Recyclers. Mem. ABA, Am. Polit. Sci. Assn., Am. Econ. Assn., Nat. Assn. Community Devel., AAAS, Nat. Council Small Bus. Devel., Nat. Acad. Mgmt. (sounding bd. manpower div.), Pitts. C. of C. Office: Calif State U Hayward Mgmt Scis Dept Hayward CA 94542

DODDS, DALE IRVIN, chemicals executive; b. Los Angeles, May 3, 1915; s. Nathan Thomas and Mary Amanda (Latham) D.; m. Phyllis Doreen Kirchmayer, Dec. 20, 1941; children: Nathan E., Allan I., Dale I. Jr., Charles A. AB in Chemistry, Stanford U., 1937. Chem. engr. trainee The Texas Co., Long Beach, Calif., 1937-39; chemist Standard Oil of Calif., Richmond, 1939-41; chief chemist Scriver and Quinn Interchem., L.A., 1941-46; salesman E.B. Taylor and Co. Mfg. Rep., L.A., 1947-53, Burbank (Calif.) Chem. Co., 1953-57, Chem. Mfg. Co./ICI, L.A., 1957-68; pres., CEO J.J. Mauget Co., L.A., 1969-97; CEO J.J. Mauget Co., Arcadia, Calif., 1998—. Inventor: Systemic Fungicide, 1976; patentee in field; contributed to devel. Microinjection for Trees. Fellow Am. Inst. Chemists; mem. Am. Chem. Soc., L.A. Athletic Club, Sigma Alpha Epsilon Alumni (pres. Pasadena, Calif. chpt. 1973, 90). Republican. Christian Scientist. Office: JJ Mauget Co 5435 Peck Rd Arcadia CA 91006-5847

DODGE, PETER HAMPTON, architect; b. Pasadena, Calif., July 1, 1929; s. Irving C. and Edna D. (Allison) D.; m. Janice Coor-Pender, Aug. 30, 1952; children: Susan Julia, Sarah Caroline. Student, Art Center Sch., Calif., 1947-49; A.B. with honors in Architecture, U. Calif., Berkeley, 1956. Cert. architect, Calif., Hawaii, Nev., Idaho, Colo., The Nat. Coun. of Archtl. Registration Bds., (NCARB). Apprentice Alvin Lustig (designer), Los Angeles, 1949-50; draftsman Joseph Esherick (AIA), 1956, architect, 1959-63; asso. architect Joseph Esherick and Assos. (architects), San Francisco, 1963-72; prin. Esherick, Homsey, Dodge and Davis (architects and planners, P.C.), San Francisco, 1972—; pres. Esherick, Homsey, Dodge and Davis (architects and planners, P.C.), 1979-85; lectr. dept. architecture U. Calif., Berkeley, 1961-64, 71; vis. lectr. dept. design San Francisco Art Inst., 1965. Prin. archtl. works include grad. residence facility U. Calif.-Davis, 1970, Shortstop Inc. markets, office and warehouse, Benicia, Calif., 1976, Ekahi Village (297 condominium units) Wailea, Hawaii, 1976, TWA and Western Airlines at San Francisco Internat. Airport, 1977, Citizens Utility Ctr., Susanville, Calif., 1983, various projects Golden Gate U., San Francisco, 1984—, additions and renovation Forest Hill Mcpl. R.R. Sta., San Francisco, 1985, Life Sci. Bldg. Mills Coll., Oakland, Calif., 1986, showroom R.A.B. Motors Mercedes-Benz, San Rafael, Calif., 1986, U.S. Embassy, La Paz, Bolivia, 1979-87, boarding area "B" expansion San Francisco Internat. Airport, 1987, additions and renovations Mills. Coll. Art Ctr., Oakland, 1987, F.W. Olin Libr. Mills Coll., Oakland, 1989, Calif. State U. at Bakersfield Walter Stiern Libr., 1993, Mills Hall restoration, Olney Hall rehab. Mills Coll., 1994 ; mem. editorial bd. Architecture Calif. mag., 1984-88, chmn. bd., 1985-88, Landscape mag., 1986—. Mem. Rockridge Community Planning Council, Oakland, Calif., 1971. Served with C.E., U.S. Army, 1957-58. Firm recipient of highest nat. honor for archtl. firm. AIA, 1986. Fellow AIA (dir. Calif. council 1979-81, dir. San Francisco chpt. 1977-78, sec. 1979, v.p. 1980, pres. San Francisco chpt. 1981, Honor award 1970, Bartlett award 1970); mem. U. Calif. at Berkeley Coll. Environ. Design Alumni Assn. (mem. founding steering com., pres. 1990-91). Office: Esherick Homsey Dodge & Davis 2789 25th St San Francisco CA 94110-3516*

DODGE, STEPHANIE LEE, vocational rehabilitation counselor; b. Phoenix, July 8, 1957; d. Robert Hollister and Mary Josephine (Dearstyne) D. BS, U. No. Colo., 1979; MS, Calif. State U., Sacramento, 1984. Fed. govt. cert. Vocat. rehab. counselor Pioneer Rehab., Elk Grove, Calif., 1982-86, Lisa Suhonos Rehab., Sacramento, 1986-91, Profl. Rehab. Svcs., Sacramento, 1991-94, Dodge & McElroy, Sacramento, 1994—. Mem. Calif. Assn. Rehab. Profls. Avocations: tennis, bowling, biking, scuba diving, roller blading.

DODS, WALTER ARTHUR, JR., bank executive; b. Honolulu, May 26, 1941; s. Walter Arthur Sr. and Mildred (Phillips) D.; m. Diane Lauren Nosse, Sept. 18, 1971; children: Walter A. III, Christopher L., Peter D., Lauren S. BBA, U. Hawaii, 1967. Mktg. officer 1st Hawaiian Bank, Honolulu, 1969, asst. v.p. mktg. div., 1969-71, v.p., chmn. mktg. and rsch. group, 1971-73, sr. v.p. mktg. and rsch. group, 1973-76, exec. v.p. retail banking group, 1976-78, exec. v.p. gen. banking group, 1978-84, pres., 1984-89, chmn., ceo, 1989—; chmn., pres., CEO First Hawaiian, Inc., 1989-90, chmn., CEO, 1989—; chmn., CEO First Hawaiian Creditcorp., 1989-92; bd. dirs. First Hawaiian Inc., 1st Hawaiian Bank, First Hawaiian Creditcorp Inc., First Hawaiian Leading, Inc., Alexander & Baldwin Inc., A&B-Hawaii Inc., Duty Free Shoppers Adv. Bd., Matson Navigation Co. Inc., 1st Ins. Co. Hawaii Ltd., GTE Calif., GTE Hawaiian Telephone Co., GTE Northwest, Grace Pacific Corp., Oceanic Cablevision Inc., Pacific Guardian Life Ins. Co., Princeville Adv. Group, RHP, Inc., Restaurant Suntory USA, Inc., Suntory Resorts, Inc. Bd. dirs. Ahahui Koa Anuenue, East-West Ctr. Found.; past sec., treas. The Rehab. Hosp. of the Pacific; exec. bd. mem. Aloha Coun., Boy Scouts Am.; trustee, past chmn., trustee Blood Bank Hawaii; past chmn. bd. Aloha United Way; past chmn. Bd. Water Supply; bd. govs., v.p. fin. Ctr. for Internat. Comml. Dispute Resolution; bd. dirs., treas. Coalition for Drug-Free Hawaii; trustee Contemporary Mus. co-chmn. corp. campaign com.; mem. Duty Free Shoppers Adv. Bd.; past chmn. Gubernatorial Inauguration, 1974, 82; bd. govs. Hawaii Employers Coun.; trustee Hawaii Maritime Ctr; mem. Gov.'s Adv. Bd. Geothermal/Inter-Island Cable Project, Gov.'s Blue Ribbon Panel on the Future of Healthcare in Hawaii; dir., past chmn. Hawaii Visitors Bur.; exec. com. Hawaiian Open; past spl. dir. Homeless Kokua Week; bd. gov. Honolulu Country Club, Japanese Cultural Ctr. Hawaii, Pacific Peace Found.; trustee Japan-Am. Inst. Mgmt. Sci., The Nature Conservancy Hawaii, Punahou Sch.; Hawaii chmn. Japan-Hawaii Econ. Coun.; chmn., dir. Pacific Internat. Ctr. for High Tech. Rsch.; past co-chmn., chmn. bldg. fund St. Louis High Sch.; treas. The 200 Club; dir. World Cup Honolulu 1994. Named Outstanding Jaycee in Nation, 1963, Outstanding Young Man Am. from Hawaii, 1972, Marketer of Yr., Am. Mktg. Assn., 1987; recipient Riley Allen Individual Devel. award, 1964, Hawaii State Jaycees 3 Outstanding Young Men award, 1971, Am. Advt. Fedn. Silver medal, 1977, St. Louis High Sch.'s Outstanding Alumnus award, 1980. Mem. Am. Bankers Assn., Bank Mktg. Assn., Hawaii Bankers Assn., Hawaii Bus. Roundtable, C. of C. of Hawaii, Honolulu Press Club. Office: 1st Hawaiian Bank PO Box 3200 Honolulu HI 96847*

DODSON, GERALD PAUL, lawyer; b. Pitts., Sept. 15, 1947; s. Paul C. and Eileen (Lebo) D.; m. Patricia Lawrence, May 31, 1981. BSME, Lafayette Coll., 1969; JD, U. Md., 1972; LLM, George Washington U., 1977. Bar: Calif., Pa., DC; registered to practice U.S. Patent and Trademark Office. Asst. county solicitor Allegheny County Law Dept., Pitts., 1972-73, staff atty. U.S. Dept. of Interior, Washington, 1976-78; chief counsel U.S. House of Reps., subcom. on Health & Environ., Washington, 1978-88; ptnr. Townsend & Townsend, San Francisco, 1988-92, Howard, Rice & Nemerovski, San Francisco, 1992-95, Arnold, White & Durkee, Menlo Park, Calif.,

1995—. Mem. San Francisco Patent & Trademark Law Assn. Democrat. Office: Arnold White & Durkee 155 Linfield Dr Menlo Park CA 94025-3741

DODSON, MATTHEW JAMES, literary agent, writer; b. Salem, Oreg., June 28, 1964; s. Frank Elmer and Linda (Mar) D.; m. Susan Elizabeth Lowry, May 18, 1991 (div. Jan. 1996); m. Beneth Anderson Browne, Oct. 31, 1997. BA, Evergreen State Coll., 1991; postgrad., U. of the Pacific, 1988—. Media cons. Dodson Media Svcs., Portland, Oreg., 1991-96; legal rschr. N.H. Atty. Gen., Concord, 1997; pub. asst. Zachary Shuster, N.Y.C., 1997; mng. ptnr. Omni Verse Literary Agy., LLC, Sacramento, 1997—. Author: (novel) Cosmopolis, 1997, (screenplay) Mocktail Nation, 1997; contbr. to periodicals; editor: Risk-Health, Safety & Environment, 1997-98. Legis. analyst Consumer Attys. of Calif., Sacramento, 1998—; mediator N.H. Office of Atty. Gen., Concord, 1996-97; bd. dirs. Evergreen State Coll. Alumni Assn., 1995-96. Mem. Sport and Entertainment Law Assn. (co-founder 1997), Intellectual Property Agts. of Calif. (pres. 1997—), Cyberlaw Group, Pro Bono Alliance (co-dir. 1996-98), Antler House Roundtable (co-founder 1991—). Democrat. Episcopalian. Avocations: painting, poetry, Vespa scooters, antitrust law. Office: Omni Verse Literary Agy LLC 2550 18th St Sacramento CA 95818-2450

DODSON, RICHARD LEE, music educator; b. Topeka, Kans., Oct. 11, 1955; s. Lee and Kathleen D. BS Journalism, U. Kans., 1978; MA Edn., No. Ariz. U., 1985, EdD Edn., 1994. Cert. prin., supr., tchr. music, journalism, social studies, K-12, Ariz. Tchr. govt., psychology Marcos de Niza High Sch., Tempe, Ariz., 1982-83; tchr., athletic dir., coach Grand Canyon (Ariz.) Schs., 1985—; presenter Internat. Network of Performing and Visual Arts Schs., Chgo., 1994. Composer symphonic music: Symphony #1 in D Minor, 1989, Symphony #2 in A Major, 1994. Mem. NEA, Ariz. Edn. Assn., Grand Canyon Edn. Assn. (v.p. 1994-95), Music Educators Nat. Conf., Nat. Interscholastic Athletic Adminstrs. Assn., Ariz. Interscholastic Athletic Adminstrs. Assn., Phi Kappa Phi. Avocations: movies, sports, jogging, fishing, travel. Home: 9009 W Mall Dr Apt 309 Everett WA 98208-2108

DOENGES, JUDITH ANN, writer; b. Elmhurst, Ill., Apr. 23, 1959. BA, U. Wis., 1981; MFA, U. Mass., 1987. Faculty mem. Ohio State U., 1987-91, Pacific Luth. U., Tacoma, 1992-98; Artist in residence Headlands Ctr. for the Arts, 1991, Hedgebrook, 1995, Ragdale, 1997. Author (short stories) What She Left Me, 1993, MIB, 1993, Disaster, 1996, God of Gods, 1997 (Bakeless Fiction Publ. Prize, 1998). Fiction fellow Ohio Arts Coun., 1990, Artist Trust, 1994; MacDowell fellow, 1997.

DOERMANN, DAVID JAMES, paralegal, writer; b. Tracy, Calif., Apr. 18, 1964; s. James Alfred and Norma Eunice (Courtright) D.; m. Rebecca Healey, June 20, 1990 (div. Jan. 1996). BS in Psychology, U. Utah, 1989, BS in Philosophy, 1989; MA in Comm., Fresno State U., 1992; postgrad. in comm., Westminster Coll., Salt Lake City, 1997—. Family tchr. Utah Youth Village, Sandy, 1987-88; dir. social svcs. Sandy Regional Hosp., 1988-89; case mgr., adminstr. Good Shepherd Luth. Homes, Fresno, Calif., 1990-92; asst. social worker CPC Sierra Gateway Hosp., Fresno, 1990-92; tchr. English, coach Grand County H.S., Moab, Utah, 1992-94; paralegal David E. Ross II, Salt Lake City, 1994-96, Legal Aid Soc., Salt Lake City, 1997-98; cons. World Play Consulting, Salt Lake City, 1998—. Mem. Utah State Bar (mem. edn. com. 1996-97). Avocations: running, writing poetry. Home: 736 S 500 E Salt Lake City UT 84102

DOERPER, JOHN ERWIN, publisher, editor; b. Wuerzburg, Germany, Sept. 17, 1943; came to U.S., 1963, permanent resident, 1973; s. Werner and Theresia (Wolf) D.; m. Victoria McCulloch, Dec. 2, 1970. BA, Calif. State U., Fullerton, 1968; MA/ABD, U. Calif., Davis, 1972. Writer/author Seattle, 1984—; food columnist Washington, Seattle, 1985-88, Seattle Times, 1985-88; food editor Wash.-The Evergreen State Mag., Seattle, 1989-94, Pacific Northwest mag., 1989-94, Seattle Home and Garden, 1989-91; pub., editor, founder Pacific Epicure, Quarterly Jour. Gastronomy, Bellingham, Wash., 1988—; dir. Annual N.W. Invitational Chef's Symposium. Author: Eating Well: A Guide to Foods of the Pacific Northwest, 1984, The Eating Well Cookbook, 1984, Shellfish Cookery: Absolutely Delicious Recipes from the West Coast, 1985; author, illustrator: The Blue Carp, 1994, Wine Country: California's Napa and Sonoma Valleys, 1996, Pacific Northwest, 1997, Coastal California, 1998; contbr. articles to profl. jours., intro. and chpts. to books; co-author: Washington: A Compass Guide, 1995. Recipient Silver medal, White award for city and regional mags. William Allen White Sch. Journalism, U. Kans. Mem. Oxford Symposium Food and Cookery (speaker 26th Ann. Pacific N.W. Writer's Conf. 1982, 92). Avocations: food, wine, travel, painting, printmaking. Home: 610 Donovan Ave Bellingham WA 98225-7315

DOERR, PATRICIA MARIAN, elementary and special education educator; b. Rochford, Essex, Eng., Mar. 14, 1947; came to U.S., 1976; d. Edward Earnest and Winifred May (Daniels) Earl; m. Hans Joachim Doerr, Dec. 17, 1983; children: Daniel, Nicholas, Carla. Cert. of Edn., Sussex U., 1968; Diploma in Edn. of Handicapped, London U., 1974; MS, Calif. Luth. U., 1986. Tchr. Long Road Jr. Sch., Canvey Island, Eng., 1968-70; tchr. scale 1 Belvedere (Kent, Eng.) Jr. Sch., 1970-71; tchr. scale 2 Bostal (Kent, Eng.) Manor Jr. Sch., 1971-73; tchr. scale 3, head remedial Warren Wood Boys Comprehensive Sch., Rochester, Kent, 1974-76; ednl. therapist Westvalley Ctr. for Ednl. Therapy, Canoga Park, Calif., 1977-79; tchr. K-2 Sundance Sch., Simi Valley, Calif., 1977-78; spl. tchr. Conejo Valley Unified Sch. Dist., Thousand Oaks, Calif., 1979-94; elem. tchr. Meadows Elem. Sch., Thousand Oaks, Calif., 1994—; ednl. cons. Scwrip & Independent, Ventura County, Calif., 1988—; mem. London Panel of Art Tutors, ILEA Evening Inst., 1969-73; mentor spl. edn. and lang. arts Conejo Valley Unified Sch. Dist., 1988-95. Recipient Award of Tchr. Excellence, AMGEN, 1996; Scwrip fellow Santa Barbara U., 1988. Mem. Calif. Assn. Mediated Learning (bd. dirs. 1991-95). Episcopalian. Home: 1933 Tamarack St Westlake Village CA 91361-1841

DOFFLEMYER, JOHN CUTLER, poet, publishing executive, editor, rancher; b. Visalia, Calif., Apr. 4, 1948; s. Robert Todd and Margaret Ross (Cutler) D.; m. Nancy Lynn Staples, Aug. 29, 1971 (div. Sept., 1981); children: Jessica, Amanda, Robert II; m. Robbin Jean Donnell, Jan. 30, 1996. Student, U. So. Calif., 1970. Cattle rancher; editor Dry Crik Rev., Lemon Cove, Calif., 1989-97; publ. Dry Crik Press, Lemon Cove, 1989—; poet-in-residence U. Redlands (Calif.), fall 1994. Author: poems; editor: Blood Trails, 1992, (anthology) Maverick Western Verse, 1994; publ. poems; contbr. poems to Between Earth & Sky, Poets of the Cowboy West, Pulpit of Bones: Perspectives on Cowboy Poetry, other anthologies. Founder Dry Creek Citizens Coalition, Lemon Cove, Calif., 1995. Wilbur S. Shepperson poetry scholar We. Folklife Ctr., 1992. Mem. Tullre County Cattlemen's Assn. (dir. 1984-86), Calif. Cattlemen's Assn. (mem. state com. pub. lands 1986-88, mem. state com. animal welfare 1988-90). Home: 37081 Dry Creek Rd Lemon Cove CA 93244

DOGLIONE, ARTHUR GEORGE, data processing executive; b. Bklyn., May 24, 1938; s. Francis and Georgia (Smith) D.; m. Maryann Laurette Bonfanti, Sept. 3, 1960; children: Dana Ann, Arthur Todd, Lora Michele. AA, Scottsdale (Ariz.) Community, 1978; AAS, Maricopa Tech. Coll., Phoenix, 1984; BS, Ariz. State U., 1985. Salesman Columbus Realty Co., Trenton, N.J., 1962-65; appraiser J.H. Martin Appraisal Co., Trenton, 1965-68; office mgr. Mcpl. Revaluations, Avon-by-the-Sea, N.J., 1968-69; pres., broker Area Real Estate Agy., Wall, N.J., 1969-76; property appraiser Ariz. Dept. Revenue, Phoenix, 1976-78; investment appraiser Continental Bank, Phoenix, 1978-79; appraisal systems specialist Ariz. Dept. Revenue, Phoenix, 1979-80; project dir. Ariz. Dept. Adminstrn., 1980-83; pres. Logical Models, Scottsdale, Ariz., 1983-95; founder Genus Tech., Scottsdale, 1989—; tax assessor Upper Freehold Twp., N.J., 1974-75, Borough of Bradley Beach, N.J., 1975; lectr. in field. Author various software. Counselor SCORE, SBA, Mesa, Ariz., 1986-90. Mem. Phi Theta Kappa. Republican. Roman Catholic. Office: Genus Tech PO Box 725 Scottsdale AZ 85252-0725

DOHERTY, BETTY JEAN, artist; b. Superior, Wis., June 24, 1935; d. Frank J. Doherty and Ethel I. Olin. BA, Mpls. Sch. Art, 1958; MA, Louis Nat. U., 1988. Chmn. visual arts Wilmette (Ill.) Pub. Schs.; represented by Winnetka (Ill.) Women's Art League, Evanston (Ill.) Art Ctr., Woodstock (Ill.) Courthouse Gallery, Woman Made Gallery, Chgo., John Martin Gallery, Scottsdale, Ariz., Dream Catcher Gallery, Ketchum, Idaho, Blue Angel Gallery, Gainesville, Ga., Marathon Gallery, Tucson; evaluator art curriculum State of Ill.; adj. instr. art North Park Coll., Chgo., Nat. Louis U., Evanston; chmn. Ill. Arts Coun. Grant. Contbg. editor Sch. Arts Mag.; prodr. Youth Art (Cablevision award 1991). Recipient Svc. award Ill. Alliance Art, 1991, First Place award Northbrook Arts Coun., Beauty Salon Digest. Home: 37383 S Arroyo Verde Dr Tucson AZ 85739-1266

DOHRING, DOUG, marketing executive. Chmn. Dohring Co., Calif. Office: Dohring Co 412 W Broadway Ste 300 Glendale CA 91204*

DOHRING, LAURIE, marketing executive. CEO Dohring Co., Glendale, Calif. Office: Dohring Co 412 West Broadway Ste 300 Glendale CA 91204*

DOI, LOIS, psychiatric social worker; b. Honolulu, Oct. 24, 1951; d. James Masato and Thelma Kimiko Miyamoto; m. Brian Doi, May 26, 1972; children: Michael, Lorian. BS, U. Hawaii, 1974, MSW, 1978. Lic. clin. social worker, Calif. Psychiat. social worker, child specialist Desert Community Mental Health Ctr., Indio, Calif., 1979-92, coordinator children's day treatment program, 1982-91; pvt. practice psychiat. social worker 1-2-1 Counseling, Palm Springs, Calif., 1992—; owner, ptnr. 1-2-1 Counseling, Rancho Mirage, Calif.; psychiat. social worker, adult case mgr. Desert Community Mental Health Ctr., Palm Springs, Calif., 1992-93; clin. dir. Barbara Sinatra Children's Ctr., Rancho Mirage, Calif., 1998; expert examiner, Bd. of Behavioral Sci. Examiners, 1987—. Vol. advisor Community Recreation Ctr. Youth Group, Hawaii, 1967-69; vol. interviewer ARC Food Stamp Program, Hawaii, 1973; vol. asst. YWCA Programs Young Mothers and Teens, Hawaii, 1973; vol. group leader YWCA Juvenile Delinquent Program, Hawaii, 1973; placement counselor Vols. In Service to Am., L.A., 1975; VISTA counselor L.A. Urban League, 1975-76. Mem. Nat. Assn. Social Workers. Avocations: needlework, reading. Office: 1-2-1 Counseling # 409 42-600 Bob Hope Dr Rancho Mirage CA 92270

DOLAN, ANDREW KEVIN, lawyer; b. Chgo., Dec. 7, 1945; s. Andrew O. and Elsie (Grafner) D.; children: Andrew, Francesca, Melinda. BA, U. Ill., Chgo., 1967; JD, Columbia U., 1970, MPH, 1976, DPH, 1980. Bar: Wash. 1980. Asst. prof. law Rutgers-Camden Law Sch., N.J., 1970-72; assoc. prof. law U. So. Calif., L.A., 1972-75; assoc. prof. pub. health U. Wash., Seattle, 1977-81; ptnr. Bogle & Gates, Seattle, 1988-93; pvt. practice law, 1993—. Commr. Civil Svc. Commn., Lake Forest Park, Wash., 1981; mcpl. judge City of Lake Forest Park, 1982-98. Russell Sage fellow, 1975. Mem. Order of Coif, Washington Athletic Club. Avocation: book collecting. Office: 5800 Columbia Ctr 701 5th Ave Seattle WA 98104-7016

DOLAN, MARY ANNE, journalist, columnist; b. Washington, May 1, 1947; d. William David and Christine (Shea) D.; BA, Marymount Coll., Tarrytown, N.Y., 1968, HHD (hon.), 1984; student Queen Mary, Royal Holloway colls. U. London, London Sch. Econs., also Kings Coll., Cambridge U., 1966-68. Reporter, editor Washington Star, 1969-77, asst. mng. editor, 1976-77; mng. editor Los Angeles Herald Examiner, 1978-81, editor, 1981—. Recipient Golden Flame award Calif. Press Women, 1980, Woman Achiever award Calif. Fed. Bus. and Profl. Women's Clubs, 1981; bd. selectors for Neiman Fellows Harvard U.; mem. Pulitzer Prize Journalism Jury, 1981, 82. Mem. Am. Soc. Newspaper Editors, NOW. Office: MAD Inc. 1033 Gayley Ave Ste 205 Los Angeles CA 90024-3417

DOLAN, MARYANNE MCLORN, small business owner, writer, educator, lecturer; b. N.Y.C., July 14, 1924; d. Frederick Joseph and Kathryn Cecilia (Carroll) McLorn; m. John Francis Dolan, Oct. 6, 1951 (dec.); children: John Carroll, James Francis McLorn, William Brennan. B.A., San Francisco State U., 1978, M.A., 1981. Tchr. classes and seminars in antiques and collectibles U. Calif., Berkeley, Davis, Santa Cruz, Coll. of Marin, Kentfield, Calif., Mills Coll., Oakland, St. Mary's Coll., Moraga, 1969-90, Solano C.C., 1990—; tch. writing Dolan Sch., 1969-90; owner antique shop, Benicia, Calif., 1970-98; lectr. Nat. Assn. Jewelry Appraisers Symposium, Tucson; lectr. Vintage Fashion Expo., Oakland, Coll. for Appraisers, Placentia, Calif. Author: Vintage Clothing, 1880-1980, 3d edit., 1983, Collecting Rhinestone Jewelry, 4th edit., 1998, Old Lace and Linens, 1989, Commonsense Collecting, 1991, 300 Years of American Sterling Silver Flatware, 1992, American Medallion Silver, 1997, The World of Dolls, 1998; weekly columnist The Collector, 1979-88, Antique Jour., 1997—; contbr. articles to profl. jours. Mem. Antique Appraisal Assn. Am. Inc., Questers, Internat. Soc. Appraisers (lectr. ann. meeting), Internat. Platform Assn., Internat. Fan Assn., Internat. Perfume Bottle Assn., No. Calif. Bead Soc. Republican. Roman Catholic. Home and Office: 138 Belle Ave Pleasant Hill CA 94523-4640

DOLD, CATHERINE ANNE, writer, editor; b. Glen Ridge, N.J., Aug. 3, 1957; d. Robert Bruce and Margaret Anne (Noll) D. BA in Biology, U. Colo., 1981; cert. in sci. and environ. reporting, NYU, 1989, MA in Journalism, 1989. Asst. dir. comm. Natural Resources Def. Coun., N.Y.C., 1982-89; sr. editor Audubon Mag., N.Y.C., 1990-91; freelance writer numerous nat. print and electronic publs., Boulder, Colo., 1991—. Mem. Am. Soc. Journalists and Authors, Soc. Environ. Journalists, Nat. Assn. Sci. Writers, Boulder Media Women. Office: PO Box 4424 Boulder CO 80306-4424

DOLGIN, STEPHEN MARK, teacher, social worker; b. San Francisco, Dec. 22, 1949; s. David Aubrey and Ruth (Ogurak) D.; B.A., U. Minn., 1972, M.S.W., 1976; M.B.A. in Health Svcs. Mgmt., Golden Gate U., 1982; postgrad., San Francisco State U., 1987—. Social caseworker Contra Costa County Social Svcs. Dept., Richmond, Calif., 1979-81; social ins. claims examiner Social Security Adminstrn., Richmond, Calif., 1982-84; vets. svc. officer Dakota County, Minn., 1987; substitute tchr. South San Francisco Sch. Dist., 1987-88; tchr. Fresno Unified Sch. Dist., 1989-98; tchr. San Francisco Unified Sch. Dist., 1989—; intern Lawrence Livermore Nat. Lab., summer 1991. Served with U.S. Army, 1976-79; maj. USAR; lt. col. Calif. Army NG. Mem. CAP (cadet program officer, Sr. Mem. of Yr. award 1980), Assn. U.S. Army, Am. Philatelic Soc., Res. Officers Assn., (v.p. med. svc. dept. Calif. 1983-84, chpt. sec.), Toastmasters Internat. (club pres., sec. 1984, Competent Toastmaster award), Air Force Assn., Mil. Order World Wars (chpt. sr. v.p. 1986), Am. Legion, Phi Delta Kappa. Home: Ste 306 1400 Carpentier St Apt 306 San Leandro CA 94577-3657

DOLGOW, ALLAN BENTLEY, consulting company executive; b. N.Y.C.; BIE, NYU, 1959, MBA, 1972; postgrad. Hunter Coll., 1976, U. Calif., 1991; divorced; children: Nicole, Marc, Ginger, Kimbie. With Republic Aviation Corp., Farmingdale, N.Y., 1959-60, Internat. Paper Co., N.Y.C., 1960-73, J.C. Penney Co. Inc., N.Y.C., 1973-76, Morse Electro Products, N.Y.C., 1976-77, Morse Electrophonic Hong Kong Ltd., 1976-77, mgr. Revlon Inc., Edison, N.J., 1977-79, SRI Internat., Menlo Park, Calif., 1979-96, Dolgow Cons. Group, Menlo Park, 1996-99. With U.S. Army, 1954-56, Germany. Office: 4777 Gouse Run Dr Apt 137 Stockton CA 95207-5375

DOLIBER, DARREL LEE, consultant, design engineer; b. Mpls., June 19, 1940; s. Russell Clifford Doliber and Helen Carol (Homa) Price; m. Ethel Lorraine Dzivi, June 17, 1962; children: Wendy Lorraine, Heather Leigh; m. Helga Renate Miggo, Oct. 31, 1986. AA, Palomar Coll., 1973. Prodn. engr. Hughes Aircraft Co., Carlsbad, Calif., 1969-74; sr. engr. I.T.T., Roanoke, Va., 1974-77; dir. mfg. Gainsboro Elec. Mfg. Co., Inc., Roanoke, Va., 1977-78; mfg. engr. Litton Industries, Tempe, Ariz., 1978-82; sr. engr. Datagraphix, Inc., San Diego, 1982-84; lab. mgr. S.A.I.C., San Diego, 1984-98; cons. in photon counting detectors UHV Systems, Cleanroom Design, Med. Devices, Alpine, Calif., 1996—; proprietor Victoria Rock Bed and Breakfast, 1995—. Contbr. articles in field; patentee in field. Mem. Soc. Photo-Optical and Instrumentation Engrs. Roman Catholic. Avocations: art, soaring. Home and Office: 2952 N Victoria Dr Alpine CA 91901-3673

DOLICH, ANDREW BRUCE, sports marketing executive; b. Bklyn., Feb. 18, 1947; s. Mac and Yetta (Weiselter) D.; m. Ellen Andrea Fass, June 11, 1972; children: Lindsey, Caryn, Cory. BA, Am. U., 1969; MEd, Ohio U., 1971. Adminstrv. asst. to gen. mgr. Phila. 76ers, NBA, 1971-74; v.p. Md. Arrows Lacrosse, Landover, 1974-76; mktg. dir. Washington Capitals, NHL, Landover, 1976-78; exec. v.p., gen. mgr. Washington Diplomats Soccer, 1978-80; v.p. bus. ops. Oakland A's Baseball, Calif., 1980-92, exec. v.p., 1993-95; pres., COO Golden State Warriors NBA, Oakland, Calif., 1995-98; pres. Dolich & Assoc. Sports Mktg., Alameda, Calif., 1996—; exec. v.p. Advantix, 1998—; nat. fundraising chmn. sports adminstrs. program Ohio U., Athens, dir., 1978-82; lectr. sports mktg. U. Calif. Ext. Bd. dirs. Bay Area Sports Hall of Fame, 1982—, Celebrate Oakland Com., Internat. Sports Mktg. Coun., Oakland Zoo Adv. Coun. Recipient Alumni of Yr. award Ohio U. Sports Adminstrs. Program, Athens, 1982; recipient Clio award Am. Advt. Fedn., 1982. E-mail: adolich@advantix.com.

DOLL, LINDA A., artist, educator; b. Bklyn., May 5, 1942; d. William James Harrington and Ann B. (Casey) Cook; m. William John Doll, Feb. 4, 1962; children: Patricia, William Jr. AA, Palomar Coll., 1974; BA, San Diego State U., 1976. chairperson Arts Adv. Com. to Congressman Jim Bates, 1983-84; U.S. Coast Guard Artist, 1985—. Exhibited in group shows with Am. Watercolor Soc., 1985-91 (selected for one yr. nat. travel show, Elsie and David Ject-key award 1988) N.Y.C., 1986, 87, 88, Canton, Ohio, 1985, Nat. Watercolor Soc., Brea, Calif., 1984-89, Watercolor West Annual, Riverside, Calif., 1982, 84-88 (E. Gene Crain Purchase Selection award 1985, Second Place Jurors award 1982), Rocky Mountain Nat., Golden, Colo., 1984-85, Midwest Annual, Davenport, Iowa, 1983, 85, Nat. Watercolor Soc., Riverside, 1985 (selected for one yr. nat. travel show) 88, Canton Ohio, 1985, Watercolor Internat., San Diego, 1978-79, 82-88 (selected for one yr. nat. travel show 1983-84), Watercolor Okla., 1982-84 (Harry Hulett Jr. award 1984), Pa. Soc. Watercolor Painters, Harrisburg, 1988, 1982 (hon. mention); represented in permanent collections including E. Gene Crain Collection, Scripps Hosp., La Jolla, Calif., Redlands Community Hosp., Riverside, Campbell River Community Art Council, Can., Simpact Assocs. Inc., San Diego. Mem. San Diego Watercolor Soc. (past pres., life), Nat. Watercolor Soc. (past pres., life), Knickerbocker Artists, Am. Watercolors Soc. (past juror, bd. dirs.). Office: 17490 Matinal Dr San Diego CA 92127-1238

DOLL, LYNNE MARIE, public relations agency executive; b. Glendale, Calif., Aug. 27, 1961; d. George William and Carol Ann (Kennedy) D.; m. David Jay Lans, Oct. 11, 1986. BA in Journalism, Calif. State U., Northridge, 1983. Freelance writer Austin Pub. Rels. Systems, Glendale, 1978-82; asst. account exec. Berkhemer & Kline, L.A., 1982-83; exec. v.p., ptnr. Rogers & Assocs., L.A., 1983—; exec. dir. Suzuki Automotive Found. for Life, Brea, Calif., 1986-91; mem. strategic planning com. Gateway to Indian Am. Corp. for Am. Indian Devel., San Francisco, 1988-90. Pub. rels. cons., Rape Treatment Ctr., L.A., 1986—. Mem. Ad Club L.A. (bd. dirs., pres. 1994-95), Pub. Rels. Soc. Am., So. Calif. Assn. Philanthropy, Coun. on Founds., Internat. Motor Press Assn., Nat. Conf. Christians and Jews (bd. dirs. 1996—). Democrat. Office: Rogers & Assocs 1875 Century Park E Ste 300 Los Angeles CA 90067-2504

DOLLARHIDE, WILLIAM WILES, genealogist, writer; b. Seattle, Apr. 17, 1942; s. Albert Raymond and Marjory Watkins (Wiles) D.; m. Mary Earlene Smith, Oct. 6, 1967 (div. July 1972); 1 child, Meredith Ann; m. Linda Kay Lawson, Aug. 24, 1988. AA, Seattle C.C., 1971; student, U. Wash., 1971-73, Western Wash. U., 1977-79. cert. engr. technician Holgate Tech. Sch., Seattle, 1965. Engrng. technician Boeing Co., Seattle/Renton, Wash., 1965-68, 70-72; assoc. architect Western Wash. U., Bellingham, 1977-85; genealogist Blaine/Bellingham, Wash., 1985-94; genealogist/mag. editor Heritage Quest, Bountiful, Utah, 1994—; nat. exhibitors rep. Fedn. Geneal. Socs., Kansas City, Mo., 1989-92; editor Genealogy Bull., Heritage Quest, 1994—, Dollarhide Systems, 1984-94; contbg. editor Heritage Quest mag., 1984—. Co-author: (with William Thorndale) Map Guide to the U.S. Federal Censuses, 1790-1920, 1987 (award of merit Am. Soc. Genealogists 1987); author: Map Guide to American Migration Routes, 1996, British Origins of American Colonists, 1629-1775, 1997, Genealogy Starter Kit, 1992, 98, Managing a Genealogical Project, 1988, (with Ronald Bremer) America's Best Genealogy Resource Centers, 1998, U.S. and Canadian Census Records: a Genealogist's Guide to Census Facts, Schedules and Indexes, 1998; contbr. more than 60 articles to profl. jours.; lectr. in field; has conducted seminar programs for more than 600 geneal. societies; spkr. at major geneal. gatherings. Mem. Blaine (Wash.) Planning Commn., 1980-81, Blaine City Coun., 1981-84, mayor pro-tem, 1982-84; chmn. Whatcom County Bd. of Health, Bellingham, Wash., 1982-84. Recipient Award of Appreciation Wash. State Geneal. Soc., 1992, Oreg. Geneal. Forum, 1993. Mem. Nat. Geneal. Soc. (Award of Appreciation 1990). Avocations: history: U.S. and local, early roads, railroads, steamboats, canals. Office: Heritage Quest 593 W 100 N PO Box 329 Bountiful UT 84011-0329

DOLLIVER, JAMES MORGAN, retired state supreme court justice; b. Ft. Dodge, Iowa, Oct. 13, 1924; s. James Isaac and Margaret Elizabeth (Morgan) D.; m. Barbara Babcock, Dec. 18, 1948; children: Elizabeth, James, Peter, Keith, Jennifer, Nancy. BA in Polit. Sci. with high honors, Swarthmore Coll., 1949; LLB, U. Wash., 1952; D in Liberal Arts (hon.), U. Puget Sound, 1981. Bar: Wash. 1952. Clk. to presiding justice Wash. Supreme Ct., 1952-53; pvt. practice Port Angeles, Wash., 1953-54, Everett, Wash., 1961-64; adminstrv. asst. to Congressman Jack Westland, 1955-61, Gov. Daniel J. Evans, 1965-76; justice Supreme Ct. State of Wash., 1976-99, chief justice, 1985-87; adj. prof. U. Puget Sound Sch. Law, 1988-92. Chmn. United Way Campaign Thurston County, 1975; chmn. Wash. chpt. Nature Conservancy, 1981-83; pres. exec. bd. Tumwater Area coun. Boy Scouts Am., 1972-73, Wash. State Capital Hist. Assn., 1976-80, 85—, also trustee, 1983-84; trustee Deaconess Children's Home, Everett, 1963-65, U. Puget Sound, 1969—, chair exec. com., 1990-93, Wash. 4-H Found., 1977-93, Claremont (Calif.) Theol. Sem., assoc. mem., Community Mental Health Ctr., 1977-84; bd. mgrs. Swarthmore Coll., 1980-84; bd. dirs. Thurston Mason Community Health Ctr., 1977-84, Thurston Youth Svcs. Soc., 1969-84, also pres., 1983, mem. exec com. 1970-84, Wash. Women's Employment and Edn., 1982-84; mem. jud. coun. United Meth. Ch., 1984-92, gen. cong., 1970-72, 80—, gen. bd. ch. and soc., 1976-84; adv. coun. Ret. Sr. Vol. program, 1979-83; pres. Wash. Ctr. Law-related Edn., 1987-89, bd. dirs. 1987-95; bd. dirs. World Assn. for Children and Parents, 1987-93; trustee U. Wash. Law Sch. Found., 1982-90, Olympic Park Inst., 1988-94; mem. bd. visitors U. Wash. Sch. Social Work, 1987-93; chair bd. visitors U. Puget Sound Sch. Law, 1988-90, bd. visitors, 1988-93; chmn. bd. dirs. Pub. Lands Employee Recognition Fund, 1994—; mem. bd. dirs. St. Peter Hosp. Med. Rehab. Community Adv. Bd., 1993—. With USN, 1943-45; ensign USCG, 1945-46. Recipient award Nat. Council Japanese Am. Citizens League, 1976; Silver Beaver award, 1971; Silver Antelope award, 1976. Mem. ABA, Wash. Bar Assn., Am. Judges Assn., Am. Judicature Soc., Pub. Broadcast Found. (bd. dirs. 1982-95), Masons, Rotary, Phi Delta Theta, Delta Theta Phi.

DOLSEN, DAVID HORTON, mortician; b. Durango, Colo., Feb. 27, 1940; s. Donald B. and Florence I. (Maxey) D.; m. Jo Patricia Johnson, Dec. 23, 1962; children: Wendy, Douglas. BA, Southwestern Coll., 1962; Mortuary Sci. degree, Dallas-Jones Coll Mortuary Sci, 1963. Apprentice Davis Mortuary, Pueblo, Colo., 1963-64; bus. mgr. George F. McCarty Funeral Home, Pueblo, 1964-65; owner Dolsen Mortuary, Lamar, Colo., 1965-72; pres., gen. mgr., dir. Almont, Inc., Pueblo, 1972-92; sec. Dolsen, Inc., 1967—; pres. Wilson Funeral Dirs. Inc., 1972-92, Carlson Travel Network/Let's Talk Travel, Inc., Pueblo/Denver. bd. dirs. Afrin U., 1989—, spl. asst. to pres. Southwestern Coll., 1997, dir. adminstr. svcs., Mt. Conference United Methodist Ch., Denver, 1995-98. Mem. Am. Soc. Travel Assn. Execs., Nat. Funeral Dirs. Assn., Nat. Selected Morticians, cremation Assn. Am., Monument Builders N.Am., Colo. Funeral Dirs. Assn., Internat. Assn. Travel Agts., Masons, Shriners, Elks, Rotary (bd. dirs., pres. 1990—, Paul Harris fellow), Pi Sigma Eta, Pi Kappa Delta, Pi Gamma Mu. Home: 1315 Plum St Winfield KS 67156-4619 Office: 100 Coll Ave Winfield KS 67156-4708

DOMENICI, PETE V. (VICHI DOMENICI), senator; b. Albuquerque, May 7, 1932; s. Cherubino and Alda (Vichi) D.; m. Nancy Burk, Jan. 15, 1958; children: Lisa, Peter, Nella, Clare, David, Nanette, Helen, Paula. Student, U. Albuquerque, 1950-52; BS, U. N.Mex., 1954, LLD (hon.); LLB, Denver U., 1958; LLD (hon.), Georgetown U. Sch. Medicine; HHD (hon.), N.Mex. State U. Bar: N.Mex. 1958. Tchr. math. pub. schs. Albuquerque, 1954-55; ptnr. firm Domenici & Bonham, Albuquerque, 1958-72; chmn., ex-officio mayor Albuquerque, 1967; mem. U.S. Senate from N.Mex. 106th Congress, N.Mex., 1972—; city commr. Albuquerque, 1966-68; mem. appropriations com., energy and natural resources com., chmn. subcom. on energy rsch. and devel.; mem. com. on environ. and pub. works, mem. govtl. affairs com.; chmn. budget com., com. on Indian affairs; mem. Presl. Adv. Com. on Federalism; senate Rep. policy com. Mem. Gov.'s Policy Bd. for

Law Enforcement, 1967-68; chmn. Model Cities Joint Adv. Com., 1967-68. Recipient Nat. League of Cities award Outstanding Performance in Congress; Disting. Svc. award Tax Found., 1986, Legislator of Yr. award Nat. Mental Health Assn., 1987, public sector leadership award, 1996. Mem. Nat. League Cities, Middle Rio Grande Council Govts. Office: US Senate 328 Hart Senate Office Bldg Washington DC 20510-3101*

DOMEÑO, EUGENE TIMOTHY, elementary education educator, principal; b. L.A., Oct. 22, 1938; s. Digno and Aurora Mary (Roldan) D. AA, Santa Monica (Calif.) City Coll., 1958; BA, Calif. State U., 1960, MA, 1966. Cert. elem. tchr., gen. sch svcs, special secondary tchr. Elem. tchr. L.A. Unified Sch. Dist., 1960-70; asst. prin. Pomona (Calif.) Unified Sch. Dist., 1970-71, prin., 1971—; cons. testing and evaluation Pomona Unified Sch. Dist., 1990—. With USNR, 1957-65. Recipient PTA Hon. Svc. award Granada Elem. PTA, Granada Hills, Calif., 1960, Armstrong Sch. PTA, Diamond Bar, Calif., 1990, Calif. Disting. Sch. Calif. Dept. Edn., 1989, Nat. Blue Ribbon Sch. U.S. Dept. Edn., Washington, 1990, Prin. and Leadership award, 1990. Mem. ASCD, Nat. Assn. Elem. Sch. Prins. (Prin. of Leadership award with Nat. Safety Com., 1991), Nat. Assn. Year Round Sch., Assn. Calif. Sch. Administrs., Pomona Elem. Prin.'s Assn., Diamond Bar C. of C. (edn. com.). Avocations: golf, dancing, tennis, playing the flute. Office: Neil Armstrong Elem Sch 22750 Beaverhead Dr Diamond Bar CA 91765-1566*

DOMINGUEZ, EDDIE, artist; b. Tucumcari, N.Mex., Oct. 17, 1957. BFA, Cleve. Inst. Art, 1981; MFA, Alfred U., 1983. Grad. asst., ceramics and visual design courses Alfred (N.Y.) U., 1981-83; artist-in-residence, lectr. Ohio State U., Columbus, 1984; artist-in-edn. N.Mex. Arts Divsn., Santa Fe, 1985-86; artist-in-residence Cleve. Inst. Art, 1986; artist-in-residence, lectr. U. Mont., Missoula, 1988; asst. prof. art U. Nebr., Lincoln, 1998—; Lectr., presenter workshops, mem. panels Ill. Arts Coun., Chgo., 1994, NEA, Washington, 1994, Ariz. Commn. on the Arts, 1994, Concordia U., Montreal, Que., Can., 1994, Mass. Coll. Art, Boston, 1994, Bennington (Vt.) Coll., 1994, 95, 96, Peters Valley, Layton, N.J., 1994, Firehouse Art Ctr., Norman, Okla., 1994, Haystack Mountain Sch. Arts & Crafts, Deer Isle, Maine, 1994, Ghost Ranch, Abiquiu, N.Mex., 1995, We. States Arts Fedn., Santa Fe, 1995, Colo. Coun. on the Arts, Boulder, 1995, Durango (Colo.) Art Ctr., 1995, Tamarind Inst., Albuquerque, 1995, 96, Kansas City (Mo.) Ar Inst., 1995, Hallmark Cards, Kansas City, 1996, Wichita (Kans.) Ctr. Arts, 1996, La. State U., Baton Rouge, 1996, Idaho State Arts Coun. Grants, Boise, 1996, Mattie Rhodes Counseling and Art Ctr., Kansas City, 1996, Southwest Ctr. Crafts, San Antonio, 1997, Very Spl. Arts, Albuquerque, 197, Topeka (Kans.) and Shawnee County Pub. Libr., 1997, numerous others. Solo exhbns. include Pro Art Gallery, St. Louis, 1990, Mobilia Gallery, Cambridge, Mass., 1990, Munson Gallery, Santa Fe, 1990, 92, 94, 95, 97, Mariposa Gallery, Albuquerque, 1990, Joanne Rapp Gallery, Scottsdale, Ariz., 1991, 93, 95, Felicita Found., Escondido, Calif., 1991, Tucumcari (N.Mex.) Area Vocat. Sch., 1992, Manchester Art Ctr., Pitts., 1993, Wetsman Collection, Detroit, 1993, Clovis (N.Mex.) C.C., 1993, Firehouse Art Ctr., 1994, Kavesh Gallery, Sun Valley, Idaho, 1995, Jan Weiner Gallery, Kansas City, 1995, 96, numerous others; group exhbns. include Fred Jones Mus. Art, U. Okla., Norman, 1995, Roswell (N.Mex.) Mus. & Art Ctr., 1995, Nancy Margolis Gallery, N.Y.C., 1995, Sharadin Art Gallery, Kutztown (Pa.) U., 1995, Richard Kavesh Gallery, 1995, Jan Weiner Gallery, 1995, Ariz. State U. Art Mus., Tempe, 1995, Islip (N.Y.) Mus., 1995, Bruce Kapson Gallery, Santa Monica, Calif., 1996, Site Sante Fe Gallery, 1996, Johnston County C.C., Overland Parks, Kans., 1996, Jane Haslem Gallery, Washington, 196, Karen Ruhlen Gallery, Santa Fe, 1996, Margo Jacobson Gallery, Portland, Oreg., 1996, Very Spl. Arts Gallery, Albuquerque, 1997, Joanne Rapp Gallery, 1997, numerous others; pub. art project include, among others, murals at Great Brook Valley Health Ctr., Worcester, Mass., 1994, Mass. Gen. Hosp., 1996; represented in many permanent collections, including Cooper-Hewitt, N.Y.C., Mus. Fine Arts, Santa Fe, Cleve. Inst. Art, Fed. Reserve Bank, Dallas, Roswell Mus. and Art Ctr., Albuquerque Mus. Fine Arts, City of Tucson (Ariz.), Phoenix Airport, Renwick Gallery Nat. Mus. Am. Art Smithsonian Inst., Washington, Detroit Inst. Art, Hallmark Cards Corp., Kansas City, State Capitol Art Collection, Santa Fe, pvt. collections. Recipient numerous grants, including NEA fellowships, 1986, 88, Kohler Arts-in-Industry grant, Sheboygan, Wis., 1988, Percent for Art Project grant, Phoenix Arts Coun., 1990, 1992; recipient various prizes, including Clay, Fiber and Wood Best in Show, Albuquerque, 1984, Clay in '87 1st place award, Albuquerque St. Fair Exhbn., 1987.

DOMINICK, ANTHONY, JR., entrepreneur, Internet consultant; b. Oakland, Calif., Jan. 6, 1963; s. Anthony Sr. and Sheery Lee (Logan) D. AA, Laney C.C., Oakland, Calif., 1998. Commd. q.m., E-5 USN, 1984, resigned, 1992; with Fremont Ford Autosales, Newark, Calif., 1992-93; computer asst. Laney C.C., 1995—. Recipient Expeditionary medal U.S. Pres.-USN, 1988. Mem. NARAS, Broadcast Music Inc., Big Bros.-Big Sisters. Home: PO Box 10441 Oakland CA 94610-0441 Office: West Ave Kingfish Internat PO Box 10441 Oakland CA 94610-0441

DONAHOO, STANLEY ELLSWORTH, orthopedic surgeon; b. St. Joseph, Mo., Dec. 3, 1933; s. Charles Ellsworth and Opal (Cole) D.; m. Cheryl R. Donahoo; children: Shan Maureen, Brian Patrick, Mary Kathleen, Jane Eileen; stepchildren: Trina Person, Kevin. MD, U. Wash., 1963. Resident, Duke U., Durham, N.C., 1967-68, U.S. Naval Hosp., Oakland, Calif., 1963-67; commd. lt., U.S. Navy, 1963 advanced through grades to lt. comdr. (orthopaedic surgeon), 1971; practice medicine, specializing in orthopaedic surgery, Roseburg, Oreg., 1971—; chief surgery Mercy Hosp., Roseburg, 1973-74; chief surgery Douglas Community Hosp., Roseburg, 1973, chief of staff, 1974—; cons. Guam Meml. Hosp., co-dir. rehab. unit, 1970-71; cons. orthopaedic surgery VA Hosp., Roseburg, 1971—; chmn. Douglas County (Oreg.) Emergency Med. Services Com., 1973-74. Trustee Douglas Community Hosp., 1975. Served with AUS, 1952-55. Diplomate Am. Bd. Orthopaedic Surgery. Fellow Am. Acad. Orthopaedic Surgeons (admissions com. region 14), North Pacific Orthopaedic Soc. (v.p. 1984-85, trustee 1991-95, pres.-elect 1996-98, pres. 1998); mem. Piedmont Orthopaedic Soc., Western Orthopedic Assn. (pres. Oreg. chpt. 1996—), Oreg. Med. Assn. (mem. sports medicine com., med. rev. com. 1981), Guam Med. Soc. (pres. 1970), Am. Trauma Soc. (founding mem.), Roseburg C. of C. (bd. govs. 1978—). Home: 173 Songbird Ct Roseburg OR 97470-9400 Office: 1813 W Harvard Ave Ste 201 Roseburg OR 97470-2752

DONAHUE, MARK FORREST, financial planner; b. St. Louis, May 11, 1951; m. Julie E. Jones; children: Richard, Suzanne. BA, Williams Coll., 1973; MBA, Wharton Sch. Fin., 1978; JD, U. Pa., 1978. CFP, CLU, ChFC. Atty. Simpson, Thacher & Bartlett, N.Y.C., 1980-82, Holtzmann, Wise & Shepard, N.Y.C., 1982-83; v.p. Merrill Lynch Capital Markets, N.Y.C., 1984-86, Whale Securities Corp., N.Y.C., 1986-87, Resource Holdings Capital Group, N.Y.C., 1988-89; atty. Kelley, Drye & Warren, N.Y.C., 1989-90, Coudert Brothers, L.A., 1990-93; pres. Compass Fin. Svcs., Laguna Hills, Calif., 1993—; instr. fin. planning U. Calif., Irvine, 1997-98. Contbr. articles to profl. jours. Lehman scholar Williams Coll., 1973. Mem. Inst. Cert. Fin. Planners, Internat. Assn. for Fin. Planning, Calif. Bar Assn., D.C. Bar Assn., N.Y. Bar Assn. Fax: 949-448-5967. E-mail: mfdonahue@earthlink.net. Office: Compass Fin Svcs 24791 Nellie Gail Rd Laguna Hills CA 92653-5817

DONAHUE, RICHARD KING, athletic apparel executive, lawyer; b. Lowell, Mass., July 20, 1927; s. Joseph P. and Dorothy F. (Riordan) D.; m. Nancy Lawson, Sept. 19, 1953; children: Gail M., Timothy J., Michael R., Nancy C., Richard K., Daniel J., Alicia A., Stephen J., Christopher P., Tara E., Philip A. A.B., Dartmouth Coll., 1948; J.D., Boston U., 1951. Bar: Mass. 1951. Ptnr. Donahue & Donahue, Attys., P.C., Lowell, Mass., 1951-60, 63-90; v.p., chmn. bd., Nike, Inc., 1990— ; asst. to Pres. Kennedy, Washington, 1960-63. Served with USNR. Recipient Herbert Harley award Am. Judicature Soc., 1981. Mem. Am. Bd. Trial Advs., ABA (gov., ho. of dels. 1972—), Am. Coll. Trial Lawyers, Mass. Bar Assn. (past pres., Gold medal 1979), New Eng. Bar Assn. (past pres.). Clubs: Union League (Boston); Vesper Country (Tyngsboro, Mass.); Fed. City (Washington); Yorick (Lowell). Office: Nike Inc 1 Bowerman Dr Beaverton OR 97005-6453

DONALDSON, GEORGE BURNEY, environmental consultant; b. Oakland, Calif., Mar. 16, 1945; s. George T. and L.M. (Burney) D.; m. Jennifer L. Bishop, Feb. 16, 1974; children: Dawn Marie, Matthew George. AS in Criminology, Porterville Coll., 1972. Registered environ. assessor, Calif.; cert. transp. specialist. Police officer City of Lindsay (Calif.), 1966-67; distbn. mgr. Ortho div. Chevron Chem. Co., Lindsay, 1967-73; safety specialist Wilbur-Ellis Co. Fresno, Calif., 1973-77, safety dir., 1977-79, dir. corporate regulatory affairs, 1979-97; sr. environ. cons. Geomatrix Conss., Inc., Fresno, 1997—; industry rep. to White House Inter-Govtl. Sci. Engring., and Tech. Adv. Panel, Task Force on Transp. of Non-Nuclear Hazardous Materials, 1980; industry rep. Transp. Rsch. Bd.'s Nat. Strategies Conf. on Transp. of Hazardous Materials and Wastes in the 1980's, NAS, 1981, Hazardous Materials Transp. Conf., Nat. Conf. of State Legislatures, 1982. speaker and moderator in field; dir. Western Fertilizer and Pesticide Safety seminar, Sacramento, 1979; speaker Southeastern Agrl. Chem. Safety seminar, Winston-Salem, N.C., 1986. Chmn. industry/govt. task force for unique on-site hazardous waste recycling, devel. task force for computerized regulatory software and data base system, devel. task force modifying high expansion foam tech. for fire suppression; hazardous materials adviser, motor carrier rating com. Calif. Hwy. Patrol, 1978-79. With U.S. Army, 1962-65. Mem. Western Agrl. Chems. Assn. (past chmn. transp., distbn. and safety com., outstanding mem. of year 1981, govtl. affairs com., regulatory affairs com., trustee polit. action com.), Nat. Agrl. Chems. Assn. (past chmn. transp. and distbn. com., occupational safety and health com., environ. mgmt. com., state affairs com., moderator spring conf. 1989), U.S. Inter-Regional Coordinating Coun. (trans. and distbn. com.), Am. Soc. Safety Engrs., Calif. Fertilizer Assn. (transp. and distbn. com., environ. com.), Fresno Agri. Round Table, Fresno City and County C. of C. (agrl. steering com., govt. affairs com.), Calif. C. of C. (environ. policy com.), Am. Legion, Elks. Republican. Office: Goematrix Cons Inc 2444 Main St Ste 215 Fresno CA 93721-2734

DONALDSON, MARY KENDRICK, nurse; b. Tifton, Ga., June 25, 1937; d. Howard Story and Trudy (Donalson) Marlin; m. Harvey Kendrick Sr., Apr. 13, 1953 (dec. 1965); children: Jerome, Micheal, Harvey Jr., Merry, Sheila, Larry; m. Isaac Hargett, Feb. 16, 1985. AA, Compton (Calif.) Coll., 1969; BS, Pepperdine U., 1972, MA, 1976; diploma in nursing, SW Coll., Los Angeles, 1984. Staff nurse St. Francis Hosp., Lynwood, Calif., 1965-67; pvt. duty nurse Profl. Nurse's Registry, L.A., 1967-82; elem. tchr. Compton Sch. Dist., Calif., 1975-80; caseworker, clk. L.A. County Probation Dept., 1980-90, dep. probation officer, 1990—; pediatric nurse companion Personal Care Health Service, Torrance, Calif., 1984—; home economist Dept. Welfare, Compton, 1970-72; asst. dir. Century Plaza Hotel, Century City, Calif., 1971-72. Chairperson Com. To Elect Garland Hardeman For Councilman, Inglewood, Calif., 1987. Exec. Housekeeping scholarship Century Plaza Hotel, Los Angeles, 1971. Mem. Fellow Am. Home Econs. Assn., Pepperdine Alumni Assn., Pepperdine's Kappa-Kappa Sorority, Am. Nurse's Assn. Democrat. Avocations: golf, bowling, sewing, fishing. Home: 4730 Falcon Ave Long Beach CA 90807-1204 Office: L A County Probation Dept 1601 Eastlake Ave Los Angeles CA 90033-1009

DONALDSON, MICHAEL CLEAVES, lawyer; b. Montclair, N.J., Oct. 13, 1939; s. Wyman C. and Ernestine (Greenwood) D.; m. Diana D., Sept. 12, 1969 (div. 1979); children: Michelle, Amy, Wendy; m. Mimi Schwied, Sept. 14, 1991. BS, U. Fla., 1961; JD, U. Calif., Berkeley, 1967. Bar: Calif. 1967, U.S. Dist. Ct. (cen. dist.) Calif. 1967, U.S. Ct. Appeals (9th cir.) 1967. Assoc. Harris & Hollingsworth, L.A., 1969-72; ptnr. McCabe & Donaldson, L.A., 1972-79; pvt. practice Law Office of M.C. Donaldson, L.A., 1979-90; ptnr. Dern & Donaldson, L.A., 1990-94, Berton & Donaldson, Beverly Hills, Calif., 1994—; lectr. in field; judge, preliminary and finalist judge Internat. Emmys; preliminary judge Night Time Emmys; gen. counsel Ind. Feature Project West, Internat. Documentary Assn. Author: EZ Legal Guide to Copyright and Trademark, 1995, (booklet) Something Funny Happened on the Way to Dinner, 1976; contg. author: Conversations with Michael Landon, 1992, Negotiating for Dummies, 1996, Clearance & Copyright What the Independent Filmmaker Needs to Know, 1997. Bd. dirs. Calif. Theatre Coun., L.A. 1st lt. USMC, 1961-64. Mem. ABA (entertainment and sports sect.), NATAS, Nat. Acad. Cable Broadcasting, Beverly Hills Bar Assn. (chmn. entertainment sect.), L.A. Copyright Soc. Republican. Avocations: photography, writing, gardening, hiking, skiing. Home: 2074 Benedict Canyon Dr Beverly Hills CA 90210-1404 Office: Berton & Donaldson 9595 Wilshire Blvd Ste 711 Beverly Hills CA 90212-2507

DONALDSON, ROBERT CHARLES, history educator; b. San Francisco, Jan. 28, 1924; s. Donald and Cora Priscilla (Donaldson) Wood; m. Persis Chapple, Jan. 4, 1975; children by previous marriage—Diane Margery. Student, U. Ariz., 1942; B.A., U. So. Calif., 1950, M.A., 1951; Ph.D., U. Mich., 1954; Fulbright scholar, U. Brussels, 1953-54. Asst. prof. Eastern Ky. State Coll., 1954-57; asst. prof. history Calif. State U., Sacramento, 1957-62; assoc. prof. Calif. State U., 1962-67, prof., 1967-94, chmn. dept., 1969-75, chmn. acad. senate, 1968-69, coll. ombudsman, 1969-70, presiding officer faculty, 1972-75, faculty emeritus, 1995-97; senator Acad. Senate of Calif. State Univs. and Colls., 1970-76; real estate broker, 1990—. Served with AUS, 1943-46. Recipient Meritorious Performance award for outstanding svc. to univ. community, 1988. Mem. Am. Hist. Assn., Faculty Emeritus Assn. (pres.), Phi Kappa Phi (pres. campus chpt. 1963-64, 74-76, 92-94), Phi Alpha Theta, Blue Key, Phi Beta Delta. Democrat. Club: Comstock. Home: 1516 Little Ct Carmichael CA 95608-5915

DONALDSON, WILBURN LESTER, property management corporation executive; b. St. Augustine, Fla., Mar. 2, 1938; s. Chester Campbell and Dovie (Pratt) D.; m. Patricia Lilias Babcock, Sept. 11, 1956; children: John Randolph, David Chester, James Robert. BA, San Francisco State U., 1968, MBA, 1971. Transp. clk. Armour Food Co., San Francisco, 1958-60, transp. mgr., 1960-65, product mgr., 1965-70; So. Calif. sales mgr. Armour Food Co., L.A., 1970-73; tng. mgr. Armour Food Co., Phoenix, 1973-77, nat. mktg. mgr., 1977-80; region sales mgr. Armour Food Co., Pitts., 1980-83; nat. tng. mgr. Armour Food Co., Phoenix, 1983-84; pres. Allied Investment Mgrs., Inc., Phoenix, 1984—. Author: How To Use Psychological Leverage, 1978, Conversational Magic, 1978, Behavioral Supervision, 1980, Human Resource Development, 1986. Republican. Avocation: writing. Home: 350 E Deepdale Rd Phoenix AZ 85022-4229 Office: Allied Investment Inc 718 E Bethany Home Rd Phoenix AZ 85014-2104

DONATO, MARY EILEEN, risk management professional; b. San Francisco, July 15, 1943; d. Roy James and Arlynn Lucille (La Bundy) Martin; m. Paul Nicholas Donato, Mar. 18, 1961 (dec. Feb. 1968); children: Nicholas, Arlynn, Anthony, Eddie. BA, U. N.Mex., 1971, MPA, 1985. Cert. assoc. in risk mgmt., Ins. Inst. Classroom tchr. Albuquerque Pub. Schs., 1971-72; claims rep. Allstate Ins. Co., Albuquerque, 1972-76, TransAmerica Ins. Co., Albuquerque, 1978-80, City of Albuquerque, 1980-85; ins./claims mgr., dir. risk mgmt. Albuquerque Pub. Schs., 1985-94; dir. risk mgmt. U. N.Mex., Albuquerque, 1994—; presenter seminar Violence in the Work Place, 1993-94. Vol. tchr. Cmty. Sch., Albuquerque, 1980-82; parent aid All Faiths Receiving Home, Albuquerque, 1982-85; tutor Cath. Social Svcs., Albuquerque, 1996—; vol. office helper St. Charles Borromeo Ch., Albuquerque. Mem. AAUW, Univ. Risk Mgmt. Assn. (conf. chair), Pub. Risk Mgmt. Assn. (v.p. 1990-92), N.Mex. Pub. Risk Mgmt. Assn. (pres. 1996-97), N.Mex. Self Insurers Assn. (pres. 1992-93). Roman Catholic. Office: Univ NMex 137 Oñate Hall Albuquerque NM 87131-3182

DONE, ROBERT STACY, criminal investigation specialist, consultant; b. Tucson, Apr. 7, 1965; s. Richard Avon Done and Nancy Jane (Meeks) Burks; m. Michele Renae Barwick, May 17, 1987 (div. Mar. 1990); m. Elizabeth Evans Robinson, Feb. 20, 1993; children: Rachel Evans, Ethan James. AS in Law Enforcement, Mo. So. State Coll., 1987, BS in Criminal Justice Adminstrn., 1987; MPA, U. Ariz., 1992, MS in Mgmt., 1998. Criminal investigator Pima County, Tucson, 1988—; pres. Data Methods Corp., Tucson, 1984—. Contbr. articles to profl. jours. Mem. Am. Evaluation Assn., Acad. Mgmt. Home: PO Box 64967 Tucson AZ 85728-4967 Office: Pima County Pub Defender 2337 E Ajo Way Tucson AZ 85713-6215

DONELSON, KENNETH LAVERN, English language educator; b. Holdrege, Nebr., June 16, 1927; s. Lester Homer Irving and Minnie Irene (Lyons) D.; m. Virginia Juanita Watts (div. 1970); children: Sheryl Lynette George, Kurt Allen; m. Annette Whetton (div. 1983); m. Marie Elizabeth Smith, May 30, 1983; 1 stepchild, Jenny. BA, U. Iowa, 1950, MA, 1951, PhD, 1963. English tchr. Glidden (Iowa) High Sch., 1951-56, Thomas Jefferson High Sch., Cedar Rapids, Iowa, 1956-63; asst. prof. English Edn. Kans. State U., Manhattan, 1963-65; asst. prof. English Ariz. State U., Tempe, 1965-67, assoc. prof. English, 1967-71, prof. English, 1971—. Co-author: Literature for Today's Young Adults, 1980, 6th edit., 1999, Inspiring Literacy, 1993; author: The Student's Right to Read, 1972. With USN, 1945-46. Mem. Nat. Coun. Tchrs. English (chmn. conf. on English edn. 1974-76, Award for Outstanding Contbn. to the Field of Adolescent Lit. 1983, pres. adolescent lit. assembly 1980-81, co-editor English Jour. 1980-87). Democrat. Episcopalian. Avocations: reading, hiking, travel.

DONENFELD, ALICE R. GREENBAUM, producer, broadcast executive; b. N.Y.C., Oct. 25, 1938; d. Lawrence Samuel and Gladys Ann (Tompkins) Greenbaum; m. Irwin Donenfeld, Apr., 1963 (div. Sept. 1970); children: Mimi Rachel Donenfeld Foss, Harry Lawrence. LLB, N.Y. Law Sch., 1965; LLM, NYU, 1969. Bar: N.Y., 1965. Assoc. Greenbaum, Wolf & Ernst, N.Y.C., 1963-67, Colton, Fembach, Weissberg, N.Y.C., 1968-70; asst. legal counsel Time Inc., N.Y.C., 1970-71; assoc. Harris & Fredericks, N.Y.C., 1973-77; v.p. Marvel Comics Group, N.Y.C., 1977-82; exec. v.p. Filmation Studios, Woodland Hills, Calif., 1982-89; pres. Alice Entertainment, Inc., L.A., 1989—; distbr. TV programs to over 100 countries worldwide. Contbr. articles to Copyright Soc.; prodr. (tv series) Internat. Outdoorsman, 1989, (tv series) The Gamesman, 1989, (tv series) Bingo & Molly, 1997. Spkr. NOW, River Head, N.Y., 1971-72; dir. Coop. Extension, River Head, 1971-72. Mem. Am. Film Market Assn., Nat. Assn. TV Prodrs. and Execs. Office: Alice Entertainment Inc 1539 Sawtelle Blvd Los Angeles CA 90025-3267

DONER, JOHN ROLAND, hospital administrator; b. Ontario, Oreg., May 6, 1949; s. L. L. and Majorie R. (Robinson) D.; m. Kathleen M. Lang, Mar. 6, 1970; children: J. R., Erica C. BA in Bus. Adminstrn., Boise (Idaho) State U., 1971. Lic. nursing home adminstr., Idaho. Disability claims adjucator Idaho Disability Determinators Unit, Boise, 1972-74, quality assurance specialist, 1974-76, unit mgr., 1976-78; mgmt. and fin. cons. Idaho Dept. Health & Welfare, Boise, 1978-81; asst. adminstr. Idaho State Sch. & Hosp., Nampa, 1981-92, adminstrv. dir., 1993—. Sec., treas. bd. dirs. Idaho Spl. Olympics, Boise, 1985-92; vice chmn. Nampa Cmty. Work Release Ctr. Bd., 1987—; mem. adv. bd. Bogus Basin Recreation Assn. Inc., Boise, 1987—; mem., pres., bd. dirs. Archie B. Teater Fund for Hanidcapped, Inc., 1991—. Mem. Profl. Ski Instrs. Am. (cert.). Avocations: snow skiing, racquetball, golf. Home: 10341 Shiloh Dr Boise ID 83704-2736 Office: Idaho State Sch & Hosp 3100 11th Ave N Ext Nampa ID 83687-3199

DONG, ZHAOQIN, materials and testing engineer, researcher; b. Dingtao, China, Apr. 19, 1963; s. Guanghan Dong and Limei Tian Dong; m. Jie Gao, Jan. 9, 1987. BS, Jiangxi (China) Inst. Metall., 1982; MS, Inst. Aero. Materials, Beijing, 1985, Calif. Inst. Tech., 1992. Engr. Inst. Aero. Materials, 1985-90; grad. rschr. Calif. Inst. Tech., Pasadena, 1990-93, U. Calif., Irvine, 1993-95; adv. bds., cons. Beijing Union Soc. Materials Testing, 1984-97, Longxiang (China) Inst. Gen. Tech., 1995-97. Author: Selection and Use of Engineering Materials, 1990; contbr. articles to profl. jours., including Acta Aero. et Astronautical Sinica, Jour. Aerospace Power, Jour. Mech. Engring. Fellow Soc. Aeronautics and Astronautics (Beijing); mem. ASME, AIAA, ASTM. Achievements include criterion: the guide of strain energy time-dependent fatigue life prediction methods, strain energy-frequency separation model, aeronautical industry criterion HB/Z 217-92.

DONLEY, DENNIS LEE, school librarian; b. Port Hueneme, Calif., July 19, 1950; s. Mickey Holt and Joan Elizabeth (Smith) D.; m. Ruth Ann Shank, June 10, 1972; children: Eric Holt, Evan Scott. AA, Ventura Coll., 1970; BA with honors, U. Calif., Santa Barbara, 1973; MLS, San Jose State U., 1976. Cert. secondary tchr., Calif. Libr. media tchr. San Diego Unified Sch. Dist., 1975—; lectr. Calif. State U., L.A., 1987-89; libr. cons. San Diego C.C. Dist., 1990; chmn. sch. adv. com. Point Loma H.S., San Diego, 1986-87; coop. book rev. bd. San Diego County, 1984-86; creator adult sch. curriculum, 1984-86; contbr. Deadbase X, Deadbase 94, The Deadhead's Taping Compendium, Vols. 1-3. Mem. ALA, Calif. Libr. Media Educators Assn. Avocations: reading, music, fitness. Office: Hoover HS 4474 El Cajon Blvd San Diego CA 92115-4312

DONLON, TIMOTHY A., cytogeneticist; b. Pasadena, Calif., Apr. 16, 1952. PhD, U. Oreg., 1984. Med. genetics fellow Children's Hosp., Boston, 1984-86; chief molecular clin. cytogenetics Kapiolani Med. Ctr., Honolulu, 1992-98, dir., 1995; assoc. prof., rschr. Cancer Rsch. Ctr. of Hawaii, 1998—; dir., lab. molecular and cytogenetics Ohana Genetics, Honolulu, 1998—; assoc. prof. U. Hawaii Burns Sch. Medicine, Honolulu, 1992—. Office: Ohana Genetics Profl Plz of the Pacific 1520 Liliha St Ste 403 Honolulu HI 96817*

DONNALLY, PATRICIA BRODERICK, newspaper editor; b. Cheverly, Md., Mar. 11, 1955; d. James Duane and Olga Frances (Duenas) Broderick; m. Robert Andrew Donnally, Dec. 30, 1977; 1 child, Danielle Christine; BS, U. Md., 1977. Fashion editor The Washington Times (D.C.), 1983-85, The San Francisco Chronicle, 1985—. Recipient Atrium award, 1984, 87-89, 90, 94, 95, 96, 97, Lulu award, 1985, 87, award Am. Cancer Soc., 1991, Aldo award, 1994. Avocation: travel. Office: Chronicle Pub Co 901 Mission St San Francisco CA 94103-2905

DONNALLY, ROBERT ANDREW, lawyer, real estate broker; b. Washington, July 10, 1953; s. Reaumur Stearnes and Katherine Ann (Sutliff) D.; m. Patricia Kane Broderick, Dec. 30, 1977; 1 child, Danielle Christine. BA in Psychology, U. Md., 1976; JD, U. Balt., 1980; cert., Stanford Grad. Sch. Bus., Palo Alto, Calif., 1996. Bar: Md. 1980, Calif. 1986. Pvt. practice Oxen Hill, Md., 1980-81; rsch. contract staff officer Dept. Def., Ft. Meade, Md., 1981-85; with legal and contractual ops. ARGOSystems, Inc., Sunnyvale, Calif., 1985-90; asst. dir. Inst. Def. Analyses, San Diego, 1990-91; dep. chief counsel ARGOSystems, Inc., 1991-93, chief counsel, corp. sec., 1993-98; chief counsel comms. and infomanagement divsn. The Boeing Co., 1997-98; gen. counsel, mng. ptnr. BT Comml. Real Estate, Palo Alto, Calif., 1998—. Editor-in-chief The Forum, 1979-80. Active The Pillars Soc./United Way, 1991—. Waxter Legal scholar U. Baltimore, 1978. Mem. Am. Corp. Counsel, Nat. Contract Mgmt. Assn., Md. Bar Assn., Calif. Bar Assn., Assn. of Silicon Valley Brokers, Tae Kwon Do Assn. (Black Belt), Black Belt, Kukkiwon World Tae Kwon Do Assn. Avocations: martial arts, hiking, traveling, reading. Office: BT Comml Real Estate 2445 Faber Pl Ste 250 Palo Alto CA 94303-3316

DONNELLY, EDWARD JAMES, JR., medical services company executive; b. Windsor, Ont., Can., May 16, 1946; s. Edward James and Hilda Rae (Cornwall) D.; m. JoDell Tamborello, Dec. 20, 1972 (div. 1982); children: Edward James III, Anna Mistelle. BS, U. Houston, 1973. Pres. Perfusion Assocs., Houston, 1970-85; pres., chief exec. officer Allied Cardiac Svcs., Houston, 1985-95; dir. ops. Tex. SETA/Baxter, Houston, 1995-96, Baxter/New Bus. Initiatives, 1996-97, Baxter CVG Perfusion Svcs., San Diego, 1997—; bd. dirs. Taylor Made Homes. Contbr. articles to profl. publs. Mem. Am. Soc. Extracorporeal Technologists (pres. so. region 1978-80, 84-86), Houston Bd. Realtors, Houston Jaycees. Republican. Episcopalian. Home: 2331 Dorrington St Houston TX 77030-3211 Office: Baxter CVG Perfusion Svcs 16818 Via Del Campo Ct San Diego CA 92127-1714

DONNELLY, RUSSELL JAMES, physicist, educator; b. Hamilton, Ont., Can., Apr. 16, 1930; s. Clifford Ernest and Bessie (Harrison) D.; m. Marian Card, Jan. 21, 1956; 1 son, James. BSc, McMaster U., 1951, MSc, 1952; MS, Yale U., 1953, PhD, 1956. Faculty U. Chgo., 1956-66, prof. physics, 1965-66; prof. physics U. Oreg., Eugene, 1966—; chmn. dept. U. Oreg., 1966-72, 82-83; vis. prof. Niels Bohr Inst., Copenhagen, Denmark, 1972; cofounder Pine Mountain Obs., 1967; cons. GM Co. Rsch. Labs., 1958-68, NSF, 1968-76, 79-84, mem. adv. panel for physics, 1970-73, chmn., 1971-72; mem. adv. coms. on matls. rsch., 1979-84; mem. Task Force on Fundamental Physics and Chemistry in Space, Space Sci. Bd., NRC; cons. Jet Propulsion Lab., Calif. Inst. Tech., Pasadena, 1973-82; chmn. Sci. Adv. Com. for Low Temp. Facilities in Space, 1990-91; mem. fluid dynamics discipline working group, NASA, 1992-95; gen. chmn. 20th Internat. Conf. on Low Temp. Physics, 1993. Author: (with Parks, Glaberson) Experimental Superfluidity, 1967, (with Francis) Cryogenic Science and Technology: Contributions of Leo Dana, 1985, Quantized Vortices in Helium II, 1991; editor: (with Herman, Prigogine) Non-Equilibrium Thermodynamics Variational Techniques and Stability, 1966, High Reynolds Number Flows Using Liquid

and Gaseous Helium, 1991, Procs. 20th Internat. Conf. Low Temperature Physics, Physica B, 1994; editor: (with Sreenivasan) Flowat Ultra-High Reynolds and Rayleigh Numbers; mem. editorial bd. Physics of Fluids, 1966-68, Phys. Rev. E, 1978-84, assoc. editor, 1987-93; mem. editorial bd. Jour. Phys. and Chem. Ref. Data, 1989-92, Handbook of Chemistry and Physics, 1989-98; contbr. articles to profl. jours. Bd. dirs. U. Oreg. Found., 1970-72, 88-91, investment com., 1990-91; bd. dirs. Oreg. Mus. Park Commn., 1975-87, chmn., 1975-82; bd. dirs. Oreg. Bach Festival, 1975-87, Oreg. Mozart Players, 1990-93. Alfred P. Sloan fellow, 1959-63; sr. vis. fellow Sci. Rsch. Coun., U.K., 1978; recipient Disting. Alumnus award McMaster U., 1992, Lars Onsager medal Norwegian U. Sci. and Tech., 1996; 1995 Chia-Shun Yih lectr. U. Mich., 1996 Fritz London Meml. lectr. Duke U, Howard Vollum award Reed Coll., 1997. Fellow AAAS, Am. Phys. Soc. (exec. com. div. fluid dynamics 1966-72, 80-84, 88-91, sec.-treas. 1967-70, 88-91, chmn. 1971-72, 82-83, APS Otto Laporte award 1974), Inst. of Physics (London); mem. Nat. Trust for Scotland, Soc. Archtl. Historians, Cosmos Club. Episcopalian. Research on physics fluids, especially hydrodynamic stability turbulence and superfluidity. Home: 2175 Olive St Eugene OR 97405-2837 Office: Univ Oreg Dept Physics Eugene OR 97403-1274

DONNELLY, TRACY ANN, biological researcher; b. Denver, Nov. 24, 1962; d. John Roland and Corrine Pauline (Wamser) D. BS in Biology, U. Calif., Riverside, 1986. Rsch. tech. Scripps Rsch. Int., La Jolla, Calif., 1987-89; rsch. asst. Immunetech Pharm., San Diego, 1989-90; applications coord. Advanced Tissue Scis., La Jolla, 1990-96; with Quidel Corp., San Diego, 1996—. Contbr. articles to profl. jours. and chpts. to books. Mem. AAAS, People to People Internat., Soc. of Toxicology. Democrat. Achievements include research in alternatives to animal testing. Avocations: music, reading, craftwork, drawing, writing poetry. Home: 515 Lands End Way Unit 179 Oceanside CA 92054-7261 Office: Quidel Corp 10165 Mckellar Ct San Diego CA 92121-4299

DONNICI, PETER JOSEPH, lawyer, law educator, consultant; b. Kansas City, Mo., Sept. 5, 1939; s. Albert H. and Jennie (Danubio) D.; m. Diane DuPlantier, July 27, 1985; children—JuliaAnn Donnici Clifford, Joseph A., Joann Donnici Powers. B.A., U. Mo.-Kansas City, 1959, J.D., 1962; LL.M., Yale U., 1963. Bar: Mo. 1963, U.S. Supreme Ct. 1966, Calif. 1969. Asst. prof. law U. San Francisco, 1963-65, assoc. prof., 1965-68, prof., 1968-91, prof. emeritus, 1992—; assoc. Law Offices Joseph L. Alioto, San Francisco, 1967-72; sole practice, San Francisco, 1974—; ptnr. Donnici & LuPo, San Francisco, 1982-92, Donnici, Kerwin, Phillips & Donnici, San Francisco, 1993—; asst. prosecutor Jackson County Prosecutor's Office, Mo., 1963; cons. to Office of Mayor of San Francisco, 1968-72; No. Calif. bd. dirs. Coun. on Legal Ednl. Opportunity, San Francisco, 1969-70; conciliator for housing discrimination cases HUD, San Francisco, 1976; cons. Calif. Consumer Affairs' Task Force on Electronic Funds Transfer, Sacramento, 1978-79; bd. dirs. Air Micronesia, Inc., DHL Internat., Ltd, Bermuda, Continental Micronesia; spl. counsel and del. to internat. confs. Commonwealth of No. Mariana Islands, 1983-84; faculty adviser U. San Francisco Law Rev., 1966-91; bd. counselors U. San Francisco, 1993—. Editor in chief U. Mo.-Kansas City Law Rev., 1961-62; contbr. articles to profl. jours., 1964—. Lawyers' Com. for Urban Affairs, San Francisco, 1965-68. Wilson scholar U. Mo.-Kansas City, 1956-62; Sterling fellow Law Sch., Yale U., 1962-63. Mem. Bench and Robe, Phi Delta Phi. Democrat. Roman Catholic. Home: 190 Cresta Vista Dr San Francisco CA 94127-1635 Office: One Post St Ste 2450 San Francisco CA 94104

D'ONOFRIO, ANTHONY, chef; b. Ann Arbor, Mich., Mar. 27, 1962; s. Dominic and Mary Ann (Clifford) D'O.; Karen Roberts, Apr. 19, 1987; 1 child, Dominique Ariana. AOS, Culinary Inst. Am., Hyde Park, N.Y., 1982. Line cook Chinois on Main, Santa Monica, Calif., 1987-88, chef de cuisine, sous chef Vincent Guerithault on Camelback, Phoenix, 1988-89; pastry chef, sous chef Citrus Restaurant, L.A., 1989-92; chef de cuisine Zenzero Restaurant, Santa Monica, 1992-95; ex-chef One Market Restaurant, San Francisco, 1995-96, Tutto Mare Restaurant, Tiburon, Calif., 1996—. Home: 4540 45th Ave NE Seattle WA 98105-3910

D'ONOFRIO, MARY ANN, medical transcription company executive; b. Detroit, Jan. 24, 1933; d. Charles Henry and Cecilia Rose (Levan) Clifford; m. Dominic Armando D'Onofrio, Apr. 19, 1958; children: Margaret Clement, Anthony, Elizabeth, Maria Spurgeon. BA, Marygrove Coll., 1954; MLS, U. Mich., 1955. Cert. med. transcriptionist. Reader's advisor Detroit Pub. Libr., 1955-58; cataloger Willow Run (Mich.) Pub. Libr., 1959-61, St. Thomas Grade and High Sch., Ann Arbor, Mich., 1968-72; med. record analyst Chelsea (Mich.) Community Hosp., 1972-79; pres. Meditranscript Svc., Ann Arbor, 1979-81; asst. office mgr. Dr. Maxfield, D.O., Tucson, 1981-82; quality assurance analyst, utilization rev. Tucson (Ariz.) Gen. Hosp., 1983-86; exec. asst. Dr. McEldoon M.D., Tucson, 1986-88; pres. Meditranscript Svc., Tucson, 1986-88; co-owner Med-Comm Assocs., Tucson, 1989—; co-owner, assoc. designer EMA of Tucson custom apparel and jewelry design co. Co-author: Psychiatric Words & Phrases, 1990, 2d edit., 1998; contbr. articles to profl. jours; co-developer Cross-Search. Block leader Infantile Paralysis Assn., Ann Arbor, 1975-80, Easter Seal Assn., Tucson, 1983-86, Am. Heart Assn., 1994, Am. Cancer Soc., 1992, 96, Leukemia Soc. of Am., 1997, 98. Mem. Am. Assn. for Med. Transcription (parliamentarian Sonora Desert chpt. 1984-86, 90-93, 95, bylaws com. 1996-97, compiler/editor AAMI Annotated Bibliography 1981, Named Disting. Mem. 1984, treas. Sonora Desert chpt. 1987, 98, 99, jour. columnist 1982-86, by-laws com. 1995-97, policies & procedures panelist 1997-98), Ednl. Honor Soc., Pi Lambda Theta (life). Avocations: desert gardening, sunset/landscape photography, reading.

DONOGHUE, JOHN CHARLES, software management consultant; b. Oswego, N.Y., Sept. 19, 1950; s. James Charles and Marion Louise (Farrell) D.; m. Ann Marie Perry, Dec. 20, 1969; children: John Charles II, Kelly Anne. BS in Electronic Tech., Chapman Coll., 1981; student, U. Calif., Irvine, 1981-82; MA, U. Redlands, 1987; postgrad., Western State U. Coll., 1988-89, Azusa Pacific U., 1991-93. Enlisted USAF, 1969, advanced through grades to staff sgt., 1977, resigned, 1979; mgr. Lockheed Aircraft, Ontario, Calif., 1979-85; project engr. Northrop Corp., Pico Rivera, Calif., 1985—; cons., Fontana, Calif., 1981—; mem. software coun. Northrop Corp., Hawthorne, Calif., 1987-97, software improvement network U. Calif., Irvine, 1988—, capability maturity model corr. group Software Engring. Inst., Pitts., 1993—, L.A. software improvement network U. So. Calif., 1994—; charter mem. Software Inspection and Rev. Orgn., Sunnyvale, Calif., 1981—. Vol. cons. S.W. Anthropol. Assn. Calif. State U., L.A., 1996-97, Resource Conservation Dist., Rancho Cucamonga, Calif., 1996—, Southwest Mus., L.A., 1997—. Mem. IEEE, Northrop Gruman Mgmt. Club, N.Y. Acad. Scis., Nat. Space Soc. Avocations: motorcycling, snorkeling. Office: Northrop Gruman Corp Mil Aircraft Sys Divsn 8900 Washington Blvd Pico Rivera CA 90660-3765

DONOGHUE, MILDRED RANSDORF, education educator; b. Cleve.; d. James and Caroline (Sychra) Ransdorf; m. Charles K. Donoghue (dec. 1982); children: Kathleen, James. Ed.D., UCLA, 1962; J.D., Western State U., 1979. Asst. prof. edn. Calif. State U.-Fullerton, 1962-66, assoc. prof., 1966-71; prof. Calif. State U., Fullerton, 1971—. Author: Foreign Languages and the Schools, 1967, Foreign Languages and the Elementary School Child, 1968, The Child and the English Language Arts, 1971, 75, 79, 85, 90; co-author: Second Languages in Primary Education, 1979; contbr. articles to profl. jours. and Ednl. Resources Info. Ctr. U.S. Dept. Edn. Mem. AAUP, AAUW, TESOL, Nat. Network for Early Lang. Learning, Nat. Coun. Tchrs. English, Am. Dialect Soc., Am. Ednl. Rsch. Assn., Nat. Soc. for Study of Edn., Am. Assn. Tchrs. Spanish and Portuguese, Internat. Reading Assn., Nat. Assn. Edn. Young Children, Orange County Med. Assn. Women's Aux., Authors Guild, Assn. for Childhood Edn. Internat., Phi Beta Kappa, Phi Kappa Phi, Pi Lambda Theta, Alpha Upsilon Alpha. Address: Prof of Education 800 State College Blvd Fullerton CA 92834

DONOHOE, JOSEPH A., V, rancher, real estate investor; b. San Francisco, Feb. 14, 1941; s. Joseph A. and Yvonne (Dibblee) D. BS in Chem., U. Calif., Berkeley, 1967, BA in Genetics, 1970. Mng. gen. ptnr. Lion Oaks Ranch, Gilroy, Calif., 1987—; pres. Donohoe Investment Co., San Francisco, 1987—; bd. dir. Parrott Investment Co.; gen. ptnr. Cunningham Investment Co., San Francisco, 1994—. Bd. dir., officer Los Californianos, San Francisco, 1967-71. Mem. Soc. Calif. Pioneers (bd. dirs., v.p. 1980—), Donohoe Clan Soc. (pres. 1991—, hereditary chief 1998—), Pacific-Union Club, Am. Assn. Sci. Republican. Roman Catholic. Avocations: genealogy, history, physical fitness, travel. Home: 2160 Leavenworth St San Francisco CA 94133-2590 Office: Lion Oaks Ranch PO Box 1085 Gilroy CA 95021-1085

DONOHUGH, DONALD LEE, physician; b. Los Angeles, Apr. 12, 1924; s. William Noble and Florence Virginia (Shelton) D.; m. Virginia Eskew McGregor, Sept. 12, 1950 (div. 1971); children: Ruth, Laurel, Marilee, Carol, Greg; m. Beatrice Ivany Redick, Dec. 3, 1976; stepchildren: Leslie Ann, Andrea Jean. BS, U.S. Naval Acad., 1946; MD, U. Calif., San Francisco, 1956; MPH and Tropical Medicine, Tulane U., 1961. Diplomate AM. Bd. Internal Medicine. Intern U. Hosp., San Diego, 1956-57; resident Monterey County Hosp., 1957-58; dir. of med. svcs. U.S. Depart. Interior, Am. Samoa, 1958-60; instr. Tulane U. Med. Sch., New Orleans, 1960-63; resident Tulane Svcs. V.A. and Charity Hosp., New Orleans, 1961-63; cons. Internat. Ctr. for Rsch and Tng., Costa Rica, 1961-63; asst. prof. medicine & preventive medicine La. State U. Sch. Medicine, 1962-63; assoc. prof., 1963-65; vis. prof. U. Costa Rica, 1963-65; faculty advisor, head of Agy. Internat. Devel. program U. Costa Rica Med. Sch., 1965-67; dir. med. svcs. Med. Ctr. U. Calif. (formerly Orange County Hosp.), Irvine, 1967-69; assoc. clin. prof. U. Calif., Irvine, 1967-79, clin. prof., 1980-85; pvt. practice Tustin, Calif., 1970-80; with Joint Commn. on Accreditation of Hosps., 1981; cons. Kauai, Hawaii, 1981—. Author: The Middle Years, 1981, Practice Management, 1986, Kauai, 1988, 4th edit., 1992, Our Ancestors, 1995, The Story of Koloa, 1999; co-translator; Rashomon (Ryonosuke Akutagawa), 1950; also numerous articles. Lt. USN, 1946-52, capt. USNR, 1966-84. Fellow Am. Coll. Physicians (life); mem. Delta Omega. Republican. Episcopalian. Home: 4890 Lawai Beach Rd Koloa HI 96756-9675

DONOVAN, THOMAS JOHN, humanities educator; b. Vancouver, Wash., Dec. 14, 1917; s. Joseph J. and Louise (Padden) D.; m. Helen F. Murphy, Dec. 29, 1953; children: Joseph, Teresa, Marcella, Elizabeth. AB, St. Edward's Coll., Seattle, 1939; MA, U. So. Calif., L.A., 1948; cert., Am. Acad. Rome, 1963. Cert. life profl. tchr., Wash. Tchr. Providence Acad., Vancouver, Wash., 1957-61, Hudson's Bay H.S., Vancouver, 1962-83, Vancouver Sch. Dist., 1983-91, U. Portland, Oreg., 1991—; cons. nat. humanities faculty, Eugene, Oreg., 1978. Sgt. M.C. U.S. Army, 1941-45, ETO. Recipient fellowship U. Chgo., 1950-52. Mem. AAUP, Classical Assn. Pacific Northwest, Classical Soc. of Am. Acad. Rome, Pi Epsilon Theta. Home: PO Box 61567 Vancouver WA 98666-1567 Office: U Portland 5000 N Willamette Blvd Portland OR 97203-5743

DONOVAN, WILLARD PATRICK, retired elementary education educator; b. Grand Rapids, Mich., Sept. 1, 1930; s. Willard Andrew and Thelma Alfreda (Davis) D.; m. Dorothy Jane Nester, Nov. 27, 1954 (dec. May 1981); children: Cindy Jane, Kimberly Sue. BS, Ea. Mich. U., 1965, MA, 1969. Cert. grades K-8, Mich. Enlisted U.S. Army, 1947, advanced through grades to master sgt., 1953; platoon sgt. U.S. Army of Occupation, Korea, 1947-48, Japan, 1948-50; platoon sgt. U.S. Army Korean War Svc., 1950-51; ret. U.S. Army, 1964; pharm. sales Nat. Drug Co., Detroit, 1964-66; tchr. Cromie Elem. Sch. Warren (Mich.) Consol. Schs., 1966—, ret., 1995; reading textbook and curriculum devel. com. Warren (Mich.) Consol. Schs., 1969-73, sci. com., 1970-95; curriculum and textbook com. Macomb County Christian Schs., Warren, 1982-95. Decorated Combat Infantry badge U.S. Army, Korea, 1950, Purple heart with three clusters U.S. Army, Korea, 1950-51, Korea-Japan Svc. medal, 1951, Presdl. citation, 1951, Korean medal with three campaign clusters, 1951, Nat. Def. Svc. medal, 1951, Bronze star, Silver star; named Chosen few Army and Marines 31st Infantry Assn. Mem. NRA, Am. Quarterhouse Assn., Assn. U.S. Army, Detroit Area Coun. Tchrs. Math., Met. Detroit Sci. Tchrs. Assn., The Chosin Few, Nat. Edn. Assn., Mich. Edn. Assn., Warren (Mich.) Edn. Assn. Avocations: theatre, arts, horsemanship, traveling, pistol shooting. Home: PO Box 563 8440 Mission Hills Arizona City AZ 85223

DONZE, JERRY LYNN, electrical engineer; b. Wauneta, Nebr., June 12, 1943; s. John Henry and Virgina May (Francis) D.; m. Marilyn Grace Bascue, Feb. 22, 1964 (div. May. 1980); children: Scott. L., Michele A.; m. Sandra Kay Morris, July 25, 1981. Cert. technician, Denver Inst. Tech., 1964; BSEE, U. Colo., 1972; postgrad., Advanced Metaphysics Inst. Religios Sci., 1986. Electronic technician A.B.M. Co., Lakewood, Colo., 1964-71; computer programmer Nat. Bur. Standards, Boulder, Colo., 1971-72; electronic engr. Autometrics Co., Boulder, Colo., 1972-76, Gates Research and Devel., Denver, 1976-77; devel. engr. Emerson Electric Co., Lakewood, 1977; engring. mgr. Storage Tech., Louisville, Colo., 1977—; cons. Sun Co., Arvada, Colo., 1974-75. Patentee in field. Mem. IEEE Student Soc. (treas. 1971-72), Eta Kappa Nu. Republican. Religious Scientist. Avocation: giving workshops and presentations. Home: 12021 W 54th Ave Arvada CO 80002-1907 Office: Storage Tech 2270 S 88th St Louisville CO 80028-0001

DOOLEY, CALVIN MILLARD, congressman; b. Visalia, Calif., Jan. 11, 1954. BS, U. Calif., Davis, 1977; MA, Stanford U., 1987. Mem. 102nd-105th Congresses (now 106th Congress) from Calif. Dist. 17 (now 20th), 1991—; mem. agriculture com., mem. natural resources com. Democrat. Methodist. Office: Ho of Reps 1201 Longworth Bldg Washington DC 20515-0520*

DOOLEY, JEFFREY EARLE, management consultant, educator; b. L.A., Apr. 6, 1946; s. George Elijah and Helen (Fitch) D.; m. Lynn Armitage Sullivan, May 14, 1982; children: Johanna Kathleen, Alison Rose. BA in Philosophy, U. Hawaii, 1971; MS in Cybernetics, San Jose (Calif.) State U., 1991. Dir. pub. info. Mental Health Assn. Santa Clara (Calif.) County, 1973-76; photo journalist Berkeley, Calif., 1971-85; sr. cons. J. Earle Assocs., Mill Valley, Calif., 1985-91, Adaptive Learning Design, Petaluma, Calif., 1991—; instr. U. Calif., Santa Cruz, 1993—; sys. seminar leader Harvard Grad. Sch. Edn., Cambridge, Mass., 1994; guest sys. lectr. Oklahoma State U., Oklahoma City, 1995; seminar co-developer Kellogg Nat. Found., San Francisco, 1995. Contbr. articles to profl. jours. Del. Hawaii UN Conf. Environment, Ont., Can., 1971. Recipient Excellence in Pub. Edn. award Calif. Assn. Mental Health, Sacramento, 1976. Mem. Soc. Orgnl. Learning (assoc.). Avocations: cycling, aikido, t'ai chi, kenpo karate, surfing. Office: Adaptive Learning Design Petaluma CA 94952

DOOLEY, MARK WAYNE, computer technologist; b. Eugene, Oreg., Oct. 24, 1960; s. Dewey Wayne and Geraldine (Edmiston) D.; m. Christine Jeanine Gadker Knoblaugh, Aug. 9, 1997; stepchild, Monica. Computer operator Dialog Info. Svcs., Palo Alto, Calif., 1984-87; computer programmer Knight-Ridder Info., Palo Alto, Calif., 1987-92; tech. lead The Dialog Corp., Mountain View, Calif., 1992—. Recipient Designer Client Svc. Product of the Yr. Infoworld Mag., 1996. Mem. IEEE, Assn. Computing Machinery. Avocation: calligraphy.

DOOLITTLE, JOHN TAYLOR, congressman; b. Glendale, Calif., Oct. 30, 1950; s. Merrill T. and Dorothy Doolittle; B.A. in History with honors, U. Calif., Santa Cruz, 1972; J.D., McGeorge Sch. Law, U. Pacific, 1978; m. Julia Harlow, Feb. 17, 1979; children: John Taylor Jr., Courtney A. Bar: Calif. 1978. Mem. Calif. State Senate, 1980-90; mem. 102nd-105th Congresses (now 106th Congress) from Calif. 4th dist., 1991—; mem. agriculture com., mem. resource com., chair water and power resources subcom. Republican. Mem. LDS Ch. Office: Ho of Reps 1526 Longworth Bldg Washington DC 20515-0504*

DOONIN, STEVEN E., university provost, officer. V.p., provost Calif. Inst. of Tech., Pasadena. Office: Calif Inst of Tech Pasadena CA 91125*

DOPP, SUSAN MARIE, artist, educator; b. Ft. Hood, Tex., May 30, 1951; d. Roy Milton Dopp and Greta Lenore (Mortensen) Wilkerson. BFA, San Francisco Art Inst., 1984, MFA, 1987. Painting instr. Acad. Art, San Francisco, 1989, Richmond (Calif.) Art Ctr., 1992-93, Oreg. Sch. Arts and Crafts, Portland, 1993, Calif. Coll. Arts & Crafts, Oakland, 1996; artist-in-residency Roswell Mus. & Art Ctr., 1988-89. One-woman shows include San Francisco Mus. Modern Art, 1988. Fleishhacker Found. Eureka fellow, 1993. Avocations: gardening, cooking, reading.

DORAN, VINCENT JAMES, steel fabricating company consultant; b. Ephrata, Wash., June 13, 1917; s. Samuel Vincent and Sarah Anastasia (Fitzpatrick) D.; B. Phil., Gonzaga U., Spokane, 1946; m. Jean Arlene Birrer, Jan. 15, 1949 (dec. Sept. 1997); children: Vincent James, Mollie Jean, Michele Lee, Patrick Michael. Mgr., Flying Service, Coulee Dam, Wash., 1947-48; mgr. constrn. Morrison-Knudsen Co., Wash. and Alaska, 1953-60; co-owner C.R. Foss Inc., constrn., Anchorage, 1961-64; mgr. Steel Fabricators, Anchorage, 1965-86. Inventor method of reducing and dewatering sewage sludge. Active Boy Scouts Am.; co-founder, pres. Chugach Rehab. Assn., 1962; mem. Alaska Gov.'s Rehab. Adv. Bd., 1962-63; mem. CAP. Served with USAAF, 1943-45, USAF, 1949-50. Decorated Air medal with 4 clusters. Mem. Welding Inst. Alaska (co-organizer, dir. 1977-78), 34th Bomb Group Assn. Roman Catholic. Club: Toastmasters. Compiler, pub. home owners' and builders' guide to sun's positions in N.Am. during solstices and equinoxes, designer packaged water, sewage treatment plants and water collection systems Arctic communities. Home: 3811 Knik Ave Anchorage AK 99517-1061 Office: 3243 Commercial Dr Anchorage AK 99501-3020

DORHOUT, MARLENE SUE, English language educator; b. Everett, Wash., Feb. 5, 1944; d. Roy and Jeanette Jacoba (Adema) VanLeeuwen; m. Marlin John Dorhout, June 17, 1967; 1 child, Bret Roy. BA, Dordt Coll., 1965; MA, Regis U., 1997. Cert. tchr. Colo. English tchr. Lake Worth (Fla.) Christian Sch., 1965-67, Watson Groen Christian Sch., Seattle, 1967-68, Denver Christian Schs., 1970-98; liaison tchr. Denver Pub. Schs., 1996-97; ednl. conf. Dordt Coll., Sioux Ctr., Iowa, 1991; conf. spkr. Christian Educators Assn., Grand Rapids, Mich., 1992; conf. presenter Nat. Middle Sch. Assn., Denver, 1998; chair fine arts com., chair English com., cmty. svc. com. chair Denver Christian Schs., 1994—. Query editor Christian Educator's Jour., 1990-98. Vol. Denver Pub. Schs., 1996-97, Denver Diaconal Conf., 1996-97, Sun Valley Cmty. Ch., Denver, 1970-98; deacon Hillcrest Christian Reformed Ch., 1997-98. Mem. Nat. Coun. of Tchrs. of English, Nat. Middle Sch. Assn. Avocations: antique collecting, traveling, reading, enjoying music, architecture. Office: Denver Christian Schs 2135 S Pearl St Denver CO 80210

DORIA, ROBIN GALIAN, financial consultant; b. L.I., N.Y., Oct. 29, 1946; s. Oswald and Helen E. (Moss) D.; m. Deborah A. Martin, June 19, 1970; children: Stacey L., Kable M., Kasy R. BS in Bus. Econs., Okla. State U., 1970; MA in Internat. Rels., Troy (Ala.) State U., 1980. Commd. 2nd lt. USAF, 1970, advanced through grades to lt. col., 1991; pilot front line fighter aircraft, F-4s and F-15s Tactical Air Command, USAF, U.S. and Germany, 1975-89; chief safety 17,000 person indsl. complex McClellan AFB, Sacramento, Calif., 1989-91; fin. cons. Merrill Lynch, Sacramento, 1991—, coord., mgr. profl. devel. program, 1995—; charter pres. LeTip of Roseville-Granite Bay, 1991-93, bd. dirs., 1991—. Decorated DFC with 4 oak leaf clusters, meritorious svc. medal with 3 oak leaf clusters. Mem. Woodcreek Oaks Golf Course, Granite Bay Tennis Club. Republican. Office: Merrill Lynch 1435 River Park Dr Ste 100 Sacramento CA 95815-4597

DORLAND, BYRL BROWN, retired civic worker; b. Greenwich, Utah, Apr. 25, 1915; d. David Alma and Ethel Myrle (Peterson) Brown; m. Jack Albert Dorland, June 11, 1944; children: Lynn Dorland Ballinger, Lee Allison. Cert. AA, Snow Jr. Coll., Ephraim, Utah, 1936; teaching cert. Brigham Young U., 1937; BS, Utah State Coll., Logan, 1940; grad.Family Inst. Vassar Coll., Poughkeepsie, N.Y., 1978; John Robert Powers Sch. Profl. Women, N.Y.C., 1980. Sch. tchr., Utah, 1937-39, 40-42; restored Washington Irving's graveplot in Sleepy Hollow (N.Y.) Cemetery (named Nat. Hist. Landmark 1972); nat. dir. Washington Irving Graveplot Restoration Program, 1968—, designer landmark plaque for grave; mem. Nat. Coun. State Garden Clubs,1959—; pres. Potpourri Garden Club, Westchester, N.Y., 1966—; nat. chmn. for graveplot programs Washington Irving Bicentennial, 1983-84; dir. Dorland Family Graveyard Restoration, N.J. Hist. Landmark, 1983—. Recipient Disting. Alumni award for Community Svc. Snow Coll., 1989; Recipient May Duff Walters trophy Nat. Coun. State Garden Clubs, 1974; nat. trophy Nat. Historic Landmark Com., 1974; citation Keep Am. Beautiful, 1974. Mem. Nat. Trust for Historic Preservation (assoc., Pres.'s award 1977), Nat. Historic Soc. Am., Gen. Soc. Mayflower Desc., Am. Mus. Natural History (hon.), Internat. Washington Irving Soc. (founder, pres. 1981—), Nat. Assn. for Gravestone Studies (hon.), Herb Soc. Am., DAR, Internat. Platform Assn., Old Dutch Churchyard Restoration Assn., Am. Mus. Natural History (hon. mem.). Home: 20802 N Cave Creek Rd Apt 60 Phoenix AZ 85024-4438

DORLAND, FRANK NORTON, art conservator, educator; b. Peru, Nebr., Oct. 11, 1914; s. Frank Norton and Marion Hope (Abbot) D.; m. Mabel Vyvyan Jolliffe, July 29, 1938 (dec. Mar. 1991); m. Vandria Rayner, Apr. 7, 1995. Student Calif. Christian Coll., 1931-33; San Diego State Coll., 1933-38. Artist preliminary design engring. Convair Co., San Diego, Calif., 1938-49; pvt. practice as art conservator, La Jolla, Calif., 1949-59, San Francisco, 1959-63, Mill Valley, Calif., 1963-73, Santa Barbara, Calif., 1973-85; head art dept. The Quaderia Inst., San Luis Obispo, Calif., 1994—; formerly engaged in authentication and classification art objects; cons. art assns. galleries, mus., collectors, chs. Author: Holy Ice: The Story of Electronic Quartz Crystal, 1992; authenticated original Our Lady of Kazan (The Black Virgin of Kazan) Russian Icon, 1963. Mem. Internat. Inst. for Conservation, Internat. Coun. Museums, Am. Mus. Assn. Pioneer in use of spl. waxes in painting; inventor oil and water mix wax mediums, first scientifically compounded fine arts wax; engaged in research and devel. waxes and resins and properties and usage of electronic quartz crystals, also pioneer biocrystallographer, researcher on crystals, the human mind and the evolution of human consciousness. Home: PO Box 6233 Los Osos CA 93412-6233

DORMAN, DANIEL, psychiatrist; b. Indpls., Aug. 13, 1936. BA, Ind. U., 1958, MD, 1961. Intern D.C. Gen. Hosp./Georgetown U., Washington, 1961-62; fellow in neurophysiology Albert Einstein Coll. Medicine, N.Y.C., 1961-63; pvt. practice gen. medicine Huntington Beach, Calif., 1963-69; resident in psychiatry UCLA, 1969-72; pvt. practice psychiatry Beverly Hills, Calif., 1972—. Capt. USAR. Office: 450 N Bedford Dr Ste 306 Beverly Hills CA 90210-4307

DORN, MARIAN MARGARET, educator, sports management administrator; b. North Chicago, Ill., Sept. 25, 1931; d. John and Marian (Petkovsek) Jelovsek; m. Eugene G. Dorn, Aug. 2, 1952 (div. 1975); 1 child, Bradford Jay. BS, U. Ill., 1953; MS, U. So. Calif., 1961. Tchr., North Chicago Cmty. H.S., 1954-56; tchr., advisor activities, high sch., Pico-Rivera, Calif., 1956-62; tchr., coach Calif. H.S., Whittier, 1962-65; prof. phys. edn., chmn. dept., coach, asst. chmn. div. women's athletic dir. Cypress (Calif.) Coll., 1966—; men's, women's golf coach; mgr. Billie Jean King Tennis Ctr., Long Beach, Calif., 1982-86; founder King-Dorn Golf Schs., Long Beach, 1984; pres. So. Calif. Athletic Conf., 1981; curriculum cons. Calif. Dept. Edn., 1989-92; spkr. Citizen Amb. Program China Conf. women, 1995; coach golf team state champions Women's Cypress Coll., 1997. Mem. del. to China Citizens Ambassador Program, 1995. Recipient cert. of merit Cypress Elem. Sch. Dist., 1976; Outstanding Svc. award Cypress Coll., 1986; named Women's Coach of Yr. Orgn. Empire Conf., 1995, Master Profl., 1996, Coll. Women's Golf Coach of Yr., Calif. Coaches Assn., 1998, L.P.G.A. Western Sect. Coach of Yr., 1998; nominated Coach of Yr., L.P.G.A. Western Sect., 1991-96. Mem. Calif. (v.p. So. dist.), San Gabriel Valley (pres.) Assns. Health, Phys. Edn. and Recreation, So. Calif. C.C. Athletic Coun. (sec., dir. pub. rels.), NEA, Calif. Tchrs. Assn., AAHPERD, Ladies Profl. Golf Assn. Conglist. Author: Bowling Manual, 1974. Office: 9200 Valley View St Cypress CA 90630-5805

DORN, NATALIE REID, consultant; b. N.Y.C.; d. John A. and Marianna (Tresenberg) Borokhovich; m. Ed Reid, July 31, 1938 (div. Apr. 1963); children: Michael John, Douglas Paul; m. Robert M. Dorn, Nov. 28, 1964. Student, Bklyn. Coll., 1937-40, Pepperdine Coll., 1969-70. Model Conover Agy., N.Y.C., 1940-54; columnist Westchester (N.Y.) Recorder, 1954-59; ptnr. Dateline, Las Vegas, Nev., 1957-61; mgr., buyer Joseph Magnin, Las Vegas, Nev., 1961-62; ptnr., cons. Personnel Placement Employment Agy. and Conv. Coords., Las Vegas, 1961-63; account exec. John A. Tetley Co., L.A., 1963-65; cons. Sport Ct. Am., Salt Lake City, 1975—; realtor, Va., Calif., 1974--. Exec. v.p. Clark County Mental Health Assn., 1961-63; ednl. chmn. Hollywood Wing, Greek Theatre Assn., 1965, mem. hospitality com. LWV, 1969; co-founder Child Abuse Listening Line, 1973—; sponsor Ashland (Oreg.) Shakespearean Festival, 1984; concertmaster Sacramento Opera;

patron, Davis Art Ctr.; docent Internat. House, Davis, 1987—; bd. dirs. El Macero Niners, Davis Art Ctr. Guild. Mem. AMA Aux., Los Angeles County Med. Assn. Aux. (chmn. publs. dist. 5, 1970-72, program chmn. 1972), Nat. Trust for Historic Preservation, Nat. Mus., Women in Arts, Crocker Art Mus., Crocker Art Mus. Assocs. Corps, Crocker Soc., El Macero Country Club. Avocations: golf, painting, writing.

DORNAN, ROBERT KENNETH, former congressman; b. N.Y.C., Apr. 3, 1933; s. Harry Joseph and Gertrude Consuelo (McFadden) D.; m. Sallie Hansen, Apr. 16, 1955; children: Robin Marie, Robert Kenneth II, Theresa Ann, Mark Douglas, Kathleen Regina. Student, Loyola U., Westchester, Calif., 1950-53. Nat. spokesman Citizens for Decency Through Law, 1973-76; mem. 95th-97th Congresses from 27th Calif. dist., 1977-83, 99th-103rd Congresses from 38th Calif. dist., 1985-93, 103rd Congress and 104th Congress from 46th Calif. dist., 1993-96; chmn. Nat. Sec. Subcom. on Military Personnel, chmn. Tech. and Tactical Intelligence. Host TV polit. talk shows in Los Angeles, 1965-73; host, producer: Robert K. Dornan Show, Los Angeles, 1970-73; combat photographer/broadcast journalist assigned 8 times to Laos-Cambodia-Vietnam, 1965-74; originator POW/MIA bracelet. Served to capt., fighter pilot USAF, 1953-58, fighter pilot, amphibian rescue pilot and intelligence officer USAFR, 1958-75. Mem. Am. Legion, Navy League, Air Force Assn., Res. Officers Assn., AMVET, Assn. Former Intelligence Officers, Am. Helicopter Soc. Special Forces Assn., AFTRA. Republican. Roman Catholic. Lodge: K.C. address: PO Box 3460 Garden Grove CA 92643

DORNBUSH, VICKY JEAN, medical billing systems executive; b. Willowick, Ohio, Aug. 12, 1951; d. Charles W. and Josephine H. (Palumbo) Rader; m. Eric D. Erickson, Oct. 22, 1972 (div. June 1974); 1 child, Dana; m. Thomas Dornbush, Dec. 29, 1979 (div. 1987). Student, Kent State U., 1969-72, San Jose State U., 1982-84. Accounts receivable clk. MV Nursery, Richmond, Calif., 1975-76; accounts receivable and computer supr. Ga. Pacific, Richmond, 1976-78; acct. Ga. Pacific, Tracy, Calif., 1978-79, Crown-Zellerbach, Anaheim, Calif., 1979-80; acct. Interstate Pharmacy Corp., San Jose, Calif., 1981-83, contr., 1983-85; gen. ptnr. Med. Billing Systems, San Jose, 1984-89; regional billing mgr., co-ordinator St. Joseph's Med. Resources, Stockton, Calif., 1997—; seminar trainer Systems Plus, Mountain View, Calif., 1987-89, MD Solutions, 1989-97; instr. med. program Sawyer Coll. Mem. San Jose Civic Light Opera, 1987—, San Jose Repertory Co., 1987-89; pres., bd. dirs. San Jose Stage Co., 1990—. Mem. AGPAM, Exec. Sales Women, Nat. Soc. Pub. Accts., Women in Bus., Univ. Women. Dem. Methodist. Office: St Joseph's Med. Resources 49 W Yokuts Ave Stockton CA 95207-5728

DORNEMAN, ROBERT WAYNE, manufacturing engineer; b. Oaklawn, Ill., Nov. 13, 1949; s. Robert John and Julia (Vorchenia) D.; M. Katrina Holland, July 30, 1977; children: Tamara, Tiana. BA in Biol. Sci., Calif. State U., Fullerton, 1974. Mfg. engr. Gen. Telephone Co., Anaheim, Calif., 1974-77, Xerox/Century Data, Anaheim, 1977-80; advance mfg. engr. MSI Data, Costa Mesa, Calif., 1980-83; sr. mfg. engr. Parker Hannifin, Irvine, Calif., 1983-86; sr. advanced mfr. engr. Western Digital, Irvine, 1986-89, mgr. advanced mfg. engring., 1989-91; mfg. engr. Pairgain Tech., Cerritos, Calif., 1991-93, mgr. mfg. engring., 1993-94; mgr. engring. svcs. Pairgain Tech., Tustin, Calif., 1994—; specialist automated assembly of circuits; cons. Base 2, Fullerton, 1980; developer surface mount tech. for computer mfg. industry; set up computer assemble plants internat. Devel. and implimented environ. safe mfg. process for computer bd. industry; contbr. articles in 3M-Alert to profl. jours. Mem. Nat. Assn. Realtors (broker), N. Orange County Bd. Realtors (broker), Calif. Assn. Realtors, Aventura Yacht Club, Internat. Soc. Hybrid Mfg., Tau Kappa Epsilon. Republican. Avocations: real estate, auto restorations, landscape architecture, billiards, bridge, sailing. Home: 21 Fair Elms Laguna Niguel CA 92677-5908 Office: Pairgain Tech 14402 Franklin Ave Tustin CA 92780-7013

DORNETTE, RALPH MEREDITH, church organization executive, educator, minister; b. Cin., Aug. 31, 1927; s. Paul A. and Lillian (Bauer) D.; m. Betty Jean Pierce, May 11, 1948; 1 child, Cynthia Anne Dornette Orndorff. AB, Cin. Bible Coll., 1948; DD (hon.), Pacific Christian Coll., 1994. Ordained to ministry Christian Ch., 1947. Min. Indian Creek Christian Ch., Cynthiana, Ky., 1946-51; assoc. prof. Cin. Bible Coll., 1948-51; sr. min. First Christian Ch., Muskogee, Okla., 1951-57; founding min. Bellaire Christian Ch., Tulsa, 1957-59; exec. dir. So. Calif. Evangelistic Assn., Torrance, Calif., 1959-62, 68-77; sr. min. Eastside Christian Ch., Fullerton, Calif., 1962-68; dir. devel., prof. ministries Cin. Bible Coll. & Sem., 1977-79; exec. dir. Ch. Devel. Fund, Inc., Fullerton, 1968-77, CEO, 1979-94; sr. preaching minister 1st Christian Ch., Downey, Calif., 1971, 91; preaching minister Hemet (Calif.) Valley Christian Ch., 1992-98; ret., 1998; pres. So. Calif. Christian Mins. Assn., Fullerton, 1975. Author: Bible Answers to Popular Questions, 1954, Walking With Our Wonderful Lord, 1955, Bible Answers to Popular Questions II, 1964. Pres. Homeowners Assn., Anaheim, Calif., 1980-81. Named Churchman of Yr. Pacific Christian Coll., Fullerton, 1973; recipient Disting. Alumni award Cin. Bible Coll. and Seminary, 1994. Mem. N.Am. Christian Conv. (conv. com. Cin. chpt. 1963, chair nat. registration 1963, v.p. 1972, exec. com. 1963, 70-72, 80-82).

DOSCHER, RICHARD JOHN, protective services official; b. Livermore, Calif., Aug. 31, 1952; s. Henry John and Violet Mary (Sutton) D.; m. Kathryn Laura Vierria, May 5, 1979; children: Cameron, Shannon. AS in Adminstrn. Justice, Yuba C.C., Maryville, Calif., 1987; BPA, U. San Francisco, 1991, MPA, 1993. From police officer to sgt. Yuba City (Calif.) Police Dept., 1977-85, sgt., watch commander, 1985-86, lt., divsn. commdr., 1986-89, lt., divsn. cmmdr. tech. svcs. and support, 1989-91, capt., divsn. cmmdr. field ops, 2d in command agy., 1991-93, capt., divsn. cmmdr. investigation, 2d in commd. agy., chief of police, 1995—; adj. prof. ethics Yuba C.C., 1997—. Bd. dirs. Yuba/Sutter Easter Seal Soc., 1988—; vol. Calif. Prune Festival, 1988—, Spl. Olympics, 1987—, Bok Kai Chinese Cultural Festival, 1993—, Yuba City Cmty. Theater, 1992—; adv. com. Adminstrn. of Justice Yuba Coll., 1993—; eucharistic min. St. Isidore's Cath. Ch., 1984—. With USAF, 1972-76. Mem. Am. Soc. for Pub. Adminstrn., Calif. Assn. Police Tng. Officers, Calif. Police Chiefs Assn. (bd. dirs. 1998—), , Calif. Peace Officers Assn., Peace Officers' Rsch. Assn. Calif., Yuba City Police Officers Assn. (past officer 1978-80), Kiwanis Club (bd. dirs., 2d v.p. Yuba City), Yuba City Health and Racquet Club. Avocation: astronomy. Office: Yuba City Police Dept 1545 Poole Blvd Yuba City CA 95993-2615

DOSSETT, LAWRENCE SHERMAN, professional services company official; b. Santa Ana, Calif., May 11, 1936; s. Wheeler Sherman and Eunice Elizabeth (Bright) D.; student U. Ariz., 1957-58, U. Calif., Irvine, 1973-75, Loyola Marymount Coll., 1974; m. Joanne Kallisch; children: Todd Sherman, Garrick Robert (dec.), Dana Shelene, Ryan William. Engring. draftsman Hughes Aircraft Co., Tucson, 1955-57, John J. Foster Mfg. Co., Costa Mesa, Calif., 1958, Standard Elec. Products, Costa Mesa, 1959; engring. mgr. Electronic Engring. Co., Santa Ana, 1959-79; product quality mgr. Farwest Data Systems, Irvine, Calif., 1979-82; dist. mgr. profl. svcs., nat. cons. mgr., sr. industry cons. Comserv/MSA/DBSoftware, L.A., 1982-92, sr. manufacturing industry cons., 1992-93; mfg. cons. Marcam Corp., Irvine, Calif., 1993-94; sr. industry cons. Cincom Sys., Inc., Irvine, Calif., 1994—. Mem. Western Electronic Mfrs. Assn., Am. Prodn. and Inventory Control Soc., Computer Mfrs. Conf., Cert. in mgmt. Am. Mgmt. Assn. Author: MRPXXI Asset/Liability Management System, 1993; co-author patent reel spindle, 1972. Office: Cincom Sys Inc 18101 Von Karman Ave Ste 1200 Irvine CA 92612-1012

DOST, JANICE E.H. BURROWS, human resources director; b. Boston, Oct. 24, 1944; d. Lloyd F. and Bernice E. (Cross) Howard; m. Quentin C. Burrows, June 25, 1966 (div. Nov. 1986); children: Matthew Howard, Christopher Lynch; m. William A. Dost, Apr. 7, 1995. BA cum laude, Harvard U., 1966; MBA, U. Calif., Berkeley, 1987. Mgr. employment, tng. U.S. Govt., Boston, 1966-72, Washington, 1966-72, N.Y.C., 1966-72; personnel specialist City of Berkeley, 1974-76; asst. dir. personnel Alta Bates Hosp., Berkeley, 1976-79; personel dir. Alta Bates Med. Ctr., Berkeley, 1979-86; human resources cons. [illegible] Berkeley, 1991 [illegible] dir. U. Calif. Libr., Berkeley, 1988—; dir. Humanities West, San Francisco, 1991—, African-Am. Mus. & Libr. of Oakland, Calif. Co-author: Minority Recruitment and Retention in ARL Libraries, 1990; author: Training Student Workers in Academic Libraries, 1994, Onward or Upward? Getting Ahead in an Unfair World, 1994. Docent Oakland Mus. Calif., 1992—; commr. personnel commn. Berkeley Unified Sch. Dist., chair, 1987-91. Nat. Merit scholar, 1962; recipient fed. funding for rsch. in continuing edn. for librs., 1994, 96. Mem. ALA (chmn. LAMA/PAS sect. 1998-99), Nat. Forum Black Pub. Adminstrs., Indsl. Rels. Rsch. Assn. Home: PO Box 40073 Berkeley CA 94704-4073

DOSTOURIAN, DICK, computer systems executive; b. L.A., Oct. 30, 1948; s. John and Elizabeth (Cholakian) D.; m. Jeanette Adrienne Torigian; children: Leslie Ann, Christopher Scott. AA in Engring., East L.A. Coll., 1968; BS in Math., Calif. State U., L.A., 1970, MS in Math., 1972. Computer engr. McDonnell Douglas, L.A., 1973-76, computing specialist, 1976-80, sect. mgr. engring. sys., 1980-83, mgr. product definition sys., 1983-89, mgr. info. tech., 1989-94; sr. mgr. software devel. Keane, Inc., L.A., 1994-95; software devel. mgr. Home Savings Am., Irwindale, Calif., 1995-96; prin. computing specialist The Boeing Co., Long Beach, Calif., 1997—. Mem. St. James Armenian Ch., L.A., 1989-94. Mem. IEEE, Assn. for Computing Machinery, Nat. Computer Graphics Soc., Data Processing Mgmt. Assn., Calif. State U. Alumni Assn. Avocations: tennis, railroading. Home: 10781 Via Jacara Stanton CA 90680-1926 Office: The Boeing Co 3855 Lakewood Blvd Long Beach CA 90846

DOTO, IRENE LOUISE, statistician; b. Wilmington, Del., May 7, 1922; d. Antonio and Teresa (Tabasso) D. BA, U. Pa., 1943; MA, Temple U., 1948, Columbia U., 1954. Engring. asst. RCA-Victor, 1943-44; research asst. U. Pa., 1944; actuarial clk. Penn Mut. Life Ins. Co., 1944-46; instr. math. Temple U., 1946-53; commd. lt. health services officer USPHS, 1954, advanced through grades to capt., 1963; statistician Communicable Disease Ctr., Atlanta, 1954-55, Kansas City, Kans., 1955-67; chief statis. and publ. services, ecol. investigations program Ctr. for Disease Control, Kansas City, 1967-73, chief statis. services, div. hepatitis and viral enteritis, Phoenix, 1973-83; statis. cons., 1984—; mem. adj. faculty Phoenix Ctr., Ottawa U., 1982-98. Mem. Am. Statis. Assn., Biometrics Soc., Am. Pub. Health Assn., Ariz. Pub. Health Assn., Ariz. Council Engring. and Sci. Assn. (officer 1982-90, pres. 1988-89), Primate Found. Ariz. (mem. animal care and use com. 1986—), Bus. and Profl. Women's Club Phoenix, The Retired Officers Assn. (state sec.-treas. 1995-96), Sigma Xi, Pi Mu Epsilon. Office: PO Box 22197 Phoenix AZ 85028-0197

DOTSON, GERALD RICHARD, retired biology educator; b. Brownsville, Tex., Sept. 8, 1937; s. Jasper William and Mary Agnes (Courtney) D.; m. Rose Delores Gonzales; children: Roberta Ana, Deborah, Matthew. BS, Coll. Santa Fe (N.Mex.), 1960; MS, U. Miss., 1966; PhD, U. Colo., 1974; postgrad., U. Tex., El Paso, 1960-61, Loyola U., New Orleans, 1962-63. Sci. tchr. Cathedral High Sch., El Paso, Tex., 1959-61; sci./math./music tchr. St. Paul's High Sch., Covington, La., 1961-62; sci./math./Spanish tchr. Christian Bros. Sch., New Orleans, 1962-63; sci. tchr., chmn. Hanson High Sch., Franklin, La., 1963-67; biology instr. Coll. Santa Fe (N.Mex.), 1967-69, U. Colo., Boulder, 1969-70, C.C. Denver, 1970-77; prof. biology and chmn. sci. Front Range C.C., Westminster, Colo., 1977-98, prof. emeritus, 1998—. Reviewer biology textbooks, media software, 1970—; contbr. articles to profl. jours. Mem. recreation dept. City of Westminster, 1971—. Mem. NSTA (regional sec. 1965), , Am. Microscopical Soc., Am. Soc. Limnology and Oceanography, Nat. Assn. Biology Tchrs., Human Anatomy and Physiology Soc., Eagles, KC (3rd and 4th deg.), Elks, Sigma Xi, Phi Sigma. Roman Catholic. Avocations: fishing, hunting, camping, golf, bowling. Home: 8469 Otis Dr Arvada CO 80003-1241

DOTY, HORACE JAY, JR., theater administrator, arts consultant; b. St. Petersburg, Fla., May 25, 1924; s. Horace Herndon and Mabel (Bruce) D.; student Sherwood Music Sch., Chgo., 1942-43; BA in Music, Pomona Coll., 1950; cert. La Verne Coll., 1969; MA in Edn., Claremont Grad. Sch., 1972; cert. in Bus. Adminstrn., 1984; m. Wanda L. Flory, Dec. 27, 1947; 1 child, Janet. Propr. Jay Doty's Inc., Claremont, 1960-68; concert mgr. Claremont Colls., 1968-73, supr. Garrison Theater, U. Ctr. Box Office, dir. Auditorium, theater events, coordinator programs, 1973-79, 81-90; exec. dir. Flint Ctr. for Performing Arts, Cupertino, Calif., 1979-81. Mem. blue ribbon com. Fox Theater Restoration, Pomona, Calif., 1982; mem. Claremont Bicentennial Com. for Performing Arts, 1975-76; mem. touring adv. panel, cons. and site visitor Calif. Arts Council; mem. exec. bd., Calif. Presenters. Served with inf. AUS, 1943-46. NEA fellow, 1986. Mem. Assn. Coll., Univ. and Community Arts Adminstrs. (dir. 1983-86), Western Alliance Arts Adminstrs. (pres. 1975-77), Internat. Assn. Auditorium Mgrs., Claremont C. of C. (pres. 1965-66). Office: Jay Doty Arts Cons 4145 Oak Hollow Rd Claremont CA 91711-2329

DOUD, CHARLES PACKARD, newspaper editor, printer; b. Preston, Idaho, Sept. 12, 1941; s. Carlton Horace D. Student, U. Mo., 1959-63, U. Wash., 1964-72, Evergreen State Coll., 1984-85. Pub. Magnolia News, Seattle, 1964-70, Skagit River Post, Burlington, Wash., 1980-92; copy editor Seattle-Post Intelligence, 1970-74; assoc. editor The News Tribune, Tacoma, Wash., 1974-86; mng. editor The Daily Courier, Prescott, Ariz., 1992-96; gen. mgr. Capital Press, Salem, Oreg., 1996-97; editor The News Guard, Lincoln City, Oreg., 1997—; pres. Think Pub. Co., 1997—. Editor: Termination with Extreme Prejudice, 1998. Bd. dirs. Phippen Mus. We. Art, 1993-96. Mem. Assoc. Press Mng. Editors (pres.-elect 1996), Bench-Bar-Press Com. (memb. bd, 1982). Episcopalian. Avocations: writing, gardening. Home: 6425 SW Inlet Ave Lincoln City OR 97367-1139 Office: The News Guard 930 SE Highway 101 Lincoln City OR 97367-2630

DOUGHERTY, GERARD MICHAEL, lawyer; b. Glen Cove, N.Y., May 11, 1959; s. Joseph John and Gina (DeGeorge) D.; m. Sherry Dougherty, Oct. 15, 1988; children: Briana Kristin, Danielle Caitlyn. BS in Mktg. and Econs., St. Johns U., 1981; JD, Southwestern U., 1984. Bar: Calif. 1985. Assoc. Matthew Biren & Assocs., L.A., 1984-87, Alfonso, Klonsky & Sternberg, Woodland Hills, Calif., 1987-89, Anderson Krehbiel McCreary, Westlake Village, Calif., 1989-95; ptnr. Dougherty and Waters, Simi Valley, Calif., 1995-97; prin. Dougherty & Landon, P.L.C., Westlake Village, Calif., 1997-98; sr. ptnr. Dougherty & Landon, P.L.C., Thousand Oaks, 1999—. Co-host Law Talk, KVEN Radio, Ventura, Calif. Coach Simi Valley Boys and Girls Club, 1995—; v.p. Simi Valley Rep. Club, 1996-97; bd. mem. Calif. Congress Reps., 1997—. Mem. Ventura County Bar Assn., Bus. Networking Internat., Westlake Village, Entrepreneurs United (Conejo Valley), Kiwanis. Roman Catholic. Avocations: ice and roller hockey, boating, camping. Office: Dougherty & Landon 2660 Townsgate Rd Ste 400 Thousand Oaks CA 91361-5715

DOUGHERTY, PATRICK, editor. Mng. editor Anchorage Daily News. E-mail: pdougherty@adn.com. Office: Anchorage Daily News 1001 Northway Dr Anchorage AK 99508-2098*

DOUGHERTY, RALEIGH GORDON, manufacturer's representative; b. Saginaw, Mich., Aug. 19, 1928; s. Raleigh Gordon and Helen Jean (McCrum) D.; 1 child, Karen Kealani. Salesman, H.D. Hudson Mfg. Co., Chgo., 1946-48; field sales rep. Jensen Mfg. Co., Chgo., 1948-50; field sales mgr. Regency Idea, Indpls., 1950-54; mgr. Brenna & Browne, Honolulu, 1954-56; owner, pres. Dougherty Enterprises, Honolulu, 1956—. With U.S. Army, 1950-52. Mem. Hawaii Hotel Assn., Internat. Home Furnishings Reps. Assn., Air Force Assn., DAV (life), Navy League U.S., Am. Legion, Hawaii Restaurant Assn., Korean Vet. Small Bus. of Hawaii, Historic Hawaii Found., Elks (past trustee Hawaii). Republican. Methodist. Home and Office: 1326 Lunalilo Home Rd Honolulu HI 96825-3216

DOUGHERTY, WILLIAM ANDERSEN, lawyer; b. Arlington, Mass., Apr. 18, 1924; s. William Leonard and Aroura Alice (Andersen) D.; m. Sharlee Sharron Powers, Apr. 14, 1961; children: Robyn, William, Shannon. AB, Bowdoin Coll., 1948; JD, Cornell U., 1955. Bar: U.S. Supreme Ct. 1952, D.C. 1955, N.Y. 1956, Calif. 1961. Asst. U.S. atty. Dept. of Justice, Washington, 1955-58, L.A., 1960-61; asst. counsel U.S. Senate Jud. Com., Washington, 1959-60; pvt. practice lawyer Orange County, Calif., 1961—. Trustee Kents Hill (Maine) Sch., 1995—; mem. Bowdoin Alumni [illegible] 1965-72, 95 [illegible] Col. USMC, 1942-76, PTO, Korea, Vietnam. Decorated 2 D.F.C., 6 Air medals. Mem. Orange County Bar Assn., Lincoln Club L.A., Lincoln Club Orange County. Republican. Episcopalian. Avocations: flying, railroads, music. Home and Office: 18352 Serrano Ave Villa Park CA 92861-2711

DOUGLAS, CHARLES HOUSE, artist, researcher; b. Milan, Tenn., July 4, 1941; s. Dave and Etolia (Wright) D.; m. Bonnie Jean Alexander, Oct. 15, 1990; 1 child, Darryl Cedric Demetrius. With Star-Kist Foods Inc., San Pedro, Calif., 1976-88, Huge Resource Ctr., Malibu, Calif., 1989-90; with mgmt. dept. U. Calif., L.A., 1990-98; graphic art specialist L.A., 1993—; cons., L.A., 1993-98. Illustrator: Face and Places, 1984. Recipient Internat. Citizen of Yr. award Hutt River Province, Australia, 1995. Avocations: walking, reading, fishing, listening to jazz music. Home: 1211 E 88th St Los Angeles CA 90002-1207

DOUGLAS, DIANE MIRIAM, museum director; b. Harrisburg, Pa., Mar. 25, 1957; d. David C. and Anna (Barron) D.; m. Steve I. Perlmutter, Jan. 23, 1991; 1 child, David Simon. BA, Brown U., 1979; MA, U. Del., 1982. Oral history editor Former Members of Congress, Washington, 1979-80; assoc. curator exhibitions John Michael Kohler Arts Ctr., Sheboygan, Wis., 1982-83; dir. arts ctr. Lill Street Gallery, Chgo., 1984-88; exec. dir. David Adler Cultural Ctr., Libertyville, Ill., 1988-91; dir. Bellevue (Wash.) Art Mus., 1992—; program chair, exec. bd. nat. Coun. for Edn. in Ceramic Arts, Bandon, Oreg., 1990-93; nat. adv. bd. Friends of Fiber Art, 1992; artists adv. com. Pilchuck Glass Sch., 1993—; mem. bd. dirs. Archie Bray Found., Helena, Mont., 1995—. Office: Bellevue Art Mus 301 Bellevue Sq Bellevue WA 98004-5000*

DOUGLAS, JOEL BRUCE, lawyer; b. L.A., Jan. 25, 1948. BA magna cum laude, Calif. State U., Northridge, 1970; postgrad., East L.A. Coll.; JD, Loyola U., L.A., 1973. Bar: Calif. 1973, U.S. Dist. Ct. (ctrl. dist.) Calif. 1974, U.S. Ct. Appeals (9th cir.) 1978, U.S. Supreme Ct. 1979. Ptnr. Bonne, Bridges, Mueller, O'Keefe & Nichols P.C., L.A.; adj. prof. sch. law Pepperdine U., Malibu, Calif., 1981-84; judge pro tempore L.A. Mcpl. Ct., 1980—, L.A. Superior Ct., 1988—. Assoc. editor Loyola U. L.A. Law Rev., 1972-73. Mem. ABA (litigation sect., tort and ins. practice sect.), State Bar Calif., L.A. County Bar Assn. (mem. legal-med. com. 1979-83, staff atty. med.-legal hot line 1979-82), Am. Bd. Trial Advocates, St. Thomas Moore Law Honor Soc., Phi Alpha Delta. Office: Bonne Bridges Mueller O'Keefe & Nichols PC 3699 Wilshire Blvd Fl 10 Los Angeles CA 90010-2719

DOUGLAS, MARION JOAN, proofreader, editor, labor negotiator; b. Jersey City, May 29, 1940; d. Walter Stanley and Sophie Frances (Zysk) Binaski; children: Jane Dee, Alex Jay. BA, Mich. State U., 1962; MSW, Sacramento State Coll., 1971; MPA, Calif. State U.-Sacramento, 1981. Owner, mgr. Linkletter-Totten Dance Studios, Sacramento, 1962-68, Young World of Discovery, Sacramento, 1965-68; welfare worker Sacramento County, 1964-67, welfare supr., 1968-72, child welfare supr., 1972-75, sr. personnel analyst, 1976-78, personnel program mgr., 1978-81, labor relations rep., 1981-89; cons. State Dept. Health, Sacramento, 1975-76; cons. in field. Author/editor: (newsletter) Thursday's Child, 1972-74. Presiding officer Cmty. Resource Orgn., Fair Oaks, Calif., 1970-72; exec. bd. Foster Parent's Assn., Sacramento, 1972-75; organizer Foster Care Sch. Dist. liaison programs, 1973-75; active Am. Lung Assn., 1983-87, 93-94; rep. Calif. Welfare Dirs. Assn., 1975-76; county staff advisor Joint Powers Authority, Sacramento, 1978-81; mem. Mgmt. Devel. Com., Sacramento, 1979-80; vol., auctioneer sta. KVIE Pub. TV, Sacramento, 1970-84, 88-90; adv. bd. Job and Info. Resource Ctr., 1976-77; spl. adv. task force coordinator Sacramento Employment and Tng. Adv. Council, 1980-81; vol. leader Am. Lung Assn., Sacramento, 1983-86, 94—, Calif. Dept. Social Welfare ednl. stipend, 1967-68, County of Sacramento ednl. stipend, 1969-70. Recipient Achievement award Nat. Assn. Counties, 1981. Mem. Mgmt. Women's Forum, Indsl. Relations Assn. No. Calif., Indsl. Relations Research Assn., Nat. Assn. Female Execs., Mensa. Republican. Avocations: real estate, nutrition. Home: 7829 Greenridge Way Fair Oaks CA 95628-4841

DOUGLAS, PATRICIA PUMP, accounting and finance educator; b. Lewistown, Mont., Apr. 20, 1941; d. Henry F. Pump and Beatrice S. Skeel; m. Robert B. Bragg, June, 1958 (div. 1967); m. Charles E. Douglas, Aug. 23, 1968. BA, U. Mont., 1963; MBA, U. Calif., Berkeley, 1964, PhD, 1967. Grad. asst., assto to dean Sch. Bus. Adminstrn. U. Mont., 1961-63, rsch. assoc. Bur. Bus. & Econ. Rsch., 1966-72, asst. prof. Sch. Bus. Adminstrn., 1966-72, dir. continuing edn. & summer programs, asst. to pres., 1972-76, assoc. prof., 1972-74, prof., 1974—, asst. to pres., 1976-78, fiscal affairs v.p., 1978-82, prof. acctg. & fin. depts., 1983—; rsch. assoc. U. Calif., Berkeley, 1963-65; dir. state tech. svcs. State Mont., 1966-70; rschr. feasibility self-ins. state owned properties Mont. Legis. Coun., 1969-71; rschr. growth profitability Mont. Banks, Helena Br. Fed. Reserve Bank Mpls., 1970-71; vis. prof. U. Calif., Berkeley, 1972; dir. Continental Nat. Bank, Harlowton, Mont., 1980—, First Security Bank, Missoula, 1981-84; Ctrl. Feed Dir., 1987—; mem. bd. investments State Mont., 1977-80; chmn. Reserve Bank Minn. Helena Br., 1977-80, bd. trustees Missoula Cmty. Hosp., 1976-77; exec. com. Missoula Cmty. Med. Ctr., 1991—, treas. UM Fed. Credit Union, 1972-77, bd. dirs., 1972-77; mem. Bus. Sch. space com. U. Mont., 1994—, chair facilities svcs. evaluation oversight com., 1992-93, Sch. Bus. Internat. com., 1992-94, bond issuance com., 1992-94, bldg. fee com., 1990—, Sch. Bus. scholarship com., 1986-95, space com., 1978-83, campus devel. com., 1978-83, adv. bd. cmty. svc. program, 1974-77, faculty senate, 1970-72, sec. budget & policy com., 1967-68, ad hoc com. curriculum acctg. & fin. dept., 1967-68, ad hoc com. Sch. Bus. Adminstrn. space, 1994-95. Contbr. articles to profl. jours. Recipient Rsch. Achievement award Assn. Govtl. Accts. At-Large, 1992-93. Mem. Am. Inst. CPAs, Nat. Assn. Accts. (dir. Western Mont. chpt. 1970-73, 91, pres. Western Mont. chpt. 1972-73, nat. dir. 1975-77, v.p. nat. com. 1994-96, nat. fin. com. 1985-86, mgmt. acctg. practices com. 1985-86, MAP com. subcom. govt. 1985-95, Outstanding Educator award 1989), Fin. Acctg. Stds. Bd. (task force nonprofits 1989-94), Western Commn. Colls. (chair fin. & ops. com. 1992-94, commr. 1989-94), Mont. Soc. CPAs (ethics com. 1985—, com. to review procedures 1987-88, com. rels. with bar 1988-90, chmn. ethics com. 1985-89, bd. dirs. 1989—, ad-hoc com. pers. policies 1994-95, ad-hoc com. by-laws changes 1992-93, v.p. 1993-94, pres.-elect 1994-95, pres. 1995-96), Northwest Assn. Schs. Colls. (accreditation pool), Data Processing Mgmt. Assn. Edn. Found. (bd. regents 1984-91, pres. 1990-91), Western Assn. Colls. & Univs. (commr. 1989-94, chair fin. com. 1991-94), Beta Alpha Psi (Outstanding Tchr. award 1985-86, 1992-93), Phi Kappa Phi. Home: Box 189 8200 Mormon Creek Rd Lolo MT 59847-9617 Office: U Mont Acctg & Fin Dept Missoula MT 59812

DOUGLAS, STEPHEN ROSS, scientist, physicist; b. Salem, Oreg., Sept. 16, 1953; s. George Frederick and Margaret Elizabeth (Evans) D. BS in Physics, Oreg. State U., 1976, MS in Math., 1980; AAS in Civil Engring. Tech., Salem, Oreg., 1992. Digitizer Oreg. State Water Res., Salem, 1992, lab. tech., 1996; surveying technologist BCM, Salem, 1996. Mem. Phi Beta Kappa. Home: 1770 Church St SE Salem OR 97302-3015

DOUGLASS, DONALD ROBERT, banker; b. Evanston, Ill., Oct. 7, 1934; s. Robert William and Dorothy (Gibson) D.; m. Susan Douglass. BBA, U. N.Mex., 1959, MBA, 1966. With Security Pacific Nat. Bank, Los Angeles, 1961—, mgmt. trainee, 1962-63, asst. mgr. Vernon (Calif.) br., 1963-64, asst. mgr. Whittier (Calif.) 1964, asst. v.p., 1965, asst. v.p., credit officer regional adminstrn., Los Angeles, 1966-69, v.p., San Francisco, 1969-74, mgr. corp. accounts credit adminstrn. No. Calif. Corp. Banking, 1974-77; group v.p. Annco Properties, Burlingame, Calif., 1977-79; v.p., sr. loan officer Borel Bank and Trust Co., San Mateo, Calif., 1979-83, sr. v.p., 1983-84, exec. v.p. mortgage banking div. comml. property sales, Los Altos, 1984-87; ptnr. Key Equities, Inc., San Mateo, 1987—; ptnr., broker Centre Fin. Group, Inc., San Mateo, 1987—, Centre Fin. Group South Inc., Menlo Park, 1987—; pres. ServiCtr. Mortgage, Inc., 1996—; instr. Am. Inst. Banking, 1963, Coll. San Mateo, 1982—. Served with AUS, 1954-56. Mem. U. N.Mex. Alumni Assn., Sigma Alpha Epsilon, Delta Sigma Phi. Republican. Presbyterian. Home: 745 Celestial Ln San Mateo CA 94404-2771

DOUGLASS, ENID HART, educational program director; b. L.A., Oct. 23, 1926; d. Frank Roland and Enid Yandell (Lewis) Hart; m. Malcolm P. Douglass, Aug. 28, 1948; children: Malcolm Paul Jr., John Aubrey, Susan Enid. BA, Pomona Coll., 1948; MA, Claremont (Calif.) Grad. Sch., 1959. Research asst. World Book Ency., Palo Alto, Calif., 1953-54; exec. sec., asst. dir. oral history program Claremont Grad. U., 1963-71, dir. oral history program, 1971 [illegible] Calif. [illegible] Commn., 1977-85, chmn. 1983-85. Contbr. articles to hist. jours. Mayor pro tem City of Claremont, 1980-82, mayor, 1982-86; mem. planning and rsch. adv. coun. State of Calif.; mem. city coun. City of Claremont, 1978-86;

founder Claremont Heritage, Inc., 1977-80; bd. dirs., 1986-95; bd. dirs. Pilgrim Pla., Claremont; founder, steering com., founding bd. Claremont Cmty. Found., 1989-95, pres., 1990-94. Mem. Oral History Assn. (pres. 1979-80), Southwest Oral History Assn. (founding steering com. 1981, J.V. Mink award 1984), Nat. Council Pub. History, LWV (bd. dirs. 1957-59, Outstanding Svc. to Community award, 1986). Democrat. Avocation: tennis. Home: 1195 N Berkeley Ave Claremont CA 91711-3842 Office: Claremont Grad U Oral History Program 710 N College Ave Claremont CA 91711-3921

DOUGLASS, RAMONA ELIZABETH, medical sales professional; b. N.Y.C., Aug. 15, 1949; d. Howard William and Lena Verona (Belle) D. Student, Colo. Sch. Mines, 1966-68; BS in Physical Sci., Colo. State U., 1970. Adminstrv. asst. S.E. Queens Community Corp., Queens, N.Y., 1970-71; research editor Encyclopedia Britannica, Chgo., 1971-73; sales rep. Scott Foresman Co., Glenview, Ill., 1973-75, Am. Sci. Products, McGaw Park, Ill., 1975-78; mgr. New Eng. territory Hollister, Inc., Libertyville, Ill., 1978-81; mgr. midwest region Precision Dynamics Corp., San Fernando, Calif., 1981-95, mgr. Western region, bar code specialist, 1995—, mng. editor sales and mktg. newsletter, 1998—; ptnr. Douglass/Sherod-Winter Assocs., Chgo., 1986-88, DMB Group, Internat., 1990-91; mem. Nat. Network Women in Sales, 1986-93, v.p. corp. rels., 1989-90; co-founder Healthy Concepts, Inc., 1993, mktg. v.p., cons., 1998—; apptd. to Fed. 2000 Census Adv. Com., 1995—, mem. Fed. Working Group on Racial and Ethnic Tabulations, 1997—; lectr., spkr. in field; appearances on radio and TV programs, including Oprah Winfrey Show, Jerry Springer Show, Mark Walberg Show, CBS Sunday Morning, Aaron Freeman Show, others. Contbr. poetry Great Am. Poetry Anthology, 1987; subject in The Rainbow Effect: Interracial Families, 1987, Heroes of Conscience: A Biographical Dictionary, 1996; contbg. author: The Multiracial Experience: Racial Borders as the New Frontier, 1995. Founding mem. The Nat. Alliance Against Racist & Polit. Repression, Chgo., 1972; bd. dirs., chair publicity The Biracial Family Network, Chgo., 1987-90, v.p., 1990-92, pres., 1992-93; v.p. pub. rels. Assn. Multi-Ethnic Ams., 1988-90, v.p. midwest region, 1991-94, pres., 1994—. Recipient Pioneer award for outstanding contbn. to multiracial issues U. Calif., Berkeley, 1997, Building Bridges award Racial Harmony award Multiracial Ams. of so. Calif., 1996. Mem. NAFE. Democrat. Avocations: creative writing, music, gourmet cooking, sailing. Office: Precision Dynamics Corp 13880 Del Sur St San Fernando CA 91340-3490

DOVE, DONALD AUGUSTINE, city planner, educator; b. Waco, Tex., Aug. 7, 1930; s. Sebert Constantine and Amy Delmena (Stern) D.; m. Cecelia Mae White, Feb. 9, 1957; children: Angela Dove Gaddy, Donald, Monica Gilstrap, Celine, Austin, Cathlyn Howze, Dianna, Jennifer. BA, Calif. State U.-L.A., 1951; MA in Pub. Adminstrn., U. So. Calif., 1966. Planning and devel. cons. D. Dove Assocs., L.A., 1959-60; supr. demographic rsch. Calif. Dept. Pub. Works, L.A., 1960-66, environ. coordinator, Sacramento, 1971-75; dir. transp. employment project State of Calif., L.A., 1966-71, chief Los Angeles Region transp. study, 1975-84; chief environ. planning Calif. Dept. Transp., L.A., 1972-75; dir. U. So. Calif. Praetors, L.A., 1984-87; panelist, advisor Pres. Conf. on Aging, Washington, 1970—, Internat. Conf. on Energy Use Mgmt., 1981; guest lectr. univs. western U.S., 1969—. Author: Preserving Urban Environment, 1976; Small Area Population Forecasts, 1966. Chmn. Lynwood City Planning Commn., Calif., 1982—; pres. Area Pastoral Coun., L.A., 1982-83; mem., del. Archdiocesan Pastoral Council, L.A., 1979-86, Compton Community Devel. Bd., Calif., 1967-71; pres. Neighborhood Esteem/Enrichment Techniques Inst., 1992-93. Served to cpl. U.S. Army, 1952-54. Mem. Am. Planning Assn., Am. Inst. Planners (transp. chmn. 1972-73), Calif. Assn. of Mgmt. (pres. 1987-88), Am. Inst. Cert. Planners, Assn. Environ. Profls. (co-founder 1973), Optimists (sec. 1978-79). Democrat. Roman Catholic. Home and Office: 11356 Ernestine Ave Lynwood CA 90262-3711

DOW, MARY ALEXIS, auditor; b. South Amboy, N.J., Feb. 19, 1949; d. Alexander and Elizabeth Anne (Reilly) Pawlowski; m. Russell Alfred Dow, June 19, 1971. BS with honors, U. R.I., 1971. CPA, Oreg. Staff acct. Deloitte & Touche, Boston, 1971-74; sr. acct. Price Waterhouse, Portland, Oreg., 1974-77, mgr., 1977-81, sr. mgr., 1981-84; CFO Copeland Lumber Yards Inc., Portland, 1984-86; ind. cons. in field, 1986-94; elected auditor Metro, Portland, 1995—; bd. dirs. Longview Fibre Co. Contbr. articles to profl. jours. Past bd. dirs., exec. com., treas. Oreg. Mus. Sci. and Industry; past chmn. bd., mem. exec. com. Oreg. Trails chpt. N.W. Regional Blood Svcs. ARC. Mem. AICPA, Pacific N.W. Intergovtl. Audit Forum (exec. com.), Am. Woman's Soc. CPAs, Oreg. Soc. CPAs (bd. dirs.), Fin. Execs. Inst. (exec. com., past pres. Portland chpt., western area v.p.), City Club (bd. govs.), Multnomah Athletic Club (trustee). Roman Catholic. Office: Office of Auditor Metro 600 NE Grand Ave Portland OR 97232-2736

DOWDLE, PATRICK DENNIS, lawyer; b. Denver, Dec. 8, 1948; s. William Robert and Helen (Schraeder) D.; m. Eleanor Pryor, Mar. 8, 1975; children: Jeffery William, Andrew Peter. BA, Cornell Coll., Mt. Vernon, Iowa, 1971; JD, Boston U., 1975. Bar: Colo. 1975, U.S. Dist. Ct. Colo. 1975, U.S. Ct. Appeals (10th cir.) 1976, U.S. Supreme Ct. 1978. Acad. dir. in Japan Sch. Internat. Tng., Putney, Vt., 1974; assoc. Decker & Miller, Denver, 1975-77; ptnr. Miller, Makkai & Dowdle, Denver, 1977—; designated counsel criminal appeals Colo. Atty. Gens. Office, Denver, 1980-81; guardian ad litem Adams County Dist. Ct., Brighton, Colo., 1980-83; affiliated counsel ACLU, Denver, 1980—. Mem. Colo. Bar Assn., Denver Bar Assn. (various coms.), Porsche Club of Am. Avocations: scuba diving, photography, wine making, travel, skiing. Home: 3254 Tabor Ct Wheat Ridge CO 80033-5367 Office: Miller Makkai & Dowdle 2325 W 72nd Ave Denver CO 80221-3101

DOWLIN, KENNETH EVERETT, librarian; b. Wray, Colo., Mar. 11, 1941; s. Ross Everett and Fern Mae (Peterson) D.; m. Janice Marie Simmons, Mar. 11, 1961; children: Kevin Everett, Kristopher Everett. BA, U. Colo., 1963, MPA, 1981; MA, U. Denver, 1966. Bookmobile libr., libr. asst. Adams County Public Libr., Westminster, Colo., 1961-63; libr. asst. II Denver Pub. Libr., 1962-64; head libr. Arvada Public Libr., Colo., 1964-68; adminstrv. asst. Jefferson County Pub. Libr., Colo., 1969; dir. Natrona County Pub. Libr., Casper, Wyo., 1969-75, Pikes Peak Regional Libr. Dist., Colorado Springs, Colo., 1975-87; city libr. San Francisco Pub. Libr., 1987-97; instr. Casper Coll., 1971-73; chmn. Colo. Librs. in Coop., 1975-76, Colo. Ad-hoc Com. Networking, 1976; libr. City of San Francisco, 1987; mem. Western Interstate Commn. Higher Edn. Libr. Network Task Force; past trustee Wyo. Dept. Libr., Archives and History; mem. Libr. of Congress Commn. on Book of Future; bd. dirs. Satellite Libr. Info. Network; bd. mem. Libr. Found. of San Francisco, 1987—, Friends of the Libr., 1987—, Bay Area Book Festival, 1988-90; mem. Calif. State Libr. Task Force on Networking, 1988—, Calif. State Libr. of Tomorrow Task Force, 1995; founding mem. Greater Bay Area Libr. Coun., 1994—; vis. instr. U. Denver, 1980, 81; vis. faculty U. Calif., Berkeley, 1993; disting. vis. prof. Sch. Libr. and Info. Sci., San Jose State U., 1997—; cons. in cable TV; dist. visiting prof. San Jose State Univ., 1997—. Editorial bd. Microcomputers for Info. Mgmt., Libr. Hi Tech., Elec. Libr. Mem. adv. bd. for series on tech. WNET, N.Y.C., 1981-83; active San Francisco Mayor's com. on Juveniles in Detention; bd. dirs. Citizens Goals for Colorado Springs, 1981-85; bd. govs. Colo. Tech. Coll., 1982-85. With USMCR, 1959-65. Recipient Disting. Alumni award U. Denver Grad. Sch. for Libr. and Info. Mgmt. Mem. ALA (coun. mem. 1985-89, commn. on equality and freedom access to info. 1984-85, chmn. awards com. 1985-86, pres.'s com. on preservation 1990—, ad hoc com. on MARC licensing, chair local arrangements com. for 1992, 1989-92, pres.'s com. on preservation policy 1989-90, edn. com. 1998—, Hammond Inc. Libr. Award Jury 1968), ALA Libr. and Info. Tech. Assn. (long range planning com. 1981-82, pres. 1983-84, com. mem. Gaylord Awards), Mountain Plains Libr. Assn., Calif. Libr. Assn. (fin. com., coun. mem. 1989—), Colo. Libr. Assn. (pres. 1968-69), Denver Coun. Govts. (chmn. librs. com. 1966), Colo. Mcpl. League (chmn. librs. sect. 1967), Bibliog. Ctr. Rocky Mountains (pres. 1972-74), Pikes Peak Area C. of C. (chmn. cultural affairs com. 1976-77). Office: San Francisco Pub Libr Civic Ctr San Francisco CA 94102

DOWNEY, JOE S., geohydrologist; b. Tempe, Ariz., Apr. 19, 1931; s. Whitehill Downey; m. Virginia L. Coxe, Sept. 12, 1954 (div. Oct. 15, 1982); children: Linda, Barbara, Ronald, Sharon; m. Shirley Mae Downey, Dec. 3, 1983. BS in Geology, U. Ariz., 1961; postgrad., Ariz. State U., 1962-63, U. N.D., 1966-70. Registered geologist, geohydrologist, Calif. Geologist U.S. Army Corps Engrs., Omaha, 1962-64; rsch. hydrologist U.S. Geol. Survey, Lakewood, Colo., 1966-92; prin. Downey & Gotentag LLC, Arvada, Colo. Author: Geohydrology of the Northern Great Plains, 1983; contbr. numerous articles to profl. jours. Staff sgt. USMC, 1950-56. Fellow AAAS, Geol. Soc. Am.; mem. ASTM, Am. Assn. Mamamulogists, Am. Geophys. Union, Am. Inst. Hydrology. Avocation: breeding Peruvian horses. Office: Downey & Gutentag LLC 6301 Eldridge St Arvada CO 80004-3610

DOWNEY, SCHEHERAZADE SHULA, academic administrator; b. Heidelberg, Germany, Aug. 19, 1952; came to U.S., 1954; d. Howard William and Dorothy Elizabeth (Mulliken) Rossow; m. John Harold Shula, Jan. 15, 1971 (div. Jan. 1976); m. Michael John Downey, July 29, 1989; 1 child, Joshua John. AA, Morgan C.C., 1979; BA magna cum laude, U. Denver, 1981, postgrad., 1988-90, 95-97. Libr. asst. Morgan C.C., Ft. Morgan, Colo., 1977-79; rsch. asst. dept. anthropology U. Denver, 1979-80, project coord. dept. anthropology, 1980-81, graduation evaluator registrar, 1981-85, functional coord. registration, 1985-89, dir. univ. registrations, 1989—; advisor, counselor U. Denver, 1986-92. Contbr. poetry to anthols. Advocate hotline Rape Awareness/Assistance Program, Denver, 1992-94; advisor Rape Awareness Counseling Edn., U. Dancer, 1991-93, S.P.E.A.K., 1993-95. Mem. Am. Assn. Collegiate Registrars and Admissions Officers (Best State Regional Profl. Activity award 1991), Colo. Collegiate Registrars Assn., Colo. Orgn. for Victims Assistance, Rocky Mountain Assn. Collegiate Registrars and Admissions Officers (com. mem. 1991—, Best State award 1991), Acad. Mgmt. Inst. (nominee Oustanding Svc. award 1996), Com. for Women on Campus (chair 1992—), Phi Beta Kappa (membership com. 1992—). Avocations: writing poetry, camping, making jewelry, gourmet cooking, wine.

DOWNIE, PAMELA, psychologist; b. Chester, Calif., Dec. 1, 1954; d. William John and June (De La Mont) D. BA, Widener U., 1980; MS, Villanova U., 1985; PhD, U. So. Calif., 1995. Counselor, trainer Del. County C.C., Media, Pa., 1985-87; counselor, instr. New Beginnings, Media, Pa., 1986-87; tchg. asst. U. So. Calif., 1989-91, instr. practicum, 1991, psychol. intern. Student Counseling Ctr., 1991-93; staff psychologist U. San Diego, 1994-95; lectr. Calif. State U., Fullerton, 1995-96, asst. prof., 1996—. Mem. APA (student), NAFE, AACD, Am. Mental Health Coun. Assn., Assn. for Multicultural Counseling, Pa. Counselors Assn., Assn. for Specialists in Group Work, Assn. for Coun. Edn. and Supervision. Home: PO Box 660582 Arcadia CA 91066-0582 Office: Calif State U Fullerton Dept Counseling EC-105 Fullerton CA 91066

DOWNING, DAVID CHARLES, minister; b. South Gate, Calif., June 24, 1938; s. Kenneth Oliver and Edna Yesobel (Casaday) D.; m. Tommye Catherine Tew, July 11, 1959 (dec. Dec. 11, 1985); children: Sheri Lynn, Teresa Kay, Carla Jeane, Michael David. BA, N.W. Christian Coll., 1961; B in Divinity, Tex. Christian U., 1966, M in Theology, 1973; DMin, San Francisco Theol. Sem., 1987. Ordained to ministry Christian Ch., 1961. Min. Marcola (Oreg.) Ch. of Christ, 1958-59; assoc. min. First Christian Ch., Lebanon, Oreg., 1960-63; min. First Christian Ch., Ranger, Tex., 1963-65, Knox City, Tex., 1966-68, Fredonia, Kans., 1968-74; min. Ctrl. Christian Ch., Huntington, Ind., 1974-77; regional min., pres. Christian Ch. Greater Kansas City, Mo., 1978-94; sr. minister Univ. Christian Ch. (Disciples of Christ), San Diego, 1994—; trustee Phillips Grad. Sem., Enid, Okla., 1988-94; bd. dirs. Ch. Fin. Coun., Indpls., Midwest Career Devel. Svc., Chgo.; v.p. bd. dirs. Midwest Christian Counseling Ctr., Kansas City. Author: A Contrast and Comparison of Pastoral Counseling in Rural and Urban Christian Churches, 1972, A Design for Enabling Urban Congregations to Cope with Their Fear of Displacement When Faced with Communities in Transition, 1987. Pres. Kansas City Interfaith Peace Alliance, 1980-82. Democrat. Avocations: swimming, camping, fishing, water skiing, collecting chalices. Home: 4325 Caminito De La Escena San Diego CA 92108-4201 Office: Univ Christian Ch (Disciples of Christ) 3900 Cleveland Ave San Diego CA 92103-3403

DOWNING, DOUGLAS ALLAN, economics educator, writer; b. Seattle, Oct. 11, 1957; s. Robert Allan and Marguerite Louise (Hayland) D.; m. Lori Rosenau, 1994. BS, Yale U., 1979, MPhil, 1982, PhD in Econs., 1987. Acting instr. Yale U., New Haven, Conn., 1981-83; asst. prof. Seattle Pacific U., 1983-91, assoc. prof., 1991—, undergrad. dir. sch. bus. and econs., 1995—. Author: Calculus the Easy Way, 1982, Algebra the Easy Way, 1983, Trigonometry the Easy Way, 1984; co-author: Dictionary of Computer Terms, 1986, and 9 others. Mem. State Com. on Teenage Parents, Olympia, Wash., 1986-88; witness Wash. State Legis., Olympia, 1991-94. Austin Howard grad. fellow Yale U., 1979. Mem. Am. Econ. Assn., Seattle Economist Club, Yale Assn. Western Wash. (treas. 1987-95), Phi Beta Kappa. Presbyterian. Avocations: astronomy, medieval history, basketball. Home: 18539 NE 184th St Woodinville WA 98072-8228 Office: Seattle Pacific U McKenna Hall Seattle WA 98119

DOYEL, CINDY M., controller; b. Stockton, Calif., Dec. 1, 1964; d. Nathan Cameron Doyel and Charlotte Blanche (Epler) Gezi. Student, Calif. State U., Sacramento, 1982-83; AA, MTI Bus. Coll., Sacramento, 1984. Supr. All Am. Mini Storage, Sacramento, 1988-89; asst. contr. Longview Devel. Corp., Sacramento, 1989-90; mng. contr. The Royce Cos., Roseville, Calif., 1990-93; contr. Calif. Comml., Sacramento, 1993-95; gen. ptnr., operator Sierra Micro, Fair Oaks, Calif., 1995—. Mem. NOW, NAFE, Nat. Abortion and Reproductive Right Action League. Presbyterian. Avocations: writing, reading, waterpolo, swimming, softball. Office: Sierra Micro 8139 Sunset Ave Ste 101 Fair Oaks CA 95628-5131

DOYLE, MICHAEL JAMES, educator, organist; b. Bell, Calif., Aug. 24, 1939; s. Joseph Edward and Irma Louise (Smith) D.; m. Mina Katherine Martensen, Feb. 8, 1964; children: Michael James II, Mary Katherine, Matthew John. BA, Whittier Coll., 1961, MEd, 1971. Tchr. El Rancho Unified Sch. Dist., Pico Rivera, Calif., 1961-79, dept. chmn., 1967-74, acting prin., 1979; tchr., asst. prin. Alta Loma (Calif.) Sch. Dist., 1979-86, summer sch. prin., 1985, prin., 1986-95; assoc. faculty Nat. U., Riverside, Calif., 1995-98; adj. prof. Calif. State U., San Bernardino, 1995—, Nat. U., Riverside, Calif., 1998—; organist, dir. various Luth. chs. in So. Calif., 1955-86; organist St. Paul's Luth. Ch., Pomona, Calif., 1986—; mem. Calif. State Program Rev., 1982-83; assoc. mem. Calif. Sch. Leadership Acad., Ontario, 1986-89; v.p. So. Calif. Luth. Music Clinic, 1978-81. Clk. Zion Luth. Sch. Bd. Edn., Maywood, Calif., 1962-64, chmn., 1966-67; mem. Downey (Calif.) City Water Bd., 1977-78; mem. Luth. High Personnel Commn., La Verne, Calif., 1988-92. Named Outstanding Tchr. of Yr., Burke Jr. High Sch. PTA, Pico Rivera, 1973; recipient hon. svc. award Jasper Sch. PTA, Alta Loma, 1983, continuing svc. award, 1988, Golden Oak Svc. award, 1996; employee recognition award Alta Loma Sch. Dist., 1985. Mem. Assn. Calif. Sch. Adminstrs., Assn. West End Sch. Adminstrs., Calif. Tchrs. Assn., Am. Guild Organists, Downey Hist. Soc., Cucamonga Hist. Soc., Casa de Rancho (Cucamonga, Calif.), Phi Delta Kappa (pres. Mt. Baldy chpt. 1993-97, advisor 1997—, found. chmn. 1991-93). Democrat. Lutheran. Home and Office: 2085 N Palm Ave Upland CA 91784-1476

DOYLE, MICHAEL JOSEPH, mining executive; b. Eveleth, Minn., Nov. 15, 1928; s. Matthew James and Lucile (McNany) D.; m. Virginia Ethel Britt, Aug. 22, 1953; children: Patricia, Matthew, Michael, Mary Anne, Thomas, Molly, Peter, Robert. BA, U. Minn., Duluth, 1952; JD, U. Minn., Mpls., 1958. Bar: Minn., U.S. Supreme Ct. Labor counsel Pickands Mather & Co., Duluth, 1959-64; asst. dir. labor Hanna Mining Co., Cleve., 1964-69, dir. environ. affairs, 1970-74, dir. govt. affairs, 1975-85; dep. dir. Ariz. Dept. Environ. Quality, Phoenix, 1987-90; pres. Nev. Mining Assn., Reno, 1990—; bus. cons. Doyle & Assocs., Chagrin Falls, 1985-87; Ariz. rep. mine waste task force EPA, Denver, 1988-90. Mem. Nev. Natural Resource Adv. Bd., Carson City, 1993—; mem. bus. and mining schs. adv. bd. U. Nev., Reno, 1992—; Nev. rep. Grand Canyon Visibility Transport Commn., Denver, 1993-96. Mem. Carlton Club (Washington). Avocations: family activities, golf. Home: 11735 E Chama Rd Scottsdale AZ 85255-5908

DOYLE, MICHAEL PHILLIP, civil engineer; b. Denver, May 7, 1955; s. Virgil Lee and Lela Virginia (Mercer) D.; m. Veronika Hertha Panholtzer; children: Kristina Michelle, Leland Collin. BSCE, U. Nev., 1985. Registered profl. engr., Calif. Staff engr. Omni Means Ltd., Reno, 1985, Sacramento, 1985-87; project engr. Carl Rodolf Engr., Sacramento, 1987; tech. dir. Sahuaro Petroleum and Asphalt Co., Phoenix, 1987-91; ptnr. Vinzoyl Petroleum Co., Phoenix, 1991—. Mem. ASCE, ASTM. Republican. Methodist. Achievements include development of a technology transfer business; research in modification of asphalt and asphalt mix to extend performance of pavements. Office: Vinzoyl Petroleum co 4665 S Ash Ave # G-6 Tempe AZ 85282-6764

DOYLE, WILFRED EMMETT, retired bishop; b. Calgary, Alta., Can., Feb. 18, 1913; s. John Joseph and Mary (O'Neill) D. B.A., U. Alta, 1935; D.C.L., U. Ottawa, Ont., Can., 1949. Ordained priest Roman Cath. Ch., 1938; chancellor Archdiocese Edmonton, Alta., Can., 1949-58; bishop Nelson, B.C., Can., 1958-89, bishop emeritus, 1989—; Chmn. bd. govs. Notre Dame U., Nelson, 1963-74. Address: 10661-82 Ave, Edmonton, AB Canada T6E 2A6

DOZIER, FLORA GRACE, civil and human rights activist, entrepreneur; b. Pineland, Tex., Apr. 5, 1937; d. Whitto G. and Agatha (Price) Grace; m. Robert Alan Dozier, Dec. 16, 1962 (div. Jan. 1967); 1 child, Martine Denise. AA in Real Estate, 1979; BA in Polit. Sci., Calif. State U., 1985; cert., Golden Gate U., 1993. Various positions Fed. Civil Svc., 1964-84; real estate saleswoman, 1971-77. Author: (poetry) Biscuits for My Man, 1997, Handwriting on the Wall, 1997. Mem. Merritt Coll. Community Ctr. Literacy Task Force; bd. dirs. Black Cowboys Assn.; advisory bd. Nat. Youth Sports Program; mem. legis. advocacy com. Alameda County Commn. on Aging. Recipient Parade Trophy Black Cowboy Assn., 1992, Golden Poet award, 1993, Golden Poet award World of Poetry, 1992, Franam Scholarship for Black Women San Francisco State U., 1992-93, Presidl. award Ctr. Black Concerns, 1994, Troy G. Grove Recognition award, cert. of recognition Calif. State Senate. Mem. NAACP, NAFE, NCNW, IPA, NCNW (life), Internat. Black Writers Assn., Ctr. for Black Concerns, Internat. Platform Assn., Oakland Black Writers Guild, Black United Front for Edn. Reform, Nat. Assn. of Black Reading and Lang. Educators (membership sec. Bay Area chpt.), Bay Area Black Journalists Assn., Help Abolish Legal Tyranny. Baptist. Avocations: shorthand speedwriting, languages, creative knitting, crocheting, sewing. Address: 484 Lake Park Ave # 442 Oakland CA 94610-2730

DRACHNIK, CATHERINE MELDYN, art therapist, artist, counselor; b. Kansas City, Mo., June 7, 1924; d. Gerald Willis and Edith (Gray) Weston; m. Joseph Brennan Drachnik, Oct. 6, 1946; children: Denise Elaine, Kenneth John. BS, U. Md., 1945; MA, Calif. State U., Sacramento, 1975. Lic. family and child counselor; registered art therapist. Art therapist Vincent Hall Retirement Home, McLean, Va., Fairfax Mental Health Day Treatment Ctr., McLean, Arlington (Va.) Mental Health Day Treatment Ctr., 1971-72, Hope for Retarded, San Jose, Calif., Sequoia Hosp., Redwood City, Calif., 1972-73; supervising tchr. adult edn. Sacramento Soc. Blind, 1975-77; ptnr. Sacramento Divsn. Mediation Svcs., 1981-82; instr. Calif. State U., Sacramento, 1975-82, 92-93, Coll. Notre Dame, Belmont, Calif., 1975-96; art therapist, mental health counselor Psych West Counseling Ctr. (formerly Eskaton Am. River Mental Health Clinic), Carmichael, Calif., 1975-93; instr. Sacramento City Coll., 1997—; instr. U. Utah, Salt Lake City, 1988-92; lectr. in field. Author: Interpreting Metaphors in Children's Drawings, 1995; one-woman shows include Vacaville (Calif.) Art Gallery, 1995, Dublier Gallery, Sacramento, 1997, Thistle Dew Gallery, Sacramento, 1998; exhibited in group shows Art of Calif. Mag., 1993, Calif. State Fair, Sacramento, 1995, 97, 98, Haggin Art Mus., Stockton, Calif. 1994, 95, 96, 97, 98, Watercolor West, Brea, Calif., 1998, West Valley Art Mus., Phoenix. Active charitable orgns. Mem. Am. Art Therapy Assn. (hon. life, pres. 1987-89), No. Calif. Art Therapy Assn. (hon. life), No. Calif. Arts, Inc., Nat. Art Edn. Assn., Am. Assn. Marriage and Family Therapists, Kappa Kappa Gamma Alumnae Assn. (pres. Sacramento Valley chpt. 1991-92), Alpha Psi Omega, Omicron Nu. Republican. Avocations: swimming, golf, theater. Home and Office: 4124 American River Dr Sacramento CA 95864-6025

DRAKE, E. MAYLON, academic administrator; b. Nampa, Idaho, Feb. 8, 1920; s. Austin Henry and Daisy Naomi (Smith) D.; m. Lois Elloise Noble, Oct. 12, 1940; children: E. Christopher, Cameron Lee. BS, U. So. Calif., Los Angeles, 1951, MS, 1954, EdD, 1963. Mgr. Frederick Post Co., San Francisco, 1943-47; asst. supt. Baldwin Park (Calif.) Schs., 1947-51; supt. Duarte (Calif.) Schs., 1951-64, Alhambra (Calif.) City Schs., 1964-70; dep. supt. Los Angeles County Schs., 1970-78; dir. Acad. Ednl. Mgmt., Los Angeles, 1978-80; pres. L.A. Coll. Chiropractic, Whittier, 1980-90, chancellor, 1990-93, chancellor emeritus, 1993—; adj. prof. U. So. Calif., 1964-90, bd. councilors, 1991—. Author Attaining Accountability in Schools, 1972; contbr. articles to profl. jours. Pres. Industry-Ednl. Council So. Calif., 1978; dir. United Way 1970; dir. Greater Los Angeles Zoo Bd., 1970; dir. Planned Parenthood of Pasadena, Calif., 1996; trustee L.A. Coll. Chiropractic Whittier, Calif., 1996. Recipient Am. Educator's medal Freedom Found.; named Educator of Yr. Los Angeles Chiropractic Soc., 1981. Mem. Coun. on Chiropractic Edn. (pres. 1988-90), Rotary (pres. Duarte 1954-56, bd. dirs. Alhambra 1964-70). Republican. Presbyterian. Avocation: performing arts. Home: Casa de Ville 206 445 S Los Robles Ave Pasadena CA 91101-3273 Office: LA Coll Chiropractic PO Box 1166 Whittier CA 90609-1166

DRAKE, LUCIUS CHARLES, JR., school administrator, university consultant, educator; b. Tacloban, The Philippines, June 29, 1946; s. Lucius Charles and Victoria (Badiles) D. BA, Fisk U., 1968; EdM, Temple U., 1970; EdD, U. No. Colo., 1995. Cert. sch. adminstr.; cert. guidance counselor. Math. tchr. Sch. Dist. of Phila., 1968-70, Gary (Ind.) City Schs., 1970-72, Dept. Defense Dependents Sch., Fed. Republic Germany and Okinawa, 1972-77; elemtary tchr. Dept. Defense Dependents Sch., Philippines, 1977-79; guidance counselor Dept. Defense Dependents Sch., Japan and Korea, 1979-83; asst. prin. Dept. Defense Dependents Sch., Seoul and Taegu, Korea, 1983-86; univ. cons. U. No. Colo., 1988-89; employment counselor Ft. Collins, Colo., 1989-90; asst. prin. Misawa, Japan, 1990-91, Philippines, 1991-92; sch. adminstr. Okinawa, 1992-93; instr./asst. prof. U. No. Colo., 1994-96; math tchr. Loveland, Colo., 1996-97; asst. prof. Midland Luth. Coll., 1997-98; dir. clin. svcs. Met. State Coll. Denver, 1998—; chmn. math dept. Sayre Jr. High Sch., Phila., 1969-70; math. curriculum rev. com., Dept. Defense Dependents Schs., Karlsruhe, Fed. Republic Germany, 1972-73; dir. Far East Basketball Tourney, Taegu, Korea, 1984-86; mem. regional mgmt. council, Dept. Defense Dependents Schs., Okinawa, 1985-86. Chairperson human rels. commn. Ft. Collins City Coun., 1990. Recipient Disting. Educator award IDEA Acad. Fellows, Denver, 1985. Fellow Am. Bd. Master Educators (disting.); mem. ASCD, Assn. Am. Sch. Adminstrs., Nat. Assn. Secondary Sch. Prins., Nat. Assn. Elem. Sch. Prins., Internat. Educator's Inst., Phi Delta Kappa, Alpha Phi Alpha (edn. sec. Seoul chpt. 1984-85). Democrat. Baptist. Avocations: weight tng., travel, chess, basketball, karate. Home: 3318 Hickok Dr Apt B Fort Collins CO 80526-2502 Office: Met State Coll Denver CO

DRAKE, RUSSELL MOORE, writer; b. San Angelo, Tex., Oct. 4, 1926; s. William Guy and Mary Clifton (Moore) D. B in Journalism, U. Tex., 1954; postgrad., Santa Monica City Coll., 1964, South Bay Adult Sch., 1980-83, Copper Mountain Campus, 1996-97. Reporter Wall Street Jour., Dallas, St. Louis, 1956-58, West Tex. Livestock Weekly, San Angelo, 1958-60; publicity mgr. Riverside Cement Co., L.A., 1960-67; asst. pub. rels. mgr. Northrop Corp., Hawthorne, Calif., 1967-70; co-founder, mgr. Ednl. Cassettes Corp., El Segundo, Calif., 1970-75; ind. writer, photographer L.A., Lake Elsinore, Yucca Valley, Calif., 1975—; speaker 3rd Annual Conf. The Ctr. for Big Bend Studies, 1996. Author (poems): Land of Man, 1987 (Golden Poet award, 1987, 88, award of Merit, 1987), The Aphrodite Song, 1988 (award of Merit, 1988, Golden Poet award, 1988, Silver Poet award, 1989). Active Friends of the Libr., Yucca Valley, Calif., 1998—, Ctr. for Big Bend Studies, 1996—. Democrat. Avocations: hiking, water aerobics. Office: PO Box 1213 Yucca Valley CA 92286

DRAPKIN, HERBERT, biology educator, consultant; b. N.Y.C., Oct. 26, 1916; m. Ethel Kaplan, Dec. 21, 1940; children: Steven, Larry. BS, CCNY, 1936; MA in Zoology, Columbia U., 1938; postgrad. in Meteorology, MIT, 1943. Cert. tchr., adminstr., supr., Calif. Rsch. asst. Columbia U. Med. Sch., N.Y.C., 1938-39; lab. asst. H.S. of Sci., Bronx, N.Y., 1939-40; tchr. biology CCNY, 1941-42, 48, 50, Bryant H.S., Queens, N.Y., 1948-54, C.C., Fullerton, Calif., 1954-82; sci. cons. County Schs. Offices, L.A. and Orange County, Calif., 1954-82; sci. tchr. Claremont (Calif.) Grad. Sch., 1956-58;

tchr. sci. tchg. methods UCLA Extension Divsn., 1955-60. Author: A Guide to Teaching and Learning, 1939, Life: Forms and Changes, 1968, Lab Manual: Biology, 1960, (autobiography) From Weather to Altitude--World War II, 1997; jour. editor Los Padres Nat. Forest Interpretive Assn., Goleta, Calif., 1988. Vol. tchr. Braille Inst., Santa Barbara, Calif., 1991—; founder Youth Sci. Ctr., Fullerton, 1961. 1st lt. USAF, 1943-44, New Guinea, Avn. Physiol. USAF Bases, 1945-46. Named Outstanding Tchr., Nat. Sci. Tchrs. Assn., 1953; NSF summer insts., 1959, 64, 65, 67. Avocations: walking, swimming, golf, poetry writing, sketching. Home: 241 Moreton Bay Ln Apt 4 Santa Barbara CA 93117-2235

DRAUR, RONALD ALVIN, retired cardiologist; b. Toledo, May 21, 1940; s. Albin and Ann Carolyn Draur; m. Georgina Anderson, 1988; children: Geri, Diana, Ronald, Thomas, Danel, Cherish. BS in Biology, Loyola U., Chgo., 1961, MD cum laude, 1965. Diplomate Am. Bd. Internal Medicine; diplomate Subspecialty Bd. Cardiovasc. Disease. Intern Mercy Hosp. and Med. Ctr., Chgo., 1965-66, resident internal medicine, 1966-67; resident internal medicine Edward G. Hines VA Hosp., Hines, Ill., 1967-68; cardiovasc. fellow Edward G. Hines VA Hosp., Hines, 1968-70; attending physician Nebr. Meth. Hosp., Omaha, 1972-96, dir. cardiovasc. svcs., 1974-95; ret.; mem., chmn. various med. staff coms. Meth. Hosp., Omaha, 1974-96; pres.-elect, pres. Nebr. Meth. Hosp., Omaha, 1991-95. Contbr. articles to profl. jours. Maj. USAF, 1970-72. Fellow Am. Coll. Cardiology (emeritus), Am. H eart Assn., Soc. for Cardiac Angiography and Interventions (emeritus); mem. Phi Sigma Tau, Alpha Sigma Nu. Republican. Roman Catholic. Avocations: photography, music, shooting, horseback riding, computers. E-mail: rdpicard@wavecom.net.

DRAZNIN, JULES NATHAN, journalism and public relations educator, consultant; b. Chgo., May 14, 1923; s. Charles G. and Goldie (Malach) D.; m. Shirley Bernstein, Apr. 9, 1950; children: Dean, Jody, Michael. Student, Wright City Coll., Chgo., 1941; BA in Journalism, Calif. State U., Northridge, 1978, MA in Higher Edn., 1984. Various journalism positions City News Bur., Chgo. Am., Chgo., 1941; promotions and publicity Balaban & Katz Theaters, Chgo., 1942-43; asst. dir pub. rels. Combined Jewish Appeal, Chgo., 1944; prin. J.N. Draznin Assocs., Chgo., 1945-50; account supr. Olian & Bronner Advt. Agy., Chgo., 1951-53; dir. advt. Chgo. Defender, Robert S. Abbott Pub. Co., 1953-55; freelance cons. Chgo., 1955-60; v.p. pub. rels. Harshe-Rotman, Chgo., 1956; pub. rels. dir. Abel and Lamensdorf Properties, Chgo., 1960-62; editor-in-chief, assoc. pub. Indsl. News Bender Publs., Calif., 1962-64; labor editor, spl. features writer Valley News and Green Sheet, Calif., 1964; ind. ins. agt. Calif., 1965-74; tch. pub. rels. UCLA and Calif. State U., L.A.; prof. journalism and pub. rels. L.A. Trade Tech. Coll., 1975-95, chmn. lang. arts dept., 1984-90; ret., 1995; prof. journalism and pub. rels. L.A. City Coll., L.A. Pierce Coll., L.A. Southwest Coll., East L.A. Coll., L.A. Mission Coll.; guest lectr. Calif. State U., Northridge. Coord. Mass Media AARP/Vote Vols., 1996—; apptd. state legis. com. AARP, 1998—. Mem. Assn. for Edn. in Journalism and Mass Comm., Soc. Profl. Journalists. Avocations: golf, classical music, travel.

DRECHSEL, EDWIN JARED, retired magazine editor; b. Bremen, Germany, Apr. 17, 1914; came to U.S., 1924, naturalized, 1935; s. William A. and Estelle Laura D.; m. Ilona Bolya, Aug. 12, 1972; children: John M., Barbara A. Grad., Dartmouth Coll., Amos Tuck Sch. Bus. Adminstrn., 1936. With Standard Oil Co., N.J., 1936-43; with U.S. News and World Report, 1943-79; regional editor, editorial ombudsman U.S. News and World Report, San Francisco, 1976-79. Author shipping company histories and fleet lists, catalogs of ship mail postal markings, including A Century of German Ship Posts, 1886-1986, 1987, Norddeutscher Lloyd, Bremen 1857-1970, vol. 1, 1994, vol. 2, 1995. Former chmn. Reed Sch. Bd., Marin County, Calif.; lay reader, former vestryman St. Stephen's Episcopal Ch., Belvedere, Calif., former mayor, City of Belvedere. Club: San Francisco Press. Home: 170 Hillcrest Rd Berkeley CA 94705-2846

DREHER, NICHOLAS C., lawyer; b. Michigan City, Ind., Nov. 15, 1948. AB magna cum laude, Harvard U., 1970; JD, Stanford U., 1973. Bar: Hawaii 1973. Ptnr. Cades Schutte Fleming & Wright, Honolulu, 1980—, chmn. of fin. and real estate dept., 1991—; vice-chmn. local rules com. U.S. Bankruptcy Ct. Mem. ABA (mem. com. foreclosure and related remedies sect. real property, probate and trust law 1991—), Am. Bankruptcy Inst. (chmn. Hawaii membership com. 1989—, mem. adv. com. bankruptcy rules 1990—), Hawaii State Bar Assn. (v.p. bankruptcy law sect. 1990-91, pres. 1991—, bd. dirs. 1990—). Office: Cades Schutte Fleming & Wright PO Box 939 1000 Bishop St Ste 1400 15th Fl Honolulu HI 96808*

DREHER, RICHARD CARL, telecommunications executive, educator; b. LaFayette, Ind., Sept. 22, 1958; s. Carl Edward and Joanne (Crowe) D.; m. Darcy Lynn Vail, July 4, 1981; children: Aubrey Joan, Austin Carl. AS, Arapahoe C.C., Littleton, Colo., 1981; BSEE, U. Colo., 1983. Registered profl. engr, Tex.; cert. automotive svc. excellence credintial. Entrepeneur Automotive Technician, Denver, 1978-83; lab. dir. U. Colo., Denver, 1981-83; lead elec. engr. Tex. Instr., Dallas, 1983-84; mem. tech. staff Adv. Bus. Comms., Dallas, 1984-87; Instr. Brookhaven Coll. of Automotive Tech., 1985-95; sr. sales support engr. DSC Comms., Plano, Tex., 1987-90; U.S. mgr., tech. sales support Ericsson Telecom., Richardson, Tex., 1990-95; dir. adv. tech. Pocket Comms., Washington, 1995-97, Evolving Sys. Inc., Englewood, Colo., 1997—; coord. telecom. Collin County C.C., Plano, Tex., 1992-95; staff mem., instr. Brookhaven Coll. Automotive Tech., 1985-97; instr. cont. edn. Ms. Automechanics various schs., 1984—. Contbr. articles to profl. jours. and public magazines on telecommunications, newspapers; inventor integrated circuit fault simulator, 1984; contr. textbook: Cellular and Personal Communications Services, 1996; co-author: (textbook) The Comprehensive Guide to Wireless Technology, 1998. Mem. com. Citizens to Keep Murphy (Tex.) Elem. Student Together, 1994-95. Recipient Outstanding Young Men of Am., 1988, IEEE Comm. Soc., Outstanding Svc., 1984, 89, 91. Mem. IEEE (sr., chmn. Comm. Soc., adv. and past pres. Dallas sect.), Soc. Automotive Engrs., Toastmasters Internat. (pres. 1983-95). Home: 3736 E Fair Pl Littleton CO 80121-3107 Office: Evolving Sys Inc 9777 Mt Pyramid Ct Englewood CO 80112-5903

DREIER, DAVID TIMOTHY, congressman; b. Kansas City, Mo., July 5, 1952; s. H. Edward and Joyce (Yeomans) D. BA cum laude, Claremont McKenna Coll., 1975; MA in Am. Govt., Claremont Grad. Sch., 1976. Dir. corp. rels. Claremont McKenna Coll., 1975-78; dir. mktg. and govt. rels. Indsl. Hydro, San Dimas, Calif., 1978-80; mem. 97th-105th Congresses (now 106th Congress) from 33rd (now 28th) Calif. dist., 1985-97; v.p. Dreier Devel. Co., Kansas City, Mo., 1985—; vice chmn. rules com., 1995—, chmn. rules of the house subcom.; bd. dirs. Internat. Rep. Inst.; mem. spkrs. steering com. Recipient Golden Bulldog award Watchdogs of the Treasury, 1981-97, Taxpayers Friends award Nat. Taxpayers Union, 1981-97, Clean Air Champion award Sierra Club, 1988. Office: US House of Reps 237 Cannon HOB Washington DC 20515-0528*

DREISBACH, JOHN GUSTAVE, investment banker; b. Paterson, N.J., Apr. 24, 1939; s. Gustave John and Rose Catherine (Koehler) D.; m. Janice Lynn Petitjean; children: John Gustave Jr., Christopher Erik. BA, NYU, 1963. With Dreyfus & Co., 1959-62, with Shields & Co., Inc., 1965-68, Model, Roland & Co., Inc., N.Y.C., 1968-72, F. Eberstadt & Co., Inc., N.Y.C., 1972-74; v.p. Bessemer Trust Co., 1974-78; pres. Community Housing Capital, Inc., 1978-80; chmn., pres. John G. Dreisbach, Inc., Santa Fe, 1980—, JGD Housing Corp., 1982—, JGD Mgmt. Corp., 1996—; gen. ptnr. numerous real estate ltd. partnerships; bd. dirs., pres. The Santa Fe Investment Conf., 1986—; assoc. Sta. KNME-TV. Mem. Santa Fe Community Devel. Commn. Served with USAFR, 1964. Mem. Internat. Assn. for Fin. Planning, Nat. Assn. Securities Dealers, Inc., NYU Alumni Assn., N.Mex. First, Friends of Vieilles Maisons Francaises Inc., Mensa, Santa Fe C. of C., Augustan Soc. Republican. Mem. Episcopalian Ch. and Lutheran Ch. Clubs: St. Bartholomew's Community, Essex, Hartford, Amigos del Alcalde. Avocations: travel, art, arch-design appreciation, classical music, Shotokan karate (1st Dan). Fax: 505-989-7381. Home: La Genvrie, La Genvrie, 49140 Jarze France Office: 369 Montezuma Ave Santa Fe NM 87501-2626

DRENNAN, MICHAEL ELDON, banker; b. Yakima, Wash., June 24, 1946; s. George Eldon and Jane (Nilsson) D.; m. Alice Marie Seabolt, May 13, 1972; children: Brian, David. BS in Fin., U. Oreg., 1968; grad., Pacific Coast Banking Sch. U. Wash., 1981. Ops. officer First State Bank, Aloha, Oreg., 1972-73, ops., loan officer First State Bank, Portland, Oreg., 1973-74; asst. mgr. First State Bank, Milwaukie, Oreg., 1974-76; asst. v.p. Citizens Bank, Corvallis, Oreg., 1976-80, v.p., 1980-81; pres., chief exec. officer Bank of Corvallis, 1981-87; v.p. dist. mgr. U.S. Bank, Corvallis, Oreg., 1987; sr. v.p. market area mgr. U.S. Bank, Bend, Oreg., 1988-94; sr. v.p., dist. mgr. U.S. Bank, Eugene, Oreg., 1994-98; v.p. bus. banking Liberty Fed. Bank, 1998—; bd. dirs. Cascades W. Fin. Svcs. Bd. dirs. United Way Benton County, 1984-88; trustee Good Samaritan Hosp. Found., 1984-88; bd. dirs. Jr. Achievement of Benton County, 1983-85, treas, 1984-85, mem. exec. bd., 1984-85; mem. budget comm. Corvallis Sch. Dist., 1987; bd. dirs. Benton County Family YMCA, 1978-80, sec. 1979, mem. fin. com., 1978-80, mem. pers. com., 1979, active sustaining membership dr.; bd. dirs. Cmty. Club, 1978-83, pres., 1978, treas., 1979-80; active Corvallis Ambs., 1976-88; mem. mgmt. com. Corvallis Conf. and Visitors Bur., 1982-85; fund raising chmn. Com. City Improvement Levy, 1980; mem. exec. com. Pack 17 Boy Scouts Am., 1984-87, treas., 1984-87; mem. adv. bd. Ctrl. Oreg. Econ. Devel. Corp., 1988-90, bd. dirs., exec. bd., treas., 1991-93, v.p., 1993, pres., 1994; bd. dirs. Regional Arts Coun. of Ctrl. Oreg., treas., 1989-92; bd. dirs. Ctrl. Oreg. Air Svc. Task Force, 1989-94, chmn. airline rels. com., 1990; mem. Bend Bus. Assistance Team, 1989-90, United Way Deschutes County, chmn. loaned exec. recruitment, 1992; mem. planning com. St. Charles Med. Ctr. Found., 1993, dir. adminstrn. capital fund drive, 1993; mem. adv. bd. Deschutes County Fair, 1993-94; bd. dirs. Birth to Three, Eugene, 1994—, treas., 1995-96, pres.-elect., 1996-97, pres. 1997-98; bd. dirs. Lane Arts Coun., 1995-98, treas. exec. bd., 1996-98; bd. dirs. Conv. and Visitors Assn. Lane County, 1995-, treas. 1998; bd. dirs. Eugene-Springfield Metro Partnership, 1995—; chmn. maj. firms campaign cabinet United Way of Lane County, 1996-97; bd. dirs. Oreg. Bach Festival, 1999—. Lt. USN, 1968-71. Named Jr. First Citizen, Corvallis, 1980. Mem. Bend C. of C. (chmn. mem. dir. task force 1988, chmn. mem. svcs. coun. 1989, chmn. chamber forums com. 1990, Outstanding Leadership award 1989), Corvallis C. of C. (v.p. fin. 1980-83, pres. 1985-86, chmn. bd. dirs. 1986-87, Econ. Devel. award 1978, Chmn. of Bd. award 1979, George award 1980-81, Devel. award 1983), Am. Inst. Banking (cert.), Rotary (bd. dirs. Corvallis club 1981-87, Bend 1988-94, Eugene, 1994—), Eugene Execs. Assn., Chi Phi, Alpha Kappa Psi, Beta Gamma Sigma. Home: 2574 W 28th Ave Eugene OR 97405-1456 Office: US Bank PO Box 10308 Eugene OR 97440-2308

DRESKIN, WENDY, environmental educator; b. N.Y.C., Feb. 21, 1950; d. Philip Rosenblatt and Freda Naomi (Osserman) Birnbaum; m. William Alan Dreskin, June 21, 1974; children: Tanya, Leila. BA, U. Calif., Berkeley, 1970. Presch. dir. The Learning Exch., Sausalito, San Anselmo, Calif., 1973-78; freelance author San Anselmo, 1978-92; environ. nature educator Terwilliger Nature Edn. Ctr., San Anselmo, 1993-96; spkr. in field Calif., 1996—. Co-author: (with W. Dreskin) The Day Care Decision, 1983; contbr. chpts. to books, articles to popular publs. Recipient tchr. recognition award Johns Hopkins U. Inst. Advancement of Youth, 1998. Mem. Calif. Native Plant Soc., Audubon Soc., Calif. Lichen Soc., San Francisco Mycol. Soc. E-mail: 70762.3212@compuserve.com.

DRESSLER, ALAN MICHAEL, astronomer; b. Cin., Mar. 23, 1948; s. Charles and Gay (Stein) Dressler. BA in Physics, U. Calif., Berkeley, 1970; PhD in Astronomy, U. Calif., Santa Cruz, 1976. Carnegie Instn. of Washington fellow Hale Obs., Pasadena, Calif., 1976-78, Las Campanas fellow, 1978-81; sci. staff Carnegie Obs. (formerly Mt. Wilson and Las Campanas Obs., formerly Hale Obs.), Pasadena, 1981—, acting assoc. dir., 1988-89. Contbr. to sci. jours. Fellow Am. Acad. Arts and Scis.; mem. NAS, Am. Astron. Soc. (councilor 1989-91, Pierce prize 1983), Internat. Astron. Union. Office: Carnegie Obs 813 Santa Barbara St Pasadena CA 91101-1232

DREVER, MARK, food products executive; b. 1956. BA, U. the Pacific; JD, Loyola U. Atty. Fresh Express Inc., Salinas, Calif., 1988—, pres. Office: Fresh Express Inc PO Box 80599 1020 Merrill St Salinas CA 93912*

DREW, CHARLES MILTON, chemist; b. McKinney, Tex., Feb. 13, 1921; s. Andrew Everett and Lutie Lella (Weger) D.; divorced; children: Darrell Everett, Donna Lee, Lynn Milton, Carl Allen. BS, U. N. Tex., 1943. Supr. chemist Columbia Southern, Corpus Christi, Tex., 1943-47; research scientist Naval Weapons Ctr., China Lake, Calif., 1947-70; cons. U. Ariz., Tucson, 1980—. Author: Principles of Gas Chromatography, 1959; contbr. articles to profl. jours.; patentee in field. Mem. Rsch. Soc. Am., Soaring Soc. Am., Colo. West Soaring Club, Glider Club (pres. China Lake, Calif. chpt. 1967-70), Rockhounds Club (pres. local chpt. 1949-50), Sigma Xi. Avocations: soaring, hot air balloons, nature, creative glass working. Home: 1420 Walker View Rd Wellington NV 89444-9326

DREW, SHARON LEE, sociologist; b. L.A., Aug. 11, 1946; d. Hal Bernard and Helen Elizabeth (Hammond) D.; children: Keith, Charmagne. BA, Calif. State U., Long Beach, 1983; postgrad., Calif. State U., Dominguez Hills, 1988—. Clerical support Compton (Calif.) Unified Sch. Dist., 1967-78; case worker L.A. County Dept. Pub. Social Svcs., 1978—. Den mother Boy Scouts Am., Compton, 1971-72; employee vol. Dominguez Sr. H.S., Compton, 1972-73; project coord. Calif. Tomorrow's Parent Edn. Leadership Devel. Project, 1990; mem. L.A. Caregiver's Network, 1993-94; vol. Calif. State U., Dominguez Hill's Older Adult Ctr., 1994. Recipient cert. Calif. Tomorrow-Parent Edn. Leadership Devel. Project, 1990. Mem. Am. Statis. Assn. (So. Calif. chpt.), Internat. Soc. Exploration of Tchg. Alternatives, Calif. Sociol. Assn. (1st gov. at large grad. student 1990-91), Dominguez Hills Gerontology Assn. (chairperson 1990-91), Sociology of Edn. Assn., Alpha Kappa Delta (Xi chpt. treas. 1992-95). Home: 12119 Elva Ave Los Angeles CA 90059-3253

DREWS, JOSEPH HARVEY, administrator; b. Milw., July 9, 1939; s. Joseph Frank and Hazel Julia D.; divorced; children: Shane, Jason, Aaron. BS, Ariz. State U., 1977. Chem. analyst Hella Mining Co., Casa Grande, Ariz., 1977; prodn. mgr. Rsch. Labs., Globe, Ariz., 1977-79; plant, prodn. mgr. Naturalife Labs., Torrance, Calif., 1979-82; mfg. mgr. Vita-Fresh Vitamin Co., Garden Grove, Calif., 1982-84; plant mgr. Gen. Rsch. Labs., Northridge, Calif., 1984-85; plant mgr., prodn. mgr. Naturalife Labs., Torrance, 1985—. Avocation: computer spreadsheet programs. Office: Naturalife Labs 20433 Earl St Torrance CA 90503-2414

DREXEL, BARON JEROME, lawyer; b. Miami Beach, Fla., Sept. 3, 1954; s. Gustave L. and Dorris J. (Haas) D. AA, U. Fla., 1973; BA, U. Calif. Berkeley, 1979; JD cum laude, U. Miami, 1985. Bar: Fla. 1985, Calif. 1987, U.S. Ct. Appeals (9th and 11th cir.), U.S. dist. Ct. (no, mid. and so. dists.) Calif., U.S. Dist. Ct. (no. and ctrl. dists.) Calif. Survey crew mem. U.S. Forest Svc., Hayfork, Calif., 1979; sales rep. real estate Allen Morris Co., Miami, Fla., 1981-82; assoc. Shutts & Bowen, Miami, 1985-88, Lasky, Haas, Cohler & Munter, San Francisco, 1988-89, Aiken, Kramer & Cummings, Oakland, Calif., 1989-92, Bostwick & Tehin, San Francisco, 1992-95; pvt. practice Oakland, 1995—. Recipient J.B. Spence award U. Miami Law Rev. Mem. ATLA, Order of Coif. Avocations: computers, travel, photography, chess, writing poetry. Office: 312 Lee St # 1 Oakland CA 94610-4356

DREXLER, KENNETH, lawyer; b. San Francisco, Aug. 2, 1941; s. Fred and Martha Jane (Cunningham) D.; BA, Stanford U., 1963; JD, UCLA, 1969. Bar: Calif. 1970. Assoc., David S. Smith, Beverly Hills, Calif., 1970, McCutchen, Doyle, Brown and Enersen, San Francisco, 1970-77; assoc. Chickering & Gregory, San Francisco, 1977-80, ptnr., 1980-82; ptnr. Drexler & Leach, San Rafael, Calif., 1982—. Served with AUS, 1964-66. Mem. Calif. State Bar (resolutions com. conf. of dels. 1979-83, chmn. 1982-83, adminstrn. justice com. 1983-89, chmn. 1987-88, adv. mem. 1990—), Marin County Bar Assn. (bd. dirs. 1985-87), Bar Assn. San Francisco (dir. 1980-81), San Francisco Barristers Club (pres. 1976, dir. 1975-76), Marin Conservation League (bd. dirs. 1985-97, 98—). Office: 1330 Lincoln Ave Ste 300 San Rafael CA 94901-2143

DREXLER, KIM ERIC, researcher, author; b. Oakland, Calif., Apr. 25, 1955; s. Allan Barry and Hazel Edna (Gassmann) D.; m. Christine Louise Peterson, June 18, 1981. BS in Interdisciplinary Sci., MIT, 1977, MS in Engring., 1979, PhD in Molecular Nanotech., 1991. Researcher, author, lectr., inventor Cambridge, Mass., 1980-85; researcher, author, lectr., cons. Palo Alto, Calif., 1985—; rsch. affiliate MIT Space Lab, Cambridge, 1980-86, MIT Artificial Intelligence Lab, Cambridge, 1986-87; sr. rsch. fellow Inst. for Molecular Mfg., 1991—; vis. scholar Stanford (Calif.) U. Computer Sci. Dept., 1986-92; bd. dirs., chmn. The Foresight Inst., Palo Alto, 1986—. Author: Engines of Creation, 1986, Nanosystems, 1992 (Assn. Am. Pubs. Best Computer Science Book, 1992); co-author: Unbounding the Future, 1991; contbr. articles to profl. jours.; inventor high performance solar sail, method for processing and fabricating metals in space. Sec. bd. dirs. L5 Soc., Tucson, 1981, bd. dirs., 1979-86, advisor, 1979-86, co-editor jour., 1983-84; bd. dirs. Nat. Space Soc., 1986-96. Grad. fellow NSF, MIT, 1977; recipient Space Pioneer award for Scientist/Engr., Nat. Space Soc., 1991, Kilby Young Innovator award Kilby Found., Dallas, 1993. Mem. AAAS, Am. Vacuum Soc., Am. Chemistry Soc. Office: The Foresight Inst PO Box 61058 Palo Alto CA 94306-6058

DREXLER, MILLARD S., retail executive; b. 1944; married. Exec. v.p. merchandising, pres. Gap Stores div. Gap Inc., San Bruno, Calif., from 1983; now pres., bd. dirs. The Gap Inc., San Bruno; pres., chief exec. officer Ann Taylor Co. Office: The Gap Inc 1 Harrison St San Francisco CA 94105-1602

DREYFOOS, DALE LEROY, director, music educator, singer, actor; b. Atlanta, June 20, 1956; s. Wallace David and Jeanne (Pinkerson) D. BM in Voice, Fla. State U., 1978; MM in Opera, U. Tex., 1980. Asst. stage dir. Des Moines Metro Opera, Indianola, Iowa, 1980, Va. Opera, Norfolk, 1981, Miss. Opera, Jackson, 1981-82; resident stage dir. Birmingham (Ala.) Civic Opera, 1982-86; asst. stage dir. Ctrl. City (Colo.) Opera, 1983, Lyric Opera Chgo., 1983; artistic dir. Charleston Opera Co., 1986-87; dir. edn. Opera Carolina, Charlotte, 1987-94; assoc. prof. opera Ariz. State U., Tempe, 1994—; stage artistry instr. Am. Inst. Musical Studies, Graz, Austria, 1996, 98; guest lectr. Ariz. Opera, Phoenix, 1995—; actor, educator Ednl. Mgmt. Group, Phoenix, 1995-97; educator, lectr. Opera Carolina Theatre, Charlotte, 1987-94; cons. Ariz. Opera Edn. Dept., 1997—. Author: (ednl. music drama) A Visit With Mr. and Mrs. Bach, 1985, (ednl. music drama) A Visit with Amadeus, 1986; co-author: (ednl. music drama) The Sound of Moosic, 1991; tenor soloist Classical Music Seminar, 1982; guest narrator Ala. Symphony, Birmingham, 1984-85. Avocations: genealogy, singing, acting. Office: Ariz State U PO Box 405 Tempe AZ 85280-0405

DREYFUSS, JOHN ALAN, health facility administrator; b. N.Y.C., Dec. 1, 1933; s. Henry and Doris (Marks) D.; m. Katharine Elizabeth Rich, June 28, 1958; children: Karen Elizabeth, James Henry, Kimberly Anne, Katharine Marks. BS in Biology, Boston U., 1959. Tchr. schs. in Montclair, Pebble Beach and Los Olivos, Calif., 1959-63; reporter, editor San Luis Obispo (Calif.) Telegram Tribune, 1963-64; advt. salesman Ventura County (Calif.) Star-Free Press, 1964-66; gen. assignment writer L.A. Times, 1966-69, 73-75, higher edn. writer, 1969-72, environment writer, 1972-73, architecture and design critic, 1975-84, feature writer View sect., 1984-87, graphics editor View sect., 1987-89, asst. to assoc. editor, 1989-93; v.p., CFO, sec. J. Dreyfuss & Assocs., Santa Monica, Calif., 1993-94; newswriter Sta. KTLA-TV, L.A., 1994-95; pub. info. officer Jonsson Comprehensive Cancer Ctr./UCLA, 1995-96, dir. for comm., 1996-98, dir. for planning and comm., 1998—. With U.S. Army, 1953-55. Office: UCLA Jonsson Comprehensive Cancer Ctr 8-684 Factor Bldg Los Angeles CA 90095-1781

DRIGGS, MARGARET, educator; b. Kansas City, Kans., June 30, 1909; d. William Foster and Lillian Edith (Landers) Brazier; m. J.W. Quarrier, Nov. 26, 1933 (div. July 1945); children: John Chilton, Philip Harrington, Camille Elizabeth; m. Howard R. Driggs, Sept. 26, 1948 (dec.). AB, U. Kans., 1930; postgrad. Hofstra Coll., 1960, Grad. Sch. Libr. Sci., Pratt Inst., 1964-65. Contbr. Kansas City Star and Johnson County (Kans.) Herald, 1930-33; editor Am. Trails Series, filmstrips; nat. dir. pub. rels. Am. Pioneer Trails Assn., 1948; chmn. pub. rels. NYU Faculty Women's Club, 1950-54; nat. 1st v.p. Assn. Parents and Friends Kings Point, 1957-58; judge Nat. Svc. Acad. Debate Tournament, 1956; hostess Kings Point Congl. Com., 1957; mem. Nat. Coun. Coll. Publs. Advisers, 1958; adminstrv. asst. to sec., dir. pub. rels. Hofstra Coll., 1956-61, staff adviser Nexus (yearbook), 1961; mem. faculty Westover Sch., Middlebury, Conn., 1964-65; dir. devel. pub. relations, asst. to dean Cathedral Sch. of St. Mary, Garden City, N.Y., 1965, also yearbook adviser; installed Duchess of Richelieu collection St. Mary's Libr., 1973; co-chmn. guides N.J. Gov.'s Mansion Morven, 1975-82; chmn. docents N.J. Hist. Soc. at Morven, Princeton, 1982-86; curator Driggs Collection of Americana. Represented in the Native North Am. Women Exhbn., Skillman Libr., Lafayette Coll., 1992. Mem. women's coun. Hofstra Coll., 1959-60; mem. U.S. Com. for UN Children's Fund, 1957; mem. Friends of Princeton U. Libr., 1975, Friends of the Winston Churchill Meml. and Lib., Westminster Coll., 1989; mem. Princeton Med. Ctr. Aux.; chair civilian hostesses 15th Ann. U.S. Army Mus. Conf., Princeton, 1986, Salute to Hall of Fame Ceremony the Voice of Am. broadcast Gould Meml. Libr., NYU, 1953; mem. Am. Farm Trust, 1992; mem. Denver Pub. Lib. Friends Found. Recipient Disting. Service citation Am. Pioneer Trails Assn., 1943, Columbia Scholastic Press Assn. medal, 1970, pin for vol. work in Princeton, 1976, French-Am. Alliance medal, cert. and hist. house tile award N.J. Hist. Soc., 1984; Margaret Brazier Driggs Collection of Americana established at U. Kans., 1953, at Hofstra Coll., 1961; advisor on placement donors' collections; Mem. Denver Pub. Lib. Friends Fdn., Colo. Hist. Soc., Governor's Mansion Guides, ALA, Internat. Platform Assn., Assn. Coll. and Rsch. Librs., Hist. Soc. Princeton, Nat. Trust Hist. Preservation, Smithsonian Assocs., Nat. Parks and Cons. Assn., Women's Bd. of N.J. Hist. Soc., Met. Mus. Art, Women's Coll. Club Princeton, Amiga of Orgn. of Am. States, NYU Faculty Club (hon. life), Libr. of Congress (charter assoc. 1994), Present Day Club (Princeton), Gold Medal Club (pin and citation for achievement 1930-1980, Kans.), Learned Club, Pi Delta Epsilon (grand councilman 1960-61). Editor: New Light on Old Glory, 1950, Pitch Pine Tales, 1951, Nick Wilson, 1951, George, The Handcart Boy, 1952, The Old West Speaks, 1956, When Grandfather Was a Boy and Western Cowkid, 1957 (all by Howard R. Driggs); contbg. editor Nat. Assn. Ind. Schs. Archives, Harvard, 1965; editor and photographer Vive Rochambeau, Vive Washington. Home: 2943 W 116th Pl Apt 107 Denver CO 80234-2519

DRINKWARD, CECIL W., construction company executive. CEO Hoffman Corp., Portland, Oreg. Office: Hoffman Corp PO Box 1300 Portland OR 97207*

DRISCOLL, DAVID LEE, chiropractor; b. Storm Lake, Iowa, Aug. 3, 1954; s. Glenn Francis and Jeannine Ann (Layer) D.; m. Joan Marie Valle, Sept. 8, 1973; children: Jennifer Marie, Matthew Bryan. D Chiropractic, Logan Coll. Chiropractic, Chesterfield, Mo., 1978. Pvt. practice Colorado Springs, 1978—. Fellow Internat. Biocranial Acad. (assoc. instr., ednl. dir.), Internat. Acad. Clin. Acupuncture; mem. Am. Chiropractic Assn., Colo. Chiropractic Assn., El Paso County Chiropractic Assn., Internat. Biocranial Acad. (ednl. dir.). Republican. Roman Catholic. Avocations: volleyball, golf, reading. Home: 813 Crown Ridge Dr Colorado Springs CO 80904-1731 Office: Driscoll Chiropractic 1819 W Colorado Ave Colorado Springs CO 80904-3836

DRISCOLL, MICHAEL P., bishop; b. Long Beach, Calif., Aug. 8, 1939. Student, St. John's Sem., Camarillo, Calif.; MSW, U. So. Calif., 1975. Ordained priest Roman Cath. Ch., 1965, titular bishop of Massita. Aux. bishop Orange, Calif., 1990—. Office: Chancery Office 2811 E Villa Real Dr Orange CA 92867-1932

DRISKILL, JAMES LAWRENCE, minister; b. Rustburg, Va., Aug. 18, 1920; s. Elijah Hudson and Annie Pharr (Carwile) D.; m. Ethel Lillian Cassel, May 28, 1949; children: Edward Lawrence, Mary Lillian. BA, Pa. State U., 1946; BD, San Francisco Theol. Sem., 1949; ThM, Princeton Sem., 1957; S.T.D., San Francisco Theol. Sem., 1969. Ordained minister in Presbyn. Ch., 1949. Missionary Presbyn. Ch. USA, Japan, 1949-72; stated supply pastor Madison Square Presbyn. Ch., San Antonio, 1973; minister Highland Presbyn. Ch., Maryville, Tenn., 1973-82; supply pastor of Japanese-Am. chs. Presbyn. Ch. USA, Long Beach, Calif., Hollywood, Calif., Altadena, Calif., 1984—; vis. prof. religion dept. Trinity U., 1972-73. Author: Adventures in Senior Living, 1997, Christmas Stories from Around the World, 1997, Worldwide Mission Stories for Young People, 1996, Cross Cultural Marriages and the Church, 1995, Mission Stories from Around the World, 1994, Japan Diary, 1993, Mission Adventures in Many Lands, 1992; contbr. articles to profl. jours. Mem. Sierra Club, Calif., 1988—; trustee Osaka (Japan) Girls Sch., 1952-65, Seikyo Gakuen Christian Sch., Japan,

1953-92. With USN, 1943-46. Mem. Am. Acad. Religion, Presbyn. Writers Guild. Democrat. Home and Office: 1420 Santo Domingo Ave Duarte CA 91010-2632

DROWN, EUGENE ARDENT, federal agency administrator; b. Ellenburg, N.Y., Apr. 25, 1915; s. Frank Arthur and Jessie Kate D.; BS, Utah State U., 1938; postgrad. Mont. State U., 1939-40; PhD in Pub. Adminstrn., U. Beverly Hills, 1979; m. Florence Marian Munroe, Mar. 5, 1938; children: Linda Harriett Oneto, Margaret Ruth Lunn. Park ranger Nat. Park Svc., Yosemite Nat. Park, 1940-47; forest ranger U.S. Forest Svc., Calif. Region, 1948-56; forest mgr. and devel. specialist U.S. Bur. Land Mgmt., Calif., 1956—; forest engring. cons., 1970—; R&D coord. U.S. Army at U. Calif., Davis., 1961-65. Mem. adv. bd. Sierra Coll., Rocklin, Calif., 1962—; active Boy Scouts Am.; instr. ARC, 1954—. With AUS, 1941-45. Decorated Bronze Star, Silver Star; registered profl. engr., profl. land surveyor, profl. forester, Calif. Recipient Nat. Svc. medal ARC, 1964. Mem. Nat. Soc. Profl. Engrs., Soc. Am. Foresters, Am. Inst. Biol. Scientists, Ecol. Soc. Am., Res. Officers Assn. U.S., NRA, Internat. Rescue and First Aid Assn., Internat. Platform Assn., Bulldog Sentinels of Superior Calif., Masons, Shriners. Methodist. Home: 5624 Bonniemae Way Sacramento CA 95824-1402

DROZD, LEON FRANK, JR., lawyer; b. Victoria, Tex., Sept. 11, 1948; s. Leon Frank and Dorothy Lucille (Smith) D.; BBA, Tex. A&M U., 1971; J.D., U. Denver, 1979. Bar: Colo., Calif., U.S. Dist. Ct. Colo. U.S. Dist. Ct. (no. dist.) Calif., U.S. Ct. Appeals (9th and 10th cirs.). Legis. asst. U.S. Ho. of Reps., also Dem. Caucus, Washington, 1971-74, chief clk. com. on sci. and tech., 1974-75; asst. to dean for devel. Coll. Law, U. Denver, 1975-79; v.p. Braddock Publs., Inc., Washington, 1975-79; land and legal counsel Chevron Shale Oil Co., Chevron Resources Co., 1980-87, ins. div., 1987-88; sr. counsel Chevron Corp. Law Dept. 1987—, Chevron Overseas Petroleum and White Nile Petroleum Co. Ltd. (Sudan), 1983, Colo. elector Anderson/Lucey Nat. Unity Campaign, 1980. Mem. ABA, Colo. Bar. Assn., San Francisco Bar Assn., Fed. Bar Assn., Am. Trial Lawyers Assn., Denver C. of C. (steering com. 1981-82). Office: Chevron Corp Law Dept PO Box 7141 555 Market St San Francisco CA 94105-2870

DROZDEK, JOSIP, computer specialist; b. NoviSad, Yugoslavia, Sept. 5, 1963; s. Lodvik and Mischelle (Miketin) D. Student, James Madison H.S., Portland, Oreg. Computer chip maker AVX Co., 1994—. Contbr. poetry to lit. publs. Home: 6215 NE 15th Ave Portland OR 97211-4805

DRUCKER, PETER FERDINAND, writer, consultant, educator; b. Vienna, Austria, Nov. 19, 1909; came to U.S., 1937, naturalized, 1943; s. Adolph Bertram and Caroline D.; m. Doris Schmitz, Jan. 16, 1937; children: Kathleen Romola, J. Vincent, Cecily Anne, Joan Agatha. Grad., Gymnasium, Vienna, 1927; LLD, U. Frankfurt, 1931; 25 hon. doctorates. Economist London Banking House, 1933-37; Am. adviser for Brit. banks, Am. corr. Brit. newspapers, 1937-42; cons. maj. bus. corps. U.S., 1940—; prof. philosophy, politics Bennington Coll., 1942-49; prof. mgmt. NYU, 1950-72, chmn. mgmt. area, 1957-62; Clarke prof. social sci. Claremont Grad. Sch. (Calif.), 1971—; prof. dept. art Pomona Coll., Calif., 1979-85. Author: The End of Economic Man, 1939, new edit. 1993, The Future of Industrial Man, 1941, new edit. 1994, Concept of the Corporation, 1946, new edit., 1993, The New Society, 1950, new edit., 1992, Practice of Management, 1954, new edit., 1992, America's Next Twenty Years, 1957, The Landmarks of Tomorrow, 1959, new edit., 1996, Managing for Results, 1964, new edit., 1996, The Effective Executive, 1966, new edit., 1996, The Age of Discontinuity, 1969, new edit., 1992, Technology; Management and Society, 1970, Men, Ideas and Politics, 1971, Management: Tasks, Responsibilities, Practices, 1974, new edit., 1992, The Unseen Revolution: How Pension Fund Socialism Came to America, 1976, new edit. (new title: The Pension Fund Revolution), 1995, People and Performance, 1977, Management, An Overview, 1978, Adventures of a Bystander, 1979, new. edit., 1998, Managing in Turbulent Times, 1980, new edit., 1992, Toward the Next Economics and Other Essays, 1981, (essays) The Changing World of the Executive, 1982, Innovation and Entrepreneurship, 1985, new edit., 1996, The Frontiers of Management, 1986, 5th edit., 1998, The New Realities, 1989, Managing the Non-Profit Organization, 1990, (essays) Managing for the Future, 1992, (essays) The Ecological Vision, 1992, Post Capitalist Society, 1993, (essays) Managing in a Time of Great Change, 1995, 4th edit., 1998, Drucker on Asia: A Dialogue With Isao Nagauchi, 1997, Peter Drucker on the Profession of Management, 1998, Management Challenges for the 21st Century, 1999; (fiction) The Last of All Possible Worlds, 1982, The Temptation to Do Good, 1984; co-author: The Song of the Brush: Japanese painting, 1979; producer: movie series The Effective Executive, 1969, Managing Discontinuity, 1971, The Manager and the Organization, 1977, Managing for Tomorrow, 1981; producer 25 audiocassette series The Non-Profit Drucker, 1988. Recipient gold medal Internat. U. Social Studies, Rome, 1957; Wallace Clark Internat. Mgmt. medal, 1963; Taylor Key Soc. for Advancement Mgmt., 1967; Presdl. citation NYU, 1969; CIOS Internat. Mgmt. gold medal, 1972; Chancellor's medal Internat. Acad. Mgmt., 1987. Fellow AAAS (council), Internat., Am., Irish Acads. Mgmt., Brit. Inst. Mgmt. (hon.), Am. Acad. Arts and Scis.; mem. Soc. for History Tech. (pres. 1965-66), Nat. Acad. Pub. Adminstrn. (hon.), Peter F. Drucker Found. Non Profit Mgmt. (hon. chmn).

DRUMMOND, MARSHALL EDWARD, business educator, university administrator; b. Stanford, Calif., Sept. 14, 1941; s. Kirk Isaac and Fern Venice (McDeritt) D. BS, San Jose State U., 1964, MBA, 1969; EdD, U. San Francisco, 1979. Adj. prof. bus. and edn. U. San Francisco, 1975-81; adj. prof. bus. and info. systems San Francisco State U., 1981-82; prof. MIS, Ea. Wash. U., Cheney, 1985—, exec. dir. info. resources, 1988, assoc. v.p. adminstrv. svcs., chief info. officer, 1988-89, v.p. adminstrv. svcs., 1989-90, exec. v.p., 1990, pres., 1990—; cons. Sch. Bus., Harvard Coll., U. Ariz. Contbg. editor Diebold Series; contbr. articles to profl. jours. Democrat. Avocations: running, water sports. Home: 10012 S Stangland Rd Medical Lake WA 99022-9409

DRURY, DORIS MARIE, economics educator, consultant, researcher; b. Louisville, Nov. 18, 1926; d. Coleman F. and Ursula P. (Darst) D. B.S., U. Louisville, 1955, M.B.A., 1957; M.A., Ind. U., Bloomington, 1962, Ph.D., 1964; postgrad., U. Denver Coll. Law, 1973-74. Asst. prof. econs. U. Wyo., Laramie, 1962-63; assoc. prof. La. State U., 1963-65; prof. econs. U. Denver, 1965-90, chmn. div. research, 1968-71, chmn. econs., 1972-79; John Sullivan prof., exec. dir. MBA programs Regis U., 1990-97; pres. Ctr. Bus. and Econs. for the Future, Littleton, Colo., 1997—; dir. Fed. Res. Bank, Kansas City, 1980-84, chmn. bd., 1985, chmn. audit, 1980-83; dir., chmn. audit com. Pub. Service Co., Denver, 1979—; dir., founder Women's Bank, Denver, 1977-78; dir. Colo. Nat. Bankshares, Equitable of Iowa; pres., chief exec. officer Ctr. for Bus. and Econ. Forecasting, Inc. Author: Accidents in Coal Producing Countries, 1964, Phase II Economic Controls, 1972, Key Public Economic Issues, 1971, Construction Industry in Colorado, 1969, 83—; editor quarterly rev. Colo. economy and econs. perspective. Mem. Gov.'s Blue Ribbon Panel on Econ. Planning, Colo., 1979-81; bd. dirs. YWCA, Denver, 1979-81. Recipient Disting. Teaching Specialist Commendation, U. Denver, 1973; Resources of the Future, Inc. fellow, 1961-62. Mem. Nat. Assn. Bus. Economists, Am. Econ. Assn., Denver C. of C. Home: 5185 S Clarkson St Littleton CO 80121-1206 Office: Ctr for Business and Economics for the Future Ste 201 1100 W Littleton Blvd Littleton CO 80120*

DRUTCHAS, GERRICK GILBERT, investigator; b. Detroit, Sept. 23, 1953; s. Gilbert Henry and Elaine Marie (Rutkowski) D.; 1 child, Gilbert Henry II. BA, Mich. State U., 1975; postgrad., U. Redlands, 1983-85. Pres. Argentum Publs., L.A., 1986—; dir. Le Baron Investigations, Pasadena. Dir. Childrens Welfare Found. Sgt. USAR, 1981-85. Named Baron, Royal House of Alabona-Ostrogojsk, 1992. Mem. Order of the Swan (chevalier), Order of St. Angilbert (chevalier), K. of P. (past chancellor 1983, 84), Delta Sigma Phi. Unitarian. Avocations: chess, coin collecting, writing fiction and non-fiction. Home: 601 E California Blvd Pasadena CA 91106-3852 Office: Le Baron Investigations Pasadena CA 91106

DRYDEN, ROBERT EUGENE, lawyer; b. Chanute, Kans., Aug. 20, 1927; s. Calvin William and Mary Alfreda (Foley) D.; m. Jetta Rae Burger, Dec. 19, 1953; children: Lynn Marie, Thomas Calvin. AA, City Coll., San Francisco, 1947; BS, U. San Francisco, 1951, JD, 1954. Bar: Calif. 1955; diplomate Am. Bd. Trial Advocates (pres. San Francisco chpt. 1997). Assoc. Barfield, Dryden & Ruane (and predecessor firm), San Francisco, 1954-60, jr. ptnr., 1960-65, gen. ptnr., 1965-89; sr. ptnr. Dryden, Margoles, Schimaneck, Kelly & Wait, San Francisco, 1989—; lectr. continuing edn. of the bar, 1971-77; evaluator U.S. Dist. Ct. (no. dist.) Calif. Early Neutral Evaluation Program; master atty. San Francisco Am. Inn of Ct. Mem. bd. counsellors U. San Francisco, 1993—. With USMCR, 1945-46. Fellow Am. Coll. Trial Lawyers, Am. Bar Found., Internat. Acad. Trial Lawyers; mem. ABA, San Francisco Bar Assn., Assn. Def. Counsel (bd. dirs. 1968-71), Def. Rsch. Inst., Internat. Assn. Ins. Counsel, Fedn. Ins. Counsel, Am. Arbitration Assn., U. San Francisco Law Soc. (mem. exec. com. 1970-72), U. San Francisco Alumni Assn. (mem. bd. govs. 1977), Phi Alpha Delta. Home: 1320 Lasuen Dr Millbrae CA 94030-2846 Office: Dryden Margoles Schimaneck Kelly & Wait 1 California St Ste 2600 San Francisco CA 94111-5432

DUARTE, HAROLD JORGE, minister; b. San Juan, Argentina, Sept. 21, 1950; came to U.S., 1972; s. A. and Laura (Bernhardt) D.; m. Johanna Ruth Nikkels, Sept. 23, 1979; children: Halcyon Johanna, Harold Johannes, Heidi Joy. BA, River Plate Coll., Argentina, 1972; postgrad., Sch. Theology at Claremont, Calif., 1990—. Ordained to ministry Seventh-day Adventists, 1979. Youth pastor Seventh-day Adventist Ch., Bakersfield, Calif., 1973-76, L.A., 1976-77; pastor Seventh-day Adventist Ch., La Crescenta, Calif., 1977-81, East Los Angeles, Calif., 1981-85; exec. dir. Listen, Seventh-day Adventist Ch., Glendale, Calif., 1985-87; assoc. pastor Downey (Calif.) Seventh-day Adventist Ch., 1987—; chmn. youth ministries com. Seventh-day Adventist Ch. in Cen. Calif. Conf., San Jose, 1974-75, Glendale, 1976-78, mem. communication steering com., 1979—. Contbr. articles to religious mags. Mem. AACD, Nat. Assn. Ch. Bus. Adminstrn., Assn. for Religious Values and Issues in Counseling. Home: 1159 Nicholas St Upland CA 91784-1288 Office: Seventh-day Adventist Ch 9820 Lakewood Blvd Downey CA 90240-3341

DUARTE, LUIZ GUILHERME, telecommunication consultant, journalist; b. Sao Paulo, Brazil, Dec. 22, 1966; came to the U.S., 1990; s. Jose Antonio Lacerda Duarte and Maria do Carmo (Giordano) Duarte; m. Flavia Camargo Junqueira, June 2, 1990; children: Amanda, Rebecca. BA in Journalism, U. Sao Paulo, 1988; MA in Telecom., Mich. State U., 1992, D in Mass Media, 1998. Asst. prof. telecom. Mich. State U., East Lansing, 1990-96; sr. cons. Galaxy Latin Am., Ft. Lauderdale, Fla., 1996—; corr. govt. elections Bandeirantes TV, Sao Paulo, 1986; mktg. cons. Horizon Cable Mid-Mich., Lansing, 1992. Author: E' Pagar Para Ver, 1996; editor L.Am. Telecom., 1993; journalist Editora Abril, Sao Paulo; contbr. articles to profl. jours. Pres. Brazilian Cmty. Assn., East Lansing, 1995. Thoman fellow Thoman Found., Lansing, 1995. Mem. Assn. Profl. Journalists (internat. corr.), Brazilian Assn. Internat. Corr. Office: Galaxy Latin America 3800 Via Oro Ave Long Beach CA 90810-1866

DUBE'-ODELL, DORICE SUZANNE, career officer; b. L.A., Sept. 2, 1958; d. Howard Ernest and Sylvia Diane (Kohler) Dube'; m. Mark Wesley Odell, Apr. 23, 1983. AS in Bus., L.A. C.C., 1981; BSBA, U. Phoenix, 1988; MS in Aeronautics and Engring., Columbia State U., 1999, postgrad., 1999—. Claims processor Blue Cross Blue Shield, Colton, Calif., 1982-84; mortgage ins. and tax specialist Shearson Lehmen Am. Express Mortgage Corp., San Bernardino, Calif., 1982-84; o-ring tech. writer Bourns Aerospace, Riverside, Calif., 1984-85; C-141 B Starlifter loadmaster (aircrew mem.) 728th Mil. Airlift Squadron, Norton AFB, Calif., 1985-89; MX rail Garrison missile project/rail & track identification Earth Tech., San Bernardino, Calif., 1987-88; aeromed. ops. evacuation officer 68th Aeromed. Evacuation Squadron, Norton AFB, 1989-94; ops. officer 452 Aeromed. Evacuation Squadron, March Air Res. Base, 1991-94; ops. group exec. officer HQ 452 Ops. Group, March Air Res. Base, Calif., 1994—. Sports planner Spl. Olympics, Calif. and Frankfurt, Germany, 1977—; charter mem. San Diego Zool. Soc., 1994—. With U.S. Army, 1976-85, capt. USAFR, 1985—. Decorated Army Commendation medal Dept. of the Army, Seoul, Korea, 1980; recipient Air Force Meritorious Svc. medal, Air Force Commendation medal, Air Force Achievement medal. Mem. Women in Mil. Svc. Assn. (charter mem.), The Bus. Press (Bus. Press Woman of Yr. nominee, 1998). Democrat. Roman Catholic. Avocations: sports, aeronautic history, folk art, researching various topics. E-mail: DOdell9313@aol.com. Home: 19339 Lambeth Ct Riverside CA 92508-6217 Office: HQ 452 Ops Group Ste 16 1250 Graeber St March Air Force Base CA 92518

DUBESA, ELAINE J., biotechnology company executive; b. Alton, Ill., July 26, 1943; m. Michael Dubesa, Oct. 28, 1967. BS in Med. Tech., Loyola U., New Orleans, 1966. Rsch. assoc. pesticides project U. Hawaii, Honolulu, 1968-69; field rep., pesticides project La. State U., New Orleans, 1970-71; lab. supr. Beaufort (S.C.) County Meml. Hosp., 1971-72; asst. supr. hematology Mayo Clinic, Rochester, Minn., 1973-75; edn. coord. Sherman Hosp., Elgin, Ill., 1975-78; sect. chief PCL (now Corning Clin. Labs.), Portland, Oreg., 1978-80; quality control supr. PCL-RIA, Inc., Portland, 1980-82; quality control mgr. Am. Bioclinical Inc., Portland, 1982-87; quality assurance mgr., regulatory affairs mgr. Epitope, Inc., Beaverton, Oreg., 1987-91, v.p. regulatory affairs, 1991-95, v.p. govt. affairs, 1995-97. Active Troutdale (Oreg.) Hist. Soc. Mem. Am. Soc. Quality Control, Regulatory Affairs Profl. Soc., Am. Soc. Clinical Pathologists, Beta Epsilon Upsilon. Avocations: hiking, gardening.

DUBOFF, LEONARD DAVID, lawyer; b. Bklyn., Oct. 3, 1941; s. Rubin Robert and Millicent Barbara (Pollach) DuB.; m. Mary Ann Crawford, June 4, 1967; children: Colleen Rose, Robert Courtney, Sabrina Ashley. JD summa cum laude, Bklyn. Law Sch., 1971. Bars: N.Y. 1974, Oreg. 1977, U.S. Dist. Cts. (so. and ea. dists.) N.Y. 1974, U.S. Ct. Appeals (2d cir.) 1974, U.S. Ct. Appeals (9th cir.) 1990, U.S. Customs Ct. 1975, U.S. Supreme Ct. 1977, U.S. Fed. Dist. Ct. 1990. Teaching fellow Stanford (Calif.) U. Law Sch., 1971-72; mem. faculty Lewis & Clark Coll. Northwestern Sch. Law, Portland, Oreg., 1972-94, prof. law, 1977-94; ptnr. DuBoff & Ross, PLLC, Portland, 1994—; instr. Hastings Coll. Law Coll. Civil Advocacy, San Francisco, summers 1978, 79. Founder, past pres. Oreg. Vol. Lawyers for Arts; mem. lawyers' com. ACLU, 1973-78, bd. dirs. Oreg., 1974-76; mem. Mayor's Adv. Com. Security and Privacy, 1974; bd. dirs. Portland Art Mus. Asian Art Council, 1976-77, Internat. Assn. Art Security, N.Y.C., 1976-80; pres. Arts Commn. of Tigard Tualatin and Sherwood, 1990-92; Gov. Oreg. Com. Employment of Handicapped, 1978-81; cons., panelist spl. projects Nat. Endowment for Arts, 1978-79; mem. Mayor's Adv. Com. on Handicapped, 1979-81; mem. Wash. State Atty. Gen's. Com. to Reorganize Maryhill Mus.; Oreg. Commn. for Blind, 1987-93; Oreg. Com. for Humanities, 1981-87. Recipient Bklyn. Law Sch. Stuart Hirschman Property, Jerome Prince Evidence, Donald W. Matheson Meml. awards, 1st scholarship prize; Hofstra U. Lighthouse scholar 1965-71; recipient Hauser award, 1967, Howard Brown Pickard award, 1967-69, Oreg. Govs. Arts award, 1990, Dist. award of merit Pioneer Dist., Boy Scouts Am., 1995, Silver Beaver award Boy Scouts Am., 1996, Vigil mem. Order of the Arrow, 1996. Mem. Am. Soc. Internat. Law, Assn. Alumni and Attenders of Hague Acad. Internat. Law, Assn. Am. Law Schs. (standing com. sect. activities 1975, chmn. sect. law and arts 1974-80, 91-93, spl. com. on disabilities 1989-91), ABA, N.Y. State Bar Assn., Oreg. Bar Assn., Delta Kappa Phi, Sigma Pi Sigma, Sigma Alpha. Spl. columnist on craft law, The Crafts Report, 1973-77; editor, contbr. materials to legal and art textbooks; author textbooks and articles for legal and art jours. Office: DuBoff & Ross PLLC Hampton Oaks 2nd Fl 6665 SW Hampton St Portland OR 97223-8357

DUBOFSKY, JEAN EBERHART, lawyer, retired state supreme court justice; b. 1942; B.A., Stanford U., 1964; LL.B., Harvard U., 1967; m. Frank N. Dubofsky; children: Joshua, Matthew. Admitted to Colo. bar, 1967; legis. asst. to U.S. Senator Walter F. Mondale, 1967-69; atty. Colo. Rural Legal Services, Boulder, 1969-72, Legal Aid Soc. Met. Denver, 1972-73; ptnr. Kelly, Dubofsky, Haglund & Garnsey, Denver, 1973-75; dep. atty. gen. Colo., 1975-77; counsel Kelly, Haglund, Garnsey & Kahn, 1977-79, 88-90, Jean E. Dubofsky, P.C., Boulder, Colo., 1991—; justice Colo. Supreme Ct., Denver, 1979-87; vis. prof. U. Colo. Law Sch., Boulder, 1987-88. Office: 1000 Rose Hill Dr Boulder CO 80302-7148

DUBOIS, CHRISTINE, writer, educator; b. Richmond Hts., Mo., Dec. 30, 1956; d. Edward N. and Jean Charlotte (Hall) D.; m. Steven E. Bourne, Sept. 16, 1979; children: Lucas, Gabriel. BA in Comm., U. Wash., 1979. Assignment editor Sta. KING-TV, Seattle, 1978-82; editor Olympia Churchman, Seattle, 1983-85; sr. editor Group Health Coop., Seattle, 1986-90; co-owner Turtledove Writers, Bothell, Wash., 1990—; instr. continuing edn. and writing North Seattle Edmonds Shoreline Cmty. Colls., 1986—; instr. writing Pacific N.W. Writers Conf., Seattle, 1993—, Write On the Sound Conf., Edmonds, 1995—. Co-author: (with Steven Bourne) Waiting In Hope, 1993 (Wash. Press Assn. 1st place award 1993); contbr. over 400 articles to jours. Bd. dirs. Mill Creek (Wash.) Coop. Presch., 1998—, Sacred Heart Shelter, Seattle, 1987-90; active Epis. Ch. Recipient Superior Performance award Wash. Press Assn., 1989, numerous awards from Cath. Press Assn., Soc. Profl. Journalists, Pub. Rels. Soc. Am., others. Mem. Nat. Writers Union, Cath. Press Assn. Avocations: music, sports, cooking. Office: Turtledove Writers PO Box 12777 Mill Creek WA 98082-0777

DU BOIS, JOLEEN DIANNE, minister; b. Des Moines, June 8, 1938; d. Joseph William and Ruth Lorene (Miller) Story; m. Marshal Kellen Du Bois, July 21, 1965 (div. June 1984); children: Jeffrey John Ayres, Joseph Todd Ayres. Student, U. Iowa, 1956-58, Simpson Coll., 1958-59; ordained min., Sancta Sophia Sem., 1981. Ordained min., Fla. Pres. White Mountain Edn. Assn., Prescott, Ariz., 1981—; pastor, sr. counselor White Mountain Edn. Assn., Prescott, 1981—, lectr., 1985—; Editor Meditation Monthly Internat., 1986-98; composer In the Temple, 1995, Gold of Love, 1996, Morning Meditation, 1997. Dir. Peace and Justice, Sarasota, Fla., 1992. Mem. AAUW, NAFE, Agni Yoga Soc., Delta Delta Delta. Avocations: composing, piano, poetry, violin, writing. Home: 543 Eastwood Dr Prescott AZ 86303-5416 Office: White Mountain Edn Assn PO Box 11975 Prescott AZ 86304-1975

DU BOIS, W.L., III, executive, writer, producer, director; b. White Plains, N.Y., Aug. 30, 1934; s. Shepard and Nellie (Staley) D.; m. Lucia L. Luciani, Oct. 16, 1975 (div. June 1979). Cert., NYU, 1960, U. West L.A., 1981. Founder, chmn., pres. Watts TV, Film and Radio Tng. Ctr., L.A., 1968; actor Father Like Son, Encino, Calif., 1972, Boss's Son, Hollywood, Calif., 1975; exec. prodr. Dr. Silkini Stage Show, North Hollywood, Calif., 1987; writer, prodr., host Video Jazz Music radio show, L.A., 1994; chmn., CEO Speed of Light Comm., Inc., L.A., 1993—; cons. Rebuild L.A., 1992. Contbg. photographer The Movement, 1964; writer, prodr.-dir.: (film) Watts Festival 69, 1969. Chmn. film program Watts Tng. Ctr., L.A., 1992-94, chmn., CEO World Youth Corp., L.A., 1988-98; founder Du Bois Found., L.A., 1968-98. With U.S. Army, 1956-58. Recipient Expert Marksman medal U.S. Army, 1956. Republican. Episcopalian. Avocations: sports, backgammon. Office: Speed of Light Communications Inc PO Box 38838 Los Angeles CA 90038-0838

DUBOSE, FRANCIS MARQUIS, clergyman; b. Elba, Ala., Feb. 27, 1922; s. Hansford Arthur and Mayde Frances (Owen) DuB.; BA cum laude, Baylor U., 1947; MA, U. Houston, 1958; BD, Southwestern Bapt. Sem., 1957, ThD, 1961; postgrad. Oxford (Eng.) U., 1972; m. Dorothy Anne Sessums, Aug. 28, 1940; children: Elizabeth Anne Parnell, Frances Jeannine Huffman, Jonathan Michael, Celia Danielle. Pastor Bapt. chs., Tex., Ark., 1939-61; supt. missions. So. Bapt. Conv., Detroit, 1961-66; prof. missions Golden Gate Bapt. Sem., 1966—, dir. World Mission Ctr., 1979—, sr. prof., 1992; lectr., cons. in 115 cities outside U.S., 1969-82; v.p. Conf. City Mission Supts., So. Bapt. Conv., 1964-66; trustee Mich. Bapt. Inst., 1963-66; mem. San Francisco Inter-Faith Task Force on Homelessness. Mem. Internat. Assn. Mission Study, Am. Soc. Missiology, Assn. Mission Profs. Co-editor: The Mission of the Church in the Racially Changing Community, 1969; author: How Churches Grow in an Urban World, 1978, Classics of Christian Missions, 1979, God Who Sends: A Fresh Quest for Biblical Mission, 1983, Home Cell Groups and House Churches, 1987, Mystic on Main Street, 1994; contbr. to Toward Creative Urban Strategy; Vol. III Ency. of So. Baptists, also articles to profl. jours. Home: 2 Carpenter Ct San Francisco CA 94124-4429 Office: Golden Gate Bapt Sem Mill Valley CA 94941

DUBROFF, HENRY ALLEN, newspaper editor; b. Neptune, N.J., Nov. 28, 1950; s. Sol and Gilda (Burdman) D.; married, 1980 (div. 1986). AB in History and Lit., Lafayette Coll., 1972; MS in Journalism, Columbia U., 1982. Staff writer Dept. Health and Human Svcs., Washington, 1972-73; tchr. English Holyoke (Mass.) St. Sch., 1974-78; employment & tng. program mgr. Knoxville (Tenn.)-Knox CY Community Action, 1978-81; bus. writer, columnist Springfield (Mass.) Newspapers, 1982-85; bus. writer, columnist The Denver Post, 1985-88, bus. editor, 1988-95; editor Denver Bus. Jour., 1995—; contbg. writer CFO Mag., Boston, 1985-90. Contbr. articles to N.Y. Times, 1982-89. Vol. Russian Resettlement Program Jewish Family & Children's Svcs., Denver, 1989-90. Recipient N.Y. Fin. Writers Assn. scholarship, 1982, Morton Margolin prize U. Denver, 1988, Bus. Story of Yr. award AP, 1989, Gen. Excellence award Am. City Bus. Jour., 1996, 97, Human Svc. award Am. Jewish Com., 1999. Mem. Soc. Am. Bus. Editors and Writers (past pres., Best in Bus. award 1995, 96, 98). Avocations: photography, writing, golf. Office: Denver Bus Jour 1700 Broadway Ste 515 Denver CO 80290-1700

DUBUQUE, CHERYL WHITMAN, film and video producer, writer; b. Oswego, N.Y., Nov. 24, 1952; d. Frederick E. and Genevieve A. (Muscalino) D. With Harrison Ford Prodns., 1980s, Embassy TV, 1980-83; Prodr./writer, owner Angel Hawk Prodns., Burbank, Calif., 1996—; casting asst. Katy & Co., Burbank, 1997—; prodn. asst. DMG Entertainment, L.A., 1997—, AIA Actors Studio, Burbank, 1997—. Scriptwriter Eldridge Way, The Adventuress; writer more than 30 poems, 1982-90. Mem. Women in Theater (bd. dirs. 1992—, publicist/prodr.). Democrat. Avocations: horseback riding, swimming. Office: Angel Hawk Prodns Cheryl Whitman Dubuque 859 N Hollywood Way Apt 246 Burbank CA 91505-2814

DUCHOW, DONNA PROMMAS, English language educator; b. Lower Merlon, Pa., July 26, 1964; d. Don C. and Sylvia V. Prommas; m. Timothy Duchow, June 6, 1992. BA, Sweet Briar Coll., 1986; MA, San Diego State U., 1991. Lang. instr. Palomar Coll., San Marcos, Calif., 1991—; participant U. Hawaii, Honolulu, 1992. Author: (textbook) En Avant, 1992, Reflets, 1996. Coun. sec. Our Redeemer Luth. Ch., San Diego, 1998. Mem. Calif. Tchrs. English to Spkrs. of Other Langs. Avocation: physical fitness.

DUCKWORTH, GUY, musician, pianist, educator; b. L.A., Dec. 19, 1923; s. Glenn M. and Laura (Lysle) D.; m. Ballerina Maria Farra, May 23, 1948. BA, UCLA, 1951; MusM, Columbia U., 1953, PhD, 1969. Piano soloist Metro Goldwyn Mayer Studios, 1936-41, Warner Bros. Studios, 1936-41, Sta. KFI, L.A., 1938, Sta. KNX, L.A., 1939, Sta. KHJ, L.A., 1940; artist Columbia Artists, 1942-49; asst. prof. music. U. Minn., Mpls., 1955-60, assoc. prof., 1960-62; prof. piano, fellow Northwestern U., Evanston, Ill., 1962-70; chmn. dept. preparatory piano Northwestern U., 1962-70; prof. music U. Colo., Boulder, 1970-88; prof. emeritus U. Colo., 1988, originator, coordinator masters and doctoral programs in mus. arts; piano concert tours in U.S., Can., Mexico, 1947-49; condr. various music festivals, U.S., 1956—; dir. Walker Art Children's Concerts, Mpls., 1957-62; nat. piano chmn. Music Educators Nat. Conf., 1965-71; vis. lectr., scholar 96 univs., colls. and conservatories, U.S. and Can., 1964—; cons. to Ill. State Dept. Program Devel. for Gifted Children, 1968-69; vis. prof. U. Colo., 1988-90. Television series "A New Dimension in Piano Instruction", 1959, rec. Natl. award from Natl. Edn. Television, creator/performer. Author: Keyboard Explorer, 1963, Keyboard Discoverer, 1963, Keyboard Builder, 1964, Keyboard Musician, 1964, Keyboard Performer, 1966, Keyboard Musicianship, 1970, Guy Duckworth Piano Library, 1974, Guy Duckworth Musicianship Series, 1975, Keyboard Musician: The Symmetrical Keyboard, 2 vols., 1987-88, Keyboard Musician: The Symmetrical Keyboard, 1988, rev. edit., 1990; contbr. to over 6 books, 23 articles on pedagogy of music to various jours.; producer, performer video tapes on piano teaching; producer, writer (film) The Person First: A Different Kind of Teaching, 1984. Nominator Irving S. Gilmore Internat. Keyboard Festival, Gilmore Artist and Young Artist Awards. With U.S. Army, 1943-46. Recipient All-Univ. Teaching award for excellence, U. Colo., 1981, Pedagogy Honors award Nat. Conf. Piano Pedagogy, Chgo., 1994; named Pioneer Pedagogue Nat. Corp. Piano Pedagogy, Princeton U. Retrospective, 1992. Mem. Music Tchrs. Nat. Assn., Colo. State Music Tchrs. Assn., Coll. Music Soc., Music Educators Nat. Conf., Music Teachers Assn. Calif., Phi Mu Alpha, Pi Kappa Lambda. Home: 6522 Ambrosia Dr Apt 5108 San Diego CA 92124-3136 Office: U Colo Coll of Music Boulder CO 80302

DUCKWORTH, KIM PELTO, marketing executive; b. Fresno, Calif., Dec. 15, 1956; d. William Armos and Marjorie Mae (Haninger) Pelto; m. David Paul Duckworth, Aug. 16, 1986; children: Heather Ann, Angela Marie, Claire Louise. BA in Communications, Stanford U., 1978. Asst. dir. membership club Westin Internat. Hotel, San Francisco, 1978; mktg. trainee IBM, Palo Alto, Calif., 1978-79, mktg. rep., 1979-82; account mktg. rep. IBM, San Francisco, 1982-83; with advt. staff IBM, White Plains, N.Y., 1983-85; mgr. mktg. IBM, Sunnyvale, Calif., 1985-88; regional mktg. mgr. software IBM, San Jose, Calif., 1989-91; CMR KidSoft, Inc., Los Gatos, Calif., 1992—. Mem. Young Reps. Los Gatos; precinct leader United Way, Palo Alto, 1985, vol. canvasser White Plains, 1984; vol. Am. Heart Assn., March of Dimes, Los Gatos, Calif., 1988—. Mem. NAFE, Stanford Alumni Assn., Roundhill Country Club. Republican. Episcopalian. Clubs: Stanford (Los Gatos), Los Gatos Athletic. Office: KidSoft Inc 718 University Ave Ste 112 Los Gatos CA 95032-7608

DUCKWORTH, TARA ANN, insurance company executive; b. Seattle, June 7, 1956; d. Leonard Douglas and Audrey Lee (Limbeck) Hill; m. Mark L. Duckworth, May 16, 1981; children: Harrison Lee III, Andrew James, Kathryn Anne. AAS, Highline C.C., Seattle, 1976. From acctg. clk. to info. sys. supr. SAFECO Ins. Co., Seattle, 1977-90, rate sys. mgr., 1990-94; sys. mgr. SAFECO Mut. Funds, SAFECO Credit, PNMR, Seattle, 1994-97, mktg. comm. and incentives, quality assurance mgr., 1997-98, dir. comml. lines sys., 1998—; mem. tech adv. com. for the computer info. svcs. program North Seattle Community Coll., 1984-96, chairperson tech. adv. com., 1988-90. Mem. Star Lake Improvement Club, 1988-94; mem. fellowship com. St. Lukes Luth. Ch., 1986—; mem. Boy Scouts Am., 1996—. Mem. NAFE, Nat. Assn. for Ins. Women, Soc. for State Filers, Nat. PTA. Office: SAFECO Ins Co SAFECO Plz Seattle WA 98185

DUCKWORTH, WALTER DONALD, museum executive, entomologist; b. Athens, Tenn., July 19, 1935; s. James Clifford and Vesta Katherine (Walker) D.; m. Sandra Lee Smith, June 17, 1955; children: Clifford Monroe, Laura Lee, Brent Cullen. Student, U. Tenn., 1953-55; BS, Middle Tenn. State U., 1955-57; MS, N.C. State U., 1957-60, PhD, 1962. Entomology intern Nat. Mus. Nat. History, Washington, 1960-62, asst. curator, 1962-64, assoc. curator, 1964-75, entomology curator, 1975-78, spl.asst. to dir., 1975-78; spl. asst. to asst. sec. Smithsonian Inst., Washington, 1978-84; dir. Bishop Mus., Honolulu, 1984-86, pres., dir., 1986—; pres., CEO Hawaii Maritime Ctr. subs. Bishop Mus.; trustee Sci. Mus. Va., Richmond, 1982-86, bd. dirs., 1982-84, Hawaii Maritine Mus., Honolulu, 1984-95; mem. Sci. Manpower Commn., Washington, 1982-84. Co-editor: Amazonian Ecosystems, 1973; Am. editor: Dictionary of Butterflies and Moths, 1976; author, co-author numerous monographs and jour. articles in systematic biology. Pres. Social Ctr. for Psychosocial Rehab., Fairfax, Va., 1975. N.C. State U. research fellow, 1957-62; recipient numerous grants NSF, Am. Philos. Soc., Smithsonian Research Found. Assn., Exceptional Service awards Smithsonian Inst., 1973, 77, 80, 82, 84, Disting. Alumnus award Middle Tenn. State U., 1984. Mem. Am. Inst. Biol. Scis (pres. 1985-86, sec.-treas. 1978-84), Entomol. Soc. Am. (pres. 1982-83, governing bd. 1976-85, Disting. Svc. award 1981), Assn. Tropical Biology (exec. dir. 1971-84, sec.-treas. 1976-81), Hawaii Acad. Sci. (coun. 1985—), Arts Coun. Hawaii (legis. com. 1986-87), Assn. Sci. Mus. Dirs., Social Sci. Assn., Assn. Systematic Collections (v.p. 1988-89, pres. 1990-91, Disting. Svc. award 1992), Pacific Sci. Assn. (pres. 1987-91, pres. Pacific Sci. Congress, Honolulu 1991). Democrat. Presbyterian. Lodges: Rotary, Masons, Order Eastern Star. Office: Bishop Mus 1525 Bernice St Honolulu HI 96817-2704*

DUCOMMUN, DEBBIE LUELLA, writer, publisher; b. Salt Lake City, Utah, Nov. 11, 1958; d. Harold Daniel and Ona Lee (Leithoff) Mertens; m. Larry John Ducommun, Apr. 21, 1990. BA, Calif. State Univ. Chico, Chico, 1980. Vet. asst. Acacia Vet. Hosp., Chico, 1981-82; mgr. Butte Humane Soc., Chico, Calif., 1982-85; lab mgr. Calif. State Univ., Chico, 1985-95; dog obedience instr. Chico Area Rec. Dist., Chico, 1987-92; self-employed Chico, 1995—. Author: Rat Health Care, 1995, Rats! A Fun & Care Book, 1998; contbr. articles to mags.; contbr. editor: Pet Business Mag., 1996—. Avocations: reading, camping, photography. Home: 857 Lindo Ln Chico CA 95973

DUDERSTADT, MACK HENRY, JR., arts educator; b. Carrolton, Mo., Mar. 17, 1958; s. Mack Henry and Katharine Sidney (Johnson) D. BA, Stanford U., 1980. Video producer KCBJ-TV, Columbia, Mo., 1980-81, WHO-TV, Des Moines, Iowa, 1981-85; pvt. practice San Francisco, 1985-95, Northern Calif., 1996—. Author: World's Weirdest Web Pages, 1996; editor: Pacific Video Resources, 1989-91. Democrat. Avocations: cooking, writing, hiking, biking. E-mail: hank@cybermeister.com. Fax: (510) 893-5609. Home: 476 Weldon Ave Apt 1 Oakland CA 94610-1500 Office: Cybermeister com PO Box 10416 Oakland CA 94610-0416

DUERIG, GILBERTE JILL, water quality engineer; b. Milw., Mar. 8, 1953; d. William R. and Germaine M. (Reback) Frey; m. Thomas W. Duerig, June 8, 1974; children: Kristin, Laura, Thomas J. BS in Fundamental Sci., Lehigh U., 1974; MSCE, U. Pitts., 1978. Registered civil engr., Calif.; cert. operator, grade 5, Calif., WA-1, Pa. Chemist Western Pa. Water Co., Pitts., 1975-77, water quality supr., 1977-79, dir. water quality, 1979-80; asst. engr. Alameda County Water Dist., Fremont, Calif., 1986-88, assoc. engr., 1988-89, divsn. engr., 1989-92, prodn. mgr., 1992—; bd. dirs. South Bay Engrs., Fremont; mem. Hazardous Waste Tech. Adv. Com., Alameda County, 1990-92; co-chair Watekeuse-Potable Reuse Subcom., San Diego, 1992-94. Mem. ASCE, Am. Chem. Soc., Am. Water Works Assn. Office: Alameda County Water Dist PO Box 5110 Fremont CA 94537-5110

DUFF, GARY NOLAN, secondary education educator; b. Butte, Mont., Apr. 1, 1939; s. Nolan E. and Frances Zita (Briggeman) D.; m. Bette Larene Kleve, Dec. 19, 1959 (separated 1993); children: Donald, Kimberly, Robyn, Ryan. BA, Carroll Coll., 1973; postgrad., Northern Mont. Coll., 1982-83. Cert. vocat. edn. tchr. 1983. Engrs. aide Milw. St. Paul & Pacific Railroad, Deer Lodge, Mont., 1957-58, Mont. Dept. Hwys., Helena, 1958-61, Utah Dept. Hwys., Salt Lake City, 1962-63; elec. sales Elec. Parts Supply, Missoula, Mont., 1963-65; draftsman Morrison-Maierle Inc., Helena, 1965-73; contractor self employed, Helena, 1973-76; engring. tech. Mont. Dept. Hwys., Helena, 1976-80; instr. drafting Capital High Sch., Helena, 1980—. Bd. dirs. Helena Housing Authority, 1985-87; advisor Vocat. Indsl. Clubs Am., Helena, 1980—. Mem. NEA, Mont. Edn. Assn. Avocations: photography, computer animation, camping, fishing, woodworking. Home: 2012 Westridge Ct Helena MT 59601-1508 Office: Capital H S 100 Valley Dr Helena MT 59601-0199

DUFF, WILLIAM LEROY, JR., university dean emeritus, business educator; b. Oakland, Calif., Sept. 14, 1938; s. William Leroy and Edna Francis (Gunderson) D.; m. Arline M. Wight, Sept. 1, 1962; children—Susan M., William Leroy III. B.A., Calif. State U.-, San Francisco, 1963, postgrad., 1963-64; M.S.Sc., Nat. Econs. Inst., U. Stockholm, 1965; Ph.D., UCLA, 1969. Research assoc. C.F. Kettering Found., 1967-69; asst. JOBS program Nat. Alliance Businessmen, 1969-70; prof. U. No. Colo., Greeley, 1970—, dir. Sch Bus., Bur Bus. and Pub. Research, 1972-75, dean Coll. Bus. Adminstrn., 1984—, interim v.p. acad. affairs, 1987; chmn. faculty senate U. No. Colo., 1981-82; on leave as UN adviser to Govt. of Swaziland, 1975-77; cons. in field. Contbr. articles to profl. jours. Mem. Greeley Planning Commn., 1972-75, chmn., 1974-75; trustee U. No. Colo., 1983; mem. Greeley Water and Sewer Bd. With U.S. Army, 1958-60. Mem. Greeley Rotary Club (bd. dirs.), Greeley Area C. of C. (bd. dirs.). Home: 1614 Lakeside Dr Greeley CO 80631-5343 Office: U No Colo Coll Bus Adminstrn Kepner Greeley CO 80639

DUFFY, GLORIA CHARMIAN, foundation administrator; b. San Francisco, Sept. 4, 1953; d. George Thomas and Gloria Sara (Cohan) D.; m. Robert L. Elder, Sept. 30, 1984 (div. Dec. 1991). AB magna cum laude, Occidental Coll., 1975; MA, Columbia U., 1977, MPhil, 1980, PhD, 1992. Rschr. The Rand Corp., Santa Monica, Calif., 1977-78; asst. dir. The Arms Control Assn., Washington, 1978-80; scholar in residence Stanford (Calif.) [illegible] 1982-84; pres. Global Outlook, Palo Alto, Calif., 1985-93; dep. asst. sec. def. U.S. Dept. Def., Washington, 1993-95; CEO The Commonwealth Club of Calif., San Francisco, 1996—. Author: Compliance and the Future of Arms Control, 1988; editor: International Arms Control, Issues and Agreements, 1984. Chair bd. dirs. Civilian R&D Found./NSF, Arlington, Va., 1997—; bd. dirs. Los Gatos (Calif.) Cmty. Hosp., 1977—, The Compton Found., Menlo Pk., Calif., 1976—, Bull. of the Atomic Scientists, Chgo., 1987-93, pres. Guadalupe River Pk. and Gardens Corp., San Jose, Calif., 1996-97; bd. dirs. Atlantic Coun. of U.S., 1997—. Recipient Spl. Merit award Bd. of Suprs. and Human Rels. Commn., Santa Clara County, Calif., 1992, outstanding pub. svc. medal Sec. of Def., Dept. of Def., Washington, 1995. Mem. Coun. on Fgn. Rels., Pacific Coun. on Internat. Policy. Avocations: hiking, tennis, skiing, ceramics, gardening. Office: The Commonwealth Club of Calif 595 Market St Ste 200 San Francisco CA 94105-2885

DUFFY, HARRY ARTHUR, violin expert and dealer; b. Eureka, Calif., Nov. 29, 1915; s. Harry Arthur and Caroline Mary (Reason) D.; m. Clara Nell Cromwell, Oct. 15, 1941 (div. 1971); children: Duane Arthur, Glenn Ellis; m. Olga Romanov, Oct. 28, 1989. AB, BS, U. Calif., Berkeley, 1939; postgrad., San Jose State U., 1939-40. Archivist, appraiser Rembert Wurlitzer, N.Y.C., 1946-70; pres. Harry A. Duffy Violins, Inc., Miami, Fla., 1970-86. 1st lt. U. S. Army, 1941-46. Mem. Westshore Music Club (L.A.). Episcopalian. Avocations: chamber music, tennis, numismatics, playing violin, string quartets.

DUFFY, IRENE KAREN, artist; b. Chgo., Mar. 10, 1942; d. Andrew Earl and Irene Margaret Kane (Barthley) James; m. James Ora Duffy, Jan. 24, 1963 (div. Oct. 20, 1993); children: Dawn Ann, James Sean, Maureen Marie. BA, Wash. State U., 1985, MFA, 1989. Juried invitational exhbns. include Gallery X "Out of the Box", Art Inst. Chgo., 1995, Wash. State U./U. Ill., 1994, Virginia Inn, Seattle, 1993, Chase Gallery, Spokane, 1992, Union Gallery, Pullman, 1991, Acad. Arts, Riga, Latvia, 1990, Galeria 5, Caracas, Venezuela, 1989; collections include Johanna Bur. for the Handicapped, Chgo., Gordon Gilkey Collection, Portland Art Mus., Modern Art Gallery, Leningrad, Russia, Neill Pub. Libr. Bd. dirs. Pullman/Moscow Regional Airport, 1981-84. Recipient Civic Appreciation award City of Pullman (Mayor Pete Butkus), 1984. Mem. Palouse Folklore Soc., Lions Club Internat. Avocations: skiing, folk dancing, flying, travel, gardening. Home: PO Box 215 Palouse WA 99161-0215 Studio: Artspace 114 E 525 Church PO Box 247 Palouse WA 99161-0247

DUFFY, LAWRENCE KEVIN, biochemist, educator; b. Bklyn., Feb. 1, 1948; s. Michael and Anne (Browne) D.; m. Geraldine Antoinette Sheridan, Nov. 10, 1972; children: Anne Marie, Kevin Michael, Ryan Sheridan. BS, Fordham U., 1969; MS, U. Alaska, 1972, PhD, 1977. Teaching asst. dept. chemistry U. Alaska, 1969-71, rsch. asst. Inst. Arctic Biology, 1974-77; postdoctoral fellow Boston U., 1977-78, Roche Inst. Molecular Biology, 1978-80; rsch. asst. prof. U. Tex. Med. Br., Galveston, 1980-82; asst. prof. neurology (biol. chemistry) Med. Sch. Harvard U., Boston, Mass., 1982-87, adv. biochemistry instr. Med. Sch., 1983-87; instr. gen. and organic chemistry Roxbury Community Coll., Boston, 1984-87; prof. chemistry and biochem. U. Alaska, Fairbanks, 1992—, head dept. chemistry and biochemistry, 1994—; coord. program biochemistry and molecular biology for summer undergrad. rsch., 1987-96. Mem. editl. bd. Sci. of Total Environ. Pres., bd. dirs. Alzheimer Disease Assn. of Alaska, 1994-95; mem. instnl. rev. bd. Fairbanks Meml. Hosp., 1990; sci. adv. bd. Am. Fedn. Aging Rsch. (AFAR); mem. Am. Soc. Circumpolar Health Bd. Lt. USNR, 1971-73. NSF trainee, 1971; J.W. McLaughlin fellow, 1981; W.F. Milton scholar, 1983; recipient Alzheimers Disease and Related Disorders Assoc. Faculty Scholar award, 1987; Carol Fiest Outstanding Advisor award, 1994, 97, Nat. Inst. Deafness & Commn. Disorders, NIH Cert. of Merit for mentoring, 1996, North Star Bough Sch. Dist. Svc. award, 1998. Fellow Am. Inst. Chemists (cert. profl. chemist, mem. editl. bd. Sci. of the Total Environment 1999); mem. Am. Soc. Neurochemists, Am. Soc. Biol. Chemists, N.Y. Acad. Sci., Am. Chem. Soc. (Analytical Chemistry award 1969), Internat. Soc. Toxinologists, Am. Soc. Circumpolar Health (bd. dirs.), Sigma Xi (pres. 1991 Alaska club, regional nominating com.), Soc. Environ. Toxicologists Chemists (SETAC), Phi Lambda Upsilon. Roman Catholic. Office: U Alaska Fairbanks Inst Arctic Biology Fairbanks AK 99775

DUFRESNE, ARMAND FREDERICK, management and engineering consultant; b. Manila, Aug. 10, 1917; s. Ernest Faustine and Maude (McClellan) DuF.; m. Theo Rutledge Schaefer, Aug. 24, 1940 (dec. Oct. 1986); children: Lorna DuFresne Turnier, Peter, m. Lois Burrell Klosterman, Feb. 21, 1987. BS, Calif. Inst. Tech., 1938. Dir. quality control, chief product engr. Consol. Electrodynamics Corp., Pasadena, Calif., 1945-61; pres., dir. DUPACO, Inc., Arcadia, Calif., 1961-68; v.p., dir. ORMCO Corp., Glendora, Calif., 1966-68; mgmt., engring. cons., Duarte and Cambria, Calif., 1968—; dir., v.p., sec. Tavis Corp., Mariposa, Calif., 1968-79; dir. Denram Corp., Monrovia, Calif., 1968-70, interim pres., 1970; dir., chmn. bd. RCV Corp., El Monte, Calif., 1968-70; owner DUFCO, Cambria, 1971-82; pres. DUFCO Electronics, Inc., Cambria, Calif., 1982-86, chmn. bd. 1982-92; pres. Freedom Designs, Inc., Simi Valley, Calif., 1982-86, chmn. bd. dirs., 1982-97; owner DuFresne Consulting, 1992—; chmn. bd., pres. DUMEDCO,Inc., 1993-95. Patentee in field. Bd. dirs. Arcadia Bus. Assn., 1965-69; bd. dirs. Cambria Community Services Dist., 1976, pres., 1977-80; mem., chmn. San Luis Obispo County Airport Land Use Commn., 1972-75. Served to capt. Signal Corps, AUS, 1942-45. Decorated Bronze Star. Mem. Instrument Soc. Am. (life), Arcadia (dir. 1965-69), Cambria (dir. 1974-75) C. of C., Tau Beta Pi. Home: 901 Iva Ct Cambria CA 93428-2913

DUHNKE, ROBERT EMMET, JR., retired aerospace engineer; b. Manitowoc, Wis., Jan. 28, 1935; s. Robert Emmet and Vivian Dorothy (Abel) D.; m. Patricia R. Ebben, 1956 (div. 1972); children: Kim Marie, Lori Ann, Dawn Diane, Robert III, Mary Lynn; m. Judy Anne Lind, Feb. 14, 1978. BS in Aero. Engring., Purdue U., 1957. Assoc. engr. Convair/Aerodyns. Group, Pomona, Calif., 1957-58; assoc. engr., instr. Boeing Co., Seattle, 1964-66, instr. maintenance tng., 1972-83, navigation sys. analyst, 1983-90, sr. specialist engr., instr. comml. maintenance tng. ctr., 1990-95; flight navigator Flying Tigers, San Francisco, 1966-68; salesman various real estate and ins. cos., Seattle, 1968-72; shuttler Hertz, Seattle, 1996-97; reservation sales agt. Alaska Airlines, Phoenix, 1997—; contract aerospace engr. Superior Design Co., Inc., Kirkland, Wash., 1996—. Author poems in English, German, French and Spanish. Sponsor World Vision, Pasadena, Calif.; mem. Citizens Against Govt. Waste. Capt. USAF, 1958-64. Recipient Hon. Freedom Fighter award Afghan Mercy Fund, 1987. Mem. Inst. Navigation, Air Force Assn. Avocations: sailing, fishing, biking, German, Spanish and French language studies. Home: 1219 30th St NE Auburn WA 98002-2471 also: 30 W Carter Dr Apt 19-206 Tempe AZ 85282-7712

DUKE, MARILYN ANN, graphic designer, educator; b. Socorro, N.Mex., Mar. 9, 1955; d. Robert Gerald Ebler and Mary Eulala (Castillo) Barber; m. Billy Joe Duke, Sept. 23, 1978; children: Manuel Anthony Anaya, Josephine Lynn Duke. Cert. Cosmetology, Lea County Beauty Coll., 1977; AAS, N.Mex. Jr. Coll., 1992; BS with honors, Ea. N.Mex. U., 1995. Cosmetologist Glamour House, Hobbs, N.Mex., 1977-85, Linda's Styling Salon, Hobbs, N.Mex., 1985-91; graphic arts asst. N.Mex. Jr. Coll., Hobbs, 1994-95, prof. comml. graphic design, 1995—; mem. faculty senate N.Mex. Jr. Coll., 1995—. Contbr. graphic designs to profl. jours. Mem. Mac Achievers of Permian Basin, Vocat. Indsl. Clubs Am. (advisor). Avocations: photography, water color, cross stitch, walking, crochet. Home: 1009 W Cain St Hobbs NM 88240-5612

DUKE, WILLIAM EDWARD, public affairs executive; b. Bklyn., July 18, 1932; m. Leilani Kamp Lattin. BS, Fordham U., 1954. City editor Middletown (N.Y.) Record, 1956-60; asst. state editor Washington Star, 1961-63; exec. asst. to U.S. Senator from N.Y. State, Jacob K. Javits, Washington, 1963-69; dir. pub. affairs Corp. Pub. Broadcasting, Washington, 1969-72; dir. fed. govt. rels. Atlantic Richfield Co., Washington, 1973-78, mgr. pub. affairs, L.A., 1978-91; mgr. external affairs We. States Petroleum Assn., 1993-95; pres. W.E. Duke and Co., 1995—; lectr. U. So. Calif. Grad. Sch. Journalism, 1988—; cons. in field. Fellow Pub. Rels. Soc. Am., Nat. Press Club, Capitol Hill Club, L.A. Athletic Club.

[illegible] and T. Henrietta Stein; m. Leo Joseph Du Lac, Apr. 20, 1941; children: Arline Du Lac Gerard, Linda Du Lac Jennings, Glen, Carl, Ralph. BA cum laude, UCLA, 1942, MA, 1962; JD, Western State U., Fullerton, Calif., 1982. Tchr. Cornelia Connelly H.S., Anaheim, Calif., 1962-63, Montebello (Calif.) Sch. Dist., 1963, Excelsior/Norwalk (Calif.) Sch. Dist., 1963-64, Garden Grove (Calif.) Unified Sch. Dist., 1964-69. Creative editor, contbg. author. Constitutional Law, 1981; contbg. author: Murder California Style, 1987, Mord in Kalifornie, 1988. Vol. law clk. Cmty. Law Ctr., Santa Ana, Calif., 1982. Mem. Mystery Writers Am. (contbg. author Edgar Ann. 1990, 92), Cath. Press. Assn., Phi Beta Kappa, Alpha Mu Gamma. Avocations: singing, reading, gardening, interior decorating, arranging flowers. Office: PO Box 403301 Hesperia CA 92340-3301

DULALIA, ZOSIMO GARCIA, physician; b. Quezon City, Philippines; s. Emilio Zuniga and Leonarda (Garcia) D.; m. Concelpcion Opinion; children: Antonio, Andrew, Alden. BS, U. Santo Tomas, Manila, 1976, MD, 1980. Diplomate Am. Bd. Internal Medicine. Intern, then resident in internal medicine Tex. Tech., El Paso, 1987-91; physician Family Med. Group, Daly City, Calif., 1992-93, DesertMed. Group, Palm Springs, Calif., 1994—. Mem. Am. Coll. Physicians. Office: Desert Med Group 275 N El Cielo Rd Palm Springs CA 92262-6972

DULBECCO, RENATO, biologist, educator; b. Catanzaro, Italy, Feb. 22, 1914; came to U.S., 1947, naturalized, 1953; s. Leonardo and Maria (Virdia) D.; m. Gulseppina Salvo, June 1, 1940 (div. 1963); children: Peter Leonard (dec.), Maria Vittoria; m. Maureen Rutherford Muir; 1 child, Fiona Linsey. M.D., U. Torino, Italy, 1936; D.Sc. (hon.), Yale U., 1968, Vrije Universiteit, Brussels, 1978; LL.D., U. Glasgow, Scotland, 1970. Asst. U. Torino, 1940-47; research asso. Ind. U., 1947-49; sr. research fellow Calif. Inst. Tech., 1949-52, asso. prof., then prof. biology, 1952-63; sr. fellow Salk Inst. Biol. Studies, San Diego, 1963-71; asst. dir. research Imperial Cancer Research Fund, London, 1971-74; dep. dir. research Imperial Cancer Research Fund, 1974-77; disting. research prof. Salk Inst., La Jolla, Calif., 1977—, pres., 1989-92; pres. emeritus Salk Inst., La Jolla, 1993—; prof. pathology and medicine U. Calif. at San Diego Med. Sch., La Jolla, 1977-81, mem. Cancer Ctr.; with Nat. Rsch. Coun. Milan; vis. prof. Royal Soc. G.B., 1963-64, Leeuwenhoek lectr., 1974; Clowes Meml. lectr. Atlantic City, 1961; Harvey lectr. Harvey Soc., 1967; Dunham lectr. Harvard U., 1972; 11th Marjory Stephenson Meml. lectr., London, 1973, Harden lectr., Wye, Eng., 1973, Am. Soc. for Microbiology lectr., L.A., 1979; mem. Calif. Cancr Adv. Coun., 1963-67; mem. vis. com. Case Western Res. Sch. Medicine; adv. bd. Roche Inst., 1968-71, Inst. Immunology, Basel, Switzerland, others; esperto Italian Nat. Rsch. Coun.; trustee Am.-Italian Fedn. for Cancer Rsch.; mem. bd. dirs. Scientific Counselors Dept. Etiology NCI; cons. Nat. Rsch. Coun. ESPERTO, 1994—. Trustee La Jolla Country Day Sch., Am.-Italian Fedn. for Cancer Rsch.; bd. mem. sci. counselors dept. etiology Nat. Cancer Inst. Recipient John Scott award City Phila., 1958, Kimball award Conf. Pub. Health Lab. Dirs., 1959, Albert and Mary Lasker Basic Med. Rsch. award, 1964, Howard Taylor Ricketts award, 1965, Paul Ehrlich-Ludwig Darmstaedter prize, 1967, Horwitz prize Columbia U., 1973, (with David Baltimore and Howard Martin Temin) Nobel prize in medicine, 1975, Targa d'oro Villa San Giovanni, 1978, Mandel Gold medal Czechoslovak Acad. Scis., 1982, Via de Condotti prize, 1990, Cavaliere di Gran Croce Italian Rep., 1991, Natale Di Roma prize, 1993, Columbus prize, 1993; named Man of Yr., London, 1975, Italian Am. of Yr., San Diego County, 1978; hon. citizen City of Imperia (Italy), 1983, City of Arezzo, City of Sommariva Perno, City of Catanzaro, City of Torino; Guggenheim and Fulbright fellow, 1957-58; decorated grand ufficiale Italian Republic, 1981; hon. founder Hebrew U., 1981. Mem. NAS (Selman A. Waksman award 1974, com. on human rights), Am. Assn. Cancer Rsch., Internat. Physicians for Prevention Nuclear War, Am. Philos. Assn., Accademia Nazionale del Lincel (fgn.), Academia Ligure di Scienze e Lettre (hon.), Royal Soc. (fgn.), Fedn. Am. Scientists, Am. Acad. Arts and Scis., Comitato di Collaborazione Culturale (hon. mem.), Alpha Omega Alpha. Home: 7525 Hillside Dr La Jolla CA 92037-3941 Office: CNR-ITBA, Via Ampere 56, Milan Italy also: Salk Inst PO Box 85800 San Diego CA 92188-5800*

DULEY, CHARLOTTE DUDLEY, vocational counselor; b. Lincoln, Nebr., Oct. 2, 1920; d. Millard Eugene and Inez Kathryn (Miller) Dudley; student U. Nebr., 1938-41; M.A. in Guidance Counseling, U. Idaho, 1977; B.S., Lewis and Clark State Coll., 1973; m. Phillip D. Duley, Mar. 28, 1942; (dec. Sept. 1984); children: Michael Dudley (dec.), Patricia Kaye; m. P. Fredrik Nordgaard, Sep.1, 1990. Tchr., Nebr. schs., 1951-56; with Dept. of Employment, Lewiston, Idaho, 1958-81, local office counselor handling fed. tng. programs, 1958-81; ind. job cons.; counselor; rep. Avon, Lewiston; part-time counselor, tester, 1981—; Avon sales rep. 1988—. Pres., bd. dirs. Civic Arts, Inc., 1972-81; mem. women's svc. league Wash.-Idaho Symphony Orch., 1972-96; bd. dirs. YWCA, 1980-88, treas., 1981-88; vol. tchr. YWCA programs, 1975—; mem. adv. bd. Salvation Army, 1980-94; dir. artist series Lewis and Clark State Coll., 1984-90. Recipient Altrusa Woman of Achievement award, 1984. Mem. Am., Idaho pers. guidance Assns., Idaho State Employees Assn., Internat. Assn. Employees in Employment Security, Am. Assn. Counseling & Devel., Idaho State Employment Counselors Assn. (pres. 1979-80), Stateline Guidance and Counseling Assn. (sec.-treas. 1964, 76-77), Lewiston Cmty. Concert Assn. (bd. dirs., 1980-96, pres. 1980-94), Greater Lewiston C. of C. (chmn. conv. and tourism com. 1984-95), Altrusa (bd. dirs.), Elks (pres. 1986-87, exec. bd. 1985-88, 1st v.p., 1993-95, ladies of elks pres. 1987-89, 95-96, bd. dirs. 1996-98, chmn. or registrar-judge 1998—). Baptist. Home: 1819 Ridgeway Dr Lewiston ID 83501-3890

DULLA, JOAN, artist; b. Hartford, Conn., Aug. 21, 1949; d. E.D. and Lois Duhamel; m. Lois Loretta Henley; children: Christopher, Emily. BA in Edn., Drake U., 1971; postgrad., Ariz. State U., 1989, 91. Cert. tchr., Ill. Tchr. kindergarten Ill., N.Mex., Dominican Republic, 1971-81; artist Chandler, Ariz., 1988—. Works included in books: Jewelry/Metalwork, 1992, 93, Bead Art, 1998. Recipient Best of Show award WIN, 1990, Juror's award ADC, 1991, Juror's award Ariz. State U., 1995, 2d Place award Steamboat Springs Arts Coun. Color., 1995. Mem. Ariz. Designer Craftsmen (treas. 1992-95, grant chairperson 1993—, pres. 1996—). Avocations: gourmet cooking, swimming. Home: 2961 S Cholla St Chandler AZ 85248-3021

DULLES, JOHN FOSTER, II, civil rights administrator; b. Tucson, June 15, 1943; s. John Watson Foster and Eleanor (Ritter) D.; m. Judith Gail Strayer, Aug. 4, 1968; children: Frank, John Patrick, Jennifer. BA cum laude, U. Tex., 1965. Rsch. asst. Libr. of Congress, Washington, 1966-67; field rep. Fed. Office of Econ. Opportunity, Austin and Dallas, 1968-73; civil rights analyst U.S. Commn. on Civil Rights, San Antonio, 1973-76, dep. regional dir. Southwestern region, 1976-86; sr. analyst Western region U.S. Commn. on Civil Rights, L.A., 1987-95; regional dir. Rocky Mountain region U.S. Commn. on Civil Rights, Denver, 1995—; chief steward Am. Fedn. Govt. Employees, Dallas, 1972; mem. adv. bd. United Way San Antonio, 1976; mem. Cmty. Housing Resource Bd., San Diego, 1987-95, Fed. Exec. Bd., Denver, 1995—. Author numerous reports on human rights issues; contbr. articles to profl. jours. Fellow Inst. Ednl. Leadership, Polit. Sci. Hon. Soc., mem. Nat. Assn. Human Rights Workers, LARASA (Colo.), Northwest Coalition Against Malicious Harassment. Avocations: running, tennis, swimming, historical research. Office: US Commn on Civil Rights 1700 Broadway Ste 710 Denver CO 80290-0701

DUMAINE, R. PIERRE, bishop; b. Paducah, Ky., Aug. 2, 1931; student St. Joseph Coll., Mountain View, Calif., 1945-51, St. Patrick Sem., Menlo Park, Calif., 1951-57; Ph.D., Cath. U. Am., 1962. Ordained priest Roman Cath. Ch., 1957; asst. pastor Immaculate Heart Ch., Belmont, Calif., 1957-58; mem. faculty dept. edn. Cath. U. Am., 1961-63; tchr. Serra High Sch., San Mateo, Calif., 1963-65; asst. supt. Cath. schs., Archdiocese of San Francisco, 1965-74, supt., 1974-78; ordained bishop, 1978, bishop of San Jose, Santa Clara, Calif., 1981—; dir. Archdiocesan Ednl. TV Ctr., Menlo Park, Calif., 1968-81. Mem. Pres.'s Nat. Adv. Council on Edn. of Disadvantaged Children, 1970-72; bd. dirs. Cath. TV Network, 1968-81, pres., 1975-77; bd. dirs. Pub. Service Satellite Consortium, 1975-81. Mem. Nat. Cath. Edn. Assn., Assn. Cath. Broadcasters and Allied Communicators, Internat. Inst. Communications, Assn. Calif. Sch. Adminstrs. Office: Diocese of San Jose 900 Lafayette St Ste 301 Santa Clara CA 95050-4966

DUMDUM, JOSEFINA MARTINEZ, chemist, researcher; b. Iloilo City, [illegible] D. BS in Chem. Engring., U. San Jose-Recoletos, Cebu City, The Philippines, 1965; MS in Chemistry, U. San Carlos, Cebu City, The Philippines, 1975. Registered profl. chem. engr., Philippines. Asst. prof. U. San José-Recoletos, Cebu City, Cebu, The Philippines, 1965-75; rsch. chemist Union

Oil Co. of Calif., Brea, 1975-83, sr. rsch. chemist, 1983-88, rsch. assoc., 1988—. Contbr. articles to profl. jours. Pres. Filipino Cath. of St. Paul, Chino Hills, Calif., 1996-98, U. San Jose-Recoletos Alumni Assn., U.S.A., 1988-92. Fellow Nat. Lubricating Grease Inst. (chairperson subcom. on govt. regulations 1988-98, columnist Govt. Regulations Update mag. 1989-94); mem. ASTM. Republican. Roman Catholic. Achievements include patents for finding use of CeF3 as a suitable extreme pressure additive for lubricants, use of tetrathiocarbonates and trithiocarbonates of K as extreme pressure additives for lubricants. Avocations: playing piano, embroidery, reading. Office: 76 Lubricants Co 1920 E Deere Ave Santa Ana CA 92705-5736

DUMITRESCU, DOMNITA, Spanish language educator, researcher; b. Bucharest, Romania; came to U.S., 1984; d. Ion and Angela (Barzotescu) D. Diploma, U. Bucharest, 1966; MA, U. So. Calif., 1987, PhD, 1990. Asst. prof. U. Bucharest, 1966-74, assoc. prof., 1974-84; asst. prof. Spanish, U. So. Calif., 1985-89; assoc. prof. Calif. State U., L.A., 1990-94, prof., 1995—. Author: Gramatica Limbii Spaniole, 1976, Indreptar Pentru Traducerea Din Limba Romana in Limba Spaniola, 1980; translator from Spanish lit. to Romanian; assoc. editor: Hispania, 1996—; contbr. articles to profl. jours. Fulbright scholar, 1993—. Mem. MLA, Am.-Romanian Acad. Arts and Scis., Linguistic Soc. Am., Internat. Assn. Hispanists, Assn. Linguistics and Philology L.Am., Am. Assn. Tchrs. Spanish and Portuguese (past pres. So. Calif. chpt.). Office: Calif State U 5151 State University Dr Los Angeles CA 90032-4226

DUMOULIN, DIANA CRISTAUDO, marketing professional; b. Washington, Jan. 5, 1939; d. Emanuel A. and Angela E. (Cogliano) Cristaudo; m. Philip DuMoulin, May 30, 1964; children: Joanmarie Patricia, John Philip. MA, U. Wis., 1967; BA, Rosary Coll., 1961. Project mgr. IDC Cons. Group, Framingham, Mass., 1982-84; sr. market analyst Cullinet, Inc., Westwood, Mass., 1984-86; prof. assoc. Ledgeway Group, Lexington, Mass., 1987-89; prin. Customer Mktg. Specialist, Brookline, Mass., 1989-93; pres. Customer Solutions Internat., Phoenix, 1994—; adj. faculty Ulster Count Community Coll., Stone Ridge, N.Y., 1967-74, Mass. Bay Community Coll., Wellesley Hills, Mass., 1983; lectr. Boston Coll., Chestnut Hill, Mass., 1976. Author: Ourselves in the Garden, 1998; contbr. articles to profl. jours. Pres. LWV, Kingston, N.Y., 1973-74. Recipient Svc. to Young Adults award 70001 Career Assn., 1977, Honorable Mention award Writers Digest Writing Competition, 1996, 98; faculty fellow U. Wis., 1964-66. Mem. Am. Field Svc. Mgrs. Internat. (software support spl. interest group, chmn. minuteman chpt. 1991-92), Nat. Assn. Women Bus. Owners, Ariz. Book Pubs. Assn. Office: Customer Solutions Internat 8441 N 1st Dr Phoenix AZ 85021-5515

DUNAWAY, JOHN ALLEN, risk management professional; b. Carlsbad, N.Mex.; s. John Albert and Grace Erline Dunaway; m. Elizabeth; children: John Arthur, Jamie Lynn, Brandy Lee. BA, U. New Mex., 1970; MA, U. Northern Colo., 1977; PhD in Comm., U. Colo., 1984. Police capt. City of Lakewood, Lakewood, Colo., 1970-86; fin. planner Littleton, Colo., 1986-87; dir. risk mgmt. dept. Jefferson County Sch. Dist., Golden, Colo., 1987—; adj. prof. human resources Webster U., St. Louis, 1986-94; mem. adv. bd. Lutheran Medical Ctr., Denver, 1988-95; bd. dirs. Yenter Cos., Inc. Morrison, 1993-94. Contbr. articles to profl. jours. Mem. Risk and Ins. Mgmt. Soc. (bd. dirs. 1992-93), Colo. Self Insurers Assn. (2d v.p. 1989-90), Pub. Risl Mgmt. Assn., Assn. Cert. Fraud Examiners. Avocations: skiing, scuba diving, tennis. Office: Jefferson County Pub Sch 1829 Denver West Dr Golden CO 80401-3120

DUNAWAY, MARGARET ANN (MAGGIE DUNAWAY), state agency consultant; b. Fresno, Calif., Feb. 10, 1943; d. Joseph John and Anna Frances (Dice) Cumero; children from previous marriage: Christian Anthony Freitag, Erika Lynn Bullard; m. Michael Earl Babcoke, Oct. 6, 1990; 1 stepchild, Jason Ethan Babcoke. Student, U. Calif., Davis, 1960-62, U. Calif., Berkeley, 1962-63. Supr. Gov's Office, Sacramento, 1969-72; office mgr. State Health and Welfare Agy., Sacramento, 1972-73; analyst regulations devel. Calif. State Depts. Health and Social Svcs., Sacramento, 1974-84, cons. adult and children's svcs., 1984-90, rep. adult svcs., 1984-90, with food drive com., 1987-88, rep. ind. living program com., 1989-90; community program specialist Calif. State Dept. Devel. Svcs., Sacramento, 1990—; project coord. SDSS study L.A. County Children's Svcs. Caseload, 1989-90; primary cons. SDDS study Family Home Agy. Program, 1998—. Active Southpark Homeowner's Assn., Sacramento 1974-78; presenter Adult Svcs. Ann. Asilomar Conf., 1987; coord., presenter 1st ann. Adult Family Home Conf., L.A., 1999. Office: Calif Dept Devel Svcs 1600 9th St Ste 320 Sacramento CA 95814-6414

DUNAWAY, PHILLIP LEE, JR., secondary school education educator; b. Asher, Okla., Jan. 29, 1936; s. Phillip L. and Jannie (Smith) D.; m. Marlene Ann Dixson, Nov. 19, 1960; children: Russell Phillip, Curtis Lee. MusB, BA, U. Pacific, 1958; postgrad., San Francisco State U., Sonoma State U. Cert. gen. elem., gen. secondary, spl. secondary music, Calif. Tchr. Benicia (Calif.) Unified Sch. Dist., 1958-66, Mt. Diablo Unified Sch. Dist., Concord, Calif., 1966—; chair social studies dept. Foothill Mid. Sch., 1978-93; gospel singer, rec. artist, 8 albums, 1966—; min. music various chs., 1961-87; pres. Philmar Ministries, Inc., Benicia, 1971—, active fgn. missions ministry, 1976—; music dir. Celebration of Life weekly TV show, San Francisco, 1975-77; mem. dist. social studies com. Mt. Diablo Unified Sch. Dist., 1978-93; tour dir. 8th grade trip to Washington Foothill Mid. Sch., 1980—. Arranger, composer: (records) Songweaver on the Move, 1967-68, Paul Weaver Chorale On Stage, Young Life Songs; arranger, composer Sacred Concert Pub., 1965-70, Lillenas Pub. Co., 1971. Counselor Am. Heritage Merit badge Boy Scouts Am., 1986-87. Recipient Nat. Evangel. Film Found. award, 1968; scholar Am. Legion Freedom Found., 1979. Mem. NEA, Mt. Diablo Edn. Assn., No. Calif./Nev. Assemblies of God, Calif. Tchrs. Assn., Phi Mu Alpha Sinfonia. Avocations: photography, gardening. Home: 2257 1st St Benicia CA 94510-2139

DUNBAR, MAURICE VICTOR, English language educator; b. Banner, Okla., May 24, 1928; s. Moyer Haywood and Louise Edna (Curry) D.; m. Carol Ann Cline, July 28, 1948 (div. 1963); children: Kurt, Karl, Karla, Karen, Kristen. AA, Compton Jr. Coll., 1948; BA, U. Calif., Berkeley, 1952; MA, Calif. State U., Sacramento, 1965. Tchr. elem. sch. Lone Tree Sch., Beale AFB, Calif., 1962-64; tchr. jr. high sch. Anna McKenney, Marysville, Calif., 1964-66; tchr. high sch. Yuba City (Calif.) High Sch., 1966-67; instr. jr. coll. Foothill Coll., Los Altos Hills, Calif., 1967-82; prof. English De Anza Coll., Cupertino, Calif., 1982-98; ret., 1998. Author: Fundamentals of Book Collecting, 1976, Books and Collectors, 1980, Collecting Steinbeck, 1983, Hooked on Books, 1997; contbr. articles to profl. jours. With U.S. Army, 1948-58, PTO. Mem. Masons, Shriners (orator, librarian San Jose Scottish Rite Temple, 1982—), K.C.C.H., Scottish Rite, B'nai B'rith. Avocations: book collecting, reading, travel, vis. univ. campuses.

DUNBAR, RICHARD PAUL, sales manager; b. Watertown, S.D., Aug. 28, 1951; s. Earl Paul and Leona Matilda (Clausen) D. Student, S.D. State U., 1969-71; BSBA, U. Ariz., 1981. Account mgr. bus. forms and supplies div. Nat. Cash Register, Phoenix, 1981-83; sales cons. Compugraphic Corp., Phoenix, 1983-84; sales rep. constrn. products div. W.R. Grace and Co., Phoenix and Tucson, 1985-87; sales rep. constrn. products div. for Ariz., so. Nev., N.Mex., El Paso (Tex.) region Pleko SW, Inc., Tempe, Ariz., 1987-92, S.W. regional sales mgr., 1992—. Recipien Robert P. Brosseau Meml. award, 1997, others. Mem. Jaycees (treas. 1977-78, recipient Outstanding Jaycee award, Pres.'s award, Jaycee of Month award), Constrn. Specifications Inst. (constrn. documents technologist, chmn. tech. documents com. Tucson chpt. 1987, program chmn. Phoenix chpt. 1988-89, Chpt. Pres.' Cert. award 1988, 90-92, 97, dir. Phoenix chpt. 1989-90achutstanding Indsl. award 1989, editor monthly newsletter Phoenix chpt. 1990-91, Inst. Publs. Commendation award 1990-91, Gem award 1990, 1st v.p. Phoenix chpt. 1991, rep. Ariz. Constrn. Industries Coalition 1991-93, chmn. S.W. region publs. 1992, pres.-elect Phoenix chpt. 1992, chmn. nominating com. 1992, CCPR inst. rev. com. 1992, past pres. Phoenix chpt. 1994, planning chmn. 1994, S.W. region membership chmn. 1994, mem. inst. awards com. 1994, inst. dir.-elect S.W. region 1994, inst. dir. 1995-97, region dir. citation 1992, S.W. region cert. thanks 1992, pres. Phoenix chpt., 1993, Individual Appreciation award 1991, Inst. Cert. Appreciation 1993, 94, Region Publ. award S.W. region 1994, Pres.'s citation Phoenix chpt. 1994, cert. thanks S.W. region 1993, 94, ad hoc internat. task force 1996, Cert. of Appreciation 1996, S.W. region cert. of appreciation 1997, Inst. region boundary task team 1997), Constrn. Products Mfrs. Coun. (treas. 1986), Alpha Mu Alpha. Republican. Congregational. Avocations: outdoor activities, photography, computers. Office: Pleko SW Inc 1824 E 6th St Tempe AZ 85281-2950

DUNBAR, SHARON KAY, controller, accountant; b. Terre Haute, Ind., Mar. 6, 1943; d. Thomas Shannon and Lillian Irene (Pipes) Parkhurst; m. Robert Michael Dunbar, Aug. 3, 1962; children: Robert Michael, Clinton Reece, Shannon Lynne. AA with honors, Modesto (Calif.) Jr. Coll., 1984; BS magna cum laude, Calif. State U., Turlock, 1987. CPA, Calif. Staff acct., auditor E. & J. Gallo Winery, Modesto, 1988-91; sr. acct. Dunker & Aced Accountancy Corp., Modesto, 1991-94, Korte & Co. CPAs, Modesto, 1994-95; asst. contr. Stanislaus Food Products, Modesto, 1995—; sole proprietor Sharon K. Dunbar, CPA, Modesto, 1995—. V.p., bd. dirs. Bravo Repertory Dance Theatre, Modesto, 1992—, pres., 1996—; bd. dirs. Downtown Arts Project, Modesto, 1993—. Modesto Jr. Coll. scholar, 1984, Women's Improvement Club scholar, 1984, Dept. Accountancy scholar Calif. State U., 1986, Bus. Adminstrn. scholar, 1985. Mem. Am. Inst. CPAs, Calif. Soc. CPAs, Inst. Mgmt. Accts. (bd. dirs., membership sec.). Avocations: reading, walking. Home: 3201 Canterbury Ct Modesto CA 95350-1419

DUNCAN, ANDREW MALCOLM, engineer; b. London, May 27, 1960; came to U.S., 1965; s. Glen Malcolm and Eleanor Jane (Watson) D.; m. Gabriella Clementine Borsay, Aug. 23, 1986 (div. Oct. 1987). BS in Engring., Calif. Inst. Tech., 1983; MA in Pure Math, U. Calif., Santa Cruz, 1989. Physics tchr. Pasadena (Calif.) Sch. Dist., 1983-84; programmer Cerwin-Vega, Simi Valley, Calif., 1984-86, 89; cons. E-mu Systems, Scotts Valley, Calif., 1987-88; engr. MAMA Found., Studio City, Calif., 1990-92; sr. engr. Philips Interactive Media, L.A., 1992-96; dept. of computer sci. U Calif., Santa Barbara, 1996—. Developer zebra bd. synthesizer, 1991. Mem. Audio Engring. Soc. (committeeman 1990-92, publ. award 1989, jour. rev. bd. 1993—), Am. Math. Soc., Assn. Computing Machinery. Avocations: competitive swimming, music theory, old maps, Shakespeare. Home: 6778 Abrego Rd Apt 4 Goleta CA 93117-4422 Office: U Calif Dept of Computer Science Santa Barbara CA 93106

DUNCAN, DORIS GOTTSCHALK, information systems educator; b. Seattle, Nov. 19, 1944; d. Raymond Robert and Marian (Onstad) D.; m. Robert George Gottschalk, Sept. 12, 1971 (div. Dec. 1983). BA, U. Wash., Seattle, 1967, MBA, 1968; PhD, Golden Gate U., 1978. Cert. data processor, systems profl., computer profl., data educator. Comm. cons. Pacific NW Bell Telephone Co., Seattle, 1968-71; mktg. supr. AT&T, San Francisco, 1971-73; sr. cons., project leader Quantum Sci. Corp., Palo Alto, Calif., 1973-75; dir. co. analysis program Input Inc., Palo Alto, 1975-76; dir. info. sci. dept. Golden Gate U., San Francisco, 1982-83, mem. info. systems adv. bd., 1983-85; lectr. acctg. and info. systems Calif. State U., Hayward, 1976-78, assoc. prof., 1978-85, prof., 1985—, coord. computer info. sys., 1994—; cons. pvt. cos., 1975—; vis. prof. U. Wash., Seattle, 1997-98; speaker profl. groups and confs. Author: Computers and Remote Computing Services, 1983; contbr. articles to profl. jours. Loaned exec. United Good Neighbors, Seattle, 1969; nat. committee woman, bd. dirs. Young Reps., Wash., 1970-71; adv. Jr. Achievement, San Francisco, 1971-72; mem. nat. bd. Inst. for Certification of Computer Profls. Edn. Found., 1990-93; mem. Editorial Rev. bd. Journal Info. Systems Edn., 1992—; bd. dirs. Computer Repair Svcs., 1992-94. Named Computer Educator of Yr., Internat. Assn. Computer Info. Syss., 1997. Mem. Data Processing Mgmt. Assn. (Meritorious Svc. award, Bronze award 1984, Silver award 1986, Gold Award 1988, Emerald award 1992, Diamond award 1994), Nat. grantee, 1984. dir., edn. chmn. San Francisco chpt. 1984-85, sec. and v.p. 1985, pres. 1986, assn. dir. 1987, bylaws chmn. 1987, chair awards com., 1992-95, nat. bd. dirs. spl. interest group in edn. 1985-87), Am. Inst. Decision Scis., 1982-83, Western Assn. Schs. and Colls. (accreditation evaluation team, 1984-85), Assn. Computing Machinery, Junior Club of Seattle (Beautiful Home award Foster City 1994, 95, winner Tournament of Christmas Lights 1996), Bus. Honor Soc., Beta Gamma Sigma. Subspecialties: Information systems (information science). Current work: curriculum development, professionalism in data processing field, professional certification, industry standards, computer literacy and user education, sys. analysis and design, design of data bases and data banks. Office: Calif State U Sch of Bus and Econs Hayward CA 94542

DUNCAN, EDWIN WILLIAMS, lawyer; b. Oakland, Calif., May 11, 1945; s. Boyd Halley and Edith Louise (Williams) D.; m. Kathie Louise Wilhelm, June 22, 1968; children: Stacie McKinnon, Marten Boyd, Ryan Scott, Courtney Marie, Marleigh Kristine. AB, U. Calif., Berkeley, 1966; JD, Hastings U., 1969. Bar: Calif. 1970, U.S. Dist. Ct. (ctrl. dist.) Calif. 1970, U.S. Dist. Ct. (so. dist.) Calif. 1990, U. S. Ct. of Appeals (9th cir.) 1992, U.S. Dist. Ct. (ea. dist.) Calif. 1993. Assoc. Lawler, Felix & Hall, L.A., 1969-76, ptnr., 1977-90; ptnr. Arter and Hadden, L.A., 1990—; editor Law Notes, Chgo., 1972-74, Hastings Law Jour., San Francisco, 1968-69. Author: Organizing Nonprofit Corporations, 1990, California Product Liability Law, 1990, 92; contbg. editor Asian Comml. Law Jour., 1995-98; contbr. articles to law journ. Bd. dirs. So. Calif. Swimming, L.A., 1982—, gen. chmn., 1984-87, treas., 1994—; counselor's com. U.S. Swimming, Colo. Springs, 1985—, chmn., 1994—. Fellow ABA; mem. Calif. Barristers Assn. (bd. dirs. 1973-75, v.p. 1975), L.A. Barristers Assn. (bd. dirs. 1972-74, v.p. 1974), L.A. County Bar Assn., Calif. Alumni Soc., Order of Coif, Thurston Soc. Presbyterian. Avocation: amateur competitive swimming, poetry and creative writing, growing roses. Fax: 213-617-9255. E-mail: edun-can2@arterhadden.com. Office: Arter & Hadden 725 S Figueroa St Ste 3400 Los Angeles CA 90017-5434

DUNCAN, ELLEN, media generalist; b. Idaho Falls, Idaho, Apr. 26, 1960; d. Robert Smith and Geraldine (Nielsen) hendricks; m. Clinton Bradley Duncan, Aug. 9, 1995; children: Hank, Michael, Katy, Nattie, Nicolas, Oliver. BA in History, Idaho State U., 1982, EdB, 1989. Media generalist Idaho Falls HS, 1989—. Author, creator: (pamphlet) Guide to the Internet, 1997. Mem. Idaho Libr. Assn. (indexed book Beautiful Bonneville). Mem. LDS Ch. Avocations: biking, reading, children, tole painting. E-mail: duncan@d91.k12.id.us. Home: 2670 Ridgecrest Dr Idaho Falls ID 83404-8312 Office: Idaho Falls HS 601 S Holmes Ave Idaho Falls ID 83401-4726

DUNCAN, GLORIA CELESTINE, elementary educator; b. Columbia, S.C., May 31, 1944; d. John DuBois and Fannie Ruby Batiste; m. (div. Dec. 1975); 1 child, Jason Ira. AA, City Coll. San Francisco, 1965; BA, U. Bridgeport, 1968; MA, U. San Francisco, 1984. Presenter Calif. State Dept., Long Beach, 1990; mentor tchr. Alum Rock Sch. Dist., San Jose, 1990-94, educator, 1972—; adv. bd. San Jose Writing Project, 1993-96; assoc. dir. San Jose State U., 1993-96. Mem. youth adv. bd. Am. Cancer Soc., Santa Clara County, 1995—, vol., 1985—; mem. edn. com. Kids Voting U.S.A., Silicon Valley, 1994—; sr. warden St. Philip's Episcopal Ch., San Jose, Calif., 1988. Mem. Informal Computer Using Educators (membership co-chair, adv. bd. mem.), Delta Kappa Gamma (co-pres. 1996, pres. Gamma Psi chpt. 1998—), Phi Delta Kappa (Stanford chpt. historian 1995-96, treas. 1996—), Beta Pi Sigma (Soror of Yr. 1996). Avocations: travel, reading, sewing, knitting, playing tennis. Office: Mildred Goss Elem Sch 2475 Van Winkle Ln San Jose CA 95116-3758*

DUNCAN, JAMES RICHARD, systems administrator; b. Little Rock, June 3, 1948; s. James Richard and Mary (Bond) D. BA in Geography, U. Calif., Berkeley, 1969; postgrad. in mass comms., Denver U., 1970. Cons. self-employed San Jose, Calif., 1972-90; broadcast engr. Nationwide Comms., San Jose, Calif., 1985-90; corp. engr. Kool Comms., San Jose, Calif., 1990-95; network adminstr. United Broadcasting, San Jose, 1995-96; v.p. info. systems Taxwright, Inc., 1996-98; gen. mgr. OKAY Multimedia, 1998—; cons. Ohlone C.C., Fremont, Calif., 1990—; chief designer Okay Multimedia, 1998—. Mem. Am. Coun. for Arts, Ariel Dance Co., Santa Clara Ballet. Avocations: LINUX, internat. folk dance, ballet performance, ice skating. E-mail: JIM@OKAY.com.

DUNCAN, JOHN WILEY, mathematics and computer educator, retired air force officer; b. San Francisco, Aug. 8, 1947; s. Vernon Alexander and Nellie May (Shaw) D.; m. Trudy Rae Hirsch, Feb. 25, 1967; children: Amber Rose, John Anthony. BS in Math. and Physics, N.W. Mo. State U., 1969; MBA, So. Ill. U., 1973; MS in Computer Sci., U. Tex., San Antonio, 1982. Tchr. Savannah (Mo.) High Sch., 1969; enlisted USAF, 1969, advanced through grades to maj.; aeromed. officer 9AES USAF, Clark Air Base, The Philippines, 1978-80; student UTSA, San Antonio, 1981-82; systems implementation team leader Sch. of Health Care Scics., Sheppard AFB, Tex., 1982-83; asst. chief med. systems Hdqrs. Air Tng. Command, Randolph AFB, Tex., 1983-86; chief med. systems Hdqrs. Pacific AF, Hickham AFB, Hawaii, 1986-89, 15 Med. Group, Hickham AFB, Hawaii, 1989; instr. Kapiolani C.C., Honolulu, 1989-94; sys. mgr. Hawaii Correctional Industries, Aiea, 1994-96, Sci. Applications Internat. Corp., Ft. Shafter, Hawaii, 1996—; computer cons., 1983—; instr. Midwestern U., Wichita Falls, 1982-83, Tex. Luth. Coll., Sequin, 1984-86, Hawaii Pacific Coll., Honolulu, 1987-89, Leeward C.C., 1989—. Cons. Ronald McDonald House, San Antonio, 1986. Presbyterian. Avocations: computing, tennis, reading, travel. Home: 2114 Aluka Loop Pearl City HI 96782-1317

DUNCAN, RICHARD FREDRICK, JR., secondary education educator, travel consultant; b. Millry, Ala., July 12, 1947; s. Richard F. and Claire Louise (Wood) D.; m. Rebecca Susan Davis, July 14, 1973. AA, Okaloosa-Walton Jr. Coll., 1967; BS, Fla. State U., 1969, MS, 1971; postgrad., Ore. State U., 1981-82. Tchr. Gadsden County Sch. Bd., Quincy, Fla., 1970-71, Leon County Sch. Bd., Tallahassee, Fla., 1972-73, Beaverton (Oreg.) Sch. Dist. No. 48, 1973—; microbiologist Washington County, Hillsboro, Ore., 1971-72; cons. on sci. edn. Northwest Regional Ednl. Lab., Portland, Ore., 1978-79; cons. on marine edn. Ore. Dept. Edn., Salem, 1980-81. Recipient award for excellence in sci. teaching Ore. Mus. Sci. and Industry, Portland, 1984, Psdl. award, 1984. Mem. Assn. Presdl. Awardees in Sci. Teaching (nat. pres. 1987-88), Nat. Assn.Biology Tchrs. (Ore. Biology Tchr. of Year award 1981), Nat. Sci. Tchrs. Assn. (Presdl. award for excellence in sci. teaching, 1983, Sheldon award 1993), Oreg. Sci. Tchrs. Assn. (pres. 1980-81, Oreg. Jr. High Tchr. of Yr. award 1982), North Assn. Marine Educators (state dir. 1978-80), Masons, Shriners. Democrat. Avocations: sports, photography, sailing, scuba diving, camping. Home: 13240 SW Juanita Pl Beaverton OR 97008-6831 Office: Beaverton Sch Dist # 48 PO Box 200 Beaverton OR 97075-0200

DUNDAS, DENNIS FRANKLIN, plastic surgeon; b. L.A., Oct. 12, 1942; s. John Arthur and Wanda (Yoakum) D.; m. Zoe Lynn Anderson, Feb. 9, 1969; children: Gregory, Denise. BA, Johns Hopkins U., 1964; MD, U. So. Calif., 1968. Diplomate Am. Bd Plastic Surgery. Pvt. practice Kirkland, Wash., 1978—. Lt. comdr. USN, 1978—. Fellow ACS; mem. Am. Soc. Plastic Surgeons. Office: 13114 120th Ave NE Kirkland WA 98034-3014

DUNGAN, SHIRLEY ANN, religious organization administrator; b. Safford, Ariz., Jan. 11, 1932; d. Guy Austin and Mabel Esther (Houck) Rhoads; m. Gerald Knox, Dec. 26, 1954 (div. Apr. 1974); children: Dirk Daniel, Kevin Knox, Delta Lynn. RN, St. Mary's Coll., Tucson, 1954; BS, St. Francis Coll., Joliet, Ill., 1986. Adminstr. St. James Presbyn. Ch., Littleton, Colo., 1985—; chaplain Swedish Med. Ctr., Englewood, Colo., 1990—. Author: Development of a Stewardship Campaign, 1989; patentee of med. equipment. Organist, choir dir., Fed. Correctional Inst., Englewood, 1965-73; reader for the blind Nat. Libr. Congress, Washington, 1970-76. Fellow Nat. Assn. Ch. Bus. Adminstrn. (v.p. Mile High chpt.); mem. WETAR Investments Club, Denver. Home: 120 N Brown Ave Tucson AZ 85710-3100 Office: St James Presbyn Ch 3601 W Belleview Ave Littleton CO 80123-1757

DUNHAM, ANNE, educational institute director. Exec. dir. Youth Sci. Inst., L.A., 1995—. Office: Youth Sci Inst 296 Garden Hill Dr Los Gatos CA 95032-7669*

DUNHAM, JOHN HANDY, II, real estate developer and broker; b. Chgo., Sept. 29, 1925; s. John H. and Lee (Yerger) D.; divorced; children: John H. III, James U. BS, Purdue U., 1950. Salesman Workman Mfg., Chgo., 1950-58, Wallace Press, Chgo., 1958-66; exec. v.p., owner tech. sales Datafold Inc., Chgo., 1967-79; co-founder, owner Datafold Inc. (merger Am. Brands), 1979; owner, CEO, founder Span, Inc., Vail, Colo., 1980—; real estate developer and broker, 1980—; internat. chair R&D, Computer Supplies Industry Worldwide, 1970-79. Developer of test equipment; patentee in field. Active for more than 55 yrs. Boy Scouts Am., dir. transp. for 2 nat. jamborees and 1 world jamboree, 1995; bd. dirs. Bravo Guild/Music Festival of Vail, 1994-97. With USN, WWII, PTO, 1942-46. Decorated 13 battle stars; recipient Vigil, Scouters Key, Scout Masters Key, Dist. award of Merit, Silver Beaver award and Silver Antelope award Boy Scouts Am., 1956—. Avocations: swimming, scuba, sailing, hunting, fishing. Home: PO Box 1875 Vail CO 81658-1875 Office: Span Inc PO Box 5830 Avon CO 81620-5830

DUNHAM, JUDITH ANN, school administrator, education educator; b. Chgo., July 27, 1952; d. Kenneth Clyde and Josephine Lucy (Celio) Kleidon; m. Richard Glen Winter, Aug. 28, 1971 (div. 1983); children: Elisabeth (Lisa) Ann, Erik Gregory; m. Thomas Wayne Dunham, June 24, 1989; stepchildren: Kristin Elaine Dunham Montgomery, Mark Thomas, Geoffrey David, Heather Elizabeth Dunham Samson. BA, Calif. State U., Bakersfield, 1977; MA in Ednl. Adminstrn., Fresno Pacific U., 1995. Cert. tchr. Spanish, adminstrv. svcs. Tchr. Bakersfield (Calif.) City Sch. Dist., 1977-94, program specialist Stiern Mid. Sch., 1994-98; asst. prin. Gilroy (Calif.) High Sch., Gilroy Unified Sch. Dist., 1998—; mem. leadership team Calif. Learning Assessment Program, Sacramento, 1994-96; tchr. trainer Kern County Supt. of Schs. Office, Bakersfield, 1995-98; evaluator Nat. Evaluation Syss., Sacramento, 1995-98, elem. disting. sch. program Calif. Dept. Edn., Sacramento, 1998; program quality rev. cons. Richland-Lerdo Sch. Dist., Shafter, Calif., 1996-98; instr. U. La Verne, Bakersfield, 1998. Singer Bakersfield Masterworks Chorale, 1990-98; lic. lay min. St. Luke's Episcopal Ch., Diocese San Joaquin, Bakersfield, 1991-92, secretariat, rectora Southeast Cursillo Secretariat, Diocese San Joaquin, Fresno, 1991-98. Grantee EITEL Project, Santa Clara County, Calif., 1996; LEA-MediCal grantee Kern County Collaborative, Bakersfield, 1996; Sch. Violence Prevention grantee Kern County Supt. Schs. Office, Bakersfield, 1997; Health Start Operational grantee, Safe Sch. grantee Calif. Dept. Edn., 1998. Mem. AAUW, ASCD, Calif. Assn. Bilingual Edn., Assn. Calif. Sch. Adminstrs. Republican. Avocations: choral singing, travel, church ministry. E-mail: dunhamja@light-speed.net. Home: 3708 Candewood Dr Bakersfield CA 93306 Office: Gilroy H S 10th St Gilroy CA 95020

DUNIPACE, IAN DOUGLAS, lawyer; b. Tucson, Dec. 18, 1939; s. William Smith and Esther Morvyth (McGeorge) D.; m. Janet Mae Dailey, June 9, 1963; children: Kenneth Mark, Leslie Amanda. BA magna cum laude, U. Ariz., 1961, JD cum laude, 1966 Bar: Ariz. 1966, U.S. Supreme Ct. 1972, Nev. 1994, Colo., 1996. Reporter, critic Long Branch (N.J.) Daily Record, 1963; assoc. firm Jennings, Strouss, Salmon & Trask, Phoenix, 1966-69; assoc. Jennings, Strouss & Salmon, PLC, Phoenix, 1969-70, ptnr., 1971-93, mem., 1993—, chmn. comml. practice dept., 1998—. Reporter Phoenix Forward Edn. Com., 1969-70; mem. Phoenix Arts Commn., 1990-93, chmn., 1992-93; bd. mgmt. Downtown Phoenix YMCA, 1973-80, chmn., 1977-78; bd. dirs. Phoenix Met. YMCA, 1976-87, 88—, chmn., 1984-85; bd. mgmt. Paradise Valley YMCA, 1979-82, chmn., 1980-81; bd. mgmt. Scottsdale/Paradise Valley YMCA, 1983, mem. legal affairs com. Pacific Region YMCA, 1978-81; chmn. YMCA Ariz. State Youth and Govt. Com., 1989-95; bd. dirs. The Schoolhouse Found., 1990-96, pres., 1990-94, Kids Voting, 1990-94, Beaver Valley Improvement Assn., 1977-79, Pi Kappa Alpha Holding Corp., 1968-72, The Heard Mus. 1993-94, Ariz. Bar Found., 1996—, treas. 1998, 99, v.p., 1999—; trustee Paradise Valley Unified Sch. Dist. Employee Benefit Trust, 1980-93, chmn., 1987-93, Sch. Theology, Claremont, Calif., 1994—; trustee First Meth. Found. of Phoenix, 1984-93; mem. Greater Paradise Valley Cmty. Coun., 1985-87; bd. dirs. Heard Mus. Coun., 1990-95, pres. 1993-94; mem. Ariz. Venture Capital Conf. Planning Com., 1994—, mem. exec. com., 1997—, vice chmn., 1999—; mem. Assn. for Corp. Growth, 1995-96, Ariz. Bus. Leadership Assn., 1996—; bd. visitors U. Ariz. Law Coll., 1996—. Capt. AUS, 1961-63. Mem. State Bar Ariz. (securities regulation sect. 1970—, chmn., 1991-92, mem. com. unauthorized practice of law 1972-84, chmn. 1975-83, mem. bus. law sect. 1981—, chmn., 1984-85), State Bar Nev., State Bar Colo., Am., Fed. (pres. Ariz. chpt. 1980-81), Maricopa County Bar Assns. (bd. dirs. Corp. Coun. Divsn. 1996—), Ariz. Zool. Soc., U. Ariz. Law Coll. Assn. (bd. dirs. 1983-90, pres. 1985-86, bd. visitors 1996—), Smithsonian Assn., U. Ariz. Alumni Assn. (bd. dirs. 1985-86), Phi Beta Kappa, Phi Kappa Phi, Phi Delta Phi, Phi Alpha Theta, Sigma Delta Pi, Phi Eta Sigma, Pi Kappa Alpha (nat. counsel 1968-72). Democrat. Methodist (mem. met. Phoenix commn. 1968-71, lay leader 1975-

78, trustee 1979-81, pres. 1981; mem. Pacific S.W. ann. conf. 1969-79, lawyer commn. 1980-85, chancellor Desert S.W. ann. conf. 1985—). Clubs: Arizona, Renaissance, Orange Tree. Lodges: Masons, Kiwanis (pres. Phoenix 1984-85, disting. lt. gov. 1986-87, SW dist. cmty. svc. chmn. 1987-88, dist. activity com. coord. 1988-89, dist. laws and regulation chmn. 1989-90, 92-93, 95-96, asst. to dist. gov. for club svcs. 1990-91, field dir. 1991-92, dist. conv. chmn., 1993-94, pub. rels. chmn. 1996-98, mem. internat. com. on Project 39, 1988-89, internat. com. On to Anaheim 1990-91, internat. com. on leadership tng. and devel. 1991-92, 93-94, trustee SW dist. found. 1987-92, 1st v.p. 1990-92). Comments editor Ariz. Law Rev., 1965-66. Home: 4147 E Desert Cove Ave Phoenix AZ 85028-3514 Office: Jennings Strouss & Salmon PLC 2 N Central Ave Fl 14 Phoenix AZ 85004-2393

DUNKLE, MICHAEL JOSEPH, mathematics and technology educator; b. Jacksonville, N.C., Nov. 29, 1950; s. Kenneth Paul and Jane Elizabeth (Travis) D.; m. Kathlyn Anice Dunkle, June 14, 1980; children: Michelle Marie, Brooke Elizabeth. BA, UCLA, 1974; tchg. credential, Chapman Coll., 1989. Cert. tchr., Calif. Youth min. Young Life, Los Altos, Calif., 1976-79; owner, contr. Oaks Constrn. Co., Carmel, Calif., 1979-83; sales mgr. various cos., Monterey Peninsula, 1977-86; tchr. math. Salinas (Calif.) H.S. Dist., 1986-88; tchr. advanced algebra and math. Gonzales (Calif.) Union H.S. Dist., 1988—, tech. mentor, 1995—, acting tech. coord., 1993-97; asst. internet educator Monterey Office Edn., Salinas, summers 1996-98; tech. cons. MJD Computing Enterprises, Salinas, 1993-98; instr. tech. repair Gonzales Union H.S., 1993-98, sch. website master, 1995-97. Chief editor tech. plan Gonzales Sch. Dist., 1996, chief editor acceptable use plan, 1995. Mem. All Am. Swim Team, Coll. and Amiture Athletics League, 1969, 70, 71. Mem. Nat. Coun. Tchrs. of Math., Calif. Ednl. Data Processing Assn., Internat. Soc. Tech. in Edn., Gonzales Mac Users Group (leader, user group amb. 1992—), Mac Advs., UCLA Alumni Assn. (life). Avocations: wood working, classic automobiles, swimming, golf, computer repair and troubleshooting. Office: Gonzales Union HS PO Box 939 Gonzales CA 93926-0939

DUNLAP, F. THOMAS, JR., electronics company executive, engineer, lawyer; b. Pitts., Feb. 7, 1951; s. Francis Thomas and Margaret (Hubert) D.; m. Kathy Dunlap; children: Bridgette, Katie. B.S.E.E., U. Cin., 1974; J.D., U. Santa Clara, Calif., 1979. Bar: Calif., 1979, U.S. Dist. Ct. (no. dist.) Calif. 1979. Mgr. engring. Intel Corp, Santa Clara, Calif., 1974-78, adminstr. tech. exchange, 1978-80, European counsel, 1980-81, sr. atty., 1981-83, gen. counsel, sec., 1983-87, v.p., gen. counsel, sec., 1987—. drafter, lobbyist Semiconductor Chip Protection Act, 1984. Republican. Roman Catholic. Avocation: jogging. Office: Intel Corp Ste 4 2200 Mission College Blvd Santa Clara CA 95054-1549

DUNLAP, JAMES RILEY, SR., former financial executive, credit manager; b. Portland, Oreg., May 21, 1925; s. William Gates and Laura (Riley) D.; m. Betty Towe; children: James R. Jr., Brian Jay, William David. BSBA, U. Oreg., 1950; postgrad., Portland State Coll., 1963-65. Sales rep. Hyster Co., Portland, 1950-61; br. asst. mgr. Reynolds Metals Co., Portland, 1961-71; corp. credit mgr. Burns Bros. Inc., Portland, 1971-79, sec.-treas., 1979-89. Contbr. articles on credit and fin. mgmt. to profl. jours. With USAAF, 1943-46. Melvin Jones fellow. Mem. Nat. Assn. Credit Mgmt. (past pres., bd. dirs.), Internat. Assn. Credit Mgmt. (past pres., bd. dirs., Disting. Svc. award 1985, Herb Barnes Meml. award 1987), Portland Retail Credit Assn. (past pres., bd. dirs.), Oreg. State Cons. Credit Assn. (past pres., lifetime bd. dirs.), Portland Jaycees, Oreg. Motor Supply Credit Assn. (past pres., bd. dirs.), Consumer Counseling Svc. Oreg. (exec. com. 1979-89), Am. Contract Bridge League (past pres. Portland chpt., gold life master), Lions (past pres. host club), Masons (life), Elks, Delta Tau Delta Alumni Assn. (past pres.). Avocations: philately, bridge.

DUNLAP, KATHLEEN JANE, public relations executive; b. Roanoke, Va., Jan. 1, 1946; d. James Grantham and Kathleen Meredith (Haggerty) D. AB in English, Greensboro Coll., N.C., 1967; grad. publishing procedures Radcliffe Coll., 1970; MA in Mass Comm. Rsch./Journalism, U. N.C., 1971. Tchr., Dept. Edn., Va., 1968-70; asst. dir. devel. Washington and Lee U., Lexington, Va., 1970-73; dir. devel., instr. So. Sem. Jr. Coll., Buena Vista, Va., 1973-74; admissions rep. Art Inst. of Ft. Lauderdale, 1974-78; pres. Dunlap Assocs., Seattle, 1979-94; dir. pub. rels. Exploration Cruise Lines, Seattle, 1985-88, Soc. Expeditions, Seattle, 1989-90; mgr. pub. rels. Windstar Cruises, Inc., 1991-94; prin. Skinner Dunlap and Stevens Internat., L.L.C., 1994—. Writer video script, 1983 (Bronze medal Internat. Film & TV festival of N.Y. 1984). Editor: Outlet, 1982-84 (Pacesetter awards Internat. Assn. Bus. Communicators 1982-84); Live Wires, 1984—. Recipient Golden Bell award Hospitality Sales Mktg. Internat. Assn., 1995, Mem. pub. rels. com. Seattle Women's Commn., 1984. Mem. Pub. Rels. Soc. Am. (chair travel and tourism sect. 1991, 92, bd. dirs. 1997—, Totem awards Puget Sound chpt. 1995, 98, APEX '98 Award of Excellence), Travel Industry Assn. Am. (press and pub. rels. com. 1989-91), Soc. Am. Travel Writers, Sound of the Baskervilles (Seattle), DAR (Va. Frontier chpt., editor Silver Anniversary Yearbook Francis Broward chpt. 1976), Va. Soc. Colonial Dames of 17th Century, Magna Carta Dames. Office: 1800 112th Ave NE Ste 220E Bellevue WA 98004-2962

DUNLAP, RILEY EUGENE, sociologist; b. Wynne, Ark., Oct. 25, 1943; s. Riley W. Dunlap Jr. and F. Eugenia (Jones) Anderson; m. Lonnie Jean Brown, Aug. 20, 1966; children: Sara Jean, Christopher Eugene. MS, U. Oreg., 1969, PhD, 1973. From asst. prof. to prof. sociology Wash. State U., Pullman, 1972-85, 85-96, Boeing Disting. prof. environ. sociology, 1996—; mem. socioeconomic peer review panel Office of Exploratory Rsch., U.S. EPA, 1991; mem. panel on aesthetic attributes in water resources planning NRC/Nat. Acad. Scis., 1982; Gallup fellow in environment George H. Gallup Internat. Inst., 1992—. Editor, author: (jour. symposium) Am. Behavioral Scientist, 1980, Internat. Sociology, 1998; editor book: American Environmentalism: The U.S. Environmental Movement, 1970-90, 92, Pub. Reactions to Nuclear Waste, 1993. Mem. AAAS (rural sociol. soc. rep. to sect. K 1986-89), Internat. Sociol. Assn. (pres., rsch. com. on environ. and soc. 1994-98), Am. Sociol. Assn. (chmn. sect. on environ. sociology 1981-83, disting. contbn. award 1986), Rural Sociol. Soc. (chmn. natural resources rsch. group 1978-79, award of merit 1985), Soc. for Study of Social Problems (chmn. environ. problems divsn. 1973-75). Achievements include being credited as co-founder of field of environmental sociology. Fax: (509) 335-2125.. E-mail: dunlap@wsu.edu. Office: Washington State Univ Dept Sociology Pullman WA 99164-4020

DUNLAP, SAM B., personnel consulting firm executive; b. Williamsport, Pa., Mar. 13, 1924; s. Lewis Weaver Dunlap and Mary Clarrisa (Bathurst) Dunlap-Stromberg; m. Mary Elizabeth Gohl, Aug. 27, 1948; children: Gary Steven, Peter Craig. BS, U. N.Mex., 1947. Cert. employment cons.; cert. pers. cons. Pres., founder N. Mex. Employment Bur. dba Exec. Search, Albuquerque, 1951—; pres. N.Mex. State Employment Agy. Bd., 1971-78. Contbr. articles to profl. firms. Past mem. Jr. C. of C.; past bd. dirs. YMCA Albuquerque; mem. Pres.'s Club, U. N.Mex. Decorated Purple Heart, Silver Star. Mem. Am. Inst. Employment Counseling (past sec.), Sales Execs. Assn. (past bd. dirs.), Nat. Office Mgmt. Assn. (past bd. dirs., v.p.), Exec. Assn. Greater Albuquerque (past pres., co-founder, chmn. nominating com.), Albuquerque C. of C. (bd. dirs.), Heights Businessmen's Assn. (past bd. dirs.), Indsl. Found. Albuquerque (past mem. exec. com.), Albuquerque Bus. Bur. (bd. dirs. 1971-78), N.Mex. Assn. Commerce and Industry (past chair pers. com.), Am. Bus. Club (past bd. dirs.), Assn. Pvt. Employment Agys. in N.Mex. (founder, past pres., bd. dirs., hon. mem. bd.), Nat. Pers. Assocs. (past sec.), Mercedes Benz Club (N.Mex. sect. bd. dirs., v.p. 1995—, pres. 1991-92), Knife and Fork Club Albuquerque (past pres.), Four Hills Country Club Albuquerque (charter and life mem.), Los Hajolotes Boat Club (1st commodore, founder, past bd. dirs.), One Hundred Club, Masons (life, Blue lodge # 6). Republican. Presbyterian. Avocation: water sports. Home: 923 Hermosa Dr SE Albuquerque NM 87108-4310 Office: N Mex Employment Bur Inc dba Exec Search 7901 Mountain Rd NE Albuquerque NM 87110-7804

DUNN, DAVID CAMERON, entrepreneur, business executive; b. Juneau, Alaska, Dec. 8, 1941; s. Robert Charles and Kay (Watson) D.; m. Karen Ann Leonard, Jan. 17, 1970 (div. 1990); children: David Cameron Jr., Paige. BA, Stanford U., 1963; MBA, U. Pa., 1968. Account exec. J. Walter Thompson, N.Y.C., 1968-70; product mgr. Gen. Foods, White Plains, N.Y., 1970-73; dir. mktg. Heublein, San Francisco, 1973-77; exec. v.p. Perelli-Minetti Winery, San Francisco, 1977-79; sr. v.p., bd. dirs. Valchris Farms, Modesto, Calif., 1980-84, DFS Advt., San Francisco, 1984-87; pres. Thomas-Rahm Advt., Oakland, Calif., 1987-89, Mktg. Comms. Assocs., Oakland, 1990—; co-founder Re-Con Systems (OTC) 1968; bd. dirs. PC Guardian, San Rafael, Calif. Trustee Oakland Symphony, 1989-90, Orinda (Calif.) Edn. Found., 1986-87. 1st lt. U.S. Army, 1964-66, Germany. Mem. Lakeview Club, Oakland Athletic Club, Oakland C. of C. (Small Bus. of Yr. 1991), Commonwealth Club. Republican. Roman Catholic. Avocation: coin collecting. Office: MCANet Inc 299 3rd St Ste 101 Oakland CA 94607-4350

DUNN, EDWARD THOMAS, JR., lawyer, educator; b. L.A., Dec. 7, 1954; s. Edward Thomas and Beverly Jean (Dixon) D.; m. Marcy Jean McNeely, Nov. 5, 1977; children: Charles Jason Thomas, Laura Brianna, Kaeli Carissa Michele, Edward Thomas IV. BA, Biola U., 1977; postgrad., U. Calif., Irvine, 1980-81; JD, Southwestern U., 1984. Bar: Calif. 1985, U.S. Dist. Ct. (cen. dist.) Calif. 1985, U.S. Dist. Ct. (ea., no. and so. dists.) Calif. 1986, U.S. Ct. Appeals (9th cir.) 1985, U.S. Supreme Ct. 1989. Mem. minority staff com. on rules Ho. of Reps., Washington, 1976-77; asst. v.p., br. mgr. Downey Savs. & Loan Assn., Rolling Hills Estates, Calif., 1977-80; sr. atty. Calif. Ct. Appeal, Santa Ana, 1989, 97—; assoc. prof. law Orange County U., Newport Beach, 1990-94; pros. Orange County Dist. Atty. Office, Santa Ana, 1985-97; adj. prof. law Western State U., Fullerton, Calif., 1991—, Whittier Law Sch., 1997—. Bd. dirs. Whittier Christian H.S., La Habra, Calif., 1995—; assoc. mem. ctrl. com. Orange County Calif. Rep. Orgn., 1997-99; candidate Orange County Superior Ct. Judge, 1996; mem. First Evang. Free Ch. of Fullerton, 1964—, elder, 1995-99. Named Atty. of Yr. Constnl. Rights Found., 1988, Vol. of Yr. Calif. Rep. Orgn., 1997. Mem. Orange County Bar Assn. (ethics com. 1992-96, Cert. of Recognition 1995, appellate com. 1992-95), Orange County Attys. Assn. (bd. dirs. 1993-94), Calif. Family Support coun. (appellate com. 1975-95). Calif. Dist. Attys. Assn. (appellate com. 1987-96), Calif. State Bar (cert. specialist in criminal law). Avocations: keyboards, writer, musical arranger, sailing. Office: Calif Ct Appeal 4th Dist Divsn 3 925 N Spurgeon St Santa Ana CA 92701-3700

DUNN, JEFFREY EDWARD, neurologist; b. Shaker Heights, Ohio, Nov. 27, 1960; s. John Kenneth and Mary Margaret (O'Neill) D.; m. Sandra Lee Judy, Feb. 3, 1990; children: Caitlin Irene, Bronwyn Leigh, Colin John Donald. *Jeff and Sandy moved from Philadelphia to Seattle in 1990. The premonition that Sandy had that their children would be Pacific Northwesterners has proven true. The couple's three children were born and are being reared in the eastside suburbs of the Emerald City.* BA in French Lit., Haverford (Pa.) Coll., 1983; MD, Temple U., 1989. Diplomate Am. Bd. Psychiatry and Neurology. Molecular immunologist Fox Chase Cancer Ctr., Phila., 1984-85; intern Ea. Va. Grad. Sch., Norfolk, 1989-90; resident in neurology U. Wash., Seattle, 1990-93; attending physician Neurol. Assocs. of Wash., Bellevue, 1993—; clin. asst. prof. neurology U. Wash., Seattle, 1993—; founder, med. dir. Overlake Multiple Sclerosis Ctr., Bellevue, Wash., 1996—. *Jeff maintains a private neurological practice on Seattle's east side. He is the founder and present medical director of the Overlake Multiple Sclerosis Center, and a clinical assistant professor in neurology at the University of Washington. His clinical research efforts helped lead to the approval of copaxone in the treatment of relapsing-remitting multiple sclerosis.* Guest physician TV: MS Update, Denver, 1994, ALS Update, Seattle, 1995. Recipient Cert. of Excellence in MS Rx, Prodigy Online Com., 1995; named to Outstanding Young Men of Am., 1996. Mem. Am. Acad. Neurology, Am. Neurol. Assn., World Congress Neurology, North Pacific Soc. of Psychiatry and Neurology. Avocations: golf, skiing, camping, outdoor recreation. Office: Neurol Assocs of Wash 1600 116th Ave NE Ste 302 Bellevue WA 98004-3057

DUNN, JEFFREY SCOTT, secondary education educator; b. Elmhurst, Ill., Aug. 10, 1956; s. Lloyd Graham and Eloise (Freeland) D.; m. Jamie Lynn Shepherd, Apr. 6, 1965; children: Wilson Steele, Beck Cameron. BA in English, Allegheny Coll., 1978, MA in Edn., 1981; MA in English Lit., U. Pitts., 1986, PhD in English Lit., Cultural Studies, 1991. Cert. English tchr. Wash., Pa. Music dir. Sta. WARC-FM, Meadville, Pa., 1977-78; tchr. English, Lorain (Ohio) Cath. H.S., 1978-80, Seton-La Salle H.S., Pitts., 1980-91, Ctrl. Cath. H.S., Pitts., 1981-93, Elma (Wash.) H.S., 1993—; performance assessment trainer Ednl. Svc. Dist. 113, Olympia, Wash., 1998—; mem. Goals 2000 com. Elma Sch. Dist., 1997—, assessment and curriculum alignment com., 1994—. Auhtor: William S. Burroughs and Technologizing Literary Studies in the Industrial Age, 1991. Elder 3d Presbyn. Ch., Pitts., 1993, mem. social justice com., 1993, chair Christian Edn. com., 1991, deacon, 1989. Recipient Svc. award Duquesne U., Pitts., 1993. Mem. NEA, Nat. Coun. Tchrs. English, Western Pa. Coun. Tchrs. English, Wash. Edn. Assn. Avocations: writing fiction and poetry, gardening, popular music, cultural criticism. Home: 1602 W Martin St Elma WA 98541-9011 Office: Elma HS 1235 Monte Elma Rd Elma WA 98541-9038

DUNN, JENNIFER BLACKBURN, congresswoman; b. Seattle, Wash., July 29, 1941; d. John Charles and Helen (Gorton) Blackburn; div.; children: Bryant, Reagan. Student, U. Wash., 1960-62; BA, Stanford U., 1963. Former chmn. Rep. Party State of Wash.; now mem. 103rd Congress (now 106th Congress) from 8th Wash. dist., Washington, D.C., 1993—; mem. house oversight com., mem. Ways and Means Com. Del. Rep. Nat. Conv., 1980, 84, 88; presdl. apptd. adv. coun. Historic Preservation; presdl. apptd. adv. coun. volunteerism SBA. Mem. Gamma Phi Beta. Office: US House of Reps 432 Cannon Bldg Washington DC 20515-4708*

DUNN, KAREN K., mental health center executive, psychotherapist; b. Clovis, N.Mex., Dec. 10, 1944; d. Kent King II and Regina Catherine (Seitz) Chesney; m. Thurman Stanley Dunn, Mar. 31, 1969; children: Michelle, Stan II. BS, Ea. N.Mex. U., 1966; MA, U. N.Mex., 1968; postgrad., U. Ariz., 1973-76, Denver Sem., 1995—. Employment counselor Ariz. State Employment Svc., Tucson, 1970-73; counselor, faculty mem. Pima C.C., Tucson, 1975-76; instr. psychology Cochise Coll., Sierra Vista, Ariz., 1976-78; pvt. practice Denver, 1979-81; pres., CEO Discovery Learning Ctr., Parker, Colo., 1981-85; mental health therapist Prince William County, Manassas, Va., 1988; substance abuse specialist Prince William County Schs., Manassas, Va., 1989; exec. dir., CEO KM Counseling and Resource Ctr., Parker, Colo., 1990—; with United Airlines, Englewood, Colo. Contbr. articles to profl. jours. Active Mile High United Way; v.p., pres. Parker Newcomers Club; health com. Douglas County Commnrs., Castle Rock, Colo., 1994-95; bd. dirs. Human Resource Coun., 1993-95, Douglas County Com. Youth and Families, 1995. Mem. Colo. Assn. Non-Profit Execs., Parker C. of C., Douglas County Srs. Avocations: community service projects, writing, Christian service projects. Home: 6281 S Netherland Way Aurora CO 80016-1327

DUNN, LARRY A., computer engineer; b. Lansing, Mich., Jan. 31, 1956; s. Fred H. and Inger K. Dunn. BA in Computer/Math., San Jose State U., 1987. Computer engr. Singer-Link, Sunnyvale, Caif., 1979-81, GE/Calma, Sunnyvale, 1981-83; sr. computer engr. KLA/Tencor, San Jose, Calif., 1984—. Shelter vol. Next Door, San Jose, 1996—. Recipient Unsung Hero award Next Door, 1998. Mem. Sierra Club, Profl. Rodeo Cowboys Assn. Mem. Green Party. Avocations: hiking, camping, rodeos. Home: 139 Action Ct Fremont CA 94539-7422

DUNN, MARIAN C., artist; b. Salt Lake City, Aug. 5, 1930; d. Arty Worth and Lillian Amanda (Quick) Clark; m. William Prescott Dunn Jr., June 11, 1951 (dec. June 1971); children: Jeff, Cary, Scott; m. James Kenneth Sweeney, Apr. 25, 1995. AS, Weber State Coll., 1949; BFA cum laude, U. of Utah, 1951. cons. in field. Bd. dirs. Salt Lake City Jr. League, 1954—; adv. bd. Salt Lake City Art Ctr., 1960-74, Mus. of Fine Arts U. of Utah, Salt Lake City, 1980-85; bd. dirs. Associated Utah Artists, Salt Lake City, 1990-98. Mem. Am. Watercolor soc., Nat. Watercolor Soc., Watercolor West. Avocations: tennis, golf, bridge, travel. Home and Studio: 2228 Bryan Cir Salt Lake City UT 84108-2711 also: 1857 Midvale Ave Apt 201 Los Angeles CA 90025-6350

DUNN, RICHARD JOSEPH, retired investment counselor; b. Chgo., Apr. 5, 1924; s. Richard Joseph and Margaret Mary (Jennett) D.; AB, Yale U., 1948; LLB, Harvard U., 1951, MBA, Stanford U., 1956; m. Marygrace Calhoun, Oct. 13, 1951; children: Richard, Marianne, Anthony, Gregory, Noelle. Admitted to Tex. bar, 1952; mem. firm Carrington, Gowan, Johnson & Walker, Dallas, 1951-54; investment counselor Scudder, Stevens & Clark, San Francisco, 1956-84, v.p., 1965-77, sr. v.p., 1977-84, gen. ptnr., 1974-84; ret. Served with AUS, 1943-46. Decorated Combat Infantry Badge, Bronze Star, Purple Heart; Knight of the Sovereign Mil. Hospitaller Order of St. John of Jerusalem of Rhodes and of Malta, Western Assn., 1978—, chancellor 1987-93, pres. 1993—, knight of obedience, 1990, comdr. Cross of Merit, 1989, Grand Cross The Sacred Mil. Constantinian Order of St. George, 1995; recipient Assumpta award Archdiocese of San Francisco, 1996. Roman Catholic. Home: 530 Junipero Serra Blvd San Francisco CA 94127-2727

DUNNE, KEVIN JOSEPH, lawyer; b. Pitts., Sept. 22, 1941; s. Matthew S. and Marjorie (Whelan) D.; m. Heather Wright Dunne, Sept. 27, 1963; children: Erin, Kevin Jr., Patrick, Sean. BA, U. Conn., 1963; JD, Georgetown U., 1966. Bar: Calif. 1967, U.S. Dist. Ct. (no. dist.) Calif., 1967, U.S. Dist. Ct. (ea. dist.) Calif. 1969, U.S. Dist. Ct. (ctrl. dist.) Calif. 1971, U.S. Ct. Appeals (9th cir.) 1971. Assoc. Sedgwick, Detert, Moran & Arnold, San Francisco, 1968-75, ptnr., 1975—; adj. prof. U. San Francisco Sch. Law, 1980-86; bd. editorial advisors Bender's Drug Product Liability Reporter, 1988-92. Author: Dunne on Depositions, 1995; editor Defense Counsel Training Manual, 1989; contbr. articles to profl. jours. Capt. U.S. Army, 1966-68, Vietnam. Recipient Bronze Star, Army Commendation medal; recipient Exceptional Performance award Def. Rsch. Inst., 1988. Fellow Internat. Acad. Trial Lawyers, Am. Coll. Trial Lawyers; mem. No. Calif. Assn. Def. Counsel (pres. 1987-88), Internat. Assn. Def. Counsel (pres. elect 1994-95), Am. Bd. Trial Advocates. Roman Catholic. Avocation: golf. Office: Sedgwick Detert Moran & Arnold 1 Embarcadero Ctr Ste 1600 San Francisco CA 94111-3716*

DUNNETT, DENNIS GEORGE, state official; b. Auburn, Calif., Aug. 5, 1939; s. George DeHaven and Elizabeth Grace (Sullivan) D. AA in Elec. Engring., Sierra Coll., 1959; AB in Econs., Sacramento State Coll., 1966. Engring. technician State of Calif., Marysville, 1961-62; data processing technician State of Calif., Sacramento, 1962-67, EDP programmer and analyst, 1967-74, staff services mgr. and contract adminstr., 1974-76, hardware acquisition mgr., 1976-86, support services br. mgr., information security officer, 1986-90, chief Office Security and Operational Recovery, 1990-92, spl. projects mgr., 1992-93, customer support ctr. mgr., 1994, procurement mgr., 1994-97, chief bur. adminstrn., 1997—. Mem. AARP, IEEE Computer Soc., Assn. Info. Tech. Profls., Assn. Inst. Cert. of Computers Profls. (certs.), Calif. Assn. Mgrs. and Suprs., Fine Arts Mus. of San Francisco, Crocker Art Mus. Home: 729 Blackmer Cir Sacramento CA 95825-4704 Office: Teale Data Ctr 2005 Evergreen St Sacramento CA 95815-3831

DUNNIGAN, MARY ANN, former educational administrator; b. St. Maries, Idaho, Sept. 7, 1915; d. William Henry and Mary Ellen (Kelly) D.; BA, Holy Names Coll., Spokane, 1942; MA, Gonzaga U., Spokane, 1957; postgrad. U. Idaho, UCLA. Tchr. rural schs. Bonner County, 1936-41, elem. schs., 1941, 45-59, high sch., 1942, 45, coordinator elem. edn., 1959-78; prin. kindergarten Sch. Dist. 271, Coeur d'Alene, Idaho, 1978-81; tchr. extension classes U. Idaho; curriculum chmn. Gov.'s Conf. on Edn.; adv. council Head Start. Mem. adv. coun. Coun. for Aging; mem. N. Idaho Mus., Community Council, Community Concerts, Community Theater, N. Idaho Booster Club, Mayor's Com. on Handicapped; mem. task force and diocesan bd. Cath. Edn. of Idaho, 1969-74; mem. Coeur d'Alene U.S. Constn. Bicentennial Com., 1986-91. Bd. dirs. Coeur d'Alene Tchrs. Credit Union, 1958-87, pres., treas., 1976-89; hist. chmn. Coeur d'Alene Centennial, 1986-89, chmn. hist. com., 1988, mem. state centennial com. for Koetenai county, 1990; parliamentarian Idaho Coun. Catholic Women State Conv., 1993, Idaho Cath. Daus. of Am. State Conv., 1994, sterring com. New Holy Famliy Cath. Sch. in Koatenai County Idaho, 1994, Parliomentation fo Idaho Coun. of Cath. Women, 1992. Named Citizen of Yr. N. Idaho Coll., 1974, Idaho Cath. Dau. of Year, 1968, Educator of Yr. Koatenai County Women's Forum, 1998; named to Idaho Retired Tchr.'s Hall of Fame, 1987; recipient Hon. Alumnus award N. Idaho Coll., 1987, Nat. Community Svc. award AARP/NRTA, 1989. Mem. Idaho Edn. Assn., NEA, Idaho Ret. Tchrs. Assn. (state chmn. pre-retirement 1985-92), Kootenai County Ret. Tchrs. Assn. (pres. 1983-87), Delta Kappa Gamma (charter, past pres Zeta chpt 1947-92; recipient Silver Bell award for 50 years, 1997). Club: Cath. Daus. Am. (state regent 1956-62, recipient 50 Year Pin, 1997). Home: 720 N 9th St Coeur D Alene ID 83814-4259

DUNNING, KENNETH LAVERNE, research physicist; b. Yale, Iowa, Sept. 24, 1914; s. Howard Grant and Gertrude Estelle (Dygert) D.; m. Ruth Ellen Pyle, Sept. 2, 1941; children: David M., Jane B., John K., Marion Leigh. BEE, U. Minn., 1938; MS in Physics, U. Md., 1950; PhD in Physics, Cath. U. Am., 1968. Engr. Western Union, N.Y.C., 1938-41; physicist U.S. Naval Research Lab., Washington, 1945-80; cons. Port Ludlow, Wash., 1981—. Contbr. articles to profl. jours. Pres. Highland Greens Condominium Assn., Port Ludlow, 1983-84, v.p. 1984-85. Served to maj. U.S. Army, 1941-45. Recipient Research Pub. award Naval Research Lab., 1971. Mem. IEEE, Am. Phys. Soc., Sigma Xi, Tau Beta Pi, Eta Kappa Nu. Home and Office: 10 Foster Ln Port Ludlow WA 98365

DUNSTAN, LARRY KENNETH, insurance company executive; b. Payson, Utah, May 26, 1948; s. Kenneth Leroy Dunstan and Verna Matilda (Carter) Taylor; m. Betty K. Limb, Sept. 23, 1966 (div. June 1975); children: Tamara, Thane; m. Jacqueline Lee Darron, Oct. 7, 1975; children: Tessa, Matthew, Bennett, Spencer, Adam. CLU, CPCU, chartered fin. cons., registered health underwriter, life underwriter tng. council fellow. Mgr. Diamond Bar Inn Ranch, Jackson, Mont., 1972-73; agt. Prudential Ins. Co., Missoula, Mont., 1973-77; devel. mgr. Prudential Ins. Co., Billings, Mont., 1977-78; div. mgr. Prudential Ins. Co., Gt. Falls, Mont., 1978-83; pres. Multi-Tech Ins. Services, Inc., West Linn, Oreg., 1983—; agy. mgr. Beneficial Life Ins. Co., Portland, Oreg., 1983-88. Mem. planning commn. City of West Linn, Oreg., 1985-87; mem. bishopric Ch. Jesus Christ of Latter Day Sts., West Linn, 1984-86, exec. sec. Lake Oswego Oreg. Stake, 1987-89; scouting coord. Boy Scouts Am., West Linn, 1984-86, scoutmaster various troops; pres. West Linn Youth Basketball Assn., 1991-97, West Linn/Wilsonville Youth Track Club, 1993-96. Named Eagle Scout Boy Scouts Am., 1965, recipient Heroism award 1965. Fellow Life Underwriter Tng. Coun. (bd. dirs. local chpt. 1980-81); mem. Gen. Agts. and Mgrs. Assn. (bd. dirs. local chpt. 1981-82), Am. Soc. CLU (pres. local chpt. 1982-83). Republican. Avocations: sports, stamp collecting, hunting, gardening, photography. Home: 19443 Wilderness Dr West Linn OR 97068-2005 Office: Multi-Tech Ins Svcs 19125 Willamette Dr West Linn OR 97068-2019

DUONG, ANDY HUE, poet, writer; b. Haiphong, Vietnam, Oct. 17, 1925; m. Bich Do Thi. BA in Pub. Adminstrn., Nat. Sch. Pub. Adminstrn., Vietnam, 1958; ND, Am. Natural Health, 1992. Cert. oriental and Chinese medicine. Tchr. Vietnam, 1946-51; apprentice Law Sch., Vietnam, 1952-55; chief exec. and fin. officer various govt. depts., Vietnam, 1958-75; writer, pub. Ctr. Oriental Studies, 1975—; founder, CEO, Oriental Studies, San Jose, 1976, Lac Viet's Poetry Forum, San Jose, 1992, Assn. Culture Exch., 1993. Author: Green Poems 19, 1955, Women's Psychology in Popular Songs, 1958, DHA Poems, 12 books, 1991-97. 1st lt. U.S. Army, 1958-75. Buddhist. Avocations: reading, writing, music, travel. Home: 1923 Mount Pleasant Rd San Jose CA 95148-1324

DUONG, TONY, electrical engineer, consultant; b. Saigon, Vietnam, June 21, 1964; came to U.S., 1975; s. Mau Duc and Hao Thi (Nguyen) D.; m. Uyen Phuong Tran; children: Jason Duc-Tien, Eric Duc-Loc. BSEE, U. Calif., Davis, 1986. Sr. staff engr. Applied Signal Tech. Inc., Sunnyvale, Calif., 1986-94; dir. engring. Jetfax Inc., Menlo Park, Calif., 1994-95; pres. Stellar Engring. Inc., San Jose, Calif., 1995—. Mem. IEEE (sr.), Phi Theta Kappa. Republican. Achievements include contributions to design, development and deployment of telecommunications, computer networking and office automation equipments; leadership in the design and development of fax/modem demodulator, FDM-to-PCM transmultiplexer T3/T1 Mux/Demux, fast ethernet switch, multifunctional products, and EMC compliance. E-mail: tonyd@stellarengineering.com. Home: 1579 Deluca Dr San Jose CA 95131-3026

DUPEE, PAMELA ANNETTE, fisheries biologist, educator, consultant; b. Lemmon, S.D., Nov. 4, 1957; d. William Morrison and Dorothy Faith (Winkowitsch) D. BS in Fisheries with honors, Oreg. State U., 1982; MS in Zoology, U. Queensland, Brisbane, Australia, 1985. Cert. coxswains powerboat, Queensland; divemaster, rescue diver, advanced diver, open-water diver, Nat. Assn. Underwater Instructors. Fish culture asst. U.S. EPA, Corvallis, Oreg., 1978-80; fish and game cadet Oreg. State Police, Medford, 1981; U.S. fgn. fisheries biologist U. Wash., Seattle, 1979, 80, 82; edn. and rsch. specialist Reef Biosearch Pty. Ltd., Pt. Douglas, Australia, 1986-89; prof. naturalist Daintree (Australia) Reef and Rainforest Ctr., 1989; profl. photographer Pt. Douglas, 1987-90; rsch. fisheries habitat biologist Ea. Oreg. State Coll. Oreg. Dept. Fish and Wildlife, Hines and LaGrande, 1990-95; cons. Market Am., Colorado Springs, 1998—; sales and mktg. rep. MCI Telecom., Inc., Colorado Springs, 1996—; cons. Market America, Colorado Springs, 1998—. Contbr. numerous articles, reports, and presentation to profl. confs. and publs. Recipient 3 photographic awards for color prints and audiovisual, 1984-87, R.E. Chambers Meml. award for outstanding rsch. and writing in environ. and ecol. concerns, 1982, Albany Kiwanis Outstanding Achievement award, 1976; rsch. grantee (2) Gt. Barrier Reef Marine Park Authority, 1983-84; Milwaukie Rod and Gun Club scholar, 1979, Albany Altrusa scholar, 1976, Fulbright scholar U. Queensland, 1982-85. Mem. NAFE, Am. Fisheries Soc. (Oreg. State U. student rep. 1979, Cert. Recognition Oreg. chpt. 1995), Ocean Realm, Mortar Board, Alpha Zeta. Avocations: photography, fishing, hunting, travel, swimming, scuba. Home: 2522 Goldrush Drive Apt 3 Colorado Springs CO 80906

DU PEN, EVERETT GEORGE, sculptor, educator; b. San Francisco, June 12, 1912; s. George E. and Novelle (Freeman) DuP.; m. Charlotte Canada Nicks, July 1, 1939; children: Stuart, Destia, Novelle, William, Ninia, Marguerite. Student, U. So. Calif., 1931-33, Chouinard Art Sch., Los Angeles, summer 1932, Harvard Sch. Architecture, summer 1933; B.F.A. (scholar), Yale, 1937; B.F.A. European traveling fellow, 1937-38. Teaching fellow Carnegie Inst. Tech. Sch. Art, 1939-39; teaching asst. sculpture Washington U. Sch. Art, St. Louis, 1939-42; marine draftsman and loftsman Sausalito Shipbldg. Corp., Calif., 1942-45; instr. sculpture U. Wash. Sch. Art, Seattle, 1945-47; asst. prof. U. Wash. Sch. Art, 1947-54, asso. prof. sculpture, 1954-60, prof. art, 1960-82, prof. emeritus, 1982—, chmn. sculpture div. One-man shows include Seattle Art Mus., 1950, Bon Marche Nat. Gallery, Seattle, 1970, Fred Cole Gallery, Seattle, 1973, Pacific Luth. U., Tacoma, 1975, Wash. Mut. Savs. Bank, Seattle, 1979-80, Frye Art Mus., Seattle, Martin and Zambito Gallery, Seattle; exhibited Prix de Rome Exhbn., Grand Central Gallery, N.Y.C., 1935-37, 39, St. Louis Mus. Ann., 1939-42, Nat. Acad. Design, N.Y.C., 1943, 49, 53-55, 57-58, Seattle Art Mus. Ann., 1945-59, Pa. Acad. Art, Phila., 1950-52, 55-58, Ecclesiastical Sculpture competition, 1950, Sculpture Ctr., N.Y.C., 1951, 53, 54, Pa. Acad. Fine Arts, 1954-58, Detroit Mus. Art, 1958, N.W. Inst. Sculpture, San Francisco Art Assn., 1959, Mainstreams, 1972, Marietta Coll., 1972, Holt Galleries, Olympia, Wash., 1980, Martin & Zambotti Gallery, Seattle, 1991-92, Freemont Art Gallery, Seattle, 1991-92, Ellensburg, Wash. Community Art Gallery, 1988, Bellevue, Wash. Invitational, Bellevue Art Mus., 1988, NAD, 1989, Wash. State Art Centennial Exhbn., Tacoma Art Mus., 1990; retrospective exhibits at Martin & Zambet Gallery, Seattle, 1994, Firye Art Mus., Seattle, 1994; represented in permanent collections Wash. Mut. Savs. Bank, Seattle, Bell Telephone Co., Seattle, Nat. Acad. Design, N.Y.C. (Saltus medal 1954), Seattle Art Mus., Safeco Ins. Co., U. Wash., also sculptures in pvt. collections; creator garden figures and portrait heads, small bronze, terra cotta, hardwood sculptures, archtl. medallions, sculpture panels for comml. bldgs. and theatres, figures and wood carvings various chs., relief panels U. Wash. campus, 1946, 83, bronze fountain Wash. State Library, Olympia, 1959, Du Pen Fountain, bronze fountain Coliseum Century 21, Seattle World's Fair, 2 walnut screens Mcpl. Bldg., Seattle, 8 large sculpture commns. Seattle chs., 1957-64, wood carving Risen Christ, St. Pius X Cath. Ch., Montlake Terrace, Wash., 1983, 3-foot wood carving St. Joseph and Mary, 1985, 6-foot wood carving Ascension, St. Elizabeth Seton Ch., Bothell, Wash., 1986, Elizabeth and Mary, 5-foot mahogany for Visitation Ctr., Fed. Way, Wash., 1990, 2-figure group for Dallas, 1982, bronze figure Edmonds, Wash., 1983-84, bronze sculpture of Charles Odegaard, pres. U. Wash., 1973, pvt. commns. Mem. U. Wash. Senate, 1952-55, exec. com., 1954-55; v.p. Allied Arts Movement for Seattle; mem. Seattle Municipal Art Commn., 1958-63. Recipient Saltus gold medal NAD, 1954, 1st prize for sculpture Bellevue (Washington) Arts and Crafts Fair, 1957; U. Wash. research grantee for creative sculpture, 1953-54. Fellow Nat. Sculpture Soc. (hon. mention Henry Herring competition); mem. Artists Equity Assn. (bd. Seattle chpt.), Nat. Acad. Design, Puget Sound N.W. Painters Group (bd.), N.W. Inst. Sculpture (pres. 1957), Allied Artists Am., U. Wash. Research Soc., Northwest Stone Sculptors, Seattle (bd. dirs. 1989—). Home: 1231 20th Ave E Seattle WA 98112-3530

DUPUY, PEDRO, film company executive; b. Guantanamo, Cuba, Feb. 22, 1922; s. Facundo and Edicta (Dupuy) Ilisastigui. Degree, U. Sci. & Philosophy, Waynesboro, Va.; student, Conservatory of Art & Music, Florence, Italy. Performer various, U.S., Europe, Asia; choreographer/dancer Sta. KTLA-TV, Sta. KCOP-TV, Paramount, L.A.; prodr./dir./choreographer/star Dupuy Prodns., N.Y.C., L.A., Las Vegas; record, video prodr. Dupuy Records/Prodns./Pub., Inc., Studio City, Calif.; prin. Moro-Landis/Dupuy Ltd. Studios, Studio City; talent mgr., cons. Dupuy Mgmt.; Glendale, Calif., 1992—; chmn., CEO F.H.S. Legacy Corp., Film Entertainment, L.A., 1998—; founder, pres. F.H.S. Legacy Corp.'s Actor-Writer Seminar, 1995—; contbg. dir./choreographer Variety Club Telethon, Easter Seals Telethon, Jerry Lewis MDA Telethon. Author: The Artist Unfolds Communication Through the Spirit, 1997, Mastery of Movement Through Dance, 1998; contbr. articles to profl. jours. Vol. prodr./dir. of stage plays Alemany Cath. Sch., L.A. Recipient Award of Commendation L.A. County Bd. Suprs., L.A. Mayor Tom Bradley. Mem. AFTRA, ASCAP, Am. Guild Variety Artists, Am. Fedn. Musicians, Nat. Assn. Recording Merchandisers, Conf. Personal Mgrs., Inc. Republican. Office: F H S Legacy Corp PO Box 9271 Glendale CA 91226-0271

DUQUE, RICARDO GERMAN, analytical chemist; b. Panama City, Panama, Nov. 14, 1970; came to U.S., 1988; s. Gabriel E. and Hilda Teresa (Soto) D. BS in Biochemistry, UCLA, 1993; MS in Analytical Chemistry, Calif. State U., Northridge, 1998. Lab. asst. Inst. Geophysics and Planetary Physics, UCLA, 1991-94, Jerry Lewis Neuromuscular Rsch. Ctr., UCLA, 1993-94; tchg. asst. Calif. State U., Northridge, 1993-98; high sch. sci. tchr. Bridges Acad., L.A., 1996-97; analytical chemist Micropolis, L.A., 1996-97, Maxtor Corp., Milpitas, Calif., 1998—. Mem. ACS, UCLA Assn. Chemists and Biochemists, UCLA Alumni Assn., Sigma Xi Sci. Rsch. Soc. (Donald Bianchi award 1996). Roman Catholic. Home: 6730 Ruffner Ave Van Nuys CA 91406-5641

DUQUETTE, DIANE RHEA, library director; b. Springfield, Mass., Dec. 15, 1951; d. Gerard Lawrence and Helen Yvette (St. Marie) Morneau; m. Thomas Frederick Duquette Jr., Mar. 17, 1973. BS in Sociology, Springfield Coll., 1975; MLS, Simmons Coll., 1978. Libr. asst. Springfield City Libr., 1975-78; reference libr. U. Mass., Amherst, 1978-81; head libr. Hopkins Acad., Hadley, Mass., 1980; instr. Colo. Mountain Coll., Steamboat Springs, 1981-83; libr. dir. East Routt Libr. Dist., Steamboat Springs, 1981-84; agy. head Solono County Libr., Vallejo, Calif., 1984; dir. libr. svcs. Shasta County Libr., Redding, Calif., 1984-87; dir. librs. Kern County Libr., Bakersfield, Calif., 1987—; chmn. San Joaquin Valley Libr. System, 1988. Contbr. articles to profl. jours. Recipient John Cotton Dana Spl. Pub. Rels. award, H.W. Wilson and ALA, 1989. Mem. ALA, Calif. Libr. Assn. (mem. coun. 1987—), Calif. County Librs. Assn. (pres. 1990). Democrat. Roman Catholic. Avocations: golf, skiing, bicycling, reading, gardening. Home: Pine Mountain Club PO Box 6595 Frazier Park CA 93222-6595 Office: Kern County Libr 701 Truxtun Ave Bakersfield CA 93301-4800

DURAN, MICHAEL CARL, bank executive; b. Colorado Springs, Colo., Aug. 27, 1953; s. Lawrence Herman and Jacqueline Carol (Ward) D. BS magna cum laude, Ariz. State U., 1980. With Valley Nat. Bank (name now Bank One, Ariz., N.A.), Phoenix, 1976—; corp. credit trainee Bank One Ariz. (formerly Valley Nat. Bank Ariz.), Phoenix, 1984-85; comml. loan officer Valley Nat. Bank Ariz. (name now Bank One Ariz.), Phoenix, 1985-86; br. mgr., asst. v.p. Valley Nat. Bank Ariz. (name now Bankone, Ariz.), Phoenix, 1986-90, comml. banking officer, asst. v.p., 1990-93, credit mgr., v.p., 1993—; cons. various schs. and orgns., 1986—; incorporator Avondale Neighborhood Housing Svcs., 1988. Mem. Cen. Bus. Dist. Revitalization Com., Avondale, Ariz., 1987-88, Ad-Hoc Econ. Devel. Com., 1988; coord. Avondale Litter Lifters, 1987-88; vol. United Way, Phoenix, 1984; bd. dirs. Jr. Achievement, Yuma, Ariz., 1989-91, vol., Phoenix, 1993—; yokefellow 1st So. Bapt. Ch. of Yuma, 1990-91; treas. Desert View Bapt. Ch., Gilbert, Ariz., 1998—. Recipient Outstanding Community Svc. award City of Avondale, 1988. Mem. Robert Morris Assocs., Ariz. State U. Alumni Assn. (life), Toastmasters, Kiwanis (local bd. dirs. 1986-88), Beta Gamma Sigma, Phi Kappa Phi, Phi Theta Kappa, Sigma Iota Epsilon. Democrat. Baptist. Avocations: art, photography, hiking, jogging. Home: 925 N Quartz St Gilbert AZ 85234-3661

DURANT, PENNY LYNNE RAIFE, author, educator; b. Albuquerque, May 22, 1951; d. John Carl and Patricia Fay (Bremermann) Raife; m. Omar Duane Durant, Jan. 2, 1971; children: Geoffrey Alan (dec.), Adam Omar. Student, Lawrence U., Appleton, Wis., 1969-70; BS, U. N.Mex., 1973, MA, 1980. Mem. adv. bd. Soc. Children's Book Writers and Illustrators/N.Mex., Albuquerque, 1996—. Author: Make a Splash!, 1991, Prizewinning Science Fair Projects, 1991, When Heroes Die, 1993 (Lambda Lit. award 1993, 1st prize juvenile novel Nat. League Am. Pen Women 1993, award of excellence N.Mex. Press Women 1993), Bubblemania!, 1995, Exploring the World of Plants, 1995, Exploring the World of Animals, 1995, More Prizewinning Science Fair Projects, 1998; works put to music, performed include We Are One, Aki's Story; conbr. articles to Parents Mag., Durango Mag., Working Parents, The Luth. Sec. bd. dirs. Albuquerque Children's Theatre, 1995—. Mem. Nat. League Am. Pen Women (v.p. Albuquerque br. 1990, sec. 1996, state letters chair 1996), S.W. Writers Workshop, Soc. Children's Book Writers and Illustrators (mem. adv. bd. N.Mex. chpt. 1997—). Democrat. Lutheran. Home: 305 Quincy St NE Albuquerque NM 87108-1344

DURDEN, ROME L., aircraft manufacturing company executive; b. L.A., Apr. 5, 1935; s. Rome and Hortense (Anderson) D.; m. Priscilla Louise Bibby, Oct. 27, 1962; children: Suzette, Steven. B in Laws, La Salle Extension U., 1971; DD (hon.), Universal Life, Modesto, Calif., 1980. Tech. writer Hughes Aircraft Co., Culver City, Calif., 1962-72; sr. tech. editor Hughes Aircraft Co., Culver City, 1972-79, sr. mgmt. systems specialist, 1979-89. Author: (Manuals) Guide for Drafting Procedure, 1981, Simplified Drawing Substitutions, 1984. Treas. Marysville United Meth. Ch., 1997—. Recipient Presentation gavel Ramona Park Adv. Coun., Long Beach, Calif., 1971. Mem. Harmony Woods Homeowners Assn. (bd. dirs., treas. 1996—). Home: PO Box 1322 Lake Stevens WA 98258-1322

DURHAM, BARBARA, state supreme court justice; b. 1942. BSBA, Georgetown U.; JD, Stanford U. Bar: Wash. 1968. Former judge Wash. Superior Ct., King County; judge Wash. Ct. Appeals; assoc. justice Wash. Supreme Ct., 1985—, chief justice, 1995-99, justice, 1999—. Office: Wash Supreme Ct Temple of Justice PO Box 40929 Olympia WA 98504-0929

DURHAM, CHRISTINE MEADERS, state supreme court justice; b. L.A., Aug. 3, 1945; d. William Anderson and Louise (Christensen) Meaders; m. George Homer Durham II, Dec. 29, 1966; children: Jennifer, Meghan, Troy, Melinda, Isaac. A.B., Wellesley Coll., 1967; J.D., Duke U., 1971. Bar: N.C. 1971, Utah 1974. Sole practice law Durham, N.C., 1971-73; instr. legal medicine Duke U., Durham, 1971-73; adj. prof. law Brigham Young U., Provo, Utah, 1973-78; ptnr. Johnson, Durham & Moxley, Salt Lake City, 1974-78; judge Utah Dist. Ct., 1978-82; assoc. justice Utah Supreme Ct., 1982—. Pres. Women Judges Fund for Justice, 1987-88. Fellow Am. Bar Found.; mem. ABA (edn. com. appellate judges' conf.), Nat. Assn. Women Judges (pres. 1986-87), Utah Bar Assn., Am. Law Inst. (coun. mem.), Nat. Ctr. State Courts (bd. dirs.). Home: 1702 Yale Ave Salt Lake City UT 84108-1836 Office: Utah Supreme Ct PO Box 140210 Salt Lake City UT 84114-0210*

DURHAM, FLETA EVELYN, educator, community volunteer; b. Nara Visa, N.Mex., May 24, 1919; d. Isaac Oren and Nellie Raye (Etheridge) D.; children: Mary Evelyn Price, Jo Beth Johnson. BA in Edn., Eastern N.Mex. U., 1953, postgrad. Elem. sch. tchr. Carlsbad (N.Mex.) Schs., 1953-75, team tchr. art, music and social studies, 1970-74; choir dir. Hillcrest Meth. Ch., Carlsbad, 1957; drama/puppet plays Meth. Chs., Carlsbad, 1978; vol. Connection Ctrs. Internat., Carlsbad, 1987-90, Hearts, Living Histories (Internat.) McDowell Pl., Phoenix, 1996. Originator, coord. children's drama, stories, 1960; composer children's songs, hymns, anthems, 1990-95; contbr. to World of Poetry, 1984. Founder Yokefellow divsn. Red Cross, Carlsbad, 1978-88; local coord. AARP Health Advocacy, 1990, AARP Vote, 1989. Named Tchr. of Yr. Carlsbad City Schs., 1975. Avocations: intergenerational projects, composing music, recording life stories of adults and children, organizing creative programs to develop and share talents. Home: 2635 N 20th Ave Phoenix AZ 85009-1936

DURHAM, HARRY BLAINE, III, lawyer; b. Denver, Sept. 16, 1946; s. Harry Blaine and Mary Frances (Oliver) D.; m. Lynda L. Durham, Aug. 4, 1973; children: Christopher B., Laurel A. BA cum laude, Colo. Coll., 1969; JD, U. Colo., 1973. Bar: Wyo. 1973, U.S. Tax Ct. 1974, U.S. Ct. Appeals (10th cir.) 1976. Assoc., Brown, Drew, Apostolos, Massey & Sullivan, Casper, Wyo., 1973-77; ptnr. Brown & Drew, 1977—. Permanent class pres. Class of 1969, Colo. Coll., Nat. Alumni Coun. Colo. Coll., 1995—; bd. dirs. Casper Amateur Hockey Club, 1970-77, sec. 1974-77; bd. dirs. Casper Symphony Assn., 1974-88, v.p., 1979-82, pres., 1983-87; bd. dirs., sec. Wyo. Amateur Hockey Assn., 1974-85, pres., 1985-88; bd. dirs. Natrona County United Way, 1974-76, pres., 1975-76; mem. City of Casper Parks and Recreation Commn., 1985-94, vice chmn., 1987-94, Nat. Alumni Coun. of The Colo. Coll., 1995—. Recipient State Heroes award SGMA, 1997. Mem. ABA, Wyo. Bar Assn., Natrona County Bar Assn., Nat. Assn. Railroad Trial Counsel, Phi Beta Kappa. Republican. Articles editor U. Colo. Law Rev., 1972-73. Home: 3101 Hawthorne Ave Casper WY 82604-4975 Office: 123 W 1st St Ste 800 Casper WY 82601-2486

DURHAM, ROBERT DONALD, JR., state supreme court justice; b. Lynwood, Calif., May 10, 1947; s. Robert Donald Durham and Rosemary Constance (Brennan) McKelvey; m. Linda Jo Rollins, Aug. 29, 1970; children: Melissa Brennan, Amy Elizabeth. BA, Whittier Coll., 1969; JD, U. Santa Clara, 1972; LLM in the Judicial Process, U. Va., 1998. Bar: Oreg. 1972, Calif. 1973, U.S. Dist. Ct. Oreg. 1974, U.S. Ct. Appeals (9th cir.) 1980, U.S. Supreme Ct. 1987. Law clk. Oreg. Supreme Ct., Salem, 1972-74; ptnr. Bennett & Durham, Portland, Oreg., 1974-91; assoc. judge Oreg. Ct. Appeals, Salem, 1991-94; assoc. justice Oreg. Supreme Ct., Salem, 1994—; mem. adv. com. to Joint Interim Judiciary Com., 1984-86; chair Oreg. Commn. on Adminstrv. Hearings, 1988-89; faculty Nat. Jud. Coll., Reno, Nev., 1992; mem. Case Disposition Benchmarks Com., 1992-93, Coun. on Ct. Procedures, 1992-93, 95—; mem. Oreg. Rules of Appellate Procedure Com., 1998—. Mem. ACLU Lawyer's Com., Eugene and Portland, Oreg., 1978-91. Recipient award for civil rights litigation ACLU of Oreg., 1988, Ed Elliott Human Rights award Oreg. Edn. Assn., Portland, 1990. Mem. Am. Acad. Appellate Lawyers (ninth cir. screening com. 1991—, rules com. 1994, co-chair appellate cts. liaison com. 1994), Oreg. Appellate Judges Assn. (pres. 1996-97), Oreg. State Bar (chair labor law sect. 1983-84, adminstrv. law com. govt. law sect. 1986), Calif. State Bar, Willamette Valley Inns of Ct. (master of bench, team leader 1994-98). Office: Oreg Supreme Ct 1163 State St Salem OR 97310-1331*

DURHAM, WARREN JOHN, television and radio producer; b. Spokane, Wash., Jan. 20, 1925; s. John J. and Esther Marion (Smith) D.; m. Lucy Maye Fleming, Apr. 8, 1950; children: James and Deborah (twins), Anne. BA, Wash. State U., 1949. Owner Sta. KLOQ, Yakima, Wash., 1956-62, Sta. KWIQ, Moses Lake, Wash., 1958-61, Sta. KDNC-AM-FM, Spokane, Wash., 1962-67, Cable Channel 9 TV, Spokane, 1977-81; host Nostalgia Cruises, 1990—. *Warren Durham founded, owned, and operated since 1954 Warren Enterprises, Inc., an international mass media marketing firm. It has served clients such as Reader's Digest, Sony Music, and others.* Host, founder (nat. TV show) Big Band Days; play-by-play announcer, disc jockey, packager, producer numerous nat. TV shows 1939—; exec. prodr. Belle of the White Star, 1996; prodr. (nat. touring prodn.) A Night to Remember; host nat. radio show Big Band Classics, 1997. Lt. (j.g.) USN, 1943-57, World War II. Home and Office: 901 W Rolland Ave Spokane WA 99218-2633

DURIS, ROBERT (ROBERT DE JONG), legal consultant, journalist; b. L.A., June 27, 1946; s. Duris W. and Evelyn Francis (Gear) de Jong; children: Desiree Roberta. BA in Journalism, U. Nev., 1978. Detective Globe Protection, L.A., 1966-67; program dir. Sta. KONE Radio, Reno, 1970-71; new anchor Sta. 11 TV, Reno, 1971-72; investigative reporter Sta. KOLO Radio, Reno, 1975-75; news dir. Sta. KWYZ Radio, Everett, Wash., 1979-80; sail news editor Boatracing Mag., Seattle, 1981-83; dir. Small Claims Legal Cons., Seattle, 1990—; host Northwest Folklife Festival, Seattle, 1983—. Contbr. articles to mags. With USN, USAR, 1963-90. Recipient Vietnam Svc. medal USN, Nat. Def. Svc. medal USN, Armed Forces Exped. medal USN, Army Achievement cert. USAR, 1984. Fellow Parents Without Partners, Inc.; mem. NRA, Nat. Writers Assn., Seattle Press., Eagles, Sigma Delta Chi. Avocations: folksinger. Office: Small Claims Legal Cons PO Box 47206 Seattle WA 98146-7206

DURKIN, JAMES BRENDAN, music publisher; b. Schenectady, N.Y., Oct. 19, 1963; s. William Thomas and Anne Marita (Deaker) D. BA, Berklee Coll. Music, 1986. Membership rels. A.S.C.A.P., L.A., 1988-91; music publ. Jobete Music, L.A., 1991-93; music agt. Ear to Ear Music, L.A., 1993-94, Vangelos Mgmt., Encino, Calif., 1994-96; A&R dir. Priority Records, Hollywood, Calif., 1996—. Author (song): Rhode Island State, 1988. Mem. Am. Ind. Music. Publ., Soc. Composers and Lycrists, ASCAP, BMI. Roman Catholic. Avocations: piano playing, music production, drawing, horseback riding, sailing. Home: 1146 N Gardner St Los Angeles CA 90046-5603 Office: Priority Records 6430 W Sunset Blvd Los Angeles CA 90028-7901

DURKOP, GEORGIA F., interior designer; b. Alexandria, La., Aug. 3; d. John D. and Nanny Landis (Barton) Freeman; m. Clarence Franklin Fielden, July 16, 1942 (wid. Dec. 1980); children: Clarence Franklin III, Landis Fielden Vance; m. Henry George Durkop, Aug. 3, 1994. BS, Vanderbilt U., 1941; postgrad., N.Y. Sch. Interior Design. Cert. designer ASID. Dept. head Camp Bon Air, Sparta, Tenn., 1939-42; art tchr. pub. schs., Jackson, Miss., 1940-41; assoc. designer J. Marshall Morin Interiors, Colorado Springs, Colo., 1953-56; owner, designer Georgia Fielden Interiors, Denver, 1956—; pub. dir. Am. Inst. Interior Design, Rocky Mountain, 1957-58, sec., 1959-60; mem. nat. com. pub. rels., ASID, N.Y., 1959-61. Exhbn. Colo. Springs Fine Art Mus., 1958; contbr. decorating and home fashion mags. Mem. ASID, DAR, PEO, Colonial Dames of Am., Soroptimist, Rotary (local v.p. 1959-60). Presbyterian. Avocations: organ, genealogy. Home: PO Box 441083 Aurora CO 80044-1083

DURYEE, DAVID ANTHONY, management consultant; b. Tacoma, Wash., July 29, 1938; s. Schuyler L. and Edna R. (Muzzy) D.; m. Anne Getchell Peterson, Nov. 26, 1966; children: Tracy Anne, Tricia Marie. BA in Bus., U. Wash., 1961, MBA, 1969; diploma, Pacific Coast Banking Schs., Seattle, 1973. Cert. fin. planner. Lending officer Seattle 1st Nat. Bank, 1964-68, v.p., trust officer, 1970-80; cons., chmn. Mgmt. Adv. Svcs., Inc., Seattle, 1980-93; mng. prin. Moss Adams Adv. Svcs., Moss Adams LLP, 1994—; bd. dirs. Lafromboise Newspapers, Inc., Seattle; lectr. in field; expert witness Wash., N.Y., Md., Calif., Mass., Ind., Fla. Author: The Business Owners Guide to Achieving Financial Success, 1994; contbr. articles to profl. jours. Capt. U.S. Army, 1962-64. Mem. Am. Soc. Appraisers, Internat. Assn. Fin. Planners, Inst. for Cert. Planners, Inst. Bus. Appraisers (speaker), Am. Bankers Assn., Nat. Retail Jewelers, Nat. Moving and Storage assn., Pacific N.W. Bankers Assn., Internat. Assn. for Fin. Planning, Estate Planning Coun. Seattle, Washington Bar Assn., Wash. State Trial Lawyers Assn., Wash. State Automobile Dealers Assn., Ky./Mo. Auto Dealers Assn., Motor Dealers Assn. B.C., Nat. Office Products Assn., Mayflower Warehousemen's Assn., Can. Movers Assn., Fedn. of Automobile Dealer Assns. of Can., Seattle Tennis Club, Seattle Yacht Club, Rotary. Avocations: tennis, boatin, skiing. Home: 3305 E John St Seattle WA 98112-4938 Office: Moss Adams Adv Svcs 1001 4th Ave Ste 2700 Seattle WA 98154-1101

DUSCHA, JULIUS CARL, journalist; b. St. Paul, Nov. 4, 1924; s. Julius William and Anna (Perlowski) D.; m. Priscilla Ann McBride, Aug. 17, 1946 (dec. Sept. 1992); children: Fred C., Steve D., Suzanne, Sally Jean; m. Suzanne Van Den Heurk, June 21, 1997. Student, U. Minn., 1943-47; AB, Am. U., 1951; postgrad., Harvard Coll., 1955-56. Reporter St. Paul Pioneer Press, 1943-47; publicist Dem. Nat. Com., 1948, 52; writer Labor's League for Polit. Edn., AFL, 1949-52, Internat. Assn. Machinist, 1952-53; editorial writer Lindsay-Schaub Newspapers, Ill., 1954-58; nat. affairs reporter Washington Post, 1958-66; assoc. dir. profl. journalism fellowships program Stanford (Calif.) U., 1966-68; dir. Washington Journalism Ctr., 1968-90; columnist, freelance journalist, West Coast corr. Presstime mag., San Francisco, 1990—; contbg. editor News Inc., San Francisco, 1998—. Author: Taxpayer's Hayride: The Farm Problem from the New Deal to the Billie Sol Estes Case, 1964, Arms, Money and Politics, 1965, The Campus Press, 1973; editor: Defense Conversion Advisory; contbr. articles to mags., including Washingtonian, N.Y. Times Mag., Changing Times. Recipient award for distinguished Washington corr. Sigma Delta Chi, 1961. Mem. Cosmos Club (Washington), Kappa Sigma. Home: 2200 Pacific Ave Apt 7D San Francisco CA 94115-1412

DUSHANE, PHYLLIS MILLER, nurse; b. Portland, Oreg., June 3, 1924; d. Joseph Anton and Josephine Florence (Eicholtz) Miller; m. Frank Maurice Jacobson, Mar. 13, 1945 (dec. 1975); children: Karl, Kathleen, Kraig, Kirk, Karen, Kent, Krista, Kandis, Kris, Karlyn; m. Donald McLelland DuShane, July 21, 1979 (dec. 1989); stepchildren: Diane DuShane Bishop, Donald III. BS in Biology, U. Oreg., 1948; BS in Nursing, Oreg. Health Scis. U., 1968. R.N., Oreg. Pub. health nurse Marion County Health Dept., Salem, Oreg., 1968-77; pediatric nurse practitioner Marion County Health Dept., Salem, 1977-91, Allergy Assocs., Eugene, Oreg., 1979-89; mem. allied profl. staff Sacred Heart Gen. Hosp., Eugene, 1979—. Named Oreg. Pediatric Nurse Practitioner of Yr., 1991. Mem. P.E.O., P.E.O. Sisterhood, Oreg. Pediatric Nurse Practioners Assn. (v.p. Salem chpt. 1977-78), Am. Nurses Assn., Oreg. Nurses Assn., Nat. Assn. Pediatric Nurse Assocs. and Practitioners, Am. Acad. Nurse Practitioners, Nurse Practitioners Spl. Interest Group, Salem Med. Aux. (sec. 1968), Oreg. Republican Women, Delta Gamma Alumni (v.p. 1979). Presbyterian. Avocations: travel, collecting clocks, aerobics, Yoga. Home: 965 E 23rd Ave Eugene OR 97405-3074 Office: Oakway Pediatrics P C 995 Willagillespie Rd # 200 Eugene OR 97401-2186 also: Eugene Pediatric Assocs 1680 Chambers St Eugene OR 97402-3655

DUSTON, ELDON CRAIG, nurse, educator; b. Colorado Springs, Oct. 13, 1955; s. Eldon Meral and Eva Florence (Chambon) D. AS, Pike Peak C.C., Colorado Springs, 1975; BS in Edn., U. Colo., 1978; BSN, Beth-El Coll. Nursing, 1995; MSN, FNP, student, U. Colo. RN, type A tchrs., Colo. Owner Craig Constrn., Colorado Springs, 1973-89; supr. Ecology Landscaping and Constrn., Colorado Springs, 1989-96; staff nurse Powers Med. Ctr., La Mar, Colo., 1997; pool nurse Nurse Finder, Colorado Springs, 1997—. Mem. Mountain Area Plain Partnership. Avocations: biking, fishing, swimming, hunting. Home: 329 S 18th St Colorado Springs CO 80904-3827

DUTT, BIRENDRA, research specialist; b. 1950. Cons. L.A.; with R & DLabs., Culver City, Calif., 1983—, now pres. Office: Research & Development Labs 5800 Uplander Way Culver City CA 90230-6608*

DUTTA, PARTHA, engineer; b. Durgapur, India, Sept. 4, 1966; came to U.S., 1990; s. Amiya Nath and Geeta (Sen) D. B in mech. engring. (hon.), Indian Inst. of Tech., 1989; MSME, U. Ky., 1991; PhD in mech. engring., Purdue U., 1995. Grad. engr. Larsen and Toubro Ltd., India, 1989; rsch. asst. U. Ky., Lexington, 1990-91; tchg. asst. U. Tex., Austin, 1991; rsch. asst. Purdue U., West Lafayette, Ind., 1992-95; sr. combustion engr. Solar Turbines, Inc., San Diego, Calif., 1995—. Contbr. articles to Atomization and Sprays, ASME Jour. of Engring. for Gas Turbines and Power, AIAA Jour., Combustion and Flame, ASME Jour. of Heat Transfer. Mem. ASME, Am. Inst. of Aeronautics and Astronautics, Combustion Inst. Achievements include significant and original contributions in the areas of radiative heat transfer predictions (ASME best paper award); application of effervescent atomization to liquid fuel atomization; application of novel statistical method to liquid dispersion predictions; application of catalytic combustion for drastic emissions reductions in industrial gas turbines, patent on application of catalytic combustion to gas turbines and innovative combustor cooling

techniques. Office: Solar Turbines Inc 2200 Pacific Hwy San Diego CA 92101-1773

DUTTON, PAULINE MAE, fine arts librarian; b. Detroit, July 15; d. Thoralf Andreas and Esther Ruth (Clyde) Tandberg; 1 child, Nancy Katherine; B.A. in Art, Calif. State U., Fullerton, 1967; M.S. in Library Sci., U. So. Calif., 1971; m. Richard Hawkins Dutton, June 21, 1969. Elem. tchr., Anaheim, Calif., 1967-68, Corona, Calif., 1968-69; fine arts librarian Pasadena (Calif.) Public Library, 1971-80; art cons., researcher, 1981—. Mem. Pasadena Librarians Assn. (sec. 1978, treas. 1979-80), Calif. Library Assn., Calif. Soc. Librarians, Art Librarians N.Am., Nat. Assn. Female Execs., Am. Film Inst., Am. Entrepreneurs Assn., Gilbert and Sullivan Soc., Alpha Sigma Phi. Club: Toastmistress (local pres. 1974).

DUVAL, BRIAN MICHAEL, art director; b. Manchester, N.H., May 7, 1972; s. Daniel Andre and Irene Doris (Tremblay) D. BFA, Colby-Sawyer Coll., 1995. Assoc. art dir. Infoworld Pub., San Mateo, Calif., 1995—. Vol. San Francisco AIDS Found., 1997. Recipient Spot Series award Soc. Pub. Design, N.Y.C., 1997. Avocations: stung kites, biking. Home: 55 Hermann St San Francisco CA 94102-6253 Office: Infoworld Pub 155 Bovet Rd San Mateo CA 94402-3108

DUVAL, JULIAN J., zoo executive; b. Oak Park, Ill., Feb. 15, 1947; s. Julian Adrian Duval and Isabel (Klawczyk) Luther; m. Becky Kotsarelis, Jan. 10, 1975 (div. Oct. 1980); m. Leslie Ann Berling, Feb. 5, 1990. AA, Coll. of Dupage, 1972; BS in Wildlife Mgmt., N.Mex. State U., 1974. Marine mammal trainer Brookfield Zoo, Chgo., 1965-71; curator, mammal and reptiles Parque Zool. Nat., Dominican Rep., 1975-78; adminstr. gen. Auto Safari Chapin, Guatemala, 1978-80; gen. curaotr Indpls. Zoo, 1980-87, v.p. zool. and botanical collections, 1987-94, v.p. scientific and program devel., 1994-95; exec. dir., CEO Quali Botanical Gardens, Encinitas, Calif., 1995—; mem. IUCN Species Survival Commn., Conservation Breeding, Specialist Group. Co-host: (TV program) At the Zoo, WRTV/ABC Indpls. Channel 6, 1989-95. Dir. Encinitas C. of C. Mem. Encinitas Rotary. Avocations: horticulture, wildlife study, photography, herpetology. Home: 325 Saxony Rd Encinitas CA 92024-2723 Office: Quail Botanical Gardens 230 Quail Gardens Dr Encinitas CA 92024-2707

DUVALL, LOURDES M., career officer; b. Neptune, N.J., Nov. 6, 1969; d. Donald and Maria Lourdes Fallace; m. Elven E. Duvall, Sept. 3, 1995. BS, U.S. Air Force Acad., 1991; M in Pub. Policy, Harvard Sch. Govt., Cambridge, Mass., 1993. Intelligence officer 8th Spl. Ops. Squadron, Ft. Walton Beach, Fla., 1994-95; from spl. security officer to chief intelligence sys. 611 Air Intelligence Flight, Elmendorf AFB, 1995-96; exec. officer 611 Air Ops. Group, Anchorage, Alaska, 1996—. Vol. tchr. English Anchorage Literacy Vols., 1997. Capt. USAF, 1991—. Mem. Assn. Grads. USAFA. Avocations: biking, cross-country skiing, hiking.

DUXLER, MICHAEL, educator; b. Chgo., Sept. 5, 1954; s. Berl Elliot and Anita Rachel (Brown) D.; m. Lisa Rebecca Duxler, Feb. 10, 1983; children: Kate, Anna. BS, Ill. State U., Normal, 1976; MSW, U. Tex., Arlington, 1981, PhD, 1994. Asst. dir. Timberlann Psychiat. Hosp., Dallas, 1977-91; dir. Los Alamos (N.Mex.) Family Coun., 1992-97; prof. N.Mex. Highlands U., Las Vegas, 1998—; pres. Canyon Inn Properties, Los Alamos, 1993-98. Avocations: weightlifhting, aviary interests. Home: 2877 Nickel St Los Alamos NM 87544-2115 Office: NMex Highlands Univ Ford Hall Las Vegas NM 87701

DUYCK, KATHLEEN MARIE, poet, musician, retired social worker; b. Portland, Oreg., July 21, 1933; d. Anthony Joseph Dwyer and Edna Elisabeth Hayes; m. Robert Duyck, Feb. 3, 1962; children: Mary Kay Boeyen, Robert Patrick, Anthony Joseph. BS, Oreg. State U., 1954; MSW, U. Wash., 1956. Cert. NASW, Oreg. Adoption worker Cath. Svcs., Portland, 1956-61, Cath. Welfare, San Antonio, 1962; musician Tucson Symphony, 1963-65; prin. cellist Phoenix (Ariz.) Coll. Orch., 1968-78, Scottsdale (Ariz.) Symphony, 1974-80; poet, 1993—. Author: (poetry cassettes) Visions, 1993 (Contemporary Series Poet 1993), Visions II, 1996 (Contemporary Series Poet 1996); contbr. to 9 Nat. Libr. of Poetry Anthologies. Rep. worker Maricopa County Reps., Phoenix, 1974; mem. Scottsdale Cultural Coun.; NASW bd. Cath. Charities Rep., Portland, 1959-61. Recipient Golden Poet award World of Poetry, 1991, 92, Editor's Choice awards Nat. Libr. Poetry, 1993—, Sec. gift Phoenix Exec. Bd., 1976. Recognition award Archbishop Howard, 1961, 5-Yr. Kathleen Duyck award Cello Congress V, 1996. Mem. Internat. Poetry Hall Fame, Ariz. Cello Soc., Nat. Libr. Poetry, Internat. Soc. Poets, Phoenix Symphony Guild (exec. bd. 1970-80). Republican. Roman Catholic. Avocations: pianist, photography, poetry, artistic collections, attending concerts. Home: 4545 E Palomino Rd Phoenix AZ 85018-1719

DUZEY, ROBERT LINDSEY, lawyer; b. Long Beach, Calif., Nov. 15, 1960; s. Donald Bohdan and Noreen (Rosen) D.; m. Susan Misook Yoon, Mar. 14, 1987; children: Dylan Grey, Zenon Drake. BA, U. Calif., Irvine, 1984; JD, Western State U., Fullerton, Calif., 1994. Bar: Calif. 1994., U.S. Dist. Ct. (so., ctrl., ea. and no. dists.) Calif., U.S. Ct. Appeals (9th cir.). Claims rep., mgr. Farmers Ins. Group, Santa Ana, Calif., 1985-89; risk mgr. Dollar Rent A Car, Irvine, 1989-93; law clk. Callahan, McCune & Willis, Tustin, Calif., 1994-96; atty. Madigan, Evans & Boyer, Costa Mesa, Calif., 1996-98, Law Offices of Robert Lindsey Duzey, Costa Mesa, 1998—. Recipient Am. Jurisprudence award, 1993. Mem. ATLA, ABA, Orange County Bar Assn., Fed. Bar Assn., Risk and Ins. Mgmt. Soc. (bd. dirs. 1991-93), Orange County Barristers, Orange County Trial Lawyers Assn., Def. Rsch. Inst., Assn. So. Calif. Def. Counsel, Am. Inns of Ct., Peter M. Elliot Inn, L.A. County Bar Assn., Long Beach Bar Assn., Delta Theta Phi. Avocations: golf, gardening, skiing, cigars. Fax: (562) 862-7721. E-mail: RDuzey@aol.com. Office: Law Offices Robert Lindsey Duzey 9900 Lakewood Blvd Ste 250 Downey CA 90240

DVORAK, RAY P., insurance company official; b. Center, N.D., Sept. 24, 1931; s. Stanley Joseph and Katherine (Schimpf) D.; m. Deanna Ellen Kern, June 1961 (div. 1974); children: Mitchell Scott, Lara Suzanne; m. Delores Marie Davis, Mar. 12, 1975 (dec. Jan. 1990). BS, U. Oreg., 1953; LLB, LaSalle Extension U., Chgo., 1964. CLU; CPCU; charter fin. cons. Claim rep. State Farm Ins. Co., Salem, Oreg., 1957-67; claim supt. State Farm Ins. Co., Medford, Oreg., 1967—. With USAF, 1953-55, lt. col. Res. ret. Mem. Soc. CPCU, Am. Soc. CLU's. Republican. Methodist. Avocations: skiing, tennis. Home: PO Box 188 840 S Oregon St Jacksonville OR 97530-9321 Office: State Farm Ins Co PO Box 790 Medford OR 97501-0217

DWIGHT, ROBERT JAMES, heavy equipment business owner; b. Fresno, Calif., Nov. 3, 1936; s. Robert Charles Dwight and Goldie Bernice Anderson; m. Nancy Ann Ferguson, June 1, 1961 (Oct. 1969); children: Laura Ann, Robert James; m. Kathy Laura Miller, Nov. 3, 1985. Student, Fresno City Coll. Aircraft mechanic Fresno Helicopters, 1955-61; auto body paint worker Dwight Auto Body, Fresno, 1961-69; blacksmith Dwight Forge, Fresno, 1969-74; equipment operator Bendix Forest Products, O'Neals and Nofork, Calif., 1975-79; equipment owner Dwight Water Trucks, O'Neals, 1979—. Avocations: street rodder, custom autos.

DWORNIK, LYNDA BEBEE, elementary school educator; b. Cripple Creek, Colo., Dec. 21, 1949; d. Alfred Henry and Wilda Louise (McGuffin) Bebee; m. Clarence Dewain Dwornik, Mar. 26, 1977. BS in Vocat. Edn., Colo. State U., 1971; MBA in Learning Disabilities, Ariz. State U., 1976; PhD in Early Childhood Edn., Walden U., 1994. Cert. tchr. grades kindergarten through 8. Tchr. sci. and math. grades 3-6, 1971-72, instr. h.s. vocat. edn., 1972-73, learning disabilities resource tchr. grades kindergarten-6, 1974-79, tchr. grade 2, 1979—; ind. ednl. cons.; author, presenter (lectures) Conceptual Devel. of Literacy in Young Children, Rsch. on Relationship of Concepts of Print in Reading Level and At-Risk Status. Home: HC 63 Box 5137 Snowflake AZ 85937-9713

DWYER, LAURAINE THERESA, ambulatory care administrator, rehabilitation nurse; b. Detroit, Feb. 29, 1948; d. Thomas Z. and Mary Alice (Parker) D. BSN, Ariz. State U., 1970, MS in Nursing, 1976; cert. nursing practitioner, Calif. State U., Long Beach, 1979. Cert. rehab. nurse. Staff and charge nurse Good Samaritan Hosp., Phoenix, 1970-75; staff nurse in neurology VA Med. Ctr., Phoenix, 1976-77, spinal cord injury nurse practitioner, 1980-85; rehab. clin. nurse specialist, 1977-85; assoc. chief nursing svc. spinal cord injury unit and ambulatory care VA Med. Ctr., San Diego, 1985-91, assoc. chief nursing svcs., ambulatory care, 1991-97, dir. abmulatory care svcs., 1997—. Mem. editorial adv. bd. Rehab. Mgmt., 1992-94. Chair logistics commn. 17th Ann. Nat. Vets. Wheelchair Games, 1997. Named Nurse of Yr., Dist. 18 Ariz. Nurses Assn., 1982. Mem. Assn. Rehab. Nurses (pres. Ariz. chpt. 1979-81, treas. San Diego chpt. 1990-94), Am. Assn. Spinal Cord Injury Nurses (bd. dirs. 1991-94, chmn. editl. bd. 1988-94, co-editor 1983-86, Disting. Svc. award 1994), Am. Acad. Ambulatory Care Nursing (sec. San Diego chpt. 1993-97, chair VA spl. interest group 1995-97), Sigma Theta Tau. Home: 8719 Ginger Snap Ln San Diego CA 92129-3715

DWYER, ROGER PATRICK, aviation executive, educator; b. Arlington, Va., Mar. 12, 1947; s. Roger Francis and Mary Francis (Pearman) D.; m. Linda Joan Simington, May 11, 1970; children: Patrick Sean, Christopher Thomas. BS, U. Md., 1974; MBA, Calif. State U., Sacramento, 1980, MS in Acctg., 1982. Title officer Safeco Title Ins. Co., Sacramento, 1975-77; budget analyst Sacramento Air Logistics Ctr., McClellan AFB, Calif., 1977-86; prodn. mgr. Sacramento Air Logistics Ctr., McClellan AFB, 1986-96, dep. dir. aircraft, 1996—; adj. prof. Golden Gate U., Sacramento, 1987—. Capt. USAF, 1967-75. Mem. Soc. Logistics Engrs. (cert. profl. logistician, chpt. pres. 1988-89), Fed. Mgrs. Assn. (dir. 1997, Calif. State Civilian of the Yr. 1994), Air Force Assn. Home: 6320 Wittenham Way Orangevale CA 95662-3722 Office: Sacramento Air Logistics Ctr Ste 3 3028 Peacekeeper Way Mcclellan AFB CA 95652

DWYER, WILLIAM L., federal judge; b. Olympia, Wash., Mar. 26, 1929; s. William E. and Ila (Williams) D.; m. Vasiliki Asimakopulos, Oct. 5, 1952; chldren: Joanna, Anthony, Charles. BS in Law, U. Wash., 1951; JD, NYU, 1953; LLD (hon.), Gonzaga U., 1994. Bar: Wash. 1953, U.S. Ct. Appeals (9th cir.) 1959, U.S. Supreme Ct. 1968. Law clk. Supreme Ct. Wash., Olympia, 1957; ptnr. Culp, Dwyer, Guterson & Grader, Seattle, 1957-87; judge U.S. Dist. Ct. (we. dist.) Wash., Seattle, 1987—. Author: The Goldmark Case, 1984 (Gavel award ABA 1985, Gov.'s award Wash. 1985). 1st lt. U.S. Army, 1953-56. Recipient Outstanding Svc. award U. Wash. Law Rev., 1985, Helen Geisness disting. Svc. award Seattle-King County Bar Assn., 1985, Disting. Alumnus award U. Wash. Sch. of Law, 1994, W.G. Magnuson award King County Mcpl. League, 1994, Judge of Yr. Wash. State Trial Lawyers, 1994, Outstanding Jurist award Am. Bd. Trial Advocates, Washington, 1998, William L. Dwyer Outstanding Jurist Award, King County Bar Assn., 1998. Fellow Am. Coll. Trial Lawyers, Am. Bar Found., Hon. Order of Coif; mem. ABA, Inter-Am. Bar Assn., Am. Judicature Soc., Supreme Ct. Hist. Soc., 9th Cir. Hist. Assn. Office: US Dist Ct 502 US Courthouse 1010 5th Ave Ste 215 Seattle WA 98104-1189

DWYRE, WILLIAM PATRICK, journalist, public speaker; b. Sheboygan, Wis., Apr. 7, 1944; s. George Leo and Mary Veronica (O'Brien) D.; m. Jill Ethlyn Jarvis, July 30, 1966; children—Amy, Patrick. B.A., U. Notre Dame, Ind. Sports copy editor Des Moines Register, 1966-68; sports writer, asst. sports editor, sports editor Milw. Jour., 1968-81; asst. sports editor, sports editor Los Angeles Times, 1981—; speaker Mark Reede's Sportstars, Los Angeles, 1986; columnist Referee Mag., 1977—; voting mem., bd. dirs. Amateur Athletic Found. Nat. Sports Hall of Fame, 1981—. Bd. dirs. Honda-Brockerick Cup Women's Collegiate Athlete of Yr.; treas. Casa Colina Hosp. Rehab., Pomona. Named Sportswriter of Yr., Wis. Nat. Sportscasters, Sportswriters Assn., 1980; Nat. Editor of Yr., Nat. Press Found., 1985; recipient award for Sustained Excellence by Individual, L.A. Times, 1985, Red Smith award AP sports Editors, 1996. Mem. Assoc. Press Sports Editors (pres. 1989), Nat. Baseball, Pro Basketball and Football Writers Assn. Club: Milw. Pen and Mike. Avocation: tennis. Office: Los Angeles Times Times Mirror Sq Los Angeles CA 90012

DYCHTWALD, MADDY KENT, public speaker, author; b. Newark, Feb. 13, 1952; d. Stanley and Sally Susan (Gordet) Kent Fusco; m. Kenneth Mark Dychtwald, Nov. 24, 1983; children: Casey, Zakary. Student, U. Wis.-Madison, 1968-70; BA, NYU, 1974. Actress, N.Y.C. and L.A., 1974-83; dir. spl. projects Dychtwald & Assocs., Emeryville, Calif., 1983-86; dir. communications Age Wave, Inc., Emeryville, 1986, v.p. communications, 1987-90, sr. v.p. communications, 1990-95; producer bus. devel. Author, speaker: Power Generation: Boomer Trends at the New Millennium, 1996. Mem. Screen Actor's Guild, Am. Fedn. TV and Radio Actors, Am. Film Inst., Internat. Assn. Bus. Communicators (Award of Merit for logo design), Nat. Assn. Female Execs. Office: Age Wave Inc 2000 Powell St Ste 1680 Emeryville CA 94608-1861

DYCUS, TERRY LEE, engineer; b. El Paso, Tex., Feb. 5, 1962; s. Joe Wesley and Jo Carrol (Austin) D.; m. Susie Marie Gritzmaker, Oct. 25, 1997. Engr. Gettings Prodns., Orlando, Fla., 1981-83; engr. Walt Disney World, Orlando, 1983-86; tech. dir. Jean Ann Ryan Prodns., Ft. Lauderdale, Fla., 1986-96; designer Rent nat. tour, Boston, 1996; engr. Walt Disney Theatrical, N.Y.C., 1996—. Mem. Internat. Alliance of Theatrical & Stage Employees. Avocations: audiophile, auto enthusiast.

DYE, ALAN, lawyer. Grad. magna cum laude, Emory U., 1975; JD, U. Ga., 1978. Spl. counsel to chmn. Securities and Exchange Commn., with divsn. corp. fin.; ptnr. Hogan & Hartson LLP, Washington. Contbr. articles to profl. jours. Mem. ABA (chmn. securities commodities and exchanges com.). Office: Exec Press Section 16 Updates PO Box 21639 Concord CA 94521-0639

DYER, ALICE MILDRED, psychotherapist; b. San Diego, July 4, 1929; d. William Silas Cann and Louise Lair (Addenbrooke) Vaile; divorced; children: Alexis Dyer Guagnano, Bryan, Christine Dyer Morales; m. James Vawter, Dec. 26, 1972. BA, Calif. State U., Fullerton, 1965, MA, 1967; PhD, U.S. Internat. U., 1980. Coord., counselor Brea (Calif.)-Olinda High Sch., 1968-72; sch. psychologist Cypress (Calif.) Sch. Dist., 1972-86; instr. North Orange County Community Coll., Fullerton, 1975-77; pvt. practice ednl. psychology Long Beach and Fountain Valley, Calif., 1978-97; pvt. practice marriage and family therapy Fullerton and Brea, Calif., 1979-97; ret., 1998; psychologist, cons. Multiple Sclerosis Soc. Orange County, 1986-95; facilitator adult mental health La Habra (Calif.) Comty. Hosp., 1988-89. Bd. dirs., officer, pres. Friends of Fullerton Arboretum, 1974-95; pres., bd. dirs. Fullerton Beautiful, 1987-88, Brea Ednl. Found., 1988-89; therapist Orange County Juvenile Connection Project, 1988-97. Recipient Appreciation award Gary Ctr., La Habra, 1975, Multiple Sclerosis Soc. Orange County, 1987. Mem. Calif. Assn. Marriage and Family Therapists, Assn. for Children and Adults with Learning Disabilities (cons. 1970—, bd. dirs., facilitator), AAUW, Soroptimists (health chmn. Brea chpt. 1987-88). Republican. Unitarian.

DYER, RICHARD HUTCHINS, risk management executive; b. Washington, Jan. 11, 1931; s. Robert Francis and Sarah Antoinette (Worley) D. BA, Yale U., 1953; JD, George Washington U., 1956. Legal liaison U. Calif. Lawrence Berkeley Lab., Berkeley, 1960-64; risk mgr. U. Calif. Lawrence Livermore Lab., Livermore, 1964-94; cons. Teknokron Inc., Berkeley, Calif., 1967; mem. Legis. Com. Calif. Self Insurer Assn., 1981-94; pres. Golden Gate Risk Mgmt. Soc., San Francisco, 1985—, legis. dir., 1986-93. Pres. PTA, Lafayette, Calif., 1970-71; bd. dirs. Berkeley Missionary Home, 1985-90; mem. Calif. Gov's Toxic Task Force, Sacramento, 1985-86; v.p. Diablo View Wellness Coun., Livermore, 1985-94, Friends Outside, 1992-94; mem. fin. com. Danville (Calif.) Sch. Dist., 1974-75; mem. Contra Costa County Rep. Ctrl. Com., Danville, 1970-82; ruling elder Danville Presbyn. Ch., 1984-93; mem. com. on preparation for ministry San Francisco Presbytery, 1993—; treas. Spinnaker Clipper Couples Club, 1993-95; docent Mus. at Blackhawk Guild, 1995. Lt. USNR, 1959-63. Recipient citation Gov.'s Toxic Task Force, 1987. Mem. Commonwealth Club San Francisco, Yale Club No. Calif., Masons, Pi Sigma Alpha., Phi Alpha Delta. Avocations: photography, travel, gymnastics, gardening, politics. Home: 1360 Brookside Dr Danville CA 94526-5148

DYMOND, RICHARDENE C., artist; b. Palisade, Nebr., Nov. 22, 1927; d. Richard Clay Repass and Carrie Eveline Erickson; m. Lloyd Charles Dymond, Jan. 9, 1948 (div. 1954); children: Frank Russel, Michael Allen. AA, Sacramento C.C., 1969. With clerical staff State of Calif. Dept. Motor Vehicles, Sacramento, 1964-87; artist Galt, Calif., 1997—. Mem. Galt C. of C., Galt. Hist. Soc. Home: 890 Village Run Dr Apt 102 Galt CA 95632

DYNAN, PHILIP EDWARD, artist; b. Kansas City, Mo., Aug. 11, 1948; s. Philip Andrew and Rosanell (Cheatham) D.; m. Ruthe Thompson, 1982, (div. 1990); children: Sara Michelle, Joseph Edward. BA, Western Ill. U., 1972. Art dir. Calif. Internat. Marathon, Sacramento, 1984-89, San Francisco Marathon, 1994-98, Lake Tahoe Marathon, 1997-98, Russian River Marathon, Ukiah, Calif., 1998, San Diego Marathon, 1998-99; art dir. Nevada City (Calif.) Classic, 1985. Author, illustrator: Enneagram Animals, 1994, The Legend of Birdtoe, 1996, Running the San Francisco Marathon, 1996, Moto & Kozo Visit the MOMA, 1998. Active Tanner Commn., Placer County, Calif., 1984-85. With U.S. Army, 1966-68, Ethiopia. Recipient Patriotic Svc. award U.S. Dept. Treasury, 1993-98. Avocations: marathon running. E-mail: phildynan@msn.com. Fax: 916-961-3320. Home: 8804 Winding Way Fair Oaks CA 95628-6439 Office: Phil Dynan Designs PO Box 188442 Sacramento CA 95818-8442

DYNES, ROBERT C., academic administrator. Prof. U. Calif., San Diego, 1991-95, sr. vice chencellor, 1995—. Office: U Calif 9500 Gilman Dr La Jolla CA 92093-5003*

DZIEWANOWSKA, ZOFIA ELIZABETH, neuropsychiatrist, pharmaceutical executive, researcher, educator; b. Warsaw, Poland, Nov. 17, 1939; came to U.S., 1972; d. Stanislaw Kazimierz Dziewanowski and Zofia Danuta (Mieczkowska) Rudowska; m. Krzysztof A. Kunert, Sept. 1, 1961 (div. 1971); 1 child, Martin. MD, U. Warsaw, 1963; PhD, Polish Acad. Sci., 1970. MD recert. U.K., 1972, U.S., 1973. Asst. prof. of psychiatry U. Warsaw Med. Sch., 1969-71; sr. house officer St. George's Hosp., U. London, 1971-72; assoc. dir. Merck Sharp & Dohme, Rahway, N.J., 1972-76; vis. assoc. physician Rockefeller U. Hosp., N.Y.C., 1975-76; adj. asst. prof. of psychiatry Cornell U. Med. Ctr., N.Y.C., 1978—; v.p., global med. dir. Hoffmann-La Roche, Inc., Nutley, N.J., 1976-94; sr. v.p. and dir. global med. affairs Genta Inc., San Diego, 1994-97; sr. v.p. drug devel. and regulatory Cypros Pharms. Corp., Carlsbad, Calif., 1997—; lectr. in field U.S. and internat. confs. Contbr. articles to profl. publs. Bd. dirs Royal Soc. Medicine Found.; mem. alumni coun. Cornell U. Med. Ctr. Recipient TWIN Honoree award for Outstanding Women in Mgmt., Ridgewood (N.J.) YWCA, 1984. Mem. AMA, AAAS, Am. Soc. Pharmacology and Therapeutics, Am. Coll. Neuropsychopharmacology, N.Y. Acad. Scis., PhRMA. (vice chmn. steering com. med. sect., chmn. internat. med. affairs com., head biotech. working group), Royal Soc. Medicine (U.K.), Drug Info. Assn. (Woman of Yr. award 1994), Am. Assn. Pharm. Physicians. Roman Catholic. Achievements include original research on the role of the nervous system in the regulation of respiratory functions, research and development and therapeutic uses of many new drugs, pharmaceutical medicine and biotechnology; molecular biology derived as well as conventional products including antisense, interferon efficacy in cancer, virology and AIDS and drugs useful in cardiovascular, immunological, neuropsychiatric, infectious diseases, and others; impact of different cultures on medical practices and clinical research; drug evaluation and development management strategies of pharmaceutical industries; treatments against cardiac and brain ischemia, cytoprotection; speaker in field. Office: Cypros Pharms Corp 2714 Loker Ave W Carlsbad CA 92008-6603

EAKIN, MARGARETTA MORGAN, lawyer; b. Ft. Smith, Ark., Aug. 27, 1941; d. Ariel Thomas and Oma (Thomas) Morgan; m. Harry D. Eakin, June 7, 1959; 1 dau., Margaretta E. B.A. with honors, U. Oreg., 1969, J.D., 1971. Bar: Oreg. 1971, U.S. Dist. Ct. Oreg. 1973, U.S. Ct. Appeals (9th cir.) 1977. Law clk. to chief justice Oreg. Supreme Ct., 1971-72; Reginald Heber Smith Law Reform fellow, 1972-73; house counsel Hyster Co., 1973-75; assoc. N. Robert Stoll, 1975-77; mem. firm Margaretta Eakin, P.C., Portland, Oreg., 1977—; tchr. bus. law Portland State U., 1979-80; speaker; mem. state bd. profl. responsibility Oreg. State Bar, 1979-82; vol. lawyer FEMA, 1995—. Mem. bd. visitors U. Oreg. Sch. of Law, 1986-93, vice chair, 1989-91, chair, 1992-93; mem. ann. fund com. Oreg. Episc. Sch., 1981, chmn. subcom. country fair, 1981; sec. Parent Club Bd., St. Mary's Acad., 1987; mem. Oreg. State. Bar Com. on Uniform State Laws, 1989-93, vol. lawyer Fed. Emergency Mgmt. Assn., 1995—. Paul Patterson fellow. Mem. ABA, Assn. Trial Lawyers Am., Oreg. Trial Lawyers Assn., Oreg. Bar Assn., Multnomah County Bar Assn. (jud. selection com. 1992-94), 1000 Friends of Oreg., City Club. Office: 30th Fl Pacwest Ctr 1211 SW 5th Ave Portland OR 97204-3713

EARL, BRYAN KENT, radio development director; b. Logan, Utah, Mar. 12, 1964; m. Robyn Derr; 1 child, Tirzah. BS in Journalism, Utah State U., 1989. Dir. of devel. Utah Pub. Radio, Logan, 1993—. Mem. Pub. Radio Assn. of Devel. Officers. Avocations: gardening, skiing, model railroading. Office: Utah Pub Radio 8505 Old Main Hill Logan UT 84322-8505

EARLEY, EDWARD JOSEPH, JR., studio musician, composer, copyist, trombonist; b. St. Louis, Mar. 16, 1952; s. Edward Joseph Earley Sr. and Frances (Hodges) May. Student, U. Mo., 1970-74, U. Mo., St. Louis, 1976-79. Copyist, musician, arranger Luther Ingram, St. Louis, 1978-80; musician, arranger, band leader Albert King Blues Band, N.Y.C., 1979-80, 83-87, 88—; musician Silver Cloud Blues Band, St. Louis, 1980-81, 87—; musician, songwriter, copyist, dir. child day-care YMCA, St. Louis, 1987—; performer Joe Louis Walker and the Boss Talkers, 1989-90; substitute tchr. music St. Louis Bd. Edn., 1974, Normandy (Mo.) Pub. Schs., 1976-79; film extra Hilzar-Roche Casting-Paramount, Chgo., 1987; freelance studio musician and vocalist, 1978—; film extra Holzar-Roche Casting Paramount, Chgo., 1987; performer rec. with Elvin Bishop, Elvin Bishop Group, 1990—. Writer (song) The Game Goes On as recorded by Albert King on Phone Booth, 1984; musician Elvin Bishop Group. Active voter registration, St. Louis, 1976, Mo. Coalition for the Environment, St. Louis, 1987. Recipient Cert. Merit Am. Songwriters Festival, 1984, Cert. Merit N.Y. Pro/Am Songwriting Festival, 1985, Cert. Music of Merit City Songwriters Festival, 1987. Mem. ASCAP, Am. Fedn. Musicians, Internat. Trombone Assn., Omega Psi Phi. Avocations: art, music, softball, playing cards, soccer. Address: PO Box 1091 Larkspur CA 94977-1091

EARLY, AMES S., healthcare system executive; b. Allison, Iowa, Apr. 18, 1937; s. W.C. and F. Eva Early; m. Beryl J. Early; 1 child, Barbara. BA, Drake U., 1959; MHA, U. Iowa, 1961. Adminstrv. resident, adminstrv. asst. U. Minn. Hosp., Mpls., 1961-67; exec. dir. Mary Francis Skiff Meml. Hosp., Newton, Iowa, 1967-68; asst. adminstr. Mercy Hosp., Miami, Fla., 1968-76; pres. Scripps Meml. Hosp., La Jolla, Calif., 1976-91; exec. v.p., COO Scripps Instns. Medicine and Sci., ScrippsHealth, 1991-93; pres., CEO Scripps Health, San Diego, 1994-98, vice chmn., CEO, 1999—. Pres. So. Fla. Hosp. Assn., 1974-75, bd. dirs., 1971-76; bd. dirs. Fla. Hosp. Assn., 1974-76, Comprehensive Health Planning of So. Fla., 1974-76, Nat. Coun. Cmty. Hosp., 1974—, Hosp. Coun. San Diego and Imperial Counties, 1978-86, Calif. Polit. Action Com., 1979-85, Calif. Health Decisions, 1994—, Catholic Healthcare West (bd. mem. 1996—), San Diego Econ. Devel. (bd. mem. 1998—), Blue Cross/Hosp. Adv. Com., 1982, Vol. Hosp. Am. West, 1986-91, San Diego Hospice (bd. mem. 1997—); mem. peer rev. panel Fla. Blue Cross Assn., 1975-76; trustee Calif. Assn. Hosp. and Health Sys., 1984-92, mem. exec. com., 1984-90, mem. legis. com., 1985, mem. hosp. med. staff bylaws com., 1985-86, treas., 1987, chmn., 1989; mem. Healthcare Forum. Recipient Headline of Yr. in Healthcare San Diego Press Club, 1987. Mem. Am. Coll. Healthcare Execs., Am. Hosp. Assn., Am. Assn. Hosp. Planning. Office: Scripps Health 4275 Campus Point Ct San Diego CA 92121-1513

EARLY, ROBERT JOSEPH, magazine editor; b. Indpls., Sept. 22, 1936; s. Robert Paul and Helen Theresa (Schluttenhofer) E.; m. Gail Louise Horvath, Sept. 6, 1958; children: Mary Jane, Joseph Robert, Jill Ann. BA, U. Notre Dame, 1958. Reporter Indpls. Star, 1958-61; reporter The Ariz. Republic, Phoenix, 1961-66, asst. city editor, 1966-69, city editor, 1969-77, asst. mng. editor, 1977-78, mng. editor, 1978-82; pres. Telesource Communication Svcs. Inc., Phoenix, 1982-90; editor Phoenix Mag., 1985-89, Ariz. Hwys., Phoenix, 1990—; lectr. Ariz. State U., 1992, 94; editor in residence No. Ariz. U., 1992, 93, 94. Chmn. Victims Bill of Rights Task Force, Phoenix [illegible] Virg Hill Newsman of Yr. award Ariz. Press Club, 1976. Mem. Soc. Profl. Journalists. Republican. Roman Catholic. Office: Ariz Hwys 2039 W Lewis Ave Phoenix AZ 85009-2819*

EASLEY, GEORGE WASHINGTON, construction executive; b. Williamson, W.Va., Mar. 14, 1933; s. George Washington and Isabel Ritchie (Saville) E.; student U. Richmond, 1952-56; children: Bridget Bland, Kathy Clark, Saville Woodson, Marie Alexis, Isabell Roxanne, George Washington, Laura Dean, Dorothy Elizabeth, Isabel Louiza. m. Bettyrae Fedje Hanner, Sep. 15, 1990. Hwy. engr. Va. Dept. Hwys., Richmond, 1956-62; dep. city mgr. City of Anchorage, 1962-68; prin. assoc. Wilbur Smith & Assos., Los Angeles, 1969-70; commr. pub. works State of Alaska, Juneau, 1971-74; exec. v.p. Burgess Internat. Constrn. Co., Anchorage, 1974, pres., 1975; pres., chmn. bd. George W. Easley Co., Anchorage, 1976-86 ; pres. Alaska Aggregate Corp., Fairbanks Sand & Gravel Co., 1986-90; constrn. mgr. Alaska Pipeline Svc. Co., 1990-96; ind. cons., 1996—; CEO Eklutna, Inc., 1997—; bd. dirs. Totem Ocean Trailer Express, Inc. Recipient commendations City of Anchorage, 1966, Greater Anchorage, Inc., 1969, Ketchikan C. of C., 1973, Alaska State Legis., 1974, Gov. of Alaska, 1974; named one of Outstanding Young Men, Anchorage Jaycees, 1964. Registered profl. engr., Calif. Mem. U.S. C. of C., Alaska C. of C. (dir. 1978—, chmn. 1982-83), Anchorage C. of C. (sec.-treas. 1976, v.p. 1977, pres.-elect 1978, pres. 1979-80, dir. 1982-88, Gold Pan award 1969, 77), Hwy. Users Fedn. Alaska (dir. 1972—, treas. 1974—), Orgn. Mgmt. of Alaska's Resources (past dir.), Am. Pub. Works Assn., Anchorage Transp. Commn. (past chmn.), Associated Gen. Contractors (dir. Alaska chpt. 1978—, chpt. treas. 1980-81, sec. 1981, pres. 1984, nat. com. labor relations, Hard Hat award, 1985), Am. Mil. Engrs. (v.p. Alaska chpt. 1978), Alaska Trucking Assn. (bd. dirs. 1986-90), Inst. Mcpl. Engrs., Inst. Traffic Engrs., Internat. Orgn. Masters, Mates and Pilots (hon.), Common Sense for Alaska (past pres.), Commonwealth North (charter). Democrat. Presbyterian. Club: San Francisco Tennis. Lodge: Rotary. Home and Office: 4921 Sportsman Dr Anchorage AK 99502-4193

EASLEY, LOYCE ANNA, painter; b. Weatherford, Okla., June 28, 1918; d. Thomas Webster and Anna Laura (Sanders) Rogers; m. Mack Easley, Nov. 17, 1939; children: June Elizabeth, Roger. BFA, U. Okla., 1943; postgrad., 1947-49; student, Art Students League, N.Y.C., 1977; postgrad., Santa Fe Inst. Fine Arts, 1985. Tchr. Pub. Sch., Okmulgee, Okla., 1946-47, Hobbs, N.Mex., 1947-49; tchr. painting N.Mex. Jr. Coll., Hobbs, 1965-80; tchr. Art Workshops in N.Mex., Okla., Wyoming. Numerous one-woman shows and group exhbns. in mus., univs. and galleries, including Gov.'s Gallery, Santa Fe, Selected Artists, N.Y.C., Roswell (N.Mex.) Mus., N.Mex. State U., Las Cruces, West Tex. Mus., Tex. Tech U., Lubbock; represented in permanent collections USAF Acad., Colorado Springs, Colo., Roswell Mus., Carlsbad (N.Mex.) Mus., Coll. Santa Fe, N.Mex. Supreme Ct, also other pvt. and pub. collections; featured in S.W. Art and Santa Fe mag., 1981, 82. Named Disting. Former Student, U. Okla. Art Sch., 1963; nominated for Gov's. award in Art, N.Mex., 1988. Mem. N.Mex. Artists Equity (lifetime mem. 1963). Democrat. Presbyterian. Home: 10909 Country Club St NE Albuquerque NM 87111-6548

EAST, DONALD ROBERT, civil engineer; b. Kimberley, South Africa, June 2, 1944; came to U.S., 1985; s. Robert George and Gladys Enid (Macintyre) E.; m. Diana Patricia Ruske, Dec. 21, 1968 (div. Mar. 1993); children: Lisa Ann, Sharon Margaret; m. Miriam B. Thompson, Mar. 16, 1996. BSCE, U. Cape Town, 1969; MSc in Found. Engring., U. Birmingham, England, 1971. Jr. engr. Ninham Shand & Ptnrs., Cape Town, South Africa, 1968-71; mgr. Civilab Ltd., Johannesburg, South Africa, 1972-74; ptnr. Watermeyer, Legge, Piesold & Uhlmann, Johannesburg, 1975-85; pres., CEO Knight Piesold LLC, Denver, 1985—; Contbr. articles to profl. jours. Fellow South Africa Instn. Civil Engrs. (chmn. 1979-85); mem. ASCE, Soc. Mining Engrs. (com. mem. 1988-89). Home: 7902 E Iowa Ave Denver CO 80231-5654 Office: Knight Piesold LLC 1050 17th St Ste 500 Denver CO 80265-0501

EAST, JOHN, computer company executive. Pres., CEO Actel, Sunnyvale, Calif. Office: Actel 955 E Arques Ave Sunnyvale CA 94086-4533

EASTAUGH, ROBERT L., state supreme court justice; b. Seattle, Nov. 12, 1943. BA, Yale U., 1965; JD, U. Mich., 1968. Bar: Alaska 1968. Asst. atty. gen. State of Alaska, 1968-69, asst. dist. atty., 1969-72; lawyer Delaney, Wiles, Hayes, Reitman & Brubaker, Inc., 1972-94; assoc. justice Alaska Supreme Ct., 1994—. Office: Alaska Supreme Court 303 K St Anchorage AK 99501-2013

EASTBY, IONE BERNICE, retired counselor; b. McHenry, N.D., Mar. 3, 1924; d. Helmer Bertinus and Synnove Juliet (Larson) Hanson; m. Franklin Lane Eastby, July 16, 1957; children: Forrest Lane, Jeff Lewis. BA, Concordia Coll., 1947; MEd, Pacific Lutheran U., 1969. Cert. elem. and secondary tchr., secondary prin., EAA counselor. Tchr. secondary bus. U. Minn., Morris, 1947-50; tchr. coll. bus. N.D. State Coll., Wahpeton, 1950-57; tchr. secondary psychology & bus. Franklin Pierce Sch. Dist., Tacoma, 1957-66, secondary counselor, 1966-89; ret., 1989; dept. chair counseling and guidance Washington High Sch., Franklin Pierce Sch. Dist., Tacoma, 1969-89. chair Ministry of Health program Christ Luth. Ch., Lakewood, Wash., 1988; pres. Luth. Social Svcs., Tacoma, 1990-93; bd. dirs. Clover Park Found., Lakewood, 1991-93. Recipient Christa McAuliffe award State of Wash., 1989, cert. of recognition Wash. Edn. Assn., 1989. Mem. Wash. State Ret. Tchrs. Assn., Greater Lakes Mental Health Found. (bd. dirs. 1981-84, plaque 1989), Delta Kappa Gamma (pres. Epsilon chpt. 1983, chair state scholarship bd. dirs. 1996). Republican. Avocations: volunteering at social service agencies and church, travel, music, crosswords, grandchildren. Home: 6410 Nyanza Park Dr SW Lakewood WA 98499-5238

EASTER, STANLEY EUGENE, musician, counselor, educator; b. Hutchinson, Kans., Mar. 4, 1932; s. Evaloe Pryntha (Johnson) E.; m. Ietje Sjoertje Hoogland, Jan. 10, 1972 (dec. Nov. 1992); 1 chld, Laura Michelle; m. Rita Walsh Reitz; 1 child, Cathrine Berlin. BMusic, Eastman Sch. Music, Rochester, N.Y., 1955; MMusic, U. Okla., 1960; EdD, Columbia U., 1969. Trombonist U.S. Mil. Acad. Band, West Point, N.Y., 1955-57, Oklahoma City Symphony, 1957-61, N.Y.C. Ballet Orch., 1962-69; instr. Tchrs. Coll., Columbia U., N.Y.C., 1966-69; music dir. Dobbs Ferry (N.Y.) Schs., 1963-65, Cañada Coll., Redwood City, Caif., 1969—. Composer, arranger numerous pieces for trombone, organ, voice. Served with U.S. Army, 1955-57. Mem. Rotary Internat., Music Assn. Calif. Cmty. Colls. Office: Cañada Coll 4200 Farm Hill Blvd Redwood City CA 94061-1030

EASTHAM, SONDRA LEE, educational consultant; b. Chester, Pa., June 15, 1934; d. Simon Martin and Cecelia Ann (Savits) Rosenthal; m. Frederick Cohn, July 16, 1954 (div. 74); children: Janice M., Lawrence S., Robert H.; m. John Perry Eastham, Dec. 30, 1979. BS, Millerville State Coll., 1955; MA, U. N.Mex., 1969. Tchr. Media (Pa.) Elem. Sch., 1955-58; mgr. internat. dept. Sunwest Bank, Albuquerque, 1978-81; commentator Sta. KGGM-TV, Albuquerque, 1981; owner Edn. Consulting and Tutoring Svcs., Albuquerque, 1982-97. Pres. LWV N.Mex., 1969-71; sec. LWV U.S., 1971-74; fin. chair, v.p. Albuquerque City Coun., 1974-81; fin. chair N.Mex. Commn. Higher Edn., 1991-97; adv. bd. Gov.'s Bus. Coun., 1994—, Western Gov.'s U., 1995—. Named Woman of Yr., State N.Mex., 1974. Home: 1805 Lafayette Dr NE Albuquerque NM 87106-1005

EASTHAM, THOMAS, foundation administrator; b. Attelboro, Mass., Aug. 21, 1923; s. John M. and Margaret (Marsden) E.; m. Berenice J. Hirsch, Oct. 12, 1946; children: Scott Thomas, Todd Robert. Student English, Northwestern U., 1946-52. With Chgo. American, 1945-56, asst. Sunday editor, 1953-54, feature writer, 1954-56; news editor San Francisco Call Bull., 1956-62, exec. editor, 1962-65; exec. editor, then D.C. bur. chief San Francisco Examiner, 1965-82; dir. pub. info,press sec. to mayor of San Francisco, 1982-88; v.p., western dir. William Randolph Hearst Founds., 1988—. Active Nat. Trust Historic Preservation; mem. Pres.'s Roundtable, U. San Francisco. Pulitzer prize nominee, 1955. Mem. Am. Soc. Newspaper Editors, Inter-Am. Press Assn., Am., Internat. press insts., White House Corres. Assn., Nat. Press Club, Ind. Sector, Coun. on Foundations, Commonwealth Club, Sigma Delta Chi. Home: 1473 Bernal Ave Burlingame CA 94010-5559 Office: Hearst Found 90 New Montgomery St Ste 1212 San Francisco CA 94105-4596

EASTMAN, FRANCESCA MARLENE, volunteer, art historian; b. Jamaica Plain, Mass., Jan. 26, 1952; d. Therald Carlton and Martha Jane (Welch) E.; m. Edward Charles Goodstein, Aug. 27, 1989. AB in Art History, Manhattanville Coll., 1972; MA in Art History, Clark Art Inst./Williams Coll., 1974; postgrad., Stanford U., 1976-80. Intern Mus. of Fine Arts, Boston, summers 1971-73; lectr. in art Regis Coll., Weston, Mass., 1974-76; sr. house assoc. Stanford (Calif.) U., 1977-80, tchg. fellow, 1978-79; student svcs. intern Menlo Coll., Atherton, Calif., 1980-81; now freelance editor. Bd. sec. Trinity Episcopal Sch., Menlo Park, Calif., 1992-96, bd. chair, 1996-98; adv. bd., chair Trinity Sch., 1998—; trustee David B. and Edward C. Goodstein Found., L.A., 1995—; vol. scholarship com. Peninsula Cmty. Found., San Mateo, Calif., 1995—; grad. Leadership Redwood City, Calif., 1995—; arts commr., co-chair Town of Atherton, Calif., 1996—, 75th ann. com. leadership coun., 1998; mem. steering com., chair edn. com. Peninsula Episcopal H.S. Project, Foster City, Calif., 1996—. Mem. Cornell Club (N.Y.C.), Williams Club (N.Y.C.), Pacific Athletic Club. Democrat. Roman Catholic. Avocations: art collecting, piano.

EASTON, ROBERT (OLNEY), author, environmentalist; b. July 4, 1915; s. Robert Eastman and Ethel (Olney) E.; m. Jane Faust, Sept. 24, 1940; children: Joan Easton Lentz, Katherine Easton Renga (dec.), Ellen Easton Brumfiel, Jane. Student, Stanford U., 1933-34, postgrad., 1938-39; BS, Harvard U., 1938; MA, U. Calif., Santa Barbara, 1960. Ranch hand, day laborer, mag. editor, 1939-42; co-pub., editor Lampasas (Tex.) Dispatch, 1946-50; instr. English Santa Barbara City Coll., 1959-65; writing and pub. cons. U.S. Naval Civil Engring. Lab., Port Hueneme, Calif., 1961-69. Author: The Happy Man, 1943, (with Mackenzie Brown) Lord of Beasts, 1961, (with Jay Monaghan and others) The Book of the American West, 1963, The Hearing, 1964, (with Dick Smith) California Condor: Vanishing American, 1964, Max Brand: The Big Westerner, 1970, Black Tide: The Santa Barbara Oil Spill and Its Consequences, 1972, Guns, Gold and Caravans, 1978, China Caravans: An American Adventurer in Old China, 1982, This Promised Land, 1982, Life and Work, 1988, Power and Glory, 1989, (with Jane Faust Easton) Love and War, 1991, Blood and Money, 1998; editor: Max Brand's Best Stories, 1967, (with Mackenzie Brown) Bullying the Moqui, 1968, (with Jane Faust Easton) Max Brand's Best Poems, 1992, (with Jane Faust Easton) Max Brand: Collected Stories, 1994, Blood and Money, 1998; contbr. to numerous mags. including Atlantic and N.Y. Times mag.; also anthologies including Great Tales of the American West. Co-chmn. Com. for Santa Barbara, 1973-81; trustee Santa Barbara Mus. Natural History, 1975-78, rsch. assoc., 1980-83; trustee Santa Barbara Community Environ. Coun., 1974-79; co-founder Sisquoc Sanctuary for Calif. Condor, 1937, also first wilderness area established under Nat. Wilderness Act, Los Padres Nat. Forest, Calif., 1968. Served to 1st lt. inf. U.S. Army, World War II. Recipient Honor award Calif. Conservation Coun., 1975.

EASTON, ROGER DAVID, art history educator; b. Douglaston, N.Y., Jan. 4, 1923; s. Spencer Garnet and Ruth Natalie (Albright) E.; m. June Marcella Healy, Dec. 21, 1953. BS, SUNY, 1949; MA, State U. Iowa, 1951; EdD, U. Denver, 1958; postgrad., U. Rochester, Fogg Mus., Harvard U. Cert. tchr., N.Y., Colo. Fellow U. Iowa, Iowa City, 1950-51; instr. to assoc. prof. SUNY, Cortland, 1951-58; prof. Ball State U., Muncie, Ind., 1958-85, ret., 1985. One-man shows include S.W. Savs. and Loan, Green Valley, Ariz., 1989; exhibited in group shows at Smithsonian Instn. Crafts Invitational Nat. Traveling Exhibit, 1960-62, Ball State U. Art Gallery, 1977-80, 80-81, Sheldon Swope Art Gallery, Terre Haute, Ind., 1979-80, 83, Ft. Wayne Mus. Art, 1981-82, Tubac Ctr. of the Arts, 1989, 90, Santa Cruz Valley Art Assn., Tubac, Ariz., 1990, 93-95, Kessel-Long Gallery, Scottsdale, Ariz., 1990, So. Ariz. Watercolor Guild, 1991, 92-95, Ariz. Aqueous, 1992, 95, 97, So. Ariz. Art Guild, 1993, 95, 96, 97, Canoa Ctr. Exhbns., 1994-95, 96, Ariz. Watercolor Assn. Phoenix Exhbn., 1990-91, 94-95, 96, and numerous others; contbr. articles to profl. jours. Mem. Nat. Watercolor Soc., So. Ariz. Watercolor Guild, Santa Cruz Valley Art Assn., Ariz. Watercolor Assn., Nat. Art Edn. Assn., Ariz. Art Edn. Assn. Avocations: travel, cinema, woodworking. Home: 3371 Placita Esconces Green Valley AZ 85614

EATON, DAVID E., II, city administrator; b. Laconia, N.H., July 15, 1959; s. David Elwell and Doris Aileen (VanBlaricum) E.; m. Judy Kuen Toy, Nov. 21, 1980; children; Meagan Mei-Lai, Nathaniel David. BA, Sangamon State U., 1982; MA, Claremont Coll., 1986. Ordained priest Soto-Zen Buddhist Ch.; lic. real estate broker, Calif. Cmty. outreach worker, caseworker Salvation Army and United Meth. Ministries, Chgo., 1977-82; youth edn. dir. Presbyn. Ch. USA, L.A., 1983-87; mil. intelligence specialist U.S. Dept. Def., 1987; mktg. rep. Anheuser Busch & Adolph Coors, L.A., 1988-90; acctg. tech. Fed. Civil Svc., DOD, L.A., 1990-93; priest, psychotherapist Shoshinkai Fellowship, Phoenix, 1993; job developer, caseworker II dislocated workers program dept. human svcs. City of Phoenix, 1994—; early head start site mgr. S.W. Human Devel. Corp., City of Phoenix, 1996—; chaplain, addictions counselor Chandler (Ariz.) Valley Hope Drug & Alcohol Treatment Ctr.; employment counselor III Ariz. Dept. Econ. Security Job Svc., Phoenix. Contbr. articles to profl. jours. Active Chinatown 10K Com., L.A., 1992, Chinese-Am. Citizens' League, Phoenix, 1993-94, Japan-Am. Citizens League, Phoenix, 1993; cons. child protective svcs. field investigations of child abuse. Recipient Citizens Svc. to Local Cmty. award Castelar Elem. Sch., 1991. Mem. ACA, Am. Mental-Health Counseling Assn., Nat. Employment Counselor Assn., Nat. Employment and Tng. Profl. Assn., Constructive Living Assn. Democrat. Avocations: reading, travel, camping, hiking, running. Home: 18836 N 15th St Phoenix AZ 85024-8200 Office: Ariz Dept Econ Security Job Svc 9801 N 7th St Phoenix AZ 85020-1701

EATON, GARETH RICHARD, chemistry educator, university dean; b. Lockport, N.Y., Nov. 3, 1940; s. Mark Dutcher and Ruth Emma (Ruston) E.; m. Sandra Shaw, Mar. 29, 1969. BA, Harvard U., 1962; PhD, MIT, 1972. Asst. prof. chemistry U. Denver, 1972-76, assoc. prof., 1976-80, prof., 1980-97, dean natural scis., 1984-88, vice provost for rsch., 1988-89, John Evans prof., 1997—; organizer Internat. Electron-Paramagnetic Resonance Symposium. Author, editor 3 books; mem. editorial bd. 4 jours.; contbr. articles to profl. jours. Lt. USN, 1962-67. Mem. AAAS, Am. Chem. Soc., Royal Soc. Chemistry (London), Internat. Soc. Magnetic Resonance, Soc. Applied Spectroscopy, Am. Phys. Soc., Internat. Electron Paramagnetic Resonance Soc. Office: U Denver Dept Chem/Biochem Denver CO 80208

EATON, GEORGE WESLEY, JR., petroleum engineer, oil company executive; b. Searcy, Ark., Aug. 3, 1924; s. George Wesley and Inez (Roberson) E.; m. Adriana Amin, Oct. 28, 1971; 1 child, Andrew. BS in Petroleum Engring., U. Okla., 1948. Registered profl. engr. Tex., N.Mex. Petroleum engr. Amoco, Longview, Ft. Worth, Tex., 1948-54; engring. supr. Amoco, Roswell, N.Mex., 1954-59; dist. engr. Amoco, Farmington, N.Mex., 1959-70; constrn. mgr. Amoco Egypt Oil Co., Cairo, 1970-81; ops. mgr. Amoco Norway Oil Co., Stavanger, 1981-84; petroleum cons. G.W. Eaton Cons., Albuquerque, 1984-94; adj. prof. San Juan Coll., Farmington, 1968-70. Bd. dirs. Paradise Hills Civic Assn., Albuquerque, 1986-89; elder Rio Grande Presbyn. Ch., Albuquerque, 1987-90; mem. Rep. Nat. Com., Washington, 1986-92. Mem. N.Mex. Soc. Profl. Engrs. (bd. dirs. 1967-70), Soc. Petroleum Engrs. (Legion of Honor), Egyptian Soc. Petroleum Engrs. (chmn. 1980-81). Home: 5116 Russell Dr NW Albuquerque NM 87114-4325

EATON, GORDON PRYOR, geologist; b. Dayton, Ohio, Mar. 9, 1929; s. Colman and Dorothy (Pryor) E.; m. Virginia Anne Gregory, June 12, 1951; children: Gretchen Maria, Gregory Mathieu. BA, Wesleyan U., 1951; MS, Calif. Inst. Tech., 1953, PhD, 1957. From instr. geology to asst. prof. Wesleyan U., Middletown, Conn., 1955-59; from asst. prof. to assoc. prof. U. Calif., Riverside, 1959-67, chmn. dept. geol. sci., 1965-67; with U.S. Geol. Survey, 1963-65, 67-81, 94-97; dep. chief Office Geochemistry and Geophysics, Washington, 1972-74; project chief geothermal geophysics Office Geochemistry Geophysics, Denver, 1974-76; scientist-in-charge Hawaiian Volcano Obs., 1976-78; assoc. chief geologist Reston, Va., 1978-81; dean Tex. A&M U. Coll. Geoscis., 1981-83; provost, v.p. acad. affairs Tex. A&M U., 1983-86; pres. Iowa State U., Ames, 1986-90; dir. Lamont-Doherty Earth Obs. Columbia U., Palisades, N.Y., 1990-94, U.S. Geol. Survey, Reston, Va., 1994-97; prin. Pac NW, SeaMountain Country, Colo., Tex., Wash., W.Va., 1997—; mem. Commn. on Internat. Edn., Am. Coun. Edn.; mem. coun. advisors World Food Prize; mem. bd. earth scis. and resources; ocean studies bd., and com. on formation of nat. biol. survey NRC, also mem. geophysics study com.; bd. dirs. Midwest Resources, Inc., Bankers Trust; mem., chair adv. com. U.S. Army Command and Gen. Staff Coll.; adv. bd. Sandia Nat. Lab. Geoscis. & Environ. Ctr.; adv. bd. Ohio State U. Ctr. Mapping. Mem. editl. bd. Jour. Volcanology and Geothermal Rsch., 1976-78; contbr. articles to profl. jours. Trustee Wesleyan U.; pres., bd. dirs. Iowa 4-H Found., 1986-90; mem. U.S. del. sci. & tech. com. Gore-Chernomyrdin Commn., 1996-97; adv. bd. Sch. Earth Sci. Stanford U. Standard Oil fellow Calif. Inst. Tech., 1953; NSF grantee, 1955-59. Fellow Geol. Soc. Am., AAAS. E-Mail: geaton@whidbey.net. Home: 709 Snowberry Ln Coupeville WA 98239-3110 Office: SeaMountain Country 705 N Snowberry Ln Ste O Coupeville WA 98239

EATON, KATHERINE GIRTON, retired library educator; b. St. Paul, Mar. 9, 1924; d. John Frances and Mary Ahleen (Peck) Girton; m. Burt Elliott Eaton, Oct. 18, 1947; children: John Girton, Marilee Eaton Warkentin, David Elliott. BA in Journalism, U. Minn., 1944; MS in Journalism, U. Oreg., 1952, MLS, 1968. Reporter Bakersfield Calif., 1945-46; women's editor Rochester (Minn.) Post Bulletin, 1946-47; legal sec. Broady Law Offices, St. Paul, 1949-51; editor Oreg. State System Higher Edn., Eugene, 1952-53; cons. Oreg. State Libr., Salem, 1968-70; head pub. affairs libr. U. Oreg., Eugene, 1970-85, assoc. prof. emerita, 1985—. Author and editor rsch. reports. Chmn. Lane County Mental Health Bd., Eugene, 1964-88, Lane County Libr. Bd., 1981-85, Eugene City Budget Com., 1988-92, Citizens for Lane County Librs., 1980—, Human Resources Planning Project, Lane County, 1986-89, Oreg. Mental Health Svcs. Planning and Mgmt. Coun., 1988—, chmn., 1996-99; founding bd. dirs. Passages, Lane County substance abuse residential program for offenders, 1990—; pres. Wil ani coun. Camp Fire Inc., 1967-68, nat. bd. dirs., 1966-70, N.W. regional chmn. 1966-70; adv. bd. Oreg. State Mental Health, 1989—, chmn. 1999—; mem. adv. bd. U.S. State Dept. Bosnia Elections Supr., 1997; coord., convener Oreg. Women's Summit, 1996—. Named Outstanding Young Woman, Eugene Jaycettes, 1956, Outstanding Women of Yr., Lane County Orgns., 1974; recipient Gulick, Seaton, Hiitina awards Camp Fire, Inc., 1959, 66, 71, Outstanding Lib. Pub. award The Wilson Co., 1993, U. Oreg. Disting. Svc. award, 1997, Soroptimist Internat. Women of Distinction award, 1998, OASIS Sr. Role Model award, 1998. Mem. AAUP (bd. dirs. U. Oreg. 1976-85, pres. 1977-78), ALA (coun. 1976-80), AAUW (del. NGO women's forum Kenya 1985, China 1995), Oreg. Libr. Assn. (hon. life, pres. 1973-74), Nat. Coun. Planning Librs. (pres. 1978-79, 88-89, Disting. Svc. award 1994), Pacific N.W. Libr. Assn. (editor, quar 1985-96, hon. life), Internat. Fedn. Univ. Women (coun. mem. 1983-85), Assn. Oreg. Faculties (state bd. dirs. 1981-89, v.p. 1983-85), AAUW (pres. Oreg. 1975-77, pres. nat. legal adv. fund 1981-85, nat. exec. v.p. 1981-85, Eugene-Lane branch pres. 1962-63), LWV Oreg. (1st v.p. 1989-91, pres. 1991-93, disting. svc. award 1995), LWV Lane County (pres. 1963-65, 97—), Oreg. Women's Rights Coalition (pres. 1994—), Va. Gildersleeve Internat. Fund (archival historian, bd. dirs. 1995—, 1st v.p. 1999—), Social Order of Beauceaut (pres. 1993, 96). Democrat. Presbyterian. Avocations: beach combing, mystery reading, lobbying.

EATON, KENT ALEXANDER, theology educator; b. Abilene, Tex., Dec. 8, 1957; s. Dorris James and Margie F. (Featherston) E.; m. Victoria Fowler Eaton, June 21, 1980; children: Stephen, Luke Alexander, Matthew Featherston. BA, Tex. Christian U., 1980; ThM, Dallas Sem., 1984; postgrad., U. Wales. Prof. of history Spanish Theol. Sem., Castelldefels, Spain, 1985-97; dir. supervised ministry Bethel Sem., San Diego, Calif., 1997—. Co-author: (book) Coming Deliverer, 1997. Bd. dirs. Ctr. for Urban Ministry, San Diego, 1998. Mem. Phi Beta Kappa. Baptist. Avocations: hiking, sports. Office: Bethel Seminary 6116 Arosa St San Diego CA 92115-3999

EATON, MARYBETH BRENDON, interior designer; b. Landstuhl, Germany, Aug. 29, 1953; came to U.S., 1954; d. Robert Kendall and Mary Elizabeth (O'Connell) Garrabrant; m. Glenn K. Eaton, Aug. 29, 1975. AA, Truckee Meadows C.C., 1991; BS, U. Nev., 1993. Interior designer Mildred Reis Interiors, Sacramento, 1994-95, Habitats Design Studio, Cameron Park, Calif., 1995—, Eaton Design Concepts, Placerville, Calif., 1995—. Mem. Am. Soc. Interior Design, Nat. Trust History Preservation, Golden Key Honor Soc. Avocations: reading, writing, snow skiing, walking, painting. Home: 5015 Thunder Head Ct Placerville CA 95667-9760

EATON, PAULINE, artist; b. Neptune, N.J., Mar. 20, 1935; d. Paul A. and Florence Elizabeth (Rogers) Friedrich: m. Charles Adams Eaton, June 15, 1957; children: Gregory, Eric, Paul, Joy. BA, Dickinson Coll., 1957; MA, Northwestern U., 1958. Lic. instr., Calif. Instr., Mira Costa Coll., Oceanside, Calif., 1980-82, Idyllwild Sch. Music and Arts, Calif., 1983—; juror, demonstarator numerous art socs. Recipient award Haywood (Calif.) area Forum for the Arts, 1986. Exhibited one-woman shows Nat. Arts Club, N.Y.C., 1977, Designs Recycled Gallery, Fullerton, Calif., 1978, 80, 84, San Diego Art Inst., 1980, Spectrum Gallery, San Diego, 1981, San Diego Jung ctr., 1983, Marin Civic Ctr. Gallery, 1984, R. Mondavi Winery, 1987; group shows include Am. Watercolor Soc., 1975, 77, Butler Inst. Am. Art, Youngstown, Ohio, 1977, 78, 79, 81, NAD, 1978, N.Mex. Arts and Crafts Fair, (Best in Show award), 1994, Corrales Bosque Gallery; represented in permanent collections including Butler Inst. Am. Art, St Mary's Coll., Md., Mercy Hosp., San Diego, Sharp Hosp., San Diego, Redlands Hosp., Riverside, 1986; work featured in books: Watercolor, The Creative Experience, 1978, Creative Seascape Painting, 1980, Painting the Spirit in Nature, 1984, Exploring Painting (Gerald Brommer); author: Crawling to the Light, An Artist in Transition, 1987, (with Mary Ann Beckwith) Best of Watercolor Texture, 1997. Trustee San Diego Art Inst., 1977-78, San Diego Mus. Art, 1982-83. Recipient Best of Show award N.Mex. Arts and Crafts Fair, 1994, Grumbacher award Conf. 96 Hill Country Art Ctr., Veloy Vigil award Watercolor USA, 1998. Mem. Nat. Watercolor Soc. (exhibited traveling shows 1978, 79, 83, 85), Rocky Mountain Watermedia Soc. (Golden award 1979, Mustard Seed award 1983), Nat. Soc. Painters in Acrylic and Casein (hon.), Watercolor West (Strathmore award 1979, Purchase award 1986), Internat. Soc. Experimental Artists (pres. 1989-92, Nautilus Merit award 1992, 98), Marin Arts Guild (instr. 1984-87), San Diego Watercolor Soc. (pres. 1976-77, workshop dir. 1977-80), Artists Equity (v.p. San Diego 1979-81), San Diego Artists Guild (pres. 1982-83), N.Mes. Watercolor Soc. (Grumbacher award), Western Fedn. Watercolor Socs. (chmn. 1983, 3d prize 1982, Grumbacher Gold medal 1983), 3d prize 1982, Grumbacher Gold medal 1983), West Coast Watercolor Socl. (exhbns. chmn. 1983-86, pres. 1989-92), Eastbay Watercolor Soc. (v.p. 1988-90), Soc. Layerists in Multi-Media (bd. dirs. 1992—), Corrales Bosque Gallery (charter mem., pres. 1996-98). Democrat. Home: 68 Hop Tree Trl Corrales NM 87048-9613

EAVES, SALLY ANN, logistics director, research administrator; b. Salt Lake City, Feb. 25, 1945; d. Frank C. and Magdalene (Buller) Winslow; m. Stephen Douglas Eaves, Apr. 27, 1974; children: Trevor Bernard, Lindsay Douglas, Christian Francis. BA in English, Gonzaga U., 1967; postgrad., Utah State U., 1980, U. So. Calif., 1985. Individual mobilization asst. to dir. of logistics U.S. Forces Korea, 1983-87; individual mobilization asst. to chief of transp., dir. distbn., dir. commodities Ogden (Utah) Air Logistics Ctr., 1987-93; individual mobilization asst. to dir. logistics N.Am. Aerospace Def. Command and U.S. Space Command, Peterson AFB, Colo., 1993-95; mobilization asst. to commdr. Okla. Air Logistics Ctr., Oklahoma City, 1995-98; mobilization asst. to dir. logistics Air Combat Command, Langley AFB, Va., 1998—; v.p. N.W. Rsch. Inst., Las Vegas, 1996—. V.p., bd. dirs. The Pond Homeowners Assn., Arvada, Colo., 1992-95; ednl./comty. vol. Jeffco Pub. Schs., 1992-95; ch. vol. Spirit of Christ Cath. Ch., Arvada, 1989—; career devel. counselor Adams County Sch. Dist. 50, Westminster, Colo., 1989—. Brig. gen. USAFR, 1967—. Decorated Def. Meritorious Svc. medal, Meritorious Svc. medal. Mem. Nat. Def. Transp. Assn., Soc. Logistics Engrs., Air Force Assn., Res. Officers Assn. (v.p. Okla. chpt. 1996-97). Home: 8708 Independence Way Arvada CO 80005-1247

EAVES, STEPHEN DOUGLAS, educator, vocational administrator; b. Honolulu, Aug. 30, 1944; s. Alfred Aldee and Phyllis Clarissa (Esty) E.; m. Sally Ann Winslow, Apr. 27, 1974; children: Trevor Bernard, Lindsay Douglas, Christian Francis. BA in Polit. Sci., U. Hawaii, 1967; MS in Bus. Mgmt., U. Ark., 1974; PhD in Edn. Adminstrn., Colo. State U., 1997. Cert. secondary tchr., prin., vocat. dir., post secondary bus. tchr., Colo. Commd. 2d lt. USAF, 1967, advanced through grades to lt. col., ret., 1989; aerospace sci. tchr. Adams County Sch. Dist. 50, Westminster, Colo., 1989-94, vocat. dir./asst. prin., 1994—; cons. Dept. of Edn., Colo., 1993—. Eucharistic min. Spirit of Christ Cath. Ch., Arvada, Colo., 1989—. Decorated Silver Star, DFC, Air medals, Commendation medals, Air Force Achievement medal; named Outstanding Tchr. Focus on Excellence Program, 1992, Outstanding Nat. Aerospace Sci. Tchr., 1994. Mem. ASCD, Coun. for Exceptional

Children, Am. Vocat. Assn., Colo. Vocat. Assn., Colo. Assn. Vocat. Adminstrs., Colo. Assn. Sch. Execs., Am. Nat. Rose Soc., Royal Nat. Rose Soc., Lions (sec. Adams Centennial chpt. 1991-92, Lion of Yr. 1992), Elks, Phi Delta Kappa, Omicron Tau Delta. Avocations: snow skiing, rose gardening. Home: 8708 Independence Way Arvada CO 80005-1247 Office: Career Enrichment Park 7300 Lowell Blvd Westminster CO 80030-4821

EBBINGA, CRYSTALLE YVONNE, social services administrator; b. Wall, S.D., Jan. 23, 1936; d. Earl Benjamin and Josie Amanda (Lee) Adamson; m. Gerald Richard Ebbinga, June 3, 1961; children: Kurtis Herm, Spencer Kirk, Brittanee Leigh. MusB, MacPhail Coll. Music, Mpls., 1960. Tchr. elem. music Boyceville (Wis.) Consol., 1960-61; tchr. and music supr. St. Louis Park (Minn.) Elem. Sch., 1961-63, St. Croix Consol. Sch. Dist., Hammond and Roberts, Wis., 1963-66; substitute tchr. Prince Albert (Sask., Can.) Pub. Schs., 1979-80; parish asst. First Luth. Ch., Pomona, Calif., 1981-86; adminstrv. asst. LaVerne (Calif.) U., 1986-87; asst. to gen. dir. YMCA, Pomona, 1988-89; dir. Hill and Dale Child Devel. Ctr., Las Vegas, Nev., 1989-90; pres., CEO St. Thomas Child and Family Ctr., Great Falls, Mont., 1990—. Editor The Supporter newsletter, 1992-96. Chmn. agy. dirs. United Way, Great Falls, Mont., 1992-95; bd. dirs. Families Count, Great Falls, 1992-95; adv. bd. Families Self-Sufficiency (Great Falls Housing Authority), 1993—; lobbyist Mont. Child Care Assn., Helena, 1992; asst. chmn. Great Falls Community Needs Assessment Com., 1993-95; mem. steering com. Dept. Family Svcs. Project; mem. Leadership Great Falls, 1991. Mem. NAFE, Soc. for Non-Profit Orgn., Nat. Parent Aide, Mont. Coun. for Families, Healthy Mothers Healthy Babies, Great Falls Advt. Club. Avocations: music (voice), reading, camping, cross-country skiing, interior decorating. Home: 6 Meadowlark Ridge Great Falls MT 59405-5532 Office: Saint Thomas Child & Family Ct 416 23rd St N Great Falls MT 59401-2847

EBEL, DAVID M., federal judge; b. 1940. BA, Northwestern U., 1962; JD, U. Mich., 1965. Law clk. assoc. justice Byron White U.S. Supreme Ct., 1965-66; pvt. practice Davis, Graham & Stubbs, Denver, 1966-88; judge U.S. Ct. Appeals (10th cir.), Denver, 1988—; adj. prof. law U. Denver Law Sch., 1987-89; sr. lectr. fellow Duke U. Sch. Law, 1992-94. Mem. Am. Coll. Trial Lawyers, Colo. Bar Assn. (v.p. 1982), Jud. Conf. U.S. (com. on codes of conduct 1991—, co-chair 10th cir. gender bias task force 1994—). Office: US Ct Appeals 1823 Stout St Rm 109L Denver CO 80257-1823

EBERHARDT, GRETCHEN ANN, lawyer, hearing officer; b. Denver, Feb. 9, 1964; d. Robert Schuler and Lusetta Mary (Bush) E. BA in Sociology, U. Colo., 1986; JD, Whittier Coll., 1991. Bar: Colo. 1992, U.S. Ct. Appeals (10th cir.) 1992. Flight attendant Continental Airlines, Denver, 1987-88; due process hearing officer Colo. Dept. Edn., Denver, 1991—; ptnr. Eberhardt & Eberhardt, Littleton, Colo., 1991—; spkr. estate planning seminars AARP, Denver, 1996; phone-in cons. Law Line 9—Legal Questions, Channel 9, Sta. KUSA, Denver, 1994—. Vol., supr. Rocky Mountain PBS, Denver, 1993—; chmn. Arapahoe County Young Reps., Aurora, Colo., 1992-97, 26th Rep. Senatorial Dist., Arapahoe County and Jefferson County, 1997—. Mem. Colo. Bar Assn., Arapahoe County Bar Assn. Republican. Roman Catholic. Avocations: traveling, skiing, swimming, reading, hiking. Office: Eberhardt & Eberhardt 8441 W Bowles Ave Ste 210 Littleton CO 80123-9501

EBERHARDT, MARTY LAMPERT, botanical garden administrator; b. Albuquerque, Aug. 6, 1952; d. Charles Lampert and Mary Elizabeth (Marty) E.; m. Thomas George Schramski, Mar. 19, 1977 (div. May 1986); children: Paul, Sam; m. Philip Alan Hastings, Dec. 12, 1987. BA, Prescott Coll., 1974; MEd, U. Ariz., 1978. Program dir. Tumamoc Hill Environ. Edn. Ctr., Tucson, 1978-79; tchr. Cmty. Psychology and Edn. Svcs., Tucson, 1985-87; asst. dir./edn. coord. Tucson Bot. Gardens, 1986-88, exec. dir., 1988—; reviewer grants Inst. Mus. and Libr. Svcs., Washington, 1994—. Tucson Cmty. Found., 1997-98; mem. adv. bd. Registree, 1993—, Project Arid, 1996—. Mem. steering com. Tucson Hasit, 1996—; mem. exec. com. Intercultural Ctr. for Study of Deserts and Oceans, Puerto Peñasco, Mex., 1998—. Recipient Women on the Move award YWCA, Tucscon, 1993, various grants from corps. and founds., 1988—. Mem. Exec. Women's Coun., Strategic Leadership in Changing Environ., Am. Assn. Bot. Gardens and Arboreta (regional coord.), Am. Assn. Museums (reviewer grants 1994-98), Native Seeds/SEARCH. Avocations: hiking, backpacking, reading, gardening. Office: Tucson Bot Gardens 2150 N Alvernon Way Tucson AZ 85712-3153

EBERHART, DAVID L., state legislator. Registered profl. engr., Ariz. Structural engr.; mem., majority whip dist. 19 Ariz. Ho. of Reps., Phoenix, 1994—; mem. environment, govt. ops., and rules coms. Republican. Office: Ariz Ho of Reps 1700 W Washington St Phoenix AZ 85007-2812

EBERLING, GEORGE GIFFORD, federal agency administrator; b. Staten Island, N.Y., Dec. 9, 1961; s. Jerome George and Jessie Theresa (White) E. BSBA, The Citadel, 1985; MS in Forensic Sci., Nat. U., San Diego, 1990; MA in Internat. Rels., U. San Diego, 1999. Commd. officer USN, San Diego, 1985-89; sales rep. ADT Security, San Diego, 1989; post enumeration supervisor U.S. Dept. Commerce, San Diego, 1990; acct. analyst U.S. IRS, San Diego, 1991-92; investigative cons. JRM Cons., San Diego, 1992; from applications adjudicator to ctr. adjudications officer U.S. Immigration & Naturalization Scs., Laguna Niguel, Calif., 1992—. Mem. U.S. Naval Res. Assn. Republican. Roman Catholic. Avocations: reading, writing poetry, computers, theater, travel. Home: 19641 133d Ave Sun City West AZ 85375

EBERTING, CORWIN H., JR., architect; b. Seattle, Mar. 9, 1924; s. Corwin H. and Annis (Jenner) E.; m. Lulleane Cutter, Apr. 11, 1946 (div. Mar. 1957); m. Joan Keith, Mar. 30, 1957; children: Casey, Kan Elise. BA, Stanford U., 1948; MArch, Harvard U., 1954. Draftsman City of Manhattan Beach (Calif.), 1948-49, Curtin & Riley, Boston, 1949-51; designer Kilham, Hopkins, Greely, Brodie, Boston, 1952-54, Kenneth Wing, Long Beach, Calif., 1954-56; owner, CEO OBerting Inc., Redondo Beach, Calif., 1957—. Lt. (j.g.) USN, 1943-46. Mem. AIA (Calif. coun. dir. 1973-74, 78-79, South Bay chpt. pres. 1974). Republican. Avocations: golf, sailing, surfing, swimming, painting. Home: 211 Yacht Club Way Redondo Beach CA 90277-2057 Office: Eberting Inc 811 N Harbor Dr # 6 Redondo Beach CA 90277-2005

EBERWEIN, BARTON DOUGLAS, construction company executive, consultant; b. Balt., Aug. 19, 1951; s. Bruce George and Thelma Joyce (Cox) E. BS, U. Oreg., 1974, MBA, 1988. Sales mgr. Teleprompter of Oreg., Eugene, 1974-75; pres., owner Oreg. Images, Eugene, 1975-80; mktg. mgr. Clearwater Prodns., Eugene, 1980-82; sales mgr. Western Wood Structures, Portland, Oreg., 1982-84, mktg. coordinator, 1984-85, mktg. dir., 1985-89; dir. bus. devel. Hoffman Constrn. Co., Portland, 1989-93, v.p., 1993—. Bd. dirs. N.W. Youth Corps, Eugene, 1984—, Police Activity League, 1991, Portland Arts and Lectrs., 1994—; vol. bd. dirs. Goodwill, Oreg. Symphony, Portland Inst. for Contemporary Art, 1997—. Mem. Soc. Mktg. Profl. Svcs., Am. Mktg. Assn., Univ. Club, Founders Club, Riverplace Athletic Club. Democrat. Presbyterian. Avocations: rare books, photography, outdoor recreation, architectural preservation. Home: PO Box 391 Portland OR 97207-0391 Office: Hoffman Constrn Co 1300 SW 6th Ave Ste 400 Portland OR 97201-3486

EBNER, ROGER SCOTT, film and television professional; b. Rochester, N.Y., Oct. 16, 1955; s. Floyd Albert and Patricia Eileen (Burke) E. BA in Biology, Trinity U., San Antonio, 1977. Freelance film and TV profl. San Antonio, 1977-92, L.A., 1992—; founder, pres., CEO Am. West Network, Toluca Lake, Calif.; mem. adv. bd. Indian Nat. Film Coun., L.A., 1998—. Avocations: American history, flying, horseback riding, history of American West. Home: 2713 W Clark Ave Burbank CA 91505-3218 Office: Am West Network PO Box 2672 Toluca Lake CA 91610-0672

EBY, DAVID EUGENE, geologist; b. Harrisburg, Pa., Sept. 26, 1947; s. Eugene Elwood and Ruth Dunkleberger (Crozier) E.; m. I. Marie Cooper, Aug. [illegible] shall Coll., 1969; MS, Brown U., 1972; PhD, SUNY, Stony Brook, 1977. Teaching asst. Brown U., Providence, 1969-71, SUNY, Stony Brook, N.Y., 1971-73; asst. prof. geology prof. L.I.U., Southampton, N.Y., 1973, Franklin and Marshall Coll., Lancaster, Pa., 1973-74, U. Tex., Dallas, 1975-79; adj. asst. prof. U. Tex., Arlington, Dallas, 1979-83; sr. research geologist Mobil Oil R&D Co., Dallas, 1979-83; geologic advisor Union Pacific Resources Co., Englewood, Colo., 1983-90; sr. rsch. geologist Marathon Petroleum Rsch. Ctr., Littleton, Colo., 1990-91; owner Eby Petrography and Cons., Inc., 1990—; speaker in field. Contbr. articles to profl. jours. Dir. Lookout Preschool Richardson, Tex., 1977-78; ch. coucil mem. Community Luth. Ch., Richardson, 1977-78; mem. Geology Adv. Com., U. Colo., Denver, 1986—. Recipient Yeakel Sedimentology award, Franklin and Marshall Coll., 1969; U. Tex. Research grantee, 1975-77. Mem. Am. Assn. Petroleum Geologist (standing com. 1979-87, chmn. 1979-87, editor, 1986-88, cert. of Merit, 1987), Soc. Econ. Minerologists and Paleontologists, Geol. Soc. Am., Internat. Assn. Sedimentologists, AAAS, Nat. Assn. Geol. Tchrs., Dallas Geol. Soc. (v.p. 1980-81), Rocky Mountian Assn. Geologists. Republican. Mem. United Church of Christ. Avocations: hiking, camping. Home: 1780 E Geddes Cir S Littleton CO 80122-1431 Office: Eby Petrography & Consulting Inc 2200 W Berry Ave Ste 2 Littleton CO 80120-1100

EBY, JOHN OLIVER, minister; b. Chgo., Aug. 28, 1940; s. John Wilbert and Gladys Anna (Palmer) E.; m. Sherrie Anne Jordan, Aug. 15, 1961; children: John Christopher, Ramona Anna-Lydia. BA, U. LaVerne, 1962; MDiv, Am. Bapt. Sem. of West, 1965. Ordained to ministry Am. Bapt. Ch., 1965. Assoc. pastor Judson Bapt. Ch., San Bernardino, Calif., 1964-68; pastor Community Bapt. Ch., Buttonwillow, Calif., 1968-74; pastor 1st Bapt. Ch., Lompoc, Calif., 1974-81, Selma, Calif., 1981—. Trustee Lompoc Unified Sch, Dist., 1979-81; mem. assessment coun. Selma Unified Sch. Dist., 1982-83; chmn. sch. site coun. Selma High Sch., 1985-87, accreditation com., 1987; chmn. blood drive Cen. Calif. Blood Bank, Selma, 1982-90; mem. delinquency prevention task force City of Selma, 1989-90; co-chmn. ICU fund drive Selma Dist Hosp. Found., 1990. Recipient Svc. award Black Leaders of San Bernardino, 1968, Buttonwillow C. of C., 1974, Hon. Svc. award Buttonwillow PTA, 1974, Scouter's Key award Boy Scouts Am., Lompoc, 1976, Continuing Svc. award Lompoc PTA, 1977, Vocat. Svc. award Rotary Club, Selma, 1988, Outstanding Citizen award Police Chief's Assn., Fresno, Calif., 1990, Svc. award Selma City Coun., 1991. Mem. Am. Bapt. Chs. of the West (moderator 1988-90, bd. mgrs. 1989-90), Am. Bapt. Chs. (mem. min. coun.), Selma Ministerial Assn. (pres. 1987-89, sec. 1990-91), porterville Area Ministerial Assn. (pres., sec. 1993-98, chaplain Porterville P.D. 1993-98). Office: 1st Bapt Ch 101 N G St Porterville CA 93257-3407

EBY, MICHAEL JOHN, marketing research and technology consultant; b. South Bend, Ind., Aug. 3, 1949; s. Robert T. and Eileen Patricia (Holmes) E.; m. Judith Alyson Gaskell, May 17, 1980; children: Elizabeth, Katherine. Student, Harvey Mudd Coll., 1969-70; BS in Biochemistry with high honors, U. Md., 1972, MS in Chemistry, 1977; postgrad., IMEDE, Lausanne, Switzerland, 1984. Product mgr. LKB Instruments Inc., Rockville, Md., 1976-79; mktg. mgr. LKB-Produkter AB, Bromma, Sweden, 1979-87; strategic planning mgr. Pharmacia LKB Biotech. AB, Bromma, 1987-88; dir. mktg. Am. Bionetics, Hayward, Calif., 1988-89; pres. PhorTech Internat., San Carlos, Calif., 1989—. Author: The Electrophoresis Explosion, 1988, Electrophoresis in the Nineties, 1990, DNA Amplification, 1993, Blotting and Hybridization, 1993, Capillary Electrophoresis, 1993, Global Laboratory Product Usage, 1994, Densitometers and Image Analysis, 1995, Microplate Equipment, 1995, Synthetic Oligonucleotides, 1995, Electrophoretic Gel Media, 1995, Visualization Reagents, 1995, U.S. Laboratory Product Usage, 1996, Cell Biology Reagent Systems, 1996, Centrifugation, 1996, Molecular Biology Reagent Systems, 1997, DNA Sequencing, 1997, DNA Diagnostics, 1997, DNA Amplification in Europe, 1998, RecombinantProtein Expression Systems, 1998, Worldwide Directory of Life Science Distributors, 1998, DNA Sequencing in Europe, 1998, Cytokines and Growth Factors, 1998, Molecular Biology Reagent Systems in the Far East, 1998, HPLC in the Life Sciences, 1998, Cytokines and Growth Factors, 1998, Cell and Tissue Culture, 1998, Monoclonal Antibodies, 1999; contbr. articles to profl. jours. Mem. AAAS, European Soc. Opinion and Mktg. Rsch., Am. Chem. Soc., Am. Soc. Cell Biology, The Electrophoresis Soc., Spirit of LKB Internat. Assn., U. Md. Alumni Assn., Am. Mensa Ltd., Calif. Separation Sci. Soc. Episcopalian. Avocations: astronomy, cheesemaking, photography, travel. Office: PhorTech Internat 238 Crestview Dr San Carlos CA 94070-1503

ECCLES, MATTHEW ALAN, golf course and landscape architect; b. Ft. Dodge, Iowa, Apr. 19, 1956; s. Guy Eldon Jr. and Mary Ellen (Baldwin) E.; m. Debra Kay Sorenson, Mar. 19, 1983; children: Stephanie Ann, Jason Alan. BS in Landscape Architecture, Iowa State U., 1978. Registered landscape architect, Kans., Minn. From project mgr. to dir. golf course design THK Assocs., Inc., Greenwood Village, Colo., 1980-94; pres. Eccles Design Inc., Englewood, Colo., 1994—. Mem. Am. Soc. Landscape Architects, U.S. Golf Assn., Golf Course Supts. Assn. Am., Nat. Golf Found., Nat. Ski Patrol, Tau Sigma Delta. Avocations: golf, skiing, fishing, photography. Home: 8120 S Monaco Cir Englewood CO 80112-3022 Office: Eccles Design Inc 8120 S Monaco Cir Englewood CO 80112-3022

ECCLES, SPENCER FOX, banker; b. Ogden, Utah, Aug. 24, 1934; s. Spencer Stoddard and Hope (Fox) E.; m. Cleone Emily Peterson, July 21, 1958; children: Clista Hope, Lisa Ellen, Katherine Ann, Spencer Peterson. B.S., U. Utah, 1956; M.A., Columbia U., 1959; degree in Bus. (hon.), So. Utah State Coll., 1982; LLB (hon.), Westminster Coll., Salt Lake City, 1986. Trainee First Nat. City Bank, N.Y.C., 1959-60; with First Security Bank of Utah, Salt Lake City, 1960-61, First Security Bank of Idaho, Boise, 1961-70; exec. v.p. First Security Corp. Salt Lake City, 1970-75, pres., 1975-86, chief operating officer, 1980-82, chmn. bd. dirs., chief exec. officer, 1982—; dir. Union Pacific Corp., Anderson Lumber Co., Zions Corp., Merc. Instn.; mem. adv. council U. Utah Bus. Coll. Served to 1st lt. U.S. Army. Recipient Pres.'s Circle award Presdl. Commn., 1984, Minuteman award Utah N.G., 1988; Named Disting. Alumni U. Utah, 1988. Mem. Am. Bankers Assn., Bankers Roundtable, Salt Lake Country Club, Alta Club. Office: 1st Security Corp PO Box 30006 79 S Main 2d Fl Salt Lake City UT 84130*

ECKELKAMP, MARYLYN, psychologist; b. Ottawa, Ont., Can., Feb. 20, 1946; came to U.S., 1960; d. Edward Joffre and Irene Ceclia (Madigan) Greenway; m. Vincent C.J. Eckelkamp, May 30, 1964; children: Lisa Ann, Vincent Edward. AA, Colo. Women's Coll., Denver, 1964; BA, U. So. Fla., 1974, MA, 1976. Nat. cert. sch. psychologist; lic. marriage and family therapist, Nev. Tchr. remedial Big Bend C.C., Afcent, The Netherlands, 1977-78; edn. counselor Civil Svc., Afcent, The Netherlands, 1978-80; psychologist Clark County Sch. Dist., Las Vegas, Nev., 1980—; intern in marriage and family therapy Family Cousneling Ctr., Las Vegas, 1988-90, HCA Montevista Hosp., Las Vegas, 1986-90, group leader eating disorders, 1987-89; pvt. practice marriage and family therapy, Las Vegas, 1991—. Parenting group leader schs. and chs., Las Vegas, 1980—. Mem. Am. Assn. Marriage and Family Therapists, Nat. Assn. Sch. Psychologists, Nev. Assn. Sch. Psychologists (pres. 1980—). Roman Catholic. Avocations: skiing, swimming, reading, traveling.

ECKELMAN, RICHARD JOEL, engineering specialist; b. Bklyn., Mar. 25, 1951; s. Leon and Muriel (Brietbart) E.; m. Janet Louise Fenton, Mar. 21, 1978; children: Christie, Melanie, Erin Leigh. Student, Ariz. State U., 1988—. Sr. engr., group leader nondestructive testing Engring. Fluor Corp., Irvine, Calif., 1979-83; sr. engr. nondestructive testing McDonnell Douglas Helicopter Co., Mesa, Ariz., 1983-91; engring. specialist Convair div. Gen. Dynamics, San Diego, 1991-94; sr. tech. specialist McDonnell Douglas Techs., Inc., San Diego, 1994-96; scientist, engr. The Boeing Co., Mesa, Ariz., 1996—. Mem. Am. Soc. Nondestructive Testing (nat. aerospace com. 1987—, sec. Ariz. chpt. 1987-88, treas. 1988—, sect. chmn. 1989—, sect. bd. dirs. 1990-91), Am. Soc. Quality Control, Soc. Mfg. Engrs., Lindbergh Yacht Club. Avocations: racquetball, sailing. Home: 11820 N 111th Pl Scottsdale AZ 85259-3070

ECKER, HOWARD, lawyer; b. N.Y.C., June 10, 1946; s. David and Sylvia (Goldstein) E.; children: David, Ashley. BA, U. Mich., 1967; JD, NYU, [illegible] 1976, U.S. Supreme Ct. 1976. Pub. defender Clark County Pub. Defender's Office, Nev., 1973-77; ptnr. Ecker & Standish, Chtd., Clark County, Nev., 1977—; apptd. settlement judge in appeals Nev. Supreme Ct., 1997—; guest lectr. in field. Mem. Nev. Employee Mgmt. Rels. Bd., Las Vegas, 1990-94. Mem. ATLA, State Bar Nev. (bd. govs. 1984-90), Clark County Bar Assn., Nev. Trial Lawyers Assn. (bd. govs. 1977-89, pres. 1985-86), Nev. Am. Inns of Ct. (barrister 1990-93, master 1993—). Avocations: travel, golf, reading. Office: Ecker & Standish Chtd 300 S 4th St Ste 611 Las Vegas NV 89101-6017

ECKER, MARC AVERY, school system administrator, educator; b. Burbank, Calif., May 31, 1949; s. Richard Earnest and Jessie (Israel) E.; m. Linda Phyllis Silverman, Dec. 17, 1972; children: Jacqueline, Michael, Molly. BA, UCLA, 1971; MS, Calif. State U., Fullerton, 1976; PhD, U.S. Internat. U., 1979. Cert. elem. tchr., secondary tchr., sch. adminstr., Calif. Tchr. Los Alamitos (Calif.) Sch. Dist., 1972-77, sch. improvement coord., 1977-78, learning coord., 1978-79; prin. elem. sch. Fountain Valley (Calif.) Sch. Dist., 1979-83, prin. mid. sch., 1983-91, asst. supt., 1991-96, supt., 1996—; cons. Mid. Sch. Assn., Columbus, 1986—. Mem. bd. dirs. Am. Cancer Soc., Orange County, Calif., 1995—, Am. Heart Assn., Orange County, 1996—, Jewish Fedn., Orange County, 1994—. Mem. Nat. Mid. Sch. Assn. (mem. exec. bd. 1995-97, Mem. of Yr. 1996), Calif. League Mid. Schs. (bd. dirs. 1984—, pres. 1991, 93), Assn. Calif. Sch. Adminstrs. (region 17 bd. dirs. 1986-91, pres. 1988-89), Calif. PTA (pres. 1995, Disting. Svc. award 1997). Democrat. Jewish. Avocations: sports, reading, racquetball. Home: 10699 El Soneto Ave Fountain Valley CA 92708-4801 Office: Fountain Valley Sch Dist 17210 Oak St Fountain Valley CA 92708-3405

ECKER, ROBERT RODGERS, fine arts educator, artist; b. Waynesboro, Pa., Apr. 30, 1936; s. Robert Garnes and Irma (Rodgers) E.; m. Jean Beard Ecker, Nov. 7, 1958; children: Cassandra, Penelope, Robert B., Jonathan. BS in Edn., Shippensburg State U., 1958; postgrad., Pa. Acad. Fine Arts, 1959-61; MFA, Pa. State U., 1965. From asst. prof. to assoc. prof. Wash. State U., Pullman, 1965-72; prof. U. Colo., Boulder, 1972—; spkr., vis. artist Denison U., Granville, Ohio, 1975, Rutgers U., Camden, N.J., 1980, U. Calif., Fullerton, 1986, U. Del., Newark, 1992. Solo exhbns. include Ban Gallery, Osaka, Japan, 1982, Am. Cultural Ctr., Bellgrade, Yugoslavia, 1983, Galleria Grafka, Tokyo, 1985, Denver Art Mus., 1991; permanent collections include Denver Art Mus.; art contbr. pub. radio and TV, 1972—. D.H. Lawrence fellow U. N.Mex., 1976, Nat. Endowment Arts artists fellow, 1981-82; recipient Recognition in Painting award Colo. Coun. Arts, Denver, 1995. Mem. Soc. Am. Graphic Artists (pres. purchase award 1980, coun. mem. 1990-92). Avocations: swimming, reading. Home: 78 Benthaven Pl Boulder CO 80303-6255 Office: U Colo PO Box 318 Boulder CO 80309-0318

ECKERSLEY, NORMAN CHADWICK, banker; b. Glasgow, Scotland, June 18, 1924; came to U.S., 1969; s. James Norman and Beatrice (Chadwick) E.; m. Rosemary J. Peters, May 23, 1986, 1 child, Anne. D Laws Strathclyde U., Scotland. With Chartered Bank, London and Manchester, 1947-48; acct., Bombay, 1948-52, Singapore, 1952-54, Sarawak, 1954-56, Pakistan, 1956-58, Calcutta, 1958-59, Hong Kong, 1959-60, asst. mgr. Hamburg, 1960-62, mgr. Calcutta, 1962-67, Thailand, 1967-69; pres. Chartered Bank London, San Francisco, 1964-74, chmn., chief exec., 1974-79; chmn. Standard Chartered Bancorp, 1978-81; dep. chmn. Union Bank, L.A., 1979-82; chmn., CEO The Pacific Bank, San Francisco, 1982-93, chmn. emeritus, 1993; chmn. Diners Club (Asia), 1967-69, Devel. Bank Thailand, 1967-69, Scottish Am. Investment Com., U. Strathclyde Found.; chmn., CEO Balmoral Capital Corp., 1994—; chmn. Balmoral Fin. Corp., 1995—. With RAF, 1940-46. Decorated D.F.C.; Comdr. Order Brit. Empire. Mem. Overseas Banks Assn. Calif. (chmn. 1972-74), Calif. Coun. Internat. Trade, San Francisco C. of C., World Trade Assn., Royal and Ancient Club, Royal Troon Golf Club (Scotland), World Trade Club, San Francisco Golf Club, Pacific Union Club (San Francisco). Mem. Ch. of Scotland. Home: 265 Casitas Ave San Francisco CA 94127-1603 Office: 20 Park Rd Burlingame CA 94010-4443

ECKERT, GERALDINE GONZALES, language professional, educator, entrepreneur; b. N.Y.C., Aug. 5, 1948; d. Albert and Mercedes (Martinez) Gonzales; m. Robert Alan Eckert, Apr. 1, 1972; children: Lauren Elaine, Alison Elizabeth. BA, Ladycliff Coll., Highland Falls, N.Y., 1970; student, U. Valencia, Spain, 1968; MA, N.Y.U., 1971; student, Instituto de Cultura Hispanica, Madrid, 1970-71. Tchr. Spanish Clarkstown High Sch. N. (N.Y.), 1971-73, Rambam Torah Inst., Beverly Hills, Calif., 1973-75; translator City of Beverly Hills, 1976-83; edn. cons. Los Angeles County of Calif. Dept. Forestry, Capistrano Beach, 1982-84; lang. services and protocol Los Angeles Olympic Organizing Com., 1983-84; pension adminstr. Pension Architects, Inc., Los Angeles, 1984-87; instr. El Camino Coll., Torrance, Calif., 1987-88, Santa Monica (Calif.) Coll., 1975—; owner, pres. Bilingual Pension Cons., L.A., 1987-89; bd. dirs. Institute for Hispanic Cultural Studies, Los Angeles; spl. asst. to Internat. Olympic Com., Lausanne, Switzerland, 1983—. V.p. Notre Dame Acad. Assoc., West L.A., 1987—; mem. L.A. March of Dimes Ambassadors Group, 1987; co-founder, pres. Blind Cleaning Express, L.A., 1989—; bd. dirs. Inst. Hispanic Cultural Studies, L.A., 1984-89; spl. asst. to pres. Internat. Olympic Com. Lausanne, Switzerland, 1983—. Democrat. Roman Catholic. Clubs: Five Ring, Los Angeles, Friends of Sport, Amateur Athletic Found., Los Angeles. Office: 8885 Venice Blvd Ste 103 Los Angeles CA 90034-3242

EDDINGTON, CAROLE ANN, writer, artist; b. Stockton, Calif., Feb. 3, 1948; d. Jack Elmer and Gladys Ester (Bartholomew) Rollins; m. James Nelson Eddington, Apr. 19, 1997. BS in Conservation of Natural Resources, U. Calif., Berkeley, 1971, AB in Arch., 1971, MA, 1974, postgrad., 1975. Coord., initiator 105 120 course U. Calif., Berkeley, 1970-74; ptnr., initiator Ca Song Records, N.Y.C., 1976-86; trustee, founder Environ. Celebration Found., Las Vegas, 1994—. *As founding trustee of the Environmental Celebration Foundation (ECF), Carole Ann Eddington is dedicated to implementing it's goals to preserve, protect and promote peace, harmony and dignity amongst all living things. ECF is preparing Ecology books and products for children, parents and teachers. ECF is also creating an Eco-Village Retreat which will showcase cutting-edge technologies in sustainable building technology and energy-saving research, and be a Center for Celebration of the Arts. It will be a place for reflection and renewal, learning to realign the balance and interdependence between people and nature. Projects will be implemented as funding is secured.* Author, illustrator: Me and My Friends, 1992, The Ecology Book, 1996; singer writer Nostalgia Goes Country, 1986; author of essays, poetry. Nat. Wildlife Fedn. fellow, 1973-74; NEA grantee, 1974-75. Avocations: singing, dancing, poetry, plants. Office: PO Box 94534 Las Vegas NV 89193

EDDY, THOMAS JOHN, landscape architect; b. Fremont, Calif., May 12, 1964; s. John Thomas and Mary Irene (Gage) E. Student, Foothill Jr. Coll., Los Altos, Calif.; BSLA, Calif. Poly. U., San Luis Obispo, 1989. Landscape arch. Dike/Runa, Irvine, Calif., 1989-91; sales rep. various organizations, Calif., 1991-96; proj. mngr. Jumpin' Junipers, Santa Rosa, Calif., 1996-97; landscape arch., owner T.E.L.C.S., Duncans Mills, Calif., 1997—; advisor San Franciso Garden Show, 1995-97. Mem. Am. Soc. Landscape Arch. (dir. Redwood Empire sect. No. Calif. chpt.). Avocations: gardening, camping travel, film, cooking, historical preservation. E-mail: tjeddy@ap.net. Fax: 707-865-9218. Office: TELCS PO Box 142 Duncans Mills CA 95430

EDEEN, WILLIAM AVERY, artist; b. San Francisco, May 13, 1973; s. John Richard and Susan (Avery) E. AA in Art History, Monterey Peninsula Coll., 1992; BA in Art, U. Calif., Santa Cruz, 1994; postgrad., Otis Coll. Art & Design, 1995. Teaching asst. Monterey (Calif.) Peninsula Coll., 1992—; graphic designer pvt. practice, Pacific Grove, Calif., 1994—; bd. dirs. Heritage Soc., Pacific Grove. One-man shows include James B. Hall Gallery, Santa Cruz, 1993, John Dizikes Gallery, Santa Cruz, 1994, Pacific Grove Mus. Natural History, 1997, The Grove Homescapes, 1997; group shows include Long Beach (Calif.) Arts, 1991, Monterey (Calif.) Peninsula Mus. art, 1991, Finegood Art Gallery, West Hills, Calif., 1991, Peconic Gallery, Riverhead, N.Y., 1992, E.P. Smith Gallery, Santa Cruz, 1993, Art at the Powerhouse, Toronto, Can., 1994, The Dancing Man Gallery, Santa Cruz, [illegible] Gallery, Santa Cruz, 1996, Monterey Peninsula Mus. Art, 1997, Calif. State U. Monterey Bay, 1997, others. Regent scholar, U. Calif., Santa Cruz, 1992-94. Mem. Am. Inst. Graphic Arts, Nat. Trust Historic Preservation, Internat. Sculpture Ctr., Artists in Print. Home. 743 Laurel Ave Pacific Grove CA 93950-3242

EDELMAN, BART, English literature educator, poet; b. Paterson, N.J., Nov. 4, 1951; s. Donald Lloyd and Beatrice (Sarver) E. BA in Polit. Sci., Hofstra U., 1973, MA in English Lit., 1974. Instr. English CUNY, Bklyn., 1974-75, Long Beach (Calif.) City Coll., 1975-76, West L.A. Coll., 1975-76, Santa Monica (Calif.) Coll., 1975-76, UCLA Extn., 1979-83; prof. Glendale (Calif.) Coll., 1975—. Author: (poetry) The Alphabet of Love, 1999, Under Damaris' Dress, 1996, Crossing the Hackensack, 1993. U. Tex. fellow, Poland, 1988, U.S. Dept. Edn., Nigeria, 1982, Egypt, 1981, India, 1980. Mem. Pen West. Home: 394 Elmwood Dr Pasadena CA 91105-1327 Office: Glendale Coll 1500 N Verdugo Rd Glendale CA 91208-2809

EDELMAN, GERALD MAURICE, biochemist, neuroscientist, educator; b. N.Y.C., N.Y., July 1, 1929; s. Edward and Anna (Freedman) E.; m. Maxine Morrison, June 11, 1950; children: Eric, David, Judith. B.S., Ursinus Coll., 1950, Sc.D., 1974; M.D., U. Pa., 1954, D.Sc., 1973; Ph.D., Rockefeller U., 1960; M.D. (hon.), U. Siena, Italy, 1974; DSc (hon.), Gustavus Adolphus Coll., 1975, Williams Coll., 1976; DSc Honoris Causa, U. Paris, 1989; LSc Honoris Causa, U. Cagliari, 1989; DSc, Georgetown U., 1989; DSc Honoris Causa, U. degli Studi di Napoli, 1990, Tulane U., 1991, U. Miami, 1995, Adelphi U., 1995, U. Bologna, 1998. Med. house officer Mass. Gen. Hosp., 1954-55; asst. physician hosp. of Rockefeller U., 1957-60, mem. faculty, 1960-92, assoc. dean grad. studies, 1963-66, prof., 1966-74, Vincent Astor disting. prof., 1974-92; mem. faculty and chmn. dept. neurobiology Scripps Rsch. Inst., La Jolla, Calif., 1992—; mem. biophysics and biophys. chemistry study sect. NIH, 1964-67; mem. Sci. Council, Ctr. for Theoretical Studies, 1970-72; assoc., sci. chmn. Neurosciences Research Program, 1980—, dir. Neurosci. Inst., 1981—; mem. adv. bd. Basel Inst. Immunology, 1970-77, chmn., 1975-77; non-resident fellow, trustee Salk Inst., 1973-85; bd. overseers Faculty Arts and Scis., U. Pa., 1976-83; trustee, mem. adv. com. Carnegie Inst., Washington, 1980-87; bd. govs. Weizman Inst. Sci., 1971-87, mem. emeritus; researcher structure of antibodies, molecular and devel. biology. Author: Neural Darwinism, 1987, Topobiology, 1988, The Remembered Present, 1989, Bright Air, Brilliant Fire, 1992. Trustee Rockefeller Bros. Fund., 1972-82. Served to capt. M.C. AUS, 1955-57. Recipient Spencer Morris award U. Pa., 1954, Ann. Alumni award Ursinus Coll., 1969, Nobel prize for physiology or medicine, 1972, Albert Einstein Commemorative award Yeshiva U., 1974, Buchman Meml. award Calif. Inst. Tech., 1975, Rabbi Shai Shacknai meml. prize Hebrew U.-Hadassah Med. Sch., Jerusalem, 1977, Regents medal Excellence, N.Y. State, 1984, Hans Neurath prize, U. Washington, 1986, Sesquicentennial Commemorative award Nat. Libr. Medicine, 1986, Cécile and Oskar Vogt award U. Dusseldorf, 1988, Disting. Grad. award U. Pa., 1990, Personnalité de l'année, Paris, 1990, Warren Triennial Prize award Mass. Gen. Hosp., 1992. Fellow AAAS, N.Y. Acad. Scis., N.Y. Acad. Medicine; mem. Am. Philos. Soc., Am. Soc. Biol. Chemists, Am. Assn. Immunologists, Genetics Soc. Am., Harvey Soc. (pres. 1975-76, Am. Chem. Soc., Eli Lilly award biol. chemistry 1965), Am. Acad. Arts and Scis., Nat. Acad. Sci., Am. Soc. Cell Biology, Acad. Scis. of Inst. France (fgn.), Japanese Biochem. Soc. (hon.), Pharm. Soc. Japan (hon.), Soc. Developmental Biology, Council Fgn. Relations, Sigma Xi, Alpha Omega Alpha. Office: Scripps Rsch Inst Dept Neurobiol SBR-14 10550 N Torrey Pines Rd La Jolla CA 92037-1000

EDELSTEIN, ROSEMARIE, nurse educator, medical-legal consultant; b. Drake, N.D., Mar. 3, 1935; d. Francis Jerome and Myrtle Josephine (Merbach) Hublou; m. Harry George Edelstein, June 22, 1957 (div.); children: Julie, Lori, Lynn, Toni Anne. BSN, St. Teresa of Avila Coll., Winona, Minn., 1956; MA in Edn., Holy Names Coll., Oakland, Calif., 1977; EdD, U. San Francisco, 1982, postgrad., 1987; postgrad. in pub. health U. Ariz., 1985—; cert. pub. health nurse U. Calif., Berkeley, 1972. Dir., clin. supr. San Francisco Sch. for Health Professions, 1971-74, Rancho Arroyo Sch. of Vocat. Nursing, Sacramento, 1974-75, intensive care nurse Kaiser-Permanente Hosp., San Rafael, Calif., 1976-77; dir. inservice edn. Ross Hosp., Calif., 1977-78; assoc. dir. nursing, nursing edn. St. Francis Meml. Hosp., San Francisco, 1978-85; med.-legal nursing cons., med.-surg. staff nurse met. hosps., San Francisco, 1985-90, St. Luke's Hosp., Duluth, Minn., 1990-91, St. Charles Hosp., New Orleans, 1992, UTMB, Galveston, Tex. 1992-94, staff RN family medicine faculty practice, 1995; med.-surg. nurse St. Anthony of Padua Hosp., Oklahoma City, Okla., 1994-95; medical medicare experience; RN medics and treatments Northgate Conv. Hosp., San Rafael, Calif., 1995—; RN, night charge nurse Creekside Conv. Hosp., Santa Rosa, Calif., 1996; RN, charge nurse medications, treatment and alzheimers unit, Fallon Conv. Ctr., Nev., 1996; RN charge medicare unit White Pine Conv. Ctr., Ely, Nev., 1997; RN emergency room and intensive care, Battle Mountain Gen. Hosp., Nev., 1997; RN supr., charge Medicare-Med. Seaview Care Ctr. Sun Corp., Eureka, Calif., 1997-98; mem. staff Walker Post Manor Oxford, NE Lantis Corp., 1998; invited mem. People to People Nursing Edn. and Adminstrn., candidate to East Asia, Philosophy, 1985; postgrad. candidate U. Zurich, Switzerland, 1988. Candidate U.S. Senate Inner Circle, 1988, 89. Lt. col. USAR Med. Res. Mem. Calif. Nurses Assn., Am. Heart Assn., Sigma Theta Tau. Roman Catholic. Author: (with Jane F. Lee) Acupuncture Atlas, 1974; The Influence of Motivator and Hygiene Factors in Job Changes by Graduate Registered Nurses, 1977; Effects of Two Educational Methods Upon Retention of Knowledge in Pharmacology, 1981.

EDENFIELD, T(HOMAS) KEEN, JR., music publishing and real estate investor; b. Chattanooga, May 8, 1943; s. Thomas Keen Sr. and Francis (Love) E.; m. Ann Louise Goodney, Jan. 24, 1976; children: Thomas Keen III, Andrew Ward, Stuart Douglas, Curtis Arthur. BS in Econs., Emory U., 1967; MS, Oxford Sch. Econs., London, 1969. Capt. Saudi Arabian Airlines, 1976-78, Air Jamaica, 1978-80; owner, pres. Mountain Hospitality, Inc., Albuquerque, 1982-86, Lamb Realty & Investment, Albuquerque, 1980-84; pres. Seeganex Internat. Ltd., London, 1986—; chmn. Seeganex N.Am., Albuquerque; defense contractor, pres. Advanced Tech. Corp., Santa Fe, 1993—; CIA aviation operative, Washington, 1974-85. Contbr. articles to profl. jours. Decorated Turkish Civilian Wings award, 1976; recipient Jamaican Disting. Citizen Humanitarian award, 1978, Nicaraguan Civilian Humanitarian award, 1984. Mem. Albuquerque Country Club, Wings Club of Arabia (pres. 1978-79), Sigma Chi. Avocations: flying, skiing, tennis. Office: Advanced Tech Corp PO Box 26026 Albuquerque NM 87125-6026

EDENS, GARY DENTON, broadcasting executive; b. Asheville, N.C., Jan. 6, 1942; s. James Edwin and Pauline Amanda (New) E.; m. Hannah Suellen Walter, Aug. 21, 1965; children: Ashley Elizabeth, Emily Blair. BS, U. N.C., 1964. Account exec. PAMS Prodns., Dallas, 1965-67; account exec. Sta. WKIX, Raleigh, N.C., 1967-69; gen. mgr. Sta. KOY, Phoenix, 1970-81; sr. v.p. Harte-Hanks Radio, Inc., Phoenix, 1978-81, pres., chief exec. officer, 1981-84; chmn., chief exec. officer Edens Broadcasting, Inc., 1984—; dir. Gt. Western Bank & Trust Ariz., 1975-86, Citibank Ariz., 1986—, Inter-Tel, Inc., 1994—; chmn. The Hanover Cos., Inc., 1995—. Bd. dirs. Valley Big Bros., 1972-80, Ariz. State U. Found., 1979—, COMPAS, 1979—, Men's Arts Coun., 1975-78. Named One of Three Outstanding Young Men, Phoenix Jaycees, 1973; entrepreneurial fellow U. Ariz., 1989. Mem. Phoenix Execs. Club (pres. 1976), Nat. Radio Broadcasters Assn. (dir. 1981-86), Radio Advt. Bur. (dir. 1981—), Young Pres. Orgn. (chmn. Ariz. chpt. 1989-90), Chief Execs. Orgn., Ariz. Pres. Orgn. Republican. Methodist. Office: Ste 1400 2400 E Arizona Biltmore Cir Phoenix AZ 85016-2114

EDGAR, JAMES MACMILLAN, JR., management consultant; b. N.Y.C., Nov. 7, 1936; s. James Macmillan Edgar and Lilyan (McCann) E.; B in Chem. Engring., Cornell U., 1959, MBA with distinction, 1960; m. Judith Frances Storey, June 28, 1958; children: Suzanne Lynn, James Macmillan, Gordon Stuart. New product rep. E.I. duPont Nemours, Wilmington, Del., 1960-63, mktg. services rep., 1963-64; with Touche Ross & Co., 1964-78, mgr., Detroit, 1966-68, ptnr., 1968-71, ptnr. in charge, mgmt. services ops. for No. Calif. and Hawaii, San Francisco, 1971-78, ptnr. Western regional mgmt. services, 1978; sr. ptnr. Edgar, Dunn & Co., San Francisco, 1978—; bd. dirs. Associated Oreg. Industries Svcs. Corp., 1991—. Active San Francisco Mayor's Fin. Adv. Com., 1976—, mem. exec. com., 1978—, Blue Ribbon com. for Bus., 1987-88, Alumnae Resources adv. bd., 1986-94, San Francisco Planning and Urban Rsch. Bd., 1986-89, mem. adv. bd., 1989-93, mem. program adv. com., 1996—; mem. alumni exec. council Johnson Grad. Sch. Mgmt. Cornell U., Cornell Coun., 1970-73; mem. steering com. Bay Area Coun., 1989-95, mem. program adv. com., 1996—; chmn. San Francisco Libr. Found., 1989-96; bd. dirs. Rosenberg Found., 1995—, dirs., Harding Lawson Assoc Group, 1996—. Recipient Award of Merit for outstanding pub. svc. City and County of San Francisco, 1978; Honor award for outstanding contbns. to profl. mgmt. Johnson Grad. Sch. Mgmt., Cornell U., 1978. CPA, cert. mgmt. cons. Mem. Assn. Corp. Growth (v.p. membership San Francisco chpt. 1979-81, v.p. programs 1981-82, pres. 1982-83, nat. bd. dirs. 1983-86), AICPA, Calif. Soc. CPAs, Inst. Mgmt. Cons. (regional v.p. 1973-80, dir. 1975-77, bd. v.p. 1977-80), San Francisco C. of C. (bd. dirs. 1987-89, 91—, mem. exec. com. 1988-89, 91-95, chmn. mktg. San Francisco program 1991-92, membership devel. 1993, chmn. bd. dirs. 1994, dir. emeritus 1995—), Bay Area Coun. (dir. 1998—), Tau Beta Pi. Clubs: Pacific Union, Commonwealth of San Francisco, Marin Rod and Gun. Patentee nonwoven fabrics. Home: 10 Buckeye Way San Rafael CA 94904-2602 Office: Edgar Dunn & Co Inc 847 Sansome St Ste 400 San Francisco CA 94111-1585

EDGERS, TRACY B., mortgage banker; b. Eugene, Oreg., June 14, 1958; s. Robert B. and Terry (Proctor) E.; m. Evelyn Rudy; 1 child, Spencer. BA in Econs., U. Wash., 1980; grad. (hon.), Pacific Coast Banking Sch., 1991. From loan adminstr. to v.p./lending officer Wash. Mut. Bank, Seattle, 1980-92; mgr. U.S. Bancorp Mortgage Co., Bellevue, Wash., 1992-94; v.p., team leader U.S. Bank, Seattle, 1994-96; asset mgr. Pacific Coast Investment Co., Seattle, 1996-97; dir. FINOVA Realty Capital, Seattle, 1997—; extension faculty Pacific Bankers Mgmt. Inst., Seattle, 1996-97. Avocations: sailing, hiking. Office: FINOVA Realty Capital 1201 3d Ave Ste 3085 Seattle WA 98101

EDGERTON, BRADFORD WHEATLY, plastic surgeon; b. Phila., May 8, 1947; s. Milton Thomas and Patricia Jane (Jones) E.; children: Bradford Wheatly Jr., Lauren Harrington; m. Louise Dungan Edgerton; stepchildren: Catherine Kelleher, Robert Kelleher. BA in Chemistry, Vanderbilt U., 1969, MD, 1973. Diplomate Am. Bd. Plastic Surgery, Am. Bd. Hand Surgery. Intern U. Calif., San Francisco, 1973-74; resident U. Va., Charlottesville, 1974-78; resident in plastic surgery Columbia-Presbyn., N.Y., 1979-81; fellow in hand surgery NYU, 1981-82, clin. instr. plastic surgery, 1981-89; ptnr. So. Calif. Permanente Med. Group, L.A., 1989—; assoc. prof. clin. plastic surgery U. So. Calif., L.A., 1989—. v.p., trustee W. Alton Jones Found., Charlottesville, Va., 1978—. Mem. Am. Assn. Hand Surgery, Am. Soc. Plastic and Reconstructive Surgery, Am. Soc. Surgery of Hand, L.A. Tennis Club. Episcopal. Home: 494 S Spalding Dr Beverly Hills CA 90212 Office: 6041 Cadillac Ave Los Angeles CA 90034-1702

EDGERTON, DEBRA, artist, educator; b. Junction City, Kans., Mar. 15, 1958; d. Hughes and Tamie E.; m. Terry Baxter, Apr. 13, 1991; children: Noah Hunter, Jesse Dylan. Student, Am. Acad. Art, Chgo., 1979; BFA, U. Kans., 1980. Artist Hallmark Cards, Kansas City, Mo., 1981-86; freelance artist Flagstaff, Ariz., 1986—; instr's. asst in printmaking U. Kans., Lawrence, 1987, instr. painting Lawrence Art Ctr., 1991-93, Sr. Citizen Ctr., Lawrence, 1992, No. Ariz. U., Flagstaff, 1993—. Mem. Round Table for Arts, Lawrence, 1991-92; mayoral appointee Lawrence Art Commn., 1992-93; pres. Lawrence Art Guild Assn., 1992. Recipient Excellence award Geary County Sch. Dist., 1991, Merit award Ariz. Aqueous, 1994; Profl. Devel. grantee Kans. Art Commn., 1992, Tech. Asst. grantee Lawrence Arts Commn., 1992. Mem. Am. Watercolor Soc., Nat. Watercolor Soc., Allied Artists Am., Midwest Watercolor Soc. (life). Office: No Ariz U PO Box 6020 Flagstaff AZ 86011

EDGERTON, LYNNE T., state agency administrator, lawyer; b. Nashville, Tenn., Oct. 26, 1947; s. Kirkland Wiley Jr. and Adrienne (Hill) Todd; m. Bradford Wheatly Edgerton, Dec. 28, 1970 (div. 1995); children: Ford, Lauren. BA, Vanderbilt U., 1969, JD, 1972; LLM, Yale U., 1979. Bar: Tenn., 1972, Va., 1975, N.Y., 1980, Calif., 1998. Atty., cons. Natural Resources Def. Coun., N.Y.C. and L.A., 1983-91; v.p. environ. and legal affairs CALSTART, Burbank, Calif., 1992-93; bd. mem. Calif. EPA Air Resources Bd., Sacramento, 1993—. Author: The Rising Tide: Global Warming and World Sea Levels, 1991. Home: 308 N Sycamore Ave Apt 107 Los Angeles CA 90036-2661 Office: Calif Air Resources Bd 2020 L St Sacramento CA 95814-4219

EDLIN, NOEL W., lawyer; b. Washington, May 14, 1956; s. William Conch and Dorothy Edlin; m. Andrea C. Olson, Dec. 27, 1997; children: Joshya R., Alexandra N. BA in Polit. Sci., U. Hawaii, 1979; JD, U. Calif., San Francisco, 1982. Asst. dist. atty. City of San Francisco; lawyer Hassal & Bonnington, San Francisco, Alexander, William & McGee, San Francisco; ptrn. Walsworth, Franklin, Bevins & McCall, San Francisco; Dir. Nat. Coun. Crime and Deliquency, San Francisco, 1989—. Bd. dirs. Wiley Manuel Law Found., Oakland, Calif., 1992-95. Avocations: golf, skiing, surfing. Office: Walsworth Franklin Bevins McCall 550 Montgomery St Fl 8 San Francisco CA 94111-2534

EDMONDO, DOUGLAS BRIAN, marine engineer; b. Plainfield, N.J., Feb. 13, 1960; s. Donald Brian and Sally Ann (Emery) E.; m. Yvonne Janssen, July 11, 1987; children: Brian James, Daniel John. BS, Calif. Maritime Coll., 1982. Lic. pvt. pilot; marine engr. Field engr. Westinghouse Marine, Sunnyvale, Calif., 1982-87, project engr., 1987-88, sr. engr., 1988-89, IPMP site mgr., 1990-92, svc. supr., 1992-95; product support mgr. Applied Materials, Santa Clara, Calif., 1995-98; prin. engr. Northrup Grumman Marine Divsn., Sunnyvale, 1998—. Mem. Soc. Naval Architects and Marine Engrs., Am. Soc. Naval Engrs. Home: 942 Dana Cir Livermore CA 94550-3782

EDMONDS, CHARLES HENRY, publisher; b. Lakewood, Ohio, Sept. 4, 1919; s. Howard H. and Mary Frances (Galena) E.; student Woodbury Bus. Coll., 1939-40; m. Ruth Audrey Windfelder, Nov. 4, 1938; children: Joan Dickey, Charles Henry, Carolyn Anne, Dianne Marie. Owner, Shoreline Transp. Co., L.A., 1946-58; mgr. transp. Purity Food Stores, Burlingame, Calif., 1958-61; supr. Calif. Motor Express, San Jose, 1961-64; account exec. Don Wright Assos., Oakland, Calif., 1964-65; sales mgr. Western U.S., Shippers Guide Co., Chgo., 1965-70; pub. No. Calif. Retailer, San Jose, 1970-83; v.p. Kasmar Publs., 1983-88; pub. Retail Observer, 1990—. Recipient journalism awards various orgns. Republican. Roman Catholic. Contbr. articles to profl. jours. Home: 1442 Sierra Creek Way San Jose CA 95132-3618

EDMONDS, IVY GORDON, writer; b. Frost, Tex., Feb. 15, 1917; s. Ivy Gordon and Delia Louella (Shumate) E.; student pub. schs.; m. Reiko Mimura, July 12, 1956; 1 dau., Annette. Freelance writer; author books including: Solomon In Kimono, 1957; Ooka the Wise, 1961; The Bounty's Boy, 1963; Hollywood RIP, 1963; Joel of the Hanging Gardens, 1966; Trickster Tales, 1966; Taiwan—the Other China, 1971; The Possible Impossibles of Ikkyo The Wise, 1971; The Magic Man, 1972; Mao's Long March, 1973; Motorcycling for Beginners, 1973; Micronesia, 1974; Pakistan, Land of Mystery, Tragedy and Courage, 1974; Automotive Tuneups for Beginners, 1974; Ethiopia, 1975; The Magic Makers, 1976; The Shah of Iran, 1976; Allah's Oil: Mid-East Petroleum, 1976; Second Sight, 1977; Motorcycle Racing for Beginners, 1977; Islam, 1977; Buddhism, 1978; The Mysteries of Troy, 1977; Big U Universal in the Silent Days, 1977; D.D. Home, 1978; Bicycle Motocross, 1979; Hinduism, 1979; Girls Who Talked to Ghosts, 1979; The Magic Brothers, 1979; (with William H. Gebhardt) Broadcasting for Beginners, 1980; (with Reiko Mimura) The Oscar Directors, 1980; The Mysteries of Homer's Greeks, 1981; The Kings of Black Magic, 1981; Funny Car Racing for Beginners, 1982; The Magic Dog, 1982; author textbooks: (with Ronald Gonzales) Understanding Your Car, 1975, Introduction to Welding, 1975; also author pulp and soft cover fiction and nonfiction under names of Gene Cross and Gary Gordon and publishers house names; pub. relations mgr. Northrop Corp., Anaheim, Calif., 1968-79, indsl. editor, Hawthorne, Calif., 1979-86. Served with USAAF, 1940-45, USAF, 1946-63. Decorated D.F.C., Air medals, Bronze Star. Home: 5801 Shirl St Cypress CA 90630-3326

EDMONDS, JAMES PATRICK (JIM EDMONDS), professional baseball player; b. Fullerton, Calif., June 27, 1970. Grad. high sch., Calif. Outfielder Calif. Angels (now Anaheim Angels), 1993—. Selected to Am. League All-Star Team, 1995. Office: Anaheim Angels 2000 E Gene Autry Way Anaheim CA 92806-6100*

EDMONDSON, W(ALLACE) THOMAS, retired limnologist, educator; b. Milw., Apr. 24, 1916; s. Clarence Edward and Marie (Kelley) E.; m. Yvette Hardman, Sept. 26, 1941. BS, Yale U., 1938, PhD, 1942; postgrad., U. Wis., 1938-39; DSc (hon.), U. Wis., Milw., 1987; HHD (hon.), Seattle U., 1996. Research assoc. Am. Mus. Natural History, 1942-43, Woods Hole Oceanographic Instn., 1943-46; lectr. biology Harvard U., Cambridge, Mass., 1946-49; mem. faculty U. Wash., Seattle, 1949—, prof., 1957-86, prof. emeritus, 1986—, Jessie and John Danz lectr., 1987; R.E. Coker Meml. lectr. U. N.C., 1977; Brode lectr. Whitman Coll., 1988. Editor: Freshwater Biology (Ward and Whipple), 2d edit, 1959; contbr. articles to profl. jours. Recipient Einar Naumann August Thienemann medal Internat. Assn. Theoretical and Applied Limnology, 1980, Outstanding Pub. Svc. award U. Wash., Seattle, 1987, commendation State of Wash., 1987; NSF sr. postdoctoral fellow Italy, Eng. and Sweden, 1959-60. Fellow AAAS; mem. NAS (Cottrell award 1973), Am. Soc. Limnology and Oceanography (G. Evelyn Hutchinson medal 1990), Internat. Assn. Limnology, Ecol. Soc. Am. (Eminent Ecologist award 1983), Yale Grad. Sch. Alumni Assn. (Wilbur Lucius Cross medal 1993). Office: U Wash Dept Zoology PO Box 351800 Seattle WA 98195-1800

EDMONSON-NELSON, GLORIA JEAN, freelance writer; b. Nowata, Okla., Oct. 7, 1938; d. Cornelius Emerson and Virginia (Cole) E.; m. Forest Nelson, Oct. 7, 1996; children: Vincent Ross, Victor Ross, Vernon Ross. AA, Labette C.C., Parsons, Kans., 1959; BS in Mgmt., U. San Francisco, 1979. Cert. securities arbitration-non-fictional writing. Adminstr. Far West Lab for Ednl. R&D, San Francisco, 1969-81; reporter The Doctor's Co. Med. Malpractice, Emeryville, Calif., 1986-89; cons. arbitrator NASD, San Francisco, 1992—. Author: How to start a medical collecting agency, 1990, Recognizing Abuse--Reclaiming Your Birthright, 1998. Telephone interviewer United Way, 1989-91, voter registrar, 1990-91. Recipient various poetry awards. Mem. AARP, Nat. Assn. of Securities Dealers. Avocations: writing poetry, traveling, jazz.

EDMUNDS, JOHN SANFORD, lawyer; b. L.A., Jan. 3, 1943; s. Arthur Edmunds and Sarah Bernadine (Miles) E.; m. Virginia Maejan Ching, Nov. 30, 1975; children: Laura, Shauna. AB, Stanford U., 1964; JD, U. So. Calif., 1967. Bar: Hawaii 1972, U.S. Dist. Ct. Hawaii, U.S. Ct. Appeals (9th cir.), U.S. Supreme Ct. Chief dep. pub. defender State of Hawaii, 1970-72, spl. dep. atty. gen., 1974-75; acting chief justice Supreme Ct., Republic of Marshall Islands, 1980-81; ptnr. Edmunds & Verga, Honolulu, 1981-97, Edmunds, Maki, Versa and Thorn, Honolulu, 1997—; adj. prof. law U. Hawaii, 1976-77, 85-89; counsel Hemmeter Investment Co., Obayashi Corp., Shell Oil Co., Nestle, U.S.A., Inc., Bank of Am. Bd. dirs. Legal Aid Soc. Hawaii, 1974-75. Fellow Internat. Acad. Trial Lawyers, Am. Coll. Trial Lawyers (state chmn. 1991-92, nat. com. legal ethics and profl. responsibility 1994—), Internat. Soc. Barristers, Am. Bar Found.; mem. ABA, ACLU (bd. dirs. 1969-73, pres. 1971-73, adv. counsel 1974-75), Hawaii Bar Assn., Assn. Trial Lawyers Am., Hawaii Acad. Plaintiffs Attys (bd. govs. 1995—), Master of Bench, Am. Inns. of Ct. E-Mail: 71330.2466@compuserve.com. Office: Edmunds Maki Verga & Thorn 841 Bishop St Ste 2104 Honolulu HI 96813-3921

EDMUNSON, JIM, political organization administrator. Chmn. Oreg. Dem. Party, Portland. Fax: (503) 224-5335. Office: Oreg Dem Party 711 SW Alder # 306 Portland OR 97205*

E'DRIE, LORRAINE, artist; b. L.A.; d. Frank G. Steiner and Leona E'drie; m. Russell C. Murphy, Sept. 26, 1948; children: Stephen Murphy, Paula Murphy Hinz. Lifetime tchg. credential, Calif. Exhibited at Salmagundi Club, N.Y., Nat. Art Club Gallery, N.Y., L.A. Artcore, Laguna Art Mus., San Bernardino Mus., Riverside Art Mus., Columbia River Maritime Mus., Oreg., San Juan Capistrano Mission Mus., Art-A-Fair Festival, 1999, Laguna Beach, Calif.; works featured in books including Yacht Portraits, Artists of Southern California Fine Arts, A Gallery of Marine Art. Mem. Nat. Watercolor Soc. (assoc.), Am. Watercolor Soc. (assoc.), Am. Soc. Marine Artists, Internat. Soc. Marine Artists, Watercolor West (asso. juried mem.), Catherine Lorillard Wolfe Art Club, Salmagundi Club (N.Y.). Home: 1809 1/2 W Bay Ave Newport Beach CA 92663-4516

EDSELL, PATRICK L., computer company executive. Pres. Spectra-Physics, Mountain View, Calif. Office: Spectra-Physics PO Box 7013 1335 Terra Bella Ave Mountain View CA 94039-7013*

EDSTROM, PAM, public relations executive; b. 1954. Pvt. practice, 1968-74; with Fred Meyer Savings and Loan, Portland, Oreg., 1974-77, Tektronix, Inc., Beaverton, Oreg., 1977-81, Micro Soft, Redmond, Wash., 1981-83; sr. v.p. Waggener Edstrom, Inc., Portland, 1983—. Office: Waggener Edstrom Inc 3 Center Point Dr Lake Oswego OR 97035*

EDWARDS, ARDIS LAVONNE QUAM, retired elementary education educator; b. Sioux Falls, S.D., July 30, 1930; d. Norman and Dorothy (Cade) Quam; m. Paul Edwards, Apr. 18, 1953 (dec. Sept. 1988); children: Kevin (dec. 1980), Kendall, Erin, Sally, Kristin, Keely. Tchg. credentials, Augustana Luth. Coll., Sioux Falls, 1949; provisional tchg. credentials, San Jose State Coll., 1953, student, 1953-57. Lic. pvt. pilot, FAA. Mgr. The Cottage Restaurant, Sioux Falls, 1943-50; one-room sch. tchr. Whaley Sch., Colman, S.D., 1949-50; one-room sch. tchr. 8 grades East Sioux Sch., Sioux Falls, 1950-51; recreation dir. City of Albany, Calif., 1951-52; first grade tchr. Decoto (Calif.) Sch. Dist., 1952-58; ret., 1958. Author Health Instrn. Unit Study Packet for Tchrs. Bible sch. tchr. East Side Luth. Ch., Sioux Falls, S.D., 1945-51, Sunday sch. tchr., 1945-51; charter mem. Our Savior Luth. Ch., Fremont, Calif., 1964—, mem. choir; Christian Week Day Sch. tchr., 1970, 87, ch. historian, 1986—, other offices; treas. PTA, Hayward, Calif., 1959; pres. Luth. Women's Missionary League, 1976; chmn. OSLC Blood Bank, 1968—; edn. officer, fraternal communicator, respecteen officer Luth. Brotherhood; officer Healthy Cmtys. Healthy Youth; mem. Am. Heart Assn., March of Dimes, Am. Cancer Soc., Arthritis Found., Tri-Cities Assn. Evangs.; rm. mother, team mother, leader Brownies.; room mother, Chadbourne Grammar Sch.; team mother, Fremont Little League. Recipient Spl. Svc. award Girl Scouts U.S., 1971, Arthritis Found., Fremont, 1974-75, Spl. Commendation March Fong Eu, 1954. Mem. NAFE, AARP, Republic Airlines Ret. Pilots Assn., Ret. Airline Pilots Assn., N.W. Airlines Ret. Pilots Assn., Aircraft Owners and Pilots Assn., S.W. Airways Pilots Wives Assn., Concerned Women for Am., World Affairs Coun., Mission Swim Club, Philomathian Lit. Soc., Tri-Cities Assn. Evangelicals. Republican. Avocations: Bible study, grandchildren, flying, history, antiques.

EDWARDS, BRUCE GEORGE, ophthalmologist, naval officer; b. Idaho Springs, Colo., Apr. 6, 1942; s. Bruce Norwood and Evelyn Alice (Kohut) Edwards. BA, U. Colo., 1964; MD, U. Colo., Denver, 1968. Diplomate Am. Acad. Ophthalmology. Commd. ensign USN, 1964; advanced through grades to capt. U.S. Naval Hosp., 1980; intern U.S. Naval Hosp., San Diego, 1968-69; USN med. officer USS Long Beach (CGN-9), 1969-70; gen. med. officer U.S. Naval Hosp., Taipei, Taiwan, 1970-72, U.S. Naval Dispensary Treasure Island, San Francisco, 1972-73; resident in ophthalmology U.S. Naval Hosp., Oakland, Calif., 1973-76, U. Calif., San Francisco, 1973-76; mem. opthalmologist staff Naval Hosp., Camp Pendleton, Calif., 1976-83; ophthalmologist, chief of med. staff Naval Hosp., Naples, Italy, 1983-85; ophthalmology head Camp Pendleton Naval Hosp., 1985-97, dir. surg. svcs., 1990-92, dir. physician advisor quality assurance, 1985-86; vol. Internat. Eye Found., Harar, Ethiopia, 1975. Fellow Am. Acad. Ophthalmology; mem. AMA, Calif. Med. Assn., Calif. Assn. Ophthalmologists, Am. Soc. Contemporary Ophthalmologists, Assn. U.S. Mil. Surgeons, Pan Am. Assn. Ophthalmology, Order of DeMolay (Colo. DeMolay of Yr. 1961, Idaho Springs Chevalier, Colo. State sec. 1961-62). Republican. Methodist. Avocations: piano, camping, hiking, biking, travel. Office: 225 E 2nd Ave Ste 310 Escondido CA 92025-4244

EDWARDS, CHARLES RICHARD, retired printing equipment and supplies company executive; b. South Bend, Ind., July 16, 1931; s. Bernard Stuart and Mary Irene (Chamberlaine) E.; student pub. schs.; m. Joanne Wood, Dec. 15, 1950; children: Timothy Stuart, Terry Lynne, David Bryan. Pressman, Toastmasters Internat., Santa Ana, Calif., 1954-60; with 3M Co., 1960-69, Salesman, Western U.S. tech. service and nat. market mgr., St. Paul, 1966-69; CEO, sec., CFO, co-owner Graphic Arts Supplies, Inc., Orange, Calif., 1969-86; owner, operator Edwards Bus. Svcs., 1987-91; bus. and trade cons., 1986-91; instr., cons. in field. Bd. dirs., treas. #1 Network, Inc., Chgo., 1982-86. Served with USAF, 1950-54; Korea. Mem. Nat. Assn. Lithographic Clubs (chpt. co-founder, officer, dir.), Nat. Assn. Printing House Craftsmen (past chpt. pres., regional officer), Toastmasters, Hobo

Golf Assn. (pres. 1985—). Republican. Home: 7221 Judson Ave Westminster CA 92683-6163

EDWARDS, DALE LEON, library director; b. Nampa, Idaho; s. Wayne Martin and Thelma Lucile Edwards; m. Julie Ann Rosa, Aug. 19, 1975; children: David, Corey, Stephen, Lisa, Russell. BA, Brigham Young U., 1980, M of Libr. and Info. Sci., 1990. Program dir., announcer Sta. KSUB, Cedar City, Utah, 1977-80; news dir. Sta. KRPX, Price, Utah, 1980-84; news writer Sun Advocate Newspaper, Price, 1984-86; dir. Learning Resource Ctr., Price Libr., Price, 1986-90; dir. libr. svcs. Treasure Valley Community Coll., Ontario, Oreg., 1990—; legis. com. mem. Utah Libr. Assn., Salt Lake City, 1986-90. Recipient Excellence in Reporting award Utah Sch. Bds. Assn., 1985. Mem. ALA, Oreg. Libr. Assn., Oreg. C.C. Libr. Assn. (pres. 1993-94), Oreg. Edn. Assn. (legis. com. 1990—), East Oreg. Libr. Assn. (pres. 1997—), Pacific N.W. Libr. Assn., Treasure Valley Chorale (pres. 1991-93), Beta Phi Mu. Mormon. Avocations: music, dancing, sports. Office: Treasure Valley CC Libr 650 College Blvd Ontario OR 97914-3423

EDWARDS, DANIEL WALDEN, lawyer; b. Vancouver, Wash., Aug. 7, 1950; s. Chester W. Edwards and Marilyn E. Russell; m. Joan S. Heller, Oct. 18, 1987; children: Nathaniel, Matthew, Stephen, Alexander. BA in Psychology magna cum laude, Met. State Coll., Denver, 1973, BA in Philosophy, 1974; JD, U. Colo., 1976. Bar: Colo. 1977, U.S. Dist. Ct. Colo. 1977. Dep. pub. defender State of Colo., Denver, 1977-79, Littleton, 1979-81, Pueblo, 1981-86; head office pub. defender State of Colo., Brighton, 1987-89; mem. jud. faculty State of Colo., 1988-91; sole practitioner Denver, 1991-93; magistrate Denver Juvenile Ct., 1993—; instr. sch. of law U. Denver, 1988-91, adj. prof., 1991—, coach appellate advocacy team, 1991—; adv. coun. Colo. Legal Svcs., 1989—; adj. mem. Colo. Supreme Ct. Grievance Com., 1991—. Author: Basic Trial Practice: An Introduction to Persuasive Trial Techniques, 1995. Mem. visual arts com. City Arts III, 1989-90, com. chmn., mem. adv. coun., 1991; bd. dirs. Metropolitan State Coll., Alumni Assn., 1991-92; vol. lectr. CSE Thursday Night Bar Pro Se Divorce Clinic, 1991—. Named Pub. Defender of Yr. Colo. State Pub. Defender's Office, 1985, Outstanding Colo. Criminal Def. Atty., 1989. Mem. ABA, Assn. Trial Lawyers Am., Colo. Bar Assn., Adams County Bar Assn., Denver Bar Assn., Met. State Coll. Alumni Assn. (bd. dirs. 1991—). Home: 2335 Clermont St Denver CO 80207-3134 Office: Denver Juvenile Ct Divsn 6 City and County Bldg Denver CO 80202

EDWARDS, DARREL, psychologist; b. San Francisco, July 9, 1943; s. Darrus and Rose Pearl (Sannar) E.; children: Alexander Hugh, Peter David, James Royce. BS in Psychology and Philosophy, Brigham Young U., 1965, MS in Psychology and Philosophy, 1967, PhD in Clin. Psychology and Philosophy, 1968. Diplomate Am. Bd. Profl. Psychology. Postdoctoral fellow in psycholinguistics Pa. State U., 1969; commd. lt. (j.g.) USN, 1970, advanced through grades to lt. comdr., 1978; dir. psychologist Tri Community Svc. Systems, San Diego, 1973-78; prof. Calif. Sch. Profl. Psychology, San Diego, 1971-78; dir. Grid Rsch., San Diego, 1978-83; pres. The Edwards Assoc., San Diego, 1983—; pres. Strategic Vision, 1987—; cons. strategist for govt. and pvt. sector, U.S., Eng., France, Germany, Italy, Mex., Brazil, Argentina, Russia, Republic of China, Japan, Can., 1978—. Co-inventor in field; contbr. articles to profl. jours. Cons., researcher U.S., U.K., France, Germany, Hungary, Japan, Brazil, Argentina, Mexico, Colombia, Kenya, Central America, India, Italy, Republic of China, Russia, numerous other countries, 1986—. Mem. Am. Psychol. Assn. Achievements include creation of Values Centered research and consulting procedures; total quality measures for the automotive industry; total customer experience measures for 30 product and service categories; Values in America bi-annual survey; four fold principles of motivation; ValueCentered theory, clinical interview, and intervention; quality research in medicine service delivery and outcomes. Office: The Edwards Assocs PO Box 420429 San Diego CA 92142-0429

EDWARDS, ERIC ALAN, director of photography; b. Portland, Oreg., Aug. 10, 1953; s. Thomas William and Nancy Naomi (Beltz) E. BFA, R.I. Sch. of Design, 1975. Ind. dir. photography, 1981—. Dir. photography: (feature films) Copland, Flirting with Disaster, Kids, To Die For, Garden of Eden, Even Cowgirls Get the Blues, My Own Private Idaho, Gift (Jane's Addiction, Last Night at the Alamo, (music videos) Good Friends by Joni Mitchell, 1985, The Boy in the Bubble by Paul Simon, 1986, Don't Give Up by Peter Gabriel, 1987, Leave Me Alone by Michael Jackson, 1987, Speed Demon by Michael Jackson, 1988, Ritual De Lo Habitual by Janes Addiction, 1990, Under the Bridge by Red Hot Chile Peppers, 1991, 57 Channels (And Nothin' On) by Bruce Springsteen, 1992, Bang, Bang, Bang by Tracy Chapman, 1992, She'a Already Made Up Her Mind by Lyle Lovett, 1992, numerous others. Mem. Internat. TV Assn., Oreg. Media Producers Assn. (founder 1984), Media Project (grants com. 1984—). Avocations: aviation, still photography, graphic design. Home and Office: 3404 SW Water Ave Portland OR 97201-4636

EDWARDS, H. BOYD, air transportation executive; b. 1956. Grad., Western State Coll., 1979. Prin. Aspen (Colo.) Aviation, 1980-84; v.p. Aspen (Colo.) Base Ops., Inc., 1984—. Office: Aspen Base Ops Inc 69 E Airport Rd Aspen CO 81611-3549*

EDWARDS, JACK LEE, secondary education educator; b. Raton, N.Mex., July 22, 1943; s. Jack and Pauline (Lee) E.; m. Dianne Carol Murray, Dec. 14, 1968; 1 child, Jennifer Lynn. Student, Fullerton Coll., 1963; grad., San Jose State U., 1966; MA, U. San Francisco, 1976; postgrad., U. Calif., Santa Cruz. Life tchg. credential, Calif. Tchr. Lincoln H.S., San José, Calif., 1968-83, Willow Glen H.S., San José, 1983—. Mem. Nat. Coun. Tchrs. English, Calif. Assn. Tchrs. English, San José Tchrs. Assn. (faculty rep. 1969-73, 85-86), Automatic Musical Instrument Collector's Assn. (founding chpt. mem.), Sierra Club. Democrat. Lutheran. Avocations: music, photography, theatre. Office: Willow Glen High Sch 2001 Cottle Ave San Jose CA 95125

EDWARDS, JOHN WESLEY, JR., urologist; b. Ferndale, Mich., Apr. 9, 1933; s. John W. and Josephine (Wood) E.; m. Ella Marie Law, Dec. 25, 1954; children: Joella, John III. Student, Alma Coll., 1949-50; BS, U. Mich., 1954; postgrad., Wayne State U., 1954-56; MD, Howard U., 1960. Internship Walter Reed Gen. Hosp., 1960-61, surg. resident, 1962-63, urol. resident, 1963-66; asst. chief urology Tripler Army Med. Ctr., 1966-69; comdr. 4th Med. Battalion, 4th Infantry Div., Vietnam, 1969; chief profl. svcs., urology 91st Evacuation Hosp., Vietnam, 1969-70; urologist Straub Clinic, Inc., 1970-74; pvt. practice, 1974-97; v.p. med. staff. svcs. Queen's Med. Ctr., Honolulu, 1993-94; v.p. physician rels. Queen's Health Sys., Honolulu, 1994-96; acting adminstr. Diagnostic Lab. Svcs., Inc., Honolulu, 1995-96, pres., 1996—; chief Dept. Surgery, Straub Clinic and Hosp., 1973; asst. chief Dept. Surgery Queen's Med. Ctr., 1977-79, chief, 1989-93; cons. in urology; chief Dept. Clin. Svcs., Kapiolani Women's and Children's Med. Ctr., 1981-83; clin. assoc. prof. U. Hawaii Sch. of Medicine; chmn. task force on phys. hosp. collaboration The Queens Health System, 1993—. Contbr. articles to profl. jours. Bd. dirs. Am. Cancer Soc., Honolulu unit, 1977-79, Hawaii Med. Svc. Assn., 1979-85, Hawaii Heart Assn., 1977-79, Hawaii Assn. for Physician's Indemnification, 1980-86; commr. City and County of Honolulu, 1990-91; mem. med. adv. bd. Nat. Kindey Found., Hawaii, 1994—; mem. adv. bd. MADD, Hawaii, 1992-96, bd. dirs., 1996-97; bd. dirs. Neighborhood Justice Ctr., 1995—. Recipient Howard O. Gray award for Professionalism, 1988, Leaders of Hawaii award, 1983; named Hawaii African-Am. Humanitarian of the Yr. by Hawaii chpt. Links, Inc., 1991. Fellow ACS (sec.-treas. Hawaii chpt. 1980-81, gov.-at-large 1986-92); mem. AMA, NAACP, Am. Urol. Assn. (alt. del. Western sect. 1991-92, gen. chmn. Western sect. 56th ann. meeting 1980, exec. com. 1983-84, del. dist. 1 1985-86, gen. chmn. 63d ann. meeting 1987, pres. 1989-90, nom. com. 1990-93, chmn. nom. 1992-93), Am. Coll. Physician Execs., Hawaii Urol. Assn., Hawaii Med. Assn., Surgicare of Hawaii (v.p. 1983-86), Alpha Phi Alpha, Chi Delta Mu, Alpha Omega Alpha. Office: Diagnostic Lab Svcs & Accupath 770 Kapiolani Blvd Ste 100 Honolulu HI 96813-5269

EDWARDS, KENNETH NEIL, chemist, consultant; b. Hollywood, Calif., June 8, 1932; s. Arthur Carl and Ann Vera (Gomez) E.; children: Neil James, Peter Graham, John Evan. BA in Chemistry, Occidental Coll., 1954; MS in Chem. and Metall. Engring., U. Mich., 1955. Prin. chemist Battelle Meml. Inst., Columbus, Ohio, 1955-58; dir. new products rsch. and devel. Dunn-Edwards Corp., L.A., 1958-72, sr. lectr. organic coatings and pigments dept. chem. engring. U. So. Calif., L.A., 1976-80; bd. dirs. Dunn-Edwards Corp., L.A.; cons. Coatings & Plastics Tech., L.A., 1972—. Contbr. articles to sci. jours. Mem. Am. Chem. Soc. (chmn. divisional activities 1988-89, exec. com. divsn. polymeric materials sci. and engring. 1963-96, chair divsn. 1970, mem. devel. adv. com. 1996—, Disting. Svc. award 1996, chair Disting. Svc. award selection 1997—, chair So. Calif. local sect. 1999), Alpha Chi Sigma (chmn. L.A. profl. chpt. 1962, counselor Pacific dist. 1967-70, grand profl. alchemist nat. v.p. 1970-76, grand master alchemist nat. pres. 1976-78, nat. adv. com. 1978—). Achievements include patents for air-dried polyester coatings and application, for process and apparatus for dispensing liquid colorants into a paint can, fluidic fillers, and for mechanical mixers. Home: Bottle Bay Rd Sagle ID 83860 also: 2926 Graceland Way Glendale CA 91206-1331 Office: Dunn Edwards Corp 4885 E 52nd Pl Los Angeles CA 90040-2884

EDWARDS, KIRK LEWIS, real estate company executive; b. Berkeley, Calif., July 30, 1950; s. Austin Lewis and Betty (Drury) E.; m. Randi Edwards, Feb. 14, 1998; children: Elliott Tyler, Jonathan Bentley. BA in Rhetoric and Pub. Address, U. Wash., Seattle, 1972; postgrad., Shoreline Coll., 1976. Cert. bus. broker. From salesperson to mgr. Rede Realty, Lynnwood, Wash., 1973-77; br. mgr. Century 21/North Homes Realty, Lynnwood, Wash., 1977-79, Snohomish, Wash., 1979-81; pres., owner Century 21/Champion Realty, Everett, Wash., 1981-82, Champion Computers, Walker/Edwards Investments, Everett, 1981-82; br. mgr. Advance Properties, Everett, 1982-87; exec. v.p. Bruch & Vedrich Better Homes & Garden, Everett, 1987-88, dir. career devel., 1988-90; pres., chief exec. officer Century 21/Champion Realty, Everett, 1991-95; pres., CEO KR Bus. Brokers, Bellevue, Wash., 1995—. Named Top Business Broker In Washington Investment Brokers Assn., 1994, 95, 96. Mem. Snohomish County Camano Bd. Realtors (chmn. 1987-88), Snohomish County C. of C., Hidden Harbor Yacht Club, Mill Creek Country Club. Republican. Avocations: travel, water skiing, scuba diving. Office: KR Business Brokers 16301 NE 8th St #223 Bellevue WA 98008

EDWARDS, LISA SIMONE, technical college administrator; b. Memphis, July 30, 1963; d. Cas Edwards and Marcelle Cohen. BA in Edn., Western Wash. U., 1987; MEd, U. Puget Sound, 1992. Cert. tchr., Wash. Instr. Puyallup (Wash.) Sch. Dist., 1987-92; health educator Virginia Mason Med. Ctr., Seattle, 1992-93; instr. ARC, Tacoma, 1992-97, Bates Tech. Coll., Tacoma, 1992-96; prog. adminstr. Pierce Partnership Network, 1996—; fundraising trainer United Way, Tacoma, 1993-94. Vol. ARC, Tacoma, 1993-95; chair Pierce County chpt. Cystic Fibrosis, 1998. NSF Tchr. Trainer grantee, 1992. Mem. U.S. Tennis Assn. Avocations: tennis, hiking, cooking, gardening. Office: Bates Tech Coll 1101 S Yakima Ave Tacoma WA 98405-4831

EDWARDS, LOUISE WISEMAN, career counselor, educator; b. Greeley, Colo., Feb. 20, 1932; d. Hunter R. and Sarah L. (Spencer) Wiseman; m. Jasin W. Edwards (div. 1975); children: Mark Hunter, Kathleen Margaret. BA, U. Colo., 1953; MA, U. N.Mex., 1983. Lic. profl. clin. counselor. Asst. dir. pub. info. Mills Coll., Oakland, Calif., 1956-57; ESL tchr. Peace Corps, Santiago, Chile, 1963-64; career counselor U. N.Mex. Career Svcs., Albuquerque, 1980-84, supr. career counseling, 1984-87, asst. dir., 1987-98, interim dir., 1992-93; pvt. counselor, 1998—; presenter U. N.Mex. Law Sch., 1982-95, Nat. Assn. Med. Schs. Admissions and Registrations Conv., 1993; instr. Anderson Sch. Mgmt. U. N.Mex., 1983—; bd. dirs. YWCA Career Divsn., Albuquerque, 1992-97. Active Dem. Women of N.Mex., 1970-80. Mem. ACA, N.Mex. Career Devel. Assn., Rocky Mt. Placement Assn. (co-chair conf. 1980—). Avocations: singing with univ. chorus, hiking, cross country skiing, bridge. Home: 2821 Tennessee St NE Albuquerque NM 87110-3707

EDWARDS, LYDIA JUSTICE, state official; b. Carter County, Ky., July 9, 1937; d. Chead and Velva (Kinney) Justice; m. Frank B. Edwards, 1968; children: Mark, Alexandra, Margot. Student, San Francisco State U. Began career as acct., then Idaho state rep., 1982-86; treas. State of Idaho, 1987-98; legis. asst. to Gov. Hickel, Alaska, 1967; conf. planner Rep. Gov.'s Assn., 1970-73; mem. Rep. Nat. Commn., 1972, del. to nat. conv., 1980. Mem. Rep. Womens Fedn. Congregationalist. Office: State Treas Office PO Box 35 Donnelly ID 83615*

EDWARDS, MARIE BABARE, psychologist; b. Tacoma; d. Nick and Mary (Mardesich) Babare; B.A., Stanford, 1948, M.A., 1949; m. Tilden Hampton Edwards (div.); 1 son, Tilden Hampton Edwards Jr. Counselor guidance center U. So. Calif., Los Angeles, 1950-52; project coordinator So. Calif. Soc. Mental Hygiene, 1952-54; pub. speaker Welfare Fedn. Los Angeles, 1953-57; field rep. Los Angeles County Assn. Mental Health, 1957-58; intern psychologist UCLA, 1958-60; pvt. practice, human rels. tng., counselor tng. Mem. Calif., Am., Western, Los Angeles psychol. assns., AAAS, So. Calif. Soc. Clin. Hypnosis. Author: (with Eleanor Hoover) The Challenge of Being Single, 1974, paperback edit., 1975. Office: 6100 Buckingham Pky Culver City CA 90230-7237

EDWARDS, PATRICIA BURR, small business owner, counselor, consultant; b. Oakland, Calif., Feb. 19, 1918; d. Myron Carlos and Claire Idelle (Laingor) Burr; m. Jackson Edwards, Nov. 14, 1942; children: Jill Forman-Young, Jan Kurzweil. AB, U. So. Calif., 1939, MSEd, 1981. Prin. Constructive Leisure, L.A., 1968—; spkr. in field; writer, prodr. counseling materials for career, leisure, life planning including computer software, audio cassettes and assessment surveys. Author: You've Got to Find Happiness: It Won't Find You, 1971, Leisure Counseling Techniques: Individual and Group Counseling Step-by-Step, 1975, 3d edit., 1980; (software) Leisure PREF, 1986, Over 50: Needs, Values, Attitudes, 1988, Adapting to Change: The NVAB Program, 1997; contbr. articles to profl. jours., mags. and books. Chmn. L.A. County Foster Families 50th Anniversary, 1962-64, L.A. Jr. League Sustainers, 1964-65, Hollywood Bowl Vols., L.A., 1960-61, Hollywood Bowl Patroness com., 1961—. Mem. Am. Counseling Assn., Calif. Assn. for Counseling and Devel., Nat. Recreation and Park Assn., Assn. for Adult Devel. and Aging, Trojan League, Travellers Aid Soc. L.A., Jr. League L.A., First Century Families of L.A., Delta Gamma. Republican. Episcopalian. Avocations: family activities, singing, dancing, pets, learning.

EDWARDS, PRISCILLA ANN, paralegal, business owner; b. Orlando, Fla., Sept. 28, 1947; d. William Granville and Bernice Royster. Paralegal cert., U. Calif., Berkeley, 1994. Paralegal Charles R. Garry Esquire, San Francisco, Calif., 1989-90, Marvin Cahn Esquire, San Francisco, 1990-91; owner, mgr. Fed. Legal Resources, San Francisco, 1991—; speaker Sonoma State U., Santa Rosa, Calif., 1993. Publisher: (book) Zero Weather, 1981. Recipient Wiley W. Manuel award for pro bono legal svcs. Bd. Govs. State Bar of Calif., 1994, 95, 96, 97, 98. Episcopalian. Avocations: horseback riding, mountain biking. Office: Fed Legal Resources 345 Franklin St San Francisco CA 94102-4427

EDWARDS, RALPH M., librarian; b. Shelley, Idaho, Apr. 17, 1933; s. Edward William and Maude Estella (Munsee) E.; m. Winifred Wylie, Dec. 25, 1969; children: Dylan, Nathan, Stephen. B.A., U. Wash., 1957, M.Library, 1960; D.L.S., U. Calif.-Berkeley, 1971. Libr. N.Y. Pub. Libr., N.Y.C., 1960-61; catalog libr. U. Ill. Libr., Urbana, 1961-62; br. libr. Multnomah County Libr., Portland, Oreg., 1964-67; asst. prof. Western Mich. U., Kalamazoo, 1970-74; chief of the Central Libr. Dallas Pub. Libr., 1975-81; city librarian Phoenix Pub. Libr., 1981-95, ret., 1996—. Author: Role of the Beginning Librarian in University Libraries, 1975. U. Calif. doctoral fellow, 1967-70; library mgmt. internship Council on Library Resources, 1974-75. Mem. ALA, Pub. Library Assn. Democrat. Home: 2884 Spring Blvd Eugene OR 97403-1662

EDWARDS, RICHARD ALAN, lawyer; b. Portland, Oreg., June 28, 1938; s. Howard A. and Kay E. (Sheldon) E.; m. Renee Rosier, June 18, 1960; children: Teri Edwards Obye, Lisa Edwards Smith, Steve. BS, Oreg. State U., 1960; JD summa cum laude, Willamette U., 1968. Bar: Oreg. 1968, U.S. Dist. Ct. Oreg. 1968, U.S. Ct. Appeals (9th cir.) 1969. Various positions 1st Interstate Bank of Oreg., Portland, 1960-65; assoc. Miller Nash Wiener Hager & Carlsen, Portland, 1968-74, ptnr., 1974—, mng. ptnr., 1991-96. Editor Willamette Law Jour., 1967-68. Mem. ABA (litigation sect. 1972), Oreg. State Bar (chairperson debtor-creditor sect. 1981-82, mem. various coms.). Republican. Presbyterian. Avocation: breeding and racing thoroughbred race horses. Office: Miller Nash Wiener Hager & Carlsen 111 SW 5th Ave Ste 3500 Portland OR 97204-3699

EDWARDS, SAMUEL ROGER, physician; b. Santa Barbara, Calif., Aug. 11 1937; s. Harold S. and Margaret (Spaulding) E.; m. Marcia Elizabeth Dutton, June 17, 1961; children—Harold S. II, Charles Dutton. B.A., Harvard U., 1960; M.D., U. So. Calif., 1964. Intern, Presbyn. Hosp., Phila., 1964-65; resident in internal medicine Presbyn. Med. Ctr., San Francisco, 1965-66, U. Calif. Hosps., San Francisco, 1968-70; fellow in cardiology Pacific Presbyn. Med. Ctr., San Francisco, 1970; pvt. practice specializing in internal medicine, Santa Paula, Calif., 1971-94; med. dir. Santa Paula Convalescent, Twin Pines Convalescent Hosps., 1974-95; pres. med. staff Ventura County Med. Ctr., Calif., 1979-80, med. dir., 1983-95, hosp. adminstr., 1995—; clin. faculty UCLA Sch. Medicine; chmn. Citizens State Bank of Santa Paula, 1975-97, Limoneira Assocs.; chief dept. medicine Ventura County Gen. Hosp., 1975; chief med. staff Santa Paula Meml. Hosp., 1977. Served to lt. comdr. USNR, 1966-68. Recipient Disting. Service award Ventura County Heart Assn., 1974. Fellow ACP; mem. AMA, Am. Soc. Internal Medicine, Am. Coll. Howp. Execs. Episcopalian. Home: 19789 E Telegraph Rd Santa Paula CA 93060-9693 Office: 243 March St Santa Paula CA 93060-2511

EDWARDS, WILLIAM H., SR., retired hotel corporation executive; b. Muskegon, Mich., May 25, 1917; s. William H. and Ruby A. (Tipson) E.; m. Ruth Ann Nolan, May 16, 1942; children: William H. Jr., Bradley N. Sr. BA, U. Mich., 1939; LLD, Northwood U., Midland, Mich., 1982. Cert. hotel adminstr. V.p., mng. dir. Palmer House Hilton, Chgo., 1966-68; v.p. Chgo. div. Hilton Hotels Corp., Chgo., 1968-70, sr. v.p., 1970-71, exec. v.p. ops., 1971-78; pres. Hilton Hotel div. Hilton Hotels Corp., Beverly Hills, Calif., 1978-89, vice chmn., 1985-89, bd. dirs., mem. exec. com., 1971-89, vice chmn. and dir. emeritus, 1989—; bd. dirs. Conrad Hilton Found., L.A., 1989—; bd. dirs. Travel and Tourism adv. bd. Dept. Commerce, Washington, 1983-88. Trustee Radiol. Soc. N.Am./Rsch. and Edn. Fund, Oak Brook, Ill., 1988-93, treas. 1988-89; trustee, v.p. So. Calif. chpt. Nat. Multiple Sclerosis Soc., 1984—. Recipient Cmty. Svc. award Brandeis U., 1975, Am. Tourism award New Sch. for Social Rsch., 1983, Amb. of Hospitality award Nat. Restaurant Assn. Ednl. Found., 1990, Convention Liaison Coun.-Hall of Leaders award, 1985. Mem. Am. Hotel Motel Assn. (pres. 1986, chmn. 1987), Travel Industry Assn. Am. (nat. chmn. 1982-84, bd. dirs. 1978—), L.A. Country Club. Republican. Roman Catholic. Avocation: golf. Home: 10350 Wilshire Blvd Los Angeles CA 90024-4700

EEN, TRUDELL ELAINE, organization administrator; b. Mankato, Minn., Feb. 2, 1950; d. Lawrence Olaf and Elaine Helen (Braun) E.; m. M. Amine Hajji, Jan. 1, 1975; children: Omar Een Hajji, Soraya Een Hajji. BA in Arch., BA in Art History, U. Minn., 1977. Constrn. project mgr. Bor-Son Bldg. Corp., Bloomington, Minn., 1977-86; owner Trudell Een Archtl. Design, Cannon Falls, Minn., 1987-94; project dir. Cannon Falls Area Recycling Project, 1987-91; owner Castle Works, San Jose, Calif., 1996-97; website project dir. LWV, San Jose, Calif., 1997—. Contbr. articles to newspapers. pres. Cannon Falls area LWV, 1985-87, San Jose and Santa Clara, Calif., 1996-97, treas. Minn., St. Paul, 1991-94. Avocation: writing. Home and Office: 1211 Quail Creek Cir San Jose CA 95120-4150

EFFORD, MICHAEL ROBERT, police administrator, educator; b. L.A., July 22, 1950; s. Robert Victor and Mary (Athens) E.; m. Jolene Lynn Buttner, Mar. 20, 1976 (dec. Jan. 1980); m. Patricia Ann Jones, Feb. 2, 1985; children: Stacy Anne, Ashley Elizabeth. AA in Criminal Justice, Western Nev. Community Coll., 1976; BA in Bus., Calif. Coast U., 1993, MBA, 1996. Trooper Nev. Hwy. Patrol, Las Vegas, 1976-80; law instr. Western Nev. Community Coll., Carson City, 1980-94; adminstrv. lt. Carson City Sheriff's Dept., 1972—, in charge of planning & tng., 1993—; sheriff Carson City, 1980-94; chief of police Sonora (Calif.) Police Dept., 1994—; instr. Reno Police Acad., 1980-94, Nev. Hwy Patrol Acad., Carson City, 1980-94, Nev. Peace Officer Stds. and Tng. Acad. Editor Carson City Sheriff's Supervisory Assn. newsletter, 1989—. Pres. Carson City Labor Coalition, 1992—, planning commr. Regional Planning Commn., Carson City, 1989—; mem. Main-street/Redevel. Authority Carson City, 1991-94; mem. Nev. Day com., Carson City, 1985-94, 4th of July com., 1985-94, Gov.'s Ball com., 1985-94; apptd. to criminal justice tech. skills com. Western Nev. C.C., 1994. Sgt. U.S. Army, 1970-73. Recipient Svc. award Carson City Bd. Suprs., 1984, Excellence in Govt. award Tuolumne County C. of C., 1997. Mem. AFL-CIO Police Assn. (pres. 1989—), Kiwanis. Republican. Roman Catholic. Avocations: golf, computers, backpacking, skiing, reading. Home: 100 S Green St Sonora CA 95370-4643

EGAN, FEROL RAYMOND, writer; b. Sonora, Calif., July 25, 1923; s. Ferol Ruoff and Verna Mae (Maddox) E.; m. Martha Toki Oshima, Mar. 6, 1965. AB, U. of the Pacific, 1946, MA, 1950; tchg. credential, U. Calif., Berkeley, 1947-48, postgrad., 1956-57. Assoc. prof. humanities Calif. Coll. Arts and Crafts, Oakland, 1957-61; sci. writer U. Calif., Berkeley, 1961-65; co-designer, text author Calif. Indian Exhibit, Oakland Mus., 1968; assoc. editor The Am. West, Palo Alto, Calif., 1970-72; prof. humanities The Fromm Inst., U. San Francisco, 1982-91. Author: The El Dorado Trail: The Story of the Gold Rush Routes Across Mexico, 1970 (Commonwealth Californiana medal 1971), Sand in a Whirlwind: The Paiute Indian War of 1860, 1972 (Commonwealth Silver medal 1973), Taste of Time, 1977 (award Merit Western Writers 1978), Fremont: Explorer for a Restless Nation, 1977 (Commonwealth Gold medal 1978), Last Bonanza Kings: The Bourns of San Francisco, 1998. Recipient Fremont award The Huntington Westerners Internat., San Marino, Calif., 1995. Mem. Friends of The Bancroft Libr., U. Calif. Home: 1199 Grizzly Peak Blvd Berkeley CA 94708-2149

EGAN, PHYLLIS REITZ, lay worker, educator; b. Buffalo, Mar. 10, 1936; d. Gerard Herman and Diana (Henrich) Reitz; m. Gerald Richard Egan, July 2, 1955; children: Sharon Lesley, Renee Denise, Kenneth Gerard, Keith Edward. BS, Christopher Newport Coll., 1980; MEd, Coll. of William and Mary, 1984; cert. in elem. and secondary teaching, guidance counseling, N.Mex. State U., 1987. Cert. secondary tchr., guidance counselor, N.Mex. Tchr. Our Lady Mt. Carmel Cath. Sch., Newport News, 1981-84, True Cross, Dickinson, Tex., 1985-86; prin. St. Mary's, League City, Tex., 1986-87; tchr. Holy Cross Cath. Sch., Las Cruces, N.Mex., 1988-91; eucharistic min. Holy Cross Parish, Las Cruces, 1987-91; instr. summer Bible sch. program Holy Cross Sch., Las Cruces, 1987-91; liturgy planner Holy Cross Cath. Sch., Las Cruces, 1988-91. Tchr. and instr. Am. Heart Assn., Va. and N.Mex., 1967-91, Am. Red Cross, Va. and N.Mex., 1967-91. Mem. ASCD, Nat. Cath. Edn. Assn. Republican. Office: Holy Cross Cath Sch 1331 N Miranda St Las Cruces NM 88005-2055

EGELI, ARTHUR BJORN, independent film director, scripwriter; b. Valley Lee, Md., Apr. 2, 1964; s. Cedric Baldwin and Joanette Astrid (Hoffman) E. Student, U. Md., 1982-83, 84-85, Coll. Design, Pasadena, Calif., 1983-84. Artist, film dir., writer Annapolis, Md., 1985-88, Pasadena, Calif., 1991—. Dir., scripwriter: (film) Unconditional Love, 1994 (Golden award 1994, 95, Starfish award Hampton's Internat. Film Festival, Gold award, Houston, Silver medal, New Delhi); art exhibited in one-man shows at Tirage Gallery, Downstairs Gallery, numerous others. Creative arts scholar U. Md., Balt., 1982. Mem. Calif. Art Club. Avocations: kickboxing, poetry. Home and Office: 914 N Michigan Ave # A Pasadena CA 91104-2956

EGER, DENISE LEESE, rabbi; b. New Kensington, Pa., Mar. 14, 1960; d. Bernard D. and Estelle (Leese) E. BA in Religion, U. So. Calif., 1982; MA in Hebrew Letters, Hebrew Union Coll., L.A., 1985; Rabbi, Hebrew Union Coll., N.Y.C., 1988. Ordained rabbi, 1988. Chaplain Rabbi Beth Chayim Chadashim, L.A., 1988-92; founding rabbi Congregation Kol Ami, West Hollywood, Calif., 1992—. Columnist Edge mag., Lesbian News; contbr. articles to religious publs., chpts. to anthologies. Exec. com. So. Calif. Bd. of Rabbis; cmty. adv. bd. Shanti Found.; treas. Women Rabbinic Network; chair Task Force on Gays and Lesbians in the Rabbinate. Recipient Rainbow Key award City West Hollywood, L.A.C.E. Spirituality award L.A. Gay and Lesbian Ctr. Mem. Cen. Conf. Am. Rabbis, Interfaith Clergy Assn. (past chair gays and lesbians bd.). Avocation: guitar. Office: Congregation Kol Ami 9056 Santa Monica Blvd Ste 100 West Hollywood CA 90069-5545

EGER, MARILYN RAE, artist; b. Offett AFB, Nebr., Jan. 2, 1953; d. John W. Shaver and Joyce Faye (Carpenter) Shaver (dec.), stepmother Myrle I. MAsoner; m. Darrell W. Masoner, Feb. 28, 1971 (div. Sept. 1977); children: William Matthew, Melissa Rae; m. Gerard J. Eger, Jan. 30, 1982. BA, Calif. State U., Turlock, 1987. Cert. art tchr. 1990, Calif., lang. devel. specialist, 1993. Freelance artist oil painting Gibson Greetings Inc., Cin., 1992-97; tchr. art, A.P. art, advanced art Bear Creek High Sch., Stockton, Calif., chmn. dept. art, 1994—, mentor tchr., 1998-2000; pvt. art tchr. One-woman shows include Stockton Fine Arts Gallery, 1984-88, Accurate Art Gallery, Sacramento, 1989-90, Sharon Gile Gallery, Isleton, Calif., 1988-91, Le Galerie, Stockton, 1989-91, Masterpiece Gallery, Carmel, Calif., 1991-95, Alan Short Gallery, Stockton, 1991, Lodi Art Ctr., 1997; represented by Iona's Gallery, Stockton, 1995-96, Heart of the Arts Gallery, Stockton, 1996—, C's Floral Gallery, Stockton, 1995-98, Lodi Art Ctr., 1984—, feature artist, 1985—; represented in permanent collections Gulf Oil Chems., Kaiser Permanente, Masterpiece Gallery; prints pub. in Mus. Edits. West. Bd. dirs. Lodi Art Ctr., 1988-91, chmn. 1989. Recipient Award of Excellence Unitarian Fall Art Festival, 1990, Award of Excellence in Oils, 1992, Ben Day Meml. award, 1993, Bank Stockton award and H.M. Haggin Mus., 1989, U.S. Nat. Collegiate Art Merit award, 1988, Lodi 31st Ann., 1st Oils, 1988, Award of Excellence in Pastel Haggin Mus., 1992, 1st Oils and Don Morrell Meml. award CCAL Gallo Show, 1993, Art of Calif. Bronze Discovery award, 1993, 1st pastel Lodi Art Ann., 1995, Hon. mention, 1998, award of merit Haggin Mus., 1997, 3rd in graphics Unitarian Fall Art Festival, 1998, 3rd Graphics award Lodi Art Ann., 1998, numerous others; Mellon grantee, 1994. Mem. Calif. Art Edn. Assn., Stockton Art League, Nat. League Am. Pen. Women, Ctrl. Calif. Art League. Republican. Methodist. Avocations: sculpting, gardening, vineyards, painting, travel. Home: 1295 E Peltier Rd Acampo CA 95220-9652 Office: 1295 1/2 E Peltier Rd Acampo CA 95220-9652

EGGENER, KEITH LEOPOLD, architectural historian; b. Portland, Oreg., Jan. 29, 1960. BA, Portland State Univ., 1985; MA, Univ. of Washington, 1989; PhD, Stanford Univ., 1995. Instr. Cleveland Mus. of Art, 1989-90; historic preservation cons. Portland, Oreg., 1984-88; asst. prof. Carleton Coll., Northfield, Minn., 1995-97, Univ. of Nevada, Las Vegas, 1997—; cons. Barragan Found., Basel, Switzerland, 1997—; referee Am. Coll. Schs. of Architecture, Washington, 1998; editorial bd. mem. Terra Firma Univ. Las Vegas, 1997-99; jury coord. Northfield Arts Guild, 1996-97. Contbr. articles to books and profl. jours. Vol., solicitor Buildings of the U.S., Las Vegas, 1998-99; vol. St. Francis Meml. Hosp., 1994-95, First Luth. Food Bank, Seattle, 1987-88, vol. instr. Oreg. Libr. Program, 1984-85. Recipient Jacob K. Javits fellowship U.S. Dept Edn., 1993-95, Sally Kress Tompkins fellowship, Soc. Arch. Historians, 1993, Samuel H. Kress Found. fellowship Samuel H. Kress Found., 1993, grad. fellowship Stanford Univ., 1990-93, Regents fellowship U. Nev. at Las Vegas, 1998-99, Best Article S.C. Hist. mag., 1997. Mem. Soc. Arch. Historians, Coll. Art Assn., Am. Collegiate Sch. of Arch., Amnesty Internat. Office: Univ Nev Las Vegas Sch Arch 4505 S Maryland Pkwy Las Vegas NV 89154-4018

EGGERT, ROBERT JOHN, SR., economist; b. Little Rock, Dec. 11, 1913; s. John and Eleanora (Fritz) Lapp; m. Elizabeth Bauer, Nov. 28, 1935 (dec. Dec. 1991); children: Robert John, Richard F., James E.; m. Annamarie Hayes, Mar. 19, 1994. BS, U. Ill., 1935, MS, 1936; candidate in philosophy, U. Minn., 1938; LHD (hon.), Ariz. State U., 1988. Research analyst Bur. Agrl. Econs., U.S. Dept. Agr., Urbana, Ill., 1935; prin. marketing specialist War Meat Bd., Chgo., 1943; rsch. analyst U. Ill., 1935-36, U. Minn., 1936-38; asst. prof. econs. Kans. State Coll., 1938-41; asst. dir. mktg. Am. Meat Inst., Chgo., 1941-43; economist, assoc. dir. Am. Meat Inst., 1943-50; mgr. dept. mktg. rsch. Ford div. Ford Motor Co., Dearborn, Mich., 1951-53; mgr. program planning Ford div. Ford Motor Co., 1953-54, mgr. bus. rsch., 1954-57, mgr. mktg. rsch. mktg. staff, 1957-61, mgr. mktg. rsch., 1961-64, mgr. internat. mktg. rsch. mktg. staff, 1964-65, mgr. overseas mktg. rsch. planning, 1965-66, mgr. mktg. rsch. Lincoln-Mercury div., 1966-67; dir. agribus. programs Mich. State U., 1967-68; staff v.p. econ. and mktg. rsch. RCA Corp., N.Y.C., 1968-76; pres., chief economist Eggert Econ. Enterprises, Inc., Sedona, Ariz., 1976—; lectr. mktg. U. Chgo., 1947-49; chmn. Fed. Statistics Users Conf., 1960-61; adj. prof. bus. forecasting No. Ariz., 1976-79; mem. econ. adv. bd. U.S. Dept. Commerce, 1969-71, mem. census adv. com., 1975-78; mem. panel econ. advisers Congl. Budget Office, 1975-76; interim dir. Econ. Outlook Ctr. Coll. Bus. Adminstrn. Ariz. State U., Tempe, 1985-86, cons., 1985—; mem. Econ. Estimates Commn. Ariz., 1979—; apptd. Ariz. Gov.'s Commn. Econ. Devel., 1991—, vice chmn. investment adv. coun. Ariz. State Retirement System, 1993-98; trustee Marcus J. Lawrence Med. Ctr. Found., 1992-96; chmn. market rsch. com. Gov.'s Strategic Partnership for Econ. Devel., Sr. Living Cluster, 1995—. Contbr. articles to profl. lit.; founder, editor emeritus: monthly Blue Chip Econ. Indicators, 1976—; exec. editor Ariz. Blue Chip, 1984—, Western Blue Chip Econ. Forecast, 1986—, Blue Chip Job Growth Update, 1990—, Mexico Consensus Econ. Forecast, 1993—. Mem. long range planning com. Ch. of Red Rocks. Recipient Econ. Forecast award Chgo. chpt. Am. Statis. Assn., 1950, 60, 68; Seer of Yr. award Harvard Bus. Sch. Indsl. Econs., 1973. Fellow Am. Statis. Assn. (chmn. bus. and econ. stats sect. 1957—, pres. Chgo. chpt. 1948-49), Nat. Assn. Bus. Economists (coun. 1969-72); mem. Coun. Internat. Mktg. Rsch. and Planning Dirs. (chmn. 1965-66), Am. Mktg. Assn. (dir., v.p. mktg. mgmt. divsn. 1972-73, nat. pres. 1974-75), Fed. Stats. Users Conf. (chmn. trustees 1960-61), Conf. Bus. Economists (chmn. 1972-74), Am. Quarter Horse Assn. (dir. 1966-73), Ariz. Econ. Roundtable, Am. Econs. Assn., Phoenix Econ. Club (hon.), Ariz. C. of C. (bd. dirs. 1991-95), Alpha Zeta. Republican. Office: Eggert Econ Enterprises Inc PO Box 2243 Sedona AZ 86339-2243

EGGLESTON, CLAUD HUNT, III, company executive, venture capitalist; b. Buffalo, June 21, 1954; s. Claud Hunt Jr. and Arlene (Shank) E.; m. Ann Pendleton, Feb. 14, 1988; children: Brett Andrew, Blake Edward Hunt. BA, Union Coll., 1976; MS, Columbia U., 1979, MEd, 1979. Pres. Checo Electronics, Schenectady, N.Y., 1974-78; chief fin. officer, bus. mgr. performing arts div. Smithsonian Inst., Washington, 1978-79; staff mgr. long lines AT&T, Washington, 1980-81; dist. mgr. strategy and product devel. Morristown, N.J., 1981-82; mgr. venture devel. consumer products Morristown, 1982-84, corp. mgr. bus. devel., 1984-85; gen. mgr. Asia Internat., Morristown, 1985-87; dir. new ventures U.S. West Inc., Denver, 1987-88, exec. dir. mergers and acquisitions, 1988-90; v.p. bus. devel. and mktg. Corel/Ventura Software Inc., San Diego, 1990-92; mng. dir. Crest Tech. Ventures, Inc., Poway, Calif., 1992—; pres. Tech. Trends Technology Focus, Inc., San Diego, 1992—. Editor: Financing Independent Education, 1978. Recipient Young Entrepreneur award Schenectady C. of C., 1975; Klingenstein fellow Columbia U., 1977-78. Mem. Am. Mgmt. Assn., Met. Club (Denver).

EGUCHI, YASU, artist; b. Japan, Nov. 30, 1938; came to U.S., 1967; s. Chihaku and Kiku (Koga) E.; m. Anita Phillips, Feb. 24, 1968. Student, Horie Art Acad., Japan, 1958-65. Exhibited exhbns., Tokyo Mus. Art, 1963, 66, Santa Barbara Mus. Art, Calif., 1972, 73, 74, 85, Everson Mus. Art, Syracuse, N.Y., 1980, Nat. Acad. Design, N.Y.C., 1980—, one-man shows, Austin Gallery, Scottsdale, Ariz., 1968-87, Joy Tash Gallery, Scottsdale, 1989—, Greyston Galleries, Cambria, Calif., 1969, 70, 72, Copenhagen Galleries, Calif., 1970-78, Charles and Emma Frye Art Mus., Seattle, 1974, 84, 98, Hammer Galleries, N.Y.C., 1977, 79, 81, 93, City of Heidenheim, W. Ger., 1980, Artique Ltd., Anchorage, 1981—; pub. and pvt. collections, Voith Gmbh, W. Ger., City of Giengen and City of Heidenheim, Fed. Republic Germany, represented, Deer Valley, Utah, Hunter Resources, Santa Barbara, Am. Embassy, Paris, Charles and Emma Frye Art Mus., Seattle, Nat. Acad. Design, N.Y.C.; author: Der Brenz Entlang, 1980; contbr. to jours in field. Active Guide Dogs for the Blind, San Raphael, Calif., 1976; active City of Santa Barbara Arts Council, 1979, The Eye Bank for Sight Restoration, N.Y., 1981, Anchorage Arts Council, 1981, Santa Barbara Mus. Natural History, 1989. Recipient Selective artist award Yokohama Citizen Gallery, 1965; recipient Artist of Yr. award Santa Barbara Arts Council, 1979, Hon. Citizen award City of Heidenheim, 1980, The Adolph and Clara Obrig prize NAD, 1983, Cert. of Merit NAD, 1985, 87. Home: PO Box 30206 Santa Barbara CA 93130-0206

EHLERT, DEWAYNE ALBERT, underwriter; b. Holstein, Iowa, Oct. 26, 1925; s. Albert and Golda M. (Leckband) E.; m. Doris B. Frasch, Aug. 6, 1951; children: Tam Jan Marek, Leslie, David. BBA, Buena Vista U., Storm Lake, Iowa, 1949; MS in secondary edn., U. Iowa, 1950. CLU. ChFC. Underwriter Stockton, Calif., 1965—; fin. cons. Stockton, 1983—; chmn. Gen. Agts. & Mgrs., Stockton, 1983-98, Life Underwriters Bd., Stockton, 1983-98; mem. Estate Planning Coun., Stockton, 1983-98. Chmn. United Way, 1989-90; vol. U. Pacific Boys and Girls Club. Mem. Rotary (pres. Stockton club 1989-90; mem. dist. bd. dirs.). Republican. Lutheran. Avocation: ranching. Home: 4084 Burge Rd Stockton CA 95215-9163

EHMAN, MICHAEL FREDERICK, electronics executive; b. Springfield, Ohio, Aug. 14, 1945; s. Burnell Frederick and Doris (Daugherty) E.; m. Carol Gampher; children: Heather Lyn, Matthew Frederick. BA in Mineralogy, Miami U., Oxford, Ohio, 1967; PhD in Solid State Sci., Pa. State U., 1970; MBA, So. Meth. U., 1982. With tech. staff Rockwell Internat., Anaheim, Calif., 1970-74; mgr. engring. Rockwell Internat., Chgo., 1975, Newport Beach, Calif., 1976; dir. engring. Rockwell Internat., Dallas, 1977-80; v.p. advt. tech. optoelectronics TRW, Carrolton, Tex., 1980-81; pres. Morgan Semiconductor Inc., Garland, Tex., 1982-85; gen. mgr. elect. materials Ethyl Corp., Garland, 1985-89; mktg. mgr. Alcoa Electronic Packaging, 1989-92, Splty. Metals div. Alcoa, New Kensington, Pa., 1992-93; gen. mgr. integrated tech. div. Bourns, Inc., Logan, Utah, 1994-95, pres. microelectronics divsn., 1995—. Contbr. 22 articles to profl. jours.; patentee in field. Mem. IEEE, Soc. Automotive Engrs. Republican. Methodist. Avocations: trains, antique cars, antique lanterns. Office: Bourns Inc Microelectronics Divsn 2355 N 1000 W Ogden UT 84414

EHMANN, ANTHONY VALENTINE, lawyer; b. Chgo., Sept. 5, 1935; s. Anthony E. and Frances (Verweil) E.; m. Alice A. Avina, Nov. 27, 1959; children: Ann, Thomas, Jerome, Gregory, Rose, Robert. BS, Ariz. State U., 1957; JD, U. Ariz., 1960. Bar: Ariz. 1960, U.S. Tax Ct. 1960, U.S. Sup. Ct. 1968; CPA, Ariz.; cert. tax specialist, trusts and estates specialist. Spl. asst. atty. gen., 1961-68; mem. Ehmann and Hiller, Phoenix, 1969—. Republican dist. chmn. Ariz., 1964; pres. Grand Canyon council Boy Scouts Am., 1987-89, mem. exec. com., 1981—; v.p. western region Boy Scouts Am., 1991—; mem. bd. dirs. Nat. Catholic Com. on Scouting, 1995—. Recipient Silver Beaver award Boy Scouts Am., 1982, Bronze Pelican award Cath. Com. on Scouting, 1981, Silver Antelope award Boy Scouts Am., 1994. Fellow Am. Coll. Trusts & Estate Counsel; mem. State Bar Ariz. (chmn. tax sect. 1968, 69), Central Ariz. Estate Planning Council (pres. 1968, 69). Republican. Roman Catholic. Clubs: KC (grand knight 1964, 65) (Glendale, Ariz.), Serra Internat. (pres. Phoenix club 1992-93, dist. gov. Ariz. 1993-95), Knight of Holy Sepulchre, Knight of Malta. Office: Ehmann & Hiller 2525 E Camelback Rd Ste 720 Phoenix AZ 85016-4229

EHRET, TERRY, writer; b. San Francisco, Nov. 12, 1955; d. Stephen Henry II and Adelaide Beatrice (O'Connor) E.; m. Donald Nicholas Moe, Apr. 7, 1979; children: Allison, Caitlin, Annelisa. AB in Psychology, Stanford U., 1977; MA in English, San Francisco State U., 1984. English tchr. Notre Dame H.S., Salinas, Calif., 1977-81, Cathedral H.S., San Francisco, 1981-83, Notre Dame H.S., Belmont, Calif., 1984-90; poet, tchr. Calif. Poets in the Schs., San Francisco, 1991—; creative writing tchr. Sonoma State U., Rohnert Park, Calif., 1993-94, San Francisco State U., 1995-97; writer-on-site Poets and Writers Inc., Oakland, Calif., 1997; English tchr. Santa Rosa (Calif.) Jr. Coll., 1991—; writer-on-site Oakland Mus. of Calif., 1997, Oakland Pub. Libr., 1997; poetry series dir. SRJC Arts and Lectures com., Santa Rosa, 1994—. Author: Suspensions, 1990, Lost Body, 1993 (Nat. Poetry Series 1992, Calif. Commonwealth Club award 1994, (poetry sequence) The Thought She Might: Picasso Portraits (Pable Neruda prize 1995). Vol. coord. McNear Elem. Sch., Petalume, Calif., 1990-94. Mem. Calif. Poets in the Schs., Acad. of Am. Arts. Home: 924 Sunnyslope Rd Petaluma CA 94952

EHRHART, JOSEPH EDWARD, retired television broadcast engineer; b. Monterey Park, Calif., Dec. 27, 1933; s. Theophile George and Catherine Louise (Spaulding) E.; m. Mary Frances Bos, Nov. 30, 1957; children: James Edward and Teresa Louise. AA in Electronics, Pasadena City Coll., 1954. 1st class lic. radiotelephone, FCC. Child actor MGM, RKO, United Artists, Republic, Warner Bros., 20th Century Fox, Universal, Hollywood, Calif., 1939-54; TV broadcast engr. Sta. KOAT-TV, Albuquerque, 1957, Sta. KOB-TV, Albuquerque, 1958, Sta. KHJ-TV, Hollywood, Calif., 1959, ABC, Hollywood, 1960-93; videotape supr. Sta. KABC-TV, Hollywood, 1987-93; ret. Sta. KABC-TV, 1993. Scoutmaster Boy Scouts of Am., Montrose, Calif., 1970-72; choir dir., Holy Redeemer Cath. Ch., Montrose, 1967-75, mem. Am. Assn. of Variable Star Observers, 1973-78. Served in USNR, 1954-56. Mem. Soc. Motion Picture and TV Engrs., Cath. Press Coun., Mensa, Pacific Pioneer Broadcasters, Soc. for Preservation and Encouragement of Barber Shop Quartet Singing in Am., L.A. Astron. Soc., Am. Legion. Lodges: KC, Order of the Alhambra. Avocations: church choir, instrumental music. Home: 1255 N Broadway Apt 348 Escondido CA 92026-2829

EHRHORN, THOMAS FREDERICK, software quality assurance engineer; b. Lebanon, Pa., Nov. 12, 1946; s. Frederick William and Evelyn Matilda (Daullary) E.; m. Elaine Mae Thernlund, Feb. 16, 1974; 1 child, Susan Marie. BA in Computer Sci., SUNY, Albany, 1981; AS in Tng. Devices Technology, C.C. of the Air Force, Maxwell AFB, Ala., 1986; MA in Edn., Chapman U., 1992. Cert. tchr. computer sci., Calif. Enlisted USAF, 1966, advanced through ranks to chief master sgt.; electronics tech. USAF, various, 1966-86; ret. USAF, 1986; electronics tech. Systems Rsch. Labs, Castle AFB, Calif., 1986-89; computer sci. USAF, Castle AFB, 1989-93; electronics engr. USAF, Kirtland AFB, N.Mex., 1994-95; software quality assurance engr. Duke Engring. and Svcs., Inc., Albuquerque, N. Mex., 1995—. Registrar Atwater (Calif.) Youth Soccer League, 1990-93; mem./pres. Winton (Calif.) Sch. Bd., 1987-91; exec. bd. Yosemite Area Coun., Boy Scouts Am., modesto, Calif., 1985-87; chmn. Fresno (Calif.) Diocese Youth Ministry Bd., 1985-86. Mem. KC, Am. Soc. Quality Control, Mensa. Democrat. Roman Catholic. Avocations: computers, youth activities. Office: Duke Engring and Svcs 1650 University Blvd NE Albuquerque NM 87102-1726

EHRLICH, JEREMY ADAM, educator, researcher; b. Ann Arbor, Mich., Nov. 22, 1970; s. Don A. and Marcia N. E. BA with hons., U. Chgo., 1993; MA with distinction, U. Birmingham, Stratford, Eng., 1996. Tchr. (summers) Aim High, San Francisco, 1990-95, co-dir., 1993-94; tchr., chmn. dept. Drew Coll. Prep Sch., San Francisco, 1993—. Recipient Coll. hons. scholarship U. Chgo., 1989-93. Office: Drew Coll Prep Sch 2901 California St San Francisco CA 94115-2432

EHRLICH, KENNETH JAMES, television producer; b. Cleve., May 11; s. Arthur A. and Lucile (Dimond) E.; m. Harriet Stromberg, Feb. 19, 1967; children: Mathew, Dori. BS in Journalism, Ohio U., 1964. Pres. Cominique, Chgo., 1970-72; dir. devel. Sta. WTTW-TV, Chgo., 1972-76; pres. Ken Ehrlich Prodns., Los Angeles, 1976—. Exec. producer (series) Showtime Coast to Coast, numerous spls. with Paul Simon, Stevie Wonder, Liza Minnelli, Phil Collins, Kenny Loggins, 1987—; producer Grammy Awards Show, 1980—, Soundstage (creator), 1974-83, Fame, 1983-85, Nelson Mandela Freedom Fest, 1988. Recipient Golden Rose of Montreax (Switzerland) Montreax Film Fest, 1975, Golden Globe award Hollywood Fgn. Press Assn., Los Angeles, 1983, Emmy award Acad. of TV Arts and Scis., Los Angeles, 1984, Emmy award nominations, 1986, 88. Mem. Nat. Assn. Cable TV (bd. dirs.). Avocations: golf, music, writing. Office: Ken Ehrlich Prodns 17200 Oak View Dr Encino CA 91316-4014

EHRLICH, SUSAN ANNE, judge; b. Dec. 26, 1948; d. Lee and Mildred Josephine (Cohen) E.; m. James C. Hair, Jr., July 16, 1978; children: Lee M.E., Caitlin A.E. AB, Wellesley Coll., 1978; JD, Ariz. State U., 1974. Bar: Ariz., D.C.; U.S. Ct. Appeals (1st, 2nd, 4th, 5th, 6th, 7th, 8th, 9th, 10th and D.C. cirs.), U.S. Dist. Ct. of Ariz., U.S. Supreme Ct. Rsch. analyst Civil Rights Divsn. U.S. Dept. Justice, Washington, 1970-71; law clk. to chief justice Ariz. Supreme Ct., 1974-76; pvt. practice Ariz., 1976-77; atty. Civil Divsn. U.S. Dept. Justice, Washington, 1978-80; asst. U.S. atty. Dist. of Ariz., 1981-89; judge Ariz. Ct. of Appeals, Phoenix, 1989—. Author: Handbook: Appeals in the Ninth Circuit, 1987, 89; co-author: The Ability of the Mentally Retarded to Plead Guilty, 1975, Tribute to Justice Jack D.H. Hays, 1995. Mem. Mayor's Task Force on Domestic Violence; mem. steering com. Phoenix Violence Prevention Initiative; bd. dirs. U. Ariz. Law Coll. Assn., others. Mem. ABA (mem. task force on the federalization of criminal law, appellate judges' conf. edn. com.), Am. Law Inst., Ariz. State, Tribal and Federal Ct. Forum, Phoenix Mcpl. Ct. Jud. Selection Adv. Bd. (chair), Ariz. Judges' Assn., Lorna E. Lockwood Inn of Ct. (past pres.), Ariz. Women Lawyers' Assn. (past pres.). Office: Ariz Ct of Appeals 1501 W Washington St Phoenix AZ 85007-3231

EHRMAN, VALERIE ANN, artist; b. Alhambra, Calif., Aug. 22, 1953; d. George Edward and Etta Permelia E. Student, Pepperdine U., 1979-82, Calif. Poly., 1985. Illustrator Shepard Design Assoc., Pasadena, 1972, Ad Rsch., L.A., 1972; cons. in field. Vol. Ch. of Christ, Alhambra, 1978. Avocations: writing, crafts, dewing, reading, sewing. Home: 425 N Marquerita Alhambra CA 91801

EHRMANTRAUT, HARRY CHARLES, medical consultant, researcher; b. Washington, Nov. 25, 1921; s. Edward Joseph and Elizabeth (Kaufmann) E.; m. Shirley Lee Anderson, Mar. 26, 1948; children: Lisa, Lynn. BA in Botany, George Washington U., 1947; MS in Chemistry, Georgetown U., 1948; PhD in Biophysics, U. Ill., 1950. Pres. Mechrolab, Inc., Mountain View, Calif., 1959-65, Videonetics, Inc., Sunnyvale, Calif., 1966-68, Gymnos corp., Los Altos, Calif., 1968-71, AVM Assocs., Inc., Los Osos, Calif., 1977-81; dir. mktg. Alpha Thermistor, Inc., San Diego, 1986-87; pres. Alchem Assocs., San Diego, 1987—; ptnr. Bus. Analysis Assocs., San Carlos, Calif., 1972-76; bd. dirs. I.I.M., Inc., San Diego, IDS, Inc. Author: Headaches, 1980, 2d ed., 1987; co-author, editor 4 books on instrumentation, 1954-65; patentee in field. Served to cpl. USAAF, 1942-46. Mem. IEEE, Biophys. Soc. (founding), Am. Chem. Soc., N.Y. Acad. Sci., Sigma Xi. Office: Alchem Assocs 985 Northridge Ave Springfield OR 97477-2393

EICHHOFF, DARRELL DEAN, retired insurance company executive, consultant; b. Piedmont, Okla., June 5, 1923; s. Hans O. and Goldie Marie (Lyle) E.; m. Corinne W. Wade, Oct. 27, 1945; children: Gay L., Sue A., Kim M. Belgarde. BS, U. Mo., 1943. CLU. Various positions to exec. v.p., chief mktg. officer Met. Life, N.Y.C., 1946-81; cons., 1981—; dir. Columbia Coll., Mo., 1968-76; chmn. bd. Life Ins. Mktg. and Rsch. Agy., Hartford, Conn., Life Underwriters Tng. Coun., 1975, Life Office Mgmt. Assn., Atlanta, 1980-81; dir. various ins. cos.; nat. dir. Gen. Agents and Mgr.'s Conf.; chmn. Agy. Officers Round Table; bd. dirs. E.F. Hutton V.I.P. Fund, Ky. Home Mutual Ins. Co., Ky. Home Capital Co. Pres., chmn. Greater N.Y. Coun. Boy Scouts, 1976-81; chmn. bd. Medic Alert Found., Turlock, Calif., 1987, 88. Republican. Presbyterian. Avocations: golf, reading. Home: 12930 Polvera Ave San Diego CA 92128-1136

EICHHORN, DENNIS PAUL, writer; b. Deer Lodge, Mont., Aug. 19, 1945; s. Elmer Norris and Catherine Eileen (Tuffley) E.; m. Joan Lee Pelley, Feb. 7, 1977 (div. June 1983); 1 child, Sarah Eileen. BA in Sociology, U. Idaho, 1968. Editor Rocket mag., Seattle, 1981-87; staff writer Turman Pub., Seattle, 1981-98; pub. Northwest EXTRA!, Olympia, Wash., 1987-89; editl. dir. Loompanics Unltd., Port Townsend, Wash., 1994-98; writer Ednl. Design, Inc., 1998—. Writer various comic books, 1988-92; editor 60 books. Mem. Fraternal Order of Eagles. Avocations: reading, writing. Home: 2318 2d Ave # 1131 Seattle WA 98121

EIFLER, CARL FREDERICK, retired psychologist; b. Los Angeles, June 27, 1906; s. Carl Frederick and Pauline (Engelbert) E.; m. Margaret Christine Aaberg, June 30, 1963; 1 son, Carl Henry; 1 adopted son, Byron Hisey. BD, Jackson Coll., 1956; Ph.D., Ill. Inst. Tech., 1962. Insp. U.S. Bur. Customs, 1928-35, chief insp., 1936-37, dep. collector, 1937-56; bus. mgr. Jackson Coll., Honolulu, 1954-56, instr., 1955-56; grad. asst. instr., research asst. Ill. Inst. Tech., Chgo., 1959-62; psychologist Monterey County Mental Health Services, Salinas, Calif., 1964-73; ret., 1973. Contbg. author Psychon. Sci., vol. 20, 1970; co-author: The Deadliest Colonel; author, pub.: Jesus Said. Served with U.S. Army, 1922-23, 40-47; col. ret. Decorated Combat Infantryman's Badge, Legion of Merit with 2 oak leaf clusters, Bronze Star medal, Air medal, Purple Heart; named to Military Intelligence Corps Hall of Fame, 1988; recipient Albert Gallatin award U.S. Treas. Dept., 1963, Gen. William J. Donovan award, 1993, Knowlton award Mil. Intelligence Corps, June 1997; Eifler Sports Plaza named in his honor, Ft. Huachuca, Ariz., June 1997. Mem. AAUP, Am. Psychol. Assn., Western States Psychol. Assn., Calif. Psychol. Assn., Res. Officers Assn. (Hawaii pres. 1947), Assn. Former Intelligence Officers (bd. govs., Western coord.), Pearl Harbor Survivors, 101 Assn., Assn. U.S. Army Vets. of OSS (past bd. govs., Western coord., v.p.), Ret. Officers Assn., Masons, KT, Shriners, Elks, Nat. Sojourners, Psi Chi. Home: 22700 Picador Dr Salinas CA 93908-1116

EIGEL, JAMES ANTHONY, environmental engineer; b. St. Louis, Mar. 1, 1939; s. Edwin George and Catherine Margaret (Rohan) E.; m. Carolyn Margaret Sudheimer, June 10, 1972 (div. 1990); 1 child, Christine. BS, St. Louis U., 1961, postgrad. Rsch. chemist Falstaff Brewing Corp., St. Louis, 1965-67; rsch. chemist water divsn. City of St. Louis, 1967-71; rsch. chemist Continental Telephone, Hickory, N.C., 1971-75; mgr. main analysis labs. Hoechst Celanese, Spartanburg, S.C., 1975-85; dir. pretreatment/lab. svcs. Macon-Bibb County (Ga.) Water Authority, 1985-89; mgr. tech. svcs. Pima County Wastewater Mgmt., Tucson, Ariz., 1989—. Contbr. articles to profl. jours. Mem. Am. Chem. Soc., Am. Water Works Assn., Water Environ. Fedn., Lions (pres. 1988-89). Mem. Am. Anglican Ch. Achievements include patent for electrical insulation protector. Office: Pima County Wastewater Mgmt 2600 W Sweetwater Dr Tucson AZ 85705-6915

EIGLER, DONALD MARK, physicist; b. L.A., Mar. 23, 1953; s. Irving Baer and Evelin Muriel (Baker) E.; m. Roslyn Winifred Rubesin, Nov. 2, 1986. BA, U. Calif., San Diego, 1975, PhD in Physics, 1984. Rsch. assoc. U. Köln (Fed. Republic Germany), 1975-76; rsch. assoc. U. Calif., San Diego, 1977-84, postdoctoral rsch. assoc., 1984, assoc. rsch. physicist dept. physics, 1986; postdoctoral mem. tech. staff AT&T Bell Labs., Murray Hill, N.J., 1984-86; rsch. staff mem. IBM, San Jose, Calif., 1986-93, IBM fellow, 1993—; Alexander M. Cruickshank lectr. in phys. sci. (Gordon Rsch. Confs.), 1994. Co-winner 1993-94 Newcomb Cleveland prize AAAS; recipient Dannie Heineman prize Göttingen Acad. Scis., 1995, Outstanding Alumnus award U. Calif. San Diego alumni Assn., 1998. Fellow Am. Phys. Soc. Office: IBM Almaden Rsch Ctr 650 Harry Rd San Jose CA 95120-6099

EIGSTI, ROGER HARRY, insurance company executive; b. Vancouver, Wash., Apr. 17, 1942; s. Harry A. and Alice E. (Huber) E.; m. Mary Lou Nelson, June 8, 1963; children: Gregory, Ann. BS, Linfield Coll., 1964. CPA, Oreg., Wash. Staff CPA Touche Ross and Co., Portland, Oreg., 1964-72; asst. to controller Safeco Corp., Seattle, 1972-78, controller, 1980; controller Safeco Life Ins. Co., Seattle, 1978-80; pres. Safeco Credit Co., Seattle, 1980-81, Safeco Life Ins. Co., Seattle, 1981-85; exec. v.p., CFO Safeco Corp., Seattle, 1985, CEO, chmn. bd. dirs. Ind. Colls. of Wash., Seattle, 1981-87, bus. dir. Seattle Repertory Theatre, 1981—, bd. dirs. 1981—. Mem. Am. Inst. CPA's, Life Office Mgmt. Assn. (bd. dirs. 1983—), Seattle C. of C. (chmn. metro budget rev. com. 1984—). Republican. Clubs: Mercer Island (Wash.) Country (treas., bd. dirs. 1981-84); Central Park Tennis. Home: 1503 Parkside Dr E Seattle WA 98112-3719*

EIKENBERRY, ARTHUR RAYMOND, writer, service executive, researcher; b. Sebring, Fla., June 5, 1920; s. Leroy Albertus and Vernie Cordelia (Griffin) E.; m. Carol Jean Parrott, June 10, 1955; children: Robin Rene, Shari LaVon, Jan Rochelle, Karyn LaRae, Kelli Yvette. Student, Pasadena (Calif.) Jr. Coll., 1939, Kunming U., China, 1944-45. MSgt. Army Air Corps, 1941-45, re-enlisted in grade of TSgt., 1947; advanced through grades to SMSgt. USAF; ret., 1973, mgmt., pers., adminstrv. and security insp.; mgr. property control, real estate agent TR Devel. Co., Englewood, Colo., 1973-74; real estate agt. The Pinery, Parker, Colo., 1974-75; mgr., patient acctg. dept. Univ. Colo. Health Scis. Ctr., Denver, 1975-89. Author: Investment Strategies for the Clever Investor, 1989, LOTTO GURU (Omni-Personal Selection Systems & Strategies), 1989. Charter mem. U.S. Congl. Adv. Bd. Fellow Internat. Biog. Ctr. (hon. life patron, dep. dir. gen.); mem. Am. Biog. Inst. (life, dep. gov., nat. adviser), World Inst. of Achievement (disting.), Masons, Eastern Star, Royal Order of the Amaranth. Address: The Lakes 9901 W Sahara Ave # 2085 Las Vegas NV 89117-1818

EILENBERG, LAWRENCE IRA, theater educator, artistic director; b. Bklyn., May 26, 1947; s. Jerome and Dorothy Vera (Natleson) E.; m. Diane Marie Eliasof, Nov. 25, 1973 (dec. Dec. 1984); children: David Joseph, Benjamin Alan; m. Judith Heiner, Nov. 10, 1990 (dec. Nov. 1994). BA, Cornell U., 1968; MPhil, Yale U., 1971, PhD, 1975. Jr. fellow Davenport

Coll., Yale U., New Haven, 1971-72; asst. prof. theatre dept. Cornell U., Ithaca, N.Y., 1972-75; vis. asst. prof. in theatre U. Mich., Ann Arbor, 1975-77; asst. prof., then assoc. prof. U. Denver, 1977-82, 83; prof. San Francisco State U., 1983—, chmn. theatre arts dept., 1984-92; artistic dir. Magic Theatre, San Francisco, 1992-93, dramaturg, 1997—; theatre corr. Sta. KCFR (NPR), Denver, 1979-82; literary mgr. Denver Ctr. Theatre Co., 1981-83; artistic dir. San Francisco New Vaudeville Festival, 1985-89; dramaturg One Act Theatre Co., San Francisco, 1986-88; bd. dirs. Theatre Bay Area, San Francisco, 1985-90, pres., 1987-89; co-dir. Congress of Clowns, 1994; speaker, lectr. in field. Editor Stage/Space mag., 1981-83; contbr. articles, book and theater revs. to profl. publs. U.S. del. Podium Festival of USSR, Moscow, 1989. Grantee Lilly Found., 1981, Idaho Humanities Assn., 1983, 84, 85, NEA, 1986, 92, Calif. Arts Coun., 1987, 88, 92; recipient Best Broadcast award Colo. Broadcasters Assn., 1982. Mem. Literary Mgrs. and Dramaturgs Am. (v.p. 1989-90), Nat. Assn. Schs. of Theatre (bd. accreditation, 1990-91, evaluator 1986—). Home: 2200 Leavenworth St Apt 606 San Francisco CA 94133-2281 Office: San Francisco State U Theatre Arts Dept 1600 Holloway Ave San Francisco CA 94132-1722

EILERMAN, DARIN LEE, writer; b. Santa Cruz, Calif., Dec. 1, 1962; s. Gregory Ward Eilerman and Christine Arlene (Bleuss) Johnson; m. Margaret Mary Critchlow, Oct. 16, 1989; children: Courie Lynn, Sarah Anna, Elizabeth Marie, Adam Gregory. Fire sci. tech., Spokane Cmty. Coll., Spokane, Wash., 1989, AAS, 1991, AA, 1994. Carpenter Calif., Idaho, Wash., 1980-89; firefighter Spokane County Fire Dept., 1989-92; freelance writer Spokane, 1993—; barometer man weather predictions Critical Date, Spokane, 1995. Author poems. Recipient Editor's Choice award Nat. Lib. of Poetry, 1995, 96. Mem. Internat. Poetry Hall of Fame, Internat. Soc. of Poets (Poet of Merit 1997). Avocations: putting music to poetry, record musical album. Home: PO Box 755 Mead WA 99021-0755

EIMERS, JERI ANNE, therapist; b. Berkeley, Calif., Jan. 20, 1951; d. Alfred D. Wallace and Marjorie E. (Nordheim) Stevens; m. Roy A. Neiman, June 12, 1969 (div. Aug. 1977); children: Lorien, Arwen; m. Richard A. Eimers, Mar. 2, 1996. AA, Palomar Jr. Coll., 1977; BA in Psychology with distinction, Calif. State U., Long Beach, 1979, MA in Psychology with distinction, 1981; postgrad. Human Sexuality Program, UCLA, 1991-92. Lic. marriage, family, child therapist, Calif.; cert. community coll. instr., counselor; cert. sex therapist. Rsch. asst. Calif. State U., 1978-82; tchr. Artesia (Calif.)-Bellflower-Cerritos Unified Sch. Dist., 1982-83; dir. Am. Learning Corp., Huntington Beach, Calif., 1983-85; social worker Los Angeles County Children's Protective Svcs., Long Beach, 1986-88; sr. social worker Orange County Social Svc. Agy., Orange, Calif., 1988-90; therapist Cypress Mental Health, Cypress, Calif., 1988—, cons., 1990—; cons., 1990—; group chair, leader Adults Abused as Children, Los Altos Hosp., Long Beach, 1991—, Coll. Hosp., Cerritos, 1993—; speaker, presenter in field. Mem. Child's Sexual Abuse Network, Orange, 1988—; mem. legis. com. Child Abuse Coun. of Orange County, 1988. Women's League scholar, 1980-81. Mem. AAUW, Am. Assn. Marriage, Family Therapists, Calif. Assn. Marriage, Family Therapists, Am. Profl. Soc. for Abused Children, Calif. Profl. Assn. for Abused Children, Phi Kappa Phi, Psi Chi. Republican. Methodist. Avocations: writing, theater, classical and jazz music, swimming. Office: Huntington Group 9191 Towne Centre Dr Ste 365 San Diego CA 92122-1229

EINSTEIN, CLIFFORD JAY, advertising executive; b. L.A., May 4, 1939; s. Harry and Thelma (Bernstein) E.; m. Madeline Mandel, Jan. 28, 1962; children: Harold Jay, Karen Holly. BA in English, UCLA, 1961. Writer Norman, Craig and Kummel, N.Y.C., 1961-62, Foote, Cone and Belding, L.A., 1962-64; ptnr. Silverman and Einstein, L.A., 1965-67; pres., creative dir. Dailey and Assos., L.A., 1968-93, chmn., CEO, 1994—, also bd dirs.; dir. Campaign '80, advt. agy. Reagan for Pres., 1980; lectr. various colls.; founder, bd. dirs. First Coastal Bank; bd. dirs. The Jewish Cmty. Found. Contbr. articles to Advertising Age; prodr.: (play) Whatever Happened to Georgie Tapps, L.A. and San Francisco, 1980; film appearances include Real Life, Modern Romance, Defending Your Life, Face/Off, 1997; T.V. appearance in Bizarre, Super Dave Show. Bd. dirs. Rape Treatment Ctr., Santa Monica Med. Ctr., Discovery Fund for Eye Rsch.; trustee Mus. Contemporary Art, L.A., 1994—. With U.S. Army, 1957. Recipient Am. Advt. award, 1968, 73, 79, Clio award, 1973, Internat. Broadcast Pub. Svc. award, 1970, 85, Nat. Addy award, 1979, Gov.'s award, 1987; named Creative Dir. of the West, Adweek Poll, 1982, Exec. of West, 1986, Western States Assn. Advt. Agys. Leader of Yr., 1992. Mem. AFTRA, ASCAP, SAG, Dirs. Guild Am., Am. Assn. Advt. Agys. (vice chmn. western region), Hillcrest Country Club, Calif. Club. Office: Dailey & Assocs 8687 Melrose Ave West Hollywood CA 90069-5701

EINSTEIN, STEPHEN JAN, rabbi; b. L.A., Nov. 15, 1945; s. Syd C. and Selma (Rothenberg) E.; m. Robin Susan Kessler, Sept. 9, 1967; children: Rebecca Yael, Jennifer Melissa, Heath Isaac, Zachary Shane. AB, UCLA, 1967; BHL, Hebrew Union Coll., L.A., 1968, DHL, 1995; MAHL, Hebrew Union Coll., Cin., 1971; DD (hon.), Hebrew Union Coll., Los Angeles, 1971. Ordained rabbi. Rabbi Temple Beth Am, Parsippany, N.J., 1971-74; rabbi Temple Beth David, Westminster, Calif., 1974-76, Congregation B'nai Tzedek, Fountain Valley, Calif., 1976—. Co-author: Every Person's Guide to Judaism, 1989; co-editor: Introduction to Judaism, 1983. Pres., trustee Fountain Valley (Calif.) Sch. Bd., 1984-90; chair Personnel Commn. Fountain Valley Sch. Dist., 1991—; chaplain Fountain Valley Police Dept. Honored for Maj. Contributions to Jewish Learning, Orange County (Calif.) Bur. Jewish Edn., 1986; recipient Micah Award for Interfaith Activities, Am. Jewish Com., 1988. Mem. Ctrl. Conf. Am. Rabbis (mem. exec. bd. 1989-91, mem. ethics com. 1993-98), Pacific Assn. Reform Rabbis (mem. exec. bd. 1987-91, 97—), Orange County Bd. Rabbis (pres. 1976-79, 97-98), Jewish Educators Assn. Orange County (pres. 1979-81), Orange County Bur. Jewish Edn. (v.p. 1982-84, 92-94, pres. 1994-97), Am. Cancer Soc. (v.p. West Orange County dist. 1994-98), Phi Beta Kappa. Democrat. Office: Congregation Bnai Tzedek 9669 Talbert Ave Fountain Valley CA 92708

EISELE, ROBERT HENRY, screenwriter, producer, playwright, educator; b. Altadena, Calif., June 9, 1948; s. Lawrence C. and Helen (Klimek) E.; m. Diana G. Ryterband, June 21, 1975; children: Nicholas A., Marissa C. BA cum laude, UCLA, 1971, MFA, 1974. Screenwriter, playwright, Los Angeles, 1975-86; assoc. prof. theater arts Rio Hondo Coll., Whittier, Calif., 1976-86; story editor Crime Story New World TV, Los Angeles, 1986-87; coproducer The Equalizer Universal TV, Los Angeles, 1987-88, supervising producer The Equalizer, 1988-89; writer, producer Warner Bros. TV, 1989-91, Universal Studios, 1991-94, Paramount Studios, 1994-97. Author: (plays) Animals Are Passing From Our Lives, 1974 (Donald Davis Dramatic Writing award 1974), West Coast Plays, vol. 3, 1979, A Dark Night of the Soul, 1979, The Murder of Einstein, 1980, (episodes for TV series) (Cagney and Lacey) Ordinary Hero, 1985 (Humanitas prize Human Family Inst. 1986, Imagen award Hispanic Task Force, NCCJ 1986), Schedule One, 1986, (Crime Story) Torello on Trial, 1987, The Pinnacle, 1987, Ground Zero, 1987, (The Equalizer) Suspicion of Innocence, Shadow Play, The Rehearsal, No Place Like Home, 1987-88, Day of the Covenant, The Visitation, Starfire, Prisoners of Conscience, 1988-89, (pilots) Cain, 1991, Darkman, 1992, (cable TV features) Last Light, 1993 (Showtime, Writers Guild award nominee 1993), Vanishing Son: The Klansman, 1994, Vanishing Son, Dragon Head, 1994, Vanishing Son: Ancestors, 1994, Lily in Winter, 1995 (Writers Guild award nominee 1995, PEN Literary award nominee 1996); also poems and short stories; exec. producer The Osiris Chronicles, 1996. Recipient Samuel Goldwyn Writing award, 1973; Oscar Hammerstein Playwriting fellow, 1974, Am. Conservatory Theatre fellow, 1975-76. Mem. Writers Guild Am. West, Dramatists Guild, Screen Actors Guild, Actors Equity Assn. Democrat. Avocations: martial arts, skiing, fishing, back-packing. Office: care Bruce Vinokour CAA 9830 Wilshire Blvd Beverly Hills CA 90212-1804

EISELE, VIRGINIA A., public accountant, investment professional; b. Bklyn., Apr. 13, 1940; d. Gustav Edward and Ruth Naomi (Wilkinson) Leistman; m. Armindo Lourenco, Aug. 5, 1968 (div. 1974); 1 child David K.; m. Gilbert Wayne Eisele, Apr. 16, 1978. Student, Antioch Coll., Yellow [illegible] Acctg., Met. State Coll., Denver, 1980. Cert. Accredit Coun. for Acctg. and Taxation. Acct., ptnr. Bloch, Eisele & Assocs., Denver, 1987-90; acct., owner G. Eisele Acctg., Denver, 1980-87, G. Eisele & Assocs., Northglenn, Colo., 1990—. Bd. dirs. Sharing and Caring Ministries, Denver, 1993—, Mem. Pub. Accts. Soc., Bus. Connections (treas. 1998—), Bus. Network Internat. (pres. 1997-98), Met. North Chamber Networking (pres. 1997). Avocations: gardening, swimming. Office: G Eisele & Assoc Inc 1412 W 104th Ave Ste 120 Northglenn CO 80234-3737

EISENBARTH, GEORGE STEPHEN, pediatrics educator; b. Brooklyn, Sept. 17, 1947; 1 child, Stephanie. BA, Columbia U., 1969; PhD, Duke U., 1974, MD, 1975. Diplomate Am. Bd. Internal Medicine, endocrinology and metabolism. Asst. prof. medicine and physiology Duke U., Durham, N.C., 1979-82; assoc. prof. medicine Harvard U., Boston, 1982-92; exec. dir. Joslin Diabetes Ctr., Bostong, 1992—, Barbara Davis Ctr. Childhood Diabetes, Denver, 1992—; prof. pediatrics, medicine and immunology U. Colo., Denver, 1992—; cons. Quest/Nichols, Calif., 1995—. Editor: Concerning Immunology; contbr. articles to profl. jours. Recipient David Rumbaugh award Juvenile Diabetes Found., 1997, Weitzman Meml. award Endocrine Soc., 1984, Don Silver Excellence Rsch. award Juvenile Diabetes Found., 1988. Mem. Am. Diabetes Assn. (chair rsch. com. 1987), Am. Assn. Physicians, Immunology Diabetes Soc. (past pres. 1990). Avocations: hiking, horseback riding. Office: U Colo Barbara Davis Ctr 4200 E 9th Ave # Denver CO 80220-3706

EISENBERG, JONATHAN MICHAEL, lawyer; b. Bklyn., May 8, 1970; s. Meyer and Elaine Marcia (Rabbiner) E. AB, Stanford U., 1992; JD, U. Calif., Berkeley, 1996. Bar: Calif. 1996. Rsch. assoc. Bus. Enterprise Trust, Palo Alto, Calif., 1992-93; assoc. Jackson, Tufts, Cole & Black LLP, San Jose, Calif., 1996-98; jud. clk. to Hon. Linda McLaughlin U.S. Dist. Ct. (cen. dist. Calif.), Santa Ana, 1998-99. Mem. ABA, Santa Clara County Bar Assn., Assn. Bus. Trial Lawyers. Democrat. Jewish. Home: 19221 Delaware St Apt 13 Huntington Beach CA 92648-2357 Office: Chambers of US Judge Linda McLaughlin US Dist Ct 751 W Santa Ana Blvd Santa Ana CA 92701-4509

EISENHAUER, DAVID THOMAS, journalist; b. Laramie, Wyo., Dec. 24, 1960; s. Thomas D. and Mary A. Eisenhauer; m. Marlene A. Tromp, Dec. 31, 1992. BA in Journalism, U. Wyo., 1991. Editor Bradford County Telegraph, Starke, Fla., 1991-94; adviser, instr. journalism U. Wyo., Laramie, 1994-97; state news editor Casper (Wyo.) Star-Tribune, 1997—. Editor, writer (mag.) Vista, 1997; contbr. (literary mag.) No. Lights, 1996. Recipient 3rd place in editl. writing and design Fla. Press Assn., 1993; Kiplinger fellow Ohio State U., Columbus, 1998. Mem. Soc. Environ. Journalists, Collegiate Media Advisers, Wyo. Press Assn. Democrat. Avocations: writing, mountain biking, running, guitar music. Office: Casper Star-Tribune 170 Star Ln Casper WY 82604-2883

EISENMAN, ATHENA JOYCE, association administrator; b. Birmingham, Ala., July 3, 1948; d. George Frank and Lillian (Crawford) Taylor; m. Alva George Eisenman, Mar. 24, 1973; children: Aaron, Adrianne. BA in Comm., Met. State Coll., Denver, 1975; MA in Orgnl. Mgmt., U. Phoenix, 1994. Social scis. instr. C.C. of Denver, 1977; pub. rels. dir. Denver Walking Tours, 1977-78; legis. aide and analyst Hon. Wm. R. Roberts, Denver City Coun., 1978-79; mem. telemktg./sales staff MCI, Denver, 1980-81; mgmt. cons. AJE Consulting Group, Denver, 1983-96; exec. dir. Colo. Sickle Cell Assn., Denver, 1995—; bd. dirs., comm. chair Speakers Bureau Tng., Nat. Voluntary Health Agencies, Denver, 1995—. Bd. dirs., sec. Adult Care Mgmt. Inc., Denver, 1993-96; pres. Montbello United Neighbors, Denver, 1993-95; mem. black edn. adv. coun. Denver Pub. Schs., 1992-95; adult edn. instr. All Nations GED Ctr., Aurora, Colo., 1996—; del. Nat. Rep. Conv., 1st Congl., Denver, 1996; named to Rep. Leadership Program, Colo. State Reps., Denver, 1989-90. Mem. Metro Denver Black Rep. Forum (bd. dirs. 1995—, pres. 1996—), Colo. Lincoln Club, Colo. H.S. Assn. (forensic judge), Nat. Forensic League (forensic judge). Republican. Avocations: fly fishing, skiing, reading. Home: 5180 Deephaven Ct Denver CO 80239-4136 Office: Colo Sickel Cell Assn Inc 4280 Hale Pkwy Denver CO 80220-3724

EISLER, DAVID L., provost; m. Patricia Johnson; children: Heather, Lindsay. BM, Univ. Mich.; MM, Yale Univ.; DMA, Univ. Mich. Coord. instrumental music Troy State, 1978-90, exec. dir. southeast band clinic, 1979-90, dir., grad. studies, 1980-90, asst. dean. of fine arts, 1982-90; dean. coll. fine arts Eastern New Mex., 1990-96; provost Weber State Univ., Ogden, Utah, 1996—; chair Fine Arts Coun., 1990-96, Univ. Comm. on Instrumental Evaluation, 1987-90, NCATE review, 1980-82. Contbr. articles to profl. jours. Concertmaster Clovis Cmty. Band.; judge Nat. Assn. Media Edn.; founding mem. High Plains Art Coun., exec.bd. Conquistador Coun., Boy Scouts Am. Named Vol. of Yr. Cmty. Svcs. Ctr., 1993-94. Mem. Ala. Music. Edn. Assn., Am. Assn. Higher Edn., Nat. Band Assn., Internat. Clarinet Soc., Coll. Band Dirs. Nat. Assn., Phi Kappa Lambda. Office: Weber State Univ 1004 University Cir Ogden UT 84408-1004

EISNER, MICHAEL DAMMANN, entertainment company executive; b. Mt. Kisco, N.Y., Mar. 7, 1942; s. Lester and Margaret (Dammann) E.; m. Jane Breckenridge; children: Breck, Eric, Anders. BA, Denison U., 1964. Began career in programming dept. CBS; asst. to nat. programming dir. ABC, 1966-68, mgr. spls. and talent, dir. program devel.-East Coast, 1968-71, v.p. daytime programming, 1971-75, v.p. program planning and devel., 1975-76, sr. v.p. prime time prodn. and devel., 1976; pres., chief operating officer Paramount Pictures, 1976-84; chmn., chief exec. officer Walt Disney Co., Burbank, Calif., 1984—; governor Mighty Ducks of Anaheim, 1993. Trustee Denison U., Calif. Inst. Arts; bd. dirs. Am. Hosp. of Paris Found., Conservation Internat., UCLA Exec. Bd. for Med. Sci. Office: Walt Disney Co 500 S Buena Vista St Burbank CA 91521-0004

EISSMANN, WALTER JAMES, consulting company executive; b. Newark, N.J., Apr. 20, 1939; s. Walter Curt Eissmann and Alice Delice (Irving) Clark; m. Dorothea Ann Donaldson, June 1, 1963; children: Patricia Helene Ridenhour, Walter William. B.S. in Indsl. Engring., Rutgers U., 1962. Account mgr. Gen. Electric, Engelwood Cliffs, N.J., 1962-67; regional sales mgr. Tymshare, Engelwood Cliffs, 1968-71, Buffalo, N.Y., 1971-73, Washington, 1973-74, v.p. mktg. service div., Cupertino, Calif., 1974-79, div. v.p., Cupertino, 1980-84; sr. v.p. McDonnell Douglas Corp., Cupertino, 1984-86; gen. ptnr. Archer Assocs., 1985-92; pres., chmn. bd. Walter J. Eissmann, Inc., La Quinta, Calif., 1989—; bd. dirs. NSF Corp., Nutri/System Franchisee Corp., 1986-90; chmn. bd. Businesswise, Inc., 1992-93; mng. gen. ptnr. Grand Tyme Partnership, 1992—. Bd. dirs. Saratoga Little League, Calif., 1976-81, Saratoga Boosters, 1981-84; active Vienna Theatre Players, Va., 1973; mem. Church Men's Choir, Saratoga, 1980-82. Named to President's Club Tymshare, Golden Circle, Nutri/System Master of the Keys. Mem. Pi Tau Sigma. Republican.

EIZENBERG, JULIE, architect. BArch, U. Melbourne, Australia, 1978; MArch II, UCLA, 1981. Lic. architect, Calif., reg. architect, Australia. Principal, architect Koning Eizenberg Architecture, Santa Monica, Calif., 1981—; instr. various courses UCLA, MIT, Harvard U.; lectr. in field; jury member P/A awards. Exhbns. incl. Koning Eizenberg Architecture 3A Garage, San Francisco, 1996, "House Rules" Wexner Ctr., 1994, "The Architect's Dream: Houses for the Next Millenium" The Contemporary Arts Ctr., 1993, "Angels & Franciscans" Gagosian Gallery, 1992, Santa Monica Mus. Art, 1993, "Broadening the Discourse" Calif. Women in Environmental Design, 1992, "Conceptional Drawings by Architects" Bannatyne Gallery, 1991, Exhbn. Koning Eizenberg Projects Grad. Sch. Architecture & Urban Planning UCLA, 1990; prin. works include Digital Domain Renovation and Screening Room, Santa Monica, Lightstorm Entertainment Office Renovation and Screening Room, Santa Monica, Gilmore Bank Addition and Remodel, L.A., 1548-1550 Studios, Santa Monica, (with RTA) Materials Rsch. Lab. at U. Calif., Santa Barbara, Ken Edwards Ctr. Cmty. Svcs., Santa Monica, Peck Park Cmty. Ctr. Gymnasium, San Pedro, Calif., Sepulveda Recreation Ctr., L.A. (Design award AIA San Fernando Valley 1995, Nat. Concrete and Masonry award 1996, AIA Calif. Coun. Honor award 1996, L.A. Bus. Coun. Beautification award 1996, AIA Los Angeles Chpt. Merit Award, 1997), PS # 1 Elem. Sch., Santa Monica, Farmers Market, L.A. Additions and Master Plan (Westside Urban Forum prize 1991), Stage Deli, L.A., Simone Hotel, L.A. (Nat. Honor award AIA 1994), Boyd Hotel, L.A., Cmty. Corp. Santa Monica Housing Projects, 5th St. Family Housing, Santa Monica, St. John's Hosp. Replacement Housing Program, Santa Monica, Liffman Ho., Santa Monica, (with Glenn Erikson) Electric Artblock, Venice (Beautification award L.A. Bus. Coun. 1993), 6th St. Condominiums, Santa Monica, Hollywood Duplex, Hollywood Hills (Record Houses Archtl. Record 1988), California Ave. Duplex, Santa Monica, Tarzana Ho. (Award of Merit L.A. chpt. AIA 1992, AIA Calif. Coun. Merit Award, 1998, Sunset Western home Awards citation 1993-94), 909 Ho., Santa Monica (Award of Merit L.A. chpt. AIA 1991), 31st St. Ho., Santa Monica (Honor award AIACC 1994, Nat. AIA Honor award 1996), others. Recipient 1st award Progressive Architecture, 1987; named one of Domino's Top 30 Architects, 1989. Mem. L.A. County Mus. Art, Westside Urban Forum, Urban Land Inst., Architects and Designers for Social Responsibility, Mus. Contemporary Art, The Nature Conservancy, Sierra Club. Office: Koning Eizenberg Architecture 1548 18th St Santa Monica CA 90404-3404

EKLUND, CARL ANDREW, lawyer; b. Denver, Aug. 12, 1943; s. John M. and Zara (Zerbst) E.; m. Nancy Jane Griggs, Sept. 7, 1968; children: Kristin, Jessica, Peter. BA, U. Colo., 1967, JD, 1971. Bar: Colo. 1971, U.S. Dist. Ct. Colo. 1971, U.S. Ct. Appeals (9th cir.) 1975, U.S. Ct. Appeals (10th cir.) 1978, U.S. Supreme Ct. 1978. Dep. dist. atty. Denver Dist. Attys. Office, 1971-73; ptnr. DiManna, Eklund, Ciancio & Jackson, Denver, 1975-81, Smart, DeFurio, Brooks & Eklund, Denver, 1982-84, Roath & Brega, P.C., Denver, 1984-88, Faegre & Benson, Denver, 1988-94, LeBoeuf, Lamb, Greene & MacRae L.L.P., Denver, 1994—; local rules com. Bankruptcy Ct. D.C., 1979-80; reporter Nat. Bankruptcy Conf., 1981-82; lectr. ann. spring meeting Am. Bankruptcy Inst., Rocky Mountain Bankruptcy Conf., Continuing Legal Edn. Colo., Inc., Colo. Practice Inst., Colo. Bar Assn., Nat. Ctr. Continuing Legal Edn., Inc., Profl. Edn. Systems, Inc., Comml. Law Inst. Am., Law Edn. Inst., Inc., Bur. Nat. Affairs, Inc., Practising Law Inst., So. Meth. U. Sch. Law, Continuing Edn. Svcs., Lorman Bus. Ctr., Inc. Author: The Probelm With Creditors' Committees in Chapter 11: How to Manage the Inherent Conflicts Without Loss of Function, 1997; contbg. author: Collier's Bankruptcy Practice Guide, Representing Debtors in Bankruptcy, Letters Formbook and Legal Opinion, Advanced Chapter 11 Bankruptcy Practice, Wiley Law Pubs.; mem. adv. bd. ABI Law Rev., 1993—. Fellow Am. Coll. Bankruptcy; mem. ABA (bus. law and corp. banking sect. 1977—, bus. bankruptcy com. 1982—, subcom. on rules 1981—), Colo. Bar Assn. (bd. govs. 1980-82, corp. banking and bus. law sect. 1977—, ethics com. 1981-82, subcom. bankruptcy cts.), Am. Bankruptcy Inst. (dir. SW Bankruptcy Conf., Rocky Mountain Bankruptcy Conf.), Denver Bar Assn. (trustee 1983-86). Office: LeBoeuf Lamb Greene & MacRae LLP 633 17th St Ste 2000 Denver CO 80202-3620

EKONG, RUTH J., nursing administrator, author; b. St. Thomas, V.I.; d. Rufus and Ruby (Maduro) Norman; m. Eno A. Ekong. Commr. spl. edn., nurse cons., dir. nurses, nurse gerontology specialist; ethnic food cons.; developer Tantie Ruth Corp. Developer Original African Salad Dressings, Tantie Ruth Foods, Uzimi cooking, Serengeti Sauce and Dressing, (TV show) Tantie Ruth.

ELAINE, KAREN, musician, educator; b. San Jose, Calif., Nov. 6, 1965; d. Gaston Ortega and Alice Lee (Ray) Sanders, III; m. John Bakunin, Dec. 21, 1998. Diploma in music, Curtis Inst. of Music, Phila., 1987; studies with Karen Tuttle, Michael Tree, Curtis Inst. Music, 1987; studies with Louis Kievman, L.A., 1988-90; MA in Music, UCSD, 1998; studies with Jann Pasler, George Lewis, Bertram Turetzky. Solo viola New Am. Chamber Orch., Detroit, 1986-87; prin. viola San Diego Symphony Orch., 1987-90; string specialist Sch. Creative & Performing Arts, San Diego, 1987-90; pvt. instr. Studio of Karen Elaine, San Diego, 1987—; viola prof. Chanterelle Music Festival, Pouidoux, Switzerland, 1989—; violin and viola prof. Utah Chamber Music Festival, 1994—; solo and prin. viola Sun Valley Summer Symphony, 1991—; viola sect. Hollywood Film and Record Industry, 1993—; asst. prin., solo viola Pro Musica Chamber Orch., Santa Fe, 1994—; vol. lectr., recitalist spl. edn. dept. Morse H.S., 1987—; adj. prof. viola San Diego State U., 1989—; featured on TV program Reflections in Music, San Diego, El Cajon, Calif., 1990; solo viola Delos Internat. Records, Paraiba Symphony Orch., Brazil, 1988, Laurel Records, London Symphony Orch., 1990, Harmonia Mundi, City of London Sinfonia, 1990; guest soloist and lectr. 19th and 25th Internat. Viola Congress, 1991, 97, solo recitalist throughout U.S.; guest speaker Sta. KFSD-FM, Sta. KPBS-FM; solo concert tour under sponsorship of Australian Broadcast Co. and Australian Arts Coun., 1994. Commissions include Concert Piece for Viola and Orch., David Baker, 1989, Cinnabar Concerto for Viola and Strings, David Ward-Steinman, 1991, Concerto for Viola and Orch., Gordon Kerry, 1993, Hetep: Tranquility #2, Ismail Wadada Leo Smith, Li'l Phrygian Rondo for Karen, Katrina Wreede, 1992; contbg. writer to The Lyre that Sings Truth: Classics in Opera; contbr. articles to Jour. of Internat. Viola Soc. Donor World Wildlife Fund, Washington, 1989—. Recipient 1st Pl. award Bruno Giurana Internat. Viola Competition, Brazil, 1988; winner numerous solo competitions Musical Merit of San Diego, 1988, 89, Rio Hondo Symphony Young Artists' Solo Competition, 1989, S.E. L.A. Young Artists Solo Competition, 1990, Nat. Assn. Negro Musicians Young Artists Solo Competition, 1992. Mem. Am. Viola Soc., Rec. Musicians Assn., Musicians Union Locals 325 (San Diego) and 47 (L.A.). Democrat. Avocations: reading, jogging, swimming, sewing, SCUBA diving (cert. PADI rescue diver). Home: 208 Welling Way San Diego CA 92114-5947

ELAM, JASON, football player; b. Ft. Walton Beach, Fla., Mar. 8, 1970. Kicker Denver Broncos. Office: Denver Broncos 13655 Broncos Pkwy Englewood CO 80112-4150

ELBAUM, JONATHAN MARTIN, performing arts director; b. Kokomo, Ind., Aug. 8, 1958; s. Jerome Kenneth Elbaum and Adele (Daab) Fox; m. Julia Lee Agnew, Aug. 24, 1991; children: Emma Rose, Lily Augusta. BA in Econs., Grinnell Coll., 1980; MBA in Finance, U. Colo., 1988. Cert. event planner. Chef Johnson & Koenig, Iowa City, Iowa, 1980-82; gen. mgr. Stouffer Restaurants, Chgo., Denver, 1982-85, Le Peep Inc., Denver, 1985-86; musician Denver, 1986-89; pres. Samphire Corp., Denver, 1989-91; dir. bldg. svcs. Denver Ctr. Performing Arts, Denver, 1991—. Composer (songs) Cowboy Song, 1986, Things Arent What They, 1987, 2 Golden Girls, 1997. Vol. Iowa Pub. Interest Rsch. Group, Grinnell, Iowa, 1978-79, Colo. Council Arts, Denver, 1998. Mem. Internat. Soc. Meeting Planners, Internat. Festival Events Assn., Denver Art Mus., Denver Mus. Natural History. Avocations: music, skiing, tennis, hiking, reading. Home: 28031 Camel Heights Cir Evergreen CO 80439-7334 Office: Denver Ctr for Performing Arts 1245 Champa St Denver CO 80204-2104

ELECCION, MARCELINO, security executive, computer consultant, music consultant, educator; b. N.Y.C., Aug. 22, 1936; s. Marcelino G. and Margaret J. (Krcha) E.; m. Marcia L. Smith, June 6, 1962; 1 child, Mark Eaton; m. Naomi E. Kor, Jan. 5, 1978; 1 child, Jordan Kai. BA, NYU, 1961; postgrad. Courant Inst. Math. Scis., 1962-64; AS, Coll. San Mateo, 1988; postgrad. San Jose State U., 1988-91. Electromech. draftsman Coll. Engring., NYU, Bronx, 1954-57, chief designer dept. elec. engring., 1957-60, tech. editor lab. for electrosci. research, 1960-62, editor publs. Sch. Engring. and Scis., 1962-67; asst. editor IEEE Spectrum, N.Y.C., 1967-69, assoc. editor, 1969-70, staff writer, 1970-76, contbg. editor, 1976—; dir. adminstrn. Internat. Bur. Protection and Investigation, Ltd., N.Y.C., 1976-78; account exec. Paul Purdom & Co., pub. relations, San Francisco, 1978-81, creative dir., 1981-83; dir. mktg. communications Am. Info. Systems, Palo Alto, 1983-85; dir. engring. Tech. Cons., Palo Alto, 1986—; cons. tech. artist, 1953—; music orchestration cons., 1956-70; cons. Ency. Britannica, 1969-70, Time-Life Books, 1973; spl. guest lectr. Napa Coll., 1979—. Aux. police officer, N.Y.C. Police Dept., 1964-70, aux. sgt., 1970-73, aux. lt., 1973-76, aux. capt., 1976-78. Recipient Mayor's commendation award N.Y.C., 1971. Mem. IEEE (sr.), N.Y. Acad. Scis., Am. Math. Soc., AAAS, Optical Soc. Am., Smithsonian Assocs., Am. Numis. Assn., Nat. Geog. Soc., U.S. Judo Fedn., Athletic Congress, AAU. Fedn. Home: 3790 El Camino Real # 2004 Palo Alto CA 94306-3314

ELGIN, GITA, psychologist; b. Santiago, Chile; came to U.S., 1968, naturalized 1987; d. Serafín and Regina (Urízar) Elguin; BS in biology summa cum laude, U. Chile, Santiago, DPs, 1964; PhD in Counseling Psychology, U. Calif., Berkeley, 1976; m. Bart Bödy, Oct. 23, 1971; children: Dio Christopher Karoly, Alma Ilona Raia Julia. Clin. psychologist Barros Luco-Trudeau Gen. Hosp., Santiago, 1964-65; co-founder, co-dir. Lab. for Parapsychol. Rsch., Psychiat. Clinic, U. Chile, Santiago, 1965-68; rsch. fellow Found. Rsch. on Nature of Man, Durham, N.C., 1968; rschr. psychol. [illegible]

holistic method of psychotherapy Psychotherapy for a Crowd of One, 1978; co-founder, clin. dir. Holistic Health Assos., Oakland, Calif., 1979—, Montclair Mediation Group, Oakland, 1994; lectr. holistic health Piedmont (Calif.) Adult Sch., 1979-80; hostess Holistic Perspective, Sta. KALW-FM, Nat. Public Radio, 1980; co-creator Holistic Renewal, The Elgin Process of Creative Self Mastery. Author: (video documentary) Taking the Risk: Sharing the Trauma of Sexual & Ritualistic Abuse in Group Therapy, 1992. Lic. psychologist, Chile, Calif. Chancellor's Patent Fund grantee U. Calif., 1976, NIMH fellow, 1976. Mem. APA, Am. Holistic Psychol. Assn. (founder 1995—), Holistic Village (pres., co-founder 1997), Alameda County Psychol. Assn., Calif. State Psychol. Assn., Montclair Health Profls. Assn. (co-founder, pres. 1983-85), Sierra Club, U. Calif. Alumni Assn. Contbr. articles in clin. psychology and holistic health to profl. jours. and local periodicals. Presenter Whole Life Expo, 1986. Office: Montclair Profl Bldg 2080 Mountain Blvd Ste 203 Oakland CA 94611-2829

ELGIN, RON ALAN, advertising executive; b. Milw., Sept. 15, 1941; s. Carl John and Vivian Elaine (Phillips) E.; m. Bonnie Kay Visintainer, Dec. 3, 1968; 1 child, Alison. BA in Advt., U. Wash., 1965. With Cole & Weber, Seattle, 1965-81; pres. Elgin Syferd, Seattle, 1981-89; chmn. Elgin Syferd/Drake, Boise, Idaho, 1987—; pres., CEO Elgin DDB, 1989—; pres. DDB Needham Retail, 1990-93; chmn. Hornall Anderson Design Works, Seattle, 1982-91; ptnr. Christiansen & Fritsch Direct, Seattle, 1988-96; bd. dirs. Hart Crowser. Bd. dirs. Ronald McDonald House, Seattle, 1984—, Big Bros., Seattle, 1986—, Spl. Olympics, Seattle, 1987-90, Pacific N.W. Ballet, Seattle, 1988-98, Poncho, Seattle, 1991—, Odyssey, 1993-99, Swedish Hosp., 1995—; mem. adv. bd. U. Wash., Wash. State U. Lt. U.S. Army, 1965-69. Mem. Am. Assn. Advt. Agencies, Am. Mktg. Assn., Mktg. Comm. Execs. Internat. Office: Elgin DDB 1008 Western Ave Seattle WA 98104-1032

ELIAS, CHARLES DAVID, psychotherapist; b. Detroit, Sept. 3, 1941; s. Charles James and Bessie Sarah (Thomas) E. BA in Psychology, Wayne State U., 1962; MSW, U. Mich., 1965; PhD in Psychotherapy, Internat. Coll., Transactional Analysis Inst., 1972. Lic. clin. social worker, Calif., Mich.; ordained to ministry Universal Life Ch., 1970. Staff counselor Foster Home Svc., Detroit, 1962-63; intern Neighborhood Svc. Orgn., Detroit, 1963-64, Jewish Family & Children Svcs., Detroit, 1964-65; clinician Jewish Family & Children Svcs., Chgo., 1965-67; co-dir. in-patient unit and outpatient svcs. Forest Hosp., Des Plaines, Ill., 1967-69; pvt. practice psychotherapy, cons., tchr. San Francisco and L.A., 1969-72; pvt. practice psychotherapy N.Y.C., Westport, Conn., Ann Arbor, Mich., 1972-79, San Francisco County, Marin County, Calif., Plymouth, Mich., 1979—; cons., tchr. orgns. including Haight/Ashbury Drug Abuse Clinic, U.S. Army Letterman Hosp., Walden Ho., Renaissance Ho. West and Milestones Drug Treatment Ctrs., Early Learning Ctr., Synectics, Inc., Cambridge, Mass., Market Pl. Pubs., San Francisco and Bay Area County Probation Depts., U.S. Probation Dept., San Francisco, Five Tigers Martial/Healing Arts; leader workshops in field, 1970-97. Bd. dirs. Paul D. Pickens II Found., 1994—; leader workshop for underground movement facilitating polit. and social evolution, Chgo., 1966-68. Recipient Appreciation and Recognition award VA Hosp., San Francisco, 1972. Mem. NASW, Internat. Transactional Analysis Assn. (clin.). Avocations: cooking, cactus cultivation, interior design, film, massage. Fax: 415-485-0239. Office: 2269 Chestnut St Ste 305 San Francisco CA 94123-2600

ELIAS, PATRICIA JOAN MILLER, research psychologist; b. Wis., Sept. 14, 1929; d. Rollin Francis and Rosetta Ellen (Ellsworth) Miller; m. Albert Elias, Oct. 16, 1954; children: Caprice Catherine. BA, U. Calif., Berkeley, 1951, MA, 1969, PhD, 1973. Project mgr. Ednl. Testing Svc., profl. assoc., dir. rsch., dir. spl. program devel.; program dir. Calif. Assessment Program, Ednl. Testing Svc., dir. writing assessment, rsch. scientist. Writer, artist. Area coordinator Am. Cancer Soc.; dir. Berkeley Mental Health fund raising. NIMH fellow. Mem. Am. Edn. Research Assn., Am. Psychol. Assn., Calif. Assn. Sch. Psychologists (chair legis. com.). Liberal Democrat. Home: 820 San Luis Rd Berkeley CA 94707-2053 Office: 1947 Center St Berkeley CA 94704-1155

ELIASON, LESLIE CAROL, comparative public policy educator; b. Portland, Oreg., Aug. 12, 1959; d. William Alexander and Nancy Carol (Kirchner) E. BA with distinction, U. Va., 1981; MA, Stanford U., 1985, PhD, 1988. Asst. prof. Scandinavian studies U. Wash., Seattle, 1988-92, asst. prof. Pub. Affairs, 1992—; lectr. U.S. Fulbright Found., Aarhus, Denmark, 1990; term mem. Coun. Fgn. Rels., 1994—. Contbr. articles to profl. publs. Coord. Hubert H. Humphrey fellowship program, U. Wash., 1993-96, mem. grad. sch. coun., 1993-96. Swedish Inst. grantee, 1989. Mem. Assn. Pub. Policy and Mgmt., Am. Polit. Sci. Assn., Western Polit. Sci. Assn., Soc. for Advancement of Scandinavian Studies (co-editor women's caucus newsletter 1989-92, adv. com. 1993-97), European Cmty. Studies Assn. Office: U Wash Grad Sch Pub Affairs PO Box 353055 Seattle WA 98195-3055

ELIKANN, LAWRENCE S. (LARRY ELIKANN), television and film director; b. N.Y.C., July 4, 1923; s. Harry and Sadye (Trause) E.; m. Corinne Schuman; Dec. 6, 1947; children—JoAnne Jarrin, Jill Barad. B.A., Bklyn. Coll., 1943; E.E., Walter Harvey Coll., 1948. Tech. dir. NBC-TV, N.Y.C., 1948-64; comml. dir. VPI-TV, N.Y.C., 1964-66, Filmex-TV, N.Y.C., 1966-68, Plus two TV, N.Y.C., 1968-70. Dir. mini-series Last Flight Out, The Great L.A. Earthquake, The Big One, The Inconvenient Woman, Fever, Story Lady, One Against the Wind, Bonds of Love, I Know My First Name is Steven, Hands of a Stranger, Kiss of a Killer, God Bless the Child, Out of Darkness, Menendez—A Killing in Beverly Hills, Tecumseh—The Last Warrior, A Mother's Prayer, Blue River, "Unexpected Family", Lies He Told. Mem. Mus. Contemporary Art of L.A., L.A. County Mus.; mem. rsch. coun. Scripps Clinic and Rsch. Found. With Signal Corps, U.S. Army, 1943-46. Recipient Emmy award, 1978-79, 89, Golden Globe award, 1989, 91, 94, Christopher award 1973-76, 77, 78-79, 91, Chgo. Internat. Film Festival award 1977, Internat. Film and TV Festival of N.Y. award, 1977, Dir. of Yr. award Am. Ctrs. for Children, 1978; Humanitas prize, 1988, 94, 96. Mem. NATAS (gov. 1961-63), Dirs. Guild Am., Am. film Inst., Nat. Hist. Preservation Soc., Smithsonian Inst., Scripps Inst. (bd. dirs.), Acad. TV Arts and Scis.

ELINSON, HENRY DAVID, artist, language educator; b. Leningrad, USSR, Dec. 14, 1935; came to U.S., 1973; s. David Moses and Fraida Zelma (Ufa) E.; m. Ludmila Nicholas Tepina, Oct. 7, 1955; 1 child, Maria Henry. Student, Herzen State Pedagogical U., Leningrad, 1954-57; BA, Pedagogical Inst., Novgorod, USSR, 1958; MA, Pedagogical Inst., Moscow, 1963. Cert. educator. Spl. edn. tchr. Leningrad Sch. Spl. Edn., 1961-64; supr. dept. speech therapy Psychoneurological Dispensary, Leningrad, 1964-73; instr. Russian lang. Yale U., New Haven, Conn., 1975-76, Def. Lang. Inst., Presidio of Monterey, Calif., 1976-94. One-man shows include The Light and Motion Transmutation Galleries, N.Y.C., 1974, Thor Gallery, Louisville, 1974, Monterey (Calif.) Peninsula Art Mus., 1977, U. Calif. Nelson Gallery, Davis, 1978, Nahamkin Gallery, N.Y.C., 1978, Nahamkin Fine Arts, N.Y.C., 1980, Gallery Paule Anglim, 1981, 85, 87, Gallery Paule Anglim, San Francisco, 1991, 93, 96, Dostoevsky's Mus., St. Petersburg, Russia, 1992, Mus. Art Santa Cruz, Calif., 1994, Duke U. Mus. Art, 1996, Mead Art Mus, 1998; exhibited in group shows at Bklyn. Coll. Art Ctr., 1974, CUNY, 1974, Galleria II Punto, Genoa, Italy, 1975, New Art From the Soviet Union, Washington, 1977, Gallery Hardy, Paris, 1978, Mus. of Fine Art, San Francisco, 1979, Santa Cruz Mus. Fine Arts, 1994, V. Morlan Gallery Transylvania U., Lexington, Ky., 1995, numerous others; represented in permanent collections Mus. Fine Arts, San Francisco, Yale U. Art Gallery, Monterey Mus. Art, U. Calif. Art Mus., Berkeley, Bochum Mus., Germany, Check Point Charlie Mus., Berlin, State Russian Mus., Leningrad, Zimmerly Art Mus., Rutgers U., N.J., Duke U Mus. Art, 1996, Mead Art Mus., 1998. Mem. Underground Anti-Soviet Govt. Students' Orgn., 1957. Recipient Gold medal Art Achievement City of Milan, 1975. Avocations: travel, writing essays and short stories. Home: 997 Benito Ct Pacific Grove CA 93950-5333

ELIOT, THEODORE LYMAN, JR., international consultant; b. N.Y.C., Apr. 14, 1951; m. Patricia F. Peters. B.A., Harvard U., 1948, M.P.A., 1956; LL.D., U. Nebr., Omaha, 1975. With U.S. Fgn. Svc., 1949-78; spl. asst. to under sec. of state, to sec. treasury; country dir. for Iran Dept. State; exec. sec. State Dept.; also spl. asst. to sec. of state Dept. State; ambassador to Afghanistan; insp. gen. Dept. State., Washington; dean Fletcher Sch. Law and Diplomacy, Tufts U., 1979-85; exec. dir. Ctr. for Asian Pacific Affairs Asia Found., San Francisco, 1985-87; bd. dirs. Neurobiol. Tech., Fiberstars, Cornell Lab. of Ornithology. Trustee Asia Found. Mem. Am. Acad. Diplomacy, Univ. Club (San Francisco).

ELKINGTON, SANDRA LOUISE, writer; b. San Francisco, Dec. 3, 1944; d. Leon Stanton and Alice Kathryn (Begert) Erickson; m. William Brice Elkinton, Oct. 17, 1987 (dec. Nov. 1995); children: Jamie, Mark, Tammy Caudy. Grad. in secretarial sci., U. Alaska, Anchorage, 1970. Trapper, dogsledder, legal sec., Chulitha and Eagle, Alaska, 1963-77; adminstrv. asst. BP Petroleum Co., Anchorage, 1977-85; disc jockey, comml. writer, broadcaster Wta. KBYR, Anchorage, 1987-91; sec., loan processor FNBA, Anchorage, 1985-92; freelance and mag. writer, Quito, Ecuador, 1993-96, Tucson, 1995—. Author: This Distant Land, 1985, Caverns of Ecuador, 1994, Trapped, 1995, Pedro in Ecuador, 1998. Avocations: hiking, travel, tennis, bridge. Home: 9950 N Stratton Saddle Trl Tucson AZ 85742-8610

ELKINS, CARL, food products executive; b. 1932. Attended, Taft Coll., 1955-57. Potato broker Higby & Sons, Bakersfield, Calif., 1957-60; office mgr. Sycamore Farms, Arvin, Calif., 1960-63; salesman, office and packing house mgr. Miller & Lux Corp., Bakersfield, 1963-72; pvt. practice, 1972-74; salesman Demont Packing Co., Victor, Calif., 1974-76; various positions Delta Packing Co., Lodi, Calif., 1976-99, pres.; now pres. Leeman Mettlar. With USAF, 1951-55. Office: Delta Packing Co 5950 E Kettleman Ln Lodi CA 95240-6410*

ELKINS, THOMAS ARTHUR, software development company executive; b. San Pedro, Calif., Jan. 25, 1965; s. Thomas O. and Carolyn M. (Bench) E. BS in computer sci., Calif. State U., 1988, BA in physics, 1988. Teaching asst. Calif. State U., Dominguez Hills, Calif., 1986-87, 88; computer scientist Air Force Astronautics Lab., Edwards Air Force Base, Calif., 1987-88; rocket propulsion analyst Air Force Phillips Lab., Edwards Air Force Base, Calif., 1988-93; computer engr. 413th Flight Test Squadron, Edwards Air Force Base, Calif., 1993-97; owner Spectrum Solutions, Palmdale, Calif., 1997—. Contbr. articles to profl. jours. With U.S. Navy, 1983-85. Recipient Profl. Performance award U.S. Air Force, 1988, 92, 93, 94, 95, 96, 97; Philip Johnson scholar Calif. State U., 1987. Mem. Am. Legion. Republican. Achievements include designed material test chamber for Australian neutron scattering device; designed, analyzed and tested an injection molded rocket nozzle using liquid crystal polymers; development of suite of software to aid flight test data analysis. Avocations: hiking, astronomy. Office: Spectrum Solutions 6804 Sycamore Ln Palmdale CA 93551-1919

ELL, TRAVIS EUGENE, electronics engineer; b. Minot, N.D., Oct. 3, 1951; s. Walter Joseph and Irene Dorthy (Ruby) E.; m. Deborah LouAnn Sorensen, Aug. 23, 1975 (div. June 1985); children: Joshua Michael, Jacob Matthew, John Thadeus; m. Sonia Ovsep Yazgulian. BSEE, N.D. State U., 1974, MSEE, 1978. Tchg. asst. N.D. State U., Fargo, 1974-77; servo engr. IBM Corp., Rochester, Minn., 1977-94; engrng. mgr. Micropolis Corp., Chatsworth, Calif., 1994-96; servo engr. Lumonics Corp., Oxnard, Calif., 1996-97, Seagate Tech., Inc., Moorpark, Calif., 1997—. Recipient IBM Market-Driven Quality award, 1993. Mem. IEEE (chmn. N.D. State U. student br. 1993-94), Sigma Phi Delta (sec. 1993-94). Unitarian-Universalist. Achievements include patent for data disk drive velocity estimator. Home: 1421 Sunnybrook Ln Oklahoma City OK 73128-4820 Office: Seagate Tech 5898 Condor Dr Moorpark CA 93021-2601

ELLENBERGER, ALLAN RALPH, insurance company special projects assistant; b. Tyrone, Pa., Sept. 9, 1956; s. Ralph Eugene and Mabel Pauline (Keller) E. AA, Ivy Sch. Profl. Art, 1976. Dist. mgr. Dist. Mktg. Del., Wilmington, 1979-85; microfilm asst. Blue Cross/Blue Shield Del., Wilmington, 1985-87; spl. projects asst. Zenith Ins. Co., Woodland Hills, Calif., 1987—; docent, historian Hollywood (Calif.) Studio Mus., 1989-96. Author: Ramon Novarro, A Biography of the Silent Film Idol, 1899-1968, 1997; contbr. articles to Classic Images, Films of the Golden Age. Avocations: cemetery history, art. Office: 15445 Ventura Blvd # 78 Sherman Oaks CA 91403

ELLINGS, RICHARD JAMES, political and economic research institution executive; b. Santa Barbara, Calif., Jan. 7, 1950; s. George MacMachan and Barbara Marie (Kollin) E.; m. Marta Anna Korduba; children: Katherine Nicole, John William, Julia Victoria, Ruric George. AB, U. Calif., Berkeley, 1973; MA, U. Wash., 1976, PhD, 1983. Lectr. Calif. Poly. State U., San Luis Obispo, 1980-81; lectr. U. Wash., Seattle, 1982-83, assoc. dir. Henry M. Jackson Sch. Internat. Studies, 1986-89; legis. asst. U.S. Senate, Washington, 1984-85; exec. dir. Nat. Bur. Asian Rsch., Seattle, 1989—; also bd. dirs.; dir. George E. Taylor Fgn. Affairs Inst., Seattle, 1986-89; lectr. USIA, 1992; cons. in field. Author: Embargoes and World Power, 1985; co-author: Private Property and National Security, 1991, (monograph) Asia's Challenge to American Strategy, 1992; editor: Americans Speak to APEC: Building a New Order with Asia, 1993, MFN Status, Human Rights and U.S.-China Relations, 1994, Access Asia: A Guide to Specialists and Current Research, 1994—, NBR Analysis, 1990—, Southeast Asian Security in the New Millenium, 1996. Del. Rep. Party State Conv., Tacoma, 1988. Grantee Dept. Def., 1990-95, 97, 98, Dept. State, 1994, Henry M. Jackson Found., 1989—, Japan Found. Ctr. for Global Partnership, 1995-98, USIA, 1992, 97. Mem. Internat. Studies Assn., Pacific Coun. on Internat. Policy. Avocations: hiking, skiing, tennis. Home: 644 NW 114th Pl Seattle WA 98177-4736 Office: Nat Bur Asian Rsch 4518 University Way NE Ste 300 Seattle WA 98105-4530

ELLINGTON, JAMES WILLARD, mechanical design engineer, retired; b. Richmond, Ind., May 26, 1927; s. Oscar Willard and Leola Lenora (Sanderson) E.; m. Sondra Elaine Darnell, Dec. 6, 1952 (dec. Jan. 1997); children: Ronald, Roxanna; m. Vada M. Jellsey, Oct. 10, 1998. BSME summa cum laude, West Coast U., L.A., 1978. Designer NATCO, Richmond, Ind., 1954-67; design engr. Burgmaster, Gardena, Calif., 1967-69; sr. mfg. engr. Xerox Co., El Segundo, Calif., 1969-84; cons. mem. engrng. staff Xerox Co., Monrovia, 1984-87; staff engr. Photonic Automation, Santa Ana, Calif., 1987-88; sr. mech. engr. Optical Radiation Co., Azusa, Calif., 1988; sr. staff engr. Omnichrome, Chino, Calif., 1988-96, ret., 1996. With USN, 1945-52. Mem. Soc. Mfg. Engrs. (sec. 1984). Republican. Baptist. Avocation: gardening.

ELLIOT, CAMERON ROBERT, legal administrator; b. Portland, Oreg., Jan. 6, 1966; s. James Addison and Dianne Louise (Youngblood) E. BS, Yale U., 1987; JD, Harvard U., 1996. Bar: Calif. 1996. Jud. clk. U.S. Dist. Ct., Reno, 1996—. Editor-in-chief: (jour.) Harvard Environ. Law Rev., 1995-96. Mem. Reno Environ. Bd., 1996—. Lt. USN, 1987-92. Home: # 1067 14625 SW Village Ln Beaverton OR 97007-3636 Office: US Courthouse 400 S Virginia St Reno NV 89501-2193

ELLIOTT, CLIFTON LANGSDALE, lawyer; b. Kansas City, Mo., Oct. 26, 1938; s. John Miller and Kate (Langsdale) E.; m. Bronwyn Ann Reese, Mar. 31, 1963 (div. Mar. 1983); children—Evan R., Kate L.; m. Marjorie A. Critten, Apr. 4, 1987. B.A., Dartmouth Coll., 1960; J.D., Northwestern U., 1963. Bar: Mo. 1963, Wash. 1991, Calif. 1992, U.S. Dist. Ct. (we. and ea. dists.) U.S. Ct. Appeals (2d, 4th, 5th, 8th, 9th, 10th, D.C. cirs.) 1980, U.S. Ct. Appeals (4th cir.) 1968, U.S. Ct. Appeals (8th cir.) 1965, U.S. Ct. Appeals (10th cir.) 1975, U.S. Ct. Appeals (D.C. cir.) 1973, U.S. Supreme Ct. 1979. Assoc., ptnr. Spencer, Fane, Britt & Browne, Kansas City, Mo., 1963-79; ptnr. Elliott & Kaiser, Kansas City, 1979-87, Smith, Gill, Fisher & Butts, Kansas City, 1987-88, Watson, Ess, Marshall & Enggas, Kansas City, 1988-91; of counsel, ptnr. Davis Wright Tremaine, Seattle, 1991—; instr. labor law U. Mo., 1966; spl. counsel Am. Hosp. Assn., 1973-75; mem. U.S. C. of C. Nat. Labor Relations Act Task Force, 1980—. Mem. ABA, Mo. Bar, Wash. State Bar, Calif. Bar, Am. Soc. Hosp. Attys. (ad hoc com. labor relations 1975—). Contbr. articles to profl. jours. Avocations: boating, fishing. Office: Davis Wright Tremaine 1501 4th Ave Ste 2600 Seattle WA 98101-1688

ELLIOTT, GORDON JEFFERSON, retired English language educator; b. Aberdeen, Wash., Nov. 13, 1928; s. Harry Cecil and Helga May (Kennedy) E.; m. Suzanne Tsugiko Urakawa, Apr. 2, 1957; children: Meiko Ann, Kenneth Gordon, Nancy Lee, Matthew Kennedy. AA, Grays Harbor Coll., 1948; BA, U. Wash., 1950; Cert. Russian, Army Lang. Sch., Monterey, Calif., 1952; MA, U. Hawaii, 1968. Lifetime credential, Calif. Community Coll. System. English prof. Buddhist U., Ministry of Cults, The Asia Found., Phnom Penh, Cambodia, 1956-62; English instr. U. Hawaii, Honolulu, 1962-68; dir., orientation English Coll. Petroleum and Minerals, Dhahran, Saudi Arabia, 1968-70; asst. prof., English/linguistics U. Guam, Mangilao, 1970-76; tchr., French/English Medford (Oreg.) Mid High Sch., 1976-77; instr., English Merced (Calif.) Coll., 1977-98, ret., 1998; cons. on Buddhist Edn., The Asia Found., San Francisco, Phnom Penh, Cambodia, 1956-62; cons. on English Edn., Hawaii State Adult Edn. Dept., Honolulu, 1966-68; conf. on English Edn. in Middle East, Am. U., Cairo, Egypt, 1969; vis. prof. of English, Shandong Tchrs. U., Jinan, China, 1984-85. Co-author: (textbooks, bilingual Cambodian-English) English Composition, 1962, Writing English, 1966, (test) Standard English Recognition Test, 1976; contbr. articles to profl. jours. Mem. Statue of Liberty Centennial Commn., Washington, 1980-86, Heritage Found., Washington, Lincoln Inst., Am. Near East Refugee Aid, Washington, Sgt. U.S. Army Security Agy., Kyoto, Japan, 1951-55. Tchr. Fellowship, U. Mich., Ann Arbor, 1956; recipient summer seminar stipend, Nat. Endowment For Humanities, U. Wash., Seattle, 1976, travel grants, People's Rep. of China, Beijing, 1984-85. Mem. NRA, Collegiate Press (editorial adv. bd.), Merced Coll. Found., Am. Assn. Woodturners, Elks. Republican. Avocations: swimming, woodturning, classical guitar, stamp/coin collecting, travel. Home: 680 Dennis Ct Merced CA 95340-2410 Office: Merced Coll 3600 M St Merced CA 95348-2806

ELLIOTT, HOLLY HALL, retired therapist for deaf; b. L.A., Jan. 20, 1920; d. Wilford Raymond and Adnee (Wright) Hall; m. James Wagner Elliott, May 7, 1944(dec. Dec. 1968); children: James Paul, Dennis Hall, Mark Andrew. BA in Music, U. Calif., L.A., 1941; MS in Counseling, Sacramento (Calif.) State U., 1970. Counselor, therapist U. Calif., San Francisco, 1970-80; instr. San Francisco State U., 1980-85; rsch., writing Laugley Porter Psychiat. Inst., San Francisco, 1985-92, retired, 1992; adv. com. Calif. State Dept. Rehab., Sacramento, 1980-84; cons. in field; lectr. in field. Author: Mental Health Assessment of Deaf Clients, 1987, Mental Health Assessment Special Conditions, 1989; contbr. articles to profl. jours. Pres. El Dorado County Bd. Edn., Placerville, Calif., 1962-68, Deaf Svcs. Network, San Francisco, 1978-85. Mem. Nat. Com. Devel. Deaf Ministries United Methodist Ch. (mem. gen. council), United Methodist Congress of the Deaf (bd. dirs., pres. 1982-98), Assn. Late Deafened Adults (I. King Jordan award 1994), Deaf Svcs. North (pres. 1974-85, Bridge award 1984), Delta Kappa Gamma (hon.). Democrat. Avocations: research, writing, disability access for churches. Home: 1300 NE 16th Ave Apt 1408 Portland OR 97232-4405

ELLIOTT, JAMES HEYER, retired university art museum curator, fine arts consultant; b. Medford, Oreg., Feb. 19, 1924; s. Bert R. and Marguerite E. (Heyer) E.; m. Judith Ann Algar, Apr. 23, 1966 (div.); children: Arabel Joan, Jakob Maxwell. BA, Willamette U., Salem, Oreg., 1947, DFA (hon.), 1978; AM, Harvard U., 1949; DFA (hon.), San Francisco Art Inst., 1991. James Rogers Rich fellow Harvard U., 1949-50; Fulbright grantee Paris, 1951-52; art critic European edit. N.Y. Herald-Tribune, 1952-53; curator, acting dir. Walker Art Center, Mpls., 1953-56; asst. chief curator, curator modern art Los Angeles County Mus. Art, 1956-63, chief curator, 1964-66; dir. Wadsworth Atheneum, Hartford, Conn., 1966-76; dir. Univ. Art Mus., Berkeley, Calif., 1976-88, chancellor's curator, 1989-90, dir. emeritus, 1990—; adj. prof. Hunter Coll., N.Y.C., 1968, U. Calif., Berkeley, 1976-90; commr. Conn. Commn. Arts, 1970-76; fellow Trumbull Coll., Yale U., 1971-75; mem. mus. arts panel Nat. Endowment Arts, 1974-77; bd. dirs. San Francisco Art Inst., 1980-90; art adv. com. Exploratorium, 1982-91; adv. com. Artists TV Access, 1987-90. Author: Bonnard and His Environment, 1964, James Lee Byars: Notes Towards a Biography, 1990. Trustee Marcia Simon Weisman Found., 1991—, 23 FIVE Found., San Francisco, 1993—, di Rosa Preserve, Napa, Calif., 1996—; mem. adv. bd. Artspace San Francisco, 1989—. With USNR, 1943-46. Mem. Am. Assn. Mus., Artists Space N.Y. (bd. dirs. 1980-84), Arts Club (Berkeley). Home: 13 Yellow Ferry Harbor Sausalito CA 94965-1327

ELLIOTT, JEANNE BATE, retired English educator, writer; b. Kearney, Nebr., May 20, 1924; d. William and Vera Grace (Clark) Bate; m. Clarence V. Lawson, Aug. 3, 1943 (div. June 1952); 1 child, Pamela; m. Stewart P. Elliott, June 20, 1969. BA in English, U. Calif., Berkeley, 1945, MA in English, 1949, PhD, 1956. Tchg. asst. dept. English U. Calif., Berkeley, 1951-54, lectr., 1956-57; instr. U. Nev., Reno, 1954-56; asst. prof. San Jose (Calif.) State U., 1957-62, assoc. prof., 1962-70, prof., 1970-91. Contbr. poetry to various publs.; editor Reed Mag., San Jose, 1962-65. Postdoctoral fellow AAUW, 1956-57. Mem. MLA, AAUP, Philological Assn. of Pacific Coast, Victorian Studies Assn. Democrat. Episcopalian. Home: 1211 N Via Vicam Green Valley AZ 85614-3926

ELLIOTT, JOHN GREGORY, aerospace design engineer; b. Surabaya, Dutch East Indies, Nov. 9, 1948; came to U.S., 1956; s. Frans Jan and Charlotte Clara (Rosel) E.; m. Jennifer Lee Austin, May 7, 1988. AA, Cerritos Coll., 1974; BS, Calif. State U., Long Beach, 1978. Design engr. Boeing Airplane Co., Long Beach, 1978-82, lead engr., 1983-89, sect. mgr. elect. installations group, 1989—. With USN, 1969-73. Mem. So. Calif. Profl. Engrng. Assn., The Boeing Co. Tennis Club, The Boeing Co. Surf Club, The Boeing Co. Mgmt. Club. Republican. Presbyterian. Avocations: sailing, guitar, reading, remote-control gliders, painting. E-mail: john.g.elliott@boeing.com. Office: Boeing Aircraft Co Long Beach Divsn Internet Mail Code D800-0053 Long Beach CA 90846-0003

ELLIS, DALE, professional basketball player; b. Marietta, Ga., Aug. 6, 1960; m. Monique E.; 1 child, Ashley. Student, U. Tenn., 1979-83. Player Dallas Mavericks, Dallas, TX, 1983-86, Seattle Supersonics, Seattle, WA, 1986-91, Milwaukee Bucks, Milwaukee, WI, 1991-98, Seattle Supersonics, Seattle, 1998—. Recipient Most Improved Player award NBA, 1987. Office: care Seattle Supersonics 190 Queen Anne Ave N Ste 200 Seattle WA 98109-9711*

ELLIS, ELDON EUGENE, surgeon; b. Washington, Ind., July 2, 1922; s. Osman Polson and Ina Lucretia (Cochran) E.; BA, U. Rochester, 1946, MD, 1949; m. Irene Clay, June 26, 1948 (dec. 1968); m. Priscilla Dean Strong, Sept. 20, 1969 (dec. Feb. 1990); children: Paul Addison, Kathe Lynn, Jonathan Clay, Sharon Anne, Eldon Eugene, Rebecca Deborah; m. Virginia Michael Ellis, Aug. 22, 1992. Intern in surgery Stanford U. Hosp., San Francisco, 1949-50, resident and fellow in surgery, 1950-52, 55; Schilling fellow in pathology San Francisco Gen. Hosp., 1955; ptnr. Redwood Med. Clinic, Redwood City, Calif., 1955-87, med. dir., 1984-87; semi-ret. physician, 1987—; med. dir. Peninsula Occupl. Health Assocs. (now Peninsula Indsl. Med. Clinic), San Carlos, Calif., 1991-94, physician, 1995—; dir. Sequoia Hosp., Redwood City, 1974-82; asst. clin. prof. surgery Stanford U., 1970-80. Pres. Sequoia Hosp. Found., 1983-92, bd. dirs.; pres., chmn. bd. dirs. Bay Chamber Symphony Orch., San Mateo, Calif., 1988-91; mem. Nat. Bd. of Benevolence Evang. Covenant Ch., Chgo., 1988-93; mem. mgmt. com. The Samarkand Retirement Cmty., Santa Barbara, Calif.; past pres. Project Hope Nat. Alumni Assn., 1992-94, bd. dirs., 1994—; med. advisor Project Hope, Russia Commonwealth Ind. States, 1992. Served with USNR, 1942-46, 50-52. Named Outstanding Citizen of Yr., Redwood City, 1987. Mem. San Mateo County (pres. 1961-63), Calif. (pres. 1965-66), Am. (v.p. 1974-75) heart assns., San Mateo Med. Soc. (pres. 1969-70), San Mateo County Comprehensive Health Planning Coun. (v.p. 1969-70), Calif., Am. med. assns., San Mateo Individual Practice Assn. (treas. 1984-97), San Mateo, Stanford surg. socs., Am. Coll. Chest Physicians, Calif. Thoracic Soc., Cardiovascular Coun. Republican. Mem. Peninsula Covenant Ch. Club: Commonwealth. Home: 2305 Wooster Ave Belmont CA 94002-1549 Office: Peninsula Indsl Med Clinic 1581 Industrial Rd San Carlos CA 94070-4111

ELLIS, EMORY LEON, retired biochemist; b. Grayville, Ill., Oct. 29, 1906; s. Walter Leon and Bertha May (Forman) W.; m. Marion Louise Faulkner, Sept. 17, 1930 (dec. Aug. 1994). BS, Calif. Inst. Tech., 1930, MS in Chemistry, 1932, PhD in Biochemistry, 1934. Registered profl. engr., Calif. Chemist U.S. FDA, L.A., 1934-35; rsch. assoc. CalTech, Pasadena, 1935-43; dept. head U.S. Navy Ordnance Test Sta., China Lake, Calif., 1943-54; dir. ordnance plan Rheem Ordnance Lab, Downey, Calif., 1954-57; project leader Inst. for Def. Analysis, Washington, 1957-63; cons. U.S. Navy

Weapons Ctr., China Lake, 1966-68; ptnr. Devcom, La Habra, Calif., 1965-68. Contbr. chpt. in books and articles to profl. jours. Recipient Alumni Disting. Svc. award Calif. Inst. Tech., 1970; Paul Harris fellow Rotary Internat., 1993. Mem. AAAS, Am. Chem. Soc., Tau Beta Pi, Sigma Xi. Avocations: writing essays, travel. Home: 506 Pioneer Ct Santa Maria CA 93454-3442

ELLIS, EUGENE JOSEPH, cardiologist; b. Rochester, N.Y., Feb. 23, 1919; s. Eugene Joseph and Violet (Anderson) E.; m. Ruth Nugent, July 31, 1943; children: Eugene J., Susan Ellis Renwick, Amy Ellis Miller. AB, U. So. Calif., L.A., 1941; MD, U. So. Calif., 1944; MS in medicine, U. Minn., 1950. Diplomate Am. Bd. Internal Medicine and Cardiovascular Diseases. Intern L.A. County Hosp., 1944, resident, 1946; fellowship Mayo Clinic, Rochester, Minn., 1947-51; dir. dept. cardiology St. Vincent's Hosp., L.A., 1953-55; dir. dept. cardiology Good Samaritan Hosp., L.A., 1955-84; ret., ret., 1984; prof. emeritus medicine U. So. Calif., 1984—; Mem. Med. Bd. of Calif., 1984-91; pres., 1988; pres. Div. of Med. Quality, State of Calif., 1985-89; exec. com. trustees U. Redlands, 1976-86. Lt. USN, 1944-46. Contbr. articles to profl. jours. Bd. dirs. Cancer Found. Santa Barbara, Casa Dorinda Retirement Facility, Alcohol Coun. Santa Barbara. Lt. USN, 1944-46. Mem. L.A. Country Club, Pauma Valley Country Club (bd. dirs. 1980-83), Birnam Wood Golf Club (bd. dirs. 1994-95), Valley Club of Montecito. Republican. Avocations: golf, fly fishing. Home: 450 Eastgate Ln Santa Barbara CA 93108-2248

ELLIS, GEORGE EDWIN, JR., chemical engineer; b. Beaumont, Tex., Apr. 14, 1921; s. George Edwin and Julia (Ryan) E.; BSChemE, U. Tex., 1948; MS, U. So. Calif., 1958, MBA, 1965, MS in Mech. Engring., 1968, MS in Mgmt. Sci., 1971, Engr. in Indsl. and Systems Engring., 1979. Rsch. chem. engr. Tex. Co., Port Arthur, Tex., 1948-51, Long Beach, Calif., Houston, 1952-53, Space and Info. div. N.Am. Aviation Co., Downey, Calif., 1959-61, Magna Corp., Anaheim, Calif., 1961-62; chem. process engr. AiResearch Mfg. Co., L.A., 1953-57, 57-59; chem. engr. Petroleum Combustion & Engring. Co., Santa Monica, Calif., 1957, Jacobs Engring. Co., Pasadena, Calif., 1957, Sesler & Assos., L.A., 1959; rsch. specialist Marquardt Corp., Van Nuys, Calif., 1962-67; sr. project engr. Conductron Corp., Northridge, 1967-68; info. systems asst. L.A. Dept. Water and Power, 1969-92. Instr. thermodynamics U. So. Calif., L.A., 1957. With USAAF, 1943-45. Mem. ASTM, ASME, AIChE, Nat. Assn. Purchasing Mgmt., Nat. Contract Mgmt. Assn., Am. Inst. Profl. Bookkeepers, Am. Soc. Safety Engrs., Am. Chem. Soc., Am. Soc. Materials, Am. Electroplaters and Surface Finishers Soc., Nat. Assn. Corrosion Engrs., Inst. Indsl. Engrs., Am. Prodn. and Inventory Control Soc., Am. Soc. Quality, Am. Indsl. Hygenists Assn., Steel Structure Painting Coun., Inst. Mgmt. Accts., Soc. Mfg. Engrs., L.A. Soc. Coating Tech., Assn. Finishing Processes, Chem. Coaters Assn. Internat., Pi Tau Sigma, Phi Lambda Upsilon, Alpha Pi Mu. Home: 1344 W 20th St San Pedro CA 90732-4408

ELLIS, GEORGE RICHARD, museum administrator; b. Birmingham, Ala., Dec. 9, 1937; s. Richard Paul and Dorsie (Gibbs) E.; m. Sherroll Edwards, June 20, 1961 (dec. 1973); m. Nancy Enderson, Aug. 27, 1975; 1 son, Joshua. BA, U. Chgo., 1959, MFA, 1961; postgrad., UCLA, 1971. Art supr. Jefferson County Schs., Birmingham, 1962-64; asst. dir. Birmingham Mus. Art, 1964-66; asst. dir. UCLA Mus. Cultural History, 1971-81, assoc. dir., 1981-82; dir. Honolulu Acad. Arts, 1981—. Author various works on non-western art, 1971—. Bd. dirs. Children's Lit. Hawaii, 1996—. Recipient Ralph Altman award UCLA, 1968; recipient Outstanding Achievement award UCLA, 1980; fellow Kress Found., 1971. Mem. Pacific Arts Assn. (v.p. 1985-89, exec. bd. 1989—), Hawaii Mus. Assn. (v.p. 1986-87, pres. 1987-88, pres. 1996-97, 97-98), Assn. Art Mus. Dirs., Am. Assn. Mus., L.A. Ethnic Arts Coun. (hon.), Friends of Iolani Palace (bd. dirs. 1989—), Pacific Club. Office: Honolulu Academy of Arts 900 S Beretania St Honolulu HI 96814-1495

ELLIS, HARRIETTE ROTHSTEIN, editor, writer; b. Memphis, Feb. 29, 1924; d. Samuel and Edith (Brodsky) Rothstein; m. Manuel J. Kaplan, June 1, 1944 (div. 1970); children: Deborah Elise Kaplan-Wyckoff, Claire Naomi Kaplan, Amelia Stephanie Kaplan; m. Theodore J. Ellis, Aug. 22, 1971 (div. Jan. 1992). Student, Memphis State U., 1941-42, Memphis Art Acad., 1940-43; BA, U. Ala., Tuscaloosa, 1944; postgrad., UCLA, 1949-50, Chouinard Art Inst., L.A., 1948. Advt. art/copy retail industry, New Orleans, Albuquerque, L.A., 1944-49; writer, graphic artist for newspapers and mags., L.A., 1944-49; editor Jewish Fedn. News, Long Beach, Calif., 1969-81; editor, writer Calif. Fashion Publs., L.A., 1982-86; editor Valley Mag., Granada Hills, Calif., 1987; pub. rels. Joan Luther & Assocs., Beverly Hills, Calif., 1988-90; editor Jewish Cmty. Chronicle, Long Beach, 1990—; dir. corp. comms. Startel Corp., Irvine, Calif., 1981-82. Active on com. to help implement infusion of fluoridated water in city water sys., mem. comty. interfaith com., Long Beach; bd. dirs. Hillel, 1994—, Camp Komaroff, 1994—, Temple Israel, Long Beach, Jewish Comty. Ctr., Long Beach. Named Woman of Yr., Temple Israel, Long Beach, Pioneer Women; recipient newspaper awards Calif. Press Women, Nat. Fedn. Press Women, Coun. of Jewish Fedns. Mem. Calif. Press Women (bd. dirs., treas., v.p., pres. 1997—), Nat. Fedn. Press Women, Women of Reform Judaism (regional and nat. bd. dirs.). Avocations: theatre, music, travel, archeology. E-mail: jchron@net999.com. Office: 3801 E Willow St Long Beach CA 90815-1734

ELLIS, JOHN W., professional baseball team executive, utility company executive; b. Seattle, Sept. 14, 1928; s. Floyd E. and Hazel (Reed) R.; m. Doris Stearns, Sept. 1, 1953; children: Thomas R., John, Barbara, Jim. B.S., U. Wash., 1952, J.D., 1953. Bar: Wash. State bar 1953. Ptnr. Perkins, Coie, Stone, Olsen & Williams, Seattle, 1953-70; with Puget Sound Power & Light Co., Bellevue, Wash., 1970—, exec. v.p., 1973-76, pres., CEO, 1976-87, also dir., chmn., CEO, 1987-92, chmn. bd., 1992—; dir., chmn. Seattle br. Fed. Res. Bank of San Francisco, 1982-88; chief exec. officer Seattle Mariners, 1992—; mem. Wash. Gov.'s Spl. Com. Energy Curtailment, 1973-74; mem. Wash. Gov.'s Coun. on Edn., 1991—; chmn. Pacific N.W. Utilities Coordinating Com., 1976-82; bd. dirs. Wash. Mut. Savs. Bank, Seattle, SAFECO Corp., Nat. Energy Found., 1985-87, FlowMole Corp., Assoc. Electric & Gas Ins. Svcs. Ltd.; chmn. Electric Power Rsch. Inst., 1984—; chmn., CEO, The Baseball Club of Seattle, L.P.; regent Wash. State U., 1992—. Pres. Bellevue Boys and Girls Club, 1969-71, Seattle/King County Econ. Devel. Council, 1984—; mem. exec. dirs. Seattle/King County Boys and Girls Club, 1972-75; bd. dirs. Overlake Hosp., Bellevue, 1974—, United Way King County, 1977—, Seattle Sci. Found., 1977—, Seattle Sailing Found., Evergreen Safety Council, 1981, Assn. Wash. Bus., 1980-81, Govs. Adv. Council on Econ. Devel., 1984—; chmn. bd. Wash. State Bus. Round Table, 1983; pres. United for Washington; adv. bd. Grad. Sch. Bus. Adminstrn. U. Wash., 1982—, Wash. State Econ. Ptnrship., 1984—; chmn. Seattle Regional Panel White Ho. Fellows, 1985—; trustee Seattle U., 1986—. Mem. ABA, Wash. Bar Assn., King County Bar Assn., Nat. Assn. Elec. Cos. (dir. 1977-79), Edison Electric Inst. (dir. 1978-80, exec. com. 1982, 2d vice chmn. 1987, 1st vice chmn. 1988, now chmn.), Assn. Edison Illuminating Cos. (exec. com. 1979-81), Seattle C. of C. (dir. 1980—, 1st vice chmn. 1987-88, chmn. 1988—), Phi Gamma Delta, Phi Delta Phi. Clubs: Rainier (Seattle) (sec. 1972, v.p. 1984, pres. 1985), Seattle Yacht (Seattle), Corinthian Yacht (Seattle); Meydenbauer Bay Yacht (Bellevue), Bellevue Athletic. Lodge: Rotary (Seattle). Home: 901 Shoreland Dr SE Bellevue WA 98004-6738 Office: Seattle Mariners PO Box 4100 83 King St Seattle WA 98104-2860 also: Puget Sound Power & Light Co PO Box 97034 Bldg Bellevue WA 98009-9734

ELLIS, LEE, publisher, editor; b. Medford, Mass., Mar. 12, 1924; s. Lewis Leeds and Charlotte Frances Ellis; m. Sharon Kay Barnhouse, Aug. 19, 1972. Child actor, dancer, stage, radio, movies, Keith-Albee Cir., Ea. U.S., 1927-37; announcer, producer, writer, various radio stas. and CBS, Boston, N.Y.C., and Miami, Fla., 1946-50; TV dir. ABC; mem. TV faculty Sch. Journalism U. Mo., Columbia, 1950-55; mgr. Sta. KFSD/KFSD-TV, San Diego, 1955-60, GM Imperial Broadcasting System, 1960-62; v.p., dir. advt., Media-Agencies-Clients, Los Angeles, 1962-66; v.p., dir. newspaper relations Family Weekly (name now USA W[illegible] editor Sharlee Publs., 1989—; voice of Nat. Date Festival, 1990-93; lectr. gen. semantics and communications Idaho State U., Utah State U., San Diego State U. Served with USN, 1941-44, PTO. Mem. San Diego Press Club, Indio C. of C. Republican. Methodist. E-mail: indiolee@the-desert.net. Home and Office: 47-800 Madison St Unit 53 Indio CA 92201-6673

ELLIS, ROBERT HARRY, retired television executive, university administrator; b. Cleve., Mar. 2, 1928; s. John George Ellis and Grace Bernice (Lewis) Ellis Kline; m. Frankie Jo Lanter, Aug. 7, 1954; children: Robert Harry Jr., Kimberley Kay Ellis Murphy, Shana Lee. BA, Ariz. State U., 1953; MA, Case Western Res. U., 1962. Newswriter, announcer Sta. KOY, Phoenix, 1953-55, continuity dir., 1955-61; dir., radio ops. Ariz. State U., Tempe, 1959-61; gen. mgr. Sta. KAET-TV, Tempe, 1961-87; assoc. v.p. Ariz. State U., Tempe, 1986-90; exec. com. bd. dirs. Pub. Broadcasting Svc., Washington, 1972-77, 80-86; founder Pacific Mountain Network, Denver, 1972, pres., 1973-75; mem. ednl. telecomm. com. Nat. Assn. Ednl. Broadcasters, Washington, 1973-77, 80-86. Mem. Sister City, Tempe, Tempe Ctr. For the Handicapped, East Valley Mental Health Alliance, Mesa, Ariz., Ariz. Acad., State Ariz. Behavior Health Bd. of Examiners, 1991-92. Recipient Bd. Govs. award Pacific Mountain Network, 1987, achievement award Ariz. State U., 1997. Mem. Nat. Assn. TV Arts and Scis. (life, v.p., bd. trustees 1969-70, bd. dirs. Phoenix chpt. 1986, silver circle award 1992), Nat. Assn. Pub. TV Stas. (bd. dirs. 1988-94), Tempe C. of C. (diplomate, bd. dirs. 1987-90), Sundome Performing Arts Assn. (bd. dirs. 1986-90), Ariz. Zool. Soc. (bd. dirs., sec. 1984-90), Ariz. State U. Alumni Assn. (life), Ariz. State U. Retirees Assn. (founder, pres. 1991-92), Tempe Conv. and Visitors Bur. (founder, sec./treas. 1988-93), Tempe Sports Authority (founder 1989-95), ASU Faculty Emeritus Orgn. (pres. 1992-93). Methodist. Avocations: tennis, racquetball, bridge.

ELLIS, SHELLEY MARIE, English writing educator; b. Billings, Mont., May 28, 1954; d. Charles Edward and Helen Marie (Standish) Hartung; 1 child, Adam James. BA, U. Mont., 1977; MEd, Mont. State U., 1983, EdD, 1997. Instr. English Mont. State U., Bozeman, 1985-97; instr. English, dir. Writing Ctr. Coll. Redwoods, Eureka, Calif., 1997—; steering com. Ink People Ctr. for Arts, Eureka, 1997. Author: Intertext, Oyster Boy, 1998. Recipient Excellence award Bozeman C. of C., 1994. Mem. AAUW, MLA, Nat. Coun. Tchrs. English, Rocky Mountain MLA, Rocky Mountain Writing Ctrs. Assn. Democrat. Office: Coll Redwoods 7351 Tompkins Hill Rd Eureka CA 95501-9302

ELLISON, CYRIL LEE, literary agent, retired publisher; b. N.Y.C., Dec. 11, 1916; m. Anne N. Nottonson, June 4, 1942. Assoc. Watson-Guptill Publs., 1939-69, v.p., advt. dir., 1939-69, assoc. pub. Am. Artist mag.; exec. v.p. Communication Channels, Inc., N.Y.C., 1969-88; pub. emeritus Fence Industry, Access Control, Pension World, Trusts & Estates, Nat. Real Estate Investor, Shopping Center World; pres. Lee Comms., 1980—; assoc. Kids Countrywide, Inc., 1987-94; literary agent, 1994—; pub. cons., book rep., advt. and mktg. cons., 1987-94; assoc. Mark Clements Rsch. N.Y., Inc., 1994—; pub. cons. Mag. Rsch. Mktg. Co., 1994—. Served with USAAF, 1942-46, PTO. Named Gray-Russo Advt. Man of Year Ad Men's Post Am. Legion, 1954; recipient Hall of Fame award Internat. Fence Industry Assn., 1985. Mem. Am. Legion (life, comdr. advt. men's post 1954, 64). Home: 6839 N 29th Ave Phoenix AZ 85017-1213 Office: Lee Communications 5060 N 19th Ave Phoenix AZ 85015-3210

ELLISON, LAWRENCE J., computer software company executive; b. 1944. BS. With Amdahl, Inc., Santa Clara, Calif., 1967-71; systems architect Amdahl, Inc.; pres. systems div. Omex Corp., 1972-77; with Oracle Corp., Redwood, Calif., 1977—, chmn., chief exec. officer, 1978—, also bd. dirs. Recipient Disting. Info. Scis. award Assn. Info. Tech. Profls., 1996. Office: Oracle Corp 500 Oracle Pkwy Redwood City CA 94065-1675*

ELLISON-ROSENKILDE, WENDY MAUREEN, psychologist, educator; b. Meadville, Pa., July 6, 1941; d. Allen Vincent and Anna Winifred (Hickman) Ellison; m. Roy N. Bidwell, May 28, 1982 (div.); m. Carl Edward Rosenkilde, May 24, 1992; step-children: Karen Louise Rosenkilde, Paul Eric Rosenkilde. AB in English, Allegheny Coll., 1962; MS in Neurol. Learning Disabilities, U. Pacific, 1974; MS, Calif. State U., 1984; PhD, U. So. Calif., 1983. Learning specialist South Bay Psychiatric Med. Clinic, Campbell, Calif., 1971-81; registered psychol. asst. Santa Clara County Mental Health, Pleasanton, Calif., 1981-84; intern in psychology Santa Clara County Mental Health, San Jose, Calif., 1982-83; psychologist Family Svc. East Bay, Livermore, Calif., 1985-86; psychologist child devel. ctr. Children's Hosp., San Francisco, 1985-86; affiliate staff psychologist CPC Walnut Creek (Calif.) Hosp., 1985-94; pvt. practice Pleasanton, 1985—; affiliate staff psychologist Valleycare Hosp., Pleasanton, Calif., 1993—; part-time instr. child devel. Foothill Coll., Los Altos, Calif., 1976-77, Los Positas Coll., Livermore, Calif., 1984-92. Co-author: Student Guide for Teaching for Learning, 1981. Mem. APA, Calif. Psychol. Assn., Alameda County Psychol. Assn. (pres. 1989, pres-elect and chair program and nomination coms., chair info. and referral 1986), Soc. Personality Assessment, San Francisco Psychoanalytic Inst., Livermore Valley Tennis Club, Rorschach Internat., Amador Valley Alumni Assn. (pres. 1996), Livermore C. of C., Contra Costa Wind Symphony, Valley Choral Soc., Kappa Kappa Gamma (pres. Amador Valley Alumni Assn.). Democrat. Presbyterian. Avocations: vocal music, piano, flute, stitchery. Home: 2604 Crater Rd Livermore CA 94550-6603 Office: 1882 Holmes St Livermore CA 94550-6014

ELLIS-VANT, KAREN MCGEE, elementary and special education educator, consultant; b. La Grande, Oreg., May 10, 1950; d. Ellis Eddington and Gladys Vera (Smith) McGee; m. Lynn F. Ellis, June 14, 1975 (div. Sept. 1983); children: Megan Marie, Matthew David; m. Jack Scott Vant, Sept. 6, 1986; children: Kathleen Erin, Kelli Christine (dec.). BA in Elem. Edn., Boise State U., 1972, MA in Spl. Edn., 1979; postgrad. studies in curriculum and instruction, U. Minn., 1985-86. Tchr. learning disabilities resource room New Plymouth Joint Sch. Dist., 1972-73, Payette Joint Sch. Dist., 1973, diagnostician project SELECT, 1974-75; cons. tchr. in spl. edn. Boise Sch. Dist., 1975-90; tchr. 1-2 combination, 1990-91, team tchr. 1st grade, 1991-92, 95—, site-based leadership team 1997—, chpt. 1 program cons., 1992-95, mem. Idaho Mgmt. Change Projet, 1997—; mem. profl. Standards Commn., 1983-86. Bd. dirs. Hotline, Inc., 1979-82; mem. Idaho Coop. Manpower Commn., 1984-85. Recipient Disting. Young Woman of Yr. award Boise Jaycettes, 1982, Idaho Jaycettes, 1983; Coffman Alumni scholar U. Minn., 1985-86. Mem. NEA (mem. civil rights com. 1983-85, state contact for peace caucus 1981-85, del. assembly rep., 1981-85), NSTA, ASCD, Internat. Reading Assn. (v.p. Boise chpt. 1996-97), NCTE, Internat. Coop. Learning Assn., Idaho Edn. Assn. (bd. dirs. region VII 1981-85, pres. region VII 1981-82), Boise Edn. Assn. (v.p. 1981-82, 84-85, pres. 1982-83), Nat. Council Urban Edn. Assn., World Future Soc., Council for Exceptional Children (pres. chpt. 1978-79), Nat. Coun. Tchrs. English, Minn. Coun. for Social Studies, Calif. Assn. for Gifted, Assn. for Grad. Edn. Students, FUMC (childcare bd. 1998—), Phi Delta Kappa. Contbr. articles to profl. jours.; editor, author ednl. texts and communiques; conductor of workshops, leadership tng. coop. learning. and frameworks. Office: Highlands Elem 3434 Bogus Basin Rd Boise ID 83702-1507

ELLSAESSER, HUGH WALTER, retired atmospheric scientist; b. Chillicothe, Mo., June 1, 1920; s. Charles Theobald and Louise Minerva (Bancroft) E.; m. Lois Merle McCaw, June 21, 1946 (dec. May 1998); children: Corbin Donald, Adrienne Sue; 1 adopted child, Robin Keith. AA, Bakersfield (Calif.) Jr. Coll., 1941; SB, U. Chgo., 1943, PhD, 1964; MA, UCLA 1947. Commd. 2d lt. USAF, 1943, advanced through grades to lt. col., 1960; weather officer USAF, Washington, Fla., Eng., 1942-63; ret., 1963; physicist Lawrence Livermore (Calif.) Nat. Lab., 1963-86, guest scientist, 1986-97; ind. atmospheric cons., 1997—. Editor: Global 2000 Revisited, 1992; contbr. numerous articles to profl. jours. Mem. Am. Meteorol. Soc., Am. Geophysics Union. Republican. Presbyterian. Avocation: languages. Home and Office: 4293 Stanford Way Livermore CA 94550-3463

ELLSWORTH, RICHARD GERMAN, psychologist; b. Provo, Utah, June 23, 1950; s. Richard Grant and Betty Lola (Midgley) E.; BS, Brigham Young U., 1974, MA, 1975; PhD, U. Rochester (N.Y.), 1979; postgrad. UCLA, 1980-84; PhD, Internat. Coll., 1983; m. Carol Emily Osborne, May 23, 1970; children: Rebecca Ruth, Spencer German, Rachel Priscilla, Melanie Star, Richard Grant, David Jedediah. Cert. Am. Bd. Med. Psychotherapy, (fellow), Am. Bd. Sexology. Instr. U. Rochester, 1976-77; asst. prof. Chapman U., 1995—; rsch. assoc. Nat. Tech. Inst. for Deaf, Rochester, 1977; instr. West Valley Coll., Saratoga, Calif., 1979-80, San Jose (Calif.) City Coll., 1980; psycholinquist UCLA, 1980-81; rsch. assoc. UCLA, 1982-85; psychologist Daniel Freeman Meml. Hosp., Inglewood, Calif., 1981-84, Broderick, Langlois & Assocs., San Gabriel, Calif., 1982-86, Beck Psychiat. Med. Group, Lancaster, Calif., 1984-87, Angeles Counseling Ctr., Arcadia, Calif., 1986-89, Assoc. Med. Psychotherapists, Palmdale, Calif., 1988—; cons. LDS Social Svcs. Calif. Agy., 1981—, Antelope Valley Hosp. Med. Ctr., 1984—, Palmdale Hosp. Med. Ctr., 1984-96, Treatment Ctrs. of Am. Psychiat. Hosps., 1985-86, Hollywood Cmty. Hosp., 1994—, Lancaster Cmty. Hosp., 1996—. Scoutmaster, Boy Scouts Am., 1976-79. UCLA Med. Sch. fellow in psychiatry, 1980-81. Mem. Am. Psychol. Assn., Am. Assn. Sex Educators, Am. Psychol. Assn., Counselors and Therapists, Assn. Mormon Counselors and Psychotherapists, Am. Soc. Clin. Hypnosis, Psi Chi. Contbr. articles to profl. jours. Office: 1220 E Avenue S Ste L Palmdale CA 93550-6196

EL MALLAKH, DOROTHEA HENDRY, editor, publishing executive; b. Emmett, Idaho, July 16, 1938; d. David Lovell Parker and Lygia Teressa (Dalton) Hendry; m. Ragaei William El Mallakh, Aug. 26, 1962 (dec. Mar. 1987); children: Helen Alise, Nadia Irene. BA in Modern Langs., Lewis and Clark Coll., 1960; MA in History, U. Colo., 1962, PhD in History, 1972; postgrad., Georgetown U., 1962-63. Exec. adminstr., treas. Internat. Rsch. Ctr. Energy & Econ. Devel., Boulder, Colo., 1973-87, exec. dir., 1987—; assoc. editor Jour. Energy & Devel., Boulder, 1975-87, mng. editor, 1987—; bd. dirs. Rocky Mountain Eye Found., Boulder. Author: The Slovak Autonomy Movement, 1979; author (with others): The Genius of Arab Civilization, 1983; editor: The Energy Watchers I-IX, 1990-98; author and editor: Saudi Arabia, 1982. Perrine Meml. fellow, U. Colo., 1960-61, Rare Lang. fellow, U.S. Govt., U. Colo., 1961-62, Rotary Internat. fellow, Boise, Idaho, 1962. Mem. Internat. Assn. Energy Econs. (v.p. internal affairs 1989-91, sec. 1988-89). E-mail: iceed@stripe.Colorado.EDU. Office: ICEED 909 14th St Boulder CO 80302-7340

ELMER, STAN, artist; b. Payson, Utah, Jan. 8, 1939; s. J. Clark and Norma (Erlandson) E.; m. JoAnne Barker, Nov. 8, 1962. BFA, U. Utah, 1962, grad. cert. in Regional Planning, 1980. City planner Salt Lake City Corp., 1962-63; county planner Weber County, Ogden, Utah, 1964-65; recreation planner State of Utah, Salt Lake City, 1966-71; environ. coord. State of Utah, Sale Lake City, 1972-81, sovereign lands coord., 1982-87; retired. Paintings pub. in art publ. including Watercolor Magic. Mem. planning commn. Bountiful City, Utah, 1971-72, 78-79. Named Best of Show, watercolor paintings, Davis County Fair, Farmington, Utah, 1996. Mem. Associated Utah Artists (pres. 1997-99)), Utah Watercolor Soc. (edn. chair 1993-95, membership chair 1991-93, Best of Show 1997), Intermountain Soc. Artists (spl. asst. to pres. 1989-92, 1st Pl. 1994), Western Fedn. Watercolor Socs. (travel exhibit award 1996). Mem. LDS Ch. Avocations: scenic photographer, golf, mountain biking. Home: 15 W 1200 S Bountiful UT 84010-6338

ELMORE, MATTHEW BRET, radio, television announcer; b. San Francisco, Oct. 26, 1951; s. Jack Prentiss and Margaret Hanna (Turnquist) E.; m. Marcia Marquez, July 14, 1973; 1 child, Nicholas Bret. Student, Coll. San Mateo, 1975-77. Announcer Sta. KCSM-TV-FM, San Mateo, Calif., 1975-81; freelance camera operator, film and video narrator San Francisco Bay Area, 1977-82, 88—, San Luis Obispo, Calif., 1982-87; announcer, program dir. Sta. KCBX-FM, San Luis Obispo, 1982-87; relief announcer Sta. KKAL, Arroyo Grande, Calif., 1984-86; staff announcer Sta. KQED-FM, San Francisco, 1987—, Sta. KQED-TV, San Francisco, 1991—; relief announcer Sta. KQED-TV/KQEC-TV, San Francisco, 1988-91. Bd. dirs. San Luis Obispo County Jazz Festival, 1985-90. Recipient Disting. Tech. Comm. award Soc. for Tech. Comm., 1985. Mem. AFTRA (bd. dirs. 1999—, bd. dirs. San Francisco chpt. 1995—), NATAS, Nat. Assn. Broadcast Employees and Technicians (alt. mem. bd. 1996—). Office: Sta KQED-FM 2601 Mariposa St San Francisco CA 94110-1426

EL-MOSLIMANY, ANN PAXTON, paleoecologist, educator, writer; b. Fullerton, Calif., Aug. 2, 1937; d. Donald Dorn and Sarah Frances (Turman) Paxton; m. Mohammed Ahmad El-Moslimany, May 31, 1962; children: Samia, Ramsey, Rasheed. BS, N.Mex. State U., 1959; MS, Am. U., Beirut, 1961; PhD, U. Wash., 1983. Tchr. various schs., 1959-83, Kuwait U., 1984-86, Seattle Ctrl. C.C., 1986-90; prin., tchr. Islamic Sch. Seattle, 1989—; paleoecological rschr. Palynological Consultants, 1987—. Author: Zaki's Ramadan Fast, 1994; contbr. articles to sci. jours.; mem. adv. bd. Muslim Kaleidescope mag., Sisters mag. Mem. Amnesty Internat., Am. Quaternary Assn., Nat. Coun. Tchrs. Math., Geog. Alliance of Wash., Seattle Islamic Sisterhood. Home: PO Box 367 Seahurst WA 98062-0367 Office: Islamic Sch Seattle PO Box 22956 Seattle WA 98122-0956

ELMSTROM, GEORGE P., optometrist, writer; b. Salem, Mass., Dec. 11, 1925; s. George and Emily Irene (Wedgwood) E.; grad. So. Calif. Coll. Optometry, 1951; m. Nancy DePaul, Apr. 29, 1973; children—Pamela, Beverly, Robert. Pvt. practice optometry, El Segundo, Calif., 1951—; mem. staff So. Calif. Coll. Optometry, 1951—; book cons. Med. Econs. Books, 1970—; instrument and forensic editor Jour. Am. Optical Assn.; comml. airplane and balloon pilot, 1968—. Served with U.S. Army, World War II. Decorated Silver Star; named Writer of Year, Calif. Optometric Assn., 1957, Man of Year, El Segundo, 1956; recipient spl. citation Nat. Eye Found., 1955. Fellow Am. Acad. Optometry, AAAS, Southwest Contact Lens Soc., Disting. Service Found. of Optometry, Internat. Acad. Preventive Medicine; mem. Am. Optometric Assn., Assn. for Research in Vision, Am. Soc. Ultrasonography, Am. Pub. Health Assn., Optometric Editors Assn., Assn. Research in Vision, Internat. Soc. Ophthalmic Ultrasound, Profl. Airshow Pilots Assn., Flying Optometrists Assn. Am., Beta Sigma Kappa, So. Calif. Coll. Optometry Alumni (pres. 1955-56). Author: Optometric Practice Management, 1963; Legal Aspects of Contact Lens Practice, 1966; Advanced Management for Optometrists, 1974; Modernized Management, 1982; mgmt. editor Optometric Monthly, 1973. Home: 484 Washington St Ste B Monterey CA 93940-3052 Office: PO Box S-3061 Carmel CA 93921-3061

EL SAYED, HATEM M., painter; b. Cairo, Apr. 10, 1954; came to U.S., 1978; s. Mohamed Mostafa El Sayed and Samira Ragib; m. Iris F. Stallworth, Dec. 8, 1978 (div. Nov. 1980); m. Rosemary Hallacy, Oct. 16, 1982. BS in Engring., Alexandria (Arab Republic Egypt) U., 1974; MFA, Egypt Coll. Fine Arts, Alexandria, 1976; PhD in Visual Arts, Helwan U., Alexandria, 1978. Founder, pres. Arabian Greetings, Ltd., San Francisco, 1980—; design cons. various firms; lectr. in field. Author: Marriage Invitation, 1976, Monk of the Violet, 1977, Posing for Red, 1978, Graphics of Pharaohs, 1979; lithography includes Beardless Jars series; designed scenery and costumes several Cairo theatre prodns.; numerous exhbns. include the Alexandria Mus., 1972, traveling sculpture show Denmark, Sweden, Greece, Fed. Republic Germany, 1973, Kerckhoff Gallery at UCLA, 1979, "Treasures of Tutankhamen", San Francisco, 1979, Involution Gallery, San Francisco, 1979, Maelstrom Gallery, San Francisco, 1980; represented in many pvt. collections. Mem. Am.-Arab Anti-Discrimination Com., Washington, 1987. Served as lt. Egyptian Commando Forces, 1973-74. Recipient Cert. Excellence in the Fine Arts Nat. Com. of the Arts, Cairo, 1977, Gold Medal Salon Annuel, Alexandria, 1977, Cert. Excellence Pres. Anwar Sadat and Presdl. Commn. on the Arts, 1978, Award of Merit Toronto (Ont.) Art Dirs. Club, 1983. Avocations: martial arts, reading, music, soccer. Office: 2215R Market St Ste 112 San Francisco CA 94114-1612 Studio: 1466 23rd Ave San Francisco CA 94122-3306

ELSBERRY, SUSAN DAVISE, computer-aided manufacturing engineer; b. Lincoln, Nebr., Oct. 27, 1953; d. Leo Herbert and Genevieve (Richards) Bischof; m. Terence Ray Elsberry, Aug. 9, 1986; 1 child, Colin Ray. BS, Brigham Young U., 1985, MS, 1992. Computer-aided mfg. engr. Northrop, Hawthorne, Calif., 1986-91; owner, tng. instr. mine safety Safety First, 1993—; ptnr. Elsberry Enterprises, 1994—; software trainer ExecuTrain, 1994—. Mem Westec Adv. Com., 1987 90, named Whirlpool Corp. fellow, 1984-86. Fellow Inst. for Advancement of Engring.; mem. Soc. Mfg. Engrs. (officer chpt. 106 1993-94). Democrat. Roman Catholic.

ELSBREE, LANGDON, English language educator; b. Trenton, N.J., June 23, 1929; s. Wayland Hoyt and Miriam (Jenkins) E.; m. Aimee Desiree Wildman, June 9, 1952; 1 child, Anita. BA, Earlham Coll., 1952; MA, Cornell U., 1954; PhD, Claremont Grad. Sch., 1963. Instr. in English Miami U., Oxford, Ohio, 1954-57, Harvey Mudd Coll., Claremont, Calif.,

1958-59; instr. humanities Scripps Coll., Claremont, Calif., 1959-60; instr., prof. Claremont McKenna Coll., 1960-94, prof. emeritus, 1994; mem. grad. faculty Claremont Grad. Sch., 1965—; part-time lectr. Calif. State U., L.A., 1968-70; vis. prof. Carleton Coll., 1987. Author: The Rituals of Life, 1982, Ritual Passages and Narrative Structures, 1991; co-author: Heath College Handbook, 6th-12th edits., 1967-90; guest editor D.H. Lawrence Rev., 1975, 87. Bd. dirs. Claremont Civic Assn., 1964-66; mem. founding com. Quaker Studies in Human Betterment, Greensboro, N.C., 1987. Fulbright Commn. lectr., 1966-67; grantee NEH, 1975, Claremont McKenna Coll., 1980, 82, 87. Mem. AAUP, MLA, Friends Assn. Higher Edn., D.H. Lawrence Soc. (exec. bd. 1990), Virginia Woolf Soc., Coll. English Assn., Sci. Fiction Rsch. Assn., Phi Beta Kappa. Democrat. Mem. Soc. of Friends. Avocations: traveling, reading, swimming, films, photography. Office: Claremont McKenna Coll Bauer Ctr 890 Columbia Ave Claremont CA 91711-3901

ELSER, DANNY RAY, financial planner; b. Butte, Mont., June 22, 1953; s. Duane Donald and Edith N.H. (Tam) E.; m. Janet L. Bottom, Dec. 1, 1974; children: Sara E., Katie V., Andrew J., Patrick M. BS, Colo. St. U., 1976. CLU. Mgr. Coll. Life, Bloomington, Ind., 1976-82, Prin. Fin. Group, Bloomington, 1982-86; prin. Fin. Strategies Corp., Bloomington, 1986-88; mgr. No. Colo. Prin. Fin. Group, 1988-89, Prin. Fin. Group, Billings, Mont., 1989—. Bd. dirs. Cmty. Svc. Coun., Bloomington, 1982-85; mem. Young Reps., Bloomington, 1982-86; mission chmn. Evang. Cmty. Ch., Bloomington, 1985-86, missions com. Faith Evang. Ch., Ft. Collins, Colo., 1987-88, 91—, mem. ch. coun., 1991—; ch. lay leader, coun. mem., missions com. Faith Evang. Ch., Billings; bd. dirs. working com. Mont. Found. Consumer Ins. Edn. Bd.; bd. dirs., coach Little Guy Football, 1993—; coach Little League, 1991—, Amateur Athletics Wrestling, 1990—; Fellowship of Christian Athletes state dir., 1995—. Mem. Nat. Assn. Life Underwriters (Nat. Quality and Sales Achievement award 1980-88, Outstanding Young Man of Am., 1983-85), Ind. State Assn. Life Underwriters (Bloomington chpt. bd. dirs. 1980-84, state bd. dirs. 1985-86), S.E. Mont. Assn. Life Underwriters (sec., prog. chmn., v.p. 1989-92, pres. 1992-93), Internat. Assn. Fin. Planning, Nat. Assn. Security Dealers (registered rep.), So. Ind. Estate Planning Forum, Million Dollar Round Table, Bloomington C. of C. (chmn. leadership Bloomington 1982-86), Ft. Collins C. of C. (bus. excellence com.), No. Rocky Mountain Chpt. CLU (sec., treas. 1988, bd. dirs. chartered fin. cons. 1988), Mont. Gen. Agts.-Mgrs. Assn. (bd. dirs. 1989—, Nat. Mgmt. award 1989, 90, 91, 92, 93, 94, 95, pres. 1992-94, past pres. 1991-92), Mont. Soc. CLU and Chartered Fin. Cons., Bloomington Jaycees (pres. 1982-86), ECC Club (mission chmn. 1985-86). Republican. Office: Prin Fin Group 401 N 31st St Ste 950 Billings MT 59101-1200

ELTON, ZOË, writer, film director; b. Hereford, U.K., Jan. 1, 1951; came to U.S., 1976; d. Ronald Charles and Christina May (Davies) E. Grad., New Coll. Speech and Drama, London, 1972. Video dir. Mill Valley (Calif.) Film Festival, 1982—; artistic dir. Platypus Theatre, San Francisco, 1984-89; resident dir. West Coast Playwrights, San Francisco, 1987-89; program dir. Mill Valley Film Festival, 1991-96, artistic dir., 1996—; mem. nat. nomination com. media arts grant NVR/Rockefeller Found., N.Y.C., 1996, 97. Author (plays) Platypus Reveals All!, 1985, Steppenwolf, Hessenwolf, 1988, Eleanor Dreams of Horses, 1989, The Secret Chronicles of Madeline Usher, 1991. Artist-in-residence Calif. Arts Coun., 1989, 91; recipient grant Zellerbach Family Fund, 1991. Avocations: film, music, design. Office: Mill Valley Film Festival 38 Miller Ave Ste 6 Mill Valley CA 94941-1939

ELTRINGHAM, THOMAS JAMES GYGER, telecommunications professional; b. Riverside, Calif., Nov. 4, 1943; s. Thomas Lamar and May Katharyn (Gyger) E.; m. Hana Libuse Strachen, Jan. 21, 1966 (Feb. 1978); m. Lydia Rose Boss, Oct. 4, 1980; children: Glenn Alexander, Eric Douglas. HSST, Hubbard Coll., Copenhagen, 1969. Ordained to ministry. Minister Ch. of Scientology, L.A. and Clearwater, Fla., 1961-83; installations mgrs. Am. Sun, Inc., Commerce, Calif., 1984-86; v.p. ops. Power Ins. Inc., Santa Fe Springs, Calif., 1986-90; dir. L.D. Svcs., Inc., Santa Fe Springs, Calif., 1990-98; CEO GCC Telecomm. Inc., 1991-98; ret., 1998. Contbr. articles to profl. jours.; developer drug rehab. program, L.A., 1966. chmn. bd. trustees Eltringham Family Found. Mem. Internat. Assn. Scientologists. Republican. Avocations: tennis, skiing, reading, computers, golf.

ELWAY, JOHN ALBERT, professional football player; b. Port Angeles, Wash., June 28, 1960; s. Jack Elway; m. Janet Elway; 2 daughters: Jessica Gwen, Jordan Marie. BA in Econs., Stanford U., 1983. Quarterback Denver Broncos, 1983—. Mem. Mayor's Council on Phys. Fitness, City of Denver; chmn. Rocky Mountain region Nat. Kidney Found. Played Super Bowl XXI, 1986, XXII, 1987, XXIV, 1989; named to Sporting News Coll. All-Am. team, 1980, 82, Sporting News NFL All-Pro team, 1987, Pro Bowl team, 1986, 87, 89, 91, 93, 94. Office: Denver Broncos 13655 Broncos Pky Englewood CO 80112-4150*

ELY, MARICA MCCANN, interior designer; b. Pachuca, Mex., May 2, 1907 (parents Am. citizens); d. Warner and Mary Evans (Cook) McCann; m. Northcutt Ely, Dec. 2, 1931; children: Michael and Craig (twins), Parry Haines. B.A., U. Calif.-Berkeley, 1929; diploma Pratt Inst. of Art, N.Y.C., 1931. Free-lance interior designer, Washington and Redlands, Calif., 1931—; lectr. on flower arranging and fgn. travel, 1931—; prof. Sogetsu Ikebana Sch., Tokyo, 1972. Art editor (calendar) Nat. Capital Garden Club League, 1957-58. Pres. Kenwood Garden Club, Md.; bd. dirs. Nat. Libr. Blind, Washington; mem. adv. bd. George C. Marshall Internat. Ctr. at Dodona Manor, Leesburg, Va.; v.p. bd. dirs. Washington Hearing and Speech Soc., 1969; co-founder Delta Gamma Found. Pre-Sch. Blind Children, Order of Delta Gamma Rose. Finalist Nat. Silver Bowl Competition, Jackson-Perkins Co., 1966; garden shown on nat. tour Am. Hort. Soc., 1985. Mem. Calif. Arboretum Found., Redlands Hort. and Improvement Soc. (bd. dirs. 1982-94), Redlands Panhellenic Soc., Redlands Country Club, Delta Gamma.

EMENHISER, JEDON ALLEN, political science educator, academic administrator; b. Clovis, N.Mex., May 19, 1933; s. Glen Allen and Mary Opal (Sasser) E.; m. Patricia Ellen Burke, Jan. 27, 1954; 1 child, Melissa Mary Emenhiser Westerfield. Student, Am. U., 1954; BA, U. Redlands, 1955; PhD, U. Minn., 1962. Cert. community coll. adminstr., Calif. Instr. to prof. polit. sci. Utah State U., Logan, 1960-77, acting dean, 1973-74; prof. Humboldt State U., Arcata, Calif., 1977—, dean, 1977-86; acting v.p. Humboldt State U., Arcata, 1984; chair Social Sci. Rsch. and Instrnl. Coun. Calif. State U., 1994-95; prof. Jr. Statesmen Summer Sch., Stanford U., 1989—; vis. instr. U. Redlands, Calif., 1959-60; vis. prof. U. Saigon, Vietnam, 1964-65; asst. dean Colgate U., Hamilton, N.Y., 1972-73; staff dir. Utah Legislature, Salt Lake City, 1967, cons., 1968-77; dir. Bur. Govt. and Opinion Rsch., Logan, 1965-70; cons. USCG, McKinleyville, Calif., 1982; v.p. Exch. Bank, New Franklin, Mo., 1970-76; reader advanced placement exam. U.S. Govt. Coll. Bd., 1990—; vis. fellow govt. divsn. Congl. Rsch. Svc. Libr. of Congress, 1996. Author: Utah's Governments, 1964, Freedom and Power in California, 1987; editor, contbr. Dragon on the Hill, 1970, Rocky Mountain Urban Politics, 1971; producer, dir. TV broadcasts The Hawks and the Doves, 1965-66; contbr. articles to profl. jours. Sec. Cache County Dem. Party, Logan, 1962-63; chmn. Mayor's Commn. on Govt. Orgn., Logan, 1973-74; campaign mgr. various candidates and issues, Logan, 1965-75; bd. dirs. Humboldt Connections, Eureka, Calif., 1986-96, pres., 1989-92; elder Presbyn. ch. Sr. Fulbright-Hays lectr. Com. Internat. Exch. of Persons, Vietnam, 1964-65; Adminstrv. fellow Am. Coun. Edn., Colgate U., 1972-73; Paul Harris fellow Rotary Internat. Mem. Am. Polit. Sci. Assn., Western Polit. Sci. Assn., Am. Studies Assn., Phi Beta Kappa, Omicron Delta Kappa. Presbyterian. Avocations: gardening, photography, travel. Home: PO Box 250 Bayside CA 95524-0250 Office: Humboldt State U Dept Polit Sci Arcata CA 95521

EMERICK, JUDSON JOHNSON, art historian; b. Kingston, N.Y., July 3, 1941; s. Benjamin Cutter and Betty Carhart (Johnson) E.; m. Betsy Ann Kruizenga, Aug. 24, 1963. BA, Hope Coll., Holland, Mich., 1963; MA in Art History, U. Mich., 1965; PhD in Art History, U. Pa., 1975. Instr. Pomona Coll., Claremont, Calif., 1973-75; asst. prof. art history Pomona Coll., 1975-81, assoc. prof. art history, 1981-97, chmn. dept. art, 1981-87, 96-99, prof. art history, 1998—; chmn. writing com. Pomona Coll., 1983-87, chmn. rsch. com., 1990-91, chmn. exec. com., 1997-99. Co-author (with C. Davis-Weyer) Monograph, Early 6th Century Frescoes of S. Martino ai Monti, Rome, 1984; author: The Tempietto del Clitunno near Spoleto, 1998. Penfield scholar, U. Pa., 1970-71, Samuel H. Kress Found. fellow, 1971-73, NEH fellow, 1981. Mem. Coll. Art Assn. Am., Soc. Archtl. Historians, Internat. Ctr. Medieval Art, Art Historians of So. Calif. (pres. 1979-80, 1989-90). Avocations: high fidelity sound systems. Home: 1421 Guadalajara Dr Claremont CA 91711-3516 Office: Pomona Coll 145 E Bonita Ave Claremont CA 91711-4429

EMERSON, ALTON CALVIN, retired physical therapist; b. Webster, N.Y., Sept. 29, 1934; s. Homer Douglas and Pluma (Babcock) E.; m. Nancy Ann Poarch, Dec. 20, 1955 (div. 1972); children: Marcia Ann, Mark Alton; m. Barbara Irene Stewart, Oct. 6, 1972. BS in Vertibrate Zoology, U. Utah, 1957; cert. phys. therapy, U. So. Calif., 1959. Staff phys. therapist Los Angeles County Crippled Children's Services, 1958-65; pvt. practice phys. therapy Los Angeles, 1966-98; ret., 1998; cons. City of Hope, Duarte, Calif., 1962-72; trustee Wolcott Found. Inc., St. Louis, 1972-86, chmn. bd. trustees, 1980-85. Recipient Cert. of Achievement, George Washington U., Washington, 1986. Mem. Masons (pres. Temple City High Twelve Club 1971, master Camellia 1973, pres. Calif. Assn. High Twelve Clubs 1986, internat. pres. High Twelve 1990-91, mem. High Twelve Internat., Pasadena Scottish Rite Bodies, Venerable Master, Lodge of Perfection 1998, KCCH, Legion Merit), Royal Order Scotland, Al Malaikah Tmeple, Ancient Arabic order Nobles Mystic Shrine, DeMolay Legion of Honor, Order of DeMolay (hon. internat. supreme coun.), Conejo-Westlake Shrine Club (pres. 1996). Home and Office: 287 W Avenida De Las Flores Thousand Oaks CA 91360-1808

EMERSON, (VIRGIL) LEON, retired judge; b. Atwood, Okla., Apr. 14, 1925; s. William Harry and Ella Rea (Pegg) E.; m. Lee Kessler Emerson, Apr. 5, 1975; children: Donald Leon, David Paul, Julia Ellen; stepchildren: Darylle Lynn Goodfield, Randall Ryan Bruno. AA, Compton C.C., 1948; JD, Southwestern U., 1951. Judge Downey Mcpl. Ct., 1961-85; judge by assignment, arbitrator; bd. mem. So. Calif. Coun. Alcohol and Drugs, Downey, 1972-74, Downey Area Counseling Ctr., 1968-71, Mcpl. Judges Cmty. Conf., Downey, 1967. Scoutmaster Troop 807, Downey, 1963-70. Named Man of Yr., Downey Coord. Coun. and N.Am. Mgmt. ASsn. Mem. Masons, Kiwanis, S.E. Bar Assn., L.A. Bar Assn., Calif. State Bar Assn. Avocations: reading, amateur radio, computers. Home: 8685 Merced Cir # 1016-C Huntington Beach CA 92646-5689

EMERSON, MARK DAVID, maternal products company executive; b. San Jose, Calif., Feb. 19, 1970; s. David Douglas and Anna Maria (Marcotte) E. BS, Santa Clara U., 1992. Pres. Maternal Concepts, Ltd., San Jose, 1992—. Mem. Theta Chi. Republican. Roman Catholic. Avocations: backpacking, rock climbing. Office: Maternal Concepts Ltd Ste 109-18 2910 Stevens Creek Blvd San Jose CA 95128-2015

EMERSON, R. CLARK, priest, business administrator; b. L.A., Mar. 9, 1945; s. George Heins and Irma Furney (Sorter) E.; m. Katharine Ann Lawrence, June 27, 1980; children: Cynthia, Holly, Angela, William, Richard. BA, San Jose State U., 1966; MDiv, Ch. Div. Sch. of Pacific, 1972. Ordained deacon Episcopal Ch., 1972, ordained priest, 1973; cert. secondary tchr., Calif. Comml. tchr. Middletown (Calif.) High Sch., 1967-69; asst. to rector St. Francis Ch., Palos Verdes, Calif., 1972-76; adminstr. Power Transistor Co., Torrance, Calif., 1977-85; priest assoc. St. John's Ch., L.A., 1976-85; adminstr. Richard B. Belli Accountancy, San Jose, Calif., 1988-96; priest assoc. St. Luke's Ch., Los Gatos, Calif., 1985—. Contr. St. John's Well Child Ctr., L.A., 1985. Republican. Episcopalian. Avocations: steam railroading, antique automobiles, hot air ballooning.

EMERT, GEORGE HENRY, biochemist, academic administrator; b. Tenn., Dec. 15, 1938; s. Victor K. Emert and Hazel G. (Shultz) Ridley; m. Billie M. Bush, June 10, 1967; children: Debra Lea Lipp, Ann Lanie Taylor, Laurie Elizabeth, Jamie Marie. BA, U. Colo., 1962; MA, Colo. State U., 1970; PhD, Va. Tech. U., 1973. Registered profl. chem. engr. Microbiologist Colo. Dept. Pub. Health, Denver, 1967-70; post doctoral fellow U. Colo., Boulder, 1973-74; dir. biochem. tech. Gulf Oil Corp., Merriam, Kans., 1974-79; prof. biochemistry, dir. biomass rsch. ctr. U. Ark., Fayetteville, 1979-84; exec. v.p. Auburn (Ala.) U., 1984-92; pres. Utah State U., Logan, 1992—; adj. prof. microbiology U. Kans., Lawrence, 1975-79. Editor, author: Fuels from Biomass and Wastes, 1981; author book chpt.; contbr. articles to profl. jours.; poet. Mem. So. Tech. Coun., Raleigh, N.C., 1985-92; dir. Ala. Supercomputer Authority, Montgomery, 1987-92, Blue Cross Blue Shield Utah, 1996—, Utah Partnership Econ. Devel.; trustee, adv. bd. First Security Bank. Capt. U.S. Army, 1963-66, Vietnam. Named to Educators Hall of Fame, Lincoln Meml. U., 1988. Fellow Am. Inst. Chemists; mem. Rotary (Paul Harris fellow, pres., v.p. 1989-90), Phi Kappa Phi, Sigma Xi. Republican. Achievements include patent for method for enzyme reutilization. Office: Utah State U 1400 Old Main Hill Logan UT 84322-1400*

EMERY, RITA DOROTHY, physical education educator; b. Berkeley, Calif., Sept. 21, 1939; d. Byron Elden and Charlotte Antoinette (Siwinski) E. AA, Contra Costa Coll., 1960; BA, Chico State Coll., 1963; MA, Wash. State U., 1977. Cert. tchr., Calif. Instr. phys. edn., coach Churchill County High Sch., Fallon, Nev., 1963-65; instr. phys. edn., coach, dept. chair Lower Lake (Calif.) High Sch., 1967-76; coach women's volleyball Contra Costa Coll., San Pablo, Calif., 1977; coach women's softball Oreg. State U., Corvallis, 1977-80; instr. phys. edn., coach, athletic dir. St. Leonard Sch., Fremont, Calif., 1985-89; instr. phys. edn. Campbell (Calif.) Unified Sch. Dist., 1989-90; elem. phys. edn. specialist, coach Vacaville (Calif.) Unified Sch. Dist., 1990-95; dir. jr. programming Club Sport of Pleasant, Calif., 1995—; intramural dir. Contra Costa Coll., 1957-60; coach, coord. recreation Holy Spirit Ch., Fremont, 1980-85; instr. youth sports Fremont Leisure Svcs., 1988-90, teen youth coord., 1988-93; girls basketball coach Wood High Sch., Vacaville, 1993-95. Speaker Alameda County chpt. Am. Heart Assn., 1983-90; vol. coach, officer, ofcl. Fremont Little League, 1983-86; vol. Hall of Health/Kids Safe Program, Berkeley, Calif., 1990—. Named Vol. of Yr. Am. Heart Assn., 1986, 88. Mem. AAHPERD (adv. com. for devel. of athletic tng. coun.), Calif. Assn. Health, Phys. Edn., Recreation and Dance. Avocations: bicycling, walking, cacti, gardening, youth activities. Office: Club Sport of Pleasant 7090 Johnson Dr Pleasanton CA 94588-3328

EMIGH, MIKE, agricultural products company executive; b. 1948. BA in Acctg., U. Las Vegas, 1973. Plant contr. Johns Manville, Fresno, Calif., 1973-79; asst. contr. Sun Maid Growers of Calif., Inc., Kingsburg, Calif., 1979-84; sec., v.p., treas. Valley Fig Growers, Inc., Fresno, Calif., 1984-97, pres., 1997—. Office: Valley Fig Growers Inc 2028 S 3rd St Fresno CA 93702-4156

EMILSSON, ELIZABETH MAYKUTH, special education educator; b. Bozeman, Mont., Feb. 23, 1936; d. Frank Leopold and Dolores Muriel (Lawrence) Maykuth; m. Robert Gunnar Emilsson, May 8, 1961 (dec.); children: Gunnar R., Ingrid L., John. BS, Mont. State Coll., 1958; MEd, Mont. State U., 1974; Spl. Edn. Cert., U. Mont., 1976, postgrad., 1978. Tchr. grades 4-8 Virginia City (Mont.) Schs., 1958-59; tchr. grades 7-8 El Camino Jr. H.S., Santa Maria, Calif., 1959-60; tchr. grade 6 Miller St. Sch., Santa Maria, 1960-61; tchr. grades 1-3 Stevenson sch., Ransomville, N.Y., 1967-72; resource tchr. Three Forks (Mont.) Unified Schs., 1974-76; spl. edn. cons. Mont. Reg. Svcs., Glendive, Mont., 1976-79; spl. edn. tchr. cons. Big Country Edn. Coop., Miles City, Mont., 1979-89; spl. edn. dir. Big Country Edn. Coop., 1990—; exec. dir. Big Country Edn./Head Start, 1991—; pres. bd. dirs. South Eastern Mont. Adv. Prog., Miles City, 1987-88. Bd. dirs. Miles City Youth Soccer Assn., 1986-88. Mem. Coun. for Exceptional Children (Mont. pres. 1985-86, Nat. Bd. Govs. 1991-94, distinguished svc. award state fedn. 1994), PEO Sisterhood, Delta Kappa Gamma. Democrat. Lutheran. Avocations: hiking, fishing, reading, gardening. Home: 2203 Main St Miles City MT 59301-3801 Office: Big Country Ednl Coop PO Box 668 Miles City MT 59301-0668

EMLET, CHARLES ARTHUR, social worker; b. Kingsburg, Calif., June 2, 1953; s. Marvin Lindsey and Catherine Marie (Gagnon) E.; m. Patricia Ann Froelich, May 7, 1977; 1 child, Rebecca Ann. AA, Reedley (Calif.) Jr. Coll., 1973, BA magna cum laude, 1975; MSW, Calif. State U., Fresno, 1979; PhD, Case Western Res. U., 1998. Lic. clin. social worker, Calif. Psychiat. social worker Sierra County, Downieville, Calif., 1979-81, mental health dir., 1981; med. social worker Solano County, Vallejo, Calif., 1981—; Commr. on Aging, Sierra County, 1980-81; instr. in gerontology Am. River Coll., Sacramento, 1982—; instr. in psychology Solano Coll., Suisun, Calif., 1984—. Author: In Home Assessment of Older Adults, 1996, (anthology) Suisun Valley Review, 1986; contbr. articles to profl. jours. Mem. Am Soc. Aging, Nat. Assn. Social Workers, Gerontol. Soc. Am. Avocations: aikido, backpacking. Home: 124 Wildflower Ave Vallejo CA 94591-8061 Office: Solano County Dept Health Health Svcs 355 Tuolumne St Vallejo CA 94590-5700

EMMANUEL, JORGE AGUSTIN, chemical engineer, environmental consultant; b. Manila, Aug. 28, 1954; came to U.S., 1970; s. Benjamin Elmido and Lourdes (Orozco) E.; 1 child, Andres Layanglawin. BS in Chemistry, N.C. State U., 1976, MSChemE, 1978; PhD in Chem. Engring., U. Mich., 1988. Registered profl. engr., Calif., environ. profl.; cert. hazardous materials mgr. Process engr. Perry Electronics, Raleigh, N.C., 1973-74; rsch. asst. N.C. State U., Raleigh, 1977-78; rsch. chem. engr. GE Corp. R & D Ctr., Schenectady, N.Y., 1978-81; Amoco rsch. fellow U. Mich., Ann Arbor, 1981-84; sr. environ. analyst TEM Assocs., Inc., Emeryville, Calif., 1988-91; pres. Environ. & Engring. Rsch. Group, Hercules, Calif., 1991—; environ. cons. to the Philippines, UN Devel. Program, 1992, 94; rsch. assoc. U. Calif., Berkeley, 1988-90. Contbr. articles to profl. jours. Mem. Assn. for Asian Studies, Ann Arbor, 1982-88; sec. Alliance for Philippine Concerns, L.A., 1983-91; assoc. Philippine Resource Ctr., Berkeley, 1988-92; bd. dirs. ARC-Ecology, San Francisco, 1990—, Asia Pacific Ctr., Washington, 1995—; bd. advisors Urban Habitat, 1995—. N.C. State U. grantee, 1976, Phoenix grantee U. Mich., 1982. Mem. NSPE, AAAS, Air and Waste Mgmt. Assn., Calif. Acad. Scis., N.Y. Acad. Sci., Filipino-Am. Soc. Architects and Engrs. (exec. sec. 1989-90, Svc. award 1990). Avocations: classical guitar, ethnomusicology, Asian studies. Office: The Environ & Engring Rsch Group 628 2nd St Rodeo CA 94572-1111

EMMELUTH, BRUCE PALMER, investment company executive, venture capitalist; b. L.A., Nov. 30, 1940; s. William J. and Elizabeth L. (Palmer) E.; children: William J. II (dec.), Bruce Palmer Jr., Carrie E.; m. Canda E. Samuels, Mar. 29, 1987. Sr. investment analyst corp. fin. dept. Prudential Ins. Co. Am., L.A., 1965-70; with Seidler Amdec Securities, Inc., 1970-90, sr. v.p., mgr. corp. fin. dept., 1974-90, also bd. dirs.; mng. dir. corp. fin., mgr. corp. fin. dept., mem. exec. com. First Securities Van Kasper, L.A., 1990—, also exec. v.p.; exec. v.p., mng. dir. corp. fin. Van Kasper & Co., L.A.; pres., bd. dirs. SAS Capital Corp., venture capital subs. Seidler Amdec Securities, 1977-90; bd. advisors Entreprenurial Studies Program, Anderson Grad. Sch. Mgmt. UCLA, 1985—, past. bd. dirs. Active Calvary Ch., Pacific Palisades, Calif. With U.S. Army N.G., 1965-71. Home: 17146 Palisades Cir Pacific Palisades CA 90272-2141 Office: First Securities Van Kasper 10877 Wilshire Blvd Ste 1700 Los Angeles CA 90024-4372

EMMONS, ROBERT JOHN, corporate executive; b. Trenton, N.J., Sept. 18, 1934; s. Charles Glunk and Ruth Marie (Heilhecker) E.; m. Christine Young Bebb, July 13, 1980; children: Bradley Thomas, Cathy Lynne, Christopher Robert, Ryan Hunter. A.B. in Econs, U. Mich., 1956, M.B.A., 1960, J.D., 1964. V.p. Baskin-Robbins Co., Burbank, Calif., 1964-68; pres. United Rent-All, Los Angeles, 1968-69, Master Host Internat., Los Angeles, 1969-71; prof. Grad. Sch. Bus., U. So. Calif., 1971-82; pres. LTI Corp., Monterey, Calif., 1982-84; chmn., chief exec. officer, dir. Casino USA/SFI Corp., Santa Barbara, Calif., 1984-9884; chmn. Casino USA/Smart & Final Inc., Santa Barbara, Calif., 1998—; chmn., CEO Casino USA/SFI Corp., 1998—. Author: The American Franchise Revolution, 1970, The American Marketing Revolution, 1980; poetry Other Places, Other Times, 1974, Love and Other Minor Tragedies, 1980. Mem. AAUP, Am. Mktg. Assn., European Mktg. Assn., Am. Econ. Assn., Calif. Yacht Club (L.A.), Hawaii Yacht Club (Honolulu), The Valley Club of Montecito (Calif.), Useppa Island Club (Fla.), St. Petersburg Yacht Club (Fla.), The Calif. Club, Beta Gamma Sigma, Pi Kappa Alpha. Office: Casino USA/Smart & Final Inc 524 Chapala St Santa Barbara CA 93101-3475

EMPEY, GENE F., real estate executive; b. Hood River, Oreg., July 13, 1923; BS in Animal Husbandry, Oreg. State U., 1949; M. of Tech. Journalism Iowa State U., 1950; m. Janet Halladay, Dec. 27, 1950; children: Stephen Bruce, Michael Guy. Publs. dir. U. Nev., Reno, 1950-55; mgr. Zephyr Cove Lodge Hotel, Lake Tahoe, Nev., 1955-65; owner Empey Co., real estate agy., Carson City and Tahoe, Nev., 1964—; land developer, owner investment and brokerage firm . Mem. Nev. Planning Bd., 1959-72, chmn., 1961-66; mem. Nev. Tax Commn., 1982—; participant People to People Program, China, 1996, Egypt, Jordan, 1997. Capt., inf. U.S. Army, 1943-47; PTO. Grad. Realtors Inst. Mem. Nat. Assn. Realtors, (cert. comml. investment mem.; pres. Nev. chpt.), Tahoe Douglas C. of C. (pres. 1962, dir.), Carson City C. of C., Carson-Tahoe-Douglas Bd. Realtors, Capital City Club, Rotary, Heavenly Valley Ski (pres. 1968) Club, The Prospector's Club (Reno). Republican. Home: PO Box 707 Zephyr Cove NV 89448-0707 Office: 512 S Curry St Carson City NV 89703-4614

ENAS, LENA MAE, research coordinator, consultant; b. Sells, Ariz., July 18, 1963; d. Floyd Michael and Lavina Mae (Segundo) Harris; m. Austin Enas, Jan. 19, 1990 (dec. Febr. 1994); children: Arlene Enas, Morris Enas. Detention officer Tohono O'Odham Nation, Sells, 1989-91, sec. I, 1990-93, rsch. coord., 1993-96, acting mgr., 1996—; acting mgr., 1996-98, mgr. 1998—, rsch. coord., cons., Avon sales rep. Rep. Baboquivari Dist., Sells; sec. Choulic Cmty., Sells. Mem. Internat. Sonoran Desert Alliance (cons. 1995—). Avocations: basket making, aerobics, reading, walking, traveling. Home: PO Box 756 Sells AZ 85634-0756 Office: Tohono O'odham Nation Hia Ced O'odham Program PO Box 837 Sells AZ 85634-0837

ENDICOTT, WILLIAM F., journalist; b. Harrodsburg, Ky., Aug. 26, 1935; s. William O. and Evelyn E.; m. Mary Frances Thomas, Dec. 27, 1956; children: Gene, Fran, Greg. Student, Am. U., 1955; BA in Polit. Sci., Transylvania U., 1957. With Lexington (Ky.) Leader, 1957; sports writer Louisville Courier-Jour., 1958-62; reporter Tulare (Calif.) Advance-Register, 1963; reporter, city editor Modesto (Calif.) Bee, 1963-66; city editor Sacramento Union, 1966-67; with Los Angeles Times, 1968-85; Capitol bur. chief Sacramento Bee, 1985-95, asst. mng. editor, 1995-98, dep. mng. editor, 1998—; Hearst vis. profl. U. Tex., 1993. Served with USMCR, 1957-58. Recipient various journalism awards Disting. Alumnus award Transylvania U., 1980. Episcopalian. Office: 21st and Q Sts Sacramento CA 95852

ENDRIZ, JOHN GUIRY, electronics executive; b. Oak Park, Ill., Jan. 10, 1942; s. John Daniel and Florence (Guiry) E.; m. Sally Jean Doubleday, July 19, 1975. BSEE, MSEE, MIT, 1965; PhD in EE, Stanford U., 1970. Guest rschr. Linkoping (Sweden) U., 1970-72; project mgr. R.C.A. Rsch. Lab., Princeton, N.J., 1972-77; engring. mgr. Varian Assocs., Palo Alto, Calif., 1977-88; v.p. engring. S.D.L., Inc., San Jose, Calif., 1988-97, v.p. power delivery bus. unit, 1997—. Contbr. over 53 articles to profl. jours.; patentee of over 29 inventions. Mem. IEEE, S.P.I.E., Soc. Information Display. Home: 5 Heritage Court Belmont CA 94002 Office: SDL Inc 80 Rose Orchard San Jose CA 94002

ENFIELD, D(ONALD) MICHAEL, insurance executive; b. L.A., Jan. 24, 1945; s. Fred Donald Jr. and Suzanne Arden (Hinkle) E.; m. Roseanne Burke, Dec. 29, 1978; children: Susan Ann, Michael David, Peter Christian. BA in Polit. Sci., U. San Francisco, 1967. Mgmt. trainee Marsh & McLennan, Inc., San Francisco, 1967-70, acct. exec., 1970-77, asst. v.p., 1977-79, v.p., 1979-81, sr. v.p., 1981-82, mng. dir., 1982-89; chmn., CEO Frank B. Hall & Co. of No. Calif., San Francisco, 1989-92; founder, chmn., CEO Metro/Risk, Inc., San Francisco, 1992—; cons. in field. Contbr. articles to profl. publs. Bd. dirs. Ronald McDonald House, San Francisco, 1989-92; chmn. bd. dirs. Midsummer Mozart Festival, San Francisco, 1985-90; trustee Lamplighters Music Theater, 1996—. Mem. San Francisco C. of C. (dir. bus./arts coun. 1987-93), Soc. Calif. Pioneers (county v.p. 1974—), Lotos Club of N.Y., City Club of San Francisco, Olympic Club of San Francisco. Avocation: classical music. Office: Metro/Risk Inc 750 Battery St Ste 550 San Francisco CA 94111-1526

ENFIELD, SUSAN ANN, secondary education educator; b. San Francisco, May 30, 1968; d. D. Michael and Julia Ann (Bettencourt) E. Student, York (Eng.) U., 1988-89; BA in English, U. Calif., Berkeley, 1990; MEd, Stanford U., 1993. Editl. asst. Jossey-Bass, Inc. Pubs., San Francisco, 1990-92; tchr. Homestead H.S., Cupertino, Calif., 1993-97; tchr. English Sir Francis Drake H.S., San Anselmo, Calif., 1997—. Contbt. author: When Tutor Meets Student. Named Outstanding Tchr., Tufts U., 1994, Carleton Coll., 1995, Coll. Wooster, 1996, U. Calif., Santa Barbara, 1997, U. Ariz., 1997. Mem.

Nat. Coun. Tchrs. English, Journalism Edn. Assn., Nat. Scholastic Press Assn. Office: Sir Francis Drake H S 1327 Sir Francis Drake Blvd San Anselmo CA 94960-1866

ENG, CHRISTOPHER KAMUELA, minister, educator; b. Honolulu, Mar. 13, 1949; s. Frank Harold and Joan (Mung) E.; m. Cheri M. Shimose, Feb. 14, 1988; children: Skye S. T., Joy S. K. BA cum laude, U. Hawaii, 1971, MA with honors, 1973; MDiv, Fuller Theol. Sem., 1977; D of Ministry, San Francisco Theol. Sem., 1985. Ordained to Am. Bapt. Ch., 1979. Campus min. Hawaii Conf. United Ch. Christ to U. Hawaii, Honolulu, 1975; asst. pastor Chinese United Meth. Ch., L.A., 1975-77; assoc. min. Japanese Bapt. Ch., Seattle, 1978-81, Nuuanu Congl. Ch. United Ch. Christ, Honolulu, 1981-85; sr. pastor Walpahu United (Hawaii) Ch. Christ, 1985—; instr. T'ai-Chi Ch'uan U. Hawaii, Leeward Community Coll., 1987—, Wahiawa Gen. Hosp., 1995—; bd. dirs. Hawaii Conf. United Ch. Christ, Honolulu, 1984—; vol. chaplain Kuakini Med. Ctr. Oncology Team, Honolulu, 1986—; pres. Oahu Assn. United Ch. Christ Mokupuni, Honolulu, 1989-90; trainer curriculum United Ch. of Christ. Contbr. articles to profl. jours. Bd. mgrs. Nuuanu YMCA, Honolulu, 1981-91, Leeward YMCA, Waipahu, 1991—; vol. Honolulu Jaycees and Jaycettes, 1982; mem. Hawaii's Plantation Village, Min.'s Coun. Masland fellow Union Theol. Sem. N.Y., 1990; recipient Pro Deo et Patria God and Country award Boy Scouts Am., 1967, Svc. award YMCA, 1987; named legis. intern Ctr. Govtl. Devel., 1971. Mem. AAUP, Nat. Assn. Underwater Instrs., Hawaii Sociological Assn., Waipahu Community Assn. Democrat. Avocations: photography, bicycling, back packing, hiking, swimming. Office: Waipahu United Ch Christ 94-330 Mokuola St Waipahu HI 96797-3313

ENGAR, RICHARD CHARLES, insurance executive, dentist, educator; b. Salt Lake City, Apr. 2, 1953; s. Keith Maurice and Amy Kathryn (Lyman) E.; m. Elizabeth Ann Willardson, June 21, 1977; children: Robert Keith, Thomas William, Julia Elizabeth. BA in Psychology, U. Utah, 1976; DDS, U. Wash., 1980. Resident gen. practice Sinai Hosp., Detroit, 1980-81; pvt. practice Salt Lake City, 1981-91; cons. Profl. Ins. Exch., Salt Lake City, 1990-91, atty.-in-fact, 1991—; clin. instr. dept. pathology, dental gen. practice residency program U. Utah Med. Ctr., Salt Lake City, 1988—. Author: Dental Treatment of the Sensory Impaired Patient, 1977; (with others) General Dentistry, 1996; contbr. articles to profl. jours. Dist. trainer Spring Creek Dist., Great Salt Lake coun. Boy Scouts Am., 1989-92. Fellow Acad. Gen. Dentistry (regional dir. 1991-97, chair regional dirs. 1995-97, trustee 1997—, publs. com. 1997—), Pierre Fauchard Acad., Utah Acad. Gen. Dentistry (pres. 1987, Dentist of Yr. 1997); mem. ADA, Salt Lake Dist. Dental Soc. (treas. 1986-88), Utah Dental Assn. (editor 1985-88), Acad. of Dentistry Internat., Utah Scale Modelers Assn. (v.p. 1992, 94, 97), Phi Beta Kappa, Phi Kappa Phi. Mem. LDS Ch. Avocations: model airplane building, backpacking, photography, painting. Home: 1806 Glenbrook Cir Salt Lake City UT 84121-1213 Office: 445 E 4500 S Salt Lake City UT 84107-3129

ENGEL, LINDA JEANNE, mining executive; b. Denver, Aug. 24, 1949; d. Thomas Mintor and Irene Evelyn (Esbenson) Kelley; m. William Stephen Engel, May 6, 1972; children: Kacey, Ryan. *Husband William Stephen (Steve) Engel is broker, manager, of ReMax West and has served as president of Denver Board of Realtors. He played professional football for two years with the Cleveland Browns. Daughter Kacey Lynn Engel (now Kacey Koonce) was recently married to Nathan Koonce, an electrical engineer. Kacey is currently employed in flight & systems operations at Lockheed Martin and is directly involved in Stardust & Genesis Satellite projects. Son Ryan Stephen Engel is currently a first-class cadet at the U.S. Coast Guard Academy in New London, Connecticut. He is studying civil engineering and would like to pursue a career in aviation.* BA in Polit. Sci., U. Colo., 1975. Statis. researcher Martin Marietta, Waterton, Colo., 1971; asst. dir. Fed. Drug Abuse Program, Denver, 1972-74; corp. sec./treas. Grayhill Exploration Co., Arvada, Colo., 1981-84; controller Western Internat. Gold-Silver, Westminster, Colo., 1985-86; investor rels. dir. and corp. sec. Canyon Resources Corp., Golden, Colo., 1986-94. Republican.

ENGEL, RACHAEL ERIN, management consultant; b. L.A., Nov. 19, 1973; d. Irwin William and Wendy Joyce (Gold) E. BS in Journalism, U. Colo., 1995. Cons. Andersen Cons., Denver, 1995—. Editor: (newsletter) Commerce Newsletter, 1997—. Mem. Jr. League Denver, 1996—. Mem. ASTD, SPI. Avocations: skiing, biking, running, volleyball, tennis. Home: 4543 E Kentucky Cir Denver CO 80246-2001

ENGEL, THOMAS P., airport executive. Dir. Sacramento Met. Airport, Calif.; dir. of airports Sacramento County Dept. of Airports, Calif. Office: Sacramento County Calif Dept of Airports 6900 Airport Blvd Sacramento CA 95837-1109

ENGELMANN, RUDOLPH HERMAN, electronics consultant; b. Hewitt, Minn., Mar. 5, 1929; s. Herman Emil Robert and Minna Louise (Kniep) E.; children: Guy Robert, Heidi Louise. BA, U. Minn., 1953. Electronic designer Lawrence Livermore (Calif.) Lab., 1959-61; cons. Atlantic Rsch. Corp., Manchester, N.H., 1961-64, Gen. Radio Co., West Concord, Mass., 1963-69, Possis Engring., Mpls., 1970—, 3M Co., St. Paul, 1977-78, Pako Photo, Mpls., 1977-78, Litton Microwave, Mpls., 1977-79; Presenter papers at confs., 1988-89, 89-90. Contbr. articles to profl. jours. 1st lt. USAF, 1946-53. Achievements include developments and patents in gigahertz digital frequency scalers and counters and time interval meters, touchtone telephone for U.S. Army, automatic photographic focus control, automatic temperature monitor and control for grain and petroleum storage safety and volume correction, optical character recognition, high efficiency battery charging systems, end-of-charge detector, rudderless flight control, ultra lightweight muscle prostheses, flight controls, power management, stealth penetrating radar, high efficiency shpae memory alloy modulation and linear circuitry, high-efficiency electronic orthetic muscle, digitally variable 90db A.C. power source, raster scanning microscope, linear wave blood pump. Office: World Effort Found 1171 Bush St Apt 2 San Francisco CA 94109-5926

ENGLAND, DAVID P., anesthesiologist, educator; b. Providence, Dec. 31, 1955; s. Norman A.W. and Edna C. (Vanasse) E.; m. Marty Jean Beck, May 29, 1987; children: Jozlyn, Addyson, Macy. Student, Providence Coll., summer 1976, U. Nebr., summer 1977; BS in Biology and Psychology, Creighton U., Omaha, 1978; MS in Physiology, Georgetown U., 1980; postgrad., No. Va. C.C., Alexandria, 1984; DO, U. Health Scis., Kansas City, Mo., 1989. Diplomate Nat. Bd. Osteopathic Med. Examiners. Intern Doctor's Hosp., Columbus, Ohio, 1989-90; resident Med. Coll. Va., Richmond, 1990-93, asst. prof. dept. anesthesiology, 1993-95; faculty No. Va. C.C., Annadale, 1983-84; emergency rm. physician Kenner Army Hosp., Ft. Lee, Va., 1991-95. Russell C. McCaughan scholar Nat. Osteopathic Found., E.F.N. Fed. scholar; Georgetown U. Nursing Sch. teaching fellow. Mem. Am. Soc. Anesthesiology, Ariz. Soc. Anesthesiology, Am. Osteo. Assn., Va. Osteo. Med. Assn., Psi Sigma Alpha, Sigma Sigma Phi, Ctrl. Va. Mustang Club. Avocations: marathon running, snow and water skiing, weight training, hunting, home improvements. Office: Canyon State Anesthesiologists PC 4820 E Mcdowell Rd Ste 101 Phoenix AZ 85008-4226

ENGLE, CINDY, medical transcriptionist; b. Denver, Aug. 12, 1958; d. Wallace Clyde and Mary Margaret (Ingram) E. AA, Arapahoe C.C., 1979; BA in Kinesiology, U. No. Colo., 1992. Cert. paralegal; former cert. paramedic, Colo. EMT/paramedic Ambulance Svc. Co., Denver, 1978-80; pers. asst. payroll Burns Security Svc., Denver, 1980-82; part-time asst. mgr. Tokoyo Bowl Restaurant, Denver, 1982-85; paramedic Platte Valley Ambulance, 1982-85; part-time flight paramedic for Air Life North Colo. Med. Ctr., Greeley, Colo., 1986-91; paramedic Weld County Ambulance, Greeley, 1985-92; intern exercise svcs. Greeley (Colo.) Med. Clinic, 1992, med. transcriptionist, 1993-94; med. transcriptionist North Colo. Med. Ctr., Greeley, 1994—; cert. bioenergetic and wellness cons. and practitioner Bio-Lines, L.L.C., 1998—; part-time EMS/criminal justice instr. Aims C.C., Greeley, 1987-96; founder The Human Factor, 1992-98. Author ednl. game: The Reality Game, 1993. Avocations: reading, walking dogs. Office: The Human Factor 2626 23rd Ave Greeley CO 80631-7918

ENGLE, ROBERT IRWIN, music educator, musician, composer, writer; b. New Kensington, Pa., Feb. 11, 1945; s. Dale Clair Engle and Rosalyn Imogene (Timblin) Erickson. BS in Music Edn., U. Cin., 1967; postgrad., Stanford U., 1967-68, Ind. U., 1969, U. So. Calif., 1969-71; MA in Music, U. Hawaii, 1973, cert. in Samoan, 1986; PhD in Music, U. Wash., 1994. Cert. tchr. music grades K-12, Calif., Wash. Choral instr. Terminal Island Prison, San Pedro, Calif., 1969-71; choral music tchr. Palos Verdes (Calif.) High Sch., 1968-72; dir. music Makiki Christian Ch., Honolulu, 1978-84, 1st United Meth. Ch., Honolulu, 1986-88; tchr. music and French Redemption Acad., Kailua, Hawaii, 1988-91; dir. music Kapiolani Community Coll., Honolulu, 1975—; dir. choral activities U. Hawaii, Hilo, 1995-96; asst. dir. music Hilo First Samoan Assembly of God, 1995-96; dir. music Good Samaritan Samoan Ch., Honolulu, 1997-98; cons. Performing Arts Abroad, Kalamazoo, 1979—, Pacific Basin Choral Festival in Hawaii, Berkeley, Calif., 1989, Gateway Music Festivals, 1997—; tchr. music theory, piano S. Seattle C.C., 1993-94; choral music tchr. Inglemoor H.S., Bothell, Wash., 1994; prof. Polynesian music and dance U. Pitts., summer 1997; spkr. Internat. Soc. Music Edn. Convention, Tampa, Fla., 1994, Pretoria, South Africa, 1998; spkr. nat. conf. Soc. Ethnomusicology, L.A., 1995, Music Educators Nat. Conf., Kansas City, 1996; spkr. in field.; accompanist Honolulu Boy Choir, 1996; coord. summer course in Tahitian dance and music, Papeete, Tahiti, 1998. Author: Taking Note of Music, 1988, Piano Is My Forte, 1989; editor Pacific Island Choral Series, 1995—; composer: Tatalo A Le Alii, 1984 (3d place state competition); composer, rec. artist Pese Pa'ia, 1988; profl. rec. Christmas Aloha; dir., composer of new repertoire New Samoan Ch. Choir Repertoire Project, Am. and Western Samoa, 1997; contbr. articles to profl. jours. Founder E Himeni Kakou Colls. Choral Festival, Honolulu, 1976—; founder, dir. Maile Aloha Singers, Honolulu, 1973-92, Carols at the Centerstage Festival, Honolulu, 1989—, Lokahi Choral Festival, Honolulu, 1989—, Aloha, America! Invitational Choral Festival, Honolulu, 1995. Dir. mus. group representing Hawaii, Cultural Office for Territorial Activity, Papeete, Tahiti, 1982, World U. Games, 1983, Casa De La Cultura, Southeastern Mex., 1984, La. World EXPO, 1984, EXPO '86, Vancouver, Hawaiian Airlines, 1987, Goodwill Tour Am. Samoa, 1989, Artists in the Schs. Auckland, N.Z., 1991; dir. mus. group representing U.S.A., U.S. Dept. State, EXPO '85, Tsukuba, Japan, 1985; Dir. award 2d pl. group Collegiate Showcase, Chgo., 1988, Dir. award 1st place Choral Groups All Am. Festival, Orlando, Fla., 1994. Mem. AAUP, Am. Choral Dirs. Assn. (Hawaii chpt. 1978—, editor newsletter 1987-89, 97-99, state pres. 1989-91, state sec. 1997-99), U. Hawaii Profl. Assembly, Samoa Fealofani Club, Delta Tau Delta (life). Republican. Mem. Pentecostal Ch. Avocations: languages, weightlifting, Polynesian dance. Home: 2901 Numana Rd Honolulu HI 96819-2904 Office: Kapiolani CC 4303 Diamond Head Rd Honolulu HI 96816-4421

ENGLERT, WALTER GEORGE, classics and humanities educator; b. Oakland, Calif., June 30, 1952; s. Walter George and Isobel Ann (O'Hearne) E.; m. Mary Ellen Mecchi; children: Francesca, Molly. BA summa cum laude, St. Mary's Coll. Calif., 1974; MA, U. Calif. Santa Barbara, 1976; postgrad., Am. Sch. Classical Studies, Athens, 1979; PhD, Stanford U., 1981. Teaching asst. U. Calif., Santa Barbara, 1974-76, Stanford U., 1977-78; vis. lectr. U. Mich., Ann Arbor, 1980-81; vis. assoc. prof. U. Calif., Berkeley, 1986, Intercollegiate Ctr. Classical Studies, Rome, 1992-93; Omar and Althea Hoskins prof. Reed Coll., Portland, Oreg., 1981—; organizer and lectr. Reed Latin Symposium for H.S. Students, 1988-97; participant TAG Spring Interdisciplinary confs., 1988; tchr. Paideia Class, 1989, 91, 96, 97, Reed MALS Seminar, 1988, 93, Reed Elderhostel Program, 1989; mem. faculty Reed Alumni Coll., 1989, 95; lectr. Seattle Reed Alumni Group, 1991; guest Town Hall TV show, 1991. Contbr. articles to profl. jours. Grantee NEH, 1983, 95, Mellon Faculty Seminar, 1986-87, Sloan Found., 1987-88. Office: Reed Coll 3203 SE Woodstock Blvd Portland OR 97202-8138

ENGLISH, CHARLES ROYAL, lawyer; b. Santa Monica, Calif., Apr. 9, 1938; s. Charles James and Antoinette Frieda (Schindler) E.; m. Marylyn Gray, Sept. 6, 1969; children: Mitchell Lloyd, Charles James, Julia Catherine. Santa Monica City Coll., 1958; BS, UCLA, 1961, UCLA, 1965. Bar: Calif. 1966. Sole practice Santa Monica, 1967; with L.A. County Pub. Defender's Office, 1967-78, sr. trial dep., 1978; ptnr. Chaleff, English and Catalano and predecessor Lafaille, Chaleff & English, Santa Monica, 1978-97; propr. Law Office of Charles R. English, 1997-98, English & Gold, Santa Monica, 1998—; lectr. in field. With USAR, 1961-67. Mem. ABA (criminal justice sect coun. 1992, chmn. standards com. 1997-98), Santa Monica Bar, State Bar Calif., Criminal Cts. Bar Assn., Bur. Automotive Repair, L.A. County Bar Assn. (trustee 1980-83, pres. found 1990-91), UCLA Law Alumni Assn. (pres. 1980), Chancery Club (treas. 1997, sec. 1998), Olde Bailey. Home and Office: 1337 Ocean Ave Santa Monica CA 90401-1029

ENGLISH, DONALD MARVIN, loss control representative; b. Raleigh, N.C., July 31, 1951; s. Marvin Lee and Lois (Woodard) E.; m. Rebecca Pritchard, Sept. 3, 1970 (div. 1977); m. Kathryn A. Sumner, July 3, 1993 (div. 1998). Student, Miami U., Oxford, Ohio, 1969-70, 73-74, U. Cin., 1977-78, Calif. State U., Fresno, 1980—; AA, Fresno City Coll., 1991. Cert. safety profl. Bd. Cert. Safety Profls. Ins. inspector Comml. Services, Cin., 1974-78, Ohio Casualty Ins. Co., Fresno, 1978-93; owner Loss Control Systems, Renton, Wash., 1993; sr. loss control specialist Scott Wetzel Svcs., Inc., Federal Way, Wash., 1993-96; loss control territory mgr. Am. States Ins. Co., Seattle, 1996—. Served with U.S. Army, 1970-73. Mem. Am. Soc. Safety Engrs., Soc. CPCU (cert.), Ins. Inst. Am. (assoc. in loss control mgmt. 1990), East Fresno Exch. Club (pres. 1984-85). Avocation: internat. traveling. Home: 6520 146th St SW Edmonds WA 98026-3523 Office: 6021 244th St SW Mountlake Terrace WA 98043-5400

ENGLISH, STEPHEN F., lawyer; b. Portland, Oreg., Jan. 17, 1948. BA with honors, U. Oreg., 1970; JD, U. Calif., San Francisco, 1973. Bar: Oreg. 1973; U.S. Dist. Ct. Oreg. 1973; U.S. Ct. Appeals (9th cir.) Oreg. 1980; U.S. Supreme Ct. 1982. Ptnr. Bullivant Houser Bailey, Portland, Oreg., 1983—; mem. faculty Hastings Coll. Trial Advocacy, 1998—. Mem. ABA (vice-chair products liability com., 1996—, chair self insurers and risk mgrs. com. 1994-95, editor Self Insurers Newsletter 1987-89, chair non-profit, charitable and religious orgns. com. 1990-92), Multnomah County Bar Assn., Oreg. State Bar Assn. (chair 1990-91, exec. com. 1987-91), Am. Bd. of Trial Adv. (treas. Oreg. chpt. 1996-98, sec. Oreg. chpt. 1998—), Oreg. Assn. of Def. Counsel (chair products liability practice group 1997-98), Def. Rsch. Inst. Office: Bullivant Houser Bailey 300 Pioneer Tower 888 SW 5th Ave Ste 300 Portland OR 97204-2089*

ENGLISH, WOODROW DOUGLAS, lawyer; b. San Antonio, Dec. 1, 1941; s. Woodie Douglas Jr. and June Louise (Wasik) E.; m. Marcia Anne Mathwig, Dec. 19, 1969 (div. Aug. 1981); children: Kristina Renee, David Douglas; m. Carol Jordan, July 11, 1987; children: Leanne Alexander Cassidy, Lisa Alexander Cook. BS in Physics, Trinity U., 1967; JD, Western State U., 1981. Bar: Calif. 1989, U.S. Patent Office 1982, U.S. Supreme Ct. 1992. Sales engr. Mfrs. Rep., Seattle, 1972-75; real estate salesperson, broker Sherwood & Roberts Realtors & Coldwell Banker, Seattle, 1975-78; safety engr. Boeing Aerospace, Seattle, 1978-79; ins. agt., broker Farmers Ins. Group, San Diego, 1979-81; U.S. patent agt. Dept. Def., China Lake, Calif., 1981-87; corp. counsel Del Mar Avionics, Irvine, Calif., 1987-97; pvt. practice Ventura, Calif., 1991—; real estate broker, Ventura, ins. broker, Ventura. Capt. USAF, 1961-65. Mem. Masons, Shriners, Elks, Kiwanis, Am. Legion, Sigma Pi Sigma, Phi Alpha Delta, Nu Beta Epsilon. Republican. Avocation: flying. Home: 1215 Lost Point Ln Oxnard CA 93030-6770 Office: County Sq Profl Offices 674 County Square Dr Ventura CA 93003-5454

ENGLISH, WOODRUFF JONES, II, physician; b. Summit, N.J., May 16, 1945; s. Woodruff Jones and Carolyn E.; m. Annie Terry, 1974; children: Woodruff Jones III, Andersen, Evelyn. AB, Princeton U., 1968; MD, Columbia U., 1972; MMM, Tulane U., 1998. Diplomate Am. Coll. Physicians. Epidemiologist Ctrs. for Disease Control & Prevention, Atlanta, 1977-80; physician Providence Med. Group, Portland, Oreg., 1980—. Office: Providence Med Group 417 SW 117th Ave Portland OR 97225-5918

ENGORON, EDWARD DAVID, food service consultant, television and [illegible] E.; m. Charlene Scott, Oct. 7, 1970 (div. July 1982). BArch., U. So. Calif., 1969, MBA, 1973, PhD, 1974; MA, Cordon Bleu, Paris, 1975. Art dir. ABC, L.A., 1964-67, Paramount Pictures, L.A., 1967-68, Warner Bros. Pictures, Burbank, Calif., 1968-69; mktg. dir. Lawry's Foods Inc., Burbank, 1969-74; v.p. Warehouse Restaurants, Marina del Rey, Calif., 1968-72; pres. Perspectives, San Francisco, 1974-82, Perspectives Comm. Syndicated Talk Shows, L.A., 1986—, China Rose Inc., Dallas, 1982-86; exec. v.p. T.G.I. Fridays Inc., Dallas, 1986-87; pres., chief exec. officer, bd. dirs. Guilt Free Goodies, Ltd., Vancouver, B.C., Can., 1986-90, Sugarless Co., L.A., 1986-90; cons. Southland Corp., Dallas, 1982-86, Pizza Hut Inc., Wichita, Kans., 1975-87, Frank L. Carney Enterprises, Wichita, 1982-87, Safeway Stores, Inc., Freemont, Calif., Romacorp, Dallas, Bel-Air Hotel Co., L.A., Capital Cities-ABC, Hollywood, Nestle Foods, White Plains, Screiber Foods, Green Bay, Rich's Food Products, Buffalo, Arby's Inc., Ft. Lauderdale, Fla., Sizzler Internat., L.A., ednl. found. Nat. Restaurant Assn., Taco Bell, Inc., Irvine, Calif., Basic Am., Inc. San Francisco, Nat. Super Markets, St. Louis, Wok Fast, Inc., L.A., The Vons Cons., L.A., 1989—; pres. Sweet Deceit, Inc., Guilt-Free Goodies, Ltd.; co-host nationally syndicated radio talk show The Super Foodies, ABC. Author: (cookbook) Stolen Secrets, 1980; patentee pasta cooking sta., 1981, micro-wave controller, 1982. Bd. govs. Los Angeles Parks, 1971-74; mem. Fine Arts Commn., Tiburon, Calif., 1974-76. Mem. Foodsvc. Cons. Soc. Internat., Soc. Motion Picture Art Dirs., Food, Wine and Travel Writers Assn., Internat. Assn. Culinary Profls., Masons. Republican. Office: 11030 Santa Monica Blvd Ste 301 Los Angeles CA 90025-7514

ENNIS, THOMAS MICHAEL, management consultant; b. Morgantown, W.Va., Mar. 7, 1931; s. Thomas Edson and Violet Ruth (Nugent) E.; m. Julia Marie Dorety, June 30, 1956; children: Thomas John, Robert Griswold (dec.). Student, W.Va. U., 1949-52; AB, George Washington U., 1954; JD, Georgetown U., 1960. With Gov. Employees Ins. Co., Washington, 1956, 59, Air Transport Assn. Am., Washington, 1959-60; dir. ann. support program George Washington U., 1960-63; nat. dir. devel. Project HOPE, People to People Health Found., Inc., Washington, 1963-66; nat. exec. dir. Epilepsy Found. Am., Washington, 1966-74; exec. dir. Clinton, Eaton, Ingham Community Mental Health Bd., Lansing, Mich., 1974-83; nat. exec. dir. Alzheimer's Disease and Related Disorders Assn., Inc., Chgo., 1983-86; exec. dir., pres. The John Douglas French Alzheimers Found., L.A., 1986-96, pres. emeritus, 1996—; clin. instr. dept. cmty. medicine and internat. health Georgetown U., 1967-74; adj. assoc. prof. dept. psychiatry Mich. State U., 1975-84; lectr. Univ. Ctr. for Internat. Rehab., 1977; cons. health and med. founds., related orgns.; cons. Am. Health Found., 1967-69, Reston, Va.-Georgetown U. Health Planning Project, 1967-70. Mem. adv. bd. Nat. Center for the Law and the Handicapped, 1971-74; advisor Nat. Reye's Syndrome Found.; mem. Nat. Com. for Research in Neurol. Disorders, 1967-72; mem. nat. adv. bd. Developmental Disabilities/Tech. Assistance System, U. N.C., 1971-78; nat. trustee Nat. Kidney Found., 1970-74, mem. exec. com. and bd. Nat. Capitol Area chpt., pres., 1972-74; bd. dirs. Nat. Assn. Pvt. Residential Facilities for Mentally Retarded, 1970-74; bd. dirs., mem. exec. com. Epilepsy Found. Am., 1977-84, Epilepsy Center Mich., 1974-83; nat. bd. dirs. Western Inst. on Epilepsy, 1969-72; bd. dirs., pres. Mich. Mid-South Health Systems Agy., 1975-78; sec. gen. Internat. Fedn. Alzheimer's Disease and Related Disorders, 1984-86; mem. panel Alzheimer's Disease Edn. and Referral Ctr., 1990-93; mem. Calif. State Coun. on Developmental Disabilities, 1997—; med. adv. bd. EdenCare Sr. Living Svcs. World Rehab. Fund fellow Norway, 1980. Mem. Nat. Epilepsy League (bd. dirs. 1977-78), Mich. Assn. Cmty. Mental Health (pres. 1977-79), Nat. Coalition Rsch. Neurol. Disorders (dir. at-large 1991—), Scan Health Plan (bd. govs.), Phi Alpha Theta, Phi Kappa Psi. Home and Office: 23740 Killion St Woodland Hills CA 91367-5822

ENNIS, WILLIAM LEE, physics educator; b. Houston, Aug. 10, 1949; s. Arthur Lee and Helen Ennis; m. Constance Elizabeth Livsey, July 20, 1991. BS, Auburn (Ala.) U., 1974, BA, 1978. Rsch. tech. Nat. Tillage Lab., Auburn, Ala., 1974-76; tchr. Stanford Jr. H.S., Hillsborough, N.C., 1979-81; physics tchr., chmn. sci. dept. East H.S., Anchorage, 1981—; chair Anchorage Sch. Dist. Physics Tchrs.; curriculum devel. sci. cons. Copper River Schs., Anchorage, 1991. Named Tandy Tech. Outstanding Tchr., 1989-90, Tchr. of Excellence Brit. Petroleum, 1996, British Petroleum Tchr. of Yr., 1996; Fermi Lab. scholar U.S. Dept. Energy, 1991; Disting Tchr., White House Commn. on Presdl. Scholars, Brit. Petroleum Tchr. of the Yr., Alaska. Fellow N.Y. Acad. Scis.; mem. AAAS, Am. Assn. Physics Tchrs., Am. Phys. Soc., Nat. Sci. Tchrs. Assn., Alaska Sci. Tchrs. (life), Am. Mountain Guides Assn., Am. Alpine Club. Avocations: mountaineering, outdoor activities, sailing, computers. Office: East HS 4025 E Northern Lights Blvd Anchorage AK 99508-3588

ENRIGHT, CYNTHIA LEE, illustrator; b. Denver, July 6, 1950; d. Darrel Lee and Iris Arlene (Flodquist) E. BA in Elem. Edn., U. No. Colo., 1972; student, Minn. Sch. Art and Design, Mpls., 1975-76. Tchr. 3d grade Littleton (Colo.) Sch. Dist., 1972-75; graphics artist Sta. KCNC TV, Denver, 1978-79; illustrator No Coast Graphics, Denver, 1979-87; editorial artist The Denver Post, 1987—. Illustrator (mag.) Sesame St., 1984, 85; illustrator, editor "Tiny Tales" The Denver Post, 1991-94. Recipient Print mag. Regional Design Ann. awards, 1984, 85, 87, Phoenix Art Mus. Biannual award, 1979. Mem. Mensa. Democrat. Home: 1210 Ivanhoe St Denver CO 80220-2640 Office: The Denver Post 1560 Broadway Denver CO 80202-5177

ENRIQUEZ, CAROLA RUPERT, museum director; b. Washington, Jan. 2, 1954; d. Jack Burns and Shirley Ann (Orcutt) Rupert; m. John Enriquez, Jr., Dec. 30, 1989. BA in history cum laude, Bryn Mawr Coll., 1976; MA, U. Del., 1978, cert. in mus. studies, 1978. Personnel mgmt. trainee Naval Material Command, Arlington, Va., 1972-76; teaching asst. dept. history, U. Del., Newark, 1976-77; asst. curator/exhibit specialist Hist. Soc. Del., Wilmington, 1977-78; dir. Macon County Mus. Complex, Decatur, Ill., 1978-81; dir. Kern County Mus., Bakersfield, Calif., 1981—; pres. Kern County Mus. Found., 1991—; advisor Kern County Heritage Commn., 1981-88; chmn. Historic Records Commn., 1981-88; sec.-treas. Arts Council of Kern, 1984-86, pres. 1986-88; county co-chmn. United Way, 1981, 82; chmn. steering com. Calif. State Bakersfield Co-op Program, 1982-83; mem. Community Adv. Bd. Calif. State Bakersfield, Anthrop. Soc., 1986-88; bd. dirs. Mgmt. Council, 1983-86, v.p., 1987, pres. 1988; bd. dirs. Calif. Council for Promotion of History, 1984-86, v.p., 1987-88. pres., 1988-90; mem. community adv. bd. Calif. State U.-Bakersfield Sociology Dept., 1986-88; mem. women's adv. com. Girl Scouts U.S., 1989-91; bd. dirs. Greater Bakersfield Conv. and Visitors Bur., 1993-95; co-chair 34th St. Neighborhood Partnership, 1994—. Hagley fellow Eleutherian Mills-Hagley Found., 1977-78; Bryn Mawr alumnae regional scholar, 1972-76. Mem. Calif. Assn. Mus. (regional rep. 1991—, v.p. legis. affairs 1992—), Am. Assn. for State and Local History (chair awards com. Calif. chpt. 1990—/regl. chair 99—), Exces. Assn. Kern County. Presbyterian. Office: Kern County Museum 3801 Chester Ave Bakersfield CA 93301-1345

ENSIGN, DONALD H., landscape architect; b. Salt Lake City, Sept. 5, 1936; s. C. Wesley and Mildred (Harker) E.; m. Kay Bateman, Sept. 9, 1959 (div. 1970); m. Nancy Ensign; children: Philip Wesley, Craig Allen, Michael Donald. B in Landscape Architecture, Utah State U., 1963; M in Landscape Architecture, U. Mich., 1968. Registered landscape architect, Mich., N.C. Landscape architect Frehner and Assocs., Salt Lake City, 1961-62; planner Roswell/Ensign and Assocs., Salt Lake City, 1962-66; instr. dept. landscape architecture and environ. planning Utah State U., Logan, 1963-66; planner Richard B. Wilkinson and Assocs., Ann Arbor, Mich., 1966-68; prin. Design Workshop, Inc., Aspen, Colo., 1970—; assoc. prof. sch. design N.C. State U., 1968-74, dir. basic design program, 1971-73. Prin. works include Aspen Inst., Grand Valley High Sch., Marolt Ranch, U. Mich., Utah State U., Estrella Lake Parks, Goodyear, Ariz., Fox River, Geneva, Ill., Lauder Residence, Aspen, Resort at Squaw Creek, Squaw Valley, Calif., 700 East Main, Aspen, Snowmass (Colo.) Club, Blackcomb Resort, Whistler, British Columbia, Early Winters Resort, Mazama, Wash., Grand Champions Resort, Aspen, many others. Avocations: fox hunting, cross country skiing, painting, golf, hiking. Office: Design Workshop 120 E Main St Aspen CO 81611-1714*

ENSLOW, ROBERT HAVEN, merchant banker; b. Seattle, June 7, 1939; s. Robert Lee and Grace Lovette (Hensler) E.; m. Janet Marie Brown, June 6, [illegible] Wash., 1961, MBA, 1963; degree preparatoire, Sorbonne, Paris, 1964. V.p. Chase Manhattan Bank, N.Y.C. and London, 1964-72; dir. Office Fgn. Direct Investments, U.S. Govt., Washington, 1972-74; v.p. Crocker Nat. Bank, San Francisco and London, 1974-81; mgr. project fin. Bechtel Group,

Inc., San Francisco, 1981-90; mng. dir. Dumas West & Co., London, 1990-97; prin. DAL Investment Co., San Francisco, 1997—. Bd. dirs. St. Francis Hosp., San Franciso, 1986-88, St. Francis Found., San Francisco, 1988-90, 97—. Mem. SAR, Mayflower Soc., Knickerbocker Club, Pacific Union Club, The Pilgrims, Royal Automobile Club (London), City of London Club. Republican. Episcopalian. Avocations: opera, sailing, shooting, English Regency furniture. Office: DAL Investment Co 235 Montgomery St Ste 662 San Francisco CA 94104-2994

ENTRIKEN, ROBERT KERSEY, retired management educator; b. McPherson, Kans., Jan. 15, 1913; s. Frederick Kersey and Opal (Birch) E.; m. Elizabeth Freeman, May 26, 1940 (div. Nov. 1951); children—Robert Kersey, Jr., Edward Livingston Freeman, Richard Davis; m. Jean Finch, June 5, 1954; 1 child, Birch Nelson. B.A., U. Kans. 1934; M.B.A., Golden Gate U., 1961; postgrad. City Univ. Grad. Bus. Sch., London, 1971-73. C.P.C.U. Ins. broker, Houston, Tex. and McPherson, Kans., 1935-39; asst. mgr. Cravens, Dargan & Co., Houston, 1939-42; br. mgr. Nat. Surety Corp., Memphis and San Francisco, 1942-54; v.p. Fireman's Fund Ins. Co., San Francisco. 1954-73; adj. prof. Golden Gate U., San Francisco, 1953-73, prof. mgmt., 1974-89; resident dean Asia Programs, Singapore, 1987-88; prof. emeritus 1989—, underwriting mem. Lloyd's of London, 1985-98; cons./expert witness gen. mgmt. and surety bonding, 1987-97; ret., 1997. Contbr. articles to trade and profl. jours. Bd. dirs., sec., treas. Northstar Property Owners Assn., Calif., 1982-86. Served to capt. USNR, 1944-73, ret., 1973. Mem. Ins. Forum San Francisco (pres. 1965, trustee 1975-78, 84-88), Surety Underwriters Assn. No. Calif. (pres. 1956), CPCU Soc. (pres. No. Calif. chpt. 1957, Ins. Profl. of Yr., San Francisco chpt. 1981, bd. dirs., 1989-93), Chartered Ins. Inst., Ins. Inst. London, Musicians' Union Local No. 6 (life), U.S. Naval Inst., Assn. Naval Aviation, Phi Delta Theta. Episcopalian. Clubs: University, Marines' Meml. (San Francisco); Commonwealth. Lodge: Naval Order U.S. Office: 109 Minna St Ste 525 San Francisco CA 94105-3728

ENZI, MICHAEL BRADLEY, senator, accountant; b. Bremerton, Wash., Feb. 1, 1944; s. Elmer Jacob and Dorothy (Bradley) E.; m. Diana Buckley, June 7, 1969; children: Amy, Bradley, Emily. BBA, George Wash. U., 1966; MBA, Denver U., 1968. Cert. profl. human resources, 1994. Pres. NZ Shoes, Inc., Gillette, Wyo., 1969-95, NZ Shoes of Sheridan, Inc., Wyo., 1983-96; acctg. mgr. Dunbar Well Svc., Inc., Gillette, 1985-97; mem. Wyo. Ho. of Reps., Cheyenne, 1987-91, Wyo. State Senate, Cheyenne, 1991-96, U.S. Senate, 1997—; chmn. bd. dirs. 1st Wyo. Bank, Gillette, 1978-88; chmn. Senate Revenue Com., 1992-96. Mayor City of Gillette, 1975-82; pres. Wyo. Assn. Mcpls., Cheyenne, 1980-82. Sgt. Wyo. Air NG, 1967-73. Mem. Wyo. Order of DeMolay (state master councilor 1963-64), Wyo. Jaycees (state pres. 1973-74), Masons (Sheridan and Gillette lodges), Scottish Rite, Shriners, Lions, Sigma Chi. Republican. Presbyterian. Avocations: fishing, bicycling, soccer. Home: 431 Circle Dr Gillette WY 82716-4903 Office: US Senate US Capitol Washington DC 20510

EPCAR, RICHARD MICHAEL, actor, writer, director; b. Denver, Apr. 29, 1955; s. George Buck and Shirley (Learner) E.; m. Ellyn Jane Stern, Aug. 15, 1982; children: Jonathan Alexander, Jacqueline Elizabeth. BFA in Performing Arts, U. Ariz., 1978; postgrad., U. So. Calif., L.A., 1980, U. Calif., L.A., 1981, Am. Film Inst., 1982. Pres. Trouble Shooter Prodns., L.A., 1986—. Actor (films) including Memoirs of an Invisible Man, D.C. Collins, Incident of War, Street Hawk, Escape to Love, Not of This World, (TV series) Diagnosis Murder Columbo, Beverly Hills 90210, Cheers, General Hospital, Guns of Paradise, Matlock, Who's the Boss?, Sonny Spoons, Moonlighting, Highway to Heaven, Amazing Stories, Fast Times, Crazy Like a Fox, Hell Town, Stir Crazy, Santa Barbara, Days of our Lives, (animated series) Teknoman 2 Lead Voices; author 7 episodes, co-dir. Robotech, Honey Bee Hutch, X-Men; co-dir., co-author, lead voice Eagle Riders; co-dir., co-author, lead voices Samurai X; (on state) Why a Hero, Dracula, An Evening with Lincoln, Real Inspector Hound, Richard II; actor, writer (play) (on stage) The Vow, Take My Wife...Please!, 1980; wrote and directed English adaptation of Acad. award winning Cinema Paradisco, Belle Epoque (Acad. Award winner), Women on the Verge of a Nervous Breakdown (Acad. Award nomination), Eat Drink Man Woman (Acad. Award nominated), Fencing Master (Acad. Award nominated); dir. (for TV) A Cowboy Christmas. Mem. L.A. Zoo Assn., 1983-90, 91, 94, Natural History Mus., L.A., 1989-91, Earth Save, L.A., 1990, L.A. Mus. Art, 1991; host fall festival Sta. KCET-Pub. TV, L.A., 1980; active Am. Cancer Soc. Recipient Haldeman Found. scholarship, U. Ariz., 1973-78; named Nat. Best Actor of Yr., Nat. Players, 1977, CPC Repertory Group, 1980; recipient Irene Ryan Soloist award, 1978. Avocations: weight lifting, tennis, music, art.

EPPELE, DAVID LOUIS, columnist, author; b. Jersey City, Apr. 4, 1939; s. Joseph Anton and Lena Marie (Tadlock) E.; m. Gladys Emily Padilla (div. 1975); children: David D., Joseph E.; m. Geneva Mae Kirsch, July 7, 1977. Student, N.Mex. State U., 1958, U. N.Mex., 1966, U. Portland, 1972. Field botanist SW Deserts and Mex., 1947-99, N.Mex. Cactus Rsch., Belen, 1953-62; dir. Ariz. Cactus and Succulent Rsch., Bisbee, 1984—; editor Ariz. Cactus News, 1984—; columnist Western Newspapers, 1987—. Author (newspaper column) On the Desert, 1986—; author: On the Desert, 1991; editor: Index of Cactus Illustrations, 1990, Desert in Bloom, 1989. Mem. Mule Mountain Dem. Party, Bisbee, 1978—. With USN, 1958-59. Mem. AAAS, Cactus and Succulent Soc. Am., N.Mex. Acad. Sci., Bisbee C. of C. Avocations: photography, music. Home and Office: Ariz Cactus 8 S Cactus Ln Bisbee AZ 85603-6356

EPPERSON, STELLA MARIE, artist; b. Oakland, Calif., Nov. 6, 1920; d. Walter Peter and Martha Josephine (Schmitt) Ross; m. John Cray Epperson, May 10, 1941; children: Therese, John, Peter. Student, Calif. Coll. Arts & Crafts, 1939, 40-41, 56, Art Inst., San Miguel d'Allende, Mex., 1972. Portrait artist Oakland Art Assn., 1956—, San Francisco Women Artists, 1962—, Marin Soc. Artists, Ross, Calif., 1971—; art docent Oakland Mus., 1969-71, mem. women's bd., 1971—, art chmn. fund raiser, 1971-89, art guild chmn., 1965-69, chmn. artists in Brazil, chmn. for honoring artist Xavier Martinez, event honoring Neil Armstrong. One-woman shows include Oakland Mus. Auction, 1993, Univ. Club, San Francisco, 1994. Recipient San Francisco Women Artists award, 1989, Oakland Art Assn. award, 1991, 97, Marin Soc. Artists award, 1992. Mem. Oakland Art Assn. (1st award in small format show 1998, 1999 Artistic award in Kaiser Ctr. Gallery Exhibit), U. Calif. Berkeley Faculty Club, Orinda Country Club. Republican. Roman Catholic. Avocations: dress design, gourmet cooking, tennis. Home: 31 Valley View Rd Orinda CA 94563-1432

EPPLING, JACQUELINE QUON, elementary school educator; b. Honolulu, Nov. 10, 1949; d. Bung Yuen and Dorothy Mew-Seong (Yap) Quon; m. John Clarence Eppling, Dec. 28, 1975; children: Natalie Kwai-Ying, Melissa Kwai-Fei. BA, Whitworth Coll., 1971; MEd, U. No. Colo., 1973. Cert. elem. tchr., Hawaii. 1st grade and lang. arts tchr. Monaco Elem. Sch., Commerce City, Colo., 1974, 2d grade tchr., 1975; 3rd grade tchr. Dupont Elem. Sch., Commerce City, Colo., 1976; 1st grade tchr. Kamehameha Schs., Honolulu, 1987-92, math. resource tchr., 1992-95, tchr. 3d grade, 1995—; site coord. Iolani Speech Festival, 1991; kindergarten admissions tester Kamehameha Schs., 1991—, judge spring festivals, 1993; guest lectr. U. Hawaii, 1991, elem. math. methods lectr., 1994; instr. Family Math. Workshops, Honolulu, 1992, 93, NCTM and math. curriculum Ahuimanu Elem. Sch., Honolulu, 1993-94; conf. presenter Hawaii Assn. for the Edn. of Young Children, Honolulu, 1994, Cath. Schs., 1994, Whole Lang. Umbrella Conf., San Diego, 1994, Hawaii Assn. for Pvt. Schs., Honolulu, 1994, Hawaii Coun. Tchrs. Math., Honolulu, 1994, Maui County Math./Sci. Conf., Kahului, 1994, Nat. Coun. Tchrs. Math., Boston, 1995; workshop presenter integrating math. and lang. arts Hawaii Coun. for Tchrs. of Math., Honolulu, 1993, Kauai and Big Island, Hawaii, 1993, Linapuni Elem. Sch., Honolulu, 1994. Mem. Nat. Coun. Tchrs. Math. Avocations: reading, shopping, children's activities. Home: 45-603 Olakino Pl Kaneohe HI 96744-1754 Office: Kamehameha Schs 225 Bishop Cir Honolulu HI 96817-1568

EPSTEIN-SHEPHERD, BEE, mental skills golf coach, hypnotist, professional speaker; b. Tubingen, Fed. Republic Germany, July 14, 1937; came to U.S., 1940, naturalized, 1945; d. Paul and Milly (Stern) Singer; student Reed Coll., 1954-57; m. Leonard Epstein, June 14, 1959 (div. 1982); children: Bettina, Nicole, Seth; m. Frank Shepherd, 1991 (dec. 1992). BA, U. Calif., Berkeley, 1958; MA, Goddard Coll., 1976; PhD, Internat. Coll., 1982, DCH, Am. Inst. Hypnotherapy, 1999. Bus. instr. Monterey Peninsula Coll., 1975-85; owner, mgr. Bee Epstein Assos., cons. to mgmt., Carmel, Calif., 1977—; pres. Success Tours Inc., Carmel, 1981—; founder, prin. Monterey Profl. Speakers, 1982; instr. Monterey Peninsula Coll., Golden Gate U., U. Calif., Santa Cruz, Am. Inst. Banking, Inst. Ednl. Leadership, Calif. State Fire Acad. Monterey Peninsula Coll., U. Calif., Berkeley, Foothill Coll., U. Alaska. Author: How to Create Balance at Work, at Home, in Your Life, 1988, Stress First Aid for the Working Woman, 1991, Free Yourself From Diets, 1994, Mental Management for Great Golf, 1996; contbr. articles to newspapers and trade mags. Research grantee, 1976. Mem. NAFE, Nat. Speakers' Assn., Peninsula Profl. Women's Network, Assn. for Advancement Applied Sports Psychology, Nat. Guild of Hypnotists. Democrat. Jewish. Office: PO Box 221383 Carmel CA 93922-1383

EPTON, GREGG, performing company executive. Prodn. and tour. mgr. Alberta Ballet, Calgary, Can., 1987, gen. mgr., 1989, exec. dir., 1991—; co-founder Alberta Ballet Sch., 1991. Mem. Can. Assn. Profl. Dance Orgns. (corp. sec. 1992-94). Office: Alberta Ballet, 141-18 Ave SW, Calgary, AB Canada T25 0B8*

ERB, RICHARD LOUIS LUNDIN, resort and hotel executive; b. Chgo., Dec. 23, 1929; s. Louis Henry and Miriam (Lundin) E.; m. Jean Elizabeth Easton, Mar. 14, 1959; children: John Richard, Elizabeth Anne, James Easton, Richard Louis II. BA, U. Calif., Berkeley, 1951, postgrad., 1952; student, San Francisco Art Inst., 1956. Cert. hotel adminstr. Asst. gen. mgr. Grand Teton Lodge Co., Jackson Hole, Wyo., 1954-62; mgr. Mauna Kea Beach Hotel, Hawaii, 1964-66; v.p., gen. mgr. Caneel Bay Plantation, Inc., St. John, V.I., 1966-75; gen. mgr. Williamsburg (Va.) Inn, 1975-78; exec. v.p., gen. mgr. Seabrook Island Co., Johns Island, S.C., 1978-80; v.p., dir. hotels Sands Hotel and Casino, Inc., Atlantic City, 1980-81; v.p., gen. mgr. Disneyland Hotel, Anaheim, Calif., 1981-82; COO Grand Traverse Resort, Grand Traverse Village, Mich., 1982-93; gen. mgr. Stein Eriksen Lodge, Deer Valley, Utah, 1993-96; pres. The Erb Group, 1996—; pres. Spruce-Park Mgmt. Co., 1989; mem. adv. bd. travel and tourism Mich. State U., 1992-96; vice-chmn. Charleston (S.C.) Tourism Coun., 1979-81; bd. dirs. Anaheim Visitors and Conv. Bur., 1981-82, Grand Traverse Conv. and Visitors Bur., 1985-90, U.S. 131 Area Devel. Assn., 1983-93; sr. cons. Cayuga Hosp. Advisors, 1996—. Contbr. articles to trade jours. Vice-pres. V.I. Montessori Sch., 1969-71, bd. dirs., 1968-76; bd. dirs. Coll. of V.I., 1976-79; adv. bd. U. S.C., 1978-82, Calif. State Poly. Inst., 1981-82, Orange Coast C.C., 1981-82, Northwestern Mich. Coll., 1983-93; adv. bd. hospitality mgmt. program Ea. Mich. U., 1989-93; trustee Munson Med. Ctr., Traverse City, 1985-93; bd. dirs. Traverse Symphony Orch., 1984-88, N.A. Vasa, 1987-89; adv. panel Mich. Communities of Econ. Excellence Program, 1984-88; mem. hospitality adv. bd. Utah Valley State Coll., 1994-98. Lt. arty. U.S. Army, 1952-54. Named hon. prof. Mich. State U. Hotel Sch., 1992—. Fellow Edn. Inst.; mem. Am. Hotel and Motel Assn. (dir. 1975-77, , 90-94, exec. bd. 1991-94, Service Merit award 1976, Lawson Odde award 1993, Gold Medalist Membership award 1993, trustee Ednl. Inst. 1977-83, mktg. com., exec. com. 1978-83, chmn. projects and programs com. 1982-83, AH&MA resort com. 1986-96, AH&MA condominium com. 1985-96, chmn. ratings com. 1988-96, Ambassador award 1986, Blue Ribbon task force 1988-89, Resort Exec. of Yr. 1988), Caribbean Hotel Assn. (1st v.p. 1972-74, dir. 1970-76, hon. life mem., Extraordinary Service Merit award 1974), V.I. Hotel Assn. (pres. chmn. bd. 1971-76, Merit award 1973), Calif. Hotel Assn. (dir. 1981-82), Caribbean Travel Assn. (dir. 1972-74), Internat. Hotel Assn. (dir. 1971-73), S.C. Hotel Assn. (dir. 1978-82), Am. Hotel Assn. Edn. Inst., (Lamp of Knowledge award 1988), Va. Hotel Assn., Williamsburg Hotel Assn. (bd. dirs. 1975-78), Atlantic City Hotel Assn. (v.p. 1981-82), Atlantic City Casino Assn. (dir. 1981-82), Cornell Soc. Hotelmen, Mich. Travel and Tourist Assn. (bd. dirs. 1983-94, treas. 1986, sec. 1987, v.p. 1988, mktg. com. 1986-93, govtl. affairs com. 1986-93, chmn. edn. com. 1983-84, chmn. bd. 1989-90, Mich. Hotelier of Yr. 1991), Mich. Restaurant Assn. (bd. dirs. 1989-91, chmn. adminstrv. com. 1989-90), Mich. Gov.'s Task Force on Tourism, 1986-87, Grand Island Adv. Commn., Grand Traverse C. of C. (bd. dirs. 1984-89), Nat. Restaurant Assn., Utah Hotel and Motel Assn. (bd. dirs. 1994-96, treas. 1996), Leadership Grand Traverse (exec. com. 1984-92, fellow 1992), Park City Lodging Assn. (bd. dirs. 1993-96), Park City C. of C. (bd. dirs. 1994-97), Tavern Club, Golden Horseshoe Club, Greate Bay Club, Seabrook Island Club, Kiawah Island Club, Grand Traverse Resort Club, Rotary (Paul Harris fellow 1990), Beta Theta Pi. Congregationalist.

ERBACHER, KATHRYN ANNE, editor, art and design writer, marketing consultant; b. Kansas City, Mo.; d. Philip Joseph and Thelma Lillian (Hines) E. BS in English Edn., U. Kans., 1970; BA magna cum laude in Art, Metro State Coll., Denver, 1983. Reporter, Kansas City Star (Mo.), 1970-72; newswriter, publicist Washington U., St. Louis, 1972-76; copy editor Kansas City Star-Times (Mo.), 1976-79; corp. comm. mgr., editor Petro-Lewis Corp., Denver, 1979-82; assoc. Artours, Inc., Denver, 1983-84; assoc. editor arts and travel editor Denver Mag., 1984-86; owner Arts Internat., 1987—; internat. editor Gates Rubber Co., Denver, 1987-90; feature writer/editor Rocky Mountain News, 1998—. Creative dir. TV shorts for contemporary art collection Denver Art Mus., 1983. Bd. dirs. Metro State Coll. Alumni Assn., 1986-87, co-chair 1987 Metro State Coll. Alumni Awards Dinner, Denver; bd. govs. Metro State Coll. Found., 1986-87; mem. program com. Colo. Bus. Com. for the Arts, 1989-90; mem. pub. affairs com. Denver Ctr. for Performing Arts., 1989-98; active Denver Art Mus. Alliance for Contemporary Art, 1984—. Recipient award for arts writing Denver Partnership, 1986, award for Artbeat column in Denver mag. Colo. MAC News, 1986, also award for spl. fashion sect. Dressing the Part; co-recipient award for Gates Rubber Co. Global Comm. Bus./Profl. Advt. Assn., 1988; Colo. Trade Mission del. to Japan, 1994. Mem. Denver Art Mus., Museo de las Ams., One West Art Ctr. Avocations: visual art, theater, films, travel, Spanish language. Office: Rocky Mountain News 400 W Colfax Ave Denver CO 80204

ERDMANN, JOACHIM CHRISTIAN, physicist; b. Danzig, June 5, 1928; s. Franz Werner and Maria Magdalena (Schreiber) E.; doctorate Tech. U. Braunschweig (Germany), 1958; m. Ursula Maria Wedemeyer, Aug. 24, 1957; children—Michael Andreas, Thomas Christian, Maria Martha Dorothea. Physicist, Osram Labs., Augsburg, Germany, 1954-60; sr. research scientist Boeing Sci. Research Labs., Seattle, 1960-72; sr. research scientist Boeing Aerospace Co., Seattle, 1972-73; prin. engr. Boeing Comml. Airplane Co., Seattle, 1973-81, sr. prin. engr., 1981-84; sr. prin. engr. Boeing Aerospace, Seattle, 1984-90; tech. cons., 1990—; vis. prof. Max Planck Inst. for Metals Research, Stuttgart, Germany, 1968-69; lectr. Tech. U. Stuttgart, 1968-69; pres. Optologics Inc., Seattle, 1973-94 . Mem. Am. Phys. Soc., Optical Soc. Am., Soc. Photo Optical Instrumentation Engrs. Author: Heat Conduction in Crystals, 1969. Contbr. articles to profl. jours. Research in cryogenics, statis. physics and opto electronics. Home: 14300 Trillium Blvd SE Apt 8 Bothell WA 98012-1300 Office: Boeing Def and Space Group PO Box 3999 Seattle WA 98124-2499

ERICKSON, CALVIN HOWARD, computer systems engineer; b. Worcester, Mass., June 18, 1946; s. Stanley Howard and Mae Harriet (Wivagg) E.; m. Radmila Frencic, June 5, 1970; children: Jennifer Joy, Melissa Mae. Student, Clark U., 1975-77; ABS in Computer Sci., Quinsigamond Community Coll., Worcester, 1971; cert. Unix System Mgmt. and Adminstrn., U. Calif., Santa Cruz, 1991. Sr. systems programmer Datatrol Inc., Hudson, Mass., 1972-76; tech. support mgr. Keane Inc., Wellesley, Mass., 1976-81; software support specialist Data Gen. Corp., Westboro, Mass., 1981-87; computer systems engr. Loral Rolm-Mil Spec Computers, San Jose, Calif., 1987-92; co devel. support engr., cons. engr. Adobe Systems, Mountain View, Calif., 1992-96; sr. tech. applications support engr. Microtec Rsch. Inc., 1996-98; mgr. advanced tech. support Mentor Graphics, San Jose, 1998—. Author: AOS/VS Internals Manual, 1986. With USN, 1965-71. Mem. Nat. Geog. Soc., San Francisco Zool. Soc., Golden Gate Nat. Park Assn., The Friends of Photography (sustaining), Smithsonian (assoc.), Alpha Nu Omega. Avocation: advanced fine arts photography. Home: 34786 Comstock Common Fremont CA 94555-2820 Office: Mentor Graphics 880 Ridder Park Dr San Jose CA 95131

ERICKSON, DENNIS, professional football coach, former university football coach; b. Everett, Wash., Mar. 24, 1947; m. Marilyn, children: Bryce, Ryan. BS Phys. Educ., Montana State U. Grad. asst. coach Montana State U., 1969, Washington State U., 1970; head football coach Billings Central H.S., Billings, Mont., 1970; backfield coach Montana State U., 1971-73; offensive coordinator, head coach U. Idaho, 1974-75, 1982-85; offensive coordinator Fresno State U., 1976-78, San Jose State U., 1979-81; head coach U. Wyoming, 1986, Washington State U., 1987-88, U. Miami Hurricanes, 1989-95, Seattle Seahawks, 1995—. All-Big Sky quarterback, 1966-68, honorable All-American; head coach NCAA Divsn. 1A football champions, 1989, co-champions (with U. Wash.), 1991; fishing, golf. Office: Seattle Seahawks 11220 NE 53rd St Kirkland WA 98033-7595

ERICKSON, RICHARD BEAU, insurance and financial company executive; b. Chgo., May 14, 1952; s. Charles Arthur and Carole Annette (Beaumont) E. BS, U. Ky., 1974, MBA, 1975. CLU. Sales rep. Met. Life and affiliated cos., Chgo. Hgts., Ill., 1975-78; sales mgr. Met. Life and affiliated cos., Flossmoor, Ill., 1978-80; mktg. specialist Met. Life and affiliated cos., Aurora, Ill., 1980-81; branch mgr. Met. Life and affiliated cos., Orland Park, Ill., 1981-84; corp. dir. Met. Life Gen. Ins. Agy. Inc., N.Y.C., 1984-86; regional sales mgr. Met. Life Gen. Ins. Agy. Inc., L.A., 1986-89, agy. v.p., sr. mktg. and sales exec., 1989-98, agy. v.p., 1989-95, regional v.p., 1996-98; CEO, pres. Greater L.A. Fin. Group, Inc., L.A., 1999—; rep. (Midwest) Sales Mgr. Adv., N.Y.C., 1979; dir. South Cook County Assn. Life Underwriters, Chgo., 1983. Author: Met. Manpower Development, 1981, Met. Manpower Development: A Guideline for Success, 1986. Mem. Nat. Assn. Securities Dealers, Life Underwriters Tng. Counsel, Chartered Life Underwriters, Nat. Assn. Life Underwriters, Gen. Agts. & Mgrs. Assn., Sigma Nu. Avocations: coaching soccer, hiking, Norwegian Elkhound dog shows, mountain climbing. Fax: 310-789-7999. Office: Met Life 15260 Ventura Blvd Ste 2240 Sherman Oaks CA 91403-5352

ERICKSON, VIRGINIA BEMMELS, chemical engineer; b. Sleepy Eye, Minn., June 19, 1948; d. Gordon Boothe and Marion Mae (Rieke) Bemmels; m. Larry Douglas Erickson, Sept. 6, 1969; children: Kirsten Danielle, Dean Michael. Diploma in Nursing, Swedish Hosp. Sch. Nursing, 1969; BSChemE, U. Wash., 1983, MChemE, 1985. RN. Asst. head nurse N. Meml. Hosp., Mpls., 1970-73; intensive care RN Swedish Med. Ctr., Seattle, 1973-83; research asst. U. Wash., Seattle, 1983-85; instrumentation and control engr. CH2M Hill, Bellevue, Wash., 1985—, mgr. dept., 1988-93, mgr. info. mgmr., 1994—, v.p., 1995—; cons. instrumentation and control engr. Mem. editorial adv. bd. Control. Leader Girl Scouts U.S., Seattle, 1985; supt. Seattle Ch. Sch., 1983; rep. United Way, 1986—. Recipient Cert. Achievement, Soc. Women Engrs., 1983, Teenfeed, 1990. Mem. AAUW, Instrument Soc. Am., Tau Beta Pi. Democrat. Mem. United Methodist Ch. Avocations: running, soccer, music, cooking. Home: 6026 24th Ave NE Seattle WA 98115-7009 Office: CH2M Hill PO Box 91500 777 108th Ave NE Bellevue WA 98009-2050

ERICKSON, WILLIAM HURT, retired state supreme court justice; b. Denver, May 11, 1924; s. Arthur Xavier and Virginia (Hurt) E.; m. Doris Rogers, Dec. 24, 1953; children: Barbara Ann, Virginia Lee, Stephen Arthur, William Taylor. Degree in petroleum engring., Colo. Sch. Mines, 1947; student, U. Mich., 1949; LLB, U. Va., 1950. Bar: Colo. 1951. Pvt. practice Denver; justice Colo. Supreme Ct., 1971-96, chief justice, 1983-86; faculty NYU Appellate Judges Sch., 1972-85; mem. exec. Commn. on Accreditation of Law Enforcement Agys., 1980-83; chmn. Pres.'s Nat. Commn. for Rev. of Fed. and State Laws Relating to Wiretapping and Electronic Surveillance, 1976. Chmn. Erickson Commn., 1997. With USAAF, 1943. Recipient Disting. Achievement medal Colo. Sch. Mines, 1990. Fellow Internat. Acad. Trial Lawyers (former sec.), Am. Coll. Trial Lawyers, Am. Bar Found. (chmn. 1985), Internat. Soc. Barristers (pres. 1971); mem. ABA, (bd. govs. 1975-79, former chmn. com. on standards criminal justice, former chmn. coun. criminal law sect., former chmn. com. to implement standards criminal justice, mem. long-range planning com., action com. to reduce ct. cost and delay), Colo. Bar Assn. (award of merit 1989), Denver Bar Assn. (past pres., trustee), Am. Law Inst. (coun.), Practising Law Inst. (nat. adv. coun., bd. govs. Colo.), Freedoms Found. at Valley Forge (nat. coun. trustees, 1986—), Order of Coif, Scribes (pres. 1978). Home: 10 Martin Ln Englewood CO 80110-4821

ERICSON, MARK FREDERICK, investment analyst; b. Colorado Springs, Colo., June 28, 1957; s. Frederick Walter and Eleanor Joan (Juraska) E. BS in Civil Engring., U. Colo., 1979, MBA, 1986. Registered profl. engr., Colo. Project mgr. JR Engring. Ltd., Englewood, Colo., 1982-86; cons. Kirkham Michael & Assocs., Greenwood Village, Colo., 1988-89, Merrick & Co., Aurora, Colo., 1989—; pres. Ericson Investors, Aurora, 1986—. Author: Follow the Crowd and Be Contrary, 1991, You Can Have Eternal Life for Certain, 1994; contbr. (book) Salvador Dali-A Retrospective of Master Prints, 1992; co-producer God's News Behind the News, 1994. Elder, lay pastor Calvary Temple, Disciple of Jesus Christ Evangelism Explosion Trainer. Mem. ASCE, Am. Assn. Individual Investors, Chi Epsilon. Avocations: ultra running, traveling, ballroom dancing, handwriting analysis, Bible prophecy. Office: 2206 Soda Creek Rd Idaho Springs CO 80452-9536

ERIKSSON, ANNE-MARIE, social services executive, educator; b. Dunkirk, N.Y., Mar. 30, 1932; d. J. Kenneth and Kate Findley; m. Erik A. Eriksson, Jan. 1, 1984; 3 children from prior marriage. BS, SUNY, Fredonia, 1955; postgrad., Hunter Coll. CUNY, 1960. Social worker N.Y. State Dept. Social Welfare, N.Y.C., 1960-64; probation officer N.Y., 1972-84; founder, pres. Incest Survivors Resource Network Internat. a Quaker witness ednl. resource, N.Y.C., 1983—; cons. mental health needs UN Hdqs., 1987; presenter 1st and 3d Internat. Conf. Incest and Related Problems, Zurich, 1987, London, 1989; founder first internat. incest tel. helpline, 1983; co-convenor Quaker Sexual Child Abuse Prevention Network. Mem. Quaker Studies Human Betterment, Internat. Soc. Traumatic Stress Studies (founding co-chair bldg. bridges between profls. and self-help interest area), World Fedn. Mental Health, others. E-mail: http://www.zianet.com/ISRNI. Office: Incest Survivors Resource Network Internat PO Box 7375 Las Cruces NM 88006-7375

ERIKSSON, LAURA KERSTIN, architect, artist; b. Detroit, Aug. 15, 1946; d. John Arthur and Maxine Pearl (McKinstry) E.; m. William Lester Pitts, Sept. 2, 1971 (div. Oct. 1986); children: Kerstin Dominique, William Lester, Richard Wayne. BS magna cum laude, Ga. Inst. Tech., Atlanta, 1981, MArch, 1984. Staff architect Thompson, Ventulett, Stainback & Assocs., Atlanta, 1983-91; architect, owner Twin Springs Studio, Manitou Springs, Colo., 1992-96; architect LKA Ptnrs., Colorado Springs, Colo., 1996—; vol. Mineral Springs Found., 7 Minute Spring design, Manitou Springs, 1992-94. Author brochure and art catalog for Manitou Art Project, 1994, 95; one-woman shows include U. Denver, 1993, Human Touch Gallery, Manitou Springs, 1992; exhibited in group shows include Bus. Art Ctr., Manitou Springs, 1994, Gallery Contemporary Art, U. Colo., Colorado Springs, 1994, Commonwheel Gallery, Manitou Springs, 1992, 93, (Artists' Choice Best of Show award), Panache, Cherry Creek Village, Denver, 1993, Colorado Springs Art Guild, 1993 (Juror's Choice award), Bus. Art Ctr., Manitou Springs, 1992, 93, Jewish Cmty. Ctr., Denver, 1993, Pikes C.C. Downtown Studio, Colorado Springs, 1996; also pvt. collections. Coun. mem. Manitou Springs City Coun., 1994—; mem. Historic Preservation Commn., Manitou Springs, 1990-93; sec. Mineral Springs Found., 1990-94, v.p., 1994—; founding mem., sec., pres. Manitou Art Project, 1991-96; mem. Clayfest Steering Com., Manitou Springs, 1991—; mem. Downtown Enhancement Master Plan Steering Com., 1996—;. Recipient Best of Show award Commonwheel Artist Coop., Manitou Springs, 1993, Juror's Choice award Colorado Springs Art Guild, 1993. Mem. Bus. and Art Ctr., Mensa (local calendar editor 1982-88, Person of Yr. award 1990, newsletter award 1987). Avocations: reading, thinking, computers, conversation, painting. Home: 121 Ruxton Ave Manitou Springs CO 80829-1914

ERISMAN, FRANK, lawyer; b. Lackawanna, N.Y., Mar. 6, 1943; s. Henry S. and Mary Lorraine (Conlin) E.; m. Judith A. Milano, Feb. 18, 1984; children: Porter, Melanie, Lindsay, Jacob. Degree in metall. engring., Colo. Sch. Mines, 1965; JD, U. Denver, 1968. Bar: Colo., 1968. Law clk. U.S. Ct. Appeals (5th cir.), Jacksonville, Fla., 1968-69; ptnr. Holme Roberts & Owen, L.L.P., Denver, 1969—. Mem. editorial bd. American Law of Mining, 2d edit., 1984; chmn. editorial bd. (periodical) The Public Land Resources Law Digest, 1985-88. Pres. bd. trustees Colo. Sch. Mines, Golden, 1996—; chmn. Colo. Sch. Mines Ann. Fund, 1990-91, Colo. Sch. Mines Pres.'s Coun., 1991-

93; trustee Western Mus. of Mining & Industry, Colorado Springs, 1991-93. Recipient Disting. Achievement medal Colo. Sch. Mines, 1993. Mem. ABA (chmn. sect. of natural resources, energy and environ. law 1993-94), Colo. Bar Assn. (chmn. mineral law sect. 1991-92), Colo. Mining Assn. (bd. dirs. 1990-92), Rocky Mountain Mineral Law Found. (trustee, exec. bd. dirs. 1986-93, pres. 1997-98), Mining and Metallurgical Soc. Am. Avocations: gardening, hiking, fishing. Office: Holme Roberts & Owen LLP 1700 Lincoln St Ste 4100 Denver CO 80203-4541

ERKILETIAN, ALEXANDER TODD, filmmaker, philanthropist; b. Washington, Jan. 23, 1974; s. Myron Parsek and Josephine (Noerr) E. Grad. high sch., Washington, 1992. Spl. effects make-up Hammond & Davis, Washington, 1989-91; writer, dir. Ha! Network, N.Y.C. 1991; writer Dudleson Prodns., L.A., 1993; prodr., writer Seed Prodns., L.A., 1995; spl. effects make-up Sheen Prodns., L.A., 1997; guest spkr. Am. Film Inst. L.A., 1995. Writer, dir.: Victim, 1994 (Best Live Action Short Film award Santa Monica Film Festival, 1995). Avocations: cryptozology.

ERLUND, JULIA ELIZABETH, artist; b. Comfort, Tex., May 23, 1947; d. Otheil Justus and Virginia Elizabeth (Lollar) E.; m. James David Hooker, Aug. 19, 1967 (div. Feb. 1982); children: Deborah Joann, Cade Derek; m. Dennis Arden Johnson, Dec. 10, 1987. BA in Zoology, U. New Orleans, 1970; Batik Tng., Okinawa, Japan, 1974-77. Rsch. asst. Tulane Med. Sch., New Orleans, 1970-74; exhibitor Okinawa Hilton Hotel, Japan, 1976; profl. artist Evergreen, Morrison, Colo., 1980—. Mus. exhbns. include: (permanent exhbns.) Nat. Wildlife Mus., Monument, Colo., 1979, Soc. Wildlife Art of Nations, Gloucester, Eng., 1993, (non-permanent) Birds in Art Exhbn./Leigh Yaw Key Woodson Art Mus., Wausau, Wis., 1991, 93, 95, 97, Brit. Mus. of Natural History, London, 1996; contbg. author: (books) Nature in Art, 1991, Owls of North America, 1997, The Best of Wildlife Art, 1997. Best of Show/Fiber award U. Miami Art Mus., 1998, Best of Show/ Exotic Animals award Ducks Unltd. Nat. Wildlife Art, Overland Park, Kans., 1998, Best of Show, Nat. Aviary Art Show, Pitts., 1994, 96. Mem. Nat. Audubon Soc., Evergreen Artists Assn. (pres. 1981, arts festival dir. 1979-80, 84-85, 90-92). Lutheran. Avocations: scuba diving, kayaking, plein air oil painting, birding, hiking. Home: 22528 Blue Jay Rd Morrison CO 80465-2662

ERNST, DONALD WILLIAM, producer; b. L.A., Jan. 25, 1934; s. William McKinley and Dorothy Elizabeth (Hast) E.; m. Janice Elaine Barber, Apr. 16, 1966; children: Stacey Dawn, Darci Lynn. BS in Civil Engring., UCLA, 1956. Apprentice editor Telemat, L.A., 1956-61; asst. editor Columbia Pictures, L.A., 1961-62, Metro-Goldwyn-Mayer, Culver City, Calif., 1962-64; film editor CBS, Studio City, Calif., 1964-72, Bakshi Prodns., L.A., 1972-79; sound editor Echo Films, L.A., 1979-82, Horta Editorial, Burbank, Calif., 1982-88; film editor Walt Disney Pictures, Glendale, Calif., 1988-89; prodn. exec. Walt Disney Pictures, Glendale, 1989—. Prodr.: (animated film) Roller Coaster Rabbit, 1990; co-prodr.: (animated film) Aladdin, 1992; exec. prodr.: (live action film) Homeward Bound: The Incredible Journey, 1993. Recipient Emmy awards TV Acad. Arts and Scis., 1977, 82. Mem. Am. Cinema Editors, Acad. Motion Picture Arts and Scis. Home: 26026 Trana Cir Calabasas CA 91302-1054 Office: Walt Disney Feature Animation 500 S Buena Vista St Burbank CA 91521-0004*

ERSKINE, JOHN MORSE, surgeon; b. San Francisco, Sept. 10, 1920; s. Morse and Dorothy (Ward) E. BS, Harvard U., 1942, MD, 1945. Diplomate Am. Bd. Surgery. Surg. intern U. Calif. Hosp., San Francisco, 1945-46; surg. researcher Mass. Gen. Hosp., Boston, 1948; resident in surgery Peter Bent Brigham Hosp., Boston, 1948-53; George Gorham Peters fellow St. Mary's Hosp., London, 1952; pvt. practice in medicine specializing in surgery San Francisco, 1954-98; asst. clin. prof. Stanford Med. Sch., San Francisco, 1956-59; asst., assoc. clin. prof. U. Calif. Med. Sch., San Francisco, 1959—; surg. cons. San Francisco Vets. Hosp., 1959-73. Contbr. articles to profl. jours., chpts. to books. Founder No. Calif. Artery Bank, 1954-58, Irwin Meml. Blood Bank, San Francisco, commr., pres., 1969-74; bd. dirs. People for Open Space-Greenbelt Alliance, 1984-98, adv. coun., 1998—; chmn. adv. coun. Dorothy Erskine Open Space Fund. Capt. with U.S. Army, 1946-48. Fellow ACS; mem. San Francisco Med. Soc. (bd. dirs. 1968-72), San Francisco Surg. Assn. (v.p. 1984), Pacific Coast Surg. Soc., Am. Cancer Soc. (bd. dirs. San Francisco br. 1965-75), Calif. Med. Assn., Olympic Club, Sierra Club. Democrat. Unitarian. Avocations: mountaineering, tree farming. Home and Office: 233 Chestnut St San Francisco CA 94133-2452

ERTEL, GRACE ROSCOE, freelance non-fiction writer, educator; b. Santa Monica, Calif., Oct. 10, 1921; d. Thomas Benedict and Grace (Kelly) Roscoe; m. Donald Joseph Ertel, Sept. 28, 1946; children: Eileen Ariel, Adrienne Marie. BA, UCLA, 1943; teaching credential, U. Calif., Sacramento, 1970. Tchr. remedial reading Grant Sch. Dist., RioTierra-Sacramento, Calif., 1965-66; tchr. English as a second lang., other subjects Sacramento City Adult Schs., 1966-86, Grant Adult Schs., North Highlands, Calif., 1986—; freelance writer, 1975—; lectr. on writing Am. River Coll., Sacramento, 1982. Author: (booklet) Plant an Ecology Garden, 1972, 76; contbr. articles to popular mags. Mem. citizens adv. Sacramento County Solid Waste Reclamation, 1975-80. Mem. Am. Soc. Journalists and Authors, Am. Med. Writers, Internat. Food, Wine & Travel Writers Assn. Avocations: photography, gardening, international cuisine. Home and office: 6350 Dorchester Ct Carmichael CA 95608-3442

ERVIN, ARDITH ANN, psychiatric social worker; b. St. Charles, Ill., June 13, 1935; d. Arden J. and Helen Mildred (Carlson) Zollers; m. Don L. Ervin, Sept. 25, 1954 (div. Mar. 1975); children: Ann Lee, Mark Richard, Daniel Arden; m. Bill D. Toland, Dec. 31, 1983 (div. Aug. 1987). Student, Presbyn. Hosp. Sch. Nursing., 1953-54; RN, Community Coll. of Denver, 1973; BSW magna cum laude, Met. State Coll., 1974; MSW magna cum laude, U. Denver, 1984. With Jefferson County Dept. Social Services, Lakewood, Colo., 1972-75, Larimer County Dept. Social Services, Ft. Collins, Colo., 1975-83; pvt. practice social work Colo., 1976-78; psychiat. social worker S.E. Wyo. Mental Health Ctr., Cheyenne, 1984-87; founder with others The Jacob Center, Inc., 1988. Organizer Parents Anonymous Groups, Ind., 1975, leader; v.p. Child Protective Service Workers, 1979-80; bd. dirs. United Day Care Ctr., Ft. Collins, 1978-79, Larico Youth Home, Ft. Collins, 1978-80, Youth Shelter Care, Ft. Collins, 1980-82. Vol. Service award, Jefferson County; named one of Agency of Yr., 1992. Mem. Nat. Assn. Social Workers. Lutheran. Home: 1217 Village Ln Fort Collins CO 80521-4232

ERVIN, MARGARET HOWIE, elementary education educator, special education educator; b. L.A., May 13, 1924; d. James Stanley and Margaret (Goff) H.; m. E. Frank Ervin, Mar. 22, 1947 (div. 1957); children: Frank, Daniel, Charles. BA, Fresno (Calif.) State U., 1958; grad. student, Purdue U., 1965-66, San Francisco State U., 1974-75. Cert. elem. and spl. edn. tchr. Elem. tchr. Clovis (Calif.) Schs., 1958-60, Fremont (Calif.) Unified Schs., 1960-83; spl. tchr. in summers Dominican Coll., San Rafael, Calif., 1972-78; asst. dir., cons. Arena Sch. and Learning Ctr., San Rafael, 1974-75; dir. Ervin Sch. and Learning Ctr., San Rafael, 1983-88; researcher, tchr. Primaria Sch. #110 PRI9745, Celaya, Mex., 1988; elem., spl. tchr. Napa (Calif.) City/County Schs. 1989—; diagnosis cons. Ervin Learning Ctr., Napa, 1989—; spl. edn. guest speaker various cities, U.S., Can., 1974-98; learning seminar Parents and Tchrs., Mexico, summer 1992, Psycho-motor Tgn. Don Bosco Home for Girls, Mexico, summer 1993. Vol. Option Inst. and Fellowship, "Sonrise" autism/devel. disabilities, Sheffield, Mass., summer 1994; pres. Children Handicapped Learning Devel., Calif., 1971-72, tchr. parents, 1970-80, 94—; bay area rep. Calif. Tchrs. Assn., Burlingame, 1970-74. Recipient cert. of merit Calif. Tchrs. Assn., Burlingame, 1974, $5,000 gift to Ervin Sch. Calif. Assn. Neurol. Handicapped Children, Fremont, 1984. Mem. AAUW, NOW, Assn. Children with Learning Abilities. Democrat. Unitarian. Avocations: tennis, biking, swimming. Home and Office: Ervin Learning Ctr 3361 Rohlffs Way Bldg 31 Napa CA 94558-4494

ERVIN, PATRICK FRANKLIN, nuclear engineer; b. Kansas City, Kans., Aug. 4, 1946; s. James Franklin and Irma Lee (Arnett) E.; m. Rita Jeanne Kingman Apr. 11, 1967; children: James R., ..., ... Engring., Kans. State U., 1969, MS in Nuclear Engring., 1971; postgrad., Northeastern U., 1988. Registered profl. engr., Ill., Colo., Calif., Idaho, Wash.; cert. paleontology paraprofl. Colo. Reactor health physicist Dept. Nuclear Engring. Kans. State U., Manhattan, 1968-69, rsch. asst. Dept. Nuclear Engring., 1969-72, sr. reactor operator, temp. facility dir. Dept. Nuclear Engring., 1970-72; system test engr. Commonwealth Edison Co., Zion, Ill., 1972-73, 73-74; shift foreman Commonwealth Edison Co., Zion, 1973, shift foreman with sr. reactor operator lic., 1974-76, prin. engr., 1976-77, acting operating engr., 1977; tech. staff supr. Commonwealth Edison Co., Byron, Ill., 1977-81; lead test engr. Stone & Webster Engring. Corp., Denver, 1982-83, project mgr., 1982-95, ops. svcs. supr., 1982-86, asst. engring. mgr., 1986-89, cons. engr., 1989-94; sr. cons., 1994-96; decommissioning program mgr. Rocky Flats Closure project Kaiser-Hill Co., Denver, 1996—. Contbr. articles to profl. jours. Served with U.S. Army N.G., 1971-77. Mem. Am. Nuclear Soc. (Nat. and Colo. chpts.), Am. Nat. Standards Inst. (working group on containment leakage testing). Independent. Roman Catholic. Avocations: paleontology, hunting, fishing, camping, stamp collecting. Home: 2978 S Bahama St Aurora CO 80013-2340 Office: Kaiser Hill Co PO Box 464 Golden CO 80402-0464

ERVING, CLAUDE MOORE, JR., career officer, pilot; b. St. John's, N.F., Can., Sept. 10, 1952; s. Claude Moore Sr. and Ingeborg (Mauss) E.; m. Donna Lee Mathis, June 17, 1978; children: Zachary C., Allyson B., Michael J. M. BS in Geography, USAF Acad., 1975. Commd. 2d lt. USAF, 1975, advanced through grades to lt. col., 1979; check pilot, instr. 85th Flying Tng. Squadron, Laughlin AFB, Tex., 1976-80; flight examiner, instr. pilot, flight comdr. 460th Fighter Interceptor Tng. Squadron, Peterson AFB, Colo., 1980-82; flight comdr. 49th Fighter Interceptor Squadron, Griffiss AFB, N.Y., 1982-85; chief of tng. 18th Tactical Fighter Squadron, Eielson AFB, Alaska, 1985-86; chief of flight safety, asst. chief of safety 343d Tactical Fighter Wing, Eielson AFB, Alaska, 1986-88; chief ops. plans div. and exec. officer to dep. comdr. ops. for 11th Air Force and Alaskan NORAD region Hdqrs. Alaskan Air Command, Elmendorf AFB, 1988-92; comdr. 94th airmanship tng. squadron USAF Acad., Colo., 1992-94; dep. dir. pub. affairs, 1994-96; rsch. 1994-96; aircraft accident investigator USAF, worldwide, 1986-96; pilot Fed. Express Corp. Mem. CAP (flight comdr. 1990-93). Republican. Avocations: hunting, fishing, camping, traithalons, flying. Home: 3811 Gunwale Ct Anchorage AK 99516-7601

ERWIN, JOAN LENORE, artist, educator; b. Berkeley, Calif., Feb. 12, 1932; d. Ralph Albert and Dorothy Christine (Wuhrman) Potter; m. Byron W. Crider, Jan. 28, 1956 (div. May 1975); children: Terry, Ray, Steve, Tim. BS, U. So. Calif., 1954; MS in Sch. Adminstrn., Pepperdine U., 1975. Cert. tchr., Calif.; registered occupational therapist, Calif. Occupational therapist Calif. State Hosp., Camarillo, 1955-56, Harlan Shoemaker Sch., San Pedro, Calif., 1956-57; tchr. Norwalk (Calif.) Sch. Dist., 1957-59, Tustin (Calif.) Sch. Dist., 1966-68, Garden Grove (Calif.) Sch. Dist., 1968-92; freelance artist Phelan, Calif., 1976—; comml. artist Morningstar Creations, Fullerton, Calif., 1982-92; substitute tchr. Snowline Sch. Dist., Phelan, Calif., 1994—; artist Y.U.G.O., Los Alamitos, 1977-87. Pet portrait artist, U.S. and Eng., 1978-85; author, artist Biblical coloring books, 1985-90; exhibited in group shows San Bernardino County Mus., Riverside, Calif., Riverside Fine Arts Mus. Bd. dirs. San Bernardino County Mus., Fine Arts Inst. Calif. Elks scholar, 1952-53; grantee Ford Found., 1957-58, Mentor Tchr. Program, 1986. Republican. Baptist. Avocations: gardening, travel. Home: 10080 Monte Vista Rd Phelan CA 92371-8371

ESHBAUGH, DAVID CHARLES, society administrator; b. Martinsville, Ind., Jan. 17, 1960; s. William Hardy III and Barbara Jean (Keller) E.; m. Dawn-Starr Crowther, Aug. 3, 1985. BA, Miami U., Oxford, Ohio, 1983; MA, Ariz. State U., 1988, postgrad., 1988-93. Grad. rsch. and tchg. asst. Ariz. State U., Tempe, 1985-91, instr., 1991; cons. zooarchaeologist Tempe, 1987-94; vol. coord. Audubon Soc. of Portland, Oreg., 1995-96, exec. dir., 1996—, mem. state office task force, 1995-96. Co-author: Summary Report: Salinas Survey, 1989; assoc. editor newsletter Cactus Wrencition, 1994-95. Mem. Am. Birding Assn., Nat. Audubon Soc. (mem. membership task force 1998), Soc. for Am. Archaeology, Cornell Lab. of Ornithology, Willamette Valley Devel. Officers, Oreg. Field Ornithologists, City Club of Portland, Sigma Xi, Phi Kappa Phi, Alpha Kappa Delta (life), Omicron Delta Kappa. Home: 2726 NE 14th Ave Portland OR 97212-3201 Office: Audubon Soc Portland 5151 NW Cornell Rd Portland OR 97210-1081

ESHOO, ANNA GEORGES, congresswoman; b. New Britain, Conn., Dec. 13, 1942; d. Fred and Alice Alexandre Georges; children: Karen Elizabeth, Paul Frederick. AA with honors, Canada Coll., 1975. Chmn. San Mateo County Dem. Ctrl. Com., Calif., 1978-82; chair Human Rels. Com., 79-82; mem. Congress from 14th Dist. Calif., 1993—, at-large minority whip; mem. commerce com. 106th Congress from 14th Dist. Calif.; chief of staff Calif. Assembly Spkr. Leo McCarthy, 1981; regional majority whip No. Calif., 1993-94. Co-founder Women's Hall of Fame; chair San Mateo County (Calif.) Dem. Party, 1980; active San Mateo County Bd. Suprs., 1982-92, pres., 1986; pres. Bay Area Air Quality Mgmt. Dist., 1982-92; mem. San Francisco Bay Conservation Devel. Commn., 1982-92; chair San Mateo County Gen. Hosp. Bd. Dirs. Roman Catholic. Office: US Ho of Reps Office of House Mems 308 Cannon 10B Washington DC 20515-0514*

ESLER, JOHN KENNETH, artist; b. Pilot Mound, Man., Can. Jan. 11, 1933; s. William John and Jennie Mae (Thompson) E.; m. Annemarie Schmid, June 26, 1964; children—William Sean, John Derek. B.F.A., U. Man., B.Ed., 1962. Mem. faculty dept. art Alta. Coll. Art, 1964-68; mem. faculty U. Calgary, Alta., Can., 1968-80; chmn. Print and Drawing Council Can., 1976-78. One-man exhbn., Gallery Moos, Toronto, Ont., 1978, Past and Present: One-Man Exhbn. Painting, Triangle Gallery, Calgary, Alberta, 1994, Retrospective/35 Years Printmaking, U. of C. Nickle Arts Mus., Calgary, Travelling exhbn., Sept. 1994; represented in permanent collections, Victoria and Albert Mus., London, Eng., Albright Knox Gallery, Buffalo, N.Y., Mus. Modern Art, N.Y.C., Nat. Gallery Can., Ottawa, Ont.; Author: Printing in Alberta. Life mem. Print and Drawing Coun. Can. Address: Box 2 Site 7, 5020 Vice Roy Dr NW, Calgary, AB Canada T2A 0V5

ESMAILZADEH, EBRAHIM, mechanical engineering educator, consultant; b. Mashhad Khorasan, Iran, Apr. 6, 1944; s. Mohammad and Fakhrolsharieh (Riaz) E.;m. Rouhangiz Daei Sadeghi, July 15, 1977; children: Reza, Ali. BSc with honours, U. London, 1967, MPhil, 1969, PhD, 1971. Chartered engr., U.K. Lab. instr. U. London, 1967-71; asst. prof. Arya-Mehr U. Tech., Tehran, 1971-75; vis. assoc. prof. MIT, Cambridge, Mass., 1976-77; prof. Sharif U. Tech., Tehran, 1980-89, univ. disting. prof., 1992-97, v.p., 1979-80; vis. prof. U. Victoria, Can., 1990-91, 97—; rsch. advisor Ministry of Heavy Industry, Iran, 1982-84; tech. cons. in field. Author textbooks and jour. articles on mech. engring.; mem. editl. bd. nat. and internat. jours.; spkr. in field. Named Excellent Prof., Iranian Soc. Mech. Engrs., 1994, Exemplar Prof. of Iranian Univs., 1993. Fellow Instn. Mech. Engrs. Eng., ASME; mem. Soc. Automotive Engrs., Iranian Acad. Scis. Tehran (chair mech. engring. dept. 1995-97), Iranian Soc. Control and Instrumentation Engrs. (dir. 1994). Avocations: chess, photography, music, ball games, skiing. Home: 29-4061 Larchwood Dr, Victoria, BC Canada

ESPARZA, RICHARD R., museum director; b. Washington; m. Lauraine Brekke, Oct. 24, 1992; 4 children. BA in Philosophy, Calif. State U. Hayward, 1969; student, Met. State Coll., 1972-73. Asst. curator Colo. State Mus. Colo. State Hist. Soc., Denver, 1972-73; exec. dir. South Park City Mus., Fairplay, Colo., 1973-74, Ventura (Calif.) County Mus. History and Art, 1974-80, San Diego Hist. Soc., 1980-87, Santa Barbara (Calif.) Hist. Museums, 1987-89, Nev. Mus. Art, Reno, 1991-95; dir. Riverside (Calif.) Mcpl. Mus., 1995—; faculty U. Calif. Santa Barbara Inst. Local History, 1981, Small Mus. Adminstrn. UCLA ext., 1981, Williamsburg Seminar for Historic Adminstrn., 1984. Mem. Riverside Downtown Assn. (bd. dirs.), Mission Inn Found. (bd. dirs.), Calif. Assn. Museums (bd. dirs.). Office: Riverside Mcpl Mus 3580 Mission Inn Ave Riverside CA 92501-3307

ESPENLAUB, MARGO LINN, women's studies educator, artist; b. Decorah, Iowa, May 1, 1944; d. Lloyd Wilson and Margaret Mary (Seegmiller) Ruidl; m. Alan Ludwig Espenlaub, Aug. 8, 1980; children: Ann D., ... in Philosophy, Wri tting, ... Humanities, 1985; PhD in Women's Studies, The Union Inst. Grad. Sch., 1995. Adj. prof. women's studies Met. State Coll., Denver, 1987-99; adj. prof. U. Denver, The Women's Coll., 1996—; colloquium coord. Front Range Feminist Studies, Denver, 1991-98; faculty coord. TWC Student Writer's Club. Co-author: Women's Studies: Thinking Women, 1993; gen. editor Voices of the Women's Coll., 1999. Mem. biomed. ethics com. Kaiser Permanente, Denver, 1986-96. Mem. Nat. Women's Studies Assn., Colo. Women's Studies An., Colo. Women's Agenda, Women's Caucus for Art (Colo. chpt., nat. bd. dirs.), Front Range Women in the Visual Arts. Avocations: drawing, writing, nature walking, snow shoeing. Office: The Womens Coll U Denver 7150 Montview Blvd Denver CO 80220-1866

ESPINOSA, JANET MAE, mathematics educator; b. Seattle, Nov. 28, 1943; children: Sidney Abel, Tami Lucila. BA, BA in Edn., Western Wash. U., 1966; MS in Tchg. Math., Santa Clara U., 1973, MA in Bilingual Cross-Cultural Edn., 1976. Cert. tchr., adminstr., bilingual specialist, C.C., Calif. Tel. operator Pacific N.W. Bell, Seattle, 1962-66; tchr. Garfield H.S., Seattle, 1966-68; tchr., counselor, coord. Overfelt H.S., San Jose, Calif., 1968-82; tchr., mentor, coord. Silver Creek H.S., San Jose, 1982-91; dir. Valdés Math. Inst., San Jose, 1991—; prof. math. Evergreen Valley Coll., San Jose, 1993—; cons. ESL, bilingual and sheltered instrn. various sch. dists., Calif., 1975-95; mentor tchr. ESL, East Side Union H.S. Dist., San Jose; evaluator for accreditation Western Assn. Secondary Schs., Calif. author, editor: Valdés Math, 1991-98. Prodr., bd. mem., actress South Valley Civic Theatre, Gilroy, Calif. Mem. Calif. Math. Coun., Sons of Norway, Gilroy Presbyn. Ch., Ea. Star, Kappa Delta Pi. Avocations: travel, photography, farming, reading, theatre.

ESPOSITO, HOLLY TYLER, secondary education educator; b. Reno, Sept. 18, 1970; d. Harry Walter Zuehlsdorff and Sally Tyler Small; m. Michael Anthony Esposito, Dec. 23, 1993. BA in English, U. Nev., 1989-92. Tchr. English Washoe County Sch. Dist., Reno, 1994—; advisor Literary Mag., Reno, 1996-97. Mem. Nat. Coun. Tchrs. of English, Internat. Reading Assn., ASCD. Avocations: skiing, reading, paint ball.

ESPOSITO, LARRY WAYNE, planetary astronomer; b. Schenectady, N.Y., Apr. 15, 1951; s. Albert and Beverly Jane (DeLaMater) E.; m. Diane Marie McKnight, July 24, 1975; children: Rhea, Ariel. SB in Math., MIT, 1973; PhD in Astronomy, U. Mass., 1977. Research assoc. Lab. Atmospheric and Space Physics U. Colo., Boulder, 1977—, lectr., 1979-84, assoc. prof. dept. astrophys., planetary and atmospheric scis., 1984-95, prof., 1995—; prin. investigator NASA, Cassini Space Mission, 1990—; investigator Pioneer Venus, Pioneer Saturn, Voyager, Galileo, Mars Observer, USSR Phobos and Mars 1994 spacecraft missions, 1977—; mem. NASA Planetary Atmospheres Mgmt. Ops. Working Group, 1981-84, Nat. Acad. Scis. Space Sci. Bd. com. on planetary and lunar exploration, 1982-86, chmn. 1989-92; dep. chmn. Nat. Acad. Scis. Space Sci. Bd. task group on planetary exploration, 1984-86. Contbr. articles to sci. publs. Recipient Exceptional Sci. Achievement medal NASA, 1986, Richtmyer Lecture award Am. Assn. Physics Tchrs. and Am. Phys. Soc., 1991. Mem. Am. Astron. Soc. (div. planetary scis. com. 1983-86, H.C. Urey prize 1985), Internat. Astron. Union, Am. Geophys. Union, Internat. Council Sci. Unions (exec. mem. com. space research). Methodist. Club: Boulder Go. Achievements include discovery of Saturn's 4th ring, 1979 (as part of the Pioneer Saturn Team). Office: U Colo CB392 Lab Atmosphere Space P Boulder CO 80309

ESQUER, DEBORAH ANNE, elementary education educator; b. Omaha, Oct. 28, 1950; d. Thomas Ross and Carolyn Mae (Wright) Woods; m. Mario H. Esquer, Aug. 21, 1971 (div. Apr. 1991); children: Mario, Michael. BA, Ariz. State U., 1972, MA in Edn., 1972, 78; postgrad., Ottawa U., Phoenix, 1990-92. Cert. elem. tchr., spl. edn. Tchr. Paradise Valley Sch. Dist., Phoenix, 1972—. Dem. precinct com. person; state Dem. com. person. Tchr. venture grantee, Phoenix, 1988. Mem. NEA, Ariz. Edn. Assn., Ariz. Reading Coun., Paradise Valley Edn. Assn., Paradise Valley Reading Coun., Phoenix Art Mus., Ariz. Hist. Soc., Ariz. Forum, Paradise Valley Jr. Women's Club (corr. sec. 1991-92), Alpha Delta Kappa (pres. 1986-88, ctrl. dist. treas. 1986-88, corr. sec. 1992-94, treas. 1994—, state com.), Alpha Phi. Democrat. Methodist. Office: Desert Springs 6010 E Acoma Dr Scottsdale AZ 85254-2599

ESQUIVEL, JOE G., food products executive; b. 1938. With Hanson Farms, Salinas, Calif., 1967-83; pres. Adobe Packing Co., Salinas, Calif., 1983—. Office: Adobe Packing Co PO Box 4940T Salinas CA 93912-4940*

ESQUIVEL, MARY, agricultural products company executive; b. 1945. Homemaker, 1976; ct. interpreter State of Calif., Salinas, 1976-83; sec., treas. Adobe Packing Co., Salinas, 1983—. Office: Adobe Packing Co PO Box 4940 Salinas CA 93902-0490*

ESSA, LISA BETH, elementary education educator; b. Modesto, Calif., Nov. 19, 1955; d. Mark Newyia and Elizabeth (Warda) E. BA, U. Pacific-Stockton, 1977, MA in Curriculum and Instrn. Reading, 1980. Cert. tchr. elem., multiple subject and reading specialist, Calif. Tchr. primary grades Delhi (Calif.) Elem. Sch. Dist., 1978-80; reading clinic tutor San Joaquin Delta Community Coll., Stockton, Calif., 1980; tchr. primary grades Hayward (Calif.) Unified Sch. Dist., Supr., San Francisco host com. Dem. Nat. Conv., 1984. Femmes Club scholar, 1973; U. Calif. Optometry Alumni Assn. scholar, 1973; Jobs Daughters scholar, 1974. Mem. Internat. Reading Assn., Calif. Tchrs. Assn., Hayward Unified Tchrs. Assn., San Francisco Jr. C. of C., Jr. League San Francisco. Democrat. Episcopalian. Home: 1960 Clay St Apt 109 San Francisco CA 94109-3435

ESTEBAN, MANUEL ANTONIO, university administrator, educator; b. Barcelona, Spain, June 20, 1940; came to U.S. 1970; s. Manuel and Julia Esteban; m. Gloria Ribas, July 7, 1962; 1 child, Jacqueline. BA with 1st class honors in French, U. Calgary, Can., 1969, MA in Romance Studies, 1970; PhD in French, U. Calif., Santa Barbara, 1976. From asst. prof. to prof. French and Spanish langs. and lit. U. Mich., Dearborn, 1973-87, assoc. dean, 1984-86, acting dean coll. arts, scis., and letters, 1986-87; dean arts and scis. Calif. State U. Bakersfield, 1987-90; provost, v.p. acad. affairs Humboldt State U., Arcata, Calif., 1990-93; pres., chief. French and Spanish Calif. State U. Chico, 1993—; bd. dirs. Calif. Joint Policy Coun. on Agr. and Edn., 1995—, Sierra Health Found., 1998—. Author: Georges Feydeau, 1983; contbr. books revs. and articles to profl. publs. Woodrow Wilson fellow, 1969, doctoral fellow U. Calif., Santa Barbara, 1970-73, Can. Coun. doctoral fellow, Govt. Can., 1970-73; Rackham grantee U. Mich., 1979, fellow, 1982-83. Mem. Am. Coun. Edn., Am. Assn. State Colls. and Univs., Greater Chico C. of C., U.S. Distance Learning Assn., Sierra Health Found. (bd. dirs. 1998—). Avocations: golf, woodworking, glassblowing. Office: Calif State Univ Office of Pres Chico CA 95929-0150

ESTES, MARK WAYNE, corporate communications writer, editor; b. Phoenix, Feb. 19, 1955; s. Wilbur Calvin and Mary Rose Elizabeth (Filchak) E.; m. Odilia Ana Altamirano, Aug. 6, 1983; children: Anna Christina, Matthew, Samuel, Roseanne. Student, No. Ariz. U., 1973-76; BA, U. Ariz., 1978; postgrad., Gateway Community Coll., Phoenix, 1989. Reporter The Ariz. Republic, 1972-73; adminstrv. reporter The Lumberjack, Flagstaff, Ariz., 1974-75; assoc. editor The Voice, Flagstaff, 1975; reporter Flagstaff News, 1975-76; assoc. editor Tucson Sports Mag., 1981; pub. rels. advisor Am. Chiropractic Assn., Tucson, 1981; staff writer Salt River Project, Phoenix, 1981-87, sr. staff writer, 1987—, internal projects editor, 1989—, fin. publs. editor, 1991—, fin. projects editor; mem. Svc. Quality Task Force Salt River Project, Phoenix, 1990, Substance Abuse Task Force Salt River Project, Phoenix, 1984-85. Contbr. numerous articles to local newspapers. Fundraiser St. Daniel's Home and Sch., Scottsdale, Ariz., 1983-89; dep. registrar Pima County Rep. Party, Tucson, 1979-80; dist. gov. Circle K Internat., Ariz., N.Mex., Tex., 1975-76, lt. gov., Ariz., N.Mex., 1974-75; publicity chair Ariz. Vocat. Indsl. Clubs Am. Industry Coun.; bd. dirs. St. Theresa Sch.; coach, bd. dirs. Arcadia Scottsdale United Soccer Club, 1991-93; active Xavier Coll. Prep. Parents' Assn. Recipient Merit award Utility Comm. Internat., 1990, News Reporting 1st Place Editor's Forum, 1989, award Utility Communicator's Assn., 1989, award of excellence Awards for Publs. Excellence (5), 1991, 92, 93, award of merits Ann. Reports. Mem. Internat. Assn. Bus. Communicators (programs com. 1990, v.p. profl. devel., ... 92, Pres. award, award of excellence Dist. 5), Salt River Project Polit. Involvement Com. Avocations: reading, traveling, camping. Home: 8233 E Edgemont Ave Scottsdale AZ 85257-1730 Office: Salt River Project PO Box 52025 Phoenix AZ 85072-2025

ESTES, RICHARD D., recording industry executive; b. El Paso, Tex., May 23, 1963; s. Thomas Keith and Donna Elaine (Thatcher) E. BBA, N.Mex. State U., 1990. Ptnr., gen. mgr. Nickelodian Amusement, La Mesa, N.Mex., 1983-89; staff acct. CBS, Inc., L.A., 1990—; co-prodr. Orchard Ave. Records, L.A., 1992—; gen. ptnr. Cactus Prophylactics, L.A., 1993—; co-published a complete reference guide to the collection of musical scores for The Carol Burnett Show, 1997; donated in 1998 to the UCLA Music Libr. Co-prodr., performer: (CD) Vacation Beach, 1995; co-prodr., co-writer, performer: (CD) 2609 Manning, 1996, Valleys, 1997, Left of Center, 1998; guitarist The Bonnie Hunt Show, 1996. Mem. Profl. Musicians (Local 47), Broadcast Music, Inc. Avocations: mem. Wattles Farm Cmty. Garden. Office: Crazy Cat George PO Box 480471 Los Angeles CA 90048-1471

ESTES, SHAWN, baseball player; b. San Bernardino, Calif., Feb. 18, 1973. Pitcher San Francisco Giants. Named All-Star. Office: c/o San Francisco Giants San Francisco CA 94124

ESTRADA, LUIS TOMÁS, artist; b. Phoenix, July 27, 1949; s. Luis and Martha (Valadez) E. children: Gabriel Tomás, Daniel Fabian. AA, Phoenix Coll., 1971; BFA in Painting, Design, No. Ariz. U., 1977. Artist, designer Upstairs Art Studios, Flagstaff, Ariz., 1974-79; art dir., coord. Valle del Sol, Inc., Phoenix, 1982-83; asst. exhibit designer Heard Mus., Phoenix, 1983-84; artist, designer Bravado Design, Tempe, Ariz., 1984-86; instr. Maricopa C.C., Phoenix, 1986-89; artist, illustrator Matson Represents, Phoenix, 1987-95; art dir., designer Mestizo Arts, Scottsdale, Ariz., 1991—; instr. Scottsdale Artists Sch., 1994-96, New Sch. for Arts, Scottsdale, 1995-96; lead instr. Visual Comm. ACGDS, Tempe, Ariz., 1997—. Represented in permanent collections Ariz. Historical Soc. Mus., Phoenix, Nat. Mus. Am. History Smithsonian Inst.; author: (7 jours.) Days and Nights, 1971-97; composer, pub. Mestizo Music, BMI. Recipient ADDY award Art Dirs. Club N.Y., 1995, Graphis Design Annual award Graphis Press Corp., Zurich, 1995, Ariz. Prizma award, Phoenix. Avocations: music, photography, writing, publishing, computers. Home and Studio: 4605 S Priest Dr #157 Tempe AZ 85282-6527 Office: Mestizo Arts 7373 Scottsdale Mall #4 Scottsdale AZ 85251

ETCHART, MIKE, agricultural products company executive; b. 1961. V.p., pres. Everkrisp Vegetables, Inc., Tolleson, Ariz. Office: Everkrisp Vegetables Inc PO Box 25 Tolleson AZ 85353-0025*

ETESSAMI, HIRBOD (HIRI ETESSAMI), endodontist, educator; b. Tehran, Jan. 31, 1965; came to U.S., 1978; s. Abdollah and Mahin Etessami; m. Jacqueline Etessami, Aug. 21, 1993; 1 child, Noah Etessami. Student, Georgetown U., 1982-85; DDS, U. So. Calif., 1989, Cert. in Advanced and Surg. Endodontics, 1991. Endodontist in pvt. practice, L.A., 1991—; clin. instr. U. So. Calif. Sch. Dentistry, 1991—, UCLA Sch. Dentistry, 1993—. Bd. dirs. Beth Jacob Congregation, Beverly Hills, Calif., 1995—; bd. dirs. L.A. Mozart Orch., 1995-96; mem. ethics com. U. So. Calif. Dental Sch., 1985-91. Mem. ADA, Calif. Dental Assn., Am. Assn. Endodontics, Alpha Omega (pres. chpt. 1989). Jewish. Avocations: playing Santour (hammer/dulcimer), Archeology, theology, politics. Office: 9201 W Sunset Blvd Ste 908 Los Angeles CA 90069-3710

ETHERIDGE, CLAYTON DENNIS, small business owner; b. Sacramento, Calif., Oct. 14, 1947; s. Clayton Demerse and Naydeen (Pitney) E.; m. Katheryn Marie Lee, Aug. 12, 1978; children: Michael, Johnathan, Michelle. Expert repairman Samsonite, Denver, 1966-70; billiard mechanic Ace Billiards, Denver, 1970-72; svc. mgr. Quality Billiards, Lakewood, Colo., 1972-78; store mgr. Home Billiards, Northglenn, Colo., 1978-80; pres., owner Showcase Billiards, Westminster, Colo., 1980—. Mem. Billiard Congress Am. (bd. dirs. 1997—), Am. Legion, Elks Lodge, Moose Lodge. Democrat. Avocations: coin & currency collecting, playing pool, Corvettes. Office: Showcase Billiards 12031 Tejon St Denver CO 80234-2303

ETSITTY, SYLVIA MAE, administrator; b. Ganado, Ariz., July 23, 1957; d. Benjamin William Harding and Evelyn (Lee) McCabe; 1 child, Bryant Loren. AA, Bacone Jr. Coll., Muskogee, 1978; student, U. N.Mex., Albuquerque, 1982-83, Ariz. State U. Researcher Navajo Nation Jud. Branch, Window Rock, Ariz., 1978-78; police planner Div. Pub. Safety, Window Rock, 1979-80; mgmt. analyst Navajo Nation Div. Soc. Services, Window Rock, 1981-81; personnel analyst Navajo Nation Personnel Dept., Window Rock, 1983-84; prog. analyst Navajo Nation Vet. Office, Window Rock, 1984-84; project dir. Navajo Dept. Health, 1984—; bd. dirs. Ft. Defiance (Ariz.) Hosp. Steering Cmty., 1984—, health planner Navajo Divsn. Health; organizer Navajo Nation Vietnam Vet. Symposium, Window Rock, 1987-84. Author: Short Story, 1975, 89, Poetry, 1978. Vice-chmn. Local Planning Bd. Ganado, Cornfields Ariz., 1988; tech. advisor Ft. Defiance Steering Com. Window Rock, 1988; Native Am. Child Welfare Advocate. Recipient Excellence in Svc. award Dept. of Health, 1986, Disting. Svcs. award Ft. Defiance Hosp. Window Rock, 1987, Photography awards Navajo Nation Window Rock, 1988, 89, Disting. Svc. award The Navajo Nation Govt. Mem. Red Cross Navajo Chpt. Window Rock. Democrat. Presbyterian. Avocations: creative writing, photography, pastel painting, reading, running, music. Home: PO Box 1432 Window Rock AZ 86515-1432 Office: Navajo Nation Dept Health PO Box 1390 Window Rock AZ 86515-1390

ETT, ALAN PAUL, composer; b. Detroit, Mar. 2, 1952; s. Seymour and Florence (Lesan) E. BA in Psychology, U. N.C., 1972; MM, New Eng. Conservatory, 1978. Faculty Berklee Coll. Music, Boston, 1976-79; internat. concert performer W. Europe, North Am., 1979-83; composer, producer various groups, L.A., 1983—; musical dir. in field; master classes W. German Kulturamt, 1979-83. Composer music for TV shows including 227, Who's the Boss, 1987-89, Unsolved Mysteries, 1989-91, Wild & Crazy Kids, 1992, How'd They Do That, 1993, Movie Magic, 1993-97, Sightings, 1995-97, Seatek, 1996, A&E Biography, 1996, Behind Closed Doors with Joan Lunden, 1994-97, Kids Say. . .with Bill Cosby, 1997-98; films including Fourth War, Cold Feet, Mob Boss, Madhouse, 1988-90, Pacific Heights, Thelma & Louise, Madonna-Truth or Dare; videos including Kareem-Reflections, 1989 (Golden Globe award); advt. campaigns including MCI, GM, Mazda, MCA Universal; owner post-prodn. facility Media City Sound. Mem. Broadcast Music Inc., Am. Fedn. Musicians. Avocations: photography, bicycling, cooking, fishing. Home: 11542 Decente Dr Studio City CA 91604-3868 Office: Alan Ett Music Group 12711 Ventura Blvd Ste 110 Studio City CA 91604-2432

EU, MARCH FONG, ambassador, former state official; b. Oakdale, Calif., Mar. 29, 1929; d. Yuen and Shiu (Shee) Kong; children by previous marriage: Matthew Kipling Fong, Marchesa Suyin Fong; m. Henry Eu, Aug. 31, 1973; stepchildren: Henry, Adeline, Yvonne, Conroy, Alaric. Student, Salinas Jr. Coll.; BS, U. Calif.-Berkeley, 1943; MEd, Mills Coll., 1947; EdD, Stanford U., 1956; postgrad., Columbia U., Calif. State Coll.-Hayward; LLD, Lincoln U., 1984; LLB (hon.), Western U., 1985; DHL (hon.), Northrup Coll., 1991; LLB (hon.), Pepperdine U., 1993. Chmn. divsn. dental hygiene U. Calif. Med. Center, San Francisco, 1948-56; dental hygienist Oakland (Calif.) Pub. Schs., 1948-56; supr. dental health edn. Alameda County (Calif.) Schs.; lectr. health edn. Mills Coll., Oakland; mem. Calif. Legislature, 1966-74, chmn. select com. on agr., foods and nutrition, 1973-74; mem. com. natural resources and conservation, com. commerce and pub. utilities, select com. med. malpractice; chief of protocol State of Calif., 1975-83, sec. of state, 1975-94; amb. to Federated States of Micronesia, Am. Embassy, Pohnpei, 1994—; chmn. Calif. State World Trade Commn., 1983-87; ex officio mem. Calif. State World Trade Commn., 1987—; spl. cons. Bur. Intergroup Relations, Calif. Dept. Edn.; ednl., legis. cons. Sausalito (Calif.) Pub. Schs., Santa Clara County Office Edn., Jefferson Elementary Union Sch. Dist., Santa Clara High Sch. Dist., Santa Clara Elementary Sch. Dist., Live Oak Union High Sch. Dist.; mem. Alameda County Bd. Edn., 1956-66, pres., 1961-62, legis. adv., 1963, Assembly Retirement Com., Assembly Com. on Govtl. Quality Com., Assembly Com. on Pub. Health; pres. Alameda County Sch. Bds. Assn., others; U.S. advisor Shenzhen Internat. Ent. Co., Ltd., Shenzhen, Guangzhou, China, 1997; internat. hon. advisor 4th World Chinese Entrepreneurs Conv., Vancouver, B.C., 1997; hon. chmn. Sino-Am. Inst. Human Resources, L.A., 1997; U.S. advisor Internat. Hort Exposition for 1999, Kunming, Yunnan, 1997; mem. exec. adv. bd. Asian Am. Policy Rev. Bd., Washington, 1998, others. Mem. budget panel Bay Area United Fund Crusade; mem. Oakland Econ. Devel. Coun.; mem. tourism devel. com. Calif. Econ. Devel. Commn.; mem. citizens com. on housing Coun. Social Planning; mem. Calif. Interagy. Coun. Family Planning; edn. chmn., mem. coun. social planning, dir. Oakland Area Baymont Dist. Cmty. Coun.; charter pres., hon. life mem. Howard Elem. Sch. PTA; charter pres. Chinese Young Ladies Soc., Oakland; mem., vice chmn. adv. com. Youth Study Ctrs. and Ford Found. Interagy. Project, 1962-63; chmn. Alameda County Mothers' March, 1971-72; bd. councillors U. So. Calif. Sch. Dentistry, 1976; mem. exec. com. Calif. Dem. Ctrl. Com., mem. ctrl. com., 1963-70, asst. sec.; del. Dem. Nat. Conv., 1968; dir. 8th Congl. Dist. Dem. Coun., 1963; v.p. Dems. of 8th Congl. Dist., 1963; dir. Key Women for Kennedy, 1963; women's vice chmn. No. Calif. Johnson for Pres., 1964; bd. dirs. Oakland YWCA, 1965; mem. nat. vice-chmn. Clinton/Gore Reelection Campaign Com., 1996; U.S. Ambassador to Federated States Micronesia, 1994; mem. exec. adv. bd. Asian Policy Review, Washington, 1994; chmn. Investment Devel. Fund Fed. States Micronesia, 1995; chmn. March Fong Eu com. to promote Asian Am. Agenda, 1996; U.S. advisor Internat. Hort. Expn., Kumming, China, 1977; hon. chmn. Sino-Am. Inst. Human Resources, L.A., 1997; internat. hon. advisor 4th World Chinese Entrepreneurs Convention, Vancouver, Can., 1997; U.S. advisor Shenzhen Internat. Enterprises Co. Ltd., China, 1997; U.S. advisor in S.E. Asia Heart to Heart Internat. Found., Olathe, Kans. and San Diego, 1997. Recipient Citizen of Yr. award Chinese-Am. United for Self Employment, 1996, Govt. Svc. award friends of Mus. of Chinese Am. History, L.A., 1997, Cmty. Svc. award Coll. of San Mateo, Ann. Humanitarian award Women's Ctr., Coll. of Law, San Diego, Asian Am. on the Move award for politics L.A. City Employees Asian Am. Assn., Outstanding Svc. to Cmty. award Irish-Israeli Italian Soc.. San Francisco, Disting. C.C. Alumni award Calif. C.C. and Jr. Coll. Assn., Outstanding Woman award Nat. Women's Polit. Caucus, Daisy award Calif. Landscape Contrs. Assn., 1980, Milton Shoong Hall of Fame Humanitarian award, 1981, Citizen of the Yr. award Coun. for Civic Unity of San Francisco Bay Area, 1982, Woman of the Yr., Dems. United, San Bernardino, 1986, Woman of Achievement Award of Distinction, San Gabriel Valley YWCA, 1987, Disting. svc. award Rep. of Honduras, 1987, Woman of the Yr. award Santa Barbara County Girls Club Coalition, 1987, Polit. Achievement award Calif. Dem. Party, Black Caucus, 1988, 1989 JFK Am. Leadership award Santa Ana Dem. Club, 1989, Cmty. Leadership award Torat-Haijun Hebrew Acad., 1990, numerous others; March Fong Eu ann. achievement award named in her honor Nat. Notary Assn., 1998. Fellow Internat. Coll. Dentists; mem. Navy League (life), Am. Dental Hygienists Assn. (pres. 1956-57), No. Calif. Dental Hygienists Assn., Oakland LWV, AAUW (area rep. in edn. Oakland br.), Calif. Tchrs. Assn., Calif. Agrl. Aircraft Assn. (hon.), Calif. Sch. Bd. Assn., Alameda County Sch. Bd. Assn. (pres. 1965), Alameda County Mental Health Assn., Calif. Pub. Health Assn. Northern Divsn. (hon.), So. Calif. Dental Assn. (hon.), Bus. and Profl. Women's Club, Soroptimist (hon.), Hadassah (life), Ebell Club (L.A.), Chinese Retail Food Markets Assn. (hon.), Chinese Women's Assn. Singapore, Am. Assn. Singapore, Pilot Club Internat., Clara Barton Soc. Am. Red Cross (L.A. chpt.), Delta Kappa Gamma, Phi Alpha Delta (hon.), Phi Delta Gamma (hon.), others. Avocation: painting.

EUBANKS, GORDON, software company executive. Pres., CEO Symantec Corp., Cupertino, Calif. Office: Sumantec Corp Office 10201 Torre Ave Cupertino CA 95014-2131*

EUBANKS, RACHEL AMELIA, music educator; b. San Jose, Calif.; d. Joseph Sylvester and Elizabeth Amelia (Gant) E. BA, U. Calif., Berkeley, 1945; MA, Columbia U., 1947; DMA, Pacific Western U., 1980. Chmn. music dept. Wilberforce (Ohio) U., 1949-50; founder, pres. Eubanks Conservatory of Music and Arts, L.A., 1951—. Author: Musicianship, 1961; composer: Cantata, 1947, Trio, 1977, Symphonic Requiem, 1980, Sonata for Piano, 1992, 5 Interludes for Piano, 1996, Easter Suite for Organ, 1995. Rosenthal fellow Columbia U., 1946; recipient Cmty. awards City of L.A., 1982, Crenshaw Chamber of Congress, 1986, Calif. Legis. Assembly, 1991, County of L.A., 1991. Mem. Ethnomusicology Soc., Music Tchrs. Nat. Assn., Nat. Piano Guild, Internat. Alliance of Women in Music, Alpha Mu. Avocation: travel. Office: Eubanks Conservatory Music & Arts 4928 Crenshaw Blvd Los Angeles CA 90043

EUFINGER, ROSALIE RIGG, public relations executive; b. St. Louis, Jan. 10, 1940; d. Dean and Helen Katherine (Grothe) Rigg; m. R. J. Eufinger Jr., Sept. 25, 1963 (dec. Jan. 1987). AB, Washington U., St. Louis, 1963. Corp. mag. editor, pub. rels. writer Oakite Products, Berkeley Heights, N.J., 1967-74; asst. advt. and pub. rels. mgr. Fleetwood Enterprises, Riverside, Calif., 1975-78; mgr. corp. news bur. Tymshare, Cupertino, Calif., 1979-83; v.p. editl. svcs. Mathews & Clark Comms., Sunnyvale, Calif., 1983—. Mng. editor: Channel, 1991—. Avocations: hiking, cooking, theater, traveling, music. Home: 10923 Canyon Vista Dr Cupertino CA 95014-3908 Office: Mathews & Clark Comms 710 Lakeway Dr Ste 170 Sunnyvale CA 94086-4013

EVANCHO, JOSEPH HAMILTON, editor, publisher, writer, fishing guide; b. Detroit, July 5, 1960; s. Joseph Andrew and Dorothy Marie (Goodrich) E. B of Applied Arts, Ctrl. Mich. U., 1985. Freelance writer, 1982—; writer, pub. Cutthroat Press, Boise, Idaho, 1995—. Author, pub.: Fishing Idaho, An Angler's Guide, 1996. Home and Office: Cutthroat Press PO Box 1471 Boise ID 83701-1471

EVANGELISTA, RAMON A., chemist; b. Manila, Philippines, June 21, 1952; s. Abelardo and Norma (Acantilado) E.; m. Purita Dionisio, Nov. 6, 1982; children: Michelle, Lisa. BS in Chemistry, U. Philippines, 1973; PhD, Ohio State U., 1978; MASc, U. Toronto, 1982. Postdoctoral rsch. assoc. U. Calif., Berkeley, 1978-80, U. Toronto, 1982-83; sr. scientist HSC Rsch. Devel. Corp., Toronto, 1983-89; group leader Kronem Systems Inc., Mississauga, Can., 1989-91; sr. scientist Beckman Instruments, Inc., Fullerton, Calif., 1992-96, prin. scientist, 1996—. Contbr. some 30 articles to profl. jours. Mem. Am. Chem. Soc. Achievements include patents on 1,10-phenanthroline derivatives and use in fluorescence immunoassays, enzyme-amplified lanthanide chelate luminescence, fluorescent labelled carbohydrates and their analysis. Office: Beckman Instruments Inc 2500 N Harbor Blvd Fullerton CA 92835-2600

EVANS, ANGELA MARIE, religious organization executive; b. L.A., Sept. 25, 1956; d. Frederick K.C. and Betty Ruth (Scott) P.; m. A. Michael Evans, Feb. 28, 1976; children: Alan Michael, Adrian Marie. Student, West L.A. City Coll., 1974-75; cert. in mgmt. effectiveness, U. So. Calif., 1988; BA in Church Adminstrn., Friends Internat., Merced, Calif., 1992. Exec. sec., office mgr. Crenshaw Christian Ctr., L.A., 1977-80, exec. asst., 1980-84, exec. adminstr., 1984-88, exec. v.p., 1988—; corp. sec. Crenshaw Christian Ctr., L.A., 1983—, Employee Med. Fund/Assist Fund, L.A., 1984-85; bd. dirs. Frederick K.C. Price III Sch. Bd., L.A., 1985—. Supporter Traditional Value Coalition, Orange County, Calif., 1990—, Life Chain of So. Calif., Orange County, 1990—, Christian Legal Soc., Annandale, Va., 1988—. Recipient Outstanding Svc. award Lung Assn., 1979, Appreciation award FKCP III Child Care Ctr., 1986; named Outstanding Young Woman of Am., 1986. Mem. Christian Mgmt. Assn. Democrat. Office: Crenshaw Christian Ctr PO Box 90000 Los Angeles CA 90009-9201

EVANS, ANTHONY HOWARD, university president; b. Clay County, Ark., Sept. 24, 1936; s. William Raymond and Thelma Fay (Crews) E.; m. Lois Fay Kirkham, Aug. 29, 1959. BA, East Tex. Bapt. Coll., Marshall, 1959; MA, U. Hawaii, 1961; PhD, U. Calif.-Berkeley, 1966. Program officer Peace Corps, Seoul, Korea, 1970-72; chief program planning Peace Corps, Washington, 1972-73, dir. planning office, 1973-75; asst. to pres. Eastern Mich. U., Ypsilanti, 1975-76, exec. v.p., 1976-79, acting pres., 1978-79, provost, v.p. acad. affairs, 1979-82; pres. Calif. State U., San Bernardino, 1982—. Mem. Orgn. Am. Historians, Phi Kappa Phi. Home: 707 S Live Oak Park Rd Fallbrook CA 92028-3683

EVANS, ANTHONY LAWRENCE, minister, educator; b. Durham, N.C., Apr. 24, 1951; s. Robert Glenn Evans and Mary LaSena (Forsyth) Polk; m. Priscilla Anne Bynum, Aug. 5, 1973; 1 child, Sean Christopher. BA, Campbell Coll., Buies Creek, N.C., 1973; MDiv., Colgate-Rochester Div. Sch., 1976, DMin., 1984. Ordained to ministry Am. Bapt. Chs. in USA, 1976. Student min., asst. pastor Greece Bapt. Ch., Rochester, N.Y., 1974-76, assoc. min., 1976-82; sr. min. 1st Bapt. Ch., Olean, N.Y., 1982-91, Colorado Springs, Colo., 1991—; adj. prof. St. Bonaventure U., Olean, 1987—; bd. dirs. Interfaith Caregivers, Olean, 1985-89; pres. Greater Olean Assn. Chs., 1985-86; moderator Allegany-Cattaraugus Bapt. Assn., Olean, 1987-88; guest chaplain U.S. Ho. of Reps., Washington, 1989. Bd. dirs. Olean YMCA, 1986—; trustee Olean Gen. Hosp., 1987—; mem. presentation team millennial celebration U.S. Congressman Amory Houghton, Moscow, 1988; pres. alumni/ae coun. Colgate-Rochester Div. Sch., 1989-90. Mem. Rotary (pres. Olean club 1990-91). Democrat. Home: 3610 Willow Creek Dr Raleigh NC 27604-6067 Office: 1st Bapt Ch 317 E Kiowa St Colorado Springs CO 80903-1799

EVANS, BERNARD WILLIAM, geologist, educator; b. London, July 16, 1934; came to U.S., 1961, naturalized, 1977; s. Albert Edward and Marjorie (Jordan) E.; m. Sheila Campbell Nolan, Nov. 19, 1962. BSc, U. London, 1955; PhD, Oxford U., Eng., 1959. Asst. U. Glasgow, Scotland, 1958-59; departmental demonstrator U. Oxford, 1959-61; asst. research prof. U. Calif., Berkeley, 1961-65; asst. prof. U. Calif., 1965-66, assoc. prof., 1966-69; prof. geology U. Wash., Seattle, 1969—; chmn. dept. geol. scis. U. Wash., 1974-79. Contbr. articles to profl. jours. Recipient U.S. Sr. Scientist award Humboldt Found., Fed. Republic Germany, 1988-89; Fulbright travel award, France, 1995-96. Fellow Geol. Soc. Am., Mineral Soc. Am. (pres. 1993-94, award 1970), Geochem. Soc., Geol. Soc. London, Mineral. Soc. Gt. Britain, Swiss Mineral. Soc. Home: 8001 Sand Point Way NE Apt 55C Seattle WA 98115-6399 Office: U Wash Dept Geol Scis PO Box 351310 Seattle WA 98195-1310

EVANS, DAVID CLARK, medical systems analyst, pharmacist; b. Lehi, Utah, Aug. 9, 1949; s. Boise J. and Carole (Nelson) E.; m. Gaylene Bradley Evans, June 6, 1970 (div. June 1981); 1 child, Shand; m. Mary Elizabeth Kearns, July 18, 1981; children: David, Joseph, Mary Margaret, Alexander. AS, Snow Coll., 1971; BS cum laude, U. Utah, 1974; PharmD, SUNY, Buffalo, 1976. Registered pharmacist, Utah; cert. poison control specialist Am. Assn. Poison Control Ctrs. Pharmacist Reams Pharmacy, Sandy, Utah, 1978-80, Alta View Hosp., Sandy, 1980-88; sales and mktg. support GTE Health Sys., Salt Lake City, 1988-94, account exec., 1992-94; poison control specialist U. Utah, Salt Lake City, 1990—; clin. products specialist Shared Med. Sys. Inc., Salt Lake City, 1994-97, sr. clin. analyst, 1997—; clin. pharmacist Vernal (Utah) Family Health Ctr., 1976-78. Advisor Order of the Arrow. Mem. Am. Soc. Health Info. Pharmacists, Utah Soc. Health Info. Pharmacists, Utah Pharm. Soc., Rho Chi (Beta Epsilon chpt.). Republican. Mem. LDS Ch. Avocations: fishing, golf, scouting. Home: 1742 Millbury Way Sandy UT 84092-3826

EVANS, DAVID HAROLD, film company executive; b. Cedar City, Utah, June 14, 1955; s. Harold B. and Melba A. (Haslam) E.; m. Karen Christene Bigler, Apr. 6, 1991; children: John, B.J., Matthew, Nicole. Student, So. Utah U., 1973-79. Various Century Cinema Corp., Cedar City, 1975-84; CEO Commedia Pictures, Inc., Salt Lake City, 1979-83, Burbank, Calif., 1983-84; prodr./dir. Monarch Video, Salt Lake City, 1983-85; nat. mktg. dir. Tilley Toys, Salt Lake City, 1985; pub. rels. Utah Home Front Gallery, Salt Lake City, 1985; dir. pub. rels. Elvis Presley Cosmetics, San Diego, 1985-87; sales/mktg. FX-BIO Med., San Diego, 1987; prodr./writer Film Street, USA, El Cajon, Calif., 1994-96; CEO/prodr./dir. Oracle Films, Inc., Cedar City, 1996—; bd. dirs. Jr. Cinema Corp., Salt Lake City, 1980-84. Author: (screenplays) The Latch Key Kid, 1996, A Hand Full of Wind, 1994, Bottom, 1979, others. Leader Boys Scouts Am., Cedar City, 1989— (cert. of merit 1992), Girl Scouts U.S., 1991-94; bd. dirs. Cedar City Arts Coun., 1995. Honored Thespian Nat. Thespian Soc., 1973. Mem. Masque Club. Republican. Mem. LDS Ch. Avocations: hunting, fishing, fencing. Office: Oracle Films Inc 620 W Industrial Rd Ste 14 Cedar City UT 84720-4159

EVANS, DAVID LYNN, management consultant; b. Red Oak, Iowa, June 26, 1941; s. John Louis and Margaret Alice (Young) E.; m. Mary Susan Ricke, Aug. 4, 1963; children: John Louis, Mary Lynn, Sarah Leigh, Michael Ricke. BS, Iowa State U., 1964; MBA, U. Pa., 1966. Mem. staff Deere & Co., Moline, Ill., 1964-92; mgr. John Deere Info Systems, Moline, 1983-87; dir. fin. Deere & Co., Moline, 1987-92; exec. v.p. Rocky Mountain Internet, Denver, 1997-98; pres. Evanwood Corp., Evergreen, Colo., 1992—; chmn. Evanwood Corp., Evergreen, 1997—; bd. dirs. Conen Internat., Inc.; v.p. John Deere Leasing Co., bd. dirs. John Deere Receivables, Inc.; bd. dirs., chmn. audit com. Mut. Selection Fund, Inc., 1977—; chmn. audit com. Data Transmission Network Corp., 1986-95; mng. dir. Evans Farms, 1972—; dir. World Federalists Assn., 1980-90, v.p. midwest region 1977-82; dir. Campaign for UN Reform, 1979-82, 1980-81, treas, 1982-88; trustee John Deere Dealer Group Ins. Trust, 1981-85; chmn. fin. rels. com. Am Fin. Svcs. Assn., 1991-92; chmn. Nat. Assn. Corp. Dirs., 1991—; cons. corp. fin. N.Am., India and China. Elder Presbyn. Ch. Mem. Quad Cities World Affairs Coun. (pres. 1984, 92), Am. Econ. Assn., UN Assn., Iowa Mfrs. Assn. (chmn. econ. edn. com. 1979-81). Republican. Home and Office: Evanwood Corp 32500 El Diente Ct Evergreen CO 80439-9773

EVANS, GREGORY, college program administrator; b. Leflore, Miss., Jan. 30, 1967; s. Willie and Marguarite (Hardimon) E. BA, Jackson (Miss.) State U., 1989. Dir. student devel. Jackson State U., 1989-91, coord. acad. skills, 1991-92; instr. English Pikes Peak C.C., Colorado Springs, 1992-94; dir. student life Trinidad (Colo.) Jr. Coll., 1994—; cons. coll. issues Fishers Peak YMCA, Trinidad, 1997—, Friendship Bapt. Ch., Colorado Springs, 1993—; cons. student devel. Jackson State U., 1990—. Advisor Colo. State Student Adv. Coun., Denver, 1994—, Trinidad State Jr. Coll. Student Govt., 1994—; bd. dirs. Fishers Peak YMCA, 1998—; sr. advisor Youth 2000, Colo., 1998—; advisor, cons. Jackson State U. Kid's Coll., 1996—. Named Advisor of Yr., Colo. Cmty. Colls. and Occupl. Edn. Sys., Denver, 1998. Mem. Assn. Coll. Unions Internat., Nat. Assn. Coll. Aux. Svcs., Nat. Assn. Campus Activities. Office: Trinidad State Jr Coll 600 Prospect St Trinidad CO 81082-2356

EVANS, JAMES HANDEL, university administrator, architect, educator; b. Bolton, Eng., June 14, 1938; came to U.S., 1965.; s. Arthur Handel and Ellen Bowen (Ramsden) E.; m. Carol L. Mulligan, Sept. 10, 1966; children: Jonathan, Sarah. Diploma of Architecture, U. Manchester, Eng., 1965; MArch., U. Oreg., 1967; postgrad., Cambridge (Eng.) U., 1969-70. Registered architect, Calif., U.K.; cert. NCARB. Assoc. dean. prof. architecture Calif. Poly. State U., San Luis Obispo, 1967-78; prof. art and design San Jose (Calif.) State U., 1979—, assoc. exec. v.p., 1978-81, interim exec. v.p., 1981-82, exec. v.p., 1982-91, interim pres., 1991-92, pres., 1992-95; vice chancellor Calif. State U System, Long Beach, CA, 1995-96; planning pres. Calif. State U. Channel Islands, Ventura; cons. Ibiza Nueva, Ibiza, Spain, 1977-80; vis. prof. Ciudad Universitaria, Madrid, 1977; vis. lectr. Herriott Watt U., Edinburgh, 1970; mem. adv. com. Army Command Staff Coll., Ft. Leavenworth, Kans., 1988. Trustee Good Samaritan Hosp., San Jose, 1987-90; bd. dirs. San Jose Shelter, 1988-90; dir. San Jose C. of C., 1991-94. Sci. Rsch. Coun. fellow Cambridge U., 1969-70. Fellow AIA; mem. Royal Inst. Brit. Architects, Assn. Univ. Architects. Avocation: golf. Office: Calif State Univ Channel Is 1878 S Lewis Rd Camarillo CA 93012-8584

EVANS, JANET, Olympic swimmer; b. Aug. 28, 1971. 3 time Gold medalist, 400m Freestyle, 800m Individual Medley Seoul Olympic Games, 1988; Gold medalist, 800m Freestyle Barcelona Olympic Games, 1992, Silver medalist, 400m Freestyle, 1992; wubber 40th nat. title-400m Freestyle Phillips 66 Nat. Swimming Championships, Indpls., 1994; competed Atlanta Olympic Games, 1996. Named U.S. Swimmer of Yr., 1987. Office: US Swimming Inc One Olympic Plaza Colorado Springs CO 80909-5724*

EVANS, LAWRENCE JACK, JR., lawyer; b. Oakland, Calif., Apr. 4, 1921; s. Lawrence Jack and Eva May (Dickinson) E.; m. Marjorie Hisken, Dec. 23, 1944; children: Daryl S. Kleweno, Richard L., Shirley J. Coursey, Donald B. Diplomate Near East Sch. Theology, Beirut, 1951; MA, Am. U. Beirut, 1951; grad. Command and Gen. Staff Coll., 1960; PhD, Calif. Coast U.; Sussex, Eng., 1968; JD, Ariz. State U., 1971; grad. Nat. Jud. Coll., 1974. Bar: Ariz. 1971, U.S. Dist. Ct. Ariz. 1971, U.S. Ct. Claims 1972, U.S. Customs Ct., 1972, U.S. Tax Ct. 1972, U.S. Ct. Customs and Patent Appeals 1972, U.S. Ct. Appeals (9th cir.) 1972, U.S. Supreme Ct. 1975. Enlisted U.S. Navy, 1938-41, U.S. Army, 1942-44, commd. 2d lt. U.S. Army, 1944, advanced through ranks to lt. col., 1962; war plans officer, G-3 Seventh Army, 1960-62, chief, field ops. and tactics divsn., U.S. Army Spl. Forces, 1963, chief spl. techniques divsn., U.S. Army Spl. Forces, 1964, unconventional warfare monitor, U.S. Army Spl. Forces, 1964-65; ops. staff officer J-3 USEUCOM, 1965-68; mem. Airborne Command Post Study Group, Joint

Chiefs of Staff, 1967; ret., 1968; mem. faculty Ariz. State U., 1968; sole practice law, cons. on Near and Middle Eastern affairs, Tempe, Ariz., 1971-72, 76—; v.p., dir. Trojan Investment & Devel. Co., Inc., 1972-75; active Ariz. Tax Conf., 1971-75; mem. adminstrv. law com., labor mgmt. rels. com., unauthorized practice of law com. Ariz. State Bar. Author: Legal Aspects of Land Tenure in the Republic of Lebanon, 1951, International Constitutional Law, (with Helen Miller Davis) Electoral Laws and Treaties of the Near and Middle East, 1951; contbr. articles to mags., chpts. to books. Chmn. legal and legis. com. Phoenix Mayor's Com. To Employ Handicapped, 1971-75; active Tempe Leadership Conf., 1971-75; chmn. Citizens Against Corruption in Govt., 1976-95; mem. Princeton Coun. on Fgn. and Internat. Studies, 1968; comdr. Ranger Area-Ariz., Ranger Region-West, 1993—. Decorated Silver Star, Legion of Merit, Bronze Star, Purple Heart, Combat Infantryman badge, Master Parachutist badge, Aircrewman badge; named Outstanding Adminstrv. Law Judge for State Service for U.S., 1974; named to U.S. Army Ranger Hall of Fame, 1981. Fellow Coll. of Rites of U.S.A.; mem. Ranger Bns. Assn. World War II (life), Tempe Rep. Mens Club (v.p., bd. dirs. 1971-72), U.S. Army Airborne Ranger Assn. (life), Mil. Order Purple Heart (life), NRA (official referee, life), Masonic Order of the Bath, The Philatethes Soc., Ye Antient and Old Order of Corks, Order of the Secret Monitor, BL (twice past master Thunderbird Lodge # 48 Phoenix, past master Ariz. Rsch. Lodge # 1), Order Ky. Colonels, Sovereign Mil. Order of Temple of Jerusalem (grand avocat pro tem 1993, grand officier 1993), Knight Commdr. Grace Sovereign Mil. Order St. John Jerusalem (Knights Hospitallers), Grand Chpt. Royal Arch Masons Ariz. (grand lectr.), Fraternal Order of Medieval Knighthood, Internat. (sovereign venerable master Ariz. Coll. 1988-93, supreme sovereign grand master 1991), YR (past high priest, past thrice illustrious master, twice eminent past comdr., Knight Templar Cross of Honor, 1988, Orator Order of High Priesthood, Grand Chpt. YRM 1989, pres. Grand Coun. Holy Order of High Priesthood of Ariz. 1996-97, York Rite Mason of Decade, Scottsdale YRB 1989), SR (32, ritual dir.), Chief Adept Ariz. Coll. Socs. Rosicruceana In Civitatibus Foederatis IX Degree, Grand Commandery of Knights Templar of Ariz. (grand insp. gen. 1990-91), Grand Royal Arch Masons Ariz. (grand lectr. 1995-96), Masons (knight U.S.A., Chevalier and Ami du Patriarchate, KCM Ordo Sancti Constantini Magni), Order of Secret Monitor, So. Calif. Rsch. Lodge, Royal Order of Scotland, Comdr. Ranger Area-Ariz. (Ranger Region- West Red 1993), Mil. Order of World Wars (historian, archivist), The Nat. Sojourners Inc., United Assn. (life, local #469 Phoenix), Phi Delta Phi, Delta Theta Phi, Alpha Rho of Theta Chi. Episcopalian. Home: 539 E Erie Dr Tempe AZ 85282-3712

EVANS, LOUISE, investor, retired psychologist, philanthropist; b. San Antonio; d. Henry Daniel and Adela (Pariser) E.; m. Thomas Ross Gambrell, Feb. 23, 1960. BS, Northwestern U., 1949; MS in Clin. Psychology, Purdue U., 1952, PhD in Clin. Psychology, 1955. Lic. Marriage, Family and Child Counselor Calif., Nat. Register of Health Svc. Providers in Psychology; lic. psychologist N.Y. (inactive), Calif.; diplomate Clin. Psychology, Am. Bd. Profl. Psychology (fellow), Am. Bd. Clin. Psychology. Intern clin. psychology Menninger Found.-Topeka (Kans.) State Hosp., 1952-53, USPHS-Menninger Found. postdoctoral fellow clin. child psychology, 1955-56; staff psychologist Kankakee (Ill.) State Hosp., 1954; head staff psychologist child guidance clinic Kings County Hosp., Bklyn., 1957-58; dir. psychology clinic Barnes-Renard Hosp., instr. med. psychology Washington U. Sch. Medicine, 1959; clin. rsch. cons. Episc. City Diocese, St. Louis, 1959; pvt. practice clin. psychology, 1960-92; fellow Internat. Coun. Sex Edn. and Parenthood, 1984; psychol. cons. Fullerton (Calif.) Community Hosp., 1961-81; staff cons. clin. psychology Martin Luther Hosp., Anaheim, Calif., 1963-70; nat., internat. lectr. clin. psychology schs. and profl. groups, 1950—; chairperson, participant psychol. symposiums, 1956—; guest speaker clin. psychology civic and cmty. orgns., 1950—. Elected to Hall of Fame, Central H.S., Evansville, Ind., 1966; recipient Svc. award Yuma County Head Start Program, 1972, Statue of Victory Personality of the Yr. award Centro Studi E. Ricerche Delle Nazioni, Italy, 1985, Alumni Merit award Northwestern U. Coll. Arts and Scis., 1997; named Miss Heritage, Heritage Publs., 1965. Fellow APA (clin. divsn., psychology of women divsn., divsn. psychotherapy, cons. divsn., dir. exec. bd. 1976-7?), Acad. Clin. Psychology, Am. Assn. Applied and Preventative Psychology (charter), Royal Soc. Health England (emeritus), Internat. Council of Psychologists (dir. 1977-79, sec. 1962-64, 73-76), AAAS (emeritus), Am. Orthopsychiat. Assn. (life), World Wide Acad. of Scholars of N.Z. (life), Am. Psychol. Soc. (charter); mem. AAUP (emeritus)L.A. Soc. Clin. Psychologists (exec. bd. 1966-67), Calif. State Psychol. Assn. (life, ins. com. 1961-65), L.A. County Psychol. Assn. (emeritus), Orange County Psychol. Assn. (charter founding mem., exec. bd. 1961-62), Orange County Soc. Clin. Psychologists (founder, exec. bd. 1963-65, pres. 1964-65), Am. Public Health Assn. (emeritus), Internat. Platform Assn., N.Y. Acad. Scis. (emeritus), Purdue U. Alumni Assn. (life, mem. pres. coun., dean's club pacesetters, Citizenship award 1975, Disting. Alumni award 1993, Old Master 1993), Northwestern U. 1851 Soc. & Wilson Soc. (Coll. Arts and Scis. Merit award 1997). Center for Study of Presidency, Soc. Jewelry Historians USA (charter), Alumni Assn. Menninger Sch. Psychiatry, Soc. Sigma Xi Nat. Rsch. Hon. (emeritus), Pi Sigma Pi (pres. 1947-48, sec. 1946-47). Contbr. articles on clin. psychology to profl. publs. Achievements include development of innovative theories and techniques of clinical practice; acknowledged pioneer in devel. psychology as sci. and profession both nat. and internat., and pioneer in marital and family therapy, and in consulting to hospitals and clinics. Office: PO Box 6067 Beverly Hills CA 90212-1067

EVANS, PAUL VERNON, lawyer; b. Colorado Springs, Colo., June 19, 1926; s. Fred Harrison and Emma Hooper (Austin) E.; m. Patricia Gwyn Davis, July 27, 1964; children—Bruce, Mike, Mark, Paul. B.A. cum laude, Colo. Coll., 1953; J.D., Duke U., 1956. Bar: Colo. 1956, U.S. Dist. Ct. Colo. 1956, U.S. Supreme Ct. 1971, U.S. Ct. Appeals (10th cir.) 1974. Field mgr. Keystone Readers Service, Dallas, 1946-50; sole practice, Colorado Springs, 1956-60; ptnr. Goodbar, Evans & Goodbar, 1960-63; sr. ptnr. Evans & Briggs Attys., Colorado Springs, 1963-95 ; city atty. City of Fountain, Colo., 1958-62, City of Woodland Park, Colo., 1962-78; atty. Rock Creek Mesa Water Dist., Colorado Springs, 1963—. Author instruction materials. Precinct com. man Republican Com., Colorado Springs, 1956-72. Served with USNR, 1944-46, PTO. Recipient Jr. C. of C. Outstanding Achievement award, 1957. Mem. Colo. Mining Assn., Am. Jud. Soc., ABA, Colo. Bar Assn. (com. chmn. 1966-67, 84), El Paso County Bar Assn. (com. chmn. 1956—), Assn. Trial Lawyers Am., Colo. and Local Trial Lawyers, Tau Kappa Alpha (pres.), Phi Beta Kappa. Republican. Club: Optimist (pres. 1966-67). Home: 244 Cobblestone Dr Colorado Springs CO 80906-7624 Office: 227 E Costilla St Colorado Springs CO 80903-2103

EVANS, PAULINE D., physicist, educator; b. Bklyn., Mar. 24, 1922; d. John A. and Hannah (Brandt) Davidson; m. Melbourne Griffith Evans, Sept. 6, 1950; children: Lynn Janet Evans Hannemann, Brian Griffith. BA, Hofstra Coll., 1942; postgrad., NYU, 1943, 46-47, Cornell U., 1946, Syracuse U., 1947-50. Jr. physicist Signal Corps Ground Signal Svc., Eatontown, N.J., 1942-43; physicist Kellex Corp. (Manhattan Project), N.Y.C., 1944; faculty dept. physics Queens Coll., N.Y.C., 1944-47; teaching asst. Syracuse U., 1947-50; instr. Wheaton Coll., Norton, Mass., 1952; physicist Nat. Bur. Standards, Washington, 1954-55; instr. physics U. Ala., 1955, U. N.Mex., 1955, 57-58; staff mem. Sandia Corp., Albuquerque, 1956-57; physicist Naval Nuclear Ordnance Evaluation Unit, Kirtland AFB, N.Mex., 1958-60; programmer Teaching Machines, Inc., Albuquerque, 1961; mem. faculty dept. physics Coll. St. Joseph on the Rio Grande (name changed to U. Albuquerque 1966), 1961—, assoc. prof., 1965—, chmn. dept., 1961—. Mem. AAUP, Am. Phys. Soc., Am. Assn. Physics Tchrs., Fedn. Am. Scientists, Sigma Pi Sigma, Sigma Delta Epsilon. Achievements include patents on mechanical method of conical scanning (radar), fluorine trap and primary standard for humidity measurement Home: 730 Loma Alta Ct NW Albuquerque NM 87105-1220 Office: U Albuquerque Dept Physics Albuquerque NM 87140

EVANS, RICHARD LLOYD, financial services company executive; b. Seattle, Oct. 16, 1935; s. Lloyd Herman and Dorleska L. (Rotta) E.; m. Judith Anne Sahlberg, Dec. 20, 1958; children: Dallas L., Douglas L., Daniel [illegible] CLU; chartered fin. cons. Agt. Phoenix Mut. Life Ins. Co., Seattle, 1960-69; chmn. R.L. Evans Co. Inc., Seattle, 1969—; mng. prin. Evans Capital Mgmt. Assocs., Seattle; speaker on ins. and fin. planning to numerous orgns., 1975—; adv. Oreas Island Found., 1996—. Mem. exec. bd. Chief Seattle coun. Boy Scouts Am., 1976—; chmn. N.W. Theol. Union, Seattle, 1984-88; chief fin. officer, vice-chmn. San Juan County Pk. Bd., 1996—. Lt. USN, 1957-59. Recipient award of merit Chief Seattle coun. Boy Scouts Am., 1984. Mem. Am. Soc. CLU, Am. Soc. Chartered Fin. Cons., Nat. Assn. Life Underwriters, Wash. State Assn. Life Underwriters (bd. dirs. 1973-79, pres. 1977-78), Seattle Assn. Life Underwriters (v.p. 1972-73), Assn. Advanced Underwriting, Million Dollar Round Table, Estate Planning Coun. Seattle, Rainier Club, Masons, Rotary (dir.). Republican. Presbyterian. Home: 871 Deer Point Rd Olga WA 98279-9702 Office: 600 Stewart St Ste 1210 Seattle WA 98101

EVANS, ROBERT VINCENT, sales and marketing executive; b. Mobile, Ala., Sept. 21, 1958; s. William Alexander Evans and Katherine Barbara (Doerr) Davidson; m. Debra Marie Winters, July 27, 1984; children: James Vernon, Chelsea Marie. BS in Computer Info. Systems, Regis U., Denver, 1987, BS in Tech. Mgmt., 1987; postgrad. in Mgmt., U. Wash., 1995. Electrician Climax (Colo.) Molybdenum Co., 1978-82; applications engr. Honeywell, Inc., Englewood, Colo., 1982-83, sales engr., 1983-87; systems engr. Apple Computer, Inc., Seattle, 1987-88; regional systems engring. mgr. Apple Computer, Inc., Portland, Oreg., 1988-96; dist. sales mgr. Apple Computer, Inc., Seattle, 1997—. Author: Anthology of American Poets, 1981. Dir. Operation Lookout, Seattle, 1989; mem. Rep. Nat. Com.; commr. dist. chmn. Boy Scouts Am. Recipient USMC Blues award, Marine Corps Assn. Leatherneck award, 1977, Denver Post Outstanding Svc. award, 1983, N.Y. Zool. Soc. Hon. medal, James West fellowship award, Paul Harris fellowship award, Silver Beaver award Boy Scouts Am., 1998. Mem. Am. Mgmt. Assn., Am. Platform Assn., Mensa, Rotary, Kiwanis. Republican. Mem. Northwest Cmty. Ch. Avocations: reading, church ministry, family activities. Office: Apple Computer Inc PO Box 40355 Bellevue WA 98015-4355

EVANS, THOMAS EDGAR, JR., title insurance agency executive; b. Toronto, Ohio, Apr. 17, 1940; s. Thomas Edgar and Sarah Ellen (Bauer) E.; BA, Mt. Union Coll., 1963; m. Cynthia Lee Johnson, Feb. 23; children: Thomas Edgar, Douglas, Melinda, Jennifer. Tchr. Lodi, Ohio, 1963-64; salesman Simpson-Evans Realty, Steubenville, Ohio, 1964-65, Shadron Realty, Tucson, 1965-67; real estate broker, co-owner Double E Realty, Tucson, 1967-69; escrow officer, br. mgr., asst. county mgr., v.p. Ariz. Title Ins., Tucson, 1969-80; pres. Commonwealth Land Title Agy., Tucson, 1980-82, also dir.; pres. Fidelity Nat. Title Agy., 1982-90; bd. govs. Calif. Land Title Assn., 1990—; exec. v.p. Fidelity Nat. Title Ins. Co., 1990-92; v.p. Inland Empire Divsn. Fidelity Nat. Title, 1991-93, pres. Orange County Divsn., 1995—; bd. dirs. Western Fin. Trust Co., Fidelity Nat. Fin. Inc., Fidelity Nat. Title Ins. Co., Fidelity Nat. Title Agy. Pinal, The Griffin Co., Computer Market Place, Inc.; bd. dirs., chmn. bd. Cochise Title Agy., TIPCO; v.p., dir. A.P.C. Corp. Named Boss of Year, El Chaparral chpt. Am. Bus. Women's Assn., 1977. Mem. Calif. Land Title Assn. (pres. 1995-96), So. Ariz. Escrow Assn., So. Ariz. Mortgage Bankers Assn. (bd. dirs. 1982-85), Ariz. Mktg. Bankers Assn., Old Pueblo Businessmen's Assn. Tucson, Tucson Bd. Realtors, Ariz. Assn. Real Estate Exchangors (bd. dirs. 1968-69), Land Title Assn. Ariz. (pres. 1984), So. Ariz. Homebuilders Assn., Blue Key, Sigma Nu. Republican. Methodist. Clubs: Pacific, Ctr., Old Pueblo Courthouse, La Paloma, Ventana Country, Centre Court, Coto de Casa Country, Elks, Pima Jaycees (dir. 1966), Sertoma (charter pres., chmn. bd. Midtown sect. 1968-70); Tucson Real Estate Exchangors (pres. 1968); Sunrise Rotary; Old Pueblo, South Coast Repertory (bd. trustees 1996—), Pacific, Ctr. Home: 28861 Glen Rdg Mission Viejo CA 92692-4301 Office: 17592 17th St Ste 200 Tustin CA 92780-7917

EVANS-SHAW, GLENDA, nursing administrator; b. Tucson, Nov. 20, 1938; d. Loran R. and Bonnie Woneda (Heller) E.; 3 children. Student, L.A. City Coll., 1956-58; Diploma in Profl. Nursing, Hollywood Presbyn. Sch., 1956-59; AA, Santa Monica Coll., 1975; BS in Nursing, Cert. Pub. Health, Calif. State U., Sacramento, 1985. RN, Calif.; cert. disability mgmt. splst., case mgr. Staff nurse St. John's Hosp., Santa Monica, Calif., 1959-60; office nurse Ross-Loos Med. Clinic, Santa Monica, 1960; staff nurse Georgetown U. Hosp., Washington, 1961; occupl. health nurse Am. Embassy Health Clinic, 1964-65; vis. home health nurse Staten Is. (N.Y.) Vis. Nurse Agy., 1966-67; staff, charge nurse Bel Air (Calif.) Hosp., 1968-70; staff nurse Santa Monica Hosp., 1970-92; sr. rehab. nurse Indsl. Indemnity Ins. Co., L.A., Stockton,, Sacramento, 1972-83; nurse, case mgr. Nursing Concepts Cons., Amador City, Calif., 1983—; co-founder, pres. Strategic Health Alliances, Inc., 1993—; Mem. adv. bd. Calif. Spinal Cord Injury Network, 1987; mem. cmty. adv. bd. Kentfield Rehab. Hosp., 1994-96, dept. nursing San Francisco State U., 1994-95; mem. adv. bd. case mgmt. Amgen, Inc., 1995; mem. ACT III Consortium Ryan White Founding for HIV/AIDS, 1996; mem. HIV/AIDS adv. bd. Calaveras and Amador Counties, Calif., 1995-96; mem. adv. coun. Learning Svcs., Inc., 1996; mem. Glaxo-Wellcome Health Cre Execs: Bldg. Interdisciplinary Health Care Collaboration, 1997; mem. guidelines rev. expert panel Aetna/Individual Case Mgmt. Assn., 1994; presenter in field. Author: proposal; mem. editl. rev. panel: Performance Criteria, 1985. Vol. Ptnrs. in Progress and Calif. chpt. Nat. Spinal Cord Injury Assn.; team sponsor Little League baseball, Amador County, Calif., 1995-97; mem. Amador County Arts Coun., Amador County Women's Network. Mem. AAUW, Am. Acad. Nurse Life Care Planning, Case Mgmt. Soc. Am. (chair sub-com. govtl. affairs com. 1992, nat. govtl. affairs com. 1993, Case Mgr. of Yr. com. 1994, nomination com. 1995, co-author white paper regarding case mgmt. 1993, Case Mgr. of Yr. 1994, bd. dirs. 1995-98, policy and procedure, com. 1997, co-founder No. Calif. chpt. 1990, mem. interim bd. 1990, bd. dirs 1991, v.p. 1992, 97, pres. 1993, chair govtl. affairs com. 1992, ednl. com. 1996, bd. sec. 1995, mem. Ctr. for Case Mgmt. Accountability outcomes project com. 1996, pres. bd. 1999), Individual Case Mgmt. Assn. Avocations: reading, music, theater, gardening, grandchildren. Fax: (209) 267-9394. Home: PO Box 506 Amador City CA 95601-0506

EVE, ELIZABETH, artist, educator; b. L.A., Oct. 11, 1959; d. Dolph and Roslyn B. (Bernstein) Shapiro; m. Kirk Fredrick Mayer, Nov. 20, 1987. BA cum laude, San Francisco State U., 1984, tchg. credential, 1985. Cert. art, English, drama, dance tchr., Calif. Artist in residence, tchr. San Francisco Sch. of Arts, McAtter H.S., 1985-87; head theater dept. James Denman Mid. Sch. of Arts, San Francisco, 1987-89; dir. Eugene Victor Debs: An American Road to Radicalism, San Francisco, 1989-91; English instr. Korean Embassy, Yochun, South Korea, 1995-96; arts dir. Esperanza Cmty. Housing Corp., L.A., 1996—; arranger trips and scholarships U. So. Calif. Head Start, L.A., 1988—, various youth orgns.; represented by L.A. County Mus. of Art Sales and Rental Gallery; adv. Getty Ctr. & Sci. Ctr., 1999. One woman shows at Brand Libr., Pasadena, Calif., San Francisco Arts Commn. Gallery, 1985, Arts Coun. San Mateo, Calif., 1986, Joseph Chowray, San Francisco, 1988, Grant's Pass Mus. of Art, Oreg., 1991, KidSpace Mus., Pasadena, 1996, Barnsdale Jr. Art Ctr., L.A., 1997, Bridge Gallery, L.A., 1997, McGroarty Arts Ctr., L.A., 1998, William Grant Stills, L.A., 1998, Twin Towers, L.A., 1998, 99, Bower Mus., Santa Anna, Calif., Esperanza Cmty. Housing Corp. executed mural Esulas Para La Vida Spain, 1997; group show Bklyn. Mus., N.Y., 1983. Art checker Nat. Mus. Women in the Arts Archive. Tides fellow, Spain, 1997. Mem. Mus. Educators of So. Calif. Avocations: travel, snorkeling, biking, nature studies. Home: 240 3d Ave # 2 Venice CA 90291 Office: Esperanza Cmty Housing Corp 2337 S Figueroa St Los Angeles CA 90007-2501

EVEN, RANDOLPH M., lawyer; b. 1943. BS, U. Calif.; JD, Calif. Western Sch. Law. Bar: Calif. 1969. Atty. Even, Crandall, Wade, Lowe & Gates and predecessor firm Genson, Even, Crandall & Wade, P.C., Woodland Hills, Calif. Mem. Am. Bd. Trial Advocates, Assn. So. Calif. Def. Counsel (bd. dirs. 1978-80, 93—). Office: Even Crandall Wade Lowe & Gates 21031 Ventura Blvd Ste 801 Woodland Hills CA 91364-2240

EVENHUIS, NEAL LUIT, entomologist; b. Upland, Calif., Apr. 16, 1952; s. Kornelus and Harmina (Vermeer) E.; m. Marilyn L. Nicholson, 1994. BS, Calif. State Poly. U., Pomona, 1974, MS, 1977; PhD, U. Hawaii, Manoa, 1988. Sci. illustrator Bishop Mus., Honolulu, 1976-78, entomologist, 1978—; chmn. dept. natural scis., 1997—; mem. internat. editorial adv. bd. [illegible] 1991—. Author: Bibliography of Bombyliidae, 1983 (Oberly award 1985), Catalog of Diptera of Australasia/Oceania, 1989 (Thomas Say award 1992); assoc. editor Pacific Insects, a publ. of Bishop Mus., 1980-85, sr. editor Internat. Jour. Entomology, 1985; contbr. 200 articles to profl. jours. Grantee Nat. Geographic Soc., 1984-85, Nat. Sci. Found., 1988-89. Fellow Royal Entomol. Soc. London, Willi Hennig Soc., Pacific Sci. Assn.; mem. Entomol. Soc. Am., Hawaiian Entomol. Soc. (sec. 1983, Disting. Service award 1984, named Entomologist of Yr., 1997). Tibetan Buddist. Avocations: reading, guitar playing, coin collecting, flying disc sports. Home: 3060 Papali St Honolulu HI 96819-3052 Office: Bishop Mus Dept Entomology 1525 Bernice St Honolulu HI 96817-2704

EVENS, TIMOTHY WALT, lawyer; b. Denver, Sept. 8, 1951. BA, Ariz. State U., 1973, JD, 1976. Bar: Ariz. 1976, U.S. Ct. Appeals 1976, U.S. Dist. Ct. Ariz. 1976, U.S. Ct. Appeals (9th cir.) 1976, Calif. 1982, U.S. Dist. Ct. (so. dist.) Calif. 1982, U.S. Supreme Ct. 1984; cert. specialist in injury and wrongful death litigation, Ariz. Bd. Legal Specialization. Ptnr. Moore & Evens, Phoenix, 1998—. Author: Lights! Camera!! Action!!! Welcome to the Cinematic Set of the Trial Attorney, 1995, Defying Injustice, 1998. Vol. Ariz. Spl. Olympics, 1997. Mem. Assn. Trial Lawyers Am., Def. Rsch. Inst., Internat. Assn. Def. Counsel, State Bar Ariz., State Bar Calif., Maricopa County Bar Assn., San Diego County Bar Assn. Republican. Lutheran. Avocations: golf, writing, coaching sports, travel. Office: Moore & Evens 1144 E Jefferson St Phoenix AZ 85034-2285

EVERETT, HOBART RAY, JR., engineer, naval officer, consultant, researcher, inventor; b. Charleston, S.C., Nov. 29, 1949; s. Hobart Ray and Ruth (Humphreys) E.; m. Rachael Patricia Lewis, Dec. 30, 1971 (div. Dec. 1995); children: Todd Ashley, Rebecca Nicole. BEE, Ga. Inst. Tech., 1973; MS in Mech. Engring., Naval Postgrad. Sch., 1982. Commd. ensign U.S. Navy, 1973, advanced through grades to comdr., 1988; asst. engr. USS Nitro, 1975-77; engring. recruiter for officer programs, Montgomery, Ala., 1977-80; robotics coordinator Naval Sea Systems Command, Washington, 1983-84, dir. Office of Robotics and Autonomous Systems, 1984-86; autonomous systems project officer Naval Ocean Systems Ctr., San Diego, 1986-88, chief engr. USMC teleoperated vehicle program, 1988-89, assoc. div. head advanced systems div., 1988-93; cons. to Computer Scis. Corp., Falls Church, Va., 1993-94; assoc. divsn. head robotics Space and Naval Warfare Systems Ctr., San Diego, 1994—; founder DoD Robotics and Artificial Intelligence Database, 1983; Navy rep. to tri-svc. Joint Tech. Panel for Robotics, 1984-86; guest lectr. in robotics U. Md., U. Pa., 1983-86, U. Calif., San Diego, 1988; robotics researcher Naval Ocean Systems Ctr., prin. tech. cons. U.S. Army Mobile Detection Assessment and Response System interior program, 1990-93; tech. dir. Joint Army-Navy Mobile Detection Assessment and Response System interior and exterior program, 1993—. Author: Sensors for Mobile Robots, 1995, (with Borenstein and Feng) Sensors and Techniques for Mobile Robot Positioning, 1996; contbg. author Robotics Age mag., 1982-86, Sensors mag., 1987—; mem. editorial bd., contbg. author Robotics and Autonomous Systems mag.; contbr. 80 tech. publs.; inventor 1st autonomous sentry robot; patentee in field. Decorated Navy Commendation,1981, 86; recipient Naval Sea Systems Command award for Acad. Excellence, 1982, Woelful award for Acad. Excellence, Naval Sea Systems Command, 1983, Gen. Dynamics award for Acad. and Mil. Accomplishment, 1973. Mem. IEEE, Soc. Mfg. Engrs. (sr.), Robotics Inst. Am., Nat. Svc. Robot Assn. (bd. dirs. 1991—), Assn. Unmanned Vehicle Systems Internat. Sigma Xi. Office: Space & Naval Warfare Sys Ctr Code D3701 53406 Woodward Rd San Diego CA 92152-7383

EVERETT, MICHAEL A., producer; b. Lawrenceville, Ga., July 2, 1960; s. Malon and Allene (Wilson) E.; m. Danielle C Christoffersen, Sept 7, 1988; children: Mitchell A., Jessica D. A in Bus. Adminstrn., McConnell Coll., 1980; BBA, Belmount U., 1982. Sr. audio engr. JSM, Baton Rouge, 1984-90; v.p. Cal Chris, Turlock, Calif., 1990—; owner Everett Video Prodns., Turlock, Calif., 1992—. Songwriter, 1980-85; engr. on several Gold records, 1984-90. Chair RNC, Washington, 1997. Republican. Home: 11577 Griffith Rd Turlock CA 95380-9624 Office: Everett Video Prodns 11577 Griffith Rd Turlock CA 95380-9624

EVERETT, PAMELA IRENE, legal management company executive, educator; b. L.A., Dec. 31, 1947; d. Richard Weldon and Alta Irene (Tuttle) Bunnell; m. James E. Everett, Sept. 2, 1967 (div. 1973); 1 child, Richard Earl. Cert. Paralegal, Rancho Santago Coll., Santa Ana, Calif., 1977; BA, Calif. State U.-Long Beach, 1985; MA, U. Redlands, 1988. Owner, mgr. Orange County Paralegal Svc., Santa Ana, 1979-85; pres. Gem Legal Mgmt. Inc., Fullerton, Calif., 1986—; co-owner Bunnell Publs., Fullerton, Calif., 1992-96, The Millennium Network, 1997; instr. Rancho Santiago Coll., 1979—, chmn. adv. bd., 1980-85; instr. Fullerton Coll., 1989—, Rio Hondo Coll., Whittier, Calif., 1992-94; advisor Nat. Paralegal Assn., 1982—, Saddleback Coll., 1985—, North Orange County Regional Occupational Program, Fullerton, 1986—, Fullerton Coll. So. Calif. Coll. Bus. and Law; bd. dirs. Nat. Profl. Legal Assts. Inc., editor PLA News. Author: Legal Secretary Federal Litigation, 1986, Bankruptcy Courts and Procedure, 1987, Going Independent--Business Planning Guide, Fundamentals of Law Office Management, 1994. Republican. Avocation: reading. Office: 406 N Adams Ave Fullerton CA 92832-1605

EVERETT, VIRGINIA SAUERBRUN, counselor; b. Newark, N.J., Mar. 24, 1939; d. Arthur Gordon and Elwyna (Van Alen) Sauerbrun; m. Chandler H. Everett, Sept. 14, 1963 (div. Feb. 1986); children: Chandler P., Alexander U. BA, Coll. Wooster, 1961; MS in Gen. Counseling, Seattle Pacific U., 1990. Cert. chem. dependency counselor I. Counselor South King County Drug & Alcohol Recovery Ctrs., Seattle, 1990—; counselor Seattle Mental Health Inst., 1988-89, King County Perinatal Treatment Program, 1992-93, King County Pub. Health Dept., 1991—. Treas. Pacific N.W. Ballet League, Seattle, 1983; chmn. publicity Seattle Opera Guild, 1984; mem. work com. Washington State Coalition on Women's Substance Abuse Issues, 1990. Mem. ACA, Nat. Assn. Alchoholism and Drug Abuse Counselors, Chem. Dependency Profls. Wash. Republican. Episcopalian. Avocations: hiking, sailing, race walking. Home: 8408 NE 19th Pl Bellevue WA 98004-3236 Office: South King County Recovery Ctrs 15025 4th Ave SW Seattle WA 98166-2301

EVERHART, LEON EUGENE, retired career officer; b. Abilene, Kans., Jan. 14, 1928; s. Charles Francis and Florence Etta (Amess) E. BS with distinction, Ariz. State U., 1957; postgrad., U. Tenn., 1965. Commd. 2d lt. USAF, 1952, advanced through grades to col., 1970, ops. officer Berlin Air Safety Ctr., 1961-63; project officer Missile Devel. Ctr. USAF, Holloman AFB, N.Mex., 1963-65, chief spl. projects div. Missile Devel. Ctr., 1965-66; tactical fighter pilot, flight commander USAF, South Vietnam, 1967-68; system program dir. Aero. Systems Div. USAF, Wright Patterson AFB, Ohio, 1968-72; dir. test engring. Devel. and Test Ctr. USAF, Eglin AFB, Fla., 1973-78; comdr. Air Force Western Test Range USAF, Vandenberg AFB, Calif., 1978-82; ret. USAF, 1982; cons. in field. Speaker on big-game hunting in Africa and wildlife conservation for various civic and ednl. orgns. Mem. Amateur Trapshooting Assn. Ohio, NRA. Avocations: golf, trapshooting, big-game hunting, deep-sea fishing.. Home: 1285 Oak Knolls Rd Santa Maria CA 93455-4302

EVERHART, THOMAS EUGENE, retired university president, engineering educator; b. Kansas City, Mo., Feb. 15, 1932; s. William Elliott and Elizabeth Ann (West) E.; m. Doris Arleen Wentz, June 21, 1953; children—Janet Sue, Nancy Jean, David William, John Thomas. AB in Physics magna cum laude, Harvard, 1953; MSc, UCLA, 1955; PhD in Engring., Cambridge U., Eng., 1958. Mem. tech. staff Hughes Research Labs., Culver City, Calif., 1953-55; mem. faculty U. Calif., Berkeley, 1958-78, prof. elec. engring. and computer scis., 1967-78, Miller research prof., 1969-70, chmn. dept., 1972-77; prof. elec. engring., Joseph Silbert dean engring. Cornell U., Ithaca, N.Y., 1979-84; prof. elec. and computer engring., chancellor U. Ill., Urbana-Champaign, 1984-87; prof. elec. engring. and applied physics, pres. Calif. Inst. Tech., Pasadena, 1987-97; pres. emeritus Calif. Inst. Tech., Pasadena, 1997—; fellow scientist Westinghouse Rsch. Labs., Pitts., 1962-63; guest prof. Inst. Applied Physics, U. Tuebingen, Germany, 1966-67, Waseda U., Tokyo, Osaka U., 1974; vis. fellow Clare Hall, Cambridge, U., 1975; chmn. Electron, Ion and Photon Beam Symposium, 1977; cons. in field; mem. sci. and ednl. adv. com. Lawrence Berkeley Lab., 1978-85, chmn., [illegible] 1989—; bd. dirs. Hewlett Packard Corp., Saint-Gobain Corp., Reveo, Inc., Raytheon Co., Hughes Electronics Co., Elec. Power Rsch. Inst., Calif. Inst. Tech.; tech. adv. com. R.R. Donnelly & Sons, 1981-89; sr. sci. advisor W.M. Keck Found., 1997—; pro-vice chancellor Cambridge U., 1998. Chmn. Sec.

of Energy Adv. Bd., 1990-93; bd. dirs. KCET, 1989-97, Corp. for Nat. Rsch. Initiatives, 1990—, Electric Power Rsch. Inst., 1998—; trustee Calif. Inst. Tech., 1998—. NSF sr. fellow, 1966-67, Guggenheim fellow, 1974-75. Fellow IEEE, AAAS, ASEE, Royal Acad. Engring.; mem. NAE (edcnl. adv. bd. 1984-88, mem. com. 1984-89, chmn. 1988, coun. 1988-94, 96—), Microbeam Analysis Soc. Am., Electron Microscopy Soc. Am. (coun. 1970-72, pres. 1977), Coun. on Competitiveness (vice-chmn. 1990-96), Assn. Marshall Scholars and Alumni (pres. 1965-68), Athenaeum Club, Sigma Xi, Eta Kappa Nu. Home: PO Box 1639 Santa Barbara CA 93116-1639 Office: Calif Inst Tech Office Pres Emeritus 1201 E California Blvd Pasadena CA 91125-0001

EVERINGHAM, HARRY TOWNER, editor, publisher; b. Memphis, Aug. 14, 1908; s. William Kirby and Ida Pauline (Towner) E.; m. Margaret Sophia Johnson; children: Martha, Barbara, Richard Kirby. Student, Northwestern U., Evanston, Ill., 1936-39, U. Chgo., 1940. Writer, dir. weekly radio drama WREC, Memphis, 1930-33; radio writer, producer Miles Lab., Chgo., Wade Advt. Agy., Chgo., 1934-35; v.p. Sehl Advt. Agy., Chgo., 1936-41; broadcasting Henry C. Lytton & Co., Chgo.; film producer, lectr. Employers Assn., Chgo., 1942; editor, pub. The Fact Finder, 1942—; pub. rels. dir. Ingalls-Shepard Div. Wyman Gordon Co., Harvey, Ill.; editor Forging Ahead Mag., 1942-45. Editor, pub. U.S.A.-Beyond the Crossroads, Chgo., The Am. Patriot, 1959-94; syndicated newspaper columnist, 1960-63. V.p. Greater Chgo. Churchmen, 1946-47; founder Pub. Club Chgo., 1942. Mem. Ariz. Breakfast Club (founder, pres.). Republican. Avocations: teaching, speaking, broadcasting. Office: We the People UNITED Box A Scottsdale AZ 85252

EVERSOLE, FINLEY TRAWEEK, arts foundation executive; b. Birmingham, Ala., Dec. 24, 1933; s. Finley Pratt and Frieda Mae (Traweek) E. AB, Birmingham-So. Coll., 1955; BD with honors, Vanderbilt U., 1958; PhD, Union Grad. Sch., 1976. Literary editor Motive Mag. Meth. Bd. Edn., Nashville, 1959-61; dir. Interseminary Movement Nat. Student Christian Fedn., N.Y.C., 1962-64; sr. book editor Nat. Coun. Chs., N.Y.C., 1964-65; exec. dir. Soc. for the Arts, Religion and Contemporary Culture, N.Y.C., 1966-69; founder, dir. The Creative Soc., Inc., N.Y.C., 1969-72, Atlanta, 1977-84; art prof. U. Ctrl. Fla., Orlando, 1972-74; pres. The Creative Age, Birmingham, 1991-97; exec. dir. The Creative Soc., Inc., Manitou Springs, Colo., 1997—. Author, editor: Christian Faith and the Contemporary Arts, 1962; pub. various fine art prints, 1991-97; contbr. numerous articles to profl. jours. Avocations: woodworking, hiking, spiritual studies. E-mail: arts@access.webcombo.net. Fax: 719-685-3626. Office: The Creative Soc Inc 441 Manitou Ave Manitou Springs CO 80829-2335

EVILSIZOR, DOUGLAS E., development director; b. Flint, Mich., June 28, 1972; s. Jerry and Pat E.; m. Angela Lynch, June 20, 1998. BA, Wheaton Coll., Ill., 1994. Dir. ann. giving Rehoboth (N.Mex.) Christian Sch., 1994-97, dir. devel., 1997—. Mem. Nat. Soc. Fund-Raising Execs., Rotary. Republican. Avocations: mountain biking, skiing, backpacking. Office: Rehoboth Christian Sch PO Box 415 Rehoboth NM 87322

EVRIGENIS, JOHN BASIL, obstetrician-gynecologist; b. Athens, Greece, Feb. 23, 1929; came to U.S., 1951; s. Basil I. and Maria (Soteriou) E.; m. Sophia M. Goritsan, June 22, 1952; children: Maryellen, E. Debbie, W. Gregory, John Jr. BA, U. Athens, 1947, MD, 1951. Diplomate Am. Bd. Ob-Gyn. Intern Providence Hosp., Portland, Oreg., 1951-52, resident in gen. practice medicine, 1952-53; resident in ob-gyn Emanuel Hosp. and U. Oreg. Med. Sch., Portland, 1953-56; pvt. practice specializing in ob-gyn Sacramento, 1956—; assoc. clin. prof. ob-gyn Med. Sch., U. Calif., Davis, 1975—; chief ob-gyn dept. Mercy Hosp., Sacramento, 1972-73. Mem. AMA, Am. Fertility Soc., Pan-Am. Med. Soc., Royal Soc. Medicine, Royal Soc. Health, Sacramento County Med. Soc., Calif. Med. Assn., So. Calif. Ob-Gyn. Assembly, Am. Soc. Gynecol. Laproscopists, Am. Soc. Abdominal Surgeons, No. Calif. Ob-Gyn. Soc. (pres. 1975-76), Dynamis Club, Ahepa, Del Paso Country Club, Northridge Country Club, Sutter Club, Sacramento Club, Lions, Elks, Masons, Rotary Club. Eastern Orthodox. Avocations: reading, travel, golf, history, statistics. Home and Office: 3615 Winding Creek Rd Sacramento CA 95864-1530

EWELL, MIRANDA JUAN, journalist; b. Beijing, Apr. 25, 1948; d. Vei-Chow and Hsien-fang Yolanda (Sun) J.; m. John Woodruff Ewell Jr., Feb. 20, 1971; children: Emily, David, Jonah. BA summa cum laude, Smith Coll., 1969; postgrad., Princeton U., 1971, U. Calif., Berkeley, 1981-82. Staff writer The Montclarion, Oakland, Calif., 1982-83; with San Jose (Calif.) Mercury News, 1984—, staff writer; now correspondent San Jose (Calif.) Mercury News, San Francisco Bureau, 1990-95; correspondent in bus. San Jose Mercury News, 1997—. Recipient Elsa Knight Thompson award Media Alliance, San Francisco, 1984, George Polk award L.I. U., N.Y., 1989, Heywood Brown award Newspaper Guild, Washington, 1989; Knight fellow Stanford U., 1995. Mem. Asian-Am. Journalists Assn. *

EWING, EDGAR LOUIS, artist, educator; b. Hartington, Nebr., Jan. 17, 1913; s. David E. and Laura (Buckendorf) E.; m. Suzanna Peter Giovan, Feb. 12, 1941. Grad., Art Inst. Chgo., 1935; studied in France, Eng., Italy, 1935-37. Mem. faculty Art Inst. Chgo., 1937-43, U. Mich., Ann Arbor, 1946; asst. prof. fine arts U. So. Calif., 1946-54, assoc. prof., 1954-59, prof., 1959-78, Disting. prof. emeritus, 1978—; Mellon prof. Carnegie-Mellon U., Pitts., 1968-69. One-man shows M.H. DeYoung Meml. Mus. Art, San Francisco, 1948,, Long Beach Mus. Art, 1955, Dalzell Hatfield Galleries, Los Angeles, 1954, 56, 58, 61, 63, 65, Hewlett Gallery-Carnegie Mellon U., Pitts., 1969, Nat. Gallery, Athens, Greece, 1973, Los Angeles Mcpl. Art Gallery, 1974, Palm Springs (Calif.) Desert Mus., 1976-77, Fisher Gallery U. So. Calif., 1978; group exhbns. Cin Art Mus., Corcoran Gallery Art, Washington, Denver Art Mus., Dallas Mus. Fine Arts, Fort Worth Art Ctr., Met. Mus., N.Y.C.; represented: San Francisco Mus. Art, Dallas Mus. Fine Arts, Ft. Worth Art Ctr., Met. Mus., N.Y.C., Sao Paulo (Brazil) Mus. Art, Wichita Art Mus., Fisher Gallery, U. So. Calif., 1994. Served with C.E., U.S. Army, 1943-46, PTO. Recipient Aberle Florscheim Meml. prize for Oil Painting, Art Inst. Chgo., 1943, Purchase award for oil painting Los Angeles County Mus. Art, 1952, Samuel Goldwyn award, 1957, Ahmanson Purchase award City of Los Angeles Exhbn., 1962, Disting. Prof. Emeritus award U. So. Calif., 1987; Edward L. Ryerson fellow, 1935; Louis Comfort Tiffany grantee, 1948-49, Jose Drudis Fund grantee, Greece, 1967; named one of 100 Artists-100 Yrs., Art Inst. Chgo., 1980. Mem. AAUP, Nat. Watercolor Soc. (v.p. 1952, pres. 1953). Democrat. Home: 4226 Sea View Ln Los Angeles CA 90065-3350

EWING, JACK ROBERT, accountant; b. San Francisco, Feb. 14, 1947; s. Robert Maxwell and Blanche Julia (Diak) E.; m. Joan Marie Coughlin Ewing, Nov. 25, 1967; children: Theresa Marie Ewing, Christina Ann Ewing. BS, U. Mo., 1969. CPA. Staff acct. Fox & Co., St. Louis, 1969-70; radio station opr. USAF, Mountain Home, Idaho, 1970-72; internal auditor Air Force Audit Agy., Warren, Wyo., 1972-74; supr. auditor Fox & Co., St. Louis, 1974-79; audit mgr. Erickson, Hunt & Spillman, P.C., Ft. Collins, Colo., 1979-82; stockholder, owner Hunt, Spillman & Ewing, P.C., Ft. Collins, Colo., 1982-93; owner Jack R. Ewing, CPA, 1993—. Mem., pres. Parent Adv. Bd., Beattie Elem. Sch., 1982-83, 86-87; mem. Entrepreneur of Yr. Selection Com., Ft. Collins, Colo., 1989-92, Suicide Resource Ctr. of Larimer County, Ft. Collins, Colo., 1992—, pres., 1998—, bd. dirs.; mem. Leadership Ft. Collins-Class of 1992, State of Colo. Mental Health Planning Coun., 1993—; dir. treas. One West Contemporary Art Ctr., 1989-97—, Ctr. for Diversity in Work Place, 1991—; pres., adv. bd. Larimer County Bd. Mental Health, 1992—; v.p. Colo. Behavioral Healthcare Coun., 1995-97; mem. mental health pro bono project, 1996-97; mem. gov.'s citizen panel on suicide prevention, 1998—. Mem. Am. Inst. CPAs, Colo. Soc. CPAs. Avocations: writing, hiking. Office: 3112 Meadowlark Ave Fort Collins CO 80526-2843

EWING, JAMES E., priest; m. Elisabeth Anne Rooney. Ordained to ministry Evang. Episcopal Chs., 1953. Sr. pastor, gen. overseer St. Matthew Living Cathedral, N.Y.C.; mem. Rand Rsch. Corp.; mem. diplomat cir. L.A. World Affairs Coun.; rsch. bd. dirs. Am. Biog. Inst./Internat. Biog. Ctr. Author, editor: Church History, The Church Visible, George Washington, Life After Death, Bible Lessons. With USAF, 1953-57. Mem. Knights of Malta, Sovereign Order St. John of Jerusalem. Office: St Matthew Cathedral Ste 145 10736 Jefferson Blvd Culver City CA 90230

EWING, MICHAEL, producer, film company executive; b. Kalamazoo, Mich., Mar. 29, 1960; s. Robert Earl and Juan Marie Snyder. Student, We. Mich. U., 1979, Am. Acad. Dramatic Arts, N.Y.C., 1980, Actors Studio, N.Y.C., 1981, Stella Adler Conservatory, N.Y.C., 1980-84. Theater dir., co-prodr. L.A., 1985, N.Y.C., 1986-87; asst. to prodr. Paramount Pictures, L.A., 1988; asst. prodr. Paramount Pictures, 1989-90, assoc. prodr., 1991-95; co-prodr. Warner Bros., 1995-96; pres. Greenhaven Films, L.A., 1995—. Dir., co-prodr. (plays) World Premiere, Tigers Wild, L.A., 1985, N.Y.C., 1986-87; asst. to prodr. (film) The Naked Gun: From the Files of Police Squad, 1988; asst. prodr.: (films) Nothing But Trouble, 1990, Crazy People; assoc. prodr.: Naked Gun 2-1/2: The Smell of Fear, 1991, Naked Gun 33 1/3: The Final Insult, 1993; co-prodr.: (films) My Fellow Americans, 1995-96, Nutty Professor 2, 1998—. Office: Nutty Professor II/Universal Studios Building 506 Ste B 100 Universal City Plz Universal City CA 91608-1002

EWING, RUSSELL CHARLES, II, physician; b. Tucson, Aug. 16, 1941; s. Russell Charles and Sue M. (Sawyer) E.; children: John Charles, Susan Lenore. BS, . Ariz., 1963; MD, George Washington U., 1967. Diplomate Am. Bd. Family Practice. Intern L.A. County-U. So. Calif. Med. Ctr., L.A., 1967-68; gen. practice medicine and surgery, Yorba Linda, Calif. and Placentia, Calif., 1970-90, Brea, Calif., 1990-96, Placentia, 1996-97; mem. staff St. Judes Hosp., Fullerton, Calif., 1970-98; mem. staff Placentia Linda Cmty. Hosp., 1972—, vice chief staff, 1977-78, chief staff, 1978-80, bd. dirs., 1974-81; sec., dir. Yorba Linda Med. Group, Inc., 1974-90; bd. dirs. Prospect Med. Group, 1984-94, Heritage Assoc. Physicians, 1995-97, Western Empire Savs. & Loan Assn. (Calif.); bd. dirs., sec. St. Judes Med. Group, 1993-98. Bd. dirs. Yorba Linda YMCA, 1973-88, pres., 1973-74, 81. With USN, 1968-70. Fellow Am. Acad. Family Practice; mem. AMA, Calif. Med. Assn. (house of del. 1978-90, 92—, trustee 1990-92), Orange County Med. Assn. (bd. dirs. 1983-90, pres. 1988-89), Am. Coll. Physician Execs. Republican. Episcopalian. Email: rce.md@juno.com. Home and Office: 2400 Natoma Station Dr Apt 286 Folsom CA 95630-8173

EXNER, ADAM, archbishop; b. Killaly, Sask., Can., Dec. 24, 1928. Ordained priest Roman Catholic Ch., 1957, consecrated bishop, 1974. Bishop of Kamloops B.C., Can., 1974-82; archbishop of Winnipeg Man., Can., 1982-91; archbishop of Vancouver B.C., Can., 1991—. Office: Archdiocese of Vancouver, 150 Robson St, Vancouver, BC Canada V6B 2A7

EXNER, JANE FRANCES, nursing administrator; b. Pitts., Nov. 20, 1958; d. Albert Francis and Jane Frances (Tweed) E. BSN, Wheeling (W.Va.) Jesuit Coll., 1980; MPH, Temple U., 1992; student nurse practitioner program, U. N.Mex., 1996—. RN, W.Va., Pa., N.Mex. Staff nurse U. Pa. Hosp., Phila., 1980-83; vol. Peace Corps, Niger, West Africa, 1984-86; emergency dept. nurse Hahnemann U. Hosp., Phila., 1987-88; perioperative nurse Thomas Jefferson U. Hosp., Phila., 1989-92; coord. nursing Internat. Med. Corps., Baidoa, Somalia, 1992-93; dir. health care CARE, Somalia/Tanzania, 1993-95; country dir. Burundi, Internat. Med. Corps, 1996; guest lectr. nutrition Temple U., Phila., 1992; nutrition cons. Peace Corps, 1986. Nurse vol. Operation Smile, Liberia, West Africa, 1989, Romania, 1992. Recipient Disting. Alumni award Wheeling Jesuit Coll., 1994. Mem. Am. Pub. Health Assn., Emergency Nurses Assn., Maternity Care Coalition (program devel. and evaluation com. 1991-92). Roman Catholic. Home: 220 Western Skies Dr SE Bldg 10 Albuquerque NM 87123-4904

EYMAN, ROGER ALLEN, minister; b. Canton, Ill., Mar. 16, 1942; s. Silbert Lionel and Ruth Maxine (Noland) E.; m. Priscilla Ann Baker, Dec. 24, 1979; 1 child, Hans Roger. AA, Orange Coast Coll., Costa Mesa, Calif., 1969; BA in Psychology, Calif. State U., L.A., 1971; MMin, Bethany Theol. Sem., 1975, DMin summa cum laude, 1991. Ordained to ministry Am. Evang. Christian Ch./Gen. Conf., 1983. Missionary Gospel Mission Ch., Liberia, Costa Rica, 1974-76, Wadi Es Sir, Jordan, 1976-79; founder, pastor Ch. of Calvary Grace of Ariz., Tucson, 1984-89, Ch. of Calvary Grace of Alaska, Anchorage, 1989—; ins. claims cons., Anchorage, 1989—. Fellow Internat. Ministerial Fellowship, AECC Gen. Conf., Internat. Chaplains Assn., Alaska Club. Republican. Office: Ch of Calvary Grace Alaska 3107 W Colorado Ave # 241 Colorado Springs CO 80904-2040

EZAKI-YAMAGUCHI, JOYCE YAYOI, renal dietitian; b. Kingsburg, Calif., Mar. 18, 1947; d. Toshikatsu and Aiko (Ogata) Ezaki; m. Kent Takao Yamaguchi, Oct. 28, 1972; children: Kent Takao, Jr., Toshia Ann. AA, Reedley Coll., 1967; BS in Foods and Nutrition, U. Calif., Davis, 1969. Dietetic intern Henry Ford Hosp., Detroit, 1969-70, staff dietitian, 1970-71; renal dietitian Sutter Meml. Hosp., Sacramento, 1971-72; therapeutic dietitian Mt. Sinai Hosp., Beverly Hills, Calif., 1972-73; clin. dietitian Pacific Hosp., Long Beach, Calif., 1973-77; consulting dietitian Doctor's Hosp., Lakewood, Calif., 1976-77; clin. dietitian Mass. Gen. Hosp., Boston, 1977-78, Winona Meml. Hosp., Indpls., 1978-80; renal dietitian Fresno (Calif.) Community Hosp., 1980—. Author: (computer program) Dialysis Tracker, 1987; author: (with others) Cultural Foods and Renal Diets for the Dietitian, 1988, Standards of Practice Guidlines for the Practice of Clinical Dietetics, 1991. Religious chair Fresno Dharma Sch., 1994—; sec. Japanese Lang. Sch. Fresno Betsuin Buddhist Temple, 1997-98. Mem. Nat. Kidney Found. (exec. com. coun. renal nutrition 1992—, region V rep., nutrition editor, chair patient and pub. edn. com. 1992-93, chair elect comms. chair 1994-95, chair 1995-96, past chair 1997-98, chair nominations com., chair rsch. grant com., Disting. Svc. award 1996, Disting. Svc. award 1996), Am. Dietetic Assn. (bd. cert. renal nutrition specialist, renal practice group 1993—), No. Calif/No. Nev. chpt. Nat. Kidney Found. (disting. achievement award coun. on renal nutrition 1993, co-chair-elect 1993-94, co-chair 1994-95, co-past chair 1995-96, treas., corr. sec.). Buddhist. Avocations: computers, cross stitch. Office: Cmty Hosps Ctrl Calif Fresno & R Sts Fresno CA 93715-2094

EZRA, DAVID ALAN, federal judge; b. 1947. BBA magna cum laude, St. Mary's U., 1969, JD, 1972. Law clk. Office of Corp. Counsel City and County Honolulu, 1972; mem. firm Greenstein, Cowen & Frey, 1972-73, Anthony, Hoddick, Reinwald & O'Connor, 1973-80, Ezra, O'Connor, Moon & Tam, 1980-88; dist. judge U.S. Dist. Ct., Hawaii, 1988-98, chief judge, 1998—; adj. prof. law Wm. S. Richardson Sch. Law, 1978—; exec. com. 9th cir. Jud. Conf. Co-editor, author: Hwaii Construction Law - What to Do and When, 1987; editor: Hawaii Collection Practices Manual. 1st lt. USAR 1971-77. Daugherty Fund scholar, 1971, San Antonio Bar Assn. Aux. scholar, 1972. Mem. ABA, U.S. Fed. Judges Assn. (bd. dirs., exec. com.), Dist. Judges Assn. (v.p. 9th cir.), Hawaii State Bar, Am. Arbitration Assn., Delta Epsilon Sigma, Phi Delta Phi. Office: US Dist Ct 300 Alamoana Blvd C-400 Honolulu HI 96803*

FABE, DANA ANDERSON, judge; b. Cin., Mar. 29, 1951; d. George and Mary Lawrence (Van Antwerp) F.; m. Randall Gene Simpson, Jan. 1, 1983; 1 child, Amelia Fabe Simpson. B.A., Cornell U., 1973; J.D., Northeastern U., 1976. Bar: Alaska 1977, U.S. Supreme Ct. 1981. Law clk. to justice Alaska Supreme Ct., 1976-77; staff atty. pub. defenders State of Alaska, 1977-81; dir. Alaska Pub. Defender Agy., Anchorage, from 1981; judge Superior Ct., Anchorage; justice Alaska Supreme Ct., Anchorage, 1996—. Named Alumna of Yr., Northeastern Sch. Law, 1983. Mem. Nat. Assn. Women Judges, Alaska Bar Assn., Anchorage Assn. Women Attys. Office: Alaska Supreme Ct 303 K St Fl 5 Anchorage AK 99501-2013

FABRICK, OLGA, lawyer; b. Havana, Cuba, Dec. 14, 1949; came to U.S., 1960; d. Morris Kantoras and Sara Hochberg; m. Martin N. Fabrick, Sept. 12, 1970; children: Tess Sharie, Laura Michelle. BA, U. Calif., Davis, 1972; MS, Cal. State U., Fullerton, 1982; JD, LaVerne Coll. Law, 1988. Tchr. L.A.U.S.D., 1974-77; resource tchr. R.U.S.D., Rowland Heights, Calif., 1978-83; adminstr. O.M.U.S.D., Ontario, Calif., 1983-84; pvt. practice Upland, Calif., 1988—; pres. East West Family Law Coun., Claremont, Calif., 1994-96; minor's coun. L.A. County Superior Ct., 1992—, San Bernardino County Superior Ct., 1992-94. Chair, bd. dirs. pers. commn. Temple Beth Israel, Pomona, Calif., 1994-96. Recipient Boss of Yr. award Ontario Inland Valley Legal Sec. Assn., 1994. Mem. Phi Beta Kappa, Phi Kappa Phi. Democrat. Jewish. Office: Law Office Olga Fabrick 409B N Central Ave Upland CA 91786-4219

FACIONE, NOREEN CAROL, nursing educator, researcher; b. Pitts., Apr. 16, 1948; d. Paul Joseph and Dolores (August) Winterhalter; m. Peter Arthur Facione, Dec. 23, 1967; children: Carol Ann Giancarlo, Christopher, Shawn, Jerome, Bethany. BS, Bowling Green State U., 1977; MSN, Calif. State U., 1981; PhD, U. Calif., San Francisco, 1994. RN, Calif. Nurse Med. Coll. Toledo, 1977-78, U. Calif. Med. Ctr., Orange, 1978-79; nurse practitioner Siegel & Kravitz, Orange, 1980-90; rschr., asst. prof. U. Calif., San Francisco, 1994—; cons., rschr. Calif. Acad. Press, Millbrae, 1991—. Author: Assessing Critical Thinking in Nursing Education, 1997; contbr. articles to profl. jours. Chancellors fellow U. Calif., 1993; Rsch. grantee Nat. Inst. for Nursing Rsch. 1992, Am. Cancer Soc., 1992-93, 97, Breast Cancer Rsch. Program, 1995. Mem. Markkula Cter. for Applied Ethics (assoc.), Sigma Theta Tau (sec. 1996-98). Democrat. Roman Catholic. Avocations: puzzles, bridge. Office: Univ Calif Sch Nursing PO Box 0610 San Francisco CA 94143

FADHLI, HUSSAM ABBAS, retired cardiovascular surgeon, sculptor, painter; b. Baghdad, Apr. 24, 1938; came to U.S., 1957; s. Abbass Mohemmed and Najia (Razzak) F.; m. Brigitte Roman, July 10, 1957; children: Delilah, Adam, Sam, Amy. MD, U. Baghdad, 1951. Intern Fairview Park Hosp., Cleve., 1957-58; resident St. Vincent Hosp., 1958-59, St. Luke's Hosp., 1959-62; resident in thoracic and cardiovasc. surgery U. Tex. Med. Br., Galveston, 1962-64, instr., 1962-65; cardiovascular surgeon Port Arthur (Tex.) Hosps., 1965-93; sculptor, painter Fadhli Arts, Port Arthur and Loveland, Colo., 1986—. Contbr. articles to profl. jours.; commd. sculpture Southwind, Internat. Arabian Horse Assn. hdqs., Aurora, Colo.; represented in permanent collections at Camanderie Mus., France, Pres. Bus. Libr., Tex. A&M U., Katten Mus., Amsterdam, Holland, Mayoralty Bldg., Beppu, Japan, The Digit Found., Golden, Colo., TAMS Mus., Port Arthur, Tex., Shadow Ridge Golf Course, Omaha, Ranchos Cedras, Chile, U. Fla., GAinesville, various ranches throughout U.S. and abroad; also pvt. collections. Recipient First Pl. award Gallery One, Reno, Nev., 1989; named one of ten most prominent Arab Am., Arab Am. Found., Houston, 1992. Fellow Am. Artist League; mem. Acad. Artists Assn. (Best in Sculpture awards 1995, 95), Western Artists Soc. Avocations: daily exercise, racketball, travel. Home: Fadhli Arts 9908 W CR 18E Loveland CO 80537

FADNER, WILLARD LEE, physics educator, researcher; b. Racine, Wis., Aug. 10, 1933; s. Glenn Roland and Evelyn Hannah (Larsen) F.; m. Alice J. Lienhard, June 27, 1959; children: Jenette Marie Dunworth, Peter Willard. BSEE, Purdue U., 1955; MS in Physics, U. Wis., 1962; PhD in Physics, U. Colo., 1971. Project engr. A.C. Electronics, Milw., 1958-62; project asst. U. Wis., Madison, 1962-64; instr. Mankato (Minn.) State U., 1964-68; from rsch. asst. to rsch. assoc. U. Colo., Boulder, 1968-72, instr., 1971-72; from asst. prof. to assoc. prof. U. No. Colo., Greeley, 1972-80, prof., 1980—, chair dept. physics, 1991—; faculty senator U. No. Colo., Greeley, 1991-98; book reviewer, jour. referee in field. Contbr. numerous articles to profl. jours. including Nuclear Physics, Phys. Rev., Physics Letters, Am. Jour. Physics; contbr. photography articles to Shutterbug mag. ElectroOptics Lab. grantee Eastman Kodak, U. No. Colo., 1988, Computer Enhanced Phys. Labs. NSF—Leadership in Lab. Devel. grantee U. No. Colo., 1992-94. Achievements include development on the Generalized Correspondence Principle; work on wave-particle duality for photons; work on educational value of undergraduate research. Avocation: photography. Office: U No Colo Dept Physics Greeley CO 80639

FAER, A.M., magazine publishing consultant, poet; b. N.Y.C., Oct. 25, 1944; s. Meyer and Violet (Shecter) F.; m. 1967 (div. 1996); children: Daniel, Stacy; m. Fran Brennan, June 1999. Prodn. mgr. McGraw Hill Publ., N.Y.C., 1969-72; customer svc. mgr., scheduling mgr. Rumford Nat. Graphics, Concord, N.H., 1972-77; v.p. mfg. LFP, Inc., L.A., 1978-82, v.p. ops., sr. v.p., 1983-84; founder, pres. The Jared Co., Scottsdale, Ariz., 1981—; spkr. in field. Contbr. to books and mags. Mem. Western Publ. Assn. (bd. dirs. 1996—). Avocations: writing, art, travel. Office: The Jared Co 7119 E Shea Blvd Ste 264 Scottsdale AZ 85254

FAGAN, FREDERIC, neurosurgeon; b. Bklyn., Oct. 18, 1935; s. Jack and Sophie (Altschuler) F.;m. Donna Fagan, Mar. 1, 1969; children: Gabrielle, Samantha. BA, Ohio State U., 1958. Intern Santa Monica (Calif.) Hosp., N.Y.C., 1959; resident N.Y. Hosp., N.Y.C., Calif., 1960; cons. AMA, L.A., 1980—. Dir. Smithsonian Assocs., Washington, 1995, U.s. Holocaust Meml. Mus., Washington, 1995. Named Surgeon of Yr. MacMillan Industries, Santa Clara, Calif., 1989. Mem. N.Y. Acad. Scis., NRA (dir. 1995). Home: 11102 Excelsior Dr Apt 9E Norwalk CA 90650-5646 Office: Woodruff Hosp 3800 Woodruff Ave Long Beach CA 90808-2125

FAGERBERG, DIXON, JR., retired accountant, weather observer; b. Prescott, Ariz., Mar. 20, 1909; s. Dixon and Amy (Nelson) F.; m. Mary Jergens, June 21, 1933 (div. Aug. 1980); children: Dick, Mary, Nelson; m. Lorraine Brenn, Sept. 22, 1980. AB in Econs. summa cum laude, Stanford U., 1931. CPA, Ariz. Valuation engr. Calif. R.R. Commn., San Francisco, 1931-32; acct. Harmon Audit Co., Prescott, 1933-34; owner, mgr. Dixon Fagerberg, Jr., CPA, Flagstaff, Kingman, Phoenix, Ariz., 1935-57; ptnr.-in-charge Peat, Marwick, Mitchell & Co., Phoenix, 1957-71; ret., 1971; vol. cons. Internat. Exec. Svc. Corps, Guatemala City, Guatemala, 1975. Co-author: 108 Sedona Westerner Trail Walks, 1979; author: Boyhood Recollections of Prescott, Arizona, 1983, Dix's Almanac of Weather and Climate, 1989; columnist Practitioner's Forum, 1954-56. Bd. dirs. Phoenix Libr., 1960-65; mem. Coconino County Planning and Zoning Commn., Flagstaff, 1973-76; councilman City of Sedona, 1988. Lt. USNR, 1944-46. Recipient medal of merit U. Ariz., 1960, Outstanding CPA award Mountain States Acctg. Conf., 1966. Mem. AICPA (nat. v.p. 1955-56), Ariz. Soc. CPA's (pres. 1938-39, columnist The Oasis 1972—), Am. Soc. Mining Engrs., Assn. Am. Weather Observers, Sedona Westerners (trail boss 1973-74), Pinewood Country Club, Masons. Avocations: orchardist, hiking, tennis.

FAIN, KAREN KELLOGG, retired history and geography educator; b. Pueblo, Colo., Oct. 10, 1940; d. Howard Davis and Mary Lucille (Cole) Kellogg; m. Sept. 1, 1961; divorced; 1 child, Kristopher. Student, U. Ariz., 1958-61; BA, U. So. Colo., 1967; MA, U. No. Colo., 1977; postgrad., U. Denver, 1968, 72-93, Colo. State U., 1975, 91, Chadron State Coll., 1975, U. No. Ill., 1977, 83, Ft. Hayes State Coll., 1979, U. Colo., 1979, 86-87, 92, Ind. U., 1988. Cert. secondary tchr., Colo. Tchr. history and geography Denver Pub. Schs., 1967-96; tchr. West H.S., Denver, 1992-96; area adminstr., tchr. coord. Close Up program, Washington, 1982-84; reviewer, cons. for book Geography, Our Changing World, 1990. Vol., chmn. young profls. Inst. Internat. Edn. and World Affairs Coun., Denver, 1980—; mem. state selection com. U.S. Senate and Japan Scholarship Com., Denver, 1981-89, Youth for Understanding, Denver; mem. Denver Art Mus., 1970—; vol. Denver Mus. Natural History, 1989—, Am. Cancer Soc. "Jail and Bail", 1996, "Climb the Mountain", 1996, Denver Conv. Bur., 1997; bd. overseas Dept. Def. Dependents Sch., Guantanamo Bay, Cuba, 1990-91; screening panelist Tchr. to Japan Program Rocky Mtn. Regional Fulbright Meml. Fund, 1997; vol. tour guide Colo. State Capitol, 1997—. Fulbright scholar Chadron State Coll., Pakistan, 1975; Geog. Soc. grantee U. Colo., 1986; recipient award for Project Prince, Colo. U./Denver Pub. Schs./Denver Police Dept., 1992. Mem. AAUW, Colo. Coun. Social Studies (sec. 1984-86), Nat. Coun. Social Studies (del. 1984), World History Assn., Fulbright Assn., Am. Forum for Global Edn., Rocky Mountain Regional World History Assn. (steering com. 1984-87), Colo. Geographic Alliance (steering com. 1986), Denver Bot. Gardens, Gamma Phi Beta, Kappa Kappa Iota. Episcopalian. Avocations: traveling, hosting international visitors, swimming, reading. Home: 12643 E Bates Cir Aurora CO 80014-3315

FAIOLA, RICHARD LOUIS, physician; b. L.A., Jan. 20, 1950; s. Louis Rocco and Leah Margaret (Klein) F.; m. Wenche Marageareth Kirk, July 30, 1972; children: Anne-Marie, Erik Louis. BS in Human Biology and Religion, Pacific Union Coll., 1972; MD, Loma Linda U., 1972. Diplomate Nat. Bd. Med. Examiners, Am. Acad. Family Physicians; cert. Am. Bd. Family Practice. Chief resident family practice Hinsdale (Ill.) Hosp., 1978-79; family practice physician Steck Med. Group, Chehalis, Wash., 1981—; pres., mng. ptnr. Steck Med. Group, Chehalis, 1993-98, med. dir., 1998—; med. dir. rehab. svcs. Providence Hosp., Chehalis, 1983-93; pres. Lewis County Med. Soc., Chehalis, 1985, 96, Lewis County Med. Svc. Orgn., Chehalis, 1994—, Noble Products, Onalaska, Wash., 1996—, Ontos, Inc., Chehalis, 1997—; sec.-dir. Pro Health Alliance, Olympia, Wash., 1996—. Lectr. human sexuality W.F. West H.S., Chehalis, 1982—; leader, tchr. Ch. Youth Divsn., Chehalis, 1985—. Capt. USAF-MC, 1979-81. Mem. Nat. Fedn. Ind. Bus., Nat. Mail Order Assn., Lewis County Econ. Devel. Coun., Lewis County C. of C. Seventh-Day Adventist. Avocations: travel, photography, reading,

gourmet foods. E-mail: rfaila@localaccess.com. and faiolar@steckmedial.com. Fax: 360-748-0950. Office: PO Box 1267 1299 Bishop Rd Chehalis WA 98532-8758

FAIR, ANNIE MAY, geological computer specialist; b. Coolidge, Ariz., Sept. 21, 1939; d. Jack C. and Birdie Geneva (Strickland) Cullins; m. Charles Leroy Fair, Sept. 12, 1964; children: Rex Lee Myers, Kathleen Ann, Rebecca Elizabeth. Student, Wichita State U., 1979-81, U. Colo., 1982-84, 94—, Met. State U., Denver, 1983-84. Cert. geol. engr. Pres., bd. dirs. Fresnal Minerals, Inc., Tucson, 1975-80; geol. technician Foxfire Exploration, Inc., Wichita, Kans., 1980-81, Coastal Oil & Gas Corp., Denver, 1981-93; stat. analyst fluid minerals, nat. applications adminstr. Bur. Land Mgmt., Canon City, Colo., 1993—, nat. help desk, 1993—; geol. cons. C.L. Fair & Assocs., Littleton, Colo., 1984-93. Active adv. bd. Masonic-Rainbow Girls-Grand Cross of Color, Denver, 1983-84; vol.- helper United Way Campaign, Denver, 1990, 91; vol. Am. Cancer Soc., Littleton, 1991, 92; art judge Reflections Nat. Art Contest, Denver, 1992, 93, Skyline Elem. Sch., Canon City, 1993. Recipient Grand Cross of Color, Masons-Order Rainbow/Girls, 1957; Music scholar U. No. Ariz., 1957, Ariz. Girls state, 1956. Mem. Am. Assn. Petroleum Geologists, Geol. Soc. Am., Rocky Mountain Assn. Geologists, Computer Oriented Geol. Soc., Alpha Lambda Delta. Avocation: artist. Home: 2853 Melvina St Canon City CO 81212-8837

FAIR, MARCIA JEANNE HIXSON, retired educational administrator; b. Scobey, Mont.; d. Edward Goodell and Olga Marie (Frederickson) Hixson; m. Donald Harry Mahaffey (div. Aug. 1976); 1 child, Marcia Anne (dec.); m. George Justin Fair, Mar. 26, 1997. BA in English, U. Wash.; MA in Secondary Edn., U. Hawaii, 1967. Cert. secondary and elem. tchr. and adminstr. Tchr. San Lorenzo (Calif.) Sch. Dist., 1958-59; tchr. Castro Valley (Calif.) Sch. Dist., 1959-63, vice prin., 1963-67; vice prin. Sequoia Union High Sch. Dist., Redwood City, Calif., 1967-77, asst. prin., 1977-91, ret., 1991; tchr. trainer Project Impact Sequoia Union Sch. Dist., Redwood City, 1986-91; mem. supr.'s task force for dropout prevention, 1987-91, Sequoia Dist. Goals Commn. (chair subcom. staff devel. 1988); mentor tchr. selection com., 1987-91; mem. Stanford Program Devel. Ctr. Com., 1987-91; chairperson gifted and talented Castro Valley Sch. Dist.; mem. family svcs. bd., San Leandro, Calif. Vol. Am. Cancer Soc., San Mateo, Calif., 1967, Castro Valley, 1965; Sunday sch. tchr. Hope Luth. Ch., San Mateo, 1970-76; chair Carlmont H.S. Site Coun., Belmont, Calif., 1977-91; mem. Nat. Trust for Hist. Preservation. Recipient Life Mem. award Parent, Tchr., Student Assn., Belmont, 1984, Svc. award, 1989, Exemplary Svc award Carlmont High Sch., 1989, 92; named Woman of the Week, Castro Valley, 1967, Outstanding Task Force Chair Adopt A Sch. Program San Mateo (Calif.) County, 1990. Mem. ASCD, AAUW, DAR, Assn. Calif. Sch. Adminstrs. (Project Leadership plaque 1985), Sequoia Dist. Mgmt.Assn. (pres. 1975, treas. 1984-85), Met. Mus. Art, Smithsonian Instn., Libr. of Congress Assocs. (charter), Am. Heritage - The Soc. of Am. Historians, Internat. Platform Assn., Animal Welfare Advocacy, Woodrow Wilson Internat. Ctr. Scholars, Nat. Geographic Soc., Am. Mus. Natural History (charter mem.), Bridle Trails Cmty. Club, Delta Kappa Gamma, Alpha Xi Delta (Order of Rose award). Avocations: oil painting, travel, tap dancing, redecorating, writing poetry.

FAIR, MARY LOUISE, retired elementary school educator; b. Emporia, Kans., July 16, 1931; d. Dale Franklin Fair and Beulah Fair (Emma) Martin. BA, Marymount Coll., 1953. Bus. edn. tchr. Geneseo (Kans.) High Sch., 1953-55, St. John (Kans.) High Sch., 1955-56; sec. YMCA, Salina, Kans., 1956-57; alumna sec. Marymount Coll., Salina, Kans., 1957-58; bus. edn. tchr. Hayden High Sch., Topeka, Kans., 1958-59; sec. Mental Health Assn., Denver, 1959-60; sec., substitute tchr. Denver Pub. Schs., 1960-62, elem. tchr., 1962-86. 1st v.p. AARP, Heather Gardens, Aurora, Colo., 1988-90, pres. 1991, parliamentarian 1994, publication com. 1994—, Heather Gardens Restaurant Comm., 1995—; tutor Aurora and Cherry Creek elem. schs., 1987—. Mem. AAUW (Aurora br., historian 1993-94), Marymount Coll. Alumnae Assn. (pres. 1956-58), Luncheon Optomist Club, Altrusa Club Aurora, Alpha Delta Kappa (state sgt.-at-arms 1982-84, state pres. 1986-88, S.W. regional sgt.-at-arms 1989-91, internat. chmn. living meml. scholarship com. 1991-93, chpt. pres. 1994-96, chpt. pres. coun. (pres. 1994-96). Republican. Baptist. Avocations: travel, reading, embroidery. Home: 3022 S Wheeling Way Apt 311 Aurora CO 80014-5607

FAIRBANK, JANE DAVENPORT, editor, civic worker; b. Seattle, Aug. 21, 1918; d. Harold Edwin and Mildred (Foster) Davenport; AB magna cum laude, Whitman Coll., 1939; postgrad. U. Wash., 1940-42; m. William Martin Fairbank, Aug. 16, 1941; children: William Martin, Robert Harold, Richard Dana. Sci. staff mem. Radiation Lab., Mass. Inst. Tech., Cambridge, 1942-45. Chmn. Second Careers for Women, Stanford, Calif., 1970-75; chmn. annual continuing edn. program Whitman Coll. Sr. Alumni Coll., 1986-96; founding mem. Bay Area Consortium on Ednl. Needs of Women. 1971; mem. Canada Coll. Citizens Adv. Com. for Community Edn., 1968; mem. organizing com. for conf. on frontiers of physics Stanford U., 1982; tchg. asst. U. Wash., 1940-42. Mem. Whitman Coll. Alumni Assn. (bd. dirs. 1986-96), Calif. Congress Parents and Tchrs. (hon. life), Mortar Bd., Phi Beta Kappa. Alpha Chi Omega. Mem. United Ch. of Christ. Mem. Stanford Univ. Women's Club (pres. 1975-76). Editor: Radar Maintenance Manual (2 vols.), 1945; co-editor Near Zero: New Frontiers of Physics, 1988; Second Careers for Women: A View from the San Francisco Peninsula, 1971; Second Careers for Women, vol. II: A View of Seven Fields from the San Francisco Bay Area, 1975. Office: 141 E Floresta Way Menlo Park CA 94028-7530

FAIRBANKS, MARY KATHLEEN, data analyst, researcher; b. Manhattan, Kans., June 4, 1948; d. Everitt Edsel and Mary Catherine (Moran) F. BS, St. Norbert Coll., 1970; postgrad., Calif. Family Study Ctr., 1981-82. Neuropsychology researcher U.S. VA Hosp., Sepulveda, Calif., 1970-76; mgr. print shop Charisma In Missions, City of Industry, Calif., 1976-77; neuropsychology researcher L.A. County Women's Hosp., 1977-79; mem. tech. staff Computer Scis. Corp., Ridgecrest, Calif., 1979-81; systems programmer Calif. State U., Northridge, 1982-84; bus. systems analyst World Vision, Monrovia, Calif., 1984-86; configuration analyst Teledyne System Co., Northridge, 1986-87; applications system analyst Internat. Telephone and Telegraph/Fed. Electric Corp., Altadena, Calif., 1987-88; supr. data analysts OAO Corp., Altadena, 1988—. Co-author, contbr.: Serotonin and Behavior, 1973, Advances in Sleep Research, vol. 1, 1974. Mem. St. Mary's Cath. Cmty. Theatre. Mem. OAO Mgmt. Assn., So. Calif. Application System Users Group, Digital Equipment Computer Users Soc. Roman Catholic. Avocations: photography, reading, music, hiking, camping. Home: 37607 Lasker Ave Palmdale CA 93550-7721 Office: OAO Corp 787 W Woodbury Rd Ste 2 Altadena CA 91001-5388

FAIRFULL, THOMAS MCDONALD, museum director; b. Greensburg, Pa., Nov. 28, 1942; s. Tom and Margaret Jane (Heasley) F. BA, U. Pitts., 1964; MA, Duke U., 1972. Dir. 82d Airborne Div. Mus., Fort Bragg, N.C., 1975-78; instr. Campbell U., Buies Creek, N.C., 1976-78; dir. U.S. Army Mus. Hawaii, Honolulu, 1978—. Co-author: (with William R. Porter) History of the 3d Brigade 82d Airborne Div. 1969. Served to capt. U.S. Army, 1965-74, Vietnam. Recipient Bronze Star with oak leaf cluster, USA. Mem. Am. Mil. Inst., Hawaii Mus. Assn., Council Am.'s Mil. Past. Home: 1950 A 9th Ave Honolulu HI 96816-2906 Office: US Army Museum of Hawaii Stop 319 APVG-GAR-LM CRD DCA USAG Fort Shafter HI 96858*

FAIRHAM-WHEELER, VICTORIA RUTH KUHNS, secondary education educator; b. Detroit, Aug. 27, 1949; d. Vernon Cecil and Doris Lillian (Bridges) Kuhns; m. Kert Roderick Fairham, Jan. 10, 1970 (div. Jan. 1985); children: Shawn (dec.), Laura; m. Kevin Royce Wheeler, July 26, 1989. BS, Eastern Mich. U., 1973; MEd, U. Portland, 1982. Tchr. Detroit Pub. Schs., 1973-75, McLoughlin Jr. H.S., Milw., 1975-93, Milwaukie (Oreg.) H.S., 1993—; adj. staff Warner Pacific Coll., Portland, 1997—. Author: Daily Writing Topics, 1996; editor: Depression is Curable, 1987, Seasons and Other Times, 1987. Mem. NEA, Nat. Coun. Tchrs. English, Oreg. Edn. Assn. Democrat. Unitarian Universalist. Avocations: travel, music, dance, hiking, art.

FAIRHURST, JEFFREY THOMAS, software consultant; b. Tacoma, Wash., May 10, 1955; s. Cyrel Jackson and Evelyn Marie Fairhurst; m. Irene Johanna Moser, Sept. 22, 1976 (div. Dec. 1982); children: Johanna Evelyn, Jeffrey Jackson. Student, Ctrl. Tex. Coll. Analyst Barclay's Bank, San Jose, Calif., 1984; ind. cons. San Jose, 1984-85; analyst GE Nuclear Energy Bus., San Jose, 1985; software developer CSC, San Diego, 1986-87; analyst Lorimar, Culver City, Calif., 1987-88, Decom Sys. Inc., San Marcos, Calif., 1988, Profl. Computer Resources, Inc., Cypress, Calif., 1989, Psicor Inc., San Diego, 1990; ind. cons. Carlsbad, Calif., 1990-92, Midcom Corp., Cypress, 1992-93, Logicorp Inc., Bingham Farms, Mich., 1994; cons. Air Touch, Irvine, Calif.; cons. Found. Health Corp., 1996, Alcatel, Richardson, Tex., 1998. With U.S. Army, 1973-84. Avocations: gold prospecting, camping, scuba diving, guitar playing, bow hunting, sky diving. Home: 3990 Scott Dr Carlsbad CA 92008-3625

FAIRLEY, PETER CARLTON, secondary education educator; b. Oakland, Calif., Oct. 17, 1958; s. Gerald R. Fairley and Elizabeth A. (Cerini) Lopez; m. Linda L. Gilmore, June 27, 1998. BS in Psychology, Wash. State U., 1981; MS in Biology, U. Calif., Irvine, 1985. Cert. tchr. in biology, earth sci., gen. sci. and math., Nev. Sci. tchr. Pyramid Lake H.S., Nixon, Nev., 1986-90, Incline H.S., Incline Village, Nev., 1990-95, Galena H.S., Reno, Nev., 1995—; project wild facilitator Nev. Divsn. Wildlife, Reno, 1992—. Writer, performer (recorded music) Pangaea Percussion Spirit Safari C.D., 1985. Mem. Earth Spirit Drum Cir., Reno, 1993—. Mem. Masons. Democrat. Eclectic. Avocations: hiking, skiing, scuba diving.

FAIRWEATHER, EDWIN ARTHUR, electronics company executive; b. London, July 21, 1916; came to U.S., 1967; s. Arthur Henry and Elizabeth (Dawson) F.; m. Joan Barbara Branson, Sept. 14, 1946; children: David Martin, Janet Elizabeth Fairweather Nelson. BSME, London Poly., 1940. Quality engr. Lucas-Rotex, Toronto (Ont., Can.) and Birmingham (Eng.), 1951-58; mfg. engr. Flight Refuelling Co., Dorset, Eng., 1958-62, Spar Aerospace, Toronto, 1962-67, Sperry Flight Systems, Phoenix, 1967-71; engr. research and devel. Ford Aerospace Co., Palo Alto, Calif., 1971-85; founder, pres., chief engr. Fairweather & Co., Sunnyvale, Calif., 1980—. Patentee in field. Served with RAF, 1940-46. Avocations: sailing, golf. Fax: (408) 773-1613. Home and Office: 1442 S Wolfe Rd Sunnyvale CA 94087-3669

FAISS, ROBERT DEAN, lawyer; b. Centralia, Ill., Sept. 19, 1934; s. Wilbur and Theresa Ella (Watts) F.; m. Linda Louise Chambers, Mar. 30, 1991; children: Michael Dean Faiss, Marcy Faiss Ayres, Robert Mitchell Faiss, Philip Grant Faiss, Justin Cooper. *Robert Faiss's grandchildren are Stephanie Jane Faiss, Branden Faiss, Khristopher Robert Faiss, Adelaide Chambers Ayres and Eliza Pennington Ayres. Son Michael Faiss is a regional restaurant manager in California. Daughter Marceline Ayres is an educator in Massachusetts. Son Robert Mitchell Faiss owns an electrical company in Nevada. Sons Philip Faiss and Justin Cooper are involved in the entertainment industry in California.* BA in Journalism, Am. U., 1969, JD, 1972. Bar: Nev. 1972, D.C. 1972, U.S. Dist. Ct. Nev. 1973, U.S. Supreme Ct. 1977, U.S. Ct. Appeals (9th cir.) 1978. City editor Las Vegas (Nev.) Sun, 1957-59; pub. info. officer Nev. Dept. Employment Security, 1959-61; asst. exec. sec. Nev. Gaming Commn., Carson City, 1961-63; exec. asst. to gov. State of Nev., Carson City, 1963-67; staff asst. U.S. Pres. Lyndon B. Johnson, White House, Washington, 1968-69; asst. to exec. dir. U.S. Travel Adminstrn., Washington, 1969-72; ptnr., chmn. adminstrv. law dept. Lionel, Sawyer & Collins, Las Vegas, 1973—; mem. bank secrecy Act Adv. Group U.S. Treasury. Co-author: Legalized Gaming in Nevada, 1961, Nevada Gaming License, 1988, Nevada Gaming Law, 1991, 95, 98. Recipient Bronze medal Dept. Commerce, 1972, Chris Schaller award We Can, Las Vegas, 1995, Lifetime Achievement award Nev. Gaming Attys. Assn., 1997; named One of 100 Most Influential Lawyers in Am. and premier U.S. gaming atty., Nat. Law Jour., 1997. Mem. ABA (chmn. gaming law com. 1985-86), Internat. Assn. Gaming Attys. (founding, pres. 1980), Nev. Gaming Attys. Office: Lionel Sawyer & Collins 300 S 4th St Ste 1700 Las Vegas NV 89101-6053

FALEOMAVAEGA, ENI FA'AUAA HUNKIN, congressman; b. Vailoatai Village, Am. Samoa, Aug. 15, 1943; m. Hinanui Bambridge Cave; children: Temanuata Tuilua'ai, Taualai, Nifae, Vaimoana, Leonne. BA in Polit. Sci. and History, Brigham Young U., 1966; JD, U. Houston, 1972; LLM, U. Calif., Berkeley, 1973. Bar: Am. Samoa, U.S. Supreme Ct. Adminstrv. asst. Am. Samoa del. to Washington, 1973-75; staff counsel to house com. on interior and insular affairs U.S. House of Reps., Washington, 1975-81; dep. atty. gen. Am. Samoa, 1981-84, lt. gov., 1984-89; territorial del. from Am. Samoa U.S. Ho. Reps., 1988; mem. 105th Congress from Samoa, 1988—, mem. internat. rels. com., resources com.; chmn. Gov.'s Task Force for Reorgn. of the Adminstrn., Am. Samoa Adv. Fisheries Council, 1985—, Gov.'s Adv. Com. on Grants Programs, 1985—; mem. nat. lt. gov.'s mission to Egypt, Jordan and Saudi Arabia, South Pacific Leaders Orientation Mission to Paris, 1987; leader Am. Samoa's del. to South Pacific Conf., Noumea New Caledonia, 1987; keynote speaker and leader Am. Samoa's del. to Pacific Trade/Omvestment Conf., 1986. With U.S. Army, 1966-69, including Vietnam, USAR, 1985—. Recipient Alumni Svc. award Brigham Young U., 1979; named Chieftain Faleomavaega, leone Village. Mem. Nat. Conf. of Lt. Govs., Nat. Assn. Secs. of State, Navy League of U.S., VFW, Nat. Am. Indian Prayer Breakfast Group, Lions (charter mem. Pago Pago chpt.), Go for Broke Assn. (life; pres. Samoa chpt.). Office: US Ho of Reps 2422 Rayburn Bldg Washington DC 20515-5201*

FALGIANO, VICTOR JOSEPH, electrical engineer, consultant; b. San Francisco, Nov. 25, 1957; s. Victor Anthony and Frances Mary Falgiano; m. Linda Maxine Owens, July 24, 1982; children; Gregory Joseph, Nicholas Rexford. BS in Elec. Engring. Tech. magna cum laude, Cogswell Coll., 1989, BS in Computer Engring. magna cum laude, 1989. Sr. design engr. Amdahl Corp., Sunnyvale, Calif., 1978-93; prin. sys. devel. engr. Nat. Semiconductor Corp., Santa Clara, Calif., 1993-98, engring. mgr. Cyrix divsn., 1998—; mem. steering com. System Design and Integration Conf., 1994; chmn. Calif.; mem. acad. adv. com. Cogswell Coll., Cupertino, Calif., 1991; evaluator Accrediting Bd. Engring. and Tech., 1995—. Contbr. articles to profl. publs. Advisor to high sch. students Jr. Achievement. Mem. IEEE (sr.), Assn. Computing Machinery, Internat. Microelectronics and Packaging Soc. Achievements include development of computer program pre-reading children, automobile digital instrumentation, speech recognition user interface for automotive applications, data aquisition circuitry used in mainframe computer power systems, high performance connector system for mainframe computers, developments in commercial/industrial multichip modules and design of personal computer systems. Office: Nat Semicondr Cyrix Divsn/Chipset Enging PO Box 58090 M/S A2-575 2900 Semiconductor Dr Santa Clara CA 95052

FALICK, ABRAHAM JOHNSON, printing company executive; b. Chgo., Oct. 11, 1920; s. Simon Falick and Ellen Martina (Johnson) Sherwood; m. Carolyn Weber, Dec. 11, 1947; 1 child, Leslie Carol Falick Koplof. BA, Ind. U., 1947; MBA, U. Chgo., 1951; MA, UCLA, 1967, PhD, 1970. Cert. pub. planner. Commd. ensign USNR, 1941, advanced through grades to lt. comdr., 1941-46, ret., 1967; mgr. sales/mktg. Webb-Linn Printing Co., Chgo., 1948-56; pres., chief exec. officer Murray and Gee, Inc., Culver City, Calif., 1956-60; planning economist City of Los Angeles, 1967-75; pres., chief exec. officer AJ Falick Assocs., Los Angeles, 1960-67, Navigator Press, Inc., Los Angeles, 1975—; mem., bd. dirs. Navigator Press. Contbr. transp. research articles to profl. jours. Chmn. Coalition Rapid Transit, L.A., 1978—, Friends of Geography UCLA, 1989—; v.p. Westwood Dem. Club, 1988—; chair L.A. Bus./Profl. Dem. Club, 1992—. Mem. Am. Econ. Assn., Am. Planning Assn., Am. Inst. Cert. Planners (counselor 1972-74), Nat. Assn. Bus. Economists (pres. L.A. chpt. 1996-98, bd. mem. L.A. chpt.). Democrat. Jewish. Avocations: photography, bowling, tennis. Office: Navigator Press Inc 516 N Fair Oaks Ave Pasadena CA 91103-3304

FALK, STEVEN B., newspaper publishing executive. Pres., CEO San Francisco Newspaper Agy. Office: San Francisco Newspaper Agy 925 Mission St San Francisco CA 94103-2905

FALKENBERG, WILLIAM STEVENS, architect, contractor; b. Kansas City, Mo., July 21, 1927; s. John Joseph and Maraba Elizabeth (Stevens) F.; m. Janis Patton Hubner, Apr. 13, 1951; children: Ruth Elizabeth, Christopher Joseph, Charles Stevens. BS in Archtl. Engring., U. Colo., 1949. Pres. Falkenberg Constrn. Co., Denver, 1951-71, 74-84, devel. cons., 1984-94; broker Hogan & Stevenson Realty, Denver, 1971-74. Chmn. constrn. Archdiocesan Housing Com., Inc., pres. 1997-98; chmn. restoration 9th Street Hist. Park; chmn. bldg. comm. Four Mile House Hist. Park; chmn. Housing Trust Coun., Denver, 1986-90; chmn. Rocky Mountain Better Bus. Bur., 1965-67; pres. Denver Friends Folk Music, 1966. Lt. (j.g.) USNR, 1945-51. Mem. AIA (bd. dirs. Denver chpt. 1978-81, treas. 1981), Home Builder Assn. Met. Denver, Colo. Hist. Soc. Found. (trustee, sec. 1987-97), Serra Internat. (pres. 1971, dist. gov. 1973), Nat. Assn. Atomic Vets., Colo. Archeol. Soc., Denver Athletic Club, Equestrian Order of Holy Sepulchre, Cactus Club (pres. 1995-98). Home and Office: 430 Marion St Denver CO 80218-3930

FALKNER, DAVID A., principal, educator; b. St. Louis, Mar. 2, 1948; s. Virgil W. and Lucille L. (Burroughs) F.; m. Margaret A. Hyder, June 4, 1979; children: Kalissa, Allen. BA, U. Ariz., 1970; MEd, Tex. Christian U., 1975; postgrad., U. Ariz. Tchr. Tucson Unified Sch. Dist.; prin. Faith Lutheran Sch., Tucson, Ariz.; prin., tchr. Lutheran Sch. of the Foothills, La Crescenta, Calif.; minister of edn. Ramona (Calif.) Luth. Sch. Lt. col. USAF, 1970—. Mem. ASCD, Nat. Guard Assn. (Calif. chpt.), Lutheran Educators Assn. Home: 3441 Gentilly Blvd New Orleans LA 70122-4933 Office: Ramona Luth Sch 520 16th St Ramona CA 92065-2622

FALKNER, JAMES GEORGE, foundation executive; b. Spokane, Wash., Dec. 24, 1952; s. Albert Andrew and Amanda Rosalia (Reisinger) F.; m. Joleen Rae Ann Brown, June 22, 1974; children: James Jr., Jayson, Jerin, Jarret. BS in Acctg., U. Wash., 1975. CPA, Wash. CPA LeMaster & Daniels, Spokane, 1975-80; treas. Dominican Sisters Spokane, 1980-95; pres. Dominican Outreach Found., Spokane, 1995—; bd. dirs. Dominican Network, Spokane, Dominican Health Svcs., Providence Svcs., Spokane; mem. Bishop's Fin. Coun. Spokane Diocese, 1990-96. Bd. dirs. sch. bd. St. Mary's Ch., Veradale, Wash., 1986-89, 90, sch. found., 1987—; active acctg. adv. com. Spokane Falls Community Coll., 1989—. Mem. Healthcare Fin. Mgmt. Assn. (bd. dirs. 1982-85), AICPA, Wash. State Soc. CPAs (Spokane Wash. bd. dirs.), Nat. Notary Assn. Avocations: coaching baseball, golf, soccer, carpentry. Office: Dominican Outreach Found 3102 W Fort George Wright Dr Spokane WA 99224-5203

FALLETTA, JO ANN, musician; b. N.Y.C., Feb. 27, 1954; d. John Edward and Mary Lucy (Racioppo) F.; m. Robert Alemany, Aug. 24, 1986. BA in Music, Mannes Coll. Music, N.Y.C., 1976; MA in Music, Juilliard Sch., N.Y.C., 1982; PhD in Musical Arts, Juilliard Sch., 1989; Honorary Doctorate, Marian Coll., Wis., 1988. Music dir. Queens Philharmonic, N.Y.C., 1978-91, Den. Chamber Orch., Colo., 1983-92; assoc. condr. Milw. Symphony, Wis., 1985-88; music dir. Women's Philharmonic, San Francisco, 1986-96; music dir., condr. Long Beach Symphony, Calif., 1989—; music dir. Va. Symphony, Norfolk, 1991—. Stokowski Conducting Competition, Toscanini Conducting award. Office: ICM Artists LTD 40 W 57th St New York NY 10019-4001*

FALTIN, BRUCE CHARLES, hotel executive; b. Cin., Mar. 7, 1947; s. Charles F. and Meryl (Gunther) F.; m. H. Ann Walker: children: Sharon, Laura, John. BS, Cornell U., 1969. Mgr. Winegardner & Hammons Inc., Cin., 1969-78; ptnr. Idahotels Ltd., Boise, Idaho, 1978—; pres. Mountain States Mgmt. Inc., Boise, 1978—, also bd. dirs; trustee Rodeway Inns Advt. Fund, Phoenix, 1985-94; chmn. Rodeway Inns Owner's Coun., Phoenix, 1986-88. Co-founder, dir., pres. Idaho Hospitality Edn. Found., 1990-91. Mem. Am. Hotel and Motel Assn. (state dir. 1983-84), Nat. Restaurant Assn., Idaho Innkeepers Assn. (bd. dirs. 1974-86, 88-94, pres. 1979, treas. 1988-91), Greater Boise C. of C. (bd. dirs. 1987), Choice Hotels Brands Adv. Coun., Idaho Hospitality Edn. Found. (pres. 1990-91), Idaho Hospitality and Travel Assn. (pres. 1994-95). Home: 2423 Hillway Dr Boise ID 83702-0933 Office: Rodeway Inn of Boise 1115 N Curtis Rd Boise ID 83706-1298

FALUDI, SUSAN C., journalist, scholarly writer. Formerly with West Mag., San Jose, Calif., Mercury News; with San Francisco Bur., Wall St. Jour.; spkr. in field. Author: Backlash: The Undeclared War Against American Women, 1991 (National Book Critics Circle award for general nonfiction 1992); contbr. articles to mags. Recipient Pulitzer Prize for explanatory journalism, 1991. Office: care Sandra Dijkstra Literary Agy 1155 Camino Del Mar Ste 515 Del Mar CA 92014-2605

FALVEY, DONALD, government official; b. Price, Utah, Mar. 22, 1942; s. Arthur Edward and Lillian Viola (Erickson) F.; m. Susan Katherine Grant, July 2, 1966 (div. Apr. 1979); children: Erik Grant, Jason Andrew; m. Carole Georgianne Longo, Feb. 10, 1984. BCE, Ga. Inst. Tech., 1963; MPA, U. Denver, 1973. Registered profl. engr., Colo. Bridge design engr. Smith Pollitte & Assocs., Columbia, S.C., 1964; civil engr. U.S. Forest Svc., Golden, Colo., 1966, Bur. Indian Affairs, Littleton, Colo., 1966-72; civil engr., sect. chief Nat. Park Svc., Lakewood, Colo., 1972-81, divsn. chief Rocky Mountain Regional Office, 1981-85; supt. Badlands Nat. Park Nat. Park Svc., Interior, S.D., 1985-87; mgr. eastern team Denver Svc. Ctr. Nat. Park Svc., Lakewood, 1987-91; supt. Zion Nat. Park, Springdale, Utah, 1991—. Planning commr. Town of Springdale, Utah, 1993—. Capt. U.S. Army, 1964-66. Recipient Partnership Leadership award Nat. Park Found., 1996. Mem. ASCE. Methodist. Avocations: hiking, camping, vintage cars. Office: Zion National Park Supt's Office Springdale UT 84767-1099*

FAN, LEE SIU, business executive and vocational training program administrator; b. Hong Kong, Aug. 5, 1948; came to U.S., 1974; s. Kwok-Kam and Po-Hang (Law) F. BSc in Bus. Mgmt. and Mktg., U. Wis., Superior, 1975; MSc in Spl. Edn., Portland State U., 1989; DBA in Bus. Mgmt., Pacific Western U., 1997. Cert. foodsvcs. mgmt. profl. Prodn. and sales mng. coord. Castle Peak Garment Factory Co., Ltd., Hong Kong, 1969-70; mng. exec. Wilson Garment Mfg. Co. Ltd., Hong Kong, 1970-74; ops. mgr. Portland State U., 1975-92; CEO Handily Enterprises (U.S.A.) Inc., Portland, 1991—, Happy Heart Foods Inc., Portland, 1992—, Lok Hop, Inc., Portland, 1996—; vocat. tng. programs coord. Portland Pub. Schs., Lake Oswego Sch. Dist., Clackamas County Employment Tng. and Bus. Svcs., Oreg. Comm. for the Blind, Westside Youth Ctr., 1986-92; adv. bd. Unicorn Fisheries Ltd., Hong Kong, 1990—. Cmty. svc. provider Loaves & Fishes Sr. Cmty. Ctr., Portland, 1991—; coord. Oreg. Gov.'s Ann. Food Dr., Salem, 1991; mem. diversity commn. Portland State U., 1992; mem. delegation on learning disabilities Citizen Ambassador of People to People Internat., Spokane, Wash., 1994. Recipient Exemplary Svc. award Portland State U., 1985, Extraordinary Svc. award, 1987, various svc. awards, 1972-92. Mem. Coun. for Exceptional Children (Beyond the Call of Duty Svc. award 1992), Nat. Assn. of Coll. and Univ. Food Svcs. (Leadership Program rep. 1986-92, named Food Svc. Mgmt. Profl. 1992), Nike Portland Running Club (2d master runner of yr. 1988, 89), Oreg. Rd. Runners Club (Inspirational Runner of Yr. 1990). Democrat. Avocations: running, community services, coin collecting. Home: 3723 SE Steele St Portland OR 97202-4260 Office: Handily Enterprises (USA) 6335 SE 82nd Ave Portland OR 97266-5607

FANARIS, JOHN MICHAEL, motion picture producer; b. Glendale, Calif., Aug. 4, 1965; s. James and Barbara (Cannan) F. BS, U. So. Calif., 1990. Office asst. Soundstorm, Hollywood, Calif., 1984-87, exec. asst., 1987-90; opers. mgr., chief fin. officer Soundstorm, Burbank, Calif., 1990-96, pres., 1996—. Mem. Apt. Owners Assn., Heal the Bay/Santa Monica. Avocations: skiing, scuba diving, travel, ecology. Home: PO Box 5786 Santa Monica CA 90409-5786 Office: Soundstorm 639 S Glenwood Pl Burbank CA 91506-2819

FANCHER, MICHAEL REILLY, newspaper editor, newspaper publishing executive; b. Long Beach, Calif., July 13, 1946; s. Eugene Arthur and Ruth Leone (Dickson) F.; m. Nancy Helen Edens, Nov. 3, 1967 (div. 1982); children: Jason Michael, Patrick Reilly; m. 2d Carolyn Elaine Bowers, Mar. 25, 1983; Katherine Claire, Elizabeth Lynn. BA, U. Oreg., 1968; MS, Kans. State U., 1971; MBA, U. Wash., 1986. Reporter, asst. city editor Kansas City Star, Mo., 1970-76, city editor, 1976-78; reporter Seattle Times, 1978-79, night city editor, 1979-80, asst. mng. editor, 1980-81, mng. editor, 1981-86, exec. editor, 1986—, now vice pres., exec. editor, 1989-95; sr. v.p., 1995—; bd. dirs. Blethen, Maine Newspapers, Walla Walla Union-Bulletin, Yakima Herald Rep. Ruhl fellow U. Oreg., 1983. Mem. Am. Soc. Newspaper Editors, Soc. Profl. Journalists, Nat. Press Photographers Assn. (Editor of Yr. 1986). Office: Seattle Times Fairview Ave N & John St PO Box 70 Seattle WA 98111-0070*

FANN, MARGARET ANN, counselor; b. Pasco, Wash., July 16, 1942; d. Joseph Albert David and Clarice Mable (Deaver) Rivard; m. Jerry Lee Fann, June 13, 1986; children: Brenda Heupel, Scott Sherman, Kristin Johnson, Robert Lack III. AA, Big Bend C.C., Moses Lake, Wash., 1976; BA in Applied Psychology magna cum laude, Ea. Wash. U., 1977, MS in Psychology, 1978. Cert. mental health counselor, Wash.; cert. chem. dependency counselor II, nat. cert. addictions counselor II, cert. in chronic psychiat. disability. Intern counselor Linker House Drug Rehab., Spokane, Wash., 1976-78; drug counselor The House drug program, Tacoma, Wash., 1978-80; exec. dir. Walla Walla (Wash.) Commn. Alcohol, 1980-82; dir. Cmty. Alcohol Svcs. Assn., Kennewick, Wash., 1982-86; primary care coord. Carondelet Psychiat. Care Ctr., Richland, Wash., 1986-90; part-time instr. Ea. Wash. U., Cheney, 1981-88; instr. Columbia Basin Coll., Pasco, 1990-93; adminstr. Action Chem. Dependency Ctr., Kennewick, 1993—; bd. dirs. Benton-Franklin County Substance Abuse Coalition, Pasco, Kennewick, Richland, 1990—. Vol. Pat Hale for Senator, Kennewick, 1994. Mem. Am. Counselors Assn., Nat. Mental Health Counselors Assn., Wash. State Mental Health Counselors Assn., Tri-Cities Counselors Assn., Phi Theta Kappa. Avocations: Triathlons (swim, bike, run), Native Am. culture and artifacts. Office: Action Chem Dependency Ctr 552 N Colorado St Ste 5525 Kennewick WA 99336-7779 also: Benton-Franklin County MICA Detoxification Ctr 1020 E 7th Ave Kennewick WA 99336-5936

FARAH, TAWFIC ELIAS, political scientist, educator; b. Nazareth, Palestine, Aug. 12, 1946; s. Elias Tawfic and Itaf Fahim F.; BA, Calif. State U., Fresno, 1970, MA, 1971; PhD, U. Nebr., 1975; m. Linda Maxwell, Apr. 24, 1969; children—Omar Lee, Aliya Jane. With Xerox Corp., Lincoln, Nebr., 1974-75; asst. prof. polit. sci. Kuwait U., 1975-79; pres., CEO polit. risk analysis Mid. East Rsch. Group Analityca, 1979—, nat. dir. internat. edn., 1989—; vis. assoc. prof. UCLA, summers 1978-83, fellow Center for Internat. and Strategic Affairs, 1980-81, Ctr. for Near Eastern Studies, 1986; trustee The Arne Nuxon Ctr. for Children's Lt./Calif. State U., Fresno. Fulbright scholar, 1983; Toyota Found. grantee, 1985. Mem. Am. Polit. Sci. Assn. Author: Reinventing Palestinian Politics: A New Order in the Middle East, 1995; co-author: Research Methods in the Social Sciences, 1977, A Dictionary of Social Analysis, 1980; author: Aspects of Modernization and Consociationalism: Lebanon as an Exploratory Test Case, 1975, 77; co-editor: Palestinians Without Palestine: Socialization of Palestinian Children, 1979, Learning to Become Palestinians, 1985; editor Political Behavior in the Arab States, 1983, Pan Arabism and Arab Nationalism: The Continuing Debate, 1986, Political Socialization in the Arab States, 1987, Survey Research in the Arab World, 1987; editor Jour. Arab Affairs, 1981-95. E-mail: tef@merganalytica.com.

FARANDA, JOHN PAUL, college administrator; b. Orange, Calif., Feb. 21, 1957; s. Paul L. and Kay S. (Wilson) F. BA cum laude, Claremont McKenna Coll., 1979. Staff liaison L.A. County Bar Assn., 1979-80; spl. programs adminstr. L.A. County Med. Assn., 1980-85; dir. corp. rels. Claremont (Calif.) McKenna Coll., 1985-87, dir. campaign and devel. svcs., 1987-89, dir. devel., 1989-96, assoc. v.p. devel., 1996—. Contbr. articles to profl. jours. Campaign chmn. United Way, Mt. Baldy Region, Ontario, Calif., 1987-90; bd. govs. Faculty Ho. of the Claremont Colls., pres. 1993-95; bd. dirs. Recording for the Blind and Dyslexic, Community Friends of Internat. Students. Recipient Gold award Mt. Baldy United Way, 1988, 91. Mem. L.A. County Bar Assn. (com. on arbitration), Coun. for Advancement and Support of Edn. (USX award 1986), Athletic Club L.A. Avocations: sailing, skiing. Office: Claremont McKenna Coll Bauer Ctr #320 500 E 9th St Claremont CA 91711-5903

FARBER, BERNARD, sociologist, educator; b. Chgo., Feb. 11, 1922; s. Benjamin and Esther (Axelrod) F.; m. Annette Ruth Shugan, Dec. 21, 1947 (div. 1970); children—Daniel, Michael, Lisa, Jacqueline; m. Rosanna Bodanis, June 10, 1971 (dec. June 1988); 1 dau., Tanya. AB, Roosevelt U., Chgo., 1943; AM, U. Chgo., 1949, PhD, 1953. Research asso. U. Chgo., 1951-53; asst. prof. Henderson State Tchr. Coll., Arkadelphia, Ark., 1953-54; mem. faculty U. I., 1954-71, prof. sociology, 1964-71; asso. dir. Inst. Research Exceptional Children, 1967-69; prof. Ariz. State U., 1971-92, prof. emeritus, 1992—, chmn. dept. sociology, 1971-75, 90-92; vis. prof. U. Tex., Austin, 1974-75, U. Ill., Chgo., 1988-95; cons. in field, 1957—. Author: Family: Organization and Interaction, 1964, Mental Retardation: Its Social Context and Social Consequences, 1968, Kinship and Class, 1971, Guardians of Virtue, 1972, Family and Kinship in Modern Society, 1973, Conceptions of Kinship, 1981; editor Sociol. Perspectives, 1985-89; co-editor: Sociological Inquiry, 1997—. Mem. mental retardation research com. Nat. Inst. Child Health and Human Devel., 1971-75. Served with AUS, 1943-46. Recipient E.W. Burgess award Nat. Council on Family Relations, 1975; Disting. Research award Ariz. State U., 1980. Mem. Am. Sociol. Assn. (coun. mem. family sect. 1966-69), Ill. Sociol. Assn. (founding pres. 1965-66), Pacific Sociol. Assn. (pres. 1986-87). Jewish. Home: 7949 E Montebello Ave Scottsdale AZ 85250-6108 Office: Ariz State U Dept Sociology Tempe AZ 85287

FARBER, GERALDINE OSSMAN, civic worker; b. Salt Lake City, May 4, 1929; d. Lawrence N. and Janet (Perkins) Ossman; m. John Val Browning, July 19, 1949 (div. June 1964); 1 child, John Allen; m. Seymour M. Farber, June 5, 1973 (dec. 1995). Student, Vassar Coll., 1947-49, U. Liege, Belgium, 1951-53, U. Utah, 1955. Tchrs. aid spl. programs elem. schs. Ogden, Utah, Los Altos and Woodside, Calif., 1962-70; cons. Glasrock Products, Inc., 1979-80. Editor: Teilhard de chardin: In Quest of the Perfection of Man, 1973. Bd. dirs. Am. Field Svc., Ogden, 1960-64, Utah Ballet, Ogden, 1963-64, Christmas Bur., Palo Alto and Los Altos, 1964-66, Jr. League Palo Alto, 1966-69; active Cmty. Com. Internat. Students, Stanford, 1965-67; dir. Ednl. TV Fgn. Student Series, Ogden, 1963-64; bd. dirs. Vol. Bur. No. Santa Clara County, 1965-68, exec. v.p., 1967-68; mem. exec. com. Paul N. McCloskey, Jr. Congl. Campaign, San Mateo, Calif., 1967; vol. parentis in locus, tubercular refugee children Caritas Catholique, Liege, 1952-55; ways and means chmn. San Francisco Ballet Assn. Aux., 1970, pres., 1974-75, trustee assn., 1974-75; co-founder, pres. bd. dirs. Performing Arts Libr. and Mus., 1975-76; bd. dirs. Am. Conservatory Theater, 1975-81; mem. Calif. Pub. Broadcasting Commn., 1975-85; vol., asst. media buyer campaign Supt. Pub. Instrn. Calif., 1970; mem. exec. planning com. and nat. adv. bd. John Muir Med. Film Festival, 1979-91; mem. program com. Kauai Found. Continuing Edn. and Hawaii Med. Assn., 1979-85. Recipient Merit awards City and County San Francisco, Vol. Bur. No. Santa Clara County, commendation Calif. State Senate, 1985. Mem. San Francisco Peninsula Vassar Alumnae Club (pres. 1968-70), Francisca Club. Home and Office: 26303 Esperanza Dr Los Altos CA 94022-2601

FARCNIK, ALEXANDER, commercial artist, portraitist; b. Hrastnik, Yugoslavia, Sept. 15, 1930; came to U.S., 1968; s. Ivan Anton and Ana (Grgurevic) F.; m. Milka Farcnik, 1955; 1 child, Zoran. Student, Piers Coll., L.A., 1973. Draftsman Dor-O-Matic, Milw., 1968-70; comml. artist Am. Art, L.A., 1970-72; draftsman Norolscok, L.A., 1972-74; freelance artist Sacramento, 1974—. Holder 2 patents. Mem. Am. Soc. Portrait Artists. Home: 1103 Canyon Terrace Ln Folsom CA 95630-1875

FARHAT, CAROL SUE, motion picture company executive; b. Santa Monica, Calif.; d. Annis Abraham Farhat; divorced; 1 child, Michael. Student, Santa Monica Coll., 1967; Assoc. degree, Inst. Audio Rsch., 1976-78; student, Otis Parsons Inst., 1980-84, UCLA, 1984-90; BA in Bus., Music, Antioch U., 1992. Recording studio mgr. The Village Recorder, L.A., 1972-78; audio engr. The Village Recorder Studio, L.A., 1978-79; music adminstr. 20th Century Fox Film Corp., Beverly Hills, Calif., 1980-82, music supr., 1983-86, music dir., 1986-92; supr. internat. music 20th Century Fox Film Corp., Tokyo, 1993; music prodr. Scopus Films, England, 1987-89; songwriter Music Experts Ltd., Santa Monica, Calif., 1989-90; v.p. music 20th Century Fox Film Corp., 1994-95; v.p. TV music and feature Am. Fedn. Musicians advisor 20th Century Fox Music, 1995-99. Author: China Diary, 1992; composer (music book) Children's Songbook, 1991; songwriter (for film) Rockin' Reindeer, 1990; prodr. (soundtrack) Ally McBeal Show (double platinum record award 1998).. Recipient Emmy award contbn. recognition for Simpson TV-show music, 1990, 96, 97, 98. Mem. BMI, NATAs, NARAS, Women in Film, Am. Film Inst., Pacific Composers Forum, Entertainment Industry Counsel. Avocation: classical ballet. Office: 20th Century Fox Film Corp Bldg 222 Rm 8 PO Box 900 Beverly Hills CA 90213-0900

FARLEY, THOMAS T., lawyer; b. Pueblo, Colo., Nov. 10, 1934; s. John Baron and Mary (Tancred) F.; m. Kathleen Maybelle Murphy, May 14, 1960; children: John, Michael, Kelly, Anne. BS, U. Santa Clara, 1956; LLB, U. Colo., 1959. Bar: Colo. 1959, U.S. Dist. Ct. Colo. 1959, U.S. Ct. Appeals (10th cir.) 1988. Dep. dist. atty. County of Pueblo, 1960-62; pvt. practice Pueblo, 1963-69; ptnr. Phelps, Fonda & Hays, Pueblo, 1970-75, Petersen & Fonda, P.C., Pueblo, 1975—; bd. dirs. Pub. Svc. Co. Colo., Denver, Norwest Pueblo, Norwest Sunset, Found. Health Systems, Inc., Colo. Public Radio. Minority leader Colo. Ho. of Reps., 1967-75; chmn. Colo. Wildlife Commn., 1975-79, Colo. Bd. Agr., 1979-87; bd. regents Santa Clara U., 1987—; commr. Colo. State Fair; trustee Cath. Found. Diocese of Pueblo, Great Outdoors Colo. Trust Fund. Recipient Disting. Svc. award U. So. Colo., 1987, 93, Bd. of Regents, U. Colo., 1993. Mem. ABA, Colo. Bar Assn., Pueblo C. of C. (bd. dirs. 1991-93), Rotary. Democrat. Roman Catholic. Office: Petersen & Fonda PC 650 Thatcher Bldg Pueblo CO 81003

FARMER, ANN DAHLSTROM, English language professor; b. South Gate, Calif., June 18, 1934; d. Merrill Xanthus and Marcia Hazel (Ross) Dahlstrom; m. Roger Lee Chandler, Aug. 19, 1956 (div. 1960); 1 child, Mark Walton Chandler; m. Malcolm French Farmer, Oct. 25, 1963. BA, Whittier Coll., 1956, MA, 1971; MA, Calif. State U., Fullerton, 1976. Prof.'s asst. Whittier (Calif.) Coll., 1960-62, gen. studies instr., 1963-70, English instr., 1970-72, dir. freshman English, 1972-87, dir. English language and lit. dept., 1978-86, asst. prof. English, 1983-95, assoc. prof. English, 1995—. Author: Jessamyn West, rev. edit., 1996; co-author: Jessamyn West: A Descriptive and Annotated Bibliography, 1998, Creative Analysis, rev. edit., 1978. Mem. AAUW (gift honoree, 1995), Western Lit. Assn., Linguistic Soc., Delta Kappa Gamma (Star in Edn., 1990), Phi Kappa Phi. Democrat. Society of Friends. Avocations: dollhouse miniatures, rubber stamps, antiques, family history, cats. Office: Whittier Coll 13406 Philadelphia St Whittier CA 90601-4446

FARMER, BARRY WAYNE, artist, art educator; b. Vinton, Iowa, Oct. 16, 1942; s. Wallace William and Doris Maxine (Berry) F.; m. Marilene Kay Beeman, June 5, 1964; children: Christen Bradley, Courtnay Shannon. BA, State Coll. Iowa, 1965; MA, U. No. Iowa, 1972. Art tchr. grades K-12 Iowa Braille and Sight Saving Sch., Vinton, 1965-66; art tchr. grade 7-12 Dysart (Iowa)-Geneseo Cmty. Sch., 1966-69; artist Hayfield, Minn., 1969-70; art tchr. grades 7-12 Monticello (Iowa) Cmty. Sch., 1970-72; artist Raymond, Minn., 1972-73, Waverly, Iowa, 1973-77; art tchr. grades K-6 Waterloo (Iowa) Cmty. Sch., 1977-79; art tchr. grades K-9 Saudi Arabian Internat. Sch., Dhahran Acad., 1979-91; art tchr. grades K-6 Valley Horizon Elem. Sch., Yuma, Ariz., 1992-93; artist Yuma, 1993-94; art tchr. grades K-6 Wellton (Ariz.) Elem. Sch., 1994-95; art tchr. grades K-12 Ash Fork (Ariz.) Unified Sch., 1995-96; artist Flagstaff, Ariz., 1996—; assoc. faculty Coconino C.C., Flagstaff, 1997—. Singer Meth. Ch. Choir, Dysart, 1966-69, Waverly, 1976-79, Cmty. Choir, Vinton, 1991; actor, set painter Yuma Cmty. Theater, 1994. Works exhibited in shows at Des Moines Art Ctr., 1977, Des Moines Art Mus., 1992, No. Ariz. Watercolor Soc., 1996, 97. Mem. Ariz. Watercolor Soc., No. Ariz. Watercolor Soc. (juried mem.), Artist's Gallery Cooperative Bd. (bd. mem. 1998—), Artist's Coalition Flagstaff.

FARMER, TERRY D(WAYNE), lawyer; b. Oklahoma City, May 1, 1949; s. Gayle V. and Allene (Edsall) F.; children: Grant L., Tyler M. BA, U. Okla., 1971, JD, 1974. Bar: Okla. 1974, N.Mex. 1975, U.S. Dist. Ct. N.Mex. 1976, U.S. Ct. Claims 1975, U.S. Ct. Appeals (10th cir.) 1977, U.S. Supreme Ct. 1980. Asst. trust officer First Nat. Bank of Albuquerque, 1974-75; assoc. Nordhaus, Moses & Dunn, Albuquerque, 1975-78, ptnr., 1978-80; dir. Moses, Dunn, Farmer & Tuthill, P.C., Albuquerque, 1980—; pres. Albuquerque Lawyers Club, N. Mex., 1982-83. Fellow N.Mex. Bar Found.; mem. N.Mex. Bar Assn. (pres. Young Lawyers div., 1978-79), Okla. Bar Assn., N.Mex. Trial Lawyers. Office: Moses Dunn Farmer & Tuthill PC PO Box 27047 Albuquerque NM 87125-7047

FARNHAM, MARY GLADE SIEMER, artist; b. Ross, Calif., Nov. 1, 1924; d. Albert Henry and Mabel Meta (Jones) Siemer; children: Thomas Ross, Evan Neil, Gwen Marie, William Blair, Hugh Porter. *Mary Farnham is a fourth generation San Franciscan. Her great grandfather, Thomas Daniel Jones, visited San Francisco in 1844, when he was seventeen. He completed his education at Cambridge and retured to San Francisco in 1848. He met his future wife, Anne Porter, dockside to tell her of the death of his friend, and her fiancé, on the voyage out. Thomas and Anne had five surviving children: Thomas, Will (grandfather of Mary Farnham), Ottiwell, Mattie, and Hubert.* Student, Marin Jr. Coll., 1942-43, Groucher Coll., 1943-44; BA, U. Calif.-Berkeley, 1947. Profl. athlete Curry Co., Yosemite, Calif., 1945; advt. prodn. mgr. City of Paris/Hale's, San Francisco, 1947; advt. artist Lipman Wolfe, Portland, Oreg., 1947-48; advt. layout artist Meir & Frank, Portland, Oreg., 1948; art dir. Olds & King, Portland, Oreg., 1948-50; free lance comml. artist Portland, Oreg., 1950-56; pres. Marin County Devel. Co., San Anselmo, Calif., 1963-78; pres., designer Mary Farnham Designs Inc., Portland, 1983-89; Mem. pub. art selection panel II, Met. Arts Commn., Portland, 1982-83, bd. dirs. N.W. Artists Workshop, Portland, 1977-78, sec. Artist Membership, Portland Art Assn., 1973-74. Exhibited in 14 one woman shows and numerous group shows, U.S. & abroad. Mem. Multnomah Athletic Club. Episcopalian. Avocations: swimming, diving, cooking.

FARNSWORTH, ELIZABETH, broadcast journalist; b. Mpls., Dec. 23, 1943; d. H. Bernerd and Jane (Mills) Fink; m. Charles E. Farnsworth, June 20, 1966; children: Jennifer Farnsworth Fellows, Samuel Mills. BA, Middlebury Coll., 1965; MA in History, Stanford U., 1966. Reporter, panelist PBS World Press, KQED, San Francisco, 1975-77; reporter InterNews, Berkeley, Calif., 1977-80; freelance TV and print reporter, San Francisco, 1980-91; fgn. corr. MacNeil/Lehrer News Hour, San Francisco, 1991-95; chief corr., prin. substitute anchor News Hour with Jim Lehrer, Arlington, Va., 1995-97, San Francisco, 1997—; mem. nat. adv. bd. Writers Corps, 1999—, U. Calif. Grad. Sch. Journalism, Berkeley, 1998—. Co-author: El Bloqueo Invisible, 1974; prodr., dir. documentary Thanh's War, 1991 (Cine Golden Eagle award); contbr. articles to various publs. Mem. adv. bd. Berkeley Edn. Found., 1990-95; bd. dirs. Media Alliance, San Francisco, 1985-87, Data Ctr., Oakland, Calif., 1993-95. Recipient Golden Gate award San Francisco Film Festival, 1984, Best Investigative Reporting award No. Calif. Radio, TV News Dirs.' Assn., 1986, Blue Ribbon, Am. Film and Video Festival, 1991. Mem. AFTRA, NATAS, World Affairs Coun. (bd. dirs. 1998—), Pacific Coun. on Internat. Policy. Presbyterian. Avocations: gardening, hiking, writing poetry.

FARNUM, NANCY ALYSON, communications executive; b. Birmingham, Ala., Mar. 2, 1949; d. Leon Vernon and Martha Reeves (McGahee) F. BA, Rockford Coll., 1971; MSLS, Case We. Reserve U., 1972. cert. health information profl. Information specialist Merrell-Nat. Lab. Pharm. Co., Cin., 1973-78; dir. and comptroller U.S. ops. Applied Human Cybernetics, London, 1975-78; asst. prof. and online search analyst Coll. Medicine E. Tenn. State U., Johnson City, Tenn., 1982-84; assoc. dir. N.W. Area Health Edn. Ctr., Salisbury, N.C., 1984-88; asst. prof. Bowman Gray Sch. Medicine, Winston Salem, 1984-88; coord. multimedia svcs. U. Ala., Birmingham, 1989-92; cons. MRM Communications, Claremont, Calif., 1988—; cons. St. George's (Grenada) U. Sch. Medicine, 1989; chmn. K-12 devel. U. of the World, La Jolla, Calif., 1989—; mem. Gov.'s Tech. Task Force on Edn. Reform, Montgomery, Ala., 1993—. Coord. Global Awareness Seminar Birmingham Pub. Schs., 1988-93, World Peace Day Friends of the City of Birmingham, 1988—. Recipient Grad. endowment Nat. Inst. Health, Bethesda, Md., 1971-72; scholarship Sch. Theology at Claremont (Calif.), 1993, Fuller Theol. Sem., Pasadena, Calif., 1996-97. Mem. NAFE, Med. Libr. Assn., Network Birmingham, Acad. Health Info. Profls. Episcopalian. Office: 260 Claremont Ave Long Beach CA 90803-3554

FARON, FAY CHERYL, private investigator, writer; b. Kansas City, Mo.; d. Albert David and Geraldine Fay (Morgan) F. Student, Glendale (Ariz.) C.C., 1967-68, Ariz. State U., 1968-71, U. Ariz., 1971-72. Lic. pvt. investigator, Calif. Owner Monogramation, San Francisco, 1976-80; assoc. prodr. Sta. KGO-TV, San Francisco, 1980-81, Power/Rector, San Francisco, 1982-83; owner Office in the City, San Francisco, 1982-83, The Rat Dog Dick Detective Agy., San Francisco, 1983—; lectr., guest spkr. San Francisco U., 1984—, San Francisco Assn. Legal Assts., 1984—, Commonwealth Club San Francisco, 1987, Calif. Collectors Coun., San Francisco, 1992—, Book Passage Mystery Writers Conf., 1997-98. Author: A Private Eye's Guide to Collecting a Bad Debt, 1991, Missing Persons, 1997; author/editor: The Instant National Locator Guide, 1991, 2nd edit., 1993, 3rd edit, 1996, Rip-Off, 1998; columnist Ask Rat Dog, 1993—. Co-founder, pres. bd. Elder Angels, San Francisco. Subject of Jack Olsen's book, Hastened to the Grave, 1998. Mem. Nat. Assn. Investigative Specialists, Nat. Assn. Bunco Investigators (asst.), Profls. Against Confidence Crimes (asst.), Sisters in Crime. Avocations: biking, camping, horseback riding, river rafting, travel. Office: The Rat Dog Dick Detective Agy PO Box 470862 San Francisco CA 94147-0862

FARQUHARSON, WALTER HENRY, retired minister, church official; b. Zealandia, Sask., Can., May 30, 1936; s. James and Jessie Ann (Muirhead) F.; m. Patricia Joan Casswell, Sept. 16, 1958; children: Scott, Michael, Catherine, Stephen. BA, U. Sask., Saskatoon, 1957, Diploma in Edn., 1969; BD, St. Andrew's Coll., Saskatoon, 1961, DD (hon.), 1975. Ordained to ministry United Ch. of Can., 1961. Min. Saltcoats-Bredenbury-Churchbridge Pastoral Charge, Sask., 1961-97; moderator United Ch. of Can., 1990-92; exec. gen. coun., pres. Sask. Conf.; head Blue Heron House Bed and Breakfast Retreat, Counseling. Contbr. numerous hymns and religious songs. Recipient Commemorative medal 125th anniversary Confedn. Can. Home: PO Box 126, Saltcoats, SK Canada S0A 3R0 Office: United Ch of Can, PO Box 58, Saltcoats, SK Canada S0A 3R0*

FARR, DONALD EUGENE, engineering scientist; b. Clinton, Iowa, July 1, 1933; s. Kenneth Elroy and Nellie Irene (Bailey) F.; m. Sally Joyce Brauer, Mar. 8, 1954; children: Erika Lyn Farr Leventis, Jolene Karyn Farr Walters. BA in Engring. Psychology, San Diego State U., 1961; MT with honors, Nat. U., 1974; postgrad., Calif. Pacific U., 1976-80. Human factors specialist Bunker Ramo Corp., Canoga Park, Calif., Germany, 1964-69; sr. design specialist Gen. Dynamics, San Diego, 1955-63, 69-76; tech. staff Sandia Nat. Labs., Albuquerque, 1977-80; group supr., sr. tech. advisor The Babcock and Wilcox Co., Lynchburg, Va., 1980-82; dir. human factors sys. Sci. Applications, Inc., Lynchburg, 1982-83; human engring. scientist Lockheed Calif. Co., Burbank, 1983-91; MANPRINT mgr. Teledyne Electronic Sys., Northridge, Calif., 1991-94; human engring. scientist, program mgr. Symvionics, Inc., Pasadena, Calif., 1994—; ergonomics safety cons. govt., industry and academia, 1977—. Contbr. articles to profl. jours. Precinct capt., voter registration vol. Rep. Party, 1963—; lectr., support group Am. Diabetes Assn., L.A., 1993—. With USN, 1952-53. Scholarship USN, 1953; recipient Admiral's award NSIA, 1963. Mem. Human Factors and Ergonomics Soc. (pres. San Diego, L.A. chpt.), Internat. Numismatic Soc. (pres. 1973-75), Am. Nuclear Soc. (human factors chair 1980-82), Am. Legion, NRA Golden Eagles (honor role). Lutheran. Avocations: bridge, numismatics, genealogy, computer graphics, travel. Home: 20054 Avenue Of The Oaks Newhall CA 91321-1361 Office: Symvionics Inc 3280 E Foothill Blvd Ste 200 Pasadena CA 91107-3187

FARR, SAM, congressman; b. Calif., July 4, 1941; m. Shary Baldwin; 1 child, Jessica. BSc Biology, Willamette U., 1963; student, Monterey Inst. Internat. Studies, U. Santa Clara. Vol. Peace Corps, 1963-65; budget analyst, cons. Assembly com. Constl. Amendments; bd. suprs. Monterey (Calif.) County; rep. Calif. State Assembly, 1980-93; mem., regional whip 103d U.S. Congress (now 106th Congress) from 17th Calif. dist., 1993—; mem. agr. com., mem. resources com. 103d U.S. Congress. Named Legislator of Yr. Calif. 9 times. Democrat. Avocations: photography, skiing, fly fishing, Spanish. Office: Ho of Reps 1221 Longworth Bldg Office Bldg Washington DC 20515-0517*

FARRAR, DANA GLAD, journalist; b. L.A., Oct. 20, 1964; d. Dain Sturgis and Betty Alexandra (Shainoff) Glad; m. Joseph Frank Farrar, Feb. 17, 1990; 1 child, Alison. B Print Journalism, U. So. Calif., 1986; M Clin. Psychology, Calif. State U., L.A., 1998. Editl. asst. Rolling Stone mag., Beverly Hills, Calif., 1984-86; copy editor Orange County Register, Santa Ana, Calif., 1986-90; copy editor, page designer L.A. Times, 1990—; freelance restaurant reviewer San Gabriel Valley Weekly, Monrovia, Calif., 1997—. Nat. merit scholar Gen. Tire Found., 1982; co-recipient Pulitzer prize Pulitzer Found., 1993, 95, 98. Mem. Soc. Newspaper Design. Home: 4935 Harriman Ave South Pasadena CA 91030-4015

FARRAR, ELAINE WILLARDSON, artist; b. L.A.; d. Eldon and Gladys Elsie (Larsen) Willardson; BA, Ariz. State U., 1967, MA, 1969, PhD, 1990; children: Steve, Mark, Gregory, JanLeslie, Monty, Susan. Tchr., Camelback Desert Sch., Paradise Valley, Ariz., 1966-69; mem. faculty Yavapai Coll., Prescott, Ariz., 1970-92, chmn. dept. art, 1973-78, instr. art in watercolor and oil and acrylic painting, intaglio, relief and monoprints, 1971-92; grad. advisor Prescott Coll. Master of Arts Program, 1993-97. One-man shows include: R.P. Moffat's, Scottsdale, Ariz., 1969, Art Center, Battle Creek, Mich., 1969, The Woodpeddler, Costa Mesa, Calif., 1979; group show Prescott (Ariz.) Fine Arts Assn., 1982, 84, 86, 89, 90-95, 96, 97, N.Y. Nat. Am. Watercolorists, 1982; Ariz. State U. Women Images Now, 1986, 87, 89, 90-92; works rep. local and state exhibits, pvt. nat. & internat. collections. Mem., curator Prescott Fine Arts Visual Arts com., 1992-97, mem. exec. com. 1996-98; bd. dirs. Prescott Fine Arts Assn., 1995-98, Friends Y.C. Art Gallery Bd., 1992-97. Mem. Mountain Artists Guild (past pres.), Women's Nat. Mus. (charter Washington chpt.), Kappa Delta Pi.

FARRELL, ANNE, opera company administrator; m. William; children: Jennifer, Rebecca. BA, Calif. Luth. U. Gen. dir. Tacoma Opera. Office: Tacoma Opera PO Box 7468 Tacoma WA 98407-0468

FARRELL, DENNIS, sports association executive; b. Orange, Calif., Feb. 23, 1951; s. Fred Bernard and Janet Louise (Crawford) F.; m. Charlene Louise Cassingham, Jan. 11, 1975; Timothy William, Michael Ted. AA in Liberal Arts, Santa Ana Coll., 1971; BA in Journalism, San Diego State U., 1973. Sports editor Saddleback Valley News, Mission Viejo, Calif., 1974-77; sports info. dir. Saddleback Coll., Mission Viejo, Calif., 1977-80; asst. commr. Pacific Coast Athletic Assn., Santa Ana, Calif., 1980-88; assoc. commr. Big West Conf., Santa Ana, Calif., 1988-92; commr. Big West Conf., Irvine, Calif., 1992—. Mem. Collegiate Commrs. Assn. Avocations: golf, music. Office: Big West Conf 2 Corporate Park Ste 206 Irvine CA 92606-5128*

FARRELL, PETER SNOW, musician, retired educator; b. Greensboro, N.C., Sept. 13, 1924; s. Charles Anderson and Anne Patricia (McKaughan) F.; m. Miriam Louise Mellott, Apr. 21, 1946; children: David Gerard, Jeffrey Bernard. MusB, U. Rochester, 1948, MusM, 1954, artists diploma, 1953. Prof. music U. Ill., Champaign-Urbana, 1954-72; prof. U. Calif., San Diego, 1972-91, prof. emeritus, 1991—; prin. cellist Columbus Philharm. Orch., 1948-49, San Diego Symphony Orch., 1969; profl. performing artist cello and viola da gamba, 1946—. Performer festivals in U.S., Germany, Poland, France, Eng.; contbr. articles and revs. to profl. jours. With U.S. Army, 1943-46, PTO. Mem. Viola da Gamba Soc. Am. (bd. dirs. 1956-60), San Diego Early Music Soc. (mem. adv. bd.), U. Calif. San Diego Emeriti Assn. (pres. 1995-96). Avocations: hiking, cross-country skiing. Office: Univ Calif San Diego Music Dept San Diego CA 92093-0326

FARRELL, THOMAS JOSEPH, insurance company executive, consultant; b. Butte, Mont., June 10, 1926; s. Bartholomew J. and Lavina H. (Collins) F.; m. Evelyn Irene Southam, July 29, 1951; children: Brien J., Susan M., Leslie A., Jerome T. Student U. San Francisco, 1949. CLU. Ptnr. Affiliated-Gen. Ins. Adjusters, Santa Rosa, Calif., 1949-54; agt. Lincoln Nat. Life Ins. Co., Santa Rosa, 1954-57, supr., 1957-59, gen. agt., 1959-74; pres. Thomas J. Farrell & Assos., 1974-76, 7 Flags Ins. Mktg. Corp., 1976-81, Farrell-Dranginis & Assocs., 1981-88, 1988-90, consultant, 1990, Specialist Dept. of developmental services, Calif.; pres., bd. dirs. Lincoln Nat. Bank, Santa Rosa, San Rafael. Pres. Redwood Empire Estate Planning Council, 1981-82, Sonoma County Council for Retarded Children, 1956-59, Sonoma County Assn. for Retarded Citizens, City Santa Rosa Traffic and Parking Commn., 1963; specialist State of Calif. Dept. Devel. Svcs., 1990—. del. Calif. State Conf. Small Bus., 1980; mem. Santa Rosa City Schs. Compensatory Edn. Adv. Bd.; bd. dirs. Santa Rosa City Schs. Consumer Edn. Adv. Bd.; pres., nat. dir. United Cerebral Palsy Assn., 1954-55; nat. coord. C. of C.-Rotary Symposia on Employment of People with Disabilities, 1985-87; v.p. Vigil Light, Inc.; chmn. bd. dirs. Nat. Barrier Awareness for People with Disabilities Found., Inc.; pres. Commn. on Employment of People with

Disabilities, 1986-92; mem. Pres.'s Com. on Mental Retardation, 1982-86; chmn. Santa Rosa Community Relations Com., 1973-76; pres. Sonoma County Young Reps., 1953; past bd. dirs. Sonoma County Fair and Expn., Inc.; bd. dirs. Sonoma County Family Service Agy., Eldridge Found., North Bay Regional Ctr. for Developmentally Disabled; trustee Sonoma State Hosp. for Mentally Retarded. Recipient cert. Nat. Assn. Retarded Children, 1962, Region 9 U.S. HHS Community Service award, 1985, Sonoma County Vendor's Human Service award, 1986, Individual Achievement award Community Affirmative Action Forum of Sonoma County, 1986. Mem. Nat. Assn. Life Underwriters, Redwood Empire Assn. CLU's (pres. 1974-75), Japanese-Am. Citizens League, Jaycees (Outstanding Young Man of Year 1961, v.p. 1955), Santa Rosa C. of C. (bd. dirs. 1974-75), Calif. PTA (hon. life). Svc. Club: Rotary (Svc. Above Self award 1996). Home: 963 Wyoming Dr Santa Rosa CA 95405-7342

FARRELL, WARREN THOMAS, author; b. N.Y.C., June 26, 1943; s. Thomas Edward and Muriel (Levy) F.; m. Ursie Otte Fairbairn, June 19, 1966 (div. 1977). BA in Social Sci., Montclair State U., 1965; MA in Political Sci., U. Calif., L.A., 1966; PhD in Political Sci., NYU, 1974; D. of Humane Letters, Profl. Sch. Psychology, San Diego, 1985. Diplomate Am. Board Sexology; cert. tchr., N.J. adj. asst. prof. Sch. Medicine U. Calif., San Diego, 1986-88; cons. HUD, U.S. Dept. Edn., Bonneville Power, NASA, 1975-98, IBM, Revlon, Ogilvy, Toyota, Beckman Labs., AT&T, Bell Atlantic, 1974-99. Author: The Liberated Man, 1975, Why Men Are The Way They Are, 1986, 87, 88, The Myth of Male Power, 1993, 94, Women Can't Hear What Men Don't Say, 1999; contbr. articles to profl. jours; TV appearances include Oprah, Donahue, The Today Show, Larry King Live, ABC World News with Peter Jennings, Crossfire, CBC's Newsworld; TV spls. ABC's 20/20, ABC (Australia), BBC (Britian), CBC (Can.), People Mag., Parade Mag., Japan Times, N.Y. Times, Wall St. Jour., Time, Forbes, Der Speigel, Mac Leans, London Times, So. China Morning Post, others. Recipient Outstanding Contribution award Calif. Assn. Marriage Family Therapists, 1988. Mem. Nat. Coalition Free Men (adv. bd. 1996—, best book 1986), Nat. Congress Fathers & Children (bd. dirs. 1992—, best book 1993), Nat. Org. Women (N.Y.C Chpt. bd. dirs. 1970-73), Children's Rights Council (adv. bd. 1985—), Am. Coalition of Fathers and Children (bd. dirs. 96-98). Unitarian. Avocations: tennis, running. Office: 103 N Hwy 101 Box 220 Encinitas CA 92024

FARRELL, WILLIAM EDGAR, sales executive, infosystems specialist, management consultant; b. Jeanette, Pa., Mar. 13, 1937; s. Arthur Richard and Lelia (Ryder) F.; m. Sara Lynnette Swing, Aug. 20, 1960; children: Wendy J., Tracy L., Rebecca J. BS in Edn., Pa. State U., 1959. Location mgr. IBM Corp., Dover, Del., 1969-72; corp. lobbyist IBM Corp., Washington, 1972-74, planning cons., 1974-78, nat. mktg. mgr., 1978-80, exec. asst., 1980-81; account exec. IBM Corp., Denver, 1981-87, policy exec., 1987-91; pres., CEO Weatherall Co., Inc., Englewood, Colo., 1993-97; CFO, Wide Horizon, Inc., Denver, 1987-92, chmn. bd. trustees, 1989-92; pres. Exec. Mgmt. Cons., 1987—; sec.-treas., bd. dirs. Electronic Shoe Enterprises Inc., 1991-94; mem. Colo. Info. Mgmt. Commn., 1992-95; bd. dirs. Energaire Corp. Founding mem. River Falls Community Assn., Potomac, Md., 1975; first reader First Ch. of Christ Scientist, Chevy Chase, Md., 1976-80; chmn. Amigo's De Ser; bd. dirs. Rocky Mountain Ser, 1991-92. Recipient Outstanding Contbn. award IBM Corp., 1968. Republican. Avocation: flying instrument S.E.L. airplanes.

FARRER, CLAIRE ANNE RAFFERTY, anthropologist, folklorist, educator; b. N.Y.C., Dec. 26, 1936; d. Francis Michael and Clara Anna (Guerra) Rafferty; 1 child, Suzanne Claire. BA in Anthropology, U. Calif., Berkeley, 1970; MA in Anthropology and Folklore, U. Tex., 1974, PhD in Anthropology and Folklore, 1977. Various positions, 1953-73; fellow Whitney M. Young Jr. Meml. Found., N.Y.C., 1974-75; arts specialist, grant adminstr. Nat. Endowment for Arts, Washington, 1976-77; Weatherhead resident fellow Sch. Am. Research, Santa Fe, 1977-78; asst. prof. anthropology U. Ill., Urbana, 1978-85; assoc. prof., coord. applied anthropology Calif. State U., Chico, 1985-89, prof., 1989—; dir. Multicultural and Gender Studies, 1994; cons. in field, 1974—; mem. film and video adv. panel Ill. Arts Coun., 1980-82; mem. Ill. Humanities Coun., 1980-82; vis. prof. U. Ghent, Belgium, spring 1990; named Hulbert Prof. S.W. Studies, Colo. Coll., Colorado Springs, Spring 1997. Author: Play and Inter-Ethnic Communication, 1990, Living Life's Circle: Mescalero Apache Cosmovision, 1991, Thunder Rides a Black Horse: Mescalero Apaches and the Mythic Present, 1994, 96; cofounder, co-editor Folklore Women's Commn., 1972; editor spl. issue Jour. Am. Folklore, 1975, 1st rev. edit., 1986; co-editor: Forms of Play of Native North Americans, 1979, Earth and Sky: Visions of the Cosmos in Native North American Folklore, 1992; contbr. numerous articles to profl. jours., mags. and newspapers, chpts. to books. Recipient numerous awards, fellowships and grants. Fellow Am. Anthrop. Assn., Royal Anthrop. Inst. (U.K.), Am. Astronomy Assn. (history divsn.); mem. Authors Guild, Am. Ethnol. Soc., Am. Folklore Soc., Am. Soc. Ethnohistory. Mem. Soc. of Friends. Office: Calif State U Dept Anthropology Butte 311 Chico CA 95929-0400

FARRIES, JOHN KEITH, petroleum engineering company executive; b. Cardston, Alta., Can., July 9, 1930; s. John Mathew and Gladys Helen (Adams); B.S. in Petroleum Engring., U. Okla., 1955; postgrad. Banff Sch. of Advanced Mgmt., 1963; m. Donna Margaret Lloyd, Dec. 30, 1960; children—Gregory, Bradley, Kent. Engr., dist. engr., joint interest supt. Pan Am. Petroleum Corp., Calgary, Edmonton, Tulsa, Drayton Valley, 1955-65; pres. Tamarack Petroleums Ltd., Calgary, Alta., 1965-70, Canadian Well Services & Tank Co. Ltd., Calgary, 1968-70, Farries Engring. Ltd., 1970—, Wave Internat. Engring., Inc., Israel, 1975-88, Westridge Petroleum Corp, 1985—, Muskeg Oilfield Services, 1987-96; v.p. Bobby Burns Petroleum Ltd., 1983-95; dir. Westgrowth Petroleums, 1983-88; dir. Pension Fund Energy Resources, 1990—, Trisol Inc., 1990—, Blue Range Resources, Inc., Exch. Resources, Inc., Storm Energy Corp. Mem. AIME, Canadian Inst. Mining and Metallurgy (dir. petroleum soc. 1966-68), Assn. Profl. Engrs. of Alta., B.C. and Sask., Canadian Assn. of Drilling Engrs. (pres. 1977-78). Clubs: Calgary Petroleum, Willow Park Golf and Country. Past pub. chmn. Jour. Canadian Petroleum Tech. Home: 10819 Willowglen Pl, Calgary, AB Canada T2J 1R8

FARRINGTON, HELEN AGNES, personnel director; b. Queens, N.Y., Dec. 1, 1945; d. Joseph Christopher and Therese Marie (Breazzano) F. AS, Interboro Inst., N.Y.C., 1965; AA, Ohio State U., 1983, BS in Human Resource Mgmt., 1987. Mgmt. cert. U. Mich., 1980. pers. adminstr. Am. Electric Power Co., N.Y.C., 1974-79; supr. human resources Ohio Power divsn. Am. Electric Power Co., Newark, Ohio, 1979-87; mgr. human resources Citizens Utilities Co., Stamford, Conn., 1987-88; mgr., exec. search firm Arthur Lyle Assocs., Norwalk, Conn., 1988-89; dir. human resources CaroLee Designs, Inc., Greenwich, Conn., 1990-92, cons. 1992-95; dir. human resources The Gartner Group, Stamford, 1993-95; prin. HFA Resources, Englewood, Colo., 1996—. Mem. NAFE, Am. Mgmt. Assn., Am. Soc. Profl. Female Execs., Soc. Human Resources Mgmt. Cons. Forum, Colo. Human Resources Assn. Office: PO Box 3527 Englewood CO 80155-3527

FARRIS, JEROME, federal judge; b. Birmingham, Ala., Mar. 4, 1930; s. William J. and Elizabeth (White) F.; widower; children: Juli Elizabeth, Janelle Marie. BS, Morehouse Coll., 1951, LLD, 1978; MSW, Atlanta U., 1955; JD, U. Wash., 1958. Bar: Wash. 1958. Mem. Weyer, Roderick, Schroeter and Sterne, Seattle, 1958-59; ptnr. Weyer, Schroeter, Sterne & Farris and successor firms, Seattle, 1959-61, Schroeter & Farris, Seattle, 1961-63, Schroeter, Farris, Bangs & Horowitz, Seattle, 1963-65, Farris, Bangs & Horowitz, Seattle, 1965-69; judge Wash. State Ct. of Appeals, Seattle, 1969-79, U.S. Ct. of Appeals (9th cir.), Seattle, 1979—; lectr. U. Wash. Law Sch. and Sch. of Social Work, 1976—; mem. faculty Nat. Coll. State Judiciary, U. Nev., 1973; adv. bd. Nat. Ctr. for State Cts. Appellate Justice Project, 1978-81, founder First Union Nat. Bank, Seattle, 1965, dir., 1965-69; mem. U.S. Supreme Ct. Jud. Fellows Commn., 1997—; mem. Jud. Conf. Com. on Internat. Jud. Rels., 1997—. Del. The White House Conf. on Children and Youth, 1970; mem. King County (Wash.) Youth Commn., 1969-70; vis. com. U. Wash. Sch. Social Work, 1977-90; mem. King County Mental Health-Mental Retardation Bd., 1967-69; past bd. dirs. Seattle United Way; mem. Tyee Bd. Advisers, U. Wash., 1984—, bd. regents, 1985—, pres., 1990-91; trustee U. Law Sch. Found., 1978-84; mem. vis. com. Harvard Law Sch., 1996—. With Signal Corps, U.S. Army, 1952-53. Recipient Disting. Service award Seattle Jaycees, 1965, Clayton Frost award, 1966. Fellow Am. Bar Found. (sec. of fellows 1998); mem. ABA (exec. com. appellate judges conf. 1978-84, 87—, chmn. conf. 1982-83, del. jud. adminstrn. coun. 1987-88), Wash. Council on Crime and Delinquency (chmn. 1970-72), Am. Bar Found. (bd. dirs. 1987, exec. com. 1989—), State-Fed. Jud. Council of State of Wash. (vice-chmn. 1977-78, chmn. 1983-87), Order of Coif (mem. law rev.), U. Wash. Law Sch. Office: US Ct Appeals 9th Cir 1030 US Courthouse 1010 5th Ave Seattle WA 98104-1130*

FARVER, SUZANNE, museum administrator; b. Pella, Iowa, Feb. 22, 1955. BA in Econs., Grinnell Coll., 1978; JD, U. Denver, 1982. Dir. pub. affaris Aspen (Colo.) Art Mus., 1990-92; exec. dir. Aspen (Colo.) Art Mus., Denver, 1992—; dir. of devel. Anderson Ranch Arts Ctr., Snowman Village, Colo., 1990-92. Trustee Denver Art Mus., 1988—. Office: Aspen Art Mus 590 N Mill St Aspen CO 81611-1510

FARWELL, HERMON WALDO, JR., parliamentarian, educator, former speech communication educator; b. Englewood, N.J., Oct. 24, 1918; s. Hermon Waldo and Elizabeth (Whitcomb) F.; A.B., Columbia, 1940; M.A., Pa. State U., 1964; m. Martha Carey Matthews, Jan. 3, 1942; children—Gardner Whitcomb, Linda Margaret (Mrs. Richard Hammer). Commd. USAF, 1940, advanced through grades to maj., various positions, 1940-66, ret., 1966; instr. aerial photography Escola Tecnica de Aviação, Brazil, 1946-48; faculty U. So. Colo., Pueblo, 1966-84, prof. emeritus speech communication, 1984—; cons., tchr. parliamentary procedure. Author: The Majority Rules-A Manual of Procedure for Most Groups: Parliamentary Motions: Majority Motions; editor The Parliamentary Jour., 1981-87, 91-93; contbr. articles to profl. jours. Mem. Am. Inst. Parliamentarians (nat. dir. 1977-87), Commn. on Am. Parliamentary Practice (chmn. 1976), Ret. Officers Assn., Nat. Assn. Parliamentarians, Am. Legion, VFW, Air Force Assn. Home and Office: 65 Macalester Rd Pueblo CO 81001-2052

FASI, FRANK FRANCIS, state senator; b. East Hartford, Conn., Aug. 27, 1920. B.S., Trinity Coll., Hartford, 1942. Mem. Hawaii Senate, 1959—; Dem. mayor City and County of Honolulu, 1969-81, Rep. mayor, 1985-94; resigned, 1994; owner Property & Bus., Honolulu, 1995. Mem. Dem. Nat. Com. for Hawaii, 1952-56; del. 2d Constl. Conv., 1968; mem.-at-large Honolulu City Coun., 1965-69. Served to capt. USMCR. Mem. Pacific-Asian Congress Municipalities (founder, past pres., exec. dir.), VFW (former comdr. Hawaii dept.), AFTRA (past v.p.). Office: 401 Waiakamilo Rd Ste 201 Honolulu HI 96817-4955

FASMAN, MARJORIE LESSER, artist, writer; b. San Francisco, Dec. 1, 1916; d. Sol Leonard and Fay (Grunauer) Lesser; m. Morris Pfaelzer III, Apr. 12, 1938 (div. 1959); children: Fay Ellen Pfaelzer Abrams, Betty Pfaelzer Rauch; m. Michael J. Fasman, Mar. 30, 1961. Student, Wellesley Coll., 1934-37; BA, U. Pa. Designer for Mercado and cmty. events L.A. Music Ctr., 1946-48. Author: The Diary of Henry Fitzwilliam Darcy, 1998. Vol. Physicians for Social Responsibility, L.A.; founder (with others) Venice Family Clinic, 1985, UCLA Med. Ctr. Auxiliary (bd. dirs.). Recipient Corit Kent Peace award Immaculate Heart Coll., 1992. Mem. Women of L.A. (Hope is a Woman award 1998). Democrat. Jewish. Avocations: tennis.

FATA, DANIEL PAUL, foreign policy specialist; b. Ayer, Mass., Jan. 24, 1972; s. Daniel Eugene Jr. and Patricia Alexandria (Waiwat) F. BA with honors, U. Conn., 1994; MA, Boston u., 1996. Fgn. policy analyst Balkan Inst., Washington, 1997; asst. to the dir. Coun. on Fgn. Rels., Washington, 1997—. Contbr. articles to profl. jours. Named one of ten outstanding youths Elk Club, Norwood, Mass., 1990. Republican. Avocations: camping, hiking, tennis. Home: 314 Constitution Ave NE Washington DC 20003 Office: Coun on Fgn Rels 1779 Massachusetts Ave NW Washington DC 20036-2109

FATERI, FARDAD, dean; b. Tehran, Iran, July 12, 1964; came to U.S., 1981; s. Mohammad and Farideh (Miri) F.; m. Farnaz Abdollahi; children: Elika Sara, Cameron Tyler. BA, U. Calif., Irvine, 1985; MA, Calif. State U., Fullerton, 1987; PhD, U.S. Internat. U., San Diego, 1990. Mgmt. of Lifelong Edn., Harvard U. Asst. dir. Orange County Ctr. U.S. Internat. U., Irvine, 1988-90, dir. Orange County Ctr., 1990-95; dean of student affairs DeVry Inst. Tech., Pomona, Calif., 1995-96; campus dean DeVry Inst. Tech., Long Beach, Calif., 1996—; cons. on higher edn., 1991-94; adj. prof. various, 1987—; bd. dirs. Hist. & Cultural Found., Irvine, 1990-93, Pomona Economic Devel. Corp., 1995—. Contbr. articles to profl. jours. Commr. Transp. & Infrastructure Commn., City of Irvine, 1996—; mem. Intellectual Adv. Com., City of Irvine, 1992-95, Multicultural Task Force, City of Irvine, 1992; organizer Iranian New Yr. Festival, Irvine, 1989—. Mem. APA, Am. Mgmt. Assn., Assn. Coll. Adminstrn. Profls., Assn. for Student Judicial Affairs, Nat. Assn. for Student Personnel Adminstrs., Soc. for Coll. & Univ. Planners. Avocations: stocks, mutual funds, sci. fiction, real estate, tennis. Office: DeVry Inst Tech 3880 Kilroy Airport Way Long Beach CA 90806-2449

FATHAUER, THEODORE FREDERICK, meteorologist; b. Oak Park, Ill., June 5, 1946; s. Arthur Theodore and Helen Ann (Mashek) F.; m. Mary Ann Neesan, Aug. 8, 1981. BA, U. Chgo., 1968. Cert. cons. meteorologist. Rsch. aide USDA No. Dev. Labs., Peoria, Ill., 1966, Cloud Physics Lab., Chgo., 1967; meteorologist Sta. WLW Radio/TV, Cin., 1967-68, Nat. Meteorol. Ctr., Washington, 1968-70, Nat. Weather Svc., Anchorage, 1970-80; meteorologist-in-charge Nat. Weather Svc., Fairbanks, Alaska, 1980-98, lead forecaster, 1998—; instr. U. Alaska, Fairbanks, 1975-76, USCG Aux., Fairbanks and Anchorage, 1974—; specialist in Alaska meteorology. Contbr. chpt to book Denali's West Buttress, 1997, Living With the Coast of Alaska, 1997; contbr. articles to weather mags. and jours. Bd. dirs. Fairbanks Concert Assn., 1988—; bd. dirs. No. Alaska Combined Fed. Campaign, 1996—, campaign chmn., 1996-97; bd. dirs. Friends U. Alaska Mus., 1993—, pres., 1993-95, sec. 1997-98; bd. visitors U. Alaska Fairbanks, 1995—; bd. dirs., sec. Fairbanks Symphony Assn., 1994—; bd. trustees U. Alaska Found., 1997—, mem. coll. fellows, 1993—, exec. com., 1997—, vice chair, 1998—; mem. adv. bd. Salvation Army Fairbanks Corps, 1997—. Recipient Outstanding Performance award Nat. Weather Service, 1972, 76, 83, 85, 86, 89, Fed. Employee of Yr. award, Fed. Exec. Assn., Anchorage, 1978. Fellow Am. Meteorol. Soc. (TV and radio seals of approval), Royal Meteorol. Soc.; mem. AAAS, Am. Geophys. Union, Western Snow Conf., Arctic Inst. N.Am. (exec. sec. U.S. Corp. 1998—), Oceanography Soc., Can. Meteorol. and Oceanographic Soc., Greater Fairbanks C. of C., Am. Sailing Assn. Republican. Lutheran. Avocations: reading, music, skiing, canoeing. Home: PO Box 80210 Fairbanks AK 99708-0210 Office: Nat Weather Svc Forecast Office Internat Arctic Rsch Ctr U Alaska PO Box 757345 Fairbanks AK 99775-7345

FATZINGER, JAMES A. S., construction educator, estimator; b. Bethlehem, Pa., Jan. 27, 1926; s. James Andrew and Cora Ellen (Steigerwalt) F.; m. Mary Lois Beckman, June 10, 1972. Student, Pa. State Coll., 1943-44, Moravian Coll., 1957-58, Fullerton Jr. Coll., 1972-73. Journeyman various cos., 1951-72; supr. 3M Co., Montpelier, Ohio, 1966-67; journeyman Endicott Brass Co., Montpelier, 1967; substation operator Pub. Svc. Elec. and Gas Co., Newark, 1959-65; constrn. estimator various cos., 1972—; contractor Calif. and Ariz., 1980-85; constrn. instr. Mesa (Ariz.) C.C., Rio Salado C.C., Mesa, 1974-78, C.C. of So. Nev., Las Vegas, 1978-97, U. Nev., Las Vegas, 1992-97; pres., owner Basic Estimating Ltd., Las Vegas, 1978—. Author: Basic Estimating for Construction, 1996, Blueprint Reading for Construction, 1997. Trustee Tech. Sch., Fullerton Jr. Coll., 1986-92; scoutmaster Boy Scouts Am., Bethlehem, 1950-60, commr., Huntington Beach, Calif., 1976-77. 1st sgt. U.S. Army, 1944-46, ETO. Mem. Am. Soc. Profl. Estimators (cert., emeritus mem.), Constrn. Specifications Inst. Republican. Avocation: motor home travel, music.

FAUGHNAN, MARGARET H., nurse; b. Dromod, Ireland, Aug. 3, 1941; d. Bernard and Catherine (Maguire) F. RN, St. Mary's Hosp., London, 1962; student, St. Gile's Hosp., London, 1962-64; supt. St. Paul's Hosp., Hemel Hempstead, England, 1964; student, Royal Coll. Nursing, London, 1965. Cert. midwife, Wash., community health nurse. Staff nurse Mt. Sinai Hosp., N.Y.C., Lenox Hill Hosp., N.Y.C., Group Health Co. Operative, Seattle; RN anesthetician Nancy Meadows Inc., Seattle; staff nurse Community Health Coop., Seattle. Mem. Am. Nurse's Assn. (polit. action com. coord. 1st Congl. dist.), Wash. Nurse's Assn. (bd. trustees), King County Nurse's Assn.

FAULKNER, SEWELL FORD, real estate executive; b. Keene, N.H., Sept. 25, 1924; s. John Charles and Hazel Helen (Ford) F.; AB, Harvard, 1949; MBA, 1951; m. June Dayton Finn, Jan. 10, 1951 (div.); children: Patricia Anne, Bradford William, Sandra Ford, Jonathan Dayton, Winthrop Sewell; m. Constance Mae Durvin, Mar. 15, 1969 (div.); children: Sarah Elizabeth, Elizabeth Jane. Product mgr. Congoleum Nairn, Inc., Kearny, N.J., 1951-55; salesman, broker, chmn., pres. Jack White Co. real estate, Anchorage, 1956-86; chmn. Faulkner, Inc.; chmn. Mem. Anchorage City Council, 1962-65, Greater Anchorage Area Borough Assembly, 1964-65, Anchorage Area Charter Commn., 1969-70. Pres., Alaska World Affairs Council, 1967-68; treas. Alyeska Property Owners, Inc., 1973-75, pres., 1977-78; pres. Downtown Anchorage Assn., 1974-75; mem. Girdwood Bd. Suprs. Served with USAAF, 1943-45. Mem. Anchorage Area C. of C. (dir. 1973-74), Alaska Notch Club. Office: Faulkner Real Estate 604 K St Anchorage AK 99501-3329

FAULKNER, THERESA ANNE, psychologist; b. Cleve., July 21, 1964; d. Chester George and Shirley Marie (Krawczewicz) Laquatra; m. Kim Knox Faulkner, Aug. 13, 1993. BA, Miami U., Oxford, Ohio, 1986; MA, Tex. Tech. U., 1990, PhD, 1993. Staff psychologist, dir. clin. tng. The Wyo. State Hosp., Evanston, 1993—; dir. adult mental health svcs. Mountain Regional Svcs., Evanston, 1993—. Mem. APA (divsn. clin. psychology, divsn. psychoanalysis), Wyo. Psychol. Assn. Avocations: gardening, weight lifting, jogging, reading, skiing. Home: 8440 State Highway 150 S Evanston WY 82930-8911 Office: Mountain Regional Svcs 50 Allegiance Cir Evanston WY 82930-3804

FAUST, MARJORIE JARETTA, nursing administrator; b. Dilliner, Pa., Apr. 29, 1937; d. Sanford and Virginia Pearle (Hart) Griffin; m. James R. Faust, Sept. 13, 1958; children: Cynthia Ann, James Christian, Frederick Allan. Diploma, Washington Sch. Nursing, 1958; BSN, W.Va. U., 1981; cert., U. Minn., 1989. RN, Pa., W.Va., N.Mex. Gen. staff nurse St. Vincent Pallott Hosp., Morgantown, W.Va., 1958-60; instr. Kings Daughter Hosp. Sch. Nursing, Martinsburg, W.Va., 1960-61; from staff nurse to DON clinical sys. W.Va. U. Hosp., Morgantown, 1961-91; DON Ea. N.Mex. Med. Ctr., Roswell, 1991-92, v.p. patient care svcs., 1992-98; adv. bd. Chavez County Ambulance, Roswell, N.Mex., 1986—. Contbr. articles to profl. jours. Bd. dirs. Chavez County United Way, Roswell, 1996-98, Southeastern Green Cmty. Health Clinic, Greensboro, Pa., 1987-90. Mem. Am. Orgn. Nurse Execs. (scholarship reviewer 1995), N.Mex. Orgn. Nurse Execs. (dist. III rep. 1997-98), Am. Coll. Health Care Execs., Sigma Theta Tau. Home: 825 Swinging Spear Rd Roswell NM 88201-7823

FAVILLI, ANDREA, designer, sculptor; b. Rome, Mar. 8, 1963; came to U.S., 1970; naturalized 1989; s. Riccardo Aldo and Bianca Idalina (De Oliveira) F.; m. Camille Anne Motz, Oct. 8, 1994. BFA (hon.), Art Ctr. Coll. Design, Pasadena, Calif., 1986. Independent designer Will Vinton Prodns., Applause, Mattel and Dakin, Pasadena, Calif., 1986-87, Walt Disney Imagineering, Glendale, Calif., 1987-92; prin. Favilli Studio, Glendale, Calif., 1992-97. Prin. works include the Disney Legends Award, the Am. Tchrs Award, Frank G. Wells Award, Calif., the Camerman, Burbank, Calif., the Madonna and child at Am. Martyrs parish, Manhattan Beach, Calif., Leg ends, Paris, Burbank, Calif., numerous theme park attractions, Paris, Tokyo, Fla., Calif., Chillicothe, Ohio, Jacarta, Indonesia. Art. Ctr. Coll. Design Alumni Orgn, Calif. Art Club. Roman Catholic. Avocations: carpentry, mountain climbing, musician. Office: Favili Studio 35 E Union St Pasadena CA 91103-3945

FAVRE, GREGORY, editor; b. New Orleans; m. Beatrice, children: Monica Kauppinen, Jeff. Asst. sports editor Atlanta Jour.; mng. editor Dayton Daily News; editor Palm Beach (Fla.) Post; news dir. WPLG-TV, Miami; mng. editor Corpus Christi Caller-Times, Chgo. Daily News, Chgo. Sun-Times; exec. editor Scramento Bee, 1984-98; v.p. News of the McClatchy Co., 1989—; bd. vis. Medill Sch. Journalism, U. Calif., Davis Med. Sch.; bd. advisors Pacific Coast Ctr. Freedom Forum. Recipient Silver Elm award U. Miss., 1996, Nat. Assn. Minority Media Execs. Catalyst award, 1997; named Calif. Press Assn. News Exec. of Yr., 1992. Mem. Am. Soc. Newspaper Editors (past pres., past chmn. program com., readership com., journalism edn. com., future newspapers com.), Found. Am. Commn. (bd. dirs.), Inter Am. Press Assn. (bd. dirs., membership chmn.), Calif. Soc. Newspaper Editors (past pres.). Office: 2100 QST PO Box 15779 Sacramento CA 95852

FAW, DUANE LESLIE, lay worker, law educator, retired career officer, author; b. Loraine, Tex., July 7, 1920; s. Alfred Leslie and Noma Leigh (Elliott) F.; m. Lucile Elizabeth Craps, Feb. 20, 1943; children: Cheryl Leigh, Bruce Duane, Debra Leoma, Melanie Loraine. Student, N. Tex. State Coll., 1937-41; J.D., Columbia U., 1947. Bar: Tex. 1948, D.C. 1969, U.S. Supreme Ct. 1969. Commd. 2d lt. USMC, 1942, advanced through grades to brig. gen., 1969, bn. comdr., 1959-61, staff judge adv., 1961-64, policy analyst Marine Hdqrs., 1964-67, dep. chief of staff III Marine Amphibious Force, 1967-68, judge Navy Ct. Mil. Rev., 1968-69; dir. Judge Ad. Div. Marine Hdqrs. USMC, Washington, 1969-71; ret. USMC, 1971; prof. law Pepperdine U. Sch. Law, Malibu, Calif., 1971-85; Bible tchr. So. Presbyn. Ch., Denton, Tex., 1948-50, Camp Pendleton, N.C., 1959-61, Quantico, Va., 1962-63, United Meth. Ch., Arlington, Va., 1963-71; Bible tchr., elder Presbyn. Ch., Van Horn, Tex., 1950-52; lay spkr., Bible tchr. United Meth. Ch., Tustin, Malibu and Laguna Hills, Calif., 1972—, lay mem. ann. conf., 1974-81, 91, 95, 98. Author: The Paramony, 1986, The Joy of Spiritual Discovery, 1995; co-author: The Military in American Society, 1978. Gen. councilor URANTIA Brotherhood, 1979-88, gen. councilor of FELLOWSHIP, 1991-94; bd. dirs. Jesusonian Found., Boulder, 1988—, Touch for Health Found., Pasadena, Calif., 1988-94. Decorated Air medal with gold star, Navy Commendation medal with gold star, Legion of Merit with combat V with gold star; UN Cross of Gallantry with gold star; VN Honor medal 1st class. Mem. ABA (adv. com. mil. justice 1969-71, adv. com. lawyers in Armed Forces 1969-71), Fed. Bar Assn. (council), Judge Advs. Assn., Am. Acad. Religion, Soc. Bibl. Lit. Club: Masons. One of original 12 judges Navy Ct. Mil. Rev.; 1st gen. officer head Marine Corps Judge Advs. Home: 2399 Via Mariposa W Laguna Hills CA 92653-2008

FAWCETT, JOHN SCOTT, real estate developer; b. Pitts., Nov. 5, 1937; s. William Hagen and Mary Jane (Wise) F.; m. Anne Elizabeth Mitchell, Dec. 30, 161; children: Holly Anne, John Scott II (dec.). BS, Ohio State U., 1959. Dist. dealer rep. Shell Oil Co., San Diego, 1962-66; dist. real estate rep. Shell Oil, Phoenix, 1967-69; region real estate rep. Shell Oil, San Francisco, 1970-71; head office land investments rep. Shell Oil, Houston, 1972-75; pres., CEO Marinita Devel. Co., Newport Beach, Calif., 1976—; lectr. in land devel. related fields. With U.S. Army, 1960-61. Named Ky. Col., Gov. Ky., 1996. Mem. Internat. Platform Assn., Internat. Coun. Shopping Ctrs., Internat. Right of Way Assn., Internat. Inst. Valuers, Inst. Bus. Appraisers, Nat. Assn. Rev. Appraisers and Mortgage Underwriters, Am. Assn. Cert. Appraisers, Urban Land Inst., Nat. Assn. Real Estate Execs. (pres. L.A. chpt. 1975), Calif. Lic. Contractors Assn., Bldg. Industry Assn., U.S.C. of C., Town Hall of Calif., Ohio State U. Alumni Assn., Toastmasters (pres. Scottsdale Ariz. club 1968, pres. Hospitality T club 1964), U. Athletic Club, Phi Kappa Tau. Republican. Roman Catholic. Avocations: antiques, tennis, skiing. Home: 8739 Hudson River Cir Fountain Vly CA 92708-5503 Office: Marinita Devel Co 3835 Birch St Newport Beach CA 92660-2600

FAY, ABBOTT EASTMAN, history educator; b. Scottsbluff, Nebr., July 19, 1926; s. Abbott Eastman and Ethel (Lambert) F.; m. Joan D. Richardson, Nov. 26, 1953; children: Rand, Diana, Collin. Grad., Scottsbluff (Nebr.) Jr. Coll.; BA, Colo. State Coll., 1949, MA, 1953; postgrad., U. Denver, 1961-63; cert. advanced study, Western State U., 1963. Tchr. Leadville (Colo.) Pub. Schs., 1950-52, elem. prin., 1952-54; prin. Leadville Jr. H.S., 1954-55; pub. info. dir., instr. history Mesa Coll., Grand Junction, Colo., 1955-64; asst. prof. history Western State Coll., Gunnison, Colo., 1964-76, assoc. prof. history, 1976-82, assoc. prof. emeritus, 1982—; adj. faculty Adams State Coll., Alamosa, Colo., Mesa State Coll., Grand Junction, Colo., 1989—; propr. Mountaintop Books, Paonia, Colo.; bd. dirs. Colo. Assoc. Univ. Press; dir. hist. tours; columnist Valley Chronicle, Paonia, Best Years Beacon, Grand Junction, Guide Lines, Denver, The Historian, Fruita, Colo.,

Grand Mesa Byway News, Delta, Colo., Agewave: Get Up & Go!, Mpls.; profl. speaker in field; cons. Colo. Welcome Ctr., 1997—. Author: Mountain Academia, 1968, Writing Good History Research Papers, 1980, Ski Tracks in the Rockies, 1984, Famous Coloradans, 1990, I Never Knew That About Colorado, 1993; playwright: Thunder Mountain Lives Tonight!; contbr. articles to profl. jours.; freelance writer popular mags. Founder, coord. Nat. Energy Conservation Challenge; travel cons. Colo. State Welcome Ctr., 1997—; project reviewer NEH, Colo. Hist. Soc.; steering com. West Elk Scenic & Historic Byway, Colo., 1994—; founder Leadville (Colo.) Assembly, pres., 1953-54; mem. Advs. of Lifelong Learning, 1994—. Named Top Prof. Western State Coll., 1969, 70, 71; fellow Hamline U. Inst. Asian Studies, 1975, 79; recipient Colo. Ind. Pubs. award, 1998. Mem. Western Writers Am., Rocky Mountain Social Sci. Assn. (sec. 1961-63), Am. Hist. Assn., Assn. Asian Studies, Western History Assn., Western State Coll. Alumni Assn. (pres. 1971-73), Internat. Platform Assn. Profl. Guides Assn. Am. (cert.), Rocky Mountain Guides Assn., Colo. Antiquarian Booksellers Assn., Am. Legion (Outstanding Historian award 1981), Phi Alpha Theta, Phi Kappa Delta, Delta Kappa Pi. Home: 1156 Bookcliff Ave Apt 4 Grand Junction CO 81501-8198

FAY, CHRISTOPHER WAYNE, mechanical engineer, consultant; b. N.Y.C., Mar. 9, 1955; s. John Henry and Marie (Erickson) F.; m. Elizabeth Brownfield, Mar. 5, 1983; children: Abigail, John, Patrick, Dana. BS in Nautical Sci., Maine Maritime Acad., 1976. Profl. engr., Wash., Alaska; lic. Master 1600 GTand Third Mate Unltd., USCG. Officer U.S. Merchant Marines, various locations, 1976-80; mech. engr. JJ Henry Co., Alexandria, Va., 1980-83, GD Quincy Shipyard, Quincy, Mass., 1983-85, Lockheed Shipbuilding, Seattle, 1985-87; pvt. practice cons. Seattle, 1987-89; mech. engr. Boeing, Seattle, 1989—. Contbr. articles to profl. pubs. including Marine Transactions, ASNE Jour., Am. Forests. Sch. vol. Seattle Pub. Schs., 1991—. Mem. ASME. Am. Soc. Naval Engrs., Soc. Naval Architects & Marine Engrs. Home: 7037 18th Ave NE Seattle WA 98115-5742

FAY, GERARD WILLIAM, quality assurance professional; b. Bklyn., Jan. 6, 1959; s. Francis M. and Theresa Mary (Johnson) F.; m. Carol Ruth Santangelo, Sept. 4, 1982; children: Ryan Christopher, Stephen Francis, Taylor Marie, Morgan Marie; m. Lea Ann Simson, Aug. 30, 1997. BS with distinction, U. Redlands, 1987. Wupr. quality assurance Gen. Dynamics/Convair, San Diego, 1987-90; chief quality assurance Hughes Missile Systems Co., San Diego, 1990-92; mgr. quality assurance McDonnell Douglas Tech., Inc., San Diego, 1992-95; dir. quality assurance Insight Electronics, San Diego, 1996—. With USN, 1977-82. Fellow AIAA; mem. Am. Soc. Quality Control (cert. quality engr.). Republican. Roman Catholic. Achievements include creation of audit-based inspection programs utilizing tuguchi and SPC techniques. Home: 937 Homestead Pl Escondido CA 92026-2370 Office: Insight Electronics 9980 Huennekens St San Diego CA 92121-2997

FAY, WILLIAM FREDERICK, film producer; b. Redmond, Wash., July 25, 1956; s. James Russell and Patricia Jean Fay; m. Jody Beth Silverman, June 14, 1987; children: Caitlin Emily, Natasha Anne, Megan Elizabeth. Student, Stanford U., 1974-76; BA, UCLA, 1978. Prodn. exec. Film Finances Ltd., London, 1988-90, New World Entertainment, L.A., 1990; pres. Boy Meets Girl Prodns., Beverly Hills, Calif., 1991—; CEO Centropolis Effects, L.L.C., Santa Monica, Calif., 1996—; pres. Centropolis Entertainment, L.A., 1996—. Exec. prodr. feature films: The Hunted, 1995, Independence Day, 1996, Godzilla, 1998; co-prodr.: CB4, 1993, Bad Girls, 1994. Avocation: tennis. Office: Centropolis Entertainment 10202 Washington Blvd Culver City CA 90232-3119

FAYAD, MIKE SAMIH, financial analyst; b. Sidon, Lebanon, Feb. 7, 1953; came to U.S., 1974; s. Samih Ali and Samia Fayad; m. Zeina Takieddine, Nov. 4, 1996. B of Elec. Engring., Am. U., 1974; M of Elec. Engring., U. So. Calif., 1976, MBA, 1984. Bus. adminstrn. trainee Elec. Constrn. Co., Wolver Hampton, England, 1973; trainer Westinghouse Corp., Jubail, Saudi Arabia, 1977; systems analyst IBM Corp., Riyadh, Saudi Arabia, 1978-81; product mktg. engr. Intel Corp., Santa Clara, Calif., 1983; mktg. mgr. SEAM Internat., Palos Verdes, Calif., 1985-86; coord. data entry dept. Webster Coll., L.A., 1988-89; mainframe specialist Andrew Corp., Torrance, 1990; sr. fin. analyst City of Hope, Duarte, 1990—; adj. faculty Nat. U., L.A., 1993-94; fin. cons. LifeCare Corp., Whittier, Calif., 1987; dir. Trader's Internat., L.A., 1991. Author of poems. Mem. Internat. Bus. Assn., L.A., 1982; v.p. Gen. Knowledge Com., Beirut, 1974, HopeMasters/Pres., Duarte, Calif., 1995-96. Mem. HBOC Users Group (speaker). Avocations: swimming, biking, soccer, volleyball, travel. Office: City of Hope 1500 Duarte Rd Duarte CA 91010-3000

FAY-SCHMIDT, PATRICIA ANN, paralegal; b. Waukegan, Ill., Dec. 25, 1941; d. John William and Agnes Alice (Semerad) Fay; m. Dennis A. Schmidt, Nov. 3, 1962 (div. Dec. 1987); children: Kristin Fay Schmidt, John Andrew Schmidt. Student, L.A. Pierce Coll., 1959-60, U. San Jose, 1960-62, Western State U. of Law, Fullerton, Calif., 1991-92. Cert. legal asst., Calif. Paralegal Rasner & Rasner, Costa Mesa, Calif., 1979-82; paralegal, adminstr. Law Offices of Manuel Ortega, Santa Ana, Calif., 1982-92; sabbatical, 1992-94; mem. editorial adv. bd. James Pub. Co., Costa Mesa, 1984-88. Contbg. author: Journal of the Citizen Ambassador Paralegal Delegation to the Soviet Union, 1990. Treas., Republican Women, Tustin, Calif., 1990-91; past regent, 1st vice regent, 2d vice regent NSDAR, Tustin, 1967—; docent Richard M. Nixon Libr. and Birthplace, 1993—, bd. dirs. Docent Guild, 1994—; docent Orange County Courthouse Mus., 1992-94. Mem. Orange County Paralegal Assn. (hospitality chair 1985-87). Roman Catholic. Avocations: theater, dance. E-mail: gabriellex@pacbel.net. Home: 13571 Hewes Ave Santa Ana CA 92705-2215

FAZIO, VIC, congressman; b. Winchester, Mass., Oct. 11, 1942; m. Judy Kern; children: Dana Fazio, Anne Fazio (dec.), Kevin Kern, Kristie Kern. BA, Union Coll., Schenectady, 1965; postgrad., Calif. State U., Sacramento. Journalist, founder Calif. Jour.; congl. and legis. cons., 1966-75; mem. Calif. State Assembly, 1975-78; mem. 96th -103rd Congresses from Calif. 3rd Dist., 1979—; former chmn. Dem. Congl. Campaign Com.; chmn. Dem. caucus, house steering policy com.; mem. legis. br. appropriations subcom., ranking mem. appropriations subcom. energy and water; mem. Ho. budget com. 97th-100th Congress; majority whip-at-large 96th-105th Congress; also co-chmn. Fed. Govt. Svcs. Task Force 96th-101st Congresses, former chmn. bipartisan com. on ethics; mem. approriations com. 105th Congress; former mem. Sacramento County Charter and Planning Commns. Bd. dirs. Asthma Allergy Found., Jr. Statesman, Nat. Italian-Am. Found. Coro Found. fellow; named Solar Congressman of Yr. Mem. Air Force Assn. Office: 2113 Rayburn Bldg Washington DC 20515-0005

FE, SONYA, artist, consultant; b. L.A., Sept. 26, 1952; d. Joseph and Ruth Martha (Goldfein) William; children: Dante, Cervantes. AA, L.A. City Coll., 1972; BA, Art Ctr. Coll. of Design, Pasadena, 1976. Conv. art exhibitor Calif. Assn. Bilingual Edn., Calif. Migrant Edn., others, 1994—; tchr. pvt. art lessons Sonya Fe Studios, 1995-97; art cons., tch. Long Beach Unified Sch. Dist., Calif., 1995—. Group shows include: Self Help Graphics, East L.A., Calif., 1998, U. La Verne, Calif., 1997, Irvine Valley Coll., Calif., 1993, Latino Festival South County Mus., L.A., 1993, Jewel Spiegel Gallery, N.J., 1990, Tokyo Fair, 1990, Paul Sorota Fine Arts, Boston, 1989, others; mus. exhbns. include: Carnegie Mus., Oxnard, Calif., Mus. of Contemporary Hispanic Art, N.Y.C., Ky. Derby Mus., San Diego Art Mus., Calif., others; work collected by Coca Cola Corp., Commn. Femenil of L.A., others.

FEARON, LEE CHARLES, chemist; b. Tulsa, Nov. 22, 1938; s. Robert Earl and Ruth Belle (Strothers) F.; m. Wanda Sue Williams, Nov. 30, 1971 (div. June 1998). Student, Rensselaer Polytech. Inst., 1957-59; BS in Physics, Okla. State U., Stillwater, 1961, BA in Chemistry, 1962, MS in Analytical Chemistry, 1969. Rsch. chemist Houston process lab. Shell Oil Co., Deer Park, Tex., 1968-70; chief chemist Pollution Engring. Internat., Inc., Houston, 1970-76; rsch. chemist M-I Drilling Fluids Co., Houston, 1976-83; cons. chemist Profl. Engr. Assocs., Inc., Tulsa, 1983-84; chemist Anacon, Inc., Houston, 1984-85; scientist III Bionetics Corp., Rockville, Md., 1985-86; sr. chemist L.A. County Sanitation Dist., Whittier, Calif., 1986; chemist Quanterra-Sacramento, West Sacramento, Calif., 1986-87; cons. chemist Branham Industries, Inc., Conroe, Tex., 1987-89; adv. laboratorian EAP/Lab Accreditation unit Wash. State Dept. Ecology, Manchester, 1989—; cons. chemist Terra-Kleen, Okmulgee, Okla., 1988-94, Excel Pacific, Inc., Camarillo, Calif., 1993-96, 97—. Patentee for environ. soil remediation tech., 1994. With U.S. Army, 1962-65. Fellow Am. Inst. Chemists; mem. AAAS, Am. Chem. Soc. Avocations: photography, travel. Home: PO Box 514 Manchester WA 98353-0514 Office: PO Box 488 Manchester WA 98353-0488

FEATHERS, ELIZABETH KELLOGG, retired secondary education educator; b. Kuliang, Fujian, China, Aug. 17, 1920; came to U.S., 1927; d. Edwin Dwight and Alice Rogers (Ropes) Kellogg; m. Joseph John Feathers, July 16, 1943; children: John Edwin, Alice Irene, James Kellogg, Joseph Marvin, Jesse Roger, Jeffrey Mark. Car, Pacific U., 1941; postgrad., U. Wash., 1954; tchr. cert., Lewis Clark State Coll., Lewiston, Idaho, 1968. Tchr. English Clatskanie (Oreg.) H.S., 1941-43; substitute tchr. Tucson (Ariz.) H.S., 1944; tchr., prin. Lexington (Oreg.) H.S., 1947-48; substitute tchr. Seattle Pub. Schs., 1954-56; postmaster replacement U.S. Postal Svc., Spalding, Idaho, 1973-96; spkr. in field. Author, editor: 50th Anniversary of Congregational Presbyterian Church, 1989; contbr. articles to newspapers. Treas. Congl. Presbyn. Ch., Lewiston, Idaho, 1976-91; registrar, chief judge primary and gen. elections, Spalding; den mother, leader Boy Scouts and Girl Scouts, Seattle, Dillon, Mont. and Lewiston, 1954-76. Mem. PEO (sec., treas., chaplain, 50-yr. membership honor), Sacajawea Study Club. Democrat. Mem. United Ch. of Christ. Avocations: stamp collecting, reading, camping, travel, history. Home: Moon Rising Ranch PO Box 254 Lewiston ID 83501

FEAVER, GEORGE ARTHUR, political science educator; b. Hamilton, Ont., Canada, May 12, 1937; came to U.S., July 4, 1967; s. Harold Lorne and Doris Davies (Senior) F.; m. Nancy Alice Poynter, June 12, 1963 (div. 1978); m. Ruth Helene Tubbesing, Mar. 8, 1986 (div. 1991); children: Catherine Fergusson, Noah George, Anthea Jane. B.A. with Honors, U. B.C., 1959; Ph.D., London Sch. of Econs., 1962. Asst. prof. Mt. Holyoke Coll., South Hadley, Mass., 1962-65; lectr., research assoc. London Sch. Econs. and Univ. Coll., London, 1965-67; assoc. prof. Georgetown U., Washington, 1967-68, Emory U., Atlanta, 1968-71; assoc. prof. U.B.C., Vancouver, B.C., Canada, 1971-74, prof., 1974—; vis. fellow Australian Nat. U., Canberra, 1987. Author: From Status to Contract, 1969; editor: Beatrice Webb's Our Partnership, 1975; editor: The Webbs in Asia: The 1911-12 Travel Diary, 1992; co-editor: Lives, Liberties and the Public Good, 1987; contbr. articles to profl. jours., books. Fellow Canada Council, 1970-71, 74-75, Am. Council Learned Socs., 1974-75, Social Scis. and Humanities Research Council of Canada, 1981-82, 86-91. Mem. Can. Polit. Sci. Assn., Am. Polit. Sci. Assn., Am. Soc. for Polit. and Legal Philosophy, Conf. for Study of Polit. Thought, Inst. Internat. de philosophie politique. Club: Travellers' (London). Avocations: hiking and wine appreciation. Home: 4776 W 7th Ave, Vancouver, BC Canada V6T 1C6 Office: Univ British Columbia, Dept Polit Sci, Vancouver, BC Canada V6T 1Z1

FEDAK, BARBARA KINGRY, technical center administrator; b. Hazleton, Pa., Feb. 7, 1939; d. Marvin Frederick and Ruth Anna (Wheeler) Siebel; m. Raymond F. Fedak, Mar. 27, 1993; children: Sean M., James Goldey. BA, Trenton State Coll., 1961; MEd, Lesley Coll., Cambridge, Mass., 1986. Registered respiratory therapist. Dept. dir. North Platte (Nebr.) Community Hosp., 1974-75; newborn coord. Children's Hosp., Denver, 1975-79; edn. coord. Rose Med. Ctr., Denver, 1979-81; program dir. respiratory tech. program Pickens Tech., Aurora, Colo., 1981-86; mktg. rep. Foster Med. Corp., Denver, 1986-87; staff therapist Porter Meml. Hosp., Denver, 1987-88; dir., br. mgr. Pediatric Svcs. Am., Denver, 1988-90; dir. clin. edn. Pickens Tech., Aurora, Colo., 1991—, divsn. chair health occupations, 1991—; site evaluator Joint Rev. Com. for Respiratory Therapy Edn., Euless, Tex. Met. coun. mem. Am. Lung Assn., 1987-91. Mem. Am. Assn. Respiratory Care (edn. sect. program com. 1992—, abstract rev. com. 1993—, alt. del. AARC Ho. Dels., 1997—), Colo. Soc. Respiratory Care (dir. at large 1983-86, 90-92, sec. 1980-81, program com. 1982-92), Colo. Assn. Respiratory Educators (chair 1991-96), Lambda Beta (faculty). Methodist. Avocations: reading, mountain biking, golf, singing, piano playing. Home: 11478 S Marlborough Dr Parker CO 80138-7318 Office: Pickens Tech 500 Airport Blvd Aurora CO 80011-9307

FEDER, JOHN NATHAN, molecular biologist; b. Bklyn., June 28, 1955; s. John Jacob and Doris Marie (Mahoney) F. BA, Calif. State U., Chico, 1977, MA, 1980; PhD, Stanford U., 1990. Lectr. Calif. State U., 1980; rsch. asst. Stanford U., 1980-84, tchg. asst., 1987; postdoctoral fellow U. Calif., San Francisco, 1990-93; sr. scientist Progenitor, Menlo Park, Calif., 1993—. Contbr. articles to profl. pubs. Fellow Am. Cancer Soc., 1990, NIH, 1990. Achievements include patents for hereditary hemochromatosis gene, methods to diagnosis and treat iron overload diseases. Home: 1450 Chestnut St San Carlos CA 94070-4717 Office: Progenitor 4040 Campbell Ave Menlo Park CA 94025-1007

FEES, NANCY FARDELIUS, special education educator; b. Santa Monica, Calif., Mar. 25, 1950; d. Carl August and Dodi Emma (Hedenschau) Fardelius; m. Paul Rodger Fees, June 4, 1971; children: Evelyn Wyoming, Nelson August. BS, Mills Coll., 1971; MA in Edn., Idaho State U., 1975. Cert. tchr., Calif., Idaho, Wyo., R.I. Specialist curriculum mgmt. Barrington (R.I.) High Sch., 1975-81; coordinator learning skills ctr. Northwest Community Coll., Powell, Wyo., 1982-84, instr., 1985—; pres. Children's Resource Ctr., 1985-89, bd. dirs., 1983-89, 91—. Editor (with others) The Great Entertainer, 1984. Vol. Buffalo Bill Hist. Ctr., Cody, Wyo., 1981—; mem. Centennial Com., Cody, 1983; mem. parent's adv. com. Livingston Sch., 1989-92, chmn., 1991-92; dir. Christian Edn. Christ Episcopal Ch., 1995—. Mem. Council Exceptional Children, Assn. Children with Learning Disabilities, Council Adminstrs. of Spl. Edn. Democrat. Episcopalian. Home: 1718 Wyoming Ave Cody WY 82414-3320

FEHR, J. WILL, newspaper editor; b. Long Beach, Calif., Mar. 8, 1926; s. John and Evelyn (James) F.; m. Cynthia Moore, Sept. 4, 1951; children—Michael John, Martha Ann. B.A. in English, U. Utah, 1951. City editor Salt Lake City Tribune, 1964-80, mng. editor, 1980-81, editor, 1981-91. Served to 1st lt. USAF, 1951-53. Mem. Am. Soc. Newpaper Editors, Sigma Chi. Home: 468 13th Ave Salt Lake City UT 84103-3229 Office: Salt Lake City Tribune 143 S Main St Salt Lake City UT 84111-1924

FEHRIBACH, RONALD STEVEN, investment executive; b. Huntingburg, Ind., Nov. 2, 1949; s. Edwin Joseph and Stella Ann (Edele) F. BS in Polit. Sci., Ind. State U., 1974; postgrad., Rose Hulman Inst. Tech., 1974, Ind. U., 1977; MA, Eastern Ky. U., Richmond, 1980. Crew supr. Ahrens and Son's Nursery, Huntingburg, Ind., 1966-70; constrn. worker Nailer Constrn. Co., Huntingburg, 1971; fin. and program analyst HEW, Chgo., Washington, 1972; investment exec. Moseley, Hallgarten, Estabrook & Weeden Inc., Chgo., 1980-87, LaSalle St. Securities, Inc., Chgo., 1987-93, F.J. Garber & Co., Mesa, Ariz., 1993-95; pres. Fehribach Investments Inc., Chgo., 1986—; owner Mama's Place - The Legend Continues, Mesa, 1991—; investment exec, First Fin. Planners, Inc., Chesterfield, Mo., 1996—; corp. comdr. Res. Officer Tng. Program, Terre Haute, 1973-74. Capt. U.S. Army, 1975-77, Korea; with Ind. Nat. Guard, 1977-79. Named Rookie of Yr., Moseley Assocs., Boston, 1983; recipient Outstanding Sales award Am. Fin. Group, Boston, 1986. Avocations: travel.

FEIGIN, PHILIP ALAN, assistant commissioner; b. Manhattan, N.Y., Mar. 7, 1949; s. William Murray and Dora (Levenkron) F. BA, U. Wis., 1971; JD, Pepperdine U., 1977. Bar: Calif. 1977, Wis. 1978, U.S. Dist. Ct. (we. dist.) Wis. 1978, U.S. Dist. Ct. (ea. dist.) Wis. 1981, Colo. 1986. Assoc. Eisenberg, Giesen, Ewers & Hayes, Madison, Wis., 1977-79; chief atty. enforcement div. Wis. Commn. of Securities, Madison, 1979-82; asst. sec. commr. Colo. Div. of Securities, Denver, 1982—. Mem. ABA (state securities regulation subcom.), N.A. Securities Adminstrn. Assn. (chmn. commodities com. 1986—). Office: Colo Div of Securities 1580 Lincoln St Ste 420 Denver CO 80203-1506

FEIL, LINDA MAE, tax preparer; b. Dallas, Oreg., Apr. 9, 1948; d. Fred Henry and Ruth Irene (Hoffman) F. AA, West Valley Community Coll., 1975; student, Golden Gate U. Ctr. for Tax Studies, 1975, Menlo Coll. Sch. Bus. Adminstrn., 1978. Enrolled agt. IRS; cert. in fed. taxation. Income tax preparer, office mgr. H & R Block, Inc., Santa Clara, Calif., 1972-74, asst. area mgr., 1974-76; propr. L.M. Feil Tax Service, Santa Clara, 1976-80; ptnr. Tennyson Tax Service, Santa Clara, 1980-81; owner McKeany-Feil Tax Service, San Jose, Calif., 1981-83; owner Feil Tax Service, San Jose, 1983-90, Richmond, Calif., 1990-96, Vallejo, Calif., 1996—. Mem. Nat. Soc. Pub. Accts., Nat. Assn. Enrolled Agts. (chpt. sec. 1981-83, chpt. v.p. 1983-84), Mission Soc. Enrolled Agts. (pres. 1984-85, Enrolled Agt. of Yr. 1985), Calif. Soc. Enrolled Agts. (bd. dirs. 1985-86). Office: Feil Tax Svc 824 Foothill Dr Vallejo CA 94591-3697

FEILER, FREDERIC CHARLES, orthopedic surgeon; b. Frankfurt, Germany, Mar. 8, 1930; came to U.S., 1939; s. Melvin and Johanna Klara (Milch) F.; m. Virginia Tatum Van Bree, Nov. 24, 1956; children: Katharine Elizabeth, Frederic Charlres, Karl Steven, Suzanne Van Bree, Stephen Matthew. PhB, U. Chgo., 1948; BS in Medicine, U. Ill., Chgo., 1952, MD, 1954. Diplomate Am. Bd. Orthopedic Surgery. Intern Augustana Hosp., Chgo., 1954-55; resident in orthopedic surgery Ill. Rsch. and Edn. Hosp., Chgo., 1955-58, chief resident in orthopedic surgery, 1958-59; orthopedic surgeon Colorado Springs Med. Ctr., 1962-66, Rustic Hills Orthopedic Assn., Colorado Sprigns, 1966-95, Front Range Orthopedics, Colorado Sprigns, 1995—; med. dir. Memorial Hosp. Wound Care Ctr., Colorado Sprgs., 1998—; chief of staff St. Francis Hosp., Colorado Springs, Meml. Hosp., Colorado Springs; asst. clin. prof. orthopedics U. Colo., Denver, 1966-97; vis .prof. Manepal Med. Sch. Pokhara, Nepal, 1993-98; vis. surgeon Green Pastures Leprosy Hosp. and Gandaki Hosp., Pokhara, Nepal, 1987—. Patentee plug for proximal cementing of total hips, hydraulic walker for stairs. Head med. divsn. United Way, Colorado Springs, 1963. Capt. M.C., U.S. Army, 1959-62. U. Chgo. scholar, 1946. Fellow Am. Acad. Orthopedic Surgeons; mem. AMA, Western Orthopedic Assn. (pres. Rocky Mountain chpt. 1986-87), Mid-Ctrl. Orthopedic Assn. (v.p. 1993-94), Rocky Mountain traumatological Soc., Clin. Club, Colo. Med. Soc., El Paso County Med. Soc. Republican. Avocations: skiing, vintage car racing, jogging and fitness, tennis. Home: 10 Mesa Ln Colorado Springs CO 80906 Office: Meml Hosp Wound Care Ctr 2121 E LaSalle Colorado Springs CO 80909

FEIN, WILLIAM, ophthalmologist; b. N.Y.C., Nov. 27, 1933; s. Samuel and Beatrice (Lipschitz) F.; m. Bonnie Fern Aaronson, Dec. 15, 1963; children: Stephanie Paula, Adam Irving, Gregory Andrew. BS, CCNY, 1954; MD, U. Calif., Irvine, 1962. Diplomate Am. Bd. Ophthalmology. Intern L.A. County Gen. Hosp., 1962-63, resident in ophthalmology, 1963-66; instr. U. Calif. Med. Sch., Irvine, 1966-69; mem. faculty U. So. Calif. Med. Sch., 1969—, assoc. clin. prof. ophthalmology, 1979—; attending physician Cedars-Sinai Med. Ctr., L.A., 1966—, chief ophthalmology clinic svc., 1979-81, chmn. div. ophthalmology, 1981-85; attending physician Los Angeles County-U. So. Calif. Med. Ctr., 1969—; chmn. dept. ophthalmology Midway Hosp., 1975-78; dir. Ellis Eye Ctr., L.A., 1984—. Mem. editorial bd. CATARACT, Internat. Jour. of Cataract and Ocular Surgery, 1992—; contbr. articles to med. publs. Chmn. ophthalmology adv. com. Jewish Home for Aging of Greater L.A., 1993—. Fellow Internat. Coll. Surgeons, Am. Coll. Surgeons; mem. Am. Acad. Ophthalmology, Am. Soc. Ophthalmic Plastic and Reconstructive Surgery, Royal Soc. Medicine, AMA, Calif. Med. Assn., L.A. Med. Assn. Home: 718 N Camden Dr Beverly Hills CA 90210-3205 Office: 415 N Crescent Dr Beverly Hills CA 90210-4860

FEINBERG, ELEN AMY, artist, educator; b. N.Y.C., Jan. 22, 1955; d. S.J. Feinberg. BFA, Cornell U., 1976; student, Tyler Sch. of Art, Rome, 1974-75; MFA, Ind. U., 1978. Regent's prof. of art U. N.Mex., Albuquerque, 1978—. One-man shows include Eason Gallery, Santa Fe, 1981, Touchstone Gallery, N.Y.C., 1984, Roger Ramsay Gallery, Chgo., 1987, Mekler Gallery, L.A., 1988, Graham Gallery, Albuquerque, 1992, Locus Gallery, St. Louis, 1996, 98, Inpost Gallery, Albuquerque, 1997, Sarah Morthland Gallery, N.Y.C., 1999, Ruth Bachofner Gallery, L.A., others; exhibited in group shows at Okun Gallery, Santa Fe, 1994, Ruth Siegel Gallery, N.Y.C., 1987, Bill Bace Gallery, N.Y.C., 1990, Locus Gallery, 1997, 98, The Works Gallery, Long Beach, Calif., 1991, Museum of Fine Arts, Santa Fe, 1992, Albuquerque Museum, 1992, Thomas Barry Fine Arts, Mpls., 1993, Gallery A., Chgo., 1995, Ruth Bachofner Gallery, Santa Monica, Calif., 1998, Dist. Fine Arts, Washington, 1998, South Bend (Ind.) Regional Mus. Art, 1998, Byron Cohen Gallery for Contemporary Art, Kansas City, Mo., 1998, U.S. Dept. of State Art in Embassies Program, Lilonque, Malawi, 1998, Cedar Rapids Mus. Art, 1998, Dist. Fine Arts, Washington, 1998, others; represented in pub. collections Israel Mus., Jerusalem, Mus. of Fine Arts, Santa Fe, Mountain Bell, Denver, IBM, Atlanta, others. Recipient Ingram Merrill Found. award in painting, 1989, Ruth Chenven Found. award in painting, 1991, Basil H. Alkazzi award in painting, 1997; fellow in painting NEA, 1987, MacDowell Colony fellow, Peterbough, N.H., 1987, Burlington rsch. fellow U. N.Mex., 1991, Va. Ctr. for the Creative Arts fellow, Sweet Briar, 1998; grantee Montalvo Ctr. for Arts, Saratoga, Calif., 1981, 84, rsch. grantee U. N.Mex. Coll. Fine Arts, 1992-97; Regents professorship U. N.Mex., 1994-97. Office: U NMex Dept Arts and Art Hist 1 Univ Campus Albuquerque NM 87131

FEINHANDLER, EDWARD SANFORD, writer, photographer, art dealer, sports mentor, consultant, educator; b. Elko, Nev., Jan. 13, 1948; s. Samuel and Sylvia (Manus) F. BA, U. Nev., 1972; EdD in Elem. Edn., Sierra Nevada Coll., 1997. Supr. underpriveledged Washoe County Extension Program, Reno, 1970-71; sports editor, writer Sagebrush Campus newspaper, Reno, 1971-72; internal salesman, mgr. Trigon Corp., Sparks, Nev., 1975-88; owner, operator Art Internat. Gallery Extraordinaire, Reno, 1981—; tennis dir. City of Sparks, 1991-93, Cmty. Edn. Program, Sparks, 1994, Sparks YMCA, 1995-96; with nat. news Top Ten radio interviews, U.S. and Can., 1978-79; freelance writer and photographer; pre. No. Nev. H.S. Tennis Assn., 1996. Contbr. articles to newspapers; extra in various movies; TV interviewee AM Chgo., AM L.A., 1979, Afternoon Exchange, Cleve., 1979, To Tell the Truth, 1975, Reno Tonight TV show, 1989, Fox Across America TV show, 1989, Wheel of Fortune, 1995. Player, coach Summer Volleyball League, Reno, 1982-85; tennis coach Cmty. Svc. Ctr., Reno, 1986-88, 94; founder softball event Make-A-Wish Found., Reno, 1985-98; active U. Nev. Journalism Dept., 1985-93, UNR Children's Svcs., Reno, 1986-88; basketball coach Little Flower Cath. Sch., 1987-89; head coach girls varsity tennis team Bishop Manogue H.S., 1989-91; coach boys varsity tennis Sparks H.S., 1993-97, spl. olympics, 1989, girls jr. varsity basketball, 1989-90; active Ptnrs. in Edn., 1988-99, Jr. Achievement, 1989-94, Animal Welfare Inst., Statue of Liberty Found., 1984-98, No. Nev. Cancer Coun., United Blood Svcs., Arthritis Found., Cancer Soc., Sta. KNPB, Ret. Sr. Citizens, Reno Fire Dept. Christmas Basket Delivery, 1991-98, Sierra Arts Found.; vol. free tennis lessons, 1993-98; fundraiser H.L.A. Testing United Blood Svcs., 1991-98; founder, dir. No. Nev. Youth Opportunistic Tennis program, 1997-99. Sgt. U.S. Army, 1968-69, Vietnam. Winner Ugly Man contest No. Nev. Bone Marrow Program, 1991-98, ind. category Ugly Bartender contest Multiple Sclerosis, 1989-90; Sparks Tennis Club singles, doubles, and mixed doublas Champion B/C divsn., 1994, STC Singles B Champion, Mixed B Doubles Champion, 1995, STC Ladder B Singles Men's Champion, 1996, 97, 3rd Ann. STC B Doubles Champion, 1996; recipient numerous tennis, billiards, volleyball and bowling awards including 1st pl. C divsn. NNCC Tennis Tournament, 1991, RTC C Mixed Doubles Champion, 1992, Sparks Recreation Open Doubles Champion, 1993; world record holder nosedarts and squint, 1972—; recipient Cmty. Svc. award United Blood Svcs., 1995, Svc. Above Self award Rotary Internat., 1995, Jocil Vowell Charity Softball award Make-A-Wish Found., 1997, Cmty. Safety award Associated Builders and Contractors, 1997, Spl. Thank You award Pine Mid. Sch. Students Concerned with Quick Thinking and Gt. Effort, 1997, Angel award Washoe County Sch. Dist., 1997. Mem. DAV, Orthodox Jewish Union. Democrat. Avocations: bowling, tennis, basketball, baseball, volleyball. Office: Art Internat Gallery Extraordinaire PO Box 13405 Reno NV 89507-3405

FEINSTEIN, DIANNE, senator; b. San Francisco, June 22, 1933; d. Leon and Betty (Rosenburg) Goldman; m. Bertram Feinstein, Nov. 11, 1962 (dec.); 1 child, Katherine Anne; m. Richard C. Blum, Jan. 20, 1980. BA History, Stanford U., 1955; LLB (hon.), Golden Gate U., 1977; D Pub. Adminstrn. (hon.), U. Manila, 1981; D Pub. Service (hon.), U. Santa Clara, 1981; JD (hon.), Antioch U., 1983, Mills Coll., 1985; LHD (hon.), U. San Francisco, 1988. Fellow Coro Found., San Francisco, 1955-56; with Calif. Women's Bd. Terms and Parole, 1960-66; mem. Mayor's com. on crime, chmn. adv. com. Adult Detention, 1967-69; mem. Bd. Suprs., San Francisco, 1970-78, pres., 1970-71, 74-75, 78; mayor City of San Francisco, 1978-88; mem. U.S. Senate from Calif., Washington, 1992—; mem. exec. com. U.S. Conf. of Mayors, 1983-88; Dem. nominee for Gov. of Calif., 1990; mem. Nat. Com. on U.S.-China Rels., mem. judiciary com., rules and adminstrn Senate Dem. Policy Com.; fgn. rels. com. Mem. Bay Area Conservation and Devel.

Commn., 1973-78; mem. Senate Fgn. Rels. Com. Recipient Woman of Achievement award Bus. and Profl. Women's Clubs San Francisco, 1970, Disting. Woman award San Francisco Examiner, 1970, Coro Found. award, 1979, Coro Leadership award, 1988, Pres. medal U. Calif., San Francisco, 1988, Scopus award Am. Friends Hebrew U., 1981, Brotherhood/Sisterhood award NCCJ, 1986, Comdr.'s award U.S. Army, 1986, French Legion of Honor, 1984, Disting. Civilian award USN, 1987; named Number One Mayor All-Pro City Mgmt. Team City and State Mag., 1987. Mem. Trilateral Commn., Japan Soc. of No. Calif. (pres. 1988-89), Inter-Am. Dialogue, Nat. Com. on U.S.-China Rels. Office: US Senate 331 Hart Senate Office Bldg Washington DC 20510-0504*

FEISS, GEORGE JAMES, III, financial services company executive; b. Cleve., June 24, 1950; s. George James Jr. and Bettie (Kalish) F.; m. Susan Margaret Cassel, May 30, 1981; children: Kalish Ilana Cassel-Feiss, Nika Catherine Cassel-Feiss. BA in Social Studies, Antioch Coll., 1973; MBA in Internat. Fin., Am. Grad. Sch. Internat. Mgmt., Phoenix, 1975. Registered investment advisor, Wash.; CFP Coll. Fin. Planning, Denver. Ptnr. Healthcare Cons., Seattle, 1976-80; pres. M2 Inc., Seattle, 1980—; CFO, bd. dirs. Vivid Image Co., San Diego, Calif., 1994—; cons. Sta. KRAB, Seattle, 1988-89, Zion Christian Acad., Seattle, 1990—. Author: Mind Therapies/Body Therapies, 1979, Hope & Death in Exile - The Economics and Politics of Cancer in the United States, 1981. Bd. dirs. B'nai Brith, Seattle, 1988-91; mem. fin. com. Univ. Child Devel. Sch., Seattle, 1989—; mem. social action com. Am. Jewish Com., Seattle, 1992. Mem. Eastside Estate Planning Coun., Inst. for CFPs, Social Investment Forum, Social Venture Network. Avocations: sailing, skiing, travel, writing, sculpture. Home: 603 38th Ave Seattle WA 98122-6423 Office: M2 Inc 1932 1st Ave Ste 614 Seattle WA 98101-2447

FEISS, HUGH BERNARD, priest, religious educator; b. Lakeview, Oreg., May 8, 1939; s. Sherman H. and Margaret I. (Furlong) F. Licentiate in Sacred Theology, Cath. U. Am., 1967, Lic. in Philosophy, 1972; STD, Anselmianum, Rome, 1976; MA, U. Iowa, Iowa City, 1987. Ordained priest Roman Cath. Ch., 1966. Asst. dean of men Mt. Angel Seminary, St. Benedict, Oreg., 1967-72, prof. philosophy, 1967-74, prof. humanities and theology, 1976-96; dir. Mt. Angel Abbey Libr., St. Benedict, 1987-96. Translator: Works of Pierre de Celle, 1988, Supplement to Life of Marie d'Oignies, 1986, Hildegard of Bingen, Explanation of the Rule of Benedict, 1990, Life of Holy Hildegard, 1996; contbr. articles to profl. jours. Mem. Am. Acad. Religion, Am. Benedictine Acad., Cath. Theol. Soc. Am., Am. Cath. Philos. Assn. E-mail: hughf@magiclink.com. Home and Office: Ascension Priory 541 E 100 S Jerome ID 83338-5655

FELDMAN, NATHANIEL E., aerospace engineering specialist; b. New London, Conn., Oct. 7, 1925; s. Morris and Frieda (Pelenberg) F.; m. Clara Klein, Oct. 20, 1946; children: Ellis Steven, Phillip Matthew, David Daniel, Pamela Caren. BS, U. Calif., Berkeley, 1949, MS, 1951. Asst. elec. engr. U. Calif., Berkeley, 1949-50; engr. Lawrence Radiation Lab., 1951-54; instr. fire control radar Hughes Aircraft Co., Culver City, Calif., 1955; leader adv. devel. def. electronic prod. div. Radio Corp. Am., 1956-60; project leader, systems analyst Rand Corp., Santa Monica, Calif., 1960-78; chief scientist Systems Rsch. Ops. Sci. Application Inc., L.A., 1978-81; systems dir. advanced space comms. Aerospace Corp., El Segundo, Calif., 1981-84, sr. engring. specialist, 1984—. Editor: Communication Satellites for the '70's: vol.1 Technology, vol. 2 Systems, 1971; contbr. numerous articles to profl. jours. Fellow AIAA (assoc.); mem. IEEE (sr., MILCOM Conf. Bd. 1986—, sec. 1987—), Sigma Xi, Tau Beta Pi, Eta Kappa Nu. Jewish. Home: 10294 Cresta Dr Los Angeles CA 90064-3431 Office: Aerospace Corp MS M1/928 PO Box 92957 Los Angeles CA 90009-2957

FELDMAN, ROBERT LEON, real estate company officer, executive; b. Chgo., Aug. 21, 1933; s. Samuel Eli and Gertrude (Kravitz) F.; m. Helen L. Fi, June 7, 1992; children: Michael, Susan Knopf. BS, UCLA, 1958. CPA. Pres. Aetua Tax Ctrs., L.A., 1958-75; sec., treas., CFO Plaza Suites Hotels, L.A., 1976-98; sec., treas.,chmn. bd. Samson Equities Corp, Las Vegas, Nev., 1998—. Reg. dir., Friends of the River, San Francisco, Calif., 1985—. With USAF, 1951-55. Jewish. Avocations: tennis, golf, camping, fishing. Fax: 702-341-7518. E-Mail: bobbyhel@aol.com. Office: Samson Equities Corp 800 S Rainbow Blvd # 200 Las Vegas NV 89128-6237

FELDMAN, STANLEY GEORGE, state supreme court justice; b. N.Y.C., N.Y., Mar. 9, 1933; s. Meyer and Esther Betty (Golden) F.; m. Norma Arambula; 1 dau., Elizabeth L. Student, U. Calif., Los Angeles, 1950-51; LL.B., U. Ariz., 1956. Bar: Ariz. 1956. Practiced in Tucson, 1956-81; ptnr. Miller, Pitt & Feldman, 1968-81; justice Ariz. Supreme Ct., Phoenix, 1982—, chief justice, 1992-97; lectr. Coll. Law, U. Ariz., 1965-76, adj. prof., 1976-81. Bd. dirs. Tucson Jewish Community Council. Mem. ABA, Am. Bd. Trial Advocates (past pres. So. Ariz. chpt.), Ariz. Bar Assn. (pres. 1974-75, bd. govs. 1967-76), Pima County Bar Assn. (past pres.), Am. Trial Lawyers Assn. (dir. chpt. 1967-76). Democrat. Jewish. Office: Ariz Supreme Ct 1501 W Washington St Phoenix AZ 85007-3231

FELL, JAMES F., lawyer; b. Toledo, Ohio, Nov. 18, 1944; s. George H. Fell and Bibianne C. (Hebert) Franklin; children from a previous marriage: Jennifer A., Brian F.; m. Betty L. Wenzel, May 23, 1981. BA, U. Notre Dame, 1966; JD, Ohio State U., 1969. Bar: N.Y. 1970, Calif. 1972, Idaho 1978, Wash. 1981, Oreg. 1984, U.S. Ct. Appeals (9th cir.) 1983, U.S. Dist. Ct. Idaho 1978. Assoc. Breed, Abbott & Morgan, N.Y.C., 1969-72; ptnr. McKenna & Fitting, L.A., 1972-78; atty. Office Atty. Gen., State of Idaho, Boise, 1978-79; dir. policy and administrn. Idaho Pub. Utilities Commn., Boise, 1979-81; gen. counsel, dep. dir. Northwest Power Planning Coun., Portland, Oreg., 1981-84; ptnr. Stoel Rives LLP, Portland, 1984—. Mem. ABA (pub. utility law sect.), Oreg. State Bar (exec. com. pub. utility law sect.). Office: Stoel Rives LLP 900 SW 5th Ave Ste 2600 Portland OR 97204-1232*

FELL, JENNIFER ANNE, writer; b. Columbus, Ohio, Nov. 6, 1968; d. James Frederick Fell and Mary Elizabeth Kelly McColl. BA in English, Santa Clara U., 1990. Pub. rels. asst. de Saisset Mus., Santa Clara, Calif., 1987-90; tech. writer Rational Software Corp., Santa Clara, 1990-94; sr. tech. writer ParcPlace-Digitalk, Inc., Sunnyvale, Calif. and Austin Tex., 1994-97; mem. tech. staff Neometron, Austin, Tex., 1997; tech. writer Expert Support, Mountain View, Calif., 1997—. Vol. Planned Parenthood, Calif. and Idaho, 1993-96. Mem. NOW, NARAL, Planned Parenthood, Soc. for Tech. Comm., Alpha Sigma Nu, Sigma Tau Delta, Phi Sigma Tau. Avocations: electric bass, dogs, poker.

FELL, KATHERINE CHRISTINE, artist; b. Tacoma, Wash., Dec. 12, 1948; d. Bobby Gene and Doris Lavonne (Abrahamson) Anderson; m. Charles Dennis Fell, Mar. 10, 1973; children: Christopher Charles, Noah Michael, Peyton Christine. AA in Comml. Art, Chabot Coll., Hayward, Calif., 1968; BA in Art, Calif. State U., Hayward, Calif., 1970. Cert. community coll. instr., Calif. Instr. watercolor workshops, Santa Rosa, Calif., 1989—. Exhibited in one-woman shows at Marin County civic Ctr., San Rafael, Calif., 1992, 95, Press House Gallery, Buena Vista Winery, Sonoma, 1992, 96, 98, Rochioli Winery, Healdsburg, Calif., 1993, J. Pedroncelli Winery, Geyserville, Calif., 1994, Hop Kiln Winery Gallery, 1995, Quicksilver Mining Co. Gallery, Sebastopol, Calif., 1995, Dolphin Gallery, Gualala (Calif.) Art Ctr., 1996, Innpressions Gallery, Healdsburg, Calif., 1997; exhibited in group shows at La Petite Gallery, Bozeman, Mont., 1986-89, Eastbay Watercolor Soc. Annual, Oakland, Calif., 1991, 92, 93, El Presidio Gallery, Sonoma, Calif., 1991-92, Ga. Watercolor Soc. Ann., 1993, Rocky Mtn. Nat. Exhbn., Golden, Colo., 1991, Nat. Watercolor Okla., Oklahoma City, 1992, 94, La. Watercolor Soc. Internat. Exhbn., New Orleans, 1992, Western Watercolor Soc. Ann., Grand Junction, Colo., 1993, Artisans Gallery, Mill Valley, Calif., 1994, 95, 96, Sonoma County Mus., Santa Rosa, Calif., 1994, Sebastopol Ctr. for the Arts, 1995, 98, Wolfard & Co., Santa Rosa, Calif., Golden Gate U., Rohnert Park, Calif., 1996. Mem. Santa Rosa Art Guild, 1990-92, Cultural Arts Coun. Sonoma County, 1992-98, Mont. Inst. Arts, 1987-88. Recipient 1st pl. Watercolors award Santa Rosa Art Guild Statewide, 1990, 3rd pl. Watercolors award Bodega Bay Allied Arts, 1990, 2nd pl. Watercolors awards Cultural Arts Art Show, 1990, Santa Rosa Art Guild Statewide, 1991, merit award Bodega Bay Allied Arts, 1991, 1st pl. Watercolors award Bodega Bay Allied Arts, 1993, Silver award Art of Calif. mag. Discovery awards, 1993, 94, 1st place Eastbay Watercolor Soc., 1994, judges award Bodega Bay Allied Arts, 1995, Award Excellece, 1997; featured artist in Am. Artist Watercolor 93 Spring, Coast and Valley July, 1998; 1st place Sebastopol C. of C., 1996. Mem. Culural Arts Coun. So. Calif., Sebastopol Ctr. Arts, Calif. Watercolor Soc.

FELLIN, OCTAVIA ANTOINETTE, retired librarian; b. Santa Monica, Calif.; d. Otto P. and Librada (Montoya) F. Student U. N.Mex., 1937-39; BA, U. Denver, 1941; BA in L.S., Dominican U., River Forest, Ill., 1942. Asst. libr., instr. libr. sci. St. Mary-of-Woods Coll., Terre Haute, Ind., 1942-44; libr. U.S. Army, Bruns Gen. Hosp., Santa Fe, 1944-46, Gallup (N.Mex.) Pub. Libr., 1947-90; post libr. Camp McQuaide, Calif., 1947; freelance writer mags., newspapers, 1950—; libr. cons.; N.Mex. del. White House Pre-Conf. on Librs. & Info. Svcs., 1978; dir. Nat. Libr. Week for N.Mex., 1959. Chmn. Red Mesa Art Ctr., 1984-88; pres. Gallup Area Arts Coun., 1988; mem. Western Health Found. Century Com., 1988, Gallup Multi-Model Cultural Com., 1988-95; v.p., publicity dir. Gallup Cmty. Concerts Assn., 1957-78, 85-95; organizer Gt. Decision Discussion groups, 1963-85; co-organizer, v.p. chair fund raising com. Gallup Pub. Radio Com., 1989-95; mem. McKinley County Recycling Com., 1990—; mem. local art selection com. N.Mex. Art Dirs., 1990; mem. Gallup St. Naming Com., 1958-59, Aging Com., 1964-68; chmn. Gallup Mus. Indian Arts and Crafts, 1964-78; mem. Eccles. Conciliation and Arbitration Bd., Province of Santa Fe, 1974; mem. publicity com. Gallup Inter-Tribal Indian Ceremonial Assn., 1966-68; mem. Gov's. Com. 100 on Aging, 1967-70; mem. U. N.Mex.-Gallup Campus Cmty. Edn. Adv. Coun., 1981-82; N.Mex. organizing chmn. Rehoboth McKinley Christian Hosp. Aux., pres., 1983, chmn. aux. scholarship com., 1989—, chmn. cmty. edn. loan selection com. 1990—, bd. dirs., corr. sec., 1991-94; mem. N.Mex. Libr. Adv. Coun., 1971-75, vice chmn., 1974-75; chmn. adv. com. Gallup Sr. Citizens, 1971-73; mem. steering com. Gallup Diocese Bicentennial, 1975-78, chmn. hist. com., 1975; chmn. Trick or Treat for UNICEF, Gallup, 1972-77, Artists Coop, 1985-89; chmn. pledge campaign Rancho del Nino San Huberto, Empalme, Mex., 1975-80; active Nat. Cath. Social Justice Lobby; bd. dirs. Gallup Opera Guild, 1970-74; bd. dirs., sec., co-organizer Gallup Area Arts Council, 1970-78; mem. N.Mex. Humanities Council, 1979, Gallup Centennial Com., 1980-81; mem. Cathedral Parish Council, 1980-83, v.p., 1981, century com. Western Health Found., 1988-89; active N.Mex. Diamond Jubilee/U.S. Constn. Bicentennial Gallup Com., 1986-87, N.Mex. Gallup Campus 25 Silver Anniversary Com., 1994. Recipient Dorothy Canfield Fisher $1,000 Libr. award, 1961, Outstanding Community Service award for mus. service Gallup C. of C., 1969, 70, Outstanding Citizen award, 1974, Benemerenti medal Pope Paul VI, 1977, Celebrate Literary award Gallup Internat. Reading 8 Assn., 1983-84, Woman of Distinction award Soroptimists, 1985, N.Mex. Disting. Pub. Svc. award, 1987, finalist Gov's award Outstanding N.Mex. Women, 1988, Edgar L. Hewett award Hist. Soc. N.Mex., 1992; Octavia Fellin Pub. Libr. named in her honor, 1990. Mem. ALA, N.Mex. Library Assn. (hon. life, v.p., sec., chmn. hist. materials com. 1964-66, salary and tenure com., nat. coordinator N.Mex. legislative com., chmn. com. to extend library services 1969-73, Librar. of Yr. award 1975, chmn. local and regional history roundtable 1978, Community Achievement award 1983, Lifetime Membership award 1994), AAUW (v.p., co-organizer Gallup br., N.Mex. nominating com. 1967-68, chmn. fellowships and centennial fund Gallup br., chmn. com. on women), Plateau Scis. Soc., N.Mex. Folklore Soc. (v.p. 1964-65, pres. 1965-66), N.Mex. Hist. Soc. (dir. 1979-85), Gallup Hist. Soc., Gallup Film Soc. (co-organizer, v.p. 1950-58), LWV (v.p. 1953-56), NAACP, Pax Christi U.S.A., Women's Ordination Conf. Network, Call to Action Nat. Ch. Renewal Org., Gallup C. of C. (organizing chmn. women's div. 1972, v.p. 1972-73), N.Mex. Women's Polit. Caucus, N.Mex. Mcpl. League (pres. libr.'s div. 1979), Alpha Delta Kappa (hon.). Roman Catholic (Cathedral Guild, Confraternity Christian Doctrine Bd. 1962-64, Cursillo in Christianity Movement, mem. of U.S. Cath. Bishop's Adv. Council 1969-74; corr. sec. Latin Am. Mission Program 1972-75, sec. Diocese of Gallup Pastoral Council 1972-73, corr. sec. liturgical commn. Diocese of Gallup 1977). Author: Yahweh the Voice that Beautifies the Land, A Chronicle of Mileposts A Brief History of the University of New Mexico, Gallup Campus. Home and Office: 513 E Mesa Ave Gallup NM 87301-6021

FELLMETH, AARON XAVIER, lawyer; b. St. Louis, May 3, 1971; s. Robert Charles and Jill Diane (Heiman) F. AB, U. Calif., Berkeley, 1993; MA, Yale U., 1997, JD, 1997. Law clk. U.S. Internat. Trade Commn., Washington, 1994, UN, N.Y.C., 1995; summer assoc. Baker & McKenzie, San Francisco, 1996, White & Case, Washington, 1996; assoc. Baker & McKenzie, 1997—. Sr. editor The Yale Law Jour., New Haven, Conn., 1994-96; editor-in-chief Yale Jour. Internat. Law, 1995-96; contbr. articles to profl. jours. Mem. ABA, Am. Soc. Internat. Law, Am. Psychology Law Soc., Internt. Law Assn. Home: 630 Mason St # 403 San Francisco CA 94108 Office: Baker & McKenzie 2 Embarcadero Ctr Fl 24 San Francisco CA 94111-3909

FELLOWS, WARD JAY, philosophy educator, minister; b. Chgo., Dec. 6, 1913; s. Norman Jay and Milfred (Myers) F.; m. Ada Louise Johnson, Sept. 18, 1937; children: Milfred L. Fellows Goodall, Catherine C. Fellows Smith, Ward J. Jr. BA, Cornell U., 1936; MDiv, Union Theol. Sem., 1939, STM, 1946, PhD, 1988; MA in Philosophy, U. Calif., Berkeley, 1964. Ordained to ministry Congregational Ch./United Ch. of Christ, 1939. Minister various Congl. chs., 1939-62; prof. in world religions and philosophy of religion Coll. San Mateo (Calif.), 1968-83, prof. emeritus, 1988—; vis. scholar Harvard U. Ctr. for Study of World Religions, Cambridge, Mass., 1982. Author: Religions East and West, 1979, 2d rev. edit., 1998. Chaplain USAAF, 1942-45, ETO. Mem. AAUP, Am. Acad. Religion, Alumni of Deep Springs and Telluride Assn. Democrat. Home: 1139 Parrott Dr San Mateo CA 94402-3626

FELSTINER, JOHN, literature educator, translator; b. Mt. Vernon, N.Y., July 5, 1936; s. Louis John and Gertrude (Shiman) F.; m. Mary Lowenthal, Feb. 19, 1941; children: Sarah, Aleksandr. BA, Harvard Coll., 1958; PhD, Harvard U., 1965. Prof. English Stanford (Calif.) U., 1965—; vis. prof. U. Chile, Santiago, 1967-68, The Hebrew U., Jerusalem, 1974-75, Yale U., New Haven, Conn., 1990. Author: The Lies of Art: Max Beerbohm's Parody and Caricature, 1972, Translating Neruda: The Way to Macchu Picchu, 1980, Paul Celan: Poet, Survivor, Jew, 1995. Lt. (j.g.) USN, 1958-61. Recipient fellowship Guggenheim, Rockefeller, NEH, NEA, Gold medal Calif. Commonwealth Club, 1981, Truman Capote award for lit. criticism, 1997, Translation prize Brit. Comparative Lit. Assn.; finalist Nat. Book Critics Cir. award, 1996, MLA James Russell Lowell prize, 1997. Office: Stanford Univ English Dept Stanford CA 94305-2087

FELT, PAUL SCHENK, lawyer; b. Salt Lake City, Aug. 16, 1947; s. Spencer P. and Barbara F.; m. Janet Hugie Smith; children: Elizabeth, Matthew. BS, U. Utah, 1969; JD, U. Mich., 1972. Bar: Utah 1972, U.S. Dist. Ct. (ctrl. dist.) Utah 1972. Ptnr. Ray, Quinney & Nebeker, Salt Lake City, 1972—; jury instruction review State of Utah. Mem. Utah State Bar (mem. exec. com. 1984-85), Def. Rsch. Inst. (pres. 1986-87), Am. Coll. Trial Lawyers. Office: Ray Quinney & Nebeker 79 S Main St Ste 400 PO Box 45385 Salt Lake City UT 84145-0385 also: Ray Quinney & Nebeker 79 S Main St Ste 400 Salt Lake City UT 84111*

FELTS, MARGARET DAVIS, librarian, bibliographer; b. Walla Walla, Wash., Jan. 26, 1917; d. Schuyler Ernest and Blanche Marie (Fischer) Davis; m. Wells Carter Felts, June 20, 1940 (div. 1966); children: Carol Margaret, Thomas William, Helen Elizabeth. StaBA, Stanford U., 1938; MLS, U. Calif., Berkeley, 1965. Libr. Mills Coll., Oakland, Calif., 1965-68; libr., bibliographer U. Calif., Santa Cruz, 1968-85; ret. Author: Archives of the South Pacific Commission and Related Papers, 1971; contbr. to Catalog of the South Pacific Collection, 1978; Selection of Library Materials for Area Studies, 1990, Part IV: The South Pacific: Polynesia, Micronesia, Melanesia, 1990.

FENG, XIANGDONG SHAWN, chemist; b. Lingling, Hunan, China, July 27, 1956; came to the U.S., 1982; s. Hui Feng and Yuying Jiang; m. Meiling Gong, Dec. 26, 1984; children: Melinda G., Stephanie G. BS, Hunan Normal U., Changsha, Hunan, China, 1978; MS, Cath. U. Am., 1984; PhD, 1988. Lectr. Hunan Normal U., Changsha, 1978-82; rsch. asst., tchg. asst. Cath. U. Am., Washington, 1982-88; postdoctoral fellow Vitreous State Lab., Washington, 1988-89, rsch. scientist, 1989-91; chemist Argonne Nat. Lab., Chgo., 1991-94; sr. rsch. scientist project mgr. Pacific N.W. Nat. Lab., Richland, Wash., 1995-97, staff scientist, project mgr., 1997-98; Glass Core Tech. chair, rsch. assoc. Ferro Corp., 1998—; mem. tech. program organizing com. Am. Nuclear Soc., La Grange Park, Ill., 1996. Contbr. chpts. to books and articles to profl. jours.; patentee in field. Named Hon. Prof., Human Normal U., 1995, China Inst. Atomic Energy, Beijing, 1995; recipient Outstanding Performance award Pacific N.W. Nat. Lab., 1997, Materials Sci. award U.S. Dept. Engry, 1998, Alumni Outstanding Achievement award in sci. Cath. U. Am., 1998; grantee Dept. Energy, Washington, 1992—. Mem. Am. Ceramic Soc. (symposium chair for tech. meetings 1989—, fed. liaison com. 1996—), Am. Chem. Soc., Materials Rsch. Soc. (tech. program com. 1995, Finalist of 1998 Discover Award for Tech. Innovation. Achievements include development of specialty glass/ceramics; development of thermodynamic models based on glass structure for the prediction of glass properties from composition; development of advanced composite and polymeric materials for water purification and recycle, catalysis, drug delivery, and industrial coatings and applications. Avocations: jogging, table tennis, swimming, bicycling, computers. Office: 8300 E Pleasant Valley Rd Independence WA 44131

FENISON, EDDIE, health science educator; b. Montgomery, Ala., Feb. 17, 1935; s. Oliver and Rachel (Boyd) F.; m. Selena Viola, July 10, 1958; children: Michel, Anthony, Michelle, Cynthia, Chantelle. BA, Calif. State U., Los Angeles, 1975, MEd, 1976. Cert. Nat. Bd. Respiratory Care, Calif.; cert. class A tchr., Calif. Mem. staff UCLA Med. Ctr. Respiratory Dept., Los Angeles, 1965-67; dir. respiratory dept. Daniel Freeman Hosp., Inglewood, Calif., 1967-68, Centinela Valley Hosp., Inglewood, 1968-69; instr. health scis. Mt. San Antonio Coll., Walnut, Calif., 1969—. Instr. CPR, ARC, 1976—. Mem. Am. Assn. Respiratory Therapy (chmn. continuing edn. subcom. 1970-71), Calif. Assn. Respiratory Therapy (pres. 1972-75). Democrat. Seventh-day Adventist. Avocations: baseball, basketball, football, travel, nature. Home: 6288 Hellman Ave Alta Loma CA 91701-3416

FENN, DAVID L., farmer; b. Centralia, Wash., Oct. 19, 1945; s. Carroll H. and Idelia C. (Carlson) F.; m. Marilyn J. Ulrikson, Nov. 21, 1947; children: Katherine, Kristina. BA in Edn., Pacific Luth. U., 1968. Permanent tchg. cert. Wash. Tchr., coach, athletic dir. Eatonville (Wash.) H.S., 1968-75; pvt. practice farmer Curtis, Wash., 1975—; pea industry adv. com. N.W. Agrl. Rsch. Found., Wash., 1992-94. Precinct com. officer Rep. Party, Lewis County, Wash., 1991—; commr. Boistfort Fire Dist., Lewis County, 1995—. Recipient Meritorious Svc. award Wash. Interscholastic Activities Assn., 1995. Mem. Western Wash. Farm Crops Assn. (bd. dirs. 1997—), Western Wash. Horticultural Assn. (bd. dirs. 1994—, pres. 1998). Republican. Lutheran. Avocations: hunting, travel, golf.

FENNELL, DIANE MARIE, marketing executive, process engineer; b. Panama, Iowa, Dec. 11, 1944; d. Urban William and Marcella Mae (Leytham) Schechinger; m. Leonard E. Fennell, Aug. 19, 1967; children: David, Denise, Mark. BS, Creighton U., Omaha, 1966. Process engr. Tex. Instruments, Richardson, 1974-79; sr. process engr. Signetics Corp., Santa Clara, Calif., 1979-82; demo lab. mgr. Airco Temescal, Berkeley, Calif., 1982-84; field process engr. Applied Materials, Santa Clara, 1984-87; mgr. product mktg. Lam Rsch., Fremont, Calif., 1987-90; dir. sales and mktg. Ion & Plasma Equipment, Fremont, Calif., 1990-91; pres. FAI, Half Moon Bay, Calif., 1990-96; v.p. mktg. Tegal Corp., Petaluma, Calif., 1997—; founder, coord. chmn. Plasma Etch User's Group, Santa Clara, 1984-87; tchr. computer course Adult Edn., Half Moon Bay, Calif., 1982-83. Founder, bd. dirs. Birth to Three program Mental Retardation Ctr., Denison, Tex., 1974-75; fund raiser local sch. band, Half Moon Bay, 1981-89; community rep. local sch. bd., Half Moon Bay, 1982-83. Mem. Am. Vacuum Soc., Soc. Photo Instrumnentation Engrs., Soc. Women Engrs., Material Rsch. Soc. Avocations: hiking, reading, gardening. Home: 441 Alameda Ave Half Moon Bay CA 94019-5337

FENTON, BRADLY NOLAN, architect; b. San Diego, Dec. 17, 1957; s. Robert D. and Evelynn Lee (Zurcher) F.; m. Caroline L., July 12, 1980. BArch, U. Calif., Berkeley; MArch. Registered architect, Calif., Nev. Project architect Strauss Breveton, San Francisco, 1984-86, Lewi-Ceta Partnership, Santa Monica, Calif., 1986-92; architect pvt. practice, Santa Monica, Calif., 1992-93; ptnr. CF&G, Inc., Van Nuys, Calif., 1993—. Calif. Alumni scholar, U. Calif., 1982. Mem. AIA, Phi Beta Kappa. Office: CF&G Inc 14931 Califa St Van Nuys CA 91411-3002

FENTON, DONALD MASON, retired oil company executive; b. L.A., May 23, 1929; s. Charles Youdan and Dorothy (Mason) F.; m. Margaret M. Keehler, Apr. 24, 1953; children: James Michael, Douglas Charles. BS, U. Calif., L.A., 1952, PhD, 1958. Chemist Rohm and Haas Co., Phila., 1958-61; sr. rsch. chemist Union Oil Co., Brea, Calif., 1962-67, rsch. assoc., 1967-72, sr. rsch. assoc., 1972-82, mgr. planning and devel., 1982-85; mgr. new tech. devel. Unocal, Brea, 1985-92; cons. AMSCO, 1967-73; co-founder, 1st chmn. Petroleum Environ. Rsch. Forum; chmn. bd. dirs. Calif. Engring. Found., 1991-92. With U.S. Army, 1953-55. Inventor in field. Fellow Am. Inst. Chemists, Alpha Chi Sigma; mem. Am. Chem. Soc. Achievements include more than 100 patents in field; co-invention of unisulf process. Home: 2861 E Alden Pl Anaheim CA 92806-4401

FENWICK, JAMES H(ENRY), editor; b. South Shields, Eng., Mar. 17, 1937; came to U.S., 1965; s. James Henry and Ellen (Tinmouth) F.; m. Suzanne Helene Hatch, Jan. 27, 1968. BA, Oxford U., Eng., 1960. Freelance lectr., writer, 1960-65; assoc. editor Playboy mag., Chgo., 1965-71; planning and features editor Radio Times, BBC, London, 1971-77; U.S. rep. Radio Times, BBC, N.Y.C., 1978-87; sr. editor Modern Maturity mag., Lakewood, Calif., 1987-90, exec. editor, 1990-91, editor, 1991—. Office: Am Assn Ret Persons 601 E St NW Washington DC 20049-0001

FERBER, NORMAN ALAN, retail executive; b. N.Y.C., Aug. 25, 1948; m. Rosine Abergel; children: Robert, Lauren, Richard. Student, L.I. U., 1965-68. Buyer, mdse. mgr. Atherton Industries, N.Y.C., 1976-79; v.p., mdse. mgr. Raxton Corp., N.Y.C., 1979-82; v.p. Fashion World, N.Y.C., 1982; v.p merchandising, mktg. and distbn. Ross Stores Inc., Newark, Calif., 1982-87, pres., COO, 1987-88, pres., CEO, 1988-93; chmn., CEO Ross Stores Inc., Newark, 1993-96, chmn., 1996—. Home: 1455 Edgewood Dr Palo Alto CA 94301-3118 Office: Ross Stores Inc PO Box 728 8333 Central Ave Newark CA 94560-3440

FERBER, ROBERT RUDOLF, physics researcher, educator; b. New Eagle, Pa., June 11, 1935; s. Rudolf F. and Elizabeth J. (Robertson) F.; m. Eileen Merhaut, July 25, 1964; children: Robert Rudolf, Lynne C. BSEE, U. Pitts., 1958; MSEE, Carnegie-Mellon U., 1966, Ph.D. in Semiconductor Physics, 1967. Registered profl. engr., Pa. Mgr. engring. dept. WRS Motion Picture Labs., Pitts., 1954-58, sec., 1959-76, v.p., 1976-79; sr. engr. Westinghouse Rsch. Labs., Pitts., 1956-67; mgr. nuclear effects group Westinghouse Elec. Corp., Pitts., 1967-71, mgr. adv. engr. energy projects, East Pittsburgh, 1971-77; photovoltaic materials and collector rsch. mgr. Jet Propulsion Lab., Pasadena, Calif. 1977-85, SP100 Project contract tech. mgr., 1985-90, asst. project mgr. Spaceborne Imaging Radar, 1990-95, Earth Observing System microwave limb sounder radiometer devl. mgr., 1995—; v.p. Executaire Inc., Pitts., 1960-64; pres. Tele-Cam Inc., Pitts., 1960-78. Editor: Transactions of the 9th World Energy Conf. 1974, Digest of the 9th World Energy Conf., 1974. Contbr. articles to profl. jours. Patentee in field. Mem. Franklin Regional Sch. Dist. Bd., Murrysville, Pa., 1975-77. Fellow Buhl Found., 1965-66, NDEA, 1976-77. Mem. IEEE (sr.), ASME (chmn. 1986 Solar Energy Div. Conf.). Republican. Lutheran. Home: 5314 Alta Canyada Rd La Canada Flintridge CA 91011-1606 Office: Jet Propulsion Lab 4800 Oak Grove Dr Pasadena CA 91109-8001

FERENTZ, TOM BART, photographer, photography workshop administrator; b. Santa Monica, Calif., Aug. 26, 1954; s. Edward Judson and Shirley (Caron) F.; m. Wanjiko Mwangi. BA, U. Ill., Chgo., 1976; MFA, U. Calif., San Diego, 1985. Dir., founder Eye Gallery, San Francisco, 1982-91, Sixth St. Photography Workshop, San Francisco, 1992—; lectr. in photography Calif. State U., Hayward, 1993—; bd. dirs. Eye Gallery, 1982-88, 509 Cultural Ctr., San Francisco, 1997. Co-author: (with B. Highley) Stories of Health and Illness, 1989; photography exhbns. include Meridian Gallery, San Francisco, Nickel Mus., Calgary, Can., Ctr. for Arts, San Francisco, Luggage Store Gallery, San Francisco, Internat. Ctr. for Nursing Scholarship, Bloomington, Ind., Am. Cultural Ctr., Taipei, Taiwan, Intersection for Arts,

San Francisco, Pontiac Hotel, San Francisco. Recipient Eureka fellowship Fleishhaker Found., 1989, Artist-in-Residence, Calif. Arts Coun., 1994, 95, 96, 98, Program of the Yr. award Golden Light Awards of Maine Photog. Workshops, 1997. Mem. Coll. Art Assn. Office: Calif State Univ Dept MCOM 25800 Carlos Bee Blvd Hayward CA 94542-3001

FERGUS, GARY SCOTT, lawyer; b. Racine, Wis., Apr. 20, 1954; s. Russell Malcolm and Phyl Rose (Muratore) F.; m. Isabelle Sabina Beekman, Sept. 28, 1985; children: Mary Marckwald Beekman Fergus, Kirkpatrick Russell Beekman Fergus. SB, Stanford U., 1976; JD, U. Wis., 1979; LLM, NYU, 1981. Bar: Wis. 1979, Calif. 1980. Assoc. Brobeck, Phleger & Harrison, San Francisco, 1980-86, ptnr., 1986—, mng. ptnr. products liability, ins. coverage, environ. and antitrust/appellat practices, 1996—, mgr. product liability/ins. coverage, environ. and antitrust, 1996—. *Since 1996, Gary Fergus has been the managing partner for the products liability, insurance coverage, envrionmental and anti-trust/appellate practices at Brobeck, Phleger & Harrison. He is responsible for approximately 100 lawyers and a staff of nearly 200 para professionals. He actively represents the firm's clients in trials throughout the U.S. In July 1997, he was selected as a participant in the San Francisco Leadership Program sponsored by the San Francisco Chamber of Commerce. The Leaderhip Program brings together private sector, public officials, and nonprofit organizations to help solve community problems.* Arch. computerized case mgmt. sys. Vol. San Francisco Leadership. Mem. ABA. Home: 3024 Washington St San Francisco CA 94115-1618 Office: Brobeck Phleger & Harrison 1 Market Plz Ste 341 San Francisco CA 94105-1193

FERGUSON, GARY L., public relations executive; b. Okarche, Okla., Sept. 17, 1949; s. Jack J. Ferguson and Joan C. (Hauser) Long; m. Georgia A. Keller, Jan. 20, 1975 (div. Nov. 1994); 1 child, Laura J. BA in English, Met. State Coll., Denver, 1980; MA in Comm., U. No. Colo., 1992. Dir. pub. rels. Assoc. Builders and Contrs., Denver, 1981-83; pres. Ferguson Comm., Inc., Littleton, Colo., 1983-88; mng. editor MacGuide Mag., Lakewood, Colo., 1988-89; sr. adminstr. pub. affairs Ball Aerospace and Technologies, Broomfield, Colo., 1989-94; journalism instr. Colo. State U., Ft. Collins, 1994-95; sr. rep., pub. rels. Storage Tech. Corp., Louisville, Colo., 1995—. Author: (book of poetry) Excavating Camelot, 1979. Mem. Pub. Rels. Soc. Am. (chair employee comm. sect. 1999, Gold Pick for feature/news writing 1991, Gold Pick Award of Merit for feature writing 1992, Silver Pick award for feature writing 1993, Silver Pick award for mag./periodicals 1994), Soc. Profl. Journalists (pres. Colo. chpt. 1992-93, 94-95, dir.-at-large 1993-94, 96-97, v.p. membership 1991-92, sec. 1990-91, Circle of Excellence award), Clan Fergusson Soc. N.Am. Office: Storage Technology Corp 2270 S 88th St Louisville CO 80028-0001

FERGUSON, LEONARD PRICE (BEAR FERGUSON), advertising executive, consultant; b. Bryan, Tex., Mar. 23, 1951; s. Thomas Morgan and Grace Evelyn (Barnett) F.; m. Kathleen Ann Winter, Feb. 15, 1986; children: Hillary Annette, Carissa Marie. BBA, Tex. A&M U., 1973; MS in Communications, U. Ill., 1975. Field supr. Agri-Systems Tex., Inc., Bryan, Tex., 1966-69; mgr., sales rep. Wang Labs., Inc., Beaumont and Houston, Tex., 1973-75; account exec. Leo Burnett Advt., Inc., Chgo., 1976-79, Clinton E. Frank Advt., Chgo., 1979-80; v.p., supr. account group Ogilvy & Mather Advt., Inc., Houston, 1980-84; co-founder, mgr. sales ops. Nat. Recycling Corp., Houston, 1984-85; sr. v.p., mgmt. supr., stockholder Eisaman, Johns & Laws Advt., Houston, 1985-95; exec. v.p. Lois/EJL, Houston, 1996—; pres. Pathfinder Cons., Houston, 1980—. Inventor glass crusher, recycling system. Chmn. Houstonians on Watch Program, Braeburn Glen and Houston, Tex., 1982-84. Grantee U. Ill., 1969, 73, Sam Houston U., 1970. Mem. Advt. Agy. Assn. Am. (affiliate), Direct Mail Mktg. Assn. Am. (affiliate), Advt. Research Found. (affiliate). Methodist. Avocations: golf, music, landscaping, wildlife, travel. Home: 1215 Redfield Rd Naperville IL 60563-0440 Office: Eisaman Johns & Laws 5700 Wilshire Blvd # 6 Los Angeles CA 90036-3659

FERGUSON, LLOYD ELBERT, manufacturing engineer; b. Denver, Mar. 5, 1942; s. Lloyd Elbert Ferguson and Ellen Jane (Schneider) Romero; m. Patricia Valine Hughes, May 25, 1963; children: Theresa Renee, Edwin Bateman. BS in Engring., Nova Internat. Coll., 1983. Cert. hypnotherapist, geometric tolerance instr. Crew leader FTS Corp., Denver, 1968-72; program engr. Sundstrand Corp., Denver, 1972-87, sr. assoc. project engr., 1987-90, sr. liaison engr., 1990-93, sr. planning engr., 1990—; v.p. Valine Corp. Lic. practitioner of religious sci. United Ch. of Religious Sci., L.A.; team capt. March of Dimes Team Walk, Danver, 1987; mem. AT&T Telephone Pioneer Clowns for Charity. Recipient recognition award AT&T Telephone Pioneers, 1990. Mem. Soc. Mfg. Engrs. (chmn. local chpt. 1988, zone chmn. 1989, achievement award 1984, 86, recognition award 1986, 90, appreciation award 1988), Nat. Mgmt. Assn. (cert., program instr. 1982—, honor award 1987, 90), Am. Indian Sci. and Engring. Soc., Colo. Clowns. Mem. United Ch. of Religious Sci. Home: 10983 W 76th Dr Arvada CO 80005-3481 Office: Sundstrand Corp 2480 W 70th Ave Denver CO 80221-2501

FERGUSON, MARILYN, writer, lecturer, consultant; b. Grand Junction, Colo., Apr. 5, 1938; d. Luke Michael and Helen Olinda (Bauer) Grasso; m. Ray Gottlieb, July 24, 1984 (div. 1992); children: Eric, Ann Kristin, Lynn. AA, Mesa Coll.; LLD (hon.), John F. Kennedy U., 1989. Pub. Brain/Mind Bull., L.A., 1975—; mem. adv. bd. Inst. Noctic Sousale Scis., Calif., 1982-84. Author: Brain Revolution, 1973, The Aquarian Conspiracy, 1980. Recipient Elmer and Allyce award for career achievement Inst. for Study of Subtle Energy Medicine, 1997. Mem. ASTD (Brain/Trainer of Yr. 1994). Home: 419 Crane Blvd Los Angeles CA 90065-5017 Office: Brain Mind 4717 N Figueroa St Los Angeles CA 90042-4406

FERGUSON, MICHAEL ROGER, newspaper executive, publisher; b. Dayton, Ohio, Oct. 15, 1951; s. Earl Roger and Betty Louise (Spahr) F.; m. Kathryn Louise Davis, July 22, 1972; children—Kellie, Stacie, Jacob. AA, Mt. San Antonio Coll., 1971; BA with honors, Calif. State Poly. U., 1973. With Progress Bull. newspaper, Pomona, Calif., 1968-82, bus. mgr. 1973-80, sales mgr., 1980-82; bus. Daily Report newspaper, Ontario, Calif., 1973-78; advt. dir. Vallejo Times-Herald (Calif.), 1982-83; gen. mgr. Woodland Daily Democrat, 1983—. Mem. Calif. Newspapers Pubs. Assn., Woodland C. of C. (dir.). Republican. Methodist. Lodge: Rotary. Home: 1080 Deborah St Upland CA 91784-1206 Office: Inland Valley Daily Bulletin PO Box 4000 Ontario CA 91761-1020*

FERGUSSON, ROBERT GEORGE, retired career officer; b. Chgo., May 20, 1911; s. Archibald Campbell and Anne (Sheehan) F.; m. Charlotte Lawrence, Nov. 18, 1937; 1 son, Robert Lawrence (dec.). Student, Beloit Coll., 1929-32; BS, U.S. Mil. Acad., 1936; MA in Internat. Rels., Boston U., 1959. Commd. 2d lt. U.S. Army, 1936, advanced through grades to maj. gen., 1962; comdg. officer 14th Inf. Regt., Hawaii, 1955-57; chief army adv. group Naval War Coll., Newport, R.I., 1957-61; asst. divsn. comdr. 24th Inf. Divsn., Augsburg, Ger., 1961-62; chief staff Hdqrs. Central Army Group (NATO), Heidelberg, Ger., 1962-65; comdg. gen. U.S. Army Tng. Center, Inf., Ft. Ord, 1965-67; comdr. U.S. Forces, Berlin, 1967-70; ret., 1970; corp. group v.p. manpower planning Dart Industries, Inc., Los Angeles, 1970-78; cons., 1978-82, ret., 1982. Decorated D.S.M., Legion of Merit with oak leaf cluster, Bronze Star with 3 oak leaf clusters, Purple Heart (U.S.); knight comdr. Cross with badge and star Order of Merit (W.Ger.); officer Legion of Honor (France). Mem. Clan Fergusson Soc. (Scotland), Beta Theta Pi. Clubs: Cypress Point (Pebble Beach); Old Capitol (Monterey, Calif.). Home: PO Box 1515 Pebble Beach CA 93953-1515

FERINI, ROBERT PAT, agricultural products company executive; b. 1963. With Betteravia Farms, Santa Maria, Calif.; now ptnr. Office: Betteravia Farms PO Box 5845 Santa Maria CA 93456-5845*

FERKO, CHRISTOPHER ANDREW, computer network engineering administrator; b. Atlanta, Aug. 13, 1957; s. Francis Andrew and margie Nell (Hollehan) F.; divorced; children: Lisa, Thomas. BS, U. Ariz., Tucson, 1980; AA, Pima Coll., Tucson, 1982. Computer applications mgr. City of Tucson, 1982-94, network engr., 1994—. Bd. dirs. Employees Combined Appeal/United Way, Tucson, 1989-93. Capt. U.S. Army, 1975-95. Recipient Pub. Svc. Excellence award Employee Recognition Com., Tucson, 1996. Mem. Project Mgmt. Inst. Republican. Roman Catholic. Avocations: volleyball, hockey, flying, scuba diving, marathons. Office: City of Tucson 480 W Paseo Redondo Tucson AZ 85701-8253

FERNÁNDEZ, CELESTINO, sociologist, educator; b. Santa Ines, Michoacan, Mex., Sept. 8, 1949; came to U.S., 1957; c. Celestino and Angelita (Barragán) F.; m. Kathryn A. Gouze, Aug. 1, 1970 (div. May 1989); children: Kristina M., Celestino III; m. Jannie L. Carter, Sept. 22, 1990; stepchildren: Carter Cox, Colin Cox, Quinn R. Cox. BA, Sonoma State U., Rohnert Park, Calif., 1973; MA, Stanford U., 1974, PhD, 1976. Asst. prof. sociology U. Ariz., Tucson, 1976-82, assoc. prof., 1982-88, affirmative action officer, 1982-84, v.p. for undergrad. edn., 1989-92, prof. sociology, 1989—, v.p. for acad. outreach and internat. affairs, 1992-94, prof. sociology, 1998—; exec. v.p., provost Ariz. Internat. Coll., Tucson, 1994-98; adv. bd. Harvard Jour. Hispanic Policy, Cambridge, Mass., 1996—, Ednl. Testing Svc., Princeton, N.J., 1988-93; commr. North Ctrl. Assn. of Colls., Chgo., 1995—; cons. in field;. Contbr. articles to profl. jours., chpts. to books. Bd. dirs. Hispanic-Jewish Dialogue, Tucson, 1989—, Project PPEP, Tucson, 1989—; mem. hon. com. AIDSwalk '98 and '98, Tucson; bd. dirs., chmn. Ariz. Humanities Coun., 1988—, Edn. Enrichment Found., 1996—, Fedn. of State Humanities Couns., 1994—. Named Hispanic Man of the Yr., Hispanic Profl. Action Com., 1997, Spirit of Excellence award Gov. Ariz., Phoenix, 1994; named disting. Alumnus, Sonoma State U., 1991. Mem. Am. Assn. for Higher Edn. (Disting. Leadership in Higher Edn. award 1998), Am. Sociol. Assn., Pacific Sociol. Assn. Roman Catholic. Avocations: basketball, bicycling, tennis, writing ballads and poetry, reading. Home: 6724 E Calle Buena Tucson AZ 85715 Office: Univ of ariz Dept Sociology PO Box 210027 Tucson AZ 85721

FERNANDEZ, FERDINAND FRANCIS, federal judge; b. 1937. BS, U. So. Calif., 1958, JD, 1963; LLM, Harvard U., 1963. Bar: Calif. 1963, U.S. Dist. Ct. (cen. dist.) Calif. 1963, U.S. Ct. Appeals (9th cir.) 1963, U.S. Supreme Ct. 1967. Elec. engr. Hughes Aircraft Co., Culver City, Calif., 1958-62; law clk. to dist. judge U.S. Dist. Ct. (cen. dist.) Calif., 1963-64; pvt. practice law Allard, Shelton & O'Connor, Pomona, Calif., 1964-80; judge Calif. Superior Ct. San Bernardino County, Calif., 1980-85, U.S. Dist. Ct. (cen. dist.) Calif., L.A., 1985-89, U.S. Ct. Appeals (9th cir.), L.A., 1989—; Lester Roth lectr. U. So. Calif. Law Sch., 1992. Contbr. articles to profl. jours. Vice chmn. City of La Verne Comm. on Environ. Quality, 1971-73; chmn. City of Claremont Environ. Quality Bd., 1972-73; bd. trustees Pomona Coll., 1990—. Fellow Am. Coll. Trust and Estate Counsel; mem. ABA, State Bar of Calif. (fed. cts. com. 1966-69, ad hoc com. on attachments 1971-85, chmn. com. on adminstrn. of justice 1976-77, exec. com. taxation sect. 1977-80, spl. com. on mandatory fee arbitration 1978-79), Calif. Judges Assn. (chmn. juvenile cts. com. 1983-84, faculty mem. Calif. Jud. Coll. 1982-83, faculty mem. jurisprudence and humanities course 1983-85), Hispanic Nat. Bar Assn., L.A. County Bar Assn. (bull. com. 1974-75), San Bernardino County Bar Assn., Pomona Valley Bar Assn. (co-editor Newsletter 1970-72, trustee 1971-78, sec.-treas. 1973-74, 2d v.p. 1974-75, 1st v.p. 1975-76, pres. 1976-77), Estate Planning Coun. Pomona Valley (sec. 1966-76), Order of Coif, Phi Kappa Phi, Tau Beta Pi. Office: US Ct Appeals 9th Cir 125 S Grand Ave Ste 602 Pasadena CA 91105-1621

FERRARI, DAVID GUY, auditor; b. Scottsbluff, Nebr., Jan. 12, 1944; s. Guy C. and Waunita E. (Bailey) F.; m. Kay Cooper, May 29, 1966; children: Brian S., Justin D. BSBA, U. Wyo., 1966, MS in Bus. Adminstrn., 1971. Fin. dir. Wyo. Dept. Edn., Cheyenne, 1967-71; budget analyst State of Wyo., Cheyenne, 1971-73, state budge dir., 1973-75, dep. state auditor, 1975-87; cons. Cheyenne, 1987-90; state auditor State of Wyo., Cheyenne, 1991-99. Author, cons.: Wyoming 1988-A Study of Revenues and Expenditures, 1988, A Study in State Government Efficiency, 1989, Accountability and Efficiency in State Government, 1990, The Final Report on Accountability and Efficiency in State Government, 1991. Elected state ofcl. Rep. Party, Cheyenne, 1991—. Mem. Rotary (hon.). Avocations: reading, writing, boating, drawing, sports. Office: State Auditors Office PO Box 2072 Cheyenne WY 82003-2072

FERRARIS, ALFRED CHARLES, JR., poet; b. S.I., N.Y., Feb. 8, 1946; s. Alfred Charles Sr. and Florence Marie (Melleby) F.; m. Mary Elizabeth Eastlake, Sept. 5, 1985; children: Elizabeth, Theodora; 1 child from previous marriage, James. Student, Hamilton Coll., 1964-67. Author: Marpa Point, 1976, Older Than Rain, 1997. Buddhist. Home: PO Box 65 226 High St Lyons CO 80540

FERRARO, RAY, hockey player; b. Trail, B.C., Can., Aug. 23, 1964. Hockey player Hartford Whalers Nat. Hockey League, 1985-91, hockey player N.Y. Islanders, 1991-96, hockey player L.A. Kings, 1996—; played All-Star Game, 1992. Office: Los Angeles Kings 3900 W Manchester Blvd Inglewood CA 90305-2200

FERRARO, ROBERT, customer service executive. BS, U. Nev., Reno, 1957, MS, 1959. Asst. county agt. U. Nev., Fallon, 1959-63, Lovelock, 1963-70; mgr. electrocytic sys. Pacific Engring. and Prodn. of Nev., Henderson, 1970-85; mgr. Pepcon sys. Pepcon Sys. Inc., Las Vegas, Nev., 1985-96; mgr. customer rels. Ampac, Las Vegas, 1996—. Pres. boulder City (Nev.) Mus. and Hist. Assn., 1980—. Address: Boulder City/Hoover Dam Mus PO Box 60516 Boulder City NV 89006-0516*

FERREE, JOHN NEWTON, JR., fundraising specialist, consultant; b. Wadesboro, N.C., Nov. 21, 1946; s. John Newton and Mary Cleo (Tice) F.; m. Ginger Ann Rogers, June 6, 1969 (div. 1991); m. Patricia Gayle Kruger, Nov. 19, 1994. AA, Bluefield (Va.) Coll., 1966; BA, Baylor U., 1968; JD, Samford U., 1975. Bar: Ala. Contr. Aetna Life Ins. Co., Seattle, 1972; atty. Ferree & Armstrong, Alabaster, Ala., 1975-82; exec. dir. Northwest Bapt. Found., Portland, Oreg., 1982-84; asst. v.p. Harris Trust Co. of Ariz., Scottsdale, 1984; v.p. Bapt. Found. of Ariz., Phoenix, 1985-89; dir. planned giving Phoenix Children's Hosp., 1989-91; pres. Scottsdale (Ariz.) Healthcare Found., 1991—; bd. dir. Nat. Com. Planned Giving, 1994-96; bd. dirs. FBI Citizen's Acad. Found., v.p. 1994-96, 98, Charitable Accord, v.p., 1996-98; instr. Cannon Sch. Found. Mgmt., 1995—; adj. prof. Ariz. State U., 1998—; cons. in field. Named Ariz. Profl. Fundraiser of Yr., 1996. Mem. Nat. Soc. Fund Raising Execs. (pres. 1990), Planned Giving Roundtable of Ariz. (pres. 1992, 97), Assn. for Healthcare Philanthropy. Republican. Baptist. Office: Scottsdale Healthcare Found Ste 121 10001 E 92nd St Scottsdale AZ 85258-4530

FERRELL, CONCHATA GALEN, actress, acting teacher and coach; b. Charleston, W.Va., Mar. 28, 1943; d. Luther Martin and Mescal Loraine (George) F.; m. Arnold A. Anderson; 1 dau., Samantha. Student, W.Va. U., 1961-64, Marshall U., 1967-68. N.Y. theater appearances The Hot L Baltimore, 1973, The Sea Horse, 1973-74 (OBIE award and Drama Desk award 1974), Battle of Angels, 1975; appeared in: Los Angeles plays Getting Out, 1978, Here Wait, 1980, Picnic, 1986; appeared in TV series: The Hot L Baltimore, 1975, B.J. and the Bear, 1979, McClain's Law, 1981, E.R., 1984, A Peaceable Kingdom, 1989, L.A. Law, 1991, Hearts Afire, 1993-94, Townies, 1996, Teen Angel, 1997; appeared in movies: Network, 1975, Dangerous Hero, 1975, Heartland, 1981, Where the River Runs Black, 1986, For Keeps,1987, Mystic Pizza, 1987, Witches of Eastwick, 1987, Chains of Gold, 1990, Edward Sissorhands, 1990, Family Prayers, 1993, True Romance, 1993, Samurai Cowboy, 1993, Heaven and Earth, 1993, Freeway, 1995, Touch, 1996, My Fellow Americans, 1996; appeared in TV movies: A Girl Called Hatter Fox, 1977, A Death in Canaan, 1977, The Orchard Children, 1978, Before and After, 1979, Bliss, 1979, Reunion, 1980, The Rideout Case, 1980, The Great Gilley Hopkins, 1981, Life of the Party, 1982, Emergency Room, 1983, Nadia, 1984, Miss Lonely Hearts, 1985, Samaritan, 1986, Northbeach and Rawhide, 1986, Picnic, 1986, Eye on the Sparrow, 1987, Runaway Ralph, 1987, Goodbye Miss Liberty (Disney Channel), 1988, Running Mates, 1990, Deadly Intentions, Again, 1990, Back Field in Motion, 1991, 120 Volt Miracle, 1992, Forget Me Not, 1996, Sweetdreams, 1996. Recipient Wrangler award Nat. Cowboy Hall of Fame, 1981, Most Promising Newcomer award Theatre World, 1974, Emmy award nomination, 1991-92. Mem. AFTRA, ACLU, NOW, Actors Equity Assn., Screen Actors Guild, Women in Films. Democrat. Office: Paradigm 10100 Santa Monica Blvd Los Angeles CA 90067-4003

FERRERI, MICHAEL VICTOR, optometrist; b. Park Ridge, Ill., May 15, 1967; s. Samuel Joseph and Dolores Jean (Liebich) F.; m. Celaine Berenda Ward, Apr. 2, 1994; children: Christopher, Anthony. BS in Biol. Scis., U. Calif., Irvine, 1989; OD, So. Calif. Coll. Optometry, 1993. Cert. therapeutic optometrist, Calif., Tex. Extern Ctr. for the Partially Sighted, Santa Monica, Calif., 1992-93; pvt. practice Long Beach, Calif., 1993—; assoc. optometrist Antelope Mall Vision Ctr., Palmdale, Calif., 1995—; color vision analysis cons. Dept. Health and Human Svcs., Long Beach, 1994-97; participating doctor Vision USA, Long Beach, 1995—. Contbr. articles to profl. jours. Mem. Rep. Nat. Com., 1991—; v.p. congregation Grace Luth. Ch., Long Beach, 1996—, also elder. Recipient Corning Low Vision award Corning Optics, Anaheim, Calif., 1993, Vision Therapy Enhancement cert. So. Calif. Coll. Optometry, Fullerton, 1993, appreciation cert. for outstanding contbns. to Save Your Vision Week, U.S. Senate, 1997, gov.'s letter of commendation for organizing coloring and essay contest for sch. children State of Calif., 1997, appreciation certificate Calif. Optometric Assn., 1998. Mem. Am. Optometric Assn. (contact lens sect.), Calif. Optometric Assn., Fellowship of Christian Optometrists, Optometric Ext. Program (clin. assoc.), Rio Hondo Optometric Soc. (treas. 1997-99). Avocations: camping, hiking, watersports. Home: PO Box 2573 Guasti CA 91743-2573 Office: Los Altos Med Ctr 1777 N Bellflower Blvd Ste 109 Long Beach CA 90815-4013

FERRIN, ALLAN HOGATE, architect; b. N.Y.C., Oct. 24, 1951; s. Allan Wheeler and Barbara (Hogate) F.; m. Barbara Lorayne Weaver, May 1, 1976; children: Leigh, Ellen. Student, Princeton U., 1969-72; BA in Chinese, U. Wis., 1973; MArch, U. N.Mex., 1975. Registered architect, Wash., Ala., Oreg. Draftsman Amrep. Corp., Albuquerque, 1975-76, Mitchell Assocs., Albuquerque, 1976-77; architect Jorge del la Torre, Albuquerque, 1977-78, John Graham Co., Seattle, 1978-79; project dir. Charles Kober Assocs., Seattle, 1979-85; ptnr. Carlson/Ferrin Assocs., Seattle, 1985-93; pres. Hogate Properties, Inc., 1994—. Bd. dirs. Gainsborough Condominium Assn., Seattle, 1986-91; trustee Bainbridge (Wash.) Performing Arts Coun., The Arboretum Found., 1996-98; planning commnr. Bainbridge Island, 1995—; chair steering com. Bainbridge Performing Arts Ctr.; vice chair comprehensive plan adv. com. Bainbridge Island. Mem. Urban Land Inst., Internat. Coun. Shopping Ctrs. Office: Hogate Properties Inc 1017 Minor Ave Apt 1001 Seattle WA 98104-1303

FERRIS, EVELYN SCOTT, lawyer; b. Detroit, d. Ross Ansel and Irene Mabel (Bowser) Nafus; m. Roy Shorey Ferris, May 21, 1969 (div. Sept. 1982); children: Judith Ilene, Roy Sidney, Lorene Marjorie. J.D., Willamette U., 1961. Bar: Oreg. 1962, U.S. Dist. Ct. Oreg. 1962. Law clk. Oreg. Tax Ct., Salem, 1961-62; dep. dist. atty. Marion County, Salem, 1962-65; judge Mcpl. Ct., Stayton, Oreg., 1965-76; ptnr. Brand, Lee, Ferris & Embick, Salem, 1965-82; chmn. Oreg. Workers' Compensation Bd., Salem, 1982-89; exec. asst. to dir. Dept. Ins. and Fin., 1989-94. Bd. dirs. Friends of Deepwood, Salem, 1979-82, Salem City Club, 1972-97, Marion County Civil Svc. Commn., 1970-75; com. mem. Polk County Hist. Commn., Dallas, Oreg., 1976-79; mem. Oreg. legis. com. Bus. Climate, 1967-69, Govs. Task Force on Liability, 1986. Recipient Outstanding Hist. Restoration of Comml. Property award Marion County Hist. Soc., 1982. Mem. Oreg. Mcpl. Judges Assn. (pres. 1967-69), Altrusa, Internat., Mary Leonard Law Soc., Western Assn. Workers Compensation Bds. (pres. 1987-89), Capitol Club (pres. 1977-79), Internat. Assn. Indsl. Accident Bds. and Commns. (pres. 1992-93), Phi Delta Delta. Republican. Episcopalian. Home: 747 Church St SE Salem OR 97301-3715

FERRIS, RUSSELL JAMES, II, freelance writer; b. Rochester, N.Y., June 11, 1938; s. Russell James and Phyllis Helen (Breheny) F.; m. Ilma Maria dos Santos, June 29, 1968. Student, St. Bonaventure U., 1956-59; BS, U. Rochester, 1967; MS, Emerson Coll., 1989; PhD, Universal Life Ch., 1983. Cert. social worker. Film inspector City of Rochester, 1962-67; social worker Tulare County, Visalia, Calif., 1967-69, Alameda County, Oakland, Calif., 1969-71; ghostwriter self-employed, San Francisco, 1971—. Author: Crescendo, 1972 and 9 other novels. With USAR, 1956-68. Recipient Botany fellowship Emerson Coll., 1989. Mem. Assn. U.S. Army, Air Force Assn., Navy League U.S., Ret. Officers Assn. (life), Res. Officers Assn. (life), Internat. Platform Assn., Am. Mensa Inc. Libertarian. Roman Catholic. Avocation: aviculture. Home and Office: 202 Font Blvd San Francisco CA 94132-2404

FERRY, MILES YEOMAN, state official; b. Brigham City, Utah, Sept. 22, 1932; s. John Yeoman and Alta (Cheney) F.; m. Suzanne Call, May 19, 1952; children: John, Jane Ferry Stewart, Ben, Helen, Sue Ferry Thorpe. BS, Utah State U., 1954. Rancher Corinne, Utah, 1952; pres. J.Y. Ferry & Son, Inc.; mem. Utah Ho. of Reps., 1965-66; mem. Utah Senate, 1967-84, minority whip, 1975-76, minority leader, 1977-78, pres. senate, 1979-84; mem. presdl. advisor commn. on intergovtl. affairs, 1984; mem. governing bd. Council State Govts., 1983-84; v.p. Legis./Exec. Consulting Firm, 1994—; chmn. Corinne Cemetery Dist., 1989—. Pres. Brigham Jr. C. of C., 1956-61, Nat. Conf. of State Legislators, 1984, v.p., 1982, pres.-elect, 1983, pres., 1984; v.p. Utah Jr. C. of C., 1960-61; nat. dir. Utah Jaycees, 1961-62; pres. Farm Bur. Box Elder County, 1958-59; food and agr. commr. USDA, commr. agr. State of Utah, 1985-93. Recipient award of merit Boy Scouts Am., 1976, Alumnusi of Yr. award Utah State U., 1981, award of merit Utah Vocat. Assn., 1981, Friend of Agr. award Utah Farm Bur., 1988, Cert. Appreciation USDA, 1988, Contbn. to Agr. award Utah-Idaho Farmers Union, 1989, Disting. Svc. award Utah State U., 1993, 94; named Outstanding Young Man of Yr., Brigham City Jr. C. of C., 1957, Outstanding Nat. Dir. U.S. Jaycees, 1963, Outstanding Young Man in Utah, Utah Jr. C. of C., 1961, Outstanding Young Farmer, 1958, One of 3 Outstanding Young Men of Utah, 1962, Rep. Legislator of Yr., 1984, One of 10 Outstanding Legislators of Yr., 1984. Mem. SAR, Sons Utah Pioneers, Gov.'s Cabinet, Utah Commn. Agr., Fed. Rsch. Com., Nat. Assn. State Depts. Agr. (bd. dirs. 1989), Western Assn. of State Depts. of Agr. (v.p. 1990-91, pres. 1991-92), Western U.S. Agr. Trade Assn. (sec. treas- elect 1987-88, pres. 1989-90), Utah Cattlemen's Assn., Nat. Golden Spike Assn. (dir. 1958—), Phi Kappa Phi, Pi Kappa Alpha. Republican. Address: 815 N 6800 W Corinne UT 84307-9737

FERRY, RICHARD MICHAEL, executive search firm executive; b. Ravenna, Ohio, Sept. 26, 1937; s. John D. and Margaret M. (Jeney) F.; m. Maude M. Hillman, Apr. 14, 1956; children: Richard A., Margaret L., Charles Michael, David W., Dianne E., Ann Marie. BS, Kent State U., 1959. CPA. Cons. staff Peat, Marwick, Mitchell, Los Angeles, 1965-69, ptnr., 1969; chmn., co-founder Korn/Ferry Internat., Los Angeles, 1969—; bd. dirs. Mellon/1st Bus. Bank, L.A., Avery Dennison, Pasadena, Calif., Dole Food Co., Calif., Pacific Life Ins. Co., Newport Beach, Calif. Trustee Calif. Inst. Tech., L.A., St. John's Health Ctr., Santa Monica, Calif.; bd. dirs. Cath. Charities, L.A., Calif. Cmty. Found., Hugh O'Brien Youth Leadership. Republican. Roman Catholic. Office: Korn/Ferry Internat 1800 Century Park E Ste 900 Los Angeles CA 90067-1512

FERY, JOHN BRUCE, former real estate property manager; b. Bellingham, Wash., Feb. 16, 1930; s. Carl Salvatore and Margaret Emily (Hauck) F.; m. Delores Lorraine Carlo, Aug. 22, 1953; children: John Brent, Bruce Todd, Michael Nicholas. BA, U. Wash., 1953; MBA, Stanford U., 1955; D of Law (hon.), Gonzaga U., 1982; D of Nat. Resources (hon.), U. Idaho, 1983. Asst. to pres. Western Kraft Corp., 1955-56; prodn. mgr., 1956-57; with Boise Cascade Corp., Idaho, 1957-94, pres., CEO, 1972-78, chmn. bd., CEO, 1978-94; chmn. Boise Cascade Corp., Boise, Idaho, 1994-95; with F&C Corp., Boise, 1996—; bd. dirs. Albertsons, Inc., Hewlett-Packard Co., The Boeing Co.; active mem. Bus. Coun. Dir. Idaho Community Found. With USN, 1950-51. Named Most Outstanding Chief Exec. Officer Fin. World, 1977, 78, 79, 80. Mem. Am. Forest and Paper Assn. (exec. com., bd. dirs.), Arid Club, Hillcrest Country Club, Arlington Club. Office: F&C Corp Rocky Mountain Mgmt PO Box 15407 Boise ID 83715-5407 also: F&C Corp 2700 Airport Way Boise ID 83705*

FERZACCA, JOHN BARRY, director, playwright; b. Green Bay, Wis., July 26, 1940; s. Faust Louis and Marion (Sullivan) F. BA, No. Mich. U., 1962; MA, Mich. State U., 1965. Playwright: The Failure to Zigzag, 1970 (Best Play award 1971), Comeback Memories, 1976, Margo and the Girls, 1978 (Jane Chambers Meml. award), Click, 1980 (Best Play award 1990), The Death of Me Yet, 1981, The Haunted One, 1986, Night Falls in L.A., 1993; prodr.: (film) Mission of the Shark, 1990; dir. Boys in the Band (South Coast Repertory), Funny Girl, Equus, Ballroom, Peter Pan, Sweet Charity (with Toni Tennille), Vanities (with Kelly McGillis), I'm Getting My Act

Together (with Teri Ralston, Laguna Moulton Playhouse). Named Orange County Man of Yr., Daily Pilot, 1978. Avocations: professional photography, newscasting.

FETLER, DANIEL GREGORY, cinematographer; b. Mpls., Aug. 21, 1952; s. Paul and Ruth Regina (Pahl) F. BFA, Mpls. Coll. Art and Design, 1974. Dir. photography Dessere Pictures, L.A., 1985; camera operator Universal Studios, Burbank, Calif., 1985, Lighthouse Films, L.A., 1987; dir. photography Lorimar Pictures, Warren Miller Prodns., Los Angeles, 1985, Western Video and Film, Laguna Niguel, Calif., 1986, Bill White Prodns., Los Angeles, 1986, Amethyst Studios, Hollywood, Calif., 1986, Whitmore Prodns., L.A., 1987—, Continental Films, Pitts., 1988, Blue Moon Prodns., L.A., 1989, A Major Find, 1991, Sightings, Fox TV, 1993, Dreamland Pictures, Hollywood, 1993, Writers Block Prodns., 1994, Discovery Channel, The New Detectives, The FBI Files, 1998; dir. photography Gold Spl. Jury award Station Time Huston Internat. Film Festival, 1988. Mem. Soc. Operating Cameramen, Ind. Feature Project West, Am. Film Inst. Avocations: writing, travel, sailing, carpentry. Home and Office: 505 S Beverly Dr Ste 302 Beverly Hills CA 90212-4514

FETTER, ALEXANDER LEES, theoretical physicist, educator; b. Phila., May 16, 1937; s. Ferdinand and Elizabeth Lean Fields (Head) F.; m. Jean Holmes, Aug. 4, 1962 (dec. Dec. 1994); children: Anne Lindsay, Andrew James. AB, Williams Coll., 1958; BA, Balliol Coll., Oxford U., 1960; PhD, Harvard U., 1963. Miller rsch. fellow U. Calif., Berkeley, 1963-65; mem. faculty dept. physics Stanford U., 1965—, prof., 1974—, chmn. dept. physics, 1985-90, assoc. chmn. dept. physics, 1998—, asso. dean undergrad. studies, 1976-79, assoc. dean humanities and sci., 1990-93, dir. Hansen Exptl. Physics Lab., 1996-97; vis. prof. Cambridge U., 1970-71; Nordita vis. prof. Tech. U., Helsinki, Finland, 1976. Author: (with J.D. Walecka) Quantum Theory of Many Particle Systems, 1971, Theoretical Mechanics of Particles and Continua, 1980. Alumni trustee Williams Coll., 1974-79. Rhodes scholar, 1958-60; NSF fellow, 1960-63; Sloan Found. fellow, 1968-72; Recipient W.J. Gores award for excellence in teaching Stanford U., 1974. Fellow Am. Physics Soc. (chmn. div. condensed matter physics 1991), AAAS; mem. Sigma Xi. Home: 904 Mears Ct Palo Alto CA 94305-1029 Office: Stanford U Physics Dept Stanford CA 94305-4060

FETTER, WILLIAM ALLAN, computer graphics executive; b. Independence, Mo., Mar. 14, 1928; s. William Herbert and Edna Katherine (Werner) F.; m. Darlene Glea Wyss, Aug. 20, 1950 (div. 1962); 1 child, William Arnold (dec.); m. Barbara Ann Shaffer, Dec. 21, 1963; children: Brant Shaffer, Elena Katherine (twins). Student, Kansas City Jr. Coll., 1945-46, Kansas City U., 1948-49; BFA, U. Ill., 1952. Supr. computer graphics The Boeing Co., Wichita, Kans. and Seattle, 1959-69; v.p. Graphcomp. Scis., Newport, Calif., 1969-70; chmn. design dept., lectr. So. Ill. U., Carbondale, 1970-77; pres. So. Ill. Rsch. and Corp. Office (SIROCO), Carbondale, Ill., 1977—; also bd. dirs. So. Ill. Rsch. and Corp. Office (SIROCO), Bellevue, Redmond, Wash.; owner ORIGIN, Bellevue, Redmond, 1982—; presenter 3D conf. U. Tokyo, 1992; spkr. in field. Author: Human figures for Designers by Computer, 1983, Computer Graphics in Communication, 1964; author (TV program) Computer Graphics, The Accurate Eye, 1975; exhibited in show Mus. Modern Art, N.Y.C., 1976; patentee in field. Bd. dirs. Com. on Handicapped, Park Forest, Ill., 1957-58, Master Resources Council Internat., Seattle, 1980—; mem. UNESCO TACT Task Force, Washington, 1975-85. With U.S. Army, 1946-48; 2nd lt. USAFR, 1952-57. Recipient Cert. Merit Internat. Graphic Design, 1967, Letter Commendation USAF, Boeing Airplane Co., 1962, Bronze Medal Nat. Soc. Art Dirs., 1963. Fellow AIAA (assoc.); mem. Internat. Design Conf. (presenter 1976, 78), Soc. Info. Display, Indsl. Designers Soc. Am., N.W. Human Factors Soc., Mus. Modern Art Club, Alfa Romeo Owner's Club.

FETTERS, DORIS ANN, retired secondary education educator; b. N.Y.C.; d. John Joseph and Loreta Gertrude (Stratford) F. BA, Calif. State Coll., L.A., 1952. Cert. gen. secondary tchr. Tchr. Temple City (Calif.) H.S., 1954-55, L.A. City Schs., 1955-56; vice consul 3d sec. of embassy Dept. of State, Washington, 1957-60; tchr. U. Rafael Landivar, Guatemala, 1960-63, L.A. Unified Schs., 1964-90. Mem. Am. Fedn. Tchrs., United Tchrs. L.A. Democrat. Roman Catholic. Avocations: gardening, arts and crafts, reading.

FIALA, ROBERT HENRY, electrical engineer; b. Ft. Dodge, Iowa, Oct. 31, 1939; s. Henry A. and Julia (Urban) F.; m. Janet Elizabeth Durke, June 12, 1971 (div. Sept. 1987); m. In Ji Yi, Dec. 5, 1987; 1 child, Sarah T. Yi. AAS, Devry Tech. Inst., Chgo., 1959; BSEE, Northrop Inst., Inglewood, Calif., 1969; MSEE, Loyola U., Westchester, Calif., 1975. Tech. supr. Hughes Aircraft Co., Fullerton, Calif., 1976-84; project engr. Raytheon Sys. Co., El Segundo, Calif., 1984—. With USN, 1962-66, Vietnam. Avocation: computers. Home: 1850 N Nordic Pl Orange CA 92865-4637 Office: Raytheon Sys Co 501 Continental Blvd El Segundo CA 90245-5036

FIBIGER, JOHN ANDREW, life insurance company executive; b. Copenhagen, Apr. 27, 1932; came to U.S., 1934, naturalized, 1953; s. Borge Rottboll and Ruth Elizabeth (Wadmond) F.; m. Barbara Mae Stuart, June 22, 1956; children: Karen Ruth McCarthy, Katherine Louise. B.A., U. Minn., 1953, M.A., 1954; postgrad., U. Wis. With Lincoln Nat. Life Ins. Co., Ft. Wayne, Ind., 1956-57; with Bankers Life Ins. Co. Nebr., Lincoln, 1959-73; sr. v.p. group Bankers Life Ins. Co. Nebr., 1972-73; with New Eng. Mut. Life Ins. Co., Boston, 1973-89; vice chmn., pres., chief operating officer New Eng. Mut. Life Ins. Co., 1981-89; with Transam Life Cos., 1991-94; exec. v.p., CFO, then pres. Transamerica Occidental Life Ins. Co., L.A., 1994-95, chmn., 1995-97; past vice chmn. Actuarial Bd. for Counseling and Discipline; bd. dirs. Transamerica Life Can., Transamerica Life N.Y., Conning Corp. Life trustee, past chmn. Mus. Sci., Boston, 1989-91; overseer New Eng. Med. Ctr.; bd. dirs. Menninger Found., L.A. Chamber Orch.; past chmn. Menninger Fund; bd. dirs., vice-chmn. U. So. Calif. Sch. Gerontology; pres. West Coast Bus. Inst. on Aging; past trustee Calif. Mus. Sci. and Industry. Fellow Soc. Actuaries (past bd. dirs.); mem. Nat. Acad. Social Ins. (founding mem.), Am. Acad. Actuaries (past pres.), Assn. Calif. Life Cos. (past bd. chmn.).

FICKINGER, WAYNE JOSEPH, communications executive; b. Belleville, Ill., June 23, 1926; s. Joseph and Grace (Belton) F.; m. Joan Mary Foley, June 16, 1951; children: Michael, Joan, Jan, Ellen, Steven. BA, U. Ill., 1949; MS, Northwestern U., 1950. Overnight editor United Press, Chgo., 1950-51; spl. project writer Sears-Roebuck & Co., Chgo., 1951-53; account exec. Calkins & Holden Advt. Agy., Chgo., 1953-56; account supr. Foote, Cone & Belding Advt. Agy., Chgo., N.Y.C., 1956-63; sr. v.p. J. Walter Thompson Co., Chgo., 1963-72; exec. v.p., dir. U.S. Western div. J. Walter Thompson Co., 1972-75, pres. N.Am. divsn., 1975-78; pres., chief operating officer J. Walter Thompson Co. Worldwide, 1978-79; pres. JWT Group, Inc., 1979-82, trustee retirement fund, dir., mem. exec. com., 1980-82; mng. dir. Spencer Stuart & Assocs., 1982-83; vice chmn., dir. Bozell, Jacobs, Kenyon & Eckhardt Inc., Chgo., 1984-89; pres. Mid-Am. Com., Chgo., 1989-93; exec. v.p., dir. Monroe Comm. Corp., 1992—; v.p., dir. Adams Comm., 1994—; advisory bd. Phase One, Susidiary, Cyberoffice Tech., 1993—; bd. dirs. Alford Group, Inc., Frankel & Assocs. Fundraising cons. Nat. Mental Health Assn., 1970; communications counselor Cook County (Ill.) Rep. Orgn., 1970; bd. dirs. Off-the-Street Club, Chgo., 1974-77, Mundelein Coll., 1985-91, United Cerebral Palsy, 1986, Chgo. Conv. and Tourists Bur., 1986-90, Columbia Coll., Chgo., 1990-95; chmn. Chgo. Funding Statue of Liberty, 1986, March of Dimes, 1987, Mayor's Chgo. Tourism Com., 1990-92. With USNR, 1943-46. Recipient Five-Year Meritorious Service award A.R.C., 1963, Service award Mental Health Assn., 1970. Mem. Am. Assn. Advt. Agys., Council on Fgn. Relations (Chgo. com.), Sigma Delta Chi, Alpha Delta Sigma. Clubs: Exmoor Country (Highland Park, Ill.); N.Y. Athletic; Mid-Am. (Chgo.), Internat. (Chgo.). Office: 350 S Beverly Dr Ste 300 Beverly Hills CA 90212-4817

FIEDLER, JOHN AMBERG, marketing scientist; b. Evanston, Ill., Nov. 11, 1941; s. George and Agnes Zoe (Amberg) F.; m. Frances Eudora Murphy, June 18, 1966 (div. 1983); children: Margaret, Neil; m. Lesley A. Bahner, Dec. 28, 1986. BA, U. Wis., 1965; MBA, U. Chgo., 1969. V.p. Leo Burnett Co., Inc., Chgo., 1969-72, 74-79; mgr. decision systems Market Facts, Inc., Chgo., 1972-73; exec. v.p. Ted Bates Co., Inc., N.Y.C., 1980-84; prin., founder, chief exec. officer POPULUS, Inc., Boise, Idaho, 1985—. Coauthor: (book) Psychological Effects of Advertising, 1985; contbr. articles to profl. jours. and confs.; inventor Ballot Box (TM) communication assessment system, 1985. Rsch. dir. Reagan-Bush '84, Wash., 1984, bd. dirs. Childreach, U.S.A., 1986-98, mem. exec. com. Mem. Am. Mktg. Assn. Republican. Roman Catholic. Office: POPULUS Inc 195 Wilderness Way Boise ID 83716-3383

FIELD, CAROL HART, writer, journalist, foreign correspondent; b. San Francisco, Mar. 27, 1940; d. James D. and Ruth (Arnstein) Hart; m. John L. Field, July 23, 1961; children: Matthew, Alison. BA, Wellesley Coll., 1961. Contbg. editor, assoc. editor, asst. editor City Mag., San Francisco, 1974-76; contbg. editor New West/Calif. Mag., San Francisco, L.A., 1975-80, San Francisco Mag., 1980-82; fgn. corr. La Gola, Milan, Italy, 1990-94; lectr. Smithsonian Inst., Washington, 1991, 95, Schlesinger Libr., Radcliffe Coll., 1995; TV appearances with Lorenza de Medici, 1992, Julia Child, 1995; bd. dirs. Lyra Corp., Bay Package Prodns. Author: The Hill Towns of Italy, 1983 (Commonwealth Club award 1984), new edit., 1997, The Italian Baker, 1985 (Internat. Assn. Culinary Profls. award 1986), Celebrating Italy, 1990 (Commonwealth Club award Internat. Assn. Culinary Profls. award 1991), paperback edit., 1997, Italy in Small Bites, 1993 (James Beard award), Focaccia: Simple Breads from the Italian Oven, 1994, In Nonna's Kitchen: Traditional Recipes and Culture from Italian Grandmothers, 1997 (main selection Good Food Club, Book of the Month Club); contbr. articles to profl. jours. Mem. lit. jury Commonwealth Club Calif., San Francisco, 1987, 88, 92; bd. dirs. Women's Forum West, San Francisco, 1990-92, Bancroft Libr. U. Calif., Berkeley, 1991-97, Headlands Inst., San Francisco, 1992-93; bd. dirs. Mechanics' Inst., San Francisco, 1987-92, pres., 1990-92. Recipient Internat. Journalism prize Maria Luigia Duchessa di Parma, Italy, 1987, Barbi Colombini prize Tuscany, 1991, Nat. Journalism prize Vanghetto d'Oro, 1997; named Alumna of Yr. Head Royce Sch, Oakland, Calif., 1991. Mem. Accademia Italia della Cucina, Authors Guild, Les Dames d'Escoffier, Internat. Assn. Culinary Profls. Home and Office: 2561 Washington St San Francisco CA 94115-1818

FIELD, CHARLES WILLIAM, metallurgical engineer, small business owner, consultant; b. Kankakee, Ill., Feb. 4, 1934; s. Euell Charles and Genevieve Thelma (Fletcher) F.; m. Barbara Sue Bird, Sept. 20, 1957; children: Charles Scott, Lynda Lois. BS in Metall. Engring., U. Ariz., 1960. Lic. real estate broker, Ariz. Research metallurgist Titanium Metals Corp. Am., Henderson, Nev., 1960-62; mgr. tech. service Titanium Metals Corp. Am., N.Y.C., 1962-67; with materials dept. for supersonic transport engine Large Jet Engine div. Gen. Electric Co., Cin., 1967-69; sr. engr. specialist, advanced tech. dept. Garrett Corp., Phoenix, 1969-76; real estate broker, prin. C.W. Field & Co., Scottsdale, 1985—; cons. titanium alloy applications, failure analysis; cons. to NASA, USAF, Secret Svc. Contbr. articles to profl. jours. Recipient commendation from U.S. Govt., 1964, Pres.'s Round Table award Phoenix Bd. Realtors, 1981, 84. Mem. American Institute of Aeronautics and Astronautics, Am. Soc. Metals, Nat. Assn. Corrosion Engrs., Space Age Materials and Process Engrs., Scottsdale Realtors (Million Dollar Club), Rotary (bd. dirs. Scottsdale), Camelback Country Club. Avocations: sci. reading, geology, Indian arts, investments. Home: 6620 E Maverick Rd Paradise Valley AZ 85253

FIELD, JEFFREY FREDERIC, designer; b. Los Angeles, July 6, 1954; s. Norman and Gertrude Clara (Ellman) F.; m. Susan Marie Merrin, Jan. 8, 1978. BA in Art, Calif. State U., Northridge, 1977, MA in Art, 1980. Cert. indsl. plastics tchr., Calif. Designer Fundamental Products Co., N. Hollywood, Calif., 1972-82; designer/model maker The Stansbury Co., Beverly Hills, Calif., 1982-84; mech. engr. Vector Electronic Co., Sylmar, Calif., 1984-87; pres., prin. Jeffrey Field Design Inc., Camarillo, Calif., 1987—; cons. MiniMed Techs., Sylmar, 1987—, Best Time Inc., Leander, Tex., 1987—, Spectrum Design, Granada Hills, Calif., 1987—, Raycom Systems Inc., Boulder, Colo., 1988-89, Alfred E. Mann Found. for Sci. Rsch., Sylmar, 1988—, Atomic Elements, L.A., E-O Products, Laguna Hills, Calif., Autogenics, Newbury Park, Calif., 1990—, Pacesetter Systems, Sylmar, 1990—, Baxter Healthcare Corp., Pharmaseal Div., Valencia, Calif., 1990—, Surgidev Corp., Goleta, Calif., 1990—, Sensor Medics Inc., Yorba Linda, Calif., 1997—, Percusurge Inc., Sunnyvale, Calif., 1996—, Whittader Safety Systems, Simi Valley, Calif., 1998—, Howard Leight Ind., San Diego, Calif., 1996—, Indsl. Strength Eyewear/Grafix Mktg. Group, Manhattan Beach & Campbell, Calif., 1991—. Democrat. Jewish. Avocations: bicycle riding, backpacking, cartooning, reading. Home and Office: 3061 Vista Grande Camarillo CA 93012-8893

FIELD, JOHN LOUIS, architect; b. Mpls., Jan. 18, 1930; s. Harold David and Gladys Ruth (Jacobs) F.; m. Carol Helen Hart, July 23, 1961; children: Matthew Hart, Alison Ellen. BA, Yale U., 1952, MArch, 1955. Individual practice architecture San Francisco, 1959-68; v.p. firm Bull, Field, Volkmann, Stockwell, Architects, San Francisco, 1968-83; ptnr. Field/Gruzen, Architects, San Francisco, 1983-86, Field Paoli Architects, San Francisco, 1986—; guest lectr. Stanford, 1970; chmn. archtl. council San Francisco Mus. Art, 1969-71; mem. San Francisco Bay Conservation and Devel. Commn., Design Rev. Bd., 1980-84; founding chmn. San Francisco Bay Architects Review, 1977-80. Co-author, producer, dir.: film Cities for People (Broadcast Media award 1975, Golden Gate award San Francisco Internat. Film Festival 1975, Ohio State award 1976); film The Urban Preserve (Calif. Council AIA Commendation of excellence 1982); co-design architect: design for New Alaska Capital City (winner design competition). Recipient Archtl. Record award, 1961, 1972; AIA, Sunset mag. awards, 1962, 64, 69; No. Calif. AIA awards, 1967, 82; Calif. Council AIA award, 1982; certificate excellence Calif. Gov.'s Design awards, 1966; Homes for Better Living awards, 1962, 66, 69, 71, 77; Albert J. Evers award, 1974, Best Bldg. award Napa (Calif.) C. of C., 1987, Design award Internat. Council Shopping Ctrs., 1988, Stores of Excellence award Nat. Mall Monitor, 1989, 92, 93, Pacific Coast Builders Gold Nugget award, 1989, 91, Urban Design award Calif. Coun. AIA, 1991, 93. Fellow AIA (com. on design); mem. Nat. Coun. Archtl. Registration Bds., Urban Land Inst. (Design award 1995), Yale Club, Lambda Alpha. Office: Field Paoli Architects 1045 Sansome St Ste 206 San Francisco CA 94111-1315

FIELDEN, C. FRANKLIN, III, early childhood education consultant; b. Gulfport, Miss., Aug. 4, 1946; s. C. Franklin and Georgia (Freeman) F.; children: Christopher Michaux (dec.), Robert Michaux, Jonathan Dutton. Student, Claremont Men's Coll., 1964-65; AB, Colo. Coll., 1970; MS, George Peabody Coll. Tchrs., 1976, EdS, 1979. Tutor Proyecto El Guacio, San Sebastian, P.R., 1967-68; asst. tchr. GET-SET Project, Colorado Springs, Colo., 1969-70, co-tchr., 1970-75, asst. dir., 1972-75; tutor Early Childhood Edn. Project, Nashville, 1975-76; pub. policy intern Donner-Belmont Child Care Ctr., Nashville, 1976-77; asst. to urban min. Nashville Presbytery, 1977; intern to prin. Steele Elem. Sch., Colorado Springs, 1977-78, tchr., 1978-86; resource person Office Gifted and Talented Edn. Colorado Springs Pub. Schs., 1986-87; tchr. Columbia Elem. Sch., Colorado Springs, 1987-92; tchr., pre-sch. team coord. Helen Hunt Elem. Sch., Colorado Springs, 1992-93; validator Nat. Acad. Early Childhood Programs, 1992—, mentor, 1994—, commr., 1996—; cons. Colo. Dept. Edn., Denver, 1993-96, sr. cons., 1996—, state coord. Even Start Family Literacy Program, 1997—; lectr. Arapahoe C.C., Littleton, Colo., 1981-82; instr. Met. State Coll., Denver, 1981; cons. Jubail Human Resources Devel. Inst., Saudi Arabia, 1982; mem. governing bd. GET-SET Project, 1969-79, 91-93. Mem. ad hoc bd. trustees Tenn. United Meth. Agy. on Children and Youth, 1976-77; mem. So. Regional Edn. Bd. Task Force on Parent-Caregiver Relationships, 1976-77; mem. day care com. Colo. Commn. Children and Their Families, 1981-82; mem. Nashville Children's Issues Task Force, 1976-77, Tenn. United Meth. Task Force on Children and Youth, 1976-77, Citizens' Goals Leadership Tng., 1986-87, Child Abuse Task Force, 4th Jud. Dist., 1986-87, FIRST IMPRESSIONS (Colo. Govs. Early Childhood Initiative) Task Force, 1987-88; mem. El Paso County Placement Alternatives Commn., 1990-96; mem. proposal rev. team Colo. Dept. Edn., 1992—; co-chair City/County Child Care Task Force, 1991-92; charter mem. City/County Early Childhood Care and Edn. Commn., 1993-96; mem. bd. dirs. Colo. Office of Resource and Referral Agys., 1996-99. Recipient Arts/Bus./Edn. award, 1983 [illegible] Tchg. award 1984; fellow NIMH 1976. Mem. [illegible] Nat. Assn. Edn. Young Children (founding mem. primary caucus 1992—, co-chair Western States Leadership Network 1993, Membership Action Group grantee 1993, mem. panel profl. ethics in early childhood edn. 1993-97), Colo. Assn. Edn. Young Children (legis. com. 1979-84, governing bd. 1980-84, 85-86, 89-95, exec. com. 1980-84, 93, sec. 1980-84, rsch. conf. chmn. 1982, tuition awards com. 1983-86, chmn. tuition awards com. 1985-86, pub. policy com. 1989-96, treas. 1993, primary grades conf. chmn. 1994), Nat. Assn. Early Childhood Specialists in State Depts. of Edn. (v.p. 1997—), Pikes Peak Assn. Edn. Young Children, Huguenot Soc. Great Britain and Ireland, Nat. Trust Hist. Preservation, Phi Delta Kappa. Presbyterian. Home: PO Box 7766 Colorado Springs CO 80933-7766 Office: 201 E Colfax Ave Denver CO 80203-1704

FIELDEN, NED LEE, librarian; b. Hartford, Conn., Aug. 30, 1954; s. Lee and Constance Fielden; m. Lucy Kuntz, June 1, 1996; children: Aaron, Gene, Maggie. BA in Liberal Arts, Hampshire Coll., 1976; MA in History, Sonoma State U., 1992; M in Libr. and Info. Sci., U. Calif., Berkeley, 1992. Reference and instrnl. libr. Sonoma State U., Rohnert Pk., Calif., 1993-95, San Francisco State U., 1995—. Author: Internet Research, 1998. Mem. ALA, Am. Soc. Info. Sci., Assn. Computing Machinery, Calif. Acad. and Rsch. Librs. Office: San Francisco State U 1630 Holloway Ave San Francisco CA 94132-1722

FIELDING, ELIZABETH BROWN, education educator; b. Ligonier, Ind., Feb. 17, 1918; d. Herbert Benjamin and Roberta (Franklin) B.; m. Frederick Allan Fielding, May 23, 1942 (wid. July 1962); children: Elizabeth Enndriss Fielding, Frederick Allan Fielding, Jr. BA, Smith Coll., 1939; MA, U. San Francisco, 1975. Cert. tchr. com. colls., Calif. Field staff mem. San Francisco Bay Girl Scout Assn., 1963-69; exec. dir. Tri-City Project on Aging, Rodeo, Calif., 1970-73; tchr., cons. various univs., 1974-98; mem. curriculum com. U. Calif., Berkeley, 1979-80; chair edn. programs Diablo Valley Found. on Aging, Walnut Creek, Calif., 1980s. Author: The Memory Manual, 1999; contbr. articles to profl. jours. Chair Mental Health Task Force, County Coun. for Aging, Contra Costa County, 1974-76; mem. Sr. Svcs. Commn., City of Lafayette, Calif., 1981-98; pres. bd. dirs. Calif. Specialists on Aging, Calif., 1976-79. Mem. Western Gerontol. Assn. (now Am. Soc. on Aging), Internat. Transactional Analysis Assn. Avocations: writing fiction, genealogy, art appreciation, bird watching. Home: 3170 Plymouth Rd Lafayette CA 94549

FIELDING, HAROLD PRESTON, bank executive; b. Roaring Springs, Tex., Oct. 18, 1930; s. Rennon Preston and Merle (Woods) F.; m. Ingrid Margarete Eva Ziegler, May 4, 1962; children: Terry Stephen, Harold Preston Jr., Rennon Preston II, Marcel Preston, Noël Preston. AA, Fresno City Coll., 1972; BA, Calif. State U., 1976. Enlisted U.S. Army, 1950, command sgt. major, 1950-72, retired, 1972; br. mgr. Bank of Am., Stockton, Calif., 1972-78; exec. v.p. Bank of Oreg., Woodburn, 1978-84; pres., chief exec. officer Calif. Valley Bank, Fresno, 1984-86; pres., chief exec. officer Am. Samoa Bank, Pago Pago, Am. Samoa, 1986—, bd. dirs. Bd. dirs. Am. Samoa Econ. Devel. Authority, Pago Pago, 1990, C. of C. of Am. Samoa, Pago Pago, 1987, Goodwill Industries of Am. Samoa, Pago Pago, 1988, Tony Solaita Scholarship Trust Fund, Pago Pago, 1990; treas. S. Pacific Mini-Games for 1997. Mem. Am. Bankers Assn., Western Ind. Bankers Assn., Calif. Bankers Assn., Oreg. Bankers Assn. Democrat. Roman Catholic.

FIELDS, ANTHONY LINDSAY AUSTIN, health facility administrator, oncologist, educator; b. St. Michael, Barbados, Oct. 21, 1943; arrived in Can., 1968; s. Vernon Bruce and Marjorie (Pilgrim) F.; m. Patricia Jane Stewart, Aug. 5, 1967. MA, U. Cambridge, 1969; MD, U. Alta., 1974. Diplomate Am. Bd. Internal Medicine. Sr. specialist Cross Cancer Inst., Edmonton, Alta., Can., 1980-85, dir. dept. medicine, 1985-88, dir., 1988—; asst. prof. medicine U. Alta., Edmonton, 1980-84, assoc. prof., 1984-98, prof., 1998—, dir. divsn. med. oncology, 1985-89, dir. divsn. oncology, 1988-93. Fellow ACP (gov. elect Alta. chpt.), Royal Coll. Physicians and Surgeons Can. (specialist cert. med. oncology, internal medicine); mem. Can. Assn. Med. Oncologists (pres. 1994-96), Am. Soc. Clin. Oncology, Am. Fedn. Clin. Rsch., Can. Soc. for Clin. Investigation, Can. Med. Assn. Avocation: photography. Office: Cross Cancer Inst, 11560 University Ave, Edmonton, AB Canada T6G 1Z2

FIELDS, BERTRAM HARRIS, lawyer; b. Los Angeles, Mar. 31, 1929; s. H. Maxwell and Mildred Arlyn (Ruben) F.; m. Lydia Ellen Minevitch, Oct. 22, 1960 (dec. Sept. 1986); 1 child, James Eldar; m. Barbara Guggenheim, Feb. 21, 1991. B.A., UCLA, 1949; J.D. magna cum laude, Harvard U., 1952. Bar: Calif. 1953. Practiced in Los Angeles, 1955—; assoc. firm Shearer, Fields, Rohner & Shearer, and predecessor firms, 1955-57, mem. firm, 1957-82; ptnr. Greenberg, Glusker, Fields, Claman & Machtinger, 1982—. Author: (as D. Kincaid) The Sunset Bomber, 1986, The Lawyer's Tale, 1992, (as B. Fields) Royal Blood Richard III and the Mystery of the Princes, 1998; mem. bd. editors: Harvard Law Rev., 1953-55. Bd. dirs. U. So. Calif. Annenberg Sch. Comm. 1st. lt. USAF, 1953-55, Korea. Mem. ABA, L.A. County Bar Assn., Coun. Fgn. Rels. Subject of profiles Calif. Mag., Nov. 1987, Avenue Mag., Mar. 1989, Am. Film Mag., Dec. 1989, Vanity Fair Mag., Dec. 1993, Harvard Law Sch. Bull., spring 1998. Office: Greenberg Glusker Fields Claman & Machtinger Ste 2000 1900 Avenue Of The Stars Los Angeles CA 90067-4590

FIELDS, CARL VICTOR, food company executive; b. Lima, Ohio, Apr. 26, 1951; s. John Cecil and Baby Doll (Harris) F.; m. Charlean Annett Hartsfield, Oct. 3, 1981. BA, U. Calif., Irvine, 1973; MA, Yale U., 1975. Mktg. officer Wells Fargo Bank, San Francisco, 1975-77; bus. planner Dart Industries, L.A., 1977-80; mgr. bus. rsch. Amfac Foods, Portland, Oreg., 1980-83; v.p. mktg. Monterey Mushrooms divsn., Amfac Foods, Watsonville, Calif., 1983—; bd. dirs. K. Jazz Ctr., U. Calif., Santa Cruz, mem. adv. com. South African career devel. program. Bd. dirs. Santa Cruz Women's Crisis Ctr. Mem. Assn. Corp. Devel., Am. Mktg. Assn., Produce Mktg. Assn. (bd. dirs.), Western Mushroom Mktg. Assn. (chmn. mktg. com.), Am. Mushroom Inst. (bd. dirs., chmn., pub. Mushroom News), North Am. Mushroom Conf. (chmn.), U. Calif. at Irvine Alumni Assn. (bd. dirs.). Baptist. Avocations: track and field. Home: PO Box 1210 Capitola CA 95010-1210 Office: Monterey Mushrooms Inc 260 Westgate Dr Watsonville CA 95076-2452

FIERRO, MICHELLE, artist; b. L.A., Jan. 6, 1967; d. William Armando and Ramona Solis Fierro. BA in Studio Art, Calif. State U., Fullerton, 1992; MFA, Claremont U., 1995. Mgr. Am. Youth Hostel, San Pedro, Calif., 1992-93; instr. painting Buck's Rock Fine Art Camp, New Milford, Conn., 1994; asst. in advanced drawing Pitzer Coll., Claremont, Calif., 1994-95; vis artist Long Beach (Calif.) Children's Museum, 1993-94, So. Calif. Inst. Design and Architecture, Mar Vista, 1996, Art Ctr. Sch. Fashion, Pasadena, Calif., 1996, UCLA, 1997. One-woman shows include Jack Tilton Gallery, N.Y.C., 1995, 97, Burnett Miller Gallery, Santa Monica, Calif., 1996, London Projects, 1999, Solo Drawing Show, 1999. Contbr., donor art work to AIDS Project, L.A., Museum of Contemporary Art, L.A., Pasadena Art Alliance. Avocations: photography, biking, running. Home: 607 N Plymouth Blvd #4 Los Angeles CA 90004

FIFE, DENNIS JENSEN, chemistry educator, career officer; b. Brigham City, Utah, Feb. 10, 1945; s. Glen Shumway and June (Jenson) F.; m. Metta Marie Gunther, June 22, 1972; children: Kimball, Kellie, Keith, Kurt, Katie, Kenton. BS in Chemistry, Weber State U., Ogden, Utah, 1969; MBA, Inter-Am. U., San German, P.R., 1973; MS in Chemistry, Utah State U., 1978, PhD in Phsy. Chemistry, 1983. Assoc. chemist Thiokol Chem. Corp., Brigham City, 1969; commd. 2d lt. USAF, 1969, advanced through grades to lt. col.; pilot, instr., flight examiner Hurricane Hunters, Ramey AFB, P.R. and Keesler AFB, Miss., 1971-76; test project pilot 6514th Test Squadron, Ogden, Utah, 1979-81; instr. chemistry USAF Acad., Colorado Springs, Colo., 1977-79, asst. prof., 1983-85, assoc. prof., 1985-90; prof. USAF Acad., 1990; pres. Select Pubs., Inc., Colorado Springs, 1985-90, also chmn. bd. dirs., 1990; mgr. analytical labs. dept. Thiokol Corp., Brigham City, Utah, 1990—. Author: How to Form a Colorado Corporation, 1986; contbr. articles to profl. jours. Active Boy Scouts Am., 1981—, sustaining mem. Rep. Nat. Com., Washington, 1983—. Decorated Air medal with oak leaf cluster; NSF research grantee, 1967-68. Mem. Internat. Union Pure and Applied Chemistry (affiliate), Am. Chem. Soc., Phi Kappa Phi. Republican. Mormon. Avocations: racketball, fly fishing, hunting. Office: Thiokol Propulsion PO Box 707 M/S 245 Brigham City UT 84302-0707

FIGLIN, ROBERT ALAN, physician, hematologist, oncologist; b. Phila., June 22, 1949; s. Jack and Helen Figlin; 1 child, Jonathan B. BA in

Chemistry, Temple U., 1970, postgrad., 1972; MD, Med. Coll. Pa., 1976. Diplomate Am. Bd. Internal Medicine, sub-bd. Med. Oncology; diplomate Nat. Bd. Med. Examiners; lic. physician, Calif. Med. intern, resident in medicine Cedars-Sinai Med. Ctr., L.A., 1976-79, chief resident in medicine, 1979-80; fellow in hematology-oncology UCLA, 1980-82, asst. prof. medicine Sch. Medicine, 1982-88, assoc. prof. Sch. Medicine, 1988-94, prof. medicine Sch. Medicine, 1994—, chmn. instnl. rev. bd., human rsch. policy bd., 1998—; dir. Bowyer Oncology Ctr., dir. outpatient clin. rsch. unit Jonsson Comprehensive Cancer Ctr., 1990-92, dir. clin. rsch. unit, 1993-98; med. dir. thoracic oncology program Jonsson Comprehensive Cancer Ctr., 1994—, genito urinary program, 1994—, solid tumor program, 1997—; prin. investigator UCLA S.W. Oncology Group, 1992—; sci. founder UroGeneSys, 1996—. Editor Interferons in Cytokines, 1988-90, Kidney Cancer Jour., 1993-94; affiliate editor Current Clin. Trials, 1992-96; mem. editorial bd. UCLA Cancer Trials Newsletter, 1990-96, Seminars on Oncology-Kidney Cancer, 1995, Cancer Therapeutics, 1997, Cancer Biotherapy and Radio Pharms., 1997; author articles and revs. Mem. med. adv. bd. Nat. Kidney Cancer Assn., 1993—; FDA cons., 1990-92. Recipient numerous awards. Fellow ACP; mem. Am. Soc. Clin. Oncology, Am. Fedn. Clin. Rsch., Am. Assn. for Cancer Rsch., Soc. for Biologic Therapy (chmn. ann. scientific meeting 1997, pres. cancer panel 1997, S.W. Oncology Group, Assn. Subsplty. Profs., Internat. Assn. for Study of Lung Cancer. Office: UCLA Ste 2333 10945 Le Conte Ave Ste 2333 Los Angeles CA 90024-2828

FIKES, JAY COURTNEY, anthropology educator, art dealer; b. San Luis Obispo, Calif., June 14, 1951; s. J. C. and Virginia Lee (Roberts) F.; m. Lebriz N. Tosuner, Apr. 17, 1979; 1 child, Leyla Tupina. BA in Comparative Culture, U. Calif.-Irvine, 1973; MEd in Bilingual Edn., U. San Diego, 1974; MA in Anthropology, U. Mich., 1977, PhD in Anthropology, 1985. Tutor Palomar Coll., Pala Indian Reservation, Calif., 1974; instr. anthropology Allan Hancock Coll., Santa Maria, Calif., 1975-76; anthropology teaching fellow U. Mich., Ann Arbor, 1976-79; land use planner Navajo Nation, Windowrock, Ariz., 1983; instr. anthropology U.S. Internat. U., Oceanside, Calif., 1985—; instr. research methods in soc. sci. Marmara U., Istanbul, Turkey, 1985-87; lobbyist Friends Com. on Nat. Legislation, 1990; postdoctoral fellow Smithsonian Instn., Washington, 1991-92; instr. anthropology Yeditepe U., Istanbul, 1998—; owner Cuatro Esquinas Traders, Carlsbad, Calif., 1979—. Author: Huichol Indian Identity and Adaptation, 1985, Carlos Castaneda, Academic Opportunism and the Psychedelic Sixties, 1993, Reuben Snake, Your Humble Serpent, 1996, Huichol Indian Ceremonial Cycle, 1997; contbr. articles on edn. and anthropology to profl. jours. Coordinator Fiestas Patrias, Carlsbad Bicentennial Com., 1975. Acad. scholar dept. anthropology U. Mich., 1981-82; doctoral dissertation grantee Rackham Grad. Sch. U. Mich., 1981. Mem. Internat. Platform Assn., Am. Anthropol. Assn., N.Y. Acad. Scis. Mem. Religious Soc. of Friends. Lodge: Rotary (dir. internat. service 1982-83). Home: 2421 Buena Vista Cir Carlsbad CA 92008-1601

FILLBROOK, FREDERICK J., newspaper publisher; b. Detroit, Feb. 10, 1937; s. John M. and Marie E. (Pelto) F.; m. Marie T. DiBasio, Dec. 31, 1957 (div.); children: Susan, Michael, Steven; m. Deborah A. Ambrosino, July 7, 1978 (div.); children: Dennis, Tiffany; m. Sally J. Holler, Aug. 8, 1988; 1 child, Kathy. AA, Macomb Coll., 1978; BA, Oakland U., Mich., 1984, MA, 1987. Dir. mktg. M & B, Mich., 1970-73; dir. security Yankee/Arnolds, Mich., 1973-80; security supr. Kings Dept. Store, N.Y.C., 1980-83; CEO Fillbrook & Assoc., Edmonds, Wash., 1977-96; pub. Mill Creek View, 1991—. Chmn. Mill Creek Bd. Appeals, 1990—. Sgt. U.S. Army, 1955-59. Avocation: playing softball. Home: 1227 141st St SE Mill Creek WA 98012-1361 Office: Mill Creek View Ste F-313 16212 Bothell Everett Hwy Mill Creek WA 98012-1235

FILLEMAN, TERESA ELLEN, technical writer; b. Columbus, Ohio, Aug. 19, 1952; d. Marion Denver and Doris Audrey (Freeland) Grow; m. John Jay Filleman, June 4, 1977; children: John Wesley, Scott Ashley. AA in Geology, Glendale C.C., 1973; BS in Geology, No. Ariz. U., 1975, postgrad., 1975-77. Hydrologist Ariz. Dept. Water Resources, Phoenix, 1977-82, 84-85, computer cons., bd. dirs. Cross Roads Presch., Ltd., Phoenix, 1984-89; computer cons. Geraghty & Miller, Inc., Phoenix, 1987-88; tech. writer Digital Equipment Corp., Phoenix, 1989-92; documentation designer ASI Solution Integrators, Phoenix, 1994-95, pres., 1994—; client svcs. rep., Web master Ref. Pathology Svcs., 1997-98; tech. writer, cons. Mt. Shadows Elem. Sch., Glendale, 1987-91, Desert Sage Elem. Sch., 1991-94. Co-author: A Study of Global Sand Seas, 1979, also various sci. studies and publs.; performer mus. CD and taps Wings Like Eagles, 1994; newsletter editor Mt. Shadows and Desert Sage Elem. Schs., 1987-94; prodr., performer on cassette tape Jammin' for Jesus, 1997, Drummin' to Beat Hell, 1998; featured in video Leading in the Spirit. Edn. coord. Dove of the Desert United Meth. Ch., Glendale, Ariz., 1990-94, dir. steel band, 1991—; parent rep. Deer Valley Unified Sch. Dist., Phoenix, 1993. Recipient Giant Slayer award Dove of the Desert United Meth. Ch., 1991, 93, Chmn.'s award City of Phoenix Electric Light Parade, 1993, Judges award for Best Theme Entry, City of Phoenix Electric Light Parade, 1994. Mem. Percussive Arts Soc., Phi Theta Kappa. Republican. Avocations: steel drums, piano, nutrition, walking, volleyball.

FILLEY, CHRISTOPHER MARK, neurologist; b. Saranac Lake, N.Y., July 31, 1951; s. Giles Franklin and Mary Brown (Klinefelter) F. BA, Williams Coll., 1973; MD, Johns Hopkins U., 1979. Diplomate Am. Bd. Psychiatry and Neurology. Intern U. Conn., Farmington, 1979-80; resident in neurology U. Colo., Denver, 1980-83; behavioral neurology fellow Boston U., 1983-84; from instr. to asst. prof. neurology U. Colo. Sch. Medicine, Denver, 1984-91, assoc. prof. neurology, 1991-97, prof. neurology, 1997—; prin. investigator studies in Alzheimers Disease NIH, Bethesda, Md., 1991-94. Author: Neurobehavioral Anatomy, 1995, Best Doctors in America, 1996-97, 1998-99; contbr. articles to profl. jours. Health com. Denver Found., 1995-98. Mem. Am. Acad. Neurology, Am. Neurol. Assn., Internat. Neuropsychol. Soc., Behavioral Neurology Soc., Colo. Soc. Clin. Neurologists. Avocations: piano, hiking, reading, guitar, skiing. Office: Univ Colo Behavioral Neurology Sect 4200 E 9th Ave Denver CO 80220-3700

FILLMORE, JOHN DILLON, fine artist; b. Canoga Park, Calif., Nov. 24, 1951; s. Herbert Peter and Patricia Louise (Dillon) F. BFA, Art Ctr. Coll. Design, Hollywood, Calif., 1973. Fine artist, designer Chris O'Connell Inc./Ancient Echoes/Martex, Santa Fe, N.Mex., 1989-95; freelance fine artist Santa Fe, Tarzana, 1974—. Recipient Hubbard Art award for excellence, 1991. Republican. Roman Catholic. Avocations: art history, collecting art and books.

FILNER, ROBERT, congressman; b. Pitts., Sept. 4, 1942; m. Jane Merrill; children: Erin, Adam. BA in Chemistry, Cornell U., 1963; MA in History, U. Del., 1969; PhD in History, Cornell U., 1973. Prof. history San Diego State U., 1970-92; legis. asst. Senator Hubert Humphrey, 1974, Congressman Don Fraser, 1975; spl. asst. Congressman Jim Bates, 1984; city councilman 8th dist. City of San Diego, 1987-92, dep. mayor, 1992; mem. 103rd Congress (now 106th Congress) from 50th Calif. dist., 1993—. Pres. San Diego Bd. Edn., 1982, mem.-elect 1979-83; chmn. San Diego Schs. of the Future Commn., 1986-87. Democrat. Office: US Ho of Reps 330 Cannon HOB Washington DC 20515-0550*

FILOSA, GARY FAIRMONT RANDOLPH V., II, multimedia executive, financier, writer; b. Wilder, Vt., Feb. 22, 1931; s. Gary F.R. de Marco de Viana and Rosaline M. (Falzarano) Filosa; m. Catherine Moray Stewart (dec.); children: Marc Christian Bazire de Villadon III, Gary Fairmont Randolph de Viana III. Grad., Mt. Hermon Sch., 1950; PhB, U. Chgo., 1954; BA, U. Americas, Mex., 1967; MA, Calif. Western U., 1968; PhD, U.S. Internat. U., 1970. Sports reporter Claremont Daily Eagle, Rutland Herald, Vt. Informer, 1947-52; pub. The Chicagoan, 1952-54; account exec., editor house publs. Robertson, Buckley & Gotsch, Inc., Chgo., 1953-54; account exec. Fuller, Smith & Ross, Inc., N.Y.C., 1955; prodr./host Weekend KCET Channel 13, N.Y.C., 1955-67; editor Apparel Arts mag. (now Gentlemen's Quar.), Esquire, Inc., N.Y.C., 1955-56; pub. Teenage, Rustic Rhythm, Teen Life, Mystery Digest, Top Talent, Rock & Roll Roundup, Celebrities, Stardust, Personalities, Campus monthly mags., N.Y.C., 1955-61; pres., chmn. bd. Filosa Publs. Internat., N.Y.C., 1956-61, L.A., 1974-83, Palm Beach, Fla., 1983-88; pres., chmn. bd. Teenarama Records, Inc., N.Y.C., 1956-62; chmn. bd., pres. Produciones Mexicanes Internationales (S.A.), Mexico City, 1957-68; assoc. pub. Laundromatic Age, N.Y.C., 1958-59; ptnr. of Warner LeRoy purchase of Broadway plays for Hollywood films, N.Y.C., 1958-61; pres. Montclair Sch., 1958-60, Pacific Registry, Inc., L.A., 1959-61; exec. prodr. Desilu Studios, Inc., Hollywood, Calif., 1959-61; exec. asst. to Benjamin A. Javits, 1961-62; proprietor Ginola of Hollywood, 1961-70; dean adminstrn. Postgrad. Ctr. for Mental Health, N.Y.C., 1962-64; chmn. bd., CEO Filosa Films Internat., Beverly Hills, Calif., 1962—; chmn. bd., pres. Filosa Films Internat., Honolulu, 1996-98; pres. Amateur Athletes Internat., Iowa City, Iowa, 1996—, Banana Chip Corp. Am., N.Y.C., 1964-67; chmn. bd., pres. Cinematografica Americana Internationale (S.A.), Mexico City, 1964-74; pres. Casa Filosa Corp., Palm Beach, Fla., 1982-87; dir. Community Savings, North Palm Beach, Fla., 1982-87; v.p. acad. affairs World Acad., San Francisco, 1967-68; asst. to provost Calif. Western U., San Diego, 1968-69; assoc. prof. philosophy Art Coll., San Francisoc, 1969-70; v.p. acad. affairs, dean of faculty Internat. Inst., Phoenix, 1968-73; chmn. bd. dirs., pres. Universite Universelle, 1970-73; bd. dirs., v.p. acad. affairs, dean Summer Sch., Internat. C.C., L.A., 1970-72; chmn. bd., pres. Social Directory Calif., 1967-75, Am. Assn. Social Registries, L.A., 1970-76; pres. Social Directory U.S., N.Y.C., 1974-76; pres. Herbert Hoover Forum, Iowa City, 1996—; chmn. bd. dirs. Internat. Soc. Social Registers, Paris, 1974—; surfing coach U. Calif. at Irvine, 1975-77; instr. history Coastline C.C., Fountain Valley, Calif., 1976-77; v.p. Xerox-Systemic, 1979-80; CEO Internat. Surfing League, Palm Beach, 1987-95; pres., CEO Filosa Harrop Internat., Phoenix, 1987-89; pres. Amateur Athletes Internat., Iowa City, 1996—; nationally syndicated columnist Conservations with Am., 1997—. Editor: Sci. Digest, 1961-62; composer: (lyrics) The Night Discovers Love, 1952, That Certain Something, 1953, Bolero of Love, 1956; author: (stage play) Let Me Call Ethel, 1955, The Bisexual, 1961, Technology Enters 21st Century, 1966, (mus.) Feather Light, 1966, No Public Funds for Nonpublic Schools, 1968, Creative Function of the College President, 1969, The Surfers Almanac, 1977, The Filosa Newsletter, 1986-92, The Sexual Continuum, 1990, Traveltalk, 1991, God's Own Prince, 1995, Holy Hawaii, 1996, (biography) A Plague on Paradise, 1994, (TV series) Danny Thomas Show, 1963, Surfing USA, 1977, Payne of Florida, 1985, Honolulu, 1991, The Gym, 1992, Sales Pitch, 1992, 810 Ocean Avenue, 1992, One Feather, 1992, Conversations with America, 1989, All American Beach Party, 1989; contbr. numerous articles, editorials, to profl. jours., newspapers, and encys., including Life, Look, Sci. Digest, Ency. of Sports, World Book Ency., New York Times, Cedar Rapids Gazete, L.A. Times, others. Trustee Univ. of the Ams., Pueblo, Mex., 1986—; candidate for L.A. City Coun., 1959; chmn. Educators for Re-election of Ivy Baker Pirest, 1970; mem. So. Calif. Com. for Olympic Games, 1077-84. With AUS, 1954-55. Recipient DAR Citizenship awrd, 1959, Silver Conquistador award Am. Assn. Social Registers, 1970, Ambassador's Cup U. Ams., 1967, resolution Calif. State Legis., 1977, Duke Kahanamoku Classic surfing trophy, 1977, gold pendant Japan Surfing Assn., 1978, Father of Olympic Surfing award Internat. Athletic Union, 1995, Father of Surfing trophy Amateur Athletes Internat., 1997; inducted into Rock & Roll Mus. & Hall of Fame, Cleve., 1995. Mem. NAACP, NCAA (bd. dels. 1977-82), AAU (gov. 1978-82), Am. Acad. Motion Picture Arts and Scis., Am. Surfing Assn. (founder, pres. 1960-92), Internat. Surfing Com. (refounder, pres. 1960-95, 96-98), U.S. Surfing Com. (founder, pres. 1960-98), Internat. Surfing League (founder, pres. 1988—), Internat. Surfing Fedn. (pres. 1998—), Am. Walking Soc. (founder, pres. 1980-92), Internat. Walking Soc. (founder, pres. 1987-93), Am. Assn. UN, Authors League, Authors Guild, Alumni Assn. U. Ams. (pres. 1967-70), Surf Club of the Palm Beaches (pres. 1983-94), Sierra Club, Surfing Hui of Hawaii, Internat. Soc. Bibliotherapists (Paris, pres. 1997—), The Corybantes (Berlin) (pres. 1998—), Commonwealth Club (San Francisco), Town Hall (L.A.), Calif. Club (L.A.), Sigma Omicron Lambda (founder, pres. 1965-92). Republican. Episcopalian. Home: PO Box 299 Beverly Hills CA 90213-0299

FILS, ELLIOTT, advertising executive. CEO Rodgers & Assocs., L.A. Office: Rodgers & Assocs 1875 Century Park E Ste 300 Los Angeles CA 90067-2504*

FILSON, JAY GORDON, art educator; b. Scott City, Kans., Nov. 22, 1939; s. George Washington and Audrey Mae (Beers) F.; m. Norma Jean Vidalovich, May 28, 1960 (div. Sept. 1989); children: Allen, Stormy, Eric. BA, U. No. Colo., 1963, MA, 1967. Instr. art Rubodoux H.S., Riverside, Calif., 1963-66, Mid. Park Jr./Sr. H.S., Granby, Colo., 1967-68, Alamesa Sr. H.S., Lakewood, Colo., 1968-96; retired, 1996. Republican. Home: 1083 S Beech Dr Lakewood CO 80228-3418

FINBERG, JAMES MICHAEL, lawyer; b. Balt., Sept. 6, 1958; s. Laurence and Harriet (Levinson) F.; m. Marian D. Keeler, June 28, 1986. BA, Brown U., 1980; JD, U. Chgo., 1983. Bar: Calif. 1984, U.S. Dist. Ct. (no. dist.) Calif. 1984, U.S. Dist. Ct. (ea. dist.) Calif. 1987, U.S. Ct. Appeals (9th and fed. cirs.) 1987, U.S. Dist. Ct. Hawaii, 1988, U.S. Supreme Ct. 1994. Law clk. to assoc. justice Mich. Supreme Ct., 1983-84; assoc. Feldman, Waldman and Kline, San Francisco, 1984-87, Morrison and Foerster, 1987-90; ptnr. Lieff, Cabraser, Heimann & Bernstein, L.L.P., San Francisco, 1991—; adv. com. local rules for securities cases U.S. Dist. Ct., Calif., 1996; lawyer rep. to 9th Cir. Jud. Conf., 1998—; lawyer rep. 9th Cir. Jud. Conf., 1999—. Exec. editor U. Chgo. Law Rev., 1982-83. Mem. ABA (chmn. securities subcom. class and derivative action com. 1998—), ACLU (bd. dirs. No. Calif. chpt. 1995), Bar Assn. San Francisco (bd. dirs. 1999—, jud. evaluation com. 1994, bd. dirs. 1998—), Calif. Bar Assn. (mem. standing com. on legal svcs. to poor 1990-94, vice-chmn. 1993-94), Lawyers Com. for Civil Rights of San Francisco Bay Area (bd. dirs. 1992-98, fin. chmn. 1992-95, sec. 1996, co-chmn. 1997-98). Office: Lieff Cabraser Heimann & Bernstein LL 275 Battery St Fl 30 San Francisco CA 94111-3305

FINCH, THOMAS WESLEY, corrosion engineer; b. Alhambra, Calif., Dec. 17, 1946; s. Charles Phillip and Marian Louisa (Bushey) F.; m. Jinx L. Heath, Apr. 1979. Student Colo. Sch. Mines, 1964-68. Assayer, prospector Raymond P. Heon, Inc., Idaho Springs, Colo., 1968; corrosion engr. Cathodic Protection Service, Denver, 1973-80, area mgr., Lafayette, La., 1980-81; area mgr. Corrintec/USA, Farmington, N.Mex., 1981-83; dist. mgr. Cathodic Protection Services Co., Farmington, 1983-98 . Served with C.E., U.S. Army, 1968-72. Mem. Nat. Assn. Corrosion Engrs., Soc. Am. Mil. Engrs., U.S. Ski Assn., Am. Security Council (nat. adv. bd. 1978—), Kappa Sigma. Republican. Lutheran. Home and Office: 2404 Municipal Dr Farmington NM 87401-3942

FINE, AUBREY HOWARD, educator; b. Montreal, Que., Can., May 15, 1955; s. Morris and Fanny Betty (Shuster) F.; m. Nya Marie Daniels, Aug. 27, 1978; children: Sean David, Corey Ryan. BA, Concordia U., Montreal, 1977; MEd, U. South Ala., 1978; EdD, U. Cin., 1982. lic. psychologist, Calif.; cert. sch. psychologist. Project dir., cons. Que. Assn. for Children with Learning Disabilities, Laval, Que., Can., 1974-77; dir. learning disability and aging program Mobile (Ala.) Jewish Ctr., 1977-78; dir. normalization project Cin. Ctr. for Developmental Disabilities, 1980-82; psychologist Our Lady of Lourdes, Cin., 1981-82; lic. psychologist/dir. Children's Diagnostic Svcs., Claremont, Calif., 1986—; prof. Calif. State Poly. U., Pomona, 1982—; cons. psychologist Charter Oak Schs., Covina, Calif., 1989-93. Author: Total Sports Experience for Kids, 1997, Therapeutic Recreation and Exceptional Children, 1996, Behavior Management and Parenting Children, 1989; assoc. cons. editor Jour. Developmental Disabilities, 1993—; cons. editor Mental Retardation, 1988—; editor Living and Learning with Attention Deficit Disorder, 1992—. Profl. advisor San Gabriel Valley Assn. for Children with Attention Deficit Disorder, 1992-97, Pomona Valley Learning Disability Assn., 1985—; bd. dirs. Temple Sholom, Ontario, 1988-92, San Gabriel Valley Regional Ctr. for Developmental Disabilities, Covina, 1989-91. Named Educator of the Yr., Learning Disability Assn. of Calif., 1989. Fellow Am. Assn. Mental Retardation (pres. region II 1992-94, Outstanding Leadership award 1994), Prescribing Psychologist Register (diplomate, bd. cert.); mem. APA, Acad. on Mental Retardation (mem.-at-large of bd. 1988-97). Avocations: racquetball, playing saxaphone, hockey, sports collecting. Office: Calif State Poly Univ 3801 W Temple Ave Pomona CA 91768-2557

FINE, J. DAVID, lawyer; b. N.Y.C., Jan. 30, 1951; s. Phillip and Irma (Miller) F.; m. Judith Lynn McMillan, June 6, 1984. BSFS, Georgetown U., 1970; LLB, McGill U., Montreal, Que., 1973, BCL, 1974; LLM, Columbia U., 1978. Bar: We. Australia, 1987, High Ct. Australia, 1987, Oreg., 1992, U.S. Dist. Ct. Oreg., 1994. Asst. prof. U. Melbourne, Australia, 1974-76; clin. instr. Osgoode Hall Law Sch., Toronto, Ont., Can., 1976-77; Jervey fellow comp. law Columbia U., N.Y.C., 1977-79; assoc. prof. Loyola U., New Orleans, 1979-84, Macquarie U., Sydney, Australia, 1984-86; prof. U. Western Australia, Perth, 1986-91; pvt. practice Ashland, Oreg., 1992—; traffic safety commr., City of Ashland, 1997—. contbr. articles to profl. jours. City councilman City of Ashland, 1999—. Mem. Internat. Trademark Assn., So. Oreg. Internat. Trade Coun. (charter mem.), Oreg. State Bar Assn. (continuing legal edn. com. 1995-98), Jackson County Bar Assn. (sec. 1999), Ashland Gun Club. Jewish. Avocations: reading, shooting, cooking, fly fishing. Home: 735 Frances Lane Ashland OR 97520-0166 Office: 50 3rd St PO Box 66 Ashland OR 97520-0166

FINESILVER, JAY MARK, lawyer; b. Denver, June 10, 1955; s. Sherman G. and Annette (Warren) F.; m. Debra K. Wilcox, Apr. 6, 1979 (div.); children: Justin, Lauren. BA, Washington U., St. Louis, 1977; JD, U. Denver, 1980. Bar: Colo. 1981, U.S. Dist. Ct. Colo. 1980, U.S. Ct. Appeals (7th and 10th cirs.) 1981. Law clk. to judge U.S. Ct. Appeals (7th cir.), Chgo., 1980-81; assoc. Rothgerber, Appel & Powers, Denver, 1981-85, Elrod, Katz, Preeo & Look, Denver, 1985-86; pvt. practice Denver, 1986-90; v.p. corp. affairs Daniels Communications Inc., Denver, 1990—; instr. Denver Paralegal Inst., 1987-88. Author: Colorado Foreclosure and Bankruptcy, 1988; contbr. articles to profl. jours. Pres. Denver Citizenship Day Com., 1983-86, Mayfair Neighbors, Inc., Denver, 1984-87. Named Outstanding Neighbor Mayfair Neighbors Inc., 1988. Mem. ABA, Washington U. Alumni Assn. (Colo. chmn. 1982-87). Avocations: fishing, skiing, photography, creative writing, Southwestern art. Office: Ste 460 3200 Chevy Creek South Dr Denver CO 80209

FINESILVER, SHERMAN GLENN, retired federal judge; b. Denver, Oct. 1, 1927; s. Harry M. and Rebecca M. (Balaban) F.; m. Annette Warren, July 23, 1954; children: Jay Mark, Steven Brad, Susan Saunders. BA, U. Colo., 1949; LLB, U. Denver, 1952; cert., Northwestern U. Traffic Inst., 1956; LLD (hon.), Gallaudet Coll., Washington, 1970, Met. State Coll., Denver, 1981, N.Y. Law Sch., N.Y.C., 1983, U. Colo., 1988. Bar: Colo. 1952, U.S. Ct. of Appeals (10th cir.) 1952, U.S. Supreme Ct. 1952. Legal asst. Denver City Atty.'s Office, 1949-52; asst. Denver city atty., 1952-55; judge Denver County Ct., 1955-62; judge Denver Dist. Ct., 2d Jud. Dist., 1962-71, presiding judge domestic relations div., 1963, 67, 68; judge U.S. Dist. Ct., Denver, from 1971, elevated to chief judge, 1982-94; ret., 1995—; spl. counsel Popham Haik Schnobrich & Kaufman, Attys. at Law, Denver, 1995—; adj. prof. U. Denver Coll. Law and Arts and Sci. Sch., 1955—, Met. State Coll., 1989—; mem. faculty Nat. Coll. Judiciary, Reno, 1967-84, Atty. Gen.'s Advocacy Inst., Washington, 1974—, seminars for new fed. judges, 1974—; elected to Jud. Conf. U.S., 1985-88; mem. Jud. Conf. Com. on Rules for Admission to Practice in Fed. Cts., 1976-79, Com. on Adminstrn. Probation System, 1983-87, Adv. Com. on Criminal Rules, 1984-87, Com. on Bicentennial of Constn., 1985-87, Com. on Criminal Law and Probation Adminstrn., 1988—. Contbr. chpt. to Epilepsy Rehabilitation, 1974; contbr. articles and publs. on law, medicine, legal rights of deaf, aging, physically impaired and many others, 1974-94. Mem. task force White House Conf. on Aging, 1972, presdl. commn., 1980-84; mem. Probation Com., U.S. Cts., 1985-88, Nat. Com. to Study Qualifications to Practice in Fed. Cts., 1976-82, bd. visitors Brigham Young U., 1977-80, Nat. Commn. Against Drunk Driving, 1982-86. Decorated Inspector Gen. 33d degree; recipient numerous awards including medallion for outstanding service by a non-handicapped person to physically disabled Nat. Paraplegia Found., 1972, cert. of commendation Sec. Transp., 1974, Norlin award for outstanding alumni U. Colo., 1988, numerous others. Fellow Am. Coll. Legal Medicine (Chgo., hon. fellow); mem. ABA (nat. chmn. Am. citizenship com. 1968, award of merit Law Day 1968), Colo. Bar Assn. (chmn. Law Day 1964, chmn. Am. citizenship com. 1963, bd. govs. 1982-94), Denver Bar Assn. (chmn. Law Day 1964), Am. Judicature Soc., Am. Amateur Radio, B'nai B'rith, Masons, Shriners, Phi Sigma Delta (trustee 1960-66, Nat. Man of Yr. Zeta Beta Tau chpt. 1989). *

FINIE, PETER HENRY, property tax manager; b. Avalon, Calif., Jan. 5, 1948; s. Philip Adam and Anita Mary Finie; m. Christina Conaway, Apr. 7, 1975 (div. Apr. 1993); m. Patricia Lynn Brown, May 17, 1997; 1 child, Patrick. B of Bus. Adminstrn., Loyola U., L.A., 1969; MBA, M of Pub. Adminstrn., U. San Francisco, 1981. Cert. marine surveyor Nat. Assn. Marine Surveyors; sys. credential UCLA; advanced appraisal cert. Calif. State Bd. Equalization. Adminstrv. asst., budget analyst L.A. County Assessor, 1969-70, asst. dir. pers., 1970-71, marine appraiser, 1971-76; sr. appraiser Ventura County Assessor, Ventura, Calif., 1976-89; tax issues mgr. Western States Petroleum Assn., Glendale, Calif., 1989-93; property tax mgr. Calmat County, L.A., 1993—; bd. dirs. Caltax, Sacramento. Mem. exec. com. Ventura coun. Boy Scouts Am., 1984-88. Mem. Inst. Property Taxation (chair steering com. 1997—), Calif. Mining Assn. (chair tax com. 1997—), Rotary Internat. (pres. 1983, 91, dist. chair 1985, interact chair 1979-92, Paul Harris fellow 1984), Delta Sigma Pi (pres. 1968-69, Alumni of Yr. 1983, 85). Republican. Roman Catholic. Avocations: antique car restoration, music, reading, wine/vineculture, antique glass collecting. E-mail: finiep@calmat.com. Home: PO Box 1686 Camarillo CA 93011-1686 Office: Calmat Co 3200 N San Fernando Rd Los Angeles CA 90065-1415

FINK, JAMES BREWSTER, geophysicist, consultant; b. Los Angeles, Jan. 12, 1943; s. Odra J. and Gertrude (Sloot) F.; m. Georgeanne Emmerich, Aug. 24, 1970; 1 child, Jody Lynn. BS in Geophysics and Geochemistry, U. Ariz., 1969; MS in Geophysics cum laude, U. Witwatersrand, Johannesburg, Transvaal, Republic of South Africa, 1980; PhD in Geol. Engring., Geohydrology, U. Ariz, 1989. Registered profl. engr., Ariz., N.Mex.; registered land surveyor, Ariz.; registered profl. geologist, Wyo.; cert. environ. inspector. Geophysicist Geo-Comp Exploration, Inc., Tucson, 1969-70; geophys. cons. IFEX-Geotechnica, S.A., Hermosillo, Sonora, Mex., 1970; chief geophysicist Mining Geophys. Surveys, Tucson, 1971-72; research asst. U. Ariz., Tucson, 1973; cons. geophysics Tucson, 1974-76; sr. minerals geophysicist Esso Minerals Africa, Inc., Johannesburg, 1976-79; sr. research geophysicist Exxon Prodn. Research Co., Houston, 1979-80; pres. Geophynque Internat., Tucson, 1980-90, hydroGeophysics, Inc., Tucson, 1990—; cons. on NSF research U. Ariz., 1984-85, adj. lectr. geol. engring., 1985-86, assoc. instr. geophysics, 1986-87, supr. geophysicist, geohydrologist, 1986-88, bd. dirs. Lab. Advanced Subsurface Imaging, 1986—; v.p. R&D Alternative Energy Engring., Inc., Tucson, 1992—, also bd. dirs.; v.p. Reclamation Svcs., Inc., 1995—, also bd. dirs.; v.p. Catalina Marble Inc., 1996—; lectr. South African Atomic Energy Bd., Pelindaba, 1979; cons. Argonne Nat. Lab., 1992-93, Los Alamos Nat. Lab., 1987—; v.p. Rincon Stock Yard, 1997—. Contbr. articles to profl. jours. Served as sgt. U.S. Air NG, 1965-70. Named Airman of Yr., U.S. Air NG, 1967. Mem. Soc. Exploration Geophysicists (co-chair internat. meetings 1980, 81, 92, sr. editor monograph 1990, reviewer), Am. Geophys. Union (reviewer), European Assn. Exploration Geophysicists, Assn. Ground Water Scientists, Nat. Water Well Assn. (reviewer), Mineral and Geotech. Explorationists, Ariz. Geol. Soc., Ariz. Water Well Assn., Environ. and Engring. Geophys. Soc., Pres.'s Club U. Ariz. Republican. Avocations: reading, computers, natural sciences, genealogy. Home and Office: Hydrogeophysics Inc 5865 S Old Spanish Trl Tucson AZ 85747-9487

FINK, KEVIN G., finance executive; b. Mankato, Minn., Feb. 25, 1959; s. John Andrew and Ruth Margaret (Budde) F.; m. Laura Susan Stufflebeam, Aug. 7, 1979; children: Heather Marie, Valerie Susan. BSBA, U. S.D., 1982; student, U. Denver, 1986. CPA, Colo., S.D. Staff acct. Deloitte, Haskins & Sells, Colorado Springs, Colo., 1982-84. sr. acct., 1984-86, mgr., 1986-87; chief fin. officer, treas. WCM Industries, Inc., Colorado Springs, Colo., 1987—, v.p. fin. Contbr. articles to mags. Mem. Citizen's Goals Leadership 2000, Colorado Springs, 1990-91; treas. Keep Colorado Springs Beautiful, 1991-93; bd. dirs. Pikes Peak Mental Health Systems, 1991-96, Western Mus. Mining and Industry, 1995—, Pikes Peak Coun. Boys Scouts Am., v.p. adminstrn., 1996—; state affairs chair Colorado Springs C. of C., bd. dirs. 1987-91. Mem. AICPA, Colo. Soc. CPAs, Gleneagle Country Club. Avocations: hunting, fishing, camping. Office: WCM Industries Inc 2121 Waynoka Rd Colorado Springs CO 80915-1602

FINK, MARK ELLIOTT, union representative; b. L.A., Aug. 19, 1947; s. Sol and Evelyn (Kraus) F.; m. Therese M. Illing, Aug. 31, 1947. Diploma in Labor Studies (hon.), L.A. Trade/Tech. Sch. Cert. Am. Arbitration.

Lithographer L.A. County Govt., 1968-87; bd. dirs. Local 660 SEIU, L.A., 1978-86, treas., 1981-82, 86, union rep., 1987—. Active 20-30 Assn., L.A., bd. dirs., 1980-83. Democrat. Jewish. Avocations: hot rods, auto racing, motor home. Home: 13025 Glasgow Pl Hawthorne CA 90250-4951

FINK, ROBERT RUSSELL, music theorist, former university dean; b. Belding, Mich., Jan. 31, 1933; s. Russell Foster and Frances (Thornton) F.; m. Ruth Joan Bauerle, June 19, 1955; children: Denise Lyn, Daniel Robert. B.Mus., Mich. State U., 1955, M.Mus., 1956, Ph.D., 1965. Instr. music SUNY, Fredonia, 1956-57; instr. Western Mich. U., Kalamazoo, 1957-62, asst. prof., 1962-66, assoc. prof., 1966-71, prof., 1971-78, chmn. dept. music, 1972-78; dean Coll. Music U. Colo., Boulder, 1978-93; retired, 1994; prin. horn Kalamazoo Symphony Orch., 1957-67; accreditation examiner Nat. Assn. Schs. Music, Reston, Va., 1973-92, grad. commr., 1981-89, chmn. grad. commn., 1987-89, assoc. chmn. accreditation commn., 1990-91, chmn., 1992. Author: Directory of Michigan Composers, 1972, The Language of 20th Century Music, 1975; composer: Modal Suite, 1959, Four Modes for Winds, 1967, Songs for High School Chorus, 1967; contbr. articles to profl. jours. Bd. dirs. Kalamazoo Symphony Orch., 1974-78, Boulder Bach Festival, 1983-90. Mem. Coll. Music Soc., Soc. Music Theory, Mich. Orch. Assn. (pres.), Phi Mu Alpha Sinfonia (province gov.), Pi Kappa Lambda. Home: 643 Furman Way Boulder CO 80303-5614

FINKELSTEIN, JAMES ARTHUR, management consultant; b. N.Y.C., Dec. 6, 1952; s. Harold Nathan and Lilyan (Crystal) F.; m. Lynn Marie Gould, Mar. 24, 1984; children: Matthew, Brett. BA, Trinity Coll., Hartford, Conn., 1974; MBA, U. Pa., 1976. Cons. Towers, Perrin, Forster & Crosby, Boston, 1976-78; mgr. compensation Pepsi-Cola Co., Purchase, N.Y., 1978-80; mgr. employee info. systems Am. Can. Co., Greenwich, Conn., 1980; mgr. bus. analysis Emery Airfreight, Wilton, Conn., 1980-81; v.p. Meidinger, Inc., Balt., 1981-83; prin. The Wyatt Co., San Diego, 1983-88; pres., chief exec. officer W. F. Corroon, San Francisco, 1988-95; chmn., CEO FutureSense, Inc., Larkspur, Calif., 1995—; founder TallyUp Software, 1996—; dir. En Wisen, Inc., 1996-98; ptnr. Arthur Andersen LLP, San Francisco, 1997—; mem. regional adv. bd. Mchts. and Mfrs. Assn., San Diego, 1986-88; instr. U. Calif., San Diego, 1984-88. Mem. camp com. State YMCA of Mass. and R.I., Framingham, 1982-86; pres. Torrey Pines Child Care Consortium, La Jolla, Calif., 1987-88; vice chmn. La Jolla YMCA, 1986-88; chmn. fin. com. YMCA, San Francisco, 1992-95, vice chmn., 1993-95, chmn., 1995—; bd. dirs. San Domenico Sch., 1994—; bd. trustees World Affairs Coun., 1998—. Avocations: music, sports, camping. Home: 17 Bracken Ct San Rafael CA 94901-1587 Office: Arthur Andersen LLP One Market Spear St Tower San Francisco CA 94105

FINLAY, ALICE SULLIVAN, writer, educator; b. Phila., Sept. 10, 1946; d. James Neely Johnston and Alice Agnes (McLaughlin) Sullivan; m. Richard Allen Finlay, Nov. 26, 1976. BA in English, Gwynedd (Pa.) Mercy Coll., 1968; MA, N.Y.U., 1974; postgrad. studies, U. Kans., 1975-76. Asst. The Literary Guild, N.Y.C., 1969-70; asst. to children's book editor E.P. Dutton, N.Y.C., 1970-72; asst. to dir., asst. tchr. Fifteenth St. Sch., N.Y.C., 1972-74; writing tchr. U. N. Mex. dept continuing edn., Albuquerque, N. Mex., 1986-93; spkr., tchr. in grammar and high schs.; guest on radio, TV shows and appearances in book stores. Author: four children's books: Laura Lee and the Monster Sea, A Victory for Laura Lee, Laura Lee and the Little Pine Tree, A Gift from the Sea for Laura Lee, all published, 1993;; contbr. short stories to The Friend, Clubhouse, Discoveries, Grit, Mature Living, True Story and True Experience, poetry and stories to anthologies; photographer: exhibited at shows in N. Mex. including N. Mex. State Fair (2d. place 1995), Albuquerque Animal Humane Soc., (2d. 1997), Kirtland AFB Photography Contest 1st, 2d and 3d places, 2d place in Air Force AMF Divsn., Finalist in Photographer's Forum Mag. Spring Contest, 1997; published in Best of Photography annual, 1997. Mem. Am. Legion Aux., Nat. League Am. Pen Women (pres. Albuquerque, 1992-94, 1st and 2d place in N. Mex. state photography shows), Soc. Children's Book Writers and Illustrators, Mystery Writers Am. Avocations: travel, camping, nature, gardening, stained glass. Home: 9215 Mickelsen Ave SE Albuquerque NM 87123-3132

FINLAY, AUDREY JOY, environmental educator, consultant, naturalist; b. Davidson, Sask., Can., Sept. 18, 1932; d. Leonard Noel and Vilhemine Marie (Rossander) Barton; m. James Campbell Finlay, June 18, 1955; children: Barton Brett, Warren Hugh, Rhonda Marie. BA, U. Man., Can., 1954; profl. diploma in edn., U. Alta., 1974, MEd, 1978. Social worker Children's Aid, Brandon, Man., 1954-55; foster home worker Social Services Province of Sask., Regina, 1955-56, City of Edmonton, Alta., 1956-59; naturalist City of Edmonton, 1965-74; tchr., cons., adminstr. Edmonton Pub. Bd., 1974-88; cons. edn., interpretation numerous projects, 1965—. Author: Winter Here and Now, 1982; co-author: Parks in Alberta, 1987, Ocean to Alpine, A British Columbia Nature Guide, 1992; contbr. nature articles to profl. jours. Chmn., chief exec. officer Wildlife '87: Canadian Centennial Wildlife Conservation, 1985-87. Named Ms. Chatelaine, Chatelaine mag., 1975; recipient Order of Bighorn award Alta Gov., Ralph D. Bird award, 1987, Can. Park Svc. Heritage award Environ. Can., 1990, Order of Can. award, 1990, Reeve's award of Distinction County of Strath, 1991, Douglas Pimlot award Can. Nat. Fedn., 1991. Fellow Alta. Tchrs. Assn. , Environ. Outdoor Coun. (founder, 1st pres., disting. mem.); mem. Canadian Nature Fedn. (v.p. 1984-90), Edmonton Natural History Soc. (Loran Goulden award 1980), Am. Nature Study Soc. (bd. dirs. 1984-91, pres. 1991-94), N.Am. Environ. Edn. Assn. (bd. dirs. 1983-89), Fedn. Alta Naturalists (bd. dirs. 1970s). Home and Office: 270 Trevlac Pl, Victoria, BC Canada V8X 3X1

FINLAY, JAMES CAMPBELL, retired museum director; b. Russell, Man., Can., June 12, 1931; s. William Hugh and Grace Muriel F.; m. Audrey Joy Barton, June 18, 1955; children: Barton Brett, Warren Hugh, Rhonda Marie. BSc, Brandon U., 1952; MSc in Zoology, U. Alta., 1968. Geophysicist Frontier Geophys. Ltd., Alta., 1952-53; geologist, then dist. geologist Shell Can., Ltd., 1954-64; chief park naturalist and biologist Elk Island (Can.) Nat. Park, 1965-67; dir. hist. devel. and archives, dir. hist. and sci. service, dir. Nature Center, dir. interpretation and recreation City of Edmonton, Alta., 1967-92; founder Fedn. Alta. Naturalists, 1969. Author: A Nature Guide to Alberta, Bird Finding Guide to Canada; (with Joy Finlay) Ocean to Alpine-A British Columbia Nature Guide, A Guide to Alberta Parks. Recipient Order of the Bighorn, Govt. of Atla., 1987, Heritage award Environment Can., 1990, Loran Goulden award Fedn. Alta Naturalists, 1991, Can. 125th Anniversary award, 1993; named to Edmonton Hist. Hall of Fame, 1976. Mem. Can. Mus. Assn. (pres. 1976-78), Alta. Mus. Assn. (founding mem., past pres.), Am. Mus. Assn. (past council), Am. Ornithol. Union. Home: 270 Trevlac Pl, RR 3, Victoria, BC Canada V8X 3X1

FINLEY, SUSIE QUANSTROM, solar energy company executive; b. Kewanee, Ill., Mar. 3, 1950; d. Melvin Dale and Annamae (Kubelius) Quanstrom; m. Dana J. Finley, July 12, 1980; 1 child, Tiffany Nicole. BS in Edn., North Tex. State U., 1972; cert. in bus. and legal secretarial, Draughan's Bus. Coll., Albuquerque, 1973, pub. relations, N.Mex. Jr. Coll., Hobbs, 1985, English Lit., U. N.Mex., 1975. Owner, dealer Solar Age Industries, Hobbs, N.Mex., 1982—, v.p. advt. and pub. relations, Albuquerque, 1986—; lobbyist N.Mex. Solar Energy Inst., 1985-86. Mem. Nat. Assn. Female Execs., N.Mex. Solar Energy Inst. Republican. Avocations: camping, reading, travel, ante-bellum Southern history. Home: 13412 Circulo Largo NE Albuquerque NM 87112-3764

FINN, GERALD ROBERT, adult education educator; b. Wayne, Nebr., Oct. 31, 1944; s. John Hugh Finn and Frances Acyntha (Verzani) Kelley; m. Sharon Ann Friesen, Apr. 4, 1970 (div. 1980); m. Nairy Partamian, Aug. 28, 1983. AA, Pasadena City Coll., 1964; BA, Pasadena Coll., 1974; MA, Loyola Marymount U., 1980. Engr. Consol. Electrodynamics, Monrovia, Calif., 1965-68, Hoffman Electronics, El Monte, Calif., 1968-69; studio technician Pasadena (Calif.) City Coll., 1969-74, prof., 1974—; faculty adv. Soc. Motion Picture TV Engrs., Pasadena, 1981—. Recipient Eastman Kodak Gold Medal, Soc. Motion Picture TV Engrs., N.Y.C., 1987. Fellow Soc. Motion Picture TV Engrs. (mem. chmn. 1990-97, citation for outstanding svc. 1989), mem. (life) Brit. Kinematography Sound TV Soc. Avocations: chess, photography. Office: Pasadena City College 1570 E Colorado Blvd Pasadena CA 91106-2041

FINN, MARY RALPHE, artist; b. St. Paul, Nov. 13, 1933; d. Wendell W. and Rose Marie (Arendt) Ralphe; m. H. Roger Finn, June 15, 1957; children: Mark W., Shelly, Scott R. BS, U. Ark., 1955; MS, U. Iowa, 1957. Workshop demonstrator and cons. in field. Exhibited in solo shows at Art Mart Gallery, 1973, 76, Brown's Gallery, Boise, 1977, 80, 85, 89, 94, St. Lukes Regional Med. Ctr., Boise, 1982, Piper Jaffray Hopwood, Boise, 1979, 85, St. Alphonsus Med. Ctr., Boise, 1981, 90, Bank of Idaho, Boise, 1975, 79, Morrison Knudsen, Boise, 1978; group shows include Browns Galleries, 1975-98, St. Lukes Regional Med. Ctr., 1976-90, Idaho State Capitol, 1978, Idaho Watercolor Soc., 1987, St. Alphonsus Hosp., 1990, Albertson Coll. Idaho, 1988-98, Boise State U., 1991; represented in permanent collections Morrison-Knudsen Corp., West One Bancorp, 1st Security Bank Idaho, Inc., St. Lukes Regional Med. Ctr., 1st Interstate Bank, Am.-Hydro Corp. Mem. Boise Art Mus., Phi Upsilon Omicron, Zeta Tau Alpha, Omicron Nu.

FINN, ROBERT, mathematician, educator; b. Buffalo, Aug. 8, 1922. PhD, Syracuse U., 1951; PhD (hon.), U. Leipzig, Germany, 1994. Rsch. assoc. U. Md., College Park, 1953-54; asst. prof. U. So. Calif., L.A., 1954-56; assoc. prof. Calif. Inst. Tech., Pasadena, 1956-59; prof. Stanford (Calif.) U., 1959-92, prof. emeritus, 1992—; math. adv. panel Fulbright Commn., 1988-91; cons. European Space Agy., Germany, 1987, Univ. Sys., Fla., 1989-90, Kans., 1994; investigator NASA, Cleve., 1990—; vis. prof. Tech. Hochschule, Berlin, 1958, U. Paris, 1966, U. Sussex, 1969, U. Bonn, U. Heidelberg, 1971-86, Scuola Normale Superiore, Pisa, 1972, U. Genova, 1973, Nat. Taiwan U., 1981, Ohio State U., 1986, U. Leipzig, 1987, 93-98, Max-Planck Inst., Bonn, 1987, Leipzig, 1997-98, Acad. Sinica, Taipei, 1996; cons. in field. Editor Archive Rational Mechanics and Analysis, 1959-68, Pacific Jour. Math., Zeitschrift für Analysis und ihre Anwendungen, Jour. Math. Fluid Dynamics, Differentiial Equations and Math. Physics, Pacific Jour. Math., 1968—, Taiwan Jour. Math., 1999—; contbr. articles to profl. jours. Guggenheim Found. fellow, Germany, 1958-59, 87, France, 1965-66, Fulbright Found. fellow, Germany, 1987; Rsch. grantee NSF, NASA, 1959-98. Mem. Sächsische Acad. Wissenschaften.

FINNBERG, ELAINE AGNES, psychologist, editor; b. Bklyn., Mar. 2, 1948; d. Benjamin and Agnes Montgomery (Evans) F.; m. Rodney Lee Herndon, Mar. 1, 1981; 1 child, Andrew Marshal. BA in Psychology, L.I. U., 1969; MA in Psychology, New Sch. for Social Rsch., 1973; PhD in Psychology, Calif. Sch. Profl. Psychology, 1981. Diplomate Am. Bd. Forensic Examiners, Am. Bd. Forensic Medicine, Am. Bd. Med. Psychotherapists and Psychodiagnosticians, Am. Bd. Disability Analysts, Am. Bd. Psychol. Specialties, Prescribing Psychologists Register; lic. psychologist, Calif. Rsch. asst. in med. sociology Cornell U. Med. Coll., N.Y.C., 1969-70; med. abstractor USV Pharm. Corp., Tuckahoe, N.Y., 1970-71, Coun. for Tobacco Rsch., N.Y.C., 1971-77; editor, writer Found. of Thanatology Columbia U., N.Y.C., 1971-76, cons. family studies program cancer ctr. Coll. Physicians &Surgeons, 1973-74; dir. grief psychology and bereavement counseling San Francisco Coll. Mortuary Scis., 1977-81; rsch. assoc. dept. epidemiology and internat. health U. Calif., San Francisco, 1979-81, asst. clin. prof. dept. family and cmty. medicine, 1985-93, assoc. clin. prof., dept. family and cmty. medicine, 1993—; active med. staff Natividad Med. Ctr., Salinas, Calif., 1984—, chief psychologist, 1984-96; profl. adv. coun. Am. Bd. Disability Analysts; asst. chief psychiatry svc. Natividad Med. Ctr., 1985-96, acting chief psychiatry, 1988-89, vice-chair medicine dept., 1991-93, sec.-treas. med. staff, 1992-94; cons. med. staff Salinas Valley Meml. Hosp., 1991—, Mee Meml. Hosp., 1996-97; dir. tng. Monterey Psychiat. Health Facility, 1996-97, chief clin. staff, 1996-97; expert cons. Calif. Bd. Psychology. Editor: The California Psychologist, 1988-95; editor Jour. of Thanatology, 1972-76, Cathexis, 1976-81. Govs. adv. bd. Agnews Devel. Ctr., San Jose, Calif., 1988-96, chair, 1989-91, 94-95. Fellow Prescribing Psychologists Register (diplomate); mem. APA, Nat. Register Health Svc. Providers in Psychology, Calif. Psychol. Assn. (Disting. Svc. award 1989), Soc. Behavioral Medicine, Mid-Coast Psychol. Assn. (sec. 1985, treas. 1986, pres. 1987, Disting. Svc. to Psychology award 1993), Forensic Mental Health Assn. Calif., Western Psychol. Assn., Assn. Advancement Behavior Therapy, Am. Med. Writers Assn., Assn. Treatment Sexual Abuses, Soc. for Personality Assessment, Internat. Rorschach. Soc., Internat. Soc. Police Surgeons, Internat. Soc. of Police Surgeons.

FINNEY, LEE, negotiator, social worker; b. Balt., Feb. 25, 1943; d. E. William and Mildred Lee (Refo) Carr; m. James Nathaniel Finney, Feb. 25, 1967 (div. Aug. 1970); 1 child, Karen Elizabeth. Student, Sweet Briar Coll., 1961-63; BA in Govt., George Washington U., 1965; MS in Counseling, Calif. State U., Hayward, 1986. Caseworker N.Y.C. Welfare Dept., 1966-68; probation officer N.Y.C. Probation Dept., 1968-74; dep. probation officer Alameda County Probation Dept., Oakland, Calif., 1974-78, child welfare social worker, 1979-80; children's svcs. social worker Contra Costa County Dept. Social Svcs., Richmond, Calif., 1980-87; social work supr. Contra Costa County Dept. Social Svcs., Antioch, Calif., 1987-88; dir. staff devel. Contra Costa County Dept. Social Svcs., Martinez, Calif., 1989-90; pay equity analyst Contra Costa County Pers. Dept., Martinez, 1988-89; labor rels. cons. Indsl. Employers and Distributors Assn., Emeryville, Calif., 1990—; instr. edn. psychology dept. Calif. State U., Hayward, 1987-89; mem. exec. bd. Contra Costa Ctrl. Labor Coun., Martinez, 1987-89; no. v.p., chief negotiator Svc. Employees Internat. Union Local 535, Oakland, 1983-88; chair Coalition for Children and Families, Richmond, Calif., 1986-88. Author booklet: First Steps to Identifying Sex and Race Based Inequities in a workplace: A Guide to Achieving Pay Equity, 1989. Bd. dirs. YWCA, Contra Costa County, 1989-91; pres., acting dir. Comparable Worth Project, Inc., Oakland, 1984-87; mem. Adv. Com. on Employment and Econ. Status for Women Contra Costa, 1984-89, chair, 1987-89. Recipient Cmty. Svc. award Vocare Found., 1976, Golden Nike award Emeryville Bus. and Profl. Women, 1986, Woman of Yr. award Todos Santos Bus. and Profl. Women, 1989, Women Who Have Made a Difference award Coalition of Labor Union Women, 1989. Democrat. Avocations: sailing, travel, natural history. Home: 6 Commodore Dr # C336 Emeryville CA 94608-1649 Office: IDEA 2200 Powell St Ste 1000 Emeryville CA 94608-1869

FINNIE, C(LARENCE) HERBERT (HERB FINNIE), aerospace company executive; b. San Marcos, Tex., Feb. 22, 1930; s. Clarence Herbert and Robbie Mary (Hinkle) F.; B.S., S.W. Tex. State U., 1951; M.A., U. Calif.-Berkeley, 1955; M.B.A., U. Santa Clara, 1968; m. Bruna Rebecchi, June 28, 1955 (dec. Feb. 1997); children: Elisa Gene, John Herbert, Mary Lea, Ann Catherine. Bur. chief, disk jockey KCNY, 1950; with Lockheed Missiles & Space Co., Inc., Sunnyvale, Calif., 1958—, supr. computer programming, systems analyst, mgr. software design and devel., advanced systems staff engr. sr; free-lance writer, photographer; pres. Creative Imagineering, Sunnyvale, 1984—; cons. in field. Scriptwriter, announcer, narrator (submarine theater) Aquarena, San Marcos, Tex., 1950-51. Served to Capt. USAF, 1951-58. Mem. Assn. Computing Machinery, Nat. Mgmt. Assn., Pentagon Players (charter), Photog. Soc. Am., Air Force Assn., Assn. Old Crows, Marquis Club, Alpha Chi, Beta Gamma Sigma, Phi Mu Alpha Sinfonia. Roman Catholic. Designed and developed first generally used compiler prepared for a digital electronic computer (Univac I), computer game package and a universally used tng. system, 1952; original documentation and reference materials deeded to the Smithsonian Institution. Home: 1582 Lewiston Dr Sunnyvale CA 94087-4148 Office: 1111 Lockheed Way Sunnyvale CA 94089-1212

FINNIE, DORIS GOULD, investment company executive; b. Mpls., Sept. 2, 1919; d. Earl Chester and Marie Ethelee (McGulpin) Gould; m. Donald Johnstone Finnie, May 23, 1939; children: Dianne Elaine Finnie Boggess, Denise Eileen Finnie-Pascento. BA in Journalism, U. Denver, 1941. Office mgr. K&P, Inc., Golden, Colo., 1965-82; exec. dir. Rocky Mountain Coal Mining Inst., Lakewood, 1982—. Editor Procs. of Rocky Mountain Coal Mining Inst., 1982—. Founder City of Lakewood, 1968; dir. Alzheimer and Kidney Found., Denver, 1970-72. Recipient Ernest Thompson Seton award Camp Fire, Inc., 1963; named Woman of Yr. Denver Area Panhellenic, 1977; Paul Harris fellow Rotary Internat., 1998. Mem. Colo. Soc. Assn. Execs., Meeting Planners Internat. (Humanitarian award 1997), Profl. Conv. Mgmt. Assn., Kappa Delta (Outstanding Alumnae award 1959, 74, Order of Emerald 1987). Avocations: gourmet cooking, playing bridge. Office: Rocky Mountain Coal Mining Inst 3000 Youngfield St Ste 324 Lakewood CO 80215-6553

FINOCCHIARO, PENNY MORRIS, secondary school educator; b. Glendale, Calif., Sept. 30, 1949; d. C. Harold and Margaret (Nelson) Morris; m. Paul D. Finocchiaro, Apr. 9, 1996; children from previous marriage: E. Pierce III, Hailey M. BA in Speech and English, Muskingum Coll., New Concord, Ohio, 1971; MA in Edn., Nat. U., Sacramento, 1991. Cert. multiple and single subject tchr., Calif. Assoc. prod. Alhecama Players, Santa Barbara (Calif.) C.C. Dist., 1972-86; docent Santa Barbara Mus. Art, 1975-86; importer Cambridge Place Corp., Santa Barbara, 1974-86; with promotions and fund raising depts. Stewart-Bergman Assocs., Nevada City, Calif., 1986-89; travel columnist The Union, Grass Valley, Calif., 1987-90; tchr. drama and English Bear River H.S., Grass Valley, 1991—, dept. chair visual and performing arts, 1993—. Art docent coord. Deer Creek Sch., Nevada City, 1986-90, pres. Parent Tchr. Club, 1987-88. Recipient award for valuable contbn. to schs. Nevada City Sch. Dist., 1990, Dir.'s award Santa Barbara C.C., 1982, Tchrs. Who Make a Difference award Assn. of Calif. Sch. Adminstrs., 1998. Mem. Nat. Coun. Tchrs. of English, Ednl. Theatre Assn., Calif. Ednl. Theatre Assn., No. Calif. Ednl. Theatre Assn. Avocations: art and antique collecting, rollerblading, travel, biking, swimming, theatre. Home: 2123 Jones St San Francisco CA 94133-2582 Office: Bear River HS 11130 Magnolia Rd Grass Valley CA 95949-8366

FINSTER, BRENT EDWIN, public safety communications administrator; b. Sept. 13, 1958; s. Arno C. and Barbara E. Finster. Student, U. Colo., 1976-77, AIMS C.C., 1986-88. Asst. store mr. Radio Shack-Tandy Corp., Boulder, Colo., 1976-77; store mgr. Radio Shack-Tandy Corp., Laramie, Wyo., 1977-79, Lakewood, Colo., 1977-79; patrol dispatcher Colo. State Patrol, Eagle, 1979-80; dispatcher Boulder County Sheriff, Boulder, 1980-85, comms. supr., 1986-88; mktg. mgr. DPZ Systems, Boulder, 1988; comms. dir. Pitkin County Sheriff, Aspen, Colo., 1989—; fire chief Lyons (Colo.) Fire Protection Dist., 1983-89; cert. peace officer Peace Officer Stds. Bd., Denver, 1993—. Co-author: Public Safety Communications Standard Operating Procedure Manual, 1986; mem. editl. bd. Radio Resource Mag., Denver, 1991—. Mem. Assn. Pub. Safety Comms. Ofcls. (Colo. pres. 1991-92, rep. exec. coun. 1997—), Nat. Emergency Number Assn. (Colo. v.p. 1995-98). Avocations: travel, bowling, RF monitoring, amateur radio, ATV's. Office: Aspen-Pitkin County Comms 506 E Main St Dept C Aspen CO 81611-2923

FIORINO, JOHN WAYNE, podiatrist; b. Charleroi, Pa., Sept. 30, 1946; s. Anthony Raymond and Mary Louise (Caramela) F.; m. Susan K. Bonnett, May 2, 1984; children—Jennifer, Jessica, Lauren, Michael. Student Nassau Coll., 1969-70; B.A. in Biology, U. Buffalo, 1972; Dr. Podiatric Medicine, Ohio Coll. Podiatric Medicine, 1978. Surg. Res., MESA Gen. Hosp., 1978-79, Bd. cert. primary podiatric medicine Am. Podiatric Med. Specialties Bd. Salesman, E. J. Korvettes, Carle Place, N.Y., 1962-65; orderly Nassau Hosp., Mineola, N.Y., 1965-66; operating room technician-trainee heart-lung machine L.I. Jewish-Hillside Med. Center, New Hyde Park, N.Y., 1967-69; pharmacy technician Feinmel's Pharmacy, Roslyn Heights, N.Y., 1969-70; mgr., asst. buyer Fortunoffs, Westbury, N.Y., 1972-73; bd. certified perfusionist L.I. Jewish-Hillside Med. Center, New Hyde Park, N.Y., 1973-74; clin. instr. cardiopulmonary tech. Stony Brook (N.Y.) Univ., 1973-74; operating room technician Cleve. Met. Hosp., 1975; lab. technician Univ. Hosp., Cleve., 1976-78; surg. resident Mesa Gen. Hosp., 1978-79; staff podiatrist, 1979—; pvt. practice podiatry, Mesa, 1979—; staff podiatrist Sacaton (Ariz.) Hosp., 1979—, Mesa Gen. Hosp., 1979, Valley Luth. Hosp., Mesa, 1985, Chandler Community Hosp., 1985, Desert Samaritan Hosp., Mesa, 1986, podiatrist U.S. Govt. Nat. Inst., Sacaton, 1980-87, Indian Health Services, Sacaton, 1980-87; cons. staff Phoenix Indian Med. Ctr., 1985. Served with USN, 1966-67. Mem. Am. Podiatry Assn., Ariz. Podiatry Assn. (treas. 1984-86), Acad. Ambulatory Foot Surgery, Am. Coll. Foot Surgeons (assoc.), Mut. Assn. Profls., Am. Acad. Pain Mgmt. (cert.), Pi Delta, Alpha Gamma Kappa. Home: 2624 W Upland Dr Chandler AZ 85224-7870 Office: 5520 E Main St Mesa AZ 85205-8793

FIROOZABADY, EBRAHIM, plant scientist; b. Kangavar, Iran, Mar. 1, 1952; came to U.S., 1976; s. Khosrow and Tavous (Gharloghi) F.; m. Nickoo Tavassoli, Oct. 2, 1976; children: Amy, Yasmin, Navid. BS, U. Tehran, Iran, 1975; MS, U. Calif., Davis, 1978, PhD, 1982. Postdoctoral assoc. U. Nebr., Lincoln, 1982-84; rsch. scientist Agrigenetics, Madison, Wis., 1984-86, sr. rsch. scientist, 1986-88; prof. U. N.Mex., Las cruces, 1989; group rsch. scientist DNA Plant Tech., Oakland, Calif., 1989-93, prin. rsch. scientist, 1993—. Contbr. chpts. to books, numerous articles to profl. jours. Mem. Soc. for In Vitro Biology (plant divsn. v.p. 1994-96, symposium chmn. congress 1991—, plant program com. 1990—). Achievements include research in genetic engineering of different crop plants including pineapple, carnation, rose, banana, papaya, chrysanthemum, cotton, tomato, sunflower, alfalfa and tobacco; production of new cultivars by genetic engineering; inventor/patentee in field. Avocations: gardening, camping, skiing. Office: DNA Plant Tech 6701 San Pablo Ave Ste B Oakland CA 94608-1275

FIRSTENBERG, JEAN PICKER, film institute executive; b. N.Y.C., Mar. 13, 1936; d. Eugene and Sylvia (Moses) Picker; m. Paul Firstenberg, Aug. 9, 1956 (div. July 1980); children—Debra, Douglas. BS summa cum laude, Boston U., 1958. Asst. producer Altman Prodns., Washington, 1965-66; media advisor J. Walter Thompson, N.Y.C., 1969-72; asst. for spl. projects Princeton (N.J.) U., 1972-74, dir. publs., 1974-76; program officer Markle Found., N.Y.C., 1976-80; dir., CEO Am. Film Inst., L.A., Washington, 1980—; bd. dirs. Trans-Lux Corp.; former chmn. nat. adv. bd. Peabody Broadcasting Awards; bd. dirs. Trans-Lux Corp. Former trustee Boston U.; mem. adv. bd. Will Rogers Inst., N.Y.C.; chmn., bd. advisors Film Dept. N.C. Sch. of Arts. Recipient Alumni award for disting. service to profession Boston U., 1982; seminar and prodn. chairs at directing workshop for women named in her honor Am. Film Inst., 1986. Mem. Women in Film (Crystal award 1990), Trusteeship for Betterment of Women, Acad. Motion Picture Arts and Scis. Office: Am Film Inst 2021 N Western Ave PO Box 27999 Los Angeles CA 90027-0999

FISCHER, EDMOND HENRI, biochemistry educator; b. Shanghai, Republic of China, Apr. 6, 1920; came to U.S., 1953; s. Oscar and Renée (Tapernoux) F.; m. Beverley B. Bullock. Lic. es Sciences Chimiques et Biologiques, U. Geneva, 1943, Diplome d'Ingenieur Chimiste, 1944, PhD, 1947; D (hon.), U. Montpellier, France, 1985, U. Basel, Switzerland, 1988, Med. Coll. of Ohio, 1993, Ind. U., 1993, U. Bochum, Germany, 1994. Pvt. docent biochemistry U. Geneva, 1950-53; research assoc. biology Calif. Inst. Tech., Pasadena, 1953; asst. prof. biochemistry U. Wash., Seattle, 1953-56, assoc. prof., 1956-61, prof., 1961-90, prof. emeritus, 1990—; mem. exec. com. Pacific Slope Biochem. Conf., 1958-59, pres., 1975; mem. biochemistry study sect. NIH, 1959-64, symposium co-chmn. Battelle Seattle Rsch. Ctr., 1970, 73, 78; mem. sci. adv. bd. Biozentrum, U. Basel, Switzerland, 1982-86; mem. sci. adv. bd. Friedrich Miescher Inst., Ciba-Geigy, Basel, 1976-84, chmn., 1981-84; memb. bd. sci. govs. Scripps Rsch. Inst., La Jolla, Calif., 1987—, Basel Inst. for Immunology, 1996—; bd. govs. Weizmann Inst. Sci., Rehovot, Israel, 1997—. Contbr. numerous articles to sci. jours. Mem. sci. council on basic sci. Am. Heart Assn., 1977-80, sci. adv. com. Muscular Dystrophy Assn., 1980-88. Recipient Lederle Med. Faculty award, 1956-59, Guggenheim Found. award, 1963-64, Disting. Lectr. award U. Wash., 1983, Laureate Passano Found. award, 1988, Steven C. Beering award, 1991, Nobel prize in Physiology or Medicine, 1992. Fellow Am. Acad. Arts and Scis.; mem. NAS, AAAS, AAUP, Am. Soc. Biol. Chemists (coun. 1989-93), Am. Chem. Soc. (adv. bd. biochemistry divsn. 1962, exec. com. divsn. biology 1969-72, monograph adv. bd. 1971-73, editl. adv. bd. Biochemistry, 1961-66, assoc. editor 1966-91), Swiss Chem. Soc. (Werner medal), Spanish Royal Acad. Scis. (fgn. assoc.), Venice Inst. Sci., Arts and Letters (fgn. assoc.), Japanese Biochem. Soc. (hon.). Achievements include cellular regulation by phosphorylation/dephosphorylation cycle. Office: U Washington Med Sch Box 357350 Seattle WA 98195-7350

FISCHER, JOEL, social work educator; b. Chgo., Apr. 22, 1939; s. Sam and Ruth (Feiges) F.; m. Renee H. Furuyama; children: Lisa, Nicole. BS, U. Ill., 1961, MSW, 1964; D in Social Welfare, U. Calif., Berkeley, 1970. Prof. sch. social work U. Hawaii, Honolulu, 1970—; vis. prof. George Warren Brown Sch. Social Work, Washington U., St. Louis, 1977, U. Wis. Sch. Social Welfare, Milw., 1978-79, U. Natal, South Africa, 1982, U. Hong Kong, 1986; cons. various orgns. and univs. Author: (with Harvey L. Gochros) Planned Behavior Change: Behavior Modification in Social Work, 1973, Handbook of Behavior Therapy with Sexual Problems, vol. I, 1977, vol. II, 1977, Analyzing Research, 1975, Interpersonal Helping: Emerging

Approaches for Social Work Practice, 1973, The Effectiveness of Social Casework, 1976, (with D. Sanders and O. Kurrem) Fundamentals of Social Work Practice, 1982, Effective Casework Practice: An Eclectic Approach, 1978, (with H. Gochros) Treat Yourself to a Better Sex Life, 1980, (with H. Gochros and J. Gochros) Helping the Sexually Oppressed, 1985, (with Martin Bloom) Evaluating Practice: Guidlines for the Helping Professional, 1982, (with Kevin Corcoran) Measures for Clinical Practice, 1987, (with Daniel Sanders) Visions for the Future: Social Work and Pacific-Asian Perspectives, 1988, (with Martin Bloom and John Orme) Evaluating Practice, 2nd edit., 1995, (with Kevin Corcoran) Measures for Clinical Practice, 2nd edit., vol. 1, 1994, Families, Children, vol. 2, 1994, Adults, 1994, East-West Connections: Social Work Practice Traditions and Change, 1992, (with Martin Bloom and John Orme) Evaluating Practice, 3d edit., 1999, (with Martin Bloom and John Orme) Teacher's Manual for Evaluating Practice, 1999; mem. editl. bd. 12 profl. jours.; contbr. over 150 articles, revs., chpts. and papers to profl. jours. With U.S. Army, 1958. Mem. Hawaii Com. for Africa, Nat. Assn. Social Workers, Coun. Social Work Edn., Acad. Cert. Social Workers, Nat. Conf. Social Welfare, AAUP, Unity Organizing Com., Hawaii People's Legis. Coalition, Bertha Reynold Soc. Democrat. E-mail: jfischer@hawaii.edu. Home: 1371-4 Hunakai St Honolulu HI 96816-5501 Office: U Hawaii 2500 Campus Rd Honolulu HI 96822-2217

FISCHER, MICHAEL LUDWIG, environmental executive; b. Dubuque, Iowa, May 29, 1940; s. Carl Michael and Therese Marie (Stadler) F.; m. Jane Pughe Rogers; children: Christina Marie, Steven Michael. BA in Polit. Sci., Santa Clara U., 1964; M in City and Regional Planning, U. Calif., Berkeley, 1967; grad. exec. program in environ. mgmt., Harvard U., 1980. Planner City of Mountain View, Calif., 1960-65; assoc. Bay Area Govts., 1966-67; planner County of San Mateo, Calif., 1967-69; assoc. dir. San Francisco Planning and Urban Rsch. Assn., nonprofit civc orgn., 1969-73; exec. dir. North Cen. region Calif. Coastal Zone Conservation Commn., San Rafael, 1973-76; chief dep. dir. Gov.'s Office Planning and Rsch., Sacramento, 1976-78; exec. dir. Calif. Coastal Commn., San Francisco, 1978-85; sr. assoc. Sedway Cooke Assocs., environ. cons., San Francisco, 1985-87; exec. dir. Sierra Club, San Francisco, 1987-93; resident fellow John F. Kennedy Sch. Govt., Inst. Politics, Harvard U., Cambridge, Mass., 1993; sr. cons. Natural Resources Def. Coun., San Francisco, 1993-95; exec. officer Calif. Coastal Conservancy, Oakland, 1994-97; program officer environ. William & Flora Hewlett Found., Menlo Park, Calif., 1997—; lectr. dept. city and regional planning U. Calif., Berkeley, 1984; chairperson environ. com. adv. coun. Calvert Social Investment Fund, 1989—; mem. Harvard Commn. Global Change Info. Policy, 1993—; mem. com. on impact of maritime facility devel. NAS/NRC, 1975-78; mem. nat sea grant review panel Nat. Oceanic and Atmosphric Adminstrn., 1998—. Co-author Calif. state plan, An Urban Strategy for Calif., 1978, Building a New Municipal Railway, 1973, Oral History, Coastal Commn. Yrs., 1973-85, Oral History, Sierra Club Yrs., 1987-93; author intro. Ansel Adams: Yosemite, 1995; contbr. papers to profl. publs. Recipient Life Achievement award Assn. Environ. Profls., 1986, Disting. Leadership award. Am. Soc. Pub. Adminstrn., 1987, Outstanding Nat. Leadership award Coastal States Orgn., 1990, Exemplary Pub. Svc. award San Francisco Bay Conservation and Devel. Commn., 1997, Spl. Recognition award Calif. State Legis., 1998. Mem. Nat. Resources Def. Coun., 1000 Friends of Fla., Calif. Planning and Conservation League (bd. dirs. 1970-76), Alliance Ethnic and Environ. Orgn. (founding bd. dirs. 1991-93), The Oceanic Soc. (bd. dirs. 1983-88), Sierra Club, Friends of the Earth (bd. dirs. 1988-94), League for Coastal Protection, Save San Francisco Bay Assn., Am. Youth Hostels, Inc. (bd. dirs. 1985-87), Yosemite Restoration Trust (bd. dirs. 1990-97), Lambda Alpha. Office: William & Flora Hewlett Found 525 Middlefield Rd Menlo Park CA 94025-3460

FISCHER, MICHELE ELIZABETH, screenwriter, actress; b. Balt., Nov. 11, 1969; d. Thomas William and Marjorie Lynne (Kadlec) F. AA in Liberal Arts with honors, Anne Arundel C.C., 1990; BA in English, Rockford Coll., 1993; student, Regent's Coll., London. Intern Medialab Film Co., London, 1992; adminstrv. work for Warner Bros., Paramount Studios, Disney Channel, Internat. Film Guarantors, The Griffin Group. Playwright/actress: The Monkee Junkee, 1988; author: (novel) Things Growing, 1996; author/creator: (screenplays) Youthquake, 1997, Reflections, 1998, (TV pilot) Sugar and Spice, 1998. Recipient Cmty. Svc. award Jamestown-Yorktown Found., 1991. Mem. Ferguson's Royal Artillery, Nat. Honor Soc.

FISCHER, ROBERT EDWARD, meteorologist; b. Bethlehem, Pa., Aug. 4, 1943; s. Frederic Philip and Muriel Winifred (Johnson) F. BS cum laude, U. Utah, 1966; MS, Colo. State U., 1969. Meteorologist Nat. Weather Svc., Fairbanks, Alaska, 1973—. Contbr. articles to profl. jours. Vol. classical music program prodr. Sta. KUAC-FM, Fairbanks. Recipient Nat. Oceanic and Atmospheric Adminstrn. Unit citation, 1989. Fellow Royal Meteorol. Soc.; mem. Am. Meteorol. Soc. (Charles L. Mitchell award 1985), Nat. Weather Assn. (Outstanding Operational Performance award 1987), Assn. Lunar and Planetary Observers, Am. Assn. Variable Star Observers, Royal Astron. Soc. Can., Sigma Xi, Phi Kappa Phi. Avocations: running, photography, astronomy, bird watching. Home: PO Box 82210 Fairbanks AK 99708-2210 Office: Nat Weather Service Forecast Office 101 12th Ave Unit 12 Fairbanks AK 99701-6237

FISCHER, RUDOLPH F., oil company chemical researcher; b. Milw., Feb. 27, 1923; s. Rudolph F. and Margaret (Shoemacher) F.; m. Marie A. Grunewald, July 29, 1944; children: Margaret, John, James, Anne. BS in Chemistry, U. Wis., 1948; PhD in Organic Chemistry, U. Ill., 1951. Rsch. chemist Shell Devel., Emeryville, Calif., 1951-58, rsch. supr., 1958-60, asst. to pres., 1960-61; dept. head Shell Devel., Emveryville, Calif., 1961-67, rsch. dir., 1967-69; product devel. mgr. Shell Chem., Houston, 1969-73; instr. Cheheketa C.C., Salem, Oreg., 1975-82. Author chpt. to book; contbr. articles to profl. jours; patentee in field. With U.S. Army, 1942-46. Mem. Nat. Audubon Soc., Am. Mus. of Natural History. Avocations: forestry, agriculture, finance. Home and Office: 13005 Jerusalem Hill Rd NW Salem OR 97304-9622

FISCHER, ZOE ANN, real estate and property marketing company executive, real estate consultant; b. L.A., Aug. 26, 1939; d. George and Marguerite (Carrasco) Routsos; m. Douglas Clare Fischer, Aug. 6, 1960 (div. 1970); children: Brent Sean Cecil, Tahlia Georgienne Marguerite Bianca. BFA in Design, UCLA, 1964. Pres. Zoe Antiques, Beverly Hills, Calif., 1973—; v.p. Harleigh Sandler Real Estate Corp. (now Prudential-Jon Douglas), 1980-81; exec. v.p. Coast to Coast Real Estate & Land Devel. Corp., Century City, Calif., 1981-83; pres. New Market Devel., Inc., Beverly Hills, 1983—; dir. mktg. Mirabella, L.A., 1983, Autumn Pointe, L.A., 1983-84, Desert Hills, Antelope Valley, Calif., 1984-85; cons. Lowe Corp., L.A., 1985. Designer interior and exterior archtl. enhancements and remodelling; designed album cover for Clare Fischer Orch. (Grammy award nomination 1962). Soprano Roger Wagner Choir, UCLA, 1963-64. Mem. UCLA Alumni Assn. Democrat. Roman Catholic. Avocations: skiing, designing jewelry, interior, landscape and new home design, antique collecting.

FISCHLER, SANDY LYNN, event producer; b. Anchorage, Alaska, Dec. 28, 1962; d. Joseph Michael Fischler and Sharon Leigh (Blodgett) Smith. Student, U. Alaska, 1980-83, Circle in Square Theatre Sch., 1983. Spl. event coord. Universal Studios Fla., Orlando, 1993-95; prodn. mgr. Headdress Ball, Orlando, 1994; assoc. prodr. Nickelodeon "Guts", Orlando, 1994; event mgr. First Night Providence, 1995; prodr. bike stunt segment 1997 Holiday Bowl Halftime Show, San Diego, 1997; event prodr. ESPN X Games, San Diego, 1995-98; ptnr. Avalanche Events Group, 1998—; owner Pagan Prodns., 1998—; event coord. NFL Experience, Super Bowl XXXIII, 1999. Exec. prodr. Colorado Board Blast, 1999. Vol. Feral Cat Coalition, San Diego, 1998. Mem. Women in Sports and Events, Internat. Festival and Events Assn., Calfest. Avocations: computer graphics, gardening. Home: 3675 Barnard Dr #256 Oceanside CA 92056

FISET, STEPHANE, hockey player; b. Montreal, Que., Can., June 17, 1970. Goaltender L.A. Kings. Office: LA Kings 3900 W Manchester Blvd Inglewood CA 90305

FISETTE, SCOTT MICHAEL, golf course designer; b. Orange, Tex., May 17, 1963; s. Roderick John and Addie Faye (Byrnes) F.; divorced; 1 child, Shane Roderick. BS in Landscape Architecture, Tex. A&M U., 1985. Registered landscape architect, Tex., Hawaii, Commonwealth of No. Mariana Islands. Project architect Dick Nugent Assocs., Long Grove, Ill., 1985-90; prin., pres. Fisette Golf Designs, Kaneohe, Hawaii, 1991—. Mem. Golf Course Supts. Assn. Am., Am. Soc. Landscape Architects, Nat. Golf Found., Hawaii Turf Grass Assn. (bd. dirs. 1991-96), Donald Ross Soc., Pacific Asia Travel Assn. Avocations: golf, fishing, water skiing, softball. Office: Fisette Golf Designs PO Box 1433 Kaneohe HI 96744-1433

FISH, RUBY MAE BERTRAM (MRS. FREDERICK GOODRICH FISH), civic worker; b. Sheridan, Wyo., July 24, 1918; d. Ryan Lawrence and Ruby (Beckwith) Bertram; R.N., St. Luke's Hosp., 1936; postgrad. Washington U., St. Louis, 1941; m. Frederick Goodrich Fish, Apr. 12, 1942; children: Bertram Frederick, Lisbeth Ann Fish Kalstein. Staff nurse Huntington Meml. Hosp., Pasadena, Calif., 1941-42; dr.'s office nurse, Denver, 1943-44; travel cons. Buckingham Travel Agy., Aurora, Colo., 1976—. Bd. dirs. Jefferson County Easter Seal Soc., 1949—, pres., 1952-53, 56-57, 66-67; pres. Colo. Easter Seal Soc., 1960-61; bd. dirs. Nat. Easter Seal Soc., 1968-69, sec. ho. of dels., 1976-77; bd. dirs. Assistance League Denver, 1968-70, 75-76, People to People for Handicapped, 1981— (Vol. of Yr. award 1991); mem. Pres.'s Com. on Employing Handicapped, 1976—; active Rehab. Internat. of U.S.A., 1972—, Rehab. Internat., 1960—. Mem. Dau. Nile-El Mejedel. Home: 6900 W Stetson Pl Apt 3 Littleton CO 80123-2419 Office: 13741 E Mississippi Ave Aurora CO 80012-3628

FISHER, BARRY ALAN JOEL, protective services official; b. N.Y.C., Sept. 11, 1944; s. George and Pearl (Newman) F.; m. Susan Joan Saperstein, Dec. 29, 1968; children: David, Michael. BS, CCNY, 1966; MS, Purdue U., 1969; MBA, Calif. State U., Northridge, 1973. With criminalistics lab. L.A. County Sheriff's Dept., 1969-79, chief sheriff's criminalistics lab., 1979-86, dir. Sci. Svcs. Bur., 1986—; lectr. U. Calif., L.A.; adj. lectr. Calif. State U., 1996. Fellow Am. Acad. Forensic Scis. (co-chmn. local arrangements com. 1981, chmn., sec. criminalistics sect. program 1981-82, sec., chmn. 1982-83, chmn. local arrangements com. 1991, chmn. sect. 1995—, pres.-elect 1997, pres. 1998-99); mem. Am. Soc. Crime Lab. Dirs. (chmn. forensic sci. ops. and program com. 1982-86, bd. dirs. 1986-89, pres. 1988-89, editor newsletter 1989-90), Forensic Sci. Found. (bd. dirs. 1985—, sec. 1988—), Forensic Sci. Soc., Internat. Assn. of Identification, Internat. Assn. Chiefs of Police, Internat. Assn. Forensic Scis. (pres. 1996—). Republican. Jewish. Avocations: computers, reading, photography. E-mail: bajfisher@earthlink.net. Office: LA County Sheriffs Crime Lab 2020 Beverly Blvd Los Angeles CA 90057-2404

FISHER, BRUCE DAVID, elementary school educator; b. Long Beach, Calif., Dec. 24, 1949; s. Oran Wilfred and Irene (May) F.; m. Mindi Beth Evans, Aug. 15, 1976; 1 child, Jenny Allison Viola. BA, Humboldt State U., 1975, standard elem. credential, 1976, learning handicapped credential, 1977. Instrnl. svcs. specialist Blue Lake (Calif.) Elem. Sch.; resource specialist Fortuna (Calif.) Union Sch. Dist., tchr. 3d grade, tchr. 5th grade, 1988—; prof. Humboldt State U., 1996—; sci. cons. Pitsco, 1995; cons. Newton's Apple, 1995-97, NASA, 1995; site leader tchr., cons., 1998-99, curriculum writer Calif. Sci. Internet, 1995-97; cons. U.S. Forest Svc., 1999; mem. J.P.L./NASA/Johns Hopkins U. Core Curriculum Devel. Team Project KidSat and CASOE; mem. ednl. adv. bd. Calif. Dairy Coun., 1998-99, advisor, 1998; rep. Calif. Tech. Assistance Project, 1998; mem. Calif. Ski Industry and U.S. Forest Svc. Vice chmn. Tchrs. Edn. and Cmty. Helpers, Arcata, Calif., 1990—; v.p. Sequoia Pk. Zool. Soc., Eureka, 1989-90, chmn. Whale Fair, 1989—; mem. selection com. Christa McAuliffe Fellowship; bd. dirs. Redwood Environ. Edn. Fair, Eureka, 1990—, Family Wellness Project, 1991; apptd. to Calif. Curriculum and Supplemental Materials Commn.; commr. Calif. Curriculum Commn., 1992-95; chairperson math. assessment Calif. Dept. Edn., 1995; cons. PITSCO Sci., 1995, NASA/JPL, 1995-97; mem. NASA/JPL and Johns Hopkins U. CORE Curriculum Devel. Team, 1995-96; lead tchr. KidSat and CASDE projects Calif. Sci. Internat. Site. Named Calif. Tchr. of Yr. Dept. Edn., 1991, Favorite Tchrs. ABC-TV, 1991, Humboldt County Tchr. of Yr., 1991; recipient Leadership Excellence award Calif. Assn. Sci. Specialists, 1990, Masonic Meritorious Svc. award for Pub. Edn., 1991, Profl. Best Leadership award Learning Mag., Oldsmobile Corp., and Mich. State U., 1991, Nat. Educator award Miliken Found. Calif. State Dept. Edn., 1991, NASA/NSTA Newest award, 1993, Newton's Apple Multimedia Inst., 1995, Lifetime Achievement award Humboldt County Bd. Edn., 1996. Mem. Calif. Tchrs. Assn., Calif. Sci. Tchrs. Assn., Calif. Assn. Health, Phys. Edn., Recreation, and Dance. Democrat. Avocations: whale watching, curriculum development, photography, sports, aviation, travel. Home: 4810 14th St Arcata CA 95519-9778 Office: Fortuna Elem Sch 843 L St Fortuna CA 95540-1997

FISHER, DELBERT ARTHUR, physician, educator; b. Placerville, Calif., Aug. 12, 1928; s. Arthur Lloyd and Thelma (Johnson) F.; m. Beverly Carne Fisher, Jan. 28, 1951; children: David Arthur, Thomas Martin, Mary Kathryn. BA, U. Calif., Berkeley, 1950; MD, U. Calif., San Francisco, 1953. Diplomate Am. Bd. Pediat. (examiner 1971-80, mem. subcom. on pediat. endocrinology 1976-79). Intern, resident in pediat. U. Calif. Med. Ctr., San Francisco, 1953-55; resident in pediat. U. Oreg. Hosp., Portland, 1957-58; from asst. prof. to assoc. prof. pediat. Med. Sch. U. Ark., Little Rock, 1960-67, prof. pediat., 1967-68; prof. pediat. UCLA, 1968-73, prof. pediat. and medicine Med. Sch., 1973-91, prof. emeritus, 1991—; chief, pediat. endocrinology Harbor-UCLA Med. Ctr., 1968-75, rsch. prof. devel. and perinatal biology, 1975-85, chmn. pediat., 1985-89, sr. scientist Rsch. and Edn. Inst., 1991—; dir. Walter Martin Rsch. Ctr., 1986-91; pres. Nichols Inst. Reference Labs, San Juan Capistrano, Calif., 1991-93; pres. acad. assocs., chief sci. officer Nichols Inst., San Juan Capistrano, Calif., 1993-94; pres. acad. assocs., chief sci. officer Quest Diagnostics-Nichols Inst., San Juan Capistrano, Calif., 1994-97, sr. sci. officer, 1997-98, chief sci. officer, 1999—; cons. genetic disease sect. Calif. Dept. Health Svcs., 1978-98; cons. genetic disease sect. Calif. Dept. Dept. Health Svcs., 1978—; mem. organizing com. Internat. Conf. Newborn Thyroid Screening, 1977-88. Co-editor: Pediatric Thyroidology, 1985, 6 other books; editor-in-chief Jour. Clin. Endocrinology and Metabolism, 1978-83, Pediat. Rsch., 1984-89; contbr. chpts. to numerous books, over 500 articles to profl. jours. Capt. M.C., USAF, 1955-57. Recipient Career Devel. award NIH, 1964-68. Mem. Inst. Medicine NAS, Am. Acad. Pediat. (Borden award 1981), Soc. Pediat. Rsch. (v.p. 1973-74), Am. Pediat. Soc. (pres. 1992-93), Endocrine Soc. (pres. 1983-84, Williams Leadership award 1998)), Am. Thyroid Assn. (pres. 1988-89), Am. Soc. Clin. Investigation, Assn. Am. Physicians, Lawson Wilkins Pediatric Endocrine Soc. (pres. 1982-83), Western Soc. Pediat. Rsch. (pres. 1983-84), Phi Beta Kappa, Alpha Omega Alpha. Home: 24582 Santa Clara Ave Dana Point CA 92629-3031 Office: Quest Diagnostics-Nichols Inst 33608 Ortega Hwy San Juan Capistrano CA 92675-2042

FISHER, DONALD G., casual apparel chain stores executive; b. 1928; married. B.S., U. Calif., 1950. With M. Fisher & Son, 1950-57; former ptnr. Fisher Property Investment Co.; co-founder, pres. The Gap Stores Inc., San Bruno, Calif., dir., now chmn., founder, 1996—. Office: The Gap Stores 1 Harrison St San Francisco CA 94105-1602*

FISHER, EARL MONTY, utilities executive; b. Chgo., June 26, 1938; s. Harry George and Fannie (Feinberg) F.; m. Joyce Leah Bender, Mar. 14, 1959 (div. Dec. 1978); children: Jan Carol, Wendy Robin; m. Teri Jean Janssen, Jan. 27, 1979. Student, La. Trade Tech. Coll., 1961. Apprentice and journeyman Comfort Air Refrigeration Corp., L.A., 1955-64; contractor Bonanza Air Conditioning and Refrigeration Corp., Van Nuys, Calif., 1964—. Bd. dirs. Hidden Hills (Calif.) Homeowners Assn., 1982-84, vice chmn., v.p., 1990; chmn. Hidden Hills Rds. Com., 1984-85, Hidden Hills Gate Ops. Commn., 1988-91; commr. emergency svcs. City of Hidden Hills, 1986—; pres. Hidden Hills Cmty. Assn., 1991-93; mem. Hidden Hills City Coun., 1994; mayor, Hidden Hills, 1996, 97, 98. Mem. Air Conditioning Sheet Metal Assn. (vice chmn. 1994-96, dir. 1996—). Democrat. Avocations: scale model aircraft, horses. Office: Bonanza Air Conditioning Heating & Refrigeration Corp 7653 Burnet Ave Van Nuys CA 91405-1081

FISHER, FREDERICK HENDRICK, oceanographer, emeritus; b. Aberdeen, Wash., Dec. 30, 1926; s. Sam (Sverre) and Astrid K. Fisher; m. Julie Gay Saund, June 17, 1955 (dec. 1993); children: Bruce Allen, Mark Edward, Keith Russell, Glen Michael; m. Shirley Mercedes Lippert, Oct. 10, 1994. BS, U. Wash., 1949, PhD, 1957. Teaching asst. U. Wash., 1949-53; rsch. asst. UCLA, 1954-55; grad. rsch. physicist Maine Phys. Lab., Scripps Inst. Oceonography, 1955-57; rsch. fellow acoustics Harvard, 1957-58; rsch. physicist, rsch. oceanographer Marine Phys. Lab., Scripps Instn. Oceanography, La Jolla, Calif., 1958-91, assoc. dir., 1975-87, dep. dir., 1987-93, acting assoc. dir., 1993-94, rsch. oceanographer emeritus, 1997—; dir. rsch. Havens Industries, San Diego, 1963-64; prof., chmn. dept. physics U. R.I., Kingston, 1970-71; mem. governing bd. Am. Inst. Physics, 1984-90. Mem. San Diego County Dem. Cen. Com., 1956-57, 60-62. NCAA nat. tennis doubles champion, 1949; named to U. Wash. Athletic Hall of Fame, 1989; recipient Disting. Svc. award IEEE Oceanic Engring. Soc., 1991, Disting. Tech. Achievement award, 1996. Midshipman U.S. Naval Acad., 1945-47; with USNR, 1945. Fellow Acoustical Soc. Am. (assoc. editor jour. 1969-76, v.p. 1980-81, pres. 1983-84, Am.'s Finest Acousticians award San Diego chpt. 1997); mem. IEEE (sr., editor Jour. of Oceanic Engring. 1988-91), Marine Tech. Soc., Am. Geophys. Union, Acoustic Soc. Am., The Oceanographic Soc., Seattle Tennis Club. Co-designer, project scientist ocean research platform FLIP, 355' long manned spar buoy with 300' draft in vertical position, 1960-62. Home: 5034 Park West Ave San Diego CA 92117-1046

FISHER, JEFF, graphic designer, artist; b. Corvallis, Oreg., May 21, 1956; s. James Gordon and Dorene Ann (Cantrall) F.; life ptnr. Edward Dale Cunningham. BA in Interdisciplinary Studies, U. Oreg., 1980. Freelance designer Jeff Fisher Logomotives, Portland, Seattle, 1979—; art dir. Multnomah County Med. Assn., Portland, 1982-84, Osborne & Assocs., Portland, 1984-86; creative dir. Internat. News, Seattle, 1985-86. Logos and designs published in books including American Hotel Identity Graphics, 1994, Graphic Design USA, 1994, Letterhead & Logo Design 4, 1996, 5, 1998, Restaurant Graphics 2, 1996, Great T-Shirt Graphics 3, 1997, International Logos and Trademarks 3, 1997, 4, 1998, Designers' Handbook of Logo and Symbols, 1998, The Best of Business Card Design 3, 1998, New Logo & Trademark Design, 1998, American Corporate Identity, 1998, LOGO 2000, 1998; contbr. articles to profl. publs. Recipient B. Joe Medley Vol. award Portland Area Theatre Alliance, 1994, 1st place Gallery of Superb Printing, 1995, Honorable Mention award Internat. Gallery Superb Printing, 1995, Cert. Design Excellence PRINT Regional Design Ann., 1995, 96, 97, 98, Drake award Ctrl. Oreg. Ad Club, 1st place Greater Palm Springs Pride Design Competition, 1997, Cert. Excellence Biennial Internat. Logos and Trademarks Award, 1996, 97, Bronze Summit award, 1998, over 100 other awards. Office: Jeff Fisher Logomotives PO Box 6631 Portland OR 97228

FISHER, JOSEPH STEWART, management consultant; b. Athens, Pa., Mar. 3, 1933; s. Samuel Royer and Agnes Corinne (Smith) F.; m. Anita Ann Coyle, May 15, 1954; 1 child, Samuel Royer. BS in Tech. Mgmt., Regis U., 1981; postgrad., U. Colo., 1986-87, Iliff Sch. Theology, 1988-89. With IBM Corp., 1956-87; cons., sole propr. Fisher Enterprises, Boulder, 1975—; bd. dirs. Vervcraft Inc., Loveland, Colo. Leadership devel. Boy Scouts Am., 1975—, chmn. long range planning, 1982-86, chaplain, 1991—; bd. dirs. Longs Peak Coun., 1983-87, Colo. Crime Stoppers, 1983-88; exec. dir. Caring About People, Inc., Colo., 1990—; v.p. Helplink, Inc., Boulder, 1991—. With USN, 1952-56, Korea. Recipient Silver Beaver award Boy Scouts Am., Boulder, 1978, God and Svc. award Boy Scouts Am. and United Meth. Ch., 1991, OES Rose award 1994; James E. West fellow Boy Scouts Am., 1997. Mem. Am. Soc. Indsl. Security (cert. CPP, treas. 1985), Colo. Crime Prevention Assn. (cert. CPS), Mason (treas. Columbia lodge #14 1969-85, 90—), Royal Arch. Masons and Commandery Knights Templar of York Rite. Republican. Methodist. Avocations: scouting, church. Home and Office: 4645 Bedford Ct Boulder CO 80301-4017

FISHER, JULIET, lawyer; b. L.A., Nov. 29, 1969; d. William Edward and Ruth Gabrielle (Pinson) F. BA in English, UCLA, 1991; JD in Law, Loyola U., 1994. Bar: Calif. 1994. Dep. pub. defender Law Offices of Pub. Defender, Riverside, Calif., 1995—. Mem. Calif. Pub. Defenders Assn., Nat. Assn. Criminal Def. Lawyers, Temple Sholom of Ont. Democrat. Jewish. Avocations: creative writing, homeopathy and herbal medicine, cooking, yoga. Office: Law Offices Pub Defender 4200 Orange St Riverside CA 92501-3827

FISHER, MARK JAY, neurologist, neuroscientist, educator; b. Bklyn., Aug. 23, 1949; s. Ralph Aaron and Dorothy Ann (Weissman) F.; m. Janeth Godeau, Aug. 5, 1994. BA in Polit. Sci., UCLA, 1970; MA in Polit. Sci., U. S.D., 1972; MD, U. Cin., 1975; JD, Loyola U., 1997. Diplomate Am. Bd. Psychiatry and Neurology. Intern UCLA Sepulveda VA Hosp., 1975-76; resident UCLA Wadsworth VA Med. Ctr., 1976-79, chief resident, 1979-80; faculty mem., dir. stroke rsch. program U. So. Calif. Sch. of Medicine, L.A., 1980-98, prof. neurology, 1995-98; dir. residency tng. program U. So. Calif. Sch. Medicine, L.A., 1992-96; chmn. dept. neurology U. Calif. at Irvine, Orange, 1998—, prof. neurology and anatomy and neurobiology, 1998—. Editor: Medical Therapy of Acute Stroke, 1989. Recipient Tchr. Investigator award NIH, Bethesda, Md., 1984-89, Program Project grantee, 1994—. Mem. Am. Acad. Neurology, Am. Neurol. Assn., Am. Heart Assn. (stroke coun.), Nat. Stroke Assn., Internat. Soc. for Thrombosis and Haemostasis. Office: U Calif Irvine Dept Neurology 101 The City Dr S Bldg 3 Orange CA 92868-3201

FISHER, NANCY LOUISE, pediatrician, medical geneticist, former nurse; b. Cleve., July 4, 1944; d. Nelson Leopold and Catherine (Harris) F.; m. Larry William Larson, May 30, 1976; 1 child, Jonathan Raymond. Student, Notre Dame Coll., Cleve., 1962-64; BSN, Wayne State U., 1967; postgrad., Calif. State U., Hayward, 1971-72; MD, Baylor Coll. of Medicine, 1976; M in Pub. Health, U. Wash., 1982, certificate in ethics, 1993. Diplomate Am. Bd. Pediatrics, Am. Bd. Med. Genetics. RN coronary care unit and med. intensive care unit Highland Gen. Hosp., Oakland, Calif., 1970-72; RN coronary care unit Alameda (Calif.) Hosp., 1972-73; intern in pediatrics Baylor Coll. of Medicine, Houston, 1976-77, resident in pediatrics, 1977-78; attending physician, pediatric clinic Harborview Med. Ctr., Seattle, 1980-81; staff physician children and adolescent health care clinic Columbia Health Ctr., Seattle, 1981-87, founder, dir. of med. genetics clinic, 1984-89; maternal child health policy cons. King County div. Seattle King County Dept Pub. Health, 1983-85; dir. genetic svcs. Va. Mason Clinic, 1986-89; dir. med. genetic svcs. Swedish Hosp., 1989-94; pvt. practice Seattle, 1994-97; med. cons. supr. office of managed care Wash. State Dept. Social and Health Svcs., Olympia, 1996-97; med. dir. Medicaid Dept. of Social and Health Svcs., Wash., 1997—; nurses aide psychiatry Sinai Hosp., Detroit, 1966-67; charge nurse Women's Hosp., Cleve., 1967; research asst. to Dr. Shelly Liss, 1976; with Baylor Housestaff Assn., Baylor Coll. Medicine, 1980-81; clin. asst. prof. grad. sch. nursing, U. Wash., Seattle, 1981-85, clin. asst. prof. dept. pediatrics, 1982-92, clin. assoc. prof. dept. pediatrics, 1992—; com. appointments include Seattle CCS Cleft Palate Panel, 1984-97; bd. dirs., first v.p. King County Assn. Sickle Cell Disease 1985-86, acting pres. 1986, pres. 1986-87; hosp. affiliation include Childrens Orthopedic Hosp. and Med. Ctr., Seattle, 1981-89, Virginia Mason Hosp., Seattle, 1985—, Harborview Hosp., Seattle, 1986—. Contbr. articles to profl. jours. Active Seattle Urban League, 1982-96, 101 Black Women, 1986-94; bd. dirs. Seattle Sickle Cell Affected Family Assn., 1984-85; mem. People to People Citizen Ambassador Group; sec. Shala Com. on Infant Mortality, 1993—, Twins Com. Inst. of Medicine, 1995—; Evaluation, Rsch. and Planning Group Ethical Legal & Social Implications Nat. Human Gerome Rsch. Inst., 1997—. Served to lt. USN Nurse Corps, 1966-70. Fellow Am. Coll. Medicine Genetics (founder); mem. Am. Acad. Physician Execs., Student Governing Body and Graduating Policy Com. Baylor Coll. Medicine (founding mem. 1973-76), Loans and Scholarship Com. Baylor Coll. Medicine (voting mem. 1973-76), Am. Med. Student Assn., Student Nat. Med. Assn., Admission Com. Baylor Coll. Medicine (voting mem. 1974-76), AMA, Am. Med. Women's Assn., Am. Acad. Pediatrics, Am. Pub. Health Assn., Am. Soc. Human Genetics, Nat. Speakers Assn., Wash. State Assn. Black Providers of Health Care, Soc. Health and Human Values, Wash. State Soc. Pediatrics, Seattle C. of C. (mem. Leadership Tomorrow 1988—), Wash. State Med. Assn. (women in medicine com., interspecialty coun., telemedicine com.), Sigma Gamma Rho, Phi Delta Epsilon. Office: PO Box 45506 Olympia WA 98504-5506

FISHER, PHILIP CONDON, artist; b. Oil City, Pa., Nov. 17, 1930; s. Raleigh Harris and Fredericka Alvina (Faaborg) F.; m. Lois Ann Paddock, Nov. 5, 1955; children: Curtis Condon, Nancy Ann, Denise Marie. Student, Graceland Coll., 1950, U. Nebr., 1955, Famous Artists Schs., Westport, Conn., 1958-61. Advt. illustrator Sioux City (Iowa) Jour., 1967-68; comml.

artist Bolstein Creative Printers, Sioux City, 1968-69; comic strip/story strip illustrator "Brenda Starr" Chgo., 1977-78; portrait painter/art dealer Denver, 1979—; art appraiser Fisher's Master Artists, Inc., Golden, Colo., 1984—; copyright registration agt. Fisher's Master Artists, Inc., 1984—; portrait painter Prince Charles Philip, Arthur George Mountbatten, Windsor, 21st Prince of Wales, 1989, others. With USAF, 1951-54. Mem. Internat. Platform Assn., Am. Legion, Am. Portrait Soc. Avocations: antiques, interior decoration, gardening, writing, reading. Home and Office: 13325 W 15th Dr Golden CO 80401-3507

FISHER, ROBERT MORTON, foundation administrator, university administrator; b. St. Paul, Minn., Oct. 15, 1938; s. S.S. and Jean Fisher; m. Elinor C. Schectman, June 19, 1960; children: Laurie, Jonathan. AB magna cum laude, Harvard Coll., 1960; JD, Harvard U., 1963; PhD, London Sch. Econs, Polit. Sci., 1967; LLD, West Coast U., L.A., 1981; DHL, Profl. Sch. Psychology, San Francisco, 1986; DPS, John F. Kennedy U., Orinda, Calif. 1988. Rsch. assoc. Mass. Mental Health Ctr., Cambridge, 1957-62; rsch. asst. Ctr. Study Juvenile Delinquency, Cambridge, 1961-63; spl. asst. to chief psychologist British Prison Dept. Home Office, London, 1963-67; prof. Sch. Criminology U. Calif., Berkeley, 1965-71; profl. race car driver, 1972-77; pres. John F. Kennedy U., Orinda, Calif., 1974-85; exec. dir. 92d St. YMHA, N.Y.C., 1984-85; dir., CEO The San Francisco Found., 1987-97; mayor, councilman Lafayette, Calif., 1968-76; mem. Minn. and Calif. Bar Specialty: charitable gift planning; CEO Fisher Cos., 1997—. Scholar-in-residence Rockefeller Found., Bellagio, 1994; Polit. Sci. vis. fellow London Sch. Econs. and Polit. Sci., 1994; named Outstanding Fundraising Exec. Nat. Soc. Fund Raising Execs. Home and Office: 85 Southwood Dr Orinda CA 94563-3026

FISHER, WESTON JOSEPH, economist; b. Glendale, Calif., Aug. 29; s. Edward Weston and Rosalie Eloise (Bailey) F. BS, U. So. Calif., 1962, MA, 1965, MS, 1971, PhD, 1989. Sr. mgr. Naval Undersea Ctr., Pasadena, Calif., 1964-69; chief exec. officer, prin. Ventura County, Ventura, Calif., 1969-73; So. Calif. dir. County Suprs. Assn., L.A., 1974-75; coord. govtl. rels. So. Calif. Assn. Govts., L.A., 1975-78; devel. dir. Walter H. Leimert Co., L.A., 1979-90; bd. dirs. Gray Energy Corp., L.A., Mission Inn Group, Riverside, Calif., Coun. of Leaders and Specialists - UN, Peterson Oil and Gas. Mem. Gov.'s Adv. Coun. for Econ. growth, Channel Islands Conservancy. Mem. Medieval Acad. Am., El Dorado Country Club, Univ. Club, South Coast Yacht Club, Cave Creek Club, Lambda Alpha. Republican. Avocation: medieval and U.S. history. Home: 28261 Westover Way Sun City CA 92586-2525

FISHMAN, ARNIE, marketing executive, consultant, film producer; b. Bklyn., 1940; married; 3 children. BS, CUNY, 1965, postgrad. in Pschology, 1966. Rsch. asst. Liberman Rsch. N.Y.C., 1966, v.p., 1971; founder Lieberman Rsch. Worldwide, L.A., 1973—; also chmn. bd. dirs.; founder, chmn. bd. dirs. Interviewing Svc. Am., 1982—; expert witness Fed. Trade Commn.; spkr. in field; cons. in field. Office: Lieberman Rsch Worldwide 1900 Ave Of Stars #1550 Los Angeles CA 90067-4483*

FISHMAN, BRUCE ELIOT, physician, surgeon, consultant; b. Detroit, Apr. 30, 1952; s. Sheldon Russel and Marilyn Loraine (Goodman) F.; m. Elissa Patricia Adler, June 30, 1974; children: Nina Heather, Rachel Michelle. BS, Wayne State U., 1974, MD, 1979; JD, Whittier Coll., 1992. Orthopaedic surgery resident Henry Ford Hosp. Med. Ctr., Detroit, 1979-83; med./legal cons. EPA Consulting Inc., Calif., 1985-90; orthopaedic cons. West Oaks Urgent Care, Canoga Park, Calif., 1990—; med. dir. Encino (Calif.) Urgent Care Med. Ctr., 1992—. Fellow Am. Acad. Neurol. and Orthopaedic Surgeons, Am. Coll. Legal Medicine, Internat. Coll. Surgeons; mem. Am. Coll. Sports Medicine, Internat. Spinal Injection Soc., N.Am. Cervicogenec Headache Soc., Alpha Omega Alpha. Avocations: karate (black belt), scuba diving. Office: Encino Urgent Care Med Ctr 15450 Ventura Blvd Ste 102 Sherman Oaks CA 91403-3061

FISHMAN, WILLIAM HAROLD, cancer research foundation executive, biochemist; b. Winnipeg, Man., Can., Mar. 2, 1914; s. Abraham and Goldie (Chmelnitsky) F.; m. Lillian Waterman, Aug. 6, 1939; children—Joel, Nina, Daniel. B.S., U. Sask., Can., Saskatoon, 1935; Ph.D., U. Toronto, Ont., Can., 1939; MDhc U. Umea, Sweden, 1983; Dir. cancer rsch. New Eng. Med. Ctr. Hosp., Boston, 1958-72; rsch. prof. pathology Tufts U. Sch. Medicine, 1961-70, prof. pathology, 1970-77, dir. Tufts Cancer Rsch. Ctr., 1972-76; pres. La Jolla Cancer Rsch. Found., Calif., 1976-89, pres. emeritus, 1989—; mem. basic sci. programs merit rev. bd. com. VA, 1971-75; mem. pathobiol. chemistry sect. NIH, Bethesda, Md., 1977-81. Author in field. Rsch. Career award NIH, 1962-77; Royal Soc. Can. rsch. fellow, 1939, 17th Internat. Physiol. Congress-U.K. Fedn. fellow, 1947. Fellow AIC, AAAS, Nat. Acad. Clin. Biochemistry; mem. Am. Assn. Cancer Rsch., Am. Soc. Biol. Chemists, Am. Soc. Cell Biology, Am. Soc. Exptl. Pathology, Histochem. Soc. (pres. 1983-84), Internat. Soc. Clin. Enzymology (hon.). Internat. Soc. Oncodevel. Biology and Medicine (hon., Abbott award 1993), Univ. Club (San Diego). Jewish. Current work: Basic rsch. on expression of placental genes by cancer cells; monoclonal antibodies; oncodevelopmental markers; immuno-cytochemistry. Home: 715 Muirlands Vista Way La Jolla CA 92037-6202 Office: The Burnham Institute 10901 N Torrey Pines Rd La Jolla CA 92037-1062

FISK, EDWARD RAY, retired civil engineer, author, educator; b. Oshkosh, Wis., July 19, 1924; s. Ray Edward and Grace O. (Meyer) Barnes; married, Oct. 28, 1950; children: Jacqueline Mary, Edward Ray II, William John, Robert Paul. BCE Marquette U., 1949; student Fresno (Calif.) State Coll., 1954, UCLA, 1957-58; BS, MBA, Calif.-Western U., Engr., Calif. Div. Hwys., 1952-55; engr. Bechtel Corp., Vernon, Calif., Detroit, 1959-61; project mgr. Toups Engring Co., Santa Ana, Calif., 1959-61; dept. head Perliter & Soring, Los Angeles, 1961-64; Western rep. Wire Reinforcement Inst., Washington, 1964-65; cons. engr., Anaheim, Calif., 1965; assoc. engr. Met. Water Dist. So. Calif., 1966-68; chief specification engr. Koebig & Koebig, Inc., Los Angeles, 1968-71; mgr. constrn. services VTN Consol., Inc., Irvine, Calif., 1971-78; pres. E.R. Fisk Constrn., Orange, Calif., 1978-81; corp. dir. constrn. mgmt. James M. Montgomery Cons. Engrs., Inc., Pasadena, Calif., 1981-83; v.p. Lawrance, Fisk & McFarland, Inc., Santa Barbara and Orange, 1983—; pres. E.R. Fisk & Assocs., Orange, 1983—; Gleason, Peacock & Fisk, Inc., 1987-92; v.p. constrn. svcs. Wilsey & Ham, Foster City, Calif., 1993-94; adj. prof. engring., constrn. Calif. State U., Long Beach, 1987-90, Orange Coast Coll., Costa Mesa, Calif., 1957-78, Calif. Poly. State U., Pomona, 1974; Instr. U. Calif., Berkeley, Inst. Transportation Studies, 1978—; engring. prof. programs U. Wash., 1994—, internationally for ASCE Continuing Edn.; former mem. Calif. Bd. Registered Constrn. Insps. Served with USN, 1942-43, USAF, 1951-52. Registered profl. engr., Ariz., Calif., Colo., Fla., Idaho, Ky., La., Mont., Nev., Oreg., Utah, Wash., Wyo.; lic. land surveyor, Oreg., Idaho; lic. gen. engring. contractor, Calif.; cert. arbitrator Calif. Constrn. Contract Arbitration Com. Fellow ASCE (life fellow, past chmn. exec. com. constrn. div., former chmn. nat. com. inspection 1978—), Nat. Acad. Forensic Engrs. (diplomate); mem. Orange County Engring. Council (former pres.), Calif. Soc. Profl. Engrs. (past pres. Orange County), Structural Engrs. Assn. Calif. (engrs. joint contracts documents com. 1993-95), Am. Arbitration Assn. (nat. panel), U.S. Com. Large Dams, Order Founders and Patriots Am. (past gov. Calif.), Soc. Colonial Wars (dep. gov. gen. Calif. chpt.), S.R. (past dir.), Engring. Edn. Found. (trustee), Tau Beta Pi. Republican. Author: Machine Methods of Survey Computing, 1958, Construction Project Administration, 1978, 82, 88, 92, 97, Construction Engineers Complete Handbook of Forms, 1981, 92, Resident Engineers Field Manual, 1992; co-author: Contractor's Project Guide, 1988, Contracts and Specifications for Public Works Projects, 1992. Home: 1792 N Ridgewood St Orange CA 92865-4454

FISK, IRWIN WESLEY, financial investigator; b. Byers, Kans., Nov. 20, 1938; s. Walter Roleigh Fisk and Mae Pearl Irwin; m. Susie Bea Walters, Sept. 9, 1973; children: Mark Christopher, Paul Steven. Student, L.A. City Coll., 1958-60, Calif. State U., L.A., 1960-64, Pasadena C.C., 1981-88. Lic. pvt. investigator, Calif. Asst. exec. dir. Stores Protective Assn., L.A., 1962-66; sr. spl. investigator Calif. Dept. Corps., L.A., 1966-83, chief investigator Multi-State Law Enforcement Task Force of Fraudulent Telemarketing, L.A., 1987-94. Contbr. articles to profl. publs. Mem. U.S. Chess Fedn. (life), Am. Radio Relay League (DXCC award 1993), Authors Guild, So. Calif. Fraud Investigators Assn. Masons. Republican. Avocations: chess,

ham radio. Home: 343 N 1st St Lindsborg KS 67456-2004 Office: Bus and Fin Investigations Inc PO Box 8246 La Crescenta CA 91224-0246

FISTELL, IRA J., newspaper editor, adult education educator, newswriter, radio and television personality; b. Chgo., Mar. 31, 1941; s. Harry and Marian L. (Wolfe) F.; m. Tonda R. Sloane, Aug. 20, 1978; children: Kelly, Christopher, Katherine, Mary Ellen, Sara, Andrea. AB with honors, U. Chgo., 1962, JD, 1964; MA in U.S. History, U. Wis., 1967. Bar: Ill. 1964. Radio personality Sta. WKOW-AM, Madison, Wis., 1968-71, Sta. WEMP-AM, Milw., 1971-77, Sta. KABC-AM, L.A., 1977-95; nat. radio personality ABC Talkradio Network, L.A., 1982-88; TV personality USA & ESPN Cable Networks, 1980-84; editor L.A. Jewish Times, 1995—; fac. mem. U. Phoenix, 1998—; mem. faculty U. Phoenix, 1998—. Author: America By Train, 1982, Oddball America, 1986, Encounters with Mark Twain, 1995. Recipient Golden Spike award for svc. to rail passengers, NARRP, Anaheim, Calif., 1987. Mem. AFTRA, SAG, Milw. Press Club. Avocations: music, reading, travel.

FITCH, BONNIE LYNN, music store owner; b. New Rochelle, N.Y., June 1, 1953; d. Harry H. and Nevair Isabelle (Gulbenkian) Shahdanian; m. Clyde James Fitch, July 22, 1978; children: James Andrew, Thomas William. BMus in Music Edn., SUNY, Potsdam, 1975. Cert. elem. and secondary music tchr., N.Y. Elem. music specialist Monticello (N.Y.) Sch. Dist., 1975-78; mgr. sheet music dept. So. Nev. Music Co., Las Vegas, Nev., 1979-81; owner Bonnie's Music Shoppe, Las Vegas, 1981—; Vocalist Saratoga Performing Arts Ctr., 1976. Named to Disting. Women in So. Nev., Careline, 1989, 90, 91, 92, 94. Mem. Retail Print Music Dealers Assn. (bd. dirs. 1996-97), Music Tchrs. Nat. Assn., So. Nev. Comty. Concert Assn. (mem. exec. bd., historian 1988-93), Social Register of So. Nev. Mem. Armenian Orthodox Ch. Office: Bonnie's Music Shoppe 1500 E Sahara Ave Las Vegas NV 89104-3439

FITCH, DONALD EVERETT, librarian; b. Miles City, Mont., Apr. 9, 1928; s. Everett Willis and Teresa Helen (Sagaser) F.; m. Dorothy Ann Lamb, June 19, 1954; children: Stephen, Charles, Robert, Jane, Alan, Hugh. BA in English, Gonzaga U., 1953; MA in English, UCLA, 1954; MLS, U. Calif., Berkeley, 1959. Tchr. Coeur d'Alene (Idaho) High Sch., 1954-56, Santa Monica (Calif.) Coll., 1958; libr. U. Calif., Santa Barbara, 1959—, head reference dept., 1963-84, asst. coll. devel. officer, 1984—. Author: Blake Set to Music, 1990; composer choral works include Ye Sons and Daughters, 1991; editor: Soundings Jour., 1969—; contbr. articles to profl. jours. Home: 7281 Butte Dr Santa Barbara CA 93117-1335 Office: U Calif Libr Santa Barbara CA 93106

FITCH, EDWARD M., JR., insurance company executive, retired; b. Phoenix, Aug. 26, 1920; s. Edward M. Fitch and Lillian Ann Piwetz; m. Beverley J. Nellis, Apr. 25; children: Edward, III, Donald Charles, Wannelle. BS, Phoenix Jr. Coll., 1941, U. So. Calif., 1947. Pres. Bayly Martin Fay, L.A., 1947-85; ret., 1985. Capt. USNR, 1941-85; active service WWII, Korea. Mem. Newport Beach County Club, Balboa Bay Club. Republican. Avocations: stamp collecting. Home: 602 Kings Rd Newport Beach CA 92663-5712

FITTERER, JOHN ANGUS, priest, church administrator, author; b. Ellensburg, Wash., July 1, 1922; s. C.J. and Violet (McMillan) F.; m. Karen L. Guthrie, Oct. 20, 1990. AB, St. Louis U., 1945, MA, 1946, Licentiate in Philosophy, 1947; Licentiate in Sacred Theology, Gregorian U., Rome, 1954. Ordained to ministry Episcopal Ch., 1978. Assoc. prof. classical langs. and philosophy, dean Coll. Arts and Scis. Seattle U., 1956-64, pres., chancellor, 1965-71; pres. Assn. Jesuit Colls. and Univs., Washington, 1971-77; rector Ch. St. John Evangelist, Highland, Mass., 1978-79; asst. to bishop Diocese of Calif., San Francisco, 1980-84; vice chmn. Episcopal Homes Found., Lafayette, Calif., 1984-86, chmn., 1986—. Translator: Thomas Aquinas Commentary on Nichomachean Ethics of Aristotle, 1965; contbr. Adminstrs. in Higher Edn., 1978; also numerous articles on higher edn., religion and life care for elderly. Chmn. Nat. Coun. on Crime and Delinquency, Wash., 1965-70; pres., chmn. bd. trustees Seattle U., 1965-70; vice chmn. Wash. Urban Affairs Coun., 1966-69; vice chmn. bd. trustees Loyola Coll., Balt., 1970-76; trustee U. Detroit, 1976-77. Recipient Disting. Civilian Svc. medal U.S. Army, 1968, 71, Disting. Citizen's award Boys' Club Am., 1972, Outstanding Svc. award Nat. Coun. on Crime and Delinquency, 1969. Mem. Bankers Club of San Francisco. Home: 2349 Franklin St Apt 1 San Francisco CA 94123-5019 Office: Episcopal Homes Found 3650 Mt Diablo Blvd PO Box 1027 Lafayette CA 94549-1027

FITZGERALD, JOHN CHARLES, JR., investment banker; b. Sacramento, May 23, 1941; s. John Charles and Geraldine Edith (McNabb) F.; BS, Calif. State U. at Sacramento, 1964; MBA, Cornell U., 1966; m. Mildred Ann Kilpatrick, June 26, 1965; children—Geraldine Kathrine, Erec John. Dir. corp. planning Bekins Co., L.A., 1966-73; mgr. corp. planning Ridder Publs., Inc., L.A., 1973-75; chief fin. officer City of Inglewood (Calif.), 1975-77; treas./contr. Inglewood Redevel. Agy., 1975-77, Inglewood Housing Authority, 1975-77; v.p. mcpl. fin. White, Weld & Co., Inc., L.A., 1977-78; v.p. pub. fin. Paine Webber Jackson & Curtis, L.A., 1978-79; v.p. and mgr. for Western region, mcpl. fin. dept. Merrill Lynch Capital Markets, L.A., 1979-82, mng. dir. Western region, mcpl. fin. dept., 1982-86; mng. dir. Seidler-Fitzgerald Pub. Fin., L.A., 1986—; sr. v.p. The Seidler Cos., Inc., L.A., 1986—, also bd. dirs, mem. exec. com.; instr. fin./adminstrn. El Camino Coll., Torrance, Calif., 1977-80; bd. dirs., mem. exec. com. The Seidler Cos., Inc. Chmn. bd. dirs., exec. com., treas., chmn. fund raising com. L.A. chpt. Am. Heart Assn., 1977—; bd. dirs. Daniel Freeman Hosps. Inc., Corondelet Health Care Corp.; trustee Mt. St. Mary's Coll., L.A., 1992—; bd. dirs. Tau Kappa Epsilon Ednl. Found., Indpls., 1995—; bd. dirs. Calif. Soc. for Biomed. Rsch., 1998; alumni coun. mem. Johnson Grad. Sch. of Mgmt. Cornell U., real estate council. Mem. Fin. Execs. Inst., Mcpl. Fin. Officers Assn., Calif. Soc. Mcpl. Fin. Officers, League Calif. Cities, So. Calif. Corp. Planners Assn. (past pres.), L.A. Bond, Beta Gamma Sigma. Republican. Clubs: Jonathan, The Calif., Lake Arrowhead Country. Lodge: Rotary. Address: PO Box 765 27447 Bayshore Dr Lake Arrowhead CA 92352

FITZGERALD, MATTISON DALY, artist; b. San Francisco, Sept. 14, 1961; d. Daniel Joseph and Ann F. BA, U. Calif., Santa Cruz, 1985; post-grad. in Mus. Studies, John F. Kennedy U., 1993. Owner M Gallery and M Landscape, San Jose, Calif., 1994—; Artist-in-residence Santa Fe Internat. Acad. of Art, 1998, San Jose Art League Beaux Artes Ball, 1996, CADartists Santa Clara County, 1996, Tamian Station Mural Project, City Yr. San Jose, 1996, M Art Studio, 1991-96, Santa Barbara Mus. Natural History, 1986. Paintings at exhbns. include: 29 East Main Street Gallery, Los Gatos, Calif., 1998, Kismet Galllery, San Jose, Calif., 1997, Works Gallery, San Jose, 1997, Los Gatos Arts Commn. Gallery, Los Gatos, 1996, San Jose Inst. Contemporary Art, San Jose, 1995, Popular Culture Libr., Bowling Green, Ohio, 1995, South First Street Billiards, San Jose, 1996, Cafe Q Billiards, Palo Alto, Calif., 1996, others, numerous other exhibits through the Bay Area; commns. include NASA, Expoo Found.; work collected in numerous pvt. collections and represented at Ridgeway Gallery, Santa Fe, N.Mex., Studio One Gallery, Gualala, Calif., Arte Club Catania, Italy, Ceres Gallery N.Y., San Jose Art League, Mexican Art, San Jose; publs. include MS NBC Washington, Studio Notes Benicia, Calif., Sunset Mag., Bio Sci. Mag., others; short film Millenium, A Time of Happiness, Pulsart, 1998, shown at Canness Film Festival. Named to Outstanding Young Women of Am., 1998; recipient award Nat. Assn. Am. Penn Women, 1996, nominee Womens Fund Achievement awards, 1996, others. Mem. Art and Technology Soc. Internat., San Jose Jaycees, Calif. Assn. of Mus., Western Mus. Conf., Am. Assn. Museums, San Jose Mus. of Art, Santa Cruz County Mus. of Art, San Jose Inst. of Contemporary Art, Triton Mus. of Art. Studio: M Art 31 Union Street San Jose CA 95110

FITZGERALD, MICHAEL L., newspaper columnist; b. San Francisco, Aug. 12, 1954; s. Leo James and Dorothy Jane (Call) F.; 1 child, Aubrey (Leigh). AB, U. Calif., Santa Cruz, 1977. Reporter-feature writer Record, Calif., 1984-90, columnist, 1990—. Recipient Best of Gannett award Gannett Newspapers Inc., Calif. Newspaper Pubs. Assn. award 1991, 93, 94, 98, AP Excis. Coun. award, 1998. Avocations: chess. Office: The Stockton Record 530 E Market St Stockton CA 95202-3097

FITZGERALD, ROBERT LYNN, small business owner; b. Indiana, Pa., Oct. 1, 1939; s. Joseph and Jean (Smith) F.; m. Tomi Higuchi, May 30, 1991; 1 child, Robert Lynn Jr. Student, Orange Coast Coll., 1985-86; BA, U. Redlands, 1990; MA, U.S. Internat. U., 1993, D in Psychology, 1997. Dist. mgr. Napco Sci., Portland, Oreg., 1981-88; prin., pub. Fitzgerald's Real Estate Yellow Pages, Santa Ana, Calif., 1987—; psychol. sales cons., 1990—. Hospice vol. Orange County (Calif.), Vis. Nurses Assn., 1980; founder Orange County HELP chpt., Santa Ana, 1982. Avocations: fishing, computers. Home: 2700 W Segerstrom Ave # D Santa Ana CA 92704-6547 Office: Fitzgerald's Real Estate Yellow Pages 3941 S Bristol St Ste 335 Santa Ana CA 92704-7400

FITZGERALD, TIKHON (LEE R. H. FITZGERALD), bishop; b. Detroit, Nov. 14, 1932; s. LeRoy and Dorothy Kaeding (Higgins) F. AB, Wayne State U., 1958. Ordained deacon, 1971, priest, 1978, bishop Eastern Orthodox, 1987. Enlisted U.S. Army, 1954-57; commd. 2 lt. USAF, 1960, advanced through grades to capt., 1971; air staff, 1966-71, released, 1971; protodeacon Holy Virgin Mary Russian Orthodox Cathedral, L.A., 1972-78, rector, archpriest, 1979-87; bishop of San Francisco Orthodox Ch. in Am., L.A., 1987—. Recipient Order of St. Vladimir II Class, Patriarch Aleksy of Moscow, 1993. Democrat. Home: 649 Robinson St Los Angeles CA 90026-3612 Office: Orthodox Ch Am Diocese of the West 650 Micheltorena St Los Angeles CA 90026-3623

FITZGERALD, TIM K., writer; b. San Jose, Calif., Jan. 3, 1946; s. Ralph George and Bernice Christine (Huston) F. *Tim is single, the oldest of three brothers. His grandfather Fitzgerald found his fortune as a baker in Nome, Alaska, during the Klondike gold rush. His mother's family date themselves to the Battle of King's Mountain in the American Revolution and further back to the early founding of Jamestown, Virginia in 1612. Tim himself pioneered first ascents in Yosemite Valley in its golden era of the sixties.* BA, San Jose State Coll., 1971, San Jose State U., 1980; MA, San Jose State U., 1985, San Jose State U., 1997. Treas. Associated Students San Jose State Coll., 1969-70; camp bus. mgr. Boy Scouts Am., Sonora, Calif., 1973; co. budget analyst Allstate Equity Investments, San Jose, 1980; adminstrv. asst. Summer Employment of Youth program CETA, San Jose, 1981; pres. Corp. for Shared Responsibility, San Jose, 1983-84; researcher San Jose, 1992-96; owner/operator Raccoon Pubs., San Jose, 1991-92; freelance writer San Jose, 1986—, researcher, 1992-96; sec. Discovery, Inc., San Jose, 1991-93; adminstrv. trustee Inst. for Social Orgnl. Rsch., San Jose, 1992-94, 98—; instr. Cerro Coso C.C., Mammoth Lakes, Calif., 1998—. *Tim has become a civic leader in his community since his undergraduate days in the mid-sixties. As a student activist, he was first elected to office on a ticket with a militant black civil rights spokesperson in a campus party of ethnic pluralism in 1969. His first writings were published as letters in the campus daily. He has been a frequent contributor to the San Jose Mercury "Letters" page since 1978. An advocate of issues of poverty, the disabled and disadvantaged, he has since become a facilitator in national issues in Green Party politics.* Author: Essays in Capitalism, 1986, Civic Community, 1992, Inner City, 1993, Twilight in the Afternoon, 1997, Prospects for a New World Order, 1998 (narrative) Trail to Black Mountain, 1978, (poetry) Impressions from Idle Rock, 1981; host. (talk show) KSJS Radio, San Jose, 1995-97; corr. Mono County Rev. Herald, 1997-98. Mgr., candidate for State Assembly, San Jose, 1994, for San Jose City Coun., 1982, for Mono County Bd. Edn., 1998; co-coord. State Green Party Platform, Calif., 1993, State Green Party campaigns and candidates, Calif., 1995-97; elected mem. Green Party County Coun., Santa Clara County, Calif., 1992-94; vol. Cmty. Companions, Inc., San Jose, 1990-91; commr. City of San Jose Disability Advisement, 1993-97, vice chair, 1997; mem. task force on poverty Santa Clara County, 1995-97; mem. Mono County Mental Health Adv. Bd., 1998—. Advanced cadet U.S. Army ROTC, 1966-67. Mem. Am. Acad. Poets, Nat. Writers Union, Fellowship of Reconciliation, Commonwealth Club, Sierra Club, Tau Delta Phi. Avocations: hiking, wilderness photography, chess, bridge, backpacking/camping. Home: PO Box 3504 Mammoth Lakes CA 93546-3504

FITZGERALD-VERBONITZ, DIANNE ELIZABETH, nursing educator; b. Tampa, Fla., July 11, 1943; d. James Gerald and Bernice Elizabeth (Creel) F.; children: Deborah Elizabeth Guilbault Starr, Fred Anthony Guilbault Jr. AA summa cum laude, Montgomery Coll., 1979; BS in Health Svcs., No. Ariz. U., 1985, MEd, 1987. Nurse in Washington Internship, 1989, Advanced Internship, 1990. Orthopaedic nurse clinician Phoenix, pvt. practice counselor; mem. faculty C.V. Mosby Co., St. Louis; nurse clinician in orthopedics; mgr. orthopedic program Kimberly Quality Care; adminstr. Staff Builders Health Svcs, Phoenix; utilization mgr. CCN, Phoenix, 1998—. Bd. dirs. Valley of Sun Sch. and Rehab. Ctr., Arthritis Found.; mem. Am. Vol. Med. Team; med. vol. Habitat for Humanity. Named one of Top Ten Bus. Women in Managed Health Care, Today's Ariz. Woman, 1998. Mem. Nat. Assn. Orthopedic Nurses (pres. 1989-90), Assn. Rehab. Nurses, Case Mgmt. Soc. Am., Phi Kappa Phi (life). Office: CCN 3636 N Central Ave Ste 950 Phoenix AZ 85012-1971

FITZGERRELL SMITH, LEE, artist, illustrator; b. Hollywood, Calif., Sept. 11, 1946; d. Ray Hartley Jr. and Marcia (James) F.; m. Brian Rees Smith; children: Graham, Leslie, Lauren. BA, Occidental Coll., 1968; MFA, Instituto Allende, Mex., 1971. Illustrator L.A. Parks and Recreation, El Monte, Calif., 1970-71; staff artist Santa Barbara (Calif.) Pub. Library, 1972-74; tchr. Howard Sch., Montecito, Calif., 1972-73; instr. Santa Barbara Art Mus., 1971-74; freelance illustrator and muralist Placerville, Calif., 1974—. Illustrator: Indian Paintbrush, 1975, Comfort Clothes, 1981, internat. stationery and giftware products, 1994—, (TV comml.) Sacramento International Airport, 1996—. Mem. Graphic Artists Guild. Studio: 1815 Woodsman Ct Placerville CA 95667

FITZPATRICK, AL W., educator; b. Widby Island, Wash., Jan. 14, 1962; s. Robert Warren and Merna (Bess) F. BS in Polit. Sci., So. Oreg. State Coll. 1974, MS in Social Sci., 1975. Tchr. Mazama High Sch., Klamath Falls (Oreg.) City Schs., 1975-78; govt. and law tchr. Newport (Oreg.) High Sch., 1978—; presenter in field. Del. Republican Nat. Conv., New Orleans, 1988, Houston, 1992, San Diego, 1996; advisor YMCA Youth & Govt., Salem, Oreg., 1989-1991; selected for German marshall insvc. Nat. Coun. Social Studies, 1991; mem. Nat. Coun. Social Studies Textbook com., 1990-1995, Nat. St. Law Conv., Washington, 1996. Recipient Leavey award Freedom Found., 1991, Levey award of Excellence in private Enterprise Edn. 1992, Arrid Tchr. Recognition award Carter-Wallace, Inc., 1992, Golden Apple award; Keizai Koho fellow Japanese C. of C., Tokyo, 1990; grantee law studies Oreg. Law Related Edn. Project, 1990; James Madison Meml. fellowship, 1992. Mem. Oreg. Theatre Arts Assn. (treas. 1985), Oreg. Speech Tchrs. Assn. (workshop presenter), Oreg. Thespians Conf. (workshop presenter), Optimists Club (dir. youth activities). Avocations: photography, bodysurfing, swimming, waterpolo, traveling. Office: Newport H S 322 NE Eads St Newport OR 97365-2894

FITZ-PATRICK, DAVID, endocrinologist, educator; b. Burnley, Lancashire, England, Sept. 1, 1951; came to U.S., 1975; s. Malcolm Milligan and Ada (Maguire) F.; m. Elizabeth Joaquin, Dec. 30, 1972; children: Ian Rodney, Claire Larissa. MB, BS, U. Newcastle-Upon-Tyne, England, 1974. House officer Newcastle (England) Gen. Hosp., 1974-75; resident in internal medicine U. Md. Hosp., Balt., 1975-77; fellow in endocrinology McGill U., Montreal, Que., Can., 1977-81; cons. physician Straub Clinic and Hosp., Honolulu, 1981-91, chief of endocrinology, 1986-91; asst. clin. prof. medicine John Burns Sch. Medicine, Honolulu, 1982-95, assoc. clin. prof., 1995—; med. dir. Diabetes and Hormone Ctr. of Pacific, Honolulu, 1990—; mem. house of dels. Hawaii Med. Assn., 1987-90; med. educ. Bd. Med. Examiners, Hawaii, 1989—; founding mem. bd. dirs. Juvenile Diabetes Found., Honolulu, 1989-92 (Geraldine Fleming Meml. fellowship 1980-81). Contbr. articles to profl. jours.; founder, editor Diabetes & Endocrinology Home Page on Internet. Dir. The Straub Found., Honolulu, 1984-90. Rsch. scholar McGill U., 1979-80. Fellow Am. Coll. Physicians (mem. coun. 1990-92, Gov.'s prize 1986), Am. Coll. Endocrinology; mem. Am. Diabetes Assn. (pres. 1984-86, 93-94), The Endocrine Soc., Am. Soc. Internal Medicine, Am. Assn. Clin. Endocrinologists (state chair 1992-96, 98—). Avocations:

FITZPATRICK, MICHAEL KIERAN, restaurant company executive, b. Saratoga Springs, N.Y., Nov. 1, 1946; s. Robert Laurance and Leola Theresa

(Russom) F.; m. Jeaneen C. Spittler, June 24, 1967; children: Stacey Fitzpatrick Herhusky, Michael Scott, Daniel Kieran, Shannon. AA, State U. N.Y., Canton, 1964; MBA, So. Meth. U., 1989. V.p. ops. P&S Mgmt., Schiller Pk., Ill., 1980-82; various KFC Nat. Mgmt. Co., Louisville, 1982-90, v.p., gen. mgr., 1990-92; exec. v.p., COO Rax Restaurants, Inc., Dublin, Ohio, 1992-94; pres., COO China Jump, Inc., Ocean, N.J., 1994-96; exec. v.p., COO Sizzler Internat., L.A., 1996-97; pres., CEO Big Springs Enterprises, Inc., Truckee, Calif., 1997—; bd. dirs. 1st Tex. Bank, Dallas, 1986-92. Presenter/lectr. How Work is Accomplished. Bd. govs. U. North Tex., 1989-92; mem. adv. bd. So. Meth. U., 1989-92. Winner 2d pl. Butoko Kai East Coast Karate Championship, Norfolk, Va., 1985. Republican. Roman Catholic. Avocations: golf, hunting, fishing, karate. Home: 1720 Grouse Rdg Truckee CA 96161-4026

FITZPATRICK, THOMAS DAVID, videographer, educator; b. Ferndale, Mich., Mar. 30, 1947; s. Thomas Robert and Julia Rose (Kaufman) F.; m. Barbara Gene Schanberger, Apr. 19, 1969; children: Brian Thomas, Erin Kathleen. BA, Met. State Coll., Denver, 1970; MA, EdS, U. No. Colo., 1979. Prodn. dir. radio and TV, media specialist, tchr. Adams County Sch. Dist. 12, Thornton, Colo., 1970—; videographer J.F.W. Prodns., Denver, 1983-85, JOYCO Prodns., Denver, 1989—. Appeared in several plays including A Man for All Seasons, Harvey, Oh Dad Poor Dad, West Side Story, and The Royal Slave, 1965—. Mem. ACA, Am. Ednl. Rsch. Assn., Colo. Lang. Arts Soc., Internat. TV Assn., Nat. Coun. Tchrs. English. Avocations: fishing, camping, hunting, photography. Home: 7557 Newton St Westminster CO 80030-4750 Office: Adams County Sch Dist 12 5321 E 136th Ave Brighton CO 80601-7714

FITZSIMMONS, (LOWELL) COTTON, professional basketball executive, broadcaster, former coach; b. Hannibal, Mo., Oct. 7, 1931; s. Clancy and Zelda Curry (Gibbs) F.; m. JoAnn D'Andrea, Sept. 2, 1978 (div.); 1 child, Gary. B.S., Midwestern Univ., Wichita Falls, Tex., 1956, M.A., 1957. Head coach, athletic dir. Moberly Jr. Coll, Moberly, Mo., 1958-67; head coach Kans. State U., Manhattan, 1967-70; head coach NBA Phoenix Suns, 1970-72, 1988-94, 96-97, dir. player personnel, 1987-88; head coach NBA Atlanta Hawks, 1972-76; dir. player personnel NBA Golden State Warriors, Oakland, Calif., 1976-77; head coach NBA Buffalo Braves, 1977-78, NBA Kansas City Kings, Mo., 1978-84, NBA San Antonio Spurs, 1984-87; sr. exec. v.p. Phoenix Suns, 1992—, head coach; coach Schick Rookies, 45th ann. All Star Game, America West Arena. Recipient Coach of the Yr. award Nat. Jr. Coll. Athletic Assn., 1966, 67, Coach of the Yr. award Big 8 Conf., 1970, Coach of the Yr. award NBA, 1979, 89, Coach of the Yr. award Sporting News, St. Louis, 1979, 89; inducted into Mo. Sports Hall of Fame, Springfield, Mo., 1981, Nat. Jr. Coll. Basketball Hall of Fame, Hutchinson, 1985. Fellow Nat. Assn. Basketball Coaches. Avocations: golf, fishing. Office: Phoenix Suns 201 E Jefferson St Phoenix AZ 85004-2412

FIX, TOBIE LYNN, special education educator; b. L.A., Aug. 25, 1961; d. Howard Jacob and Pearl (Bram) Berger; m. Thomas Fix, Aug. 25, 1985. AA, Nat. U., L.A., 1992, student, 1992—. Substitute tchr. asst. of trainable mentally handicapped Los Angeles County, Calif., 1980-85, tchr. asst. trainable mentally handicapped, 1985—; substitute preschool tchr. Los Angeles County, Los Angeles County, Calif., 1996—; coaching asst. Spl. Olympic State Games, Los Angeles County. Recipient Vol. awards in spl. edn. Mem. Mus. of Tolerance, Huntington Libr./Gardens, L.A. Zool. Found. Democrat. Jewish. Avocations: photography, art appreciation, music, antiques, gardening. Home: 1628 Carlson Ln Redondo Beach CA 90278-4711

FIX, WILBUR JAMES, department store executive; b. Velva, N.D., Aug. 14, 1927; s. Jack J. and Beatrice D. (Wasson) F.; m. Beverly A. Corcoran, Sept. 20, 1953; children: Kathleen M., Michael B., Jenifer L. BA, U. Wash., 1950. Credit mgr. Bon Marche, Yakima, Wash., 1951-54; controller, ops. mgr. Bon Marche, Boise, Idaho, 1954-58; sr. v.p. Bon Marche, Seattle, 1970-76; exec. v.p. Bon Marche, 1976-77, pres., chief exec. officer, 1978-87; chmn., chief exec. officer, sr. v.p. Allied Stores Corp., 1987-93; chmn. Fix Mgmt. Group, 1993—; chmn. Wash. Retail Coun., 1983-84; bd. dirs., vice chmn. Wash. Telecomm. Corp.; bd. dirs. BMC West Corp., Vans, Inc., Swirland Apparel Ventures, Inc. Mem. pres.'s adv. com. Allied Stores Corp., N.Y., 1968-72; mem. citizens adv. com. Seattle Pub. Schs., 1970-71, v.p. Citizens Council Against Crime; chmn. Seattle King County Conv. & Visitors Bur., 1990. With AUS, 1946-47. Mem. Nat. Retail Mchts. Assn., Controllers Congress, Seattle Retail Controllers Group (past pres.), Fin. Execs. Inst., Western States Regional Controllers Congress (past pres.), Seattle C. of C. (exec. com., bd. dirs.), Assn. Wash. Bus. (fin. adv.), Downtown Seattle Devel. Assn. (exec. com., trustee), Wash. Round Table, Wash. Athletic Club, Mission Hills Country Club (Rancho Mirage, Calif.), Elks, Pi Kappa Alpha, Alpha Kappa Psi, Phi Theta Kappa. Episcopalian. Address: 149 Racquet Club Dr Rancho Mirage CA 92270-1461 Office: The Bon Marché 3rd and Pine St Seattle WA 98181 also: 5403 W Mercer Way Mercer Island WA 98040-4635

FLÄATEN, WAYNE RICHARD, principal; b. Culver City, Calif., Dec. 27, 1940; s. John Oscar and Clara Jensine (Sorenson) F.; m. Lynn Ellen Chappel, Feb. 17, 1962; children: Todd Gilbert, Brent Douglas, Kana Kristine. BA, Calif. State U., Northridge, 1965, MA, 1969; EdD, Brigham Young U., 1972. Cert. tchr. and adminstr. Tchr. L.A. Unified Sch. Dist., Woodland Hills, Calif., 1965-67, Pleasant Valley Sch. Dist., Camarillo, Calif., 1967-73; prin. Moorpark (Calif.) Unified Sch. Dist., 1973-77, Hueneme Sch. Dist., Port Hueneme, Calif., 1977-79, 93—; adminstrv. asst. Hueneme Sch. Dist., Port Hueneme, 1979-91, dean, 1991-93, prin., 1993—. Vol. Bowlful of Blues Festival, Ojai, Calif., 1986-97, Ojai Music Festival, 1986-97, Habitat for Humanity, Ventura County, Calif., 1993-97. Mem. Assn. Calif. Sch. Adminstrs., Ventura County Scottish Rite, Ojai Masonic Lodge. Avocations: birding, hiking, distance running, stone sculpting, gardening. Home: 2295 Valley Meadow Dr Oak View CA 93022-9562 Office: Hueneme Sch Dist 205 N Ventura Rd Port Hueneme CA 93041-3084

FLACHMANN, MICHAEL CHARLES, English language educator; b. St. Louis, Nov. 3, 1942; s. Charles Randall and Charlotte W. (Widen) F.; m. Josephine Kumbera Marschel, June 30, 1969; children: Christopher Michael, Laura Marschel. BA, U. of the South, 1964; MA, U. Va., 1965; PhD, U. Chgo., 1972. Asst. prof. English So. Ill. U., Edwardsville, 1965-68; from asst. prof. to prof. English Calif. State U., Bakersfield, 1972—; dir. univ. honors programs Calif. State U., 1985—; dir. Camp Shakespeare Utah Shakespeare Festival, 1986—, company-dramaturg, 1985—; vis. prof. Calif. Inst. Arts, Valencia; mem. Western Region Adv. Coun. Shakespeare Globe Ctr., 1983—; mem. Internat. Com. for the Bibliography of Shakespeare Quarterly, 1985—. Author: Sharkespeare's Lovers, 1983, Teaching Excellence, 1998; co-author: Shakespeare's Women, 1986, The Prose Reader, 1986, 89, 92, 95, 98, Beware the Cat, 1988; editor: Image of Idleness, 1990; contbr. articles to profl. publs. Recipient 4th degree black belt U.S. Judo Fedn., 1990; named CSU System-Wide Outstanding Prof., 1993, Carnegie Found. U.S. Prof. of Yr., 1995. Mem. MLA, Shakespeare Assn. Am., Early English Text Soc., Renaissance Soc. Am., Assn. for Theatre in Higher Edn., So. Calif. Ednl. Theatre Assn. Avocations: judo, tennis, antiques, kids. E-mail: mflachmann@csubak.edu. Home: 1236 Fairway Dr Bakersfield CA 93309-2422 Office: Calif State U Dept English 9001 Stockdale Hwy Bakersfield CA 93311-1099

FLACK, DORA DUTSON, writer, performing artist, lecturer; b. Kimberly, Idaho, July 9, 1919; d. Alonzo Edmund and Iona (James) Dutson; student Brigham Young U., U. Utah, Utah State U.; m. A. LeGrand Flack, Jan. 7, 1946; children: Marc Douglas, Lane LeGrand, Kent Dutson, Marlane, Karen, Marie. Exec. sec. Utah State Nat. Bank, Salt Lake City, 1938-46; author: (with Vernice G. Rosenvall and Mabel H. Miller) Wheat for Man...Why and How, 1952; England's First Mormon Convert, 1957; (with Louise Nielson) Dutson Family History, 1957, 2d rev. edit, 1998; What About Christmas?, 1971; Fun with Fruit Preservation, 1972; (with others) The Joy of Being a Woman, 1972; (with Lula P. Betenson) Butch Cassidy, My Brother, 1975; Dry and Save, 1976 (U.S. Info. Service selection for Internat. Book Fair, Cairo, 1978); (with Janice T. Dixon) Preserving Your Past, 1977; Christmas Magic, 1977; Testimony in Bronze, 1980; (with Karla C. Erickson) Gifts Only You Can Give, 1984; Bread Baking Made Easy, 1984; (with others) Flood Fighters, 1984, (with others) Celebration of Christmas, 1988, Christmas Magic All Year Long, 1991, Bountiful Centennial Cemetery Historical Walking Tour, 1992, Centennial Contest Collection, 1992, Dwellings— 90 Homes in Bountiful Built Before 1900, 1992; author: History of Bountiful Centennial, 1995; History of League of Utah Writers, 1996; contbr. numerous articles, stories to hist., religious and homemaking mags.; performing artist western U.S.; TV and radio appearances; mem. lit. panel Utah Arts Council, 1979-81; mem. faculty Brigham Young U. Edn. Week, 1976-83; mem. faculty World Conf. on Records, Salt Lake City, 1980. Mem. Utah Gov.'s Com. on Employment Handicapped, 1975-81. Recipient numerous state and nat. writing awards, including Utah Arts Coun., 1969, 73-75, 77, 80, 84, Bountiful Total Citizen award Utah C. of C., 1993; named Bountiful's Citizen of Yr. BPOE Elks Lodge 2442, 1998. Mem. League Utah Writers (Writer of Yr. award 1982), Nat. League Am. Pen Women, Daus. Utah Pioneers. Republican. Mormon. Home and Office: 448 E 775 N Bountiful UT 84010-3538

FLAGG, NORMAN LEE, retired advertising executive; b. Detroit, Jan. 21, 1932; s. Frank and Harriet (Brown) F.; m. Carolanne Flagg; children: James, Suzanne. BFA, U. Miami, Miami, Fla., 1958. Advt. supr. Smithkline Beckman, Phila., 1970-75, creative dir., 1975-80; owner Illusions Restaurants, Bryn Maur, Pa., 1979-87, Illusions Restaurant, Tucson, Ariz., 1984-88. Author: Shooting Blanks, 1994. With USMC, 1954-56. Recipient Diana awards Whlse Druggest Assn. 1977, Aesculapius award Modern Medicine 1978. Mem. Acad. Magical Arts.

FLAMMANG, SUSANN, author, publisher; b. Kenosha, Wis., June 2, 1950; d. Leslie James and Beatrice (Woodward) Flammang Sampe. Pres. The Family of God, Las Vegas, 1984—, World Harvest, 1985—, pub., editor The Family of God Newsletter, Poets for Africa, 1986—; pres. World Harvest, 1986—; producer, broadcaster Heart-to-Heart, Sta. KUNV-TV, Las Vegas; v.p. Art Affair. Author of 30 books, numerous works of poetry. Recipient numerous poetry awards including Calif. Fedn. of Poets award, 1983, Humanitarian award Clark County, 1986, Woman of Achievement award, 1987, Gov's Art award, 1985, 86. Mem. Internat. Women's Writing Guild, Internat. PEN Assn., Acad. Am. Poets. Office: The Family of God/World Harvest 8436 Kawala Dr Las Vegas NV 89128-7170

FLANAGAN, JOHN MICHAEL, editor, publisher; b. Bangor, Maine, Mar. 8, 1946; s. Joseph F. and Dorothy Elizabeth (Albert) F.; m. Mary Katherine Fastenau, June 22, 1990. Student, U. Notre Dame, 1963-65; BJ, U. Mo., 1970. With The News-Jour. papers, Wilmington, Del., 1970-84, mng. editor, 1982-84; editor Marin Ind. Jour., San Rafael, Calif., 1984-87; exec. editor Honolulu Star-Bulletin, 1987-93; editor, pub. Honolulu Star-Bull., 1993—. With U.S. Army, 1965-68. Office: Honolulu Star Bull PO Box 3080 Honolulu HI 96802-3080

FLANAGAN, LATHAM, JR., surgeon; b. Pitts., Dec. 2, 1936; s. Latham and Elizabeth Lansing (Bunting) Kimbrough; m. Elizabeth Ruth Losaw, June 26, 1961 (dec. May 1971); 1 child, Jennifer Ruth; m. Mary Jane Flanagan, Mar. 28, 1975; children: Sahale Ann, David Nooroa. MD, Duke U., 1961, student, 1957, MD, 1961. Diplomate Am. Bd. Surgery. Intern U. Calif., San Francisco, 1961-62; resident in surgery U. Oreg., Portland, 1962-66, chief resident in surgery, 1965-66; pvt. practice surgery Sacred Heart Hosp., Eugene, Oreg., 1968-84, 85—; clin. sr. instr. in surgery Oreg. Health Scis. U., Portland, 1968-84; assoc. prof. surgery U. Otago, Dunedin (New Zealand) Pub. Hosp., 1984-85; nat. surgeon Cook Islands, 1985; founder Oreg. Ctr. for Bariatric Surgery, Eugene, 1993—. Contbr. articles to profl. jours. Founder White Bird Clinic, Eugene, 1969-71; mem. adv. com. Planned Parenthood of Lane County, 1979-84, Lt. comdr. USNR, 1966-68, Vietnam. Fellow ACS (pres. Oreg. chpt. 1991-92); mem. AMA, Oreg. Med. Assn., Lane County med. Soc. (com. chair 1970s), Am. Soc. Bariatric Surgery (chair ins. com. 1991-94, councillor 1994-96, sec.-treas. 1996-98, pres.-elect 1998—), North Pacific Surg. Soc., Eugene Surg. Soc. (pres. 1981). Republican. Avocations: mountaineering, photography, river running, scuba, raising llamas. Home: 31033 Foxridge Ln Eugene OR 97405-9589 Office: 655 E 11th Ave Ste 8 Eugene OR 97401-3621

FLANIGAN, JAMES J(OSEPH), journalist; b. N.Y.C., June 6, 1936; s. James and Jane (Whyte) F.; m. Patricia Quatrine, Nov. 28, 1997; children: Michael, Siobhan Jane. BA, Manhattan Coll., 1961. Fin. writer N.Y. Herald Tribune, 1957-66; bur. chief, asst. mng. editor Forbes Mag., 1966-86; bus. columnist, sr. econs. editor L.A. Times, 1986—. Office: LA Times Times Mirror Sq Los Angeles CA 90053

FLANNELLY, KEVIN J., psychologist, research analyst; b. Jersey City, Nov. 26, 1949; s. John J. and Mary C. (Walsh) F.; m. Laura T. Adams, Jan. 10, 1981. BA in Psychology, Jersey City State Coll., 1972; MS in Psychology, Rutgers U., 1975; PhD in Psychology, U. Hawaii, 1983. Rsch. asst. dept. psychology U. Ill., Champaign, 1972-73; rsch. intern Alcohol Behavior Rsch. Lab. Rutgers U., New Brunswick, N.J., 1973-75; rsch. scientist Edward R. Johnstone Tng. and Rsch. Ctr., Bordentown, N.J., 1975-78; teaching asst. dept. psychology U. Hawaii, Honolulu, 1980-81, rsch. asst. Pacific Biomed. Rsch. Ctr., 1981-83, asst. prof. Bekesy Lab. Neurobiology, 1983-85; rsch. statistician, statewide transp. planning office Hawaii Dept. Transportation, Honolulu, 1986-89; researcher Office of Lt. Gov., Honolulu, 1989-93; legis. dir., policy analyst energy and environ. protection com. State House of Reps., 1994; planning and policy analyst Gov.'s Office of State Planning, Honolulu, 1994-96; with office of planning Hawaii Dept. Bus., Econ. Devel. and Tourism, Honolulu, 1996-97; with Office of Gov. of State of Hawaii, Honolulu, 1997—; statis cons. U. Hawaii Sch. Nursing, Honolulu, 1986, Hawaii Dept. Health, Honolulu, 1986; staff mem. gov's. subcabinet on early childhood edn. and childcare, 1989, Hawaii task force on ednl. governance, 1991-92; mem. Gov's. Office State Planning, environ. scanning project, 1992-94; v.p., rsch. dir. Ctr. Psychosocial Rsch., Honolulu, 1987—; instr. dept. social scis. Honolulu Community Coll., 1981; ptnr. Flannelly Cons., 1991—; rsch. dir. Mktg. Rsch. Inst., 1992—; mem. State Ridesharing Task Force, 1987. Editor: Biological Perspective on Aggression, 1984, Introduction to Psychology, 1987; reviewer 8 sci. and profl. jours., 1978—; grant reviewer NSF, 1984-92; contbr. numerous articles to profl. jours. Polit. survey cons., Honolulu, 1988—; transp. cons., Honolulu, 1989—; mktg. cons., Honolulu, 1990—. Grantee NIH, 1984, Fed. Hwy. Adminstrn., 1987; N.J. State scholar N.J. Dept. Higher Edn., 1968-72. Fellow Internat. Soc. Rsch. on Aggression; mem. AAAS, APA, Am. Psychol. Soc., Am. Statis. Assn., Internat. Soc. Comparative Psychology, N.Y. Acad. Scis., Psychonomic Soc., Sigma Xi. Achievements include research on aggression, educational testing, mental-health services, social and emotional behavior, transportation planning, stochastic models of decision-making. Home: 445 Kaiolu St Apt 1006 Honolulu HI 96815-2239 Office: Office of Gov Hawaii State Capitol Honolulu HI 96813

FLANNELLY, LAURA T., mental health nurse, nursing educator, researcher; b. Bklyn., Nov. 7, 1952; d. George A. Adams and Eleanor (Barragry) Mulhearn; m. Kevin J. Flannelly, Jan. 10, 1981. BS in Nursing, Hunter Coll., 1974; MSN, U. Hawaii, 1984, PhD in Ednl. Psychology, 1996. RN, N.Y., Hawaii. Psychiat. nurse Bellevue Hosp., N.Y.C., 1975, asst. head nurse, 1975-77; psychiat. nurse White Plains (N.Y.) Med. Ctr., 1978-79; community mental health nurse South Beach Psychiat. Ctr., N.Y.C., 1979-81; psychiat. nurse The Queen's Med. Ctr., Honolulu, 1981-83; crisis worker Crisis Response Systems Project, Honolulu, 1983-86; instr. nursing U. Hawaii, Honolulu, 1985-92, asst. prof., 1992—, assoc. grad. faculty, 1998—; adj. instr. nursing Hawaii Loa Coll., Honolulu, 1988, Am. Samoa Community Coll., Honolulu, 1987, 89, 90; mem. adv. bd., planning com. Psychiat. Day Hosp. of The Queen's Med. Ctr., Honolulu, 1981-82; program coord. Premenstrual Tension Syndrome Conf., Honolulu, 1984; dir. Ctr. Psychosocial Rsch., Honolulu, 1987—; program moderator 1st U.S-Japan Health Behavioral Conf., Honolulu, 1988; faculty Ctr. for Asia-Pacific Exch., 1995-99, Internat. Conf. on Transcultural Nursing, Honolulu, 1990; mem. bd. dirs. U. Hawaii Profl. Assembly, 1994-97; mem. Hawaii State Coun. Mental Health, 1997—. Contbr. articles to profl. jours. N.Y. State Bd. Regents scholar, 1970-74; NIH nursing trainee, 1983-84; grantee U. Hawaii, 1986, 91, Hawaii Dept. Health, 1990. Fellow Internat. Soc. Rsch. on Aggression; mem. AAAS, APA, Am. Ednl. Rsch. Assn., Am. Psychol. Soc., Am. Psychiat. Nurses Assn., Am. Statis. Assn., Nat. League for Nursing, N.Y. Acad. Scis., Sigma Theta Tau (rec. sec. chpt. 1995-97). Achievements include research on aggressive behavior, educational testing, learning styles, problem-based learning, cross-cultural differences, statistical modeling. Home: 445 Kaiolu St Apt 1006 Honolulu HI 96815-2239 Office: U Hawaii Sch Nursing Webster Hall Honolulu HI 96822

FLECK, RAYMOND ANTHONY, JR., retired university administrator; b. Bklyn., Mar. 9, 1927; s. Raymond Anthony and Dorothy (Canavan) F.; m. Dorothy Marie Rossow, Aug. 22, 1970; children: Andrew Jerome, Casey Thomas. Student, Manhattan Coll., 1946-48; BS, U. Notre Dame, 1951, PhD, 1954. Brother of Holy Cross, 1949-70. Prof. chemistry St. Edward's U., 1954-69, pres., 1957-69; assoc. research chemist dept. environ. toxicology U. Calif. at Davis, 1969-72; pres. Marygrove Coll., Detroit, 1972-79; acting dir. Food Protection and Toxicology Center, U. Calif., Davis, 1979-83; dir. research Calif. State Poly. U., Pomona, 1983-95; assoc. Anver Biosci. Design, Inc., Sierra Madre, Calif., 1995—; cons. EPA, La. Bd. Regents, U. Wis., Eau Claire, NSF; dir. Monterey Basin Pilot Monitoring Project, 1971-72; rep. Primerica Fin. Svcs., 1996—. Vice pres., bd. dirs. Harmony Village Home Corp. N.W., Detroit, 1977-79. Served with USN, 1945-46. NSF fellow, 1952, 1969; recipient U. Notre Dame Centennial of Sci. medal, 1965; sci. bldg. at St. Edward's U. named Fleck Hall. Home: 4273 Guava St La Verne CA 91750-3010

FLECK, RICHARD FRANCIS, English language educator, writer; b. Phila., Aug. 24, 1937; s. J. Keene and Anne M. (DeLeon) F.; m. Maura B. McMahon, June 29, 1963; children: Richard Sean, Michelle Marie, Ann Maureen. BA, Rutgers U., 1959; MA, Colo. State U., 1962; PhD, U. N.Mex., 1970. Park ranger naturalist Rocky Mountain Nat. Pk., Colo., 1959; instr. English North Adams (Mass.) State Coll., 1963-65; prof. of English U. Wyo., Laramie, 1965-90; prof. intercultural studies, dir. humanities div. Teikyo Loretto Heights U., Denver, 1990-93, dir. humanities div., 1991-93; exch. prof. Osaka (Japan) U., 1981-82; vis. prof. SUNY, Cortland, 1988-89; dean arts and humanities C.C. Denver, 1993—. Author: Thoreau and Muir Among the Indians, 1985, Earthen Wayfarer, 1988, Critical Perspectives on Native American Fiction, 1993, (with others) John Muir: His Life and Works, 1993, (with others) World Without Violence: Essays in Honor of the 125th Anniversary of Gandhi's Birth, 1993, (with others) Stories and Stone: Writing the Anasazi Homeland, 1996, Where Land is Mostly Sky: Essays on The American West, 1997; asst. editor Sage U. Wyo., 1965-67; editor Thoreau Jour. Quar., 1975-77; contbg. editor Paintbrush, 1986—. Dem. precinct committeman, Laramie, 1968. With USN, 1961-63. Grantee U. Wyo., 1967, 71, Wyo. State Hist. Soc., 1973, Wyo. Humanities Coun., 1979, 80, Colo. Coun. Arts, 1995. Mem. Thoreau Soc., Sierra Club. Roman Catholic. Avocations: Alpine skiing, cross country skiing, mountaineering. Office: CC Denver Office of Dean Arts & Humanities 1111 W Colfax Ave Denver CO 80204-2026

FLEISCHER, HUGH WILLIAM, lawyer; b. Riverside, Calif., Aug. 14, 1938; s. Frederick John and Helen Marie (Bendorf) F.; m. Lanie Lacey, May 31, 1960; children: Robin, Erin, Ian. BA, Washington U., St. Louis, 1961; JD, U. Denver, 1964. Bar: Colo. 1964, U.S. Supreme Ct. 1970, Alaska, 1971, Mo. 1972. Atty. U.S. Dept. Justice, Washington, 1964-70, Alaska Legal Svcs. Corp., Anchorage, 1971-72; atty., adviser St. Louis Legal Aid Soc., 1972; ptnr. Hedland, Fleischer, Friedman, Brennan & Cooke, Anchorage, 1972-96. Co-dir., McGovern for Pres. campaign, Anchorage, 1972; pres. Bartlett Dem. Club, Anchorage, 1987; bd. dirs. Alaska Pub. Interest Group, 1974—, Out North Theater, 1988-94; pres. Anchorage Friends of Library, 1989-92. Avocations: reading, mountain climbing. Home: 1401 W 11th Ave Anchorage AK 99501-4248 Office: 310 K St Ste 200 Anchorage AK 99501-2064

FLEISCHMANN, ERNEST MARTIN, music administrator; b. Frankfurt, Germany, Dec. 7, 1924; came to U.S., 1969; s. Gustav and Antonia (Koch) F.; children: Stephanie, Martin, Jessica. B of Commerce, U. Cape Town, South Africa, 1950, MusB, 1954; postgrad., South African Coll. Music, 1954-56; MusD (hon.), Cleve. Inst. Music, 1987. Gen mgr. London Symphony Orch., 1959-67; dir. Europe CBS Masterworks, 1967-69; exec. v.p., mng. dir. L.A. Philharm. Assn. and Hollywood Bowl, 1969-88; artistic cons. L.A. Philharm. Assn., 1998—; pres. Fleischmann Arts, Intl. Arts Mgmt. Cons. Svc., 1998—; mem. French Govt. Commn. Reform of Paris Opera, 1967-68; steering com. U.S. nat. commn. UNESCO Conf. Future of Arts, 1975; pres. Fleischmann Arts Internat. Arts Cons., 1998—. Debut as condr. Johannesburg (Republic of South Africa) Symphony Orch., 1942; asst. condr. South African Nat. Opera, 1948-51, Cape Town U. Opera, 1950-54; condr. South African Coll. Music Choir, 1950-52, Labia Grand Opera Co., Cape Town, 1953-55; music organizer Van Riebeeck Festival Cape Town, 1952; dir. music and drama Johannesburg Festival, 1956; contbr. to music publs. Recipient award of Merit, L.A. Jr. C. of C., John Steinway award, Friends of Music award, Disting. Arts Leadership award U. So. Calif., 1989, L.A. Honors award, L.A. Arts Coun., 1989, Live Music award Am. Fedn. Musicians Local 47, 1991, Disting. Authors/Artists award U. Judaism, 1994, Treasures of L.A. award, Ctrl. City Assn. L.A., 1996, Los Amigos de Los Angeles award, L.A. Conv. and Vis. Cur., 1996, Comdrs. Cross of Order of Merit, Germany, 1997, Knight, First Class, of the Order of the White Rose of Finland, Jan., 1999, Officer, Ordre des Arts et Lettres (Legion of Honor), France, 1998, Honored by Mayor and City Counc. as First living Cultural Treasure of Los Angeles, 1998. Mem. Assn. Calif. Symphony Orchs., Major Orch Mgrs. Conf., Am. Symphony Orch. League, L.A. Philharm. Assn. (bd. dirs. 1984—), L.A. Arts Leaders (exec. com.), Nat. Endowment for Arts. Office: Fleischmann Arts 707 Wilshire Blvd Ste 1850 Los Angeles CA 90017-3507

FLEISHER, MARK, health care executive. Student, U. N.Mex. Prodr. info. commls. Twin Star Prodns., Scottsdale, Ariz., 1987-93; real estate assoc. Coldwell Banker, Phoenix, 1993-96; pres. Pain Care Clinic, 1996. Chmn. Dem. Party Ariz. State. Mem. Assn. State Dem. Chairs (chmn.). Home: 13635 N 49th St Scottsdale AZ 85254 Office: Ste 105 1337 S Gilbert Mesa AZ 85204*

FLEISHMAN, ALAN MICHAEL, marketing consultant; b. Berwick, Pa., June 28, 1939; s. Benjamin Bennet and Ruth (Sadock) F.; m. Ann Arrasmith, Aug. 3, 1963; children: Elizabeth, Gregory, Keith. BA, Dickinson Coll., 1961; postgrad., Xavier U., 1966-67, Calif. State U., Fullerton, 1968-69. Sales and mktg. planning Procter & Gamble, Cin., 1963-67; sr. product mgr. Baxter Internat., Costa Mesa, Calif., 1967-70; dir. mkgt. Allergan, Inc., Irvine, Calif., 1970-76; exec. v.p. Hudson Vitamins, West Caldwell, N.J., 1976-77; v.p. mktg. and sales Cooper Vision, Inc., Mountain View, Calif., 1977-80; pres. Alan M. Fleishman, Mktg. Cons., San Carlos, Calif., 1980—; instr. U. Calif., Berkeley, 1990—. With U.S. Army, 1961-63. Mem. Am. Mktg. Assn., Med. Mktg. Assn. Democrat. Jewish. Home and Office: 3 Bluebell Ln San Carlos CA 94070-1526

FLEMING, JANE WILLIAMS, retired educator, author; b. Bethlehem, Pa., May 26, 1926; d. James Robert and Marion Pauline (Melloy) Groman; m. George Elliott Williams, July 2, 1955 (div. July 1965); children: Rhett Dorman, Santee Stuart, Timothy Cooper; m. Jérome Thomas Fleming, Sept. 25, 1980. BS, UCLA, 1951; MA, Calif. State U., Long Beach, 1969. Tchr. San Diego Unified Sch Dist., 1951-55, Costa Mesa (Calif.) Sch. Dist., 1955-56, Long Beach (Calif.) Sch. Dist., 1956-58, 62-87, 1990-92; ret. Author: Why Janey Can't Teach, 1999. Mem. Mus. of Tolerance. Fellow Phi Kappa Phi; mem. Ret. Tchrs. Assn., UCLA Alumni Assn., Planetary Soc. (charter), Mus. of Tolerance. Avocations: theater, travel, ancient history, mysteries, reading about outer space. E-mail: jwilli5687@aol.com. Address: PO Box 13053 Belmont Shore CA 90803-8053

FLEMING, LAURA CHRISTINE, software engineer; b. Oakland, Calif., May 8, 1953; d. Glen Thomas and Maxine B. (Stracner) F.; m. John Ignacio Cruz, Sept. 17, 1972 (div. 1979); m. Mark Paul von Gnechten, May 3, 1981; children: Paul Fleming, Thomas von Gnechten, Martin von Gnechten. BS in Computer Sci., Calif. State U., Hayward, 1989. Sys. design engr. Amdahl, Sunnyvale, Calif., 1978-85; sr. mem. tech. staff Cadence Design Sys., San Jose, 1985-94; sr. software engr. Dow Jones Telerate, Palo Alto, Calif., 1994-95; sr. engr. Chordiant Software, Inc., Palo Alto, 1995—. Sec. Citizen Action Com. for Spl. Edn., Fremont, Calif., 1988, Parent Faculty Assn., Fremont, 1992-93. Mem. IEEE, Soc. Women Engrs. Democrat. Avocations: computers, photography, tennis. Home: 40010 Dolerita Ave Fremont CA 94539-3014 Office: Chordiant Software Inc 20400 Stevens Creek Blvd # 400 Cupertino CA 95014-2217

FLEMMING, STANLEY LALIT KUMAR, family practice physician, mayor, state legislator; b. Rosebud, S.D., Mar. 30, 1953; s. Homer W. and Evelyn C. (Misra) F.; m. Martha Susan Light, July 2, 1977; children: Emily Drisana, Drew Anil, Claire Elizabeth Misra. AAS, Pierce Coll., 1973; BS in Zoology, U. Wash., 1976; MA in Social Psychology, Pacific Luth. U., 1979; DO, Western U., 1985. Diplomate Am. Coll. Family Practice; cert. ATLS. Intern Pacific Hosp. Long Beach (Calif.), 1985-86; resident in family practice Pacific Hosp. Long Beach, 1986-88; fellow in adolescent medicine Children's Hosp. L.A., 1988-90; clin. preceptor Family Practice Residency Program Calif. Med. Ctr., U. So. Calif., L.A., 1989—; clin. instr. Sch. Medicine U. So. Calif., L.A., 1989-90; clin. instr. Western U. Health Sci., Pomona, Calif., 1989-90; clin. asst. prof. Family Medicine Western U. Health Sci., Pomona, 1987—; exam. commr., expert examiner Calif. Osteo. Med. Bd., 1987-89; med. dir. Cmty. Health Care Delivery System Pierce County, Tacoma, Wash., 1990—; mayor City of University Place, Wash.; clin. instr. U. Wash. Sch. Medicine, 1990—; bd. dirs. Calif. State Bd. Osteo. Physicians Examiners, 1989—, cons., 1989. Mayor, City of University Place, Wash. Col. M.C., U.S. Army, 1976—,. Named one of Outstanding Young Men of Am., U.S. Jaycees, 1983, 85, Intern of Yr. Western U. Health Sci. Coll., 1986, Resident of Yr., Greater Long Beach Assn., 1988, Alumnus of Yr., Pierce Coll., 1993, 97; recipient Pumerantz-Weiss award, 1985. Mem. Fedn. State Bds. Licensing, Am. Osteopathic Assn., Am. Acad. Family Practice, Soc. Adolescent Medicine, Assn. Military Surgeons U.S., Assn. U.S. Army (chpt. pres.), Soc. Am. Military Engrs. (chpt. v.p.), Calif. Med. Assn., Wash. Osteopathic Med. Assn. (Physician of Yr. 1993), Calif. Family Practice Soc., Long Beach Med. Assn. (com. mem.), N.Y. Acad. Sci., Calif. Med. Review Inc., Sigma Sigma Phi, Am. Legion. Episcopalian. Home: 7619 Chambers Creek Rd W University Place WA 98467 Office: Family Health Ctr University Place WA 98466

FLETCHER, BETTY B., federal judge; b. Tacoma, Mar. 29, 1923. B.A., Stanford U., 1943; LL.B., U. Wash., 1956. Bar: Wash. 1956. Mem. firm Preston, Thorgrimson, Ellis, Holman & Fletcher, Seattle, 1956-1979; judge U.S. Ct. Appeals (9th cir.), Seattle., 1979—. Mem. ABA (Margaret Brent award 1992), Wash. State Bar Assn., Am. Law Inst., Fed. Judges Assn. (past pres.), Order of Coif, Phi Beta Kappa. Office: US Ct Appeals 9th Cir 1010 5th Ave Ste 1000 Seattle WA 98104-1130*

FLETCHER, HOMER LEE, librarian; b. Salem, Ind., May 11, 1928; s. Floyd M. and Hazel (Barnett) F.; m. Jacquelyn Ann Blanton, Feb. 7, 1950; children—Deborah Lynn, Randall Brian, David Lee. B.A., Ind. U., 1953; M.S. in L.S, U. Ill., 1954. Librarian Milw. Pub. Library, 1954-56; head librarian Ashland (Ohio) Pub. Library, 1956-59; city librarian Arcadia (Cal.) Pub. Library, 1959-65, Vallejo (Calif.) Pub. Library, 1965-70; city librarian San Jose, Calif., 1970-90, ret., 1990. Contbr. articles to profl. jours. Pres. S. Solano chpt. Calif. Assn. Neurol. Handicapped Children, 1968-69; mem. Presbyn. Ch. Sunnyvale, 1997. Served with USAF, 1946-49. Mem. ALA (intellectual freedom com. 1967-72), Calif. Library Assn. (pres. pub. libraries sect. 1967), Phi Beta Kappa. Democrat. Presbyterian. Home: 7921 Belknap Dr Cupertino CA 95014-4973

FLETCHER, JAMES ALLEN, video company executive; b. Toledo, Sept. 18, 1947; s. Allen Rae and Ruth Helen (Scharf) F.; m. Kathy Jane Barrett, Jan. 25, 1975. AS, West Coast U., 1977, BSEE, 1979. Electronic technician Hughes Aircraft Co., El Segundo, Calif., 1970-72; engring. technician Altec Corp., Anaheim, Calif., 1972-75, Magna Corp., Santa Fe Springs, Calif., 1975-76; engring. technician Odetics Inc., Anaheim, 1976-79, electronic engr., 1979-86; pres., founder F & B Technologies, Orange, Calif., 1986—. Served as sgt. U.S. Army, 1967-69. Mem. Soc. Motion Picture and TV Engrs., Mensa. Libertarian. Avocations: record collecting, automobile restoration and customization. Office: F & B Technologies 630 N Tustin St Ste 1516 Orange CA 92867-7127

FLETCHER, LELAND VERNON, artist; b. Cumberland, Md., Sept. 18, 1946; s. Kenneth L. and Marjorie L. (Benecke) F.; m. Janis Traub, July 19, 1978; children: Nathan Fletcher, Joshua Traub. BS, U. Minn., 1972. One man shows include U. Minn. Exptl. Gallery, 1972, La Mamelle Art Ctr., San Francisco, 1976, San Jose State U. Union Gallery, 1978, Place des Nations, Maubeuge, France, 1987, Univ. Art Gallery, Calif. State U., Hayward, 1989, McHenry County Coll. Art Gallery, Crystal Lake, Ill., 1991, Lake County Mus., Calif., 1995; group exhbns. include Mus. Contemporary Art, Sao Paulo, Brazil, 1977, Urbanart '77, Vancouver, Can., 1977, L.A. Inst. Contemporary Art, 1978, Inst. Modern Art, Brisbane, 1978, Hansen Gallery, N.Y.C., 1978, Fendrick Gallery, Washington, 1979, 8th Internat. Print Bienale, Cracow, Poland, 1980, Cooper-Hewitt Mus., N.Y.C., 1980, Sch. Art Inst. Chgo., 1981, Metronome Gallery, Barcelona, 1981, 16th Bienal de Sao Paulo, 1981, Neue galerie der Stadt Linz, 1982, Bienal de Pontevedra, Spain, 1983, Lyng by Kunstbibliotek, Denmark, 1984, Otis Art Inst./Parsons Sch. Design, Los Angeles, 1984, 10th Internat. Print Bienale, Cracow, Poland, 1984, Mus. Arte da Univ. Fed. de Mato Grosso, Brazil, 1984, 11th Biennal Internat., Mus. Art Contemporani d'Eivissa, Spain, 1984, Intergrafik '84 Triennale, Berlin, Fiatel Muveszek Klubja Budapest, 1985, Intersection Gallery, San Francisco, 1985, Mus. Petit Format, Couvin, Belgium, 1985, 9th British Internat. Print Biennale, Bradford, Eng., 1986, Victoria and Albert Mus., London, 1986, Sculpt 87/3, Maubeuge, 1987, Fundacio la Caixa, Valencia, Spain, 1987, Acad. Belles Arts Sabadell, Barcelona, 1987, Taliesin Ctr. for Arts, Swansea, Eng., 1987, Worcester (Eng.) City Art Gallery, 1987, Symposium Sculpture en Plein Air, Maubeuge, France, 1987, Richards Gallery, Northeastern U., Boston, 1987, Montserrat Coll. Art, Beverly, Mass., 1987, 11 Internat. Print Biennale, Krakow, 1986, Skulptur Biennale '88 Royal Gardens, Copenhagen, Internat. Biennale Palais des Roi de Majorque, Peripignan, France, 1988, Fine Art Mus., Budapest, Hungary, 1988, Works gallery, San Jose Calif., 1988, Palthehuis Mus., Oldenzaal, The Netherlands, 1989, Budapest Galeria, Hungary, 1989, Stedelijk Hoger Institut, Cultural Ctr., Genk, Belgium, 1989, Inst. Contemporary Art, Clocktower Gallery, N.Y.C., 1989, Corporacion GOG, Pontevedra, Spain, 1989, Ea. Washington U., Spokane Ctr. Gallery, 1989, Munson-Williams-Proctor Inst., Sch. Art Gallery, Utica, N.Y., 1989, 44th Salon des Realities Nouvelles, Grand Palais, Paris, 1990, Buda Castle Palace, Budapest, 1990, Pensacola (Fla.) Mus. Art, 1990, Anchorage (Alaska) Mus. Art, 1990, Fundacao Democrito Rocha, Fortaleza, Brazil, 1991, Miejski Osrodek Kultury, Chelm, Poland, 1991, Bharat Bhavan, Bhopal, India, 1991, Chabot Coll., Hayward, Calif., 1992, Lake County Arts Coun., Lakeport, Calif., 1992, Artisans Gallery, Mill Valley, Calif., 1992, Greenville Mus. Art, N.C., Centro Civico Social, Alcorcon, Madrid, 1994, Lake Co. Mus., 1995, Muscarelle Mus. Art, Coll. William and Mary, Williamsburg, Va., 1998, Mus. Internat. Contemporary Art, Florianopolis, Brazil, 1998, Manchester Met. U. Art Dept. Gallery, England, 1998, Helsinki Fine Arts Acad., Finland, 1998, numerous others; represented in permanent collection at Mus. Contemporary Art, Sao Paulo, Mpls. Inst. Arts, Art Mus. of Calif. State U., Long Beach, deSaisset Mus., U. Santa Clara (Calif.), Art Inst. Chgo., Victoria and Albert Mus., London, Museen der Stadt Koln, Ludwig Mus., Cologne, Mus. Plantin-Moretus, Antwerp, Mus. de Arte Moderno, Barcelona, Bradford Mus., Eng., Kunsthalle, Hamburg, Galleria D'Arte Moderna, Trieste, Ecole des Beaux-Arts, Mus. Maubeuge, Musee de la Sculpture en plein Air, Maubeuge, Musee de Maubeuge, FMK Galeria, Budapest, Bur. for Artistic Exhibitions, Cracow, Poland, Kunsthalle Bremen, West Germany, Museu de Arte da Universidad Federal de Mato Grosso, Brazil, others. Address: 3288 Konocti Ln Kelseyville CA 95451-9131

FLICK, WILLIAM FREDRICK, surgeon; b. Lancaster, Pa., Aug. 18, 1940; s. William Joseph and Anna (Volkl) F.; m. Jacqueline Denise Phaneuf, May 21, 1966; children: William J., Karen E., Christopher R., Derrick W., Brian A. BS, Georgetown U., 1962, MD, 1966; MBA, U. Colo., 1990. Cert. Am. Bd. Surgeons, 1976. Self employed surgeon Cheyenne, Wyo., 1973-84; pres., surgeon Cheyenne Surgical Assocs., 1984-94; med. dir. Blue Cross Blue Shield of Wyo., Cheyenne, 1994—. Trustee Laramie County Sch. Dist. #1, Cheyenne, 1988-92. Maj., chief of surgery USAF, 1971-73. Fellow ACS; mem. Am. Coll. Physician Execs., Nat. Assn. Managed Care. Republican. Roman Catholic. Office: Blue Cross Blue Shield Wyo 400 House Ave Cheyenne WY 82007-1468

FLINN, ROBERTA JEANNE, management and computer applications consultant; b. Twin Falls, Idaho, Dec. 19, 1947; d. Richard H. and Ruth (Johnson) F. Student Colo. State U., 1966-67. Cert. Novell netware engr. Ptnr., Aqua-Star Pools & Spas, Boise, Idaho, 1978—, mng. ptnr., 1981-83; ops. mgr. Polly Pools, Inc., Canby, Oreg., 1983-84, br. mgr. Polly Pools, Inc., A-One Distributing, 1984-85; comptr., Beaverton Printing, Inc., 1986-89; mng. ptnr. Invisible Ink, Canby, Oreg., 1989—. Mem. Nat. Appaloosa Horse Club, Oreg. Dressage Soc., NetWare Users International (Portland chpt.). Home: 24687 S Central Point Rd Canby OR 97013-9743

FLINT, LOU JEAN, retired state education official; b. Ogden, Utah, July 11, 1934; d. Elmer Blood and Ella D. (Adams) F.; children: Dirk Kershaw Brown, Kristie Susan Brown Felix, Flint Kershaw Brown. B.S., Weber State Coll., 1968; M.Ed., U. Utah, 1974, Ed.S, 1981. Cert. early childhood and elem. edn., Utah Bd. Edn., 1968, edn. adminstrn., 1981. Master tchr. Muir Elem., Davis Sch. Dist., Farmington, Utah, 1968-77; edn. specialist Dist. I, Dept. Def., Eng., Scotland, Norway, Denmark, Holland, Belgium, 1977-79; ednl. cons. Office Higher Edn. State of Utah, Utah System Approach to Individualized Learning, Tex., S.C., Fla., Utah, 1979-81; acad. affairs officer Commn. Higher Edn. Office State of Utah, Salt Lake City, 1982-98; mem. Women's Politics Caucus; adv. bd. Women and Bus. Conf.; mem. MHCS Centennial Com., 1995-96, welfare reform demonstration project State of Utah, 1992-96, foster care citizen review pilot project State of Utah. Named Exemplary Tchr., Utah State Bd. Edn., 1970-77, Outstanding Educator, London Central High Sch., 1979; recipient Appreciation award, Gov. of Utah, 1983-85, 93, Woman of Achievement award Utah Bus. and Profl. Women, 1985, Pathfinder award C. of C., 1988, Outstanding Educator award YWCA, 1989, Silver Apple award Utah State U., 1992, award for svcs. Utah Mental Health Assn., 1996. Mem. AAUW (Edn. Found. award given in her honor, 1986, named Woman Who Makes History, 1994), Nat. Assn. Women's Work/Women's Worth (Disting. Woman award 1987), Women's Polit. Caucus (Susa Young Gates award 1987), Nat. Assn. Edn. Young Children, Utah Assn. Edn. Young Children (past pres.), Women Concerned About Nuclear War, Utah Jaycee Aux. (past pres. Centerville), Crones Coun., Math Sci. Network. Mormon. Author: The Comprehensive Community College, 1980; others.

FLINT, WILLIS WOLFSCHMIDT (WILLI WOLFSCHMIDT), artist, sculptor; b. Kenton, Ohio, Dec. 27, 1936; s. Wilbur Henry and Ilo Edna (Obenour) F. Student, Art Career Sch., N.Y.C., 1957-60, Ins. Allende, San Miguel Allende, Mexico, 1961. Artist trainee Kossack Advt., Tucson, 1961; gen. boardman Mithoff Advt., El Paso, 1962-63; tech. illustrator Volt Tech. Corp., N.Y.C., 1967; gen. illustrator Salesvertising Advt., Denver, 1968; gen. boardman/cons. Burr-Brown Rsch. Corp., Tucson, 1969-71; musician, actor Paul Barons Harmonica Rascals, Bklyn., 1965-85; musician The Wild Ones, Tucson, 1982-83; muralist, San Diego, Tucson, N.Y.C., 1976-80; artist, Tucson, 1985—; originator Fantasy-Expressionism, 1984; pvt. tchr. art, Tucson, 1981-85; cons. muralist Yaqui Indian-Pascua Ctr., Tucson, 1989; freelance muralist and graphic artist Wolfschmidt & Washburn, 1994-96. Poetry included in: Best-Loved Contemporary Poems, 1979, Famous Poems of Today, 1995, A Delicate Balance, 1996, three edits. of Poetic Voices of America, 1996, Best Poems of the '90s, 1996, Best Poems of the 20th Century, 1996, Best Famous Poems of '96, 1997, Best Poems of '97, 1997, Soaring with the Wind, 1998, Ten Years of Excellence, 1998; one man show (sculptor) at Old Pascua Village, Tucson, 1996; paintings exhibited in group shows at United Way Fund Drive Exhibit, Tucson, United Servicemen's Orgn. Exhibit, Mobile, Ala., Student Union Exhibit U. Ariz., Tucson, La Galeria Instituto, San Miguel de Allende, Margarita De Mena Gallery, N.Y.C.; represented in permanent collection So. Ariz. Hist. Soc., Tombstone, also pvt. collections. With USN, 1954-57, 1979-81. Recipient scholarship Latham Found., 1958, award of merit Latham Found., 1958, letter commendation U. Ariz. Family Practice, Tucson, 1978, letter commendation Dept. Navy, San Diego, 1979. Mem. The Maverick Artists, Internat. Soc. Poets. Avocations: antique vehicles, international travel, motorcycling. Home: 707 W Calle Progreso Tucson AZ 85705-6446

FLOCK, ROBERT ASHBY, retired entomologist; b. Kellogg, Idaho, July 16, 1914; s. Abraham Lincoln and Florence Louise (Ashby) F.; m. Elsie Marie Ronken, Apr. 8, 1950; children: Karen Marie, Anne Louise Checkai. BS, U. Ariz., 1938, MS, 1941; PhD, U. Calif., Berkeley, 1951. Inspector Ariz. Commn. Agriculture and Horticulture, Phoenix, 1938-41, asst. entomologist, 1941-46; lab. tech. U. Calif., Riverside, 1947-52, asst. entomologist, 1952-63; entomologist Imperial County Dept. Agriculture, El Centro, Calif., 1963-85, part-time entomologist, 1985—. Contbr. articles to profl. jours. Mem. Entomol. Soc. Am., Am. Phytopathol. Soc., Pan-Pacific Entomol. Soc., AAAS, Ctr. for Process Studies, Kiwanis (pres. Imperial Valley chpt. 1984-86, Man of Yr. 1986), Sigma Xi. Republican. Methodist. Avocations: taxonomy and biology of Homoptera, desert ecology, science, religion. Home: 667 Wensley Ave PO Box 995 El Centro CA 92244-0995 Office: Imperial County Dept Agricu 150 S 9th St El Centro CA 92243-2801

FLOCK, ROBERTA RAE, real estate executive; b. Seattle, Nov. 14, 1937; d. Boyd Wilbur and Pearl C. Anderson; m. Larry Jay Flock, Apr. 4, 1964; children: Tony J., Shane M. Grad., Lincoln H.S., Seattle. Owner Real Estate Investments, Seattle, 1970—, Flock Apts., Seattle, 1970—; ins. agt. Seattle, 1968-73, real estate agt., 1970—. Vol. Seattle Art Mus., Rental/Sales Gallery, Seattle, 1989-99, vol. chmn., 1991-92. Mem. Apt. Assn. Seattle and King County, Fremont C. of C., Laguna Art Mus., Seattle Art Mus., Tacoma Art Mus., Mus. of Northwest Art, Frye Mus., Pratt Fine Arts Ctr. Republican. Avocations: antiques, art collecting, boating. Office: PO Box 60065 Seattle WA 98160-0065

FLOM, ROBERT MICHAEL, interior designer; b. Grand Forks, N.D., Oct. 27, 1952; s. John Nicholai and Irene Magdaline (Miller) F.; m. Holly Suzanne Schue, July 20, 1975 (div. June 1986); m. Margaret Elizabeth Moon, Oct. 15, 1988; children: Amy Michelle Moon, Jamie Bryant Moon. Student, Western Tech., 1970-71, U. N.D., 1980-83, LaSalle U., 1994-95, Century U., 1996—. Asst. food and beverage mgr. Holiday Inn/Topeka Inns, Denver, 1970-71; interior designer, fl. mgr. Crossroads Furniture, Grand Forks, 1972-85; store mgr. Greenbaums, Tacoma, 1986-88, interior designer, 1986—; tng. advisor Greenbaums, Bellevue, Wash., 1988—. Mem. Am. Soc. Interior Designers (allied mem.), Autism Soc. Tacoma-Pierce County (treas. 1991—). Avocations: reading, cycling, cross-country skiing, hiking, woodworking. Home: 6816 47th St W Tacoma WA 98466-4912 Office: Greenbaums 929 118th Ave SE Bellevue WA 98005-3889

FLOOD, JAMES TYRRELL, broadcasting executive, public relations consultant; b. Los Angeles, Oct. 5, 1934; s. James Joseph and Teresa (Rielly) F.; m. Bonnie Carolyn Lutz, Mar. 25, 1966; children: Hilary C., Sean L. BA in Liberal Arts, U. Calif., Santa Barbara, 1956; MA in Communications, Calif. State U., Chico, 1981. Publicist Rogers & Cowan, 1959-60, Jim Mahoney & Assocs., 1960-61, ABC-TV, San Francisco and Hollywood, Calif., 1961-64; cons. pub. relations, Beverly Hills, Calif., 1964-72; pub. relations, advt. dir. Jerry Lewis Films, 1964-72; dir. pub. rels. MTM Prodns., 1970-72; pub. relations cons. Medic Alert Found. Internat., 1976-83; owner, mgr. Sta. KRIJ-FM, Paradise, 1983-88; instr. Calif. State U. Sch. Communications, Chico, 1982-89; gen. mgr. KIXE-TV (PBS), Redding-Chico, Calif., 1991-92; media cons., 1993—. represented numerous artists including Pearl Bailey, Gary Owens, Ruth Buzzi, Allen Ludden, Betty White, Celeste Holm, Jose Feliciano, Tom Kennedy, Shirley Jones, David Cassidy, others. Pub. rels. dir. Warren Miller Prodns., 1967—, Mary Tyler Moore Prodns., 1971. Calif. media cons. Carter/Mondale campaign, 1976; mem. Calif. Dem. Fin. Com., 1982-83. Served with USNR, 1956-58. Mem. Calif. Broadcasters Assn. (bd. dirs. 1986-88).

FLOR, LOY LORENZ, chemist, corrosion engineer, consultant; b. Luther, Okla., Apr. 25, 1919; s. Alfred Charles and Nellie M. (Wilkinson) F.; BA in Chemistry, San Diego State Coll., 1941; m. Virginia Louise Pace, Oct. 1, 1946; children: Charles R., Scott R., Gerald C., Donna Jeanne, Cynthia Gail. With Helix Water Dist., La Mesa, Calif., 1947-84, chief chemist, 1963—, supr. water quality, 1963—, supr. corrosion control dept., 1956—. 1st. lt. USAAF, 1941-45. Registered profl. engr., Calif. Mem. Am. Chem. Soc. (chmn. San Diego sect. 1965—), Am. Water Works Assn. (chmn. water quality div. Calif. sect. 1965—), Nat. Assn. Corrosion Engrs. (chmn. western region 1970), Masons. Republican. Presbyterian.

FLORENCE, KENNETH JAMES, lawyer; b. Hanford, Calif., July 31, 1943; s. Ivy Owen and Louella (Dobson) F.; m. Verena Magdalena Demuth, Dec. 10, 1967. BA, Whittier Coll., 1965; JD, Hastings Coll. Law, U. Calif.-San Francisco, 1974. Bar: Calif. 1974, U.S. Dist. Ct. (cen. dist.) Calif. 1974, U.S. Dist. Ct. (ea. and so. dists.) Calif., 1976, U.S. Dist. Ct. (no. dist.) Calif. 1980, U.S. Ct. Appeals (9th cir.) 1975, U.S. Supreme Ct. 1984. Dist. mgr. Pacific T&T, Calif., 1969-71; assoc. Parker, Milliken, et al, Los Angeles, 1974-78; ptnr. Dern, Mason, et al, 1978-84, Swerdlow, Florence & Sanchez, A Law Corp., Beverly Hills, 1984—; pres. Westside Legal Services, Inc., Santa Monica, Calif., 1982-83. Served to lt. USNR, 1966-69, Vietnam. Col. J.G. Boswell scholar, 1961. Mem. ABA (co-chmn. state labor law com. 1988-91). Democrat. Office: Swerdlow Florence & Sanchez 9401 Wilshire Blvd Ste 828 Beverly Hills CA 90212-2921

FLORENCE, LINDA SUE, secondary school educator; b. Greenville, S.C., Nov. 26, 1957; d. Charles Jr. and Alice Christine (Johnson) Bartley; m. Dennis Jay Florence, July 25, 1992; 1 child, James Nolan. BS in Biology, We. Ky. U., 1980; MA in Bilingual Multicultural Edn., No. Ariz. U., 1994. Tchr. Frederick Fraize H.S., Cloverport, Ky., 1980, Gila Bend (Ariz.) Unified Sch. Dist., 1981-82; biology tchr. Yuma (Ariz.) Union H.S. Dist., 1982—; co-dir. Summer Sci. Acad., Yuma, Ariz., 1996—. Contbr. article to profl. jour. Mem. Nat. Biology Tchrs. Assn., NEA, Ariz. Sci. Tchrs. Assn., Phi Delta Kappa. Democrat. Mem. So. Bapt. Ch. Avocations: reading, crafts, travel, golf. Home: 2038 S 10th Ave Yuma AZ 85364-8311 Office: Cibola H S 4100 W 20th St Yuma AZ 85364-4800

FLORENCE, MICHAEL GLENN, medical educator; b. Atlanta, Sept. 15, 1949; s. Thomas James and Glenna Louise (Smith) F.; m. Gwen Yvonne Kawabata, Aug. 10, 1980; children: Jameson Michael, Kelsey Anne. BS, Washington and Lee U., 1971; MD, Emory U., 1975. Diplomate Nat. Bd. Med. Examiners, Am. Bd. Surgery; lic. physician, Wash. Intern then resident U. Wash., Seattle, 1975-80, acting instr., 1980-93, clin. assoc. prof. surgery, 1993—; mem. staff Providence Med. Ctr., Seattle, Swedish Hosp. Med. Ctr., Seattle; presenter and instr. in field. Contbr. numerous articles to profl. jours. Mem. AMA, ACS (program chmn. 1993, sec.-treas. 1994—), Wash. Med. Soc., King County Med. Soc. (membership com. 1982, 84-86), Seattle Surg. Soc. (trustee 1985, program chmn. 1986-89, sec. 1992-94), Henry Harkins Surg. Soc. (pres. 1990-91), North Pacific Surg. Soc., Pacific Coast Surg. Assn. Avocations: water skiing, snow skiing, computers in medicine. Office: Arnold Pavilion 1221 Madison St Ste 1411 Seattle WA 98104-3555

FLORENCE, VERENA MAGDALENA, business and computer consultant; b. Interlaken, Switzerland, Nov. 4, 1946; came to U.S., 1967; d. Paul Robert and Marie (Raess) Demuth; m. Kenneth James Florence, Dec. 10, 1967. BA, U. Calif., Berkeley, 1974; MS, UCLA, 1979, PhD, 1982. Research scientist Procter & Gamble, Cin., 1983; adminstr. Swerdlow & Florence, Beverly Hills, Calif., 1984-89; pres., chief exec. officer, chmn. of bd. Böl Designs, Inc., L.A., Calif., 1989—. Contbr. articles to profl. jours. Mem. L.A. Computer Soc. (SIG leader). Democrat. Home and Office: 9401 Wilshire Blvd Ste 828 Beverly Hills CA 90212-2921

FLORES, JOHN A., internist; b. Indio, Calif., Jan. 17, 1957; m. Gladys Dolores Flores; children: Angelina, Jacob, Matthew, Marisa, Lauren. BS in Biochemistry, U. Calif., Riverside, 1980, MS in Biochemistry, 1981; MD, U. Minn., 1986. Intern internal medicine San Fernando Valley Program UCLA, 1986-87, resident internal medicine San Fernando Valley Program, 1988-90; resident anesthesiology U. Kans. Med. Ctr., 1987-88; dir. Pain Mgmt. Clinic Beaver Med. Clinic, Redlands, Calif., 1990—, physician internal medicine, 1990—; mem. active staff Redlands Community Hosp., 1990—; instr. advanced coronary life support cert. San Fernando Valley program UCLA, 1988-89; mentor sci. ednl. enhancement svcs. health profl. mentor program Calif. Poly. State U., 1991—; preceptor med. student edn. Osteo. Sch. Medicine Coll. of Pacific, 1993-94; lectr. Med. Sch. U. Minn., 1982-84, San Fernando Valley program UCLA, 1988-89, Beaver Med. Clinic, 1992, Calif. Poly. State U., Pomona, 1992, Redlands Com. Hosp., 1994. Recipient Appreciation award Chicano/Latino Pre-Med. Student Assn. Calif. Poly State U., 1993, Appreciation award Beverly Manor Convalescent, 1993, Recognition award Coll. Osteopathic Medicine Pacific, 1993—. Mem. AMA, ACP (assoc.), Am. soc. Anesthesiologists, Am. Soc. Pain Mgmt., Am. Soc. Regional Anesthesia, Calif. Med. Assn. (alt. del. for San Bernardino County Med. Soc. 1993-94, tech. adv. com. on pain mgmt. 1994—), San Bernardino County Med. Soc. (young physicians com. 1992—, chmn. 1993—, exec. com. 1993—), Redlands C. of C. Home: 2 W Fern Ave Redlands CA 92373-5916

FLORES, VERA JACOBSON, theater arts educator; b. San Francisco, Jan. 14, 1952; d. Leo David and Doris Bush (Mulford) Jacobson; m. Paul Vasiliy Kopeikin, Nov. 27, 1975 (div. Feb. 1990); 1 child, Katie Elizabeth Kopeikin; m. Leonard Flores, Jr., Dec. 29, 1993. BA in Theatre Arts, Calif. State U., Hayward, 1992; M in Arts Edn., San Francisco State U., 1998. Cert. tchr. English/drama, also mid. sch., Calif. Realtor Trotter Realty, Burlingame, Calif., 1977-79; bookkeeper Vorsatz & Vorsatz, Burlingame, Calif., 1981-86; med. transcriptionist Mills Meml. Hosp., San Mateo, Calif., 1986-94, 94-96; tchr. Visitacion Valley Sch., San Francisco, 1994-96; tchr. drama, media, coord. arts Potrero Hill Mid. Sch. of the Arts, San Francisco, 1996-98; tchr. drama, media edn. Carlmont H.S., Belmont, Calif., 1998—; mem. leadership team Visitacion Valley Sch., 1995-96; judge Shakespeare Festival, Calif. State U., Hayward, 1994-95. Dir. (musical theatre) The Wiz, 1995, Little Shop of Horrors, 1996, Around the World, 1998, Murder for Rent, 1998. Mem. AAUW, Autism Soc. Am., San Francisco Mus. Modern Art, Calif. Ednl. Theatre, Epilepsy Soc. Am., Women in Arts, Performing Arts Libr. Mus., Nat. Urban Alliance, Calif. Ednl. Theatre Assn. (bd. dirs., New Tchr. of Yr. 1998), Calif. Arts Project. Democrat. Episcopalian. Avocations: running, tap dancing, gardening, oil painting, travel. E-mail: vjflores@postoffice.pacbell.net. Office: Carlmont H S 1400 Alameda de las Pulgas Belmont CA 94002

FLORES, WILLIAM VINCENT, Latin American studies educator; b. San Diego, Jan. 10, 1948; s. William J. and Velia (Aldrete) F.; m. Carole Mary Dische, July 3, 1973 (div. Jan 1986); children: Antonio Ramon, Diana Maria. BA, UCLA, 1970; MA in Polit. Sci., Stanford U., 1971, PhD in Social Theory/Pub. Policy, 1987. Teaching & rsch. fellow Stanford (Calif.) U., 1971-72; lectr. in polit. sci. Calif. State U., Hayward, 1972-75; program coord. Project Intercept, San Jose, Calif., 1976-78; assoc. dir. Gardner Cmty. Health Ctr., San Jose, 1979-84; lectr. U. Santa Clara, Calif., 1985-87; asst. dir. Inter-Univ. Program for Latino Rsch., Stanford, 1987-88; chair dept. Chicano/Latin Am. studies Calif. State U., Fresno, 1988-92, assoc. dean Sch. of Social Scis., 1992-94; dean Coll. Soc. and Behavioral Scis. Calif. State U., Northridge, 1996—; v.p., bd. trustees Arte Americas, 1995-96. Author: Latino Cultural Citizenship, 1997. Mem. CSU Northridge Found. Bd. CSUN pres.'s bus. coun., 1996-98, exec. com. Chicano/Latino Faculty Assn. Calif. State Univ. Sys., 1994-95; chair Com. for Hispanic Ednl. Equity, Fresno, 1990-92; mem. nat. adv. bd. U.S. Students Assn., Washington, 1991-93; v.p. Latino Agenda Coalition Calif., L.A., 1984-86. Chicano Fellows Program fellow Stanford U., 1971-72; Ford Found. fellow Stanford U., 1970-74; Compton-Danforth fellow Stanford U., 1984-85.; Rockefeller Humanities fellow, 1993-94; Am. Coun. on Edn. fellow, 1993-94. Mem. Am. Anthropol. Assn., Am. Studies Assn., Nat. Assn. Chicano Studies (co-chair polit. action com. 1986), Internat. Platform Assn. Democrat. Avocations: poetry, music, racquetball, hiking. Office: Coll Social Behav Scis 18111 Nordhoff St Northridge CA 91330-0001

FLORESCU, JOHN MAURICE, broadcast executive; b. Boston, Apr. 14, 1954; s. Radu Radu and Nicole (Michel) F.; m. Gina Diane Christensen, July 31, 1993; 1 child, Peter Vlad. Degree, Campion Hall, Oxford U., England, 1974; BA, Boston Coll., Chestnut Hill, 1976, MA. Correspondent Associated Press, Paris, 1977-79; staff Sen. Edward Kennedy Presdl. Campaign, Washington, 1979-80; exec. prodr. Great Confrontations at Oxford Union/PBS-BBC, 1982-85; v.p. Am. Program Bur., Boston, 1981-85; dir. comms. Dem. Nat. Com., Washington, 1985-86; exec. prodr. PBS Talking with D. Frost, L.A., 1991-; CEO David Paradine TV, Inc., L.A., 1987-; exec. prodr. A&E George Bush: A President's Story, 1998; commentator U.S. Politics TFI-French Television, N.Y.C., 1984; mem. bd. dirs. [illegible] Bucharest, Romania, 1991—. Election observer Nat. Dem. Inst., Romania, 1990, Kenya, 1992. Mem. Oxford-Cambridge Soc. Calif., Boston Coll. Alumni Soc. Democrat. Roman Catholic. Avocations: tennis, skiing. Office: David Paradine TV Inc 9000 W Sunset Blvd Ste 1020 Los Angeles CA 90069-5810

FLORIE, TERRY LYNN, career officer; b. NAS Sangley Pt., Philippines, May 18, 1956; s. Julian and Hazel Savannah (Byrd) F.; m. Deborah Louise Murchison, Aug. 31, 1985. BBA, Augusta Coll., 1977. Lt. comdr. USN, 1987—, Augusta, Ga., 1978; lt. comdr. USN, Aviation Schs. Command, Pensacola, Fla., 1978; naval officer USN, Patrol Squadron Five, Jacksonville, Fla., 1979-82, USN, Naval Air Tng. Unit, Sacramento, 1982-85, USN, USS Constellation, San Diego, 1985-88, Fleet Tng. Group, San Diego, 1988-90; naval flight officer Patrol Squadron Nine, Moffett Field, Calif., 1990—. Mem. Civil Air Patrol, Sacramento, 1984-85. Mem. U.S. Naval Inst., Aircraft Owners and Pilots Assn., Cessna Pilots Assn. Republican. Methodist. Avocation: flying.

FLOYD, BRETT ALDEN, mortgage banker; b. Las Vegas, Nev., Nov. 12, 1963. Branch mgr. Transamerica Fin., West Covina, Calif., 1984-89, Assocs. Fin., San Gabriel, Calif., 1989; area sales mgr. Long Beach Bank, F.S.B., Woodland Hills, Calif., 1989-94; divsn. mgr. Royal Thrift & Loan Co., L.A., 1994-96; v.p. Royal MortgageBanc, Orange, Calif., 1996-97; sr. v.p. retail prodn. mgr. WMC Mortgage Corp., Woodland Hills, Calif., 1997—. Assoc. Ctl. Com., L.A., 1992. Republican. Avocation: snow skiing. Home: 12433 Sebastian Pl Tustin CA 92782-1510 Office: WMC Mortgage Corp 6320 Canoga Ave Ste 720 Woodland Hills CA 91367-2526

FLUKE, LYLA SCHRAM (MRS. JOHN M. FLUKE), publisher; b. Maddock, N.D.; d. Olaf John and Anne Marie (Rodberg) Schram; m. John M. Fluke, June 5, 1937; children: Virginia Fluke Gabelein, John M. Jr., David Lynd. BS in Zoology and Physiology, U. Wash., Seattle, 1934, diploma teaching, 1935. High sch. tchr., 1935-37; tutor Seattle schs., 1974-75; pub. Portage Quar. mag., Hist. Soc. Seattle and King County, 1980-84. Author articles on history. Founder N.W. chpt. Myasthenia Gravis Found., 1953, pres., 60-66; obtained N.W. artifacts for destroyer Tender Puget Sound, 1966; mem. Seattle Mayor's Com. for Seattle Beautiful, 1968-69; sponsor Seattle World's Fair, 1962; charter mem. Seattle Youth Symphony Aux., 1974; bd. dirs. Cascade Symphony, Salvation Army, 1985-87; benefactor U. Wash., 1982-88, nat. chmn. ann. giving campaign, 1983-84; benefactor Sterling Circle Stanford U., MIT, 1984, Wash. State Hist. Soc., Pacific Arts Ctr.; mem. condr.'s club Seattle Symphony, 1978—. Fellow Seattle Pacific U., 1972—; mem. Wash. Trust for Hist. Preservation, Nat. Trust for Hist. Preservation, N.W. Ornamental Hort. Soc. (benefactor, life, hon.), Nat. Assn. Parliamentarians (charter mem., pres. N.W. unit 1961), Wash. Parliamentarians Assn. (charter), IEEE Aux. (chpt. charter mem., pres. 1970-73), Seattle C. of C. (women's div.), Seattle Symphony Women's Assn. (life, sec. 1982-84, pres. 1985-87), Hist. Soc. Seattle and King County (exec. com. 1975-78, pres. women's mus. league 1975-78, pres. Moritz Thomsen Guild of Hist. Soc., 1978-80, 84-87), Highlands Orthopedic Guild (life), Wash. State Hist. Soc, Antiquarian Soc. (v.p. 1986-88, pres. 1988-90, hon. mem. John Fluke Mfg. Co. 20 Year club, 1987—), Rainier Club, Seattle Golf Club, Seattle Tennis Club, U. Wash. Pres.'s Club. Republican. Lutheran. Address: 1206 NW Culbertson Dr Seattle WA 98177-3942 also: Vendovi Island PO Box 703 Anacortes WA 98221-0703

FLYGARE, KATHLEEN TIFFENI, elementary education educator, piano educator; b. Ogden, Utah, Apr. 7, 1951; d. Jay Golwyn and Norene Sylvia (Carter) Page; m. Mark E. Flygare, Feb. 15, 1974; children: Christopher Mark, Jeremy Page. BS, Weber State U., 1976. Cert. spl. edn., resource tchr., Utah. Intern tchr. WSU Tchr. Corp., Ogden, 1974-76; dir. YWCA Presch., Salt Lake City, 1978-87; tchr. 1st grade Davis County Sch. Dist., Farmington, Utah, 1987-90, tchr. 2d grade, 1990—; chmn. joint staff study com. Monte Vista Sch., Farmington, 1988-90, reading implementor, 1990-92, self-esteem implementor, 1992-93, music implementor, 1993—. Composer/dir. Utah State Centennial Musical for Monte Vista Sch., 1996; mem. Celebration Chamber Ensemble, 1994-96. Mem. gov.'s adv. com. Utah Sch. for Deaf and Blind, Salt Lake City, 1982-84, mem. instnl. coun., 1984-90, chmn. instnl. coun., 1990-92. Mem. ASCD, Assn. for Childhood Edn. Internat., Internat. Reading Assn., Phi Delta Kappa. Republican. Mem. LDS Ch. Avocations: composing music, playing piano and dulcimer, singing, reading, going to Disneyland. Home: 1142 Little Valley Rd Farmington UT 84025-3301 Office: Monte Vista Sch 100 S 200 E Farmington UT 84025-2316

FLYNN, RALPH MELVIN, JR., sales executive, marketing consultant; b. Winchester, Mass., May 2, 1944; s. Ralph Melvin and Mary Agnus (Giuliani) F.; m. Rose Marie Petrock (div. 1988); children: John Patrick, Marc Jeffery; m. Carolyn F. Lee; 1 child, Sean Michael. Engr. Bell Tel. Labs., Holmdel, N.J., 1966-68; tech. coord. Expts. in Art and Tech., N.Y.C., 1968-69; exec. v.p. Bestline Products, San Jose, Calif., 1969-73; pres. Internat. Inst. for Personal Achievement, Palo Alto, Calif., 1975-76, Diamite Corp., Milpitas, Calif., 1977-84; dir. mktg. IMMI, Campbell, Calif., 1973-77; v.p. internat. Neo-Life Co., Fremont, Calif., 1984—; pres. Ultra Promotions, Los Gatos, Calif., 1988-89, Score Publishing, Saratoga, Calif., 1987—; tech. cons. Robert Rauschenberg, N.Y.C., 1968; cons. Std. Oil Co., San Francisco, 1975, I.B.C., Geneva, 1984-88, 1st Interstate Bank, L.A., 1985, Ray Rossi, Design Environs., Los Altos Hills, Calif., 1995; lectr. in field. Author: The Only Variable, 1985, Navigating towards Success, 1986; contbr. articles to profl. publs. Named adm. State of Nebr., 1987; Joseph Kaplan Trust scholar, 1961. Mem. Direct Selling Assn., Coffee Soc. (founder 1988), Rolls Royce Owners Club. Republican. Avocations: music, sailing, art, interior design, classic automobiles. Office: Coffee Soc 21265 Stevens Creek Blvd Cupertino CA 95014-5715

FOCH, NINA, actress, creative consultant, educator, director; b. Leyden, The Netherlands, Apr. 20, 1924; came to U.S. 1927; d. Dirk and Consuelo (Flowerton) F.; m. James Lipton, June 6, 1954; m. Dennis de Brito, Nov. 27, 1959; 1 child, Dirk de Brito; m. Michael Dewell, Oct. 31, 1967 (div.). Grad., Lincoln Sch., 1939; studies with Stella Adler. Adj. prof. drama U. So. Calif., 1966-68, 78-80, adj. prof. film, 1987—; creative cons. to dirs., writers, prodrs. of all media; artist-in-residence U. N.C., 1966, Ohio State U., 1967, Calif. Inst. Tech., 1969-70; mem. sr. faculty Am. Film Inst., 1974-77; founder, tchr. Nina Foch Studio, Hollywood, Calif., 1973—; founder, actress Los Angeles Theatre Group, 1960-65; bd. dirs. Nat. Repertory Theatre, 1967-75. Motion picture appearances include Nine Girls, 1944, Return of the Vampire, 1944, Shadows in the Night, 1944, Cry of the Werewolf, 1944, Escape in the Fog, 1945, A Song to Remember, 1945, My Name Is Julia Ross, 1945, I Love a Mystery, 1945, Johnny O'Clock, 1947, The Guilt of Janet Ames, 1947, The Dark Past, 1948, The Undercover Man, 1949, Johnny Allegro, 1949, An American in Paris, 1951, Scaramouche, 1952, Young Man with Ideas, 1952, Sombrero, 1953, Fast Company, 1953, Executive Suite, 1954 (Oscar award nominee), Four Guns to the Border, 1954, You're Never Too Young, 1955, Illegal, 1955, The Ten Commandments, 1956, Three Brave Men, 1957, Cash McCall, 1959, Spartacus, 1960, Such Good Friends, 1971, Salty, 1973, Mahogany, 1976, Jennifer, 1978, Rich and Famous, 1981, Skin Deep, 1988, Sliver, 1993, Morning Glory, 1993, 'Til There Was You, 1996, Hush, 1998, Shadow of Doubt, 1998; appeared in Broadway plays including John Loves Mary, 1947, Twelfth Night, 1949, A Phoenix Too Frequent, 1950, King Lear, 1950, Second String, 1960; appeared with Am. Shakespeare Festival in Taming of the Shrew, Measure for Measure, 1956, San Francisco Ballet and Opera in The Seven Deadly Sins, 1966; also many regional theater appearances including Seattle Repertory Theatre (All Over, 1972 and The Seagull, 1973); actress on TV, 1947—, including Playhouse 90, Studio One, Pulitzer Playhouse, Playwrights 56, Producers Showcase, Lou Grant (Emmy nominee 1980), Mike Hammer; series star: Shadow Chasers, 1985, War and Remembrance, 1988, LA Law, 1990, Hunter, 1990, Dear John, 1990, 91, Tales of the City, 1993, Dharma and Greg, 1999; many other series, network spls. and TV films; TV panelist and guest on The Dinah Shore Show, Merv Griffin Show, The Today Show, Dick Cavett, The Tonight Show; TV moderator: Let's Take Sides, 1957-59; assoc. dir. (film) The Diary of Anne Frank, 1959; dir. (nat. tour and on-Broadway) Tonight at 8:30, 1966-67, Family Blessings, 1997; assoc. producer re-opening of Ford's Theatre, Washington, 1968. Hon. chmn. Los Angeles chpt. Am. Cancer Soc., 1970. Recipient Film Daily award, 1949, 53. Mem. AAUP, Acad. Motion Picture Arts and Scis. (co-chair exec. com. fgn. film award, membership com.), Hollywood Acad. TV Arts and Scis. (bd. govs. 1976-77). Avocation: work. Office: PO Box 1884 Beverly Hills CA 90213-1884

FOCHT, MICHAEL HARRISON, health care industry executive; b. Reading, Pa., Sept. 16, 1942; s. Benjamin Harrison and Mary (Hannahoe) F.; m. Sandra Lee Scholwin, May 14, 1964; 1 child, Michael Harrison. Archtl. estimator Caloric Corp., Topton, Pa., 1964-65, cost acct., 1965-66, indsl. engr., 1966-68, mgr. wage rates and standards, 1968-70; indsl. engr. Am. Medicorp. Inc., Fort Lauderdale, Fla., 1970-71; exec. dir. midwest region Am. Medicorp. Inc., Chgo., 1977-78; asst. adminstr. Cypress Community Hosp., Pompano Beach, Fla., 1971-73, adminstr., 1975-77; adminstr. Doctor's Hosp. Hollywood, Fla., 1973-75; v.p. Medfield Corp., St. Petersburg, Fla., 1978-79; v.p. ops. hosp. group Nat. Med. Enterprises, Inc., Los Angeles, 1979-81; regional sr. v.p. hosp. group Nat. Med. Enterprises, Inc., Tampa, Fla., 1981-83; pres., chief exec. officer internat. group Nat. Med. Enterprises, Inc., Los Angeles, 1983-86, pres. chief exec. officer hosp. group, 1986-91; sr. exec. v.p., dir. ops. Nat. Med. Enterprises, Inc., 1991-93, pres., 1993-95; pres., COO Tenet Healthcare Corp., Santa Barbara, 1995—. Mem. Fedn. Am. Hosps. (bd. govs. 1983—), Fla. League Hosps. (bd. dirs. 1982-83). Republican. Roman Catholic. Home: PO Box 703 Santa Ynez CA 93460-0703 Office: Tenet Healthcare Corp 3820 State St Santa Barbara CA 93105-3112

FOLDEN, NORMAN C. (SKIP FOLDEN), information systems executive, consultant; b. San Francisco, July 28, 1933. BS in Math./English/Engring., U.S. Mil. Acad., 1956. With IBM, various locations, 1966-83; U.S. program mgr. I/S tech. IBM, Sommers, N.Y., 1983-86; owner Folden Mgmt. (Palladin Advocacy), Westchester, N.Y., 1986-91, Folden Mgmt., Las Vegas, 1991—. Author: Drug Criminalization: Organized Crime Cash Cow, Prime Cause of U.S. Victim Crime and Threat to National Sovereignty, 1996, Delegation of Legislative Authority, 1997. Mem. Internat. Platform Assn., Assn. Grads. U.S. Mil. Acad., The Federalist Soc., Little Big Horn Assocs., Calif. Scholarship Fedn. Avocations: ancient history/teachings/exploration, organized crime and drug policy, antiquities, constitutional law. Home and Office: 4329 Silvercrest Ct North Las Vegas NV 89030-0116

FOLDES, LAWRENCE DAVID, film producer, director, writer; b. L.A., Nov. 4, 1959; s. George and Valerie (Keller) F.; m. Victoria Paige Meyerink, Apr. 24, 1983. Student, San Bernardino Valley Coll., 1975, UCLA, 1976, Calif. Inst. of the Arts, 1977; BA with hons., Brooks Inst. Photography, 1978. Pres. Star Cinema Prodn. Group, 1981-85; chmn. bd. Star Entertainment Group, Inc., 1985—; faculty mem. UCLA, Internat. Film and TV Workshops, Internat. Coll., William Lyon U.; instr ., film lectr. The Learning Network, UCLA; exec. dir. Malibu Film and TV Workshops. Producer, dir., writer: (motion pictures) Struggle for Israel, 1977, Malibu High, 1979, Don't Go Near the Park, 1980, The Great Skycopter Rescue, 1982, Lovely but Deadly, 1983, Young Warriors, 1984, Night Force, 1987, Prima Donnas, 1996. Recipient mayoral proclamation for Outstanding Achievement City of L.A., Cert. of Merit Paris Internat. Film Festival, Outstanding Achievement award Acad. of Family Films. Mem. Acad. Motion Picture Arts and Scis. (acad. awards exec. com.), Los Angeles Film Tchrs. Assn., Acad. Sci. Fiction, Fantasy and Horror Films (chmn. membership and direction coms., dir. Acad. film expn., Humanitarian award). Avocations: scuba diving, travel, photography. Office: Star Entertainment Group Inc 13601 Ventura Blvd Ste 500 Sherman Oaks CA 91423-3701

FOLEY, JANE DEBORAH, foundation executive; b. Chgo., May 30, 1952; d. Colin Gray Stevenson and Bette Jane (Cullenbine) Coleman; m. George Edward Foley, Jan. 29, 1972; 1 son, Sy Curtis. BA, Purdue U., 1973, MS, 1977, PhD, 1992. Cert. elem. adminstr., Ind., cert. elem. adminstrn. and supervision. Tchr. phys. edn. and health Lafayette (Ind.) Jefferson H.S., 1973-74; tchr. music and phys. edn. Valparaiso (Ind.) Cmty. Schs., 1974-79, tchr. elem. phys. edn., 1979-90; prin. South Ctrl. Elem. sch., Union Mills, Ind., 1990-93, Flint Lake Elem. Sch., Valparaiso, 1993-98; v.p. Milken Family Found., Santa Monica, Calif., 1998—; mem. panel of experts The Master Tchr., 1996—; key note spkr., presenter state and nat. confs. Contbr. articles to profl. jours. Mem. Valparaiso Sch. Sys. PTA, mem. exec. bd., 1993-98. Recipient Hoosier Sch. award, 1992, Ind. 2000 Designation award 1994, Outstanding Dissertation award Internat. Soc. Ednl. Planning, 1993, Nat. Educator award, Milken Family Found., 1994, Ind. Bell Ringer award Ind. Dept. Edn., 1994, Ind. 4 Star Sch. award, 1995, 96, 97, 98, Internat. Tech. Edn. Assn. award, 1995, Cmty. Improvement award Valparaiso C. of C., 1994, NCREL Pathways to Improvement Pilot Site, 1995, Ind. Sch. Improvement award, Ind. Dept. Edn., 1998, others; Ind. 2000 Planning grantee, 1993, Milken Educator Tech. Project leader, 1997, other grants. Mem. ASCD (assoc.), NAESP, Ind. Assn. Sch. Prins., Valparaiso Tchrs. Assn. (treas. 1989-90), Phi Kappa Phi. Avocations: running, reading, writing, computers. Office: Milken Family Found 1250 4th St Santa Monica CA 90401-1353

FOLEY, JOHN V., water company executive. Chmn. Met. Water Dist. of So. Calif., L.A., bd. dirs. Office: Office of the Bd of Dirs PO 54153 Los Angeles CA 90054-0153*

FOLEY, MARTIN JAMES, lawyer; b. Nebr., Nov. 7, 1946; s. James Gleason and Mary Elizabeth (O'Brien) F.; m. Linda Sivyer; children—James Gleason II, Daniel Patrick, Ryan Edward, Michelle Sivyer. Cert Completion, Cambridge U., 1967; B.A. in Philosophy, U. So. Calif. 1968, M.B.A., 1975, J.D., 1974. Bar: Calif. 1975, U.S. Dist. Ct. (cen. dist.) Calif. 1975, U.S. Dist. Ct. (ea., so. and no. dists.) Calif. 1980, U.S. Ct. Appeals (9th cir.) 1980, U.S Ct. Federal Claims, U.S. Supreme Ct. Acct., Ford Motor Co., San Jose, Calif., 1968, cost analyst, 1970-71; assoc. Adams, Duque & Hazeltine, 1975-80; sr. ptnr. Bryan, Cave, McPheeters & McRoberts, Los Angeles, 1980-89, sr. ptnr. Sonnenschein Nath & Rosenthal, Los Angeles, 1990—. Mem. bd. govs. Gen. Alumni Assn., U. So. Calif., 1982-84, ct. appt. settlement officer Calif. State, 1992-94, U.S. Dist. Ct. (ctr. dist.), 1998—. Served to lt. (j.g.) USNR, 1968-70. Mem. ABA (numerous coms.), Calif, Bar Assn. (conf. of del. 1979-93), Los Angeles County Bar Assn. Republican. Roman Catholic. Clubs: Jonathan (Los Angeles); Annandale Golf (Pasadena, Calif.). Contbr. articles to profl. jours.; lectr. groups and profl. confs. Office: Sonnenschein Nath Rosenthal 601 S Figueroa St Ste 1500 Los Angeles CA 90017-5720

FOLEY, RITA VIRGINIA, computer company executive; b. Boston, Mar. 20, 1953; d. Francis Michael and Rita Claire (Martin) F.; m. Peter G. Buckley, May 15, 1976; children: Michael E., Nathaniel R. Grad., U. Geneva, 1974; AB in Psychology, Smith Coll., 1975. Sales rep. Polaroid, St. Albans, England, 1975-77; br. mgr. Harris Lanier, N.Y.C., 1977-82; various mgmt. positions Digital Equipment Corp., N.Y., N.J., 1982-89; dist. mgr. Digital Equipment Corp., Piscataway, N.J., 1989-91, group mgr. northwest telecom & utilities, 1991-92; U.S. mktg. mgr. high performance systems Digital Equipment Corp., Marlboro, Mass., 1992-93; v.p. northeast regional ctr. Digital Equipment Corp., N.Y.C., 1993-94; v.p., regional mgr. western region Digital Equipment Corp., Santa Clara, Calif., 1994—. Head various coms. Pratt Area Cmty. Coun., Bklyn., 1982—, co-chair bd. dirs., 1983-85; mem. exec. devel. forum N.Y.C. C. of C., 1993; mem. svc. com. children with learning disabilities Mary McDowell Cmty. Ctr., Bklyn., 1990—; sponsor Spl. Olympics, N.Y. and Conn., 1990, 91; cmty. crime patroller Pratt Area Crime Patrol, Bklyn., 1983-89. Mem. Am. Womens Elec. Devel. Corp., Smith Coll. Club. Avocations: gardening, golf, tennis, skiing, reading. Office: Digital Equipment Corp 19333 Vallco Pkwy Cupertino CA 95014-2506

FOLKERTH, THEODORE LEON, cardiovascular surgeon, educator; b. Darke County, Ohio, Nov. 24, 1937; s. L.D. and Lenore Abigail (Carpenter) F.; m. Lenora Lee Wallace, Dec. 22, 1963 (div. 1981); children: Theodore Wesley, Elizabeth Anne, Geoffrey Wallace; m. Jean Mary Macfarlane, Feb. 17, 1995. AB in Chemistry, Earlham Coll., 1959; MS in Biochemistry, Ind. U., Indpls., 1962, MD, 1965. Commd. officer USN, 1964, advanced through grades to comdr.; intern Naval Hosp., Phila., 1965-66; resident in gen. thoracic surgery Naval Hosp., San Diego, 1967-72; resident in cardiac surgery Stanford VA Hosp., Palo Alto, Calif., 1972-73; staff thoracic and cardiovasc. surgeon, fellow Naval Regional Med. Ctr., San Diego, 1973-77; ret., 1978; staff cardiovasc. surgeon Good Samaritan Hosp., San Jose, Calif., 1978-81; chief cardiac surgery Meml. Hosp., Santa Rosa, Calif., 1979-87; pvt. practice, Oceanside, Calif., 1987—; mem. staff Scripps Meml. Hosp., LaJolla, Calif., 1996—; cardiac surgeon Tri City Med Ctr., Oceanside, Calif., 1987—; chmn. div. cardiovasc. surgery Tri-City Med. Ctr., Oceanside, 1987—; asst. clin. prof. U. Calif., San Diego, 1975-77, assoc. clin. prof., 1987—; program dir. seminar Current Controversies in Cardiac Surgery, 1993. Contbr. over 30 articles to profl. jours. Named One of Otstanding Young Men. of Am., 1974. Fellow ACS, Soc. Thoracic Surgeons (pub. affairs com. 1997-98); mem. Western Thoracic Surg. Assn. Avocations: woodworking, golf, tennis, breeding thoroughbreds. Office: 3998 Vista Way Ste C204 Oceanside CA 92056-4515

FOLLETT, NANCY CROUTHAMEL, publishing executive; b. Albany, N.Y., Feb. 1, 1932; d. J. Ralph and Laura (Buckland) Crouthamel; m. Robert J. R. Follett, Dec. 30, 1950; children: Brian, Kathryn, Jean, Lisa. Grad. h.s., Endicott, N.Y. Dir. Follett Corp., River Grove, Ill., 1958-96; v.p. Alpine Guild, Inc., Dillon, Colo., 1977—; co-chair Colo. Mountain Coll. Campaign for Excellence, 1998—; chair Mountain Art Gathering, 1998—. Supr. Oak Park Twp., Ill., 1973-81; pres. Cmty. Welfare Coun., Cmty. Chest, Oak Park, Suburban Cook-DuPage Counties Health Sys. Agy., Oak Park, Ill.; vice-chmn. Cook County Coun. Govts., Ill.; chmn. Oak Park-River Forest Cmty. Found., Oak Park Fire and Police Commn., 1986-92; mem. Gov.'s Commn. on Mandates, Springfield, Ill.; dir. Nat. Repertory Orch., Denver, 1994—; dir., treas. Summit Found., Summit County, Colo., 1997—. Mem. Ill. Assn. Health Sys. Agys. (pres.), Am. Health Planning Assn. (dir.), Keystone (Colo.) Ranch Assn. (pres. 1997—). Fax: (970) 262-9378. Home: 1 Kinnikinnik Rd Keystone CO 80435-8394 Office: Alpine Guild Inc PO Box 4848 Dillon CO 80435-4848

FOLLICK, EDWIN DUANE, law educator, chiropractic physician; b. Glendale, Calif., Feb. 4, 1935; s. Edwin Fulfford and Esther Agnes (Catherwood) F.; m. Marilyn K. Sherk, Mar. 24, 1986. BA, Calif. State U., L.A., 1956, MA, 1961; MA, Pepperdine U., 1957, MPA, 1977; PhD, DTh, St. Andrews Theol. Coll., Sem. of Free Prot. Episc. Ch., London, 1958; MS in Libr. Sci., U. So. Calif., 1963, MEd in Instructional Materials, 1964, AdvMEd in Edn. Adminstrn., 1969; postgrad., Calif. Coll. Law, 1965; LLB, Blackstone Law Sch., 1966, JD, 1967; DC, Cleve. Chiropractic Coll., L.A., 1972; PhD, Academia Theatina, Pescara, 1978; MA in Organizational Mgmt., Antioch U., L.A., 1990. Tchr., libr. adminstr. L.A. City Schs., 1957-68; law librarian Glendale U. Coll. Law, 1968-69; coll. librarian Cleve. Chiropractic Coll., L.A., 1969-74, dir. edn. and admissions, 1974-84, prof. jurisprudence, 1975—, dean student affairs, 1976-92, chaplain, 1985—, dean of edn., 1989—; assoc. prof. Newport U., 1982; extern prof. St. Andrews Theol. Coll., London, 1961; dir. West Valley Chiropractic Health Ctr., 1972—. Contbr. articles to profl. jours. Chaplain's asst. U.S. Army, 1958-60. Decorated cavaliere Internat. Order Legion of Honor of Immaculata (Italy); Knight of Malta, Sovereign Order of St. John of Jerusalem; knight Order of Signum Fidei; comdr. chevalier Byzantine Imperial Order of Constantine the Gt.; comdr. ritter Order St. Gereon; chevalier Mil. and Hospitaller Order of St. Lazarus of Jerusalem (Malta); numerous others. Mem. ALA, NEA, Am. Assn. Sch. Librarians, L.A. Sch. Libr. Assn., Calif. Sch. Libr. Assn., Assn. Coll. and Rsch. Librarians, Am. Assn. Law Librarians, Am. Chiropractic Assn., Internat. Chiropractors Assn., Nat. Geog. Soc., Internat. Platform Assn., Phi Delta Kappa, Sigma Chi Psi, Delta Tau Alpha. Democrat. Episcopalian. Home: 6435 Jumilla Ave Woodland Hills CA 91367-2833 Office: 590 N Vermont Ave Los Angeles CA 90004-2115 also: 7022 Owensmouth Ave Canoga Park CA 91303-2005

FOLLMER, JOHN SCOTT, visual effects producer, supervisor; b. Chgo., Apr. 3, 1951; s. Frank Joseph and Lucille Caroline (Fink) F.; m. Carol Jean Lewittes, Feb. 9, 1974; children: Sean Weston, Brian Matthew, Kevin Jeremy. *Parents Frank and Lucille studied in the late 1920s at the Art Institute of Chicago where she also exhibited paintings. Frank was an art editor and illustrator for magazines between 1929-73. Lucille was an illustrator and author including 1949's humorous book "Your Sports are Showing". For the Depression's WPA, Frank oversaw the Ilinois murals project and both taught teachers art and puppetry. Lucille's 1933 Chicago World's Fair marionette performances led to creating and performing their own puppet theater, "Kukla, Gus and Oscar" was created with their young protege who brought his version to television as "Kukla, Fran and Ollie".* BS with honors, Ill. Inst. Tech., 1973. Animator, designer Crocus Prodns., Evanston, Ill., 1973-75; asst. dir. Phase 5 Prodns., Chgo., 1976; dir., designer Goldsholl Assocs., Northfield, Ill., 1977-84; dir., producer Moore Films, Inc., Hollywood, Calif., 1985; v.p., exec. producer Calico Entertainment, Chatsworth, Calif., 1986-94; v.p., head of prodn., co-exec. producer Metrolight Studios, Hollywood, 1994—. *John Follmer studied film and animation. Early involvement with the computer in film led to his supervising the production of the "largest, projected computer animated film in the world" for Disney in 1985. Increasingly involved in international production, John supervised the visual effects on a project shot in Tokyo in 1994. In 1995, he produced the Grammy nominated "Best Music Video", Herbie Hancock's "Dis Is Da Drum" using advanced techniques in computer animation including motion-capture and cyberscanning of humans. Involved in the development of feature film and television projects, Follmer has received over 50 honors for producing and directing.* Supervising producer visual effects (films) Batman Forever, Warner Bros., 1995, Mortal Kombat New Line Cinema, 1995, Under Siege II-Dark Territory, Warner Bros., 1995, Virtuosity, Paramount Pictures, 1995, Broken Arrow, 20th Century Fox, 1996, Happy Gilmore, Universal Pictures, 1996, Matilda, Tristar Pictures, 1996, Daylight, Universal Pictures, 1996, Eraser, Warner Bros., 1996, Batman & Robin, Warner Bros., 1997, Kull the Conqueror, Universal Pictures, 1997, Leave it to Beaver, Universal Pictures, 1997, McHale's Navy, Universal Pictures, 1997, Baseketball, Universal Pictures, 1998, From the Earth to the Moon, Imagine Entertainment, 1998, Dragon Heart II, Universal Pictures, 1999. Mem. Acad. TV Arts and Scis. Office: Metrolight Studios 5724 W 3rd St Ste 400 Los Angeles CA 90036-3078

FOLTZ, JOHN CLARK, agricultural economics educator; b. Newport, R.I., May 15, 1957; s. John Charles and Anne (Clark) F.; m. Barbara Elizabeth Haffner, Aug. 16, 1980; children: John Richard, James Clark. BS in Agrl. Econs., Ohio State U., 1979, MS in Agrl. Econs., 1981; PhD in Agrl. Econs., Purdue U., 1991. Intern DeKalb Agresearch, Inc., London, Ohio, 1978; sales asst. Elanco Products Co., Worthington, Ohio, 1979; terr. mgr. Ralston Purina Co., Circleville, Ohio, 1981-83; dist. mgr. Purina Mills, Circleville, 1983-87; grad. rsch./tchg. asst. dept. agrl. econs. Purdue, West Lafayette, Ind., 1987-91; asst. prof. dept. agrl. econs. U. Idaho, Moscow, 1991-97, assoc. prof., 1997—; chmn. Coop. Leadership Seminar, Spokane, 1993—; cons. Harvey A. Meier Co., Spokane, 1992—; expert witness Snyder, Matthews & Nelson, Boise, Idaho, 1996, Quane, Smith, Howard & Hull, Boise, 1996-97. Contbr. articles to profl. publs., chpt. to book. Bd. dirs., chair Moscow/Latah County Libr. Bd., 1993-97; cubmaster Boy Scouts Am., Moscow, 1996-97, asst. scoutmaster, 1994—; swim team ofcl. Moscow Swim Team, Inland Empire Swimming, 1994—; ex-officio mem. Idaho Coop. Coun., 1997—; co-chmn. Leadership Idaho Agr., 1997-98. Mem. Am. Agrl. Econs. Assn., Nat. Eagle Scout Assn., Masons, Alpha Zeta (chancellor 1978-79), Gamma Sigma Delta (treas., v.p., pres. 1993-97). Republican. Methodist. Avocations: collecting Boy Scout patches, political campaign buttons, Lionel trains; swimming, camping. Home: 905 Fort Stevens Moscow ID 83843-2471 Office: U Idaho Dept Agrl Econs Moscow ID 83844-2334

FONG, HIRAM LEONG, former senator; b. Honolulu, Oct. 15, 1906; s. Lum Fong and Chai Ha Lum; m. Ellyn Lo; children, Hiram, Rodney, Marie-Ellen Fong Gushi, Marvin-Allan (twins). AB with honors, U. Hawaii, 1930, LLD, 1953; JD, Harvard U., 1935; LLD, Tufts U., 1960, Lafayette Coll., 1960, Lynchburg Coll., 1970, Lincoln U., 1971, U. Guam, 1974, St. John's U., 1975, Calif. Western Sch. Law, 1976, Tung Wu (Soochow) U., Taiwan, 1978, China Acad., Taiwan, 1978; LHD, L.I. U., 1968. With supply dept. Pearl Harbor Navy Yard, 1924-27; chief clk. Suburban Water System, 1930-32; dep. atty. City and County of Honolulu, 1935-38; founder, ptnr. law firm Fong, Miho, Choy & Robinson, until 1959; founder, chmn. bd. emeritus Finance Factors, Grand Pacific Life Ins. Co.; founder, chmn bd. Finance Investment Co., Market City, Ltd., Fin. Enterprises Ltd.; pres. Ocean View Cemetery, Ltd.; owner, operator Sen. Fong's Plantation and Gardens, Honolulu; dir. numerous firms, Honolulu; hon. cons. China Airlines. Mem. Hawaii Legislature, 1938-54, speaker, 1948-54; mem. U.S. Senate, 1959-77, Post Office and Civil Service Com., Judiciary Com., Appropriations Com., Spl. Com. on Aging; U.S. del. 150th Anniversary Argentine Independence, Buenos Aires, 1960, 55th Interparliamentary Union (World) Conf., 1966, Ditchley Found. Conf., 1967, U.S.-Can. Inter-Parliamentary Union Conf., 1961, 65, 67, 68, Mex.-U.S. Inter-Parliamentary Conf., 1968, World Interparliamentary Union, Tokyo, 1974; mem. Commn. on Revision Fed. Ct. Appellate System, 1975—; Active in civic and service orgns.; v.p. Territorial Constl. Conv., 1950; del. Rep. Nat. Conv., 1952, 56, 60, 64, 68, 72; founder, chmn. bd. Fin. Factors Found.; founder, pres. Hiram & Ellyn Fong Found.; founder, pres., chmn. bd. Market City Found.; hon. co-chmn. McKinley

High Sch. Found., 1989; bd. visitors U.S. Mil. Acad., 1971—, U.S. Naval Acad., 1974—. Served from 1st lt. to maj. USAAF, 1942-44; ret col. USAF Res. Recipient award NCCJ, 1960, Meritorious Svc. citation Nat. Assn. Ret. Civil Employees, 1963, Horatio Alger award, 1970, citation for outstanding svc. Japanese Am. Citizens League, 1970, award Am. Acad. Achievement, 1971, Outstanding Svc. award Orgn. Chinese Ams., 1973, award Nat. Soc. Daus. Founders and Patriots Am., 1974, cert. Pacific Asian World, 1974, Citizen Among Citizens award Boys & Girls Clubs of Hawaii, 1991, Disting. Alumnus award U. Hawaii Alumni Assn., 1991, Kulia I Ka Nu'u award Pub. Schs. Hawaii Found., 1992, Dedication and Support Svc. award McKinley Found., 1995, ABOTA-Hawai'i Ha'aheo award, 1997; named to Jr. Achievement Hawaii Bus. Hall of Fame, 1995; decorated Order of Brilliant Star with Grand Cordon Republic of China, 1976, Order of Diplomatic Svc. Merit, Gwanghwan Medal Republic of Korea, 1977; Univ. of Hawaii Colls. of Arts and Scis. Hiram L. Fong Endowment in Arts and Scis., 1995; recipient nat. Outstanding Citizen Achievement award Orgn. Chinese Ams., Inc., 1996; named Model Chinese Father of Yr., United Chinese Soc., 1996. Mem. Am. Legion, VFW, Lambda Alpha Internat. (Aloha chpt.), Phi Beta Kappa. Congregationalist. Home: 1102 Alewa Dr Honolulu HI 96817-1507

FONG, MATTHEW KIPLING, state official; b. Oakland, Calif., Nov. 20, 1953; s. Chester and March Fong; m. Paula Fong, May 28, 1978; children: Matthew II, Jade. Grad., U.S. Air Force Acad., 1975; MBA, Pepperdine U., 1982; JD, Southwestern Law. Sch., 1985. Former vice chmn. State Bd. Equalization; treas. State Calif. Regent Pepperdine U., Children's Hosp. L.A.; Rep. nominee State Controller, 1990. Lt. col. Air Force Res. Office: State Treasurer PO Box 942809 Sacramento CA 94209-0001*

FONG, WEI-MING NICKSON, film special effects expert; b. Singapore, Nov. 1, 1969; came to U.S., 1992; s. Kim Yong Fong and Siew Siong Chong; m. Joyce Tsai, July 7, 1998. Diploma in graphic design, Nanyang Acad. Arts, Singapore, 1990; MFA in Computer Art, Savannah Coll. Art & Design, 1996. Digital artist Computer Graphics Imaging Tech., Singapore, 1993-94; animator Future Pirates Inc., Tokyo, 1994, Dreamworks SkG, L.A., 1996-97; tech. dir. Sony Picture Imageworks, L.A., 1997, Motion Syndicate, Santa Monica, Calif., 1997-98; lead tech. dir. Centropolis Effect Co., L.A., 1998—; advisor Savannah Coll. Art and Design, 1996—. Dir., prodr. computer graphics ScreamScape (Computer Art award for animation 1995), Wacky Racer (Aesthetic CG Still award 1995), Dreamaker, 1996 (Siggraph, Sydney Intermedia Network Festival, Art Futura Computer Graphics Show, Spain, 1996). Lance cpl. Singapore armed forces, 1990-92. Recipient Young Designer's award, Singapore, 1990,. Mem. United Asian Artists Network (bd. trustees 1997-98), Assn. for Computing Machinery, Chinese Student Assn. (vice chmn. 1994). Avocations: tennis, woodworking, painting, movies, photography.

FONOIMOANA, ROXANN PUANANI, school district education specialist; b. Honolulu, Sept. 14, 1954; d. Sentuli Laie and Victoria Moana (Kekauoha) F.; m. Leroy A. Christensen, July 2, 1974 (div. Feb. 1996); children: Tawna, Jesse, Teage, Brett, Sunni, Brook. Student, Olympic C.C., Bremerton, Wash., 1987-92; BA, Pacific Luth. U., 1992-95. Vol. coord. South Kitsap Sch. Dist., Port Orchard, Wash., 1990-92, tchr., 1995—; tchr. Ctrl. Kitsap Sch. Dist., Silverdale, Wash., 1995—. Pres. South Kitsap Citizens for Quality Edn., Port Orchard, 1986-87; campaign chairperson Jud. Race David C. Hill, Superior Ct., Port Orchard, 1996. Recipient undergrad. felllowship and faculty merit award Pacific Luth. U. Coll. Edn., 1994-95, Hawaiian Civic Club award, Honolulu, 1994-95, Hawaiian Cmty. Club award, Honolulu, 1994-95. Mem. Nat. Fedn. Ofcls., PTA (legis. rep. 1985-86, pres. 1984, 90, Golden Apple award 1991-92, 92-93), Pacific Luth. Alumni. Avocations: gardening, sewing, volleyball, tennis, basketball.

FONTENOTE-JAMERSON, BELINDA, museum director. Pres. Mus. African Am. Art, L.A. Office: Mus African Am Art 4005 S Crenshaw Blvd Fl 3 Los Angeles CA 90008-2534*

FONVILLE-WILLIAMS, DEBRA MARIE, religious organization executive; b. St. Paul, Jan. 18, 1960; d. Charles B. and Deena (Salter) Fonville; m. Stanley L. Williams, June 8, 1996; children: Rory, ShaDeena. BRE, Citadel Bapt. Coll., 1986; BTh, Pacific Coast Coll., 1996; M in Ministry, Trinity Evang. Sem., Naples, Fla., 1997. Cert. in income tax preparation, Federated Tax Svc. Pres. Empowering Youth for Outreach, St. Paul, 1987-95; customer svc. assoc. Van Waters & Roger, Phoenix, 1995-98; pres., CEO Clergy United Internat., Phoenix, 1998—. Author: Understanding the Work of God's Ministering Angels, 1996. Mem. Glendale (Ariz.) Com. for Disabled, 1991. Avocations: reading, writing. Office: PO Box 1563 Phoenix AZ 85001-1563

FOOTE, BARBARA AUSTIN, civic foundation executive; b. Seattle, Mar. 26, 1918; d. Edwin Charles and Marion (Roberts) A.; m. Robert Lake Foote, June 14, 1941; children: Markell Foote Kaiser, Marion Roberts, Helen Foote Schloerb. AB, Vassar Coll., 1940. Tchr. Shady Hill Sch., Cambridge, Mass., 1942-43, Madeira Sch., Greenway, Va., 1943-44, North Shore Country Day Sch., Winnetka, Ill., 1960-71; mem. exec. com. Chgo. Community Trust, 1970-85, chmn. exec. com., 1978-85; bd. dirs. Harris Bank, Glencoe and Northbrook, Ill., The New Eng. (name formerly New Eng. Mut. Life Ins. Co.), Boston. Author book of verse, 1948. Pres. Jr. League Chgo., 1947-49, Assn. Jr. Leagues Am., 1954-56, Glencoe Bd. Edn., 1957-63; trustee Vassar Coll., 1966-74; bd. dirs. Presbyn. Home, Evanston, Ill. Mem. Vassar Alumni Assn. (nat. pres. 1975-78), Phi Beta Kappa. Congregationalist. Clubs: Fortnightly of Chgo.; Cosmopolitan (N.Y.C.). Home: PO Box 1157 Bellingham WA 98227-1157 also: Wausaukee Club Box 8-A HCR Hwy 1 Athelstane WI 54104

FOOTE, KAY REBBER, artist; b. Long Beach, Calif., Mar. 3, 1923; d. Leland Lester Rebber and Mary Alice Thomas; m. John Taintor Foote, Dec. 24, 1943; children: Carol Ann, John Taintor Jr., Ellen Jackson. BFA, U. So. Calif., Los Angeles, 1943; postgrad., Art Ctr. Coll., Los Angeles, 1943-45, Chouinard Art Inst., Los Angeles, 1943-45. Co-owner Gallery Xyst, Laguna Beach, Calif., 1975-84; juror Calif. State Fair, 1979, Laguna Hills Art Assn., 1980. Works exhibited Laguna Beach Art Mus., 1976-79, City of Newport Beach (Calif.) Ann. Juried Show, 1976-77, Dafca Show, Disney Studios, L.A., 1977, Laguna Beach Festival Art, 1976-98, Brea (Calif.) Mcpl. Art Gallery, 1987, Designs Recycled Gallery, Brea, 1984, San Bernardino County (Calif.) Mus. Art, 1983, Laguna Beach Art Mus. Invitational, 1983, Realism Exhbn. John Wayne Airport, 1991. Donated works to Laguna Beach Boys' Club, Our Lady of Angels, Junior League, Children's Home Soc. Recipient Past Pres. award Nat. Watercolor Soc., Los Angeles, 1987, Spl. award Laguna Beach Art Mus., 1983; named Best of Show Laguna Niguel Echoes & Visions, 1997. Signature mem. Nat. Watercolor Soc. (Past Pres. award 1987). Home: 74 Emerald Bay Laguna Beach CA 92651-1266

FOOTMAN, GORDON ELLIOTT, educational administrator; b. L.A., Oct. 10, 1927; s. Arthur Leland and Meta Fay (Neal) F.; m. Virginia Rose Footman, Aug. 7, 1954; children: Virginia, Patricia, John. BA, Occidental Coll., 1951, MA, 1954; EdD, U. So. Calif., 1972. Tchr., Arcadia, Calif., 1952, Glendale, Calif., 1956; psychologist Burbank (Calif.) Schs., 1956-64, supr., 1964-70, dir. pupil personnel svcs., 1970-72; dir. div. ednl. support svcs. L.A. County Office Edn., Downey, Calif., 1972-91; cons. ednl. adminstrn., counseling and pscyhol. svcs., 1991—; pres. Calif. Assn. Adult Devel. and Aging, 1994-95; lectr. ednl. psychology U. So. Calif., 1972-75, asst. prof. ednl. psychology, 1976-85. Pres. Coun. for Exceptional Children, 1969-70; pres. Burbank Coordinating Coun., 1969-70; mem. Burbank Family Svc. Bd., 1971-72. Served with AUS, 1945-47. Mem. Am. Edn. Rsch. Assn., Am. Counseling Assn. (senator 1983-86, gov. coun., 1989-93, exec. com. 1990-93, parliamentarian 1991-92, western region br. assembly publs. editor 1985-87, chair 1988-89, chair bylaws com. 1995-97), Am. Assn. for Humanistic Edn. and Devel. (bd. dirs., treas. 1996—), Calif. Personnel and Guidance Assn. (pres. 1981-82, exec. coun. 1996—), Nat., Calif. (monograph editor 1977-80), Assns. Pupil Personnel Adminstrs., Calif. Assn. Counselor Educators and Suprs. (trustee), Calif. Soc. Ednl. Program Auditors and Evaluators (sec. 1975-76, v.p. 1976-77, [illegible]), Calif. Assn. [illegible] Evaluation in Counseling and Devel. (sec. 1976, pres. 1979-80, 96-97, pres. 1997-98, cons. ednl. and pupil svcs. adminstrn. 1991—), Calif. Inst. Tech. Assocs., Assn. Humanistic Ed. and Devel. (bd. dirs. 1996—, treas. 1996—), Huntington Libr. Soc. Fellows, Coun. Exceptional Children (pres. Foothill chpt. 1969-70), Phi Beta Kappa, Phi Alpha Theta, Psi Chi. Republican. Presbyn. Home and Office: 1259 Sherwood Rd San Marino CA 91108-1816

FORBES, ALFRED DEAN, religious studies researcher, biomedical consultan; b. Pomona, Calif., Mar. 2, 1941; s. Paul Edward and Lela Irene (Randall) F.; m. Ellen Moss, May 8, 1971. BA in Physics, Harvard Coll., 1962; MDiv, Pacific Sch. Religion, 1969. With U.S. Peace Corps, Nigeria, 1962-64; prin. med. dept. scientist Hewlett-Packard Labs., Palo Alto, Calif., 1971-98; vis. scholar U. Calif., San Diego, 1999—; vis. scholar religious studies Stanford (Calif.) U., 1986-89; adj. prof. Jewish studies Pa. State U., 1998—. Author: (with F.I. Andersen) Spelling in the Hebrew Bible, 1986, The Vocabulary of the Old Testament, 1989; (with F.I. Andersen and D.N. Freedman) Studies in Hebrew and Aramaic Orthography, 1992, others; algorithms editor Jour. Clin. Monitoring and Computing; contbr. articles to profl. jours. Trustee, v.p. Whitney Edn. Found., Los Altos, Calif., 1981-88. Mem. Soc. Bibl. Lit., IEEE (sr. mem.). Avocations: travel, magic. E-mail: adforbes@ix.netcom.com. Home: 820 Loma Verde Ave Palo Alto CA 94303-4112

FORBES, DAVID CRAIG, musician; b. Seattle, Feb. 12, 1938; s. Douglas James and Ruby A. (Niles) F.; m. Sylvia Sterling, Aug. 29, 1965 (div. Apr. 1973); 1 child, Angela Rose. Grad., USN Sch. Music, 1957; student, Western Wash. U., 1960-64. Prin. horn La Jolla (Calif.) Civic Orch., 1958-60, Seattle Worlds Fair Band, 1962, Seattle Opera Co., 1964—, Pacific Northwest Ballet, Seattle, 1964—; asst. prin. horn Seattle Symphony Orch., 1964—; prin. horn Pacific Northwest Wagner Fest., Seattle, 1975—; instr. horn Western Wash. State U., 1969-81, Cornish Inst., Seattle, 1964-78. Served with USN, 1956-60. Mem. NARAS, Internat. Horn Soc. Avocations: piano, golf, fishing. Home: 9050 15th Ave NW # 2 Seattle WA 98117-3429

FORBES, KENNETH ALBERT FAUCHER, urological surgeon; b. Waterford, N.Y., Apr. 28, 1922; s. Joseph Frederick (dec.) and Adelle Frances (Robitaille) Faucher; adopted s. James Peter Forbes; m. Jeanne Ann Bonacci, June 18, 1947 (dec.); 1 child: Michael; m. Eileen Ruth Gibbons, Aug. 4, 1956; children: Diane, Kenneth E., Thomas, Maureen, Daniel. BS cum laude, U. Notre Dame, 1944; MD, St. Louis U., 1947. Diplomate Am. Bd. Urology. Intern St. Louis U. Hosp., 1947-48; resident in urol. surgery Barnes Hosp., VA Hosp., Washington U., St. Louis. U. schs. medicine, St. Louis, 1948-52; asst. chief urology Letterman Army Hosp., San Francisco, 1952-54; fellow West Roxbury (Harvard) VA Hosp., Boston, 1955; asst. chief urology VA Hosp., East Orange, N.J., 1955-58; practice medicine specializing in urology Green Bay, Wis., 1958-78, Long Beach, Calif., 1978-85; mem. cons. staff Fairview State Hosp. U. Calif. Med. Ctr., Irvine, VA Hosp., Long Beach; chmn. Legal Def. Com., State Med. Soc. Wisc., 1976-77; pres. Wisc. Urological Soc., 1977-78; asst. clin. prof. surgery U. Calif., Irvine, 1978-85; cons. Vols. in Tech. Assistance, 1986—. Contbr. articles to profl. jours. Served with USNR, 1944-46, ensign 1947-51; capt. U.S. Army, 1952-54. Named Outstanding Faculty Mem. by students, 1981. Fellow ACS, Royal Soc. Medicine, Internat. Coll. Surgeons; mem. AMA, AAAS, Calif. Med. Assn., Am. Urol. Assn. (exec. com. North Ctrl. sect. 1972-75, Western sect. 1980—), N.Y. Acad. Scis., Surg. Alumni Assn. U. Calif.-Irvine, Justin J. Cordonnier Soc. Washington U., Urologists Corr. Club, Notre Dame Club (Man of Yr. award 1965), Union League Club of Chgo., Miles City Club (Mont.), Phi Beta Pi. Republican. Roman Catholic. Home and Office: 14425 W Via Tercero Sun City West AZ 85375-2741

FORBES, LEONARD, engineering educator; b. Grande Prairie, Alta., Can., Feb. 21, 1940; came to U.S., 1966; s. Frank and Katie (Tschetter) F.; B.Sc. with distinction in Engring. Physics, U. Alta., 1962; M.S. in E.E., U. Ill., 1963, Ph.D., 1970. Staff engr. IBM, Fishkill, N.Y. and Manassas, Va., 1970-72; IBM vis. prof. Howard U., Washington, 1972; asst. prof. U. Ark., Fayetteville, 1972-75; assoc. prof. U. Calif.-Davis, 1976-82; prof. Oreg. State U., Corvallis, 1983—; with Hewlett-Packard Labs., Palo Alto, Calif., 1978; cons. to Telex Computer Products, D.H. Baldwin, Hewlett-Packard, Santa Rosa, Fairchild, United Epitaxial Tech., Naval Ocean Systems Ctr., Hewlett-Packard Corvallis, Micron Tech. Boise; organizer Portland Internat. Conf. and Exposition on Silicon Materials and Tech., 1985-87. Served with Royal Can. Air Force, 1963-66. Mem. IEEE. Contbr. articles to profl. jours. Home: 965 NW Highland Ter Corvallis OR 97330-9706 Office: Oreg State U Dept Elec Engring Corvallis OR 97331

FORBIS, RICHARD GEORGE, archaeologist; b. Missoula, Mont., July 30, 1924; s. Clarence Jenks and Josephine Marie (Hunt) F.; m. Marjorie Helen Wilkinson, Nov. 12, 1960; children: Michael, David, Amanda. B.A., U. Mont., 1949, M.A., 1950; Ph.D., Columbia U., 1955. Sr. archeologist Pacific N.W. Pipeline Corp., Western U.S., 1955-56; archeologist Glenbow Found., Calgary, Alta., Can., 1957-63; mem. faculty U. Calgary, 1963—, prof. archaeology, 1968-88, prof. emeritus, 1988—, interim chmn. dept., Killam Meml. fellow, 1977; chmn. Alta. Public Adv. Com. Hist. and Archeol. Resources, 1971-74; mem. Alta. Historic Sites Bd., 1974-78; vis. scientist Can. Nat. Museum Man, 1970. Author: Cluny: An Ancient Fortified Village in Alberta, 1977; co-author: An Introduction to the Archaeology of Alberta, Canada, 1965. Served with AUS, 1943-46. Mem. AAAS, Soc. Am. Archaeology, Can. Archaeol. Assn. (Smith-Wintemberg award 1984), Am. Anthrop. Assn., Plains Anthrop. Conf., Champlain Soc., Sigma Chi. Office: U Calgary Dept Archeology, 2500 University Dr NW, Calgary, AB Canada T2N 1N4

FORD, ALONZO ANTHONY, minister; b. Tallahasee, Aug. 15, 1953; s. Rath Wesley Sr. and Josephine Louise (Nicks) F.; m. Chancey M. Lamb, Mar. 27, 1976; 1 child, Amanda Chanel. AD, U. Md., 1984; B, U. Md. U. Coll., 1986; Mdiv, Howard U., 1991. Lic. to ministry Greater Little Rock Missionary Bapt. Ch., 1970, ordained, 1981. Assoc. min. Greater Little Rock Bapt. Ch., Pensacola, Fla., 1970-81; lay leader, pastor Hardt Chapel, Schwaebisch, Gmuend, Fed. Republic of Germany, 1981-83; assoc. min. Bethlehem Bapt. Ch., 1983-85; youth min. 1st Mt. Zion Bapt. Ch., Dumfries, Va., 1985-89; pastor Olive Branch Bapt. Ch., Haymarket, Va., 1989-91; analyst Resource Mgmt. Directorate, Ft. Belvoir, Va., 1987—. Staff sgt. U.S. Army, 1972-84. Named to Nat. Dean's List, Howard U., 1987. Mem. Am. Soc. Mil. Comptrollers, Kiwanis (chaplain 1989-90).

FORD, BETTY BLOOMER (ELIZABETH FORD), health facility executive, wife of former President of United States; b. Chgo., Apr. 8, 1918; d. William Stephenson and Hortence (Neahr) Bloomer; m. Gerald R. Ford (38th Pres. U.S.), Oct. 15, 1948; children: Michael Gerald, John Gardner, Steven Meigs, Susan Elizabeth. Student, Sch. Dance Bennington Coll., 1936, 37; LL.D. (hon.), U. Mich., 1976. Dancer Martha Graham Concert Group, N.Y.C., 1939-41; fashion dir. Herpolscheimer's Dept. Store, Grand Rapids, Mich., 1943-48; dance instr. Grand Rapids, 1932-48; chmn. bd. dirs. The Betty Ford Ctr., Rancho Mirage, Calif. Author: autobiography The Times of My Life, 1979, Betty: A Glad Awakening, 1987. Bd. dirs. Nat. Arthritis Found. (hon.); trustee Martha Graham Dance Ctr., Eisenhower Med. Ctr., Rancho Mirage; hon. chmn. Palm Springs Desert Mus.; nat. trustee Nat. Symphony Orch.; bd. dirs. The Lambs, Libertyville, Ill. Episcopalian. Home: PO Box 927 Rancho Mirage CA 92270-0927*

FORD, CHRIS, professional basketball coach; b. Atlantic City, NJ, Jan. 11, 1949; m. Kathy Ford; children: Chris, Katie, Anthony, Michael. Ed., Villanova Univ. Player Detroit Pistons, NBA, 1973-78; player Boston Celtics, NBA, 1978-82, broadcaster, 1982-83, asst. coach, 1983-90, head coach, 1990-95; head coach Milw. Bucks, NBA, 1996-98, L.A. Clippers, NBA, 99-. Mem. NBA Championship teams, as player, 1981, as coach, 1984, 86. Office: Los Angeles Clippers 3939 S Figueroa St Los Angeles CA 90037-1200*

FORD, CLYNN ROBERTS, thoracic and cardiovascular surgeon, lab director; b. Centerville, Utah, Apr. 30, 1926; s. Rulon Garn and Arvilla (Roberts) F.; m. Katherine Garrett, Aug. 19, 1951; children: Cheri Lynn, Michelle, Randon, Shawna, Mary Ann. BA, Northwestern U., Evanston, Ill., 1946; MB, Northwestern U., Chgo., 1950, MD, 1951. Diplomate Am. Bd. Surgery, Am. Bd. Thoracic Surgery; lic. medicine Utah, Ill., Calif., Ohio. [illegible] Hosp., 1951-52; asst. surg. resident, 1955-58; asst. attending surgeon, 1958-59, chief surg. resident, 1959-60, surg. rsch. fellow, 1959-60; asst. chief surg. svc. Salt Lake VA Hosp., 1960-64, acting chief surg. svc., 1964-67; asst. surgeon, attending staff Univ. Hosp., Salt Lake City, 1960-70; attending surgeon thoracic/cardiovascular and gen. surgery LDS Hosp., Salt Lake City, 1965—; dir. peripheral vascular lab. LDS Hosp., 1976—, attending surgeon trauma surgery, 1977-84, instr. surgery U. Cin., 1958-59, U. Utah, 1960-64; asst. prof. surgery U. Utah, 1964-67, assoc. clin. prof. surgery, 1979; presenter in field. Contbr. articles to profl. jours. Lt. U.S. Naval Res. Med. Corps, 1951-65. Fellow ACS; mem. AMA, Utah State Med. Soc., Utah Thoracic Soc., Salt Lake Surg. Soc., Salt Lake County Med. Soc., Alpha Omega Alpha, Phi Beta Pi.

FORD, FREDERICK JAY, clergyman; b. Franklin, Ind., Aug. 11, 1960; s. William Frederick and Janice Marie (Houston) F.; m. Wendi Carol Platt, Feb. 19, 1983; children: Tonya Dawn, Clint Boone. BS in Ministry and Bible Studies, Platte Valley Bible Coll., 1988; diploma in fin. counseling, Christian Fin. Concepts, 1989; diploma in behavior analysis, Inst. for Christian Living, 1989. Ordained to ministry Christian Ch., 1987; Automotive Svc. Excellence cert. mechanic. Min. Glenrock (Wyo.) Christian Ch., 1987-88; youth min. Cen. Christian Ch., Claremore, Okla., 1988-95; dir. Ctrl. Youth Mission Programs, 1990—; owner Ford Imaging - Slides for Praise and Worship; assoc., youth min. First Christian Ch., Sierra Vista, Ariz., 1996—; organizer T.L.C. Autocare Ministry, 1990; dean, asst. dean H.S. Wilderness Challenge, 1989-95; dean So. Ariz. H.S. Wilderness Challenge, 1997—; dean Camp Christian Echoes Christian Svc. Camp, 1997—, bd. sec., 1996—; trustee and mem. exec. bd. Agape Christian Youth Ctr., Sierra Vista, Ariz., 1998—. Town councilman City Coun., Hartman, Colo., 1987. With U.S. Army, 1979-83. Republican. Office: First Christian Ch 55 Kings Way Sierra Vista AZ 85635-3619

FORD, GAIL, library administrator; b. Sacramento, Mar. 5, 1952; d. R. Eugene and Jeanne P. Ford; m. Clive Matson, Jan. 15, 1993; 1 child, Ezra John Matson-Ford. AB in Philosophy, Stanford U., 1973. Adminstrv. analyst U. Calif. Berkeley Libr., 1984—; pub. Broken Shadow Publs., Oakland, Calif., 1993—. Pub.: (book) Emptiness That Plays So Rough, 1995, Under a Gibbons Moon, 1996. Home: 472 44th St Oakland CA 94609-2136

FORD, GERALD RUDOLPH, JR., former President of United States; b. Omaha, July 14, 1913; s. Gerald R. and Dorothy (Gardner) F.; m. Elizabeth Bloomer, Oct. 15, 1948; children: Michael, John, Steven, Susan. A.B., U. Mich., 1935; LL.B., Yale U., 1941; LL.D., Mich. State U., Albion Coll., Aquinas Coll., Spring Arbor Coll. Bar: Mich. 1941. Practiced law at Grand Rapids, 1941-49; mem. law firm Buchen and Ford; mem. 81st-93d Congresses from 5th Mich. Dist., 1949-74, elected minority leader, 1965; v.p. U.S., 1973-74, pres., 1974-77; del. Interparliamentary Union, Warsaw, Poland, 1959, Belgium, 1961, Bilderberg Group Conf., 1962; dir. The Travelers, Inc.; adv. dir. Tex. Commerce Bancshares, Inc., Am. Express Co.; mem. internat. adv. coun. Inst. Internat. Studies. Served as lt. comdr. USNR, 1942-46. Recipient Grand Rapids Jr. C. of C. Distinguished Service award, 1948; Distinguished Service Award as one of ten outstanding young men in U.S. by U.S. Jr. C. of C., 1950; Silver Anniversary All-Am. Sports Illustrated, 1959; Distinguished Congressional Service award Am. Polit. Sci. Assn., 1961. Mem. Am., Mich. State, Grand Rapids bar assns., Delta Kappa Epsilon, Phi Delta Phi. Republican. Episcopalian. Clubs: University (Kent County), Peninsular (Kent County). Lodge: Masons. Home: PO Box 927 Rancho Mirage CA 92270-0927*

FORD, JAMES CARLTON, human resources executive; b. Portland, Mar. 10, 1937; s. John Bernard and Margaret (Reynolds) F.; m. Carolyn Tadina, Aug. 22, 1959; children: Scott, Michele, Mark, Brigitte, Deidre, John. BA in History, U. Portland, 1960; MS in Edn., Troy State U., 1969; MPA, U. Puget Sound, 1976. Cert. sen. profl. in human resources. Commd. 2d lt. USAF, 1960, advanced through grades to lt. col., 1976, adminstr., tng. officer, 1960-70, personnel mgmt. officer, 1971-76; dep. inspector gen. U.S. Air Force Acad., Colorado Springs, Colo., 1977-80; ret. U.S. Air Force Acad., 1980; employment mgr. Western Fed. Savs. (name changed to Bank Western), Denver, 1980-82, v.p. human resources, 1982-88, sr. v.p. mgmt. svcs., 1988-92; dir. career mgmt. AIM Exec., Inc., Cons. Svcs., 1992-95; owner Orgn./Individual Strategies, Inc., Cons., 1995—; bd. dirs. Rocky Mountain chpt. Am. Inst. Banking, Denver, 1988-92; adj. prof. U. Colo., Colorado Springs, 1978-79, USAF Acad., Colorado Springs, 1978-80; adv. bd. U. Colo. Contemporary Mgmt. Program, Regis Coll. Career Svcs.; mem. faculty U. Phoenix, Colo., 1995—; mediator Pikes Peak Better Bus. Bur., 1995—. Mediator Neighborhood Justice Ctr., Colorado Springs, 1980; vol. allocations com. Pikes Peak United Way, Colorado Springs, 1978-79; vol. campaign exec. Mile Hi United Way, Denver, 1986-89; vol. mgmt. cons. Tech. Assistance Svc., Denver, 1991. Mem. Assn. for Mgmt. of Orgn. Design, Soc. for Human Resource Mgmt. (state dir. certification 1996-97). Republican. Roman Catholic. Office: Orgn/Individual Strategies, Inc 975 Tari Dr Colorado Springs CO 80921-2256

FORD, JOHN T., JR., art, film and video educator; b. Rotan, Tex., Feb. 17, 1953; s. John T. and Lala Fern (Shipley) F.; m. Betty Jean Crawford; children: Casey, Craig, Kirk. BA, U. Redlands, 1975. Cert. tchr., Calif. Tchr. art, film, video Yucaipa (Calif.) Joint Unified Sch. Dist., 1976-88; tchr. art and crafts Vacaville (Calif.) Unified Sch. Dist., 1990-92, tchr. video prodn., 1992—, sr. prodn. video, 1994—; cons. Dist. Fine Arts Insvc., Yucaipa, 1987; co-sponsor Art Club, Will C. Wood High Sch., Vacaville, sponsor Video Club. Creator, coord. (conceptual art) Whole School Environments, Caves, Tubes and Streamers, Forest Edge, 1980-84; creator (comml. art prints) Toy Horse Series, 1982-83; prodr. ann. sr. video, 1994—. Mem. Yeoman Svc. Orgn., U. Redlands, 1972, Vacaville Sch. Dist. Tech. Com., Dist. Fine Arts Task Force, Yucaipa, 1984-87, Dist. Task Force for Vocat. Edn., 1992; interim dir. Hosanna House, Redlands, Calif., 1975; liaison Sch. Cmty. Svc./San Bernardino County (Calif.) Fire Dept., 1980-81. Recipient Golden Bell award Calif. Sch. Bd. Rsch. Found., 1987, Ednl. Svc. award Mason's, 1987-88; named one of Outstanding Young Men of Am., 1987, Tchr. of Yr. Calif. Continuation Edn. Assn., 1987-88; grantee Calif. Tchrs. Instructional Improvement Program, 1985; scholar U. Redlands, 1975. Mem. Am. Film Inst. Avocations: art, media fabrication, writing, collecting books, backpacking. Office: Will C Wood High Sch 998 Marshall Rd Vacaville CA 95687-5735

FORD, MARYELLEN, reporter; b. Orange, Calif., Apr. 10, 1957; d. James Henry Lee, Jr. and Maureen (Morrissey) F.; m. John Ross Elliott, mar. 7, 1998. BS in Bus., Ind. U., 1979. Model Ford Models, L.A., 1985-98; comml. actress J. Michael Bloom, L.A., N.Y.C., 1985-98; news writer KNSD-TV/NBC, San Diego, 1995-96; reporter, anchor KDCI-TV, Carlsbad, Calif., 1996-97; reporter KGET-TV/NBC, Bakersfield, Calif., 1997—. Author/editor/reporter: TV-Reports, Incontinenance, 1998, Quest for the Best, 1998 (awards in field 1998). Vol. Sch. of Am. Ballet, N.Y.C., 1989-91; recognition chair United Way, Bakersfield, 1998. Mem. Nat. Acad. TV Arts and Scis., Radio and TV News Dirs. Found., Am. Women in Radio and TV, Radio and TV News Assn., Screen Actors Guild, Am. Fed. TV and Radio Artists. Avocations: sailing, skiing, bicycling, tennis, jogging. Home: 8200 Kroll Way Apt 137 Bakersfield CA 93311-1108

FORD, MICHAEL Q., not-for-profit association administrator; b. Washington, Dec. 12, 1949; s. Milton Q. and Jeanne Louise (Goltman) F.; m. Christine Ann Davies, Apr. 24, 1971 (div. June 1980); m. Elizabeth Julia Ginsberg, June 1, 1984; 1 child, Jennifer. BS in Journalism, Ohio U., 1971. Writer, reporter TV Digest, Washington, 1971-72; staff writer Coun. Better Bus. Burs., Washington, 1972-74; staff assoc. Ctr. for Study of Responsive Law, Washington, 1974; exec. dir. Coalition for Health Funding, Washington, 1975-77; dir. Office of Pub. Policy Nat. Coun. on Alcoholism, Washington, 1977-80; pres. Nat. Assn. Addiction Treatment Providers, Irvine, Calif., 1980-93; exec. dir. Nat. Nutritional Foods Assn., Newport Beach, Calif., 1994—; trustee Commn. on Accreditation of Rehab. Facilities, Tucson, 1985-91. Chmn. legis. com. Nat. Coalition for Adequate Alcoholism Programs, Washington, 1978-80, chmn., 1981. Fellow Am. Coll. of Addiction Treatment Adminstrs. Jewish. Avocations: music, exercise, gardening. Home: 3013 Nestall Rd Laguna Beach CA 92651-2026 Office: Nat Nutritional Foods Assn 3931 Macarthur Blvd Ste 101 Newport Beach CA 92660-3013

FORD, VICTORIA, public relations executive, author, oral historian; b. Carroll, Iowa, Nov. 1, 1946; d. Victor Sargent and Gertrude Francis (Headlee) F.; m. John K. Frans, July 4, 1965 (div. Aug. 1975); m. David W. Keller, May 2, 1981 (div. Nov. 1985); m. Jerry W. Lambert, Mar. 30, 1991. AA, Iowa Lakes Community Coll., 1973; BA summa cum laude,

Buena Vista Coll., 1974; MA in Journalism, U. Nev., Reno, 1988. Juvenile parole officer Iowa Dept. Social Services, Sioux City, 1974-78; staff reporter Feather Pub. Co., Quincy, Calif., 1978-80; tng. counselor CETA, Quincy, 1980; library pub. info. officer U. Nev., Reno, 1982-84; pub. relations exec. Brodeur/Martin Pub. Relations, Reno, 1984-87; pub. relations dir. Internat. Winter Spl. Olympics, Lake Tahoe (Calif.) and Reno, 1987-89; owner Ford Factor Pub. Rels. cons. firm, Reno, 1989—. Author: Making Their Mark: Reno-Sparks YWCA History, 1997, (with R.T. King and Ken Adams) War Stories, 1995; contbr. articles to profl. jours. Mem. adv. bd. Reno Philharm., 1985-87, Reno-Sparks Conv. and Visitors Authority, 1985-93; bd. dirs. Truckee Meadows Habitat for Humanity, 1992-93, half-time exec. dir., 1994; mem. Gov.'s Com. on Fire Prevention, 1991-92; mem. U. Nev. Reno Oral History Program, 1994; bd. dirs. Nev. Women's Archives, 1996; state sec. Nev. Women's History Project, 1998, com. Nev. Writers Hall of Fame, 1993-96; bd. dirs. Friends of the U. Nev. at Reno Libr., 1995-98. Mem. NOW, Pub. Rels. Soc. Am. (charter v.p. Sierra Nev. chpt. 1986-87, pres. 1987-88), Southwest Oral History Assn., Sigma Delta Chi. Democrat. Home and Office: The Ford Factor PO Box 6715 Reno NV 89513-6715

FORDEMWALT, JAMES NEWTON, microelectronics engineering educator, consultant; b. Parsons, Kans., Oct. 18, 1932; s. Fred and Zenia (Chambers) F.; m. Suzan Lynn Hopkins, Aug. 26, 1958 (div. June 1961); m. Elizabeth Anna Hoare, Dec. 29, 1963; children: John William, James Frederick. BS, U. Ariz., 1955, MS, 1956; PhD, U. Iowa, 1960. Sr. engr. GE Co., Evandale, Ohio, 1959-60, U.S. Semcor, Inc., Phoenix, 1960-61; sect. mgr. Motorola Semiconductor Products Div., Phoenix, 1961-66; dept. mgr. Philco-Ford Microelectronics Div., Santa Clara, Calif., 1966-68; assoc. dir. R & D Am. Microsystems Inc., Santa Clara, 1968-71; assoc. rsch. prof. U. Utah, Salt Lake City, 1972-76; dir. microelectronics lab. U. Ariz., Tucson, 1976-87; assoc. prof., lab. mgr. Ariz. State U., Tempe, 1987—, assoc. chair microelectronics, 1992—, asst. chair dept. electronic and computer tech., 1993—; cons. Integrated Cirs. Engring., Scottsdale, Ariz., 1976—, Western Design Ctr., Mesa, Ariz., 1980—; mem. semiconductor com. United Techs. Corp., Hartford, Conn., 1978-87. Author: Silicon Wafer Processing Technology, 1979; editor: Integrated Circuits, 1965; contbr.: MOS Integrated Circuits, 1972. Mem. IEEE, Internat. Soc. for Hybrid Microelectronics (chpt. pres. 1982-83), Electrochem. Soc. Avocations: pilot, photographer. Home: 613 W Summit Pl Chandler AZ 85224-1556

FORE, ANN, counselor, educator, country dance instructor; b. Artesia, N.Mex., July 16, 1948; d. Stanley William and Jackie (Hightower) Blocker; divorced; 1 child Richard Todd. BS, Eastern N.Mex. U., Portales, 1971, MA, 1976. Instr. sociology Eastern N.Mex. U., Clovis, 1974; counselor, instr. So. Plains Jr. Coll., Plainview, Tex., 1975-76; drug and alcohol counselor U.S. Dept. Army, Ft. Hood, Tex., 1976-77; group leader Forest Svc., USDA, Estacada, Oreg., 1980-81; owner Women's Issues Counseling Svcs., Salem, 1985—; tchr. country western ptnr. dancing and line dancing various ednl. settings, Salem, Oreg., Portland C.C., Salem Keizer Schs. Author: founder, adminstr. award-winning, nationally televised country dance team Koda Kountry Drifters. U. N.Mex. rsch. dept. grantee, 1972; recipient Star award United Country/Western Dance Coun., 1998. Mem. APGA, Willamette Writers Assn., Nat. Tchrs. Assn. for Country/Western Dance Instrs., Internat. Platform Assn. Republican. Christian. Avocations: reading, camping, photography, public speaking. Home and Office: PO Box 13851 Salem OR 97309-1851

FOREMAN, DALE MELVIN, lawyer, state official; b. Los Angeles, May 1, 1948; s. C. Melvin and Sylvia (Ahnlund) F.; m. Gail Burgener, June 24, 1972; children: Mari Elizabeth, Ann Marie, James Sterling. AB cum laude, Harvard U., 1970, JD, 1975. Bar: Wash. 1976, U.S. Dist. Ct. (we. dist.) Wash. 1977, U.S. Ct. Claims 1977, U.S. Dist. Ct. (ea. dist.) Wash. 1981, U.S. Ct. Appeals (9th cir.) 1981, Calif. 1986, U.S. Ct. Appeals (3rd cir.) 1987. Ptnr. Jeffers, Danielson & Foreman, Wenatchee, Wash., 1975-81, Jardine, Foreman & Arch, Wenatchee, 1981-88; sr. ptnr. Foreman, Arch, Dodge, Volyn & Zimmerman, Wenatchee, 1988—; mem. 12th legis. dist. Wash. Ho. of Reps., 1993-96, majority leader, 1995-97; mem. Spl. Adv. Commn. on Pub. Opinion, U.S. Dept. of State, 1970-72. Author: Washington Trial Handbook, 1988, Dental Law, 1989, How to Become an Expert Witness, 1989, Crucify Him! A Lawyer Looks at the Trial of Jesus, 1989. Chmn. Chelan County Rep. Cen. Com., Wenatchee, 1977-79, 82-84; bd. dirs. Am. and Fgn. Christian Union, N.Y.C., 1985—, Greater Wenatchee Community Found., 1987—. Mem. ABA, Assn. Trial Lawyers Am., Wash. State Bar Assn., State Bar Calif., Wash. State Trial Lawyers Assn. (bd. govs. 1990—), Harvard Club, Rotary. Presbyterian. Avocation: horticulture. Home: 323 Chatham Hill Rd Wenatchee WA 98801-5931 Office: Foreman Arch Dodge & Volyn 124 N Wenatchee Ave # A Wenatchee WA 98801-2239*

FOREST, MICHEL, computer software company executive; b. Indre-et-Loirem, France, Aug. 15, 1952; s. Jean-Claude Forest and Mireille du-Pont. MS, U. Toulouse, France, 1977. Mng. ptnr. Forest and Webster, Palo Alto, Calif., 1989—. Author: Musée des Beaux-Arts, 1978. E-mail: forest@glx.com. Office: Forest and Webster PO Box 735 Palo Alto CA 94302-0735

FORGAN, DAVID WALLER, retired career officer; b. Chgo., Sept. 28, 1933; s. Harold Nye and Ruth Ada (Waller) F.; m. Shirley Dobbins, Oct. 18, 1958; children—Bruce Dobbins, Todd Macmillan. B.S. in Mktg., U. Colo., 1955; M.S. in Mgmt., George Washington U., 1966. Commd. 2d lt. U.S. Air Force, 1956, advanced through grades to maj. gen., 1985, various positions worldwide, 1956-77; dir. programs hdqrs. tactical air command U.S. Air Force, Langley AFB, Va., 1977-79; dir. force devel. U.S. Air Force, Washington, 1979-80; dep. comdr. spl. ops. command U.S. Air Force, Fort Bragg, N.C., 1980-82; asst. chief staff ops. Allied Forces Central Europe, Brunssum, The Netherlands, 1982-85; dep. chief staff ops. U.S. Air Force Europe, Ramstein Air Base, Fed. Republic Germany, 1985-87; comdr. Sheppard Tech. Tng. Ctr. Sheppard AFB, Tex., 1987-89; ret., 1989. Decorated Silver Star, D.F.C. (3), Legion of Merit, Air medal, Def. Disting. Svc. medal, Def. Superior Svc. medal; Aero Cross of Merit (Spain). Mem. Delta Tau Delta. Republican. Avocations: military history, skiing, golf. Home: 4935 Newstead Pl Colorado Springs CO 80906-5978

FORMAN, ADINE OBERLANDER, religious organization administrator; b. Chgo., June 22, 1968; d. Morton Barry and Renee Oberlander; m. Dan Mark Forman, Jan. 14, 1996. BA, U. Ariz., 1989; JD, Loyola Law Sch., 1992. Aide Calif. State Assemblyman Barbara Friedman, Sherman Oaks, 1994-95; dir. govt. rels. The Jewish Fedn., L.A., 1995—. Contbr. articles to profl. jours. Bd. dirs. Ctr. for Health Care Rights, L.A.; mem. steering com. L.A. Non-Profit Policy Coun.; commr. City of Santa Monica (Calif.), 1997; mem. L.A. County Welfare Reform Task Force, L.A. County, 1997; mem. legis. com. L.A. County Domestic Violence Coun., 1994—; mem. Westside Women's Health Ctr., Santa Monica, 1994—; pres. L.A. County Young Dems., 1992-95. Recipient Wiley W. Manuel award for pro-bono legal svcs. Calif. State Bar, 1992, Spl. award Jewish Communal Profls. of So. Calif., 1997. Democrat. Jewish. Avocations: swimming, reading, travel, investing in the stock market. E-mail: AdineDan@aol.com. Home: 1910 Westridge Ter Los Angeles CA 90049-2219

FORMBY, BENT CLARK, immunologist; b. Copenhagen, Apr. 3, 1940; naturalized, 1991; s. John K. and Gudrun A. (Dinesen) F.; m. Irene Menck-Thygesen, June 28, 1963 (div. May 1980); children: Rasmus, Mikkel; m. Florence G. Schmid, June 28, 1980. BA in Philosophy summa cum laude, U. Copenhagen, 1959, PhD in Biochemistry, 1968, DSc, 1976. Asst. prof. U. Copenhagen, 1969-73, assoc. prof., 1973-79, prof., 1979-83; vis. prof. U. Calif., San Francisco, 1979-84; sr. scientist, dir. lab. of immunology Sansum Med. Rsch. Found., Santa Barbara, Calif., 1984—; cons. Cell Tech., Inc., Boulder, Colo., 1989—, Immunex Corp., Seattle, 1989—; med. adv. bd. Biocellular Rsch. Orgn., Ltd., London, Childrens Hosp. of Orange County, Lautenburg Ctr. for Gen. and Tumor Immunology, Hebrew U., Hadassah Med. Sch., Jerusalem, 1993—, Loran Med. Sys., Inc. Editor: Fetal Islet Transplantation, 1988, 2d edit. 1995; contbr. articles to profl. jours.; patentee on non-invasive glucose measurement; BH55 Hyaluronidase. Grantee Juvenile Diabetes Found., 1987, 88, E.L. Wiegand Found., 1993, Santa Barbara Cottage Hosp. Rsch., 1993-94, Breast Cancer Rsch. U. Calif., 1995-96, 96-97, 97-98. Mem. N.Y. Acad. Scis., Am. Diabetes Assn. (grantee 1985, 86, 89, pres. Santa Barbara chpt. 1995), Am. Fedn. Clin. Rsch., European Assn. for the Study of Diabetes. Avocations: painting, swimming. Office: Sansum Med Rsch Found 2219 Bath St Santa Barbara CA 93105-4321

FORNELLI, PAUL KEVIN, video producer, educator; b. Torrance, Calif., June 10, 1961; s. James Sperto and Marilyn Fornelli. BA, Calif. State U., Long Beach, 1990; MFA, Loyola Marymount U., 1995. Prodr. Simmons Cable TV, Long Beach, 1989-91; lighting supr. Loyola Marymount U., L.A., 1990-93; pres. Blatant Image Group, L.A., 1990-95; media instr. El Camino Coll., Torrance, 1994—; video coord. City of Torrance, 1992—; advisor Torrance Unified Sch. Dist., 1997—; mem. adv. bd. La Puente Valley Sch. Dist., Torrance, 1997—; state coord. Alliance for Cmty. Media, Calif., 1997—. Exec. prodr. (video) ECC Sports, 1995-98, South Bay 360 degrees, 1996-98, Bourbon St. Musician, 1997, Pet Talk, 1997. Mem. SMPTE. Home: 3637 Emerald St Apt 17 Torrance CA 90503-3511 Office: Torrance Cmty TV 3350 Civic Center Dr N Torrance CA 90503-5016

FORNEY, RONALD DEAN, elementary school educator, consultant, educational therapist; b. Kearney, Nebr., June 28, 1954; s. Carl Roger and Florence Alyce (Gordon) F. Student, Community Coll. Denver, 1972-73; BA in Liberal Arts, Loretto Heights Coll., Denver, 1975; AS in Devel. Psychology, Arapahoe Community Coll., Denver, 1977; MBA, Calif. State Coll., San Bernardino, 1992; MS in Ednl. Adminstrn., Nat. U., 1993. Cert. tchr., English tchr., Calif.; cert. ednl. therapist. Tchr. Lake Elsinore (Calif.) Sch. Dist., 1985-87; tchr. Banning (Calif.) Unified Sch. Dist., 1987—, master tchr., classroom mgmt.-assertive discipline cons., 1990—, asst. prin. Ctrl. Elem. Sch., 1996-98; cons. visual and performing arts, motivation and self-esteem bldg; ednl. therapist in pvt. practice, 1998—. Recipient cert. in affective domain Lake Elsinore Sch. Dist., 1986, Outstanding Tchr. award Hemmerling Sch., Banning, 1989. Avocations: theatre, reading, writing and reading Haiku poetry.

FORREST, KENTON HARVEY, science educator, historian; b. Fort Lauderdale, Fla., Oct. 3, 1944; s. Harvey William and Marjorie A. (Boxrud) F. BA, Colo. State Coll., 1968; MA, U. No. Colo., 1981. Science tchr. Dunstan Middle Sch., Jefferson County Pub. Schs., Lakewood, Colo., 1968-98, dept. chmn., 1994-98; pres. Tramway Press, Inc., 1983-98. Author: Denver's Railroads, 1981; (with William C. Jones) Denver-A Pictorial History, 1973; (with others) The Moffat Tunnel, 1978; Rio Grande Ski Train, 1984, History of the Public Schools of Denver, 1989, Route 3 Englewood, 1990, The Railroads of Coors Field, 1995. Trustee Colo. Railroad Hist. Found., Golden, 1975-98, trustee emeritus, 1998—, pres. 1994-95; archivist Richardson Railroad Libr., 1998—; mem., 1st pres. Lakewood Hist. Soc. (Colo.), 1976; office Jeffco Credit Union. Mem. NEA (life) Colo. Assn. Sci. Tchrs., Nat. Railway Hist. Soc. (Intermountain chpt. pres. 1980-83, chmn. hist. plaque commn.), Mobile Post Office Soc. Home: PO Box 15607 Lakewood CO 80215-0007

FORREST, NANCY L., journalist, writer; b. Redondo Beach, Calif.. AA in Liberal Studies, El Camino Coll., 1986; BA, BA in Journalism, Calif. State U., Fresno, 1989. Cert. in CPR and first aid; trained in disaster relief; ARC jr. lifeguard. City reporter Redondo Beach News, 1990-91; corr. South Bay and S.E. edits. L.A. Times, Torrance and Cerritos, Calif., 1991-92; staff writer Palisadian-Post, Pacific Palisades, Calif., 1992-93; edn. editor Palos Verdes Peninsula News, Rolling Hills Estates, Calif., 1993-96; freelance writer Nat. Tech. Mags., Redondo Beach, 1996-97; panorama editor Lodi (Calif.) News-Sentinel, 1997-98; edn. writer Our Times L.A. Times, Ventura, Calif., 1998—; vol. judge writing competitions Journalism Assn. of C.C.s, 1990—, Assn. H.S. Journalists, 1990—, Shell Scholarship Writing Competition, 1990—. V.p. membership, state dir., mem. Redondo Beach Jaycees, 1994-97; campaign worker Candidate City Coun. Health Dist., Redondo Beach, 1992-97; mem., vol. Cheer for Children, Redondo Beach, 1992-97; mem. Kenny Nickelson Meml. Found. for Homeless Vets, 1992—. Recipient Excellence in Edn. Coverage award Peninsula PTA Coun., 1995, Cert. of Appreciation, Kenny Nickelson Meml. Found. for Homeless Vets., Cert. of Merit, Redondo Beach Jaycees. Mem. Soc. Profl. Journalists. Avocations: reading, photography, distance running, bicycling, gourmet cooking. Home: PO Box 305 Ventura CA 93002-0305

FORRESTER, DAVID MARK, graphic designer; b. Santa Ana, Calif., Oct. 18, 1946; s. Joseph Holden and Eleanor Maxine (Munson) F.; m. Ana Maria Crespo, Aug. 23, 1968 (div. 1971); 1 child, Sean David. BA in Art, Calif. State U., Long Beach, 1971, MA in Art, 1979. Signmaker Coast Sign Display, Santa Ana, 1967-68; silk screen printer and spray painter T-C Etching Corp., Long Beach, 1973-75; silk screen printer Super Screen, Signal Hill, Calif., 1975-78; graphic artist Golf Design, Inc., Los Alamitos, Calif., 1977-80, Fad'en Design, Irvine, Calif., 1978, Leisure World News, Seal Beach, Calif., 1978, Lienett Graphics, Los Alamitos, 1978-81, Viking Office Products, L.A., 1981—. Supporter Calif. State U. Found., Long Beach, 1987—. With U.S. Army, 1971-72, Vietnam. Recipient Bank of Am. award, 1964. Democrat. Avocations: painting, sculpture, swimming. Home: 454 Exeter Ln Cambria CA 93428-1914 Office: Viking Office Products Inc 950 W 190th St Torrance CA 90502-1001

FORRESTER, STAN, retired mechanical engineer, writer; b. Carlisle, Eng., Oct. 21, 1931; came to U.S., 1963; s. Robert Edward and Annie (Farish) F.; m. Ann Judith Round, Apr. 21, 1951 (dec. Sept. 1984); m. Linda Jean Lidgett, Apr. 15, 1991. BS in Mech. Engring., Glasgow (Scotland) U., 1953. Profl. engr., N.J. cons. paper mill, 1962-94, ret. Author, pub.: (novels) Fool Circle, 1993, Fool Square, 1994, Fool Triangle, 1995, Fool Deck, 1997, Freedom on Choice, 1998. Mem. Masons. Avocations: bridge, sailing. Home: 19593 Beaver Dike Rd Clatskanie OR 97016-2019

FORSBERG, CHARLES ALTON, computer, information systems engineer; b. Wilmette, Ill., May 6, 1944; s. Delbert Alton and Margery (McCleary) F. Student, Rensselaer Poly. Inst.; BSEE, U. Wis., 1966, MSEE, 1968; postgrad., various univs. and colls. From design engr. to project leader Tektronix, Portland, Oreg., 1968-74; mgr. R&D Sidereal, Portland, 1974-80; chief engr. Computer Devel. Inc., Portland, 1980-84; pres. Omen Tech. Inc., Portland, 1984—. Developer YMODEM and ZMODEM Protocols for worldwide data transfer. Recognized for outstanding contbn. to field IBM-PC Users Group, Madison, Wis., 1988, Alamo PC Orgn., San Antonio, 1988. Home and Office: 10255 NW Old Cornelius Pass Rd Portland OR 97231-2515

FORSDALE, (CHALMERS) LOUIS, education and communication educator; b. Greeley, Colo., Mar. 8, 1922; s. John Aaron and Wilhelmina (Thorkildsen) F.; m. Elinor Wulfekuhler, Aug. 22, 1947 (dec. 1963); children: Lynn, John; m. Joan Ida Rosengren, May 28, 1964 (div. 1966). B.A., Colo. State Coll., 1942; M.A., Columbia U. Tchrs. Coll., 1947; Ed.D., Columbia U., 1951. Instr. English Tchrs. Coll., Columbia U., N.Y.C., 1947-51; asst. prof. Tchrs. Coll., Columbia U., 1951-55, assoc. prof., 1955-58, prof. communication and edn., 1958-87, prof. emeritus, 1987; vis. assoc. prof. edn. U. So. Calif., Los Angeles, 1957; cons. in communication various businesses, industries and schs., 1965—; vis. scholar Iran Communication and Devel. Inst., Tehran, 1977. Author: Nonverbal Communication, 1974, Perspectives on Communication, 1981; Editor: (with others) Communication in General Education, 1961, 8MM Sound Film and Education, 1962. Served to 1st lt. USAAF, 1943-45. Recipient Tchrs. Coll. Disting. Alumni award Merit, 1989. Democrat. Home: 330 Otero St Santa Fe NM 87501-1906

FORSETH, JON EDWARD, consultant; b. Tacoma, Oct. 12, 1948; divorced; children: Erik Logan, Jennifer Menoy, Lana Rashelle. Degree in tech. arts on energy mgmt., Tacoma Coll., 1985. Mem. Internat. Laborers Union, Tacoma, 1969-85; owner Rainshine Constrn., Tacoma, 1980-85; cons. Investment Realty Svcs., Tacoma, 1985-94, Tagar, Tacoma, 1994—; mem. advisor Pierce Co. Comml. Investment Realtors Coun., 1991-94. Fellow Fraternal Order of Eagles (pres. 1995-96, numerous awards), Elks; mem. Tenn. Squires Assn. Avocations: woodworking, sport fishing, gardening. Home: PO Box 843 Home WA 98349 Office: Tagar 3505 6th Ave Tacoma WA 98406

FORSHEY, TIMOTHY ALLAN, lawyer; b. Urbana, Ill., Apr. 25, 1961; s. Thomas Collins Forshey and Paula Jean (Upp) Baker; m. Shannon Marie Gillham, May 11, 1996. BA, Ill. Wesleyan U., 1983; MS, N.E. Mo. State U., 1986; JD, U. Ill., 1989. Bar: Ariz. 1990, Ill. 1990. Student prosecutor Champaign County State's Atty. Office, Champaign, Ill., 1987-89; atty. Jones, Skelton and Hochuli, Phoenix, 1989-91, Goldstein, Kingsley & McGroder, Phoenix, 1991-93, Matz & Rubin, Phoenix, 1993-95, Timothy A. Forshey P.C., Phoenix, 1995-97, Davis, McKee & Forshey P.C., Phoenix, 1997—. Vol. Am. Kidney Found., Phoenix, 1989—, March of Dimes, Phoenix, 1989—; approved atty. NRA, Washington, 1995—; head coach, mem. adv. bd. Pop Warner Football, Phoenix, 1990. Mem. ATLA, U.S. Practical Shooting Assn., Ariz. State Bar Assn., Ill. State Bar Assn., Maricopa County Bar Assn., Mensa. Republican. Avocations: target shooting, hunting, camping, reading, theater. Office: Davis McKee & Forshey 5333 N 7th St Ste A201 Phoenix AZ 85014-2821

FORSHIER, RICHARD STEVEN, physics and biology educator; b. Greeley, Colo., May 13, 1949; s. Richard Glenn and Elsie Mae (Daniels) F.; m. Cindi Batko, Nov. 27, 1991. BS in Edn., Ea. Ill. U., 1971; M in Natural Scis., Ariz State U., 1983, supr. cert., 1988, prin. cert., 1989. Cert. tchr., adminstr., prin. Ariz. Sci. tchr. Hoopeston (Ill.) Jr. H.S., 1971-75; biology tchr. Agua Fria Union H.S., Avondale, Ariz., 1975-76; chemistry, biology tchr. Paradise Valley Schs., Phoenix, 1976-81, tchr., chmn. dept. sci., 1981-87, sci. curriculum coord., 1987-91, tchr. physics and biology, 1991—; mem. Hoopeston, Ill. Youth Bd., 1971-75. Author: (videos) How to Do a Science Project, 1988, How to Use the StarLab Planetarium, 1989; (handbook) Safety and Emergency Procedures in the Science Classroom, 1988; (books) Outdoor Education Guidebook, 1990, Introduction to Ecology Concepts, 1991. Runner-up Ariz. Tchr. of Sci. award, 1981; grantee Energy and Phys. Sci., 1978, NSF Biology, 1983, GTE Greenhouse Bldg., 1986, AAAS, Astronomy Rsch., 1993; named Outstanding Biology Tchr. for Ariz., 1980. Mem. Ariz. Sci. Olympics (bd. dirs. 1978-81), Outstanding Biology Tchrs. Soc. (bd. dirs. 1981-86, Outstanding Biology Tchr. award for Ariz. 1979), Ariz.-Nev. Jr. Acad. Sci. (bd. dirs. 1981-86), Phi Kappa Phi. Office: North Canyon H S 1700 E Union Hills Dr Phoenix AZ 85024-3033

FORSTER, BRUCE ALEXANDER, dean; b. Toronto, Ont., Can., Sept. 23, 1948; m. Margaret Jane Mackay, Dec. 28, 1968, (div. Dec. 1979); 1 child, Kelli Elissa; m. Valerie Dale Pendock, Dec. 8, 1979; children: Jeremy Bruce, Jessica Dale. BA in Math., Econs., U. Guelph, Ont., 1970; PhD in Econs., Australian Nat. U., Canberra, 1974. Asst. prof. U. Guelph, 1973-77, assoc. prof., 1977-83, prof. econs., 1983-88; vis. assoc. prof. U. B.C., Vancouver, 1979; vis. fellow U. Wyoming, 1979-80, vis. prof., 1983-84, 87; prof. econs., 1987—, dean Coll. Bus., 1991—; vis. prof. Profl. Tng. Ctr., Ministry of Econ. Affairs, Taiwan, 1990-97; acad. assoc. The Atlantic Coun. of the U.S., cons. in field. Author: The Acid Rain Debate: Science and Special Interest in Policy Formation, 1993; co-author: Economics in Canadian Society, 1986; assoc. editor Jour. Applied Bus. Rsch., 1987, editorial adv. bd., 1987—; editorial coun. Jour. Environ. Econs. and Mgmt., 1989, assoc. editor, 1989-91; contbr. articles to profl. jours. Trustee Wyo. Retirement Sys., 1995—, Laramie Sr. Housing, Inc., 1995-96. Jayes-Qantas Vis. scholar U. Newcastle, Australia, 1983. Mem. Am. Econ. Assn., Assn. Environ. and Resource Economists, Mid-West Assn. Bus. Deans and Divsn. Heads (pres. 1995-96), Internat. Assn. Mgmt. Edn. (bus. accreditation com. 1995-98), Faculty Club U. Guelph (treas. 1981-82, v.p. 1982-83, 85- 86, pres. 1986-87). Avocations: weight lifting, swimming, skiing, scuba diving. Home: 3001 Sage Dr Laramie WY 82070-5751 Office: U Wyo Coll Bus Laramie WY 82071

FORSTER, ROBERT, actor, speaker; b. Rochester, N.Y., July 13, 1941; s. Robert Wallace and Grace (Montanarella) F.; m. June Carol Provenzano (div.); children: Robert, Elizabeth, Kathrine, Maeghen; m. Tsvia Mizrahi (div.). BA in History and Psychology, U. Rochester, 1964; student, Heidelberg Coll., Tiffin, Ohio, 1959-60, Alfred (N.Y.) U., 1960-62. Actor, 1966 ; motivational speaker Interacting, L.A.; instr. actor workshops. Appeared in Broadway plays Mrs. Dally Has a Lover, 1965, Streetcar Named Desire; Off-Broadway plays include Glass Menagerie, Twelve Angry Men, The Sea Horse, others; films include Reflections in a Golden Eye, 1966, Medium Cool, 1968, The Don is Dead, Stunts, Avalanche, Jackie Brown, 1997 (Acad. award nominee), American Perfekt, Psycho, 1998, others; T.V. appearances in Banyon, 1972, Nakia, 1974, Death Squad, Standing Tall, Police Story, Once a Hero, others, TV movie Rear Window, 1998; prodr., dir. Hollywood Harry, 1985.

FORSYTH, BEN RALPH, academic administrator, medical educator; b. N.Y.C., Mar. 8, 1934; s. Martin and Eva (Lazansky) F.; m. Elizabeth Held, Aug. 19, 1962; children: Jennifer, Beverly, Jonathan. Attended, Cornell U., 1950-53; MD, NYU, 1957. Diplomate Am. Bd. Internal Medicine. Intern, then resident Yale Hosp., New Haven, 1957-60; postdoctoral fellow Harvard U. Med. Shc., Boston, 1960-61; rsch. assoc. NIH, Bethesda, Md., 1963-66; assoc. prof. med. microbiology, prof. med. coll. U. Vt., Burlington, 1966-90, assoc. dean div. health scis., 1971-85, assoc. v.p. acad. affairs, 1977-78, v.p. adminstrn., 1978-85, sr. v.p., 1985-90; sr. exec. asst. to pres. Ariz. State U., Tempe, 1990—, prof. health adminstrn. and policy, 1991—, interim v.p. adminstrv. svcs., 1991-93; interim provost Ariz. State U. West, Phoenix, 1992-93, Ariz. State U. East, Mesa, 1994-96, provost, v.p. Ariz. State U. West, Phoenix, 1993-96; sr. cons. Univ. Health Ctr., Burlington, 1986-90. Contbr. articles to profl. jours. V.p., chmn. United Way Planning Com., Burlington, 1974-75, Ops. Com., 1975-76, bd. dirs., officer, 1977-89; bd. trustees U. Vt., Burlington, 1996—; mem. New England Bd. Higher Edn. Com., Burlington, 1985-89; chmn. U. Vt. China Project Adv. Bd., Burlington, 1989-90. Lt. comdr. USN, 1962-63. Sinsheimer Found. faculty fellow, 1966-71. Fellow ACP, Infectious Diseases Soc. Am.; mem. Phi Beta Kappa, Alpha Omega Alpha. Avocations: hiking, gardening. Office: Arizona State Univ PO Box 872203 Tempe AZ 85287-2203

FORSYTH, G. VAUGHN, artist; b. Provo, Utah, May 8, 1948; s. Gordon James and Nadene (Dow) F. BFA, U. Utah, 1974. Mem. various performing groups, Washington, 1960-67; trumpet soloist UN Army Band, Seoul, Republic of Korea, 1967-69; watercolorist Salt Lake City, 1976-87; travelling watercolorist Springville Mus., 1984; digital printmaker Pacesetter Labs, Palo Alto, Calif., 1987—; artists in schs. Utah Arts Council, Salt Lake City, 1979-80; consulting curator Utah Mus. Fine Arts, Salt Lake City, 1980-84. Illustrator: The Modern Chair Escapes Moab 77, 1997; travelling exhbn. NEA Utah Mus. Fine Arts, 1986-87; inventor front-end profl. large-print graphics software. Spkr. Utah Watercolor Soc., 1979-84. Recipient Visual Arts award Utah Arts Coun., 1984. Mem. LDS Ch. Avocations: mountain biking, motorcycling, art-critic. Office: Pacesetter Labs 546 Oxford Ave Palo Alto CA 94306-1137

FORSYTH, RAYMOND ARTHUR, civil engineer; b. Reno, Mar. 13, 1928; s. Harold Raymond and Fay Exona (Highfill) F.; BS, Calif. State U., San Jose, 1952; M.C.E., Auburn U., 1958; m. Mary Ellen Wagner, July 9, 1950; children: Lynne, Gail, Alison, Ellen. Jr. engr., asst. engr. Calif. Div. Hwys., San Francisco, 1952-54; assoc. engr., sr. supervising, prin. engr. Calif. Dept. Transp., Sacramento, 1961-83, chief geotech. br., 1972-79, chief soil mechanics and pavement br., 1979-83, chief Transp. Lab., 1983-89; cons., lectr. in field. Served with USAF, 1954-56. Fellow ASCE (pres. Sacramento sect., chmn. Calif. council 1980-81); mem. Transp. Research Bd. (chmn. embankments and earth slopes com. 1976-82, chmn. soil mechanics sect. 1982-88, chmn. group 2 council 1988-91), ASTM. Contbr. articles to profl. publs. Home: 5017 Pasadena Ave Sacramento CA 95841-4149

FORT, LEE EARTHMON, financial services representative; b. Detroit, Sept. 15, 1950; s. Esmar Earthmon and Leona Mary Ann (Lucky) F.; m. Mary Elizabeth Thomas, Aug. 26, 1972. BA in Psychology, U. Notre Dame, 1972; EdM in Clin. Psychology, Harvard U., 1973; postgrad., Ind. U., 1973-75. Donor cons. ARC, Louisville, 1975-77; asst. dir. donor resources ARC, San Jose, Calif., 1977-78; dir. donor resources ARC, San Jose, 1978-88; with Lee E. Fort & Assocs., 1988—; bd. dirs. Inn Vision, chmn. mktg. & devel. com. Fundraiser East Valley YMCA, San Jose, 1987-88; co-devel. Ethics Check-Youth Ethics Workshop, 1994. Named co-winner Donor Recruiter of Yr. Am. Assn. Donor Recruitment Profls. Mem. San Jose Life Underwriters, Nat. Assn. Securities Dealers, Pres.'s Club (Penn. Mut.), Interact Club, Rotary (treas. 1987-88, bd. dirs. community svc. 1988-89 San Jose chpt., vocat. svcs. 1989-90, area rep. dist. 517 Youth Leadership Camp 1989-90, pres. San Jose East club 1991-92, Rotarian of Yr. San Jose East club 1989-90, Paul Harris fellow 1990, sponsor San Jose East Interact Clubs 1986—), Chmn.'s Club (Penn Mut.). Democrat. Roman Catholic. Avocations: stamp collecting, nature photography, classical music, jazz. Home: 1720 Quimby Rd San Jose CA 95122-1223

FORT, ROBERT BRADLEY, minister; b. Portsmouth, Va., Dec. 27, 1948; s. Richard Gould and Hazel Naomi (McBride) F.; m. Esther Faith Hardin, June 10, 1967; children: Yvonne René, Nathan Michael. Ordained to ministry United Evang. Ch., 1973. Evangelist United Evang. Chs., Monrovia, Calif., 1966, nat. youth dir., 1968-70, asst. to the pres., 1970-73, Calif. dist. supt., 1973-75; evangelist Assemblies of God, Springfield, Mo., 1976-78; sr. pastor Lynden (Wash.) Assembly of God, 1978-81, County Christian Ctr., Bellingham, Wash., 1981-87, First Assembly of God, Salinas, Calif., 1988—; exec. dir. Life Mgmt. Sems., Salinas, 1989—; pres. Fort Ministries, Salinas, 1967—; exec. v.p., chmn. bd. United Evang. Chs., Hollister, Calif., 1996—; plenary spkr. World Congress Evang. Chs., Nairobi, Kenya, Africa, 1993. Composer Love was the Color, 1980 (Grand prize 1981); singer, musician 15 records. Republican. Office: Fort Ministries PO Box 1000 San Juan Bautista CA 95045-1000

FORTH, KEVIN BERNARD, beverage distributing industry consultant; b. Adams, Mass., Dec. 4, 1949; s. Michael Charles and Catherine Cecilia (McAndrews) F.; children: Melissa, Brian. AB, Holy Cross Coll., 1971; MBA with distinction, NYU, 1973. Div. rep. Anheuser-Busch, Inc., Boston, 1973-74, dist. sales mgr., L.A., 1974-76, asst. to v.p. mktg. staff, St. Louis, 1976-77; v.p. Straub Distbg. Co., Ltd., Orange, Calif., 1977-81, pres., 1981-93, chmn., CEO, 1986-93, also bd. dirs. Commr. Orange County Sheriff's Adv. Coun., 1988—; mem. adv. bd. Rancho Santiago C.C. Coll. Dist. 1978-80; bd. dirs. Children's Hosp. of Orange County Padrinos Found., 1983-85, St. Joseph's Hosp. Found., Orange County Sports Hall of Fame, 1980-89; exec. com., bd. dirs. Nat. Coun. on Alcoholism, 1980-83; mem. pres. coun. Holy Cross Coll., 1987-91; bd. dirs., pres. Calif. State Fullerton Titan Athletic Found., 1983-85, 89-90 (vol. of yr., 1991),mem. Calif. Beer Wholesalers Assn., dir., 1978-89, v.p., 1984, chmn, 1985,; bd. dirs. Freedom Bowl, 1984-93, v.p., 1984-85, pres., 1986, chmn., 1986-87, Anaheim Vis. and Conv. Bur., 1989-93; bd. dirs. Orangewood Children's Found., 1988-93; mem. Calif. Rep. State Cen. Com., 1988-93, Orange County Probation Dept. Cmty. Involvement Bd., 1992-93. Benjamin Levy fellow NYU, 1971-73; recipient Founders award Freedom Bowl, 1993. Mem. Industry Environ. Coun., Holy Cross Alumni Assn., NYU Alumni Assn., Nat. Assn. Stock Car Auto Racing, Sports Car Club Am. (Ariz. state champion 1982), Beta Gamma Sigma. Roman Catholic. Club: Holy Cross (So. Calif.), Nat. Beer Wholesalers Assn. (bd. dir. 1986-93, asst. sec. 1989-90, sec. 1989-91, vice-chmn. 1992, chmn. 1993). Home: 27750 Tamara Dr Yorba Linda CA 92887-5840

FORTI, WILLIAM BELL, sports products executive, inventor; b. Washington, Dec. 6, 1941; s. Francis and Margaret Lee (Bell) F.; m. Martha Louise Goding; children: Scott, Jennifer, Meredith, Kimberly, Mark, Andrea. BS, U. Richmond, 1963, MComm., 1964. Fin. analyst Securities and Exch. Commn., Washington, 1964-66; staff economist Joint Tax Com., House Judiciary Com., U.S. Congress, Washington, 1966-71; from sr. staff exec. to exec. v.p. Bendix Corp., Southfield, Mich., 1971-75; mgr. bus. devel. projects Internat. Paper Co., N.Y.C., 1975-78; dir. planning, bus. devel. positions Gen. Dynamics, St. Louis, 1978-92; founder, chmn. William Mark Corp., Claremont, Calif., 1992—. Patent for flying gyroscope, 1997, 98. Mem. World Affairs Coun., L.A., 1997, Rep. Nat. Com., Washington, 1997, chmn. adv. bc., 1997; co-chmn. L.A. County Aerospace Task Force, L.A., 1997; participant nat. security forum Air War Coll., Maxwell AFG, Ala., 1997. Recipient Recognition of Dedicated Svc. County of L.A., 1992, Recognition of Contribution Naval War Coll. Found., 1997. Mem. Nat. Sci. Tchrs. Assn., Def. Orientation Conf. Assn., Claremont U. Club (asst. treas. 1994—), Radio Controlled Hobby Trade Assn., Kite Trade Assn., C. of C. (Claremont, Calif.). Republican. Avocations: travel, reading, hiking, golf, skiing. Office: William Mark Corp 112 Harvard Ave Claremont CA 91711-4716

FORTIER, DANA SUZANNE, psychotherapist; b. Fresno, Calif., Jan. 15, 1952; d. Dan and Louise (Metkovich) Ninkovich; m. Timothy Fortier, Jan. 29, 1994. BA in Journalism summa cum laude, Calif. State U., Fresno, 1974; BSN, Calif. State U., 1979, MSW with distinction, 1986. Registered nurse, Calif; lic. social worker, Calif. Staff nurse Valley Med. Ctr., Fresno, 1980-81; pub. health nurse Fresno County Health Dept., 1981-83; therapist II Sierra Community Hosp., Fresno, 1986-87; women's svcs. coord. Turning Point Youth Svcs., Visalia, Calif., 1987-89; psychotherapist and cons. in pvt. practice Visalia, 1989—; instr. San Joaquin Valley Coll., 1994—; clins. cons. in field. Contbr. articles to profl. jours. Mem. Task Force on Pregnant Mothers, 1990—. Mem. Calif. Women's Commn. on Drugs and Alcohol, Calif. Advocacy for Pregnent Women, Soc. for Clin. Social Wk., Nat. Assn. Social Workers, Visalia Bus. and Profl. Women's Clubs. Republican. Office: 304 S Johnson St Visalia CA 93291-6136

FORTIER, SAMUEL JOHN, lawyer; b. Spokane, Wash., Mar. 30, 1952; s. Charles Henry and Mary (Petersen) F.; m. Dagmar Christine Mikko, Sept. 15, 1983; children: Nova Marie, Matthew Theodore. BA cum laude, Boston U., 1974; JD magna cum laude, Gonzaga U., 1982. Bar: Alaska 1982, U.S. Dist. Ct. Alaska 1983, U.S. Ct. Appeals (9th cir.) 1987. Acting exec. dir. Bristol Bay Native Assn., Dillingham, Alaska, 1974-76; fin. analyst Alaska Fedn. of Natives, Anchorage, Alaska, 1976-78; loan analyst State of Alaska, Anchorage, 1978-79; law clk. consumer protection div., atty. gen.'s office State of Wash., Spokane, 1980-82; assoc. Cummings & Routh P.C., Anchorage, 1982-84; ptnr. Fortier & Mikko, Anchorage, 1984—; adj. prof. U. Alaska, Anchorage, 1982-85; speaker workshop Small Bus. Adminstrn., Anchorage, 1982-85; manpower dir. VISTA. Mem. ABA, Alaska Bar Assn. (native law sect.), Anchorage Bar Assn. Democrat. Avocations: reading, writing, camping, skiing. Home: 6800 Sequoia Cir Anchorage AK 99516-3755 Office: Fortier & Mikko 2550 Denali St Ste 1500 Anchorage AK 99503-2737

FORTIER, SHARON MURPHY, special education educator; b. Alice, Tex., July 22, 1939; d. Henry Barcus and Burnice Ruth (Clifft) Murphy; m. James Robert Fortier, Sept. 30, 1967; children: Mikaron, Robynlea. BS in Elem. Edn., Tex. Woman's U., Denton, 1961; MEd in Early Childhood Spl. Edn., U. Wash., 1988. Cert. tchr., Tex., K-12 spl. edn. tchr., Wash. Ctrl. Agy. dir. Tex. Intercollegiate Student Assn., Austin, 1960-61; tchr. Denver Pub. Schs., 1961-62, Deer Park (Tex.) Sch. Dist., 1962-66; tchr. Anchorage Sch. Dist., 1966-70, spl. reading tchr., 1970-72; dir. St. Mary's Creative Playsch., Anchorage, 1976-79; resource specialist/coord. Alaska Resource Access Project, Anchorage, 1981-83, co-dir., 1983-86; spl. edn. tchr. Northshore Sch. Dist., Bothell, Wash., 1988—; mem. task force on regulation Nat. Head Start Nat. Resource Access Project, Washington, 1982; presenter workshops. Compiler, editor: (libr. catalog) Alaska Special Services Resource Library Catalog and Addenda, 1979-81; co-editor, producer: (video) Like Any Child, 1993-94; editor newsletter Rapline, 1981-86. Troop leader Girl Scouts U.S., Anchorage, 1978-84; block chmn. Am. Cancer Soc., Seattle, 1992-93; asst. in organizing telethon Easter Seals, Anchorage, 1985-86. Kindergarten Inclusion grantee Assn. Wash. Sch. Prins., 1993-94. Mem. AAUW, Coun. for Exceptional Children (divsn. early childhood), Early Childhood Devel. Assn. Wash. Democrat. Episcopalian. Avocations: camping, travel, reading, sewing. Home: 15316 Old Redmond Rd Redmond WA 98052-6837 Office: Woodmoor Elem Sch 12225 NE 160th St Bothell WA 98011-4167

FORTNER, HUESTON GILMORE, lawyer, writer, composer; b. Tacoma, Nov. 1, 1959; s. Hueston Turner Jr. and Deborah Hewes (Berry) F. BS, Tulane U., 1981; JD, U. Miss., 1985. Bar: Miss. 1986, La. 1987, U.S. Dist. Ct. (no. and so. dists.) Miss. 1986, U.S. Dist. Ct. (ea., mid. and we. dists.) La., 1987, U.S. Ct. Appeals (5th cir.) 1986, Calif. 1989, U.S. Dist. Ct. (cen. dist.) Calif. 1989. Clk. Farrer and Co., London, Miss., 1985; assoc. Cliff Finch & Assocs., Batesville, Miss., 1986; pvt. practice New Orleans, 1987-88; atty. Parker, Milliken, Clark, O'Hara & Samuelian, L.A., 1989-90; pvt. prctice L.A., 1990—; vis. lectr. Anhui U., Hefei, People's Rep. of China, Bejing Inst. of Petrochem. Tech., 1994; participanted in Leicester vs. Leicester Rugby Union, House of Lords, Eng., 1985; assisted Queen's Counsel in Yussuf Islam (Cat Stevens) vs. Bank of Westminster P.L.C. royalties litigation 1985, Newton vs. NBC, 1988; temporary judge L.A. County mcpl. ct., 1991—; dep. investigator State Bar (Calif.) Trial Ct., 1999—; pres., CEO Orange Records, 1997—. Contbg. photographer Flix mag., 1993—; contbr. editor Rental, 1987-89. Recipient Space Devel. Strategies award NASA/U. Houston Advanced Rsch. Ctr., 1995; grantee NSF, 1976. Mem. Miss. Bar Assn., La. Bar Assn., State Bar Calif., Broadcast Music Internat., Phi Alpha Delta. Presbyterian. Avocations: music, film, scuba diving.

FORTUNA, ANTHONY FRANK, retired educator, consultant; b. Thomas, W.Va., Apr. 8, 1914; s. Anton and Rose (Secna) F.; m. Ann Marie Barthel, Sept. 27, 1938; children: Richard, Eugene. Student, L.A. Trade Tech. Coll., Pierce Coll., Valley Coll.; grad. Warren Sch. Astronautics, L.A. Coll.; student, U.S. Aviation Cadets. Registered profl. engr., Calif. Leadman Vultee Aircraft, Downy, Calif., 1939-40; gen. supr. Hindustan Aircraft, Bangalore, India, 1942-44; supr., inspector U.S. Air Corp., Long Beach, Calif., 1945-46; tng. supr. Douglas Aircraft Co., El Segundo, Calif., 1946-55; mgr. Northrop Ventura Div., Newberry Park, Calif., 1955-79; devel. engr. Hughes Space, El Segundo, 1981-86; dir. Talley Corp., Newberry, 1980-81; tchr., instr. Pierce Coll., Woodland Hills, Calif., 1962-98; source engr. BQS, Inc., 1982-98; cons. in field. Mem. Am. Inst. Astronautic/Aeronautic. Republican. Mormon. Avocations: teaching, reading. Home and Office: 3415 Loadstone Dr Sherman Oaks CA 91403-4513

FORTUNE, JAMES MICHAEL, network analyst; b. Providence, Sept. 6, 1947; s. Thomas Henry and Olive Elizabeth (Duby) F.; m. G. Suzanne Hein, July 14, 1973. Student, Pikes Peak Community Coll., Colorado Springs, Colo., 1981-83; BSBA, BS in Computer Info. Systems, Regis Coll., 1991. Owner Fortune Fin. Svcs., Colorado Springs, Colo., 1975-79; ptnr. Robert James and Assocs., Colorado Springs, 1979-81; pres. Fortune & Co., Colorado Springs, 1981-88; sr. v.p. mktg. and editorial Phoenix Communications Group, Ltd., Colorado Springs, 1985-95, also bd. dirs.; sr. network analyst Coastal States Mgmt. Corp., 1995—; bd. dirs. Interstate Gas Credit Union, Inc., N.Am. Internet, LLC; talk show host Sta. KRCC, fin. commentator Wall Street Report, Sta. KKHT, 1983-84. Editor Fortune newsletter, 1981-85, The Can. Market News, 1981-83; editor, pub. Penny Fortune newsletter, 1981-95, The Low Priced Investment newsletter, 1986-87, Women's Investment Newsletter, 1987-95; pub. Internal Revenue Strategies, 1990, Tax and Investment Planning Strategies for Medical Professionals, 1991; contbr. articles to profl. jours. Cons. Jr. Achievement bus. project, Colorado Springs, 1985, 97-98. Sgt. U.S. Army, 1968-70, Vietnam. Mem. Direct Mktg. Assn., Elks. Avocations: fly fishing, skiing, hiking, backpacking. Office: 1837 S Nevada Ave Ste 223 Colorado Springs CO 80906-2516

FOSS, LINDA GRAY, English writing educator, writer; b. Greenwich, Conn., Feb. 25, 1953; d. Clifton Tenney and Susan Frances (Collins) F.; m. Douglas Hitch, Sept. 12, 1992. Student, Seattle Ctrl. C.C., 1972-74; AA, Shoreline C.C., 1989; BA in English, U. Wash., 1991; postgrad., Antioch U., 1998—. Freelance writing and design Seattle, 1974-79; advt. mgr. Tone Commander Systems, 1980-81; customer svc. mgr. Color Control, Redmond, Wash., 1982-88; writing ctr. tutor Shoreline C.C., Seattle, 1988-90, U. Wash., 1990-91; calendar dir. Bainbridge Island (Wash.) Arts Coun., 1991-92; writing ctr. coord., adj. faculty Centralia (Wash.) Coll., 1993-98. Contbr. articles to publs. Bd. dirs. Friends of Evergreen Libr, Olympia, 1996-98, chair Celebration of Written Word, 1995-97. Mem. Nat. Coun. Tchrs. English, Olympia Poetry Network, Seattle Group Theatre, Wash. Poets Assn., Women's Writing Circle. Avocations: reading, writing, gardenign. Office: Centralia Coll 600 Locust Centralia WA 98531

FOSSEEN, NEAL RANDOLPH, business executive, former banker, former mayor; b. Yakima, Wash., Nov. 27, 1908; s. Arthur Benjamin and Florence (Neal) F.; m. Helen Witherspoon, Sept. 26, 1936; children: Neal Randolph Jr., William Roger. BA, U. Wash., 1930; LLD (hon.), Whitworth Coll., 1967. With Wash. Brick, Lime & Sewer Pipe Co., 1923-32, v.p., 1932-38; pres. Wash. Brick & Lime Co., 1938-58; dir. Securities Intermountain Co., 1954-71; v.p., dir. Old Nat. Bank Wash., 1958-68; v.p., dir. Wash. Bancshares, 1968-71, vice chmn., 1971-72, chmn. bd., pres., 1972-73; dir. Utah-Idaho Sugar Co., 1968-79, 1st Nat. Bank Spokane, 1972-79, dir., Spokane Indsl. Park, 1959-72, (treas. 1959-66), dir. North Coast Life Ins. Co., 1965-76; chmn. emeritus, dir. Old Nat. Bancorp., 1973-77; pres. 420 Investment Co., 1982-84; hon. dir. Metropolitan Mortage Co., 1995—; dir. Quarry Tile Co., 1965-68, Day Mines, Inc., 1968-81. Mem. exec. com. Expo '74; adv. bd. Mus. Native Am. Culture, 1957-81; mayor City of Spokane, 1960-67, mayor emeritus, 1967—; mem. adv. bd. emeritus Spokane Intercollegiate Rsch. and Tech. Inst., 1993-96. Past chmn. adv. bd. Wash. State Inst. Tech.; bd. dirs., past pres. council Boy Scouts Am.; bd. dirs. Wash. Rsch. Coun., sec., 1968-74; bd. dirs. YMCA, 1969-80, Pacific Sci. Found., 1970-73, Mountain States Legal Found., 1979-85; mem. adv. bd. Grad. Sch. Bus., U. Wash., 1974-81, emeritus, 1981—; mem. adv. bd. dept. History, 1981—; chmn. Regent Gonzaga U., 1948-61, emeritus, 1961—; mem. adv. bd. Coll. Engring., Wash. State U., 1949-79; hon. trustee Found. N.W.; trustee Rockwood Cmty. Found., 1993-97, Gonzaga Dussault Found., Fosseen-Kusaka Disting. Professorship, Jackson Found. Scholaarship U. Wash., 1998; mem. adv. bd. Advanced Tech. Ctr., 1989-94, Mukogawa Fort Wright Inst., Whitworth Coll. Internat. Mgmt.; founding dir. Athletic Round Table; adv. bd. City Innovation. Col. USMCR, ret. Recipient Shrine award El Katif Temple, 1974, Disting. Eagle Scout award Boy Scouts Am., 1976, Silver Beaver award, Silver Antelope award; Non Sibi, Sed Patriae award Marine Corps Res. Officers Assn.; Outstanding Svc. award Fairchild AFB, Spokane Mcpl. League; Forward Spokane award Spokane County Hotel and Restaurant Coun.; Liberty Bell award Spokane County Bar Assn.; Book of Golden Deeds, Exchange Club; Sister City Outstanding Svc. award Town Affiliation Assn.; Disting. Citizen award Eastern Wash U., 1982, Founders Day award, 1994; Disting. Citizen award Air Force Air Mobility Command, 1995, Cit. Lg. Lifetime Svc. award, 1997; named hon. citizen, Nishinomiya, Japan. Mem. VFW, Ret. Officers Assn., Assn. Wash. Bus. (past pres.), Spokane C. of C. (v.p. 1946-51), Spokane-Nishinomiya Sister City Soc. (pres.), Srs. N.W. Golf Assn. (gov.), Mil. Order World Wars (Perpetual), Order of the Rising Sun (Japan), Balboa de Mazatlan Club (Mex), Spokane Club (life), Spokane Country Club (life), Prosperity Club, Travellers Century Club, Spokane Ski Club, Rotary (Paul Harris fellow), Beta Theta Pi. Home: Rockwood Forest Estates 2609 E Foxwood Ct Spokane WA 99223-3410 Office: 1420 US Bank Bldg Spokane WA 99201

FOSSLAND, JOEANN JONES, professional speaker, personal coach; b. Balt., Mar. 21, 1948; d. Milton Francis and Clementine (Bowen) Jones; m. Richard E. Yellott III, 1966 (div. 1970); children: Richard E. IV, Dawn Joeann; m. Robert Gerard Fossland Jr., Nov. 25, 1982. Student, Johns Hopkins U., 1966-67; cert., Hogan's Sch. Real Estate, 1982. Cert. values coach, behaviors coach, 1998, GRI. Owner Kobble Shop, Indiatlantic, Fla., 1968-70, Downstairs, Atlanta, 1971; seamstress Aspen (Colo.) Leather, 1972-75; owner Backporch Feather & Leather, Aspen and Tucson, 1975-81; area mgr. Welcome Wagon, Tucson, 1982; realtor assoc. Tucson Realty & Trust, 1983-85; mgr. Home Illustrated mag., Tucson, 1985-87; asst. pub., gen. mgr. Phoenix, Scottsdale, Albuquerque, Tricities Tucson Homes Illustrated, 1990-93; pres. Advantage Solutions Group, Cortaro, Ariz., 1993—; power leader Darryl Davis Seminars Power Program, 1995—; personal and profl. coach. Designer leather goods (Tucson Mus. Art award 1978, Crested Butte Art Fair Best of Show award 1980); author: Personal and Professional Coaching: Coach University, Certified Training Program, 1996. Voter registrar Recorder's Office City of Tucson, 1985-91; bd. dirs. Hearth Found., Tucson, 1987-96, pres., 1994; bd. dirs. Ariz. Integrated Residential & Ednl. Svcs., Inc., 1989-95, pres. 1994-95). Mem. NAFE, Internat. Fedn. Coaches, Women's Coun. Realtors (leadership tng. grad. designation, pres. Tucson chpt. 1995, Ariz. state gov. 1997-98, Tucson Affiliate of Yr. award 1991), Tucson Assn. Realtors (Affiliate of Yr. award 1988). Democrat. Presbyterian. Avocations: tennis, gardening, reading, traveling, public speaking. Office: Advantage Solutions Group PO Box 133 Cortaro AZ 85652-0133

FOSTER, DAVID RAMSEY, soap company executive; b. London, May 24, 1920; (parents Am. citizens); s. Robert Bagley and Josephine (Ramsey) F.; m. Anne Firth, Aug. 2, 1957 (dec. June 1994); children: Sarah, Victoria; m. Alexandra Chang, May 24, 1996. Student in econs., Gonville and Caius Coll., Cambridge (Eng.) U., 1938. With Colgate-Palmolive Co. and affiliates, 1946-79, v.p., gen. mgr. Europe, Colgate-Palmolive Internat., 1961-65, v.p., gen. mgr. household products div. parent co., N.Y.C., 1965-68, exec. v.p., 1968-70, pres., 1970-75, chief exec. officer, 1971-79, chmn., 1975-79. Author: Wings Over the Sea, 1990. Trustee Woman's Sport Found. Served to lt. comdr. Royal Naval Vol. Res., 1940-46. Decorated Disting. Service Order, D.S.C. with bar, Mentioned in Despatches (2); recipient Victor award City of Hope, 1974, Herbert Hoover Meml. award, 1976, Adam award, 1977, Harriman award Boys Club N.Y., 1977, Charter award St. Francis Coll., 1978, Walter Hagen award, 1978, Patty Berg award, 1986, Commr.'s award LPGA, 1995. Mem. Soc. Mayflower Descs. Clubs: Hawks (Cambridge U.); Royal Ancient Golf (St. Andrews, Scotland); Royal Cinque Ports Golf (life), Sunningdale Golf, Swinley Forest Golf (U.K.); Sankaty Head Golf; Racquet and Tennis (N.Y.C.); Mission Hills Country, Bally Bunion Golf. Home: 540 Desert West Dr Rancho Mirage CA 92270-1310

FOSTER, DUDLEY EDWARDS, JR., musician, educator; b. Orange, N.J., Oct. 5, 1935; s. Dudley Edwards and Margaret (DePoy) F. Student Occidental Coll., 1953-56; AB, UCLA, 1957, MA, 1958; postgrad. U. So. Calif., 1961-73. Lectr. music Immaculate Heart Coll., L.A., 1960-63; dir. music Holy Faith Episcopal Ch., Inglewood, Calif., 1964-67; lectr. music Calif. State U., L.A., 1968-71; assoc. prof. music L.A. Mission Coll., 1975-83, prof., 1983—, also chmn. dept. music, 1977—; mem. dist. acad. senate L.A. Community Colls., 1991-92; mem. acad. senate L.A. Mission Coll., 1993-97; dir. music 1st Luth. Ch., L.A., 1968-72. Organist, pianist, harpsichordist; numerous recitals; composer O Sacrum Convivium for Trumpet and Organ, 1973, Passacaglia for Brass Instruments, 1969, Introduction, Arioso & Fugue for Cello and Piano, 1974. Fellow Trinity Coll. Music, London, 1960. Recipient Associated Students Faculty award, 1988. Mem. Am. Guild Organists, Am. Musicol. Soc., Nat. Assn. of Scholars, Acad. Senate, Town Hall Calif., L.A. Coll. Tchrs. Assn. (pres. Mission Coll. chpt. 1976-77, v.p., exec. com. 1982-84), Mediaeval Acad. Am. Republican. Anglican. Office: LA Mission Coll Dept Music 13356 Eldridge Ave Sylmar CA 91342-3200

FOSTER, LAWRENCE, concert and opera conductor; b. Los Angeles, 1941. Student, Bayreuth Festival Masterclasses; studied with, Fritz Zweig. Debut as condr., Young Musicians' Found., Debut Orch., 1960; condr., mus. dir., 1960-64, condr., San Francisco Ballet, 1961-65, asst. condr., Los Angeles Philharmonic Orch., 1965-68, chief guest condr., Royal Philharmonic Orch., Eng., 1969-75, guest condr., Houston Symphony, 1970-71, condr. in chief, 1971-72, music dir., 1972-78, Orch. Philharmonique of Monte Carlo, 1979, gen. music dir., Duisburg & Dusseldorf Opera (Ger.), 1982-86, former music dir. Lausanne Chamber Orch., 1991-96, music dir. Aspen (Colo.) Music Festival and Sch.; currently music dir. Orquestra Ciutat de Barcelona; artistic dir. Bucharest Festival and Competition; guest condr. orchs. in, U.S., Europe, Australia and Japan; recorded, condr. world premiere Paul McCartney's Standing Stone, 1997; (Recipient Koussevitsky Meml. Conducting prize 1966, Eleanor R. Crane Meml. prize Berkshire Festival, Tanglewood, Mass. 1966); condr. Jerusalem Symphony Orch., 1990. Address: ICM Artists Ltd c/o Jenny Vogel 8942 Wilshire Blvd Beverly Hills CA 90211-1934

FOSTER, MARY FRAZER (MARY FRAZER LECRON), anthropologist; b. Des Moines, Feb. 1, 1914; d. James and Helen (Cowles) LeCron; B.A., Northwestern U., 1936; Ph.D., U. Calif., Berkeley, 1965; m. George McClelland Foster, Jan. 6, 1938; children—Jeremy, Melissa Foster Bowerman. Research asso. dept. anthropology U. Calif., Berkeley, 1955-57, 75—; lectr. in anthropology Calif. State U., Hayward, 1966-75; mem. faculty Fromm Inst. Lifelong Learning, U. San Francisco, 1980. Fellow AAAS, Am. Anthropol. Assn.; mem. Linguistic Soc. Am., Internat. Linguistic Assn., Southwestern Anthrop. Assn., Soc. Woman Geographers. Democrat. Author: (with George M. Foster) Sierra Popoluca Speech, 1948; The Tarascan Language, 1969; editor: (with Stanley H. Brandes) Symbol As Sense: New Approaches to the Analysis of Meaning, 1980, (with Robert A. Rubinstein) Peace and War: Cross-Cultural Perspectives, 1986, (with Robert A. Rubinstein) The Social Dynamics of Peace, 1988 (with Lucy J. Botscharow) The Life of Symbols, 1990. Home: 790 San Luis Rd Berkeley CA 94707-2030

FOSTER, MICHAEL WILLIAM, librarian; b. Astoria, Oreg., June 29, 1940; s. William Michael and Margaret Vivian (Carlson) F. BA in History, Willamette U., 1962; MA, U. Oreg., 1965; postgrad., So. Oreg. Coll., 1976. Tchr. Astoria High Sch., 1963-66, librarian, 1970-96; tchr. Am. Internat. Sch. of Kabul (Afghanistan), 1966-70; bd. dirs. Astoria H.S. Scholarships, Inc., AG-BAG Internat. Ltd., Astoria Pacific Industries, Inc., Asta Ltd. Mem. Oreg. Arts Commn., Salem, 1983-91; commr. Oreg. Coun. Humanities, 1994—, chmn., 1995-97; commr. Oreg. Advs. for the Arts, 1994-97; bd. dirs. Am. Cancer Soc., Clatsop County, Oreg., 1980-87, Luth. Family Svcs., 1994-96, Oreg. Arts Advocates Found., 1994-98, Columbia Meml. Hosp. Found., 1992—, Edward Hall Scholarship Bd., pres. Clatsop C.C. Found.; bd. dirs. U. Oreg. Art Mus. Coun., 1991—, pres., 1993-95; bd. dirs., treas. Astoria Cmty. Concert Assn., 1964-88, pres., 1989—; bd. dirs., treas. Ed and Eda Ross Scholarship Trust; bd. dirs., pres. Clatsop C.C. Found., 1997—; mem. Oreg. Econ. Devel. Dept. Task Force, 1995-97; mem. adv. bd. Oreg. Symphony, 1992—. Mem. NEA, Oreg. Edn. Assn., Oreg. Edn. Media Assn., Clatsop County Hist. Soc. (bd. dirs., pres. 1983-87), Ft. Clatsop Hist. Assn. (treas. 1974-91, pres. 1991—, bd. dirs.), Astoria C. of C. (bd. dirs. 1982-88, George award 1985, pres. 1987), Lewis and Clark Trails Heritage Found., Rotary (pres. Astoria Club 1986), Astoria Golf and Country Club, Beta Theta Pi. Republican. Roman Catholic. Avocations: antique dealer, art collector, oil painter, golf, tennis. Home: 1636 Irving Ave Astoria OR 97103-3621

FOSTER, NORMAN MCDANIEL, artist; b. Smithville, Tex.; s. James McDaniel and Irene (Owens) McDaniel; m. Muriel Long Foster; children: Douglas, Victoria. BA, Mex. City Coll.; MA, U. Mo. Lt. USAF, 1941-45. Avocation: gardening. Home: 48 Del Mesa Carmel CA 93923 Office: 418 Orange Ave Sand City CA 93955-3517

FOSTER, RUTH MARY, dental association administrator; b. Little Rock, Jan. 11, 1927; d. William Crosby and Frances Louise (Doering) Shaw; m. Luther A. Foster, Sept. 8, 1946 (dec. Dec. 1980); children: William Lee, Robert Lynn. Grad. high sch., Long Beach, Calif. Sr. hostess Mon's Food Host of Coast, Long Beach, 1945-46; dental asst., office mgr. Dr. Wilfred H. Allen, Opportunity, Wash., 1946-47; dental asst., bus. asst. Dr. H. Erdahl, Long Beach, 1948-50; office mgr. Dr. B.B. Blough, Spokane, Wash., 1950-52; bus. mgr. Henry G. Kolsrud, D.D.S., P.S., Spokane, 1958—, Garland Dental Bldg., Spokane, 1958—. Sustaining mem. Spokane Symphony Orch. Mem. NAFE, Nat. Assn. Dental Assts., DAV Aux., DAV Comdrs. Club, Wash. State Fedn. Bus. and Profl. Women (dir. dist. 6), Spokane's Lilac City Bus. and Profl. Women (past pres.), Nat. Alliance Mentally Ill, Wash. Alliance Mentally Ill, Internat. Platform Assn., Spokane Club, Credit Women's Breakfast Club, Dir.'s Club, Inland N.W. Zool. Soc., Pioneer Circle of Women Helping Women. Democrat. Mem. First Christian Ch. Avocations: gardening, reading, continuing education studies. Office: Henry G Kolsrud DDS PS 3718 N Monroe St Spokane WA 99205-2850

FOSTER, WILLIAM SILAS, JR., minister; b. Kansas City, Mo., Nov. 5, 1939; s. William Silas and Edna LaResta (Scott) F.; m. Susan Jean Mannle, June 5, 1983; children Robert Light, Beth Light, Stacey Light; children from previous marriage, Beth Ann, Amy Lynne. BA, Mo. Valley Coll., 1962; MDiv, McCormick Sem., 1966. Ordained to ministry Presbyn. Ch. (USA), 1966. Asst. min. 1st Presbyn. Ch., Edwardsville, Ill., 1966-68; min. St. Paul's Presbyn. Ch., St. Louis, 1968-71, Moro (Ill.) Presbyn. Ch., 1971-83; min. 1st Presbyn. Ch., North Kansas City, Mo., 1983-84, Worland, Wyo., 1985—; commr. to Gen. Assembly Presbyn. Ch. (U.S.A), Omaha, Balt., Albuquerque, 1973, 91, 95; stated clk. Presbytery Wyo., Casper, 1990—, Com. of the Office of Gen. Assembly; instr. calligraphy Synod Sch., 1982-83; pres. Presbyn. Alcohol Info. Network, 1982-83, Ill. Impact Bd., 1983. Resource person 1980 Youth Triennium, Bloomington, Ind., 1980; bd. dirs. Edwardsville Sch. Bd., 1976-83, Mental Bd. Washakie County, 1989—. Recipient M. Keith Upson award U.S. Jaycees, 1974; named Outstanding New Mem., Ill. Jaycees, 1972, Outstanding Mem., 1973. Mem. Lions (2d v.p. 1989-91). Home: 1515 Yellowstone Ave Worland WY 82401-2206 Office: 1st Presbyn Ch PO Box 53 Worland WY 82401-0053

FOTSCH, DAN ROBERT, elementary education educator; b. St. Louis, May 17, 1947; s. Robert Jarrel and Margaret Louise (Zimmermann) F.; m. Jacquelyn Sue Rotter, June 12, 1971; children: Kyla Michelle, Jeffrey Scott, Michael David. BS in Edn. cum laude, U. Mo., 1970; MS in Edn., Colo. State U., 1973. Cert. K-12 phys. edn. and health tchr., Mo., Colo. Tchr. phys. edn., coach North Callaway Schs., Auxvasse, Mo., 1970-71; grad. teaching asst., asst. track coach Colo. State U., Ft. Collins, 1971-73; tchr. elem. phys. edn., coach Poudre R-1 Sch. Dist., Ft. Collins, 1973—; tchr. on spl. assignment Elem. Phys. Edn. Resource, 1990; adminstrv. asst. Moore

Sch., Ft. Collins, 1990—, acting prin., 1997; tchr. on spl. assignment dist. phys. edn. coord. Moore Sch., 1998, k-12 coord. dist. phys. edn., 1998—; co-dir. Colo. State U. Handicapped Clinic, Ft. Collins, 1973-93; dir. Moore Elem. Lab. Sch., Ft. Collins, 1979—; dir. Colo. State U. Super Day Camp, 1979—; presenter for conf. in field. Contbr. articles to profl. jours. State dir. Jump Rope for Heart Project, Denver, 1981. Recipient Scott Key Acad. award, Sigma Phi Epsilon, 1969, Honor Alumni award, Coll. of Profl. Studies of Colo. State U., 1983; grantee Colo. Heart Assn., 1985; recipient Coaching Excellence award Ft. Collins Soccer Club, 1991-92. Mem. NEA, AAHPERD (exec. bd. mem. coun. on phys. edn. for children 1983-86, reviewer Jour. Phys. Edn., Recreation and Dance 1984—, fitness chairperson, conv. planner 1986), ASCD, Poudre Edn. Assn., Colo. Edn. Assn., Colo. Assn. Health, Phys. Edn., Recreation and Dance (pres. 1979-82, Tchr. award 1977, Honor award 1985), Internat. Platform Assn., Ctrl. Dist. Alliance for Health, Phys. Edn., Recreation and Dance (elem. divsn. chairperson for phys. edn. 1989—), Phi Delta Kappa (found. rep. 1985), Phi Epsilon Kappa (v.p. 1969, pres. 1970). Republican. Avocations: marathons, triathlons, racketball, volleyball, swimming (Colo. State Swimming Championship Village Green Team, 1987, 89). Home: 2807 Blackstone Dr Fort Collins CO 80525-6190 Office: Moore Elem Sch 1905 Orchard Pl Fort Collins CO 80521-3210

FOULIARD, PAUL EMILE, journalism educator, author; b. New Rochelle, N.Y., June 3, 1948; s. Georges Guillaume and Lucie Marie (Harrison) F.; m. Nicole Jan Freed, Dec. 19, 1993; children: Heath, Morgan, Eric, Emily, Alexandria, Bretagne. AA, Lakeland Coll., 1974; postgrad., Ea. Ill. U., 1980. C.C. tchg. cert. in journalism. Curriculum devel. staff Bell Helicopter Internat., Isfahan, Iran, 1977-78; freelance writer, 1980—; lectr. Ea. Ill. U., Charleston, 1980, Lakeland Coll., Mattoon, Ill., 1981; prof. journalism Mesa (Ariz.) C.C., 1991—; instr. YMCA, Scottsdale, Ariz., 1997. Editor Family Pet, 1980-82; author: Waltz With The Devil, 1993; contbr. articles to profl. jours. Sgt. USMC, 1966-72. Recipient Nat. Newspaper Pacemaker award Newspaper Assn. Am., 1995. Mem. Maricopa County Adj. Faculty, Amnesty Internat., The Authors Guild Inc., Natural Resources Def. Coun. Roman Catholic. Avocation: restoring antique motorcycles. Office: Mesa Cmty Coll 1833 W Southern Ave Mesa AZ 85202-4822

FOUNTAIN, LINDA, secondary education educator; b. LaPorte, Ind., Dec. 2, 1950; d. Richard Raymond and Myrtle Irene (Sigle) Hartwick; m. Donald Henry Nebelung, Dec. 23, 1972 (div. June 1991); children: Michele Lynette, Trent Howard; m. Franklin C. Fountain, Jan. 20, 1996. BS, Purdue U., 1972; MA, U. Ariz., 1996. Cert. secondary tchr., Ariz. Tchr. math. Williamsport (Ind.) Jr. High Sch., 1973-74, Jefferson County Schs., Louisville, Ky., 1974-75; substitute tchr. Crawford County Schs., Bucyrus, Ohio, 1975-77; tchr. math. Emily Gray Jr. High Sch., Tucson, Ariz., 1989—, basketball coach, 1991-94; pvt. math. tutor, Tucson, 1985—. Mem. choir Tanque Verde Luth. Ch., Tucson, 1980—, chmn. presch. com., 1982-89, leader Sunday sch., 1984—. GIFT fellow, 1993. Mem. Nat. Coun. Tchrs. Maths., Ariz. Assn. Tchrs. Maths. Lutheran. Avocations: tennis, golfing, hiking. Home: 6280 E Placita de Fuego Tucson AZ 85750-1285 Office: Emily Gray Jr H S 4201 N Melpomene Way Tucson AZ 85749-9330

FOURNIER, DONALD FREDERICK, dentist; b. Phoenix, Oct. 16, 1934; s. Dudley Thomas and Margaret Mary (Conway) F.; m. Sheila Ann Templeton, Aug. 5, 1957 (div. 1972); children: Julia Marguerite, Donald Frederick, John Robert, Anne Marie Selin, James Alexander; m. Nancy Colleen Hamm, July 10, 1976; children: Catharine Jacinthe, Jacques Edouard. Student, Stanford U., 1952, U. So. Calif., L.A., 1952-54; BSc, U. Nebr., 1958, DDS, 1958. Pvt. practice restorative dentistry Phoenix, 1958—; pres. Hope Mining and Milling Co., Phoenix, 1970—; chief dental staff St. Joseph's Hosp., Phoenix, 1968; vis. prof. periodontology Coll. Dentistry U. Nebr., 1985; faculty Phoenix Coll. Dental Hygiene Sch., 1968-71; investigator Ariz. State Bd. Dental Examiners, 1978-89; mem. Meml. Dental Clinic Staff, 1968-70; dir. Canadian Am. Inst. Cariology, 1986—. Contbr. articles to profl. jours. Pres. bd. trustees Osborn Sch. Dist., Phoenix, 1976; dir. Lukesmen, Phoenix, 1978-81; patrolman Nat. Ski Patrol, Phoenix, 1974-79; pres. Longview PTA, 1969; mem. adv. bd. Phoenix Crime Commn., 1969-71, Phoenix Coll. Dean's Adv. Bd., 1968-75; mem. The Phoenix House Am. Indian Rehab., 1985-86. Lt. col. (retired) Ariz. Army Res. N.G., 1958—. USPHS fellow, 1956-57, 57-58. Fellow Am. Coll. Dentists, Internat. Coll. Dentists; mem. ADA, Ariz. State Dental Assn., Pacific Coast Soc. Prosthodontists, Am. Acad. Restorative Dentistry (pres. 1991-92), Am. Acad. Gold Foil Operators, Craniomandibular Inst. (dir.), Internat. Assn. Dental Rsch., Acad. Operative Dentistry (charter), U.S. Croquet Assn., Ariz. Croquet Club, Downtown Croquet Club (pres. 1993—), Phoenix Country Club, Am. Acad. Orofacial Pain (pres. 1988-89), Phi Delta Theta, Xi Psi Phi. Republican. Roman Catholic. Avocations: snow skiing, croquet, fly fishing. Home: 86 E Country Club Dr Phoenix AZ 85014-5435 Office: 207 E Monterey Way Phoenix AZ 85012-2619 also: 26450 N Alma School Rd Scottsdale AZ 85255-8172

FOWLES, CARL S., human resources executive; b. Salt Lake City, Nov. 24, 1948; s. George Donald and Lavee (Brady) F.; m. Martha Fellows, July 29, 1952; children: Jordan T., John B., Jenavee, Aaron S., Adam C., Austin B. BA in English, Brigham Young U., 1974, MPA, 1978, EdD, 1986. Cert. sr. profl. of human resources, Human Resource Cert. Inst. Salesman, supr. Leven's, Inc., Provo, Utah, 1970-74; instr., adminstr. LDS Edn. Sys., Brigham Young U., Salt Lake City and Provo, 1974-80; orgn. devel. coord. Conoco, Inc., Houston, 1980-81; dir. human resources Trammell Crow Co., Dallas, 1982-83; asst. v.p. human resources healthcare divsn. Cigna Corp., Dallas and Hartford, Conn., 1983-88; sr. v.p., mng. dir. Drake Beam Morin, Inc., Dallas and Salt Lake City, 1988-96; sr. v.p. orgn. and profl. devel. 1st Security Corp., Salt Lake City, 1996—; cons. Fowles Assocs., Hartford, 1988. Mem. Soc. for Human Resource Mgmt., Rotary Internat., Brigham Young U. Alumni Assn. (regional dir. 1985-86). Home: 9414 S 2100 W South Jordan UT 84095-9276 Office: 1st Security Corp 405 S Main St Ste 400 Salt Lake City UT 84111-3417

FOWLKES, DONALD IRWIN, mechanical engineer; b. Spokane, Wash., Oct. 2, 1959; s. Donald Edward Fowlkes and Marjorie (Gibbs) O'Connor; m. Karen Lynn Zotcavage, June 19, 1985 (div. 1989). BSME, Gonzaga U., 1982. Eng.-in-tng., Calif. Mech. engr. IBM, San Jose, Calif., 1982-93; sr. mech. engr. Antex Data Systems, Union City, Calif., 1994, Cybeg Systems, Menlo Park, Calif., 1994-95, AG Assocs., San Jose, 1995-97, Applied Komatsu Tech., Santa Clara, 1997—. Mem. ASME, Materials Info. Soc.

FOX, FRANCES JUANICE, retired librarian, educator; b. Vicksburg, Miss., Aug. 17, 1916; d. Willie Amercy Thaxton and Fannye Lou (Spell) Hepfer; m. Leonard John Fox, Feb. 25, 1937; children: Frances Juanice, L. John Jr., Kenneth L., Robert T., William E., Elizabeth Jean. AA, Phoenix Coll., 1959; BS in Edn., Ariz. State U., 1963, MS in Edn., Libr., 1972. Cert. kindergarten, primary, and elem. tchr., cert. libr., cert. religious edn. Diocese of Phoenix. Substitute tchr. Escambia County Sch. Dist., Pensacola, Fla., 1936-38; kindergarten tchr. Lollipop Ln. Sch., Phoenix, 1960-61, 1st United Meth. Day Sch., Phoenix, 1961-62; tchr. grade 3 Wilson Elem. Sch., Phoenix, 1962-63; summer libr. R.E. Simpson Elem. Sch., Phoenix, 1964, 65; preschool tchr. Jewish Community Ctr., Phoenix, 1967-68; libr. Audio Visual Ctr. Sts. Simon and Judge Elem. Sch., Phoenix, 1969-82; cataloger First Untied Meth. Ch. Libr., Phoenix, 1963, Baker Ctr. Ariz. State Univ. Meth. and Hillel Students Libr., Tempe, 1969; tchr. ch. sch., 1942-69, ret., 1969. Contbr. poetry to varius publs., including Nat. Libr. Poetry, 1995, Poetic Voices of Am., 1990, 95, World Book of Poetry. 1990; co-compiler: (libr. manual) Diocese of Phoenix, 1980-81. Organizer, leader Girl Scouts USA, Birmingham, Ala., 1951, 52, Phoenix, 1976-83; leader cub scouts Boy Scouts Am., Birmingham, 1950-52, Phoenix, 1952-55; swim instr. ARC, Fla., Ariz., 1933, 34, 53, 54; dance instr. Circle Game and Beginning Dance, Wesley Cmty. Ctr., Phoenix, 1966, 67; sch. tchr. Meth. Ch., 1939-69. Scholar Phoenix Coll., Ariz. State Coll., 1959; recipient Gold Poet award World Book of Poetry, 1990, Honorable Mention Poetic Voices of Am., 1990, Internat. Twentieth Century Achievement award Cambridge Edn., 1994. Mem. ALA, Ariz. State Libr. Assn. (com. on continuing edn. 1979-81), Gold Star Wives of Am. Inc. (pres. 1993-94, nat. parlementarian 1990-91), DAV Aux. (life), Ariz. PTA (life mem., organizer, v.p.), Phi Theta Kappa, Iota Sigma Alpha Honor Soc. Methodist. Avocations: dancing, photography, genealogy, sewing, music composition. Home: 2225 W Montebello Ave Phoenix AZ 85015-2327

FOX, HAROLD LAVAR, computer executive; b. Provo, Utah, Aug. 24, 1923; s. George James and Jennie (Holdaway) F.; m. Lucy Grant, May 16, 1942 (dec. Apr. 1968); children: James Harold (dec.), Nancy Jane, Kathleen (dec.), Caroline (dec.); m. Joyce Benson, Aug. 20, 1968. BS, U. Utah, 1951, MBA, 1972; cert. in meterology, UCLA, 1952; PhD, Found. for Advancement and Mastery of Edn., 1984. Commd. USAF, 1951-59, advanced through grades to capt., resigned, 1959; missile system engr. Hughes Aircraft Corp., Sperry Corp., Los Angeles and Salt Lake City, 1959-71; dir. project ops. IRMP U. Utah, Salt Lake City, 1972-73; founder D.C.P.S., Salt Lake City, 1973-83; pres. Trenergy, Salt Lake City, 1983—; founder CITE Nat., Inc., 1987—; cons. hydroponics industry, 1960-80, tar sand processing, 1975-84, advanced computer software devel., 1973—; founder, pres. Fusion Info. Ctr., 1989—. Co-author: Modern Science and Technology, 1965, Fluidic Systems Design Guide, 1966; editor Jour. New Energy, New Energy News; contbr. articles to profl. jours.; patentee in field. Mormon. Avocations: writing sci. fiction, poetry, gardening, inventing. Office: Trenergy 3084 E 3300 S Salt Lake City UT 84109-2154

FOX, KELVIN MORGAN, rancher, writer; b. Stamford, Conn., Aug. 17, 1912; s. Frederick Pierce and Josephine (Morgan) F.; m. Patricia Anne Grady, Sept. 25, 1951; two children: Geoffrey, Grady. BA, Princeton U., 1935; DSc (hon.), U. Ariz., 1973. Exec. sec. Gov. Ariz., Phoenix, 1939-41; mem. Ariz. Ho. of Reps., Phoenix, 1947-52, Ariz. State Senate, Phoenix, 1953-55; chmn. State Water Commn., Phoenix, 1974-80, Land De't Bd. Appeals, Phoenix, 1981-91. Named to Ariz. Agrl. Hall of Fame, U. Ariz. Coll. Agr., 1995. Avocation: tournament tennis. Home and Office: PO Box 25912 Munds Park AZ 86017-5912 *Died May 11, 1998.*

FOX, KENNETH L., retired newspaper editor, writer; b. Kansas City, Mo., Mar. 18, 1917; s. Henry Hudson and Margaret Patience (Kiely) F.; m. Mary Harbord Manville, June 20, 1975. A.B., Washington U., St. Louis, 1938; student, U. Kansas City, 1939-40. With Kansas City Star, 1938-78, asso. editor, 1966-78; news analyst Sta. WDAF, Kansas City, 1948-53; war corr., Vietnam and Laos, 1964, corr., No. Ireland, 1973. Served to col. AUS, 1940-46, vet. Normandy Invasion, Battle of the Bulge, Liberation of Paris, 1945. Decorated Bronze Star, Commendation medals with Oak Leaf Cluster; recipient 1st place editl. div. nat. aviation writing contest, 1957, 58, 59, 60, 67, Disting. Alumnus award Washington U. (St. Louis), 1998; named Aviation Man of Yr. for Kansas City, 1959; Kenneth L. Fox Day proclaimed by Gov. of Ariz., 1998. Mem. Am. Legion, 40 and 8, Res. Officers Assn., Ret. Officers Assn., Mil. Order World Wars, Phi Beta Kappa, Beta Theta Pi, Pi Sigma Alpha, Sigma Delta Chi. Clubs: Kansas City Press; Ariz. Home: 9796 E Ironwood Dr Scottsdale AZ 85258-4728

FOX, MATTHEW ADRIAN, political campaign consultant, musician; b. N.Y.C., Oct. 8, 1966; s. Michael Alan and Leslie Anne Fox. BA with honors, U. Wash., 1988. Chair, founder Seattle Commons Opponents Com., 1995-96; campaign mgr. Chong for City Coun., Seattle, 1996; legis. asst. Office Seattle City Councilmember Charlie Chong, Seattle, 1996-97; pres. U. Dist. Cmty. Coun., Seattle, 1998—; freelance campaign cons. Seattle, 1998—; mem. Office of Ethics and Elections Lobbying Taskforce, City of Seattle, 1996-97. Guitarist, vocalist with Bitter End (rec.) Harsh Realities-Metal Blade, 1990; guitarist, vocalist with Dr. Unknown, 1992-95, Dinsdale, 1998—; writer Backlash Mag., 1988-89. Mem. Phi Beta Kappa. Home: 1409 NE 56th Seattle WA 98105

FOX, MAXINE RANDALL, banker; b. Yates Ctr., Kans., Feb. 18, 1924; d. Carey Holaday and Nettie Myrrl (Herder) Randall; m. Joseph Marlin Fox, Aug. 25, 1946 (dec. 1992); children: Kathryn Lynette Fox Wilz, Jonathan Randall Fox. A in Fine Arts, Colo. Woman's Coll., 1942; B Music Edn., U. Denver, 1946. Pub. sch. music. tchr. Barr Lake (Colo.), 1942-43, Independence Sch., Fort Lupton, Colo., 1943-44, Fowler Pub. Schs., Fowler, Colo., 1944-48, 1952-54; employee The Fox Ins. Agy., Fowler, Colo., 1948-55, co-owner, 1955-86; with The Fowler (Colo.) State Bank, 1949—, vice chmn. bd. dirs., 1987—. Former mem. Fowler Libr. Bd.; mem. PEO. Named woman of Yr., Eta Tau chpt. Beta Sigma Phi, 1997. Mem. AAUW, DAR, First Families Ohio, Descendants Colonial Clergy (life), Fowler Hist. Soc. (past treas.), Fowler C. of C., Friends of Libr., Fowler Women's Club, Order Ea. Star, Fowler Golf Club, Pueblo Golf and Country Club. Republican. Methodist. Avocations: genealogy, reading, fishing, gardening, bridge. Home: 3308 County Road Kk.75 Fowler CO 81039-9713 Office: Fowler State Bank 201 Main St Fowler CO 81039-1132

FOX, MICHAEL J., museum director. Pres., CEO Mus. of No. Ariz., Flagstaff. Office: Mus of No Ariz 3101 N Fort Valley Rd Flagstaff AZ 86001-8348*

FOX, STUART IRA, physiologist; b. Bklyn., June 21, 1945; s. Sam and Bess F.; m. Ellen Diane Berley; 1 child, Laura Elizabeth. BA, UCLA, 1967; MA, Calif. State U., L.A., 1967; postgrad., U. Calif., Santa Barbara, 1969; PhD, U. So. Calif., 1978. Rsch. assoc. Children's Hosp., L.A., 1972; prof. physiology L.A. City Coll., 1972-85, Calif. State U., Northridge, 1979-84, Pierce Coll., 1986—; cons. William C. Brown Co. Pubs., 1976—. Author: Computer-Assisted Instruction in Human Physiology, 1979, Laboratory Guide to Human Physiology, 2d edit., 1980, 7th edit., 1996, 8th edit., 1999, Textbook of Human Physiology, 1986, 5th edit., 1996, 6th edit., 1999, Human Anatomy and Physiology, 1986, 4th edit., 1995, 5th edit., 1999, Perspectives on Human Biology, 1991, Laboratory Manual for Anatomy and Physiology, 1986, 4th edit., 1996, 5th edit., 1999; contbg. author: Biology, 4th edit., 1995, Synopsis of Anatomy and Physiology, 1997. Mem. AAAS, So. Calif. Acad. Sci., Am. Physiol. Soc., Sigma Xi. Home: 5556 Forest Cove Ln Agoura Hills CA 91301-4047 Office: Pierce Coll 6201 Winnetka Ave Woodland Hills CA 91371-0001

FOXLEY, WILLIAM COLEMAN, cattleman; b. St. Paul, Jan. 7, 1935; s. William Joseph and Eileen (Conroy) F. BA, U. Notre Dame, 1957. Pres., chmn. bd. Foxley Cattle Co., Omaha, 1960—. Chmn. bd. Mus. Western Art, Denver. Served with USMCR, 1957-60. Republican. Roman Catholic. Office: Foxley Cattle Co 7480 La Jolla Blvd La Jolla CA 92037-5029*

FOXX, DANIEL LEROY, JR., history educator; b. Gaffney, S.C., Mar. 19, 1939; s. Daniel LeRoy and Lois Olena (Brown) Fox; m. Mary-Helen Sears, May 30, 1964; children: Wade Patrick, Matthew Paul, Ethan Alexander, Reagan McNeill. BA, Brigham Young U., 1969, MA, 1970; MHL (hon.), Ottawa (Kans.) U., 1989. Instr. East Carolina U., Greenville, N.C., 1970-73; visiting prof. Glendale (Ariz.) Community Coll., 1973—; ops. mgr. Danner Industries, Inc., Phoenix, 1973-74; v.p. MFR Enterprises, Inc., Phoenix, 1974-76; rsch. assoc. Ariz. State Legis. Coun., Phoenix, 1976-77; rsch. coord. Ariz. Med. History Project, Phoenix, 1977-79; assoc. prof. Ottawa U. Phoenix, 1982—. Author: I Only Laugh When It Hurts, 1995; contbg. author: Applying Adult Development Strategies, 1990;editor: Forward, 1990-94. Speaker Ariz. State Atty. Gen., 1987. With U.S. Army, 1958-61. Republican. LDS Ch. Avocations: painting, photography, travel. Office: Ottawa U Phoenix 2340 W Mission Ln Phoenix AZ 85021-2807

FRAITAG, LEONARD ALAN, project and manufacturing engineer; b. N.Y.C., Dec. 23, 1961; s. David and Lucille Reneé (Jay) F.; children: Shoshana Elizabeth, Aaron Joseph. BSME, San Diego State U., 1987; AA, Grossmont Coll., 1983. Design engr. Restaurant Concepts, San Diego, 1987; mech. engr. Vantage Assocs., Inc., San Diego, 1988-89; design engr. Mainstream Engring. Co., Inc., San Diego, 1989; project engr. Pilkington Barnes Hind, San Diego, 1989-96, Advanced Structures, Inc., Escondido, 1996-99; product devel. engr. Sybron Dental Spltys., A Co., San Diego, 1999—. Inventor safe product moving device for contact lens. Mem. Shriners (Al Bahr shrine), Masons (past master), Pi Tau Sigma. Avocations: computers, sports, camping, skiing, scuba diving. Office: Advanced Structures Inc 2181 Meyers Ave Escondido CA 92029-1002

FRAKER, MARK ARNOTT, environmental scientist; b. Columbus, Ind., Dec. 13, 1944; s. Ralph Waldo and Carol (Arnott) F.; m. Pamela Norton, May 27, 1967 (div. Feb. 1985); 1 child, Russell; m. Donice Horton, Aug. 23, 1986. BA with honors, Ind. U., 1967, MA, 1969. Biologist, project mgr. F.F. Slaney and Co., Vancouver, Can., 1972-78; biologist, project dir. LGL Ltd., Sidney, B.C., Can., 1978-82; sr. environ. scientist BP Exploration (Alaska) Inc., Anchorage, 1982-91; wildlife, restoration program mgr. divsn. oil spill impact assessment & restoration Alaska Dept. Fish and Game, Anchorage, 1991-93; pres. TerraMar Environ. Rsch. Ltd., Sidney, B.C., Can., 1993—; broadcaster CBC, Vancouver, 1970-72; mem. sci. com. Internat. Whaling Com., Cambridge, Eng., 1982-91; adj. prof. U. Alaska, Anchorage, 1985-89; mem. panel NAS, 1987-92; mem. rescue team Barrow Gray Whale Rescue, 1988; mem. adv. com. on polar programs NSF, 1988-90; mem. Pacific Sci. Rev. Group for Marine Mammal Stock Assessments, 1994—; mem. Ballard Locks Pinniped-Fishery Interaction Task Force, 1994—. Author: Balaena mysticetus, 1984; also articles; mem. editorial bd. Biol. Papers of the U. of Alaska. Amb. to Peru, Anchorage Olympic Organizing Com., 1986-89. Woodrow Wilson fellow, Princeton, N.J., 1967. Mem. AAAS, Am. Soc. Mammalogists, Arctic Inst. N.Am., Ottawa Field Naturalists' Club, Can. Soc. Zoologists, Soc. for Marine Mammalogy, The Wildlife Soc., Sigma Xi. Avocations: Latin Am. affairs, bird watching, backpacking, hunting, Spanish.

FRAM, MICHAEL LEWIS, graphic and fine artist; b. Cambridge, Mass., Nov. 15, 1942; s. Nathan Irving and Harriet (Kline) F.; m. Livia Stein, Mar. 20, 1983; 1 child, Theo Vincent. AA in Painting and Drawing, L.A. City Coll., 1973; BA in Painting and Drawing, Calif. State U., Northridge, 1975. Graphic artist Met. Transp. Commn., Oakland, Calif., 1984—. Oil and acrylic paintings exhibited in numerous solo and group shows in San Francisco Bay area, 1981—. Studio: 5212 Shattuck Ave Oakland CA 94609-1915 Office: Met Transp Commn 101 8th St Oakland CA 94607-4707

FRAME, TED RONALD, lawyer; b. Milw., June 27, 1929; s. Morris and Jean (Lee) F.; student UCLA, 1946-49; AB, Stanford U., 1950, LLB, 1952; m. Lois Elaine Pilgrim, Aug. 15, 1954; children: Kent, Lori, Nancy, Owen. Bar: Calif. 1953. Gen. agri-bus. practice, Coalinga, Calif., 1953—; sr. ptnr. Frame & Matsumoto, 1965—. Trustee, Baker Mus.; dir. West Hills Coll. Found. Mem. ABA, Calif. Bar Assn., Fresno County Bar Assn., Am. Agrl. Law Assn., Coalinga C. of C. (past pres.), Masons, Shriners, Elks. Avocations: bicycling, hiking. Home: 1222 Nevada St Coalinga CA 93210-1239 Office: 201 Washington St Coalinga CA 93210-1645

FRANCESCHI, ERNEST JOSEPH, JR., lawyer; b. L.A., Feb. 1, 1957; s. Ernest Joseph and Doris Cecilia (Beluche) F. BS, U. So. Calif., 1978; JD, Southwestern U., L.A., 1980. Bar: Calif. 1984, U.S. Dist. Ct. (cen. dist.) Calif. 1984, U.S. Dist. Ct. (ea. dist.) Calif. 1986, U.S. Dist. Ct. (no. and so. dists.) Calif. 1987, U.S. Ct. Appeals (9th cir.) 1984, U.S. Supreme Ct. 1989. Pvt. practice law L.A., 1984—. Mem. Assn. Trial Lawyers Am., Calif. Trial Lawyers Assn., L.A. Trial Lawyers Assn., Trial Lawyers for Pub. Justice, Fed. Bar Assn. Office: 445 S Figueroa St Ste 2600 Los Angeles CA 90071-1630

FRANCHINI, GENE EDWARD, state supreme court justice; b. Albuquerque, May 19, 1935; s. Mario and Lena (Vaio) F.; m. Glynn Hatchell, Mar. 22, 1969; children: Pamela, Lori (dec.), Gina, Joseph James, Nancy. BBA, Loyola U., 1955; degree in adminstrn., U. N.Mex., 1957; JD, Georgetown U., 1960; LLM, U. Va., 1995. Bar: N.Mex. 1960, U.S. Dist. Ct. N.Mex. 1961, U.S. Ct. Appeals (10th cir.) 1970, U.S. Supreme Ct. 1973. Ptnr. Matteucci, Gutierrez & Franchini, Albuquerque, 1960-70, Matteucci, Franchini & Calkins, Albuquerque, 1970-75; judge State of N.Mex. 2d Jud. Dist., Albuquerque, 1975-81; atty.-at-large Franchini, Wagner, Oliver, Franchini & Curtis, Albuquerque, 1982-90; chief justice N.Mex. Supreme Ct., Santa Fe, 1990-99, justice, 1999—. Chmn. Albuquerque Pers. Bd., 1972, Albuquerque Labor Rels. Bd., 1972, Albuquerque Interim Bd. Ethics, 1972. Capt. USAF, 1960-66. Mem. Bd. Trial Advocates, N.Mex. Trial Lawyers (pres. 1967-68), N.Mex. Bar Assn. (bd. dirs. 1976-78), Albuquerque Bar Assn. (bd. dirs. 1976-78). Democrat. Roman Catholic. Avocations: fishing, hunting, golf, mushroom hunting. Home: 4901 Laurene Ct NW Albuquerque NM 87120-1026 Office: NMex Supreme Ct PO Box 848 Santa Fe NM 87504-0848*

FRANCIS, RELL GARDNER, artist, photographer, writer; b. Lake Shore, Utah, Jan. 27, 1928; s. S. Evan and Barbara (Ferguson) F.; m. Janet Oaks Francis, July 18, 1958; children: Sean Francis, Lewis Francis, Dana Francis Le Pore. BA, Brigham Young U., 1954, MA, 1963; postgrad., Ill. Sch. Design, Chgo., summer 1957, Ohio State U., summer 1968, U. Utah, 1968-69. Cert. tchr. Monument designer A.H. Child & Son Monuments, Springville, Utah, 1945-54; art and English tchr. Nebo Sch. Dist., Springville, 1954-74; home study art instr. Brigham Young U., Provo, Utah, 1964-70; photo tchr. European Art Acad., Paris, summer 1966; dir. art mus. Springville Mus. Art, 1976; dir. City Spirit art Nat. Endowment for Arts, Springville City, Utah, 1974-75; owner Photo Gallery, Heritage Prints Photography, Provo, 1977-90; cons. photography PBS (Judy Crichton) Am. 1900, Boston, N.Y.C., 1996-97; lectr. Cyrus E. Dallin at Rockwell Mus. Exhibit, Corning, N.Y., 1995. Author: Cyrus E. Dallin, 1976, The Utah Photographs of George Edward Anderson, 1979; film prodr.: Stoneman Sheepherder, 1969, Que Bonita, 1972; contbr. articles to profl. jours.; one-person show at Provo Utilities Gallery, Provo, 1969; exhibited in group shows at Springville Mus. Art, 1982, 88, LDS Ch. Mus. Art and History, Salt Lake City, 1985, Amon Carter Mus., Ft. Worth, 1979, Brigham Youung U. and Springville Mus. Art, 1974, Segnali de Fumo, Italy, 1994. Trustee Springville Mus. Art, 1958-74; environ. activist Audubon Soc., Provo, 1995—. Recipient Best of Show, photography Utah State Fair, 1966, 67, Meritorious Svc. award in photography Brigham Young U., Provo, 1974, Morris Rosenblatt award Utah Hist. Quar., Salt Lake City, 1976. Mem. Utah Hist. Soc., Springville Hist. Soc. (trustee 1975-99). Mem. LDS Ch. Avocation: writing poetry. Home: 750 Chase Ln Springville UT 84663-2053

FRANCIS, TIMOTHY DUANE, chiropractor; b. Chgo., Mar. 1, 1956; s. Joseph Duane and Barbara Jane (Sigwalt) F. Student, U. Nev., 1974-80, We. Nev. C.C., 1978; BS, L.A. Coll. Chiropractic, 1982, Dr. of Chiropractic magna cum laude, 1984; postgrad., Clark County C.C., 1986—; MS in Bio/Nutrition, U. Bridgeport, 1990. Diplomate Internat. Coll. Applied Kinesiology, Am. Acad. Pain Mgmt., Am. Naturopathic Med. Bd.; cert. kinesiologist, applied kinesiology tchr.; lic. chiropractor, Calif., Nev. Instr. dept. recreation and phys. edn. U. Nev., Reno, 1976-80; from tchng. asst. to lead instr. dept. principles & practice L.A. Coll. Chiropractic, 1983-85; pvt. practice Las Vegas, 1985—; asst. instr. Internat. Coll. Applied Kinesiology, 1990, chmn. exam review com., 1993, chmn. syllabus review com., 1994; adj. faculty The Union Inst. Coll. of Undergrad. Studies, 1993; joint study participant Nat. Olympic Tng. Ctr., Beijing, China, 1990. Mem. editl. rev. bd. Alternative Medicine Rev., 1996; contbr. articles to profl. jours. including Internat. Coll. Applied Kinesiology. Charles F. Cutts scholar, 1980. Fellow Internat. Acad. Clin. Acupuncture, British Inst. Homeopathy (homeopathy diploma 1993); mem. Am. Chiropractic Assn. (couns. on sports injuries, mutrition, roentgenology, technic, and mental health), Nev. State Chiropractic Assn., Nat. Strength and Conditioning Assn., Gonsted Clin. Studies Soc., Found. for Chiropractic Edn. and Rsch., Internat. Chiropractors Assn., Internat. Coll. Applied Kinesiology, Internat. Fedn. Practitioners Natural Therapeutics, Nat. Inst. Chiropractic Rsch., Nat. Strength and Conditioning Assn., Am. Naturopathic Med. Assn., Nat. Acad. Rsch. Biochemists, Phi Beta Kappa, Phi Kappa Phi (v.p. 1979-80, Scholar of the Yr. award, 1980), Delta Signa. Republican. Roman Catholic. Avocations: karate, weightlifting. Home: 3750 S Jones Blvd Las Vegas NV 89103-2283

FRANCISCO, WAYNE M(ARKLAND), automotive executive; b. Cin., June 14, 1943; s. George Lewis and Helen M. (Markland) F. Student, Ohio State U., 1962-63; BS in Mktg. and Acctg., U. Cin., 1967; m. Susan Francisco; children: Diana Lynn, W. Michael. Unit sales mgr. Procter & Gamble, Cin., 1967-69; mktg. mgr. Nat. Mktg. Inc., Cin., 1969-70; pres. Retail Petroleum Marketers, Inc., Cin., 1970-72, chmn. bd., chief exec. officer, Phoenix, 1972-85; chmn. bd., chief exec. officer DMC Industries, Inc., 1985—; pres., chief exec. officer Cassia Petroleum Corp., Vancouver, B.C., Can., 1980-84; bd. dirs. P.F.K. Enterprises, F.I.C. Inc., Internat. Investment and Fin. Enterprises, Inc., Alpha Realty, Inc. Class agt. 62G Culver Mil. Acad., 1987-91. Mem. Culver Legion (bd. trustees 1990—), Eugene C. Eppley Club, Phoenix Bd. Appeals, 1978-80; v.p. Cuernavaca Homeowners Assn., 1982, pres., 1983-86. Recipient Image Maker award Shell Oil Co., 1979; Top Performer award Phoenix dist. Shell Oil Co., 1979, 80. Mem.

Petroleum Retailers Ariz. (pres. 1977-79), Nat. Congress Petroleum Retailers (adv. bd.), Automotive Svc. Excellence (cert.), Culver Legion (life), Studebaker Drivers Club (zone coord. Pacific S.W. 1983, nat. v.p. 1986, 87, 88, nat. pres. 1989-90, Grand Canyon chpt. pres. 1986), Avanti Owners Assn. (nat. bd. dirs. 1975-96, internat. pres. 1986-89). Republican. Lodge: Optimists (bd. dirs. Paradise Valley club 1984, sec.-treas. 1984). Fax: (602) 948-4535. Office: PO Box 4793 Scottsdale AZ 85261-4793

FRANCKE, UTA, medical geneticist, genetics researcher, educator; b. Wiesbaden, Germany, Sept. 9, 1942; came to U.S., 1969; d. Kurt and Gertrud Müller; m. Bertold Richard Francke, May 27, 1967 (div. 1982); m. Heinz Furthmayr, July 27, 1986. MD, U. Munich, Fed. Republic Germany, 1967; MS, Yale U., 1985. Diplomate Am. Bd. Pediatrics, Am. Bd. Med. Genetics (bd. dirs. 1981-84). Asst. prof. U. Calif., San Diego, 1973-78; assoc. prof. Yale U., New Haven, 1978-85, prof., 1985-88; prof. genetics Stanford (Calif.) U., 1989—; investigator Howard Hughes Med. Inst., Stanford, 1989—, mem. sci. rev. bd., Bethesda, Md., 1986-88; mem. mammalian genetics study sect. NIH, Bethesda, 1990—; bd. dirs. Am. Soc. Human Genetics, Rockville, Md., 1981-84. Profl. advisor March of Dimes Birth Defects Found., White Plains, N.Y., 1990, Marfan Assn., Port Washington, N.Y., 1991. Mem. Inst. Medicine of NAS (fgn. assoc.), Human Genome Orgn., Soc. for Pediatric Rsch., Soc. for Inherited Metabolic Disorders. Avocation: piloting. Office: Stanford U Med Sch Howard Hughes Med Inst Beckman Ctr Stanford CA 94305-5323*

FRANK, ANN-MARIE, sales administration executive; b. Omaha, July 27, 1957; d. Joseph Anthony and Louise Virginia (DiMauro) Malingagio; m. Jon Lindsay Frank, July 13, 1985; 1 child, Jon L. BA in Fine and Communication Arts, Loyola Marymount U., L.A., 1980, MBA, 1988. Region adminstrv. mgr. Data Gen. Corp., Manhattan Beach, Calif., 1986-90; contracts/sales adminstrn. mgr. Candle Corp., Santa Monica, Calif., 1991-96; dir. records and royalties Herbalife Internat., Inglewood, Calif., 1996-98; dir. customer svc. and internat. ops. G.B. Data Sys., Marina del Rey, Calif., 1998—. Dir., editor: (creative drama) Patchwork, 1982 (Rochester, N.Y. trophy). Republican. Roman Catholic. Avocations: travel, Victorian architecture, music, antiques. Home: 3311 Raintree Ave Torrance CA 90505-6618 Office: GB Data Sys 330 Washington Blvd Marina del Rey CA 90292

FRANK, DEBRA WILSON, retail manager and trainer; b. Seattle, Nov. 14, 1961; d. Melvin Edmond W. and Deanna May Sanner; m. Thomas S. Frank, Aug. 6, 1994. BA in Bus. Adminstrn. cum laude, U. Wash., 1984. Asst. buyer, dept. mgr. Frederick & Nelson, Seattle, 1985-86; gen. mgr. Borders Book Shop, Indpls., 1986-87; regional mgr. Borders Book Shop, Ann Arbor, Mich., 1987-89, v.p. ops., 1989-92, mgmt. trainer, 1993—. Pres. Brownstones Condominium Assn., Ann Arbor, 1992-93. Mem. Am. Soc. Tng. & Devel., Phi Beta Kappa, Beta Gamma Sigma. Avocations: reading, cooking.

FRANK, GARY WAYNE, broadcast technician, broadcast station executive; b. Dexter, Mo., Feb. 2, 1951; s. Robert Wayne and Beulah Berniece (Oakley) F.; m. Berta deSanti, Nov. 23, 1978 (div. Sept. 1986); children: Keri Berniece Pellerin, Gary Jeffrey Frank; m. Lisa Catherine Schlink, Dec. 17, 1993. Student, Glendale (Ariz.) Coll., 1969-71, Bailie Sch. of Broadcast, Phoenix, 1977-78. On-air announcer Sta. KYCA, Prescott, Ariz., 1978-79; on-air announcer Sta. KNIX-AM-FM, Phoenix, 1979-80; engr. Sta. KPAZ-TV, Phoenix, 1979-83, Sta. KNXV-TV, Phoenix, 1983-84; prodn. mgr. Sta. KUSK-TV, Prescott, 1984-85, Sta. KPAZ-TV, Phoenix, 1985-88; prodn./ops. supr. Sta. KUTP-TV, Phoenix, 1988—; licensee/owner Sta. KIHX-FM, Prescott, 1985; co-owner Sta. WYXE, Gallatin, Tenn., 1997—. Republican. Baptist. Avocation: music. Home: 4521 W Greenway Rd Glendale AZ 85306-3621 Office: Sta KUTP TV 4630 S 33rd St Phoenix AZ 85040-2812

FRANK, GERALD WENDEL, civic leader, journalist; b. Portland, Oreg., Sept. 21, 1923; s. Aaron Meier and Ruth (Rosenfeld) F. Student, Stanford U., 1941-43, Loyola U., L.A., 1946-47; BA with honors, Cambridge U., 1948, MA, 1953; D Bus. Adminstrn. (hon.), Greenville (Ill.) Coll., 1971; LLD (hon.), Pacific U., 1983. Mgr. Meier & Frank Co., Salem, Oreg., 1955-65; v.p. Meier & Frank Co., Ltd., 1948-65; also bd. dirs.; pres. Gerry's Frankly Speaking, Salem, Oreg., 1965—; co-owner Gerry Frank's Konditorei, Salem, Oreg., 1982—; bd. dirs. Oreg. Baking Co., U.S. Bancorp, World Masters Games 1998, Inc. Author: Where to Find It, Buy It, Eat It in New York, 10 edits., 1980—, Joan and Gerry's Little Black Book of Shopping Secrets, 1991, Friday Surprise, 1995; sr. corres. Northwest Reports, 1992-96; commentator/reporter Morning news shows KPTV, Portland, 1993—. Trustee Lorene Sails Higgins Charitable Trust, 1993—; chief of staff to Sen. Mark O. Hatfield, 1973-92; gen. chmn. Mark Hatfield for U.S. Sen., 1966, 72, 78, 84, 90; mem. Culver Commn. on Reorganization of U.S. Senate, 1975-76; mem. mgmt. com. U.S. Senate, 1978; active Nat. Found. Infantile Paralysis, Arthritis and Rheumatism Found., Portland C. of C., Salem Area C. of C., Sunshine Divsn., Portland Police Res., Portland Area Coun., Cascade Area Coun., Cascade Pacific Coun., Nat. Coun., Boys Scouts Am., Portland Rose Festival Assn., Jr. Achievement, Travelers Aid Soc. Portland, Nat. Mcpl. League, Salem Pub. Libr. Found., Portland United Fund, Marion-Polk Counties United Good Neighbors, Salem Gen. Hosp., Nat. Retail Merchants Assn., Citizens' Conf. for Govtl. Coop., Gov.'s Econ. Devel. Commn., Oreg. Retail Distributors' Inst., Am. Heart Soc., Oreg. Rsch. Assn., Salem 4-H Club, Willamette River Days, Salem YWCA, Willamette U. bd. trustees, League Women Voters, Oreg. Grad. Inst. Sci. & Tech., Portland Met. Futures Unltd., Inc., Marion-Salem Bldg. Study Com., Oreg. Symphony Soc., Am. Legion, Oreg. Coast Aquarium, 1990—, exec. com., U.S. Com. for UNICEF, 1990—, Oreg. High Desert Mus., Salvation Army, Salem Art Assn., Parry Ctr. for Children, St. Vincent Hosp. & Med. Ctr., Oreg. Health Scis. U., OMSI, chair, dir., 1996-97, Oreg. Tourism Coun., chair, 1996—, Oreg. Hist. Soc., 1990—, Oreg. Coll. Found., AAA of Oreg., Oreg. Assn. Nurserymen, Oreg. State Bar Ho. Dels., Miss Oreg. Scholarship Program. Recipient numerous awards including Silver Beaver Boy Scouts Am., 1963, Reginald H. Vincent trophy United Good Neighbor of Yr., 1980, Brotherhood Nat. Conf. Christians and Jews, Portland, 1984, Glenn Jackson leadership Willamette U., 1984, Tom Lawson McCall fellowship Pacific U., 1987. Mem. Am. Legion, Elks, Rotary (Paul Harris fellow 1986). Avocations: travel, gourmet dining. Home: 3250 Crestview Dr S Salem OR 97302-5959 Office: Gerry's Frankly Speaking Inc Ste 130 475 Cottage St NE Salem OR 97301-3825 also: PO Box 2225 Salem OR 97308-2225

FRANK, STEPHEN RICHARD, lawyer; b. Portland, Oreg., Dec. 13, 1942; s. Richard Sigmund Frank and Paula Anne (Latz) Lewis; divorced; children: Richard Sigmund II, Theresa Anne; m. Patricia Lynn Graves, Aug. 20, 1988; stepchildren: Brian Kinney, Mathew Kinney. AB in Econs., U. Calif., Berkeley, 1964; JD, Willamette U., 1967. Bar: Oreg., U.S. Ct. Appeals (9th cir.), U.S. Supreme Ct. Assoc. Tooze, Duden, Creamer, Frank and Hutchison, Portland, 1967-72, ptnr., 1972—; mem. audit com. Seligman & Latz NYSE, 1981-85, bd. dirs. 1976-85. Editor Willamette Law Jour., 1967. Trustee, sec. Oreg. High Desert Mus., 1977-86; sec., bd. dirs. Palatine Hill Water Dist., 1973-77; bd. dirs. Emanuel Hosp. Found., 1980-83, Portland Ctr. for Visual Arts, 1977-82. Mem. ABA, Assn. Trial Lawyers Am., Oreg. Trial Lawyers Assn., Oreg. State Bar Assn. (dir., sec. minority scholarship program 1981—, sec.-chmn. com. worker's compensation 1974-77), Oreg. Assn. Ins. Def. Counsel, Oreg. Assn. Workers Compensation Def. Counsel. Clubs: Multnomah Athletic; City (Portland). Avocations: snow skiing, bicycling, running, mountain climbing, sailing. Home: 3103 SW Cascade Dr Portland OR 97201-1813 Office: Tooze Duden Creamer Frank & Hutchison 333 SW Taylor St Portland OR 97204-2413

FRANK, THOMAS, design, construction and management executive; b. Salt Lake City, Nov. 23, 1937; s. Simon and Suzanne (Seller) F. BFA, U. Utah, 1963. Lic. contractor, Utah. Owner Thomas Frank Designers & Specifiers, Salt Lake City, 1962—; owner, pres. OmmiComputer West, Salt Lake City; bd. dirs. Silver Eagle Refining, Inc.; pres. Nova Devel. Corp.; cons. in field; instr. design, textiles and drafting LDS Jr. Coll., Salt Lake City, 1963-80, lectr. on interior design for jr. and high schs. Bus. & Industry Coop. Edn. Program; profl. adviser interior design curriculum devel. program U. Utah; mem. inter-profl. adv. coun. Utah State Bldg. Bd.; lectr., presenter seminars in field. Contbr. articles to profl. publs. Exec. v.p. Salt Lake Art Ctr., 1977-80; spl. advisor Children's Ctr.; co-chmn. spl. events Utah divsn. Am. Cancer Soc., 1978. Recipient awards U. Utah, 1962, Utah Designers Craftsman Guild, 1962, State Fair Fine Arts, 1962. Fellow Am. Soc. Interior Designers; mem. N.Am. Autocadd Users Group, Nat. Kitchen and Bath Assn. (pres. mountain states chpt. west 1991-92), Am. Soc. Interior Designers (nat. long-range planning com. 1985-87, nat. comms. area coord. 1985, nat. membership devel. com. 1986-87, nat. regional dir. 1991-92, nat. edn. com. 1981, nat. chmn. energy conservation 1980-82, nat. chpt. pres.' orientation task force 1980, nat. bd. dirs. 1977-82, chmn. regional indsl. rels. 1977-78, numerous other offices, numerous awards), AID (sec. Utah 1969-71, bd. govs. 1970-74, Utah pres. 1973-75). Avocations: tennis, skiing, art collecting. Home: 2360 Oakhill Dr Salt Lake City UT 84121-1520 Office: Thomas Frank Designers 3369 Highland Dr Salt Lake City UT 84106-3356

FRANKE, JACK EMIL, foreign language educator; b. Pine Bluff, Ark., July 8, 1965; s. Ernest Rudolph and Charlotte (Harris) F.; m. Lyudmila Veniaminovna Vagun, Aug. 30, 1996; 1 child, Maria. BA, U. Tex., 1987; MA, Monterey Inst. Internat. Studies, 1992; PhD, St. Petersburg (Russia) State U., 1995. Interpreter/at-sea rep. Marine Resource Corp., Seattle, 1988-90; tng. specialist-Russian Def. Lang. Inst., Monterey, Calif., 1990-94, assoc. prof., 1997—; computer-aided lang. instrn. dir. Dept. Fgn. Langs. George C. Marshall Ctr., Garmisch-Partenkirchen, Germany, 1994-97; pres. Ganbaru Yudanshakai, Monterey. Co-author: Russian Topical Reader, 1992, (CD-ROM) Basic Military Language Course-Russian, 1993, (monograph) Multimedia as a Means of Intensifying Self-Study in the Russian Language for Foreigners, 1995, (web site) American-Russian POW/MIA Commn., 1996. With U.S. Army, 1983-85. Mem. Am. Legion, U.S. Judo Fedn., Computer-Aided Lang. Instrn. Consortium, Phi Sigma Iota. Republican. Russian Orthodox. Avocations: judo, weightlifting, racquetball, travel. Fax: (831) 373-2721. E-mail: drfranke@geocities.com. Home: 370 Clay St Apt 13 Monterey CA 93940-2254 Office: Def Lang Inst PO Box 5818 Monterey CA 93944-0818

FRANKEL, EDWARD IRWIN, financial consultant; b. Aug. 26, 1941. Student, NYU, 1962-68, N.Y. Inst. Fin., 1960-62. Founder, chmn. bd. United Resources, Inc., 1976-84; pres. Syndicates Underwriting Svcs., 1984-87; founder, pres. Edward I. Frankel & Assocs., Rolling Hills Estates, Calif., 1988—; mem. N.Y. Stock Exch., 1966-71. Bd. advisors South Bay Hosp.; past pres. The Wellness Community of South Bay Cities; bd. dirs. South Bay Cancer Found; bd. dirs. LCMHF Bay Harbor Hosp. Found. Mem. Internat. Assn. Fin. Planners, Pres. Assn. Am. Mgmt. Assn., Nat. Assn. Life Underwriters, South Bay Estate Planning Coun., Palos Verdes Breakfast Club.

FRANKEL, JENNIE LOUISE, writer, composer, playwright; b. Chgo., Aug. 7, 1949. Student, Roosevelt U., 1968, U. Hawaii, 1969-71, Golden West Law Sch., 1976. bd. govs. Hollywood Scriptwriting, Authors Guild. Author: You'll Never Make Love in this Town Again, 1996 (N.Y. Times Bestseller), Unfinished Lives, 1996; co-author: Tales From the Casting Couch, 1996; publisher Page Turner Publishing. With USO Vietnam Tour, 1968. Mem. Acad. TV Arts & Scis., L.A. Women in Music (bd. dirs. 1991-92), Circumnavigators Club. Avocation: travel. Office: PO Box 346 Sedona AZ 86339

FRANKEL, TERRIE MAXINE, author, composer, playwright, publisher; b. Chgo., Aug. 7, 1949; d. David Frankel and Jewell Hennigan. Student, Roosevelt U., 1968, U. Hawaii, 1971, U. Hong Kong, 1979-80. Entertainer USO, 1968; performer, 1969-79; writer, producer, performer Sta. WTTV, Indpls., 1982; pres. Page Turner Pub., Scottsdale, Ariz. Author: You'll Never Make Love in this Town Again, 1996 (N.Y. Times Best Seller List); co-author: Unfinished Lives, 1996; author, editor: Tales from the Casting Couch, 1996. Mem. Producers Guild of Am. (bd. dirs., sr. editor POV mag. 1990—), Hollywood Script Writing Inst. (bd. govs.), Authors Guild, Circumnavigators Club. Avocations: Cantonese and Mandarin Chinese. Address: PO Box 346 Sedona AZ 86339

FRANKFORT, JAMES, artist; b. Brussels, Belgium, May 11, 1930; s. Jack and Hillegonda (Frank) F.; children: Michelle,, Jacob, Daniel, Reina. Grad., Parson's Sch. Design. Freelance artist, 1953—. Mem. Visual Arts Ctr., 1993—. With U.S. Army, 1952-53. Home: PO Box 871 Waldport OR 97394-0871

FRANKISH, BRIAN EDWARD, film producer, director; b. Columbus, Ohio, July 28, 1943; s. John (Jack) Fletcher Frankish and Barbara Aileen (Tondro) Gray; m. Tannis Rae Benedict, Oct. 13, 1985; children: Merlin L. Reed III, Michelle Lynn Reed. AA, Chaffey Coll., 1964; BA, San Francisco State U., 1967. Freelance producer L.A.; prin. Frankish-Benedict Entertainment, L.A. Prodr. (film) Vice Squad, 1981, (TV series) Max Headroom, 1987; assoc. prodr.: (films) Elephant Parts, 1981, Strange Brew, 1982, The Boy Who Could Fly, 1985, In the Mood, 1986; exec. prodr., unit prodn. mgr. (film) Field of Dreams, 1989, Flight of the Intruder, 1990, American Me, 1991; prodr. visual effects for film Turbulence, 1996; prodr., dir. (theatrical play) Timing is Everything, 1991; 1st asst. dir.: (TV shows) Big Shamus, 1979, Skag, 1979, Why Me?, 1983, Making Out, 1984, Berrengers, 1984, (films) Strange Brew, 1982, Uncle Joe Shannon, 1978, Savage Harvest, 1980, Dead and Buried, 1980, Spring Break, 1982, Brainstorm, 1982-83, The Last Starfighter, 1983, The New Kids, 1983, Aloha Summer, 1984, The Best of Times, 1985, Odd Jobs, 1985, The Fugitive, 1993, Demolition Man, 1993, Roswell, 1994; unit prodn. mgr. Second Serve, 1986, The Net, 1995; distbr.'s rep. and completion bond rep. Made in Heaven, 1986; prodn. mgr.: The Net, 1995; other prodn. credits include: Play it Again, Sam, 1971, Everything You Always Wanted to Know About Sex..., 1972, Time to Run, 1972, Haunts, 1975, Mahogany (Montage), 1975, King Kong, 1976, The Betsy, 1977. Mem. Dirs. Guild Am., Calif. Yacht Club.

FRANKLIN, JON DANIEL, writer, journalist, educator; b. Enid, Okla., Jan. 12, 1942; s. Benjamin Max and Wilma Irene (Winburn) F.; m. Nancy Sue Creevan, Dec. 12, 1959 (div. 1976, dec. 1987); children: Teresa June, Catherine Cay; m. Lynn Irene Scheidhauer, May 20, 1988. B.S. with high honors, U. Md., 1970; LHD (hon.), U. Md., Balt. County, 1981, Coll. Notre Dame, Balt., 1982. With USN, 1959-67; reporter/editor Prince Georges (Md.) Post, 1967-70; sci. and feature writer Balt. Evening Sun, 1970-85; assoc. prof. U. Md. Coll. Journalism, 1985-88, prof., 1988-89; prof., chmn. dept. journalism Oreg. State U., Corvallis, 1989-91; prof. creative writing, dir. U. Oreg., Eugene, 1991—. Author: Shocktrauma, 1980, Not Quite a Miracle, 1983, Guinea Pig Doctors, 1984, Writing for Story, 1986, The Molecules of the Mind, 1987. pub.: *Bylines*, WriterL. Recipient James T. Grady medal Am. Chem. Soc., 1975, Pulitzer prize for feature writing, 1979, Pulitzer prize for explanatory journalism, 1985, Carringer award Nat. Mental Health Assn., 1984, Penney-Mo. Spl. award for health reporting, 1985; named to Newspaper Hall of Fame, Md.-Del.-D.C. Press Assn. Mem. Nat. Assn. Sci. Writers, Soc Profl. Journalists, The Writers Guild, Investigative Reporters and Editors.

FRANKLIN, ROBERT BLAIR, cardiologist; b. Buffalo, Dec. 18, 1919; s. Wilson Gale and Frances Eunice (Sullivan) F.; m. Anne W., Jan. 16, 1969; children: Virginia, Richard, Victor, George, Robert, Kathleen. BA, Canisius Coll., Buffalo, 1940; MD, U. St. Louis, 1943. Diplomate Am. Bd. Internal Medicine, Am. Bd. Cardiovascular Diseases. Commd. U.S. Army, advanced through grades to col.; chief med. svc. 130th Sta. Hosp. U.S. Army, Heidelberg, Germany, 1955-58, comdg. officer 5th Surg. Hosp., 1958-59; chief gen. med. svc. Fitzsimons Gen. Hosp. U.S. Army, Denver, 1959-60, chief cardiology svc., 1962-65; comdg. officer 121st Evacuation Hosp. U.S. Army, Seoul, Korea, 1965-66; chief cardiology svc. Letterman Gen. Hosp. U.S. Army, San Francisco, 1966-68; chief cardiology dept. Kaiser Permanente Med. Group, Santa Clara, Calif., 1968-79; dep. comdg. officer 130th Sta. Hosp. U.S. Army, Heidelberg/Seoul/Vicenza, Italy, 1979-89; asst. clin. prof. Med. Coll. Ga., Augusta, 1953-54, U. Colo., Denver, 1963-65, Seoul Nat. U., 1965-66; guest lectr. Phy Yonsei U., Seoul, 1965-66; asst. clin. prof. U. Calif. Med. Sch., San Francisco, 1966-68, 74-79, 89—. Contbr. 35 articles to profl. jours. Decorated Legion of Merit with 3 oak leaf clusters. Roman Catholic. Avocations: handball, golf. Home: 30 Palomino Cir Novato CA 94947-3619

FRANKLYN, AUDREY POZEN, talent promoter, television personality; b. Detroit, Dec. 8, 1930; d. Sidney Pozen and Rachel (Slobasky) F. AA, Los Angeles City Coll., 1952; BA, UCLA, 1955. Dir. pub. rels., radio disc jockey Gene Norman, L.A., 1957-60; owner Franklyn Agy. Pub. Rels. Firm, L.A., 1960—; ptnr. A & E Prodns. Host (cable TV show) The Franklyn Interview, 1977—; promoter numerous celebrities; promoter Ella Fitzgerald, 1966-94, prepared her memorabilia for Smithsonian; promoter Pablo Records; prodr. various comedy albums and talk shows for cable. Mem. L.A. Press Club. Office: 1010 Hammond St Apt 312 West Hollywood CA 90069-3853

FRANKS, DONALD RICHARD, writer, website designer; b. Chgo., June 18, 1945; s. Richard William and Edith Kathleen (Emerick) F.; m. Dana Lorraine Stimpson, June 10, 1989; children: Dorothy Kathleen, Linnaea Barbara. BA magna cum laude, City U., Bellevue, Wash., 1984, MA, 1985. Lic. 1st class radio-telephone operator, FCC. Film editor WGN-TV, Chgo., 1969-70, WLS-TV, Chgo., 1970-76; news program coord. KIRO-TV, Seattle, 1977-85; instr. City U., 1987-90, Highline C.C., Des Moines, 1986-90; audio-visual mgr. Mus. Flight, Seattle, 1990-96; writer/webmaster Method Consultants, Seattle, 1996—; pres. Method Consultants, Seattle, 1985—. Author, artist, photographer: Skin Diving for Kids, 1980; author: Tony, Grammy, Emmy, Country, 1985, Entertainment Awards, 1996; contbg. author: Building Mental Muscle, 1998; editor (newsletter) Sunnydale Elem. Sch., Seattle, 1998. Rec. sec. Alumni Assn. City U., Bellevue, 1984-87; designer website AVANTA-The Va. Satir Network, Burien, Wash., 1997, Highline C.C., 1998. Recipient Instr. award Twenty-Fathom Scuba Club, 1975, Svc. award Alumni Assn. City U., 1987. Mem. Author's Guild, HTML Writers Guild, Assn. Internet Profls., Am. Assn. Museums, N.W. Oral History Assn., Prison Awareness Project (vol./sponsor 1985—). Democrat. Avocations: scuba diving, photography, classical music listening, camping, hiking.

FRANTZ, GILDA GLORIA, Jungian analyst; b. Bklyn., Dec. 29, 1926; d. Jack Feldrais and Ruth (Gersten) Striplin; m. Kieffer Evans Frantz, Apr. 21, 1950 (dec. May 1975); children: Carl Gilbert (dec.), Marlene Maris. MA, Antioch U., L.A., 1978. Founding editor Psychol. Perspectives C.G. Jung Inst. of L.A., 1969-76, interviewer, adv. com. Matter of Heart, 1975-81, pres., 1980-83, chmn., 1980-83, tng. analyst, 1977—; adv. coun. Paul Brunton Philos. Found.; lectr. and workshop presenter in field. Editorial bd. Jour. of Contemporary Jungian Psychology; editorial adv. bd. Chiron, A Rev. of Jungian Analysis; contbr. articles to profl. jours. Co-facilitator support group for significant others of people with AIDS, Sherman Oaks (Calif.) Hosp.; keynote speaker Nat. Conf. Jungian Analysts, Lake Tahoe, 1994. Mem. Soc. of Jungian Analysts of So. Calif., Internat. Assn. Analytical Psychology (spkr. 13th congress 1995, Internat. Symposium on Grief and Bereavement (adv. bd. 1983—), Nat. Archive for Rsch. in Archetypal Symbolism (exec. bd., sec. 1984-89).

FRANZ, MARCIA KAY, foundation administrator; b. Grayling, Mich., July 18, 1948; d. Harold G. and Orissa D. (Knapp) Forman; m. Karl D. Franz, Oct. 21, 1967; children: David, Jason, Christopher. Student, U. Mich., 1966-67, SUNY, Albany, 1973-74; BS cum laude, U. Ark., 1982. Exec. dir. SCAN Svcs., Inc., Little Rock, 1981-83; dir. Drew County Hist. Soc., 1983-84; cmty. planning specialist Ark. Social Svcs., 1984-85; dir. West Women's and Children's Shelter, 1985-88; pub. rels. devel. dir. Edgefield Children's Ctr., 1989-94; CEO Make A Wish Found. Org., 1994—. Bell ringer St. Bartholomew Episcopal Ch. Bell Choir. Mem. Nat. Soc. Fund Raising Execs. (cert. fund raising exec.), Willamette Valley Devel. Officers, Women In Comms. Inc. Avocations: dogs, walking, golf, reading, boating. Home: 10625 SW Wedgewood St Portland OR 97225-5126 Office: Make A Wish Found Org 5319 SW Westgate Dr Ste 113 Portland OR 97221-2432

FRAPPIA, LINDA ANN, management executive; b. St. Paul, May 14, 1946; d. Orville Keith Ferguson and Marilyn Ardis (Morris) Bidwell; 1 child, Jennifer Frappia Barrett. Grad. high sch., Seattle. Cert. claims adminstr. Claims rep. Fireman's Fund Ins., L.A., 1965-68; adminstrv. asst. to v.p. Employee Benefits Ins., Santa Ana, Calif., 1969-72; claims specialist Indsl. Indemnity Ins., Orange, Calif., 1972-83; claims supr. CNA Ins., Brea, Calif., 1983-85; claims mgr. EBI Ins. Svcs., Tustin, Calif., 1985; v.p. United Med. Specialists, Santa Ana, Calif., 1985-91; chief exec. officer United Ind. Specialists, Santa Ana, 1990—; chief executive officer United Chiropractic Specialists, Santa Ana, 1987—; instr. Ins. Edn. Assn., Brea, 1988—; speaker Western Ins. Info. Svc., Orange, 1976-83. Mem. Calif. Mfrs. Assn., Pub. Agencies Risk Mgmt. Assn., Calif. Self-Insured Assn., Toastmasters Internat. (v.p. Orange chpt. 1978). Republican. Avocations: sailing, reading, traveling.

FRASER, BRUCE DOUGLAS, JR., architect, artist; b. Corvallis, Oreg., Dec. 1, 1948; s. Bruce Douglas and Betty Adele (Lively) F.; m. Laura Jane Wells, June 18, 1972. BArch, Calif. Poly. State U., 1972. Registered architect, Calif. Artist, illustrator Hopkins Assocs., San Luis Obispo, Calif., 1972-73; planner U.S. Peace Corps, Mashhad, Iran, 1973-75; mem. archtl. staff Meyer-Merriam Assocs., San Luis Obispo, 1975-77; prin. MDW Assocs., San Luis Obispo, 1977-85, Merriam-Fraser Architecture and Planning, San Luis Obispo, 1985-87, Archtl. Office Bruce Fraser, San Luis Obispo, 1987—. Chair Bldg. Appeals Bd., Pismo Beach, Calif., 1990, Planning Commn., Pismo Beach, 1991-92, vice chair, 1990. Recipient various design awards Obispo Beautiful Assn., 1977—, Downtown Assn., 1990—. Mem. AIA (v.p. Calif. Ctrl. Coast chpt. 1985, pres. 1986). Office: Archtl Office of Bruce Fraser AIA 971 Osos St San Luis Obispo CA 93401-3212*

FRASER, CATHERINE ANNE, Canadian chief justice; b. Campbellton, N.B., Can., Aug. 4, 1947; d. Antoine Albert and Anne (Slevinski) Elias; m. Richard C. Fraser, Aug. 17, 1968; children: Andrea Claire, Jonathan James. BA, U. Alta., Can., 1969, LLB, 1970; ML, U. London, 1972. Assoc., ptnr. Lucas, Bishop & Fraser, Edmonton, Alta., 1972-89; justice Ct. Queen's Bench Alta., Edmonton, 1989-91; justice Ct. Appeal Alta., Edmonton, 1991-92, chief justice Alta. and NW Ter., 1992—; dir. Can. Inst. Adminstrn. Justice, 1991-95. Recipient Tribute to Women award YWCA, 1987. Mem. Can. Bar Assn., Edmonton Bar Assn., Law Soc. Alta. Office: Ct Appeal Alta, Law Courts Bldg, Edmonton, AB Canada T5J OR2*

FRASSINELLI, GUIDO JOSEPH, retired aerospace engineer; b. Summit Hill, Pa., Dec. 4, 1927; s. Joseph and Maria (Grosso) F.; m. Antoinette Pauline Clemente, Sept. 26, 1953; children: Lisa, Erica, Laura, Joanne, Mark. BS, MS, MIT, 1949; MBA, Harvard U., 1956. Treas. AviDyne Rsch., Inc., Burlington, Mass., 1958-64; asst. gen. mgr. Kaman AviDyne divsn. Kaman Scis., Burlington, 1964-66; asst. dir. strategic planning N. Am. ACFT OPNS, Rockwell Internat., L.A., 1966-69; from mgr. program planning to project mgr. advanced programs Rockwell Space Sys. Divsn., Downey, Calif., 1970-94; ret. Rockwell Space Systems Div., Downey, 1994. Mem. Town Hall of Calif., L.A., 1970—; treas. Ecology Devel. and Implementation Commitment Team Found., Huntington Beach, Calif., 1971-75; founding com. mem. St. John Fisher Parish Coun., Rancho Palos Verdes, Calif., 1978-85. Recipient Tech. Utilization award, NASA, 1971, Astronaut Personal Achievement award, 1985. Fellow AIAA (assoc.; tech. com. on econs. 1983-87, exec. com. L.A. sect. 1987-91, 94-98), Inst. for Advancement of Engring.; mem. Sigma Xi, Tau Beta Pi. Roman Catholic. Achievements include determination of aircraft damage limits and atomic-weapon-delivery capabilities of aircraft; development of cost models to account for advances in engineering state of art, of cost prioritization techniques for space shuttle improvements, of software to produce business plans. Home: 29521 Quailwood Dr Palos Verdes Peninsula CA 90275-4930

FRASZ, GEOFFREY BRYCE, philosophy educator; b. Chgo., Nov. 18, 1947; s. Edward Richard and Marie Emily (Gullidge) F.; m. Linnea Jonnson (div. May, 1976); m. Marjorie Rae Conderman, Feb. 8, 1997; stepchildren: Stephanie, Samantha, Jerry. BA in Philosophy, Ill. Benedictine U., 1972; MA in Philosophy, U. Ga., 1986, PhD in Philosophy, 1995, grad. cert. in Environ. Ethics, 1986. Prof. of philosophy C.C. of So. Nev., Las Vegas, 1990—; senator C.C. So. Nev. Faculty Senate, Las Vegas, 1994-98. Contbr. articles to profl. jours. Mem. AAUP, Am. Philos. Soc., Internat. Soc. for Environ. Ethics, Nev. Faculty Alliance (grievance officer 1997-98), Nat. Speleological Soc. Avocations: cave exploring, hiking, camping. Office: Comty Coll So Nev 6375 W Charleston Blvd Las Vegas NV 89146-1139

FRAUTSCHI, STEVEN CLARK, physicist, educator; b. Madison, Wis., Dec. 6, 1933; s. Lowell Emil and Grace (Clark) F.; m. Mie Okamura, Feb. 16, 1967; children—Laura, Jennifer. B.A., Harvard U., 1954; Ph.D., Stanford U., 1958. Research fellow Kyoto U., Japan, 1958-59, U. Calif.-Berkeley, 1959-61; mem. faculty Cornell U., 1961-62, Calif. Inst. Tech., Pasadena, 1962—; prof. theoretical physics Calif. Inst. Tech., 1966—, exec.

officer physics, 1988-97, master student houses, 1997—; vis. prof. U. Paris, Orsay, 1977-78. Author: Regge Poles and S-Matrix Theory, 1963, The Mechanical Universe, 1986. Guggenheim fellow, 1971-72. Mem. Am. Phys. Soc. Research, publs. on Regge poles, bootstrap theory, cosmology. Home: 1561 Crest Dr Altadena CA 91001-1838 Office: 1201 E California Blvd Pasadena CA 91125-0001

FREAS, FRANK KELLY, illustrator; b. Hornell, N.Y., Aug. 27, 1922; s. Francis Matthew and Miriam Eudora (Sylvester) K.; m. Pauline H. Bussard, Mar. 26, 1952 (dec. Jan. 1987); children: Jacqueline Deborah, Jeremy Patrick; m. Laura Brodian, June 30, 1988. Grad., Pitts. Art Inst., 1951. Freelance illustrator books and mags., cover artist, 1950—, art dir., cons. pubs., 1952—; cover artist Mad mag., 1955-62, Religious Art Franciscans, 1958-76; designer space posters Smithsonian Instn., 1971; designer crew insignia Slylab I, 1974; v.p. Environ Assocs., Inc., Virginia Beach, Va., 1974—; artist NASA, 1975; pres. Greenswamp Publs., Virginia Beach, 1984—; illustration dir. Writers of the Future, 1987-92; coordinating judge Illustrators of future, 1987-92; dir. Kelly Freas Studios, 1988—; lectr., cons. colls., art schs.; guest of honor confs. including EuroCon IV, Brussels, 1978, World Sci. Fiction Conv., Chgo., 1982, Chattacon, Chattanooga, 1988, AmigoCon, El Paso, 1989, Archcon, St. Louis, 1989, As Astra, Toronto, Can., 1990, WindyCon, Chgo., 1993, Internat. Assn. for Fantastic in the Arts, ConClave, Southfield, Mich., 1994, AGOH Conf., Irvine, Calif., Internal'l Assoc. for the Fantastic in the Arts conf., Eaton Conf. U. Calif., Riverside, 1995, Midsouthcon, Memphis, 1996, BalitCon., Balt., 1997; numerous others. Contbr. Child Welfare League poster, A Voice for Children, 1985-86; pub.: Astounding Fifties, 1971, rev. ltd. edit., 1990, Six-to-go, 1971, Science Fiction Art Print Portfolios, 1972-79, Photoprint Series, 1983—, Ltd. Edit. Prints (6), 1991, Transition, Spl. Limited Edit., 1993; author: Frank Kelly Freas: The Art of Science Fiction, 1977, A Separate Star, 1985; editor, illustrator: Starblaze Editions, 1978-79; designer, promoter research and devel. in microbiologicals, cancer research, nutritional therapies, 1985—, DNA Molecule, Ltd. Edit. Print Pharmacia, 1986; designer covers 3d Internat. Conf. on Monoclonal Antibodies, San Diego Cancer Ctr., 1988, 1st Internat. Conf. on Human Antibodies & Hybridomas, 1990, Jour. Human Hyrbidomas, 1990—; one-man show Chrysler Mus. at Norfolk, 1977, 82, 84, Am. Renaissance Gallery, Portland, Oreg., 1990; retrospective exhbn. Am. Mus. Natural History, N.Y.C., 1974, Coos Art Mus., Coos Bay, Oreg., 1988, Orlando (Fla.) Sci. Ctr., 1988, Del. Art Mus., Wilmington, 1989—, Park Ave. Atrium, N.Y.C., 1990 , Canton Art Museum, 1996—. Bd. govs. Internat. Star Found., Vienna, Va., 1981—. Served with USAAF, 1941-46. Recipient Hugo Achievement award World Sci. Fiction Soc., 1955-56, 58-59, 70, 72-76, Frank R. Paul award, 1977, Ink Pot award, 1979, Skylark award New Eng. Sci. Fiction Assn., 1981, ROVA award, 1981, Lensman award, 1982, Phoenix award, 1982, Kelly & Polly Freas Art scholar award established, Roanoke, 1982, L.A. Sci. Fantasy Soc. Svc. award, 1993, Neographics award, 1985, Daedalos Life Achievement award, 1987, Art Tchr. Emeritus award, 1988, Chesley award (best mag. cover) Am. Sci. Fiction and Fantasy Artists, 1990, Analog Readers' Poll award (best cover), 1991, LA Sci. Fantasy Soc. Art award, 1992; named Dean Sci. Fiction Artists, 1972, Nat. Hall of Fame, Nat. Assn. Trade and Tech. Schs., 1991. Mem. Nat. Caricaturists Network, Soc. Illustrators L.A., Sci. Fiction Writers Am., So. Fandom Confedn., Assn. Sci. Fiction and Fantasy Artists (pres. 1982-83), L-5 Soc. (life), Internat. Assn. Astron. Artists, L.A. Sci. Fiction Assn., Nat. Cartoonists Soc., Soc. Illustrators L.A.. Comic Arts Profl. Soc., Graphic Artists Guild, Dorsai Irregulars. Address: 7933 Quimby Ave West Hills CA 91304-4444

FREDERICK, SHERMAN, publishing executive. Pub. Las Vegas (Nev.) Rev.-Jour. Office: Las Vegas Rev-Journal 1111 W Bonanza Rd Las Vegas NV 89106-3545*

FREDERICKS, MICHAEL KARL, freelance artist, writer, magazine publisher; b. Warner Robbins AFB, Ga., May 21, 1955; s. Leslie Lloyd and Barbara Lee (Lacy) F.; m. Judith Claire Novinsky, June 22, 1985; children: Lara, Erik, Edward. BA, U. Calif., Davis, 1983. Freelance artist, writer; editor, pub. Prehistoric Times, Folsom, Calif., 1993—. With USN, 1974-78. Republican. Avocation: collecting. Home and Office: Prehistoric Times 145 Bayline Cir Folsom CA 95630-8077

FREDERICKS, PATRICIA ANN, real estate executive; b. Durand, Mich., June 5, 1941; d. Willis Edward and Dorothy (Plowman) Sexton; m. Ward Arthur Fredericks, June 12, 1960; children: Corrine Ellen, Lorraine Lee, Ward Arthur II. BA, Mich. State U., 1962. Cert. Grad. Real Estate Inst., residential broker, residential salesperson; cert. real estate broker. Assoc. Stand Brough, Des Moines, 1976-80; broker Denton, Tuscon, 1980-83; broker-trainer Coldwell Banker, Westlake Village, Calif., 1984-90; broker, br. mgr. Brown, Newbury Park, Calif., 1990-94; dir. tng. Brown Real Estate, Westlake Village, Calif., 1994—; gen. mgr., dir. mktg. Coldwell Banker Town & Country Real Estate, Newbury Park, Calif., 1994—; dir. mktg. Coldwell Banker Town and Country, 1995—; bd. sec. Mixtec Corp., Thousand Oaks, 1984—. Contbr. articles to profl. jours. Pres. Inner Wheel, Thousand Oaks, 1991, 96-97; bd. dirs. Community Leaders Club, Thousand Oaks, 1991, Conejo Future Found., Thousand Oaks, 1989-92, Wellness Community Ventura Valley, 1994—. Mem. Calif. Assn. Realtors (dir. 1988-95 regional chairperson 1995, vice chairperson expn. 1997, chair Calif. Expo 1998), Conejo Valley Assn. Realtors (sec., v.p., pres.-elect 1989-92, pres. 1993, Realtor of Yr. 1991), Pres.'s Club Mich. State U., Com. 100, Cmty. Concerts Assn., Alliance for the Arts, Conejo Valley Symphony Guild, Wellness Cmty., Indian Wells Country Club, North Ranch Country Club, Sherwood Country Club. Office: 2235 Michael Dr Newbury Park CA 91320-3340

FREDERICKS, WARD ARTHUR, venture capitalist, food industry consultant; b. Tarrytown, N.Y., Dec. 24, 1939; s. Arthur George and Evelyn (Smith) F.; BS cum laude, Mich. State U., 1962, MBA, 1963, PhD. m. Patricia A. Sexton, June 12, 1960; children: Corrine E., Lorrine L., Ward A. Assoc. dir. Technics Group, Grand Rapids, Mich., 1964-68; gen. mgr. logistics systems Massey-Ferguson Inc., Toronto, 1968-69, v.p. mgmt. svcs., comptr., 1969-73, sr. v.p. fin., dir. fin. Americas, 1975—; comptr. Massey-Ferguson Ltd., Toronto, Ont., Can., 1973-75; prin. W.B. Saunders & Co., Washington, 1962—; sr. v.p. mktg. Massey/Ferguson, Inc., 1975-78, also pres., gen. mgr. Tractor div., 1978-80; gen. mgr. Rockwell Graphic Sys., 1980-82; pres. Goss Co.; v.p. ops., Rockwell Internat., Pitts., 1980-84; v.p. Fed. MOG., 1983-84; chmn. MIXTEC Group LLC, 1998—, also dir., chmn.; principal Venture Assocs., 1993—. dir. Polyfet RF, Inc., Venture Assocs., Badger Northland Inc., MST, Inc., Calif., Tech-Mark Group Inc., Spectra Tech., Inc., Mixtec Group-Venture Capital, Inc., Unicorn Corp., Mixtec Food Group Calif., Mixtec Signal Tech., Harry Ferguson Inc., M.F. Credit Corp., M.F. Credit Co. Can. Ltd. Bd. dirs., mem. exec. com. Des Moines Symphony, 1975-79; exec. com. Conejo Symphony, pres. 1988-90, pres. Westlake Village Cultural Found., 1991; mem. exec. com. Alliance for Arts.; pres. Conejo Valley Indsl. Assn., 1990, 93; mem. Constn. Bicentennial Com., 1987-88, Ventura County Airport Commn., 1995—, LaQuinta Arts Found.; bd. dirs. Ventura County Bus. Incubator, 1996—; v.p. Com. Leaders Club, 1988, pres., 1989-90, pres. Westlake Cultural Found. 1991; vice chair Alliance for the Arts; regent Calif. Lutheran U., 1990—, exec. com. 1993—, chmn. acad. affairs 1993—, exec. com. 1992—, chmn. acad. affairs, 1992—, vice chmn., 1997—; v.p. Aviation C.C. of Calif. Fellow Am. Transp. Assn., 1962-63, Ramlose, 1962-63; mem. AAAS, IEEE, SAR, Am. Mktg. Assn., Nat. Council Phys. Distbn. Mgmt. (exec. com. 1974), Produce Mktg. Assn., United Fresh Fruit and Vegetable Assn., Internat. Fresh-cut Produce Assn., Soc. Automotive Engrs., U.S. Strategic Inst., Tech. Execs. Forum (Tech. Corridor 100 award, 1989), Internat. Food Mfg. Assn., Produce Mktg. Assn., Toronto Bd. Trade, Westlake Village C. of C. (chmn. 1990), Cochella Valley Community Concerts Assn. (bd. dirs. 1992-95), Old Crows, Assn. for Advanced Tech. Edn., Air Force Assn., Aerospace Soc., Experimental Aircraft Assn., Mil. Order World Wars, Conf. Air Force (col.), Westlake Village C. of C. (chmn. bd. 1990-91), Republican Ctrl. Com., State of Calif., 1993-97, Community Leaders Club, Pres.'s Club Mich. State U., North Ranch Country Club, Indian Wells Country Club, Sherwood Country Club, St. Georges Club (U.K.), Aviation Country Club of Calif. (v.p. 1999), Rotary, Flying Rotarians, Beta Gamma Sigma. Author: (with Edward W. Smykay) Physical Distribution Management, 1974; author: Management Vision, 1988, Competitive Advantage in Technology Organizations, 1996, Competitive Advantage in Technology Organizations, 1996; contbr. articles to profl. jours. Lutheran. Home: 1640 Aspenwall Rd Westlake Vlg CA 91361-1704 also: 48143 Vista Cielo La Quinta CA 92253-2256 Office: 31255 Cedar Valley Dr Westlake Village CA 91362-4014

FREDERICKSON, ARTHUR ROBB, physicist; b. Rahway, N.J., July 5, 1941; s. Arthur Raymond and Bertine Lavinia (Beecher) F.; m. Christine Magnuson, June 6, 1970; children: Timothy R., Nathan B., Julie H. BSc, Rensselaer Poly. Inst., 1965; PhD, U. Mass., Lowell, 1991. Physicist Cambridge Rsch. Labs., Bedford, Mass., 1967-80, Rome Air Devel. Ctr., Bedford, 1980-87, Air Force Geophysics Lab., Hanscom AFB, Mass., 1987-91, Air Force Phillips Lab., Hanscom AFB, Mass., 1992-97, Calif. Inst. Tech. Jet Propulsion Lab., Pasadena, 1997—; mem. spl. topics rev. groups, panels Dept. Def., 1980—. Author: Spacecraft Dielectric Material Properties, 1986; contbr. articles to Jour. Applied Physics, Jour. Elec. Materials, numerous other jours., conf. procs. Chmn. Town Ctr. Com. Planning Bd., Stow, Mass., 1974-75; adult leader Carlisle (Mass.) area Boy Scouts Am., 1981-90. Mem. IEEE (sr., chmn. Boston sect. nuclear and plasma soc. 1983-92), Am. Phys. Soc., Sigma Xi. Achievements include patent on device to aid centering of high-energy beams, method and system for secondary emission detection, charge accumulation gamma radiation detector, process for prevention of spontaneous discharging in irradiated insulators. E-mail: robb@ieee.org. Home: 781 S Mentor Ave Pasadena CA 91106-4037 Office: Jet Propulsion Lab Mail Stop 303-217 Pasadena CA 91109

FREDMANN, MARTIN, ballet artistic director, educator, choreographer; b. Balt., Feb. 3, 1943; s. Martin Joseph and Hilda Adele (Miller) F.; m. Kaleriya Fedicheva, Jan. 2, 1973 (div.); m. Patricia Renzetti, June 12, 1980. Student, Nat. Ballet Sch., Washington, 1962-64, Vaganova Sch., Leningrad, 1972. Prin. dancer The Md. Ballet, Balt., 1961-64; dancer The Pa. Ballet, Phila., 1964-65, Ballet of the Met. Opera Co., N.Y.C., 1965-66; prin. dancer Dortmund (Fed. Republic Germany) Ballet, 1973-75, Scapino Ballet, Amsterdam, Holland, 1975-76; tchr. German Opera Ballet, West Berlin, Fed. Republic Germany, 1979, Netherlands Dance Theater, 1979, Royal Swedish Ballet, 1980, San Francisco Ballet, 1981; tchr., coach Australian Ballet, 1982; tchr. Tokyo City Ballet, Hong Kong Ballet, 1985, 86, 87, London Festival Ballet, 1981-83; dir. ballet Teatro Comunale, Florence, Italy, 1984-85; artistic dir. Tampa (Fla.) Ballet, 1984-90; artistic dir. in alliance with The Tampa Ballet Colo. Ballet, Denver, 1987-90; artistic dir. Colo. Ballet, 1987—; tchr. German Opera Ballet, 1982, Ballet Rambert, London, Bat Dor summer course, Israel, 1983, Cullberg Ballet, Sweden, 1983, Hong Kong Acad. For Performing Arts, 1985, 86, 87, 89, 91, Tokyo City Ballet, 1985, 86, 87, 89, 90, Ballet West, 1990, Nat. Ballet Korea, 1991, Dance Divsn. Tsoying High Sch., Kaohsiung, Taiwan, R.O.C., 1992; guest lectr., tchr. Cen. Ballet China, Beijing Dancing Acad., P.L.A. Arts Coll., Beijing, 1990; tchr. Legat Sch., 1978, examiner, 1980; tchr. Eglevsky Sch., N.Y.C., 1980; asst. dir., ballet master Niavaron Cultural ctr., Tehran, Iran, 1978; tchr. Ballet Arts Sch. Carnegie Hall, N.Y.C., 1979-81, choreographer Estonia Nat. Theatre, USSR, 1991; dir. Marin Ballet, Calif., 1981. Choreographer Romeo and Juliet, 1983, Sachertorte, 1984, A Little Love, 1984, Ricordanza, 1986, Cinderella, 1986, Coppelia, 1987, The Nutcracker, 1987, Beauty and the Beast, 1988, Masquerade Suite, 1989, Silent Woods, 1989, The Last Songs, 1991, Centenial Suite, 1994. Mem. Am. Guild Mus. Artists, Fla. State Dance Assn., Nat. Assn. Regional Ballet. Avocations: cooking, cook book collecting, travel, opera. Home: 836 E 17th Ave Apt 3A Denver CO 80218-1449 Office: Colo Ballet 1278 Lincoln St Denver CO 80203-2114

FREEBURG, GARY L., art educator; b. Mpls., Apr. 20, 1948; s. Garold W. and Marilyn R. (Hall) F.; m. Katherine A. Schwartz, May 14, 1987; children: Andrea, Ava. BFA, Mankato State Univ., 1974, MA, 1977; MFA, Univ. Iowa, 1978. Art prof. Univ. Alaska, Soldotna, Alaska, 1980—. Bd. dirs. KDLL Pub. Radio, Kenai, Alaska, 1996—, Alaska Alliance for Arts Edn., 1997—. With Navy, 1969-73, Vietnam. Recipient grant Alaska State Coun. on the Arts, 1983. Mem. Coll. Arts Assn., Nat. Art Edn. Assn. (art edn. higher edn. award, 1989), Alaska Art Edn. Assn. Office: Kenai Peninsula Coll 34820 College Dr Soldotna AK 99669-8245

FREECE, DAVID WARREN, museum director; b. Seattle, June 22, 1951; s. Kenneth Robert and Thelma Louise (Broad) F.; m. Janet Louise Morton, Jan. 23, 1979; children: Emily Amanda, Cheryl Louise. BA in Philosophy, Western Wash. U., 1980, BEd in History and Social Studies, 1980; MA in Pub. History, Portland State U., 1985. Dir. Cowlitz County Hist. Mus., Kelso, Wash. Contbr. articles to profl. jours. Bd. dirs. Cowlitz County Hist. Mus., 1986—; bd. dirs. Clark County Mus., Vancouver, WA, 1985-86, curator, 1981-85; chmn. Cowlitz County Centennial Com., 1986-89; vice chmn. Longview (Wash.) Hist. Preservation Com. Mem. Am. Assn. Mus., Am. Assn. State and Local History, Washington Mus. Assn., Rotary Internat. (historian 1989—). Avocations: bicycling, hiking, camping. Home: 911 Crestline Dr Longview WA 98632-5679

FREED, PETER QUENTIN, amusement park executive; b. Salt Lake City, Jan. 8, 1921; s. Lester David and Jasmine (Young) F.; B.A. with honors, U. Utah, 1947; children—David Wicker, Michael Stahlc, Howard Eldred, Anne, Kristen, Jennifer. Pres., Freed Corp., 1952-74; v.p., sec., Freed Co., 1952-74; exec. v.p. Amusement Service, Salt Lake City, 1947—; v.p. Terrace Co., Salt Lake City, from 1952; exec. v.p. Patio Gardens, Farmington, Utah, from 1956; v.p. Westworld Corp., Salt Lake City, from 1974, Pioneer Village Campground, Farmington, from 1975; dir. Pioneer Village, Farmington; pres. Lagoon Corp., Salt Lake City, 1974—. Mem. Union Sta. Theatre Bd. Served with USNR, 1942-45. Mem. Nat. Assn. Amusement Parks, Utah Mus. Assn. Republican. Christian Scientist. Clubs: Salt Lake Tennis, New Yorker. Home: 642 Aloha Rd Salt Lake City UT 84103-3329 Office: Lagoon Theme Park 375 Lagoon Dr Farmington UT 84025*

FREEDMAN, BART JOSEPH, lawyer; b. New Haven, Sept. 27, 1955; s. Lawrence Zelic and Dorothy (Robinson) F.; m. Esme Detweiler, Sept. 28, 1985; children: Luke Edward, Samuel Meade, Benjamin Zelic. BA, Carleton Coll., 1977; JD, U. Pa., 1982. Bar: Wash. 1984, U.S. Dist. Ct. (we. dist.) Wash. 1984, U.S. Ct. Appeals (9th cir.) 1985, U.S. Dist. Ct. (ea. dist.) Wash. 1988. Law clk. to chief justice Samuel Roberts Supreme Ct. Pa., Erie, 1982-83; asst. city solicitor City of Phila., 1984; assoc. Perkins Coie, Seattle, 1984-90; ptnr. Preston Gates & Ellis, Seattle, 1990—. Editor: Natural Resource Damages, 1993. Bd. dirs. Seattle Metrocenter YMCA, 1988-97, chmn. 1993-97; bd. dirs. Leadership Tomorrow, 1996-97; chair Sierra Club Inner City Outings Program, Seattle, 1986-90; chmn. bd. advisors Earth Svc. Corps/YMCA, Seattle, 1990-97. Mem. ABA (com. on corp. counsel 1985—), Wash. State Bar Assn., Seattle-King County Bar Assn. (participant neighborhood legal clinics 1985-94). Office: Preston Gates & Ellis 701 5th Ave Ste 5000 Seattle WA 98104-7078

FREEDMAN, DAVID NOEL, religion educator; b. N.Y.C., May 12, 1922; s. David and Beatrice (Goodman) F.; m. Cornelia Anne Pryor, May 16, 1944; children: Meredith Anne, Nadezhda, David Micaiah, Jonathan Pryor. Student, CCNY, 1935-38; AB, UCLA, 1939; BTh, Princeton Theol. Sem., 1944; PhD, Johns Hopkins U., 1948; LittD, U. Pacific, 1973; ScD, Davis and Elkins Coll., 1974. Ordained to ministry Presbyn. Ch., 1944; supply pastor in Acme and Deming, Wash., 1944-45; tchg. fellow, then asst. instr. Johns Hopkins U., 1946-48; asst. prof., then prof. Hebrew and Old Testament lit. Western Theol. Sem., Pitts., 1948-60; prof. Pitts. Theol. Sem., 1960-61, James A. Kelso prof., 1961-64; prof. Old Testament San Francisco Theol. Sem., 1964-70, Gray prof. Hebrew exegesis, 1970-71, dean of faculty, 1966-70, acting dean of sem., 1970-71; prof. Old Testament Grad. Theol. Union, Berkeley, Calif., 1964-71; prof. dept. Nr. Ea. studies U. Mich., Ann Arbor, 1971-92, Thurnau prof. Bibl. studies, 1984-92, dir. program on studies in religion, 1971-91; prof., endowed chair in Hebrew Bibl. studies U. Calif., San Diego, 1987—; dir. religious studies program U. Calif., 1989-97; Danforth vis. prof. Internat. Christian U., Tokyo, 1967; vis. prof. Hebrew U., Jerusalem, 1977, Macquarie U., N.S.W., Australia, 1980, U. Queensland (Australia), 1982, 84, U. Calif., San Diego, 1985-87; Green vis. prof. Tex. Christian U., Ft. Worth, 1981; dir. Albright Inst. Archeol. Rsch., 1969-70, dir., 1976-77; centennial lectr. Johns Hopkins U., 1976; Dahood lectr. Loyola U., 1983; Soc. Bibl. Lit. meml. lectr., 1983, Smithsonian lectr., 1984; prin. bibl. cons. Reader's Digest, 1984, 88, 89, 90, 94; disting. faculty lectr. Univ. Mich., 1988; Stone lectr. Princeton Theol. Sem., 1989; Mowinckel lectr., Oslo U., 1991; lectr. Uppsala U., Sweden, 1991; vis. lectr. Brigham Young Ctr. Near Eastern Studies, Jerusalem, 1993. Author: Divine Commitment and Human Obligation, 1997; co-author: (with J.D. Smart) God Has Spoken, 1949, (with F.M. Cross, Jr.) Early Hebrew Orthography, 1952, (with John M. Allegro) The People of the Dead Sea Scrolls, 1958, (with R.M. Grant) The Secret Sayings of Jesus, 1960, (with F.M. Cross, Jr.) Ancient Yahwistic Poetry, 1964, rev. edit., 1975, 97, (with M. Dothan) Ashdod I, 1967, The Published Works of W.F. Albright, 1975, (with L.G. Running) William F. Albright: Twentieth Century Genius, 1975, 2d edit., 1991, (with B. Mazar, G. Cornfeld) The Mountain of the Lord, 1975, (with W. Phillips) An Explorer's Life of Jesus, 1975, (with G. Cornfeld) Archaeology of the Bible: Book by Book, 1976, Pottery, Poetry and Prophecy, 1980, (with K.A. Mathews) The Paleo-Hebrew Leviticus Scroll, 1985, The Unity of the Hebrew Bible, 1991, (with D. Forbes and F. Andersen) Studies in Hebrew and Aramaic Orthography, 1992,(with Sara Mandell) The Relationship between Herodotus' History and Primary History, 1993; co-author, editor: (with F. Andersen) Anchor Bible Series Hosea, 1980, Anchor Bible Series Amos, 1989; editor: (with G.E. Wright) The Biblical Archaeologist, Reader I, 1961, (with E.F. Campbell, Jr.) The Biblical Archaeologist, Reader 2, 1964, Reader 3, 1970, Reader 4, 1983, (with W.F. Albright) The Anchor Bible, 1964—, including, Genesis, 1964, James, Peter and Jude, 1964, Jeremiah, 1965, Job, 1965, 2d edit., 1973, Proverbs and Ecclesiastes, 1965, I Chronicles, II Chronicles, Ezra-Nehemiah, 1965, Psalms I, 1966, John I, 1966, Acts of the Apostles, 1967, II Isaiah, 1968, Psalms II, 1968, John II, 1970, Psalms III, 1970, Esther, 1971, Matthew, 1971, Lamentations, 1972, 2d edit., 1992, To the Hebrews, 1972, Ephesians 1-3, 4-6, 1974, I and II Esdras, 1974, Judges, 1975, Revelation, 1975, Ruth, 1975, I Maccabees, 1976, I Corinthians, 1976, Additions, 1977, Song of Songs, 1977, Daniel, 1978, Wisdom of Solomon, 1979, I Samuel, 1980, Hosea, 1980, Luke I, 1981, Joshua, 1982, Epistles of John, 1983, II Maccabees, 1983, II Samuel, 1984, II Corinthians, 1984, Luke II, 1985, Judith, 1985, Mark, 1986, Haggai-Zechariah 1-8, 1987, Ecclesiasticus, 1987, 2 Kings, 1988, Amos, 1989, Titus, 1990, Jonah, 1990, Leviticus I, 1991, Deuteronomy I, 1991, Numbers 1-20, 1993, Romans, 1993, Jude and 2 Peter, 1993, Zechariah 9-14, 1993, Zephaniah, 1994, Colossians, 1995, Joel, 1995, James, 1995, Obadiah, 1996, Tobit, 1996, Ecclesiastes, 1997, Ezekiel 21-37, 1997, Galatians, 1997, Malachi, 1998, Acts, 1998; editor Anchor Bible Ref. Libr., Jesus Within Judaism, 1988, Archeology of the Land of the Bible, 1990, The Tree of Life, 1990, A Marginal Jew Vol. 1, 1991, The Pentateuch, 1991, The Rise of Jewish Nationalism, 1992, History and Prophecy, 1993, Jesus and the Dead Sea Scrolls, 1993, The Birth of the Messiah, 1993, The Death of the Messiah, 2 vols., 1994, Introduction to Rabbinical Literature, 1994, A Marginal Jew, vol. 2, 1994, The Scepter and the Star, 1995, An Introduction to the New Testament, 1997, Education in Ancient Israel, 1998, Warrior, Dancer, Seductress, Warrior, 1998, (with J. Greenfield) New Directions in Biblical Archaeology, 1969, (with J.A. Baird) The Computer Bible, 1971, A Critical Concordance to the Synoptic Gospels, 1971, An Analytic Linguistic Concordance to the Book of Isaiah, 1971, I, II, III John: Forward and Reverse Concordance and Index, 1971, A Critical Concordance to Hosea, Amos, Micah, 1972, A Critical Concordance of Haggai, Zechariah, Malachi, 1973, A Critical Concordance to the Gospel of John, 1974, A Synoptic Concordance of Aramaic Inscriptions, 1975, A Linguistic Concordance of Ruth and Jonah, 1976, A Linguistic Concordance of Jeremiah, 1978, Syntactical and Critical Concordance of Jeremiah, 1978, Synoptic Abstract, 1978, I and II Corinthians, 1979, Zechariah, 1979, Galatians, 1980, Ephesians, 1981, Philippians, 1982, Colossians, 1983, Pastoral Epistles, 1984, 1 & 2 Thessalaians, 1985, Density Plots in Ezekiel, 1986, Exodus, 1987, Hebrews, 1988, Ruth, 1989, James, 1991, 1 & 2 Peter, 1991, 1, 2 & 3 John and Jude, 1991, Psalms, Job and Proverbs, 1992, Apocalypse, 1993, The Pentateuch, 1995, Aramaic Inscriptions, 1975, (with T. Kachel) Religion and the Academic Scene, 1975, Am. Schs. Oriental Research publs; co-editor: Scrolls from Qumran Cave I, 1972, Jesus: The Four Gospels, 1973, Pomegranates and Golden Bells, 1995; Reader's Digest editor: Atlas of the Bible, 1981, Family Guide to the Bible, 1984, Mysteries of the Bible, 1988, Who's Who in the Bible, 1994, The Bible Through the Ages, 1996, The Leningrad Codex, 1998; assoc. editor Jour. Bible Lit., 1952-54, editor, 1955-59; cons. editor Interpreter's Dictionary of the Bible, 1957-60, Theologisches Wörterbuch des Alten Testaments, 1970-92, English Translation Theological Word-Book of the Old Testament, 1975—; editor in chief The Anchor Bible Dictionary, 6 vols., 1992; co-editor (with W.H. Propp and Baruch Halpern) The Hebrew Bible and Its Interpreters, 1990; contbr. numerous articles to profl. jours. Recipient prize in New Testament exegesis Princeton Theol. Sem., 1943, Carey-Thomas award for Anchor Bible, 1965, Layman's Nat. Bible Com. award, 1978, 3 awards for Anchor Bible Bibl. Archaeol. Soc., 1993; William H. Green fellow in Old Testament, 1944, William S. Rayner fellow Johns Hopkins U., 1946, 47, Guggenheim fellow, 1959, Am. Assn. Theol. Schs. fellow, 1963; Am. Coun. Learned Socs. grantee-in-aid, 1967, 76. Fellow U. Mich. Soc. Fellows (sr., chmn. 1980-82); mem. Soc. Bibl. Lit. (pres. 1975-76), Am. Oriental Soc., Am. Schs. Oriental Rsch. (v.p. 1970-82, editor bull. 1974-78, editor Bibl. Archeologist 1976-82, dir. publs. 1974-82), Archaeol. Inst. Am., Am. Acad. Religion, Bibl. Colloquium (sec.-treas. 1960-90). Office: U Calif San Diego Dept History 0104 9500 Gilman Dr La Jolla CA 92093-0104

FREEDMAN, GREGG, real estate appraisal company executive; b. Burbank, Calif., Feb. 1, 1957; s. Morton Ira and Charlotte (Chernick) F.; m. Laura Jean Anderson, May 20, 1989; 1 child, Hillary Anne. Student, U. So. Calif., Calif. State U., L.A. Cert. gen. real estate appraiser Calif.; cert. rev. appraiser, sr. cert. prof. appraiser, cert. comml. property appraiser, cert. real estate owned appraiser, cert. appraiser; independent fee appraiser-senior ASA. Appraiser, mgr. Freedman and Freedman Cons., Monrovia, Calif., 1984-88; pres. Gregg Freedman and Assocs., Inc., Sierra Madre, Calif., 1988—; Tchr. real estate appraisal classes Monrovia H.S. Adult Edn.; chmn., bd. dirs. Pacific Commerce Credit Union. Prodr. Music Theater of So. Calif. Former commr. City of Duarte Econ. Devel. Coun.; bd. dirs. Meth. Hosp. Arcadia Found. Fellow Coll. Real Estate Appraisers; mem. Appraisal Inst. (assoc.), U. So. Calif. Alumni Assn. Avocations: gourmet food and wines, international travel, community service. E-mail: gfreedman@gfassociates.com. Home: 195 S Canon Ave Sierra Madre CA 91024-2601 Office: G Freedman & Assocs 124 N 1st Ave Arcadia CA 91006

FREEDMAN, JONATHAN BORWICK, journalist, author, lecturer; b. Rochester, N.Y., Apr. 11, 1950; s. Marshall Arthur and Betty (Borwick) F.; m. Maggie Locke, May 4, 1979; children: Madigan, Nicholas. AB in Lit. cum laude, Columbia Coll., N.Y.C., 1972. Reporter AP of Brazil, Sao Paulo and Rio de Janeiro, 1974-75; editorial writer The Tribune, San Diego, 1981-90; syndicated columnist Copley News Service, San Diego, 1987-89; free-lance opinion writer L.A. Times, 1990—; free-lance editorial writer N.Y. Times, 1990-91; dir. Hope Lit. Project, 1998—; dist. vis. lectr. and adj. faculty San Diego State U., 1990—; mem. U.S.-Japan Journalists Exch. Program, Internat. Press Inst., 1985. Author, illustrator: The Man Who'd Bounce the World, 1979; author: The Editorials and Essays of Jonathan Freedman, 1988; contbg. author: Best Newspaper Writing, From Contemporary Culture, 1991, (nonfiction) From Cradle to Grave: The Human Face of Poverty in America, 1993; freelance columnist, 1979-81; contbr. articles to N.Y. Times, Chgo. Tribune, San Francisco Examiner, Oakland Tribune, others. Moderator PBS, San Diego, 1988; bd. dirs. Schs. of the Future Commn., San Diego, 1987. Recipient Copley Ring of Truth award, 1983, Sigma Delta Chi award, 1983, San Diego Press Club award, 1984, Spl. citation Columbia Grad. Sch. Journalism, 1985, Disting. Writing award Am. Soc. Newspaper Editors, 1986, Pulitzer prize in Disting. Editorial Writing, 1987; Cornell Woolrich Writing fellow Columbia U., 1972, Eugene C. Pullian Editorial Writing fellow Sigma Delta Chi Found., 1986, Media fellow Hoover Instn., Stanford, Calif., 1991, Kaiser Media fellow, 1995. Mem. Soc. Profl. Journalists (Disting. Svc. award 1985, Casey medal for meritorious journalism 1994), Nat. Conf. Editl. Writers, Authors Guild, Phi Beta Kappa. Jewish. Avocations: skiing, tai chi. Office: 4506 Adair St San Diego CA 92107-3804

FREEDMAN, SARAH WARSHAUER, education educator; b. Wilimington, N.C., Feb. 23, 1946; d. Samuel Edward and Miriam (Miller) Warshauer; m. S. Robert Freedman, Aug. 20, 1967; 1 child, Rachel Karen. BA in English, U. Pa., 1967; MA in English, U. Chgo., 1970; MA in Linguistics, Stanford U., 1976, PhD in Edn., 1977. Tchr. English Phila. Sch. Dist., 1967-68, Lower Merion H.S., 1968-69; instr. English U. N.C., Wilmington, 1970-71; instr. English and linguistics Stanford U., 1972-76; asst. and assoc. prof. English San Francisco State U., 1977-81; asst. prof. edn. U. Calif., Berkeley, 1981-83, assoc. prof. edn., 1983-89; dir. Nat. Ctr. for the Study of Writing and Literacy, 1985-96; prof. edn. U. Calif., 1989—; resident Bellagio Conf. and Study Ctr., Rockefeller Found., 1997; mem. nat. task force Nat. Writing Project, 1998—. Author: Response to Student Writing, 1987, Exchanging

Writing, Exchanging Cultures, Lessons in School Reform from the United States and Great Britain, 1994, (with E.R. Simons, J.S. Kaluin) Inside City Schools, Investigating Literacy in Multi-cultural Classrooms, 1999; editor: The Acquisition of Written Language: Response and Revision, 1985; contbr. chpts. to books and articles to profl. jours. Recipient Richard Meade award for Pub. Rsch. in Tchr. Edn. Nat. Coun. Tchrs. English, 1989, 94, Ed Fry book award, 1996; fellow Nat. Conf. on Rsch. in English, 1986; Rockefeller Found. grantee Bryn Mawr Coll., 1992, Nat. Ctr. for Study of Writing and Literacy grantee Office Ednl. Rsch. and Improvement, 1985-95, Minority Undergrad. Rsch. Program grantee U. Calif., 1988, 89, 92, 93, numerous other grants. Mem. Nat. Coun. Tchrs. English (mem. standing com. on rsch. 1981-87, ex-officio 1987—, chair bd. trustees rsch. found. 1990-93), Am. Ednl. Rsch. Assn. (chair spl. interest group on rsch. in writing 1983-85, numerous other coms.), Linguistic Soc. Am., Am. Assn. Applied Linguistics, Internat. Reading Assn. Office: U Calif Dept Edn Berkeley CA 94720

FREEHLING, ALLEN ISAAC, rabbi; b. Chgo., Jan. 8, 1932; s. Jerome Edward and Marion Ruth (Wilson) F.; m. Lori Golden; children: Shira Susman, David Matthew, Jonathan Andrew. Student, U. Ala., 1949-51; AB, U. Miami, Fla., 1953; B of Hebrew Letters, Hebrew Union Coll., 1965, MA, 1967; PhD, Kensington U., 1977; DD (hon.), Hebrew Union Coll., 1992. Ordained rabbi, 1967. Asst. to pres. Stylaneze, Inc., 1953-54, Univ. Miami, 1954-56; exec. dir. Temple Israel, Miami, 1956-57; asst. to pres. Stevens Markets, Inc., 1957-59; acct. exec. Hank Meyer Assocs., 1959-60; exec. dir. Temple Emanu-El, Miami Beach, Fla., 1960-62; assoc. rabbi The Temple, Toledo, Ohio, 1967-72; sr. rabbi Univ. Synagogue, L.A., 1972—; adj. prof. Loyola-Marymount U., St. Mary's Coll.; v.p. Westside Ecumenical Coun., 1979-81; v.p. Bd. Rabbis of So. Calif., 1981-85, pres., 1985-87; mem. com. on rabbinic growth Cen. Conf. Am. Rabbis; chair Regional Synagogue Coun., 1984-86; bd. dirs., mem. several coms. and commns. Jewish Fedn. Coun.; cons. social actions Union of Am. Hebrew Congregations, mem. nat. and Pacific-S.W. region coms. on AIDS; mem. Rabbinic Cabinet, United Jewish Appeal; bd. dirs. Israel Bonds Orgn., Nat. Jewish Fund; bd. govs. Synagogue Coun. Am.; bd, dirs., newsletter editor Am. Jewish Com. Guest columnist L.A. Hearld Examiner (Silver Angel award Religion in Media, 1987, 88); guest religion progs. Sta. KCBS, KABC; radio/TV host Nat. Conf. Christians and Jews. Chaplain L.A. Police Dept., 1974-86; bd. dirs., mem. exec. com., chair com. on pub. policy, chair govt. affairs com. AIDS Project L.A.; founding chair, exec. com. chairperson AIDS Interfaith Coun. So. Calif.; mem. adv. bd. L.A. AIDS Hospice Com.; apptd. mem., founding chair L.A. County Commn. on AIDS, 1987-89, chair svcs. com., 1989-91, L.A. County Commn. on Mental Health, 1992-95; mem. AIDS-related grants proposal rev. com. Robert Wood Johnson Found., AIDS Task Force of United Way; mem. com. on ethics, medicine and humanity Santa Monica Hosp., L.A. County Commn. on Pub. Social Svcs., 1984-86, Gate Ways Hosp. bd dirs., 1992-95, Jewish Big Bros., 1994—; City of L.A. Task Force on Diversity of Families, Commn. to Draft Ethics Code for L.A. City Govt.; mem. L.A. County Commn. on Juvenile Delinquency and Adult Crime, 1991—; bd. dirs. Jewish Homes for Aging of Greater L.A., NCCJ, 1989, Health of the Bay ; adv. bd. Westside Children's Mus., Interreligious Info. Ctr.; chmn. com. on fed. legislation commn. on law and legislation L.A. Jewish Cmty. Rels. Com., trustee; chair CCAR/UAHC com. on HIV AIDS, Progressive Religious Alliance, City of L.A. 1998 Vol. Festival Adv. Com., First Internat. Conf. on Allocation of Health Resources, Washington, 1997; mem. exec. com., bd. dirs. Heal the Bay; mem. adv. com. Disability Rights Advocates; hon. bd. mem. Jewish Fedn. Western Region Bd. Recipient Bishop Daniel Corrigan commendation Episcopal Diocese, 1987, Humanitarian award NCCJ, 1988, Social Responsibility award L.A. Urban League, 1988, Nat. Friendship award Parents and Friends of Lesbians and Gays, 1989, AIDS Hospice Found. Gene La Pietra Leadership award, 1989, Cath. Archdiocese's Serra Tribute award, 1989, Univ. Synagogue's Avodah award for Cmty. Svc., 1990, Am. Jewish Congress Tzedek award for Cmty. Leadership and Svc., 1990, Crystal Achievement award AIDS Project L.A., 1996, Planned Parenthood Disting. Svc. award, 1996, Cmty. Leadership award Beeth Chayim Chadashim Congregation. Mem. Am. Jewish Congress (pres. 1977-80, 82-84), Physicians Assn. for AIDS Care (nat. adv. bd.), AIDS Nat. Interfaith Network (bd. dirs.), Jr. C. of C. (chair internat. rels. com.), Sigma Alpha Mu, Omnicron Delta Kappa, Phi Mu Alpha. Office: Univ Synagogue 11960 W Sunset Blvd Los Angeles CA 90049-4200

FREELAND, DARRYL CREIGHTON, psychologist, educator; b. Omaha, Feb. 22, 1939; s. Elverson Lafayette and Lauretta Joyce (Coffelt) F.; m. Tina Anne Richmond, July 21, 1979; children—Adam Daniel, Noah Nathan, Sarah Eileen. B.S., U. Nebr., 1961; S.T.B., Fuller Theol. Sem., 1965; M.A., Calif. State U.-Fullerton, 1966; Ph.D., U. So. Calif., 1972. Lic. psychologist, Calif. Tchr. elem. schs., Calif., 1961-66; instr. Glendale Community Coll., Calif., 1966-67, Citrus Community Coll., Glendora, Calif., 1967-79; pvt. practice psychology, Laguna Niguel, Calif., 1969—; field faculty and vis. prof. Calif. State U.-Los Angeles, 1970, San Marino Community Presbyterian Ch., 1972, Calif. Sch. Profl. Psychology, Los Angeles, 1972-73, U. Calif.-Riverside, 1973, Humanistic Psychology Inst., San Francisco, 1976-79, U. Humanistic Studies, San Diego, 1983; tenured assoc. prof. psychology and family U.S. Internat. U., 1986—; dir. MFT tng. Univ. Ctr., Orange County, 1998—; asst. dir. clin. psychology tng. Marriage and Family Therapy Tng., 1986-89; pvt. post-secondary com. for qualitative rev. and assessment of licensure Calif. Dept. Edn., 1989-97. Finisher, Newport Beach-Irvine Marathon, 1981, San Francisco Marathon, 1982, Long Beach Marathon, 1988. Office: 30131 Town Center Dr Ste 298 Laguna Niguel CA 92677-2086

FREELAND, ROBERT FREDERICK, retired librarian; b. Flint, Mich., Dec. 20, 1919; s. Ralph V. and Susan Barbara (Goetz) F.; m. June Voshel, June 18, 1948; children: Susan Beth Visser, Kent Richard. BS, Eastern Mich. U., 1942; postgrad., Washington & Lee U., 1945; MS, U. So. Calif., 1948, postgrad., 1949; postgrad., U. Mich., 1950-52, Calif. State U., 1956-58, UCLA, 1960; LittD (hon.), Linda Vista Bible Coll., 1973. Music supr. Consol. Schs. Warren, Mich., 1946-47; music dir. Carson City (Mich.) Pub. Schs., 1948-49; librarian, audio-visual coord. Ford Found., Edison Inst., Greenfield Village, Dearborn, Mich., 1950-52, Helix High Sch. Library, 1952-77; librarian, prof. library sci. Linda Vista Bible Coll., 1976—; reference libr. San Diego Pub. Libr. System, 1967-97; cons. edn., libr. and multimedia. Editor book and audio-visual aids review, Sch. Musician, Dir. and Teacher, 1950-75. Former deacon and elder Christian Reform Ch., libr., 1969-72, Classis archivist, 1991—; pub. affairs officer, sr. program officer, moral leadership officer Sq. 57 GP III, Calif. wing CAP. With USAAF, 1942-46. Named Scholar Freedoms Found., Valley Forge, Pa., 1976-80. Mem. NEA (life), ALA, Nat. Music Camp, Calif. Tchrs. Assn., Music Libr. Assn. So. Calif. (adviser exec. bd.), Calif. Libr. Assn. (pres. Palomar chpt. 1972-73), Sch. Libr. Assn. Calif. (treas. 1956-73), Calif. Media and Libr. Educators (charter mem.), Am. Legion (Americanism chmn. 22d dist. San Diego County, chmn. oratorical contest com. La Mesa post), Ret. Officers Assn., San Diego Aero Space Mus., San Diego Mus. Art, Alumnia Assn. Ea. Mich. U. Home: 4800 Williamsburg Ln Apt 223 La Mesa CA 91941-4651

FREEMAN, J. P. LADYHAWK, underwater exploration, security and transportation executive, educator, fashion model; b. Berkley, Calif., Feb. 21, 1951; d. Gilbert Richard Freeman (dec.) and P. M. (Ann) Raistrick; m. B.M. McGlynn, Feb. 9, 1974; children: Jennifer Patricia (dec.), Schne F. (dec.). BA in English, Davis & Elkins Coll., W.Va., 1973; grad., USAF Air Weapons Controller Sch., Tyndall AFB, Fla., 1973, USAF Air Command and Staff Coll., 1982, U.S. Marine Corps Command and Staff Coll., 1982, Dept. Def. Computer Inst., 1984; M in Aviation Mgmt., Embry-Riddle Aeronautical U., Daytona Beach, Fla., 1986, postgrad., 1986; grad., USAF Air War Coll., Montgomery, Ala., 1988. Cert. EMT. Mem. 56th spl. ops. rescue for Southeast Asia NKP Royal Thai Air Force Base, 1974, 75; chief wing radar standardization/evaluation RAF Alconbury, England, 1980-83; commdr. joint U.S. forces Operation Raleigh, 1986; support chief of staff Hdqs. NORAD, Colorado Springs, Colo., 1987-89; dep. base commdr. NATO Hdqs. Allied Forces No. Europe, Norway, 1989-91; chief airport mgmt. divsn. Whiteman AFB, Knob Noster, Mo., 1991-93; dir. spl. projects USAF Acad. Regional Hosp., Colorado Springs, 1993-94; systems performance specialist Colo. Sport & Spine Rehab., Colorado Springs, 1994-95; dir. FLEET Internat. Explorations and Svcs. Co., Colorado Springs, 1995-97; fashion model, 1990—; spl. adv. for anti and counter terrorist security design for 1994 Internat. Olympic Games, Oslo, Norway, 1989-91; designer Automated Provider Credentialing System USAF Acad. Regional Hosp., USAF Acad., Colo., 1993-94; spl. adv. comms. NATO German High Commd., 1977-80; experience in 37 countries. *After careers spanning the stage and folk singing to White House reporter for Associated Press during the Nixon Administration to serving America in uniform, she has been to every continent, including Antarctica. She is now semiretired in Colorado Springs, spending her spare time doing what she calls "appreciating rainbows" and visiting her mother, brother John, and sister Jill in England. Her hobbies are as eclectic as her careers have been. An avid traveler, she is forever off to the familiar and/or the exotic. She also enjoys riding horses and motorcycles, writes both poetry and prose, and her paintings continue to appear in private collections.* Poet, poems included in numerous anthologies. Mem. bd. dirs. Johnson County (Mo.) United Way, 1991-93; surgery life support specialist ARC, USAF Acad. Regional Hosp., 1993-95; mem. nat. scholarship com. Red River Valley Fighter Pilots Assn., 1993—; hosp. vol., med. technician, provider credentialing system designer, oral surgery life support system specialist. Recipient 53 awards and decorations including Defense Meritorious svc. medal with 1 oak leaf cluster, Meritorious Svc. medal with 2 oak leaf clusters, Joint Svc. Commendation medal with 1 oak leaf cluster, air force commendation medal, Armed Forces Expeditionary medal with 2 bronze stars, 2 Humanitarian Svc. medals, 2 Kuwait Liberation medals, 2 Southwest Asia medals; named Adminstrsn. Officer of Yr. USAF, 1986; named one of the six top Support Officers USAF, 1986-87; 1st woman named dir. Fleet Internat. Mem. VFW, DAV, Am. Legion, Air Force Assn., Soc. of Profl. Journalists, Assn. of Old Crows, Lambda Lambda, Alpha Phi Omega, Iota Beta Sigma. Mem. Anglican Ch. Avocations: writing, skiing, horseback riding, oil painting, music. Home: 4861 Chaparral Rd Colorado Springs CO 80917-1413 Office: FLEET Internat Explorations & Svcs Co PO Box 14192 Colorado Springs CO 80914-0192

FREEMAN, NEIL, accounting and computer consulting firm executive; b. Reading, Pa., Dec. 27, 1948; s. Leroy Harold and Audrey Todd (Dornhecker) F.; m. Janice Lum, Nov. 20, 1981. BS, Albright Coll., 1979; MS, Kennedy-Western U., 1987, PhD, 1988. Cert. systems profl., data processing specialist, info. system security profl. Acct. Jack W. Long & Co., Mt. Penn, Pa., 1977-78; comptroller G.P.C., Inc., Bowmansville, Pa., 1978-79; owner Neil Freeman Cons., Bowmansville, 1980-81; program mgr., systems cons. Application Systems, Honolulu, 1981-82; instr. Chaminade U., Honolulu, 1983-96; owner Neil Freeman Cons., Kaneohe, Hawaii, 1982-96, Grand Junction, Colo., 1996—; instr. Mesa State Coll., Grand Junction, 1997—. Author: (computer software) NFC Property Management, 1984, NFC Mailing List, 1984; (book) Learning Dibol, 1984. Served with USN, 1966-68, Vietnam. Mem. Nat. Assn. Accts., Am. Inst. Cert. Computer Profls., Assn. Systems Mgmt. Office: PO Box 60070 Grand Junction CO 81506-8758

FREEMAN, PATRICIA ELIZABETH, library and education specialist; b. El Dorado, Ark., Nov. 30, 1924; d. Herbert A. and M. Elizabeth (Pryor) Harper; m. Jack Freeman, June 15, 1949; 3 children. BA, Centenary Coll., 1943; postgrad., Fine Arts Ctr., 1942-46, Art Students League, 1944-45; BSLS, La. State U., 1946; postgrad., Calif. State U., 1959-61, U. N.Mex., 1964-74; EdS, Peabody Coll., Vanderbilt U., 1975. Libr. U. Calif., Berkeley, 1946-47; libr. Albuquerque Pub. Schs., 1964-67, ind. sch. libr. media ctr. cons., 1967—. Painter lithographer; one-person show La. State Exhibit Bldg., 1948; author: Pathfinder: An Operational Guide for the School Librarian, 1975, Southeast Heights Neighborhoods of Albuquerque, 1993; compiler, editor: Elizabeth Pryor Harper's Twenty-One Southern Families, 1985; editor: SEHNA Gazette, 1988-93. Mem. task force Goals for Dallas-Environ., 1977-82; pres. Friends of Sch. Librs., Dallas, 1979-83; v.p., editor Southeast Heights Neighborhood Assn., 1988-93. With USAF, 1948-49. Honoree AAUW Ednl. Found., 1979, 96; vol. award for outstanding service Dallas Ind. Sch. Dist., 1978; AAUW Pub. Service grantee 1980. Mem. ALA, AAUW (dir. Dallas 1976-82, Albuquerque 1983-85), LWV (sec. Dallas 1982-83, editor Albuquerque 1984-88), Nat. Trust Historic Preservation, Friends of Pub. Libr., N.Mex. Symphony Guild, Alpha Xi Delta. Home: 3016 Santa Clara Ave SE Albuquerque NM 87106-2350

FREEMAN, ROBIN D., manufacturers company executive, actress; b. Cleve., Feb. 3, 1951; d. George and Shirley (Landau) Kassoff; m. Duey R. Freeman, Sept. 13, 1996. BFA, Columbus Coll. Art and Design, 1975; M, U. Colo., 1978. Comm. dir. Colo. Assn. Pub. Employees, Denver, 1979-80; mktg. dir. Proctor Cos., Denver, 1994-95; editor Sch. Food Svc. Jour., Denver, 1986-88; publicist Am. Lamb Coun., Denver, 1988-91; v.p. 2 Group, Denver, 1995-98; account mgr. Millikan, Denver, 1998—; pres. Statements, Denver. Contbr. articles to fin. jours. Mem. Network Exec. Women in Hospitality (newsletter editor, 1995), Evergreen players. Avocations: ballet, music, theatre. Office: PO Box 496 Kittredge CO 80457-0496

FREEMAN, VAL LEROY, geologist; b. Long Beach, Calif., June 25, 1926; s. Cecil LeRoy and Marjorie (Austin) F.; BS, U. Calif., Berkeley, 1949, MS, 1952; m. June Ione Ashlock, Sept. 26, 1959 (div. June 1962); 1 child, Jill Annette Freeman Michener; m. Elizabeth Joann Sabia, Sept. 4, 1964 (div. Oct. 1972); 1 child, Rebecca Sue Freeman Shepard; 1 stepchild, Frank J. Sabia; m. Betty M. Avey, Oct. 9, 1993. Geologist, U.S. Geol. Survey, 1949-85, Fairbanks, Alaska, 1955-57, Denver, 1957-70, 74-85, Flagstaff, Ariz., 1970-74, dep. chief coal resources br., until 1985. With USNR, 1943-45. Fellow Geol. Soc. Am. Contbr. articles to profl. jours. Home: 26 S Indiana Pl Golden CO 80401-5082

FREEMAN, WILLIAM TAFT, JR., minister; b. L.A., Aug. 28, 1937; s. William Taft and Virginia (Sabella) F.; m. Patricia Ann Moomjean, Feb. 25, 1956; children: Renee, Jennifer, William Taft III, Desiree, Jonathan. BA, Asuza Pacific U., 1960; MA, Fuller Theol. Sem., 1979. Min. Evang. Tabernacle Ch., 1957; asst. min. Alamitos Friends Ch., Garden Grove, Calif., 1957-60; co-pastor Yorba Linda Friends Ch., 1960-64; min. Ch. in Yorba Linda, Calif., 1964-70, Ch. in Seattle, 1970-87, Ch. in Scottsdale, Ariz., 1987—; conf. speaker Ministry of Word Inc., Scottsdale, 1969—, pres., 1981—; instr. ch. history Ariz. State U., Tempe, 1988; radio Bible instr. Seattle, Scottsdale, 1981—. Author: The Testimony of Church History Regarding the Mystery of the Triune God, 1976, The Testimony of Church History Regarding the Mystery of the Mingling of God with Man, 1977, In Defense of Truth, 1981, The Dividing of Soul and Spirit, 1984, The Triune God in Experience, 1984, The Love Life of the Bride, 1990, God's Eternal Purpose, 1991, Experiential Outlines of the Old Testament Books, 1991, Experiential Outlines of the Gospel of Matthew, 1991, Experiential Outlines of the Gospel of John, 1991, The Father's Good Pleasure, 1991, (booklets) Inward and Outward Christians, 1983, How the Church Met in the New Testament, 1982, The Assurance Christ is In You, 1984; editor: How They Found Christ: In Their Own Words, 1983, Spending Time with the Lord, 1990. Mem. Am. Soc. Ch. History. Republican. Avocation: reading, computer. Home: 7125 E Paradise Dr Scottsdale AZ 85254-5157 Office: Ministry of Word Inc 7135 E Sunnyside Dr Scottsdale AZ 85254-5169

FREEMAN-ZUNIGA, ROCHELLE ELLEN LASKOV, electrologist, medical technologist; b. Chgo., June 25, 1943; d. Bernard M. and Harriet (Itzkowitz) Laskov; m. Leonard Irwin Freeman, Mar. 1, 1964 (div. Dec. 1969); m. Jorge Clemente Zuniga, Jan. 4, 1992; children: Irma Squires, Jorge Jr. Cert. Med. Technologist, Cook Cty. Grad. Sch. Med. Tech, Chgo., 1962; BA in Bus. & Biology, North Park Coll., 1978; Assoc. of Selective Studies, Mesa Coll., San Diego, 1980; Assoc., Coll. Electrology, San Diego, 1985. Registered electrologist, Bd. Barbering and Cosmetology, Calif. Owner, operator New Image Ctr. AKA New Image Electrolysis Ctr., San Diego, 1985—. Precinct asst. Dem. Orgn., Chgo., 1970. Mem. Internat. Soc. Clin. Lab. Tech. (cert.), Electrologist Assn. Calif., Am. Electrology Assn., Internat. Guild of Profl. Electrologist, Clin. Lab. Scientists. Home: 7807 Nightingale Way San Diego CA 92123-2726 Office: New Image Ctr AKA New Image Electolysis Ctr 7677 Ronson Rd Ste 200 San Diego CA 92111-1538

FREIBOTT, GEORGE AUGUST, physician, chemist, priest; b. Bridgeport, Conn., Oct. 6, 1954; s. George August and Barbara Mary (Schreiber) F.; m. Jennifer Noble, July 12, 1980 (div.); children: Jessica, Heather, George; m. Arlene Ann Steiner, Aug. 1, 1982. BD, Am. Bible Coll., Pineland, Fla., 1977; BS, Nat. Coll. NHA, International Falls, Minn., 1978; ThM, Clarksville (Tenn.) Sch. Theology, 1979; MD, [illegible] Am. Coll., 1979; MsT, Fla. Sch. Massage, 1977. Diplomate Nat. Bd. Naturopathic Examiners; ordained priest Ea. Orthodox Ch., 1983. Chief mfg. cons. in oxidative chemistry Am. Soc. Med. Missionaries, Priest River, Idaho, 1976-88; mfg. cons. Oxidation Products Internat. div. ASMM, Priest River, 1974—; chemist/oxidative chemistry Internat. Assn. Oxygen Therapy, Priest River, 1985—; oxidative chemist, scientist, priest A.S. Med. Missionaries, Priest River, 1982—; CEO Internat. Oxydative Products Techs., Ltd., Las Vegas, Nev., 1996—; massage therapist Fla. Dept. Profl. Registration, Tallahassee, 1977-91; cons. Benedict Lust Sch. Naturopathy; cons. mem. World Natural Health Orgn., Washington, Internat. Colon Hydrotherapy Found., London; lectr. in field. Author: Nicola Tesla and the Implementation of His Discoveries in Modern Science, 1984, Warburg, Blass and Koch: Men With a Message, 1990, Free Radicals and Their Relationship to Complex Oxidative Compounds, 1991, Complex Oxidative Molecules: Their Implication in the Rejuvenation of the Human Cell, 1994, History of Naturopathy or Pseudomedicalism: Naturopathy's Demise?, 1990, 95; contbr. articles to profl. jours. Recipient Tesla medal of Scientific Merit, Benedict Lust Sch. Natural Scis., 1992. Mem. Am. Chem. Soc., Tesla Meml. Soc., Tesla Coil Builder's Assn., Internat. Bio-Oxidative Med. Found. (Disting. Spkr. award 1994), Brit. Guild Drugless Practitioners, Internat. Assn. for Colon Therapy, Am. Massage Therapy Assn., Am. Naturopathic Med. Assn., Am. Soc. Med. Missionaries, Am. Coll. Clinic Adminstrs., Nat. Assn. Naturopathic Physicians, Am. Psychotherapy Assn., Am. Soc. Metals, Am. Naturopathic Assn. (trustee, pres.), Internat. Traders. Achievements include research conducted in organic and inorganic oxidative chemistry, thermoelectric/thermionic materials in relation to oxygen, oxygen as related to superconductivity and molecular makeup, energy studies, material science, archaeology, ancient Biblical and medical studies; developer and co-designer advanced oxidative equipment and testing apparatus of oxidation and oxidative studies. Home: PO Box 1360 Priest River ID 83856-1360

FREIHEIT, CLAYTON FREDRIC, zoo director; b. Buffalo, Jan. 29, 1938; s. Clayton John and Ruth (Miller) F. Student, U. Buffalo, 1960; DHL (hon.), U. Denver, 1996. Caretaker Living Mus., Buffalo Mus. Sci., 1955-60; curator Buffalo Zool. Gardens, 1960-70; dir. Denver Zool. Gardens, 1970—. Contbr. articles to profl. jours. Named Outstanding Citizen, Buffalo Evening News, 1967. Mem. Internat. Union Dirs. Zool. Gardens, Am. Assn. Zool. Pks. and Aquariums (pres. 1967-68 Outstanding Svc. award). Home: 3855 S Monaco Pky Denver CO 80237-1271 Office: Denver Zool Gardens City Park Denver CO 80205

FREITAG, KURT B., trucking executive; b. San Antonio, Oct. 1, 1958; s. Gunther H. and Hilda (Martin) F.; m. Barbara J. Freitag, June 20, 1981; children: William, Michelle, Kevin. BSBA, City U., Bellevue, Wash., 1993; MBA, Seattle U., 1997. Garage supr. Sweeney & Co., Inc., San Antonio, 1978-83; svc. mgr., dir. maintenance Trans Lease Corp., San Antonio, 1983-90; port ops. mgr. Paccar Sales N.Am., Houston, 1990-91; v.p. maintenance TSI Equipment Co., Dallas, 1991-92; mktg. mgr. Paccar Parts, Renton, Wash., 1992-97; dir. customer svc. Kenworth Truck Co., Kirkland, Wash., 1997—. Mem. bus. adv. com. Kent (Wash.) Ind. Sch. Dist., 1987—; mentor students Seattle U., 1997—; asst. scoutmaster Boy Scouts Am. Troop 711, Maple Valley, Wash., 1995—; treas., com. mem. Cub Scout Pack 711, Maple Valley, 1992—. Eagle Scout, San Antonio, 1973. Mem. Truck Maintenance Coun.

FREITAG, PETER ROY, transportation specialist; b. L.A., Dec. 19, 1943; s. Victor Hugo and Helen Veronica (Burnes) F. Student, U. Fla., 1961-63, George Washington U., 1964-65. Chief supr. Eastern Airlines, L.A., 1965-77; tariff analyst, instr. United Airlines, San Francisco, 1977-84; mng. ptnr. Bentdahl, Freitag & Assoc., San Francisco, 1984-86; v.p. ops. PAD Travel, Inc., Mountain View, Calif., 1985-86; travel mgr. Loral Aerospace Corp, San Jose, Calif., 1986-95; pres. Capital Fin. Ptnrs. Corp., San Francisco, 1995—. Co-editor: (textbook) International Air Tariff and Ticketing, 1983. Vol. San Francisco Bay chpt. Oceanic Soc., 1984-95. Mem. Silicon Valley Bus. Travel Assn., Bay Area Bus. Travel Assn. Episcopalian. Avocations: travel, cooking, oenology, hiking. Office: Capital Fin Ptnrs Corp 3145 Geary Blvd Ste 708 San Francisco CA 94118-3316

FREITAS, DAVID PRINCE, lawyer; b. San Francisco, Oct. 21, 1940; s. Walter Francis and Marno Catherine (Prince) F.; m. Alice Urrutia, June 24, 1961 (div. 1972); children: Diane Phillips, Nancy Freitas, Megan Neale; m. Patricia Garbarino, June 20, 1996. BS, U. San Franciso, 1964; JD, San Francisco Law Sch., 1968. Bar: Calif. 1969. Atty. Freitas Law Firm, San Rafael, Calif., 1969-96, Ragghianti, Freitas, Montobbio & Wallace LLP, San Rafael, 1996—; bd. dirs. St. Vincent's Sch.; lectr. in field; judge pro tempore San Francisco and Marin Counties; spl. master Superior Cts. of Marin and Sonoma. Contbr. articles to profl. jours. Bd. dirs. Guide Dogs for the Blind, San Rafal, 1994-95, Marin Agrl. Land Trust, 1991-92, Marin County Humane Soc., 1967-71. Fellow Am. Coll. Trial Lawyers, Internat. Acad. Trial Lawyers, Internat. Soc. Barristers; mem. Internat. Assn. Def. Counsel, Am. Bd. Trial Adv. (San Francisco chpt., pres. 1993, nat. bd. dirs. 1992—, exec. com. 1990—), Nat. Bd. Trial Adv. (diplomate), Assn. Def. Counsel N.C. (pres. 1985, bd. dirs. 1977-86), Calif. State Bar Assn. (adminstrn. justice com. 1982, jury instrns. com. 1977), Calif. Def. Counsel (bd. dirs. 1984), Marin County Bar Assn. (secr. 1987, treas. 1984), Def. Rsch. Inst. (Nat. Execptional Performance award 1985), Cal-ABOTA (bd. chair 1995), Edward J. McFetridge Am. Inn Ct. (pres. 1993, exec. com. 1990—), San Rafal C. of C. (bd. dirs. 1995—). Home: 90 Convent Ct San Rafael CA 94901-1334 Office: Ragghianti Freitas Montobbio Wallace LLP 874 4th St San Rafael CA 94901-3246

FREIWALD, DAVID ALLEN, physicist, mechanical engineer; b. Cleve., June 4, 1941; s. Harry Herman and Arline Mildred (Woehrman) F.; m. Karen Lee Eaton, Aug., 1960 (div. 1976); children: Wesley, Todd, Christopher; m. Joyce Darlyne Gross, Apr. 3, 1976. BSME, Northwestern U., 1963, PhD, 1968. Rsch. scientist Sandia Nat. Labs., Albuquerque, 1967-72; scientist, staff dir.'s office Los Alamos (N.Mex.) Nat. Lab., 1972-81; program mgr. SEA, Inc., McLean, Va., 1981-82, MRJ, Inc., Oakton, Va., 1982-85; dir., gen. mgr. Gen. Dynamics, San Diego, 1985-90; v.p., F2 Assocs., San Diego, 1991-92, Albuquerque, 1992—; adv. bd. USAF, Washington, 1985; team leader 20-Yr. Look Ahead Study Gen. Dynamics, St. Louis, 1986-87; SMES adv. bd. Bechtel, Inc., San Francisco, 1986-87. Active N.Mex. Gov.'s Land Use Legislation Com., Santa Fe, 1971, Energy Task Force, 1973-74; pres. Whispering Ridge Homeowners Assn., 1988. Mem. Am. Def. Preparedness Assn., Marine Corps Assn., N.Mex. Acad. Sci. (pres. 1981), Tau Beta Pi, Pi Tau Sigma, Sigma Xi. Republican. Methodist. Achievements include patents pending for magnetically protected laser fusion cavity, burst laser communication mode for satellite-submarines, explosive driven shock tubes for top-atmosphere weapon effects simulation, numerous patent applications for robotic laser-based industrial decoating systems. Home: 1708 Soplo Rd SE Albuquerque NM 87123-4485 Office: 14800 Central Ave SE Albuquerque NM 87123-3905

FREMOUW, EDWARD JOSEPH, physicist; b. Northfield, Minn., Feb. 23, 1934; s. Fred J. and Marion Elizabeth (Drozda) F.; m. Rita Lorraine Johnson, June 26, 1960; children: Thane Edrik, Sean Fredrik; 2nd marriage: Marilyn Call Allred, Feb. 15, 1998. BSEE, Stanford U., 1957; MS in Physics, U. Alaska, 1963, PhD in Geophysics, 1966. Asst. prof. geophysics U. Alaska, Fairbanks, 1966-67; physicist Stanford Research Inst., Menlo Park, Calif., 1967-70, sr. physicist, 1970-75; program mgr. SRI Internat., Menlo Park, 1975-77; v.p. Phys. Dynamics, Inc., Bellevue, Wash., 1977-86; pres. Northwest Research Assocs., Inc., Bellevue, Wash., 1986—, also bd. dirs.; cons. Geophys. Inst., College, 1967-68; assoc. La Jolla (Calif.) Inst., 1981-89. Contbr. articles to profl. jours. Trustee East Shore Unitarian Ch., 1984-86; co-chair adv. com. on econ. diversification Wash. State, 1991-96; bd. dirs., pres. Banchero Friends Svcs., Inc., 1994-95. Geographic feature Fremouw Peak named in his honor, 1968. Mem. IEEE, Am. Geophys. Union (Excellence in Refereeing award 1984, 89), Union Radio Sci. Internat., Stanford Club of Western Wash. (trustee 1984-86). Democrat. Unitarian Universalist. Avocations: hiking, skiing. Home: 2873 W Lk Sammamish Pkwy NE Redmond WA 98052-5913 Office: Northwest Rsch Assocs Inc PO Box 3027 Bellevue WA 98009-3027*

FRENCH, EDWARD GLEN, artist; b. Denver, Oct. 30, 1940; s. Elby Edward and Eleanor Lilian (Forst) F.; m. Suzie Broadstreet, Sept. 8, 1961; children: [illegible] Art Ctr., 1961-62, Coll. of Design. Artist Martin Lockheed, 1960-61, New Tribes Mission, Sanford, Fla., 1964-79; sr. artist Walt Disney World, Orlando, Fla., 1979-94; freelance artist Cotopaxi, Colo., 1994—; art show judge

Walt Disney's Festival of the Masters, Orlando, 1993; artist S.O.A.R. Bald Eagle Restoration, Fla., 1983-90. Artist (calendar) Nat. Wildlife Fedn., 1982, (L.E. print) Eurodisney, 1992. Bible tchr., preacher, spkr. various chs., Kenosha, Wis., 1964-78, Sanford, Fla., 1979-89, Salida, Colo., 1996—; 4H art tchr., Kenosha, 1969. Recipient 15 Yr. Trophy Walt Disney World, 1994. Avocations: hiking, photography, flying, wildlife study, hunting. Home and Office: Box 300 Cotopaxi CO 81223

FRENCH, JAMES L., performing company executive. Music dir. condr. Maui Symphony Orch., Hawaii. Office: Maui Symphony Orchestra 40 Hana Hwy Kahului HI 96732*

FRENCH, JAMES ROWLEY, radio dramatist, writer; b. Pasadena, Calif., Sept. 23, 1928; s. James Forrest and Mabelle Olive (Rowley) F.; m. Patricia Anne Soule, June 17, 1950; children: Leslie Anne, James Forrest. Student, Pasadena City Coll., 1945-49. Radio personality Radio KPOA, Radio KIKI, Honolulu, 1950-52; program host Radion KING, Seattle, 1952-58, Radio KIRO, Seattle, 1958-71; program host, prodr. Radio KVI, Seattle, 1971-78; film writer, prodr. Cinevista Prodns., Boeing Co., Seattle, 1978-80; program host, prodr. Radio KIRO, Seattle, 1980-94; pres. Jim French Prodns., Inc., Bellevue, Wash., 1994—; instr. Sch. Comm., U. Wash., Seattle, 1965-66; instr. radio-TV Bellevue C.C., 1966-68. Author: Nauvoo, 1980, The Outcasts, 1981, Seattle, Pacific Gem, 1997; creator, writer (radio drama series) KIRO Mystery Playhouse, 1987—. Rep. Bellevue Cmty. Coun., 1955; pres., bd. dirs. Seattle Civic Light Opera, 1972-74; v.p., bd. dirs. History House, Seattle, 1996-97. With U.S. Army, 1946-47. Mem. LDS Ch. Avocation: playing piano. Home and Office: Jim French Prodns Inc 16215 SE Roanoke Pl Bellevue WA 98006-4529

FRENCH, KIRBY ALLAN, transportation engineer, computer programmer; b. San Angelo, Tex., Oct. 12, 1948; s. Leland Wayne French and Helen Lois (Stennett) French-Vance; m. Verda Jane Amyl Schaffer, Oct. 11, 1970; children: Tammy Lyrae, Adrian Allyn. Diploma in Computer Programming, Mkt. Tng. Inst., 1968. Transp. engr. Calif. Dept. Transp., San Bernardino, 1969-98; ret., 1998. Author: Speed Math, 1991, Trigonometric Formulas, 1991, Speed Reading, 1994, Microsoft Word 6 Macros for Spec Writers, 1996, Power Macintosh Apple Script Programs, 1996. Avocations: computer programming, writing, painting, Star Trek conventions. Home: 1257 Poplar St San Bernardino CA 92410-2522

FRENCH, LAURENCE ARMAND, social science educator, psychology educator; b. Manchester, N.H., Mar. 24, 1941; s. Gerald Everett and Juliette Teresa (Boucher) F.; m. Nancy Picthall, Feb. 13, 1971. BA cum laude, U. N.H., 1968, MA, 1970, PhD, 1975; postdoctorate, SUNY, Albany, 1978; PhD, U. Nebr., 1981; MA, Western N.M. U., 1994. Diplomate Am. Bd. Forensic Medicine, Am. Bd. Forensic Examiners, Am. Bd. Psychol. Specialties in Forensic Psychology; lic. psychologist, Ariz. Instr. U. So. Maine, Portland and Gorham, 1971-72; asst. prof. Western Carolina U., Cullowhee, N.C., 1972-77, U. Nebr., Lincoln, 1977-80; psychologist I N.H. Hosp., Concord, 1980-81; psychologist II Laconia (N.H.) State Sch., 1981-88; sr. psychologist N.H. Divsn. for Children & Youth Svcs., Concord, 1988-89; prof., chair dept. social scis. Western N.Mex. U., Silver City, 1989—; Psi Chi Nat. Honor Soc. in psychology Western N.Mex. faculty adviser; adj. assoc. prof. U. So. Maine, 1980-84; cons. N.C. Dept. Mental Health, 1972-77, Nebr. Indian Commn., Lincoln, 1977-80, Cherokee (N.C.) Indian Mental Health Program, 1974-77; cons. alcohol program Lincoln Indian Ctr., 1977-80; profl. adv. bd. Internat. Coll. Prescribing Psychologists. Author: The Selective Process of Criminal Justice, 1976, (with Richard Crowe) Wee Wish Tree: Special Qualla Cherokee Issue, 1976, (with Hornbuckle) Cherokee Perspective, 1981, (with Letman et al) Contemporary Issues in Corrections, 1981, Indians and Criminal Justice, 1982, Psychocultural Change and the American Indian, 1987, The Winds of Injustice, 1994, Counseling American Indians, 1997, The Qualla Cherokee Surviving in Two Worlds, 1998; spl. issue editor Quar. Jour. Ideology, Vol. II, 1987; contbr. articles to profl. jours. Commr. Pilsbury Lake Village Dist., Webster, N.H., 1985-90. With USMC, 1959-63. U. N.H. fellow, 1971-72, Nebr. U. System fellow, 1978. Fellow APA, Prescribing Psychologists Register (diplomate); mem. NASP, VFW, Am. Soc. Criminology (life), Internat. Coll. Prescribing Psychologists Inc. (profl. adv. bd.), Nat. Assn. Alcohol and Drug Abuse Counselors (nat. chmn., clin. issue com. 1996-98), N.Mex. Alcohol and Drug Abuse Counselors Assn. (educator of the yr. award 1997), Phi Delta Kappa (treas. 1990-91, pres. 1991-92). Office: Western NMex U Dept Social Scis Silver City NM 88062

FRENCH, STEPHEN WARREN, art educator, university official; b. Seattle, Sept. 6, 1934; s. George Warren and Madge Evelyn (Marshall) F. m. Hanna Clara Misch, June 10, 1956 (div. May 1971); children: Alexandra, Kenneth, Katharine; m. Toni Virginia Thunen, Aug. 14, 1974 (div. June 1979); 1 child, Elly Kinsell Thunen-French; m. Wanda Waldera, Oct. 19, 1990. BA, U. Wash., 1956, MFA, 1960. Instr. art dept. San Jose (Calif.) State U., 1960-61; from instr. to asst. prof. art dept. U. Wis., Madison, 1961-66; from asst. prof. to prof. art San Jose State U., 1966—, chmn. dept., 1986-90, assoc. dean Coll. Humanities and Arts, 1990—, acting dean Coll. Humanities and the Arts, 1998—; vis. artist U. Wash., Seattle, 1972, 73, Mont. State U. Boseman, 1970; mem. collections com. San Jose Mus. of Art, 1990—, mem. arts commn. City of San Jose, 1990-93, chair, 1993-94; vice chmn. conv. ctr. art selection com. City of San Jose, 1986-93; chmn. Art in Pub. Places Adv. Panel City of San Jose, 1991-93; mem. long range planning com. San Jose Mus. Art, 1997-98. One man show San Jose Mus., 1980; exhibited in group shows at Smithsonian Inst., Washington, 1965, Palace of the Legion of Honor, San Francisco, 1967, British Biennial of Graphic Art, 1969, 71, San Francisco Mus. of Modern Art, 1970. Mem. adv. com. San Jose Inst. of Contemporary Art. Sarah Denny fellow U. Wash., 1958. Mem. Coll. Art Assn., Nat. Assn. Schs. of Art & Design, Nat. Conf. of Art Adminstrs., Phi Beta Kappa, Phi Kappa Phi. Unitarian. Home: 736 N 17th St San Jose CA 95112-3030 Office: San Jose State U 1 Washington Sq San Jose CA 95112-3613

FRENKEL, EDWARD VLADIMIR, mathematician, educator; b. Kolomna, Russia, May 2, 1968; came to U.S., 1989; s. Vladimir Iosifovich and Lidia Vladimirovna Frenkel; m. Zvezdelina Stankova. BA, Gubkin Inst., Moscow, 1989; PhD, Harvard U., 1991. Jr. fellow Soc. Fellows, Harvard U., Cambridge, Mass., 1991-94, assoc. prof. math., 1994-97; prof. U. of Calif., Berkeley, 1997—; vis. prof. Kyoto (Japan) U., 1992, 93, 95, U. Paris VII, 1992, U. Paris VI, 1996, Ecole Normale Superieure, Paris, 1998, Weizmann Inst., Israel, 1992; invited spkr. Internat. Congress Mathematicians, Zurich, Switzerland, 1994, Internat. Congress Math. Physics, Paris, 1994; mem. Inst. for Advanced Study, Princeton, 1997. Editl. bd. Inventiones Mathematical, Internat. Math. Rsch. Notices; contbr. articles to profl. jours. Harvard prize fellow, 1989, Packard Found. fellow, 1995; grantee NSF, 1992, 95, Sloan Found., 1995. Mem. Am. Math. Soc. Office: U Calif at Berkeley Evans Hall Berkeley CA 94720

FRENZEL, FRANCES JOHNSON, registered nurse, educator, lecturer; b. Bedford, Va., Feb. 2, 1911; d. J. James and Willie Calpernia (Markham) Johnson; m. Paul H. Frenzel, Dec. 21, 1933 (dec. 1990); children: Virginia Lee Frenzel Lawrence, Helen Marie Frenzel LaGourgue. RN, Wash. Adventist Hosp., Takoma Park, Md., 1932; BS, Columbia Union Coll., 1933; real estate license, Glendale (Calif.) C.C., 1968. Cert. real estate broker. RN supr. Glendale (Calif.) Adventist Med. Ctr., 1933-34; instr. various flower show schs., Nat. Coun. State Garden Clubs, U.S. & Mex., 1951-98; flower design instr. Edinburg (Tex.) Coll., 1953; founder, chmn. World Flower Festival L.A. Garden Club and Greater L.A. Dist. Calif. Garden Clubs, Inc., 1962-98; lectr. in many states including Hawaii. Author: Arrangements on Parade, 1950; co-author: Wildflower Expression, 1995; contbr. photographs of flower arrangements to profl. jours. Mem. City of Glendale Beautification adv. council, 1974—, L.A. County Med. Auxillary, Glendale, 1956—; election precinct officer L.A. County, Glendale, 1956—; founder The Golden Garden Angel fund, 1998. Recipient numerous Garden Club awards 1962-89. Mem. Ikabana Internat. (L.A. chpt.), Judges Council So. Calif., Judges Council Orange County, L.A. Garden Club., Inc. Avocations: flower arranging, gardening, gourmet cooking, interior decorating, happy family.

FREUD, NICHOLAS S., lawyer; b. N.Y.C., Feb. 6, 1942; s. Frederick and Fredericka (von Rothenburg) F.; m. Elsa Doskow, July 23, 1966; 1 child, Christopher. AB, Yale U., 1963, JD, 1966. Bar: N.Y. 1968, Calif. 1970, U.S. Tax Ct. 1973. Ptnr. Chickering & Gregory, San Francisco, 1978-85, Russin & Vecchi, San Francisco, 1986-93, Jeffer, Mangels, Butler & Marmaro, LLP, San Francisco, 1993—; Mem. joint adv. bd. Calif. Continuing Edn. of Bar, chair taxation subcom. 1987-87; mem. fgn. income adv. bd. Tax Management Internat. Jour., mem. bd. advs. The Jour. of Internat. Taxation; mem. adv. bd. NYU Inst. on Fed. Taxation. Author: (with Charles G. Stephenson and K. Bruce Friedman) International Estate Planning, rev. edit., 1997; contbr. articles to profl. jours. Fellow Am. Coll. of Tax Counsel (cert. specialist in taxation law) mem. ABA (tax sect. coun. dir. 1995-97, chair com. on U.S. activities of foreigners and tax treaties 1989-91, vice chair 1987-89, chair subcom. on tax treaties 1981-87), Calif. State Bar Assn. (taxation sect. exec. com. 1981-85, vice chair 1982-83, chair 1983-84, vice chair income tax com. 1981-82, chair 1982-83, vice chair personal income tax subcom. 1979-80, chair 1980-81, co-chair fgn. tax subcom. 1978-79), N.Y. State Bar Assn. (taxation sect., mem. com. on U.S. activities of fgn. taxpayers and fgn. activities of U.S. taxpayers), Bar Assn. of San Francisco, Bar Assn. of City of N.Y., San Francisco Tax Club (pres. 1988), San Francisco Internat. Tax Group. Office: Jeffer Mangels Butler & Marmaro LLP 1 Sansome St Fl 12 San Francisco CA 94104-4430

FREUDENTHAL, DAVID D., prosecutor. U.S. atty. for Wyo. U.S. Dept. Justice, Cheyenne. Office: US Atty Dist Wyo 2120 Capitol Ave Rm 4002 Cheyenne WY 82001-3633*

FREY, GERRARD RUPERT (GARY FREY), management executive; b. Medicine Hat, Alta., Can., June 7, 1943; s. Walter and Margaret (Materi) F.; m. Karen Martha Johnson, Aug. 27, 1968; children: Samantha Elizabeth, Jonathan Edward. B of Comm. with Distinction, U. Calgary, Alta., 1970; MBA, Harvard U., 1972. Sr. exec. Prin. Group, Edmonton, Alta., 1972-73; dir., v.p. Collective Securities Ltd., Edmonton, 1972-73; program mgr. Banff (Alta.) Ctr. for Mgmt., 1974-75; mgr. fin. svcs. The Banff Ctr., 1976-81, v.p. fin. and adminstrn., 1981-87; v.p. Banff Ctr. for Mgmt., 1981-83; acting pres. The Banff Ctr., 1991-93, exec. v.p., 1987—; chmn., pres., Exdev Cons. Ltd., Banff, 1974—; chmn. Sunshine Village Corp., Banff, 1983-89. Councillor Can. West Found., Calgary, 1983-95; founding dir., chmn. Banff/Lake Louise Tourism Bur., 1990-91; chmn. Assn. for Mountain Parks Protection and Enjoyment, 1994-96; elected trustee Banff Sch. Dist., 1990-92. Capt. Royal Can. Armoured Militia Corps, 1967-70. Recipient Commemorative medal 125th Anniversary of Can. Confedn., 1992. Mem. Can. Com. for Triple E. Senate, Can. Assn. Univ. Bus. Officers, Banff-Lake Louise C. of C. (pres. 1988-90), Banff Springs Golf Club, Harvard Bus. Sch. Club of Calgary, Riverside Golf and Country Club. Avocations: golf, skiing, music, books. Home: Box 698, 115 St Julien Rd, Banff, AB Canada TOL OCO Office: The Banff Ctr, Box 1020, Banff, AB Canada TOL OCO

FREY, KATIE MANCIET, educational administrator; b. Tucson, Ariz., Dec. 31, 1952; d. Hector Encinas and Lilian Eloisa (Hanna) Manciet; m. Richard Patrick Frey, Jul. 20, 1974; 1 child, Stacy Ann. BS, U. Ariz., 1974, MEd, 1982, PhD, 1987. Tchr. physical edn. Amphitheater Pub. Schs., Tucson, 1974-81, rsch. specialist, 1982-85, dir. rsch. & devel., 1985-88, asst. supt., 1988-89, assoc. supt., 1989-98; gymnastics coach Amphitheater Pub. Schs., Tucson, 1974-81, rsch chair Ad Hoc Adv. Coun. on Sch. Dropouts, Ariz., 1987, mem. Gov. Edn. Conf., Ariz., 1989, mem. State Supr. Task Force on Sch. Violence, Ariz., 1993-94, Mayor's Sch. Dist. Action Task Force, Tucson. 1993—; mem. NCAA recertification equity subcom. U. Ariz., 1997-98. Mem. APEX, Tucson, 1987—, Traveler's Aid Soc. of Tucson, 1993-98, Citizen's Adv. Coun. U. Ariz., 1994—; mem. tech. adv. bd. Town of Oro Valley, 1995-96; mem. exec. steering com. K-16 Edn. Coun. So. Ariz.; bd. dirs. YWCA, 1999—. Recipient APEX Apple award U. Ariz., 1994. Mem. Assn. for Supervision and Curriculum Devel., Nat. Organ. for Women, Am. Assn. of U. Women, U. Ariz. Hispanic Alumni Assn., Coll. Assn. for the Devel. and Renewal of Edn., U. Ariz. Letterwinners Club. Avocations: reading, traveling, family, Tai Chi.

FREYD, WILLIAM PATTINSON, fund raising executive, consultant; b. Chgo., Apr. 1, 1933; s. Paul Robert Freyd and Pauline Margaret (Pattinson) Gardiner; m. Diane Marie Carlson, May 19, 1984. BS in Fgn. Svc., Georgetown U., 1960. Field rep. Georgetown U., Washington, 1965-67; campaign dir. Tamblyn and Brown, N.Y.C., 1967-70; dir. devel. St. George's Ch., N.Y.C., 1971; assoc. Browning Assocs., Newark, 1972-73; regional v.p. C.W. Shaver Co., N.Y.C., 1973-74; founder IDC, Henderson, Nev., 1974—. Inventor PHONE/MAIL program. Bd. dirs. Nev. Symphony Orch., 1994—, N.J. Symphony Orch., 1991-94; apptd. Nev. Charitable Solicitation Task Force, 1994. Mem. Nat. Soc. Fund Raising Execs. (nat. treas. 1980-81, pres. N.Y. chpt. 1974-76, cert. 1982), Am. Assn. Fund Raising Counsel (sec. 1984-86), World Fund Raising Coun. (bd. dirs. 1995—, treas. 1998—), Georgetown U. Regional Club Coun., N.Y. Yacht Club, Union League Club N.Y., Masons, Nassau Club, Circumnavigators Club (regional club coun. 1996—). Achievements include the invention of the Phone Mail Program. Office: IDC The IDC Ctr 2920 N Green Valley Pkwy Henderson NV 89014-0406

FREYER, JAMES PAUL, tumor biologist, educator; b. Pitts., Nov. 4, 1954; s. Albert M. and Mary F.; m. Shari Elliott; children: Emily Anne, Kevin Michael, Dylan Edward. BA in Physics, LaSalle Coll., Phila., 1976; MS in Biophysics, U. Rochester, N.Y., 1978, PhD in Biophysics, 1982. Grad. fellow dept. radiation biology and biophysics U. Rochester, 1976-81; dir.'s postdoctoral fellow Toxicology Group Los Alamos (N.Mex.) Nat. Lab., 1982-84, staff mem., 1984-87, staff mem. Cell Biology Group, 1987—, chairperson instl. biosafety com., 1988—; clin. prof. dept. cell biology and physiology U. N.Mex., 1998—; instr. Coll. Sci., Rochester Inst. Tech., 1978-81; instr. pharmacology dept. U. N.Mex., Albuquerque, 1982-86; judge N.Mex. Regional Sci. Fair, 1987—; tchr. Los Alamos Student Sci. Program, 1988-92; presenter to outside groups through Los Alamos Nat. Lab. Ednl. Outreach Office, 1990—; mentor Los Alamos Nat. Lab.-sponsored programs for H.S., undergrad. and grad. students, H.S. and coll. tchrs., 1990—; presenter N.Mex. Acad. Scis. Vis. Scientist Program, 1992—; NIH site rev. com. U. Tex., San Antonio, 1990; ad hoc reviewer radiation study sect., diagnostic radiology study sect. NIH, 1992—, NIH site rev. com. Core Grant, NMR Facility, Fox Chase Cancer Ctr., 1996; ad hoc reviewer Nat. Cancer Inst. Can., 1996. Assoc. editor Internat. Jour. Radiation Oncology, Biology and Physics, 1989—; reviewer manuscripts Cancer Rsch., Radiation Rsch., Internat. Jour. Oncology, Biology and Physics, Internat. Jour. Radiation Biology, Internat. Jour. Cancer, Jour. Cellular Physiology, Brit. Jour. Cancer, Cytometry, Cellular Proliferation, Magnetic Resonance in Medicine; contbr. articles to profl. jours.; chpts. to books. Grantee Nat. Cancer Inst., 1984, 87, 91, 96, 98, Los Alamos Nat. Lab., 1994, U.S.-Israeli Binat. Sci. Found., 1994, Nat. Inst. Environ. Health Scis., 1996. Mem. AAAS, Radiation Rsch. Soc., Internat. Soc. Magnetic Resonance Medicine, Am. Assn. Cancer Rsch. Achievements include patent on method for rapid isolation of sensitive mutants; avocations: skiing, National Ski Patrol, soccer referee. Office: Los Alamos Nat Lab Mail Stop M888 Los Alamos NM 87545

FREYERMUTH, GUNDOLF S., writer; b. Hannover, Germany, Jan. 3, 1955; s. Georg and Ursula (Toennies) Schneider-Freyermuth; m. Elke M.M. Waldvogel, Dec. 23, 1983; children: Leon Sebastian, George Samuel. MA in Comparative Lit., Free U., Berlin, 1979. Sr. editor TransAtlantik, Munich, 1981-82; sr. editor, writer Stern Mag., Hamburg, Germany, 1983-90; advisor to editor-in-chief Elle Mag., Munich, 1990-92; head reporter Tempo Mag., Hamburg, 1992-94; lectr. Free U., Berlin, 1985-90. Author: The Way Out, 1989, Bogart's Brother (writing as John Cassar), 1997, A Travel Into a Past Lost, 1990, Endgamer, 1993, Spy Among the Stars, 1994, Cyberland, 1996, That's It. Last Words with Charles Bukowski, 1996. Home and Office: PO Box 1001 Canyon Creek Ranch Snowflake AZ 85937

FRICK See GROEBLI, WERNER FRITZ

FRICK, OSCAR LIONEL, physician, educator; b. N.Y.C., Mar. 12, 1923; s. Oscar and Elizabeth (Ringger) F.; m. Mary Hubbard, Sept. 2, 1954. A.B., Cornell U., 1944, M.D., 1946; M.Med. Sci., U. Pa., 1960; Ph.D., Stanford U., 1964. Diplomate: Am. Bd. Allergy and Immunology (chmn. 1967-72). Intern Babies Hosp., Columbia Coll. Physicians and Surgeons, N.Y.C., 1946-47; resident Children's Hosp., Buffalo, 1950-51; pvt. practice medicine specializing in pediatrics Huntington, N.Y., 1951-58; fellow in allergy and immunology Royal Victoria Hosp., Montreal, Que., Can., 1958-59; fellow in allergy U. Calif.-San Francisco, 1959-60, asst. prof. pediatrics, 1964-67, assoc. prof., 1967-72, prof., 1972—, dir. allergy tng. program, 1964—; fellow immunology Inst. d'Immunobiologie, Hosp. Broussais, Paris, France, 1960-62. Contbr. articles papers to profl. publs. Served with M.C., USNR, 1947-49. Mem. Am. Assn. Immunologists, Am. Acad. Pediatrics (chmn. allergy sect. 1971-72, Bret Ratner award 1982), Am. Acad. Allergy (exec. com. 1972—, pres. 1977-78), Internat. Assn. Allergology and Clin. Immunology (exec. com. 1970-73, sec. gen. 1985—), Am. Pediatric Soc. Club: Masons. Home: 370 Parnassus Ave San Francisco CA 94117-3609

FRIDAY, KATHERINE ORWOLL, artist; b. Granite Falls, Minn., Dec. 3, 1917; d. Melvin Sylvester and Anna Elizabeth (Hustvedt) Orwoll; m. Erling Bjarne Struxness, May 8, 1943 (div. 1961); children: John Eric Struxness, Mimi Ann McNicholas, Martha Jane Begin; m. George Edward Friday, Apr. 12, 1969 (dec. Jan. 1997). Student, U. Minn., 1935-36, 40-41, Frederick Mizen Sch. of Art, Chgo., 1941. Designer, illustrator Josten's, Owatonna, Minn., 1936-39, 42-43; layout artist Tempo Inc., Chgo., 1941-42, Vogue-wright Studios, Chgo., 1943-44; layout, illustration Allan D Parson Advt. Agy., Chgo., 1945, Ad-Art, Wichita, Kans., 1952-54, 63; indsl. designer Harold W. Darr Assoc., Mpls., 1959-61; layout, illustration Lydiard Assoc., Mpls., 1961-64; owner Skyline Studio, Mpls., 1964-66; layout, illustration Comm. Cons., Wilmington, Del., 1971; freelance illustration, med. illustration dept. pathology U. Chgo., Chgo., 1946-48; freelance illustrator Hutchinson, Kans., 1948-58; art dir. SPF Adv., Intermedia, Mpls., 1966-69, Arne Westerman Adv., Portland, Oreg., 1970-71, Battle Advt., Wyncote, Pa., 1971-72; creative dir., owner A'La Carte Advt./Art, Bellevue, Wash., 1973-77; graphic illustration Courseware, Moffat Field, Mountain View, Quantic, Los Altos, Calif., 1978-81; ret., 1981. Exhibited at Westminster Gallery, London, 1995; represented by Northridge Art Gallery, Ridgefield, Conn., Gallery 33, Portland, Rental Sales Gallery, Portland Art Mus. Recipient Best of Show award Internat. Miniature Art Show, Kirkland, Wash., 1997. Mem. Colored Pencil Soc. Am., Miniature Artists of Am. (signature), Miniature Art Soc. Fla. (1st pl. 1189-90, 97-98, 2d pl. 1994, 95, 99), Ga. Miniature Artist Soc. (1st pl. 1991, 94, 2d pl. and 3d pl. 1990, Merit award 1997), Miniature Painters, Sculptors, Gravers Soc. (assoc.; Washington, 1st pl. 1996, 3rd pl. 1990, 1st of show 1998), Oreg. Soc. of Artists, Main St. Artists, Cider Painters of Am. (1st in floral 1993, still life 1995, protrait 1998, award of excellence 1992, 93, 94, 97), NorthWest Watercolor Soc. (assoc.), Watercolor Soc. Oreg. (assoc., Award of Achievement spring show 1998), Colored Pencil Soc. Oreg. Avocations: painting, drawing, reading, music.

FRIDLEY, SAUNDRA LYNN, internal audit executive; b. Columbus, Ohio, June 14, 1948; d. Jerry Dean and Esther Eliza (Bluhm) F. BS, Franklin U., 1976; MBA, Golden Gate U., 1980. Accounts receivable supr. Internat. Harvester, Columbus, Ohio, San Leandro, Calif., 1972-80; sr. internal auditor Western Union, San Francisco, 1980; internal auditor II, County of Santa Clara, San Jose, Calif., 1980-82; sr. internal auditor Tymshare, Inc., Cupertino, Calif., 1982-84, div. contr., 1984; internal audit mgr. VWR Scientific, Brisbane, Calif., 1984-88, audit dir., 1988-89; internal audit mgr. Pacific IBM Employees Fed. Credit Union, San Jose, 1989-90, Westaff, Inc., Walnut Creek, Calif., 1990—, dir. quality assurance, 1992-98, v.p. audit and investigations, 1998—; owner Dress Fore the 9's, Brentwood, Calif., 1994—; pres., founder Bay Area chpt. Cert. Fraud Examiners, 1990. Mem. NAFE, Friends of the Vineyards, Internal Auditors Speakers Bur., Assn. Cert. Fraud Examiners (founder, pres. Bay area chpt., we. regional gov. 1996-97, Disting. Achievement award 1997), Inst. Internal Auditors (pres., founder Tri-Valley chpt.), Internal Auditor's Internat. Seminar Com., Internal Auditor's Internat. Conf. Com. Avocations: woodworking, gardening, golfing. Home: 19 Windmill Ct Brentwood CA 94513-2502 Office: Western Staff Svcs 301 Lennon Ln Walnut Creek CA 94598-2418 also: Dress Fore The 9's 613 1st St Ste 19 Brentwood CA 94513-1322

FRIED, ELAINE JUNE, business executive; b. L.A., Oct. 19, 1943; grad. Pasadena (Calif.) H.S.; various coll. courses; m. Howard I. Fried, Aug. 7, 1966; children: Donnoven Michael, Randall Jay. Agt., office mgr. Howard I. Fried Agy., Alhambra, Calif., 1975—; v.p. Sea Hill, Inc., Pasadena, 1973-95. Publicity chmn., unit telephone chmn. San Gabriel Valley unit Am. Diabetes Assn., past chmn., vol. lobbyist, mem. patient edn. com. region II Calif. chpt., 1998; past publicity chmn. San Gabriel Valley region Women's Am. Orgn. for Rehab. Tng. (ORT); chmn. spl. events publicity, Temple Beth Torah Sisterhood, Alhambra, membership chmn., 1991-92, v.p. membership, 1991-93; former mem. bd. dirs., pub. relations com., pers. com. Vis. Nurses Assn., Pasadena and San Gabriel Valley; chmn. outside Sisterhood publicity Congregation Shaarei Torah, 1993, pub. rels. chmn., 1993—. Recipient Vol. award So. Calif. affiliate Am. Diabetes Assn., 1974-77, 25 Yr. Vol. Svc. award, 1996, cert. of appreciation, 1987; co-recipient Ner Tamid award Temple Beth Torah. Contbr. articles to profl. jours. Mem. ORT, Hadassah, Greater Pasadena Assn. Life Underwriters (co-v.p. cmty. affairs 1998—). Speaker on psycho-social aspects of diabetes, insurance and the diabetic, ins. medicine. Home: 404 N Hidalgo Ave Alhambra CA 91801-2640

FRIED, IAN NATHAN, writer; b. Akron, Ohio, Dec. 17, 1974; s. Michael I. and Dorothy Maxine (Nathan) F. Cert., U. Amsterdam, The Netherlands, 1995; BA, Miami U. Oxford, Ohio, 1996. Bus. writer Glendale (Calif.) News Press, Calif, 1994; fed. ct. reporter City News Svc., L.A., 1995; reporting intern The Cin. Enquirer, 1995-96, The Plain Dealer, Cleve., 1996; staff writer The Orange County Register, Anaheim, Calif., 1996-97, Orange County Bus. Journ., Newport Beach, Calif., 1997-99; semicondr. writer Bridge News, San Francisco, 1999—. Recipient 3d pl. Best Environ. Reporting, Orange County Fair, 1997, 2d pl. Breaking News story, Orange County Fair, 1997. Mem. Soc. Profl. Jounalists, Orange County Press Club (2d pl. Best Reporting 1997). Office: 44 Montgomery St Ste 2410 San Francisco CA 94104

FRIED, LOUIS LESTER, information technology and management consultant; b. N.Y.C., Jan. 18, 1930; s. Albert and Tessie (Klein) F.; m. Haya Greenberg, Aug. 15, 1960; children: Ron Chaim, Eliana Ahuva, Gil Ben. BA in Pub. Adminstrn., Calif. State U., Los Angeles, 1962; MS in Mgmt. Theory, Calif. State U., Northridge, 1965. Mgr. br. plant data processing Litton systems, Inc., Woodland Hills, Calif., 1960-65; dir. mgmt. info. systems Bourns, Inc., Riverside, Calif., 1965-68, Weber Aircraft Co., Burbank, Calif., 1968-69; v.p. mgmt. services T.I. Corp. of Calif., Los Angeles, 1969-75; dir. advanced computer systems dept. Stanford Research Inst., Menlo Park, Calif., 1976-85, dir. ctr. for info. tech., 1985-86, dir. worldwide info. tech. practice, 1987-90; v.p. info. tech. cons. Stanford Rsch. Inst., Menlo Park, Calif., 1990-97; spl. advisor to pres. TELUS Corp., Edmonton, Alta., Can., 1997-98; info. tech. mgmt. cons., 1998—; lectr. U. Calif., Riverside, 1965-69, lectr. mgmt. and EDP. Contbr. numerous articles to profl. jours., 2 textbooks. E-mail: LLFRIED@aol.com. Fax: 650-493-8712. Home: 788 Loma Verde Ave Palo Alto CA 94303-4147 also: King George V St 16B 7th Fl #14, Jerusalem 94229, Israel

FRIEDEWALD, WILLIAM R., animator, consultant; b. N.Y.C., June 12, 1969; s. Walter Maxemillian and Ligia (Davilas) F. BA, Hampshire Coll., 1991. Image processing artist Intouch Group, San Francisco, 1992-93; illustrator Soft Ad Group, Mill Valley, Calif., 1992-93; 2 dimensional character animator Equilibrium, Sausalito, Calif., 1993, Software Toolworks, San Rafael, Calif., 1993; 2 dimensional interface designer, illustrator, photoprocessor Books Than Work, Palo Alto, Calif., 1993; 3 dimensional illustrator, online interface designer Apple, Inc., Cupertino, Calif., 1993; digital art and designer NOVO Media, San Francisco, 1993; 3 dimensional animator, character designer PF Magic, San Francisco, 1993-94; instr. 3 dimensional animation Acad. Art Coll., San Francisco, 1996—. Creator 3 dimensional proto type E World on-line svc. Apple, Inc., 1993; interactive advertisement Kohler Bathroom Products, 1993; 3 dimensional animation for various video and computer games, 1995-96. Avocations: scuba diver, musician, martial arts. Office: PF Magic 501 2nd St San Francisco CA 94107-1469

FRIEDHOFF, RICHARD MARK, computer scientist, entrepreneur; b. N.Y.C., Dec. 2, 1953; s. Arnold Jerome and Frances (Galanter) F.; m. Livia R. Antola, May 5, 1988 (div. 1995). BA, Columbia U., 1976; MA, Yale U., 1978. Sci. cons. PBS's The Brain, N.Y.C., 1978-80; industry adviser Polaroid Corp., Cambridge, Mass., 1981-82; v.p. Internat. Sci. Exch., N.Y.C., 1982-85;, 1986-93; CEO, dir. rsch. InGen Corp., San Francisco, 1994—, 1994—; pres., dir. rsch. Visicom Corp.; cons. U. Calif., 1990-91, Silicon Graphics Inc., Rowland Inst. Sci., Polaroid Corp. Dolby Labs. Edge Sci.; spkr. Smith-

sonian Instn., also various corps. and sci. socs., 1989—. Author: Visualization: The 2nd Computer Revolution, 1989, 2d edit., 1991; contbr. articles to profl. jours. Dir. S & A Friedhoff Found. Fellow AAAS; mem. IEEE, Soc. for Photo Optical Instrumentation, Assn. for Computing Machinery, Authors Guild of Am., N.Y. Acad. Scis., Phi Beta Kappa. Office: InGen Corp 235 Montgomery St Ste 300 San Francisco CA 94104-2905

FRIEDKIN, NOAH ENTON, sociologist, educator; b. Chgo., Mar. 31, 1947; s. Morris Enton and Roberta F.; m. Ellen Anne, Dec. 10, 1978; children: Jessica, Anna. BA, U. Chgo., 1969, PhD, 1977. Prof. U. Calif., Santa Barbara, 1978—. Author: A Structural Theory of Social Influence, 1998. Mem. Am. Sociol. Assn. Office: Univeristy of California Dept of Sociology Santa Barbara CA 93106

FRIEDL, RANDALL RAYMOND, environmental scientist; b. San Fernando, Calif., Jan. 18, 1957; s. Raymond Joseph and Ione Louise (Anderson) F.; m. Myrna Wijmer, Dec. 20, 1980. BS, UCLA, 1978; MA, Harvard U., 1980, PhD, 1984. From rsch. assoc. to group supr. JPL, Pasadena, Calif., 1984-94, rsch. scientist, 1997—; lead scientist Jet Propulsion Lab., 1998—; project scientist NASA, Washington, 1994-96. Assessment chairperson (NASA publ.) Atmospheric Effects of Subsonic Aircraft, 1997; coord. lead author: Intergovernmental Panel on Climate Change Special Report on Aviation and the Global Environment, 1999; contbr. over 30 articles to profl. jours., chpts. to books. Mem. ACS, Am. Geophys. Union, Sigma Xi. Achievements include research on chemistry of importance to understanding anthropogenic impacts on earth's atmosphere. Office: Jet Propulsion Lab Mailstop 183-901 4800 Oak Grove Dr Pasadena CA 91109-8001

FRIEDLANDER, CHARLES DOUGLAS, space consultant; b. N.Y.C., Oct. 5, 1928; s. Murray L. and Jeane (Sottosanti) F.; m. Diane Mary Hutchins, May 12, 1951; children: Karen Diane, Lauren Patrice, Joan Elyse. BS, U.S. Mil. Acad., 1950; exec. mgmt. program, NASA, 1965; grad., Command and Staff Coll. USAF, 1965, Air War Coll. USAF, 1966. Commd. 2d lt. U.S. Army, 1950, advanced through grades to 1st lt.; officer inf. U.S. Army, Korea, 1950-51; resigned U.S. Army, 1954; mem. staff UN Forces, Trieste, Italy, 1953-54; chief astronaut support office NASA, Cape Canaveral, Fla., 1963-67; space cons. CBS News, N.Y.C., 1967-69; exec. asst. The White House, Washington, 1969-71; v.p. bd. dirs. Internat. Aerospace Hall of Fame, San Diego; space program cons., various cos., Boca Raton, Fla., 1967-69; mem. staff First Postwar Fgn. Ministers Conf., Berlin, 1954; radio/TV cons. space program. Author: Buying & Selling Land for Profit, 1961, Last Man at Hungnam Beach, 1952. V.p. West Point Soc., Cape Canaveral, Fla., 1964. Served to lt. col. USAFR, maj. USAR. Decorated Bronze Star V, Combat Inf. badge; co-recipient Emmy award CBS TV Apollo Moon Landing, 1960; recipient medal of honor N.Y.C., 1951. Mem. Explorer's Club, West Point Soc., Chosin Few Survivors Korea, NASA Alumni League, Nat. Space Soc. Avocations: fishing, travel.

FRIEDMAN, ALAN E., lawyer; b. N.Y.C., May 5, 1946. BA, Amherst Coll., 1967; JD, Stanford U., 1970. Bar: Calif. 1971. Atty. Tuttle & Taylor, L.A., 1970—. Note editor: Stanford Law Rev., 1969-70. Office: Tuttle & Taylor 355 S Grand Ave Fl 40 Los Angeles CA 90071-1560*

FRIEDMAN, MILTON, economist, educator emeritus, author; b. Brooklyn, N.Y., July 31, 1912; s. Jeno Saul and Sarah Ethel (Landau) F.; m. Rose Director, June 25, 1938; children: Janet, David. AB, Rutgers U., 1932, LLD (hon.), 1968; AM, U. Chgo., 1933; PhD, Columbia U., 1946; LLD (hon.), St. Paul's (Rikkyo) U., 1963, Loyola U., 1971, U. N.H., 1975, Harvard U., 1979, Brigham Young U., 1980, Dartmouth Coll., 1980, Gonzaga U., 1981; DSc (hon.), Rochester U., 1971; LHD (hon.), Rockford Coll., 1969, Roosevelt U., 1975, Hebrew Union Coll., L.A., 1981, Jacksonville U., 1993; LittD (hon.), Bethany Coll., 1971; PhD (hon.), Hebrew U., Jerusalem, 1977; DCS (hon.), Francisco Marroquin U., Guatemala, 1978; D honoris causa, Econ. U. Prague, 1997. Assoc. economist Nat. Resources Com., Washington, 1935-37; mem. research staff Nat. Bur. Econ. Research, N.Y.C., 1937-45, 1948-81; vis. prof. econs. U. Wis., Madison, 1940-41; prin. economist, tax research div. U.S. Treasury Dept., Washington, 1941-43; assoc. dir. research, statis. research group, War Research div. Columbia U., N.Y.C., 1943-45; assoc. prof. econs. and statistics U. Minn., Mpls., 1945-46; assoc. prof. econs. U. Chgo., 1946-48, prof. econs., 1948-62, Paul Snowden Russell disting. service prof. econs., 1962-82, prof. emeritus, 1983—; Fulbright lectr. Cambridge U., 1953-54; vis. Wesley Clair Mitchell research prof. econs. Columbia U., N.Y.C., 1964-65; fellow Ctr. for Advanced Study in Behavioral Sci., 1957-58; sr. research fellow Hoover Inst., Stanford U., 1977—; mem. Pres.'s Commn. All-Vol. Army, 1969-70, Pres.'s Commn. on White House Fellows, 1971-74, Pres.'s Econ. Policy Adv. Bd., 1981-88; vis. scholar Fed. Res. Bank, San Francisco, 1977. Author: (with Carl Shoup and Ruth P. Mack) Taxing to Prevent Inflation, 1943; (with Simon S. Kuznets) Income from Independent Professional Practice, 1946; (with Harold A. Freeman, Frederic Mosteller, W. Allen Wallis) Sampling Inspection, 1948, Essays in Positive Economics, 1953, A Theory of the Consumption Function, 1957, A Program for Monetary Stability, 1960, Price Theory: A Provisional Text, 1962; (with Rose D. Friedman) Capitalism and Freedom, 1962, (with R.D. Friedman) Free To Choose, 1980, Tyranny of the Status Quo, 1984, Two Lucky People: Memoirs, 1998; (with Anna J. Schwartz) A Monetary History of the United States, 1867-1960, 1963; (with Schwartz) Monetary Statistics of the United States, 1970, Monetary Trends in the U.S. and the United Kingdom, 1982, Inflation: Causes and Consequences, 1963; (with Robert Roosa) The Balance of Payments: Free vs. Fixed Exchange Rates, 1967, Dollars and Deficits, 1968, The Optimum Quantity of Money and Other Essays, 1969; (with Walter W. Heller) Monetary vs. Fiscal Policy, 1969, A Theoretical Framework for Monetary Analysis, 1972; (with Wilbur J. Cohen) Social Security, 1972, An Economist's Protest, 1972, There's No Such Thing As A Free Lunch, 1975, Price Theory, 1976; (with Robert J. Gordon et al.) Milton Friedman's Monetary Framework, 1974, Tax Limitation, Inflation and the Role of Government, 1978, Bright Promises, Dismal Performance, 1983, Money Mischief, 1992; (with Thomas S. Szasz) Friedman & Szasz on Drugs: Essays on the Free Market and Prohibition, 1992; editor: Studies in the Quantity Theory of Money, 1956; bd. editors Am. Econ. Rev, 1951-53, Econometrica, 1957-69; adv. bd. Jour. Money, Credit and Banking, 1968-94; columnist Newsweek mag, 1966-84, contbg. editor, 1971-84; contbr. articles to profl. jours. Chmn. bd. dirs. Milton and Rose D. Friedman Found. Decorated Grand Cordon of the 1st Class Order of the Sacred Treasure (Japan); recipient Nobel prize in econs., 1976, Pvt. Enterprise Exemplar medal Freedoms Found., 1978, Presdl. medal of Freedom, 1988, Nat. Medal of Sci., 1988, Prize in Moral-Cultural Affairs, Instn. World Capitalism, 1993; named Chicagoan of Yr., Chgo. Press Club, 1972, Educator of Yr., Chgo. Jewish United Fund, 1973, Source award for lifetime achievement The Primary Source, Tufts U., 1997, Robert Maynard Hutchins History Maker award for distinction in edn. Chgo. Hist. Soc., 1997, Templeton Honor Rolls Lifetime Achievement award, 1997, Goldwater award, 1997. Fellow Inst. Math. Stats., Am. Statis. Assn., Econometric Soc.; mem. NAS, Am. Econ. Assn. (exec. com. 1955-57, pres. 1967; John Bates Clark medal 1951), Am. Enterprise Inst. (adv. bd. 1956-79), Western Econ. Assn. (pres. 1984-85), Royal Economic Soc., Am. Philos. Soc., Mont Pelerin Soc. (bd. dirs. 1958-61, pres. 1970-72), Quadrangle Club. Office: Stanford U Hoover Instn Stanford CA 94305-6010

FRIEDMAN, PAULA NAOMI, museum public relations director; b. Washington, Feb. 22, 1939; d. Melvin Hillard and Beatrice Patricia (Zisman) F.; children: Carl, Joseph. BA, Cornell U., 1961; MA, San Francisco State U., 1965; MLS, U. Calif., Berkeley, 1975. Asst. libr. Woodward-Clyde Corp., Emeryville, Calif., 1976-77; freelance editor Berkeley, Calif., 1978-82, 88—; prodn. editor Ednl. Products Info. Exch. Western Office, Berkeley, 1984-85; libr. Berkeley Pub. Libr., 1984-93; pub. rels. dir. Judah L. Magnes Mus., Berkeley, 1985—; publicist Caring Ctr., Univ. Ave. Coop. Homes, Berkeley, 1979-92; dir. nationwide Rosenberg Poetry Award, 1986—.. Author: (story) Prayer, Roses, Merry Christmas, and others, 1969—, (poem) Inside the Axioms, Minotaur, and others, 1969—; founding and coordinating editor, Open Cell rev., 1969-75; editor: Sam Hamburg, 1989, In Their Own [illegible] Dreams, 1998 and others; reporter Grassroots, Berkeley Barb, other weekly newspapers, 1966-69, 76-78; poetry editor Berkeley Insider, 1994-96; author essays. Publicist Bay Area Adoption Registration Day Coalition, 1996. Mem. Am. Assn. Mus., Bay Area Mus. Publicists' Roundtable, No. Calif. Book Publicists' Assn., Sierra Club, Gray Panthers. Avocations: writing, photography, Sierra hiking.

FRIEDMAN, SHELLY ARNOLD, cosmetic surgeon; b. Providence, Jan. 1, 1949; s. Saul and Estelle (Moverman) F.; m. Andrea Leslie Falchook, Aug. 30, 1975; children: Bethany Erin, Kimberly Rebecca, Brent David, Jennifer Ashley. BA, Providence Coll., 1971; DO, Mich. State U., 1982. Diplomate Nat. Bd. Med. Examiners, Am. Bd. Dermatology. Intern Pontiac (Mich.) Hosp., 1982-83, resident in dermatology, 1983-86; assoc. clin. prof. dept. internal med. Mich. State U., 1984-89, adj. clin. prof., 1989—; med. dir. Inst. Cosmetic Dermatology, Scottsdale, Ariz., 1986—; pres. Am. Bd. Hair Restoration Surgery. Contbr. aritcles to profl. jours. Mem. B'nai B'rith Men's Council, 1973, Jewish Welfare Fund, 1973. Am. Physicians fellow for medicine, 1982. Mem. AMA, Am. Osteopathic Assn., Am. Assn. Cosmetic Surgeons, Am. Acad. Cosmetic Surgery, Internat. Soc. Dermatologic Surgery, Internat. Acad. Cosmetic Surgery, Am. Acad. Dermatology, Am. Soc. Dermatol. Surgery, Frat. Order Police, Sigma Sigma Phi. Jewish. Avocations: karate, horseback riding. Office: Scottsdale Inst Cosmetic Dermatology 5206 N Scottsdale Rd Scottsdale AZ 85253-7006

FRIEND, DAVID ROBERT, chemist; b. Vallejo, Calif., Aug. 10, 1956; s. Carl Gilbert and Roberta (Schwarzrock) F.; m. Carol Esther Warren, Dec. 17, 1983; 1 child, Ian, Michael. BS in Food Biochemistry, U. Calif., Davis, 1979; PhD in Agrl. Chemistry, U. Calif., Berkeley, 1983. Polymer chemist SRI Internat., Menlo Park, Calif., 1984-87, sr. polymer chemist controlled release and biomed. polymers dept., 1987-90, assoc. dir. controlled release and biomed. polymers dept., 1990-92, dir. controlled release and biomed. polymers dept., 1992-93; exec. dir. rsch. and product devel. Cibus Pharm., Burlingame, Calif., 1993-94; v.p. rsch. and product devel. Cibus Pharm., Redwood City, Calif., 1994-96, v.p., chief scientific officer, 1996—; leader Biopharms. Rsch. Group, 1990; lectr. U. Calif. Sch. Pharmacy, San Francisco. Assoc. editor Jour. Controlled Release; contbr. articles to scholarly jours.; patentee in field. Mem. Controlled Release Soc., Am. Assn. Pharm. Sci. Democrat. Jewish. Avocations: piano, swimming. Home: 454 9th Ave Menlo Park CA 94025-1802

FRIES, LITA LINDA, school system administrator; b. Merced, Calif., Feb. 16, 1942; d. Alfred Earl and Juanita Lora (Brown) Griffey; m. George Richard Fries, Feb. 3, 1962; 1 child, Damon Brant. BA, U. Calif., Berkeley, 1966; MS, Calif. State U., 1976. Cert. elem. tchr., secondary tchr., ednl. administrator, reading specialist. Tchr. Peace Corps, Mwanza, Tanzania, 1963-65; tchr. Oakland (Calif.) Unified Sch. Dist., 1966-74, tchr. spl. assignment, 1974-84, principal, Burckhalter, 1984-85, program mgr., 1985-90, administr., 1990-92, coord. state and fed. programs, 1992-97, dir. elem. edn., 1997—. Mem. Assn. Calif. Sch. Adminstrs., East Bay Reading Assn. (editor 1982-83), Pi Lamda Theta (membership chairperson 1986-88), Delta Kappa Gamma, Phi Delta Kappa. Democrat. Office: Oakland Unified Sch Dist 1025 2nd Ave Oakland CA 94606-2296

FRIESECKE, RAYMOND FRANCIS, health company executive; b. N.Y.C., Mar. 12, 1937; s. Bernhard P. K. and Josephine (De Tomi) F.; BS in Chemistry, Boston Coll., 1959; MS in Civil Engring., MIT, 1961. Product specialist Dewey & Almy Chem. div. W. R. Grace & Co., Inc., Cambridge, Mass., 1963-66; market planning specialist USM Corp., Boston, 1966-71; mgmt. cons., Boston, 1971-74; dir. planning and devel. Schweitzer div. Kimberly-Clark Corp., Lee, Mass., 1974-78; v.p. corp. planning Butler Automatic, Inc., Canton, Mass., 1978-80; pres. Butler-Europe Inc., Greenwich, Conn. and Munich, Germany, 1980; v.p. mktg. and planning Butler Greenwich Inc., 1980-81; pres. Strategic Mgmt. Assocs., San Rafael, Calif., 1981-96; chmn. Beyond Health Corp., 1994—; corp. clk., v.p. Bldg. Research & Devel., Inc., Cambridge, 1966-68. Host, prodr. The Ounce of Prevention Show, Sta. KEST, San Francisco, 1994-98, Stas. KBPA and WNN, 1998—; author: Management by Relative Product Quality, The New Way to Manage; editor Beyond Health News, 1995—; contbr. articles to profl. jours. State chmn. Citizens for Fair Taxation, 1972-73; state co-chmn. Mass. Young Reps., 1967-69; chmn. Ward 7 Rep. Com., Cambridge, 1968-70; vice chmn. Cambridge Rep. City Com., 1966-68; vice-chmn. Kentfield Rehab. Hosp. Found., 1986-88, chmn., 1988-91; Rep. candidate Mass. Ho. of Reps., 1964, 66; pres. Marin Rep. Coun., 1986-91; chmn. Calif. Acad., 1986-88; sec. Navy League Marin Coun., 1984-91, v.p. 94—; bd. dirs. The Marin Ballet, 1996-98. 1st lt. U.S. Army, 1961-63. Mem. NRA, Nat. Health Fedn., Am. Chem. Soc., Physicians Com. for Responsbile Medicine, Marin Philos. Soc. (v.p. 1991-92), Ctr. for Sci. in Pub. Interest, Health Medicine Forum, Orthomolecular Health Medicine Soc., The World Affairs Coun. Home: 141 Convent Ct San Rafael CA 94901-1335 Office: 60 Belvedere St San Rafael CA 94901

FRIESS, DONNA LEWIS, children's rights advocate, writer; b. L.A., Jan. 16, 1943; d. Raymond W. Lewis, Jr. and Dorothy Gertrude (Borwick) McIntyre; m. Kenneth E. Friess, June 20, 1964; children: Erik, Julina, Daniel. BA in Comm., U. So. Calif., 1964; MA in Comm., Calif. State U., Long Beach, 1966; PhD in Psychology, U.S. Internat. U., San Diego, 1993. Cert. tchr., Calif. Prof. human comm. Cypress (Calif.) Coll., 1966—; lectr. survivors of abuse, 1990—, mental health profls., 1990—; CEO Hurt Into Happiness Publishing, 1990—, Hurt Into Happiness Seminars, 1993—; presenter and keynote presenter in field of child abuse, various confs., convs., cmty. groups, workshops, and lawmakers' groups; guest expert (TV shows) Sally Jessy Raphael, 1993, Leeza Gibbons Talk Show, 1994, Sonja: Live, 1994, Oprah Winfrey Show, 1991, many others. Author: Relationships, 1995, Just Between Us: A Guidebook for Survivors of Childhood Trauma, 1995, Cry the Darkness, 1993, European edits. 1995, Danish edit., 1999, Korean edit., 1995, Norwegian edits., 1998, Circle of Love: Secrets to Successful Relationships, 1996, Whispering Waters: The Story of Historic Weesha, 1998; contbr. articles to mags. Recipient Author's award U. Calif. Friends of Libr., 1996, recognition from U.S. Justice Dept. for outstanding efforts to stop child abuse, 1995; nominee for Pres.'s Am. Svc. award, 1996. Mem. Am. Coalition Against Child Abuse (founder), Task Force for ACCA to Educate American Judges on Issues of Sexual Abuse, One Voice, Calif. Psychol. Assn., Western Social Sci. Assn., Child Abuse Listening and Mediating (bd. dirs.), Am. Profl. Soc. on Abuse of Children, Mother Against Sexual Abuse (bd. dirs.), Laura's House for Battered Women (bd. dirs.), Calif. Tchrs. Assn., Faculty Assn. Calif. C.Cs., Speech Communication Assn. of Am., U.S. Internat. U. Alumni Assn. (bd. dirs.). Avocation: painting on porcelain. Office: Cypress College Dept Human Communications Cypress CA 90630

FRIIS, ROBERT HAROLD, epidemiologist, health science educator; b. San Jose, Calif., July 15, 1941; s. Harold Hector and Florence Marie (Brant) F.; m. Carol Ann Speer, Oct. 28, 1966; children: Michelle Alanna, Erik Adler. BA, U. Calif., Berkeley, 1964; MA, Columbia U., N.Y.C., 1966, PhD, 1969. Postdoctoral fellow U. Mich., Ann Arbor, 1969-71; asst. prof. Sch. Pub. Health Columbia U., 1971-74, Albert Einstein Coll. Medicine, Bronx, N.Y., 1974-76; assoc. prof. CUNY, Bklyn. Coll., 1976-78; dir. field epidemiology Orange County Pub. Health, Santa Ana, Calif., 1978-79; assoc. clin. prof. U. Calif., Irvine, 1979-93; prof., chairperson dept. health sci. Calif. State U., Long Beach, 1988—; vis. rschr. Karolinska Inst., Stockholm, Sweden, 1993; dir. Joint Studies Inst., Calif. State U. and VA Med. Ctr. Long Beach, 1995—; mem. vol. faculty Coll. Medicine, U. Calif., Irvine, 1993—; ind. cons. epidemiology, Irvine, 1970—. Sr. author: Epidemiology Public Health Practice, 1996; contbr. articles to sci. jours. Faculty mentor Ptnrs. for Success, Long Beach, 1992—. Grantee, U. Calif., Irvine, 1995, Mexus com. U. Calif., 1988, U. Calif. systemwide, 1988, U. Calif. Tobacco Related Disease Rsch. Program, 1998. Mem. APHA, Am. Parkinsons Disease Assn., Am. Statis. Assn. (So. Calif. sect.), Soc. Epidemiol. Rsch., U. Calif. Berkley Alumni Assn. Democratic. Avocations: reading, travel, coin collecting, computers, gardening. Office: Calif State U Long Beach Dept Health Sci 1250 N Bellflower Blvd Long Beach CA 90840-0006

FRISBEE, DON CALVIN, retired utilities executive; b. San Francisco, Dec. 13, 1923; s. Ira Nobles and Helen (Sheets) F.; m. Emilie Ford, Feb. 5, 1947; children: Ann, Robert, Peter, Dean. BA, Pomona Coll., 1947; MBA, Harvard U., 1949. Sr. investment analyst, asst. cashier investment analysis dept. 1st Interstate Bank Oreg., N.A., Portland, 1949-52; treas. PacifiCorp, Portland, 1958-60, then v.p., exec. v.p., pres., 1966-73, chief exec. officer, 1973-89, chmn., 1973-94; chmn. emeritus PacifiCorp., Portland, 1994-97; bd. dirs. Wells Fargo Bank. Chmn. bd. trustees Reed Coll.; trustee Safari Game Search Found., High Desert Mus.; mem. cabinet Columbia Pacific coun. Boy Scouts Am.; founder Oreg. chpt. Am. Leadership Forum; mem. exec. com. Oreg. Partnership for Internat. Edn. 1st lt. AUS, 1943-46. Mem. Arlington Club, Univ. Club Multnomah Athletic Club, City Club. Office: 1500 SW 1st Ave Portland OR 97201-5815

FRISCHKNECHT, LEE CONRAD, retired broadcasting executive; b. Brigham City, Utah, Jan. 4, 1928; s. Carl Oliver and Geniel (Lund) F.; m. Sara Jean McCulloch, Sept. 3, 1948; children: Diane Frischknecht Etherington, Jill Frischknecht Taylor, Ellen Frischknecht DePola, Amy Frischknecht Blodgett. BS in Speech, Utah State U., 1951; MA in Radio-TV, Mich. State U., 1957. Announcer sta. KID Radio, Idaho Falls, Idaho, 1951-52; producer-director sta. WKAR-TV, East Lansing, Mich., 1953-57, prodn. mgr., 1958-59, program mgr., 1960-61, gen. mgr., 1962-63; dir. sta. rels. Nat. Ednl. TV, N.Y.C., 1964-67; dir. univ. rels. Utah State U., 1969-70; dir. network affairs Nat. Pub. Radio, Washington, 1971, v.p., 1972, pres., 1973-77; communications cons., 1978—; mgr. ed. telecommunications sta. KAET-TV, Phoenix, Ariz., 1980-86; asst. gen. mgr. sta. KAET-TV, Phoenix, 1987-93; assoc. prof. radio-TV, Mich. State U., 1962-63; assoc. prof. speech Utah State U., 1968-69; lectr. Ariz. State U., 1981-82. Bd. dirs. Nat. Pub. Radio, 1973-78, Ariz. Sch. Svcs. Through Ednl. Tech., 1984-93, PSSC Legacy Fund, 1993—; bd. dirs. Pub. Svc. Satellite Consortium, 1982-90, chmn., 1987-90. Recipient Outstanding Alumnus in Communications award Mich. State U., 1973, Meritorious Svc. award in Communications, Brigham Young U., 1974, Disting. Svc. award Pacific Mountain Network, 1987. Mem. LDS Ch. Home: 8100 E Camelback Rd # 180 Scottsdale AZ 85251-2729

FRISK, JACK EUGENE, recreational vehicle manufacturing company executive; b. Nampa, Idaho, Jan. 22, 1942; s. Steinert Paul and Evelyn Mildred (Letner) F.; m. Sharon Rose Caviness, Aug. 3, 1959; 1 dau., Toni. With Ideal of Idaho, Inc., Caldwell, purchasing mgr., 1969-75, gen. mgr., sec.-treas., 1975-82; sales mgr. Traveleze Industries div. Thor Industries, Sun Valley, Calif., 1982-88; owner, pres. Crossroads Industry div. Cross Enterprises Inc., Mesa, Ariz., 1988-92; dir. mktg. western divsn. Chariot Eagle, Inc., Ocala, Fla., 1992-95; gen. mgr. Chariot Eagle West, Inc., Phoenix, 1995-96; tool coord. III The Boeing Co., 1996—. Episcopalian. Home: 1430 N Parsell Cir Mesa AZ 85203-3713 Office: The Boeing Co 5000 E Mcdowell Rd # D178 Mesa AZ 85215-9707

FRITCHER, EARL EDWIN, civil engineer, consultant; b. St. Ansgar, Iowa, Nov. 24, 1923; s. Lee and Mamie Marie (Ogden) F.; m. Dorsille Ellen Simpson, Aug. 24, 1946; 1 child, Teresa. BS, Iowa State U., 1950. Registered civil engr., Calif. Project devel. engr. dept. transp. State of Calif., Los Angeles, 1950-74, traffic engr. dept. transp., 1974-87; pvt. practice cons. engr. Sunland, Calif., 1987—; consulting prin. traffic engr. Parsons DeLeuw Inc., 1990—; cons. traffic engr. DeLeuw Cather Internat., Dubai, United Arab Emerates, 1994. Co-author: Overhead Signs and Contract Sign Plans, 1989; patentee in field. Served to 2d lt. USAF, 1942-46, 50-51. Mem. Iowa State U. Alumni Assn. (life). Republican. Methodist. Clubs: Verdugo Hills Numismatic (Sunland), Glendale Numismatic.

FRITH, ANNA BARBARA, artist; b. Fort Collins, Colo., Jan. 3, 1925; d. Adam Christian and Rose Virginia (Ayers) Tepfer; m. Donald Eugene Frith, May 7, 1949; children: Eugenia, Martin, Johanna, Juliet. ABFA in Painting, Colo. Women's Coll., Denver, 1944; Cert. in Illustration, Cleve. Sch. of Art, 1946; BFA in Painting (Hon.), Cleve. Western Reserve U., 1947; MA in Painting, Denver U., 1950; attended, U. Ill., Champaign, 1975-89. Tchr. figure drawing Denver Art Mus., Chappell House, Denver, 1942, 43, 44, 45; tchr. ceramic sculpture San Bernardino (Calif.) Jr. Coll., 1950, 51, 52; tchr. art H.S. San Bernardino, 1953; part-time tchr. women's classes U. Ill., Champaign, 1955-80; tchr. Sat. and pvt. classes; conductor workshops in field. Exhbns. include Gilman/Gruen Gallery, Chgo., The Peoria (Ill.) Art Guild, Prairie House Gallery, Springfield, Ill., Mus. Modern Art, N.Y.C., 1950; one-woman shows include Julian McPhee Univ. Gallery, San Luis Obispo, Calif., Calif. Poly. U., 1996; participant 1998 Mural-in-a-Day, Lompoc, Calif. Recipient Mary Agnes Page award Cleve. Inst. of Art, 1946, 5th Yr. Scholarship award, 1946. Republican. Presbyterian. Avocations: tennis, swimming, dancing, biking, music. Home: 310 Poppinga Way Santa Maria CA 93455-4204

FRITJOFSON, SARAH MARIE, reporter, columnist; b. Roswell, N.Mex., July 8, 1908; d. Robert Seabury and Gena Vera (Nichols) Cook; m. Hjalmar Peter Fritjofson, Dec. 16, 1939 (dec. 1964). BA, Wellesley Coll., 1930; art studied with Winold Reiss, N.Y.C., Glacier Park, 1936-39; studied with Hipolito Hidalgo de Caviedes, N.Y.C., 1939-40; studied with Adolf Spohr, 1950. Soc. editor Muscatine (Iowa) Jour., 1930-31; reporter, columnist Cody (Wyo.) Enterprise, 1962—; participated in seminars and workshops Buffalo Bill Hist. Ctr., Cody. Contbr. to Smithsonian Catalog on Winold Reiss Show, 1989, South Fork Jour., Smoke Signals. Lay reader Christ Ch., 1973—; pres. pub. Cody Music Club; patron Buffalo Bill Hist. Assn.; hon. mem. Cody Country Art League. Mem. AAUW (sec.), Wellesley Alumnae Assn. Republican. Episcopalian. Avocations: singing, swimming, dancing, reading, walking. Home: 715 Sheridan Ave # 20E Cody WY 82414-3409

FRITZ, THOMAS DONALD, artist; b. San Fernando, Calif., Nov. 21, 1957; s. Arthur Evenson and Virginia Mary (Burcham) F.; m. Molly Lynn Taylor, Nov. 1, 1962; children: Emily Dustinne, Wesley Thomas. BA in Art, Calif. State U., Northridge, 1980. Illustrator ITT Gilfillan, Van Nuys, Calif., 1980-83; staff artist Litton Data Sys., Agoura Hills, Calif., 1983—. Artist: (mags.) Street Rodder, 1996, Rodder's Jour., 1996, Road & Track, 1997, 98, Classic Automobile Registry, 1998, Automobiles Classiques, 1998, Automobile, 1998. Recipient Ada Callahan Meml. award Ventura County Fair Bd., 1996, Peter Helck award, 1997, 98, Athena award of excellence, 1997, 98, Strother McMinn award, 1998. Mem. Automotive Fine Arts Soc. (Peter Helck award 1997, Athena award of excellence 1997). Office: Tom Fritz Automobile Fine Art PO Box 800 Newbury Park CA 91319-0800

FROELICH, BEVERLY LORRAINE, foundation director; b. Vancouver, B.C., Can., Oct. 23, 1948; came to U.S., 1968; d. Kenneth Martin and Ethel (Seale) Pulham; m. Eugene Leonard Froelich, Dec. 26, 1971; children: Craig, Grant. Cert. in fundraising, U. So. Calif., 1986; profl. designation in pub. rels., UCLA, 1987. Cert. fund raising exec. Contract analyst Universal Studios, Calif., 1968-71; exec. dir. Olive View, UCLA Med. Ctr. Found., Sylmar, Calif., 1987—; pres. Beverly Froelich Pub. Rels., Sherman Oaks, Calif., 1988-90; prin. Tracy Susman & Co., Sherman Oaks, 1986-88. Co-author: (program) Overcoming Chronic Arthritis Pain, 1989; contbg. writer hosp. earthquake preparedness guidelines Hosp. Coun. So. Calif., 1991. Founder San Fernando Valley br. Arthritis Found., Encino, 1983, pres., 1983-87, mktg. com.; bd. dirs. health care com. Valley Industry and Commerce Assn. Recipient Nat. Vol. Svc. award Arthritis Found., 1986, Jane Wyman Humanitarian award Arthritis Found., 1991, Disting. Svc. award Arthritis Found., 1990, Marilyn Magaram award for Cmty. Svc., 1997. Mem. AAUW, Nat. Soc. Fund Raising Execs. (exec. com. San Fernando Valley chpt.), Valley Industry and Commerce Assn., UCLA Alumni Assn. Avocations: hockey, music. Home: 14152 Valley Vista Blvd Sherman Oaks CA 91423-4043 Office: Olive View Med Ctr Found North Annex 14445 Olive View Dr Sylmar CA 91342-1437

FROGLEY, CRAIG RONALD, data processing educator, chiropractor; b. Salt Lake City, Aug. 9, 1948; s. H. Ronald and Donna Lee F.; m. Janet Ruth Haggard, May 27, 1972; children: Stephanie, Stephen, Michael, David, Kristyan, Mark, Matthew, Adam. BS, Brigham Young U., Provo, Utah, 1972; D.Chiropractic summa cum laude, Palmer Coll., Davenport, Iowa, 1975. Tchg. faculty neurophysiology Palmer Coll. Chiropractic, Davenport, 1975; pvt. practice Phoenix, 1975-79, Fairfield, Calif., 1979-93, Salt Lake City, 1993—; tchr. LDS Ch. Ednl. Sys., Tempe, Ariz., 1976—; computer specialist LDS Ch. Ednl. Sys., Fairfield, 1985-93; mgr. sys. tng. and adminstrn. LDS Ch. Ednl. Sys., Salt Lake City, 1993—; mem. teaching faculty U. Utah LDS Inst. Religion. Active Boy Scouts Am., Utah and Calif., 1986-96; membership chmn. J.S. Sr. Internat. Family Found., 1994. Mem. Pi Tau Delta. Mem. LDS Ch. Avocations: geneology, music, organizational psychology, camping, sports. Office: LDS Church Educational System 50 E North Temple Salt Lake City UT [illegible]

FROHMADER, FREDERICK OLIVER, lawyer; b. Tacoma, Wash., Mar. 12, 1930; s. Frederick William and Elizabeth May (Farrell) F.; m. Brenda

Frohmader (dec.); children: Fred Albert Aubert, Frederick William, Lisa Kim. BCS, Seattle U., 1953; LLB, Gonzaga U., 1960, JD, 1967. Bar: Wash. Lawyer in pvt. practice, Tacoma, 1960—; with Pierce County Prosecutor, Tacoma, 1961-62; represented various Wash. Indians and Indian tribes in their fishing and hunting rights under various treaties signed with U.S., 1962-83. Served to 1st lt. U.S. Army, 1953-56. Mem. Wash. State Bar Assn., Wash. State Trial Lawyers Assn., Elks. Christian. Avocations: history, military history and military science, western history, western art. Home: 629 S Winnifred St Tacoma WA 98465-2538 Office: 1130 S 11th St Tacoma WA 98405-4017

FROHNEN, RICHARD GENE, journalism educator; b. Omaha, Mar. 26, 1930; s. William P. and Florence E. (Rogers) F.; student U. Nebr., Omaha, Mo. Valley Coll., 1948-52; BA, Calif. State U., 1954; MS, UCLA 1961; EdD, Brigham Young U., 1976; grad. Army War Coll., 1982 m. Harlene Grace LeTourneau, July 4, 1958; children: Karl Edward, Eric Eugene. Bus. mgr. athletics and sports publicity dir. U. Nebr., Omaha, 1951-52; pub. rels. dir. First Congl. Ch. Los Angeles, 1953-54, 58-59; writer Los Angeles Mirror News, 1959; gen. assignment reporter, religion editor Los Angeles Times, 1959-61; prof. journalism, dean men Eastern Mont. State Univ., Billings, 1961-65; N.W. editor, editorial writer Spokesman-Review, Spokane, 1965-67, also editor Sunday mag.; prof. journalism U. Nev., Reno, 1967-79; exec. dir. devel. Coll. of Desert/Copper Mountain, 1982-85, Ariz. Health Scis. Ctr., Tucson, 1986-90; pub. rels. devel. officer Sch. Med. Scis. U. Nev., 1969-75; adj. prof. mgmt., dir. grad. pros. in Mgmt. U. Redlands (Calif.), 1979-85, 91-95; adj. prof. comm. Calif. State U., Dominguez Hills, 1991-95; cons. Instl. Advancement, Long Beach, Calif., Everett, Wash., 1990—. Mem. exec. bd. Nev. area coun. Boy Scouts Am., 1968-76, coun. commr., 1973-74, v.p., 1975-76; mem. exec. bd. Yellowstone Valley coun. Boy Scouts Am., 1961-65, coun. pres. 1963-64; v.p. Catalina coun. Boy Scouts Am., 1987-90; mem. exec. bd. Long Beach Area Coun., 1990-93; founder, mng. dir. Ch. Western Expdns., 1958-90; adminstrv. asst. to Gov. of Nev., 1985; active Nat. Eagle Scout Assn. Served to 1st lt. USMC, 1954-58; now col. Res., ret. Recipient Silver Beaver award Boy Scouts Am., 1974, Pres.' Vol. Action award Coll. Desert/Copper Mountain, 1984, Outstanding Faculty award U. Redlands, 1984; named to Benson High Sch. Hall of Fame, Omaha, 1988. Mem. Assn. Edn. Journalism, Am. Legion, Res. Officers Assn. U.S., Marine Corps Assn., Marine Corps Res. Officers Assn., Am. Humanics Found., Internat. Platform Assn., Nat. Soc. Fund Raising Execs., N.W. Devel. Officers Assn., Snohomish, Whatcom, Island, Skagit County Devel. Officers Assn., Planning Execs. Inst., Internat. Communication Assn., Religion Newswriters Assn., Navy League, Semper Fidelis Soc., Am. Mgmt. Assn., Assn. Am. Med. Colls. Group on Pub. Affairs, Counc. for Advancement and Support Edn., The Ret. Officers Assn., U.S., Assn. for Healthcare Philanthropy, Kiwanis, Lions, Rotary (club pres.), Kappa Tau Alpha, Alpha Phi Omega, Soc. Profl. Journalists, Sigma Delta Chi (sec.-treas. chpt.). Episcopalian. Office: 1614 Meadow Pl Snohomish WA 98290-1860

FROHNMAYER, DAVID BRADEN, university president; b. Medford, Oreg., July 9, 1940; s. Otto J. and MarAbel (Fisher) B F.; m. Lynn Diane Johnson, Dec. 30, 1970; children: Kirsten (dec.), Mark, Kathryn (dec.), Jonathan, Amy. AB magna cum laude, Harvard U., 1962; BA, Oxford (Eng.) U., 1964, MA (Rhodes scholar), 1971; JD, Calif., Berkeley, 1967; LLD (hon.), Willamette U., 1988; D Pub. Svc. (hon.), U. Portland, 1989. Bar: Calif. 1967, U.S. Dist. Ct. (no. dist.) Calif. 1967, Oreg. 1971, U.S. Dist. Ct. Oreg. 1971, U.S. Supreme Ct. 1981. Assoc. Pillsbury, Madison & Sutro, San Francisco, 1967-69; asst. to sec. Dept. HEW, 1969-70; prof. law U. Oreg., 1971-81, spl. asst. to univ. pres., 1971-79; atty. gen. State of Oreg., 1981-91; dean Sch. Law U. Oreg., 1992-94, pres., 1994—; chmn. Conf. Western Attys. Gen., 1985-86; chmn. Am. Coun. Edn. Govtl. Rels. commn, 1996-98; bd. dirs. South Umpqua Bank. Mem. Oreg. Ho. of Reps, 1975-81; bd. dirs. Fred Hutchinson Cancer Rsch. Ctr., Nat. Marrow Donor Program, Fanconi Anemia Rsch. Fund, Inc., Tax Free Trust of Oreg. Fund; active Oreg. Progress Bd. Recipient awards Weaver Constl. Law Essay competition Am. Bar Found., 1972, 74; Rhodes scholar, 1962. Mem. ABA (Ross essay winner 1980), Oreg. Bar Assn., Calif. Bar Assn., Nat. Assn. Attys. Gen. (pres. 1987, Wyman award 1987), Round Table Eugene, Order of Coif, Phi Beta Kappa, Rotary. Republican. Presbyterian. Home: 2315 McMorran St Eugene OR 97403-1750 Office: U Oreg Johnson Hall Office of Pres Eugene OR 97403

FROST, EVERETT LLOYD, academic administrator; b. Salt Lake City, Oct. 17, 1942; s. Henry Hoag Jr. and Ruth Salome (Smith) F.; m. Janet Owens, Mar. 26, 1967; children: Noreen Karyn, Joyce Lola. BA in Anthropology, U. Oreg., 1965; PhD in Anthropology, U. Utah, 1970. Field researcher in cultural anthropology Taveuni, Fiji, 1968-69; asst. prof. in anthropology Ea. N.Mex. U., Portales, 1970-74, assoc. prof., 1974-76, asst. dean Coll. Liberal Arts and Scis., 1976-78, dean acad. affairs and grad. studies, 1978-80, v.p. for planning and analysis, dean rsch. 1980-91, dean grad. studies, 1983-88, pres., 1991—; cons., evaluator N. Ctrl. Assn. Accreditation Agy. for Higher Edn., 1989—, mem. rev. bd., 1993—; bd. dirs. Quality N.Mex., 1st Savs. Bank of Clovis and Portales, N.Mex., Plains Regional Med. Ctrs., Clovis and Portales; bd. mem. emeritus N.Mex. First; commr. Western Interstate Commn. for Higher Edn., 1993—; pres. Lone Star Athletic Conf. Pres.'s Commn., 1992—; chmn. rsch. com. N.Mex. First, 1989-91. Chmn. N.Mex. Humanities Coun., 1980-88; mem. N.Mex. Gov.'s Commn. on Higher Edn., 1983-86; mem. exec. bd. N.Mex. First, 1987—; bd. dirs. Roosevent Gen. Hosp., Portales, 1989—; pres. bd. dirs. San Juan County Mus. Assn., Farmington, 1979-82; vice chair Portales Pub. Schs. Facilities Com., 1990—. NDEA fellow, 1969-70; grantee NEW, 1979-80, NSF, 1968-69, Fiji Forbes, Ltd., 1975-76, others. Fellow Am. Anthropol. Assn., Am. Assn. Higher Edn., Soc. Coll. and Univ. Planning, Assn. Social Anthropologists Oceania, Anthropol. Soc. Washington, Sch. Am. Rsch., Western Assn. Grad. Deans, Current Anthropology (assoc.) Polynesian Soc., Phi Kappa Phi. *

FROST, STERLING NEWELL, arbitrator, mediator, management consultant; b. Oklahoma City, Dec. 21, 1935; s. Sterling Johnson and Eula Dove (Whitford) F.; m. Patricia Joyce Rose, Aug. 18, 1957; children: Patricia Diane Wiscarson, Richard Sterling, Lindy Layne Harrington. BS Indsl. Engring., U. Okla., Norman, 1957; MS Indsl. Engring., Okla. State U., 1966. Registered indsl. engr. Okla. Calif. Asst. mgr. acctg. Western Electric, Balt., 1972-73, mgr. indsl. engring., Chgo., 1973-75, mgr. devel. engring., 1975-76, mgr. acct. mgmt., San Francisco, 1976-78, dir. staff, Morristown, N.J., 1978-79; gen. mgr. distbn. & repair AT&T Techs., Sunnyvale, Calif., 1979-85, area v.p. material mgmt. svcs. AT&T Info. Systems, Oakland, Calif., 1985-87, ops. v.p. material mgmt. svcs., San Francisco, 1988-89; dir. configuration ops. Businessland, Inc., San Jose, Calif., 1989-90, dir. svcs. support, 1990-91; exec. v.p. Isotek, Tiburon, Calif., 1991; v.p., gen. mgr. Tree Fresh, San Francisco, 1991-92; CFO Prima Pacific, Inc., Tiburon, 1992-93; mgmt. cons., arbitrator/mediator, Sterling Solutions, Santa Cruz, 1993—; bd. dirs. Contract Office Group, San Jose, 1983—, chmn., 1984—. Bd. dirs. Santa Clara County YMCA, San Jose, Calif., 1981-84, bd. dirs. Northern Calif. Medication Assn., 1995—, Recipient Man of Day citation Sta. WAIT Radio, Chgo. Mem. Nat. Soc. Prof. Engrs. (chmn. com. 1969-70), Am. Inst. Indsl. Engrs. (pres. bd. dirs. 1966-68), Okla. Soc. Profl. Engrs. (v.p. 1968-69), No. Calif. Mediation Assn. (bd. dirs. 1996-98), Am. Arbitration Assn., Soc. Profls. in Dispute Resolution. Republican.

FROST, W. GREGORY, mortgage company executive; b. San Mateo, Calif., Mar. 17, 1949; s. James Homer and Mary Viola (Rael) F.; m. Devon Tyler Young, Aug. 7, 1988; children: W. Gregory Jr., Derek Adam. BS, U. N.Mex., 1971; postgrad., Tex. Tech U., 1979. V.p. Am. Savs. & Loan, Albuquerque, 1972-77; pres., chief exec. officer Devargas Savs. & Loan, Santa Fe, N.Mex., 1977-80; regional v.p. Citi Fed Mortgage, Albuquerque, 1981-84; v.p. Foster Mortgage Corp., Albuquerque, 1985-87; sr. v.p. Bane Plus Mortgage Corp., Albuquerque, 1987-91; pres. Frost Mortgage Banking Group, Albuquerque, 1991—; lectr., mortgage banking sales trainer; profl. motivational sales trainer The Duncan Group, 1990—. Author: Cross Selling the Listing Agent, 1991, Selling to First Time Home Buyers, 1992, The Assistant System, 1994. Chmn. N.Mex. Dem. rules com., 1977-80; mem. pres.'s coun. Dem. Nat. Com., 1977-80; bd. dirs. Albuquerque Civic Light Opera, 1989-92; bd. dirs., pres. U. N.Mex. Alumni Lettermen, Albuquerque, 1990—; N.Mex. state dir. Fellowship Christian Athletes, 1994—; dir. Nat. Football Found., 1996—; bd. dirs., treas. Albuquerque Sports Coun., 1994—, Fellowship Christian Athletes; dir. Nat. Football Found.; treas. Am. Equity Found. Named one of Outstanding Young Men Am., 1980, 81.

Mem. Albuquerque Petroleum Club, Albuquerque Country Club, UNM Lobo Club (bd. dirs.), Sigma Alpha Epsilon (eminent dep. archon). Roman Catholic. Avocations: water skiing, snow skiing, weight training, public speaking. Home: 5425 Eakes Rd NW Albuquerque NM 87107-5531 Office: Frost Mortgage Banking Grp 2051 Wyoming Blvd NE Albuquerque NM 87112-2615

FRUCHTER, JONATHAN SEWELL, research scientist, geochemist; b. San Antonio, June 5, 1945; s. Benjamin and Dorothy Ann (Sewell) F.; m. Cecelia Ann Smith, Mar. 31, 1973; children: Diane, Daniel. BS in Chemistry, U. Tex., 1966; PhD in Geochemistry, U. Calif., San Diego, 1971. Research assoc. U. Oreg., Eugene, 1971-74; research scientist Battelle Northwest, Richland, Wash., 1974-79, mgr. research and devel., 1979-87, staff scientist, 1987-91, 94—, tech. group leader, 1991-94. Contbr. numerous articles to profl. jours. Mem. AAAS, Am. Chem. Soc., Phi Beta Kappa, Phi Kappa Phi. Avocations: fishing, skiing, boating. Office: Battelle NW PO Box 999 Richland WA 99352-0999

FRUCHTERMAN, JAMES ROBERT, JR., computer company executive; b. Washington, May 1, 1959; s. James R. Sr. and Ellen Patricia (Fallon) F.; m. Virginia Belwood, Aug. 11, 1984; children: James David, Richard Andrew, Katherine Elizabeth. BS in Engring., MS in Applied Physics, Calif. Inst. Tech., 1980. Chief elec. engr. G.C.H. Inc., Sunnyvale, Calif., 1981; v.p. Phoenix Engring. Inc., Redwood City, Calif., 1981-82; v.p., chief fin. officer Calera Recognition Systems, Inc. (formerly Palantir Corp.), Santa Clara, Calif., 1982-88; v.p. mktg. The Palantir Corp., Santa Clara, Calif., 1987-89; pres. RAF Tech., Inc., Palo Alto, Calif., 1989-95; v.p., 1995—; chmn. Arkenstone, Inc., Moffett Field, Calif., 1989—; tech. co-founder Calera Recognition Systems; chief elec. engr. and chmn. definitions subcomm. 1st pvt. U.S. launch vehicle venture. Mem. IEEE, AAAS, AAES, AHEAD, RESNA, Am. Inst. Aeros. and Astronautics (fed. adv. com. on telecomm. access 1996-97), Electronic and Info. Tech. Access Adv. Comm. Achievements include development of the most accurate optical character recognition technology in the world, and of leading reading machine for the blind and people with reading disabilities. Office: NASA Ames Moffett Complex Bldg 23 Moffett Field CA 94035-0215

FRUSH, JAMES CARROLL, JR., real estate development company executive; b. San Francisco, Oct. 18, 1930; s. James Carroll and Edna Mae (Perry) F.; m. Patricia Anne Blake, Oct. 29, 1960 (div. 1977); children: Michael, Gloria; m. Carolyn Fetter Bell, Aug. 23, 1978; 1 child, Stephen. BA, Stanford, 1953; postgrad., U. Calif., San Francisco, 1957-58; MA, Saybrook Inst., 1981, PhD, 1985. Ptnr. James C. Frush Co., San Francisco, 1960-70; v.p., bd. dir. Retirement Residence, Inc., San Francisco, 1964-70; pres., 1971—; pres. Nat. Retirement Residence, San Francisco, 1971-89, Casa Dorinda Corp., 1971-89, Retirement Residence Inc. Ala., Daphne, 1995—; pres. Marin Shakespeare Festival, 1971-73, James C. Frush Found., 1972-78; adj. prof. gerontology, psychology and theology Spring Hill Coll., Mobile, Ala., 1988—; adj. prof. counseling edn. U. South Ala., Mobile. Author (with Benson Eschenbach): The Retirement Residence: An Analysis of the Architecture and Management of Life Care Housing, 1968, Self-Esteem in Older Persons Following a Heart Attack: An Exploration of Contributing Factors, 1985, Kind Hearts, Reflections on Being an Elder; contbr. articles to profl. jours.; producer ednl. films. Bd. dirs. San Francisco Sr. Ctr., 1973-78, Found. to Assist Calif. Tchrs. Devel. Inc., 1987-89; mem. adv. bd. Christus Theol. Inst., Mobile, Ala., 1992-95; mem. ethics com. adv. bd. Westminster Village, Spanish Ft., 1994—; bd. dirs. com. affirmative aging Episc. Diocese Ctrl. Gulf Coast, 1996—. Mem. Gerontol. Soc., Southeastern Psychol. Assn., Assn. for Anthropology and Gerontology, Stanford Alumni Assn., RSVP (adv. bd. Mobile chpt. 1988-94), C.G. Jung Soc. of Gulf Coast (pres.), Ala. Humanities Found. Speakers Bur. (presenter 1993-94, 94-95), Gulf Coast Storyteller's Guild. Office: care T Pimsleur 2155 Union St San Francisco CA 94123-4003

FRY, EDWARD BERNARD, retired education educator, publishing executive; b. L.A., Apr. 4, 1925; s. Eugene Bernard and Frances (Dreier) F.; m. Carol Addison Adams, 1950 (div. 1970); m. Cathy Ruwe, Jan. 8, 1974; children: Shanti, Christopher. BA, Occidental Coll., 1949; MS in Edn., U. So. Calif., 1954, PhD, 1960. Asst. prof. Loyola U., L.A., 1953-63; prof. edn. Rutgers U., New Brunswick, N.J., 1963-86; prof. emeritus Rutgers U., New Brunswick, 1986—; pub., author Laguna Beach Ednl. Books; Fulbright lectr., Uganda, 1961, Zimbabwe, 1985; pub., owner Laguna Beach Ednl. Books, 1991—. Author: How to Teach Reading, 1992; co-author: Reading Teachers Book of Lists, 3d edit., 1993; author of over 25 textbooks for schs. and colls. With U.S. Mcht. Marine, 1943-46. Recipient Disting. Svc. award N.J. Reading Assn., 1979. Mem. Nat. Reading Conf. (pres. 1974-76, Oscar Causey award 1980), Internat. Reading Assn. (Reading Hall of Fame 1992). Democrat. Methodist. Avocations: skiing, docent in Greenbelt Park. Home: 245 Grandview St Laguna Beach CA 92651-1518

FRYE, HELEN JACKSON, judge; b. Klamath Falls, Oreg., Dec. 10, 1930; d. Earl and Elizabeth (Kirkpatrick) Jackson; m. William Frye, Sept. 7, 1952; children: Eric, Karen, Heidi; 1 adopted child, Hedy; m. Perry Holloman, July 10, 1980 (dec. Sept. 1991). BA in English with honors, U. Oreg., 1953, MA, 1960, JD, 1966. Bar: Oreg. 1966. Public sch. tchr. Oreg., 1956-63; with Riddlesberger, Pederson, Brownhill & Young, 1966-67, Husband & Johnson, Eugene, 1968-71; trial judge State of Oreg., 1971-80; U.S. dist judge Dist. Oreg. Portland, 1980-95; sr. judge U.S. Dist. Ct., Portland, 1995—. Office: 1107 US Courthouse 1000 SW 3rd Ave Portland OR 97204-2930*

FRYE, JUDITH EILEEN MINOR, editor; b. Seattle; d. George Edward and Eleen G. (Hartelius) Minor; student UCLA, 1947-48, U. So. Calif., 1948-53; m. Vernon Lester Frye, Apr. 1, 1954. Acct., office mgr. Colony Wholesale Liquor, Culver City, Calif., 1947-48; credit mgr. Western Distbg. Co., Culver City, 1948-53; ptnr. in restaurants, Palm Springs, L.A., 1948, ptnr. in date ranch, La Quinta, Calif., 1949-53; ptnr., owner Imperial Printing, Huntington Beach, Calif., 1955—; editor, pub. New Era Laundry and Cleaning Lines, Huntington Beach, 1962—; registered lobbyist, Calif., 1975-84. Mem. Textile Care Allied Trade Assn., Calif. Coin-op Assn. (exec. dir. 1975-84, Cooperation award 1971, Dedicated Svc.award 1976), Nat. Automatic Laundry & Cleaning Coun. (Leadership award 1972), Women Laundry & Drycleaning (past pres., Outstanding Svc. award 1977), Printing Industries Assn., Master Printers Am., Nat. Assn. Printers & Lithographers. Office: 22031 Bushard St Huntington Beach CA 92646-8409

FRYER, GLADYS CONSTANCE, retired physician, medical director, educator; b. London, Mar. 28, 1923; came to U.S., 1967; d. William John and Florence Annie (Dockett) Mercer; m. Donald Wilfred Fryer, Jan. 20, 1944; children: Peter Vivian, Gerard John, Gillian Celia. MB, BS, U. Melbourne, Victoria, Australia, 1956. Resident Box Hill Hosp., 1956-57; postdoctoral fellow Inst. of Cardiology, U. London, 1958; med. registrar Queen Victoria Hosp., Melbourne, Australia, 1958; cardiologist Assunta Found., Petaling Jaya, Malaysia, 1961-64; fellow in advanced medicine London Hosp., U. London, 1964; clin. research physician U.S. Army Clin. Research Unit, Malaysia, 1964-66; physician to pesticide program U. Hawaii, 1967-68; internist Hawaii Permanente Kaiser Found., Honolulu, 1968-73; practice medicine specializing in internal medicine Honolulu, 1973-88; med. dir. Hale Nani Health Ctr., Honolulu, 1975-89, Beverly Manor Convalescent Ctr., Honolulu, 1975-89; vis. pediatric cardiac depts. Yale U., Stanford U., U. Calif., 1958; asst. clin. prof. medicine John Burns Sch. Medicine U. Hawaii, 1968-89; vis. geriatrics dept. U. Capetown, 1990; med. cons. Salvation Army Alcohol Treatment Facility, Honolulu, 1975-81; physician to skilled nursing patients Va, Honolulu, 1984-88; preceptor to geriatric nurse practitioner program U. Colo., Honolulu, 1984-85; lectr. on geriatrics, Alzheimer's disease, gen. medicine, profl. women's problems and neurosci., 1961—; mem. ad hoc due process bd. Med. Care Evaluation Com., 1982-88, Hospice Adv. Com., 1982-88; mem. pharmacy com. St. Francis Hosp. Clin. Staff, 1983-89, chmn. 1983-84. Contbr. articles to med. and sci. jours. Mem. adv. com. Honolulu Home Care St. Francis Hosp., 1977-87; mem. adv. bd. Honolulu Gerontology Program, 1983-89, Straub Home Health Program, Honolulu, 1984-87; mem. sci. adv. bd. Alzheimers Disease and Related Disorders Assn., Honolulu, 1984-89; mem. long term care task force (Health and Community Svcs. Coun. Hawaii, 1978-88. Special Ops. Exec., War Office, London, 1943-44. Recipient Edgar Rouse Prize in Indsl. Medicine, U. Melbourne, 1955, Outstanding Supporter award Hawaii Assn. Activity

Coordinators, 1987. Fellow ACP; mem. AAAS, AMA, Hawaii Med. Assn. (councillor 1984-89), Honolulu County Med. Soc. (chmn., mem. utilization rev. com. 1973-89), World Med. Assn., Am. Geriatrics Soc., N.Y. Acad. Sci. Episcopalian. Avocations: needlepoint, Celtic mythology, mediaeval history, gardening.

FRYMAN, CHERIE MARIE, video graphic artist; b. Burbank, Calif., Dec. 19, 1955; d. Jamed Clarence and Patricia Ann (Meis) F.; m. Karel Roland Armstorff, Nov. 10, 1990; children: Genevieve Ilse Armstorff, Griffin Van Armstorff. AA. LA. Valley Coll., 1977; student, Calif. State U., Northridge, 1979-80; BA, San Francisco State U., 1982. Page Merv Griffin Enterprises, Hollywood, Calif., 1982; tape vault supr. Trans-Am. Video, Hollywood, 1982-83, asst. editor, 1983—; graphic artist All Post, Burbank, 1993-95, Matchframe Video, Burbank, 1995—; cons. Cassidy and Assocs., Hollywood, 1987. Presenting team Engaged Encounter, L.A., 1991—; troop leader Girl Scouts U.S., 1998—. Mem. Internat. Alliance Theatrical Stage Employees, Moving Picture Machine Operators of the U.S. and Can., Acad. TV Arts and Scis. Democrat. Roman Catholic. Avocations: photography, sculpting, traveling, reading, painting. Office: Matchframe Video 610 N Hollywood Way Burbank CA 91505-3167

FRYMER, MURRY, columnist, theater critic, critic-at-large; b. Toronto, Ont., Can., Apr. 24, 1934; came to U.S., 1945; s. Dave and Sylvia (Spinrod) F.; m. Barbara Lois Grown, Sept. 4, 1966; children: Paul, Benjamin, Carrie. BA, U. Mich., 1956; student Columbia U., 1958; MA, NYU, 1964. Editor Town Crier, Westport, Conn., 1962-63, Tribune, Levittown, N.Y., 1963-64; viewpoints editor, critic Newsday, L.I., N.Y., 1964-72; asst. mng. editor Rochester Democrat & Chronicle, N.Y., 1972-75; Sunday and feature editor Cleve. Plain Dealer, 1975-77; editor Sunday Mag., Boston Herald Am., 1977-79; film and TV critic San Jose Mercury News, 1979-83, theater critic, 1983—, columnist, 1983—; instr. San Jose State U., Cleve. State U. judge Emmy awards NATAS, 1968. Author: dir. musical revue Four by Night, N.Y.C., 1963; author (play) Danse Marriage, 1955 (Hopwood prize 1955); author, dir. Hello U. S. Army show A Dozen and One, 1958. Served with U.S. Army, 1956-58. Recipient Best Columnist/Critic award Calif. Publishers Assn., 1993; named Best Columnist, Peninsula Calif. Press Club, 1993. Home: 1060 Moongate Pl San Jose CA 95120-2031 Office: San Jose Mercury News 750 Ridder Park Dr San Jose CA 95131-2432

FUCHS, VICTOR ROBERT, economics educator; b. N.Y.C., Jan. 31, 1924; s. Alfred and Frances Sarah (Scheiber) F.; m. Beverly Beck, Aug. 29, 1948; children: Nancy, Fredric, Paula, Kenneth. BS, NYU, 1947; MA, Columbia U., 1951, PhD, 1955. Internat. fur broker, 1946-50; lectr. Columbia U., N.Y.C., 1953-54, instr., 1954-55, asst. prof. econs., 1955-59; assoc. prof. econs. NYU, 1959-60; program assoc. Ford Found. Program in Econ. Devel. and Adminstrn., 1960-62; prof. econs. Grad. Ctr., CUNY, 1968-74; prof. community medicine Mt. Sinai Sch. Medicine, 1968-74; prof. econs. Stanford U. and Stanford Med. Sch., 1974-95, Henry J. Kaiser Jr. prof., 1988-95, prof. emeritus, 1995—; v.p. research Nat. Bur. Econ. Research, 1968-78, mem. sr. research staff, 1962—. Author: The Economics of the Fur Industry, 1957; (with Aaron Warner) Concepts and Cases in Economic Analysis, 1958, Changes in the Location of Manufacturing in the United States Since 1929, 1962, The Service Economy, 1968, Production and Productivity in the Service Industries, 1969, Policy Issues and Research Opportunities in Industrial Organization, 1972, Essays in the Economics of Health and Medical Care, 1972, Who Shall Live? Health, Economics and Social Choice, 1975, expanded edit., 1998, (with Joseph Newhouse) The Economics of Physician and Patient Behavior, 1978, Economic Aspects of Health, 1982, How We Live, 1983, The Health Economy, 1986, Women's Quest for Economic Equality, 1988, The Future of Health Policy, 1993, Individual and Social Responsibility: Child Care Education, Medical Care, and Long-term Care in America, 1996.; contbr. articles to profl. jours. Served with USAAF, 1943-46. Fellow Am. Acad. Arts and Scis., Am. Econ. Assn. (disting.; pres. 1995); mem. Inst. Medicine of NAS, Am. Philos. Soc., Sigma Xi, Beta Gamma Sigma. Home: 796 Cedro Way Stanford CA 94305-1032 Office: NBER 204 Alta Rd Stanford CA 94305-8006

FUHLRODT, NORMAN THEODORE, retired insurance executive; b. Wisner, Nebr., Apr. 24, 1910; s. Albert F. and Lena (Schafersman) F.; student Midland Coll., 1926-28; A.D., U. Nebr., 1930, M.A., U. Mich., 1936; m. Clarice W. Livermore, Aug. 23, 1933; 1 son, Douglas B. Thir., athletic coach high schs., Sargent, Nebr., 1930-32, West Point, Nebr., 1932-35; with Central Life Assurance Co., Des Moines, 1936-74, pres., chief exec. officer, 1964-72, chmn. bd., chief exec. officer, 1972-74, also dir. Named Monroe St. Jour. Alumnus of Month, U. Mich. Grad Sch. Bus. Adminstrn. Gen. chmn. Greater Des Moines United campaign United Community Service, 1969-70. Former bd. dirs. Des Moines Symphony Orch. and Industry. Fellow Soc. Actuaries. Home: 760 E Bobier Dr # 116B Vista CA 92084-3806

FUHRMAN, KENDALL NELSON, software engineer; b. Evansville, Ind., Aug. 1, 1962; s. Ronald Charles and Mildred Elaine (Gulley) F.; m. Susan Ann Bagstad. BS in Computer Sci. and Math., U. Denver, 1984; postgrad., Colo. State U., 1988. Assoc. engr. Am. TV & Communications, Englewood, Colo., 1982-84; mem. tech. staff Hughes Aircraft Corp., Englewood, 1984-85; software engr. Ampex Corp., Golden, Colo., 1985-87, sr. software engr., 1987-88, project leader, 1988-92; project leader Ohmeda, Louisville, Colo., 1992-94; pres. founder Evolving Video Techs., 1994—; cons. in field, Arvada, Colo., 1990—. Contbr. articles to profl. jours.; patentee antialising algorithm, graphics rendering. Mem. Assn. for Computing Machinery, IEEE, Spl. Interest Group Graphics, Spl. Interest Group Computer Human Interaction, Phi Beta Kappa. Avocations: skiing, hiking, reading. Home: 8417 Pierson Ct Arvada CO 80005-5238 Office: Evolving Video Tech Corp 100 Technology Dr Ste 100 Broomfield CO 80021-3414

FUHS, G(EORG) WOLFGANG, environmental research manager; b. Cologne, Germany, May 19, 1932; came to U.S., 1964; s. Friedrich Karl and Lisette I. (Stayen) F.; children: Lisette Fuhs Mallary, H. Georg, Dagmar Ariane Serota. Diploma in biology, D in Nat. Scis., U. Bonn, Germany, 1956; postdoctoral, Tech. U. Delft, The Netherlands, 1956-57. Sch. employee dept. botany U. Frankfurt, Germany, 1957-58; research asst. dept. hygiene U. Bonn Sch. Medicine, 1958-63; fellow dept. genetics U. Cologne, 1963-64; sr., prin. research scientist div. labs. and research N.Y. State Dept. Health, Albany, 1964-72, dir. environ. health labs., 1973-85; chief div. labs. Calif. Dept. Health Services, Berkeley, 1985-89; rsch. scientist Calif./EPA Dept. Toxic Substances Control Lab., Berkeley, 1989-93, mgr. technology evaluation, 1993—; vis. prof. U. Wis., Milw., 1973; rsch. assoc. U. Minn. Sch. Pub. Health, Mpls., 1970-74; adj. prof. biology SUNY, Albany, 1984-86; mem. explt. com. on human health effects of Great Lakes water quality U.S./Can. Internat. Joint Commn. 1978-88; tech. adv. com. San Francisco Estuary Project, 1987-92; mem. Calif. Environ. Technol. Partnership, Calif. Comparative Risk Project, 1993-94. Contbr. articles to profl. jours. (Inst. Sci. Info. award 1969); mem. editorial bd. Jour. Phycology, 1972-74, Limnology and Oceanography, 1973-76, Microbial Ecology, 1974-89. Mem. AAAS, Am. Soc. Microbiol. (past chmn. Eastern N.Y. br.), Internat. Assn. Theoretical Applied Limnology.$Dm. Pub. Health Assn., Water Pollution Control Fedn. Office: Calif-EPA Dept Toxic Substances Control Lab 2151 Berkeley Way Berkeley CA 94704-1011

FUJIMOTO, E. TED, management consultant; b. Vallejo, Calif., Mar. 10, 1970; s. Edward K. and Karen K. (Lematsu) Fujimoto; m. Rebecca L. Den, Oct. 6, 1992. BBA, Pacific Union Coll., Angwin, Calif., 1991. Pres. Landmark Cons. Group, Napa, Calif., 1988—; cons. Airtouch Comm., 1992-94, Napa New Tech. H.S., 1993-96, Calif. C. of C., 1995-96. Recipient award of appreciation Business Education Partnership, 1994; grantee Lotus/IBM, 1996. Mem. Napa C. of C., Calif. C. of C. Avocations: golf, boating, cars, family. Office: Landmark Consulting 477 Devlin Rd Ste 107 Napa CA 94558-7511

FUJITA, JAMES HIROSHI, history educator; b. Honolulu, July 24, 1958; s. George Hideo and Teruko (Miyano) F. BA, U. Hawaii, 1980, MA, 1983. Grad. asst. U. Hawaii at Manoa, Honolulu, 1980-85, lectr. history, 1986—; lectr. history Kapiolani C.C., Honolulu, 1987—; lectr. Elderhostel Program, Honolulu, 1992. Mem. NEA, Hawaii State Tchrs. Assn., World History Assn., U. Hawaii Profl. Assembly, Phi Alpha Theta. Office: Kapiolani C C 4303 Diamond Head Rd Honolulu HI 96816-4421

FUJITANI, MARTIN TOMIO, software quality engineer; b. Sanger, Calif., May 3, 1968; s. Matsuo and Hasuko Fujitani. BS in Indsl. and Systems Engring., U. So. Calif., 1990. Sec. Kelly Svcs., Inc., Sacramento, 1987; receptionist Coudert Bros., L.A., 1988; rsch. asst. U. So. Calif., L.A., 1988-89; math. aide Navy Pers. Rsch. and Devel. Ctr., San Diego, 1989; quality assurance test technician Retix, Santa Monica, Calif., 1989-90; software engr. Quality Med. Adjudication, Inc., Rancho Cordova, Calif., 1990-92; test engr. Worldtalk Corp., Los Gatos, Calif., 1993-94; quality engr. Lotus Devel. Corp., Mountain View, Calif., 1994-95, Gen. Magic, Sunnyvale, Calif., 1995-96; software engr. Sun Microsys. Inc., Palo Alto, Calif., 1996—. Assemblyman Am. Legion Calif. Boys State, 1985. Recipient Service Above Self award East Sacramento Rotary, 1986. Mem. Gen. Alumni Assn. U. So. Calif. (life). Avocations: dancing mambo, watching ballet, listening to jazz music, bicycling, windsurfing, cooking. Home: 205 Milbrae Ln Apt 2 Los Gatos CA 95032-7382 Office: Sun Microsys Inc MS UMPK 17-204 901 San Antonio Rd Palo Alto CA 94303-4900

FUKUHARA, HENRY, artist, educator; b. L.A., Apr. 25, 1913; s. Ichisuke and Ume (Sakamoto) F.; m. Fujiko Yasutake, Aug. 18, 1938; children: Joyce, Grace, Rackham, Helen. Student with Edgar A. Whitney, Jackson Heights, N.Y., 1972, Rex Brandt, Corona del Mar, Calif., 1974, Robert E. Wood, 1975, Carl Molno, Woodside, N.Y., 1976. Exhibited in group shows at Friends World Coll., Lloyds Neck, N.Y., 1980, Elaine Benson Gallery, Bridgehampton, N.Y., 1979, 83, Nat. Invitational Watercolor, Zaner Gallery, Rochester, N.Y., 1981, Fire House Gallery, 1982, Parrish Art Mus., 1982, Japan-R.I. Exchange Exhibit, Provincetown, R.I., 1986, Kawakami Gallery, Tokyo, 1986, Setagaya Mus. Art, Tokyo, 1988-91, 5th Ann. Rosoh Kai Watercolor Exhbn. Meguro Mus. Art, Tokyo, 1991, 6th Ann. Rosoh Kai Watercolor Exhbn. Meguro Mus. Art, 1992, Shinju ku Bunka Ctr., Tokyo, 93-96, 10th ann., 1997, Stary Sheets Galleries Exhbn., Irvine, Calif., 1992-94, Laguna Beach, 1996—, Living Legends, Mira Mesa Colls., 1994, Miracosta Coll., 1997; represented in permanent collections at Heckscher Mus., Huntington, N.Y., Abilene Mus. Fine art, Nassau Community Coll., SUNY-Stony Brook, Los Angeles County Mus. Art, Blaine County Mus., Chinook, Mont., Ralston Mus., Sydney, Mont., San Bernardino County Mus., Redlands, Calif., 1984, Riverside Mus. Art, Calif., 1985, Gonzaga U., Spokane, Wash., 1986, Nagano Mus. Art, Japan, 1986, Contemporary Mus. of Art, Hiroshima, 1988, Santa Monica (Calif.) Coll., 1988; instr. Watercolor Venice (Calif.) Adult Sch., 1992-93, tchr. watercolor. Recipient Purchase award Nassau Community Coll., 1976; Best in Show, Hidden Pond, Town of Islip, 1978, Strathmore Paper Co., 1979, Creative Connections Gallery award Foothills Art Ctr., Golden, Colo., 1984, Judges Choice, Mont. Minature Art Soc. 7th Ann International Show, Working with Abandoned Control, 1993, Splash 3 and 4 1995/96 in watercolor series, 1996, The Best of Watercolor 2, 1997, others. Mem. Nat. Watercolor Soc., Ala. Watercolor Soc., Pitts. Watercolor Soc., Nat. Drawing Assn., Valley Water Color Soc. Subject of profl. publs. Address: 1214 Marine St Santa Monica CA 90405-5815

FUKUI, NAOKI, theoretical linguist; b. Tokyo, Oct. 9, 1955; s. Tatsuo and Masako (Kabuyama) F. BA, Internat. Christian U., Tokyo, 1979, MA, 1982; PhD, MIT, 1986. Postdoctoral fellow Ctr. for Cognitive Sci., MIT, Cambridge, 1986-87; asst. prof. Keio U., Tokyo, 1987-89; asst. prof. theoretical linguistics U. Pa., Phila., 1989-90; asst. prof. theoretical linguistics U. Calif., Irvine, 1990-94, assoc. prof., 1994-98, grad. dir. linguistics, 1992—, prof., 1998—. Author: Theory of Projection in Syntax, 1995, Generative Grammar, 1998; mem. editl. bd. Jour. Japanese Linguistics, 1989, The Linguistic Rev., 1992, Jour. East Asian Linguistics, 1992, Linguistic Inquiry, 1995; contbr. articles to profl. jours. Fulbright grantee, 1982-87. Office: U Calif Dept Linguistics 3151 Social Science Plz Irvine CA 92697-5100

FULCO, WILLIAM JAMES, archaeology educator; b. L.A., Feb. 24, 1936; s. Herman John and Clelia Marie (DeFeo) F. MA in Philosophy, Gonzaga U., 1959; M in Sacred Theology, Santa Clara U., 1967; PhD in Near Ea. Studies, Yale U., 1970. Joined Jesuit Order, ordained Roman Cath. priest 1954. Tchr. Greek, Latin Bellarmine Coll. Prep., San Jose, Calif., 1960-63; prof. theology Jesuit Sch. Theology, Berkeley, Calif., 1971-84; prof. Old Testament Grad. Theol. Union, Berkeley, Calif., 1971-84; dir. Archaeol. Mus. Pntifical Bibl. Inst., Jerusalem, 1974—; prof. classics, Loyola Marymount U., L.A., 1984—; adj. prof. archaeology U. So. Calif., L.A., 1989—; NEH chair in ancient Mediterranean studies Loyola Marymount U., L.A., 1998—; vis. prof. Near Ea. langs. U. Calif., Berkeley, 1971-84, Ecole Biblique Francaise, Jerusalem, 1974-75, mem. Am. Schs. of Oriental Rsch. Syrian Archaeol. Survey Team summer 1977, Am. Ctr. Oriental Rsch., Amman, Jordan, 1977-78, U. Judaism, L.A., 1984-90. Author: Maranatha: Mystical Theology of John the Evangelist, 1973, The Canaanite God Resep, 1986, (with Bikai and Marchand) Tyre: The Shrine of Apollo, 1997; contbr. chpts. to books and articles to profl. jours. Mem. Cath. Bibl. Assn. (assoc. editor, chair archaeol. com. 1996—), Am. Numismatic Assn., Am. Oriental Assn., Soc. Bibl. Lit., Nat. Assn. Afroasiatic Linguistics, Numismatic Soc. India, Am. Schs. Oriental Rsch. Democrat. Roman Catholic. Avocations: antiquities, numismatics, orchidculture, hiking, classical music. Home: PO Box 45041 Los Angeles CA 90045-0041 Office: Dept of Classics Loyola Marymount U 7900 Loyola Blvd Los Angeles CA 90045-8400

FULD, FRED, III, computer consultant, financial consultant; b. San Pedro, Calif., July 31, 1952; s. Fred Jr. and Gloria Mary F.; m. Sharon Elizabeth Fuld; 1 child, Fred IV. BA in Bus., Rockford Coll., 1974, BA in Econs., 1974; postgrad., Heriot-Watt U., Berkeley/Edenburgh. Cert. tchr. credential, Calif.; Registered Investment Advisor, SEC, 1981. Investment mgr. San Diego Securities, 1974-78; market maker Pacific Stock Exch., San Francisco, 1978-79; v.p. CGR Conss., San Francisco, 1979-83; pvt. practice fin., computer cons. Concord, Calif., 1983—; exec. prodr. Mt DTV Ednl. TV series. Author: (software) Personal Financial Planning, 1984, (software) Asset Allocation, 1986, (software) Business Valuation, 1986; author: Stock Market Secrets, 1985, 101 Most Asked Questions about the MAC, 1992. Mem. Mensa Soc. (life), The Magic Castle (life). Avocations: swimming, jogging, boating, collecting antique stock certificates. Office: 3043 Clayton Rd Concord CA 94519-2730

FULKERSON, CHRISTOPHER ALLEN PAUL, composer, conductor; b. Sacramento, Calif., Nov. 13, 1954; s. William Spencer and Rosemarie Elizabeth (Neuburger) Githens. B, Univ. Pacific, 1976; MA, Univ. Calif., 1979, PhD, 1986; BMus, U. Pacific. Lectr. Calif. State Univ., San Jose, 1982; founder, dir. Musicianship Program San Francisco Girls Chorus, San Francisco, 1982-91; assoc. conductor San Francisco Contemporary Music Players, 1981-84; founder, dir. The Berkeley Opera Chorus, 1985-88; founder, music dir. The Composers Chamber Players, San Francisco, 1986-88, Ariel Vocal Ensemble, San Francisco, 1982-88; pres. White Sphere Group Publ., San Francisco, 1994—; chmn., music com. Waterfront Theater, 1986-88; cons. American Inst. of Architects, 1984-85. Composer: Concerto for Harpsichord and Seven Instruments, 1979, So That, 1981, Scritti di Leonardo, 1983, Symphony the Recognitions, 1985, The Childermass, 1986, Magica Mezza Musica, 1995, Celestial Sixties, 1990, Michelangelo Fantasies, 1994-96; author: Art C riticism, 1992; composer over 45 works. Founder The Party of Universal Responsibilty, San Francisco, 1997, mem. arts policy planning com. The San Francisco Arts Commn., 1988-89; bd. dirs. Am. Concert Assn., 1985-88; founding mem., planning com. San Francisco New Music Calendar. Recipient Schroeder & Crofts fellow Tanglewood Music Festival, 1988, numerous travel grants. Mem. The Wagner Soc., Phi Mu Alpha. Roman Catholic. Avocations: reading, languages. Home: 307 Capp St Apt 2 San Francisco CA 94110-1834 Office: White Sphere Group Publ 307 Capp St Apt 2 San Francisco CA 94110-1834

FULKERSON, WILLIAM MEASEY, JR., college president; b. Moberly, Mo., Oct. 18, 1940; s. William Measey and Edna Frances (Pendleton) F.; m. Grace Carolyn Wisdom, May 26, 1962; children: Carl Franklin, Carolyn Sue. BA, William Jewell Coll., 1962; MA, Temple U., 1964; PhD, Mich. State U., 1969. Asst. to assoc. prof. Calif. State U., Fresno, 1981—; asst. to pres. Calif. State U.-Fresno, 1971-73; assoc. exec. dir. Am. Assn. State Colls., Washington, 1973-77; acad. v.p. Phillips U., Enid, Okla., 1977-81; pres. Adams State Coll., Alamosa, Colo., 1981-94, State Colls. in Colo., 1994—; interim pres. Met. State Coll., Denver, 1987-88, Western State Coll., 1996. Author: Planning for Financial Exigency, 1973; contbr. articles to profl. jours. Commr. North Ctrl. Assn., Chgo., 1980—; bd. dirs. Acad. Collective Bargaining Info. Svc., Washington, 1976, Office for Advancement Pub. Negro Colls., Atlanta, 1973-77, Colo. Endowment for Humanities, 1988—, pres., 1998-99. Named Disting. Alumni William Jewell Coll., 1982, Outstanding Alumnus Mich. State U. Coll. Comm., Arts & Scis., 1987. Mem. Am. Assn. State Colls. and Univs. (parliamentarian, bd. dirs. 1992-94), Am. Coun. on Edn. (bd. dirs.), Assn. Pub. Coll.s and Univs. Pres.s (pres. 1994-95), Nat. Assn. Sys. Heads, Alamosa C. of C. (dir., pres. 1984 Citizen Yr. award), Rotary. Office: State Colls in Colo 1580 Lincoln St Ste 750 Denver CO 80203-1505

FULLENWIDER, NANCY VRANA, music composer, dance educator; b. Sheridan, Wyo., May 9, 1940; d. Jacob Allen and Edith Martha (Tripp) Fullenwider; m. Linsfred Leroy Vrana, Apr. 26, 1980. BA summa cum laude, U. Denver, 1962, MA, 1971, postgrad., 1974. Prin. dancer, instr. Colo. Ballet and Colo. Ballet Ctr., Denver, 1958-80; owner, instr. Idaho Springs (Colo.) Sch. Ballet, 1962-67, Sch. Ballet, Parker, Colo., 1974-79; curriculum developer Career Edn. Ctr., Denver Pub. Schs., 1973; grad. asst. U. Denver, 1974; guest artist, choreographer, composer Young Audiences, Denver, 1975-80; instr. ballet Ballet Arts Ctr., Denver, 1992-98, Colo. Dance Ctr., Littleton, 1992—; music dir., accompanist for Western Chamber Ballet, Denver, 1994-98. Composer (CD) To the Pointe, 1997. Commissioned ballet works performed at Arvada Ctr. for Performing Arts, Colo., 1991, Aurora (Colo.) Fox Arts Ctr., 1989-92, Buell Theatre, Colo., 1993, Cleo Parker Robinson Dance Theatre, Colo., 1992, Colo. Springs Fine Arts Ctr., 1991, Houston Fine Arts Ctr., Colo., 1971, San Luis Arts Festival, Colo., 1990, Bonfils Theatre, Colo., 1971. Grantee Douglas County Schs., Colo., 1998. Mem. Phi Beta Kappa, Alpha Lambda Delta. Avocations: hiking, fly fishing, theatre, concerts.

FULLER, AMEENAH RASHEDAH, medical record consultant; b. Oklahoma City, July 10, 1962; d. Norman Martin and Zakiyyah (Holmes) Abdul-Raheem; m. Garry W. Fuller, Aug. 18, 1985 (div. Apr. 1987). AA, Chaffey Coll., 1994; BA, Calif. Coll. Health Sci., 1998. Pres. Charts Personell Svcs., Pomona, Calif., 1987-93; corp. cons. Longwood Mgmt. Corp., L.A., 1994-96; dir. SNF cons. Laguna Med. Sys., San Clemente, Calif., 1997-98; publ. Looking-In Publs., Chino Hills, Calif., 1996-98; pres. Chart Smarts, Upland, Calif., 1998—; spkr. in field.j. Author: Stop the Blackman Now!, 1996. Vol. L.A. Urban League, 1990-93. Recipient merit award Writers Digest, 1996. Mem. Calif. Assn. Health Facilities. Avocations: travel, writing, cooking, skating.

FULLER, EDWIN DANIEL, hotel executive; b. Richmond, Va., Mar. 15, 1945; s. Ben Swint and Evelyn (Beal) F.; m. Denise Kay Perigo, July 18, 1970. Student, Wake Forest U., 1965; BSBA, Boston U., 1968; postgrad., Harvard Sch. Bus., 1987. Security officer Pinkerton Inc., Boston, 1965-68; with sales dept. Twin Bridges Marriott Hotel, Arlington, Va., 1972-73; nat. sales mgr. Marriott Hotels & Resorts, N.Y.C., 1973-76; dir. nat. and internat. sales mgr. Marriott Hotels & Resorts, Washington, 1976-78; v.p. mktg. Marriott Hotels & Resorts, 1978-82; gen. mgr. Marriott Hotels & Resorts, Hempstead, N.Y., 1982-83, Marriott Copley Place, Boston, 1983-85; v.p. ops. Midwest region Marriott Corp., Rosemont, Ill., 1985-89; v.p. ops. Western and Pacific regions Marriott Corp., Santa Ana, Calif., 1989-90; sr. v.p., mng. dir. Marriott Hotels & Resorts-Internat., Washington, 1990-93; exec. v.p., mng. dir. internat. lodging Marriott Lodging Internat., Washington, 1994-97, pres., mng. dir., 1997—; chmn. bd. dirs. SNR Reservation Sys., Zurich, Switzerland, 1979-81; bd. dirs. Boston U. Hotel Sch., 1984—, Mgmt. Engrs. Inc., Reston, Va., Barnby Books, Barnaby Books, Honolulu, 1997—; treas. MEI Pacific Honolulu, 1985—; chmn. Fuller Properties, Laguna Hills, Calif., 1990—. Pres. Boston U. Gen. Alumni Assn., 1993—, v.p., 1990-93; v.p. Boston U. Sch. Mgmt. Alumni Bd., 1985—; mem. adv. bd. Boston U. Hospitality Mgmt. Sch., 1985—; trustee Boston U., mem. exec. com. bd. trustees, 1994—. Capt. U.S. Army, 1968-72, Vietnam. Decorated Bronze Star. Mem. Boston U. Alumni Coun. (v.p.), Harvard Sch. Bus. Advanced Mgmt. Program (fund agt.), Sigma Alpha Epsilon, Delta Sigma Pi. Republican. Avocations: real estate, travel, golf, history. Home: 25362 Derbyhill Dr Laguna Hills CA 92653-7835 Office: Marriott Hotels & Resorts 1 Marriott Dr Washington DC 20058-0001

FULLER, JANICE MARIE, secondary school educator; b. Flagler, Colo., Feb. 7, 1948; d. William Harrison and Ruth Elsie (Jensen) Martin; m. William Edward Fuller, Sept. 16, 1966; children: James Edward, David William, John Justin. A.Gen. Studies, Pikes Peak C.C., Colorado Springs, Colo., 1982; BS in Biology, Met. State Coll., Denver, 1986. Gen. office mgr. Schmidt Environ. Enterprises, Commerce City, Colo., 1972-77; v.p., sec. Fuller Constrn., Inc., Larkspur, Colo., 1993—; tchr. math. and sci. Douglas County Schs., Castle Rock, Colo., 1988-92; tchr. sci. Christ the King Sch., Denver, 1992-96; tchr. biology Ellicott Jr.- Sr. High Sch., Calhan, Colo., 1996—; tutor math./sci.; coach track, gymnastics, volleyball Castle Rock Jr. H.S., 1990-92; nominated 1st U.S./Russia Joint Conf. on Edn. in Moscow, U. Iowa Citizen Ambassador Program, 1994; mem. dist. accountability com. Ellicott Sch. Dist., 1996—. Mem. dist. accountability commn. Douglas County Sch. Dist., Castle Rock, 1987-91, dist. comm. com., 1990. Mem. ASCD, NAFE, AAUW, Nat. Assn. Student Activity Advisors, Nat. Sci. Tchrs. Assn., Met. State Coll. Alumni Assn. Avocations: cooking, sewing, country living. Office: Ellicott Jr-Sr H S 375 S Ellicott Hwy Calhan CO 80808-8838

FULLER, MICHELLE COSTELLO, interior designer; b. Omaha, Mar. 13, 1964; d. Jack Martin and Carol Ann (McCreary) Costello; children: Cameron, Madeline. BA in Internat. Rels., U. San Diego, 1987; BFA in Interior Design, Design Inst. San Diego, 1993. Cert. interior designer, Calif. Pres. Design Maison, Inc., San Diego, 1987—. Contbr. articles to popular mags. Event coord. Jr. League, San Diego, 1998—; active Solana Beach Presbyn., 1998—, Rep. Womens Fedn., Rancho Santa Fe, Calif., 1992—, Friends of Newt Gingrich, Macon, Ga., 1998, Elderhelp, San Diego, 1998. Mem. Am. Soc. Interior Designers (bd. dirs., bd. mem., pres., Peoples Choice award 1996), Internat. Interior Design Assn., San Diego Hist. Soc. (Peoples Choice award 1996), Am. Cancer Soc., Epilepsy Soc., Gamma Phi Beta. Republican. Presbyterian. Avocations: tennis, dance, sailing, swimming, reading. Office: Design Maison Inc 3525 Del Mar Heights Rd Ste 424 San Diego CA 92130-2122

FULLER, PAUL NORMAN, retired aerospace executive; b. Highland Park, Ill., Sept. 14, 1927; s. Paul Max and Friedel (Schaer) F.; m. Elizabeth Szajko; children: Janet Fuller Lawrence, Jean Elizabeth. BS in Aero. Engring., U. Ill., 1950. Supr. Thor program Rocketyne, Canoga Park, Calif., 1953-58, project engr. Redstone program, 1958-60, project engr. J-2 engine program, 1960-70, program mgr. J-2 engine program, 1970-73, dir. Nat. Space Tech. Lab. shuttle program, 1974-76, chief program engr. space shuttle engine, 1976-83, program mgr. peacekeeper program, 1983-87, v.p., 1987-94; ret., 1994; cons. Rocket Systems Svcs, Colorado Springs, Colo., 1994—, pres.; mem. external adv. bd. propulsion space engring. Pa. State U., 1990; sec. adv. com. U.S. Dept. Transp., Washington, 1988—, chmn. to sec. adv. com., 1990-92. With U.S. Army, 1950-52. Recipient Pub. Svc. award NASA, 1973, 81, Pub. Svc. medal NASA, 1981, Engring. Achievement award San Fernando Valley Engring. Coun., L.A., 1982, Disting. Alumni award U. Ill., 1983. Mem. Colorodo Springs C. of C. (mem. task forces 1995—). Avocations: golf, travel, gardening. Home: 2640 Trevor Ln Colorado Springs CO 80919-4877 Office: Boeing NAm Inc Internat-Rockedyne 6633 Canoga Ave Canoga Park CA 91303-2703

FULLER, ROBERT KENNETH, architect, urban designer; b. Denver, Oct. 6, 1942; s. Kenneth Roller and Gertrude Ailene (Heid) F.; m. Virginia Louise Elkin, Aug. 23, 1969; children: Kimberly Kirsten, Kelsey Christa. BArch, U. Colo., 1967; MArch and Urban Design, Washington U., St. Louis, 1974. Archtl. designer Fuller & Fuller, Denver; architect, planner Urban Research and Design Ctr., St. Louis, 1970-72; prin. Fuller & Fuller Assocs., Denver, 1972—. Past pres. Denver East Ctrl. Civic Assn., Country Club Hist. Dist.; bd. dirs. Cherry Creek Steering Com.; pres. Horizon Adventures, Inc. Mem. AIA (past pres. Denver chpt.), Colo. Arlberg Club (past pres.), Phi Gamma Delta, Delta Phi Delta. Home: 2211 E 4th Ave Denver CO 80206-4107 Office: 3320 E 2nd Ave Denver CO 80206-5302

FULLMER, DANIEL WARREN, psychologist, educator, retired; b. Spoon River, Ill., Dec. 12, 1922; s. Daniel Floyd and Sarah Louisa (Essex) F.; m. Janet Satomi Saito, June 1980; children: Daniel William, Mark Warren. B.S., Western Ill. U., 1947, M.S., 1952; Ph.D., U. Denver, 1955. Postdoctoral intern psychiat. div. U. Oreg. Med. Sch., 1958-61; mem. faculty U. Oreg., 1955-66; prof. psychology Oreg. System of Higher Edn., 1958-66; faculty Coll. Edn. U. Hawaii, Honolulu, 1966-95, retired, 1995, prof. emeritus, 1974—; pvt. practice psychol. counseling; cons. psychologist Grambling State U., 1960-81; founder Free-Family Counseling Ctrs., Portland, Oreg., 1959-66, Honolulu, 1966-74; co-founder Child and Family Counseling Ctr., Waianae, Oahu, Hawaii, Kilohana United Meth. Ch., Oahu, 1992, v.p., sec., 1992; pres. Human Resources Devel. Ctr., Inc., 1974—; chmn. Hawaii State Bd. to License Psychologists, 1973-78. Author: Counseling: Group Theory & System, 2d. edit., 1978, The Family Therapy Dictionary Text, 1991, MANABU, Diagnosis and Treatment of a Japanese Boy with a Visual Anomaly, 1991; co-author: Principles of Guidance, 2d. edit., 1977; author (counselor/cons. training manuals) Counseling: Content and Process, 1964, Family Consultation Therapy, 1968, The School Counselor-Consultant, 1972, Family Therapy as the Rites of Passage, 1998; editor: Bulletin, Oreg. Coop Testing Service, 1955-57, Hawaii P&G Jour., 1970-76; assoc. editor: Educational Perspectives, U. Hawaii Coll. Edn. Served with USNR, 1944-46. Recipient Francis E. Clark award Hawaii Pers. Guidance Assn., 1972, Thomas Jefferson award for Outstanding Pub. Svc., 1993; named Hall of Fame Grambling State U., 1987. Mem. Am. Psychol. Assn., Am. Counseling Assn. (Nancy C. Wimmer award 1963), Masons. Methodist. Office: 1750 Kalakaua Ave Apt 809 Honolulu HI 96826-3725

FULLMER, DONALD KITCHEN, insurance executive; b. Rockyford, Colo., Apr. 11, 1915; s. George Clinton and Florence E. (Kitchen) F.; m. June 5, 1934 (dec. 1987); children: Robert E., Maxine Fullmer Vogt, Phyllis R. Fullmer Danielson. CLU, Am. Coll. Life Underwriting, 1962. Lic. ins. agt., Wash. Life underwriter N.Y. Life, Aberdeen, Wash., 1954-74; ind. gen. agt. Aberdeen, Wash., 1974-81; life underwriter MONY, Bellingham, Wash., 1983-88; ret. County chmn. Rep. Party, Grays Harbor, Wash., 1964-69, mem. state exec. com., 1971-72. With U.S. Army, 1945. Mem. N.W. Wash. Assn. Life Underwriters, Wash. State Assn. Life Underwriters (pres. 1968-69), Twin Harbor Life Underwriters, Masons. LDS. Home: 5464 Bell West Dr Bellingham WA 98226-9033

FULLMER, STEVEN MARK, systems engineer; b. San Francisco, Mar. 15, 1956; s. Thomas Patrick and Patricia Ann (Carroll-Boyd) F.; m. Rhonda Lynnette Bush, Nov. 8, 1992; children: Wesley Stevenson, Sierra Marin. BA in Chemistry, Willamette U., 1978, BA in Biology, 1978; MBA, Ariz. State U., 1993. Sr. engr., project leader Honeywell Large Computer Products, Phoenix, 1981-86; bank officer, cons., infosecurity cons. First Interstate Bank/Wells Fargo Bank, Phoenix, 1987-96; project mgr. Wells Fargo Bank, 1996; systems engr. AG Comm. Systems, 1996—; cons. J.A. Boyd & Assoc., San Francisco, 1985-96, ImaginInc. Consulting, Phoenix, 1985—. Contbr. articles to profl. jours. Mem. exec. bd. Grand Canyon coun. Boy Scouts Am., scoutmaster, 1983-88, commr., 1988-92, dist. chmn., 1995-96; founder, lt. comdr. Maricopa County Sheriff's Adj. Posse, 1982-93; pres. Heard Mus. Coun., 1995-96; dept. head, lead Liberty Wildlife. Recipient Order of Merit Boy Scouts Am., 1988, Nat. Disting. Commr. award Boy Scouts Am., 1990, Nat. Founder's award Boy Scouts Am., 1991, Silver Beaver award Boy Scouts Am., 1994. Mem. Am. Inst. for Cert. Computer Profls. (cert. data processor 1985), Mensa, KC (membership dir. 1988), Knights Cross (Sovereign Order of St. Stanislas), Phi Lambda Upsilon, Phi Eta Sigma, Kappa Sigma, Alpha Chi Sigma, Sigma Iota Epsilon, Beta Gamma Sigma. Republican. Roman Catholic. Avocations: Am. Indian history, science fiction, scuba diving, hiking, camping. Office: AG Comm Systems 2500 W Utopia Rd Phoenix AZ 85027-4129

FULMER, LISA MICHELLE, marketing director, graphic arts consultant; b. Sacramento, July 9, 1962; d. Fred William and Scharlene Faye (Oling) F. BA in Mktg., Calif. State U. Stanislaus, Turlock, 1983. Promotions mgr. Unisource, Inc., Dublin, Calif., 1985-90, Noland Paper Co., San Jose, Calif., 1990; sales exec. Conservatree Paper, San Francisco, 1991; sales rep. Golden State Embossing, San Francisco, 1992; mktg. dir. Automatrix, Inc., San Francisco, 1993—; pvt. practice graphic arts cons. San Francisco, 1985—; bd. mem. Artists in Print, San Francisco, 1987-91; vis. lectr. Acad. Art Coll., San Francisco, 1987—; vol. Bus. Vols. for the Arts, San Francisco. Coeditor: Papers for Printing, 1991. Mem. San Francisco Creative Alliance, Western Art Dirs. Club, Print Buyers Assn. Democrat. Avocations: reading, writing, traveling. Office: Automatrix Inc 530 Hampshire St Ste 404 San Francisco CA 94110-1466

FULSHER, ALLAN ARTHUR, lawyer; b. Portland, Oreg., July 5, 1952; s. Rémy Walter and Barbara Lee (French) F.; m. Karen Louise Schmid, Dec. 28, 1974 (dec. Sept. 1990); children: Brian Rémy, Louise Katherine, Elizabeth Alane. BA in Biology, U. Oreg., 1974, BA in Econs., 1976; JD, U. of Pacific, 1979. Bar: Oreg. 1979, Calif. 1980, U.S. Dist. Ct. Oreg. 1980, U.S. Dist. Ct. (ea. dist.) Calif. 1981, U.S. Ct. Appeals (9th cir.) 1982, U.S. Dist. Ct. (no. dist.) Calif. 1985, U.S. Dist. Ct. (so. dist.) Calif. 1986. Assoc. Law Offices of Jacques B. Nichols P.C., Portland, 1979-82, Ragen, Roberts, O'Scannlain, Robertson & Neill, Portland, 1982-83; shareholder Bauer, Hermann, Fountain & Rhoades P.C., Portland, 1983-87, v.p., 1984-87; shareholder, v.p. Fulsher and Weatherhead P.C., Portland, 1987-88, pres., 1988—; gen. counsel Peregrine Holdings, Ltd., Beaverton, Oreg., 1993-97, Peregrine Capital, Inc., Beaverton, 1993—; mgr. Stamford Bridge, LLC, 1995—; pres., mgr. Portland Profl. Soccer, L.L.C., Tigard, Oreg., 1998—; gen. counsel Premier Soccer Alliance, L.L.C., Dallas, 1998—. Mem. Audi Quattro Club U.S.A. Republican. Roman Catholic. Avocations: basketball, automobile racing and restoration, coaching youth and adult sports. Home: 16399 SE Sager Rd Portland OR 97236-5509 Office: Peregrine Capital Inc 9725 SW Beaverton Hillsdale Hw Beaverton OR 97005-3305

FULTON, JEFFREY C., sales executive; b. Denver, June 3, 1970; s. Larry Calvin Fulton and Sandra Jean (Engelking) Glaviano; m. Joelle Elizabeth Casteix, Aug. 6, 1994 (div. Nov. 1997). BA in polit. sci., U. Calif., Santa Barbara, 1992. Prin. Avenir Industries, Denver, 1992-97; sales rep. Analytical Reference Materials, Evergreen, Colo., 1994, Advanced Software Techs., Inc., Littleton, Colo., 1995-97; dir. sales Advanced Software Tech., Littleton, 1997—; cons. French bus. translation, Denver, Bordeaux, France, 1991—; cons.-broker U.S./Mexico, Denver, Guadalajara, 1993. Mem. Chinese Shoto-Lin Ctr. Avocations: karate. Home: 2778 S Meade St Denver CO 80236-2244 Office: Advanced Software Techs Inc 7851 S Elati St # 102 Littleton CO 80120-4481

FULTON, LEROY MARCUS, academic administrator; b. Nov. 13, 1931; s. William Marcus and Esther (Baker) F.; m. Jean Wilson, Sept. 9, 1931; children: William Douglas, Kevin Neale, Mark Eric. BA, Anderson (Ind.) Coll., 1953; MDiv, Anderson Sch. Theology, 1960, DD, 1977. Pres. Warner So. Coll., Lake Wales, Fla., 1969-91, chancellor, 1991-92; v.p. Hope Internat. U., 1992—. Pres. Assn. Ch. of God of So. Calif., 1998—. Mem. Fla. Assn. Evangelicals (1980—), Ind. Colls., Univs. Fla. (pres. coun. 1982), Fullerton Rotary (dist. heart chmn., pres. elect 1998—). Mem. Ch. of God. Home: 211 Condessa Ct Oceanside CA 92057

FULTON, NORMAN ROBERT, credit manager; b. L.A., Dec. 16, 1935; s. Robert John and Fritzi Marie (Wacker) F.; AA, Santa Monica Coll., 1958; BS, U. So. Calif., 1960; m. Nancy Butler, July 6, 1966; children: Robert B., Patricia M. Asst. v.p. Raphael Glass Co., L.A., 1960-65; credit adminstr. Zellerbach Paper Co., L.A., 1966-68; gen. credit mgr. Carrier Transicold Co., Montebello, Calif., 1968-70, Virco Mfg. Co., L.A., 1970-72, Superscope, Inc., Chatsworth, Calif., 1972-79; asst. v.p. credit and adminstrn. Inkel Corp., Carson, Calif., 1980-82; corp. credit mgr. Gen. Consumer Electronics, Santa Monica, Calif., 1982-83; br. credit mgr. Sharp Electronics Corp., Carson, Calif., 1983-96; credit mgr. Rocheux Internat. Inc., Carson, 1997—. With AUS, 1955-57. Fellow Nat. Inst. Credit (cert. credit exec.); mem. Credit Mgrs. So. Calif., Nat. Notary Assn. Home: 6437 Kanan Dume Rd Malibu CA 90265-4037

FULTZ, PHILIP NATHANIEL, management analyst; b. N.Y.C., Jan. 29, 1943; s. Otis and Sara Love (Gibbs) F.; m. Bessie Learleane McCoy, Mar. 11, 1972 (dec. Oct. 1996). AA in Bus., Coll. of the Desert, 1980; BA in Mgmt., U. Redlands, 1980, MA in Mgmt., 1982. Enlisted USMC, 1967, advanced through grades to capt., 1972, served in various locations, 1964-78, resigned commn., 1978; CETA coord. County of San Bernardino, Yucca Valley, Calif., 1978-85; contract analyst Advanced Technology, Inc., Twentynine Palms, Calif., 1985-88, spl. transit analyst Omintrans, San Bernardino, Calif., 1988-89; tech. analyst Atlantic Rsch. Corp. (formerly

Calculon Corp.), Twentynine Palms, Calif., 1988—; mgmt. analyst Marine Corps Base, Twentynine Palms, Calif., 1991—; adj. asst. prof. mgmt. Chapman U., Orange, Calif., 1992—. Founding dir. Unity Home Battered Women's Shelter, Joshua Tree, Calif., 1982, Morongo Basin Adult Literacy; bd. dirs. Twentynine Palms Water Dist., 1991-95. Mem. Rotary (sec. Joshua Tree chpt. 1983-85). Republican. Home: 73477 Desert Trail Dr Twentynine Palms CA 92277-2218 Office: Morale Walfare & Recreation Marine Corps Base Twentynine Palms CA 92277-2302

FUNG, ROSALINE LEE, educator; b. China, May 14, 1944; came to U.S., 1962; d. Frank Kwok-Wai and Teresa Wai-Hing (Cheung) Lee; m. Stephen Ying-Chung Fung, Aug. 23, 1968. BA, Briar Cliff Coll., 1966; MA, Idaho State U., 1968. Instr. Highland C.C., Freeport, Ill., 1968-69, Merced (Calif.) Coll., 1969-70; tchr. Linden (Calif.) High Sch., 1970-84; prof. San Joaquin Delta Coll., Stockton, Calif., 1984—; cons. in field. *Upon completion of her post graduate education as an International Peace Scholar in 1968, Rosaline Lee Fung launched a widely varied teaching career. Drawing from her multilingual background, she published numerous textbooks on writing. Recent accomplishments include a series of eight textbooks entitled Patterns for Success. Her teaching materials are used in schools all over the world, including the US, Canada and Hong Kong. Aside from teaching, she currently serves on the International Educational Advisory Council of U-CANDU Learning Centres (Canada) and coordinates ESL programs for visiting educators from China.* Author: (textbooks) ESL Writing Manual, 1992, Patterns for Success, 1997, Basic Composition, 1997, Writing Essays, 1998, Writing Paragraphs, 1999. Coord. cultural exch. San Joaquin Delta Coll., 1995, 96, 98. Mem. NEA, Calif. Tchrs. Assn. Avocations: reading, writing, concerts, theater, surfing the net. E-mail: rfung@sjdccd.cc.ca.us. Office: San Joaquin Delta Coll 5151 Pacific Ave Stockton CA 95207-6304

FUNK, CLARENCE JOHN, physicist; b. Logan, Utah, Jan. 5, 1941; s. Cyril Reed and Hazel Marie (Jensen) F.; m. Joan Leslie Henderson, Mar. 19, 1965; children: Nancy Wilson, Christopher, Catherine Cvetko, James. BS in Physics, Utah State U., 1966; MS in Physics, UCLA, 1968, PhD in Engring., 1972. Scientist Spawar Sys. Ctr., San Diego, 1966—; mem. J7, Ltd. Liability Co., Dayton, Idaho, 1988—, Springhill Ranch, Ltd. Liability Co., Richmond, Utah, 1976—; sci. advisor Naval Security Group, Edzell, Scotland, 1986-87. Author: Handbook on Underwater Optics, 1969; patentee in field. Cubmaster Boy Scouts Am., San Diego, 1979-82; counselor LDS, San Diego, 1993-98. Recipient bronze medal Am. Def. Preparedness Assn., 1987, Naval Ocean Sys. Ctr. Exemplary award, 1988. Mem. IEEE Computer Soc. Democrat. Avocation: photography. Home: 5370 Burford St San Diego CA 92111-4602 Office: SPAWAR Systems Ctr Code D73A San Diego CA 92152

FUNSTON, GARY STEPHEN, publishing and advertising executive; b. Phila., July 7, 1951; s. Ralph Gaylord and Adele Rose (DeCintio) F.; m. Nancy Eileen Clark (div. 1974); 1 child, Stephen Blake. Student, DeAnza Coll., 1969-73, San Jose State U., 1973-75, London Bus. Sch., 1995; student exec. devel. program, Cornell U., 1996. Store mgr. Smith & Foley Shoes Inc., Sunnyvale, Calif., 1970-75; sales rep. The Hoover Co., San Jose, Calif., 1975-78, GTE Directories Corp., Santa Clara, Calif., 1978-81; ptnr., sec., treas. Mailco Advt. Inc., Milpitas, Calif., 1981-83; owner, cons. ADCOM, San Jose, 1983-85; dir. sales mgr. Lomar Trans Western Publs., Ft. Lauderdale, Fla., 1985-87; mgr. sales, mktg. Ameritel, San Diego, 1987-89; regional sales dir. United Advt. Publs., San Leandro, Calif., 1989-98; dist. sales mgr. Web Svc. Co., Hayward, Calif., 1998—; sales cons. Republic Telecom, San Jose, 1983-84; mgmt. cons. Norcal Directory Co., San Jose, 1984-85; advt. cons. Yellow Page Programs, San Jose, 1983-85; owner West Coast Aircraft, Hayward, Calif., 1996—. Contbr. articles to profl. jours. Mem. CAP, Mountain View, Calif., 1983-84; com. mem. Housing Ind. Found., San Jose, 1991-97, dinner sponsor, 1991-97, fundraiser, 1991-97. Mem. Calif. Apt. Assn. (suppliers coun. 1990—, chmn. suppliers com. 1993, 95, 96, industry stds. com. 1994, mem. exec. com. 1995, 96, bd. dirs. 1995, 96), Solano-Napa Rental Housing Assn., Tri-County Apt. Assn. (com. mem. 1989—), Rental Housing Owners Assn. So. Alameda County (bd. dirs. 1994, Mem. of Yr. award 1992), Highland Swingers Golf Club (treas. 1990—). Republican. Roman Catholic. Avocations: golf, health club, concerts, dining out, flying. Home: 22135 Sevilla Rd Apt 36 Hayward CA 94541-2861 Office: West Coast Aircraft 21593 Skywest Dr Hayward CA 94541

FUREN, SHIRLEY ANN, small business owner, art dealer; b. Pomona, Calif., Sept. 12, 1936; d. Orville Emmett and Mary Evelyn (Carmack) Strickland; m. Ralph R. Rickel, Sept. 3, 1954 (div.); children: Lynda Diane, Lorrie Anne, Stanley Rupert; m. Walter E. Furen, Sept. 25, 1976. B Univ. Studies with distinction, U. N.Mex., 1975; Massage Therapist, Healing Arts Inst., Roseville, Calif., 1994; student, Santa Fe C.C. Cert. massage therapist, Calif. Adminstrv. asst. Psychiat. Inst. Am., Washington, 1977; exec. sec. Am. Assn. Schs. Podiatric Medicine, Washington, 1978-79; real estate broker Snider Bros/Merrill Lynch Realty, Washington, Calif., 1980-88; owner Spheres, Santa Fe, N.Mex., 1991—; model Julie Nation Acad., Santa Rosa, 1996. Vol. Andrea Lambert, M.F.C.C., Gold River, Calif., 1992-95, United Way Santa Fe, 1997—, Santa Fe Opera; vol. hostess Ted Gaines for City Coun., Roseville, 1993; vol. fundraiser Matrix Gallery, Sacramento, Crocker Art Mus., Sacramento; staffer Matrix Gallery Aux., 1994-97; wedding coord. Culinary Guild, Trinity Cathedral, 1989-97; mem. coun. internat. rels., 1998, Santa Fe Opera (docent), 1998. Mem. ASCE (chmn. 1992, 93), Sacramento Capital Club, Santa Fe C. of C. (hospitality com. Coun. Internat. Rels.), Bus. and Profl. Women's Club. Episcopalian. Avocations: travel, arts. Home and Office: Spheres 644 Alto St Santa Fe NM 87501-2563

FURIMSKY, STEPHEN, JR., freelance writer; b. Coalton, Ill., Aug. 4, 1924; s. Stephen Sr. and Anna (Petricko) F.; m. Dorothy Conrad, June 8, 1946 (dec. Nov. 1989); children: Stephen III, Karen Ann Segal, Daniel Michael, Melany; m. Janet Fay Green, Dec. 16, 1991; step-children: Bruce Emerson, Peni Emerson, Kara Welliver, Beth Emerson Levine. AB, U. Chgo., 1951; MS in Internat. Affairs, George Washington U., 1967; grad., Air War Coll., 1967. Instr. in polit. sci. Craven Community Coll., New Bern, N.C., 1975-80; owner San Diego Sod, San Marcos, Calif., 1981-84; spl. advocate juvenile ct. Voices for Children, San Diego, 1985-91; sports editor, health and fitness editor Enterprise Newspaper, Fallbrook, Calif., 1989-91. Candidate state senate, N.C., 1978. Col. USMC, 1942-73. Decorated Legion of Merit, D.F.C., Bronze Star, Air Medal, Cross of Gallantry (Vietman). Mem. VFW (life), Am. Legion, The Order of Daedalians, Mil. Order of World Wars. Republican. Eastern Orthodox. Avocation: shark tooth fossil collecting. Home: 58 Desert Rain Ln Henderson NV 89014-2915

FURLOTTI, ALEXANDER AMATO, real estate development company executive; b. Milan, Italy, Apr. 21, 1948; came to U.S., 1957; s. Amato and Polonia Concepcion (Lopez) F.; m. Nancy Elizabeth Swift, June 27, 1976; children: Michael Alexander, Patrick Swift, Allison Nicole. BA in Econs., U. Calif. Berkeley, Berkeley, 1970; JD, UCLA, 1973. Bar: Calif. 1973, U.S. Dist. Ct. (9th cir.) 1973. Assoc. Alexander, Inman, Kravetz & Tanzer, Beverly Hills, Calif., 1973-77, ptnr., 1978-80; ptnr. Kravetz & Furlotti, Century City, Calif., 1981-83; pres. Quorum Properties, L.A., 1984—; dir., CEO Transmar N.V., Netherland Antilles, 1984—. Trustee Harvard-Westlake Sch., L.A., 1989-97, Yosemite Nat. Inst., San Francisco, 1990-92. Recipient Grand award Pacific Coast Bldrs. Conf., 1993, 98, Golden Nugget award, 1993, 98, Grand award Nat. Assn. Home Builders, 1993, Platinum award, 1997, Best Attached Housing award, 1998, Residential Project of Yr., 1998. Mem. Am. Bar Assn., Urban Land Inst., The Beach Club. Republican. Episcopalian. Office: Quorum Properties 1875 Century Park E Los Angeles CA 90067

FURLOW, MARY BEVERLEY, English language educator; b. Shreveport, La., Oct. 14, 1933; d. Prentiss Edward and Mary Thelma (Hasty) F.; divorced, 1973; children: Mary Findley, William Prentiss, Samuel Christopher; m. William Peter Cleary, Aug. 1, 1989. BA, U. Tenn., 1955, MEd, 1972; MA, Governors State U., 1975; cert. advanced study, U. Chgo., 1987. Mem. faculty Chattanooga State C.C., 1969-73, Moraine Valley C.C., Palos Hills, Ill., 1974-78; mem. English faculty Pima C.C., Tucson, 1978—; cons. in field. Contbr. author: Thinking on the Edge, 1993. Named one of Outstanding Educators of Am., 1973. Fellow Internat. Soc. Philos. Enquiry; mem. DAR, Internat. Soc. Appraisers, Internat. Soc. Philos. Enquiry, Ariz. Antiquarian Guild, Cincinatus Soc., Jr. League, Mensa, Holmes Socs., Clan Chattan Soc., Daus. of Confederacy, Alpha Phi Omega (Tchr. of Yr. 1973), Pi Beta Phi. Democrat. Episcopalian. Home: 1555 N Arcadia Ave Tucson AZ 85712-4010 Office: Pima CC 8202 E Poinciana Dr Tucson AZ 85730-4645

FURMAN, MELVIN D., insurance company executive; b. Urbana, Ill.; s. L.G. Wayne and Caroline (Neiger) F.; m. Mary-Ethel Schell, June 12, 1948; children—Wayne Lee, April Furman Bromfield, David. B.A., Allegheny Coll.; J.D., U. Pitts.; Bar: Ohio, Pa., U.S. Supreme Ct. Sole practice, Butler, Pa., 1955-56; gen. atty. Erie Ins. Exchange, Pa., 1957-65; gen. counsel Prudent Am. Life Ins. Co., Cleve., 1965-67; corp. risk mgr. Figgie Internat., Willoughby, Ohio, 1967-76; sr. counsel Outboard Marine Corp., Waukegan, Ill., 1977-78; dir. risk and ins. mgmt. Manville Corp., Devner, 1978—; exec. v.p. Rocky Mountain Ins. Ltd., Hamilton, Bermuda; chmn. ins. coun. Machinery and Allied Products Inst., Washington, 1978-80; sec. Nat. Product Liability Council, Washington, 1977-80; pres. Waite Hill Assurance Ltd., Hamilton, 1976. Sec. Erie Traffic Commn., 1964-66. Mem. ABA, Captive Ins. Co. Assn. (bd. dirs.). Methodist. Office: PO Box 595 505 W Ramshorn St Dubois WY 82513

FURNAS, DAVID WILLIAM, plastic surgeon; b. Caldwell, Idaho, Apr. 1, 1931; s. John Doan and Esther Bradbury (Hare) F.; m. Mary Lou Heatherly, Feb. 11, 1956; children: Heather Jean, Brent David, Craig Jonathan. AB, U. Calif.-Berkeley, 1952, MS, 1957, MD, 1955. Diplomate Am. Bd. Surgery, Am. Bd. Plastic Surgery (dir. 1979-85, sr. examiner 1986—), Royal Coll. Surgeons Found. (trustee 1995—). Intern U. Calif. Hosp., San Francisco, 1955-56, asst. resident in surgery, 1956-57; asst. resident in psychiatry, NIMH fellow Langley Porter Neuropsychiat. Inst. U. Calif., San Francisco, 1959-60; resident in gen. surgery Gorgas Hosp., C.Z., 1960-61; asst. resident in plastic surgery N.Y. Hosp., Cornell Med. Center, N.Y.C., 1961-62; chief resident in plastic surgery Cornell U. Svc., VA Hosp., Bronx, N.Y., 1962-63; registrar Royal Infirmary and Affiliated Hosps., Glasgow, Scotland, 1963-64; assoc. in hand surgery U. Iowa, 1964-68, sr. resident, faculty assoc. in surgery, 1964-65, asst. prof. surgery, 1966-68, assoc. prof., 1968-69; assoc. prof. surgery, chief div. plastic surgery U. Calif., Irvine, 1969-74, prof., chief div. plastic surgery, 1974-80, clin. prof., chief div. plastic surgery, 1980—; surgeon East Africa Flying Drs. Svc., African Med. and Rsch. Found., Nairobi, Kenya, 1972-73; plastic surgeon S.S. Hope, Nicaragua, 1966, Sri Lanka, 1968; mem. Balakbayan med. mission Mindanao and Sulu, The Philippines, 1980, 81, 82; overseas vis. prof. plastic surgery Ednl. Found., 1994. Contbr. chpts. to textbooks, articles to med. jours.; author, editor 6 textbooks; assoc. editor Jour. Hand Surgery, Annals of Plastic Surgery, Jour. Craniofacial Surgery. Expedition leader Explorer's Club Flag 171 Skull Surgeons of the Kisii Tribe, Kenya, Flag 44 Skull Surgeons of the Marakwet Tribes, Kenya, 1987. Capt. Med. Corps, USAF, 1957-59; col. Med. Corps., USAR, 1989-92, ret. Recipient Golden Apple award for teaching excellence U. Calif.-Irvine Sch. Medicine, 1980, Kaiser-Permanente award U. Calif.-Irvine Sch. Medicine, 1981, Humanitarian Service award Black Med. Students, U. Calif. Irvine, 1987, Sr. Research award (Basic Sci.) Plastic Surgery Ednl. Found., 1987; named Orange County Press Club Headliner of Yr., 1982, Physician of the Year, Orange County Med. Assn., 1998. Fellow ACS, Royal Coll. Surgeons Can., Royal Soc. Medicine, Explorers Club, Royal Geog. Soc.; mem. AMA, Calif. Med. Assn., Orange County Med. Assn. (Physician of Yr. 1998), Am. Soc. Plastic and Reconstructive Surgeons (bd. dirs. 1970-73), Am. Soc. Reconstructive Microsurgery, Soc. Head and Neck Surgery, Am. Cleft Palate Assn., Am. Soc. Surgery of Hand, Soc. Univ. Surgeons, Am. Assn. Plastic Surgeons (trustee 1983-86, treas. 1988-91, v.p. 1993-94, pres.-elect 1994, pres. 1995), Am. Soc. Aesthetic Plastic Surgery, Am. Soc. Maxillofacial Surgeons, Assn. Acad. Chairmen Plastic Surgery (bd. dirs. 1986-89), Assn. Surgeons East Africa, Assn. Plastic & Reconstructive Surgeons So. Africa (hon.), Pacific Coast Surg. Assn., Internat. Soc. Aesthetic Plastic Surgery, Internat. Soc. Reconstructive Microsurgery, Internat. Soc. Craniomaxillofacial Surgery, Pan African Assn. Neurol. Sci., African Med. and Rsch. Found. (bd. dirs. U.S.A. 1987—), Muthaiga Club, Ctr. Club, Club 33, Univ. Club, Phi Beta Kappa, Alpha Omega Alpha. Office: U Calif Div Plastic Surgery Irvine Med Ctr 101 City Dr S Orange CA 92868-3201

FURNIVAL, GEORGE MITCHELL, petroleum and mining consultant; b. Winnipeg, Man., Can., July 25, 1908; s. William George and Grace Una (Rothwell) F.; m. Marion Marguerite Fraser, Mar. 8, 1937; children: William George, Sharon (Mrs. John M. Roscoe), Patricia M., Bruce A. BSc, U. Man., Can., 1929; MA, Queens U., Can., 1933; PhD, MIT, 1935. Field geologist in Man., Ont., N.W.T., and Que., 1928-36; asst. mine supt. Cline Lake Gold Mines, Ltd., 1936-39; geologist Geol. Survey Can., No. and Southwestern Sask., 1939-42; from 1942-70 employed by the Standard Oil Co. Calif. (Chevron) subs. including following positions: dist. geologist Standard Oil Co. of Calif. (Chevron Standard, Ltd.), Calgary, Alta., 1942-44, asst. to chief geologist, 1944-45, field supt. So. Alta., 1945-46, mgr. land and legal dept., 1948-50, v.p. land and legal, dir., 1950-52, v.p. legal, crude oil sales, govt. rels., dir., 1952-55; pres., dir. Dominion Oil, Ltd., Trinidad and Tobago, 1952-60; v.p. exploration, dir. Calif. Exploration Co. (Chevron Overseas Petroleum, Inc.), San Francisco, 1955-63; staff asst. land to corp. v.p. exploration and land Standard Oil Co. of Calif., 1961-63; chmn. bd., mng. dir. West Australian Petroleum Pty., Ltd. (Chevron operated), Perth, 1963-70, retired 1970; dir. mines Dept. Mines and Natural Resources, Man., 1946-48; v.p., dir. Newport Ventures, Ltd., Calgary, 1971-72; v.p. ops., dir., mem. exec. com. Brascan Resources subs. Brascan Ltd. (formerly Brazilian Traction Ltd., Calgary, 1973-75, sr. v.p., dir., 1975-77, sr. cons., 1977-78; pres., CEO, dir. Western Mines Ltd. (Brascan), 1978-80, exec. v.p., divsn. gen. mgr. Westmin Resources Ltd. (Brascan), also dir., mem. exec. com., 1981-82; pres., acting gen. mgr. Coalition Mining, Ltd.; pres., COO, dir. Lathwell Resources Ltd., 1983-84; cons. petroleum and mining, 1985—; founder Man. Geol. Survey, 1946; dir. Cretaceous Pipe Line Co., Ltd., Austen & Butta Pty., Ltd., Western Coal Holdings, Inc., Quest Explorations Ltd., San Antonio Resources Inc.; del. Interprovincial Mines Ministers Conf., several years; sec. Winnipeg Conf., 1947. Elected to Order of Can., 1982. Scholarship in mining geology named in his honor, U. B.C., Can. Fellow Royal Soc. Can., Geol. Soc. Am., Geol. Assn. Can., Soc. Econ. Geologists, Am. Assn. Petroleum Geologists (hon. life); mem. Engring. Inst. Can., Canadian Inst. Mining, Metallurgy and Petroleum (hon. life mem., past br. chmn., dist. councillor, v.p., chmn. petroleum div., Distinguished Service award 1974, Selwyn G. Blaylock gold medal 1979), Australian Petroleum Producing Exploration Assn. (hon. life mem., chmn. com. West Australian petroleum legislation, councillor, state chmn. for Western Australia), Australian Am. Assn. in Western Australia (councillor), Assn. Profl. Engrs., Geologists and Geophysicists of Alta. (hon. life mem., Centennial award 1985), Coal Assn. of Can. (bd.dirs.). Clubs: Calgary Golf and Country, Calgary Petroleum, Ranchmen's. Author numerous govt. and co. papers, reports, reference texts, also sci. articles to profl. jours. Home: 1315 Baldwin Cres SW, Calgary, AB Canada T2V 2B7

FURR, JAMES WILLIAM, JR., financial planner, consultant; b. High Point, N.C., July 11, 1938; s. James William and Lois (Chidester) F.; m. Lola Dawson, Mar. 19, 1960 (div. Nov. 1971); children: James III, Karen Kristin. BS, U. N.C., 1960, MBA, 1962. CLU, CFP. Sales dir. Deering Milliken, Spartanburg, S.C., 1962-68; trading officer Soloman Bros., N.Y.C., 1968-73; sales mgr. Mutual of New York, N.Y.C., 1973-82; site mgr. Mutual of New York, San Jose, Calif., 1982-89; pres. Pan Pacific Ins. Co., Fresno, Calif., 1989-90; nat. bus. cons. Surety Life, Salt Lake City, 1991—. Fellow Life Underwriters Tng. Coun. (instr. Fresno, Calif. 1988-90); mem. Nat. Assn. Life Underwriters, CLU Soc., Internat. Assn. Fin. Planners (charter), Estate Planning Coun. Avocations: raising and showing cats. Home: 1528 Emerson Ave Salt Lake City UT 84105-2728 Office: Surety Life Ins Co 111 E Broadway Salt Lake City UT 84111-5225

FURST, ARTHUR, toxicologist, educator; b. Mpls., Dec. 25, 1914; s. Samuel and Doris (Kolochinsky) F.; m. Florence Wolovitch, May 24, 1940; children: Carolyn, Adrianne, David Michael, Timothy Daniel. AA, L.A. City Coll., 1935; AB, UCLA, 1937, AM, 1940; PhD, Stanford U., 1948; ScD, U. San Francisco, 1983. Mem. faculty, dept. chemistry San Francisco City Coll., 1940-47; asst. prof. chemistry U. San Francisco, 1947-49, assoc. prof. chemistry, 1949-52; assoc. prof. medicinal chemistry Stanford Sch. Medicine, 1952-57, prof., 1957-61; with U. Calif. War Tng., 1943-45, San Francisco State Coll., 1945; rsch. assoc. Mt. Zion Hosp., 1952-82; clin. prof. pathology Columbia Coll. Physicians and Surgeons, 1969-70; dir. Inst. Chem. Biology; prof. chemistry U. San Francisco, 1961-80, prof. emeritus, 1980—, dean grad. div., 1976-79; vis. fellow Battelle Seattle Research Center, 1974; Michael vis. prof. Weizmann Inst. Sci., Israel, 1982; cons. toxicology, 1980—; cons. on cancer WHO; mem. com., bd. mineral resources NRC; sr. mem. scientific advisory bd., GNLD, Internat. Author: Toxicologist as Expert Witness, 1997; contbr. over 300 articles to profl. and ednl. jours. Recipient Klaus Schwartz Commemorative medal Internat. Toxological Congress, Tokyo, 1986, Profl. Achievement award UCLA Alumni Assn., 1992, Henry Hall Clay award U. San Francisco, 1977. Fellow Acad. Toxicological Scis. (diplomate), AAAS, Am. Coll. Nutrition, Am. Coll. Toxicology (nat. sec., pres. 1985), N.Y. Acad. Scis., Am. Inst. Chemists; mem. Am. Soc. Pharmacology and Exptl. Therapeutics, Am. Soc. Pharmacology and Exptl. Therapeutics, Am. Chem. Soc., Am. Assn. Cancer Research, Soc. Toxicology, Sigma Xi, Phi Lambda Upsilon. Research activities on organic synthesis, chemotherapy cancer, carcinogenesis of metals and hydrocarbons. Home: 23500 Cristo Rey Dr Cupertino CA 95014-6503 Office: U San Francisco Inst Chem Biology San Francisco CA 94117-1080

FURTWANGLER, VIRGINIA W. See COPELAND, ANN

FURUYA, DANIEL KENSHO, aikido instructor, priest; b. L.A., Apr. 25, 1948; s. Tetsuo and Kimiye (Kuromma) F.:. BA, U. So. Calif., 1970. Ordained priest. Soto Zen Buddhism. Master instr. Aikido, Iaido Japanese Swordsmanship Aikido Ctr L.A.; resident chief instr., dir. Aikan Ctr. of L.A., 1974—; presenter demonstrations and workshops in field. Author (video series): Art of Aikido, 1996, author (book): KODO: Ancient Ways-Lessons in the Spiritual Life of the Warrior-Martial Artist, 1997, contbr. articles on martial arts. Served three terms grant com. panel City of L.A. Multi-Cultural Grants Com.; pres. L.A. Japanese Sword Soc., So. Calif. Yamanashi Prefectural Assn., bd. dirs. U.S. Japanese Sword Soc., Greater Little Tokyo Anti-Crime Assn., Little Tokyo Community Gymnasium, So. Calif. Japan Prefectional Assn.; mem. Community Adv. Bd. Da Camera Soc., Exec. Com. Civilian Martial Artist Adv. Panel L.A. Police Dept. Grantee Brody Multi-Cultural Arts,1990-93, Nat. Def. Act Carnegie project grant, Harvard U., 1969. Mem. Nisei Week Festival Com., Soto Zen Internat. Dept. Zen Buddhist. Home: 940 E 2nd St #7 Los Angeles CA 90012 Office: Aikido Ctr Los Angeles 940 E Second St #7 Los Angeles CA 90012

GABALDON, PAUL JAMES, high school principal; b. Jerome, Ariz., July 25, 1946; s. Paul G. and Mercedes M. (Gonzales) G.; m. Diana N. Jenkins, Aug. 31, 1968; children: Paul Jr., Adam, Jill. BS in Edn., Ariz. State U., 1969; MA in Counseling, No. Ariz. U., 1973; EdS in Adminstrn., U. Ariz., 1980. Tchr., coach Lyle (Wash.) H.S., 1969-71; tchr., coach Amphitheater H.S., Tucson, 1971-75, counselor, coach, 1975-81; asst. prin., athletic dir. Nogales (Ariz.) H.S., 1981-83; asst. prin. Prescott (Ariz.) H.S., 1983-89; prin. Westview H.S., Avondale, Ariz., 1989-92, Monte Vista (Colo.) H.S., 1992—. Coach Little League Baseball, Prescott, 1988, Babe Ruth Baseball, Monte Vista, 1993; treas. White Tonks Rotary, Avondale, Ariz., 1992; vol. Big Bros., Big Sisters, Prescott, 1985-87. Named Ariz. Baseball Coach of Yr., Ariz. Republic, 1980, Ariz. Daily Star, 1980, Tchr. of Yr., Oreg. Mus. Sci. and Industry, 1970. Mem. ASCD, Nat. Assn. Secondary Sch. Prins., Colo. H.S. Activities Assn. (mem. com. 1984—), Inter Mountain League (pres. 1994-95), Monte Vista C. of C. (conquistadores br.), Phi Delta Kappa. Democrat. Roman Catholic. Avocations: fishing, hunting, reading, camping. Home: 1109 E Laurel Dr Casa Grande AZ 85222-2909 Office: Monte Vista HS 349 Prospect Monte Vista CO 81144

GABER, JASON LEE, social worker; b. Boston, June 18, 1957; s. Louis L. and Anita (Shalachman) G. Student, Tel-Aviv U., 1974, Hebrew U., 1976-77; BS in Edn., Northeastern U., Boston, 1979; MSW, San Francisco State U., 1981. Ordained rabbi, 1991; cert. religious sch. tchr. Jewish program coord. San Francisco Jewish Community Ctr., 1981-84, adult svcs. dir., 1985-88, ctr.-wide program dir., 1989-91, asst. exec. dir., 1991—; rabbinical pastor, tchr., counselor Morenu, 1991—; Sun. sch. tchr. Peninsula Temple Sholom, Burlingam, Calif., 1982-85; high sch. tchr. Congregation Beth Shalom, San Francisco, 1979-81; foster care social worker Dept. Social Welfare, Boston, 1978-79; sr. svcs. rsch. analyst Dept. Elder Affairs, Boston, 1978; summer day camp counselor Young Israel Day Camp, Chelsea, 1973; field supr. San Francisco State U. Grad. Dept. Social Work Edn., 1987-91, community adv. coun., 1987-91. Contbr. articles to profl. jours. Policy planning com. Arts Edn. Focus Group, San Francisco Arts Commn., 1988-89; Jewish Community Rels. Coun., Soviet Jewry Commn., 1982-88, others. Named Louis Kraft Young Profl. Leadership awardee, Nat Conf. Jewish Communal Svcs., 1986; named Profl. of the Yr., United Jewish Community Ctrs., 1986, Program Achievement awardee, 1985, 89, others. Mem. Assn. Jewish Ctr. Profls. (nat. social action com. chpt. rep. 1990, exec. com. 1988-90, v.p., 1986-88, bd. dirs. 1983), Conf. of Jewish Communal Svc., Coalition for Alternatives in Jewish Edn., Jewish Humanists Community Fund (sec.-treas. 1983-87). Home: 700 Church St Apt 203 San Francisco CA 94114-3003 Office: San Francisco Jewish Ctr 3200 California St San Francisco CA 94118-1904

GABRIEL, EARL A., osteopathic physician; b. Phila., Aug. 13, 1925; s. John and Rose (Cohen) G.; m. Fredelle, Feldman, Dec. 19, 1948; children: Debra Mae, Barbara Lynn, Sheri Ann, Michael David. B.S., Muhlenberg Coll., 1950; D.O., Phila. Coll. Osteo. Medicine, 1954. Gen. practice osteo. medicine Allentown, Pa., 1955-78; chief of staff Allentown Osteo. Hosp., 1967-68, chmn. intern tng., 1956-58; prof., chmn. family practice medicine, assoc. dean clin. affairs Coll. Osteo. Medicine of Pacific, Pomona, Calif., 1978-88, assoc. dean clin. affairs for postdoctoral tng., 1983-88; med. dir. clinics, 1986-88, ret., 1988; pvt. practice gen. medicine Claremont, Calif., 1988-90, Rancho Cucamonga, Calif., 1990-94; dir. med. edn. San Bernardino (Calif.) County Med. Ctr., 1994—; mem. Pa. Gov.'s Sci. Adv. Com. on Health Care Delivery, 1970, 71; preceptor in gen. practice Phila. Coll. Osteo. Medicine; mem. ad hoc profl. group FDA, HEW, 1976-77; mem. Pa. Profl. Services Rev. Orgn. Council, 1977. Editorial adviser Family Practice News, 1976—. Active Lehigh Valley Cancer Soc. Served with USNR and USMCR, 1943-46, PTO, CBI. Recipient cert. of honor Phila. Coll. Osteo. Medicine, 1981, Alumni Achievement award Muhlenberg Coll., 1983; elected Physicians Hall of Fame John Shankwiler Soc. Muhlenberg Coll., 1995; Shankweiler fellow, 1995. Fellow Am. Coll. Gen. Practice in Osteo. Medicine and Surgery (cert., pres. div. 1959, Disting. Svc. award, life mem. Pa. div. 1978); mem. Lehigh Valley Osteo. Soc. (pres. 1959-60), Pa. Osteo. Med. Assn. (pres. 1970, Disting. Svc. award 1975), Am. Osteo. Assn. (cert., ho. dels. 1966—, trustee 1970—, pres. 1975-76, cons. family gen. practice com. on osteo. colls. and bur. profl. edn. 1988), Osteo. Physicians and Surgeons of Calif. (trustee 1981—, pres. 1985), Calif. Bd. Osteo. Examiners, Phi Epsilon Pi (pres. 1950), Sigma Sigma Phi. Republican. Jewish. Clubs: Masons, Shriners, Jester, Lions (Host Pomona), Lehigh Valley. Address: 1551 Marjorie Ave Claremont CA 91711-3545

GABRIEL, RENNIE, financial planner; b. L.A., July 27, 1948; s. Harry and Milly (Broder) Goldenhar; m. Judi Robbins, Nov. 24, 1968 (div. Feb. 1989); children: Ryan, Davida; m. Lesli Gilmore, May 5, 1990 (div. Aug. 1998). BA, Calif. State U., Northridge, 1971; CLU, Am. Coll., 1979, Cert. Fin. Planner, 1988. Ins. agt. Prudential and Provident Mutual, Encino, Calif., 1972-78; pension cons. Shadur LaVine & Assocs., Encino, 1978-81; owner Artist Corner Gallery Inc., Encino, 1977-82; pension and fin. planner Gabriel Tolleson & Stroum, Tarzana, Calif., 1983-87; pension cons., fin. planner Shadur LaVine/Integrated Fin., Encino, 1987-90; dir. pensions U.S. Life of Calif., Pasadena, Calif., 1983; fin. planner Pension Alternatives, Encino, 1990-92, The Fin. Coach Inc., Encino, 1993—; instr. UCLA, 1992—; pub. Gabriel Publs., 1996—. Contbr. articles to fin. publs. Mem. Internat. Assn. Fin. Planning (pres. San Fernando Valley chpt. 1992), Nat. Assn. Life Underwriters (Achievement award 1974, Nat. Quality award 1975, Million Dollar Round Table 1990), Internat. Assn. Fin. Planning, CLUs, Inst. Cert. Fin. Planners, Employee Assistance Profls. Assn. (treas. San Fernando Valley chpt. 1992), Apt. Assn. San Fernando Valley-Ventura County (bd. mem. 1992). Avocations: jogging, skiing, real estate management, psychology.

GABRIELSON, SHIRLEY GAIL, nurse; b. San Francisco, Mar. 17, 1934; d. Arthur Obert and Lois Ruth (Lanterman) Ellison; m. I. Grant Gabrielson, Sept. 11, 1955; children: James Grant, Kari Gay. BS in Nursing, Mont. State U., 1955. RN, Mont. Staff and operating room nurse Bozeman (Mont.) Deaconess Hosp., 1954-55, 55-56; staff nurse Warm Springs State Hosp., 1955; office nurse, operating room asst. Dr. Craft, Bozeman, 1956-57; office nurse Dr. Bush, Beach, N.D., 1957-58; pub. health nurse Wibaux

County, 1958-59; staff and charge nurse Teton Meml. Hosp., Choteau, Mont., 1964-65; staff pediatric and float nurse St. Patrick Hosp., Missoula, Mont., 1965-70; nurse, insvc. dir. Trinity Hosp., Wolf Point, Mont., 1970-79; ednl. coord. Community Hosp. and Nursing Home, Poplar, Mont., 1979-96; coord. staff devel. Faith Luth. Home, Wolf Point, 1980-81; risk mgr. Northeast Mont. Health Svcs., Inc., Poplar, 1996—; CPR instr. ARC, Am. Heart Assn., Great Falls, Mont., 1979-97; condr. workshops and seminars; program coord., test proctor for cert. nursing assts., 1989-96; risk mgr. N.E. Mont. Health Svcs., Poplar, Wolf Point, 1996—; preceptor for student nurses in rural health nursing clin. U. N.D., 1993-96. Author: Independent Study for Nurse Assistants, 1977. Former asst. camp leader Girl Scouts U.S.A.; former mother advisor, bd. dirs. Rainbow Girls; pres. Demolay Mothers Club, 1977; bd. dirs. Mont. div. Am. Cancer Soc., 1984-90, mem. awards com., 1986-89; founder Tri-County Parkinson's Support Group, N.E. Mont. Recipient Lifesaver award Am. Cancer Soc., 1987, Svc. award ARC, 1989, Health and Human Svcs. award Mont. State Dept., 1990, U.S. Dept. Health award, 1990, Outstanding award, U.S. HHS, Mont. Health Promotion award Dept. Health and Environ. Scis. Mem. ANA, Mont. Nurses Assn. (mem. commn. on continuing edn. 1977-91, chmn. 1984-86), Order Eastern Star (Worthy grand matron 1995-96), Alpha Tau Delta (alumni pres. 1956). Presbyterian. Avocations: music, travel, writing prose and poetry. Home: 428 Hill St Wolf Point MT 59201-1244 Office: NE Mont Health Svcs Inc PO Box 38 Poplar MT 59255-0038

GADAL, LOUIS STEPHEN, artist; b. L.A., Apr. 10, 1936; s. Louis A. and Lois Anna (Northup) G.; m. Lynn M. Gary, May 15, 1966; children: Eric Spencer, Stephanie Jenet. Cert., Chouinard Art Inst., L.A., 1959; postgrad., Otis Art Inst., L.A., 1962-63. Painter Walt Disney, Anaheim, Calif., 1960; freelance illustrator Louis Gadal Illustration, L.A., 1959-62; illustrator QA Archtl. Illustration, L.A., 1962-68, Carlos Diniz Assocs., L.A., 1968-70; drawing instr. Calif. Inst. Arts, Valencia, Calif., 1980-88, Otis Parsons Art Inst., L.A., 1988-90; illustrator Louis Gadal/Archtl. Illustrator, L.A. and Santa Monica, 1970—. 1st sgt. USNG, 1954-62. Recipient Cert. of Excellence San Bernardino Mus., Redlands, Calif., 1980, 2d Prize Sea Heritage Marine Art, Glen Oaks, N.Y., 1990, Liquitex Watercolor award Pa. Watercolor Soc., Mechanicsburg, Pa., 1990, Bronze Maritime Merit award Nat. Park Acad. of Arts, Jackson Hole, Wyo., 1992, Philip D'Huc Dressler Meml. award Pa. Watercolor Soc., Somerset, Pa., 1993, Combined Donors award Nat. Watercolor Soc., 1994, Dagmar Tribble award, Am. Watercolor Soc., 1995, Maritime Merit award Arts for the Parks 10th annual top 100, 1996, Region One Silver medal Arts for the Parks 12th annual top 100, 1998; included in traveling exhbn. Am. Watercolor Soc. 126th Internat. Exhibit, 1993, Nat. Watercolor Soc. 74th annual Exhibit, 1994, Am. Watercolor Soc. 128th Internat. Exhibit, 1995; contbr. to publs. including Best of Watercolor 2, Best of Watercolor Painting Light & Shadow. Mem. Niagara Frontier Watercolor Soc., Pa. Watercolor Soc., Watercolor West Soc., Nat. Watercolor Soc., Am. Soc. Marine Artist, Northwest Watercolor Soc. Republican. Roman Catholic. Avocations: printmaking, archaeology, history, poetry, writing. Home: 3648 Coolidge Ave Los Angeles CA 90066-3310 Office: Louis Gadal Archtl Illus 3107 Pico Blvd Ste H Santa Monica CA 90405-2061

GADBOIS, LINDA D., artist; b. Torrence, Calif., May 9, 1958; 1 child, Cody Lyons. AA in Comml. Art, El Paso C.C., Colorado Springs, Colo., 1976. Mgr., mktg. dir. Nor-Mar Inc., Boulder, Colo., 1980-92; owner, mgr. Legend Graphics, Ft. Collins, Colo., 1992—. Office: PO Box 454 Red Feather Lakes CO 80545

GAFFNEY, EDWARD STOWELL, scientist, technology executive; b. Bklyn., Jan. 28, 1943; s. William S. and Elizabeth Gaffney; m. Margaret Grace Walker, 1967 (div. Sept. 1975); 1 child, Sean P.; m. Susan Carroll Wasgatt, Oct. 19, 1975; children: Paul S., Joel A. BS, Yale U., 1964; AM, Dartmouth Coll., 1966; PhD, Calif. Inst. Tech., 1973. Rsch. scientist Systems, Sci. and Software, La Jolla, Calif., 1972-77, Pacifica Tech., San Diego, 1977-79; staff mem. Los Alamos (N.Mex.) Nat. Lab., 1979-86; sr. rsch. scientist Ktech Corp., Albuquerque, 1986-92; pres., chief scientist GRE Inc., Albuquerque, 1992—. Sec. Poway (Calif.) Planning and Devel. Program, 1977-79; vice chmn., chmn. Rep. Ctrl. Com., Los Alamos County, 1983-86; dir. N.Mex. Conf. of Chs., Albuquerque, 1994-95, S.W. Conf., United Ch. of Christ, Phoenix, 1994—. Mem. Am. Geophys. Union. Achievements include patent for piezoluminescent sensors. Office: GRE Inc PO Box 30863 Albuquerque NM 87190-0863

GAGARIN, DENNIS PAUL, advertising agency executive; b. Long Beach, Calif., July 9, 1952. BS in Graphic Design, San Jose State U., 1976. Art dir. Brower, Mitchell, Gum Advt., Los Gatos, Calif., 1976-79, Offield & Brower Advt., Los Gatos, 1979-82; sr. art dir. Tycer, Fultz, Bellack Advt., Palo Alto, Calif., 1982-85; head art dir. TFB/BBDO Advt., Palo Alto, 1985-87; creative dir. Lena Chow Advt., Palo Alto, 1987-90; prin., ptnr. Gagarin/McGeoch Advt. and Design, Redwood City, Calif., 1989—; prof. San Jose (Calif.) State U., 1987-90, now guest lectr.; guest art dir. Western Art Dirs. Club, Palo Alto. Recipient awards for graphic design, art direction. Office: Gagarin/McGeoch Advt-Design 493 Seaport Ct Ste 102 Redwood City CA 94063-2788

GAGE, THOMAS EVANS, English language educator, author; b. Oakland, Calif., July 16, 1937; s. William Richard and Alice Frances (Farmer) G.; m. Janet Lee Streets, June 18, 1961 (div. June, 1986); children: Ondine, Shelley, Tyche; m. Anita Lyons, Aug. 4, 1986. BA, U. Calif., Berkeley, 1961, MA, 1971, PhD, 1973. Tchr. of English Fremont H.S., Oakland, Calif., 1961-66; chmn. English dept. Concord (Calif.) H.S., 1966-69; cons. in English Mt. Diablo Unified Sch. Dist., Concord, Calif., 1969-76; dean Scholastic Internat. Scholastic Publs., Italy, France, Eng., Germany, 1973-75; prof. in English Humboldt State U., Arcata, Calif., 1976—; dir. Redwood Writing Project, Humboldt State U., 1977-86, Hooper Rsch. and Writing Projects, 1981-91; mythology lectr. Aegean Sch. Classic Studies, Nousso, Paros, Greece, 1985-87; lectr. Shandong Inst. Mining and Tech., People's Rep. China, 1992; Faulkner lectr. grad. sch. Guangxi U., Nounig, People's Rep. China, 1992, resident lectr. China, Travel and Learn, Scranton, Pa., 1993. Author: (books) America Reads Series, 1969-73, Mind, Myth and Movement, 1973; contbr. articles to Encyclopedia of English Language Studies, 1996. Mem. del. Humboldt County to Guensxi, China, Humboldt County Bd. Suprs., 1991. Recipient Redwood Writing project Bay Area Writing Project U. Calif., Berkeley, 1976-89; named sr. lectr. Am. Studies, Fulbright Scholars, Aleppo, Syria, 1982-83. Mem. Nat. Coun. Tchrs. of English, (bd. dirs., chmn. task force on English standards Calif. N. Coast, 1992-95), Calif. Assn. Tchrs. of English (v.p., award of excellence 1991), Ctrl. Calif. Coun. Tchrs. of English (pres. 1976-89). Office: Humboldt State U Rm 172 English Dept Founders Hall Arcata CA 95521

GAGNE, MARGARET LEE, accounting educator; b. Miller, S.D., June 23, 1953; d. E.A. and Helen A. (Simonds) Andersen; m. Ronald W. Gagne, Jan. 2, 1988. B summa cum laude, Huron Coll., 1975; MBA, U. S.D., 1979; PhD, Ind. U., 1989. Tchr. Hitchcock (S.D.) Ind. Schs., 1975-77; staff auditor Banco, Inc., Sioux Falls, S.D., 1979-81; instr. acctg. U. S.D., Vermillion, 1981-83; from instr. to asst. prof. U. Colo. at Colorado Springs, 1987-96, assoc. prof., 1996—; cons. Walter Drake, Colorado Springs, 1994. Contbr. articles to profl. jours. Treas. St. Luke's Luth. Ch., Colorado Springs, 1987-88; vol. Ecumenical Social Ministries, Colorado Springs, 1995-96. Ind. U. fellow, 1983-86. Mem. Am. Acctg. Assn., Inst. Internal Auditors (bd. govs. 1980-81). Republican. Avocations: reading, walking, crocheting. Office: U Colo at Colorado Springs 1420 Austin Bluffs Pkwy Colorado Springs CO 80918-3733

GAHUNGU, ATHANASE, education educator, researcher; s. Melas Kida and Gloriose Ntakiyica; m. Olive Ndacasaba, Aug. 6, 1988; children: Jessica M., Clive D., Colin A. Primary sch. tchg. diploma, Normal Sch., Gitega, Burundi, 1978; student, Dar-Es-Salam (Tanzania) U., 1983; BA, U. Burundi, 1983; postgrad., Sussex U., Brighton, Eng., 1986, No. Ariz. U., 1990, U. Pa., 1992; diploma in English Lang. Tchr., U. Leeds, U.K., 1987; MEd, No. Ariz. U., 1993, EdD, 1996. Tchr. math., English, Kirundi and phys. edn. [illegible] 1978-79; tchr. English and civic edn. Jr. Sem. Mureke, Ngozi, Burundi, 1983-86; lang. trainer, cross-cultural coord. U.S. Peace Corps, Bujumbura and Bubanza, Burundi, 1984-85; tchr. English H.S. of Rohero, Bujumbura, 1987-88, U.S. Info. Svc., Bujumbura, 1988-92; asst. prof. reading skills, tchr. trainer U. Burundi Pedagogical Inst., Bujumbura, 1988-89; instr. edn. No. Ariz. U., Flagstaff, 1994-96, instr. internat. edn., comparative edn., role of edn. in soc., ednl. rsch., multicultural edn., 1996—; instrnl. supr. Nat. Bur. Curriculum and Rsch. for Secondary Schs., Ministry of Primary and Secondary Edn., Burundi, 1988-89, asst. dir., 1989-91, rschr. and instnl. advisor, 1988-89; dir. cabinet Ministry of Interior, Govt. of Republic of Burundi, 1991-92; adminstrv. intern Flagstaff Unified Sch. Dist., 1996; interim dir. tng. and dissemination Am. Indian Rehab. Rsch. and Tng. Ctr., 1997-98; rsch. asst. No. Ariz. U., 1994-96, sr. rsch. specialist Inst. Human Devel., 1996—; presenter, organizer workshops in field; investigator in field. Mem. rep. coun. U. Burundi, 1980-83; mem. adminstrv. coun. Sem. of Mureke, 1983-86; mem. No. Ariz. Peace and Justice Network, 1996; mem., recorder South Beaver Elem. Sch. site coun. Flagstaff Unified Sch. Dist., 1995-96; mem. exec. bd. No. Ariz. Coun. Govt., 1994-95; pres. Cultural Ambassadors to Pres., No. Ariz. U., 1994; coach Am. Youth Soccer Orgn., Flagstaff, 1994-98; mem. Nat. Commn. for Recruitment to Pub. Function, Republic of Burundi, 1989-92; mem. Martin Luther King Found. for Non-Violence, 1990-92; mem. Pedagogical Bur. Coun., 1989-91; ednl. rep. Workers' Union Nat. Com., Burundi, 1989-91. Fax: (520) 523-9127. E-mail: jan.ucc.nau.edu. Home: 2520 E Joshua Ln Flagstaff AZ 86004 Office: No Ariz U Inst for Human Devel PO Box 5630 Flagstaff AZ 86011

GAINER, MICHAEL EDWARD, legal assistant; b. East Chicago, Ind., Aug. 24, 1956; s. James E. and Dorothy (Purnell) G. Grad., West Side High Sch., 1974. Stock and acctg. specialist U.S. Army, 1976—; cleaner/finisher Blow Knox Foundry & Mill, East Chicago, 1975-77; telemarketer Gold and Miller, Mesa, Ariz., 1988-92, Jobs for the Handicap, Phoenix, 1992-94. Author numerous poems. With U.S. Army, 1975. Recipient Editor's Choice award Nat. Lib. Poetry, 1997. Mem. Poetry Guild. Democrat. Avocations: coin collecting, firearms, astronomy. Home and Office: 461 W 9th St Apt 329 Mesa AZ 85201-4159

GAINES, FRANCIS PENDLETON, III, lawyer; b. Lexington, Va., Sept. 24, 1944; s. Francis Pendleton Jr. and Dorothy Ruth (Bloomhardt) G.; m. Mary Chilton, Dec. 19, 1967 (div. Aug. 1992); children: Elizabeth Chilton, Edmund Pendleton, Andrew Cavett. BA in Hist., U. Ariz., 1967; LLB, U. Va., 1969. Bar: U.S. Dist. Ct. (Ariz.) 1969, Ariz. 1969, U.S. Ct. Appeals (9th cir.) 1972, U.S. Supreme Ct. 1975. Assoc. Evans, Kitchel & Jenckes, Phoenix, 1969-75, ptnr., 1975-89; ptnr. Fennemore Craig, Phoenix, 1989—; mem. panel arbitrators N.Y. Stock Exch., 1984—, NASD, 1984—; judge pro tem Ariz. Ct. Appeals, 1994-95, Maricopa County (Ariz.) Superior Ct., 1994—; mem. State Bar Disciplinary Hearing Com., 1991—, chair, 1995-97; mem. nat. litig. panel U. Va. Sch. Law; lectr. and panelist various CLE programs. Author: Punitive Damages-A Railroad Trial Lawyers Guide, 1985. Sr. warden All Saints' Episcopal Ch., 1994-97, parish chancellor, 1997—; mem. standing com. Episcopal Diocese of Ariz., 1997—; chmn. bd. govs. All Saints' Day Sch., Phoenix, 1990-91; chmn. Phoenix planned giving subcom. U. Ariz., 1985. Fellow Am. Bar Found., Ariz. Bar Found.; mem. ABA, State Bar Ariz., Maricopa County Bar Assn., Nat. Assn. Railroad Trial Coun. (exec. com. Pacific region, v.p. 1997—), Ariz. Assn. Def. Coun., Securities Industry Assn. (law and compliance divsn.), Univ. Club, Internat. Wine & Food Soc. (Phoenix br.). Republican. Episcopalian. Office: Fennemore Craig 3003 N Central Ave Ste 2600 Phoenix AZ 85012-2913

GAINES, JEAN HUNT, healthcare administrator; b. L.A., Dec. 12, 1932; d. Robert George and Phyllis Julia (Tracy) Hunt; m. Kenneth Carnahan Gaines Jr., June 26, 1954; children: Katharine A., Elizabeth T. Gaines Pavloff. BA, UCLA, 1954; cert., U. Calif., Irvine, 1993. Assoc. dir. Delta Delta Delta Fraternity, Arlington, Tex., 1974-78, fin. dir., 1978-80, v.p. collegiate pers., 1980-84, pres., 1984-88, del. nat. Panhellenic conf., 1988-93, cons., 1993—; dir. vols. Community Hospice Care, Sherman Oaks, Calif., 1993—; area advisor So. Calif. Nat. Panhellenic Conf., Indpls., 1988-93; bd. dirs. Gamma Sigma Alpha, L.A. Author: (manuals) Advisory Committee Manual, 1973, House Corporation Guide, 1976; editor: (manuals) Finance Manual, 1980, Delta Delta Delta Chapter Manual, 1984. Chair svc. unit Orange County coun. Girl Scouts Am., 1974-78; bd. dirs. Nat. Charity League, South Coast, Calif., 1975—, Assistance League, Long Beach, Calif., 1976-91. Mem. AAUW, Nat. Assn. Female Execs., Hospice Vol. Mgrs. Assn., So. Calif. Assn. Dir. of Vol. Svcs., Phi Beta Kappa. Republican. Episcopalian. Avocations: traveling, reading and studying European history, needlework.

GAINES, STANLEY O.D., JR., psychology educator; b. Dallas, Mar. 21, 1961; s. Stanley O. Sr. and Juanita Rhea (Earls) G. BS in Psychology with honors, U. Tex., 1985, PhD, 1991. Predoctoral fellow MacAlester Coll., St. Paul, 1989-90; acad. counselor U. Tex., Austin, 1990-92; postdoctoral fellow U. N.C., Chapel Hill, 1992-93; asst. prof. Pomona Coll., Claremont, Calif., 1992—; adj. asst. instr. Coll. St. Catherine, Mpls., 1990, adj. asst. prof., 1991; scholar-in-residence Franklin & Marshall Coll., Lancester, Pa., 1991-92. Mem. cabinet of coll. couns. U. Tex., 1988-89. U. Tex. grantee, 1988-89. Mem. AAUP, Am. Psychol. Soc., Nat. Assn. Ethnic Studies, Nat. Assn. African-Am. Studies, Assn. Black Psychologists, Internat. Soc. for Study Personal Relationships, Internat. Network on Personal Relationships. Home: 1325 N College Ave # E131 Claremont CA 91711-3154

GAJOWSKI, EVELYN JACQUELINE, English language educator; b. Cleve.; d. Frank Nicholas and Genevieve Gajowski; m. Harvey Joseph Berenberg, Aug. 23, 1979. BA, Cleve. State U., 1971; MA, Case Western Res. U., 1974, PhD, 1987. Vis. asst. prof. Wittenberg U., Springfield, Ohio, 1979-81; lectr. U. Calif., Santa Cruz, 1988-91; asst. prof. U. Nev., Las Vegas, 1991-94, assoc. prof. English, 1994—. Author: The Art of Loving: Female Subjectivity and Male Discursive Traditions in Shakespeare's Tragedies, 1992. Mem. exec. bd. Arts Coun. Henderson/Green Valley. Mem. MLA, Shakespeare Assn. Am., Internat. Shakespeare Assn., Rocky Mountain MLA (mem. exec. bd. 1994-96, v.p. 1994, pres. 1995, past pres. 1996, Best Feminist Essay 1989), Pacific Ancient and MLA, Renaissance Conf. So. Calif. Office: U Nev Dept English 4505 S Maryland Pkwy Las Vegas NV 89154-5011

GALANE, MORTON ROBERT, lawyer; b. N.Y.C., Mar. 15, 1926; s. Harry J. and Sylvia (Schenkelbach) G.; children: Suzanne Galane Ash, Jonathan A. B.E.E., CCNY, 1946; LL.B., George Washington U., 1950. Bar: D.C. 1950, Nev. 1955, Calif. 1975. Patent examiner U.S. Patent Office, Washington, 1948-50; spl. partner firm Roberts & McInnis, Washington, 1950-54; practice as Morton R. Galane, P.C., Las Vegas, Nev., 1955—; spl. counsel to Gov. Nev., 1967-70. Contbr. articles to profl. jours. Chmn. Gov.'s Com. on Future of Nev., 1979-80. Fellow Am. Coll. Trial Lawyers; mem. IEEE, ABA (council litigation sect. 1977-83), Am. Law Inst., State Bar Nev., State Bar Calif., D.C. Bar. Home: 2019 Bannie Ave Las Vegas NV 89102-2208 Office: 302 Carson Ave Ste 1100 Las Vegas NV 89101-5909

GALDA, DWIGHT WILLIAM, financial company executive; b. Bklyn., Dec. 19, 1942; s. Fred C. and Audrey D. G.; m. Margaret L., Mar. 21, 1992; children: Cynthia A., Gregory J. BA, Widener U., 1964; postgrad., Am. U., 1965-67, Tex. Christian U., 1997—. Cert. Nat. Assn. Securities Dealers; registered prin. and Natl. Panal Arbitration. Rep. United Svcs. Planning Assn. and Ind. Rsch. Agy., Ft. Worth, 1983-86; dist. exec. USPA and IRA, Ft. Worth, 1986-92, regional exec., 1992-96, prin., 1990-96; prin. Carefree (Ariz.) Capital Mgmt. and Rsch., Carefree, Ariz., 1997—; ind. cons. Dwight W. Galda Consultancy, 1985—; spkr. in field. Contbr. articles profl. jours.; creator U.S. Army Opposing Force Program, 1976. Lt. col. U.S. Army, 1964-82; Army attache U.S. Embassy, Cambodia, 1973-75. Recipient Pace award Dept. of Army, 1976, 77, Legion of Merit, Bronze star, Meritorious Svc. medal, air medal, Vietnamese Cross of Gallantry with Silver star, Cambodian Nat. Def. Svc. medal. Fellow Assn. Investment Mgmt. and Rsch. (adv. advocacy com.), Phoenix Soc. Investment Analysts. Episcopalian. Avocations: running, chamber music, travel. Home: 2741 Manorwood Trl Fort Worth TX 76109-5589 Office: Drawer 1168 100 Easy St Carefree AZ 85377-0180

GALE, ARNOLD DAVID, pediatric neurologist, consultant; b. Chgo., Nov. 2, 1949; s. Benjamin and Revelle Frances (Steinman) G. AB summa cum laude Stanford U., 1971; MD, Johns Hopkins U., 1976. Diplomate Am. Bd. Pediatrics, Nat. Bd. Med. Examiners; med. lic., Calif. Resident in pediatrics Mass. Gen. Hosp., Boston, 1976-78; postdoctoral fellow Johns Hopkins Hosp., Balt., 1978-79, resident in neurology, 1979-82; asst. prof. pediatrics and neurology George Washington U. Sch. Medicine, Washington, 1982-89; dir. neurology tng. program Children's Hosp. Nat. Med. Ctr., Washington, 1982-89; med. info. officer Muscular Dystrophy Assn., Tucson, 1992—; consulting neurologist Vaccine Injury Program U.S. Dept. HHS, Rockville, Md., 1989—, Inst. Vaccine Safety Sch. Hygiene and Pub. Health Johns Hopkins U., Balt., 1998—; adv. panel FDA, Rockville, 1983-89; reviewer Am. Jour. Diseases of Children, 1991, New Eng. Jour. Medicine, 1986. Author: Pediatric Emergency Medicine, 1989; contbr. articles to profl. jours. Support group coord. Muscular Dystrophy Assn., San Jose, Calif., 1989—, v.p., 1992-94; mem. Pres.'s Com. Employment of People Disabilities, Washington, 1992—; med. adv. bd. Multiple Sclerosis Soc., Santa Clara, Calif., 1990—; bd. dirs. Muscular Dystrophy Assn., Tucson, 1993—. Recipient Nat. Rehab. award Allied Svcs., Scranton, Pa., 1994. Fellow Am. Acad. Pediatrics; mem. Am. Acad. Neurology, Am. Soc. Neurol. Investigation (founding mem.), Child Neurology Soc., Muscular Dystrophy Assn. (v.p. 992-94), Nat. Alumni Coun. (Johns Hopkins U.), Phi Beta Kappa, Alpha Omega Alpha. Jewish. Avocations: writing, travel. Office: 335 Elan Village Ln Unit 107 San Jose CA 95134-2540

GALE, DANIEL BAILEY, architect; b. St. Louis, Nov. 6, 1933; s. Leone Caryll and Gladys (Wotowa) G.; student Brown U., 1951-53, Ecole Des Beaux Arts, Paris, 1954-55; BArch., Washington U., 1957; m. Nancy Susan Miller, June 15, 1957; children: Caroline Hamilton, Rebecca Fletcher, Daniel Bailey With Gale & Cannon, Architects and Planners, Hellmuth, Obata & Kassabaum, Inc., Architects, St. Louis, and exec. v.p. corp. devel., dir. HOK, Inc., St. Louis, 1961-79; ptnr. Heneghan and Gale, architects and planners, Aspen, Colo., 1967-69; pres., chief exec. officer Gale Kober Assocs., San Francisco, 1979-83; pvt. practice architecture, Belvedere, Calif., 1984—; pres. Program Mgmt. Inc., Belvedere, 1984—. Recipient Henry Adams prize Washington U., 1957. Mem. AIA, Singapore Inst. Architects. Home and Office: 280 Belvedere Ave Belvedere CA 94920-2425

GALE, ROBERT MARTIN, research scientist, consultant; b. Teaneck, N.J., Oct. 14, 1946; s. John Martin and Evelyn Anna (Cease) G.; m. Cathleen Elizabeth Plough, May 7, 1977; children: Christopher, Melissa, Alexander. BS in Chemistry, San Jose State U., 1969, MS in Chemistry, 1975. Chemist Food Machinery Corp., San Jose, Calif., 1969-71; sr. rsch. fellow ALZA Corp., Palo Alto, Calif., 1971—. Contbr. articles to profl. jours., chpt. to book; inventor pharmaceuticals. Mem. ACS (sec. 1964-97), Am. Assn. Pharm. Sci. (honored spkr. 1982), Controlled Release Soc., Palo Alto Hills Golf and Country Club. Home: 1276 Russell Ave Los Altos CA 94024-5541

GALE, THOMAS MARTIN, university dean; b. Green Bay, Wis., May 16, 1926; s. Thomas Griswold and Carrie (Danz) G.; m. Mary Margaret Hardman, May 28, 1960; children—Thomas Hardman, John Martin. B.A., U. Calif. at Berkeley, 1949, M.A., 1950; Ph.D., U. Pa., 1958. Dean Coll. Arts and Scis. N.Mex. State U., 1971-91, bd. dirs. Acad. for Learning in Retirement, 1991-96, ret., 1991; with Border Books Festival, 1996—. Chmn. N.Mex. Humanities Coun., NEH, 1972-77; chmn. Las Cruces Am. 2000 Task Force, 1991—; vice-chmn. N.Mex. Commn. on Higher Edn.; bd. dirs. exec. com. N.Mex. State U. Found. With AUS, 1944-46. Social Sci. Research fellow, 1952-53, 53-54; Huntington Library fellow, 1959; Fulbright fellow Peru, 1960. Mem. Phi Beta Kappa, Phi Alpha Theta. Club: Rotarian. Home: 3115 Majestic Rdg Las Cruces NM 88011-4603

GALES, SAMUEL JOEL, retired civilian military employee, counselor; b. Dublin, Miss., June 14, 1930; s. James McNary McNeil and Alice Francis (Smith) Broadus-Gales; m. Martha Ann Jackson (div. Jan. 1978); children: Samuel II (dec.), Martha Diane Townsend, Katherine Roselein, Karlmann Von, Carolyn B. Ratcliff, Elizabeth Angelica McCain. BA, Chapman Univ., 1981, MS, 1987. Ordained Eucharist minister, Episcopal Ch., 1985; cert. tchr., Calif. Enlisted U.S. Army, 1948, advanced through grades to master 1st sgt., 1969, ret., 1976; tchr. Monterey (Calif.) Unified Sch. Dist., 1981-82; civilian U.S. Army Directorate of Logistics, Ft. Ord, Calif., 1982-93; collateral EEOC counselor Dept. Def., U.S. Army, 1987-93; peer counselor, 1982-84. Active Family Svc. Agy., Monterey, 1979-85; rep. Episc. Soc. for Ministry on Aging, Carmel, Calif., 1980-86, Task Force on Aging, Carmel, 1983-87, vestryman, 1982-85, 91-94; ombudsman Monterey County Long-Term Care Program, Calif. Dept. for the Aging, 1993-97; vol. guide Monterey Bay Aquarium Found., 1994—, vol. docent Bay Net, Ctr. for Marine Conservation, Monterey Bay Nat. Marine Sanctuary, 1997—. Decorated Air medal. Mem. Nat. Assn. Ret. Fed. Employees (pres. chpt. 579 1999—), Am. Legion (post comdr. 1973-74), Forty and Eight (chef-de-gare 1979, 80), Monterey Chess Club, Comdr.'s Club Calif. (pres. Outpost 28 1981-82). Republican. Avocation: classical music. Home: PO Box 919 1617 Lowell St Seaside CA 93955-3811

GALIN, ROBERT BARRY, writer, park ranger; b. L.A., Jan. 3, 1957; s. Lawrence and Bertie (Lloyd) G.; m. Deborah Lee Kelley, July 1, 1997. AA, L.A. Valley Coll., 1977; BA, SUNY, Albany, 1984; MA, U. San Francisco, 1989. Cert. EMT, Calif.; cert. law enforcement specialist, Nat. Pk. Svc. Exec. editor Pulp & Paper WEEK, San Francisco, 1986-94; humane officer Peninsula Humane Soc., San Mateo, Calif., 1995-96; pk. ranger Nat. Pk. Svc., Mesa Verde, Colo., 1997, 98, Alcatraz, San Francisco, 1997-98; freelance journalist, 1976—; CEO Rutabaga Enterprises, Mancos, Colo., 1998—; chmn. bd. Rutabaga Enterprises, 1998—. Author: Footsteps of Winter, 1998. Bd. dirs., newsletter editor Sierra Club, San Francisco, 1992-94; vice comdr., edn. officer USCG Aux., San Francisco, 1994-96; bd. dirs. Innovative Housing, San Francisco, 1994; mem. organizing com. Christmas in April Program, San Francisco, 1994. Recipient Presdl. Environ. award The White House, 1974. Mem. Soc. Profl. Journalists (bd. dirs. 1992-95), Western Writers Am., Fraternal Order Police, Am. Hist. Assn., N.Am. Assn. Environ. Edn., George Wright Soc. Avocation: educational travel. Home: PO Box 27 Cortez CO 81321-0027

GALL, A. PHILIP, recording engineer; b. Sioux City, Iowa, June 29, 1952; s. Arthur C. and LaVonne P. (Phillips) G. Student, Westmar Coll., 1971-73, No. Ariz. U., 1973, 76-79. Announcer various radio stas., Flagstaff and Williams, Ariz., 1976-82; engr. Mudshark Rec. Studios, Flagstaff, 1979—. Democrat. Avocations: cross-country skiing, hiking. Home and Office: Mudshark Rec Studios 7055 N Chambers Dr Flagstaff AZ 86001-8139

GALL, DONALD ALAN, data processing executive; b. Reddick, Ill., Sept. 13, 1934; s. Clarence Oliver and Evelyn Louise (McCumber) G.; m. Elizabeth Olmstead, June 25, 1960 (div. 1972); children: Christopher, Keith, Elizabeth; m. Kathleen Marie Insogna, Oct. 13, 1973; 1 child, Kelly Marie. BSME, U. Ill., 1956; SM, MIT, 1958, ME, 1960, ScD, 1964. Rsch. engr. GM, Detroit, 1956-57; staff engr. Dynatech Corp., Cambridge, Mass., 1959-60; mgr. ctr. systems Dynatech Corp., Cambridge, 1962-63; asst., assoc. prof. Carnegie-Mellon U., Pitts., 1964-69; rsch. assoc. prof. surgery and anesthesiology U. Pitts. Sch. Medicine, 1969-73; vis. fellow IBM Research Lab., Rueschlikon, Switzerland, 1970-71; pres. Omega Computer Systems, Inc., Phoenix, 1973—; CEO Omega Legal Systems, Inc., Phoenix, 1995—; bd. dirs. TTI Technologies, Inc., Omaha, 1996—; chmn. bd. dirs. M Tech. Assn. Contbr. articles to profl. jours.; inventor fuel injection system. Bd. dirs. Scottsdale Boys and Girls Club, 1982-93; mem. Scottsdale Head Honchos, 1978-87; mem. Verde Vaqueros, 1987—. Recipient Taylor medal Internat. Conf. on Prodn. Rsch., Disting. Alumnus award dept. mech. and indsl. engring. U. Ill., 1997. Mem. AAAS, ASME, M Tech Assn. (exec. dir., bd. dirs. 1996-98, chmn. bd. dirs. 1998—), Sigma Xi, Pi Tau Sigma, Tau Beta Pi, Phi Kappa Phi. Avocations: horseback riding, skiing, golf. Home: 9833 E Cortez St Scottsdale AZ 85260-6012 Office: Omega Computer Sys Inc 3875 N 44th St Ste 200 Phoenix AZ 85018-5486

GALLAGHER, MICHAEL L., lawyer; b. LeMars, Iowa, Apr. 14, 1944. BA, Ariz. State U., 1966, JD, 1970. Bar: Ariz. 1970. judge pro tem Maricopa County Superior Ct., 1979, Ariz. Ct. Appeals, 1985. Chmn. gov.'s adv. com. profl. football, 1981-87, mayor's adv. com. profl. sports, 1984-91; bd. dirs. Maricopa County Sports Authority, 1989; bd. visitors law sch. Ariz. State U., 1979; dir. Valley of the Sun YMCA, chmn., 1995, Phoenix Suns Charities; trustee Peter Kiewit Found.; dir. Ariz. Pub. Svc. Co., Omaha World Herald Co. [illegible] 1988), Fedn. Ins. and Corp. Counsel, Internat. Assn. Defense Counsel, Ariz. Assn. Defense Counsel (pres. 1978), Ariz. C. of C. (dir.). Office: Gallagher & Kennedy PC 2600 N Central Ave Ste 1800 Phoenix AZ 85004-3099

GALLAGHER, SHERRY E., artist; b. Great Falls, Mont., Feb. 1, 1951; d. Mike and Ina (Hanson) Morris; m. Ron Gallagher, Nov. 8, 1969 (div. Sept. 1986); children: Tonya, Ronald Paul; m. Peter Northcott, Aug. 29, 1987. instr. various workshops. Exhibited in group shows at Mus. Native Am. Culture, Spokane, Wash., 1985 (Art Com. award), 1989 (Best of Show-Traditional), Gov's. Mansion Mont., 1989-90, Las Vegas Art Mus., 1992. Recipient 3d place award Safari Club Internat. Art Competition, Reno, Nev., 1992, Juror's award and Best of Show Western Art Assn., Ellensburg, Wash., 1992, Best of Show Olfield Prodns. Celebration of Western Art, Popular Vote award-profl. div. Mont. State Fair Fine Arts, 1983-85, 90, Best of Show, 1987, 89, 98. Home and Office: PO Box 3122 Great Falls MT 59403-3122

GALLAGHER, THOMAS EDMUND, hotel executive; b. Detroit, Dec. 10, 1944; s. Edmund James and Monica F. Gallagher; m. Mary Kay Stoegbauer; children: Meighan, Kevin, Erin, Ryan. AB magna cum laude, Holy Cross, 1966; JD cum laude, Harvard Law, 1969. Bar: Calif. 1970. Legis. asst. U.S. Senate, Washington, 1970-72; ptnr., assoc. Gibson Dunn & Crutcher, L.A., 1969-79; ptnr. Gibson Dunn & Crutcher, London and Riyadh, Saudi Arabia, 1979-87, N.Y.C., 1987-92; pres., CEO Griffin Gaming (Amex-GGE), Atlantic City, N.J., 1995-96, The Griffin Group, Inc., N.Y.C., 1992-97; exec. v.p., gen. counsel Hilton Hotels Corp., Beverly Hills, Calif., 1997—; dir., chmn. exec. com. Resorts Internat., Atlantic City, 1993-95; dir., chmn. comp. com. Players Internat. Inc., Las Vegas, Nev., and Atlantic City, 1992-97. Trustee Greylock Found., N.Y.C., 1992—. Mem. Urban Land Inst. Office: Hilton Hotels Corp 9336 Civic Center Dr Beverly Hills CA 90210-3604

GALLAGHER, TIM, editor, newspaper. Editor Ventura (Calif.) County Star, 1995—. Office: Ventura County Star 5250 Ralston St Ventura CA 93003-7318*

GALLEGLY, ELTON WILLIAM, congressman; b. Huntington Park, Calif., Mar. 7, 1944; married; four children. Attended, Calif. State U., L.A. Businessman, real estate broker Simi Valley, Calif., from 1968; mem. Simi Valley City Coun., 1979; mayor City of Simi Valley, 1980-86; mem. 100th-106th Congresses from the 21st (now 23d) Calif. dist., 1986—; chmn. internat. rels. subcom. on the western hemisphere, mem. judiciary com., mem. resources com.; mem. exec. com. U.S. Ho. Reps. Rep. Study Com.; mem. Congl. Human Rights Caucus, Congl. Fire Svcs. Caucus; formerly vice-chmn., chmn. Ventura County Assn. govts., Calif. Bd. dirs. Moorpark Coll. Found. Office: US Ho of Reps 2427 Rayburn HOB Washington DC 20515*

GALLEN, WILLIAM JOSEPH, pediatrician, cardiologist; b. Columbus, Ohio, July 4, 1924; s. Francis Thomas and Marguerite Helen (Farmer) G.; m. Patricia Mary Bachman, Sept. 28, 1932; children—Jeanne, William, Thomas, Julie, Mary Pat, Michael, John (dec.). B.A., Ohio State U., 1945, M.D., 1948. Diplomate Am. Bd. Pediatrics, Am. Bd. Pediatric Cardiology. Intern Harper Hosp., Detroit, 1948-51; resident in pediatrics Milw. Children's Hosp., 1953-55; fellow pediatric cardiology Johns Hopkins U., Balt., 1955-56; fellow Karolinska Sjkhuset, Stockholm, 1956-57; developer, dir. Cardiac Ctr., Milw. Children's Hosp., 1957-91; prof. pediatrics Med. Coll. Wis., Milw., 1970-86; cons. in field. Contbr. articles to profl. jours.; presenter exhibits in field. Served to capt. USAF, 1951-53. Fellow Am. Acad. Pediatricians, Am. Coll. Cardiologists (bd. govs. Wis. 1983-86); mem. Am. Heart Assn., Wis. Heart Assn. (outstanding pediatrician Wis. 1978, outstanding physician 1980), Milw. Pediatric Soc., Midwest Pediatric Cardiologists Assn., Alpha Omega Alpha, Alpha Epsilon Delta. Roman Catholic. Home: 5462 N Via Arancio Tucson AZ 85750-6050

GALLETTA, JOSEPH LEO, physician; b. Bessemer, Pa., Dec. 21, 1935; s. John and Grace (Galletta) G.; m. Teresita Suarez Soler, Feb. 19, 1961; children: John II, Angela, Eric, Christopher, Robert Francis, Michael Angelo. Student, U. Pitts., 1953-56; MD, U. Santo Tomas, Manila, 1962. Intern, St. Elizabeth Hosp., Youngstown, Ohio, 1963-64; family practice medicine, 29 Palms, Calif., 1967-77, Hemet, Calif., 1977—; chief of staff 29 Palms Cmty. Hosp., 1970-71, 73-76; vice chief of staff Hi-Desert Med. Center, Joshua Tree, Calif., 1976-77; chmn. dept. family practice Hemet Valley Hosp., 1981-83, med. dir. chem. dependency dept., 1985-88; med. dir. Loma Linda (Calif.) U. Behavioral Medicine Ctr. Recovery Svc., 1994-96; pres. Flexisplint, Inc.; founding mem. Hemet Hospice; former cons. Morongo Basin Mental Health Assn.; mem. adv. com. on substance abuse Riverside County, 1995—. Hon. mem. 29 Palms Sheriff's Search and Rescue, 1971-77. Bd. dirs. 29 Palms Cmty. Hosp. Dist., Morongo Unified Sch. Dist. Served with M.C. USN, 1964-67. Diplomate Am. Bd. Family Practice. Fellow Am. Geriatric Soc. (founder West Coast chpt.), Am. Acad. Family Practice; mem. Calif. Med. Assn., Riverside County Med. Assn., Am. Holistic Med. Assn. (charter), Am. Soc. Addiction Medicine, Calif. Soc. Addiction Medicine (mem. exec. coun. 1995-98), Am. Acad. Family Practice, Calif. Acad. Family Practice. Roman Catholic. Established St. Anthonys Charity Clinic, Philippines, 1965; inventor Flexisplint armboards. Home: 27691 Pochea Trl Hemet CA 92544-8180 Office: Westside Medical Pla 4020 W Florida Ave Hemet CA 92545-5279

GALLI, DARRELL JOSEPH, management consultant; b. Ft. Bragg, Calif., Nov. 10, 1948; s. Joseph Germain and Esther Edith (Happajoki) G.; B.A. in Transp./Internat. Bus., San Francisco State U., 1975; BS in Computer Info. Systems, 1985; MBA Golden Gate U., 1980; m. Rondus Miller, Apr. 23, 1977 (div. 1981); 1 dau., Troyan Hulda. With Pacific Gas & Electric Co., Santa Cruz, Calif., 1972-73; with Calif. Western R.R., Ft. Bragg, 1975-77, Sheldon Oil Co., Suisun, Calif, 1978-80; mgr. House of Rondus, Suisun, 1974-79; mgmt. cons., Suisun City, 1979—; instr. Solano Coll., 1979-81, Golden Gate U., 1981; mem. faculty U. Md. European div., Heidelberg, W.Ger., 1982-88; owner, mgr. Old Stewart House Bed and Breakfast, Fort Bragg, Calif., 1990—; lectr. Coll. Redwoods, Ft. Bragg, 1989—; coord. Small Bus. Mgmt. Seminar, 1980. Asst. coordinator Sr. Citizens Survey for Solano Coll. and Sr. Citizens Center, 1980; mem. Ft. Bragg City Coun., 1994—. Served with U.S. Army, 1969-71. Lic. Calif. real estate agt. Mem. Am. Assn. M.B.A. Execs., World Trade Assn., Bay Area Elec. R.R. Assn. Democrat. Episcopalian. Club: Odd Fellows. Home and Office: 511 Stewart St Fort Bragg CA 95437-3226

GALLI, STANLEY WALTER, artist; b. San Francisco, Jan. 18, 1912; s. Ismene and Laura (Frediani) G.; m. Frances Margaret Salvato, May 18, 1941; children: Timothy Alonzo, Thomas Ramon. Ptnr. Patterson & Hall, San Francisco, 1938-41, 45-49; freelance illustrator San Francisco, 1950-72, freelance painter, 1969—; advanced illustration prof. San Francisco City Coll., 1967-73. One-man shows include Palm Springs (Calif.) Desert Mus., 1978, Crocker Art Mus., Sacramento, 1980, Frye Art Mus., Seattle, 1982, Riverside Mus., Baton Rouge, 1992, Museo Italo Americano, San Francisco, 1995,; exhibited in group shows at Oakland (Calif.) Mus., N.Y. Hist. Soc., N.Y.C., Smithsonian Inst., Washington, DeYoung Mus., San Francisco, Museo Italo Americano, San Francisco Mus. Art, Hall of Fame/N.Y. Soc. Illustrators, U.S. Postal Svc. Archives, Pentagon, San Francisco Art Initiative, others. With USN, 1942-45. Mem. Soc. Illustrators N.Y. (award 1962), Soc. Illustrators San Francisco. Office: Stanley W Galli Ltd PO Box 66 Kentfield CA 94904-2629

GALLIANI, ROBERT, marketing professional; b. L.A., Sept. 9, 1950; s. Louis Frank and Jeanne Murial (Faulk) G.; m. Mara Janel Anastasi, Nov. 12, 1988; children: Anthony Milo, Gina Lin, Enzo Luigi. AA, Coll. of San Mateo (Calif.), 1971. Promotion mgr. Warner Bros. Records, San Francisco, 1972-76; promotion mgr. Am. Broadcasting Records, San Francisco, 1976-78, RSO Records, San Francisco, 1978-80, Atlantic Records, San Francisco, 1980-84; prin. Galliani Bros. Mktg., San Francisco, 1984-94; COO Gavin/Miller Freeman, San Francisco, 1994—. Democrat. Roman Catholic. Avocation: gardening. Office: Gavin 140 2d St San Francisco CA 94105-3727

GALLIGANI, DENNIS JOHN, academic administrator, educator; b. Chgo.; s. Nelo John and Josephine Galligani; m. Jane A. Galligani; children: Christine, Michael, Daniel. BS, Quincy Coll., 1966; MS, Western Ill. U., 1972; PhD, UCLA, 1978. Asst. vice chancellor, registrar U. Calif., Irvine; assoc. v.p. student acad. svcs. U. Calif., Oakland. Lt. USN, 1966-70. Avocations: soccer, coach. Office: Univ Calif 1111 Franklin St Oakland CA 94607-5201

GALLIVAN, JOHN WILLIAM, publisher; b. Salt Lake City, June 28, 1915; s. Daniel and Frances (Wilson) G.; m. Grace Mary Ivers, June 30, 1938; children: Gay, John W. Jr., Michael D., Timothy. B.A., U. Notre Dame, 1937. With Salt Lake Tribune, 1937—, promotion mgr., 1942-48, asst. pub., 1948-60, pub., 1960-84; pres. Kearns-Tribune Corp., 1960-86, chmn. bd., 1984-89; dir., exec. com. Tele-Communications, Inc., 1989—; pres. Silver King Mining Co., 1960—. Pres. Utah Symphony, 1964-65. Mem. Sigma Delta Chi, Bohemian Club (San Francisco). Clubs: Nat. Press (Washington); Alta (Salt Lake City), Salt Lake Country (Salt Lake City), Rotary (Salt Lake City). Home: 17 S 12th E Salt Lake City UT 84102-1607 Office: Kearns-Tribune Corp 143 S Main St Salt Lake City UT 84111-1924

GALLO, JON JOSEPH, lawyer; b. Santa Monica, Calif., Apr. 19, 1942; s. Philip S. and Josephine (Sarazan) G.; m. Jo Ann Broome, June 13, 1964 (div. 1984); children: Valerie Ann, Donald Philip; m. Eileen Florence, July 4, 1985; 1 child, Kevin Jon. BA, Occidental Coll., 1964; JD, UCLA, 1967. Bar: Calif. 1968, U.S. Ct. Appeals (9th cir.) 1968, U.S. Tax Ct. 1969. Assoc. Greenberg, Glusker, Fields, Claman & Machtinger, L.A., 1967-75, ptnr., 1975—; bd. dirs. USC Probate and Trust Conf., L.A., 1980—, UCLA Estate Planning Inst., chmn. 1992—. Contbr. articles to profl. jours. Fellow Am. Coll. Trust and Estate Counsel; mem. ABA (chair Generation Skipping Taxation com. 1992-95, co-chair life ins. com. 1995—), Internat. Acad. Estate and Trust Law, Assn. for Advanced Life Underwriting (assoc. mem.). Avocation: photography. Office: Greenberg Glusker Fields Claman & Machtinger LLP Ste 2100 1900 Avenue Of The Stars Los Angeles CA 90067-4502*

GALLOWAY, PAMELA EILENE, university official emeritus; b. Tucson, Dec. 2, 1952; d. David Barnes and Nancy (Harrison) Galloway. BA in Journalism, U. Nev., 1974. Feature writer Reno Gazette Jour., 1973-74; feature writer Reno Newspapers, Inc., 1974-78, lifestyle editor, 1978-80, mem. copy desk/gen. assignment, 1980-81, edn. beat reporter, 1981-84; stataírds dir. pub. info. U. Nev. System, 1984-94; dir. student advisement, Coll. Edn. U. Nev., Reno, 1994-97, dir. student advisement emeritus, 1997—. Mem. First United Meth. Ch., 1982—; publicity chair Homeowners Assn.; bd. dirs. prison program Kairos, 1984-86; bd. dirs., fund raising chmn. Cursillo Interdenom. Group, 1981-84; no. Nev. publicity chair Gov's. Conf. Women, 1987. Active Citizen's Alert, Friends of the Libr. Recipient Planned Parenthood Pub. Svc. award for no. Nev., 1983. Mem. ACLU, Nev. State Press Assn. (numerous writing awards 1977-78), Nat. Fedn. Press Women (two nat. interview awards), Inc., Internat. Assn. Press Women, Inc., Toastmasters (10 Most Watchable Women No. Nev. 1984).

GALLUS, CHARLES JOSEPH, journalist; b. Havre, Mont., Jan. 24, 1947; s. Raymond Charles and Anna Jo (Mack) G. BA in Polit. Sci. cum laude, Carroll Coll., 1969; MA in Polit. Sci., U. Mont., 1972. Bookkeeper's asst. Ellen Solem, CPA, Chinook, Mont., 1972; circulation asst. Havre Daily News, 1972-73, wire editor, reporter, photographer, 1973-97. Mem. 2 study comms. Havre local govt., 1974-77, 84-86; mem. Hill County Dem. Ctrl. Com., Havre, 1974—. Mem. AP, Glacier Natural History Assn., Northwinds Athletic Club, Soc. Profl. Journalists, KC, Sigma Delta Chi. Roman Catholic. Avocations: outdoor recreation, travel, reading, dancing. Home: 112 3rd St # 746 Havre MT 59501-3532

GALTON, STEPHEN HAROLD, lawyer; b. Tulare, Calif., Dec. 23, 1937; s. Harold Parker and Marie Rose (Tuck) G.; m. Grace Marilyn Shaw, Aug. 15, 1964; children—Mark, Bradley, Jeremy, Elisabeth. B.S., U. So. Calif., 1966, J.D., 1969. Bar: Calif. 1970, U.S. Ct. Appeals (9th cir.) 1973, U.S. Dist. Ct. (no. dist.) Calif. 1973, U.S. Dist. Ct. (cen. dist.) Calif. 1970, U.S. Dist. Ct. (ea. and so. dists.) Calif. 1973. Assoc. Martin & Flandrick, San Marino, Calif., 1970-71, ptnr., 1971-72; assoc. Booth, Mitchel, Strange & Smith, Los Angeles, 1973-77, ptnr., 1978-85; ptnr. Galton & Helm, Los Angeles, 1986—. Mem. ABA (litigation, tort, insurance sects.), Am. Bd. Trial Advs. (assoc.), Calif. State Bar Assn. (del. 1974-81, chair fed. cts. com.), Wilshire Bar Assn. (pres. 1986-87), Los Angeles County Bar Assn. (bd. of trustees 1987—). Republican. Presbyterian. Contbr. articles to profl. jours. Office: Galton & Helm 500 S Grand Ave Ste 1200 Los Angeles CA 90071-2624

GALVAO, LOUIS ALBERTO, import and export corporation executive, consultant; b. Ponta Delgada, Sao Miguel, Portugal, July 5, 1949; came to U.S., 1969; s. Jeremias B. and Margarida M. G.; m. Antonieta A. Galvao, Oct. 26, 1966 (div. 1984); children: Marlene, Vanessa. Degree in Bus. Mgmt., Indsl. & Commerce Sch., Azores, Portugal, 1968; Dr. Universal Life (hon.), Universal Life Ch., 1991. Asst. mgr. sales J.B. Galvao Imports, Azores, 1964-68; asst. supr. Union Carbide Corp., Peabody, Mass., 1969-70, Container Corp. Am., Wakefield, Mass., 1970-73; sales dir. McCulloch Oil Corp., Lake Havash City, Ariz., 1972-74; pres. Sunset Investments Corp., Phoenix, 1974—; v.p. United Universal Enterprises Corp., Phoenix, 1985—; pres. Universal Imports, Inc., Phoenix, 1977—; dir. Global Savings & Loan Ltd., London, 1990—. mem. Nat. Rep. Congl. Com., Washington, 1982— (cert. recognition 1981, 84, 85, Campaign Kickoff award 1984, cert. merit 1992), Rep. Presdl. Task Force, Washington, 1984— (Am. flag dedicated in his honor at Rotunda of U.S. Capital bldg. 1986, life mem., mem. presdl. electiom registry 1992), Rep. Nat. Com. (cert. recognition 1990, 92), European Movement, U.K., 1990—, Social Dem. Party, Portugal, 1990—, Washington Legal Found.; charter mem. U.S. Def. Com.; del. The Presl. Trust, Washington, 1992. Recipient award U.S. Def. Com., 1984; inducted to Rep. Nat. Hall Honor Rep. Nat. Candidate Trust, 1992. Mem. Am. Mgmt. Assn., Nat. Assn. Export Cos., Profl. Fin. Assts., Heritage Bus. Club, Senatorial Club, Universal Life Ch. Roman Catholic. Avocations: reading, traveling, biking, movies.

GAMBARO, ERNEST UMBERTO, lawyer, consultant; b. Niagara Falls, N.Y., July 6, 1938; s. Ralph and Teresa (Nigro) G.; m. Winifred Sonya Porter, June 3, 1961 (div.); m. Monica Cuellar, Sept. 30, 1994. B.A. in Aero. Engring. with honors, Purdue U., 1960, M.S. with honours, 1961; Fulbright scholar, Rome U., 1961-62; J.D. with honors, Loyola U., L.A., 1975. Bar: Calif. 1975, U.S. Tax Ct. 1976, U.S. Supreme Ct. 1979, U.S. Ct. Apppeals (9th cir.). With Aerospace Corp., El Segundo, Calif., 1962-80, counsel, 1975-80; asst. gen. counsel, asst. sec. Computer Scis. Corp., El Segundo, 1980-88; sr. v.p., gen. counsel, sec. INFONET Svcs. Corp., El Segundo, 1988—; cons. bus. fin. and mgmt., 1968—; bd. dirs. STM Wireless, Govt. Systems, Inc., Networks Telephony Corp. Recipient U.S. Air Force Commendation for contbns. to U.S. manned space program, 1969; Purdue U. Pres.'s scholar, 1959-60. Mem. ABA (internat., taxation sects.), Los Angeles Bar Assn. (exec. com. 1976—, founder chmn. sect. law and tech. 1976-78, chmn. bar reorgn. com. 1981-82), Am. Arbitration Assn. Los Angeles Ctr. Internat. Comml. Arbitration (founder, bd. dirs.), Internat. Law Inst. (faculty), St. Thomas More Law Soc., Phi Alpha Delta, Omicron Delta Kappa (past pres.), Tau Beta Pi, Sigma Gamma Tau (past pres.), Phi Eta Sigma. Republican. Newspaper columnist Europe Alfresco; contbr. articles to profl. publs. Home: PO Box 3033 Crest Dr Palos Verdes Peninsula CA 90274 Office: 2100 E Grand Ave El Segundo CA 90245-5024

GAMBI, JASON GILBERT, baseball player; b. West Covine, Calif., Jan. 8, 1971. 1st baseman Oakland (Calif.) A's. Office: c/o Oakland A's 7677 Oakport St Ste 200 Oakland CA 94621-1933

GAMBINO, JEROME JAMES, nuclear medicine educator; b. N.Y.C., Sept. 13, 1925; m. Jacquelyn Ann Mazzola, Mar. 27, 1948; children: Charles, John, Mary Ellen, Jacquelyn. BA, U. Conn., 1950, MS, 1952; PhD, U. Calif., 1957. Asst. prof. natural scis. SUNY, New Paltz, 1957-59; research radiobiologist UCLA, 1959-61; mem. research staff Northrop Corp., Hawthorne, Calif., 1961-69; dir. edn. nuclear medicine dept. VA Med. Ctr., Los Angeles, 1969-96; rsch. cons. VA Med. Ctr., L.A., 1996—; lectr. anatomy U. So. Calif., L.A., 1963-89, radiol. scis. UCLA, 1978—. Mem. Radiation Research Soc., Soc. Nuclear Medicine (pres. So. Calif. chpt. 1981-82). Avocations: watercolor painting, pen and pencil sketching. Office: West LA VA Med Ctr Nuclear Medicine 115 11301 Wilshire Blvd Los Angeles CA 90073-1003

GAMBOA, GEORGE CHARLES, oral surgeon, educator; b. King City, Calif., Dec. 17, 1923; s. George Angel and Martha Ann (Baker) G.; m. Winona Mae Collins, July 16, 1946; children: Cheryl Jan Gamboa Granger, Jon Charles, Judith Merlene Gamboa Hiscox. Pre-dental cert., Pacific Union Coll., 1943; DDS, U. Pacific, 1946; MS, U. Minn., 1953; AB, U. So. Calif., 1958, EdD, 1976. Diplomate Am. Bd. Oral and Maxillofacial Surgery. Fellow oral surgery Mayo Found., 1950-53; clin. prof. grad. program oral and maxillofacial surgery U. So. Calif., L.A., 1954—; assoc. prof. Loma Linda (Calif.) U., 1958-94, chmn. dept. oral surgery, 1960-63; pvt. practice oral and maxillofacial surgery, San Gabriel, Calif., 1955-93; dir. So. Calif. Acad. of Oral Pathology, 1995—. Mem., past chmn. first aid com. West San Gabriel chpt. ARC. Fellow Am. Coll. Dentists, Am. Coll. Oral and Maxillofacial Surgeons (founding fellow), Pierre Fauchard Acad., Am. Inst. Oral Biology, Internat. Coll. Dentists, So. Calif. Acad. Oral Pathology; mem. Am. Assn. Oral and Maxillofacial Surgeons, Internat. Assn. Oral Surgeons, So. Calif. Soc. Oral and Maxillofacial Surgeons, Western Soc. Oral and Maxillofacial Surgeons, Am. Acad. Oral and Maxillofacial Radiology, Marsh Robinson Acad. Oral Surgeons, Profl. Staff Assn. Los Angeles County-U. So. Calif. Med. Ctr. (exec. com. 1976—), Am. Cancer Soc. (Calif. div., profl. edn. subcom. 1977-90, pres. San Gabriel-Pomona Valley unit 1989-90), Am. Dental Assn. (scientific session chmn. section on anesthesiology, 1970), Calif. Dental Soc. Anesthesiology (pres. 1989-94), Calif. Dental Found. (pres. 1991-93), Calif. Dental Assn. (jud. coun. 1990-96), San Gabriel Valley Dental Soc. (past pres.), Xi Psi Phi, Omicron Kappa Upsilon, Delta Epsilon. Seventh-day Adventist. Home: 1102 Loganrita Ave Arcadia CA 91006-4535

GAMBOA, LUCITO G., physician; b. Pampanga, The Philippines, Jan. 7, 1929; came to U.S., 1952; s. Serapion M. and Jacinta L. Gamboa; m. Sylvia V. Roque, Sept. 18, 1953; children: Richard, Virginia Majer, Debra Jorgensen. MS, U. Colo., 1955; MD, U. Santo Tomas, Manila, The Philippines, 1952. Diplomate Am. Bd. Pathology. Dir. pathology and clin. labs. Edgewater Hosp., Chgo., 1958-69, 80-90; dir. blood bank and sr. pathologist Little Co. of Mary Hosp., Evergreen Park, Ill., 1969-80; mem. staff Ctrl. Valley Gen. Hosp., Hanford, Calif., 1990—. Contbr. numerous articles to profl. jours. Bd. dirs. Chgo. Dist. Tennis Assn., 1973-76. Recipient Disting. Physician award Philippine Med. Soc. Chgo., 1966. Mem. Assn. Philippine Physicians in Am. (pres., founder 1972-74, Disting. Svc. award 1975), Assn. Philippine Pathologists in Am. (pres., founder 1970-72), Dove Canyon Country Club. Avocations: golf, tennis, photography, travel. Home: 18 Golf View Dr Dove Canyon CA 92679-3802 Office: Ctrl Valley Gen Hosp 1025 N Douty St Hanford CA 93230-3722

GAMBRELL, THOMAS ROSS, investor, retired physician, surgeon; b. Lockhart, Tex., Mar. 17, 1934; s. Sidney Spivey and Nora Katherine (Rheinlander) G.; m. Louise Evans, Feb. 23, 1960. Student summa cum laude, U. Tex., 1953, MD, 1957. Intern Kings County Hosp., Bklyn., 1957-58; company physician Hughes Aircraft, Fullerton, Calif., 1958-65, Chrysler Corp., Anaheim, Calif., 1962-65, L.A. Angels Baseball Team, Fullerton, 1962-64; pvt. practice medicine Fullerton, 1958-91; with St. Jude Hosp., Anaheim Meml. Hosp., Fullerton Cmty. Hosp., Martin Luther Hosp.; mem. utilization rev. com. St. Mary's Convalescent Hosp., Fullerton Convalescent Hosp., Sunhaven and Fairway Convalescent Hosp.; owner Ranching (Citrus) & Comml. Devel., Ariz., Tex., N.Y., 1962-94. Contbr. articles to profl. jours. Organizer of care for needy elderly, North Orange County, 1962-65; sponsor numerous charity events. Fellow Am. Acad. Family Physicians; mem. AMA, Am. Geriats. Soc., Calif. Med. Assn., Tex. Med. Assn., Tex. Alumni Assn., Orange County Med. Assn., Mayflower Soc., Plantagenet Soc., Sons of Confederacy, SAR, Order Royal Descendants Living in Am. (col., listed in Living Descendants of Blood Royal), Order Crown (col.), Baronial Order Magna Carta, Order of Aesculaepius, Phi Eta Sigma, Delta Kappa Epsilon, Phi Chi. Avocations: collecting, travel, history. Office: PO Box 6067 Beverly Hills CA 90212-1067

GAMMELL, GLORIA RUFFNER, professional association administrator; b. St. Louis, June 19, 1948; d. Robert Nelson and Antonia Ruffner; m. Doyle M. Gammell, Dec. 11, 1973. AA in Art, Harbor Coll., Harbor City, Calif., 1969; BA in Sociology, Calif. State U., Long Beach, 1971. Cert. fin. planner. Bus. analyst Dun & Bradstreet, Los Angeles, 1971-81; sales rep. Dun & Bradstreet, Orange, Calif., 1971-93; rep. sales Van Nuys, Calif., 1981-90; pres. sec. Gammell Industries, Paramount, Calif., 1993-95, also bd. dirs.; regional v.p. Am. Mgmt. Assn., 1995—. Mem. Anne Banning Assistance League, Hollywood, Calif., 1981-82; counselor YWCA, San Pedro, Calif., 1983-84; fundraiser YMCA, San Pedro, 1984-85; mem. womens adv. coun. Calif. State Assembly, 1984-89. Recipient Best in the West Presdl. Citation, 1981-86, 89, 90. Home: 991 W Channel St San Pedro CA 90731-1415

GANDHI, OM PARKASH, electrical engineer; b. Multan, Pakistan, Sept. 23, 1934; came to U.S., 1967, naturalized, 1975; s. Gopal Das and Devi Bai (Patney) G.; m. Santosh Nayar, Oct. 28, 1963; children: Rajesh Timmy, Monica, Lena. BS with honors, Delhi U., India, 1952; MSE, U. Mich., 1957, Sc.D., 1961. Rsch. specialist Philco Corp., Blue Bell, Pa., 1960-62; asst. dir. Cen. Electronics Engring. Rsch. Inst., Pilani, Rajasthan, India, 1962-65, dep. dir., 1965-67; prof. elec. engring., rsch. prof. bioengring. U. Utah, Salt Lake City, 1967—; chmn. elec. engring., 1992—; cons. U.S. Army Med. R & D Command, Washington, 1973-77; cons. to microwave and telecom. industry and govtl. health and safety orgns.; mem. Commns. B and K, Internation Union Radio Sci.; mem. study sect. on diagnostic radiology NIH, 1978-81. Author: Microwave Engineering and Applications, 1981; editor: Engineering in Medicine and Biology mag., 1987, Electromagnetic Biointeraction, 1989, Biological Effects and Medical Applications of Electromagnetic Energy, 1990; contbr. over 200 articles to profl. jours. Recipient Disting. Rsch. award U. Utah, 1979-80; grantee NSF, NIH, EPA, USAF, U.S. Army, USN, N.Y. State Dept. Health, others. Fellow IEEE (editor spl. issue Procs. IEEE 1980, co-chmn. com. on RF safety stds. 1988-97, Tech. Achievement award Utah sect. 1975, Utah Engr. of Yr. 1995), Am. Inst. for Med. and Biol. Engring.; mem. Electromagnetics Acad., Bioelectromagnetics Soc. (bd. dirs. 1979-82, 87-90, v.p., pres. 1991-94, d'Arsonval award 1995). Office: Univ Utah Dept Elec Engring 3280 Merrill Engring Salt Lake City UT 84112

GANDSEY, LOUIS JOHN, petroleum and environmental consultant; b. Greybull, Wyo., May 19, 1921; s. John Wellington and Leonora (McLaughlin) G.; m. Mary Louise Alviso, Nov. 10, 1945; children: Mary M., Catherine K., John P., Michael J., Laurie A. AA, Compton Jr. Coll., 1941; BS, U. Calif. Berkeley, 1943; M in Engring., UCLA, 1958. Registered profl. engr., Calif. With Richfield Oil Corp., L.A., 1943-65, process engr., processing foreman, sr. foreman, mfg. coord., 1943-61, project leader process computer control, 1961-63, light oil oper. supt., 1963-64, asst. refinery supt., 1964-65; mgr. planning Richfield div. Atlantic Richfield Co., L.A., 1966-68, mgr. evaluation products div., L.A., 1968-69, mgr. supply and transp., Chgo., 1969-71, mgr. planning and mgmt. sci., N.Y.C., 1971, mgr. supply and transp., L.A., 1971-72, mgr. coordination and supply, 1972-75, mgr. domestic crude, 1975-77; v.p. refining Lunday-Thagard Oil Co., South Gate, Calif., 1977-82; petroleum cons. World Oil Corp., L.A., 1982-85; gen. petroleum cons., 1986—; instr. chem. and petroleum tech. L.A. Harbor Coll., 1960-65; cons. on oil crops, Austria, 1991; U.S. del. in environ. affairs to Joint Inter-Govtl. Com. for Environ. Protection, USSR, 1991, asphalt tech. to Joint Inter-Govtl. Com. for Highway Design CWS, 1992; U.S. del. Econ. and Environ. Affairs, Portugal, Spain, 1994, Hist. & Econ. Affairs, Mexico, 1995, Basque Country, Spain, 1996. Contbr. articles to profl. jours. Served with C.E., AUS, 1944-45. Mem. AICE, Am. Chem. Soc., Calif. Soc. Profl. Engrs., Environ. Assessment Assn. Home: 2340 Neal Spring Rd Templeton CA 93465-8413

GANI, SCARLETT, language educator; b. Alexandria, Egypt, Dec. 24, 1941; came to U.S., 1957; d. Isaac and Lucie (Hakim) G. BA with honors, UCLA, 1964, MA, 1966; diplome d'études linguistiques, Sorbonne, Paris, 1983. Cert. cmty. coll. educator, Calif. Tchg. asst. UCLA, 1964-66; French instr. Riverside (Calif.) City Coll., 1966-67; French/Spanish instr. L.A. cmty. colls., 1967—; dept. chair English and fgn. langs. L.A. Southwest Coll., 1984-85; French instr. L.A. Pierce Coll., Woodland Hills, Calif., 1985—; dept. chair modern langs. L.A. Pierce Coll., 1993-96; translator/proofreader Agnew-Techtran, Continental Comm., L.A., others, 1965—; adminstr. Eric Morris Workshop, Hollywood, Calif., 1988-92; coord. internat. edn. Summer in Paris program, 1998. Copy editor, rschr.: (books) Irreverent Acting, 1987, Acting from Ultimate Consciousness, 1988, Acting, Imaging & Unconscious, 1997, 98. Recipient French govt. cultural svcs. grant, 1975. Mem. Am. Assn. Tchrs. of French (v.p., pres. 1973-77), Analytical Psychology Club of L.A. (bd. dirs. 1992-95), Modern Lang. Assn. of So. Calif. (French sect.

1973-80, chair 1974-75), Phi Beta Kappa. Avocation: theater. Office: Los Angeles Pierce Coll 6201 Winnetka Ave Woodland Hills CA 91371-0001

GANNETT, DAMON L., lawyer; b. Amarillo, Tex., Apr. 29, 1947; s. Willard L. Gannett and Patricia L. (Restine) Taber; m. Carol A. Leggate, Aug. 30, 1969; children: Amy, Tyler, Jessica, Lindsey, Tobin, Tucker. BBA, U. Mont., 1969, JD, 1972. Bar: Mont. 1972. Assoc. Sandall, Cavan & Edwards, Billings, Mont., 1976, Jones, Olsen & Christensen, Billings, 1976-78; ptnr. Olsen Christensen & Gannett, Billings, 1978-82, Olsen, Christensen, Gannett & Waller, Billings, 1983-84, Olsen, Christensen & Gannett, Billings, 1985-90, Gannett & Ventrell, Billings, 1990-93; pvt. practice Gannett Law Firm, Billings, 1993—; Atty. Child Protection Team, 1978—. Capt. USAF, 1972-76. Recipient Commrs. award Fed. Dept. HHS, 1985. Mem. ABA, State Bar Mont. (chmn. bd. 1987-89, pres. 1990-91), Nat. Assn. Counsel Children (v.p. 1989—). Home: 3222 Durland Dr Billings MT 59102-0443 Office: Gannett Law Firm PO Box 1375st Billings MT 59103*

GANS, EUGENE HOWARD, cosmetic and pharmaceutical company executive; b. N.Y.C., Dec. 17, 1929; m. 1953; 2 children. BS, Columbia U., 1951, MS, 1953; PhD, U. Wis., 1956. Lab. asst. Columbia U., 1951-53; sr. scientist group leader Hoffman-LaRouche, Inc., N.J., 1956-60; head new product devel. sect. Vick Div. Research and Devel. Labs. Richardson-Merrell, N.Y., 1960-64, asst. dir. devel., 1964-67, dir., 1967-71; assoc. dir. Alza Inst. Pharm. Chemistry, 1971-72; dir. research Vicks Personal Care div. Richardson-Vicks div. Proctor-Gamble, Shelton, Conn., 1972-76, v.p., dir. research and devel., 1976-87; pres. Hastings Assocs., Westport, Conn., 1987—, Lincoln Techs., Westport, Conn., 1989—; chmn. ctrl. rsch. Medicis Pharm. Co., Phoenix, 1992—; chmn. proprietary drug task group FDA, 1976-86, chmn. non-prescription drug mfg. assn. task group, 1996—; chmn. sci. adv. com. Cosmetic, Toiletry and Fragrance Assn., Washington, 1984-86. Mem. Am. Pharm. Assn., Am. Chem. Soc., Am. Acad. Dermatology, Soc. Investigative Dermatology, Sigma Xi. Western Office: 5101 N Casa Blanca Dr #223 Scottsdale AZ 85253-6988

GANTENBEIN, REX EARL, computer science educator; b. Muscatine, Iowa, Feb. 21, 1950; s. Earl Christopher and E. Louise (Hirschi) G.; m. Judith K. Powers, May 13, 1983. BS in Math., Iowa State U., 1972; MS in Computer Sci., U. Iowa, 1983, PhD in Computer Sci., 1986. Prof. dept. computer sci. U. Wyo., Laramie, 1985—; prof. biomed. unformatics U. Wash., 1998—; instr. IBM Corp., Boulder, Colo., 1987-98; advisor Assn. Computing Machinery, U. Wyo., 1986-94; vis. scientist NASA JSC, 1994-95; adj. prof. health scis. U. Wyo., 1998—; lectr. in field. Contbr. articles to profl. jours. Recipient Faculty Growth award U. Wyo. Alumni Assn., 1986, Ellbogen Teaching award U. Wyo., 1991; Motorola computer X equipment grantee, 1988, NSF grantee, 1989, Air Force Office of Sci. Rsch. rsch. assoc., 1991, 92, NASA summer rsch. fellow, 1993, 94, NASA grantee, 1995, 98. Mem. IEEE, Assn. Computing Machinery, Internat. Soc. Computers and Their Applications (bd. dirs. 1993-96, pres. 1996-98), Computer Profls. for Social Responsibility, Sigma Xi. Democrat. Avocations: jazz, travel, basketball, cooking. Home: 150 Butte Loop Laramie WY 82070-6825 Office: U Wyo Dept Computer Sci Laramie WY 82071-3682

GAO, LUJI, foreign language educator, columnist; b. Tian Jin, China, May 18, 1941; s. Shaohua and Guoqin (Yang) G.; m. Leiping Ding, Feb. 3, 1969; children: Grace Jie, Yang. BS in Civil Engring., Qing Hua U., Beijing, 1965, MS in Arch., 1980. Chief civil engr. First Constrn. Corp., Beijing, 1965-80; gen. mgr. Golden East Products Com., Morton Grove, Ill., 1981-82; corr. Wen Wei Po, Hong Kong, 1983-97; Mandarine Chinese instr. Coll. San Mateo, Calif., 1989—. Author: The Bronze Sword, 1981 (award Nat. Sci. Short Story Contest, Ministry of Culture, China 1981), editor-in-chief Hua Sheng TV, San Mateo, 1991-98; pres., editor-in-chief China Jour., San Francisco, 1994-95; columnist Hong Kong Econ. Jour., 1997—; contbr. articles to profl. jours. Deacon San Francisco Mandarin Bapt. Ch., 1997—. Avocations: art appreciation, art collection, travel, watching movies, singing. Home: 185 Santa Cruz Ave Daly City CA 94014

GARBARINO, JOSEPH WILLIAM, labor arbitrator, economics and business educator; b. Medina, N.Y., Dec. 7, 1919; s. Joseph Francis and Savina M. (Volpone) G.; m. Mary Jane Godward, Sept. 18, 1948; children: Ann, Joan, Susan, Ellen. B.A., Duquesne U., 1942; M.A., Harvard U., 1947, Ph.D., 1949. Faculty U. Calif., Berkeley, 1949—; prof. U. Calif., 1960-88, dir. Inst. Bus. and Econ. Research, 1962-88, prof. emeritus, 1988—; vis. lectr. Cornell U., 19S9-60, UCLA, 1949, SUNY, Buffalo, 1972; Fulbright lectr. U. Glasgow, Scotland, 1969; vis. scholar U. Warwick; mem. staff Brookings Instn., 1959-60; vis. lectr. U. Minn., 1978; labor arbitrator. Author: Health Plans and Collective Bargaining, 1960, Wage Policy and Long Term Contracts, 1962, Faculty Bargaining: Change and Conflict, 1975, Faculty Bargaining in Unions in Transition. Served with U.S. Army, 1942-45, 51-53. Decorated Bronze Star. Democrat. Roman Catholic. Home: 7708 Ricardo Ct El Cerrito CA 94530-3344

GARBER, ANNE THERESA, television and radio personality; b. Toronto, Ont., Can., Nov. 14, 1946; d. Jack and Rhodelle Byrde (Sapera) Hershoran; m Simon John Garber, Feb. 14, 1971 (div. Nov. 1977); m. H. Edward Johnson, Nov. 14, 1977 (div. June 1982); children: Becky, Kit. Dep. supr. pub. rels. and market reports Toronto Stock Exchange, 1968-70; supr. account group Dunsky Advt. Ltd., Vancouver, B.C., 1973-76; head writer films Asta Prodns. Ltd., Vancouver, 1977-82; commentator Consumers Report CBC-TV, Vancouver, 1983; consumer commentator Sta. BCTV-TV News, Vancouver, 1984; producer, Dave Barrett Show, talk show host Sta. CJOR, Vancouver, 1984-87; consumer commentator Sta. CKVU-TV, Vancouver, 1986-89; communications officer Office of the Mayor City of Vancouver, 1987-88, film commr., 1987-88; exec. dir. Associated Prodrs. Bur., Vancouver, 1988—; advisor media relations Commonwealth Summit Conf., Vancouver, 1987. Author: Shopping the World, 1990, The Serious Shopper's Guide to Vancouver, 1992, Victoria's Best Bargains, 1995, Vancouver's Best Bargains, 1995, Exploring Ethnic Vancouver, 1996, Cheap Eats Vancouver, 1997; columnist, restaurant critic Vancouver Province newspaper, 1989—; on-air restaurant and shopping columnist radio Sta. CKNW, 1995—; content provider/food and dining site, Mybc.com., 1998—. Mem. Alliance of Can. Cinema, TV and Radio Artists, The Fedn. B.C. Writers, The Newspaper Guild, Internat. Fedn. Journalists, B.C. Motion Picture Assn. Avocations: collecting advertising art, children's books, mail order catalogues. Office: care The Province Newspaper, 200 Granville St Ste 1, Vancouver, BC Canada V6C 3N3

GARBER, HELEN KOLIKOW, photographer, artist; b. Bklyn., Aug. 9, 1954; d. Alex and Geraldine (Rubin) Kolikow; m. Stuart Garber, Aug. 12, 1979. BS, SUNY, New Paltz, 1976. Cover and 45 interior photographs in Parents at Last, 1998; photography work has appeared in Penguin U.S.A., Doubleday, Hollywood Reporter, Am. Photo, Popular Photography, N.Y. Times, N.Y. Mag., L.A. Times, Travel Holiday, Buzz; one-woman shows include Santa Monica Mus. of Flying, 1990, Paul Kopeikin Gallery, L.A. Mem. Advt. Photographers Am., Am. Soc. Picture Profls. Avocations: travel.

GARCIA, CHERYL LINDA, sales professional; b. Huntington Park, Calif., Aug. 27, 1952; d. Charles Daniel Woodworth and Lorraine La Rue (Hoard) Ralston; m. Jeffrey Curtis Walgren, June 26, 1971 (div. Feb. 1978); 1 child, Jeffrey Travis; m. Donald Rios Garcia, Sept. 2, 1991; stepchildren: Anne E., Charles M. BSN, San Diego State U., 1981; postgrad., Grossmont Coll., 1982. Cert. pub. health nurse, Calif. Staff nurse Alvarado Hosp., San Diego, 1981-84; divisional lead nurse dept. hematology/oncology Scripps Clinic, La Jolla, Calif., 1984-86; oncology sales rep. Lederle Labs., San Diego, 1986-94; sr. sales rep. Immunex, San Diego, 1994-96; profl. sales rep. Amgen, San Diego, 1996—; mem. oncology adv. bd. Lederle Labs., 1990-94; [illegible] Amgen, 1996—. [illegible] Cancer Survivorship, San Diego, 1997—. Recipient Lederle Labs. Gold Cup award, 1987. Mem. Oncology Nursing Soc., Sigma Theta Tau. Avocations: walking, gardening, playing piano, reading. Office: Amgen One Amgen Center Dr Thousand Oaks CA 91320-1789

GARCIA, CRISOSTOMO BAUTISTA, portfolio manager, management science educator; b. Manila, Oct. 4, 1948; s. Emmanuel S. and Fe (Bautista) G.; m. Cristina F. Certeza, Sept. 21, 1970; children: Margarita, Melissa. BS in Math., U. Philippines, 1967; MS in Computer Sci., Rensselaer Poly. Inst., 1970, PhD in Ops. Rsch., 1973. Computer analyst IBM, 1968; asst. prof. math. Clemson (S.C.) U., 1973; asst. prof. mgmt. sci. Grad. Sch. Bus. U. Chgo., 1974-76, assoc. prof., 1976-78, prof., 1978-92; prin., portfolio mgr. Investment Rsch. Co., Chgo., 1985—. Author: Pathways to Solutions, Fixed Points and Equilibria, 1983; editor: Seminar on Complementary Theory, 1974; contbr. articles to profl. jours., 1970—. Chmn. Asian Am. Adv. to Gov., State of Ill., Springfield, 1987; founding mem. Asian Am. Inst., 1992. NSF fellow, 1970-74, rsch. grantee, 1976. Mem. AAUP, Ops. Rsch. Soc. Am., Math. Programming Soc., Mgmt. Sci., Philippine Am. Assn. Sci. (pres. 1990). Avocations: golf, jogging, chess, skiing. Office: Investment Rsch Co PO Box 9210 Rancho Santa Fe CA 92067-4210

GARCIA, DAVID, agricultural products executive; b. 1953. Graduate, U. Wyo., 1975. With We. Nuclear Mining, Lander, Wyo., 1976-78, Diamond Fruit Growers, Inc., Hood River, Oreg., 1978—; now contr. Office: Diamond Fruit Growers Inc PO Box 180 Hood River OR 97031-0060*

GARCIA, DON (GARCE), television and video producer, videographer; b. Newburgh, N.Y., Aug. 14, 1956; s. Antonio S. and June (Hunt) G.; m. Deborah Brush, May 17, 1998. BS in Civil Engring. and Surveying, Clarkson U., 1978; postgrad., Aurora (Colo.) C.C., 1986, Colo. U., 1981. Mem. U.S. Disabled Ski Team, Park City, Utah, 1985-91; prodr., videographer J.S.D., Inc., Denver, 1991-95; pres. Garce Works, Denver, 1995—. Prodn. coord., sound work World Youth Day, Portuguese TV, Vancouver Summit, Sta. WTN, Coll. Game Day, ESPN; photojournalist numerous stories Inside Edit., interviews for CNN, Dennis Miller Show, other programs including Am. Jour., Action Sports Video, indsl. prodns. for Intelegard Fire Def. Sys., Jimmie Huega Ctr., Disabled Sports U.S.A.; prodr. segment of Paralympics, Disability Channel, Tigne, France, 8 episodes of Ski the Rockies, Travel Channel, Colo. Off Rd. Points Series, Prime Network, 1993-97, U.S. Frisbee Open, Prime Network, 1994, 96, World Mountain Mike Championships, Home Video, 1994, U.S. Extreme Snowboarding Championships, Prime Network, 1995-96, World Extreme Skiing Championships, Prime Network, 1992-96 (Best of Competition award Internat. Ski Film Festival 1992, 93, Best Spl. Skiing Category award, Best Instrnl. Video award), Rocky Mountain Nat. Speedway, Home Video, 1996, 2 nat. press confs. U.S. Forest Svc.; videographer, prodr. U.S. Extreme Ski Championships, JSP, Inc./Fox Sports, 1993-98; prodr., camera work Mile High Adventures & Entertainment, Pay per View, Hartford Ski Spectacular, JSP, Inc./Fox Sports (Telly award 1998); prodr., dir. Montezuma's Revenge (Telly award 1998); prodr. Denver Summit of 8, Sta. WTN, '96 U.S. Extreme Ski Championships (Internat. Ski Film award 1997, Telly award 1997); dir. Customer Svc. CDI, U.S. Forest Svc.; field engr. Oklahoma City Bombing Trial, Ct. TV. 10 time Nat. Champion slalom competitor U.S. Disabled Ski Team, 1985-92, World Downhill Champion, 1986, Bronze medalist Paralympics, 1988, Gold medalist French Nats., 1988, Bronze medalist World Championships 1990; recipient Golden Camera award EDS Computer, 1995. Mem. N.Am. Ski Journalists, Colo. Film/Video Assn., Disabled Sports U.S.A., Durango Purgatory Handicapped Sports Assn. E-mail: garceworks@aol.com. Home: 473 S Lamar St Lakewood CO 80226-3413

GARCIA, EDWARD J., federal judge; b. 1928. AA, Sacramento City Coll., 1951; LLB, U. Pacific, 1958. Dep. dist. atty. Sacramento County, 1959-64, supervising dep. dist. atty., 1964-69, chief dep. dist. atty., 1969-72; judge Sacramento Mcpl. Ct., 1972-84; judge U.S. Dist. Ct. (ea. dist.) Calif., Sacramento, 1984-96, sr. judge, 1996—. Served with U.S. Army Air Corps, 1946-49. Office: US Dist Ct US Courthouse Clerk Office 501 I St Rm 4-200 Sacramento CA 95814-4707*

GARCIA, MARA LUCY, Spanish educator, researcher; b. Trujillo, Peru, June 9; came to U.S., 1986; d. Juan Garcia and Tarcila (Sevilla) Osaki. BA in Spanish Lit., Brigham Young U., 1990, MA in Spanish Lit., 1992; PhD in Philosophy, U. Ky., 1997. Asst. prof. spanish Brigham Young U., Provo, Utah, 1996—; vis. instr. U. Ky., Lexington, 1996. Author: la casa de calamina, 1997; author (short stories) Ceremonia Privada, 1996 (Minaya Alvar Fanez award 1996), Letras Femeninas, 1997; editor Ariel, 1992-95. Mem. Assn. Ecuatorianistas, Assn. Lit. Femenina Hispanica, Modern Language Assn. Am., Latin Am. Studies Assn., New Novel Assn., Sigma Delta Pi (premio Gabriela Mistral award 1994, juror 1997, assessor 1998). Avocations: reading, dancing, travel.

GARCIA, MICHAEL JOSEPH, telecommunications company executive; b. Alameda, Calif., July 23, 1949; s. Manuel Oliviera and Mary (Gonzales) G.; m. Patti Ann Tognetti, July 22, 1972; children: Michael Joseph II, Jennifer Anne. Degree in maths., econs., U. Calif., Berkeley, 1971. Cert. employee benefits specialist. From dir. customer billing to dir. benefit adminstrn. Pacific Tel., San Francisco, 1971-87; dir. fin. mgmt. Pacific Telesis, San Francisco, 1987-89; from exec. dir. info. sys. to exec. dir. technology svcs. Pacific Bell, San Francisco, 1989—; chmn. adv. bd. Contra Costa Health Plan, Martinez, Calif., 1985-95. Chmn. bd. dirs. Managed Care Commn., Martinez, 1997. Col. USANG, 1967—. Mem. Am. Mgmt. Assn., Nat. Guard Assn., Air Force Assn. Roman Catholic. Avocations: golf, reading, gardening. Home: 2409 Saddleback Dr Blackhawk CA 94506-3112 Office: Pacific Bell #1E501 2600 Camino Ramon San Ramon CA 94583

GARCIA, ROBERTO AYALA, college admissions director; b. Corpus Christi, Tex., Apr. 6, 1956; s. Joel Ledesma and Emilia (Ayala) G.; m. Petra La-Verne Pecos, Dec. 26, 1978; children: Lisa Jeanette San Juanita, Roberto Michael Xavier. AB, Princeton U., 1979; EdM, Harvard U., 1980. Coll. counselor Albuquerque Job Corps Ctr., 1980-81; ednl. program coord. All Indian Pueblo Coun., Albuquerque, 1981-83; admission officer Princeton (N.J.) U., 1987-89; assoc. dir. admissions Colo. Coll., Colorado Springs, 1989—; bd. dirs. Denver Ednl. Excellence Program, 1997—; advisor Assn. Spl. Programs in Region 8, Spearfish, S.D., 1998; mem. adv. bd. Colo. State U. Talent Search/Upward Bound, Fort Collins, 1998—. Capt. USMCR, 1983-87, USMCR, ret. Mem. Nat. Assn. Coll. Admission Counselors (panelist/spkr.), Rocky Mountain Assn. Coll. Admission Counselors, Coll. Bd. Summer Admission Inst. (faculty). Democrat. Roman Catholic. Avocations: woodworking, jogging, hunting. Home: 2404 Balboa St Colorado Springs CO 80907 Office: Colo Coll 14 E Cache La Poudre Colorado Springs CO 80903-3243

GARCIA-BORRAS, THOMAS, oil company executive; b. Barcelona, Spain, Feb. 2, 1926; came to U.S., 1955, naturalized, 1961; s. Thomas and Teresa (Borras-Jarque) Garcia-Julian; MS, Nat. U. Mex., 1950; postgrad. Rice U., 1955-56; m. Alia Castellanos Lima, Apr. 30, 1952; children: Erik, Angelica, Laureen, Cliff. Chief chemist Petroleos Mexicanos, Veracruz, Mex., 1950-55; rsch. engr. Monsanto, Texas City, Tex., 1956-60; pilot plant mgr. Cabot and Foster Grant Co., 1960-69; engring. mgr. Signal Chem. Co., Houston, 1969-71; mgmt. and engring. cons., Covina, Calif., 1971-73; project mgr. Occidental Petroleum Co., Irvine, Calif., 1973-79; fleet and indsl. mgr. internat. ops. Wynn Oil Co., Fullerton, Calif., 1979-87; dir. export Sta-Lube, Inc., Rancho Dominguez, Calif., 1987-91; prin. U.S. Products Corp., Las Vegas, Nev.; internat. bus. and energy cons. Covina, Calif. Mem. Internat. Mktg. Assn., Am. Inst. Chem. Engrs., Am. Chem. Soc. Author: Manual for Improving Boiler and Furnace Performance, 1983; contbr. articles to profl. jours. Home: 1430 E Adams Park Dr Covina CA 91724-2925 Office: 516 S 4th St Las Vegas NV 89101-6513

GARCIA Y GRIEGO, RENIE C., state agency administrator; b. Albuquerque, Mar. 14, 1948; d. Vincent and Renie Viola (Griego) Garcia; 1 child, Kathryn Ann Garcia. Degree, Albuquerque Tech-Vocat. Inst., 1968; AAS, U. Albuquerque, 1981, degree in bus., psychology and sociology, 1982. Lic. mental health counselor, cert. nursing asst., N.Mex. Group counselor, caseworker Girls' Tng. Sch., Albuquerque, 1969-70; pers. asst. Albuquerque Pub. Sch. Sys., 1970-72; placement sys. officer Albuquerque Tech-Vocat. Inst., 1972-79; area coord. City Pks. and Recreation, Albuquerque, 1979-80; program specialist city, state and fed. govt., Albuquerque, 1984-85; staff devel. specialist N.Mex. Commn. on Status of Women, Albuquerque, 1985—, acting dep. dir., 1995-96. Author: (brochure) Start From Where You Are!, 1985. Mem. Albuquerque Native Am. Network, 1995-98; vice chair membership com. Job Svc. Employers Com. N.Mex. Dept. Labor, 1995-98; mem. adv. bd. Albuquerque SANE Collaborative, 1996-98, Bridges for Women, Inc., Albuquerque, 1997-98; v.p., liaison region VI Women Work! Nat. Network, Washington, 1995. Recipient Women on the Move award YWCA, 1992, Leadership Women Work! award WDC, 1993, Keep the Dream Alive award, 1994, El Gran Abrazo award LULAC, Albuquerque, 1994. Roman Catholic. Home: 4321 San Pedro Dr NE Apt H5 Albuquerque NM 87109-2680 Office: NMex Commn on Status of Women 2401 12th St NW Albuquerque NM 87104-2302

GARDINER, T(HOMAS) MICHAEL, artist; b. Seattle, Feb. 5, 1946; s. Thomas Scott Gardiner and Carolyn Virginia (Harmer) Bolin; m. Kelly Michelle Floyd, Mar. 7, 1981 (div. Dec. 1983); m. Diana Phyllis Shurtlieff Rainwater, Sept. 26, 1986; children: Rita Em, Nigel Gus. BA in Philosophy, Sulpician Sem. N.W., Kenmore, Wash., 1969; student, Cornish Inst. Arts, 1971-73. Seaman Tidewater Barge, Camas, Wash., 1969; pari-mutuel clk. Longacres Racetrack, Renton, Wash., 1969-92; dock worker Sealand, Inc., Seattle, 1970; tchr. Coyote Jr. H.S., Seattle, 1989-95, Sch. Visual Concepts, Seattle, 1990-95; tchr., vis. artist Ctrl. Wash. U., Ellensburg, 1991. Represented in permanent collections Seattle Water Dept., Nordstrom, Seattle City Light, Sultan (Wash.) Sch. Dist., King County Portable Works Collection, SAFECO Ins. Co., Seattle, City of Portland Collection, 1988, Highline Sch. Dist., Seattle; commns. include ARTp Metro Art Project, Seattle, interior painting Villa del Lupo restaurant, Vancouver, B.C., Can.; illustrations included in The New Yorker Mag., Am. Illustration 13, The Seattle Times. Recipient Best Design award Print Mag., 1985; Nat. Endowment for Arts Fellowship grantee, 1989. Democrat. Roman Catholic. Home and Office: 3023 NW 63rd St Seattle WA 98107-2566

GARDNER, ARTHUR SPEEDIE, engineering executive; b. Port Chester, N.Y., Dec. 16, 1939; s. Angus John and Mercedes Adele (Speedie) G.; m. Estelle Kulakowski, June 8, 1963 (div. Sept. 1, 1980); children: Keith Speedie, Slade Havelock, Kess Elizabeth; m. Cathy Ann Pfost, Aug. 1, 1981; children: Colby Cameron Hughes, Brennan Allen Hughes. BSChemE, Bucknell U., Lewisburg, Pa., 1963; BAChemE, Bucknell U., 1963; LLB, LaSalle Ext. U., Chgo., 1968. Cert. profl. engr., Colo. Engring. supr., safety dir., environ. staff engr. Mobil Oil Corp., Paulsboro, N.J., 1963-74; dir. govt. and environ. affairs Buckeye Pipeline Co., Allentown, Pa., 1974-77; sr. technologist ChemDesign (subsidiary ChemShare), Houston, 1977-78; chem. engring. supr. Occidental Shale Co., Grand Junction, Colo., 1978-82; v.p. engring., gen. mgr. Wesfrac Inc., Charterhall Refining & Mktg., Wescourt Group, Grand Junction, 1982-91; tech. editor Today's Refinery Percy Pub. Co., Chappaqua, N.Y., 1989—; engring. exec., one of three founders NGL Ptnrs., NGL Inc., Farstad Gas & Oil L.L.C., Minot, N.D., 1991—; chief engr. George Bros. Fabrication, Inc., Midland, Tex., 1995—; mem. tech. sect. (measurement & product handling) Gas Processors Assn., Tulsa, 1986-91, 96—. Contbr. over 100 tech. articles to Today's Refinery. Mem., chpt. pres., state v.p., nat. dir. Jaycees, 1964-74 (Outstanding awards 1968, 69, 70); mem. Indian Guides, 1975-77, Indian Princesses, 1977-78, coach and referee Grand Mesa Soccer Assn., 1979-90; mem. Bus-Edn. Partnership, Grand Junction, 1992—; tutor Sch. Dist. 51 high schs., Mesa St. Coll., 1992—. Recipient Individual award Colo. Assn. Ptnrs. in Edn., 1993. Mem. AIChE, NSPE (Ute chpt. treas. 1996). Home: 935 Bader Dr Grand Junction CO 81501-2931 Office: Farstad Gas & Oil LLC PO Box 9093 Grand Junction CO 81501-9030

GARDNER, DAVID CHAMBERS, education educator, psychologist, business executive, author; b. Charlotte, N.C., Mar. 22, 1934; s. James Raymond and Jessica Mary (Chambers) Bumgardner m. Grace Joely Beatty, 1984; children: Joshua Avery, Jessica Sarah. BA, Northeastern U., 1960; MEd, Boston U., 1970, EdD, 1974; PhD, Columbia Pacific U., 1984. Diplomate Am. Bd. Med. Psychotherapists. Mgr. market devel. N.J. Zinc Co., N.Y.C., 1961-66, COMINCO, Ltd., Montreal, Que., Can., 1966-68; dir. alumni Ann. Giving Program, Northeastern U., Boston, 1968-69; dir. career and spl. edn. Stoneham (Mass.) Pub. Schs., Boston, 1970-72; assoc. prof. div. instructional devel. and adminstrn. Boston U., 1974—; sr. ptnr. Gardner Beatty Group, 1990—; chmn. bd. CyberHelp, Inc., 1995—; v.p. for edn. and mktg. Kaleidoscope Software, Inc., 1997-98; exec. v.p. ISMChina, Ltd., Rancho La Costa, Calif., 1998—; coord. program career vocat. tng. for handicapped, 1974-82, chmn. dept. career and bus. edn., 1974-79, also dir. fed. grants, 1975-77, 77-79; co-founder Am. Tng. and Rsch. Assocs., Inc., chmn. bd., 1979-83, pres., chief exec. officer, 1984—; dir. La Costa Inst. Lifestyle Mgmt., 1986-87. Author: Careers and Disabilities: A Career Approach, 1978; co-author: (with Grace Joely Beatty) Dissertation Proposal Guidebook: How to Prepare a Research Proposal and Get It Accepted, 1980, Career and Vocational Education for the Mildly Learning Handicapped and Disadvantaged, 1984, Stop Stress and Aging Now, 1985, Never Be Tired Again, 1990; co-author: The Visual Learning Guide Series, 1992, 93, 94, 95, 96, 97, Internet for Windows: America Online Edition, 1995, Cruising America Online for Windows, 1995, Windows 95: The Visual Learning Guide, 1995, Quicken 5 for Windows, 1995, The Visual Learning Guide, 1995, Excel for Windows 95: The Visual Learning Guide, 1995, Word for Windows 95, The Visual Learning Guide, 1995, Windows NT 4.0 Visual Desk Reference, 1997, Discover Netscape Communicator, 1997, Discover Internet Explorer, 1997; editor Career Edn. Quar., 1975-81; contbr. articles to profl. jours. With AUS, 1954-56. U.S. Office Edn. fellow Boston U., 1970, U.S. Office Edn.-Univ. Boston rsch. fellow, 1974. Fellow Am. Assn. Mental Deficiency (Ann. Profl. Tchr. and Rsch. award Region X 1979); mem. Nat. Assn. Career Edn. (bd. dirs., past pres.), Coun. for Exceptional Children, Ea. Ednl. Rsch. Assn. (founding dir.), Am. Vocat. Assn., Phi Delta Kappa, Delta Pi Epsilon. Home and Office: 7618 Nueva Castilla Way Carlsbad CA 92009-8137

GARDNER, JERRY LEE, financial consultant; b. Long Beach, Calif., Sept. 8, 1943; s. Don Gerard and Carol (Sorenson) G.; m. Rita Frandsen, May 29, 1969; children: Marc Don, Edward David, Victor John, Denise, Joyce, John Mackay, Michael Christopher. BA, Brigham Young U., 1971; MA, Calif. State U., Sacramento, 1973. Account exec. duPont Glore Forgan & Co., Sacramento, 1973-74, E.F. Hutton & Co., Sacramento, 1974-84; sr. investment advisor Am. Savs., Sacramento, 1984-89; fin. cons. The Golden 1 Credit Union, Sacramento, 1989—; mem. Leaders Coun., Mass. Fin. Svcs., Boston, 1993-98; mem. Commerce Club, Franklin Templeton Group, San Mateo, Calif., 1993-98. With U.S. Army, 1965-68, Vietnam. Recipient MVP award Fin. Network Investment Corp., 1994-95. Mem. Internat. Assn. Fin. Planners, BYU Mgmt. Soc. (bd. dirs. 1990—), LDS Bus. Group (v.p. 1992-94). Mormon. Avocations: travel, history of California, violin, guitar. Office: The Golden 1 Credit Union 6507 4th Ave Sacramento CA 95817-2611

GARDNER, NORD ARLING, management consultant administrator; b. Afton, Wyo., Aug. 10, 1923; s. Arling A. and Ruth (Lee) G.; BA, U. Wyo., 1945; MS, Calif. State U., Hayward, 1972, MPA, 1975; postgrad. U. Chgo., U. Mich., U. Calif.-Berkeley; m. Thora Marie Stephen, Mar. 24, 1945; children: Randall Nord, Scott Stephen, Craig Robert, Laurie Lee. With U.S. Army, 1941-46, 1950-52; commd. 2d lt., 1945, advanced through grades to lt. col., 1964; ret., 1966; personnel analyst Univ. Hosp., U. Calif.-San Diego, 1966-68; coordinator manpower devel. U. Calif.-Berkeley, 1968-75; univ. tng. officer San Francisco State U., 1975-80, personnel mgr., 1976-80; exec. dir. CRDC Maintenance Tng. Corp., non-profit community effort, San Francisco, 1980-85; pres., dir. Sandor Assocs. Mgmt. Cons., Pleasant Hill, Calif., 1974-86, 91-96; gen. mgr. Vericlean Janitorial Service, Inc.; in-charge bus. devel. East Bay Local Devel. Corp., Oakland, Calif., 1980-85; incorporator and pres. Indochinese Community Enterprises, USA, Ltd., Pleasant Hill, Calif., 1985-87; freelance writer, grantsmanship cons., 1987—; ptnr. Oi Kit Bldg. Maint. Svc., 1988-91; dir. univ. rels. Internat. Pacific U., San Ramon, Calif., 1990—, exec. dir., bd. dirs. Internat. Pacific Inst., 1994— ; cons. Phimmasone Internat. Import-Export, Richmond, Calif., Lao Lanx-Xang Assn., Oakland Refugee Assn., 1988-90; instr. Japanese, psychology, supervisory courses, 1977-78; bd. dirs. New Ideas New Imports, Inc. Author: To Gather Stones, 1978. Adv. council San Francisco Community Coll. Dist. Decorated Army Commendation medal. Mem. Ret. Officers Assn., Am. Soc. Tng. and Devel., No. Calif. Human Resources Council, Am. Assn. Univ. Adminstrs., Internat. Personnel Mgrs. Assn., Coll. and Univ. Personnel Assn., Commonwealth Club of Calif., U. Calif.-Berkeley Faculty Club, San Francisco State U. Faculty Club, Army Counter Intelligence Corp Vets., Inc. Republican. Home: 2995 Bonnie Ln Pleasant Hill CA 94523-4547 Office: Internat Pacific Inst 2995 Bonnie Ln Pleasant Hill CA 94523-4547

GARDNER, ROBERT ALEXANDER, career counselor, career management consultant; b. Berkeley, Calif., Sept. 16, 1944; s. Robert Sr. and Eleanor Ambrose (Starrett). BA, U. Calif., Berkeley, 1967; MA, Calif. State U., Chico, 1974; MS, San Francisco State U., 1992. Registered profl. career counselor; nat. cert. career counselor, counselor. Divsn. personnel officer Wells Fargo Bank, San Francisco, 1977-80; dir. personnel Transamerica Airlines, Oakland, Calif., 1980-84; career counselor, career mgmt. cons. Gardner Assocs., Oakland, 1984—; bd. dirs. Vocats. Svcs.; adj. faculty mem. John F. Kennedy U., Walnut Creek, Calif., 1995-96; career counselor, outplacement cons. Forty Plus of No. Calif., Oakland, 1988-93; instr. Armstrong U., Berkeley, 1980-81, U. Calif. Univ. Ext. Divsn., 1984-96, extended edn., 1981-86, internat. cons., 1984-87. Author: Achieving Effective Supervision, 1984, rev. edit. 1989, Managing Personnel Administration Effectively, 1986, Career Counseling: Matching Yourself to a Career, 1987. Mem. ACA, Nat. Career Devel. Assn., Calif. Career Devel. Assn., Calif. Assn. for Counseling and Devel., Internat. Assn. Career Mgmt. Profls., Rotary (Paul Harris fellow). Home: 335 Columbia Cir Benicia CA 94510-3911 Office: Gardner Assocs 3873 Piedmont Ave Ste 12 Oakland CA 94611-5370

GARDNER, SANDRA LEE, nurse, outreach consultant; b. Louisville, Dec. 1, 1946; d. Jane Marie (Schwab) Gardner. Nursing diploma, Sts. Mary and Elizabeth Hosp., Louisville, 1967; BSN magna cum laude, Spalding Coll., 1973; MS, U. Colo., 1975, Pediatric Nurse Practitioner, 1978. RN. Premature coordinator Meth. Evang. Hosp., Louisville, 1967-71; charge nurse Children's Hosp., Louisville, 1971-73; staff/charge nurse Children's Hosp., Denver, 1973-74, perinatal outreach coord., 1974-76; asst. prof. U. Colo. Sch. Nursing, 1976-79; co-founder, vice chmn. bd. dirs. Denver Birth Ctr., 1977-79; dir., cons. Profl. Outreach Consultation, Aurora, Colo., 1980—; founding mem. Colo. Perinatal Car Council, Denver, 1975—; founding dir. Neonatal Nursing Edn. Found., Aurora, 1982—. Co-editor: Handbook of Neonatal Intensive Care, 1985, 89, Legal Aspects of Maternal-Child Nursing Practice, 1997; contbr. articles to profl. jours. Foster parent educator Dept. Social Svcs., 1976-78; in pub. edn. KVOD Radio/Channel 2, Denver, 1978; nursing supr. 9 Health Fair, Denver, 1980. Recipient Gerald L. Hencemann award March of Dimes, Denver, 1978. Mem. ANA (Book of Yr. 1986, 89), Nat. Neonatal Nurses Assn. Democrat. Avocations: downhill skiing, hiking, biking, gardening, reading, travel. Home: 12095 E Kentucky Ave Aurora CO 80012-3233

GARDNER, SONIA KAY, writer; b. Council, Idaho, Nov. 27, 1956; d. Kenneth A. and Vera E. (Jones) White; m. William D. Gardner, Aug. 7, 1982; 1 child, Shane. BA in edn., BSU, 1979. Elem. tchr. Cambridge Elem., Cambridge, Idaho, 1980-94; writer New Meadows, Idaho, 1994—. Author: Eagle Feathers, 1997. Mem. Soc. Childrens Books Writers and Illustrators.

GAREN, KENNETH BRUCE, software company executive, software designer; b. Chgo., Sept. 5, 1947; s. Jerome and Marian Garen; m. Diana Bandlin, Feb. 11, 1987 (div. June 1988); m. Andrea Ellis, Dec. 16, 1990 (div. Sept. 1998). BA in Bus., Edn., So. Ill. U., 1970. CPA, Ill. Supr. Garen & Assocs., Skokie, Ill., 1970-82; pres. Ken Garen Inc., Skokie, Ill., 1982-87, Universal Bus. Computing Co., Taos, N.Mex., 1981—. Bd. dirs. Los Altos Homeowners Assn., 1995-98; bd. advisors San Cristobal (N.Mex.) Ranch Found., 1997, 98; fin. advisor Rocky Mountain Youth Corps, Taos, 1997, 98; mem. County of Taos Telecom. Task Force, 1997, 98. Mem. Am. Payroll Processors Assn. (bd. dirs. 1994-98), Am. Payroll Assn. (govt. liaison com. 1995-97). Avocations: photography, golf. Home: PO Box 3263 Taos NM 87571-3263 Office: Universal Bus Computing Co PO Box 768 Taos NM 87571-0768

GAREY, DONALD LEE, pipeline and oil company executive; b. Ft. Worth, Sept. 9, 1931; s. Leo James and Jessie (McNatt) G.; m. Elizabeth Patricia Martin, Aug. 1, 1953; children: Deborah Anne, Elizabeth Laird. BS in Geol. Engring., Tex. A&M U., 1953. Registered profl. engr., Tex. Reservoir geologist Gulf Oil Corp., 1953-54, sr. geologist, 1956-65; v.p., mng. dir. Indsl. Devel. Corp. Lea County, Hobbs, N.Mex., 1965-72, dir., 1972-86, pres., 1978-86; v.p., dir. Minerals, Inc., Hobbs, N.Mex., 1966-72; pres., dir. Minerals, Inc., Hobbs, 1972-86, CEO, 1978-82; mng. dir. Hobbs Indsl. Found. Corp., 1965-72, dir., 1965-76; v.p. Llano, Inc., 1972-74, exec. v.p., COO, 1974-75, pres., 1975-86, CEO, also dir., 1978-82; pres., CEO Pollution Control, Inc., 1969-81; pres. NMESCO Fuels, Inc., 1982-86; chmn., pres., CEO Estacado, Inc., 1986—, Natgas Inc., 1987—; pres. Llano Co2, Inc., 1984-86; cons. geologist, geol. engr., Hobbs, 1965-72. Chmn. Hobbs Manpower Devel. Tng. Adv. Com., 1965-72; mem. Hobbs Adv. Com. ofr Metal Health, 1965-67; chmn. N.Mex. Mapping Adv. Com., 1968-69; mem. Hobbs adv. bd. Salvation Army, 1967-78, chmn., 1970-72; mem. exec. bd. Conquistador coun. Boy Scouts Am., Hobbs, 1965-75; vice chmn. N.Mex. Gov's Com. for Econ. Devel., 1968-70; bd. regents Coll. Southwest, 1982-85. Capt. USAF, 1954-56. Mem. AIPG, AAPG, SPE of AIME. Home: 315 E Alto Dr Hobbs NM 88240-3905 Office: Broadmoor Tower PO Box 5587 Hobbs NM 88241-5587

GAREY, JUDITH FREEMAN, theatre educator; b. Balt., Mar. 30, 1949; d. Harold and Devorah (Jaffe) Freeman; m. Charles Thomson Garey, June 27, 1971; children: Kirsten Anne, Scott Charles. BS, U. Md., 1970; MA, U. Ill., 1971. Cert. tchr. (lifetime) Calif. Comty. Colls. Theatre instr. Walter Johnson H.S., Bethesda, Md., 1971-73; adj. faculty in theatre Santa Barbara (Calif.) City Coll., 1975-90; assoc. prof. theatre Ventura (Calif.) Coll., 1991—; regional adjudicator Am. Coll. Theatre Festival, 1989—; mem faculty senate Ventura Coll., 1997—. Dir. Biloxi Blues (Winner Am. Coll. Theatre Festival, 1988). Grantee Ventura Coll. Found., 1997. Fellow S. Coast Writers Conf., Am. Coll. Theatre Festival, So. Calif. Ednl. Theatre Assn. Office: Ventura Coll 4667 Telegraph Rd Ventura CA 93003-3872

GARIBOTTO-MINNESS, CARLOS FERNANDO, writer, translator; b. Lima, Peru, May 30, 1932; came to U.S., 1985; s. Pablo Enrique Garibotto and Ana Minness; m. Rosa Ariza, June 19, 1963 (dec. Mar. 1980); children: Carlos Enrique, Miguel Angel; m. Rosita Henao, Feb. 26, 1985; 1 child, Victor Hugo. Student, U.N.M.S.M., Lima, 1950-52, C.I.D.C.A., Bogota, Colombia, 1981, City Coll., San Francisco, 1993. Prof. C.I.D.C.A., Bogota, 1981-84; sys. analyst Key Software, Hayward, Calif., 1985; translator in pvt. practice, San Francisco, 1988-93, Oakland, Calif., 1994—. Author, editor: Ja, Ja, Ja, 1989, Esto si es poesia, 1994, Wonderful Revelation, 1996, Book of the Funny People, 1998. Mem. Federacion Periodistas Latinos, Masons.

GARLAND, FRANK CALDWELL, epidemiologist, educator; b. San Diego, Calif., June 20, 1950. BA in History, UCLA, 1972; PhD in Epidemiology, Johns Hopkins U., 1981. Preceptor students in MPH in epidemiology program San Diego State U. Grad. Sch. Pub. Health, 1981—; guest instr. basic epidemiology U. Calif.-San Diego Sch. Medicine, 1984—; coord. Epidemiology Rsch. Exch., San Diego, 1986-91; rsch. coord. Def. Women's Health Rsch. Program Naval Med. Rsch. and Devel. Command, Naval Health Rsch. Ctr., 1994-98; mem. epidemiology program Cancer Ctr. U. Calif.-San Diego, La Jolla, 1988—; cons. faculty divsn. epidemiology and biostats. San Diego State U. Grad. Sch. Pub. Health, 1985—; assoc. adj. prof. dept. family and preventive medicine Sch. Medicine U. Calif.-San Diego, 1988—; head dept. health scis. and epidemiology Naval Health Rsch. Ctr., San Diego, 1989—; prin. investigator various rsch. projects Naval Health Rsch. ctr., 1986—, Sch. Medicine U. Calif., San Diego, 1983-88. Mem. editl. bd. Jour. Nutritional Medicine; reviewer Am. Jour. Epidemiology, Internat. Jour. Epidemiology, Cancer Causes and Control, Jour. AMA, Preventive Medicine, Am. Inst. Biol. Scis.; contbr. articles to profl. jours. Fellow Am. Coll. Epidemiology; mem. Nat. Rsch. Coun. Advisors, Soc. Epidemiologic Rsch., Internat. Epidemiol. Assn., Physicians for Social Responsibility. Home: 2938 Renault St San Diego CA 92122-2240 Office: Naval Health Research Ctr PO Box 85122 San Diego CA 92186-5122

GARLAND, G(ARFIELD) GARRETT, sales executive, golf professional; b. Lakewood, Ohio, Dec. 17, 1946; s. Garfield George and Lois Marie (Calavan) G.; m. Debra Ann Threlkel; children, Brandon Palmer, Blake Hamilton. BA, U. Colo., 1974. Broker Marcus & Millichap, Newport Beach, Calif., 1982-84; v.p. Pacific Coast Fed., Encino, Calif., 1984-85; dir. of acquisitions Prudential Investment Fund, L.A., 1985-86; v.p. A.S.A.I., L.A. and Tokyo, 1986-89; dir. sales Lojack Corp., L.A., 1989—; pres. Collegiate Scholarship Svcs. of Am., 1991-92; cons. Centinela Hosp. Fitness Inst. Mem. Pres.'s Coun. on Competitiveness, 1992, Childhelp USA. Capt. U.S. Army, 1967-71. Mem. VFW, PGA of Am., L.I.F.E. Found., Am. Legion, World Affairs Coun., Internat. Platform Assn., U.S. Ski Team, Natural Historic Preservation Trust. Avocations: golf, reading. Home: 17638 Raymer St Northridge CA 91325 Office: Lojack Corp 9911 W Pico Blvd Ste 1000 Los Angeles CA 90035-2700

GARLAND, ROBERT LEE, educator, writer; b. Chgo., Feb. 26, 1932. BA, UCLA, 1953; MA, Calif. State U., 1962; postgrad., U. Calif., Berkeley, Nat. U. Mex., Mexico City, Stanford U., Singapore U., U. N.C., Charlotte. Educator L.A. Sch. Dist., 1957-91; mem. various coms. Los Angeles Schs., 1970-91. Contbr. articles on travel and edn. to jours. Served with U.S. Army, 1955-57. Nat. Def. Edn. Act scholar U.S. Govt., 1966, Fulbright scholar, U.S. Govt., 1967, Freedoms Found. scholar, 1982, 86; Robert Taft fellow, 1977, 81, 86, 88; NEH fellow Carnegie-Mellon U., 1990. Mem. NEA, Nat. Council Social Studies (com. chmn. 1980—), Fulbright Alumni Assn., Navy League of U.S., Steamship Hist. Soc., Am. Film Inst., Naval Inst., Big Band Soc. Am., Calif. Hist. Soc. Club: Travelers Century.

GARLICK, LARRY, executive. Chmn., pres., CEO Pemedy Corp., Mountain View, Calif. Office: 1505 Salado Dr Mountain View CA 94043-1110*

GARLOUGH, WILLIAM GLENN, marketing executive; b. Syracuse, N.Y., Mar. 27, 1924; s. Henry James and Gladys (Killam) G.; m. Charlotte M. Tanzer, June 15, 1947; children: Jennifer, William, Robert. BEE, Clarkson U., 1949. With Knowlton Bros., Watertown, N.Y., 1949-67, mgr. mfg. svcs., 1966-67; v.p. planning, equipment systems divsn. Vare Corp., Englewood Cliffs, N.J., 1967-69; mgr. mktg. Valley Mould divsn. Microdot Inc., Hubbard, Ohio, 1969-70; dir. corp. devel. Microdot Inc., Greenwich, Conn., 1970-73, v.p. corp. devel., 1973-76, v.p. adminstrn., 1976-77, v.p. corp. devel., 1977-78; v.p. corp. devel. Am. Bldg. Maintenance Industries, San Francisco, 1979-83; pres. The Change Agts., Inc., Walnut Creek, Calif., 1983—; bd. dirs. My Chef Inc.; mem. citizens adv. com. to Watertown Bd. Edn., 1957. Bd. dirs. Watertown Cmty. Chest, 1958-61; ruling elder Presbyn. Ch. With USMCR, 1942-46. Mem. Am. Mgmt. Assn., Inst. Mgmt. Cons. (cert.), Bldg. Svc. Contractors Assn., Internat. Sanitary Supply Assn., Mensa, Am. Mktg. Assn., TAPPI, Assn. Corp. Growth (pres. San Francisco chpt. 1984-85, v.p. chpts. west 1985-88), Lincoln League (pres. 1958), Marine's Meml. Club, Am. Contract Bridge League (life master), Clarkson Alumni Assn. (Watertown sect. pres. 1955), No. N.Y. Contract Club (pres. 1959), No. N.Y. Transp. Club, Tau Beta Pi. Office: The Change Agts Inc 2557 Via Verde Walnut Creek CA 94598-3451

GARONE, ELIZABETH, writer; b. New Rochelle, N.Y., Jan. 27, 1967; d. Vincent Anthony and Dorothea Angela (Healy) G. BA in Am. Studies, U. Calif., 1990; MS in Journalism, Columbia U., 1996. Reporter The World newspaper, Coos Bay, Oreg., 1991-93; editor AJET mag., Omachi, Japan, 1993-95; English tchr. JET Programme, Omachi, 1993-95; grad. asst. Columbia U., N.Y.C., 1995-96; online editor New Times, Phoenix, 1996—; guest spkr. Ariz. State U., Tempe, 1996—; bd. dirs. electronic village, Ariz. State U. Author: (anthology) Prized Writing, 1990 (1st place award 1990). Mem. Sierra Club, Ariz., Calif., 1990—, Homeless Children's Program, Phoenix, 1997—, Amnesty Internat., 1990—. Recipient scholarships Women in Internat. Journalism, 1995, Columbia U., 1995, fellowship Finland Govt., Helsinki, 1996, Pres.'s Undergrad. fellowship U. Calif. Davis, 1990. Mem. Soc. Profl. Journalists, Columbia U. Alumni Orgn., JET Alumni Orgn., U. Calif. Davis Alumni Orgn., Writer's Voice. Avocations: travel, fgn. langs., painting. Home: 1712 Baker St San Francisco CA 94115 Office: San Mateo County Times PO Box 5400 San Mateo CA 94402

GARRA, RAYMOND HAMILTON, II, marketing executive; b. Chgo., Apr. 2, 1934; s. Raymond Hamilton and Dorothy (Gardner) G.; student Duke, 1951-53; BA, U. Calif. at Los Angeles, 1956; m. Sandra Beatrice Pheasant, Dec. 27, 1962 (div. May, 1970); children: Terese Helene, Raymond Hamilton III. Gen. mgr. fine paper div. Noland Paper Co., Inc., Buena Park, Calif., 1959-67; v.p. sales Western Lithograph Co., Inc., Los Angeles, 1967-71; pres. Los Angeles Lithograph Co., 1971-73; pres. World Sports Mktg., Inc., also Miss Calif. Teen-ager, Inc., 1974-79; pres. Westaire Properties, Inc., Westaire Travel and Tours, 1975-93; pres. Teragar Mktg., 1994—; pres. Gamra Graphics, Inc., 1998—. Mem. Republican State Central Com., 1966-67; exec. bd. U. Calif., Irvine Sports Assocs.; founder Internat. Divers Festivals, 1979, West Coast Challenge Cup Yacht Regatta, 1983; participant Nat. Sr. Olympics (swimming), 1995, 97. Served with USCGR, 1956-59; lt. comdr. Res. Flotilla Comdr., USCG Aux., 1990. Recipient Sports Family of Year award, 1975. Mem. Nat. Coronado 25 Assn. (pres. 1969-70; Yachtsman of Year award 1971), Buena Park C. of C. (sec. 1967), Mensa (founder Orange County Soc. 1964), Balboa Bay, Bahia Corinthian Yacht, Shriner (pres. El Bandito Shrine Club 1992), Pacific Golf and Country Club, Phi Kappa Psi (pres. Orange County Alumni Assn. 1994—). Home: 3 Sea Island Dr Newport Beach CA 92660-5100

GARRETSON, OWEN LOREN, chemical engineer; b. Salem, Iowa, Feb. 24, 1912; s. Sumner Dilts and Florence (White) G.; m. Erma Mary Smith, Jan. 23, 1932; children: John Albert, Owen Don, Susan Marie, Leon Todd. Student, Iowa Wesleyan Coll., 1930-32; BSME, Iowa State U., 1937. Registered profl. engr., Okla., N.Mex., Iowa, Mo. Engr. Bailey Meter Co., Cleve., 1937, St. Louis, 1937-38; engr., dist. mgr. Phillips Petroleum Co., Bartlesville, Okla., 1938-39, Amarillo, Tex., 1939-40; engr., dist. mgr. Phillips Petroleum Co., Detroit, 1940-41, wholesale mgr. liquified petroleum gas sales divsn., 1941-42; mgr. product supply and transp. divsn. Phillips Petroleum Co., Bartlesville, 1942-44, mgr. engring. devel. divsn., 1944-46, mgr. spl. products engring. devel. divsn., 1946-47; pres. Gen. Tank & Steel Corp., Roswell, N.Mex., United Farm Chem. Co.; pres., dir. Garretson Equipment Co., Mt. Pleasant, Iowa; v.p., dir. Valley Industries, Inc., Mt. Pleasant; pres., dir. Garretson Carburetion of Tex., Inc., Lubbock; v.p., dir. Sacra Gas Co. Roswell, 1957-58; exec. v.p., dir. Arrow Gas Co. & Affiliated Corps., Roswell, N.Mex., Tex., Utah, 1958-60; asst. to pres. Nat. Propane Corp., Hyde Park, N.Y.; pres., chmn. bd. Plateau, Inc. Oil Refining, Farmington, N.Mex., 1960-82, also bd. dirs.; chmn. bd. S.W. Motels, Inc., Farmington; organizing dir. Farmington Nat. Bank, 1964; cons. Suburban Propane Gas Corp. Whippany, N.J. Contbr. articles to profl. jours.; 42 patents issued in several fields; inventor WWII aircraft engine power boost sys., 1942. Mem., past pres. Farmington Indsl. Devel. Svc., N.Mex. Lidquefied Petroleum Gas Commn., 1955-76, chmn., 1956-58; mem. Iowa Gov.'s Trade Commn. to No. Europe, 1970, Iowa Trade Mission to Europe, 1979; mem. com. natural gas/liquefied natural gas Internat. Petroleum Expn. and Congress, 1970-71; mem. Nat. Coun. Crime and Delinquency. Recipient Merit award Iowa Wesleyan Coll. Alunmi Assn., 1968, Profl. Achievement Engring. citation Iowa State U., 1986. Mem. ASME, NSPE, Nat. Liquefied Petroleum Gas Assn. (bd. dirs., Disting. Svc. award 1979), Am. Petroleum Inst., Nat. Petroleum Refiner's Assn. (bd. dirs., pres.), Ind. Refiners Assn. Am., Agrl. Ammonia Inst. Memphis (bd. dirs.), N.Mex. Liquefied Petroleum Gas. Assn. (pres., bd. dirs.), Ind. Petroleum Assn. Am., N.Mex. Acad. Sci., Am. Soc. Agrl. Engrs., Am. Soc. Automotive Engrs., N.Mex. Amigos., Am. Inst. Chem. Engrs., Newcomen Soc. N.Am., Soc. Indsl. Archeology, Ancient Gassers (sec., pres.), 25 Yr. Club Petroleum Industry, Masons, Rotary, Phi Delta Theta, Tau Beta Pi. Home: 500 E La Plata St Farmington NM 87401-6940 Office: PO Box 108 Farmington NM 87499-0108

GARRETSON, STEVEN MICHAEL, elementary education educator; b. L.A., Nov. 2, 1950; s. Fredrick Harmon and Mildred (Mason) G.; m. Candice Kay Clouse, Sept. 23, 1972; children: Joshua Steven, Amanda Jeanine. BA, U. Calif., Irvine, 1972, tchr. credential, 1974; postgrad., U. Calif., Santa Barbara, 1973; MA, U. San Francisco, 1980. Cert. tchr., adminstr., Calif. Tchr. Irvine Unified Sch. Dist., 1974—; energy conservation cons. Irvine Unified Sch. Dist., 1981-85, grant writer, 1983—, archtl. design cons., 1975—, mentor tchr., 1984-86; presenter state social studies conf., 1980. Mem. Irvine Tchrs. Assn. (grievance chmn. 1980-82, treas., 1977-78, v.p., 1978-79, contract negotiator, 1976-84, 89-93, benefits mgmt. bd. 1990—, pres. 1993-97, technology support 1997—), Phi Delta Kappa. Roman Catholic. Avocations: volleyball, woodworking, computers, antique cars. Office: Irvine Unified Sch Dist 5050 Barranca Pkwy Irvine CA 92604-4698

GARRETT, DEAN, basketball player; b. Nov. 27, 1966. Center Denver Nuggets. Office: c/o Denver Nuggets 1635 Clay St Denver CO 80204-1743

GARRETT, THOMAS MONROE, chemist; b. San Francisco, Mar. 10, 1961; s. Walter Norman and Sally Ann (Sharpless) G.; m. Karen Lynn Garcia, June 7, 1987; children: Andrew Henry, Alexander Monroe. BS with hons., Stanford U., 1983; PhD, U. Calif., Berkeley, 1988. Postdoctoral fellow U. Louis Pasteur, Strasbourg, France, 1988-90; part owner, dir. of rsch. MCP Industries, Inc., Corona, Calif., 1990—. Contbr. articles to profl. jours.; patentee in field. Chmn. scholarship and speech, Rotary, Corona. Recipient Bourse Chateubriand, France. Fellow Am. Inst. Chemists; mem. Am. Chem. Soc., N.Am. Soc. Trenchless Tech., L.A. Soc. Coatings Technology, Phi Lambda Upsilon, Sigma Xi. Republican. Episcopalian. Achievements include co-discovery of first perfect trigonal prismatic iron (III) complex; strongest bidentate iron chelating agts.; self-assembling pentameric silver (I) complex; a process to make sand bounce like a superball; co-developer first U.S.-made clay microtunneling pipe; invented smart materials for redistribution of .5 kiloton construction forces. Office: MCP Industries Inc 1660 Leeson Ln Corona CA 91719-2061

GARRIGUS, CHARLES BYFORD, retired literature educator; b. Benton, Ill., June 13, 1914; s. Charles Byford and Ailene Marie (Fowler) G.; m. Ferne Marie Fetters, Dec. 28, 1936 (dec.); children: Marmarie (dec.), Charles, Richmond, Karis, Rose Ann. AB, U. Ill., 1936, MA, 1937. Prof. humanities King's River Coll., Reedley, Calif., 1949-73; Calif. poet laureate for life, 1966—. Author: California Poems, 1955, (poems) Echoes of Being, 1975, Soundings, 1999, (novels) Brief Candel, 1987, Chas and The Summer of '26, 1994; editor: Modern Hamlet, 1950, An Evangel, 1998. Mem. Calif. Assembly, 1958-66. Democrat. Methodist. Avocations: lecturing, poetry readings. Home: 1623 Morgan Dr Kingsburg CA 93631-2619

GARRISON, EVA HEIM, school counselor; b. Dettingen, Bavaria, Germany, Sept. 23, 1940; came to U.S., 1964; d. Josef Fridrich and Barbara Fridericke (Vogt) Heim; m. Floyd Garrison, Sept. 15, 1962; children: Cindy Elizabeth, Michele Maria. AA, Solano C.C., 1973; BA in Spl. Edn., Cen. Wash. U., 1983; MEd in Counseling, City U., Bellevue, Wash., 1994. Cert. sch. counselor, tchr. 2d and 3d yr. high sch. German. Police officer Vallejo (Calif.) Police Dept., 1970-77; interim sch. instr. Ctrl. Kitsap Sch. Dist., Silverdale, Wash., 1983-84, interim sch. coord., 1984-87, instr. h.s. German, 1987-88, substance abuse coord., 1992-93; coord. in-sch. suspension program Camden County H.S., St. Mays, Ga., 1988-89; sch. counselor, tchr. 2d and 3d yr. German Olympic H.S., Silverdale, 1995—. Mem. Substance Abuse Adv. Bd., Kitsap County, Wash., 1989-92, At-Risk Task Force, Kitsap County, 1985-87; chair Cen. Kitsap Comty. Coalition, Silverdale, 1989-93; comty. vol. Recipient Gov.'s award in substance abuse prevention, 1992. Mem. Wash. State Sch. Counselors Assn., Wash. Mental Health Counselors Assn. Avocations: swimming, biking, gardening, traveling, hiking, walking. Home: 4709 Chico Way NW Bremerton WA 98312-1219

GARRITY, RODMAN FOX, psychologist, educator; b. Los Angeles, June 10, 1922; s. Lawrence Hitchcock and Margery Fox (Pugh) G.; m. Juanita Daphne Mullan, Mar. 5, 1948; children—Diana Daphne, Ronald Fox. Student, Los Angeles City Coll., 1946-47; B.A., Calif. State U., Los Angeles, 1950; M.A., So. Meth. U., Dallas, 1955; Ed.D., U. So. Calif., 1963. Tchr. elem. sch. Palmdale (Calif.) Sch. Dist., 1952-54; psychologist, prin. Redondo Beach (Calif.) City Schs., 1954-60; asst. dir. ednl. placement lectr., ednl. adviser U. So. Calif., 1960-62; asso. prof., coordinator credentials programs Calif. State Poly. U., Pomona, 1962-66; chmn. social sci. dept. Calif. State Poly. U., 1966-68, dir. tchr. preparation center, 1968-71, coordinator grad. program, 1971-73, prof. tchr. preparation center, 1968—, coordinator spl. edn. programs, 1979—; cons. psychologist, lectr. in field. Pres. Redondo Beach Coordinating Council, 1958-60; mem. univ. rep. Calif. Faculty Assns., 1974-76. Served with Engr. Combat Bn. AUS, 1942-45. Mem. Prins. Assn. Redondo Beach (chmn. 1958-60), Nat. Congress Parents and Tchrs. (hon. life), Am. Psychol. Assn., Calif. Tchrs. Assn. Democrat. Office: Calif State U Dept Special Edn Pomona CA 91768

GARRITY, THOMAS JOHN, pharmaceutical executive; b. Connellsville, Pa., Feb. 19, 1949; s. John Peter and Helen (Russo) G.; m. Susan Lucille Maddox, Sept. 10, 1977; children: Stephen Thomas, Laura Christine. SB in Aeros. and Astronautics, MIT, 1970; MBA, U. Chgo., 1974. Mgr. mgmt. reporting Mellon Nat. Corp., Pitts., 1974-78; various positions Eli Lilly & Co., Indpls., 1978-85, dir. mktg. Elanco div., 1985-86; European area dir. Elanco divsn. Eli Lilly & Co., London, 1986-90; dir. fin. planning Eli Lilly & Co., Indpls., 1990-92, dir. pub. policy, 1992-94; exec. v.p., CFO PCS Health Syss., Scottsdale, Ariz., 1994—. Vice pres. Zionsville (Ind.) Planning Commn., 1984-86; trustee Orchard Country Day Sch., 1991-95. Office: PCS Health Systems 9501 E Shea Blvd Scottsdale AZ 85260-6719

GARROP, BARBARA ANN, elementary education educator; b. Chgo., Sept. 2, 1941; d. Marshall and Esther (Barbakoff) Stickles; widowed; children: Alana Beth, Stacy Lynn. AA with honors, Wright Jr. Coll., Chgo., 1961; BA with honors, Roosevelt U., 1963; MS with honors, Calif. State U., Hayward, 1982. Cert. elem. tchr., reading specialist, Calif. Tchr. Von Humboldt Sch., Chgo., 1963-64, Haugan Sch., Chgo., 1964-67; primary grades reading specialist Mt. Diablo Sch. Dist., Concord, Calif., 1979-80, Mills Elem. Sch., Benicia, Calif., 1980-87, Mary Farmar Sch., Benicia, 1987—; mentor tchr. Benicia Unified Sch. Dist., Benicia, 1989, 92, 96—; inst. tchr. leader Calif. Lit. Project, 1991-93; instr. Chapman U. Acad. Ctr., Fairfield, Calif., spring, 1992; mem. reading delegation to China citizen amb. program People to People Internat., 1993, Russia & Czech citizen amb. program, 1998. Author phonic manual, 1982; featured in article Woman's Day mag., 1982; contbr. reading program to Excellence In Educational Programs Throughout Solano County, 1994-97; contbg. author Celebrating The National Reading Initiative, 1988. Bd. dirs. Sisterhood of Congregation B'nai Shalom, Walnut Creek, Calif., 1987-88. Named Benicia Tchr. of Yr., 1998, 99; grantee Reading Is Fundamental, 1979-80, Golden Bell award Calif. Sch. Bd. Assn., 1997. Mem. NEA, AAUW, Internat. Reading Assn., Calif. Reading Assn. (Achievement award 1984), Constra Costa Reading Assn., Calif. Tchrs. Assn., Pi Lambda Theta. Jewish. Lodge: B'nai Brith Women (v.p. Columbus, Ohio 1971-72, pres. Walnut Creek 1973-74). Avocations: singing, theater, reading, drawing, painting. Office: Mary Farmar Sch 901 Military W Benicia CA 94510-2598

GARRUTO, JOHN ANTHONY, cosmetics executive; b. Johnson City, N.Y., June 18, 1952; s. Paul Anthony and Katherine Helen (DiMartino) G.; m. Denise Kitty Conlon, Feb. 19, 1971 (div. May 1978); 1 child, James Joseph; m. Anita Louise, May 12, 1979 (div. Sept. 1984); 1 child, Christopher Russell; m. Debra Lynn Brady (div. Dec. 1986); m. Michelle Bartok, Apr. 2, 1988; children: Catherine Michelle, Gabrielle. BS in Chemistry, SUNY, Binghamton, 1974; AAS in Bus. Adminstrn., Broome Coll., 1976. Rsch. chemist Lander Co. Inc., Binghamton, 1974-77; rsch. dir. Lander Co. Inc., St. Louis, 1977-79, Olde Worlde Products, High Point, N.C., 1979-81; v.p. rsch. and devel. LaCosta Products Internat., Carlsbad, Calif., 1981-89; chief ops. officer Randall Products Internat., Carlsbad, 1989-91; pres. Dermasearch Internat., 1991-92; chief tech. officer Innovative Bioscis. Corp., Oceanside, Calif., 1992-95; v.p. rsch. Garden Botanika, Oceanside, Calif., 1995—; cons. Trans-Atlantic Mktg., Binghamton, 1975-78; instr. cosmetic sci UCLA, 1991—, UCLA Ext.; lectr. to cosmetic industry. Patentee in field. Mem. AAS, Soc. Cosmetic Chemists (newsletter editor 1980-81, publicity chmn. 1984—, edn. chmn. 1987, employment chmn. 1994—, sec. beauty industry west, chmn. elect 1999—), Fedn. Am. Scientists, N.Y. Acad. Scis. Office: Garden Botanika # 115 4168 Avenida De La Plata Oceanside CA 92056-6031

GARRY, JOEL E., computer database analyst; b. L.A., Dec. 24, 1956; s. Edward I. and Rose Garry; m. Laurie Garry, May 16, 1993; 1 child, Allan. BS, U. Calif., Santa Barbara, 1979. Cert. in sys. mgmt., Calif. Sr. programmer API Alarm Sys., Culver City, Calif., 1983-84; cons. Beck Computer Sys., Long Beach, Calif., 1984-88; database cons. CSC, San Diego, 1989-93, United Source Svcs., Thousand Oaks, Calif., 1994, BCSI, Irvine, Calif., 1993; sr. support analyst Ross Sys., Escondido, Calif., 1994-97; database adminstr. Info. Quest, Carlsbad, Calif., 1997-98. Mem. Internat. Oracle Users Group, DEC Users Soc., North Coast Vettes (newsletter editor 1995-97). Office: Garry Multiuser Computer Sys Box 2831 Vista CA 92085

GARSH, THOMAS BURTON, publisher; b. New Rochelle, N.Y., Dec. 12, 1931; s. Harry and Matilda (Smith) G.; m. Beatrice J. Schmidt; children: Carol Jean, Thomas Burton, Janice Lynn. B.S., U. Md., 1955. Edn. rep.

McGraw Hill Book Co., N.Y.C., 1959-68; mktg. mgr. D.C. Heath & Co., Boston, 1969-71; dir. mktg. Economy Co., Oklahoma City, 1971-72; sr. v.p. Macmillan Pub. Co., N.Y.C., 1972-78; pres. Am. Book Co., N.Y.C., 1978-81; founder, pres., dir. Am. Ednl. Computer, Inc., Palo Alto, Calif., 1981-86; founder, chmn., chief exec. officer OmnyEd Corp., Palo Alto, 1987-91; pres. Silver Burdett & Ginn divsn. of Simon and Schuster, 1991-92; dir. Fifty Plus Fitness Assn., Palo Alto, Calif. Publ. Homes and Land of Santa Clara, 1998—. Mem. county council Boy Scouts Am., 1963-65; mem. ch. council on Interracial Affairs, 1966-68, pres., 1967; vice-chmn. Madison County Democratic Party, 1967. Mem. Assn. Am. Pubs., Profl. Bookman's Assn., Omicron Delta Kappa, Sigma Alpha Epsilon. Club: Cazenovia Country (founder). Home: 401 Old Spanish Trl Portola Valley CA 94028

GARSTANG, ROY HENRY, astrophysicist, educator; b. Southport, Eng., Sept. 18, 1925; came to U.S., 1964; s. Percy Brocklehurst and Eunice (Gledhill) G.; m. Ann Clemence Hawk, Aug. 11, 1959; children—Jennifer Katherine, Susan Veronica. B.A., U. Cambridge, 1946, M.A., 1950, Ph.D., 1954, Sc.D., 1983. Research assoc. U. Chgo., 1951-52; lectr. astronomy U. Coll., London, 1952-60; reader astronomy U. London, 1960-64, asst. dir. Obs., 1959-64; prof. astrophysics U. Colo., Boulder, 1964-94, chair faculty assembly, 1988-89, prof. emeritus, 1994—; chmn. Joint Inst. for Lab. Astrophysics, 1966-67; cons. Nat. Bur. Standards, 1964-73; v.p. commn. 14 Internat. Astron. Union, 1970-73, pres., 1973-76; Erskine vis. fellow U. Canterbury, N.Z., 1971; vis. prof. U. Calif., Santa Cruz, 1971. Editor: Observatory, 1953-60; Contbr. numerous articles to tech. jours. Recipient Excellence in Svc. award U. Colo., 1990. Fellow Am. Phys. Soc., AAAS, Optical Soc. Am., Brit. Inst. Physics, Royal Astron. Soc.; mem. Am. Astron. Soc., Royal Soc. Scis. Liege (Belgium). Achievements include rsch. on atomic physics and astrophys. applications; calculation of atomic transition probabilities, atomic spectra in very high magnetic fields and magnetic white dwarf stars; modelling of light pollution. Home: 830 8th St Boulder CO 80302-7409 Office: U Colo JILA Boulder CO 80309-0440

GARTNER, HAROLD HENRY, III, lawyer; b. L.A., June 23, 1948; s. Harold Henry Jr. and Frances Mildred (Evans) G.; m. Denise Helene Young, June 7, 1975; children: Patrick Christopher, Matthew Alexander. Student, Pasadena City Coll., 1966-67, George Williams Coll., 1967-68, Calif. State U., Los Angeles, 1969; JD cum laude, Loyola U., Los Angeles, 1972. Bar: Calif. 1972, U.S. Dist. Ct. (cen. dist.) Calif. 1973, U.S. Ct. Appeals (9th cir.) 1973. Assoc. Hitt, Murray & Caffray, Long Beach, Calif., 1972; dep. city atty. City of L.A., 1972-73; assoc. Patterson, Ritner & Lockwood, L.A., 1973-79; mng. ptnr. all offices Patterson, Ritner, Lockwood, Gartner & Jurich, L.A., Ventura, Bakersfield, and San Bernardino, Calif., 1991—; instr. law Ventura Coll., 1981. Recipient Am. Jurisprudence award Trusts and Equity, 1971. Mem. ABA, Calif. Bar Assn., Ventura County Bar Assn., Nat. Assn. Def. Counsel, Assn. So. Calif. Def. Counsel, Ventura County Trial Lawyers Assn., Direct Relief Internat. (bd. trustees). Republican. Club: Pacific Corinthian Yacht. Avocations: sailing, scuba diving, skiing. Home: 6900 Via Alba Camarillo CA 93012-8279 Office: Patterson Ritner Lockwood Gartner & Jurich 260 Maple Ct Ste 231 Ventura CA 93003-3570

GARVER, RICHARD ALVIN, investment advisor; b. Covina, Calif., Aug. 6, 1956; s. Alson Eugene and Lorna Lorraine (McClean) G.; m. Anahid Ghazaros Kademian, Nov. 14, 1981; children: Felicia, Richard. Student, Citrus Coll., 1975-80; BS, U. Commns. BSA, 1984, MS, 1984, PhD, 1986. Registered fin. planner; cert. fin. planner, fund specialist, investment specialist. Territory mgr. Combined Ins. Co., Chgo., 1980-82; registered rep. Prudential Co. Securities Corp., Phoenix, 1982-86; br. office mgr. Mutual Svc. Corp., Detroit, 1986-88; regional v.p. USA Capital Mgmt. Group, Las Vegas, Nev., 1988-90; prin. Bear Valley Ins. Agy. and Fin. Svcs., Fawnskin, Calif., 1985—, Wealth Resource Capital, Newport Beach, Calif., 1990—. Recipient Merit award U.S. Congress, 1974; named Rotarian of Yr., Rotary Club of Big Bear, 1988. Mem. NRA, Internat. Assn. Fin. Planners, Inst. Cert. Fin. Planners, Internat. Assn. Registered Fin. Planners, Boy Scouts Am. (Silver Palm Eagle Scout award, 1974), Friends Accordian, Moose, Elks, Masons, Scottish Rite, Shriners, High Twelve Club (pres. 1985-86), N.Am. Hunting Club, Big Bear Valley Sportman's Club. Republican. Avocations: working with youth, fishing, hunting, music. Office: Bear Valley Ins Agy and Fin Svcs PO Box 69 39397 North Shore Dr Fawnskin CA 92333

GARVEY, DORIS BURMESTER, environmental administrator; b. N.Y.C., Oct. 3, 1936; d. William Henry and Florence Elizabeth (Sauerteig) Burmester; m. Gerald Thomas John Garvey, June 6, 1959; children: Deirdre Anne, Gerald Thomas John Jr., Victoria Elizabeth. BA with honors, Wilson Coll., 1958; MA with honors, Yale U., 1959. Rsch. assoc. Princeton U., N.J., 1967-76; environ. scientist Argonne (Ill.) Nat. Lab., 1976-84; staff mem. Los Alamos (N.Mex.) Nat. Lab., 1984-86, regulatory compliance officer, 1986-89, sect. leader environ. protection group, 1989-92, dep. group leader, environ. protection group, 1992-94, leader sitewide Environ. Impact Statement project, 1994—, leader land transfer project, 1998—. Contbr. articles to profl. jours. Bd. dirs. N.Mex. Repertory Theater, Santa Fe, 1987-88; mem. Environ. Improvement Bd., Glen Ellyn, Ill., 1980-82. Mem. AAUW, N.Mex. Hazardous Waste Soc., Women in Sci., Gov.'s Task Force Emergency Response, Nat. Assn. Environ. Profls., Phi Beta Kappa. Democratic. Roman Catholic. Avocations: backpacking, cross-country skiing, gourmet cooking. Home: 368 Calle Loma Norte Santa Fe NM 87501-1278 Office: Los Alamos Nat Lab PO Box 1663 Los Alamos NM 87544-0600

GARVEY, EVELYN JEWEL, retired mental health nurse; b. Carrizozo, N.Mex., Aug. 23, 1931; d. Everett E. and Jewel A. (Bullard) Bragg; m. Robert J. Garvey, July 10, 1949; children: Nancy, Annie, Catherine, Robert, Michael, Betty. AD, Ea. N.Mex. Coll., 1972. RN, N.Mex.; cert. EMT., N.Mex. Staff nurse N.Mex. Rehab. Ctr., Roswell, 1972; staff nurse Villa Solano State Sch., Roswell, 1972-79, DON, 1979-81; staff nurse Ft. Stanton (N.Mex.) Hosp., 1981-95, Sunset Villa Nursing Home, Roswell, N.Mex., 1995-96; ret., 1996.

GARVEY, KATHERINE HESTON, gerontology nurse; b. Galesburg, Ill., Dec. 28, 1944; d. Ernest Edwin and Eunice Corinne (Hollister) Heston; m. Edward Anthony Garvey, Nov. 25, 1967; children: Travler Franklin, Edward Anthony II, Anne Elizabeth, Michael Joseph, Thomas Heston. BS, U. Md., 1981; MA, John F. Kennedy U., 1993. RN, Calif. Staff nurse ICU Children's Meml. Hosp., Chgo., 1967-68; staff nurse pediatrics St. Joseph's Hosp., Chgo., 1968-70; staff nurse neonatal ICU Prentice Woman's Hosp., Chgo., 1970-73; staff nurse newborn nursery Anne Arundel Gen. Hosp., Annapolis, Md., 1974-82; advisor/counselor Group Health, Washington, 1982-83; patient/home care educator John Muir Med. Ctr., Walnut Creek, Calif., 1984-92; minimun data set coord. Jewish Home for Aged, San Francisco, 1992—. Youth educator St. John Vlanney Ch., Walnut Creek, 1985; vol. St. Anne's Crisis Nursery, Concord, Calif., 1993. Recipient Contbg. scholarship Contra Costa Alternative Sch., Orinda, Calif., 1988-93. Mem. AAUW (sec. 1985, 86, membership v.p. 1987, 88, program v.p. 1989, 90, ednl. found. v.p. 1995-96). Roman Catholic.

GARY, KARL, law educator; b. Winston-Salem, N.C., Feb. 5, 1957; s. Frances Gary; children: Daniel Favela-Gary, Olivia Favela-Gary. BA, Occidental Coll., 1979; JD/MM, Willamette Univ., 1984. Medical/legal Spanish/Eng. interpreter Favela Interpreters, L.A., 1985-96; educator L.A. U.S.D., L.A., 1996—; lawyer L.A., 1992—; mock trial competition coach L.A.U.S.D., 1996—; pro bono atty., L.A. Author poems. Mem. L.A. County Bar., Calif. State Bar. Avocations: martial arts, tae kwon do, hapkido. Home and office: 1615 Amberwood Dr Apt E South Pasadena CA 91030-1937

GARZA, OSCAR, newspaper editor. Daily calendar editor-arts L.A. Times, Calif. Office: Los Angeles Times Times Mirror Sq Los Angeles CA 90053*

GASICH, WELKO ELTON, retired aerospace executive, management consultant; [illegible] G.; m. Patricia Ann Gudgel, Dec. 28, 1973; 1 child, Mark David. A.B. cum laude in Mech. Engring. (Bacon scholar), Stanford U., 1943, M.S. in Mech. Engring., 1947, cert. in fin. and econs. (Sloan exec. fellow), 1967; Aero. Engr., Calif. Inst. Tech., 1948. Aerodynamicist Douglas Aircraft Co., 1943-44, supr. aeroelastics, 1947-51; chief aero design Rand Corp., 1951-53; chief preliminary design aircraft div. Northrop Corp., Los Angeles, 1953-56; dir. advanced systems Northrop Corp., 1956-61, v.p., asst. gen. mgr. tech., 1961-66, corp. v.p., gen. mgr. Northrop Ventura div., 1967-71, corp. v.p., gen. mgr. aircraft div., 1971-76, corp. v.p., group exec. aircraft group, 1976-79, sr. v.p. advanced projects, 1979-85, exec. v.p. programs, 1985-88, ret., 1988; aerospace cons., Encino, Calif., 1988—. Author: 40 Years of Ferrari V-12 Engines, 1990; patentee in field. Chmn. adv. council Stanford Sch. Engring., 1981-83; past mem. adv. council Stanford Grad. Sch. Bus.; chmn. United Way, 1964; chmn. Scout-O-Rama, Los Angeles council Boy Scouts Am., 1964; chmn. explorer scout exec. com., 1963-64. Served to lt. USN, 1944-46. Fellow AIAA, Soc. Automotive Engrs.; mem. NAE, Navy League, Stanford Grad. Sch. Bus. Alumni Assn. (pres. 1971), Conquistadores del Cielo Club, Bel Air Country Club. Republican. Office: 3517 Caribeth Dr Encino CA 91436-4103

GASKILL, HERBERT LEO, accountant, engineer; b. Seattle, July 1, 1923; s. Leo Dell and Vesta Rathbone (Dahlen) G.; m. Margaret Helen Jenkins, Mar. 1, 1944 (div.); children—Margaret V., Herbert Leo; m. Opal Jordan, June 13, 1992; 1 child, Ann. B.S. and M.S. in Chem. Engring., U. Wash., 1949, M.B.A., 1976. C.P.A., Wash. Asst. prof. dental materials, exec. officer dept. dental materials Sch. Dentistry, U. Wash., 1950-56; ops. analyst The Boeing Co., Seattle, 1958-71, mktg. cons. govt. programs, 1972-74; pvt. practice acctg., Seattle, 1976-80; hazardous waste mgr. Boeing Co., Seattle, 1980-86, project mgr. Western Processing Remediation, 1986-95, ret. 1995. Active Seattle Art Mus., Pacific Northwest Aviation Hist. Found. Served to lt. (j.g.) USNR, 1941-46. TAPPI fellow, 1956; U. Wash. Engring. Expt. Sta. fellow, 1957. Mem. Wash. Soc. C.P.A.s. Contbr. articles to profl. jours. Home: 1236 NE 92nd St Seattle WA 98115-3135

GASSMAN, DIANE LYNNE, interior designer; b. Sioux Falls, S.D., Mar. 2, 1962; d. Donald Dale and Paula-cherie (Fox) G. AA, Brooks Coll. Kitchen/bath designer The Kitchen Shoppe/Kitchens by Ingrid, Portland, Oreg., 1982-85, Kitchens, Kitchens, Beaverton, Oreg., 1985-88; designer, mgr. Siematic Corp., Portland, 1988-92, Builders Appliance Supply Co., Portland, Oreg., 1992-93; designer, owner Interior Dimensions, Portland, 1993—. Mem. ASID, Nat. Kitchen and Bath Assn. Office: Interior Dimensions 5319 SW Westgate Dr Ste 145 Portland OR 97221-2430

GAST, NANCY LOU, retired chemical company executive; b. Appleton, Wis., Aug. 13, 1941; d. Harvey William Gast and June Louella (Mohr) Webster. Med. technologist Palo Alto/Stanford (Calif.) Hosp., 1963-65; med. technologist St. Vincent Hosp., Portland, Oreg., 1965-70, chemistry supr., 1970-81; tech. rep. DuPont-Diagnostic Systems, Claremont, Calif., 1981-83; sales rep. DuPont-Diagnostic Systems, Wilmington, Del., 1983-85; account rep. DuPont-Diagnostic Systems, Claremont, Calif., 1985-87, acct. mgr., 1987-96, exec. coun. med. products sales, 1995-96, territory mgr., 1996; account rep. Dade Internat., Inc., Deerfield, Ill., 1996-98. Vol. med. technologist Health Help Ctr., Portland, 1984-88; bd. dirs. Assocs. ofSisters of Holy Names of Jesus and Mary, 1984-93, co-dir, 1994—. Mem. Am. Soc. Med. Technologists, Assn. Oreg. Med. Technologists (treas. 1976-78, chmn. sci. assembly for industry 1992-95), Am. Soc. Clin. Pathologists (cert. med. technologist assoc.). Republican. Roman Catholic. Office: 5727 SW Corbett Ave Portland OR 97201-3705

GASTON, RANDALL WALLACE, police chief; b. Lake Charles, La., Mar. 18, 1944; s. Wallace Howard and Mary Jean (Hubbs) G.; m. Linda Lou Lockwood; children: Debora Gaston Ricks, Aaron, Bryan, Allison. BS, Long Beach State Coll., 1971; MPA with honors, U. So. Calif., 1974; grad., FBI Nat. Acad., 1982. Police officer Anaheim (Calif.) Police Dept., 1965-69, police sgt., 1969-73, police lt., 1973-83, police capt., 1983-94, police chief, 1994—; instr. Orange County (Calif.) C.C.s, 1971-94. Mem. Internat. Police Chiefs Assn., Calif. Police Chiefs Assn., Orange County Police Chiefs Assn., FBI Nat. Acad. Assocs., Kiwanis Club of Greater Anaheim (bd. dirs. 1990-95), Phi Kappa Phi. Avocations: gardening, bicycling. Office: Anaheim Police Dept 425 S Harbor Blvd Anaheim CA 92805-3773

GATES, CHARLES CASSIUS, rubber company executive; b. Morrison, Colo., May 27, 1921; s. Charles Cassius and Hazel LaDora (Rhoads) G.; m. June Scowcroft Swaner, Nov. 26, 1943; children: Diane, John Swaner. Student, MIT, 1939-41; BS, Stanford U., 1943; DEng (hon.), Mich. Tech. U., 1975, Colo. Sch. of Mines, 1985. With Copolymer Corp., Baton Rouge, 1943-46; with Gates Rubber Co., Denver, 1946-96, v.p., 1951-58, exec. v.p., 1958-61, chmn. bd., 1961-96, CEO; chmn. bd. The Gates Corp., Denver, 1982-96, CEO, 1982-96, also bd. dirs.; pres. The Gates Corp., 1994-96; chmn. Cody Co., Denver, 1996—, Gates Capital Mgmt., LLC, Denver, 1996—; bd. trustees Gates Found. Trustee Denver Mus. Natural History, Calif. Inst. Tech., Pasadena, Denver Art Mus. Found., Graland Country Day Sch. Found. Recipient Cmty. Leadership and Svc. award Nat. Jewish Hosp., 1974; Mgmt. Man of Year award Nat. Mgmt. Assn., 1965; named March of Dimes Citizen of the West, 1987; inductee Colo. Bus. Hall of Fame, 1998. Mem. Conf. Bd. (dir.), Conquistadores del Cielo, Denver Country Club, Outrigger Canoe Club, Waialae Country Club, Boone and Crockett Club, Club Ltd., Old Baldy Club, Country Club of Colo., Roundup Riders of Rockies, Shikar-Safari Internat., Augusta Nat. Golf Club, Castle Pines Golf Club, The Wigwam Club. Office: Cody Co Ste 680 3773 Cherry Creek North Dr Denver CO 80209-3816

GATES, MILO SEDGWICK, retired construction company executive; b. Omaha, Apr. 25, 1923; s. Milo Talmage and Virginia (Offutt) G.; m. Anne Phleger, Oct. 14, 1950 (dec. Apr. 1987); children: Elena Motlow, Susan Gates, Virginia Lewis, Anne Symington, Milo T.; m. Robin Templeton Quist, June 18, 1988; stepchildren: Robert L. Quist, Catherine Quist, Sarah Mazzocco. Student, Calif. Inst. Tech., 1943-44; B.S., Stanford U., 1944, MBA, 1948. With Swinerton & Walberg Co., San Francisco, 1955—, pres., 1976—, chmn., 1988-96; ret. Bd. dirs., trustee Children's Hosp. San Francisco; trustee Grace Cathedral, San Francisco; bd. dirs. Calif. Acad. Scis. Lt. (j.g.), USNR, 1944-46. Mem. Pacific-Union Club, Bohemian Club. Republican. Home: 7 Vineyard Hill Rd Woodside CA 94062-2531

GATES, MIMI GARDNER, museum administrator. Dir. Seattle Art Mus., Wash. Office: Seattle Art Museum PO Box 22000 Seattle WA 98122-9700*

GATES, THEODORE ALLAN, JR., database administrator; b. Washington, May 24, 1933; s. Theodore Allan and Margaret (Camp) G.;m. Anne Bissell, Sept. 8, 1955; children: Virginia Anne, Nancy Bissell, Theodore Allan III (dec.), Margaret Kenyon. Student, U. Md., 1951-53, 56-57, 68-69. Mem. staff Arthur D. Little Sys., Burlington, Mass., 1976-77, Corp. Tech. Planning, Portsmouth, N.H., 1977-78; project mgr. Honeywell Info. Sys., Phoenix, 1978-81; tech. mgr. Honeywell Info. Sys., Seattle, 1981-83; mgr. data and software engring. ISC Sys. Corp., Spokane, Wash., 1983-90; project mgr. Boeing Computer Svcs., Richland, Wash., 1990-96, The Boeing Co., Bellevue, Wash., 1996—. With U.S. Army, 1953-56, Korea. Recipient Superior Performance award Census Bur., 1958. Mem. IEEE, Assn. Computing Machinery, Air Force Assn., U.S. Naval Inst., Smithsonian Assocs., Internat. Oracle Users Group, Woodland Park Zoo, Mus. of Flight, Commodores Club (Boston), Masons, Shriners. Lutheran. Avocations: photography, sailing, music. Home: 3208 168th Pl SE Bellevue WA 98008-5730 Office: The Boeing Co m/s 7W-43 PO Box 3707 Seattle WA 98124-2207

GATES, WILLIAM HENRY, III, software company executive; b. Seattle, Wash, Oct. 28, 1955; s. William H. and Mary M. (Maxwell) G.; m. Melinda French, January 1, 1994. Grad. high sch., Seattle, 1973; student, Harvard U., 1975. With MITS, from 1975; founder, chmn. bd. Microsoft Corp., Redmond, Wash., 1976—, now also chief exec. officer. Author: The Future, 1994, The Road Ahead, 1996. Recipient Howard Vollum award, Reed Coll., Portland, Oreg., 1984, Nat. medal Tech. U.S. Dept. Commerce Tech. Adminstrn., 1992; named CEO of Yr., Chief Executive mag., 1994. Office: Microsoft Corp 1 Microsoft Way Redmond WA 98052-8300*

GATEWOOD, CHARLES ROBERT, photographer, writer, video artist; b. Elgin, Ill., Nov. 8, 1942; s. John Jay and Clarene (Hall) G.; m. Virginia Hamilton, Jan. 1, 1975 (div. Sept. 1978). BA in Anthropology, U. Mo., 1963. Staff photographer Manhattan Tribune, N.Y.C., 1969-73, Rolling Stone, N.Y.C., 1973-74; owner Flash Video, Flash Publs., San Francisco, 1988—. One man shows include Clayton Gallery, N.Y.C., Anon Salon, San Francisco, 1995, Komm Ausstellungswerkstatt, Nurenberg, Germany, 1995, U. Tubingen, Germany, 1995, Morphos Gallery, San Francisco, 1996, Clayton Gallery, N.Y.C., 1996, Rita Dean Gallery, San Diego, 1996, Williamsburg Art Ctr., Bklyn., 1997, many others; group shows include Kalamazoo Inst. Arts, 1975, Third Eye Gallery, N.Y.C., 1976, Fine Arts Bldg., N.Y.C., 1976, Floating Fountain for Photography, N.Y.C., 1976, others; pub.: Discovery in Song, 1969, (with W.S. Burroughs) Sidetripping, 1975, People in Focus, 1977, (with S. Webb and M. Vassi) X-1000, 1977, (with S. Webb and M. Vassi) Pushing Ink: The Fine Art of Tattooing, 1979, Forbidden Photographs, 1981, 2nd edit., 1996, How to Take Great Pictures with Your Simple Camera, 1982, Wall Street, 1984, Hellfire, 1987, Primitives, 1992, Charles Gatewood Photographs, 1993, True Blood, 1997. Address: PO Box 410052 San Francisco CA 94141-0052

GAUBY, KARL MARTIN, lawyer, educator; b. Dayton, Ohio, Apr. 15, 1958; s. Carl William and Georgetta (Hulett) G.; m. Lola David, June 20, 1986; children: Stephanie, Brandon. BA, Berea Coll., 1980; MS, Eastern Ky. U., 1983, Eastern Ky. U., 1984, Golden Gate U., 1987; JD, Ariz. State U., 1990, PhD, 1998. Bar: Ariz. 1992, D.C. 1992, U.S. Dist. Ct. Ariz. 1992. Lab. dir. U.S. Pub. Health Svc., Fort Defiance, Ariz., 1983-84, USAF, Luke AFB, Ariz., 1984-88; lawyer Cates & Holloway, Scottsdale, Ariz., 1990-95; sr. counsel U. Phoenix, 1995—. Co-author: (with others) State Trademark and Unfair Competition Law, 1991-95; lectr. in field. Referee Am. Youth Soccer Assn., Phoenix, 1995—; active Phoenix Boys Choir, 1995—, Phoenix Indian Medical Ctr., 1993—. Lt. Col. USAF, 1997—. Recipient Alumni award Ariz. State U., 1997. Mem. Nat. Cert. Agy. (lab. mgmt. exam. writer 1988-90), Am. Soc. Clinical Pathologists (state adv., southwest region 1988-90), Sigma Xi, Phi Sigma, Phi Kappa Phi. Republican. Protestant. Avocations: scuba, skiing, travel, music. E-mail: karl@phoenix.edu. Fax: (602) 968-1159. Home: 3839 E Cathedral Rock Dr Phoenix AZ 85044-6626 Office: Univ Phoenix 4615 E Elwood St Phoenix AZ 85040-1908

GAULKE, MARY FLORENCE, library administrator; b. Johnson City, Tenn., Sept. 24, 1923; d. Gustus Thomas and Mary Belle (Bennett) Erickson; m. James Wymond Crowley, Dec. 1, 1939; 1 son, Grady Gaulke (name legally changed); m. 2d, Bud Gaulke, Sept. 1, 1945 (dec. Jan. 1978); m. 3d, Richard Lewis McNaughton, Mar. 21, 1983 (div. 1995). BS in Home Econs., Oreg. State U., 1963; MS in L.S., U. Oreg., 1968, PhD in Spl. Edn., 1970. Cert. std. pers. supr., std. handicapped learner, Oreg. Head dept. home econs. Riddle Sch. Dist. (Oreg.), 1963-66; libr. cons. Douglas County Intermediate Edn. Dist., Roseburg, Oreg., 1966-67; head resident, head counselor Prometheus Project, So. Oreg. Coll., Ashland, summers 1966-68; supr. librarians Medford Sch. Dist. (Oreg.), 1970-73; instr. in psychology So. Oreg. Coll., Ashland, 1970-73; libr. supr. Roseburg Sch. Dist., 1974-91; resident psychologist Black Oaks Boys Sch., Medford, 1970-75; mem. Oreg. Gov.'s Coun. Librs., 1979. Author: Vo-Ed Course for Junior High, 1965; Library Handbook, 1967; Instructions for Preparation of Cards For All Materials Cataloged for Libraries, 1971; Handbook for Training Library Aides, 1972. Coord. Laubach Lit. Workshops for H.S. Tutors, Medford, 1972. Fellow Internat. Biog. Assn. (life); mem. ALA, So. Oreg. Libr. Fedn. (sec. 1971-73), Oreg. Library Assn., Pacific N.W. Libr. Assn., Am. Biog. Inst. (lifetime dep. gov. 1987—), Internat. biog. Ctr. (hon., adv. coun. 1990), Delta Kappa Gamma (pres. 1980-82), Phi Delta Kappa (historian, research rep.). Democrat. Methodist. Clubs: Lodge: Order Eastern Star (worthy matron 1956-57). Home: 976 29th St Vero Beach FL 32960-6905 Office: 119 Orchard Ln Ashland OR 97520-9627

GAULT, ROSETTE FORD, artist, writer, inventor; b. N.Y.C., 1951. BA in Comm., U. Colo., 1975; MFA in Ceramics, U. Puget Sound, 1978. Acting dir. Pottery N.W., Seattle, 1986; instr. ceramics Oreg. Coll. Arts and Crafts, Portland, 1993-94; artist-in-residence Banff (Can.) Centre for Arts, 1990-91, 98; spkr. in field. Author: Paperclay for Ceramic Sculptors, 1993, Paper Clay, 1998; exhibited in numerous group shows; patentee in field; contbr. articles to profl. jours. Mem. Wash. Potters Assn. (sec. 1988-89), N.W. Designer Craftsmen, Coll. Art Assn. Office: New Century Arts Inc PO Box 9060 Seattle WA 98109-0060

GAUTIER, ELIZABETH JOLENE, accountant, consultant; b. Claremore, Okla., Apr. 15, 1958; d. Jack Milton and Beverly Jo (Duke) Miller; m. Roger Allen Gautier, June 19, 1980; 1 child, Heather Dawn. AD in Bus., Tulsa Jr. Coll., 1988; B in Bus., Langston U., 1989. Acct. Am. Airlines Inc., Tulsa, Okla., 1979-81; computer operator JR Norton Co., Phoenix, 1981-83; full charge bookkeeper REC Specialties, Inc., Camarillo, Calif., 1983-84; acct. Sandstone, Inc., Tulsa, 1984-89; acctg. and DP mgr. Colorgraphics Corp., Tulsa, 1989-90; mgr. cost acctg. Springtime Growers, San Diego, 1991-93; adminstr. cost acctg. GTE Interactive Media, Carlsbad, Calif., 1993-96; acctg. mgr. Airline Interiors, Simula Co., San Diego, 1996—; tax cons. Elizabeth Gautier's Tax Svc., San Diego, 1992—; tchr. Becker CPA/CMA Rev., 1996—. Auditor Carl Sandburg PTA, San Diego, 1994-95, treas., 1995-96, pres., 1996—; leader Girl Scouts of U.S., Troop 8103, San Diego, 1993-95. Fellow mem. Int. Mgmt. Accts. (cert.). Republican. Avocations: swimming, water skiing, camping. Office: Airline Interiors 12325 Kerran St Poway CA 92064-6801

GAVER, FRANCES ROUSE, lawyer; b. Lexington, Ky., Mar. 13, 1929; d. Colvin P. Rouse and Elizabeth Turner Sympson; m. Donald Paul Gaver, Jan. 24, 1953; children: Elizabeth, Donald, William. BA, Wellesley Coll., 1950; MA, U. Pitts., 1968; JD, Monterey (Calif.) Coll. of Law, 1986. Bar: Calif. 1986, U.S. Dist. Ct. (no. dist.) Calif. 1986; cert. specialist in probate, estate planing and trust law, Calif. Assoc. Hoge, Fenton, Jones & Appel, Monterey, 1986-93, Fenton & Keller, Monterey, 1993-97; ptnr. Johnson, Gaver & Leach, Monterey, 1997—. Bd. dirs. Carmel (Calif.) Unified Sch. Dist., 1973-81, Monterey Coll. of Law, 1991-97, Legal Svcs. for Srs., Pacific Grove, Calif., 1994—. Mem. Monterey County Bar Assn. Avocations: playing recorder, swimming. Office: Johnson Gaver & Leach LLP 2801 Monterey Salinas Hwy Monterey CA 93940-6401

GAVIN, DELANE MICHAEL, television writer, producer, director; b. Pierre, S.D., Oct. 6, 1935; s. Daniel Everett and Evelyn Agnes (Michaelson) G.; m. Paula Ethel Handelman, Feb. 22, 1969. BA in Journalism, San Francisco State U., 1962; MA in Journalism, UCLA, 1971; MBA in Organizational Behavior, U. So. Calif., 1982. With San Francisco Examiner, 1961-62; corr. AP, San Francisco, Reno and Las Vegas, Nev., 1962-64; reporter Las Vegas Rev.-Jour. Sun, 1964-65; editor suburban sect. Los Angeles Times, 1965-66; writer, producer news Sta. KNXT-TV, Hollywood, Calif., 1966-68; writer, reporter, dir., producer news Sta. KNBC-TV, Burbank, Calif., 1968-76; documentary writer, producer, dir. NBC-News, N.Y.C., 1976-78; med. producer KABC-TV, Hollywood, 1978—; instr. journalism U. So. Calif., 1978-90; sr. lectr. Calif. State U., Northridge, 1994-95. Served with USNR, 1955-57. Recipient Christopher award for directing Sta. NBC News TV The Christophers, 1973, for producing, 1976, Golden Mike award Radio and TV Assn., 1968, 69, 70, 72, 74, 75. Mem. Acad. TV Arts and Scis. (bd. govs. 1976-80, 82-86, 88-92, Emmy award 1968, 69, 70, 72, 73, 74), Dirs. Guild Am., Writers Guild Am., AFTRA, Nat. Assn. Broadcast Employees and Technicians, Wire Service Guild, Am. Newspaper Guild, Sigma Delta Chi. Home: 12508 Sarah St Studio City CA 91604-1112 Office: 4151 Prospect Ave Los Angeles CA 90027-4524

GAWTHROP, DAPHNE WOOD, performing company executive; b. Houston, July 22, 1940. Dir. programs and devel. Houston Mus. Natural Sci., 1987-89; dir. Inst. Mus. Svcs., Washington, 1989-91; dir. spl. projects Houston Grand Opera, 1991-92; dep. chmn. (pub. partnership) Nat. Endowment for the Arts, Washington, 1991-92; interim dir. Fotofest Ctr. for Photography, Houston, 1992; exec. dir. Sacramento Ballet, 1994—. Mem. Pres. Com. Arts and Humanities, Arts in Embassies coun. U.S. Dept. of State; adv. Arts Indemnity Program U.S. Info. Agy.; trustee Houston Ballet, Mus. of Fine Arts, Houston, Contemporary Arts Mus., Alley Theater. Recipient Nat. Devel. award Am. Assn. Museums; citation of Highest Achievement Nat. Endowment Arts. Office: Sacramento Ballet 1631 K St [illegible]

GAY, GEORGE ARTHUR, religion educator, minister; b. Niagara Falls, Ont., Can., Apr. 13, 1916; s. Robert Marshal and Marie (Copp) G.; m. Mary Thomas Bellah, May 16, 1942; children: Robert Stephen, Lloyd

Thomas. BA, U. Toronto, Can., 1942; BD magna cum laude, Fuller Theol. Sem., 1952, MTh, 1958; PhD, U. Manchester, Eng., 1971. Ordained to ministry Associated Gospel Chs. Can., 1942. Sec., field rep. InterVarsity Christian Fellowship, Alta., Can., 1942-43; missionary Evang. Union of S.Am., Bolivia, 1944-49; sem. prof. Latin Am. Mission, San Jose, Costa Rica, 1953-74, Fuller Theol. Sem., Pasadena, Calif., 1974—; acting dir. Hispanic Ministries, 1974-77, 82-85. Contbr. articles to religious jours. Active YMCA, Pasadena, 1975—. Mem. Soc. Bibl. Lit., Acad. Evangelism, Tyndale Fellowship, Inst. Bibl. Rsch., Hispanic Assn. for Theol. Edn. (sec.-treas. 1973—), Alberto Mottesi Evangelistic Assn. (bd. dirs.). Home: 3440 Youngfield St Wheat Ridge CO 80033-5245 Office: Fuller Theol Sem 135 N Oakland Ave Pasadena CA 91182-0001

GAYDOS, GREGORY GEORGE, political scientist, educator; b. Marblehead, Ohio, July 17, 1941; s. George Joseph Gaydos and Dorothy Margaret (Vargosick) Saunders; m. Yoko Okuda, Feb. 14, 1977. BS in Edn., Bowling Green State U., 1963, MA in History, 1965; PhD in Polit. Sci., U. Hawaii, 1977. Rsch. asst. Agy. for Internat. Devel., Honolulu, 1968-69; assoc. prof. polit. sci. Hawaii Pacific U., Honolulu, 1970—; invited participant Hawaii Com. for Humanities, Honolulu, 1979, East-West Ctr. conf. on Asian classics curriculum, Honolulu, 1995, conf. on Confucianism and human rights, Honolulu, 1996. Contbr. articles to profl. jours. Active Mayor's Com. on Pub. TV, Honolulu, 1987—. 1st lt. U.S. Army, 1965-67. Recipient award for Best French Poem of Yr., Vers Jour., 1981, Most Disting. Screenplay, Hawaii Internat. Film Festival, 1983. Mem. Lanikai Lit. League, Hawaii Sociol. Assn. (invited panelist and presenter 1979), Am. Polit. Sci. Assn., Western Polit. Sci. Assn. (invited panelist and presenter 1994). Republican. Roman Catholic. Avocations: marathon races, tennis. Office: Hawaii Pacific U 1166 Fort Street Mall Honolulu HI 96813-2708

GAZELL, JAMES ALBERT, public administration educator; b. Chgo., Mar. 17, 1942; s. Albert James and Ann Marion (Bloch) G. BA in Polit. Sci. with honors, Roosevelt U., 1963, MA in Polit. Sci., 1966; PhD in Govt., So. Ill. U., 1968. Instr. Roosevelt U., Chgo., 1965, 67, So. Ill. U., Carbondale, 1966-68; asst. prof. San Diego State U., 1968-72, assoc. prof., 1972-75, prof., 1975—; cons. County San Diego, 1973, Ernst and Ernst, Detroit, 1973, Wadsworth Pub. Co., 1995, McGraw-Hill Pub. Co., 1997. Author books; contbr. articles to profl. jours. Mem. ACLU, Am. Soc. Pub. Adminstrn., Nat. Ctr. for State Cts., Nat. Assn. Ct. Mgmt., Western Govt. Rsch. Assn. Inst. for Ct. Mgmt. Home: 4319 Hilldale Rd San Diego CA 92116-2135 Office: San Diego State U 5500 Campanile Dr San Diego CA 92182-0002

GEARRING, JOANNE, secondary school educator; b. East Chicago, Ind., Aug. 29, 1942; d. John William Gearring and Julius (stepfather) and Rosie Lee (Williams) McKinley. BA in English, San Francisco State U., 1967; MA in English, Calif. State U., Hayward, 1990; EdD in Internat. Multicultural Edn., U. San Francisco, 1994. Cert. secondary sch. tchr. Tchr. English and composition Portola & Roosevelt Jr. High Sch., El Cerrito and Richmond, Calif., 1965-69, Willard Jr. High Sch., Berkeley, Calif., 1969-70; tchr., English dept. chair Berkeley H.S., 1970-73; tchr. English composition and lit. Mills Coll., Oakland, Calif., 1968-70, 75-76; tchr. reading, composition, lit. Contra Costa C.C. Dist., San Pablo, Calif., 1973-76, 84-89; cofounder, co-dir., tchr. McKiley Ednl. Inst., Oakland, El Cerrito, 1976-85; tchr. composition and lit. San Francisco State U., 1987—, project and curriculum developer/cons. Sch. Ethnic Studies, 1992; workshop panelist and lectr. Rschr., editor, prodr. audio visual: Historical Overview of African-American Heritage, 1970 (Epoch award 1971); rschr., scriptwriter TV video: Don't Leave Out the Cowboys, 1988 (KTOP-TV award 1988, Black Filmmakers Hall of Fame award 1989). Recipient Disting. Leadership award Am. Biog. Inst., 1994. Mem. ASCD, NEA, Nat. Black Child Devel. Inst., Calif. FAculty Assn., Calif. Tchrs. Assn., Phi Delta Kappa. Democrat. Roman Catholic. Avocations: reading, theater, film. Home: 590 Boden Way Apt 2 Oakland CA 94610-3628

GEARY, DAVID LESLIE, communications executive, educator, consultant; b. Connellsville, Pa., Sept. 30, 1947; s. Harry and Edith Marie (Halterman) G. BA, Otterbein Coll., 1969; MSJ, W.Va. U., 1971; DLitt (hon.), Fairfax U., 1998; postgrad., U. Denver, 1974-75; diploma, Def. Info. Sch., 1971, exec. communications curriculum, U. Okla., 1978, Def. Dept. Sr. Pub. Affairs Officers Course, 1984, Fgn. Svc. Inst., U.S. Dept. State, 1984, Nat. Def. U., 1986; postgrad., U. Sarasota, 1992-95, U. N.Mex., 1998, U. San Jose, 1998—; D Lit. (hon.), Fairfax U., 1998. Admissions counselor Otterbein Coll., 1968-69; instr. English, staff counselor Office of Student Ednl. Svcs. W.Va. U., Morgantown, 1969-71; dir. info. Luke AFB, Ariz., 1971-72; course dir. English and comm. U.S. Air Force Acad., Colo., 1972-76; dir. pub. affairs Loring AFB, Maine, 1976-79; spl. asst. pub. affairs Seymour Johnson AFB, N.C., 1980; dir. pub. affairs USAF Engring. and Svcs., Tyndall AFB, Fla., 1980-84, UN and US Air Forces, Korea, 1984-85; asst. prof., asst. dept. chmn., mem. coun. of assoc. and asst. deans U. Ala., 1985-88; dir., nat. cmty. rels. dir., acting dir. pub. affairs USAFR, 1988-92; prin. Leadership Comm. Counsel, 1992-95; comm. program mgr., dir. pub. affairs U.S. Dept. Energy, Albuquerque, 1995—; adj. prof. pub. rels. Ga. State U., Atlanta, 1993-95; guest lectr. U. Maine, 1976-79, USAF Inst. Tech., 1981-82, Fla. State U., 1982-83, U. Md., 1984-85, U.So. Calif., 1984-85, Seoul (Korea) Nat. U., 1985, U. Ala., 1988, Ga. State U., 1991, U. Ga., 1991, U. N.Mex., 1997—; profl. advisor Pub. Rels. Student Soc. Am. Contbr. articles to profl. jours.; mem. bd. profls. Pub. Rels. Rev.: A Jour. of Rsch. and Comment, 1996—; mem. editl. bd. Jour. of Employee Comm. Mgmt., 1996—. Decorated 4 U.S. Meritorious Svc. medals, 2 Air Force Commendation medals, Air Force Achievement medal, Armed Forces Res. medal, Humanitarian Svc. medal, 2 Nat. Def. Svc. medals, Pres.'s Extradinary Svc. award Otterbein Coll., 1969, Hon. Citizen of Ariz. award, 1971, Mayor's Community Svc. medallion, Songtan, Korea, 1985, Nat. Disting. Svc. medal Arnold Air Soc., 1986, Nat. citation Angel Flight, 1986, George Washington Honor medal from Freedom's Found., 1988, Outstanding Faculty Advisor award U. Ala. Student Govt. Assn., 1988, Exemplary Svc. award Nat. Com. for Employer Support of Guard and Res., 1991, U.S. Dept. Energy Quality award, 1995, U.S. Dept. Energy Spl. Orgnl. Achievement Recognition, 1995, 96, 97, 98; Readers Digest Found. grantee, 1970. Mem. NATAS, VFW, Assn. for Edn. in Journalism and Mass Commn., Internat. Comm. Assn., Pub. Rels. Soc. Am. (profl. advisor U.N.Mex.), Internat. Assn. Bus. Communicators (bd. dirs. N.Mex. chpt. 1998—), SAR, Am. Legion, N.Mex. Pub. Affairs Roundtable (founding), Air Force Pub. Affairs Alumni Assn. Republican. Episcopalian. Office: Office Pub Affairs US Dept Energy PO Box 5400 Albuquerque NM 87185-5400

GEBB, SHELDON ALEXANDER, lawyer; b. Long Beach, Calif., Jan. 12, 1935. AB, U. Calif., Berkeley, 1957; LLB, U. Calif., 1963. Bar: Calif. 1964. Mng. ptnr. Baker & Hostetler, L.A., Long Beach and Beverly Hills, Silicon Valley, Calif. Chmn. bd. trustees Southwestern U. Sch. Law, 1985-91. Mem. ABA, State Bar Calif., Maritime Law Assn. U.S. Office: Baker & Hostetler 600 Wilshire Blvd Los Angeles CA 90017-3212

GEBBIA PINETTI, KAREN MARIE, lawyer, educator; b. Chgo., July 21, 1958; d. Stephen L. and Doris A. (Melendez) G. BA magna cum laude, Villanova U., 1980; JD cum laude, Georgetown U., 1983. Bar: Ill. 1983, Hawaii, 1995, U.S. Dist. Ct. (no. dist.) Ill. 1983, U.S. Ct. Appeals (7th cir.) 1985. With Nachman, Munitz & Sweig, Chgo., 1983-87, Winston & Strawn, Chgo., 1987-93; asst. prof. law U. Hawaii, Honolulu, 1993—. Contbr. numerous articles to profl. jours. Vol. N.W. Youth Outreach, Chgo., 1990-93, Lakeview Homeless Shelter, 1990-93, La Rabida Children's Hosp., 1991-93; mem. Chgo. Coun. on Fgn. Rels., People to People Internat.; mem. project adv. bd. World Without War Coun.-Midwest; mem. bd. dirs., 2d v.p. Hawaii Ctrs. for Ind. Living, 1995-96, first v.p., 1997, pres., 1998; mem. Hawaii Cath. Diocesan Women's Concerns Com., 1995—, co-chair, 1996-98. Mem. ABA (bus. law sect., bus. bankruptcy com., comml. fin. svcs. com.), Ill. Bar Assn., Hawaii State Bar Assn., Seventh Cir. Bar Assn., Chgo. Bar Assn., Assn. Am. Law Schs. (consumer and comml. law sect., debtors' and creditors' rights sect.). Avocations: running, swimming, travel, human services. Office: U Hawaii W S Richardson Sch Law 2515 Dole St Honolulu HI 96822-2328

GEBERT, HERMAN JOHN, Christian radio station executive; b. Mpls., Mar. 29, 1949; s. Charlie Lewis and Pearl Evelyn (Anderson) G.; m. Margaret Ann Ray, July 3, 1971; children: Angelene Michelle, Herman John Jr. BA in Psychology, U. Minn., 1971. Cert. 1st class engr. Announcer Sta. KNOF, Selby Broadcasting, St. Paul, 1974-76, Sta. WDLM, Moody Bible Inst., East Moline, Ill., 1979-80; gen. mgr. Sta. KHEP Radio Christian Communications, Phoenix, 1980—; bd. dirs. Christian Communications, Inc., Phoenix, 1984—, v.p., 1989—; v.p., bd. dirs. Grand Canyon Broadcasters, Inc., Phoenix, 1989—. Pub. rels. chmn. Galesburg (Ill.) Exch. Club, 1979; chmn. bd. dirs., moderator Branch of Hope Ch., Phoenix, 1987-89. Mem. Nat. Assn. Broadcasters, Ariz. Broadcasters Assn., Met. Phoenix Broadcasters, Nat. Religious Broadcasters, Western Religious Broadcasters. Republican. Office: Sta KHEP Radio 100 W Clarendon Ave Ste 720 Phoenix AZ 85013-3528

GEBHARD, BOB, professional baseball team executive. Gen. mgr. Colorado Rockies. Office: Colo Rockies 2001 Blake St Denver CO 80205-2008

GEBHART, FRED, journalist; b. Nampa, Idaho, Nov. 22; s. Lloyd F. and Lou E. (Evans) G.; m. Maxine Cass, 1974. BA, Univ. Calif., 1973. Tax auditor Internal Revenue Svc., 1974-78; Eng. tchr. Peace Corps, Ziguinchor, Senegal, 1978-80; freelance photo journalist San Francisco, 1981—. Co-author: Touring the Canadian Rockies, 1998, On the Road Around the Pacific Northwest, 1997, On the Road Around Florida, 1996, On the Road Around California, 1995, Signpost Guide: California, 1999, Discover Guide: California, 1999, Discover Guide: Florida, 1999, Signpost Guide: Vancouver-British Columbia, 1999. Mem. Am. Soc. Journalist & Authors, Soc. Am. Travel Writers, Internat. Soc. for Travel Medicine, Travel Journalists Guild.

GEDDES, BARBARA SHERYL, communications executive, consultant; b. Poughkeepsie, N.Y., May 27, 1944; d. Samuel Pierson and Dorothy Charlotte (Graham) Brush; m. James Morrow Geddes, Feb. 24, 1968 (div. Dec. 1980); 1 child, Elisabeth. BA, Skidmore Coll., 1968. Project leader Four-Phase Systems, Cupertino, Calif., 1976-77, Fairchild Co., San Jose, Calif., 1979-80; mgr. tech. publs. Mohawk Data Scis., Los Gatos, Calif., 1977-79, Sytek Inc., Mountain View, Calif., 1981-83; project mgr. Advanced Micro Computers, Santa Clara, Calif., 1980-81; v.p. communications systems Strategic Inc., Cupertino, 1983-86; pres., mng. ptnr. Computer and Telecommunications Profl. Services, Mountain View, Calif., 1986—; v.p. corp. mktg., sec. First Pacific Networks, Sunnyvale, Calif., 1988-94; pres., Auration, Inc., Palo Alto, 1994—; cons. H-P, Varian, Aydin Energy, Chemelex, also others, 1972—; v.p. Conf. Recorders, Santa Clara, 1975-77; advisor Tele-PC, Morgan Hill, Calif., 1983—. Editor: Mathematics/Science Library, 7 vols., 1971. Contbr. numerous articles to mags. Mem. Santa Clara County Adoptions Adv. Bd., 1971-73, Las Cumbres Archtl. Control Commn., Los Gatos, 1983; advisor Los Altos Hills Planning Commn., Calif., 1978-79. N.Y. State Regents merit scholar, 1962. Mem. Assn. for Computing Machinery (editor 1970-72), Nat. Soc. for Performance and Instrn., Bus. and Profl. Advt. Assn., Women in Communications (pres. San Jose 1983—). Democrat. Home: 10072 Senate Way Cupertino CA 95014-5710

GEER, DEREK HUNTER, electronic engineer, musician; b. Albuquerque, Dec. 17, 1957; s. Hunter Lee Geer and Mary Louise (Shambaugh) Maes; m. Jennifer Dovre Schilling, May 25, 1985. BSEE, U. N. Mex., 1985. Electronics engineer Hewlett Packard, San Diego, 1986-91, 94-98, VORAD Safety Sys., San Diego, 1992-93. Pres. Citizens Commn. on Human Rights, San Diego, 1994; tutor Literacy Campaign, San Diego, 1995. Recipient Internat. Youth Achievement award Internat. Biographical Ctr., Cambridge, England, 1985; mem. design team of first comml. radar for cars, 1993, main electronics designer first Hewlett Packard color copier, 1996. Mem. IEEE. Mem. Ch. Scientology. Office: Geer & Geer Engring Ste 100 11835 Carmel Mountain Rd # 1304201 San Diego CA 92128-4609

GEFFEN, DAVID, recording company executive, producer; b. Bklyn., Feb. 21, 1943; s. Abraham and Batya (Volovskaya) Geffen. U of Texas, Austin, Brooklyn Coll. of CUNY. Agt. with William Morris, N.Y.C., 1964-68; agt. with Ashley Famous, 1968; exec. V.P. and agent Creative Management Associates, 1969; founder (with Laura Nyro) and pres. Tuna Fish publishing co.; pres. Asylum Records, 1970-73, Geffen-Roberts, Inc., 1970-71, Elektra-Asylum Records, 1973-76; founder and pres. Geffen Records, L.A., 1980—; vice-pres. Warner Bros. Pictures, 1975; chmn. Geffen Records, L.A.; head Geffen Film Co.; vice-chmn. Warner Brothers Pictures, 1974; exec. asst. to chmn. Warner Communications, 1977; co-founder Dreamworks SKG, Universal City, 1995—; mem. music faculty Yale U., 1978; apptd. Regent U. Calif., Gov. Calif., 1980-87. Producer films including After Hours, Lost in America, Personal Best, 1982, Risky Business, 1983, Little Shop of Horrors, 1986, Social Security, 1986, Beetlejuice, 1988, Men Don't Leave, 1990, Interview with the Vampire, 1994; co-producer Master Harold...and the Boys, 1982, Cats, 1982, Good, 1982, Dreamgirls, 1983, Madam Butterfly, 1988 (9 Tony award, Best Play); musical Miss Saigon. Bd. dirs. Los Angeles County Art Mus. Avocations: collector modern art. Office: Dreamworks SKG 100 Universal City Plz Bldg 477 Universal City CA 91608-1002*

GEGELIYA, DMITRIY ILICH, chemist, researcher; b. Tbilisi, Republic of Georgia, May 24, 1933; came to U.S., 1993; s. Ilia Gegeliya and Ketevan Dahulabishvili; m. Natalia Kopelvich, Dec. 15, 1961 (div. Feb. 1987); 1 child, Ketevan. Engr., Tech. U., Tbilisi, 1958; PhD, Postgrad. Cours, Moscow, 1974. Engr. Road Project Inst., Tbilisi, 1958-61; sr. engr. Phys. Chem. Inst., Moscow, 1961-63; sr. rschr. Road Rsch. Inst., Moscow, 1963-80, lab. chief, 1980-83; dep. dir. Road Rsch. Inst., Tbilisi, 1983-93; prof. Peninsula Inst., Mountain View, Calif., 1995. Author: Asphalt Concrete Pavement for Roads, Bridges and Airports, 1978 (Gold medal 1981), Directions for Optimal Regime of Asphalt Concrete Production, Storage and Transportation, 1989. Mem. Ho. of Scientists (pres. 1996), Internat. Acad. Scis., Edn. Industry & Arts (pres. 1997). Roman Catholic. Avocations: wood decoration, inlay. Home: 1120 Hyde St Apt 102 San Francisco CA 94109-3990

GEHB, MICHAEL, public relations executive. CFO Copithorne & Bellows, San Francisco. Office: Copithorne & Bellows 100 1st St Ste 2600 San Francisco CA 94105-2637*

GEHLMANN, SHEILA CATHLEEN, psychologist, research analyst; b. Lorain, Ohio, Mar. 25, 1958; d. Donald Eugene and Barbara Ann Gehlmann. BSBA and Psychology, Aquinas Coll., 1986; MS in Applied Indsl./Orgnl. Psychology, Stevens Inst. Tech., 1991. Grad. intern selection and testing divsn. AT&T, Morristown, N.J., 1989-90; projects mgr. Stevens Inst. Tech., Hoboken, N.J., 1988-90; test and measurement specialist Dept. Pers. City of New York, 1990-91; rsch. analyst APA, Washington, 1991-97; rsch. cons. Denver, 1997—; pvt. practice Highlands Ranch, Colo., 1998—. Author: (with others) Stress and Well Being at Work: Assessments and Interventions for Occupational Mental Health, 1992; assoc. editor Jour. Psychol. Practice, 1995—. Vol. Sta. WCTC Cable Channel 9, Wyoming, Mich., 1980-85; participant K-9 walk, Muscular Dystrophy Assn., Fairfax, Va., 1993-94. Named one of Outstanding Women of Am., 1988. Mem. APA (assoc.), NAFE, Soc. Indsl. Orgnl. Psychology, N.Am. Assn. Masters in Psychology, Am. Psychol. Soc., Mid-Atlantic Camaro Club. Avocations: photography, camping, cross-country skiing, needlepoint, tennis. Home and Office: 600 W County Line Rd Bldg 14 Highlands Ranch CO 80126-6512

GEHRES, JAMES, lawyer; b. Akron, Ohio, July 19, 1932; s. Edwin Jacob and Cleora Mary (Yoakam) G.; m. Eleanor Agnew Mount, July 23, 1960. B.S. in Acctg., U. Utah, 1954; M.B.A., U. Calif.-Berkeley, 1959; J.D., U. Denver, 1970, LL.M. in Taxation, 1977. Bar: Colo. 1970, U.S. Dist. Ct. Colo. 1970, U.S. Tax Ct. 1970, U.S. Supreme Ct. 1973, U.S. Ct. Appeals (10th cir.) 1978, U.S. Ct. Claims 1992. Atty. IRS, Denver, 1965-80, atty. chief counsel's office, 1980—. Served with USAF, 1955-58, capt. Res. ret. Mem. ABA, Colo. Bar Assn., Am. Inst. C.P.A.s, Colo. Soc. C.P.A.s, Am. Assn. Atty.-C.P.A.s, Am. Judicature Soc., Am. Acctg. Assn., Order St. Ives, The Explorers Club, Am. Alpine Club, Colo. Mountain Club (bd. dirs.), Colo. Mountain Club Found. (bd. dirs.), Beta Gamma Sigma, Beta Alpha Psi. Democrat. Contbr. articles to profl. jours. Office: 935 Pennsylvania St Denver CO 80203-3145

GEHRING, GEORGE JOSEPH, JR., dentist; b. Kenosha, Wis., May 24, 1931; s. George J. and Lucille (Martin) G.; m. Ann D. Carrigan, Aug. 2, 1982; children: Michael, Scott. DDS, Marquette U., 1955. Pvt. practice dentistry, Long Beach, Calif., 1958—. Author: The Happy Flosser. Chmn. bd. Long Beach affiliate Calif. Heart Assn.; mem. Long Beach Grand Prix com. of 300; ind. candidate for pres. of the U.S., 1988, 92. Served with USNR, 1955-58. Fellow Internat. Coll. of Denists, Am. Coll. Dentists; mem. Harbor Dental Soc. (dir.), Pierre Fauchard Acad., Delta Sigma Delta. Club: Rotary. Home: 1230 E Ocean Blvd Unit 603 Long Beach CA 90802-6908 Office: 532 E 29th St Long Beach CA 90806-1617

GEHRY, FRANK OWEN, architect; b. Toronto, Ont., Can., Feb. 28, 1929; came to U.S., 1947; s. Irving and Thelma (Caplan) G.; children: Leslie, Brina; m. Berta Aguilera, Sept. 11, 1975; children: Alejandro, Samuel. B. in Architecture, U. So. Calif., 1954; postgrad., Harvard U., 1956-57. Registered profl. architect, Calif. Designer Victor Gruen Assocs., L.A., 1953-54, planning, design and project dir., 1958-61; project designer, planner Pereira & Luckman, L.A., 1957-58; prin. Frank O. Gehry & Assocs., Santa Monica, Calif., 1962—. Architect Loyola Law Sch., L.A., 1978-92, Temporary Contemporary Mus., L.A., 1983, Calif. Aerospace Mus., L.A., 1984, Frances Goldwyn Regional Br. Libr., Hollywood, Calif., 1986, U.C.I. Info. and Computer Sci./Engring. Rsch. Lab. and Engring. Ctr., Irvine, Calif., 1986-88, Vitra Internat. Mfg. Facility and Design Mus., Weil am Rhein, Germany, 1989, Chiat/Day Hdqs., Venice, Calif., 1991, Am. Ctr., Paris, 1994, Advanced Tech. Labs. Bldg., Iowa City, 1992, U. Toledo Ctr. for Visual Arts, 1992, Walt Disney Concert Hall, L.A., Frederick R. Weisman Art Mus., Mpls., 1993, Vitra Internat. Hdqs., Basel, Switzerland, 1994, Disney Ice, Anaheim, Calif., 1995, EMR Communication and Tech. Ctr., Bad Oeynhausen, Germany, 1995, Team Disneyland Adminstrn. Bldg., Anaheim, 1996, Nationale-Nederlanden Bldg., Prague, Czech Republic, 1996, Guggenheim Mus., Bilbao, Spain, 1997. Trustee Hereditary Disease Found., Santa Monica, Calif., 1970—. Recipient Arnold W. Brunner Meml. prize in architecture, 1983, Eliot Noyes Design chair Harvard U., 1983, Charlotte Davenport Professorship in architecture Yale U., 1982, 85, 87-89, Pritzker Architecture prize, 1989, Wolf prize in art, 1992, Praemium Imperiale, 1992, Dorothy and Lilian Gish award, 1994. Office: Frank O Gehry & Assocs 1520B Cloverfield Blvd Santa Monica CA 90404-3502*

GEIBEL, JOHN JOSEPH, biologist; b. Tacoma, Feb. 12, 1944; s. Gustav Emanuel and Mary Jane (O'Hagan) G.; m. Barbara Eileen Nichols, July 29, 1972; children: Bridget Stacy, Christine Marie. BS in Zoology, U. Calif., Davis, 1965; MS in Stats., Stanford U., 1983. Fish and game asst. Dept. Fish and Game, State of Calif., Rancho Cordova, 1965; aquatic biologist Dept. Fish and Game, State of Calif., Terminal Island, 1966-69; asst. marine biologist Dept. Fish and Game, State of Calif., Monterey, 1969-72; assoc. marine biologist Dept. Fish and Game, State of Calif., Menlo Park, 1972-89, statis. methods analyst, 1989—; mem. sci. and statis. com. Pacific Fisheries Mgmt. Coun., Portland, Oreg., 1986-98; v.p. Cambria Corp., Palo Alto, Calif., 1984—. Contbr. articles to Fish and Game Bull. (Wildlife Soc. award 1973). Mem. bd. edn. Nativity Parish, Menlo Park, 1990-93; mem. parent and tchrs. group Nativity Grammar Sch., Menlo Park, 1993-94. With USAF, 1965-66. Mem. Am. Geophys. Union, Am. Fisheries Soc., Am. Inst. Fishery Rsch. Biologists. Avocations: fishing, hunting, golf, photography, hiking/backpacking. Home: 425 Central Ave Menlo Park CA 94025-2804 Office: Calif Dept Fish and Game 411 Burgess Dr Menlo Park CA 94025-3408

GEIS, EDWARD MICHAEL, photographer, film producer; b. Portland, Oreg., Mar. 9, 1944; s. Leo Francis and Clarabelle (Nelson) G.; m. Lynn Geis, June 15, 1966; children: Aaron, Jordan, Gretchen. BA in Art History, U. Oreg., 1966, MFA in Graphics, 1968. Photographer, graphic artist Oreg. Pub. Broadcasting, Portland, 1969-76; photographer Tektronix, Inc., Beaverton, Oreg., 1977-79; owner, photographer Cloudy Bright Prodns., Portland, 1980-81; prodn. mgr. Will Vinton Prodns., Portland, 1981-82; coord. arts channel Rogers Cable TV, Portland, 1982-85; dir. pub. rels. Pacific U., Forest Grove, Oreg., 1985-89; photographer, dir. Ibex Comm., Portland, 1990-97; prodr., dir. Edges Comm., Portland, 1997; tchr. animation N.W. Film Ctr., Portland, 1972, 80, tchr. video prodn. 1985; tchr. film prodn. Portland State U., 1980. Cinematographer documentary History of Blacks in Oregon, 1976; creator, writer animation Yo-Yo, 1980; prodr., dir. exptl. art series Video Verite: The Art of Television, 1984 (Ace award Nat. Fedn. Local Cable Programmers 1984); prodr. writer (video) Pioneer Courthouse Square, 1990. Active Portland Art Mus., 1991-97. Recipient Picture Am. award Agfa-Gevert, N.Y., 1986, Grand award C.A.S.E., 1987, Vancouver, B.C., Can., Silver award, 1987. Mem. Japanese Garden Soc.

GEISELHARDT-HEAD, BARBARA THERESA, nursing administrator; b. Denver, Sept. 6, 1961; d. Alfred and Helene Marie (Birkofer) Geiselhardt; m. Mark Dean Head, Aug. 29, 1992. BSN, Creighton U., 1984; MSN, U. Colo., Denver, 1992. Cert. ABLS, BLS. Charge nurse med. oncology Univ. Hosp., Denver, 1985-87, staff nurse med. ICU, 1987-88, sr. staff nurse med. ICU, 1988-89, nurse mgr. med. ICU, 1989-90, nurse mgr. bone marrow transplant unit, 1990—, bone morrow transpalnt program, 1990—, dir. oncology svcs., 1996—; clin. faculty U. Colo. Sch. Nursing, Denver, 1992 ; clin. teaching assoc. Univ. Hosp., 1985-87. Mem. AACCN, Oncology Nursing Soc., Spl. Interest Group-Bone Marrow Transplantation, Spl. Interest Group-Mgmt. Adminstrn., S.W. Oncology Group (nurse oncologist com. 1991—), Sigma Theta Tau. Roman Catholic. Avocations: skiing, running. Office: Univ Hosp 4 West BMTU 4200 E 9th Ave Denver CO 80220-3706

GEISERT, OTTO, food products executive; b. 1928. Various positions Balcom & Moe Inc., Pasco, Wash., 1958—, now pres. *

GEISINGER, WILLIAM LOUIS, art educator; b. Cheyenne, Wyo., Mar. 29, 1951; m. William Louis Geisinger and Maydene Virginia Matts. BA, San Jose (Calif.) State U., 1974, MA, 1975. Instr. DeAnza Coll., Cupertino, Calif., 1975—. With USAF, 1969. Mem. Assn. Clay and Glass Artists Calif. (v.p. 1997-98, pres. 1999—), Nat. Coun. on Edn. for Ceramic Arts. Office: DeAnza Coll 21250 Stevens Creek Blvd Cupertino CA 95014-5702

GEISLER, SHERRY LYNN, magistrate; b. Durango, Colo., Aug. 18, 1956; d. George Walter and Evelyn Ruth (MacLean) Geisler; m. Harvey Lee Slade, June 6, 1981 (div. Aug. 11, 1993); 1 child, Sherry (Rachel) Orona. Grad. H.S., Springerville, Ariz., 1974; student, Northland Pioneer Coll., Springerville, Ariz., 1986-90, Res. Police Acad., 1986. Clk. Round Valley Justice Ct., Springerville, 1981-84; chief clk. Round Valley Justice Ct., 1984-88, office mgr., judge pro tem, 1988-93, justice of the peace, 1993—; city magistrate City of Springerville and Eagar, Ariz., 1993—; mentor judge Ariz. Supreme Ct., 1994—; edn. chair Ariz. Justice Ct. Assn, 1994-96. Mem. Nat. Judges Assn., Am. Judges Assn., Ariz. Cts. Assn., State of Ariz. Justice of the Peace Assn. (pres.). Ariz. Magistrates Assn. Democrat. Avocations: crafts, gardening, travel, scuba diving. Home: PO Box 1202 Springerville AZ 85938-1202 Office: Round Valley Justice Ct PO Box 1356 Springerville AZ 85938-1356

GEIST, KARIN RUTH TAMMEUS MCPHAIL, secondary education educator, realtor, musician; b. Urbana, Ill., Nov. 23, 1938; d. Wilber Harold and Bertha Amanda Sofia (Helander) Tammeus; m. David Pendleton McPhail, Sept. 7, 1958 (div. 1972); children: Julia Elizabeth, Mark Andrew; m. John Charles Geist, June 4, 1989 (div. 1995). BS, Juilliard Sch. Music, 1962; postgrad., Stanford U., 1983-84, L'Academia, Florence and Pistoia, Italy, 1984-85, Calif. State U., 1986-87, U. Calif., Berkeley, 1991, 92. Cert. tchr., Calif.; lic. real estate agt., Calif. Tchr. Woodstock Sch., Musoorie, India, 1957, Canadian, Tex., 1962-66; tchr. Head Royce Sch., Oakland, Calif., 1975-79, 87—, Sleepy Hollow Sch., Orinda, Calif., 1985—; realtor Freeholders, Berkeley, Calif., 1971-85, Northbrae, Berkeley, Calif., 1985-92, Templeton Co., Berkeley, 1992—; organist Kellogg Meml., Musoorie, 1956-57, Mills Coll. Chapel, Oakland, 1972—; cashier Trinity U., San Antonio, 1957-58; cen. records sec. Riverside Ch., N.Y.C., 1958-60; sec. Dr. Rollo May, N.Y.C., 1959-62, United Presbyn. Nat. Missions, N.Y.C., 1960, United Presbyn. Ecumenical Mission, N.Y.C., 1961, Nat. Coun. Chs., N.Y.C., 1962; choral dir. First Presbyn. Ch., Canadian, Tex., 1962-66; assoc. in music Montclair Presbyn. Ch., Oakland, 1972-88; site coord., artist, collaborator Calif. Arts Coun. Artist; cons. music edn. videos and CD Roms Clearvue EAV, Chgo., 1993—. Artist: produced and performed major choral and orchestral works, 1972-88; prodr. Paradiso, Kronos Quartet, 1985, Magdalena, 1991, 92, Children's Quest, 1993—. Grantee Orinda Union Sch. Dist., 1988. Mem. Berkeley Bd. Realtors, East Bay Regional Multiple

Listing Svc., Calif. Tchrs. Assn., Commonwealth Club (San Francisco). Democrat. Home: 7360 Claremont Ave Berkeley CA 94705-1429 Office: Templeton Co 3070 Claremont Ave Berkeley CA 94705-2630

GELBER, DON JEFFREY, lawyer; b. L.A., Mar. 10, 1940; s. Oscar and Betty Sheila (Chernitsky) G.; m. Jessica Jeasun Song, May 15, 1967; children: Victoria, Jonathan, Rebecca, Robert. Student UCLA, 1957-58, Reed Coll., 1958-59; AB, Stanford U., 1961, JD, 1963. Bar: Calif. 1964, Hawaii 1964, U.S. Dist. Ct. (cen. and no. dists. Calif.) 1964, U.S. Dist. Ct. Hawaii 1964, U.S. Ct. Appeals (9th cir.) 1964, U.S. Supreme Ct. 1991. Assoc. Greenstein, Yamane & Cowan, Honolulu, 1964-67; reporter Penal Law Revision Project, Hawaii Jud. Council, Honolulu, 1967-69; assoc. H. William Burgess, Honolulu, 1969-72; ptnr. Burgess & Gelber, Honolulu, 1972-73; prin. Law Offices of Don Jeffrey Gelber, Honolulu, 1974-77; pres. Gelber & Wagner, Honolulu, 1978-83, Gelber & Gelber, Honolulu, 1984-89, Gelber, Gelber, Ingersoll, Klevansky & Faris, Honolulu, 1990—; legal counsel Hawaii State Senate Judiciary Com., 1965; adminstrv. asst. to majority floor leader Hawaii State Senate, 1966, legal csl. Edn. Com., 1967, 68; majority counsel Hawaii Ho. of Reps., 1974; spl. counsel Hawaii State Senate, 1983. Contbr. articles to legal publs. Mem. State Bar Calif., ABA (sect. bus. law), Am. Bankruptcy Inst., Hawaii State Bar Assn. (sect. bankruptcy law, bd. dirs. 1991-93, pres. 1993). Clubs: Pacific, Plaza (Honolulu). Office: Gelber Gelber Ingersoll Klevansky & Faris 745 Fort Street Mall Ste 1400 Honolulu HI 96813-3877

GELFER, JEFFREY IAN, early childhood education educator; b. Bklyn., June 18, 1952; s. George Ralph and Ruth (Seltzer) G.; m. Peggy Gardner Perkins, Dec. 7, 1980; children: Sacha, Daniel. BA, Wilmington Coll., 1974; MS, U. Oreg., 1975; PhD, Fla. State U., 1981. Reading and learning disability specialist Columbia County Schs., Westport, Oreg., 1975-77; kindergarten tchr. Creative Presch., Tallahassee, 1978-79; asst. prof. SUNY, Fredonia, 1985-87; dir. Easter Seal Soc. of S.W. Fla., Sarasota, 1987-89; assoc. prof. Univ. Nev., Las Vegas, 1989—; vis. asst. prof. U. S. Fla., Tampa, 1981-85; cons. Clark County Sch. Dist., Las Vegas, 1991, Sarasota County Sch. Dist., 1984-85, Fla. State U., Tallahassee, 1979; presenter/participant workshops in field. Contbr. articles to profl. jours. Grantee Health Rehab. Svcs. of State of Fla., 1987, 88, Sarasota County Sch. Dist., 1988, Frank Stanley Beveridge Foun., 1989, Univ. Nev. Las Vegas, 1991. Mem. Assn. Childhood Edn. Internat. (mem. rev. com. 1991—), Nat. Assn. Edn. Young Children, ASCD, Coun. Exceptional Children, Nat. Coalition Campus Child Care, Am. Evaluation Assn., Phi Delta Kappa. Avocations: mountain climbing, piano, film making, jogging, golf. Home: 401 Donner Pass Dr Henderson NV 89014-3401 Office: Univ Nev Las Vegas 4505 S Maryland Pky Las Vegas NV 89154-9900

GELLMAN, GLORIA GAE SEEBURGER SCHICK, marketing professional; b. La Grange, Ill., Oct. 5, 1947; d. Robert Fred and Gloria Virginia (McQuiston) Seeburger; m. Peter Slate Schick, Sept. 25, 1978 (dec. 1980); 2 children; m. Irwin Frederick, Gellman, Sept. 9, 1989; 3 children. BA magna cum laude, Purdue U., 1969; student, Lee Strasberg Actors Studio; postgrad., UCLA, U. Calif.-Irvine. Mem. mktg. staff Seemac, Inc. (formerly R.F. Seeburger Co.); v.p. V.I.P. Properties, Inc., Newport Beach, Calif.; pres. Glamglo Prodns.; host radio show Orange County Art Bytes, Sneak Previews from the Orange County Performing Arts Ctr. Profl. actress, singer, artist, writer; television and radio talk show hostess, Indpls., late 1960s; performer radio and television commls., 1960s—. Mem. Orange County Philharm. Soc., bd. dirs. women's com.; mem. Orange County Master Chorale, Orange County Performing Arts Ctr., v.p., treas. Crescendo chpt. OCPAC Ctr. Stars, 1st v.p. membership; bd. dirs. Newport Harbor (Calif.) Art Mus., v.p. membership, mem. acquisition coun.; bd. dirs., mem. founders soc. Opera Pacific, mem. exec. com. bd. dirs.; patron Big Bros./Big Sisters Starlight Found.; mem. Visionaries Newport Harbor Mus., Designing Women of Art Inst. Soc. Calif.; pres. Opera Pacific Guild Alliance; immediate past pres. Spyglass Hill Philharm. Com.; v.p. Pacific Symphony Orch. League, chair endowment sect., spl. events chair; bd. dirs. Pacific Symphony Orch.; mem. Calif. State Libr. Found. Bd., U. Calif. Irvine Found. Bd., mem. devel. com., honors com., pub. affairs and advocacy com.; mem. social scis. dean's adv. coun. U. Calif., Irvine; chmn. adv. coun. Cold War Studies Ctr., Chapman U.; chmn. numerous small and large fundraisers; mem. com. Red Cross; bd. dirs. Pacific Symphony Orch.; mem. Fashionables of Chapman U. Recipient Lauds and Laurels award U. Calif., Irvine, 1994, Gellman Courtyard Sculpture honoring contbn. to Sch. of Humanities, U. Calif., Irvine. Mem. AAUW, AFTRA, SAG, Internat. Platform Assn., Actors Equity, U. Calif.-Irvine Chancellor's Club, U. Calif.-Irvine Humanities Assocs. (founder, pres., bd. dirs.), Mensa, Orange County Mental Health Assn., Balboa Bay Club, U. Club, Club 39, Islanders, Covergirls, Pacific Symphony Supper Club (founder), Alpha Lambda Delta, Delta Rho Kappa. Republican. Home: PO Box 1993 Newport Beach CA 92659-0993

GELL-MANN, MURRAY, theoretical physicist, educator; b. N.Y.C., Sept. 15, 1929; s. Arthur and Pauline (Reichstein) Gell-M.; m. J. Margaret Dow, Apr. 19, 1955 (dec. 1981); children: Elizabeth, Nicholas; m. Marcia Southwick, June 20, 1992; 1 stepson, Nicholas Levis. BS, Yale U., 1948; PhD, Mass. Inst. Tech., 1951; ScD (hon.), Yale U., 1959, U. Chgo., 1967, U. Ill., 1968, Wesleyan U., 1968, U. Turin, Italy, 1969, U. Utah, 1970, Columbia U., 1977, Cambridge U., 1980; D (hon.), Oxford (Eng.) U., 1992. Mem. Inst. for Advanced Study, 1951, 55, 67-68; instr. U. Chgo., 1952-53, asst. prof., 1953-54, assoc. prof., 1954; assoc. prof. Calif. Inst. Tech., Pasadena, 1955-56; prof. Calif. Inst. Tech., 1956-93, now R.A. Millikan prof. physics; vis. prof. MIT, spring 1963, CERN, Geneva, 1971-72, 79-80; dir. physics Santa Fe Inst., 1993—; Mem. Pres.'s Sci. Adv. Com., 1969-72, Pres.'s Adv. Com. on Sci. and Tech., 1994—; mem. sci. and grants com., Leakey Found., 1977—; chmn. bd. trustees Aspen Ctr. for Physics, 1973-79; founding trustee Santa Fe Inst., 1982, chmn. bd. trustees, 1982-85, co-chmn. sci. bd. 1985—. Author: (with Y. Ne'eman) Eightfold Way. Citizen regent Smithsonian Instn., 1974-88; bd. dirs. J.D. and C.T. MacArthur Found., 1979—. NSF post doctoral fellow, vis. prof. Coll. de France and U. Paris, 1959-60; recipient Dannie Heineman prize Am. Phys. Soc., 1959; E.O. Lawrence Meml. award AEC, 1966; Overseas fellow Churchill Coll., Cambridge, Eng., 1966; Franklin medal, 1967; Carty medal Nat. Acad. Scis., 1968; Research Corp. award, 1969; named to UN Environ. Program Roll of Honor for Environ. Achievement, 1988; Nobel prize in physics, 1969. Fellow Am. Phys. Soc.; mem. NAS, Royal Soc. (fgn.), Am. Acad. Arts and Scis. (v.p., chmn. Western ctr. 1970-76), Council on Fgn. Relations, French Phys. Soc. (hon.). Clubs: Cosmos (Washington); Century Assn., Explorers (N.Y.C.); Athenaeum (Pasadena). Address: Santa Fe Institute 1399 Hyde Park Rd Santa Fe NM 87501-8943

GELNAK, LEONARD, electronics executive; b. Leningrad, USSR, Apr. 2, 1969; came to U.S., 1979; s. Alexander and Galina (Murmisky) G. BS in Computer Engring., UCLA, 1991. Automobile electronics installer Mobile Sound & Security, North Hollywood, Calif., 1986-87, owner, mgr., 1987-92; pres. U.S.A. Electronics, Inc., Sherman Oaks, Calif., 1992—; computer cons. GALE Industries, North Hollywood, 1991-95; tech. adv. bd. 12 Volts Mag., Moscow, 1995—; tech. cons. designer alarm divsn. L.V. Tech., North Hollywood, 1996—. Republican. Jewish. Avocations: martial arts, computers, automobile racing, motorcycles. Office: USA Electronics, Inc 4517 Mammoth Ave Sherman Oaks CA 91423-2916

GELPI, MICHAEL ANTHONY, entrepreneur; b. Columbus, Ohio, Dec. 28, 1940; s. Andre and Eleanor (Amorose) G. AB, Georgetown U., 1962. Store mgr. Swan Cleaners, Columbus, 1964-65, dist. supr., 1965-68, v.p., 1968-76, exec. v.p., treas., 1976-81, also dir.; v.p. Rainbow Properties, Columbus, 1971-83, pres., 1983-85, chmn. bd., dir. The Neoprobe Corp., Columbus, 1985-89; pres., dir., CEO M.D. Personal Products, Hayward, Calif., 1992-95; bd. dirs. Health Options; owner The Treasure House, San Francisco. Trustee Am. Cancer Soc., 1978-92 , crusade chmn., 1979-84, 1st v.p., 1981-84, pres., 1984-85, chmn., 1985-87, trustee Ohio div., 1984-86, state spl. gifts chmn., 1984-86. Mem. City of Columbus AIDS Adv. Coalition, 1987-92, chmn., 1988-92; trustee Players Theatre of Columbus, 1981-88, v.p., 1985-86, pres. 1986-87; trustee German Village Hist. Soc., 1980-81; trustee Cen. Ohio Radio Reading Svc., 1982-88, pres., 1983-85, trustee Town-Franklin Hist. Neighborhood Assn., 1979-85, v.p., 1983-85; chmn. advance gifts Bishops Ann. Appeal, 1981-86; bd. dirs. Human Rights Campaign Fund, 1985-88; trustee Geriatric Svc. Orgn., 1988-92, devel. chair, 1988-92; candidate for Ohio 12th dist. U.S. Congress, 1988, 90. 1st lt. U.S. Army, 1962-64. Roman Catholic. Recipient Vol. of Yr. award Am. Cancer Soc., 1981, Community Svc. award Columbus Dispatch, 1984, Mayor's award for Vol. Svc. to City of Columbus, 1982, 84.

GELT, THEODORE ZVI, lawyer, director; b. Denver, Jan. 29, 1950; s. Louis Eleazar and Betty Goldie (Hellerstein) G.; (div. Apr. 1987); children: Timothy, Sarah; m. Sharon Gelt, July 30, 1993. BA, U. Colo., 1972; JD, U. Denver, 1975; LLM, NYU, 1976. Assoc. Atler, Zall & Haligman, P.C., Denver, 1975-77, Head, Moye, Carver & Ray, Denver, 1977; mem., dir. Silver and Gelt, Denver, 1977-81, Theodore Z. Gelt, P.C., Denver, 1981-82, Roath & Brega, Denver, 1982-88, Gelt, Fleishman & Sterling, Denver, 1989—; adj. prof. grad. tax program U. Denver, asst. prof., 1978. Mem. ABA (partnership com. of tax sect.), Colo. Bar Assn. (exec. coun. of tax sect., sec., treas. 1980-81, vice chmn. 1981-82, chmn. 1982-83, unauthorized practice of law com.), Denver Bar Assn., Denver Tax Assn. Office: 1600 Broadway Ste 2600 Denver CO 80202

GENEGO, WILLIAM JOSEPH, lawyer; b. Albany, Mar. 27, 1950; s. William Joseph and Olga Alice (Sultan) G. BS in Bus. and Pub. Adminstrn. magna cum laude, NYU, 1972; JD, Yale U., 1975; LLM, Georgetown U., 1977. Bar: D.C. 1975, Calif. 1982, U.S. Supreme Ct. 1984, other dist. and appellate cts. Spl. asst. state's atty. Cir. and Dist. Cts. Montgomery County, Md., 1975-77; staff atty. legal intern program Georgetown U. Law Ctr., Washington, 1975-77, adj. prof., dep. dir. legal intern program, 1977-79; cons., vis. supervising atty. Yale Legal Svcs. Orgn., Law Sch. Yale U., New Haven, 1977; with Baker & Fine, Cambridge, Mass., 1980-81; asst. clin. prof. Law Ctr. U. So. Calif., L.A., 1981-83, assoc. clin. prof., 1983-86, clin. prof., 1986-89, adj. prof., 1990-92; vis. prof. law Boston U., 1990, UCLA, 1991-92; pvt. practice Law Offices of William J. Genego, Santa Monica, Calif., 1990—; mem. practitioners' adv. group U.S. Sentencing Commn., 1989—; presenter in field. Mem. adv. bd. Criminal Practice Manual, Bur. Nat. Affairs, 1987—; editor Yale Law Jour., 1974-75; contbr. articles to legal publs. Bd. dirs. Nat. Network for Right to Counsel, 1986-88. Recipient Ann. Humanitarian award inmate rep. com. Fed. Correctional Instn., Danbury, Conn., 1974. Mem. NACDL (chairperson com. on rules of practice and procedure 1991—, Pres.'s award 1988), ABA (mem. ad hoc com. on U.S. Sentencing Commn. 1986—, chairperson competency com. sect. criminal justice 1983-85), Nat. Legal Aid and Defender Assn. (chairperson def. counsel competency com. 1984-87), Calif. Pub. Defenders Assn., Calif. Attys. for Criminal Justice. Office: Law Offices of William J. Genego 100 Wilshire Blvd Ste 1000 Santa Monica CA 90401-1113

GENÊT, BARBARA ANN, accountant, travel counselor; b. N.Y.C., Oct. 14, 1935; d. Arthur Samuel and Louise Margaret (Scheider) G. Profl. cert. in acctg., U. Calif., La Jolla, 1995, student, 1996—. Asst. to chmn. bd., asst. v.p. pub. rels. Brink's Inc., Chgo., 1976-78; co-owner, pres. Ask Mr. Foster, Chgo., 1982-90; with Profl. Cmty. Mgmt., Laguna Hills, Calif., 1990-92; travel counselor E.J. Brown & Assocs., San Diego, 1992-94; tchr.'s asst. U. Calif-San Diego, La Jolla, 1996—; rep. Becker CPA-CMA Rev., San Diego, 1995—. Becker scholar, 1995, scholr Marks CPA Rev., 1996. Mem. Am. Soc. Woman Accts., Inst. Mgmt. Accts., Inst. Cert. Travel Agts., Rancho Santa Fe Bus. and Profl. Women's Club, Order Ea. Star, Ladies of Shrine N.Am., Zonta Internat. of La Jolla (treas. 1998—), Internat. Platform Assn. Office: U Calif Dept Bus and Mgmt 9500 Gilman Dr La Jolla CA 92093-5003

GENGLER, SUE WONG, health educator, consultant, speaker, trainer; b. Hong Kong, Apr. 6, 1959; came to U.S., 1966; d. Tin Ho and Yuet Kum (Chan) Wong; m. Clayton J. Gengler, 1995. BS, UCLA, 1981; MPH, Loma Linda (Calif.) U., 1990; DrPH, Loma Linda U., 1995. Cert. health edn. specialist. Asst. to the dir. Project Asia Campus Crusade for Christ, San Bernardino, Calif., 1982-83, Campus Crusade for Christ-Internat. Pers., San Bernardino, 1983-90; health educator San Bernardino County Pub. Health, 1990-92; community lab. instr., rsch. asst. dept. health promotion and edn. Loma Linda (Calif.) U. Sch. Pub. Health, 1992-95; behaviorist/educator Anaheim Hills Med. Group/St. Jude Heritage Med. Group, Anaheim, Calif., 1995-96; direct svcs. dir. Alternatives to Domestic Violence, Riverside, Calif., 1997—. Mem. Minority Health Coalition, San Bernardino, 1990-92, Com. for the Culturally Diverse, San Bernardino, 1990-92; vol. Am. Cancer Soc.; chair Gt. Am. Smokeout, Inland Empire, 1991; bd. dirs. Family Svcs. Agy., San Bernardino, 1994-96. Selma Andrews scholar Loma Linda U., 1994; named Outstanding Young Woman of Yr., 1983, Hulda Crooke Scholar, Loma Linda U., 1989; recipient Am. Cancer Soc. Rose award, 1991 (Calif.), Gaspar award, 1991 (nat.). Mem. APHA, Nat. Coun. for Internat. Health, Soc. Pub. Health Edn. Avocations: travel, reading, volleyball, calligraphy, music.

GENGOR, VIRGINIA ANDERSON, financial planning executive, educator; b. Lyons, N.Y., May 2, 1927; d. Axel Jennings and Marie Margaret (Mack) Anderson; m. Peter Gengor, Mar. 2, 1952 (dec.); children: Peter Randall, Daniel Neal, Susan Leigh. AB, Wheaton Coll., 1949; MA, U. No. Colo., Greeley, 1975, 77. Chief hosp. intake service County of San Diego, 1966-77, chief Kearny Mesa Dist. Office, 1977-79, chief Dependent Children of Ct., 1979-81, chief child protection services, 1981-82; registered rep. Am. Pacific Securities, San Diego, 1982-85; registered tax preparer State of Calif., 1982—, registered rep. (prin.) Sentra Securities, 1985—; assoc. Pollock & Assocs., San Diego, 1985-86; pres. Gengor Fin. Advisors, 1986—; cons. instr. Nat. Ctr. for Fin. Edn., San Diego, 1986-88; instr. San Diego Community Coll., 1985-88. Mem. allocations panel United Way, San Diego, 1976-79, children's circle Child Abuse Prevention Found., 1989—; chmn. com. Child Abuse Coordinating Council, San Diego, 1979-83; pres. Friends of Casa de la Esperanza, San Diego, 1980-85, bd. dirs., 1980—; 1st v.p. The Big Sister League, San Diego, 1985-86, pres., 1987-89. Mem. NAFE, Inst. Cert. Fin. Planners, Internat. Assn. Fin. Planning, Inland Soc. Tax Cons., AAUW (bd. dirs.), Nat. Assn. Securities Dealers (registered prin.), Nat. Ctr. Fin. Edn., Am. Bus. Women's Assn., Navy League, Freedoms Found. Valley Forge, Internat. Platform Assn. Presbyterian. Avocations: community service, travel, reading. Home: 6462 Spear St San Diego CA 92120-2929 Office: Gengor Fin Advisors 4950 Waring Rd Ste 7 San Diego CA 92120-2700

GENINI, RONALD WALTER, history educator, historian; b. Oakland, Calif., Dec. 5, 1946; s. William Angelo and Irma Lea (Gays) G.; m. Roberta Mae Tucker, Dec. 20, 1969; children: Thomas, Justin, Nicholas. BA, U. San Francisco, 1968, MA, 1969. Cert. secondary edn. tchr., Calif.; adminstrv. svcs. credential. Tchr. Ctrl. Unified Sch. Dist., Fresno, Calif., 1970—; judge State History Day, Sacramento, 1986-94; mem. U.S. history exam. devel. team Golden State, San Diego, 1989-93; securer placement of state-registered landmarks. Author: Romualdo Pacheco, 1985, Darn Right It's Butch, 1994, Theda Bara, 1996; contbr. articles to profl. jours. Bd. dirs. Fresno Area 6 Neighborhood Coun., 1973-74, Fresno City and County Hist. Soc., 1975-78, St. Anthony's sch. bd., Fresno, 1980-84. Named one of Outstanding Young Educators Am., Fresno Jaycees, 1978; recipient recognition for Tchr. Cares award Calif. State Assembly and Fresno City Coun., 1996. Mem. Calif. Hist. Soc. Democrat. Avocations: writing history 19th century Calif. and early Hollywood, motion picture scriptwriter. Home: 1486 W Menlo Ave Fresno CA 93711-1305 Office: Ctrl HS 3535 N Cornelia Ave Fresno CA 93722-7020 also: Cinema Talent Agency 2609 W Wyoming Ave Apt A Burbank CA 91505-1950

GENN, NANCY, artist; b. San Francisco; d. Morley P. and Ruth W. Thompson; m. Vernon Chathburton Genn; children: Cynthia, Sarah, Peter. Student, San Francisco Art Inst., U. Calif., Berkeley. lectr. on art and papermaking Am. Ctrs. in Osaka, Japan, Nagoya, Japan, Kyoto, Japan, 1979-80; guest lectr. various univs. and art mus. in U.S., 1975—; vis. artist Am. Acad. in Rome, 1989, 94. One woman shows of sculpture, paintings include, De Young Mus., San Francisco, 1955, 63, Gumps Gallery, San Francisco, 1955, 57, 59, San Francisco Mus. Art, 1961, U. Calif., Santa Cruz, 1966-68, Richmond (Calif.) Art Center, 1970, Oakland (Calif.) Mus., 1971, Linda/Farris Gallery, Seattle, 1974, 76, 78, 81, Los Angeles Inst. Contemporary Art, 1976, Susan Caldwell Gallery, N.Y.C., 1976, 77, 79, 81, Nina Freudenheim Gallery, Buffalo, 1977, 81, Annely Juda Fine Art, London, 1978, Inoue Gallery, Tokyo, 1980, Toni Birckhead Gallery, Cin., 1982, Kala Inst. Gallery, Berkeley, Calif., 1983, Ivory/Kimpton Gallery, San Francisco, 1984, 86, Eve Mannes Gallery, Atlanta, 1985, Richard Iri Gallery, L.A., 1990, Harcourts Modern and Contemporary Art, San Francisco, 1991, 93, 96, Am. Assn. Advancement of Sci., Washington, 1994, Anne Reed Gallery, Ketchum, Id., 1995, Michael PeTronko Gallery, N.Y., 1997, Mills Coll. Art Mus., Oakland, Calif., 1999, Takada Gallery, San Francisco, 1999, group exhbns. include San Francisco Mus. Art, 1971, Aldrich Mus., Ridgefield, Conn., 1972-73, Santa Barbara (Calif.) Mus., 1974, 75, Oakland (Calif.) Mus. Art, 1975, Susan Caldwell, Inc., N.Y.C., 1974, 75, Mus. Modern Art, N.Y.C., 1976, traveling exhbn. Arts Coun. Gt. Britain, 1983-84, Inst. Contemporary Arts, Boston, 1977, J.J.Brookings Gallery, San Francisco, 1997, Portland (Oreg.) Art Mus., 1997—; represented in permanent collections Mus. Modern Art, N.Y.C., Albright-Knox Art Gallery, Buffalo, Libr. of Congress, Washington, Nat. Mus. for Am. Art, Washington, L.A. County Mus. Art, Art Mus. U. Calif., Berkeley, McCrory Corp., N.Y.C., Mus. Art, Auckland, N.Z., Aldrich Mus., Ridgefield, Conn., (collection) Bklyn. Mus., (collection) U. Tex., El Paso, Internat. Ctr. Aesthetic Rsch., Torino, Italy, Cin. Art Mus., San Francisco Mus. Modern Art, Oakland Art Mus., L.A. County Mus., City of San Francisco Hall of Justice, Harris Bank, Chgo., Chase Manhattan Bank, N.Y.C., Modern Art Gallery of Ascoli Piceno, Italy, Mills Coll. Art Mus., Oakland, Calif., Mills Coll. of Art, Oakland, Calif., various mfg. cos., also numerous pvt. collections; commd. works include, Bronze lectern and 5 bronze sculptures for chancel table, 1st Unitarian Ch., Berkeley, Calif., 1961, 64, bronze fountain, Cowell Coll., U. Calif., Santa Cruz, bronze menorah, Temple Beth Am, Los Altos Hills, Calif., 1981, 17, murals and 2 bronze fountain sculptures, Sterling Vineyards, Calistoga, Calif., 1972, 73, fountain sculpture, Expo 1974, Spokane, Wash; vis. artist Am. Acad., Rome, 1989. U.S./Japan Creative Arts fellow, 1978-79; recipient Ellen Branston award, 1952; Phelan award De Young Mus., 1963; honor award HUD, 1968. Home: 1515 La Loma Ave Berkeley CA 94708-2033

GENNARO, ANTONIO L., biology educator; b. Raton, N.Mex., Mar. 18, 1934; s. Paul and Mary Lou (Gasperetti) G.; m. Virginia Marie Sullivan, May 15, 1955 (div. 1979); children: Theresa Ann, Carrie Marie, Janelle Elizabeth; m. Marjorie Lou Cox, Sept. 27, 1980. BS, N.Mex. State U., 1957; MS, U. N.Mex., 1961, PhD, 1965. Tchr. biology Las Cruces H.S., N.Mex., 1957-58; asst. prof. biology St. John's U., Collegeville, Minn., 1964-65; prof. biology Eastern N.Mex. U., Portales, 1965—. Contbr. articles to profl. jours. Bd. trustees N.Mex. Mus. of Natural History, 1996—. Served to capt. U.S. Army, 1958-59; mem. Res., 1959-66. Recipient Presdl. Faculty award Eastern N.Mex. U., 1970, Pres.'s Faculty award for excellence in rsch., 1988, Spirit of Ea. award, 1995; Outstanding Sci. award N.Mex. Acad. Sci., 1975. Mem. Southwestern Naturalists (treas. 1974-78), Am. Soc. Mammalogists, Herpetologists League, Sigma Xi, Phi Kappa Phi (pres. 1970-74). Roman Catholic.

GENOW, RICHARD MARTIN, lawyer; b. Anaheim, Calif., Aug. 29, 1963; s. Laurence Gregory G. and Janet Roberta Shaw. BA, U. Calif., Santa Barbara, 1985; JD, Harvard U., 1989; postgrad., UCLA, 1993-95. Lawyer Mirkell Silberberg & Knum, L.A., 1989-92; dir. bus. affairs Paramount Pictures Corp., Hollywood, Calif., 1992-95; assoc. Hansen, Jacobson, Teller & Hoberman, Beverly Hills, Calif., 1995-97, Stone & Co., Beverly Hills, 1997—. Bd. dirs. Entertainment Industry Found. Office: Law Office of Doug Stone 9601 Wilshire Blvd Beverly Hills CA 90210-5213

GENRICH, MARK L., newspaper editorial writer, columnist; b. Buffalo, Aug. 28, 1943; m. Allison Forbes, 1967; children: Audrey, Liza, Colby. BA, Bucknell U., 1966. Editl. writer Palladium-Item, Richmond, Ind., 1970; writing exec. Bruce Eberle & Assocs., Inc., Vienna, Va., 1975-77; dep. editor editl. pgs. Phoenix Gazette, 1977-96; editl. writer, columnist The Ariz. Republic, Phoenix, 1996-98; dir. Warne Ctr. Goldwater Inst., Phoenix, 1998—; participant U.S. Army War Coll., Carlisle, Pa., U.S. Naval War Coll., Newport, R.I.; participant arms control, disarmament programs including Space & Arms talks, Geneva; chmn. New Tech. Com., Journalism in Edn. Com.; mem. various coms. Created, hosted cable TV program focus on polit. figures; regional editor The Masthead. Grantee European Cmty. Visitor Programme, 1993; recipient highest honors editl. writing, newspaper design Ariz., Western Region; highest honor Maricopa County Bar Assn.; Stanford U. media fellow, 1985. Mem. Nat. Conf. Editl. Writers (bd. dirs., included vol. Editl. Excellence), First Amendment Cong. (bd. dirs.), Soc. Profl. Journalists/Sigma Delta Chi, ABA (com. prisons, sentencing). Avocations: coaching competitive soccer, tennis, photography, riding. Office: The Goldwater Inst 201 N Central Ave Phoenix AZ 85004

GENTILE, ROBERT DALE, optometrist, consultant; b. Pottsville, Pa., Oct. 24, 1946; s. Joseph and Evelyn Marie (Warfield) Gentile; m. Patricia Diane Fernsler, June 20, 1969; 1 child, Heather Ly Luxon. BA in Sci., Pa. State U., 1968; BS in Optometry, Pa. Coll. of Optometry, Phila., 1974, OD, 1977; MA in Human Resources, Webster U., 1985. Bd. cert. Am. Acad. Optometry. Advanced through ranks to lt. col. AUS, 1968-94; chief optometry 9th Gen. Dispensary, Aschaffenburg, Germany, 1977-80; optometrist Brook Army Med. Ctr., Ft. Sam Houston, Tex., 1980-82; chief eye sect., medicine and surgery divsn. Acad. Health Scis., Ft. Sam Houston, 1982-84; chief optometry Dunham Army Health Clinic, Carlisle Barracks, Pa., 1984-88, Med. Dept. Activity, Berlin, 1988-91, 121st Evacuation Hosp., Seoul, Republic of Korea, 1991-93; optometry cons. 18th Med. Command, Seoul, 1991-93; chief optometry Raymond W. Bliss Army Cmty. Hosp., Ft. Huachuca, Ariz., 1993-94; optometrist Naval Hosp., Camp Pendleton, Calif., 1994-96; cons. New Vision Internat., Escondido, Calif., 1996—; adj. prof. U. Houston Coll. Optometry, 1980-84, Pa. Coll. Optometry, 1980-84, New England Coll. Optometry, Boston, 1980-84. Decorated Legion of Merit, Meritorious Svc. medal with 3 Oak Leaf Clusters, Army Commendation medal with 4 Oak Leaf Clusters. Fellow Am. Acad. Optometry; mem. Am. Optometric Assn., Armed Forces Optometric Assn., Calif. Optometric Assn., Berlin Internat. Med. Soc., 38th Parallel Med. Soc., Silver Caduceus Soc. of Korea. Avocations: golf, gymnastics, table tennis, nutrition, exercise. Home and Office: 2241 Canyon View Gln Escondido CA 92026-5020

GENTRY, SHARON L., journalism educator; b. Litchfield, Ill., Mar. 19, 1943; d. Ernest Bernard and J. Eileen (Langly) Hall; m. Floyd Lee Gentry, May 2, 1964; children: Janis Louise Gentry Wallner, Kathryn Marie. BS in edn., Southwest Miss. State Univ., 1965; M in liberal Arts, Southern Meth. Univ., 1979. Tchr. Eng. and drama Marshfield (Mo.) H.S., 1965-67; tchr. Eng. and journalism Grandview (Mo.) H.S., 1968-72, Raymore Peculiar H.S., Peculiar, Mo., 1978-83, Valley H.S., Albuquerque, N.M., 1984-86, Highland H.S., Albuquerque, N.M., 1986—. Active First Bapt. Ch. Recipient Harry Lancaster award New Mex. Scholastic Press, 1985, Friend of Journalism award, 1998, Dedicated Svc. award Cen. Mo. Scholastic Press, 1982. Mem. Journalism Edn. Assn. (nat. contest co-chair, 1990-97, nat. local chair for conv. 1991), New Mex. Scholastic Press Assn. (bd. dirs. 1984—), New Mex. Press Women, Nat. Tchr. of Eng., Alpha Delta Kappa. Avocations: needlework, reading, photography, travel. Home: 1115 Castellano Rd SE Albuquerque NM 87123-4213 Office: Highland H S 4700 Coal Ave SE Albuquerque NM 87108-2804

GENTRY, WARREN MILLER, investment company executive; b. Manville, Wyo., Oct. 3, 1921; s. William George and Ina Ella (Miller) G.; m. Billie Jean Axline, Aug. 15, 1948; children—Edward, Thomas, Bradley. A.A., Curtiss Wright Tech. Inst. Aeronautics, 1940; B.A. with distinction, Ariz. State U., 1950, M.A., 1955. Tchr., Miami High Sch., Ariz., 1950-53; art supply salesman Elquest & Son, Phoenix, 1953-55; tchr. Phoenix Union High Sch. Dist., 1955-63; from asst. prof. to prof. humanities Glendale Community Coll., Ariz., 1963-83, founding dir. art collection, 1963—, founding chmn. dept. art, 1963-68; owner, operator Gentry Gallery, Scottsdale, Ariz., 1984-90; co-owner, operator Gentry Enterprises, Scottsdale, 1990—; cons. art silk screen U.S. Army, Ft. Huachuca, Ariz. One-man shows: Phoenix Art Mus., 1954, Sombrero Playhouse, 1955, Phoenix Coll., 1963; group shows include De Young Mus., San Francisco, 1956, Artists U.S.A., Wynnewood, Pa., 1970-71. First Chmn. Scottsdale Beautification Com., 1960s; mem. first Scottsdale Fine Arts Com., 1960s; mem. West Coast Air Tng. Command. Recipient Painting awards Ariz. State Fair, 1950s, Purchase award Valley Bank Sister City, Orange, France, 1958. Mem. Internat. Netsuke Collectors Soc., Humanities Coun. Western Colls. and Univs., Masons. Republican. Office: Gentry Enterprises PO Box 4082 Scottsdale AZ 85261-4082

GEORGAKAKOS, KONSTANTINE PETER, research hydrologist; b. Athens, Greece, Sept. 12, 1954; came to U.S., 1977; MS, MIT, 1980, ScD, 1982. Postdoctoral rschr. NOAA-Nat. Rsch. Coun., Silver Spring, Md., 1982-85, rsch. hydrologist Office Hydrology, 1985; asst. prof. CEE U. Iowa,

Iowa City, 1986-89, assoc. prof., 1989-94; dir., sr. rsch. hydrologist Hydrologic Rsch. Ctr., San Diego, 1994—; full rsch. hydrologist IV Inst. Oceanography U. Calif., San Diego, 1994—; cons. Food & Agriculture Orgn. UN, Rome, 1995—; sci. rev. panelist Nat. Oceanography Atmosphere Adminstrn., Silver Spring, 1996; reviewer NSF, NOAA, NASA, Washington, 1986—. Editor Jour. Applied Meteorology, 1995, Jour. Hydrology, 1996; contbr. articles to profl. jours. Coach Little League Soccer Club Del Mar, San Diego, 1994—. Rsch. associateship Nat. Rsch. Coun., Washington, 1982; recipient Presdl. Young Investigator award NSF, Washington, 1987. Mem. ASCE (assoc. editor 1996—), Am. Geophys. Union (chair hydrology 1991-93), Am. Meteor. Soc. (chair hydrology sect. 1991-93, elected expert on the WMO Commn. Hydrology Working Group on Applications). Achievements include development of flash flood prediction system used nationally by U.S. Nat. Weather Svc., elucidated dynamics and scaling of rainfall and soil water, role of soil water in development of future land surface hydrologic response; performed integrated impact assessments of climate variability and temperature change. Office: Hydrologic Rsch Ctr 12780 High Bluff Dr Ste 250 San Diego CA 92130-2069

GEORGE, LESLIE EARL, protective services official; b. Eldrado, Okla., July 12, 1930; s. Earl Haskel and Cuba Mae (Huddleston) G.; m. Eleanor Mae Hart, Nov. 20, 1955; children: Leslie Earl Jr., Rickie Dwayne, Jeffery Scott, Gregory Allen. AA, East L.A. Coll., 1966; BA in Mgmt., Redlands U., 1983. Reinforcing iron worker Blue Diamond Corp., L.A., 1949-51; reinforcing ironworker foreman Triangle Steel Co., Vernon, Calif., 1953-54; fire fighter City of El Monte (Calif.) Fire Dept., 1955-56, fire engr., 1956-57, fire capt., 1957-61, adminstrv. capt., 1961-66, fire battalion chief, 1966-91, fire chief, 1988—. Bd. dirs., pres. Boys' Club El Monte, 1993. With U.S. Army, 1951-53. Mem. Calif. Conf. Arson Investigators (life, pub., editor), Rotary (pres., sec., program chmn.). Home: 2627 E Maureen St West Covina CA 91792-2215 Office: 3615 Santa Anita Ave El Monte CA 91731-2428*

GEORGE, LLOYD D., federal judge; b. Montpelier, Idaho, Feb. 22, 1930; s. William Ross and Myrtle (Nield) G.; m. LaPrele Badouin, Aug. 6, 1956; children: Douglas Ralph, Michele, Cherie Suzanne, Stephen Lloyd. BS, Brigham Young U., 1955; JD, U. Calif., Berkeley, 1961. Ptnr. Albright, George, Johnson & Steffen, 1969-71, George, Steffen & Simmons, 1971-74; judge U.S. Bankruptcy Ct. (Nev. dist.), 1974-84, U.S. Dist. Ct. Nev., 1984—, chief judge, sr. judge, 1997—; justice of peace Clark County, Nev., 1962-69. Served with USAF, 1955-58. Office: US Dist Ct Foley Fed Bldg Rm 316 300 Las Vegas Blvd S Fl 3 Las Vegas NV 89101-5833*

GEORGE, NICHOLAS, lawyer, entrepreneur; b. Seattle, July 11, 1952; s. Harry and Mary (Courounes) G.; children: Harry Nicholas, James Michael. BA in Polit. Sci. cum laude, Whitman Coll., 1974; MBA in Mktg. and Corp. Planning, U. Chgo., 1979; JD, U. Puget Sound, 1989. Bar: Wash. 1991, U.S. Dist. Ct. (we. dist.) Wash. 1991, U.S. Ct. Appeals (9th cir.) 1991, U.S. Tax Ct. 1992, U.S. Dist. Ct. (ea. dist.) Wash. 1994, U.S. Supreme Ct. 1994. Fin. cons. Pacific Western Investment Co., Lynnwood, Wash., 1975-77; planning dir. Clinton Capital Ventures, Seattle, 1979-81; corp. planning mgr. Tacoma Boatbldg., 1981-83; pres. MegaProf Investors, Bellevue, Wash., 1983-89; practice trial-settlement law bus., Seattle, 1989—; free-lance coll. counselor, Seattle, 1980—. Author: Legitimacy in Government: Ideal, Goal, or Myth? 1974. Bd. auditor St. Demetrios Greek Orthodox Ch., Seattle, 1982-83; bd. dirs. Hellenic Golfers Assn., Seattle, 1981-83. Mem. ABA, Assn. Trial Lawyers Am., Wash. State Bar Assn., Wash. Assn. Criminal Def. Lawyers, Wash. State Trial Lawyers Assn., Fed. Bar Assn., Nat. Assn. Criminal Def. Lawyers, Tacoma-Pierce County Bar Assn., Seattle-King County Bar Assn., Wash. Defender Assn., Wash. State Hist. Soc., Am. Inst. Archeol., Rotary, Wash. Athletic Club, Phi Alpha Delta. Greek Orthodox. Avocations: weightlifting, travel, family history, football coaching, writing. Home: 5007 80th St SW Lakewood WA 98499-4077 Office: 1201 Pacific Ave Ste 1502 Tacoma WA 98402-4322

GEORGE, PETER T., orthodontist; b. Akron, Ohio; s. Tony and Paraskeva (Ogrenova) G.; BS Kent State U., 1952; DDS, Ohio State U., 1956; cert. in orthodontics Columbia U., 1962; children: Barton Herrin, Tryan Franklin. Pvt. practice orthodontics, Honolulu, 1962—; cleft palate cons. Hawaii Bur. Crippled Children, 1963—; asst. prof. Med. Sch., U. Hawaii, Honolulu, 1970—; lectr. in field. Mem. Hawaii Gov.'s Phys. Fitness Com., 1962-68; mem. Honolulu Mayor's Health Coun., 1967-72; mem. med. com. Internat. Weightlifting Fedn., 1980-84; chmn. bd. govs. Hall of Fame of Hawaii, 1984; bd. dirs. Honolulu Opera Theatre, 1986-91, chmn. bd. Hawaii Internat. Sports Found., 1988-91. Served to capt. Dental Corps, U.S. Army, 1956-60. Olympic Gold medallist in weightlifting, Helsinki, 1952, Silver medallist, London, 1948, Melbourne, 1956; six times world champion; recipient Disting. Service award Hawaiian AAU, 1968; Gold medal Internat. Weightlifting Fedn., 1976; named to Helms Hall of Fame, 1966; named mem. 100 Golden Olympians, 1996. Diplomate Am. Bd. Orthodontics. Fellow Am. Coll. Dentistry, Internat. Coll. Dentistry, mem. Hawaii Amateur Athletic Union (pres. 1964-65), U.S. Olympians (pres. Hawaii chpt. 1963-67, 80—), Am. Assn. Orthodontists, Honolulu Dental Soc. (pres. 1967-68), Hawaii Dental Assn. (pres. 1978), Hawaii Soc. Orthodontists (pres. 1972). Editor Hawaii State Dental Jour., 1965-67. Inventor appliance to prevent sleep apnea. U.S. weightlifting coach USSR, 1979, asst. coach Olympic weightlifting team, 1980. Home and Office: 1649 Kalakaua Ave Ste 204 Honolulu HI 96826-2494

GEORGE, RONALD M., state supreme court chief justice; b. L.A., Mar. 11, 1940. AB, Princeton U., 1961; JD, Stanford U., 1964. Bar: Calif. 1965. Dep. atty. gen. Calif. Dept. Justice, 1965-72; judge L.A. Mcpl. Ct., L.A. County, 1972-77; judge Superior Ct. Calif., L.A. County, 1977-87, supervising judge criminal divsn., 1983-84; assoc. justice 2d dist., divsn. 4 Calif. Ct. Appeal, L.A., 1987-91; assoc. justice Calif. Supreme Ct., San Francisco, 1991-96, chief justice, 1996—. Mem. Calif. Judges Assn. (pres. 1982-83). Avocations: hiking, skiing, running. Office: Calif Supreme Court 350 McAllister St 5th fl San Francisco CA 94102-3600

GEORGE, ROSEMARY MARANGOLY, literature educator; b. New Delhi; came to U.S., 1984; d. Varkey Mathai and Mary (Thomas) M.; m. Badri Swaminathan, July 15, 1989. BA with honors, Delhi U., 1983; MA, Northeastern U., Boston, 1986; PhD, Brown U., 1992. Assoc. prof. lit. U. Calif.-San Diego, LaJolla, 1992—. Author: The Politics of Home, 1996; editor: Burning Down the House, 1998. Mem. MLA, Am. Studies Assn. Avocation: painting. Office: U Calif Dept Lit 9500 Gilman Dr Dept 410 La Jolla CA 92093-0410

GEORGE, ROY KENNETH, minister; b. Haskell, Tex., Sept. 23, 1934; s. Roy F. and Jimalee (Scott) G.; m. Patsy Sue Brasher, May 14, 1955; children: Janis Sue, Cheryl Anne. Ordained to ministry Assemblies of God Ch., 1959. Evangelist U.S., Africa, Europe, Asia, 1954-63; pastor Highland Assembly of God Ch., Bakersfield, Calif., 1964-65, 1st Assembly of God Ch., Carlsbad, N.Mex., 1966-67, Sem. South Ch., Ft. Worth, 1968-73, Christian Ctr., Ashland, Oreg., 1973-74, 1st Family Ch., Albuquerque, 1974-93; broadcaster religious radio and TV programs, including Moments with the Master, Sta. KKIM, Albuquerque, 1975-85; state exec. presbyter Assemblies of God N.Mex., 1976—; asst. dist. supt. Assemblies of God, 1981-93, dist. supt. N.Mex. dist., 1993—, mem. Gen. Presbytery, 1981—; mem. exec. bd. Am. Indian Coll. of the Assemblies of God, Phoenix, Ariz., 1993—. Contbr. articles to profl. jours. Bd. regents Southwestern Assemblies of God U. at Waxahachie, Tex., 1981—. Mem. Albuquerque Ministerial Assn., Greater Albuquerque Pentecostal Fellowship (pres. 1975-76), Rogue Valley Nat. Assn. Evangels. (v.p. 1974-75), Civitains (chaplain 1969-73), Kiwanis (pres. Albuquerque club 1982-83, lt. gov. S.W. dist. 1985-86). Office: Assemblies of God NMex Dist 6640 Caminito Coors NW Albuquerque NM 87120-3119

GEORGE, RUSSELL LLOYD, lawyer, legislator; b. Rifle, Colo., May 28, 1946; s. Walter Mallory and Eleanora (Michel) G.; m. Neal Ellen Moore, Nov. 24, 1972; children: Russell, Charles, Thomas, Andrew. BS in Econs., Colo. State U., 1968; JD, Harvard Law Sch., 1971. Bar: Colo. Shareholder Stuver & George, P.C., Rifle, 1976—. state rep. dist. 57 Colo. Gen. Assembly, 1993—, speaker of the House, Colo Gen.Assembly. Fellow Colo. Bar Found.; mem. Colo. Bar Assn., Rotary Internat., Masonic Lodge. Republican. Methodist. Home: 1300 E 7th St Rifle CO 81650-2123 Office: Stuver & George PC PO Box 907 120 W 3rd St Rifle CO 81650-2297*

GEORGE, SARA B., museum director. Dir. Utah Mus. of Natural History, Salt Lake City. Office: Utah Mus of Natural History care U of Utah Pres Cir Salt Lake City UT 84112*

GEORGE, SUZANNE HELEN, shoe designer, consultant; b. Montebello, Calif., Sept. 4, 1962; d. James and Odette Barbara (Zogob) G. BA in Comm., U. Calif., Santa Barbara, 1985; postgrad., San Francisco State U., 1988, Cordwainers Tech. Coll., London, 1993. With Hellman & Friedman, San Francisco, Richard C. Blum & Assoc., San Francisco, Scholastic, Inc., Palo Alto, San Francisco AIDS Found.; shoe designer, cons. Suzanne George Shoes, San Francisco, 1994—; cons. Gale Rsch. and Pub., Renaissance Entrepreneurship Ctr., Davis Shoe Therapeutics, Wilson & Dean Shoes at Wilkes Bashford. Developer, designer, mfr. made-to-order footwear Richard Tyler Fall 1996 and Spring 1997 N.Y. runway shows; commd. to produce men's boots Fall 1996, Esquire Mag.; featured in GQ Mag., Esquire Mag., Harper's Bazaar Mag., Details Mag., N.Y. Times (fashion sect.), Bergdorf Goodman, Bus. Start-Ups Mag. Active Lyon's Blind Ctr., Contact-Care Ctr., Inst. Healing Arts and Scis., U. Calif., San Francisco, Family Counseling & Comty. Svcs. Avocations: reading, photography, writing, film and filmmaking, travel, music.

GEORGE, THOM RITTER, conductor, composer; b. Detroit, June 23, 1942; s. Robert Murray and Virginia Flowers (Ritter) G.; m. Patricia Imogene Dengler , Aug. 14, 1965; children: Samantha, Clara, Alexander. MusB, Eastman Sch. Music, 1964, MusM, 1968; D in Mus. Arts, The Cath. U. Am., 1970. Lectr. music The Cath. U. Am., Washington, 1966-70; music dir., condr. Quincy (Ill.) Symphony Orch., 1970-83; lectr. music John Wood Community Coll., Quincy, 1980-83; assoc. prof. Idaho State U., Pocatello, 1983-88, prof., 1988—; music dir., condr. Idaho State Civic Symphony, Pocatello, 1983—. Composer: Concerto for Bass Trombone, 1964, Proclamations, 1965, Sextet, 1980, numerous others. Bd. dirs. Civic Music Assn., Quincy, 1970-74; bd. sec. Vol. Action Ctr., Quincy, 1976-78. Served with USN, 1966-70. Recipient citation Quincy Coll., 1973, Sigvald Thompson award Fargo (N.D.) Moorhead Symphony, 1975, Composer-in-Residence Elkhorn Music Festival, Sun Valley, Idaho, 1986. Mem. ASCAP, Am. String Tchrs. Assn., Nat. Band Assn. Lodges: Rotary (Quincy membership chmn. 1975-83, mem. Pocatello fine arts com. 1985—). Avocations: reading, traveling, photography. Office: Idaho State U Dept Music PO Box 8099 Pocatello ID 83209

GEORGE, VANCE, conductor; b. Bremen, Ind., Sept. 30, 1933. BA in Music Edn., Goshen Coll., Ind., 1955; Grad., Bhatkande Sch. Music and Dance, India, 1959; student, Goethe Inst., Germany, 1961; MusM in Conducting, Ind. Univ., 1963, Mus D in Conducting, 1965; Mus D (hon.), Kent State U., 1998. Chorus master Opera Theater, Ind. Univ., Bloomington, Ind., 1963-65; dir. Women's Chorus, Ind. Univ., Bloomington, Ind., 1963-65; dir. choral activities Univ. Wis., Madison, 1965-71; instr. Choral Inst., Am. Choral Found., Madison, 1967, 69; dir. choral activities Kent State Univ., Ohio, 1971-82; assoc. chorus conductor Cleveland Orch. Chorus, Cleveland Orch. Chamber Chorus, Ohio, 1977-83; prof. conducting Festival of the Rockies, Whitefish, Mont., 1987; conductor Phoenix Bach Soc., Ariz., 1988-90; dir. San Francisco Symphony Chorus, Calif., 1983—; bd. dirs. Choris Am.; former chmn. Cleve. Orch. Chorus, Sch. of the Cleve. Orch.; guest chorus dir. Kent State Univ. Chorus, Canton Symphony Orch., 1976-77, 80-81; vis. assoc. prof. Univ. Calif., Berkeley, 1983, 85, 87, 88. Condr. San Francisco Symphony, San Francisco Symphony Chorus, oratorio, seasonal concerts, pops, Asian Youth Orch., Asian Youth Chorus, Ein Deutsches Requiem (Grammy award Best Choral Performance 1995); studies in U.S., Europe, Canada, India. Recipient Grammy award for Best Choral Performance, 1992; nominee Grammy award Mahler Symphony #2, 1994. Mem. IFCM, ACDA, Pi Kappa Lambda. E-mail: vygeorg@aol.com. Office: San Francisco Symphony Chorus 201 Van Ness Ave Ste 107 San Francisco CA 94102-4585

GEORGE, WILFRED RAYMOND, financial advisor, portfolio manager; b. Grinnell, Iowa, Apr. 1, 1928; m. Ann Ingraham, Sept. 5, 1987. BS in Engring., Iowa U., 1950; MBA, Harvard U., 1955; PhD, Golden Gate U., 1979. Registered profl. engr., Va.; chartered market technician. Engr. Westinghouse Electric, Pitts., 1950-51; mech. design engr. 5th Naval Dist., Norfolk, Va., 1952-53; budget supr. sales and employment adminstr. Lockheed Missile and Space Div., Sunnyvale, Calif., 1955-59; registered rep. Shearson Hammill and Co., Menlo Park, Calif., 1963; v.p., mgr. Bache and Co., San Francisco, 1964-72; v.p. investments Prudential Securities, San Francisco, 1972—; concert flutist, piccoloist. Author: Profit Box System for Forecasting Stock Prices, 1976, Tight Money Timing, 1982; patentee in field. Pres. San Francisco Virtuosi, 1991—; trustee Brit. Benevolent Soc., San Francisco, 1979—; chmn. bd. trustees St. Andres Soc. San Francisco, 1983-89. Served to lt. (j.g.) USNR, 1951-52. Mem. Tech. Securities Soc. of San Francisco (founder 1970, pres. 1974, bd. dirs. 1975—). Mem. Harvard Bus. Sch. (San Francisco), Fremont Hills Country Club (bd. dirs. 1968-70), Bohemian Club. Republican. Avocations: chrematistics, music, writing. Home: 15 Niven Way Larkspur CA 94939-1525

GEORGINO, SUSAN MARTHA, city redevelopment services administrator; b. Phila., Apr. 1, 1950; d. Joseph Francis and Eleanor (Kelley) Boyle; m. Richard Romano (div.); 1 child, Sean; m. Victor Georgino. BA, Calif. State U., L.A., 1975, MPA, 1983. Adminstrv. officer Maravilla Found., Montebello, Calif., 1978-81; adminstrv. analyst City of Burbank (Calif.), 1982-84, project mgr., 1984-87, asst. dir. community devel., redevel. adminstr., 1987-89; dir. redevel. svcs. City of Brea (Calif.), 1989—; bd. dirs., v.p. Calif. Redevel. Assn. Bd. dirs. Soroptimist Internat., Brea, 1991; active La Providencia Guild, Burbank, 1990, Parks and Recreation Commn., Burbank, 1991, 93; vice chair City of Burbank's Performing Arts Grant Awards Program, 1994. Mem. Nat. Assn. Redevel. and Housing Ofcls. (bd. dirs. 1986-87), Calif. Assn. Econ. Devel. Ofcls., Orange County Bus. Coun. (adv. bd.), Bus. Coun. Econ. Devel., Lambda Alpha Internat. (v.p. Orange County chpt. 1996—). Roman Catholic. Avocations: reading, golf, opera. Office: City of Brea One Civic Ctr Circle Brea CA 92621

GER, SHAW-SHYONG, accountant; b. Kaohsiung, Taiwan, Nov. 19, 1959; s. Jing-Ru and Jui-Mei (Lee) G. BA in econs., Nat. Taiwan U., Taipei, 1981; MBA, Ariz. State U., 1986, M in acctg., 1989. CPA, Ariz.; CMA, CFM, Novell MCNE, Microsoft MCP. Rsch. asst. Ariz. State U., Tempe, 1988-89; contr. CLH Internat., Inc., Tempe, 1989—. Recipient All Am. Scholar award U.S. Achievement Acad., 1989. Mem. Assn. MBA Exec., Nat. Geog. Soc., Inst. Cert. Mgmt. Accts., Beta Gamma Sigma. Address: PO Box 601 Tempe AZ 85280-0601

GERAGHTY, JOHN VINCENT, public relations consultant; b. Seattle, Feb. 23, 1934; s. John V. and Gladys I (Johnson) G.; children: Marcella Maile, Sheila Leek, Brigid Krause, Nora Lipton. BA in Comm., U. Wash., 1956; MPA (hon.), Ea. Washington U., 1994. Reporter Spokane (Wash.) Daily Chronicle, 1959-62; sec. to mayor/coun. City of Spokane, 1962-64; county commr. Spokane (Wash.) County, 1964-71; vp. guest rels. EXPO '74 Corp., Spokane, 1971-74; publisher, owner The Falls Newspaper, Spokane, 1974-76; v.p. Haworth & Anderson, Inc., Spokane, 1976-83; owner, pres. Jack Geraghty & Assocs., Spokane, 1983—; prin. Alliance Pacific, Inc., Spokane, 1985—; mayor City of Spokane, 1994-98; bd. dirs., past pres. Future Spokane, 1983-89; cons. Citizens League of Greater Spokane. Bd. dirs. and past pres., Spokane Comty. Mental Health Ctr., 1980-95; mem. and past chmn. bd. trustees Ea. Wash., Cheney, Wash., 1985-97; mem. and vice chair Spokane Centennial Projects Com., 1988. Mem. Pub. Rels Soc. Am. (pres. Spokane chpt. 1983), Spokane Pub. Rels. Coun. (past pres.), Spokane Club, Beta Theta Pi. Democrat. Roman Catholic. Avocations: golf, sailing, cooking. Home: PO Box 251 Spokane WA 99210-0251 Office: Jack Geraghty and Assoc 621 W Mallon Ave Spokane WA 99201-2163

GERBA, CHARLES PETER, microbiologist, educator; b. Blue Island, Ill., Sept. 10, 1945; s. Peter and Virginia (Roulo) G.; m. Peggy Louise Scheitlin, June 6, 1970; children: Peter, Phillip. BS in Microbiology, Ariz. State U., 1969; PhD in Microbiology, U. Miami, 1973. Postdoctoral fellow Baylor Coll. Medicine, Houston, 1973-74, asst. prof. microbiology, 1974-81; assoc. prof. U. Ariz., Tucson, 1981-85, prof., 1985—; cons. EPA, Tucson, 1980—, World Health Orgn., Pan Am. Health Orgn., 1989—; advisor CRC Press, Boca Raton, Fla., 1981—. Editor: Methods in Environmental Virology, 1982, Groundwater Pollution Microbiology, 1984, Phage Ecology, 1987, Pollution Sci., 1996; contbr. numerous articles to profl. and sci. jours. Mem. Pima County Bd. Health, 1986-92; mem. sci. adv. bd. EPA, 1987—. Recipient McKee medal Water Environ. Fedn., 1996; named Outstanding Research Scientist U. Ariz., 1984, 92, Outstanding Rsch. Team, 1994. Fellow AAAS (environ. sci. and engring.), Am. Acad. Microbiology, Am. Soc. Microbiology (divsn. chmn. 1982-83, 87-88, pres. Ariz. chpt. 1984-85, councilor 1985-88); mem. Internat. Assn. Water Pollution Rsch. (sr. del. 1985-91), Am. Water Works Assn. (A.P. Black award 1997), Water Quality Assn. (Hom. Mem. award 1998). Achievements include research in environmental microbiology, colloid transport in ground water, wastewater reuse and risk assessment. Home: 1980 W Paseo Monserrat Tucson AZ 85704-1329 Office: U Ariz Dept Microbiol & Immunol Water & Soils Tucson AZ 85721

GERBRACHT, ROBERT THOMAS (BOB GERBRACHT), painter, educator; b. Erie, Pa., June 23, 1924; s. Earl John and Lula Mary (Chapman) G.; m. Delia Marie Paz, Nov. 27, 1952; children: Mark, Elizabeth, Catherine. BFA, Yale U., 1951; MFA, U. So. Calif., 1952. Cert. tchr., Calif. Art tchr. William S. Hart Jr. and Sr. High Sch., Newhall, Calif., 1954-56; stained glass artist Cummings Studios, San Francisco, 1956-58; art tchr. McKinley Jr. High Sch., Redwood City, Calif., 1958-60, Castro Jr. High Sch., San Jose, Calif., 1960-79; portrait artist, tchr. San Jose, San Francisco, 1979—; instr. art Coll. of Notre Dame, Belmont, Calif., 1955-60, San Jose City Coll., 1967-71, Notre Dame Novitiate, Saratoga, 1976-79, U. Calif., Santa Cruz, 1980-81; art cons. Moreland Sch. Dist., Campbell, Calif., 1979-80; instr. nationwide workshops, Calif., Colo., Fla., Kans., Mass., Nebr., N.Mex., N.Y., Oreg., S.C., Vt., Wash., Wis., Mex., 1980—. Exhibited in Charles and Emma Frye Mus. Fine Art, Seattle, Rosicrucia Mus., San Jose, Calif., San Jose Mus. of Art, Denver Art Mus., Erie Mus. Art, Triton Mus. of Art, Santa Clara, Calif., Israel, Austria, China; represented in permanent collection Triton Mus. Art, Santa Clara, Calif.; portraits include Marie Gallo, Mrs. Bruce Jenner, Austin Warburton, Rev. Jack La Rocca, Rev. Cecil Williams; subject of articles in Today's Art and Graphics, Art and Antique Collector, Am. Artist, U.S. ART; work reproduced and included in Best of Pastel, Best of Oil Painting, 1996, Postal Highlights, 1996, Portrait Inspirations, The Best of Portrait Painting, 1997, Best of Pastel 2, 1998. Cpl. U.S. Army, 1943-46. Recipient Am. Artist Achievement award Tchr. of Pastels, 1993. Mem. Pastel Soc. Am. (master pastellist), Pastel Soc. West Coast (advisor, Best of Show 1988), Soc. Western Artists (trustee 1989-97, Best of Show 1982, 85, 90, Best Portrait award 1984), Oil Painters Am. Home: 1301 Blue Oak Ct Pinole CA 94564-2145

GERHART, DOROTHY EVELYN, insurance executive, real estate professional; b. Monett, Mo., Apr. 20, 1932; d. Manford Thomas and Norma Grace (Barrett) Ethridge; m. Robert H. Gerhart, Apr. 11, 1952 (div. Dec. 1969); children: Sandra Gerhart Kreamer, Richard A., Diane Gerhart Lacey. Grad. high sch., Tucson; student, U. Ariz., 1950-53. Lic. real estate broker. Owner, pres. Gerhart Ins., Inc., Tucson, 1967-70, 89—; agt. Mahoney-O'Donnell Agy., Tucson, 1970-73, Gerhart & Mendelsoh Ins., Tucson, 1973-78; agt., mgr. personal lines dept. Tucson Realty and Trust, 1978-83; ins. agt. San Xavier Ins. Agy., Tucson, 1985-89; pres. Gerhart Ins., Inc., Tucson, 1989-93, Koty-Leavitt Ins., Inc. (formerly Gerhart Ins., Inc.), Tuscon, 1993—, Gerhart Realty, Inc., Tuscon, 1993—. Vol. Palo Verde Psychiat. Hosp. Mem. Nat. Fedn. Ind. Bus., Ind. Ins. Agts. Tucson (bd. dirs. 1973, 74, v.p. 1975, pres. 1976, First Woman Pres.), Fed. Home Life Ins. Co. (Pres.'s Club award 1986), Nat. Fedn. Small Bus., Altrusa Club of Tucson (bd. dirs. 1984, membership chmn. 1985, fund raising chmn. 1986). Republican. Avocations: arts, crafts, antiques. Address: PO Box 13421 Tucson AZ 85732-3421 Office: Gerhart Realty Inc 6339 E Speedway Blvd Ste 200 Tucson AZ 85710-1147

GERHART, JAMES BASIL, physics educator; b. Pasadena, Calif., Dec. 15, 1928; s. Ray and Marion (van Deusen) G.; m. Genevra Joy Thomesen, June 21, 1958; children: James Edward, Sara Elizabeth. B.S., Calif. Inst. Tech., 1950; M.A., Princeton, 1952, Ph.D., 1954. Instr. physics Princeton, 1954-56; asst. prof. physics U. Wash., Seattle, 1956-61; asso. prof. U. Wash., 1961-65, prof., 1965-98, prof. emeritus, 1998—; exec. officer Pacific Northwest Assn. for Coll. Physics, 1972-94, bd. dirs., 1965—, chmn., 1970-72; governing bd. Am. Inst. Physics, 1973-76, 78-81. Recipient Disting. Teaching award U. Wash. Regents and Alumni Assn., 1982, Ann. Gerhart lectr., 1997. Fellow Am. Phys. Soc, AAAS; mem. Am. Assn. Physics Tchrs. (sec. 1971-77, v.p. 1977, pres.-elect 1978, pres. 1979, Millikan medal 1985). Home: 2134 E Interlaken Blvd Seattle WA 98112-3433

GERI, LAURANCE RUDOLPH, educator; b. Snoqualamie, Wash., Oct. 10, 1958; s. Rudolph Ilario and Kathleen Ruth (Higgins) G. BA, U. Wash., 1980; MPA, George Washington U., 1982; DPA, U. So. Calif., 1996. Mgmt. analyst USDA, Animal and Plant Health Inspection Svc., Hyattsville, Md., 1981-82; program analyst USDA, Animal and Plant Health Inspection Svc., Hyattsville, 1983-88, activity dir., 1989-94; faculty mem. public adminstrn. The Evergreen State Coll., Olympia, Wash., 1994—; coord. soc. scis., 1998—. Mem. Internat. Inst. Pub. Adminstrn., Am. Soc. Pub. Adminstrn., Am. Evaluation Assn. Office: Lab I The Evergreen St Coll Olympia WA 98505

GERINGER, JAMES E., governor; b. Wheatland, Wyo., Apr. 24, 1944; m. Sherri Geringer; children: Jen, Val, Rob, Meri, Beckie. BS in Mechanical Engring., Kans. State U., 1967. Commd. officer USAF; with contract administration Mo. Basin Power Project's Laramie River Sta., 1977-79; elected mem. Wyo. Legislature, 1982; farm owner, 1987—; Governor State of Wyoming, 1994—; participant in various space devel. programs, Calif., devel. variety Air Force and NASA space boosters including launches of reconnaissance satellites, the NASA Viking Mars lander, an upper stage booster for the space shuttle and the Global Positioning Satellite System; chief of computer programming at a ground receiving station for early warning satellites. Mem. Nat. Fedn. Ind. Bus., Am. Legion, Farm Bur., Farmer's Union, Rotary, Lions, Ducks Unlimited, Pheasants Forever, C. of C. Lutheran. Office: Office of the Gov State Capitol Bldg 124 200 W 24th St Cheyenne WY 82002-0010*

GERKEN, WALTER BLAND, insurance company executive; b. N.Y.C., Aug. 14, 1922; s. Walter Adam and Virginia (Bl) G.; m. Darlene Stolt, Sept. 6, 1952; children: Walter C., Ellen M., Beth L., Daniel J., Andrew P., David A. BA, Wesleyan U., 1948; MPA, Maxwell Sch. Citizenship and Pub. Affairs, Syracuse, 1958. Supr. budget and adminstrv. analysis Wis., Madison, 1950-54; mgr. investments Northwestern Mut. Life Ins. Co., Milw., 1954-67; v.p. finance Pacific Mut. Life Ins. Co., L.A., 1967-69, exec. v.p., 1969-72, pres., 1972-75, chmn. bd., 1975-87; chmn. exec. com. Pacific Mut. Life Ins. Co., Los Angeles, 1987-95, also dir.; sr. advisor Boston Consulting Group; chmn. PIMCO Advisors, L.P.; bd. dirs. Mullin Cons., Inc. Bd. dirs. Keck Found., Hoag Meml. Presbyn. Hosp.; trustee emeritus Occidental Coll. L.A., Wesleyan U., Middletown, Conn.; bd. dirs. Nature Conservancy Calif., Exec. Svc. Corp.; mem. Calif. Citizens Budget Com., Calif. Commn. Campaign Fin. Reform, Calif. Commn. on Higher Edn.; chair Exec. Svc. Corps. So. Calif.; v.p. Orange County Cmty. Found.; mem. adv. bd. The Maxwell Sch. Citizenship and Pub. Affairs, Syracuse U. Decorated D.F.C., Air medal. Mem. Calif. Club, Dairymen's Country Club (Boulder Junction, Wis.), Balboa Bay Club (Newport Beach, Calif., former bd. dirs.), Automobilce Club So. Calif. (bd. dirs.), Calif. Ind. Coll. Network (co-chair), Pauma Valley Country Club, Edison Internat., Times Mirror Co. Office: Pimco Advisors LP 800 Newport Center Dr Newport Beach CA 92660-6309

GERMAN, DONALD FREDERICK, physician; b. San Francisco, Oct. 2, 1935; m. Marilyn Sue King; children: Susan, Charles, Donald. BS, U. San Francisco, 1956; MD, U. Calif., San Francisco, 1960. Diplomate Am. Bd. Pediats., Am. Bd. Allergy and Immunology. Intern Kaiser Found. Hosp., San Francisco, 1960-61, resident in pediats., 1963-65, resident, fellow in allergy, 1966-68; staff pediatrician Kaiser Med. Ctr., Santa Clara, Calif., 1965-66, staff allergist, 1968-69; chief dept. allergy Kaiser Permanente Med. Ctr., San Francisco, 1969—; clin. prof. pediatrics U. Calif. Med. Sch., San Francisco, 1991—. Capt. USAF, 1961-63. Fellow Am. Acad. Pediats., Am. Coll. Allergy and Immunology, Am. Acad. Allergy and Immunology; mem. Calif. Soc. Allergy and Immunology (sec./treas.). Avocations: running, hiking, fly fishing, travel. Office: Kaiser Permanente Med Ctr Allergy Dept 1635 Divisadero St Ste 101 San Francisco CA 94115-3000

GERMAN, KATY, artist; b. Jamaica, N.Y., Dec. 19, 1968; d. John and MaryAnn (Koch) G.; m. James Norris. BA, CUNY, 1992. Creative dir. Cinegraphique Prodns., N.Y.C., 1989-93; art dir. BoldType, Emeryville, Calif., 1993-96; prod. sys. mgr. IDG Books Worldwide, Foster City, Calif., 1996-99. Co-editor Medieval Assn. of the Pacific, 1993-94. Mem. San Francisco Ctr. for the Book, Bookbuilders West, Hand Bookbinders of Calif., Pacific Ctr. for the Book Arts. Avocations: Greco-Roman literature, letterpress book arts, calligraphy, astronomy. Office: Heliac Press PO Box 297 Shore Island Heights NY 11965

GERMAN, WILLIAM, newspaper editor; b. N.Y.C., Jan. 4, 1919; s. Sam and Celia (Norack) G.; m. Gertrude Pasenkoff, Oct. 12, 1940; children: David, Ellen, Stephen. B.A., Bklyn. Coll., 1939; M.S., Columbia U., 1940; Nieman fellow, Harvard U., 1950. Reporter, asst. fgn., news, mng., exec. editor, editor San Francisco Chronicle, 1940—; editor Chronicle Fgn. Service, 1960-77; mng. editor KQED, Newspaper of the Air, 1968; lectr. U. Calif., Berkeley, 1946-47, 68-70. Editor: San Francisco Chronicle Reader, 1962. Bd. trustees World Affairs Coun. Served with AUS, 1943-45. Mem. AP Mng. Editors Assn., Am. Soc. Newspaper Editors, Commonwealth Club of Calif. (pres. 1995). Home: 150 Lovell Ave Mill Valley CA 94941-1883 Office: San Francisco Chronicle 901 Mission St San Francisco CA 94103-2905

GEROU, PHILLIP HOWARD, architect; b. Natick, Mass., July 20, 1951; s. James Francis and Enid (Meymaris) G.; m. Cheri Rodgers, Nov. 24, 1979; children: Gregory Bedford, Sara Christine. BArch, U. Nebr., 1974, MArch, 1975. Architect Colo., 1975-77; project mgr. Henningson, Durham, Richardson, Denver, 1978-82; dir. architecture Daniel Mann Johnson Mendenhall, Denver, 1982-85; v.p., dir. comml. design Downing Leach Architects, Boulder, 1985-86; prin., designer, owner Gerou & Assocs. Ltd., Evergreen, Colo., 1986—; design cons. Kilimanjaro Children's Hosp., Tanzania, 1988-91, World Alpine Ski Championships, Vail, Colo., 1988. Pres. Colo. Soc. of Architects Ednl. Fund., Denver, 1986; del. State Rep. Assembly, Denver, 1986; trustee Rockland Community Ch., Denver, 1986-89. Recipient Citation award Nat. Assn. of Remodeling Industry, 1991, 96, Design Excellence Wood, Inc., 1990, Citation award, 1990. Fellow AIA (pres. Colo. chpt. 1986, bd. dirs. 1981-87, nat. dir. 1991-94, v.p. 1995, dir. Nat. Ethics Coun. 1997—, chmn., 1998—, conf. chair Western Mtn. region design conf. 1990, Spl. Recognition award 1990), Nat. Coun. Archl. Adminstrn. Bds. (examiner 1985). Republican. Mem. United Ch. of Christ. Avocations: skiing, travel, architectural design.

GERRODETTE, CHARLES EVERETT, real estate company executive, consultant; b. Alderwood Manor, Wash., June 18, 1934; s. Honoré Everett and Marjorie Violet (Stapley) G.; m. Laurine Carol Manley, Mar. 16, 1956 (div. 1977); children: Stephen Everett, Suzanne Gerrodette Prince; m. Diane Marie Drumm, Dec. 6, 1984. BA in Bus. Adminstrn., U. Wash., 1956, postgrad., 1959; postgrad., NYU, 1956-57. Credit analyst and corr. comml. credit dept. Chase Manhattan Bank, N.Y.C., 1956-57; reviewing appraiser Prudential Ins. Co. Am., Seattle, 1959-67; v.p., sr. loan officer real estate group Seattle 1st Nat. Bank, 1967-90; pres., CEO, Portal Pacific Co., Inc., Seattle, 1990—; real estate advisor, fin. cons. Charles E. Gerrodette, MAI, Seattle, 1990—; instr. appraising Shoreline C.C., Seattle, 1974-76. Contbg. author: Prentice Hall Ency. of Real Estate Appraising, 3d edit., 1978. Mem. blue ribbon com. for planning Shoreline Sch. Dist., Seattle, 1974-75. With U.S. Army, 1957-59. Mem. Am. Arbitration Assn. (panel of arbitrators), Appraisal Inst. (MAI designation 1972, officer, bd. dirs. Wash.-B.C. chpt. 1980-89, pres. 1984, nat. fin. and adminstrn. com. 1982-87, nat. governing counselor 1987-89, nat. fin. com. 1990-96), Mortgage Bankers Assn. (income property com.), Columbia Tower Club, Lambda Alpha, N.W. Grad. Assn. Theta Delta Chi (trustee 1960-70, past pres.). Episcopalian. Avocations: travel, investing, architectural appreciation, photography. Office: 2125 1st Ave Ste 1204 Seattle WA 98121-2118

GERRY, DEBRA PRUE, psychotherapist; b. Oct. 9, 1951; d. C.O. and Sarah E. Rawl; m. Norman Bernard Gerry, Apr. 10, 1981; 1 child, Gisele Psyche Victoria. BS, Ga. So. U., 1972; MEd, Armstrong State U., 1974; PhD, U. Ga., 1989. Cert. Ariz. Bd. Behavioral Health Examiners. Spl. edn. tchr. Chatham County Bd. Edn., Savannah, Ga., 1972-74; edn. and learning disabilities resource educator Duval County Bd. Edn., Jacksonville, Fla., 1974-77; ednl. resource counselor spl. programs adminstr. Broward County Bd. Edn., Ft. Lauderdale, Fla., 1977-81; pvt. practice Scottsdale, Ariz., 1990—. Contbr. author coll. textbooks; contbr. articles to profl. jours. Vol., fundraiser, psychol. cons., group leader Valley AIDS Orgns., Phoenix, 1990-96; fundraiser Hosp. Health Edn. Programs, Scottsdale, 1992-93; mem. com. for women's issues Plz. Club, Phoenix, 1992-93; pres. Laissez Les Bon Temps Rouler, Wrigley Club, Phoenix, 1993-96; exec. bd. Sojourner's Ctr., Phoenix, 1997-98, Breast Found., Inc., Phoenix, 1997-98; appointee Ariz. Supreme Ct., Foster Care Rev. Bd., Phoenix, 1996-99. Recipient Rudy award Shanti Orgn., 1991. Mem. APA, NOW, ACA, Internat. Soc. Poets (disting., Poet of Merit award 1996), Nat. Assn. Women Bus. Owners, Assn. for Multicultural Coun., Assn. for Specialists in Group Work, Mensa, Phi Delta Kappa, Kappa Delta Epsilon, Sigma Omega Phi, Kappa Delta Pi. Avocations: ballroom dancing, playing musical instruments, singing, travel, air sports.

GERSTELL, A. FREDERICK, aggregates and asphalt and concrete manufacturing executive; b. 1938. AB, Princeton U., 1960. Vice pres. mktg., dir. Alpha Portland Cement Co., 1960-75; v.p. Calif. Portland Cement Co., L.A., 1975-81, pres., chief operating officer, 1981-84; pres., chief operating officer CalMat Co., L.A., 1984-88, pres., chief exec. officer, chief operating officer, 1988-90, chmn.bd., pres., chief exec. officer/chief operating officer, 1990-96, chmn. bd., CEO, 1996-98, vice chmn., dir., 1998—. Trustee emeritus The Lawrenceville (N.J.) Sch. With USAR 1960-66. Mem. Merchants and Mfrs. Assn. (dir.), Nat. Stone Assn. (bd. dirs., vice chmn., exec. com.), Calif. C. of C. (bd. dirs.), Ameron, Inc. (dir.). Office: CalMat Co 3200 N San Fernando Rd Los Angeles CA 90065-1415*

GERTH, DONALD ROGERS, university president; b. Chgo., Dec. 4, 1928; s. George C. and Madeleine (Canavan) G.; m. Beverly J. Hollman, Oct. 15, 1955; children: Annette, Deborah. BA, U. Chgo., 1947, AM, 1951, PhD, 1963. Field rep. S.E. Asia World Univ. Svc., 1950; asst. to pres. Shimer Coll., 1951; Admissions counselor U. Chgo., 1956-58; assoc. dean students, admissions and records, mem. dept. polit. sci. San Francisco St. U., San Francisco, 1958-63; assoc. dean instnl. relations and student affairs Calif. State Univ., 1963-64; chmn. commn. on extended edn. Calif. State Univs. and Colls., 1977-82; dean of students Calif. State U., Chico, 1964-68, prof. polit. sci., 1964-76, assoc. v.p. for acad. affairs, dir. internat. programs, 1969-70, v.p. acad. affairs, 1970-76; co-dir. Danforth Found. Research Project, 1968-69; coordinator Inst. Local Govt. and Public Service, 1968-70; pres., prof. polit. sci. and public adminstrn. Calif. State U., Dominguez Hills, 1976-84; pres., prof. govt. and adminstrn. Calif. State U., Sacramento, 1984—; past chair Accrediting Commn. for Sr. Colls. and Univs. of Western Coll. Assn.; chmn. admissions coun. Calif. State U.; bd. dirs. Ombudsman Found., L.A., 1968-71; com. continuing edn. Calif. Coordinating Coun. for Higher Edn., 1963-64; lectr. U. Philippines, 1953-54, Claremont Grad. Sch. and Univ. Ctr., 1965-69; chair Sacramento World Trade Ctr.; vice chmn. Calif. State U. Inst. Co-author: The Learning Society, 1969; author, editor: An Invisible Giant, 1971; contbg. editor Education for the Public Service, 1970, Papers on the Ombudsman in Higher Education, 1979. Mem. pers. commn. Chico Unified Sch. Dist., 1969-76, chmn., 1971-74; adv. com. on justice pgorams Butte Coll., 1970-76; mem. Varsity Scouting Coun., 1980-84; chmn. United Way campaign Calif. State Univs., L.A. County, 1981-82; bd. dirs. Sacramento Area United Way, campaign chmn., 1991-92, exec. com., 1991-96, vice chmn., 1992-94, chmn.-elect, 1994-95, chmn., 1995-96; mem. bd. dirs. South Bay Hosp. Found., 1979-82; mem. The Cultural Commn., L.A., 1981-84; mem. com. govtl. rels. Am. Coun. Edn. Capt. USAF, 1952-56. Mem. Internat. Assn. Univ. Pres. (pres. 1996—), Am. Polit. Sci. Assn., Am. Soc. Pub. Adminstrn., Soc. Coll. and Univ. Planning, Western Govtl. Rsch. Assn., World Affairs Coun. No. Calif., Assn. Pub. Adminstrn. Edn. (chmn. 1973-74), Western Polit. Sci. Assn., Am. Assn. State Colls. and Univs. (bd. dirs.), Calif. State C. of C. (edn. com.), Assn. Governing Bds. of Univs. and Colls., Calif. State U. Inst. (chmn. bd. dirs.), UN Ednl., Sci. and Cultural Orgn. (mem. adv. com.), UN Univ. Coun., World Trade Ctr. Sacramento, (chmn.), Sacramento Club (bd. dirs.), Comstock Club. Democrat. Episcopalian. Avocations: tennis, skiing, reading. Home: 417 Websters Ct Roseville CA 95747-8339 Office: Calif State U 6000 J St # 206 Sacramento CA 95819-2605

GERTZ, DAVID LEE, homebuilding company executive; b. Denver, July 30, 1950; s. Ben Harry and Clara (Cohen) G.; m. Bonnie Lee Schulein, June 2, 1973; children: Joshua, Eva. BS, U. Colo., 1972; MBA, U. Colo., Denver, 1993. Real estate broker Crown Realty, Denver, 1972-73; pres. Sunshine Plumbing Co., Lakewood, Colo., 1974-76, Sunshine Diversified, Inc., Lakewood, 1976—, Sunshine Master Builders, Ltd., Lakewood, 1990—; sec.-treas. Wight Lateral Ditch Co., Lakewood, 1987-91. *David Gertz is founder and president of Sunshine Master Builders Ltd., a 22 years old company listed in the Denver Business Journal as the 22nd largest homebuilding company in the Denver Metro area. Sunshine has built over 400 custom homes, an office building and a 50,000 sq. ft. commercial project. It employs 20 full time people, and engages over 150 trade contractor companies. Currently, it's building over 60 homes valued at over 25 million dollars. David earned an MBA at the University of Colorado at Denver in 1993, and serves on the board of the Denver Home Building Association and chairman of the 1999 Parade of Homes.* Builder of custom and semi-custom homes. Cub master Boy Scouts Am., Lakewood, 1989-91, asst. scout master, 1991-94; co-chair bldg. com. Hebrew Ednl. Alliance, bd. dirs., Denver, 1991-94; mem. Anti-Defamation League, Denver, 1989—; chmn. Parade of Homes com., 1999. Scholar, Evans Scholars, U. Colo., 1968-72. Mem. Home Builders Assn. of Denver (bd. dirs., legis. com.), Colo. Assn. Home Builders (alt. dir.). Avocations: skiing, golf, softball. Office: Sunshine Master Builders 8125 W Belleview Ave Littleton CO 80123-1203

GERWICK-BRODEUR, MADELINE CAROL, marketing and timing professional; b. Kearney, Neb., Aug. 29, 1951; d. Vern Frank and Marian Leila (Bliss) Gerwick; m. David Louis Brodeur; 1 child, Maria Louise. Student, U. Wis., 1970-72, U. Louisville, 1974-75; BA in Econs. magna cum laude, U. N.H., 1979; postgrad., Internat. Trade Inst., Seattle. Cert. profl. cycles cons., 1995; cert. bus. astrologer. Indsl. sales rep. United Radio Supply Inc., Seattle, 1980-81; mfrs. rep. Ray Over Sales Inc., Seattle, 1981-82; sales engr. Tektronix, Inc., Kent, Wash., 1982-83; mktg. mgr. Zepher Industries, Inc., Burien, Wash., 1983-85, Microscan Systems Inc., Tukwila, Wash., 1986.; market devel. URS Electronics, Inc., Portland, 1986-88; sr. product specialist Fluke Corp., 1989-95; owner Astro Cycles Cons. L.L.C., Seattle, 1995—; bd. dirs., sec. Starfish Enterprises Inc., Tacoma, 1984-87; com. chmn. Northcon, Seattle and Portland, 1984-86, 88, 90; speaker to Wash. Women's Employment and Edn., Tacoma, 1983—. *Since not all days are created equal, Madeline Gerwick-Brodeur offers good timing for new business ventures, product introductions, new team starts or major events, to get them off to a good start and assure the best possible outcomes. Her 15 years of business experience, 20 years of cycle and timing experience, plus astrological certification, uniquely qualifies her for this work. Her Good Timing Guide provides daily cycles for all types of business activities and includes quarterly newsletters with trends and special opportunity days.* Writer daily column for Zodiac Zone, 1995-96, Online Noetic Network; pub. The Good Timing Guide; co-author The Complete Idiot's Guide To Astrology, 1997, Pocket Idiot's Guide to Horoscopes, 1998. Bd. dirs. Kepler Coll. of Astrol. Arts and Scis. Recipient Jack E. Chase award for Outstanding Svc. and Contbr. Northcon Founder's Orgn., 1988. Mem. Electronic Mfrs. Assn. (sec. 1982, sec.-treas. 1988, v.p. 1989), Inst. Noetic Scis., Internat. Soc. for Astrol. Rsch., Wash. State Astrol. Assn. (bd. dirs. 1996-98), Phi Kappa Phi. Avocations: writing, healing arts, metaphysics. E-mail: madelinegb@aol.com. Office: Astro Cycles PO Box 27065 Seattle WA 98125-1465

GERYE, ROBERT ALLEN, secondary school administrator; b. Topeka, Oct. 6, 1953; s. Allen Francis and Marye Ruth (Webster) G.; m. Cathy Jean Dunaway, June 19, 1981; 1 child, Rebecca Ann; stepchildren: Zachary Shelton, Gabriel Shelton. BA, Washburn U., 1974; MA, U. Kans., 1977, postgrad., 1991. Cert. principal, Kans., tchr., Colo. Tchr., chmn. dept. lang. arts Blue Valley High Sch., Overland Park, Kans., 1974-81; pres. Kids' Express, Inc., Topeka, 1981-87; asst. prin., dir. lang. arts Ft. Scott (Kans.) High Sch., 1987-88; prin. Jefferson West High Sch., Meriden, Kans., 1988-91; adminstr. Bonanza High Sch., Las Vegas, Nev., 1991; asst. prin. Western High Sch., Las Vegas, 1992—; prin. Las Vegas Acad. Internat. Studies, Performing & Visual Arts, Las Vegas; prof. edn. U. Phoenix, Las Vegas, 1996—; adj. instr. English Johnson County C.C., Overland Park, 1977-91; adj. asst. prof. Washburn U., Topeka, 1981-87; lectr. English U. Kans., Lawrence, 1985-87; speaker at profl. confs; adj. prof. English, C.C. So. Nev., 1991—, adj. prof. English and Edn., 1992—; presenter Writing Process in Action North Cen. Kans. Regional Svc. Ctr., 1990, 97, 98, Nat. Effective Schs. Conf., Phoenix, 1991, Kans. Dept. Edn. Effective Sch. Conf., Wichita, 1991; facilitor Adminstrs. Retreat, 1991. Author: Grasping the Sunset, 1978, Auroral Spring, 1979; developer Ft. Scott Writing Program, 1987-88. Recipient Community Svc. Edn. award Las Vegas C.C., 1998. Mem. United Sch. Adminstrs. (speaker 1989), Nat. Assn. Secondary Sch. Prins., ASCD, Nat. Coun. Tchrs. of English, Nat. Sch. Conf. Inst. Exec. Leadership Acad. Office: Las Vegas Acad Internat Studies and Performing Arts 315 S 7th St Las Vegas NV 89101-5894

GERZSO, GUNTHER, painter, graphic artist; b. Mexico City, June 17, 1915. Exhbns. include FIAC Art Contemporain, Grand Palais, Paris, 1978, Inst. Fine Arts, Mex., 1980, El Arbol Fla., 1981-82, Mus du Petit Palais, 1982, Mary-Ann Martin Fine Arts, N.Y.C., 1984, Galeria de Arte Mex., 1990, others. Guggenheim fellow, 1973; recipient Nat Prize Fine Arts, Mex., 1978. Office: care George Belcher Gallery 74 New Montgomery St Ste 750 San Francisco CA 94105-3411*

GESHELL, RICHARD STEVEN, lawyer; b. Colorado Springs, Colo., Aug. 6, 1943; s. Peter Steven and Ann Elizabeth (Irwin) G.; m. Carol Ann Reed, Sept. 6, 1965; 1 child, Carmen Marie. BA in Chemistry, Ariz. State U., 1965; JD, U. Nebr., 1968. Bar: Nebr. 1968, U.S. Dist. Ct. Nebr. 1968, Hawaii 1983, U.S. Dist. Ct. Hawaii 1983, U.S. Ct. Appeals (9th cir.) 1984, U.S. Supreme Ct. 1986. Mem. Robak and Geshell, Columbus, Nebr., 1968-83; ptnr. R. Steven Geshell, Honolulu, 1983—. Served to capt. USAR, 1974-83. Mem. Assn. Trial Lawyers Am., Nebr. Bar Assn., Hawaii Bar Assn., Blue Key (pres. 1964-65), Elks (chief forum 1984, past exalted ruler, trustee), Phi Sigma Kappa (past house mgr, past v.p.). Republican. Home: 1155 Kaluanui Rd Honolulu HI 96825-1357 Office: 6600 Kalanianaole Hwy Ste 116 Honolulu HI 96825-1282

GESSNER, CHERYL ANN, project manager, consultant; b. Perkasie, Pa., Dec. 2, 1954; d. Robert Earl and Myrna Loi (Chappell) Moore; m. Robert James Gessner, Sept. 9, 1972 (div. Jan. 1990); children: Robert J. Jr., William Edward, LisaMarie. BSBA in Internat. Bus. and Mgmt., Regis U., 1995. Prototype mgr. Pittman Corp., Harleysville, Pa., 1971-76; svc. rep. U.S. West Comms., Denver, 1981-83; svc. rep. consumer products AT&T, Denver, 1983-88, phone ctr. mgr. consumer products divsn., 1988-92, field supplier mgr. NCS-competitive access providers mgmt., 1993-95, access performance profl./bus. developer of new vendors, 1995-96, project mgr. local infrastructure and access mgmt., 1996-98, program mgr. local svcs. initiatives, 1998—. Parent mem. steering com. Aurora (Colo.) Pub. Schs., 1996—; foster parent Adams County Dept. Social Svcs., Denver, 1991-94; chmn. AT&T Colo. State phone ctrs. consumer products United Way, Colo., 1988-92. Recipient Cert. of Appreciation USAF, 1984. Democrat. Avocations: camping, grandchildren, cooking, fishing. Fax: (303) 749-6595. E-mail: cgessner@att.com. Home: 2371 Joliet St Aurora CO 80010-1307 Office: AT&T 7630 S Chester St Ste 300 Englewood CO 80112

GETREU, IAN E(DWIN), electronics engineer; b. Melbourne, Australia, Sept. 14, 1943; s. Leo and Matylda Getreu; m. Beverly S. Salmenson, June 5, 1983. BE with honors, U. Melbourne, 1965, M Engring. Sci., 1967; postgrad., UCLA, 1966-67; PhD, U. Calif., Berkeley, 1972. Sr. engr. Tektronix Inc., Beaverton, Oreg., 1972-79, mgr. integrated cir. computer aided design devel., 1979-83, mgr. advanced products mktg., 1983-85, scientist advanced products, 1985-86; v.p., modeling Analogy Inc., Beaverton, 1986-92, v.p. engring., 1992-94, v.p. tech. devel., 1994—, also bd. dirs., 1986-90; lectr. U. New South Wales, Sydney, Australia, 1974-75; chmn. Computer Aided Network Design Com., 1980-82. Author: Modeling the Bipolar Transistor, 1976. Bd. dirs. Jewish Fedn. of Portland, 1986-93, v.p., 1989-93; chair Oreg. Am. Israel Pub. Affairs Com., 1994-96. Mem. IEEE (sr.) (cirs. and systems soc. v.p. confs. 1990-91), Internat. Conf. Computer Aided Design (chmn. 1986). Home: PO Box 1356 Beaverton OR 97075-1356

GETREU, SANFORD, city planner; b. Cleve., Mar. 9, 1930; s. Isadore and Tillie (Kuchinsky) G.; B.A. in Architecture, Ohio State U., 1953; M.A. in Regional Planning, Cornell U., 1955; m. Gara Eileen Smith, Dec. 8, 1952 (div. Feb. 1983); children—David Bruce, Gary Benjamin, Allen Dana; m. Kelly Heim, Aug. 8, 1988. Resident planner Mackesey & Reps., consultants, Rome, N.Y., 1955-56; planning dir., Rome, 1956-57; dir. gen. planning, Syracuse, N.Y., 1957-59, dep. commr. planning, 1959-62, commr. planning, 1962-65; planning dir. San Jose, Calif., 1965-74; urban planning cons., 1974—; pres. Sanford Getreu, AICP, Inc., vis. lectr., critic Cornell U., 1960-65, Syracuse U., 1962-65, Stanford, 1965, San Jose State Coll., 1965, Santa Clara U., Calif. State Poly. Coll., DeAnza Coll., San Jose City Coll., U. Calif. at Berkeley; pres. planning dept. League of Calif. Cities, 1973-74; advisor State of Calif. Office of Planning and Research. Past bd. dirs. Theater Guild, San Jose, Triton Mus., San Jose. Mem. Am. Soc. Cons. Planners, Am. Planning Assn., Am. Inst. Cert. Planners, Bay Area Planning Dirs. Assn. (v.p. 1965-74, mem. exec. com. 1973-74), Assn. Bay Area Govts. (regional planning com. 1967-74). Club: Rotary. Home: 105 Coronado Ave Los Altos CA 94022-2222 Office: 4966 El Camino Real Ste 101 Los Altos CA 94022-1406

GETTY, GORDON PETER, composer, philanthropist; b. Los Angeles, Dec. 20, 1933; s. J. Paul and Ann Rork (Light) G.; m. Ann Getty; 4 children. Studied, voice with Easton Kent, piano with Robert Vetlesen, theory with Sol Joseph, 1961-62; BS, San Francisco Conservatory Music, hon. music degree, 1981; hon. music degree, Pepperdine U., 1985; hon. doctorate, Mannes Coll. Music, N.Y.C., 1986. Former cons. Getty Oil Co., dir.; former chmn. LSB Leakey Found., Pasadena, Calif., now trustee. Works include opera in two acts Plump Jack, commnd. by Globe Shakespeare Ctr., London, performed by San Francisco Symphony, 1985, also Scene One broadcast live from Davies Symphony Hall, San Francisco, Mar. 1985; Emily Dickinson Song Cycle The White Election, 30 performances U.S. and abroad, 1981-85, also broadcast live from Nat. Gallery Art, Washington, 1985; Victorian Scenes, performed San Francisco Girls Chorus U. Calif., Berkeley, WInifred Baker Choral, 1985; Nine Piano Pieces performed by Stewart Gordon, 1985; A Cappella Choruses and Piano Works broadcast live Georgetown U., Washington, Apr., 1985; author monograph on White Election, poems My Uncle's House, 1984, other poetry. Adv. dir. Met. Opera, 1977—; trustee Mannes Coll. Music, 1982—; dir. San Francisco Symphony, 1979—. Recipient Golden Plate award Am. Acad. Achievement, 1985, Achievement Arts award Northwood Inst., 1985. Office: Rork Music Publ 1 Embarcadero Ctr Ste 1050 San Francisco CA 94111-3698*

GETZ, JOSEPHINE ARLENE, english educator; b. Pocatelo, Idaho, Mar. 25, 1944; d. James K. and Edna D. (Panel) Bratton; divorced; children: Richard, Scott, Matthew; m. Frank V. Salata, Oct. 16, 1996. BA, U. Calif., L.A., 1967; MA in Edn., Calif. Luth. U., 1975. Cert. life tchrr., Calif.; cert. adminstrv., Calif. Tchr. Sylmar H.S., 1968-69, 79-80, North Hollywood H.S., 1970-72, Kennedy H.S., 1974-75, San Fernando H.S., 1976-77, Van Nuys H.S., 1981-82, Chatsworth H.S., 1984—. Contbr. articles to profl. jours. Field trip coord. Boy Scouts Am., Woodland Hills, Calif., 1988-92. Name Outstanding Tchr. U. Calif., San Diego, 1993, 94, U. Calif., Santa Barbara, 1995. mem. Nat. Coun. Tchrs. Engl. Avocations: stained glass, skiing, tole painting, tennis. Office: Chatsworth H S 10027 Lurline Ave Chatsworth CA 91311

GEYSER, LYNNE M., lawyer, writer; b. Queens, N.Y., Mar. 28, 1938; d. Henry and Shirley Dannenberg; m. Lewis P. Geyser, 1956 (div. 1974); 1 child, Russell B. Geyser. BA, Queens Coll., 1960; JD, UCLA, 1968. Bar: Calif. 1969. Atty. Zagon, Schiff, Hirsch & Levine, Beverly Hills, Calif., 1969-70; atty., registered legis. advocate Beverly Hills, Malibu, Calif., 1973-75; atty. Freshman, Marantz, Comsky & Deutsch, Beverly Hills, Malibu, Calif., 1971-74; prof. law Glendale (Calif.) U. Law, 1974-76, U. Iowa Sch. Law, Iowa City, 1976-77, Pepperdine U., Malibu, 1977-78; pvt. practice Newport Beach, Calif., 1978-81, San Clemente, 1978—; part-time prof. law Western State Law Sch., Fullerton, Calif., 1978; cons. atty. The Irvine Co., Newport Beach, 1981-86, Std. Mgmt. Co., L.A., 1987-88; instr. Saddleback Coll., Mission Viejo, Calif., early 1990's; lectr., instr. Calif. Assn. Realtors Grad. Realty Inst., 1972-78, U. So. Calif. brokers tng. courses, L.A., 1978-80, UCLA real estate and corp. courses for paralegals, 1973-76; creator and lectr. course on disclosure for licensees, L.A., San Diego and Orange Counties, Calif., 1978-81; faculty advisor, rev. advisor Glendale U. Coll. Law, 1975-76. Chief articles editor UCLA Law Rev., 1967; adv. bd. The Rsch. Jour., 1976; contbr. poetry and short stories to jours. Mem. exec. bd. L.A. County Art Mus. Contemporary Art Coun., L.A., 1971-73; bd. trustees Westwood (L.A.) Art Assn., 1974; bd. govs. La Costa Beach Homeowners Assn., Malibu, 1975; pres. Dana Point (Calif.) Coastal Arts Coun., 1989-90; teaching participant Jr. Achievement, Newport Beach, 1985. Recipient 6 Am. Jurisprudence awards, 1966-68, 2 West Hornbook awards, 1967; nom. Douglas Law Clk. UCLA Law Sch., 1967. Fellow The Legal Inst.; mem. AALS (chair-elect environ. law sect. 1977), San Clemente Sunrise Rotary, Order of Coif. Avocations: world travel, fine arts, writing, computers, performing arts, graphics. Office: PO Box 4715 San Clemente CA 92674-4715

GHANTI, CHANDRA RATILAL, engineering executive; b. Surat, India, Mar. 23, 1947; came to U.S., 1970; s. Ratilal and Taraben G.; m. Renuka Ghanti, Mar. 8, 1950. BSEE, W.Va. Inst. Tech., 1974; MSEE, Ohio U., 1978. Test engr. Memorex Corp., Santa Clara, Calif.; cons. engr. Moon Assocs., San Jose, Calif.; v.p. JIP Products Finishing, Santa Clara. Home: 1120 Machado Ln San Jose CA 95127-4409 Office: JIP Products Finishing 1500 Norman Ave Santa Clara CA 95054-2028

GHARDA, LAURENT KIRK, software company executive. AB in Computer Sci., U. Calif., Berkeley, 1979. 3d party mgr. Hewlett Packard, Palo Alto, Calif., 1980-90; v.p. sales Veritas Software, Mountain View, Calif., 1990-95; pres., CEO QualSoft, Palo Alto, 1995-96; v.p. sales and mktg. Willows Software, Saratoga, Calif., 1996-97; v.p. mktg. Award Software (now Phoenix Tech.), Mountain View, 1997-98, Phoenix Tech., San Jose, 1998—. Office: Phoenix Tech Ltd 411 E Plumeria Dr San Jose CA 95134

GHENT, GREGORY LOUIS, art appraiser, artist; b. Fort Collins, Colo., July 25, 1949; s. Dwight and Amy (Irwin) G. BA, U. of the Pacific, 1971. Dir. modern art Butterfields Auction House, San Francisco, 1994—; curator African and Pre-Colombian Art various univ. mus. Author: John Haley Biography, 1993, African Alchemy, 1994; contbg. editor Visual Dialog, 1975-78, Arts D'Afrique Noire, 1980. Pres. Friends Ethnic Art, San Francisco, 1989-93; chmn. adv. bd. The Hearst Art Gallery, St. Mary's Coll., Moraga, Calif., 1990-92; trustee The Haley Charitable Fund, San Francisco, 1994—, San Francisco Craft and Folk Art Mus., 1998—. Office: PO Box 70031 Point Richmond CA 94807

GHIRAGOSSIAN, ALICIA, poetess in Armenian, Spanish, English; came to U.S., 1971; adj. instr. in modern poetry, UCLA; lectr., conductor of seminars in universities world wide. Author: 39 volumes of poetry. Nominated for Nobel prize in literature. E-mail: PoetAlicia@aol.com. Office: Modern Poetry Ctr 1147 E Broadway Ste 245 Glendale CA 91205

GHISELIN, BREWSTER, author, English language educator emeritus; b. Webster Groves, Mo., June 13, 1903; s. Horace and Eleanor (Weeks) G.; m. Olive F. Franks, June 7, 1929; children: Jon Brewster, Michael Tenant. A.B., UCLA, 1927; M.A., U. Calif.-Berkeley, 1928, student, 1931-33; student, Oxford U., Eng., 1928-29. Asst. in English U. Calif., Berkeley, 1931-33; instr. English U. Utah, 1929-31, 34-38, lectr., 1938-39, asst. prof., 1939-46, assoc. prof., 1946-50, prof., 1950-71, prof. emeritus, 1971, Distinguished Research prof., 1967-68; dir. Writers' Conf., 1947-66; poetry editor Rocky Mt. Rev., 1937-46; assoc. editor Western Rev., 1946-49; lectr. creativity, cons. Inst. Personality Assessment and Research, U. Calif., Berkeley, 1957-58; editorial adv. bd. Concerning Poetry, 1968—. Author: Against the Circle, 1946, The Creative Process, 1952, new paperback edit., 1985, 95, The Nets, 1955, Writing, 1959, Country of the Minotaur, 1970, (with others) The Form Discovered: Essays on the Achievement of Andrew Lytle, 1973, Light, 1978, Windrose: Poems, 1929-1979, 1980, (with others) Contemporary Authors, 1989; (poems) Flame, 1991. Bd. advisors Silver Mountain Found.

Ford Found. fellow, 1952-53; recipient award Nat. Inst. Arts and Letters, 1970; Blumenthal-Leviton-Blonder prize Poetry mag., 1973; Levinson prize, 1978; William Carlos Williams award Poetry Soc. Am., 1981; Gov.'s award for arts Utah Arts Council, 1982; LHD hc. U of Utah, 1994. Mem. MLA, Utah Acad. Scis., Arts and Letters (Charles Redd award), Phi Beta Kappa, Phi Kappa Phi. Home (winter): 1115 Jefferson Way Laguna Beach CA 92651-3022 also (summer): 1747 Princeton Ave Salt Lake City UT 84108-1810

GHORMLEY, WILLIAM FREDERICK, elementary school educator, music educator; b. Yakima, Wash., Oct. 5, 1954; s. John Thomas and Eileen Marie (Clyde) G. B in Music Edn., U. Portland, 1977; MS in Tchg. and Music, Portland State U., 1992. Cert. tchr., Wash. Elem. music specialist Evergreen Sch. Dist., Vancouver, Wash., 1977—, mem. bldg. project team, 1990-92; grad. tchg. asst. Portland (Oreg.) State U., 1990-92. Composer, arranger (choral music) Spirit of God, 1986, Peace Like a River, 1990, Blow Ye Winds, 1991. Mem. sect. chair Portland Symphonic Choir, 1990-92; conductor Vancouver's (Wash.) Men's Chorus, 1993—, Centennial Civic Chorale, Vancouver, 1984-89; mem. S.W. Wash. Fairness Coalition, 1993—. Recipient Conductor's award Vancouver's Men's Chorus, 1994. Mem. Wash. Music Educators Assn. (conf. planning team 1993-94), Music Educators Nat. Conf., Soc. for Gen. Music (adv. bd. 1983-85). Office: Evergreen Sch Dist PO Box 8910 Vancouver WA 98668-8910

GHYMN, ESTHER MIKYUNG, English educator, writer; b. Seoul; d. Yong Shik and Kyung hee (Park) Kim; m. Kyung-Il Ed Ghymn; children: Jennifer, Eugene. MA, U. Hawaii; MAT, U. Pitts.; PhD, U. Nev., Reno, 1990. Lectr. English, U. Nev., Reno, 1993—, ESL coord., 1996—, mem. ethnic studies bd., 1998—. Author: The Shapes and Styles of Asian American Prose Fiction, 1990, Images of Asian American Women Writers, 1995; editor APANN News. Bd. dirs. Asian Americans N. Nev., 1992-95, Multicultural Office, Truckee Meadows C.C., Reno, 1994-96, mem. steering com. Access to Success, 1996; mem. affirmative action adv. bd. U. Nev., Reno, 1998, ethnic studies bd., 1997—, women's studies bd., 1998—; series editor Peter Lang Pub. Mem. Phi Beta Delta (sec.). Avocations: teaching, writing, reading, travel.

GIACOLINI, EARL L., agricultural products company executive. Vice-chmn. Sun Diamond Growers of Calif., Pleasanton; chmn., bd. dirs. Sun Sweet Growers, Yuba City, CA. Office: Sun Sweet Growers Inc 901 N Walton Ave Yuba City CA 95993-8634

GIANNULLI, MOSSIMO, designer, apparel business executive. Owner, chmn. bd. Mossimo Inc., Irvine, Calif. Office: Mossimo Inc 2450 White Rd 2nd Fl Irvine CA 92614-6250*

GIARELLI, ANDREW LINO, publisher, educator; b. Bridgeport, Conn., June 3, 1953; s. Andrew Fleming and Concetta (Caporelli) G.; m. Kimberley Anne Miske, Sept. 25, 1993. BA, Yale U., 1975; PhD, SUNY, Buffalo, 1984. Reporter Middleton (Conn.) Press, 1975-76; asst. prof. dept. comm. Utah State U., Logan, 1988-93; editor, pub. Edging West mag., Portland, Oreg., 1995—; adj. asst. prof. dept. journalism and mass comm. NYU, N.Y.C., 1984-88, dept. English Portland State U., 1996—. Contbr. articles to profl. jours. Faculty Rsch. grantee Utah State U., 1991-92; Fulbright prof. Coun. Internat. Exch. Scholars, 1993, Oreg. Chautauqua scholar Oreg. Coun. Humanities, 1998—. Office: Edging West Mag 2539 SW Spring Garden St Portland OR 97219-3974

GIBB, ROBERTA LOUISE, lawyer, artist; b. Cambridge, Mass., Nov. 2, 1942; d. Thomas Robinson Pieri and Jean Knox Gibb. Student, Boston Mus. Fine Arts, 1962-65; BS, U. Calif., La Jolla, 1969; JD, N.E. Sch. Law, 1978. Bar: Mass. 1978. Rsch. asst. in epistemology MIT, Cambridge, 1972—; legis. aid Mass. State Legislature, 1973-75; pvt. practice law, 1980—; cert. title examiner Mass. Land Ct., Boston, 1987—; assoc. Cohen & Burg Attys., Boston, 1988-89; founder, pres. Inst. for the Study of Natural Sys., 1978—, R.L. Gibb Enterprises, 1994. Author: The Art of Inflation, 1978, To Boston With Love, 1980; sculptor and painter. Named to Road Runner's Hall of Fame, Alexandria, Va., Acad. of Women Achievers YWCA, Spl. Recognition, 1996. Mem. U.S. Assn. Club Rome, Boston Athletic Assn., Rockport Art Assn., Alumni Assn. Univ. Calif. Avocation: long-distance running, first woman to run in Boston Marathon, 1966, 1st woman finisher, 1967, 68.

GIBBON, TIM, communications executive. Chmn., pres., CEO JWT Specialized Comm., Inc., L.A. Office: JWT Specialized Comm Inc 6500 Wilshire Blvd 21st Fl Los Angeles CA 90048-4920*

GIBBONS, JAMES ARTHUR, congressman; b. Reno, Dec. 16, 1944; s. Leonard A. and Matilda (Hancock) G.; m. T. Dawn Sanders-Snelling, June 21, 1986; children: Christopher, Jennifer, James A. Jr. BS in Geology, U. Nev., Reno, 1967, MS in Mining Geology, 1973; JD, Southwestern U., 1979. Bar: Nev. 1982, U.S. Dist. Ct. Nev. 1982. Hydrologist U.S. Fed. Water Master, Reno, 1963-67; geologist Union Carbide Co., Reno, 1972-75; comml. pilot Western Airlines, Inc., L.A., 1979-88; pilot Delta Airlines, Salt Lake City, 1988—; sr. land mgr., atty. Homestake Mining Co., Reno, 1980-82; pvt. practice Reno, 1982—; mem. 105th Congress from Nev. 2nd Dist., 1997—; environ. atty. Alaskan Wilderness Soc., Anchorage, 1982-83; mem. Congressional Com. on Nat. Security, 1997—, Resources, 1997—, Intelligence, 1998—. Contbr. articles to profl. pubs. Mem. Nev. Coun. on Econ. Edn., 1986; mem. Nev. State Assembly, 1988—. Lt. col. Nev. Air Nat. Guard, Persian Gulf, 1990-91; with USAF, 1967-72. Decorated DFC. Mem. Assn. Trial Lawyers of Am., Nev. Trial Lawyers Assn., Rocky Mt. Mineral Law Found., Comml Law League Am., Am. Inst. Mining Engrs., Nev. Landman's Assn. (chmn. 1981-82, cons. atty. 1982-83). Republican. Avocation: flying. Office: US Ho Reps 100 Cannon Washington DC 20515-2802

GIBBS, DENIS LAUREL, radiologist; b. Wayne, Mich., Mar. 6, 1945; s. Laurel Pierce and Alwyn Marie (Larson) G.; m. Paula Kay Lynn, Sept. 6, 1974 (div. Aug. 1988); children: Jeremy Paul, Matthew Ryan, Kevin Christopher, Denis Patrick; m. Kathleen Marie DeLaFuente, July 9, 1989; 1 child, Andrew Zachery. BS, Andrews U., Berrien Springs, Mich., 1967, postgrad., 1967-69; DO, Kansas City Coll. Osteopathic Medicine, 1974. Bd. cert. radiology, bd. cert. nuclear medicine Am. Osteo. Coll. Radiology. Intern, radiology resident Doctors' Hosps., Columbus, Ohio, 1974-78, staff radiologist, 1978; chmn. dept. radiology Rocky Mountain Hosp., Denver, 1978-88, vice chief of staff, 1982, chief of staff, 1983, 84; chmn. dept. radiology Colo. Plain Med. Ctr. Regional Trauma Ctr., Ft. Morgan, 1988—, vice chief of staff, 1992; med.-legal cons., Colo., Calif., Fla., 1979—; consulting radiologist East Morgan Hosp., Luth. Health Sys., Brush, colo., 1988—; CEO IRS Radiology Cons., P.C., Ft. Morgan, 1988—. Med. reviewer Post Grad. Medicine. Acad. booster Fort Morgan H.S./Morgan C.C. Mem. Am. Osteopathic Assn., Am. Osteopathic Coll. Radiology, Nat. Assn. Seventh-Day Adventist Osteopaths, Colo. Med. Soc., Colo. Osteopathic Soc., Ft. Morgan Med. Soc., Colo. Radiology Soc. Republican. Avocations: snorkeling, skin diving, racquetball, sports car enthusiast and owner. Home: PO Box 1243 Fort Morgan CO 80701-1243 Office: IRS Radiology Cons PC 1000 Lincoln St Fort Morgan CO 80701-3210

GIBBS, DOROTHY SCOTT, retired Latin educator; b. Chgo., May 8, 1927; d. Ewing Carruth and Dorothy Eleanor (Carnine) Scott; m. George Minnis Gibbs, Apr. 16, 1949; 1 child, Peter Carnine. Student, Colo. Coll., 1944-45; BA magna cum laude, Syracuse (N.Y.) U., 1948; MAT in French, U. Va., 1964. Cert. French, German and Latin tchr., Ohio. Tchr. English Aoyama Gakuin U., Tokyo, 1950-51; sec. Sch. of Nursing U. Va., Charlottesville, 1953-54; sec. Westminster Presbyn. Ch., Charlottesville, 1954-56; asst. dir. pub. rels. Internat. Christian U., Tokyo, 1957-59; tchr. Brookville (Ohio) High Sch., 1960-61, Fairmont High Sch., Kettering, Ohio, 1968-90; sponsor Jr. Classical League, Kettering, 1972-90; state and nat. officers sponsor Ohio Jr. Classical League, 1978, 80, 84, 87, 88, 89; sponsor Ohio Sr. Classical League, 1990-92; team mem. North Cen. Accrediting Team, Bellbrook, Ohio, 1984; founder Arthur Rackham Soc., 1984, pres., 1984-97, pres. emeritus, 1997—. Editor Newsletter, 1984-97. French coach Dayton Opera Fun-atics, 1979-86; host family for fgn. students, Kettering, 1968, 81-83, 85; tchr. in space candidate NASA, 1985; vol. trail worker Am. Hiking Assn., Mont., Alaska, 1986, 87, Calif., 1992. Jennings Found. scholar, 1986-87; recipient Tchr. Achievement award Ashland Oil, 1988, Ed Phinney Book award Nat. Jr. Classical League, 1990; named to Chester A. Roush Ednl. Hall of Fame, 1992. Mem. Am. Classical League (McKinley scholar 1985), Ohio Classical Conf. (coun. mem. 1979-82, 85-88, Hildesheim Vase 1975, 82), Ohio Fgn. Lang. Assn. (Leona Glenn award 1984), NEA, Kettering Classroom Tchrs. Assn. (workshop organizer 1973, 78, 88), Delta Zeta (sec. Syracuse chpt. 1947-48), Delta Kappa Gamma (com. chmn., Ruth Grimes scholar 1985). Republican. Presbyterian. Home: 1240 Devils Gulch Rd Estes Park CO 80517-9500

GIBBS, WILLIAM HAROLD, finance company executive; b. Evanston, Ill., Apr. 10, 1950; s. Harold William and Margaret Rose (Heidbreder) G. BS, Ariz. State U., 1973; MBA, U. Ill., 1975. CPA. Mgr. Price Waterhouse, Phoenix, 1975-82; chief fin. officer Apollo Group Inc., Phoenix, 1983-87; pres. U. Phoenix, 1987-98; sr. v.p. Apollo Group, Inc., Phoenix, 1998—. Office: Apollo Group Inc 4615 E Elwood St Phoenix AZ 85040-1958*

GIBLETT, PHYLIS LEE WALZ, middle school educator; b. Denver, July 17, 1945; d. Henry and Leah (Pabst) Walz; B.S.B.A. (Estelle Hunter scholar 1963, Denver Classroom Tchr.'s scholar 1963, Outstanding Bus. Edn. Student scholar 1967), U. Denver, 1967, MBA, 1969; m. Thomas Giblett, May 31, 1975; children: Leann Ruth, Douglas Henry, John Peter. Tchr. bus. Aurora (Colo.) South Middle Sch., info. specialist, 1996—; tchr. Aurora Pub. Schs., 1967-80, 82-86, 88-96, on leave, 1980-82, 86-88, chmn. bus. dept., 1972-79; evening tchr. S.E. Met. Bd. Coop Services, 1967-68, post secondary/adult classes Aurora Pub. Schs., 1972-75, C.C. Denver, North Campus, 1973, Aurora Pub. Schs. Adult Edn., 1983-84; mem. Aurora Pub. Sch. System, mem. tech. com. 1991—, dist. tech. trainer, 1992—, Program Cadre mem., 1995-97, tech. cadre facilitator, 1996—, steering com. shared decision making, 1990-96, zero tolerance com., 1992-94, facilitator Mentor com., 1991-92, exploratory tchr. facilitator, 1992-96; mem. dist. tech. com. South Middle Sch., Aurora Dist. Tech. Com., 1975-79; adviser chpt. Future Bus. Leaders Am., 1976-78; mem. Colo. Curriculum Specialist Com., 1976-77. Treas. Aurora Coun. PTA, 1987-89, Century Elem. Sch. PTA, 1988-89, reflections chmn., 1987-89, 90-93; mem. PTA. Named Miss Future Bus. Tchr., Phi Beta Lambda of Colo., 1965. Mem. Nat., Mountain-Plains (participant leadership conf. 1977), Colo. Bus. Edn. Assns. (pres. 1976-77), Colo. Educators for/About Bus., Am., Colo. vocat. assns., NEA, Colo., Aurora edn. assns., Delta Pi Epsilon (pres.-elect Eta chpt. 1978, pres. 1980-81). Republican. Lutheran.

GIBNEY, FRANK BRAY, publisher, editor, writer, foundation executive; b. Scranton, Pa., Sept. 21, 1924; s. Joseph James and Edna May (Wetter) G.; m. Harriet Harvey, Dec. 10, 1948 (div. 1957); children: Alex, Margot; m. Harriet C. Suydam, Dec. 14, 1957 (div. 1971); children: Frank, James, Thomas; m. Hiroko Doi, Oct. 5, 1972; children: Elise, Josephine. BA, Yale U., 1945; DLitt (hon.), Kyung Hee U., Seoul, Korea, 1974. Corr., assoc. editor Time mag., N.Y.C., Tokyo and London, 1947-54; sr. editor Newsweek, N.Y.C., 1954-57; staff writer, editorial writer Life mag., N.Y.C., 1957-61; pub., pres. SHOW mag., N.Y.C., 1961-64; pres. Ency. Brit. (Japan), Tokyo, 1965-69; pres. TBS-Brit., Tokyo, 1969-75, vice chmn., 1976—; v.p. Ency. Brit., Inc., Chgo., 1975-79; vice chmn., bd. editors Ency. Brit., Chgo., 1978—; pres. Pacific Basin Inst., Pomona Coll., Claremont, Calif., 1979—; prof. Pomona Coll., 1997—; bd. dirs. U.S. Com. for Pacific Econ. Cooperation, 1988—, v.p., 1993-95; cons. com. on space and aeros. U.S. Ho. of Reps., Washington, 1957-59; vice chmn. Japan-U.S. Friendship Commn., 1984-90, U.S.-Japan Com. Edn. and Cultural Interchange, 1984-90. Author: Five Gentlemen of Japan, 1953, The Frozen Revolution, 1959, (with Peter Deriabin) The Secret World, 1960, The Operators, 1961, The Khrushchev Pattern, 1961, The Reluctant Space Farers, 1965, Japan: The Fragile Super-Power, 1975, rev. edit., 1996, Miracle by Design, 1983, The Pacific Century, 1992, Korea's Quiet Revolution, 1993; co-author: The Battle for Okinawa, 1995; editor: The Penkovskiy Papers, 1965, Senso, 1995, Unlocking The Bureaucrats' Kingdom, 1998. Served to lt. USNR, 1942-46. Decorated Order of the Rising Sun 3d Class Japan, Order of Sacred Treasure 2d Class Japan. Mem. Council on Fgn. Relations, Tokyo Fgn. Corr. Club, Am. C.of C. (Tokyo), Japan-Am. Soc., Japan Soc. Roman Catholic. Clubs: Century Assn., Yale (N.Y.C.); Tokyo; Tavern, The Arts (Chgo.). Home: 1901 E Las Tunas Rd Santa Barbara CA 93103-1745

GIBSON, BEATRICE ANN, retired systems analyst, artist; b. Canton, Ohio, Feb. 4, 1926; d. Paul Cummins Gibson and Luella Mae (Clements) Gibson Ward. Student, Cleve. Sch. Art, 1941-44, Carnegie Mellon U., 1945-47; BA, U. Chgo., 1951; postgrad., Northwestern U., 1955-57, Oxbow Summer Sch., 1957-59, Sch. Art Inst. Chgo., 1956-60; ind. study, Italy, Greece, Spain, France, England, 1960-61, France, Netherlands, England, 1987; postgrad., EBA Sch. Art, San Francisco, 1988. Procedure analyst U.S. Steel Corp., Chgo., 1955-61; methods analyst Continental Ins. Cos., San Francisco, 1962-64; forms, methods analyst Ins. & Securities Inc., San Francisco, 1964-74; sr. systems analyst Calif. State Automobile Assn., San Francisco, 1974-91; ret., 1991; mem., editor, officer San Francisco Ins. Women's Assn., 1962-68. One-woman exhibits include Diablo Valley Coll., Pleasant Hill, Calif., 1983, EBA Sch. Art, San Francisco, 1991; group exhbns. include Old Town Art Fair, Chgo., 1955, Navy Pier Exhbn., 1956, Laguna Beach (Calif.) Gallery, 1963, San Francisco Civic Ctr. Exhbn., 1964, Hayward (Calif.) Art Show, 1983, EBA Sch. Art, 1988-93. Recipient Recognition award Calif. State Automobile Assn., 1991. Mem. Assn. Systems Mgmt. (emeritus, editor, sec. 1968—, v.p. 1973-74, pres. San Francisco chpt. 1975-76, Disting. Svc. Merit award 1978, Achievement award 1985).

GIBSON, ELISABETH JANE, principal; b. Salina, Kans., Apr. 28, 1937; d. Cloyce Wesley and Margaret Mae (Yost) Kasson; m. William Douglas Miles, Jr., Aug. 20, 1959 (div.); m. Harry Benton Gibson Jr., July 1, 1970. AB, Colo. State Coll., 1954-57; MA, San Francisco State Coll., 1967-68; EdD, U. No. Colo., 1978; postgrad. U. Denver, 1982. Cert. tchr., prin., Colo. Tchr. elem. schs., Santa Paula, Calif., 1957-58, Salina, Kans., 1958-63, Goose Bay, Labrador, 1963-64, Jefferson County, Colo., 1965-66, Topeka, 1966-67; diagnostic tchr. Ctrl. Kans. Diagnostic Remedial Edn. Ctr., Salina, 1968-70; instr. Loretto Heights Coll., Denver, 1970-72; co-owner Ednl. Cons. Enterprises, Inc., Greeley, Colo., 1974-77; resource coord. Region VIII Resource Access Project Head Start Mile High Consortium, Denver, 1976-77; exec. dir. Colo. Fedn. Coun. Exceptional Children, Denver, 1976-77; asst. prof. Met. State Coll., Denver, 1979; dir. spl. edn. N.E. Colo. Bd. Coop. Edn. Svcs., Haxtun, Colo., 1979-82; prin. elem. jr. h.s., Elizabeth, Colo., 1982-84; prin., spl. projects coord. Summit County Schs., Frisco, Colo., 1985-92; prin. Frisco Elem. Sch., 1985-91; cons. Montana Dept. Edn., 1978-79, Love Pub. Co., 1976-78, Colo. Dept. Inst., 1974-75; cons. Colo. Dept. Edn., 1984-85, mem. proposal reading com., 1987—; pres. Found. Exceptional Children, 1980-81; pres. bd. dirs. N.E. Colo. Svcs. Handicapped, 1981-82; bd. dirs. Dept. Ednl. Specialists, Colo. Assn. Sch. Execs., 1982-84; mem. Colo. Title IV Adv. Coun., 1980-82; mem. Mellon Found. grant steering com. Colo. Dept. Edn., 1984-85; mem. Colo. Dept. Edn. Data Acquisition Reporting and Utilization Com., 1983, Denver City County Commn. for Disabled, 1978-81; chmn. regional edn. com. 1970 White House Conf. Children and Youth; bd. dirs. Advocates for Victims of Assault, 1986-91; mem. adv. bd. Alpine Counseling Ctr., 1986-92; mem. placement alternatives commn. Dept. Social Svcs., 1986—; mem. adv. com. Colo. North Ctrl. Assn., 1988-91; sec. Child Care Resource and Referral Agy., 1992—; mem. Child Care Task Force Summit County, 1989-92; mem. tchr. cert. task force Colo. State Bd. Edn., 1990-91; chair Summit County Interagy. Coord. Coun., 1989-93. Recipient Vol. award Colo. Child Care Assn., 1992, Ann. Svc. award Colo. Fedn. Coun. Exceptional Children, 1981; San Francisco State Coll. fellow, 1967-68. Mem. Colo. Assn. Retarded Citizens, Assn. Supervision Curriculum Devel., Nat. Assn. Elem. Sch. Prins., North Cen. Assn. (state adv. com. 1988-91), Order Eastern Star, Kappa Delta Pi, Pi Lambda Theta, Phi Delta Kappa. Republican. Methodist. Author: (with H. Padzensky) Goal Guide: A minicourse in writing goals and behavioral objectives for special education, 1975; (with H. Padzensky and S. Sporn) Assaying Student Behavior: A minicourse in student assessment techniques, 1974; contbr. articles to profl. jours. Home: 14354 E Caley Ave Aurora CO 80016-1090 Office: Orchard Valley Learning Ctr 15100 E Orchard Rd Aurora CO 80016-3001

GIBSON, GEOF CHARLES, audio engineer; b. San Diego, Aug. 18, 1965; s. William Randolph Gibson and Judith Anne (Aquaviva) Kemp; m. Trebor Laurie Biss, July 4, 1989 (div. June 1992). BS, San Diego State U., 1992. Gen. ptnr. Variable Prodns., San Diego, 1993—; ptnr. Sound Surgeon, San Diego, 1998—. Sound mixer (feature films) Bound, 1996 (Best Fla. Made Feature award Ft. Lauderdale Internat. Film Festival 1996), To Hell With Love, 1998 (Best Romantic Comedy award N.Y. Internat. Film Festival 1998); sound designer (tv comml.) Western Towing/To The Rescue, 1997 (Telly award 1998). Recipient Cert. of Appreciation, White House Comm. Agy., Washington, 1997. Libertarian. Avocations: model airplanes, surfing. E-mail: nagra4@ix.netcom.com. Office: Variable Prodns PO Box 17168 San Diego CA 92177-7168

GIBSON, GEORGE, retired scenic art director; b. Edinburgh, Scotland, Oct. 16, 1904; came to U.S., 1930; s. George and Elizabeth Lawson (Gilchrist) G.; m. Alice Carolyn Milligan, Aug. 9, 1908; 1 child, Jean. Student, Edinburgh Coll. Art, Scotland, 1923-25, Glasgow Sch. Art, Scotland, 1923-25, W.E. Gloyer, Scotland, 1923-28, F. Tolles Chamberlain, Pasadena, Calif., 1934-38. Scenic art dir. Metro Goldwyn Mayer Studios, Culver City, Calif., 1934-69; artist Calif., 1969—. Contbr. articles to profl. jours. Recipient Life Achievements in Arts award Laguna (Calif.) Art Mus. Historical Collections Council, 1991. Fellow Nat. Acad. (Nat. Acad. award 1959); mem. Nat. Watercolor Soc. (life, sec., v.p., pres., Am. chpt. Verda McCracken award 1972, Calif. chpt. 1st award 1953), Am. Watercolor Soc. Protestant. Avocations: watercolor art. Home and Office: 1449 Santa Maria Ave Los Osos CA 93402-1447

GIBSON, L. JAMES, organization administrator, biology educator; b. Brawley, Calif., Sept. 13, 1944; s. Lloyd J. and Adaline R. Gibson; married; children: Deborah, Karina. BA, Pacific Union Coll., Angwin, Calif., 1966, MA, 1968; PhD, Loma Linda U., 1984. Tchr. Bakersfield (Calif.) Adventist Acad., 1967-72, Rio Lindo Adventist Acad., Healdsburg, Calif., 1972-76, Yele SDA Secondary Sch., Sierra Leone, 1976-80; asst. rsch. scientist Geosci. Rsch. Inst., Loma Linda, Calif., 1984-94, dir., 1994—; field conf. organizer Geosci. Rsch. Inst., Loma Linda, 1987, 93, 94, 97, 98. Assoc. editor Origins, 1990-97. Recipient Edmund Jaeger award Loma Linda U. Dept. Biology, 1983. Mem. Am. Soc. Mammalogists, Soc. for Systematic Biology, Soc. for the Study of Evolution. Avocation: birding. Office: Geosci Rsch Inst Loma Linda CA 92350

GIBSON, LAURIE ANN, editor, freelance journalist; b. L.A., Dec. 24, 1962; d. John Alfred and Mary Lorraine (Kinney) G. AA, Pasadena City Coll., 1984, San Diego City Coll., 1992; BA, Calif. State U., Northridge, 1990. Banquet asst., receptionist, sec. The Pasadena Ctr., 1984-90; litigation document analyst Volt Temps., Pasadena, Calif., 1989; proposal writer Community Care Network, San Diego, 1992-94; copy editor Fresno Bee, 1995, North County Times, 1995-96; pres. Word Assn. Editing Svc., San Diego, 1997—; freelance journalist San Diego Community Newspaper Group, 1991-92, Irish Am. Press, L.A., 1991-92; editor The City Times, 1992. Contbr. over 150 articles to various newspapers. Scholar Copley Newspapers, 1991. Mem. Soc. Profl. Journalists, Kappa Tau Alpha. Avocations: sports, photography, outdoor activities, theater, aviation, writing. Home: 811 Agate St Apt 6 San Diego CA 92109-1115 Office: c/o Word Assn Editing Svc 968 Emerald St Ste 62 San Diego CA 92109-2709

GIBSON, MELVIN ROY, pharmacognosy educator; b. St. Paul, Nebr., June 11, 1920; s. John and Jennie Irene (Harvey) G. BS, U. Nebr., 1942, MS, 1947, DSc (hon.), 1985; PhD, U. Ill., 1949. Asst. prof. pharmacognosy Wash. State U., Pullman, 1949-52, assoc. prof., 1952-55, prof., 1955-85, prof. emeritus, 1985—. Editor: Am. Jour. Pharm. Edn, 1956-61; editorial bd., co-author: Remington's Pharm. Sci, 1970, 75, 80, 85; editor, co-author: Studies of a Pharm. Curriculum, 1967; author over 100 articles. Served as arty. officer AUS, 1942-46. Decorated Bronze star, Purple Heart; sr. vis. fellow Orgn. for Econ. Cooperation and Devel., Royal Pharm. Inst. (now part of Uppsala U.) Stockholm, Sweden and U. Leiden (Holland), 1962; recipient Rufus A. Lyman award, 1972, Wash. State U. Faculty Library award, 1984, Disting. Alumnus award U. Nebr., 1999; named Wash. State U. Faculty Mem. of Yr., 1985. Fellow AAAS; assoc. fellow Am. Coll. Apothecaries; mem. AAUP, VFW (life), N.Y. Acad. Scis., Am. Pharm. Assn., Am. Soc. Pharmacognosy (pres. 1964-65), Am. Assn. Coll. Pharmacy (exec. com. 1961-63, bd. dirs. 1977-79, chmn. coun. faculties 1975-76, pres. 1979-80, Disting. Educator award 1984), U.S. Pharmacopeia (revision com. 1970-75), Am. Found. Pharm. Edn. (hon. life, bd. dirs. 1980-85, exec. com. 1981-85, vice chmn. 1982-85), Am. Inst. History of Pharmacy (sponsor), U. Nebr. Chancellor's Club, U. Nebr. Pres. Club, Sigma Xi, Phi Kappa Phi, Omicron Delta Kappa, Rho Chi, Spokane Club, Kappa Psi (Nat. Svc. citation 1961). Democrat. Presbyterian. Home: 707 W 6th Ave Apt 41 Spokane WA 99204-2813

GIBSON, MITCHELL EARL, painter, consultant, psychiatrist; b. Pinehurst, N.C., Aug. 24, 1959; s. Willie James and Mary Magdalene (Barnett) G.; m. Bernice Tripp, June 24, 1990 (div. Aug. 1996). BS magna cum laude, Fla. A&M U., 1981; MD in Psychiatry with honors, U. N.C., 1985. Diplomate Am. Bd. Psychiatry and Neurology, Am. Bd. Forensic Medicine. Intern, then resident Albert Einstein Med. Ctr., Phila., 1985-89, chief resident, 1987-88, chief of staff, 1988-89; chief of staff East Valley Camelback Hosp., Mesa, Ariz., 1990-92; pvt. practice Mesa, Ariz., 1989—; presenter in field. One-man shows include Scottsdale (Ariz.) Ctr. for Arts, 1991, Hyatt Regency Conf. Ctr., Phoenix, 1992, Wrigley Mansion Ctr., Phoenix, 1997; exhibited in group shows at Lucien Crump Art Gallery, Phila., 1989, Chosen Image Gallery, Phila., 1989, Ariz. State U. Ctr. Gallery, 1992, Gallery Q, 1996, Tucson, Deland Internat. Fall Festival of Arts, 1996, Mahogany Gallery, L.A., 1997, Agora Gallery, N.Y.C., 1997; represented in permanent collections African Am. Mus. Art, Agora Gallery Visual Registry; represented in numerous pvt. collections and ongoing internet exhbns. Mem. citizens adv. bd. Cox Publishing, 1992. Recipient NAACP Image award, Phoenix chpt., 1991, Svc. award Samaritan Health Sys., 1992; scholar U. N.C. Sch. Medicine, 1981-85. Mem. AMA, AM. Soc. Addiction Medicine, Am. Psychiat. Assn., Ariz. Med. Assn., Ariz. Psychiat. Soc., Pa. Psychiat. Assn., Pa. Psychiat. Soc., Alpha Kappa Mu. Home: 75226 S 20th Pl Phoenix AZ 85048 Office: 2600 E Southern Ave Ste C2 Tempe AZ 85282-7609

GIBSON, PAULA LAUREN, lawyer; b. Denver, 1956. BA, UCLA, 1978; JD, Southwestern U., 1981. Bar: Calif. 1981. Assoc. Potter, Bradish and Ellinghouse, Encino, Calif., 1981-82; sr. corps. counsel Calif. Dept. of Corps., Los Angeles, 1982-84; dep. atty. gen. State of Calif., Los Angeles, 1984—; gen. counsel Twilight Films div. Nefertiti Entertainment Group, Beverly Hills, Calif., 1985-93. Recipient Outstanding Achievement in civil litigation award Atty. Gen., 1994. Mem. L.A. County Bar Assn. Avocations: underwater photography, snorkeling, bicycling, computers.

GIEDT, WALVIN ROLAND, epidemiologist, educator; b. Eureka, S.D., Aug. 17, 1905; s. Theodore John Peter and Augusta Elizabeth (Pritzkau) G.; m. Lois Della Hosking, Nov. 4, 1932; children: Carol Augusta, Barbara Ellen. BS in Medicine, U. S.D., 1933; MD, U. Chgo., 1937; MPH, Johns Hopkin's U., 1941. Lab. instr. Sch. of Medicine U. S.D., Vermillion, 1933-36, asst. prof. microbiology Sch. of Medicine, 1938-40; chief epidemiologist div. S.D. Dept. Health, Pierre, 1941-43; chief epidemiologist div. Wash. State Dept. Health, Seattle, 1943-71, ret., 1971. Contbr. articles to profl. jours. With USPHS, 1941-66. Mem. Wash. State Pub. Health Assn. (past pres). Democrat. Avocations: travel, photography, reading, politics and foreign affairs, antiwar activist and supporter United Nations. Address: 409 30th Ave S Seattle WA 98144-2507

GIEM, ROSS NYE, JR., surgeon; b. Corvallis, Oreg., May 23, 1923; s. Ross Nye and Goldie Marie (Falk) G.; children: John, David, Paul, James, Ross N. III, Matthew John, Julie; student U. Redlands, Walla Walla Coll.; BA, MD, Loma Linda U. Intern, Sacramento Gen. Hosp., 1952-53; resident in ob-gyn, Kern County Gen. Hosp., Bakersfield, Calif., 1956-57, in gen. surgery, 1957-61; practice medicine specializing in gen. surgery, Sullivan, Mo., 1961-70; staff emergency dept. Hollywood Presbyn. Med. Center, 1971-73, Meml. Hosp., Belleville, Ill., 1973-87, St. Elizabeth Hosp., Belleville, Ill., 1973-90; St. Luke Hosp., Pasadena, Calif., 1973-89, Doctors Hosp., Montclair, Calif. 1990-93, Harriman Jones Med. Group, Long Beach, Calif., 1993—; instr. nurses, physicians, paramedics, emergency med. technicians,

1973-91. Served with AUS, 1943-46. Diplomate Am. Bd. Surgery. Fellow ACS, Am. Coll. Emergency Physicians; mem. AMA, Ill. Med. Assn., Pan Am. Med. Assn., Pan Pacific Surg. Assn., Royal Coll. Physicians (Eng.) Home: PO Box 5767 Pasadena CA 91117-0767 also: 834 W Huntington Dr Apt 4 Arcadia CA 91007-6610

GIER, KARAN HANCOCK, counseling psychologist; b. Sedalia, Mo., Dec. 7, 1947; d. Ioda Clyde and Lorna (Campbell) Hancock; m. Thomas Robert Gier, Sept. 28, 1968. BA in Edn., U. Mo., Kansas City, 1971; MA Teaching in Math/Sci. Edn., Webster U., 1974; MA in Counseling Psychology, Western Colo. U., 1981; MEd Guidance and Counseling, U. Alaska, 1981; PhD in Edn., Pacific Western U., 1989. Nat. cert. counselor. Instr. grades 5-8 Kansas City-St. Joseph Archdiocese, 1969-73; ednl. cons. Pan-Ednl. Inst., Kansas City, 1973-75; instr., counselor Bethel (Alaska) Regional High Sch., 1975-80; ednl. program coord. Western Regional Resource Ctr., Anchorage, 1980-81; counselor U. Alaska, Anchorage, 1982-83; coll. prep. instr. Alaska Native Found., Anchorage, 1982; counselor USAF, Anchorage, 1985-86; prof. U. Alaska, Anchorage, 1982—; dir. Omni Counseling Svcs., Anchorage, 1984—; prof. Chapman Coll., Anchorage, 1988—; workshop facilitator over 100 workshops on the topics of counseling techs., value clarification, non-traditional teaching approaches, peer-tutor tng. Co-author: Coping with College, 1984, Helping Others Learn, 1985, The Tutor Training Handbook, 1996; editor, co-author: A Student's Guide, 1983; contbg. author developmental Yup'ik lang. program, 1981; contbr. photographs to Wolves and Related Canids, 1990, 91; contbr. articles to profl. jours. Mem. Am. Bus. Women's Assn., Blue Springs, Mo., 1972-75, Ctr. for Environ. Edn., Beta Sigma Phi, Bethel, Alaska, 1976-81. Recipient 3d place color photo award Yukon-Kuskokwim State Fair, Bethel, 1978, Notable Achievement award USAF, 1986, Meritorious Svc. award Anchorage Community Coll., 1984-88, Robert Griffin long & outstanding svc. award Coll. Reading & Learning Assn. Mem. Coll. Reading and Learning Assn. (editor, peer tutor sig leader 1988—, Cert. of Appreciation 1986-93, bd. dirs. Alaska state, coord. internat. tutor program, Spl. Recognition award 1994-95), AACD, Alaska Assn. Counseling and Devel. (pres. 1989-90), Alaska Career Devel. Assn. (pres.-elect 1989-90), Nat. Rehab. Assn., Nat. Rehab. Counselors, Human Soc. of U.S. Wolf Haven Am., Wolf Song of Alaska. Avocations: travel, wolf preservation, photography, classical music, British mysteries. Home and Office: Omni Counseling Svcs 8102 Harvest Cir Anchorage AK 99502-4682

GIER, NICHOLAS FRANCIS, philosophy educator; b. North Platte, Nebr., Mar. 17, 1944; s. Nicholas Francis and Verlena (McVey) G.; m. Lisbeth Bindsler, Aug. 14, 1971 (div. Feb. 1988); 1 child, Christina Bindsley. BA with honors, Oreg. State U., 1966; MA, Claremont (Calif.) Grad. Sch., 1969, PhD, 1973. Prof. philosophy U. Idaho, Moscow, 1972—. Author: Wittgenstein and Phenomenology, 1981, God, Reason and the Evangelicals, 1987. Pres. Idaho Fedn. Tchrs., Mascow, 1982—. Rotary Found. fellow, Copenhagen, 1966-67, Fulbright Commn. fellow, Heidelberg, Germany, 1970-71; peace studies grantee Niwano Peace Found., Kyoto, Japan, 1993. Democrat. Unitarian. Avocations: cooking, backpacking, international travel, snorkeling. Office: U Idaho Dept Philosophy Moscow ID 83843-4016

GIFFIN, HERB KENT, architect; b. Richmond, Calif., Mar. 3, 1950; s. Herb S. and Edith Opal (Moore) G.; m. Sandra Lee Peterson, May 6, 1989; children: Jamen Kent, Jody Kay. BArch, Wash. State U., 1973. Registered architect, Oreg., Wash. Architect intern Brooks Hensley Creager, Spokane, 1972; assoc. Skidmore Owings & Merril, Portland, 1973-83; architect, owner Giffin Bolte Jurgens, Portland, 1983—, pres., 1984—. Bd. dirs. YMCA, Portland, 1985-93; mem. adv. bd. Portland Marathon Com., 1985-86; advisor Archtl. Explorer Post, Portland, 1976-83; mem. Northwest Architects for Health Panel, 1986—, bd. dirs., 1996—, pres., 1998. Mem. AIA (bd. dirs. 1987-90). Avocations: running, biking, skiing, hiking, reading. Home: 3110 NE Rocky Butte Rd Portland OR 97220-3658 Office: Giffin Bolte Jurgens 815 SW 2d Ave Ste 600 Portland OR 97204

GIFFIN, MARGARET ETHEL (PEGGY GIFFIN), management consultant; b. Cleve., Aug. 27, 1949; d. Arch Kenneth and Jeanne (Eggleton) G.; m. Robert Alan Wyman, Aug. 20, 1988; 1 child, Samantha Jean. BA in Psychology, U. Pacific, Stockton, Calif., 1971; MA in Psychology, Calif. State U., Long Beach, 1973; PhD in Quantitative Psychology, U. So. Calif., 1984. Psychometrist Auto Club So. Calif., L.A., 1973-74; cons. Psychol. Svcs., Inc., Glendale, Calif., 1975-76, mgr., 1977-78, dir., 1979-94; rschr. Social Sci. Rsch. Inst., U. So. Calif., L.A., 1981; dir. Giffin Consulting Svcs., L.A., 1994—; instr. Calif. State U., Long Beach, 1989-90; mem. tech. adv. com. on testing Calif. Fair Employment and Housing Commn., 1974-80, mem. steering com., 1978-80. Mem. Soc. Indsl. Organizational Psychology, Am. Psychol. Assn., Personnel Testing Coun. So. Calif. (pres. 1980, exec. dir. 1982, 88, bd. dirs. 1980-92). Home and Office: 260 S Highland Ave Los Angeles CA 90036-3027

GIFFORD, ARTHUR ROY, publishing executive; b. Buffalo, Jan. 27, 1937; s. William Howard and Dorothy Ellen (Logan) G.; m. Anna Marie Boone, July 9, 1960 (div. Feb. 1974); 1 child, Douglas Alan; m. Carolyn Elaine Crowe, Dec. 20, 1974; children: Christine Michelle, Stephen Michael. BA, Butler U., 1964; postgrad., Pacific Luth. U., Tacoma, 1970; MA, U. Wash., 1975. Cert. provisional and standard secondary tchr., Wash. Passenger svc. agt. United Airlines, Seattle, 1966-67; indsl. engr. The Boeing Co., Seattle, 1967-70, prog. mgr. engring. div. Boeing Community Connection, 1987-91; mgr. assessment reports, corp. safety, health and environ. affairs The Boeing Co., 1991-94; tchr., theatre dir. Fed. Way (Wash.) Sch. Dist., 1971-87; pres. Creative Approaches, Kent, Wash., 1994—. Bd. dirs. Lyric Theatre and Conservatory, Midway, Wash., 1980-82; treas. Wash. Edn. Theatre Assn., 1973-77, 85-89; treas. ArtsTime '89, Wash. State Centennial All-Arts Conf., 1987-89, long-range planning com., Kent (Wash.) View Christian Sch., 1987—; pres. PTA, Kent View Christian High Sch., 1992—; mem. precinct com. Dem. Orgn. King County, Wash., 1973-75, 93—. Democrat. Methodist. Avocations: theater, classical music, filmography. Home: 13904 SE 241st St Kent WA 98042-3315 Office: Creative Approaches PO Box 1363 Issaquah WA 98027-0056

GIFFORD, CHRISTOPHER SCOTT, electronic design engineer; b. Rochester, N.Y., July 24, 1964. BSEE, Calif. Poly., San Luis Obispo, 1990. Video design engr. Prime Image, San Jose, Calif., 1990—. Patentee in field of double video standards converter. Democrat. Office: Prime Image 662 Giguere Ct San Jose CA 95133-1742

GIGRAY, MARGARET ELIZABETH, foundation trustee; b. Portland, Oreg., Sept. 17, 1918; d. Frank Augustus and Anna (Cameron) King; m. William Franklin Gigray, Jr., Jan. 10, 1941; children: William Franklin III, Sherman Cameron. BA in Journalism and Philosophy, U. Idaho, 1940, postgrad., 1940. Vice chmn. Whittenberger Found., Caldwell, Idaho, 1972—; sec., chair nominating com. Friends of Idaho Pub. TV, 1994—; bd. dirs, mem. grants com. Idaho Cmty. found., 1988—; mem. devel. com. Albertson Coll. Idaho, Caldwell, 1984—, coun. founds. membership com., Washington, D.C.; mem. edn. com. C. of C., 1978—; chmn. Idaho State Devel. Disabilities Coun., Boise, 1976-79; chmn. Coll. of Idaho Women's Conf., Caldwell, 1968. Editor handbook for Ladies Golf Assn., Boise, 1996-98; author, editor brochurres, pub. rels. work; writer newspaper column, 1951-54. Chmn. Heart, Cancer, Stroke and Related Illness Bd., Boise, 1967-69; mem. exec. bd. Pacific N.W. Grantmakers Forum, Seattle, 1985-91; chair nominating com. BoiseArt Mus., 1978-84. Recipient Women Helping Women award Soroptimist Internat., 1984, Silver and Gold award U. Idaho, 1997; named Disting. Citizen, Idaho Daily Statesman, 1968, Woman of Yr., Beta Sigma Phi, 1998. Mem. Ninety-Nines, Idaho Ninety-Nines (charter mem.), PEO, Daus. of the Nile, Gamma Phi Beta. Democrat. Presbyterian. Avocations: golf, painting, dancing, catalysting.

GILB, CORINNE LATHROP, history educator; b. Lethbridge, Alta., Can., Feb. 19, 1925; d. Glen Hutchison and Vera (Passey) Lathrop; m. Tyrell Thompson Gilb, Aug. 19, 1945; children: Lesley Gilb Taplin, Tyra. BA, U. Wash., 1946; MA, U. Calif., [illegible] Harvard U., 1957. History lectr. Mills Coll., Oakland, 1957-61; prof. humanities San Francisco State U., 1964-68; rsch. assoc. U. Calif., Berkeley, 1953-68, prof. history Wayne State U., Detroit, 1968-94, co-dir. Liberal Arts Urban Studies program, 1976-86; dir. planning City of Detroit, 1979-85; pres. Atherton Press, 1997—; spl. cons. Calif. Legislature, 1963, 64; vis. scholar Hoover Instn., Stanford U., fall 1993; UN Nongovtl. Orgn. rep. Internat. Orgn. for Unification of Terminological Neologisms, 1995—. Author: Conformity of State to Federal Income Tax, 1964, Hidden Hierarchies, 1966, numerous chpts. in books; vol. writer Silicon Valley Global Trading Ctr., 1995-96, Silicon Valley Def./Space Consortium, 1996-97; contbr. articles to profl. jours. Vol. writer Silicon Valley Global Trading Ctr., 1995-96, Silicon Valley Def./Space Consortium, 1996-97. Guggenheim fellow, 1957; grantee Social Sci. Rsch. Coun. Mem. Internat. Soc. Comparative Study of Civilizations (five terms exec. coun., 1st v.p. 1995-98), No. Calif. World Affairs Coun., various acad. assns. Presbyterian.

GILBERT, DONALD ROY, lawyer; b. Phila., June 6, 1946. BA, Stanford U., 1968; JD, U. Calif., 1971. Bar: Calif. 1972, Ariz. 1972. Ptnr., dir. Fennemore Craig, Phoenix, 1972—. Mem. ABA, State Bar Ariz., State Bar Calif., Maricopa County Bar Assn. Office: Fennemore Craig 3003 N Central Ste 2600 Phoenix AZ 85012-2913*

GILBERT, GREGORY L., accountant. BS in Bus. cum laude, Calif. State U., Northridge; postgrad. studies in Taxation, Golden State U., 1980-82. CPA, Calif., Nev.; lic. real estate broker, Nev. Sr. acct. Deloitte, Haskins & Sells, L.A., 1978-80; acctg. supr. Hutchinson & Bloodgood, Glendale Calif., 1980-82; CFO, treas. Lands of Sierra, Subsidiary Sierra Pacific Resources, Reno, Nev., 1984-91; owner, mgr. Greg L. Gilbert, Reno, Nev., 1983-84, 91—; speaker at tax law seminars, legal assn. meetings, Nat. Judicial Coll. in Reno. Mem AICPA, Nev. Soc. CPAs (chmn. bus. and econ. devel. com.1993-94), Nat. Assn. Cert. Valuation Analyst, U. Nev. Reno, The Acctg. Cir. (pres. 1994-95). Office: Greg L Gilbert & Assocs 423 W Plumb Ln Ste 7 Reno NV 89509-3766

GILBERT, HEATHER CAMPBELL, manufacturing company executive; b. Mt. Vernon, N.Y., Nov. 20, 1944; d. Ronald Ogston and Mary Lodivia (Campbell) G.; BS in Math. (Nat. Merit scholar), Stanford U., 1967; MS in Computer Sci. (NSF fellow), U. Wis., 1969. With Burroughs Corp., 1969-82, sr. mgmt. systems analyst, Detroit, 1975-77, mgr. mgmt. systems activity, Pasadena, Calif., 1977-82; mgr. software product mgmt. Logical Data Mgmt. Inc., Covina, Calif., 1982-83, dir. mktg., 1983, v.p. bus. devel., 1983-84; v.p. profl. svcs., 1984-85; mgr. software devel. Unisys Corp., Mission Viejo, Calif., 1985—. Founding bd. dirs., treas. Breast Cancer Survivors Non-profit Orgn. Mem. Assn. Computing Machinery, Am. Prodn. and Inventory Control Soc., Breast Cancer Survivors Non-Profit Orgn. (founding bd. dirs., treas.), Stanford U. Alumni Assn. (life), Stanford Profl. Women Los Angeles County (pres. 1982-83), NAFE, Town Hall. Republican. Home: 21113 Calle De Paseo Lake Forest CA 92630-7037 Office: Unisys Corp 25725 Jeronimo Rd Mission Viejo CA 92691-2792

GILBERT, KAREN ANN, commodities trader; b. Chgo., Sept. 3, 1965; d. Stephen Jerome and Juanita J. (Adamski) Allen; m. Edward Michael Gilbert Dec. 7, 1991; children: Robert Michael, Victoria Marie. MS, U. Utah, 1992. Agy. adminstr. State Farm Ins., Elmhurst, Ill., 1984-87; rsch. coord. U. Utah Health Sci. Ctr., Salt Lake City, Utah, 1987-92; commodity trader pvt. practice, Salt Lake City, 1990—. V.p. Canyon Cove Homeowners Assn., Salt Lake City, 1998—. Democrat. Roman Catholic. E-mail: yukong@worldnet.att.net. Home and Office: 6484 Heughs Canyon Dr Salt Lake City UT 84121-6308

GILBERT, KERI LEE, computer analyst, educator; b. Roseburg, Oreg., June 13, 1963; d. James Steven and Karen Lee (Anderson) G. BS in Computer Tech., Oreg. Tech. Inst., 1983; MS in Computer Sci., U. Oreg., 1986. Microsoft cert. systems engr. Systems analyst Microsoft Corp., Redmond, Wash., 1987-96; gen. mgr. Awakenings and Co., Roseburg, Oreg., 1996—. Co-author: (instrnl. manual) Windows NT Advanced Programming, 1997. Mem. Profl. Bus. Women Am., Roseburg; advisor Future Bus. Leaders Am., Roseburg, 1991—. Mem. Inst. Certification of Computer Profls. (Author of Yr. award 1997), Assn. for Computing Machinery. Republican. Roman Catholic. Avocations: studies piano, fly fishing, computer programming. Office: Awakenings and Co 908 SE Pine St Roseburg OR 97470-4810

GILBERT, PAUL ENSIGN, lawyer; b. San Diego, Sept. 16, 1943; s. Arthur Gene Gilbert and Mary Dean (Peterson) Andrew; m. Susan Ann Carlson, Apr. 4, 1968; children: Clark, Emily, James, Elizabeth. BS, Brigham Young U., 1968; Jd, U. Calif., 1971. Bar: Ariz. 1972. Ptnr. Jennings, Strouss & Salmon, Phoenix, 1971-81, Beus, Gilbert & Devitt PLLC, Phoenix, 1981—. Mem. Nat. Assn. Christians & Jews (bd. dirs. 1980—), BYU Alumni Assn. (nat. pres., chmn. nat. conf.). Democrat. Mormon. Home: 5317 N 46th St Phoenix AZ 85018-1732 Office: Beus Gilbert Wake & Devitt 3200 N Central Ave Ste 1000 Phoenix AZ 85012-2430

GILBERT, PAUL THOMAS, chemical development engineer; b. Chgo., July 29, 1914; s. Paul T. and Ilse (Forster) G.; m. Phyllis A. Simons, Oct. 17, 1942 (div. July 1955); children: Susan R. Sorensen, John (dec.), Brian (dec.), Wendy E. Levy; m. Hazel L. Dalton, July 9, 1955; children: Michael L. Pinizzotto, Michele L. Urquhart. BS in Chemistry, Northwestern U., 1936; postgrad., U. Wis., 1936-38; MA in Math., U. Minn., 1940; postgrad., Calif. Inst. Tech., 1941, U. Calif., Santa Barbara, 1971-74. Tchg. asst. math. U. Minn., Mpls., 1939-41; instr. math. Utah State Agrl. Coll., Logan, 1941, 43-44, U. Minn., Mpls., 1943; rsch. chemist Metalloy Corp., Mpls., 1944-46; rsch. scientist Beckman Instruments, South Pasadena, Calif., 1946-52, N.Am. Aviation, Downey, Calif., 1952-55, Beckman Instruments, Fullerton, Palo Alto, Calif., 1955-71; devel. engr. Chemistry Dept. U. Calif., Santa Barbara, 1971-93; tchr. math. NW Mil. and Naval Prep. Sch., Mpls., 1939-41, 45; tech. translator, 1946—; cons. Atomics Internat., Canoga Park, Calif., 1956-59, lectr. Fullerton Youth Mus., 1963-65, bd. dirs. Co-author (translator) Chemical Analysis by Flame Photometry, 1963; translator: Fundamentals of Analytical Flame Spectroscopy, 1979; patentee in field; contbr. articles to profl. jours. Racecourse measurer Santa Barbara Athletic Assn., 1978—. Cadet USAF, 1941-43. Mem. AAAS, Am. Chem. Soc., Am. Math. Soc., Phi Beta Kappa, Sigma Xi, Phi Eta Sigma. Avocations: running, surfing, natural history, indexing, piano. Home: 715 Via Miguel Santa Barbara CA 93111-2743 Office: Univ Calif Dept Chemistry Santa Barbara CA 93106

GILBERT, ROBERT WOLFE, lawyer; b. N.Y.C., Nov. 12, 1920; s. L. Wolfe and Katherine L. (Oestreicher) Wolfe; m. Beatrice R. Frutman, Dec. 25, 1946; children: Frank Richard, Jack Alfred. BA, UCLA 1941; JD, U. Calif., Berkeley, 1943. Bar: Calif. 1944, U.S. Ct. Appeals. (9th cir.) 1944, U.S. Ct. Appeals. (D.C. cir.) 1976, U.S. Supreme Ct. 1959. Pres. Gilbert & Sackman, P.C. and predecessors, L.A., 1944—; judge pro tem Los Angeles Mcpl. and Superior Ct., Commr. City of L.A. Housing Authority 1953-63; bd. dirs. Calif. Housing Coun. 1955-63; U.S. faculty mem. Moscow Conf. on Law and Econ. Cooperation, 1990. Sr. editor Internat. Labor and Employment Laws, 1997. Mem. Internat. Bar Assn., Interam. Bar Assn. (co-chmn. labor law and social security com.), ABA (co-chmn. internat. labor law com.), Fed. Bar Assn., L.A. Bar Assn. (past chmn. labor law sect.), Am. Judicature Soc., Coll. Labor & Employment Lawyers, Order of Coif, Pi Sigma Alpha. Contbr. articles to profl. jours. Home: 7981 Hollywood Blvd Los Angeles CA 90046-2611 Office: 6100 Wilshire Blvd Ste 700 Los Angeles CA 90048-5114

GILBERT, SCOTT, advertising executive. Co-chmn. bd., CEO Team One Advertising, El Segundo, Calif. Office: Team One Advertising 1960 E Grand Ave Ste 700 El Segundo CA 90245-5059*

GILBERTSON, OSWALD IRVING, marketing executive; b. Bklyn., Mar. 23, 1927; s. Olaf and Ingeborg (Aase) Gabrielsen; m. Magnhild Hompland, Sept. 11, 1954; 1 child, Jan Ivar. Electrotechnician, Sorlandets Tekniske Skole, Norway, 1947; BSEE, Stockholms Tekniska Institut, Stockholm, Sweden, 1956. Planning engr. test equipment design and devel. Western Electric Co., Inc., Kearny, N.J., 1957-61, planning engr. new prodn., 1963-67, engring. supr. test equipment, 1963-67, engring. supr. submarine repeaters and equalizers, 1967-69; engring. mgr. communication cables ITT [illegible] Standard Telefon og Kabelfabrik A/S (STK), 1971-87, STK Factory rep., 1987-89, Alcatel Kabel Norge AS Factory rep., 1989-92, Alcatel Can. Wire Inc. Factory rep., 1992-95; div. mgr. Eswa Heating Systems, Inc., 1980-87, pres., 1987-89. Hon. Norwegian consul, 1981—; apptd. Knight First Class Norwegian Order Merit, 1989. Served with AUS, 1948-52. Registered profl. engr., Vt. Mem. IEEE, Norwegian Soc. Profl. Engrs., Soc. Norwegian Am. Engrs., Sons of Norway. Patentee in field. Home and Office: 6240 Brynwood Ct San Diego CA 92120-3805

GILBERTSON, ROBERT G., computer company executive; b. Madison, Wis., May 18, 1941; s. Palmer B. and Agnes E. (Ericson) G.; m. Ellen L. Podell; children: David Scott, Jeffrey Allan. Student, MIT, 1959-62; MBA, U. Chgo., 1970; PhD, Stanford U., 1973. Arch. designer various firms, 1963-66; mktg. exec. IBM, Chgo., White Plains, N.Y., 1966-71; asst. prof. Harvard Grad. Sch. Bus., Cambridge, Mass., 1973-78; sr. v.p. Data Archs. Inc., Waltham, Mass., 1978-83; pres., CEO, Channel Net Corp., Southport, Conn., 1983-85, Data Switch Corp., Shelton, Conn., 1985-92; pres., CEO, CMX Sys. Inc., Wallingford, Conn., 1993-96, also bd. dirs.; pres., CEO Network Computing Devices, Inc., Mountain View, Calif., 1996—; bd. dirs. Network Computing Devices, DSL.Net; adj. prof. Brandeis U., Walthama, 1976-80. Contbr. articles to profl. jours. Bd. dirs. Griffin Hosp., Seymour, Conn., 1987-92, Conn. Bus. Industry Assn., 1995-96; bd. dirs., vice chmn. Mfr. Assn. Conn., 1992-96. Named Turnaround Mgr. of Yr., 1988. Mem. IEEE, Am. Electronics Assn. (treas., sec., chmn. 1991-92), Assn. for Computing Machinery, Soc. Info. Mgmt., Inst. Mgmt. Scis., Conn. Com. Bus. Opportunity, Def. Diversified and Indsl. Policy, S.W. Area Commerce and Industry Assn. (bd. dirs. 1988-93 (chmn. regional transp. coun. 1990-93). Lutheran. Avocations: tennis, racquetball, skiing, golf, bridge.

GILBERTZ, LARRY E., state legislator, entrepreneur; b. Gillette, Wyo., Feb. 3, 1929; s. Jacob A. and Lena E. (Schlautmann) G.; m. Verna Ann Howell, June 18, 1955; children: Katerine, L.D., Susan, Jay. Mgr. Gilbertz Ranch, Gillette, 1953-62, owner, 1963—; sr. ptnr. Gilbertz Co., Gillette, 1971—; pres. Gilbertz Enterprises, Gillette, 1988—; mem. Wyo. Senate, Cheyenne, 1993—; chmn. U. Wyo. Exptl. Farm, Campbell County, 1970-74. Treas. Sch. Bd. Dist. # 9, Campbell County, 1969-71; active Sch. Dist. Reorgn., Campbell County, 1970, Wyo. Ct. Reform, 1971. With U.S. Army, 1951-53, PTO. Recipient Performance Testing award U. Wyo., 1969-74, Chem. Weed Control award, 1969-74. Mem. Am. Farm Bur., Am. Legis. Exch. Coun., Am. Legion. Republican. Roman Catholic. Avocation: world travel. Home: 3934 Highway 50 Gillette WY 82718-9201

GILDNER, GARY THEODORE, writer; b. West Branch, Mich., Aug. 22, 1938; s. Theodore Edward and Jean (Szostak) G.; m. Judith Ann McKibben, Jan. 5, 1963 (div. 1980); 1 child, Gretchen; m. Elizabeth Mary Sloan, July 6, 1991; 1 child, Margaret. BA, Mich. State U., 1960, MA, 1961. Sports info. dir. Wayne State U., Detroit, 1962; instr. English dept. No. Mich. U., Marquette, 1963-66; instr., to prof. Drake U., Des Moines, 1966-93; writer-in-residence Reed Coll., Portland, Oreg., 1983-85, Mich. State U., East Lansing, 1987; McGee Prof. of Writing Davidson (N.C.) Coll., 1992; sr. Fulbright lectr. Warsaw U., Poland, 1987-88, Safarik U., Presov, Slovakia, 1992-93. Author: (poetry books) First Practice, 1969, Digging for Indians, 1971, Eight Poems, 1973, Nails, 1975, Letters from Vicksburg, 1976, The Runner, 1978, Jabon, 1981, Blue Like the Heavens, 1984, Clackamas, 1991, The Swing, 1996, The Bunker in the Parsley Fields, 1997, (short stories) The Crush, 1983, A Week in South Dakota, 1987, Pavol Hudak, The Poet, is Talking, 1996, (novel) The Second Bridge, 1987, (memoir) The Warsaw Sparks, 1990; editor: (poetry book) Out of This World, 1975, others. Recipient William Carlos Williams prize New Letters mag., 1977, Helen Bullis prize Poetry Northwest mag., 1979, Pushcart prize, 1986, Nat. Mag. award Am. Soc. Mag. Editors, 1986, Iowa Poetry prize, U. Iowa Press, 1996; Yaddo fellow 1972, 73, 75, 76, 78, MacDowell Colony fellow MacDowell Colony, 1974, Robert Frost fellow Bread Loaf, 1970, fellow Nat. Endowment for Arts, 1971, 76. Home: RR 2 Box 219 Grangeville ID 83530-9615

GILES, GERALD LYNN, psychology, learning enhancement, computer educator; b. Manti, Utah, Jan. 2, 1943; s. Bert Thorne and Sarah Jenett (Carlen) G.; m. Sharon Ruth Bleak, June 12, 1967; children: Kim, David, Kristie, Becky, Michael, Andrew, Brent, Amber. BA, U. Utah, 1968, MA, 1971. Tchr. Granite Sch. Dist., Salt Lake City, 1968-72; prof. Salt Lake C.C., Salt Lake City, 1972—; cons. QUE Enterprises, Salt Lake City, 1976—; faculty U. Phoenix, Salt Lake City, 1986—; presenter in field. Author: The Vicious Circle of Life, 1988. Chmn. Rep. voting dist., Salt Lake City, 1984-86; bishop LDS Ch., 1986-91; adviser Explorer Scouts. Named Outstanding Tchr. of Yr., 1986; recipient Teaching Excellence award, 1986, Excellence award Nisod, 1994, Local Svc. aard UAACLE, 1998. Mem. ASCD, Nat. Assn. Devel. Edn., Southwestern Assn. Devel. Edn. (sec.), Utah Assn. Adult Cmty. and Continuing Edn. (Local Svc. award 1998). Avocations: videotaping, computers, writing, public speaking and presentation. Home: 4342 Beechwood Rd Taylorsville UT 84123-2206 Office: Salt Lake C C PO Box 30808 Salt Lake City UT 84130-0808

GILES, MELVA THERESA, nursing educator; b. Balt.; 1 child, Meya Elizabeth. AA in Nursing, Catonsville (Md.) Community, 1970; BSN, Calif. State U., L.A., 1981; MSN, Calif. State U., Dominguez Hills, 1988; EdD, Pepperdine U., 1993. RN, Calif. Guest lectr. Rsch. Edn. Inst. UCLA, 1987-89; DON and in-svc. edn. CompCare Corp., 1986-87; clin. nurse specialist, educator County of L.A., 1987-89; assoc. prof. nursing L.A. Pierce Coll., 1989—; lectr. Calif. State U., Dominguez Hills Statewide Grad. Sch. Nursing, 1990—. Fellow Nightingale Soc.; mem. Calif. Nurses Assn., Coun. Black Nurses, Future Soc., Assn. Pan-African Doctoral Scholars Inc., Phi Delta Kappa, Sigma Theta Tau, Chi Eta Phi (Delta chpt.).

GILES, WALTER EDMUND, alcohol and drug treatment executive; b. Omaha, Aug. 9, 1934; s. Walter Edmund and Julia Margaret (Shively) G.; m. Ellen M. Garton, June 13, 1953; m. Dona LaVonne Foster, Sept. 29, 1970 (dec. 1990); children: Sue, Stephen, Theresa, Marcy, Kim, Tim, Nadine, Charles; m. Yvonne Marie Fink, Nov. 29, 1991; children: Jessica Nicole Farr, Walter Edmund III, David Michael. BA, U. Nebr., Lincoln, 1972, MA, 1977. Counselor VA Hosp., Lincoln, Nebr., 1969-70; coord. alcohol programs Mcpl. Ct., Lincoln; dir. Orange County Employee Assistance, Santa Ana, Calif., 1977-79; adminstr. Advanced Health Ctr., Newport Beach, Calif., 1979-81; pres. Great West Health Svcs. Inc., Orange, Calif., 1982-86, Pine Ridge Treatment Ctr. Inc., Running Springs, Calif., 1986—. Author (book) The Workbook, 1985, Intervention, 1986; host (radio show) Addictions, 1984. Mem. Nat. Assn. Alcoholism Counselors, Calif. Assn. Alcoholism Counselors.

GILGER, PAUL DOUGLASS, architect; b. Mansfield, Ohio, Oct. 13, 1954; s. Richard Douglass and Marilyn Joan (Hawkins) G. BArch, U. Cin., 1978. Registered architect, Ohio. Architect Soulen & Assocs., Mansfield, Ohio, 1976-81, PGS Architecture/Planning, Los Gatos, Calif., 1981-82, Bottomline Systems, Inc., San Francisco, 1983-85; pvt. practice San Francisco Bay Area, 1985-90; set designer Nomad Prodns. Scenic Studios, San Francisco, 1985-87; architect James Gillam, Architect, San Francisco, 1987-90, Hedgpeth Architects, Santa Rosa, Calif., 1990—, Home Planners, Inc., Tucson, 1994—; booking mgr. 1177 Club, San Francisco, 1985-86, City Cabaret, San Francisco, 1986-87; bd. dirs San Francisco Coun. Entertainment, 1987-90; project architect Lucasfilm Movie Studio Indsl. Light and Magic, San Rafael, Calif., 1991. Author: "The Best of Times", the Jerry Herman Musical Revue. Recipient Ohio Cmty. Theatre Assn. award, 1980, Theatrewest Acting award, 1983, 3 Bay Area Critics Cir. award, 1984, 85, 4 Cabaret Gold awards San Francisco Coun. Entertainment, 1985, 86, 3 Hollywood Dramalogue awards, 1985, 5 awards. 1996; San Francisco Focus award, 1985. Avocations: traveling, piano, automobiles. Home: 530 Julliard Park Dr Santa Rosa CA 95401-6312 Office: Hedgpeth Architects 2321 Bethards Dr Santa Rosa CA 95405-8536

GILHOOLY, DAVID JAMES, III, artist; b. Auburn, Calif., Apr. 15, 1943; s. David James and Gladys Catherine (Schulte) G.; m. Camille Margot Chang, Aug. 23, 1983; children: David James, Andrea Elizabeth, Abigail Margaret, Peter Rodney, Hakan Yuatutsu, Kiril Shintora, Sorgan Subetei. BA, U. Calif., Davis, 1965, MA, 1967. tchr. San Jose (Calif.) State Coll., 1967-69, U. Sask. (Can.), Regina, 1969-71, York U., Toronto, Ont., Can., 1971-75, 76-77, U. Calif.-Davis, summer 1971, 75-76, Calif. State U.-Sacramento, summers 1970-75; lectr. in field. One-man shows include San Francisco Museum Art, 1967, M. H. deYoung Meml. Mus., San Francisco, 1968, Matrix Gallery, Wadsworth Athenuem, Hartford, Conn., 1976, Mus. Contemporary Art, Chgo., 1976, Vancouver (B.C., Can.), Art Gallery, 1976, ARCO Ctr. for Visual Arts, Los Angeles, 1977, Mus. Contemporary Craft,

N.Y.C., 1977, E.B. Crocker Art Mus., Sacramento, 1980, St. Louis Mus. Art, 1981, Smith-Anderson Gallery, Palo Alto, 1985, San Jose Mus. Art, 1992, Solomon Dubnick Gallery, Sacramento, 1997; group shows include U. Calif.-Berkeley Art Mus., 1967, Inst. Contemporary Art, Boston, 1967, Whitney Mus. Am. Art, N.Y.C., 1970, 74, 81, Musee d'art de la Ville Paris, 1973, Chgo. Art Inst., 1975, San Francisco Mus. Art and Nat. Collection Fine Art, Washington, 1976-77, Stedelijk Mus., Amsterdam, The Netherlands, 1979, Everson Mus. Art, Syracuse, N.Y., 1979, Whitney Mus. Am. Art, N.Y.C., 1981, Palm Springs Desert Art Mus., 1984, Oakland Mus., 1985, Stanford Mus. Art, 1987, Inst. Contemporary Art, Boston, 1994; represented in permanent collections S. Bronfman Collection Can. Art, Montreal, Que., San Francisco Mus. Art, Phila. Mus. Art, Vancouver Art Gallery, Art Gallery Greater Victoria (B.C.), Albright-Knox Art Gallery, Buffalo, San Antonio Mus. Art, Oakland (Calif.) Mus. Art, Stedelijk Mus., Stanford U., Palo Alto, Calif., Australian Nat. Gallery, Canberra, Govt. Can., Calgary, Alta., Whitney Mus. Am. Art, Eugene (Oreg.) Ctr. Performing Arts. Can. Council grantee, 1975, 78. Mem. Royal Can. Acad. Republican. Mem. Ch. of Scientology. Office: 11140 SE Oak Dr Dayton OR 97114-7447

GILKEY, GORDON WAVERLY, curator, artist; b. Albany, Oreg., Mar. 10, 1912; s. Leonard Ernest and Edna Isabel (Smith) G.; m. Vivian Malone, Oct. 17, 1938 (dec. Sept. 1995); 1 son, Gordon Spencer. BS, Albany Coll., 1933; MFA, U. Oreg., 1936; ArtsD (hon.), Lewis and Clark Coll., 1957. Mem. art staff Stephens Coll., Mo., 1939-42; prof. art, head dept. Oreg. State U., 1947-64; dean Oreg. State U. (Sch. Humanities and Social Scis.), 1963-73, Oreg. State U. (Coll. Liberal Arts), 1973-77; curator prints and drawings Portland (Oreg.) Art Mus., 1978—; prof. and printmaker-in-resident Pacific N.W. Coll. Art, 1978—; spl. asst. to exec. dir. Portland Art Mus., 1988-94; dir. Internat. Exc. Print Exhibits, 1956-78; U.S. adviser IV Bordighera Biennale, Italy, 1957; chmn. Gov.'s Planning Coun. for Arts and Humanities in, Oreg., 1965-67; mem. Gov.'s Commn. on Fgn. Lang. and Internat. Studies. Ofcl. etcher New York World's Fair, 1939, 1937-39; etcher Nat. Broadcasting Co., Radio City, N.Y.C., 1937-39; artist-author: Etchings: New York World's Fair, 1939; contbr. articles on art; major work in permanent collection, Met. Mus. Art, others. Trustee Oreg. State U. Found.; bd. govs. Pacific N.W. Coll. Art. Col. U.S. Army Air Corps, 1942-47, ret. Decorated Palmes Academiques (France), officer's cross and comdr.'s cross Order of Merit (Fed. Republic Germany), Order Star of Solidarity (Italy), comdr. Order of Merit (Italy), officer Order Acad. Palms (France), officer Legion of Honor (France), Grand Cross Order St. Gregory the Illuminator, comdr. Order Polonia Restituta, chevalier Order of Holy Sepulchre, chevalier mil. and hospitaller Order of St. Lazarus, chevalier mil. and hospitaller Order of Our Lady of Mt. Carmel, chevalier St. Dennis of Zante, knight Grand Cross Order of St. Basil the Great, knight Imperial Order of St. Eugene of Trebizond, Order of the Knights of Sinai, order of Temple of Jerusalem, comdr. Order St. Stephan the Martyr; recipient King Carl XVI Gustaf's Gold Commemorative medal in art Sweden, German Friendship award; Soc. Mayflower Descendants, Aubrey R. Watzek award; named AIA-Carnegie Corp. fellow, summers 1930, 32. Mem. Am. Print Alliance (bd. dirs.), Portland Art Mus. (founder), Soc. Am. Graphic Artists, Calif. Soc. Printmakers, Coll. Art Assn., UN Assn. Oreg. (past pres.), Oreg. Internat. Coun. (bd. dirs.), Print Coun. of Am., N.W. Print Coun. (trustee), NW Coll. Art (bd. govs.), Oreg. St. U. Fdn. (trustee), Phi Kappa Phi, Kappa Pi. Home: 1500 SW 5th Ave Apt 2401 Portland OR 97201-5437 Office: 1219 SW Park Ave Portland OR 97205-2430

GILL, BECKY LORETTE, addictionist, psychiatrist; b. Phoenix, Mar. 16, 1947; d. David Franklin and Lorette (Cooper) Brinegar; m. Jim Shack Gill, Jr., Aug. 5, 1978. *Father David F. Brinegar served as a Captain in the Army in World War II and was stationed in the Persian Gulf. After the war, he worked with the Central Arizona Project, and then as an editor of The Arizona Daily Star. Mother Lorette C. Brinegar served in the Red Cross in France in World War II, and then was a high school physical education teacher, counselor, and vice principal at various Arizona high schools. She was a ranked Arizona and Southwest tennis player. Husband Jim S. Gill is a retired Marine Corps Gunnery Sergeant who works as a high school teacher. He graduated magna cum laude from Memphis State University.* BA in Biology, Stanford U., 1968; MD, U. Ariz., 1973. Diplomate Am. Bd. Psychiatry and Neurology; cert. addiction counselor; substance abuse residential facility dir., addictions specialist, clin. supr. Clerk typist Ariz. Med. Ctr. Med. Libr., Tucson, Ariz., 1970; asst. ref. libr. Ariz. Med. Ctr. Med. Libr., Tucson, 1971; surg. extern Tucson Med. Ctr., summer 1970; med. extern Fed. Reformatory for Women, Alderson, W.Va., 1972-73; commd. lt. USN, 1974, advanced through grades to capt., 1992; intern in medicine USPHS Hosp., Balt., 1973-74; resident in psychiatry Nat. Naval Med. Ctr., Bethesda, Md., 1974-77; head alcohol rehab. svc./substance abuse dept., staff psychiatrist Naval Hosp., Camp Lejeune, N.C., 1977-85; head alcohol rehab. svc./substance abuse dept., head psych. Naval Hosp., Millington, Tenn., 1985-88; head alcohol rehab. dept. Naval Hosp., Long Beach, Calif., 1988-94; head Navy Addictions Rehab. and Edn. Dept., Camp Pendleton, Calif., 1994—; mem. tumor bd. Naval Hosp., Camp Lejeune, 1977-85, cons. Tri-Command Consolidated Drug and Alcohol Counseling Ctr. Agy., 1977-85, phys. fitness program com., 1980-85, med. liaison on substance abuse, 1982-85, drug/alcohol program advisor, 1983-85, Tri-Command Consolidated Drug and Alcohol Adv. Coun., 1983-85, controlled substance abuse review subcom. of pharmacy and therapeutics com., 1984-85; watch officer Acute Care Clinic, Naval Hosp., Millington, 1985-86, cons. Counseling and Assistance Ctr., 1985-88, mem. bioethics com., chmn. med. records, utilization review com., 1985-88, exec. com. med. staff, chmn., 1986-87, psychiatric cons. to NAS Brig, 1986-88, mem. quality assurance com., 1986, mem. credentials com., 1986-87, pharmacy and therapeutics com., 1986, pos. mgmt. com., 1986-87, dir. med. svcs., 1986-88, dir. surgical svcs., 1986, commd. duty watch officer, 1986-87, watch officer acute care clinic, 1987-88, mem. Navy Drug and Alcohol adv. coun., 1987-88, preceptor to social worker, 1987-88, pos. mgmt. com., 1988, mem. commd. retention coun., 1988; also, numerous coms. at Naval Hosp., Long Beach, Calif., Naval Hosp., Camp Pendleton, Calif. *While serving as a career officer and physician, Becky Gill became the only board certified addictionist in the Navy. She was instrumental in establishing the Navy's new Continuum of Care model for identifying and treating alcohol abuse and dependence. This model has become the standard for Department of Defense (DoD) treatment programs world-wide and for the civilian health care system (Tri-Care) treating DoD personnel.* Capt. USN. Recipient Commendation medal USN, 1988, meritorious svc. medal, 1994. Mem. Am. Acad. of Psychiatrists in Alcoholism and Addictions (founding mem.), Am. Soc. of Addiction Medicine, Assn. Mil. Surgeons of U.S., Addiction Profls. of N.C. (chmn. pub. info. com. 1979-80, ea. regional v.p. 1981-82, chmn. fall meeting planning com. 1983, sec. 1984-85), Nat. Assn. of Alcoholism and Drug Abuse Counselors, Calif. Assn. Alcohol and Drug Abuse Counselors, Am. Legion, VFW Aux. U.S. Lawn Tennis Assn. (hon. life), Stanford Cap and Gown, Stanford Alumni Assn., U. Ariz. Alumni Assn., Stanford Cardinal Club. Democrat. Avocations: tennis, swimming, jogging. Home: 32155 Corte Florecita Temecula CA 92592-6319

GILL, DAVID, food products executive; b. 1949. Student, Cal Poly San Luis Obispo, 1970-75. With Almaden Vineyards, Napa Valley, Calif., 1975-78; ptnr. Rio Farms, Oxnard, Calif., 1978—. Office: Rio Farms 1051 S Pacific Oxnard CA 93030*

GILL, FRANKLIN EDWARD, law professor; b. Sioux City, Iowa, Apr. 22, 1926; s. Franklin E. and Gertrude (Meloy) G.; m. Mary Crawford, May 16, 1958; children: Anne Garrison, Franklin Crawford. BA, Columbia U., 1950, MA, 1953; JD, Northwestern U., 1956. Bar: Ill. 1956, N.Y. 1968, Pa. 1972. Assoc. Schiff, Hardin & Waite, Chgo., 1956-58; rsch. fellow Columbia U., N.Y.C., 1958-59; vis. asst. prof. Cornell U., Ithaca, N.Y., 1960; internat. law counsel Abbott Labs., North Chgo., Ill., 1960-68; assoc. Davis, Polk & Wardwell, N.Y.C., 1968-71; chief corp. securities counsel Sun Co., Inc., Phila., 1971-89; vis. prof. U. N.Mex. Law Sch., Albuquerque, 1986-89, rsch. prof., 1989—; exec. dir. U.S. Mexico Law Inst., Inc., Albuquerque, 1991—. Editor-in-chief: U.S. Mex. Law Jour., 1994—; editor: Federal Securities Law, 1991. Chmn. Ann. Rev. of Fed. Securities Law for Am. Bar Assn., 1980-91. Sgt. U.S. Army, 1945-47. Named to Order of the Coif, Northwestern U. Law Sch., 1956; Ford Found. fellow Columbia U., 1958-59, Fulbright fellow Rostov State U. Law Faculty, Russia, 1995. Mem. ABA. Democrat. Episcopalian. Avocations: tennis, painting. Home: PO Box 9288 Santa Fe NM 87504-9288 Office: U NMex Law Sch 1117 Stanford Dr NE Albuquerque NM 87106-3721

GILL, GEORGE WILHELM, anthropologist; b. Sterling, Kans., June 28, 1941; s. George Laurance and Florence Louise (Jones) G.; BA in Zoology with honors (NSF grantee), U. Kans., 1963, M.Phil. Anthropology (NDEA fellow, NSF dissertation research grantee), 1970, PhD in Anthropology, 1971; m. Pamela Jo Mills, July 26, 1975 (div. 1988); children: George Scott, John Ashton, Jennifer Florence, Bryce Thomas. Mem. faculty U. Wyo., Laramie, 1971—, prof. anthropology, 1985—, chair dept. anthropology, 1993-96; forensic anthropologist law enforcement agys., 1972—; sci. leader Easter Island Anthrop. Expdn., 1981; chmn. Rapa Nui Rendezvous: Internat. Conf. Easter Island Rsch., U. Wyo., 1993. Served to capt. U.S. Army, 1963-67. Recipient J.P. Ellbogen meritorious classroom teaching award, 1983; research grantee U. Wyo., 1972, 78, 82, Nat. Geog. Soc., 1980, Center for Field Research, 1980, Kon-Tiki Mus., Oslo, 1987, 89, 94, 96, World Monuments Fund, 1989. Diplomate Am. Bd. Forensic Anthropology (bd. dirs. 1985-90). Fellow Am. Acad. Forensic Scis. (sec. phys. anthropology sect. 1985-87, chmn. 1987-88); mem. Am. Assn. Phys. Anthropologists, Plains Anthrop. Soc., Wyo. Archael. Soc. Republican. Presbyterian. Author articles, monographs; editor: (with S. Rhine) Skeletal Attribution of Race, 1990. Home: 649 Howe Rd Laramie WY 82070-6885 Office: U Wyo Dept Anthropology Laramie WY 82071

GILL, HARDAYAL SINGH, electrical engineer; b. Amritsar, Punjab, India, Aug. 18, 1952; came to U.S., 1974; BSc with honors, Punjabi U., Patiala, 1971, MSc, 1973; PhD, U. Minn., Mpls., 1978. Sr. engr. Nat. Semiconductor, Santa Clara, Calif., 1978-81; mem. tech. staff Hewlett-Packard, Palo Alto, Calif., 1981-83, project leader, 1983-85, project mgr., 1985-90; sr. engr. IBM, San Jose, Calif., 1990-94, sr. tech. staff, 1994-97; IBM Disting. engr., 1997—. Contbr. articles to profl. jours. Fellow IEEE (chmn. Magnetics Soc. 1987-88, chmn. Santa Clara sect. 1992-93, adminstrv. com. Magnetics Soc. 1992-94); mem. Am. Phys. Soc. Achievements include 40 patents on computer storage/memory devices; avocations: tennis, bike riding. Office: IBM Corp MS N17/142 5600 Cottle Rd San Jose CA 95123-3696

GILL, NILLY, artist; b. Tel Aviv, Israel, Oct. 31, 1943; came to U.S., 1963; d. Benjamin and Rose (Fuchs) Epstein; div.; children: Iris, Daniel Gill. Student Fine Art, Eliahu Gat Atelier, Jaffa, Israel, 1957-60, L.A. City Coll., 1965-67; student Fine Art, Painting, Bill Ainsley Studio, Johannesburg, S. Africa, 1970-77; drawing student, Johannesburg Coll. Art, 1970-77; student Fine Art Painting, U. Calif., San Diego, 1981-82. exhbiting artist R.B. Stevenson Gallery, La Jolla, Calif., 1993—. Artist: solo exhbns. include The Ordinary and The Unexpected, Unicorn Gallery, La Jolla, Calif., 1981, Nilly Gill on Paper, Stratford Gallery, Del Mar, Calif., 1983, "The Echo Series", Kruglak Art Gallery, Mira Costa Coll., Oceanside, Calif., 1993, Interior Echoes, Orange Coast Coll. Art Gallery, Costa Mesa, Calif., 1994, Staged Lives, R.B. Stevenson Gallery, La Jolla, Calif., 1994, Stage Fright, 1995, Cameo Appearances, 1998, The Green Room, "Intimate Spaces", Anaheim Mus., 1997, Boehm Gallery, Palomar Coll., San Marcos, Calif., 1998; group shows: San Diego Mus. of Art, 1993, 5 Work on Paper, San Diego State U. Art Gallery, "Beyond the Line", 1993, 3 person show, Southwestern Coll. Art Gallery, Chula Vista, Calif., 1996.; press coverage of her shows included; Visions Art Quarterly Mag., L.A., 1995, Clipps Jour. Calif. Lit. Project, La Jolla, 1996, Headline News, Century Comm. TV, Anaheim Mus., Calif., 1997, San Diego Union Tribune, 1998, others. Democrat. Jewish. Avocations: walking, museums, movies, ocean swimming, wild animals. Home and Studio: 199 La Mesa Ave Encinitas CA 92024

GILL, REBECCA LALOSH, aerospace engineer; b. Brownsboro, Tex., Sept. 17, 1944; d. Milton and Dona Mildred (Magee) La Losh; m. Peter Mohammed Sharma, Sept. 1, 1965 (div.); m. James Fredrick Gill, Mar. 9, 1985; children: Erin, Melissa, Ben. BS in Physics, U. Mich., 1965; MBA, Calif. State U., Northridge, 1980. Tchr., Derby, Kans., 1966; weight analyst Beech Aircraft, Wichita, Kans., 1966; weight engr. Ewing Tech. Design, assigned Boeing-Vertol, Phila., 1966-67, Bell Aerosystems, Buffalo, 1967; design specialist Lockheed-Calif. Co., Burbank, 1968-79; sr. staff engr. Hughes Aircraft Missile Systems, Canoga Park, Calif., 1979-82, project mgr. AMRAAM spl. test and tng. equipment, 1982-85, project mgr. GBU-15 guidance sect., Navy IR Maverick Missile, Tucson, 1985-89, project mgr. Navy IR Maverick Missile, SLAM Seeker Prodn., 1989-92, TOSH and FOD Internat. program mgr., 1992—; sec. Nat. Cinema Corp. Com. chmn. Orgn. for Rehab. through Tng., 1971-75; speaker ednl. and civic groups. Pres. Briarcliffe East Homeowners Assn.; coord. support group Am. Diabetes Assn., chmn. com. fundraising, coun. mem. Tucson chpt., walk team capt., 1997, 98; active NOW; block leader Neighborhood Watch. Recipient Lockheed award of achievement, 1977. Mem. NAFE, Soc. Allied Weight Engrs. (dir., sr. v.p., chmn. pub. rels. com.), Aerospace Elec. Soc. (dir.), Tucson Zool. Soc. (bd. dirs.), Hughes Mgmt. Club (bd. dirs., chmn. spl. events, chmn. programs, parliamentarian, 1st v.p., pres.), Women in Def. (sec., Ariz. chpt.), Las Alturas Homeowners Assn. (v.p., pres.), Raytheon Mgmt. Club (chmn. elections com.), Tucson Racquet Club. Republican. Office: Raytheon Missile Syss Co Bldg 801 MS G25A Tucson AZ 85734

GILL, SHELLEY R., writer; b. Albuquerque, June 2, 1954; d. John J. Gill and Caroline C. Erskine; 1 child, Kiana Klamser. Author: (children's books) Kiana's Iditarod, 1983, Mammoth Magic, 1984, Alaska Mother Goose, 1986, Thunderfeet, 1987, Danger the Dog Yard Cat, 1988, Alaska's Three Bears, 1989, Daddy Sing to Me, 1990, North Country Christmas, 1992, Iditarod Curriculum, 1993, Swimmer—The Life of an Alaskan Salmon, 1995, Tongass—The Last American Rainforest, 1997; pub., editor: Frontiersman Newspaper (Nat. Newspaper Assn. Best Reporting award). Home: PO Box 2364 Homer AK 99603-2364

GILL, STEVEN, food products executive; b. 1949. Student, Cal Poly San Luis Obispo, Calif., 1970-75. With Bud Antle Inc., Salinas, Calif., 1975-78; ptnr. Rio Farms, L.A., 1978—. Office: Rio Farms 1051 S Pacific Oxnard CA 93030*

GILLEN, ARTHUR FITZPATRICK, retired lawyer; b. So. St. Paul, Minn., Oct. 10, 1919; s. Leonard Peter and Cecelia (Koppy) G.; m. Louise Rosemary Powers, April 28, 1945; children: Robert, Anne Marie, Theodore, Janice, Peter, Mary. BS, U. Minn., 1941, JD, 1943. Bar: Minn., 1943. Sr. partner LeVander Gillen & Miller, PA Attys., So. St. Paul, Minn., 1943-95, LeVander Gillen & Miller PA Attys., So. St. Paul, 1943-95; bd. dirs., pres. Jr. C. of C., C. of C., and Kiwanis; bd. dirs. Gemstone Products Co. and Twin City Concrete, So. St. Paul, 1982—. State rep Minn. Legislature, 1943-51; state senator, Minn. Legislature, 1951-59. Named Man of Year, So. St. Paul Jr. C. of C., 1951. Named to hall of fame, So. St. Paul (Minn.) C. of C., 1992. Republican. Roman Catholic. Avocations: photography, computers, travel, autos. Home: 21043 N 124th Ave Sun City West AZ 85375-1953

GILLESPIE, ADRIENNE AMALIA, artist, editor, researcher; b. N.Y.C., Feb. 26, 1937; d. Quirino and Anne (De Borrello) Galante; m. Gerald Ernest Paul Gillespie, Sept. 5, 1959. BA, Barnard Coll., 1958; MA, Ohio State U., 1960; student, U. Paris, 1960-61; MLS, U. Pitts., 1967. Tchg. asst. Ohio State U., Columbus, 1958-60; libr. State U. N.Y., Binghamton, 1968-73; reviewer Choice, N.Y., 1968-73; artist Palo Alto, Calif.; rschr. hist. preservation City of Palo Alto, 1997—. Exhibited in numerous one-woman and group shows in midwest and on west coast, 1990—. Featured artist Encyclopedia Living Artists, 10th ed. Mem. Pacific Art League (1st v.p. 1993-98). Featured artist Encyclopedia Living Artists, 10th ed. Office: Pacific Art League 668 Ramona St Palo Alto CA 94301-2545

GILLESPIE, GEORGE HUBERT, physicist; b. Dallas, Sept. 9, 1945; s. Hubert W. and Frieda S. Gillespie; children: James S., Colin H., Ian G. BA, Rice U., 1968, MSEE, 1968; MS, U. Calif., San Diego, 1969, PhD, 1974. Rsch. asst. U. Calif., San Diego, 1969-74; staff scientist Phys. Dynamics, Inc., San Diego, 1975-88; pres. G. H. Gillespie Assocs., Inc., San Diego, 1988—; assoc. La Jolla Inst., San Diego, 1976-88; cons. Sci. Applications Internat., McLean, Va., 1985-87; mem. rev. com. for ANL, U. Chgo., 1991-93; mem. and/or chmn. program and organizing coms. for internat. sci. confs. Editor: Supernovae Spectra, 1980, High Current, High Brightness and High Duty Factor Ion Injectors, 1985; contbr. articles to profl. jours. Trustee Sky Mountain Life Sch., Vista, Calif., 1983-86. Capt. USAR, 1968-76. Mem. AAAS, Am. Nuclear Soc., Am. Phys. Soc. Office: G H Gillespie Assocs Inc Ste 201 10855 Sorrento Valley Rd San Diego CA 92121-1616

GILLESPIE, MARILYN, museum administrator. Dir. Las Vegas Natural History Mus., 1991—; pres. Bd. Mus. and Attractions, Nev., sec. 1997—. Vol. promoting environ. concerns, homelessness issues, spl. edn. Mem. Am. Assn. Mus., Nev. Mus. Assn., Allied Arts Coun., S.W. Marine Educators Assn., Kiwanis Club (bd. dirs. Las Vegas Territory, program dir. Uptown). Office: Las Vegas Natural History Mus 900 Las Vegas Blvd N Las Vegas NV 89101*

GILLETT, PATRICIA, pulmonary nurse practitioner, clinical nurse specialist; b. Mass., Jan. 2, 1948; d. Clyde and Estelle (Carter) Gleason; m. Warren Gillett, July 1968; children: Michael, James. ADN, Berkshire Community Coll.; BSN, U. N.Mex.; MSN, U. Tex., El Paso; FNP, Tex. Tech. Univ. Nursing instr. U. Albuquerque, Albuquerque T-VI; critical care edn. coord. St. Joseph Med. Ctr., Albuquerque VA Med. Ctr. Mem. ANA, AACN (Outstanding Cricital Care Educator 1989), Am. Acad. Nurse Practitioners, N.Mex. Nurses Assn. (award for clin. excellence 1994), Coun. Clin. Nurse Specialists, Sigma Theta Tau.

GILLETT, PAULA, humanities educator; b. N.Y.C., July 15, 1934; d. Ira and Sophie (Silvershein) Levy; m. Eric Gillett, June 23, 1956; children: Walter, Nadia, Noel. BA, Bklyn. Coll., 1955; MA, Yale U., 1956; PhD, U. Calif., Berkeley, 1979. Project dir. Grad. Sch. Edn., U. Calif., Berkeley, 1984-89; prof. San Jose (Calif.) State U., 1989—; co-chair Com. on History in the Classroom, 1992-96. Author: Worlds of Art: Painters in Victorian Society, 1990. Project dir. New Faces of Liberty, San Francisco, 1985-89. Summer fellow Am. Coun. Learned Socs., 1994; Mellon fellow Harry Ransom Humanities Rsch. Ctr., U. Tex., Austin, 1996. Mem. Am. Hist. Assn., Phi Beta Kappa. Avocation: choral singing. Office: Humanities Dept San Jose State Univ San Jose CA 95192-0092

GILLETTE, FRANKIE JACOBS, retired savings and loan executive, social worker, government administrator; b. Norfolk, Va., Apr. 1, 1925; d. Frank Walter and Natalie (Taylor) Jacobs; m. Maxwell Claude Gillette, June 19, 1976. BS, Hampton U., 1946; MSW, Howard U., 1948. Lic. clin. social worker; cert. jr. coll. tchr., life. Youth dir. YWCA, Passaic, N.J., 1948-50; dir. program Ada S. McKinley Community Ctr., Chgo., 1950-53; program dir. Sophie Wright Settlement, Detroit, 1953-64; dir. Concerted Services Project, Pittsburg, Calif., 1964-66, Job Corps Staff Devel., U. Calif., Berkeley, 1966-69; spl. program coordinator U.S. Community Services Adminstrn., San Francisco, 1969-83; pres. G & G Enterprises, San Francisco, 1985—; chmn. bd. dirs. Time Savs. and Loan Assn., San Francisco, 1986-87. Commr. San Francisco Human Rights Commn., 1988-93; bd. dirs. Urban Econ. Devel. Corp., 1980-93, San Francisco Conv. and Visitors Bur.; trustee Fine Arts Mus. of San Francisco, 1993—; chmn. San Francisco-Abidjan Sister City Com., 1990—. Mem. Nat. Assn. Negro Bus. and Profl. Women's Clubs (pres. 1983-87), The Links, Inc., Delta Sigma Theta, Inc. Office: G & G Enterprises 85 Cleary Ct Apt 4 San Francisco CA 94109-6518

GILLETTE, RICHARD GARETH, neurophysiology educator, researcher; b. Seattle, Feb. 17, 1945; s. Elton George and Hazel I. (Hand) G.; m. Sally A. Reams, Feb. 17, 1978 (div. Nov. 1988); 1 child, Jesse Robert. BS, U. Oreg., 1968; MS, Oreg. Health Sci. U., 1976, PhD, 1993. Rsch. asst. dept. otolaryngology Oreg. Health Sci. U., Portland, 1969-72, grad. rsch. asst., 1973-80; instr. physiology Western State Chiropractic Coll., Portland, 1981-85, asst. prof. physiology, 1985-93, assoc. prof. physiology, 1993-99, prof. physiology, 1999—; lectr. neurosci. sch. optometry Pacific U., Forest Grove, Oreg., 1985-86; grad. rsch. asst. Neurol. Sci. Inst. OHSU, Portland, 1988-93, vis. scientist, 1993—. Contbr. articles to profl. jours. NIH Predoctoral Tng. fellow Oreg. Health Sci. U., 1973-76, Tarter fellow Med. Rsch. Found. Oreg., 1989; NIH grantee, 1990-99. Mem. AAAS, Soc. for Neurosci., Am. Pain Soc., Internat. Assn. for Study of Pain, N.Y. Acad. Scis. Avocations: history studies, vocal music performance. Office: WSCC 2900 NE 132nd Ave Portland OR 97230-3014

GILLETTE, W. MICHAEL, state supreme court justice; b. Seattle, Dec. 29, 1941; s. Elton George and Hazel Irene (Hand) G.; m. Susan Dandy Marmaduke, 1989; children: Kevin, Saima, Ali, Quinton. AB cum laude in German, Polit. Sci., Whitman Coll., 1963; LLB, Harvard U., 1966. Bar: Oreg. 1966, U.S. Dist. Ct. Oreg. 1966, U.S. Ct. Appeals (9th cir.) 1966, Samoa 1969, U.S. Supreme Ct. 1970, U.S. Dist. Ct. Vt. 1973. Assoc. Rives & Rogers, Portland, Oreg., 1966-67; dep. dist. atty. Multnomah County, Portland, 1967-69; asst. atty. gen. Govt. of Am. Samoa, 1969-71, State of Oreg., Salem, 1971-77; judge Oreg. Ct. Appeals, Salem, 1977-86; assoc. justice Oreg. Supreme Ct., Salem, 1986—. Avocation: officiating basketball. *

GILLIAM, EARL B., federal judge; b. Clovis, N.Mex., Aug. 17, 1931; s. James Earl and Lula Mae G.; m. Rebecca L. Prater; children: Earl Kenneth, Derrick James. B.A., Calif. State U., San Diego, 1953; J.D., Hastings Coll. Law, 1957. Bar: Calif. 1957. Dep. dist. atty. San Diego, 1957-62; judge San Diego Mcpl. Ct., 1963-74, Superior Ct. Calif., San Diego County, 1975-80; judge U.S. Dist. Ct. (so. dist.) Calif., San Diego, 1980-93, sr. judge, 1993—; head Trial Practice Dept. Western State U. Law Sch., San Diego, 1969—. Recipient Trial Judge of Yr. award San Diego County Trial Lawyers Assn., 1981. Office: US Dist Ct 940 Front St San Diego CA 92101-8994

GILLIAM, JACKSON EARLE, bishop; b. Heppner, Oreg., June 20, 1920; s. Edwin Earle and Mary (Perry) G.; m. Margaret Kathleen Hindley, Aug. 11, 1943; children—Anne Meredith, Margaret Carol, John Howard; m. MarKatheryn Allender Brooks, Oct. 17, 1988. A.B., Whitman Coll., 1942; B.D., Va. Theol. Sem., 1948, S.T.M., 1949, D.D., 1969. Ordained to ministry Episcopal Ch., 1948; rector in Hermiston, Ore., 1949-53; canon St. Mark's Cathedral, Mpls., 1953-55; rector Ch. Incarnation, Great Falls, Mont., 1955-68; bishop Episcopal Diocese Mont., 1968-86; vicar St. Jude's Episcopal Ch., Hawaiian Oceanview Estates, 1987—; asst. bishop of Hawaii, 1997—; chmn. com. on pastoral devel., chmn. council on ministry, mem. program, budget and fin. com. Episc. Ch., 1978, pres. Province VI. Served to 1st lt. AUS, World War II. Decorated companion Order of Cross of Nails, companion Coventry Cathedral, Eng., 1974. Home: PO Box 6502 Ocean View HI 96737-6502

GILLIAM, VINCENT CARVER, religion educator, minister, writer; b. Boston, Mar. 24, 1944; s. Wayland Westfield and Belle (Vincent) G.; m. Linda Hassan, June 22, 1970 (div. 1979); children: Halima K., Sumaiya B., Fatimah Z.; m. Nandini Vasudev Katre, Sept. 1, 1991; children: Raphael K. AB in English Lit., Stanford U., 1968; M of Religion, Claremont Sch. Theology, 1970; MA, PhD in Religious Studies and Humanities, Stanford U., 1990. Ordained to ministry United Ch. of Christ, 1982. Asst. and youth min. Lincoln Meml. Congl. Ch., L.A., 1968-69, adj. assoc. min., 1982-86; exec. dir. Coalition for Haitian Asylum, Oakland, Calif., 1983-84; rsch. asst. Martin Luther King Jr. Papers Project, Stanford, Calif., 1985-87; President's fellow U. Calif., Berkeley, 1990-92, rsch. fellow, 1992-95; bd. dirs. United East Oakland Clergy, 1982-84, Am. Friends Svc. Com., San Francisco, 1983—, exec. com., 1990—. Pres.'s fellow U. Calif., Berkeley, 1990-92. Fellow Soc. for Values in Higher Edn.; mem. Am. Acad. Religion, Soc. Bibl. Lit., Am. Hist. Assn., Am. Soc. Ch. History, Medieval Acad. Am., MLA, Renaissance Soc. Am. Democrat. Office: PO Box 1002 Solana Beach CA 92075-1002

GILLIGAN-IVANJACK, CLAUDIA MARLENE, motion picture set artist, writer; b. Indpls., Mar. 21, 1947; d. James Emmitt Gilligan and Pearl Helen (Bodfield) Webster; m. Melvin Chilcoat, Feb. 18, 1966 (div. Sept. 1972); children: Tami Mel-lene, Andy Martin; m. Thomas Robert Ivanjack, Aug. 18, 1988. Forman set artist Internat. Alliance Theatrical Stage Employees and Moving Picture Machine Operators Local 729, Hollywood, Calif., 1976—. Author: (poetry) Penelope Noise, 1981, Imagination, 1986, (movie script) Monopoly, 1989, (short stories) The Fish Pond, 1990 (Pen Women award 1990). Rent mediation bd. City Hawthorne, Calif., 1978-79. Mem. MENSA, Am. Nat. Hygiene Soc., N.Am. Fishing Club., Japan Karate Assn.

(brown belt 1983). Republican. Avocation: fishing. Home and Office: T&C Set Art 1540 Rosita Dr Simi Valley CA 93065-3030

GILLILAND, THOMAS JOE, retired mining executive, educator; b. Globe, Ariz., June 18, 1927; s. James O. Gilliland and Bertha E. (Ikenberry) Elsworth; m. Betty J. Walker, Aug. 9, 1947 (dec. Oct. 1995); m. Mody R. Meredith, Sept. 10, 1997; 1 child, Cheryl J. Earven. Apprentice Miami Copper Co., Miami, Ariz., 1951-55, journeyman mechanic, 1955-68; truckshop foreman Cities Svc. Co., Miami, Ariz., 1968-79, mem. devel. and tng. staff, 1979-88; instr. Gilliland's Safety Enterprises, Eagar, Ariz., 1988-92; diesel instr. Eastern Ariz. Jr. Coll., Globe, Ariz., 1973-77; crane safety instr., fork lift safety instr. Gilliland's Safety Enterprises, Eagar, Ariz., 1988-92; ret. Author: Crane Safety & Rigging, 1988, Fork Lift Safety, 1988, (poetry) A Little Bit of Rhyming, 1995. Recipient Lit. award Iliad Press, 1997. Mem. Top Records Songwriters Assn. Democrat. Baptist. Avocations: fishing, hiking, writing, traveling. Home: PO Box 1678 Eagar AZ 85925

GILLIS, JOHN SIMON, psychologist, educator; b. Washington, Mar. 21, 1937; s. Simon John and Rita Veronica (Moran) G.; m. Mary Ann Wesolowski, Aug. 29, 1959; children: Holly Ann, Mark, Scott. B.A., Stanford U., 1959; M.S. (fellow), Cornell U., 1961; Ph.D. (NIMH fellow), U. Colo., 1965. Lectr. dept. psychology Australian Nat. U., Canberra, 1968-70; sr. psychologist Mendocino (Calif.) State Hosp., 1971-72; asso. prof. dept. psychology Tex. Tech U., Lubbock, 1972-76; prof. psychology Oreg. State U., Corvallis, 1976—, chmn. dept. psychology, 1976-84; cons. VA, Ciba-Geigy Pharms., USIA, UN High Commn. for Refugees; commentator Oreg. Ednl. and Pub. Broadcasting System, 1978-79; Fulbright lectr., India, 1982-83, Greece, 1992; vis. prof. U. Karachi, 1984, 86, U. Punjab, Pakistan, 1985, Am. U., Cairo, 1984-86. Contbr. articles to profl. jours. Served with USAF, 1968-72. Ciba-Geigy Pharms. grantee, 1971-82. Mem. Am. Psychol. Assn., Western Psychol. Assn., Oreg. Psychol. Assn. Roman Catholic. Home: 7520 NW Mountain View Dr Corvallis OR 97330-9106 Office: Oreg State U Dept Psychology Corvallis OR 97331

GILLIS, PAUL LEONARD, accountant; b. Montevideo, Minn., Nov. 20, 1953; s. Joseph Hans and Verna Ruth (Sjolie) G.; m. Deborah Ann Roller, Sept. 9, 1978. BA, Western State Coll., 1975; MS, Colo. State U., 1976. CPA, Colo. Tax cons. Price Waterhouse, Denver, 1976-78; tax mgr. Price Waterhouse, Singapore, 1978-82; internat. tax mgr. Price Waterhouse, San Francisco, 1982-84; sr. mgr. Price Waterhouse, Denver, 1984-88, mng. tax ptnr., 1988—, chmn. mining industry practice, 1993—; mem. adv. coun. Colo. State U.; bd. dirs. World Trade Ctr.; mem. Dist. Export Coun.; pres. Forest Hills Metro Dist.; lectr. World Trade Inst., San Francisco, 1982-84. Author: Accounting for Income Tax, 1988. Pres. Forest Hills Metro Dist., 1992—. Recipient 50 for Colo. award, Colo. Assn. Commerce and Industry, Disting. Alumni award Colo. State U., 1996. Fellow Colo. Soc. CPAs; mem. AICPA, Am. Club (Singapore) (treas. 1981-82), Nat. Mining Assn., Glenmoor Country Club, Denver Athletic Club, Harley Owners Group (Denver chpt.), Chatfield Yacht Club. Avocations: skiing, scuba diving, sailing. Home: 24106 Currant Dr Golden CO 80401-9250

GILLMAR, JACK NOTLEY SCUDDER, real estate company executive; b. Honolulu, Oct. 18, 1943; s. Stanley Eric and Ruth Dorothy (Scudder) G.; m. Janet Thebaud, June 12, 1967; children: Emily, Bennett. BA, U. Pa., 1965; MA, Harvard U., 1967, Pacifica Grad. Inst., 1994. Vol. Peace Corps/Micronesia, East Caroline Islands, 1967-70; trustee Scudder Gillmar Estate, Honolulu, 1973—; trustee, sec. Parker Sch. Trust, Kamuela, Hawaii, 1991—. Author: Impact of an In-country Peace Corps Training Program, 1970, Specimens of Hwaiian Kapa, 1979, Beauty as Experience and Transcendence, 1994. Trustee, pres. Friendship Graden Found., Honolulu, 1971—; owner Nanue (Hawaii) Forest Preserve, 1986—. Fulbright grantee, 1990. Mem. Pacific Club. Office: Scudder Gillmar Estate PO Box 2902 Honolulu HI 96802-2902

GILLMAR, STANLEY FRANK, lawyer; b. Honolulu, Aug. 17, 1935; s. Stanley Eric and Ruth (Scudder) G.; m. Constance Joan Sedgwick; children: Sara Tamsin, Amy Katherine. AB cum laude with high honors, Brown U., 1957; LLB, Harvard U., 1963. Bar: Calif. 1963. Ptnr. Graham & James, San Francisco, 1970-92; of counsel Mackenzie & Albritton, 1993—. Co-author: How To Be An Importer and Pay For Your World Travels, 1979; co-pub.: Travelers Guide to Importing, 1980. Sec. Calif. Council Internat. Trade, 1973-92, hon. counsel, 1980-92, exec. com., 1985-92; mem. Mayor San Francisco Adv. Council Econ. Devel., 1976-82; mem. Title IX Loan Bd., 1982-96, sec. 1986-92; dir. The San Francisco Ministry to Nursing Homes, 1992-94, treas., 1992-94; dir. Inverness Assn., 1995—, pres., 1996—. Served with USNR, 1957-60. Mem. ABA, Calif. State Bar, Bar Assn. San Francisco, Bankers Club (San Francisco); Villa Taverna Club, Inverness Yacht Club. Office: One Post St Ste 500 San Francisco CA 94104

GILLMOR, HELEN, federal judge; b. 1942. BA, Queen's Coll. of CUNY, 1965; LLB magna cum laude, Boston U., 1968. With Ropes & Gray, Boston, 1968-69, Law Offices of Alexander R. Gillmor, Camden, Maine, 1970, Torkildson, Katz, Jossem, Fonseca, Jaffe, Moore, et. al., Honolulu, 1971-72; law clk. to Chief Justice William S. Richardson/Hawaii State Supreme Ct., 1972; dep. pub. defender Office of Pub. Defender, Honolulu, 1972-74; dist. ct. judge per diem Family Ct. (1st cir.), Hawaii, 1977-83; with Dist. Ct., 1st cir., 1983-85; pvt. practice Honolulu, 1985-94; dist. judge U.S. Dist. Ct. Hawaii, 9th cir., 1994—; counsel El Paso Real Estate Investment Trust, 1969; lectr. U.S. Agy. Internat. Devel., Seoul, South Korea, 1969-70, U. Hawaii, 1975. Office: Prince JK Kuhio Fed Bldg 300 Ala Moana Blvd Rm C-435 Honolulu HI 96850-0435

GILMARTIN, KEVIN JARVUS, social scientist; b. Morristown, N.J., Dec. 16, 1947; s. Thomas Maran and Cornelia Kahle (Peck) G.; m. Barbara Lynn Bessey, Jan. 18, 1975. BA, Lawrence U., 1970; MS, Carnegie-Mellon U., 1971, PhD, 1974. Postdoctoral fellow Carnegie-Mellon U., Pitts., 1974-75; assoc. rsch. scientist Am. Insts. for Rsch., Palo Alto, Calif., 1975-77, rsch. scientist, 1977-79, sr. rsch. scientist, 1979-83, prin. rsch. scientist, 1983-88, sr. rsch. fellow, 1988-96, v.p., 1996—; dir. Social Indicators Rsch. Program, Palo Alto, Litigation Support Program, Palo Alto; dir. Applied Behavioral Sci. Group, Palo Alto, 1988-96; dir. John C. Flanagan Rsch. Ctr., Palo Alto, 1996—. Author: Social Indicators: An Annotated Bibliography of Current Literature, 1979, Handbook of Social Indicators, 1980, Monitoring Educational Outcomes and Public Attitudes, 1982, Agencies Working Together: A Guide To Coordination and Planning, 1982. Vol. ranger Henry W. Coe State Park, Morgan Hill, Calif., 1989—. NSF fellow, 1970-74. Mem. Law and Soc. Assn., Pine Ridge Assn. (bd. dirs.), Calif. Acad. Sci., Phi Beta Kappa, Sigma Xi, Phi Kappa Tau (pres. 1969-70). Democrat. Avocations: scuba diving, bird watching, backpacking, cooking. Home: 127 Glenwood Ave Woodside CA 94062-3512 Office: Am Insts for Rsch PO Box 1113 Palo Alto CA 94302-1113

GILMORE, A. DOUGLAS, retail sales executive; b. Kittery, Maine, July 21, 1947; s. Allen Johnston and Margaret Nell (McIntosh) G.; m. Joy Carolyn Gustafson, Aug. 23, 1969; children: Chelsea Jay, Allison Anne. BA, Willamette U., 1969; M Internat. Mgmt., Am. Grad. Internat. Mgmt., 1971. Acct. exec. Levi Strauss & Co., various locations, 1971-75; dist. sales mgr. Levi Strauss & Co., L.A., 1975-76; regional sales mgr. Levi Strauss & Co., San Francisco, 1977-80; dir. sales and mtkg. Levi Strauss & Co., Edmonton, Alta., Can., 1980-82; asst. gen. mgr., mktg. dir. Levi Strauss & Co., Sydney, Australia, 1982-86; v.p. mktg. Winmore Products, Bellevue, Wash., 1986-87; v.p. ops. Trans Am. Glass, Seattle, 1987-93; pres. Mail Movers, Inc., Seattle, 1993—; dir. internat. sales Eddie Bauer, Redmond, Wash., 1993—. Mem. Sydney/San Francisco Sister City Com., Sydney, 1982-85; mem. Boys and Girls Club of Mercer Island. Mem. Internat. Mktg. Soc., Am. Mktg. Assn., Sales and Mktg. Execs., Am. Nat. Club (Sydney). Avocations: skiing, boating, jogging. Home: 445 Beacon St Apt 1 Boston MA 02115-1340 Office: Eddie Bauer PO Box 97000 Redmond WA 98073-9700

GILMORE, JAMES CLAUS, museum curator; b. N.Y.C., July 31, 1954; s. Leonard Earl and Joan Marie (Claus) G.; 1 child, [illegible] Torri Raylyn Pratt, May 26, 1998. BFA, U. San Francisco, 1979; MFA, Univ. of the Arts, Phila., 1992. Exhibit planner, designer Nev. State Mus., Carson City, 1982-88; exhibit planner Harvard U., Cambridge, Mass., 1988-90; mus. curator Campbell (Calif.) Mus., 1990-92; exec. dir. Cupertino (Calif.) Mus., 1992-94; curator of art Redding (Calif.) Mus. of Art, 1994—; cons. Monterey County Dept. Parks, Salinas, Calif., 1994, Los Altos (Calif.) History House, 1994, Old Shasta (Calif.) State Historic Park, 1997; art instr. Shasta Coll., Redding, 1997—. Group shows include Shasta Coll., 1995, 97, Images from the Comstock, 1992. Mem. Leadership Redding, 1995—; bd. dirs. Viva Downtown Redding, 1996—; organizer, founder MarketFest Redding, 1996. Mem. Am. Assn. Museums, Am. Art Historians, Western Museums Assn. Office: Turtle Bay Museums & Arboretum 625 Overhill Dr Redding CA 96001

GILMORE, TIMOTHY JONATHAN, paralegal; b. Orange, Calif., June 24, 1949; s. James and Margaret (Swanson) G.; m. Blanche Jean Panter, Sept. 3, 1984; children: Erin, Sean and Brian (twins). BA, St. Mary's Coll., Moraga, Calif., 1971; grad., Denver Paralegal Inst., 1996. Adminstrv. asst. Gov. Ronald Reagan, Sacramento, Calif., 1971-73; salesman Penn Mutual, Anaheim, Calif., 1973-76; asst. devel. dir. St. Mary's Coll., Moraga, 1976-81; devel. dir. St. Alphonsus Hosp., Boise, Idaho, 1981-83; adminstr. Blaine County Hosp., Hailey, Idaho, 1983-86; exec. dir. Poudre Hosp. Found., Ft. Collins, Colo., 1986-87; nat. recruiting dir. Power Securities Corp., Denver, 1987-89; cons. Horn, Fagan & Lund Exec. Search Cons., Ft. Collins, 1989; v.p. Jackson & Coker Locum Tenens, Inc., Denver, 1990-93; pres. Gilmore and Assocs., Ft. Collins, Colo., 1993-98; paralegal Brownstein, Hyatt, Farber & Strickland, P.C., Denver, 1998—. Republican. Mem. LDS Ch. Avocation: fishing. E-mail: TG1527FC@aol.com. Home and Office: 1527 River Oak Dr Fort Collins CO 80525-5537

GIMBEL, HERVEY WILLIS, medical administrator; b. Calgary, Alta., Can., Nov. 25, 1926; s. Jacob Allan Gimbel and Ruth Helen Johnson; m. Ann Matterand Gimbel, Dec. 23, 1951; children: Shirley Tetz, Denise Ayoub, Kenneth, Marlin, Beverly Kramer. *Wife, Ann Matterand, BS Atlantic Union College (MA), MPH Loma Linda University, (CA), registered nurse, health educator and diabetes educator. Worked in the field of health education for Kaiser Permanente Medical Group, Fontana, CA. Numerous trips to China to conduct training health education workshops with the U.S.-China Health Project. Named consultant to the China National Health Education Institute 1992.* BA, Walla Walla Coll., 1950; MD, Loma Linda U., 1955, MPH, 1978. Diplomate Nat. Bd. Medicine; cert. Am. Bd. Preventive Medicine. Med. dir. North Hill Med. Clinic, Calgary, 1957-82; assoc. prof. Loma Linda (Calif.) U., 1982-84; med. dir. Parkview Ctr. for Occupl. Medicine, Riverside, Calif., 1985-91, Rancho Canyon Occupl. Medicine, Temecula, Calif., 1991—; cons. China Nat. Health Edn. Inst., Beijing, 1992—; dir. U.S.-China Health Project, Redlands, Calif., 1991—, Health Edn. Ctr., Calgary, 1969-82. Contbr. articles to periodicals. Flight lt. Royal Can. Air Force Res., 1958-60. Fellow Am. Coll. Preventive Medicine; mem. Am. Coll. Environ. and Occupl. Medicine, Med. Coll. Can. (licentiate), Delta Omega. Avocations: traveling, photography, history. Home: PO Box 1167 Redlands CA 92373 Office: Prime Care Med Group 27699 Jefferson Ave Temecula CA 92373

GIMBOLO, ALEKSEI FRANK CHARLES (CIMBOLO), artist, philosopher, author; b. Portland, Oreg., Mar. 29, 1956; s. Frank Charles and Elisabeth McFarlane Gimbolo; m. Lilli M. Colipapa, Dec. 16, 1985; children: Niko Alexander, Romaneé Alexander. Student, U. Hawaii, 1976-78, Coll. Charleston, 1979-80. Winemaker Chateau LaCaia, Hazel Green, Ala., 1980-87; artist, philosopher Portland, 1987—. Author: Illuminati-Wisdom of the Enlightened Ones, 1995; painting pub.: Encyclopedia of Living Artist, 7th edit., 1992, 8th edit., 1993; featured in Voice of Am.; exhibits include Seattle Art Resource, Perimeter Gallery, Houston, Signature Galleries, Calif., Hotel Vintage Plz., Portland, Oreg. Vice-chmn. Pre-Law Soc., Charleston, S.C., 1979; exec. com. chmn. Young Reps. of Am., Charleston, 1979; fencing coach Portland (Oreg.) State U., 1993. Avocations: fencing, antique collecting, martial arts.

GINELL, CARY DAVID, music historian, radio broadcaster; b. Glen Cove, N.Y., Jan. 15, 1956; s. William Seaman and Sally Ginell; m. Gail Ellen Ginell, Sept. 2, 1990; children: Brian, Adam. BS in Radio TV Broadcasting, Calif. State U., Northridge, 1978; MA in Folklore and Mythology, UCLA, 1985. Job programmer Drake-Chenault Enterprises, Canoga Park, Calif., 1981-85; broadcast engr. KFAC Radio, Hollywood, Calif., 1986-87; programming cons. AEI Music Network, Orange, Calif., 1987-91; pres. Sound Thinking Music Rsch., Thousand Oaks, Calif., 1991—. Author: Milton Brown and the Founding of Western Swing, 1994 (ARSC award for excellence 1995, Belmont U. award 1995), (discography) The Decca Hillbilly Discography, 1989. Mem. Calif. Traditional Music Soc. (mem. adv. bd.). Fax: (805) 495-3306. E-mail: cginell@gte.net. Office: Sound Thinking Music Rsch 1534 N Moorpark Rd Ste 333 Thousand Oaks CA 91360-5129

GINN, SAM L., telephone company executive; b. Saint Clair, Ala., Apr. 3, 1937; s. James Harold and Myra Ruby (Smith) G.; m. Meriann Lanford Vance, Feb. 2, 1963; children: Matthew, Michael, Samantha. B.S., Auburn U., 1959; postgrad., Stanford U. Grad. Sch. Bus., 1968. Various positions AT&T, 1960-78; with Pacific Tel. & Tel. Co., 1978—; exec. v.p. network Pacific Tel. & Tel. Co., San Francisco, 1979-81, exec. v.p. services, 1981-82, exec. v.p. network services, 1982, exec. v.p., strategic planning and adminstrn., 1983, vice chmn. bd., strategic planning and adminstrn., 1983-84; vice chmn. bd., group v.p. PacTel Cos. Pacific Telesis Group, San Francisco, 1984-86; pres. Air Touch Commn., San Francisco, 1984-87; vice chmn. bd., pres., chief exec. officer PacTel Corp. Pacific Telesis Group, San Francisco, 1986; pres., chief operating officer Pacific Telesis Group, San Francisco, 1987-88, former chmn., pres., chief exec. officer; chmn. Air Touch Commn., San Francisco, 1993—; now chmn. bd., CEO Air Touch Commn., San Francisco, Calif.; mem. adv. bd. Sloan program Stanford U. Grad. Sch. Bus., 1978-85, mem. internat. adv. council Inst. Internat. Studies; bd. dir. 1st Interstate Bank, Chevron Corp., Safeway, Inc. Trustee Mills Coll., 1982—. Served to capt. U.S. Army, 1959-60. Sloan fellow, 1968. Republican. Clubs: Blackhawk Country (Danville, Calif.); World Trade, Pacific-Union; Rams Hill Country (Borrego Springs, Calif.), Bankers. Office: Air Touch Commn 1 California St San Francisco CA 94111-5401

GINOSAR, D. ELAINE, elementary education educator; b. Red Lodge, Mont., June 14, 1937; d. Alvin Henry and Dorothy Mary (Roberson) Wedemeyer; children: Nathan B., Daniel M., David M. BA, Calif. State U., Northridge, 1964, MA, 1977. Cert. elem. tchr., reading and learning disabilities. Tchr. Sacramento City Unified Sch. Dist., 1977—; math. leader, 1992-95; owner, operator rental properties. Pres. Davis (Calif.) Flower Arrangers, 1993-96. Host family for U. Calif. Davis to 15 fgn. students from Japan, Thailand, Mexico, South Korea, 1990-95. Named Woman of Yr. Am. Biog. Soc., 1996. Mem. AAUW (edn. equity chair 1993-95, edn. chair 1965-93, readers theater, women's history week 1990, 91, treas. 1993-98, pres. 1990-91, 98—), Calif. Tchrs. Assn. Republican. Presbyterian. Home: 3726 Chiles Rd Davis CA 95616-4346

GINTER, CAROL(YN) AUGUSTA ROMTVEDT, retired bond underwriter; b. Toledo, Oreg., May 24, 1926; d. Fred and Mary Elizabeth (Whitney) Romtvedt; m. Paul Peter Ginter, June 2, 1951 (dec. Dec. 1995); children: Joan Paula, Teresa Ginter Ward, Philip M., Jeffrey G. Student, U. Oreg., 1945-46. Office and dispatch clk. Oregonian Newspaper, Portland, 1943-45; clk. typist USN Supt. of Ships, Portland, 1945; gen. ins. clk. Fidelity & Deposit Co., Portland, 1946-48; bond clk. Aetna Casualty & Surety Fireman's Fund, Transamerica, Portland, 1956-65; surety bond underwriter Cole, Clark & Cunningham/Rollins, Burdick Hunter, Portland, 1965-79; freelance publicity specialist Waldport, Oreg., 1986—. Pub., coord. family history: Fred Romtvedt, His Life and Loves, 1980. Publicity specialist ARC, 1991—; publicity/sec., lay min. Altar Soc., St. Anthony's Cath. Ch., 1990—. Mem. South County Women's Club (sec. 1984-94, 96, 98), Waldport C. of C. (vol. visitors ctr. 1995—), Lincoln County Hist. Soc., Alsi Hist. Soc. Republican. Avocations: family reunion organization, water exercise, travel, gardening. Home: 1802 NW Canal St Waldport OR 97394-9414

GINZBERG, ABIGAIL, video producer; b. N.Y.C., June 6, 1950; d. Eli and [illegible] Econs., 1969-70; BA, Cornell U., 1971; JD, U. Calif., San Francisco, 1975. Bar: Calif. 1975, D.C. 1979, U.S. Supreme Ct. 1979. Instr. Boalt Hall Law Sch., Berkeley, Calif., 1975-76; atty. Zaks and Harris, San Francisco, 1976-79; litigation counselor U.S. Dept. Labor, Washington, 1979-80; staff counsel Cal/OSHA/Dept. Indsl. Rels., San Francisco, 1979-80; instr. New Coll. Sch. Law, San Francisco, 1980-84; video prodr. Ginzberg Video Prodns., Albany, Calif., 1983—; pres. Nat. Lawyers Guild, San Francisco, 1988-91; cons. Dept. Labor, Washington, 1980-81, Dept. Health Svcs., Calif. and N.J., 1988-90, Bar Assn. of San Francisco, 1990-91. Prodr., dir.: (videos) Those Who Know Don't Tell, 1989 (Finalist award John Muir Med. Film Festival 1990, Silver Apple award Nat. Ednl. Film Festival 1990, Blue Ribbon award Am. Film and Video Festival 1990, Bronze award Houston Internat. Film Festival 1991, U.S. Environ. Film Festival award 1991), All Things Being Equal, 1989 (Golden Eagle award 1990, Finalist award Internat. Film and TV Festival N.Y. 1990), A Firm Commitment, 1990 (San Francisco AFTRA/SAG Am. Scene award 1991, silver plaque INTERCOM/Chgo. Film Festival 1991, Com. on Partnership award ABA 1992, Am. Scene award AFTRA/SAG 1992), All in A Day's Work, 1992 (E. Smythe Gambrell/ABA award 1993), Doing Justice: The Life and Trials of Arthur Kinoy, 1994 (Best of Festival award Vt. Internat. Film Festival 1994, CINE Golden Eagle award 1994, Silver Apple award Nat. Ednl. Film Festival, 1994), Inside/Out: A Portrait of Lesbian and Gay Lawyers, 1994, Breaking Down Barriers: Overcoming Discrimination Against Lawyers with Disabilities, 1994 (Silver plaque Intercom Film Festival 1995), Pulp Ethics, 1995 (Gold award World Fest Houston 1996, Gold plaque Intercom Film Festival 1996), The Unfinished Agenda: NIOSH's First 25 Years and Beyond, 1996 (Cert. of Merit, Intercom Film Festival 1996), Keeping the Door Open: Women and Affirmative Action, 1996 (Honorable mention Columbus Internat. Film Festival 1996), A Voice for Children, 1996, Movin' On Up, 1977, The Public's Health, 1997 (Gold award World Fest Houston 1998), Obstacle Courts, 1997 (Gold award Charleston World Fest 1997, others), Outlooks, 1998, others. bd. advisors KPFA, 1986-92; active Coalition for Civil Rights, San Francisco, 1988—; bd. dirs. Meiklejohn Civil Liberties Inst., 1991—; adv. bd. Impact Fund, 1993—. Recipient Cert. Recognition, Calif. Assembly, 1988, award Alice Toklas Dem. Club, 1988, Award of Merit from Bar Assn. San Francisco, 1994, Bronze Apple award Nat. Ednl. Media Network, 1997. Mem. ABA (standing com. Gavel awards 1997—), APHA, State Bar Assn. Calif., D.C. Bar Assn. Jewish. Avocations: swimming, photography. Home and Office: Ginzberg Video Prodns 1136 Evelyn Ave Albany CA 94706-2316

GIORDANO, LAURA ANN, quality management professional; b. Bronx, N.Y.; d. Joseph P. and Viola N. (Seymour) Morrissey; m. Joseph P. Giordano. BS in Nursing, Molloy Coll., Rockville Centre, N.Y., 1978; MBA, Adelphi U., Garden City, N.Y., 1985. RN, N.Y., Ariz.; cert. profl. in health care quality. Staff nurse Winthrop U. Hosp., Mineola, N.Y., 1978-79; staff nurse nursing supr. alcohol treatment ctr. Creedmoor Psychiat. Ctr., Queens, N.Y., 1979-80, asst. adminstr., cen. systems coord. acute admissions div., 1980-84, asst. dir. edn. and tng., 1984-85; community program rep. Office Community Behavioral Health Ariz. Dept. Health Svcs., Phoenix, 1985-87; clin. quality assurance coord. Ariz. State Hosp., Ariz. Dept. Health Svcs., Phoenix, 1987-90; dir. quality mgmt. svcs. div. behavioral health svcs. Ariz. Dept. Health Svcs., 1990-93; health outcomes project mgr., coop. projects specialist Health Svcs. Adv. Group Inc., Phoenix, 1994—. Mem. Am. Coll. Med. Quality, Ariz. Assn. for Healthcare Quality, Nat. Assn. for Healthcare Quality, Sigma Theta Tau, Delta Mu Delta.

GIOVALE, VIRGINIA GORE, medical products ecexutive, civic leader; b. Salt Lake City, Oct. 12, 1943; d. Wilbert Lee and Genevieve (Walton) Gore; m. John Peter Giovale, June 20, 1965; children: Peter, Daniel, Michael, Mark. BS in Math., Westminster Coll., Salt Lake City, 1965. With W.L. Gore & Assocs., Inc., Flagstaff, Ariz., 1976-84; bd. dirs. W.L. Gore & Assocs., Inc., Newark, 1976—. Trustee, Westminster Coll., Salt Lake City, 1977—, chair, 1988—; dir. Flagstaff (Ariz.) Festival of Sci., 1990—, Ariz. Cmty. Found., 1995—. Recipient Heritage award Westminster Coll., 1994. Avocations: travel, backpacking, skiing, family fun. Office: WL Gore & Assocs Inc 1505 N 4th St Flagstaff AZ 86004-6102

GIRARDEAU, MARVIN DENHAM, physics educator; b. Lakewood, Ohio, Oct. 3, 1930; s. Marvin Denham and Maude Irene (Miller) G.; m. Susan Jessica Brown, June 30, 1956; children—Ellen, Catherine, Laura. B.S., Case Inst. Tech., 1952; M.S., U. Ill., 1954; Ph.D., Syracuse U., 1958. NSF postdoctoral fellow Inst. Advanced Study, Princeton, 1958-59; research assoc. Brandeis U., 1959-60; staff mem. Boeing Sci. Research Labs., 1960-61; research assoc. Enrico Fermi Inst. Nuclear Studies, U. Chgo., 1961-63; assoc. prof. physics, research assoc. Inst. Theoretical Sci., U. Oreg., Eugene, 1963-67; prof. physics, research assoc. Inst. Theoretical Sci., U. Oreg., 1967—, dir., 1967-69, chmn. dept. physics, 1974-76. Contbr. articles to profl. jours. Recipient Humboldt Sr. U.S. Scientist award, 1984-85. NSF research grantee, 1965-79; ONR research grantee, 1981-87. Fellow Am. Phys. Soc.; mem. AAUP. Rsch. on quantum-mech. many-body problems, statis. mechanics, atomic, molecular and chem. physics, nonlinear dynamics and chaos. Home: 2398 Douglas Dr Eugene OR 97405-1711 Office: U Oreg Dept Physics Eugene OR 97403

GIRARDELLI, RONALD K., food products executive; b. 1949. BA, Oreg. State U., 1971. With Blue Cross, Portland, Oreg., 1971-73; pres. Diamond Fruit Growers, Inc., 1973—. Office: Diamond Fruit Growers Inc PO Box 180 Hood River OR 97031-0060*

GIRITLIAN, JAMES SARKIS, film producer, director, editor; b. N.Y.C., Feb. 27, 1948; s. Sahag Sarkis and Alice (Sahakian) G.; m. Joan Mina Schaeffer, June 3, 1984; children: Justin Michael, Katie Madeline. BA in Arts and Scis., U. Miami, 1970. Cameraman Sta. WTVJ-TV, Miami, 1969-76; editor Sta. KHJ-TV, Los Angeles, 1977; asst. editor 20th Century Fox, Inc., Los Angeles, 1977, Universal Studios, Los Angeles, 1978-80; trailer editor Stephen J. Cannell Prodns., Los Angeles, 1980-83; editor, dir. Stephen J. Cannell Prodns., 1984-86; assoc. producer Cannell Films of Can., Vancouver, B.C., 1986-87; co-producer 21 Jump Street Cannell Films of Can., Stephen J. Cannell Prodns., 1987-90; assoc. producer Quantum Leap Universal Studios, Universal City, Calif., 1990—; assoc. producer Tequila and Bonetti Universal Studios. Cinematographer (documentary) A Seed of Hope, 1972 (Alfred I. DuPont award, Emmy nomination); asst. editor (TV pilot film): The Greatest American Hero; editor (TV series): The A Team, Hardcastle and McCormick (1980-86), Hunter, Sting Ray, 21 Jump Street, Moloney, 1996-97, Nowhere Man, 1995-96, SeaQuest, 1994-95, Two (pilot), Melrose Place, 1993-94, The Hat Squad, 1992-93, Three, 1997-98, The Net, The Profiler. Mem. Motion Picture Editor's Guild, Dirs. Guild Am., Acad. of Motion Pictures, TV, Arts and Scis. (blue ribbion Emmy award com. judge 1985, 88), Am. Film Inst., Cousteau Soc., Am. Cinema Editors. Democrat. Congregationalist. Avocations: tennis, golf, skiing, scuba-snorkeling, piano. Home: 5647 Jumilla Ave Woodland Hills CA 91367-6910

GIROD, FRANK PAUL, retired surgeon; b. Orenco, Oreg., Aug. 13, 1908; s. Leon and Anna (Gerig)úG.; m. Nadine Mae Cooper, Aug. 26, 1939; children: Judith Anne, Janet Carol, Franklin Paul, John Cooper. AB, Willamette U., Salem, Oreg., 1929; MD, U. Colo., 1938. Diplomate Am. Bd. Family Practice. Tchr. physics and chemistry, athletic coach Cortez High Sch., Colo., 1929-34; intern U. Colo., Denver, 1938-39; resident surgeon U.S. Marine Hosp., Balt., 1939-41; pvt. practice specializing in family practice and surgery Lebanon, Oreg., 1946-95; ret., 1995; bd. dirs. Lebanon Hosp., 1960—, pres. med. staff. Trustee, sec. Blue Shield Ops., Oreg., 1950-60; grand marshal Lebanon Strawberry Festival, 1988; mem. bd. Coun. of Govts. Sr. Svcs., 1991, 92-97. Maj. Army Med. Corp, 1942-45. Decorated Bronze Star; recipient Disting. Svc. First Citizen award Lebanon, Oreg., 1989; Frank P. Girod Med. Scholarship named in his honor, 1995. Mem. AMA, Oreg. Med. Assn. (trustee), Am. Acad. Family Practice, Kiwanis (pres. 1947-48). Republican. Methodist. Avocation: travel. Home: 625 E Rose St Lebanon OR 97355-4544

GIROUX, PAUL HENRY, retired music educator, musician; b. Humboldt, Ariz., May 24, 1916; s. Frank William and Adda Jenny Mae (Gilbert) G.; m. Flo Annette Carroll, Dec. 26, 1945 (dec. June 1996); 1 child, Nicki Suzette Giroux de Navarro. Student, No. Ariz. U., 1934-39, BA in Music Edn., 1947; BS in Psychology, U. Wash., 1952, MA in Music Edn., 1952. Cert. secondary tchr., Wash. Music dir. Radio KTAR, Phoenix, 1939-49; cantor Temple Beth Israel, Phoenix, 1939-49; grad. asst. music and psychology U. Wash., Seattle, 1950-52; music tchr. Jefferson Jr. H.S., Olympia, Wash., 1953-55; chmn. arts divsn. Everett (Wash.) C.C., 1955-78; ret. Flute soloist Everett Cmty. Band, 1960-78, Nat. Champion Shrine Band, Tucson, 1978-98. Condr. Everett Symphony, 1955-65; choir master Trinity Episcopal Ch.,

Everett, 1963-69; band master of ceremonies Sabbar Shrine, Tucson, 1979-98, band flute soloist, 1979-98. Capt. U.S. Army Ordnance, 1942-45. Decorated Bronze star U.S. Army, Philippines, 1945; Contemporary Music grantee Ford Found., Eastman Sch., Rochester, N.Y., 1969; Theodore Presser fellow Theodore Presser Pub., U. Wash., Seattle, 1952-53. Mem. NEA (life), Am. Fedn. Musicians (life), Music Educators Nat. Conf. (life), VFW (life), Elks (life), Masons (life), Phi Delta Kappa (emeritus), Phi Mu Alpha Sinfonia (life). Episcopalian. Avocations: teaching bible class, studying child psychology, reading.

GIRVIGIAN, RAYMOND, architect; b. Detroit, Nov. 27, 1926; s. Manoug and Margaret G.; m. Beverly Rae Bennett, Sept. 23, 1967; 1 son, Michael Raymond. AA, UCLA, 1947; BA with honors, U. Calif., Berkeley, 1950; M.A. in Architecture, U. Calif.-Berkeley, 1951. With Hutchason Architects, L.A., 1952-57; owner, prin. Raymond Girvigian, L.A., 1957-68, South Pasadena, Calif., 1968—; co-founder, advisor L.A. Cultural Heritage Bd., 1961—; vice chmn. Hist. Am. Bldgs. Survey, Nat. Park Svc., Washington, 1966-70; co-founder, mem. Calif. Hist. Resources Commn., 1970-78; co-founder, chmn. governing bd. Calif. Hist. Bldgs. Code, 1976-91, chmn. adminstrv. law, 1992—, chmn. emeritus, 1993—; chmn. Calif. State Capitol Commn., 1985-98, chmn. emeritus, 1998—. *Raymond Girvigian's pioneering work in the Post War II Historic Preservation Movement includes many firsts. He initiated or assisted in creating over a score of California's (and the nation's) earliest laws, codes, and regulations for historical landmarks. He served as a pro-bono preservation official at local, state, and federal levels (e.g., California Landmark Commisssion's first historical architect) and led many preservation campaigns in the public interest. His professional resume includes hundreds of landmark examples. He is currently a consulting historical architect. Girvigian's numerour honors and awards recognize his years of innovative contributions to this field.* Co-editor, producer: film Architecture of Southern California for Los Angeles City Schs, 1965; historical monographs of HABS Landmarks, Los Angeles, 1958-80; historical monographs of Califs. State Capitol, 1974, Pan Pacific Auditorium, 1980, L.A. Meml. Coliseum, 1984, Powell Meml. Libr., UCLA, 1989; designed: city halls for Pico Rivera, 1963, LaPuente, 1966, Rosemead, 1968, Lawndale, 1970 (all Calif.); hist. architect for restoration of Calif. State Capitol, 1975-82, Workman/Temple Hist. Complex, City of Industry, Calif., 1974-81, Robinson Gardens Landmarks, Beverly Hills, Calif., 1983-92, Pasadena (Calif.) Ctrl. Libr., 1982-92, 95—, Mt. Pleasant House Mus., Heritage Sq., L.A., 1972-95. Mem. St. James Episcopal Ch., South Pasadena, Calif. Served with U.S. Army, 1945-46. Recipient Archtl. Design medal U. Calif., Berkeley, 1947, Outstanding Achievement in Architecture award City of Pico Rivera, Calif., 1968, Neasham award Calif. Hist. Soc., 1982, Preservationist of Yr. award Calif. Preservation Found., 1987, L.A. Mayor's award for archtl. preservation, 1987, Gold Crown award for advancement of arts Pasadena Arts Coun., 1990, Golden Palm award Hollywood Heritage, 1990; named Hist. Architect Emeritus, Calif. Legislature, 1998, Commendation for state and national career achievemtns hist. preservation, Calif. Legislature, 1998. Fellow AIA (Calif. state preservation chmn. 1970-75, state preservation coord. 1970-89, co-recipient nat. honor award for restoration Calif. State Capitol 1983, co-recipient honor award for restoration Pasadena Cen. Libr., Pasadena chpt. 1988); mem. Soc. Archtl. Historians, Nat. Trust for Historic Preservation, Calif. Preservation Found., Calif. Hist. Soc. Independent Democrat. Office: PO Box 220 South Pasadena CA 91031-0220

GISH, ROBERT FRANKLIN, English language educator, writer; b. Albuquerque, Apr. 1, 1940; s. Jesse Franklin and Lillian J. (Fields) G.; m. Judith Kay Stephenson, June 20, 1961; children: Robin Elaine Butzier, Timothy Stephen, Annabeth. BA, U. N.Mex., Albuquerque, 1962, MA, 1967, PhD, 1972. Tchr. Albuquerque Pub. Schs., 1962-67; prof. U. No. Iowa, Cedar Falls, 1968-91; dir. ethnic studies, prof. English Calif. Poly. State U., San Luis Obispo, 1991—, prof., 1992—. Author: Hamlin Garland: Far West, 1976, Paul Horgan, 1983, Frontier's End: Life of Harvey Fergusson, 1988, William Carlos Williams: The Short Fiction, 1989, Songs of My Hunter Heart: A Western Kinship, 1992, Frist Horses: Stories of the New West, 1993, North American Native American Myths, 1993, When Coyote Howls: A Lavaland Fable, 1994, Nueva Granada: Paul Horgan and the Southwest, 1995, Bad Boys and Black Sheep: Fateful Stories from the West, 1996, Beyond Bounds: Cross-Cultural Essays, 1996, Beautiful Swift Fox: Erna Fergusson and the Modern Southwest, 1996, Dreams of Quivira: Stories in Search of The Golden West, 1997. Avocation: guitarist. Office: Calif Poly State U Ethnic Studies San Luis Obispo CA 93407

GIST, JOHN MONTFORT, publishing executive; b. Denver, Oct. 26, 1963; s. Christopher Gist and Phyllis Ann (Angevine) Jozwik. BA, U. Wyo., 1992; MFA, U. Alaska, 1996. Editor, pub. Exegesis Writing Svcs., Laramie, Wyo., 1992-96; tchr. English U. Alaska, Fairbanks, 1994-96. Author: Crow Heart, 1999; editor: Plants for Profit, 1998, Perennial Plants for Profit, 1998; editor: The Greenhouse & Nursery Handbook, 1999. Tchr. Acad. Decathlon, Fairbanks, 1994-96, Upward Bound, Laramie, 1998—. Mem. Poets and Writers, U. Alaska Alumni Assn., U. Wyo. Alumni Assn. Avocations: hunting, fishing, reading, quantum theory.

GITT, CYNTHIA E., lawyer; b. York, Pa., Nov. 14, 1946. BA, Wheaton Coll., 1968; JD with high honors, George Washington U., 1971. Bar: D.C. 1971, Calif. 1974, Mich. 1976, U.S. Supreme Ct. 1976, Ariz. 1978. Legis. asst. to Hon. Bella Abzug, 1971; trial atty. Equal Employment Opportunity Commn., Washington, San Francisco, 1971-75; asst. prof. Wayne State Law Sch., Detroit, 1975-77; atty. Morgan, Lewis & Bockus, L.A., 1977-84; mem. Ford & Harrison, L.A., 1984-91, Epstein, Becker & Green, L.A., 1991—. Mem. ABA (labor and employment sect.), Assn. Trial Lawyers Am., State Bar Calif., D.C. Bar, Los Angeles County Bar Assn. (sect. labor law, sect. litigation), Order Coif. Office: Epstein Becker & Green 1875 Century Park E Ste 500 Los Angeles CA 90067-2506*

GITTLEMAN, MORRIS, consultant, metallurgist; b. Zhidkovitz, Minsk, Russia, Nov. 2, 1912; came to U.S., 1920, naturalized; s. Louis and Ida (Gorodietsky) G.; B.S. cum laude, Bklyn. Coll., 1934; postgrad. Manhattan Coll., 1941, Pratt Inst., 1943, Bklyn. Poly. Inst., 1946-47; m. Clara Konefsky, Apr. 7, 1937; children—Arthur Paul, Michael Jay. Metall. engr. N.Y. Naval Shipyard, 1942-47; chief metallurgist, chemist Pacific Cast Iron Pipe & Fitting Co., South Gate, Calif., 1948-54, tech. mgr., 1954-57, tech. and prodn. mgr., 1957-58; cons. Valley Brass, Inc., El Monte Calif., 1958-61, Vulcan Foundry, Ltd., Haifa, Israel, 1958-65, Anaheim Foundry Co. (Calif.), 1958-63, Hollywood Alloy Casting Co. (Calif.), 1960-70, Spartan Casting Co., El Monte, 1961-62; Overton Foundry, South Gate, Calif., 1962-70, cons., gen. mgr., 1970-71; cons. Familian Pipe & Supply Co., Van Nuys, Calif., 1962-72, Comml. Enameling Co., Los Angeles, 1963-68, Universal Cast Iron Mfg. Co., South Gate, 1965-71; pres. MG Coupling Co., 1972-79; instr. physics Los Angeles Harbor Coll., 1958-59; instr. chemistry Western States Coll. Engring., Inglewood, Calif., 1961-68. Registered profl. engr., Calif. Mem. Am. Foundrymen's Soc., Am. Foundrymen's Soc. So. Calif. (dir. 1955-57), AAAS, Am. Soc. Metals, N.Y. Acad. Scis., Internat. Solar Energy Soc. (Am. sect.). Contbr. to tech. jours.; inventor MG timesaver coupling, patents worldwide. Home: 17635 San Diego Cir Fountain Valley CA 92708-5243

GIUDICI, FRANCIS, food products executive; b. 1956. Pres. L.A. Heame Co., 1975—. Office: L A Hearne Co 512 Metz Rd King City CA 93930-2503*

GIULIANO, CHERYL FALLON, English educator; b. Geneva, N.Y., Jan. 17, 1948; d. Dale George and Sybil Lull (Manson) F.; m. Armando E. Giuliano, June 21, 1970; children: Christopher F., Amanda C. BA, NYU, 1969; MA, U. Chgo., 1973, PhD in English Lit., 1984. Lectr. Stanford U., Palo Alto, Calif., 1979-80; lectr. UCLA, 1980-92, dir. writing program, 1992—; faculty fellow UCLA, 1997. Author, editor: Manuscripts of Younger Romantics: Byron, 1997; manuscript reviewer for various pubs. Recipient Luckman Disting. Tchg. award 1986; rsch. grantee Office Instrnl. Devel., UCLA, 1988. Mem. MLA, Byron Soc., Nat. Coun. Tchrs. English, Writing Program Adminstrs. Avocations: dancing, jogging, singing, 6-yr. old twins. Home: 267 N Tigertail Rd Los Angeles CA 90049-2803

GIVANT, PHILIP JOACHIM, mathematics educator, real estate investment executive; b. Mannheim, Germany, Dec. 5, 1935; s. Paul and Irmy (Dinse) G.; m. Kathleen Joan Porter, Sept. 3, 1960; children: Philip Paul, Julie Kathleen, Laura Grace. BA in Math., San Francisco State U., 1957, MA in Math., 1960. Prof. math. San Francisco State U., 1958-60, Am. River Coll., Sacramento, 1960—; pres. Grove Enterprises, Sacramento, 1961—; pres. Am. River Coll. Acad. Senate, Sacramento, 1966-69; v.p. Acad. Senate for Calif. Community Colls., 1974-77; mem. State Chancellor's Acad. Calendar Com., Sacramento, 1977-79. Founder, producer Annual Sacramento Blues Music Festival, 1976—; producer Sta. KVMR weekly Blues music program, 1978—, music festivals Folsom Prison, 1979-81, Vacaville Prison, 1985. Pres. Sacramento Blues Festival, Inc., 1985—; mem. Lake Tahoe Keys Homeowners Assn., 1983—, Sea Ranch Homeowners Assn., 1977—. Recipient Spl. Service Commendation, Acad. Senate Calif. Community Colls., 1977, Spl. Human Rights award Human Rights-Fair Housing Commn., Sacramento, 1985, W.C. Handy award for Blues Promoter of Yr. Nat. Blues Found., Memphis, 1987, 1st Critical Achievement award Sacramento Area Mus. Awards Commn., 1992. Mem. Faculty Assn. Calif. Community Colls., Am. Soc. Psychical Research, Nat. Blues Found. (adv. com., W.C. Handy Blues Promoter of Yr. 1987). Avocations: tennis, racquetball, reading, music, boating. Home and Office: 3809 Garfield Ave Carmichael CA 95608-6631

GIVENS, EILEEN HADLEY, mayor. Councilmem. City of Glendale, Calif., 1991-95, 95—; chair Glendale Housing Authority City of Glendale, 1992-93, 96-97, chair Glendale Redevel. Agy., 1993-94; mayor City of Glendale, Calif., 1995—. Office: Mgmt Svcs 613 E Broadway Rm 200 Glendale CA 91206-4391*

GLAD, DAIN STURGIS, retired aerospace engineer, consultant; b. Santa Monica, Calif., Sept. 17, 1932; s. Alma Emanuel and Maude La Verne (Morby) G.; BS in Engring., UCLA, 1954; MS in Elec. Engring., U. So. Calif., 1963. Registered profl. engr., Calif. m. Betty Alexandra Shainoff, Sept. 12, 1954 (dec. 1974); 1 child, Dana Elizabeth; m. Carolyn Elizabeth Giffen, June 8, 1979. Electronic engr. Clary Corp., San Gabriel, Calif., 1957-58; with Aerojet Electro Systems Co., Azusa, Calif., 1958-72; with missile systems div. Rockwell Internat., Anaheim, Calif., 1973-75; with Aerojet Electrosystems, Azusa, 1975-84; with support systems div. Hughes Aircraft Co., 1984-90; with Electro-Optical Ctr. Rockwell Internat. Corp., 1990-94; cons., 1994—; operating mgr., sec. V.C.D. Techs. LLC, 1997—. Contbr. articles to profl. jours. Ensign, U.S. Navy, 1954-56; lt. j.g. Res., 1956-57. Mem. IEEE. Home: 1701 Marengo Ave South Pasadena CA 91030-4818

GLAD, SUZANNE LOCKLEY, retired museum director; b. Rochester, N.Y., Oct. 2, 1929; d. Alfred Allen and Lucille A. (Watson) Lockley; m. Edward Newman Glad, Nov. 7, 1953; children: Amy, Lisanne Glad Lantz, William E. BA, Sweet Briar Coll., 1951; MA, Columbia U., 1952. Exec. dir. New York State Young Reps., N.Y.C., 1951-57; mem. pub. rels. staff Dolphin Group, L.A., 1974-83; scheduling sec. Gov.'s Office, Sacramento, 1983-87; dep. dir. Calif. Mus. Sci. and Industry, L.A., 1987-94; ret. Mem. Calif. Rep. League, Pasadena, 1969—; mem. Assistance League of Flintridge, 1970—, Flintridge Guild Children's Hosp., 1969-89. Mem. Sweet Briar Alumnae of So. Calif. (pres. 1972), Phi Beta Kappa, Tau Phi. Episcopalian. Avocations: reading, gardening.

GLADNER, MARC STEFAN, lawyer; b. Seattle, July 18, 1952; s. Jules A. and Mildred W. (Weller) G.; m. Susanne Tso (div. Feb. 1981); m. Michele Marie Hardin, Sept. 12, 1981; 1 child, Sara Megan. Student, U. Colo., 1970-73; JD, Southwestern U., 1976. Bar: Ariz. 1976, Navajo Tribal Ct. 1978. Law clk. jud. br. Navajo Nation, Window Rock, Ariz., 1976-77, gen. counsel jud. br., 1977-79; pvt. practice law Phoenix, 1979-83; ptnr. Seplow, Rivkind & Gladner, Phoenix, 1983-86, Crosby & Gladner, P.C., Phoenix, 1986—; adj. instr. Coll. Ganado, Ariz., 1978-79. Democrat. Jewish. Avocation: stamp collecting. Office: Crosby & Gladner PC 1726 E Thomas Rd Phoenix AZ 85016-7604

GLADNEY, KENNETH EDWARD, construction executive, consultant; b. Toronto, Ont., Can., Nov. 18, 1954; came to U.S., 1984; s. William Edward and Margaret Kathleen G.; Lynne M. Williams, Sept. 1984; children: Sara, Christina. BArch, Ryerson Poly. Inst., Toronto, Can., 1976. Cons. purchasing mgr. Coscan Ltd., Toronto, Ont., Can., 1976-80; cons. field representative F.W. Woolworth Co., Toronto, Ont., Can., 1980; project mgr. Bldg. Resource Group, Toronto, Ont., Can., 1980-82; project coord., estimator Tasis Cons. Ltd., Toronto, Ont., Can., 1982-84; sr. project mgr. Feiler Bros./Marchetti Cons., Southern Calif., 1984-86; prin., owner T & C Gen. Contractors, Orange, Calif., 1986—. Mem. L.A. Athletic Club, Thornhill Country Club. Episcopalian. Avocations: golf, tennis, skiing. Office: T & C Gen Contractors Inc PO Box 3942 Orange CA 92857-0942

GLADSTONE, ARTHUR ABRAHAM, judge, educator; b. N.Y.C., Nov. 15, 1911; s. Phillip L. and Rena (Kaplan) G.; m. Beatrice Thatch, Oct. 3, 1978 (dec. Oct. 1991); children: Kenneth M., Donald E. AB, Columbia Coll., 1932, JD, Columbia U., 1934. Bar: N.Y. 1934, D.C. 1948, U.S. Supreme Ct. 1942. Pvt. practice N.Y.C., 1934-39; atty. U.S. Govt., Washington, 1939-60, adminstrv. law judge, 1960-75; Indian tribal judge Reno, 1992—; settlement judge Supreme Ct. Nev., Reno, 1997—; mem. faculty Nat. Jud. Coll., Reno, 1974—; cons. adminstrv. law, Washington, 1975-92; chmn. bd. Inst. for Study of Regulation, Washington, 1978-87; fellow Coun. on Econ. Regulation, Washington, 1987-91; chmn. Conf. of Adminstrv. Law Judges, ABA, Washington, 1973-74. Contbr. articles to law jours. 2d lt. U.S. Army, 1940-42. Avocations: fishing, amateur radio. Office: Nat Jud Coll U Nev-Reno Reno NV 89557

GLASCOE, WILLIAM OLIVER, III, career officer; b. Washington, Dec. 2, 1969; s. William Oliver Jr. and Louise Elizabeth (Taylor) G.; m. Tanya Marie McCrea, May 13, 1993. BS in Physics, USAF Acad., 1991. Commd. 1st lt. USAF, 1991; navigation sys. test analyst 746th Guidance Test Squadron, Holloman AFB, N.Mex., 1991—. Sec. Alamogordo (N.Mex.) Solid Waste Reduction Com., 1992.

GLASER, CAROL GROVEMAN, psychologist, marriage and family therapist; b. Bronx, N.Y., June 30, 1949; d. M. Arnold and Margaret (Moskowitz) Groveman; m. Donald Howard Glaser, Aug. 5, 1979; children: Ryan Elizabeth, Morgan Alexandra, Eden Victoria, Doren Juliana. BA, CUNY, 1971; MA, Calif. Sch. Profl. Psychology, 1977, PhD, 1979. Tchr. pub. schs. Bronx, 1971-73; tchr., ednl. coordinator Southwood Mental Health Ctr., Chula Vista, Calif., 1973-75; pvt. practice psychotherapy San Diego, 1978—. Mem. APA, Calif. Psychol. Assn., Acad. San Diego Psychologists (assoc.), Calif. Assn. Marriage and Family Therapists, Am. Assn. Marriage and Family Therapists. Office: 4330 La Jolla Village Dr San Diego CA 92122-6201

GLASER, DONALD ARTHUR, physicist; b. Cleveland, Ohio, Sept. 21, 1926; s. William Joseph Glaser. BS, Case Inst. Tech., 1946, ScD, 1959; PhD, Calif. Inst. Tech., 1949. Prof. physics U. Mich., 1949-59; prof. physics U. Calif., Berkeley, 1959—; prof. physics, molecular and cell biology, divsn. neurobiology U. Calif., 1964—. Recipient Henry Russel award U. Mich., 1955, Charles V. Boys prize Phys. Soc., London, 1958, Nobel prize in physics, 1960, Gold Medal award Case Inst. Tech., 1967, Golden Plate award Am. Acad. of Achievement, 1989; NSF fellow, 1961, Guggenheim fellow, 1961-62, fellow Smith-Kettlewell Inst. for Vision Rsch, 1983-84. Fellow AAAS, Fedn. Am. Scientists, The Exploratorium (bd. dirs.), Royal Soc. Sci., Royal Swedish Acad. Sci., Assn. Rsch. Vision and Ophthalmology, Neuroscis. Inst., Am. Physics Soc. (prize 1959); mem. Nat. Acad. Scis., Am. Assn. Artificial Intelligence, N.Y. Acad. Sci., Internat. Acad. Sci., Am. Philos. Soc., Sigma Xi, Tau Kappa Alpha, Theta Tau. Home: 41 Hill Rd Berkeley CA 94708-2131 Office: U Calif Dept Molecular & Cell Biology Univ Calif 337 Stanley Hall Berkeley CA 94720*

GLASS, DAVID D., department store company executive, professional baseball team executive; b. Liberty, Mo., 1935; married. Gen. mgr. Crank Drug Co., 1957-67; v.p. Consumers Markets Inc., 1967-76; exec. v.p. fin. Wal-Mart Stores Inc., Bentonville, Ark., to 1976, vice chmn., CFO, 1976-84, pres., 1984—, COO, 1984-88, CEO, 1988—, also bd. dirs.; CEO, chmn. bd. dirs. Kansas City Royals, 1993—. Office: Wal-Mart Stores Inc 702 SW 8th St Bentonville AR 72716 also: Kansas City Royals PO Box 419969 Kansas City MO 64141-6969*

GLASS, JEAN ANN, special education services professional; b. Phoenix, Ariz., Mar. 15, 1934; d. James Leslie Giffin and Helen Lucille Griffith; m. Dwaine Charles Glass, Nov. 26, 1952; children: Michael James, Stephen Charles, Daphne Ann, Diona Lynn, Helen Louise, Geoffrey Giffin. *A sample of pioneers in Jean's family genealogy include John Flood arriving in America at Jamestown on the "Swan" in 1610, Margaret, the widow of William Flinch, on the "Supply" in 1620, and Edward Fuller and his son, Samuel, arriving at Plymouth on the "Mayflower" in November 1620. Jean's father, Major James Leslie Giffin, was a lawyer and pioneer flyer in all of the Americas, Hawaii, the Philippine Islands, and WWI and WWII. Her mother, Helen Lucille Griffith Giffin VerBrugghen, was one of the earliest Registered Nurses in Arizona and later a pioneer specialist taking electroencephalograms in Nevada.* Student, U. Nev., 1950-52; AA in Psychology, Mt. San Antonio Coll., 1973, AS in Mental Health, 1974; BA in Behavioral Sci., Calif. Polytechnic U., 1975; MA in Spl. Edn., Calif. State U., L.A., 1979, MA in Psychology, 1983; MS in Devel. Disabilities Programming, U. La Verne, 1981, postgrad., 1981-85; postgrad., Azusa Pacific U., 1989. Instr. devel. disabled Chaffey C.C., Alta Loma, Calif., 1975-79; program dir. sch.-age parenting and infant devel. El Monte (Calif.) Union High Sch. Dist., 1981-95, tchr., 1981—; family life educator Nat. Coun. Family Rels., Mpls., 1988—; therapeutic recreation specialist Nat. Coun. Therapeutic Recreation, Thiells, N.Y., 1975—; rschr., psychiat. technician Frank D. Lanterman State Hosp. & Devel. Ctr., Pomona, Calif., 1981-94. Recipient cert. commendation State of Calif., 1985, City of El Monte, 1993. Mem. DAR, AAUW, Nat. Geneal. Soc., Coun. Exceptional Children, Archaeol. Survey Assn. So. Calif., Inc., Bibl. Archaeology Soc., L.A. World Affairs Coun., El Monte Cmty. Cultural Commn.'s Sister City Assn., Pomona Valley Personal Ancestral File Users Group, San Gabriel/Pomona Valley Alumnae Panhellenic Assn., Calif. Fedn. Chaparral Poets, Internat. Biograph. Ctr. (Order of Internat. Fellowship 1998—), Gamma Phi Beta. Republican. Mem. LDS Ch. Avocations: genealogy, archaeology, history, the arts. Office: El Monte Union H S Dist 3537 Johnson Ave El Monte CA 91731-3290

GLASS, KRISTI LYN, magazine publisher, writer; b. St. Paul, Apr. 2, 1947; d. Roy Wilford and Marguerite Francis (Lampman) Hawkinson; m. Dean Karl Hedstrom, Apr. 30, 1971 (div. 1986); m. Dwight Richmond Glass, Nov. 11, 1989; children: Dwight Ian, Bonnie Jean. BA in English/Journalism, Macalester Coll., 1969. Asst. dir., editor, yearbook critical svc. dir. Nat. Scholastic Press Assn., Associated Collegiate Press, Mpls., 1969-75; sales rep. Delmar Co., Charlotte, N.C., 1975-84; owner Mainframe Connection, Metro-Net, Mainframe Games, St. Paul, 1982-86; edition layout editor Stable Sheet Publs., Osceola, Wis., 1986; documentation mgr. Pub. Bus. Systems, St. Paul, 1986-93; tech. writer St. Paul, Elko, Nev., 1993—; pub., editor Gothic Jour., St. Paul, Elko, Nev., 1991—; author ann. report to Gov. Nev., Commn. on Alcohol and Substance Abuse Treatment, Edn. Enforcement and Prevention, 1996, 97. Author, editor various tech. manuals, 1986—. Founder Grant Trail Rangers, St. Paul, 1981; pres. Elko County Art Club, 1997. Recipient Journalism award North Ctrl. Pub. Co., 1965, Territory Growth award Delmar Co., 1977, 78, Employee Recognition award LAN Systems, Inc., 1969. Mem. Elko County Art Club (pres. 1997), Romance Writers Am. Avocations: horseback riding, fox hunting, sailing, artistic works. E-mail: Kglass@GothicJournal.com. Home and Office: PO Box 6340 Elko NV 89802

GLASSER, SELMA G., writer, columnist; b. N.Y.C., Jan. 2, 1920; d. Morris and Clara (Dlugash) Goldstein; widowed. instr. Bklyn (N.Y.) Coll., until 1985, Valley Coll., 1985—, Van Nuys, Calif. Author: The Complete Guide to Prize Contests, Sweepstakes and How to Win Them, Prize Winning Recipes, The Complete Guide to Selling Fillers-Verse-Short Humor and Winning Contests, Your Secret Shortcut to Power Writing--Analogy Book of Related Words, Analogy Anthology, Rhyming Dictionary. Pres. Bklyn. Contest Club. Recipient $4000 Cruise Prize 1997, $5000 1st place prize Aspen Essay Contest, 1997. Mem. Sr. Singles (treas. 1997-98). Avocations: bridge, lectures, hiking, speaking. Home: 10204 Camarillo St Toluca Lake CA 91602-1604

GLASSHEIM, JEFFREY WAYNE, allergist, immunologist, pediatrician; b. Far Rockaway, N.Y., Sept. 16, 1958; s. Ronald Alan and Glenda (Deitch) G.; m. Paulette Renée, Apr. 16, 1989; children: Elyssa Gwen, Brenna Chase. BA, Temple U., 1980; DO, U. New Eng., 1984. Diplomate Am. Bd. Allergy and Clin. Immunology, Am. Bd. Pediatrics. Commd. 2d lt. U.S. Army, 1980, advanced through grades to maj., 1989, resigned, 1992; intern Winthrop-Univ. Hosp., Mineola, N.Y., 1984-85; resident Madigan Army Med. Ctr., Tacoma, Wash., 1985-87; fellow Fitzsimons Army Med. Ctr. and Nat. Jewish Ctr. Immunology, Aurora, Colo., 1990-91, chief fellow allergy-clin. immunology, 1990-91; chief allergy-clin. immunology and immunizations svcs. Silas B. Hays Army Community Hosp., Fort Ord, Calif., 1991-93; resigned USAR, 1993; pvt practice Fresno, 1993—; dir. allergy-immunology dept. Pediatric Med. Group of Fresno, Calif., 1994-95; dir. allergy-immunology Northwest Med. Group, Fresno, 1995-97; pvt. practice allergy and immunology, 1997—. Contbr. articles to profl. jours. Fellow Am. Acad. Pediatrics (allergy and immunoogy sect.), Am. Acad. Allergy Asthma and Immunology, Am. Coll. Allergy, Asthma and Immunology; mem. AMA, Am. Osteo. Assn., Am. Physicians Fellowship for Medicine in Israel, Calif. Soc. Allergy, Asthma and Clin. Immunology, Ctrl. Calif. Allergy Soc., Fresno-Madera Med. Soc., Calif. Med. Assn., Osteo. Physicians and Surgeons of Calif. Republican. Jewish. Avocations: meteorology, sports, reading/current events, gardening, walking. Office: Valley Med Plz Herndon 1646 E Herndon Ave Ste 106 Fresno CA 93720-3305

GLASSMAN, ARTHUR JOSEPH, software engineer; b. N.Y.C., Apr. 4, 1948; s. Max Samuel and Ruth Rae (Gold) G. SB in Physics, MIT, 1968; MS, Yale U., 1969; PhD, Columbia U., 1977. Sr. programmer Cubic, San Diego, 1978-79; engr. Linkabit, San Diego, 1979-80; sr. scientist Jaycor, San Diego, 1980-91; sr. software engr. SuperSet, San Diego, 1992-93, Document Scis. Corp., San Diego, 1994—. Mem. IEEE, Am. Phys. Soc., Am. Geophys. Union, Am. Stats. Assn., Math. Assn. Am.

GLATZER, ROBERT ANTHONY, marketing and sales executive; b. N.Y.C., May 19, 1932; s. Harold and Glenna (Beaber) G.; m. Paula Rosenfeld, Dec. 20, 1964; m. Mary Ann Murphy, Dec. 31, 1977; children: Gabriela, Jessica, Nicholas. BA, Haverford Coll., 1954. Br. store dept. mgr. Bloomingdale's, N.Y.C., 1954-56; media buyer Ben Sackheim Advt., N.Y.C., 1956-59; producer TV commls. Ogilvy, Benson & Mather Advt., N.Y.C., 1959-62; dir. broadcast prodn. Carl Ally Advt., N.Y.C., 1962-63; owner Chronicle Prodns., N.Y.C., 1963-73; dir. Folklife Festival, Smithsonian Inst., Washington, 1973, Expo 74 Corp., Spokane, Wash., 1973-74; pres. Robert Glatzer Assocs., Spokane, 1974—; ptnr. Delany/Glatzer Advt., Spokane, 1979-84; dir. sales/mktg. Pinnacle Prodns., Spokane; adj. faculty Ea. Wash. U., 1987—. Bd. dirs. Riverfront Arts Festival, 1977-78; bd. dirs. Comprehensive Health Planning Council, 1975-78, Spokane Quality of Life Council, 1976-82, Allied Arts of Spokane, 1976-80, Art Alliance Wash. State, 1977-81, Spokane chpt. ACLU, 1979-83, Wash. State Folklife Council, 1983—, chair 1998—; commr. Spokane Arts, 1987—; mem. Spokane Community Devel. Bd., 1988—; mem. Shorelines Update Commn., 1988—; mem. Wash. State Small Bus. Improvement Coun., 1994—, chair 1998—. Recipient CINE Golden Eagle award (2). Mem. Dirs. Guild Am. Democrat. Jewish. Author: The New Advertising, 1970; co-scenarist Scorpio and other TV prodns.

GLAZER, JACK HENRY, lawyer; b. Paterson, N.J., Jan. 14, 1928; s. Samuel and Martha (Merkin) G.; m. Zelda d'Angleterre, 1979. BA, Duke U., 1950; JD, Georgetown U., 1956; postgrad. U. Frankfurt (W.Ger.), 1956-57; S.J.D. U. Calif.-Berkeley, 1977. Bar: D.C. 1957, Calif. 1968. Atty., GAO and NASA, 1958-60; mem. maritime div. UN Internat. Labour Office, Geneva, Switzerland, 1960; spl. legal adv. UN Internat. Telecommunication Union, Geneva, 1960-62; atty. NASA Washington, 1963-66; chief counsel NASA-Ames Research Center, Moffett Field, Calif., 1966-88; gov. Calif. Maritime Acad., 1975-78; asst. prof. Hastings Coll. Law, 1985-87; prof., assoc. dean bus. sch. San Francisco State U., 1988-92. Dir. San Francisco Palace of Fine Arts, 1995. Comdr. Calif. Naval Militia, ret. Capt. JAGC, USNR, ret. Mem. Calif. Bar Assn., D.C. Bar Assn., White's Inn (reader). Contbr. articles on internat. law to profl. jours. Office: White's Inn 37 White St San Francisco CA 94109-2609

GLAZER, REA HELENE See KIRK, REA HELENE

GLAZIER, RON, zoological park administrator. Dir. Santa Ana Zoo, Santa Ana, Calif. Office: Santa Ana Zoo 1801 E Chestnut Ave Santa Ana CA 92701-5001*

GLAZOV, BEVERLY, controller; b. St. Louis, Aug. 11, 1943; d. Leo and Dorothy (Eiche) Gibstein; divorced; children: David, Kenneth, Michelle. Student, UCLA, 1985. Stockbroker Oppenheimer & Co., L.A., 1980-91; adminstr. asst. El Pollo Loco, L.A., 1991—; contr. Citiwide Cellular, L.A., 1992-94; adminstr. Western Internat. Media Corp., 1994; pres. Westside Investors Group, L.A., 1994—; fin. advisor Baraban Securities, L.A., 1980—. Office: W Internat Media & Baraban Sec 11611 San Vicente Blvd Los Angeles CA 90049-5106

GLEESON, JAMES JOSEPH, artist, educator; b. San Francisco, Sept. 17, 1959; s. James Joseph and Geraldine Marie (Finney) G. Student, City Coll., San Francisco, 1978-79; BFA, U. San Francisco, 1983; BFA, cert. in illustration, Acad. of Art Coll., San Francisco, 1983. Artist Stratford Design, Brisbane, Calif., 1984-86; owner J. Gleeson Studio, San Francisco, 1986—; cert. artist Grumbacher Corp., N.J., 1996—; tchr. art Acad. of Art Coll., San Francisco, 1997—; tchr. LEAP program Baywood Sch., San Mateo, Calif., 1997—; mem. artist adv. coun. Artspan/Open Studios, San Francisco, 1996—, also bd. dirs.; presenter workshops, demonstrator various orgns. One-man shows include U. Calif., San Francisco, 1989, 901 Gallery, 1991, Rosicrucian Mus., 1992, Stanford U., 1993, World Trade Club, San Francisco, 1994, Calif. Pacific Med. Ctr., 1995, Gordon Biersch Brewery, 1995, Virtual Gallery, 1996, Thomas Moser Furniture, 1997, Acad. Art Coll. Exhibit, 1998; group shows include L.A. Art Expo, 1998 (art calender finalist); contbr. articles to profl. publs. Recipient Jurors watercolor award, 1992, 1st pl. award Kaiser Show, 1993, Gold medal for watercolor Ea. Wash. Watercolor Soc., 1993, Jack Richeston award San Diego Watercolor Soc., 1993. Mem. Soc. Western Artists (juror's award 1992, pres. 1993-95, 1st pl. watercolor award 1993, Grumbacher award 1993, Best in Show award 1994), Artists Guild San Francisco. Democrat. Roman Catholic. Avocations: music, baseball, gardening, conversation, public speaking. Home and Studio: James Gleeson Studio 148 Precita Ave San Francisco CA 94110-4621

GLEN, NIKI, artist; b. Milw., Nov. 14, 1950; d. Alan and Janet (Marx) G.; m. Mark Knops, Jan. 19, 1981; children: Dana Alan Knops, Laramie Ann Glen. BS in Art Edn., U. Wis., 1973. Cert. in art edn. K-12. Pub. artist, muralist numerous orgns. various locations, 1973—; co-founder Madison (Wis.) Graphics, 1973-76; art educator various schs. various locations, 1973—; dir. S.W. Pub. Art Group, Phoenix, Ariz., 1996—. Exhibited in group shows Corcoran Gallery, Washington, 1986, Williams Ratliff Gallery, Sedona, Ariz., 1988, Veneble Neslage Galleries, Washington, 1989-92, Spirit of N.Mex. Art Exhbn., Washington, 1990, Marin-Price Galleries, Bethesda/Chevy Chase, Md., 1992, Am. Bank Gallery, Chevy Chase, 1994, Artisimo Gallery, Scottsdale, Ariz., 1995, Nat. Soc. Mural Painters Centennial Exhibit, N.Y.C., 1996, 1st Internat. Pub. Art and Mural Congress, Mexico City, 1998; featured in publs. including Community Murals, 1984, Street Murals: The Most Exciting Cities of America, Britain and Western Europe, 1982, also numerous covers and illustrations for textbooks and periodicals. Pres. Arts and Creativity in Early Childhood, 1993-96; bd. dirs. Gaynor Mus. and Found., 1993—; mem. Ariz. Alliance for Art Edn., 1990-95. Recipient Orchid award City of Madison, 1975, Tempe Diablo award of excellence in edn., 1996, 97; Ariz. Artist Project grantee Ariz. Commn. on Arts, 1994; grantee numerous orgns. including Atlantic Richfield, City of Whitewater, The Mills Corp., Phoenix Arts Commn. Mem. Nat. Soc. Mural Painters. Avocations: swimming, skiing, reading.

GLENDINNING, CHELLIS, author, psychologist; b. Cleve., June 18, 1947; d. Paul and Mary Hooker (Daoust) G. BA in Social Scis., U. Calif., Berkeley, 1969; PhD in Psychology, Columbia Pacific U., 1984. Lic. profl. clin. counselor. mem. adv. bd. Earth Island Inst., San Francisco, 1987-98, Earth Ways Found., Malibu, Calif., 1996—, Dept. Peace and Conflict Studies, U. Calif.-Berkeley, 1984-90, Loka Inst., Amherst, Mass., 1992—. Author: Waking Up in the Nuclear Age, 1987, When Technology Wounds, 1990 (nomination for Pulitzer prize 1991), My Name is Chellis and I'm in Recovery From Western Civilizations, 1994, Off the Map (An Expedition Deep into Imperialism, The Global Economy, and Other Earthly Wherabouts), 1999. Bd. dirs. Elmwood Inst., Berkeley, 1986-93. Recipient Billy award San Francisco Examiner, 1983, First Times award N.Mex. Coun. for Humanities, Albuquerque, 1989, Zero Injustice award Rio Arriba County Commn., 1997. Avocations: sustainable living, gardening, fishing, herb gathering. Home: PO Box 130 Chimayo NM 87522-0130

GLENN, BETH, sales and marketing executive; b. Petersburg, Va., Sept. 3, 1952; d. William Francis and Helen Elizabeth (Martin) G. BA cum laude, Kent State U., 1976. Systems analyst Raytheon, N.Y.C., 1980-81; office mgr. Chem. Bank, N.Y.C., 1981-82; sr. mktg. cons. Honeywell, Boston, 1982-87; worldwide mktg. mgr. Groupe Bull, Paris, 1987-91; dir. internat. sales Nynex, White Plains, N.Y., 1991-94; telecom. & media mktg. & mgmt. rep. Hewlett-Packard, Cupertino, Calif., 1995—. Mem. NAFE, Assn. Mgmt. Women, Alliance Francais Newport, Millbrook Equestrian Ctr., Nat. Trust for Hist. Preservation, Preservation Soc. Newport, Friends of Vielles Maisons Francaises. Episcopalian. Avocations: equitation, skiing.

GLENN, CONSTANCE WHITE, art museum director, educator, consultant; b. Topeka, Oct. 4, 1933; d. Henry A. and Madeline (Stewart) White; m. Jack W. Glenn, June 19, 1955; children: Laurie Glenn Buckle, Caroline Glenn Galey, John Christopher. BFA, U. Kans., 1955; grad., U. Mo., 1969; MA, Calif. State U., 1974. Dir. Univ. Art Mus. & Mus. Studies program, from lectr. to prof. Calif. State U., Long Beach, 1973—; art cons. Archtl. Digest, L.A., 1980-89. Author: Jim Dine Drawings, 1984, Roy Lichtenstein: Landscape Sketches, 1986, Wayne Thiebaud: Private Drawings, 1988, Robert Motherwell: The Dedalus Sketches, 1988, James Rosenquist: Time Dust: The Complete Graphics 1962-92, 1993, The Great American Pop Art Store: Multiples of the Sixties, 1997; contbg. author: Encyclopedia Americana, 1995—; contbg. editor: Antiques and Fine Arts, 1991-92. Vice-chair Adv. Com. for Pub. Art, Long Beach, 1990-95; chair So. Calif. adv. bd. Archives Am. Art, L.A., 1980-90; mem. adv. bd. ART/LA, 1986-94, chair, 1992. Recipient Outstanding Contbn. to Profession award Calif. Mus. Photography, 1986. Mem. Am. Assn. Mus., Assn. Art Mus. Dirs., Coll. Art Assn., Art Table, Long Beach Pub. Corp. for the Arts (arts adminstr. of yr. 1989), Kappa Alpha Theta. Office: Univ Art Mus 1250 N Bellflower Blvd Long Beach CA 90840-0006

GLENN, GUY CHARLES, pathologist; b. Parma, Ohio, May 13, 1930; s. Joseph Frank and Helen (Rupple) G.; m. Lucia Ann Howarth, June 13, 1953; children: Kathryn Holly, Carolyn Helen, Cynthia Marie. BS, Denison U., 1953; MD, U. Cin., 1957. Intern, Walter Reed Army Med. Center, Washington, 1957-58; resident in pathology Fitzsimons Army Med. Center, Denver, 1959-63; commd. 2d lt. U.S. Army, 1956, advanced through grades to col., 1977; demonstrator pathology Royal Army Med. Coll., London, 1970-72; chief dept. pathology Fitzsimons Army Med. Center, Denver, 1972-77; past pres. med. staff St. Vincent Hosp., Billings, Mont.; past mem. governing bd. Mont. Health Systems Agy. Diplomate Am. Bd. Pathology, Am. Bd. Radioisotopic Pathology. Fellow Coll. Am. Pathologists (chmn. chemistry resources com., chmn. commn. sci. resources, mem. budget program and review com., council on quality assurance, chmn. practice guidelines com., outcomes com., bd. govs., chmn. nominating com.), Am. Soc. Clin. Pathology, Soc. Med. Cons. to Armed Forces (chair emeritus legal and legis. com.), Midland Empire Health Assn. (past pres.), Rotary (bd. dirs. local chpt.). Contbr. to profl. jours. Home: 3225 Jack Burke Ln Billings MT 59106-1113

GLENN, KATHRYN IRENE (KK GLENN), computer company professional; b. Santa Ana, Calif., May 13, 1952; d. Kenneth Elmer Glenn and Irene Mae (Jones) Cross. Grad., Indio H.S., 1970. Key punch operator Master Computer, Indio, Calif., 1970-75; data input specialist Valley Meml. Hosp., Indio, 1973-77; key punch operator Indio Community Hosp., 1977-81; infosystems ops. staff Eisenhower Med. Ctr., Rancho Mirage, Calif., 1981-84; data processing mgr. John F. Kennedy Meml. Hosp., Indio, 1984-89; owner, operator KK At Your Svc., La Quinta, Calif., 1993—. Mem. NAFE, Am. Bus. Womens Assn. (Trendsetter chpt. 1996—).

GLICKMAN, ELAINE JEANNE, artist; b. Des Moines, Jan. 21, 1922; d. Isaac Davidson and Rae (Miller) Ginsberg; m. Eugene David Glickman, Mar. 15, 1942; children: Richard Lorin, James Allan. Student, Northwestern U., 1939-41, Am. Acad. Art Chgo. Columnist, illustrator Register Tribune, Des Moines, 1942-44; art tchr. Solo shows include Bernard Heights Country Club, 1994-95, Remington, 1996; group shows include La Jolla Art Assn., Poway Ctr. Performing Arts, 1994-95, San Diego Med. Soc., 1995. Bd. dirs., past pres. Davenport Mus. of Art; vol. nurse's aide Camp Dodge Iowa, Des Moines, Cook County Hosp., Chgo., Broadlawn County Hosp., Des Moines, 1943-44. Mem. LWV. Democrat. Avocations: museums, art, painting, drawing. Home: 12876 Circulo Dardo San Diego CA 92128-1703

GLICKMAN, HARRY, professional basketball team executive; b. Portland, Oreg., May 13, 1924; s. Sam and Bessie (Karp) G.; m. Joanne Carol Matin, Sept. 28, 1958; children: Lynn Carol, Marshall Jordan, Jennifer Ann. B.A., U. Oreg., 1948. Press agt., 1948-52; pres. Oreg. Sports Attractions, 1952—; mgr. Multnomah (Oreg.) Civic Stadium, 1958-59; pres. Portland Hockey Club, 1960-73; former exec. v.p. basketball team Portland Trail Blazers, now pres. emeritus. Trustee B'nai B'rith Jr. Camp, 1965; bd. dirs. U. Oreg. Devel. Fund. Served with AUS, 1943-46. Named to Oreg. Sports Hall of Fame, 1986. Mem. Portland C. of C. (bd. dirs. 1968-72), Sigma Delta Chi, Sigma Alpha Mu. Jewish. Office: Portland Trail Blazers 1 Center Ct Ste 200 Portland OR 97227-2103*

GLOCK, CHARLES YOUNG, sociologist; b. N.Y.C., Oct. 17, 1919; s. Charles and Philippine (Young) G.; m. Margaret Schleef, Sept. 12, 1950; children: Susan Young, James William. B.S., N.Y. U., 1940; M.B.A., Boston U., 1941; Ph.D., Columbia U., 1952. Research asst. Bur. Applied Social Research, Columbia U., 1946-51, dir., 1951-58, lectr., then prof. sociology, 1956-58; prof. sociology U. Calif. at Berkeley, 1958-79, prof. emeritus, 1979—, chmn., 1967-68, 69-71; dir. Survey Research Center, 1958-67; adj. prof. Grad. Theol. Union, 1971-79; Luther Weigle vis. lectr. Yale U., 1968. Co-author: Wayward Shepherds, The Anatomy of Racial Attitudes, Anti-Semitism in America, American Piety; sr. author: Adolescent Prejudice, To Comfort and To Challenge, Religion and Society in Tension, Christian Beliefs and Anti-Semitism, The Apathetic Majority; contbg. editor Rev. Religious Rsch. Sociological Analysis; editor: The New Religious Consciousness, Survey Research in the Social Sciences, Beyond the Classics, Religion in Sociological Perspective, Prejudice U.S.A., Unison-Newsletter of One Voice, 1990-96; contbr. numerous articles on social scis. Active parish edn. Luth. Ch. Am., 1970-72; mem. mgmt. com. Office Rsch. and Planning, 1973-80; bd. dirs. Pacific Luth. Theol. Sem., 1962-74, 80-86, Inst. Rsch. in Social Behavior, 1962-90, Interplayers, 1990-92, Sandpoint Christian Connection, 1995-97; pres. Cornerhouse Fund, 1982-92, One Voice, 1994-95, bd. dirs., 1995-97; mem. adv. com. Office Rsch. and Evaluation Evang. Luth. Ch. Am., 1988—; mem. history com. Soc. Study of Religion, 1993-94. Capt. USAAF, 1942-46. Decorated Bronze Star, Legion of Merit; recipient Roots of Freedom award Pacific bd. Anti-Defamation League, 1977; Berkeley citation U. Calif., Berkeley, 1979; Rockefeller fellow, 1941-42; fellow Center Advanced Study Behavioral Scis., 1957-58; fellow Soc. for Religion in Higher Edn., 1968-69. Fellow Soc. Sci. Study Religion (Western rep., pres. 1968-69); mem. Am. Assn. Pub. Opinion Research (v.p., pres. 1962-64, pres. Pacific chpt. 1959-60), Am. Sociol. Assn. (v.p. 1978-79), Religious Research Assn., Sociol. Research Assn. Home: 319 S 4th Ave Sandpoint ID 83864-1219

GLOSS, LAWRENCE ROBERT, fundraising executive; b. Colorado Springs, Colo., Oct. 31, 1948; s. Kenneth Edwin and Clara U. (Haeker) G.; m. Carol Berg, June 4, 1977; children: Alexander Edwin, Carolyn Claire. BA, U. Denver, 1970. Dir. natl. congress on volunteerism and citizenship NCVA, Washington, 1975-76; dir. devel. Vis. Nurses Assn., Washington, 1976-77; devel. cons. Am. Lung Assn., Washington and N.Y.C., 1977-78; exec. dir. Colo. Conservation Fund, Denver, Colo., 1978-79, Rose Med. Ctr., enver, 1985-86; dir. devel. Rose Found., Denver, 1979-86; sr. campaign dir. J. Panas, Young and Ptnrs., San Francisco, 1986-88; pres. Gloss and Co., Denver, 1988—; mem. adv. coun. non-profit mgmt. Metro State Coll., Denver, 1994; cons. Native Am. Rights Fund, Boulder, Colo., Arts at the Sta., Denver, 1994, Up With People, 1995, 96, Emily Griffith Ctr. Found., 1995, 96, Colo. CASA, 1998-99, Women of the West Mus., 1998, Sister Cities-Denver and Kumming, China, 1999. Guest spkr. Tech. Assistance Ctr., Denver, 1992-94; bd. dirs. Alzeimer's and Related Disorders Assn., Denver, 1985-86; bd. dirs. Woman's Sch. Network, Denver, 1984-85, Colo. PTA, Englewood, 1991-92; active Emily Griffith Ctr. Found., 1997, U. Denver, Episcopal Ministries of U. Colo., Boulder, 1996, Colo. Pub. Expenditure Coun., 1998—, Srs. Resource Ctr., 1998—, Am. Humane Assn., 1998—. Mem. NSFRE (Colo. chpt. 1992-94, bd. dirs.), Arapahoe House, Englewood Hist. Soc., Am. Humane Assn., Women of the West Mus. Nat. Assn. of Mus. Exhibitors, Colo. Planning Giving Roundtable, Nat. Com. on Planned Giving, Am. Prospect Rsch. Assn., Am. Humane Assn., Colo. Pub. Expenditure Coun., Assn. of Healthcare Philanthropy (regional XII 1993-94), Assn. Profl. Rschrs. Advancement, Rotary Club of Denver. Lutheran. Avocations: dressage, art, soccer. Home: 11126 E Stagecoach Dr Parker CO 80138-8424 Office: Gloss and Company 2755 S Locust St Ste 113 Denver CO 80222-7131

GLOVER, KAREN E., lawyer; b. Nampa, Idaho, Apr. 14, 1950; d. Gordon Ellsworth and Cora (Frazier) G.; m. Thaddas L. Alston, Aug. 17, 1979; children: Samantha Glover Alston, Evan Glover Alston. AB magna cum laude, Whitman Coll., 1972; JD cum laude, Harvard U., 1975. Bar: Wash. 1975, U.S. Dist. Ct. (we. dist.) Wash. 1975. Assoc. Preston, Thorgrimson Ellis & Holman, Seattle, 1975-80; ptnr. Preston Gates & Ellis, Seattle, 1981—. Chmn. bd. dirs. United Way King County, Seattle, 1993-94; chair bd. overseers Whitman Coll., Walla Walla, Wash., 1995—; mem. bd. trustees King County Libr. Sys., Seattle, 1992—. Mem. Wash. State Bar Assn. (corp. and tax sects.), Seattle Pension Roundtable, Columbia Tower Club, Sand Point Country Club, Rainier Club. Episcopalian. Office: Preston Gates & Ellis 701 5th Ave Fl 50 Seattle WA 98104-7016*

GLOVSKY, MYRON MICHAEL, medical educator; b. Boston, Aug. 15, 1936; m. Carole Irene Parks; five children. BS magna cum laude, Tufts U., 1957, MD, 1962. Bd. cert. Nat. Bd. Med. Examiners, Am. Bd. Allergy & Immunology, Am. Bd. Diagnostic Lab. Immunology. Intern Balt. (Md.) City Hosp., 1962-63; resident New Eng. Med. Ctr., Boston, 1965-66; spl. NIH fellow allergy and immunology Walter Reed Army Inst. Rsch., Washington, 1966-68; fellow hematology and immunology U. Calif., San Francisco, 1968-69; staff physician dept. internal medicine So. Calif. Permanente Med. Group, L.A., 1969-72, dir. allergy & immunology lab., 1970-84, chief dept. allergy and clin. immunology, co-dir. residency program in allergy & clin. immunology, 1974-84, dir. pheresis unit, 1978-80; dir. L.A. County Gen. Hosp./U. So. Calif. Asthma Clinic; prof. medicine, head allergy and immunology labs. pulmonary divsn., head allergy and clin. immunology divsn. pulmonary medicine. U. So. Calif., Sch. Medicine, 1984-89, prof. pathology, 1986-89; clin. prof. medicine, clin. prof. pathology U. So. Calif., 1989—; dir. asthma and allergy referral ctr. Huntington Meml. Hosp., Pasadena, 1989—; head fellowship and career devel. program Nat. Heart Inst., NIH, Bethesda, Md., 1963-65, fellowship bd. mem., 1964-65; vis. assoc. in chemistry Calif. Inst. Tech., Pasadena, 1977—; acad. assoc. complement and allergy Nichols Inst., San Juan Capistrano, Calif., 1980—, med. dir. immunology, 1980-89; clin. prof. medicine U. Calif., L.A., 1983-84; vis. prof. clin. scholars program Eli Lilly & Co., Indpls., 1988; mem. steering com. Aspen Allergy Conf., 1988—. With USPHS, 1963-65. Fellow Am. Acad. Allergy; mem. AAAS, Am. Assn. Immunologists, Am. Thoracic Soc., Am. Fedn. for Clin. Rsch., Am. Coll. Allergy, Reticuloendothelial Soc., L.A. Soc. Allergy and Clin. Immunology (pres. 1979-80), Collegium Internat. Allergolicum. Home: 1961 Oak St South Pasadena CA 91030-4957 Office: Huntington Meml Hosp Asthma & Allergy Ctr 39 Congress St Ste 302 Pasadena CA 91105-3022

GLUECK, MARY A., retired psychiatric and mental health nurse; b. Bridgetown, Barbados; came to U.S., 1952; d. Hubert and Christina Cumming; m. Stephen G. Glueck (dec.). Grad. sch. nursing, St. Joseph's Mercy Hosp., Georgetown, Guyana. RN, Calif. Asst. nursing educator in new employee orientation San Mateo County Gen. Hosp., San Mateo, Calif., also facilitator video insvcs. for nursing staff, tchr. safety and emergency response procedures to staff; ret. San Mateo County Gen. Hosp., San Mateo, 1998. Mem. Mid. Mgrs. Assn., Am. Psychiat. Nurses Assn. Home: 4505 Sandra Ct Union City CA 94587-4853

GLYER, MICHAEL DALE, tax specialist; b. Chgo., Feb. 16, 1953; s. Harry and Katharine Glyer; m. Diana Lynn Pavlac, Dec. 31, 1994. BA, U. So. Calif., 1974; MA, Bowling Green State U., 1975. Appeals officer IRS, Glendale, Calif., 1987—. Editor (newsletter) File 770, 1978-98 (Hugo award 1984, 85, 88). Co-chmn. Westercon, L.A., 1978; chmn. World Sci. Fiction Conv., Anaheim, Cal. 1996. Mem. Mythopoeic Soc. (sec. 1995—), L.A. Sci. Fantasy Soc. (scribe 1978-98). Avocations: science fiction, Civil War, Biblical archeology.

GLYNN, GARY J., writer; b. Tacoma, Nov. 8, 1956; s. Don M. and Margaret (Myles) G.; m. Mary E. Lyndes, July 21, 1990; children: Kelsey Jean, Connor James. BS in Forest Resource Mgmt., U. Mont., 1980. Timber cruiser U.S. Forest Svc., 1978-81; pvt. practice, 1981—. Author: Montana's Home Front During WWII, 1994. sec. Friends of Hist. Mus. at Ft. Missoula, 1996-98, pres., 1998—, constrn. supr. Ft. Missoula Amphitheater, 1998. Office: PO Box 4092 Missoula MT 59806-4092

GLYNN, JOHN W., JR., investment manager; b. Leavenworth, Kans., Aug. 23, 1940; s. John W. and Dorothy A. (Martin) G.; m. Barbara A. Glynn, Sept. 5, 1965; children: Jacqueline, Alexandra, David, Elizabeth. BA, U. Notre Dame, 1962; LLB, U. Va., 1965; MBA, Stanford U., 1970. Owner Glynn Capital Mgmt., Menlo Park, Calif., 1975—; prof. Darden Sch., U. Va., Charlottesville, 1991—, Grad. Sch. Bus., Stanford U., Palo Alto, Calif., 1991—. Chmn. bd. dirs. Menlo Sch., Menlo Park, 1995—; mem. fin. com. Castellega Sch., Palo Alto, 1995—. Mem. Calif. State Bar. Republican. Roman Catholic. Avocations: golf, fly fishing, photography. Home: 88 Laburnum Rd Atherton CA 94027-2124 Office: Glynn Capital Mgmt 3000 Sand Hill Rd Ste 235 Menlo Park CA 94025-7113

GLYNN, ROBERT D., JR., energy-based holding company; b. Orange, N.J., 1942. BSME, Manhattan Coll.; MS in Nuclear Engring., L.I. U.; postgrad., U. Mich., Harvard U. With L.I. Lighting Co.; officer, prin. Woodward Clyde Cons.; with PG&E Corp., San Francisco, 1984—, CEO, pres., 1997, chmn. bd., 1998—; chmn. bd. dirs. Pacific Gas and Electric Co. subs. PG&E Corp.; bd. dirs. URS Corp. Mem. adv. coun. St. Mary's Coll. Calif. Sch. Edn.; bd. govs. San Francisco Symphony. Office: PG&E Corp Spear Tower One Market St Ste 2400 San Francisco CA 94105*

GOATES, DELBERT TOLTON, child psychiatrist; b. Logan, Utah, Apr. 14, 1932; s. Wallace Albert and Roma (Tolton) G.; m. Claudia Tidwell, Sept. 15, 1960 (div. Apr. 1994); children: Jeanette, Byron, Rebecca Lynn, Alan, Paul, Jonathan Phillip, Kendra, Michelle, George Milton; m. Julie Anderson Headley, Dec. 29, 1994. BS, U. Utah, 1953, MD, 1962; postgrad., U. Nebr., 1965, 67. Intern Rochester (N.Y.) Gen. Hosp., 1962-63; resident Nebr. Psychiat. Inst., Omaha, 1963-67; pvt. practice medicine specializing in child psychiatry Omaha, 1963-67, Albuquerque, 1967-71, Salt Lake City, 1971—; dir. psychiatry Riverdell Psychiat. Ctr., 1986-92, staff psychiatrist, 1992—; asst. prof. child psychiatry U. N.Mex., 1967-71, dir. children's svcs., 1967-71, asst. prof. pediatrics, 1969-71; clin. dir. Children's Psychiat. Ctr., Primary Children's Med. Ctr., Salt Lake City, 1971-77; med. dir. Life Line, 1990-93, Brightway Adolescent Psychiat. Hosp., 1992—; pres. Magic Mini Maker, Inc., Salt Lake City, 1972-78; chmn. bd. Intermountain Polytex, Inc. Bishop Ch. Jesus Christ Latter-day Sts., 1968-71; bd. dirs. Utah Cancer Soc., Great Salt Lake Mental Health. Served with MC, AUS, 1953-55. Mem. AMA, Orthopsychiat. Assn. Am., Utah Psychiat. Assn., Intermountain Acad. Child Psychiatry (pres. 1974-76), Pi Kappa Alpha, Phi Kappa Phi. Home: 4187 Abinadi Rd Salt Lake City UT 84124-4001 Office: 2738 S 2000 E Salt Lake City UT 84109-1737

GOBAR, ALFRED JULIAN, economic consultant, educator; b. Lucerne Valley, Calif., July 12, 1932; s. Julian Smith and Hilda (Millbank) G.; B.A. in Econs., Whittier Coll., 1953, M.A. in History, 1955; postgrad. Claremont Grad. Sch., 1953-54; Ph.D. in Econs., U. So. Calif., 1963; m. Sally Ann Randall, June 17, 1957; children—Wendy Lee, Curtis Julian, Joseph Julian. Asst. pres. Microdot Inc., Pasadena, 1953-57; regional sales mgr. Sutorbilt Corp., L.A., 1957-59; market research assoc. Beckman Instrument Inc., Fullerton, 1959-64; sr. marketing cons. Western Mgmt. Consultants Inc., Phoenix and L.A., 1964-66; ptnr., prin., chmn. bd. Darley/Gobar Assocs., Inc., 1966-73; pres., chmn. bd. Alfred Gobar Assocs., Inc., Placentia, Calif., 1973—; asst. prof. finance U. So. Calif., L.A., 1963-64; assoc. prof. bus. Calif. State U., L.A., 1963-68, 70-79, assoc. prof. Calif. State U.-Fullerton, 1968-69; mktg., fin. adviser 1957—; bd. dirs. Quaker City Bancorp, Inc.; pub. speaker seminars and convs. Contbr. articles to profl. publs. Trustee Whittier Coll., 1992—. tee Whittier Coll., 1992—. Home: 1100 W Valencia Mesa Dr Fullerton CA 92833-2219 Office: 721 W Kimberly Ave Placentia CA 92870-6343

GOBUS, BARBARA CHATTERTON, secondary education educator; b. Leeds, Yorkshire, Eng., Dec. 30, 1941; d. Ernest and Gertrude Emma (Balmforth) Chatterton; 1 child, Roger Eggers. AA with hons., Santa Monica Coll., 1987; BA summa cum laude, Calif. State U., Northridge, 1991; MA, 1994. Exec. sec., office mgr. Med. and Legal Field, L.A., 1966-82; docent Greater L.A. Zoo Assn., 1983-92; tutor, lang. lab. Calif. State U., Northridge, 1990-91, tchg. assoc., 1991-92; English tchr. Marlborough Sch., L.A., 1993—; bd. dirs. The Doheny Sch., L.A., 1984—. Founder, contbg. editor: Inform. and Ednl. mag., 1983-85. Reader recordings for blind, Braille Inst., L.A., 1992-93; sec. PTSA Palms Jr. High Sch., L.A., 1987-89. Mem. Nat. Coun. Tchrs. of English, Golden Key, Phi Kappa Phi, Sigma Tau Delta. Avocations: music, Jungian psychology, walking, nature, reading. Office: Marlborough Sch 250 S Rossmore Ave Los Angeles CA 90004-3739

GODAGER, JANE ANN, social worker; b. Blue River, Wis., Nov. 29, 1943; d. Roy and Elmyra Marie (Hood) G. BA, U. Wis., 1965; MSW, Fla. State U., 1969. Lic. clin. social worker. Social worker III State of Wis. Dept Corrections, Wales, 1965-71; supervising psychiat. social worker I State of Calif., San Bernardino, 1972-75, La Mesa, 1975-77; psychiat. social worker State of Calif., San Bernardino, 1978-85; supr. mental health services Riverside (Calif.) County Dept. Mental Health, 1985-86; mental health counselor Superior Ct. San Bernardino County, 1986—; mem. adv. bd. Grad. Sch. Social Work Calif. State U., San Bernardino, Mental Health Assn. Mem. Nat. Assn. Social Workers, Acad. Cert. Social Workers (diplomate), Kappa Kappa Gamma Alumnae Assn. Avocations: travel, reading, music. Office: Office Mental Health Counselor 700 E Gilbert St Bldg 1 San Bernardino CA 92404-5413

GODDARD, HAZEL BRYAN, religious organization executive; b. Mineral, Ill., Aug. 17, 1912; d. Thomas Benton and Maude Carrie (Riley) B.; m. John Howard Goddard; children: David Bryan, Joan Kathryn. BA, Judson Coll., 1966; MS, No. Ill. U., 1973; LittD (hon.), Calif. Grad. Sch. Theology, 1981. Lic. Marriage and family therapist, Fla., Colo. Clin. counselor Warrenville (Ill.) Med. Clinic, 1958-78; pres. Christian Counseling Ministries, Buena Vista, Colo., 1978—, lectr., cons., 1978—. Auhtor: Can I Hope Again, 1971, Mama, Are You There?, 1996, Somebody Else's Girl, Connie, Bob Bronson; contbr. articles to jours. Mem. Am. Pychotherapy Assn. (diplomat), Am. Assn. Marriage and Family Therapists (clin.), Nat. Assn. Social Workers, Am. Assn. Counseling and Devel. Republican. Baptist. Avocations: writing, music, hiking, fishing, travel. Home: PO Box 1366 Buena Vista CO 81211-1366

GODDART, MICHAEL, writer; b. Chgo., Sept. 3, 1949. BA in History with honors, U. Calif., Berkeley, 1971; MFA in Writing, Bowling Green State U., 1987. Author: Spiritual Revolution: A Seeker's Guide, 1998, Bliss: 33 Simple Ways to awaken Your Spiritual Self, 1999; contbr. numerous articles on tax and spirituality to local, nat., and internat. jours. Youth for Understanding scholar, 1967; History fellow U. Calif., Berkeley, 1969.

GODFREY, RICHARD GEORGE, real estate appraiser; b. Sharon, Pa., Dec. 18, 1927; s. Fay Morris and Elizabeth Marguerite (Stefanak) G.; m. Golda Fay Goss, Oct. 28, 1951; children: Deborah Jayne, Gayle Rogers, Bryan Edward. BA, Ripon Coll., 1949. V.p. 1st Thrift & Loan Assn., Albuquerque, 1959-61; pres. Richard G. Godfrey & Assocs., Inc., Albuquerque, 1961-93, owner, 1993—. Mem. Appraisal Inst. (v.p. 1981-82),

Counselors of Real Estate. Baptist. Home: 1700 Columbia Dr SE Albuquerque NM 87106-3311 Office: 523 Louisiana Blvd SE Albuquerque NM 87108-3842

GODSIL, RICHARD WILLIAM, minister; b. Estherville, Iowa, Mar. 8, 1953; s. Richard Lee and Shirley Ann (Diamond) G.; m. Laurel Christine Webster, July 17, 1971; children: Richard II, Joshua, Rebekah. AA, Okaloosa Walton Jr. Coll., 1977; BS, Okla. Christian Coll., 1980; postgrad., Pepperdine U., 1984; MS in Family Devel. & Edn., Friends U., 1997. Ordained to ministry Christian Ch., 1989. Youth min. Ch. of Christ, Derby, Kans., 1981-82; assoc. min. Ch. of Christ, Redlands, Calif., 1982-84; youth min. religious edn. Twin Cities Christian Ch., Oceanside, Calif., 1987-88; assoc. min. Montrose (Colo.) Christian Ch., 1988-94; youth min. 1st Christian Ch., Dodge City, Kans., 1994-96, West Valley Christian Ch., West hills, Calif., 1996—; pres. Colo. Christian Concerts, Montrose, 1990—; tchr. 6th grade bible West Valley Christian Sch., 1997—. V.p. Gallerya Youth Ctr., Montrose, 1990; advisor home econs. bd. high sch., Montrose, 1990—; mem. budget task force Montrose United Sch. Dist., 1993, mem. dist. accountability com., 1992-94; mem. assessment testing com. Dodge City United Sch. Dist., 1995, mem. dist. accountability com., 1995. Sgt. USAF, 1971-75. Named Young Min. of Yr. Standard Pub. Co., 1989. Mem. Mountain Area Christian Educators (v.p. Montrose chpt. 1989—), Assn. Montrose Chs. (pres. 1990), Nat. Network Youth Mins., Campus Life Club (bd. dirs. 1987 Oceanside). Republican. Home: 7831 Ponce Ave West Hills CA 91304-4629 Office: West Valley Christian Ch 22944 Enadia Way West Hills CA 91307-2206

GODWIN, BRUCE WAYNE, nurse corps officer; b. Del Rio, Tex., June 28, 1954; s. Owen Wilson and Thelma Jean (Dill) G.; m. Barbara Houston; 1 child, Brandon Bosworth. BS, Austin Peay, 1976; MSA, Cen. Mich., 1985; BSN, St. Louis U., 1990. RN, BLS instr., ACLS. Supply corps officer USN, 1976-90, nurse corps officer, 1990—; head Naval Med. Clinic Pearl Harbor, commdr. edn. and tng., chmn., mem. ethics com., chmn. navy nurse edn. com. Lt. cmdr. USN, 1976—. Recipient Navy Achievement medal USN, 1994. Mem. Am. Assn. Nurse Anesthetists, Am. Soc. Post-Anesthesia Nurses, Internat. Anesthesia Rsch. Soc., Navy Nurse Corps. Assn. Avocations: reading, computers. Fax: 808-473-3137. E-mail: PRL1BWG@PRL10.med.navy.mil. Home: 14 Hekau St Aiea HI 96701-4201 Office: Command Edn and Tng Naval Med Clin 480 Central Ave Pearl Harbor HI 96860-4908

GODWIN, MARY JO, editor, librarian consultant; b. Tarboro, N.C., Jan. 31, 1949; d. Herman Esthol and Mamie Winifred (Felton) Pittman; m. Charles Benjamin Godwin, May 2, 1970. BA, N.C. Wesleyan Coll., 1971; MLS, East Carolina U., 1973. Cert. libr., N.C. From libr. asst. to asst. dir. Edgecombe County Meml. Library, Tarboro, 1970-76, dir., 1977-85; asst. editor Wilson Library Bull., Bronx, N.Y., 1985-89, editor, 1989-92; dir. govt. sales The Oryx Press, Phoenix, 1993-95, dir. mktg. svc., 1995-96, dir. mktg., sales and promotional svcs., 1996—; mem. White House Conf. on Librs. and Info. Svcs. Task Force; bd. dirs. Libr. Pub. Rels. Coun., 1992-95. Bd. dirs. Friends of Calvert County Pub. Libr., 1994, Osborn Edn. Found., sec., 1997-98; mem. Ariz. Ctr. for the Book. Recipient Robert Downs award for intellectual freedom U. Ill. Grad. Sch. of Libr. Sci., 1992. Mem. ALA (3M/Jr. Mem. Roundtable Profl. Devel. award 1981), N.C. Libr. Assn. (sec. 1981-83), Info. Futures Inst., Ind. Librs. Exchange Roundtable (v.p., pres. elect 1994, pres. 1995-96). Democrat. Episcopalian. Office: The Oryx Press 4041 N Central Ave Ste 700 Phoenix AZ 85012-3397

GOEDDE, ALAN GEORGE, financial company executive; b. Irvington, N.J., Feb. 27, 1948; s. Albert and Herta (Konrad) G.; m. Julie S. Withers, June 30, 1981. BS in Engring., Duke U., 1970, PhD in Econs., 1978. Economist U.S. Treasury, Washington, 1976-79, Export-Import Bank, Washington, 1979-81; mgr. Arthur Andersen & Co., Chgo., 1981-84; v.p. bus. planning 1st Nat. Bank Chgo., 1984-86; dir. strategic planning The NutraSweet Co., Chgo., 1986-87; pres., CEO Mentor Internat., Northbrook, Ill., 1987-88; cons. Coopers & Lybrand, Chgo., 1988-90, Freeman & Mills, L.A., 1990-94, Putnam, Hayes and Bartlett, L.A., 1994—. Office: Putnam Hayes Bartlett Inc 520 S Grand Ave Los Angeles CA 90071-2600

GOEHRING, KENNETH, artist; b. Evansville, Wis., Jan. 8, 1919; s. Walter A. and Ruth I. (Rossman) G.; m. Margretta M. MacNicol, Dec. 1, 1945. Student, Cass Tech. Inst., 1933-35, Meinzinger Sch. Applied Art, 1945-46, Colorado Springs Fine Arts Ctr., 1947-50. Works have appeared in over 100 exhibitions in 17 states and 20 museums; 17 one-man shows; exhibitor, Terry Inst., Miami, Symphony Hall, Boston, de Cordova Mus., Fitchburg Mus., Mass., Farnsworth Mus., Maine, Corcoran, Washington, Joslyn Meml. Mus., Nebr., Detroit Inst. Arts, Nebr. Galleries, Stanford U. Galleries, Calif, De Young Mus., San Francisco, Denver Art Mus., Okla. Art Ctr., La Jolla Art Ctr., Calif., others; represented in permanent collections, Sheldon Art Ctr., Lincoln, Nebr., Colorado Springs Fine Arts Ctr., Foothills Gallery, Golden Colo., Canon City Fine Arts Ctr., Colo., Washburn U. Gallery, Wichita, Kans., Swedish Consulate, Washington, El Pomar Found., Colo. Springs, in many pvt. collections throughout U.S. Purchase awards include Colorado Springs Fine Arts Ctr., 1958; Washburn U., 1957; Am. Acad. Design, 1977. Address: 2017 W Platte Ave Colorado Springs CO 80904-3429

GOEI, BERNARD THWAN-POO (BERT GOEI), architectural and engineering firm executive; b. Semarang, Indonesia, Jan. 27, 1938; came to U.S., 1969; naturalized, 1976; s. Ignatius Ing-Khien Goei and Nicolette Giok-Nio Tjioe; m. Sioe-Tien Liem, May 26, 1966; children: Kimberley Hendrika, Gregory Fitzgerald. BA in Fine Arts, Bandung Inst. Tech. State U. Indonesia, 1961, MA in Archtl. Space Planning, 1964; postgrad., U. Heidelberg, Germany, 1967-68. Co-owner, chief designer Pondok Mungil Interiors Inc., Bandung, 1962-64; dept. mgr., fin. advisor Gumarna Architects, Engrs. and Planners, Inc., Bandung, Jakarta, Indonesia, 1964-67; shop supr., model maker Davan Scale Models, Toronto, Ont., Can., 1968-69; chief archtl. designer George T. Nowak Architects and Assocs., Westchester, Calif., 1969-72; sr. archtl. designer Krisel & Shapiro Architects and Assocs., L.A., 1972-74; sr. supervising archtl. designer The Ralph M. Parsons A/E Co. (now Parsons Infrastructure and Tech. Group Inc.), Pasadena, Calif., 1974—; v.p. United Gruno U.S.A. Corp. Import/Export, Monterey Park, Calif., 1980-89. Mem. Rep. Presdl. Task Force, Washington, 1982—, Nat. Rep. Senatorial Com., Washington, 1983—, Nat. Rep. Congrl. Com., Washington, 1981—, Rep. Nat. Com., Washington, 1982—; active Am. Indonesian Cath. Soc. Recipient Excellent Design Achievement commendation Magneto-Hydro-Dynamics Program, 1976, Strategic Def. Initiative "Star Wars" Program, 1988, USAF Space Shuttle Program, West Coast Space-Port, 1984; scholar U. Heidelberg, 1967-68. Mem. NRA, Am. Air Gunner Assn., Tech. Comm. Soc., Indonesian Am. Soc., Dutch Am. Soc., Second Amendment Found., The Right to Keep and Bear Arms Com. Republican. Roman Catholic. Avocations: fire arms and daggers, photography, hi-tech electronics, stamps and coins, world travel. Home: 154 Ladera St Monterey Park CA 91754-2125 Office: Parsons Infrastructure & Tech Group Inc 100 W Walnut St Pasadena CA 91124-0001

GOELTZ, THOMAS A., lawyer. BA in Econs. summa cum laude, DePauw U., 1969; JD magna cum laude, Mich. U., 1973. Assoc. Riddell, Williams, Ivie, Bullitt & Walkinshaw, Seattle, 1973-75; dep. prosecuting atty. civil divsn. King County Prosecuting Atty.'s Office, Seattle, 1976-79; prin. Cohen, Keegan & Goeltz, Seattle, 1979-86; ptnr. Davis Wright Tremaine, Seattle, 1986—; cons. state and local govt. agencies on environ. land use issues; adv. shoreline mgmt. City of Seattle; part-time lectr. Law Sch. U. Wash., Seattle, 1976-79. Editor Mich. Law Rev. Active Gov. Task Force on Regulatory Reform, 1993-95. Mem. ABA (urban, state & local govt. law sect.), Wash. State Bar Assn. (real property sect., past chair land use and environ. law sect.), Seattle-King County Bar Assn., Am. Coll. Real Estate Lawyers, Nat. Assn. Indsl. and Office Park, ICSC, Order of Coif. Office: Davis Wright Tremaine 2600 Century Sq 1501 4th Ave Seattle WA 98101-1688*

GOETSCHEL, ROY HARTZELL, JR., mathematician, researcher; b. Oak Park, Ill., Apr. 19, 1930; s. Roy Hartzell and Elizabeth Wilhelmina Johanna (Gaude) G.; m. Jane Peterson, June 6, 1971. *Personal gratitude necessitates acknowledgement of several influencial people: Former principal oboist Chicago Symphony Orchestra Alfred Bartel instilled the importance of dedication to excellence; Mentor and beloved teacher Dr. Guido Weiss opened the rigorous and wonderous world of mathematics inspiring amazement, imagination and joy; Major professor Dr. Wolfgang Wasow graciously guided first efforts into mathematical writing and research; Uncle George Gaude uniquely trusted warm gentle counselor, dearly missed; Mom and dad with unequaled love and devotion made all things possible; Wife Jane educator and necessary editor supported personal mathematical research above everything else and continues to be an inspiration and joy.* BS, Northwestern U., 1954; MS, DePaul U., 1958; PhD, U. Wis., 1966. Asst. prof. math. Sonoma State U. of Calif., Rohnert Park, Calif., 1966-69; prof. math. U. Idaho, Moscow, Idaho, 1969-97; prof. emeritus math. U. Idaho, Moscow, 1997—. Author: Advanced Calculus, 1981; contbr. articles to Fuzzy Sets and Systems. Mem. N.Y. Acad. Scis. Achievements include introduction and development of concept of fuzzy darts and fuzzy dart representations of fuzzy numbers; introduction of the topic of fuzzy hypergraphs including methodology and applications (especially Hebbian structures) to the literature through papers published in Fuzzy Sets and Systems; conceptualization and development of the basis of a fuzzy matroid theory. Avocation: music (vocal and instrumental). Home: 1721 Atsirk St Moscow ID 83843-9302

GOETZ, ALEXANDER FRANKLIN HERMANN, geophysicist, educator; b. Pasadena, Calif., Oct. 14, 1938; s. Alexander and Sylvia (Scott) G.; m. Rosamaria Cyrus, Aug. 22, 1982 (div. July 1996); children: Freya E., Julian F.C. BS in Physics, Calif. Inst. Tech., 1961, MS in Geophysics, 1962, PhD in Planetary Sci., 1967. Mem. staff Bell Telephone Labs, Washington, 1967-70; sr. scientist, mgr. Jet Propulsion Lab, Pasadena, Calif., 1970-85; prin., owner Geoimages Inc., Altadena, Calif., 1974-78; prof., dir. ctr. study earth from space U. Colo., Boulder, 1985—; chmn., CEO Analytical Spectral Devices Inc., Boulder, Colo., 1990—; cons. in field; vis. sci. Jet Propulsion Lab., Pasadena, Calif., 1989-90. Assoc. editor Jour. Remote Sensing of Environment, 1984—. Pres. Spaceship Earth Fund, Boulder, 1987-89; trustee San Juan Inst., San Jaun Capistrano, Calif., 1986-92. Recipient Exceptional Scientific Achievement medal NASA, Washington, 1982, William T. Pecora award NASA/Dept. of Interior, Washington, 1982, Space Act award NASA, Washington, 1987. Mem. IEEE (geosci., remote sensing chpt.), AAAS, Am. Geophysical Union, Soc. Photo Instrumentation Engrs., Transpacific Yacht Club, Sigma Xi. Avocations: ocean sailing, hiking, skiing, woodworking. Office: U Colorado CSES/CIRES CB216 Boulder CO 80309

GOETZEL, CLAUS GUENTER, metallurgical engineer; b. Berlin, July 14, 1913; came to U.S., 1936; s. Walter and Else (Baum) G.; m. Lilo Kallmann, Nov. 19, 1938; children: Rodney G., Vivian L. Holley. Dipl.-Ing., Technische Hochschule, Berlin, 1935; PhD, Columbia U., 1939. Registered profl. engr., Calif. Research chemist, lab. head Hardy Metall. Co., 1936-39; tech. dir., works mgr. Am. Electro Metal Corp., 1939-47; v.p., dir. research Sintercast Corp. Am., 1947-57; adj. prof. NYU, N.Y.C., 1945-57, sr. research scientist, 1957-60; cons. scientist Lockheed Missiles & Space Co., Sunnyvale, Calif., 1960-78; cons. metall. engring. Portola Valley, Calif., 1978—; lectr., vis. scholar Stanford (Calif.) U., 1961-88; vis. prof. Tech. Univ. Karlsruhe, Germany, 1978-80. Author: Treatise on Powder Metallurgy, 5 vols., 1949-63; co-author: (with Lilo Goetzel) Dictionary of Materials and Process Engineering, vol. 1 English-German, 1995, vol. 2, German-English, 1997; inventor or co-inventor of over 40 U.S. patents; contbr. over 50 articles to profl. jours. and handbooks. Recipient Alexander von Humboldt Sr. U.S. Scientist award, Fed. Republic Germany, 1978. Fellow AIAA (assoc.), Am. Soc. Materials Internat.; mem. AIME (life), Am. Powder Metallurgy Inst. (sr.), Materials Sci. Club N.Y. (life, past pres.), Inst. Materials (life, London).

GOETZKE, GLORIA LOUISE, social worker, income tax specialist; b. Monticello, Minn.; d. Wesley and Marvel (Kreidler) G. BA, U. Minn., 1964; MSW, U. Denver, 1966; MBA, U. St. Thomas, 1977. Cert. enrollment to practice before IRS. Social worker VA Med. Ctr., L.A., 1980—; master tax preparer and instr. H&R Block, Santa Monica, Calif.; clin. instr. UCLA Grad. Sch. Social Welfare; field instr. Calif. State U., Long Beach Grad. Sch. of Social Work. Chairperson parish edn., Sunday Sch. tchr., vacation Bible Sch. tchr. Westchester Luth. Ch., L.A. Mem. Nat. Assn. Social Workers (cert.). Lutheran. Avocations: crochet designing, food designing, flowers.

GOFMAN, JOHN WILLIAM, health-research physician, educator; b. Cleve., Sept. 21, 1918; s. David Martin and Sarah (Kaplan) G.; m. Helen Fahl, Aug. 10, 1940; 1 child, John David. AB in Chemistry, Oberlin Coll., 1939; PhD in Nuclear Chemistry, U. Calif., Berkeley, 1943; MD in Internal Medicine, U. Calif., San Francisco, 1946. Co-leader Plutonium Project for Manhattan Project U. Calif., Berkeley, 1941-43, from asst. to assoc. prof. med. physics, 1947-54, prof. med. physics/molecular and cell biology, 1954-73; founder, dir. Biomed. Rsch. divsn. Lawrence Livermore (Calif.) Nat. Lab., 1963-64, assoc. dir., 1963-68; lectr. dept. medicine U. Calif. Med. Sch., San Francisco, 1947—; prof. emeritus molecular and cell biology U. Calif., Berkeley, 1973—; med. cons. Aerojet-Gen. Nucleonics, San Ramon, Calif., 1960-68; rsch. cons. Lederle Labs., N.Y., 1952-55, Riker Labs., Northridge, Calif., 1962-66; sci. cons. heart monitor Vida Med. Systems, Dublin, Calif., 1970-74. Author: Coronary Heart Disease, 1959, Radiation and Human Health, 1981, Preventing Breast Cancer, 1996; patentee in field of fission-ability of uranium-233 for weapons and electric power. Chmn. Com. for Nuclear Responsibility, San Francisco, 1971—. Recipient Lyman Duff Lectureship award Am. Heart Assn., 1965, Stouffer prize Stouffer Found., 1972, Right Livelihood award Right Livelihood Award Found., 1992; named 1 of 25 Leading Rschrs. in Cardiology, Am. Coll. Cardiology, 1974. Avocations: clarinet, piano, ocean salmon-fishing. Office: Univ Calif 229 Stanley Hall # 3206 Berkeley CA 94720-3206

GOFORTH, NATHAN DAN, police officer; b. Phoenix, Sept. 12, 1951; s. Nathan and Mabel Lettie (Deal) G.; m. Lori Ann Petersen (div. 1984). AA in Bus. Adminstrn., Glendale Community Coll., Ariz., 1974, AA in Adminstrn. Justice, 1976; BS in Pub. Programs, Ariz. State U., 1985. Second asst. mgr. Smittys Big Town, Phoenix, 1967-73, sales rep., 1975-76; sr. inventory auditor Motorola Semiconductor, Phoenix, 1973-74; police officer City Glendale, Ariz., 1976—; Interpreter for deaf Glendale Police Dept., 1976—, peer counselor, 1989—, field tng. officer, 1980—; vol. tchr. Glendale Community Coll. Police Res. Acad., 1989-94. Res. hwy. patrolman Ariz. Dept. Pub. Safety, Phoenix, 1975-76; advisor Glendale Explorer Post 469, 1978—, instl. head, 1992; bd. dirs. Theater Works, 1994-97, v.p., 1995-97. Recipient Dedication to DAV award, 1990-91, Cert. of Appreciation award Independence High Sch., 1990, Outstanding Vol. Svc. award MADD, 1991. Mem. NRA, Ariz. State U. Alumni Assn., Internat. Police Assn., Frat. order of Police (treas. 1990-94, v.p. 1994-95, 96—, trustee 1995—), Ariz. Cts. Assn., Critical Incident Stress Debriefing (S.W. region), Sons of Am. Legion. Avocations: volleyball, racquetball, camping, traveling Europe. Office: Glendale Police Dept 6835 N 57th Dr Glendale AZ 85301-3218

GOGOLADZE, ARCHIE, special effects artist, animator; b. Tbilisi, Ga., Nov. 25, 1972; s. Tom and Mzia Gogoladze; m. Alys Anne Urwiler, Sept. 6, 1996. Cert. interpreter, Inst. of Fgn. Langs., 1991; MA in Fine Arts, Sch. of Arts, 1992; BA in Film/animation, Film Inst., 1994. Dir., animator Georgian Film Studios, 1992-94; monitor, humanitarian Premier Urgence, France, Ga., 1993-95; facilitator, animator Animaction Am., L.A., 1995-97; digital editor L2 Comms., L.A., 1996; animator VisionArt, L.A., 1997—. Avocations: writing, music. Office: Santa Monica Studios/Vision Art 3025 Olympic Blvd Santa Monica CA 90404-5001

GOGOLIN, MARILYN TOMPKINS, educational administrator, language pathologist; b. Pomona, Calif., Feb. 25, 1946; d. Roy Merle and Dorothy (Davidson) Tompkins; m. Robert Elton Gogolin, Mar. 29, 1969. BA, U. LaVerne, Calif., 1967; MA, U. Redlands, Calif., 1968; postgrad., U. Washington, 1968-69; MS, Calif. State U., Fullerton, 1976. Cert. clin. speech pathologist; cert. teaching and sch. adminstrn. Speech and lang. pathologist Rehab. Hosp., Pomona, 1969-71; diagnostic tchr. L.A. County Office of Edn., Downey, Calif., 1971-72, program specialist, 1972-74, cons. lang., 1975-76, cons. orgns. and mgmt., 1976-79, dir. administrv. affairs, asst. to supt., 1979-95; dep. supt., 1995—; cons. lang. sch. dists., Calif., 1975-79; cons. orgn. and mgmt. and profl. assns., Calif., 1976—; exec. dir. L.A. County Sch. Trustees Assn., 1979—; treas. L.A. County Edn. Found, 1996—. Founding patron Desert chpt. Kidney Found., Palm Desert, Calif., 1985. Doctoral fellow U. Washington, 1968; named One of Outstanding Young Women Am., 1977. Mem. Am. Mgmt. Assn., Am. Speech/Hearing Assn., Calif. Speech/Hearing Assn., Am. Edn. Research Assn. Baptist. Avocation: tennis. Office: LA County Office Edn 9300 Imperial Hwy Downey CA 90242-2813

GOHRES, MARC PHILLIP, construction company executive; b. Orange, Calif.; s. Phillip Hubert and Judith Jerilyn (Moon) G.; m. Daylene Renee Hoekstra, Feb. 27, 1996. Pilot's Diploma, King Schs., San Diego, Calif., 1998. Foreman Gohres Constrn. Co., Orange, Calif., 1983-91; v.p. Gohres Constrn. Co., Las Vegas, 1991-97, pres., CEO, 1997—; pres., CEO Omni Corp., Las Vegas, 1992—, corp. pilot, 1998—. Author: (software) Electric Crayon, 1981. Mem. AOPA. Avocations: flying aircraft, water sports, computer programming, electronics. Home: 5030 Norte Del Sol Ln North Las Vegas NV 89031-1056 Office: Gohres Constrn Co 6150 Palmyra Ave Las Vegas NV 89146-6648

GOIN, MARCIA KRAFT, physician; b. Portsmouth, N.H., June 27, 1932; d. Wendell Everett and Dorothy (Spurr) Kraft; m. John Morehead Goin, Mar. 5, 1960 (dec. May 1995); children: Suzanne J., Jessica M. BA, Middlebury Coll., 1954; MD, Yale U., 1958; PhD, So. Calif. Psycho-Analytic Inst., 1972. Intern in medicine U. Calif., San Francisco, 1958-59; resident in psychiatry U. So. Calif. Med. Sch., L.A., 1959-62; pvt. practice psychiatry and psychoanalysis L.A., 1962—; dir. residency edn. psychiat. outpatient dept. L.A. County/U. So. Calif. Med. Ctr., 1980—; clin. prof. psychiatry and behavioral scis. U. So. Calif. Sch. Medicine, 1980—. Co-author: Changing the Body: Psycholotic Effects of Plastic Surgery, 1981; author (med. jour. column) Practical Psychiatry and Behavioral Health, 1998—; contbr. articles to profl. jours. Mem. L.A. Coun. World Affairs. Recipient Humanitarian Svc. award AMA, 1964, Cert. of Merit, Am. Soc. Plastic Surgeons, 1985. Fellow Am. Psychiat. Assn. (cons. commn. on psychotherapy 1993—, cons. steering com. practice guidelines 1993—, com. on grad. edn. 1997-99, elected trustee-at-large bd. trustees 1997—), Am. Coll. Psychiatrists; mem. Am. Soc. Aesthetic Surgery (assoc.), So. Calif. Psychoanalytic Inst. (faculty), So. Calif. Psychiat. Soc. (Disting. Svc. award 1991). Episcopalian. Avocations: tennis, travel, international politics. Office: 1127 Wilshire Blvd Ste 1115 Los Angeles CA 90017-4002

GOIN, PETER JACKSON, art educator; b. Madison, Wis., Nov. 26, 1951; children: Kari, Dana. BA, Hamline U., 1973; MA, U. Iowa, 1975, MFA, 1976. Prof. art. U. Nev., Reno, 1984—. Author: Tracing the Line: A Photographic Survey of the Mexican-American Border, 1987, Nuclear Landscapes, 1991, Arid Waters: Photographs from the Water in the West Project, 1992, Stopping Time: A Rephotographic Survey of Lake Tahoe, 1992, Humanature, 1996, Atlas of the West, 1997; one-man shows include Nora Eccles Harrison Mus. Art, Logan, Utah, 1992, Duke U. Mus. Art, Durham, N.C., 1992, Phoenix Mus. Art, 1992, Indpls. Mus. Art, 1992, Savannah (Ga.) Coll. Art and Design, 1992, Nev. Humanities Com. Traveling Exhibit, 1992, NICA, Las Vegas, Nev., 1997, Mus. for Photographie, Braunschweig, Germany, 1997, U. Oreg. Mus. of Art, Eugene, 1997, Nev. Mus. Art, Reno, 1996, Princeton (N.J.) U. Art Mus., 1996, Whitney Mus. Am. Art, N.Y.C., 1996, among others. Recipient grant NEA, 1981, 90. Office: Univ Nev Dept Art Reno NV 89557

GOLCHAN, FREDERIC ALFRED, film producer, director; b. Paris, Nov. 20, 1953; came to U.S., 1971; s. Raymond and Georgette (Farahnick) G. BA in Econs. and M.P., UCLA, 1976; MBA in Fin., NYU, 1978; postgrad., London Bus. Sch., 1978, HEC, Paris. Exec. trainee Am. Express Bank, N.Y.C., 1979-80; pres. TEPCO Investment Banking, Beverly Hills, Calif., 1981-84, Frederic Golchan Prodns., L.A., 1985—. Dir. (documentary) Victory of the Deaf, 1975, (play) Devil and the Good Lord, 1976; co-producer film Flagrant Desire, 1987; producer TV movie Freedom Fighter, 1988; exec. producer films Dream Date, 1989, Quick Change, 1990, Intersection, 1993, The Associate, 1996, writer, producer, dir. Kimberly, 1998. Recipient Internat. Mgmt. Cert. award, 1978. Mem. Am. Film Inst., French Hollywood Circle (v.p.). Avocation: photography. Home: 1043 Maybrook Dr Beverly Hills CA 90210-2715 Office: 8787 Shoreham Dr Apt 1001 West Hollywood CA 90069-2230

GOLD, ANNE MARIE, library director; b. N.Y.C., Feb. 24, 1949; d. James Raymond and Marion Rita (Magner) Scully; m. Steven Louis Gold, Aug. 9, 1974; 1 child, Lauren Z. BA in English, St. Lawrence U., 1971; MS in Libr. Svc., Columbia U., 1972. Libr. N.Y. Pub. Libr., N.Y.C., 1972-74, Oakland (Calif.) Pub. Libr., 1975-80; libr. Solano County Libr., Fairfield, Calif., 1980-90, dir. libr. svcs., 1986-90; county libr. Contra Costa County Libr., Pleasant Hill, Calif., 1990—. Mem. Lafayette Sch. Dist. Sch. Bd., 1993-97. Mem. ALA, Pub. Libr. Assn. (bd. dirs. 1992-93, met. librs. sect., pres. 1992-93), Libr. Adminstrn. and Mgmt. Assn. (various coms.), Calif. Libr. Assn. (coun. mem. 1985-87, 90-92, exec. bd. 1991-92, co-chair legis. com. 1992-94, pres. 1998, Mem. of Year award, 1994), Calif. Inst. Librs. (v.p. 1990-91), Restructuring Calif. Pub. Librs. Task Force (1994-95).. Office: Contra Costa County Libr 1750 Oak Park Blvd Pleasant Hill CA 94523-4412

GOLD, BETTY VIRGINIA, artist; b. Austin, Tex., Feb. 15, 1935; d. Julius Ulisses and Jeffie Mae (Meek) Lee; 1 child, Laura Lee Gold Bousquet. Student, U. Tex. lectr. Gazi U., Ankara, Turkey, 1988, NAshida Gallery, Nara, Japan, 1989, Met. State Coll. Denver, 1992, Downey Mus., Calif., 1993, Foothills Art Ctr., Golden, Colo., 1994, Triskel Art Ctr., Cork, Ireland, 1994, ARmand Hammer Mus., L.A., 1994, Austin Art Mus., 1996. One-woman shows include Sol Del Rio Gallery, San Antonio, 1971, Parkcrest Gallery, Austin, 1972, Rubicon Gallery, L.A., 1973, Downtown Gallery, Honolulu, 1974, Esther Robles Gallery, L.A., 1975, Laguna Gloria Art Mus., Austin, 1976, Charles W. Bowers Meml. Mus., Santa Ana, Calif., 1977, Phoenix Art Mus., 1979, Baum-Silverman Gallery, L.A., 1988, Del. Art Mus., Wilmington, 1981, Univ. Art Mus., Austin, 1981, Decias Art, LaJolla, Calif., 1982, Patrick Gallery, Austin, 1983, Jan Baum Gallery, L.A., 1984, Boise State U., 1985, Purdue U., West Lafayette, Ind., 1986, Walker Hill Art Ctr., Seoul, Korea, 1987, Nishida Gallery, Nara, Japan, 1989, Armeson Fine Arts, Ltd., Vail, Colo., 1991, Downey Mus., Calif., 1993, ARt Mus. South Tex., Corpus Christi, 1995, Austin Art Mus., Austin, 1996, The Czech Mus. Fine Arts, Prague, 1998, Elite Gallery, Venice, 1998, others; group shows include Enhol Gallery, Dallas, 1971, Bestart Fallery, Houston, 1972, Gargoyle, Inc., Aspen, Colo., 1975, Aronson Gallery, Atlanta, 1976, Shidoni Gallery, Sante Fe, N.Mex., 1977, Elaine Horwich Gallery, Scottsdale, Ariz., 1981, Fordham U., Bronx, 1983, NAt. Mus. Contemporary Art, Seoul, 1987, John Thomas Gallery, Santa Monica, Calif., 1989, La Quinta Sculpture Park, Calif., 1994, Bova Gallery, L.A., 1995, Museo Nacional Centro de Arte Reina Sofia, Madrid, Spain, 1997, Threshold Gallery, Santa Monica, 1998, others; represented in permanent collections at RCA Bldg., Chgo., Cedars Sinai Hosp., L.A., Sinai Temple, L.A., Hawaii State Fond. Arts, Apollo Plastic Corp., Chgo., Houston First Savs., Pepperdine U., Malibu, Calif., No. Ill. U., Dekalb, Mus. Nacional-Centro de Arte Reina Sofia, Madrid, Texas U., Austin, others.

GOLD, HYMAN, cellist; b. Cleve., Aug. 26, 1914; s. Isaac and Fanny (Liebenson) g.; m. Ruth Olgin, Feb. 4, 1936; 1 child, Ronald Kenneth; m. Sue DiCicco, Oct. 2, 1982. Student, Cleve. Inst. Music, 1932-38; studies with Victor DeGomez, Cleve., 1938-40; studies with Leonard Rose, 1941-43. Cellist Gold Trio, Cleve., 1935-46, Paul Whiteman and Cleve. Orch., 1940; musician, actor 170 films numerous studios, Los Angeles and Las Vegas, Nev., 1947—, Jack Benny TV Show, L.A., 1953-70; cellist numerous symphonies and ballet cos., L.A., 1955-65; condr. Beverly Hills (Calif.) Ensemble, Las Vegas, 1965—; cellist TV comms., L.A., 1960-73; condr. Las Vegas Pops Orch., 1977—; prin. cellist/soloist Nat. Sr. Symphony, New London, Conn., 1990-95; prin. cellist, soloist Las Vegas Civic Symphony, 1994—; pres. Gold 'N' Cello Rec. Co., 1964—. Performer numerous recs. and club shows, Los Angeles and Las Vegas, 1947—. Grantee Cleve. Inst. Music, 1935, 36, Nev. State Council for Arts, 1977-80. Mem. SAG, Am. Fedn. Musicians, B'nai B'rith. Democrat. Jewish. Club: Scrabble (Las Vegas). Avocations: gardening, tennis, bowling, travel. Home and Office: 2416 Laurie Dr Las Vegas NV 89102-2104

GOLD, MICHAEL NATHAN, investment banker, management consultant; b. Chgo., May 3, 1952; s. Julius and Sarah (Blitzblau) G.; m. Cynthia Bilicki, June 19, 1976; children: Aaron Michael, Nathan Matthew. BA, Kalamazoo Coll., 1976; cert. in exec. mgmt., UCLA, 1989. Rsch. fellow Sinai Hosp., Detroit, 1976; rsch. assoc. Molecular Biological Inst., UCLA, L.A., 1976-77; lab mgr., adminstr. Biomed. Engring. Ctr. U. So. Calif., L.A., 1977-80; asst.

dir. Crump Inst. for Med. Engring. UCLA, 1980-84, assoc. dir., exec. officer Crump Inst. for Med. Engring., 1984-89; chmn., pres. Therapeutic Environments Inc., Van Nuys, Calif., 1989-91; pres., mng. dir. Michael Gold & Assocs., Van Nuys, 1989—; investment banker Crimson Capital Corp., 1991—; Govt. of Czech Repub., 1992-96. Mem. IEEE, Assn. Advancement Med. Instrumentation, Am. Assn. Med. Systems and Informatics, Sea Edn. Assn., Biomed. Engring. Soc., Internat. Soc. Optical Engring. Office: Michael Gold & Assocs 236 W Mountain St Ste 101 Pasadena CA 91103-2968

GOLD, RICK L., federal government executive; b. Rexburg, Idaho, June 25, 1946; s. Raymond Russell and Thelma (Lee) G.; m. Anamarie Sanone, May 14, 1988; children: Nanette Phillips, Russell. BSCE, Utah State U., 1968, MSCE, 1970. Registered profl. engr., Colo., Mont., Utah. Hydraulic engr. U.S. Bur. Reclamation, Provo, Utah, 1969-73; project hydrologist U.S. Bur. Reclamation, Durango, Colo., 1973-75; regional hydrologist U.S. Bur. Reclamation, Billings, Mont., 1975-81; spl. asst. to regional dir. U.S. Bur. Reclamation, Washington, 1981-82; asst. planning officer U.S. Bur. Reclamation, Billings, 1982-83; projects mgr. U.S. Bur. Reclamation, Durango, Colo., 1983-88; regional planning officer U.S. Bur. Reclamation, Salt Lake City, 1988-90, asst. regional dir., 1990-94, deputy regional dir., 1994—; mem. water quality com. Internat. Joint Commn. Study on Garrison Divsn. Unit, Billings, 1975-77; fed. negotiator Cost Sharing and Indian Water Rights Settlement, Durango, 1986-88; chmn. Cooperating Agy. on Glen Canyon Dam EIS, Salt Lake City, 1990-94. Contbr. articles to profl. jours.; author papers. Mem. Rotary Internat., Durango, 1985-87; bd. dirs. United Way of La Plata County, Durango, 1983-88; chmn. Combined Fed. Campaign, La Plata County, 1985. Mem. ASCE, bd. dirs. U.S. Com. on Irrigation and Drainage. Office: US Bur Reclamation 125 S State St Salt Lake City UT 84138-1102

GOLD, STANLEY P., diversified investments executive; b. 1942. AB, U. Calif., 1964; JD, U. So. Calif., 1967. Ptnr. Gang Tyre and Brown, 1967-85, Shamrock Holdings Inc., Burbank, Calif., 1985—; pres., CEO, Shamrock Holdings, Burbank. Office: Shamrock Holdings Inc 4444 W Lakeside Dr Burbank CA 91505-4054

GOLD, STEVEN, dentist; b. Washington, Nov. 13, 1967; s. Benjamin A. and Mary T. (Tafarella) G. BS, Syracuse U., 1989; DDS, U. So. Calif., 1993. Instr. U. So. Calif. Sch. Dentistry, L.A., 1993-95; pvt. practice Santa Monica, 1993—. Rschr. Jour. Dental Rsch., 1994; guitarist with Creepazoid, 1995—. Mem. Sam Shepher Conservation Soc. Mem. ADA, Calif. Dental Assn. (del. 1997—, Outstanding Editl. and Publ. 1997), Western L.A. Dental Soc. (editor Westviews 1996—), Newport Harbor Acad. Dentistry (Carl E. Rieder scholarship 1992), Omicron Kappa Upsilon. Avocations: snowboarding, surfing, in-line skating, musician. Home: 129 Seaview St Manhattan Beach CA 90266-3046 Office: 2901 Wilshire Blvd Ste 336 Santa Monica CA 90403-4912

GOLDAPER, GABRIELE GAY, clothing executive, consultant; b. Amsterdam, The Netherlands, May 4, 1937; came to U.S., 1949; d. Richard and Gertrud (Sinzheimer) Mainzer; married, 1957; children: Carolyn, Julie, Nancy. BA in Econs., Barnard Coll., 1959; BS in Edn., U. Cin., 1960; postgrad., Xavier U., 1962. V.p. planning, systems and material control High Tide Swimwear div. Warnaco, Los Angeles, 1974-79; v.p., customer support cons. Silton AMS, Los Angeles, 1979-80; exec. v.p., ptnr. Prisma Corp., Los Angeles, 1980-84; exec. v.p. Mindstar Prods., Los Angeles, 1984-85; gen. mgr. Cherry Lane, Los Angeles, 1985-86; dir. inventory mgmt. Barco Uniforms, Los Angeles, 1986; mgmt. cons. to clothing industry Santa Monica, Calif., 1986—; dir. corp. operation svcs. Authentic Fitness, L.A., 1993; exec. v.p. corp. LCA Intimates, 1994—; instr. Calif. State U., 1978-79, UCLA Grad. Bus. Mgmt. Sch., 1979-86, Fashion Inst. Design and Merchandising, 1985—; chmn. data processing com. Calif. Fashion Creators, 1980; mediator Los Angeles County Bar Assn.; cons. Exec. Service Corps; lectr. various colls. Author: A Results Oriented Approach to Manufacturing Planning, 1978, Small Company View of the Computer, 1979; also articles. Elected mem. Commn. on Status Women, 1985-89. Mem. Apparel Mfrs. Assn. (mgmt. systems com. 1978-80), Calif. Apparel Industries Assn. (exec. com., bd. dirs. 1980), Am. Arbitration Assn. Home: 4342 Redwood Ave # C309 Marina Del Rey CA 90292

GOLDBERG, FRED SELLMANN, advertising executive; b. Chgo., Jan. 22, 1941; s. Sydney Norman and Birdie (Cohen) G.; m. Jerrilyn Toby Tager, Apr. 12, 1964; children—Robin Lynn, Susanne Joy. B.S., U. Vt., 1962; M.B.A., NYU, 1964. Mktg. research mgr. P. Ballantine & Sons, Newark, 1964-67; sr. v.p., mgmt. supr. Young & Rubicam, N.Y.C., 1967-78; sr. v.p., gen. mgr. Young & Rubicam, Los Angeles, 1978-82; exec. v.p., gen. mgr. Chiat-Day, Inc., San Francisco, 1982-85; exec. v.p., chief operation officer Chiat-Day, Advt., L.A., 1985-87; pres., chief exec. officer San Francisco office Chiat-Day, Inc., San Francisco; vice chmn. Chiat/Day Advt., Inc., L.A., 1987-90; founder, chmn., CEO Goldberg Moser O'Neill Advt., San Francisco, 1990—. Republican. Jewish. Avocations: tennis, music, running. Office: Goldberg Moser O'Neill 77 Maiden Ln San Francisco CA 94108-5414

GOLDBERG, HERB, psychologist, educator; b. Berlin, Germany, July 14, 1937; came to U.S., 1941; s. Jacob and Ella (Nagler) G.; 1 child, Amy Elisabeth. BA cum laude, CUNY, 1958; PhD, Adelphi U., 1963. Lic. psychologist, Calif. Pvt. practice, L.A., 1965—; prof. Calif. State U., L.A. Author: Creative Aggression, 1972, The Hazards of Being Male, 1976, Money Madness, 1978, The New Male, 1979, The Inner Male, 1986, The New Male/Female Relationship, 1982, What Men Really Want, 1991. Mem. APA, Phi Beta Kappa. Office: 3739 Mayfair Dr Los Angeles CA 90065-3208

GOLDBERG, HILLEL, rabbi, educator; b. Denver, Jan. 10, 1946; s. Max and Miriam (Harris) G.; m. Elaine Silberstein, May 19, 1969; children: Tehilla, Temima, Mattis, Shayna, Tiferet, Chaim. BA, Yeshiva U., 1969; MA, Brandeis U., 1972, PhD, 1978. Ordained rabbi, 1976. Lectr. Machzeke Torah Inst., Brookline, Mass., 1971-71, 75, Jerusalem Coll. for Women, 1973-75, 77, The Hebrew U., 1978-85, Jerusalem Torah Coll., 1979-82; Halakhic adviser Torah MaMidbar and Pardes Israel, Santa Fe, 1986-96; exec. editor Intermountain Jewish News, Denver, 1966—; bd. dirs. Rofeh Internat., Boston. Author: Israel Salanter: Text, Structure, Idea (Acad. Book of Yr. 1982), The Fire Within, 1987, Between Berlin and Slobodka, 1989, Illuminating the Generations, 1991; editor: In Honor of Walter Wurzburger, 1989; assoc. editor Tradition, 1988—; contbg. editor Jewish Action, 1987—; mem. editorial bd. Jewish Tradition, Jerusalem, 1990—. Vol. Head Start, Oakland, Calif., 1964-65, Harlem, N.Y., 1965-66; founder Torah Cmty. Project, Denver, 1986—; legis. com. mem. Colo. Press Assn., 1990—; sci. adv. com. mem. Nat. Assn. for Rsch. and Therapy of Homosexuality, 1997—; bd. dirs. Open Door Youth Gang Alternatives. Grantee Meml. Found. for Jewish Culture, 1972-74. Mem. Am. Hist. Assn., Am. Jewish Press Assn. (Rockower awards 1983, 85, 89, 91-94, 96-97, rec. sec. 1989-91), Rabbinical Coun. Am., Nat. Assn. Rudimental Drummers, Assn. for Jewish Studies. Office: Intermountain Jewish News 1275 Sherman St #214 Denver CO 80203

GOLDBERG, HOWARD ALAN, writer; b. Glen Cove, N.Y., Apr. 21, 1948; s. Louis and Theodora Sheila (Ellner) G. BFA, Phila. Coll. Art, 1971; postgrad., NYU, 1979. Pres. Aumont Prodns., 1974—. Author: (screenplays) The Diabolical Despot, 1976, 9 rue de la Baseball, 1977, Helen Kunen, 1980, Don't Bug Me, 1985, Eden, 1991, Orpheus, 1996, Motion for Judgment, 1997, (with Howard Himelstein) Rockmalion, A Million to One, The King of Clubs, 1988, (with Tobe Hooper) Spontaneous Combustion, 1988, (with Steven Lisberger) Made in Japan, Mr. Justice, 1989, Databoy, 1990, (novel) The King of Clubs, 1982; exec. prodr., dir., writer (film) Eden, 1996; producer, dir., writer (mus.) Buskers, 1986; dir. (play) Welcome to the Moon; producer, dir., writer (film) Apple Pie, 1975; dir., cameraman (TV documentary) Davian, (video) Rod Stewart's Sailing, 1976; assoc. producer (film) Spontaneous Combustion, 1989. Avocations: skiing, tennis.

GOLDBERG, LEE WINICKI, furniture company executive; b. Laredo, Tex., Nov. 20, 1932; d. Frank and Goldie (Ostrowiak) Winicki; student San Diego State U., 1951-52; m. Frank M. Goldberg, Aug. 17, 1952; children: Susan Arlene, Edward Lewis, Anne Carri. With United Furniture Co., Inc., San Diego, 1953-83, corp. sec., dir., 1963-83, dir. environ. interiors, 1970-83; founder Drexel-Heritage store Edwards Interiors, subs. United Furniture, 1975; founding ptnr., v.p. FLJB Corp., 1976-86, founding ptnr., sec. treas., Sea Fin., Inc., 1980, founding ptnr., First Nat. Bank San Diego, 1982. Den mother Boy Scouts Am., San Diego, 1965; vol. Am. Cancer Soc., San Diego, 1964-69; chmn. jr. matrons United Jewish Fedn., San Diego, 1958; del. So. Pacific Coast region Hadassah Conv., 1960, pres. Galilee group San Diego chpt., 1960-61; supporter Marc Chagall Nat. Mus., Nice, France, U. Calif. at San Diego Cancer Ctr. Found., Smithsonian Instn., L.A. County Mus., San Diego Mus. Contemporary Art, San Diego Mus. Art; pres. San Diego Opera, 1992-94. Recipient Hadassah Service award San Diego chpt., 1958-59; named Woman of Dedication by Salvation Army Women's Aux., 1992, Patron of Arts by Rancho Sante Fe Country Friends, 1993. Democrat. Jewish.

GOLDBERG, MARK ARTHUR, neurologist; b. N.Y.C., Sept. 4, 1934; s. Jacob and Bertha (Grushlawska) G.; 1 child, Jonathan. BS, Columbia U., 1955; PhD, U. Chgo., 1959, MD, 1962. Resident neurology N.Y. Neurol. Inst., N.Y.C., 1963-66; asst. prof. neurology Columbia U. Coll. Phys. and Surgs., N.Y.C., 1968-71; assoc. prof. neurology and pharmacology UCLA, 1971-77, prof. neurology and pharmacology, 1977—; chair dept. neurology Harbor UCLA Med. Ctr., Torrance, 1977—. Contbr. articles to profl. jours., chpts. to books. Capt. U.S. Army, 1966-68. Fellow Am. Neurol. Assn., Am. Acad. Neurology; Am. Soc. Neurochemistry, Assn. Univ. Profs. Neurology. Avocation: oriental cusine.

GOLDBERG, MICHAEL ARTHUR, land policy and planning educator; b. Bklyn., Aug. 30, 1941; s. Harold and Ruth (Abelson) G.; m. Rhoda Lynne Zacker, Dec. 22, 1963 (div. 1987); children: Betsy Anne, Jennifer Heli; m. Deborah Nelson, Sept. 7, 1991. B.A. cum laude, Bklyn. Coll., 1962; M.A., U. Calif., Berkeley, 1965, Ph.D., 1968. Acting instr. Sch. Bus. Adminstrn., U. Calif., Berkeley, 1967-68; asst. prof. Faculty of Commerce and Bus. Adminstrn., U. B.C., Vancouver, 1968-71, assoc. prof., 1971-76, prof., 1976—, assoc. dean, 1980-84, dean, 1991-97, Herbert R. Fullerton prof. urban land policy, 1981—; mem. Vancouver Econ. Adv. Commn., 1980-82, Can. dept. Fin. Deposit Ins. adv. group, 1992-94, Can. dept. Internat. Trade, Strategic Adv. Group on Internat. Trade in Fin. Svcs., 1991-96; vice chmn. B.C. Real Estate Found., 1985-87, chmn. 1987-91; mem. IFC Vancouver, 1985—, vice chmn., 1985-88, chmn., 1988-89, exec. dir., 1989-91; bd. dirs. Imperial Parking Ltd., 1991-94, VLC Properties Ltd., 1991-93, Redekop Properties, 1993—, Catamaran Ferries, Inc., 1996-97, Sinorank Petroleum, 1996-98; vice chmn. Can. Fedn. Deans of Mgmt. and Adminstrv. Scis., 1991-92, chair, 1992-94, Securities Industry Policy Adv. Con., 1995—; pub.-pvt. partnership task force, 1995-96. Author: (with G. Gau) Zoning: Its Costs and Relevance for 1980's, 1980, The Housing Problem: A Real Crisis?, 1983, (with P. Chinloy) Urban Land Economics, 1984, The Chinese Connection, 1985, (with J. Mercer) The Myth of the North American City, 1985, On Balance, 1989; editor: Recent Perspectives in Urban Land Economics, 1976, (with P. Horwood) North American Housing Markets into the Twenty-first century, 1983, (with E. Feldman) The Rites and Wrongs of Land Use Policy, 1988. Trustee Temple Sholom, 1980-84. Can. Coun. fellow, 1974-75, Social Scis. and Humanities Rsch. Coun. fellow, 1979-80, 84-85, Inst. Land Policy fellow, 1979-80, Urban Land Inst. fellow, 1984—, Homer Hoyt Inst. fellow, 1988—, recipient Can. 125th anniversary medal for service to Can., 1993. Mem. Canadian Regional Sci. Assn., Am. Real Estate and Urban Econs. Assn. (dir. 1978—, pres. 1984), Vancouver Bd. Trade, Lambda Alpha. Home: 4625 Puget Dr, Vancouver, BC Canada V6L 2V9 Office: U BC, Faculty Commerce & Bus, Vancouver, BC Canada V6T 1Z2

GOLDBERG, MORRIS, internist; b. N.Y.C., Jan. 23, 1928; s. Saul and Lena (Schanberg) G.; BS in Chemistry cum laude, Poly. Inst. Bklyn., 1951; MD, SUNY, Bklyn., 1956; m. Elaine Shaw, June 24, 1956; children: Alan Neil, Seth David, Nancy Beth. Intern, Jewish Hosp. Bklyn., 1956-57, resident, 1957-58, 61-62, renal fellow, 1958-59; practice medicine, specializing in internal medicine, N.Y.C., 1962-71, Phoenix, 1971—; instr. to asst. clin. prof. internal medicine State U. N.Y. Coll. Medicine, Bklyn., 1962-71; clin. investigator, metabolic research unit Jewish Hosp. Bklyn., 1962-71; cons. in field; mem. staff Phoenix Bapt., Maryvale Samaritan, Good Samaritan, St. Joseph's Hosp., Vets. Affairs Med. Ctr., Phoenix. Served to capt. M.C., U.S. Army, 1959-61. Diplomate Am. Bd. Internal Medicine. Fellow ACP; mem. AMA, Am. Soc. Internal Medicine, Am. Coll. Nuclear Physicians (charter mem.), Am. Soc. Nephrology, Am. Soc. Hypertension (charter mem.), Ariz. Med. Assn., 38th Parallel Med. Soc. S. Korea, Ariz., Maricopa County Med. Assn., Sigma Xi, Phi Lambda Upsilon, Alpha Omega Alpha. Contb articles to med. jours. Office: Vets Affairs Med Ctr 650 E Indian School Rd Phoenix AZ 85012-1839

GOLDBLATT, HAL MICHAEL, photographer, accountant; b. Long Beach, Calif., Feb. 6, 1952; s. Arnold Phillip and Molly (Stearns) G.; m. Shawn Naomi Doherty, Aug. 27, 1974; children: Eliyahu Yonah, Tova Devorah, Raizel, Shoshana, Reuven Lev, Eliezer Noach, Esther Bayla, Rochel Leah, Zalman Ber, Perle Sara. BA in Math., Calif. State U., Long Beach, 1975. Owner Star Publs., Las Vegas, 1975—; treas. Goldblatt, Inc., Las Vegas, 1980—; pres. SDG Computer Svc., Las Vegas, 1985—; chief fin. officer Martin & Mills Ltd., Las Vegas, 1992-93; controller Amland Devel., Las Vegas, 1993-95; CFO Stewart Constrn., Las Vegas, 1995-96; CEO Goldblatt, Inc., Las Vegas, 1996-97; cost acct. Ameristar Casinos, Inc., Las Vegas, 1997—. Photographer: (photo essays) Mikveh Yisroel, 1978, Chassidic Fabrengen, 1979, A Day at Disneyland, 1985, Shavous Trek, 1997, Garth Brooks World Tour, 1998, Care for Kids Telethon, 1998, Chanukah - Festival of Lights, 1998; prodr., engr.: (audio cassettes) From the Heart of My Dreams, 1980, Middle Class Dreams, 1981, Uforatzta Trio, 1982. Founder, pres. Jews for Judaism, Long Beach, 1975-82, v.p., 1983—; fundraising chmn. Friends of Lubavitch, Long Beach, 1977; bd. dirs. Congregation Lubavitch, Long Beach, 1987, 91-92; treas. Actor's Repertory Theatre, 1995-98, mem. adv. bd., 1998—. Recipient Gold Press Card award Forty Niner Newspaper, 1973, 74, Floyd Durham Meml. award for Outstanding Community Svc., 1973, Georgie award Actor's Repertory Theatre, 1995, ART Disting. Svc. award, 1996. Office: Ameristar Casinos Inc 3773 Howard Hughes Pkwy Las Vegas NV 89109-5940

GOLDEN, JUDITH GREENE, artist, educator; b. Chgo., Nov. 29, 1934; d. Walter Cornell and Dorothie (Cissell) Greene; m. David T. Golden, Oct. 10, 1955 (div.); children: David T. Golden III, Lucinda Golden Rizzo. BFA, Inst. Chgo., 1973; MFA, U. Calif., Davis, 1975; PhD Art, Moore Coll. Art, 1990; PhD (hon.), Moore Coll. Art. Assoc. prof. art U. Ariz., Tucson, 1981-88, prof. art, 1989-96, prof. emerita, 1996—; NEA forum pub. grants panelist, 1987; project dir. U. Calif. L.A. NEA Lecture series, 1979, 84. One woman shows include Women's Bldg., L.A., 1977, G. Ray Hawkins Gallery, L.A., 1977, Quay Gallery, San Francisco, 1979, 81, A. Nagel Galerie, Berlin, 1981, Ctr. Creative Photography, U. Ariz., 1983, Colburg Gallery, Vancouver, Can., 1985, Etherton Gallery, Tucson, 1985, 89, 91, 95, Mus. Photog. Arts, San Diego, 1986, Friends of Photography, Carmel, Calif., 1987, Tucson Mus. Art, 1987, Mus. Contemporary Photography, Chgo., 1988, Visual Arts Ctr., Anchorage, Alaska, 1990, Temple Music and Art, Tucson, 1992, 97, Scottsdale (Ariz.) Ctr. Arts, 1993, Arte de Oaxaca, Mex., 1995, Etherton Gallery, Tucson, 1995, Columbia Art Ctr., Dallas, 1997; exhibited in group shows at Centre Georges Pompidou, Paris, 1981, Security Pacific Bank, L.A., 1985, Phoenix Mus. Art, 1985, L.A. County Mus. Art, 1987, Tokyo Met. Mus. Photography, 1991, Laguna Art Mus., 1992, U. N.M. Art Mus., 1993, L.A. County Mus., 1994, Hara contemporary Mus., Tokyo, 1995, Mus. Women in Arts, Washington, 1997, Santa Barbara Mus. Art, Calif., 1997, numerous others; represented in permanent collections at Art Inst. Chgo., Calif. Mus. Photography, Ctr. Creative Photography U. Ariz., Denver Art Mus., Fed. Reserve Bank San Francisco, Fogg Mus. Art, Grunwald Ctr. Graphic Arts, Internat. Mus. Photography George Eastman House, L.A. County Mus. Art, Mpls. Inst. Arts, Mus. Photographic Arts, Newport Harbor Mus. Art, Oakland Mus. Art, Photography Mus. Osaka, Polaroid Corp., San Francisco Mus. Modern Art, Security Pacific Bank, Tokyo Met. Mus. Photography, Tucson Mus. Art, Weisman Collection, L.A., Mus. Photography, Chgo. Individual artist grantee Tucson Pima Arts Coun., 1987; faculty rsch. grantee U. Ariz., 1986-87, 93-94; Ariz. Found. grantee U. Ariz., 1984; fellow Ariz. Commn. Arts, 1984; individual photography fellow NEA, 1979; Regent's faculty fellow Creative Rsch. U.Calif. L.A., 1977.

GOLDEN, JULIUS, advertising and public relations executive, lobbyist, investor; b. N.Y.C., Feb. 25, 1929; s. Nathan and Leah (Michlin) G.; m. Constance Lee Carpenter, Dec. 31, 1954 (div. Mar. 1965); children: Andrew Mitchell, Juliet Deborah; m. Diana Zana George, Apr. 30, 1973; 1 child, Jeremy Philip. BA, U. N.Mex., 1952. Asst. dir. info. U. N.Mex., Albuquerque, 1952-53; writer AP, Albuquerque, part-time 1952-53, staff writer, 1953-55, fgn. corr., S.Am., 1956-59; pres. Group West Advt./Pub. Relations Albuquerque, 1959—; dir. Auto Lend Group, Inc., Electrical Products Co., Albuquerque. Author: A Time to Die, 1975. Active Bernalillo County Lung Assn., 1961-64; mem. Met. Crime Commn., Albuquerque, 1967-71; chmn., 1970-71; mem. Albuquerque Police Commn. Task Force, 1988-89. Served with AUS, 1945-48, PTO, Korea. Recipient Nat. Feature Writing award Sigma Delta Chi, 1952, E.H. Shaffer award N.Mex. Press Assn., 1953. Mem. Pub. Rels. Soc. (pres. N.Mex. chpt. 1972), Profl. Journalism Soc. (pres. 1969-70), Pub. Rels. Soc. N.Mex. pres. 1972), Am. Advt. Fedn., Overseas Press of Am. Club, Albuquerque Press Club, Petroleum Club, 4 Hills Country Club, Sigma Delta Chi. Democrat. Jewish. Home: 1408 Stagecoach Ln SE Albuquerque NM 87123-4429 Office: Group West 1110 Pennsylvania NE Albuquerque NM 87110

GOLDEN, T. MICHAEL, state supreme court justice; b. 1942. BA in History, U. Wyo., 1964, JD, 1967; LLM, U. Va., 1992. Bar: Wyo. 1967, U.S. Dist. Ct. 1967, U.S. Ct. Appeals (10th cir.) 1967, U.S. Supreme Ct. 1970. Mem. firm Brimmer, MacPherson & Golden, Rawlins, Wyo., 1971-83, Williams, Porter, Day & Neville, Casper, Wyo., 1983-88; justice Wyo. Supreme Ct., Cheyenne, 1988—, chief justice, 1994—, assoc. justice; mem. Wyo. State Bd. Law Examiners, 1977-82, 86-88. Capt. U.S. Army 1967-71. Office: Wyo Supreme Ct Bldg PO Box 1737 2301 Capitol Ave Cheyenne WY 82002*

GOLDFARB, TIMOTHY MOORE, hospital administrator; b. Jerome, Ariz., Dec. 15, 1949; married. B, Ariz. State U., 1975, MHA, 1978. Adminstrv. resident Univ. Med. Ctr., Tucson, 1977-78, mgr. patient accts., 1978-79; asst. adminstr. Tucson Gen. Hosp., 1979; asst. adminstr. Univ. Med. Ctr., Tucson, 1979-83, assoc. adminstr., 1983-84; assoc. hosp. dir. Oreg. Health Scis. Univ. Hosp., Portland, 1984-89, health care sys. dir., 1989—. Office: Oreg Health Scis Univ Hosp 3181 SW Sam Jackson Park Rd Portland OR 97201-3011

GOLDFIELD, EMILY DAWSON, finance company executive, artist; b. Bklyn., May 31, 1947; d. Martin and Renee (Solow) Dawson; m. Stephen Gary Goldfield, June 17, 1973; children—Stacy Rose, Daniel James. B.S., U. Mich., 1969; M.Ed., Pa. State U., 1971; Ph.D., U. So. Calif., 1977. Chmn. bd. Union Home Loan, Inc. Author: The Value of Creative Dance, 1971; Development of Creative Dance, 1977. U. Mich. scholar, 1969; Pa. State U. fellow, 1970, U. So. Calif. fellow, 1972. Mem. PTA, Mortgage Assn. of Calif., Calif. Trust Deed Brokers Assn., South Orange County Assn. of Realtors, Am. Small Bus. Assn., Nat. Assn. Realtors, Calif. Assn. Realtors, Visual Arts Assn., Friend of the Orange County Performing Arts Ctr., U.S. Tennis Assn., Am. Horse Show Assn., Sierra Club, Nat. Audobon Soc., Golf and Racquet Club, Ferrari Owners Club. Office: 3200 Bristol St Ste 650 Costa Mesa CA 92626-1843

GOLDIE, RAY ROBERT, lawyer; b. Dayton, Ohio, Apr. 1, 1920; s. Albert S. and Lillian (Hayman) G.; student U. So. Calif., 1943-44, JD magna cum laude, 1957; student San Bernardino Valley Coll., 1950-51; m. Dorothy Roberta Zafman, Dec. 2, 1941; children: Marilyn, Deanne, Dayle, Ron R. Elec. appliance dealer, 1944-54; teaching asst. U. So. Calif. Law Sch., 1956-57; admitted to Calif. bar, 1957; cert. specialist, estate planning, trusts, and probate law, State of Calif. Assn. Bd. Legal Specialization; dep. atty. gen. State Bar of Calif., 1957-58; pvt. practice, San Bernardino, 1958-87, Rancho Mirage, 1987—. Pres., Trinity Acceptance Corp., 1948-53. Mem. World Peace Through Law Ctr., 1962—; regional dir. Legion Lex, U. So. Calif. Sch. Law, 1959-75; chmn. San Bernardino United Jewish Appeal, 1963; v.p. United Jewish Welfare Fund San Bernardino, 1964-66, Santa Anita Hosp., Lake Arrowhead, 1966-69. Bd. dirs. San Bernardino Med. Arts Corp.; trustee McCallum Theater, Bob Hope Cultural Ctr., 1996—, Friends of Cultural Ctr. Found.; bd. dirs. Palm Canyon Theater, 1998—, legal counsel Lake Arrowhead Skating Found. Served with AUS, 1942-43. Fellow Internat. Acad. Law and Sci.; mem. ABA, Assn. Naval Aviation Desert Storm Sqdn. (adminstrv. officer, sec.), San Bernardino County Bar Assn., Riverside County Bar Assn., State Bar Calif., Am. Judicature Soc., Am. Soc. Hosp. Attys., Calif. Trial Lawyers Assn. (v.p. chpt. 1965-67, pres. 1967-68), Am. Arbitration Assn. (nat. panel arbitrators), Coachella Valley Desert Bar Assn. (chmn. taxation and estate planning, trusts, wills & probate com. 1992-94), Order of Coif, Lake Arrowhead Country Club (pres. 1972-73, 80-81), Lake Arrowhead Yacht Club, Club at Morningside (CFO 1992-93, sec. 1993-94), Nu Beta Epsilon (pres. 1956-57). Home and Office: 1 Hampton Ct Rancho Mirage CA 92270-2585

GOLDING, GEORGE EARL, journalist; b. Oakdale, Calif., Aug. 26, 1925; s. Herbert Victor and Elva M. (Leydecker) G.; m. Joyce Mary Buttner, July 15, 1948 (dec. Oct. 1997); children: Earlene Golding Bigot, Brad Leslie, Dennis Lee, Frank Edwin, Charlton Kenneth, Daniel Duane. AA, Modesto Jr. Coll., 1950; BA San Francisco State Coll., 1959. Advt. salesman Riverbank News, 1949; galley bank boy, cub reporter San Bernardino Sun, 1951; editor Gustine Standard, 1952; photographer-reporter Humboldt Times, 1952-56; reporter, asst. city editor San Mateo (Calif.) Times, 1956-90; staff writer, corr. UPI; contbg. writer, photographer Nat. Motorist mag.; aviation writer, columnist Flight Log; co-author: (with Joyce Golding) Empire of Cousins, 1995; co-editor (with Joyce Golding) Empire of Cousins Newsletter, 1996. Pub. relations adviser Powder Puff Derby start. 1972. Served with U.S. Maritime Service, 1943, USAAF, 1944-46, AUS, 1950. Recipient John Swett award Calif. Tchrs. Assn., 1964; nominee McQuaid award Cath. Newsmen, 1965, 68; A.P. and Ency. Brit. photography awards, 1954-55, A.P. newswriting award, 1964. Mem. Am. Newspaper Guild, San Francisco-Oakland News Guild, Aviation/Space Writers Assn. (various awards 1983-84), Peninsula Press Club (founding dir., pres. 1976, co-chmn. awards and installation 1986-87), San Mateo County Arts Council (charter). Home: 1129 Balboa Ave Burlingame CA 94010-4930

GOLDING, SUSAN, mayor; b. Muskogee, Okla., Aug. 18, 1945; d. Brage and Hinda Fay (Wolf) G.; children: Samuel, Vanessa. Cert. Pratique de Langue Francaise, U. Paris, 1965; BA in Govt. and Internat. Rels., Carleton Coll., 1966; MA in Romance Philology, Columbia U., 1974. Asssoc. editor Columbia U. Jour. of Internat. Affairs, N.Y.C., 1968-69; teaching fellow Emory U., Atlanta, 1973-74; instr. San Diego Community Coll. Dist., 1978; assoc. pub., gen. mgr. The News Press Group, San Diego, 1978-80; city council mem. City of San Diego, 1981-83; dep. sec. bus., transp., housing State of Calif., Sacramento, 1983-84; county supr. dist. 3 County of San Diego, 1984-92; mayor City of San Diego, 1992—; chmn. San Diego Drug Strike Force, 1987-88, Calif. Housing Fin. Agy., Calif. Coastal Commn.; bd. dirs. San Diego County Water Authority; trustee So. Calif. Water Com., Inc.; founder Mid City Comml. Revitalization Task Force, Strategic Trade Alliance, 1993, Calif. Big 10 City Mayors, 1993; mem. Gov. Calif. Mil. Base Reuse Task Force, 1994; established San Diego World Trade Ctr., 1993, San Diego City/State/County Regional Permit Assistance Ctr., 1994; mem. adv. bd. U.S. Conf. of Mayors, 1994; chair Gov. Wilson's Commn. on Local Governance for 21st Century. Bd. dirs. Child Abuse Prevention Found., San Diego Conv. and Vis. Bur., Crime Victims Fund, United Cerebral Palsy, San Diego Air Quality Bd., San Diego March of Dimes, Rep. Assocs.; adv. bd. Girl Scouts U.S.; trustee So. Calif. Water Comm.; mem. Rep. State Cen. Com.; co-chair com. Presidency George Bush Media Fund, Calif.; chair San Diego County Regional Criminal Justice Coun., race rels. com. Citizens Adv. Com. on Racial Intergration, San Diego Unified Sch. Dist.; hon. chair Am. Cancer Soc's. Residential Crusade, 1988. Recipient Alice Paul award Nat. Women's Polit. Caucus, 1987, Calif. Women in Govt. Achievement award, 1988, Willie Velasquez Polit. award Mex. Am. Bus. and Profl. Assn., 1988, Catalyst of Chance award Greater San Diego C. of C., 1994, Woman Who Means Bus. award San Diego Bus. Jour., 1994, Internat. Citizen award World Affairs Coun., 1994; named One of San Diego's Ten Outstanding Young Citizens, 1981, One of Ten Outstanding Rep. County Ofcls. in U.S.A., Rep. Nat. Com., 1987, San Diego Woman of Achievement Soroptimists Internat., 1988. Mem. Nat. Assn. of Counties (chair Op. Fair Share, mem. taxation and fin. com.), Nat. Women's Forum. Jewish. Office: Office

of the Mayor City Administration Bldg 11th Fl 202 C St San Diego CA 92101-4806

GOLDMAN, CHARLES, electromechanical engineer; b. N.Y.C., Sept. 19, 1968; s. Ira and Marilyn Goldman. BSME, Rutgers U., 1995, BSEE, 1998. Chem. coater Nat. Starch Corp., Bridgewater, N.J., 1992-93, engring. asst., 1994; engring. asst. Rsch. Devel. and Engring. Ctr., Dover, N.J., 1995. Tutor math and physics CCM Ambs., 1992-93, video mgr., 1992-93. Rsch. Coun. N.J. engring. scholar, 1993, Coll. Morris scholar, 1992. Mem. NSPE, ASME, AIAA, The Planetary Soc., Am. Phys. Soc., Phi Theta Kappa, Tau Alpha Pi. Avocations: travel, space science, astrophysics,. Home: PO Box 64371 Phoenix AZ 85082-4371

GOLDMAN, PAUL, mechanical engineer, researcher; b. St. Petersburg, Russia, Sept. 8, 1953; came to U.S., 1989; s. Simon and Anna (Notkina) G.; m. Alla Donigakhi, Apr. 27, 1978; children: Michael, Leo. MSME, State Tech. U., St. Petersburg, Russia, 1976, PhD in Applied Math., 1985. Mech. engr. Rsch. and Devel., St. Petersburg, Russia, 1976-79; sr. mech. engr. Mining Corp., St. Petersburg, Russia, 1979-85; sr. scientist Mechanobr, St. Petersburg, Russia, 1985-89; from scientist to sr. scientist Bently Nev. Corp., Minden, 1990—. Contbr. over 50 articles to profl. jours.; patentee in field. Mem. ASME, Russian Engring. Acad. (fgn.). Achievements include developer in the field of vibroexcitation, vibroisolation, theory of synchronization, rotor dynamics and machinery diagnostics. Avocations: skiing, martial arts, tennis. Home: 1748 Westwood Dr Minden NV 89423-4715 Office: Bently Nev Corp PO Box 157 Minden NV 89423-0157

GOLDMAN, RICHARD MARTIN See GOULD, R(ICHARD) MARTIN

GOLDSMITH, DONALD WILLIAM, lawyer, astronomer, writer; b. Washington, Feb. 24, 1943; s. Raymond William and Selma Evelyn (Fine) G.; m. Rose Marien, Apr. 10, 1975 (div. 1978); 1 child, Rachel Evelyn. BA, Harvard U., 1963; PhD, U. Calif., Berkeley, 1969, JD, 1983. Asst. prof. earth and space sci. SUNY, Stony Brook, 1972-74; vis. prof. Niels Bohr Inst., Copenhagen, 1977; vis. instr. physics Stanford (Calif.) U., 1983; vis. lectr. astronomy U. Calif., Berkeley, 1980-88, vis. assoc. prof., 1990-93; assoc. Pillsbury, Madison and Sutro, San Francisco, 1985-87; cons. Cosmos TV program, Los Angeles, 1978-80; pres. Interstellar Media Publs., Berkeley, 1978—. Author: Nemesis, 1985, The Evolving Universe, 1985, Supernova!, 1989, Space Telescope, 1989, The Astronomers, 1991, The Hunt for Life on Mars, 1997, Worlds Unnumbered, 1997, The Ultimate Einstein, 1997, The Ultimate Planets, 1998, Voyage to the Milky Way, 1999; (with others) The Search for Life in the Universe, 1980, 2d edit. 1992, Cosmic Horizons, 1982, Mysteries of the Milky Way, 1991; co-writer (TV programs) Is Anybody Out there, 1986, The Astronomers, 1991. Recipient 1st prize popular essays in astronomy Griffith Obs./Hughes Aircraft Corp., L.A., 1983, Best Popular Writing by a Scientist award Am. Inst. Physics, 1986, Klumpke-Roberts award for lifetime achievement Astronomy Soc. Pacific, 1990, Annenberg Found. award for edn. Am. Astron. Soc., 1995. Home: 2153 Russell St Berkeley CA 94705-1006

GOLDSMITH, HARRY, podiatrist, practice management company executive; b. Hadera, Israel, May 10, 1951; s. William and Helena G.; m. Susan C. Weber, June 28, 1973; children: Jon, Mark, Brian. DPM, Ohio Coll. Podiatric Medicine, Cleve., 1976. Diplomate Am. Bd. Podiatric Surgery, Am. Bd. Quality Assurance and Utilization Rev. Physicians. Pvt. practice podiatry Paramount, Calif., 1977-92; group practice podiatry Gallatin Med. Corp., Downey, Calif., 1992-97; med. cons. Podiatric Med. Rev. Consultants, Cerritos, Calif., 1980—; exec. v.p. Footcare Ctrs. of Am., L.A., 1997—; mem. Nat. Health Care Anti-Fraud Assn., 1992—. Author: (book) Medical and Surgical Foot Care Services Guidelines, 1994; contbr. chpt. to Economic Ethics of Medical Practice, 1997. Inducted Nat. Acads. of Practice, 1998. Fellow Am. Coll. Podiatric Med. Rev. (pres. 1991-93, 96-98), Am. Coll. Foot and Ankle Surgeons, Am. Coll. Foot Orthopedics and Podiatric Medicine, Am. Coll. Med. Quality; mem. Am. Podiatric Med. Assn. (health policy com. 1990-93, chmn. CPT coding com., 1993-95), Calif. Podiatric Med. Assn. Office: Podiatric Med Rev Cons 13337 E South St Ste 325 Cerritos CA 90703

GOLDSTEIN, BARRY BRUCE, biologist, food company executive, lawyer; b. N.Y.C., Aug. 2, 1947; s. George and Pauline (Kolodner) G.; m. Jacqueline Barbara Aboulafia, Dec. 21, 1968; children: Joshua, Jessica. BA, Queens Coll., 1968; MA, CCNY, N.Y.C., 1974; PhD, CUNY, N.Y.C., 1980; JD, U. N.Mex., 1994. Microbiologist CPC Internat., Yonkers, N.Y., 1968-71; rsch. scientist U. Tex., Austin, 1977-80; v.p. SystemCulture Inc., Honolulu, 1980-83; bioenergy/aquaculture program mgr. N.Mex. Solar Energy Inst., Las Cruces, 1983-89; pres. Ancient Seas Aquaculture Inc., Roswell, N.Mex., 1989-92, Desert Seas Aquaculture Inc., Roswell, 1990-92, Hawaii Shellfish Co., Las Cruces, 1991—; prin. mem. tech. staff Sandia Nat. Labs., Carlsbad, N.Mex., 1994—. Editl. bd. Natural Resources Jour.; contbr. articles to profl. jours. Recipient Nat. Energy Innovation award Dept. Energy, Washington, 1985; Grad. fellow CUNY, 1971, Jesse Smith Noyes fellow, 1975, Regents scholar SUNY, 1964. Mem. World Aquaculture Soc., Am. Bar Assn., N.Mex. State Bar Assn., AAAS. Avocations: aquaculture, gardening, reading, inventing. Office: PO Box 1349 Carlsbad NM 88221-1349

GOLDSTEIN, BERNARD, biology educator; b. San Francisco, Oct. 21, 1935; s. Jacob and Sarah Goldstein; m. Estelle L. Blumberg, Aug. 21, 1962; 1 child, David E. BA in Biology, San Francisco State Coll., 1962, MA in Biology, 1964; PhD in Zoology, U. Calif., Davis, 1968. Asst. prof. biology San Francisco (Calif.) State U., 1968-72, assoc. prof. biology, 1972-76, prof. biology, 1976—, chair dept. physiology and behavioral biology, 1972-75, chair acad. senate, 1980-82, dir. rsch. and profl. devel., 1989-91; head tchg. asst. dept. zoology U. Calif., Davis, 1965-66, lectr., coord. tchg. assts., 1967; vis. prof. Western Wash. State Coll., Bellingham, 1976; chair Statewide Acad. Senate, Calif. State U., 1984-87; assessment specialist Acad. Senate, Calif. State U., 1987-90; chair Chancellor's Adv. Com. on Student Outcomes Assessment, 1988; faculty trustee, various com. positions Calif. State U. Bd. Trustees, Long Beach, 1990—; cons. and presenter in field; others. Author: General Zoology Laboratory Manual, 1974, Introduction to Human Sexuality, 1976, General Zoology Laboratory Text, 3d edit., 1979; contbg. editor: Healthline, 1988; contbr. chpts. to books and articles to profl. jours.; host: (radio show) Speaking About Human Nature, 1983. V.p. comm. Calif. State U. Alumni Coun., 1990-91; chair Bay Area Homelessness Project Steering Com., San Francisco State U., 1991; v.p. programs San Francisco State U. Alumni Coun., 1993; mem. Alumni Assocs. Adv. Coun., Lowell H.S., 1994. NSF summer fellowship, 1966, NIH doctoral fellowship, 1967-68; grantee San Francisco State U., 1977, 78, U.S. Fish and Wildlife Svc., 1984; named Alumnus of Yr., San Francisco State U., 1986. Fellow AAAS; mem. AFTRA, Am. Soc. Zoologists (divsn. morphology), Soc. for the Sci. Study Sex (nat. bd. dirs. 1988, nat. exec. com. 1988, pres. Western region 1988, chair liason com. AAAS 1991), Am. Assn. Sex Educators Counselors and Therapists, Assn. for Integrative Studies, Calif. State Student Assn. (hon. mem.), Associated Students San Francisco State U. (hon. life mem.), Phi Kappa Phi, Sigma Xi (v.p. San Francisco State U. 1977-78, pres. 1978-79). Office: Sonoma State U 1600 Holloway Ave San Francisco CA 94132-1722

GOLDSTEIN, IRA STEVEN, publishing company executive, consultant; b. Red Bank, N.J., June 2, 1963; s. Denne and Anne (Ziswasser) G. Sales mgr. Gold Trade Publs., Van Nuys, Calif., 1983-90; pres. ISG Comms., Hollywood, Calif., 1993—; instr. Income Builders Internat., Ala., 1995-97. Avocations: woodworking, art, music, cooking, boating. Office: ISG Comms Inc 916C N Formosa Ave Los Angeles CA 90046-6702

GOLDSTEIN, MICHAEL SAUL, sociologist; b. N.Y.C., Aug. 1, 1944; s. Abraham J. and Rose G.; m. Laura Geller, Dec. 23, 1979 (div. May 1992); children: Joshua, Adam, Elana. BA, Queens Coll., Flushing, N.Y., 1965; MA, Brown U., Providence, 1967, PhD, 1971. Lectr. Brown U., Providence, 1970-71; asst. prof. Sch. Pub. Health, UCLA, 1971-78, assoc. prof., 1978-88, prof., 1988—, chair dept. community health, 1988-91. Author: The Health Movement, 1992; author, editor: 50 Simple Things You Can Do to Save Your Life, 1992. Mem. APHA, Am. Sociol. Assn. Soc. for Study Social Problems, Hastings Inst. Soc. Ethics and the Life Scis. Office: UCLA Sch Pub Health Los Angeles CA 90095*

GOLDSTEIN, SIR NORMAN, dermatologist; b. Bklyn. July 14, 1934; s. Joseph H. and Bertha (Docteroff) G.; B.A., Columbia Coll., 1955; M.D., SUNY, 1959; m. Ramsay, Feb. 14, 1980; children: Richard, Heidi. Intern, Maimonides Hosp., N.Y.C., 1959-60; resident Skin and Cancer Hosp., 1960-61, Bellevue Hosp., 1961-62, NYU. Postgrad. Center, 1962-63 (all N.Y.C.); ptnr. Honolulu Med. Group, 1967-72; practice medicine specializing in dermatology, Honolulu, 1972—; clin. prof. dermatology U. Hawaii Sch. Medicine, 1973—; bd. dirs. Pacific Laser. Bd. dirs. Skin Cancer Found., 1979—; trustee Dermatol. Found., 1979-82, Hist. Hawaii Found., 1981-87; pres. Hawaii Theater Ctr., 1985-89, Hawaii Med. Libr., 1987; mem. Oahu Heritage Council, 1986-94. Served with U.S. Army, 1960-67. Recipient Henry Silver award Dermatol. Soc. Greater N.Y., 1963; Husik award NYU, 1963; Spl. award Acad. Dermatologia Hawaiiana, 1971, Outstanding Scientific Exhibit award Calif. Med. Assn., 1979, Special award for Exhibit Am. Urologic Assn., 1980, Svc. to Hawaii's Youth award Adult Friends for Youth, 1991, Nat. Cosmetic Tattoo Assn. award, 1993, Cmty. Svc. award Am. Acad. Dermatology, 1993; named Physician of Yr., Hawaii Med. Assn., 1993. Fellow ACP, Am. Acad. Dermatology (Silver award 1972), Am. Soc. Lasers Medicine & Surgery, Royal Soc. Medicine; mem. Internat. Soc. Tropical Dermatologists (Hist. and Culture award), Soc. Investigative Dermatologists, AAAS, Am. Soc. Photobiology, Internat. Soc. Cryosurgery, Am. Soc. Micropigmentation Surgery, Pacific and Asian Affairs Council, Navy League, Assn. Hawaii Artists, Biol. Photog. Assn., Health Sci. Communication Assn., Internat. Pigment Cell Soc., Am. Med. Writers Assn., Physicians Exchange of Hawaii (bd. dirs.), Am. Coll. Cryosurgery, Internat. Soc. Dermatol. Surgery, Am. Soc. Preventive Oncology, Soc. for Computer Medicine, Am. Assn. for Med. Systems and Info., Japan Am. Soc. Hawaii (bd. dirs.), Pacific Telecom Council, Hawaii State Med. Assn. (mem. public affairs com.), Hawaii Dermatol. Soc. (sec.-pres.), Hawaii Public Health Assn., Pacific Dermatol. Assn., Pacific Health Research Inst., Honolulu County Med. Soc. (gov.), Nat. Wildlife Fedn., C. of C., Preservation Action, Am. Coll. Sports Medicine, Rotary, Hemlock Soc. USA (med. bd.), Hawaii Govs. Blue Ribbon Panel on Living and Dying with Dignity, Ancient Gaelic Nobilitary Soc. (named Knight of the Niadh Nask, 1995), Outrigger Canoe Club, Plaza Club (pres. bd. dirs. 1990-92), Chancellor's Club, Oahu Country Club. Editor: Hawaii Med. Jour.; contbr. articles to profl. jours. Office: Tan Sing Bldg 1128 Smith St Honolulu HI 96817-5197

GOLDSTEIN, NORTON MAURICE (GOLDY NORTON), public relations consultant; b. Cleve., Apr. 11, 1930; s. Jacob N. and Phyllis Ruth (Weinstein) G.; m. Judith Marcia Morris, Oct. 29, 1955; 1 child, Ann Dee. Reporter L.A. Daily News, 1952-54; writer, producer Cleve Hermann Radio-TV Sports, L.A., 1952-59; exec. v.p. Kennett Pub. Rels. Assocs., L.A., 1959-71; writer, producer Vin Scully Sports Program, L.A., 1959-64; owner, oper. Goldy Norton Pub. Rels., L.A., 1971—. Author: Official Frisbee Handbook, 1972. Founding dir. U.S. Acad. Decathlon, L.A., 1982. With U.S. Army, 1949-52, Korea. Named to Frisbee Hall of Fame, Internat. Frisbee Assn., Hancock, Mich., 1979. Mem. So. Calif. Sports Broadcasters Assn. (charter). Avocations: sports, reading, travel. Office: Goldy Norton Pub Rels 6200 Wilshire Blvd Ste 903 Los Angeles CA 90048-5810

GOLDSTON, BARBARA M. HARRAL, editor; b. Lubbock, Tex., Jan. 26, 1937; d. Leonard Paul and Olivette (Stuart) Harral; m. John Rowell Toman (div. 1963); 1 child, Stuart Rowell; m. Olan Glen Goldston, 1989. BE, Tex. Christian U., 1959; MLS, U. Hawaii, 1968; postgrad., Golden Gate U., 1980-82. Tchr. pub. elem. schs., various cities, Tex. and Hawaii, 1959-66; contracts abstractor, indexer Champlin Oil Co., Ft. Worth, 1963-64; adminstrv. asst. engring. Litton Industries, Lubbock, Tex., 1964-65; mgr. rsch. library Hawaii Employers' Coun., Honolulu, 1968-72; rsch. cons. Thailand Hotel Study, Touche-Ross Assocs., Honolulu, 1974; dir. med. library U. S.D.-Sacred Heart Hosp., Yankton, 1977-79; editor, adminstrv. coord. book div. ABC-Clio, Inc., Santa Barbara, Calif., 1981-88; free-lance rsch./editorial cons. Albuquerque, 1988-89; instr. Santa Fe Community Coll., 1989—; owner Sandbar Prodns., Albuquerque, 1993—; ptnr. Broome-Harral, Inc., Albuquerque, 1989—. Author, editor with others Hist. Periodical Dir., 5 vols., World Defense Forces compendium. Contbr. Boy's Ranch, Amarillo, Tex., 1987—; mem. Lobero Theater Group, Santa Barbara, 1975-76; mem., treas. Yankton Med. Aux., 1977-79. Mem. ALA, Spl. Libraries Assn., Med. Libraries Assn., Am. Soc. Info. Sci., Albuquerque C. of C., Albuquerque Conv. and Visitors Bur., Better Bus. Bur. Albuquerque, Tex. Christian U. Alumni Assn., Delta Delta Delta. Republican. Episcopalian. Avocations: bridge, theater, music, skiing, dance. Home: 11137 Academy Ridge Rd NE Albuquerque NM 87111-6868 Office: PO Box 3824 Albuquerque NM 87190-3824

GOLDSTRAND, DENNIS JOSEPH, business and estate planning executive; b. Oakland, Calif., July 12, 1952; s. Joseph Nelson and Frances Marie (Royce) G.; m. Judy A. Goldstrand. BSBA, Calif. State U., Chico, 1975; CLU, Am. Coll., 1986, CFC, 1988. Accredited estate planner, Nat. Assn. Estate Planners Couns. Asst. mgr. Household Fin. Corp., San Leandro, Calif., 1975-76; registered rep. Equitable Fin. Svcs., San Francisco, 1976-79, dist. mgr., 1979-85; ptnr. Goldstrand & Small Ins. and Fin. Svcs., Stockton, Calif., 1986-89; owner Goldstrand Fin. & Ins. Svcs. (now Goldstrand Planning Group), Stockton, 1989—; spkr. taxation course Law Sch. Humphreys Coll., 1997, 98. Spkr. Calif. Assn. Life Underwriters, 1986, 95, San Joaquin chpt. Calif. CPA Soc., 1997; contbr. articles to Life Ins. Selling mag., 1986, 88. Mem. Stockton Estate Planning Coun., bd. dirs. 1995—, pres. 1998-99, spkr., 1996, 97; past pres. United Way San Joaquin County Endowment Found., Inc., 1994, bd. dirs. Keel Club; mem. endowment devel. com. U. Pacific; charter mem. planned giving com. U. of Pacific; assoc. mem. scholarship adv. coun. Bldr.'s Exch. of Stockton. Mem. Nat. Assn. Life Underwriters, pres. Stockton chpt. 1990-91, chair ethics com. 1993-94, Life Underwriter of Yr. 1994, Soc. Fin. Svc. Profls. (formerly Soc. CLU ChFC, pres. Stockton chpt. 1989-90), Calif. Assn. Life Underwriters (trustee 1995-96), Calif. Restaurant Assn. (assoc.), Million Dollar Round Table, Greater Stockton C. of C., Rotary, Golden Key Soc. Avocation: tennis. Home: 9215 Stony Creek Ln Stockton CA 95219-4910 Office: Goldstrand Planning Group 2800 W March Ln Ste 326 Stockton CA 95219-8218

GOLDWATER, ROBERT WILLIAMS, III, lawyer; b. Phoenix, Oct. 31, 1966; s. Robert Williams Jr. and Dianne (Gain) G. BS, Ariz. State U., 1989, JD, 1992. Bar: Ariz. 1989, U.S. Dist. Ct. 1989. Assoc. Gust Rosenfeld, Phoenix, 1992-94, Campana & Vieh, Scottsdale, Ariz., 1994-96; owner, ptnr. Goldwater Law Offices, Scottsdale, Ariz., 1996—. Republican. Episcopalian. Avocations: tennis, golf, snow skiing, flying, auto racing.

GOLDY, DANIEL LOUIS, economist, consultant; b. Butler, N.J., Aug. 7, 1915; s. Morris A. and Gussie (Silverman) G.; m. Genevieve Beatrice Rustvold, Aug. 14, 1944; 1 child, Daniel Rustvold. BA in Econs. summa cum laude with honors, U. Wis., 1936. Spl. asst. to dir. U.S. Employment Service, Washington, 1946-47; dep. asst. sec. U.S. Dept. Interior, Washington, 1947-48; regional adminstr. Bur. of Land Mgmt., Washington, 1949-51; adminstr. econ. coop. Office of the Spl. rep. of Pres. for Europe, Paris, 1951-52; regional dir. bur. of employment security U.S. Dept. of Labor, Seattle and N.Y.C., 1952-58; v.p. Pacific No. Lumber Co., Wrangell (Alaska) and Portland, Oreg., 1959-61; dep. adminstr. area redevel. adminstrn. U.S. Dept. of Commerce, Washington, 1961-62, adminstr. bus. and def. services, adminstr. and dep. asst. sec. of commerce, 1962-64; nat. export expansion coordinator, exec. dir. cabinet com. on export expansion The White House, Washington, 1964-65, mem. Pres.'s adv. coun. for trade negotiations, 1975-80; pres., dir. Internat. Systems and Controls Corp., Houston, 1965-76; dir. dept. of econ. devel. State of Oreg., Portland, 1976-78; pres. Daniel L. Goldy, Cons. Economists, Portland, Oreg., 1979—; ptnr. Mountain Fir Lumber Co., Independence, Oreg., 1955-69; bd. overseers World Affairs Council, Portland, 1987—. Bd. govs. Portland City Club, 1997—; bd. dirs. Marquam Nature Park, Portland, 1986—. Served to lt. USN, 1943-46. Recipient John Lendrum Mitchell Meml. award U. Wis., 1936. Mem. Nat. Assn. Bus. Economists, U.S. C. of C. (chmn. internal com., past bd. dirs.). Democrat. Home: 2225 SW Scenic Dr Portland OR 97225-4014

GOLITZ, LOREN EUGENE, dermatologist, pathologist, clinical administrator, educator; b. Pleasant Hill, Mo., Apr. 7, 1941; s. Ross Winston and Helen Francis (Schupp) G.; MD, U. Mo., Columbia, 1966; m. Deborah Burd Frazier, June 18, 1966; children: Carrie Campbell, Matthew Ross. Intern, USPHS Hosp., San Francisco, 1966-67, med. resident, 1967-69; resident in dermatology USPHS Hosp., Staten Island, N.Y., 1969-71; dep. chief dermatology, 1972-73; vis. fellow dermatology Columbia-Presbyn. Med. Ctr., N.Y.C., 1971-72; asst. in dermatology Coll. Physicians Surgeons, Columbia, N.Y.C., 1972-73; vice-chmn. Residency Rev. Com. for Dermatology, 1983-85. Earl D. Osborne fellow dermal. pathology Armed Forces Inst. Pathology, Washington, 1973-74; assoc. prof. dermatology, pathology Med. Sch. U. Colo., Denver, 1974-88, prof., 88-97, clin. prof. patholoIgy, dermatology, 1997—; chief dermatology Denver Gen. Hosp., 1974-97; med. dir. Ambulatory Care Ctr., Denver Gen. Hosp., 1991-97. Diplomate Am. Bd. Dermatology, Nat. Bd. Med. Examiners. Fellow Royal Soc. Medicine; mem. Am. Soc. Dermatopathology (sec., treas. 1985-89, pres.-elect 1989, pres. 1990), Am. Acad. Dermatology (chmn. coun. on clin. and lab. svcs., coun. sci. assembly 1987-91, bd. dirs. 1987-91, chmn. 1991, chmn. task force dermatopathology, 1998—), Soc. Pediatric Dermatology (pres. 1981), Soc. Investigative Dermatology, Pacific Dermatol. Assn. (exec. com. 1979-89, sec.-treas. 1984-87, pres. 1988), Noah Worcester Dermatol. Soc. (publs. com. 1980, membership com. 1989-90), Colo. Dermatol. Soc. (pres. 1978), Am. Bd. Dermatology Inc. (chmn. part II test com. 1989—, exec. com. 1993—, v.p. 1994, pres.-elect 1995, pres. 1996, dir. Emeritus, cons. to bd. 1997—), Colo. Med. Soc., Denver Med. Soc., AMA (residency rev. com. for dermatology 1982-89, dermatopathology test com. 1979-85), Denver Soc. Dermatopathology, Am. Dermatol. Assn. Editorial bd. Jour. Cutaneous Pathology, Jour. Am. Acad. Dermatology, Advances in Dermatology (editorial bd. Current Opinion in Dermatology), Women's Dermatologic Soc., So. Med. Assn., Internat. Soc. Pediatric Dermatology, Am. Contact Dermatitis Soc., Am. Soc. Dermatologic Surgery, Physicians Who Care, Am. Bd. Med. Specialties (del.), N.Y. Acad. Scis., AAAS, Brit. Assn. Dermatologists (hon.), Brazilian Soc. Dermatology (hon.), U. Mo. Med. Alumni Orgn. (bd.govs. 1993—); contbr. articles to med. jours. Home: 130 S Elm St Denver CO 80246-1131 Office: Dermatopathology Svc PO Box 6218 Denver CO 80206-0218

GOLLEHER, GEORGE, food company executive; b. Bethesda, Md., Mar. 16, 1948; s. George M. and Ruby Louise (Beecher) G.; div.; 1 child, Carly Lynn. BA, Calif. State U., Fullerton, 1970. Supr. acctg. J.C. Penney, Buena Park, Calif., 1970-72; systems auditor Mayfair Markets, Los Angeles, 1973, v.p., CFO, 1982-83; controller Fazio's, Los Angeles, 1974-78; group controller Fisher Foods, Ohio, 1978-79; v.p. fin. Stater Bros. Markets, Colton, Calif., 1979-82; sr. v.p., CFO Boys Markets Inc., Los Angeles, 1983—; CEO Ralph Grocery Co., Compton, Calif., 1995—. Office: Ralph Grocery Co 1100 W Artesia Blvd Compton CA 90220-5108

GOLSTON, JOAN CAROL, psychotherapist; b. Vancouver, B.C., Can., Aug. 10, 1947; came to U.S., 1958; d. Stefan and Lydia Barbara (Fruchs) G. Student, Reed Coll.; BA, U. Wash., 1977, MSW, 1979. Cert. social worker; bd. cert. diplomate in clin. social work Am. Bd. Examiners in Clin. Social Work. Clin. supr. Crisis Clinic, Seattle, 1975-77; psychiatric social worker Valley Gen. Hosp., Renton, Wash., 1979-82; psychotherapist pvt. practice, Seattle, 1981—; sch. counselor Northwest Sch., Seattle, Seattle Acad.; clin. cons. outpatient dept. Valley Cities Cmty. Mental Health, Renton, 1991, Seattle Counseling Svcs., 1991-96, emergency svcs., 1975-89; cons., trainer and presenter in field. Contbr. articles to profl. jours. Bd. dirs. Open Door Clinic, Seattle, 1975-76, Northwest Family Tng. Inst., Seattle, v.p., 1990, pres., 1991, mem. exec. com., 1988-91; mem. adv. bd. Ctr. Prevention of Sexual and Domestic Violence, 1993—, AIDS Risk Reduction Project Sch. Social Work U. Wash., 1988-93. Nat. Merit scholar, 1964. Mem. NASW (diplomate), Wash. State chpt. NASW (chmn. com. on inquiry ethics 1996—, mem. com. 1992—), Internat. Soc. Study of Dissociation, Internat. Soc. Trauma Stress Studies, Acad. Cert. Social Workers. Avocations: athletics, antiquities. Office: 726 Broadway Ste 303 Seattle WA 98122-4337

GOLUB, SIDNEY HARRIS, dean, educator; b. Hartford, Conn., July 28, 1943; s. Morris and Lillian (Pollin) G.; m. Judith Stern, Aug. 21, 1966; 1 child, Brian. BA, Brandeis U., 1965; PhD, Temple U., 1969. Postdoctoral rsch. fellow Royal Karolinska Inst., Stockholm, 1969-71; from asst. prof. to assoc. prof. UCLA, 1971-83, prof., 1983—, assoc. dean, acad. affairs, 1986-92, vice provost, dean acad. affairs, 1991-92, provst, former dean interim, now acting dean; vis. prof. Sloan Kettering Inst., N.Y.C., 1978-79. Contbr. articles to profl. jours., chpts. to books. Recipient Jonsson prize for rsch. UCLA Jonsson Comprehensive Cancer Ctr. Mem. Am. Soc. for Microbiology, Am. Assn. for Cancer Rsch., Am. Assn. Immunologists, Soc. for Leukocyle Biology, Soc. for Natural Immunology. Office: UCLA Sch Medicine 3148 Murphy Hall Los Angeles CA 90095-3075*

GOLUBIC, THEODORE ROY, sculptor, designer, inventor; b. Lorain, Ohio, Dec. 9, 1928; s. Ivan and Illonka (Safar) G.; m. Rose Andrina Ieraci-Golubic, Nov. 27, 1958; children: Vincivan, Theodore E., Victor, Georjia. Student Ohio State U., Columbus, 1947-48; BFA in Painting, Miami U., Oxford, Ohio, 1951; student Syracuse U., 1955; MFA in Sculpture, U. Notre Dame, 1957. Asst. to Ivan Mestrovic, 1954-60; guest tchr. U. Notre Dame, 1959; urban planner redevel. dept., South Bend, Ind., 1960-65, sculpture cons., Rock of Ages Corp., 1965-67; instr. Cen. Mo. State U., 1969; instr. San Diego Sculptors' Guild, 1970-71; artist-in-residence Roswell (N.Mex.) Mus. and Art Ctr., 1971-72; sculptor, designer, inventor, 1958-98; works include: 4 dimensional sun environ. design, South Bend, Ind., limestone relief sculpture Cathedral of the Nativity, Dubuque, Iowa, The Crypt Series, ROA Corp., Barre, Vt., bronze St. John Bapt., Lorain, Ohio, 4 pt. surface pick-up, 3 dimensional interconnected integrated cir., multilevel S.I.P. package, isolated heatsink bonding pads, lead form as test, semiconductor chip module (Eureka award Motorola, Inc.), Phoenix, mahogany bas relief U. San Diego. With U.S. Army, 1951-53. Mem. Coll. Art Assn. Am., Internat. Sculpture Ctr. Contbr. articles to profl. jours. Home and Studio: 4015 W Topeka Dr Glendale AZ 85308-7536

GOMBOCZ, ERICH ALFRED, biochemist; b. Vienna, Austria, Aug. 29, 1951; came to U.S., 1990; s. Erich and Maria (Mayer) G.; m. Gisela M. Dorner, June 12, 1973 (div. Apr. 1992); 1 child, Manfred Alexander (dec.). Cert., T.U., Vienna, 1970-75. With Fed. Inst. for Food Analysis and Rsch., Vienna, 1975-90, head of sect. dept. biochem. analysis, 1980-90, contbr. Cen. Lab. Info. Mgmt. System, 1987-90; chmn. scientific adv. bd. LabIntelligence, Inc., Menlo Park, Calif., 1989—, COO, v.p. R & D, 1989—; speaker and lectr. in field. Editor: Computers in Electrophoresis; contbr. articles to profl. jours.; patentee in field. Postdoctoral Rsch. award NIH, Bethesda, Md., 1985-86, 88. Mem. Internat. Assn. for Cereal Chemistry, Internat. Electrophoresis Soc., Am. Electrophoresis Soc. Roman Catholic. Office: LabIntelligence Inc 101 Industrial Way Ste 14 Belmont CA 94002-8207

GOMEZ, DAVID FREDERICK, lawyer; b. Los Angeles, Nov. 19, 1940; s. Fred and Jennie (Fujier) G.; m. Kathleen Holt, Oct. 18, 1977. BA in Philosophy, St. Paul's Coll., Washington, 1965, MA in Theology, 1968; JD, U. So. Calif., 1974. Bar: Calif. 1975, U.S. Dist. Ct. (cen. dist.) Calif. 1975, U.S. Dist. Ct. (ea. dist.) Calif. 1977, Ariz. 1981, U.S. Dist. Ct. Ariz. 1981, U.S. Ct. Claims 1981, U.S. Ct. Appeals (9th cir.) 1981, U.S. Supreme Ct. 1981; ordained priest Roman Cath. Ch., 1969. Staff atty. Nat. Labor Relations Bd., Los Angeles, 1974-75; ptnr. Gomez, Paz, Rodriguez & Sanora, Los Angeles, 1975-77, Garrett, Bourdette & Williams, San Francisco, 1977-80, Van O'Steen & Ptnrs., Phoenix, 1981-85; pres. David F. Gomez, PC, Phoenix, 1985—; faculty Practicing Law Inst., 1989; instr. contracts law Peoples Coll. Law., L.A., 1975-76. Author: Somos Chicanos: Strangers in Our Own Land, 1973; co-author: Advanced Strategies in Employment Law, 1988, Arizona Employment Law Handbook, 1995. Mem. ABA, Maricopa County Bar Assn., Los Abogados Hispanic Bar Assn., Nat. Employment Lawyer's Assn., Calif. State Bar Assn., Ariz. Employment Lawyers Assn. (bd. dirs. 1996—), Ariz. State Bar Assn. (com. on rules of profl. conduct 1991-97, civil jury instructions com. 1992-94, peer rev. com. 1992—). Democrat.

GOMEZ, LOUIS SALAZAR, college president; b. Santa Ana, Calif., Dec. 7, 1939; s. Louis Reza and Mary (Salazar) G.; m. Patricia Ann Aboytes, June 30, 1962; children: Louis Aboytes, Diana Maria, Ramon Reza. Student, Calif. State Poly. U., 1959-65; BA, Calif. State U., San Bernardino, 1971; MA, Calif. State U., 1975; EdD, U. So. Calif., L.A., 1987. Cert. tchr., counselor, adminstr., Calif. Tchr., counselor San Bernardino City Schs., 1971-76; human rels. coord. San Bernardino Valley Coll., 1976-78, counselor, 1978-82, coord. of counseling, 1982-87; asst. dean student svcs. Crafton Hills

Coll., Yucaipa, Calif., 1987-89, dean student svcs., 1989-90, acting pres., 1990-92, pres., 1992—; lectr. Calif. State U., San Bernardino, 1976-81, mem. adv. bd., 1987-95. Bd. dirs. Redlands YMCA, 1995—; pres. San Bernardino Regional Emergency Tng. Ctr. Joint Power Authority, 1998—. Mem. San Bernardino Valley Coll. Faculty Assn. (treas. 1980-82), Faculty Assn. Calif. Community Colls., San Bernardino Community Coll. Dist. Mgmt. Assn., Kiwanis (pres. San Bernardino chpt. 1982). Democrat. Roman Catholic. Avocations: financial planning, photography, treasure hunting. Home: 10682 Berrywood Cir Yucaipa CA 92399-5924 Office: Crafton Hills Coll 11711 Sand Canyon Rd Yucaipa CA 92399-1742

GOMEZ, ROMAN I., producer, cameraman, editor; b. Uruapan, Michoacan, Mex., Mar. 12, 1961; came to U.S., 1975; s. Rosalio C. and Loreta (Paz) G. Student, Rancho Santiago Coll., 1991-93. Tv exec. prodr. Santa Ana (Calif.) Cable TV, 1994-97; editor Comcast TV, Santa Ana, Calif., 1996-97; prodr., cameraman, editor R.G. Prodns., Santa Ana, Calif.; bd. dirs. Cmty. TV Adv. Bd., Santa Ana. Freelance reporter: (newspaper) El Sol Latino, 1995-96, prodr., over 100 music video shows in 3 years. Avocations: music video producing and directing, computers, internet. Home: 2208 W Wilshire Ave Santa Ana CA 92704-3245 Office: RG Prodns 2208 W Wilshire Ave Santa Ana CA 92704-3245

GONG, LIPING, computer engineer, consultant; b. Beijing, May 21, 1956; came to U.S., 1987; s. Xuezheng Gong and Xiuzheng Yan; m. Hui Wang, Dec. 16, 1986. BS in Computer Engring., Northeastern U., Shengyang, China, 1982. Diplomate Computer Sci. & Engring. Dir. Computing & Analytic Ctr. Beijing Med. U., 1985-87; rsch. fellow Geotech Inst., Hong Kong, 1987; project mgr., R&D engr. CMC Corp., Foster City, Calif., 1987-88; mgr., design engr. GCM Computer Sys., Mountain View, Calif., 1988-92; sr. engr. Synnex/MiTAC, Fremont, Calif., 1992-95; prin. engr. Elitegroup, Fremont, 1995—; cons. Beijing Med. U., 1985-87. Recipient State 3d Class award Beijing Mcpl. Govt., 1985. Avocations: music, tennis, ice skating, travel. Office: Elitegroup 45401 Research Ave Fremont CA 94539-6111

GONG, MAMIE POGGIO, elementary education educator; b. San Francisco, June 26, 1951; d. Louis and Mary Lee (Lum) G.; m. Andy Anthony Poggio. BA, U. Calif., Berkeley, 1973, postgrad., 1981-83, MEd, 1982. Tchr. Oakland (Calif.) Unified Sch. Dist., 1974-84, Palo Alto (Calif.) Unified Sch. Dist., 1984-91; cons., writer Nat. Clearinghouse for Bilingual Edn., Washington, 1984; cons. ARC Assocs., Oakland, 1983; rsch. asst. dept. edn. Stanford U., 1987-89. Co-author: Promising Practices: A Teacher Resource, 1984. Recipient Kearney Found. award, 1969, others. Mem. Tchrs. English to Speakers Other Langs. (presenter 1990 conf.), Calif. Assn. Tchrs. English to Speakers Other Langs. Democrat. Office: Palo Alto Unified Sch Dist 25 Churchill Ave Palo Alto CA 94306-1099

GONSALVES, PAMELA YVONNE, artist, educator, graphic designer; b. Turlock, Calif., Apr. 14, 1953; d. Morris Joseph Gonsalves and Ava Madeleine (Gunnels) Mueller; m. Milton Murry Schild, Dec. 24, 1972 (div.); children: Zedekiah Philip, Isaac Woodrow; m. John Arthur McLean, June 23, 1996. BFA, Pacific Northwest Coll. of Art, 1985; Tchg. Cert., Portland State U., 1986. Art educator Portland (Oreg.) Pub. Schs., 1988-96; gallery mem. Blackfish Gallery, Portland, 1997—; tchr. mono print, Pacific Northwest Coll. of Art, 1986, basketry and fiber arts, Eugene Parks and Recreation, Oreg., 1973, 74, Rock Creek Campus, Portland C.C., Beaverton, Oreg., 1977, 78; judge fibers Washington County Fair, Beaverton, 1977; art lectr. Art Beat, Portland C.C. Art Celebration, 1991; graphic designer, art dir. PJ Artlines, Portland, 1997—. Artist: (multi-media sculptures) South Africa/Any Tapestry is Only as Strong as Warp, 1989, Sarcophogus, 1991, Connections, 1997. Mem., promoter Culture Shock Gallery, Portland, 1991-92. Named to 50 Women in the Arts, The Women's Found. of Oreg., Portland, 1992; recipient award of Merit, Pacific Northwest Coll. of Art, 1984, Undergrad. award in printmaking, U. Tex., San Antonio, 1983, Libr. Print competition, 1983. Mem. Humbolt Arts Coun., Portland Art Mus. Avocations: hiking, swimming. Office: Blackfish Gallery 420 NW 9th Ave Portland OR 97209-3309

GONZALES, HILARIO DURAN (LARRY GONZALES), insurance company executive, finance educator; b. Almagordo, N.Mex., Aug. 2, 1938; s. Jesus Lujan and Margarita Duran (Duran) G.; m. Ingrid Elizabeth Indseth, July 25, 1965 (div. July 1985; children: Eric, Sonja, Inger, Kirstin, Alicia; m. Dawn Nicole Lawrence, Oct. 25, 1993; stepchildren: Chad and Cameron Melkus. BS, San Diego State U., 1963; MBA, U. Dallas, Irvine, Tex., 1965; MPH, UCLA, 1978. Cert. ins. broker, Calif. Project mgr. Tex. Instruments, Dallas, 1965-69, Sci. Control, Dallas, 1969-71, Gen. Dynamics, Pomona, Calif., 1971-74; dep. dir. Los Angeles County, L.A., 1974-79; dir. gen. svcs. San Diego County, San Diego, 1979-84; pres. Prestige Bus. Enterprises, San Diego, 1984-90; ptnr. Evergreen Fin., San Diego, 1990-92; CEO, pres. Employee Ins. Svcs., Fallbrook, Calif., 1992—; adj. prof. health adminstrn. Webster U., 1994-98; prof. fin. Nat. U., 1980-98, U. Phoenix, 1989-98, chair fin. undergrad., 1996-98, fin. grad., 1998-99. Author: (textbooks) Accounting and Finance, 1997, Managerial Finance, 1997, Managerial Finance, Vol. II, 1997, Finance: Profit, Planning, Control, 1998. Mem. integration task force bd. City of San Diego Schs., 1980; bd. dirs., treas. St. Clare's Home, Inc., Escondido, Calif.; bd. dirs. New Haven, Vista, Calif.; chair fin. grad. com. U. Phoenix, San Diego, also chair acctg., 1994-96. With USMC, 1957-60. Named Outstanding Instr. Grad. Fin., U. Phoenix, 1998. Roman Catholic. Avocations: camping, golf, jogging, weight lifting, fishing. Office: Employee Ins Svc PO Box 1974 Fallbrook CA 92088-1974

GONZALES, RICHARD L., fire department chief. AA in Fire Sci. Tech., Red Rocks C.C., 1988; BS summa cum laude in Bus. Adminstrn., Regis U., 1991; MA, Harvard U., 1991; student, U. Colo. Firefighter Denver Fire Dept., 1972-75, mem. fire prevention bureau, dist. 5 roving officer, 1976-79, mem. training divsn., 1980-81, dist. roving officer firefighter, 1981-82, capt. firefighter pumper 2 and 27, 1982-85, asst. chief, 1985-87, chief fire dept., 1987—; Mem. Nat. Fire Protective Assn. Urban Fire Forum, Internat. Assn. Fire Chiefs, Metro Fire Chiefs Assn., Denver Metro Fire Chiefs Assn., Colo. State Fire Chiefs Assn., Urban Fire Forum, IAFF Local 858 Negotiating Team; bd. trustees Nat. Fire Protection Assn., 1992-95. Mem. adv. bd. U. Colo. Denver Sch. of Pub. Affairs, Red Rocks C.C., Denver Ptnrs., KAZY Denver Marathon; bd. trustees Nat. Multiple Sclerosis Soc.; bd. dirs. Rocky Mountain Poison Drug Found., Chic Chicana, Golden Gloves Charity. Recipient Outstanding Achievement award Hispanics of Colo., 1987; named Young Firefighter of the Yr., 1981. Office: Denver Fire Dept 745 W Colfax Ave Denver CO 80204-2612*

GONZALES, RICHARD ROBERT, academic administrator; b. Palo Alto, Calif., Jan. 12, 1945; s. Pedro and Virginia (Ramos) G.; m. Jennifer Ayres; children: Lisa Dianne, Jeffrey Ayres. AA, Foothill Coll., 1966; BA, San Jose (Calif.) State U., 1969; MA, Calif. Poly. State U., San Luis Obispo, 1971; grad. Def. Info. Sch., Def. Equal Opportunity Mgmt. Inst. Counselor student activities Calif. Poly. State U., San Luis Obispo, 1969-71, instr. ethnic studies, 1970-71; counselor Ohlone Coll., Fremont, Calif., 1971-72, coord. coll. readiness, 1971; counselor De Anza Coll., Cupertino, Calif., 1972-78, mem. community speakers bur., 1975-78; counselor Foothill Coll., Los Altos Hills, Calif., 1978—, mem. community speakers bur., 1978—; instr. Def. Equal Opportunity Mgmt. Inst., 1984—. Mem. master plan com. Los Altos (Calif.) Sch. Dist., 1975-76; vol. worker, Chicano communities, Calif.; active mem. Woodside (Calif.) Recreation Commn. With Calif. Army N.G., now maj. Adj. Gen. Corps, USAR. Recipient Counselor of Yr. award Ohlone Coll., 1971-72; Masters and Johnson Inst. fellow. lic. marriage family child counselor, Calif. Mem. ACA, Am. Coll. Counseling Assn., Calif. Assn. Marriage and Family Therapists, Calif. Community Coll. Counselor Assn. (former pres.), Calif. Assn. Counseling and Devel. (former pres. Hispanic Caucus), Calif. Assn. for Humanistic Edn. and Devel., Calif. Assn. for Multi-Cultural Counseling, Res. Officers Assn., La Raza Faculty Assn. Calif. Community Colls., Nat. Career Devel. Assn., Phi Delta Kappa, Chi Sigma Iota. Republican. Office: Foothill Coll Los Altos CA 94022

GONZALES, RON, mayor, former county supervisor; b. San Francisco; m. Alvina Gonzales; 3 children: Miranda, Rachel, Alejandra. BA in Community Studies, U. Calif., Santa Cruz. Formerly with Sunnyvale (Calif.) Sch. Dist., City of Santa Clara, Calif.; then human resource mgr. Hewlett-Packard Co.; market program mgmt. cons. state and local govts.; mem. city coun. City of Sunnyvale, 1979-87, mayor, 1982, 87; mem. bd. suprs. Santa Clara County, 1989-96; edn. program mgr. Hewlett Packard Co., 1996-98; mayor San Jose, Calif., 1999—; bd. chair, 1993; bd. transit suprs. Santa Clara County, 1989—; bd. dirs. Joint Venture: Silicon Valley, The Role Model Program, Bay Area Biosci. Ctr., Am. Leadership Forum, Santa Clara County. Office: Office of the Mayor City Hall 801 N 1st St Rm 600 San Jose CA 95110-1704*

GONZALES, STEPHANIE, state official; b. Santa Fe, Aug. 12, 1950; 1 child, Adan Gonzales. Degree, Loretto Acad. for Girls. Office mgr. Jerry Wood & Assocs., 1973-86; dep. sec. of state Santa Fe, 1987-90, sec. of state, 1991; state dir. rural devel. U.S. Dept. of Agriculture, Albuquerque, 1999—; bd. dirs. N.Mex. Pub. Employees Retirement, N.Mex. State Convassing Bd., N.Mex. Commn. Pub. Records. Mem. exec. bd. N.Mex. AIDS Svc.; mem. Commn. White House Fellowships. Mem. Nat. Assn. Secs. State, United League United Latin Am. Citizens (women's coun.), Nat. Assn. Latin Elected and Appointed Ofcls. Office: Rural Devel State Office 6200 Jefferson St NE Rm 255 Albuquerque NM 87109*

GONZALES-DAY, KENNETH ROBERT, artist, educator; b. Santa Clara, Calif., Nov. 11, 1964; s. Peter Jose and Nancy Dea (Mabbitt) Gonzales. BFA, Pratt Inst., 1987; MA, CUNY, N.Y.C., 1990; postgrad., Whitney Mus. Am. Art, 1993, NYU, 1995; MFA, U. Calif., Irvine, 1995. Preparator New Mus. Contemporary Art, N.Y.C., 1985-90, Am. Craft Mus., N.Y.C., 1985-90; asst. curator Bklyn. Mus., 1987-88; personal asst. Charles Cowles Gallery, N.Y.C., 1990-92; devel. officer Alternative Mus., N.Y.C., 1991-92, Pub. Art Fund, N.Y.C., 1993; asst. prof. Scripps Coll., Claremont, Calif., 1995—; mem. adv. bd. L.A. Freewaves, 1997; mem. artist adv. bd. Mcpl. Art Gallery, Barnsdall Art Park, L.A., 1998. Author: St. James Press Gay and Lesbian Almanac, 1998; contbr. articles to profl. jours.; works exhibited at Christine Rose Gallery, N.Y.C., 1996, White Columns, N.Y.C., 1996, Post, L.A., 1997, Barnsdall Art Park-Mcpl. Gallery, L.A., 1998. Recipient New Genre Individual Artist award NEA WESTAF, 1996; Van Lee fellow Whitney Mus., ISP, N.Y.C., 1992; faculty rsch. grantee Scripps Coll., Claremont, 1996, 97. Mem. Soc. for Photographic Edn. (co-chair), Coll. Art Assn. Office: Scripps Coll 1030 Columbia Ave Claremont CA 91711-3986

GONZALEZ, IRMA ELSA, federal judge; b. 1948. BA, Stanford U., 1970; JD, U. Ariz., 1973. Law clk. to Hon. William C. Frey U.S. Dist. Ct. (Ariz. dist.), 1973-75; asst. U.S. atty. U.S. Attys. Office Ariz., 1975-79, U.S. Attys. Office (ctrl. dist.) Calif., 1979-81; trial atty. antitrust divsn. U.S. Dept. Justice, 1979; assoc. Seltzer Caplan Wilkins & McMahon, San Diego, 1981-84; judge U.S. Magistrate Ct. (so. dist.) Calif., 1984-91; ct. judge San Diego County Superior Ct., 1991-92; judge U.S. Dist. Ct. (so. dist.) Calif., San Diego, 1992—; adj. prof. U. San Diego, 1992; trustee Calif. Western Sch. Law; bd. visitors Sch. Law U. Ariz. Mem. Girl Scout Women's Adv. Cabinet. Mem. Lawyers' Club San Diego, Thomas More Soc., Inns of Ct. Office: Edward J Schwartz US Courthouse 940 Front St Ste 5135 San Diego CA 92101-8994*

GONZALEZ, KIMBERLY REGINA, controller; b. Walnut Creek, Calif., Nov. 5, 1964; d. Earl Glenn and Marilynn Mae (Roberts) Kramar; m. George Gonzalez, May 30, 1987; children: Joshua Alan, Nathaniel James, Matthew Jacob. BS in Internat. Bus. summa cum laude, Woodbury U., 1986. Controller Charisma Missions Inc., L.A., 1985—, dir., treas., 1986—. Assoc. producer (TV program) Alabare, L.A., 1988—. Mem. NAFE, Am. Soc. Profl. and Exec. Women, Am. Mgmt. Assn., Cath. Communicators Assn. (vice chmn. 1990-92), Am. Mktg. Assn. Republican. Roman Catholic. Avocation: Catholic missionary evangelization. Home: 15625 New Hampton St La Puente CA 91745-4120 Office: Charisma in Missions Inc 1059 S Gage Ave Los Angeles CA 90023-2505

GONZALEZ, MANUEL GEORGE, IV, architect; b. Santa Monica, Calif., Dec. 30, 1954; s. Manuel George III and Mary Mac (Short) G.; m. Martha Lynn Hutchcraft, June 28, 1980; children: Megan, M.G., Matthew. B. U. Calif., Berkeley, 1977; M, U. So. Calif., 1980. Architect pvt. practice, Malibu, Calif., 1980-85; ptnr. Van Tilburg & Ptnrs., Santa Monica, Calif., 1985-94; dir. architecture Kaufman & Broad, L.A., 1994—. Mem. AIA. Avocations: coaching baseball, skiing, roto games. Home: 1014 Crater Camp Dr Calabasas CA 91302-2126 Office: Kaufman & Broad Ste 2060 100 Bayview Cir Newport Beach CA 92660

GONZALEZ, MICHAEL JOE, multimedia producer; b. North Hollywood, Calif., Mar. 6, 1959. AA in Journalism, L.A. Valley Coll., Van Nuys, Calif., 1984; postgrad. in mgmt., Master's U., 1998—; student, Master's Coll., 1998—. Cert. graphic designer. Pub. Martial Arts Mag., North Hollywood, 1982-87; tng. instr. Great Western Bank, Northridge, Calif., 1987-92; multimedia prodr. Calif. Fed. Bank, L.A., 1992-96; prodr. Martial Arts Entertainment, Valencia, Calif., 1995—; multimedia prodr. Blue Cross Calif., Woodland Hills, 1996—; art dir. Scott Advt., Van Nuys, Calif., 1984-87. Author: Monkey Kung-Fu Book, 1984, Monkey Kung-Fu Book, Vol. Z, 1998; freelance writer Inside Kung-Fu Mag., 1983—, Black Belt Mag., 1983—, Whu Shu Kung-Fu Mag., 1998—; art dir. Traveling Times mag., 1982-84. Recipient hon. black belt Universal Soc. Martial Arts, 1986. Mem. Am. Film Inst., Internat. Interactive Comm. Soc., Tau Alpha Epsilon. Avocations: Kung-Fu instr., studying martial arts. E-mail: Michael.Gonzalez@wellpoint.com. Office: Blue Cross Calif 21555 Oxnard St 3J Woodland Hills CA 91367-4943

GONZALEZ, TRUDY ANN, television producer; b. Grand Rapids, Mich., Mar. 29, 1941; d. Frederick Wilhelm Heinrich Lomker and Betty Leticius (McCabe) Jensen; m. Val Riccardo Fernengel, Feb. 20, 1970 (div. Oct. 1977); children: Michelle, Lynne, Joseph, Daniel; m. Regino Melquiades Camacho Polanco Gonzalez, May 14, 1994. Student, Western Mich. U., 1960-61, Mt. Hood C.C., Gresham, Oreg., 1993-94; cert., Western Bus. Coll., 1984. Ind. TV prodr. Vancouver, Wash., 1991-93, Multnomah Cmty. TV, Gresham, 1993—, TCI of So. Wash., Vancouver, 1994—, Tualatin Valley Cmty. Access, Hillsboro, Oreg., 1994-97; propr., exec. prodr. One Hundredth Psalm Prodns., Vancouver, 1991—. Creator, prodr. TV series People Need The Lord, 1992— (Telly award 1996). Sponsor Christian Children's Fund, Richmond, Va., 1997-98, 99. Mem. Multnomah Cmty. TV, Internat. Traders, Highlander Club. Mem. Foursquare Ch. Avocations: writing radio and TV scripts, novel and poetry, immigration counseling. Office: One Hundredth Psalm Prodns 11919 N Jantzen Dr # 362 Portland OR 97217-8195

GONZÁLEZ-TRUJILLO, CÉSAR AUGUSTO, Chicano studies educator, writer; b. L.A., Jan. 17, 1931; s. José Andalón and Camerina (Trujillo) González; m. Bette L. Beattie, Aug. 30, 1969. BA, Gonzaga U., 1953, MA, Licentiate in Philosophy, 1954; MST, Licentiate in Sacred Theology, U. Santa Clara, 1961; postgrad., UCLA, 1962-65. Tchr. Instituto Regional Mex., Chihuahua, Mex., 1954-57; community devel. specialist Centro Laboral Méx., México D.F., Mex., 1965-68; supr. ABC Headstart East L.A., L.A., 1968-69; employment counselor Op. SER, San Diego, 1969-70; prof., founding chair dept. Chicano studies San Diego Mesa Coll., 1970—; founding chairperson Raza Consortium, San Diego, 1971-72; cons. Chicano Fedn. San Diego, Inc., 1987-89. Author poetry, short fiction and criticism, 1976—; contbr. numerous articles to profl. jours. Mem. Ednl. Issues Coordinating Com., L.A., 1968-69; founding bd. dirs. Mex.-Am. Adv. Com. to Bd. of Edn., L.A., 1969. Fulbright-Hays fellow, Peru, 1982, NEH fellow, 1984; recipient Cmty. Svc. award Chicano Fedn. San Diego Inc., 1982, Teaching Excellence award Nat. Inst. Staff and Orgnl. Devel., 1993, Outstanding Tchr. San Diego Mesa Coll., 1985, 95, Editor's Choice award Poet Mag., 1993, Cesar Chavez Social Justice award, 1994, Latina Latino Indigenous People Coalition award, 1995; named Outstanding Tchr. and Scholar, Concilio of Chicano Studies for San Diego, Imperial Valley and Baja, Calif., 1990; Spl. Congl. recognition Congressman Bob Filner, 1995; AVID Writer of the Yr. award San Diego Imperial Counties, 1997. Mem. Am. Fedn. Tchrs., Nat. Assn. Chicano Studies, Chicano Fedn. San Diego County, Centro Cultural De La Raza (past bd. dirs.), Poets and Writers, Asociacion Internacional de Hispanistas, C. C. Humanities Assn. Democrat. Roman Catholic. Avocations: reading, travel. Office: San Diego Mesa Coll 7250 Mesa College Dr San Diego CA 92111-4902

GOOCH, LAWRENCE BOYD, accounting executive; b. L.A., Oct. 20, 1942; s. John Elmer and Roberta Alice (Grant) G.; m. Barbara Ann Buehrig, June 21, 1970; children: Brenda, Timothy, Ted. BSCE, Stanford U., 1965, MBA, 1970. Cons. Am. Appraisal Co., Milw., 1970-71; v.p. Am. Valuation Cons., Chgo., 1971-78, Stone Webster Appraisal, Woodland Hills, Calif., 1979-80; sr. v.p. Arthur D. Little Valuation, Woodland Hills, 1980-88; prin. Pricewaterhouse Coopers LLP, L.A., 1988—. Capt. USMC, 1965-67, Vietnam. Mem. Stanford Alumni Assn., Stanford Bus. Sch. Alumni Assn., Am. Soc. Appraisers (sr.). Avocations: golf, biking, reading. Home: 3939 Freshwind Cir Westlake Vlg CA 91361-3804 Office: Price Waterhouse 400 S Hope St Ste 2300 Los Angeles CA 90071-2889

GOOCH, MICHAEL THOMAS, television production professional, writer; b. Durham, N.C., June 21, 1953; s. Thomas Alva and Clara Lee (Harper) G. BA, Prescott (Ariz.) Coll., 1985. Range technician Bur. Land Mgmt., Eulu, Nev., 1984; rsch. U. Calif., Berkeley, 1987; wildlife technician Ariz. Dept. Game and Fish, Phoenix, 1988; maintenance technician Don Horl's Cabins, Flagstaff and Sedona, Ariz., 1988-92; master control technician KNAZ-KMOH-TV, Flagstaff, 1994-96; master control technician KBPX-TV, Flagstaff, 1996—, prodn. mgr., 1998—. Contbr. articles to profl. jours.; host, prodr.: (TV program segment) Community Coffee Break-Nature Notes. Recipient 3 Gold Key awards Eastman Kodak/Scholastic Mag., Durham, 1972. Democrat. Avocations: fly fishing, reading, writing, drawing and painting, nature study. Home: 230 E Camille Dr Flagstaff AZ 86001-8338 Office: KBPX-TV 2158 N 4th St Flagstaff AZ 86004-4235

GOOD, REBECCA MAE WERTMAN, learning and behavior counselor, grief and loss counselor, hospice nurse, therapeutic touch practitioner, educator; b. Barberton, Ohio, May 13, 1943; d. Frederick Daniel Wertman and Freda Beam Wertman Lombardi; m. William Robert Good Jr., Aug. 15, 1964; children: William Robert III, John Joseph, Matthew Stephan. RN diploma, Akron Gen. Med. Ctr., Ohio, 1964; BS in Psychology, Ramapo Coll., Mahwah, N.J., 1986; MA in Counseling, NYU, 1990. RN, Utah; nat. cert. counselor; cert. psychiat. and mental health nurse; lic. profl. counselor, AIDS cert. RN. Staff nurse Green Cross Gen. Hosp., Cuyahoga Falls, Ohio, 1965-68; staff nurse, relief supr., psychiat. nurse F.D.R. VA Hosp., Montrose, N.Y., 1971-72; geriatric staff and charge nurse Westledge Extended Care Facility, Peekskill, N.Y., 1972-77; infirmary and ICF nurse St. Dominics Home, Orangeburg, N.Y., 1981-83; allergy and immunology nurse Dr. Andre Codispoti, Suffern, N.Y., 1979-89; rsch. asst. counselor NYU, N.Y.C., 1989-90; Rockland advocate Student Advocacy Inc., White Plains, N.Y., 1989-90; exec. dir. Rockland County Assn. for Learning Disabled, Orangeburg, 1990-91; life skills counselor Bd. Coop. Edn., West Nyack, N.Y., 1991-93; learning and behavior disorders counselor, Suffern, 1991-93, Salt Lake City, 1994—; hospice nurse United Hospice Rockland, 1991-93; assessment and referral counselor/case mgr. CPC Olympus View Hosp., Salt Lake City, 1994-97; practitioner, tchr. Therapeutic Touch, 1990—; outcomes coord. U. Utah Med. Ctr., 1997—. Co-chmn. Rockland County Coordinating Coun. for Devel. Disabled Offenders, New City, N.Y., 1990-93; bd. visitors Rockland Children's Psychiat. Ctr., Orangeburg, 1991-93, sec., 1992; mem. U.S. Congressman Benjamin Gilman's Handicapped Adv. Com., Rockland County, 1985-94; pres. Ramapo Ctrl. Sch. Dist. Spl. Edn. PTA, 1982-86. Ramapo Coll. of N.J. Pres.'s scholar, 1986. Mem. ACA, Utah Counselors Assn., Children and Adults with Attention Deficit Disorders (coord. Rockland chpt. 1992-93), Hospice Nurses Assn., Nurse Healers Profl. Assn., Internat., Inc. (trustee, Utah networker), Learning Disabilities Assn. of Utah (profl. adv. bd. 1997—), Assn. Nurses in AIDS Care. Episcopalian. Avocations: gardening, nature, golf, skiing, choir. Office: 1100 E Quicksilver Dr Salt Lake City UT 84405

GOODALL, JACKSON WALLACE, JR., restaurant company executive; b. San Diego, Oct. 29, 1938; s. Jackson Wallace and Evelyn Violet (Koski) G.; m. Mary Esther Buckley, June 22, 1958; children: Kathleen, Jeffery, Suzanne, Minette. BS, San Diego State U., 1960. With Foodmaker, Inc., San Diego, 1963—, pres., 1970—, CEO, 1979—, also chmn. bd. dirs.; founder, bd. dir. Grossmont Bank, La Mesa, Calif.; bd. dirs. Thrifty Drug Stores Inc., Van Camp Seafood Inc., Ralcorp.; owner, dir., bd. dirs. San Diego Padres Baseball Club. Bd. dirs. Greater San Diego Sports Assn.; mem. Pres.'s Coun. San Diego State U.; chmn. Child Abuse Prevention Found.; dir. San Diego Hall Champions. Recipient Golden Chain award, 1982, Silver Plate award Internat. Foodsvc. Mfg. Assn., 1985; named Disting. Alumni of Yr. San Diego State U., 1974, 89, Golden Chain Operator of Yr. Multi Unit Food Svc. Operators, 1988, State of Israel Man of Yr., 1987, Citizen of Yr. City Club of San Diego, 1992, Marketer of Yr. Acad. Mktg. Sci., 1992, Manchester Cmty. Svc. award, 1997; inducted into San Diego Bus. Hall of Fame, 1992. Mem. Am. Restaurant Assn., Fairbanks Ranch Country Club (founder), Univ. Club of San Diego, San Diego Intercollegiate Athletic Coun., Kadoo Club of N. Am., La Jolla Country Club. Republican. Office: Foodmaker Inc 9330 Balboa Ave San Diego CA 92123-1598

GOODBY, JEFFREY, advertising agency executive. Grad., Harvard Univ., 1973. Political reporter Boston; began advt. career with J. Walter Thompson; with Hal Riney & Ptnrs. San Francisco; co-chmn., creative dir. Goodby, Silverstein & Ptnrs., San Francisco, 1983—. *

GOODEY, ILA MARIE, psychologist; b. Logan, Utah, Feb. 1, 1948; d. Vernal P. and Leona Marie (Williams) Goodey. BA with honors in English and Sociology, U. Utah, 1976; Grad. Cert. Criminology, U. Utah, 1976, MS in Counseling Psychology, 1984, PhD in Psychology, 1985. Speech writer for dean of students U. Utah, Salt Lake City, 1980-89, psychologist Univ. Counseling Ctr., 1984—; cons. Dept. Social Services, State of Utah, Salt Lake City, 1983—; pvt. practice psychology Consult West, Salt Lake City, 1985-86; pub. relations coordinator Univ. Counseling Ctr., 1985—; cons. Aids Project, U. Utah, 1985—; pvt. practice psychology, Inscapes Inst., Salt Lake City, 1987-88; writer civic news Salt Lake City Corp., 1980—; mem. Senator Orrin Hatch's Adv. Com. on Disability Oriented Legis., 1989—. Author book: Love for All Seasons, 1971, Poemspun, 1994, Echoes, 1995, Rapture, 1996; play: Validation, 1979; musical drama: One Step, 1984. Contbr. articles to profl. jours. Chmn. policy bd. Dept. State Social Service, Salt Lake City, 1986—; campaign writer Utah Dem. Party, 1985; appointed to Utah State Legis. Task Force on svcs. for people with disabilities, 1990; chmn. bd. Utah Assistive Tech. Program, 1990—. Recipient Creative Achievement award Utah Poetry Soc., 1974, English SAC, U. Utah, 1978, Leadership award YWCA, 1989, Nat. Golden Rule award J.C. Penny, Washington, 1989, 90, Volunteerism award State of Utah, 1990; Ila Marie Goodey award named in honor. Mem. AAUW, Am. Psychol. Assn., Utah Psychol. Assn., Internat. Platform Assn., Mortar Board, Am. Soc. Clin. Hypnosis, Utah Soc. Clin. Hypnosis, Soc. Psychol. Study Social Issues, League of Women Voters, Phi Beta Kappa, Phi Kappa Phi, Alpha Lambda Delta. Mormon. Clubs: Mormon Theol. Symposium, Utah Poetry Assn. Avocations: theatrical activities, creative writing, travel, political activities. Office: U Utah Counseling Ctr 2450 SSB Salt Lake City UT 84112

GOODIN, EVELYN MARIE, writer; b. Fullerton, Calif.; d. Theodore Hopper and Nellie Mary (Henger) DeWitt; m. Robert Delmer Goodin, Feb. 23, 1950; 1 child, Michael Warren. AA, Fullerton Jr. Coll., 1942; BA, U. Calif., Santa Barbara, 1946. Tchr. Bakersfield (Calif.) City Schs., 1947-50, Stockton (Calif.) City Schs., 1950-58, San Juan Unified Schs., Carmichael, Calif., 1958-82. Author: (poetry) The Young West Sings, 1940, (children's book) The Greatest Living Scientist, 1993; editor: (poetry anthology) First the Blade, 1942; writer radio show Uncle Punkle Show, 1951. Registrar Selective Svc. Sys., Bakersfield, 1948; vol. tchr. Sacramento Safety Ctr., 1985; sec. Suburban Writers Club, Sacramento, 1986-87; mem. Fremont Presbyn. Fremont Presbyterian Inspiration Recreation Svc., 1992-96; with Friendship Inspiration Recreation Svc. Recipient First Prize in Poetry, Creative Arts Coun. Fullerton Jr. Coll., 1942, Recognition award for extended profl. svc. San Juan Tchrs. Assn., 1982. Mem. Whitney Lunch Bunch, Calif. Ret. Tchrs. Assn. (mailing com. N.E. sect. 1994-96), Sports Leisure Travel Club. Avocations: music, reading, politics, decorating, travel. Home: 5705 River Oak Way Carmichael CA 95608-5549

GOODLEY, PAUL HARVEY, physician; b. Bklyn., Feb. 6, 1932; s. Israel Harry and Ruth (Reiter) G.; m. Dolores Henrietta Ledfors, Apr. 2, 1955; children—Mark David, Pamela Susan, Diane Deborah, Caryn Lynn, Lisa Louise. B.A. cum laude, U. So. Calif., 1955; M.D., UCLA, 1959. Diplomate Am. Bd. Phys. Medicine and Rehab., Am. Bd. Family Practice. Intern,

Harbor Gen. Hosp., Torrance, Calif., 1959-60; gen. practice indsl. medicine, Torrance, 1960, Wilmington, Calif., 1961-72; resident physician medicine and rehab. U. So. Calif.-Los Angeles County Med. Ctr., 1972-73, instr. dept. emergency medicine, 1973-74; resident physician U. Calif.-Davis, 1974; practice medicine specializing in phys. medicine and rehab., Los Angeles, 1975—; med. dir. rehab. ctr. Glendale (Calif.) Adventist Med. Ctr., 1975-76; pvt. practice Glendale, Calif., 1976-78; founder, med. dir. Pain Diagnostics and Rehab. Inst., L.A., 1977-83; pvt. practice Edwards Med. Plz., Phoenix, 1983-84, Bear Valley Orthopaedic Medicine, Big Bear Lake, Calif., 1987-90; pvt. practice, Redlands, Calif., 1991; pvt. practice in orthopaedic medicine, San Bernandino, Calif., 1993-94; med. cons. orthopedic medicine U.S. VA, 1981-84; adj. prof. orthopedic medicine Coll. Osteo. Medicine of Pacific, 1984—; exam. physician Los Angeles County Sheriff's Dept., 1962-79; founder MET (Med. Emergency Team). Inventor Goodley Polyaxial Cervical Traction System, A Goodley/Lumbar Lift, A Goodley Lift, A Goodley Stretch; author Goodley Stories, Goodley Medicine. Recipient Award of Valor, Los Angeles County Sheriff's Dept., 1968. Fellow Am. Assn. Orthop. Medicine (founder, pres. emeritus 1982—); mem. Am. Acad. Phys. Medicine and Rehab. (former chmn. task force and spl. interest group musculoskeletal medicine), AMA, Am. Assn. Electromyography and Electrodiagnosis, Nat. Rifle Assn. (life master, Gold medal Calif. championships 1968), Goodley Dirs. (formerly Traction Theraputics, pres. 1997—), Phi Delta Epsilon.

GOODMAN, BEATRICE MAY, real estate professional; b. Rehoboth, Mass., Nov. 12, 1933; s. Manuel Silva and Mercy Elizabeth (Mayers) Bettencourt; m. Sam R. Goodman, Sept. 15, 1957; children: Mark, Stephen, Christopher. BS, Marymount Coll., 1980. Pres. Bettencourt Draperies, Rehoboth, Mass., 1955-56; asst. mgr. Leo H. Spivack Furniture, L.I., N.Y., 1956-57; asst. designer Lillian Decorators, L.I., N.Y., 1957-58; asst. buyer Macy's N.Y., N.Y.C., 1958-59; pres. Beatrice & Beverly, Mt. View, Calif., 1980-82; realtor Coldwell Banker, Menlo Park, Calif., 1984—; pres. The Added Touch, Atherton, Calif., 1984-91; realtor Cornish & Carey Realtors, Menlo Park, Calif., 1991—. Den mother Boy Scouts Am., N.Y.C., 1970-76; active Peninsula Vols., Palo Alto, 1974—, Internat. Friendship Force. Mem. Nat. Bd. Realtors, Orgn. for Rehab. Tng. Avocations: gardening, travel, physical fitness activities, vol. work for the arts. Home: 60 Shearer Dr Atherton CA 94027-3957 Office: Coldwell Banker 1000 El Camino Real Ste 150 Menlo Park CA 94025-4327

GOODMAN, CHARLES SCHAFFNER, JR., food product executive, consultant; b. Phila., Nov. 15, 1949; s. Charles Schaffner Sr. and Dorothy Ruth (Irwin) G. BA, U. Pa., 1971. Warehouse and distb. mgr. Odyssey Records, Santa Cruz, Calif., 1974-75; mgr. Paradiso's, Santa Cruz, Calif., 1978-79; sales mgr. Mask Prodns., Chatsworth, Calif., 1980; regional sales mgr. Harmony Foods, Inc., Santa Cruz, 1981-83, nat. sales mgr., 1983-85, nat. sales mgr. foodsvc., 1985-88, v.p. foodsvc., 1988-90; owner, pres. Creative Mktg. Group, Soquel, Calif., 1990—; bd. dirs. Noema Software. Mem. No. Calif. Food Svc. Mktg. Assn., The Foodsters. Avocations: scuba diving, golf. Home: 4713 Soquel Creek Rd Soquel CA 95073-9657 Address: PO Box 5271 Santa Cruz CA 95063-5271 Office: Creative Mktg Group PO Box 1736 Soquel CA 95073-1736

GOODMAN, GWENDOLYN ANN, nursing educator; b. Davenport, Iowa, Aug. 7, 1955; d. Merle Erwin and Loraine Etta (Mahannah) Langfeldt; m. Mark Nathan Goodman, Oct. 24, 1982; children: Zachary Aaron, Alexander Daniel. BS in Nursing, Ariz. State U., 1977. RN, Ariz. Staff nurse surg. fl. and intensive care unit St. Luke's Hosp. and Med. Ctr., Phoenix, 1977-81; staff nurse intensive care unit Yavapai Regional Med. Ctr., Prescott, Ariz., 1981-82; instr. nursing Yavapai Coll., Prescott, 1982-88, cons., 1986; part-time staff nurse Ariz. Poison Control Ctr., Phoenix, 1980-81; mem. profl. adv. com. Home Health Agy. Yavapai Regional Med. Ctr., 1988-93. Mem. Sigma Theta Tau. Democrat. Home: PO Box 450 Prescott AZ 86302-0450

GOODMAN, JACK, journalist; b. Bklyn., Oct. 23, 1913; s. Joseph and Anna (Birnbaum) G.; m. Marjorie, May 10, 1942; children: Nathaniel, Kathryn, Jean. BS, NYU, 1936, MA, 1937. News editor Radio Sta. WNYC, N.Y.C., 1938-45, Radio Sta. KALL, Salt Lake City, 1946-49; reporter, feature writer Salt Lake Tribune Telegram, Salt Lake City, 1949-51; news dir. KTVT-Channel 4, Salt Lake City, 1951-55, KUTA-Channel 2, Salt Lake City, 1955-60; writer Evans Advt. Agy., Salt Lake City, 1960-70; stringer corr. for Utah, N.Y. Times and Newsweek, Engring. and Mining Jour., 1947-75; interim dir. Utah State Travel Commn., 1960-61; columnist Salt Lake Tribune, 1980—. Author, illustrator: As You Pass By, 1996. Bd. dirs. Marriott Libr., Salt Lake City, 1980, Utah State Hist. Soc., 1992. Democrat. Jewish. Home: 6053 S 23rd E Salt Lake City UT 84121-1439

GOODMAN, MARY A., photographer; b. Hartford, Conn., July 24, 1934; d. Allan S. and Carlyn Rhoda (Leicher) G. BS in Edn., NYU, 1958; MA in Spl. Edn., Columbia U., N.Y.C., 1961; MSW, Simmons Coll. Social Wk., Boston, 1965. Free lance photographer various locations, 1975—. Photography of notable persons include His Royal Highness Prince of Wales, Her Majesty, Queen Elizabeth, The Queen Mother, Sir Michael Tippett, O.M., Sir Yehudi Menuhin, Dame Morgot Fonteyn, Dame Alicia Markova, many others; CD cover pub. If I Should Lose You, 1997. Mem. Friends of Photography, Ansel Adams Ctr., San Francisco. Mem. Nat. Soc. Arts and Letters (Tucson br.), N.Y. Acad. Sci., Internat. Ctr. Photography, The Photographer's Gallery, Ctr. for Creative Photography, Soc. Southwestern Authors, Resources for Women. Avocations: classical music, sketching, drawing, watercolors. Home: 6266 N Campbell Ave Tucson AZ 85718-3150

GOODMAN, MATTHEW MORTENSEN, dermatologist, educator; b. Tucson, Feb. 10, 1955; s. Vance Herbert and Ethel Mae (Mortensen) G.; m. Kay Arlene Norvell, Mar. 18, 1978; children: Jared Norvell, Seth Matthew, Joel Pierce, Brett Joseph, Sarah Joy. BS, U. Ariz., 1979, MD, 1983. Diplomate Am. Bd. Dermatology. From asst. clin. prof. dermatology to assoc. clin. prof. UCI Med. Ctr., Orange, Calif., 1988—; dermatologist Rehlan, Bartlow, Goodman, Santa Ana, Calif., 1992—. Stake pres. LDS Ch., Orange, 1996. Mem. Am. Soc. Mohs Surgery (pres. 1990-92). Republican. Avocations: water and snow skiing, flying, hiking, family. Home: 13261 Cromwell Dr Tustin CA 92780-4705 Office: Rehlen Bartlow and Goodman Santa Ana CA 92711

GOODMAN, MAX A., lawyer, educator; b. Chgo., May 24, 1924; s. Sam and Nettie (Abramowitz) G.; m. Marlyene Monkarsh, June 2, 1946; children: Jan M., Lauren A. Packard, Melanie Murez. AA, Herzl Jr. Coll., 1943; student, Northwestern U., 1946-47; JD, Loyola U., 1948. Bar: Calif. 1948; cert. family law specialist, 1980, 85, 90. Pvt. practice L.A., 1948-53; ptnr. Goodman, Hirschberg & King, L.A., 1953-81; prof. Southwestern U. Sch. Law, L.A., 1966—; lectr. Calif. Continuing Edn. of the Bar, 1971—; editorial cons. Bancroft Whitney, San Francisco, 1986—. Contbr. articles to profl. jours. Served to cpl. U.S. Army, 1943-45. Mem. ABA (chmn. law sch. curriculum com. family law sect. 1987-88, family law sect. 1988-89, 97-98), State Bar Calif. (del. conf. dels. 1972, 80-87, 91, exec. com. family law sect. 1981-85), Los Angeles County Bar Assn. (chmn. family law sect. 1971-72, editor family law handbook). Avocation: contract bridge. Office: Southwestern U Sch of Law 675 S Westmoreland Ave Los Angeles CA 90005-3905

GOODMAN, MURRAY, chemistry educator; b. N.Y.C., July 6, 1928; s. Louis and Frieda (Bercun) G.; m. Zelda Silverman; Aug. 26, 1951; children: Andrew, Joshua, David. BS magna cum laude with honors in Chemistry, Bklyn. Coll., 1949; PhD, U. Calif., Berkeley, 1953; DSc honoris causa, CUNY, Staten Island, 1995; DSc (hon.), U. Ioannina, Greece, 1995. Asst. prof. Polytechnic Inst., Bklyn., 1956-60, assoc. prof., 1960-64, prof. chemistry, 1964-71, dir. polymer rsch. inst., 1967-71; prof. chemistry U. Calif.-San Diego, La Jolla, 1971—, chmn. dept. Chemistry, 1976-81; vis. prof. U. Alta., Can., 1981, Lady Davis Vis. Prof., Hebrew U., Jerusalem, 1982; William H. Rauscher lectr. Rensselaer Poly. Inst., 1982; BioMega lectr. McGill U., 1998. Editor Biopolymers Jour., 1963—; contbr. numerous articles to profl. jours. Recipient Alumnus medal Bklyn. Coll., 1964, Scoffone medal U. Padova, 1980, Humboldt award 1986, Max-Bergmann medal 1991, Givaudan-Roure award Assn. Chemo-reception Scis., 1992, Ralph Hirschmann award for peptide chemistry Am. Chem. Soc., 1997, Chem. Pioneer award Am. Inst. Chemists, 1997; NRC fellow Cambridge (Eng.) U., 1955-56. Fellow AAAS; mem. IUPAC, Am. Chem. Soc., Am. Peptide Soc. (Pierce award 1989), Am. Soc. Biol. Chemists, Chem. Soc., Biophys. Soc., Protein Soc., Phi Beta Kappa, Sigma Xi. Home: 9760 Blackgold Rd La Jolla CA 92037-1115 Office: U Calif San Diego Dept Chemsitry/Biochemistry Mail Code 0343 La Jolla CA 92093

GOODMAN, WILLIAM LEE, commercial pilot; b. Butte, Mont., May 15, 1946; s. William Lonzo and Phyllis Hilma (White) G.; m. Susan Margaret Thompson, Nov. 29, 1969; children: Kathryn, Margaret, William. BS in Computer Sci., Oreg. State U., 1968; MBA, City U., Seattle, 1982; postgrad., Seattle U.; postgrad. in def. econs., U.S. Naval War Coll., 1986. Cert. airline transport pilot, flight engr., control tower operator, flight instr., FAA. Systems analyst Mohawk Data Scis. Corp., Portland, Oreg., 1974-76; air traffic controller FAA, Pendleton, Oreg., 1976-78; pilot Trans Internat. Airlines, Oakland, Calif., 1978; aerospace engr. Boeing Comml. Airplane Co., Seattle, 1978-86; pilot USAirways, Washington, 1986—. Editor Boeing Tng. Ctr. newsletter Intercom, 1980-82; contbg. editor Boeing Customer Service mag. Advisor, 1982-86. V.p. Homeowners Assn., Auburn, 1982-85. Served to comdr. USNR, 1968-89, Vietnam. Mem. Airline Pilots Assn. (chmn. local air safety 1994-95). Republican. Avocations: skiing, auto restoration, racquetball. Home: 2912 202nd Avenue Ct E Sumner WA 98390-9022

GOODWIN, JOHN ROBERT, law educator, author; b. Morgantown, W.Va., Nov. 3, 1929; s. John Emory and Ruby Iona G.; m. Betty Lou Wilson, June 2, 1952; children: John R., Elizabeth Ann Paugh, Mark Edward, Luke Jackson, Matthew Emory. B.S., W.Va. U., 1952, LLB, 1964, J.D., 1970. Bar: W.Va., U.S. Supreme Ct. Formerly city atty., county commr., spl. pros. attys., then mayor City of Morgantown; prof. bus. law W.Va. U.; prof. hotel and casino law U. Nev., Las Vegas; Author: Legal Primer for Artists, Craftspersons, 1987, Hotel Law, Principles and Cases, 1987. Served with U.S. Army, Korea. Recipient Bancroft-Whitney award in Constl. Law'; named Outstanding West Virginian, State of West Virginia. Democrat. Author: Twenty Feet From Glory; Business Law, 3d edit.; High Points of Legal History; Travel and Lodging Law; Desert Adventure; Gaming Control Law; editor Hotel and Casino Letter; past editor Bus. Law Rev., Bus. Law Letter. Home: Casa Linda 48 5250 E Lake Mead Blvd Las Vegas NV 89115-6751

GOODWIN, MARTIN BRUNE, radiologist; b. Vancouver, B.C., Can., Aug. 8, 1921; came to U.S., 1948; m. Cathy Dennison, Mar. 7, 1980; 1 child, Suzanne; stepchildren: Chuck Glikas, Dianna; 1 child from previous marriage, Nancijane Goodwin Hilling. BSA in Agriculture, U. B.C., 1943, postgrad., 1943-44; MD, CM, McGill U. Med. Sch., Montreal, Can., 1948. Diplomate Am. Bd. Med. Examiners, lic. Med. Coun. Can.; cert. diagnostic and therapeutic radiology Am. Bd. Radiology; cert. Am. Bd. Nuclear Medicine. Intern Scott & White Hosp., Temple, Tex., 1948-49; fellow radiology Scott & White Clinic, 1949-52, mem. staff, 1952-53; instr. U. Tex., Galveston, 1952-53; radiologist Plains Regional Med. Ctr., Clovis, N.Mex.; radiologist Plains Regional Med. Ctr., Portales, N.Mex., pres. med. staff; chief radiology De Baca Gen. Hosp., Ft. Sumner, N.Mex.; cons. Cannon AFB Hosp., Clovis; pvt. practice radiology Clovis, Portales, Ft. Sumner and Tucumcari, 1955—; adj. prof. health scis. Ea. N.Mex. U., 1976-77; adj. clin. prof. health scis. We. Mich. U., 1976-78. Apptd. N.Mex. Radiation Tech. Adv. Coun., N.Mex. Bd. Pub. Health; former chmn. N.Mex. Health and Social Svcs. Bd.; mem. Regional Health Planning Coun.; treas. Roosevelt County Rep. Ctrl. Com. Capt. U.S. Army M.C., 1953-55; Col. USAF M.C., 1975-79. Fellow AAAS, Am. Coll. Radiology, Am. Coll. Radiology (past councillor); mem. Am. Soc. Thoracic Radiologists (founder), Radiol. Soc. of N.Am. (past councillor), N.Mex. Med. Soc. (various coms., chmn. joint practice com., councillor bd. dirs.), N.Mex. Radiol. Soc. (past pres.), N.Mex. Thoracic Soc. (past pres.), N.Mex. Med. Review Assn. (bd. dirs. 1970-93), N.Mex. Med. Soc. Found. for Med. Care (bd. dirs. 1975—, former v.p., former treas.), County Med. Soc. (past pres., past v.p., past sec.), Clovis C. of C. (chmn. civic affairs com., bd. dirs.), Clovis Elks Lodge (past exalted ruler), Clovis Noonday Lions Club (past sec.). Republican. Presbyterian. Home: 505 E 18th St Portales NM 88130-9201

GOODWIN, RICHARD CYRUS, judge; b. Annapolis, Md., Feb. 6, 1942; s. Ralph Abijah and Margaret Anne (Curry) G.; m. Pauline Claire Woeste, Jan. 20, 1970 (div. Feb. 1987); m. Susan Walters, July 15, 1997; children: Richard Andrew, Daniel Eugene, Deric Walters, Derin Walters. BA, Coll. William and Mary, 1964; MBA, Xavier U., 1971; JD, No. Ky. U., 1975; postgrad. in law, George Washington U., 1977-78. Bar: Ohio 1976, Md. 1978, D.C. 1979. Enlisted U.S. Army, 1964, commd. capt., 1976; advanced through grades to col. USAR, 1979—; pvt. practice in law Annapolis, 1979-96; adminstrv. law judge Social Security Adminstrn., Fresno, Calif., 1996—; lectr. Sch. Law Ctrl. Calif. Coll., trial advocacy workshop Coll. Law Stanford U. Co-author: Legal Representation and Fee Agreements for the Maryland Lawyer, 1995. Pres. Rotary Internat., Annapolis, 1988, March of Dimes, 1989-96. Col. judge advocate U.S. Army res. Paul Harris fellow Rotary Internat., 1991. Home: 326 E Buckingham Way Fresno CA 93704-4144 Office: Office Hearing and Appeals Soc Security Administrn 155 E Shaw Fresno CA 39710-8115

GOODY, WILLIAM KEITH, lawyer; b. Milw., June 7, 1948; s. James W. and Marjorie (Ferguson) G.; m. Mary C. Costanzi, Aug. 4, 1995; children: Grant, Greyson, Elliott, James. BA, U. Calif., Berkeley, 1970; postgrad., Duke U., 1970-71; JD, U. Wyo., 1975. Bar: Wyo. 1975. Pvt. practice Jackson, Wyo., 1975—; sr. asst. pub. defender State of Wyo., Jackson, 1978—; lectr. on mental health and criminal law and other subjects. Avocations: mountaineering, skiing, kayaking. Home and Office: PO Box 2488 Jackson WY 83001-2488

GOOKIN, THOMAS ALLEN JAUDON, civil engineer; b. Tulsa, Aug. 5, 1951; s. William Scudder and Mildred (Hartman) G.; m. Sandra Jean Andrews, July 23, 1983. BS with distinction, Ariz. State U., 1975. Registered profl. engr., Calif., Ariz., Nev., land surveyor Ariz., hydrologist. Civil engr., treas. Gookin Engrs. Ltd, Scottsdale, Ariz., 1968—. Chmn. adv. com. Ariz. State Bd. Tech. Registration Engring., 1984—. Recipient Spl. Recognition award Ariz. State Bd. Tech. Registration Engring., 1990. Mem. NSPE, Ariz. Soc. Profl. Engrs. (sec. Papago chpt. 1979-81, v.p. 1981-84, pres. 1984-85, named Young Engr. of Yr. 1979, Outstanding Engring. Project award 1988), Order Engr., Ariz. Congress on Surveying and Mapping, Am. Soc. Civil Engrs., Ariz. Water Works Assn., Tau Beta Pi, Delta Chi (Tempe chpt. treas. 1970-71, sec. 1970, v.p. 1971), Phi Kappa Delta (pres. 1971-73). Republican. Episcopalian. Avocations: Disneyana, science fiction, computer gaming. Home: 10760 E Becker Ln Scottsdale AZ 85259-3868 Office: Gookin Engrs Ltd 4203 N Brown Ave Ste A Scottsdale AZ 85251-3990

GOPALAKRISHNAN, SUDHAKAR, engineer; b. Madras, India, June 5, 1964; s. Sathanencheri Ragagopalan and Nirmala (Kuppuswamy) G.; m. Vaidehi Ramamoorthy Sudhakar, Aug. 23, 1993. B Tech. ceramics engring., Benaras Hindu Univ., Benaras, India, 1986; MS in ceramics engring., Alfred Univ., 1990, PhD in ceramics engring., 1994. Jr. mgr. Indian Iron & Steel Co., Burnpur, India, 1986-89; fellow Alfred Univ., Alfred, N.Y., 1994-95; sr. engr. Alcoa Elec. Packaging, San Diego, 1995-96; engr. Candescent Tech. Corp., San Jose, 1997—; cons. Alfred Univ., 1996-97. Inventor in field. Mem. Am. Ceramic Soc. Avocations: gardening, photography, travel. Office: Candescent Tech Corp 6320 San Ignacio Ave San Jose CA 95119

GORANS, GERALD ELMER, accountant; b. Benson, Minn., Sept. 17, 1922; s. George W. and Gladys (Schneider) G.; m. Mildred Louise Stallard, July 19, 1944; 1 child, Gretchen. BA, U. Wash., Seattle, 1947. CPA, Wash. With Touche, Ross & Co., CPAs and predecessor, Seattle, 1947-88; ptnr. Touche, Ross & Co. (name changed to Deliotte & Touche 1989), 1957-88, in charge Seattle office, 1962-82, mem. policy group, adminstrv. com., 1964-69, dir., 1974-83, sr. ptnr., 1979-88, chmn. mgmt. group, 1982-88, ret., 1988; trustee Washington Inst., 1994-96. V.p. budget and fin. Seattle Worlds Fair, 1962; chmn. budget and fin. com. Century 21 Ctr., Inc., 1963-64; mem. citizens adv. com. Seattle Lic. and Consumer Protection Com., 1965; head profl. div. United Way King County, Seattle, 1963-64, head advanced gifts div., 1965, exec. v.p., 1966, pres., 1967; trustee United Way Endowment Fund, 1984-90; adv. bd. Seattle Salvation Army, 1965-80, treas., 1974-80; fin. com. Bellevue Christian Sch., 1970-77; citizens adv. bd. pub. affairs Sta. KIRO-TV, 1970-71; treas., bd. dirs., exec. com. Scandinavia Today in Seattle, 1981-83; treas., bd. dirs. Seattle Citizens Coun. Against Crime, 1972-80, pres., 1976, 77; bd. dirs. U. Wash Alumni Fund, 1967-71, chmn., 1971; trustee U. Wash. Pres.'s Club, 1980-83; bd. dirs., chmn. devel. com. N.W. Hosp. Found., 1977-83; bd. dirs., treas. N.W. Hosp., 1981-86; chmn. fin. com., vice chmn. bd. Health Resources N.W., 1986-89, bd. dirs., 1986—, chmn. bd., 1989-90; chmn. fin. com. Com. for Balanced Regional Transp., 1981-91; co-chmn. United Cerebal Palsy Seattle Telethon, 1986; chmn. fin. com. fund raising Mus. Flight, 1983-87; mem. assoc. bd. Pacific Scis. Ctr., Seattle, 1986-95; active Japanese/Am. Conf. Mayors and C. of C. Pres. vice chmn. U.S. del., 1989-91; chmn. fin. com. Napa Valley Club Homeowners Assn.; bd. dirs., chmn. fin. com. Napa Valley Club Homeowners Assn., 1992-95; bd. dirs., 1st pres. 600 Pk. Ter. Condominium Assn., 1993—. Lt. (j.g.) USNR, 1943-45. Recipient Honor award Sr. Svcs. of Seattle and King County, 1990. Mem. AICPA (chmn. nat. def. com. 1969-75, spl. investigation com. 1984-87), Wash. Inst. for Policy Study (bd. dirs. 1994-96), Nat. Office Mgmt. Assn. (past pres.), Wash. Soc. CPAs (Outstanding Pub. Svc. award 1988), Seattle C. of C. (chmn. taxation com. 1970-71, bd. dirs. 1971-74, 76-79, 80-81, 85—, exec. com. 1980-83, v.p. 1981-84, 1st vice chmn. 1983-84, chmn. 1984-85, vice chmn. facilities fund dr. 1982-84), Nat. Club Assn. (bd. dirs. 1984-93, sec., exec. com. 1991-93), Assn. Wash. Bus. (bd. dirs. 1983-86), Wash. Athletic Club (life, bd. dirs. 1971-77, pres. 1975), Rainier Club (treas. 1978). Home: 612 Bellevue Way SE Bellevue WA 98004-6633 also: 18222 N Petrified Forest Dr Surprise AZ 85374-6284 Office: Deloitte & Touche 700 5th Ave Ste 4500 Seattle WA 98104-5044

GORDON, FLORENCE IRENE, graphic artist, illustrator; b. L.A., Oct. 22, 1928; d. Harry and Etta (Goldstein) Gronoff; widowed; 1 child. Student, Chounard Art Inst., L.A., Santa Monica City Coll.; BA, Art Ctr., L.A. Graphic artist Ned North Enterprises, L.A.; artist Hawaii Newspaper, Oahu; tech. illustrator Northrop-Aircraft, L.A., McDonnell Douglas, L.A. Exhibited in group shows. Art scholar Chounard Art Inst., 1950. Home: 5166 Sepulveda Blvd Apt 208 Culver City CA 90230-5235

GORDON, FORREST LYLE, minister; b. Rich Hill, Mo., Feb. 4, 1926; s. Fay Ward and Martha Blanche (Caton) G.; m. Onie Elizabeth Orr, Sept. 11, 1946; children: Carol Diane Gordon Kobe, David Ward. CLU, Am. Coll., 1977. Lic. as min. First Bapt. Ch., 1976; ordained to ministry Evang. Ch. Alliance, 1987. Capt. (ret.) L.A. City Fire Dept., 1951-62; pastor of adminstrn. and missions First Bapt. Ch., Reseda, Calif., 1986—; mem. fin. com. S.W. Bapt. Conf., West Covina, Calif., 1987-90. Author: Church Safety, 1990. chmn. Reseda Cen. Bus. Dist. Citizens Adv. com., 1987-89. With USCG, 1943-46. Fellow Nat. Assn. Ch. Bus. Adminstrn.; mem. Christian Mgmt. Assn., Reseda C. of C. Republican. Office: First Bapt Ch Reseda 18644 Sherman Way Reseda CA 91335-4138

GORDON, HUGH SANGSTER, JR., fire services administrator; b. Winnipeg, Manitoba, Can., July 6, 1949; s. Hugh Sangster Sr. and Margaret Forbes (Johnston) G. BS, U. N.D., 1973, MS, 1975. Cert. arena and pool mgr., fireman. Gen. mgr. recreation commn. City of Flin Flon, Can., 1978-81; supr. field house City of Saskatoon, Can., 1982-84, arena mgr., 1984-85; mgr. facility ops. dept. park and recreation City of Regina, Can., 1985-87, acting. dir. parks and recreation dept., 1986-87, dir. fire svcs., 1987—. Recipient Cert. of Devoted Civil Svc., City of Saskatoon, 1985. Mem. Can. Assn. Fire Chiefs., Saskatchewan Assn. Fire Chiefs (v.p. 1987—). Mem. United Ch. Can. Avocations: skiing, fishing, swimming, mountain biking. Office: Regina Fire Dept, Box 1790, Regina, SK Canada S4P 3C8*

GORDON, JUDITH, communications consultant, writer; b. Long Beach, Calif.; d. Irwin Ernest and Susan (Perlman) G.; m. Lawrence Banka, May 1, 1977. BA, Oakland U., 1966; MS in Libr. Sci., Wayne State U., 1973. Researcher Detroit Inst. of Arts, 1968-69; libr. Detroit Pub. Libr., 1971-74; caseworker Wayne County Dept. Social Svcs., Detroit, 1974-77; advt. copywriter Hudson's Dept. Store, Detroit, 1979; mgr. The Poster Gallery, Detroit, 1980-81; mktg., corp. communications specialist Bank of Am., San Francisco, 1983-84; mgr., consumer pubs. Bank of Am., 1984-86; prin. ACTIVE VOICE, San Francisco, 1986—. *Judith Gordon brings a singular combination of capabilities to ACTIVE VOICE, a company she founded in 1986. Since then, she has provided editorial, project management, consulting, and marketing services to diverse clients nationwide. Gordon is the former manager of consumer publications at Bank of America where she directed an award-winning publications program within strict time and cost constraints. Among the publications were the bank's account disclosures, considered models of plain language. The name of Gordon's company reflects its key focus: to communicate clearly and compellingly to specialists and laypersons alike. Her company's primary emphasis is financial services collateral, consumer information/education materials, and customer documents that satisfy legal, compliance, and marketing objectives. For these efforts, Gordon has received frequent recognition.* Contbr. edit. The Artist's Mag., 1988-93; contbr. to book Flowers: Gary Bukovnik, Watercolors and Monotypes, Abrams, 1990. Vol. From the Heart, San Francisco, 1992, Bay Area Book Festival, San Francisco, 1990, 91, Aid & Comfort, San Francisco, 1987, Save Orch. Hall, Detroit, 1977-81, NOW sponsored abortion clinic project. Recipient Nat. award Merit. Soc. Consumer Affairs Profls. in Bus., 1986, Bay Area Best award Internat. Assn. Bus. Communicators, 1986, Internat. Galaxy awards, 1992, 95, 97, Internat. Mercury awards, 1995. Mem. AAUW, Internat. Assn. Bus. Communicators, Nat. Writers Union, Freelance Editl. Assn., Clarity, Achenbach Graphics Arts Coun., Women's Nat. Book Assn., Assn. for Women in Comms., FIMA West (bd. dirs.), ZYZZYVA (bd. dirs., v.p.). Office: 899 Green St San Francisco CA 94133-3756

GORDON, LEONARD, sociology educator; b. Detroit, Dec. 6, 1935; s. Abraham and Sarah (Rosen) G.; m. Rena Joyce Feigelman, Dec. 25, 1955; children: Susan Melinda, Matthew Seth, Melissa Gail. B.A., Wayne State U., 1957; M.A., U. Mich., 1958; Ph.D., Wayne State U., 1966. Instr. Wayne State U., Detroit, 1960-62; research dir. Jewish Community Council, Detroit, 1962-64; dir. Mich. area Am. Jewish Com., N.Y.C., 1964-67; asst. prof. Ariz. State U., Tempe, 1967-70, assoc. prof., 1970-77, prof., 1977—, chmn. dept. sociology, 1981-90, assoc. dean for acad. programs Coll. Liberal Arts and Scis., 1990—; cons. OEO, Maricopa County, Ariz., 1968. Author: A City in Racial Crisis, 1971, Sociology and American Social Issues, 1978, (with A. Mayer) Urban Life and the Struggle To Be Human, 1979, (with R. Hardert, M. Laner and M. Reader) Confronting Social Problems, 1984, (with J. Hall and R. Melnick) Harmonizing Arizona's Ethnic and Cultural Diversity, 1992. Sec. Conf. on Religion and Race, Detroit, 1962-67; mem. exec. bd. dirs. Am. Jewish Com., Phoenix chpt., 1969-70. Grantee NSF, 1962, Rockefeller found., 1970, 84. Fellow Am. Sociol. Assn.; mem. AAUP, Pacific Sociol. Assn. (v.p. 1978-79, pres. 1980-81), Soc. Study Social Problems (chair C. Wright Mills award com. 1988, treas. 1989-96), Ariz. State U. Alumni Assn. (faculty dir. 1981-82). Democrat. Jewish. Home: 13660 E Columbine Dr Scottsdale AZ 85259-3753 Office: Ariz State U Coll Liberal Arts and Scis Office for Acad Programs Tempe AZ 85287

GORDON, MARK JAMES, film producer and director; b. L.A., July 17, 1966; m. Lisa Faye Remland; 1 child, Ryley Frances. Grad. Degree in Cinematography, Am. Film Inst., Hollywood, Caif., 1992. Pres. Preferred Stock Photography, L.A., 1981-88, Mark Gordon Photography, Calabasas, Calif., 1981—; pres., prodr. Wildcat Entertainment Inc., Calabasas, 1994—; producer feature films Pub. Enemy, 1997, Vegas Run, 1998; dir. feature films Sunset After Dark, 1994, Point Dume, 1995. Sheryl C. Corwin/Tommy Gross scholar Am. Film Inst., 1992. Mem. Ind. Feature Project. Avocations: skiing, surfing. Office: Wildcat Entertainment Inc 22287 Mulholland Hwy # 201 Calabasas CA 91302-5157

GORDON, MILTON ANDREW, academic administrator; b. Chgo., May 25, 1935; s. Herrmann Andrew Gordon and Ossie Bell; m. Margaret Faulwell, July 18, 1987; children: Patrick Francis, Vincent Michael; 1 stepchild, Michael Faulwell. BS, Xavier U. La., New Orleans, 1957; MA, U. Detroit, 1960; PhD, Ill. Inst. Tech., 1968; postgrad., Harvard U., 1984. Teaching asst. U. Detroit, 1958-59; mathematician Lab. Applied Scis. U. Chgo., 1959-62; part-time tchr. Chgo. Pub. Sch. System, 1962-66; assoc. prof. math. Loyola U., Chgo., 1966-67; dir. Afro-Am. Studies Program Loyla U., Chgo., 1971-77; dean Coll. Arts and Scis., prof. math. Chgo. State U., 1978-86; v.p. acad. affairs, prof. math. Sonoma State U., Rohnert Park, Calif., 1986-90; pres., former prof. math. Calif. State U., Fullerton, 1990—; bd. dirs. Associated We. Univs., Inc.; hon. admissions counselor United States Naval Acad., 1979; mem. exec. coun. Calif. State U., 1990; rep. for Calif. univs.Am. Assn. State Colls. and Univs., 1992; commn. on leadership devel. Am. Coun. on Edn., 1992; nat. task force on gender equality Nat. Collegiate Athletic Assn., 1992-94, pres.'s commn., 1994—; commr. joint commn. on ac-

coutability reporting project Am. Assn. of State Colls. and Univs./Nat. Assn. of State Univs. and Land Grant Colls., 1994—. Am. Assn. Applied Ethics. Contbr. articles to profl. jours. Chmn. Archdiocese of Chgo. Sch. Bd., 1978-79; bd. govs. Orange County Community Found., Costa Mesa, Calif., 1990—, NCCJ, 1991—; bd. dirs. United Way of Orange County, Irvine, Calif., 1991, Pacific Symphony Orch., Santa Ana, 1993—; bd. adv. St. Jude Med. Ctr., Fullerton, Calif., 1992, Partnership 2010, Orange County, 1994, Black Leadership in Orange County, 1995—; bd. dirs. Orange County Bus. Coun., 1996—. Recipient cert. of appreciation Community Ch. Santa Rosa, Calif., 1988, Tree of Life award Jewish Nat. Fund, 1994, Humanitarian of Yr. award North Orange County YMCA, 1995; named Adminstr. of Yr., Chgo. State U., 1979. Mem. Am.conf. Acad. Deans (chmn. bd. dirs. 1983-85), Am. Assn. Univ. Adminstrs. (bd. dirs. 1983-86), Calif. Coalition of Math., Sigma Xi, Phi Beta Delta. Roman Catholic. Avocations: photography, sports, walking, movies. Office: Calif State Univ 800 N State College Blvd Presidents Office Lh900 Fullerton CA 92834-6810*

GORDON, ROBERT EUGENE, lawyer; b. L.A., Sept. 20, 1932; s. Harry Maurice and Minnie (Shaffer); 1 child, Victor Marten. BA, UCLA, 1954; LLB, U. Calif., Berkeley, 1959, JD, 1960; cert., U. Hamburg, Fed. Republic Germany, 1960. Bar: Calif. 1960. Assoc. Lillick, Geary, McHose, Roethke & Myers, Los Angeles, 1960-64, Schoichet & Rifkind, Beverly Hills, Calif., 1964-67; ptnr. Baerwitz & Gordon, Beverly Hills, 1967-69, Ball, Hunt, Hart, Brown & Baerwitz, Beverly Hills, 1970-71; of counsel Jacobs, Sills & Coblentz, San Francisco, 1972-78; ptnr. Gordon & Hodge, San Francisco, 1978-81; sole practice San Francisco, 1981-84, Sausalito, Calif., 1985-89; pvt. practice Corte Madera, Calif., 1989—; adj. prof. entertainment law Hastings Coll. of Law, San Francisco, 1990-91, U. Calif., Berkeley, 1992. Served to 1st lt. U.S. Army, 1954-56. Mem. ABA (forum com. on entertainment and sports law), Los Angeles Copyright Soc. (bd. trustees 1970-71), Copyright Soc. of the USA. Avocations: cycling, skiing. Home: 35 Elaine Ave Mill Valley CA 94941-1014 Office: 5725 Paradise Dr Ste 250 Corte Madera CA 94925-1222

GORDON, SHARON J., special education educator; b. Calif., 1972; m. Ted H. Gordon, 1972; 1 child, Matthew. BA, San Jose State U., 1969, MA, 1973. Cert. tchr., Calif. Speech lang. pathologist Walnut Creek (Calif.) Elem. Sch. Dist., 1969, San Ramon Unified Sch. Dist., Danville, Calif., 1969-75; speech lang. pathologist Cotati-Rohnert Park (Calif.) Sch. Dist., 1975-80, spl. edn. educator lang. handicapped students, 1980-92, spl. edn. educator, 1992—; mem. leadership team Waldo Rohnert Sch., 1993—. Pres. Congregation Rodef Sholom, San Rafael, Calif., 1989-91; social action chair no. Calif. Union Am. Hebrew Congregations, San Francisco, 1985-88; chair Jewish Cmty. Rels. Coun., San Rafael, 1992-94. Named Woman of Yr. ORT, 1991. Mem. Am. Speech Lang. Hearing Assn., Calif. Speech Lang. Hearing Assn., Calif. Tchrs. Assn. Avocation: community service projects. Office: Waldo Rohnert Sch 550 Bonnie Ave Rohnert Park CA 94928-3897

GORDON, STEVEN ERIC, animator, designer; b. Hollywood, Calif., Mar. 23, 1960; s. Wilfred Isadore and Tamara (Bernstein) G.; m. Judith Katherine Ball, June 27, 1981; children: Scott Conrad, Eric Alexander, Natalie Michelle. Grad. high sch., Granada Hills, Calif. Asst. animator Bakshi Prodns., Hollywood, 1977-79, animator, 1979-80; animation dir. Bakshi Prodns., Sun Valley, Calif., 1981-82; layout artist Filmation Studios, Hollywood, 1980-81; animator Disney Pictures, Burbank, Calif., 1982-87; dir. animation Rich Animation, Burbank, Calif., 1987-96; owner The Animator's Gallery, 1994—; story bd. artist Disney TV, Burbank, 1984-91, DIC Enterprises, Burbank, 1986-88, designer, 1994; comml. animator Playhouse Pictures, Hollywood, 1986-88, Baer Animation Co., Inc., Hollywood, 1989-90, Cool Prodn., Burbank, 1990-92, Film Roman, North Hollywood, 1991; designer Saban Ctr., L.A., 1993-96; story board artist Fox Animation, 1995—. Democrat. Avocation: skiing, golfing. Home: 32449 Scandia Dr Running Springs CA 92382 Address: PO Box 2829 Running Springs CA 92382-2829

GORDON, TIMOTHY WAYNE, database administrator; b. Luling, Tex., Apr. 5, 1957; s. Gerald Arthur and Carol June (Ady) G.; m. Maura Lee Cahill, July 24, 1981 (div. Feb. 1995); children: Caleen Marie, Ashley Elizabeth, Jonathan David, Adam Lee Wright; m. Judith Louise Lindstrom, Nov. 16, 1996; 1 child, Robert Kirk Hanson. BA, Ea. N.Mex. U., 1982, MA, 1983; MPA, Troy State U., 1992; MS, Nova Southeastern U., Ft. Lauderdale, Fla., 1997; PhD in Theology, Trinity Theol. Seminary, 1998. Grocery clk. Big Star Foods, Roanoke Rapids, N.C., 1973-76; entomologist specialist USAF, Fayetteville, N.C., 1976-78; Entomology technician USAF Res., Clovis, N.Mex., 1978-85; naval officer USN, Mayport, Fla., 1985-92; tech. salesman Electronic Data Solutions, Jerome, Idaho, 1993; database adminstr. Micron Tech., Inc., Boise, 1993—; commdg. officer Naval Res. Naval Beach Group 1, Detachment 119, NRC Port Hueneme, Calif., 1998—; computer cons. Discount Computer Cons., Boise, 1993-96. Min. Cole Cmty. Ch., Boise, 1995—. Lt. comdr. USNR, 1976—. Recipient Navy Commendation medal, Navy Achievement medal. Mem. Naval Res. Assn., Soc. Christian Philosophers, Evangelical Philosophical Soc. Republican. Avocations: ministry, bible study, weightlifting, reading, education. Office: Micron Tech Inc Box 6 8000 S Federal Way Boise ID 83707

GORDON-BROWN, NICHOLAS, editor, consultant author; b. London, Dec. 31, 1947; s. Gavin Muspratt and Dorothy Jean (McLaren) G.-B.; m. Jane Frances Cattell, July 20, 1955; children: Piers Alexander, Hugh Gavin, Guy Benedict. Degree in Botany and Zoology with honors, Sir John Cass Coll., London, 1971. Tech.mgr. Britover Ltd., Bedfordshire, Eng., 1973-78; press officer Brit. Road Fedn., London, 1978-80; dir. Lloyd-Hughes Assocs., London, 1982-84, Edelman Pub. Rels. Ltd., London, 1984-92; cons. Chelgate Pub. Rels. Ltd., London, 1992-94, Barzilay Ltd., London, 1994-97; editor U.S. Borax Inc., Valencia, Calif., 1997—. Editor/author numerous tech. and semitech. booklets, pamphlets and articles. Chmn. Kingsley Parish Coun., Hampshire, Eng., 1994-95. Mem. Inst. Pub. Rels. (Sword of Excellence award 1987, 89). Office: US Borax Inc 26877 Tourney Rd Valencia CA 91355-1847

GORDY, BERRY, entrepreneur, record company executive, motion picture executive; b. Detroit, Nov. 28, 1929; m. Grace Eaton, July 17, 1990; children: Berry IV, Hazel Joy, Terry James, Kerry A., Kennedy W., Stefan K. Founder Motown Record Corp., from 1961; chmn. bd. dirs. The Gordy Co.; exec. producer motion pictures; chmn. bd. dirs. West Grand Media, 1998—. Dir. motion picture Mahogany, 1975; exec. producer films Lady Sings the Blues, 1972, Bingo Long Traveling All-Stars and Motor Kings, 1975, The Last Dragon, 1984; author: To Be Loved: The Music, the Magic, the Memories of Motown, 1994. Recipient Bus. Achievement award Interracial Coun. for Bus. Opportunity, 1967, 2d Ann. Am. Music award for outstanding contbn. to mus. industry, 1975, Whitney M. Young Jr. award L.A. Urban League, 1980, NARAS Trustees award, 1991; named one of Five Leading Entrepreneurs of Nation Babson Coll., 1978; inducted into Rock and Roll Hall of Fame, 1988; Gordon Grand fellow Yale U., 1985. Mem. Guild Am. (bd. dirs.). Office: West Grand Media 6255 W Sunset Blvd Ste 1100 Los Angeles CA 90028-7412

GORE, ANDREW, editor-in-chief, periodical. Editor-in-chief Mac World, San Francisco. Office: Mac World 301 Howard St San Francisco CA 94105-2252

GORELICK, ELLEN CATHERINE, museum director, curator, artist, educator, civic volunteer; b. Chgo., Jan. 2, 1946; d. Martin Francis and Doris Harriet (Adams) Heckmann; m. Walter Lee Gorelick, Dec. 19, 1970. AA cum laude, Coll. of Sequoias, 1976; BA cum laude, Calif. State U., Fresno, 1979, MA in Art, 1982. Book divsn. corr. Time, Inc., Chgo., 1964-68; accounts receivable supr. Tab Products Co., San Francisco, 1968-69; exec. sec. Foremost-McKesson, Inc., San Francisco, 1969-71, McCarthy Land Co., Visalia, Calif., 1972-74; adminstrv. dir. Creative Ctr. for Handicapped, Visalia, 1979-80; curator Tulare (Calif.) Hist. Mus., 1984-87, dir., curator, 1994—, mem. adj. faculty Coll. of Sequoias, Visalia, 1983-96, gallery dir. Calif. State U., Fresno, 1997—, adj. faculty, 1998—. Bd. dirs. Tulare-Kings Regional Arts Coun., pres., 1989-90; bd. dirs. Tulare County Art League, pres., 1977-78; bd. dirs. Leadership Tulare, founding CORE com., 1991-93, alumni chair, 1992-93; bd. dirs. Tulare County U. Calif. Campus Expansion task force, Visalia, 1988-91, Tulare City Sch. Dist. Classrooms for Kids Campaign, co-chair, 1989; mem. Tulare City Hist. Soc. long range planning com., 1995; mem. Tulare County Symphony Assn., 1992-95, sec., 1993—; founding bd. dirs., v.p., program chair Tulare Cultural Arts Found., 1997—. Named Artist of Yr., Tulare-Kings County Arts Coun., 1988; recipient cert. of appreciation City of Tulare, 1989, Tulare County Bd. Suprs., 1991, Woman of Distinction award Soroptimists, Tulare, 1994. Mem. Tulare Palette Club (pres. 1984-85, Artist of Yr. award 1985). Democrat. Roman Catholic. Avocations: photography, travel, gourmet cooking. Office: Tulare Hist Mus 444 W Tulare Ave Tulare CA 93274-3831

GORENBERG, ALAN EUGENE, physician; b. Japan, Apr. 30, 1959; s. Daniel and Louise Gorenberg. BS in Biology, U. Calif., Irvine, 1981; MD, Loma Linda U., 1986. Diplomate Am. Bd. Internal Medicine, Am. Bd. Allergy and Immunology. Pvt. practice San Bernardino, Calif., 1991—, Victorville, Calif., 1991—; asst. clin. prof. medicine Loma Linda (Calif.) U. Sch. Medicine, 1996—, Western U. Sch. Medicine, 1997—. Office: 2130 N Arrowhead Ave Ste 101 San Bernardino CA 92405-4023 also: 12408 Hesperia Rd Ste 7 Victorville CA 92392-5839

GORHAM, DANIEL JOHN, priest; b. Miami, Fla., Mar. 4, 1929; s. Vincent Raymond and Ruth Leola (McSweeny) G. AA, Palm Beach Jr. Coll., Lake Worth, Fla., 1952; BA, Santa Fe (N.Mex.) Coll., 1957; BS, Fla. State U., 1959; MA, George Washington U., 1966. Ordained priest Greek Orthodox Ch., Old Calendar, 1960. Pastor St. Vincent Orthodox Ch., Fullerton, Calif., 1979—; editor, pubr. Axios, The Orthodox Jour., Fullerton, 1981—; dir. Nat. Bd. of Greek Orthodox Ch., 1985—; trustee St. Michael Fund, Fullerton, 1980—; del. Greek Orthodox Ch., Astoria, 1965—; dir. Western Am. Deanery, Orthodox Ch., 1979—. Author: St. Vincent Calendar, 1981, The Orthodox Year, 1982, Saints of the Orthodox, 1984, The Liturgical Year, 1990; contbr. articles to profl. jours. Bd. dirs. Libertarian Party, Orange County, Santa Ana, Calif., 1991—; supr. registration Palm Beach County, Fla., 1960-65. Named Outstanding Pastor, Greek Orthodox Ch., 1990. Fellow Orthodox Univ. Assn.; mem. Nat. Orthodox Clergy Assn., Assoc. Ch. Press, Santa Fe Coll. Alumni Assn. (dir. 1990), Fla. State U. Alumni Assn., Irish-Am. Soc. (dir. 1989), Alpha Phi Omega (Outstanding Alumni), Sons of Confederate Vets., Esperanto Assn., Kiwanis. Home: 1501 E Chapman Ave # 345 Fullerton CA 92831-4013

GORMAN, MICHAEL STEPHEN, construction executive; b. Tulsa, Aug. 3, 1951; s. Lawrence Matthew and Mary Alice (Veith) G.; m. Sheryl Lane McGee, Feb. 19, 1972; children: Kelley Lane, Michael Ryan. Student, Colo. State U., 1970, 71. With McGee Constrn. Co., Denver, 1972-74, with sales and estimating dept., 1974-78, gen. mgr., 1978-80, pres., owner, 1980-91; pres. Wisor Group, Boulder, 1990—; cons., author, columnist in remodeling and custom home building; mortgage banker, ins. cons., 1995—; presenter seminars in field. Mem. Nat. Assn. Remodeling Industry (chmn. membership svcs. com. 1987-91, bd. dirs. 1982-91, regional v.p. 1987-89, nat. sec. 1990-91, Man of Yr. 1982, Regional Contractor of Yr. 1988). Avocations: running, racquetball, sailing, skiing, pilot.

GORMAN, RUSSELL WILLIAM, marketing executive, consultant; b. Glen Ridge, N.J., Aug. 17, 1927; s. William Francis and Emily (Weldon) G.; m. Mieko Deguchi, June 19, 1956. BS, U.S. Merchant Marine Acad., 1949. Lic. mcht. marine, chief mate. Lic. officer Moore McCormack Lines Inc., N.Y., 1949-53; dir. tng. Chevron Shipping Co., San Francisco, 1957-77; mgr. orgn., adminstrn. Utah Internat. Corp., San Francisco, 1977-84; pres. Lumier Inc., San Francisco, 1984-85; v.p. John F. Perry Assocs., Concord, Calif., 1986; pres. Market Devel. Assocs., Danville, Calif., 1986-92; sr. v.p. Aegis Fin. Svcs., 1993—; pres., dir. Perfect Wash US, 1993-96; ptnr. Two Star Internat., Oakland, Calif., 1993—; bd. dirs., v.p. Norlock Tech. Inc., San Mateo, Calif., 1989—; bd. dirs. INTA, Inc., Santa Clara, Calif., 1986—. Chmn. Calif. Vets. Coalition for Bush, 1988; mem. Sec. of Def. Adv. Bd. on Naval History, 1990-97; vice chmn. Sec. of Interior Adv. Commn. on San Francisco Maritime Hist. Park, 1992—; chmn., CEO U.S.S. Missouri and Allied Forces Meml., 1995—; adv. speaker Peter Wilson for Senate Campaign, 1988; bd. dirs. Calif. Mil. Mus., Sacramento, 1996—; trustee VFW Post 75, 1997—. Lt. USN, 1954-57, rear adm. USNR, 1980-87. Decorated Legion of Merit with gold star, Navy Commendation medal. Mem. Navy League of U.S. (v.p. Pacific Ctrl. region 1989—), Res. Officer Assn. of U.S. (v.p. Navy sect. 1990-92, chmn. long range planning 1992-97), Naval Res. Assn. (nat. v.p. surface/subsurface 1990-95, co-chair long range plan 1995—), Oakland C. of C. (vice chmn. mil. affairs com. 1990-95). Republican. Methodist. Home: 46 Willowview Ct Danville CA 94526-1945

GORMÈZANO, KEITH, arbitrator, writer, marketer; b. Madison, Wis., Nov. 22, 1954; s. Isadore and Miriam Gormèzano; m. Emma Lee Rogers, Aug. 17, 1986 (div. Nov. 1990). BGS, U. Iowa, 1977, postgrad. in pub. affairs, 1979-80; postgrad. in law, U. Puget Sound, 1984-86. Pub. Le Beacon Presse, Seattle, 1980-89; real estate agt. Jim Stacy Realty, Seattle, 1988-89; owner A Better Temporary, 1989—; arbitrator Better Bus. Bur. Greater Seattle, 1987-93; arbitrator Puget Sound Multi-Listing Assn., 1988-89, Nat. Assn. Securities Dealers, 1989-92, Ford Consumer Appeals Bd., 1991-92, Harborview Med. Ctrs., 1990-91, 92-93, Up. Improvement Found., 1980-81; joint labor mgmt. com. Puget Fin. Svcs., U. Wash. Med. Ctr., 1990-91, 92-93; pub. info. officer; vol. VISTA, 1982-83; dir. ACJS, Inc., 1981-82; mem. steering com. Seattle Polyfidelity Group, 1994-98, mem. No Safeword Writers Group, 1996-98. Editor M'godolim, 1980-81, Funding Bull. U. Wash. Health Scis. Grantseekers, 1991; pub., editor Beacon Rev., 1980-89. Vice chmn. Resource Conservation Commn., Iowa City, 1979-80; bd. dirs. Seattle Mental Health Inst., 1981-83, Youth Advocates, Seattle, 1984, Atlantic St. Ctr., 1984; mem. City of Seattle Animal Control Commn., 1984-86, vice chmn., 1985-86, chmn., 1986; mem. Selective Svc. System, 1982—, vice chmn. civilian rev. bd. 742, 1985—; mem. Wash. State Local Draft Bd. # 18, 1982-84, controlled choice appeals bd. Seattle Sch. Dist., 1989; patient collection rep. U. Wash., 1990-91, Harborview Med. Ctrs., 1990-91, 92-93; mem. Ford Consumer Appeals Bd., 1991-93, Ford Motor Co. Dispute Settlement Bd., 1991-93, Joint Labor-Mgmt. Com., Patient Fin. Svcs., U. Wash. Med. Ctr., 1990-91, 92-93, Temple B'nai Torah, 1986-96, Congregation Eitz Or, Phinney Neighborhood Assn.; mem. coordinating com. edn. after dark program Jewish Fedn. Greater Seattle, 1991-92, young leadership divsn.; mem. exec. bd. thirty-something plus Jewish Community Ctr., 1991-92; coord. Seattle BiPolar Support Group, 1992-93; coordinating chair Seattle BiPolar Disorder Support Grp, 1992-93; co-facilitator Polyfidelity Group, 1995-98; amb. Wash. State Basic Health Program, 1996—. Named Citizen of the Day Sta. KIXI Radio, 1982. Mem. Am. Assn. for Nude Recreation, Self Help for the Hard of Hearing, The Naturist Soc., Hosteling Internat., League United Latin Am. Citizens Amigos (chair 1984-86), U. Iowa Alumni Assn., No Safeword Writers' Group, Wandering Jews Hiking Club, Seattle Cmty. Network Assn., Mensa, Sierra Club. Democrat. Jewish. E-mail: bb822@scn.org. Office: 501 N 36th St Ste 330 Seattle WA 98103-8653

GORMLEY, FRANCIS XAVIER, JR., social worker; b. Boston, Apr. 27, 1953; s. Francis Xavier and Catherine Caroline (Ireland) G. Student, Massasoit Community Coll., 1973; BA in Psychology, U. Mass., Boston, 1981; MSW, U. Wash., 1984. Lic. social worker, Hawaii. Coordinator Gerontology Career Program Elder Fest, Chico, Calif., 1981; mgr. Arnold's Restaurant, Cardiff, Wales, 1981-82; med. social worker Harborview Med. Ctr., Seattle, 1983-84; psychotherapist Seattle Counseling Svc., 1982-88; clin. social worker Pain Ctr. Swedish Hosp., Seattle, 1984-88, Valley Med. Ctr., Renton, Wash., 1987-88; clin. social worker AIDS program, virology clinic Univ. Hosp., Seattle, 1988-94; mgr. clin. ops. dept. social work The Queen's Med. Ctr., Honolulu, 1994—; speaker U. Wash Sch. Social Work Graduation Class, 1984, Social Sensitivity in Health Care U. Wash., 1985—; coord. Coping with AIDS Swedish Hosp. Tumor Inst., 1985; participant Coun. of Internat. Fellowship Italia, Placement Servizi Socio-Sanitari AIDS-Roma, 1991; guest speaker Sta. KIRO-TV, Seattle, 1985, Sta. KPLZ, Seattle, 1985; presentor psychosocial aspects HIV/AIDS Northwest AIDS Edn. & Tng. Ctr. Program, U. Wash. Med. Ctr., 1992, clin. mgmt. of patient with HIV/AIDS El Rio Health Ctr., Pima Colo. Pub. Health Dept., 1992, Queen's Cancer Inst. Symposium, 1996; cons. Assn. Workers Resources, Seattle, 1983—, practicum instr. U. Wash. Seattle Sch. Social Work, 1989—; preceptor, intern Residency Tng. Project Sch. of Medicine/Health Scis., Univ. Wash; HIV/AIDS planning coun. Seattle/King County Pub. Health Dept., 1993; com. for the 26th health fair, open house U. Wash.; trainer, cons. Queen's Med. Ctr. Mind/Body Med. Inst. Editor abstract form Comprehensive Multi-Disciplinary Documentation, Western U.S.A. Pain Soc., 1986, contbr. articles to profl. jours. Mem. Seattle Aids Network, 1985—. Mem. NASW (bd. dirs. Wash. chpt. 1988-90), Occupl. Social Work Orgn. of NASW, Acad. Cert. Social Workers, Leukemia Soc. Am. (co-facilitator family support group Hawaii chpt., trustee San Diego/Hawaii chpt., Man and Woman of Yr. com. 1997), Coun. Internat. Fellowship, U. Wash. Alumni Assn., U. Mass. Alumni Assn., Green Key Soc. Democrat. Avocations: travel, reading, swimming. Office: Queen's Med Ctr Social Work Dept 1301 Punchbowl St Honolulu HI 96813-2413

GORNE, IVAN LEROY, academic administrator; b. Faulkton, S.D., July 22, 1947; s. Emil Gotlieb and Viola Violet (Miller) G.; m. Marsha Ann Norberg, Aug. 24, 1969; children: Anneliese Elizabeth, Nicholas Ivan Peter. BA in Edn., Pacific Luth. U., 1970, MA in Edn., 1973; JD, Seattle U., 1988. Bar: Wash.; cert. tchr., Wash. Tchr. Steilacoom (Wash.) Sch. Dist., 1970-72; grad. asst. Pacific Luth. U., Tacoma, 1972-73; tchr. placement Ctrl. Wash. U., Ellensburg, 1973-77; assoc. dean students Edmonds C.C., Lynnwood, Wash., 1977-98; v.p. for student affairs So. Oreg. U., Ashland, 1998—; pres. Coun. for Unions and Student Programs, Wash., 1982. Sch. dir. Mukilteo (Wash.) Sch. Dist., 1988-95, pres., 1991-93. Recipient Am. Jurisprudence award Bancroft-Whitney Co., U. Puget Sound, 1988, Profl. Excellence award Woodring Coll. Edn., Western Wash. U., 1995, Christa McAuliffe award Wash. State Legis., Olympia, 1995. Mem. Lynnwood Rotary Club (treas. 1992-93, 93-94, pres. 1995-96). Avocations: reading, choral music, skiing, tennis, weight lifting. Office: 1250 Siskiyou Blvd Ashland OR 97520-5010

GORNIK, HOLLY LEE, musician, educator; b. Ogden, Utah, Dec. 1, 1946; d. Kenneth L. and Jacqueline (Ohrel) Lee; m. Edward J. Gornik, Apr. 6, 1972; children: Edward Joseph III, Alexei Jacqueline. BM, Univ. Utah, 1965-69; MM, Northwestern Univ., Evanston, Ill., 1970-71. English horn and asst. first oboe San Antonio Symphony, 1971-74; assoc. first oboe and English horn Utah Symphony, Salt Lake City, 1974—; adj. prof. U. Utah, 1980—, Weber Coll., Ogden, Utah, 1992—, Westminster Coll., Salt Lake City, 1996—; recording artist (movie scores, albums), Salt Lake City, 1980—; Soloist Internat. double reed Conf., Las Vegas, 1987. Recipient Nat. Found. Advancement in the Arts award, 1996. Avocation: metal sculpture. Home: 7561 Bridgewater Ct Salt Lake City UT 84121-5266

GORRY, CONNER CLOUGH, writer; b. Port Chester, N.Y., Nov. 7, 1969; s. Peter Edward and Sandra Jaekel (Clough) G. BA, NYU, 1991; MA, Monterey Inst. Internat. Studies, 1994. Writer Gale Rsch., Detroit, 1994—, San Francisco Chronicle, 1997—, Lonely Planet Pubs., Oakland, 1998—. Vol. Am. Friends Svc. Com., Havana, Cuba, 1993. Mem. S.Am. Explorers Club, Ctr. Cuban Studies. Avocations: traveling, reading, crossword puzzles.

GORSLINE, RUSSELL ELVIN, production company executive; b. Portland, Oreg., Oct. 30, 1943; s. Elvin Donald and Margaret (Heddle) G.; m. Janet Elizabeth Garland, May 25, 1968; 1 child, Taralynn. BS in Music, Lewis and Clark Coll., 1965. Producer, rec. engr. Sta. KBPS, Portland, 1965-67; rec. engr. Northwestern, Inc., Portland, 1967-69; gen. mgr. Rex Rec. Co., Portland, 1969—; pres. Sunny Day Prodns., Portland, 1972—; mem. adv. bd. beaverton Sch. Dist., Portland Community Coll., 1984-88. Recipient Clio, Addy, Best in West, Rosy, IBA and Telly awards. Mem. AFTRA (N.W. signators com. 1988—), Audio Engring. Soc., Portland Advt. Fedn. (bd. dirs. 1991). Republican. Baptist. Avocations: music, biking. Home: 13431 SW Scotts Bridge Dr Portland OR 97223-1609 Office: Rex Rec Co 1931 SE Morrison St Portland OR 97214-2732

GORSUCH, EDWARD LEE, chancellor. Degree in Econ. & Cmty. Devel., U. Mo. Dir. Inst. Social and Econ. Rsch., 1976-94; dean Sch. Pub. Affairs U. Alaska, Anchorage, 1988-94, chancellor, 1994—; commr. U.S. Arctic Rsch. Commn.; bd. dirs. Commonwealth North; mem. adv. bd. Alaska Airlines Anchorage Cmty.; mem. civilian adv. bd. ALCOM; mem. Fiscal Policy Coun. Alaska. Office: Office of Chancellor Univ AK Anchorage 3211 Providence Dr Anchorage AK 99508-8060*

GORSUCH, RICHARD LEE, psychologist, educator, minister; b. Wayne, Mich., May 14, 1937; s. Culver C. and Velma L. Gorsuch; m. Sylvia S. Coalson, Aug. 18, 1961; children: Eric, Kay. BA, Tex. Christian U., 1959; MA, U. Ill., 1962, PhD, 1965; MDiv, Vanderbilt U., 1968. Lic. psychologist, Calif; ordained 1968. Asst. prof. of psychology Vanderbilt U., 1966-68, dir. statis. consultation, 1966-68; asst. prof., then assoc. prof. psychology George Peabody Coll. for Tchrs., 1968-73; assoc. prof. Inst. Behavioral Rsch. Tex. Christian U., 1973-75; assoc. prof., then prof. psychology U. Tex., Arlington, 1975-79; prof. psychology Fuller Theol. Sem., Pasadena, 1979—. Author: Factor Analysis, 2d edit., 1983; co-author: Psychology of Religion, 1983, 2nd edit., 1990; editor Jour. For. Sci. Study of Religion, 1975-78; cons. editor Ednl. and Psychol. Measurement, Multivariate Behavioral Rsch.; contbr. article to Ann. Rev. Psychology, 1988. Fellow APA (coun. of reps. 1984-85, 89-90, pres. divsn. 36, 1990-91, William James award 1986), Soc. Sci. Study Religion; mem. Religious Rsch. Assn., Soc. of Multivariate Exptl. Psychology. Mem. Disciples of Christ Ch. Achievements include development of UniMult statistics package. Office: Fuller Theol Sem Grad Sch Psychology 180 N Oakland Ave Alhambra CA 91001

GORTON, SLADE, senator; b. Chicago, Ill., Jan. 8, 1928; s. Thomas Slade and Ruth (Israel) G.; m. Sally Jean Clark, June 28, 1958; children: Tod, Sarah Jane, Rebecca Lynn. AB, Dartmouth Coll., 1950; LLB with honors, Columbia U., 1953. Bar: Wash. 1953. Assoc. law firm Seattle, 1953-65; ptnr. law firm, 1965-69; atty. gen. State of Wash., Olympia, 1969-81; U.S. senator from Wash., 1981-87, 89—; ptnr. Davis, Wright & Jones, Seattle, 1987-89; mem. Wash. Ho. of Reps., 1959-69, majority leader, 1967-69, nat. Rep. senatorial com., Indian affairs/labor and human resources com., budget com., appropriations com., commerce/sci. and transp. com., energy and natural resources com.; chmn. commerce, sci., & transp. subcom. on consumer affairs, fgn. commerce & tourism, appropriations subcom. interior & related agys. Trustee Pacific Sci. Center, Seattle, found. mem., 1977-78; mem. Pres.'s Consumer Adv. Council, 1975-77; mem. Wash. State Law and Justice Commn., 1969-80, chmn., 1969-76; mem. State Criminal Justice Tng. Commn., 1969-80, chmn., 1969-76. Served with AUS, 1946-47; to 1st lt. USAF, 1953-56; col. USAFR (ret.). Mem. ABA, Wash. Bar Assn., Nat. Assn. Attys. Gen. (pres. 1976-77, Wyman award 1980), Phi Delta Phi, Phi Beta Kappa. Clubs: Seattle Tennis, Wash. Athletic (Seattle). Office: US Senate 730 Hart Senate Bldg Washington DC 20510

GOSE, RICHARD VERNIE, lawyer; b. Hot Springs, S.D., Aug. 3, 1927. MS in Engring., Northwestern U., 1955; LLB, George Washington U., 1967; JD, George Washington U., 1968. Bar: N.Mex. 1967, U.S. Supreme Ct. 1976, Wyo. 1979; registered prof. engr., Wyo.; children: Beverly Marie, Donald Paul, Celeste Marlene. Exec. asst. to U.S. Senator Hickey, Washington, 1960-62; mgr. E.G. & G., Inc., Washington, 1964-66; asst. atty. gen. State of N.Mex., Santa Fe, 1967-70; pvt. practice law, Santa Fe, 1967—, Santa Fe/Prescott, 1989—; assoc. prof. engring. U. Wyo., 1957-60; owner, mgr. Gose & Assocs., Santa Fe, 1967-78; pvt. practice law, Casper, Wyo., 1978-83; pres. Argosy Internat., Inc., 1994—; ranch mgr., foreman, 1945-49; mem. Phoenix com. on fgn. rels., 1980—; co-chmn. Henry Jackson for Pres., M.Mex., 1976, Wyo. Johnson for Pres., 1960. With U.S. Army, 1950-52. Mem. N.Mex. Bar Assn., Wyo. Bar Assn., Yavapai County Bar Assn., Masons, High Country Hounds, Phi Delta Theta, Pi Tau Sigma, Sigma Tau. Methodist. Home and Office: PO Box 3998 Prescott AZ 86302-3998

GOSS, EILEEN ABEL, editor; b. Cleve., Nov. 12, 1942; d. Henry and Faye (Zelivyansky) Abel; m. Lawrence Allan, Dec. 20, 1964; children: Melissa, Deborah. BS, Ohio U., Athens, 1964. Tchr. Cleve. Bd. of Edn., 1964-68; substitute tchr. Cleve. U. Hts., 1968-72; tchr. Hebrew Acad., Cleve., 1972-77; prodn. editor Am. Metal Mkt. Metalworking News, Des Plaines, Ill.; asst. editor Shelby Report of the SE/SW, Atlanta, 1980-85; editor Leisure Times, 1985-91; recorder Leads Inc., 1988; program chmn. Career Connections, 1988. Editor: Leisure Times, 1985-91; publisher North County Active Lifestyles, 1991-93; copy editor Bamboo Telegraph, Singapore, 1993-94. Tutor Carlsbad Adult Learning Program, 1988-90; mng. editor Jewish Cmty. News, Los Gatos, Calif., 1996—. Mem. Soroptimist Internat., Hadassah Women, B'nai B'rith Women (co-pres. 1992-93), Rotary Internat. (bd. dirs. 1992-93). Avocations: tennis, sailing, exercising, bridge. Home: 13 Trillium Ln San Carlos CA 94070-1525 Office: 14855 Oka Rd Los Gatos CA 95032-1919

GOSS, JEROME ELDON, cardiologist; b. Dodge City, Kans., Nov. 30, 1935; s. Horton Maurice and Mary Alice (Mountain) G.; m. Lorraine Ann Sanchez, Apr. 20, 1986. BA, U. Kans., 1957; MD, Northwestern U., 1961. Diplomate Am. Bd. Internal Medicine, Am. Bd. Cardiology (fellow, bd. govs. 1981-84). Intern Met. Gen. Hosp., Cleve., 1961-62; resident in internal medicine Northwestern U. Med. Ctr., Chgo., 1962-64; fellow in cardiology U. Colo., Denver, 1964-66; asst. prof. medicine U. N.Mex., Albuquerque, 1968-70; pvt. practice N.Mex. Heart Clinic, Albuquerque, 1970—; bd. alumni counsellors Northwestern U. Med. Sch., 1977-89, nat. alumni bd., 1991-97; chief dept. medicine Presbyn. Hosp., Albuquerque, 1978-80, exec. com., 1980-82, dir. cardiac diagnostic svcs., 1970-96. Contbr. articles to profl. jours. Bd. dirs. Presbyn. Heart Inst., Ballet West N.Mex., N.Mex. Symphony Orch.; pres. Albuquerque Mus. Found. Lt. comdr. USN, 1966-68. Nat. Heart Inst. research fellow, 1965-66; named one of Outstanding Young Men Am., Jaycees, 1970; recipient Alumni Service award Northwestern U. Med. Sch., 1986, Disting. Achievement award Albuquerque Mus. Found., 1997. Fellow ACP, ACC, Coun. Clin. Cardiology of Am. Heart Assn., Soc. Cardiac Angiography; mem. Albuquerque-Bernalillo County Med. Soc. (sec. 1972, treas. 1975, v.p. 1980), Alpha Omega Alpha. Republican. Methodist. Office: NMex Heart Clinic 1001 Coal Ave SE Albuquerque NM 87106-5205

GOSS, PATRICIA ELIZABETH, secondary education educator; b. Cheyenne, Wyo., June 6, 1958; d. Alan Robert and Donna Jean (Hirst) G.; m. Michael Holland Argall, Nov. 6, 1993. BA, Colo. Women's Coll., 1979; MA, U. Denver, 1980; postgrad., U. Colo., 1986. Cert. secondary tchr., Colo. Exec. dir. Denver Dem. Com., 1980-82; coord. 3d Congl. dist. Mondale for Pres. Campaign, Colo., 1984; tchr. mid. sch. gifted and talented Denver Pub. Schs., 1988-90, tchr. history, 1991—; supr. student tchrs. Regis Coll., Denver, 1996. Contbr. articles to profl. jours. Chmn. precinct com. Denver Dem. Com., 1980—, mem. exec. com., 1980-86. Mem. NEA (congl. contact team 1993—, rep. assembly del. 1993, 96), Colo. Edn. Assn. (legis. action team 1991—, bd. dirs. 1992—), Denver Classroom Tchrs. Assn. (dir. govtl. rels. 1991—), DAR, Order Ea. Star, Alpha Delta Kappa. Presbyterian. Avocations: travel, photography, cooking, miniature dollhouses. Home: 1378 Locust St Denver CO 80220-2831 Office: George Washington HS 655 S Monaco Pkwy Denver CO 80224-1228

GOSSARD, EARL EVERETT, physicist; b. Eureka, Calif., Jan. 8, 1923; s. Ralph Dawson and Winifred (Hill) G.; m. Sophia Poignand, Nov. 21, 1948; children: Linda Margaret, Kenneth Earl, Diane Winifred. BA, UCLA, 1948; MS, U. Calif., San Diego, 1951; PhD in Phys. Oceanography, Scripps Instn. Oceanography, 1956. Meteorologist Navy Electronics Lab., San Diego, 1949-55, head radio meteorol. sect., 1955-61; head radio physics div. Navy Electronics Lab. (name now Naval Ocean Systems Ctr.), San Diego, 1961-71; chief geoacoustics program Wave Propagation Lab., NOAA, Boulder, Colo., 1971-73, chief meteorol. radar program, 1973-82; sr. rsch. assoc. Coop. Inst. for Rsch. in Environ. Scis. U. Colo., Boulder, 1982-98; sr. rsch. assoc. Sci. and Tech. Corp., Colorado Springs, Colo., 1998—. Co-author: (with Hooke) Waves in the Atmosphere (Disting. Authorship award Dept. Commerce 1975), 1973; (with Strauch) Radar Observation of Clear Air and Clouds (Disting. Authorship award Dept. Commerce 1985); editor: Radar Observation of the Clear Air, 1980; contbr. over 74 articles to profl. jours. 1st lt. USAAF, 1943-46, CBI. Recipient Silver medal Dept. Commerce, 1976, Citation Am. Geophys. Union, 1986. Fellow Am. Meteorol. Soc.; mem. Nat. Acad., Internat. Union Radio Sci. (past chmn. U.S. Commn. F.). Republican. Presbyterian. Home: 1088 Kelly Rd W Sugarloaf Star Rt Boulder CO 80302 Office: Sci and Tech Corp 2140 Broken Circle Rd Colorado Springs CO 80915-1321

GOSSELL, TERRY RAE, advertising agency executive, small business owner; b. Rockford, Ill., Jan. 24, 1947; d. Virgil Houston and Wilma Beatrice (Cox) Pierce; m. Ronald Richard Gossell, Mar. 3, 1979 (div. Apr., 1983); children: Cameo Ann Elliott, Ronica Rae. Grad. high sch., Loves Park, Ill.; arts cert., U. Kans., 1962. Artist Rockford (Ill.) Silk Screen Process, 1967-72, Grocery Co-op Advt., Ocala, Fla., 1973-74; art dir. Carlson & Co. Advt., Rockford, Ill., 1975-76; co-owner R.S.S.P. Graphics & Typesetting, Rockford, 1975-76; owner Graphic Comm., Inc., Rockford, 1976-79, T.R. Gossell Advt., Rockford, 1979-82, TR Gossell Advt. & Mktg. Svcs., Phoenix, 1982-88, 97—, The Gossell Agy., Rockford, 1988-97. Author, artist: (comic book) The Gang from Carl Hayden High Sch., 1986-87. Advisor No. Ill. Advt. Coun. Explorer Post #423, Rockford, 1990-92. Recipient Merit and 1st Place awards Rockford Advt. Club, 1978, 79, 1st Place award of Excellence, Nat. Assn. Pers. Cons., San Diego, 1985, Cert. of Merit, BMA Tower awards, 1994. Mem. Am. Advt. Fedn., No. Ill. Advt. Coun. (pres. 1992-94, merit, 1st and 2nd pl. awards 1980, 81, 91, 93, 94, 95, 96, 97), Greater Rockford Ad Club (bd. dirs. 1996-98). Democrat. Lutheran. Avocations: fishing, photography, horses, outdoors, classic cars. Office: TR Gossell Advt & Mktg Svcs 5131 N 6th St Phoenix AZ 85012

GOSZCZYNSKI, STEFAN, chemistry educator; b. Radomsko, Poland, Apr. 14, 1924; came to U.S., 1987, s. Tadeusz and Zofia (Nowak) G.; m. Hanna Jaroslawska, June 28, 1953; children: Peter, Thomas. MSc, Silesian Tech., Gliwice, Poland, 1950; PhD, Silesian Tech., 1960, DSc, 1964. Asst., reader Silesian Tech. U., 1948-60, from asst. to assoc. prof., 1962-68; postdoctoral fellow Birmingham (Eng.) U., 1960-61; from assoc. prof. to prof. Poznan (Poland) Tech. U., 1968-87; vis. prof. U. Idaho, Moscow, 1987—; dir. Inst. Tech. and Engring. Poznan Tech. U., 1968-70, head dept., 1977-80. Patentee in field. Named to Order of Merit Polonia Restituta, 1978, Disting. Prof. Republic of Poland, 1980; recipient medal Nat. Edn. Com., 1984. Home: 115 S Lilley St Apt 201 Moscow ID 83843-2082 Office: U Idaho Food Rsch Ctr 103 Moscow ID 83843

GOTHOLD, STUART EUGENE, school system administrator, educator; b. L.A., Sept. 20, 1935; s. Hubert Eugene and Adelaide Louise (Erickson) G.; m. Jane Ruth Soderberg, July 15, 1955; children: Jon Ernest, Susan Louise, Eric Arthur, Ruth Ann. BA, Whittier Coll., 1956, MA in Edn., 1961, LLD (hon.), 1988; EdD, U. So. Calif., 1974. Tchr. grades 1-9 El Rancho Sch. Dist., Pico Rivera, Calif., 1956-61, prin. jr. h.s., 1961-66; curriculum cons. L.A. County Office Edn., 1966-70; asst. supt. South Whittier (Calif.) Sch. Dist., 1970-72, supt., 1972-77; asst. supt. L.A. County Office Edn., Downey, 1977-78, chief dep. supt., 1978-79, supt., 1979-94; clin. prof. U. So. Calif., L.A., 1994—; mem. adv. bd. Nat. Ctr. Fgn. Lang., 1984—; charter mem. Edn. Insights, Detroit, 1990—; bd. dirs. Fedco, KCET. Author: (book) Inquiry, 1970, Decisions-A Health Edn. Curriculum, 1971. Recipient Alumni Merit award USC, 1993, Alumni Achievement award Whittier Coll., 1986; named Dist. Educator Calif. State U., 1993. Republican. Roman Catholic. Avocations: tennis, choral singing, photography, hiking. Home: 10121 Pounds Ave Whittier CA 90603-1649 Office: U So Calif WPH 902c Los Angeles CA 90089-0031

GOTSHALL, CORDIA ANN, publishing company executive, distributing executive; b. Greenwood, Ark., Jan. 21, 1931; d. Harrison Wages and Mabel Magdalene (Boswell) Wages Moreland; m. Daniel W. Gotshall, Apr. 12, 1952. AA with honors, Foothill Jr. Coll., Los Altos Hills, Calif., 1966; BA magna cum laude, Humboldt State U., Arcata, Calif., 1969; student, Humboldt State U., 1969-71. Clk., typist Indentification Bur. Stanislaus County Sheriff's Office, Modesto, Calif., 1950-55; credit dept. mgr. Brizard's Dept. Store, Arcata, 1955-56; sec.-coord. City of Eureka (Calif.) Recreation Dept., 1956-60; seasonal aide State of Calif. Dept. Fish and Game, Palo Alto, 1961; owner, v.p. Sea Challengers Pub. Co., Monterey, Calif., 1976-83, pres., 1983—; co-editor (with Daniel W. Gotshall) Fishwatcher's Guide, 1977; U.S. rep. Moscow Internat. Book Fair, 1985. Mem. Chi Sigma Epsilon. Avocations: reading, travel, hiking, nature studies, exploring. Office: 4 Sommerset Rise Monterey CA 93940-4112

GOTTFREDSON, MICHAEL RYAN, criminal justice educator; b. Oakland, Calif., Jan. 16, 1951; s. Don Martin and Betty Jane (Hunt) G.; m. Karol Ann Schmalenberger, Sept. 20, 1970; children: Katherine, Bryan. AB, U. Calif., Davis, 1973; MA, SUNY, Albany, 1974; PhD, SUNY, 1976. Dir. Criminal Justice Rsch. Ctr., Albany, 1976-79; asst. prof. Sch. Criminal Justice, SUNY, Albany, 1979-81; assoc. prof. Dept. Sociology, U. Ill., Urbana, 1981-83, Claremont (Calif.) Grad. Sch., 1983-85; prof. mgmt. and pub. policy U. Ariz., Tucson, 1985—; head dept. mgmt. and policy U. Ariz., 1988—, from vice provost to v.p., 1994—; bd. dirs. Criminal Justice Rsch. Inst., Phila., 1989—; vis. disting. prof. N.Mex. State U., 1986. Co-author: A General Theory of Crime, 1990, Decisionmaking in Criminal Justice, 1988, Policy Guideline for Bail, 1985, Victims of Crime, 1978. Mem. Am. Soc. Criminology, Phi Beta Kappa. Office: U Ariz 501 Adminstrn Bldg Tucson AZ 85721

GOTTLIEB, ALAN MERRIL, advertising, fundraising and broadcasting executive, writer; b. L.A., May 2, 1947; s. Seymour and Sherry (Schutz) G.; m. Julie Hoy Versnel, July 27, 1979; children: Amy Jean, Sarah Merril, Alexis Hope, Andrew Michael. Grad. Georgetown U., 1970; BS, Nuclear Engring., U. Tenn., 1971. Press sec. Congressman John Duncan, Knoxvill, Tenn., 1971, regional rep., Young Ams. for Freedom, Seattle, 1972, nat. dir. Young Ams. for Freedom, Washington, 1971-72; nat. treas. Am. Conservative Union, Washington, 1971—, bd. dirs., 1974—; pres. Merril Assocs., 1974—; chmn. Citizens Com. for Right to Keep and Bear Arms, Bellevue, Wash., 1972—, exec. dir., 1973; pres. Ctr. Def. of Free Enterprise, Bellevue 1976—, Second Amendment Found., Bellevue, 1974—; pub. Gun Week, 1985—, The Gottlieb-Tartaro Report, 1995—; bd. dirs. Nat. Park User Assn., 1988—, Am. Polit. Action Com., 1988—, Coun. Nat. Policy, bd. govs., 1985—, Svc. Bureau Assn., pres., dir., 1974—, Chancellor Broadcasting, Inc, Las Vegas, Nev., 1990-93; pres. Sta. KBNP Radio, Portland, 1990—, Pres. Station KZTY Radio, Las Vegas, NV, Evergreen Radio Network, Bellevue, 1990-93, Westnet Broadcasting Inc., Bellevue, 1990, Sta. KSBN Radio, Spokane, 1995—; chmn. Talk Am. Radio Networks, 1994—. With U.S. Army, 1968-74. Recipient Good Citizenship award Citizens Home Protective Assn., Honolulu, 1978, Cicero award Nat. Assn. Federally Licensed Firearms Dealers, Fla., 1982, Second Amendment award Scope, 1983, 91, Outstanding Am. Handgunner award, Am. Handgunners Award Found., Milwaukee, Wisc., 1984, Roy Rogers award, Nat. Antique Arms Collectors Assn., Reno, Nev., 1987, Golden Eagle award, Am. Fedn. Police, Washington, 1990. Mem. NRA. Republican. Author: The Gun Owners Political Action Manual, 1976, The Rights of Gun Owners, 1981, Rev. edit., 1991, The Gun Grabbers, 1988, Gun Rights Fact Book, 1989, Guns For Women, 1988, The Wise Use Agenda, 1989, Trashing the Economy, 1993, Things You Can Do To Defend Your Gun Rights, 1993, Alan Gottlieb's Celebrity Address Book, 1994, More Things You Can Do To Defend Your Gun Rights, 1995, Politically Correct Guns, 1996, She Took a Village, 1998.

GOTTLIEB, JEFFREY PAUL, journalist; b. L.A., Oct. 15, 1953; s. Irvin Mathews and Zelda (Grossman) G. AB, Pitzer Coll., 1975; MS, Columbia U., 1980. Reporter Simi Valley (Calif.) Enterprise, 1979, Riverside (Calif.) Press-Enterprise, 1980-82; assoc. editor Ofcl. Olympic Souvenir Program, L.A., 1983-84; reporter L.A. Herald Examiner, 1985-88; staff writer/asst. city editor San Jose (Calif.) Mercury News, 1988-97, L.A. Times, 1997—; mem. panel advisors George Polk Awards, Bklyn., 1992—. Contbr. articles to profl. jours. Recipient Spanish Lang. fellowship Nat. Press Club, 1982, George Polk award L.I. U., 1991. Mem. Investigative Reporters and Editors. Democrat. Jewish. Avocations: sports, music, movies, reading, skiing. Home: 235 Belmont Ave Apt 7 Long Beach CA 90803-1521 Office: LA Times 1375 Sunflower Ave Costa Mesa CA 92626-1697

GOTTLIEB, LEONARD, foundation administrator; b. Santa Monica, Calif., Apr. 12, 1923; s. Charles and Sarah Gottlieb; m. M. Elizabeth Gottlieb, 1943; children: Thomas Byron, Robert John, Mary Lou. AA, L.A. Trade Tech. Coll., 1943; student, UCLA, 1958, Calif. State U., L.A., 1960. Chief field dep. L.A. City Coun., 1957-67; campaign mgr. Spencer-Roberts & Assocs., L.A., 1967-69; exec. dir. So. Calif. Kidney Found., L.A., 1969-75; dir. devel. Nat. Kidney Found., N.Y.C., 1975-79; regional dir. Nat. Kidney Found., L.A., 1983-91, dir. planned giving, 1991—; legis. analyst II City of L.A., 1980-83. Author: Fund Raising: The How To's, 1976. Mem. life Calif. PTA, 1954; mem. Friends of Sport. Recipient L.A. City Coun. commendation resolution, 1969. Fellow Nat. Kidney Found. Profl. Staff Assn., Planned Giving Coun. So. Calif., Nat. Com. on Planned Giving, Nat. Health Agys. Planned Giving Roundtable, Ephebian Soc., Venice H.S. Alumni Assn. Avocations: reading, gardening, music. Office: Nat Kidney Found 3140 Grand View Blvd Los Angeles CA 90066-1027

GOTTLIEB, MICHAEL B., computer consultant; b. Portland, Oreg., Nov. 12, 1975; s. Arthur and Jeanette (Zuercher) G. BS in Psychology, Portland State U., 1997. Engr. Microsoft, Portland, 1997—; cons. MG Consulting, Inc., Beaverton, Oreg., 1995—. Sysop adminstr. Disk Jockey Online, Lake Oswego, Oreg., 1990-97. Recipient Oreg. Laurels scholarship Portland State U., 1993. Office: MG Consulting Inc PO Box 872 Lake Oswego OR 97034-0141

GOTTRY, STEVEN ROGER, communications executive, author, screenwriter; b. Mpls., Dec. 7, 1946; s. Roger Eugene and Helen Viola (Johnson) G.; m. Joanne Moritz (div. Nov. 1983); children: Jonathan, Michelle; m. Karla Mae Styer, Nov. 7, 1984; 1 child, Kalla Paige. BA in Advt. and Radio-TV Prodn., U. Minn., 1970. With promotion dept. Sta. WCCO-TV, Mpls., 1967-69; pres. Visual Communications, Inc., Mpls., 1970-87, The Gottry Comm. Group, Inc., Bloomington, Minn., 1987-96; pub. Priority Multimedia Group, Mesa, Ariz., 1995—. Author: Commonsense Business in a Nonsense Economy, 1994; co-author: The Spirit of Tocayo, 1995, Options, 1996, The Screenwriter's Story Planning Guide, 1999, several scripts for cable TV movies; contbr. articles to mags. and newspapers. Recipient Internat. Advt. Festival N.Y. award, 1988, three Silver Microphone Nat. Radio awards, 1990, Internat. Travel Competition award, 1991. Mem. Advt. Fedn. Minn. (award 1974, 75), Bloomington C. of C. (winner Bloomington Small Co. of Yr. 1991, Small Bus. Advocate of Yr. 1995), Rotary (bd. dirs., named New Rotarian of Yr. 1990). Avocations: boating, camping, biking, tennis, aviation. Office: 2339 W Lomita Cir Mesa AZ 85202-6458

GOTTSTEIN, BARNARD JACOB, retail and wholesale food company executive, real estate executive; b. Des Moines, Dec. 30, 1925; s. Jacob B. and Anna (Jacobs) G.; children: Sandra, James, Ruth Anne, David, Robert; m. Rachel Landau, July, 1986. BA in Econs. and Bus., U. Wash., 1949; LLD (hon.), U. Alaska, Fairbanks, 1991. Pres. J.B. Gottstein & Co., Anchorage, 1953-90; chmn. bd. Carr-Gottstein Inc., Anchorage, 1974-90; ret., 1990—; dir. United Bank Alaska, Anchorage, 1975-86. Commr. Alaska State Human Rights Commn., 1963-68; del. Dem. Nat. Conv., 1964, 68, 76, 88, 92; committeeman Dem. Nat. Com., 1976-80; v.p. State Bd. Edn., Alaska, 1983-87, pres., 1987-91. Served with USAF, 1944-45. Jewish. Office: Carr-Gottstein Properties 550 W 7th Ave Ste 1540 Anchorage AK 99501-3567

GOULD, EILEEN TRACY, interior designer, general contractor; b. Phila., July 7, 1955; d. Herman and Jeannette (Shorr) Luboff; m. Fred Joel Gould, Aug. 4, 1979; children: Jeff, Aly. BA, Pa. State U., 1976; postgrad., UCLA Contractors Sch., Van Nuys, Calif., 1997. Set dir. AFI, L.A., 1979-80; ind. set designer L.A.; owner Lifestyles Interior Design and Constrn., Westlake, Calif., 1980—; editl. dir. Loompanics Unltd. Appeared on KABC TV, 1997; author 12 books, 1981-98, Northwest EXTRA! tabloid, 1987-89, comic books, Stars mag. Pres. Women's Referral Svc., L.A., 1993-98, Jewish Fedn., L.A., 1998. Mem. Am. Soc. Interior Design, Interior Designers Guild (cert.), Calif. Assn. Profl. Designers. Office: Lifestyles Interior Design and Constrn 2612 Grandlakes Dr Westlake Village CA 91361

GOULD, MARTHA BERNICE, retired librarian; b. Claremont, N.H., Oct. 8, 1931; d. Sigmund and Gertrude Heller; m. Arthur Gould, July 29, 1960; children: Leslie, Stephen. BA in Edn., U. Mich., 1953; MS in Library Sci., Simmons Coll., 1956; cert., U. Denver Library Sch. Community Analysis Research Inst., 1978. Childrens librarian N.Y. Pub. Libr., 1956-58; adminstr. library services act demonstration regional library project Pawhuska, Okla., 1958-59; cons. N.Mex. State Libr., 1959-60; childrens librarian then sr. childrens librarian Los Angeles Pub. Libr., 1960-72; acctg. dir. pub. srvices, reference librarian Nev. State Libr., 1972-74; pub. services librarian Washoe County (Nev.) Libr., 1974-79, asst. county librarian, 1979-84, county librarian, 1984-94; ret., 1994; cons. Nev. State Libr. and Archives, 1996—; part-time lectr. in libr. adminstrn. U. Nev.; cons. Nev. State Libr. and Archives; acting dir. Nev. Ctr. for the Book. Contbr. articles to jours. Exec. dir. Kids Voting/USA, Nev., 1996; treas. United Jewish Appeals, 1981; bd. dirs. Temple Sinai, Planned Parenthood, 1996-97, Truckee Meadows Habitat for Humanity, 1995—; trustee RSVP, North Nevadans for ERA; No. Nev. chmn. Gov.'s Conf. on Libr., 1990; mem. bd. Campaign for Choice, No. Nev. Food Bank, Nev. Women's Fund (Hall of Fame award 1989); mem. No. Nev. NCCJ, Washoe County Quality Life Task Force, 1992—; chair Sierra (Nev.) Comty. Access TV; presdl. appointee vice-chair Nat. Comn. on Librs. and Info. Sci., 1993—; mem. adv. bd. Partnership Librs. Washoe County; co-chair social studies curriculum adv. task force Washoe County Sch. Dist.; mem. Nev. Women's History Project Bd.; chair Downtown River Corrodiro Com., 1995-97; vice chair Dem. Party Washoe Dem. Party. Recipient Nev. State Libr. Letter of Commendation, 1973, Washoe County Bd. Commrs. Resolution of Appreciation, 1978, ACLU of Nev. Civil Libertarian of Yr. 1988, Freedom's Sake award AAUW, 1989, Leadership in Literacy award Sierra chpt. Internat. Reading Assn., 1992, Woman of Distinction award 1992, Nev. Libr. Assn. Libr. of Yr., 1993. Mem. ALA (bd. dirs., intellectual freedom roundtable 1977-79, intellectual freedom com. 1979-83, coun. 1983-86), ACLU (bd. dirs. Civil Libertarian of Yr. Nev. chpt. 1988, chair gov.'s conf. for women 1989), Nev. Libr. Assn. (chmn. pub. info. com. 1972-73, intellectual freedom com. 1975-78, govt. rels. com. 1978-79, v.p., pres.-elect 1980, pres. 1981, Spl. Citation 1978, 87, LIbr. of Yr. 1993).

GOULD, R(ICHARD) MARTIN (RICHARD MARTIN GOLDMAN), marketing consultant, researcher; b. Auburn, N.Y., Aug. 19, 1941; s. Max and Lillian (Kanter) Goldman. *Maternal grandparents Joseph and Ida Kanter settled in Auburn, New York from Poland. Joseph was an antique dealer. Three children Lillian, Jane, Emma. Paternal grandparents Israel and Bella Packard, changed to Goldman, settled in Auburn, New York, ten children. Founded Princess Manufacturers, Inc., women's apparel. Father, Max, trial attorney, special county Judge, vehicle examiner, trusts and estate attorney, family owned footwear store. Mother Lillian, county school teacher, homemaker. Sister, Carole, school teacher, first woman president of Temple Rodef Shalom. Husband Mark, CPA firm, two children. Brother Robert, retired FBI agent, wife Ellen, school teacher, screen printer, homemaker. Biographee, bachelor.* Grad., Auburn East H.S., 1959; student, U. Buffalo, 1961; AB, Ohio No. U., 1963, JD, 1966; postgrad., U. Ariz., 1966. Dir. response mktg. Rep. Orgn., Tucson, 1966-67; legal rschr. ICC, Washington, 1967; asst. bank examiner Comptr. of the Currency, N.Y.C., 1967-68; pub. bond securities salesman Henry Harris & Sons, Inc., N.Y.C., 1968-69; pub. bond salesman Chester Harris & Co., Inc., N.Y.C., 1970-93; land surveyor Interstate Gen. Corp., San Juan, P.R., 1969; with Gen. Devel. Corp., San Juan, 1969; marketer, new bus. rep. Canadaigua Enterprises, Inc., Farmington, N.Y.; assoc. Law Offices of Max Goldman, Auburn, N.Y., 1972-77; sales mktg. cons. G. Enterprises, Gould & Assocs., San Rafael, Calif., 1972—, pub. rels. exec., 1993-96, sales mktg. cons., 1996—. *Devised method to market to various customers, government and corporate securities, activity that promotes development and growth in government, economics, social and culture fields, through blueprint dealing-trading corporation portfolio securities or government portfolio securities. Introduced government officials to process of inflation prevention. Proposed process to eradicate federal, state and local taxes or related ones; to increase new rewarding government programs, budget surplus. Consults legal industry on legal issues. Proposed to soap manufacturers a method D for shaving body hair. Promoted to have manufacturer reps and eliminate salesmen. Promoted to sports commissioner, ways to increase fan interest and excitement, adapt coaching strategy. Proposed to vehicle makers seat and floor massage units.* Mem. Internat. Platform Assn., Alpha Epsilon Pi, Phi Alpha Delta, Phi Beta Lambda. Mem. Humanism Ch. Avocations: walking, tennis, table tennis, golf, reading. Home and Office: Gould Consultants PO Box 6701 128 La Perdiz Ct San Rafael CA 94903-3541

GOULDTHORPE, KENNETH ALFRED PERCIVAL, publisher, state official; b. London, Jan. 7, 1928; came to U.S., 1951, naturalized, 1956; s. Alfred Edward and Frances Elizabeth Finch (Callow) G.; m. Judith Marion Cutts, Aug. 9, 1975; children: Amanda Frances, Timothy Graham Cutts. Student U. Westminster (formerly Regent St. Poly.), 1948-49, Bloomsbury Tech. Inst., 1949-50; diploma City and Guilds of London, 1949; student, Washington U., 1951-52. Staff photographer Kentish Mercury, London, 1949-50, St. Louis Post-Dispatch, 1951-55, picture editor, 1955-57; nat. and fgn. corr. Life mag., Time, Inc., N.Y.C., 1957-61, Paris Bur., 1961-65, regional editor Australia-New Zealand, 1966-68, editorial dir. Latin Am., 1969-70; editor Signature mag., N.Y.C., 1970-73; mng. editor Penthouse mag., N.Y.C., 1973-76, pub. cons., 1976-79; editor, exec. pub. Adventure Travel mag., Seattle, 1979-80; sr. ptnr. Pacific Pub. Assocs., Seattle, 1981-83; editor, pub. Washington mag., 1984-89; vice chmn. Evergreen Pub. Co., 1984-89; dir. tourism, State of Wash., 1989-91; pub./cons., writer, 1991—; dir. Grand Fir Pub. Corp., 1994—; tchr. design, editorial techniques Parsons Sch. Design, N.Y.C.; lectr., contbr. elementary schs. lit. progs. Served with Royal Navy, 1946-48. Decorated Naval Medal and bar; recipient awards of excellence Nat. Press Photographers Assn., AP and UP, 1951-57, Pres.' medal Ea. Wash. U., 1986; certs. excellence, Am. Inst. Graphic Arts, 1971, 72, 73, Communication Arts, 1980, 81, 84; spl. award, N.Y. Soc. Publs. Designers, 1980. Mem. Regional Pubs. Assn. (v.p., pres., Best Typography award 1985, Best Spl. Issue 1989), Western Publs. Assn. (Best Consumer Mag. award, Best Travel Mag. awards, 1980, Best Regional and State Mag. award 1985, 86, 88, Best New Publ. award 1985, Best Column award 1985, Best Signed Essay 1986, 87, Best Four-Color Layout 1985, Best Four Color Feature Design), City and Regional Mag. Assn. (William Allen White Bronze awards), Time/Life Alumni Soc., Assn. Washington Gens. (gen. of state 1995, bd. dirs.), Sigma Delta Chi. Episcopalian. Nominated for Pulitzer Prize for coverage of Andrea Doria disaster, 1956; contbr. articles, photographs to nat. mags., books by Life mag.; author: Design for Music, 1998. Home: 3049 NW Esplanade Seattle WA 98117-2624

GOURAS, MARK STEVEN, lawyer; b. Seattle, Apr. 21, 1961; s. Robert N. and Suzanne Marie Gouras; m. Elvira Pilar Lipio, July 27, 1984. BA in English, U. Wash., 1983; JD, U. Puget Sound, 1986. Bar: Wash. 1986, U.S. Dist. Ct. (we. dist.) Wash. Assoc. Albert & Slater, P.S., Federal Way, Wash., 1986-88, Taylor, Kiefer & Bartlett, Seattle, 1988-93; pvt. practice Seattle, 1993-96; ptnr. Hillman & Gouras, LLP, Tukwila, Wash., 1997—. Mem. ABA, Wash. State Bar Assn., Seattle-King County Bar Assn. Republican. Office: 16040 Christensen Rd Ste 215 Tukwila WA 98188-2966

GOVAN, GLADYS VERNITA MOSLEY, retired critical care and medical/surgical nurse; b. Tyler, Tex., July 24, 1918; d. Stacy Thomas and Lucy Victoria (Whitmill) Mosley; m. Osby David Govan, July 20, 1938; children Orbrenett K. (Govan) Carter, Diana Lynn (Govan) Mosley. *Grandson Akili John Carter IV is a member of the Centaurs football team at Culver City High School. He is interested in professional football, and will be graduating June 19, 1998. He plans to attend the University of California, San Diego.* Student, East Los Angeles Coll., Montebello, Calif., 1951; lic. vocat. nurse, Calif. Hosp. Med. Ctr., L.A., 1953; cert., Western States IV Assn., L.A., 1978. Lic. vocat. nurse, Calif.; cert. in EKG. Intravenous therapist Calif. Hosp. Med. Ctr., cardiac monitor, nurse; ret. Past pres. PTA, also hon. mem., 1963—; charter mem. Nat. Rep. Presdl. Task Force.

GOVERNAL, ROBERT ANDREW, technology executive; b. Jersey City, Dec. 18, 1964; s. George J. and Roberta A. Governal. BS, Rutgers U., 1986; PhD, U. Ariz., 1992. Asst. engr. Maxwell House divsn. Gen. Foods, Hoboken, N.J., 1986-87; process engr., staff microbiologist ABIC Internat., Fairfield, N.J., 1987-88; intern engr. Motorola, Mesa, Ariz., 1989; tech. strategies mgr. U.S. Filter Corp., Rockford, Ill., 1992-94; tech. dir. Internat. Innovative Techs., Tucson, 1995—; vis. scholar U. Ariz., 1995—. Author: The Multi-Professional Planner, 1997, World War 5, 1998; inventor ultrapure water sys. IBM rsch. fellow Thomas J. Watson Rsch. Ctr., Yorktown Heights, N.Y., 1991. Mem. AIChemE, ASTM, Inst. Environ. Scis. and Tech., Electrochem. Soc. Fax: (520) 578-3124. E-mail: Governal@ag.arizona.edu. Home: 5761 W Creda St Tucson AZ 85735-9383 Office: Internat Innovative Techs 2709 W San Paulus Rd Tucson AZ 85746-6342

GOZANI, TSAHI, nuclear physicist; b. Tel Aviv, Nov. 25, 1934; came to U.S., 1965; s. Arieh and Rivcca (Meiri) G.; m. Adit Soffer, Oct. 14, 1958; children: Mor, Shai Nachum, Or Pinchas, Tal. BSc, Technion-Israel Inst. Tech., Haifa, 1956, MSc, 1958; DSc, Swiss Fed. Inst. Tech. (ETH), Zurich, Switzerland, 1962. Registered profl. nuclear engr., Calif.; accredited nuclear material mgr. Rsch. physicist Israel Atomic Energy Commn., Beer-Sheva, 1962-65; rsch. assoc. nuclear engring. dept. Rensselaer Poly. Inst., Troy, N.Y., 1965-66; sr. staff scientist General-Atomic & IRT, San Diego, 1966-70, 71-75; prof. applied physics Tel Aviv U., 1971; chief scientist, divsn. mgr. Sci. Applications Internat. Corp., Palo Alto and Sunnyvale, Calif., 1975-84; v.p., chief scientist Sci. Applications Internat. Corp., Sunnyvale, 1984-87;

corp. v.p. Sci. Applications Internat. Corp., Santa Clara, Calif., 1987-93, sr. v.p., 1993-97; pres., CEO Ancore Corp., Santa Clara, 1997—; Lady Davis vis. prof. Technion-Israel Inst. Tech., 1983-84; bd. dirs. Radiation Sci. Inst., San Jose State U. Author: Active Non-Destructive Assay of Nuclear Materials, 1981; co-author: Handbook of Nuclear Safeguards Measurement Methods, 1983; contbr. over 170 articles to profl. jours. Recipient 1989 Laurel award Aviation Week Jour., R&D 100 award, 1988, Most Innovative New Products. Fellow Am. Nuclear Soc.; mem. Am. Phys. Soc., Inst. Nuclear Materials. Achievements include patents for explosive detection system, explosive detection system using an artificial neural system, multi sensor explosive detection system, composite cavity structure for an explosive detection system, apparatus and method for detecting contraband using fast neutron activation, contraband detection system using direct imaging pulsed fast neutrons; invention of method to measure nuclear reactor's reactivity. Office: Ancore Corp 2950 Patrick Henry Dr Santa Clara CA 95054-1813

GRAB, FREDERICK CHARLES, lawyer; b. N.Y.C., Aug. 1, 1946; s. Daniel Justin and Elizabeth (Kam) G. BS in Aerospace Engring., Polytech U. N.Y., 1967; JD, U. So. Calif., 1977. Bar: Calif. 1978, U.S. Dist. Ct. (cen. dist.) Calif. 1978, U.S. Supreme Ct. 1988, U.S. Ct. Appeals (9th cir.) 1989. Deputy atty. gen. Calif. Atty. Gen., L.A., 1977—. Contbr. articles to profl. jours. Avocations: playwright, author, composer, musican. Office: Office of Atty Gen 300 S Spring St Los Angeles CA 90013-1230

GRABARZ, DONALD FRANCIS, pharmacist; b. Jersey City, Sept. 18, 1941; s. Joseph and Frances (Zotynia) G.; m. Joan Isoldi, Aug. 13, 1966; children: Christine, Robert, Danielle. BPharm, St. Johns U., N.Y.C., 1964. Lic. pharmacist, N.Y., Vt. Dir. qualtiy control and assurance Johnson and Johnson Co., New Brunswick, N.J., 1965-72; dir. quality assurance and regulatory affairs Bard Parker div. Becton Dickinson, Franklin Lakes, N.J., 1972-76; asst. corp. dir. regulatory affairs Becton Dickinson, 1976-80; corp. dir. regulatory affairs C.R. Bard Inc., Murray Hill, N.J., 1980-85; v.p. regulatory affairs, qualtiy assurance Symbion Inc., Salt Lake City, 1985-86; cons., pres. DFG & Assocs., Inc., Salt Lake City, 1986—; mem., mng. dir. Internat. Regulatory Consultants, L.C., Sale Lake City, 1987—; adj. prof. Salt Lake C. C., 1993—; lectr. Inst. for Applied Tech., Inst. Internat. Rsch., Ernst & Young, Salt Lake C.C. Co-author, technical advisor, editor Inspection and Recall Film; co-author: Science, Technology, and Regulation in a Competetive Environment, 1990; contbr. articles to profl. jours. Bd. dirs. v.p., asst. treas. Am. Lung Assn., N.J., 1972-75; chmn. Drug Edn., DuPage County, Ill., 1968. Mem. Health Industry Mfg. Assn. (chmn. Legal and Regulatory commn. 1983), Regulatory Affairs Profl. Soc. (lectr.), Am. Soc. Quality Control, Am. Mfr. Med. Instrumentation Assn., Am. Pharm. Assn., Food and Drug Law Inst., Cottonwood Country Club (bd. dirs., treas. 1995—, v.p. 1996—, pres. 1997). Avocations: soccer, tennis, baseball, skiing, music. Office: Internat Regulatory Cons, LC PO Box 17801 Salt Lake City UT 84117-0801

GRABER, SUSAN P., judge; b. Oklahoma City, July 5, 1949; d. Julius A. and Bertha (Fenyves) G.; m. William June, May 3, 1981; 1 child, Rachel June-Graber. BA, Wellesley Coll., 1969; JD, Yale U., 1972. Bar: N.Mex. 1972, Ohio 1977, Oreg. 1978. Asst. atty. gen. Bur. of Revenue, Santa Fe, 1972-74; assoc. Jones Gallegos Snead & Wertheim, Santa Fe, 1974-75, Taft Stettinius & Hollister, Cin., 1975-78; assoc., then ptnr. Stoel Rives Boley Jones & Grey, Portland, Oreg., 1978-88; judge, then presiding judge Oreg. Ct. Appeals, Salem, 1988-90; assoc. justice Oreg. Supreme Ct., Salem, 1990-98; judge U.S. Ct. Appeals (9th cir.), Portland, 1998—. Mem. Gov.'s Adv. Coun. on Legal Svcs., 1979-88; bd. dirs. U.S. Dist. Ct. of Oreg. Hist. Soc., 1985—, Oreg. Law Found., 1990-91; mem. bd. visitors Sch. Law, U. Oreg., 1986-93. Mem. Oreg. State Bar (jud. adminstrn. com. 1985-87, pro bono com. 1988-90), Ninth Cir. Jud. Conf. (chair exec. com. 1987-88), Oreg. Jud. Conf. (edn. com. 1988-91, program chair 1990), Oreg. Appellate Judges Assn. (sec.-treas. 1990-91, vice chair 1991-92, chair 1992-93), Am. Inns of Ct. (master), Phi Beta Kappa. Office: US Ct Appeals 9th Cir Pioneer Courthouse 555 SW Yamhill St Portland OR 97204-1336*

GRABILL, JAMES R., JR., educator, writer; b. Bowling Green, Ohio, Nov. 29, 1949; s. James R. Sr. and Bette L. (Baker) G.; ptnr. Marilyn Burki. BFA, Bowling Green State U., 1974; MA, Colo. State U., 1984, MFA, 1988. Poet, writer, 1968—; instr. CCC, PCC, OWW, CSU, Ft. Collins, Colo., 1985-87, CCC, PCC, OWW, Portland, Oreg., 1990—; Editor, pub. Leaping Mountain Press, Ft. Collins, 1985-86; author: (poems) Poem Rising Out of the Earth, 1995 (Oreg. Book Award), Listening to the Leaves Form, 1997, (poems and essays) Through the Green Fire, 1995; contbr. numerous poems and essays to lit. publs. Coord. readings Power Plant Arts Ctr., Ft. Collins, 1984-86. Grad. fellow Colo. State U., 1981-83, 87-88, Nat. Presbyn. fellow, 1967-70. Avocations: art, drawing, running reading.

GRABOWSKI, MARILYN, photo editor; d. Julia Szlosek.; V.p., photo editor Playboy Mag., Santa Monica, Calif., 1964—. Office: Playboy Enterprises Inc 2112 Broadway Santa Monica CA 90404-2912

GRACE, JOHN WILLIAM, electrical company executive; b. Swissville, Pa., May 29, 1921; s. Joseph and Ruth Margaret (Bailey) G.; student Am. TV Inst. Tech., 1950; BEE, Drexel U., 1960; m. Ruth Delores Schroeder, Nov. 25, 1950; children: Martha, Joan, Nancy, John William. Technician missiles and surface radar div. RCA, Moorestown, N.J., 1950-56, design engr., 1956-60, project engr., 1960-66; mgr. engring. and sci. exec. EG & G, Inc., Las Vegas, Nev., 1966-73, mgr. bus. devel. operational test and evaluation, Albuquerque, 1973-77; engring. mgr. Instrumentation div., Idaho Falls, Idaho, 1977-79, mgr. systems project office, 1979, mgr. instrumentation program office, 1979-82, mgr. engring. spl. products div., 1982-84, dir. tech. resources, 1984-91, retired 1991. Active Boy Scouts Am., 1969-71. Served with USNR, 1941-45. Mem. IEEE, Instrument Soc. Am. (dir. sci. instrumentation and research div.), Assn. Old Crows, Am. Legion (post adj. vice comdr. 1950). Episcopalian (pres. couples retreat 1969-70). Patentee contradirectional waveguide coupler. Home: 8311 Loma Del Norte Dr NE Albuquerque NM 87109-4901 Office: EG&G Spl Projects Divsn PO Box 93747 Las Vegas NV 89193-3747

GRACE, RICH JOSEPH, writer; b. L.A., Mar. 30, 1959; s. Richard Joseph, Sr. and Carol June (Rosenthal) G.; m. Elisabeth Anne Parker. Tech. journalist, freelance writer, 1990—. Author: The Benchmark Book, 1996, The Sound and Music Workshop, 1996, The Lingo Handbook, 1997, (with Andy Rathbone) Dummies 101: Windows NT 4, 1997; contbr. articles to mags. Avocations: martial arts, jazz. Home and Office: 1455 Clay St Apt 6 San Francisco CA 94109-3928

GRACE, WILLIAM PERSHING, petroleum geologist, real estate developer; b. Mineral Point, Mo., Sept. 19, 1920; s. William Francis and Bertha Luciel (Nephew) G.; m. Jeannette Marie Grace, March 28, 1942 (dec.); children: Joyce Medaris, Pamela Grace, Sonia Scott, Patricia Lawser. Student, Corpus Christi U., 1946-47; B in Geology, Tex. Tech. U., 1947-50; student (GRI), U. Colo. Extension, 1968-69. Capt. USAF, 1940-46; regional geologist Anderson-Prichard Oil Corp., San Antonio, Tex., 1950-62; real estate broker Grace Reality, Aurora, Colo., 1963-66; pres. Kimberley Homes, Construction, Aurora, 1966-72; pres., broker Grace-Scott-Cooper Corp., Aurora, 1972—. pres. Friends of the Aurora Pub. Library, 1967, trustee mem. 1978; chmn. Adams County Rep. Party, 1970-72; mem. vocat. edn. coun. Sch. Dist. 28J, 1989—. Named Colorado of Yr. Colo. State Libr. Assn., 1988. Mem. Am. Assn. Petroleum Geologists (del. House of Dels. 1961-62), Nat. Assn. Realtors, Rocky Mountain Assn. Petroleum Geologists, Colo. Assn. Realtors, Colo. State Friends and Trustee Assn., Denver Petroleum Club, Aurora Bd. Realtors (treas. 1979, Realtor of Yr. 1980), Aurora C. of C. (dir. 1966-68, Man of Yr. 1980), Aurora Kiwanis (internat. del. in Nice, France, 1993, lt. gov. Rocky Mountain divsn. 1992, sec. 1965, pres. 1972), Sixty Five Roses Found., Sigma Gamma Epsilon. Lutheran. Avocations: geologic exploration, flying, golfing, skiing, traveling. Home: PO Box 440169 Aurora CO 80044-0169

GRADY, CHERYL RAE, telecommunications executive; b. Texas City, Tex., Nov. 19, 1958; d. William J. III and Marjorie L. (McAleer) G.; m. John M. Kelly, Dec. 19, 1981 (div. Jan. 1987). BS in Engring. Tech., Tex. A&M U., 1981. Engr. Pacific Bell, San Ramon, Calif., 1982-93; dir. mktg. Pacific Bell, San Ramon, 1993-98; dir. data strategy SBC, San Ramon, 1998-99; dir. data product devel. SBC Long Distance, Pleasanton, Calif., 1999—. Roman Catholic. Avocations: scuba diving, rollerblading, bicycling. Office: SBC Ops 2600 Camino Ramon Rm 1s155 San Ramon CA 94583-5000

GRADY, DOLORES ANNE, academic administrator, educator, consultant; b. Wiesbaden, Germany, Apr. 24, 1958. BA, U. No. Colo., Greeley, 1980, MA, 1983. Cert. tchr., 1987, trainer, 1996. Instr. Adelphi Bus. Coll., 1984-87; assoc. prof. Colo. Tech. Coll., 1987-91; project mgr. Advanced Skills Edn. Program/Basic Skills Edn. Program Pikes Peak C.C., Ft. Carson, Colo., 1991-93; tng. mgr. Matrix Mktg., Colo., 1993-96; dir. tng. and devel. Ent Fed. Credit Union, 1996-97; dir. training FutureCall, 1998—; adj. prof. Chapman U., Colorado Springs, Colo., 1991-93, Pikes Peak C.C., 1991—, Univ. Phoenix, 1997—. Bd. dirs. Pikes Peak Mental Health Action League, Jr. League Colorado Springs. Mem. Internat. Bd. Cert. Trainers, Internat. Soc. Performance Improvement, Am. Soc. Tng. and Devel. Home: 2111 Lockhaven Dr Colorado Springs CO 80909-2037

GRAF, ERVIN DONALD, municipal administrator; b. Crow Rock, Mont., Mar. 9, 1930; s. Emanuel and Lydia (Bitz) G.; m. Carolyn Sue Robinson, Mar. 15, 1956 (div. 1958); m. Eleanor Mahlein, Apr. 13, 1959 (dec. Oct. 1990); children: Debra, Belinda, Corrina, Melanie (dec.), Ervin Jr. (dec.). Enlisted U.S. Army, 1948; served two tours of duty in Vietnam; ret. U.S. Army, 1972; with office and maintenance staff Greenfields Irrigation Dist., Fairfield, Mont., 1972-77, sec. to Bd. Commrs., 1977-95; ret., 1995. Decorated Bronze star with oak leaf cluster. Mem. Am. Legion (all offices Post #80 and Dist. 8 incl. dist. comdr.). Democrat. Lutheran. Avocations: bowling, coin collecting, fishing, camping. Home: 211 6th St N Fairfield MT 59436-0565

GRAF, HANS, conductor; b. Austria, Feb. 15, 1949. Studied with Franco Ferrera and Arvid Jonsons. Music dir. Mozarteum Orch., Salzburg, Austria, 1984-94, Calgary Philharm. Orch., 1995—; guest condr. Vienna Symphony, Vienna Philharm., Orchestre Nat. de France, Leningrad Philharm., Pitts. Symphony, Boston Symphony. Office: Calgary Philharmonic Orchestra, 205 8th Ave SE, Calgary, AB Canada T2G 0K9

GRAFE, WARREN BLAIR, cable television executive; b. N.Y.C., June 22, 1954; s. Warren Edward and Maree Lee (Ahn) G.; m. Pamela Arden Rearick, Mar. 8, 1980 (div. Nov. 1982). Student Kendall Coll., 1974-75, U. Wis., Platteville, 1975-76; BA, Ind. U., 1979. Sales rep., Sta. WGTC-FM, Bloomington, Ind., 1979-84, account exec., coop. coord., 1980-84; nat. sales rep. Stas. WTTS-WGTC, Bloomington, 1984; sales rep. Sta. KLFF-KMZK, Phoenix, 1985; account exec. Rita Sanders Advt. and Pub. Rels. Agy., Tempe, Ariz., 1985, Am. Cable TV, Phoenix, 1985-86, Dimension Media Svcs., Phoenix, 1986-89, Greater Phoenix Interconnect, 1989-95, CableRep/Phoenix, 1995—. Recipient Nat. Sales awards, Cable TV Advt. Bur., 1986, 87, 91, 94, 96, 98, finalist, 1995; named one of Cable's Best Top Ten Cable Advt. Sales Reps. in Country, Cable Avails, 1995. Mem. Tempe C. of C. (ambassador 1986), Chandler (Ariz.) C. of C., Mesa (Ariz.) C. of C. Home: 9616 N 26th Pl Phoenix AZ 85028-4708 Office: CableRep/Phoenix 2020 N Central Ave Ste 400 Phoenix AZ 85004-4510

GRAFFEO, FRANCIS, artistic director. Artistic dir. Eugene Opera. Office: Eugene Opera PO Box 11200 Eugene OR 97440-3400*

GRAFFIS, JULIE ANNE, entrepreneur, retail consultant, interior designer; b. Houston, Jan. 4, 1960; d. Robert B. and Dorothy Gean (Weempe) Hyde; m. William B. Graffis, May 29, 1988; 1 child, Aaron James Hehr. Student, U. St. Thomas, Houston, 1977, Portland C.C., The Dalles, Oreg., 1984-85; AA, North Seattle C.C., 1987. Cert. window fashions profl. assoc., specialist, master Window Fashions Cert. Program. Co-owner Mosier (Oreg.) Shell Svc., 1981-85; quality control mgr. Town & Country Jeep-Eagle, Seattle, 1986-87; cons. Giovi Ford-Mercury, Pullman, Wash., 1988-89; prin., CEO, Interiors by JAG, Houston, 1990—; mem. Allied Bd. of Trade; cons. Habitat for Humanity, Vancouver, 1992-93; lectr., presenter interior design workshops; retail cons. Bus. ptnr. Hough Elem. Found. and Sch.; patron Pilchuck Glass Sch. Mem. NAFE, Window Fashions Edn. and Design Resource Network, Greater Vancouver C. of C. (liaison bus. and edn. partnership 1992—, amb. 1993-95), Inst. Managerial and Profl. Women. Avocations: furniture and landscape design, jewelry design, classic automobiles, art collecting, travel, architecture, interior renovations.

GRAHAM, ANITA LOUISE, correctional and community health nurse; b. Casa Grande, Ariz., Sept. 17, 1959; d. Therman Louis (dec. 1995) and Anne Clessie (Dornan) Nichols; m. Richard Arthur Christy, Aug. 27, 1990; children: Amanda Sue Foster-Wells, Kristi Lynn Foster. AS in Practical Nursing, Ctrl. Ariz. Coll., 1982; AAS, RN, Gateway C.C., Phoenix, 1985, Degree in Health Svc. Mgmt., 1992. RN, Ariz., Okla.; cert. BLS, ACLS, Chemotherapy. Cert. nursing asst. Hoemako Hosp., Casa Grande, 1977-82; lic. practical nurse Mesa (Ariz.) Luth. Hosp., 1982-85; RN Mesa Gen. Hosp., 1985-86, East Mesa Care Ctr., 1986-88; RN, case mgr. Interim Healthcare, Phoenix, 1988-93; RN, nurse clinician PDR Carum Care, Phoenix, 1991-97; correctional RN Ariz. Dept. Corrections, Florence, 1993-95; IV nurse clinician Signature Home Care, 1994-97; RN, unit mgr., home health IV specialist Select Care, Globe, Ariz., 1997—; mem. RN adv. bd. Interim Healthcare, 1990-93. Mem. Ariz. Nurses Assn., Internat. Platform Assn. Republican. Avocations: stitchery, reading. Home: 1646 N Pennington Dr Chandler AZ 85224-5115

GRAHAM, ANNA REGINA, pathologist, educator; b. Phila., Nov. 1, 1947; d. Eugene Nelson and Anna Beatrice (McGovern) Chadwick; m. Larry L. Graham, June 29, 1973; 1 child, Jason. BS in Chemistry, Ariz. State U., 1969, BS in Zoology, 1970; MD, U. Ariz., 1974. Diplomate Am. Bd. Pathology. With Coll. Medicine U. Ariz., Tucson, 1974—, asst. prof. pathology, 1978-84, assoc. prof. pathology, 1984-90, prof. Pathology, 1990—. Fellow Am. Soc. Clin. Pathologists (bd. dirs. Chgo. chpt. 1993—, sec. 1995—), Internat. Acad. Pathology, Internat. Acad. Telemedicine, Coll. Am. Pathologists; mem. AMA (alt. del. Chgo. chpt. 1992—), Ariz. Soc. Pathologists (pres. Phoenix chpt. 1989-91), Ariz. Med. Assn. (treas. Phoenix chpt. 1995-97). Republican. Baptist. Avocations: motorcycles, piano, choir. Office: Ariz Health Scis Ctr Dept Pathology Tucson AZ 85724

GRAHAM, BILL, opera company director. Artistic dir. Spokane (Wash.) Opera, Spokane, Wash. Vet. dir. over 50 shows ranging from grand opera to musical theatre; active vocal coach. Office: Spokane Opera 643 S Ivory Ste 2 Spokane WA 99202*

GRAHAM, BRUCE EDWARD, video specialist; b. Bluefield, W.Va., Dec. 31, 1953; s. Marvin Arthur Graham and Phyllis Jean (Walters) Coffey. BS in Communications, Ohio U., 1977. Computer programmer Churchill area sch. dist., Pitts., 1971-73; staff engr. Sta. WOUB-TV, Athens, Ohio, 1973-77, Sta. KDKA-TV, Pitts., 1977; asst. chief engr. TPC Communications, Inc., Pitts., 1977-79, tech. ops. mgr., 1979-80, tech. support mgr., 1980-81; chief engr. Fla. Prodn. Ctr., Jacksonville, 1981-83, dir. engring., 1983-84; chief engr. Video Tape Assocs., Hollywood, Fla., 1984-88; dir. engring. Post Edge, Hollywood, 1988-89; product mgr. da Vinci Sys., Ft. Lauderdale, Fla., 1989-95; telecine engr. Modern Videofilm, Burbank, Calif., 1996-98; dir. engring. CIS/EFILM, Hollywood, Calif., 1998—. Mem. Soc. Motion Picture and TV Engrs. Avocations: electronic design, computer programming, aviation. Office: Modern Videofilm 4411 W Olive Ave Burbank CA 91505-4219

GRAHAM, CARY MARK, architect; b. Glendora, Calif., May 27, 1962; s. Jesse Albert and Carolyn Janette (Drake) G.; m. Cindy Ann Good, Jan. 24, 1997. Registered architect, Calif. Draftsman Forum Assn., Culver City, Calif., 1981-82; project mgr. Taylor & Taylor, Covina, Calif., 1982-87, Robert Kubicek, Santa Ana Heights, Calif., 1987-91; arch. McLean & Schultz, Brea, Calif., 1991-97, Sverdrup Facilities, Costa Mesa, Calif., 1997—. Sunday sch. jr. high tchr, Yorba Linda (Calif.) Friends, 1995—. Mem. AIA. Republican. Avocations: skiing, hiking, travel, bible study tchr., tng. Office: Sverdrup Facilities 675 Anton Blvd Ste 400 Costa Mesa CA 92626

GRAHAM, DENIS DAVID, [illegible] marriage and family therapist, education counsultant; b. Santa Rosa, Calif., Oct. 21, 1941; s. Elbert Eldon and Mildred Bethana (Dyson) G.; m. Margaret Katherine Coughlan, Aug. 31, 1968; children: Kathleen Ann, Todd Cameron (dec.). BS in Edn., U. Nev., 1964, MEd, 1973, MA, 1982. Cert. for ednl. personnel; lic. marriage and family therapist, Nev.; nat. cert. counselor Nat. Bd. for Cert. Counselors. Tchr. vocat. bus. edn. Earl Wooster High Sch., Reno, 1964-66, chmn. dept. bus. edn., 1966-67; state supr. bus. and office edn. Nev. Dept. Edn., Carson City, 1967-70, adminstr. vocat. edn. field svcs., 1970-74, asst. dir., 1974-78, vocat. edn. cons., 1978-85; edn. curriculum specialist Washoe County Sch. Dist., Reno, 1985-89, curriculum coord., 1989-94; ret., 1994; pres. Midpoint Inc., 1995—. marriage and family counselor Severance & Assocs., Carson City, 1983-85, Mountain Psychiat. Assocs., 1985-87; mem. tng. and youth employment council S.W. Regional Lab. for Ednl. Research and Devel., Los Alamitos, Calif., 1982, mem. career edn. council, 1980-81. Editor Council of Chief State Sch. Officers' Report: Staffing the Nation's Schools: A National Emergency, 1984. Contbr. articles to profl. jours. bd. dirs. U. Nev.-Reno Campus Christian Assn., 1988-90, 97; adv. com. Truckee Meadows Community Coll., Reno, 1988-94; mem. Gov.'s Crime Prevention Com., Carson City, 1979-83, Atty. Gen.'s Anti-Shoplifting Com., Carson City, 1974-78, Gov.'s Devel. Disabilities Planning Council, Carson City, 1977-79; bd. dirs. Jr. Achievement No. Nev., 1989-92, sec., mem. exec. com., 1990-91; bd. dir. Friends of the Coll. of Edn. U. Nev., Reno, 1995—. Recipient award for svc. Bus. Edn. Assn. of No. Nev., 1973, Svc. award YMCA, 1962, 63, Helping Hand award Procter R. Hug High Sch., 1993-94. Mem. Am. Vocat. Assn., Nat. Assn. Vocat. Edn. Spl. Needs Pers. (Outstanding Svc. award region V 1982), Assn. Suprs. & Curriculum Devel., Am. Assn. Marriage and Family Therapy, Am. Counseling Assn., Nev. Vocat. Assn. (Outstanding Svc. award 1991, Bill Trabert Meml. award Excellence in Occupational Edn. 1994), Internat. Assn. Marriage and Family Counselors, U. Nev. Reno Alumni Assn. (exec. com. 1971-75), Phi Delta Kappa, Phi Kappa Phi. Democrat. Methodist. Home: 3056 Bramble Dr Reno NV 89509-6901 Office: PO Box 33034 Reno NV 89533-3034

GRAHAM, JAN, state attorney general; b. Salt Lake City. BS in Psychology, Clark U., Worcester, Mass., 1973; MS in Psychology, U. Utah, 1977, JD, 1980. Bar: Utah. Ptnr. Jones, Waldo, Holbrook & McDonough, Salt Lake City, 1979-89; soliciter gen. Utah Atty. Gen.'s Office, Salt Lake City, 1989-93; atty. gen. State of Utah, 1993—; adj. prof. law U. Utah Law Sch.; bar commr. Utah State Bar, 1991; master of bench Utah Inns Ct. VII; mem. Utah Commn. on Justice in 21st Century; bd. dirs. Jones, Waldo, Holbrook & McDonough; bd. trustees Coll. Law U. Utah (pres.). Fin. devel. chair YWCA; chair Ctrl. Bus. Improvement Dist.; mem. Salt Lake City Olympic Bid Com. 1988 Games. Named Woman Lawyer Yr. Utah, 1987. Mem. Am. Arbitration Assn. (nat. panel arbitrators), Women Lawyers Utah (co-founder, mem. exec. com.). Office: Office of Attorney General 236 State Capitol Building Salt Lake City UT 84114-1202*

GRAHAM, JUDITH TAYLOR, poet; b. Pasadena, Calif., July 28, 1944; d. Kenneth Maynard and Selma Clarisse (Heilmann) T.; m. Hatch Graham, Feb. 22, 1972. BA, Calif. Luth. U., 1966; MA, U. So. Calif., 1968. Reporter/photographer Rialto Record, 1971-72; freelance writer Copley News Svc., 1972-74; editor SAR Dog Alert, 1982-92; staff writer DogSports, 1984-88. Author: (book of poetry) Casualties, 1995. Search and rescue dog handler DOGS, Alaska, 1975-77, VSRDA & DOGS-East, Va., 1977-81, WOOF & Calif. Rescue Dog Assn., 1982—. Mem. Nat. Assn. for Search and Rescue, Calif. Rescue Dog Assn. (bd. dirs. 1984, 89), El Dorado Writer's Guild (editor 1993—). Avocations: hiking, travel. Home: PO Box 39 Somerset CA 95684-0039

GRAHAM, LOIS CHARLOTTE, retired educator; b. Denver, Mar. 20, 1917; d. James Washington and Martha Wilhemina (Raukohl) Brewster; m. Milton Clinton Graham, June 30, 1940 (dec.); children: Charlotte, Milton, Charlene, James. Student, Okla. City U., 1935-36; AB, Ouachita Bapt. U., 1939; postgrad., U. Nev., Reno, 1953, 63, 68, Ark. State U., 1954, 59. Cert. tchr., Colo., Nev., Ark. Tchr. Fairmount Sch., Golden, Colo., 1939-40, Melbourne (Ark.) Sch., 1940-41, Blytheville (Ark.) Jr. H.S., 1944-45, Hawthorne (Nev.) Elem. Sch., 1952-81; substitute tchr. Mineral County Sch. Dist., Hawthorne, 1988-94; sr. resource cons. dept. geriatrics U. Nev.-Reno Med. Sch., 1988-90, del. to Rural Health Conf., Hawthorne, 1990; officer Mineral County Tchrs. Assn., 1955-65; ad hoc com. Nev. State Tchrs., 1965. Mem. Mineral County Emergency Planning Com., 1991—; asst. to pres. High Sch. PTA, Hawthorne, 1958, Elem. PTA, Hawthorne, 1961; pianist, choir dir., tchr. various chs., 1927—; active Older Am. Friends of Libr. Recipient Disting. Svc. award. Mem. AAUW (membership v.p. 1988-91, pres. 1991-92, 94-96), AARP (pres. 1995-98), Ret. Pub. Employees of Nev. (membership v.p. 1994-96, pres. 1995—), Older Ams., Friends Libr., Delta Kappa Gamma (v.p. 1991-92). Republican. Baptist. Avocations: volunteer work, reading, writing, knitting, crochet. Home: PO Box 1543 Hawthorne NV 89415-1543

GRAHAM, PETER MARK, multimedia producer; b. Tucson, Sept. 3, 1965; s. Tad Laury Graham and Margaret Ann (Fox) Yslas; m. Sylvia Ann Davis, Oct. 27, 1990; children: Matthew Tad, Christopher Henry. BA in Visual Arts, U. Calif., San Diego, 1997. Musician Private Practice, San Diego, Calif., 1986-89; multimedia producer ARINC, Inc., San Diego, 1989—. Producer, animator, Computer Animation Proxy Kiosk Animation, 1997 (Comm. award of distinction 1997): (interactive CD) Accel Electronic Design Automation Multimedia Tour, 1998 (Bronze Telly award 1998). Mgr. Youth Baseball, San Diego , 1998. Avocations: golf, music composition. Office: Arinc Inc 4055 Hancock St San Diego CA 92110-5107

GRAHAM, STEVEN PIDDINGTON, entertainment production company executive; b. San Juan, P.R., May 26, 1962; s. Charles Paul and Gayle Ann (Piddington) G. BA in Motion Picture and Video, Brooks Inst. Photography, Santa Barbara, Calif., 1988. Freelance photographer, 1980—; prodn. asst. Handmade Films, L.A., 1989; operator, technician Lynn Greenberg Teleprompting, Newhall, Calif., 1989-91; pres. PC Prompting Sys., Sherman Oaks, Calif., 1992—. Author teleprompting software Scrollmaster, 1992; creator, inventor portable jib arm teleprompting equipment, 1992, wireless portable steadicam teleprompting equipment, 1996. Vol. L.A. Works, 1993. Mem. Nat. Assn. Broadcast Employees and Technicians (Local 53), Nat. Parks Assn., Sierra Club. Republican. Lutheran. Avocations: photography, treking, horseback riding, camping, paragliding. Home: 4261 Dixie Canyon Ave Apt 4 Sherman Oaks CA 91423-3970

GRAHAM, TONI, writer; b. San Francisco, June 24, 1945; d. Joseph Foster and Maxine E. (Johnson) Avila; m. J. Richard Graham, Nov. 23, 1972 (div. 1987); 1 child, Salvatore Z. BA, New Coll. Calif., 1989; MA in English, San Francisco State U., 1992, MFA in Creative Writing, 1995. Lectr. creative writing San Francisco State U., 1992, 98; adj. prof. MA writing program U. San Francisco, 1994—; lectr. U. Calif., Santa Cruz, 1995-97, Chabot Coll., 1996-97, Dominican Coll., 1996-97, Santa Clara U., 1997-98. Author: The Daiquiri Girls, 1998; contbr. short fiction to mags., including Playgirl, Am. Fiction 88, Five Fingers Rev., Miss. Rev., Ascent, Clockwatch Rev., Miss. Mud, SFSU Rev., Worcester Rev., ZIPZAP mag., Green Mountain Rev., Chiron Rev., others. Harrold scholar, 1986; recipient Calif. Short Story Competition award, 1987, Herbert Wilner Meml. Short Story award, 1994; story Shadow Boxing cited in Pushcart Prize XIV-Best of the Small Presses, 1989; recipient Associated Writing Programs Fiction award 1997. Mem. MLA, Assoc. Writing Programs, Hemingway Soc., Golden Key Honor Soc. Home: 345 Prospect Ave San Francisco CA 94110-5509

GRAINGER-HAYNES, LESLIE, foreign language video producer, translator; b. Taos, N. Mex., May 7, 1951; d. Dick and Margo (Noble) Grainger; m. Kenneth Haynes. Student, U. N. Mex., 1970, U. Colo., 1971-73, Sorbonne U., Paris, 1975, U. Colo., Denver, 1990. Pres. Internat. Translation Svcs., Nashville, Tenn., 1980-85; pres. Internat. Transition Svcs., Denver, 1990—, Taos, N. Mex., 1998—. Producer: (videos) John Denver Special, Country Roads Take Me Home, Japan, 1985, various fgn. lang. mktg. videos. Mem. Am. Translators Assn., Colo. Translators Assn., Colo. Film and Video Assn., Denver C. of C. (ambassador). Avocations: cooking, langs.

GRAMER, ROD EUGENE, journalist; b. Boise, Feb. 26, 1953; s. Harold [illegible] and Virginia Ruth (Greenwood) G.; m. Julie Ann Simis, June 25, 1977; children: Jennifer Ann Helen, Robert Thomas Simis. BA in History and Jouralism, U. Idaho, 1975. Reporter The Idaho Statesman, Boise, 1975-81, city editor, 1981-83, polit. editor, 1983-86, editorial page editor, 1986-88;

news dir. Sta. KTVB-TV, Boise, 1988—. Co-author: Fighting The Odds: TheLife of Sevador Frank Church, 1994. Chmn. Boise Com. on Fgn. Rels., 1986-87; bd. dirs. Easter Seal of Idaho, Boise, 1986, Discovery Ctr. of Idaho, Boise, 1989—, Red Cross of Idaho, 1990—. Recipient numerous journalism awards. Mem. Idaho Press Club (pres. 1978, 81, bd. dirs. 1978-83), Idaho Associated Press Broadcast Assn. (pres.), Radio TV New Dirs. Assn. Avocations: fishing, hiking, reading, gardening, golf. Office: Sta KTVB-TV 5407 Fairview Ave Boise ID 83706-1162

GRAMES-LYRA, JUDITH ELLEN, building engineering inspector, artist, educator; b. Inglewood, Calif., Feb. 7, 1938; d. Glover Victor and Dorothy Margaret (Burton-Bellingham) Hendrickson; children: Nansea Ellen Ryan, Amber Jeanne Shelley-Harris, Carolyn Angel Longmire, Susan Elaine Gomez, Robert Derek Shallenberger; m. Jon Robert Lyra, Feb. 14, 1997. Cert in journalism, Newspaper Inst. Am., N.Y.C., 1960; AA, Santa Barbara City Coll., 1971; BA, U. Calif., Santa Barbara, 1978, cert. in teaching, 1979. Cert. bldg. inspector, plumbing inspector, Calif. Editor, reporter, photographer Goleta Valley Sun Newspaper, Santa Barbara, 1968-71; editor, team asst. Bur. of Ednl. Rsch. Devel., Santa Barbara, 1971; bus. writer, graphics cons. Santa Barbara, 1971-77; art and prodn. dir. Bedell Advt. Selling Improvement Corp., Santa Barbara, 1979-81; secondary sch. tchr. Coalinga (Calif.) Unified Sch. Dist., 1981-83; bldg. inspector aide Santa Barbara County, Lompoc, 1983-88, from bldg. engring. inspector I to III, 1988—. Exhibited in group shows at Foley's Frameworks and Interiors, 1984, 98, Grossman Gallery, 1984, Lompoc Valley Art Assn., 1984— (numerous awards including Best of Show 1985, 1st place 1984, 94, 2d place 1984, 86, 88, 96, 97, 3d place 1987, 89, 97, Hon. Mention 1986, 90, 91, 97), Brushes and Blues Invitational, 1997; featured artist Harvest Arts Festival, 1989, Cypress Gallery, 1994; contbr. poetry to anthologies. Mem. disaster response team Calif. Bldg. Ofcls., 1992—; exec. bd. dirs. Lompoc Mural Soc., 1991—. Delta Kappa Gamma scholar. Mem. NOW, Nat. Abortion Rights Action League), Nat. Mus. of Women in the Arts (charter), Internat. Conf. Bldg. Ofcls., Engrs. and Technicians Assn., Lompoc Valley Art Assn., Toastmasters Internat. (Outstanding Speaker awards 1991-93). Avocations: painting, glass fusing and leading, home improvement activities, writing poetry, bicycling. Office: Santa Barbara County 624 W Foster Rd Santa Maria CA 93455-3623

GRAMMATER, RUDOLF DIMITRI, retired construction executive; b. Detroit, Nov. 29, 1910; s. D.M. and Amelia (Busse) G.; m. Fredricka W. Cook, Aug. 18, 1943, 1 child, Douglas. Student, Pace Inst., 1928-32; LLB, Lincoln U., 1937. Bar: Calif. 1938; CPA, Calif. With Bechtel Corp., San Francisco, 1941-73, treas., v.p., 1955-62, v.p., 1962-71, dir., 1960-73, cons., 1973, v.p., dir. subsidiaries, 1955-71. Mem. ABA, AICPA, Calif. Soc. CPAs, Calif. Bar Assn., Menlo Country Club. Home: The Peninsula Regent # 819 One Baldwin Ave San Mateo CA 94401-3852

GRAMS, THEODORE CARL WILLIAM, librarian, educator; b. Portland, Oreg., Sept. 29, 1918; s. Theodore Albert and Emma Elise (Boehne) G. B.A., U. Wash., 1947; postgrad. Harvard Law Sch., 1947-48; M.S. in L.S., U. So. Calif., 1951. Land title asst. U.S. Bonneville Power Adminstrn., Portland, 1939-45, accountant, 1948-50, librarian, 1951-52; head cataloger, lectr. Portland State U. Library, 1952-59, dir. processing services, 1960-83, prof., 1969-87, prof. emeritus, 1988—. Pres. Portland Area Spl. Librns., 1954-55; panelist on impact new tech. on info. scis. Am. Soc. Info. Sci., 1974, panelist on Libr. Congress svcs., 1976. Author: Allocation of Joint Costs of Multiple-Purpose Projects, 1952, Textbook Classification, 1968; editor: Procs. 4th Am. Soc. Info. Scis. Midyear Meeting, 1975, Special Collections in the Libraries of the Pacific Northwest, 1979, Disaster Preparedness and Recovery, 1983, Technical Services: The Decade Ahead (in Beyond 1984: The Future of Technical Services), 1983. Panelist on community action N.W. Luth. Welfare Assn. Conf., 1969; mem. adv. council Area Agy. on Aging, 1974-75; commr. City-County Commn. Aging, Portland-Multnomah County, 1975-80. Bd. dirs. Hub-Community Action Program, Portland, 1967-70, Project ABLE, 1972-74. HEW Inst. fellow, 1968-69. Mem. ALA, AAUP, Beta Phi Mu. Lutheran. Home: 6653 E Carondelet Dr Tucson AZ 85710-2155

GRAN, ROBERT, engineering company executive; b. 1941. PhD, Calif. Inst. Tech., 1970. Sec. head TRW Sys., Redondo Beach, Calif., 1970-73; sr. rsch. engr., divsn. mgr. Flow Rsch. Inc., L.A., 1973-76; chief sci. Dynamics Tech., Inc., Torrance, Calif., 1976—. Office: Dynamics Tech Inc 21311 Hawthorne Blvd Ste300 Torrance CA 90503-5610*

GRANDY, JAY FRANKLIN, fruit processing executive; b. Murray, Ky., July 21, 1939; s. Rodney Leon and Marion Elizabeth (Birchall) G.; m. Jane Ann Howard, June 26, 1965; children—Joanna, Sharon. B.S. in Physics, Auburn U., 1961; M.B.A., Siena Coll., 1969. With Gen. Electric, 1961-77; mktg. mgr. FMC, Cedar Rapids, Iowa, 1977-81, gen. mgr., Fresno, Calif., 1981-82; pres. Snokist Growers, Yakima, Wash., 1984-95; gen. mgr. Seneca Foods Corp., Prosser, Wash., 1996-98; mgr. Washington-Oreg. Canning Pear Assn., 1998—. Served to 1st lt. U.S. Army, 1962-64. Home: 4203 Fellows Dr Yakima WA 98908-2266

GRANGER, CLIVE WILLIAM JOHN, economist, educator; b. Swansea, Wales, Sept. 4, 1934; came to U.S., 1974.; s. Edward John and Evelyn Agnes (Hessey) G.; m. Patricia Anne Loveland, May 14, 1960; children: Mark, Claire. BA, U. Nottingham, Eng., 1955; PhD in Stats., U. Nottingham, 1959, DSc, 1992; DSc (hon.), Carlos III, Madrid, 1997; D. Econ. (hon.), Stockholm Sch. Econs., 1998. Lectr. in maths. U. Nottingham, 1956-64; prof. stats., 1964-74; prof. econs. U. Calif., San Diego, 1976—; chancellor's assoc. chair, 1994—. Author: Forecasting Stock Markets, 1970; editor: Commodity Markets, 1973. Fellow Harkness Fund, 1959-60, Econometric Soc., 1973, Guggenheim Found., 1988. Fellow Am. Acad. Arts and Scis, Royal Statis. Soc.; mem. Am. Econ. Soc., Am. Statis. Assn. (bd. dirs. 1985-87). Avocations: hiking, swimming, travel, reading. Office: U Calif San Diego Econs Dept D-008 La Jolla CA 92093

GRANLUND, THOMAS ARTHUR, engineering executive, consultant; b. Spokane, Wash., Mar. 1, 1951; s. William Arthur and Louise (Urie) G.; m. Jean MacRae Melvin, May 25, 1974 (div. Feb. 1991). BS, Wash. State U., 1973, BA, 1973; MBA, Gonzaga U., 1982. Engring. adminstr. Lockheed Aeronautical Systems Co., Burbank, Calif., 1978-91; mgmt. cons., 1991—. Co-author: (screenplay) Identities, 1988, Flash, 1989. 1st lt. USAF, 1973-78. Mem. Wash. State U. Alumni Assn. Avocations: skiing, golf, tennis. Home: 20924 Ben Ct Santa Clarita CA 91350-1418

GRANQUIST, OSKAR ADAM, sales professional; b. Sacramento, Oct. 21, 1962; s. Ronald O. and Laurel (Whitman) G.; divorced; 1 child, Emma. BS in Criminal Sci., San Diego State U., 1989; JD, Western State U. Internat. sales mgr. Hoke Inc., Latin Am., 1995-98, SSP Corp., 1997—; cons. Petroleos Mexicanos, Mexico City, 1996-98; advisor/analyst SSP/GIH, Latin Am., 1996—. Mem. Long Beach (Calif.) Police Assn., 1996—. With USAF, 1983-86. Recipient Energy Conservation award Dept. of Energy, 1997. Fellow Instrumentation Soc. Am.; mem. SAG, Aircraft Owners and Pilots Assn. (pilot), U.S. Naval Inst., U.S. Propeller Club (sec./v.p. 1996—). Home: # 1012 12190 Cuyamaca College Dr E El Cajon CA 92019

GRANT, EARL E., minister, educator; b. San Diego, Mar. 12, 1931; s. Earl and Ora Maude (Bolding) G.; m. Marilyn Jane Masters, July 3, 1953; children: Keving, Kim, Holly, Christopher, Sarajane, Ian. BA, Biola U., 1965; MA, Wheaton Grad. Sch., 1972, postgrad., 1972-73; postgrad., U. Chgo., 1972-73, Biola U., 1973-74; MDiv, Fuller Theol. Sem., 1977, DMin, 1978, ThM, 1982, PhD, 1986. Assoc. pastor Village Bible Ch., Garden Grove, Calif., 1964-65; sr. pastor Naperville (Ill.) Free Ch., 1973-74, Village Ch., Burbank, Calif., 1977-83; English pastor Phila. Presbyn. Ch., 1993-96, Sam Sung Presbyn. Ch., 1996—; dir. D of Ministry program, assoc. dean Haggard Grad. Sch. Theology Azusa Pacific U., 1994—, chmn. dept. ministry, 1983-96; dir. Asian Theol. Studies Korea and Asian Ctr., L.A., 1983—; intern pastor Emmanuel Faith Cmty. Ch., Escondido, Calif., 1961-64; missionary 1965-71; lectr. Old Testament Wheaton Grad. Sch., 1978-79; adj. prof. Zwemer Inst., William Crey Internat. U., 1979-83, Biola U., 1983-84, Sch. World Mission Fuller Theol. Sem., 1989—; dir. urban studies, The Urban Ctr., 1983-93. With USN, 1950-63. Contbr. articles to profl. jours. Avocations: fishing, gardening. Home: 20133 Rancherias Rd Apple Valley CA 92307-5219 Office: Azusa Pacific U Haggard Grad Sch Theology 721 E Acosta Ave Azusa CA 91702

GRANT, JOHN CARRINGTON, advertising executive; b. St. Louis, Feb. 2, 1937; s. George Nelson Whitfield and Mary Frances (Tissier) G.; m. Judith Ann Thompson, Oct. 20, 1962; children: Christopher, Susan. Student Westminister Coll., 1960; BS, Washington U., St. Louis, 1969. Account mgr. Darcy, McManus & Masius, St. Louis, N.Y.C. and San Francisco, 1960-68; with Gardner Advt., St. Louis, 1963-66, McCann-Erickson, Seattle, 1974-75; stockbroker Dean Witter, San Francisco, 1968-74; with Tracy-Locke/BBDO, 1975-80; pres. Grant Pollack Advt., Denver, 1980-85; v.p. Brock & Assocs., Denver, 1985-86; dir. Univ. rels. U. Denver, 1987-89; pres. Grant & Assocs., 1989—; pres. CEO The Advertising Consortium, 1989—; mem. faculty Met. State Coll., Denver, 1981-82. Mem. Denver Advt. Fedn. Clubs: Denver Athletic, Oxford.

GRANT, KENNETH RICHARD, technologist; b. Monterey, Calif., Feb. 21, 1962; s. Lawerence Joseph and Sandra Love (Smith) G.; m. Virginia Lovell Ryan, Aug. 16, 1986; children: Katharine, Diana. SB, MIT, 1984. Rsch. assoc. MIT, Cambridge, Mass., 1984-86; sr. tech. staff mem. Oracle Corp., Redwood Shores, Calif., 1987-93; product mgr., co-founder TenFold Corp., San Francisco, 1993-94; cons. engr. Migration Software, San Jose, Calif., 1995; prin. architect Eloquent, Inc., San Mateo, Calif., 1995—. Contbr. numerous articles to profl. jours., chpts. to books. Sunday sch. tchr. Ch. of the Epiphany, San Carlos, Calif., 1997-98. Episcopalian. Avocations: music, adventure travel. E-mail: kgrant@alum.mit.edu. Office: Eloquent Inc 2000 Alameda De Las Pulgas San Mateo CA 94403-1269

GRANT, LAURIE LOUISE, physician assistant, health educator, consultant, biofeedback and neurofeedback therapist; b. York, Nebr., Dec. 24, 1953; d. Donald Eugene and Mae Louise (McDill) G.; m. Rory R. Hein, May 26, 1973 (div. Feb. 1993); children: Misty Louise, Miles Jeffrey. AS, Allegheny Coll., 1980; BA in Health & Natural Sci., La Roche Coll., 1981; MS, U. Colo., 1983; postgrad., Loyola U., New Orleans, 1990—. Physician asst. Vista Grande Family Medicine, Colorado Springs, Colo., 1980-84, Erindale Family Medicine, Colorado Springs, 1984-86, Front Range Family Medicine, Colorado Springs, 1986-88, Exec. Park Med. Arts, Colorado Springs, 1988-94, USAF Acad. Hosp., Colo., 1994—; health educator, pres., founder Profl. Health Providers Health Consulting, Colorado Springs, 1984—; tchr., facilitator Nat. Inst. Inner Healing, Colorado Springs, 1991—; biofeedback/neurofeedback therapist, founder Awareness Assocs. Contbr. articles to profl. jours. Mem. pastoral coun. Corpus Christi Ch., Colorado Springs, 1991—, eucharistic min., 1990—; tchr. religious edn. seminars, Colorado Springs, 1986—; inner healing specialist Nat. Inst. Inner Healing, 1988—; co-founder Single Mothers and Children Found. Fellow Am. Acad. Physician Assts., Am. Coll. Sports Medicine; mem. Colo. Acad. Physician Assts., Nat. Inst. Inner Healing Specialists, Assn. Applied Psychophysiology and Biofeedback, Colo. Assn. Applied Psychophysiology and Biofeedback, Am. Counseling Assocs. Republican. Avocations: karate, teaching, cross-country skiing, scuba diving, snorkeling. Office: USAF Academy Hospital U S A F Academy CO 80840

GRANT, LEWIS O., agricultural products executive, meteorology educator; b. Washington, Pa., Mar. 29, 1923; s. Lewis F. and Rita J. (Jacqmain) G.; m. Patricia Jean Lovelock, July 23, 1949; children: Ann, Nancy, Brenda, Andrew, Laura. BS, U. Tulsa, Okla., 1947; MS, Calif. Inst. Tech., Pasadena, 1948. Meteorological cons. Water Resources Devel. Corp., Pasadena, Calif., 1948-54, Denver, 1948-54; rschr. and rsch. dir. Am. Inst. Aerological Rsch., Denver, 1954-59; asst. prof., assoc. prof., prof. atmospheric sci. dept. Colo. State U., Ft. Collins, 1959-93, emeritus prof., 1993—; pres. Piedmont Farms, Inc., Wellington, Colo., 1975-98, Grant Family Farms, Wellington, 1998—; cons. Colo. Legis., Denver, 1971-73. Contb. to profl. jours. Scout master, com. chmn. Boy Scouts of Am.; pres. Partner Communities, Ft. Collins, Colo., 1988; elder Presbyn. Ch., 1980—; 1st lt. U.S. Field Artillery and USAF, 1943-46. Recipient Vincent J. Schaefer award Weather Modification Assn., 1991. Fellow Am. Meterological Assn.; mem. Nat. Acad. Sci. (sect. chmn. 1975-76, mem. climate com.), Organic Farming Rsch. Found. (bd. mem. 1995—). Republican. Presbyterian. Avocation: organic farm-scale gardening. Office: Grant Family Farms 1020 W County Road 72 Wellington CO 80549-1912 also: Colo State U Dept Atmospheric Sci Fort Collins CO 80523

GRANT, NEWELL M., real estate investment manager; b. Denver, Nov. 2, 1941; s. Edwin Hendrie and Mary Belle (McIntyre) G.; m. Judith G. Wilson, June 19, 1971; children: Margaret, James, Newell, Caroline. BA, Dartmouth Coll., 1964; postgrad, U. Pa., 1967-68. Assoc. Kidder Peabody Realty, N.Y.C., 1969-74; ptnr. Borden, Danielson & Grant, Denver, 1975; cons. N.M. Grant & Co., Denver, 1976-78; ptnr. Grant Mgmt. Co., Denver, 1978—; gen. ptnr. Grant Properties, Denver, 1977-93; chmn. bd. Colo. Nat. Bank Southwest, Littleton, Colo., 1983-89, pres. bd. trustees, 1990-91, pres. Denver Botanical Garden Endowment Inc., 1991—. Trustee vol. for outdoor Colo., 1993—. Pres. bd. trustees Denver Bot. Gardens, 1976—; active Gov.'s Task Force for Efficiency and Economy in Colo. State Govt., Denver, 1976. Served to 1st lt. U.S. Army, 1965-66. Mem. Urban Land Inst. (assoc.). Democrat. Episcopalian. Clubs: Denver; Garden of the Gods (Colo. Springs). Avocations: hunting, gardening, reading. Home: 1325 Cherryville Rd Littleton CO 80121-1221

GRANT, RICHARD EARL, medical and legal consultant; b. Spokane, Wash., Aug. 27, 1935; s. Conrad Morrison and Sylva Celeste (Sims) G.; m. Susan Kimberly Hawkins, Mar. 17, 1979; children: Paaqua A., Camber Do'otsie O. BSc cum laude, U. Wash., 1961; MEd, Whitworth Coll., 1974; PhD, Wash. State U., 1980. Cert. ins. rehab. specialist; cert. case mgr. Supr. nursing Providence Hosp., Seattle, 1970-72; asst. prof. nursing Wash. State U., Spokane, 1972-78; dir. nursing Winslow (Ariz.) Meml. Hosp., 1978-79; adminstr. psychiat. nursing Ariz. State Hosp., Phoenix, 1979-80; asst. prof. Ariz. State U., Tempe, 1980-83; assoc. prof. Linfield Coll., Portland, Oreg., 1983-86, Intercollegiate Ctr. for Nursing Edn., Spokane, 1986-88; sr. med. care coord. Fortis Corp., Spokane, 1988-92; med. svcs. cons. CorVel Corp., Spokane, 1992-94; owner Richard Grant & Assoc., Spokane, 1995-99; med./voc. case mgr. Genex Svcs., Seattle, 1999—; cons. Ariz. State Hosp., 1980-82, Pres.'s Commn., Washington, 1981-83, U. No. Colo., Greely, 1985-86; area med. svcs. cons., 1992—. Author: The God-Man-God Book, 1976, Publications of the Membership (Conaa), 1983, 3d rev. edit., 1985, 4th rev. edit., 1988, Predetermined Careplan Handbook-Nursing, 1988, Duhikya: The Hopi Healer, 1996; contbr. articles to profl. jours. Judge Student Space Shuttle Project, Portland, 1983, N.W. Sci. Expo, Portland, 1983. With U.S. Army, 1953-56. Grantee NIMH, U. Wash., 1961; named one of top Hopi Scholars, Hopi Tribe, Second Mesa, Ariz., 1981. Mem. AAAS, Nat. League for Nursing, Wash. League for Nursing (v.p. 1988-90), Coun. on Nursing and Anthropology (editor 1982-90), N.Y. Acad. Scis., Case Mgmt. Soc. Am., Sigma Theta Tau. Avocations: painting, scuba diving.

GRANT, ROBERT NOEL, lawyer; b. Cairo, Ill., Dec. 23, 1945; m. Joan D'Angelo, June 29, 1968; children: Tyler, Ryan. BA, Princeton Univ., 1967; JD, MBA, Stanford Univ., 1972. Bar: Calif. Assoc. McCutchen, Doyle Brown & Enersen, San Francisco, 1972-76, Gray Cary Ware & Freidenrich, Palo Alto, Calif., 1976-80; founding pntr. Grant & Gordon, Palo Alto, Calif., 1995—. Author: Untangling Some of the Wrights of Bedford County, Virginia, 1977, The Robert Noel Grant Family Tree, 1986, Identifying the Wrights in the Goochland County, Virginia Tithe Lists, 1993. Nat. Bd. Govs. Am. Red Cross, 1995—, bd. dirs., 1985-92, 93—, chpt. chmn., 1990-92, adv. coun. mem., 1992-93, exec. com. mem., 1985-92; bd. visitors Stanford Univ. Law Sch., 1987-93, planned adv. coun. Stanford Univ., 1993—, bus. sch. fund vol., 1976—, planned adv. com. Princeton Univ., 1996—, planned giving coun. El Camino Hosp., 1993, bd. dirs. Altos Found., 1988—, profl. adv. coun. Peninsula Cmty. Found., 1997—; mem. City of Palo Alto Dream Team. Recipient Lifetime Achievement award Palo Alto Red Cross, 1998. Mem. ABA, Santa Clara County Bar Assn., San Mateo County Bar Assn., Palo ALto Bar Assn., Am. Coll. Trust & Estate Coun. Office: Grant & Gordon 525 University Ave Ste 1325 Palo Alto CA 94301-1913

GRANT, THOMAS ARTHUR, television journalist; b. Toasket, Wash., Sept. 19, 1953; s. Joseph Charles and Lorraine (Wiswell) G.; m. Mary Ann Connery, Sept. 1, 1941; children: Sean Connery, Patrick Connery, Thomas Connery. BA in English, Wash. State U., 1975; MS in Journalism, Columbia U., 1986. Vol. VISTA, Mpls., 1978-79; reporter Seaside (Oreg.) Signal, 1979-80; editor News-Guard, Lincoln City, Oreg., 1980-82, Silverton (Oreg.) Appeal-Tribune, 1982-85; reporter KCAU TV, Sioux City, Iowa, 1986-87; reporter/anchor WCAX TV, Burlington, Vt., 1987-91; reporter KREM TV, Spokane, Wash., 1991-97, KXLY-TV, Spokane, 1998—. Recipient Feature Reporting prize Nat. Newspaper Assn., 1984, Oscars In Agrl., U. Ill., 1988, Pub. Svc. award Soc. Profl. Journalists, 1992, George Polk award Long Island U., N.Y.C., 1995, Edward R. Murrow award RTNDA, 1997, Mike Wallace Fellow for Investigative Reporting U. Mich. Journalism Fellows, 1997-98. Avocations: jogging, biking, triathalons. Office: KXLY-TV 500 W Boone Ave Spokane WA 99201-2497

GRANT, WILLIAM WEST, III, banker; b. N.Y.C., May 9, 1932; s. William West and Katherine O'Connor (Neelands) G.; m. Rhondda Lowery, Dec. 3, 1955. BA, Yale U., 1954; postgrad., NYU Grad. Sch. Bus., 1958, Columbia U. Grad. Sch. Bus., 1968, Harvard U. Grad. Sch. Bus., 1971. With Bankers Trust Co., N.Y.C., 1954-58; br. credit adminstr. Bankers Trust Co., 1957-58; with Colo. Nat. Bank, Denver, 1958-93; pres. Colo. Nat. Bank, 1975-86, chmn. bd., 1986-93; chmn. bd. Colo. Capital Advisors, 1989-94; bd. dirs. Barrett Resources Corp. Trustee Denver Mus. Natural History, Gates Found. Denver, Midwest Rsch. Inst., Kansas City, Episc. Ch. Found., Nat. Trust for Hist. Preservation; bd. dirs. Mountain State Employers Coun., World Trade Ctr. Mem. Colo. Bankers Assn., Metro. Denver C. of C. (dir. Internat. Gateway Com.). Episcopalian. Clubs: Denver Country, Denver. Home: 545 Race St Denver CO 80206-4122 Office: KRMA-TV 1089 Bannock St Denver CO 80204-4066

GRASS, GEORGE MITCHELL, IV, pharmaceutical executive; b. Bryn Mawr, Pa., Dec. 31, 1957; s. George Mitchell III and Irma Lucy (Schaffer) G. PharmD, U. Nebr., Omaha, 1980; PhD, U. Wis., 1985. Lic. pharmacist. Staff rschr. Syntex Rsch., Palo Alto, Calif., 1985-91; pres. Precision Instrument Design, Tahoe City, Calif., 1987-96, NaviCyte Inc., San Diego, 1996—; cons. Costar Corp., Cambridge, Mass., 1990-96, various pharm. cos., 1991—; co-founder Raptor Graphics, Snohomish, Wash. Contbr. numerous articles to profl. jours. Recipient Ebert prize Jour. Pharm. Sci., 1989. Mem. AAAS, Am. Assn. Pharm. Scientists, Sigma Xi. Avocations: skiing, bicycling, music.

GRAUBART, JEFFREY LOWELL, entertainment lawyer; b. Chgo., Aug. 18, 1940; s. John H. and Florence R. G.; m. Mary Linda Carey, June 24, 1973; children: Joshua Gordon, Noah Carey. BS in Fin., U. Ill., 1962; JD, Northwestern U., Chgo., 1965. Bar: Ill. 1965, Calif. 1968, N.Y. 1980. Assoc. Curtis Friedman & Marks, Chgo., 1965-67, Capitol Records, Inc., Los Angeles, 1968-70; prin. Hadfield, Jorgensen, Graubart & Becker, San Francisco, 1970-81; counsel Frankfurt, Garbus, Klein & Selz, P.C., N.Y., 1981-85; prin. Strote, Graubart & Ashley, P.C., Beverly Hills, Calif. and N.Y., 1986-87; counsel Cohen & Luckenbacher, L.A., 1988-90, Engel & Engel, L.A., 1991-92; pvt. practice L.A., 1992—; sec. Paramount Growers, Inc., Delano, Calif., 1968-70; v.p., dir. London Internat. Artists, Ltd., Los Angeles, 1969-70, Jazz Images, Inc., N.Y.C., 1983-86; adj. prof. NYU, 1982-85; lectr. Columbia U. Sch. Law, N.Y.C., 1982-85, UCLA, 1988—, U. So. Calif., 1988—. Contbr. articles to profl. jours. and mags. Counsel San Francisco Jazz Found., 1980-81. Recipient Deems Taylor award ASCAP, 1981. Mem. NARAS (San Francisco chtp. legal counsel 1973-93, gov. 1973-85, gov. and legal counsel N.Y. chpt. 1982-85, gov. L.A. chpt. 1988-92), Calif. Copyright Conf. (dir. 1995—), Internat. Fedn. Festival Orgns. (dir. 1994—), Inter-Pacific Bar Assn., Beverly Hills Bar Assn. (chair internat. law sect. 1995—), Internat. Radio and TV Soc., Country Music Assn., Assn. of the Bar of the City of N.Y., Soc. Preservation of Film Music (trustee 1989—), v.p. 1991-94). Lodges: B'nai Brith (N.Y. and Los Angeles); Golden Gate (San Francisco) (v.p. 1974-75), Entertainment Industry Unit L.A. (founder, trustee 1988—). Office: 2029 Century Park E Ste 2700 Los Angeles CA 90067-3013*

GRAUER, RONALD GENE, artist; b. St. Joseph, Mo., Nov. 2, 1927; s. Lisle Siegmond Grauer and Erma Floy (Anderson) Gilbert; m. LeMoyne W. Schaufel, June 2, 1952 (div. 1983); 1 child, Mark Elliot; m. Carole Anne Ball Minou, Dec. 26, 1984 (div. 1987). Student, Washburn M.U., 1946-47, Kansas City Art Inst., 1947-49, Ringling Sch. Art, 1949-50, Art Ctr. Coll., 1952-54, Chounard Art Inst., 1955, UCLA, 1966. Ptnr., illustrator Advt. Illustrators, Pasadena, Calif., 1954-60; owner, art dir. Ron Grauer Studio, Pasadena, Calif., 1960-65; L.A., 1965-70; painter Ron Grauer Studio, Carmel, Calif., 1970-71, Ben Lomond, Calif., 1984—; owner, painter Ron Grauer Gallery, Carmel, Calif., 1971-77; ptnr., creative dir. Grauer & Fingerote Advt., Monterey, Calif., 1977-80; pres., CEO, creative dir. G & F/F & G, Inc., Monterey, Calif., 1980-84. One-person shows include Carmel Art Assn., Christopher Bell Gallery, Monterey, numerous others; exhibited in group shows at Monterey County Fair, 1971-74 (1st pl. award (2), 2d pl. award, 3d pl. award), Santa Cruz Art League, 1979 (2d pl. award) Pacific Grove Mus., 1975 (2d pl. award), Hist. Com. for Salinas (Calif.) Conf. Ctr., 1976; represented in collections in U.S. and Europe. Chmn. Monterey County Fair Art Exhibit, 1975. Mem. Carmel Art Assn. (bd. dirs. 1983-85), Oil Painters Am., Quiet Birdmen. Avocations: aviation, music, reading, physics, science fiction. Studio: Ron Grauer Studio PO Box 153 Ben Lomond CA 95005-0153

GRAU-TWENA, PAMELA, artist, writer; b. Santa Monica, Calif., Feb. 15, 1955; d. Mel and Mary Grau; m. Yacov Twena, July 16, 1981; children: Satya, Jonathan, Claire. BA, Mills Coll., 1977; postgrad., Art Ctr. Coll. Design, 1979. Author: Memories and Tradition, 1992, The Sephadic Table, 1998, A Woman's Painted Journey, 1998; sculpture Laguna Beach Art Mus., 1998. Office: 3822 Campus Dr Ste 111 Newport Beach CA 92660-2636

GRAVES, EARL WILLIAM, JR., journalist; b. Kodiak, Alaska, June 30, 1950; s. Earl William Graves, Sr. and Lola (Olson) Raab; m. Karin Ann Steichen, July 30, 1972; children: Emma, Mark, Max. BA in English with honors, U. Puget Sound, 1972; MA in English, Western Wash. State U., 1976. Tchr. English Naselle (Wash.) High Sch., 1972-74, Clatskanie (Oreg.) High Sch., 1975-77; police reporter Coeur d'Alene (Idaho) Press, 1978-79, city editor, 1980-82, mng. editor, 1983-84; sr. reporter Bulletin, Bend, Oreg., 1984-86; edn. reporter News and Observer, Raleigh, N.C., 1986-87; state edn. reporter News and Observer/Raleigh Times, 1987-89; edn. reporter The Oregonian, Portland, 1990—. Author: Poisoned Apple, 1995. Recipient Outstanding Svc. award N.C. chpt. Phi Delta Kappa, 1988, Third Prize So. Journalism Feature Reporting award Inst. for So. Studies, 1989, N.C. Sch. Bell award N.C. Assn. Educators, 1989, Benjamin Fine award Nat. Assn. Secondary Sch. Prins., 1989, First Pl. Gen. News Reporting award N.C. Press Assn., 1990, First Pl. Edn. Reporting award Pacific Northwest Excellence in Journalism, Soc. Profl. Journalists, 1991, 92, Media award Assn. Retarded Children Oreg., 1992, Seconad Pl. Spot News Reporting award Best of West, 1992, Second Pl. Best Writing award Oreg. Newspaper Pubs. Assn., 1993, Excellence in Edn. award Oreg. Assn. Supervision and Curriculum Devel., 1993; Nieman fellow Harvard U., 1998-99. Mem. Edn. Writers Assn. (pres., sec., bd. dirs. 1990—, Spl. Citation Nat. Awards for Edn. Reporting 1987, 91, Second Pl. Newspaper Series award 1989, Second Pl. Nat. Awards Edn. Reporting 1989). Democrat. Avocations: gardening, photography, outdoors, running, travel. Office: Oregonian 1320 SW Broadway Portland OR 97201-3499

GRAVES, KAREN LEE, high school counselor; b. Twin Falls, Idaho, Dec. 9, 1948; d. Isaac Mason and Agnes Popplewell; m. Frederick Ray Graves, Apr. 2, 1987. BA, Idaho State U., 1971; MEd, Coll. of Idaho, 1978. Cert. tchr. secondary edn., english 7-12, vocat. home econs. 7-12, pupil pers. svcs. K-12, Idaho. Tchr. Filer (Idaho) Sch. Dist., 1971-74, 76-80, Twin Falls (Idaho) Sch. Dist., 1974-76; counselor Mountain Home (Idaho) Sch. Dist., 1980—, dept. chairperson, dir.; bldg. coord. student assistance program, parent newsletter. Mem. probation and parole screening com. Mountain Home; sponsor mem. Rocky Mountain Elk Found.; support person Donor Network. Mem. NEA, ACA, ASCD, Am. Sch. Counseling Assn., Idaho Counseling Assn., Idaho Sch. Counseling Assn., Idaho Edn. Assn., Idaho Affiliation Supervision and Curriculum Devel. Avocations: painting ceramics, crafting, reading, crossword puzzles. Home: 1105 Maple Dr Mountain Home ID 83647-2027 Office: Mountain Home H S 300 S 11th E Mountain Home ID 83647-3263

GRAVES, LENNIE KEITH, animator; b. Bklyn., June 20, 1957; s. Lone and Genevieve (Bowens) G.; m. Shu Hua Lin, Dec. 29, 1993; 1 child, Leondra Lin. BFA, The Sch. of Visual Arts, 1979. Asst. animator DePatie/Freeling Inc., Reseda, Calif., 1979; animator Ralph Bakshi Prodns., Wittareywood, Calif., 1979; asst. animator Nepenthe Prodns., San Francisco, 1981-82; animator Filmation, Woodland Hills, Calif., 1984-86; head animator Bajus-Jones Co., Edina, Minn., 1987-88; flower planet head animator Bob Rogers & Co., Burbank, Calif., 1988-89; animator Walt Disney, Glendale, Calif., 1989-91; directing animator Hyperion Animation Co., Glendale, Calif., 1992-93; supr. animator Hanna-Barbera, Hollywood, Calif., 1993-94; lead animator Turner Feature Animation, Hollywood, 1994-96, Warner Bros. Feature Animation, Glendale, 1996—. Illustrator: How To Draw Flower Planet, 1989; screenwriter (Animaniacs episode) It, 1997. Vol. lectr. on animation L.A. Juvenile Hall, 1997, First A.M.E. Bapt. Ch., L.A., 1997. Mem. AFTRA. Avocations: racquetball, chess.

GRAVES, MELISSA JUNE, elementary school educator; b. Gt. Lakes, Ill., Mar. 7, 1956; d. Robert Eugene and Bettyelou G. BA, Calif. State U., Fresno, 1979, Calif. State U., Fresno; postgrad., Fresno Pacific Coll., Chapman Coll. Cert. life elem. Ryan Act teaching credential, Calif., lang. devel. specialist. Elem. tchr. Columbine Elem. Sch., Delano, Calif., 1980-88, St. James Cathedral Sch., Fresno, 1988-89; tchr. Mayfair Elem. Sch., Fresno Unified Sch. Dist., 1989—. Calif. State scholar, 1974-79. Mem. Mu Phi Epsilon (internat. chmn.). Office: Mayfair Elem Sch 3305 E Home Ave Fresno CA 93703-4044

GRAW, LEROY HARRY, purchasing-contract management company executive; b. Dupree, S.Dak., Jan. 10, 1942; s. Harry Fred and Luella (Eichmann) G.; m. Kyong Hee Yuk, Sept. 25, 1969 (div. Feb. 1979); 1 child, Natasha; m. Anat Harari, July 3, 1981; children: Byron, Karen. BS, U.S. Mil. Acad., 1964; M Commerce, U. Richmond, 1974; EdD, U. So. Calif., 1980. Govt. contracting officer worldwide, 1971-88; mgr. govt. contracts Fluor Corp., Dallas, 1988-89; mgr. contracts Superconducting Super Collider, Dallas, 1989-95; dir. contract adminstrn. Los Angeles County MTA, L.A., 1995-96; pres. Internat. Resource Mgmt. Assocs., Upland, Calif., 1996—; ccons., Dallas, 1991-95; adj. prof. U. Dallas, 1990-95, U. Calif., Riverside, 1996—, UCLA, Westwood, 1996—, Keller Grad. Sch., 1997—. Author: Service Purchasing, 1994, Cost/Price Analysis, 1994; editor: Global Purchasing, 1990; contbr. articles to profl. jours. Dist. commr. Boy Scouts Am., Portland, Oreg., 1987, mem. troop com. troop 608, La Crescenta, 1997. Capt. U.S. Army, 1964-70, Vietnam. Recipient dist. award of merit Boy Scouts Am., Honolulu, 1985. Fellow Nat. Contract Mgmt. Assn. (cert., chpt. pres. 1997—); mem. Nat. Assn. Purchasing Mgmt. (cert., nat. officer 1992—). Avocations: skiing, hiking, camping, chess. Home and Office: 1667 N Vallejo Way Upland CA 91784-1934

GRAY, ALFRED ORREN, retired journalism educator, communications specialist; b. Sun Prairie, Wis., Sept. 8, 1914; s. Charles Orren and Amelia Katherine (Schadel) G.; m. Nicolin Jane Plank, Sept. 5, 1947; children—Robin, Richard. B.A., U. Wis.-Madison, 1939, M.A., 1941. Reporter-correspondent-intern U. Wis.-Madison and Medford newspapers, 1937-39; free-lance writer, 1938-41, 51-57; intelligence investigator U.S. Ordnance Dept., Ravenna, Ohio, 1941-42; hist. editor, chief writer U.S. Office Chief Ordnance Service, ETO, Paris and Frankfurt, Germany, 1944-46; asst. prof. journalism Whitworth Coll., Spokane, Wash., 1946-48, assoc. prof., 1948-56, head dept. journalism, adviser student publs., 1946-80, prof., 1956-80, prof. emeritus, 1980—, chmn. div. bus. and communications arts, 1958-66, chmn. div. applied arts, 1978-79; rschr. writer Spokane, 1980—; dir. Whitworth News Bur., 1952-58; prin. researcher, writer 12 hist. and ednl. projects. Author: The History of U.S. Ordnance Service in the European Theater of Operations, 1942-46, Not by Might, 1965, Eight Generations From Gondelsheim: A Genealogical Study, 1980; co-author: Many Lamps, One Light: A Centennial History, 1984; editor: The Synod Story, 1953-55; mem. editl. adv. bd. Whitworth Today mag., 1989-90; contbr. articles to newspapers, mags., jours.; reader Am. Presbyns.: The Jour. of Presbyn. History, 1992-94. Scoutmaster Troop 9, Four Lakes Coun., Boy Scouts Am., Madison, Wis., 1937-41; chmn. Pinewood Addition Archtl. Com., Spokane, 1956—; dir. Inland Empire Publs. Clinic, Spokane, 1959-74; mem. ho. of dels. Greater Spokane Council of Chs., 1968-71; judge Goodwill Worker of Yr. awards Goodwill Industries Spokane County, 1972; vice-moderator Synod Wash.-Alaska, Presbyn. Ch. (U.S.A.), 1966-67; bd. dirs. Presbyn. Hist. Soc., 1984-90, 91-94, exec. com., 1986-90, chmn. hist. sites com., 1986-90; mem. Am. Bd. Mission Heritage Commn. for Sesquicentennial of Whitman Mission, 1986; elder Spokane 1st Presbyn. Ch., 1962—, clk. of session, 1984-86, mem. Inland Empire Presbytery Com. for Bicentennial of Gen. Assembly, 1988-89; mem. com. justice and peacemaking Presbytery of the Inland Northwest, 1988-95; mem. Care and Equipping of Congregations Com., 1995—; Dem. precinct official, Spokane, 1988-92. Served with AUS, 1942-46. Decorated Bronze Star and Army Commendation medals; recipient Printers Ink trophy Advt. Assn. West, 1953, citation Nat. Coun. Coll. Publ. Advisers, 1967, Outstanding Teaching of Journalism award Whitworth Coll. Alumni Assn., 1972; named Disting. Newspaper Adviser in U.S. among colleges and univs., Nat. Coun. Coll. Publ. Advisers, 1979. Mem. Assn. for Edn. in Journalism and Mass Comms., Ea. Wash. Hist. Soc., Coll. Media Advisors (hon.), Ea. Wash. Geneal. Soc., N.Am. Mycol. Assn., U. Wis. Alumni Assn. Half Century Club, Phi Beta Kappa (pres. profl. chpt. 1949-50, 67-68, 70-71), Sigma Delta Chi, Phi Eta Sigma. Democrat. Avocations: genealogy, travel. Home: 304 W Hoerner Ave Spokane WA 99218-2124

GRAY, BARBARA BRONSON, nurse, writer, editor; b. Van Nuys, Calif., June 3, 1955; d. Gerald M. and Jane Marie (Strauss) Bronson; m. Thomas Stephen Gray, Aug. 27, 1977; children: Jonathan Thomas, Katherine Marie. BS, UCLA, 1977, M in Nursing, 1981. RN, Calif. Staff nurse Valley Presbyn. Hosp., Van Nuys, Calif., 1977-80; asst. adminstr. Calif. Med. Ctr., L.A., 1981-84; freelance writer Agoura, 1984—; exec. dir. Nurseweek, 1995-96, editor-in-chief, 1996—; cons. St. John's Hosp. and Health Ctr., Santa Monica, Calif., 1986-90, Los Robles Regional Med. Ctr., Thousand Oaks, Calif., 1993-95; lectr. UCLA Sch. Nursing, 1991-98, clin. prof., 1998—. Author: 120 Years of Medicine in Los Angeles County, 1991; contbr. articles to jours., mags. and newspapers; syndicated by L.A. Times Syndicate. Recipient Outstanding Achievement award Perinatal Network, Santa Clara County, Calif., 1994, named Witer of Yr. Nurseweek, 1991; Kellogg fellow, 1979-81. Mem. Nat. Assn. Sci. Writers, Am. Orgn. Nurse Execs., Assn. Calif. Nurse Leaders (bd. dirs. 1999—), Sigma Theta Tau (Cert. of Appreciation 1994, Internat. Media award 1995). Republican. Episcopalian. Avocations: swimming, tennis, hiking, kayaking.

GRAY, BRUCE, computer and electronics company executive. Pres. Xicor, Milpitas, Calif. Office: Xicor 1511 Buckeye Dr Milpitas CA 95035-7431*

GRAY, CHRIS HABLES, adult education educator, writer; b. Bishop, Calif., Aug. 23, 1953; s. George Edward and Edna Benita (Hables) G.; m. Jane Lovett Wilson, Mar. 3, 1986; children: Corey Alexander Grayson, Zackary Hables Grayson. BA, Stanford U., 1975; PhD in the History of Consciousness, U. Calif. (Santa Cruz), 1991. Cons. various computer firms, Oreg., Calif., 1984-94; tech. asst. U. Calif. (Santa Cruz), 1987-90, lectr., 1989-91; vis. prof. Ore. State U., Corvallis, 1992-95, Musaryk U., Brno, Czech Republic, 1995; assoc. faculty Goddard Coll., Plainfield, Mass., 1994—; assoc. prof. U. Great Falls (Mont.), 1996—; student rep. History Consciousness Bd., U. Calif. (Santa Cruz), 1989-90; mem. History Consciousness Bd. Admissions Com., 1990; panel organizer Soc. Lit. Sci. conf., 1990, Soc. Social Studies Sci. meeting, 1994; chmn. Internet Com., U. Great Falls, 1996-98; mem. faculty devel. com., U. Great Falls, 1997-98, Accreditation Self-Study Com., U. Great Falls, 1997-98. Author: Power-Learning: Developing Effective Study Skills, 1992, Postmodern War: The New Politics of Conflict, 1997; editor: The Cyborg Handbook, 1995, Technohistory: Using the History of American Technology in Interdisciplinary Research, 1996; contbr. articles to profl. jours; spkr. numerous colls. and univs. Active mem. Columbae, Stanford, Calif., 1977-83; organizer Abalone Alliance, Calif., 1981-90; del. 5th Internat. Student Pugwash Conf., 1987, soccer coach Ayso, Mini-Bolts, Corvallis, Great Falls, 1994—; treas., bd. dirs. Guardians ad Litem Cascade County, Mont., 1997-99. Recipient U. Calif. Regents fellow, 1986, 91, Smithsonian Instn. summer fellow, Washington, 1990, NEH summer fellow, Cleve., 1992, Ore. State U. fellow, 1992-94, NASA History fellow, Washington, 1993-94, Eisenhower Found. fellow, Czech Republic, 1995, Silicon Valley Rsch. Group grantee, 1986, IGCC Rsch. grantee, 1987-88. Mem. Am. Studies Assn., Computer Profls. Social Responsibility, Assn. Advancement Computing Edn., Soc. History Tech., History Sci. Tech., Soc. Social Studies Sci., Cultural Studies Sci. Tech. Rsch. Group, Circus Numicus. Avocations: gardening, writing, soccer. E-mail: cgray@ugf.edu. Home: 606 5th Ave N Great Falls MT 59401-2334 Office: University of Great Falls 1301 20th St S Great Falls MT 59405-4934

GRAY, GAVIN CAMPBELL, II, computer information engineer, computer consultant; b. Levittown, N.Y., Sept. 16, 1948; s. Gavin Campbell Gray and Pauline Louise (Bauerschmidt) Gowen; m. Catherine Ann West, Aug. 23, 1969; children: Jeffrey William, Tamara Pauline. Student, U. Wis., Milw., 1966-71. Programmer, analyst Equitable Variable Life Ins., Farmingdale, N.Y., 1975-77; analyst, programmer Atty.'s Title Svcs., Orlando, Fla., 1977-78; systems analyst Cert. Grocers, Ocala, Fla., 1978-80; supr. R & D, Clay Electric Coop., Keystone Heights, Fla., 1980-86; mgr. info. svcs. Coldwell Banker Relocation Svcs., Mission Viejo, Calif., 1986-96; knowledge mgr. Oracle Corp., San Diego, 1996—; mem. Guide Internat. Bus. Rules Stds. Project, 1994—, Am. Nat. Stds. Inst. Accredited Stds. Com. X12, 1994-96, Asymetrix Corp. Adv. Coun. Author: IBM GIS Usage for IMS/DLI, 1979; developer software Map-Paint for CICS, methodology Path Evaluation Method (PEM), TRANS-FLOW Programming, Tier Diagramming Method; contbr. articles to profl. jours. Mem. IEEE, Project Mgmt. Inst., Assn. Computing Machinery, Data Adminstrn. Mgmt. Assn. Internat., Data Warehousing Inst., Software Program Mgrs. Network, Math. Assn. Am., Internat. Platform Assn., IEEE Computer Soc., IEEE Engring. Mgmt. Soc., N.Y. Acad. Scis., Am. Mus. Natural History, Zool. Soc. San Diego, Am. Mensa Ltd., Nat. Eagle Scout Assn., Intertel. Office: Oracle Corp 12230 El Camino Real San Diego CA 92130-2090

GRAY, GEORGE EDWARD, transportation planner, engineer, consultant; b. Fullerton, Calif., Oct. 3, 1927; s. Sabin Verbal and Mary Thelma (Hammett) G.; m. Edna Benita Hables, Dec. 30, 1951; children: Kenneth Edward, Chris Hables, Dana George. BSCE, Stanford U., 1951; MA in Pub. Adminstrn., Calif. State U., San Diego, 1972; MSCE, U. Calif., Davis, 1975. Registered profl. engr., Calif. Hwy. engr. Calif. Dept. Transp., Bishop, 1951-54, San Bernardino, 1954-58; hwys. engr. Capitol Engring., Vietnam, 1958-60; engr., planner Calif. Dept. Transp., San Diego, 1960-70; divsn. chief Calif. Dept. Transp., Sacramento, 1970-81; advisor U.S. Dept. Transp., Riyadh, Saudi Arabia, 1981-85; adminstr. Calif. Dept. Transp., San Francisco, 1985-91, San Diego, 1991-95; ind. transp. cons. San Diego, 1995—. Co-editor: (textbook) Public Transportation, 1979, 2nd edit., 1989; contbr. over 50 articles and reports to profl. publs. With USAF, 1945-47, Japan. Recipient Purcell award Calif. Transp. Found., Sacramento, 1992. Fellow ASCE; mem. Am. Pub. Works Assn., Nature Conservancy, Native Plant Soc. Avocations: environment, gardening, genealogy. Fax: 619-538-4929. E-mail: gegray@aol.com.

GRAY, JAN CHARLES, lawyer, business owner; b. Des Moines, June 15, 1947; s. Charles Donald and Mary C. Gray; 1 child, Charles Jan. BA in Econs., U. Calif., Berkeley, 1969; MBA, Pepperdine U., 1986; JD, Harvard U., 1972. Bar: Calif. 1972, D.C. 1974, Wyo. 1992. Law clk. Kindel & Anderson, L.A., 1971-72; assoc. Halstead, Baker & Sterling, L.A., 1972-75; sr. v.p., gen. counsel and sec. Ralphs Grocery Co., L.A., 1975-97; pres. Am. Presidents Resorts, Custer, S.D., Casper/Glenrock, Wyo., 1983—; owner Big Bear (Calif.) Cabins-Lakeside, 1988—; pres. Mt. Rushmore Broadcasting, Inc., 1991—; owner Sta. KGOS/KERM, Torrington, Wyo., 1993—, Sta. KRAL/KIQZ, Rawlins, Wyo., 1993—, Sta. KZMX, Hot Springs, S.D., 1993—, Sta. KFCR, Custer, S.D., 1992—, Sta. KQLT-FM, Casper, Wyo., 1994—, Sta. KASS-FM, Casper, 1995—, Sta. KVOC-AM, Casper, 1997—, KAWK-FM, Rapid City, S.D., 1997—; judge pro tem L.A. Mcpl. Ct., 1977-85; instr. bus. UCLA, 1976-85, Pepperdine MBA Program, 1983-85; arbitrator Am. Arbitration Assn., 1977—; media spokesman So. Calif. Grocers Assn., 1979-90, Calif. Grocers Assn., 1979-97, Calif. Retailers Assn., 1979-97; real estate broker, L.A., 1973—. Contbg. author: Life or Death, Who Controls?, 1976; contbr. articles to profl. jours. Trustee South Bay U. Coll. Law, 1978-79; mem. bd. visitors Southwestern U. Sch. Law, 1983—; mem. L.A. County Pvt. Industry Coun., 1982—, exec. com. 1984-88, chmn. econ. devel. task force, 1986-89, chmn. mktg. com. 1991-93; mem. L.A. County Martin Luther King, Jr. Gen. Hosp. Authority, 1984—; mem. L.A. County Aviation Commn, 1986-92, chmn., 1990-91; L.A. Police Crime Prevention Adv. Coun., 1986—; Angelus Plaza Adv. Bd., 1983-85; bd. dirs. RecyCAL of So. Calif., 1983-89; trustee Santa Monica Hosp. Found., 1986-91, adv. bd., 1991—; mem. L.A. County Dem. Cen. Com., 1980-90, L.A. City Employees' Retirement System Comsn., 1993—; del. Dem. Nat. Conv., 1980. Recipient So. Calif. Grocers Assn. award for outstanding contbns. to food industry, 1982, appreciation award for No on 11 Campaign, Calif./Nev. Soft Drink Assn., 1983; Tyler Price Meml. award Mex.-Am. Grocers Assn., 1995. Mem. ABA, Calif. Bar Assn., L.A. County Bar Assn. (exec. com. corp. law depts. sect. 1974-76, 79—, chmn. 1989-90, exec. com. barristers sect. 1974-75, 79-81, trustee 1991-93, jud. evaluation com. 1993—, nominating com. 1994), San Fernando Valley Bar Assn. (chmn. real property sect. 1975-77, L.A. Pub. Affairs Officers Assn., L.A. World Affairs Coun., Calif. Retailers Assn. (supermarket com.), Food Mktg. Inst. (govt. rels. com. 1977-97, benefits coun. 1993-97, chmn. lawyers and economists 1993-95), So. Calif. Bus. Assn. (bd. dirs. 1981—, mem. exec. com. 1982—, sec. 1986-91, chair 1991—), Town Hall L.A., U. Calif. Alumni Assn., Ephebian Soc. L.A., Harvard Club of So. Calif., Phi Beta Kappa. Home: 2793 Creston Dr Los Angeles CA 90068-2209 Office: PO Box 2515 Casper WY 82602-2515

GRAY, KARLA MARIE, state supreme court justice. BA, Western Mich. U., MA in African History; JD, U. Calif., San Francisco, 1976. Bar: Mont. 1976, Calif. 1977. Law clk. to Hon. W. D. Murray U.S. Dist. Ct., 1976-77; staff atty. Atlantic Richfield Co., 1977-81; pvt. practice law Butte, Mont., 1981-84; staff atty., legis. lobbyist Mont. Power Co., Butte, 1984-91; justice Supreme Ct. Mont., Helena, 1991—. Mem. Mont. Supreme Ct. Gender Fairness Task Force. Fellow Am. Bar Found., Am. Judicature Soc., Internat. Women's Forum; mem. State Bar Mont., Silver Bow County Bar Assn. (past pres.), Nat. Assn. Women Judges. Avocations: travel, reading, piano, family genealogy, cross-country sking. Office: Supreme Ct Mont Justice Bldg 215 N Sanders St Helena MT 59620*

GRAY, KATHERINE, marriage and family counselor and support therapist; b. Los Angeles, July 6, 1941; d. Edward David and Marjorie Ross; m. Daniel C. Gray, Feb. 5, 1965; children: Michael, Lisa. BA, Calif. State U., Sacramento, 1983, MS in Ednl. Cons. and Counseling, 1987, MS in Sch. Counseling. Instr. Shasta Coll., Redding, Calif., 1965-69; owner Water Ojai Valley Chapel, Ojai, Calif., 1971-77, Lipp & Sullivan, Marysville, Calif., 1977—; instr. Yuba Coll., 1988—; pres. Interagy. Council, 1988—; cons. and organizer various community outreach programs in edn. Contbr. articles to profl. jours. and newspapers. County coordinator, bd. dirs. Am. Cancer Soc., Marysville, 1980—; mem. exec. com., bd. dirs., com. chairperson Gateway Projects, Yuba City, Calif., 1980—; bd. dirs. Mercy Guild, Yuba City, 1980—, Easter Seals; past bd. dirs., com. chairperson Campfire Inc., Yuba City and Morro Bay, Calif., 1979-80; past pres. Ojai Valley-Oxnard Symphony Orch. Assn., Ventura County, Calif., 1975; Sacramento focus program coordinator 4-H, Yuba and Sutter Counties, 1985—; exec. officer, bd. dirs. Gateway Projects, 1985-87; pres. Interagy. Council of Yuba & Sutter Counties, 1988—. Mem. Calif. Funeral Dirs. Assn. (mem. legis. bd. com., edn., ethics and mem. bd. com.), Calif. Assn. for Counseling and Devel., Sacramento Area Gifted Assn., Children's Home Soc. (chpt. bd. sec.). Lodges: Soroptimists (past bd. dirs.), Rainbow for Girls (pres., bd. dirs. 1985-87). Avocations: music, art, travel, historical studies. Home: PO Box 611 Yuba City CA 95992-0611 Office: PO Box 148 629 D St Marysville CA 95901-5527

GRAY, LONNA IRENE, indemnity fund executive; b. Forsyth, Mont., Nov. 10, 1944; d. John Jr. and Inga (Hill) Gray; m. James Dodd, Nov. 26, 1964 (div. Oct. 1988); children: Sheri Dodd, James Dodd, Thaddeus Dodd. BS, Mont. State U., 1967; MPA, Boise State U., 1997. Workers compensation claims monitor Idaho State Ins. Fund, Boise, 1990-92; workers compensation claims examiner Indsl. Spl. Indemnity Fund, Boise, 1992-94, [illegible] Compensation, Boise, 1995—. Mem. Boise City Comprehensive Plan Com., 1993-96; founding mem. Log Cabin Lit. Ctr., Boise, 1996—; mem. Beaux Arts Soc./Boise Art Mus., 1976—; mem. Boise City Planning and Zoning Commn., 1985—. Mem. Workers Compensation Surety Group (sec. 1994-95, pres. 1995-96), Bosie Adjusters Assn. (treas. 1995-96, v.p. 1996-97, pres. 1997—), City Club, Idaho Women's Network. Avocations: skiing, landscape design. Office: Indsl Spl Indemnity Fund 650 W State St Boise ID 83702-7701

GRAY, MARK MICHAEL, political scientist; b. San Bernardino, Calif., Aug. 16, 1970; s. Michael Harry and Patricia Hazal (Garrett) G.; m. Shoshannah Sioban Victorine, July 25, 1998. AA cum laude, Saddleback Coll., 1991; BA magna cum laude, UCLA, 1993; MA, U. Calif., Irvine, 1998. Facilties mgr. Wesierski & Zurek, Irvine, 1993-96; film maker The Cardamon Group, Santa Ana, Calif., 1997—; polit. scientist, rschr. U. Calif., Irvine, 1995—; assoc. editor, writer Ability mag., Costa Mesa, Calif., 1996—; rsch. asst. Unthinkable Democracy Project, Irvine, 1997—. Editor, writer Ability mag., 1996—. Mem. Am. Polit. Sci. Assn., Western Polit. Sci. Assn., Theta Chi (athletic chmn. 1991-93). Roman Catholic. Avocation: quantum physics. Office: Ability Mag 1001 W 17th St Costa Mesa CA 92627-4512

GRAY, NICOLIN JANE PLANK, botanist, educator; b. Yakima, Wash., Apr. 24, 1921; d. Laurence Lubin and Clara Nicoline (Larsen) Plank; B.S., U. Wash., 1942, M.S. (Alpha Chi Omega scholar), 1945; m. Alfred Orren Gray, Sept. 5, 1947; children—Robin, Richard. Instr. biology Yakima Valley (Wash.) Jr. Coll., 1942-44; instr. Whitworth Coll., Spokane, Wash., 1944-46, asst. prof., 1946-48, 1956-72, asso. prof., 1972-78, prof. biology, 1978-80, prof. emeritus, 1980—, chmn. natural sci. div., 1977-79; bot. cons. Inland Empire Poison Center, Spokane, 1963—; herbarium curator Whitworth Coll., 1963—; cons. Ragged Ridge Outdoor Ednl. Opportunities Center, Spokane, 1973-80; cons. mycologist to various groups, 1975—; bot. illustrator, 1981—. Elder Presbyn. Ch., 1983—. Whitworth faculty research grantee, 1960, 64, 69; NSF grantee, 1962, 65, 71-72; NIH grantee, 1960-61; recipient Woman of Distinction award Women in Communications, 1987. Mem. N.Am. Mycol. Assn., Washington Native Plant Soc., Eastern Wash. State Hist. Soc. (trustee 1979-85), Phi Beta Kappa (sec.-treas. Inland Empire assn. 1951-52, 66-67, 70-71), Sigma Xi, Pi Lambda Theta. Democrat. Presbyterian. Author: A Manual of Common Fungi of the Inland Northwest, 1982; Many Lamps, One Light, A Centennial History of First Presbyterian Church, Spokane, Washington, 1984; An Illustrated Key to Plants of the Spokane Area, 1985. Contbr. articles to profl. jours.

GRAY, PATRICIA JOYCE, court administrator; b. Carlsbad, N.Mex., Feb. 5, 1951; d. Owen Corbett and Bobby Jo (Jones) G.; m. Patrick A. Edwards, Oct. 29, 1981 (div. June 1990). Student, U. Nev., Las Vegas, 1974-77. Receptionist, clk. Nationwide Fin., Las Vegas, 1969-70; dep. clk. U.S. Bankruptcy Ct. for Dist. Nev., Las Vegas, 1970-74, chief dep. clk., 1974-75, chief clk., 1975-79, clk. of ct., 1979—; mem. bankruptcy work measurement subcom. of com. on adminstrn. bankruptcy system Jud. Conf. U.S., 1989-91; mem. tng. and edn. com. U.S. Bankruptcy Cts. Adminstrv. Office U.S. Cts., 1990-91; mem. Bankruptcy Work Measurement subcom. of Clerk's adv. com. Adminstrv. Office U.S. Cts., 1992-93, local rules subcom. Dist. Nev., 1991—. Mem. Space and Facilities Ad Hoc Task Force on Personnel of Adminstrv. Office of U.S. Cts., 1994-95, 9th Cir. Task Force on Race, Religious, and Ethnic Fairness, 1994-97; mem. bd. dirs. of Clark County, Nev. chpt. ARC, 1994-98. Mem. Nat. Conf. Bankruptcy Clks., Fed. Ct. Clks. Assn., Nat. Assn. Ct. Mgrs. Rebublican. Avocations: reading, pottery, gardening. Office: US Bankruptcy Ct Foley Fed Bldg 300 Las Vegas Blvd S Las Vegas NV 89101-5833

GRAY, PAUL WESLEY, university dean; b. Cicero, Ill., Jan. 30, 1947; s. Harry B. and Audrey (Tong) G.; m. Rachel E. Boehr, June 3, 1967; children: John M., Janel E., Robert B. BA, Faith Baptist Bible Coll., Ankeny, Tex., 1970; ThM, Dallas Theol. Sem., 1975; MS in Libr. Sci., East Tex. State U., 1977, EdD, 1980; MA, Tex. Woman's U., 1989. Dorm dir. Buckner Baptist Benevolences, Dallas, 1971-75; dir. community living residence IV Dallas County Mental Health/Mental Retardation, Dallas, 1975-78; cataloger W. Walworth Harrison Pub. Libr., Greenville, Tex., 1978-81; v.p. Golden Triangle Christian Acad., Garland, Tex., 1979-83; dir. libr. LeTourneau U., Longview, Tex., 1983-88; dean computer svc. and univ. libr. Azusa (Calif.) Pacific U., 1989—. Mem. ALA, Calif. Libr. Assn., So. Calif. Area Theol. Libr. Assn., Foothill Libr. Consortium. Republican. Baptist. Office: Azusa Pacific U 901 E Alosta Ave Azusa CA 91702-2769

GRAY, PHILIP HOWARD, retired psychologist, educator; b. Cape Rosier, Maine, July 4, 1926; s. Asa and Bernice (Lawrence) G.; m. Iris McKinney, Dec. 31, 1954; children: Cindelyn Gray Eberts, Howard. M.A., U. Chgo., 1958; Ph.D., U. Wash., 1960. Asst. prof. dept. psychology Mont. State U., Bozeman, 1960-65; assoc. prof. Mont. State U., 1965-75, prof., 1975-92; ret., 1992; vis. prof. U. Man., Winnipeg, Can., 1968-70, U. N.H., 1965, U. Mont., 1967, 74, Tufts U., 1968, U. Conn., 1971; pres. Mont. Psychol. Assn., 1968-70 (helped write Mont. licensing law for psychologists); chmn. Mont. Bd. Psychologist Examiners, 1972-74; spkr. sci. and geneal. meetings on ancestry of U.S. presidents; presenter, instr. grad. course on serial killers and the psychopathology of murder. Organizer folk art exhbns. Mont. and Maine, 1972-79; author: The Comparative Analysis of Behavior, 1966, (with F.L. Ruch and N. Warren) Working with Psychology, 1963, A Directory of Eskimo Artists in Sculpture and Prints, 1974, The Science That Lost Its Mind, 1985, Penobscot Pioneers vol. 1, 1992, vol. 2, 1992, vol. 3, 1993, vol. 4, 1994, vol. 5, 1995, vol. 6, 1996, Mean Streets and Dark Deeds: The He-Man's Guide to Mysteries, 1998, Ghoulies and Ghosties and Long-Leggety Beasties, 1998; contbr. numerous articles on behavior to psychol. jours.; contbr. poetry to lit. jours. With U.S. Army, 1944-46. Recipient Am. and Can. research grants. Fellow AAAS, APA, Am. Psychol. Soc., Internat. Soc. Rsch. on Aggression; mem. NRA (life), SAR (v.p. Sourdough chpt. 1990, pres. 1991-99, trustee 1989, v.p.-gen. intermountain dist. 1997-98, pres. state soc. 1996-98), Nat. Geneal. Soc., New Eng. Hist. Geneal. Soc., Gallatin County Geneal. Soc. (charter, pres. 1991-93), Deer Isle-Stonington Hist. Soc., Internat. Soc. Human Ethology, Descs. Illegitimate Sons and Daus. of Kings of Britain, Piscataque Pioneers, Order Desc. Colonial Physicians and Chirugiens, Flagon and Trencher, Order of the Crown of Charlemagne, Bozeman Rifle and Pistol Club. Republican. Avocations: collecting folk art, first and signed editions of novels, pistol shooting. Home: 1207 S Black Ave Bozeman MT 59715-5633

GRAY, RALPH GARETH, architect and structural engineer; b. Stockton, Calif., Aug. 21, 1929; s. Ralph Nichols and Louise (Noack) G.; m. Alice Wirth, July 16, 1954; children: Mary Louise, Elizabeth Katherine. BS, U. Calif., 1953; MS, MIT, 1957. Rsch. engr., rsch. asst. MIT, Cambridge, Mass., 1955-57; archtl. draftsman John Lyon Reid & Parts, San Francisco, 1957-59; structural designer, civil engr. Akol Engring. Co., Berkeley & San Francisco, 1959-62, Gerald McCue & Assocs., Berkeley, 1962-63; project sr. engr. Nicholas Forell & Assocs., San Francisco, 1963-64; assoc. architect Jacob Robbins, Berkeley, 1964-66; architect pvt. practice, Berkeley, 1966-68, 76-80; prin. Hirsch & Gray, San Francisco, 1968-76, Overstreet Rosenberg & Gray, San Francisco, 1980-86; architect pvt. practice, Berkeley, 1986—. Mem. AIA, ASCE, Structural Engrs. Assn. Calif., Internat. Congress Bldg. Ofcls., Western Constrn. Cons. Assn., Earthquake Engring. Rsch. Inst. Avocations: history, WWII, history of architecture. Home and office: 1001 Merced St Berkeley CA 94707-2521

GRAY, RICHARD ARDEN, transportation executive; b. Ft. Bragg, Calif., Oct. 29, 1935; s. Arden Howard and Marion Florence (Coolidge) G.; m. Roberta Jeanne Montna, Feb. 5, 1955; children: Mark Alan, Laura Ann, Deborah Marie, Lisa Lynn. AA, Yuba Coll., 1955; BA, Calif. State U., 1957. Cert. coll. instr., Calif. Deputy sheriff Yuba County Sheriffs Dept., Marysville, Calif., 1957; traffic officer Calif. Hwy. Patrol, Ventura, 1958-60, Yuba City, 1961-68; sgt. field ops. officer Calif. Hwy. Patrol, Gardena, 1969-71; lt. exec. officer Calif. Hwy. Patrol, Van Nuys, 1972-76; lt. area comdr. Calif. Hwy. Patrol, Chico, 1977-88; wholesale, retail distbr. Dick Gray Enterprises, Chico, 1989-94, 95—; instr. Yuba Coll., Marysville, 1965-67, Calif. fish and game hunter safety program, Chico, 1982-86; profl. driver, transporter motor homes, 1989—. Chmn. citizen rev. com. United Way of Butte County, Chico, 1984 (outstanding achievement 1984-86), fundraising [illegible] ties Exch. Club Child Abuse Prevention Ctr., Chico, 1987-91. With USNR, 1953-61. Recipient Individual Excellence Outstanding Cmty. Svc. award United Way Butte and Glenn Counties, 1994-95. Mem. Calif. Hwy. Patrolmen Assn., RV Club, Elks (honors 1988, pres. 1988-89), Breakfast Exch.

Club (pres., bd. dirs. 1980-81), Exch. Club Greater Chico (sponsor 1983). Republican. Avocations: travling in recreational vehicle, tennis, golf.

GRAY, RICHARD MOSS, retired college president; b. Washington, Jan. 25, 1924; s. Wilbur Leslie and Betty Marie (Grey) G.; m. Catherine Claire Hammond, Oct. 17, 1943; children: Janice Lynn Gray Armstrong, Nancy Hammond Gray Schultz. BA, Bucknell U., 1942; MDiv summa cum laude, San Francisco Theol. Sem., 1961; PhD, U. Calif., Berkeley, 1972; doctorate degree (hon.), World Coll. West, 1988. Writer, creative dir. N.W. Ayer & Son, Phila., 1942-58; univ. pastor Portland State U., Oreg., 1961-68; founder, pres. World Coll. West, Petaluma, Calif., 1973-88, pres. emeritus, 1988—; bd. dirs. World Centre, San Francisco, Lifelplan Ctr.; founder Presidio World Coll., 1992—. Author poetry Advent, 1989. Bd. dirs. Citizens Found. Marin, San Rafael, Calif., 1988—, Marin Ednl. Found., 1989-92; ruling elder Presbyn. Ch. U.S.A. Named Disting. Alumnus of Yr. San Francisco Theol. Sem., 1988, Marin Citizen of Yr. Citizens Found., 1988; recipient Svc. to Humanity award Bucknell U., 1992. Mem. Phi Beta Kappa. Avocations: song-writing, poetry.

GRAY, ROBERT DONALD, retired mayor; b. Quincy, Ill., May 6, 1924; s. James Arthur and Katherine Elnora (Moore) G.; m. Marie Dolores Albert, July 15, 1951; children: Michael S., Sheilah C. Student, Washington & Jefferson Coll., 1945-47; BSEE, Okla. State U., 1949; postgrad., Northwestern U. Electrolysis engr. Sinclair Refining Co., 1949-50; North Atlantic field mgr. navigation/communication systems USAF, 1950-51; cons. Lockheed Aircraft Ga. Co., 1951-52; sr. devel. engr. Harris Corp., 1952-54; dir. Gen. Telephone Electronics, Mountain View, Calif., 1954-66; dir. reliability and quality control Gen. Dynamics/Electronics, Rochester, N.Y., 1961-62; v.p. rsch./devel. Lockheed Missiles/Space Co., Sunnyvale, Calif., 1966-79; pres. Gray Assocs., Internat. Air Traffic Control System, Los Altos, Calif., 1980-87; mem. Los Altos City Coun., 1993-97; mayor City of Los Altos, Calif., 1994-95. With USN, 1941-45; ETO. Mem. IEEE (sr.), Phi Kappa Psi. Republican. Avocations: golf, amateur radio, electronics, aircraft. Home: 7307 Lost Lake Ln Roseville CA 95747-8312

GRAY, THOMAS STEPHEN, newspaper editor; b. Burbank, Calif., Aug. 22, 1950; s. Thomas Edgar and Lily Irene (Ax) G.; m. Barbara Ellen Bronson, Aug. 27, 1977; children: Jonathan Thomas, Katherine Marie. BA, Stanford U., 1972; MA in English, UCLA, 1976. Teaching assoc. UCLA, 1976-77; reporter L.A. Daily News, 1977-79, editorial writer, 1979-84, editorial page editor, 1984-95; sr. editor Investor's Bus. Daily, L.A., 1995-98. Recipient 1st Place award Editorial Writing Greater L.A. Press Club, 1988, Inland Daily Press Association, 1993.

GRAY, WALTER P., III, archivist, consultant; b. San Francisco, Aug. 8, 1952; s. Walter Patton II and Elsie Josephine (Stroop) G.; m. Mary Amanda Helmich, May 23, 1980. BA in History, Calif. State U., Sacramento, 1976. Rschr. Calif. State R.R. Mus., Sacramento, 1977-80, curator, 1980-81, 85-90, archivist, 1981-85, mus. dir., 1990-98; Calif. state archivist, 1998—; cons. in field, 1976—. Contbr. articles to profl. jours. Democrat. Buddhist. Avocations: woodworking, antique automobiles, photography. Office: California State Archives 1020 O St Sacramento CA 95814-5704

GRAY, WILLIAM R., lawyer; b. Peoria, Ill., Aug. 25, 1941; s. John J. and Alverna K. (Kennedy) G.; m. Tiana M. Yeager, June 12, 1982; children: Ann Katherine, Thomas William. BA, U. Colo., 1963, JD, 1966. Bar: Colo. 1966; U.S. Dist. Ct. Colo. 1966; U.S. Ct. Appeals (10th cir.) 1976. Dep. dist. atty. Dist. Atty.'s Office/10th Jud. Dist., Pueblo, Colo., 1967-69, Dist. Atty.'s Office/20th Jud. Dist., Boulder, Colo., 1969-70; dep. state pub. defender Colo. State Pub. Defender, Boulder, 1970-72; ptnr. Miller & Gray, Boulder, 1973-85, Purvis, Gray & Gordon, LLP, Boulder, 1985—; mem./vice chair, chmn., Colo. Supreme Ct. grievance com., 1983-88, mem. criminal rules com., 1982-84; adj. prof. law U. Colo. Sch. of Law, Boulder, 1984. Bd. dirs. Mental Health Ctr. of Boulder County, 1972-78. Fellow Am. Coll. Trial Lawyers (Courageous Advocacy award 1985), Internat. Soc. Barristers, Am. Bar Found., Colo. Bar Foun., Colo. Bar Assn. (Professionalism award 1995), Am. Bd. Trial Advocates. Democrat. Office: Purvis Gray & Gordon LLP 1050 Walnut St Ste 501 Boulder CO 80302-5144

GRAYBEAL, LYNNE ELIZABETH, lawyer; b. Seattle, May 21, 1956; d. John Olin and Janice Marie (Everly) G.; m. Scott Harron, Oct. 7, 1989. Student, Pomona Coll., 1974-76; BA, Colby Coll., 1979; JD, U. Puget Sound, 1983. Bar: Wash. 1983, U.S. Dist. Ct. (we. dist.) Wash. 1983. Rsch. asst. Charles River Assocs., Boston, 1979-80; assoc. Bogle & Gates, Seattle, 1982, 83-85, 83-85; assoc. Monroe, Stokes, Eitelbach & Lawrence, P.S., Seattle, 1986-89, prin., 1990-92; ptnr. Riddell, Williams, Bullitt & Walkinshaw, 1992-94, Foster Pepper & Shefelman, 1994—. Sec. Bathhouse Theatre, 1984-86, v.p., 1987; bd. dirs. Wash. Vol. Lawyers for Arts, 1985-89; v.p., bd. dirs. Seattle Found. for Motion Picture Arts, 1988-89. Mem. ABA (chmn. unfair competition trade identity subcom. 1987-88), Wash. State Bar Assn. (chmn. intellectual and indsl. property sect. 1988-89), Wash. State Patent Law Assn., Wash. Women Lawyers (treas. 1989-91, pres. 1992), Greater Seattle C. of C. (curriculum com. 1989-91, Leadership Tomorrow class 1988-89). Avocations: travel, music, jazz dance, hiking, bicycling. Home: 3037 38th Ave W Seattle WA 98199-2512 Office: Foster Pepper & Shefelman PLLC 1111 3rd Ave Ste 3400 Seattle WA 98101-3299*

GRAYESKI, MARY LYNN, chemist, foundation administrator. BS in Chemistry, Kings Coll., 1974; PhD in Analytical Chemistry, U. N.H., 1982. Tchg., rsch. asst. U. N.H., Durham, 1979-82; asst. prof. Seton Hall U., S. Orange, N.J., 1982-87, assoc. prof., 1987-93, chair chemistry dept., 1991-93; program officer Rsch. Corp., Tucson, 1993—; mem. govning. bd. Ea. Analytical Symposium, N.J., 1985-93. Contbr. over 30 articles to profl. jours. Vol. ACTION/VISTA, Midland, Tex., 1975; vol. recruiter ACTION, San Francisco, 1976; vol. ACTION/Peach Corps, Ghana, 1977-78; judge Internat. Sci. and Engring. Fair, 1996. Mem. Am. Chem. Soc., Delta Epsilon Sigma. Office: Rsch Corp 101 N Wilmot Rd Ste 250 Tucson AZ 85711-3361

GRAY-FUSON, JOAN LORRAINE, lawyer; b. Glendale, Calif., Mar. 25, 1938; d. Stanley Wayne Brune and Maxine Lorraine (Falconer) Talkin; m. Darrell Herbert Gray, June 26, 1959 (div. 1972); children: Michael Herbert Gray, Thomas Edward Gray; m. Arnold Max Fuson, Dec. 18, 1977; children: Marie Fuson Hudson, Karen Fuson, Gregory J. Fuson. BA in Edn., Calif. State U., 1960; JD, U. of the Pacific, 1978. Bar: Calif. 1978, U.S. Dist. Ct. (ea. dist.) Calif. 1978. Tchr. Rio Linda Union Sch. Dist., Sacramento, Calif., 1960-65; pvt. practice Sacramento, 1978-81; staff counsel State of Calif. Water Resources Control Bd., Sacramento, 1982-91; sr. staff counsel State of Calif. Dept. of Conservation, Sacramento, 1991—. Elder on session Fremont Presbyn. Ch., Sacramento, 1995-97. Avocations: gardening, folk dancing, fitness. Office: Dept of Conservation 801 K St # Ms24-3 Sacramento CA 95814-3500

GRAYSON, MARGARET MARION, association executive, anthropologist; b. Lynwood, Calif., Oct. 12, 1949; d. William Mac and Margaret Marian (Clark) Summerlin; m. Lawrence Marion Martin, June 18, 1967 (div.); 1 son, Jay Scott; m. 2d James Lee Grayson, Feb. 18, 1977. A.A. in Liberal Arts, Pasadena City Coll., 1972; B.A. in Anthropology, Calif. State U.-Los Angeles, 1975, M.A. in Anthropology, 1975. Dep. dir. L.S.B. Leakey Found., Pasadena, Calif., 1977-81; exec. dir. Santa Fe Trail council Camp Fire Inc., Temple City, Calif., 1981-83; assoc. exec. dir. Camp Fire Council Foothills, Inc., Pasadena, 1983—. Vol. United Way, Arcadia, Calif., 1981-83; mem. exec. bd. El Monte/South El Monte Community Coordinating Council (Calif.), 1983, rec. sec., 1984—. Mem. AAUW, Nat. Soc. Fundraising Execs., Women in Communications, Women in Mgmt. (corr. sec. San Gabriel Valley chpt. 1983-84, v.p. pub. relations 1984—), Camp Fire Assn. Profls. Democrat. Office: Neighborhood Partnership 9916 Central Ave Montclair CA 91763-3201

GREASER, CONSTANCE UDEAN, automotive industry executive; b. San Diego, Jan. 18, 1938; d. Lloyd Edward and Udean Greaser. BA, San Diego State Coll., 1959; postgrad. U. Copenhagen Grad. Sch. Fgn. Students, 1963, Georgetown U. Sch. Fgn. Service, 1967; MA, U. So. Calif., 1968; Exec. MBA, UCLA, 1981. Advt., publicity mgr. Crofton Co., San Diego, 1959-62; supr. Mercury Publs., Fullerton, Calif., 1962-64; supr. engring. support services div. Arcata Data Mgmt., Hawthorne, Calif., 1964-67; mgr. computerized typesetting dept. Continental Graphics, Los Angeles, 1967-70; v.p., editorial dir. Sage Publs., Inc., Beverly Hills, Calif., 1970-74; head publs. RAND Corp., Santa Monica, Calif., 1974-90; mgr. communications Am. Honda Motors Co., Torrance, Calif., 1990—. Mem. nat. com. Million Minutes of Peace Appeal, 1986, Nat. Info. Standards Orgn., 1987-93, nat. com. Global Cooperation for Better World, 1988. Recipient Berber award Graphic Arts Tech. Found., 1989. Mem. Women in Bus. (pres. 1977-78), Graphic Comm. Assn. (bd. dirs. 1994—), Soc. for Scholarly Pubs. (nat. bd. dirs.), Women in Communication, Soc. Tech. Communication, Brahma Kumaris World Spiritual Orgn. Co-author: Quick Writer-Build Your Own Word Processing Users Guide, 1983; Quick Writer-Word Processing Center Operations Manual, 1984; editor: Urban Research News, 1970-74; mng. editor Comparative Polit. Studies, 1971-74; contbr. articles to various jours. Office: Am Honda Motor Co 1919 Torrance Blvd Torrance CA 90501-2722

GREAT, DON CHARLES, composer, music company executive; b. Medford, Oreg., Mar. 11, 1951; s. Donald Charles Sr. and Anna Marie (Huff) G.; m. Andrea Louise Gerber, Oct. 31, 1970. Student, UCLA, 1975-76, 83-86, Dick Grove Sch. Music, 1983-87. Freelance songwriter Metro-Goldwyn-Mayer Records, 20th Century Records, Bell Records, Los Angeles, 1968—; pres. Don Great Music, Inc., Los Angeles, 1972—. Composer music for TV shows including Who's the Boss? (ABC), 227 (NBC), The Jeffersons (CBS), Gimme a Break (NBC), A Different World (NBC), Fact of Life (NBC), Unsolved Mysteries (NBC), Amen (NBC), Freddie's Nightmares (Lorimar-Warner Bros. TV), Saved By the Bell (NBC Disney), One Day at a Time (CBS), Married With Children (Fox/Columbia Pictures), Small Wonder (Fox TV), 1978—, Different Strokes (NBC), BJ and the Bear (NBC), Silverspoons (NBC), Sheriff Lobo (NBC), Incredible Hulk (CBS), Sanford (NBC), Real People (NBC), Crimetime After Primetime (CBS), The Promised Land (CBS), Candid Camera, Tales From the Crypt, In Living Color (Fox-TV), Laugh-In, Baby Races, Walker: Texas Ranger (CBS); composer music score Pres. Reagen Libr. Video, Pres. Carter Presdl. Libr. CD-ROM, 1994. Mem. Broadcast Music, Inc. (Best Music Score of Yr. award 1986, named TV Composer of Yr. 1986). Avocations: playing piano, going for Sunday drives.

GREAVER, HARRY, artist; b. L.A., Oct. 30, 1929; s. Harry Jones and Lucy Catherine (Coons) G.; m. Hanne Synnestvedt Nielsen, Nov. 30, 1955; children—Peter, Paul, Lotte. BFA, U. Kans., 1951, MFA, 1952. Assoc. prof. art U. Maine, Orono, 1955-66; exec. dir. Kalamazoo Inst. Arts, 1966-78; dir. Greaver Gallery, Cannon Beach, Oreg., 1978—; mem. visual com. Mich. Coun. Arts, 1976-78. One-man exhbns. include Baker U., Baldwin, Kans., 1955, U. Maine, Orono, 1958, 59, Pacific U., 1985; group exhbns. include U. Utah Mus. Fine Arts, 1972-73, Purdue U., 1977, Drawings/U.S.A, St. Paul, 1963, San Diego Mus., 1971, Rathbun Gallery, Portland, Oreg., 1988; 10-yr. print retrospective Cannon Beach Arts Assn., 1989, 20-yr. retrospective, 1998. Mem. adv. bd. Haystack Ctr. for the Arts, Cannon Beach, 1988-91. Recipient Purchase award Nat. Endowment Arts, 1971; grantee U. Maine, 1962-64. Mem. Cannon Beach Arts Assn., 1986-88. Address: PO Box 120 Cannon Beach OR 97110-0120

GREAVES, JOHN ALLEN, lawyer; b. Kansas City, Mo., Feb. 18, 1948; s. John Allen Greaves and Nancy Lee (Farmer) Greaves-Meltzer; m. Sharon Louise Peace Ventura, Dec. 23, 1967 (div. Mar. 1971); 1 child, Karen Christine Greaves Calogne; m. Jerri Lynn Crawford, Sept. 5, 1981. BA in Polit. Sci., U. Mo., 1976; MPA, JD with honors, Drake U., 1992. Bar: Iowa 1992, U.S. Dist. Ct. (so. dist.) Iowa 1992, Calif. 1994, U.S. Dist. Ct. (no. and cen. dists.) Calif. 1994, U.S. Dist. Ct. (so. and ea. dists.) Calif. 1995, U.S. Dist. Ct. N.Mex. 1995, U.S. Ct. Appeals (9th cir.) 1995, U.S. Dist. Ct. (no. dist.) N.Y. 1996, U.S. Dist. Ct. S.C. 1995, U.S. Ct. Appeals (4th and 10th cirs.) 1996. Pres., CEO VIPilot Svcs., Inc., Kansas City, 1980-83; pilot Air Illinois, Carbondale, Ill., 1983-84, Wright Airlines, Cleve., 1983-84, ComAir Airlines, Cin., 1984-88; jud. law clk. to Hon. Arthur E. Gamble Iowa Dist. Ct., Des Moines, 1990-91; pvt. practice Des Moines, 1992-94; assoc. Baum, Hedlund, Aristei, Guilford & Downey, L.A., 1994—. Mem. ABA, ATLA, Airline Pilots Assn. (chmn. contract adminstrn. com. 1985-87, Disting. Svc. award 1987), Lawyer/Pilot Bar Assn., State Bar Calif., State Bar Iowa, Iowa Trial Lawyers Assn., Delta Theta Phi. Avocations: aviation, snow and water skiing, boating and sailing, tennis, golf. Home: 3664 May St Los Angeles CA 90066-3606 Office: Baum Hedlund Aristei Gilford & Downey 12100 Wilshire Blvd Ste 950 Los Angeles CA 90025-7107

GREBER, ROBERT MARTIN, financial investments executive; b. Phila., Mar. 15, 1938; s. Joseph and Golda (Rubin) G.; m. Judith Ann Pearlstein, Dec. 23, 1962; children: Matthew, Jonathan. B.S. in Fin., Temple U., 1962; grad., Sch. Mgmt. and Strategic Studies, 1982-84. Account exec. Merrill Lynch, Phila., 1962-68; portfolio mgr. v.p. Afuture Funds Inc., Lima, Pa., 1968-70; instl. account exec. Merrill Lynch, Phila., 1970-75; officer, mgr.-v.p. Merrill Lynch, Los Angeles, 1975-79; chief fin. officer Lucasfilm Ltd., Los Angeles, 1979-80; pres., CEO Lucasfilm Ltd., San Rafael, Calif., 1980-84, Diagnostic Networks, Inc., San Francisco, 1984-87; ptnr. Leon A. Farley Assocs., San Francisco, 1988-90; pres., COO The Pacific Stock Exch., 1990-95, chmn., CEO, 1996—; bd. dirs. Bay View Capital Group. Bd. dirs. KQED Pub. Broadcasting Sys., San Francisco, 1983, chmn. bd., 1988; bd. dirs. Film Inst. No. Calif., Marin Symphony Orch., 1981-83, Sonic Solutions, 1993—; trustee Western Behavior Scis. Inst., La JOlla, 1982-89; vice chmn. Assn. Am. Pub. TV, 1992-94; trustee Beryl Buck Inst. for Edn., 1990-93. With Army NG, 1959-60. Office: Pacific Stock Exchange Inc 115 Sansome St San Francisco CA 94104-3601

GREEN, BETH INGBER, intuitive practitioner, counselor, musician, composer; b. N.Y.C., Feb. 28, 1945; d. Frank and Lillian Ingber; m. Jonathan Ingber Green, 1995. BA, Bklyn. Coll., 1970; MA, UCLA, 1978. Cert. in intuitive consulting, counseling, tchg. and learning, body and kinetic intervention. Spiritual dir. and founder The Stream, L.A., 1980-86; ptnr., co-founder The Healing Partnership, L.A. and Ramona, 1986-90; spiritual dir. and founder The Triple Eye Found., Escondido, Calif., 1990-93; intuitive practitioner, counselor, cons. and tchr. Talent, Oreg., 1980—; owner Beth & Friends Spiritual Counseling, Talent, Oreg.; spiritual activist, co-founder Rising Mountains Setting Suns, Ramona, 1993-95; co-founder Spiritual Activist Movement, L.A. and Ramona, 1993-95; owner Treehouse Music. Author: The Autobiography of Mary Magdalene, 1988; spoken tapes include: The Healing of God, The Alienation of Love, Spirituality: The Last Block to Freedom; music tapes include Beyond the Mystery, Sara in the Clouds; videotapes include Breaking the "I" Barrier. West Coast coord. Wages for Housework Campaign, L.A., 1974-78; co-founder The Looseleaf Directory: Linking Bodies, Minds and Spirits in the Healing Arts, 1994-95.

GREEN, BETTY JEAN, hotel executive; b. Dublin, Ga., Aug. 14, 1946; d. Napoleon and Dorine (Wright) Stanley; m. Eddie Green III, June 1, 1979 (div. May 1988); children: Yolanda Nicole, Orlando Ray, Tonya Guyton. Student, Apollo Bus. Tech. Slot floor person Harrah's Hotel and Casino, Las Vegas, Nev. Author: Children's Poetry Book, 1998. Pentacostal. Avocations: bowling, playing drums, writing poetry, children's short stories. Home: 4550 W Sahara Ave Apt 2235 Las Vegas NV 89102-3617

GREEN, BRIAN GERALD, marketing executive; b. Missoula, Mont., Sept. 5, 1954; s. Gerald Jay and Ruth Anne (Althaus) G.; m. Robin Lee McIntyre, May 10, 1980; 1 child, Sean Brian. ASEE, Clark Coll., 1976; BS in Electronics Engring. Tech., Oreg. Inst. Tech., Klamath Falls, 1978; MBA, U. Hartford, 1988. Cert. electronic technician. Field engr. Triad Systems Corp., Hartford, Conn., 1978-79; midwest regional mgr. Triad Systems Corp., Chgo., 1979-81; Northwest regional mgr. Triad Systems Corp., Portland, Oreg., 1981-83; northeast area mgr. Triad Systems Corp., Bristol, Conn., 1983-88, Canadian svc. mgr., 1987-88; western area mgr. Triad Systems Corp., Tracy, Calif., 1988-89; world wide svc. mgr. Sysgen, Inc., Milpitas, Calif., 1989-91; svc. mktg. mgr. Sony Corp. Am., San Jose, 1991-93; self employed cons., 1993; bus. mgr. REPAC, Inc., Forest Park, Ga., 1993-94; dir. authentication AirTouch Cellular, Walnut Creek, Calif., 1994—. Mem. Assn. for Svcs. Mgmt. Internat., Masons (Southington, Conn. and Vancouver, Wash. chpts.), Scottish Rite (Hartford), Sphinx Shrine (Hartford). Republican. Methodist. Avocations: skiing, camping, family. Home: 12140 Carnegie Dr Tracy CA 95376-9149

GREEN, CYRIL KENNETH, retired retail company executive; b. Portland, Oreg., June 11, 1931; s. Lionel and Nora Evelyn (Walker) G.; m. Beverly Ann Hutchinson, July 24, 1950; children: Kenneth James, Teri Ann, Tamara Jo Green Easton, Kelly Denise Green Van Horn. Student pub. schs., Portland. Salesperson Fred Meyer Inc., Portland, Oreg., 1947-53, mgr. food dept., 1953-57, supr. food div., 1957-60, buyer food div., 1960-64, head buyer food div., 1964-67; gen. mgr. Roundup Co. subs. Fred Meyer Inc., Spokane, Wash., 1967-70; dir. ops. Fred Meyer Inc., Portland, Oreg., 1970-72, pres., 1972-96, chief operating officer, 1972-96; ret. Fred Meyer Inc., Portland, 1996; vice chmn., bd. dirs. Oreg. Trail chpt. ARC, Portland, 1984-89; bd. dirs. Marylhurst Coll., Portland, 1987—.

GREEN, DAVID OLIVER, JR., sculptor, designer; b. Enid, Okla., June 29, 1908; s. David Oliver Green and Ina (Christmas) McBride; m. Jaxine Rhodes Green, Aug. 20, 1929 (dec. Dec. 1983); m. Lilian Stone DeLey, Mar. 15, 1986 (dec. May 1986). Student, Am. Acad. Art, Chgo., 1926, Nat. Acad. Art, 1927. Letterer Nat. Playhouses, Chgo., 1925-30; with lettering/layout Chgo. Herald-Examiner, Chgo., 1931-32; freelance designer London Guarantee Bldg., Chgo., 1932-33; layout artist Charles Daniel Frey Advt., Chgo., 1933-36; package designer Sears Roebuck, Chgo., 1936-37; art dir. advt. Mills Industries, Chgo., 1947-40; prodn. illustrator McDonald Douglas Aircraft, Long Beach, Calif., 1940-42; draftsman Calif. Inst. Tech., Pasadena, Calif., 1943-45; prof. sculpture Otis Art Inst., L.A., 1946-69; Prin. works include Altadena Libr. Bldg., Calif., Lytton Savs. and Loan, Hollywood, Calif.; author: La Partida/The Contest, 1957. Recipient Golden Crown award Pasadena Arts Coun., 1984. Mem. Pasadena Soc. Artists, Soc. for Calligraphy, Pasadena Photochrome Soc. Avocations: reading, nature study, languages. Home and Studio: 176 Jaxine Dr Altadena CA 91001-3818

GREEN, FRANCIS WILLIAM, investment consultant, former missile scientist; b. Locust Grove, Okla., Mar. 17, 1920; s. Noel Francis and Mary (Lincoln) G.; B.S., Phoenix U., 1955; M.S. in Elec. Engring., Minerva U., Milan, Italy, 1959; M.S. in Engring., West Coast U., Los Angeles, 1965; m. Alma J. Ellison, Aug. 26, 1950 (dec. Sept. 1970); children: Sharmon, Rhonda; m. Susan G. Mathis, July 14, 1973 (div. July 1979). With USN Guided Missile Program, 1945-49; design and electronic project engr. Falcon missile program Hughes Aircraft Co., Culver City, Calif., 1949-55; sr. electronic engr. Atlas missile program Convair Astronautics, San Diego, 1955-59; sr. engr. Polaris missile program Nortronics div. Northrop, Anaheim, Calif., 1959-60; chief, supr. electronic engr. data systems br. Tech. Support div. Rocket Propulsion Lab., USAF, Edwards AFB, Calif., 1960-67, dep. chief tech. support div., 1967-69; tech. adviser Air Force Missile Devel. Ctr., Holloman AFB, N.Mex., 1969-70, 6585 Test Group, Air Force Spl. Weapons Ctr., Holloman AFB, from 1970; pvt. investment cons., 1978—. Bd. examiners U.S. CSC; mem. Pres.'s Missile Site Labor Relations Com.; cons. advanced computer and data processing tech. and systems engring.; mem. USAF Civilian Policy Bd. and Range Comdrs. Coun; brig. gen., comdr. 2d brigrade State Mil. Forces; comdr. State Mil. Forces, 1989—; mem. Nat. Guard Assn. U.S. Served as pilot USAAF, 1941-45. Fellow Am. Inst. Aeros. and Astronautics; mem. IEEE, Nat. Assn. Flight Instrs. Contbr. articles to profl. jours. Home and Office: 2345 Apache Ln Alamogordo NM 88310-4851

GREEN, JAMES CRAIG, retired data systems company executive; b. Gladstone, Mich., Apr. 19, 1933; s. Albert Keene and Margaret Josephine (Craig) G.; student Coll. of Gt. Falls, 1951-53, UCLA, 1962; m. Catherine Maxwell, Nov. 1, 1957; children: Cindi, Shelley, Nancy, James W., Robert. Clk., carrier U.S. Post Office, Gt. Falls, Mont., 1951-57; clk. office and sales Mont. Liquor Control Bd., Gt. Falls, 1957-59; payroll clk. Herald Examiner, Hearst Publs., L.A., 1959-67, data processing mgr., 1967-75, data processing ops. mgr. corp. hdqrs. Hearst Publs., N.Y.C., 1975-78; gen. mgr., v.p. Computer/Data Inc., Billings, Mont., 1978-83; mgr. customer service Big Sky Data Systems, Billings, Mont., 1983-84; pres. FACTS, Inc., 1985-95; tax cons., L.A., 1962-75. Cub Scout leader, com. chmn., L.A. coun. Boy Scouts Am., 1973-75; pres. Bus. Office Employees Assn. L.A., 1963-66. Area commr. Black Otter coun. Boy Scouts Am., 1982-84, com. chmn., 1982-84; exec. bd. dirs. Family Svcs. Inc.; bd. dirs. Big Sky Air Show 1990—; sec. Yellowstone Valley Model Railway; bd. govs. Spokane unit Shrine Hosp. Crippled Children, 1993—, hosp. chmn. Al Bedoo Shrine, 1992—. With USNR, 1951-59. Recipient degree of Chevalier, De Molay Cross of Honor, Legion of Honor degree.; cert. data processing mgr. Mem. Data Processing Mgrs. Assn., Rainbow Girls Grand Cross of Colors Shrine, L.A. Masonic Press Club. Clubs: Masons, Blue Lodge, York Rite, Scottish Rite, Shrine, Grotto (charter mem. Gt. Falls), DeMolay (chpt. advisor 1983-92, state advisor 1982-92). Writer, negotiator contract Bus. Office Employees Assn., L.A., 1965.

GREEN, JONATHAN WILLIAM, museum administrator and educator, artist, author; b. Troy, N.Y., Sept. 26, 1939; s. Alan Singer and Frances (Katz) G.; m. Louise Lockshin, Sept. 16, 1962 (div. 1985); children: Raphael, Benjamin; m. Wendy Hughes Brown, Aug. 12, 1988. Student, MIT, 1958-60, Hebrew U., 1960-61; BA, Brandeis U., 1963, postgrad., 1964-67; MA, Harvard U., 1967. Photographer Jonathan Green, Photography, Boston, 1966-76, Ezra Stoller Assocs., Mamaroneck, N.Y., 1967-68; prof. MIT, Cambridge, Mass., 1968-76; dir. Creative Photography Lab MIT, Cambridge, 1974-76; editor Aperture Books and Periodical, N.Y.C., 1972-76; prof. Ohio State U., Columbus, 1976-90; dir. Univ. Gallery Fine Arts, Columbus, 1981-90; founding dir. Wexner Ctr. for the Arts, Columbus, 1981-90; dir. Calif. Mus. Photography, U. Calif., Riverside, 1990—, prof., 1990—; cons. Nat. Endowment for Arts, Washington, 1975-76, 85, 88, 94, Harry N. Abrams, Pubs., N.Y.C., 1982-84, Oxford U. Press, N.Y.C., 1977-82, Polaroid Corp., Cambridge, 1976; co-founder Visible Lang. Workshop, MIT Media Lab., 1973. Author: American Photography, 1984 (Nikon Book of Yr. award 1984, Benjamin Citation 1986), The Snapshot, 1974 (N.Y. Type Dirs. Club award 1974), Camera Work: A Critical Anthology, 1973 (Best Art Book award 1973), Continuous Replay: The Photographs of Arnie Zane, 1999; editor, essayist Re-framing History in Jean Ruiter Photo Works, 1985-1995, 1996, The Garden of Earthly Delights: Photographs by Edward Weston and Robert Mapplethorpe, 1995, New Photographs by Pedro Meyer: Truths & Fictions, An Interactive CD-ROM, 1993, 5 Celebrations of Leslie J. Payne in Leslie Payne: Visions of Flight, 1991, Algorithms for Discovery, 1989, Pink Noise: Three Conversations concerning a Collaborative acoustic Installation with Philip Glass, Richard Serra, Kurt Munacsi, 1987, Rudolf Baranik Elegies: Sleep Napalm Night Sky, 1987, Straight Shooting in America, 1985, James Friedman: Rephotographing the History of the World in James Friedman, Color Photographs 1979-1982, 1982, Aperture in the 50's: The Word and the Way, in Afterimage, 1979, others; represented in permanent collections Mus. Fine Arts, Boston, Mus. Fine Art, Houston, Cleve. Mus. Art, Va. Mus. Fine Art, Richmond, Princeton U. Art Mus., Bell System Collection, Moderna Museet, Stockholm, Ctr. for Creative Photography, Tucson, De Saisset Art Gallery and Mus., Internat. Ctr. Photography, N.Y.C., MIT, Mpls. Inst. Arts; photographs pub.: American Images: New Work by Twenty Contemporary Photographers, 1979, Aperture, 1972, 73, 74, 25 Years of Record Houses, 1981, Architectural Record, Architecture and Urbanism, Progressive Architecture, A Field Guide to Modern American Architecture. Danforth fellow, 1963-67, NEA Photographer fellow, 1978, AT & T fellow, 1979. Office: UCR/California Museum Of Photography Downtown Hist Pedestrian Mall 3824 Main St Riverside CA 92501-3624

GREEN, JUDSON C., marketing agency executive. Pres. Attractions Divsn. Walt Disney Co., Burbank, Calif. Office: Walt Disney Attractions Team Disney 531 500 S Buena Vista St Burbank CA 91521-0004*

GREEN, KENNETH CHARLES, education educator, researcher; b. N.Y.C., Feb. 2, 1951; s. Gilbert and Shirley (Milter) G.; m. Rika Rosemary van Dam, June 29, 1980; children: Aaron Hans, Mara Claire. BA, New Coll., 1973; MA, Ohio State U., 1977; PhD, UCLA, 1982. Assoc. dir., operating officer Higher Edn. Rsch. Inst., assoc. dir. Am. coun. Edn. Coop. Instl. Rsch. Program. UCLA, 1984-89; sr. rsch. assoc. James Irvine Found. Ctr. Scholarly Tech. U. So. Calif., 1989-94, dir. Ctr. Scholarly Tech., 1992-95; rschr., author Campus Computing Nat. Survey Info. Tech. Am. Higher Edn., 1990-98; cons. in field; lectr., various colls. and universities; vis. scholar Claremont Grad. (Calif.) U., 1995—. Author: (with F.R. Kemerer and J.V. Baldridge) Strategies for Effective Enrollment Management, 1982, Government Support for Minority Participation in Higher Education, 1982, (with

Daniel Seymour) Whose Going to Run General Motors, 1992, and numerous research publs.; reviewer Jour. Higher Edn., also monograph series; rschr.; contbr. articles to profl. jours. Mem. Am. Assn. Higher Edn., Assn. for Study of Higher Edn., Am. Edn. Research Assn., Fund for Improvement of Postsecondary Edn. (reviewer), Policy Studies Orgn. Fax: 818-784-8008. E-mail: cgreen@earthlink.net. Office: PO Box 261242 Encino CA 91426-1242

GREEN, LORA MURRAY, immunologist, researcher, educator; b. Redfield, S.D., Feb. 8, 1955; d. Everett k. and Marlene Y. (Palm) Murray; m. Timothy W. Green, Jan. 24, 1976; 1 child, Keigm W. BS in Biochemistry, U. Calif., Riverside, 1981, MS in Biochemsitry, 1982, PhD in Immunology, 1987. Fellow in immunology U. Calif., Riverside; fellow in cell biology Loma Linda (Calif.) U.; rsch. immunologist JL Pettis VA Med. Ctr., Loma Linda, 1991—; assoc. prof. medicine Loma Linda Med. Ctr., 1996—; bd. dirs. Dept. Micro and Molecular Genetics, Loma Linda. Contbr. articles to profl. jours. Grantee VA, 1991-94, Loma Linda, 1995-96. Fellow Am. Assn. Immunology, Assn. Cell Biologists. Achievements include research in the role of the target tissue in autoimmune disease. Office: JL Pettis Vets Hosp 11201 Benton St Loma Linda CA 92357-1000

GREEN, MELANIE JANE, speech-language pathologist; b. Fremont, Calif., Nov. 23, 1968; d. Robert Lucian and Frances Eileen (Jones) G. BA in Communicative Disorders, Calif. State U., Fullerton, 1992; MS in Speech Lang. Pathology, U. Redlands, 1994. Child care coord. Calvary Chapel of Fullerton (Calif.), 1986-87; speech pathologist aide Providence Speech and Hearing Ctr., Orange, Calif., 1988-90; activities asst. Western Neuro Care Ctr., Tustin, Calif., 1989-90; speech-lang. pathology paraprofl. Long Beach, Calif., 1990—; speech-lang. pathologist Newport Lang., Speech, and Audiology Ctr., Newport Beach, 1994—. Mem. Autism Soc. Am., Am. Speech and Hearing Assn. Avocations: rock climbing, surfing, volleyball. Home: PO Box 5679 Newport Beach CA 92662-5679

GREEN, NANCY BALDWIN, marketing consultant; b. Cin., Oct. 25, 1947; d. Robert S. and Mary O'Neill (McDevitt) G.; children: Adrian Alexandra Burns, Alexander Anthony. BFA, Stanford U., 1970, MBA, 1975. Creative dir. Moorhead Mktg., Palo Alto, Calif., 1970-73; mng. dir. The Fields Investment Group, Mrs. Fields' Cookies, Portola Valley, Calif., 1975-83; prin. Green, Schleck & Stoller, Palo Alto, 1983-88, The William Baldwin Group, Palo Alto, 1988—. Co-author: Price Trends and Strategic Response, 1985. Office: The William Baldwin Group 2190 Saint Francis Dr Palo Alto CA 94303-3113

GREEN, PETER, mayor, biological sciences educator. BSc in Biology, St. Benedict's Coll., 1952; BS in Theology, St. Gregory's Sem., 1956; BS in Zoology, U. Okla., 1959; MS in Zoology, Okla. State U., 1961, PhD in Ecology, 1964. Acad. dean St. Gregory's Coll., Shawnee, Okla., 1964-69, founding pres., 1968; pres. St. Gregory's Coll., Shawnee, 1969-70; prof. biol. scis. Golden West Coll., Huntington Beach, Calif., 1970—; now mayor City of Huntington Beach, 1998—; post-doctoral fellow higher edn. U. Okla., Norman, 1970; cons. Environ. Planners, Linesch and Assocs., Long Beach, Calif., Wintersburg High Sch. Sci. Program, 1982-83; coun. mem. City of Huntington Beach, 1984—, mayor pro tempore, 1989-90. Contbr. articles to profl. jours. Chmn. curriculum com. for regional accreditation Golden West Coll., 1975-76, resdl. search com., 1977, parliamentarian, senator at large Acad. Senate of Golden West Coll., 1976-78, pres., 1978-79; liaison allied arts bd., libr. bd., environ. rev. bd., A & R design com., pub. facilities corp., toxic waste com. Huntington Beach City Coun., 1989—; rep. state-wide environ. issues com. Orange County div. Calif. League of Cities, 1988—; founding chmn. bd. Bolsa Chica Found., 1983—. NSF grantee, 1965, 68-69, 70-71, Kellogg grantee, 1966, 67; fellow Golden West Coll., 1973-77; named one of Outstanding Educators of Am., 1969-70, 74-75. Mem. Bosa Chica Conservancy (founding bd. mem. 1990), Amigos De Bolsa Chica (governing bd. mem., past pres. 1975-84). Office: Office of Mayor & City Coun City Hall 2000 Main St Huntington Beach CA 92648*

GREEN, PHYLLIS HARTMAN, writer, playwright; b. Pitts., June 24, 1932; d.Victor Geyer and Phyllis (Sailer) Hartman; m. Robert Bailey Green, Aug. 15, 1959; children: Sharon Buell, Bruce. BS in Edn, Westminster Coll., 1953; MEd, U. Pitts., 1955. Writer, playwright, 1972—. Author: The Fastest Quitter in Town, 1972, Nantucket Summer, 1974, Ice River, 1975, Wild Violets, 1977, Grandmother Orphan, 1977, Mildred Murphy, How Does Your Garden Grow?, 1977, Walkie-Talkie, 1978, Nicky's Lopsided, Lumpy, But Delicious Orange, 1978, A New Mother for Martha, 1978, Gloomy Louie, 1980, Bagdad Ate It, 1980 (Calif. Young Reader Medal 1984), The Empty Seat, 1980, Uncle Roland, The Perfect Guest, 1983, Eating Ice Cream with a Werewolf, 1983 (Maud Hart Lovelace award 1989), Bummer Summer, 1988, Chucky Bellman Was So Bad, 1991; playwright: Deer Season, 1980, Physically Handicapped Singles Dance, 1983, Acapulco Holiday, 1988. Named Best Actress in Del., Del. Play Festival, 1956.

GREEN, RICHARD FREDERICK, astronomer; b. Omaha, Feb. 13, 1949; m. Joan Auerbach; children: Alexander Simon, Nathaniel Martin. AB in Astronomy magna cum laude, Harvard U., 1971; PhD in Astronomy, Calif. Inst. Tech., 1977. Physics lab instr. Harvard U., Cambridge, 1970-71; NSF trainee Calif. Inst. Tech., Pasadena, 1971-72, grad. teaching asst. in astronomy, 1972-74, grad. rsch. asst. in astronomy, 1974-77, rsch. fellow in astronomy, 1977-79; asst. astronomer Steward Observatory, U. Ariz., Tucson, 1979-83; asst. astronomer Kitt Peak Nat. Observatory, Tucson, 1983-85, assoc. astronomer, 1986-90, astronomer, 1990—, dir., 1997—; acting dir. Nat. Optical Astronomy Observatories, Tucson, 1992-93, acting dep. dir., 1993-94, dep. dir., 1994—; rsch. asst. Smithsonian Astrophys. Observatory, 1970-71; adj. asst. prof. Steward Observatory, U. Ariz., 1983-85, adj. assoc. astronomer and prof., 1986-90, adj. astronomer, 1990—; mem. users' com. Internat. Ultraviolet Explorer Satellite, NASA, 1979-81, chair proposal rev. panel, 1986-88, 93, final sci. program com., 1993, mem. sci. team Far Ultraviolet Spectroscopic Explorer Satellite, 1981—, Space Telescope Imaging Spectrograph, 1982—, guest observer working group Extreme Ultraviolet Explorer Satellite, 1988-92, chair proposal rev. panel ROSAT Guest Observer Program, 1989, 92, ROSAT Users' Coms., 1990-93, chair HST Cycle 2 Porposal Rev. Panel, mem. time allocation com., 1991, STSDAS users' com., 1991-92, Hubble Space Telescope Program Rev., 1997; mem. panel ultraviolet and optical astronomy from space, astronomy survey com. Nat. Acad. Scis., 1989-90; mem. panel HST and Beyond AURA, 1994-95; mem. proposal rev. panels NSF, 1996-97; instrument scientist Gemini 8-m Telescopes Project, 1991-92; mem. U.S. Gemini sci. adv. com., Gemini (Internat.) sci. com. U.S. Gemini Project Office, 1991-93, acting U.S. Gemini Project scientist, 1992-93, mem. instrument forum, optical instrumentation sci. working group, chair multi-object spectrograph critical design rev., 1997. Nat. Merit scholar; Hon. scholar Harvard U. Mem. AAAS (astronomy divsn. nominating com. 1992, coun. astronomy rep. com. coun. affairs 1995-97), Am. Astronomical Soc., Internat. Astronomical Union, Astronomical Soc. of the Pacific, Phi Beta Kappa. Office: Kitt Peak Nat Observatory 950 N Cherry Ave PO Box 26732 Tucson AZ 85726-6732*

GREEN, ROBERTA HELEN, rancher, writer, historian; b. Challis, Idaho, Sept. 4, 1919; d. Robert Weir and Ethel Belle (Thompson) Philps; children: Joann, Judith, Ronald, Gary, Melissa. Cattle rancher Idaho, 1934—; historian Custer County, Challis, Idaho, 1980. Author: (books) They Passed This Way, They Followed Their Dreams, The Glory Trail. Mem. Idaho Press Women (Communicator of Yr. Idaho 1997, nominated for Nat. Communicator of Yr., 1997), Cowboy Poets of Idaho. Republican. Mem. Congregational Ch. Avocations: painting, cowboy poetry. Home: PO Box 213 Challis ID 83226-0213

GREEN, TRAVIS, professional hockey player; b. Castlegar, B.C., Can., Dec. 20, 1970; m. Sherry Ragan, July 18. Center New York Islanders, 1989-98, Mighty Ducks of Anaheim, 1998-; mem. Team Canada at World Championships, Vienna, 1995-96/. Office: Mighty Ducks of Anaheim P.O.Box 61077 2695 E Katella Ave Anaheim CA 92803-6177*

GREEN, WILLIAM PORTER, lawyer; b. Jacksonville, Ill., Mar. 19, 1920; s. Hugh Parker and Clara Belle (Hopper) G.; m. Rose Marie Hall, Oct. 1, 1944; children: Hugh Michael, Robert Alan, Richard William. BA, Ill. Coll., 1941; JD, Northwestern U., Evanston, Ill., 1947. Bar: Ill. 1947, Calif. 1948, U.S. Dist. Ct. (so. dist.) Tex. 1986, U.S. Ct. Customs and Patent Appeals, U.S. Patent and Trademark Office 1948, U.S. Ct. Appeals (fed. cir.) 1982, U.S. Ct. Appeals (5th and 9th cir.), U.S. Supreme Ct. 1948, U.S. Dist. Ct. (cen. dist.) Calif. 1949, (so. dist.) Tex.1986. Pvt. practice L.A., 1947—; mem. Wills, Green & Mueth, L.A., 1974-83; of counsel Nilsson, Robbins, Dalgarn, Berliner, Carson & Wurst, L.A., 1984-91; of counsel Nilsson, Wurst & Green L.A., 1992—; del. Calif. State Bar Conv., 1982—, chmn., 1986. Bd. editors Ill. Law Rev., 1946; patentee in field. Mem. L.A. world Affairs Coun., 1975—; deacon local Presbyn. Ch., 1961-63. Mem. ABA, Calif. State Bar, Am. Intellectual Property Law Assn., L.A. Patent Law Assn. (past. sec.-treas., mem. bd. govs.), Lawyers Club L.A. (past treas., past sec., mem. bd. govs., pres. 1985-86), Los Angeles County Bar Assn. (trustee 1986-87), Am. Legion (past post comdr.), Northwestern U. Alumni Club So. Calif., Big Ten Club So. Calif., Town Hall Calif. Club, PGA West Golf Club (La Quinta, Calif.), Phi Beta Kappa, Phi Delta Phi, Phi Alpha. Republican. Home: 3570 Lombardy Rd Pasadena CA 91107-5627 Office: 707 Wilshire Blvd Ste 3200 Los Angeles CA 90017-3514

GREENBAUM, ROBERT STRAUSS, recreational facility executive; b. New Orleans, Dec. 29, 1955; s. James R. and Peggy (Strauss) G.; m. Andrea Lynn Siegel, June 30, 1985; children: Jolene, Hannah, Charlotte. BA, Tulane U., 1978. Events coord. Pace Mgmt., Houston, 1978-79; pres. Greenbaum Realty, Palm Springs, Calif., 1980-96; founder Telemarketing Comm. of Las Vegas, Inc. (merged into Access Long Distance), 1985-87; pres. Andrea's Calif. Farms, Palm Springs, 1985-93; owner/chmn. Par-Tee Golf, Palm Springs, 1993-96; founder/pres. Uprising Rock Climbing Ctr., Palm Springs, 1995—. Bd. dirs., sec. Jewish Fedn. of Desert, Palm Springs, 1987—; bd. dirs. Ctr. for Learning and Leadership, N.Y.C., 1995—, Turner's Syndrome Soc., Wayzata, Minn., 1994-96. Mem. Tamarisk Country Club, Palm Valley Country Club. Avocations: golf, running, skiing, swimming, climbing. Home: 38-105 Via Fortuna Palm Springs CA 92264 Office: 69-844 Hwy 111 Ste H Rancho Mirage CA 92270

GREENBERG, BARRY MICHAEL, talent executive; b. Bklyn., Nov. 9, 1951; s. Aaron Herbert and Alice Rhoda (Strauss) G.; m. Susan Kay Greenberg, Feb. 19, 1990; 1 child, Samuel Jacob; 1 child by previous marriage: Seth Grahame-Smith. BA, Antioch U. Dir. B'nai B'rith, Phila., 1976-80; acting dir. Jewish Nat. Fund, L.A., 1980-81; chmn. Celebrity Connection, Beverly Hills, Calif., 1981—; co-founder Beverly Hills Air Force Co.; ptnr. U.S. Film Force Co. Emeritus mem. Air Force adv. bd. USAF; mem. Wilshire cmty. police adv. bd. L.A. Police Dept.; fin. co-chair, past chair Cmty.-Police Adv. Bd. Summit; mem. 50th Anniversary of WWII com. U.S. Dept. Def.; mem. pub. safety steering com. L.A. 4th Councilmanic Dist.; mem. exec. bd. CDC Bus. Responds to AIDS program; co-founder Windsor Watch; adv. bd. Windsor Sq. Assn.; charter past pres. entertainment industry unit B'nai B'rith. With USAF, 1969-75. Recipient Chief of Chaplains Meritorious Svc. award, USAF. Mem. Def. Orientation Conf. Assn., Air Force Pub. Affairs Alumni Assn. Jewish. Avocations: pilot, music. Office: Celebrity Connection 4311 Wilshire Blvd # 300 Los Angeles CA 90010

GREENBERG, BYRON STANLEY, newspaper and business executive, consultant; b. Bklyn., June 17, 1919; s. Albert and Bertha (Getleson) G.; m. Helena Marks, Feb. 10, 1946; children: David, Eric, Randy. Student, Bklyn. Coll., 1936-41. Circulation mgr. N.Y. Post, 1956-62, circulation dir., 1962-63, bus. mgr., 1963-72, gen. mgr., dir., 1973-79; sec., dir. N.Y. Post Corp., 1966-75, treas., dir., 1975-76, v.p., 1976-81; v.p., dir. Leisure Systems, Inc., 1978-80; pres., chief exec. officer, dir. Games Mgmt. Services, Inc., 1979-80. Bd. dirs. 92d St YMHA, 1970-71, Friars Nat. Found., 1981-82. Served with AUS, 1942-45. Mem. Friars Club. Home and Office: 2560 S Grade Rd Alpine CA 91901-3612

GREENBERG, EDWARD SEYMOUR, political science educator, writer; b. Phila., July 1, 1942; s. Samuel and Yetta (Kaplan) G.; m. Martha Ann Baker, Dec. 24, 1964; children: Joshua, Nathaniel. BA, Miami (Ohio) U., 1964, MA, 1965; PhD, U. Wis., 1969. Asst. prof. polit. sci. Stanford (Calif.) U., 1968-72; assoc. prof. Ind. U., Bloomington, 1972-73; prof. U. Colo., Boulder, 1973—, dir. research program polit. and econ. change Inst. Behavioral Sci., 1980—, chair dept. polit. sci., 1985-88. Author: Serving the Few, 1974, Understanding Modern Government, 1979, Capitalism and the American Political Ideal, 1985, The American Political System, 1989, Workplace Democracy, 1986 (Dean's Writing award Social Scis. 1987), The Struggle for Democracy, 1993, 95, 97, 99, brief edit., 1996, 99; contbr. articles to profl. jours. Recipient fellowship In Recognition of Disting. Tchg., 1968, Jeffrey Pressman award Policy Studies Assn.; grantee Russell Sage Found., 1968, U. Wis., 1968, NSF, 1976, 82, 85, NIH, 1991-94, 96-2000. Mem. Internat. Polit. Sci. Assn., Am. Polit. Sci. Assn., Western Polit. Sci. Assn. (mem. exec. bd. 1986-89). Avocations: skiing, reading, bicycling, travel. E-mail: edward.greenberg@colorado.edu. Home: 755 11th St Boulder CO 80302-7512 Office: U Colo Inst Behavioral Sci PO Box 487 Boulder CO 80309-0487

GREENBERG, IRA ARTHUR, psychologist; b. Bklyn., June 26, 1924; s. Philip and Minnie (S.) G.; m. Martha Estella Cantrell, 1949 (div. 1950); m. Judith Linda Burgard-Rials, 1952 (div. 1954); m. Monita Ruth Nibord, 1961 (div. 1965). BA in Journalism, U. Okla., 1949; MA in English, U. So. Calif., 1962; MS in Counseling, Calif. State U. L.A., 1963; PhD in Psychology, Claremont (Calif.) Grad Sch., 1967; Grad. Marine Corps Inst.'s Command and Staff Coll., 1992. Editor, Ft. Riley (Kans.) Guidon, 1950-51; copy editor, reporter Columbus (Ga.) Enquirer, 1951-55; reporter Louisville Courier-Jour., 1955-56, L.A. Times, 1956-62; free-lance writer, L.A., Montclair, Camarillo, Calif., 1960-69, 76—; counselor Claremont Coll. Psychol. Clinic and Counseling Ctr., 1964-65; lectr. psychology Chapman Coll., Orange, Calif., 1965-66; psychologist Camarillo State Hosp., 1967-69, supervising psychologist, 1969-73, part-time clin. psychologist, 1973-93; part-time asst. prof. edn. San Fernando Valley State Coll., Northridge, Calif., 1967-69, lectr. psychodrama, social welfare U. Calif. Extension Div., Santa Barbara, 1968-69; vis. prof. edn. U. Nev., Reno, 1977—; vol. psychologist Free Clinic, L.A., 1968-70; staff dir. Calif. Inst. Psychodrama, 1969-71; tng. cons. Topanga Ctr. for Human Devel., 1970-75, bd. dirs., 1971-74, faculty Calif. Sch. Profl. Psychology, 1970-80; founder, exec. dir. Behavioral Studies Inst., mgmt. cons., L.A., 1970—; pvt. practice cons. in psychology, psychodrama, hypnosis, 1970—; founder, exec. dir. Psychodrama Ctr. for L.A., Inc., 1971—, Group Hypnosis Ctr., L.A., 1976—; producer, host TV talk show Crime and Pub. Safety, Century Comm., Channel 77, 1983—. Vol. humane officer State of Calif., 1979-89; res. officer L.A. Police Dept., 1980-86; bd. dirs. Humane Educators Coun., 1982-86; mem. Nat. Coun. Employer Support of Guard and Res., 1998—. With AUS 11th engr. combat bn., XXI Corps, Seventh Army, ETO, 1943-46; USAR, 1950-51; capt. Calif. State Mil. Res., 1986-93, maj. 1993—. Fellow Am. Soc. Clin. Hypnosis, Am. Soc. Group Psychotherapy and Psychodrama; mem. Am. Psychol. Assn., Calif. Psychol. Assn., L.A. County Psychol. Assn., So. Calif. Soc. Clin. Hypnosis (pres. 1977-78), Group Psychotherapy Assn. So. Calif. (pres. 1987-88), So. Calif. Psychotherapy Affiliation (dir. 1976-85), Am. Soc. Psychical Rsch., Assn. Rsch. and Enlightenment. Peace Officers Assn., L.A. County, Acad. TV Arts and Scis., Nat. Acad. Cable Programming, Fraternal Order of UDT/SEAL, Navy Amphibious Scouts and Raiders Assn., 11th Engr. Combat Battalion Assn., 78th Infantry Divsn. Assn., VFW, Am. Legion, Jewish War Vets., State Def. Forces Assn. Am., State Def. Forces Assn. Calif., Mensa, Am. Zionist Fedn., NRA, Calif. Rifle and Pistol Assn., SW Pistol League, Animal Protection Inst. Am., L.A. SPCA, Hebrew Nat. Orphan Home Alumni Assn., Sigma Delta Chi. Clubs: Sierra, Greater L.A. Press; B'nai B'rith; Beverly Hills Gun. Author: Psychodrama and Audience Attitude Change, 1968. Editor, author: Psychodrama: Theory and Therapy, 1974; Group Hypnotherapy and Hypnodrama, 1977. Office: BSI & Group Hypnosis Ctr 8939 S Sepulveda Blvd Ste 318 Los Angeles CA 90045-3605

GREENBERG, LENORE, public relations professional; b. Flushing, N.Y.; d. Jack and Frances Orenstein. BA, Hofstra U.; MS, SUNY. Dir .pub. rels. Bloomingdale's, Short Hills, N.J., 1977-78; dir. comms. N.J. Sch. Bds. Assn., Trenton, 1978-82; dir pub. info. N.J. State Dept. Edn., Trenton, 1982-90; assoc. exec. dir. Nat. Sch. Pub. Rels. Assn., Arlington, Va., 1990-91, pres. Lenore Greenberg & Assocs., Inc., 1991—; adj. prof. pub. rels. Rutgers U. Freelance feature writer N.Y. Times. Mem. bd. assocs. McCarter Theatre, Princeton, N.J.; mem. Franklin Twp. Zoning Bd. Adjustment; mem. Franklin Twp. Human Rels. Commn.; chair Somerset County LWV; instr. Bus. Vols. for the Arts. Recipient award Am. Soc. Assn. Execs., award Women in Comms., award Internat. Assn. Bus. Communicators; Gold Medallion awrd Nat. Sch. Pub. Rels. Assn. Mem. Pub. Rels. Soc. Am. (accredited; pres. N.J. State chpt., nat. nominating and accreditation coms., Silver Anvil award), Nat. Health/Edn. Consortium. Home and Office: 30971 Carrara Rd Laguna Niguel CA 92677-2757

GREENBERG, MYRON SILVER, lawyer; b. L.A., Oct. 17, 1945; s. Earl W. and Geri (Silver) G.; m. Shlomit Gross; children: David, Amy, Sophie, Benjamin. BSBA, UCLA, 1967, JD, 1970. Bar: Calif. 1971, U.S. Dist. Ct. (cen. dist.) Calif. 1971, U.S. Tax Ct. 1977; cert. specialist in taxation law; CPA, Calif. Staff acct. Touche Ross & Co., L.A., 1970-71; assoc. Kaplan, Livingston, Goodwin, Berkowitz, & Selvin, Beverly Hills, 1971-74; ptnr. Dinkelspiel, Pelavin, Steefel & Levitt, San Francisco, 1975-80; ptnr. Steefel, Levitt & Weiss, San Francisco, 1981-82; pres. Myron S. Greenberg, a Profl. Corp., Larkspur, Calif., 1982—; professional lectr. tax. Golden Gate U.; instr. U. Calif., Berkeley, 1989—; mem. taxation law adv. commn. Calif. Bd. Legal Specialization, 1998—. Author: California Attorney's Guide to Professional Corporations, 1977, 79; bd. editors UCLA Law Rev., 1969-70. Mem. San Anselmo Planning Commn., 1976-77; Marin County chpt. Am. Heart Assn. (bd. dirs., pres. 1984-90); mem. adv. bd. cert. program in personal fin. planning U. Calif., Berkeley, 1991—. Mem. ABA, AICPA, Los Angeles County Bar Assn., Marin County (Calif.) Bar Assn. (bd. dirs. 1994—, pres. 1999), Real Estate Tax Inst. of Calif. Continuing Edn. Bar (planning com.), Larkspur C. of C. (bd. dirs. 1985-87). Democrat. Jewish. Office: # 205 700 Larkspur Landing Cir Larkspur CA 94939-1715

GREENBERG, PAMELA THAYER, public policy specialist; b. Denver, May 16, 1959; d. Paul Burton and Betty Mae (Clint) Thayer; m. Alan Greenberg, Aug. 7, 1988. BA, U. Colo., 1981, MS, 1994. Rsch. asst. Nat. Assessment of Ednl. Progress, Denver, 1982-83; rsch. coord. Regis Coll., Denver, 1983-86; program prin. Nat. Conf. State Legislatures, Denver, 1986—. Author: Guide to Legislative Information Technology, 1995; contbr. articles to profl. jours. Named one of Outstanding Young Women of Am., 1984. Mem. LWV (bd. dirs. 1990-91). Office: Nat Conf State Legislatures 1560 Broadway Ste 700 Denver CO 80202-5176

GREENBERG, RICHARD ALAN, film designer; b. Chgo.; s. Louis Hyman and Ruth (Glass) G.; m. Paula Diane Silver, Mar. 25, 1980; children: Jessica, Morgan, Luke. BFA, U. Ill., 1970, MFA, 1972. Founding ptnr. R. Greenberg Assocs., N.Y.C., 1978-94, Greenberg/Schluter, Venice, Calif., 1994—. Dir.: (film) Stop, 1970 (Best Student Film); one-man shows include U. Ill., Chgo., 1995. Bd. dirs. Am. Inst. Graphic Arts, N.Y.C., 1980-82. Grantee Program for Film on Art, N.Y.C., 1988; recipient Clio award, 1986-88. Mem. NATAS, Acad. Motion Pictures Arts and Scis. Office: Greenberg/Schluter 215 1/2 Windward Ave Venice CA 90291-3764

GREENE, ALVIN, service company executive, management consultant; b. Pitts., Aug. 26, 1932; s. Samuel David and Yetta (Kroff) G.; BA, Stanford U., 1954, MBA, 1959; m. M. Louise Sokol, Nov. 11, 1977; children: Sharon, Ami, Ann, Daniel. Asst. to pres. Narmco Industries, Inc., San Diego, 1959-62; adminstrv. mgr., mgr. mktg. Whittaker Corp., L.A., 1962-67; sr. v.p. Cordura Corp., L.A., 1967-75; chmn. bd. Sharon-Sage, Inc., L.A., 1975-79; exec. v.p., chief operating officer Republic Distbrs., Inc., Carson, Calif., 1979-81, also dir.; chief operating officer Memel, Jacobs & Ellsworth, 1981-87, 87—; pres. SCI Cons., Inc.; dir. Sharon-Sage, Inc., True Data Corp.; vis. prof. Am. Grad. Sch. Bus., Phoenix, 1977-81. Chmn. bd. commrs. Housing Authority City of L.A., 1983-88 . Served to 1st lt., U.S. Army, 1955-57. Mem. Direct Mail Assn., Safety Helmet Mfrs. Assn., Bradley Group. Office: 11990 San Vicente Blvd Ste 300 Los Angeles CA 90049-6608

GREENE, FRANK SULLIVAN, JR., investment management executive; b. Washington, Oct. 19, 1938; s. Frank S. Sr. and Irma O. Greene; m. Phyllis Davison, Jan. 1958 (dec. 1984); children: Angela, Frank, Ronald; m. Carolyn W. Greene, Sept. 1990. BS, Washington U., St. Louis, 1961; MS, Purdue U., 1962; PhD, U. Santa Clara, Calif., 1970. Part-time lectr. Washington U., Howard U., Am. U., 1959-65; pres., dir. Tech. Devel. Corp., Arlington, Tex., 1985-92; pres. Zero One Systems (formerly Tech. Devel. of Calif.), Santa Clara, Calif., 1971-87, Zero One Systems Group subs. Sterling Software Inc., 1987-89; asst. chmn., lectr. Stanford U., 1972-74; bd. dirs. Beyond Software, Inc., ZNYX Corp.; bd. dirs. Networked Picture Systems Inc., 1986-94, pres. 1989-91, chmn. 1991-94; mng. mem. New Vista Capital, LLC, Palo Alto, Calif., 1993—. Author two indsl. textbooks; also articles; patentee in field. Bd. dirs. NCCJ, Santa Clara, 1980—, NAACP, San Jose chpt., 1986-89, Am. Musical Theatre of San Jose, 1995—; bd. regents Santa Clara U., 1983-90, trustee, 1990—; mem. adv. bd. Urban League, Santa Clara County, 1986-89, East Side Union High Sch., 1985-88. Capt. USAF, 1961-65. Mem IEEE, IEEE Computer Soc. (governing bd. 1973-75), Assn. Black Mfrs. (bd. dirs. 1974-80), Am. Electric Assn. (indsl. adv. bd. 1975-76), Fairchild Rsch. and Devel. (tech. staff 1965-71), Bay Area Purchasing Coun. (bd. dirs. 1978-84), Security Affairs Support Assn. (bd. dirs. 1980-83), Sigma Xi, Eta Kappa Nu, Sigma Pi Phi.

GREENE, JOHN THOMAS, judge; b. Salt Lake City, Nov. 28, 1929; s. John Thomas and Mary Agnes (Hindley) G.; m. Dorothy Kay Buchanan, Mar. 31, 1955; children: Thomas Buchanan Greene, John Buchanan Greene, Mary Kay Greene Platt. BA in Polit. Sci., U. Utah, 1952, JD, 1955. Bar: Utah 1955, U.S. Dist. Ct. (10th cir.) 1955, U.S. Supreme Ct. 1966. Pvt. practice Salt Lake City, 1955-57, asst. U.S. atty., 1957-59; ptnr. Marr, Wilkins & Cannon (and successor firms), Salt Lake City, 1959-75; ptnr., pres., chmn. bd. dirs. Greene, Callister & Nebeker, Salt Lake City, 1975-85; judge U.S. Dist. Ct., Salt Lake City, 1985—. Author: (manual) American Mining Law, 1960; contbr. articles to profl. jours. Chmn. Salt Lake City Cmty. Coun., 1970-75, Utah State Bldg. Authority, Salt Lake City, 1980-85; Regent Utah State Bd. Higher Edn., Salt Lake City, 1982-86. Recipient Order of Coif U. Utah, 1955, Merit of Honor award, 1994, Utah Fed. Bar Disting. Svc. award, 1997. Fellow ABA Found. (life; ABA ho. of dels. 1972-92, bd. govs. 1987-91); mem. Dist. Judges Assn. (pres. 10th cir. 1998—), Utah Bar Assn. (pres. 1971-72, Judge of Yr. award 1995), Am. Law Inst. (life, panelist and lectr. 1980-85, advisor 1986-98), Phi Beta Kappa. Mormon. Avocations: travel, reading, tennis. Office: US Dist Ct 350 S Main St Ste 150 Salt Lake City UT 84101-2180

GREENE, LAURENCE WHITRIDGE, JR., surgical educator; b. Denver, Jan. 18, 1924; s. Laurence Whitridge Sr. and Freda (Schmitt) G.; m. Frances Steger, Sept. 16, 1950 (dec. Dec. 1977); children: Charlotte Greene Kerr, Mary Whitridge Greene, Laurence Whitridge III; m. Nancy Kay Bennett, Dec. 7, 1984. BA, Colo. Coll., 1945; MD, U. Colo., 1947; postgrad., U. Chgo., 1948-50. Diplomate Am. Bd. of Surgery. Intern St. Lukes Hosp., Denver, 1947-48; sr. intern in ob./gyn. U. Chgo. Lying-In Hosp., 1948-49; surg. resident U. Cin. Gen. Hosp., 1952-55, sr. surg. resident, 1955-57, chief surgery resident, 1957-58; clin. surgery asst. Sch. of Medicine U. Colo., Denver, 1958-61, clin. instr. Sch. of Medicine, 1961-67, asst. clin. prof. Sch. of Medicine, 1967-75, assoc. clin. prof. Sch. of Medicine, 1975-87, clin. prof. Sch. of Medicine, 1987—; adj. prof. zoology and physiology U. Wyo., Laramie, 1970-80; mem. staff Ivinson Meml. Hosp., Laramie, 1958—; chmn. Wyo chpt. Com. on Trauma, 1973-89; tchr., mem. adv. staff U. Colo. Med. Sch., Denver, 1958-83; mem. advisor, surgeon U. Wyo. Athletics, Laramie, 1975-80, Wyo. Hwy. Patrol, 1950—. Contbr. numerous articles to profl. jours. Lt. M.C. (s.g.) USN, 1950-52, Korea. Fellow ACS; mem. Am. Assn. for Surgery of Trauma, Southwestern Surgery Congress, Western Surg. Assn., Mont Reed Soc., Masons, Shriners, Sigma Xi. Republican. Episcopalian. Avocations: golf, sports, hunting, fishing.

GREENE, RICHARD BOYD, JR., marketing and sales executive; b. Boston, July 31, 1962; s. Richard B. and Joy C. (Cudd) G.; m. Lynn Susan Lippoldt, Aug. 24, 1991. BBA, U. Wis., Milw., 1985; MBA, U. Phoenix, San Jose, Calif., 1994. Sales rep. Campbell Soup Co., Des Plaines, Ill., 1985, sales specialist, 1985-87; mgr. trade svcs. Selling Areas Mktg., Inc., Chgo., 1987-88; regional dir. Selling Areas Mktg., Inc., San Ramon, Calif., 1988-91; dir. Info. Resources, Inc., San Francisco, 1991-94; v.p. A.C. Nielsen, Fremont, Calif., 1994-97; v.p. bus. devel. Planet U., San Francisco, 1997-98; v.p. sales Spence Info. Svcs., San Francisco, 1998—. Mem. Am. Mktg. Assn. Republican. Methodist. Avocations: golfing, suba diving.

GREENLAW, ROGER LEE, interior designer; b. New London, Conn., Oct. 12, 1936; s. Kenneth Nelson and Lyndell Lee (Stinson) G.; children: Carol Jennifer, Roger Lee. BFA, Syracuse U., 1958. Interior designer Cannell & Chaffin, 1958-59, William C. Wagner, Architect, L.A., 1959-60, Gen.

Fireproofing Co., L.A., 1960-62, K-S Wilshire, Inc., L.A., 1963-64; dir. interior design Calif. Desk Co., L.A., 1964-67; sr. interior designer Bechtel Corp., L.A., 1967-70; sr. interior designer, project mgr. Daniel, Mann, Johnson, & Mendehall, L.A., 1970-72, Morganelli-Heumann & Assos., L.A., 1972-73; owner, prin. Greenlaw Design Assos., Glendale, Calif., 1973—, Greenlaw Interior Planning & Design, 1996—; lectr. UCLA; mem. adv. curriculum com. Mt. San Antonio Coll., Walnut, Calif., Fashion Inst. Design, L.A.; bd. dirs. Calif. Legis. Conf. Interior Design. Past scoutmaster Verdugo council Boy Scouts Am.; pres. bd. dirs. Unity Ch., La Crescenta, Calif., 1989-91. Mem. Am. Soc. Interior Designers (treas. Pasadena chpt. 1983-84, 1st v.p. 1985, pres. 1986-87, chmn. So. Calif. regional conf. 1985, nat. dir. 1987—, nat. com. legis., nat. com. jury for catalog award, speaker ho. dels., nat. bd. dirs., medallist award, regional v.p., nat. chair ethics com., nat. exec. com., v.p., treas. 1992 Calif. legislative conf. interior design, chmn. standards task force, pres. 1994-98), Glendale C. of C. (bd. dirs. 1998), Adm. Farragut Acad. Alumni Assn., Delta Upsilon. Republican. Lodge: Kiwanis (bd. dirs.). Home: 2100 Valderas Dr Apt F Glendale CA 91208-1340 Office: 2155 Verdugo Blvd Montrose CA 91020-1628

GREENLEAD, JUDITH CAROL, artist, art educator; b. Newark, Dec. 7, 1936; ds. Charles and Esther (Satz) Robin; children: Brandon Katter, Jud Yaski (div. 178). BA in Fine Arts cum laude, UCLA, 1959, MA in Fine Arts, 1964; postgrad., Sonoma State U., Rohnert Park, N.Y., 1978. Cert. lifetime tchr. art, Calif. Cons. in arts The Midtown Sch., L.A., 1963-64; art instr. El Camino (Calif.) Jr. Coll., 1967-68, L.A. Trade Tech. Coll., 1966-70, Coll. of Redwoods, Ft. Bragg, Calif., 1974-91; founder, dir. Escape to Baja, Little River and San Jose, Calif., 1989—, Del Cabo, Mexico, 19896; art instr., workshop leader Mendocino (Calif.) Art Ctr., 1973—; art instr. Santa Rosa (Calif.) Jr. Coll., 1985—; curator sculpture Ft. Bragg (Calif.) Ctr. for Arts, 1993-94; dir. art tours Europe and Mexico Coll. Redwoods, Santa Rosa Jr. Coll., 1981-98; dir. resident student program Mendocino Art Ctr., 1974-75; art cons. Am. Savs. & Loan, Van Nuys, Calif., 1984; art lectr. various schs., arts orgns. and socs., 1970-98. Author, presenter lecture series/video Art, Style and Society, 1995. Recipient awards Mendocino Art Ctr., Gualala Art Ctr., 1972-97. Democrat. Avocations: camping, snorkeling, rafting, gardening, travel. Home and Office: 6034 Airport Rd Little River CA 95456

GREENLEY, KENNETH J., writer; b. N.Y.C., Feb. 4, 1958; s. Langdon John and Anne Margaret (Hoffman) G.; m. Vicki Diana Marrows, Oct. 1, 1993. Author: Son of Mass Production, 1992, Magnetic Colfax, 1994, Clouds But No Rain, 1997. Avocations: hiking, basketball, bicycling.

GREENSTEIN, MERLE EDWARD, import and export company executive; b. Portland, Oreg., June 22, 1937; s. Sol and Tillie Germaine (Schnitzer) G.; m. Nasi Jenab; 1 child, Todd Aaron. BA, Reed Coll., 1959. Pres. Acme Trading and Supply Co., Portland, 1963-82; chmn. MMI Group, Portland, 1982-91, Internat. Devel. Assocs., Portland, 1991—; com. mem. ISRI, Washington, 1987-89; mem. dist. export coun. U.S. Dept. Commerce, 1980—, mem. first USA trade Missions to Vietnam, 1996. Chmn. fin. Portland Opera, 1966; bd. dirs. Met. YMCA, 1964-67; del. to China, State of Oreg. Ofcl. Trade Mission, 1979; chmn. Western Internat. Trade Group, 1981-82; mem. State of Oreg. Korea Commn., 1985-90; fin. chmn. Anne Frank exhibit, Portland; joint chmn. bldg. campaign Oreg. Mus. Sci. and Industry; bd. dirs. Waverly Children's Home; bd. cons. Unilearn Corp.; chmn. fin. Oreg. Holocaust Mem.; mem. Food Bank Relocation Com., property task force com. Oreg. Food Bank Property. Recipient President's E for Export, U.S. Dept. Commerce, 1969; named Citizen of the Week, City of Portland, 1953. Mem. Rolls Royce Owners Club (London), City Club, Tualatin Country Club, Masons, Shriners. Avocations: antique autos, Arabian horses, cross country skiing. Office: Internat Devel Assocs 6731 NE 47th Ave Portland OR 97218-1205

GREENWOOD, VAL DAVID, church administrator; b. Murray, Utah, July 14, 1937; s. David Hartley and Mary Thelma (Cox) G.; m. Margaret (Peggy) Turner, July 3, 1964; children: Yvonne Israelsen, Cherie Halladay, Karen Labrum. BS, Brigham Young U., 1962; JD, U. Idaho, 1974. Bar: Utah 1975; accredited genealogist Geneal. Soc. of Utah. Geneal. rschr. LDS Ch., Salt Lake City, 1962-65; faculty Ricks Coll., Rexburg, Idaho, 1965-74; publs. specialist, Gen. Dept. LDS Ch., Salt Lake City, 1974-76, mgr. spl. svcs., Gen. Dept., 1976-80, mgr. spl. svcs., Temple Dept., 1980-88, dir. spl. svcs. Temple Dept., 1988-98; dir. temple facilities, Temple Dept. LDS Ch., 1999—; faculty Samford U. Inst. Geneal. Rsch., Birmingham, Ala., 1976, 78, Brigham Young U. Genealogy Seminars, Provo, Utah, 1970, 74-79, 82; lectr. Nat. Geneal. Soc. Seminars, 1978, 85, 86. Author: The Researcher's Guide to American Genealogy, 1973, 2d edit., 1990. Mem. Heritage Found., Washington, 1993—. S/Sgt. U.S. Army N.G., 1959-65. Winner 4th pl. Nathan Burkam Meml. Competition ASCAP, 1974, award of merit Nat. Geneal. Soc., 1978. Fellow Utah Geneal. Assn. (bd. dirs. 1975-80, pres. 1977-79). Republican. Mem. LDS Ch. Avocations: home repair, books. Home: 2422 Surrey Rd Taylorsville UT 84118-2028

GREER, CYNTHIA FAYE, university administrator, legal educator, mediator; b. Madison, Tenn., Oct. 22, 1954; d. Leo Curtis Sr. and Vera Evelyn (Dickens) G. BA, David Lipscomb U., Nashville, 1976; MEd, Ga. State U., 1978; EdD, Pepperdine U., 1988, M in Dispute Resolution, 1997. Cert. in dispute resolution; cert. counselor and mediator. Secondary English tchr. Greater Atlanta Christian Sch., 1977-80; dir. career svcs. David Lipscomb U., Nashville, 1980-81; dir. career svcs. and alumni rels. Pepperdine Sch. Law, Malibu, Calif., 1981-82, asst. dean, 1982-92, assoc. dean instnl. advancement, 1992—. Editor Pepperdine Law Quar., 1981—. Mem. Malibu Vol. Patrol, 1994—. Mem. ABA, Calif. State Bar (com. on continuing legal edn. 1990-93), Am. Assn. Law Schs. (sec. sects. on student svcs. 1995, exec. com. 1995). Office: Pepperdine Sch Law 24255 Pacific Coast Hwy Malibu CA 90263-0001

GREER, HOWARD EARL, retired career officer; b. Tyler, Tex., May 1, 1921; s. Earl Abner and Ollie (Lightfoot) G.; m. Dale Price, Nov. 1, 1986; children—Margaret, Darby, David, Briand, Holly, Howard. Student, Tyler Jr. Coll., 1939-40; B.S., U.S. Naval Acad., 1943; M.B.A., George Washington U., 1965. Commd. ensign U.S. Navy, 1943, advanced through grades to vice adm., 1975; comdr. Aircraft Carrier Hancock, 1967-69, Carrier Force, Vietnam, (4 tours), Naval Air Forces, U.S. Atlantic Fleet, Norfolk, Va., 1975-78; mem. CEDAM Internat. Decorated D.S.M. (2), Legion of Merit (4), Knights of Malta Order St. John of Jerusalem. Mem. Assn. Naval Aviation, Golden Eagles (early pioneer naval aviators), Tailhook Assn., Naval Res. Assn., Lomas Santa Fe Country Club. Republican. Methodist. Home: 8539 Prestwick Dr La Jolla CA 92037-2025

GREEVER, JANET GROFF, history educator; b. Philadelphia, Sept. 12, 1921; m. William St. Clair Greever, Aug. 24, 1951; 1 child. BA, Bryn Mawr Coll., 1942, MA, 1945; MA, Harvard U., 1951, PhD, 1954. Resident head grad. houses Radcliffe Coll., Cambridge, Mass., 1947-48; resident head undergrad. hall Bryn Mawr (Pa.) Coll., 1949-51, instr. history, 1949-50; asst. prof. history Wash. State U., Pullman, 1962-63, U. Idaho, Moscow, 1965-66; ind. rschr., lectr. history Moscow, Idaho, 1954—; interim lectr. history Whitman Coll., Walla Walla, Wash., 1978; Idaho regional admissions cons. and interviewer Bryn Mawr COll., 1955-81. *After graduation in 1942, before the organization of the WAVES, Janet worked for the U.S. Navy Communications Division in Washington D.C. (details restricted). Her foreign travel from 1976 to the present includes one or more trips to Canada, Mexico, Panama, Great Britain, The Netherlands, Ireland, Belgium, France, Portugal, Spain, Balearic Islands, Sardinia, Italy, Malta, Greece, Turkey, and North Africa.* Author: Jose Ballivian y El Oriente Boliviano, 1987. bd. dirs. U. Idaho Libr. Assocs., Moscow, 1979-81, pres. 1980-81. Pa. State scholar, 1938-42, History fellow Bryn Mawr (Pa.) Coll., 1944-45, Margaret M. Justin fellow AAUW, Washington, 1948-49; grantee Lucius N. Littauer Found., N.Y.C., 1948-49. Mem. Am. Hist. Assn. (life), Conf. on Latin. Am. History (life), Latin Am. Studies Assn., Soc. for Am. Archaeology (life), Archaeol. Inst. Am. (life), Phi Alpha Theta. Avocations: travel, photography. Home: 315 S Hayes St Moscow ID 83843-3419

GREEVER, MARGARET QUARLES, retired mathematics educator; b. Wilkensburg, Pa., Feb. 7, 1931; d. Lawrence Reginald and Ella Mae (LeSueur) Quarles; m. John Greever, Aug. 29, 1953; children: Catherine Patricia, Richard George, Cynthia Diane. Cert. costume design, Richmond Profl. Inst., 1952; student, U. Va., 1953-56; BA in Math., Calif. State U., L.A., 1963; MA in Math., Claremont Grad. Sch., 1968. Cert. tchr. specializing in Jr. Coll. math., Calif. Tchr. math. Chaffey Unified H.S. Dist., Alta Loma, Calif., 1963-64, L.A. Unified Sch. Dist., 1964-65, Chino (Calif.) Unified Sch. Dist., 1965-81; from asst. prof. to prof. Chaffey Coll., Rancho Cucamonga, 1981-96; phys. sci. divsn. chmn. Chaffey Coll., Alta Loma, 1985-92, dean, phys., life, health sci., 1992-96. Mem. AAUW (pres. local chpt. 1998—), Orcas Island Garden Club (treas. 1997—), Orcas Island Yacht Club, Pi Lambda Theta. Avocations: quilting, cooking, sewing, gardening.

GREGER, KENNETH RICHARD, executive recruiter; b. Vancouver, Wash., Mar. 4, 1953; s. Leonard R. and E. Jay (Gamer) G.; m. Cindy Richards, Sept. 6, 1992. BS in Bus. Adminstrn., Portland (Oreg.) State U., 1975. CPA, Oreg., Calif. Auditor Touche Ross & Co., Portland, 1975-78; search profl. Murphy, Symonds & Stowell, Portland, 1978-80; mgr. exec. search KPMG Peat Marwick, L.A., 1980-87; dir. exec. search svcs., western region Laventhol & Horwath, L.A., 1987-90; prin., exec. search Greger/Peterson Assocs., Inc., Portland and L.A., 1990—; Disting. prof. U. Houston, 1990. Contbr. articles to profl. jours. Bd. dirs. Portland Creative Conf., 1996—; mem. Red Herring Editorial Adv. Bd., 1995—; sponsor Oreg. Multimedia Alliance, 1995—. Mem. Calif. Soc. CPAs (chmn. entertainment and sports industry com. 1982-85). Avocations: people, family, music, new media, travel. Office: Greger/Peterson Assocs Inc 5335 Meadows Rd Ste 401 Lake Oswego OR 97035-3115

GREGERSEN, R(ONALD) GEORGE, newspaper publishing executive; b. Copenhagen, Mar. 14, 1935; came to U.S., 1948; s. Richard Vilhelm and Eva (Giertsen) G.; m. Gayle Froerer Richards, May 1, 1964 (div. 1978); m. Penny Losse, Dec. 21, 1982; children: Mary Anne Georgia, John Christian. Student, U. Utah, 1953-55. Pres., CEO Mortgage Investment Corp., Salt Lake City, 1955-68; pres., CEO Gregersen & Co., Salt Lake City, 1968-74; pub., CEO The Enterprise (weekly), Salt Lake City, 1974—. Editl. writer The Enterprise, 1974—. Bd. dirs. Utal Mil. & Vets. Affairs com., Salt Lake City, 1982-92. Named Utah Mil. Citizen of Yr., 1986; recipient Assn. U.S. Army Exceptional Svc. award, 1990. Mem. Alta Club (bd. dirs. 1993-96), Rotary. Republican. Episcopalian. Avocation: flyfishing. Home: 1427 Circle Way Salt Lake City UT 84103-4433 Office: Enterprise Newspaper Group Inc 136 S Main St Ste 721 Salt Lake City UT 84101-1676

GREGG, NADINE MARIE, pastor; b. Flushing, N.Y., Apr. 17, 1948; d. Joseph Martin and Estelle Marie (Andereya) Simeone; m. Thomas Gary Gregg, Aug. 2, 1969; children: Christopher, Derek, Marnie. Student, So. Calif. Sch. Prophetic Min., Carson, 1990. Sunday sch. spvr. Mission Hills Christian Ch., Laguna Hills, Calif., 1978-79; prayer coord. Faith Fellowship, Laguna Hills, Calif., 1983-84; prophet, pastor Fellowship of Jesus, Laguna Hills, Calif., 1987—; sec., co-owner Loves Alot, Laguna Hills, 1990—; counselor Saddleback Christian, Mission Viejo, Calif., 1986. Author: Derek's Story, 1990, The Truth, The Whole Truth, and Nothing But The Truth, So Help Me, God., 1991; broadcaster Sta. KLNG, 1991—, Pan Am. Broadcasting to East Africa and Israel, 1991. Home: 25103 Southport St Laguna Beach CA 92653-4922 Office: Loves Alot 25103 Southport St Laguna Beach CA 92653-4922

GREGGS, ELIZABETH MAY BUSHNELL (MRS. RAYMOND JOHN GREGGS), retired librarian; b. Delta, Colo., Nov. 7, 1925; d. Joseph Perkins and Ruby May (Stanford) Bushnell; m. Raymond John Greggs, Aug. 16, 1952 (dec. 1994); children: David M., Geoffrey B., Timothy C., Daniel R. BA, U. Denver, 1948. Children's librarian Grand Junction (Colo.) Pub. Library, 1944-46, Chelan County Library, 1948, Wenatchee (Wash.) Pub. Library, 1948-52, Seattle Pub. Library, 1952-53; children's librarian Renton (Wash.) Pub. Library, 1957-61, dir., 1962, br. supr. and children's services supr., 1963-67; area children's supr. King County Library, Seattle, 1968-78, asst. coordinator children's services, 1978-86; head librarian Valley View Library of King County Library System, Seattle, 1986-90, cons., organizer Tutor Ctr. Library, Seattle South Community Coll., 1969-72; mem. Puget Sound (Wash.) Council for Reviewing Children's Media, 1974—, chmn., 1974-76; cons. to children's TV programs. Editor: Cayas Newsletter, 1971-74; cons. to Children's Catalog, Children's Index to Poetry. Chmn. dist. advancement com. Kloshee dist. Boy Scouts Am., 1975-78; mem. Bond Issue Citizens Group to build new Renton Libr., 1958, 59; mem. exec. bd. Family Edn. and Counseling Ctr. on Deafness, 1991-94; mem. children's lit. tour People to People, South Africa, 1996. Recipient Hon. Service to Youth award Cedar River dist. Boy Scouts Am., 1971, Award of Merit Kloshee dist., 1977, winner King County Block Grant, 1990. Mem. ALA (Newbery-Caldecott medal com. 1978-79, com. chmn. 1983-84; membership com. 1978-80, Boy Scouts com. children's svcs. div. 1973-78, chmn. 1976-78, exec. bd. dirs. Assn. for Libr. Svc. to Children 1979-81, mem. coun. 1985-92, chmn. nominating com. 1986-87, councillor 1989-92, exec. bd. 1989-92, exec. com. 1989-92, coun. orientation com. 1987-89), Wash. Libr. Assn. (exec. bd. children's and young adult svcs. div. 1970-78, chmn. membership com. 1983-90, publs. com. 1988-92, emeritus 1991, mem. elections com.), King County Right to Read Coun. (co-chmn. 1973-77), Pierce-King County Reading Coun., Wash. State Literacy Coun. (exec. bd. 1971-77), Wash. Libr. Media Assn. (jr. high levels com. 1980-84), Pacific N.W. Libr. Assn. (young readers' choice com. 1981-83, chmn. div. 1983-85, exec. bd. 1983-85). Methodist. Home: 11448 Rainier Ave S Seattle WA 98178-3940

GREGOIRE, CHRISTINE O., state attorney general; b. Auburn, Wash.; m. Michael Gregoire; 2 children. BA, U. Wash.; JD cum laude, Gonzaga U., 1977. Clerk, typist Wash. State Adult Probation/ Parole Office, Seattle, 1969; caseworker Wash. Dept. Social and Health Scis., Everett, 1974; asst. atty. gen. City of Spokane, Wash., 1977-81, sr. asst. atty. gen., 1981-82; dep. atty. gen. City of Olympia, Wash., 1982-88; atty. gen. Washington St., 1992—; dir. Wash. State Dept. Ecology, 1988-92. chair Puget Sound Water Quality Authority, 1990-92, Nat. Com. State Environ. Dirs., 1991-92, States/B.C. Oil Spill Task Force, 1989-92. Mem. Nat. Assn. Attys. Gen. (consumer protection and environment com., energy com., children and the law subcom.). *

GREGOR, DOROTHY DEBORAH, librarian; b. Dobbs Ferry, N.Y., Aug. 15, 1939; d. Richard Garrett Heckman and Marion Allen (Richmond) Stewart; m. A. James Gregor, June 22, 1963 (div. 1974). BA, Occidental Coll., 1961; MA, U. Hawaii, 1963; MLS, U. Tex., 1968; cert. in Library Mgmt., U. Calif., Berkeley, 1976. Reference libr. U. Calif., San Francisco, 1968-69; dept. libr. Pub. Health Libr. U. Calif., Berkeley, 1969-71, tech. services libr., 1973-76; reference libr. Hamilton Libr., Honolulu, 1971-72; head serials dept. U. Calif., Berkeley, 1976-80, assoc. univ. libr. tech. svcs. dept., 1980-84, univ. libr., 1992-94; ret., 1994; chief Shared Cataloging div. Libr. of Congress, Washington, 1984-85; univ. libr. U. Calif.-San Diego, La Jolla, 1985-92, OCLC asst. to pres. for acad. and rsch. libr. rels., 1995-98; instr. sch. libr. and info. studies U. Calif., Berkeley, 1975, 76, 83; cons. Nat. Libr. of Medicine, Bethesda, Md., 1985, Ohio Bd. Regents, Columbus, 1987; trustee Online Computer Libr. Ctr., 1988-96; dir. Nat. Coordinating Com. on Japanese Libr. Resources, 1995-98. Mem. ALA, Libr. Info. Tech. Assn., Program Com. Ctr. for Rsch. Librs. (bd. chair 1992-93, Hugh Atkinson award 1994).

GREGORY, CALVIN, insurance service executive; b. Bronx, N.Y., Jan. 11, 1942; s. Jacob and Ruth (Cherchian) G.; m. Rachel Anna Carver, Feb. 14, 1970 (div. Apr. 1977); children—Debby Lynn, Trixy Sue; m. 2d, Carla Deane Deaver, June 30, 1979. AA, L.A. City Coll., 1962; BA, Calif. State U.-L.A., 1964; MDiv, Fuller Theol. Sem., 1968; MRS, Southwestern Sem., Ft. Worth, 1969; PhD in Religion, Universal Life Ch., Modesto, Calif., 1982; DDiv (hon.), Otay Mesa Coll., 1982. Notary pub., real estate lic., casualty lic., Calif.; ordained to ministry Am. Baptist Conv., 1970. Youth minister First Bapt. Ch., Delano, Calif., 1964-65, 69-70; youth dir. St. Luke's United Meth. Ch., Highland Park, Calif., 1969-70; tchr. polit. sci. Maranatha High Sch., Rosemead, Calif., 1969-70; aux. chaplain U.S. Air Force 750th Radar Squadron, Edwards AFB, Calif., 1970-72; pastor First Bapt. Ch., Boron, Calif., 1971-72; ins. agt. Prudential Ins. Co., Ventura, Calif., 1972-73, sales mgr., 1973-74; casualty ins. agt. Allstate Ins. Co., Thousand Oaks, Calif., 1974-75; pres. Ins. Agy. Placement Svs., Thousand Oaks, 1975—; head youth minister Emanuel Presbyn. Ch., L.A., 1973-74; owner, investor real estate, U.S., Wales, Eng., Can., Australia. Counselor YMCA, Hollywood, Calif., 1964, Soul Clinic-Universal Life Ch., Modesto, Calif., 1982. Mem. Apt. Assn. L.A., Life Underwriter Tng. Coun., Forensic Club (L.A.), X32 Club (Ventura, Calif.), Kiwanis (club spkr. 1971). Republican. Office: Ins Agy Placement Svc PO Box 4407 Thousand Oaks CA 91359-1407

GREGORY, ELEANOR ANNE, artist, educator; b. Seattle, Jan. 20, 1939; d. John Noel and Eleanor Blanche G.; BA, Reed Coll., 1963; MFA, U. Wash., 1966; MEd, Columbia U., 1978, EdD., 1978. Art tchr. Seattle Pub. Schs., 1970-75; instr. N.Y.C. C.C., 1977, Manhattan C.C., N.Y.C., 1978; asst. prof. N.Mex. State U., Las Crucas, 1978-79; asst. prof. art Purdue U., West Lafayette, Ind., 1979-82, West Tex. State U., Canyon, 1982-84; mgr. Watson's Crick Gallery, West Lafayette, 1982-83; lectr. Calif. State U., Long Beach, 1985-87, L.A. Unified Sch. Dist., 1988—. One woman shows: Columbia U. Tchrs. Coll., 1976, Watson's Crick Gallery, West Lafayette, 1980, 81, Gallery I, Purdue U., 1980, W. Tex. State U., 1983, Amarillo Art Ctr., 1984, Sch. Visual Concepts, Seattle, 1985; group shows include: El Paso (Tex.) Art Mus., 1979, Ind. State Mus., Indpls., 1980, Lafayette (Ind.) Art Mus., 1982, T. Billman Gallery, Long Beach, 1987; represented in permanent collection: Portland (Oreg.) Art Mus. Mem. Nat. Art Edn. Assn. (pres. women's caucus chpt. 1988-90, v.p.-elect Pacific region 1994-96, v.p. 1996-98, Pacific region sect. award 1997), N.Y. Soc. Scribes, L.A. Soc. Calligraphy, Internat. Soc. Edn. Through Art, Art Educators of L.A. (pres. 1993-95). Episcopalian. Died Sept. 3, 1997.

GREGORY, JAMES, retired actor; b. N.Y.C., Dec. 23, 1911; s. James Gillen and Axemia Theresa (Ekdahl) G.; m. Ann Catherine Miltner, May 25, 1944. Grad. high sch. Actor, 1936—. Actor: (summer stock prodns.) Deer Lake, Pa., 1936-37, 39, Millbrook, N.Y., 1938, Braddock Heights, Md., 1940, Buck's County Playhouse, New Hope, Pa., 1941, Ivy Tower Playhouse, Spring Lake, N.J., 1951, (Broadway shows) Key Largo, 1939, Journey to Jerusalem, 1940, In Time to Come, 1941, Dream Girl, 1945, All My Sons, 1947, Death of a Salesman, 1948-49 (played Biff on Broadway with 5 Willy Lomans), Dead Pigeon, 1954, Fragile Fox, 1955, Desperate Hours, 1956-57, (films) The Young Strangers, 1955, Al Capone Story, 1955, Gun Glory, 1956, Nightfall, 1956, The Big Caper, 1956, A Distant Trumpet, 1961, Underwater Warrior, 1962, PT-109, 1965, The Sons of Katie Elder, 1967, The Manchurian Candidate, 1967, Captain Newman, M.D, 1967, Million Dollar Duck, 1968, Clam Bake, 1967, Secret War of Harry Frigg, 1968, Beneath the Planet of the Apes, 1970, The Hawaiians, 1970, Shoot Out, 1971, The Late Liz, 1971, $1,000,000. Duck, 1971, The Strongest Man in the World, 1974, The Main Event, 1979, Wait Til Your Mother Gets Home, 1982, X-15, Death of a Salesman, also 5 Matt Helm pictures, (TV shows) Big Valley, Bonanza, Gunsmoke, Rawhide, Playhouse 90, Climax, Alfred Hitchcock Presents, Twilight Zone, Quincy, as Inspector Luger in Barney Miller, Mr. Belvedere, 1986. Served with USNR, USMCR, 1942-45, PTO. Mem. Soc. Preservation and Encouragement Barber Shop Quartet Singing Am. Club: Hollywood Hackers, Golf. Home: 55 Cathedral Rock Dr Unit 33 Sedona AZ 86351-8624*

GREGORY, LEONARD, publishing executive. Mng. editor Pueble (Colo.) Chieftan. Office: Pueblo Chieftan 825 W 6th St Pueblo CO 81003-2390*

GREGORY, NELSON BRUCE, motel owner, retired naval officer; b. Syracuse, N.Y., Aug. 4, 1933; s. Nelson Bruce and Josephine (Sully) G.; m. Bonnie K. Bannowsky, May 2, 1961 (div. 1970); children: Elizabeth Jo, Jennifer Kay; m. Patricia Ann Greenhalgh, Oct. 15, 1977 (div. 1994); m. Serita Lamoreaux; children: Peter Ward, Annette Frances, Michael John, Geoffrey Charles, Natasha, Secrita Lamoreaux. BS, N.Y. Maritime Coll., 1955; postgrad., USN Pilot Tng., Pensacola, Fla., 1955-57; grad., NATO Weapons Sch., Oberammergau, Fed. Republic of Germany, 1966; diploma, Joint Warfare Sch., Salisbury, Eng., 1967, USN Counter Insurgency, Little Creek, Va., 1968, USAF Space Ops., Montgomery, Ala., 1969. Commd. ens. USN, 1955, advanced through grades to lt. comdr., 1964; operational pilot airborne Early Warning Squadron 2 USN, Patuxent River, Md., 1957-60; flight instr. Airborne Early Warning Tng. Unit USN, Patuxent River, 1960-63; command pilot Air Devel. Squadron 6 USN, McMurdo Sound, Antarctica, 1963-64; airspace control officer NATO, Naples, Italy, 1964-68; chief pilot Naval Support Activity, Danang, Vietnam, 1968-69; space intelligence analyst NORAD, Colorado Springs, Colo., 1969-71; operational pilot Electronic Warfare Squadron 33 USN, Norfolk, Va., 1971-74; ops. officer Nat. Parachute Test Range USN, El Centro, Calif., 1974-75, ret. USN, 1975; owner, gen. mgr. Bonneville Motel, Idaho Falls, Idaho, 1975—; bd. dirs. Am. Travel Inns, 1976-78. Decorated Air medals (3) USN; recipient Vietnamese Gallantry Cross Republic of Vietnam, 1969; Gregory Ridge in Antarctica named for him, 1964. Mem. Ret. Officers Assn. (life), Elks. Republican. Presbyterian. Avocations: yachting, camping, travel, golf. Home: PO Box 51501 Idaho Falls ID 83405-1501 Address: 221 W 3rd N Rexburg ID 83440-1532

GRENFELL, GLORIA ROSS, freelance journalist; b. Redwood City, Calif., Nov. 14, 1926; d. Edward William and Blanch (Ross) G.; m. June 19, 1948 (div. Nov. 15, 1983); children: Jane, Barbara, Robert, Mary. BS, U. Oreg., 1948, postgrad., 1983-85. Coll. bd., retail sales Meier & Frank Co., Portland, Oreg., 1945; book sales retailer J.K. Gill & Co., Portland, Oreg., 1948-50; advisor Mt. Hood Meadows Women's Ski Program, Oreg., 1968-78; corp. v.p. OK Delivery System, Inc., Oreg., 1977-82; ski instr. Willamette Pass, Oreg., 1983-85, Mt. Shasta, 1986; Campfire girls leader Portland, 1958-72; freelance journalist Marina, Calif., 1986—. Mem. Assn. Jr. League Internat., 1957-87; mem. Monterey County Mental Health Commn., 1994—, So. Poverty Law Ctr., No. Mariposa County History Ctr., Calif. Recipient Golden Poles award Mt. Hood Meadows, 1975. Mem. Soc. Profl. Journalists, Profl. Ski Instrs. Am., U.S. Ski Assn., Calif. State Sheriffs' Assn. (assoc.), Monterey History and Art Assn., Monterey Sports Ctr., Carmel Women's Club, Mariposa County C. of C., Monterey Bay Area Nat. Alumnae Panhellenic. Order Ea. Star, DAR (Commodore Sloat chpt.), Citizens for Law and Order, Mortar Bd., Kappa Alpha Theta. Democrat. Episcopalian. Home and Office: 3128 Crescent Ave Lot 9 Marina CA 93933-3131

GREY, ROBERT DEAN, academic administrator, biology educator; b. Liberal, Kans., Sept. 5, 1939; s. McHenry Wesley and Kathryn (Brown) G.; m. Alice Kathleen Archer, June 11, 1961; children: Erin Kathleen, Joel Michael. BA, Phillips U., 1961; PhD, Washington U., 1966. Asst. prof. Washington U., St. Louis, 1966-67; from asst. prof. to full prof. zoology U. Calif., Davis, 1967—, chmn. dept., 1979-83, dean biol. scis., 1985—, interim exec. vice chancellor, 1993-95, provost, exec. vice chancellor, 1995—. Author: (with others) A Laboratory Text for Developmental Biology, 1980; contbr. articles to profl. jours. Recipient Disting. Tchg. awrd Acad. Senate U. Calif., Davis, 1977, Magnar Ronning award for tchg. Associated Students U. Calif., Davis, 1978, Disting. Alumnus award Phillips U., 1991. Mem. Am. Soc. Cell Biology, Soc. Developmental Biology, Phi Sigma. Avocations: music, hiking, gardening. Office: U Calif Office of the Provost 5th Flr Mrat Hall 1 Shields Ave Davis CA 95616*

GRIEGO, JUAN LAWRENCE, federal agency administrator; b. Española, N. Mex., Apr. 9, 1963; s. Juan Santiago Griego and Marcia Kay (Clapper) Richardson; m. Katherine Therese McReynolds, Sept. 15, 1981 (div. Oct. 15, 1986); 1 child, John; m. Philippa Marie Sanchez, Jan. 11, 1992; children: Marisa, Eliana. BS in Civil Engring., N. Mex. State U., 1986. Project mgr. U.S. Dept. Energy, Los Alamos, N. Mex., 1986-92; project mgmt. br. chief U.S. Dept. Energy, Los Alamos, 1992-94, team leader project mgmt. office, 1994—; sec.-treas. Fast Ditch, Inc., Española, N. Mex., 1997—. Major N. Mex. Nat. Guard. Mem. Nat. Guard Assn. U.S., Project Mgmt. Inst. (cert. profl. project mgr., v.p. programs Otowi chpt., 1996-97). Avocations: farming, ranching, auto sports, skiing. Home: 1151 Calle Verde Espanola NM 87532-3385 Office: US Dept Energy 528 35th St Los Alamos NM 87544-2201

GRIER, JAMES EDWARD, hotel company executive, lawyer; b. Ottumwa, Iowa, Sept. 7, 1935; s. Edward J. and Corinne (Bailey) G.; m. Virginia Clinker, July 4, 1959; children: Michael, Susan, James, John, Thomas. BSc, U. Iowa, 1956, JD, 1959. Bar: Iowa 1959, Mo. 1959. Mng. ptnr. Hillix, Brewer, Hoffhaus & Grier, Kansas City, Mo., 1964-77, Grier & Swartzman, Kansas City, 1977-89; pres. Doubletree Hotels Corp., Phoenix, 1989-94; chmn. Sonoran Hotel Capital, Inc., Phoenix, 1994-96; mng. ptnr. Copa Investments, 1996—; bd. dirs. Iowa Law Sch. Found., Iowa City, Mercy Healthcare Ariz., Phoenix, Homeward Bound, Phoenix. Home: 3500 E

Lincoln Dr Phoenix AZ 85018-1010 Office: Copa Investments Ste 169 7300 E Gainey Suites Dr Scottsdale AZ 85258

GRIESCHE, ROBERT PRICE, hospital purchasing executive; b. Berkeley, Calif., July 21, 1953; s. Robert Bowen and Lillian (Price) G.; m. Susan Dawn Albers, June 8, 1985 (div. Apr. 1989); 1 child, Sara Christine. AA, Coll. of the Canyons, Valencia, Calif., 1984. Warehouse supr. John Muir Hosp., Walnut Creek, Calif., 1973-82; purchasing mgr. Henry Mayo Newhall Hosp., Valencia, 1982-85; materials mgr. Foothill Presbyn. Hosp., Glendora, Calif., 1985-87; materials mgmt. dir. Huntington Meml. Hosp., Pasadena, Calif., 1987-96; sys. dir. purchasing So. Calif. Healthcare Sys., Pasadena, 1996—; chmn. Huntington Employee Campaign, 1990-92. V.p. Coll. of Canyons Found., Valencia, 1985-90. Named to Outstanding Young Men of Am., 1988. Mem. Am. Soc. Healthcare Materials Mgmt., Calif. Cen. Svc. Assn. (charter). Republican. Presbyterian. Avocations: swimming, gardening, photography. Home: 3651 Cosmos Ct Palmdale CA 93550-5748 Office: So Calif Healthcare Sys 1300 E Green St Pasadena CA 91106-2606

GRIESEMER, ALLAN DAVID, retired museum director; b. Mayville, Wis., Aug. 13, 1935; s. Raymond John and Leone Emma (Fisher) G.; m. Nancy Jean Sternberg, June 6, 1959; children: David, Paul, Steven. A.B., Augustana Coll., 1959; M.S., U. Wis., 1963; Ph.D., U. Nebr., 1970. Curator; coordinator ednl. services U. Nebr., Lincoln State Museum, 1965-77, assoc. prof., assoc. dir., 1977-79, acting dir., 1980-81, assoc. dir. and coordinator, 1981-82, interim dir., 1982-84; dir. San Bernardino County Mus., Calif., 1984-97, dir. emeritus, 1997—; mem. faculty dept. geology U. Nebr., Lincoln, 1968-80; lectr. geology U. Nebr., Lincoln State Mus., 1968-80; CEO, dir., curator Mousley Mus. Natural History, San Bernardino County Mus., Yucaipa, Calif.; adj. prof. Calif. State U., San Bernardino, 1986. Contbr. articles to sci. jours., mus. publs., 1965—. Bd. dirs. Redland Music Assn., Prospect Pk., Boys and Girls Club, Inland Harvest, Calif. Desert Studies Consortium; mem. adv. bd. Redlands Cmty. Hosp., brd. mem., Habitat Humanity San Bernardino, adv. mem., Montessori in Red Lands. Recipient Hon. award Sigma Gamma Epsilon, 1958. Mem. Paleontol. Soc., Nebr. Mus. Conf. (pres. 1976-79), Nebr. Geol. Soc., Nebr. Acad. Scis., Mountain Plains Conf., Mountain Plains Mus. Assn. (pres. 1979), Am. Assn. Museums (v.p. 1983), Am. Assn. State and Local History, Western Museums Conf., Rotary. Lutheran. Home: 306 La Colina Dr Redlands CA 92374-8247

GRIESSMAN, BENJAMIN EUGENE, author, professional speaker; b. Spartanburg, S.C., Aug. 12, 1934. BA, Tenn. Temple Coll., 1956; MA, Baylor U., 1958; MDiv, New Orleans Bapt. Theol. Sem., 1962; PhD, La. State U. Asst. prof. N.C. State U., assoc. prof., Auburn U.; head dept. sociology and anthropology; with Ga. Inst. Tech., regional dir., external affairs. Fellow Am. Anthrop. Assn.; mem. Ga. Speakers Assn. (pres.), So. Sociol. Soc., Phi Kappa Phi. Author: Minorities, 1975; co-editor: The Southern Mystique, 1977; Technology, Human Values, and the Southern Future, 1977; Images and Memories: Georgia Tech 1885-1985, The Achievement Factors, 1987 (transl. into Japanese, 1991, Winner 1991 Benjamin Franklin Award), Diversity, 1993, Time Tactics of Very Successful People, 1994; contbr. articles to newspapers and profl. jours. including USA Today, N.Y. Times. Office: 17352 W Sunset Blvd Ste D-604 Pacific Palisades CA 90272-4120

GRIFFEY, KEN, JR. (GEORGE KENNETH GRIFFEY, JR.), professional baseball player; b. Donora, Pa., Nov. 21, 1969. Grad. high sch., Cin. Outfielder Seattle Mariners, 1987—. Recipient Gold Glove award, 1990-96; named to All-Star team, 1990-95, All-Star game MVP, 1992, , Sporting News Am. League Silver Slugger team, 1991, 93-94, 96 Sporting News All-Star team, 1991, 93-94. Office: Seattle Mariners/The Kingdome PO Box 4100 83 King St Seattle WA 98104-2860*

GRIFFIN, GLORIA JEAN, elementary school educator; b. Emmett, Idaho, Sept. 10, 1946; d. Archie and Marguerite (Johnson) G. AA, Boise (Idaho) Jr. Coll., 1966; BA, Boise Coll., 1968; MA in Elem. Curriculum, Boise State U., 1975. Cert. advanced elem. tchr., Idaho. Tchr. music, tutor, Boise; sec. Edward A. Johnson, atty., Boise; tchr. Head Start, Boise; elem. tchr. Meridian (Idaho) Sch. Dist., 1968—; developer multi-modality individualized spelling program; co-developer program for adapting curriculum to student's individual differences. Author: The Culture and Customs of the Argentine People As Applied to a Sixth Grade Social Studies Unit. Sec. PTA. Named Tchr. of Yr., Meridian Sch. Dist., 1981. Mem. NEA, Idaho Edn. Assn., Meridian Edn. Assn. (bldg. rep.), Internat. Reading Assn., Idaho Reading Coun., Horizons Reading Coun., Alpha Delta Kappa (rec. sec.). Office: Silver Sage Elem Sch 7700 Snohomish St Boise ID 83709-5975

GRIFFIN, JAMES EDWARD, real estate consultant; b. Fall River, Mass., Jan. 27, 1941; s. James Edward and Marion Beatrice (Johnsen) G. AA, Napa (Calif.) Coll., 1965; BS, Calif. State U., Sacramento, 1967. CPA, Calif., Nev. Auditor Arthur Young & Co., San Francisco, 1967-69, Providence, 1969-71; v.p. fin. R.I. Land Co., Providence, 1971-79; treas. Moss Land Co., Sacramento, 1979-82; chief fin. officer Equi-Real Devel. Co., Sacramento, 1982-84, Am. Nev. Co., Henderson, Nev., 1984-90; exec. v.p., chief oper. officer Am. Nev. Co., 1990-93; prin. cons. Griffin & Co., Las Vegas, 1993—; sec.-treas. acctg. adv. coun. UNLV, 1991, chmn. 1993. Recipient Bus. Adminstrn. award Bank Am., 1965. Fellow Nev. Soc. CPAs; mem. AICPA, Inst. Mgmt. Accts. (treas. Las Vegas chpt. 1991, bd. dirs. 1990), Beta Alpha Psi, Beta Gamma Sigma. Office: Griffin & Co 7550 Pearwood Ct Las Vegas NV 89123-0546

GRIFFIN, (ALVA) JEAN, entertainer; b. Detroit, June 1, 1931; d. Henry Bethel White and Ruth Madelyn (Gowen) Durham; m. Francis Jay Griffin, July 8, 1958 (dec.); stepchildren: Patra, Rodney; 1 adopted child, Donald; children: Rhonda Jean, Sherree Lee. Student, Anderson Coll., 1952-53; DD (hon.), Ministry of Salvation, Chula Vista, Calif., 1990, Ministry of Salvation, 1990. Ordained minister, 1990. Supr. Woolworth's, Detroit, 1945-46; operator, supr. Atlantic Bell Tel. Co., Detroit, 1947-51, Anderson, Ind., 1952-56; sec. to div. mgr. Food Basket-Lucky Stores, San Diego, 1957-58; owner, mgr. Jay's Country Boy Markets, Riverside, Calif., 1962-87; entertainer, prodr., dir., singer Mae West & Co., 1980—; past owner The Final Touch, Colorado Springs; owner Omega Communique Co., 1997—; tchr. art Grant Sch., Riverside, 1964-65; tchr., adviser Mental Retarded Sch., Riverside, 1976-77; instr. Touch for Health Found., Pasadena, Calif., 1975-79; cons., hypnotist, nutritionist, Riverside, 1976-79; mem., tchr. Psi field parapsychology. Writer children's stories and short stories. Mem. Rep. Presdl. Task Force, 1983. Recipient svc. award Rep. Presdl. Task Force, 1986. Mem. Parapsychology Assn. Riverside (pres. 1981-82). Mem. Ch. of Religious Science New Thought. Avocations: arts and crafts, photography, hiking, horseback riding, travel. Home: 201 W Chapel Rd Sedona AZ 86336-7031

GRIFFIN, KENYON NEAL, retired academic administrator; b. Natoma, Kans., Aug. 8, 1939; s. Leslie Tillman and Elizabeth Alice (Hobrock) G.; m. Leah Gwen Sharp, Mar. 2, 1962; children: Karol Rene, Shari Lene. BA in History, Ft. Hays (Kans.) State U., 1961; MA in Polit. Sci., Kans. State U., 1968; PhD in Polit. Sci., U. Ky., 1972. Edn. officer Govt. Tanzania, Dodoma, 1961-63; tchr. Garden City (Kans.) Pub. Schs., 1964-66; prof. polit. sci. U. Wyo., Laramie, 1970-83, dir. extended credit program, 1983-88, acting dean sch. extended studies and pub. svc., 1988-89, assoc. provost acad. affairs, 1989-98, interim provost acad. affairs, 1998, prof. emeritus, 1999—; cons. Wyo. State Bar, Cheyenne, 1978-98; mem. Wyo. Jud. Supervisory Commn., Cheyenne, 1982-85; mem. Statewide Wyo. Info. Adv. Coun., 1988-95. Contbr. articles to profl. jours. Mem. Western Polit. Sci. Assn., Western Social Sci. Assn. Avocations: photography, hiking, camping, horseback riding.

GRIFFIN, KIRSTEN BERTELSEN, nursing educator; b. Oakland, Calif., Mar. 23, 1940; d. Elmer V. and Helen E. (Hansen) Bertelsen; children: Colleen Hime Risvold, Sean W., Patrick C., m. John R. Griffin. Diploma, Samuel Merritt Coll. Nursing, 1961; BA, U. Redlands, 1982; A in Bus., Advantage-Health Edn., 1992. Pvt. practice cons./stress trainer San Jacinto, Calif.; cons. Calif. State Dept. Edn., Sacramento, 1979 ; program dir. nursing asst. program Riverside (Calif.) County Office Edn., 1984—; part-time instr. Mt. San Jacinto (Calif.) Coll., 1989; part-time staff nurse acute psychiat. unit Hemet (Calif.) Med. Ctr.-Behavioral Health; advisor, judge Health Occupation Students Am., 1990—; rater Nurse Asst. Tng. Assessment Program, 1992—. Youth advisor, judge Vocat. Indsl. Clubs Am., 1977-88; instr. ARC, Am. Heart Assn. Recipient Women Helping Women award Soroptimists, 1989. Mem. Calif. Assn. Health Career Educators (pres.-elect 1984-85, pres. 1985-86), Beta Sigma Phi (Order of Rose award, Laureate 1995). Home: 3109 La Travesia Dr Fullerton CA 92835-1421

GRIFFIN, MERV EDWARD, former entertainer, television producer, entrepreneur; b. San Mateo, Calif., July 6, 1925; s. Mervyn Edward and Rita (Robinson) G.; m. Julann Elizabeth Wright, May 18, 1958 (div. June 1976); 1 son, Anthony Patrick. Student, San Mateo Coll., 1942-44; L.H.D., Emerson Coll., 1981. Owner Teleview Racing Patrol Inc., Miami, Fla., Video Racing Patrol Inc., Seattle, Beverly Hilton Hotel, Beverly Hills, Calif., The Scottsdale (Ariz.) Hilton, Wickenburg (Ariz.) Inn; chmn. bd. Griffin Group, Inc., Beverly Hills, Givenchy Hotel and Spa, Palm Springs, Calif., Merv Griffin Prodns., Beverly Hills; owner Merv Griffin Entertainment, Beverly Hills, 1996—. Performer Merv Griffin Show radio sta. KFRC, San Francisco, 1945-48, vocalist Freddy Martin's Orch., 1948-52; contract player, star So This is Love, Warner Bros., 1953-55; TV master ceremonies, 1958—, Merv Griffin Show, NBC-TV, 1962-63, Westinghouse Broadcasting Co., 1965-69, CBS-TV, 1969-72, syndication, 1972-86; currently exec. producing: Wheel of Fortune, Jeopardy. Club: Bohemian (San Francisco). Office: Merv Griffin Enterprises 3000 31 St Santa Monica CA 90405 also: The Griffin Group 780 3rd Ave New York NY 10017-2024*

GRIFFIN, SYLVIA GAIL, reading specialist; b. Portland, Oreg., Dec. 13, 1935; d. Archie and Marguerite (Johnson) G. AA, Boise Jr. Coll., 1955; BS, Brigham Young U., 1957, MEd, 1967. Cert. advanced teaching, Idaho. Classroom tchr. Boise (Idaho) Pub. Schs., 1957-59, 61-66, 67-69, reading specialist, 1969-90, 91-95, 98—, inclusion specialist, 1995-98, early childhood specialist, 1990-91; tchr. evening Spanish classes for adults, 1987-88; lectr. in field; mem. cons. pool U.S. Office Juvenile Justice and Delinquency Prevention, 1991—. Author: Procedures Used by First Grade Teachers for Teaching Experience Readiness for Reading Comprehension, The Short Story of Vowels, A Note Worthy Way to Teach Reading. Advisor in developing a program for dyslexics Scottish Rite Masons of Idaho, Boise. Mem. NEA, AAUW, Internat. Reading Assn., Orton Dyslexia Soc., Horizon Internat. Reading Assn., Idaho Edn. Assn. (pub. rels. dir. 1970-72), Boise Edn. Assn. (pub. rels. dir. 1969-72, bd. dirs. ednl. polit. involvement com. 1983-89), Alpha Delta Kappa. Avocations: music, creative writing. Office: 5007 Franklin Rd Boise ID 83705-1188

GRIFFIN, W. C., bishop. Bishop Ch. of God in Christ, Albuquerque. Office: Ch of God in Christ 3322 Montclaire Dr NE Albuquerque NM 87110-1702

GRIFFIN-HOLST, (BARBARA) JEAN, marketing professional; b. Pasadena, Calif., May 20, 1943; d. DeWitt James and Jean Marie (Donald) Griffin; m. Rodney C. Holst, Mar. 22, 1969 (div. May 1975); 1 child, Justin D. Griffin-Holst. BA cum laude, San Jose State U., 1967. Designer integrated cir. mask Fairchild Semicondr., Mountain View, Calif., 1967-69; sr. custom integrated cir. mask designer Nat. Semicondr., Santa Clara, Calif., 1969-71; sr. specialist Advanced Micro Devices, Sunnyvale, Calif., 1971-75; mgr. mask design and computer-aided design groups Precision Monolithics, Santa Clara, 1975-76; mgr. analog mask design and graphic services Signetics Corp., Sunnyvale, 1976-82; dist. mgr. tech. mktg. Computervision Corp., Santa Clara, 1982-84, dist. mgr. sales, 1984-85, mgr. distbr. sales, 1985-87; dir. U.S. field mktg. Sun Microsystems Inc., Mountain View, 1987—; bd. dirs. U.S. Thin Film Products, Inc., Campbell, Calif. Mem. NAFE, AAUW, Navy League U.S., San Francisco Mus. Modern Art, St. Francis Yacht Club (San Francisco), Commonwealth Club of San Francisco. Republican. Avocations: sailing, skiing, refurbishing antique furniture, painting, photography. Office: Sun Microsystems Inc 2550 Garcia Ave Mountain View CA 94043-1100 Address: 455 Park Ave S Ph 4 New York NY 10016-7329

GRIFFIS, STANLEY DOUGLAS, county manager; b. Odum, Ga., Oct. 25, 1942; s. John Randall and Hattie Lou (Dubberly) G.; m. Pamela Stewart, Aug. 8, 1945; children: David, Jeffery, Michelle. BBA, U. Okla., 1966; MBA, Mich. State U., 1969; PhD, St. Louis U., 1981. Commd. 2d lt. USAF, 1968, advanced through grades to maj., 1981; assoc. prof. USAF Acad., 1976-81; ret. USAF, 1982; pres. Griffco, Colorado Springs, 1982-87; dir. fin. and adminstrv. svcs. El Paso County, Colorado Springs, 1987-89; dir. fin. Douglas County, Castle Rock, Colo., 1989; county mgr. Pinal County, Florence, Ariz., 1989—; grad. prof. Regis Coll., Colorado Springs, 1983-87; adj. prof. Ctrl. Ariz. Coll., Florence, 1989—. Decorated with Vietnamese Cross of Gallantry, Bronze star. Democrat. Avocations: building clocks. Office: Pinal County PO Box 827 Florence AZ 85232-0827

GRIFFITH, CARL DAVID, civil engineer; b. Hill City, Kans., Mar. 1, 1937; s. Wilfred Eugene and Veda May (Jackson) G.; m. Mariana Segall, Mar. 26, 1988; stepchildren: Laurie Ann Segall, Allen Segall. BSCE summa cum laude, West Coast U., 1978; MSCE in Water Resources, U. So. Calif., 1980, MS in Engring. Mgmt., 1983. Profl. engr., Calif. Chief draftsman Bear Creek Mining Co., Spokane, Wash., 1959-64; right-of-way technician So. Calif. Edison Co., Los Angeles, 1964-65; engr. treatment plant design of treatment plants br. Metropolitan Water Dist. So. Calif., Los Angeles, 1965—; assoc. prof. Sch. Engring., West Coast U. Sustaining mem. Calif. Republican party. Served with USAF, 1957-58. Mem. ASME, ASCE, NSPE, Am. Water Works Assn., Nat. Mgmt. Assn., Metropolitan Water Dist. Mgmt. Club. Lodge: Masons. Home: 11043 Pender Ave Granada Hills CA 91344-4910 Office: PO Box 54153 Los Angeles CA 90054-0153

GRIFFITH, MARY C., community college vice president; b. Amarillo, Tex., June 3, 1943; d. Earl A. and Mattie Dean (Holland) M.; 1 child, Ben Patterson. BS in Edn., Biology, Chemistry, Abilene (Tex.) Christian U., 1967; MS in Biology, U. Oreg., 1971; PhD in C.C. Adminstrn., U. Tex., 1980. Secondary tchr. permanent cert., Tex. Reader, supr. Luce-Romeike Press Clipping Bur., Mesa, Ariz., 1963-64; tng. tchr. Abilene (Tex.) State Sch., 1964-65; sci. tchr. Sudan (Tex.) H.S., 1967-69, Springlake-Earth H.S., Earth, Tex., 1969-70; phys. sci. tchr. Burkburnett (Tex.) H.S., 1971-72; divsn. chmn. math./sci., instr. biology, project dir. Vernon (Tex.) Regl Jr. Coll., 1972-77; adminstrv. intern Office Exec. V.P. Tarrant County Jr. Coll., Fort Worth, 1978; staff devel. specialist Nat. Inst. Staff and Orgnl. Devel., U. Tex., Austin, 1979-80; coord., cons. c.c. and continuing edn. Tex. HIgher Edn. Coordinating Bd., Austin, dir., asst. dir. Office Rsch., program dir. health affairs, program dir. c.c. and tech. insts., 1980-88; v.p. instrnl. affairs Paris (Tex.) Jr. Coll., 1988-94; v.p. instrn. Pueblo (Colo.) C.C., 1994-96, v.p. ednl. devel., 1996—; adj. prof. East Tex. State U., Commerce, 1988-94; cons. Tex. State Coordinating Bd., Austin, 1995-97; officer long range planning Paris Jr. Coll., 1988-94, computer resource com., 1990-94. Bd. mem. Tex. Common Course Numbering Sys., 1992-94. Recipient ednl. leadership fellowship Sir Richardson Found., U. Tex., 1977-79, grants NSF, 1976, Post-Secondary Edn. Fund, 1987, Rotary Internat., India, 1998; acad. yr. inst. fellow U. Oreg. Molecular Biology Inst., NSF, 1970-71, summer inst. fellow earth sci. program Tex. A&M, NSF, 1968. Mem. Am. Assn. Higher Edn., Tex. Assn. Jr./C.C. Instrnl. Adminstrn. (bd. mem. 1992-94), Tex. Assn. Post Secondary Occupl. Adminstrn., Phi Kappa Phi, Phi Delta Kappa. Avocations: singing barbershop harmony. Office: Pueblo CC 900 W Orman Ave Pueblo CO 81004-1430

GRIFFITHE, TODD ALLEN, television associate director; b. Lakewood, Calif., Aug. 24, 1966; s. Thomas Delano and Rosemary Pearl (Lowery) G.; m. Lisa Jill Mandarino, June 8, 1991. BA in Comms., Calif. State U., Fullerton, 1992. Prodn. staff mem. Comcast Cablevision, Seal Beach, Calif., 1988-92; ENG camera/editor Sta. KDOC-TV, Anaheim, Calif., 1988-91; prodn. staff mem. Fin. News Network, L.A., 1990-91; videotape oper. Johnson Controls, San Bernardino, Calif., 1991-94; assoc. dir., dir. Sta. KTLA-TV, L.A., 1992—, E! Entertainment Tel., L.A., 1994-97; assoc. dir. Sta. KTTV-TV (Fox), L.A., 1996. Mem. Serrano Hills Cmty. Ch., Tustin, Calif., 1994 . Recipient ACE award Cable ACE Awards, 1989, 90, Best ENG Feature Story award Orange County Press Club, 1990. Mem. Nat. Assn. Broadcast Employees and Technicians. Office: KTLA-TV 5800 W Sunset Blvd Los Angeles CA 90028-6607

GRIFFITHS, ARTHUR R., professional hockey team executive. Vice-chmn., alt. gov. Vancouver (Can.) Canucks. Office: Vancouver Canucks, Gen Motors PL 800 Griffiths Way, Vancouver, BC Canada V6B 6G1

GRIGG, SUSAN LESLIE, library administrator; b. Chgo., June 27, 1947; d. Wallace and Loretta (Mittman) G.; m. Justin G. G. Kahn, Sr., Jan. 1, 1994. AB, Oberlin Coll., 1968; MSLS, Simmons Coll., 1993; MA, U. Wis., 1970, PhD, 1978. Archivist Yale U., New Haven, 1976-81; asst. prof., curator U. Minn., St. Paul, 1981-85; head Sophia Smith collection coll. archives Smith Coll., Northampton, Mass., 1985-92; mus. libr., archivist Strawbery Banke Mus., Portsmouth, N.H., 1993-96; prof. U. Alaska, Fairbanks, 1996—. Editor: Historic Portsmouth, 1995; contbr. articles to profl. jours. Fellow Soc. Am. Archivists; mem. Am. Libr. Assn., Orgn. Am. Historians, Acad. Cert. Archivists. Avocation: contra dancing. Office: U Alaska PO Box 756808 Fairbanks AK 99775

GRIGGS, EMMA, management executive; b. Cleveland, Ark., Feb. 8, 1928; d. James and Frazier (Byers) Wallace; m. Augusta Griggs, Mar. 20, 1954 (dec.); children: Judy A., Terri V. *My two professional daughters, Judy A. Griggs and Terri V. Griggs have been and are still extremely influential in my professional career success. We, my daughters and I, have influenced one another's respective careers and in one another's personal lives.* Grad. H.S., Chgo. Pres., CEO Burlington No. Inc., Inglewood, Calif., 1986—. *I am privileged to be President and C.E.O of a successful company, "Burlington Northern, Inc.". My career began at BNI in January of 1986. Because of my contribution to the Republican Presidential Task Force in 1996, my name will be permanently enshrined on the National Republican Victory Monument, Ronald Reagan Republican Center, 425 Second Street N.E., Washington, D.C. I received the 1998 National Republican Victory Campaign Certificate of Valor for my outstanding devotion and loyalty to the Republican party. In 1997, I received from the Speaker of the House, the honorable Newt Gingrich, The Speaker's Citizen Task Force Certificate of Merit.* Republican. Avocations: reading, gardening, housekeeping.

GRIGGS, GAIL, marketing executive; b. 1937. Grad., U. Oreg., U. Chgo. Instr. Chgo. Art Inst., Roosevelt U., Chgo., Evergreen State U., Olympia, Wash.; with Griggs-Anderson, Inc., 1979—; now pres. Griggs-Anderson, Inc./Gartner Group. Office: Griggs-Anderson Inc/Gartner Group 308 SW 1st Ave Fl 4 Portland OR 97204-3400*

GRILLO, LEO, actor, photographer, animal rescuer; b. Lawrence, Mass., Feb. 6, 1949; s. Leo F. Sr. and Carmela M. (DeLucia) G.; m. Stacy Grillo; children: Erica, McGuire. BS in speech, Emerson Coll., Boston, 1970. Actor Glendale, Calif., 1965—; pres., founder Dedication and Everlasting Love to Animals Inc., Glendale, 1979—, Living Earth Prodns., 1990—, Horse Rescue Am., 1991—; founder, pres. DELTA Rescue Netherlands, DELTA Rescue Italy; pres. Leo Grillo Prodns. Inc., 1995. Author: (with others) Landscam, 1988, Is This the Place?; producer, host Safe House, (TV show) Delta Rescue Story; actor (feature film) The Crap Game. Mem. Screen Actors' Guild, AFTRA, Actors Equity Assn. Office: DELTA Rescue PO Box 9 Glendale CA 91209-0009

GRILLY, EDWARD ROGERS, physicist; b. Cleve., Dec. 30, 1917; s. Charles B. and Julia (Varady) G.; m. Mary Witholter, Dec. 14, 1942 (dec. 1971); children: David, Janice; m. Juliamarie Andreen Langham, Feb. 1, 1973. BA, Ohio State U., 1940, PhD, 1944. Rsch. scientist Carbide & Carbon Chemicals Corp., Oak Ridge, Tenn., 1944-45; asst. prof. Chemistry U. N.H., Durham, 1946-47; mem. staff U. Calif. Nat. Lab., Los Alamos, N.Mex., 1947-80, cons., 1980—. Contbr. articles to books and profl. jours. Mem. N.Mex. House of Reps., Santa Fe, 1967-70, Los Alamos County Coun., Los Alamos, 1976-78. Mem. Am. Physical Soc., Kiwanis Club, Los Alamos Golf Club (pres. 1974-75). Republican. Avocation: golf. Home: 705 43rd St Los Alamos NM 87544-1807

GRIM, MARK ROBERT, newspaper editor; b. Bellingham, Wash., Feb. 12, 1962; s. Gary Lee Grim and Diane Carol (Behme) Scansen. BA in Philosophy, Humanities, Eastern Wash. U., 1991, student Gonzaga Sch. of Law, 1992, BA in Journalism, 1993. Law clk. Lukins & Annis, Spokane, 1990-91; staff writer West Plains Tribune, Spokane, 1993; sports corr. Spokesman-Review, Spokane, 1993; part-time sportswriter Seattle Times, 1993-94; corr. Lake Stevens (Wash.) Jour., 1993-94; reporter-sportswriter Willapa Harbor Herald, Raymond, Wash., 1995; editor Othello (Wash.) Outlook, 1995—. Mem. Soc. Profl. Journalists. Avocations: computers and technology, golf, theology, philosophy, movies. Home: 420 S 4th St Othello WA 99344 Office: Othello Outlook 180 E Main PO Box 0 Othello WA 99344

GRIMES, BRYAN KELLY, artist; b. Gresham, Oreg., Oct. 21, 1970; s. Steve Patrick Grimes and Linda (Zito) Rogers. BA magna cum laude, Western Oreg. State Coll., 1993. Photographer South Salem Times, Salem, Oreg., 1988-89; profl. artist Portland, Oreg., 1993—; prin. Frame of Mind, Portland, 1996—; represented artist Three Sisters Folk Art Gallery, Sisters, Oreg., Omni Gallery, Portland, 1997—. Editor: (periodical) Official Graffiti; artist: (exterior mural) Yellow Etblank, 1991, Main St. Pk., 1994; author: Good Fences Make Good Neighbors but Fire Hydrants Make Better Friends, 1992. Co-recipient art scholarship Western Oreg. State Coll., 1992; named Cmty. Artist of Yr. Monmouth-Independence Cmty. Arts Assn., 1993. Mem. Beaverton (Oreg.) Arts Commn. (visual arts com. 1996—, Artist Mem. of Yr. 1998), Phi Kappa Phi, Sigma Tau Delta. Democrat. Home and Office: 7644 Crystal Springs Blvd Portland OR 97206-8612

GRIMES, DAPHNE BUCHANAN, priest, artist; b. Tulsa, Apr. 12, 1929; d. George Sidney and Dorothy Elnora (Dodds) Buchanan; m. Thomas Edward Grimes, Nov. 6, 1964 (dec. Oct., 1986). BFA, U. Houston, 1952; MA, Columbia U., 1954; MA in Religion, Episcopal Seminary of the Southwest, 1985. Ordained deacon Episcopalian Ch., 1982, priest, 1986. Tchr. history Rockland County Day Sch., Nyack, N.Y., 1959-61; dir. Am. Sch., Tunis, Tunisia, 1962-64; priest vicar St. Andrew's Ch., Meeteetse, Wyo., 1987-90; dir. Thomas the Apostle Ctr., Cody, Wyo., 1990—; stewardship chmn. Diocese Wyo., 1979-85, mem. bd. diocesan coun., 1987-90, chmn. social svcs., 1987-91. Author of poems. Chaplain West Park County Hosp., Cody, Wyo., 1981-84, West Park County Long Term Care Ctr., Cody, 1982—; bd. dirs. Park County Arts Coun., 1995-98. Mem. Cody Country Arts League, Cmty. of Celebration (spiritual adv. 1990—), Order of Julian of Norwich (assoc.), St. Andrew's Cmty. (assoc.), Compass Rose Soc. Avocations: reading science, theology, fiction, journaling, travel, skindiving, animals. Home and Office: Thomas the Apostle Ctr 45 Road 3cx S Cody WY 82414-9601

GRIMES, JOSEPH EDWARD, computer science educator; b. Bloomington, Ill., Sept. 28, 1941; s. Edward A. and Mary C. (Kleemann) G.; m. Mary Rae Tures, Aug. 8, 1964; children: Joe, Therese, Christine, Michael, Matthew, Mark. BA, St. Ambrose U., Davenport, Iowa, 1963; MS, Ill. State U., 1968; PhD, Iowa State U., 1973. Tchr., coach Ctrl. Cath. H.S., Bloomington, 1963-66; civil engr. McLean County Hwy. Dept., Bloomington, 1966-68; instr. Iowa State U., Ames, 1968-73; prof. computer sci. Calif. Poly. State U., San Luis Obispo, 1973—, mgr. computer svcs., 1986-87, dir. computer engring., 1997—; cons. NASA, Moffett Field, Calif., 1974-91, Xerox Corp., Santa Clara, Calif., 1984-91; mem. Naval Ship Weapons Engring. Sta., Port Huename, Calif., 1987-90; expert witness NCR Corp., 1984-89, Ford Motor Corp., 1989, State of Calif., 1992; chairperson instrnl. adv. com. on computing Calif. Poly. State U., 1994—, chairperson UNIX team, 1995-97. Contbr. articles to profl. jours. Dir. referees San Luis Obispo Youth Soccer, 1982—; chmn. fin. coun., mem. pastoral coun. Old Mission, San Luis Obispo, 1985-89. Mem. Am. Statis. Assn., Assn. for Computing Machinery, Computing Soc. of IEEE, Mu Sigma Rho. Roman Catholic. Avocations: racquetball, running, gardening, carpentry, family. Home: 650 Evans Rd San Luis Obispo CA 93401-8121 Office: Dept Computer Sci Calif Poly State U San Luis Obispo CA 93407

GRIMM, BOB, food products executive; b. 1954. With Grimmway Enterprises, Inc., Bakersfield, Calif., 1973—, v.p., 1973-98, pres., 1998—. Office: Grimmway Enterprises Inc PO Box 81498 Bakersfield CA 93380*

GRIMM, JANE BOLLES, [illegible] d. John Savage and Mary Vande Water (Piper) Bolles; m. Rupert Edwin Grimm, Aug. 1968; children: Jacqueline, John Piper. AB, Sarah Lawrence Coll., 1965; MFA, Calif. Coll. Arts & Crafts, 1992. Pres. Jane Bolles, Inc., N.Y., 1965-70; pres., designer Bolles Jewelry, San Francisco, 1975-89; artist San

Francisco, 1989—. Trustee Cambridge Sch. Weston, Weston, Mass., 1992—, Calif. Coll. Arts & Crafts, 1996—. Recipient Murphy fellowship San Francisco Found., 1991, Merit award Calif. State Fair, 1994. Avocation: tennis. Office: 1777 Yosemite Ave # 320 San Francisco CA 94124

GRIMM, LARRY LEON, psychologist; b. Goshen, Ind., Aug. 16, 1950; s. Warren Arden and Elizabeth Ann (Rassi) G.; m. Ann Mae Nelson, July 16, 1977; 1 child, Kirsten Ann. BS in Elem. Edn., No. Ariz. U., 1975, MA in Early Childhood Edn., 1977, EdD in Ednl. Psychology, 1983. Lic. psychologist; cert. sch. psychologist, elem. tchr. Ariz., Nat. Tchr. elem. sch. Page (Ariz.) Unified Dist., 1975-76; grad. asst. Coll. Edn., No. Ariz. U., Flagstaff, 1976; tchr. elem. sch. Litchfield Sch. Dist., Litchfield Park, Ariz., 1976-80; grad. assoc. dept. ednl. psychology No. Ariz. U., Flagstaff, 1980-81; sch. psychologist intern Peoria (Ariz.) Unified Dist., 1981-82; adj. faculty Grand Canyon Coll., Phoenix, 1982; sch. psychologist Child Study Services, Prescott (Ariz.) Unified Sch. Dist., 1982-87; adj. assoc. prof. No. Ariz. U., Flagstaff, 1984—, vis. faculty, 1987-88; postdoctoral fellow in pediatric psychology Child Devel. Ctr. Georgetown U. Med. Ctr., Washington, 1988-89; pvt. practice, 1989—; cons. in field; presenter at convs. Contbr. articles to profl. jours. Chmn. project devel. com. Infant & Toddler Network, 1989-92; mem. family resource ctr. adv. bd. Yavapai Regional Med. Ctr., 1990—. Mem. Am. Psychol. Assn. (publs. com. div. 16), Ariz. Assn. Sch. Psychologists (bd. dirs. No. Ariz., regional dir. 1983-84, pres. 1986-87, newsletter editor, 1986-87, Pres.'s award 1985, 88, 89), Nat. Assn. Sch. Psychologists (Ariz. del. fiscal adv. com. 1987-88, Capitol Network 1988-89), Soc. Pediatric Psychologists, Christian Assn. Psychol. Studies. Republican.

GRIMMER, BEVERLEY SUE, consumer products executive; b. Olathe, Kans., June 9, 1950; d. Edward Mathines Rice and Jessie LaVaun (Cade) Waymire; m. Danny Joe San Romani, June 4, 1977 (div. May 1991); 1 child, Justin (dec.); m. Gary G. Grimmer, June 21, 1992. Student, Kans. State Tchrs. Coll., 1968-71, U. Kans., 1975-77. Employee trainer, dept. mgr. T.G.&Y. Stores, Emporia, Kans., 1968-70; office mgr. Office of Staff Judge Adv. 3d Armored Div., Frankfurt, Fed. Republic of Germany, 1971-75, Don W. Lill, Atty. at Law, Emporia, 1976-77; instr., sub. tchr. Kodiak (Ala.) C.C. and Kodiak Pub. Sch. System, 1979-81; legal sec. Kaito & Ishida, Honolulu, 1983-84; adminstr. Alcantara & Frame, Honolulu, 1984-86; ind. contractor Hughes Hubbard & Reed, N.Y., Honolulu, 1986-88; paralegal Carlsmith, Ball, Wichman, Murray, Case, Mukai & Ichiki, Honolulu, 1988-91; spl. agt. Vanuatu (Hawaii) Maritime Agy., 1989—; ch. adminstr. Ctrl. Union Ch., Honolulu, 1991-94; owner Gentle Memories, Kailua, Hawaii, 1995—; Gubernatorial coun. appointee Juvenile Justice State Adv. Coun., 1993-94; mem. women's health week com. State of Hawaii, Commn. on Status of Women, 1994. 1st v.p. Christmas in April Oahu, 1995, bd. dirs., 1995—; auction pub. chair Acad. Arts Guild, 1993; mem. Contemporary Arts Mus.; cmty. rels. and arrangements chairs for Tuxes 'n Tails Black and White Ball, Hawaiian Humane Soc., 1993, 94; mem. Hawaii Lupus Found.; bd. dirs. Armed Forces YMCA, 1995—; mem. vestry St. Christopher's Ch., 1995—. Recipient Order of Golden Swivel Shot award Comdt. USCG, 1981, 89, 1st Runner-up Maritime Week Maritime Employee award Propeller Club U.S., 1986, Letter of Appreciation, Dept. Navy, 1983, Cert. of Commendation, U.S. Army, 1975. Mem. Am. Heart Assn. (chair Celebrity Celebration 1994, silent auction co-chair 1996 Heart Ball, co-chair 1997 Heart Ball), Coast Guard Officers' Spouses Club (nominating chair 1989, pres. 1982, 87, 88), Awa Lau Wahine (Coast Guard rep. 1988, 87, corr. sec. 1983, Boutiki chair 1982), Rotary (vice chair Friends of Foster Kids Picnic 1994, chair 1995), Jr. League (cmty. v.p. 1993, rec. sec. 1990), Navy League, Propeller Club Port of Honolulu (bd. govs. alt. 1990), Hawaii Legal Aux. (v.p. 1994, pub./publs. chair 1994). Republican. Episcopalian. Avocations: golf, tennis, needlepoint, reading, community voluntarism. Home and Office: 159 Kakahiaka St Kailua HI 96734-3474

GRIMSBO, RAYMOND ALLEN, forensic scientist; b. Portland, Oreg., Apr. 25, 1948; s. LeRoy Allen and Irene Bernice (Surgen) G.; m. Barbara Suzanne Favreau, Apr. 26, 1969 (div. 1979); children: John Allen, Kimberly Suzanne; m. Charlotte Alice Miller, July 25, 1981 (div. 1994); children: Sarah Marie, Benjamin Allen. BS, Portland State U., 1972; D of Philosophy, Union for Experimenting Colls. & Univs., Cin., 1987. Diplomate Am. Bd. Criminalistics; cert. profl. competency in criminalistics DEA Rschr. Registration. Med. technician United Med. Labs., Inc., Portland, 1969-74; criminalist Oreg. State Police Crime Lab., Portland, 1975-85; pvt. practice forensic science Portland, 1985-87; pres. Intermountain Forensic Labs., Inc., Portland, 1987—; adj. instr. Oreg. Health Scis. U., Portland, 1987-95; adj. prof. Portland State U., 1986-88, adj. asst. prof., 1988—; clin. dir. Intermountain Forensic Labs., Inc., 1988-92, Western Health Lab., Portland; adj. faculty Union Inst.; mem. substance abuse methods panel Oreg. Health Divsn. Contbr. articles to profl. jours. Fellow Am. Acad. Forensic Scientists; mem. ASTM, STM, Soc. Forensic Haemogenetics, N.W. Assn. Forensic Scientists, Internat. Assn. Bloodstain Pattern Analysis, Electrophoresis Soc., Internat. Assn. Identification, internat. Assn. Forensic Toxicologists, Pacific N.W. Forensic Study, New Horizons Investment Club. Avocations: gardening, camping, photography, forensic science, study of ritualistic crime. Home: 16936 NE Davis St Portland OR 97230-6239 Office: Intermountain Forensic Labs Inc 11715 NE Glisan St Portland OR 97220-2141

GRIMWADE, RICHARD LLEWELLYN, lawyer; b. Chgo., Apr. 26, 1945; s. Eric Illingworth and Pauline J. (Crandall) G.; m. Alexandra M. Galbraith, Feb. 22, 1981; children: Eric Montgomery, Sarah Elizabeth. BA, Lawrence U., 1967; JD cum laude, U. Wis., 1971. Bar: Wis. 1971, N.Y. 1971, Ill. 1978, Calif. 1981, U.S. Dist. Ct. (so. dist., ea. dist.) N.Y., 1971, U.S. Dist. Ct. (no. dist.) Wis., 1978, U.S. Dist. Ct. (no. dist.) Ill., 1981, U.S. Dist. Ct. (ctrl. dist.) Calif., U.S. Ct. Appeals (2d, 7th and 9th cirs.). Atty. Davis Polk, N.Y.C., 1971-75; ptnr. Barton Klugman, L.A., 1983-93; pvt. practice L.A., 1993—. Mem. U. Wis. Law Rev., 1969-71. Bd. mgrs. Ketchum Downtown YMCA, L.A., 1991-97; trustee Reform L.A. Pub. Schs. (LEARN). Recipient 3 Am. Jurisprudence awards for evidence, legis., and acctg. and law Bancroft-Whitney, 1970. Mem. State Bar Calif., State Bar Wis., State Bar N.Y., State Bar Ill., Rotary L.A. (bd. dirs. 1991-93, sec. 1994), Toastmasters (Best Spkr. award, Best Performer award 1996, Best Table Topics award 1997), Order of Coif. Avocations: gardening, poetry, running, public speaking. Home: 23362 Park Hacienda Calabasas CA 91302-1715 Office: MCI Center 700 S Flower St Ste 1100 Los Angeles CA 90017-4113

GRIN, LEONID, conductor; b. Dniepropetrovsk, Ukraine, June 19, 1947; came to U.S., 1981; s. Gavriil and Ita (Sklar) Grinshpun; m. Marina Gusak, Apr. 25, 1970; children: Radmila, Daniel. BMus, Dniepropetrovsk Music Coll., 1966; MusM, Onesin's Music Inst., 1971; MusM in Conducting, Moscow State Conservatory, 1975, DMus, 1977. Assoc. condr. Moscow Philharm. Symphony Orch., 1977-79; prof. conducting U. Houston, 1983-86; prin. guest condr. Tampere (Finland) Philharm Orch., 1988-90, music dir., condr., 1990-94; music dir., condr. San Jose (Calif.) Symphony Orch., 1992—; guest condr. various orchs. in Denmark, Sweden, Norway, Finland, Eng., Scotland, Israel, Germany, The Netherlands, Italy, Belgium, Spain, Portugal, New Zealand, USA, Can., many others. Recs. include music by Tchaikovsky, Procofrev, Shostakovitch, all 6 symphonies by Erkki Mellartin. Office: San Jose Symphony Orchestra 495 Almaden Blvd San Jose CA 95110*

GRINDAL, MARY ANN, former sales professional; b. Michigan City, Ind., Sept. 9, 1942; d. James Paxton and Helen Evelyn (Koivisto) Gleason; m. Bruce Theodore Grindal, June 12, 1965 (div. Sept. 1974); 1 child, Matthew Bruce. BSBA, Ind. U., 1965. Sec. African studies program Ind. U., Bloomington, 1965-66; rsch. aide Ghana, West Africa, 1966-68; exec. sec. divsn. biol. scis. Ind. U., Bloomington, 1968-69; office asst. Dean of Students office Middlebury (Vt.) Coll., 1969-70; exec. sec. Remo, Inc., North Hollywood, Calif., 1974-76; sec., asst. to product mgrs. in cosmetic and skin care Redken Labs., Canoga Park, Calif., 1976-79; various sec. and exec. sec. positions L.A., 1979-81, 85-89; exec. sec. Sargent Industries, Burbank, Calif., 1981-85; sales asst. Chyron Graphics, Burbank, Calif., 1989-97; adminstrv. sec. divsn. instructional svcs. Burbank Unified Sch. Dist., 1998—. Author of poems and essays. Mem. U.S. Navy Meml. Found. Mem. DAR (chpt. registrar 1988-91, chpt. regent 1991-94, chpt. chmn. pub. rels. and pub. 1994—, chpt. chaplain 1994—, mem. spkrs. staff 1995—, state chmn. Am. Heritage 1994-96, state chmn. Calif. DAR scholarship com. 1996-98), Daus. of Union Vets. of Civil War, 1861-65, Inc., Nat. Soc. Dames of the Ct. of Honor (state chaplain 1997—). Episcopalian. Avocations: travel, writing, genealogy.

GRINELL, SHEILA, museum director; b. N.Y.C., July 15, 1945; d. Richard N. and Martha (Mimiless) G.; m. Thomas E. Johnson, July 15, 1980; 1 child, Michael; stepchildren: Kathleen, Thomas. BA, Radcliffe Coll., 1966; MA, U. Calif., Berkeley, 1968. Co-dir. exhibits and programs The Exploratorium, San Francisco, 1969-74; promotion dir. Kodansha Internat., Tokyo, 1974-77; traveling exhbn. coord. Assn. Sci. Tech. Ctrs., Washington, 1978-80, exec. dir., 1980-82, project dir. traveling exhbn. Chips and Changes, 1982-84; assoc. dir. N.Y. Hall of Sci., 1984-87; exec. dir. Ariz. Sci. Ctr., Phoenix, 1993—; cons. Optical Soc. Am., 1987, Nat. Sci. Ctr. Found., 1988, Interactive Video Sci. Consortium, 1988, Assn. Sci. Tech. Ctrs., 1988-89, Found. for Creative Am., 1989-90, Am. Assn. for World Health, 1990, Children's TV Workshop, 1991, Sciencenter, 1991, SciencePort, 1991, The Invention Factory, 1992, N.Y. Bot. Garden, 1992-93. Author: Light, Sight, Sound, Hearing: Exploratorium '74, 1974; editor A Stage for Science, 1979, A New Place for Learning Science: Starting and Running A Science Center, 1992, (with Mark St. John) Vision to Reality: Critical Dimensions in Science Center Development, Vol. I, 1993, II, 1994. Fulbright teaching asst., 1966; hon. Woodrow Wilson fellow, 1967. Fellow AAAS; mem. Am. Assn. Mus., Phi Beta Kappa. Office: Ariz Sci Ctr 600 E Washington St Phoenix AZ 85004-2303

GRINNELL, CHRISTOPHER WADE, photographer, art educator; b. Newport News, Va., Dec. 13, 1959; s. Alvin Wade Grinnell and Elizabeth Stewart (Edwards) Sclater. BA, Rochester Inst., N.Y., 1989; MA, U. N.Mex., 1991, MFA, 1999. Cert. tchr., N.Mex. Prin. Chris Grinnell photography, Albuquerque, 1990—; art tchr. Rio Grande H.S., Albuquerque, 1995—; photo instr. N.Mex State U., Grants, N.Mex., 1994-95. photography series pub.in Albuquerque Monthly mag. Bd. dir Albuquerque United Artists, 1993-95. Mem. Coll. Art Assoc., Soc. Photographic Edn. Avocations: imaging tech., student assistance. Office: Rio Grande HS 2300 Arenal Rd SW Albuquerque NM 87105-4160

GRISEZ, JAMES LOUIS, physician, plastic surgeon; b. Modesto, Calif., Feb. 25, 1935; s. John Francis and Josephine Marie (Tournahu) G.; m. Diane Madeline Skidmore, Mar. 7, 1989; children: James, Stephen, Suzanne, Kathleen. MD, St. Louis Sch. Medicine, 1960. Diplomate Am. Bd. Plastic and Reconstructive Surgery. Intern D.C. Gen. Hosp., Washington, 1960-61; resident med. ctr. Georgetown U., Washington, 1961-64; resident plastic and reconstructive surgery ctr. St. Francis Meml. Hosp., San Francisco, 1964-66; military surgeon Brook Army Med Ctr., San Antonio, 1966, Second Gen. Hosp., Landstuhl, Germany, 1966-69; pvt. practice Napa, Calif., 1969-82, Salinas, Calif., 1982-90, Kailua-Kona, Hawaii, 1990-93; pvt. practice South Valley Plastic Surgery, Gilroy, Calif., 1993—; active staff mem. St. Louise Hosp.; chief of staff South Valley Med. Ctr., Hazel Hawkins; chief staff St. Helena Hosp., 1977-78, exec. com. 1973-80; radio talk show host All About Plastic Surgery, sta. KRNY, 1986-88. Contbr. articles to med. jours. Mem. Am. Cancer Soc. (pres. 1988-90), Am. Soc. Plastic and Reconstructive Surgeons, Calif. Soc. Plastic and Reconstructive Surgeons, Hawaii Plastic Surgery Soc. Home: 8675 Muir Dr Gilroy CA 95020-3725 Office: 8375 Church St Gilroy CA 95020-4406

GRISHAM, ANDREW FLETCHER, aerospace engineer, consultant; b. Nashville, Feb. 23, 1937; s. Albert Harding and Gladys Katella (Harmon) G.; m. Marilyn Jean Crerar, Sept. 2, 1967; children: David Andrew Fletcher Grisham, Mary Kathryn Grisham, Elizabeth Ann Grisham Volz. BSCE, Vanderbilt U., 1958; MSCE, U. Calif., Berkeley, 1960, postgrad., 1958-60. Civil engrng. tchg. asst. U. Calif., Berkeley, 1958-59; sr. structural engr. B52, B70, Dyna-Soar, SST, Apollo The Boeing Co., Seattle, New Orleans, 1958-73; sr. specialist engr. 727, 737, SST, 757, 767, 777 The Boeing Co., Renton, Everett, Wash., 1973-82; prin. engr. Boeing Space Group/Marine Sys., Kent, Renton, Wash., 1982-89; sr. prin. engr. A6, B2, F22 Boeing Mil. Airplane Group, Seattle, 1989-94; cons. joint strike fighter Boeing Def. and Space Group Rsch., Seattle, 1994-96; cons. The Raisbeck Group, Rockwell Internat., Seattle, 1977, Superior Design Co., Bellevue, Wash., 1994-96, The Boeing Co., Bellevue, 1994-96; instr. finite element methods Boeing grad. engr. tng., Kent, Wash., 1979; chmn. cross-corp. maj. structural analysis sys., The Boeing Co., Phila., Wichita, Kans., Renton, Wash., Kent, Wash., Everett, Wash., Seattle, 1988-91. Author: (Boeing mainframe sys. handbooks and software) Interfaced Structural Analysis System, 1965-87, (Boeing workstation sys. handbooks and software) Multidisciplinary Design, Analysis and Optimization System, 1987-96; author papers. Chmn. worship and music com. Trinity Methodist Ch., Seattle, 1969-75, mem. Rep. precinct com., Seattle, 1978-86, ch. organist, Seattle, 1954-73. U. Calif. grantee NSF, 1959-60; A.J. Dyer scholar Vanderbilt U., 1954-58, scholar U. Calif., 1958-60. Mem. Seattle Prof. Engring. Employees Assn., Queen City Yacht Club, Holiday Ramblers, Tau Beta Pi. Republican. Presbyterian. Achievements include devel. of Boeing finite element pre- and post-processors for modeling, analysis, optimization and commonality for joint (Marine, Navy, Air Force) strike fighter; developed methods for nonlinear analysis of Apollo, Saturn booster tank penetrations including post buckling in aerospace structural finite element models for multiple load conditions using pre-strains. Avocations: travel, boating, music, politics, restoration of 1961 Rolls Royce. Home and Office: 8713 Golden Gardens Dr NW Seattle WA 98117-3942

GRISHAM, JEANNIE, artist; b. Opportunity, Wash., June 26, 1942; d. Lyle Gordon and Lela Georgia (Miller) Jacklin; m. John Paul Grisham, July 4, 1965; children: Jill Jacklin Grisham Ross, Jennifer Jean Grisham Marks, John Paul Jr. Attended, Wash. State U., 1960-62; grad., Burnley Sch. Profl. Art (now Seattle Art Inst.), 1962-64; postgrad., Lyme (Conn.) Acad. Fine Art, 1981-82; studied with, Gerald Brommer, Jerry Caron, Brent Heighton, Katherine Chang Liu, Marilyn Hughy Phillis, Barbara Nechis, Carol Orr, Lou Taylor, Alex Powers, Irving Shapiro, Frank Webb. Exhibits include U.S. Naval Acad., Annapolis, Md., 1974, San Diego Watercolor Soc., 1982-83, San Diego Art Inst., 1982-83, Western Fedn. Watercolor Soc., 1982-83, Deerpath Art Festival, Lake Forest, Ill., 1985-88, Deerpath Art Gallery, Lake Forest, 1985-88, David Adler Show, Libertyville, Ill., 1987-88, Curtis Gallery, Libertyville, 1987-88, Eastside Assn. Fine Art, Kirkland, Wash., 1989, 90, Ea. Wash. Watercolor Soc., Richland, 1989, Mercer Island (Wash.) Art Festival, 1989, Frye Art Mus., Wash., 1990, 91, 93, Bainbridge Arts and Crafts Solo Show, 1989, 91, 93, 94, N.W. Watercolor Soc., 1991, 92, 94, 95, 96, 97, Women Painters Wash., 1993-98, Midwest Watercolor Soc., 1992, 93, 97, 98, NWWS Waterworks, 1992, 94-97, Nat. Watercolor Soc., 1996, 97, Nat. Acad. 1998, many others; works included in various publs. Recipient A and C. Obrig award NAt. Acad. Mem. Am. Watercolor Soc. (assoc.), Midwest Watercolor Soc. (signature mem.), Nat. Watercolor Soc. (signature mem.), N.W. Watercolor Soc. (pres. emeritus, signature mem.), Women Painters Wash., Watercolor West Juried Assn. Home: 10044 Edgecombe Pl NE Bainbridge Island WA 98110-4333

GRISHMAN, LEE HOWARD, college program administrator; b. L.A., Dec. 16, 1946; s. Milton and Sadie Edith (Kisner) G.; children: Melissa Leigh, Julia Anne, Andrea Joy. BA, Brigham Young U., 1973; MA in Religion, Yale U., 1975; AM in Higher Edn., Columbia U., 1977, EdD in History of Am. Edn., 1983. Instr., religion and edn. U. Utah, 1978-79, Columbia U.; dir. admission and acad. svcs. Sch. Bus. and Econs., Calif. State U., L.A., 1984-88; dir. counseling and matriculation Chaffey Coll., Rancho Cucamonga, Calif., 1988-90; asst. vice chancellor for student devel. Pima County C.C. Dist., Tucson, AZ, 1991-93; coord. transfer edn. and articulation Antelope Valley Coll., 1995—; adj. sr. lectr., dept. policy, planning and adminstrn. U. So. Calif. Contbr. articles to profl. jours. Fellow Yale U., 1974, Union Theol. Sem., Columbia U., 1976-78. Mem. ASTD, Phi Delta Kappa.

GRISMORE, ROGER, physics educator, researcher; b. Ann Arbor, Mich., July 12, 1924; s. Grover Cleveland and May Aileen (White) G.; m. Marilynn Ann McNinch, Sept. 15, 1950; 1 child, Carol Ann. BS, U. Mich., 1947, MS, 1948, PhD, 1957; BS in Computer Sci., Coleman Coll., 1979. From asst. to assoc. physicist Argonne (Ill.) Nat. Lab., 1956-62; assoc. prof. physics Lehigh U., Bethlehem, Pa., 1962-67; specialist in physics Scripps Inst. Oceanography, La Jolla, Calif., 1967-71, 75-78; prof. physics Ind. State U., Terre Haute, 1971-74; from mem. staff to sr. scientist JAYCOR, San Diego, 1979-84; lectr. Calif. Poly. State U., San Luis Obispo, 1984-92, rsch. prof., 1992—, lunar sample investigator, 1994—. *Experimental research scientist and educator specializing in measurements of natural and manmade gamma radioactivities in environmental and lunar samples. Codiscoverer of the radioisotope Silver-108m in the general marine environment. Developed the technique of radiosilver dating.* Contbr. numerous articles to profl. jours. Served as ensign USNR, 1945-46, PTO. Mem. Am. Phys. Soc., Am. Geophys. Union, N.Y. Acad. Scis., Sigma Xi. Home: 535 Cameo Way Arroyo Grande CA 93420-5574 Office: Calif Poly State U Dept Physics San Luis Obispo CA 93407

GRISSOM, GARTH CLYDE, lawyer; b. Syracuse, Kans., Jan. 24, 1930; s. Clyde and Bernice Minnie (Eddy) G.; m. Elena Joyce Kerst, Aug. 17, 1958; children: Colin, Grady, Cole, Kent. B.S., Kans. State U., 1951; LL.B., Harvard U., 1957. Bar: Colo. 1957, U.S. Dist. Ct. (fed. dist.) Colo., 1957, U.S. Ct. Appeals (10th crct.) 1957, U.S. Supreme Ct. 1989. Ptnr., mem., counsel Sherman & Howard, L.L.C., Denver, 1963—. Sec., counsel, trustee Mile High United Way, Denver, 1985-88; trustee Kans. State U. Found., Manhattan, 1962-89; mem. Colo. Gov.'s Commn. on Life and the Law, 1990—, chmn., 1996—. Mem. ABA, Colo. Bar Assn., Denver Bar Assn. (pres. 1985-86, award of merit 1994), Rotary (sec. Denver 1983-84, bd. dirs. 1983-86, pres. 1989-90), Pi Kappa Alpha (pres. 1968-70). Home: 1777 Larimer St Apt 1610 Denver CO 80202-1548 Office: Sherman & Howard LLC 633 17th St Ste 3000 Denver CO 80202-3665

GRISWOLD, DOUGLAS A., engineer; b. Columbus, Ohio, June 28, 1957; s. Byron D. and Elizabeth A. Russell; m. Deborah A. Thomas Bowman, June 10, 1978 (div. Nov. 1985); 1 child, Amy Ranee; m. Karen A. Freshour, July 20, 1996; children: Anthony Freshour, Amanda Freshour. BS in Aeronautics, Miami U., Oxford, Ohio, 1979; AS in Electronics, Cochise Coll., 1997. Field engr. Eaton Corp./Contel, Honolulu, 1987-90; field svc. rep. GTE, Sierra Vista/Ft. Huachuca, Ariz., 1990-91; site mgr. Whittaker Electronics, Sierra Vista, 1991-94; field engr. Telos, Sierra Vista, 1994-95; sr. Lan/Wan engr. SAIC, Sierra Vista, 1995—. Sgt. U.S. Army, 1983-87. Republican. Lutheran. Avocations: amateur radio, pvt. pilot, computer. Home: 3084 Thunderbird Dr Sierra Vista AZ 85650-6686 Office: US Army Meddac Bldg 45001/Rm 1161 Raymond W Bliss Army Hlth Fort Huachuca AZ 85613

GRISWOLD, MARTHA KERFOOT, social worker; b. Oklahoma City, Mar. 22, 1930; d. John Samuel III and Frances (Mann) Kerfoot; m. George Littlefield Griswold, Jan. 28, 1967. AB, Occidental Coll., 1951; MRE, U. So. Calif., 1956, postgrad., 1962. Cert. social worker. Teen dir. Toberman Settlement, San Pedro, Calif., 1954-56; social worker County of L.A., 1956-62; cons. community orgn. L.A., 1962-84; dir. LIV Disability Resources Ctr., Altadena, Calif., 1984—; instr. Calif. State U., L.A., 1966-68, 1983-84; chair Childrens' Adv. Com. L.A. County Dept. Mental Health, 1985-86; coordinator So. Calif. Conf. on Living Long Term with Disability, 1985-87. Co-host, prodr. radio program on disability Access Unlimited, Sta. KPFK-FM, 1987—, host. prodr. cable TV program on disability issues LIVstyles, 1992—. Mem. Pasadena (Calif.) City disability Issues Com., 1984-86, Pasadena Strategic Planning Task Force, 1985-86, City of Pasedena commn. disability access 1990-97; com.on aging and long-term care Region 2 United Way, L.A., chairperson, 1989-90, Pasadena Awareness: A Cmty. Effort for Disabled (PACED v.p.), 1983—. Recipient award So. Calif. Rehab. Assn., 1986, Disting. Alumna award Claremont Sch. Theology, 1996. Mem. AAUW, NASW, Californians for Disability Rights, Acad. Cert. Social Workers, Health and Social Svc. Workers with Disabilities. Congregationalist (UCC). Office: LIV Ctr 943 E Altadena Dr Altadena CA 91001-2033

GRODY, MARK STEPHEN, public relations executive; b. Milw., Jan. 1, 1938; s. Ray and Betty (Rothstein) G.; m. Karen Goldstein, Mar. 6, 1965 (div. 1972); 1 child, Laura; m. Susan Tellem, Mar. 25, 1979 (div. 1989); 1 child, Daniel. BS, U. Wis., 1960. Pub. rels. exec. GM, Detroit, 1961-74; v.p. pub. affairs Nat. Alliance of Businessmen, Washington, 1973-74; v.p. Carl Terzian & Assocs., L.A., 1974-75; chmn. Mark Grody Assocs. and Grody Tellem Comm., Inc. (now The Rowland Co.), L.A., 1975-90; pres. Mark Grody Assocs., L.A., 1990-93; exec. v.p., gen. mgr. Ogilvy Adams & Rinehart, L.A., 1993-96; pres. Mark Grody Assocs., L.A., 1996—; ptnr. Mktg. Golf Resources, L.A., 1996—, thegolfspot.com, 1998. Co-author: Corporate Golf: How to Play the Game for Business Success, 1996. Capt. U.S. Army, 1960. Mem. Pub. Rels. Soc. Am., Industry Edn. Coun. of Calif. (bd. dirs.), Nat. Alliance of Bus./West (bd. dirs.), Mountain Gate Country Club, L.A. Sports Club . Avocations: golf, bridge.

GRODY, WAYNE WILLIAM, physician; b. Syracuse, N.Y., Feb. 25, 1952; s. Robert Jerome and Florence Beatrice (Kashdan) G.; m. Gaylen Ducker, July 8, 1990. BA, Johns Hopkins U., 1974; MD, Baylor Coll. Medicine, 1977, PhD, 1981. Diplomate Am. Bd. Pathology, Am. Bd. Med. Genetics; lic. physician, Calif. Intern/resident UCLA Sch. Medicine, 1982-85, postdoctoral fellow, 1985-86, asst. prof., 1987-93, assoc. prof., 1993-97; prof., 1997—; panelist Calif. Children's Svcs., 1987—, U.S. FDA, Washington, 1989—; mem. DNA tech. com. Pacific Southwest Regional Genetics Network, Berkeley, Calif., Coll. Am. Pathologists, Am. Coll. Med. Genetics, NIH Task Force on Genetic Testing, others, 1987—; med., tech. cons. and writer Warner Bros., NBC, Tri-Star, CBS, Twentieth Century Fox, Universal, others, 1987—; mem. molecular genetics com. Coll. Am. Pathology, Am. Coll. Med. Genetics, Nat. Com. on Clin. Lab. Stds., others; also TV/movie consulting and writing. Contbg. editor: MD Mag., 1981-91; assoc. editor Diagnostic Molecular Pathology, 1993—; contbr. articles to profl. jours. Recipient best paper award L.A. Soc. Pathology, 1984, Joseph Kleiner Meml. award Am. Soc. Med. Technologists, 1990; Basil O'Connor scholar March of Dimes Birth Defects Found., 1989, Nakamura Lectureship Scripps Clinic, 1996, Mass. Lectureship LSU, 1998, Stop Cancer Fdn. Rsch. Award, 1998. Mem. AAAS, AMA, Am. Soc. Clin. Pathology (DNA workshop dir. 1988—), Am. Soc. Human Genetics, Coll. Am. Pathologists (scholar award 1987), Soc. Inherited Metabolic Disorders, Soc. Pediat. Rsch., Am. Coll. Med. Genetics (mem. DNA com.). Democrat. Jewish. Achievements include application of molecular biology to clinical diagnosis, molecular genetics research and AIDS research. Avocation: classical music. Office: UCLA Sch Medicine Divsn Med Genetics & Molecular Pathology Los Angeles CA 90095-1732

GROEBLI, WERNER FRITZ (FRICK), professional ice skater, realtor; b. Basel, Switzerland, Apr. 21, 1915; s. Fritz and Gertrud (Landerer) G.; m. Yvonne Baumgartner, Dec. 30, 1954. Student architecture, Swiss Fed. Inst. Tech., 1934-35. Lic. realtor, Calif. Chmn. pub. relations com. Profl. Skaters Guild Am., 1972—. Performed in ice shows, Patria, Brighton, Eng., 1937; command performance in Marina, London, 1937, Symphony on Ice, Royal Opera House, 1937; mem. Ice Follies, 1939-81, partner (with Hans Mauch) in comedy team Frick & Frack, 1939-53; solo act as Mr. Frick (assisted by comedy team), 1955-81; numerous TV appearances including Snoopy on Ice, 1973, Snoopy's Musical on Ice, 1978, Sportsworld, NBC-TV, 1978, Donnie and Marie Osmond Show, 1978, Mike Douglas Show, 1978, Dinah Shore Show, 1978; films include Silver Skates, 1942, Lady Let's Dance, 1943, Jinxed, 1981; interviewed by Barbara Walters NBC Today, 1974; appeared in Christmas Classics on Ice at Blue Jay Ice Castle, 1991. Served with Swiss Army, 1934-37. Named Swiss jr. skating champion, 1934; named to Madison Sq. Garden Hall of Fame for 10,000 performances in Ice Follies, 1967, U.S. Figure Skating Assn. World Hall of Fame, 1984; recipient Hall of Fame Ann. award Ice Skating Inst. Am. Mem. SAG, Profl. Skaters Guild Am., Swiss Club of San Francisco (hon.). Lasted 15,000 performances in Ice Follies; originator of "Frick" cantilever spread-eagle skating movement; comedic choreography consultant. Office: care US Figure Skating Assn 20 1st St Colorado Springs CO 80906*

GROEZINGER, LELAND BECKER, JR., investment professional; b. San Francisco, Dec. 6, 1941; s. Leland Becker Sr. and Clara Catherine (Hudson) G. BS and BA, U. Ariz., 1964, MS in Fin., 1967. Asst. legis. adv. Leland B. Groezinger Sr., Sacramento, 1970-78; personal investor Sacramento, 1978—. Mem. Episcopal Cmty. Svcs. for the Diocese of No. Calif., Sacramento, 1983-91, bd. dirs., 1984-91, treas., 1985-91; mem. Sacramento Traditional Jazz Soc., Sacramento, 1985—, bd. dirs., 1992—, treas., 1994-95, v.p., 1996-97, pres. 1998—. Republican.

GROFMAN, BERNARD NORMAN, political science educator, consultant; b. Houston, Dec. 2, 1944; s. Dave and Fannie (Pachter) G. BS in Math., U.

Chgo., 1966, PhD in Polit. Sci., 1972. Asst. prof. polit. sci. SUNY, Stony Brook, 1970-76; assoc. prof. polit. sci. U. Calif., Irvine, 1976-80, prof., 1980—. Editor: (with others) Representation and Redistricting Issues, 1982, Choosing an Election System, 1984, Electoral Laws and Their Political Consequences, 1986, Information Pooling and Group Decision Making, 1986, The "Federalist Papers" and the New Institutionalism, 1988, Race and Redistricting, 1998. Research grantee NSF 1974-76, 77-79, 84-85, 85-86, 87-88, 92-93, 98—; Fellow Ctr. for Advanced Study in the Behavioral Scis., Stanford, Calif., 1985-86, 1989—. Mem. Am. Polit. Sci. Assn., Pub. Choice Soc., Law and Soc. Assn. Avocation: folk art. Office: U Calif Sch Social Scis Irvine CA 92697

GROGAN, STANLEY JOSEPH, educational and security consultant; b. N.Y.C., Jan. 14, 1925; s. Stanley Joseph h and Marie (Di Giorgio) G.; AA, Am. U., 1949, BS, 1950, MA, 1955; grad. FEMA Staff Coll., 1970; degree, Industrial Coll. of Armed Forces Air War Coll., 1972; MS, Calif. State Coll., Hayward, 1973; EdD, Nat. Christian U., 1974; m. Mary Margaret Skroch, Sept. 20, 1954; 1 child, Mary Maureen. Pers. asst., recruitment asst. CIA, Washington, 1954-56; disting. grad. acad. instr., allied officer course, Maxwell AFB, Ala., 1962; asst. prof. air sci. U. Calif., Berkeley, 1963-64, Chabot Coll., 1964-70, Oakland Unified Sch. Dist., 1962-83, Hayward Unified Sch. Dist., 1965-68; instr. ednl. methods, edn. rsch. methods of instrn. Nat. Christian U., 1975—, Nat. U. Grad. Studies, Belize, 1975—; pres. SJG Enterprises, Inc., cons., 1963—. Asst. dir. Nat. Ednl. Film Festival, 1971. Pub. rels. cons., 1963—. Bd. dirs. We T.I.P., Inc., 1974. With AUS, 1945; lt. col. USAFR, 1948-76; col. Calif. State Mil. Res. Decorated Air medal with oak leaf cluster; recipient citation Korea, 1963; RCVP Korean Vets. Assn. medal, 1994; named to Hon. Order Ky. Cols. Commonwealth of Ky., 1970, Outstanding Secondary Educators of Am. 1972. Fellow Internat. Inst. of Security and Safety Mgmt.; mem. NRA (life), VFW (life), DAV (life), Am. Def. Preparedness Assn. (life), Internat. Inst. Security and Safety Mgmt. (v.p. 1998), Assn. Nat. Def. and Emergencdy Resources (bd. dirs. 1995-98), Night Fighter Assn. (nat. publicity chmn. 1967), Air Force Assn. (life), Res. Officers Assn. (life), Phi Delta Kappa, Am. Soc. Indsl. Security (cert. protection profl.), Nat. Def. Exec. Res./FEMA, Marines Meml. Contbr. articles to profl. jours. and newspapers. Home: 2585 Moraga Dr Pinole CA 94564-1236

GROH, CLIFFORD JOHN, SR., lawyer; b. Ramapo, N.Y., Apr. 1, 1926; s. Marcel and Helen (Jaworski) G.; m. Lucy Bright Woodruff, Aug. 22, 1949; children: Clifford John II, Paul Woodruff, Lucy Elizabeth. BS, St. Lawrence U., 1948; JD, U. N.Mex., 1951. Bar: N.Mex. 1952, Alaska 1953. Ptnr. firm Groh, Eggers & Price, Anchorage, Alaska, 1955-96; of counsel Groh, Eggers, LLC, Anchorage, Alaska, 1996—; mem. Alaska Senate, 1970-74. First pres. Operation Statehood, 1953; chmn. Alaska Constl. Rsch. Com., 1955; mem., pres. Anchorage Ind. Sch. Bd., 1955-59, 62-63; assemblyman Greater Anchorage Area Borough, 1964-66; mem. Anchorage City Coun., 1963-67, acting mayor, 1966-67; chmn. Greater Anchorage Charter Com., 1968-69; mem. Rep. Nat. Com., 1976-78; mem. sr. adv. bd. 9th Jud. Cir., 1991-96; Alaska campaign co-chmn. Bush/Quayle, 1988, chmn., 1992; mem. U.S. Arctic Rsch. Commn., 1991-96; advisor Arctic Rsch. Commn., 1997—. Served to lt. USNR, 1943-46, 50-52. Named Outstanding Legislator, 1972, Alaska Rep. of Yr. 1995; recipient Life Service award, Alaska Rep., 1997. Fellow Am. Bar Found.; mem. ABA, Alaska Bar Assn. (bd. govs. 1958-61, pres. 1960-61), Anchorage Bar Assn., Am. Judicature Soc., Lincoln Soc. of Alaska (pres. 1995-97), Rotary. Episcopalian. Home: 1576 Coffey Ln Anchorage AK 99501-4977 Office: Groh Eggers LLC 3201 C St Ste 400 Anchorage AK 99503-3967

GRONEMEIER, DEAN WARREN, music educator, musician; b. Elgin, Ill., May 24, 1963; s. Harvey William and Loretta Ann (Giambelluca) G.; m. Martha Jean Hubbard, Jan. 3, 1987. BA, No. Ill. U., 1985; MusM, U. Ariz., 1987, D of Musical Arts, 1991. Lectr. U. Nev., Las Vegas, 1989-92, asst. prof., 1992-95, assoc. prof., 1995—. Composer numerous persussion pieces; contbr. articles to profl. jours. Mem. Percussive Arts Soc., Internat. Assn. Rudimental Percussionists. Home: 2815 Via Avanti St Henderson NV 89014-1421 Office: Univ Nev 4505 S Maryland Pkwy Las Vegas NV 89154-9900

GRONLI, JOHN VICTOR, college administrator, minister; b. Eshowe, South Africa, Sept. 11, 1932; s. John Einar and Marjorie Gellet (Hawker) G.; came to U.S., 1934, naturalized, 1937; BA, U. Minn., 1953; MDiv, Luther Theol. Sem., 1958, DMin, 1978; MA, Pacific Luth. U., 1975; m. Jeanne Louise Ellertson, Sept. 15, 1952; children: Cheryl Marie Mundt, Deborah Raechel Hokanson, John Timothy, Peter Jonas, Daniel Reuben. Ordained to ministry, 1958; pastor Brocket-Lawton Luth. Parish, Brocket, N.D., 1958-61; Harlowton (Mont.) Luth. Parish, 1961-66; sr. pastor St. Luke's Luth. Ch., Shelby, Mont., 1966-75; missionary Paulinum Sem., Otjimbingwe, Namibia, 1975-76; dean, chmn. dept. philosophy and humanities Golden Valley Luth. Coll., Mpls., 1976-85; dir. Summer Inst. Pastoral Ministry, Mpls., 1980-85, sr. pastor Pella Luth. Ch., Sidney, Mont., 1985-95; pres., CEO Ctrl. Mont. Concrete, Harlowton, GEHM Inc., Martinsdale, Mont., 1991—, cons. for orgnl. comms., 1995—. Bd. dirs. Mont. Assn. Chs., 1973-75, Richland Homes, Sidney, Mont., 1990-94, Ea. Mont. Mental Health Assn., 1993-94; sec. bd. for comm. and mission support Am. Luth. Ch., 1973-75; mem. dist. coun. Rocky Mountain Dist., 1963-75, sec., 1963-70; mem. S.African affairs task force SEM Dist., 1978-79; dean S.W. Mont. Conf. Evang. Luth. Ch. in Am.; faculty No. Rockies Inst. Theology, 1986—; trustee Luth. Bible Inst., Seattle, 1986-92. Mem. personnel and guidance assns., Am., Minn. coll. personnel assns. Editor: Rocky Mountain Dist. Yearbook, 1963-70; Rocky Mountain Views, 1973-75; contbr. to Lutheran Standard, 1973-77; contbr. articles to religious jours. Home and Office: HC 83 Box 630 Martinsdale MT 59053-9710

GRONNING, LLOYD JOSEPH, engineering company executive, civil engineer; b. Tacoma, July 12, 1951; s. Neil Roland and Marie Sarafica (Buettner) G.; m. Robyn Mary McAtavey, May 29, 1971; children: John, Jenny, Margaret. BSCE, U. Notre Dame, 1973; MSCE, Colo. State U., 1976; MBA, U. Denver, 1983. Registered profl. engr. Colo., Wyo., N.Mex. Design engr., resident insp. Nelson, Haley, Patterson and Quirk, Greeley, Colo., 1972-76; project engr. M&I Cons. Engrs., Ft. Collins, Colo., 1976-77; mgr. water resources City of Thornton, Colo., 1977-80, utilities dir., 1980-84; pres. Gronning Engring. Co., Denver, 1984-96; v.p. Montgomery Watson, Denver, 1996. Mem. ASCE, Cons. Engrs. Council Colo., Am. Waterworks Assn., Colo. Water Congress, Internat. Water Supply Assn. Democrat. Roman Catholic. Home: 9916 Wagner Ln Westminster CO 80030-2527 Office: 1401 17th St Ste 600 Denver CO 80202-1244

GROOMS, HENRY RANDALL, civil engineer; b. Cleve., Feb. 10, 1944; s. Leonard Day and Lois (Pickell) G.; m. Tonie Marie Joseph; children: Catherine, Zayne, Nina, Ivan, Ian, Athesis, Shaneya, Yaphet, Rahsan, Dax, Jevay, Xava. BSCE, Howard U., 1965; MSCE, Carnegie-Mellon U., 1967, PhD, 1969. Hwy. engr. D.C. Hwy. Dept., Washington, 1965; structural engr. Peter F. Loftus Corp., Pitts., 1966; structural engr., engring. mgr. Rockwell Internat. (now Boeing), Downey, Calif., 1969—. Contbr. articles to profl. jours. Scoutmaster Boy Scouts Am., Granada Hills, Calif., 1982-87; basketball coach Valley Conf., Granada Hills, 1984—; coach Am. Youth Soccer Orgn., Granada Hills, 1985-90, 94—; tutor Watts Friendship Sports League, 1989—; co-founder Project Reach, 1993. Recipient Alumni Merit award Carnegie-Mellon U., 1985; named Honoree Black History Project Western Res. Hist. Soc., 1989. Mem. ASCE, Tau Beta Pi, Sigma Xi. Office: Boeing Mail Code AD 69 12214 Lakewood Blvd Downey CA 90242-2693

GROSCOST, JEFF, state legislator, small business owner; b. Tooele, Utah, Apr. 29, 1961; m. Dana Groscost; 4 children. Student, Ariz. State U., Mesa C.C., Brigham Young U. Mem. Ariz. Ho. of Reps., 1993—; past chmn. ways and means com., past mem. appropriations com., past mem. block grants com., past mem. joint legis. budget com. Ariz. Ho. of Reps., Phoenix, past mem. joint legis. tax com., past majority whip, past chmn. apropriations sub-com. gen. gov., past com. states rights and mandates, house spkr.; gem broker; mem. adv. bd. Gov.'s Motion Picture and TV. Bd. dirs. S.W. Shakespeare Fest.; vol. youth coach Mesa Family YMCA, East Valley; chmn. Cub pack com. Boy Scouts Am. Mem. State Bd. Chartered Schs., Constl. Def. Coun. LDS. E-mail: igroscos@azleg.state.az.us. Fax: 602-542-0102. Office: State Capitol 1700 W Washington Phoenix AZ 85007 also: 2425 E Florian Ave Mesa AZ 85204

GROSE, ANDREW PETER, foundation executive; b. Washington, July 16, 1940; s. Peter Andrew and Mildred (Holston) G.; m. Jacqueline Stamm, Aug. 17, 1963; children: Peter Andrew II, Tracey Christine. BS with high honors, U. Md., 1962, MA, 1964. Mem. legis. staff Fla. Ho. of Reps., Tallahassee, 1972-74; rsch. dir. Nev. Legislature, Carson City, 1974-83; chief of staff Office of Gov. Nev., Carson City, 1983-84, dir. econ. devel., 1984-90; dir. Western region Coun. of State Govt., San Francisco, 1990-95; pres. Westrends, 1990-95; CFO Pub. Policy Inst. Calif., 1995—; mem. exec. com. Nat. Conf. State Legislatures, Denver, 1982-83. Author: Florida Model City Charter, 1974; mem. editl. bd. Nev. Rev. of Bus. and Econs., Reno, 1976-90. Chair trustees Temple United Meth. Ch., San Francisco, 1998—; active Habitat for Humanity. Capt. USAF, 1964-70, to brig. gen., Res. Recipient Spl. citation Nev. Libr. Assn., Carson City, 1981. Mem. Air Force Assn., Res. Officers Assn., Nat. Assn. State Devel. Agys. (1st v.p.), Western Govt. Rsch. Assn. (pres. 1993-95), Kiwanis (pres. 1981-82, bd. dirs. 1994-97, treas. 1997—). Democrat. Home: 405 Hazelwood Ave San Francisco CA 94127-2129 Office: Public Policy Inst of California 500 Washington St Ste 800 San Francisco CA 94111-2934

GROSE, ELINOR RUTH, retired elementary education educator; b. Honolulu, Apr. 23, 1928; d. Dwight Hatsuichi and Edith (Yamamoto) Uyeno; m. George Benedict Grose, Oct. 19, 1951; children: Heidi Diane Hill, Mary Porter, John Tracy, Nina Evangeline. AA, Briarcliff Jr. Coll., 1948; postgrad., Long Beach State U., 1954-55; BS in Edn., Wheelock Coll., Boston, 1956; MA in Edn., Whittier Coll., 1976. Cert. tchr., Mass., N.Y., Calif. Reading tchr. Cumberland Head Sch., Plattsburgh, N.Y., 1968-70; master tchr. Broadoaks Sch., Whittier (Calif.) Coll., 1971; reading tchr. Phelan/Washington Schs., Whittier, 1971-73; elem. tchr. Christian Sorensen Sch., Whittier, 1977-94, ret., 1994; cons. Nat. Writing Projet, 1987—, South Basin Writing Project, Long Beach, 1987—; team tchr. first Young Writers' Camp, Long Beach State U., 1988. Author: Primarily Yours, 1987, Angel Orchid Watercolor, 1994. First v.p. Women's League of Physicians Hosp., Plattsburgh, 1970; asst. to Christian, Jewish and Muslim pres., v.p.s of Acad. Judaic, Christian and Islamic Studies 6th Assembly World Coun. Chs., Vancouver, 1983. Mem. AAUW (assoc. in dialogue 1996—), NEA, Calif. Tchrs. Assn., Whittier Elem. Tchrs. Assn., English Coun. of Long Beach, Acad. Judaic, Christian and Islamic Studies (named companion Order of Abraham 1987), Orange County Soc. Calligraphy. Presbyterian. Avocations: travel, painting, gardening, gym. Home: 171 N Church Ln Condo 619 Los Angeles CA 90049-2068

GROSECLOSE, WANDA WESTMAN, retired elementary school educator; b. Clarks, Nebr., Oct. 5, 1933; m. B. Clark Groseclose; children: D. Kim, Byron C. Jr., Eric P., A. Glenn. B degree, Brigham Young U., 1976; M in Tchg., St. Mary's Coll., Moraga, Calif., 1981. Cert. tchr., Calif., life credential. 5th grade tchr. Brentwood (Calif.) Union Sch. Dist., 1977-97; ret.; art tchr., mentor tchr. Contra Costa County Program of Excellence. Mem. human rels. bd. dirs. City of Livermore, Calif., 1968-70. Republican. Mem. LDS Ch. Avocations: oil painting, sewing, gardening. Home: 83 Payne Ave Brentwood CA 94513-4701

GROSS, BRIAN A., art dealer; b. Havre de Graces, Md., June 30, 1953. AB, Oberlin Coll, 1975. Intern ept. drawings Mus. Modern Art, N.Y.C., 1973; staff intern Whitley Mus. Modern Art, N.Y.C., 1974; asst. dir. edn. Akron (Ohio) Art Inst., 1975-76; curator fellow Tamarind Inst., Albuquerque, 1976-78; dir. Endrick Gallery, Washington, 1978-81; v.p. Fuller Goldeen Gallery, San Francisco, 1983-86, Fuller Goss Gallery, San Francisco, 1987-90; pres. Brian Gross Fine Art, Inc., San Francisco, 1990—. Washington Commn. on Arts & Humanities, 1980. Mem. Art Dealers Assn. Am., San Francisco Art Dealers Assn., Am. Frneids Svc. Com. (hon.). Office: Brian Gross Fine Art 49 Geary St Fl 5 San Francisco CA 94108-5731

GROSSEN, BONNIE J., research scientist; b. Hillsboro, Oreg.; d. Elmer J. Grossen and Lillie M. Wagner. BA in German, Lewis and Clark Coll., 1969; MA in German Lit., U. Wash., 1970; MA in Spl. Edn., Mildly Handicapped, U. Oreg., 1977, PhD in Spl. Edn., 1988. Cert. basic prin., Oreg., std. handicapped learner K-12, Oreg., std. extreme learning problems K-12, Oreg., std. reading K-12, Oreg., std. German K-12, Oreg., basic secondary edn., Oreg., secondary life, Tex., spl. edn., Idaho. Tchr. secondary edn. McAllen (Tex.) H.S., 1970-73; instr. Gymnasium Damme, Lower Saxony, Germany, 1973-74; Title I reading tchr., dir. cultural curriculum devel. proj. Coeur d'Alene Indian Tribal Sch., DeSmet, Idaho, 1975-76; tchr. secondary spl. edn. Junction City (Oreg.) H.S., 1977-85; instr. English as Second. Lang. Junction City, 1979-82, tchr. talented and gifted, 1982; instr. U. Oreg., Eugene, 1985-89; head of English dept. Hoxani Coll., South Africa, 1989-90; instrnl. designer Sys. Impact, Eugene, 1990-93; rsch. assoc. U. Oreg., Eugene, 1990—; rsch. scientist Oreg. Ctr. for Applied Sci., Inc., Eugene, 1995-96; leader numerous nat. workshops and conf. presentations; spkr. in field. Contbr. articles to profl. jours. Recipient award for outstanding rsch. in learning disabilities Coun. for Learning Disabilities, 1989, Nat. Young Rschr. award Assn. for Computers and Ednl. Tech., 1989. Mem. Assn. for Direct Instrn. (bd. dirs. 1992—, editor Effective Sch. Practices quar. 1992—), Oreg. Edn. Assn. (rep. assembly del. 1981-85, cons. for budget analysis 1983-85), Junction City Edn. Assn. (pres. 1980-81, faculty rep. to sch. bd. budget com. 1981-85), Junction City C. of C. (mem. edn. com. 1985). Office: Assn for Direct Instrn Effective Sch Practices PO Box 10252 Eugene OR 97440-2252

GROSSETETE, GINGER LEE, retired gerontology administrator, consultant; b. Riverside, Calif., Feb. 9, 1936; d. Lee Roy Taylor and Bonita (Beryl) Williams; m. Alec Paul Grossetete, June 8, 1954; children: Elizabeth Gay Blech, Teri Lee Zeni. BA in Recreation cum laude, U. N.Mex., 1974, M in Pub. Adminstrn., 1978. Sr. ctr. supr., Office of Sr. Affairs, City of Albuquerque, 1974-77, asst. dir. Office of Sr. Affairs, 1977-96; conf. coord. Nat. Consumers Assn., Albuqueruqe, 1978-79; region 6 del. Nat. Coun. on Aging, Washington, 1977-84; conf. chmn. Western Gerontol. Soc., Albuquerque, 1983; N.Mex. del. White House Conf. on Aging, 1995; mem. adv. coun. N.Mex. Agy. on Aging, 1996-99. Contbr. articles to mags. Campaign dir. March of Dimes N.Mex., 1966-67; pres. Albuquerque Symphony Women's Assn., 1972; mem. exec. com. Jr. League Albuquerque, 1976; mem. Gov.'s Coun. on Phys. Fitness, 1987-91, chmn. 1990-91; mem. bd. dirs. N.Mex. Sr. Olympics, 1995—. Recipient N.Mex. Disting. Pub. Service award N.Mex. Gov.'s Office, 1983, Disting. Woman on the Move award YWCA, 1986, Outstanding Profl. award N.Mex. State Conf. on Aging, 1995, Presdl. citation S.W. Soc. on Aging, 1995; inductee Albuquerque Sr. Citizens Hall of Fame, 1998. Fellow Nat. Recreation and Pk. Assn. (bd. dirs. S.W. regional coun. rep., bd. dirs. leisure and aging sect., pres. N.Mex. chpt. 1983-84, 97-98, bd. dirs. N.Mex. Sr. Olympics, 1994—, Outstanding profl. award 1982, pres. leisure and aging sect. 1997-98); mem. ASPA (pres. N.Mex. coun. 1987-88), S.W. Soc. on Aging (pres. 1984-85, bd. dirs., Outstanding Profl. award 1991, Presdl. citation 1996), U. N.Mex. Alumni Assn. (bd. dirs. 1978-80, Disting. Alumni award 1985), Las Amapolas Garden Club (pres. 1964), Phi Alpha Alpha, Chi Omega (pres. alumni 1959-60). Avocations: tennis, water skiing, snow skiing, racewalking, arts and crafts. Home: 517 La Veta Dr NE Albuquerque NM 87108-1403

GROSSMAN, MARC RICHARD, media consultant; b. L.A., Sept. 11, 1949; s. Morris Grossman and Esther Beatrice (Wishnow) Goldstein; m. Maria Luisa Lopez, Sept. 23, 1987; children: Joshua, Aaron, Matthew. BA, U. Calif., Irvine, 1972; M of Journalism, UCLA, 1973. Press sec., personal aide to Pres. Cesar Chavez, United Farm Workers, 1975-81; legis. cons. to Spkr. Willie Brown, Calif. Assembly, Sacramento, 1981-87; media cons. Words in Public, Sacramento, 1987—. Ghostwriter speeches, columns and pieces for dozens of pub. figures; contbr. articles to daily newspapers and mags. Democrat. Jewish. Office: Words in Public 1700 L St Sacramento CA 95814-4024

GROSSMANN, RONALD STANYER, lawyer; b. Chgo., Nov. 9, 1944; s. Andrew Eugene and Gladys M. Grossmann; m. Jo Ellen Hanson, May 11, 1968; children: Kenneth Frederick, Emilie Beth. BA, Northwestern U., 1966; JD, U. Mich., 1969. Bar: Oreg., 1969. Law clk. Oreg. Supreme Ct., Salem, 1969-70; assoc. Stoel Rives Boley Jones & Grey, Portland, Oreg., 1970-76, ptnr., 1976—. Mem. ABA, Oreg. Bar Assn. Office: Stoel Rives LLP 900 SW 5th Ave Ste 2600 Portland OR 97204-1268

GROSZ, PHILIP J., lawyer; b. Oshkosh, Wis., Feb. 1, 1952; s. Joseph Otto and Marjorie (Berkhoel) G.; m. Linda Marie Ondrejka, Dec. 29, 1973. BA with honors, U. Wis., 1973; JD, Yale Law Sch., 1977. Bar: Calif. Ptnr. Loeb & Loeb, L.A., 1983-92, mng. ptnr., 1992-96. founder, bd. dirs. Love is Feeding Everyone, L.A., 1983-94. Mem. Calif. Bar Assn. Democrat. Office: Loeb & Loeb 10100 Santa Monica Blvd Ste 2200 Los Angeles CA 90067-4164*

GROTH, DAVID MIKAEL, artist; b. Scotia, Calif., June 6, 1950; s. Bruno and Nita (Emsley) G. BA in Studio Arts, Sociology, Humboldt State U., 1973. Artist Trinidad, Calif., 1971—, designer, builder custom homes, 1976-95. Exhibited in group exhibitions at mendocina (Calif.) Woodworking Assn., 1982, Gallery Fair, Mendocino, 1982, 83, 84, 85, 86, Humboldt County Fair, Ferndale, Calif., 1983, Art Ctr. Gallery, Eureka, Calif., 1983, Humboldt Cultural Ctr., Eureka, 1983, 84, Redwood Arts Assn. Show, Eureka, 1984, Ankrums Gallery, L.A., 1985, Elaine Potter Gallery, San Francisco, 1985, Neiman-Marcus, Dallas, 1985, Neiman-Marcus, San Francisco, 1986, The Dairy Barn, Athens, Ohio, 1986, 87, Syntex Gallery, Palo Alto, Calif., 1987, Humboldt Arts Coun., 1989, 93, 98, del Mano Gallery, L.A., 1997, 98, McAllen (Tex.) Internat. Mus., 1997, Oakland (Calif.) Mus., 1997, Reese Bullen Gallery, Humboldt State U., Calif., 1997, SOFA Exposition, Chgo., 1997, Am. Craft Mus., N.Y.C., 1998, Heller Gallery, N.Y.C., 1998.

GROTH, OLAF JONNY, communications executive; b. Viersen, Germany, Sept. 12, 1967; came to U.S., 1991; s. Guenther and Sophia (Kaufmann) G. BA, MA, Monterey Inst., 1993; MA, Tufts U., 1995, PhD, 1997. Freelance author Wirtschaftswoche, Duesseldorf, Germany, 1991; devel. asst. Monterey (Calif.) Inst., 1993; rsch. asst. Fletcher Sch.-Tufts U., Medford, Mass., 1994; govt. rels. cons. Air Touch Comm., San Francisco, 1995; rsch. assoc. Ctr. for Tech. and Internat. Affairs, Medford, 1995; tchr. Kuwaiti Diplomats Program, Medford, 1996; staff dir. internat. devel. and govt. rels. Airtouch Satellite Svcs., San Francisco, 1997—; alumni adv. bd. Monterey Inst. Med. aide Catastrophe Relief Corp., Nettetal, Germany, 1988-91; vol. Little Bros. of the Rose, San Francisco, 1998. German Acad. Exch. Svc. fellow, Bonn, 1991, Girardet fellow Fletcher Sch.-Tufts U., Medford, 1993-95; Merit scholar Monterey Inst., 1991-93. Mem. World Affairs Coun., Internat. Inst. for Strategic Studies, Internat. Studies Assn., Assn. for Internat. Bus., Internat. Assn. Conflict Mgmt., German-Am. C. of C. (bd. dirs. 1998—), Heidelberg Club, Rotary Club San Francisco, Pacific Counsel. Avocations: skiing, cooking, reading, martial arts, jazz. Home: 44 Calhoun Terr San Francisco CA 94133 Office: Airtouch Satellite Svcs Inc One California St San Francisco CA 94111

GROVE, ANDREW S., electronics company executive; b. Budapest, Hungary, 1936; married; 2 children. B.S., CCNY, 1960, DSc (hon.), 1985; Ph.D., U. Calif.-Berkeley, 1963; DEng (hon.), Worcester Poly. Inst., 1989. With Fairchild Camera and Instrument Co., 1963-67; pres., COO, Intel Corp., Santa Clara, Calif., 1967-87, pres., CEO, 1987—, also bd. dirs. Recipient medal Am. Inst. Chemists, 1960, Merit cert. Franklin Inst., 1975, Townsend Harris medal CCNY, 1980, Enterprise award Profl. Advt. Assn., 1987, George Washington award Am. Hungarian Found., 1990, Citizen of Yr. award World Forum Silicon Valley, 1993, Exec. of Yr. award U. Ariz., 1993, Achievement medal Am. Electronics Assn., 1993, Heinz Family Found. award for tech. and economy, 1995, John von Neumann medal Am. Hungarian Assn., 1995, Steinman medal City Coll. N.Y., 1995, Statesman of the Yr. award Harvard Bus. Sch., 1996, Internat. Achievement award World Trade Club, 1997, Cinema Digital Technols. award Internat. Film Festival, 1997, Cinema Digital Tech. award Cannes Film Festival, 1997, Tech. Leader of Yr. award Industry Week, 1997, Man of Yr. award Time mag., 1997; named CEO of Yr. CEO mag., 1997. Fellow IEEE (Achievement award 1969, J.J. Ebers award 1974, Engring. Leadership Recognition award 1987, Computer Entrepreneur award 1997), Acad. Arts and Scis.; mem. Nat. Acad. Engring. Office: Intel Corp PO Box 58119 2200 Mission College Blvd Santa Clara CA 95054-1549

GROVE, DOUGLAS DAVID, insurance company executive; b. Corona, Calif., Aug. 6, 1957; s. David Malley and Kathleen Lillian (Hogan) G.; m. Gail DeBenedictis, Sept. 12, 1992. BS in Bus. Adminstrn., U. Pacific, Stockton, Calif., 1980. CPCU, ARM. Package underwriter Kemper Group, San Francisco, 1980-85; comml. account underwriter Northbrook Property & Casualty Co., San Francisco, 1985-86, Chubb Ins. Cos., San Francisco, 1986-87; sr. underwriter nat. accounts Fireman's Fund Ins. Cos., San Rafael, Calif., 1987-88, exec. underwriter nat. accounts, 1989-93; exec. underwriter nat. brokerage unit Fireman's Fund, Novato, Calif., 1993-96; comml. lines product mgr. product mgmt. dept. Home Office Product Devel. Dept., 1996-97; underwriter Am. Internat. Group, San Francisco, 1997—. Mem. Underwriters Forum of San Francisco (sec. 1987, v.p. 1988, pres. 1989), Nat. Assn. Clock and Watch Collectors, Commonwealth Club of San Francisco, Alpha Kappa Lambda (chpt. sec., v.p., pres.). Avocations: boating, antique collection, real estate, travel, car collection. Office: Am Internat Group Nat Accts 2 Viver Plzstries 1 Spear St San Francisco CA 94105-1504

GROVER, HANK L., motion picture producer; b. Phila.; s. William Oliver and Dorothy May G. BA Lit., U. Pa.; BA in Film, Columbia Coll., Chgo. Writer, prodr. of nationally-syndicated TV/radio series U. Ill., Chgo., 1980-85, 85-89; free-lance motion picture prodr. L.A., 1989—. 2d asst. dir.: (motion picture) Stand Ins, 1997, (network TV series) Mighty Morphin Power Rangers, 1994-96; prodr. (nat. TV series) Consultation, 1980-85; prodn. supr. (motion picture) High Voltage, 1997; line prodr. (motion pictures) Flamingo Dreams, Big Monster on Campus, Error in Judgement, I'll Remember April; assoc. prodr. (motion picture) Shattered Illusions. Mem. Doing Something, L.A., 1996—, Ind. Feature Project, L.A., 1995—. Lt. (j.g.) USN. Decorated Nat. Def. medal USN. Mem. Dirs. Guild of Am. Avocations: weightlifting, tennis, golf.

GROVER, JAMES ROBB, chemist, editor; b. Klamath Falls, Oreg., Sept. 16, 1928; s. James Richard and Marjorie Alida (van Groos) G.; m. Barbara Jean Ton, Apr. 14, 1957; children: Jonathan Robb, Patricia Jean. BS summa cum laude, valedictorian, U. Wash., Seattle, 1952; PhD, U. Calif., Berkeley, 1958. Rsch. assoc. Brookhaven Nat. Lab., Upton, N.Y., 1957-59, assoc. chemist, 1959-63, chemist, 1963-67, chemist with tenure, 1967-77, sr. chemist, 1978-93, rsch. collaborator, 1993—; cons. Lawrence Livermore (Calif.) Nat. Lab., 1962; assoc. editor Ann. Rev. of Nuclear Sci., Ann. Revs., Inc., Palo Alto, Calif., 1967-77; vis. prof. Inst. for Molecular Sci., Okazaki, Japan, 1986-87; vis. scientist Max-Planck Inst. für Strömungsforschung, Göttingen, Fed. Republic Germany, 1975-76. Contbr. numerous articles to profl. jours. With USN, 1946-48. Mem. Am. Chem. Soc. (chmn. nuclear chemistry and tech. 1989), Am. Phys. Soc., Triple Nine Soc., Sigma Xi, Phi Beta Kappa, Phi Lambda Upsilon, Zeta Mu Tau, Pi Mu Epsilon. Libertarian. Presbyterian. Achievements include naming of the nuclear yrast levels and discovery of their importance in nuclear reactions; invention of use of short-lived radioactivity in molecular beams; first to successfully use radioactivity for detection in chemically reactive scattering experiments; invention of threshold photoionization method for measuring the dissociation energies of neutral weak complexes in molecular beams. Home and Office: 1536 Pinecrest Ter Ashland OR 97520-3427

GROVER, LAURA DIANE, marketing professional; d. Martin M. and Inez Learner G. AB magna cum laude, Brown U., 1979. Exec. chief Citizens Bank Corp., Providence, R.I., 1980-82; dir. spl. projects Infinity Broadcasting/WBCN-FM, Boston, 1983-87, Infinity Broadcasting KROQ-FM, L.A., 1988-89; owner, project mgr., cons. Kitchen Sync, L.A., 1990-97; dir., spl. projects and entertainment House of Blue Mktg., L.A., 1994-97; contbg. editor Venice Mag., L.A., 1996—; dir. mktg. A&M Records, L.A., 1998—. Treas. DLZIC, L.A., 1993-94; transp. coord. Clinton Campaign, L.A., 1992. Democrat. Jewish. Avocations: chef, cross-country travel, photography, music, art. Home: 8530 Holloway Dr Los Angeles CA 90069-2475 Office: A&M Records 1416 N La Brea Ave Los Angeles CA 90028-7596

GROVES, MARTHA, newspaper writer. Computer writer L.A. Times, 1992-93, staff writer, 1985—. Office: LA Times Times Mirror Sq Los Angeles CA 90053*

GROVES, SHERIDON HALE, orthopedic surgeon; b. Denver, Mar. 5, 1947; s. Harry Edward Groves and Dolores Ruth (Hale) Finley; m. Deborah

Rita Threadgill, Mar. 29, 1970 (div. Apr. 1980); children: Jason, Tiffany; m. Nanely Marie Lamont, July 1, 1980 (div. Dec. 1987); 1 child, Dolores; m. Elaine Robbins, Feb. 7, 1991. BS, U.S. Mil. Acad., 1969; MD, U. Va., Charlottesville, 1976. Commd. 2nd lt. U.S. Army, 1969, advanced through grades to maj., 1979, ret., 1992; surg. intern U.S. Army, El Paso, Tex., 1976-77, resident in orthop. surgery, 1977-80; staff orthop. surgeon U.S. Army, Killeen, Tex., 1980-83; ret. U.S. Army, 1992; staff emergency physician various emergency depts. State of Tex., 1983-84, 87; emergency dept. dir. Victoria (Tex.) Regional Med. Ctr., 1984-86; med. dir. First Walk-In Clinic Victoria, 1986-87; tchr. U. Tex. Med. Br., Galveston, 1986-90; emergency dept. dir. Gulf Coast Med. Ctr., 1988-89; with Amerimed Corp., 1990-92, Primedex Corp., 1992-93; clinic med. dir, staff orthop. surgeon Pain Relief Network, 1993—; lectr. Spkrs. Bur., Victoria, 1984-86, Cato Inst., Ludwig Von Mises Inst. Contbr. articles to profl. jours. Mem. Victoria Interagy. Coun. Sexual Abuse, 1984-86; treas. bd. dirs. Youth Home Victoria, 1986-90. Recipient Physician's Recognition award, AMA, 1980, 83, 86, 89, 92, 95. Fellow Am. Acad. Neurologic and Orthop. Surgeons; mem. Soc. Mil. Orthop. Surgeons, Am. Coll. Emergency Physicians, Tex. Med. Found., Assn. Grads. of U.S. Mil. Acad. (life), Am. Assn. Disability Evaluation Physicians, Coalition of Med. Providers, Am. Coll. Sports Medicine, Am. Running and Fitness Assn. (cert. of recognition 1987), Internat. Coll. Surgeons (pres., vice regent), Internat. Martial Arts Assn., Hurricane Sports Club of Houston, Smithsonian Assocs., So. Calif. Striders Track Club. Avocations: track and field masters (3-time nat. champion), martial arts.

GRUBAUGH, KARL DAVID, secondary education educator; b. Edwards AFB, Calif., Feb. 15, 1958; s. Kenneth Wayne and Lou Ellen (Gatlin) G.; m. Tanya Ruth Gangursky, Aug. 28, 1982; children: Lauren, Connor, Garrett. BA in Social Sci., Calif. State U., 1981; BA in Am. Studies, U. Canterbury, Christchurch, New Zealand, 1988; postgrad., U. Mo., 1989-91. Cert. secondary tchr., Calif. Tchr. Santa Cruz (Calif.) City Schs., 1981-89; asst. instr., editor U. Mo., Columbia, 1989-91; tchr. Moss Landing (Calif.) Mid. Sch., 1991-92, Harden Mid. Sch., Salinas, Calif., 1992-93, Oak Ridge H.S., El Dorado Hills, Calif., 1993-97, Granite Bay (Calif.) H.S., 1997—; cons., writer Tchr.'s Curriculum Inst., Palo Alto, Calif., 1997—. Rotary Found. scholar, 1988. Mem. Nat. Scholastic Press Assn., Columbia Scholastic Press Assn. (bd. judges), Journalism Edn. Assn., Nat. Interscholastic Swimming Coaches Assn. Home: 3077 Granada Ct Cameron Park CA 95682-8140

GRUBB, DAVID H., construction company executive; b. 1936; married. BSCE, Princeton U.; MSCE, Stanford U. With Swinerton and Walberg Co., San Francisco, 1964—, then exec. v.p. Structural divsn., exec. v.p. ops., pres., also bd. dirs.; pres. Swinerton Incorp., 1993-96, CEO and chmn. bd.; chmn. bd. Swinerton & Walberg Co., SW Indsl., Inc., Westwood Swinerton Constrn., Swinerton & Walberg Property Svcs., Inc., chmn. William P. Young Construction, Inc., Bud Bailey Constrn., Inc. Office: Swinerton Incorp 580 California St Ste 1200 San Francisco CA 94104-1045

GRUCHALLA, MICHAEL EMERIC, electronics engineer; b. Houston, Feb. 2, 1946; s. Emeric Edwin and Myrtle (Priebe) G.; m. Elizabeth Tyson, June 14, 1969; children: Kenny, Katie. BSEE, U. Houston, 1968; MSEE, U. N.Mex., 1980. Registered profl. engr., Tex. Project engr. Tex. Instruments Corp., Houston, 1967-68; group leader EG&G Washington Analytical Services Ctr., Albuquerque, 1974-88; sr. staff engr. EG&G Energy Measurements Inc., Albuquerque, 1988-94; engring. specialist Allied Signal FM&T, Albuquerque, 1994—; cons. engring., Albuquerque; lectr. in field, 1978—; expert witness in field; presenter sci. testimony before Ho. of Reps. Sci. Com., 1996. Contbr. articles to tech. jours.; patentee in field. Judge local sci. fairs, Albuquerque, 1983—. Served to capt. USAF, 1968-74. Recipient R&D 100 award, 1991, Gen. Mgr.'s Vision award Dept. Energy, 1994. Mem. IEEE, Instrumentation Soc. Am., Planetary Soc., N.Mex. Tex. Instruments Computer Group (pres. 1984-85), Electric Auto Assn. (v.p. Albuquerque chpt. 1994—), Sigma Xi, Tau Beta Pi, Eta Kappa Nu. Avocations: electro-optics, photography, woodworking. Office: Allied Signal KCD PO Box 4339 Albuquerque NM 87196-4339

GRUDEN, JON, professional football coach; b. Sandusky, Ohio, Aug. 17, 1963. Student, U. Dayton. Asst. coach U. Tenn., 1986-87, U. Southeast Mo., 1988-89, San Francisco 49ers, 1990, U. Pitts., 1991, Green Bay Packers, 1992-94; offensive coord. Phila. Eagles, 1994-97; head coach Oakland Raiders, 1998—. Office: Oakland Raiders 1220 Harbor Bay Pky Alameda CA 94502*

GRUENWALD, GEORGE HENRY, new products development management consultant; b. Chgo., Apr. 23, 1922; s. Arthur Frank and Helen (Duke) G.; m. Corrine Rae Linn, Aug. 16, 1947; children: Helen Marie Gruenwald Orlando, Paul Arthur. BS in Journalism, Northwestern U., 1947; student, Evanston Acad. Fine Arts, 1937-38, Chgo. Acad. Fine Arts, 1938-39, Grinnell Coll., 1940-41. Asst. to pres. UARCO, Inc., Chgo., 1947-49; creative dir., mgr. mdse. Willy-Overland Motors Inc., Toledo, 1949-51; new products, brand and advt. mgr. Toni Co./Gillette, Chgo., 1951-53; v.p., creative dir., account supr. E.H. Weiss Agy., Chgo., 1953-55; exec. v.p., mgmt. supr. North Advt., Chgo., 1955-71; pres., treas., dir. Pilot Products, Chgo., 1963-71; pres., dir. Advance Brands, Inc., Chgo., 1963-71; owner Venture Group, 1971—; exec. v.p., dir. Campbell Mithun Inc., Mpls. and Chgo., 1971-72; pres., dir. Campbell Mithun Inc., 1972-79, chmn., dir., 1979-81, CEO, dir., 1981-83, chief creative officer, dir., 1983-84; vice-chmn., dir. Ted Bates Worldwide, N.Y.C., 1979-80, mgmt. cons. new product devel., 1984—. Author: New Product Development-What Really Works, 1985, 2d edit., New Product Development-Responding to Market Demand, 1992, How to Create Profitable New Products, 1997, Creative Choices-How to Make Them, 1999, (workbook) New Product Development Checklists: From Mission to Market, 1991, (videos) New Products Seven Steps to Success, 1988, New Product Development, 1989; editor-in-chief Oldsmobile Rocket Cir. mag., 1955-65, Hudson Family mag., 1953-56; feature writer Mktg. News, 1988—; contbr. articles to profl. jours. Trustee Chgo. Pub. TV Assn., 1969-73, Mpls. Soc. Fine Arts, 1975-83, Linus Pauling Inst. Sci. and Medicine, Palo Alto, 1984-92, 95-96; advisor Linus Pauling Inst., Oreg. State U., Corvallis, 1996—; chmn., v.p., chmn. class reps. Northwestern U. Alumni Fund Coun., Chgo., 1965-68; trustee, chmn., chmn. exec. com. Twin Cities Pub. TV Corp., 1971-84; trustee Minn. Pub. Radio Inc., 1973-77, vice chmn., 1974-75; bd. dirs., mem. exec. com. PBS, Alexandria, Va., 1978-86, 88-94, mem. comm. adv. com., 1993-95, vice chmn. task force on funding, 1991-92; chmn. task force on tech. applications, lay rep., 1971—; del. Am.'s Pub. TV Stas., Washington, 1971—; bd. dirs. St. Paul Chamber Orch., 1982-84, San Diego Chamber Orch., 1986-88; mem. adv. bd. San Diego State U. Pub. Broadcasting Comty., 1986—, pub. rels. specialist, editor. With USAAF, 1943-45, MTO. Recipient Hermes award Chgo. Federated Advt. Clubs, 1963, Ednl. TV awards, 1969, 71, 86, Best of the Best award San Diego Book Awards, 1997; charter mem. Medill Sch. Journalism Hall of Achievement, 1997. Mem. Am. Mktg. Assn., Am. Assn. Advt. Agys. (mgmt. com. 1976-84), Nat. Soc. Profl. Journalists, Am. Inst. Wine and Food (bd. dirs. 1985-92), So. Calif. Advt. Media Soc., Rancho Santa Fe Art Guild. Office: PO Box 1696 Rancho Santa Fe CA 92067-1696

GRUENWALD, OSKAR, research institute executive, consultant; b. Yugoslavia, Oct. 5, 1941; came to U.S., 1961; s. Oskar and Vera (Wolf) G. AA, Pasadena City Coll., 1964; BA, U. Calif., Berkeley, 1966; MA, Claremont Grad. U., 1967, PhD, 1972. Cert. life standard teaching credential, Calif. Internat. economist U.S. Treasury Dept., Washington, 1967-68; vis. rsch. assoc. U. Erlangen, Nürnberg, Fed. Republic Germany, 1971-72; lectr. Pepperdine U., Malibu, Calif., 1972-73, Santa Monica (Calif.) Coll., 1973-76; ind. researcher and writer, Santa Monica, 1976-83; founder, pres. Inst. for Interdisciplinary Rsch., 1983—; guest lectr. in U.S. and fgn. countries, 1976—; rsch. assoc. Ctr. for Russian and East European Studies, U. Ill., Champaign-Urbana, summers 1976, 79; cons. Inst. for Advanced Philosophic Rsch., Boulder, Colo., 1977—, Com. To Aid Dem. Dissidents in Yugoslavia, Washington, 1980—, Pub. Rsch., Syndicated, Claremont, Calif., 1982—, Freedom House Exch., N.Y.C., 1985—; participant NEH Summer Seminar on Polit. Cultures, U. Calif., 1989. Author: The Yugoslav Search for Man, 1983; co-editor: Human Rights in Yugoslavia, 1986; founder, editor Jour. Interdisciplinary Studies: Internat. Jour. Interdisciplinary and Interfaith Dialogue, 1989—. Recipient Best Pub. Paper in Sci. and Religion award Templeton Found., 1992, 94; grantee Ludwig Vogelstein Found., 1976-77. Mem. Am. Philos. Assn., Am. Assn. for Advancement Slavic Studies (cons. Slavic Rev. 1986—), Am. Sci. Affiliation, Inst. for Study Internat. Problems (bd. dirs. 1988—), Internat. Christian Studies Assn. (founder, pres. 1983—, editor newsletter 1983—), Delta Tau Kappa. Home and Office: Inst Interdisciplinary Rsch 1065 Pine Bluff Dr Pasadena CA 91107-1751

GRUENWALD, T. MELISSA, healthcare communications specialist; b. Tucson, Oct. 3, 1967; d. Thomas Michael and Elizabeth Sharon (Buzan) Fredrick; m. Michael Kevin Gruenwald, June 10, 1989 (div. May 1994); children: Brianna Michelle, Amanda Paige. BBA, U. Ariz., 1989, MBA, 1995. Staff planner TMC Healthcare, Tucson, 1993-95, cmty. devel. specialist, 1995-97, coord. cmty. partnerships, 1997—. Mem. staff Cmty. Action Network, Tucson, 1994-95; mem. com. Success by 6-Children's Action Alliance, Tucson, 1998; bd. dirs. Vol. Ctr. Tucson, 1997—; vol. So. Ariz. Rescue Assn., Tucson, 1991-94; vol. mentor Catalina H.S., Tucson, 1995—. Named Person of Yr., Ariz. Supreme Ctr. LEARN Ctr., Catalina H.S., 1995-96. Avocations: equestrian events, scuba diving, hiking, music, arts. Office: TMC Healthcare Patio Bldg 5301 E Grant Rd Tucson AZ 85712-2805

GRUHL, JAMES, energy scientist; b. Milw., Apr. 9, 1945; s. Alfred and Helen (Vanderveer) G.; m. Nancy Lee Huston, July 4, 1974; children: Amanda Natalie, Steven Christopher. SB, MIT, 1968, SM, 1968, PhD, 1973. Lectr., MIT, 1969-83; rsch. sci. MIT. Energy Lab., Cambridge, 1973-83, program mgr., 1978-83, rsch. affiliate, 1984, U.S. EPA, sci. adv. bd., 1986-93; energy cons. U.S. Congress, rsch. insts. internat. energy industries, 1973—. Ednl. counselor MIT, 1978—. Recipient Silver Beaver award Boy Scouts Am., 1986, numerous art awards, 1990—. NSF grantee. Mem. IEEE, AAAS, Math. Programming Soc., MIT Alumni Assn. (officer 1978—), Tau Beta Pi, Eta Kappa Nu. Rsch. on uncertainties and validity of analytic models, validity of govt. and industry energy policy models, and climate change models. Office: Gruhl Assocs PO Box 36524 Tucson AZ 85740-6524

GRUNER, GEORGE RICHARD, secondary education educator; b. Springfield, Mo., Apr. 6, 1940; s. George Fredrick and Elsie Rachel (Souders) G.; m. Grayce Anne Hartman, Mar. 29, 1957 (div. June 1977); children: Mark Randall, Stephen Eric; m. Rita Marie Torres, May 31, 1982; children: Gregory Lee, Dawn Marie. BA in History, Lincoln U. of Mo., 1961; tchg. credentials, U. Puget Sound, 1965; MS in Edn., Calif. State U., Fullerton, 1972; postgrad., U.S. Army War Coll., Carlisle, Pa., 1986. Cert. tchr. Calif. History tchr. Huntington Beach (Calif.) High Sch., 1965-69; tchr., coord. for gifted/talented edn. Edison High Sch., Huntington Beach, 1969-81, English tchr., 1983-90, chmn. English dept., 1991—, chmn. site restructuring com., 1992-97, cross-curricular integration mentor, 1993-95; commandant Calif. Mil. Acad., Sacramento, Calif., 1986-90; dep. dir. Nat. Interagy. Counterdrug Inst., San Luis Obispo, Calif., 1991; acad. bd. dirs. Calif. Mil. Acad., Sacramento, 1986-91; mem., nat. rep. State Mil. Acad. Adv. Coun., Region VII, Calif., Nev., Utah, Ariz., Hawaii, 1986-90; cons. Calif. Army Nat. Guard, L.A., 1992—; mem. Orange County Vital Link Assessment Com., 1993—; adminstrv. coord. Ctr. for Internat. Bus. and Comm. Studies, 1994—. Contbr. articles to regional and nat. jours., author publs. in field. Exec. bd. PTA Edison High Sch., 1971-75; adult leader, cubmaster Boy Scouts Am., Huntington Beach, 1967-74; mem. Huntington Beach Dist. Tech. Coun., 1994-95, Action Planning Com., 1993-95; steering com. CIBACS Found., 1995—. Col. U.S. Army, 1962-92. Decorated Legion of Merit, Order of Calif., 1992; grantee AST Rsch. Corp., 1993, Calif. Dept. Edn., 1994-98; recipient Hon. Svc. award Calif. Congress of Parents, Tchrs. and Students, 1995. Mem. Dist. Educators Assn. (faculty rep.), Calif. Tchrs. Assn., NEA, Nat. Coun. Tchrs. English, Nat. Guard Assn. U.S. and Calif., Am. Legion. Avocations: hiking, camping, nature study. Home: 9055 Caladium Ave Fountain Vly CA 92708-1418 Office: Edison H S 21400 Magnolia St Huntington Beach CA 92646-6306

GRUZALSKI, MARION MAY, health care administrator, artist; b. Blackpool, Eng., Mar. 9, 1936; d. George William and Elsie (Hume) Lines; m. Ronald Eugene Wilson, July 27, 1962 (div. May 1979); m. Bartholomew Karl Gruzalski, Aug. 19, 1987; children: Laura O'Pella, Heather Prichard. AS, Harris County Jr. Coll., Houston, 1975; student, Rice U., 1975-79. Founder, exec. dir. Hospice at the Tex. Med. Ctr., Houston, 1979-85; exec. dir. Cranberry Hospice, Plymouth, Mass., 1986-89; founder, exec. dir. St. Joseph Hospice, Houston, 1994-96; exec. dir. Redwoods Rural Health Ctr., Redway, Calif., 1997—; pres. Pacific Ctr. for Sustainable Living, Redway, 1995—. Pres. North Pembroke Civic Assn., Pembroke, Mass., 1987. Named Woman of Yr., Found. for Sci. and Man, 1985, 95. Avocations: writing, art. Home: PO Box 2224 Redway CA 95560-2224

GRYGUTIS, BARBARA, sculptor; b. Hartford, Conn., Nov. 7, 1946; m. Lawrence Evers; 1 child, Noah Zion Evers. BFA, U. Ariz., 1968, MFA, 1971. One woman show at Scottsdale Ctr. for the Arts, 1988; exhibited in group exhibns. U. Ariz., Tucson, 1998, N.J. Transit Authority, Hamilton, 1998, Internat. 94 Socrates Sculpture Park, L.I. City, N.Y., 1994, Arts Festival of Atlanta, 1993, U. Ala. Nat. Site Sculpture Invitational, 1993, The Found. for Architecture and The Clay Ctr., 1993, Quadriennal Competition, Faenza, Italy, 1989, Scottsdale Ctr. for the Arts, 1986, The Vice-Pres.'s House, 1978, Herbert Johnson Mus. of Art, Cornell U., 1978, Renwick Gallery, Smithsonian Inst., 1977, Mus. of Contemporary Crafts, 1977, Mus. of Folk Art and Crafts, 1977, Everson Mus. of Art, 1977, John Michael Kohler Arts Ctr., 1977, The Bronx Mus., Cornell U.; Radisson Suites Hotel, Tucson, 1986, Williams Ctr. Comml. Office Complex, Phoenix, Ariz., 1987, U. No. Colo., Greeley, 1987, St. Paul Tech. Coll., 1991-92, 3 mini-parks for San Mateo St., Albuquerque, 1991-92, Martin Luther King Jr. Memorial, 1992, "Earth and Water" sculpture for parks, Kent, Wash., 1993, Columbia, Mo., Sculpture Garden, Ohio State U. Garden of Constrants, 1994, Sculptural Gateway, Los Indios, Tex., 1995, Park Earthwork, Santa Fe, N.Mex., 1996, "Tribute" Bench for Martin Luther King Dr., Chgo., 1996, Collaborative Design, College Grove Dr., Road Improvement Project, San Diego, 1998. El Presidio Nat. Register Historic Dist. adv. coun. Architecture and Design Rev. Bd., 1978-90; artist cons. to project for pub. places Urban Design, Mgmt. and Devel. Strategies for the Tucson Arts Dist., 1988; mem. nat. adv. com. Pub. Art Review, 1993-97. Recipient Govs. award Ariz. Women's Partnership, 1985, Award of Merit The Albuquerque Conservations Assn., 1991, Second prize Ceramics in the Urban Setting, the Second Internat. Quadrennial Competition, 1988, Individual Project Design Arts award Nat. Endowment for the Arts, 1988, Individual Artist award, 1975; project grant Tuscon Pima Arts Coalition, 1984, Ariz. Commn. on the Arts, 1984, Individual Artist fellow, 1997. Home: 273 N Main Ave Tucson AZ 85701-8219

GRZANKA, LEONARD GERALD, writer, consultant; b. Ludlow, Mass., Dec. 11, 1947; s. Stanley Simon and Claire Genevive Grzanka; m. Christine Duncan Pearson, May 15, 1997. BA, U. Mass., 1972; MA, Harvard U., 1974. Asst. prof. Gakushiun U., Tokyo, 1975-78; pub. rels. specialist Pacific Gas and Electric Co., San Francisco, 1978-80; sales promotion writer Tymshare Transaction Svcs., Fremont, Calif., 1980-81; account exec. The Strayton Co., Santa Clara, Calif., 1981-82; mng. editor Portable Computer Mag., San Francisco, 1982-84; prin. Grzanka Assocs., San Francisco, 1984-86; San Francisco bur. chief Digital News, 1986-91; battery program cons. Bevilacqua Knight Inc., Oakland, Calif., 1991-97; staff asst. Electric Power Rsch. Inst./U.S. Advanced Battery Consortium, Palo Alto, Calif., 1991-96; lectr. Golden Gate U., San Francisco, 1985-87. Author: Neither Heaven Nor Hell, 1978; translator, editor: (art catalog) Masterworks of Japanese Crafts, 1977; translator: (book chpt.) Manajo: The Chinese Preface to the Kokinwakashu, 1984 (Literary Transl. award 1984), Spanish translation, 1994. Sgt. USAF, 1965-69. Fellow Danforth Found., 1974. Mem. United Anglers Calif., Harvard Club of San Francisco (bd. dirs. 1984-88, Cert. Appreciation 1986, 88), Phi Beta Kappa, Phi Kappa Phi. Avocations: writing, fishing. Home: 2909 Madison St Alameda CA 94501-5426

GUAJARDO, ELISA, counselor, educator; b. Roswell, N. Mex., Nov. 13, 1932; d. Alejo Najar and Hortensia (Jiminez) Garcia; m. David Roberto Guajardo, Oct. 15, 1950; 1 child, Elsie Edith. BS, Our Lady of the Lake U., 1962, MEd, 1971; MA, Chapman U., 1977. Cert. tchr., adminstr., counselor, Calif. Elem. tchr. San Antonio (Tex.) Sch. Dist., 1962-63; tchr. social sci. Newport Mesa Sch. Dist., Costa Mesa, Calif., 1963-67; tchr. social sci. Orange (Calif.) Unified Sch. Dist., 1967-70, project dir., 1970-71, tchr. English, 1972-73, counselor, 1973—; pres. Bilingual, Bicultural Parent Adv. Bd., Orange, Calif., 1971-72; reader bilingual projects Calif. State Dept. Edn., Orange, 1971-72; vis. lectr. We. Wash. Univ., Bellingham, 1972-73; mem. curriculum and placement couns., Orange Unified Sch. Dist., 1973-78, 95-96. Author: (Able)Adaptations of Bilingual/Bicultural Edn. Fed. Project Proposal. Mem. NEA, AAUW, Calif. Tchrs. Assn., Orange Unified Edn. Assn, Hon., Alpha Chi, Our Lady of Lake U., Tex. chpt. Democrat. Mem. Assemblies of God Church. Avocations: choir and solo singing, piano, marimba, organ. Home: 335 E Jackson Ave Orange CA 92867-5743 Office: Canyon HS 220 S Imperial Hwy Anaheim CA 92807-3945

GUARDALABENE, JEANNINE SUE, marriage and family therapist; b. Walton, N.Y., June 14, 1952; d. James Harby and Ruth Louise (Le Tourneur) Courtney; m. Anthony E. Guardalabene. AA, Citrus Coll., Azusa, Calif., 1972; BA, Azusa Pacific Coll., 1974; MA, N.W. Christian Coll., 1994. Elementary sch. tchr. Azusa Unified Schs., 1974-78; sales rep. Red Carpet Real Estate, Claremont, Calif., 1978-79; pres. Statewide Transmissin Svc., Inc., Elmira, Oreg., 1982-94; owner, cons. ReGard, Eugene, Oreg., 1992—; family therapist pvt. practice, Eugene, 1994—. Co-author: (workbook) ReGard: Men and Women Working Together, 1992. Case mgr. United Way, Eugene, 1991-93; crisis phone vol. Women Space, Eugene, 1991-93; vol., contbr. ARC, Oreg., 1994. Mem. AAUW, Women in the Arts, Women's Bus. Network. Republican. Avocations: snow skiing, backpacking. Office: Re Gard 350 E 11th Ave Apt 3 Eugene OR 97401-3226

GUARDINO, SAL, food executive; b. 1922. Farmer Stockton, Calif., 1942—; v.p. Sunniland Fruit Inc., Stockton. Office: Sunniland Fruit Inc 1350 Report Ave Stockton CA 95205-3054*

GUAY, GORDON HAY, postal service executive, marketing educator, consultant; b. Hong Kong, Aug. 1, 1948; came to U.S., 1956; s. Daniel Bock and Ping Gin (Ong) G. AA, Sacramento City Coll., 1974; BS, Calif. State U., Sacramento, 1976, MBA, 1977; PhD, U. So. Calif., 1981. Mgmt. assoc. U.S. Postal Svc., Sacramento, 1980-82, br. mgr., 1982-83, fin. mgr., 1983-84, mgr. quality control, 1984-86, mgr. tech. sales and svcs. divsn., 1986-91, dir. mktg. and comm., 1991-95, postmaster, 1996—; assoc. prof. bus. adminstrn., mktg. and mgmt. Calif. State U., Sacramento, 1981-85; prof. mktg. Nat. U., San Diego, 1984—; pres. Gordon Guay and Assocs., Sacramento, 1979—; cons. Mgmt. Cons. Assocs., Sacramento, 1977-79. Author: Marketing: Issues and Perspectives, 1983; also articles to profl. jours. With U.S. Army, 1968-70. Recipient Patriotic Svc. award U.S. Treasury Dept., San Francisco, 1985. Fellow Acad. Mktg. Sci.; mem. NEA, AAUP, Am. Mgmt. Assn., Am. Mktg. Assn. (Outstanding Mktg. Educator award 1989), Am. Soc. Pub. Adminstrn., Soc. Advancement Mgmt. (Outstanding Mem. 1976), Assn. MBA Execs. Democrat. Avocations: photography, golf, tennis, fishing, camping. Office: US Postal Svc 4131 S Shingle Rd Shingle Springs CA 95682-9341

GUDERIAN, RONALD HOWARD, pathologist; b. Morden, Man., Can., Jan. 31, 1942; s. Harry Fred and Edna Elizabeth (Hildabrand) G.; m. Eleanor Joy Corey, Dec. 27, 1966; children: Jeffrey, Joy, Janell. BSc, Seattle Pacific U., 1967, DSc (hon.), 1990; PhD, U. Wash., 1970; MT, U. Calif., San Francisco, 1972; MD, Cath. U., Cuenca, Ecuador, 1978. Cir. clin. lab. Hosp. Vozandes, Quito, Ecuador, 1975-80, dir. dept. clin. investigation, 1980—, dir. primary health care program, 1980—; dir. nat. control program onchocerciasis Ministry of Health, Quito, 1990-96; assoc. prof. medicine Cath. U., Cuenca, 1986—; adj. prof. medicine U. Miami, Fla., 1995—; mem. expert com. on parasitic diseases WHO, Geneva, 1985—, cons. on onchocerciasis, 1981-95; cons. for malaria U.S. AID, Quito, 1984-85; internat. cons. on tropical medicine Cath. U., 1995—. Author: Oncocerosis en el Ecuador, 1996; patentee use of electric shock with venemous snake bites; contbr. over 150 articles to profl. jours. Pres. Healing Fund, Seattle, 1990-92. Named Alumnus of Yr. Seattle Pacific U., 1987, Hon. Citizen of Ecuador, 1995. Fellow Royal Soc. Tropical Medicine and Hygiene; mem. World Fedn. Parasitologists, Am. Soc. Tropical Medicine, Ecuadorian Acad. Medicine, Lions. Avocations: hiking, camping, fishing, gardening. Office: Northwest Med Teams Internat 6955 SW Sandburg St Portland OR 97223-8081

GUEDEL, JOHN BIMEL, radio and television writer, producer; b. Portland, Ind., Oct. 9, 1913; s. Walter Morris and Hazel McKee (Bimel) G.; m. Beth Pingree, Aug. 15, 1936; children—John Kenneth, Heidi Beth; m. Helen Parrish, Aug. 3, 1956; m. Valerie McDonald, June 27, 1968. Student, UCLA, 1931-32. V.p. in charge radio Dan B. Miner Advt. Co., Los Angeles, 1937-41, Russel M. Seeds Advt. Co., Chgo., 1942-44; pres. John Guedel Radio Prodns., Hollywood, 1942—; partner Peterson-Guedel Family Center, 1959-72; chief exec. officer Tanner Electronics Systems Tech., Inc., 1973-78; chmn., mfr. Suboccipital Ice-Pillo, 1987—. Motion picture writer Bohemian Girl, Chimes of Normandy (Laurel and Hardy), 10 Our Gang shorts, General Spanky feature Hal Roach Studio, Culver City, Calif., 1933-37; writer, producer, creator People Are Funny, 1938-60, House Party, 1945-70 (Emmy award 1954), Tommy Dorsey show, 1943-44, Charlotte Greenwood show, 1944, Life With Linkletter TV show, 1950-52, Johnny Carson, Earn Your Vacation show, 1949-50, 59-60; co-creator Ozzie and Harriet, 1943; producer, writer Inside Beverly Hills, 1956, Love Is Funny, 1962, Kids Are Funny, 1962; creator, producer (radio and TV shows) Groucho Marx You Bet Your Life, 1947-61 (Emmy and Peabody awards 1952), Red Skelton show, 1943-46, Anybody Can Play, 1958, For Better or Worse, 1959-60, Kids Say the Darndest Things for U.S. Armed Forces, 1982-85; author: Tornado, 1942; originator singing comml. radio spots, 1938, radio stunt game show Pull Over Neighbor, 1938, multi-camera simultaneous TV filming You Bet Your Life, 1950. Cons. U.S. Dept. State, 1952; founder Guedel Dinky Found., 1949—. Mem. Radio Writers Guild, Radio and TV Dirs. Guild (pres. 1949-50), Nat. Acad. TV Arts and Scis. (pres. Hollywood chpt. 1964-66), Pacific Pioneer Broadcasters (pres. 1973-74). Home: 8455 Fountain Ave West Hollywood CA 90069-2536

GUENTHER, ROBERT STANLEY, II, investment and property executive; b. Orange, Calif., Sept. 29, 1950; s. Robert Stanley and Fanny Newman (Shaw) G. BA in Psychology, U. Calif., Santa Barbara, 1975; BA in Sociology, U. Calif., 1975. Cert. radio telephone 3rd class operator. Pvt. practice Templeton, Calif., 1975—. Mem. Templeton Hist. Soc. (life), Space Explorers Network, Internat. Platform Soc. Assn., The Planetary Soc., Nat. Geog. Soc., Canine Companions for Independence, U. Calif. Santa Barbara Alumni Assn., San Francisco Soc. for Prevention of Cruelty to Animals (life). Home and Office: 5340 El Pomar Dr Templeton CA 93465-8628

GUENTHER, SHEILA WALSH, sales and promotion executive; b. Hamilton, Mont., Sept. 19, 1933; d. Leo Frederick and Edith Frances (Leonard) W.; James William Guenther, June 29, 1957; children: Kurt Dennis, Kelly David, Gayla Koleen. BA cum laude, Wash. State Coll., 1955. Layout artist The Bon Marche, Spokane, Wash., 1955-56; sales promotion mgr. The Bon Marche (formally The Paris), Great Falls, Mont., 1956-57; faculty staff artist info. and pub. rels. Mont. State Coll., Bozeman, 1958-61; sales promotion mgr. David's House Name Brands, Wichita, Kans., 1961-65; writer, graphic artist Warren Printing, Chamberlain Graphics, Olympia, Wash., 1965-73; art instr. Wichita State U.; writer, graphics freelancer Prescott Co. Advt. Pub. RelS., Olympia, Wash., 1970-77; instr. Clark Coll., Vancouver, Wash., 1979-81; sales promotion dir. Vancouver Furniture, 1974-94; pres. Walsh Guenther & Assocs., Inc., Vancouver, 1982—; Printer's Ink juror; mem. adv. coun. Columbian newspaper, 1996—. Co-author: Vancouver on the Columbia Business History, 1986. Columbian People in Need Adv. Com., Ellen Goodman Project for YWCA Emergency Shelter, Hands Across Clark County Stop Hunger Campaign; co-founder Swift Charity Auction, 1977. Recipient Spokane and Wichita Newspaper and TV Advt. award, Sertoma, Benjamin Franklin Svc. award, 1984, Woman of Achievement award YWCA, 1988. Mem. Wichita Press Women, Advt. Fedn., Oreg. Women in Comms., Retail Advt./Mktg. Assn., Columbian Newspaper Adv. Coun., Delta Phi Delta. Democrat. Office: PO Box 61628 Vancouver WA 98666-1628

GUERARD, ALBERT JOSEPH, retired modern literature educator, author; b. Houston, Nov. 2, 1914; s. Albert Leon and Wilhelmina (McCartney) G.; m. Mary Maclin Bocock, July 11, 1941; children: Catherine Collot, Mary Maclin, Lucy Lundie. AB, Stanford U., 1934, PhD, 1938; AM, Harvard U., 1936. Instr. Amherst (Mass.) Coll., 1935-36; mem. faculty Harvard U., Cambridge, Mass., 1938-61, successively instr. English, asst.

prof., assoc. prof., 1948-54, prof., 1954-61; prof. Stanford (Calif.) U., 1961-85, Albert L. Guerard prof. lit., 1965-85. Author: The Past Must Alter, 1937, Robert Bridges, 1942, The Hunted, 1944, Maquisard, 1945, Joseph Conrad, 1947, Thomas Hardy, 1949, Night Journey, 1950, Andre Gide, 1951, Conrad the Novelist, 1958, The Bystander, 1958, The Exiles, 1963, The Triumph of the Novel: Dickens, Dostoevsky, Faulkner, 1976, The Touch of Time: Myth, Memory and the Self, 1980, Christine/Annette, 1985, Gabrielle, 1992, The Hotel in the Jungle, 1996, Suspended Sentences, 1999; co-editor: The Personal Voice, 1964. Served as tech. sgt. psychol. warfare br. AUS, World War II. Recipient Paris Rev. Fiction prize, 1963, Lit. award Am. Acad. Arts and Letters, 1998; Rockefeller fellow, 1946-47; Fulbright fellow, 1950-51; Guggenheim fellow, 1956-57; Ford fellow, 1959-60; Nat. Found. Arts fellow, 1967-68; Nat. Found. Humanities fellow, 1974-75. Mem. Am. Acad. Arts and Scis., Pen Ctr. West, Phi Beta Kappa. Home: 635 Gerona Rd Stanford CA 94305-8452

GUERBER, STEPHEN CRAIG, historical society director; b. Corvallis, Oreg., Oct. 2, 1947; s. Allen Lewis and Thelma Mae (Gilson) G.; m. Donna Kay Panko, Feb. 4, 1968; children: Dani Mofit, Patrick Jason, Suzanne Crupper. BA, Idaho State U., 1969. Bus. editor The Idaho Statesman, Boise, 1970-73; info. svcs. dir. Jim Hawkes Advt., Boise, 1973-74; asst. alumni dir. Idaho State U., Pocatello, 1974-76; pub. rels. mgr. U.S. West Communications, Boise, 1978-88; dir. info. U.S. West Found., Boise, 1988-91; mgr. community affairs U.S. West Communications, Boise, 1991-93; exec. dir. Idaho Cmty. Found., 1993-96; dir. Idaho State Hist. Soc., 1996—. Councilman City of Eagle, 1984-88, mayor, 1988-96; bd. dirs. Assn. Idaho Cities, 1988-94, Silver Sage coun. Girls Scouts USA, 1990-93, Am. Festival Ballet, 1984-88; mem. Ada Planning Assn., 1985-96, Fourth Idaho Dist. Jud. Coun., 1988-96, Ada County Centennial Commn., 1989-90. Recipient Outstanding Pub. Svc. award Social Svc. Adminstrn., 1983, Profl. Achievement award Idaho State U. Coll. Arts and Scis., 1991, Simplot Vol. award, 1988; named Idaho Disting. Citizen The Idaho Statesman, 1988. Democrat. Baptist. Avocations: free-lance sports writer, carpentry, landscaping. Home: 699 Ranch Dr Eagle ID 83616-5115 Office: Idado State Hist Soc 1109 Main St Ste 250 Boise ID 83702-5642

GUERIN, CHARLES ALLAN, museum director, artist; b. San Francisco, Feb. 27, 1949; s. John Warren and Charlene (Roovaart) G.; m. Katherine Riccio. BFA, No. Ill. U., 1971, MA, 1973, MFA, 1974. Co-dir. Guerin Design Group, Colorado Springs, Colo., 1972-77; dir. exhbns. Colorado Springs Fine Arts Ctr., 1977-80, curator fine arts, 1980-86; dir. U. Wyo. Art Mus., Laramie, 1986—. Author catalogues including various Colorado Springs Fine Arts Ctr. catalogues; contbg. author The Encyclopedia of Crafts, 1974; exhbns. include Purdue U. West Lafayette, Ind., 1974, 76, DePauw U., Greencastle, Ind., 1976, Colorado Springs Fine Arts Ctr., 1977, Mus. of Fine Arts, Santa Fe, N.Mex., 1978, Wis. State U., Platteville, 1972, Suburban Fine Arts Ctr., Highland Park, Ill., 1974, Colo. Woodworking Invitational, Silver Plume, 1977, Colo. Craft Invitational, Arvada, 1981, Leslie Levy Gallery, Scottsdale, Ariz., 1983, Robischon Gallery, Denver, 1983, Adams State Coll., Alamosa, Colo., 1984, U. Wyo. Art Mus., 1986—, Elaine Horwitch Gallery, Scottsdale, 1990; represented in permanent collections Lloyds of London, Dallas, Art Inst. Chgo., Marriott Hotel, Albany, N.Y., Ill. State Mus., Springfield, U.S. West Corp., Denver, Thresholds, Chgo., others. Grantee Nat. Endowment for the Arts, Ill. Arts Council, 1973. Mem. Coll. Art Assn. Am., Am. Assn. Mus., Western Mus. Conf. Office: U Wyo Art Mus PO Box 3807 U Laramie WY 82071-3807

GUERRA, JUAN E., news correspondent; b. Santiago, Region V, Chile, Jan. 9, 1963; came to U.S., 1990; s. Jorge Ernesto and Rita Nelly (Rojas) G.; m. Nidia Elisabeth Rubilar, July 10, 1987; 1 child, Natalia Carolina. Grad. high sch., Quilpue, Chile, 1980. Dir., prodr. A.I.E.P., Viña del Mar, Chile, 1980-83; cameraman, editor H.E.S., Studio City, Calif., 1990-92; news cameraman Sta. KMEX-TV, L.A., 1992-94; news cameraman, editor Sta. KVEA-TV, Glendale, Calif., 1994—. Prodr. En la linea de Fuego (TV spl.), 1997 (Crystal award, Omni award, Videograph award, Communicator award). Mem. NABET, L.A. Press Photographers. Avocations: computers, aviation. Office: KVEA TV Channel 52 4125 W Hood Ave Burbank CA 91505-4011

GUGGENHEIM-BOUCARD, ALAN ANDRE ALBERT PAUL EDOUARD, business executive, international consultant; b. Paris, May 12, 1950; came to U.S., 1981, naturalized, 1991; s. Jacques and Micheline (Raffalovich) Guggenheim; m. Suzanne Marton, Mar. 20, 1974; 1 child, Valerie. BS, U. Paris, 1971; MSCE, Ecole Speciale des Travaux Publics, Paris, 1974; MBA in Finance, U. Paris, 1975; grad., French Command-Gen. Staff Res. Coll., 1981. Asst. prof. math. Nat. Sch. Arts and Architecture, Paris, 1972-75; civil engr. Societe Routiere Colas, Paris, 1976-77, French Antilles, 1977-78; chief exec. officer, exec. dir. C.R.P.G., Pointe A Pitre, Guadeloupe, 1978-81; chief exec. officer, chmn. San Joaquin Software Systems, Inc., Stockton, Calif., 1982-86, CalCar Investment Svcs., Inc., Newbury Park, Calif., 1983—; chmn., CEO CYCOM Tech. Corp., 1996—; bd. mem. Sucmanu, Paris, 1976-82; bd. of organizers Pacific State Bank, Stockton, Calif., 1985-87. Exec. Editor newsletter L'Action Universitaire, 1970-76. Mem. French Res. Policy Rev. Bd., Paris, 1971-77; mem. Ventura County Rep. Cen. Com., Rep. Presdl. Task Force, Rep. Campaign Coun.; mem. bd. Calif. Rep. Assembly; candidate Rep. 37th Assembly Dist., Calif.; mem. cen. com. Calif. Rep. Party, 1992—. Maj. French Res., 1981. Recipient Gold Medal Omnium Technique Holding, 1975. Fellow Engr. and Scientist France; mem. AAAS, ADPA, Assn. U.S. Army, Rotary. Roman Catholic. Avocations: skiing, boating, classical music. E-mail: agugqenheim@cis.tech.com. Home: 3265 Peppermint St Newbury Park CA 91320-5039 Office: 1560 Newbury Rd # 204 Newbury Park CA 91320-3452

GUGGENHIME, RICHARD JOHNSON, lawyer; b. San Francisco, Mar. 6, 1940; s Richard E. and Charlotte G.; m. Emlen Hall, June 5, 1965 (div.); children: Andrew, Lisa, Molly; m. Judith Perry Swift, Oct. 3, 1992. AB in Polit. Sci. with distinction, Stanford U., 1961; JD, Harvard U., 1964. Bar: Calif. 1965, U.S. Dist. Ct. (no. dist.) Calif. 1965, U.S. Ct. Appeals (9th cir.) 1965. Assoc. Heller, Ehrman, White & McAuliffe, 1965-71, ptnr., 1972—; spl. asst. to U.S. Senator Hugh Scott, 1964; bd. dirs. Comml. Bank of San Francisco, 1980-81, Global Savs. Bank, San Francisco, 1984-86, North Am. Trust Co., 1996-99. Mem. San Francisco Bd. Permit Appeals, 1978-86; bd. dirs. Marine World Africa USA, 1980-86; mem. San Francisco Fire Commn., 1986-88, Recreation and Parks Commn., 1988-92; chmn. bd. trustees San Francisco Univ. High Sch., 1987-90; trustee St. Ignatius Prep. Sch., San Francisco, 1987-96. Mem. Am. Coll. Probate Counsel, San Francisco Opera Assn. (bd. dir.), Bohemian Club, Wine and Food Soc. Club, Olympic Club, Chevaliers du Tastevin Club (San Francisco), Thunderbird Country Club (Rancho Mirage, Calif.). Home: 2621 Larkin St San Francisco CA 94109-1512 Office: Heller Ehrman White & McAuliffe 333 Bush St San Francisco CA 94104-2806

GUGLIELMO, EUGENE JOSEPH, software engineer, consultant; b. Bklyn., Nov. 23, 1958; s. Anthony and Carlotta Sylvia (Grossi) G.; m. Nancy Eleanor Booth, Aug. 13, 1983; children: Tiffany, Trevyn, Kyle, Quentyn. BS in Computer Sci., St. John's U., 1979; MS in Computer Sci., Calif. State U., Chico, 1987; PhD in Computer Sci., Naval Postgrad. Sch., 1992. Computer asst. St. John's U., Jamaica, N.Y., 1977-79; mem. tech. staff Bell Telephone Labs., Whippany, N.J., 1979-80; sys. designer AT&T Comm., Piscataway, N.J., 1980-85; computer scientist Naval Air Warfare Ctr., China Lake, Calif., 1985-94; sr. cons. IBM Cons. Group, Boulder, Colo., 1994; prin. investigator Monterey Bay Aquarium Rsch. Inst., Moss Landing, Calif., 1994-96; prin. cons. BEA Systems, San Jose, Calif., 1996-99; v.p. Media Knowledge Decisions, Inc., San Jose, Calif., 1999—. Contbr. articles to profl. jours. Mem. IEEE, IEEE Computer Soc., Assn. for Computational Linguistics, Assn. Computing Machinery (Info. Retrieval, Artificial Intelligence), N.Y. Acad. Scis. Roman Catholic. Avocations: model building, baseball, basketball, reading, coaching. Home: 35 Bayview Rd Castroville CA 95012-9725

GUHA, ALOKE, information technology company executive, electrical engineer; b. London, Dec. 18, 1957; s. Amitabha and Ketaki Guha. B of Tech. in Elec. Engring., Indian Inst. Tech., Kanpur, 1980; MSEE, U. Minn., 1982, PhD in Elec. Engring., 1985. Sr. prin. rsch. engr. Honeywell Inc., Mpls., 1985-94; sr. consulting engr. Network Systems Corp., Mpls., 1994-95, chief tech. officer, 1995-97; chief arch. Storage Tech. Corp., Louisville, Colo., 1997—. Contbr. over 60 articles to profl. jours.; patentee in field. Mem. IEEE, Assn. for Computing Machinery. Avocations: singing, travel. Home: 814 W Mulberry St Louisville CO 80027-9404

GUICE, JOHN THOMPSON, retired career officer; b. Kosciusko, Miss., Nov. 5, 1923; s. Gustave Nathaniel and Anne Mae (McCool) G.; m. Charlotte Webb, Mar. 8, 1949; children—John Thompson, James G., Steven L., Thomas A., Joseph D. B.S. in Engring, U.S. Mil. Acad., 1947; M.S. in Internat. Relations, George Washington U., 1966; disting. grad., Air Command and Staff Coll., 1962, Air War Coll., 1966. Commd. 2d lt. U.S. Army, 1947; advanced through grades to maj. gen. USAF, 1974; tactical and interceptor pilot, 1947-55; officer Air N.G. and N.G., 1956—; dep. dir. Air N.G., 1974-77, dir., 1977-81, ret., 1981. Decorated Legion of Merit, Air Force D.S.M. Mem. Air Force Assn., N.G. Assn., Sigma Chi. Home: 4901 N Calle Luisa Tucson AZ 85718-4925

GUILIANI, RICHARD JAMES, judge; b. Stockton, Calif., Aug. 31, 1949; s. Richard James and Beatrice Marie (Larranaga) G.; m. Krista Jean Kmetz, Aug. 16, 1980 (div. 1981); m. Millicent Elizabeth Rudd, Nov. 5, 1983; children: Anthony, William. BA, U. San Francisco, 1974; JD, Humphrey's Sch. Law, 1979. Correctional officer Calif. Dept of Corrections San Quentin State Prison, 1972-74; correctional program supr. Calif. Dept of Corrections, Soledad, 1974-75; atty. San Joaquin County Pub. Defender, Stockton, Calif., 1980-92; mcpl. ct. commr. Stockton Mcpl. Ct., Stockton, Calif., 1992-96; judge San Joaquin County Superior Ct., Stockton, Calif., 1996—; law clk. San Joaquin County Pub. Defender, 1976-80. Cpl. USMC, 1970-72. Named Peacemaker of Yr. Mediation Ctr. Stockton, 1996. Mem. Calif. Judges' Assn. Avocations: reading, golf, spectator sports, travel. Office: Superior Ct 222 E Weber Ave Stockton CA 95202-2709

GUILLEMIN, ROGER C. L., physiologist; b. Dijon, France, Jan. 11, 1924; came to U.S., 1953, naturalized, 1963; s. Raymond and Blanche (Rigollot) G.; m. Lucienne Jeanne Billard, Mar. 22, 1951; children: Chantal, Francois, Claire, Helene, Elizabeth, Cecile. B.A., U. Dijon, 1941, B.Sc., 1942; M.D., Faculty of Medicine, Lyons, France, 1949; Ph.D., U. Montreal, 1953; Ph.D. (hon.), U. Rochester, 1976, U. Chgo., 1977, Baylor Coll. Medicine, 1978, U. Ulm, Germany, 1978, U. Dijon, France, 1978, Free U. Brussels, 1979, U. Montreal, 1979, U. Man., Can, 1984, U. Turin, Italy, 1985, Kyung Hee U., Korea, 1986, U. Paris, Paris, 1986, U. Barcelona, Spain, 1988, U. Madrid, 1988, McGill U., Montreal, Can., 1988, U. Claude Bernard, Lyon, France, 1989, Laval U., Quebec, Can., 1990, Sherbrooke U., Quebec, 1997. Intern, resident univs. hosps. Dijon, 1949-51; asso. dir., asst. prof. Inst. Exptl. Medicine and Surgery, U. Montreal, 1951-53; asso. dir. dept. exptl. endocrinology Coll. de France, Paris, 1960-63; asst. prof. physiology Baylor Coll. Medicine, 1953-57, assoc. prof., 1957-63, prof., dir. labs. neuroendocrinology, 1963-70, adj. prof., 1970—; resident fellow, chmn. labs. neuroendocrinology Salk Inst., La Jolla, Calif., 1970-89, adj. rsch. prof., 1989-94; Disting. Scientist Whittier Inst., 1989-97, med. and sci. dir., 1993-94; adj. prof. medicine U. Calif., San Diego, 1995-97; disting. prof. Salk Inst., La Jolla, Calif., 1997—; adj. prof. medicine U. Calif., San Diego, 1995-97. Decorated chevalier Legion d'Honneur (France), 1974, officer, 1984; recipient Gairdner Internat. award, 1974; U.S. Nat. Medal of Sci., 1977; co-recipient Nobel prize for medicine, 1977; recipient Lasker Found. award, 1975; Dickson prize in medicine, 1976; Passano award sci., 1976; Schmitt medal neurosci., 1977; Barren Gold medal, 1979; Dale medal Soc. for Endocrinology U.K., 1980, Ellen Browning Scripps Soc. medal Scripps Meml. Hosps. Found., 1988, Disting. Scientist award Nat. Diabetes Rsch. Coalition. Fellow AAAS; mem. NAS, Am. Physiol. Soc., Am. Peptide Soc. (hon.), Assn. Am.Physicians, Endocrine Soc. (pres. 1986), Soc. Exptl. Biology and Medicine, Internat. Brain Rsch. Orgn., Internat. Soc. Rsch. Biology Reprodn., Soc. Neuro-scis., Am. Acad. Arts and Scis., French Acad. Scis. (fgn. assoc.), Academie Internationale de Medecine (fgn. assoc.), Swedish Soc. Med. Scis. (hon.), Academie des Scis. (fgn. assoc.), Academie Royale de Medecine de Belgique (corr. fgn.), Internat. Soc. Neurosci. (charter), Western Soc. Clin. Rsch., Can. Soc. Endocrinal Metabolism, (hon.), Club of Rome. Office: The Salk Inst 10010 N Torrey Pines Rd La Jolla CA 92037-1099

GUILMET, GEORGE MICHAEL, cultural anthropologist, educator; b. Seattle, Feb. 8, 1947; s. Michael D. and Avis M. (Digerness) G.; m. Glenda J. Black, May 24, 1980; children: Michelle R., Douglas J. BS in Metallurg. Engrng., U. Wash., Seattle, 1969; MA in Anthropology, U. Wash., 1973; PhD in Anthropology, UCLA, 1976. Lectr. anthropology Calif. State U., Bakersfield, 1976-77, program dir. urban anthropology internship program, 1977-78; asst. prof. comparative sociology U. Puget Sound, Tacoma, Wash., 1977-82; assoc. prof. U. Puget Sound, Tacoma, 1982-88, prof., 1988—; reader dept. anthropology UCLA, 1974-75; rsch. cons. dept. psychiatry UCLA, 1975-76; rsch. assoc. Nat. Ctr. Am. Indian Alaska Native Mental Health Rsch., U. Colo., 1986—; disting. prof. anthropology San Diego State U., 1991; grant reviewer NIMH, Bethesda, 1991, 92; spkr. in field. Author, co-author: (chpts.) Research in Philosophy and Technology, vol. 8, 1985, Technology and Responsibility: Philosophy and Technology, vol. 3, 1987, Behavioral Health Issues among American Indians and Alaska Natives: Explorations on the Frontiers of the Biobehavioral Sciences, 1988, Native America in the Twentieth Century: An Encyclopedia, 1994, (rsch. monograph) The People Who Give More, 1989; contbr. articles to profl. jours.; keyboardist, vocals Brave New World; singles released include It's Tomorrow, 1967. Evaluation cons. Chief Leschi Sch., Puyallup Tribe Indians, Tacoma, 1989, 96—, vol. musician Puyallup Tribe Indians, Tacoma, 1996, 97, cultural needs assessment cons., 1996-97, juvenile justice program cons., 1997-98. Kaiser Aluminum Chem. Corp. scholar, 1968-69; grantee Carnegie Found., 1974, U. Puget Sound, 1977-79, 83-84, 86, 88, 89, 91, 93. Fellow Am. Anthrop. Assn. (bd. dirs. coun. anthropology edn. 1983-85); mem. Soc. Psychol. Anthropology, Soc. Philosophy Tech., Fedn. Small Anthropology Programs, Pacific N.W. Historians Guild. Home: 1211 S Tyler St Tacoma WA 98405-1135 office: Dept Comparative Sociology U Puget Sound Tacoma WA 98416-0130

GUINN, KENNY C., governor; b. Garland, Ark., Aug. 24, 1936; married. BA, Calif. State U., Fresno, MA; EdD, Utah State U. Supt. Clark County Sch. Dist.; v.p. adminstrn. Nev. Savs. and Loan Assn. (PriMerit Bank), 1978-80, pres., chief operating officer, 1980-85, chief exec. officer, 1985-92, now chmn. bd.; pres. Southwest Gas Corp., 1987-88, chmn., chief exec. officer, 1988-93; chmn. bd. S.W. Gas Corp.; gov. State of Nev., Carson City, 1999—. Office: Office of the Governor Capitol Complex 101 N Carson St Carson City NV 89710*

GUINN, STANLEY WILLIS, lawyer; b. Detroit, June 9, 1953; s. Willis Hampton and Virginia Mae (Pierson) G.; m. Patricia Shirley Newgord, June 13, 1981; children: Terri Lanae, Scott Stanley. BBA with high distinction, U. Mich., 1979, MBA with distinction, 1981; MS in Taxation with distinction, Walsh Coll., 1987; JD cum laude, U. Mich., 1992. CPA, Mich.; cert. mgmt. acct., Mich. Tax mgr. Coopers & Lybrand, Detroit, 1981-87; tax cons. Upjohn Co., Kalamazoo, 1987-89; litigation atty. Brobeck, Phleger & Harrison, 1992-94, Coughlan, Semmer & Lipman, San Diego, 1994-95; consumer fin. atty. Bank Am. NT & SA, San Francisco, 1995-98, Green Point Credit Corp., San Diego, 1998—. Served with USN, 1974-77. Mem. AICPA, ABA, Calif. State Bar Assn., Inst. Cert. Mgmt. Acctg., Phi Kappa Phi, Beta Gamma Sigma, Beta Alpha Psi, Delta Mu Delta. Republican. Presbyterian. Avocations: tennis, racquetball, running. Home: 3125 Crystal Ct Escondido CA 92025-7763 Office: Green Pt Credit Corp 10089 Willow Creek Rd San Diego CA 92131-1603

GUINOTTE, HENRY PAUL, clergyman; b. Omaha, June 16, 1930; s. Henry P. and Pearl (Eisele) G.; m. Martha Jean Marling, June 7, 1953; children: Diana, Henry. BA, Hastings Coll., 1953; BD, U. Dubuque, 1956. Ordained to ministry United Presbyn. Ch. in U.S.A., 1956. Pastor Divide Center, Lyons, Nebr., 1955-60, Presbyn. Ch., Craig, Nebr., 1955-60, Neola (Iowa) Presbyn. Ch., 1960-66, Cedar Bluffs (Nebr.) Presbyn. Ch., 1966-72, United Protestant Ch., Palmer, Alaska, 1972-90; dir. youth caravans, Nebr. and Alaska, 1963-74; mem. NW mission evangelism com. Synod of Alaska, 1975—; mem. camp and conf. com. Synod of Iowa,1962-66; dir. Alaska youth teams Wellington Ch. Scotland, Glasgow, 1987-91. Organizer, tchr. dir. vol. rescue squads Neola Fire Dept., 1961-66, Cedar Bluffs Fire Dept., 1967-72; mem. Palmer City Coun., 1991; mayor City of Palmer, 1995. Named Lion of Yr., 1976; recipient joint resolution of commendation Alaska Legislature, 1986, Excellency in Ministry award Dubuque Sem., 1991. Mem. Rotary (Paul Harris fellow 1990). Address: PO Box 579 Palmer AK 99645-0579

GUINOUARD, DONALD EDGAR, psychologist; b. Bozeman, Mont., Mar. 31, 1929; s. Edgar Arthur and Venabell (Ford) G.; m. Irene M. Egeler, Mar. 30, 1951; children: Grant M., Philip A., Donna I. BS, Mont. State U., Bozeman, 1954; MS, Mont. State U., 1955; EdD, Wash. State U., Pullman, 1960; postdoctoral, Stanford U., 1965; grad., Indsl. Coll. of the Armed Forces, 1964, Air War Coll., 1976. Lic. psychologist, Ariz., counselor, Wash., Mont.; cert. secondary tchr. and sch. adminstr., Wash., Mont. Advanced through grades to col. USAFR, 1946-84, ret., 1984; dir. counseling Consol. Sch. Dist., Pullman, Wash., 1955-60; assoc. prof. Mont. State U., Bozeman, 1960-66; field selection officer Peace Corps, U.S., S.Am., 1962-68; prof. counseling, counseling psychologist Ariz. State U., Tempe, 1966-90; prof. emeritus, 1990; co-owner Forensic Cons. Assocs., Tempe, 1970—; pvt. practice, 1990—; admissions liaison officer USAF Acad., Colo. Springs, 1967-84; assessment officer Fundamental Edn. Ctr. for the Devel. of the Latin American Community, Patzcuaro, Mex., 1963-64; expert witness on vocat. and psychol. disability for fed. and state cts. Contbr. articles to profl. jours. Mem. Ariz. Psychol. Assn., Am. Assn. Counseling & Devel., Reserve Officers Assn. Democrat. Methodist. Avocations: photography, woodworking, camping, fishing, silversmithing. Home and Office: 112 E Cairo Dr Tempe AZ 85282-3606

GUINOUARD, PHILIP ANDRE, restaurant executive; b. Pullman, Wash., Apr. 9, 1960; s. Donald Edgar and Irene (Egeler) G.; m. Miquela Teresa Padilla, Feb. 16, 1988; children: Mia, Angela. Student, Mesa (Ariz.) Community Coll. Dir. quality Garcia's, Phoenix, 1978-84; area spr. El Pollo Asado Inc., Phoenix, 1985-89; gen. mgr. Quinto Patio, Evergreen, Colo., 1989-90, Garcia's, Littleton, Colo., 1990—, Quila's Fresh Mexican Cantina, 1993-94; field tng. mgr. Internat. House of Pancakes, 1994-95; pres., CEO Sub & Munch, 1995—; pres. S.W. Automated Payment Svc., 1997—. Mem. Colo. Restaurant Assn. Avocations: sports, photography. Home: 1714 W Manor St Chandler AZ 85224-5105 Office: 230 W Baseline Rd Ste 103B Tempe AZ 85283-1261

GUIROY, DON CAMANCE, psychiatrist; b. Basilan, Philippines, Apr. 22, 1952; came to U.S., 1985; s. Flaviano Kiamco Guiroy and Leoncia Awing Camance; m. Bernadette Diekmann, May 30, 1981; 1 child, Ilang Mae. BS, U. San Carlos, 1972; MD, Southwestern U., Cebu City, Philippines, 1976; MSc, Hood Coll., 1991. Resident in pediat. Silliman U. Med. Ctr., Dumaguete City, Philippines, 1977-79; fellow in neurology U. Munich, 1979-81; resident in psychiatry Kreiskrankenhaus, Tauberbischofsheim, Germany, 1982-84; neurologist in postgrad. tng. Nat. Hosp. Nervous Disease, London, 1984-85; vis. rsch. fellow, vis. rsch. assoc. NIH, Bethesda, Md., 1985-92; vis. rsch. scientist U. Dusseldorf, Germany, 1992-93; psychiatrist U. Calif.-Davis, Sacramento, 1995-96, Stanford (Calif.) U., 1996—; clin. rsch. physician Eli Lilly, Bad Hamburg, Germany, 1993-94; rsch. dir. Southwestern U., 1995—. Vol. psychiatrist Franciscans, San Francisco, 1997. Named most outstanding med. grad. Philippine Med. Assn., Manila, 1976. Mem. Am. Acad. Psychiatry, N.Y. Acad. Sci. Roman Catholic. Avocations: painting, cello, antique furniture restoration, tennis, gardening. Achievements include demonstration that brains of Guamanian patients with Parkinsonism-dementia and amyotrophic lateral sclerosis and neurologically normal Guamanians with neurofibrillary degeneration contain abnormal fibrils composed of protein similar to Alzheimer's Disease; described the ultrastructural, biochemical and molecular characterization of prion in captive mule deer and elk with chronic wasting disease highly related to bovine spongiform encephalopathy. Office: Stanford U 401 Quarry Rd MC 5543 Stanford CA 94305

GUITTAR, LEE JOHN, retired newspaper executive; b. St. Louis, May 4, 1931; s. LeRoy and Edna Mae (Johnston) G.; m. Elizabeth Madden Shedrick, Aug. 23, 1980; children—David Lee, Stephen Joseph, Mitchell John, Jeanne Marie, Richard Laughran; step-children: Elisabeth F. Shedrick, Kathryn S. Shedrick, Daniel C. Shedrick. AB, Columbia U., 1953; postgrad., U. Mass., 1962; MA, Columbia U., 1993. With Gen. Electric Co., 1955-65; mgr. community and govt. relations programs Gen. Electric Co., N.Y.C., 1963-65; mgr. employee and pub. relations Tidewater Oil Co., N.Y.C., 1965-66; from personnel dir. to circulation dir. Miami (Fla.) Herald, 1967-71; v.p., bus. mgr. Detroit Free Press, 1972-74, v.p., gen. mgr., 1974-75, pres., dir., 1975-77; pub. Dallas Times Herald, 1977-80; Publisher The Denver Post, 1980-83; chmn. Denver Post, 1983; pres. U.S.A. Today, 1984-86; v.p. group exec. newspapers The Hearst Corp., N.Y.C., 1986-98; editor, pub. San Francisco Examiner, 1995-98, ret., 1998. Lt. (j.g.) USNR, 1953-55, Korea. Mem. Am. Newspaper Pubs. Assn., Am. Mgmt. Assn., Am. Press Inst., Dallas C. of C. (dir.), Farm Neck Golf Club (Martha's Vineyard, Mass.), Phi Beta Kappa. Republican. Roman Catholic.

GULKAROV, ILIA SEMENOVICH, physicist, researcher; b. Buchara, Russia, June 18, 1939; came to U.S., 1992; s. Semen Yunaevich Gulkarov and Sonya Chi Zarkiev; m. Lidia R. Kalendarev, Feb. 5, 1971; children: Lina Gulkarov, Rita Nisanov. MS in Physics, Moscow State U., 1963; postgrad., Physico-Tech. Inst., Kharkov, Ukraine, 1965-68; PhD in Physics, Math., Moscow State U., 1969; DSc in Physics, Math., St. Petersburg (Russia) State U., 1990. Cert. physics tchr., math. tchr., Ariz. Instr. dept. physics Poly. U., Tashkent, Russia, 1963-65, from asst. prof. to prof., 1968-92; faculty dept. math./sci. Maricopa C.C., Phoenix, 1993—. Author: Investigation of Nuclei by Electrons, 1977; contbr. over 100 articles to profl. jours. Avocations: chess, creative arts, classical music, literature, reading. Home: 7601 E Chaparral Rd Scottsdale AZ 85250-7751 Office: Maricopa CC 2411 W 14th St Tempe AZ 85281-6941

GULL, PAULA MAE, renal transplant coordinator, nephrology nurse, medical-surgical nurse; b. L.A., Mar. 7, 1955; d. Gerald Henry and Artemis (Cubillas) Balzer; m. Randell Jay Gull, July 10, 1976. AA, Cypress (Calif.) Coll., 1976; AS with high honors, Rancho Santiago Coll., Santa Ana, Calif., 1985; BSN with high honors, Calif. State U., 1993; MSN, Long Beach U., 1996. Cert. med. surg. nurse, nephrology nurse, nurse practitioner, clin. transplant coord. Staff RN U. Calif. Irvine Med. Ctr., Orange, Calif., 1986-87, asst. nurse mgr., 1987-88, nurse mgr., 1988; med.-surg. nurse N000, 1990—; coord. renal transplant U. Calif.-Irvine Med. Ctr., Orange, 1992—, St. Joseph Hosp., Orange. Mem. Am. Nephrology Nurses Assn., N.Am. Transplant Coord. Orgn., Calif. Coalition Nurse Practitioners. Mormon. Home: 24974 Enchanted Way Moreno Valley CA 92557-6410

GUMAN, WILLIAM F., landscape architect, city councilman; b. Troy, N.Y., July 19, 1956; s. William John and Elsie (Kramer) G.; m. Cathy Cramer, Nov. 29, 1980; children: William R., Courtney A. AAS, SUNY, Farmingdale, 1976; BS, Colo. State U., 1978. Landscape architect Russett Industries, Colorado Springs, Colo., 1978-79, Landscape Enterprises, Colorado Springs, 1979-80; prs. MDC, Inc., Colorado Springs, 1980-88; pres. Guman & Assocs., Ltd., Colorado Springs, 1988—; mem. city coun. City of Colorado Springs, 1993—, commr. Utility Bd., 1993—, planning commr., 1992, mem. hort. adv. bd., 1983-89. Author city ordinances. Co-chair Youth Violence Action Plan, Colorado Springs, 1995-96; hon. bd. dirs. Teen Ct., City of Colorado Springs, 1996—; pres. Bethel Luth. Ch. Coun., 1988-93. Mem. AIA (assoc.), Am. Soc. Landscape Arthitects, Housing and Bldg. Assn. Republican. Lutheran. Avocations: 4X4ing, camping, motocross, photography, creative writing. Home: 4825 Seton Pl Colorado Springs CO 80918-5205 Office: City of Colorado Springs 30 S Nevada Ave Colorado Springs CO 80903-1825

GUND, GEORGE, III, financier, professional sports team executive; b. Cleve., May 7, 1937; s. George and Jessica (Roesler) G.; m. Mary Theo Feld, Aug. 13, 1966; children: George, Gregory. Student, Western Res. U., Menlo (Calif.) Sch. Bus. Engaged in personal investments San Francisco, 1967—; cattle ranching Lee, Nev., 1967—; partner Calif. Seals, San Francisco, 1976-77; pres. Ohio Barons, Inc., Richfield, 1977-78; chmn. bd. Northstar Fin. Corp., Bloomington, Minn., from 1978; formerly chmn. bd. Minn. North Stars, Bloomington; chmn., co-owner San Jose Sharks, NHL, San Jose, CA, 1991 [illegible] Francisco; dir. Ameritrust Cleve.; vice-chmn. Gund Investment Corp., Princeton, N.J.; chmn. North Stars Met Center Mgmt. Corp., Bloomington; v.p. hockey Sun Valley Ice Skating, Inc., Idaho. Chmn. San Francisco Internat. Film Festival, 1973—; mem. sponsors council Project for Popula-

tion Action; adv. council Sierra Club Found.; mem. internat. council Mus. Modern Art, N.Y.C.; collectors com. Nat. Gallery Art; bd. dirs. Calif. Theatre Found., Bay Area Ednl. TV Assn., San Francisco Mus. Art, Cleve. Health Museum, George Gund Found., Cleve. Internat. Film Festival, Sun Valley Center Arts and Humanities, U. Nev. Reno Found., Sundance Inst. Served with USMCR, 1955-58. Clubs: Calif. Tennis (San Francisco), University (San Francisco), Olympic (San Francisco); Union (Cleve.), Cleve. Athletic (Cleve.), Kirkland Country (Cleve.), Rowfant (Cleve.); Ranier (Seattle). Office: 1821 Union St San Francisco CA 94123-4307*

GUND, JEFFREY RAINIER, composer, sound designer; b. Las Vegas, Feb. 17, 1965; s. Rainier G. W. and Muriel Sarah (Drabkin) G. Cert. in Electronics, Area Tech. Trade Ctr., 1983; BM in Composition, U. So. Calif., 1990. Supervising sound designer 7th Level Multimedia, Glendale, Calif., 1995-97. Compositions include music for tv shows such as Entertainment Tonight, World of Wonder, various episodes of Earth's Fury, Without Warning, film scores include Postmark Paradise, Angel's Dance, Soft Toilet Seats, Neon City, Eric's Monster, trailers include Even Cowgirls Get the Blues, Playing God, Frank & Jesse, Best of the Best, Best of the Best 2, Night Heat, Candid Camera, Multimedia titles include: Disney's Tarzan Activity Center, My Disney Kitchen, Wild World of Madison Jaxx, Codename: Gallahad, musical theatre includes Down, But Not Out, (W)holes, various advertising compositions; music prodr., arranger: (trailers) Dances with Wolves (Clio award best music in film trailer 1990), White Fang 2, Young Guns 2, Silence of the Lambs, Radio Flyer, (radio spot) Back to the Future 3, (tv spot) 1990 Academy Awards Show; sound designer: (CD ROMs) The Lion King: Timon & Pumbaa's Game Break, The Lion King 2: Simba's Pride, Monty Python and the Quest for the Holy Grail (Software Publishers Assn. Codie award best use of music and sound in multimedia), The Hunchback of Notre Dame: Game Break, Ace Ventura, Arcade America, The Universe Acording to Virgil Reality, Reader Rabbit First Grade, others, (website) PythOnLine; sound designer, sound editor, asst. dialogue editor: (tv show) VR-5. Mem. Soc. Composers and Lyricists, BMI, Women in Film (male mem.), Computer Game Developers Assn., MIDI Mfrs.'s Assn. Interactive Audio Special Interest Group, Film Music Network. Avocations: skiing, backpacking, tennis, collecting animation art. Office: Jeffrey R Gund Music and Sound Design 2532 Lincoln Blvd Ste 108 Venice CA 90291-5978

GUNDERMAN, WILLIAM JEROME, III, insurance executive; b. Lenardtown, Md., Mar. 17, 1957; s. William Jerome Jr. and Joan M. (Hendy) G.; m. Deborah A. Fisher, Aug. 14, 1982; children: William Jerome IV, Erica Mary. BBA, U. San Diego, 1979; MBA, Seattle U., 1987. Rep. John Hancock Inst., San Diego, 1979; ops. mgr. Allstate Inst., Seattle, 1980-87, Home Ins., Seattle & Milw., 1987-93; asst. v.p. field ops. Home Ins., N.Y.C, 1990-93; br. mgr. USF&G Ins., Denver & Balt., 1993-96; northwest regional v.p. Northwestern Nat. Ins., Denver, 1997—. Assoc. mem. Owings Mills (Md.) Corp. Coun. Avocations: golf, baseball. Office: Northwestern Nat Ins Co Ste 501 5670 Greenwood Plaza Blvd Englewood CO 80111-2409

GUNDERSON, CLEON HENRY, management consultant corporation executive; b. Great Falls, Mont., June 5, 1932; s. Leon H. and Mona (Emmett) G.; m. Virginia Ellen Hudson, Aug. 26, 1972; children: Craig H., Robert S., Laura E. BS, Inst. Tech., Dayton, Ohio, 1971, Mont. State U., 1957; MAPA, U. Okla., 1975. Communications engr. Mountain States Tel & Tel, Helena, Mont., 1953-54; aerospace engr. Boeing Co., Seattle, 1957-58; commd. 2nd lt. USAF, 1958, advanced to col., 1974, ret., 1976; pres. Precision Prodn. & Engring., Walla Walla, Wash., 1976-79, Western Skies Energy Systems, Spokane, Wash., 1979-88, Computer Central, Olympia, Wash., 1988-90, C.H. Gunderson & Assocs., Littlerock, Wash., 1990—; Mem. Am. Inst. Elec. Engrs., Seattle, 1957-60, Am. Inst. Indsl. Engrs., Spokane, 1982-85. Inventor heatexchange solar panels, comml. solar panels. V.p. Tumwater Lions Club. Decorated Silver Stars, Disting. Flying Crosses, Purple Heart, Air medals. Mem. Soc. Mfg. Engrs. (sr. mem.), Soc. Mil. Engrs., Nat. Assn. Small Businesses, Toastmasters Internat., Walla Walla C. of C., Canto Blanco Gun Club (Madrid, v.p. 1973-75, Scott Air Force Base Gun Club (v.p. 1975-76), Spokane Gun Club. Republican. Avocations: hunting, fishing, competitive shooting. Home: 13001 Littlerock Rd PO Box 246 Littlerock WA 98556-0246 Office: C H Gunderson & Assocs PO Box 246 Littlerock WA 98556-0246

GUNNERSON, CHARLES GILBERT, environmental engineering and policy educator; b. LeMars, Iowa, June 5, 1920; s. Gilbert and Florence May (Holm) G.; m. Betty Ann Brown, Dec. 24, 1943; children: Barbara Lynn, Beverly Joan, Eric Charles. BA, U. Calif., L.A., 1947; MA, U. Colo., 1990. Registered profl. engr., Calif.; diplomate Am. Acad. Environmental Engrs. Sanitary engr. Bur. Sanitation, L.A., 1947-60; sr. engr. Dept. Water Resources, Sacramento, Calif., 1960-63; dep. dir. rsch. and devel. solid wastes program USPHS, Cin., 1963-66, 68-70; chief sanitary engr. Daniel, Mann, Johnson & Mendenhall/WHO, Istanbul, Turkey, 1967-68; dir. Great Lakes office U.S.-Can. Internat. Joint Commn., Windsor, Ont., Can., 1973-74; cons. World Bank, Washington, 1974-76, 76-80, 85—, project officer, 1976-78, 81-85; program dir. Dept. Commerce, Nat. Oceanic and Atmospheric Assn., Boulder, Colo., 1974-76, 78-81, 85-87; lectr. U. Calif., Irvine, 1991—; sr. advisor Motor Columbus Engrs., Baden, Jakarta, 1988. Advisor Mus. Nat. Sci., Aliso Viejo, Calif., 1990—. Served to capt. U.S. Army, 1941-46, PTO, 1950-53, Panama. Fellow ASCE (chmn. Environ. Impact Analysis Rsch. Coun. 1976-90, Hering award 1960, 67, 75, Horner medal 1975); mem. Am. Pub. Works Hist. Soc., Mid. East Studies Assn., Nat. Inst. of Engring. Ethics, Soc. for Internat. Devel., Found. for Advancements in Sci. and Edn. (bd. dirs. 1985—). Democrat. Avocations: photography, Middle Eastern art and music, bicycling,. Office: 2399-3D Via Mariposa Laguna Hills CA 92653

GUNTER, ROBERT L., lawyer; b. Tacoma, Wash., Aug. 25, 1945. BA cum laude, Seattle Pacific U., 1967; JD, U. Wash., 1970. Bar: Wash. 1970. Law clk. to Hon. Walter T. McGovern Wash. State Supreme Ct., 1970-71, U.S. Dist. Ct. Wash., 1970-71; with Preston Gates & Ellis, Seattle. Mem. Wash. Law Rev., 1969-70. Mem. ABA (forum com. constrn. industry, pub. contracts sect.), Wash. State Bar Assn. (pub. procurement and pvt. constrn. sect.), Christian Legal Soc. Office: Preston Gates & Ellis 5000 Columbia Seafirst Ctr 701 5th Ave Ste 5400 Seattle WA 98104-7078

GUNTHER, BARBARA, artist, educator; b. Bklyn., Nov. 10, 1930; d. Benjamin and Rose (Lev) Kelsky; m. Gerald Gunther, June 22, 1949; children: Daniel Jay, Andrew James. BA, Bklyn. Coll., 1949; MA, San Jose State U., 1975. Instr. printmaking, drawing, painting Cabrillo Coll., Aptos, Calif., 1976-93; instr. lithography Calif. State U., Hayward, 1978-79; instr. studio arts Calif. State U., San Jose, summer 1977, 78, 80; co-founder San Jose Print Workshop, 1975. One-woman shows include Palo Alto (Calif.) Cultural Ctr., 1981, Miriam Perlman, Inc., Chgo., 1984, D.P. Fong & Spratt Galleries, San Jose, 1991, 93, Branner/Spangenburg Gallery, Palo Alto, U. Calif., Santa Cruz, 1991, Frederick Spratt Galleries, San Jose, 1996, Cabrilto Coll., 1997; exhibited in numerous group shows; represented in permanent collections at San Jose Art in Pub. Places Program, Hilton Towers Hotel, GM, Found. Press, Inc. Recipient Purchase award Palo Alto Cultural Ctr., 1975, Judges' Merit award Haggin Mus., 1988. Mem. Calif. Printmakers Soc., Women's Caucus for Art, San Jose Inst. of Contemporary Art. Studio: 199 Martha St Ste 22 San Jose CA 95112-5878

GUNTY, CHRISTOPHER JAMES, newspaper editor; b. Hometown, Ill., Oct. 13, 1959; s. Harold Paul and Therese Agnes (Kohs) G.; m. Nancy Louise Blanton, July 10, 1982; children: William, Amy, Timothy. BA, Loyola U., Chgo., 1981. Circulation mgr. The Chgo. Catholic, 1981-83, assoc. mnging. editor, 1983, mng. editor, 1983-85; editor, mng. editor The Catholic Sun, Phoenix, 1985-96; assoc. pub. The Cath. Sun, Phoenix, 1996—. Author: He Came to Touch Us, 1987; co-author videotape script The Pope in Arizona, 1987. Contbr. articles to spl. Catholic news svcs. as well as papers where employed. Mem. Fiesta Bowl Com., Phoenix, 1987-92; bd. dirs. Catholic Journalism Scholarship Fund, 1990—, pres., 1995-96. Named Honoree Summer U. Internat. Cath. Union of the Press, Switzerland, 1988. Mem. Cath. Press Assn. (bd. dirs. 1988—, sec. 1990-92, v.p. 1994-96, pres. 1996-98), Assoc. Ch. Press, Ariz. Newspapers Assn., Soc. Profl. Journalists. Roman Catholic. Avocations: bicycling, sci. fiction. Office: The Catholic Sun 400 E Monroe St Phoenix AZ 85004-2336

GUO, XUANCHANG, sculptor, educator; b. Ching Qing, China, Dec. 25, 1953; came to U.S., 1993; s. Han Zhong Guo and Fangbi Liu; m. Qun Cao, Jan. 31, 1982 (div.); 1 child, Dao Xi Guo; m. Hong Zhao, May 16, 1996; 1 child, Shirley D. BA in Art, Sichuan Fine Art Inst., Chong Qing, China, 1982; student, Sichuan Fine Art Inst., 1978-82. Mem. staff Chong Qing (China) Ctr. Co., 1968-71; prof. Sichuan Fine Art Inst., Chong Qing, China, 1981-91; rschr. Germany Kassel U. Art Dept., Kassel, 1991-92; master sculptor Sculpture USA, L.A., 1993. Creator Logo Sculpture of Chamber, 1995 (Pres. appreciation award), monument Sun President in US, 1997 (L.A. award of art achievement 1997); portrait statues include George Bush, 1991, Bill Clinton, 1996, Arnold Schwarzenegger, others; public sculptures include Monument of the Longmuch, Sichuan, China, 1989, Journey to the West, China Town, Las Vegas, Nevada, 1994, The Silk Way, Las Vegas, 1996, Sun Zhong Shan in Am.-1911, L.A., 1997, 300 foot statue of Deng Xiao Ping in China, 1999; permanent displays include Nat. Art Mus., Beijing, Sichuan Art Mus., Chong Qing, China; exhibitions include Art Exhibition for six Famous Sculptures of China, Hong Kong, 1991, 14th World of Art Under One Roof, N.Y.C., 1992, Asian Art Exhibition, Korea, 1994, Nat. Chinese Sculpture Exhibition, Beijing, 1995, Sculpture Exhibition of Guo XuanChang, L.A., 1996. Recipient The Columbus Gold award L.A., 1994, Outstanding award Fine Art Assn. of China, 1994, Sculpture Achievement award L.A., 1998; featured in books including Selected Sculpture by Guo XuanChang, 1987, Encyclopedia of Living Artists, 1992, The World Famous Chinese Artists Almanac, 1996, The Eloqent Sculpture of Guo XuanChang, 1997, Calligraphy and Painting Collection of Eminent Chinese of World Over, 1998. Mem. World Assn. Chinese Artists (v.p. 1997, art achievement award 1997), Internat. Sculpture Ctr., China Sculpture Rsch. Inst. (dir. 1987), City Sculpture USA (pres. 1992). Avocations: outdoor sports, music, movies. E-mail: city@gus.net. Fax: (626) 333-2087. Home: 16151 La Monde St Hacienda Heights CA 91745-4253

GUPTA, BIMLESHWAR PRASAD, mechanical engineer, manager; b. Jaipur, Raj, India, May 17, 1946; s. Hari Prasad and Sarla D. (Agarwal) G.; m. Rajni Garg, Dec. 10, 1974; children: Anjli, Neeraj. BSME, U. Jodhpur, India, 1968; MSME, U. Minn., 1971, MBA, 1974. Registered profl. engr., Colo. Engr. Honeywell Inc., Mpls., 1971-76, sect. mgr., 1976-78; program and div. ops. mgr. Nat. Renewable Energy Lab., Golden, Colo., 1978—; lectr. in field; chairperson nat. and internat. confs. on solar thermal rsch. Guest editor spl. edit. The Energy Jour., 1987; contbr. articles to profl. jours. Mem. ASME (assoc. editor jour. 1983-85, guest editor spl. issue 1984), Internat. Solar Energy Soc., India Assn. Colo. (exec. com. 1983-84, pres. 1991), U. Minn. Alumni Assn., Toastmasters (pres. Lakewood 1985, bd. govs. F-2 area 1988-89). Home: 14373 W Bayaud Pl Golden CO 80401-5339 Office: Nat Renewable Energy Lab 1617 Cole Blvd Golden CO 80401-3305

GUPTA, GOUTAM, biologist, biophysicist; b. Calcutta, India, Jan. 15, 1953; came to U.S., 1983; s. Kalyan and Kumar Gupta; m. Swapna Sen, Sept. 2, 1987. BS in Physics, Calcutta U., 1973; MA in Physics, Visva Bharati U., Santiniketan, India, 1975; MPhil in Molecular Biophysics, Indian Inst. Sci., Banglore, 1976, PhD in Molecular Biophysics, 1981. Postdoctoral fellow SUNY, N.Y.C., 1983-87; collaborator Los Alamos (N.Mex.) Nat. Lab., 1987-89, mem. staff theoretical biology and biophysics, 1989—. Reviewer jours. Biochem., Jour. Biomolecular Str. and Dyn. Grantee NIH, 1992-95, U.S. Army, 1992-93. Mem. Biophys. Soc. Achievements include research in structure and structure-function correlation of the repetitive DNA sequences in the human genome and thermodynamics of surface recognition. Office: Los Alamos Nat Lab MS K710 T-10 PO Box 1663 Los Alamos NM 87544-0600

GUPTA, SUDHIR, immunologist, educator; b. Bijnor, India, Apr. 14, 1944; came to U.S., 1971; s. Tej S. and Jagdishwari Gupta; m. Abha, Jan. 28, 1980; children: Ankmalika Abha, Saurabh Sudhir. MD, King George's Med. Coll., Lucknow, India, 1966, PhD, 1970. Diplomate Am. Bd. Allergy and Immunology, Am. Bd. Diagnostic Lab. Immunology, Clin. Immunology Bd., Royal Coll. Physicians and Surgeons Can. Intern King George's Med. Coll., Lucknow, 1966, resident in medicine, 1967-70; teaching faculty fellow dept. medicine Tufts U. Med. Sch., Boston, 1971-72; vis. fellow in medicine Columbia U., N.Y.C., 1972-74; rsch. fellow Sloan-Kettering Inst. Cancer Rsch., N.Y.C., 1974-76, asst. prof., 1976-78, assoc. prof., 1978-82; instr. Cornell U., N.Y.C., 1976-77, asst. prof., 1977-79, assoc. prof., 1979-82; prof. medicine U. Calif., Irvine, 1982—, prof. microbiology and molecular genetics, 1984—, prof. pathology, 1986—, prof. neurology, 1988—, vice chair Dept. Medicine, 1994—; mem. adv. panel FDA, Washington, 1989—; sci. advisor Inst. Immunopathology, Kohn, Germany, 1990—; mem. allergy-immunology subcom. NIH, Bethesda, Md., 1985-89; vis. prof. Hematologic Rsch. Found., Roslyn, N.Y., 1992. Editor-in-chief Jour. Clin. Immunology, 1980—; editor: Immunology of Clinical and Experimental Diabetes, 1984, Mechanisms of Lymphocyte Activities and Immune Regulation I-VII, 1985-98, New Concepts in Immunbodeficiency Diseases, 1993, Multidrug Resistance in Cancer, 1996, Immunology of HIV Infections, 1996. Pres. Nargis Dutt Meml. Found., So. Calif., 1990; vice-chair AIDS Task Force, Orange County (Calif.) Med. Assn., 1987-95; mem. Indo-Am. Republican Club, Orange County, 1991—. Recipient Arthur Manzel Rsch. award R.A. Cooke Inst., N.Y.C., 1976, Outstanding Achievement award in med. scis. Nat. Fedn. Asian Indians in N.Am., 1986, Lifetime Achievement award Jeffrey Modell Found., N.Y.C., 1990, Disting. Scientists award Assn. Scientists Indian Origin in Am., 1994, Disting. Physician award Indian Med. Assn. Master ACP; fellow Royal Coll. Physicians and Surgeons Can., Am. Soc. Medicine (London); mem. Am. Assn. Immunologists. Achievements include description of the presence of $K+$ channels in human T cells, their role in T cell function and assn. with exptl. autoimmune diseases, reversal of multidrug resistance of cancer cells by cyclosporin A both in vitro and in vivo, described a new human intracisternal retrovirus associated with CD4+ cell deficiency without HIV infection; increased apoptosis in T cells in human aging. Fax: 949-824-4362. E-mail: sgupta@uci.edu. Office: U Calif Dept Medicine C240 Med Sci I Irvine CA 92697

GURWITZ-HALL, BARBARA ANN, artist; b. Ayer, Mass., July 7, 1942; d. Jack and Rose (Baritz) Gurwitz; m. James M. Marshall III, Mar. 12, 1966 (div. 1973); m. William D. Hall, May 3, 1991; 1 ward: Samantha Hollinger, 1994-96. Student, Boston U., 1960-61, Katherine Gibbs Sch., Boston, 1961-62. Represented by Karin Newby Gallery, Tubac, Ariz.; represented by Wilde-Meyer Gallery, Scottsdale, Ariz.; Artist-in-residence Desert House of Prayer, Tucson, 1989-91; oblate mem. Benedictine Sisters Perpetual Adoration, 1986—. One-woman show Henry Hicks Gallery, Bklyn., 1978, Misty-Mountain Gallery, Tubac, Ariz., 1987, Karin Newby Gallery, Tubac, 1989, West Ctr. Gallery, Green Valley, 1998, CCGV Artist of Month 1998, Martin and Roll Gallery, Durango, 1998; exhibited in group shows YWCA, Bklyn., 1977, Henry Hicks Gallery, 1977-79, Becket (Mass.) Art Ctr., 1978, Winter Gallery, Tucson, 1980, Johnson Gallery, Bisbee, Ariz., Hilltop Gallery, Nogales, Ariz., 1981, Scharf Gallery, Santa Fe, 1982, Data Mus., Ein Hod, Israel, 1985, C.G. Rein Gallery, Santa Fe, 1986, Tubac Ctr. for Arts Invitational, 1985, Mesquite Gallery, Patagonia, Ariz., 1986, Beth O'Donnell Gallery, Tucson, 1989, Karin Newby Gallery, 1989—, Wilde-Meyer Gallery, Scottsdale, Ariz., 1991—, Art Collector's Gallery, Tulsa, 1992, Contemporary Landscape Show Wilde-Meyer, 1996, Mountain Oyster Club, Tucson, 1994, Phoenix Mus. League, 1994, Brewster Ctr., 1994-98, Tubac Ctr. for Arts Biennial Gala, 1994, 96, Tubac Ctr. for Arts Ann. Members Show, 1980-94, 96, 97, 25th Anniversary Invitational SCV/aa, 1997, Juried Exhibit, Tucson Mus. Art, 1997, NLAPW/GV Juried Exhibit (2d prize) 1997, (hon. mention) 1998, Santa Cruz Valley Art Assn. juried show 1989-94, 96-98, (Best of Show award 1989, award for excellence 1992, Hon. Mention 1990), Tucson Mus. of Art, 1998, Marathon-Milagro, 1998, Wilde-Meyer, 1998, U. Tampa juried exhibit, award of Honor, 1998, Wilde-Meyer, 1999, Courtyard Gallery, New Buffalo, Mich., 1999, Sophia Georg Gallery, Denver, 1999; represented in permanent collections Diocese of Tucson, Data Mus., Desert House of Prayer, Tucson, Ethical Culture Soc., Bklyn., St. Andrews Episcopal Ch., Nogales, Tubac Elem. Sch., Sheraton Corp., also numerous corp. and pvt. collections in U.S. and Europe. Mem. Tubac Village Coun., 1979-86; bd. dirs. Pimeria Alta Hist. Soc., Nogales, Ariz., 1982-84, Rose and Jack Baritz Gurwitz Found.; creator Children's Art Walk, Tubac Sch. Sys. and Village Coun., 1980; set designer, choreographer DeAnza Ann. Pageant, Tubac Ctr. Arts, 1982—; pastoral asst. St. Ann's Parish, Tubac, 1986-89, religious edn. com., 1996-97; team mem. R.C.I.A. Our Lady of the Valley Parish, Green Valley, Ariz., 1994—. Mem. Nat. League Am. PEN Women, Inc. (Sonoran Desert br.), Rose and Jack Baritz Gurwitz Found. (bd. dirs.), Assn. Contemplative Sisters, Tuscon Mus. Art, Santa Cruz County Art Assn., Los Angeles County Mus., Women's Mus. Washington. Avocations: golf, teaching, theater, singing, travel.

GUST, GREGORY JOHN, meteorologist, educator; b. Grand Forks, N.D., May 14, 1957; s. Amos Joseph and Ann (Vanyo) G.; m. Cynthia Ann Shaw, Oct. 18, 1980; children: Christopher Shaw, Bethany Joy, Moriah Noelle. Grad., U. Montpellier, France, 1979; BS, St. John's U., Collegeville, Minn., 1979; MS, Pa. State U., 1992. Farm mgr. Gust Agricorp. Inc., East Grand Forks, N.D., 1975-82; tchr. Grand Forks Pub. Schs., 1980-84; staff meteorologist USAF, Offutt AFB Omaha, Nebr., 1986-88, Luke AFB Phoenix, 1988-90, State College, Pa., 1990-92; meteorologist intern Nat. Weather Svc., Helena and Great Falls, Mont., 1992-95; sci. officer Dept. Commerce Nat. Weather Svc., Glasgow, Mont., 1995-98; sr. meteorologist Nat. Weather Svc., Grand Forks, N.D., 1998—; area coord. Gideon's Internat., Great Falls, 1994-96; v.p. Gust Agricorp. Inc., East Grand Forks, 1975-80. Author, editor: Western Region Technical Attachments, 1996-98. Mem. Am. Meteorol. Soc., Nat. Weather Assn., Kiwanis Internat., Gideon's Internat. (camp pres.), Chi Epsilon Pi, Mil. Ops. Rsch. Soc. Avocations: theatre, vocal music. Office: Nat Weather Svc 4797 Technology Cir Grand Forks ND 58203

GUSTAFSON, KIRK, performing company executive. Student, U. Colo.; D in Mus. Arts, U. Wash. Music dir. Grand Junction (Colo.) Symphony Orch.; guest condr. Rogue Valley (S.D.) Symphony, Salt Lake Symphony, Boulder Philharmonic, Arapahoe Philharmonic, Arvada Chamber Orch., Colo. Festival Orch.; soloist various orchs.; lectr. Mesa State Coll. Boeing fellow U. Wash. Office: Grand Junction Symphony Orch PO Box 3039 Grand Junction CO 81502-3039

GUSTAFSON, LEWIS ALLAN, engineering geologist; b. Lansing, Mich., Dec. 12, 1931; s. Palmer Leonard and Erma Beryl (Washburn) G.; m. Mary Joanne Porter, Oct. 1, 1955; children: Lori, Steven, Leslie. BS in Geology, Mich. State U., 1955, MS in Geology, 1960; postgrad., U. Minn., 1974. Cert. engring. geologist, Oreg., Calif. Staff geologist Walla Walla Dist. U.S. Army Corps Engrs., 1963-68, Omaha Dist. U.S. Army Corps Engrs., Omaha, 1968-74; resident geologist RIRIE Dam U.S. Army Corps Engrs., Idaho Falls, 1974-75; chief, geology sect. Portland Dist. U.S. Army Corps Engrs., 1975-81; divsn. geologist North Pacific Divsn. U.S. Army Corps Engrs., Portland, 1981-88; chief geologist Hdqtrs. U.S. Army Corps of Engrs., Washington, 1988-92; cons. engring. geologist Bend, Oreg., 1992—. *During his government career, Mr. Gustafson was closely associated with foundation investigations and geotechnical studies for Dworshak Dam, Idaho, John Day Dam, Oregon, Chatfield Dam, Colorado, Bear Creek Dam, Colorado, Bonneville Second Powerhouse and Railroad Tunnel, Washington, Applegate Dam, Oregon, and Snettisham Second Power Tunnel, Alaska. His review responsibilities involved numerous additional construction projects throughout the United States and possessions.* Lt. U.S. Army, 1956. Mem. Soc. Am. Mil. engrs., Assn. Engring. Geologists, Am. Underground Constrn. Assn., U.S. Com. on Large Dams. Avocations: hunting, shooting, fishing, hiking, history. Home: 1275 NE Paula Dr Bend OR 97701-6058

GUSTAFSON, RANDALL LEE, city manager; b. Sidney, Nebr., Nov. 11, 1947; s. Robert John and Hilda Lydia (Sims) G.; m. Cynthia Ann Taylor, Oct. 18, 1974. Student, U. Kans., 1965-68, Rockhurst Coll., 1968-70; BS in Pub. Adminstrn., Upper Iowa U., 1992; MS in Pub. Adminstrn., Hamilton U., Jackson, Wyo., 1998, PhD in Pub. Adminstrn., 1998. City mgr. City of Bonner Springs, Kans., 1970-77; bus. owner Lambquarters, Dix, Nebr., 1977-83; city mgr. City of Aurora, Mo., 1983-85, City of Sterling, Colo., 1985—; bd. dirs. Logan Area Devel. Co., Sterling. Bd. dirs. Fire and Police Pension Assn. Colo., Denver, 1987-95, 13th Jud. Dist. Cmty. Corrections, Brush, Colo., 1988-90; mem. Colo. Mcpl. League Policy Com., Denver, 1987-89. Recipient Disting. Svc. award Jaycees, 1976. Mem. Internat. Assn. City Mgmt. (full mem.), Colo. Assn. City Mgmt., Am. Soc. for Pub. Adminstrn., Govs. Fin. Assn., Rotary, Elks, Mensa. Republican. Lutheran. Office: Centennial Sq Sterling CO 80751

GUSTAFSON, RICHARD PAUL, utilities administrator; b. St. Paul, July 20, 1957; s. Clarence John and Grace Esther (Benson) G.; m. Joan Kay Barnett, Apr. 23, 1977; children: Kari, Jennifer. BBA, Western Internat. U., Phoenix, 1982; MBA, Westen Internat. U., Phoenix, 1988. Teller Valley Nat. Bank, Phoenix, 1976-77; with Ariz. Pub. Svc., Phoenix, 1978-90, credit analyst, 1984-85, office mgr., 1985-86, adminstr. credit and collections, 1986-89, bus. office supr., 1989-90; supr. adminstrv. svcs. Citizen's Utilities, Sun City, Ariz., 1991-92; adminstrv. svcs. supr., 1992—. Mem. Am. Mgmt. Assn., Nat. Assn. Software Consultants and Programmers. Republican. Avocations: tennis, hockey, family. Office: Citizen's Utilities 15626 N Del Webb Blvd Sun City AZ 85351-1602

GUSTAT, MATTHEW PETER, III, health care executive; b. Logansport, Ind., Oct. 27, 1938; s. Matthew Peter and Emily Amelia (Schmidt) G.; m. Nicole Marie Marraccini, Oct. 26, 1964 (dec. Feb. 1993); 1 child, Matthew Peter IV; m. Kathleen Claire Robison, Nov. 25, 1994. B.S. in Commerce, U. Ky., 1961; M.A. in Health Care Adminstrn., Central Mich. U., 1978. Commd. officer U.S. Army, 1961, advanced through grades to col.; health-care adminstr. and logistician U.S. Army, Washington and Europe, 1961-76; project mgr. health automation, dir. Dept. Def., Bethesda, Md., 1977-84, ret., 1985; exec. v.p. Healthcare Concepts, Riverdale, Md., 1985-91; chmn. Mgmt. Assistance and Concepts Corp., Bethesda, Md., 1991—; cons., lectr. in field. Editor Materials & Fin. Strategy newsletter, 1985—. Contbr. articles to profl. jours. Mem. Republican Presdl. Task Force, 1982—; soccer coach Wheaton Boys and Girls Club, Md., 1979-83; v.p. Am. Nat. Standards Inst., 1980-82. Decorated Bronze Star, Commendation medal. Fellow Health Care Materials Mgmt. Soc. (disting. cert., v.p. 1978—, pres. 1986-87); mem. Am. Assn. Med. Systems and Informatics, Am. Mgmt. Assn., Am. Numis. Assn., Am. Legion. Methodist. Avocations: coins; stamps; golf; soccer. Office: Mgmt Assistance & Concepts Corp 203 Calle Del Oaks # A Monterey CA 93940-5710

GUSTAVSON, CARRIE, museum director. Dir. Bisbee (Ariz.) Mining and Hist. Mus. Office: Bisbee Mining and Hist Mus PO Box 14 Bisbee AZ 85603*

GUTERMAN, SHERYL LEVINE, screenwriter, producer; b. Harlingen, Tex.; d. Lewis Milton and Dena Fai (Mayers) Levine; m. Barry Lee Guterman; children: Marisa Tiffany, Travis Mayers. BS in Radio-TV-Film, U. Tex. Pres. The Manna Co., L.A., 1986-91; chmn., founder Test Pilot Prodns., 1991—. Screenwriter: (TV show) Diff'rent Strokes, 1981, One Day at a Time, 1982, The Twilight Zone, 1986, Diabolik, 1997; (film) They'll Be Sorry When I'm Gone, 1984, Happy Anniversary, Mr. Wrong, 1987 (Gold award Houston Internat. Film Festival 1987), Irresistible, 1989; producer: (stage plays) Hannah Senesh, 1987 (Excellence in Arts award B'nai Brith 1987), Loot, 1987 (Robby award L.A. Dispatch 1987), A Shayna Maidel, 1990-91 (L.A. Drama Critics Circle award 1990, Drama Logue award 1990, Robby award 1990, L.A. Weekly award 1990). Active Big Sisters of Los Angeles, 1981-82; fundraising event chair Pro-Peace, Los Angeles, 1985. Mem. Writers Guild Am. (vice-chair women's com. 1982-86), Women in Film (chair retreat), Bus. and Profl. Women (bd. dirs. 1984-85, 86-87), U. Tex. Alumni Assn. (bd. dirs. 1984-85, 86-87). Avocation: dance, photography, swimming. Office: Test Pilot Prodns 1093 Broxton Ave Ste 546 Los Angeles CA 90024-2831

GUTHRIE, DAVID NEAL, marketing executive; b. Paris, Tex., Feb. 12, 1941; s. Wesley Neal and Marie (Oliver) G.; m. Ramona Jeanne Busch, Feb. 6, 1959; children: David Jr., Scott, Laure. Student, San Antonio Coll., 1959-62, U. Tex., 1962-63, U. Tex., Arlington, 1965-66, U. Mo., 1970-72. From systems analyst to sales mgr. Sperry Univac, St. Louis, 1967-80; sales rep. Computer Sharing Svcs. Inc., St. Louis, 1980-83, Tandem Computers, Inc., St. Louis, 1983-84, Sykes Dataronics, Inc., St. Louis, 1984-85; sales rep. Cray Rsch., Inc., Colorado Springs, 1985-88, mktg. mgr., 1988-93; sales mgr. Thinking Machines Corp., 1993—. With USMCR, 1957-59. Fellow Mensa. Republican. Avocations: astronomy, photography, music, European history, reading. Home and Office: NCR Govt Sys Corp 42 Jessana Heights Colorado Springs CO 80906-7902

GUTHRIE, EDGAR KING, artist; b. Chenoa, Ill., May 12, 1917; s. David McMurtrie and Emily Henrietta (Streid) G.; m. Eva Ross Harvey, Dec. 8, 1945 (dec. Jan. 1978); children: Melody Bliss Johnson, Mark King Guthrie. BEd, Ill. State U., 1939; MA, Am. U., 1958; graduate, Command and General Staff Coll., Ft. Leavenworth, Kan., 1967. Artist W.L. Stensgaard Co., Chgo., 1939-40, The Diamond Store, Phoenix, 1941-42; presentation artist CIA, Washington, 1955-72; instr. Columbia Tech. Inst., Arlington, Va., 1966-72; owner, later ptnr. Guthrie Art & Sign Co., Winchester, Va., 1976—; instr. U. Hawaii, Lihue, 1980-81; cartoonist The Kauai Times, Lihue, 1981-90; owner Alo-o-oha-ha-ha Caricatures, Lihue, Honolulu, 1980—; cons., artist Shenandoah Apple Blossom Festival, Winchester, 1975-78; cartoonist Internat. Salon of Caricature, Montreal, Can., 1976-77; co-chmn. Kauai Soc. of Artists Art Show, Lihue, 1981. One man shows include 50 Yrs. of Painting-A Retrospective, Lihue, 1984; inventor Artists' Kit; Filmic Artist: (documentary film) The River Nile, 1960 (NBC Emmy Award). Bd. dirs. Civil Def., Virginia Hills, 1954; publicity com. Frederick County Taxpayers Assn., Winchester, 1973, Exch. Club, Winchester, 1977. Lt. col. U.S. Army, 1942-54. Decorated Purple Heart, Bronze Star with oak leaf cluster; recipient Spl. Merit award Boy Scouts Am. Aloha Coun., Lihue, 1982. Mem. Mus. of Cartoon Art, U.S. Naval Combat Artist, Daniel Morgan Mus. (contbr. 1976), Nat. Soc. Mural Painters (contbr. 1976), Allied Artists of Am. (contbr. 1977), Pastel Soc. Am. (contbr. 1977-78), Am. Watercolor Soc. (contbr. 1982—), Greek Expeditionary Forces (hon.). Mem. Ch. LDS. Avocations: animation, cinematography, hiking, swimming, genealogy. Home and Office: 2444 Hihiwai St Apt 703 Honolulu HI 96826-5104

GUTKIN, PETER ALAN, furniture designer, sculptor; b. Bklyn., Apr. 23, 1944; s. Samuel Sholom; m. Vicky Doubleday, June 16, 1974; 1 child, Miles Alpine. BFA, Temple U., 1966; MFA, San Francisco Art Inst., 1968. Furniture and design mfr. through showrooms throughout U.S. Trustee San Francisco Art Inst., 1970-74. Recipient Graduation award NEA, Washington, 1966, Artist fellowships NEA, 1980, 84, Product Design award Resources Coun., 1986. Avocation: hiking. Office: Peter Gutkin Furniture & Design Inc 2250 Jerrold Ave Ste 13 San Francisco CA 94124

GUTSCHE, STEVEN LYLE, physicist; b. St. Paul, Nov. 10, 1946; s. Lyle David and Phyllis Jane (Stubstad) G.; divorced; children: Kristina, Angela; m. Marilyn D. Maloney, Oct. 4, 1980; children: Taylor Steven, Daniel Mark. BS, U. Colo., 1968; MS, U. Calif., Santa Barbara, 1970. Physicist USN Pacific Missile Range, Point Mugu, Calif., 1968-71; staff scientist Mission Rsch. Corp., Santa Barbara, 1971-76, group leader, 1977-79, div. leader, 1979—, v.p., 1987-89; pres., 1989—; also bd. dirs. Mission Rsch. Corp., Santa Barbara. Contbr. articles to tech. publs. Presbyterian. Avocations: collecting oriental rugs, soccer, long distance running, reading. Office: Mission Rsch Corp 735 State St Santa Barbara CA 93101-3351*

GUTTERSEN, MICHAEL, ranching and investments professional; b. San Francisco, Mar. 26, 1939; s. William L. and Grace Tooee (Smith) Vogler; m. Penny Leonora Quinn, Aug. 29, 1959; children: Michael William, Arthur Roy, Shawn Patrick. Student, U. Col., 1957-58. Foreman Crow Creek Ranch, Ault, Colo., 1960-61; owner/mgr. Flying G Ranch, Briggsdale, Colo., 1961-86; pres. Two E Ranches Inc., Greeley, Colo., 1969-86, PX Ranch, Elko, Nev., 1969-71, Indian Creek Ranch, Encampment, Wyo., 1970-83, Lake Farms Co., Eaton, Colo., 1969-86; gen. ptnr. Guttersen & Co./Guttersen Ranch, Kersey, Colo., 1986—; mgr. ins. agy. Am. Nat. Ins. Co., Greeley, 1962-70; owner FGF Ins. Brokers, Inc., Greeley, 1962-70. Bd. dirs. United Way, Weld County, Colo., 1979-81, Greeley Philharmonic Orch., 1991-94, Nat. Cowboy Hall of Fame, Oklahoma City, 1994—. With U.S. Army, 1958-60. Mem. Nat. Cattlemens Assn., Colo. Cattlemens Assn., Colo. Cattle Feeders Assn., Tex. and S.W. Cattle Raisers Assn., Weld County Livestock Assn., Greeley Country Club. Republican. Roman Catholic. Avocations: fishing, hunting in Africa. Home: Woods Lake Farm 13696 RD 74 Eaton CO 80615 Office: Guttersen and Co PO Box 528 Kersey CO 80644-0528

GUTTMAN, IRVING ALLEN, opera stage director; b. Chatham, Ont., Can., Oct. 27, 1928; s. Shea and Bernetta (Schaffer) G. Opera student, Royal Conservatory Music, Toronto, 1947-52; LittD (hon.), U. Winnipeg, 1996. Asst. to Herman Geiger Torel of Can. Opera Co., Toronto, 1948-52; dir., under Pauline Donalda Montreal (Que., Can.) Opera Guild, 1959-68; artistic dir. Edmonton Opera, Manitoba Opera; mem. adv. com. Can. Coun. Founding artistic dir., Vancouver (B.C., Can.) Opera Assn., 1960-74, artistic dir., Edmonton (Alta., Can.) Opera Assn., from 1966, Man. (Can.) Opera Assn., Winnipeg, from 1972; dir. numerous TV productions of opera, including first full-length TV opera for, CBC French Network, 1953, operatic productions for numerous U.S. opera cos., also Can. and European cos.; founding artistic dir., Opera Group, Courtenay Youth Music Camp; author: The Unlikely Pioneer-David Watmough, 1987. Decorated Centennial medal, Queen Elizabeth Jubilee medal, Order of Can., Alberta Govt. award of Excellence, 1989, Gov. Gen.'s Can.'s 125th medal for contbn. to arts in Can., Opera Am. Achievement award for 25 yrs. of disting. svc., 1996; named to Edmonton Hall of Fame, 1989, Vancouver Hall of Fame, 1994, Montreal Hall of Fame, 1996. Mem. Canadian Equity, Am. Guild Musical Artists. *

GUY, ANDREW A., lawyer; b. Kansas City, Mo., May 11, 1952. AB summa cum laude, Princeton U., 1974; JD, U. Va., 1979. Bar: Wash. 1979. With firm Bogle & Gates, P.L.L.C., Seattle, 1979—, ptnr., 1987—. Mem. ABA (litigation sect.), Wash. State Bar Assn. (litigation sect.), King County Bar Assn. (litigation sect., creditors' rights, real property, probate and trust sects.). Office: Bogle & Gates PLLC Two Union Sq 601 Union St Ste 4700 Seattle WA 98101-2346

GUY, MILDRED DOROTHY, retired secondary school educator; b. Brunswick, Ga.; d. John and Mamie Paul (Smith) Floyd; BA in Social Sci., Savannah State Coll., 1949; MA in Am. History, Atlanta U., 1952; postgrad. U. So. Calif., U. Colo.; m. Charles H. Guy, Aug. 18, 1956 (div. 1979); 1 child, Rhonda Lynn. Tchr. social studies L.S. Ingraham H.S., Sparta, Ga.; tchr. English and social studies North Jr. H.S., Colorado Springs, 1958-84; ret., 1984; cooperating tchr. Tchr. Edn. Program, Col. Coll., 1968-72. Fund raiser for Citizens for Theatre Auditorium, Colorado Springs, 1979; bd. dirs. Urban League, 1971-75; del. to County and State Dem. Conv., 1972, 76, 80, 84, 92; mem. Pike's Peak C.C. Coun., 1976-83; mem. Colo. Springs Opera Coun. of 500, 1984-88; mem. nominating com. Wagon Wheel coun. Girl Scouts U.S.A., 1985-87; active Fine Arts Ctr., Pikes Peak Hospice; mem. St. John's Bapt. Ch. Recipient Viking award North Jr. H.S., 1973, Woman of Distinction award Girls Scouts Wagon Wheel Coun., 1989, 94; Outstanding Black Woman of Colorado Springs award, 1975; named Pacesetter, Atlanta U., 1980-81, Outstanding Black Educator of Yr., Black Educators of Dist. II, Colorado Springs, 1984; Outstanding Ednl. Service award Colo. Dept. and State Bd. Edn., 1983, Dedicated Svc. award Pikes Peak C.C., 1983; Outstanding Community Leadership award Alpha Phi Alpha, 1985; award Colo. Black Woman for Polit. Action, 1985, Sphinx award, 1986; named in recognition sect. Salute to Women, Colorado Springs Gazette Telegraph, 1986; Wall of Fame honoree Nat. Women's Hall of Fame, 1997. Mem. LWV (Colo. chpt.), Negro Hist. Assn., Women's Found. Colo.; life mem. NAACP (Golden Heritage), NEA, AAUW, Colo. Coun. Social Studies, Assn. Study Afro-Am. Life and History, Women's Ednl. Soc. Colo. Coll. (bd. mgrs. 1992—), St. John's Baptist Ch. (former Sanctuary Choir mem.), Services of Charity (local and nat.), Alpha Delta Kappa, Alpha Kappa Alpha (pres. Iota Beta Omega chpt. 1984-85, Chpt. Pres. award 1985). Home: 3132 Constitution Ave Colorado Springs CO 80909-2177

GUY, RICHARD P., state supreme court justice; b. Coeur d'Alene, Idaho, Oct. 24, 1932; s. Richard H. and Charlotte M. Guy; m. Marilyn K. Guy, Nov. 16, 1963; children: Victoria, Heidi, Emily. JD, Gonzaga U., 1959. Bar: Wash. 1959, Hawaii 1988. Former judge Wash. Superior Ct., Spokane, from 1977; chiefjustice Wash. Supreme Ct., Olympia, 1998—. Capt. USAS. Mem. Wash. State Bar, Spokane County Bar Assn. Roman Catholic. Office: Wash Supreme Ct Temple of Justice PO Box 40929 Olympia WA 98504-0929*

GUYOT, GARY WAYNE, psychology educator; b. Cape Girardeau, Mo., Nov. 12, 1945; s. Earnest J. and Lynetta J. (Berkbiegler) G.; children: Sean, Angela. BS in Psychology, Colo. State U., 1970, MS in Exptl. Psychology, 1973, PhD in Exptl. Psychology, 1975. Instr. Colo. State U., Ft. Collins, 1973-75; asst. prof. West Tex. State U., Canyon, 1975-79, assoc. prof., 1979-84, prof., 1984-87; prof., chmn. dept. psychology Regis U., Denver, 1987—. Contbr. chpts. to books: Species Identity and Attachment, 1980, Service Learning, 1994, Attachment in Mammals, 1998, also numerous articles to profl. jours. With U.S. Army, 1965-68. Grantee NSF, 1976-78, 89-91, Mabel Y. Hughes Charitable Trust Fund, 1989-91. Mem. APA, Am. Psychol. Soc., Southwestern Comparative Psychology (pres. 1989-90), Sigma Xi, Phi Kappa Phi, Psi Chi. Home: 3843 W Temple Pl Denver CO 80236 Office: Regis U Dept Psychology 3333 Regis Blvd Denver CO 80221

GUYTON, SAMUEL PERCY, retired lawyer; b. Jackson, Miss., Mar. 20, 1937; s. Earl Ellington and Eulalia (Reynolds) G.; m. Jean Preston, Oct. 11, 1959; children: Tamara Reynolds, William Preston, David Sage. BA, Miss. State U., 1959; LLB, U. Va., 1965. Bar: Colo. 1965, U.S. Dist. Ct. Colo. 1965, U.S. Tax Ct. 1977, U.S. Ct. Appeals (10th cir.) 1965, U.S. Ct. Appeals (5th cir.) 1981. Ptnr., Holland & Hart, Denver, 1965-92; ret., 1992; faculty Am. Law Inst. ABA, 1976-88. Sec., trustee Colo. Hist. Found., 1971-92, pres., 1983-87; trustee Music Assn. Aspen and Aspen Music Festival, 1980-88; precinct com. chmn. Dem. Party, 1968-70; mem. Gov.'s mansion preservation com., 1989-92, mem. adv. com., 1989-92; bd. advisors Coll. Arts and Scis., Miss. State U.; mem. com. govt. and legal affairs Hampshire Coll.; chmn. com. on legis. Woodmen of the World, 1972—. Capt. USAF, 1959-62. Fellow Am. Coll. Tax Counsel (bd. regents 1985-92, chmn., pres. 1989-91), Am. Tax Policy Inst. (trustee 1989-92, v.p. 1989-92); mem. ABA (sect. taxation 1967-92, chmn. sect.'s com. on agr. 1980-82), Colo. Bar Assn. (tax coun. 1983-86, sec. 1983, chmn. 1985-86), Colo. Bar Found., Greater Denver Tax Csls. Assn. (chmn. 1978), Law Club Denver, Little River Lectures Assn. (bd. dirs., v.p. 1985-96, pres. 1996—), Am. Alpine Club (life), Colo. Mountain Club (life, planned giving com.), Eleanore Mullen Weckbaugh Found. (trustee 1983-95), Humphreys Found. (sec., treas., trustee), Colo. Trail Found. (trustee), Colo. Mountain Club Found. (dir., asst. sec. 1998), Colo. Hist. Soc. (mem. bd. dirs., chmn. nominating com. 1996), bd. dirs. Royal Street Corp., Royal Street Utah, Inc., bd. dirs. Deer Valley Ski Resort. Mem. Unity Ch. Co-author: Cattle Owners Tax Manual, 1984, Supplement to Federal Taxation of Agriculture, 1983, Colorado Estate Planning Desk Book, 1984, 90; contbr. articles to jours., mags.; bd. advs. Agrl. Law Jour., 1978-82; mem. editorial bd. Jour. Agrl. Tax and Law, 1983-92. Home and Office: 12345 W 19th Pl Lakewood CO 80215-2516

GUZMAN, ARMANDO, electrical research engineer; b. Mazatlan, Mexico, Jan. 15, 1958; came to U.S., 1993; s. Armando and Concepcion (Casillas) G.; m. Claudia Uribe, Dec. 5, 1992; 1 child, Elizabeth Andrea. BSEE with honors, U. Autonoma de Guadalajara, Mexico, 1979. Product engr. Burroughs of Mexico, Guadalajara, 1979-80; regional supr. Fed. Electricity Commn., Guadalajara, 1980-84; application engr. GE, Malvern, Pa., 1984-85; regional supr. Fed. Electricity Commn., Guadalajara, 1985-93; application engr. Schweitzer Engrng. Labs., Pullman, Wash., 1993-94, rsch. engr., 1994—. Co-author, editor: Extra-High Voltage Transmission Line Protection, 1990. Mem. IEEE. Achievements include patent for development of a new ground directional relay for transmission line protection, of a very economical digital relay for transformer protection. Home: 525 NW Robert St Pullman WA 99163-3691 Office: Schweitzer Engrng Labs 2350 NE Hopkins Ct Pullman WA 99163-5600

GUZY, MARGUERITA LINNES, middle school education educator; b. Santa Monica, Calif., Nov. 19, 1938; d. Paul William Robert and Margarete (Rodowski) Linnes; m. Stephen Paul Guzy, Aug. 25, 1962 (div. 1968); 1 child, David Paul. AA, Santa Monica Coll., 1959; student, U. Mex., 1959-60; BA, UCLA, 1966, MA, 1973; postgrad. in psychology, Pepperdine U., 1988-92; cert. bilingual competence, Calif., 1994. Cert. secondary tchr., quality review team ednl. programs, bilingual, Calif. Tchr. Inglewood (Calif.) Unified Sch. Dist., 1967—, chmn. dept., 1972-82, mentor, tchr., 1985-88; clin. instr. series Clin. Supervision Levels I, II, Ingelwood, 1986-87; clin. intern Chem. Dependency Ctr., St. John's Hosp., Santa Monica, 1988-92; lectr. chem. and codependency St. John's Hosp., Santa Monica, 1992—; tchr. Santa Monica Coll., 1975-76; cons. bilingual edn. Inglewood Unified Sch. Dist., 1975—, lead tchr. new hope program at-risk students, 1992; cons. tchr. credentialing fgn. lang. State of Calif., 1994; sch. rep. restructuring edn. for state proposal, 1991-93; mem. Program Quality Rev. Team Pub. Edn., Calif., 1993; mem. Supt.'s Com. for Discrimination Resolution, 1994-95, tech. com. for integrating multimedia in the classroom, 1997—. Author: Elementary Education: "Pygmalian in the Classroom", 1975, English Mechanics Workbook, 1986. Recipient Teaching Excellence cert. State of Calif., 1986; named Tchr. of Yr., 1973, 88. Mem. NEA, Calif. Tchrs. Assn., Inglewood Tchrs. Assn. (local rep. 1971-72, tchr. edn. and profl. svcs. com. 1972-78), UCLA Alumnae Assn. (life), Prytanean Alumnae Assn. (bd. dirs. 1995-96, 1960's rep., 2d v.p. membership 1996-98). Republican. Avocations: reading, travel, swimming, dancing, cooking. Office: Monroe Magnet Mid Sch 10711 S 10th Ave Inglewood CA 90303-2015

GUZZETTI, BARBARA JEAN, education educator; b. Chgo., Nov. 15, 1948; d. Louis Earnest and Viola Genevive (Russell) G. BS, No. Ill. U., 1971, MS, 1974; PhD, U. Colo., 1982. Title I reading tchr. Harlem Consolidated Sch. Dist., Loves Park, Ill., 1971-72; elem. classroom tchr. Rockford (Ill.) Pub. Schs., 1972-77; diagnostic tchr. Denver Pub. Schs., 1977-78; secondary reading tchr. Jefferson County Pub. Schs., Lakewood, Colo., 1979-81, secondary reading specialist, 1983-84; rsch. and program assoc. Mid-Continent Regional Ednl. Lab., Aurora, Colo., 1983-84; evaluation specialist N.W. Regional Ednl. Lab., Denver, 1984-85; assoc. prof. Calif. State U., Ponoma, 1985-88; prof. Ariz. State U., Tempe, 1988—; chair, tech. com. Nat. Reading Conf., 1994-96. Author: Literacy Instruction in Content Areas, 1996; editor: Perspectives on Conceptual Change; mem. editl. bd. The Reading Tchr., Jour. of Reading Behavior, Nat. Reading conf. Yearbook; contbr. articles to profl. jours. Mem. Am. Ednl. Rsch. Assn., Nat. Reading Conf., Internat. Reading Assn. (chair studies and rsch. grants com. 1992-95). Democrat. Lutheran. Avocations: reading, oenology, raising a pot-bellied pig, Piglet. Home: 2170 E Aspen Dr Tempe AZ 85282-2953 Office: Ariz State U Coll of Edn Tempe AZ 85287-0311

GUZZO, ANTHONY VICTOR, sculptor; b. Newark, Oct. 31, 1934; s. Anthony and Julia (Bianco) G.; m. Sandra Elizabeth, June 22, 1963; children: Phillip Anthony, Anne Marie. BA, U. N.Mex., 1956; PhD, Washington U., St. Louis, 1960. Tech. collaborator U. Montpellier, France, 1964; prof. U. Wyo., Laramie, 1965-97; v.p. Wyo. Territorial Park Corp., Laramie, 1994-97. Home: 810 S 12th St Laramie WY 82070-4630

GUZZO, SANDRA ELIZABETH, newspaper columnist, writer; b. Berkeley, Calif., May 14, 1941; d. Frederick Joseph and Eva Maria (Weiskopf) Schmitz; m. Anthony Victor Guzzo; children: Phillip Anthony, Anne Marie. BA, U. Ariz., 1963; postgrad., U. Montpllier, France, 1963-64, U. Chgo., 1965. Sec. classics dept. U. Ariz., Tucson, 1961-63; women's news editor Laramie (Wyo.) Newspapers, Inc., 1973-79, columnist Laramie Rendezvous, 1986—, life styles editor, 1994—; originator co-ed Picket Pin Supplement, Laramie Newspapers, Inc., 1976-79. Author: (children's books), Fox and Heggie, 1983, Miguel and the Santero, 1986, The Days Before Christmas, 1994; (book) Chickens in the Greenhouse, 1993. Columnist for Pen Pals (group for preservation of Wyo. Territorial Prison), Laramie, 1985, 90. Named Fulbright fellow U. Montpellier, France, 1963-64. Mem. Wyo. Writers, Inc., Laramie Writers Group, Children's Book Writers (sec. Rocky Mt. chpt. 1994-98), Rocky Mt. Fiction Writers. Avocation: watercolor and pastel artist. Home: 810 S 12th St Laramie WY 82070-4630 Office: Laramie Daily Boomerang 320 Grand Ave Laramie WY 82070-3712

GWINN, MARY ANN, newspaper reporter; b. Forrest City, Ark., Dec. 29, 1951; d. Lawrence Baird and Frances Evelyn (Jones) G.; m. Richard A. King, June 3, 1973 (div. 1981); m. Stephen E. Dunnington, June 10, 1990. BA in Psychology, Hendrix Coll., 1973; MEd in Spl. Edn., Ga. State U., 1975; MA in Journalism, U. Mo., 1979. Tchrs. aide DeKalb County Schs., Decatur, Ga., 1973-74, tchr., 1975-78; reporter Columbia (Mo.) Daily Tribune, 1979-83; reporter Seattle Times, 1983—, internat. trade and work- [illegible] editor Times Books (formerly Seattle Times); instr. ext. divsn. U. Wash., Seattle, 1990; journalism instr., Seattle U., 1994. Recipient Charles Stewart Mott Found. award for edn. reporting, 1980, C.B. Blethen award for enterprise reporting Blethen Family, Seattle, 1989, Pulitzer Prize for nat. reporting, 1990. Mem. Newspaper Guild. Avocations: writing fiction, gardening, reading, wilderness camping. Office: Seattle Times PO Box 70 1120 John St Seattle WA 98109-5321*

GWINN, MARY DOLORES, business developer, philosopher, writer, speaker; b. Oakland, Calif., Sept. 16, 1946; d. Epifanio and Carolina (Lopez) Cruz; m. James Monroe Gwinn, Oct. 23, 1965; 1 child, Larry Allen. Student, Monterey Peninsula Jr. Coll., 1965. Retail store mgr. Consumer's Distbg. divsn. May Co., Hayward, Calif., 1973-78; mktg. rep. Dale Carnegie Courses, San Jose, Calif., 1978-79; founder, pres. Strategic Integrations, Ariz.'s Innovative Bus. Devel. Ctr., Scottsdale, 1985—, Gwinn Genius Inst., Scottsdale, 1998—; speaker St. John's Coll. U. Cambridge, England, 1992, INC. Mag., U.S.A., 1996, Clemson Univ., 1996, Antelope Valley Coll., Lancaster, Calif., 1998; founder, pres. Internat. Inst. for Conceptual Edn., Scottsdale, 1993—; chairperson Keble Coll., Oxford (Eng.) U., 1997. *President of Gwinn Genius Institute and Gwinn Genius, Mary is world authority in "The Thought Process of Genius." A business developer, author, international speaker, management consultant and mentally ambidextrous genius, Mary shows today's CEO's how to put their business together from the perspective of the whole brain - a convergence of vision, conceptual design, and strategic market plans. Corporate missions are clarified, followed by a purposeful launch and execution ofunique business ideas. Mary's trademark confidence, graciousness, warmth and poise are known across the globe as she instructs executives how to capitalize on her secrets to structure and synchronize their business.* Founder new fields of study Genestics and NeuroBus.; profiled the Thought Process of Genius; conceived Whole Brain Business Theory, 1985; author: Genius Leadership Secrets from the Past for the 21st Century, 1995; writer bus. column Gwinn on Bus., IMAGE Networker, Pa., 1996; contbr. articles to profl. jours. Chairperson Keble Coll., Oxford (Eng.) U. Republican. Avocations: reading, imagination games, playing with grandchildren. Home and Office: 5836 E Angela Dr Scottsdale AZ 85254-6410

GWYNN, ANTHONY KEITH (TONY GWYNN), professional baseball player; b. L.A., May 9, 1960; m. Alicia; children: Anthony, Anisha Nicole. Student, San Diego State U. Player minor league teams Walla Walla and Amarillo, Hawaii, 1981-82; with San Diego Padres, 1981—. Winner Nat. League batting title, 1984, 87, 88, 89, 95; recipient Gold Glove award, 1986-87, 89-91; mem. All-Star team, 1984-87, 89-96; named MVP N.W. League, 1981, Sporting News Nat. League Silver Slugger team, 1984, 86-87, 89, 94, Sporting News Nat. League All-Star Team, 1984, 86-87, 89, 94. Office: San Diego Padres Qualcomm Stadium PO Box 2000 San Diego CA 92112-2000*

GYLSETH, DORIS (LILLIAN) HANSON, retired librarian; b. Helena, Mont., May 26, 1934; d. Richard E. and Lillie (Paula) Hanson; m. Arlie Albeck, Dec. 26, 1955 (div. Apr. 1964); m. Hermann M. Gylseth, Apr. 29, 1983 (dec. Aug. 1985). BS in Edn., Western Mont. Coll. Edn., 1958; MLS, U. Wash., 1961. Tchr. Helena Sch. Dist., 1955-56, Dillon (Mont.) Elem. Sch., 1957-59, Eltopia (Wash.) Unified Sch. Dist., 1959-60; sch. libr. Shoreline Sch. Dist., Seattle, 1960-64, Dept. of Def., Chateauroux, France, Hanau, Fed. Republic Germany, Tachikawa, Japan, 1964-68, Long Beach (Calif.) Unified Sch. Dist., 1968-70; br. libr. Long Beach Pub. Libr., 1970-74, coord. children's svcs., 1974-85; libr. Long Beach (Calif.) Unified Sch. Dist., 1986-94; realtor Century 21, All Pacific, 1994-96. Bd. dirs. Children's Svcs. divsn. Calif. Libr. Assn., 1985, Literary Guild of Orange County, 1993—; co-chmn. Long Beach Authors Festival, 1978-86; mem. planning coun. Third Pacific Rim Conf. on Children's Lit., UCLA, 1986. Mem. So. Calif. Coun. on Lit. for Children and Young Poeple (bd. dirs. 1974-88, pres. 1982-84), Helen Fuller Cultural Carrousel (bd. dirs. 1985—), Friends of Long Beach Pub. Libr. (bd. dirs. 1988—), Zonta (pres. 1978-80). Avocations: cats, traveling. Home: 5131 Kingscross Rd Westminster CA 92683-4832

HA, CHONG WAN, information technology executive; b. Chin-ju, Kyung-Nam, South Korea, Oct. 25, 1938; came to U.S., 1963; s. Kyung-sik and Kyung-Nam (Park) H.; m. Karen Hye-Ja Han, Aug. 19, 1968; children: Jean Frances, Julie Ann. BA in Econs., UCLA, 1970; cert. in exec. mgmt., The Peter F. Drucker Mgmt. Ctr., 1984; MA in Mgmt., Claremont (Calif.) Grad. Sch., 1985; PhD in Bus. Mgmt., La Salle U., La., 1995. Sr. systems analyst Atlantic Richfield Co., Los Angeles, 1972-78; asst. v.p. 1st Interstate Services Co., Los Angeles, 1978-85; v.p. Ticor Title Ins. Co., Los Angeles, 1985-91; assoc. dir. MCA/Universal Studios, 1991; dir. State of Calif. Stephen P. Teale Data Ctr., Sacramento, 1991-97; v.p. LCS, Inc., Sacramento, 1997—; mem. exec. com. Calif. Forum on Info. Tech.; mem. adv. bd. Govt. Tech. Conf., 1994. Res. police officer Monterey Park (Calif.) Police Dept., 1981-82; bd. dirs. Asian Pacific Alumni Assn., UCLA, 1988, Asian Pacific Am. Legal Found., L.A., 1988, Korean Youth Ctr., Korean Am. Music Acad.; mem. alumni coun. Claremont Grad. Sch., 1993. Recipient Peter Drucker Ctr. Alumni award, 1994, Calif. State Atty. Gen. award, 1994, Carnegie Mellon U. and AMS Achievement award in mng. info. tech., 1995. Mem. Soc. of Info. Mgmt., Leadership Edn. for Asian Pacifics, UCLA Chancellers Circle. Avocations: golf, classical music, reading. Home: 5625 Adobe Rd Rocklin CA 95765-4529

HAAG, JANIS LINN, journalism and creative writing educator, writer; b. Long Beach, Calif., July 30, 1958; d. Roger Edwin and Dorothy Marlene (Keeley) H.; m. Clifford Polland, Dec. 17, 1983. BA in English, Journalism, Calif. State U., Sacramento, 1982, MA in Journalism, English, 1992. Reporter, copy editor The Sacramento Bee, 1983-85; instr. journalism Calif. State U., Sacramento, 1984-86, 88-89, Am. River Coll., Sacramento, 1986-87; Sacramento C.C., 1989-93; reporter UPI, Sacramento, 1986-88; assoc. editor Sacramento Mag., 1988-89, editor, 1989-92; prof. journalism and creative writing Sacramento City Coll., 1993—. Author: (anthology) included in From Mothers to Daughters: I've Always Meant to Tell You, 1997, An Ear to the Ground, 1997; editor/adviser (jour.) Susurrus, 1995—; contbg. editor Sacramento News and Review, 1996—. Recipient Arts Edn. grant Sacramento Met. Arts Commn., 1996. Mem. Sacramento Press Club (bd. dirs. 1990-92), Soc. Profl. Journalists. Office: Sacramento City Coll 3835 Freeport Blvd Sacramento CA 95822-1318

HAAGE, ROBERT MITCHELL, retired history educator, organization leader; b. Garden City, Kans., Mar. 10, 1924; s. William Russell and Mayme Levice (Mitchell) H.; m. Lila Marie Baker, Sept. 7, 1947; children: Lori Deane, Lisa Anne, Melanie Sue. BA, Southwestern Coll., 1947; MDiv, Garrett Bibl. Inst., 1952. Cert. tchr., Kans., Calif. Min. Meth. Ch., Copeland, Kans., 1947-48, Meth. Chs., Ingleside, Spring Grove, Ill., 1948-50; asst. min. First Meth. Ch., Emporia, Kans., 1952-53; tchr. core curriculum Marshall Intermediate Sch., Wichita, Kans., 1953-56; tchr. U.S. history Bellflower (Calif.) High Sch., 1956-57; tchr. math. Chaffey Joint Union High Sch. Dist., Ontario, Calif., 1957-59, tchr. U.S. history and econs. Chaffey Joint Union High Sch. Dist., 1959-85; 1st faculty pres. Montclair High Sch., 1959-60; founding pres. Inland Empire Counties Coun. for Social Studies, San Bernardino, Calif., 1961-62; dean student activities Western CUNA Mgmt. Sch., Pomona Coll., Claremont, Calif., 1980-84; treas. Tchrs. Adv. Group/Tchrs. Farm and Ranch Co-op, 1984-93. Conservation editor Desomount Dustings Newsletter, 1990-92, gen. editor, 1993—. Founding officer Chaffey Dist. Employees Fed. Credit Union, Ontario, 1964-69; chair, bd. dirs. Chaffey Fed. Credit Union, Ontario, 1979-87, dir., 1969—; officer, bd. govs. Mt. Baldy chpt. Calif. Credit Union League, Pomona, 1977-86; bd. dirs., treas. Upper Westwood Homeowners Assn., Pomona, 1982-84, 91-92; conservation chair Desomount Environ. Orgn.; mem. Nat. Wildlife Fedn. Recipient We Honor Ours award Calif. Tchrs. Assn., 1985, Outstanding Svc. award Associated Chaffey Tchrs., 1985. Mem. Univ. Club Claremont (sec.-v.p.-pres. 1986-92, editor newsletters 1986-90, bd. dirs. 1993-96, chair fin. com. 1993-97, Leadership award 1992), Toastmasters Club 12 (pres. 1964-65, Best Evaluator award 1982, 83, 85), Sierra Club, Fedn. of Western Outdoor Clubs (v.p. So. Calif. chpt. 1990—, gen. v.p. 1994-95, treas. 1995-98, mem. Sequoia strategy com. 1998—), Phi Delta Kappa (pres. 1977-78, Disting. Svc. award 1978), Kappa Delta Pi (hon. soc. in edn. 1953—), Democrat. Avocations: woodworking, reading, camping, hiking, photography. Home: 9541 Tudor Ave Montclair CA 91763-2219

HAAS, BRADLEY DEAN, pharmacy director, clinical pharmacist, consultant; b. Albion, Nebr., Nov. 24, 1957; s. Ernest Duane Jr. and Joy Lou (Fusselman) H. Student, Kearney State Coll., 1976-78; PharmD with distinction, U. Nebr. Coll. Pharmacy, Omaha, 1981. Registered pharmacist, Nebr., Colo.; cert. hosp. pharmacy residency, basic life support instr. and

provider, advanced cardiac life support instr. and provider. Resident hosp. pharmacy U. Nebr. Med. Ctr., Omaha, 1981-82; intensive care clin. pharmacist Mercy Med. Ctr., Denver, 1982-85; home care pharmacist Am. Abbey Homecare, Englewood, Colo., 1985; pharmacy dir. Charter Hosp. of Aurora, Colo., 1989-90; clin pharmacy coord. Porter Meml. Hosp., Denver, 1987-92; asst. dir. clin. pharmacy svcs. Luth. Med. Ctr., Wheat Ridge, Colo., 1992-94; dir. pharmacy Integrated Pharmacy Solutions, Inc./Pru Care Pharmacies, Denver, 1994-96; med. info. scientist Astra Pharmaceuticals, LP (formerly Astra-Merck), 1996—; cons. Porter Meml. Hosp. Chronic Pain Treatment Ctr., 1987-89, Charter Hosp., 1989-90; adj. asst. prof. pharmacy U. Colo., 1983—; mem. leadership adv. coun. sch. pharmacy U. Colo., 1987-89; mem. adv. bd. Instl. and Managed Healthcare, Ortho Biotech, Inc., 1992-93; mem. State Colo./ Medicare D.U.R. Com., 1992-96. Author, co-author in field. Vol. Colo. Hosp. Pharmacists Week, Poison Prevention Week, KUSA-TV Health Fair; active Colo. Trust. Named Disting. Young Pharmacist of the Year Marion Labs., Colo., 1987, one of Outstanding Young Men of Am., 1987; recipient Acad. Scholarship U. Nebr. Med. Ctr, 1978-81, Excellence in Pharmacy Practice award U. Colo. Sch. Pharmacy, 1988; Marjorie Merwin Simmons Meml. scholar U. Nebr. Found. Fund., 1980; scholar VFW, 1978-81. Mem. Am. Soc. Hosp. Pharmacists (state chpt. grants program selection com. 1989, nominations com. 1990-91, ho. of dels. 1987, 90-92), Acad. Managed Care Pharmacy, Colo. Managed Care Pharmacy Dirs., Colo. Soc. Hosp. Pharmacists (presdl. officer 1987-89, chmn. numerous couns. and coms., Hosp. Pharmacy Practitioner Excellence award 1988, 89), Sertoma Club (charter). Avocations: snow/water skiing, bicycling, photography, golf, community service activities. Home: 10115 Granite Hill Dr Parker CO 80134-9515 Office: Astra Pharm LP 10115 Granite Hill Dr Parker CO 80134-9515

HAAS, JUNE F., special education educator, consultant; b. Burien, Wash., June 5, 1934; d. Carl Edwin and Mary Rebecca (Best) Flodquist; m. Frank M. Haas, June 21, 1958; children: Michael Edward, Katherine June Haas Dunning. BA in Elem. Edn., Psychology, U. Wash., 1956; MS in Early Childhood Edn., Oreg. Coll. Edn., 1975. Tchr. Haines (Alaska) Borough Sch. Dist., 1956-76, spl. edn. tchr., 1976-86, gifted, talented coord., 1978-87, migrant edn. tchr., 1986-87; instr. U. Alaska, Haines, 1984-85; cons. Ednl. Cons. Svcs., Haines, 1987—; instr. World Conf. Gifted/Talented Children, Hamburg, Germany, 1985, Sydney, Australia, 1989, 2d Gifted Asian Conf. on Giftedness, Taipei, Taiwan, 1992, World Conf. Gifted/Talented Children, Toronto, Can., 1993 ; coach Alaska Future Problem Solving Program, 1982-87; del. Citizen Ambassador Program Russia, Siberia, Hungary, 1991; del./ presentor U.S./Russia Joint Conf. Edn., Moscow, 1994. Pres. Bus. and Profl. Women's Clubs, Alaska, 1973-74; pres. Am. Legion Aux., Alaska, 1990-91, nat. exec. com., 1991-92, mem. nat. edn. com., 1991-92; bd. dir. Am. Cancer Soc., Alaska, 1976—; chmn. we divsn. Nat. Edn. Com., 1992-93. Mem. World Coun. Gifted/Talented Children, Coun. Exceptional Children, Bus. and Profl. Women's Club (v.p. 1972-73, Woman of Yr. 1972), Am. Legion Aux. (nat. jr. activities com., western divsn. chmn. 1993-94, mem. citizens flag alliance 1994-95), Lynn Canal Community Players (nat. drama festival com. 1983), Haines Women's Club (pres. 1988-90), Pioneers of Alaska (pres. 1990-91). Methodist. Avocations: photography, community theater, flying, bridge, travel. Home and Office: Ednl Cons Svcs PO Box 97 Haines AK 99827-0097

HAAS, PETER E., SR., company executive; b. San Francisco, Dec. 20, 1918; s. Walter A. and Elise (Stern) H.; m. Josephine Baum, Feb. 1, 1945; m. Mimi Lurie, Aug., 1981; children: Peter E., Michael Stern, Margaret Elizabeth. Student, Deerfield Acad., 1935-36; A.B., U. Calif., 1940; MBA cum laude, Harvard, 1943. With Levi Strauss & Co., San Francisco, 1945—, exec. v.p., 1958-70, pres., 1970-81, CEO, 1976-81, chmn. bd., 1981-89, chmn. exec. com., 1989—, also bd. dirs.; chmn. exec. com., bd. dirs. Levi Strauss Assocs. Inc. Holding Corp.; dir. emeritus AT&T. Trustee San Francisco Found., 1984—; assoc. Smithsonian Nat. Bd., 1988—; bd. dirs. No. Calif. Grantmakers, 1989—; former mem. exec. com. Strive for Five; former mem. Golden Gate Nat. Recreation Area Adv. Com.; Former pres. Jewish Welfare Fedn.; former trustee Stanford U.; former dir., vice chmn. San Francisco Bay Area Council; former trustee United Way of San Francisco Bay Area; former pres. Aid to Retarded Children; former bd. govs. United Way of Am. Recipient Alexis De Tocqueville Soc. award, United Way Am., 1985; named CEO of Yr., Fin. World mag., 1981, Bus. Statesman of Yr., Harvard Bus. Sch., 1982; Baker scholar, 1940. Office: Levi Strauss & Co 1155 Battery St San Francisco CA 94111*

HAAS, RAYMOND P., lawyer; b. Corpus Christi, Tex., Dec. 9, 1942. BA cum laude, Yale U., 1964, LLB, 1967. Bar: Calif. 1967. Law clk. to Hon. Roger J. Traynor Supreme Ct. of Calif., 1967-68; atty. Howard, Rice, Nemerovski, Canady, Falk & Rabkin, San Francisco. Trustee San Francisco U. High Sch., 1973-78, 85-88, chmn., 1973-76, treas., 1986-88; trustee Pacific Presbyn. Med. Ctr., 1979-91, vice chmn. 1986-91. Mem. ABA (forum com. on franchising, antitrust law sect., bus. law sect., internat. law sect., patent, copyright and trademarks sect., sci. and tech. sect.), State Bar Calif., Bar Assn. San Francisco (computer law sect.), Licensing Execs. Soc., Computer Law Assn., Order of Coif. Office: Howard Rice Nemerovski Canady Falk & Rabkin 3 Embarcadero Ctr Ste 7 San Francisco CA 94111-4003

HAAS, ROBERT DOUGLAS, apparel manufacturing company executive; b. San Francisco, Apr. 3, 1942; s. Walter A. Jr. and Evelyn (Danzig) H.; m. Colleen Gershon, Jan. 27, 1974; 1 child, Elise Kimberly. BA, U. Calif., Berkeley, 1964; MBA, Harvard U., 1968. With Peace Corps, Ivory Coast, 1964-66; fellow White House, Washington, 1968-69; assoc. McKinsey & Co., 1969-72; with Levi Strauss & Co., San Francisco, 1973—, sr. v.p. corp. planning and policy, 1978-80, pres. new bus. group, 1980, pres. operating groups, 1980-81, exec. v.p., COO, 1981-84, pres., CEO, 1984-89, CEO, chmn. bd., 1989—, also bd. dirs.; pres. Levi Strauss Found., mem. global leadership team. Hon. dir. San Francisco AIDS Found.; trustee Ford Found.; bd. dirs. Bay Area Coun.; past bd. dirs. Am. Apparel Assn. White House fellow, 1968-69. Mem. Brookings Inst. (trustee), Bay Area Com., Conf. Bd., Coun. Fgn. Rels., Trilateral Commn., Calif. Bus. Roundtable, Meyer Freidman Inst. (bd. dirs.), Phi Beta Kappa. Office: Levi Strauss & Co 1155 Battery St San Francisco CA 94111-1256*

HABBESTAD, KATHRYN LOUISE, writer; b. Spokane, Wash., Sept. 29, 1949; d. Bernard Malvin and Gertrude Lucille (Westberg) H. BA, U. Wash., 1971; postgrad., Seattle U., 1981-82. Mgr. bus. Seattle Sun, 1974-75; analyst, dep. dir. Research and Planning Office, Seattle, 1975-83; account exec. Southmark Fin. Services, Seattle, 1983-84; stockbroker Interstate Securities, New Bern, N.C., 1985-86; co-founder, assoc. pub. Havelock (N.C.) News, 1986-87; owner ISIS Enterprises, Spokane, 1988—; writer Spokane; sec.-treas. Seattle Sun Pub. Co., 1974-75, Veritas Services, Seattle, 1978-83; chmn. Energy Com. Nat. Congress for Community Econ. Devel., Washington, 1979-82; pub. The Gnus, 1988. Treas. Havelock Chili Festival, 1985-87. Mem. Internat. Platform Assn., Mensa. Avocation: wordsmith. Home and Office: 12819 SE 30th #340 Bellevue WA 98006

HABER, RALPH NORMAN, psychology consultant, researcher, educator; b. Lansing, Mich., May 15, 1932; s. William and Fannie (Gallas) H.; m. Ruth Lea Boss, 1961 (div. 1974); children—Sabrina Beth, Rebecca Ann; m. Lyn R. Roland, 1974. B.A., U. Mich., 1953; M.A., Wesleyan U., Middletown, Conn., 1954; Ph.D., Stanford U., 1957; Postdoctoral fellow, Med. Research Council, Applied Psychology Unit, Cambridge, Eng., 1970-71. Rsch. assoc. Inst. for Comm. Rsch., Stanford, 1957-58; instr. psychology San Francisco State Coll., Calif., 1957-58; asst. prof. psychology Yale, 1958-64; assoc. prof. psychology U. Rochester, N.Y., 1964-67, prof. psychology, 1967-70, prof. psychology and visual sci., 1970-79, chmn. dept. psychology, 1967-70, mem. faculty senate, 1968-70, sec., mem. steering com., 1969-70; prof. psychology U. Ill., Chgo., 1979-91, rsch. prof., 1991-94, rsch. prof. emeritus, 1994—; ptnr. Human Factors Cons., Bishop, Calif., 1988—; rsch. assoc. psychology U. Calif., Santa Cruz, 1995—; adj. prof. U. Calif., Riverside, 1997—; vis. prof. Air Force Human Resources Lab., Williams AFB, Ariz., 1981-83; ptnr. Human Factors Cons., Highland Park, Ill.; vis. scientist Med. Rsch. Coun. Applied Psychology Unit, Cambridge, Eng., 1970-71; chmn., divisional maj. III Yale, 1959-64; vis. asst. prof. New Sch. for Social Research, 1963; research cons. VA, 1967-71; adv. editor for exptl. psychology Holt, Rinehart & Winston Book Pubs., 1969-77. Author: (with Hershenson) The Psychology of Visual Perception, 1973, 2d edit., 1980, (with Fried) An Introduction to Psychology, 1975, (with others) Discovering Psychology, 1977; editor: Current Research on Motivation, 1966, Contemporary Theory and Research on Visual Perception, 1968, Information Processing Approaches to Visual Perception, 1969; Contbr. articles to profl. jours. Committeeman 18th Ward, Brighton (N.Y.) Democratic Com., 1967-70; founding mem., trustee Coll. Admission Prep. Program, Rochester, 1968-70; commr. Wheeler Crest Fire Prevention Dist., Bishop, Calif., 1995—. Recipient Outstanding Achievement award U. Mich., 1977; Behavioral Sci. fellow Ford Found., 1953-54; grantee NSF, NIH, Nat. Inst. Edn., Air Force Office Sci. Research, Dept. Army. Fellow APA, AAAS; mem. Am. Psychol. Soc., Psychonomics Soc., Midwestern Psychol. Assn., Brit. Psychol. Assn., Optical Soc. Am., Human Factors and Ergonomics Soc., Am. Contract Bridge League (dir. Bishop unit 517 1996—), Sigma Xi, Pi Lambda Phi.

HABERBERGER, RICHARD LOUIS, JR., microbiologist, epidemiologist; b. East St. Louis, Ill., June 2, 1951; s. Richard Louis Sr. and Patricia Ann (Henderson) H.; m. Cynthia Anne Irby, June 30, 1973; children: Lori, Sarah, Amy. BS, Rockhurst Coll., 1973; MS, N.E. La. U., 1975; PhD, So. Ill. U., 1983. Microbiology supr. Wellborn Bapt. Hosp., Evansville, Ind., 1983; commd. lt. USN, 1983, advanced through grades to comdr.; staff scientist Naval Bioscis. Lab., Oakland, Calif., 1983-86; head bacteriology dept. Naval Med. Rsch. Unit # 3, Cairo, 1986-89, exec. officer, 1998—; head pathogen characterization Naval Med. Rsch. Inst., Bethesda, Md., 1989-92, head microbiology lab., 1992-94; head microbiology lab. Naval Med. Ctr., San Diego, 1995-98. Contbr. over 35 articles to sci. publs. Pres. PTA San Francisco Unified Sch. Dist., Treasure Island, Calif., 1985-86, Cairo Am. Coll., 1988. Mem. Am. Coll. Epidemiology (reviewer 1991—), Am. Soc. Microbiology (mentor, proctor 1975—). Republican. Roman Catholic. Avocations: gardening, travel, photography, collecting. Address: NAMRU-3 PSC 452 Box 102 FPO AE 09835-0007

HACK, DAVID FRANK, art director; b. Rochester, N.Y., Nov. 6, 1957; s. Harold F. and Arlene (Witmeyer) H. BFA, Rochester Inst. Tech., 1973. Art dir. ICE Comm., Rochester, N.Y., 1973-78, BBDO Healthcare, L.A., 1978-80; sr. art dir. Lowe Marschalk Healthcare, N.Y.C., 1980-87; art group supr. Kallir, Phillips & Ross, N.Y.C., 1987-90; sr. art group supr. FCB Healthcare, N.Y.C., 1990-92; art supr. David Hack Assocs., N.Y.C., 1992-93; ptnr., sr. art group supr. Bozell Healthcare, N.Y.C., 1993-98; creative dir. Koppes & Ptnrs., Irvine, Calif., 1998—. Avocations: skiing, golf, tennis, travel. Home: 72-81 113th St 6N Forest Hills NY 11375 Office: Koppes & Ptnrs 19900 Macarthur Blvd Irvine CA 92612-2445

HACKER, KENNETH RUSSELL, insurance executive; b. Sharon, Pa., June 28, 1947; s. Russ Edward and Stella (Hibler) H.; children: Tammy, Todd. Student, Penn-Ohio Coll., 1966-68, Youngstown State U., 1968-70. Cert. Wealth Practitioner, WTES Inst., 1998. Steel mill worker Westinghouse Electric, Sharon, Pa., 1966-70; ins. agt. N.Y. Life, Youngstown, Ohio, 1970-82, Phoenix, 1982-85; regional dir. First Del. Life, Phoenix, 1985-87; pres. Estate Planning Concepts, Inc., Phoenix, 1987—. Selected del. People Internat. Citizen Amb. Program to Republic of China, 1994. Recipient disting. sales award Sales and Mktg. Execs. of Greater Phoenix, 1984. Mem. Ariz. Estate Planning Coun., CLU Soc., Nat. Assn. Life Udnerwriters (pres. Phoenix chpt. 1987-88), Phoenix Assn. Life Underwriters (Man of Yr. 1994), Million Dollar Roundtable (life, state chmn. 1985-92, mem. found., mem. Ct. of Table 1976—). Republican. Avocation: racquetball. Office: Estate Planning Concepts PO Box 26812 Phoenix AZ 85068-6812

HACKER, THOMAS OWEN, architect; b. Dayton, Ohio, Nov. 4, 1941; s. Homer Owen and Lydia (McLean) H.; m. Margaret (Brooks) Stewart, Mar. 21, 1965; children: Jacob, Sarah, Alice. BA, U. Pa., 1964, MArch, 1967. Registered arch., Oreg.; registered Nat. Coun. Archtl. Registration Bds. Intern architect Office of Louis I. Kahn, Phila., 1964-70; mem. faculty architecture U. Pa., Phila., 1967-69, U. Oreg., Eugene, 1970-84; design prin. Thomas Hacker and Assocs. Architects P.C., Portland, Oreg., 1983—; vis. profl. architecture, U. Oreg., 1985—. Prin. works include Biomed. Info. Comm. Ctr., Oreg. Health Scis. U., Sch. Nursing, Oreg. Health Scis. U. (Regional Honor award AIA 1993), Portland Art Mus., High Desert Mus., Bend, Oreg.; designer crystal vase for Steuben Inc., Spokane Pub. Libr., Yellowstone Art Mus., Billings, Mont., Lewis & Clark Coll. Signature Project, Multnomah County Midland Libr., Columbia Gorge Interpretive Ctr., Portland State U. Urban Ctr., Whitman Coll. Penrose Meml. Libr., Portland 1st Unitarian Ch. Office: 34 NW 1st Ave Ste 406 Portland OR 97209-4017 Home: 2762 SW Montgomery Dr Portland OR 97201-1693*

HACKETT, SUZANNE F., cultural organization administrator; b. Burbank, Calif., Apr. 12, 1961; d. David Woollan and Krystyna Barbara (Skalmowski) H.; m. Jack Martin Katzantek, Jan. 9, 1988 (div. Sept. 1997). BA in English, We. Wash. U., 1982; posrgrad., Calif. State U., Northridge, 1998—. Exec. dir. Custer County Art Ctr., Miles City, Mont., 1987-89; devel. assoc. Exploratorium, San Francisco, 1989-90; exec. dir. Marine World Found., Vallejo, Calif., 1990-92; dir. devel. Lied Discovery Children's Mus., Las Vegas, 1992-94; v.p. advancement Calif. Sci. Ctr., L.A., 1994-98; exec. dir. Valley Cultural Ctr., Woodland Hills, Calif., 1998—; mgmt. assistance program cons. L.A. Women's Found., 1995-97; bd. dirs. Saving and Preserving Arts and Cultural Environs., L.A. Editor: Jeopardy Jour., 1982, Cutbank Jour., 1983, The Hot Springs Gazette, 1984-87; curator: Women's Work The Montana Womens' Centennial Survey, 1989, Under Other Circumstances, 1996. Pres. Contemporary Arts Collective, Las Vegas, 1994-95. Recipient grant-in-aid U. Nev. Las Vegas Women's Ctr., 1995. Avocation: painting. Home: 1040 N Cordova St Burbank CA 91505

HACKNEY, ROBERT WARD, plant pathologist, nematologist, parasitologist, molecular geneticist, commercial arbitrator; b. Louisville, Dec. 11, 1942; s. Paul Arnold and Ovine (Whallen) H.; m. Cheryl Lynn Hill, June 28, 1969 (div. Dec. 1995); 1 child, Candice Colleen; m. Jacqueline Monica Eisenreich, Dec. 27, 1995. BA, Northwestern U., 1965; MS, Murray State U., 1969; PhD, Kans. State U., 1973. Postgrad. rsch. nematologist U. Calif., Riverside, 1973-75; plant nematologist Calif. Dept. Food and Agr., Sacramento, 1975-85, sr. plant nematologist, supr. 1985-89, sr. plant nematologist, specialist, 1989—; comml. arbitrator Am. Arbitration Assn., 1980—; chmn. Calif. Nematode Diagnosis Adv. Commn., Sacramento, 1981—. Contbr. articles to profl. jours. Hon. dep. Sheriff, Sacramento, 1982-83. Served with USMC, 1966. NSF grantee, 1974. Mem. Soc. Nematologists, Internat. Council Study of Viruses and Virus Diseases of the Grape, Delta Tau Delta, Sigma Xi. Democrat. Baptist. Office: Calif Dept Food & Agriculture Plant Pest Diagnostic Ctr 3294 Meadowview Rd Sacramento CA 95832-1437

HACKWORTH, MICHAEL L., executive; m. Joan. Chmn., pres., CEO Cirrus Logic, Fremont, Calif. Office: 3100 W Warren Ave Fremont CA 94538-6423

HACKWORTH, THEODORE JAMES, JR., city official; b. Denver, Nov. 7, 1926; s. Theodore James and Thelma B. (Hill) H.; m. Doris Evelyn Larson, Dec. 31, 1947; children—James Robert, Joan Evelyn Grady, Linda Jean Hoffman. B.A., U. Denver, 1955. Sales mgr. Continental Baking Co., Denver, 1950-64; mktg. exec. Sigman Meat Co., Denver, 1964-76; v.p. sales Pierce Packing Co., Billings, Mont., 1976-79; city councilman City of Denver, 1979—, pres., 1983-84; cons. EPA. Mem. Denver pub. schs. bd. edn., 1971-77; dir. Urban Drainage and Flood Control Dist., 1981-84; dir. Met. Wastewater Reclamation Dist., 1982—, sec., 1984-85, chmn. elect 1988-89, chmn., 1989-91; mem. Denver Regional Council Govts., 1979-94, vice chmn., 1981-83, chmn., 1984-86; neighborhood commr. Boy Scouts Am., 1968-69, Western Dist. commr., 1970-71; pres. Harvey Park Improvement Assn., 1969; chmn. Denver Met. Library Task Force, 1982. Served with USAF, 1945-47. Recipient Individual Achievement award for pub. svc. Assn. Met. Sewerage Agys., 1996, Paul Swalm Lifetime Achievement award Denver County Reps., 1998. Mem. Nat. Assn. Regional Coun. (bd. dirs., chmn. surface trans. task force, pres. 1987-89, Tom Bradley Regional Leadership award 1993), Mt. Vernon Country Club. Republican. Contbr. articles to EPA jours. Home: 3955 W Linvale Pl Denver CO 80236-2212 Office: 3110 S Wadsworth Blvd Ste 304 Denver CO 80227-4810

HADA, JOHN JUJI, East Asian international affairs educator; b. San Francisco, Apr. 16, 1927; s. Jutaro James and Katsuyo (Noma) H.; m. Mitzi Mutsumi Egusa, May 27, 1951; children: Elayne Naomi, Matthew Stuart Jun, Sterling Theodore, Leslie Anne. BA in Philosophy and History, U. San Francisco, 1972, MA in History, 1973, EdD in Edn., 1981; PhD in Anthrop. Linguistics, U. Tokyo, Japan, 1986. Col. U.S. Army, 1944-71; fgn. svc. officer Embassy of U.S.A., Tokyo, 1982-86; sr. Fulbright fellow Nat. Lang. Rsch. Inst., Tokyo, 1986-88; prof. Tohoku Nat. U., Sendai, Japan, 1988-93, U. San Francisco, 1993—, Coll. of Notre Dame, Belmont, Calif., 1994—; rschr. Ctr. for the Pacific Rim, U. San Francisco, 1993—. Author: The Anatomy of the All Japan Federation of Self-Governing Students: Its Evolution and Dimensions of Japanese Student Activism in the Postwar Period, Indictment and Trial of Iva Ikuko Toguri D'Aquino, 1973, The Romanization Movement of the Japanese Language During the Allied Occupation of Japan, 1981. Decorated D.S.C., Legion of Merit; recipient Dr. Edward J. Griffin award U. San Francisco Alumni Assn., 1996, Disting. Faculty award U. San Francisco, 1995. Mem. Nat. Japanese Am. Hist. Soc. (dir. 1994—). Democrat. Roman Catholic. Avocation: tennis. Home: 1429 23rd Ave San Francisco CA 94122-3305 Office: U San Francisco 2130 Fulton St San Francisco CA 94117-1080

HADAS, ELIZABETH CHAMBERLAYNE, publisher; b. Washington, May 12, 1946; d. Moses and Elizabeth (Chamberlayne) H.; m. Jeremy W. Heist, Jan. 25, 1970 (div. 1976); m. Peter Eller, Mar. 21, 1984 (div. 1998). A.B., Radcliffe Coll., 1967; postgrad. Rutgers U., 1967-68; M.A., Washington U., St. Louis, 1971. Editor U. N.Mex. Press, Albuquerque, 1971-85; dir., 1985—. Mem. Assn. Am. Univ. Presses (pres. 1992-93). Democrat. Home: 2900 10th St NW Albuquerque NM 87107-1111 Office: U New Mexico Press 1720 Lomas Blvd NE Albuquerque NM 87106-3807

HADDAD, EDMONDE ALEX, public affairs executive; b. Los Angeles, July 25, 1931; s. Alexander Saleeba and Madeline Angela (Zail) H.; m. Harriet Ann Lenhart; children: Mark Edmonde, Brent Michael, John Alex. AA, Los Angeles City Coll., 1956; BA, U. Southern Calif., 1958; MA, Columbia U., 1961. Staff writer WCBS Radio News, New York, 1959-61; news commentator, editor KPOL AM/FM Radio, Los Angeles, 1961-67, dir., pub. affairs, 1967-73; exec. dir. Los Angeles World Affairs Council, 1973-84; pres. L.A. World Affairs Coun., 1984-88; deputy asst. sec. of State for Pub. Diplomacy Dept. State, U.S. Govt., Wash., 1987-88; mem. steering com., moderator Conf. environ., L.A., 1989-90; pres. Nat. Coun. World Affairs Orgns., 1981-83; pres. Radio and TV News Assn. So. Calif., 1965-66; sr. fellow Ctr. Internat. Rels., U. Calif., L.A., 1991-94; bd. dirs. Pen Ctr. USA West. Author: Look to the Rainbow, 1997; contbg. author: How Peace Came to the World,, 1985; founder, pub. World Affairs Jour. Quar., 1981. Bd. dirs. PEN Ctr. USA West, 1994—, World Affairs Coun., Ventura County, 1995-97. Recipient Am. Polit. Sci. Assn. award for Disting. Reporting of Pub. Affairs, 1967. Mem. Am. Assn. Ret. Persons (team mem. congl. dist. 23 AARP/Vote 1995—), Friends of Wilton Park (exec. com. So. Calif.), Brit. Fgn. Office Conf. Ctr. Democrat. Avocations: writing poetry, nonfiction, and op-ed articles for newspapers, public speaking, travel. Home: 582 Pacific Cove Dr Port Hueneme CA 93041-2175

HADDAD, EDWARD RAOUF, civil engineer, consultant; b. Mosul, Iraq, July 1, 1926; came to U.S., 1990.; s. Raouf Sulaiman Haddad and Fadhila (Sulaiman) Shaya; m. Balquis Yousef Rassam, July 19, 1961; children: Reem, Raid. BSc, U. Baghdad, Iraq, 1949; postgrad., Colo. State U., 1966-67; PhD (hon.), 1995. Project engr., cons. Min. Pub. Works, Baghdad, 1949-63; arbitrator Engring. Soc. & Ct., Kuwait City, Kuwait, 1963-90; tech. advisor Royal Family, Kuwait, 1987-90; cons. pvt. practice Haddad Engring., Albuquerque, 1990-95; owner, pres. Overseas Contacts-Internat. Bus. and Consulting, Albuquerque, 1995—; organizer reps abroad, Kuwait, 1990. Pres. Parents Assn., U. N.Mex., 1995. Recipient Hon. medal Pope Paul VI of Rome, 1973, Men of Achievement award Internat. Biog. Ctr., 1994. Mem. ASCE, NSPE, ABA (assoc.), Am. Arbitration Assn. (mem. adv. bd.), Sierra Cath. Internat. (trustee), Lions (bd. dirs. 1992), Inventors Club (bd. dirs. 1992), KC (chancellor 1992). Address: 1425 Monte Largo Dr NE Albuquerque NM 87112-6378

HADGES, THOMAS RICHARD, media consultant; b. Brockton, Mass., Mar. 13, 1948; s. Samuel Charles and Ethel Toli (Prifti) H.; m. Beth Evelyn Rastad, Oct. 22, 1988. BA in Biology magna cum laude, Tufts U., 1969; student, Harvard Sch. Dental Med., 1969-71. Announcer Sta. WOKW, Brockton, 1965-67, Sta. WTBS-FM, MIT, Cambridge, 1966-68; announcer, program dir. Sta. WTUR, Medford, Mass., 1967-69; announcer Concert Network, Sta. WBCN-FM, Boston, 1968-78, program dir., 1977-78; program dir. Sta. WCOZ-FM, Blair Broadcasting, Boston, 1978-80, Sta. KLOS-FM, ABC, L.A., 1980-85; sr. programming advisor Pollack Media Group, Pacific Palisades, Calif., 1985-89, pres., 1989—; pres. Pollack/Hadges Enterprises, Pacific Palisades, 1985-89. Named Program Dir. of Yr., L.A. Times, 1981. Mem. Phi Beta Kappa. Avocations: jogging, electronics. Office: Pollack Media Group 860 Via De La Paz Ste D2 Pacific Palisades CA 90272-3663

HADLEY, PAUL BURREST, JR. (TABBIT HADLEY), domestic engineer, photographer; b. Louisville, Apr. 26, 1955; s. Paul Burrest and Rose Mary (Ruckert) H. Grad. in Computer Ops. and Programming, No. Ky. Vocat. Sch., 1975. Floor mgr. reconciling dept. Cen. Trust Co., Cin., 1974-76; freelance photographer Ky., Ohio, Colo., 1975—; chef mgr. The Floradora, Telluride, Colo., 1978-96; domestic engr. Telluride Resort Accomodations, 1996—; pres. Tabbit Enterprises; freelance recipe writer, Telluride, 1978—. Author poetry (Golden Poet award 1989, Silver Poet award 1990); actor: (plays) Of Mice and Men, The Exercise, Crawling Arnold, A Thousand Clowns, The Authentic Life of Billy The Kid, others. Actor The Plunge Players, Telluride; v.p. Telluride Coun. for Arts and Humanities, 1989. Mem. Plan Internat. USA, Christian Children's Fund. Avocations: mountain climbing, hiking, photography, travel. Home: PO Box 923 Telluride CO 81435-0923

HADLEY, SUSAN R., accountant; b. Boise, Idaho, Mar. 30, 1969; d. Douglas Gene and Sonja K. (Philliber) H. BA, Boise State U., 1992. CPA. Adminstrv. asst. Boise Printer Divsn. Hewlett Packard, 1988-92; audit assoc. Coopers & Lybrand, 1992-93; asst. contr. St. Mary Lodge & Resort, 1993-94; payroll/benefits mgr. Sun Valley (Idaho) Resort, 1994—. Vol. Idaho Foodbank Warehouse, Idaho Shakespeare Festival, Arts in the Park. Mem. Inst. Mgmt. Accts. (bd. dirs.). Home: 11938 W Silverking Dr Boise ID 83709-2253 Office: Sun Valley Co PO Box 10 Sun Valley ID 83353-0010

HADREAS, PETER JAMES, philosophy educator; b. San Diego, Apr. 22, 1945; s. James D. and Catherine (Mountanos) Hadreas. BA, U. Calif., Berkeley, 1966, MA, 1969, PhD, 1975. Lectr. U. Calif., Berkeley, 1978-86; assoc. prof philosophy San Jose (Calif.) State U., 1986—; actor (stage play) One Flew Over the Cuckoo's Nest, San Francisco, 1970-75; composer, 20th Century Fox, L.A., 1979; assoc. dir. Inst. for Social Responsibility, San Jose, 1993-98. Author: In Place of Flawed Diamond, 1986; contbr. articles to profl. jours.

HAENEL, HAL H., JR., film and TV studio executive; b. St. Louis, Oct. 18, 1958; s. Hal H. and Lietta (Braun) H. BA in Film, Columbia Coll., 1981; DFA (hon.), Piedmont Coll., 1997. Dir. prodn. svcs. Cine-Pro/ Panavision, Hollywood, Calif., 1981-85; v.p., gen. mgr. Hollywood Ctr. Studios, 1985—; formerly Olympic star athlete in yachting. Athlete rep. Athletes Adv. Coun., U.S. Olympic Com., 1996—, team leader U.S. sailing com., 1996—, v.p., 1998—. Recipient Olympic Silver medal, 1988, Olympic Gold medal, 1992; named Male Athlete of Yr. U.S. Olympic Yachting Com., 1989, 92; world champion Internat. Star Class Yacht Racing, Laredo, Spain, 1995. Mem. Internat. Star Class Yacht Racing Assn. (life). Avocations: sailing, photography, automobiles, motorcycles. Office: Hollywood Ctr Studios 1040 N Las Palmas Ave Hollywood CA 90038

HAFEY, EDWARD EARL JOSEPH, precision tool company executive; b. Hartford, Conn., June 7, 1917; s. Joseph Michael and Josephine (Pyne) H.; B.S. in Mech. Engring., Worcester Poly. Inst., 1940; postgrad. Johns Hopkins U., 1943, 44; m. Loyette Lindsey, Oct. 21, 1971; children—Joseph M., Barbara Hafey Beard, Edward F. Instr. dept. mech. enging. Worcester Tech. Inst., 1940-41; mgr. Comfort Air Inc., San Francisco, 1946-47; owner, mgr. Hafey Air Conditioning Co., San Pablo, Calif., 1947—, pres. Hafey Precision Tool, Inc., Laguna Beach, Calif., 1982—; cons. air conditioning U.S. Navy, C.E., Japan, Korea, Okinawa. Served to comdr. USNR, 1941-46. Registered profl. engr., Calif.; named Man of Year, San Pablo, 1962. Mem. Assn. Energy Engrs., Calif. Air Conditioning Service Engring. Soc., Am. Legion, Ret. Officers Assn., Sigma Alpha Epsilon. Republican. Roman

Catholic. Clubs: Exchange of Laguna Beach, Marine's Meml. Office: PO Box 417 Laguna Beach CA 92652-0417

HAFNER-EATON, CHRIS, health services researcher, educator; b. N.Y.C., Dec. 9, 1962; d. Peter Robert and Isabelle (Freda) Hafner; m. James Michael Eaton, Aug. 9, 1986; children: Kelsey James, Tristen Lee, Wesley Sean. BA, U. Calif., San Diego, 1986; MPH, UCLA, 1988, PhD in Health Svcs., 1992. Cert. health edn. specialist; internat. bd. cert. lactation cons. Cons. dental health policy UCLA Schl. Dentistry, 1989; grad. teaching asst. UCLA Sch. Pub. Health, 1987-92; health svcs. researcher UCLA, 1987-92; cons. health policy U.S. Dept. Health & Human Svcs., Washington, 1988—; analyst health policy The RAND/UCLA Ctr. Health Policy Study, Santa Monica & L.A., 1988-94; asst. prof. health care adminstrn. Oreg. State U. Dept. Pub. Health, Corvallis, 1992-95; pres. Health Improvement Svcs. Corp., 1994—; dir. rsch. rev. La Leche League Internat., 1996—; adj. faculty pub. health Linn-Benton Coll., 1995—; bd. dirs. Benton County Pub. Health Bd., Healthy Start Bd.; mem. Linn-Benton Breastfeeding Task Force, Samaritan Mother-Baby Dyad Team., Am. Public Hlth. Assn. (sect. Council Med. Care). Peer reviewer for NIH jours., others; contbr. articles to profl. jours. Rsch. grantee numerous granting bodies, 1988-97. Mem. AAUW, NOW, La Leche League Internat. (area profl. liaison for Oreg.), Am. Pub. Health Assn. (med. care sect. coun., women's caucus), Am. Assn. World Health, Oreg. Pub. Health Assn., Oreg. Health Care Assn., Assn. Health Svcs. Rsch., Soc. Pub. Health Edn., Physicians for Social Responsibility, UCLA Pub. Health Alumni Assn., Pub. Health Honor Soc., Delta Omega. Home: 1807 NW Beca Ave Corvallis OR 97330-2636

HAGA, ENOCH JOHN, computer educator, author; b. L.A., Apr. 25, 1931; s. Enoch and Esther Bouncer (Higginson) H.; student Sacramento Jr. Coll., 1948-49; AA, Grant Tech. Coll., 1950; student U. Colo., Denver, 1950, U. Calif., Berkeley, 1954, Midwestern U., 1950-54; AB, Sacramento State Coll., 1955, MA, 1958; PhD, Calif. Inst. Integral Studies, 1972, diploma tchr. Asian Culture, 1972; m. Elna Jo Wright, Aug. 22, 1957. Tchr. bus. Calif. Med. Facility, Vacaville, 1956-60; asst. prof. bus. Stanislaus State Coll., Turlock, Calif., 1960-61; engring. writer, publs. engr. Hughes Aircraft Co., Fullerton, Calif., 1961-62, Lockheed Missiles & Space Co., Sunnyvale, Calif., 1962, Gen. Precision, Inc., Glendale, Calif., 1962-63; sr. adminstrv. analyst Holmes & Narver, Inc., L.A., 1963-64; tchr., chmn. dept. bus. and math. Pleasanton Unified Dist., Pleasanton, Calif., 1964-92, coordinator computer svcs., adminstrn. and instrn., 1984-85; vis. asst. prof. bus. Sacramento State Coll., 1967-69; instr. bus. and computer sci. Chabot Coll., Hayward, Calif., 1970-89; instr. bus. and philosophy Ohlone Coll., Fremont, Calif., 1972; prof., v.p., mem. bd. govs. Calif. Inst. Asian Studies, 1972-75; pres., prof. Pacific Inst. East-West Studies, San Francisco, 1975-76, also mem. bd. govs.; dir. Certification Councils, Livermore, Calif., 1975-80; mem., chmn. negotiating team Amador Valley Secondary Educators Assn., Pleasanton, Calif., 1976-77, pres., 1984-85. With USAF, 1949-52, with USNR, 1947-49, 53-57. Mem. Internat. Assn. for Computer Information Systems (exec. dir. 1970-74). Coordinating editor Total Systems, 1962; editor Automation Educator, 1965-67, Automated Educational Systems, 1967, Data Processing for Education, 1970-71, Computer Techniques in Biomedicine and Medicine, 1973; contbg. editor Jour. Bus. Edn., 1961-69, Data Processing mag., 1967-70; author and compiler: Understanding Automation, 1965; author: Simplified Computer Arithmetic, Simplified Computer Logic, Simplified Computer Input, Simplified Computer Flowcharting, 1971-72, Before the Apple Drops, 15 Essays on Dinosaur Education 2nd edition, 1997, Exploring Prime Numbers on Your PC 2nd edition, 1997, TAROsolution, A Complete Guide to Interpreting the Tarot, 1994, The 2000-Year History of the Haga-Helgøy and Krick-Keller Families, Ancestors and Descendants, 1994; editor Data Processor, 1960-62, Automedica, 1970-76, FBE Bull., 1967-68. Home: 983 Venus Way Livermore CA 94550-6345

HAGAN, ALFRED CHRIS, federal judge; b. Moscow, Idaho, Jan. 27, 1932; s. Alfred Elias and Irene Lydia (Wells) H.; m. Doreen M. Auve, July 10, 1953; children: Chris E., Martha Ann, Peter M. BA, U. Idaho, 1953, JD, 1958. Bar: Idaho 1958, U.S. Dist. Ct. Idaho 1958. Asst. atty. gen. State of Idaho, Boise, 1958, dist. judge, 1967-77; dep. pros. atty. Ada County, Boise, 1959; pvt. practice Boise, 1960-67, 77-84; U.S. bankruptcy judge Dist. of Idaho, Boise, 1985—. 1st lt. USAF, 1953-55. Mem. Nat. Conf. Bankruptcy Judges. Office: MSC 040 550 W Fort St Boise ID 83724-0101

HAGELSTEIN, WILLIAM C., executive. Exec. v.p. Rubin Postaer & Assocs., Santa Monica, Calif. Office: Rubin Postaer & Assocs 1333 2d St Santa Monica CA 90401

HAGEN, DAVID WARNER, judge; b. 1931. BBA, U. Wis., 1956; LLB, U. San Francisco, 1959. Bar: Washoe County 1981, Nev. 1992. With Berkley, Randall & Harvey, Berkeley, Calif., 1960-62; pvt. practice Loyalton, Calif., 1962-63; with Guild, Busey & Guild (later Guild, Hagen and Clark Ltd. and Guild & Hagen Ltd.), Reno, 1963-93; judge U.S. Dist. Ct. Nev., Reno, 1993—, chmn. 9th Cir. Art. III, judge edn. com., 1998—; lectr U. Nev., 1968-72; acting dean Nev. Sch. of Law, 1981-83, adj. prof., 1981-87; mem. Nev. Bd. Bar Examiners, 1972-91, chmn., 1989-91; chmn. Nev. Continuing Legal Edn. Com., 1967-75; mem. Nev. Uniform Comml. Code Com. S/sgt. USAF, 1949-52. Fellow Am. Coll. Trial Lawyers (state chmn. 1983-85); mem. VFW, Nev. Bar Assn., Calif. Bar Assn., Washoe County Bar Assn., Am. Bd. Trial Advocates (advocate), Nat. Maritime Hist. Soc., U.S. Sailing Assn. Office: US Dist Ct Fed Bldg & US Courthouse 400 S Virginia St Reno NV 89501-2193

HAGEN, LARRY WILLIAM, manufacturing and retail executive; b. Pyote, Tex., May 5, 1945; s. Lawrence Herbert and Marjorie Fern (MacFarland) H.; m. Lynda Barbara Rogers; children: Bret William, Adam Richard. AA, Highline Coll., 1965; BS cum laude, Seattle U., 1969; MBA, Pacific Luth. U., 1987. Dir. ops. group III The Bon Marche, Seattle, 1967-75; dir. distbn. Brittania Sportswear, Seattle, 1975-77; exec. v.p., chief oper. officer, chief fin. officer, ptnr. Mallory & Church Corp., Seattle, 1977—, also bd. dirs., 1984—; bd. dirs. Mallory & Church Ltd., London, 1985—; cons. Jeans Warehouse, Seattle, 1979-81. Loaned exec. United Way, Seattle, 1966-69; collector YMCA Disadvantaged Youth, Seattle, 1983-86. Served with USNG, 1964-74. Mem. Am. Prodn. Inventory Control Soc., Pacific NW Personnel Mgmt. Assn., Am. Soc. Personnel Adminstrn. (v.p. Seattle chpt. 1970-71, pres. Columbian Basin 1981-82). Democrat. Lutheran. Avocations: golf, fishing, music. Home: 5731 111th Ave SE Bellevue WA 98006-2609 Office: Mallory & Church Corp 676 S Industrial Way Seattle WA 98108-5236

HAGENBUCH, JOHN JACOB, investment banker; b. Park Forest, Ill., May 31, 1951; s. David Brown and Jean Iline (Reeves) H.; m. Christy Ann Nichols; children: Henry, Hunter, Hilary, Hunter Scott, Will. AB magna cum laude, Princeton U., 1974; MBA, Stanford U., 1978. Assoc., Salomon Bros., N.Y.C., 1978-80, v.p., San Francisco, 1980-85; gen. ptnr. Hellman & Friedman, 1985-93; owner, John J. Hagenbuch & Co., San Francisco, 1993—; gen. ptnr. M&H Realty Ptnrs., L.P., 1993—. Bd. govs. Town Sch. for Boys. Mem. Burlingame Country Club, Pacific-Union Club, Calif. Tennis Club, Villa Taverna Club, Menlo Circus Club, Bohemian Club, Valley Club. Office: M&H Realty Ptnrs 353 Sacramento St Fl 21 San Francisco CA 94111-3620

HAGENBUCH, RODNEY DALE, stock brokerage house executive; b. Saxville, Wis.; s. Herbert Jenkin and Minnie Leona (Hayward) Hagenbuch; children: Kris, Beth, Patricia; m. LaVerne Julia Scoonover, Sept. 1, 1956. BS, Mich. State U., 1980. Cert. fin. mgr. Designer Olds div. Gen. Motors, Lansing, Mich., 1960-66; institutional account exec. Merrill Lynch, Lansing, 1966-75, institutional mgr., 1975-80; sales mgr. Merrill Lynch, Columbus, Ohio, 1980-82; sr. resident v.p. Merrill Lynch, Tacoma, 1982-93, L.A., 1993-98; ret., 1998; Bd. dirs. Merrill Lynch Trust Co. Mem. adv. bd. L.A. Bus. Jour. Bd. dirs. Tacoma Club, 1989-93, treas. 1990, pres. 1993, L.A. Acad. Finance, 1993-98, L.A. United Cerebral Palsey, 1994—; adv. bd. Charles Wright, 1989-93; bd. dirs. L.A. Red Cross, 1996—; mem. econ. devel. bd. City of Tacoma, 1986-93, chmn. 1987-88; pres. Downtown Tacoma Assn., 1986; chmn. Corp. Coun. for the Arts, 1986, L.A. United Way, 1993—; pres. Tacoma Symphony, 1988; chmn. Human Resources Commn., Meridian Twp., 1972-74, Meridian Planning Commn., Lansing, 1964-70, Meridian Police and Fire Com., Lansing, 1964-70; pres. adv. bd. U. Wash., Tacoma, chmn. 1992; mem. State Wash. Arts Stabilization Bd., Tacoma Art Mus. Bd., sec. 1992; legis. chmn. N.W. Securities Industry Assn.; campaign chmn. Pierce County United Way Bd., 1991-92; non-resident dir. Tacoma Art Mus., 1994—, Tacoma Urban League, 1983-93; bd. mem. New L.A. Mktg. Plan; bd. mem., dist. 2 com. NASD; bd. mem. L.A. Red Cross, 1997—; mem. bd. govs. L.A. Town Hall, 1996; mem. fraternity of friends L.A. Music Ctr. Recipient Outstanding Citizen award Mcpl. League Pierce County, 1988; named Nat. Vol. of Yr., Urban League Western Divsn., 1987. Mem. Tacoma C. of C. (bd. dirs.), Forward Washington (bd. dirs.), L.A. Children's Hosp. Rsch. Inst. (bd. govs. 1994—). Avocations: running, skiing. Home: 16826 Monte Hermoso Dr Pacific Palisades CA 90272-1910

HAGENS, WILLIAM JOSEPH, state official, public health educator; b. Bay City, Mich., June 3, 1942; s. Francis Bernard and Lillian May (O'Neill) H.; m. Noel Scantlebury, Apr. 15, 1967; children: Clara O'Neill, Nicholas Barlow. BA, Saginaw Valley Coll., 1969; MA, Wayne State U., 1971. Mem. adj. faculty Wayne State U., Detroit, 1971; VISTA vol. Pierce County Legal Assistance, Tacoma, 1971-73; sr. policy analyst Wash. Ho. of Reps., Olympia, 1974—; instr. Pacific Luth. U., Tacoma, 1979-81; clin. prof. Sch. Pub. Health U. Wash., Seattle, 1984—, mem. vis. com. Sch. Nursing, 1993; mem. health policy project George Washington U., Washington, 1985—; bd. dirs. Area Health Edn. Ctr., Seattle, 1988-90; mem. Nat. Acad. State Health Policy, 1990—; mem. adv. com. Wast. State Ctr. Health Stats.; mem. Nat. Conf. State Legislatures' Forum for Health Policy Leadership. Contbg. author: Analyzing Poverty Policy, 1975. Participant AIDS symposium Pasteur Inst., Paris, 1987; mem. North End Neighborhood Coun., Tacoma. Recipient Pres. award Wash. State Pub. Health Assn., 1986, Animal award Wash. State Pub. Health Assn., 1994; NIMH fellow, 1979, WHO internat. travel fellow, 1992. Mem. Am. Pub. Health Assn., Am. Polit. Sci. Assn., Policy Studies Orgn., English Speaking Union, World Affairs Coun., Pi Sigma Alpha. Avocations: opera, classical music, history, birdwatching, paintings and engravings. Home: 3214 N 27th St Tacoma WA 98407-6208 Office: Wash State Ho of Reps PO Box 40600 Olympia WA 98504-0600

HAGENSTEIN, WILLIAM DAVID, forester, consultant; b. Seattle, Mar. 8, 1915; s. Charles William and Janet (Finigan) H.; m. Ruth Helen Johnson, Sept. 2, 1940 (dec. 1979); m. Jean Kraemer Edson, June 16, 1980. BS in Forestry, U. Wash., 1938; MForestry, Duke, 1941. Registered profl. engr., Wash., Oreg. Field aid in entomology U.S. Dept. Agr., Hat Creek, Calif., 1938; logging supt. and engr. Eagle Logging Co., Sedro-Woolley, Wash., 1939; tech. foreman U.S. Forest Svc., North Bend, Wash., 1940; forester West Coast Lumbermen's Assn., Seattle and Portland, Oreg., 1941-43, 45-49; sr. forester FEA, South and Central Pacific Theaters of War and Costa Rica, 1943-45; mgr. Indsl. Forestry Assn., Portland, 1949-80; exec. v.p. Indsl. Forestry Assn., 1956-80, hon. dir., 1980-87; pres. W.D. Hagenstein and Assocs., Inc., Portland, 1980—; H.R. MacMillan lectr. forestry U. B.C., 1952, 77; Benson Meml. lectr. U. Mo., 1966; S.J. Hall lectr. indsl. forestry U. Calif. at Berkeley, 1973; cons. forest engr. USN, Philippines, 1952, Coop. Housing Found., Belize, 1986; mem. U.S. Forest Products Trade Mission, Japan, 1968; del. VII World Forestry Congress, Argentina, 1972, VIII Congress, Indonesia, 1978; mem. U.S. Forestry Study Team, West Germany, 1974; mem. sec. Interior's Oreg. and Calif. Multiple Use Adv. Bd., 1975-76; trustee Wash. State Forestry Conf., 1948-92, Keep Oreg. Green Assn., 1957—, v.p., 1970-71, pres., 1972-73; adv. trustee Keep Wash. Green Assn., 1957-95; co-founder, dir. World Forestry Ctr., 1965-89, v.p., 1965-79; hon. Dir. for Life, 1990. Author: (with Wackerman and Michell) Harvesting Timber Crops, 1966; Assoc. editor: Jour. Forestry, 1946-53; columnist Wood Rev., 1978-82; contbr. numerous articles to profl. jours. Trustee Oreg. Mus. Sci. and Industry, 1968-73. Served with USNR, 1933-37. Recipient Hon. Alumnus award U. Wash. Foresters Alumni Assn., 1965, Forest Mgmt. award Nat. Forest Products Assn., 1968, Western Forestry award Western Forestry and Conservation Assn., 1972, 79, Gifford Pinchot medal for 50 yrs. Outstanding Svc., Soc. Am. Foresters, 1987, Charles W. Ralston award Duke Sch. Forestry, 1988, Lifetime Achievement award Oreg. Soc. Am. Foresters, 1995. Fellow Soc. Am. Foresters (mem. coun. 1958-63, pres. 1966-69, Golden Membership award 1989); mem. Am. Forestry Assn. (life, hon. v.p. 1966-69, 74-92, William B. Greeley Forestry award 1990), Commonwealth Forestry Assn. (life), Internat. Soc. Tropical Foresters, Portland C. of C. (forestry com. 1949-79, chmn. 1960-62), Nat. Forest Products Assn. (forestry adv. com. 1949-80, chmn. 1972-74, 78-80), West Coast Lumbermen's Assn. (v.p. 1969-79), David Douglas Soc. Western N. Am., Lang Syne Soc., Hoo Hoo Club, Xi Sigma Pi (outstanding alumnus Alpha chpt. 1973). Republican. Home: 3062 SW Fairmount Blvd Portland OR 97201-1439 Office: 921 SW Washington St Ste 803 Portland OR 97205-2826

HAGGARD, JOEL EDWARD, lawyer; b. Portland, Oreg., Oct. 10, 1939; s. Henry Edward and Kathryn Shirley (O'Leary) H.; m. Mary Katherine Daley, June 8, 1968; children: Kevin E., Maureen E., Cristin E. BSME, U. Notre Dame, 1961; M in Nuclear Engring., U. Okla., 1963; JD, U. Wash., 1971. Bar: Wash. 1971, U.S. Dist. Ct. (we. dist.) Wash. 1971, U.S. Ct. Appeals (9th cir.) 1971, U.S. Supreme Ct. 1971. Nuclear engr. Westinghouse Corp. Bettis Atomic Power Lab., Pitts., 1963-67; research engr. aerospace div. The Boeing Co., Seattle, 1968; engr., mgmt. cons. King County Dept. Pub. Works, Seattle, 1969-71; assoc. Houghton, Cluck, Coughlin & Riley, Seattle, 1971-74, ptnr., 1975-76; pvt. practice law Seattle, 1977, 85—; ptnr. Haggard, Tousley & Brain, Seattle, 1978-84; judge marriage tribunal, Archdiocese of Seattle, 1975-90; chmn. Columbia River Interstate Compact Commn., 1975—; arbitrator King County Superior Ct., 1986—. Contbr. articles to profl. jours. Past trustee, mem. exec. com., past sec. Seattle Symphony. Mem. ABA, Wash. Bar Assn. (past chmn. environ. law sect., fee arbitration com., past mem. rules of profl. conduct com.), Seattle-King County Bar Assn., Rainier Club, Wash. Athletic Club, Astoria Golf and Country Club, Magnolia Cmty. Club (past pres., bd. dirs.). Office: 1200 5th Ave #1200 Seattle WA 98101-1127

HAGIWARA-NAGATA, ERIK SUMIHARU, landscape consultant and designer; b. Seattle, Feb. 23, 1958; s. Frederick S. and Frances K. (Yamashita) Nagata. AA in Gen. Edn., City Coll., San Francisco, 1985; BA in Landscape Architecture, U. Calif., Berkeley, 1988. Gardener San Francisco, 1983-88; pvt. practice Concord, Calif., 1988—; chmn. bamboo dept. Strybing Arboretum and Botanical Gardens, (former chmn. horticulture display com., former docent). Donated 1,000 flowering cherry trees to Arlington Nat. Cemetery for centennial aniv. Japanese Tea Garden, 1994. Mem. Constractor's State Lic. Bd. Calif. E-mail: www.HaNaSCAPE.com.

HAGMEIER, CLARENCE HOWARD, retired anesthesiologist; b. Pitts., Dec. 23, 1914; s. Clarence Howard and Bertha May (Rogers) H.; m. Hilda Marie Bronder, Oct. 30, 1942; children: Clarence, Roberta, Susan, David, Michael. BS with honors, U. Pitts., 1943, MD, 1950. Diplomate Am. Bd. Anesthesiology; Oreg. State Bd. Med. Examiners. Intern Good Samaritan Hosp., Portland, Oreg., 1950-51; resident Oreg. Med. Sch. and Hosp., 1951-53; pvt. practice Portland, 1953-87; ret., 1987. Chmn. Multnomah County Rep. Com., 1980-82; pres. Portland Ronald McDonald House, 1991-93; mem. internat. adv. bd. Ronald McDonald House, 1993-95; mem. exec. com. Oreg. Presch. Immunization Consortium 1992—; sr. role model OASIS, 1993; Vols. of Am. Allstar, 1996. With USN, World War II. Fellow Am. Coll. Anesthesiologists, Internat. Coll. Surgeons; mem. Oreg. Med. Assn. (pres. 1976-77), Multnomah County Med. Soc. (pres. 1974), Rotary (pres. Portland club 1979-80, dist. gov. 1983-84, nat. coord. PolioPlus, 1986-88, mem. exec. com. Nat. PolioPlus Immunization Task Force 1992-94, Found. citation for meritorious svc. 1991, Svc. Above Self award 1993, Found. Disting. Svc. award 1995, del. to Coun. on Legis. 1995, 98), PolioPlus Partners Com., Theta Chi, Chi Rho Nu, Phi Rho Sigma. Republican. Avocation: gardening. Home: 4907 SW Canterbury Ln Portland OR 97219-3326

HAGNER, JOHN GILBERT, artist; b. Balt., Dec. 6, 1927; s. Frank Raymond Hagner and Mary Veronica Cochran; m. Eleanor Mae Alther (div. 1980); m. Dorothy Rose Holyoak; children: Don Carter, Desiree Clarice, Doricca Lyn Brewer. Student, Md. Inst. Art, 1949-50. Comml. artist Balt. Sunpapers, 1950-55; freelance artist Harrison-Landauer Art Studio, 1956; artist Mowinckle Art Studio, Moab, Utah, 1973; stuntman, 1960—; founder Hollywood Stuntmen's Hall of Fame, Moab, Utah, 1973; mem. Antarctic expedition to South Pole with Rear Admiral Richard E. Byrd, 1946-47. With U.S. Navy, 1945-47. Mem. Screen Actors Guild. Home: Hollywood Stuntmens Hall of Fame 81 W Kane Creek Blvd # 12 Moab UT 84532

HAHN, BETTY, artist, photographer, educator; b. Chgo., Oct. 11, 1940; d. Eugene Joseph and Esther Josephine (Krueger) H.; widowed. A.B., Ind. U., 1963, M.F.A., 1966. Asst. prof. photography Rochester (N.Y.) Inst. Tech., 1969-75; prof. art U. N.Mex., Albuquerque, 1976-97, prof. emeritus, 1997—. One-woman shows include Smithsonian Instn., Washington, 1969, Ctr. Photographic Studies, Louisville, 1971, Focus Gallery, San Francisco, 1974, Sandstone Gallery, Rochester, N.Y., 1978, Blue Sky Gallery, Portland, Oreg., 1978, Susan Spiritus Gallery, Newport Beach, Calif., 1977, 82, Witkin Gallery, N.Y.C., 1973, 79, Washington Project for the Arts, 1980, Ctr. Creative Photography, Tucson, 1981, Columbia Coll. Gallery, Chgo., 1982, Port Washington Pub. Library, N.Y., 1984, Mus. Fine Arts, Mus. N.Mex, Santa Fe, 1986, Lehigh U., 1988, U. Mass., Amherst, 1989, Andrew Smith Gallery, Santa Fe, 1991, U. N.Mex. Art Mus., Albuquerque, 1994. Named Honored Educator, Soc. for Photog. Edn., 1984; Nat. Endowment Arts grantee, 1977-78, 82-83; N.Y. State Council Arts grantee, 1976. Mem. Soc. Photog. Edn., Coll. Art Assn., Evidence Photographers Internat. Council. Office: Univ N Mex Art Dept Albuquerque NM 87131

HAHN, ELLIOTT JULIUS, lawyer; b. San Francisco, Dec. 9, 1949; s. Leo Wolf and Sherry Marion (Portnoy) H; m. Toby Rose Mallen; children: Kara Rebecca, Brittany Atira Mallen, Michael Mallen, Adam Mallen. BA cum laude, U. Pa., 1971, JD, 1974; LLM, Columbia U., 1980. Bar: N.J. 1974, Calif. 1976, D.C. 1978, U.S. Dist. Ct. N.J. 1974, U.S. Dist. Ct. (cen. dist.) Calif. 1976, U.S. Supreme Ct. 1980. Assoc. von Maltitz, Derenberg, Kunin & Janssen, N.Y.C., 1974-75; law clk. L.A. County Superior Ct., 1975-76; atty. Atlantic Richfield Co., L.A., 1976-79; prof. Summer in Tokyo program Santa Clara Law Sch., 1981-83; assoc. prof. law Calif. Western Sch. Law, San Diego, 1980-85; atty. Morgan, Lewis & Bockius, L.A., 1985-87; assoc. Whitman & Ransom, L.A., 1987-88, ptnr., 1989-93; ptnr. Sonnenschein Nath & Rosenthal, L.A., 1993-97; ptnr. Hahn, Bolson & Mendelson LLP, 1997—; vis. scholar Nihon U., Tokyo, 1982; vis. lectr. Internat. Christian U., Tokyo, 1982; adj. prof. law Southwestern U. Sch. Law, 1986—, Pepperdine U. Law Sch., 1986—, U. So. Calif. Law Sch., 1997—; lectr. U. Calif., Davis, Law Sch. Orientation in U.S.A. Law Program, 1994-97. Author: Japanese Business Law and the Legal System, 1984; contbr. chpt. on Japan to The World Legal Ency.; internat. law editor Calif. Bus. Law Reporter. Vice-chmn. San Diego Internat. Affairs Bd., 1981-85; bd. dirs. San Diego-Yokohama Sister City Soc., 1982-85, L.A.-Nagoya Sister City Soc., 1986—; mem. master planning com. City of Rancho Palos Verdes, Calif., 1989-91; advisor, exec. com. Calif. Internat. Law Sect., 1990-91, 95, appointee exec. com., 1991-94, vice-chmn., 1992-93, chair, 1993-94; appointee, trustee Palos Verdes Libr. Dist., 1993-94; bd. dirs. Internat. Student Ctr. UCLA. Mem. ABA, State Bar of Calif., L.A. County Bar Assn. (bd. dirs. internat. sect., exec. com. Internat. Legal Sec. 1987—, sec. 1995-96, 2d v.p. 1996-97, 1st v.p., 1997-98, chmn. 1998—, appointee pacific rim com. 1990—, chmn. 1991-92, 95-98, trustee 1997-98), Assn. Asian Studies, U. Pa. Alumni Club (pres. San Diego chpt. 1982, pres. coun. Phila., 1983), Anti-Defamation League, Japanese-Am. Soc. Legal Studies (book rev. editor Seattle 1983-85). Jewish. Office: Hahn & Bolson LLP 601 S Figueroa St Ste 3700 Los Angeles CA 90017-5742

HAHN, HAROLD THOMAS, physical chemist, chemical engineer; b. N.Y.C., May 31, 1924; s. Gustave Hahn and Lillie Martha (Thomas) H.; m. Bennie Joyce Turney, Sept. 5, 1948; children: Anita Karen, Beverly Sharon, Carol Linda, Harold Thomas Jr. Student, Hofstra U., 1941-43; BSChemE, Columbia U., 1943-44; PhD in Chemistry, U. Tex., 1950-53. Chem. engr. Manhattan Dist. U.S. Army, Los Alamos, N.Mex., 1945-47; chem. engr. U. Calif., Los Alamos, 1947-50; sr. scientist Gen. Electric Co., Hanford, Wash., 1953-58; sect. chief, chem. research dept. Phillips Petroleum Co., Idaho Falls, Idaho, 1958-64; sr. staff scientist Lockheed Missiles & Space Co., Palo Alto, Calif., 1964-92; private cons., 1992—. Contbr. articles to profl. jours.; patentee in field. Pres. Edgemont Gardens PTA, Idaho Falls, 1963-64; commr. cub scout div. Stanford area council Boy Scouts Am., Palo Alto, 1973-76, also cubmaster pack 36, 1973-80, chmn. troops 36 and 37, 1975-77; mem. adminstrv. bd. Los Altos Meth. Ch. Served to col. U.S. Army, 1944-46, with res., 1946-84, col. res. ret. Humble Oil Co. fellow, 1952, Naval Bur. Ordnance fellow, 1953. Fellow Am. Inst. Chemists; mem. AIAA, Magnetics Soc. IEEE (elected sr. mem.), Calif. Acad. Scis., Internat. Platform Assn., Am. Chem. Soc., Sigma Xi, Phi Lambda Upsilon, Kappa Rho. Home and Office: 661 Teresi Ln Los Altos CA 94024-4162

HAHN, JENNIFER LYNN, accountant; b. Dover, Del., Dec. 29, 1972; d. Dennis Calvin and Sandra Faith (Skinner) H. BS in Acctg., Elizabethtown (Pa.) Coll., 1994. CPA, Calif. Assoc. Pricewaterhouse Coopers LLP, Harrisburg, Pa., 1994-96; sr. assoc. Pricewaterhouse Coopers LLP, San Francisco, 1996—. Mem. AICPA, Calif. Soc. CPAs, Elizabethtown Coll. Alumni Assn. Democrat. Christian Scientist. Avocations: skiing, roller-blading, travelling. Home: 2224A Rivera St San Francisco CA 94116-1631

HAHN, JOAN CHRISTENSEN, retired drama educator, travel agent; b. Kemmerer, Wyo., May 9, 1933; d. Roy and Bernice (Pringle) Wainwright; m. Milton Angus Christensen, Dec. 29, 1952 (div. Oct. 1, 1971); children: Randall M., Carla J. Christensen Teasdale; m. Charles Henry Hahn, Nov. 15, 1972. BS, Brigham Young U., 1965. Profl. ballroom dancer, 1951-59; travel dir. E.T. World Travel, Salt Lake City, 1969—; tchr. drama Payson High Sch., Utah, 1965-71, Cottonwood High Sch., Salt Lake City, 1971-95; retired, 1995; dir. Performing European Tours, Salt Lake City, 1969-76; dir. Broadway theater tours, 1976—. Bd. dirs. Salem City Salem Days, Utah, 1965-75; regional dir. dance Latter-day Saints Ch., 1954-72. Named Best Dir. High Sch. Musicals, Green Sheet Newspapers, 1977, 82, 84, 90, Utah's Speech Educator of Yr., 1990, 91, named to Nat. Hall of Fame Ednl. Theatre Assn., 1991; recipient 1st place award Utah State Drama Tournament, 1974, 77, 78, 89, 90, 91, 94, 95, Tchr. of Yr. award Cottonwood High Sch., 1989-90, Limelight award, 1982, Exemplary Performance in teaching theater arts Granite Sch. Dist., Salt Lake City, 1982; named to Nat. Hall of Fame, Ednl. Theatre Assn., 1991, Cottonwood H.S. Hall of Fame, 1995; Joan C. Hahn Theatre named in her honor Cottonwood H.S., 1997; named Outstanding Educator, Utah Ho. Reps., 1995. Mem. Internat. Thespian Soc. (sponsor 1968—, internat. dir. 1982-84, trustee 1978-84), Utah Speech Arts Assn. (pres. 1976-78, 88-90), NEA, Utah Edn. Assn., Granite Edn. Assn., Profl. Travel Agts. Assn., Utah High Sch. Activities Assn. (drama rep. 1972-76), AAUW (pres. 1972-74). Republican. Mormon. Avocations: reading; travel; dancing. Home: PO Box 36 Salem UT 84653-0036

HAHN, WOODY, sports association executive. Grad., Wash. State U. Athletic dir. Ea. Mont. Coll., until 1987; commr. Great Northwest Conf., 1988—, Continental Divide Conf., 1989—, Pacific West Conf., Billings, Mont.; active NCAA West Region Men's Basketball Adv. Com. Mem. Nat. Assn. Collegiate Dirs. Athletics, Volleyball Coaches' Assn., Basketball Coaches' Assn., NCAA Divsn. II Commrs. Assn. Office: Pacific West Conf PO Box 2002 Billings MT 59103-2002

HAHNER, LINDA R. R., artist, creative director; b. Healdsburg, Calif., Dec. 4, 1952; d. Ellison and Joan (Prenderville) Ruffner; m. Thomas G. Russell, Dec. 23, 1971 (div.); 1 child, Thomas Kristian Russell, 1 foster child, Eric J. Miklas; m. Wolfgang Andreas Hahner, Dec. 21, 1989. BA Fine Art/Creative Writing with honors, Principia Coll., Elsah, Ill., 1980; MFA, Washington U., St. Louis, 1986; student, Skowhegan Sch. Painting/Sculp., 1985, Acad. Fine Art, Helsinki, 1987. Painter, prof., artist London, Helsinki, Freiburg, 1986-95; pres., founder Out of the Blue Design Ltd., San Francisco, 1995—. One-person shows include The Am. Ctr., Helsinki, 1986, Helsinki Art Hall, 1987, Millikin Gallery, Decatur, Ill., 1988, Hagelstam Gallery, Helsinki, 1990, Zimmerman Gallery, Breisach, Germany, 1994; exhibited in group shows Steinberg Gallery, St. Louis, 1986, B Z Wagman Gallery, St. Louis, 1988, Rislakki Collection, Helsinki, 1991; represented in permanent collections Boatman's Bank, 1st Nat. Bank of Columbia, Finland/U.S. Ednl. Exch. Commn., Trade-off OY, KOP Bank Finland, Veikko Savolainen, Arja and Kari Antilla. Fulbright fellow and travel grantee, 1986; Skowhegan award and grantee, 1985. Mem. Women in Multimedia, Multimedia Devel. Group., ACM & Siggraph. Office: Out of the Blue Design Ltd 601 4th St Ste 212 San Francisco CA 94107-1641

HAIGHT, WARREN GAZZAM, investor; b. Seattle, Sept. 7, 1929; s. Gilbert Pierce and Ruth (Gazzam) H.; m. Suzanne H., Sept. 1, 1951; children—Paula Lea, Ian Pierce; m. Ottina Mehau, June 25, 1985. A.B. in Econs, Stanford U., 1951. Asst. Treas. Hawaiian Pineapple Co., Honolulu,

1955-64; v.p., treas. Oceanic Properties, Inc., Honolulu, 1964-67; pres., dir. Oceanic Properties, Inc., 1967-85, chmn., 1983-85; pres. Hawaii, Castle & Cooke Inc., 1983-85, Warren G. Haight & Assocs., 1985—; chmn. Molokai Ranch, Ltd., 1996—; bd. dirs. Round Hill Enterprises, Inc., Las Positas Land Co., Inc., Baldwin Pacific Properties, Inc., Hawaii Project Mgmt., Inc., Transamerica Realty Advisors, Inc., Queen Emma Corp., Queens Devel. Corp., Dole Corp., Standard Fruit and Steaship Co., Inc., Bumble Bee Seafoods, Inc. Bd. dirs. Downtown Improvement Assn., Oahu Devel. Conf., Hawaii Island Econ. Devel. Bd., Econ. Devel. Corp. Honolulu, Intellect, Inc., Hawaii Resort Developers Conf., Homeless Solutions, Inc., Mutual Housing of Hawaii, Inc.; mem. Transit Coalition, Honolulu, Govs. Com. on Econ. Futures; pres., bd. dirs. Land Use Rsch. Found. of Hawaii, Pacific Found. for Cancer Rsch., Hawaii Nature Ctr.; mem. policy adv. bd. for elderly affairs State of Hawaii. Lt. USNR, 1951-55. Mem. Housing Coalition, Calif. Coastal Council. Clubs: Outrigger Canoe, Round Hill Country, Plaza, Pacific. Home: 319 Lala Pl Kailua HI 96734-3224 Office: 220 S King St Ste 1465 Honolulu HI 96813-4542

HAILE, LAWRENCE BARCLAY, lawyer; b. Atlanta, Feb. 19, 1938; children: Gretchen Vanderhoof, Eric McKenzie (dec.), Scott McAllister, m. Carole Chimko, Dec.1, 1998. BA in Econs, U. Tex., 1958, LLB, 1961. Bar: Tex. 1961, Calif. 1962. Law clk. to U.S. Judge Joseph M. Ingraham, Houston, 1961-62; pvt. practice law San Francisco, 1962-67, L.A., 1967—; instr. UCLA Civil Trial Clinics, 1974, 76; lectr. law Calif. Continuing Edn. of Bar, 1973-74, 80-89; mem. nat. panel arbitrators Am. Arbitration Assn., 1965—. Assoc. editor: Tex. Law Rev, 1960-61; Contbr. articles profl. publs. Mem. State Bar Calif., Tex., U.S. Supreme Ct. Bar Assn., Internat. Assn. Property Ins. Counsel (founding mem., pres. 1980), Vintage Auto Racing Assn. (bd. dirs.), Vintage Motorsports Coun. (pres.), Phi Delta Phi, Delta Sigma Rho. Office: 9925 Lancer Ct Beverly Hills CA 90210-1419

HAILE, MARCUS ALFRED, retired chemistry educator; b. Haviland, Kans., Oct. 14, 1930; s. William Oral and Myrna May (Stotts) H.; m. Lynne Helene Hunsucker, Mar. 20, 1964; children: Marta Helene, Cavan William. BS, Pepperdine U., 1955; Master, U. No. Iowa, 1968. Cert. secondary tchr., Calif. Tchr. chemistry Hamilton High Sch., L.A., 1957-67; prof. chemistry L.A. City Coll., 1969-94, also pres. acad. senate, 1972-73. Author: Experimental General Chemistry, 1973, 76, Gen. Analytical Chemistry, 1987; contbr. articles to profl. jours. Chmn. Amateur Athletic Union So. Calif. Swimming U.S. Swim, Los Angeles, Ventura and Santa Barbara Counties, Calif., 1980-81. Served with U.S. Army, 1950-52. NSF grantee, 1967-68. Mem. Am. Chem. Soc., Am. Fedn. Tchrs., Thoroughbred Owners Calif. Democrat. Avocations: race horse owner, skiing, fishing. Home: PO Box 3295 Wrightwood CA 92397-3295

HAINING, JEANE, psychologist; b. Camden, N.J., May 2, 1952; d. Lester Edward and Adina (Rahn) H. BA in Psychology, Calif. State U., 1975; MA in Sch. Psychology, Pepperdine U., 1979; MS in Recreation Therapy, Calif. State U., 1982; PhD in Psychology, Calif. Sch. Profl. Psychology, 1985. Lic. clin. psychologist 1987, lic. ednl. psychologist 1982. Crisis counselor Calif. State U., Northridge, 1973-74; recreation therapist fieldwork Camarillo (Calif.) State Hosp.-Adolescent/Children's Units, 1974; Intern recreation therapist UCLA Neuropsychiatric Inst., L.A., 1975-76; substitute tchr./recreation therapist New Horizons Sch. for Mentally Retarded, Sepulveda, Calif., 1976-79; sch. psychologist Rialto (Calif.) Unified Sch. Dist., 1979-82; clin. psychologist field work San Joaquin County Dept. Mental Health, Stockton, Calif., 1982-83; intern clinical psychologist Fuller Theol. Sem. Psychology Ctr., Pasadena, Calif., 1984-85; clin. psychologist U.S. Dept. Justice, Terminal Island, Calif., 1985-86; cmty. mental health psychologist L.A. County Dept. Mental Health, 1987-89; clin. psychologist Calif. Dept. Corrections, Parole Outpatient Clinic, L.A., 1990—, Mary Magdeline Project, Commerce, Calif., 1992—; mem. psychiat.-psychol. panel adult and juvenile Superior Ct., L.A., 1992—; mem. psychiat. panel U.S. Dist. Ct. (cen. dist.) Calif., L.A., 1989—; clin. psychologist O. Carl Simonton Cancer Ctr., Pacific Palisades, Calif., 1993—. Adv. bd. Camarillo (Calif.) State Hosp., 1994-97, vice-chmn. adv. bd., 1996-97; examiner Lic. Ednl. Psychologist Oral Examinations, Calif. Bd. Behavioral Sci. Examinations, Sacramento, 1985. Recipient award Outstanding Achievement Western Psychology Conf., Calif., 1974. Mem. APA, Forensic Mental Health Assn. (con. planning com. 1993). Democrat. Lutheran. Avocations: rock climbing, skiing, skating, tennis, piano.

HAIR, KITTIE ELLEN, secondary educator; b. Denver, June 12, 1948; d. William Edward and Jacqueline Jean (Holt) H. BA, Brigham Young U., 1971; MA in Social History, U. Nev., Las Vegas, 1987, cert. paralegal, 1995. cert. tchr., Nev. Health educator Peace Corps, Totota, Liberia, 1971-72; tchr. Clark County Sch. Dist., Las Vegas, Nev., 1972-77, 1979—; chair dept. social studies Clark County Sch. Dist., Las Vegas, 1993-95; missionary Ch. Jesus Christ Latter-Day Saints, Alta., Can., 1977-79. Recipient Outstanding Faculty award U. Nev./Southland Corp., Las Vegas, 1991. Mem. Phi Kappa Phi, Phi Alpha Theta, Delta Kappa Gamma (pres. Chi State, Iota chpt. 1996-98). Democrat. Avocations: collecting western and Native American art, gardening. Office: Advanced Technologies Acad 2501 Vegas Dr Las Vegas NV 89106-1643

HAIRE, JAMES, sculptor; b. Crawfordsville, Ind., Feb. 14, 1951; s. James T. and Audrey N. (Manion) H.; m. Patricia M. Sellers, Sept. 16, 1980; children: Keaton E., Calen A., Quiten O. BFA in Painting, No. Ill. U., 1978. Patineur Art Castings of Colo., Loveland, 1983-89. Home: 924 Rocky Mountain Way Fort Collins CO 80526-2625

HAISCH, BERNHARD MICHAEL, astronomer; b. Stuttgart-Bad Canstatt, Federal Republic of Germany, Aug. 23, 1949; s. Friedrich Wilhelm and Gertrud Paula (Dammbacher) H.; m. Pamela S. Eakins, July 29, 1977 (div. 1986); children: Katherine Stuart, Christopher Taylor; m. Marsha A. Sims, Aug. 23, 1986. Student, St. Meinrad (Ind.) Coll., 1967-68; BS in Astrophysics, Ind. U., 1971; PhD in Astronomy, U. Wis., 1975. Rsch. assoc. Joint Inst. Lab. Astrophysics, U. Colo., 1975-77, 78-79; vis. scientist space rsch. lab. U. Utrecht, The Netherlands, 1977-78; rsch. scientist Lockheed Rsch. Lab., Palo Alto, Calif., 1979-83, staff scientist, 1983—; dep. dir. Ctr. for EUV Astrophysics U. Calif., Berkeley, 1992-94; guest investigator Internat. Ultraviolet Explorer, Einstein Obs., Exosat, ROSAT Obs., EUVE Obs., Astro-D (ASCA), X-Ray Timing Explorer, 1980—; vis. fellow Max Planck Inst. Extraterr. Physik, Garching, Germany, 1991-94. Editor-in-chief Jour. Sci. Exploration, 1988—, Solar and Stellar Flares, 1989; sci. editor The Astrophys. Jour., 1993—; monograph The Many Faces of the Sun, 1999; mem. editl. bd. Solar Physics, 1992-95, Speculations in Sci. and Tech., 1995—; contbr. articles to profl. jours. Fellow Royal Astron. Soc., AIAA (assoc.); mem. Internat. Astron. Union, Am. Astron. Soc., European Astron. Soc., Commonwealth Club Calif., Sigma Xi, Phi Beta Kappa, Phi Kappa Phi. Avocations: Tae Kwon Do, international folk dance, downhill skiing, songwriting. Office: Lockheed Martin Solar and Astrophys Lab Div H1-12 Bldg 252 3251 Hanover St Palo Alto CA 94304-1121

HAKIM, BESIM SELIM, architecture and urban design educator, researcher; b. Paris, July 31, 1938; came to U.S., 1978; s. Selim D. and Meliha M. (Yamulki) H.; m. Fatina S. Hijab, Oct. 31, 1963 (div. July 1983); children: Omar, Lena, Sara; m. Mariam B. Bashayan, Dec. 31, 1984; 1 child, Malak. BArch, Liverpool (Eng.) U., 1962; MArch in Urban Design, Harvard U., 1971. Registered architect, Ariz. Asst. prof. Tech. U. of Nova Scotia, Halifax, Can., 1967-74, assoc. prof., 1974-80, adj. rsch. prof., 1980-83; adj. assoc. prof. U. N.Mex., Albuquerque, 1982-83; assoc. prof. King Fahd U. of Petroleum and Minerals, Dhahran, Saudi Arabia, 1984-85; assoc. prof. Coll. of Architecture and Planning King Faisal U., Dammam, Saudi Arabia, 1985-93; ind. scholar and cons., 1994—; vis. prof. McGill U., Montreal, 1974, Tech. Inst. Architecture and Urbanism, Tunis, Tunisia, 1975, King Saud U., Riyadh, Saudi Arabia, 1982, 87, 89, 92, MIT, 1977; vis. scholar MIT, 1981, Cornell U., 1995; cons. to Skidmore, Owings and Merrill, Architects/Engrs., Chgo., Keith Graham & Assocs., Architects, Halifax, Nova Scotia, others; architect, engr. King Khaled Internat. Airport, Riyadh, Saudi Arabia, 1983-84; lectr. in field. Prin. works include urban design downtown Halifax, N.S., Coors Corridor Study, Albuquerque, Hist. Old Town, Albuquerque, 11 custom-built houses, 8-story office bldg., hosp. renovations/additions, apt. bldgs. and a religious facility, U.S., Can., Mid-East; author: Arabic-Islamic Cities: Building and Planning Principles, 1986, 2d edit., 1988, Japanese edit., 1990; contbr. articles to profl. jours. Recipient citation for rsch. Progressive Architecture, 1987, Edn. Honors award AIA, 1990. Mem. AIA, Am. Inst. Cert. Planners, Am. Planning Assn., Assn. Collegiate Schs. of Architecture, Middle East Studies Assn. N.Am., Halifax Bd. Trade (civic affairs com.). Home: 1832 Field Dr NE Albuquerque NM 87112-2834

HAKKILA, EERO ARNOLD, retired nuclear safeguards technology chemist; b. Canterbury, Conn., Aug. 4, 1931; s. Jack and Ida Maria (Lillquist) H.; m. Margaret W. Hakkila; children: Jon Eric, Mark Douglas, Gregg Arnold. BS in Chemistry, Cen. Conn. State U., 1953; PhD in Analytical Chemistry, Ohio State U., 1957. Staff mem. Los Alamos (N.Mex.) Nat. Lab., 1957-78, assoc. group leader safeguard systems, 1978-80, dep. group leader, 1980-82, group leader, 1982-83, project mgr. internat. safeguards, 1983-87, program coord., 1987-95; ret., 1995. Editor: Nuclear Safeguards Analysis, 1978; contbr. numerous articles to profl. jours. Fellow Am. Inst. Chemists; mem. N.Mex. Inst. Chemists (pres. 1971-73), Am. Chem. Soc., Am. Nuclear Soc. (exec. com. fuel cycle and waste mgmt. div. 1984-86), Inst. Nuclear Materials Mgmt. Avocations: skiing, fishing, rockhounding. Office: Los Alamos Nat Lab PO Box 1663 Los Alamos NM 87544-0600

HALASZ, STEPHEN JOSEPH, retired electro-optical systems engineer; b. Eger-Csehi, Hungary; s. Sandor and Ilona (Huszák) H.; children: Stephen S., Christopher L. Jacqueline R. BS, Columbia U., 1955. Test engr. J.A. Maurer, Inc., N.Y.C., 1955-56; project engr. GE Co., Utica, N.Y., 1956-58; sr. physicist Avion divsn. ACF Industries, Paramus, N.J., 1958-65; head IR and Display Lab. Aerojet Gen., 1965-72; sr. specialist Xerox Electro-Optical, Pasadena, Calif., 1972-75, Ford Aeronutronic, Newport Beach, Calif., 1975-83; chief scientist Hughes Aircraft, El Segundo, Calif., 1983-92. Contbg. author: (handbook) IR Handbook, 1969. With U.S. Army, 1945. NRA. Republican. Roman Catholic. Achievements include numerous designs and research projects including optical guidance for satellite interception; IR moving target tracker; handheld thermal imager; scanned matrix for IR pattern recognition; high speed target acquisition with fused senors; others; patentee in field. Avocations: photography, antique guns. Home: 66887 San Carlos Rd Desert Hot Springs CA 92240-2622

HALBERSTADT, DEB LEE, producer, photographer. BA in Liberal Arts, Lawrence U. Creator, pub. Westmont (Ill.) Challenger, 1974-76; photo editor AP, Chgo., 1976-80, L.A., 1976-80; mgr. media svc. photography corp. comm. NBC, 1980-88; owner, prodr. HalfCity Prodns., 1989—. Recipient Diamond award So. Calif. Cable Assn. Mem. Radio TV News Assn., Nat. Assn. TV Prodn. Execs, Nat. Assn. women Bus. Owners (bd. dirs.). Office: HalfCity Prodns # 137 115 W California Blvd # 137 Pasadena CA 91105-3005

HALBROOK, JANE, writer; b. Murrayville, B.C., Can., Jan. 3, 1957; d. Edward Hansen and Evelyn (Gillingwater) Paizk; children: Nicole Lana Groen, Michael Spencer Halbrook. Grad. h.s., Nooksack Valley, 1975. Retail clerk K-Mart, Bellingham, Wash., 1976-78, Pacific Grocery, Bellingham, Wash., 1978-80; hairdresser Woodwards, Victoria, B.C., Can., 1980-84, Lynden, Wash., 1984—. Author poems. Recipient Internat. Poetry Hall of Fame, Libr. of Congress, 1997, Best Poems of 1998. Mem. Internat. Soc. Poets. Avocations: drawing, gardening, sewing, pictures.

HALE, BRUCE DONALD, retired marketing professional; b. Oak Park, Ill., Dec. 21, 1933; s. Edward Garden and Mildred Lillian (Pelc) H.; m. Nancy Ann Novotny, July 2, 1955 (div. 1976); children: Jeffrey Bruce, Karen Jill Hale; m. Connie Luella Green Gunderson, Apr. 21, 1979. BA in Econs., Wesleyan U., Middletown, Conn., 1955. Trainee Caterpillar Tractor Co., Peoria, Ill., 1955-56, dealer tng. rep., 1956-59; dist. rep. Caterpillar Tractor Co., Albuquerque, 1959-62; asst. sales mgr. Rust Tractor Co., Albuquerque, 1962-65; gen. sales mgr. Rust Tractor Co., Albuqerque, 1965-71, v.p. sales, 1971-81, v.p. mktg., 1981-96; ret., 1996. Mem. Am. Mining Congress, Soc. Mining Engrs., Associated Contractors N.Mex., Associated Equipment Distbrs., Rocky Mountain Coal Mining Inst., N.Mex. Mining Assn., Albuquerque Country Club. Avocations: golf, fishing, music, classic cars. Home: 9508 Layton Pl NE Albuquerque NM 87111-1368

HALE, DAVID FREDRICK, health care company executive; b. Gadsden, Ala., Jan. 8, 1949; s. Millard and Mildred Earline (McElroy) H.; BA, Jacksonville State U.; m. Linda Carol Sadorski, Mar. 14, 1975; children: Shane Michael, Tara Renee, Erin Nicole, David Garrett. Dir. product mgmt. Ortho Pharm. Corp. Divsn. Johnson & Johnson, Raritan, N.J., 1978-80; v.p. mktg. BBL Microbiology Systems divsn. Becton Dickenson & Co., Cockeysville, Md., 1980-81, v.p., gen. mgr., 1981-82; sr. v.p. mktg. and bus. devel. Hybritech, Inc., San Diego, 1982, pres. 1983-86, CEO, 1986-87; pres., CEO Gensia Sicor, Inc., San Diego, 1987-97, also bd. dirs.; pres., CEO Women First HealthCare, Inc., 1998—, also bd. dirs.; bd. dirs. Gensia Sicor, Dura Pharmaceuticals, LMA N.Am., Metabasis Therapeutics, Collateral Therapeutics, Children's Hosp., Francis Parker Sch., U. Calif. San Diego Found., San Diego Econ. Devel. Corp., Biocom San Diego; founder CONNECT. Mem. Young Pres.'s Orgn. Republican. Episcopalian Home: PO Box 8925 16596 Via Lago Azul Rancho Santa Fe CA 92067 Office: Women First HealthCare Inc 12220 El Camino Real Ste 400 San Diego CA 92130-2091

HALE, DEAN EDWARD, social services administrator; b. Balt., Aug. 4, 1950; s. James Russell and Marjorie Elinor (Hoerman) H.; m. Lucinda Hoyt Muniz, 1979; children: Christopher Deane, Lydia Alice JeeSoo. BASW, U. Pa., 1975; postgrad. U. Oreg., 1976, U. London, 1974, U. Mont., 1968-71, Portland State U., 1993, 95—. Dir. recreation Hoffman Homes for Children, Gettysburg, Pa., 1970; social worker Holt Adoption Program, Inc., Eugene, Oreg., 1975-78; supr. social svcs. Holt Internat. Children's Svcs., Eugene, 1978-84, Asia rep., 1984-90, program mgr., 1990-94, interim dir. internat. programs, 1994-95, dir., China, 1995—; guest lectr. U. Oreg.; cons. internat. child welfare, 1982—; co-founder Family Opportunities Unltd. Inc., 1981—. Author: Adoption, A Family Affair, 1981, When Your Child Comes Home, 1986. Pres. Woodtique Heights Homeowners Assn., 1980-91, bd. dirs.; pres. Our Saviour's Luth. Ch., 1981-85; bd. dirs. Greenpeace of Oreg., 1979-84; cons., campaign worker Defazio for Congress 1988, 1987-90; mem. Westside Neighborhood Quality Project, 1988—. Named Outstanding New Jaycee, Gettysburg Jaycees, 1971. Mem. Nat. Assn. Social Workers (bd. dirs. 1978-80, sec. 1979-80), Nat. Assn. Christian Social Workers, Acad. Cert. Baccalaureate Social Workers. Fax: (541) 683-4339. E-mail: hale1@juno.com. Home: 931 Taylor St Eugene OR 97402-4451 Office: PO Box 2880 1195 City View St Eugene OR 97402-3325

HALE, HEATHER JANE, contract writer; b. Santa Maria, Calif., June 1, 1967; d. Daniel James and Cynthia Foster (Brown) H. BA in Creative Writing, San Diego State U., 1989. Screenwriter various videos; writer newsletters. Founder, v.p. Swallows Found., 1993-97. Recipient Senate Commendation San Juan Capistrano C. of C., 1995. Mem. Ind. Writers of So. Calif., Writers Connection, Paladin Writers and Artists' Freelance Assn., Internat. TV Assn., Cassell Network of Freelance Writers, Profl. Writers of Orange County, Assn. of Profl. Mortgage Women (founder, v.p. 1989-93), Orange County Profl. Bus. Group, 1993-97. E-mail: creativeHH@aol.com. Home: 18051 Joyful Ln Apt 102 Huntington Beach CA 92648-5667

HALER, LAWRENCE EUGENE, technology educator, councilman; b. Iowa City, Iowa, Jan. 24, 1951; s. Eugene Hilbert and Mary Elizabeth (Hans) H.; m. Jenifer Lea Leitz, June 1, 1974. BA, Pacific Luth. U., 1974. Reactor operator UNC Nuclear Industries, Richland, Wash., 1974-80, lead cert. instr., 1980-81, mgr. tng. adminstrn., 1981-82, sr. ops. analyst, 1982-85; sr. specialist Gen. Physics Corp., Columbia, Md., 1985-86; sr. instr. Rockwell Hanford Ops., Richland, 1986-88; tech. instr. Westinghouse Hanford Co., Richland, 1988-89, sr. specialist instr., 1989-96, Fluor Daniel Hanford team leader, 1996—; chmn. bd. dirs. Benton-Franklin County Bd. Health, Richland, 1994-95, Sci. and Tech. Park, Richland; vice chmn. Benton-Franklin Regional Coun. Govts., 1994. Chmn. Benton County Reps., Richland, 1976-78, state committeeman, 1988-90; councilman, mayor pro-tem City of Richland, 1990-96, mayor, 1996—, chmn. Richland ctrl. bus. dist. revitalization com.; active cmty. econ. devel. steering com. Nat. League of Cities. Mem. Richland C. of C. (chmn. legis. affairs com. 1988-93), Richland Kiwanis (pres. 1994-95). Lutheran. Avocations: swimming, photography. Home: PO Box 1319 Richland WA 99352-1319 Office: Richland City Coun 505 Swift Blvd Richland WA 99352-3510

HALES, ALFRED WASHINGTON, mathematics educator, consultant; b. Pasadena, Calif., Nov. 30, 1938; s. Raleigh Stanton and Gwendolen (Washington) H.; m. Virginia Dart Greene, July 7, 1962; children—Andrew Stanton, Lisa Ruth, Katherine Washington. B.S., Calif. Inst. Tech., 1960, Ph.D., 1962. NSF postdoctoral fellow Cambridge U., Eng., 1962-63; Benjamin Peirce instr. Harvard U., 1963-66; faculty mem. UCLA, 1966-92, prof. math., 1973-92, prof. emeritus, 1992—; dir. Inst. Def. Analyses, Ctr. Comms. Rsch., La Jolla, Calif., 1992—; cons. Jet Propulsion Lab., La Canada, Calif., 1966-70, Inst. for Def. Analyses, Princeton, N.J. and LaJolla, Calif., 1964-65, 76, 79-92; vis. lectr. U. Wash., Seattle, 1970-71; vis. mem. U. Warwick Math. Inst., Coventry, Eng., 1977-78, Math. Sci. Rsch. Inst., Berkeley, 1986-87. Co-author: Shift Register Sequences, 1967, 82; contbr. articles to profl. jours. Bd. trustees Math. Sci. Rsch. Inst., Berkeley, 1995—. Mem. Am. Math. Soc., Math. Assn. Am., Soc. Indsl. and Applied Math. (Polya prize in combinatorics 1972), Sigma Xi. Clubs: Pasadena Badminton. Office: Ctr for Comm Rsch 4320 Westerra Ct San Diego CA 92121-1969

HALEY, ARTHUR JOSEPH, recreation management educator, consultant; b. Boston, Oct. 7, 1942; s. Arthur Bernard and Anne (Sullivan) H. AB, Stonehill Coll., 1964; MEd, Springfield Coll., 1966; PhD, Tex. A&M U., 1974. Asst. prof. U. Wyo., Laramie, 1974-76; asst. prof. Ariz. State U., Tempe, 1976-80, assoc. prof., 1980-83, charter asst. dean Coll. Pub. Programs, 1980-83, prof., 1983—, chair dept. recreation mgmt. and tourism, 1983-91; founder recreation and tourism mgmt. program Ariz. State U.-West, Phoenix, 1986; vis. prof. Brunell U., High Wycombe, Eng., 1996. Mem. editl. bd. Anatolia: Internat. Jour. Tourism and Hospitality Rsch., 1997—, Jour. Tourism, Culture and Comm., 1998—, The Sport Jour.; contbr. numerous articles to profl. jours. Docent Stickney Collection of Art, Ga. So. U., Statesboro, Ga., 1996—; mem. cmty. and curriculum adv. com. Shipyard Coll., Phila., 1998—; mem. Nat. Faculty, U.S. Sports Acad., 1998—. Mem. Nat. Intramural-Recreational Sports Assn. (editl. bd. 1998—), Nat. Trust for Hist. Preservation, Calif. Am. Studies Assn., Wester Social Sci. Assn., Rocky Mountain Am. Studies Assn., Gamma Sigma Delta. Avocations: reading, golf, basketball, travel, cycling. Office: Dept Recreation Mgmt PO Box 874905 Tempe AZ 85287-4905

HALEY, JOHN DAVID, petroleum consulting company executive; b. Denver, Mar. 16, 1924; s. Peter Daniel and Margaret Dorothy (O'Haire) H.; m. Annie Loretta Breeden, June 20, 1951; children: Laura, Patricia, Brian, Sharon, Norine, Kathleen. Profl. engr. Colo. Sch. Mines, 1948. Registered profl. engr., Colo., Okla. Petroleum engr. Creole Petroleum, Venezuela, 1948-50, field engr. Texaco Inc., La., 1950-52; staff engr. Carter Oil (Exxon), Tulsa, 1954-56; petroleum cons. Earlougher Engring., Tulsa, 1956-61, resident mgr., Denver, 1961-62; v.p. prodn. Anschutz Corp., Denver, 1962-86; v.p. Circle A Drilling, Denver, 1967-78; dir. Circle A Mud, Denver, 1983-86; pres. Greylock Pipeline, Denver, 1983-86, Anschutz Pipeline, Denver, 1984-86; pres. Haley Engring. Inc., 1987—; mem. pres.'s council Colo. Sch. Mines, 1985—; bd. dirs. Alumni Assn., 1992-97, pres., 1995. Bd. dirs. CSM Found., 1996-98; Rep. committeeman, Littleton. Lt. comdr. USNR, 1943-46, 52-54. Recipient Outstanding Alumnus award Alumni Assn., 1997. Mem. Soc. Petroleum Engrs. (bd. dirs. Denver chpt. 1965), Soc. Petroleum Evaluation Engrs. (bd. dirs. 1992-95), Ind. Petroleum Assn. Mountain States, Am. Petroleum Inst. (citation for service), Internat. Assn. Drilling Contractors, Rocky Mountain Oil & Gas Assn. (bd. dirs. 1988—), Soc. Profl. Well Log Analysts, Petroleum Club (Denver chpt.). Roman Catholic. Home: 561 E Caley Dr Littleton CO 80121-2212

HALEY, MICHAEL CABOT, English educator, researcher; b. Birmingham, Ala., Dec. 30, 1947; s. John Hendon and Margaret Reece (Beavers) H.; m. Linda Joan McCarriston, June 15, 1996 (div. July 1997). BA, U. Ala., 1969, MA, 1969; PhD, Fla. State U., 1975. Instr. Fla. Coll., Temple Terrace, Fla., 1969-72; tchg. asst. Fla. State U., Tallahassee, Fla., 1972-75; asst. prof. North Ctrl. Coll., Naperville, Ill., 1975-79; from adj. prof. to prof. U. Alaska, Anchorage, 1979-93, prof., 1993—. Author: the Semeiosis of Poetic Metaphor, 1988, Noam Chomsky, 1994; editor: Linguistic Perspectives on Literature, 1980; mng. editor Peirce Seminar Papers, Providence, R.I., Oxford, England, N.Y.C., 1993—. Named Moss Chair of Excellence U. Memphis, 1998. Mem. Semiotic Soc. am., S.E. Conference Linguistics, Phi Beta Kappa. Republican. Avocations: motorcycling, camping, fishing. Home: 3550 W Dimond Blvd Apt 311 Anchorage AK 99515-1256 Office: English Dept Univ AK 3211 Providence Dr Anchorage AK 99508-4614

HALEY, SALLY FULTON, artist; b. Bridgeport, Conn., June 29, 1908; d. John Poole and Elizabeth (Akers) H.; m. Michele Russo, June 29, 1935; children: Michael Haley, Gian Donato. BFA, Yale U., 1931. One-woman shows include Marylhurst Coll., 1965, Maryhill Mus. Fine Arts, Washington, 1975, Portland Art Mus., 1960, 75, Woodside Gallery, Seattle, 1971, 76, 79, Gov's. Office, Oreg. State Capitol, 1976, Wentz Gallery, Pacific N.W. Coll. Art, 1984, Fountain Gallery Art, Portland, 1962, 72, 77, 80, 81, 84, 86; exhibited in group shows Stewart Gallery, Boston, 1947, San Francisco Mus. Art, 1949, Walker Art Ctr., Mpls., 1954, Denver Art Mus., 1956, 57, 3d Pacific Coast Biennial Exhbn., 1960, Francis J. Newton's Collection, Bush House, 1964, Seattle Ctr. Art Pavilion, 1976, Womans Bldg., L.A., 1977, Laura Russo Gallery, 1993, 97, Oreg. Group Show, Expn. '86 World's Fair, Vancouver, B.C., Mus. N.W. Art, Conner, Wash., 1998; represented in permanent collections Fred Myer Trust, Wash. State U., State Capitol Bldg., Salem, Portland Art Mus., The Laura Russo Gallery, Portland, Lynn McAllister Gallery, Seattle, Barby Investment Co., AT&T, Kaiser Found., numerous others; retrospective, Marylhurst Coll., 1993, Mus. Northwest Art Ha Conner, Washington, 1998. Named Artist of Yr. Neighbor Newspaper Community, Portland, 1984; recipient Woman of Achievement award YWCA, 1988, Govs. award for the Arts, 1989, Poster award, 1982, Hubbard award Hubbard Mus., Ruidoso Downs, N.Mex., 1990-91.

HALL, ALICE AVERETTE, college administrator, counselor; b. Gastonia, N.C., June 13, 1957; d. Richard Glenn and Juanita Wanda (Watkins) Averette; m. Kenneth Eldridge Hall, June 16, 1979; children: Aryn Leigh, Lindsey Ann, Lauren Ashley. BA in Psychology & Music, Coll. of William and Mary, 1979; MEd in Counselor Edn., Auburn U., 1981; postgrad., Va. Poly. Inst., 1986—. Counselor II Mt. Rogers Mental Health Clinic, Marion, Va., 1983-85, acting clinic dir., 1984-85; asst. prof., support svcs. counselor Wytheville (Va.) C.C., 1985-91; dir. student devel. ctr. Western Wyo. C.C., Rock Springs, 1991—; presenter various workshops, seminars at state, regional & nat. confs. Bd. dirs. Family Resource Ctr., Wytheville, 1982-85, Task Force on Sexual Assault, Sweetwater County, Wyo., 1992. Named Woman of Yr. Bus. & Profl. Women, Rock Springs, 1992. Mem. ACA, Am. Coll. Pers. Assn., Am. Coll. Counseling Assn., Nat. Career Devel. Assn., Wyo. Counseling Assn., Phi Kappa Phi. Methodist. Avocation: collecting teddy bears. Office: Western Wyoming CC 2500 College Dr Rock Springs WY 82901-5802

HALL, BLAINE HILL, retired librarian; b. Wellsville, Utah, Dec. 12, 1932; s. James Owen and Agnes Effie (Hill) H.; m. Carol Stokes, 1959; children: Suzanne, Cheryl, Derek. BS, Brigham Young U., 1960, MA, 1965, MLS, 1971. Instr. English, Brigham Young U., Provo, Utah, 1963-72, humanities librarian, 1972-96; book reviewer Am. Reference Book Ann., 1984—. Author: Collection Assessment Manual, 1985, Saul Bellow Bibliography, 1987, Jerzy Kosinski Bibliography, 1991, Jewish American Fiction Writers Bibliography, 1991, Conversations with Grace Paley, 1997; editor: Utah Libraries, 1972-77 (periodical award ALA 1977); contbr. articles to profl. jours. Bd. dirs. Orem (Utah) Pub. Libr., 1977-84; mem. Orem Media Rev. Commn., 1984-86; chmn. Utah Adv. Commn. on Librs. With U.S. Army, 1953-54, Korea. Mem. ALA (coun. 1988-92), Utah Libr. Assn. (pres. 1980-81, Disting. Svc. award 1989), Mountain Plains Libr. Assn. (bd. dirs. 1978-83, editor newsletter 1978-83, pres. 1994-96, grantee 1979, 80, Disting. Svc. award 1991), Phi Kappa Phi. Mormon. Avocations: writing, photography, carpentry, family history, reading. Home: 230 E 1910 S Orem UT 84058-8161

HALL, BRENDA, human resources executive. CEO Hall, Kinion and Assocs., Cupertino, Calif. Office: Hall Kinion and Assocs 19925 Stevens Creek Blvd Cupertino CA 95014-2305*

HALL, CHARLES FREDERICK, space scientist, government administrator; b. San Francisco, Apr. 7, 1920; s. Charles Rogers and Edna Mary (Gibson) H.; m. Constance Vivienne Andrews, Sept. 18, 1942; chil-

dren—Steven R., Charles Frederick, Frank A. B.S., U. Calif., Berkeley, 1942. Aero. research scientist NACA (later NASA), Moffett Field, Calif., 1942-60; mem. staff space projects NACA (later NASA), 1960-63; mgr. Pioneer Project, NASA, 1963-80. Recipient Disting. Service medal NASA, 1974, Achievement award Am. Astronautical Soc., 1974, Spl. Achievement award Nat. Civil Service League, 1976, Astronautics Engr. award Nat. Space Club, 1979. Rsch., reports on performance of wings and inlets at transonic and supersonic speeds, on conical-cambered wings at transonic and supersonic speeds, 1942-60; pioneer project launched 4 solar orbiting, 2 Jupiter and 2 Venus spacecraft. Home: 817 Berry Ave Los Altos CA 94024-5416

HALL, CYNTHIA HOLCOMB, federal judge; b. Los Angeles, Feb. 19, 1929; d. Harold Romeyn and Mildred Gould (Kuck) Holcomb; m. John Harris Hall, June 6, 1970 (dec. Oct. 1980);. A.B., Stanford U., 1951, J.D., 1954; LL.M., NYU, 1960. Bar: Ariz. 1954, Calif. 1956. Law clk. to judge U.S. Ct. Appeals 9th Circuit, 1954-55; trial atty. tax div. Dept. Justice, 1960-64; atty.-adviser Office Tax Legis. Counsel, Treasury Dept., 1964-66; mem. firm Brawerman & Holcomb, Beverly Hills, Calif., 1966-72; judge U.S. Tax Ct., Washington, 1972-81, U.S. Dist. Ct. for central dist. Calif., Los Angeles, 1981-84; cir. judge U.S. Ct. Appeals (9th cir.), Pasadena, Calif., 1984—. Served to lt. (j.g.) USNR, 1951-53. Office: US Ct Appeals 9th Cir 125 S Grand Ave Pasadena CA 91105-1621

HALL, DAVID RAMSAY, architect; b. Lansing, Mich., Oct. 24, 1945; s. Harold Wendell and Sarah Katherine (Schlademan) H.; m. Catherine Anne Weeks, Dec. 23, 1967; children: Sarah Catherine, Rebecca Jane. BArch, Wash. State U., 1968. Registered architect, Wash. Designer, draftsman Earl Flansburgh & Assocs., Cambridge, Mass., 1968-70, NBBJ, Seattle, 1970, Mel Streeter & Assoc., Seattle, 1971-72; designer, ptnr. Henry Klein Partnership, Architects, Mt. Vernon, Wash., 1972—. Author, designer, contbr. articles to profl. publs. Commr. Dike Dist. # 19, Skagit County, Wash., 1984-95; mem. adv. bd. Wash. State U., Pullman, 1990-96; bd. dirs. Self Help Housing, Mt. Vernon, 1980-84. Recipient Prograssive Architecture Design award, 1972, Honor award Cedar Shake & Shingle, 1991, Am. Wood Coun., 1993, Sunset Mag. Western Home award. 1995. Mem. AIA (bd. dirs. N.W. chpt. 1985-88, Honor award Seattle chpt. 1991, N.W. chpt. 1991, 94, 96, Commendation award Seattle chpt. 1987). Avocations: watercolor painting, photography, hiking, gardening, fishing. Home: 585 Farm To Market Rd Bow WA 98232-9213 Office: Henry Klein Partnership 314 Pine St Ste 205 Mount Vernon WA 98273-3852*

HALL, ELEANOR WILLIAMS, public relations executive; b. Boston; d. James Murray and Julia Eleanor (Williams) H. AB cum laude, Radcliffe Coll., 1945. Exec. sec. Am. Express Co., N.Y.C., 1950-62, adminstrv. asst. corp. mktg., 1963-65, mgr. corp. mktg., 1965-69, mgr. corp. pub. rels., 1969-71; mgr. mktg. svcs. Am. Express Internat. Banking Corp. (now Am. Express Bank Ltd.), N.Y.C., 1971-72, asst. treas. advt. and pub. rels., 1972-76, asst. v.p. advt. and pub. rels., 1976-82; pres. Eleanor Hall Assocs., Inc., 1982-90. Mem. Harvard-Radcliffe Club. Address: 342 102d Ave SE Ste 218 Bellevue WA 98004-6165

HALL, GORDON R., retired state supreme court chief justice; b. Vernal, Utah, Dec. 14, 1926; s. Roscoe Jefferson and Clara Maud (Freestone) H.; m. Doris Gillespie, Sept. 6, 1947; children: Rick Jefferson, Craig Edwin. B.S., U. Utah, 1949, LL.B., 1951. Bar: Utah 1952. Solo practice Tooele, Utah, 1952-69; county atty. Tooele County, 1958-69; judge 3d Jud. Dist. Utah, 1969-77; assoc. justice Supreme Ct. Utah, 1977-81, chief justice, 1981-94; of counsel Snow, Christensen & Martineau, Salt Lake City, 1994-98; chmn. Utah Jud. Coun., 1983-94; pres. Conf. Chief Justices, 1988-89; chmn. Nat. Ctr. State Cts., 1988-89; pres. Utah Assn. Counties, 1965; mem. Pres.'s Adv. Com. OEO, 1965-66. Served with U.S. Maritime Svc., 1944-46. Mem. ABA, Utah Bar Assn. Office: 250 N Sandrun Rd Salt Lake City UT 84103-2239

HALL, GUINIVERE (GUIN) BRYAN, retired telephone company manager; b. Sand Coulee, Mont., Nov. 8, 1918; d. Charles Stanley and Blanche Verniere (Meehan) H. Student, St. Helen's Hall Jr. Coll., Portland, 1936-38; BS, NYU, 1974, MS, 1977. Newspaper reporter N.Y. Herald Tribune, N.Y.C., 1947-59; dep. commr. N.Y. State Dept. Commerce, Albany, 1959-71; dist. staff mgr. N.Y. Telephone, N.Y.C., 1971-84; ret., 1984. Editor (newsletter) Terwilliger Times, Portland, Oreg., 1993—; contbr. articles to profl. publs. Founder, bd. dirs. Salute to Women, YWCA, N.Y.C., 1975-79; founder Elder Craftsmen, Inc., N.Y.C. Served with USCG, 1943-45. Mem. Soc. of Silurians, Newswomen's Club of N.Y. (pres. 1956-58). Republican. Episcopalian. Avocations: watercolor painting. Home: 2545 SW Terwilliger Blvd Portland OR 97201-6302

HALL, HAROLD ROBERT, retired computer engineer; b. Bakersfield, Calif., Feb. 7, 1935; s. Edward Earl and Ethel Mae (Butner) H.; m. Tenniebee May Hall, Feb. 20, 1965. BS, U. Calif., Berkeley, 1956, MS, 1957, PhD, 1966. Chief engr. wave-filter div. Transonic, Inc., Bakersfield, 1957-60; chief design engr. Circuit Dyne Corp., Pasadena and Laguna Beach, Calif., 1960-61; sr. devel. engr. Robertshaw Controls Co., Anaheim, Calif., 1961-63; research engr. Naval Command, Control and Ocean Surveillance Ctr., rsch. and devel. divsn. Navy Research Lab., San Diego, 1966-95; bd. dirs. Circuit Dyne Corp., Pacific Coil Co. Treas. Pacific Beach Town Coun., San Diego, 1996-98, Friends of Ostomates Worldwide-U.S.A., Akron, Ohio, 1992—. Recipient Thomas Clair McFarland award U. Calif., Berkeley, 1956, NSF fellow, 1957. Mem. IEEE, Acoustical Soc. Am., Phi Beta Kappa. Home: 8585 Via Mallorca Unit 7 La Jolla CA 92037-2585

HALL, HOWARD PICKERING, engineering and mathematics educator; b. Boston, July 8, 1915; s. George Henry and Elizabeth Isabel (McCallum) H.; m. Ellen Marguerite Ide, June 25, 1945 (dec. 1984); children: Charlotte McCallum, Stephanie Wilson, Lindsey Louise, Gretchen Elizabeth. AB, Harvard U., 1936, MS, 1937, DSc, 1951. Registered structural engr., Ill., 1953. Instr., civil engring. Brown U., Providence, 1937-38; structural analyst Mark Linenthal, Engr., Boston, 1938-39; instr., asst. prof., assoc. prof. civil engring. Northwestern U., Evanston, Ill., 1939-56; design engr, field engr. Porter, Urquart, Skidmore, Owings, Merrill, Casablanca, Fr. Morocco, 1951-53; dean, sch. engring., acad. v.p. Robert Coll., Istanbul, Turkey, 1956-68; dir. of studies, acting headmaster St. Stephen's Sch., Rome, 1968-72; prof. math. Iranzamin Internat., Tehran, Iran, 1973-80; math. tchr. Vienna Internat. Sch., 1980-83, Copenhagen Internat. Sch., 1983-86; cons. S.J. Buchanan, Bryan, Tex., Eng., 1955. Contbr. articles to profl. jours. Served to Capt. U.S. Army, 1942-46, ETO. Recipient Clemens Herschel award Boston Soc. Civil Engrs., 1954. Mem. Sigma Xi. Home: 301 SW Lincoln St Apt 1401 Portland OR 97201-5033

HALL, LARRY D., energy company executive, lawyer; b. Hastings, Nebr., Nov. 8, 1942; s. Willis E. and Stella W. (Eckoff) H.; m. Jeffe D. Bryant, July 5, 1985; children: Scott, Jeff, Mike, Bryan. BA in Bus., U. Nebr., Kearney; JD, U. Nebr. Bar: Nebr., Colo. Ptnr. Wright, Simmons, Hancock & Hall, Scottsbluff, Nebr., 1967-71; atty., asst. treas. KN Energy Inc., Hastings, 1971-73, dir. regulatory affairs, 1973-76; v.p. law divsn. KN Energy Inc., Lakewood, Colo., 1976-82, sr. v.p., 1982-85, exec. v.p., 1985-88, pres., COO, 1988-94, pres., CEO, 1994—, also bd. dirs., 1988-94, chmn., CEO, pres., 1996—; bd. dirs. Colo. Assn. Commerce and Industry, Gas Rsch. Inst., Colo. Alliance for Bus., MLA, Rocky Mountain Oil and Gas Assn.; chmn. Natural Gas Coun., 1998. Mem. ABA, Interstate Natural Gas Assn. Am. (chmn. 1997), Midwest Gas Assn., CAB (bd. dirs.), Fed. Energy Bar Assn., Nebr. Bar Assn., Colo. Bar Assn., Pres. Assn., Midwest Gas Assn. (chmn.), Hiwan Country Club, Desert Mountain, Elks, Club 30. Presbyterian. Avocations: skiing, golf, photography. Home: 1892 Sugarbush Dr Evergreen CO 80439-9415 Office: KN Energy Inc PO Box 15265 Lakewood CO 80215

HALL, LOIS RIGGS, former state senator, former symphony orchestra administrator; b. Beeville, Tex., May 22, 1930; d. Ira Franklin and Pearl Ophelia (McCoy) Riggs; m. Walter William Hall, Dec. 28, 1950 (dec.); children: Robert Macfarlane, Elaine Denise, Judith Lea. Student, Tex. Women's U., 1947-49, U. Tex., Austin, 1949-50. Exec. sec. N.Mex. Symphony Orch., Albuquerque, 1975-93; mem. N.Mex. Senate, 1980-85, ret. . Active Boy Scouts Am., Girl Scouts U.S.A., Officers Wives Clubs; 2d v.p. Albuquerque Symphony Women's Assn.; bd. dirs. Friends of Music, 1986-88; treas., publicity dir. N.Mex. Aviation Assn. Republican. Home: 620 Ortiz Dr NE Albuquerque NM 87108-1447

HALL, LYNDA LEE, legal transcription service executive; b. Detroit, Nov. 11, 1941; d. Kenneth Kirk and Nova Lee (Grant) H. AA in English, El Camino Coll., 1975. Office mgr. Computer Svc. Bur., Torrance, Calif., 1976-78; engring. charge proposal writer Hughes Aircraft Corp., El Segundo, Calif., 1978-81; legal sec. ACLU Found.-So. Calif. Chpt., L.A., 1982-84; temporary legal sec. various orgns., 1987-89; legal sec. Stephen E. Traverse, 1990-91; owner Westword Legal Transcription Svc., Inglewood, Calif., 1995—; Editor, tchr. (children's poetry and sci. fiction stories with their personal illustrations) S.F. and Fantasy, 1974 (Smiles award 1974). Founding mem. NOW Beach Cities Chpt., 1972, consciousness raising coord., 1973, chpt. pres., 1975; mem. at large Alliance for Democracy So. Calif., 1998. Finalist N.Am. Open Poetry Contest, 1995, semi-finalist Sparrowgrass Poetry Contest, 1996. Unitarian. Avocations: writing poetry, essays, fiction and non-fiction books. Fax: (310) 673-9992. E-mail: gowestword@worldnet.att.net. Office: Westword Legal Transcription Svc PO Box 4313 Inglewood CA 90309

HALL, MARIAN ELLA See ROBERTSON, MARIAN ELLA

HALL, PAUL J., lawyer; b. San Diego, Jan. 13, 1951. AB with highest honors, U. Calif., Santa Cruz, 1972; postgrad, Yale U.; JD, U. Calif., Berkeley, 1975. Bar: Calif. 1975. Mem. Manatt, Phelps & Phillips, L.A., 1975-94, Stein & Lubin LLP, San Francisco, 1995-98, Lillick & Charles LLP, San Francisco, 1998—; bd. regents U. Calif., 1992-93, regent designate, 1991-92. Trustee U. Calif. Santa Cruz Found., 1986—. Mem. Calif. State Bar, Boalt Hall Alumni Assn. (bd. dirs. 1983-90, treas. 1985-86, sec. 1986-87, v.p. 1987-89, pres.-elect 1989-90, pres. 1990-91), U. Calif. Santa Cruz Alumni Assn. (bd. dirs. 1983-90, pres. 1986-90). Address: 2 Embarcadero Ctr Ste 2700 San Francisco CA 94111-3996

HALL, ROBERT EMMETT, JR., investment banker, realtor; b. Sioux City, Iowa, Apr. 28, 1936; s. Robert Emmett and Alvina (Faden) H.; m. Marna Thiel, 1969. BA, U. S.D., 1958, MA, 1959; MBA, U. Santa Clara, 1976; grad. Am. Inst. Banking, Realtors Inst. Grad. asst. U. S.D., Vermillion, 1958-59; mgr. ins. dept., asst. mgr. installment loan dept. Northwestern Nat. Bank of Sioux Falls, S.D., 1959-61, asst. cashier, 1961-65; asst. mgr. Crocker Nat. Bank, San Francisco, 1965-67, loan officer, 1967-69, asst. v.p., asst. mgr. San Mateo br., 1969-72; v.p., Western regional mgr. Internat. Investments & Realty, Inc., Washington, 1972—; owner Hall Enterprises Co., 1976—; pres. Almaden Oaks Realtors, Inc., 1976—; instr. West Valley Coll., Saratoga, Calif., 1972-82, Grad. Sch. Bus., U. Santa Clara (Calif.), 1981-82, Evergreen Valley Coll., San Jose, Calif. Treas., Minnehaha Leukemia Soc., 1963, Lake County Heart Fund Assn., 1962, Minnehaha Young Republican Club, 1963. Mem. Am. Inst. Banking, Calif. Assn. Realtors (vice chmn.), Beta Theta Pi. Republican. Clubs: Elks, Rotary (past pres.), K.C., Almaden Country. Home: 6951 Castlerock Dr San Jose CA 95120-4705 Also: 8864 Rubicon Dr Rubicon Bay CA 96142 Office: Hall Enterprises 6501 Crown Blvd Ste 106 San Jose CA 95120-2903

HALL, TENNIEBEE M., editor; b. Bakersfield, Calif., May 21, 1940; d. William Elmer and Lillian May (Otis) Hall; m. Harold Robert Hall, Feb. 20, 1965. BA in Edn., Fresno State Coll., 1962; AA, Bakersfield Coll., 1960. Cert. tchr., Calif. Tchr. Edison (Calif.) Sch. Dist., 1962-65; substitute tchr. Marin and Oakland Counties (Calif.), Berkeley, 1965-66; engring. asst. Pacific Coil Co., Inc., Bakersfield, 1974-81; editor United Ostomy Assn., Inc., Irvine, Calif., 1986-91. Co-author: Treating IBD, 1989, Current Therapy in Gastroenterology, 1989; author, designer: Volunteer Leadership Training Manuals, 1982-84; contbr. articles to Ostomy Quar., 1973—. Mem. Pacific Beach Town Coun., San Diego, 1977—; campaign worker Maureen O'Connor (1st woman mayor of city), San Diego, 1986; mem. Nat. Digestive Diseases Adv. Bd., NIH, Washington, 1986-91; mem. planning and devel. bd. Scripps Clinic and Rsch. Found. Inflammatory Bowel Disease Ctr., San Diego, 1993—; various vol. activities, 1966-74, 81-86. Recipient Outstanding Svc. award VA Vol. Svc., Bur. of Vets. Affairs, Washington, 1990. Mem. Nat. Assn. Parliamentarians, United Ostomy Assn. Inc. (regional program dir. 1980-84, pres. 1984-86, Sam Dubin award 1983, Industry Adv. award 1987), Crohn's and Colitis Found. Am. (nat. trustee 1986-95, nat. v.p. 1987-92). Avocations: travel, volunteerism. Home and Office: 8585 Via Mallorca Unit 7 La Jolla CA 92037-2585

HALL, WENDY LAPIC, program director; d. Gregory T. and Margaret (Keiter) L.; m. Thomas Inwood Hall, Aug. 21, 1993. BA, Whitman Coll., 1987; MPA, U. Wash., 1991. Staff asst. U.S. Congress, Washington, 1988-89; program asst. Internat. Trade Inst., Seattle, 1989-90; rsch. asst. Dept. Cmty., Trade and Econ. Devel., Seattle, 1990-91; grants coord. North Seattle C.C., 1991-94, dir. grants, planning, and rsch., 1994—. Author: NSCC Institutional Effectiveness Plan, 1998; co-author, co-editor: NSCC Accreditation Self-Study, 1997. Voter registrar League of Women Voters, Seattle, 1994-95. Recipient grant U.S. West, 1996, grant NSCC Telecomms. Project Econ. Devel. Adminstrn. Dept. Commerce, 1998. Democrat. Avocation: gardening. Office: North Seattle CC 9600 College Way N Seattle WA 98103-3514

HALL, WILLIAM DAVID, aerospace engineer; b. Newark, Jan. 1, 1924; s. Edward Milton and Mary (Bice) H.; m. Patricia Lin Hodge, Sept. 25, 1948 (div. 1979); children: Kerrida Anne Leskey, Jaye Alison. BS in Engring., West Coast U., 1060. Aerospace engr. Rockwell Internat., Seal Beach and L.A., Calif., 1948-66, Boeing Co., Seattle, Phila., 1966, 67-68, 80-82, 85, 86—, Lockheed Aircraft, Burbank, Calif., 1968-70, various cos., various cities, 1970-86. Lt. USAF, 1942-45, ETO. Decorated Air Medal with 6 oak leaf clusters. Mem. Caterpillar Club, Elks. Republican. Mem. Science of Mind. Avocations: sculpting, jogging, reading, crossword puzzles. Home: 3112 Haddon Dr Las Vegas NV 89134-8990

HALL, WILLIAM E., engineering and construction company executive; b. Washington, Sept. 5, 1942; s. George W. and Jane F. (Brogger) H.; m. Lavinia Swift, Sept. 21, 1974; children: Deborah A., Douglas E., L. Jane, Elizabeth D. BSChemE, Va. Poly. Inst. and State U., 1963, MSChemE, 1964; postgrad., Stanford U., 1991. Process engr. Stone & Webster Engring. Co., Boston, 1967-70; project mgr. Stone & Webster Engring. Co., London, 1970-76, N.Y.C., 1976-78; regional bus. devel. mgr. Stone & Webster Engring. Co., Houston, 1978-79; prin. project mgr. RM Parsons Co., Pasadena, Calif., 1979-81, sr. v.p., 1989-92; pres. Ralph M. Parsons Co., Pasadena, Calif., 1992—; prin. project mgr. Saudi Arabia Parsons Ltd., Yanbu, 1981-84, mng. dir., 1984-89; bd. dirs. Proye Parsons, Caracas, Venezuela, Latisa; alt. dir. Constrn. Industry Inst., Austin, Tex., 1990-92, dir. 1992—. CHmn. Tournament of Life, Pasadena, 1990-92. Mem. Am. Inst. Chem. Engrs. Republican. Lutheran. Avocations: golf, bridge. Office: Ralph M Parsons Co 100 W Walnut St Pasadena CA 91124-0002 also: Parsons Process Group 5 E Greenway Plz Houston TX 77046-0500*

HALLA, BRIAN, electronics company executive; b. Springfield, Ill., 1946. BSEE, U. Nebr., 1969. Applications engr. Control Data Corp., 1969-74; dir. mktg. Intel Corp., 1974-78; exec. v.p. LSI Logic, 1988-96; chmn. bd., pres., CEO Nat. Semiconductor Corp., Santa Clara, Calif., 1996—. Mem. Semi-Conductor Indsl. Assn. (bd. dirs.). Office: National Semiconductor Corp 2900 Semiconductor Dr Santa Clara CA 95051-0695*

HALLAHAN, KIRK EDWARD, journalism educator; b. Cleve., Feb. 16, 1950; m. Jean Sheppard, Jan. 8, 1977. BA magna cum laude, UCLA, 1971; MA, U. Wis.-Madison, 1974, PhD, 1995. Project asst. U. Wis.-Madison, 1972; account supr. Harshe-Rotman & Druck, Inc., L.A., 1973-79; v.p. pub. rels. Calif. Fed. Savs. and Loan, L.A., 1979-84; sr. v.p. pub. affairs Calif. League of Savs. Instns., L.A., 1984-89; v.p. pub. affairs Coast Savs., L.A., 1989-91; asst. prof. Colo. State U., Ft. Collins, 1996—; sr. lectr. U. So. Calif. Sch. Journalism, 1977-84. Author: The Consequences of Mass Communication, 1997. Mem. Pasadena Tournament Roses, Calif., 1979-93; adv. com. L.A. City Fire Dept., United Way Region V, Cen. City Assn. State dept. fellow Internat. Communication Seminar, Yugoslavia, 1971. Fellow Pub. Rels. Soc. Am. (Silver Anvil award 1974, South Pacific dist. chmn. 1984, fin. svcs. sect. chmn. 1986, 87, L.A. Outstanding Profl. 1988); mem. Publicity Club L.A. (pres. 1978-79), Soc. Profl. Journalists, Phi Beta Kappa. Democrat. Presbyterian. Home: 3230 Pepperwood Ln Fort Collins CO 80525-2943 Office: Colo State U C-225 Clark Fort Collins CO 80523-1785

HALLAM, JUANITA MAY, visual artist, poet, writer; b. Denver, Aug. 6, 1920; d. Aura Duane and Buda Gladys (Hansen) Shirley; m. Irvin Hallam, Aug. 14, 1939; children: Ilona Shirley, Kent. Student, Colo. Women's Coll.; studied with R. Idris Thomas, Paris; studied with Enrique Montenegro; studied with Akiba Emmanuel, N.Y.C.; studied with Oksana Ross, N.Y.C., Denver. Pvt. practice Colo., 1948—. One-woman shows include Internat. House, 1961, 64, Neusteters Gallery, 1970, May D&F Gallery, 1972, Bonfil's Theatre, 1983, Boettcher Concert Hall-Gallery One, 1985, Wilshire Presby. Ch. Gallery, 1986, others; exhibited in group shows at Mile High Ctr., 1962, Las Georges Gallery, San Francisco, 1963, Tucson Fine Arts Mus., Santa Fe Mus. Art, Okla. City Mus., Colo. Springs Fine Arts Mus., Joslyn Mus., Denver Art Mus., others. Recipient Carter Meml. prize, 1938, Art award poster design Nat. Theatre Guild, 1963, Invisage award Denver, 1979, 80; art scholar Colo. Women's Coll., 1939. Mem. Western Watercolor Soc. (Colo. chpt.). Baptist. Avocations: counseling, writing, travel to see art.

HALLAM, ROBERT J., performing company executive, consultant; b. Edmonton, Alta., Can., Oct. 24, 1952; s. Donald Robert and Mary (Dutton) H.; m. Sydney Ann Scott, Oct. 5, 1984; 1 child, Robert Ian. MusB, U. Alta., 1976, MBA, 1983. Adminstrv. mgr. Edmonton Opera, 1983-85, gen. mgr., 1985-89, gen. dir., 1989-91; gen. dir. Vancouver (B.C.) Opera, Can., 1991—; dir. Opera Am., Washington, 1987-93, treas., 1990-93; bd. dirs. Tourism Vancouver, Vancouver Cultural Alliance, vice chmn., 1994-95, chmn., 1995—. Office: Vancouver Opera, 845 Cambie St Ste 500, Vancouver, BC Canada V6B 4Z9*

HALLAS-GOTTLIEB, LISA, film and television assistant director; b. Rahway, N.J., Feb. 22, 1950; d. Taras and Mary (Lapchinski) Hallas; m. David N. Gottlieb, May 2, 1980; children: Gabriel, Jamie. BA in Broadcasting, Stanford U., 1972. Asst. dir. numerous T.V. series and pilots, movies, 1976—; owner, prodr. Never A Dull Moment Prodns., Topanga, Calif., 1986—; line prodr., prodn. mgr. Pizza Prodns., L.A., 1997. Mem. Women in Film. Avocations: reading, theater, bicycling, hiking. Home and Office: 1406 N Topanga Canyon Blvd Topanga CA 90290-4274

HALL-BARRON, DEBORAH, lawyer; b. Oakland, Calif., Oct. 7, 1949; d. John Standish Hall and Mary (Swinson) H.; m. Eric Levin Meadow, Feb. 1973 (div. June 1982); 1 child, Jesse Standish Meadow Hall; m. Richie Barron, 1997. Paralegal cert., Sonoma State U., Rohnert Park, Calif., 1984; JD, John F. Kennedy U., Walnut Creek, Calif., 1990. Bar: Calif. 1991. Paralegal Law Offices Marc Libarle/Quentin Kopp, Cotati, Calif., 1983-84, MacGregor & Buckley, Larkspur, Calif., 1984-86, Law Offices Melvin Belli, San Francisco, 1987-88, Steinhart & Falconer, San Francisco, 1988; mgr. Computerized Litigation Assocs., San Francisco, 1986; law clk. Morton & Lacy, San Francisco, 1989-91, assoc., 1991-96; atty. Law Offices of Charlotte Venner, San Francisco, 1996-97, Plastiras & Terrizzi, San Francisco, San Rafael, Calif., 1998, Bishop, Barry, Howe, Haney & Ryder, San Francisco, Calif., 1998—. Atty. Vol. Legal Svcs., San Francisco, 1991-96; judge San Francisco Youth Ct., 1995-97; com. chmn. Point Richmond (Calif.) coun., 1994-96. Recipient Whiley Manuel Pro Bono award State Bar Calif., 1993. Mem. Nat. Assn. Ins. Women, Def. Rsch. Inst., Bar Assn. San Francisco (del. 4th world conf. on women 1995, chair product liability com.), Internat. Com. Lawyers for Tibet (litigation com. 1991-97, co-chair women's com.), Ins. Claims Assn. (chmn. membership com. 1994-96), Hon. Order of Blue Goose Internat., Queen's Bench (chmn. employment com. 1994-97, bd. dirs. 1996—), BASF intellectual property/entertainment law). Democrat. Avocations: sailing, playing guitar and saxaphone, home brewing, mountain biking, human rights advocate.

HALLBERG, CLAUDIA SKYE, marketing executive, consultant; b. Huntington Park, Calif., May 6, 1951; d. Ted Ulf and Lynn (Hansen) H. Student U. London, 1971-72; B.A., Scripps Coll., 1973. Brand mgr. Procter & Gamble Co., Cin., 1973-76; account exec., account supr. Needham, Harper & Steers Advt., Chgo., 1976-78; account supr., mgmt. supr. Tracy Locke Advt., Dallas, 1978-80; mgmt. supr. Young & Rubicam, San Francisco, 1980-82; exec. v.p. worldwide dir., 1982-87; pres. Hallberg, Schireson & Co., San Francisco, 1987—. Mem. Older Women's League, Confrérie des Chevaliers du Tastevin, Phi Beta Kappa. Office: Hallberg Schireson & Co 2044 Union St San Francisco CA 94123-4103

HALLENBECK, HARRY C., architect. Dir. State of Calif., Sacramento, 1997; dir. planning and design svc. Vanir Constrn. Mgmt., Inc., Sacramento, 1997—. Recipient Edward C. Kemper award Archtl. Inst. Am., 1994. Office: Vanir Constrn Mgmt Inc State & Consumer Svc Agy 980 9th St Ste 900 Sacramento CA 95814-2719 also: 7485 Rush River Dr # 333 Sacramento CA 95831-5259*

HALLENBECK, POMONA JUANITA, artist; b. Roswell, N.Mex., Nov. 12, 1938; d. Cleve and Juanita Henriette (Williams) H.; children: Cheryl Ellis, Cynthia Ellis-Ralph, Catherine Ellis-Timmons. AA, Ea. N.Mex. U., 1965; BFA, Art Student's League, 1976; postgrad., Pan Am. Art Sch., 1976-77. Mgr. Paul Anderson Photography, San Antonio, Tex., 1951-54; tchr. Roswell (N.Mex.) Ind. Sch. Dist., 1960-64; dir., instr. Sketchbox Sch. Art, Galveston, Tex., 1965-71; monitor etching class Art Student's League, N.Y.C., 1975-77; dir., instr. Alleyworks Atlier, Austin, Tex., 1978-81; dir., proprietor, artist Sketchbox Studio, Roswell, 1982-94; instr. Elderhostel program Ghost Ranch, Abiquiu, N.Mex, 1984-94; coord. Calender project Ghost Ranch, Abiquiu, N.Mex., 1992—; owner, proprietor Pomona's Accent Line, Roswell, 1986-94, cons., 1988-94; artist, demonstrator Roswell (N.Mex.) Mus. and Art Ctr., 1981-90, Roswell (N.Mex.) Ind. Sch., 1982-90, Wonder of Watercolor Workshops, Austin, Tex., 1997-98, Art After Sch., Bastrop, Tex., 1997-98. Illustrator: (book covers) Julian of Norwich, Nachman, Pseudo Dionysius, Classics of Western Spirituality, Naming the Powers, Unmasking the Powers, Engaging the Powers, Ghost Ranch Cookbook, Savoring the Southwest; exhibited in Southwest Expressions Gallery, Chgo., 1990, 91, Claire's Mountain Village, Ruidoso, N.Mex., 1990-94, Roswell Fine Art Mus., 1994, Artisan Gallery, Austin, 1995, Cimmaron (N.Mex.) Art Gallery, 1995, Trading Post, 1995, Bitzer & Johnson, Roswell, 1996, 97, Potter's Guild Sho, 1997, The Gallery Bastrop, Tex., Teeks Gallery, Wimberley, Tex., Laughing at the Sun Gallery, Austin, Artisan's, Austin, 1998. Mem. World Wildlife, 1996, Roswell Assurance Home for Children, 1990, Ghost Ranch Compadres, Santa Fe, 1990-96, People for the Ethical Treatment of Animals, 1996; arts convener silent auction, Ghost Ranch, 1995, New Art Bldg., 1998. Recipient purchase award Am. Artist, 1975; named Best of Show, Ghost Ranch Compadre Show, 1990, Altusa Fashion Show, 1990; scholar Altrusa Club, 1973; grantee Whitney Enterprises, 1990, artist-in-residence grantee Ghost Ranch, 1992, McKee grantee, 1995-96. Mem. Internat. Platform Assn., Nat. Platform Assn., Soc. Illustrators, Taos Fine Arts Assn., N.Mex. Watercolor Soc., Western Colo. Watercolor Soc., Supts. Salon of Paris (Bronze medal 1988), Ghost Ranch Found. Ctr., Roswell Mus. and Art Ctr., U.S. Humane Soc., Tex. Watercolor Soc., Mus. Women Artists, Washington, Knickerbocher (N.Y.C.). Democrat. Avocation: photography. Office: Sketchbox Studio of Art 3737 E Grand Plains Rd Roswell NM 88201-9005

HALLIDAY, JOHN MEECH, investment company executive; b. St. Louis, Oct. 16, 1936; s. William Norman and Vivian Viola (Meech) H.; m. Martha Layne Griggs, June 30, 1962; children: Richard M., Elizabeth Halliday Traut. BS, U.S. Naval Acad., 1958; MBA, Harvard U., 1964. Dir. budgeting and planning Automatic Tape Control, Bloomington, Ill., 1964-66; dir. planning Ralston-Purina, St. Louis, 1966-67, v.p. subsidiary, 1967-68, dir. internat. banking, 1967-68; v.p. Servicetime Corp., St. Louis, 1968-70; assoc. R.W. Halliday Assocs., Boise, Idaho, 1970-87; v.p. Sawtooth Comm. Corp., Boise, 1970-73, Comdr. Corp., 1979-81; pres., CEO, bd. dirs. ML, Ltd., San Francisco, 1979—, H.W.L. Inc., San Francisco, 1985-93; pres. Halliday Labs., Inc., 1980-91; exec. v.p., bd. dirs. Franchise Fin. Corp. Am., Phoenix, 1980-85; bd. dirs., v.p. Harvard Bus. Sch. Assn. No. Calif., 1980-87; pres., CEO, bd. dirs. Cycletorl Diversified Industries, Inc., 1992—; guest lectr. U. Calif. Berkeley, 1991—, Calif. Bus.-Higher Edn. Forum, 1995-98; mem. Senator Bill Lockyer's Ad-Hoc Bus. Adv. Group on Corrections, 1995-96. Pres. Big Bros. San Francisco, 1978-81; trustee, pres. U. Calif.-Santa Cruz Found., 1988—; mem. ad hoc com. on corrections Calif. State Senate, 1995-96. Mem. Restaurant Assn. (v.p. 1969-70), Olympic Club (San Francisco), Scott Valley Tennis Club (Mill Valley, Calif.). Republican. Episcopalian. Home: 351 Corte Madera Ave Mill Valley CA 94941-1013 Office: 44 New Montgomery St Ste 317 San Francisco CA 94105-3402

HALLOCK, C. WILES, JR., athletic official; b. Denver, Feb. 17, 1918; s. Claude Wiles and Mary (Bassler) H.; m. Marjorie Louise Eldred, Mar. 23, 1944; children: Lucinda Eldred Hallock Rinne, Michael Eldred. A.B., U. Denver, 1939. Sports info. dir. U. Wyo., 1949-60, track coach, 1952-56; sports info. dir. U. Calif., Berkeley, 1960-63; dir. pub. relations Nat. Collegiate Athletic Assn., 1963-68; dir. Nat. Collegiate Sports Services, 1967-68; commr. Western Athletic Conf., 1968-71; exec. dir. Pacific-8 Conf. (now Pacific-10 conf.), San Francisco and Walnut Creek, Calif., 1971-83; historian Pacific 10 Conf., 1983. Mem. Laramie (Wyo.) City Council, 1958-60. Served to lt. comdr. USNR, World War II. Decorated Air medal; mem. Nat. Football Found. and Hall of Fame Honors Ct. Mem. Nat. Collegiate Athletic Assn., Nat. Assn. Collegiate Dirs. Athletics (Corbett award 1983), Collegiate Commrs. Assn., Coll. Sports Info. Dirs. Am. (Arch Ward award 1963), Football Writers Assn. Am. (past dir.), U.S. Basketball Writers Assn., Lambda Chi Alpha. Presbyn. Home: 235 Western Hills Dr Pleasant Hill CA 94523-3167 Office: 800 S Broadway Walnut Creek CA 94596-5218*

HALLORAN, JAMES VINCENT, III, technical writer; b. Greenwich, Conn., May 12, 1942; s. James Vincent and Rita Lucy (Keator) H.; m. Barbara Sharon Case, Sept. 7, 1974. BME, Cath. U. Am., 1964; MBA, U. Chgo., 1973. Mktg. rep. Rockwell Internat., El Segundo, Calif., 1973-76, bus. area mgr., 1976-80, bus. analysis mgr., 1980-84; asst. dir. market analysis H. Silver & Assocs. Inc., Torrance, Calif., 1984-87, dir. mktg., 1987-90; program mgr. Tech. Tng. Corp., Torrance, 1990-91; prin. Bus. Info. & Analysis, Redondo Beach, Calif., 1991-94; mgr. spl. projects Wyle Labs., El Segundo, Calif., 1994—. Commr. Redondo Beach Housing Adv. and Appeals Bd., 1985-89; mem. citizens adv. bd. South Bay Union High Sch. Dist., Redondo Beach, 1983; dir. Project Tomahawk, Curtiss-Wright Hist. Assn., 1995—, newsletter editor, 1995-98, spl. events chmn., 1998— . Capt. USAF, 1964-68. Libertarian. Avocations: cycling, photography, traveling abroad. Home: 612 S Gertruda Ave Redondo Beach CA 90277-4245 Office: Wyle Labs 128 Maryland St El Segundo CA 90245-4115

HALLOWELL, JOHN H, minister; b. L.I., Oct. 30, 1953; s. John Wentworth and Ann Marie (Burkhard) H.; m. Kathryn Margaret Allen, Dec. 30, 1978; children: David, Marke, Matthew. BA in Classical Langs., Calif. State U., Long Beach, 1979. Ordained min. Calvary Chapel, Capistrano Beach, Calif., 1985—, pastoral rschr., 1985—. Mem. Am. Acad. Religion, Soc. Bibl. Lit. Home: 27251 Rosario Mission Viejo CA 92692-3512 Office: Calvary Chapel 25975 Domingo Ave Capo Beach CA 92624-1115

HALLSTROM, ROBERT CHRIS, government actuary; b. Sacramento, June 8, 1953; s. Clifford Clarence and Billee June (Plunkett) H.; m. Pamela Jane Pracht, Apr. 25, 1987; 1 child, Kelsey Kathlene. BA in Math. with honors, Calif. State U., Sacramento, 1974, MS in Math., 1976. Cert. math. tchr. c.c., Calif. Asst. actuary Transam. Ins. Co., L.A., 1976-80; actuary Cal-Farm Ins. Co., Sacramento, 1980-84; instr. math. Sacramento City Coll., 1985, Sierra Coll., Rocklin, Calif., 1985; sr. casualty actuary Calif. Dept. Ins., San Francisco, 1985—. Fellow Casualty Actuarial Soc.; mem. Internat. Actuarial Assn. Avocations: mathematics, collecting books and phonograph records, reading. Office: Calif Dept Ins 45 Fremont St Fl 24 San Francisco CA 94105-2204

HALLUIN, ALBERT PRICE, lawyer; b. Nov. 8, 1939; children: Russell, Marcus. BA, La. State U., 1964; JD, U. Balt., 1969. Bar: Md. 1970, N.Y. 1985, Calif. 1991. Assoc. Jones, Tullar & Cooper, Arlington, Va., 1969-71; sr. patent atty. CPC Internat. Inc., Englewood Cliffs, N.J., 1971-76; counsel Exxon Rsch. & Engring. Co., Florham Park, N.J., 1976-83; v.p., chief intellectual property counsel Cetus Corp., Emeryville, Calif., 1983-90; ptnr. Fleisler, Dubb, Meyer & Lovejoy, San Francisco, 1990-92, Limbach & Limbach, San Francisco, 1992-94, Pennie & Edmonds, Menlo Park, Calif., 1994-97, Howery & Simon, Menlo Park, 1997—; pres., CEO, chmn. Halzyme Tech., Inc., 1995—. Contbr. articles to legal jours. Pres. Belle Roche Homeowners Assn., Redwood City, Calif., 1995—. Named One of Top 20 Intellectual Property Lawyers, Calif. Lawyer's mag., 1993. Mem. ABA, Am. Intellectual Property Law Assn. (chmn. chem. practice com. 1981-83, sec. 1984-85, bd. dirs. 1984-89, founding chmn. biotech. com. 1990-92), Licensing Exec. Soc., Assn. Corp. Patent Counsel, Bar Assn. San Francisco, San Francisco Patent Assn. Republican. Episcopalian. E-mail: HalluinA@Howrey.com. and Halzym@Earthlink.net. FAX: 650-463-8400. Office: Howery & Simon 301 Ravenswood Ave Menlo Park CA 94025

HALOPOFF, WILLIAM EVON, industrial designer, consultant; b. Los Angeles, May 31, 1934; s. William John Halopoff and Dorothy E. (Foote) Lawrence; m. Nancy J. Ragsdale, July 12, 1960; children: Guy William and Carolee Nichole. BS, Art Ctr. Coll. Design, 1968. Internat. indsl. design cons. FMC Corp. Cen. Engring. Lab., Santa Clara, Calif., 1969-81; mgr. indsl. design Tandem Computers, Cupertino, Calif., 1981-93; design cons. Halopoff Assocs., San Jose, Calif., 1984—. Patentee in field. Served with U.S. Army, 1957-59. Mem. Indsl. Designers Soc. Am., Soc. Automotive Engrs. (chmn. subcom. 29 1979-85). Avocation: fine art. Home and Office: 17544 Holiday Dr Morgan Hill CA 95037-6303

HALSELL, GEORGE KAY, music educator; b. Bryan, Tex., 1956; s. Kay and Jo Inez (Wootten) H.; m. Melanie Lynn Marsh, 1984. MusB, Johns Hopkins Univ., 1979; MusM, U. Tex., 1980, DMA, 1989. Instr. music West Va. Univ., Morgantown, 1983-84; adj. instr. music Essex C.C., Balt., 1985-90, Frederick (Md.) C.C., 1985-90; asst. prof. music Adams State Coll., Alamosa, Colo., 1990-91; adj. instr. music Pikes Peak C.C., Colorado Springs, 1992-94, U. So. Colo., Pueblo, 1992-94; asst. prof. music Coll. So. Idaho, Twin Falls, 1994—; freelance musician; lectr. Pueblo Symphony Orch., 1992-94. Office: Coll So Idaho 315 Falls Ave Twin Falls ID 83301-3367

HALTERMAN, HAROLD LELAND, lawyer; b. Vallejo, Calif., Oct. 11, 1950; s. Harold Prescott and Lorraine Edna (Lowery) H.; m. Margaret M. Russell, June 23, 1991; children: Alexander Cheff, Kimiko Lorraine; 1 stepchild, Joshua L. Brooks. AB, U. Calif., Berkeley, 1973, JD, 1979. Bar: Calif. 1979, U.S. Dist. Ct. (no. dist.) Calif. 1979. Precinct coord. Com. to Elect Ronald V. Dellums, Oakland, Calif., 1970; adminstrv. aide U.S. Rep. Ronald V. Dellums, Oakland, 1971-80, dist. counsel, 1980-92, dist. dir., gen. coun., 1993; counsel, policy dir. House Armed Svcs. Com., 1994-95; precinct coord. Com. to Re-elect Ronald V. Dellums, Oakland, 1972, mgr. campaign, 1974; Dem. counsel Ho. Nat. Security Com., Washington, 1995-98; campaign chmn. Barbara Lee for Congress Com., 1998—; pres., dir. Surviving in the '80s, Oakland, 1979-92. Author: Defense Sense, 1983; writer, critic San Francisco Bay Guardian, 1981-85. Mem. com. Dems. United, Oakland, 1972-76; chair Mayor's Adv. Com., Berkeley, 1974-76, 79-81; mem. steering com. Berkeley Citizens Action, 1974-76, 81; mem. Human Rigths Advs., 1979-92; mem. ctrl. com., exec. com. Calif. Dem. Party, 1986-92; bassist, vocalist Third Pary (rhythm and blues band), 1989-92, Fabulous Jackalopes, 1992-93. Recipient Svc. award Lions Club, 1966. Mem. ACLU (local chpt., bd. dirs. 1983-92, pres. 1988-91), Ctrl. Com. for Conscientious Objectors, State Bar Assn. Calif., Alameda Dem. Lawyers Com., Nat. Lawyers Guild, Boalt Hall Alumni Assn. Avocations: tennis, music, fatherhood. Office: Offices of H Lee Halterman 405 14th St Ste 208 Oakland CA 94612-2705

HALVORSEN, JAN LA RAYNE, library services manager; b. Chgo., Aug. 30, 1941; d. La Vern Grant and Dorothy Ethelyn (Johnston) Kelley; m. Wayne Lee Halvorsen, Nov. 5, 1958 (div. Feb. 1975); children: Jon Alan, Kathryn Lynn. BA in Polit. Sci. with honors, Calif. State Poly. U., 1975; M in Pub. Adminstrn., U. Calif., Riverside, 1977; MLS, UCLA, 1990. Ops. supr. City of Huntington Beach (Calif.) Libr., 1984-90, libr. svcs. mgr. circulation, tech. svcs., branches, 1991—; guest lectr. mcpl. fin. Calif. State Poly. U., Pomona, 1986, 87; guest lectr. libr. mgmt. UCLA, 1989; intenr devel. office UCLA, 1988, Mayor Tom Bradley's city econ. devel. office City of L.A., 1989; spkr. Women's Fedn. for World Peace, Anjo, Japan, 1996. Founder family literacy program U.S. Dept. Health Edn. and Welfare, Huntington Beach, 1993, svc. club for teenage girls Valley (Vista H.S.) Club, Fountain Valley, Calif., 1996; dir. ARIDAY, Costa Mesa, Calif., 1994; v.p. Mgmt. Employees Orgn., Huntington Beach, 1986, pres., 1987; sister city rep. from Huntington Beach to Anjo, Japan, 1996. Community Devel. grantee Huntington Beach Dept. Housing Urban Devel., 1994, 97, Calif. League of Cities Helen Putnam award for Excellence, Top award for Cultural Diversity for New Oak View Branch, 1995, Internat. award for svc. for founding Teen Svc. Club, Soroptimist Internat. of Americas, 1997. Mem. ALA, Am. Soc. Pub. Adminstrn., Calif. Libr. Assn. (chair women's devel. conf. 1991-92), Acad. Polit. Sci., Soroptimist Internat. (newsletter, del. 1991-92, 92-93, v.p. 1993-94, pres. 1994-95, Desert Coast region dist. II sec. 1996-98, rep. UN 4th World Women's Conf. Beijing 1995, Internat. Youth Citizen award, DCR/dist. II chair 1998—), UN Assn. (Orange County edn. chair 1997-99, v.p. 1999—). Avocations: scuba diving, piloting small aircraft, swimming. Home: 15682 Mayflower Ln Huntington Beach CA 92647-2807 Office: Huntington Beach Libr 7111 Talbert Ave Huntington Beach CA 92648-1232

HALVORSON, ALFRED RUBIN, retired mayor, consultant, education educator; b. Milan, Minn., Jan. 22, 1921; s. Chris and Alice (Kleven) H.; m. Dorothy F. Boxrud, Apr. 23, 1944; children: Gary A., Joan D. Halvorson Felice. BS, U. Minn., 1944, PhD, 1949. County extension agt. Agr. Extension Svc. of Minn., St. Paul, 1945; soil fertility researcher Oreg. State U., Klamath Falls, 1949-54; extension agronomist Purdue U., Lafayette, Ind., 1954-57; extension soil scientist Wash. State U., Pullman, 1957-86, prof. emeritus, 1986—; cons. ACF & Shirley Fetilizer Ltd., Brisbane, Australia, 1964, Saudi Arabia Farming Ops., Riyadh, 1984, U.S. AID, Sanaa, North Yemen, 1987. City councilman, City of Pullman, 1987-91, mayor, 1991-95. With M.C. U.S. Army, 1945. Mem. Kiwanis (chair com. Pullman chpt.). Republican. Lutheran. Avocations: hiking, backpacking, gardening, reading, classics. Home and Office: 325 SE Nebraska St Pullman WA 99163-2239

HALVORSON, MARJORY, opera director. Pvt. studies with, Sister Marietta Coyle, Jerry Daniels, Dolores Ravich. Dir. vocal studies Whitworth Coll., Spokane; artistic dir. Spokane Opera, Spokane; dir. vocal master classes iwth Thomas Hampson, Richard Miller, Dale Moore, John Shirley-Quirk, James Maddalena, Armen Guzlimien; tchr. pvt. lesons in voice, vocal pedagogy, diction and lit.; director opera workshop. Named Woman of Achievement in Arts and Culture, City of Spokane, 1996; recipient outstanidng cmty. svc. award Westminster United Ch. of Christ. Office: Spokane Opera 643 S Ivory Spokane WA 99202*

HAM, GARY MARTIN, psychologist; b. Lincoln, Nebr., Feb. 6, 1940; s. Wendell E. and Sally Bertha (Lind) H.; children: Jeffery M. BS in Psychology, Wash. State U., 1963, MS in Psychology, 1965; PsyD, Newport U., 1988. Diplomate Am. Psychotherapy Assn., Am. Bd. Psychol. Spltys. in Med. Psychology; lic. psychologist, Calif.; cert. tchr., Calif, counselor. Clin. psychologist Riverside (Calif.) County Dept. Mental Health, 1967—; tchr., cons., pub. speaker, researcher Riverside County Dept. Mental Health, 1967—; instr. U. Calif. Riverside, Chapman U. Clin. psychologist Riverside County, Critical Incidents Disaster Response Team, 1985—, ARC Disaster Team. 1st lt. USAF, 1964-67. Mem. APA, ASCD, Am. Mental Health Counselors Assn., Am. Critical Incident Stress Found., Calif. Psychol. Assn., Air Force Soc. Psychologists, Am. Coll. Forensic Examiners, Psi Chi, Sigma Phi Epsilon. Office: Riverside County Dept Mental Health PO Box 52567 Riverside CA 92517-3567

HAMADA, DUANE TAKUMI, architect; b. Honolulu, Aug. 12, 1954; s. Robert Kensaku and Jean Hakue (Masutani) H.; m. Martha S.P. Lee, Dec. 22, 1991; children: Erin, Robyn, David. BFA in Environ. Design, U. Hawaii, 1977, BArch, 1979. Registered architect, Hawaii, Guam, Florida, Puerto Rico, Saipan. Intern Edward Sullam, FAIA & Assocs., Honolulu, 1979-80; assoc. Design Ptnrs., Inc., Honolulu, 1980-86; prin. AM Ptnrs., Inc., Honolulu, 1986-98; dir. Design Ptnrs. Inc., Honolulu, 1998—. Chmn. 31st Ann. Cherry Blossom Festival Fashion Show, Honolulu, 1982, 32d Ann. Cherry Blossom Festival Cooking Show, 1983, mem. steering com., 1982, 83. Recipient Gold Key award for Excellence in Interior Design Am. Hotel and Motel Assn., 1990, Renaissance '90 Merit award Nat. Assn. Home Builder's Remodeler Coun., Merit award Honolulu mag., 1990, Cert. of Appreciation PACDIV USN, 1992, Gold Nugget award of Merit, 1997. Mem. AIA (jury student awards 1997), Constrn. Specifications Inst., Nat. Coun. Archtl. Registration Bds., Colegio de Arcquitectos de P.R., Japanese C. of C. Hawaii, Japan-Am. Soc., Hawaiian Astron. Soc. Avocations: astronomy, music. Office: Design Ptnrs Inc 1580 Makaloa St Ste 1100 Honolulu HI 96814*

HAMAI, JAMES YUTAKA, business executive; b. L.A., Oct. 14, 1926; s. Seizo and May (Sata) H.; B.S., U. So. Calif., 1952, M.S., 1955; postgrad. bus. mgmt. program industry exec., UCLA, 1963-64; m. Dorothy K. Fukuda, Sept. 10, 1954; 1 child, Wendy A. Lectr. chem. engring. dept. U. So. Calif., Los Angeles, 1963-64; process engr., sr. process engr. Fluor Corp., Los Angeles, 1954-64; sr. project mgr. central research dept. Monsanto Co., St. Louis, 1964-67, mgr. research, devel. and engring. graphic systems dept., 1967-68, mgr. comml. devel. New Enterprise div., 1968-69; exec. v.p., dir. Concrete Cutting Industries, Inc., Los Angeles, 1969-72, pres., dir. Concrete Cutting Internat., Inc., Los Angeles, 1972-78, chmn. bd., 1978—; cons. Fluor Corp., Los Angeles, 1970-72; dir. Intech Systems Co., Ltd., Tokyo, Cutting Industries Co., Ltd., Tokyo, Unity Five Industries, Ltd., Tokyo; internat. bus. cons. Served with AUS, 1946-48. Mem. Am. Inst. Chem. Engrs., Am. Mgmt. Assn., Tau Beta Pi, Phi Lambda Upsilon. Club: Rotary (gov. dist. 1982-83). Home: 6600 Via La Paloma Rancho Palos Verdes CA 90275-6449 Office: PO Box 700 Wilmington CA 90748-0700

HAMBRECHT, WILLIAM R., retired venture capitalist; b. 1935; married; 5 children. Student, Princeton U. Broker Francis I. DuPont & Co., San Francisco; mng. ptnr. Hambrecht & Quist, San Francisco, pres., chief exec. officer, dir., now chmn.; ret., 1997; bd. dirs. People Express, Inc.

HAMBURGER, ROBERT N., pediatrics educator, consultant; b. N.Y.C., Jan. 26, 1923; s. Samuel B. and Harriet (Newfield) H.; m. Sonia Gross, Nov. 9, 1943; children: Hilary, Debre (dec.), Lisa. BA, U. N.C., 1947; MD, Yale U., 1951. Diplomate Am. Bd. Pediatrics, Am. Bd. Allergy and Immunology. Instr., asst. clin. prof. sch. medicine Yale U., New Haven, 1951-60; assoc. prof. biology U. Calif. San Diego, La Jolla, 1960-64, assoc. prof. pediatrics, 1964-67, prof., 1970-90, prof. emeritus, 1990—, asst. dean sch. medicine, 1964-70, lab. dir., 1970—, head fellows tng. program allergy and immunology divsn., 1970-90; pres. RNA and Co., Inc., 1997—; cons. various cos., Calif., Sweden, Switzerland, 1986—; bd. dirs. La Jolla Diagnostics, Inc. Author 1 book; contbr. articles to profl. jours.; patentee allergy peptides, allergen detector. Vol. physician, educator Children of the Californias, Calif. and Baja California, Mex., 1993—. 1st lt. Air Corps, U.S. Army, 1943-45. Grantee NIH and USPHS, 1960-64, 64-84; Fulbright fellow, 1980, Disting. fellow Am. Coll. Allergy, Asthma, Immunology, 1986. Mem. U. Calif. San Diego Emeriti Assn. (pres. 1992-94). Avocations: flying, skiing, writing. Office: U Calif San Diego Allergy Immunology Lab La Jolla CA 92093-0950

HAMBY, BARBARA JEAN, writer, poet; b. Chico, Calif., Apr. 20, 1929; d. Frank Llewellyn Fairfield and Grace Ellen Mann; separated; children: Gail D. Wilson Anderson, Kurt E. Deutscher. Student, U. Wash., 1947-48, Clark Coll., 1990—. Author: My Muse Has Many Moods, 1995, Trilogy: Love Lines, Life Lines, Laugh Lines, 1998. Named Golden Poet, World of Poetry, 1987, 91, Silver Poet, 1989, People to People Amb. to South Africa, Women Writers, 1995. Mem. NOW, Older Women's League, Oreg. State Poetry Assn. (2nd prize 1995), Wash. State Poets (3rd prize 1995), Southwest Wash. Writers, Columbia Poets (1st prize 1990). Democrat. Unitarian. Avocations: swimming, walking, traveling. Office: Drummer Pub PO Box 65596 Vancouver WA 98665

HAMEL, BERNARD HENRI, publisher; b. Tupperware, N.Y., Nov. 11, 1927; s. Joseph Emile and Irene (Martineau) H.; m. Leonor Kahanoff, Aug. 5, 1965; children: Carlos, Bernard Jr. BA, U. de las Americas, Mex., 1955; MA, UCLA, 1959; PhD, U. Madrid, 1962. Prof. Calif. State U., L.A., 1962-66, Occidental Coll., L.A., 1966-69; pres., owner Bernard Hamel Spanish Book Corp., L.A., 1967—, Bilingual Book Press, L.A., 1994—. author: Bilingual Dictionary of Mexican Spanish, 1994, Bilingual Dictionary of Latin American Spanish, 1996, Bilingual Dictionary of Spanish False Cognates, 1998. Pres. Argentinian Sch. of L.A. Office: Bernard Hamel Spanish Book Corp 10977 Santa Monica Blvd Los Angeles CA 90025-4538

HAMER, JEANNE HUNTINGTON, soprano, educator; b. Lovell, Wyo., Mar. 1, 1933; d. Edward Olney and Francine M. (Clavier) Huntington; Mus.B. with honors, U. Wyo., 1955, postgrad., 1976-82, MA with honors, 1984; postgrad. U. Denver, 1976; m. Roger F. Hamer, Aug. 19, 1955; children: Michael Edward, Kathryn Louise. Grad. teaching asst. U. Wyo., 1955-56; pvt. vocal tchr., Billings, Mont., 1957-58, Miles City, Mont., 1958-59, Grand Rapids, Minn., 1959-61, Torrington, Wyo., 1962—; instr. music Eastern Wyo. Coll., 1968—, chmn. dept. music, 1978—, faculty emerita, 1992—; part-time instr., 1992—; lead roles in operas, including: The Medium, The Telephone, Cavalleria Rusticana, I Pagliacci, Baby Doe; soloist with Billings (Mont.) Symphony, Casper (Wyo.) Symphony, Scottsbluff (Nebr.) Symphony, Nebr. Panhandle Symphony, U. Wyo. Symphony, Wyo. chorus for Wyo. Centennial at Teton Music Festival with Orch.; soprano Barta Trio, 1972-89; mem. Cheyenne Chamber Singers, 1992—, soloist, adjudicator for music festivals, Wyo., Mont., Nebr.; organist, choir dir. All Saints Episcopal Ch., Torrington, 1974-82, 86-98; dir. Torrington Community Chorus, 1975-93. Mem. Nat. Assn. Tchrs. Singing (gov. Wyo.), Am. Choral Dirs. Assn., Music Educators Nat. Conf., Wyo. Am. Choral Dirs. (pres. 1988-91). Episcopalian. Clubs: PEO, Order Eastern Star. Home: 515 E 23rd Ave Torrington WY 82240-2529 Office: 3200 W C St Torrington WY 82240-1603

HAMERLY, RANDALL ALAN, architect; b. Walla Walla, Wash., July 28, 1961; s Elray and Sharon Louise (Sjoboen) H.; m. Patricia Suzanne Floyd, July 15, 1990. BArch, Calif. Polytech. State U., 1984. Lic. architect, Calif., Nev., Idaho. Intern architect ROM Assocs., Riverside, Calif., 1984-87; architect, project mgr. Dan Smith Assocs., Redlands, Calif., 1987-91; architect pvt. practice, Highland, Calif., 1991—; mem. Meadow Oaks design rev. bd. Chair Planning Commn., City of Loma Linda, Calif., 1994-95; bd. dirs., assoc. head elder Univ. Ch., Loma Linda, 1992—. Mem. AIA (bd. dirs. 1995—, treas. 1997—), Tau Sigma Delta. Avocations: skiing, tennis, cycling. Office: 7353 Silkwood Ln Highland CA 92346-6225

HAMILTON, ALLEN PHILIP, financial advisor; b. Albany, Calif., Oct. 17, 1937; s. Allen Philip Sr. and Barbara Louise (Martin) H.; m. Mary Williams, July 18, 1981 (div. Mar. 1987). BA in Bus. Mgmt., St. Mary's U., San Jose, Calif., 1961; AA, Contra Costa State Coll., 1957; Bus. Assoc. degree, NW Mo. State U., 1969; postgrad., San Jose State U., 1959-61. Cert. fin. planner. Fin. advisor Consol. Investment Svcs., Kansas City, Mo., 1968-70; pres., CEO, Balanced Mgmt. Assn., Mission, Kans., 1969-72, Advanced Svc. Assn., Overland Park, Kans., 1971-78; divisional mgr. Waddell & Reed, Inc., Kansas City, 1978-81; sr. v.p., regional dir. WZW Fin. Svcs., Kansas City, 1981-86; exec.v.p. Skaife & Co., Orinda, Calif., 1986-88; v.p., mktg. dir. Consol. Securities Corp., Walnut Creek, Calif., 1988; sr. dir. and cert. trainer Club Am., Inc., L.A., 1990—; CFP, prin. Hamilton Fin. Adv., Am. Investment Svcs., Pleasant Hill., Calif., 1989—; silver mktg. distbr., corp. trainer, Can. mktg. distbr. and trainer Nikken, Inc. Internat., numerous fgn. countries, 1991—; sales mgr., ind. distributor, sales trainer Alpine Industries, 1992—; prin. advisor Environ. Solutions Internat.; exec. dir., C.E.O. Environ. Air Quality and Health Found. (Environ. Solutions Internat.), 1998—; sales, mktg. dir. Exthel Wireless Communications Inc., 1998—; trainer, presdl. dir. Builders Referral Inc., Orange County, Calif., 1998—; sr. dir. Club Am. OTC Pink Shts., L.A., 1990-92; presdl. dir. FundAmerica, Irvine, Calif., 1988—; guest speaker in field. Author: (with others) The Financial Planner A New Profession, 1986. Asst. dist. commr. Boy Scouts Am., Kansas City, Kans., 1970-79; corp. dir. United Campaign, Overland Park, Kans., 1965-73; active TV show Kidney Found., Kansas City, Mo., 1969-70; sr. arbitrator San Francisco Bay Area Better Bus. Bur., 1986—. Lt. U.S. Army, 1963-65. Recipient Citation Nat. Campaign Re-election 1992, 1992m Senatorial Commn. Rep. Senatorial Inner Circle, 1991. Mem. Inst. Cert. Fin. Planners, Internat. Assn. for Fin. Planning (v.p., bd. dirs. 1982-87, practitioner div.), Registry of Fin. Planning Practitioners, Mt. Diablo Distbrs. Assn. Republican. Avocations: cars, outdoors, tennis, travel, boating. Home: 8 Robin Ridge Aliso Viejo CA 92656

HAMILTON, CHARLES HOWARD, metallurgy educator; b. Pueblo, Colo., Mar. 17, 1935; s. George Edwin and Eva Eleanor (Watson) H.; m. Joy Edith Richmond, Sept. 7, 1968; children: Curtis Gene, Krista Kathleen, Brady Glenn. BS, Colo. Sch. Mines, 1959; MS, U. So. Calif., 1965; PhD, Case Western Res. U., 1968. Research engr. Space div. Rockwell Internat., Downey, Calif., 1959-65; mem. tech. staff Los Angeles div. Rockwell Internat., 1968-75; tech. staff, phys. metallurgy Sci. Ctr., Thousand Oaks, Calif., 1975-77, group mgr. metals processing, 1977-79, prin. scientist, 1979-81, dir. materials synthesis and processing dept., 1982-84; assoc. prof. metallurgy Wash. State U., Pullman, 1984-87, prof., 1987—; chmn. Rockwell Corp. tech. panel, materials research and engring; co-organizer 1st Internat. Symposium Superplastic Forming, 1982, Internat. Conf. on Superplasticity and Superplastic Forming, 1988. Sr. editor Jour. Materials Shaping Tech.; dep. editor Scripta Metallurgica et Materialia, 1989—; contbr. tech. articles to profl. publs.; patentee advanced metalworking and tech. Named Rockwell Engr. of Yr., 1979; recipient IR 100 award Indsl. Research mag., 1976, 80. Fellow Am. Soc. Metals; mem. AIME (shaping and forming com.), Sigma Xi. Home: 410 SE Crestview St Pullman WA 99163-2213

HAMILTON, DARDEN COLE, flight test engineer; b. Pitts., Nov. 28, 1956; s. Isaac Herman Hamilton and Grace Osborne (Fish) Thorp; m. Linda Susanne Moser, Aug. 7, 1976; children: Christopher Moser Hamilton, Elijah Cole Hamilton. BS in Aeronautics, St. Louis U., Cahokia, Ill., 1977; postgrad., Ariz. State U. Lic. pilot, airframe and power mechanic. Engr. McDonnell Douglas Aircraft Co., St. Louis, Mo., 1977-80; group leader, engring. Cessna Aircraft Co., Wichita, Kans., 1980-83, sr. flight test engr., 1983-85; sr. flight test engr. Allied-Signal Aerospace Co., Phoenix, 1986-92, flight test engr. specialist, 1992-98, prin. engr., 1998—. Editor Family Proponent Newsletter, 1994-98. Mem. Ariz. Gov.'s Constnl. Commemoration Com., 1997-99; bd. dirs. Ariz. House and Senate Chaplaincy, 1997-98, chmn. bd. advisors, 1998—; Desert Sky precinct committeeman Glendale Rep. Com.; vol. coord. legis. dist. 16 campaign John Shadegg for Congress, 1994-96; elected dist. 16 for Ariz. Senate, 1999—; mem. adult edn. dept. Rivers Cmty. Ch.; del. Ariz. dist. 16 Ariz. Rep. Conv., 1995—; resolutions com. Ariz. Rep. Com. Mem. NRA (life, cert. instr.), Soc. Flight Test Engrs., Am. Helicopter Soc., Ariz. State Rifle and Pistol Assn. (life). Avocations: horses, target shooting, camping. Home: 5533 W Christy Dr Glendale AZ 85304-3889 Office: Allied-Signal Aerospace Co Allied Signal Engines Inc 111 S 34th St Phoenix AZ 85034-2802

HAMILTON, DAVID ARTHUR, performing arts educator, actor; b. Pocatello, Idaho, Oct. 20, 1956; s. David A. and Margaret Katherine (Keesey) H. BA, Calif. State U., Sacramento, 1980; MA, San Diego State U., 1985; MFA, U. Calif., Davis, 1989. Actor Great Am. Melodrama, Bakersfield, Calif., 1985, Berkeley Repertory Theatre, Shakespeare, San Francisco, 1985-87; instr. San Joaquin Delta Coll., Stockton, Calif., 1988-90; dir. theatre Lake Tahoe (Calif.) Cmty. Coll., 1989—. Film critic Tahoe Mountain News, 1995—; actor in various companies. Pres. Lake Tahoe (Calif.) Theatre Co., 1989-94; bd. dirs. Tahoe Arts Project, Lake Tahoe, 1990-92. Recipient Contributions to Theatre award El Dorado Arts Council, 1993. Mem. Assn. Theatre Higher Edn., Calif. Tchrs. Assn., Calif. Ednl. Theater Assn. (bd. dirs. 1993—, pres. No. Calif. chpt. 1993-95). Avocations: mountain biking, kayaking, skiing. E-mail: Hamiltonda@LTCC.cc.ca.us. Fax: 530-541-7852. Office: Lake Tahoe Community Coll 1 College Dr South Lake Tahoe CA 96150-4500

HAMILTON, DAVID MIKE, publishing company executive; b. Little Rock, 1951; s. Ralph Franklin and Mickey Garnette H.; m. Carol Nancy McKenna, Oct. 25, 1975; children: Elisabeth Michelle, Caroline Ellen. BA, Pitzer Coll., 1973; MLS, UCLA, 1976. Cert. tchr. library sci., Calif. Editor Sullivan Assocs., Palo Alto, Calif., 1973-75; curator Henry E. Huntington Library, San Marino, Calif., 1976-80; mgr. prodn., mktg. William Kaufmann Pubs., Los Altos, Calif., 1980-84; pres. The Live Oak Press, Palo Alto, 1984—; cons. editor, gen. ptnr. Sensitive Expressions Pub. Co., Palo Alto, 1985—; consulting dir. AAAI Press, 1994—; mng. editor and pub. AI Mag. Author: To the Yukon with Jack London, 1980, The Tools of My Trade, 1986, Making A Digital Book, 1994; contbg. editor and webmaster AAAI world-wide web site, 1995—; contbg. author Small Press jour., 1986, Making a Digital Book, 1995, (books) Book Club of California Quarterly, 1985, Research Guide to Biography and Criticism, 1986. Sec. vestry Trinity Parish, Menlo Park, 1986, bd. dirs., 1985-87; trustee Jack London Ednl.

Found., San Francisco; bd. dirs. ISYS Forum, Palo Alto, 1987-96; pres. site coun., mem. supt.'s adv. com. Palo Alto Unified Sch. Dist. Mem. ALA, Coun. on Scholarly, Med. and Ednl. Publs., Am. Assn. Artificial Intelligence (bd. dirs. 1984—, dir. publs.), Bookbuilders West (book show com. 1983), Author's Guild, Soc. Tech. Communication (judge 1984), Assn. Computing Machinery (chmn. pub. com. 1984), Soc. Scholarly Pubs., Sierra Club (life), Book Club Calif. Democrat. Episcopalian. Avocations: backpacking, camping, hiking, book collecting. Home: 2620 Emerson St Palo Alto CA 94306-2310 Office: The Live Oak Press PO Box 60036 Palo Alto CA 94306-0036

HAMILTON, EARL, artist; b. Tokyo, Aug. 20, 1956; s. George and Satsuko (Yamaguchi) H. Represented by Attic Gallery, Portland, Lawrence Gallery, Sheridan, Oreg., Foster White Gallery, Kirkland, Wash., Bush Art Ctr., Salem, Oreg., Mack Gallery, Seattle, 1996—, Coda Gallery, Palm Desert, Calif., 1999—; asst. art tchr. Oreg. State U., Corvallis; demonstrator, lectr. in field. One man shows include Thelma Pearsons Gallery, Lincoln City, Oreg., 1979, Portland (Oreg.) Art Mus., 1991; two man show includes Georgetown Manor, Portland, Oreg., 1979; group shows include Mt. Hood C. C., Gresham, Oreg., 1974, Wilson Hall Oreg. State U., Corvallis, Oreg., 1975, Equitable Savings and Loan Assn., Portland, Oreg., 1976, Rental Sales Galery Portland Mus. Art, 1979, Lakewood Ctr. Lake Oswego, Oreg., 1981-82, Willamette U., Salem, Oreg., 1981, Lakewood Art Ctr., Lake Oswego, 1982-87, Lawrence Gallery, Sheridan, Oreg., 1988-89, 90, 91, 92, 93, 94, 95, 97, Saif Corp. Gallery, Salem, Oreg., 1988, Salem Art Assn., 1988, Waikiki Fence Sale, Honolulu, 1989, Raindance Gallery, Portland, 1989-90, 91, 92, 93, 94, 95, 96, Thelma Pearsons Gallery, 1989, Foster White Gallery, Seattle, 1988-90, 93, Corner Gallery Bush Barn, Salem, 1990, Attic Gallery, Portland, 1991-92, 93, 94, 95, 96, 97, Forcast Gallery, Portland, 1991-92, Coin Gallery, Portland, 1992, Oreg. State Capital Bldg., 1992, Oreg. Coun. Galleria Gallery, Portland, 1992, Gallery at Salishan, Gleneden Beach, Oreg., 1996, Mack Gallery, Seattle, 1996, Earthenworks Gallery, Laconner, Wash., 1997; represented in collections including La. Corp., Hilton Hotel, Hilman Properties, Fidelity Nat. Title, St. Vincent's Hosp., Keizer Hosp., Capital Cons., Inc., Stroebe Zinc and Assocs., U.S. Nat. Bank, Mt. Hood C.C., First Interstate Bank, Oreg. Trailblazers Basketball players Kenny Carr, Wayne Copper, Buck Williams. Recipient Scholastic Cert. of Merit State of Oreg., 1969, Scholastic Gold Key Nat. Graphic Design Contest State of Oreg., 1970, Nat. Gold Medal Scholastic Art award Competition, 1970, 2nd Place scholarship Oreg. State U., 1976, The Grumbacher award N.W. Watercolor Soc., 1980, First Place Sweepstake award Watercolor Soc., 1981, First Place profl. category Oreg. State Fair, 1991, Third Place profl. category, 1993. Mem. Amnesty Internat., Covenant House. Home: 137 E Pine St Lebanon OR 97355-3456

HAMILTON, ELEANOR LEIGH, writer, therapist; b. Portland, Oreg., Oct. 6, 1909; d. Kenneth and Clara Belle (Cunningham) Poorman; m. Albert Edward Hamilton, Aug. 12, 1932, (wid. 1969); children: Heather, Mark, Wendy, April. AB, U. Oreg., 1930; MA, Columbia U., 1939, PhD, 1953. Marriage counselor, psychologist, sex educator and therapist. Dir. girl reserves YWCA, San Jose, Calif., 1930-32; dir., founder Hamilton Sch., Inc., N.Y.C., 1933-48, Sheffield, Mass., 1948-83; marriage counselor, sex therapist Hamilton Sch., Inc., N.Y.C. and Sheffield, 1955-83; dir., founder Inverness Ridge Counseling Ctr., Inverness, Calif., 1983-93; Cons. Inst. for Advanced Study of Sex, San Francisco, 1979—, Pt. Reyes Light, Pt. Reyes Station, Calif., 1986—. Author: Partners In Love, 1961, Sex Before Marriage, 1969, Sex With Love: A Guide for Young People (ALA award 1979, Soc. Sci. Study of Sex Achievement of Yr. award 1979); columnist The Point Reyes Light, 1989—. Fellow Am. Assn. Marriage and Family Therapists; diplomate Am. Coll. Sexology; mem. Soc. for Scientific Study of Sex, Am. Soc. Journalists and Authors, Am. Fedn. TV and Radio Artists, Soroptomist (v.p. Pt. Reyes Station chpt. 1988-89), Garden Club. Avocations: camping, house building, massage therapy, dogs for the handicapped and companion dogs. Home: 2069 Marylhurst Dr West Linn OR 97068-1422

HAMILTON, JODY ANN, personal manager, film producer; b. Santa Monica, Calif., Jan. 18, 1967; d. Joseph Henry and Carol Creighton (Burnett) H. BA, U. Pacific, Stockton, Calif., 1988; assoc. degree, Colo. Inst. Art, Denver, 1990. Exec. asst. Cinema Music Group, Hollywood, Calif., 1990-91; CEO JH Entertainment, Valley Village, Calif., 1991—. Author, producer (film) Relativity 3 The Movie, 1995; prodr. Conway/Steckler Show for Real Radio, L.A., 1997. Mem. AFI.

HAMILTON, JOE, executive. BA in Math., Fordham U. Chief operating officer Cunningham Comm., Inc., Palo Alto, Calif. Office: 1510 Page Mill Rd Palo Alto CA 94304-1125*

HAMILTON, PENNY RAFFERTY, research executive, writer, educator; b. Altoona, Pa., Feb. 18, 1948; d. William E. and Lois B. (Noel) Rafferty; m. William A. Hamilton, Dec. 21, 1971. AA, Temple U., 1968; BA, Columbia (Mo.) Coll., 1976; MA, U. Nebr., 1978, PhD, 1981; postdoctoral studies, Menninger Found., Topeka, 1984. Community educator U.S. Forces in Europe, Fulda, Fed. Republic of Germany, 1972-74; health educator Nebr. State Govt., Lincoln, 1974-84; v.p. Advanced Rsch. Inst., Winter Park, Colo., 1984—; spl. features editor, newspaper columnist Sun Newspapers/Capital Times, Lincoln, 1982-91; dir. pub. affairs Sta. KHAT-KMXA, Lincoln, 1986-92. Bd. dirs. Grand County Pet Pals, 1992—, Grand County Aviation Assn., 1992—, Friends of Granby Airport, 1992—. Set world and nat. aviation speed record, 1991. Home: PO Box 2001 Granby CO 80446-2001 Office: Advanced Rsch Inst PO Box 3499 Winter Park CO 80482-3499

HAMILTON, SCOTT SCOVELL, professional figure skater, former Olympic athlete; b. Toledo, Aug. 28, 1958; adopted s. Ernest Scovell and Dorothy (McIntosh) H. Grad. high sch., Bowling Green, Ohio, 1976; student, Metro State Coll., 1979. nat. spokesman Discover Card youth programs, 1995—. Amateur competitive career includes Nat. Figure Skating Championships: jr. men's 1st pl., 1976, sr. men's 9th pl., 1977, 3d pl., 1978, 4th pl., 1979, 3d pl., 1980, 1st pl., 1981, 82, 83, 84, Mid-Western Figure Skating Championships: sr. men's 3d pl., 1977, 78, 79, Norton Skate Championships (now Skate Am.): men's divsn. 1st pl., 1979, 80, 81, 82, South Atlantic Figure Skating Championships: sr. men's divsn. 1st pl., 1980, Eastern Figure Skating Championships: sr. men's 1st pl., 1980, 81, 82, 83, 84, World Figure Skating Championships: men's divsn. 5th pl., 1980, 1st pl. 81, 82, 83, 84, Nat. Sports Festival Championships: 1st pl. men's divsn., 1981; Winter Olympics: men's divsn. 5th pl., Lake Placid, N.Y., 1980, 1st pl., Sarajevo, Yugoslavia, 1984, Nippon Hoso Kykai Figure Skating Championships, men's divsn. 1st pl., 1982, Golden Spin of Zagreb Championships, men's divsn. 1st pl., 1983; Profl. competitive career includes Nutrasweet/NBC-TV World Profl. Figure Skating Championships mens. divsn., 1st pl., 1984, 86, 2d pl., 85, 87, 88, 89, 91; World Challenge Champions/ABC-TV men's divsn., 2d pl., 1985, 1st pl., 1986; U.S. Open men's divsn. 1st pl., 1990, 2d pl., 1991, Diet Coke Profl. Skaters Championship men's divsn. 1st pl., 1992, Hershey's Kisses Pro-Am. Figure Skating Championships 2d Place Men's divsn. 1993, Sun Valley Men's Outdoor Championship 2d pl., 1994, The Gold Championship men's divsn. 1st pl., 1994, Can. Profl. Skating Championship men's divsn. 1st pl., 1994, Fox's Rock and Roll Skating Championship men's divsn. 1st pl., 1994; profl. performances include Nat. Arena Tour Ice Capades, 1984-85, 85-86, star Scott Hamilton's Am. Tour, 1986-87, 1990-91, co-star Concert On Ice, Harrah's Hotel, Lake Tahoe, Nev., 1987, spl. guest star Festival On Ice, Nat. Theatre Tour, 1987, star Discover Card Stars On Ice Nat. Arena Tour, 1987-88, 88-89, star Festival On Ice, Harrah's Hotel, 1988, guest star ABC-TV spl. Ice Capades With Kirk Cameron, 1988, A Very Special Christmas, ABC-TV, 1988, An Olympic, Calgary Christmas, ABC-TV, 1988, star and mus. comedy and acting debut Broadway On Ice, Harrah's Hotel and Nat. Theatre Tour, 1989; CBS-TV Sports Figure Skating Commentator 1984-91 various skating competitions and CBS-TV coverage Winter Olympics, Albertville, France, 1992, Lillehammer, Norway, 1994; star, dir., producer Scott Hamilton's Celebration On Ice, Sea World of Calif., 1988, Scott Hamilton's Time Traveler: An Odyssey On Ice, Sea World of Calif., 1989; host, guest star TV spl. A Salute To Dorothy Hamill, 1988; star, co-producer Discover Card Stars On Ice, Nat. Arena Tour, 1989-91; guest star CBS-TV spl. Disney's Christmas on Ice, 1990; co-producer, star Discover Card Stars on Ice Nat. Arena Tour, 1991-92; co-host, star HBO TV spl. Vail Skating Festival, 1992; co-prodr., star Discover Card Stars on Ice Nat. Arena Tour, 1992-93, 93-94, 94-95, Canadian Nat. Tour, 1995; guest TV spl. A Disney Christmas on Ice, 1992, CBS-TV spl. Disney on Ice, 1992, HBO-TV spl. Vail Skating Festival, 1993, Skates of Gold I, Boston, 1993, Skates of Gold II, Cin., 1994, CBS-TV Disney Fantasy on Ice, 1993, CBS TV spl. Nancy Kerrigan & Friends, 1994, CBS-TV spl. Disney's Greatest Hits, 1994, CBS-TV spl. Dreams on Ice, 1995; creator original concepts in arena figure skating. Cons. Friends of Scott Hamilton Found. named in his honor to fundraise and benefit youth oriented causes throughout U.S., 1988, Scott Hamilton's Friends and Legends 1st Annual Celebrity Charity Golf Tournament, Ford's Colony, Williamsburg, Va., 1991; participant fund-raising Athletes for Reagan, March of Dimes, Am. Cancer Soc., Spl. Olympics, Starlight Found., United Way Adoption Home Socs., Make A Wish Found, Big Bros., 1984—, Athletes For Bush, Adult and Ped. AIDS Rsch., Edn. and Funding, 1988—, Homeless, 1989—, Great Am. Workout for Pres.'s Coun. Phys. Fitness & Sports, 1990, 92; nat. spokesman Discover Card youth programs, 1995—. Winner Olympic Gold medal, Sarajevo, 1984; U.S. Olympic Com. awards and honors include carrier Am. Flag in opening ceremonies Lake Placid, 1980, Figure Skating Athlete of Yr., 1981, 82, 83, 84, Athlete of Yr., 1981, Olympic Spirit award, 1987; recipient Olympia award Southland Corp., 1984, Achievement award March of Dimes, 1984, Colo. Athlete of Yr. award Denver Athletic Club, 1984, Most Courageous Athlete award Phila. Sportswriters Assn., 1985, Profl. Skater of Yr. award Am. Skating World mag., 1986, Jacques Favart award Internat. Skating Union, 1988, The Crown Royal Achievement award from House of Seagrams and Jimmy Heuga Ctr., 1991, Clairol's Personal Best award, 1991, Spirit of Giving award U.S. Figure Skating Assn., 1993, 9th Ann. Great Sports Legends award Nick Buonoconti Fund The Miami Project, 1994, Ritter F. Shumway award U.S. Figure Skating Assn., 1994; inducted U.S. Olympic Hall of Fame, 1990, World Figure Skating Hall of Fame, 1990; honoree nat. com. for adoption, 1992. Hon. mem. Phila. Skating Club, Humane Soc. Republican. Avocation: golf. Office: 4242 Van Nuys Blvd Sherman Oaks CA 91403-3710 Address: CBS Sports/CBS Inc 7800 Beverly Blvd Los Angeles CA 90036-2112*

HAMILTON, SOLOMON MAXIMY, physiologist, educator; b. Marigot, Dominica; came to U.S., 1992; s. Samuel and Euthelie (Joseph) H. AA, Caribbean Union Coll., Trinidad and Tobago, 1983, BA, 1987; PhD, Loma Linda (Calif.) U., 1996. Asst. mgr. Ebenezer Mktg. Corp., Caribbean, Dominica, 1977-78, mgr., 1978-81; tchr. chemistry/physics Dominica SDA H.S., 1988-91; rsch. asst. Loma Linda U., 1992-93, rsch. assoc., 1993-96; asst. prof. physiology La Sierra U., Riverside, Calif., 1996—. Contbr. articles to profl. jours. Pres. No. Dist. Youth Assn., Caribbean, 1980; elder SDA Ch., 1979-90. Mem. AAAS, N.Y. Acad. Scis., Nat. Teaching & Learning Forum. Avocations: hiking, travel, classical music, gardening. Office: La Sierra U Dept Biology 4700 Pierce St Riverside CA 92505-3331

HAMIT, FRANCIS GRANGER, freelance writer; b. N.Y.C., Oct. 6, 1944; s. Harold Francis and Ethel Cordelia (Granger) H.; m. Doris Elaine Pratt Kaesser, May 31, 1974 (div. Mar. 1978). B of Gen. Studies, U. Iowa, 1972, MFA in English, 1976. Freelance writer Iowa City, Chgo., L.A., 1975—; area capt. RRS Security, Ill., 1977; sales rep. Wells Fargo Co. Inc., Chgo., 1979-80; assoc. editor Video Action Mag., Chgo., 1982; factory rep. Hoover Co., L.A., 1987-88; v.p. sales and mktg. EPIC Pvt. Security, West Covina, Calif., 1989-90. Author: Virtual Reality and the Exploration of Cyberspace, 1993; author, dir.: (play) Marlowe: An Elizabethan Tragedy, 1988; contbg. editor: Security Technology and Design Mag., 1993—, Advanced Imaging Mag., 1994—; contbr. 15th edit. Ency. Britannica, 1981-82. With U.S. Army, 1967-71, Vietnam, Germany. Mem. Am. Soc. Indsl. Security, Nat. Mil. Intelligence Assn., L.A. Sci. Fantasy Soc., Assn. Former Intelligence Officers. Democrat. Buddhist.

HAMLIN, DOUG, publishing executive. Pub. Motor Trend, subs. Petersen Pub. Co., L.A. Office: Petersen Pub Co LLC 6420 Wilshire Blvd Los Angeles CA 90048-5502*

HAMLIN, EDMUND MARTIN, JR., engineering manager; b. Utica, N.Y., June 9, 1949; s. Edmund Martin and Catherine Mary (Humphreys) H.; m. Nancy Ann Christensen, June 26, 1971; children: Benjamin John (dec.), Eleanor Mary, Edmund Alexander. BSEE, Clarkson U., 1971; MBA, UCLA, 1993. Lic. airframe and powerplant mechanic, 1994. Engr. NASA Flight Rsch. Ctr., Edwards, Calif., 1971-75; sr. engr. NASA Flight Rsch. Ctr., Edwards, 1976-79; project engr. Sundstrand Energy Systems Div., Belvidere, Ill., 1975-76; sr. engr. Teleco Oilfield Svcs., Meriden, Conn., 1979-80, mgr. electronic systems, 1980-83, the sr. staff engr., 1984; sr. engr. NASA Ames-Dryden, Edwards, Calif., 1984-85; asst. chief flight sys. NASA Ames-Dryden, Edwards, 1985-90, chief flight instrumentation, 1990-94, asst. dir. rsch., 1994-98, asst. dir. safety & flight assurance, 1998—. Inventor: position measurement system, 1976, method for determining and correcting magnetic interference in boreholes, 1988, method for computing borehole azimuth while rotating, 1989. Pres. bd. trustees Tehachapi (Calif.) Unified Sch. Dist., 1989-94. Mem. AIAA, Instrument Soc. Am., Aircraft Owners and Pilots Assn., Exptl. Aircraft Assn., Ea. European Adoption Coalition (dir.). Avocations: flying, aircraft restoration, fly fishing, camping, carpentry. Office: NASA Ames-Dryden Flight Rsch Facility PO Box 273 Edwards CA 93523-0273

HAMMAN, STEVEN ROGER, vocational rehabilitation specialist; b. Santa Monica, Calif., Nov. 2, 1946; s. Roy Ernest H. and Joan Barbara (Werner) Scott; m. Christine Frances Solomon, May 29, 1976; children: Zachary Charles, Tamara Edith, Bryan Joseph. AA, Northeastern Colo. U., 1967; BA, Colo. State Coll., 1970; MA, U. No. Colo., 1972; MS, Drake U., 1981. Cert. vocat. expert, rehab. counselor, ins. rehab. specialist. Social worker Poudre-Thompson Transp. Corps, Ft. Collins, Colo., 1974-78; placement specialist Missoula (Mont.) Rehab. Ctr., 1978-80; rehab. counselor Adolph Coors Co., Golden, Colo., 1981; rehab. counselor, br. mgr. Nat. Rehab. Cons., Duluth, Minn., 1981-82; Mont. case svcs. dir. Nat. Rehab. Cons., Missoula, 1982-83; case svcs. dir. Northwest U.S. Nat. Rehab. Cons., Spokane, Wash., 1983-86; rehab. cons., pres., chief exec. officer Vocability, Inc., Post Falls, Idaho, 1986—; pvt. practice as Social Security claimant's rep.; counselor, trainer Community Corrections Program, Ft. Collins, 1976. Chmn. organizer VISTA, Clay, W.Va., 1973-74; pres., bd. dirs. Mountain Van Spl. Transp., Missoula, 1980; bd. dirs. Heritage Place I and II, Coeur d'Alene Homes Inc., 1991-94; advanced master gardner Univ. Idaho Coop. Extention Ctr. Mem. Nat. Assn. Rehab. Practitioners in the Private Sector., Vocat. Evaluation and Work Adjustment Assn. (registered cons. Americans with Disabilities Act), Am. Bd. Disability Analysts (diplomate, sr. disability analyst), Nat. Orgn. Social Security Claimants Reps. Avocations: fly fishing, chess, cert. Kootenai county master gardener (Idaho). Office: Vocability Inc PO Box 772 Post Falls ID 83877-0772

HAMMARGREN, LONNIE, former lieutenant governor; b. Dec. 25, 1937; married. BA, U. Minn., 1958, MA in Psychol., 1960, BS, 1964, MD, 1964, MS in Neurosurgery, 1974. Diplomate Am. Bd. Neurological Surgery; med. license Nev., Minn. Flight surgeon for the astronauts NASA Manned Space Craft Ctr.; former lt. gov., pres. of the senate State of Nev., 1995-98; med. pvt. practice Las Vegas, 1998—; assoc. clin. prof. neurosurgery U. Nev. Sch. Medicine, Reno; clin. assoc. prof. surgery U. Calif., San Diego, 1982; chair Commn. Econ. Devel., Commn. Tourism; bd. dirs. Nev. Dept. Transp. Bd. regents U. and C.C. Sys. Nev., 1988-94; adv. bd. mem. Gov.'s com. for Employment of Handicapped; mem. State Bd. Edn., 1984-88; bd. mem. March of Dimes, Aid to Adoption of Spl. Kids. Mem. Spinal Cord Injury Program of Nev. (pres.), Cancer Soc., Aerospace Med. Assn., U Med. Ctr. Rehabilitation Unit (dir.), U. Med. Ctr. (chmn. neurosurgery dept.), Help Them Walk Again Found. (Nat. Dir.), Spina Bifida and Hydrocephalus Soc. (med. dir.), Internat. Ctr. for Rehabilitation Engring. (med. dir.), Pacific World Med. Found. (treas.), Paramed. and Emergency Care Bd. (adv.). Office: 3196 Maryland Pkwy Ste 106 Las Vegas NV 89109*

HAMMER, JOHN LEVERING, IV, film propmaster; b. Annapolis, Md., May 17, 1969; s. John Levering and Dorrice (Griffith) H. BS, Bentley Coll., 1991. Acct. exec. Earle, Palmer Brown, Phila., 1991-92; acct. exec., copywriter Foote, Cone Belding, Phila., 1992-94; propmaster, art dir. L.A., 1994—. Avocations: surfing, sailing. Home: PO Box 12862 Marina Del Rey [illegible]

HAMMER, SUSAN M., lawyer; b. Salem, Oreg., Dec. 14, 1948. BA, U. Puget Sound, 1971; JD, Willamette U., 1976. Bar: Oreg. 1976, Wash. 1977. Law clk. to Hon. James Dolliver Wash. State Supreme Ct., 1976-77; mem. Stoel Rives LLP, Portland, Oreg.; investigator Wash. State Human Rights Commn., 1971; mem. Oreg. State Bd. Bar Examiners, 1981-84. Mem. ABA (labor and employment law sect.), Tri-County Affirmative Action Assn. (bd. dirs.). Office: Stoel Rives LLP 900 SW 5th Ave Ste 2300 Portland OR 97204-1235

HAMMER, SUSAN W., mayor; b. Altadena, Calif., Dec. 21, 1938; d. James Nathan and Katrine (Krutzsch) Walker; m. Philip Hammer, Sept. 4, 1960; children: Philip, Hali, Matthew. BA in History, U. Calif., Berkeley, 1960. Svc. rep. Pacific Telephone Co., Berkeley, 1960-61; staff asst. Peace Corps, Washington, 1962-63; councilwoman City of San Jose, Calif., 1980-81, 83-90, spl. asst. to mayor, 1981-82, vice mayor, 1985-87, mayor, 1991—; chair, pres. Adv. Com. on Trade Policy and Negotiations, 1994—. Bd. dirs. San Jose Mus. Art, 1971-90, pres., 1978-80; mem. governing bd. NCCJ, 1978—; mem. adv. bd. Cmty. Found. Santa Clara County, 1978—; mem. Santa Clara County Transp. Com., 1976-77, Santa Clara County Juvenile Justice Commn., 1980, Victim-Witness Adv. Bd., 1977-90, Children's Health Coun., San Jose, 1981-89, Santa Clara Valley Leadership Program, 1986-90, Childrens Shelter Project, 1991—, Am. Leadership Forum, 1992—; past chmn. parents adv. com. Trace Sch.; chair Pres.' Adv. Com. on Trade Policy and Negotiation; mem. San Jose Fine Arts Commn., 1980. Recipient Rosalie M. Stern Community Svc. award U. Calif., 1975, Disting. Citizen of San Jose award Exch. Club, 1979, Investment in Leadership award Coro Found., 1985, Tzedek award for honor, compassion and community svc. Temple Emanu-El, 1987, Recognition award YWCA, Santa Clara County, 1989, resolution of commendation Assn. for Responsible Alcohol Control, 1990, Woman of Achievement award The Women's Fund, 1990, Dox Quixote award Nat. Hispanic U., 1991, Friends of Bay Area Mcpl. Elections Com. award, 1991. Democrat. Office: Office of Mayor 801 N 1st St Rm 600 San Jose CA 95110-1704

HAMMER, TERENCE MICHAEL, physician; b. Chgo., May 7, 1946; s. Albert S. and Minnetta Elizabeth (Nichols) H.; 1 child, Kathryn Gyo Hammer. BS, U. Ill., 1968; MD, Stanford U., 1973. Diplomate Am. Bd. Family Practice. Intern L.A. County-U. So. Calif. Med. Ctr., 1973-74; med. dir. Long Beach (Calif.) Health Dept. Drug Program, 1974-75; resident in family medicine Contra Costa Med. Svcs., Martinez, Calif., 1975-77; pvt. practice in family medicine Redondo Beach (Calif.) Med. Group, 1977-81, Family Practice Assocs., Torrance, Calif., 1981-96, Med. Inst. Little Co. of Mary Hosp., Torrance, 1996—; lectr. in field. Bd. trustees Peninsula Edn. Found., Palos Verdes, Calif., 1991—. Mem. Am. Coll. Physician Execs., Premier Health Med. Group (pres. 1991—), South Bay Ind. Physicians Med. Group (pres. emeritus), Phi Beta Kappa. Lutheran. Avocations: white water rafting, skiing, modern art collecting, swimming. Office: Med Inst Little Co Mary Hosp 20911 Earl St Ste 400 Torrance CA 90503-4355

HAMMETT, BENJAMIN COWLES, psychologist; b. L.A., Nov. 18, 1931; s. Buell Hammett and Harriet (Cowles) Graham; m. Ruth Finstrom, June 18, 1957; children: Susan Hood, Sarah, Carol Bress, John. BS, Stanford U., 1957; PhD, U. N.C., 1969. Lic. psychologist, Calif. Staff psychologist Children's Psychiat. Ctr., Butner, N.C., 1965-67; sr. psychologist VA Treatment Ctr. for Children, Richmond, Va., 1968-71; asst. prof. child psychiatry Va. Commonwealth U., Richmond, 1968-71; instr. psychology Western Grad. Sch. Psychology, 1980-87; pvt. practice clin. psychology Palo Alto, Calif., 1972-92; rsch. psychologist, 1992—; affiliate staff mem. O'Connor Hosp., San Jose, Calif., 1980-84; v.p. bd. dirs. Mental Rsch. Inst., Palo Alto, 1982-83, pres. bd. dirs., 1983-85, treas., 1990-92, mem. staff, 1992—, bd. dirs. emeritus, 1992—, rsch. affiliate, 1992-95, rsch. assoc., 1995—; bd. dirs. Western Grad. Sch. Psychology, 1993-97. Co-author chpts. two books. Scoutmaster Boy Scouts Am., 1952-54; 1st lt. Civil Air Patrol, 1969; vol. Peninsula Conservation Ctr., Palo Alto, 1983—, Calif. Acad. Scis., San Francisco, 1987—; treas. John B. Cary Sch. PTA, Richmond, Va., 1969-70; trustee Nat. Parks and Conservation Assn., 1995-98. Named Eagle Scout, 1947; grantee NIMH, 1970. Mem. AAAS, APA, Am. Psychol. Soc., Am. Group Psychotherapy Assn., Internat. Transactional Analysis Assn. (cert. clin. mem.), Assn. Applied Psychophysiology and Biofeedbck, Biofeedback Soc. Calif., Calif. Psychol. Assn., Assn. for the Advancement of Gestalt Therapy, El Tigre Club Stanford U. (sec. 1954). Democrat. Unitarian. Avocations: photography, computers, environmental volunteer, international ecological traveler. Home: 301 Lowell Ave Palo Alto CA 94301-3812

HAMMOND, JUDY MCLAIN, business services executive; b. Downey, Calif., June 24, 1956; d. Ernest Richard and Bernice Elaine (Thompson) McLain; m. Dennis Francis Hammond, Aug. 15, 1981. BS in Mgmt., Pepperdine U., 1982; MBA, U. So. Calif., 1986. Br. mgr. Kelly Svcs., Encino, Calif., 1978-81; mktg. mgr. Payco Am. Corp., Encino, 1981-83, GC Svcs. Corp., Santa Ana, Calif., 1983-86; pres. Resource Mgmt. Svcs. Inc., Norwalk, Calif., 1986—; founder, pres. The Debt Marketplace, Inc., Norwalk, 1994—; founder, pres. The Debt Marketplace, Inc., 1994—; cons., expert in collection and recovery. Author: Collect More From Collection Agencies. Mem. Toastmasters. Avocations: scuba diving, underwater photography. Office: 10440 Pioneer Blvd Ste 2 Santa Fe Springs CA 90670-8235

HAMMOND, LARRY AUSTIN, lawyer; b. Wichita, Kans., Sept. 17, 1945. BA, U. Tex., 1967, JD, 1970. Bar: Calif. 1971, Ariz. 1975. Law clk. to Hon. Carl McGowan U.S. Ct. Appeals (D.C. cir.), 1970-71; law clk. to Hon. Hugo L. Black U.S. Supreme Ct., 1971, law clk. to Hon. Lewis F. Powell Jr., 1971-73; asst. spl. prosecutor Watergate spl. prosecution force U.S. Justice Dept., 1973-74, dep. asst. atty. gen. office legal counsel, 1977-80; mem. Osborn Maledon P.A., Phoenix, 1995—; adj. prof. law Ariz. State U., 1977, 85—, U. Ariz., 1983, U. Mex., 1983; judge pro tempore Ariz. Ct. Appeals, 1992. Editor-in-chief Tex. Law Rev., 1969-70. Mem. ABA, Order of Coif. Office: Osborn Maledon PO Box 36379 2929 N Central Ave Ste 2100 Phoenix AZ 85067*

HAMMOND-BLESSING, DIANN A., elementary education educator; b. Cedar Rapids, Iowa, May 24, 1943; d. Russell Irving and Ola Arline (Leonard) Hammond; m. Dale Fredrick Blessing, June 10, 1979. BA in Edn., U. Wyo., 1966, MEd, 1973. Cert. elem. tchr., Colo. Tchr. German and social studies Deaver-Frannie Schs., Deaver, Wyo., 1966-68, Alliance (Nebr.) City Schs., 1968-70; tchr. elem. Jefferson County Schs., Arvada, Colo., 1971—; del. Colo. Del. Assembly, 1974-79; sec. Argonauts Investment Group, 1986-87, v.p., 1989, pres., 1990, treas.-elect, 1993, treas., 1994. Co-author curriculum units Our Changing Langauge, 1978. mem. Record Keeping Task Force, Jefferson County, Colo., 1974-75, 84; del. Dem. County and State Convention, Colo., 1976, 80; mem. polit. action com. Jefferson County Schs., 1979-80; precint chair Dem. Com., Colo., 1984. Mem. NEA, AAUW (editor newspaper 1985-87), PTA, Internat. Reading Assn. (Colo. coun., Colo. Edn. Assn., Colo. Reading Assn., Jefferson County Edn. Assn. (mem. com., rep. 1973-82, 94-95, 96-97, 97-98, bd. dirs. 1974-79), Jefferson County Internat. Reading Assn., Instrnl. Profl. Devel. Avocations: special event and interior decorating, assembly and design of clothing, elegant crafts. Home: 6626 S Yukon Way Littleton CO 80123-3070 Office: Warder Elem Sch 7840 Carr Dr Arvada CO 80005-4420

HAMPTON, BRET DOUGLAS, videotape editor; b. Santa Monica, Calif., Feb. 14, 1950; s. George Leroy and Ann Louise (Brinson) H.; 1 child, Shane. BA in English Lit., Calif. State U., 1975; student in film prodn., UCLA, 1981, Am. Film Inst., L.A., 1982. Cameraman, editor Tosco Corp., L.A., 1981-83; videotape editor One Inch Video, Burbank, Calif., 1983-85; freelance editor, 1985-88; mgr. Midtown Video, L.A., 1987-88; editor, prodr. Hollywood Stars, L.A., 1988-90; sr. video editor Image Entertainment, Chatsworth, Calif., 1990—; video cameraman/editor Deaf West Theatre, L.A., 1997; sign lang. interpreter for the deaf Whole Life Expo, L.A., 1990, L.A. Pierce Coll., Woodland Hills, Calif., 1977-80; judge ITVA Monitor Awards, 1988. Video editor Voices of Hope, Lifetime T.V., 1998, The Star Wars Trilogy, Fox Video, 1994; videotape editor, restorer Sunrise, Fox [illegible] 1996 [illegible] Big Bros., L.A., 1992-96. Mem. Ind. Feature Project West, Women in Film, L.A. MacIntosh Users. Home: 25710 Leticia Dr Valencia CA 91355 Office: Image Entertainment 9333 Oso Ave Chatsworth CA 91355

HAMPTON, STEPHEN DREW, law clerk; b. Jacksonville, Fla., July 20, 1952; s. James Jarrel and Margaret Francis (Bell) H. BA, Duke U., 1973; MA, U. Nev. Las Vegas, 1979; JD, Southwestern U., 1991. Law clk. Kegal Tobin Harriety & Truce, L.A., 1989-91; legal writer Mark Oring, L.A., 1992-94; law clk. Dena Patti & Assocs., Las Vegas, 1994-95, Paul Kirst & Assocs., Las Vegas, 1996—. Mem. county ctrl. com. Dem. Party Nev., 1984-88, del. to state conv., 1984, 88, del. to county conv., 1984, 86, 88. Avocations: chess, bicycling, swimming. Office: Paul R Kirst & Assocs 701 Bridger Ave Ste 502 Las Vegas NV 89101-5555

HAMREN, NANCY VAN BRASCH, bookkeeper; b. L.A., Feb. 2, 1947; d. Milton Carl and Winifred (Taylor) Van Brasch; m. Jerome Arthur Hamren, Feb. 14, 1981; children: Emily Allison, Meredith Ann. Student, Pasadena City Coll., 1964-65, San Francisco State Coll., 1966-67, U. Oreg., 1975-79. Bookkeeper/office mgr. Springfield Creamery, Eugene, Oreg., 1969—, also bd. dirs.; originator Nancy's Yogurt, Nancy's Cultured Dairy Products. Active mem. Oreg. Shakespearean Festival, Ashland, 1986, Oreg. Nat. Abortion Rights Action League, Planned Parenthood, Sta. KLCC-PBS Radio; bd. dirs. BRING Recycling. Mem. Oreg. Dairy Assn., Audubon Soc., N.Am. Truffling Soc., The Wilderness Soc., Oreg. Pub. Broadcasting, Buhl (Idaho) Arts Coun., Conservation Internat, Provender Alliance (bd. dirs.). Democrat. Unitarian. Avocations: gourmet cooking, gardening, walking, wine tasting. Home: 1315 Ravenswood Dr Eugene OR 97401-1912 Office: Springfield Creamery 29440 Airport Rd Eugene OR 97402-9524

HAMRICK, JOSEPH EUGENE, JR., information services specialist; b. Chapel Hill, N.C., Feb. 4, 1954; s. Joseph Eugene Sr. and Emily Southerland (Cole) H.; m. Elaine Kay Metcalf, Oct. 2, 1982; children: Aubrie Nicole, Allison Laurel, Wendy-Anne Alisa, Claire Elise. BS in Computer and Mmt. Sci, Met. State Coll., Denver, 1989. Cert. system profl. Inst. for Cert. Computer Profls. Programmer, analyst Aviation Mgmt. Systems, Denver, 1980-83; mgr., AVsoft devel. PHH Aviation Systems, Golden, Colo., 1983-86; programmer, analyst Columbine Systems, Inc., Golden, 1986-88; dir., info. svcs. Property Asset Mgmt., Denver, 1988—; cons., pres. Bridgeware, Denver, 1985—. Cons. Terry Considine U.S. Senate Campaign, Denver, 1985-86. Sgt. USAF, 1975-79. Presbyterian. Avocations: golf, bowling, reading. Home: 2272 S Grape St Denver CO 80222-6263 Office: Property Asset Mgmt 1873 S Bellaire St Ste 1700 Denver CO 80222-4300

HAN, ITTAH, lawyer, political economist, high technology, computer engineering and financial strategist; b. Java, Indonesia, Jan. 29, 1939; came to U.S., 1956, naturalized, 1972; s. Hongtjioe and Tsuiying (Chow) H. BS in Mech. Engring. and Elec. Engring., Walla Walla Coll., 1960; MA in Math., U. Calif., Berkeley, 1962; BA in French, U. Colo., 1965, MS in Elec. Engring., 1961; MSE in Computer Info. and Control Engring., U. Mich., 1970; MS in Computer Sci., U. Wis., 1971; MBA in Mgmt., U. Miami, Fla., 1973; BA in Econs., U. Nev., 1977; MBA in Tax, Golden Gate U., 1978, MBA in Real Estate, 1979, MBA in Fin., 1979, MBA in Banking, 1980, MPA in Adminstrv. Orgn. and Mgmt., 1984, ME in Computer Engring. U. Idaho, 1991, JD, Whittier Coll., 1991, PhD. in Ethics & Tech. The Union Inst., 1994; MS in Computer-Based Learning Nova Southeastern U., 1994, MA in Edn. & Human Devel. George Washington U., 1995, MS in Instructional & Performance Tech. Boise State U., 1995, MA in Humanities Calif. State U., Dominguez Hills, 1995. Bar: Calif. 1992; M.A. in Human Res. Devel., Webster Univ., 1997, M.S. in Space Studies, U. of North Dakota, Grandforks, 1998, cert. fin. planner. Salesman, Watkins Products, Walla Walla, Wash., 1956-60; instr. Sch. Engring. U. Colo., Denver, 1964-66; systems engr. IBM Corp., Oakland, Calif., 1967-69, Scidata Inc., Miami, Fla., 1971-72; chief of data processing Golden Gate Bridge, Hwy. and Transp. Dist., San Francisco, 1973-74; mgr. info. systems tech. and advanced systems devel. Summa Corp., Las Vegas, Nev., 1975-78; mgr. systems devel. Fred Harvey Inc., Brisbane, Calif., 1978-80; chmn. corp. systems steering com., mgr. systems planning Amfac Hotel & Resorts, Inc., 1978-80; tax strategy planner, innovative turnaround fin. strategy planner, chief exec. Ittahhan Corp., 1980-95; exec. v.p. Developers Unltd. Group, Las Vegas, 1982-84; v.p. Fidelity Fin. Co., Las Vegas, 1984-85; exec. v.p. John H. Midby and Assocs., Las Vegas, 1982-84, 1986-95; sec., treas., dir. River Resorts Inc., Las Vegas, 1983-84; sec., treas. Goldriver Ltd., Las Vegas, 1983-84; pres. Weststar Gen. Ptnr. Co., 1984-85, Developers Group Service Co., 1984-86; chief exec. officer, pres. Very High Tech. Polit. Economy Turnaround Management Strategist, Inc., 1986-95, chief exec. officer, pres. Artificial Intelligence Computer Engring. and Expert Systems Engring., Inc. (name changed to Turnaround Strategist & Artificial Intelligence Engring., Inc.), 1986—; pres. Orion Land Devel. Co., Las Vegas, 1987-89, Very High Tech. Computer Engring., Inc., Las Vegas, 1988-95; instr. U. Nev. Sch. Elec. Engring., Reno, 1981; systems designer, cons. in field. Mem., Internat. Bd. of Stds. and Practices for CFP, Inc., Calif. Bar Assn., Am. Contract Bridge League. Republican. Home and Office: 2501 Fulano Way Las Vegas NV 89102-2034

HAN, JIAWEI, computer scientist, educator; b. Shanghai, China, Aug. 10, 1949; came to U.S., 1979; arrived in Can., 1987; s. Yu-chang Han and Jia-zhi Wang; m. Yandong Cai, July 3, 1979; 1 child, Lawrence. BSc, USTC, Beijing, China, 1979; MSc, U. Wis., 1981, PhD, 1985. Asst. prof. Northwestern U., Evanston, Ill., 1986-87, Simon Fraser U., Burnaby, B.C., Can., 1987-91; assoc. prof. Simon Fraser U., Burnaby, 1991-95, prof., 1995—. Editor Jour. Intelligent Info. Sys., Jour. of Knowledge Discovery and Data Mining, IEEE Trans. Knowledge and Data Engring.; contbr. articles to profl. jours. Mem. IEEE, ACM, Spl. Internet Group on Mgmt. of Data. Office: Simon Fraser Univ, Sch Computing Sci, Burnaby, BC Canada V5A 1S6

HAN, MAO-TANG, surgeon, researcher; b. Jinan, Shandong, China, Aug. 28, 1934; came to U.S., 1989; s. Houngwen Han and Shie Sun; m. Hui-Fong Wang, Aug. 28, 1960; children: Han Qiang, Han Shan. Student, Chee-Loo U., 1951-52; MD, Tongj Medical Sch., Wuhan, China, 1952-57. Resident gen. surgery Simo (Province of Yunan) Dist. Hosp., 1957-60, Tonjee Teaching Hosp. Medical U. Tonjee, Wuhan, Province of Hubei, 1960-61; resident in pediatric surgery Tianjin Children's Hosp., Tianjin, 1963-64, chief resident in pediatric surgery, 1964-65, attending surgeon, 1965-79; postgrad. fellow Shanghai Chest Hosp., 1975-76; vis. physician, fellow dept. surgery The Mayo Clinic, Rochester, Minn., 1979-82; chief surgeon dept. surgery Tianjin Children's Hosp., Tianjin, 1984-89; assoc. editor Chinese Jour. Pediat. Surgery; organizer 1st and 2d Internat. Symposia on Pediat. Surgery of China, 1984, 88. Contbr. chpts. to books; contbr. articles to profl. jours. Mem. Assn. of Chinese Pediatric Surgery, Chinese Medical Assn., Am. Coll. Chest Physicians, Asian Assn. Pediatric Surgeons, Pacific Assn. Pediatric Surgeons. Achievements include pioneering of clinical surgery in neonatal esophageal atresia, hypoglycemic hyperinsulinemia, and pediatric hepatic cancer surgery. Home: 4009 NE 70th St Seattle WA 98115-6021

HAN, SOMA, artist; b. Choongnam-do, Korea, Jan. 13, 1942; came to U.S., 1976; d. Tok-Kyo and Tok-Myong (Song) H.; m. John C. Stickler; children: Stephen H., Alexander H. BA in Korean Lit., Korea U., 1969; BFA, Calif. Coll. Arts and Crafts, 1978; studied with Lee Il Young, 1969-73. Exhibited in galleries including CCAC Gallery, Claremont Hotel Gallery, Berkeley, Calif., Rosequist Gallery, Wolfe Gallery, Gyrols Fine Art Gallery, Tucson, Copenhagen Gallerie, Calif., Harkness House, E. Ives Bartholet Gallery, N.Y.C., also Hong Kong, Korea; represented in nat. registry at Nat. Mus. Women in Arts, Washington, Very Spl. Arts Gallery, Kennedy Ctr., Washington; illustrator: Tigers, Frogs and Rice Cakes: A Book of Korean Proverbs, 1998. Bd. dirs. Very Spl. Arts Ariz., 1995-96. Mem. Soc. Children's Book Writers and Illustrators. Avocation: gardening. Home and Studio: 16550 Twin Lakes Dr Royal Oaks CA 95076-9068

HANAN, LAURA MOLEN, artist; b. Ft. Monmouth, N.J., Jan. 30, 1954; d. Richard Eugene Molen and Agnes Arlene (Stahlhacke) Rose; m. John Morris Hanan, Apr. 26, 1985; 1 child, Whitney Anne. BS, U. Calif. Berkeley, 1978; BA in Journalism, Humboldt State U., 1980; AOS in Visual Comm., Northwest Coll. Art, 1992. Reporter, city editor Contra Costa Sun, Moraga, Calif., 1980-81; sports reporter, photographer The Canby (Oreg.) Herald, 1981-82; sr. technical writer MDS Qantel Bus. Computers, Hayward, Calif., 1982-84; bus. mgr., owner, designer Hanan Constrn. and Design Co., Inc., Alameda, Calif., 1986-90; dir. admissions Northwest Coll. Art, Poulsbo, Wash., 1992-93; fine artist, graphic artist Laura Hanan Art, Gig Harbor, Seattle, Wash., 1993—; creative dir. Pacific Pipeline, Kent, Wash., 1992-93; co-owner The Watermark Gallery, Village Art Gallery, Freighthouse Gallery, Gig Harbor, Tacoma, 1993-96; art dir., cons. Exec. Office Svcs., Gig Harbor, Beaverton, Oreg., 1996-97. Exhibited in group shows Emerald City Fine Art Gallery, Seattle, 1996-97, Nicholas Joseph Fine Art, N.Y.C., 1997-98, Hastings-Ray Gallery, Southern Pines, N.C., 1997—, Peninsula Br. Libr., Gig Harbor, 1994, 95, 96, Tacoma Art Mus., 1999; represented in permanent collection Pierce County Libr., also pvt. collections. Recipient First Place prize Peninsula Art League, 1995, 2d place, 1996, 3d place, 1997, Peoples Choice award Peninsula Art League, 1997; nominated for 1999 Tacoma Art Mus. juried fundraiser "The Night Tacoma Danced". Avocations: swimming, fishing, sewing, computers, walking.

HANCE, ANTHONY JAMES, retired pharmacologist, educator; b. Bournemouth, Eng., Aug. 19, 1932; came to U.S., 1958; s. Walter Edwin and Jessie Irene (Finch) H.; m. Ruth Anne Martin, July 17, 1954; children: David, Peter, John. BSc, Birmingham U., 1953, PhD, 1956. Rsch.fellow in electrophysiology Birmingham U., Eng., 1957-58; rsch. pharmacologist UCLA, 1959-62; rsch. assoc. pharmacology Stanford U., Palo Alto, Calif., 1962-65, asst. prof., 1965-68; assoc. prof. U. Calif., Davis, 1968-94, ret. prof. emeritus, 1994. Contbr. articles to profl. jours. Mem. Am. Soc. for Pharmacology and Exptl. Therapeutics, Biomed. Engring. Soc., Assn. for Computing Machinery. Home: 1103 Radcliffe Dr Davis CA 95616-0944 Office: U Calif Med Sch Dept Med Pharmacology & Toxicology Davis CA 95616-8654

HANCOCK, NANNETTE BEATRICE FINLEY, mental health educator, consultant; b. Birmingham, Ala., Aug. 24, 1937; d. James L. and Minnie (Mason) Finley; m. Frank J. Hancock Jr., Dec. 27, 1958 (div. May 1976); children: Andria Denise, Frank J. III, Cheryl René. BSN, Dillard U., 1958; MPH in Pub. Health, U. Calif., Berkeley, 1970; PhD in Psychology, Western Colo. U., 1977; MA in Clin. Psychology, John F. Kennedy U., 1991. Lic. marriage, family and child therapist. 2d lt. staff nurse U.S. Army Nurse's Corp, Denver, 1958-59; staff nurse, head nurse St. Francis Hosp., Evanston, Ill., 1960-64, Richmond (Calif.) Hosp., 1964-65; sch. nurse Richmond Unified Sch. Dist., 1965-69; prof. Contra Costa Coll., San Pablo, Calif., 1970—; pvt. practice mental health cons. Richmond, 1977—; founder, owner Nannette's Beauty and Figure Salon, 1982-86; head mental health component Bay Area Black Consortium for Quality Health Care AIDS Minority Health Initiative, Oakland, Calif., 1994—. Mem. Social Heritage Group, 1964—, human rels. com., 1966-70, Easter Hill Meth. Ch., 1964—. Col. Army Nurse's Corp. USAR, 1978—. Mem. Calif. Assn. Marriage and Family Therapy, Calif. Nurse's Assn., Bay Area Assn. Black Psychologists, Res. Officer's Assn. Avocations: water skiing, opera, symphony, theatre, reading. Home: 4801 Reece Ct Richmond CA 94804-3444 Office: 1440 Broadway Ste 209 Oakland CA 94612-2022

HANCOCK, N(EWELL) LES(LIE), accountant; b. Pitts., Apr. 13, 1943; s. Newell Francis and Mildred Helen (Bouverot) H.; m. Margaret Ann Kendrick, Nov. 30, 1968; children: Michelle Lynn, Jennifer Ann, Marie Noelle. BSBA, U. Denver, 1966; postgrad., various schs., 1969—. CPA, Colo. Supr. Pannell, Kerr, Forster, Denver and Atlanta, 1969-78; mgr. Wolf & Co. of Colo., Inc., Denver, 1978-79, 83-84; supr. Kafoury, Armstrong & Co., Reno, 1979-82; pvt. practice acctg. Arvada, Colo. and Reno, 1982—; mgr. Ashby, Armstrong & Co., Denver, 1984-87; asst. contr. 1st Resorts Inc. and Great Am. Mgmt. Group Inc., Lakewood, Colo., 1987-89; team leader subcontract audit Nat. Renewable Energy Lab., Golden, Colo., 1989—. Served to 1st lt. U.S. Army, 1966-69. Mem. AICPA, Colo. Soc. CPAs (report rev. com. 1984-90, pvt. co. practice com. 1990-93, accountancy regulation com. 1993-94, mem. rels. com. 1994-96, mem. svcs. com. 1996-97), Nev. Soc. CPAs (bd. dirs. Reno chpt. 1982-83, auditing stds. com. 1981-82, vice chmn. acctg. principles com. 1981-83), Hospitality Accts. Assn. (sec. 1976-77). Republican. Baptist. Avocations: summer sports, collections. Office: PO Box 740535 Arvada CO 80006-0535

HANCOCKS, DAVID MORGAN, museum director, architect; b. Kinver, Worcestershire, Eng., May 5, 1941; came to U.S., 1972; s. Cecil and Eva Alice (Morgan) H.; m. Anthea Page Cook, Feb. 16, 1982; children: Samuel Morgan, Thomas David, Morgan Page. BSc with honors, U. Bath, Eng., 1966, BArch with honors, 1968. Registered architect, U.K. Architect Zool. Soc. London, 1968-69, West of Eng. Zool. Soc., Bristol, 1970-72; design coord. Woodland Pk. Zool. Gardens, Seattle, 1973-74, dir., 1975-84; pvt. practice design Melbourne, Australia, 1985-89; exec. dir. Ariz.-Sonora Desert Mus., Tucson, 1989-97; cons. Singapore Zool. Gardens, 1979-89, Zool. Soc. Victoria, Australia, 1986-89, Mus. of Victoria, 1994. Author: Animals and Architecture, 1971, Master Builders of the Animal World, 1973 (writing award State of Wash. Govs. 1974), 75 Years: A History of Woodland Park Zoological Gardens, 1979. Bd. dirs. Allied Arts, Seattle, 1976-85, Chamber Music Soc., Seattle, 1984-85; adv. coun. Sch. of Renewable Natural Resources, U. Ariz.; adv. bd. U. Ariz. Press. Fellow Discovery Inst., Seattle; recipient Disting. Svc. award Am. Soc. Landscape Architects, 1975, Outstanding Pub. Employee of Yr. award Seattle Mcpl. League, 1983, WPZS medal Woodland Pk. Zool. Soc., 1991. Mem. Am. Assn. Mus., Am. Assn. Zool. Pks. and Aquariums, Am. Assn. Bot. Gardens and Arboreta, Internat. Coun. Mus., Royal Inst. Brit. Architects (assoc.). Avocations: photography, gardening, music. Home: c/o Vorz K Rd, Werribee 3030, Australia Office: Ariz-Sonora Desert Mus 2021 N Kinney Rd Tucson AZ 85743-9719

HAND, DALE L., pharmacist; b. Boise, Idaho, Oct. 21, 1947; s. Robert Ray and Evelyn Mabel (McKenzie) H.; m. Gloria J. Lassen, Dec. 19, 1970; children: Travis D., Jason D. Student, Walla Walla Coll., 1965-66; B Pharmacy, Idaho State U., 1970; MS in Health Svcs. Adminstrn., Coll. St. Francis, Joliet, Ill., 1985. Intern Clinic Pharmacy, Pocatello, Idaho, 1968-70; pharmacognosy lab. tchng. asst. Idaho State U., 1969-70; hosp. pharmacy internship St. Luke's Hosp., Boise, 1970-71, clin. staff pharmacist, 1971-77; various to dir. pharmacy svcs. Porter Meml. Hosp., Denver, 1981-92, adminstrv. dir. dept. pharm. care, 1992—; pharmacy extern preceptor U. Colo., 1981—; cons. pharmacist McNamara Hosp. and Nursing Home, Fairplay, Colo., 1981-83; cons. Edn. Design, Inc., 1993—; lectr. in field.; chmn. various hosp. coms. Contbr. articles to profl. jours. Bd. dirs. Arapahoe Sertoma, 1991-98. Mem. Am. Soc. Health Sys. Pharmacists, Colo. Soc. Health Sys. Pharmacists. Seventh-Day Adventist. Avocations: golf, softball, snow-skiing, landscape design, music. Home: 7269 W Chestnut Dr Littleton CO 80128-5699 Office: Porter Adventist Hosp 2525 S Downing St Denver CO 80210-5817

HANDEL, WILLIAM KEATING, advertising and sales executive; b. N.Y.C., Mar. 23, 1935; s. Irving Nathaniel and Marguerite Mary (Keating) H.; m. Margaret Inez Sitton; children: William Keating II, David Roger. BA in Journalism, U. S.C., 1959, MA in English Lit., 1960. Account supr. Ketchum, MacLeod & Grove, Pitts., 1960-67; mgr. advt. and pub. rels. ITT Gen. Controls, Glendale, Calif., 1967-80; mgr. corp. comm. Fairchild Camera and Instrument Corp., 1980-84; dist. mgr. Cahners Pub. Co., 1984-90; western regional sales mgr. Quality Publ. Co., 1990—; pub. rels. counsel Calif. Pvt. Edn. Schs., 1978-87; chmn. exhibits Mini/Micro Computer Conf. Bd. dirs. West Valley Athletic League, L.A. chpt. USMC Scholarship Found.; pub. rels. cons. Ensenada, Mexico Tourist Commn., 1978; chmn., master of ceremonies USMC Birthday Ball, L.A., 1979-82. With USMC, 1950-53. Decorated Silver Star, Bronze Star, Purple Heart (4), Navy Commendation medal with combat V; recipient Pub. Svc. award L.A. Heart Assn., 1971-73. Mem. Bus. and Profl. Advt. Assn. (cert. bus. communicator, past pres.), 1st Marine Divsn. Assn., Navy League (bd. dirs.), AdLinx Golf Club of So. Calif., Torrey Pines Golf Club, Griffith Pk. Golf Club, Nueva España Boat Club, Bajamar Country Club, Ensenada Country Club, Baja Country Club, Ensenada Fish and Game Club (Baja, Mex.), U. S.C. Alumni Club (founder/pres. L.A. chpt.), Sigma Chi (chpt. adv.). Republican. Roman Catholic. Home: 2428 Badajoz Pl Rancho La Costa CA 92009-8006

HANDLER, EVELYN, science administrator; b. Budapest, Hungary, May 5, 1933; U.S. citizen; m. 1965; two children. BA, Hunter Coll., 1954; MSc, NYU, 1962, PhD in Biology, 1963; LHD (hon.), Rivier Coll., 1982, U. Pitts., 1987, Hunter Coll., 1988. Rsch. assoc. Sloan-Kettering Inst., 1958-60, Merck Inst. Therapeutic Rsch., 1958-60; lectr. Hunter Coll., 1962-64, from asst. to prof. biol. sci., 1965-80, dean sci. and math., 1977-80; pres. U. N.H., 1980-83, Brandeis U., 1983-91; exec. dir. Calif. Acad. Scis., San Francisco, 1994-98; ret.; vis. scientist Karolinska Inst., 1971-72; evaluator Com. Higher Edn., Middle States Assn., 1972—; vice chmn. univ. faculty senate CUNY, 1974-76; generalist, mem. Am. Coun. Pharm. Edn., 1978-83; bd. dirs. New Eng. Life Ins. Co., Student Loan Corp. Trustee Bay Area Biosci. Ctr., 1995—, Mills Coll., 1995—. Sr. fellow Carnegie Found. Advanced Tchg., 1990-92; scholar in residence Harvard U., 1991-92, assoc. in edn. 1992-93; rsch. grantee NIH, 1964-69, 73-76, NSF, 1965-67, 70-72, CUNY, 1972-74. Fellow AAAS, N.Y. Acad. Sci.; mem. Internat. Soc. Hematology, Harvey Soc. Office: Calif Acad Scis Golden Gate Park San Francisco CA 94118*

HANDLEY, MARGIE LEE, business executive; b. Bakersfield, Calif., Sept. 29, 1939; d. Robert E. and Jayne A. (Knoblock) Harrah; children: Steven Daniel Lovell, David Robert Lovell, Ronald Eugene Lovell; m. Leon C. Handley, Sr., Oct. 28, 1975. Grad. high sch., Willits, Calif. Lic. gen. engring. contractor. Owner, operator Shasta Pallet Co., Montague, 1969-70; owner, operator Lovell's Tack 'n Togs, Yreka, Calif., 1970-73; v.p. Microphor, Inc., Willits, 1974-81; pres. Harrah Industries, Inc., Willits, 1981—, Hot Rocks, Inc., Willits, 1983-89; gen. ptnr. Madrone Profl. Group, Willits, 1982—; co-ptnr. Running Wild Ostriches, 1994—; bd. dirs. Nat. Bank of the Redwoods, NBR Mortgage Co., Howard Found., Willits Electronics Assembly, Inc.; active State of Calif. Employment Tng. Panel, 1993-95, coord. State Calif. Timber Transition, 1994-95, State of Calif. Econ. Strategy Panel, 1995—; apptd. mem. State of Calif. Econ. Strategy Panel, 1995—. Sec. Willits Cmty. Scholarships, Inc., 1962; trustee Montague Meth. Ch., 1966-73; sec. Montague PTA, 1969; clk. bd. trustees Montague Sch. Dist., 1970-73; del. Calif. State Conf. Small Bus., 1984; alt. del. Rep. Nat. Conv., Kansas City, Detroit, 1976, 80; 3d dist. chmn. Mendocino County Rep. Ctrl. Com., 1978-84; mem. Calif. State Rep. Ctrl. Com., 1985, 86, 87; Rep. nominee for State Senate Calif. 2nd Senate Dist., 1990, 93; mem. Rep. Congl. Leadership Coun., 1980-82; Mendocino County chmn. Reagan/Bush, 1980, 84; Mendocino County co-chmn. Deukmejian for Gov., 1982; mem. Region IX Small Bus. Adminstrn. Adv. Coun., 1982-93; mem. Gov.'s Adv. Coun., 1983-90; Rep. nominee State Assembly 1st Assembly dist.; del., asst. sgt. of arms Rep. Nat. Conv., Dallas, 1984, del., New Orleans, 1988, San Diego, 1996; vice chmn. Mendocino County Rep. Ctrl. Com., 1985; mem. Willits C. of C. (hon.), Calif. Transp. Commn., 1986-90; state dir. North Bay Dist. Hwy. Grading and Heavy Engring. divsn. 1986; dir. Lit. Vols. Am. Named Mendocino 12th Dist. Fair Woman of the Year, 1987. Mem. No. Coast Builders Exch., Soroptimist Internat., Rotary Club (Willits). Home: PO Box 1329 Willits CA 95490-1329 Office: Harrah Industries Inc 42 Madrone St Willits CA 95490-4206

HANDSCHUMACHER, ALBERT GUSTAVE, retired corporate executive; b. Phila., Oct. 20, 1918; s. Gustave H. and Emma (Streck) H.; children: Albert, David W., Megan, Karin, Melissa. B.S., Drexel Inst. Tech., 1940; diploma, U. Pitts., 1941, Alexander Hamilton Inst., 1948. Prodn. mgr. Jr. Motors Corp., Phila., 1938-40; sales engr. Westinghouse Electric Co., Pitts., 1941; with Lear, Inc., Grand Rapids, Mich., 1945-57; beginning as sales mgr. central dist., successively asst. to pres., asst. gen. mgr., v.p. and gen. mgr., sr. v.p., dir. sales, pres., dir. Lear, Inc., 1959-62; v.p., gen. mgr. Rheem Mfg. Co., 1957-59; pres., dir. Lear Siegler, Inc., 1962-65; underwriting mem. Lloyd's of London. Trustee Drexel U., Am. Heart Assn. Maj. USAAF, 1942-45. Recipient 60th Anniversary Alumni award for outstanding achievements and services field of indsl. mgmt. Drexel U., 1951, Outstanding Alumni award, 1971; Man of Year award City of Hope, 1970; Man of Year award Nat. Asthma Assn., 1978; named to Abington High Sch. Hall of Fame, 1989. Mem. Astro Club (Phila.). Home: 321 18th St Manhattan Beach CA 90266-4652

HANDZLIK, JAN LAWRENCE, lawyer; b. N.Y.C., Sept. 21, 1945; s. Felix Munso and Anna Jean Handzlik; children: Grant, Craig, Anna. BA, U. So. Calif., 1967; JD, UCLA, 1970. Bar: Calif. 1971, U.S. Dist. Ct. (cen. dist.) Calif. 1971, U.S. Ct. Appeals (9th cir.) 1971, U.S. Supreme Ct. 1975, U.S. Tax Ct. 1979, U.S. Dist. Ct. (no. dist.) Calif. 1979, U.S. Dist. Ct. (ea. dist.) Calif. 1981, U.S. Dist. Ct. (so. dist.) Calif. 1982, U.S. Ct. Appeals (2d cir.) 1984, U.S. Ct. Internat. Trade 1984. Law clk. to Hon. Francis C. Whelan, U.S. Dist. Ct. (cen. dist.) Calif., L.A., 1970-71; asst. U.S. atty. fraud and spl. prosecutions unit criminal div. U.S. Dept. Justice, L.A., 1971-76; assoc. Greenberg & Glusker, L.A., 1976-78; ptnr., prin. Stilz, Boyd, Levine & Handzlik, P.C., L.A., 1978-84; prin. Jan Lawrence Handzlik, P.C., L.A., 1984-91; ptnr. Kirkland & Ellis, L.A., 1991—; del. U.S. Ct. Appeals for 9th cir. Jud. Conf., L.A., 1983-85; counsel to ind. Christopher Commn. Study of the L.A. Police Dept., 1991; dep. gen. counsel to Hon. William H. Webster, spl. advisor to L.A. Police Commn. for Investigation of Response to Urban Disorders, 1992; mem. adv. com. for Office of L.A. County Dist. Atty., 1994-96. Mem. editl. adv. bd. DOJ Alert, 1994-95. Bd. dirs. Friends of Child Advs., L.A., 1987-91, Inner City Law Ctr., L.A., 1993—; mem. bd. judges Nat. and Calif. Moot Ct. Competition Teams, UCLA Moot Ct. honors program. Mem. ABA (sect. criminal justice nat. com. on white collar crime 1991—, vice-chair 1998—, co-chair securities fraud subcom. 1994-98, west coast white collar crime com., exec. com. 1993—, vice-chair 1994-96, chair 1996-98, mem. sect. litigation, criminal litigation com. 1989—), Fed. Bar Assn., State Bar Calif. (sects. on criminal law and litigation), L.A. County Bar Assn. (mem. exec. com. criminal justice sect. 1997—, coms. on fed. cts. 1988—, chair criminal practice subcom. 1989-90, fed. appts. evaluation 1989-93, white collar crime com. 1991-97, exec. com. 1991-97), Nat. Assn. Criminal Def. Lawyers. Office: Kirkland & Ellis 300 S Grand Ave Ste 3000 Los Angeles CA 90071-3140

HANES, JOHN WARD, sculptor, civil engineer consultant; b. San Francisco, June 5, 1936; s. Ward Herbert and Ruth Florence (Jacks) H.; m. Virginia Rae Meadows, Nov. 27, 1957 (div. Feb. 1966); children: Derek S., Kim R., Mark A.; m. Meda Lee Walter, June 29, 1968; 1 child, Ward W. BS in Engring., U. Calif., Davis, 1979. Registered civil engr., Calif. From engr. technician to civil engr. Soil Conservation Svc., USDA, Berkeley, Calif., 1960-79; civil engr. Soil Conservation Svc., USDA, Davis, 1979-83, hydraulic engr., 1983-90; sculptor, consulting civil engr. Boonville, Calif., 1990—. Pres. Santa Rosa (Calif.) Ski Club, 1971. Mem. Gualala Arts Ctr., Mendocino Arts Ctr., Nat. Sculpture Soc. Avocations: private pilot, multi media art, hunting, camping, fishing. Home: Box 510 29000 Mountain View Rd Boonville CA 95415

HANEY, ROBERT LOCKE, retired insurance company executive; b. Morgantown, W.Va., June 14, 1928; s. John Ward and Katherine Eugenia (Locke) H. BA, U. Calif., Berkeley, 1949. Sr. engr. Pacific Telephone Co., San Francisco, 1952-58; mgmt. analyst Lockheed Missiles & Space Co., Sunnyvale, Calif., 1958-64; sr. cons. John Diebold, N.Y.C., 1964-65; sr. indsl. economist Mgmt. & Econs. Research, Inc., Palo Alto, Calif., 1965-67; prin. economist Midwest Research Inst., Kansas City, Mo., 1967-69; dir. mktg. coordination Transam. Corp., San Francisco, 1969-73; staff exec. Transam. Ins. Corp., L.A., 1974-82; 2d v.p. Transam. Life Cos., L.A., 1982-93; ret., 1993; cons. in field. Co-author: Creating the Human Environment, 1970. Lt. (j.g.) USN, 1949-52. Mem. Scabbard & Blade. Republican. Episcopalian. Avocations: photography, gardening, cycling. Home: 2743 Tiburon Ave Carlsbad CA 92008-7908

HANF, JAMES ALPHONSO, poet, government official; b. Chehalis, Wash., Feb. 3, 1923; s. William G. and Willa DeForest (Davis) H.; m. Ruth G. Eyler, Aug. 16, 1947; 1 child, Maureen Ruth. Grad. Centralia Jr. Coll., 1943, DLitt (hon.) World U. Ariz., 1980 Naval architect technician P.F. Spaulding, naval architects, Seattle, 1955-56, Puget Sound Bridge & Dredge Co. (Wash.), 1953-55, Puget Sound Naval Shipyard, 1951-53, 56-93; cons. Anderson & Assocs., ship bldg.; cons. The Rsch. Bd. Advs., Am. Biographical Inst., Inc.; guest lectr. on poetry and geneal. rsch. methods to various lit. socs., 1969—; contbr. hundreds of poems to lit. jours., anthologies and popular mags.; poetry editor Coffee Break, 1977-82. Recipient Poet Laureate Recognition award Internat. Biog. Centre of Cambridge, Eng., grand prize World Poetry Soc. Conv., 1985, 86, , 90, Golden Poet award World of Poetry in Calif., 1985-90, Silver Poet award Calif. sponsored nat. contest, 1989, numerous other awards. Judge poetry contest, Australia and India, 1985; named Man of Yr. Abaas, 1989—; named Internat. Eminent Poet Internat. Poet Acad. of Madras, India, 1987. Mem Internat. Poetry Soc. (Poet Laureate Wash. State award 1981), World of Poetry Soc. (Golden Poet award 1985-88, Poet Laureate award 1979), Kitsap County Writers Club (pres. 1977-78), Internat. Fedn. Tech. Engrs., Nat. Hist. Locomotive Soc., Kitsap County Hist. Soc., Puget Sound Geneal. Soc., Western World Haiku Soc., Olympic Geneal. Soc. (pres. 1974-75), N.Y. Poetry Forum, World Poets Resource Ctr., Literarische Union, Académie

Européenne des Scis., Des Arts Et Des Letters (corr.), Internat. Soc. Poets Md. (hon. charter), Internat. Platform Assn., Calif. Fedn. Chaparral Poets, World Sadhak Soc. (hon.), Nat. Libr. Poetry (hon. mem.). Baptist. Home: PO Box 374 Bremerton WA 98337-0075

HANIFEN, RICHARD CHARLES, bishop; b. Denver, June 15, 1931; s. Edward Anselm and Dorothy Elizabeth (Ranous) H. B.S., Regis Coll., 1953; S.T.B., Cath. U., 1959, M.A., 1966; J.C.L., Pontifical Lateran U., Italy, 1968. Ordained priest Roman Catholic Ch., 1959; asst. pastor Cathedral Parish, Denver, 1959-66; sec. to archbishop Archdiocese Denver, 1968-69, chancellor, 1969-76; aux. bishop of Denver, 1974-83; 1st bishop of Colorado Springs, Colo., 1984—. Office: Bishop of Colo Springs 29 W Kiowa St Colorado Springs CO 80903-1403

HANKINS, HESTERLY G., III, computer systems analyst, inventor, educator; b. Sallisaw, Okla., Sept. 5, 1950; s. Hesterly G. and Ruth Faye (Jackson) H. BA in Sociology, U. Calif., Santa Barbara, 1972; MBA in Info. Systems, UCLA, 1974; postgrad., Golden Gate U., 1985-86, Ventura Coll., 1970, Antelope Valley Coll., 1977, La Verne U., 1987, NRI McGraw-Hill Sch. Writing, Washington, 1993—; PhD (hon.). Cert. community coll. tchr., Calif. Applications programmer Xerox Corp., Marina Del Rey, Calif., 1979-80; spl. asst. to CEO Naval Air Sta. of Moffett Field, Mountain View, Calif., 1984-85; mgr. computer systems project Pacific Missile Test Ctr., Oxnard, 1985-88; mgr. computer systems project MIS Def. Contract Adminstrn. Svcs. Region, L.A., 1988-94, ret., 1994; instr. writing Nat. U., Inglewood, Calif., 1994—; instr. bus. West Coast U., Camarillo, Calif., 1985; core adj. faculty Nat. U., L.A., 1988—; lectr. bus. Golden Gate U., Los Altos, Calif., 1984; instr. computer sci. Chapman Coll., Sunnyvale, 1984, Ventura (Calif.) Coll., 1983-84; lectr. tchr. computers De Anza Coll.; cons. L.A. Police Dept., Allison Mortgage Trust Investment Co.; minority small bus. assn. cons. UCLA. Author: Campus Computing's Accounting I.S. As A Measurement of Computer Performance, 1973, Campus Computer, 1986, Network Planning, 1986, Satellites and Teleconferencing, 1986, Quotable Expressions and Memorable Quotations of Notables, 1993, Idea Bank, 1993, Product Rating System, 1993, Training Base Model, 1993, Sound Seal/Shield, 1994, My Biographical Profile. Mem. St. Paul United Meth. Ch., Oxnard, Calif., 1986-87; fundraiser YMCA Jr. Rodeo, Lake Casitos, Calif.; key person to combine fed. campaign United Way. Named One of Outstanding Young Men in Am., U.S. Jaycees, 1980. Mem. Nat. Assn. Accts., Calif. Assn. Accts., Intergovtl. Coun. on Tech. Info. Processing, Assn. Computing Machinery (Smart Beneficial Suggestion award 1984), IEEE Computer Soc., Fed. Mgrs. Assn., Alpha Kappa Psi (sec. 1972-73).

HANKS, EUGENE RALPH, land developer, cattle rancher, forester, retired naval officer; b. Corning, Calif., Dec. 11, 1918; s. Eugene and Lorena B. Hanks; m. Frances Elliot Herrick, Mar. 4, 1945; children: Herrick, Russell, Stephen, Nina. Student, Calif. Poly. Coll., 1939-41, U. So. Calif., 1949-50, Am. U., 1958-59; grad., Command and Staff Coll., Norfolk, Va., 1960. With Naval Aviation Flight Tng.,V-5 Program USN, 1941-42, commd. ensign, 1942, advanced through ranks to capt., 1963; carrier fighter pilot, Am. Ace, six victories, 1942-45; test pilot Naval Air Test Ctr., 1946-48; mem. Navy Flight Exhbn. Team Blue Angels, 1950; commdg. officer three fighter squadrons including Navy's 1st squadron of F4 Phantoms, Mach II Missile Fighters, Miramar, Calif., 1952-61; 1st ops. officer U.S.S. Constellation, 1961-62; dir. ops. Naval Missile Test Ctr., 1963-66; test dir. Joint Task Force Two, Albuquerque, 1966-69; ret., 1969; owner, developer Christmas Tree Canyon, Cebolla Springs and Mountain River subdivs., Mora, N.Mex., 1969-98. Decorated Navy Cross, DFC with star (2), Air medal (7), Legion of merit; named Citizen of Yr., Citizen's Com. for Right to Bear Arms, 1987. Mem. Ret. Officers Assn., Am. Fighter Aces Assn., Combat Pilots Assn., Assn. Naval Aviation, Am. Forestry Assn., NRA, Blue Angels Assn., Naval Aviation Museum Found., Am. Aviation Mus. Gt. Britain, Legion of Valor. Republican. Home and Office: Christmas Tree Canyon PO Box 239 Mora NM 87732-0239

HANKS, MERTON EDWARD, professional football player; b. Dallas, Tex., Mar. 12, 1968. BA, liberal arts, U. Iowa, 1990. With San Francisco 49ers, 1991—. Named to Sporting News NFL All-Pro Team, 1994-95, Pro Bowl, 1994-96. Dr. Z's All-Pro team, 1994; played in Super Bowl XXVIV, 1994. Office: San Francisco 49ers 4949 Centennial Blvd Santa Clara CA 95054-1229

HANLEY, KEVIN LANCE, maintenance manager; b. Oil City, Pa., Nov. 25, 1961; s. Harold Edward and Helen Louise (Banta) H.; m. Patricia Yolanda DeLeon, Sept. 29, 1984; children: Jennifer Jessica, Kevin Lance Jr. Grad. high sch., Titusville, Pa.; diploma, McDonald's Regional Hdqs., L.A., 1986. Maintenance supr. Paschen Mgmt. Corp. McDonald's, Camarillo, Calif., 1980-86, asst. mgr., 1986-88, 95, maintenance cons., 1988-89; mgr. phys. plant Westmont Coll., Santa Barbara, Calif., 1988—; apartment mgr. Bartlein & Co., Ventura, Calif., 1990-97; 3rd class petty officer USNR, Port Hueneme, Calif., 1994—; gen. cons. "R" Cleaning Maintenance, Santa Paula, Calif., 1989-91; owner Custodial-Plus Svcs., Ventura, Calif., 1996—. Sec.-treas. Ch. of God of Prophecy, Carpinteria, Calif., 1987-95, 98—, co-pastor, 1988-95. With USNR, 1994—. Recipient Navy and Marine Corp Achievement Medal, 1998. Republican. Avocations: backpacking, bowling, camping. Office: Westmont Coll 955 La Paz Rd Santa Barbara CA 93108-1023

HANNA, NABIL, biomedical engineer; b. 1944. PhD in Immunology, Hebrew U., Israel. Lectr. Hebrew U., Israel, 1973-78; rsch. sci. NCI-Frederick Cancer Rsch. Ctr., 1978-81; dir. SmithKline Beecham, 1981-90; now with IDEC Pharm. Corp., San Diego, 1991—. Office: IDEC Pharm Corp 11011 Torreyana Rd San Diego CA 92121-1104*

HANNA, PHILIP, civil engineer; b. Alexandria, Egypt, Oct. 31, 1934; came to U.S., 1969; s. Abedu Hanna and Nazipa (Sedra) Soliman; 1 child, Suzan. BSc, Alexandria (Egypt) U., 1960. Registered profl. engr., N.Y., Calif. Civil engr. N.Y.C. Transit Authority, 1970-80, Calif. Dept. Transp., Colton, 1980—. Home: # 157 1043 Santo Antonio Dr Apt 157 Colton CA 92324-8166

HANNUM, GERALD LUTHER (LOU HANNUM), retired tire manufacturing company official; b. Syracuse, N.Y., May 31, 1915; s. Ralph Charles and Coral (Snyder) H.; m. Carolyn Russell Osgood, Nov. 29, 1941; children: Nancy, Susan, Jean. AB, Syracuse U., 1937; MA, Kent State U., 1971. Supr. forecasting and inventory control B.F. Goodrich, Arkon, Ohio, 1961-67; econ. planning specialist, staff for v.p. planning B.F. Goodrich Co., 1967-75, econ. planner, 1946-75; ret., 1975. Councilman City of Medford, Oreg., 1977-82, 89-92, mayor, 1983-86, water commr., 1997—; bd. dirs. United Way, Medford, 1986—; pres. Crater Lake coun. Boy Scouts Am., 1987-90. Lt. USNR, 1943-52, PTO. Recipient Silver Beaver award Boy Scouts Am., 1987. Mem. League Oreg. Cities (pres. 1983, Richards award 1989), Rotary. Avocations: hiking, photography. Home: 2900 Seckel St Medford OR 97504-8150

HANOWELL, ERNEST GODDIN, physician; b. Newport News, Va., Jan. 31, 1920; a. George Frederick and Ruby Augustine (Goddin) H.; m. Para Jean Hall, June 10, 1945; children: Ernest D., Deborah J. Hanowell Orick, Leland H., Dee P. Hanowell Martinmaas, Robert G. Diplomate Am. Bd. Internal Medicine. Intern USPHS Hosp., Norfolk, Va., 1948-49; resident in internal medicine USPHS Hosp., Seattle, 1952-55; fellow in cardiology New Eng. Ctr. Hosp., Boston, 1961-62; chief medicine USPHS Hosp., Ft. Worth, 1955-57; dept. chief medicine USPHS Hosp., Boston, 1957-59; chief medicine USPHS Hosp., Memphis, 1964-65, Monterey County Gen. Hosp., 1969-70; ret. med. dir., col. USPHS; mem. internal medicine and cardiology staff Kaiser Permanente Med. Group, Sacramento, 1971-87; writer, Auburn, Calif., 1987--; clin. asst. Tufts Med. Sch., 1960-61; cons. chest disease Phila. Gen. Hosp., 1960-61, asst. prof. U. Md. Med. Sch., 1961-64; instr. U. Tenn. Med. Sch., 1964-65; asst. clin. prof. Sch. Medicine, U. Calif., Davis, 1973-81; mem. attending staff Cardiac Clinic Stanford U. Med. Sch. 1967-69; mem. sr. adv. bd. Area 4 Agy. on Aging. Mem. sch. bd. Salinas, Calif., 1968-69; bd. dirs. Am. Heart Assn., Tb and Health Assn. Served with AUS, 1943-46. Fellow ACP, Am. Coll. Chest Diseases; mem. Crocker Art Mus. Assn., Rotary, Phi Chi. Home and Office: 1158 Racquet Club Dr Auburn CA 95603-3042

HANSELL, WALTER WHITE, lawyer; b. Phila., Sept. 16, 1959; s. Norris and Margaret White (Corry) H.; m. Amy Lottman, Sept. 23, 1989; children: Abigail Jean, Marian White. BA, U. Ill., 1981; JD, U. Calif., Berkeley, 1984. Bar: Calif. 1984, U.S. Dist. Ct. (no. dist.) Calif. 1984, U.S. Dist. Ct. (ea. dist.) Calif. 1992. Investment adviser self-employed, Urbana, Ill., 1980-81, San Francisco, 1981-84; assoc. atty. Cooper, White & Cooper, San Francisco, 1984-90, ptnr., 1991—; govt. rels. com. chair, dir. Women in Cable, San Francisco Bay Area Chpt., 1988-92. Vol. atty. Vol. Legal Svcs. Project and Homeless Assistance Project Bar Assn., San Francisco, 1985-96; trustee Philos. Rsch. Soc., L.A., 1993—. Recipient Wiley Manuel Pro Bono Svc. award State Bar Calif., 1990-95. Mem. ABA, Women in Cable, Bay Area Cable Club, Communications Law Forum, State Bar Calif., Bar Assn. San Francisco, Internat. C. of C. (mem. group legal experts elec. commerce working group 1997-98). Home: 1049 Harvard Rd Piedmont CA 94610-1128 Office: Cooper White & Cooper 201 California St Ste 1500 San Francisco CA 94111-5017

HANSEN, ALEXANDER E., advertising agency executive. Pres., CEO Bravant LLC, L.A. E-mail: alex.hansen@bravant.com. Office: Bravant LLC 6500 Wilshire Blvd 21st fl Los Angeles CA 90048-4920*

HANSEN, ANNE KATHERINE, poet, retired elementary education educator; b. Coulter, Iowa, Oct. 29, 1928; d. Carl Christian and Else Katherine (Paulsen) H. BA, Chapman U., 1958; MA, U. Redlands, 1971. Life credential, Calif. Elem. tchr. Bloomington (Calif.) Schs., 1958-60, San Bernardino (Calif.) Unified Sch. Dist., 1960-87; ret., 1987. *She has published in 1998 Book of Poetry from Minerva Press in London "Listen to my Heart". Entered into International Biographical Centre, Cambridge, England for "Outstanding People of the 20th Century". Included in "Who's Who in the World" as well as "Who's Who in the West" and "Who's Who in America".* Contbr. poetry to anthologies. Recipient Golden Poet award World of Poetry, 1988, 89, 90, 91, 92, Poet of Merit award Internat. Soc. Poets, plaque, 1993, 94, 96, medallion, 1996. Home: 1632 Sepulveda Ave San Bernardino CA 92404-4702

HANSEN, CARL FREDERICK, chemistry educator; b. Owatonna, Minn., June 11, 1921; s. Clifford Franklin and Lumetta Gladys (Swanson) H.; m. Alice Adelaide Underleak, July 11, 1946 (div. 1968); children: David R., Richard F., George H. BA, Carleton Coll., 1943; MS, Stanford U., 1948; D of Engring., Nagoya U., 1982. Aeronautical rsch. scientist Ames Aerospace Lab. NACA, Mountain View, Calif., 1950-59; chief physics br. Ames Rsch. Ctr. NASA, Mountain View, Calif., 1959-61, 67-82; head earth & astro scis. GM Defense Rsch. Lab., Santa Barbara, Calif., 1961-67; pres. JAI Assoc., Inc., Mountain View, 1985-89; rsch. prof. chem. physics inst. U. Oreg., Eugene, 1989—; vis. prof. aerospace engring. Nagoya (Japan) U., 1982, Indian Inst. Sci., Bangalore, 1983, Nat. Cheng Kung U., Taiwan, 1984-85, vis. prof. mech. engring. MIT, Cambridge, 1965-66; pres. Hansen Rsch. Assocs., Eugene, 1989—. Author: Molecular Physics of Equilbrium Gases, 1976, Rate Process in Gas Phase, 1983; contbr. articles to profl. jours. Treas. Com. Sch. Improvement, Palo Alto, Calif., 1958-59; bd. dirs. Orchard Farms Assn., San Jose, Calif., 1969-81. Sgt. USAF, 1943-46. Fellow AIAA (assoc., v.p. No. Calif. chpt. 1960); mem. Aircraft Owners and Pilots Assn., Elks. Independent. Avocations: flying, back packing, skiing, golf, swimming. Office: U Oreg Physics Dept Eugene OR 97403

HANSEN, CAROL LOUISE, English language educator; b. San Jose, Calif., July 17, 1938; d. Hans Eskelsen and Thelma Josephine (Brooks) Hansen; m. Merrill Chris Davis, July 17, 1975 (div. 1978). BA in English, San Jose State U., 1960; MA in English Lit., U. Calif., Berkeley, 1968; PhD in English Lit., Ariz. State U., 1975. Asst. prof. English City Coll. San Francisco, Calif., 1985—, Coll. San Mateo, Calif., 1987—, De Anza Coll., 1998—; coord. writing Calif. State U., Monterey Bay, 1996; presenter in field. Author: Woman as Individual in English Renaissance Drama, 1993, 2nd edit., 1995, Beyond Evil: Cathy and Cal in East of Eden, 1998. Active Grace Cathedral, San Francisco. NDEA fellow, English-Speaking Union fellow for rsch. in Eng. Ariz. State U., 1972. Mem. MLA (chair exec. com. discussion group on two-yr. colls. 1999), Virginia Woolf Soc. Episcopalian. Avocation: animal welfare. Office: City Coll San Francisco 50 Phelan Ave San Francisco CA 94112-1821

HANSEN, CURTIS LEROY, federal judge; b. 1933. BS, U. Iowa, 1956; JD, U. N.Mex., 1961. Bar: N.Mex. Law clk. to Hon. Irwin S. Moise N.Mex. Supreme Ct., 1961-62; ptnr. Snead & Hansen, Albuquerque, 1962-64, Richard C. Civerolo, Albuquerque, 1964-71, Civerolo, Hansen & Wolf, P.A., 1971-92; dist. judge U.S. Dist. Ct., N.Mex., 1992—. Mem. State Bar N.Mex., Albuquerque Bar Assn., Am. Coll. Trial Lawyers, Am. Bd. Trial Advocates, Albuquerque Country Club. Office: US Courthouse Chambers 660 333 Lomas Blvd NW Albuquerque NM 87102

HANSEN, DONALD CURTIS, retired manufacturing executive; b. Marinette, Wis., Mar. 13, 1929; s. Curtis Albert and Dagmar Anne (Johnson) H.; m. Joan Mary Crant, Nov. 9, 1973. BBA, Carroll Coll., 1952. Purchasing agt. Prescott/Sterling Co., Menominee, Mich., 1954-62; mfrs. rep. Don C. Hansen Assocs., Phoenix, 1962-63; sales mgr. Karolton Envelope Co., San Francisco, 1964-72; owner, pres. San Francisco Envelope Co., 1972-79; owner Curtis Swann Cards, San Francisco, 1977-79; pres., owner Don C. Hansen, Inc. (doing bus. as The Envelope Co.), Oakland, Calif., 1979-95; ret., 1995. Mgr., organizer Twin City Civic Chorus, Menominee, 1959; bd. dirs. Menominee C. of C., 1958. Served with U.S. Army, 1952-54. Mem. Envelope Printing Specialists Assn. (bd. dirs. 1983—, pres. 1983-84), Envelope Mfrs. Assn. Am., San Francisco Lithograph and Craftsmans Club, Printing Industries of No. Calif. (bd. dirs. 1980-94), San Francisco Tennis Club (bd. govs. 1989-92), Terravita Country Club (Scottsdale, Ariz.; bd. dirs. 1997-98), Masons, Shriners, Desert Foothills Bridge Club (mgr. 1998—). Republican. Avocations: tennis, skiing, bridge, golf, dominoes.

HANSEN, EDWARD ALVIN CHARLES, feature animation executive; b. Berkeley, Calif., Sept. 7, 1925; s. Einar Aage Christian and Agnes (Beck) H.; m. Lorna Ida Tierney, Apr. 24, 1958; children: Candice Annette, Robert Paul, Janice Marie. Student, Miami U., Oxford, Ohio, 1944; AA, Hartnel Coll., 1950; student, UCLA, 1972, Los Angeles Valley Coll., 1979. Animation artist Walt Disney Prodns., Burbank, Calif., 1952-54, asst. dir., 1955-71, mgr., 1972-79, dir., 1980-83; v.p. Walt Disney Pictures, Burbank, 1984-87, prodn. cons., 1988-89; curator Disney Traveling Mus. Show, 1988; nat. judge Nissan Focus Awards, N.Y., 1982—; lectr. Royal Viking Line, San Francisco, 1987—; creator Seemore the C'ni Bee, Nat. Inst. for the Blind, Vancouver, B.C., Nisse Mand, logo Solvang annual Danish Days; Welcome Home Logo, USS Enterprise, CVN 65, 1996. Asst. dir. 7 feature films, 1955-71; prodn. mgr. (feature film) The Fox and the Hound, 1981; prodn. exec.: (feature films) The Black Cauldron, 1985, The Great Mouse Detective, 1986. Bd. dirs. Solvang Heritage Assocs. Elverhoj Mus.; com. Solvang Danish Days Found. Served with USN, 1943-46, PTO, 1950-51, Korea. Mem. Motion Picture Acad. Arts and Scis., Danish Brotherhood in Am., Am. Legion (past comdr. Santa Ynez Valley), Alisal Golf. Club: Alisal Golf. Avocations: art, golf.

HANSEN, GEOFFREY, magician, actor, composer, journalist; b. Richmond, Calif., Sept. 1, 1953; s. Robert Andrew von Oldenburg and Doris Carlene (O'Dell) H.; m. Josephine Lugnasin, June 12, 1998. Organized own prodn. mgmt. pub. co., World Artist Mgmt., 1972; past dir. cons. to several internat. bus. corps., U.S. and Far East. Began theatrical career in 1958 as child actor in TV commercials; later profl. magician with headline appearances in night clubs, theaters and TV shows in over 40 countries; tours of U.S., nat. TV appearances on ABC, NBC, CBS, others. Appeared in films Mandrake, The Dragon's Eye, Midnight in Transylvania, Fighting Dragon, Funny Kung Fu; narrator for radio and TV, U.S., Can., Japan, others. Composer musical works including commercial record This Is Hilo, Hawaii. Author numerous mag. articles, polit. essays, short stories, screen plays. Recipient Karate Black Belt award, 1977, Charles Atlas Internat. Phys. Fitness Championship award, 1968; inducted into Magicians Hall of Fame, 1981; decorated Knight Grand Cross, Order of Honored Saints, 1997, Knight Grand Comdr., Chivalrous Order of Jerusalem, 1997; named Best Magician in the World, Internat. Congress of Magicians, 1998. Mem. Universal Magic Assn. (Monarch of Mystery award 1971, 73), Hawaii Magic Circle (hon.), Shinobu Ninjutsu Soc. (Am. rep.), Am. Prodrs. Assn. (pres. 1987), Entertainers and Musicians' Assn. (bd. dirs. 1987), N.Am. Fedn. Showmen (trustee 1987), Internat. Magicians Soc. (life), Showman's League of Am., Soc. Am. Magicians, Am. Showman's Alliance (Entertainer of Yr. 1995, Lifetime Achievement award 1996), Am. Friends of the Philippines. Jewish. Office: Central Booking Office 855 E Twain #123411 Las Vegas NV 89109

HANSEN, GLEN ARTHUR, scientist, researcher; b. Thermopolis, Wyo., June 28, 1961; s. Glen Arthur and Ilene Lois (Haynes) H.; m. Paula Dee Rathbun, May 23, 1998. AAS in Petroleum Engring. Tech., Casper Coll., 1982; BS in Petroleum Engring., U. Wyo., 1985; MS in Mech. Engring., U. Nebr., 1991; PhD in Computer Sci., U. Idaho, 1996. Rsch. asst. U. Nebr., Lincoln, 1989-90, tchg. asst., 1990-91; sr. engr. Idaho Nat. Engring. Lab., Idaho Falls, 1991-95, engring. specialist, 1995-96; tech. staff mem. Los Alamos Nat. Lab., 1996—, project leader, 1997—; prin. investigator Los Alamos (N. Mex.) Nat. Lab., 1998—. Mem. Am. Soc. Mech. Engrs., Am. Nuclear Soc. (Idaho chpt.), Soc. Indsl. Applied Math., Assn. Computing Machinery. Home: 945 San Ildefonso Rd Trlr 57 Los Alamos NM 87544-2849 Office: Los Alamos National Lab MSF645 PO Box 1663 Los Alamos NM 87545

HANSEN, J. WOODFORD, agricultural products supplier; b. 1948. Owner of affiliate Hansen Ranch, Camarillo, Calif., 1968—; with Seaboard Produce, Oxnard, Calif., 1979—, now pres. Office: Seaboard Produce PO 6229 Oxnard CA 93031*

HANSEN, JAMES LEE, sculptor; b. Tacoma, Wash., June 13, 1925; s. Hildreth Justine and Mary Elizabeth Hansen; m. Annabelle Hair, Aug. 31, 1946 (dec. Sept. 1993); children: Valinda Jean, Yauna Marie; m. Jane Lucas, May 13, 1994. Grad., Portland Art Mus. Sch. Faculty Oreg. State U., Corvallis, 1957-58, U. Calif., Berkeley, 1958, Portland State U., 1964-90. One-man shows include Fountain Gallery, Portland, Oreg., 1966, 69, 77-81, U. Oreg. Art Mus., Eugene, 1970, Seligman (Seders Gallery), Seattle, 1970, Portland Art Mus., 1971, Cheney Cowles Meml. Mus., Spokane, Wash., 1972, Polly Freidlander Gallery, Seattle, 1973, 75-76, Smithsonian Instn., Washington, 1974, Hodges/Banks Gallery (now Linda Hodges Gallery), Seattle, 1983, Abanté Gallery, Portland, 1986, 88, 92, Maryhill Mus. of Art, Goldendale, Wash., 1997-98, Bryan Ohno Gallery, Seattle, 1997; exhibited in group shows at N.W. Ann. Painters and Sculptors, Seattle, 1952-73, Oreg. Ann. Painters and Sculptors, Portland Art Mus., 1952-75, Whitney Mus. Am. Art, N.Y.C., 1953, Santa Barbara (Calif.) Mus. Art, 1959-60, Denver Art Mus., 1960, San Francisco Art Mus., 1960, Smithsonian Instn., Washington, 1974, Wash. State U., Pullman, 1975, Benton County Hist. Mus., 1998; represented in permanent collections Graphic Arts Center, State Capitol, Olympia, Wash., U. Oreg., Eugene, Salem (Oreg.) Civic Center, Clark Coll., Vancouver, Wash., Portland Art Mus., Transit Mall, Portland, Seattle Art Mus., Gresham Town Fair (Oreg.), Oreg. Health Scis. U., Portland, Vancouver Sculpture Park, others; represented by Abanté Gallery, Portland, Hansen Studio, Vancouver, Peter Bartlow Gallery, Chgo., Bryan Ohno Gallery, Seattle. Address: 28219 NE 63rd Ave Battle Ground WA 98604-7107

HANSEN, JAMES VEAR, congressman; b. Salt Lake City, Aug. 14, 1932; s. J. Vear and Sena H.; m. Ann Burgoyne, 1958; children: Susan, Joseph James, David Burgoyne, Paul William, Jennifer. BS, U. Utah, 1960. Mem. Utah Ho. of Reps., 1973-80; spkr. of the house U.S. Ho. of Reps., 1979-80; mem. 97th-105th Congresses from 1st Utah dist., Washington, 1981—; pres. James V. Hansen Ins. Agy., Woodland Springs Devel. Co. Office: Ho of Reps 2466 Rayburn Bldg Washington DC 20515-4401*

HANSEN, LELAND JOE, communications executive; b. Spokane, Wash., Mar. 26, 1944; s. Herman Johnny and Emma Irene (Borth) H.; m. Jonni Krajeski, Apr. 15, 1979. Creative dir., dir., producer Mel Blanc and Assocs., Beverly Hills, Calif., 1971-73; creative dir., writer, producer, dir. nat. TV and radio commls. and entertainment programs ABC Watermark, Universal City, Calif., 1973-80; pres., chief exec. officer, writer, producer, dir. film and TV GDE Prodns. Inc., Sherman Oaks, Calif., 1980-87; sr. writer, dir. video svcs. Rockwell Internat., Canoga Park, Calif., 1987-95; ind. film, video and multimedia audio prodr. specializing in mktg. videos for corps., 1995—; voice-over artist nat. TV and radio. Dir. American Top Forty, 1973-77, The Elvis Presley Story, Soundtrack of the Sixties; creator, producer, dir. Alien Worlds, 1973-80. Founding mem. Am. Forces Radio, Saigon, Socialist Republic of Vietnam, 1963-64. Served with U.S. Army, 1962-65, Vietnam. Recipient Belding award The Advt. Club Los Angeles, 1977. Mem. AFTRA. Avocations: pilot, architectural design, model builder.

HANSEN, LEONARD JOSEPH, author, journalist; b. San Francisco, Aug. 4, 1932; s. Einar L. and Margie A. (Wilder) H.; m. Marcia Ann Rasmussen, Mar. 18, 1966 (div.); children: Barron Richard, Trevor Wilder. AB in Radio-TV Prodn. and Mgmt., San Francisco State U., 1956, postgrad. 1956-57; cert. IBM Mgmt. Sch., 1967. Jr. writer Sta. KCBS, San Francisco, 1952-54; assoc. producer and dir. Ford Found. TV Rsch. Project, San Francisco State U., 1955-57; crew chief on live and remote broadcasts Sta. KPIX-TV, San Francisco, 1957-59, air promotion dir. and writer Sta. KPIX-TV, San Francisco, 1959-60; pub. rels. mgr. Sta. KNTV-TV, San Jose, Calif., 1961; radio and TV promotion mgr. Seattle World's Fair, 1962; pub. relations and promotion mgr. Century 21 Ctr., Inc., Seattle, 1963-64; pub. rels. dir. Dan Evans for Gov. Com., Seattle, 1964; propr., mgr. Leonard J. Hansen Pub. Rels., Seattle, 1965-67; campaign mgr. Walter J. Hickel for Gov. Com., Anchorage, 1966; exec. cons. to Gov. of Alaska, Juneau, 1967; gen. mgr. No. TV, Inc., Anchorage, 1967-69; v.p. mktg. Sea World, Inc., San Diego, 1969-71; editor, pub. Sr. World Publs., Inc., San Diego, 1973-84; chmn. Sr. Pubs. Group, 1977-89; speaker and mktg. cons. to sr. citizens, 1984-92; panelist, pub. affairs radio programs, 1971-92; lectr. journalism San Diego State U., 1975-76. Writer weekly syndicated column Mainly for Seniors, 1984—, syndicated column Travel for Mature Adults, 1984—; writer, journalist The Mature Market; contbg. editor Mature Life Features, news/feature syndicate, 1987-90; chmn. Mature Mkt. Seminars, 1987-90; author Life Begins at 50-The Handbook for Creative Retirement Planning, 1989; pres., pub. Mature Market Editorial Svcs., 1991—. Founding mem. Housing for Elderly and Low Income Persons, San Diego, 1977-78; mem. Mayor's Ad Hoc Adv. Com. on Aging, San Diego, 1976-79; vice chmn. Housing Task Force, San Diego, 1977-78; bd. dirs. Crime Control Commn., San Diego, 1980; del. White House Conf. on Aging, 1981. Served with U.S. Army, 1953-55. Nat. Press Found. fellow, 1994, Alicia Patterson Found. fellow in Journalism, 1999; recipient Longterm Achievement award Am. Soc. on Aging., 1999; recipient numerous service and citizenship awards from clubs and community orgns. Fellow Nat. Press Found.; mem. Pub. Rels.Soc. Am. (accredited), Soc. Profl. Journalists (Best Investigative Reporting award 1979), Internat. Platform Assn., San Diego Press Club (Best Newswriting award 1976-77, Headliner of Yr. award 1980), Nat. Press Club (profl. mem.) Home and Office: 10 Town Plz Ste 313 Durango CO 81301-5104

HANSEN, MATILDA, state legislator; b. Paullina, Iowa, Sept. 4, 1929; d. Arthur J. and Sada G. (Thompson) Henderson; m. Robert B. Michener, 1950 (div. 1963); children: Eric J., Douglas E.; m. Hugh G. Hansen. BA, U. Colo., 1963; MA, U. Wyo., 1970. Tchr. history Englewood (Colo.) Sr. High Sch., 1963-65; dir. Albany County Adult Learning Ctr., Laramie, Wyo., 1966-78, Laramie Plains Civic Ctr., 1979-83; treas. Wyo. Territorial Prison Corp., Laramie, 1988-93, also bd. dirs.; bd. dirs. Wyo. Territorial Park. Author: (textbooks) To Help Adults Learn, 1975, Let's Play Together, 1978. Legislator Wyo. Ho. of Reps., Cheyenne, 1975-95, minority whip, 1987-88, asst. minority leader, 1991-92, 93-94; mem. mgmt. coun. Wyo. State Legislature, Cheyenne, 1983-84; chair Com. for Dem. Legislature, Cheyenne, 1990-94, Wyo. State Dems., 1995—. GE fellow in econs. for high sch. tchrs., 1963; named Pub. Citizen of Yr., Wyo. Assn. Social Workers, 1980-81. Mem. LWV Wyo. (v.p. 1966-68), LWV Laramie (bd. dirs. 1966-72, Nat. Conf. State Legislators (vice chair human resources 1983, nat. exec. com. 1990-94), Laramie Area C. of C., Laramie Women's Club, Faculty Women's Club. Mem. Soc. of Friends. Avocations: gardening, quilting, mountaineering. Home: 1306 E Kearney St Laramie WY 82070-4142 Office: 1306 E Kearney St Laramie WY 82070-4199*

HANSEN, REX COSSEY, mechanical engineer; b. Salt Lake City, Dec. 23, 1952; s. Alvin Leo and Norma Dean (Cossey) H.; m. Gloria Lyn Haslam, May 18, 1978; children: Karen, Angela, Staci, Kayla. AA, Snow Coll.,

1975; BS, Brigham Young U., 1977. Mech. engr., gas res. engr. Pacific Gas & Electric Co., San Francisco, 1977-81; sr. reservoir engr. Northwest Pipeline Corp., Salt Lake City, 1981-93; sr. petroleum engr. Williams Prodn. Co., Salt Lake City, 1993-95; compression engr. Northwest Pipeline Co., Salt Lake City, 1995—; mem. gas storage steering com. Gas Rsch. Inst., Chgo., 1990—; mem. natural gas res. com. Am. Gas Assn., Chgo., 1979-88. Mem. Soc. Petroleum Engrs. (tech. com. chair 1993-94, sect. chair 1990-91). Avocations: sailing, snow skiing, gardening. Office: Northwest Pipeline Corp PO Box 58900 Salt Lake City UT 84158-0900

HANSEN, ROBERT DENNIS, educational administrator; b. San Francisco, July 17, 1945; s. Eiler Cunnard and Muriel Lenore (Morrison) H.; BA, U. San Francisco, 1967, MA in Counseling and Guidance, 1971, MA in Supervision and Adminstrn., 1973; EdD, U. La Verne, 1988; children from a previous marriage: April Michelle, Alison Nicole, Andrew Warren. Tchr., dept. chmn., counselor, dir. student affairs, attendance officer South San Francisco Unified Sch. Dist., 1968-74, coord., asst. prin. Jurupa Unified Sch. Dist., Riverside, Calif., 1974-78; prin., asst. supt. San Gabriel (Calif.) Sch. Dist., 1978-91; supt. Rosemead (Calif.) Sch. Dist., 1991—; adj. prof. U. La Verne, Calif., 1988—. Mem. exec. bd. South San Francisco PTA, 1968-74; bd. dirs. West San Gabriel YMCA; mem. parade formation com. Pasadena (Calif.) Tournament of Roses. Recipient Hon. Svc. award Calif. State PTA. Mem. U. San Francisco Edn. Alumni Soc. (pres. 1972-73), Nat. Assn. Year-Round Edn., U. San Francisco Alumni Assn., ASCD, Am. Assn. Sch. Adminstrs., Assn. Calif. Sch. Adminstrs., Phi Delta Kappa. Republican. Presbyterian. Masons (32 degree). Office: Rosemead Sch Dist 3907 Rosemead Blvd # 213 Rosemead CA 91770-1951 Address: 1624 3rd St Manhattan Beach CA 90266-6304

HANSEN, ROBERT GUNNARD, philatelist, entrepreneur; b. Chgo., Aug. 16, 1939; s. Earl F. and Mildred E. (Hargrave) H.; A.A., Lincoln Coll., 1960; B.A., Culver Stockton Coll., 1962; M.B.A., U. So. Calif., 1966; postgrad. UCLA Extension, 1962-67; m. Bertha Golds, Aug. 10, 1960; children—Karin Lee, Lisa Marie. With Litton Industries, 1962-63, Sterer Engring., 1963-69; mktg. and contracts ofcl. Santa Barbara Research Ctr., 1969-73; pres., chief exec. officer, R.G. Hansen & Assocs., Santa Barbara, 1974— ; pres., owner The Silver Penny and Santa Barbara Stamp & Coin, 1969—; owner, CEO, pres. Univ. Travel Bureau, 1990-95; guest lectr. Santa Barbara City Coll. Mem. Am. Vacuum Soc., Am. Philatelic Soc. (life), Am. Numismatic Assn., Hawaii Numismatic Assn., Sci. and Engring. Coun. Santa Barbara (pres. 1989), Token and Medal Soc., Masons, York Rite. Scottish Rite, Shriners, Royal Order of Scotland, Channel City, Royal Arch Masons, trustee Santa Barbara Historical Soc., Rotary Internat. (Paul Harris fellow 1990, 96). Research and publs. on cryogenics, electro-optics, infrared radiation; patentee in field. Republican. Presbyterian. Office: 631 Chapala St Santa Barbara CA 93101-3311

HANSEN, RONALD GORDON, retired research administrator, consultant; b. Gisborne, New Zealand, May 23, 1924; came to U.S., 1929; s. Leo and Vesta Merle (Bull) H.; m. Inez Merrel Carter, Feb. 21, 1945 (dec. Aug. 1991); children: Sandra, Ronald C., Julie, Karen, Hettie Ann, Melinda, Melanie, Pamela; m. Bliss Jarvis Brimley, June 26, 1992. BS in Bacteriology and Pub. Health, Utah State U., Logan, 1949; MA in Speech and Hearing, Ohio State U., 1950, PhD in Speech Sci., 1954. Commd. t/sgt. USAF, 1943, advanced through grades to lt. col., 1960, ret., 1965; project scientist bioacoustics unit biophysics br., aeromedical lab., Wright Air Devel. Ctr. USAF, Wright AFB, 1950-52, asst. chief/project scientist biol. acoustics sect., bioacoustics br., aeromedical lab., Wright Air Devel. Ctr., 1954-56, chief phys. acoustics bioacoustics br.,aerospace med. lab., Wright Air. Devel. Ctr., 1956-58, chief biol. acoustics bioacoustics br. Aerospace Med. Lab., 1958-59; chief audiology lab. Sch. Aviation Medicine Aerospace Med. Ctr., 1960-62; chief programs divsn. aerospace med. AF sys. comd., 1962-63; dir. applied scis. Tech., Inc., Dayton, Ohio, 1963-65; asst. provost internal, external rsch. So. Ill. U., Carbondale, 1965-73, prof. speech pathology, audiology, 1965-73; founding pres., ceo Eyring Rsch. Inst., Provo, Utah, 1973-86; adj. prof., founding assoc. dir. Ctr. of Excellence for Signal Processing, Brigham Young U., 1986-90; mgmt. cons., 1990—; Chmn. adv. bd. Harding & Harris, Orem, Utah, 1981—; founding bd. dirs. Lifestory, Inc., Orem; chmn. bd. Imagen, San Diego; presenter in field. Contbr. numerous articles to profl. jours. Pres., v.p., bd. dris. United Way, Utah County, 1978-84; pres. AHA, Utah County, 1993-95. Lt. col. USAFR, 1950-65. Decorated 12 medals and ribbons for combat flying USAF, 1943-45; recipient Govt. Citizen Svc. award Govs. Bus. Devel. State of Utah, 1986. Mem. Am. Speech and Hearing Soc., Kiwanis Club (pres., v.p., bd. dirs. 1980-85 Utah County, pres. Provo 1978—), Mgmt. Soc.)pres. adv. bd. Utah chpt. 1993-95), Scientific Soc., Acoustical Soc., Utah Valley Speech and Hearing Soc., Utah C. of C. (Total Citizen award 1986). Republican. Mem. LDS Ch. Avocations: hunting, fishing, reading. Home: 1799 Cobblestone Dr Provo UT 84604-1174

HANSEN, THOMAS CARTER, college athletics conference commissioner; b. Seattle, Nov. 30, 1937; s. Herbert and Marjorie Jean (Jordan) H.; m. Melva Marie Fuhr, Oct. 11, 1962; children: Sarah Marie Hansen Reeves, Bryan Thomas. BA, U. Wash., 1959. Reporter The Columbian, Vancouver, Wash., 1959-60; dir. pub. rels. Pacific-10 Conf., San Francisco, 1960-67; dir. pub. rels. NCAA, Kansas City, Mo., 1967-71, asst. exec. dir., 1971-83; commr. Pacific-10 Conf., Walnut Creek, Calif., 1983—. Author: (chpt.) Administration for Athletic Programs, 1987. Mem. Kiwanis Club, Vancouver, 1959-60, San Francisco, 1960-67, Kansas City, 1967-83. Mem. Nat. Assn. Collegiate Dirs. of Athletics (exec. com. 1988-92, Adminstrv. Excellence award 1994), Collegiate Commrs. Assn. (pres. 1992, 93), Football Found. Hall of Fame (honors ct. 1994—). Republican. Lutheran. Avocations: golfing, reading, music. Office: Pacific 10 Conf 800 S Broadway Ste 400 Walnut Creek CA 94596-5278*

HANSEN, WAYNE W., lawyer; b. Clintonville, Wis., June 7, 1942; s. William W. and Berniece M. (Kuehn) H.; m. Carolyn M. Lemke, Dec. 21, 1969; children: Drew D., Janna J. BBA, U. Wis., 1965, JD, 1967. Bar: Wis. 1967, U.S. Dist. Ct. (we. dist.) Wis. 1971, U.S. Ct. Appeals (7th cir.) 1972, U.S. Dist. Ct. (ea. dist.) Wis. 1975, Wash. 1979, U.S. Dist. Ct. (we. dist.) Wash. 1979, U.S. Ct. Appeals (9th cir.) 1982, U.S. Dist. Ct. (ea. dist.) Wash. 1986. Atty. NLRB, Mpls., 1967-70, Schmitt Nolan Hansen & Hartley, Merrill, Wis., 1970-79; ptnr. Lane Powell Spears Lubersky, Seattle, 1979-98; mng. ptnr. Jackson Lewis Schnitzler & Krupman, Seattle, 1998—. Contbg. author: Developing Labor Law, 1971, Doing Business in Washington State—Guide for Foreign Business, 1989. Office: Jackson Lewis Schnitzler & Krupman 1420 5th Ave Ste 2000 Seattle WA 98101-4087

HANSEN-KYLE, LINDA L., managed health care nurse; b. Selma, Calif., Aug. 24, 1947; d. Ernest L. and Mary Hansen; m. Kenton L. Kyle, Feb. 16, 1974. BA in History summa cum laude, Humboldt State, 1969, MA in Psychology, 1972; ASN, Saddleback Coll., 1976; MS in Human Resources and Mgmt. Devel., Chapman U., 1993. RN, Calif. ICU nurse supr. Scripps Clinic and Rsch., San Diego, 1978-81; asst. dir. nursing Maric Coll., San Diego, 1980-85; mgr. of ops. MetraHealth, San Diego, 1985—. Mem. ASTD, ACCN, AAUW.

HANSEY, RENEE JEANNE, retired communications executive; b. Tacoma, Apr. 24, 1927; d. Francis J. and Genevieve (Hewitt) Payette; m. James Burpee, Mar. 13, 1947 (dec. 1950); children: James, Victoria; m. Orville D. Hansey (div. 1987); children; Dan, Terri, John, Bill; m. Ralph Edward Lecky Sr., June 26, 1989 (div. Dec. 1993). Student in Layout and Design, Art Inst. Chgo., 1943; BS in Psychology, St. John's U., 1988; MS in Psychology, St John's U., 1991; postgrad. in Graphics, U. Alaska, 1985. Copy writer Sta. KIT, Yakima, Wash., 1942-44; program mgr. Sta. KING, Seattle, 1945-47; advt. mgr. Sequim (Wash.) Press, 1967-70, editor, 1970-76; TV producer Municipality of Anchorage, 1976-86; pub. Voice, Port Angeles, Wash., 1986-89; cons. on media rels. and sr. citizens; coord. Lifeline Olympic Meml. Hosp., Pt. Angeles, Wash., 1994—; founder Widowed Persons Svc., Anchorage, 1983-85; owner Frontier Pub., Anchorage, 1983-85; dir. Far North Network, Anchorage, 1982-86. Author: Go to the Source, 1977, One Way to the Funny Farm, 1978; producer (TV show) Opportunities for Seniors, 1981-86 (TV Prodn. award, 1982-85). Sec. Dem. Ctrl. Com., Clallam County, Wash., 1965-76; founder Olympic Women's Resource Ctr., Port Angeles, 1966-75; councilwoman City of Sequim, 1973-76, 95—; active Affirmative Action Clallam County, Wash., 1974, Sr. Companions, Elder Abuse Task Force, Wash. Commn. on Salaries and Compensation for Elected Ofcls. and Judiciary, Wash. State Coun. on Aging; chmn. bd. dirs. Port Angeles Sr. Ctr.; mem. Peninsula Regional Transp. Policy Bd. With WAC, 1944. Mem. AAUW, Alaska Press Women (pres. 1981-82, 85-86), Nat. Fedn. Press Women, Alaska Press Club. Roman Catholic. Avocations: woodworking, sewing, knitting, hiking, traveling. Home: 150 Melrose Ave E Apt 502 Seattle WA 98102-5535

HANSON, GEORGE, music director, conductor; m. Dawn Hanson. Degree, Ind. U. Resident conductor Atlanta Symphony; asst. to Leonard Bernstein Vienna Stae Opera; asst. Giuseppe Patane La Scala, Covent Garden, Munich Opera Houses; mus. dir. Anchorage Symphony; asst. conductor N.Y. Philharmonic; conductor Tucson Symphony Orchestra; appeared with sixty orchestras and operas in sixteen countries. Named Winner of the Leopold Stokowski Competition at Carnegie Hall, N.Y.C., Hungarian Internat. Coducting Competition, Budapest, Young Musician of 1990 Musical Am. Address: Tucson Symphony Orchestra-TSO 2175 N 6th Ave Tucson AZ 85705-5606*

HANSON, GEORGE PETER, retired research botanist, real estate investor; b. Conde, S.D., July 20, 1933; s. George Henry and Rosa Wilhelmina (Peterson) H.; m. Barbara Jean Graves, Aug. 20, 1958; children: David, Carole, Heather, Peter; m. Gloria Ann Gauntt, June 1, 1969. BS in Agronomy, S.D. State U., 1956, MS in Plant Breeding, 1958; PhD in Genetics, Ind. U., 1965. Asst. prof. biology Thiel Coll. Greenville, Pa., 1962-65; asst. prof. botany Butler U., Indpls., 1965-67; sr. biologist L.A. State and County Arboretum, Arcadia, Calif., 1968-82; real estate investor, 1971—. Mem. Apt. Assn. of Greater L.A. Methodist. Contbr. numerous articles in field to profl. jours. Home: 1345 W Haven Rd San Marino CA 91108-2018

HANSON, GERALD EUGENE, oral and maxillofacial surgeon; b. Lincoln, Nebr., July 18, 1947; s. Gerald Stephen and Ferne Althea (Russell) H. DDS, MPH, Loma Linda U., 1973; oral & maxillofacial surgery cert., U. Minn., 1976. Diplomate Am. Bd. Forensic Dentistry. Pvt. practice Palm Desert, Calif., 1976-78, Las Vegas, Nev., 1978—; mem. com. edn. & rsch. Eisenhower Med. Ctr., Rancho Mirage, Calif., 1977, dir. continuing dental edn. program, 1977-78; chief divsn. oral & maxillofacial surgery Sunrise Hosp., 1984-94, Columbia Mountain View Hosp., 1995—. Rep. environ. reference com. joint policy coun. APHA, Washington, 1977; bd. dirs. Clark County chpt. Am. Cancer Soc., 1979-83; chmn. oral cancer screening clinics Jaycees State Fair & Annual Health Fair, Las Vegas, 1981; adv. bd. Clark County C.C., Las Vegal, 1979; mem. Nev. State Bd. Health, 1990-95; bd. dirs. Am. Assn. Oral and Maxillofacial Surgery Found., 1995—. Fellow Pierre Fauchard Acad., Internat. Coll. Dentists, Western Soc. Oral & Maxillofacial Surgeons (bd. dirs. 1981-83, 91-97, pres. 1995-96), Am. Assn. Oral & Maxillofacial Surgeons (trustee Dist. VI 1984-88, Nev. del. 1979-83, sec.-treas. 1988-91), Am. Coll. Dentistry; mem. ADA (chmn. sci. session 1982, mem. coun. hosp. affairs 1985-89, AAOMS rep. interprofl. rels. com. 1987), Nev. Dental Assn. (co-chmn. group care & hosp. svcs. com. 1979-84, Clark County del. Ho. Dels. 1980-84, pres. 1987), Am. Coll. Oral & Maxillofacial Surgeons, Nev. Soc. of Oral and Maxillofacial Surgeons (pres. 1983-85), Am. Assn. Oral and Maxillofacial Surgery Found. (bd. dirs. 1995—), Las Vegas Execs. Assn., Clark County Aviation Assn., Clark County Dental Soc. (pres. 1982-83). Avocations: flying, antique airplane collecting, music, diving, skiing. Office: 2585 S Jones Blvd Ste 1A Las Vegas NV 89146-5604

HANSON, GERALD WARNER, retired county official; b. Alexandria, Minn., Dec. 25, 1938; s. Lewis Lincoln and Dorothy Hazel (Warner) H.; m. Sandra June Wheeler, July 9, 1960; 1 child, Cynthia R. AA, San Bernardino Valley (Calif.) Coll., 1959; BA, U. Redlands (Calif.), 1979; MA, U. Redlands, 1981; EdD, Pepperdine U., 1995. Cert. advanced metrication specialist. Dep. sealer San Bernardino (Calif.) County, 1964-80, div. chief, 1980-85, dir. weights and measures, 1985-94; CATV cons. City of Redlands, 1996—, City of Yucaipa, 1998—; substitute tchr. Redlands Unified Sch. Dist., 1996—. Chmn. Redlands Rent Rev. Bd., 1985-99; bd. dirs. House Neighborly Svc., Redlands, 1972-73, Boys Club, Redlands, 1985-86; mem. Redlands Planning commn., 1990-98. With USN. Fellow U.S. Metric Assn. (treas. 1986-88, 92—); mem. NRA (life), Nat. Conf. on Weights and Measures (asst. treas. 1986-94), Western Weights and Measures Assn. (pres. 1987-88), Calif. Assn. Weights and Measures Ofcls. (1st v.p. 1987), Calif. Rifle and Pistol Assn. (life), Masons, Shriners, Kiwanis (treas. Redlands club 1983-95), Over the Hill Gang (San Bernardino). Avocations: golf, hunting, mechanics, microcomputers. Home: 225 E Palm Ave Redlands CA 92373-6131

HANSON, JANICE CRAWFORD, artist, financial analyst; b. Norwalk, Conn., Oct. 8, 1952; d. Arthur James and Jean Alice (MacKinnon) Crawford; m. Jeffrey Becker Hanson, May 29, 1976; children: Forrest James, Shane Crawford. BA, Wellesley Coll., 1974; MBA, U. Denver, 1979. CFA. Sec. to assoc. dean Yale Sch. of Music, New Haven, Conn., 1975-76; adminstrv. asst. to dir. of internships Inst. Policy Scis. Duke U., Durham, N.C., 1976-78; fiscal analyst Denver Water Bd., 1979-84; fin. analyst Englewood, Colo., 1984; part-time fin. analyst Jeffrey B. Hanson M.D., P.C., Granger, Ind., 1989-92; part-time watercolorist Englewood, Colo., 1989—. Exhibited in group shows at Watercolor West XXVII Exhbn., Riverside, Calif., 1995, Western Colo. Watercolor Soc. Nat. Juried Exhbn., Grand Junction, 1994, 95, 96, Rocky Mountain Nat. Watermedia Exhbn., Golden, Colo., 1996, 98, Pikes Peak Watercolor Soc. Nat. Exhbn., Colorado Springs, Colo., 1997, 98. Vol. Denver Dumb Friends League, 1986-88, Cherry Creek Schs., Englewood, Colo., 1992—. Recipient Best of Show award Nat. Greeley Art Mart, 1994, Platinum award, Nat. Greeley Art Mart, 1995, Dean Witter award for originality Colo. Watercolor Soc. State Juried Exhbn., Denver, Colo., 1996. Mem. Assn. for Investment Mgmt. and Rsch., Watercolor West (juried assoc.), Colo. Watercolor Soc. (signature), Western Colo. Watercolor Soc. (signature), Denver Soc. Security Analysts. Avocations: running, fiber arts, needlework, photography.

HANSON, NOEL RODGER, management consultant; b. L.A., Jan. 19, 1942; s. Albert and Madelyne Gladys (Pobanz) H.; B.S. in Indsl. Mgmt., U. So. Calif., 1963, M.B.A. in Fin., 1966; m. Carol Lynn Travis, June 17, 1967 (div.); 1 son, Eric Rodger. Asst. dir. alumni fund, then dir. ann. funds U. So. Calif., 1964-66; asst. to Walt Disney for Cal-Arts, Retlaw Enterprises, Glendale, Calif., 1966-68; asst. dir. joint devel. Claremont U. Center, 1968-69; v.p. adminstrn. Robert Johnston Co., Los Angeles, 1969-70; partner Hale, Hanson & Co., Pasadena, Calif., 1970-82, Hanson, Olson & Co., 1982—; pres. Pasadena Services, Inc., 1977—; dir. Pasadena Fin. Cons., Inc., Wilhire Funding, Inc., 1988—. Mem. Pasadena City Traffic Adv. Commn., 1997—; trustee Oakhurst Sch., Pasadena, 1973-75; bd. advisers Girls Club Pasadena, 1977—; mem. U. So. Calif. Assos., 1979—, U. So. Calif. Commerce Assos., 1965—. Republican. Presbyterian. Club: Jonathan (Los Angeles). Home: 1051 La Loma Rd Pasadena CA 91105-2208 Office: Hanson & Co 21 W Dayton St Pasadena CA 91105-2001

HANTUSCH, MARK JOHN, traffic administrator; b. San Francisco, Sept. 26, 1950; s. Fred and Larrita (King) H.; children: Mark, David. AA in Electronics, West Valley Coll., 1978; BSEE, San Jose State U., 1992; cert. in engring., DeAnza Coll., 1994. Mem. printer/circuit assembly staff Hewlett-Packard Co., Mountain View, Calif., 1972-82; svc. rep., buyer Hewlett-Packard Co., San Jose, Calif., 1982-85, traffic mgr., 1985-92; distbr., rep. rels. Amway Corp., Long Beach, Calif., 1992—. Bd. dirs. Goodwill Industries; active Bixby Highlands Assn., Rigley Assn. Long Beach; v.p. Calif. Disability Rights Assn.; counselor Disabled Resource Ctr.; mem. coun. Disabled Action Network; program mgr. Ind. Living Ctr.; mem. folk music group area ch. Named Vol. of Yr., Bixby Assn. Mem. Bixby Bus. Assn. Democrat. Roman Catholic. Home and Office: Amway Corp 1165 E Carson # 4 Long Beach CA 90807

HAO, LAWRENCE KAHOLO, state official, clinical hypnotherapist; b. Paahau, Hawaii, Aug. 24, 1937; s. Louis Kanoa and Mona Doris (Kaholo) H.; m. Ramona Kay Newton, Apr. 15, 1960; children: Debra Lynn Kelani, Melanie Pualani, Lance Kanoa, Sean Lani Newton. BS, Ind. U., 1962, MS, 1970. Cert. internat. travel agt., pvt. pilot, scuba, charter boat capt., USCG. Recreational therapist Beatty Meml. Hosp., Westville, Ind., 1962-63; tchr. Russiaville (Ind.) Elem. Sch., 1963-65; tchr. phys. edn. Western Elem. Sch., Russiaville, 1965-67; aquatic dir. Ea. H.S., Greentown, Ind., 1967-69; grad. asst. Ind. U., Bloomington, 1969-70; asst. prof. Western Ill. U., Macomb, 1970-72, U. Hawaii, Honolulu, 1973-76; asst. coord. hwy. safety Hawaii Dept. Transp., Honolulu, 1972-76, adminstr. motor vehicle safety, 1976—. Mem., chmn. Med. Adv. Bd. Hawaii, 1972—, Hawaii Hwy. Safety Coun., 1972—, Lt. Sheriff reserve program Sheriff Dept. State of Hawaii, 1984—. With USAR, 1956-62. Mem. MADD (profl.), Am. Assn. Motor Vehicle Adminstrs. (profl., regional rep. 1978—), Nat. Hwy. Traffic Safety Adminstrn. (profl., regional rep. 1972—). Avocations: swimming, spear and sport fishing, scuba diving, ukulele. Fax: 808-832-5830. Office: Motor Vehicle Safety Office Kakuhihewa Bldg 601 Kamokila Blvd Rm 511 Kapolei HI 96707

HAPNER, MARY LOU, securities trader and dealer; b. Fort Wayne, Ind., Nov. 9, 1937; d. Paul Kenneth Brooks and Eileen (Summers) H. BS with honors, Ariz. State U., 1966, MS, 1967. Stockbroker Young, Smith & Peacock, Phoenix, Ariz., 1971-76, v.p., 1976-89; v.p. Peacock, Hislop, Staley & Given, Phoenix, 1989-90, 1st v.p., 1990—. Author: Career Courage, 1984; author numerous poems. Chmn. March of Dimes, Sun City, Ariz., 1983; trustee St. Lukes, Phoenix, 1978; mem. fin. com. YWCA, Phoenix, 1975; chair budget com. Ch. of Beatitudes, Phoenix, mem. exec. coun., 1991; bd. dirs. Ariz. Children's Found., 1998. Recipient Spirit of Philanthropy award, 1997. Mem. Charter 100 (chair membership 1979-81, pres. 1980, pres. 1982, v.p. 1981, treas., membership chair 1995). Republican. Lutheran. Avocations: golf, singing with concert choirs, writing poetry.

HAPPEL, KENNETH MALCOLM, computer scientist; b. N.Y.C., June 8, 1949; s. Carl Frederick and Katherine King (Kehlor) H.; m. Riemke Rip, 1974 (div. 1977); m. Marie-Jose Kaasenbrood, Feb. 14, 1990 (div. 1995); 1 child, Lieneke. Student, U. Calif., Santa Barbara. Quality engr. EMI Holland Prodns., Haarlem, Netherlands, 1975-77; tech. dir. Technovation, Arnhem, Netherlands, 1978-82, Synterials Plc., London, 1982-83; CEO, founder Devtech Bv., Heerlen, 1984-89; sr. staff engr. Gen. Dynamics Electronics, San Diego, 1989-91; CEO, chmn. Omnigon, San Diego, 1991—. Mem. IEEE, Assn. for Computing Machinery, Eurographics. Republican. Achievements include invention of Hyperknowledge; research in artificial intelligence, virtual reality and advanced materials; construction of 1st European ful C.I.M. facility for advanced composites; development of autonomous reading systems for Opendoc applications.

HAQUE, MOHAMMED SHAHIDUL, electrical engineer; b. Dhaka, Bangladesh, May 12, 1965; came to U.S., 1991; s. Shamsul and Hafiza (Akter) H.; m. Aynun Naher, June 14, 1994; children: Afsara, Sakib. BSEE, Bangladesh U. Engring. & Tech., Dhaka, 1989; MSEE, U. Ark., 1992, PhD, 1997. Tchg. asst., dept. elec. engr. Bangladesh U. Engring. and Tech., 1990; rsch. asst., dept. elec. engr. U. Ark., Fayetteville, 1991-92; sr. rsch. asst. U. Ark., 1993-97, rsch. asst. prof., 1997; key account process support engr. Novellus Syss. Inc., Phoenix, 1997—; lectr. in field. Contbr. articles to Jour. Applied Physics, Solar Energy Materials and solar Cells, Jour. Elec. Materials, others. Mem. IEEE, Electrochemical Soc., Internat. Microelectronics Packaging Soc. Islamic. Achievements include research in microelectronic materials for solar cell applications and multichip module packaging technology; invention of a low temperature silicon solar cell fabrication process; contribution to understanding and quality improvement of chemical vapor deposited silicon dioxide and diamond dielectric films. Avocations: music, philately, photography. Home: 233 NW Gina Loop Apt 219 Beaverton OR 97006-8863 Office: Novellus Sys Inc 410 N 44th St Ste 1140 Phoenix AZ 85008-7617

HAR, LI (ANITA DICK), artist; b. Floral Park, N.Y., Aug. 26, 1931; d. Henry Dick and Annie Leung; m. Gilbert Wong, Feb. 24, 1957; children: Glenn, Craig. Student, Munson Coll. for Secs., Coll. San Mateo (Calif.). Sec. City of San Mateo, U. Calif. Med. Ctr., San Francisco, U. Extension, L.A. Author: Names for Your Personal License Plates, 1990; shows include Burlingame Libr., Belmont Libr., Belmont Art Coun., San Mateo County Fair, Bay Area Meadows Exhibn., Peninsula Hosp., Mariposa Stained Glass Studio, Susan's Beauty Salon, San Francisco, Peninsula Gallery, San Mateo, San Carlos Libr., Arguello Gallery, San Mateo, Mariner's Island Med. Ctr., Foster City Gallery San Mateo Garden Club, Chinese Cultural Ctr., Millbrae, Women's Caucus for Art, Foster City Recreation, Redwood City Cmty. Ctr., Art-U-Form, Pacifica Gallery, Hall of Flowers Golden Gate Park, San Francisco, 1995 Soc. We. Artists, Monterey Gallery, Dario's Cafe, Redwood City, Cafe La Tosca, San Carlos, Eight County Country Bldg., Redwood City, Equine Arts and Craft Show, Bay Meadows Derby Exhibn., San Mateo; permanent collections include Imperial Florist, Kathy Kreative Kakes, Dazzling Digits, Fox and Carskadon, Realtors, Safeway Store, Pacific Rsch., Art and Wine Festivals, Bay Meadows, Woodside Ch., Hi-Start Inc., numerous pvt. collections; featured in Evening Mag. Bay Area, Good Morning Bay Are, KTEH Fine Art Auction. Recipient award Hall of Flowers Golden Gate Park Mus., award Homeless Cat Network, 1sp place, hon. mention Millbrae Arts, 2nd place juried show Redwood City, 1st award Homeless Cat Network, 1995, Older Am.'s Art Show, 1995, Grumbacher Gold Medal Medallion award Soc. We. Art, 1990, named Milbrae (Calif.) Artist of Yr., 1996, Artist of the Mo. Mem. Soc. We. Art (Signature award 1998), Women's Caucus fo Art, Sequoia Arts (1st, 2nd, 3rd place watercolor), Peninsula Art Assn., Thirty Plus One, Burlingame Art Soc. E-mail: lihar@juno.com. Home: 3400 Caxton Ct San Mateo CA 94403-3832

HARA, TADAO, educational administrator; b. Shimonoseki, Japan, Oct. 21, 1926; s. Ikuhisa and Chitose Hara; m. Suzuko Hara, May 12; children: Nobumichi, Izumi. BA, Tamagawa U., Machida, Japan, 1952; MA in Bibl. Theology, N.W. Coll., 1958; MA in Ednl. Psychology, Calif. State U., Long Beach, 1965; LittD (hon.), N.W. Coll., 1990. Ordained to ministry Assembly of God Ch. Fgn. student counselor Calif. State U., Long Beach, 1965-68; prof. edn. Tamagawa U., 1969-79, dean students, 1973-77, dir. internat. edn., 1976-79; founder, prin. Internat. Bilingual Sch., Palos Verdes Estates, Calif. Mem. adv. bd. Calif. State U. Long Beach Coll. Edn., 1985-88. Recipient Disting. Alumnus award Coll. Edn., Calif. State U., Long Beach, 1994. Mem. ASCD, Nat. Assn. Internat. Educators, Delta Upsilon Chi. Home: 3992 Toland Cir Los Alamitos CA 90720-2261 Office: 300 Paseo Del Mar # B Palos Verdes Estates CA 90274

HARAD, GEORGE JAY, manufacturing company executive; b. Newark, Apr. 24, 1944; m. Beverly Marcia Harad, June 12, 1966; children: Alyssa Dawn, Matthew Corde. BA, Franklin and Marshall Coll., 1965; MBA with high distinction, Harvard Bus. Sch., 1971. Staff cons. Boston Cons. Group, 1970-71; asst. to sr. v.p. housing Boise (Idaho) Cascade Corp., 1971; asst. to v.p. Boise Cascade Corp., Palo Alto, Calif., 1971; fin. mgr. Boise Cascade Realty Group, Palo Alto, Calif., 1972-76; mgr. corp. devel. Boise Cascade Corp., Palo Alto, Calif., 1976-80; dir. retirement funds, risk mgmt. Boise Cascade Corp., 1980-82, v.p., contr., 1982-84, sr. v.p., chief fin. officer, 1984-89, exec. v.p., chief fin. officer, 1989-90, exec. v.p. paper, 1990-91; pres., COO Boise Cascade Corp., Palo Alto, Calif., 1991-94, pres., CEO, 1994-95; chmn., bd. dirs. Boise Cascade Corp., 1995; chmn., dir. Boise Cascade Office Products Corp.; CEO, chmn. Boise Cascade Corp., Palo Alto, Calif., 1995—; bd. dirs. Allendale Ins. Co., Inst. Paper Sci. and Tech.; bd. govs. Nat. Coun. of Paper Industry for Air and Stream Improvement Inc. Founder, pres. Boise Coun. for Gifted and Talented Students, 1977-79; bd. dirs. Boise Philharm. Assn., 1983-84; dir. bd. trustees Coll. Idaho, 1986-91. Grad. Prize fellow Harvard Grad. Sch. Arts and Scis., 1965-69, Frederick Roe fellow Harvard U. Sch. Bus., 1971; George F. Baker scholar, 1970-71. Mem. NAM (bd. dirs.), Am. Forest and Paper Assn. (bd. dirs., mem. exec. com. 1984-94), Century Club (Boston), Arid Club, Crane Creek Country Club, Phi Beta Kappa. Home: 224 E Braemere Rd Boise ID 83702-1710 Office: Boise Cascade Corp PO Box 50 Boise ID 83728-0001*

HARARI, ELI, executive. Pres., CEO San Disk Corp., Sunnyvale, Calif. Office: 140 Caspian Ct Sunnyvale CA 94089-1000*

HARARY, KEITH, psychologist, researcher, writer; b. N.Y.C., Feb. 9, 1953; s. Victor and Lillian (Mazur) H.; m. Darlene Moore, Oct. 22, 1985. BA in Psychology, Duke U., 1975; PhD, Union Inst., 1986. Crisis counselor Durham (N.C.) Mental Health Ctr., 1972-76; rsch. assoc. Psychical Rsch. Found., Durham, 1972-76; rsch. assoc. dept. psychiatry Maimonides Med. Ctr., Bklyn., 1976-79; dir. counseling Human Freedom Ctr., Berkeley, Calif., 1979; rsch. cons. SRI Internat., Menlo Park, Calif., 1980-82; design cons. Atari Corp., Sunnyvale, Calif., 1983-85; pres., rsch. dir. Inst. for Advanced Psychology, San Francisco, 1986—; freelance sci.

journalist, 1988—; editor-at-large Omni Mag., 1996-98; sr. v.p., rsch. dir. Capital Access/Resource Group Internat., 1996—; invited lectr. Duke U., 1995; lectr. in field; adj. prof. Antioch U., San Francisco, 1985, 86; guest lectr. Lyceum Sch. for Gifted Children, 1985-89; vis. rschr. USSR Acad. Scis., 1983; rsch. cons. Am. Soc. for Psychical Rsch., 1971-72, Found. for Rsch. on Nature of Man, 1972, sci. applications Internat. Corp., 1991-93; psychol. cons., nat. media spokesperson Budget Rent A Car Corp., 1997—, Sears Corp., 1997; psychol. cons. Microsoft Corp., 1998—. Co-author: The Mind Race, 1984, 85, 30-Day Altered States of Consciousness Series, 1989-91, rev. edits., 1999, Who Do You Think You Are? Explore Your Many-Sided Self With the Berkeley Personality Profile, 1994, CD-ROM edit., 1996; featured monthly columnist in The Omni Mind Brain Lab in Omni Mag., 1995-98; contbr. over 100 articles to profl. jours., other publs. Mem. APA, Am. Psychol. Soc., Assn. for Media Psychology, Am. Soc. for Psychical Rsch. (bd. dirs. 1994—). Achievements include first to develop reflective approach to personality profiling; development of advanced human perception research, including original training methodologies in altered states induction, and extended perception; development of original scientific terminology adapted and used in specialized theoretical areas in advanced perceptual research, including extended perception, extended human abilities, mental noise, paranormal hysteria, stress apparitions, others; development of original clinical approaches to crisis intervention. Home and Office: 98 Main St Apt 637 Tiburon CA 94920-2517

HARBAUGH, DANIEL PAUL, lawyer; b. Wendell, Idaho, May 18, 1948; s. Myron and Manuelita (Garcia) H. BA, Gonzaga U., 1970, JD, 1974. Bar: Washington 1974, U.S. Dist. Ct. (ea. dist.) Wash. 1977, U.S. Ct. Appeals (9th cir.) 1978. Asst. atty. gen. State of Wash., Spokane, 1974-77; ptnr. Richter, Wimberley & Ericson, Spokane, 1977-83, Harbaugh & Bloom, P.S., Spokane, 1983—; bd. dirs. Spokane Legal Svcs., 1982-86; bd. govs. LAWPAC, Seattle, 1980-92. Bd. dirs. Spokane Ballet, 1983-88; chpt. dir. Les Amis du Vin, Spokane, 1985-88; mem. Spokane County Civil Svc. Commn., 1991—, Gonzaga U. Pres'. Coun., 1991—. Mem. ABA, ATLA, Wash. State Bar Assn. (spl. dist. counsel 1982-95, mem. com. rules for profl. conduct 1989-92, mem. legis. com. 1995-96), Spokane County Bar Assn. (chair med.-legal com. 1991), Wash. State Trial Lawyers Assn. (v.p. 1988-89, co-chair worker's compensation sect. 1992, 93, spl. select. com. on workers' corp. 1990—, forum 1994—, vice-chmn. 1994-97, mem. legis. com. 1995—), Nat. Orgn. Social Security Claimants Reps., Internat. Wine and Food Soc. (pres. local chpt. 1989-91, cellar master 1994-96), Spokane Club, Spokane Country Club (adminstrv. com. 1995-98, chmn. 1991-98, trustee 1996—, sec.-treas. 1997-98, pres. 1998—), Alpha Sigma Nu, Phi Alpha Delta. Roman Catholic. Office: Harbaugh & Bloom PS PO Box 1461 Spokane WA 99210-1461

HARBAUGH, JAMES MICHAEL, psychology educator; b. St. Louis, Oct. 30, 1945; s. Harold and Rita (Brennan) H. BA in English, St. Louis U., 1969, MA in English, 1970; MDiv, Jesuit Sch. Theology, Berkeley, Calif., 1976; PhD, U. Chgo., 1981. English tchr. Regis H.S., Denver, 1970-73, Regis Coll., Denver, 1982-89; addictions counselor intern Ctrl. Seattle Recovery Ctr., 1990-91; addictionology tchr., campus minister Seattle U., 1993—. Author: A 12-Step Approach to the Spiritual Exercises of St. Ignatius, 1998; editor Dionysos, 1996—. Chair King County Alcohol & Substance Abuse Adv. Bd., Seattle, 1995—; trustee Seattle U., 1998—. Democrat. Roman Catholic. Avocations: opera, classical music, weightlifting. Office: Seattle U 900 Broadway Seattle WA 98122-4340

HARBAUGH, JOHN PAUL, music educator; b. Waterloo, Iowa, Nov. 6, 1953; s. John Wesley and Marjorie Roberta (Schmolt) H.; m. Teresa Lee Thompson, Jan. 8, 1977; children: Ingrid, Heidi, John Eric, Tom, Ben. BA, U. No. Iowa, 1975; M in Mus. Edn., N. Tex. State U., 1977; postgrad. studies in Music, Ind. U., 1981-83. Asst. prof. music U. Idaho, Moscow, 1977-81; assoc. instr. music Ind. U., Bloomington, 1981-83; trumpet player Buddy Rich Band, Great Britain tour, 1981-82; musician Paul Anka Prodns., on tour, 1983-86, Tom Jones Brass, on tour, 1986-87; free lance musician Las Vegas, 1983-88; assoc. prof. music U. Alaska, Fairbanks, 1988—; trumpet player Lettermen Summer Tour, 1982; instr. U. Alaska, Fairbanks Summer Fine Arts Camp, 1989—; clinician for United Musical Instrument/ Conn Corp., 1990—; mem. faculty Yellowstone Jazz Camp, 1990—, Idyllwild Jazz Camp, 1994—, Fairbanks Summer Arts Festival, 1996—; back up musician for: Sammy Davis Jr., Tony Bennett, Woody Herman, Stan Getz, Andy Williams, Bob Hope, Ray Charles, Mel Torme, Gerry Mulligan, Jim Nabors, Clark Terry, Lionel Hampton Big Band and others. Recorded album with Ashley Alexander's Big Band, 1980 (nominated for 2 Grammy awards), 1980; guest soloist at Banff Internat. Festival, 1995, with Fairbanks Symphony, 1996, with London Symphony, 1996 (recording). Recipient 2d runner up prize, Women's Assn. Minn. Symphony Orch. Contest, 1973, Outstanding Soloist award, Wichita Jazz Festival, 1975, U. Alaska Nat. award, 1996; semi-finalist McMahon Internat. Music Competition, 1993. Mem. Music Educators Nat. Conf., Internat. Trumpet Guild, Pi Kappa Phi, Phi Mu Alpha. Home: 5150 Hardland Ave Fairbanks AK 99709-4527 Office: U Alaska Fairbanks Music Dept Fairbanks AK 99775

HARBORD, ANNE MARIE, consulting dietetics company executive; b. Detroit, Nov. 9, 1954; d. Lionel Joseph and Mary Ellen (Beaushaw) H.; m. Scott H. Reed, May 27, 1978 (div. Apr. 1980); m. Charles Bloom, June 18, 1988; children: Erica, Mark Alexander. BS in Dietetics, Mich. State U., 1976; MS Nutrition, Food Mgmt., Calif. Poly. U., 1985. Registered dietition, Calif. Clin. dietitian Saga Foods Co., Kalamazoo, 1976-78; cardiac dietition Anaheim (Calif.) Meml. Hosp., 1978; dir. dietary svcs. Care Enterprises, Orange, Calif., 1978-88; owner, mgr. Geriatric Nutrition Mgmt., Oceanside, Calif., 1988—; dir. nutrition svcs. Kennon Shea & Assoc., El Cajon, Calif., 1988—; speaker in field; quality assurance cons. Health Care div. ARA Living Ctrs. and Retirement Homes, Verduga Hills, Calif., 1979; spl. project coord. Calif. Dieticians in Health Care, 1995—. Pub. (continuing edn. prog.) Nutritional Problems in the Elderly; co-author: (with Christine Hansen) Dietary Policy and Procedure Manual for Long-Term Care, 1998, Recipes Standardized for Long-Term Care, 1986. Calif. Dietetic Assn. grad. scholar, 1984. Mem. Am. Dietetic Assn., Calif. Assn. Health Facilities (chmn. cons. dietitian practice group 1981-85, treas. 1990-91), Am. Soc. Enteral and Parenteral Nutrition, San Diego Dietetic Assn. (edn. chmn. 1988-89, dist. rep. 1989-91). Roman Catholic. Avocations: walking, swimming, interior design, cooking, travel. Home and Office: Geriatric Nutrition Mgmt 5027 Nighthawk Way Oceanside CA 92056-5447

HARCOURT, MICHAEL FRANKLIN, retired premier of Province of British Columbia, lawyer, educator; b. Edmonton, Alta., Can., Jan. 6, 1943; s. Frank Norman and Stella Louise (Good) H.; m. Mai-Gret Wibecke Salo, June 26, 1971; 1 son, Justen Michael. BA, U. B.C., 1965, LLB, 1968. Bar: B.C. 1969. Founder dir. Vancouver Cmty. Legal Assistance Soc., 1969-71; ptnr. firm Lew, Fraser & Harcourt, 1971-79; pres. Housing and Econ. Devel. Cons. Firm, Vancouver, from 1977; alderman City of Vancouver, 1972-80, mayor, 1980-86; mem. Legis. Assembly, 1986-96; leader New Dem. Party of B.C., 1987-96; premier Province of B.C., 1991-96, ret., 1996; former leader of opposition, leader of govt.; sr. assoc. Sustainable Devel. Inst., Vancouver, B.C., 1996—; asst. dir. Justice Devel. Commn., Vancouver; dir. Housing Corp. B.C.; adj. prof. faculty grad. studies U. B.C., 1996—. Bd. dirs. Asia-Pacific Found. Mem. Law Soc. B.C., Nat. Rountable Environ. and Economy (chmn. fgn. rels. com.), Jericho Tennis Club. New Democrat. Mem. United Ch. Can. Avocations: tennis, golf, skiing, jogging, basketball. Office: HU B5-2202 Main Mall, Vancouver, BC Canada V6T1Z4

HARCOURT, ROBERT NEFF, educational administrator, journalist, genealogist; b. East Orange, N.J., Oct. 19, 1932; s. Stanton Hinde and Mary Elizabeth (Neff) H. BA, Gettysburg Coll., 1958; MA, Columbia U., 1961. Cert guidance, secondary edn., career and vocational guidance, N.Mex. Social case worker N.J. State Bd. Child Welfare, Newark and Morristown, 1958-61; asst. registrar Hofstra U., 1961-62; asst. to evening dean of students CCNY, 1961-62; housing staff U. Denver, 1962-64; fin. aid and placement dir. Inst. Am. Indian Arts (IAIA), Santa Fe, 1965-95; appointed by corp. pres. to adv. bd. Genre Ltd. Art Pubs., L.A., 1986—; nat. color ad participant The Bradford Exchange, Chgo., 1986—. *In 1955-56 Mr. Harcourt was the personnel and public relations specialist with the U.S. Army's first Atomic Cannon Unit. He presented his research paper, "Cyclic Regeneration" to the International Conference on General Semantics in Denver, Colorado, in August, 1968, S.I. Hayakawa Honorary Chairman. Using photographic works, he participated in the spring 1973 Institute of American Indian Arts Faculty Exhibit at the Kennedy Center, Washington D.C. Mr. Harcourt took selected graduate courses at the University of Denver (Post Master's Fellowship), Northern Arizona University, San Francisco State University, University of Hawaii, Rutgers University and Worcester College of Oxford University in England.* Donor Am. Indian Lib. collection Gettysburg (Pa.) Coll., active Santa Fe Civic Chorus, 1977-78, art judge, 3d and 4th ann. Aspen Fundraiser Nat. Mus. Am. Indian, 1993, 94, vol. Inst. for Preservation Original Langs. Am. (IPOLA). With U.S.Army, 1954-56. Ger. Named Hon. Okie, Gov. Okla. (decorated Nat. Def. medal), 1970, postmasters fellow U. Denver, 1962-64, col. a.d.c. to N.Mex. Gov. David F. Cargo, 1970, IAIA Truman scholar; recipient disting. Alumni award Gettysburg Alumni Assn., 1995. Mem. Am. Contract Bridge League (exec. bd., v.p., Santa Fe unit, life master, ACBL dist. 17 rep.), SAR, Santa Fe Coun. Internat. Rels., Am. Assn. Counseling and Devel., New England Historic Genealogical Soc., Assn. Specialists in Group Work (charter), Adult Student Personnel Assn. (charter), Southwestern Assn. Indian Affairs, Neff Family Hist. Soc., St. Andrew Scottish Soc. of N.Mex., Gen. Soc. Mayflower Descendents, Pilgrim John Howland Soc., Upson Family Assn., Order of the Founders and Patriots of Am., Mil. Order of the Loyal Legion of the U.S., Military Order of Fgn. Wars of U.S., Phi Delta Kappa (past mem. exec. bd. local chpt.), Alpha Tau Omega, Alpha Phi Omega, Safari Club Internat. Home: 2980 Viaje Pavo Real Santa Fe NM 87505-5344

HARDCASTLE, MARCIA E. (MARCIA E. TEMME), newspaper editor; b. Oakland, Calif., Nov. 28, 1945; d. Charles Frederick and Lillian Callita (Johnson) Temme; children: Glenn Arthur Hardcastle, Jason Roger Hardcastle. BA, San Jose State U. Society editor Los Altos (Calif.) News, 1967-70; reporter, lifestyle editor Santa Maria (Calif.) Times, 1979-82; adminstrv. asst. sr. Diablo Canyon Nuclear Power Plant, Calif., 1983-86; lifestyle editor 5-Cities Times Press Recorder, Arroyo Grande, Calif., 1987-98; arts and entertainment features editor Pulitzer Cmty. Newspapers, 1998—; cons. pub. rels., Pismo Beach, Calif., 1977—; chair bd. dirs. publicity Am. Heart Assn., San Luis Obispo, Calif. Press sec. Assemblyman Eric Seastrand, Calif., 1982; campaign mgr. Tris Colman for State Assembly, Calif., 1994; founder Five Cities Women's Network, 1987—; worthy advisor Girl Scouts Am. Recipient Cmty. Svc. award Santa Maria Mental Health Assn., 1980, Media award Calif. Mental Health Assn., 1980, Hon. Mention award Nat. Newspaper Assn., 1989, 2d Place award Best Lifestyle/Family Life Pages Calif. Newspaper Assn., 1991. Avocations: photography, painting, piano, swimming, traveling.

HARDER, KELSIE T., artist, educator; b. Trenton, Tenn., Mar. 8, 1942; s. Kelsie Brown Harder and Geneva Lee (Tomlin) Carlson; m. Kumiko Tanaka, Oct. 2, 1991; children: Michon Skyler, Samuel Armstrong, Tsunami Tomlin and Tanaka Solomon (twins). Student, Claremont (Calif.) Men's Coll., 1960-61, Escuela de Bellas Artes, Morelia, Mex., 1961, Ventura (Calif.) Coll., 1961-62; BA, U. Nev., 1973-75. Cert. illustrator technician, USAF. Artist self-employed, 1957—; prof. Truckee Meadows C.C., Reno, 1978—; chmn. art dept. Truckee Meadows C.C., 1982-91; art exhibit judge over 30 regional competitions. Contbr. articles to profl. jours., mags., textbooks; 28 one-man shows; represented in over 100 collections. Recipient numerous regional and nat. awards including YWCA Silver cert. for Outstanding Cmty. Svc., No. Nev., 1972, 88. Office: Truckee Meadows CC 7000 Dandini Blvd Reno NV 89512-3901

HARDER, KRISTINE, civic worker; b. Seattle, Dec. 13, 1949; d. Ole Gregors and Mary Frances (Hinde) H.; m. William Chapin Heumann, Apr. 9, 1983 (div. 1989); children: Michael Paul, Laura Chapin; m. Anthony Michael Sholty, 1990. BA in Comparative Lit., Alaska Meth. U., 1973. Staff aide U.S. senator Mike Gravel, Washington, 1973-74; legis. aide Alaska Ho. of Reps., Juneau, 1975-81; vol. coord. KTOO-TV/Pub. Broadcast, Juneau, 1981-83; owner, mgr. Alaskawear Clothing Co., Juneau, 1986-92; owner Kristine Harder Tile Design, Juneau, 1996—. Lobbyist, Advocates for Comprehensive Health Edn., Juneau, 1988-92. Mem. DAR, AAUW (pres. local chpt. 1988-89, v.p. 1990-92, state v.p. 1992-94), Gastineau Humane Soc. (editor 1988-89). Democrat. Episcopalian. Home: 1015 Otter Run Juneau AK 99801

HARDING, JACK, executive. BA in Chemistry & Econs., Drew U. Pres., CEO Cadence Design Systems, Inc., San Jose, Calif. Bd. trustees Drew U. Office: San Jose River Oaks Campus 555 River Oaks Pkwy San Jose CA 95134-1917*

HARDING, JAMES GEORGE, financial executive; b. Iowa City, Iowa, Oct. 3, 1949; s. Joe Petsel and Florence Lorena (Yarwood) H.; children from previous marriage: Paige Annette, Pamela Suzanne; m. Cynthia Gail Balzer, Feb. 14, 1987; children: Kelly Kristin Cannon, Matthew Patrick Perry Cannon. BBA in Fin., U. Iowa, 1972, BBA in Ins., 1972; postgrad. in acctg., Colo. State U., 1974-76. Asst. nat. bank examiner U.S. Dept. Treasury, Albuquerque, 1972-74; dir. fin. City of Ft. Collins, Colo., 1974-76; fin. dir., city treas., city clk. City of Canon City, Colo., 1977-79; bus. dir. West Central Mental Health Ctr., Canon City, 1979-81; dir., exec. v.p., chief fin. officer Peak Health Care, Inc., Colorado Springs, Colo., 1981-87; v.p., dir. Talis Corp., Colorado Springs, 1986—; dir. Sunset Met. Dist., Colorado Springs, 1988—; dir., sr. v.p., chief fin. officer Excell, Inc., Colorado Springs, 1988—, also bd. dirs.; cons. in field. Co-treas. Rep. Party of Fremont County, Canon City, 1978; officer United Way, Canon City, 1978. Mem. Winter Night Club, Lions (officer Canon City chpt. 1977-80). Mem. Christian Ch. (Disciples of Christ). Avocations: raising Arabian show horses, outdoor activities.

HARDING, JOHN EDWARD, lawyer; b. San Francisco, Sept. 5, 1963; s. Merle Lewis and Trudy (Evertz) H.; m. Lisa Elliott; children: Jack Joseph, Ryan Elise. BA, St. Mary's Coll., Moraga, Calif., 1986; JD, Golden Gate U., 1989. Bar: Calif. 1989, U.S. Dist. Ct. (no. dist.) Calif. 1989, U.S. Ct. Appeals (9th cir.) 1989, D.C. 1991, Wyo. 1996, U.S. Dist. Ct. (ctrl. dist.) Calif. 1997. Assoc. Law Offices of Merle L. Harding, Pleasanton, Calif., 1989; ptnr. Harding & Harding, Pleasanton, 1990—. Bd. dirs. Tri-Valley br. Am. Heart Assn., Oakland, Calif., 1992-93, Valley Community Health Ctr., Pleasanton, 1992-96. Mem. ABA, ATLA, Consumer Atty. Calif., State Bar Calif., D.C. Bar Assn., Wyo. Bar Assn., Pleasanton C. of C. (bd. dirs. 1993-96, v.p. pub. affairs 1994). Avocations: golf, softball, backpacking, fishing, spectator sports, reading, travel. Office: Harding & Harding 78 Mission Dr Ste B Pleasanton CA 94566-7683

HARDING, KAREN ELAINE, chemistry educator and department chair; b. Atlanta, Sept. 5, 1949; d. Howard Everett and Ruth Evangeline (Lund) H.; m. Bruce Roy McDowell, Aug. 30, 1975. BS in Chemistry, U. Puget Sound, Tacoma, 1971; MS in Environ. Chemistry, U. Mich., 1972; postgrad., Evergreen State Coll., 1972, 84, Yale U., 1986, Columbia U., 1991. Chemist Environ. Health Lab., Inc., Farmington, Mich., 1972-73, U. Mich. Med. Sch., Ann Arbor, 1973-75; instr. chemistry Schoolcraft Coll., Livonia, Mich., 1975-77; chair chemistry dept. Pierce Coll., Tacoma, 1977—; adj. prof. U. Mich., Dearborn, 1974-77; instr. S.H. Alternative Learning Ctr., Tacoma, 1980-83, Elderhostel, Tacoma, 1985-89; mem. exec. com. Chemlinks project NSF. Mem. County Solid Waste Adv. Com., Tacoma, 1989—, Superfund Adv. Com., Tacoma, 1985-89, Sierra Club, Wash., 1989—; mem., past pres. Adv. Com. Nature Ctr., Tacoma, 1981-87. Faculty Enhancement grantee Pierce Coll., 1990; recipient Nat. Teaching Excellence award, 1991. Mem. NW Assn. for Environ. Studies (treas. 1985—), Am. Chem. Soc., Ft. Steilacoom Running Club (race dir. 1986—). Avocations: running, skiing, backpacking, bicycling, reading. Office: Pierce Coll 9401 Farwest Dr SW Tacoma WA 98498-1919

HARDING, MARIE, ecological executive, artist; b. Glen Cove, N.Y., Nov. 13, 1941; d. Charles Lewis and Marie (Parish) H.; m. John P. Allen, Jan. 29, 1965 (div. Oct., 1991); 1 child, Eden A. Harding. BA, Sarah Lawrence Coll., 1964; postgrad., Arts Students League, N.Y.C., 1965. Founder Synergia Ranch for Wellness, Innovation, Retreats and Confs., Santa Fe, 1969; founding mem., actress Theater of All Possibilities, Santa Fe, 1971-86; founding mem., dir. Inst. Ecotechnics, Santa Fe, also London, 1974—; bd. dirs. Synopco Corp., N. Mex., 1974-81; bd. dirs., founding mem. Savannah Systems Pty., Ltd., Kimberly region, Australia, 1976—, Outback Sta. Pty. Ltd., Kimberly region, Australia, 1976-94; chair, dir. EcoWorld, Inc., Santa Fe, 1982-94; dir., founding mem., CFO Space Biospheres Ventures, Biosphere 2, Ariz., 1984-94; chair, CEO Oceans Expdns., Inc., 1986-92; pres. ecol. and biosphere devel./implementation Global Ecotechnics Corp., Santa Fe, 1994—; pres. Decisions Team, Inc. Ecol. Project Mgmt., Santa Fe, Ariz., 1994—, Syneco LLC, retreats and confs.; particpant in constrn. and fin. Capt. R. Heraclitus rsch. vessel, Oakland, Calif., 1974; bd. dirs. Hotel Vajra, Kathamdu, Nepal, 1976-94, Caravan of Dreams Performing Arts Ctr., Ft. Worth, 1983-94, Synergetic Press, London and Ariz., 1984—. Artist: paintings shown in exhibitions San Francisco, London, Ft. Worth, Santa Fe, Biosphere 2, Ariz., 1979-93, Biosphere 2 Paintings Exhbn., London, 1996; project dir., artist mural project History of Jazz, Dance, Theater, Ft. Worth, 1982-83; producer, dir. (films) Bryon Gysin Loves ya, Project Charlie, The Search, Synergia History, Planet Earth Conf. Vol. Swallows, Madras, India, 1964, Project Concern, Vietnam, Hong Kong, 1964-65; artist, founder, trustee October Gallery Trust, internat. artists forum, London, 1979; mem. Planetary Coral Reef Found., Inc., 1993—. Mem. Friends of Tibet, N.Mex. Black Belt Club, Tae Kwon Doe Inst. N.Mex. Avocations: ecological project implementation, endangered lifestyles/cultures, painting, landscape gardening, retreat faciliatation. Home and Office: Synergia Ranch 26 Synergia Rd Santa Fe NM 87505-0900

HARDING, WAYNE EDWARD, III, software company executive, accountant; b. Topeka, Sept. 29, 1954; s. Wayne Edward and Nancy M. (Gean) H.; BS with honors in Bus. Adminstrn., U. Denver, 1976, MBA, 1983; m. Janet Mary O'Shaughnessy, Sept. 5, 1979 (div. Mar. 1985); m. Karen Ruttan, Oct. 10, 1987. Partner, HKG Assocs., Denver, 1976-77; staff auditor Peat, Marwick, Mitchell & Co., Denver, 1976-78; auditor Marshall Hornstein, P.C., Wheat Ridge, Colo., 1978-79; sr. auditor Touche Ross & Co., Denver, 1979-80; controller Mortgage Plus Inc., 1980-81; sec.-treas. Sunlight Systems Energy Corp., 1980-81; ptnr. Harding, Newman, Sobule & Thrush, Ltd., Denver, 1981-82; pvt. practice specializing in microcomputer applications and litigation support, 1982-89; acct., v.p. Great Plains Software, Fargo, N.D., also dir. CPA ptnr. rels.; founder Discount Computer Rentals, Inc., 1985; dir. Harding Transp., Harding Tech. Leasing, Crown Parking Products; lectr. to various profl. groups on computer tech. Class agt., mem. alumni council Phillips Exeter Acad., Exeter, N.H., 1973-83, class agt., 1993—; bd. dirs., treas. Legal Center for Handicapped Citizens, Denver, 1979-80; vol. Denver Bridge, 1984-85. Mem. AICPA (instr., mem. tech. rsch. com. 1994—), Colo. Soc. CPAs (chmn. CPE com. 1987-89, instr., mem. bd. dirs. 1994-97, v.p. 1996-97), Beta Alpha Psi, Pi Gamma Mu, Beta Gamma Sigma. Libertarian. Mem. editorial bd. Practical Acct. Mag.; contbr. articles in field of microcomputers to profl. jours. including Jour. of Accountancy. Home and Office: 5206 S Hanover Way Englewood CO 80111-6240

HARDMAN, SEAN KEVIN, catering company executive; b. Bountiful, Utah, Sept. 11, 1971; s. Glen Charles and Christine (Eddington) H.; m. Megan Ann Tsukamoto, Nov. 18, 1995. BFA, Weber State U., 1994. Gardener Malnove Inc. of Utah, Clearfield, Utah, 1985-87; mgr. banquets and catering Best Western, Ogden, Utah, 1987—. Asst. art dir. Mountain High Kids Charity, Kaysville, Utah, 1998—; art donor Mountain High Kids for Make A Wish, Kaysville, 1998, Saint Josephs H.S., Ogden, 1998, Utah Arts Festival, Salt Lake City, 1992. Turscott Trust scholarship Weber State U., 1990, 92, 93, 94, Farrell Colleti scholarship, 1991, Douglas McFarland Art scholarship, 1993-94. Mem. Ogden C. of C., Utah Arts Coun., Son of the Utah Pioneers, SAR. Democrat. Roman Catholic. Avocations: painting, photography, geology, running, snowboarding. Home: 5776 S 2000 W Roy UT 84067-2349 Office: Best Western 1307 W 1200 S Ogden UT 84404-5417

HARDWAY, JAMES EDWARD, vocational and rehabilitative specialist; b. Pueblo, Colo., Nov. 26, 1944; s. William Jeremiah and Margaret Ann (Rinker) H.; m. Mary Frances Walker, Sept. 9, 1967; children: Tina Marie, Catherine Ann, William James. BA, U. So. Colo., 1969; MS, U. Wis.-Stout, Menomonie, 1971; postgrad., U. Toledo, 1972—. Cert. vocat. evaluator, work adjustment specialist. Counselor Pueblo (Colo.) Diversified Industries, 1969-70; vocat. evaluator Penta County Vocat. Schs., Perrysburg, Ohio, 1971-82; dept. mgr. Magic City Enterprises, Cheyenne, Wyo., 1982-88; case mgr. Profl. Rehab. Mgmt., Cheyenne, 1989-91, regional mgr., 1992-94; pvt. practice vocational expert Cheyenne, 1994—; speaker State of Ohio Spl. Needs Conf., Ohio, 1972-80; cons. Wyo. State Tng. Sch., Lander, 1977. Pres. bd. dirs. Laramie County Community Action, Cheyenne; bd. dirs. Handicapped Employment Agy., Cheyenne, Wyo. Alzheimer's Assn. With U.S. Army, 1962-65. Fellow Am. Bd. Vocat. Experts; mem. Kiwanis (bd. dirs.). Home: 12309 White Eagle Rd Cheyenne WY 82009-8640

HARDY, BEN(SON B.), orchid nursery executive; b. Oakland, Calif., Nov. 22, 1920; s. Lester William and Irene Isabell (Bliss) H.; student pub. schs., Oakland, Calif., Concord, Calif.; grad. photo Intelligence Sch., Denver, 1949. Served as enlisted man U.S. Navy, 1942-48; joined USAF, 1948, advanced through grades to capt., 1957; with 67th Reconnaisance Squadron, Korea, 1951-52, Hdqrs. Squadron, Thule AFB, 1956, resigned, 1957; material requirements analyst-coord. Teledyne Ryan Aero. Co., San Diego, 1958-73, 83—; dispatcher-coord. Cubic Western Data Co., San Diego, 1977-80; owner-ptnr. orchid nursery. Pres. Exotic Plant Soc., 1976-78, 81-84, San Diego Gesneriad Soc., 1978; dir. 23d Western Orchid Congress, 1979. Author: (with John Klemme) The Orchid Badge Collector's Guide, 1993. Decorated Bronze Star; recipient Letter of Commendation NASA, also others. Mem. Am. Orchid Soc. (life), N.Z. Orchid Soc., San Diego County Orchid Soc. (life, pres. 1972-73, 75-76), Pacific Orchid Soc. Hawaii, Hoya Soc. Internat. (pres. 1981-83, 95—), Cymbidium Soc. Am., Orchid Digest Corp., Auckland Orchid Club, Orchid Badge Club Internat. (found. 1988, pres. 1991—), VFW (life). Home: 9443 E Heaney Cir Santee CA 92071-2919

HARDY, BYRON LYNN, medical physicist; b. L.A., Aug. 3, 1950; s. Lynn William and Marjorie (Mitchell) H.; m. Judy Lynne Christensen, May 1, 1978. BS in Biology, U. Utah, 1975, BS in Med. Tech., 1978, MS in Nuclear Engring., 1992, PhD in Nuclear Engring., 1996. Cert. mammography imaging med. physicist, Utah, environ. health scientist, Utah; qualified expert diagnostic radiology, Utah. Radiation analyst U. Utah, Salt Lake City, 1979-80; environ. scientist Salt Lake City-County Health Dept., 1980-81; radiation safety officer Rio Algom Corp., LaSal, Utah, 1981-84; environ. health scientist Utah Dept. Health, Salt Lake City, 1984-89; health physicist U. Utah, 1989-94, interim dir./radiation safety officer, 1994, alt. radiation safety officer, 1994—; med. physicist Tooele (Utah) Regional Med. Ctr., 1990—, Columbia St. Mart's Hosp., Salt Lake City, 1990—, Talbat Med. Group, Salt Lake Regiona, 1994—; med. physicist/consulting radiation safety officer FHP/PHC Ragional Hosps., Salt Lake, West Valley Cities, 1994—. Contbr. articles to profl. jours. Mem. Am. Assn. Phyhsicists in Medicine (assoc.), Am. Nuclear Soc., Am. Indsl. Hygiene Assn., Nat. Fire Protection Assn., Health Physics Societies (Great Salt Lake chpt., pres. 1988-90, sch. sci. tchr.'s workshops 1994-97), Phi Kappa Phi, Sigma Xi, Alpha Nu Sigma. Avocations: music, photography, martial arts, gardening. Office: Univ Utah Dept Radiol Health 100 Orson Spencer Hall Salt Lake City UT 84112

HARDY, DEL, lawyer; b. Jan. 19, 1954. BA, U. Nev., 1976; JD, U. of the Pacific, 1982. Bar: Calif. 1983, Nev. 1983, U.S. Dist. Ct., U.S. Ct. Appeals (9th cir.), U.S. Tax Ct.; lic. Nev. Gaming Commn. Bd. Dep. atty. gen. State of Nev., Carson City, 1983-86; atty., owner Hardy & Assocs., Reno, 1986—. Mem. ABA, ATLA, Nev. Trial Lawyers. Office: Hardy & Assocs 96 Winter St Reno NV 89503-5605

HARDY, LOIS LYNN, educational training company executive; b. Seattle, Aug. 20, 1928; d. Stanley Milton and Helen Berniece (Conner) Croonquist; m. John Weston Hardy, July 29, 1951 (div. 1974); children: Sarah Lynn, Laura Lynn; m. Joseph Freeman Smith, Jr., Apr. 18, 1981. BA, Stanford U., 1950, MA, 1952; postgrad., U. Calif., Berkeley, 1957-78, U. San Francisco, 1978-81. Cert. life secondary tchr., life counselor, adminstr., Calif.; lic. career and ednl. counselor, Calif. Tchr., counselor Eastside Union High Sch. Dist., San Jose, Calif., 1951-55; dir. Lois Lynn Hardy Music Studio, Danville, Calif., 1955-69; high sch. tchr. San Ramon Unified Sch. Dist., Danville, 1969-71, counselor, 1971-83; dir. Growth Dynamics Inst., Alamo, Calif., 1976—; instr. Fresno (Calif.) Pacific Coll., 1976-79, Dominican Coll., San Rafael, Calif., 1979—; cons., trainer Personal Dynamics Inst., Mpls., 1976—, Performax Internat., Mpls., 1979—, San Jose Unified Sch. Dist., 1986-86, Novato (Calif.) Unified Sch. Dist., 1985-86, IBM, San Francisco, 1984, corp. and ednl. cons.,

1951—. Author: How To Study in High School, 1952, 3d edit., 1973; (with B. Santa) How To Use the Library, 1954; How To Learn Faster and Succeed: A How to Study Workbook For Grades 1-14, 1982, rev., 1985; author various seminars; contbr. numerous articles to profl. jours. Choir dir., organist Community Presbyn. Ch., Danville, 1966-68, elder, 1974-75; speaker to numerous orgns., 1955—. Named Musician of Yr., Contra Costa County, 1978, Counselor of Yr., No. Calif. Personnel and Guidance Assn., 1980; Olive S. Lathrop scholar, 1948, AAUW scholar, 1950; recipient Colonial Dames prize in Am. History, 1950. Mem. Am. Assn. Counseling and Devel., Calif. Assn. Counseling and Devel., Calif. Tchrs. Assn., Calif. Career Guidance Assn., Nat. Speakers Assn., Am. Guild Organists, Stanford U. Alumni Assn., Calif. Assn. for the Gifted, Delta Zeta. Democrat. Presbyterian. Avocations: writing, music, art, building houses. Office: Growth Dynamics Inst PO Box 1053 Alamo CA 94507-7053

HARDY, WAYNE RUSSELL, insurance and investment broker; b. Denver, Sept. 5, 1931; s. Russell Hinton and Victoria Katherine (Anderson) H.; m. Carolyn Lucille Carvell, Aug. 1, 1958 (July 1977); children: James Russell Hardy, Jann Miller Hardy. BSCE, U. Colo., 1954; MS in Fin. Svcs., Am. Coll., 1989. Chartered Life Underwriter; ChFC. Western dist. mgr. Fenestra, Inc., San Francisco, 1956-63; ins. and investment broker John Hancock Fin. Svs., Denver, 1963—, Wayne R. Hardy Assocs., Denver, 1963—; speaker convs. and sales seminars, 1977, 81, 84, 85, 89; v.p. CLU assn. John Hancock, 1979-80, chmn. agt.'s adv. com., 1983-84; active State of Colo. Ins. Adv. Bd., 1991-93. Chmn. Colo. Coun. Camera Clubs, Denver, 1962; bd. dirs. Porter Charitable Found., Denver, 1983-85; deacon, class pres. South Broadway Christian Ch., 1961-65; mem. Denver Art Mus., Denver Botanic Gardens, Rocky Mountain Estate Planning Coun., Mensa, Alliance Francaise. Capt. U.S. Army, 1954-56, Korea, USAR, 1956-80. Mem. Am. Soc. CLU and ChFC (pres. Rocky Mountain chpt. 1990-91), Nat. Assn. Life Underwriters (pres. Denver chpt. 1983-84, Nat. Quality award 1968—, expert witness ins. litigation, Disting. Life Underwriters award 1970-83), Nat. Football Found. (bd. dirs. Denver chpt. 1992—), Million Dollar Round Table (life), U. Colo. Alumni (bd. dirs. 1990-92), U. Colo. Alumni C Club (bd. dirs. 1972-74), Univ. Club, Greenwood Athletic Club, Village Tennis Club, Rocky Mountain Optimist Club (pres. 1984-85). Republican. Avocations: tennis, photography, foreign languages, art, travel. Home and Office: 6178 E Hinsdale Ct Englewood CO 80112-1534

HARDY-LEE, MARTHA MARIA, mental health nurse; b. Montgomery, Ala., Apr. 18, 1936; d. Charlie Hardy and Delsie (King) Hardy; m. Dalton C. Lee, Feb. 1964. RN, St. Helena Sch. Nursing, Deer Park, Calif., 1959; BSN, Sonoma (Calif.) State U., 1973; MA, John F. Kennedy U., Orinda, Calif., 1983. Pub. health nurse, nurse practitioner Contra Costa County, Pittsburg, Calif.; charge nurse Brookside Hosp., San Pablo, Calif.; crisis intervention charge nurse Merrithaw Meml. Hosp., Martinez, Calif.; pvt. practice psychotherapist Benicia, Calif.; conductor workshops in field. Mem. Calif. Nurses Assn., Calif. Assn. Marriage Family and Child Therapists, Am. Assn. Christian Counselors, Nat. Coun. Negro Women, Mariners Internat. Tng. in Communication (charter).

HARE, PAUL DEHAVEN, public safety director; b. Salamanca, N.Y., Feb. 3, 1936; s. Edwin Lawrence and Mary Elizabeth (DeHaven) H.; m. Gene Marie Hurlbut, May 5, 1959; children: Scott, Shawn, Shelly. BS in Sociology, U. Rochester, 1973. Cert. polygraphist Nat. Acad. Lie Detection. Investigator L.A. Sheriff's Dept., 1962-70, Palm Springs (Calif.) Police Dept., 1976-83; security cons. Paul Hare & Assocs., Palm Springs, 1984-90; dir. pub. safety Cabazon Band Mission Indians, Indio, Calif., 1991—; bd. advisor Calif. Polygraph Examination Assn., 1984-88; security advisor, cons. Cabazon Band Mission Indians, 1984-90. City commr., mem. personnel bd. City of Palm Springs, 1983-86. Sgt. USAF, 1954-62. Mem. Internat. Assn. Chiefs of Police, Masons (sr. deacon 1973—), Royal Arch (high priest 1975-76), Scottish Rite, Am. Legion (comdr. 1973—), Rotary (Palm Springs pres. 1988-89, Indio bd. dirs. 1993-94). Avocations: golf, fishing, hunting. Office: Cabazon Pub Safety Dept 84-245 Indio Springs Dr Indio CA 92203-3405

HARGISS, JAMES LEONARD, ophthalmologist; b. Manhattan, Kans., June 15, 1921; s. Meade Thomas and Julia Baldwin (Wayland) H.; m. Helen Natalie Berglund, July 19, 1947; children: Phillip M., Craig T., D. Reid. BS, U. Wash., 1942; MD, St. Louis U., 1945; MSc in Medicine, U. Pa., 1952. Diplomate Nat. Bd. Med. Examiners, Am. Bd. Ophthalmology. Intern U.S. Naval Hosp., PSNS Bremerton, Washington, 1945-46; resident physician G.F. Geisinger Meml. Hosp. and Foss Clinic, Danville, Pa., 1949-51; practice medicine specializing in ophthalmic surgery Seattle, 1951-58; ophthalmic surgeon Eye Clinic of Seattle, 1958-94, pres., 1962-91, CEO, 1985-91; ophthalmic cons. Eye Assocs. N.W., Seattle, 1994—; asst. clin. prof. Sch. Medicine, U. Wash., 1995—. Contbr. chapter to book, 1987, articles to Ophthalmology, 1964-80. Dist. chmn. King County Rep. Cen. Com., 1962-70. Served as physician/surgeon with USNR, 1945-48. Recipient Citation of Merit Washington State Med. Assn., 1959; Wendell F. Hughes fellow, 1960. Fellow AMA (Cert. of award 1960), Am. Coll. Surgeons (fellows leadership soc.), Leadership Soc., Am. Acad. Ophthalmology (Honor award 1975), Am. Soc. Ophthalmic Plastic and Reconstructive Surgery (charter) (Lester T. Jones award 1979), De Bourg Soc. of St. Louis U., Pacific Coast Oto-Ophthalmology Soc. (v.p.), Lions (Lake City pres. 1960-61), Gullwing Group Internat., Alpha Omega Alpha. Avocations: golf, skiing, art, classic cars. Office: Eye Assocs NW 1101 Madison St Ste 600 Seattle WA 98104

HARGITT, ROLLIN JERRY, retired telecommunications company executive; b. Burlington, Iowa, Aug. 4, 1931; s. Robert Leslie and Mildred H.; m. Marilyn Jean Anton, Dec. 28, 1956; children: Laurie, Bradley, Christopher, Andrew. BA in Edtl. Journalism, U. Iowa, 1955. From installer to v.p., CEO Nebr. Northwestern Bell, Omaha, 1955-85; mng. dir., v.p. Internat. Exec. Svc. Corps, Cairo, Egypt, Jakarta, Indonesia, 1988-95. Pres. State Bd. Edn., Lincoln, Nebr., 1972-76; chmn. bd. Bellevue (Nebr.) Coll.; pres. Nebr. Arts Coun., Lincoln; chmn. Omaha C. of C., 1985-86. Sgt. U.S. Army, 1952-54, Korea. Named citizen of yr. United Way of the Midlands, Omaha, 1985; recipient Americanism citation B'nai B'rith, Omaha, 1985, Gov.'s arts award Nebr. Arts Coun., Lincoln, 1985, svc. to mankind award Sertoma Club, Omaha, 1973, disting. svc. award Omaha Cmty. Playhouse, 1981. Republican. Avocations: photography, golf, woodworking, antiquing.

HARKEN, ALDEN HOOD, surgeon, thoracic surgeon; b. Boston, 1941. MD, Case Western Reserve U., 1967. Diplomate Am. Bd. Surgeons, Am. Bd. Thoracic Surgeons. Intern Peter Bent Brigham Hosp., Boston, 1967-68, resident surgery, 1968-70, resident thoracic surgery, 1971-73; fellow cardio-vascular surgery Boston Children's Hosp., 1970-71; surgeon U. Colo. Hosp., Denver; prof., chmn. surgery dept. U. Colo. Sch. Medicine, Denver; part time pvt. practice surgery Denver. Mem. Am. Assn. Thoracic Surgeons, Soc. Univ. Surgeons. Office: U Colo Med Sch Dept Surg 4200 E 9th Ave Denver CO 80220-3706

HARKINS, CRAIG, management consultant; b. Boston, May 1, 1936; s. Edwin Craig and Shirley Nadine (Pike) H.; m. Betty Letitia Hester, June 17, 1961 (div. 1985); children: Daniel, Sean, Lance; m. Donna Marie Hamlin, Sept. 1, 1990; 1 child Angelika. BA, Colby Coll., Waterville, Maine, 1958; MA, NYU, 1959; Profl. Dipl., Columbia U., N.Y.C., 1963; PhD, Rensselaer Poly. Inst., Troy, N.Y., 1978. Computer operator Pacific Mutual, L.A., 1957; reporter Evening Independent, St. Petersburg, Fla., 1960-61; pub. rels. mgr. IBM, N.Y./Calif, 1961-82; mgmt. cons. Hamlin Harkins Ltd., San Jose, 1982—. Co-editor: Guide to Writing Better Technical Papers, 1982; contbr. numerous articles to profl. jours. Sec. Hudson River Sloop Restoration, Poughkeepsie, N.Y., 1972-76; communications/mktg. com. United Way, Santa Clara, Calif., 1981—; mem. mktg. com. San Jose Cleve. Ballet, 1991—. With USMCR, 1961-66. Mem. Internat. Communication Assn., Peninsula Mktg. Assn., Soc. for Tech. Communication (bd. dirs. 1980-81), IEEE Profl. Communications Soc. (sec. 1977-80). Democrat. Roman Catholic. Avocations: gardening, swimming, poetry, hockey. Home: 1010 Villa Ave Apt 52 San Jose CA 95126-2452 Office: Hamlin Harkins Ltd 1611 The Alameda San Jose CA 95126-2202

HARLAN, KATHLEEN TROY (KAY HARLAN), business consultant, professional speaker and seminar leader; b. Bremerton, Wash., June 9, 1934; d. Floyd K. and Rosemary (Parkhurst) Troy; m. John L. Harlan, Feb. 16, 1952 (div. 1975); children: Pamela Kay, Kenneth Lynwood, Lianna Sue; m. Stuart Friedman, Nov. 10, 1991. Chair Kitsap-North Mason United Way, 1968-70; owner, operator Safeguard N.W. Systems, Tacoma, 1969-79; devel., mgr. Poulsbo (Wash.) Profl. Bldg., 1969-75; pres. Greenapple Graphics, Inc., Tacoma, 1976-79; owner, mgr. Iskrem Hus Restaurant, Poulsbo, 1972-75; pres. Bus. Seminars, Tacoma, 1977-82; owner, mgr. Safeguard Computer Ctr., Tacoma, 1982-91; owner Total Systems Ctr., Tacoma, 1983-88; mem. Orgnl. Renewal, Inc., Tacoma, 1983-88; assoc. mem. Effectiveness Resource Group, Inc., Tacoma, 1979-80; pres. New Image Confs., Tacoma, 1979-82; spkr. on mgmt. and survival in small bus.; CEO Manage Ability, Inc., profl. mgmt. firm, 1991-97; exec. dir. Another Door to Learning, 1996-97; dir. ops. CEO Read Inc., , 1997-98, pres., 1998—. Contbg. author: Here is Genius!, 1980; author small bus. manuals. Mem. Wash. State br. Boundary Rev. for Kitsap County, 1970-76, Selective Svc. Bd. 19, 1969-76; co-chair Wash. State Small Bus. Improvement Coun., 1986; del. White House Conf. on Small Bus., 1986; chair Wash. State Conf. on Small Bus., 1987; founder, mem. exec. bd. Am. Leadership Forum, 1988-94; dir. Bus. Leadership Week, Wash. State, 1990-96; chair Pro-Tech Pierce County, 1992-94; chair Allenmore Hosp., 1993-96; founding mem. Multicare Health Found., 1995-98. Recipient Nellie Cashman award; named Woman Entrepreneur of Yr. for Wash. State, 1986, 87. Mem. Tacoma-Pierce County C. of C. (lifetime exec. bd. 1985—, chair spl. task force on small bus. for Pierce County 1986-89, treas. 1987-88, chair-elect 1988-90, chair 1990-91).

HARLAN, RAYMOND CARTER, communication executive; b. Shreveport, La., Nov. 13, 1943; s. Ross E. and Margaret (Burns) H.; m. Nancy K. Munson, Sept. 3, 1966 (div. 1978); children: Kathleen Marie, Patrick Raymond; m. Sarah J. Kinzel, Sept. 1, 1979 (div. 1982); m. Linda Frances Gerdes, Mar. 30, 1985; stepchildren: Kimberly Jo Gillis, Kellie Leigh Raffa, Ryan William Gerdes. BA in Speech and Drama cum laude, Southwestern U., 1966; MA in English, U. Tex., 1968; MA in Speech & Theatre Arts, Bradley U., 1976. Commd. 2d lt. USAF, 1968, advanced through grades to maj., 1980, ret., 1988; pres. ComSkills Tng., Aurora, Colo., 1988—; asst. prof. Bradley U., Peoria, Ill., 1972-76; instr., asst. prof., course dir. Air Force Acad., Colorado Springs, 1976-81; asst. prof. Air Force Inst. Tech., Dayton, Ohio, 1987-88; internat. trainer Inst. for Internat. Rsch., London, 1990-92; presenter in field. Author: The Confident Speaker, 1993; co-author: Telemarketing That Works, 1991, Interactive Telemarketing, 1995; contbr. articles and revs. to profl. jours. Decorated Air Force Commendation medal with three oak leaf clusters, Air Force Meritorious Svc. medal with one oak leaf cluster; recipient George Washington Honor Medal Freedom Found., 1983, Leo A. Codd award Am. Def. Preparedness Assn., 1st Prize ann. poetry contest Ariz. State Poetry Soc., 1979. Mem. ASTD, Air Force Assn., Ret. Officers Assn., Soc. for Tech. Comm. Lutheran. Avocations: skiing, cycling, gardening. Office: ComSkills Tng 17544 E Wesley Pl Aurora CO 80013-4174

HARLEY, ROBISON DOOLING, JR., lawyer, educator; b. Ancon, Panama, July 6, 1946; s. Robison Dooling and Loyde Hazel (Goehenauer) H.; m. Suzanne Purviance Bendel, Aug. 9, 1975; children: Arianne Erin, Lauren Loyde. BA, Brown U., 1968; JD, Temple U., 1971; LLM, U. San Diego, 1985. Bar: Pa. 1971, U.S. Ct. Mil. Appeals 1972, Calif. 1976, U.S. Dist. Ct. (cen. and so. dists) Calif. 1976, N.J. 1977, U.S. Dist. Ct. N.J. 1977, U.S. Supreme Ct. 1980, D.C. 1981, U.S. Ct. Appeals (9th cir.) 1982, U.S. Dist. Ct. (ea. dist.) Pa. 1987, U.S. Ct. Appeals (3rd cir.) 1986. Cert. criminal law specialist Calif. Bd. Legal Specialization, 1981, recertified 1986, 91, 96; cert. criminal trial adv. Nat. Bd. Trial Advocacy, 1982, recertified, 1987, 92, 97. Asst. agy. dir. Safeco Title Ins. Co., L.A., 1975-77; ptnr. Cohen, Stokke & Davis, Santa Ana, Calif., 1977-85; prin. Harley Law Offices, Santa Ana, Calif., 1985—; adj. prof. Orange County Coll. Trial Advocacy, adj. prof., paralegal program U. Calif., trial adv. programs U.S. Army, USN, USAF, USMC; judge pro-tem Orange County Cts. Author: Orange County Trial Lawyers Drunk Driving Syllabus; contbr. articles to profl. jours. and reports. Bd. dirs. Orange County Legal Aid Soc. Served to lt. col. JAGC, USMCR, 1975-94; trial counsel, def. counsel, mil. judge, asst. staff judge adv. USMC, 1971-75, regional def. counsel Western Region, 1986-90, instr., program coord. Army, Navy, Air Force, Marines, Coast Guard Trial Adv. Programs worldwide. Recipient Commendation medal U.S. Navy, Nat. Defense Svc. medal, Reserve medal, 23 Certs. of Commendation and/or Congratulations. Mem. ABA, ATLA, Orange County Bar Assn. (judiciary com., criminal law sect., adminstrn. of justice com.), Orange County Trial Lawyers Assn., Calif. Trial Lawyers Assn., Calif. Attys. for Criminal Justice, Calif. Pub. Defenders Assn., Nat. Assn. for Criminal Def. Attys., Assn. Specialized Criminal Def. Advs., Orange County Criminal Lawyers Assn. (found. com.), Res. Officers Assn., Marine Corps Reserve Officers Assn., Marine Corps Assn. Republican. Avocations: sports, physical fitness, reading. Home: 31211 Paseo Miraloma San Juan Capistrano CA 92675-5505 Office: Harley Law Offices 825 N Ross St Santa Ana CA 92701-3419

HARLOW, CHARLES VENDALE, JR., finance educator, consultant; b. Long Beach, Calif., May 18, 1931; s. Charles Vendale and Lucille (Morris) H.; m. Luann Jones, July 6, 1956; children: Jeffrey, Pamela, John. BA, Stanford U., 1953; MBA, U. So. Calif., 1960, DBA, 1968. Ptnr. Harlow & Harlow Investments, Long Beach, 1955-68; pres. Cambistics, Inc., Long Beach, 1968-88; asst. prof. Calif. State U., Long Beach, 1968-71, assoc. prof., 1971-75, prof. fin., 1975-94; prof. fin. Pepperdine U., 1995—; mng. dir. Cambistics Securities Corp., Long Beach, 1990—. Co-author: The Commodity Futures Trading Guide, 1969 (100 Best Books in Bus. award), The Futures Game, 1974, How to Shoot From the Hip Without Getting Shot in the Foot: Making Smart Strategic Choices Every Day, 1990. 1st lt. USMC, 1953-55. NSF grantee, 1968. Republican. Avocations: running, golf, amateur radio, writing.

HARMAN, JANE, congresswoman, lawyer; b. N.Y.C., June 28, 1945; d. A. N. and Lucille (Geier) Lakes; m. Sidney Harman, Aug. 30, 1980; children: Brian Lakes, Hilary Lakes, Daniel Geier, Justine Leigh. BA, Smith Coll., 1966; JD, Harvard U., 1969. Bar: D.C. 1969, U.S. Ct. Appeals (D.C. cir.) 1972, U.S. Supreme Ct. 1975. Spl. asst. Commn. of Chs. on Internat. Affairs, Geneva, Switzerland, 1969-70; assoc. Surrey & Morse, Washington, 1970-72; chief legis. asst. Senator John V. Tunney, Washington, 1972-73; chief counsel, staff dir. Subcom. on Rep. Citizen Interests, Com. on Judiciary, Washington, 1973-75; adj. prof. Georgetown Law Ctr., Washington, 1974-75; chief counsel, staff dir. Subcom. on Constl. Rights, Com. on Judiciary, Washington, 1975-77; dep. sec. to cabinet The White House, Washington, 1977-78; spl. counsel Dept. Def., Washington, 1979; ptnr. Manatt, Phelps, Rothenberg & Tunney, Washington, 1979-82, Surrey & Morse, Washington, 1982-86; of counsel Jones, Day, Reavis & Pogue, Washington, 1987-92; mem. 103rd-105th Congresses from 36th Calif. dist., 1992—, mem. nat. security com., intelligence com.; mem. vis. coms. Harvard Law Sch., 1976-82, Kennedy Sch. Govt., 1990-96. Counsel Dem. Platform Com., Washington, 1984; vice-chmn. Ctr. for Nat. Policy, Washington, 1981-90; chmn. Dem. Nat. Com. Nat. Lawyers' Coun., Washington, 1986-90. Mem. Phi Beta Kappa. Democrat. Office: US House Reps 325 Cannon Bldg Ofc Bldg Washington DC 20515-0003 also: 1217 El Prado Ave Torrance CA 90501-2708*

HARMAN, KENNETH R., counseling administrator; b. Balt., Nov. 10, 1927; s. Clarence L. and Madeline M. (Geaslen) H.; m. Linda Harman, June 5, 1965; children: Kenneth, Wendy, Jory, Jennifer, John. BD, Reformed Episcopal Sem., 1949; BS, Temple U., 1951; MA, John F. Kennedy U., 1987; MDiv, Phila. Theol. Sem., 1990. V.p. Drake Beam Morin, Walnut Creek, Calif.; dist. sales mgr. Pacific Northwest; regional adminstrv. mgr. San Leandro, Calif. Home: 9519 Davona Dr San Ramon CA 94583-4014

HARMEL, HILDA HERTA See PIERCE, HILDA

HARMENING, GAIL JOAN, craft pattern designer; b. Mt. Clemens, Mich., Mar. 16, 1943; d. Ross Henry and Olive E. (Gardner) Fox; m. Lewis Martin Harmening, Sept. 2, 1961 (div. May 1987); children: Christopher, Carrie Williams, Kathleen. AA, Grossmont Coll., El Cajon, Calif., 1991. Adminstr. asst. Chevron Corp., La Habra, Calif., 1962-64, 81-86; pers. clk. North Orange County Regional Occup. Program, Anaheim, Calif., 1973-75; payroll/pers. clk. Fullerton Elem. Schs., Los Angeles county Schs., Fullerton, Calif., 1976-80; adminstr. asst. Grossmont Coll., 1987-89; counseling sec. Grossmont Union H.S. Dist., La Mesa, Calif., 1989-91; entrepreneur craft pattern designs, La Mesa, 1991-98; distbr. personal care products NEWAYS, Inc., La Mesa, 1992—. Designer clown doll Clancey; designer quilted wall-hanging patterns Gail's Fabric Puzzles. Recipient award for best original design Del Mar (Calif.) Fair, 1995. Republican. Christian. Avocations: reading, walking, swimming. Home: # 211 5700 Baltimore Dr Unit 211 La Mesa CA 91942-1644

HARMONY, PATRICIA STARR, writer, poet; b. Odessa, Tex., Oct. 9, 1955; d. Lennis Paul and Juanita Outawa (Nelson) Walls; children: Cody Reed Christopher Paul Cox, Lennis Elijah Vincent Isaiah Walls; m. Gerald Lloyd Harman, Nov. 4, 1973 (div. Feb. 1986); children: Leland Jenean Salyn Harman-Block, Alisha Beth Lorraine Harman-Wynant. Degree in art/English, South Oreg. State U., 1978, degree in art, 1982. Writer, poet, 1966—; editor, pub. Calliopes Corner, 1980-88; self-employed PS Cleaning Co., Index, Wash., 1988-98; installer S. Nagy Co., Sultan, Wash., 1998—. Editor, pub. poetry book, 1980—; poetry editor: (newspaper) Index Eagle, 1996-98. Avocations: musician, songwriting, poet, artist. Home: PO Box 328 Index WA 98256-0328

HARNACK, BARBARA WOOD, artist, sculptor; b. N.Y.C., Oct. 9, 1957; d. William and Phyllis Claire (Mitchell) H.; m. Michael N.J. Dean Lancaster; 1 child, Amrit Ringling Mitchell. Cert. of graduation, Parson's Sch. Design, N.Y.C., 1980. Co-founder Malden Bridge (N.Y.) Pottery, 1979-86; co-founder, sec. bd. dirs. Historic Malden Bridge Playhouse Soc., 1983-86; owner Woods Gallery, Malden Bridge, N.Y., 1982-86; curator exhibits Malden Bridge Arts Ctr., 1979-86; adv. bd. Internat. Friends Transformative Art, Scottsdale, Ariz., 1991-92; bd. dirs. Children's Workshop, Cerrillos, N.Mex., 1995; exhibits coord. N.J. Lancaster Fine Art, Madrid, N.Mex., 1997. Vol. Meals on Wheels, Westchester County, 1972; founder Scarecrow Day, Malden Bridge, 1984-85; vol. flood victim support ARC, Elmira, N.Y., 1973; vol. Holiday Project Internat., N.Y., N.Mex., 1990—; vol. child tchr. Hudson River Mus., N.Y., 1973. Recipient Macy's Merit award Albany (N.Y.) Inst. History and Art, 1978, Purchase prize Feats of Clay Lincoln Arts, 1998. Mem. Am. Craft Coun. Avocations: gardening, backpacking, birding, building adobe home. Home: 98 B Gold Mine RD Cerrillos NM 87010

HARNEY, PATRICIA RAE, nuclear analyst; b. Oklahoma City, Sept. 8, 1960; d. Donald R. Thompson and Donaleen L. (Turner) Robinson; m. Timothy D. Harney, Dec. 2, 1997; 1 child, Adrian. AAS in Ct. Reporting, Mile Hi Coll. Ct. Reporting, 1985; student, Front Range C.C., Westminster, Colo., 1993—. Cert. in hazardous materials; cert. Dept. Transp. Pvt. practice ct. reporter Denver, 1985-91; facility adminstr. Allen Bradley Co., Englewood, Colo., 1990-91; nuc. analyst Rocky Flats Environ. Tech. Site, Golden, Colo., 1991-95; tech. writer/analyst Y-12 Nuc. Plant, Oak Ridge, Tenn., 1995-96; nuc. safety sys. engr. Rocky Flats Environ. Tech. Site, Golden, 1996—; com. mem. Pro Bono Com., Denver, 1989-91. Mem. Non-Profit Orgn. for Abused Children, Denver, 1984-86. Recipient Productivity Improvement award for centralized waste storage facility EG&G Rocky Flats, 1994. Mem. Am. Nuc. Soc., Phi Theta Kappa. Avocations: reading, skiing, scuba diving, biking. Home: 8722 W Ute Dr Littleton CO 80128-6964

HARNSBERGER, THERESE COSCARELLI, librarian; b. Muskegon, Mich.; d. Charles and Julia (Borrell) Coscarelli; B.A. cum laude, Marymount Coll., 1952; M.L.S., U. So. Calif., 1953; postgrad. Rosary Coll., River Forest, Ill., 1955-56, U. Calif., Los Angeles Extension, 1960-61; m. Frederick Owen Harnsberger, Dec. 24, 1962; 1 son, Lindsey Carleton. Free-lance writer, 1950—; librarian San Marino (Calif.) High Sch., 1953-56; cataloger, cons. San Marino Hall, South Pasadena, Calif., 1956-61; librarian Los Angeles State Coll., 1956-59; librarian dist. library Covina-Valley Unified Sch. Dist., Covina, Calif., 1959-67; librarian Los Angeles Trade Tech. Coll., 1972—, mem. acad. senate, 1996—; med. librarian, tumor registrar Alhambra (Calif.) Community Hosp., 1975-79; tumor registrar Huntington Meml. Hosp., 1979—; pres., dir. Research Unltd., 1980—; free lance reporter Los Angeles' Best Bargains, 1981—; med. library cons., 1979—; reviewer various cookbooks, 1991—. Author numerous poems. Chmn. spiritual values com. Covina Coordinating Council, 1964-66; chmn. Neighborhood Watch, 1976—. Winner poetry contest Pasadena Star News, 1993. Mem. ALA, Internat. Women's Writing Guild, Calif. Assn. Sch. Librarians (chmn. legis. com.), Acad.Com. Partimers Rep., 1996 Covina Tchrs. Assn., AAUW (historian 1972-73), U. So. Calif. Grad. Sch. Libr. Sci. (life), Am. Nutrition Soc. (chpt. Newsletter chmn.), Nat. Tumor Registrars Assn., So. Calif. Tumor Registrars Assn., Med. Libr. Assn., So. Calif. Libr. Assn., So. Calif. Assn Law Libr., Book Publicists So. Calif., Am. Fedn. Tchrs. (exec. bd. part-timers 1994, alt. exec. bd. local # 1521 coll. guild 1994—, acad. senate part-timers rep. 1996—, reporter, co-editor Pen & Quill, 1997—), Coll. Guild, Calif. Libr. Assn., Assn. Poetry Bibliographers, Faculty Assn. Calif. Community Colls., Immaculate Heart Coll. Alumnae Assn., Assistance League Pasadena, Loyola Marymount Alumnae Assn. (coord. 1986), Pi Lambda Theta. Author: (poetry) The Journal, 1982, To Julia: in Memoriam; author: (words to choral music by Lindsay C. Harnsberger) Haiku Poem for Vanigals, 1996; cookbook rev. columnist Citizen's Voice, 1997—; contbr. articles to profl. jours., poems to newspapers. Office: 2809 W Hellman Ave Alhambra CA 91803-2737

HARP, GRADY ESTLE, art dealer, curator, poet; b. Enid, Okla., Apr. 13, 1941; s. Merle Fisher and Ruby Lorene (Lambert) H.; div.; children: Thomas Fisher, Alexander Lockwood. AB, Occidental Coll., 1963; MD, U. So. Calif., 1967. Genitourinary surgeon Pasadena, Calif., 1974-81; chief dept. urology Cigna Healthplans, L.A., 1982-92; dir. Lizardi/Harp Gallery, Pasadena and L.A., 1981—; chair ednl. policy and student life Otis Coll. Art and Design, L.A., 1994-98; curator Art Inst. So. Calif., Laguna Beach, Calif., 1997; guest curator Fresno (Calif.) Art Mus., 1996; artist in residence Nev. Mus. Art, Reno, 1997, Cleve. State U., 1997; mus. artist Nat. Vietnam Vets. Art Mus., Chgo., 1997-98. Exhibited War Songs, Nev., Ill., Ohio and Calif., 1997-98; poet: War Songs, 1996, Rustling Leaves, 1998, Vietnam: Reflexes and Reflections, 1998; contbg. editor Provocateur Mag., 1996-97. Bd. govs. Otis Coll. Art and Design. Lt. comdr. USNR, 1968-74. Diplomate Soc. of the Cir. of Spanish Am. Poets; mem. Coll. Arts Assn., Am. Acad. Poets, Am. Assn. Museums, Art Dealers Assn. of Calif., L.A. Conv. and Visitors Bur. Office: Lizardi/Harp Gallery PO Box 91895 Pasadena CA 91109-1895

HARP, JAMES LUTHER, mechanical engineer; b. Muskogee, Okla., Dec. 31, 1922; s. James Luther and Maude Diana (Burns) H.; m. Bette Rose Koenig, Oct. 16, 1948 (dec. May 1988); children: Thomas Allen, Linda Louise; m. Joyce Olsen Riddell, Nov. 23, 1994. BS in mech. engr. cum laude, Univ. Ill., 1948. Aeronautical rsch. scientist Nat. Adv. COm. Aeronautics Lewis Lab, Cleve., 1948-56; mng. mem. adv. tech. staff The Marquardt Corp., Van Nuys, Calif., 1956-69; pres. Thermo Mech. Systems Inc., Canoga Park, Calif., 1969—, also chmn. bd. dirs.; rsch. engr. on turbojet engines, NACA, Cleve., 1948-56; speaker in field. Contbr. articles to profl. jours. Commodore Malibu Yacht Club, 1965. With USAF, 1942-45, ETO. Decorated Disting. Flying Cross, Air medal, Meritorious Svc. medal, USAF, 1942-45; recipient 5th pl. award Bendix Transcontinental Trophy Race in a Lockheed P=38 Fighter, 1946. Fellow Am. Inst. Aero. and Astro.; mem. AIAA Ground Test & Simulation Com., Soc. of Automotive Engrs., Am. Soc. Mech. Engrs., Air Force Assn., P-47 Pilots Assn. Republican. Baptist. Achievements include program manager that solved combustion screech problem in turbojet after burners; developed a 3 stage turbocharged spark engine for NASA unmanned flight at 90,000 feet to study ozone problem. Avocations: yacht racing, golf, hiking, tennis. Home: 21900 Marylee St Apt 293 Woodland Hills CA 91367-4827 Office: Thermo Mech Systems Co 20944 Sherman Way Ste 210 Canoga Park CA 91303-3643

HARPER, ANTHONY, counselor, singer; b. Clarksville, Tenn., Jan. 6, 1952; s. Hal L. and Kathryn A. (Reding) H.; m. Mary K. McGrane, July 1972 (div. Nov. 1974); 1 child, Amy; m. Mary J. Breshears, Aug., 1980. BA, USNY, 1984; MEd, Coll. Idaho, 1986; postgrad., Liberty U., Calif. Coast U., 1989—; PhD, Calif. Coast U., 1996. Tv switcher engr. KISU TV, Pocatello, Idaho, 1977-78, KIFI TV, Idaho Falls, Idaho, 1979; singer various locations, 1978—; co-founder, exec. dir., counselor Shiloh Counseling Ctr., Boise, Idaho, 1987—; guest spkr. in field; co-founder, exec. dir. Children of Hope Family Hosp., 1997—. Author: (test and manual) Spiritual Relationship Scale, 1990. Republican. Avocations: playing trumpet, piano, hiking, ice skating. E-mail: aharper1952@juno.com. Office: PO Box 1829 Boise ID 83701-1829

HARPER, DONALD CALVIN, social services administrator; b. Claresholm, Alta., Can., Oct. 31, 1942; s. William James and Effie Mabel (Slonaker) H.; m. Kathleen Ann Paton, May 18, 1968; children: Christopher Bradley, Angela Dawn. BA, U. Alta., Edmonton, 1963, MA, 1970. Rsch. asst. exec. coun. Province of Alta., 1966-67, rsch. asst. dept. of youth, 1967-69; instr. sociology Grande Prairie Regional Coll., Alta., 1969-71, registrar, 1971-74, registrar, dir. student svcs., 1974-79, dir. student and community svcs., 1979-80, instr. humanities and social scis., 1980-81, chairperson acad. devel., 1981-84, dean acad. and applied studies, 1984-93; exec. dir. S. Peace Soc. Planning Coun., 1998—; project coord. Aboriginal Head Start, Grande Prairie Friendship Ctr., 1996-98; instl. mediator/family and divorce, 1995-87; mem. task force Worth Royal Com. Ednl. Planning, 1970-71; mem. Alta Coun. Admissions & Transfer, 1974-77, 79-82, 89-92; chairperson com. Sr. Acad. Officers, Alta, 1990-92; exec. dir. South Peace Social Planning Coun., 1998—. Pres. Grande Prairie Little Theatre, 1978-80, 94-95, Crohn's and Colitis Found. of Can., G.P. chpt.; bd. dirs. Prairie Gallery, 1980-81, 84-86, other community bds.; regional dir. Alta. Fedn. Home and Sch. Assns., 1990-92; mem. Can. Program adv. com. Assn. Can. C.C., 1991-93. Avocations: amateur theatre, gardening. Home: 8517 100A St, Grande Prairie, AB Canada T8V 3C4

HARPER, ED, computer company executive. Pres., CEO Sy Quest Tech., Fremont, Calif. Office: Sy Quest Tech 47071 Bayside Pkwy Fremont CA 94538*

HARPER, GLORIA JANET, artist, educator; children: Dan Conyers, Jan Girvan. Student, Famous Artists Sch., 1967-69, 69-71; BA in Comml. Art, Portland C.c., 1981; postgrad., Valley View Art Sch., 1982-89, Carrizzo Art Sch., 1983-89, Holdens Portrait Sch., 1989; studied with Daniel Greene, 1989, postgrad. in paralegal studies. Cert. art educator. Artist, art instr. Art By Gloria, 1980—; owner Art By Gloria Art Sch. and Gallery, Pendleton, Oreg., 1991—; lectr., workshop presenter in field, 1980—. Paintings and prints included in various mags. Mem. NAFE, Nat. Assn. Fine Artists, Water Color Soc. Am., Nat. Mus. Women in Arts, So. Career Inst. Profl. Legal Assts. (area rep.), Northwest Pastel Soc., Profl. Legal Assts., Pendleton C. of C. Avocations: photography and art of nature, hiking, gardening, learning. Home: PO Box 1734 Pendleton OR 97801-0570 Office: Art By Gloria 404 SE Dorion Ave Ste 204 Pendleton OR 97801-2531

HARPER, JENNIFER JUANITA, art historian; b. L.A.; d. John Bert and Bessie Alberta (Cobb) H. BA, Carleton Coll., Northfield, Minn.; MA, U. Va., 1993; postgrad., Yale U. Pub. rels. rep. William Grant Still Cmty. Arts Ctr., L.A., 1980; adminstrv. asst. S.W. Mus., L.A., 1984; sec. L.A. County Mus. Art, 1984-88; asst. curator Laguna Art Mus., Laguna Beach, Calif., 1994-96; Otelia Cromwell fellow Yale U. Art Gallery, New Haven, 1994-96, Rose Herrick Jackson fellow, 1998-99, Marcia Brady Tucker fellow, 1999—; Grad. Dean's fellow, Commonwealth fellow U. Va. DuPont fellow U. Va., 1991-93, Paul Mellon fellow, Yale U., 1998, Luce Found. for Am. Art fellow, 1998. Mem. Am. Soc. 18th Century Studies, Coll. Art Assn.

HARPER, KENNETH CHARLES, clergyman; b. Detroit, Aug. 31, 1946; s. Charles Burdett and Marion Anna (Pankau) H.; m. Charlene Elizabeth Gates, Apr. 14, 1996; children: Charles William, David Peter, Andrew Scott. BS in Edn., Ill. State U., 1969; MDiv, Trinity Evang. Div. Sch., Deerfield, Ill., 1973; ThM, Princeton (N.J.) Theol. Sem., 1976; D of Ministry, San Francisco Theol. Sem., San Anselmo, Calif., 1986; postgrad., Pepperdine U., 1989-93. Ordained to ministry Presbyn. Ch., 1974. Edn. advisor Amwell Valley Comm., Reaville, N.J., 1973-74; asst. pastor 1st Presbyn. Ch., Mt. Holly, N.J., 1974-77; pastor 1st Presbyn. Ch., Herrin, Ill., 1977-82; sr. pastor 1st Presbyn. Ch., Westminster, Calif., 1982-94; pastor Chula Vista (Calif.) Presbyn. Ch., 1994—. Contbr. book revs. and articles to religious jours. Mem. Evang. Theol. Soc., Presbyns. for Renewal, Assn. Psychol. Type. Democrat. Office: Chula Vista Presbyn Ch 940 Hilltop Dr Chula Vista CA 91911-2235

HARPER, RICHARD HENRY, film producer, director; b. San Jose, Calif., Sept. 15, 1950; s. Walter Henry and Priscilla Alden (Browne) H.; m. Ann Marie Morgan, June 19, 1976; children: Christine Ann, Paul Richard, James Richard. Show designer Walt Disney Imagineering, Glendale, Calif., 1971-76; motion picture producer, dir. Harper Films, Inc., La Canada, Calif., 1976—. Producer, dir. (films) Impressions de France, Disney World, Fla., 1982, Magic Carpet Round the World, Disneyland, Tokyo, 1983, American Journeys, Disneyland, Calif., 1985, Collecting America, Nat. Gallery Art, Washington, 1988, Hillwood Mus., Washington, 1989, Journey Into the 4th Dimension for Sanrio World, Journey Into Nature for Sanrio World, Japan, 1990, Masters of Illusion, Nat. Gallery of Art, Washington, 1992. Recipient more than 150 awards world-wide for outstanding motion picture prodn. including Silver trophy Cannes Internat. Film Festival, 2 Gold awards Internat. Festival of the Ams., 1981, 82, 14 Golden Eagle C.I.N.E. awards, 1977-92, Emmy award Nat. Acad. TV Arts and Scis., 1993. Mem. Acad. of Motion Picture Arts and Scis.

HARPER, ROBERT LEVELL, pharmaceutical company executive; b. Wichita, Kans., Nov. 11, 1942; s. Cleo Levell and Mary Florence (Weaver) H.; m. Margaret Lucille Madden, Jan. 20, 1961 (div. 1980); children: Douglas Warren, Susan Denise; m. Maria Elain Davis, June 20, 1981; stepchildren: Laura Elaine Emery, Melissa MacAlpin Emery. Cert. med. rep., Sterling Mgmt. Inst. Sales rep. Dorsey Labs. div. Sandoz Pharms., Tulsa, 1967-70; mgr. key accounts Sandoz Pharms., Houston, 1970-72; div. mgr. Dorsey Pharms. div. Sandoz Pharms., Kansas City, Mo., 1972-85; mgr. govt. affairs Sandoz Pharms., Sacramento, 1985—; rotating mgr. Sandoz Pharms., East Hanover, N.J., 1985. Donor Kansas City Coll. Osteo. Medicine, 1973; co-founder first aid program state CAP, Oklahoma City, 1973; leader youth program YMCA, Johnson County, Mo., 1977-79; leader youth baseball Johnson County, 1976-79; del. Nat. Baseball Congress, Houston, 1971, 72, 73; mem. med. edn. for srs. SRx Regional Program, 1985—. With USAFR, 1960-64. Recipient appreciation award Calif. State Firemen's Assn., Sacramento, 1987. Mem. Nat. Assn. Legis. Svcs., Calif. Medication Edn. Coalition, Calif. Mfrs. Assn., Pharm. Mfrs. Assn., Calif. Derby. Avocations: racquetball, softball, tennis. Home: 7418 Manchester Ct Castle Rock CO 80104-8809

HARRELL, GARY PAUL, lawyer; b. Texas City, Tex., July 8, 1952; s. James Eugene Jr. and Mary Alice Harrell; m. Leigh Evans, May 27, 1978. BS, U. Tex., 1977, MA, 1979; cert. mgmt. healthcare facilities, UCLA, 1984; JD cum laude, Lewis & Clark Coll., 1991. Bar: Oreg. 1991, U.S. Dist. Ct. (fed. dist.) Oreg. 1991; diplomate Am. Coll. Healthcare Execs. Staff/charge nurse Healthcare Facilties, Austin, Tex., 1972-78; gen. mgr. Nursing Support Svcs., Austin, 1978-80; dir. edn. Downey (Calif.) Cmty. Hosp., 1980-84; v.p. patient care Grande Ronde Hosp., La Grande, Oreg., 1984-88; assoc. Lane Powell Spears Lubersky, Portland, Oreg., 1990-94; ptnr. Harrell & Nester, LLP, Portland, 1994—; adj. prof., asst. prof. Calif. State U., Long Beach, 1980-84; pres. Oreg. State Bd. Nursing, Portland, 1987-90. Contbr. chpts. to books. With USNR, 1970-74. Recipient Am. Jurisprudence award, 1989. Fellow Healthcare Fin. Mgmt. Assn. (v.p. Oreg. chpt.); mem. Oreg. Assn. Nurse Attys. (treas., past. pres.), Am. Coll. Health Care Adminstrs. (past pres. Oreg. chpt.), Am. Health Lawyers Assn., Oreg. Health Care Assn. (chair assoc. com.). Avocations: flying, sailing, motorcycling. E-mail: gharrell@health-law.net. Office: Harrell & Nester LLP 1515 SW 5th Ave Ste 510 Portland OR 97201-5450

HARRELL, IRIS FAYE, general contractor; b. Franklin, Va., Apr. 1, 1947; d. Alton Joseph and Evelyn Pearl (Goodwin) H.; life ptnr.: Anne Elizabeth Benson, May 12, 1979. BA, Mary Washington Coll., 1969; M in Edn. Adminstrn., Va. Commonwealth U., 1975. Tchr. Henrico County Schs., Varina, Va., 1969-71, Richmond (Va.) City Schs., 1972-73, Rough Rock Navajo Reservation, Ariz., 1974-75; tribunal adminstr. Am. Arbitration Assn., Dallas, 1979-80; regional dir. Women in Cmty. Svc., Dallas, 1980-81; owner, gen. contractor Harrell Remodeling, Dallas, 1981-84, Harrell Remodeling, Inc., Menlo Park, Calif., 1984—. Named female entrepreneur of the year Nat. Assn. Women Bus. Owners, 1996. Mem. Nat. Assn. Remodelers (nat. contractor of yr. award-bathrooms 1995), Nat. Kitchen & Bath Assn., Menlo Park C. of C. Democrat. Mem. Christian Sci. Ch. Avocations: running, music. Office: Harrell Remodeling 103 Gilbert Ave Menlo Park CA 94025-2832

HARRIGAN, ROSANNE CAROL, nursing educator; b. Miami, Feb. 24, 1945; d. John H. and Rose (Hnatow) Harrigan; children: Dennis, Michael, John. BS, St. Xavier Coll., 1965; MS in Nursing, Ind. U., 1974, EdD in Nursing and Edn., 1979. Staff nurse, recovery rm. Mercy Hosp., Chgo., 1965, evening charge nurse, 1965-66; head nurse Chgo. State Hosp., 1966-67; nurse practitioner Health and Hosp. Corp. Marion County, Indpls., 1975-80; assoc. prof. Ind. U. Sch. Nursing, Indpls., 1978-82; nurse practitioner devel. follow-up program Riley Hosp. for Children, Indpls., 1980-85; chief nursing sect. Riley Hosp. Child Devel. Ctr., Indpls., 1982-85; prof. Ind. U. Sch. Nursing, Indpls., 1982-85; chmn., prof. maternal child health Loyola U. Niehoff Sch. Nursing, Chgo., 1985-92; dean U. Hawaii, Honolulu, 1992—; lecturer Ind. U. Sch. Nursing, 1974-75, chmn. dept. pediatrics, family and women's health, 1980-85; adj. prof. of pediatrics Ind. U. Sch. Med., 1982-85; editorial bd. Jour. Maternal Child Health Nursing, 1984-86, Jour. Perinatal Neonatal, 1985—, Jour. Perinatology, 1989—, Loyola U. Press, 1988—; adv. bd. Symposia Medicus, 1982-84, Proctor and Gamble Rsch. Adv. Com. Blue Ribbon Panel; scientific review panel NIH, 1985; cons. in field. Contbr. articles to profl. jours. bd. dirs. March of Dimes Cen. Ind. Chpt., 1974-76, med. adv., 1979-85; med. and rsch. adv. March of Dimes Nat. Found., 1985—, chmn. Task Force on Rsch. Named Nat. Nurse of Yr. March of Dimes, 1983; faculty research grantee Ind. U., 1978, Pediatric Pulmonary Nursing Tng. grant Am. Lung Assn., 1982-85, Attitudes, Interests and Competence of Ob-Gyn Nurses Rsch. grant Nurses Assn. Am. Coll. Ob-Gyn., 1986, Attitudes, Interests and Priorities of Neonatal Nurses Rsch. grant Nat. Assn. Neonatal Nurses, 1987, Biomedical Rsch. Support grant, 1988; Doctoral fellow Am. Lung Assn. Ind. Tng. Program, 1981-86. Mem. AAAS, ANA (Maternal Child Nurse of Yr. 1983), Assn. Women's Health, Obstetrical and Neonatal Nursing (chmn. com. on rsch. 1983-86), Am. Nurses Found., Nat. Assn. Neonatal Nurses, Nat. Perinatal Assn. (bd. dirs. 1978-85, rsch. com. 1986), Midwest Nursing Rsch. Soc. (theory devel. sect.), Ill. Nurses Assn. (commn. rsch. chmn. 1990-91), Ind. Nurses Assn., Hawaii Nurses Assn., Ind. Perinatal Assn. (pres. 1981-83), N.Y. Acad. Sci., Ind U. Alumni Assn. (Disting. Alumni 1985), Sigma Xi, Pi Lambda Theta, Sigma Theta Tau (chpt. pres. 1988-90).

HARRINGTON, CHARLES LEE, retired judge; b. Berkeley, Calif., Feb. 5, 1932; s. Harris Clifford and Thelma Aileen (Lee) H.; m. Febe Forster, Dec. 29, 1956; children: Kathleen Harrington Guerra, Aileen Harrington Parsons, Jane Harrington Erdiakoff, Charles Lee II. BSBA, U. Calif., Berkeley, 1953; JD, U. Calif., San Francisco, 1963. Bar: N.Mex., Calif. Pvt. practice Albuquerque and Roswell, N.Mex., 1964-68; dep. county counsel Alameda County Counsel's Office, Oakland, Calif., 1969-86; ct. commr./judge pro tem Alameda County Superior Ct., Oakland, 1986-94; mem. bioethics com. Alameda-Contra Costa Med. Assn., Oakland; panelist on continuing edn. of the Bar, Berkeley, calif., 1972-80; panelist The Rutter Group, Encino, Calif., 1989. Bd. dirs., pres. Moraga (Calif.) Hist. Soc., 1975-78; bd. dirs. Big C Soc., Berkeley, 1979-83; bd. dirs., v.p., sec. Friends of Cal Crew, Berkeley, Calif., 1987—; bd. dirs. Oakland (Calif.) Strokes, 1975-83. 1st lt. USAF, 1954-58; lt. col. USAF Res., retired 1984. Decorated 2 Air Force Commendation medals. Mem. Friends of Cal Crew (bd. dirs., sec. 1987—), Moraga Hist. Soc. (pres. 1975—), Alameda County Bar Assn., State Bar of N.Mex., Calif. State Bar. Republican. Avocations: mil. and U.S. history, travel, jogging, grandchildren. Home: 105 La Quinta St Moraga CA 94556-1024 Office: PO Box 185 Moraga CA 94556-0185

HARRINGTON, MARK ELLIS, lawyer; b. Bakersfield, Calif., Dec. 9, 1966. BA, UCLA, 1990; JD, Southwestern U., 1995. Dir. sales Ticketmaster Inc., L.A., 1990-94; law clk. Ticketmaster, Inc., L.A., 1994-95; atty. Munger, Tolles & Olson, L.A., 1995-97; sr. counsel Trillium Digital Sys., L.A., 1997—. Republican. Roman Catholic. Office: Trillium Digital Sys 12100 Wilshire Blvd Ste 1800 Los Angeles CA 90025-7107

HARRINGTON, MARY EVELINA PAULSON (POLLY HARRINGTON), religious journalist, writer, educator; b. Chgo.; d. Henry Thomas and Evelina (Belden) Paulson; m. Gordon Keith Harrington, Sept. 7, 1957; children: Jonathan Henry, Charles Scranton. BA, Oberlin Coll., 1946; postgrad., Northwestern U., Evanston, Ill., Chgo., 1946-49, Weber State U., Ogden, Utah, 1970s, 80s; MA, U. Chgo.-Chgo. Theol. Sem., 1956. Publicist Nat. Coun. Chs., N.Y.C., 1950-51; mem. press staff 2d assembly World Coun. Chs., Evanston, Chgo., 1954; mgr. Midwest Office Communication, United Ch. of Christ, Chgo., 1955-59; staff writer United Ch. Herald, N.Y.C., St. Louis, 1959-61; affiliate missionary to Asia, United Ch. Bd. for World Ministries, N.Y.C., 1978-79; freelance writer and lectr., 1961—; corr. Religious News Svc., 1962—; prin. lectr. Women & Family Life in Asia series to numerous librs., Utah, 1981, 81-82; pub. rels. coord. Utah Energy Conservation/Energy Mgmt. Program, 1984-85; tchr. writing Ogden Cmty. Schs., 1985-89; adj. instr. writing for publs. Weber State U., 1986—; instr. Acad. Lifelong Learning, Ogden, 1992—, Eccles Cmty. Art Ctr., Ogden, 1993—; dir. comm. Shared Ministry, Salt Lake City, 1983—; chmn. comm. Intermountain Conf., Rocky Mountain Conf., Utah Assn. United Ch. of Christ, 1970-78, 82—, Ind. Coun. Chs., 1960-63; chmn. comm. Ch. Women United Utah, 1974-78, Ogden rep., 1980—, hostess Northern Utah, 1998. Editor: Sunshine and Moonscapes: An Anthology of Essays, Poems, Short Stories, 1994, (booklet) Family Counseling Service: Thirty Years of Service to Northern Utah, 1996; contbr. numerous articles and essays to religious and other publs. Pres. T.O. Smith Sch. PTA, 1976-78, Ogden City Coun. PTA, 1983-85; assoc. dir. Region II, Utah PTA, Salt Lake City, 1981-83, mem. State Edn. Commn., 1982-87; chmn. state internat. hospitality and aid Utah Fedn. Women's Clubs, 1982-86; v.p. Ogden dist., 1990-92, pres. Ogden dist., 1992-96, state resolutions com., 1996—; trustee Family Counseling Svc. No. Utah, Ogden, 1983-95, emeritus trustee, 1995—; Utah rep. to nat. bd. Challenger Films, Inc., 1986—; state pres. Rocky Mountain Conf. Women in Mission, United Ch. of Christ, 1974-77, sec., 1981-84, vice moderator Utah Assn., 1992-94. Recipient Ecumenical Svc. citation Ind. Coun. Chs., 1962, Outstanding Local Pres. award Utah PTA, 1978, Outstanding Latchkey Child Project award, 1985, Cmty. Svc. award City of Ogden, 1980, 81, 82, Celebration of Gifts of Lay Woman Nat. award United Ch. of Christ, 1987, Excellence in the Arts in Art Edn. award Ogden City Arts Commn., 1993, Spirit of Am. Woman in Arts and Humanities award Your Cmty. Connection, Ogden, 1994; Utah Endowment for Humanities grantee, 1981, 81-82. Mem. Nat. League Am. Penwomen (chmn. Utah conv. 1973, 11 awards for articles and essays 1987-95, 1st pl. news award 1992, 1st pl. short stories 1997, 3d pl. articles 1997), AAUW (state edn. rep. 1982-86), League of Utah Writers (Publ. Quill award 1998). Democrat. Avocation: building miniature world of peace each Christmas by family in the home. Home and Office: 722 Boughton St Ogden UT 84403-1152

HARRINGTON, WALTER HOWARD, JR., judge; b. San Francisco, Aug. 14, 1926; s. Walter Howard and Doris Ellen (Daniels) H.; BS, Stanford, 1947; JD, Hastings Coll., U. Calif., 1952; m. Barbara Bryant, June 1952 (div. 1973); children: Stacey Doreen, Sara Duval; m. 2d, Hertha Bahrs, Sept. 1974. Admitted to Calif. bar, 1953; dep. legislative counsel State of Calif., Sacramento, 1953-54, 55; mem. firm Walner & Harrington, Sacramento, 1954; dep. dist. atty. San Mateo County, Redwood City, Calif., 1955-62; pvt. practice in Redwood City, 1962-84; judge San Mateo County Mcpl. Ct., 1984-90, Superior Ct., 1990-96. Chmn., San Mateo County Criminal Justice Council, 1971-76, San Mateo County Adult Correctional Facilities Com., 1969-71; pro tem referee San Mateo County Juvenile Ct., 1967-72. Ensign USNR, 1944-46. Mem. San Mateo County Bar Assn. (pres. 1969, editor publs. 1964-74), State Bar Calif. (editorial bd. 1968-81, vice chmn. 1969, 74-75, chmn., editor 1975-76), San Mateo County Legal Aid Soc. (pres. 1971-72), Order of Coif, Delta Theta Phi. Republican. Episcopalian. Office: Hall of Justice 400 County Ctr Redwood City CA 94063-1636

HARRIS, BARBARA HULL (MRS. F. CHANDLER HARRIS), social agency administrator; b. L.A., Nov. 1, 1921; d. Hamilton and Marion (Eimers) Baird; m. F. Chandler Harris, Aug. 10, 1946; children: Victoria, Randolph Boyd. Pres., Victoria Originals, 1955-62. Student, UCLA, 1939-41, 45-47. Ptnr.J.B. Assocs., cons., 1971-73; statewide dir. vols. Children's Home Soc. Calif., 1971-73. L.A. County Heart Sunday chmn. L.A. County Heart Assn., 1965, bd. dirs., 1966-69; mem. exec. com. Hollywood Bowl Vols., 1966-84, chmn. vols., 1971, 75; chmn. Coll. Alumni of Assistance League, 1962; mem. exec. com. Assistance League So. Calif., 1964-71, 72-80, 83-89, pres., 1976-80; bd. dirs. Nat. Charity League, L.A., 1965-69, 75, sec., 1967, 3d v.p., 1968; ways and means chmn., dir. L.A. Am. Horse Show, 1969; dir. Coronet Debutante Ball, 1968, ball bd. chmn., 1969-70, 75, 84, 96—, mem. ball bd., 1969—; pres. Hollywood Bowl Patroness com., 1976; v.p. Irving Walker aux. Travelers Aid, 1976, 79, pres., 1988-89; pres. So. Calif. alumni council Alpha Phi, 1961, fin. adviser to chpts. U. So. Calif., 1961-72, UCLA, 1965-72; benefit chmn. Gold Shield, 1969, 1st v.p., 1970-72; chmn. Golden Thimble III Needlework Exhbn., Hosp. of Good Samaritan, 1975; bd. dirs. UCLA Affiliates, 1976-78, KCET Women's Council, 1979-83, Region V United Way, 1980-83; pres. Jr. Philharmonic Com., 1981-82; bd. dirs. L.A. Founder chpt. Achievement Rewards for Coll. Scientists, 1980-91, pres., 1984-85; pres. L.A. County chpt. Freedom Found. of Valley Forge; mem. com. for the Hollywood Bowl 75 yr. history, 1994-96. Recipient Outstanding Svc. award L.A. County Heart Assn., 1965, Outstanding Alumna Ivy award Alpha Phi, 1969, Outstanding Alumni award for community service UCLA, 1978, Mannequin's Eve award, 1980, Outstanding Bd. Mem. of Yr. award Assistance League of So. Calif., 1989-90. Mem. Hollywood C. of C. (dir. 1980-81). Home: 7774 Skyhill Dr Los Angeles CA 90068-1232

HARRIS, BILL H., computer software company executive. Pres., CEO Intuit, Inc., Mountain View, Calif. Office: 2535 Garcia Ave Mountain View CA 94043-1111

HARRIS, CLAUDE, fire department chief. Fire chief Seattle Fire Dept., ret., 1996. Office: Seattle Fire Dept Office of the Chief 301 2nd Ave S Seattle WA 98104-2680

HARRIS, DALE RAY, lawyer; b. Crab Orchard, Ill., May 11, 1937; s. Ray B. and Aurelia M. (Davis) H.; m. Toni K. Shapkoff, June 26, 1960; children: Kristen Dee, Julie Diane. BA in Math., U. Colo., 1959; LLB, Harvard U., 1962. Bar: Colo. 1962, U.S. Dist. Ct. Colo. 1962, U.S. Ct. Appeals (10th cir.) 1962, U.S. Supreme Ct. 1981. Assoc. Davis, Graham & Stubbs, Denver, 1962-67, ptnr., 1967—, chmn. mgmt. com., 1982-85; spkr., instr. various antitrust seminars; bd. dirs. Lend-A-Lawyer, Inc., 1989-94. Mem. campaign cabinet Mile High United Way, 1986-87, chmn., atty. adv. com., 1988, sec., legal counsel, trustee, mem. exec. com. 1989-94, chmn. bd. trustees, 1996, 97; trustee The Spaceship Earth Fund, 1986-89; trustee, Legal Aid Found. Colo., 1989-95; mem. devel. coun. U. Colo. Arts & Scis. dept., 1985-93; area chmn. law sch. fund Harvard U., 1978-81; bd. dirs. Colo. Jud. Inst., 1994— (vice chair 1998—), Colo. Lawyers Trust Account Found., 1996—; steering com. Youth-At-Work, 1994, School-To-Work, 1995. With USAR, 1962-68. Fellow Am. Bar Found.; mem. ABA (antitrust and litigation sects., Colo. State chmn., 1998—), Colo. Bar Found., Colo. Bar Assn. (chmn. antitrust com. 1980-84; coun. corp. banking and bus. law sect. 1978-83, bd. govs. 1991-95, exec. com. 1993-94, chmn. family violence task force 1996—, pres.-elect, 1999), Denver Bar Assn. (chmn. Centennial Com. 1990-91, pres.-elect 1992-93, pres. 1993-94, bd. trustees 1992-95, Merit award, 1997), Colo. Assn. Corp. Counsel (pres. 1973-74), Denver Law Club (pres. 1976-77, Lifetime Achievement award, 1997), The Two Percent Club (exec. com., 1994—), Citizens Against Amendment 12 Com. (exec. com. 1994). Phi Beta Kappa, Univ. Club, Rotary (Denver). Home: 2032 Bellaire St Denver CO 80207-3722 Office: Davis Graham & Stubbs 370 17th St PO Box 185 Denver CO 80201-0185

HARRIS, DAVID JACK, artist, painter, educator; b. San Mateo, Calif., Jan. 6, 1948; s. Jack McAllister and Audrey Ellen (Vogt) H. BA, San Francisco State U., 1971, MA, 1975. Dir. Galerie de Tours, San Francisco, 1971-72; lectr. Chabot Coll., Hayward, Calif., 1975-80; interior designer David Harris Assocs., San Mateo, 1975-85; freelance artist, painter San Mateo, 1975—; ptnr. Harris & Kasten, Archs. & Designers, 1990—; art cons. David Harris Assocs., Belmont, Calif., 1980—; v.p. Coastal Arts League Mus., Half Moon Bay, Calif., 1988—; ptnr., art dir. Fine Art Pub., Palo Alto, Calif., 1989—; bd. dirs. 1870 Gallery and Studios, Belmont, 1978—, gallery dir., 1989—, owner, partner HSW Gallery, San Francisco. Painter murals Chartered Bank of London, 1979, Caesar's Hotel, Las Vegas, 1984, Pacific Telephone, San Francisco; author mus. catalog California Concepts, 1988; represented in permanent collections at Ask Computer, Palo Alto, shared Fin., Harris Corp., Bain and Co., San Francisco, Verilink, Litton Industries, Foothill Bank, Los Altos, Chartered Bank of London, San Francisco, Stanford U., Palo Alto, Golden Nugget Hotel, Atlantic City, Nat. Bank of Detroit, Crisafi, Sciabica, Woodward, D.J. Crisafi and Co., Sheraton Grande, L.A., 1st am. Title Guaranty Co., Walt Disney, Voysys Corp., Spieker Pntrs., Storm & Co., Menlo Park, Calif., Royal family, Saudi Arabia, others. Recipient Purchase award North Cen. Washington Mus., 1988. Mem. Internat. Soc. Interior Designers, Coastal Arts League Mus. (v.p. 1988—, Zoe Tierny award 1988). Avocations: travel, photography, hiking. Home and Office: 485 Miramar Half Moon Bay CA 94019

HARRIS, DAVID JAKE, writer, educator; b. Phila., June 2, 1945; s. Herbert Harris and Gertrude (Ansel) Cohen; 1 child, Morgan Lee; m. Cindy Lee Muntwyler, Apr. 25, 1976 (div. Feb. 1995). BSBA, N.Y. Inst. Tech., 1969. Lic. massage technician Oreg. Bd. Massage Technicians. Gen. contractor Basic Home Repair, Eugene, Oreg., 1971-78; ptnr. Back Therapy Rehab. Ctr. Herwyler Ctr., Eugene, 1978-91; freelance writer, 1992—; coord. Solar Ctr., U. Oreg., Eugene, 1974-75; tchr. Lane C.C., Eugene, 1975-76, 98. Author: Almost Anyone Can Ride a Bike, 1995, And, Poseidon Smiled, 1996, Tales From the Plumbing Zone, 1997; song writer (song book) Songs With You in Mind, 1992; art and entertainment editor Torch, 1994-95. Tchr. cmty. plumbing workshops Project Self-Reliance, Eugene, 1976. Mem. Rails to Trails Conservancy, Sierra Club, Willamette Writers. Avocations: blues keyboard playing, sailing, adventure activities, spiritual exploration.

HARRIS, DAVID JOEL, financial planner; b. Miller, S.D., Sept. 22, 1950; s. Joel Chips and Amy Ruth (Rietz) H.; m. Susan Claire Hagius, June 30, 1979 (div. 1997); children: John, Jennifer. BA, Earlham Coll., Richmond, Ind., 1972; MS, Purdue U., 1975; PhD, U. Hawaii, 1983. Vis. rsch. asst. Internat. Ctr. Tropical Agr., Cali, Colombia, 1975-76; sr. rsch. fellow Internat. Ctr. Tropical Agr., 1984-87; rsch. assoc. U. Hawaii, Honolulu, 1976-83; sr. rsch. fellow Internat. Ctr. Tropical Agr., 1984-87; mgr. Calif.-Nev. United Meth. Found., San Francisco, 1988-92; exec. v.p. Calif.-Nev. United Meth. Found., Sacramento, 1992-97; charitable trust planner Legacy Solutions, Santa Rosa, Calif., 1997—; treas. Nat. Assn. United Meth. Found., 1992-94. Contbr. articles to profl. jours. Pres. Mothers Against Drunk Driving, Sonoma County, Calif., 1989-91. Grad. fellow Purdue U., 1972, fellow NSF, 1973, 75-77. Mem. Nat. Com. on Planned Giving, Commonwealth Club Calif., Phi Beta Kappa. Methodist. Avocations: travel, computers, dogs, environment. Home: 355 Gemma Cir Santa Rosa CA 95404-2733 Office: David Harris Co Legacy Sols 1275 4th St Ste 388 Santa Rosa CA 95404-4049

HARRIS, DAVID THOMAS, immunology educator; b. Jonesboro, Ark., May 9, 1956; s. Marm Melton and Lucille Luretha (Buck) H.; m. Francoise Jacqueline Besencon, June 24, 1989; children: Alexandre M., Stefanie L., Leticia M. BS in Biology, Math. and Psychology, Wake Forest U., 1978, MS, 1980, PhD in Microbiology and Immunology, 1982. Fellow Ludwig Inst. Cancer Rsch., Lausanne, Switzerland, 1982-85; rsch. asst. prof. U. N.C., Chapel Hill, 1985-89; assoc. prof. U. Ariz., Tucson, 1989-96, prof., 1996—; cons. Teltech, Inc. Mpls., 1990—, Advanced Biosci. Resources, 1994-95; bd. sci. advisors Cryo-Cell Internat., 1992-95; bd. dirs. Ageria, Inc., Tuscon; dir. Cord Blood Stem Cell Bank, 1992—; mem. Ariz. Cancer Ctr., Steele Meml. Children's Rsch. Ctr., Ariz. Arthritis Ctr. Program, sci. adv. bd. Cord Blood Registry, Inc., chief sci. div. Cord Blood Registry, Inc. Coauthor chpts. to sci. books, articles to profls. jours.; reviewer sci. jours.; coholder 4 scientific patents. Grantee local and fed. rsch. grants, 1988—. Mem. AAAS, Am. Assn. Immunologists, Reticuleondothelial Soc., Internat. Soc. Hematotherapy and Graft Engring., Internat. Soc. Devel. and Comparative Immunology, Scandanavian Soc. Immunology, Sigma Xi,. Democrat. Mem. Ch. of Christ. Avocations: tennis, hiking, jogging, skiing, travel. Office: U Ariz Dept Microbiology Bldg 90 Tucson AZ 85721

HARRIS, DEL WILLIAM, professional basketball coach; b. Plainfield, Ind., June 18, 1937. BA, Milligan Coll., Tenn., 1959; MA, Ind. U., 1965. Ordained minister, Christian Ch., 1958. High sch. coach, 1959-64; head basketball coach Earlham Coll., Richmond, Ind., 1965-74; asst. coach Utah Stars, Am. Basketball Assn., 1974-75, U. Utah, 1975-76; asst. coach Houston Rockets, NBA, 1976-79, basketball coach, 1979-83; scout Milw. Bucks, Nat. Basketball Assn., 1983-86, asst. coach, 1986-87, head coach, 1987-91; v.p. ops. Milw. Bucks, from 1987; head coach Los Angeles Lakers, 1994—; asst. coach Team USA World Games, 1998; speaker on motivation Intercon-

tinental Tng. Systems Inc., 1982-84. Author: Multiple Defenses, 1971, Zone Offense, 1975, Winning Defense, 1995; juvenile novel Playing the Game, 1982; appeared in (movie) Space Jam, 1996, (TV) Diagnosis Murder, 1996, In the House, 1997 (TV), Over The Top, 1997 (TV). Bd. dirs. Wis. Leukemia Soc., 1989, Milw. Athletes Against Childhood Cancer Fund; hon. chairperson Easter Seals Milw. High Sch. Classic, Vince Lombardi Golf Classic, Leukemia 6 Hours for Life Telethon; spokesperson St. Francis Children's Ctr., Milw., Spl. Olympics. Recipient Disting. Houstonian award, 1981, Coach of Yr. award NBA, 1995; Eli Lilly fellow, 1965. Office: Los Angeles Lakers PO Box 10 3900 W Manchester Blvd Inglewood CA 90306*

HARRIS, ELIHU MASON, mayor; b. L.A., Aug. 15, 1947; m. Kathy Neal, Aug. 14, 1982. BS in Polit. Sci. with honors, Calif. State U., 1968; M in Pub. Adminstrn., U. Calif., Berkeley, 1969; JD, U. Calif., Davis, 1972. Bar: Calif., D.C. Pvt. practice Calif., 1977-78; formerly mem. Calif. Legis. Assembly, from 1978; now mayor City of Oakland, Calif.; prof. pol. sci. and adminstrn. of justice Calif. State U., Hayward and Sacramento campuses. Former chmn. Joint Legis. Audit Com., Assembly Com. on Fair Employment Practices and the Select Com. on Judicial Efficiency and Improvement, also former mem. Ways and Means, Judiciary, and Health and Transp. coms.; mem. Niagara Movement Dem. Club. Dr. Martin Luther King Rsch. fellow U. Calif. Davis Sch. Law; finalist White House Fellowships competition, 1977-78. Mem. ABA (exec. dir. 1975-77), NAACP, Charles Houston Bar Assn., Calif. Assn. Black Lawyers, Black Am. Polit. Assn. Calif. (former chmn.), Kappa Alpha Psi. Office: Office of Mayor 1 City Hall Plz Oakland CA 94612-1932

HARRIS, EMMA EARL, nursing home executive; b. Viper, Ky., Nov. 6, 1936; d. Andrew Jackson and Zola (Hall) S. children: Debra, Joseph, Wynona, Robert Walsh. Grad. St. Joseph Sch. Practical Nursing. Staff nurse St. Joseph Hosp., Bangor, Maine, 1973-75; office nurse Dr. Eugene Brown, Bangor, 1975-77; dir. nurses Fairborn Nursing Home, Ohio, 1977-78; staff nurse Hillhaven Hospice, Tucson, 1979-80; asst. head nurse, 1980. Author: Thoughts on Life, 1988. Vol. Heart Assn., Bangor, 1965-70, Cancer Assn., Bangor, 1965-70. Mem. NAFE. Democrat. Avocations: theatre, opera. Home: 2818 N Campbell Ave # 232 Tucson AZ 85719-2811

HARRIS, F. CHANDLER, retired university administrator; b. Neligh, Nebr., Nov. 5, 1914; s. James Carlton and Helen Ayres (Boyd) H.; m. Barbara Ann Hull, Aug. 10, 1946; children: Victoria Williams, Randolph Boyd. AB, UCLA, 1936. Assoc. editor Telegraph Delivery Spirit, L.A., 1937-39; writer, pub. svc. network radio programs Univ. Explorer, Sci. Editor, U. Calif., 1939-61; pub. info. mgr. UCLA, 1961-75, dir., 1975-82, dir. emeritus, 1982—. Mem. pub. rels. com., western region United Way, 1972-75; bd. dirs. Am. Youth Symphony, L.A., 1978-98, v.p., 1983-98; bd. dirs. Hathaway Home for Children, 1982-88. Recipient 1st prize NBC Radio Inst., 1944; Harvey Hebert medal Delta Sigma Phi, 1947, Mr. Delta Sig award, 1972; Adam award Assistance League Mannequins, 1980, Univ. Service award UCLA Alumni Assn., 1986; bd. dirs. Western L.A. Regional C. of C., 1976-80. Mem. U. Calif. Retirees Assn. L.A. (pres. 1985-87), Sigma Delta Chi, Delta Sigma Phi (nat. pres. 1959-63), UCLA Faculty Club (sec. bd. govs. 1968-72). Editor Interfraternity Rsch. Adv. Coun. Bull., 1949-50, Carnation, 1969-80, Royce Hall, 1985. Home: 7774 Skyhill Dr Los Angeles CA 90068-1232

HARRIS, FRED ORIN, retired director; b. Sumpter, Oreg., Jan. 24, 1901; s. Orin Icabod and Mary Ellen (Murphy) H.; m. Mary Harris, July 26, 1931 (dec. Jan. 1994). BFA cum laude, U. Wash., 1924; MA, N.Y.U., 1939. With wife, dir. of plays mainly for student U. Calif., Berkeley, 1940-69; ret., 1969; advisor Auditorium Theater (honor roll U. Calif. Berkeley Centennial Yr.); play dir. Bohemian Club, 1942-80 (List of 50). Author: (unpublished) Letters to a Young Director (in the Bancroft Libr., U.S. Berkeley). Democrat. Episcopalian. *Died Aug. 28, 1998.*

HARRIS, FREDERICK PHILIP, retired philosophy educator; b. Portland, Oreg., Aug. 28, 1911; s. Philip Henry and Nellie Louise (Humpage) H.; m. Hester Almira Larson, July 15, 1943; children: Judith, Jacquelyn, Jennifer, Elizabeth, Marcia, Frederick (dec.). AB, Willamette U., 1935; MA, Columbia U., 1937, PhD, 1944; cert. in Japanese, U. Mich., 1944. Tutor Horace Mann Sch. for Boys, N.Y.C., 1935-41; instr. English Rutgers U., New Brunswick, N.J., 1941-42; psychologist Bur. Psychol. Svcs., U. Mich., Ann Arbor, 1946; assoc. prof. philosophy Case Western Res. U., Cleve., 1946-55, chmn. dept., 1948-57; headmaster Am. Sch. in Japan, Tokyo, 1957-66; prof. Oreg. State U., Corvallis, 1967-80, chmn. dept. philosophy, 1967-76; Fulbright vis. prof. faculty edn. Kyoto (Japan) U., 1955-57; prof. Rockefeller Found. Am. Studies Seminar, Doshisha U. Japan, 1956; vis. prof. U. Oreg., Eugene, summer 1950, U. Hawaii, Honolulu, summer 1966, Lewis & Clark Coll., Portland, 1966-67; dir. Oreg. Study Ctr. Waseda U., Tokyo, 1977-80; vis. prof. Grad. Sch. Commerce Waseda U., 1980, Open Coll., 1982-92; pres. Tokyo Internat. Co., 1986 92; advisor Japan Intercultural Comm. Soc., Tokyo, 1980-82. Author: The Neo-Idealist Political Theory, 1944; editor: The Teaching of Philosophy, 1950; editor Perspectives, Japan Intercultural Comm. Soc., 1981-82. Trustee Internat. Sch., Nagoya, Japan, 1963-66, Sendai Am. Sch., Japan, 1963-65. Staff sgt. U.S. Army, 1942-45. Fulbright grantee Kyoto U., 1955, 56; Frederick Philip Harris Libr. named in his honor Am. Sch. in Japan, Tokyo, 1966. Mem. Am. Philos. Assn., Asiatic Soc. Japan (counselor 1986-89), Japan English Forensics Assn., Dem. Nat. Com., Common Cause, Nature Conservancy, Wilderness Soc., Nat. Wildlife Fedn. Methodist. Avocations: swimming, hiking, mountain climbing, pottery, travel. Home: 3050 SW Ridgewood Ave Portland OR 97225-3363

HARRIS, GWEN MOYERS, artist, homemaker; b. Ardmore, Okla., Oct. 7, 1924; d. Earl Claude and Iva May (Benson) Moyers; m. Howard Hunter Harris, Dec. 31, 1945; children: Howard Sidney, Rodney Craig. BA, U. Okla., 1947; postgrad. studies, U. Tulsa, 1962, Findlay Coll., 1963-65; BFA, Bowling Green State U., 1974; postgrad. studies, Toledo U./ Toledo Mus. of Art, 1977-78. Artist: works exhibited in juried shows: (drawings) Findlay (Ohio) Coll. Student Art Exhibit, 1964 (1st pl.), Bowling Green (Ohio) State U., 1972 (1st pl.), Hancock County Show, Findlay, 1977 (merit, purchase award); (paintings) Findlay Coll. Student Art Exhibit, 1964 (1st pl.), Lima (Ohio) Art Assn. Show (Doris Brown Meml. award), 1965, Bowling Green State U., 1974 (2d pl.), Hancock County Show, Findlay, (purchase award 1978, merit award 1979); (collages) Hancock County Show, 1981 (1st pl.), Findlay Area Arts Coun., 1982, 84, Nat. Coll. Soc., Hudson, Ohio, 1985 (signatory mem., Judges Spl. merit award 1988, merit award 1996), Findlay Art League, 1987, (1st pl.); (photography) Findlay Art League Photo (1981 2 awards, 1982 1st pl., 1983 3 awards, 1984 2d pl., Honorable Mention, 1985 2 awards, 1986 Photo Ctr. award), Wassenberg Photo Exhbn., Van Wert, Ohio, 1982 (1st pl.), Festival, Findlay, 1982 (1st pl.), 1984 (Best of Show), Toledo Area Artists' Ann. Exhbt, 1984 (2d pl.), Women Alive, 1986 (Elizabeth Norse award). Mem. Nat. Collage Soc., Shemer Art Ctr. Republican. Episcopalian.

HARRIS, HARRY H., television director; b. Kansas City, Mo., Sept. 8, 1922; s. Harry Howard Sr. and Jennie Harris; m. Patricia A. Pulici, Aug. 18, 1939; children: Susanne and Joanne. Student, UCLA, 1940-41. film editor Desilu Prodns., 1949-57. Prodr., dir. (TV movie): Eight is Enough Reunion, 1987; dir (TV movies): Alice in Wonderland, 1984, The Waltons Thanksgiving Special, 1993, The Runaways, 1974, Swiss Family Robinson,1976, Rivkin Bounty Hunter, 1980, The Young Pioneers, 1978; dir. (TV pilots): House Detective, 1985, Private Life of T.K. Dearing, 1975, Carousel Horse, 1986 (Emmy nomination), Kowalski Loves Ya, 1986, Tom Swift, 1982, Apple's Way, 1975, The Home Front, 1980, Scamps, 1969; dir (TV episodes): In the Heat of the Night, 1988-93, Remington Steele, 1984-88, Magnum P.I., 1985-88, Cagney & Lacey, 1983, Bodies of Evidence, 1992, Spenser for Hire, Jake and the Fatman, 1991, MacGyver, 1989-90, Father Dowling Mysteries, 1990, Scarecrow and Mrs. King, 1984, Hawaii 5-0, 1976, Blue Knight, 1985, Hunter, 1976, Oldest Rookie, 1987, Naked City, 1972, Mission Impossible, 1972, Perry Mason, 1972, Shell Game, 1976, Shaft, 1975, The D.A., Adam-12, 1974, T.H.E. Cat, 1965, Fame, 1982 (Emmy award 1982), The Waltons, 1972-82 (Emmy award nominee 1973, Humanitas award 1976), Eight is Enough, 1977-80, Our House, 1986, Boone, Apple's Way, 1975, Sisters, 1992-96 (Genesis award 1992, Golden Reel award 1995), Tom Swift, 1982, Falcon Crest, 1982-87, Dallas, 1981, 85, Hotel, 1983, Kung-Fu, 1975, A Fine Romance, 1989, Nurse, 1981, Mississippi, 1983, Supercarrier, 1988, Love American Style, 1968, Doc Elliot, 1975, Gibbsville, 1976, Spencer's Pilots, 1976, The Islanders, 1959, McCall of the Wild, 1989, Hearts are Wild, 1982, Dante's Inferno, 1968, Stick With Me Kid, 1994, The Cape, 1996, 7th Heaven, 1988-89, Beverly Hills 90210, 1988-89, Eight Is Enough Reunion, 1987, University Hospital, 1994-95, Savannah, 1995, Dr. Quinn Medicine Woman, 1994, Gunsmoke, 1961-66, Guns of Paradise, 1991, Wanted Dead or Alive, 1958-60, Rawhide, 1963-64, Jesse James, 1963, Wells Fargo, High Chapparral, 1967-70, Bonanza, 1968, Daniel Boone, 1964-68, Pistols N' Petticoats, 1967, Hondo, 1968, Stagecoach West, 1959, MacKenzies of Paradise Cove, 1978, Swiss Family Robinson, 1976, Man from Atlantis, 1977, Voyage to the Bottom of the Sea, 1968-72, Land of the Giants, 1968-70, Lost in Space, 1965-68, Time Tunnel, 1966, Road West, 1969, The Texan, 1958-59, Death Valley Days, 1968, Man Called Shenandoah, 1965, The Virginian, 1970, Men of Shiloh, 1970, Branded, 1964-66, Young Pioneers, 1978. 2nd Lt. USAF, 1944. Mem. Dirs. Guild Am., Motion Picture Film Editors (life). Avocation: amateur radio.

HARRIS, HOWARD JEFFREY, marketing and printing company executive; b. Denver, June 9, 1949; s. Gerald Victor and Leona Lee (Tepper) H.; m. Michele Whealen, Feb. 6, 1975; children: Kimberly, Valerie. BFA with honors, Kansas City Art Inst., 1973; M of Indsl. Design with honors, Pratt Inst., 1975; postgrad. Graphic Arts Rsch. Ctr., Rochester Inst. Tech., 1977; cert. mktg. exec., U. Utah, 1987. Indsl. designer Kivett & Myers, Architects, 1970-71; indsl. designer United Rsch. Corp., Denver, 1971-72; indsl. designer, asst. to v.p., pres. JFN Assos., N.Y.C., 1972-73; dir. facility planning Abt & Assos., Cambridge, Mass., 1973-74; v.p. design, prodn., and rsch. Eagle Direct, Denver, 1974—; pres. Eagle Direct, Denver. Vol., chmn. dirs. Stepping Stones (multi-religious orgn.). Recipient SBA Small Bus. Person of the Year award for Ste of Colo., 1997. Mem. Indsl. Designers Soc. Am., Graphic Arts Tech. Found., Design Methods Group, Cable TV Adminstrn. Mktg. Assn., Mail Advt. Assn., Am. Advt. Fedn., Nat. Assn. Printers and Lithographers (bd. dirs., chmn. mktg. com.). Democrat. Jewish. Office: 5105 E 41st Ave Denver CO 80216-4420

HARRIS, JAMES MICHAEL, sales executive; b. San Francisco, Mar. 24, 1947; s. Alfred James and Pearl Olga (Slavich) H.; m. Vivian Toni Ferrara, Mar. 20, 1987 (div. Mar. 1992); 1 child, Michael James. BA, San Diego State U., 1971. Rsch. assoc. San Diego State U., 1971-73; assoc. dir. San Diego Taxpayers Assn., 1973-75, exec. dir., 1976-79; govt. rels. dir. Rohr Industries, San Diego, 1975-76; chief of staff City of San Diego, 1979-83; CEO Harris & Lee, San Diego, 1983-90; exec. dir. San Diego Auto Mus., 1990-96; dir. corp. sales Rely, Inc., San Diego, 1996—; cons. Souplantation Restaurants, San Diego, 1977-83, Fuego Zero, San Diego, 1989-90, Couveé Comm., San Diego, 1989-90, Deanna Kay Products, Carlsbad, Calif., 1989-90; bd. dirs. Ctrl. Balboa Park Assn., Inter-Mus. Promotional Coun. Rschr. (book) Public Finance in the San Diego S.M.S.A., 1972, Shifting Public Functions and the Distribution of Tax Burden by Economic Class, 1972. Bd. dirs. Alumni Assn. San Diego State U., 1977-79; San Diego county coord. Yes on Lottery Campaign, Woodward/McDowell, San Diego, 1984; expert witness San Diego County Grand Jury, 1977, 78; charter rev. com. mem. San Diego County, 1984. Recipient 20 Outstanding Young Citizens of San Diego award San Diego Jr. C. of C., 1977, Man of Distinction award San Diegans Inc., 1979. Avocation: old cars. Office: 1610 Windsor St San Diego CA 92103

HARRIS, JAY TERRENCE, newspaper editor; b. Washington, Dec. 3, 1948; s. Richard James and Margaret Estelle (Burr) H.; m. Eliza Melinda Dowell, June 14, 1969 (div.); 1 child, Taifa Akida; m. Anna Christine Harris, Oct. 25, 1980; children: Jamarah Kai, Shala Marie. BA, Lincoln U., 1970, LHD (hon.), 1988. Reporter Wilmington (Del.) News-Jour., 1970-73, spl. project editor, 1974-75; instr. journalism and urban affairs Medill Sch. Journalism, Northwestern U., Evanston, Ill., 1973-75, asst. prof., 1975-82, asst. dean, 1977-82; nat. corr. Gannett News Service, Washington, 1982-84, columnist Gannet newspapers and USA Today, 1984-85; exec. editor Phila. Daily News, 1985—; v.p. Phila. Newspapers, Inc., 1987—; chmn., pub. San Jose Mercury News, 1995—; asst. dir. Frank E. Gannett Urban Journalism Ctr., Northwestern U., 1977-82; founder, exec. dir. Consortium for Advancement of Minorities in Journalism Edn., Evanston, 1978-81; dir. Dow Jones Newspaper Fund, Princeton, N.J., 1980—; bd. visitors John S. Knight Profl. Journalism Fellowships, Palo Alto, Calif., 1982—, head Minorities and Communication Div. Assn. for Edn. in Journalism, 1982-83. Author: (annual census) Minority Employment in Daily Newspapers, 1978-82; co-author series articles on drug trafficking in Wilmington, 1972 (Pub. Service awards AP Mng. Editors Assn. 1972, Greater Phila. chpt. Sigma Delta Chi 1973). Past mem. bd. advisors Sch. Journalism U. Mo. Frank E. Gannett Urban Journalism fellow, 1973-74; recipient Pub. Service award Greater Phila. chpt. Sigma Delta Chi, 1973; Pub. Service award AP Mng. Editors Assn., 1972; Spl. Citation Nat. Urban Coalition, 1979; Par Excellence Disting. Service in Journalism award Operation PUSH, 1984; Drum Maj. for Justice award Southern Christian Leadership Conf., 1985. Mem. Am. Soc. Newspaper Editors (chmn. readership and rsch. com.), Women in Communication, Nat. Assn. Black Journalists, Omega Psi Phi. Office: San Jose Mercury News 750 Ridder Park Dr San Jose CA 95190*

HARRIS, JEFFREY SAUL, physician executive, consultant; b. Pitts., Mar. 13, 1949; s. Aaron Wexler and Janet Mary (Szerlip) Harris; m. Mary V. Anderson, Jan. 2, 1981; children: Sarah Ariel, Noah Aaron, Susannah Leia. BS in Molecular Biophysics/Biochemistry, Yale U., 1971; MD, U. N.Mex., 1975; MPH, U. Mich., 1982; MBA, Vanderbilt U., 1988. Diplomate Am. Bd. Preventive Medicine in Occupl. Medicine & Gen. Preventive Medicine & Pub. Health, Am. Bd. Emergency Medicine, Am. Bd. Medicine Quality, Am. Bd. Ind. Med. Examination; lic. Md., Calif., Tenn., Alaska. Gen. med. officer USPHS, Juneau, Alaska, 1976-78; clin. dir. S.E. Alaska Native Health Corp., Juneau, 1978-79; asst. to commr. Tenn. Dept. Health and Environment, Nashville, 1980-83; dir. health care mgmt. Northern Telecom Inc., Nashville, 1983-88; pres. HDM, Inc., Nashville, 1988-90; med. dir. Aetna Health Plans of Tenn., Nashville, 1990-91; leader nat. practice, health strategy Alexander & Alexander Cons. Group, San Francisco, 1991-94; chief prevention, health and disability officer Indsl. Indemnity, San Francisco, 1994-97; pres. J. Harris Assocs., Inc., Mill Valley, Calif., 1979—. Author: Strategic Health Management, 1994, Best Practices in Occupational Medicine, 1999, Integrated Health Management, 1998; author, editor: Managing Employee Health Care Costs, 1992, Occupational Medicine Practice Guidelines: Evaluation and Management of Common Health Problems and Functional Recovery in Workers, 1997, Quick Reference to Practice Guidelines in Occupational Medicine, 1998, Managed Care in Occupational Medicine, 1998; author, co-editor: Manual of Occupational Health and Safety, 1992, 96, Health Promotion in the Work Place, 1994, Integrated Health Management, 1998; mem. editl. bd. Am. Jour. Health Promotion, 1985—, Occupl. Environment Med. Report, 1988—; contbg. editor JAMA, Am. Jour. Pub. Health, 1988—; contbr. articles to profl. jours. Fellow Am. Acad. Family Practice, Am. Coll. Occupl. Environ. Medicine (dir., chmn. practice guidelines com., Presdl. award 1996), Am. Coll. Preventive Medicine, Am. Coll. Med. Quality, Am. Bd. Ind. Med. Examiners. Avocations: skiing, running, playing music, painting, writing children's stories. Home: 386 Richardson Way Mill Valley CA 94941-4053 Office: J Harris Assocs Inc 386 Richardson Way Mill Valley CA 94941-4053

HARRIS, JEREMY, mayor; s. Ann Harris; m. Ramona Sachiko Akui Harris. BA, BS in Marine Biology, U. Hawaii, 1972; M in Population and Environmental Biology and Urban Ecosystems, U. Calif., Irvine. Lectr. oceanography, biology Kauai C.C.; instr. on reef walks on Kauai U. Hawaii Sea Grant Program; del. Hawaii Constl. Conv., 1978; chmn. Kauai County Council; exec. asst. to Mayor Frank F. Fasi City and County of Honolulu, 1985-86, mng. dir. of Honolulu, 1986-94, mayor, 1994—. Named Pub. Adminstr. of Yr. Am. Soc. Pub. Adminstrn., 1993, 94; recipient Merit award Internat. Downtown Assn., others. Office: Office of the Mayor 530 S King St Rm 300 Honolulu HI 96813-3019*

HARRIS, LARRY B., academic administrator, dean; b. Kingman, Kans., May 25, 1947; s. Loren M. and Beatrice A. (Reinoldt) H.; m. Carmen E. Glidewell, June 15, 1968; children: Todd J., Ryan M., Kelly R., Kyle D. BA, Friends U., 1969; MEd, Wichita State U., 1977; PhD, Kans. State U., 1985. English/reading tchr. Wichita Pub. Schs., 1970-77, Haven (Kans.) Pub. Schs., 1977-78; instr. Wichita State U., 1978-83; asst. prof. Mount Marty Coll., Yankton, S.D., 1985-87; assoc. prof., prof., divsn. head Wayne (Nebr.) State Coll., 1987-93; dean Sch. Edn. U. Ark., Monticello, 1993-97; dean Coll. Edn. Idaho State U., Pocatello, 1997—. Active Boy Scouts Am., Yankton, 1987. Mem. Phi Delta Kappa (pres. 1992-93), Kappa Delta Pi, Phi Kappa Phi. Avocations: fishing, reading, traveling, gardening. E-mail: harris@isu.edu. Fax: 208-235-4697. Home: 140 N 19th Ave Pocatello ID 83201-3311 Office: Idaho State Univ Box 8059 Pocatello ID 83209

HARRIS, MICHAEL GENE, optometrist, educator, lawyer; b. San Francisco, Sept. 20, 1942; s. Morry and Gertrude Alice (Epstein) H.; m. Dawn Block; children: Matthew Benjamin, Daniel Evan, Ashley Beth, Lindsay Meredith. BS, U. Calif., 1964, M. Optometry, 1965, D. Optometry, 1966, MS, 1968; JD, John F. Kennedy U., 1985. Bar: Calif., U.S. Dist. Ct. (no. dist.) Calif. Assoc. practice optometry, Oakland, Calif., 1965-66, San Francisco, 1966-68; instr., coord. contact lens clinic Ohio State U., 1968-69; asst. clin. prof. optometry U. Calif., Berkeley, 1969-73, dir. contact lens extended care clinic, 1969-83, chief contact lens clinic, 1983—, assoc. clin. prof., 1973-76, asst. chief contact lens svc., 1970-76, assoc. chief contact lens svc., 1976—, lectr., 1978-80, sr. lectr., 1980—, vice chmn. faculty Sch. Optometry, 1983-85, 95—, prof. clin. optometry, 1984-86; clin. prof. optometry, 1986—, dir. residency program, 1993—, asst. dean, 1994-95, assoc. dean, 1995—; John de Carle vis. prof. City U., London, 1984; vis. rsch. fellow U. New South Wales, Sydney, Australia, 1989; sr. vis. rsch. scholar U. Melbourne, Australia, 1989, 92; pvt. practice optometry, Oakland, Calif., 1973-76; mem. ophthalmic devices panel, med. device adv. com. FDA, 1990—, interim chair, 1994; lectr., cons. in field; mem. regulation rev. com. Calif. State Bd. Optometry; cons. hypnosis Calif. Optometric Assn., Am. Optometric Assn.; cons. Nat. Bd. Examiners in Optometry, Soflens div. Bausch & Lomb, 1973—, Barnes-Hind Hydrocurve Soft Lenses, Inc., 1974-87, Pilkinton-Barnes Hind, 1987—, Contact Lens Rsch. Lab., 1976—, Wesley-Jessen Contact Lens Co., 1977—, Palo Alto VA, 1980—, Primarius Corp., Cooper Vision Optics Alcon, 1980—; co-founder Morton D. Sarver Rsch. Lab., 1986; Planning commr. Town of Moraga, Calif., 1986, vice-chmn., 1987-88, chmn. 1988-90; mem. Town Coun., Moraga, Calif., 1992—, vice mayor, 1994-95, Medi-Cal. Adv. Planning Commn., 1993-95, chair, 1994—; with Managed Care Commn., 1995—, chair, 1996—; with City County Rels. Com., Contra Costa County; founding mem. Young Adults div. Jewish Welfare Fedn., 1965—, chmn. 1967-68; commr. Sunday Football League, Contra Costa County, Calif., 1974-78. Charter Mem. Jewish Community Ctr. Contra Costa County; founding mem. Jewish Community Mus. San Francisco, 1984; Para-Rabbinic, Temple Isaiah, Lafayette, Calif., 1987, bd. dirs., 1990; life mem. Bay Area Coun. for Soviet Jews, 1976; bd. dirs. Jewish Community Rels. Coun. of Greater East Bay, 1979—, Campolindo Homeowners Assn., 1981-85; pres. student coun. John F. Kennedy U. Sch. Law, 1984-85. Fellow U. Calif., 1971; Calif. Optometric Assn. Scholar 1965, George Schneider Meml. scholar, 1964, Max Shapero Meml. Lectr., 1995. Fellow Am. Acad. Optometry (diplomate cornea and contact lens sect.; chmn. contact lens papers; mem. contact lens com. 1974—, vice chmn. contact lens sect. 1980-82, chmn. 1982-84, immediate past chmn. 84-86, chmn. jud. com. 1989—, chmn. by-laws com. 1989—), Assn. Schs. and Colls. Optometry (coun. on acad. affairs), AAAS, Prentice Soc. (pres.-elect 1994-96, pres. 1996—); mem. Assn. for Rsch. in Vision and Ophthalmology, Am. Optometric Assn. (proctor 1969—, cons. on hypnosis, mem. contact lens sect., mem. position papers com., com. on ophthalmic standards, sub-com. on testing and certification, cons. editor Jour.), Calif. Optometric Assn., Assn. Optometric Contact Lens Educators, Am. Optometric Found., Mexican Soc. Contactology (hon.), Nat. Coun. on Contact Lens Compliance, Internat. Soc. Contact Lens Rsch., Calif. State Bd. Optometry (regulation rev. com.), Calif. Acad. Scis., U. Calif. Optometry Alumni Assn. (life), ABA, Calif. Young Lawyers Assn., Contra Costa Bar Assn., Mus. Soc., JFK U. Sch. Law Alumni Assn., Benjamin Ide Wheeler Soc. U. Calif., Mensa. Democrat. Lodge: B'nai B'rith. Editor current comments sect. Am. Jour. Optometry, 1974-77; editor Eye Contact, 1984-86, assoc. editor The Video Jour. Clin. Optometry, 1988—, consulting editor Contact Lens Spectrum, 18—; author: Contact Lenses: Treatment Options for Ocular Disease, Contact Lenses for Pre & Post-Surgery; editor: Problems in Optometry, Special Contact Lens Procedures; Contact Lenses and Ocular Disease, 1990; mem. hon. internat. edtl. bd. Contact Lens and Anterior Eye Jour.; contbr. chpts. to books; author various syllabi; contbr. articles to profl. pubs. Office: U of Calif Sch of Optometry Berkeley CA 94720

HARRIS, NICHOLAS TODD, architect; b. Kingston, Jamaica, July 27, 1954; came to U.S., 1955; s. Paul and Marguerite (Kirk) H.; m. Monica Jane Williams, May 17, 1981; children: Rebecca Marie, Katie Grace, Peter Augustin. BA in Philosophy, Haverford Coll., 1977; MArch, MIT, 1982. Registered architect, Calif., Mont., Oreg. Architect Computerland, Oakland, Calif., 1983; controller Teevan, Inc., San Francisco, 1984; architect U. Ill., Champaign, 1985; sr. project mgr. Am. Saving Bank, Stockton, Calif., 1986-90; v.p. architecture & design 1st Nationwide Bank, West Sacramento, Calif., 1990-93; facilities planning mgr. U.S. Bank, Portland, 1993-95, Nike, Inc., Beaverton, Oreg., 1995-97; architecture. engrng. divsn. mgr. Shimizu Am. Corp., Tigard, Oreg., 1997—. Rsch. grantee NEA, Cambridge, Mass., 1981. Mem. AIA, Nat. Coun. Archtl. Registration Bds., Inernat. Facilities Mgmt. Assn. Avocation: chess. Home: 3918 SW Jerald Way Portland OR 97221-4064

HARRIS, ROBERT DALTON, history educator, researcher, writer; b. Jamieson, Oreg., Dec. 24, 1921; s. Charles Sinclair and Dorothy (Cleveland) H.; m. Ethel Imus, June 26, 1971. BA, Whitman Coll., Walla Walla, Wash., 1951; MA, U. Calif., Berkeley, 1953, PhD, 1959. Tchg. asst. U. Calif., Berkeley, 1956-59; instr. history U. Idaho, Moscow, 1959-61, asst. prof., 1961-68, assoc. prof., 1968-74, prof. history, 1974-86, prof. emeritus, 1986—. Author: (Book) Necker, Reform Statesman of Ancient Regime, 1979, Necker & Revolution of 1789, 1986. 1st lt., U.S. Army, 1942-46; Ballet Folk of Moscow, Idaho, (bd. dirs., 1971-73), Historian, First United Methodist Church, Moscow, Idaho, 1989—. Mem. Am. Hist. Assn., Am. Assn. of U. Prof. Democrat. Methodist. Avocations: social dancing, violinist. Home: 928 E 8th St Moscow ID 83843-3851

HARRIS, ROBERT GAYLEN, art director, graphic designer, illustrator; b. Tacoma, Nov. 29, 1960; s. Gaylen Amon and Janelle Lee (Hinton) H.; m. Chelene Hope Ward, Sept. 24, 1988 (div. Nov. 1995). AD, Tacoma C.C., 1981; student, Brigham Young U., 1981-84. Graphic artist Phone Directories, Provo, Utah, 1983-84; graphic designer Clark Pub., Tacoma, 1984-89; art dir. Bringhurst Corp., Tacoma, 1989-98; owner Images, Tacoma, 1987—, Art Haus Harris Gallery, Tacoma, 1997—; art dir. Web-X, Tacoma, 1998—; pres. Art Haus, Inc., Tacoma; curator The Pierce County Playwrights Festival, Tacoma, 1995-97; cons. in field. Designer holiday poster Tacoma C. of C., 1991-97; designer fire safety poster Tacoma Fire Dept., 1992; designer food safety awareness posters Domani Labs., Tacoma, 1997; mem. Tacoma Art Mus., Seattle Art Mus., Bellevue Mus. Art. Named Regional winner Corel/Egghead Software Nat. Design Contest, 1995, 2nd place original concept-digital PIP Corp. Masters Competition, 1998; winner Corp. Identification Corel $3,000,000 World Design Contest, 1996; featured artist Reader Gallery, Corel Mag., Mar. 1996, June 1998. Mem. Allied Artists Am. Avocations: painting, writing, reading, computing, travel. Home and office: 1119 E 53rd St # D Tacoma WA 98404-2720

HARRIS, ROBERT W., lawyer; b. Hindsdale, Ill., Feb. 5, 1948. BA, U. Kans., 1970; JD, U. Denver, 1973. Bar: Colo. 1973. Formerly ptnr. Hall & Evans, Denver; pres., sr. ptnr. Harris, Karstaedt, Jamison & Powers, P.C., Englewood, Colo., 1995—. Mem. ABA. Office: Harris Karstaedt Jamison & Powers 5299 Dtc Blvd Ste 1130 Englewood CO 80111-2761*

HARRIS, ROGER J., mortgage company executive, entrepreneur; b. Chgo., Nov. 20, 1930; s. Stanley and Mary (Koba) Pokwinski; married, 1948 (div. Jan. 1970); 1 child, Linda; m. Betty J. Henry, Nov. 21, 1971. BS in Commerce, Roosevelt U., Chgo., 1956; postgrad., Loyola U. Law Sch., Chgo., 1959-62. Systems sales rep. Univac, Chgo., 1953-55; merchandising systems analyst Montgomery Ward, Chgo., 1956-62; cons. Haskins & Sells, Chgo., 1962-65; prin. A.T. Kearney, L.A., 1965-70; bus. cons. Roger J. Harris and Assocs., Inc., Calif. and Alaska, 1970—; chmn. bd. dirs., CEO Mortgage Co. Alaska; chmn. bd. dirs. MBI Corp.; conf. reader Am. Mgmt. Assn., L.A., 1970-82. Mem. Am. Soc. of Accts., Small Bus. Adminstrn. (chmn. score/ ACE program 1990-91). Office: PO Box 210707 Anchorage AK 99521-0707

HARRIS, SIGMUND PAUL, physicist; b. Buffalo, Oct. 12, 1921; s. Nathan N. and Ida (Lebovitz) H.; m. Florence Katcoff, Sept. 19, 1948; 1 child, Roslyn. BA cum laude, SUNY, Buffalo, 1941, MA, 1943; postgrad., Yale U., 1943; PhD, Ill. Inst. Tech., 1954. Physicist Metall. Lab. U. Chgo., 1943-44; jr. scientist Los Alamos (N.Mex.) Nat. Lab., 1944-46; assoc. physicist Argonne Nat. Lab., Chgo., 1946-53; sr. physicist Tracer Lab., Inc., Boston, 1954-56; sr. research engr. Atomics Internat., Canoga Park, Calif., 1956-64; head physics sect. research div. Maremont Corp., Pasadena, Calif., 1964-66; from asst. prof. to full prof. L.A. Pierce Coll., Woodland Hills, Calif., 1966-86, prof. physics emeritus, 1986—; cons. Space Scis. Inc., Monrovia, Calif., 1968—. Author: Introduction to Air Pollution, 1973. Patentee method for measuring power level of nuclear reactor, apparatus for producing neutrons. Mem. Am. Nuclear Soc., Am. Assn. Physics Tchrs., Am. Phys. Soc., Phi Beta Kappa, Sigma Xi. Home: 5831 Saloma Ave Van Nuys CA 91411-3018 Office: 6201 Winnetka Ave Woodland Hills CA 91371-0001

HARRIS, WARREN LYNN, development engineer; b. Albuquerque, May 8, 1966; s. Jerry Dale and Viola Guadalupe (Gutierrez) H. BS, Ariz. State U., 1988. Programming mgr. I.P.C. Computer Svcs., Inc., Tempe, Ariz., 1985-89; software sys. engr. Intel Corp., Chandler, Ariz., 1990; dir. software R & D Pics, Inc., Tempe, 1990-91; dir. software R & D parics divsn. Ansoft Corp., Tempe, 1991-94; devel. engr. Ansoft Corp., Phoenix, 1994—. Mem. IEEE, Assn. for Computing Machinery, Mortar Bd., Golden Key, Upsilon Pi Epsilon. Avocations: racquetball, model building, chess, pool, Star Trek collecting. Office: Ansoft Corp 4949 W Phelps Rd Glendale AZ 85306-1426

HARRISON, ALLEN C., artist, educator; b. L.A., Mar. 5, 1947; s. R.S. and Dorothy Dean (Duncan) H. BFA, Chouinard Art Sch., L.A., 1971; MFA, Otis Art Inst., L.A., 1975. Instr. painting and drawing Canada Coll., Redwood City, Calif., 1975-76; instr. drawing, design and painting Fullerton (Calif.) Coll., 1975-87; instr. drawing, painting, 2-dimensional and exhibit design Pasadena (Calif.) City Coll., 1989—; Gallery dir. Pasadena City Coll., 1994—; instr. painting Citrus Coll., Azuza, Calif., 1981; designer Cover Design for Math. Texts (4), Addison-Wesley Pub. Co., 1989; illustrator Avante, MDP Distbn., for film promotion (character drawings), 1994; juror, Calif. State U. Liberal Arts Competition, LaHabra (Calif.) Comty. Art Ctr. Juried Art Exhbn., 1991, Conejo Valley Art Mus. Ann. Juried Art Exhbn., Thousand Oaks, Calif., 1996. Artist: solo exhibitions include Janus Gallery, L.A., 1974, Stage One Gallery, Orange, Calif., 1981, Fullerton (Calif.) Coll., 1981, Tortue Gallery, Santa Monica, Calif., 1982, 84, 85, 87, 89, 92, 95, L.A. Inst. Contemporary Art, 1983, OK Harris Works of Art, N.Y.C., 1983, 86, 88, 91, 94, 97, Salathe Gallery, McDonnell Ctr., Pitzer Coll., Claremont, Calif., 1985, Gallery 2020 at Riviera Fine Arts Ctr., Santa Barbara, Calif., 1994, Rio Hondo Coll. Art Gallery, Whittier, Calif., 1995; paintings in group exhibitions include Three Painters Santa Anna (Calif.) Coll., 1973, Allen Harrison and Joel Smith, Ea. Washington State Coll., 1974, Cerritos Coll. Open, Norwalk, Calif., 1976, Business Not as Usual, Newport Harbor Art Mus., Newport Beach, Calif., Three Painters, Arco Ctr. for Visual Arts, L.A., 1977, Allen Harrison and Diana Hobson, Long Beach City Coll., Calif., 1977, Allen Harrison and Percy Gibbar, Janus Gallery, Venice, Calif., 1978, Allen Harrison and Robert Alderette, El Camino Coll., Torrance, Calif., 1979, In Celebration, Tortue Gallery, Santa Monica, Calif., 1984, Ten California Colorists, Redding Mus., Shasta Coll., Redding Calif. (travels), 1985, Black and White Drawings from the David Nellis Collections, Fine Arts Gallery, Calif. State U., L.A., 1985, The Artists of OK Harris, Helander Gallery, Palm Beach, Fla., 1986; many in public and private collections including Goldman-Sachs, L.A., Jonathan Tisch, N.Y.C., ARCO collection, Frederic Weisman, L.A., Byer Mus. of Art, San Francisco Mus. of Modern Art and others. Home and Studio: 903 N Ford St Burbank CA 91505-2718

HARRISON, CANDACE J., physician assistant; b. Reno, June 19, 1949; d. Robert George and Gleva T. (Trevenen) H. BA, Ind. U., 1971; M in Health Sys. Leadership, U. San Francisco, 1989. Cert. physician asst., Stanford Primary Care Assoc. program. Physician asst. Stanislaus County Family Practice Residency, Modesto, Calif., 1978-81, Merced (Calif.) County, 1981-92; clinic coord., physician asst. John C. Fremont Med. Clinic, Mariposa, Calif., 1992—; advisor Area Health Edn. Com., Modesto, 1980-85, Mariposa (Calif.) Peri-natal Coun., 1992—. Bd. dirs. New Directions for Women, Modesto, 1979-81; pres., bd. dirs. YMCA Rehab. Com., Modesto, 1980-81. Recipient Women Helping Women award Soroptimist Internat., 1994. Fellow Am. Acad. Physician Assts., Calif. Assn. Physician Asst. Avocation: camping, fishing. Office: John C Fremont Med Clinic 5186 Hospital Rd Mariposa CA 95338-9524

HARRISON, CAROLE ALBERTA, museum curator, restaurateur, civic worker; b. Dayton, Ohio, Jan. 16, 1942; d. Chester Arthur and Mildred Irene (Focke) Shaw; student U. Dayton, 1959-60, U. Colo., 1960-61; children: Amelia Holmes, Ann Elizabeth, Abigail Shaw. With Council for Pub. TV, Channel 6, Inc., Denver, 1972-78, Hist. Denver, Inc., 1973-93; owner Harrison Enterprises, Inc., 1982—; general mgr. The Denver Petroleum Club, The Denver Club; dir. devel. Sewall Rehab. Center, Denver, 1979-80; exec. v.p. Marilyn Van Derbur Motivational Inst., Inc., 1980-82. Bd. dirs. Center for Public Issues, Denver, 1979-82, Passages, 1982-88, Hall of Life, 1981-83, Historic Denver, 1982-84, Denver Firefighters Mus., 1979—; bd. dirs. KRMA-TV Vols., 1970—, pres., 1973-74; founder Com. for Support of Arts, Denver, 1978-79; chmn. Graland Country Day Sch. Auction, 1979, 80, Channel 6 Auction, 1971, 72, Colo. Acad. Auction, 1980, The Hundred Most Interesting Women in Denver, 1988; mem. Denver Mayor's Task Force on Infrastructure Fin., 1988-90; bd. dirs. Met. Denver and Colo. Conv. and Visitors Bur. Named Outstanding Bus. Woman of the Yr. Colo. Woman's C. of C., 1991. Mem. Leadership Denver Alumni Assn. (dir. 1980-82), Colo. Restaurant Assn., Denver C. of C. (govt. relations com. 1983-87, state local affairs council 1987-88, urban affairs), Women's Forum. Home: 1625 E 5th Ave Denver CO 80218-4029 Office: 555 17th St Ste 3700 Denver CO 80202-3906

HARRISON, CHARLES WAGNER, JR., applied physicist; b. Farmville, Va., Sept. 15, 1913; s. Charles Wagner and Etta Earl (Smith) H.; m. Fern F. Perry, Dec. 28, 1940; children—Martha R., Charlotte J. Student, U.S. Naval Acad. Prep. Sch., 1933-34, U.S. Coast Guard Acad., 1934-36; BS in Engring., U. Va., 1939, EE, 1940; SM, Harvard U., 1942, M of Engring., 1952, PhD in Applied Physics, 1954; postgrad., MIT, 1942, 52. Registered profl. engr., Va. Engr. Sta. WCHV, Charlottesville, Va., 1937-40; commd. ensign U.S. Navy, 1939, advanced through grades to comdr., 1948; research staff Bur. Ships, 1939-41, asst. dir. electronics design and devel. div., 1948-50; research staff U.S. Naval Research Lab., 1944-45, dir.'s staff, 1950-51; liaison officer Evans Signal Lab., 1945-46; electronics officer Phila. Naval Shipyard, 1946-48; mem. USN Operational Devel. Force Staff, 1953-55; staff Comdg. Gen. Armed Forces Spl. Weapons project, 1955-57; ret. U.S. Navy, 1957; cons. electromagnetics Sandia Nat. Labs., Albuquerque, 1957-73; instr. U. Va., 1939-40; lectr. Harvard U., 1942-43, Princeton U., 1943-44; vis. prof. Christian Heritage Coll., El Cajon, Calif., 1976. Author: (with R.W.P. King) Antennas and Waves: A Modern Approach, 1969; contbr. numerous articles to profl. jours. Fellow IEEE (Electronics Achievement award 1966, best paper award electromagnetic compatibility group 1972); mem. Internat. Union Radio Sci. (commn. B), Electromagnetics Acad., Famous Families Va., Sigma Xi. Home: 2808 Alcazar St NE Albuquerque NM 87110-3516

HARRISON, E(RNEST) FRANK(LIN), management educator, consultant, author, former university president and chancellor; b. Seattle, July 1, 1929; s. Ernest and Ethel (Stutler) H.; m. Monique Adrienne Pelletier. B.A. magna cum laude, U. Wash., 1956, M.B.A., 1961, Ph.D., 1970. With Shell Oil Co., 1956-58; in mgmt. positions Boeing Co., 1958-70; lectr. Grad. Sch. Bus. Adminstrn., U. Wash., 1968-71; lectr. Seattle U., 1968-74, dir. Sch. Bus. Pub. Adminstrn.; dir. grad. programs, prof. mgmt. U. Puget Sound, 1970-74, dean Coll. Bus.; prof. mgmt. Ill. State U., 1974-78; chancellor, prof. mgmt. U. Alaska, Anchorage, 1978-81; pres., disting. prof. So. Conn. State U., New Haven, 1981-84; prof. mgmt. San Francisco State U., 1984—; cons. in field. Author: The Managerial Decision Making Process, 1975, 5th edit., 1999, Management and Organizations, 1978, Policy, Strategy, and Managerial Action, 1986, 94; contbr. more than 35 articles to profl. jours. Mem. bd. visitors Air Force Inst. Tech., 1992-96, Air Force U., 1995-96. With USMC, 1946-49. Mem. IEEE, Acad. Mgmt., Phi Beta Kappa, Beta Gamma Sigma. Address: 124 Canyon Dr Napa CA 94558-1255 also: San Francisco Univ Coll Sch Bus San Francisco CA 94132

HARRISON, ETHEL MAE, financial executive; b. Ft. Dodge, Iowa, June 11, 1931; d. Arthur Melvin and Grace Gwendolyn (Hall) Cochran; m. Cleo Arden Goss, June 17, 1951 (div. 1962); m. Clarence Hobert Harrison, Dec. 23, 1965 (dec. Feb. 1993). Dipl., Internat. Corres. Schs., Riverside, Calif., 1986. Tax preparer Goss Tax Svc., Riverside, 1953-61; tax preparer H & R Block, Inc., Riverside, 1972-84, supr./bookkeeper, 1974-79; owner, pres. Ethel Harrison's Tax Svc., Riverside, 1984—. Mem. NAFE, Riverside Tax Cons. Assn. (sec. 1988—), Am. Soc. Profl. and Exec. Women, Am. Inst. Profl. Bookkeepers, Soc. of Calif. Tax Profls., Nat. Assn. Tax Cons., Nat. Soc. Tax Profls., Nat. Assn. Tax Preparers, Inland Soc. Tax Cons., Nat. Taxpayers Union. Avocations: camping, fishing, photography, auto racing. Home and Office: 10460 Gramercy Pl Riverside CA 92505-1300

HARRISON, GARTH TREVIER, artist, retired social worker; b. Hiawatha, Utah, Jan. 24, 1928; s. George Trevier and Alda L. (Jackson) H.; m. Norma Muir, Oct. 2, 1956 (div. June 1977); m. Carmen Ramirez-Perez; children: Rosemary Carter, Celeste Moss, Annette Ross, Theresa Cook, Victor T. BS in Sociology, U. Utah, 1952, MSW in Psychiat., 1954. Child welfare worker Utah State Dept. Pub. Welfare, Provo, 1953-56; clin. social worker Idaho Dept. Mental Health, Blackfoot, Pocatello, 1957-60; psychiat. social worker, dir. pub. edn. South Ctrl. Mental Health Ctr., Owatonna, Minn., 1961-65; dir. Josephine County Child Guidance Clinic, Grants Pass, Oreg., 1965-68; mgr. pub. info. svcs. Utah State Dept. Pub. Welfare, Salt Lake City, 1968-70; dist. mental health specialist Utah State Dept. Social Svcs., Vernal, 1970-78, adult svcs. worker, 1978-90. Chmn. rsch. com. Utah Coun. Family Rels., Provo, 1964-65; mem. Wintah County Sheriff's Adv. Com., 1996—. With USN, 1946-48; Capt. USAR. Mem. Am. Soc. Classical Realism, Knickerbocker Artists, Utah Sheriffs' Assn. (hon.). Avocations: gardening, bee keeping, alpine backpacking, traveling, fishing. Home: PO Box 745 Vernal UT 84078-0745 Office: Alpine Studio 659 N 500 E Vernal UT 84078-1864

HARRISON, GEORGE HARRY, III (HANK HARRISON), publishing executive, author; b. Monterey, Calif., June 17, 1940; s. Edith Cooke; 1 child, Courtney Love. BA in Psychology, San Francisco State Univ., 1965; postgrad., Univ. London, 1978-81. Mgr. Grateful Dead (formerly Warlocks), Palo Alto, Calif., 1965-66; founder, counselor LSD rescue Inst. Contemporary Studies, San Francisco, 1967; pvt. practice counselor San Francisco, 1967-78; pub., founder Archives Press, San Francisco, 1979—; writer-in-residence Montalvo Ctr. Arts, Saratoga, Calif., 1974; founder Media Assocs., Los Altos, Calif., 1991—; presenter, expert witness, lectr. in field. Author: The Dead Trilogy, 1972-97, Quest for Flight, 1975, 2nd edit., 1995, The Cauldron and the Grail, 1992, Mysteries of the Grail, 1998, Ace of Cups The Grail in Tarot, 1998, Confessions of a Naked Beekeeper, 1996, The Stones of Ancient Ireland, 1996; contbr. VSD (Paris), San Francisco Oracle, The Berkeley Barb, The Ga. Straight and L.A. Free Press, Dragon's Quest, The Green Knight; editor emeritus Doctor Dobb's Jour.; tech., staff writer Info World, A Plus; Vancouver Magazine, radio, TV guest including Geraldo, Am. Jour., Inside Edition, Hard Copy, Maury Povitch Show, America's Most Wanted, Fox News Contribution, 1998; editor: Vancouver Mag., 1974-75, Las Vegas Sun, 1976-77, Jour. Psychedelic Drugs, 1967; contbg. editor High Times, 1996-97. With USN Med. Corps., 1958-61. Rocky Mountain Writer's Conf. scholar, 1968, Frances Yates scholar Warburg Inst. Univ. London, 1981, Applied Materials Corp. scholar, 1984. Mem. Press Club, Ind. Pub. Assn., San Francisco Press Club, Las Vegas Press Club, Masons. Democrat. Avocations: motorcycle repair, horse breeding, dog breeding. E-mail: hank@arkives.com. Home & Office: PO Box 46 Wilton CA 95693-0046

HARRISON, JEANETTE KEMCHICK, business executive; b. Point Pleasant, N.J., Sept. 2, 1954; d. Patrick John Kemchick and Gloria E. (Stensland) Martin; m. Roger Anthony Piantadosi, Aug. 4, 1975 (div. Mar. 1982); m. John G. Harrison, Mar. 1989. BA in Sociology magna cum laude, Am. U., 1977, MEd, 1979; postgrad., Va. Poly. Inst. and State U., 1980, George Washington U., 1981, UCLA Extension, 1983; D in Pub. Adminstrn. U. So. Calif., 1994. Dir. fin. aid Am. U., Washington, 1977-81; Revson fellow to Rep. Patricia Schroeder, Washington, 1981-82; dir. fed. and state rels. Systems Rsch., Inc., Washington, 1981-84; v.p. mktg. Sigma Systems, Inc., L.A., 1982-84; v.p. The Wyndgate Group, Sacramento, 1984-89; v.p. adminstrn. Noel/Levitz Ctrs., Inc., Coralville, Iowa, 1989-90; ind. cons., 1990-91; coord. projects Iowa Program Assistive Tech., 1991-93; dir. strategic planning and bus. devel. Info. Tech. divsn. Nat. Computer Sys., 1992-93, v.p. edn. strategic planning and bus. sys., 1993-95; dir. components tng. Intel Corp., 1996—, TMG Tng., 1996—. Recipient Meritorious Svc. award Am. U., 1977, 80; Gen. U. scholar, 1975-76, Mathas scholar, 1975-77; Charles Revson fellow, 1981-82. Mem. Nat. Assn. Women Deans, Adminstrs. and Counselors (chmn. div. govt./agy. spl. programs 1984). Democrat. Roman Catholic. Home: 2132 E Calle De Arcos Tempe AZ 85284-3536 Office: Intel Corp TMG Tng 5000 W Chandler Blvd Chandler AZ 85226-3699

HARRISON, JOHN CONWAY, state supreme court justice; b. Grand Rapids, Minn., Apr. 28, 1913; s. Francis Randall and Ethlyn (Conway) H.; m. Ethel M. Strict; children—Nina Lyn, Robert Charles, Molly M., Frank R., Virginia Lee. LLD, George Washington U., 1940. Bar: Mont. 1947, U.S. Dist. Ct. 1947. County atty. Lewis and Clark County, Helena, Mont., 1934-60; justice Mont. Supreme Ct., Helena, 1961-98, ret., 1998. Pres. Mont. TB Assn., Helena, 1951-54, Am. Lung Assn., N.Y.C., 1972-73, Mont. coun. Boy Scouts Am., Great Falls, Mont., 1976-78. Col. U.S. Army. Mem. ABA, Mont. Bar Assn., Kiwanis (pres. 1953), Sigma Chi. Home: 215 S Cooke St Helena MT 59601-5143

HARROP, THOMAS, publishing company executive; b. Salt Lake City, Apr. 30, 1954; s. Raymond William and Fern Pearse (Wheelwright) H.; m. Diane Louise Hokans, July 15, 1995; children: Anne Rochelle, Catherine Lindsay, Kyle. BA, Brooks Inst., 1983, MS, 1994. Mng. editor Petersenis Photographic, L.A., 1983-84; photographer NASA, Edwards AFB, Calif., 1987-88; editl. dir. Cameras & Darkroom, L.A., 1988-92; mng. editor Outdoor Photograph, L.A., 1992-93; pub., editor PhotoWork, Whitefish, Mont., 1996—. Author: (book) Getting Info Print, 1996. Mem. Am. MENSA Soc. Avocations: photography, web design, book publishing. Office: PhotoWork PO Box 4753 Whitefish MT 59937-4753

HARROW, SUSAN A., publicist; b. Kenton, Ohio, Feb. 24, 1957; d. Herman and Noreen Harrow. BA in English, U. Calif., Berkeley, 1979; Moyen Superieure Degree Grammar & Lit., Sorbonne, Paris, 1980; secondary edn. tchg. credential, San Francisco State U., 1982. Tchr. Mission H.S., San Francisco, 1981-82; mktg. rsch. analyst Cunningham & Walsh Advt. Agy., San Francisco, 1981-83; office mgr. Sundara Industries, San Francisco, 1983-84; sales rep. Nova Sys., Point Richmond, Calif., 1984-85, GCE Telecom., Oakland, Calif., 1985-86; sales rep. Centex Telemanagement, San Francisco, 1986-87, account exec., 1986-89, 88-89; writer, spkr. Oakland, 1989—; pub. rels. specialist, media coach Harrow Comm., Oakland, 1990—; cons. Pacific Bell Directory, San Francisco, 1991—. Avocations: tennis, conversational French, classical piano, speaking. Home: 4200 Park Blvd Ste 333 Oakland CA 94602-1312

HARRUS, ALAIN SIMON, marketing professional; b. Casablanca, Morocco, Aug. 25, 1955; came to U.S., 1979; s. David and Helen (Ifergan) H.; m. Carol Beth Ronis, July 26, 1981; children: Isaac Alexander, Rachel Beth Julie. BS in Math. and Physics, U. Paris, 1978, MS in Physics, 1979; PhD, Temple U., 1984. Tech. staff AT&T Bell Labs., Allentown, Pa., 1985-89; sr. tech. Novellus Systems, San Jose, Calif., 1989-90, dir. chem. vapor deposition, 1990-93, dir. strategic mktg., 1994-96; v.p., chief tech. officer, 1996—; dir. chem. vapor desosition LAM Rsch., Fremont, Calif., 1993-94. Patentee in field; contbr. articles to profl. jours. Mem. IEEE, Am. Phys. Soc., Electrochem. Soc. Home: 517 Patricia Ln Palo Alto CA 94303-2856 Office: Novellus Systems 81 Vista Montana San Jose CA 95134-1510

HARSHA, PHILIP THOMAS, aerospace engineer; b. N.Y.C., Feb. 22, 1942; s. Palmer and Catherine (Redinger) H.; m. Jean Ann Quinn, Oct. 23, 1966 [illegible] BS in Engring. Sci., SUNY, Stony Brook, 1962, MS in Engring. Sci., 1964; PhD in Aerospace Engring., U. Tenn., 1970. Combustion rsch. engr. Gen. Electric Co., Cin., 1964-67; lead rsch. engr. Aro, Inc., Arnold Engring. Devel. Ctr., Tenn., 1969-74; rsch. specialist R&D Assoc., Marina Del Rey, Calif., 1974-76; div. mgr. Sci. Applications Internat. Corp., Chatsworth, Calif., 1976-85; chief aero. scientist Lockheed Aero. Systems Group, Burbank, Calif., 1985-88; chief project engr. Rocketdyne div. Rockwell Internat., Canoga Park, Calif., 1988-90; dep. program dir. Nat. Aero-Space Plane Program, 1990-95; program mgr. Boeing North American, Inc., Seal Beach, Calif., 1994—. Contbr. articles to profl. jours. Recipient Disting. Alumnus award U. Tenn. Space Inst., 1984. Mem. AIAA, ASME, N.Y. Acad. Sci., Sigma Xi. Republican. Methodist. Home: 1607 Ocean Ave Seal Beach CA 90740-6548 Office: The Boeing Co 2401 E Wardlow Rd Long Beach CA 90807-5309

HARSHMAN, VIRGINIA ROBINSON, writer, historical researcher; b. L.A., June 29, 1920; d. Paul Edward and Hazel (Reed) Robinson; m. Walter Neill Harshman, Jr., Apr. 24, 1942; children: Loren James, Walter Neill III, David Alan, Anne Elizabeth. Grad. h.s., Inglewood, Calif., 1937. Draftsman So. Calif. Edison, San Bernardino, Calif., 1961-76; freelance writer Lytle Creek, Calif., 1950-94, Rialto, Calif., 1994—. Author: The Story of Lytle Creek Canyon, 1992. Mem. com. Lytle Creek Comty. Plan, 1980-82; docent spl. collections Feldhym Libr., San Bernardino, Calif., 1985-95, 97—; historian, dir. Citizens for a Safe Environment, Rialto, 1996—, reorganized Citizen Advocates of Rialto, 1997—. Mem. San Bernardino Valley Geneal. Soc. (editor, bd. dirs.), Lytle Creek Cmty. Ctr. (editor The Canyon, 1956-59, 79-81). Avocations: genealogy, gardening, ecology.

HARSTAD, MARK GEORGE, operations research analyst; b. Belview, Minn., Jan. 13, 1954; s. Norman Bjug and Martha Leona (Thorpe) H. BS, Univ. Wis., 1976; MS in engr., Univ. Calif., 1984. Cert. profl. engr. Industrial engr. Naval Telecommunications, Washington, 1977-80; industrial engr. Navy Manpower, San Diego, 1980-83, Waipahu, Hawaii, 1984-86; ops. rsch. anaylst Commander In Chief Pacific, Camp Smith, Hawaii, 1987—. Author: South China Sea Reference Book, 1996, Burma Reference Book, 1996; co-author: Asia-Pacific Economic Update, 1994, 95, 96, 98, Philippine Bases Relocation Study, 1988. Mem. IIE (sr., chpt. pres. 1998), Operations Rsch. Soc. of Am. Lutheran. Home: 3045 Pualei Cir Apt 210 Honolulu HI 96815-4908 Office: USCINCPAC PO Box 64015 Camp H M Smith HI 96861-4015

HART, BROOK, lawyer; b. N.Y.C., Aug. 24, 1941; s. Walter and Julie H.; m. Barbara Ingersoll, Nov., 1980; children—Morgan M., Lauren L., Ashley I., Ariel J. BA Johns Hopkins U., 1963; LL.B., Columbia U., 1966. Bar: N.Y. 1966, U.S. Ct. Appeals (9th cir.) 1967, Hawaii 1968, U.S. Supreme Ct. 1972, Calif. 1973. Law clk. to chief judge U.S. Dist. Ct. Hawaii, 1966-67; assoc. counsel Legal Aid Soc. Hawaii, 1968; assoc. Greenstein and Cowan, Honolulu, 1968-70; chief pub. defender State of Hawaii, 1970-72; co-founder, ptnr. Hart, Leavitt, Hall and Hunt, Honolulu, 1972-80; co-founder, ptnr. Hart and Wolff, Honolulu, 1980-96; sr. ptnr. Law Offices of Brook Hart, 1996—. instr. course U. Hawaii, 1972-73, lectr. Sch. Law, 1974—; apptd. Nat. Commn. to Study Def. Services, 1974, Planning Group for U.S. Dist. Ct. Hawaii, 1975; spl. counsel City Council of City and County of Honolulu, 1976-77, spl. investigative counsel to trustee in bankruptcy THC Fin. Corp., 1977; mem. Jud. Council State of Hawaii com. on revision state penal codes, 1984—; lectr. schs., profl., civic groups; mem. com. to select Fed. Pub. Defender Dist. of Hawaii, 1981, 95. Recipient Reginald Heber Smith award Nat. Legal Aid and Defender Assn., 1971; named Bencher, Am. Inn of Ct., Hawaii, 1982—. Fellow Am. Bd. Criminal Lawyers; mem. ABA, Hawaii Bar Assn., State Bar Calif., Am. Judicature Soc., Nat. Legal Aid and Defender Assn., Nat. Assn. Criminal Def. Lawyers, Calif. Attys. for Criminal Justice. Contbr. chpts. to books, articles to profl. publs. Office: Law Offices of Brook Hart 333 Queen St Honolulu HI 96813-4726

HART, EDWARD LEROY, poet, educator; b. Bloomington, Idaho, Dec. 28, 1916; s. Alfred Augustus and Sarah Cecilia (Patterson) H.; m. Eleanor May Coleman, Dec. 15, 1944 (dec. Dec. 1990); children: Edward Richard, Paul LeRoy, Barbara, Patricia; m. Leah Yates Bryson, Apr. 30, 1993. BS, U. Utah, 1939; MA, U. Mich., 1941; DPhil (Rhodes scholar), Oxford (Eng.) U., 1950. Instr. U. Utah, Salt Lake City, 1946; asst. prof. U. Wash., Seattle, 1949-52; asst. prof. Brigham Young U., Provo, Utah, 1952-55, assoc. prof., 1955-59, prof., 1959-82, prof. emeritus, 1982—; vis. prof. U. Calif., Berkeley, 1959-60, Ariz. State U., summer 1968. Author: Minor Lives, 1971, Instruction and Delight, 1976, Mormom in Motion, 1978; (poems) To Utah, 1979, Poems of Praise, 1980; More Than Nature Needs, 1982, God's Spies, 1983; contbr. articles to profl. jours. Lt. USNR, 1942-46. Am. Philos. Soc. grantee, 1964; First prize in poetry and biography Utah State Arts Coun., 1973, 75; Fulbright-Hays sr. lectr. Pakistan, 1973-74; recipient Charles Redd award Utah Acad., 1976, Coll. Humanities Disting. Faculty award Brigham Young U., 1977. Fellow Am. Coun. Learned Socs., Found. Econ. Edn.; mem. Phi Beta Kappa, Phi Kappa Phi. Democrat. Mormon. Home: 1401 Cherry Ln Provo UT 84604-2848 Office: Brigham Young U Dept English Provo UT 84602

HART, JOHN LEWIS (JOHNNY HART), cartoonist; b. Endicott, N.Y., Feb. 18, 1931; s. Irwin James and Grace Ann (Brown) H.; m. Bobby Jane Hatcher, Apr. 26, 1952; children: Patti Sue, Perri Ann. Ed. pub. schs. Freelance cartoonist, 1954-58; commerical artist GE, Johnson City, NY, 1957-58; syndicated cartoonist, 1958—. Comic strip, B.C., nationally syndicated, 1958—, (with Brant Parker) The Wizard of Id, 1964—; collections include: Hey B.C., 1958, Hurray for B.C., 1958, Back to B.C., 1959, B.C. Strikes Back, 1961, What's New B.C., 1962, B.C.- Big Wheel, 1963, B.C. is Alive and Well, 1964, The King is a Fink, 1964, Take a Bow, B.C., 1965, The Wonderous Wizard of Id, 1965, B.C. on the Rocks, 1966, The Peasants are Revolting, 1966, B.C. Right On, 1967, B.C. Cave In, 1967, Remember the Golden Rule, 1967, There's A Fly in My Swill, 1967, The Wizard's Back, 1968, B.C., 1972, B.C. Cartoon Book, 1973. Served with USAF, 1950-53, Korea. Recipient Best Humor Strip awards, Nat. Cartoonists Soc., 1967-71; Reuben Award, Nat. Cartoonist Soc., 1969, named Outstanding Cartoonist of Year, 1968; Yellow Kid award, 1970; Internat. Congress Comics for best cartoonist, Lucca, Italy; Best Humor Strip award, French Comics Council, 1971; Public Service Award, NASA, 1972. Mem. Nat. Comics Council, Nat. Cartoonists Soc. Premiered nationally pub. cartoon in Sat. Eve. Post, 1954. Office: care Creators Syndicate 5777 W Century Blvd Ste 700 Los Angeles CA 90045-5677*

HART, JOHN WILLIAM, theology educator; b. N.Y.C., Oct. 5, 1943; s. Thomas Esmond and Veronica Frances (Merz) H.; m. Jane Helen Morell, Aug. 16, 1975; children: Shanti, Daniel. BA, Marist Coll., 1966; STM, Union Theol. Sem., 1972, MPhil, 1976, PhD, 1978. Dir. Heartland Project, Midwestern Cath. Bishops, 1979-81; asst. prof. religious studies Mt. Marty Coll., Yankton, S.D., 1981-82; assoc. prof. religious studies Coll. of Great Falls (Mont.), 1983-85; prof. theology Carroll Coll., Helena, Mont., 1985—; vis. asst. prof. religion Howard U., Washington, 1978-79; dir., founder environtl. studies program Carroll Coll., 1997—; lectr. in field in U.S., Brazil, Can. and Italy, 1980—. Author: The Spirit of the Earth: A Theology of the Land, 1984, Ethics and Technology: Innovation and Transformation in Community Contexts, 1997; ghost author various ch. documents, 1979—; contbr. articles to profl. publs., chpts. to books. Del. Internat. Indian Treaty Coun., Geneva, 1987, 90, UN Internat. Human Rights Commn. Recipient Templeton Sci.-Religion award, 1995; Danforth Found. fellow, 1973-74, Lilly tchg. fellow, 1997-98; NEH grantee, 1985, 86; named Oxford Sci. and Christianity scholar, 1999—. Mem. Soc. Christian Ethics, Am. Acad. Religion. Democrat. Roman Catholic. Office: Carroll Coll Theology Dept Helena MT 59625

HART, JOSEPH H., bishop; b. Kansas City, Mo., Sept. 26, 1931. Ed., St. John Sem., Kansas City, St. Meinrad Sem., Indpls. Ordained priest Roman Catholic Ch., 1956; consecrated titular bishop of Thimida Regia and aux. bishop Cheyenne Wyo., 1976; apptd. bishop of Cheyenne, 1978. Office: Bishop's Residence Chancery Office PO Box 426 Cheyenne WY 82003-0426*

HART, MARIAN GRIFFITH, retired reading educator; b. Bates City, Mo., Feb. 5, 1929; d. George Thomas Leon and Beulah Winiferd (Hackley) Griffith; m. Ashley Bruce Hart, Dec. 23, 1951; children: Ashley Bruce Hart II, Pamela Cherie Hart Gates. BS, Cen. Mo. State Coll., 1951; MA, No. Ariz. U., 1976. Title I-chpt. I reading dir. Page (Ariz.) Sch. Dist.; Title I dir. Johnson O'Malley Preschool; dist. reading dir. Page Sch. Dist.; bd. dirs. Lake Powell Inst. Behavioral Health Svcs., sec., 1993-95, chmn. fin. com., 1995-96. Contbr. articles to profl. jours., childrens mags. Vol., organizer, mgr., instr. Page Cmty. Adult Literacy Program, 1986-91, Marian's Literacy Program, 1991-95; lifetime mem. Friends of Page Pub. Libr., sec. bd., 1990-

91. Mem. Delta Kappa Gamma (pres. chpt. 1986-90, historian 1990-92, Omicron state coms., scholarship 1988-89, nominations 1991, Omicron State Comms. com. 1995—, Tau chpt. nominations com. chair 1998), Beta Sigma Phi (pres. chpt., v.p. chpt., pvt. reading tutor 1997—). Home and Office: 66 S Navajo Dr PO Box 763 Page AZ 86040-0763

HART, MICHAEL JOHN, environmental management; b. Manchester, N.H., July 7, 1946; s. Wilfred Norman and Agnes Hedvega (Filipowitz) H.; m. G. Mary Falvey, Aug. 15, 1976; children: Jocelyn Elizabeth, Catherine Mary. BA, Colo. U., 1968; MBA, Denver U., 1989. Radio announcer Sta. KRNW, Boulder, Colo., 1971-73; resource mgr. Flatiron Cos., Boulder, Colo., 1973-79; v.p. Flatiron Sand & Gravel, Boulder, Colo., 1979-89; pres. Hart Environ., Boulder, Colo., 1989—; chmn. of bd. Thorne Ecol. Inst., Boulder, 1991-93; pres. Colo. Rock Products Assoc., Denver, 1989; bd. dirs. Nat. Aggregates Assoc., Silver Springs, Md., 1992, Nat. Sand and Gravel Assoc., Silver Spring, 1983-86, bd. dirs. M&S div. Nat. Stone Assn. Contbr. articles to profl. jours. Mem. LWV, BOulder, 1992, Pvt. Industry Coun., Boulder, 1989, Sch. Dist./Capital Needs Com., Boulder, 1990-92. Named Man of Yr., Colo. Sand & Gravel Assoc., 1979. Mem. Soc. for Ecol. Restoration, Assn. State Wetland Mgrs., Environ. Law Inst., Colo. Water Congress, Nat. Stone Assn. (bd. dirs. 1995), Nat. Aggregates Assn., Beta Gamma Sigma. Avocations: outdoor recreation, camping, hiking, fishing. Office: Hart Environ 2255 Meadow Ave Boulder CO 80304-1626

HART, RUSS ALLEN, telecommunications educator; b. Seguin, Tex., June 30, 1946; s. Bevelly D. and Hattie V. (Reeh) H.; m. Judith Harwood, 1984 (div. 1986); m. Patricia Barrios, Mar. 22, 1987. BA, Tex. Tech. U., 1968; MA, U. Ariz., 1976; PhD, U. Wyo., 1984. Chief cinematographer, producer-dir. dept. med-TV-film, health sci. ctr. U. Ariz., Tuscon, 1973-77; instr., coord. ednl. TV and cinematography U. Wyo., Laramie, 1977-81; assoc. prof., dir. biomed. communication Mercer U., Macon, Ga., 1981-84; prof., dir. instructional telecommunications Calif. State U., Fresno, 1984-92, prof., assoc. dir. computing, comm. and media svcs., 1992-95, prof., assoc. dir. Acad. Innovation Ctr., 1995-98, prof. mass comm., 1998—; condr. ednl. confs.; tech. cons. for distance edn. Contbr. articles to profl. jours. Served to capt. USAF, 1968-73. Recipient Cert. Merit, Chgo. Internat. Film Festival, 1975, 1st pl. INDY Indsl. Photography award, 1976, 2d pl. INDY Indsl. Photography award, 1975, Silver plaque Chgo. Internat. Film Festival, 1978, Winner of case study competition Internat. Radio and TV Soc., 1989, Bronze Telly award, 1992-93, 95, Crystal Shooting Star award, 1993, 94, Cine Golden Eagle award, 1994. Mem. Assn. for Ednl. Comms. and Tech. (rsch. session chmn. 1983), Am. Assn. Adult and Continuing Educators (mem. eval. task force 1986), Broadcast Edn. Assn., Health Sci. Comms. Assn. (mem. continuing edn. subcom. 1983), Biol. Photog. Assn. (film judge 1975), Alliance for Distance Edn. in Calif. (founding mem. 1991), Ednl. Telecom. Consortium of Ctrl. Calif. (founding mem. 1993), Phi Delta Kappa, Phi Kappa Phi. Office: Calif State U Acad Innovation Ctr Fresno CA 93740

HART, TIMOTHY RAY, lawyer, dean; b. Portland, Jan. 5, 1942; s. Eldon V. and Wanda J. (Hillyer) H.; m. Mary F. Barlow, Aug. 31, 1964 (div. Dec. 1975); children: Mark, Matthew, Marisa, Martin; m. Annette Bryant, Aug. 8, 1981. AA, San Jose City Coll., 1968; BA, San Jose State U., 1970; MA, Wash. State U., 1973; JD, San Joaquin Coll. Law, Fresno, Calif., 1983. Bar: Calif. 1983, U.S. Dist. Ct. (ea. dist.) Calif. 1983. Police officer City of Santa Clara, Calif., 1965-71; chief of police U. Idaho, Moscow, 1971-73; crime prevention officer City of Albany, Oreg., 1973-75; instr. criminal justice Coll. of Sequoias, Visalia, Calif., 1975-81, dir. paralegal dept., 1981-83, chmn., dir. adminstrn. justice div., 1983-88; assoc. dean instruction, 1988—; sole practice, Visalia, 1983—; apptd. dep. chief police City of Sanger (Calif.), 1996-97. Chair nonprofit com. Sanger Interagy. Youth and Cmty. Svcs., Inc. With USAF, 1960-63. Mem. ABA, Calif. Bar Assn., Assn. Trial Lawyers Am., Assn. Criminal Justice Educators, Am. Criminal Justice Assn., Delta Phi. Mennonite. Home: 1012 W Hemlock Ave Visalia CA 93277-7435 Office: Coll of Sequoias 915 S Mooney Blvd Visalia CA 93277-2214

HART-DULING, JEAN MACAULAY, clinical social worker; b. Bellingham, Wash.; d. Murry Donald and Pearl N. (McLeod) Macaulay; m. Richard D. Hart, Feb. 3, 1940 (dec. Mar. 1973); children: Margaret Hart Morrison, Pamela Hart Horton, Patricia L. Hart-Jewell; m. Lawrence Duling, Jan. 20, 1979 (dec. May 1992); children: Lenora Daniel, Larry, Jayne Munch. BA, Wash. State U., 1938; MSW, U. So. Calif., 1961. Lic. clin. social worker, Calif.; accredited counselor, Wash. Social worker Los Angeles County, 1957-58; children's svc. worker Dept. Children's Svcs., L.A., 1958-59; program developer homemakers svcs. project Calif. Dept. Children's Svcs., L.A., 1962-64; developer homemaker cons. position State of Calif., L.A., 1964-66; supr. protective svcs. Dept. Children's Svcs., L.A., 1966-67; dep. regional svc. adminstrn. Dept. Los Angeles County Children's Svcs., 1967-76; adminstr. Melton Home for Developmental Disability, 1985-86; pvt. practice pro bono therapy Calif. and Wash.; therapist various pro bono cases. Mem. Portals Com., L.A., 1974, Travelers Aid Bd., Long Beach, Calif. 1969. Recipient Nat. award work in cmty., spl. award for work with emotionally disturbed Com. for Los Angeles, 1974. Mem. AAUW, NASW, Acad. Cert. Social Workers, Calif. Lic. Clin. Soc. Workers, Wing Point Golf and Country Club (Bainbridge Island, Wash.). Republican. Congregationalist. Avocations: golf, bridge. Office: 7300 Quill Dr # 212 Downey CA 90242-2031

HARTENBACH, DAVID LAWRENCE, school system administrator; b. St. Louis, Dec. 6, 1934; s. Henry Charles and Loretta S. (Schwarz) H. BA, St. Louis U., 1958, MEd, 1960; EdD in Sacred Theology, U. No. Colo., 1981. Cert. adminstr., Colo. Adminstrv. intern St. Louis U. H.S., 1966-67, asst. prin., 1967-68; prin. Regis H.S. Archdiocese of Denver, 1968-70; prin. Benton Harbor (Mich.) H.S., 1970-72; prin. W.C. Hinkley H.S. Aurora (Colo.) Pub. Schs., 1972-77, exec. dir. H.S.'s, 1977-86, assoc. supt. instrn., 1986-89, assoc. supt. aux., 1989-93, supt. schs., 1993—; mem. state com. Colo. North Ctrl. Assn., Greeley, 1976-83. Membership chmn. Centennial Dist. Unit PTA, Aurora, 1993—; mem. human rels. com. City of Aurora, 1978-84. Named Colo. Supt. of Yr., Nat. Sch. Bds. Assn., 1995; grantee Ford Found., 1965-66, Nat. Acad. Rsch. in Vocat. Edn., 1979. Mem. ASCD, Nat. Assn. Secondary Sch. Prins. (nat. com. large secondary schs. 1980-83, adminstrv. intern J. Lloyd Trump grantee 1966-67), Am. Assn. Sch. Adminstrs., Colo. Assn. Sch. Bds., Colo. Assn. Sch. Execs., Kiwanis (past pres. Centennial chpt.). Avocations: golfing, fishing, sports, music. Office: Aurora Pub Schs 1085 Peoria St Aurora CO 80011-6203*

HARTER, CAROL CLANCEY, university president, English language educator; m. Michael T. Harter, June 24, 1961; children: Michael R., Sean P. BA, SUNY, Binghamton, 1964, MA, 1967, PhD, 1970; LHD, Ohio U., 1989. Instr. SUNY, Binghamton, 1969-70; asst. prof. Ohio U., Athens, 1970-74, ombudsman, 1974-76, v.p., dean students, 1976-82, v.p. for adminstrn., assoc. prof., 1982-89; pres., prof. English SUNY, Geneseo, 1989-95; pres. U. Nev., Las Vegas, 1995—. Co-author: (with James R. Thompson) John Irving, 1986, E.L. Doctorow, 1990; author dozens of presentations and news columns; contbr. articles to profl. jours. Office: U Nev Las Vegas Office of Pres 4505 S Maryland Pkwy # 1001 Las Vegas NV 89154-9900

HARTER, LAFAYETTE GEORGE, JR., economics educator emeritus; b. Des Moines, May 28, 1918; s. Lafayette George and Helen Elizabeth (Ives) H.; m. Charlotte Mary Toshach, Aug. 23, 1950; children—Lafayette George III, James Toshach, Charlotte Helen. B.A. in Bus. Adminstrn, Antioch Coll., 1941; M.A. in Econs, Stanford, 1948, Ph.D., 1960. Instr. Menlo Coll., Menlo Park, Calif., 1948-50; instr. Coll. of Marin, Kentfield, Calif., 1950-60; prof. econs. dept. Oreg. State U., 1960-85, prof. emeritus, 1985—, chmn. dept., 1967-71; mem. panel arbitrators Fed. Mediation and Conciliation Svc., 1965-84, Oreg. Conciliation Svc., 1967-84; mem. Univ. Ctrs. for Rational Alternatives. Author: John R. Commons: His Assault on Laissez-faire, 1962, Labor in America, 1957, Economic Responses to a Changing World, 1972; editorial bd. Jour. Econ. Issues, 1981-84. Assoc. campaign chmn. Benton United Good Neighbor Fund, 1970-72, campaign chmn., v.p., 1972-73, pres., 1973-74, vice chmn.; pub. mem. Adv. Commn. on Unemployment Compensation, 1972, 73, chmn., 1974-78; Bd. dirs. Oreg. Coun. Econ. Edn., 1971-89; pub. mem. local profl. responsibilities Oreg. State Bar Assn., 1980-83; pub. mem. Oreg. Coun. on Ct. Procedures, 1985-93, bd. mem. Community Econs. of Corp., Community Econ. Stabilization Corp. Lt. comdr. USNR, 1941-46. Mem. AAUP, Am. Arbitration Assn. (pub. employment disputes panel 1970-92), Am. Western Econ. Assns., Indsl. Rels. Rsch. Assn., Am. Assn. for Evolutionary Econs., Oreg. State Employees Assn. (v.p. faculty chpt. 1972, pres. 1973), Am. Assn. Ret. Persons (pres. local chpt. 1992-93), Corvallis Retirement Village (fin. com., bd. dirs.). Democrat. Mem. United Ch. of Christ (moderator 1972, 73; mem. fin. com. Oreg. conf. 1974-82, dir. 1978-81, mem. personnel com. 1983-85). Home: 3755 NW Van Buren Ave Corvallis OR 97330-4952

HARTFORD, MARGARET ELIZABETH (BETTY HARTFORD), social work educator, gerontologist, writer; b. Cleve., Dec. 12, 1917; d. William A. and Inez (Logan) H. BA, Ohio U., 1940; MS, U. Pitts., 1944; PhD, U. Chgo., 1962. Dir. youth svc. YWCA, Canton, Ohio, 1940-42; program cons. Intercultural Rels. Am. Svc. Inst., Pitts., 1943-48, exec. dir., 1948-50; prof. social work Case Western Res. U., Cleve., 1950-75; founding dir. Sch. Gerontology U. So. Calif., L.A., 1975-77, prof. gerontology, social work, 1977-83, prof. emeritus, 1983—; instr. Claremont (Calif.) Adult Sch. Dist., 1983—, mentor/tchr. adult edn., 1990-95; instr. retirement Pasadena (Calif.) City Coll., 1983-84, Mt. San Antonio Coll., 1988-90; cons. pre-retirement, retirement planning to corps. and ednl. systems, various cities, 1980—; cons., lectr. 1970—; instr. gerontology/mental health Kaiser Permanente, 1997-99. Author: Groups in Social Work, 1973, (workbook) Making the Best of the Rest of Your Life, 1982, rev. edit., 1998, Leaders Guide to Making the Best of the Rest of Your Life, 1986; contbr. monthly column on successful aging Pomona Valley Cmty. Svcs. on Aging Newsletter, 1988—; contbr. numerous articles to profl. publs. Commr. human svcs. City of Clairmont, 1986-89, city coun. observer LWV, 1994-95; trustee Mt. San Antonio Gardens Retirement Com., 1985-92, sec., 1988-91; v.p. Mt. San Antonio Gardens Club Coun., bd. dirs. admissions com. 1996-99, nominating com. 1992-97, health svcs. com. 1996-98, chmn. task force on wellness/fitness, historian 1996—; trustee Corp. Pilgrim Pl. Ret. Cmty., chmn. health and svcs. com., 1987-94, 96—; bd. dirs., trustee Vol. Assn. Rancho Santa Ana Bot. Gardens, 1991—; chmn. vol. pers. com., goals and evaluation com. St. Ambrose Episcopal Ch., Claremont, 1988—, mem. TRAM com., 1996—, chmn., 1998—, trail steward, 1999; chmn. bd. Friends of Claremont Srs., 1997—. Named Outstanding Contbn. to Social Work, Alumni Assn. Schs. Social Work U. So. Calif., 1984, Outstanding Contbr. Social Group Work, Com. Advancement of Group Work, Toronto, Ont., Can., 1985, Woman of Yr., Trojan Women U. So. Calif., 1976, Woman of Yr., YWCA of Pomona Valley, 1989, Vol. of Yr., L.A. County Coun. on Aging, 1990; recipient Dart award for Innovative Tchg., U. Soc. Calif., 1974, 1st pl. award at juried show Am. Assn. Chinese Brush Painting, 1987, 2nd pl. short story Sedona Writers Contest, Hon. Mention non-fiction, 1989, County Commr. Citation State of Calif. Ho. of Reps., Outstanding Contbn. award Mt. San Antonio Gardens Retirement Cmty., 1994, 99, Contbn. to Srs. award Pomona Valley Cmty. Svcs., 1994, Spl. Recognition award, Social Work, U. So. Calif., 1996, Jo Smith award for outstanding contbrs. to Claremont Srs., 1998, Mt. San Antonio Gardens award for svc., 1999. Fellow Gerontol. Soc. Am.; mem. AAUW, Nat. Assn. Social Workers (cert., nat. chmn. 1962-64, group work sect., chmn. Cleve. chpt. 1969-72), Am. Soc. Aging (chmn. program com. 1983-85, City of Claremont com. on aging 1983—, chmn. 1991, program chair 1985-94), Rembrandt Soc., Scripps Fine Arts Assn., Harvey Mudd Gallilio Soc. Episcopalian. Avocations: botanical gardens docent, birdwatching, watercolor painting, sculpturing, poetry writing. Home: 918 Harrison Ave Claremont CA 91711-4129

HARTH, ROBERT JAMES, music festival executive; b. Louisville, June 13, 1956; s. Sidney and Teresa O. H.; m. Melanie Lynn Pope; 1 child, Jeffrey David Harth Curtis. B.A. in English, Northwestern U., 1977. Assoc. mgr. Ravinia (Ill.) Festival Assn., 1977-79; v.p., gen. mgr. Los Angeles Philharm. Assn., 1979-89, Hollywood Bowl, 1979-89; pres., chief exec. officer Aspen (Colo.) Music Festival and Sch., Music Assocs. of Aspen, Inc., 1989—. Office: Aspen Music Festival Sch 2 Music School Rd Aspen CO 81611-8500

HARTH-BEDOYA, MIGUEL, conductor; b. Lima, Peru, 1968. Degree, Curtis Inst. Music, Juilliard Sch. Music dir. Eugene (Oreg.) Symphony Orch.; music dir., condr. N.Y. Youth Symphony Carnegie Hall; guest condr. N.Y. Philharm., L.A. Philharm., Florida Orch., Seattle Symphony, Colorado Symphony, Quebec Symphony, Auckland Philharmonia, New Zealand, Puerto Rico Symphony, Buenos Aires Philharmonia, Evansville Philharm. Orch., Ind., others; condr. Juilliard Orch. tour, France, 1993, Japan, 1995, St. Luke's Orch., 1995; founder, artistic dir. New Opera Co. Peru, Orquestra Filarmonica de Lima; mem. conducting faculty Juilliard Sch. Condr. (opera) Il Tutore Burlato, 1994, Italy, recording, 1995. Office: Eugene Symphony Orch 45 W Broadway Ste 201 Eugene OR 97401-3002*

HARTLAND, NANCI JEAN, communications executive, educator; b. Passaic, N.J., Feb. 3, 1944; d. Irvin Correll and Maureen Victory (Elmer) H.; m. Frederick Emerson Gilbert, May 30, 1962 (div. June 1968); children: Jacqueline Jean, Juré Noel, Frederick Thomas II. BS in Psychology, U. Maine, Orono, 1978; BA in Art, U. Maine, 1978. Human resources profl. Woolco Dept. Stores, Bangor, Maine, 1966-72; asst. to pres. Fransway Realty, Bangor, Maine, 1972-78; pres. Mgmt. Pro-Tem, Bangor, Maine, 1978-82; owner, pres. LifeTracks, San Diego, 1982—; trainer, developer Global Leaders Programs, Vacations with a Conscience, planting fruit trees in small villages in East Africa, San Diego, 1992—, Ethnics & Ethics, San Diego, 1992—; leader Tree Pals Project Safaris; relief worker small villages in Tanzania. Author: My Spirit Speaks, 1985, Future Perfect, 1991, Some Places I Will Kiss You, 1992; assoc. producer Winnervision, Inward Bound, 1983-84; assoc. producer Renaissance Films, 1985-86; producer Suzy Prudden Show, 1987—; contbr. articles to profl. jours. Vol. Consumers of Maine Bringing Action, Bangor, 1978-82, Maine Nuclear Referendum, Bangor, 1978-82, Global Energy Network Internat., San Diego; bd. dirs. Earthvision, 1994—. Mem. Optimist Club (v.p. 1990-93), Liason League. Democrat. Avocations: fencing, beach walking, hiking, dancing, rollerblading. Address: 3075 Redwood St San Diego CA 92104-4613

HARTLEY, BOB, hockey coach; b. Hawesbury, Ont., Can., Sept. 7, 1960. Head coach Colo. Avalanche, 1998—. Office: care Colo Avalanche McNichols Arena 1635 Olay St Denver CO 80204*

HARTLEY, CORINNE, painter, sculptor, educator; b. L.A., July 24, 1924; d. George D. and Marjorie (Fansher) Parr; m. Thomas L. West, Sept. 3, 1944 (div. 1970); children: Thomas West III, Tori West, Trent West; m. Clabe M. Hartley, Aug. 27, 1973 (div. 1997). Attended, Chouinard Art Inst., L.A., 1942-44, Pasadena (Calif.) Sch. Fine Arts, 1952-54. Paste up artist Advt. Agy., L.A., 1944; fashion illustrator May Co., L.A., 1944-45; freelance fashion illustrator Bullock's, L.A., 1946-76; art tchr. Pasadena Sch. Fine Arts, 1965-71; pvt. art tchr., owner studio, Venice, Calif., 1971—; presenter art workshops; works pub. and distributed by Art in Motion, Prints and Cards, Vancouver, B.C., Can., 1990—. Gallery representation includes Dassin Gallery, L.A., 1981—, Legacy Gallery, Scottsdale, Ariz., 1989—, G. Stanton Gallery, Dallas, 1990—, Coda Gallery, Palm Desert, Calif., 1993—, Huntsman Gallery, Aspen, Colo., 1995—, Carol Kavanaugh Gallery, Des Moines, 1996—, Jones & Terwilliger Gallery, Carmel, Calif., 1997—, Lee Youngman Gallery, Calistoga, Calif., 1997—, Coda Gallery, Park City, Utah, 1997—, Terbush Gallery, Santa Fe, 1997—. Recipient Purchase award Nat. Orange Show, San Bernardino, Honor award All City Art Festival, Barnsdall Park, L.A., Best of Show award Clumer Mus. Wash., 3d pl. award still life Calif. Art Club, others. Mem. Am. Acad. Women Artists, Calif. Art Club, Oil Painters Am. Republican. Avocation: singing in ch. choir. Studio: 411 N Venice Blvd Venice CA 90291-4534

HARTMAN, JEANNETTE MARIE, marketing specialist; b. Wichita Falls, Tex., Apr. 20, 1952; d. Jean F. and Betty J. (Logan) Hartman. BS in Journalism, U. Kans., 1974; MBA, Pepperdine U., 1998. Publs. specialist Caudill, Rowlett Scott, Houston, 1974-76; reporter Evening Outlook, Santa Monica, Calif., 1976-80; pub. info. officer Santa Monica Coll., 1980-87; sr. media relations specialist Blue Cross Calif., Woodland Hills, 1987-88, pub. relations supr., 1988-89, pub. relations mgr., 1989; news bur. mgr. Jewish Fedn. Council Greater L.A., 1989-92, sr. asst. dir. comms., 1992-93; mgr. mktg. & comms. Jewish Community Found., L.A., 1993-98; sr. mktg. assic. Cedars-Sinai Med. Ctr., L.A., 1998-99; mgr. mktg. Cedars Sinai Med. Network, 1999—. Recipient 2d place for newsletters Calif. Community and Jr. Coll. Assn., 1982, John Swett award Calif. Tchrs. Assn., 1978, Silver award for ann. reports Coun. Jewish Fedns., 1991, 1st place for ann. reporters Publicity Club L.A., 1992. Mem. Am. Mktg. Assn., Pub. Rels. Soc. Am. (recipient 1st place for non-profit newsletters 1992, award of merit for ann. reports 1992), Internat. Assn. Bus. Communicators (Ace Award Merit overall achievement ann. reports 1992). Office: Ste112 200 N Robertson Blvd Beverly Hills CA 90211

HARTMAN, ROBERT LEROY, artist, educator; b. Sharon, Pa., Dec. 17, 1926; s. George Otto and Grace Arvada (Radabaugh) H.; m. Charlotte Ann Johnson, Dec. 30, 1951; children: Mark Allen, James Robert. BFA, U. Ariz., 1951, MA, 1952; postgrad., Colo. Springs Fine Arts Center, 1947, 51, Bklyn. Mus. Art Sch., 1953-54. Instr. architecture, allied arts Tex. Tech. Coll., 1955-58; asst. prof. art U. Nev., Reno, 1958-61; mem. faculty dept. art U. Calif., Berkeley, 1961—, prof., 1972-91, prof. emeritus, 1991—, chmn. dept., 1974-76; mem. Inst. for Creative Arts, U. Calif., 1967-68. One man exhbns. include, Bertha Schafer Gallery, N.Y.C., 1966, 69, 74, Santa Barbara Mus. Art, 1973, Cin. Art Acad., 1975, Hank Baum Gallery, San Francisco, 1973, 75, 78, San Jose Mus. Art, 1983, Bluxome Gallery, San Francisco, 1984, 86, U. Art Mus., Berkeley, 1986, Instituto D'Arte Dosso Dossi, Ferrara, Italy, 1989, Victor Fischer Galleries, San Francisco, 1991, Triangle Gallery, San Francisco, 1992, 93, 95, 97, Augusta State U., 1998; group exhbns. include Richmond Mus., 1966, Whitney Mus. Biennial, 1973, Oakland Mus., 1976, San Francisco Arts Commn. Gallery, 1985 (award), Earthscape Expo '90 Photo Mus., Osaka, Japan, 1990, In Close Quarters, American Landscape Photography Since 1968, Princeton Art Mus., 1993, Facing Eden: 100 Years of Landscape Art in The Bay Area, San Francisco, 1995, Colorado Springs Fine Arts Ctr., 1998; represented in permanent collections, Nat. Collections Fine Arts, Colorado Springs Fine Arts Center, Corcoran Gallery, San Francisco Art Inst., Roswell Mus., Princeton Art Mus. U. Calif. humanities research fellow, 1980. Office: U Calif Dept Art Berkeley CA 94720

HARTMAN, ROSEMARY JANE, special education educator; b. Gainesville, Fla., Aug. 24, 1944; d. John Leslie and Irene (Bowen) Goddard; m. Alan Lynn Gerber, Feb. 1, 1964 (div. 1982); children: Sean Alan, Dawn Julianne Silva, Lance Goddard; m. Perry Hartman, June 27, 1992. BA, Immaculate Heart Coll., 1967; MA, Loyola U., 1974. Cert. resource specialist. Tchr. L.A. Unified Schs., 1968-78; resource specialist Desert Sands Unified Sch. Dist., Palm Desert, 1978-83, Palm Springs Unified Schs., 1983—. Co-author: The Twelve Steps of Phobics Anonymous, 1989, One Day At A Time in Phobics Victorious, 1992, The Twelve Steps of Phobics Victorious, 1993; founder Phobics Victorious, 1992. Mem. Am. Assn. Christian Counselors (charter), Internat. Platform Assn., Nat. Assn. of Christian Recovery, Anxiety Disorders Assn. Am. Office: Phobics Victorious PO Box 695 Palm Springs CA 92263-0695

HARTMAN, SUSAN P(ATRICE), adult education administrator. Dir. adult edn. Front Range C.C., Westminster, Colo., 1995—. Recipient Regional Person of Yr. award, 1992. Office: Front Range Community Coll Westminster CO 80030*

HARTMAN-IRWIN, MARY FRANCES, retired language professional; b. Portland, Oreg., Oct. 18, 1925; d. Curtiss Henry Sabisch and Gladys Frances (Giles) Strand; m. Harry Elmer Hartman, Sept. 6, 1946 (div. June 1970); children: Evelyn Frances, Laura Elyce, Andrea Candace; m. Thomas Floyd Irwin, Apr. 11, 1971. BA, U. Wash., 1964-68; postgrad., Seattle Pacific, 1977-79, Antioch U., Seattle, Wash., 1987, Heritage Inst., Seattle, Wash., 1987. Lang. educator Kennewick (Wash.) Dist. # 17, 1970-88; guide Summer Study Tours of Europe, 1971-88. Sec. Bahai Faith, 1971-94, libr., Pasco, Washington, 1985-88; trustee Mid. Columbia coun. Girl Scouts U.S. Fulbright scholar, 1968. Mem. NEA, Wash. Edn. Assn., Kennewick Edn. Assn., Nat. Fgn. Lang. Assn., Wash. Fgn. Lang. Assn., Literacy Coun. (literacy tutor Tillamook Bay C.C.). Avocations: painting, sewing, writing essays and short stories. Home: PO Box 247 Netarts OR 97143-0247

HARTNETT, GARY J., architect; b. Holyoke, Mass., June 20, 1954; s. James R. and Rita R. (Sullivano) H.; m. Kristine Hansen, Nov. 12, 1983 (div. Sept. 1992); children: Molly, Wendy. A, Dean Jr. Coll., Franklin, Mass., 1974; BArch, Boston Architecture Ctr., 1979. Archtl. designer Keyes Assocs., Waltham, Mass., 1974-77, Eisenberg Haven, Boston, 1977-78, Cambridge (Mass.) Seven, 1978-79; arch. McKinley Archs., Cambridge, 1979-82, L.M.N. Archs., Seattle, 1982-83, Eric Heng Assocs., Seattle, 1983-84, John Graham Archs., Seattle, 1984-85, Parsons Brinckerhoff, Seattle, 1985-95; dir. arch. Otak, Inc., Seattle, 1995—. Prin. works include Transit Sta., Seattle, 1990 (design award of merit AIA, 1990). Mem. AIA. Office: Otak Archs Inc 117 S Main St Seattle WA 98104-2540

HARTNETT, KATHLEEN CAMBLIN, counselor; b. N.Y.C., July 17, 1942; d. John Hutchinson and Margaret (Donovan) Camblin. BA, St. Mary's Coll., 1964; MEd, Lewis &Clark Coll., 1977; postgrad., Portland State U., 1996—. Lic. profl. counselor, Oreg. Missionary Extension Lay Vols., Anadarko, Okla., 1964-65; social worker Cook County Pub. Aid, Chgo., 1965-67, Cath. Svcs. for Children, Portland, 1967-68; dir. social work Patterson (N.J.) Orphanage, 1968-69; cancer counselor St. Vincent Med. Ctr., Portland, 1974-79; asst. dir. cancer counseling Kaiser Permanente, Portland, 1979-84; dir. cancer counseling Providence Health System, Portland, 1984—; cons. in field. cons. pub. edn. Portland Pub. Schs., Am. Cancer Soc., Portland, Lewis and Clark Coll., Portland, Portland Ctr. Hearing and Speech, Oreg. Comprehensive Cancer Program, Nat. Psoriasis Assn., all 1976—. Mem. Am. Counseling Assn. (mental health spl. interest 1990—), Oreg. Counseling Assn. Avocations: outdoor activities, music, theatre. Office: Providence Health System care Cancer Counseling Svcs 5050 NE Hoyt Level B Portland OR 97213

HARTSBURG, CRAIG WILLIAM, professional hockey coach; b. Stratford, Ont., Can., June 29, 1959. Grad. H.S., Sault Ste. Marie, Ont., Can. Profl. hockey player Minn. North Stars, 1979-89, asst. coach, 1989-90; asst. coach Phila. Flyers, 1990-94; head coach Chgo. Blackhawks, 1995-98, Mighty Ducks of Anaheim, 1998—. Recipient Max Kaminsky Meml. trophy, 1978-77; named OHA All-Star 2d team, 1978-77; played in NHL All-Star Game, 1980, 82, 83. Office: Mighty Ducks of Anaheim 2695 E Katella Ave PO Box 61077 Anaheim CA 92803-6177*

HARTWICK, THOMAS STANLEY, technical management consultant; b. Vandalia, Ill., Mar. 19, 1934; s. William Arthur and Bernice Elizabeth (Daniels) H.; m. Alberta Elaine Lind, June 10, 1961; children: Glynis Anne, Jeffrey Andrew, Thomas Arthur. BS, U. Ill., 1956; MS, UCLA, 1958; PhD, U. So. Calif., 1969. Mgr. quantum electronics dept. Aerospace Corp., El Segundo, Calif., 1973-75, asst. dir. electronics research lab., 1975-79; mgr. electro-optical devel. lab. Hughes Aircraft Co. subs. Gen. Motors Corp., El Segundo, 1979-82, chief sci. advanced tactical programs, 1982-83; mgr. electro-optics research ctr. TRW Corp., Redondo Beach, Calif., 1983-86, mgr. microelectrics ctr., 1986-90, program mgr., 1990-96; chmn., bd. dirs. Laser Tech., Inc., Hollywood, Calif., 1990-94; cons. mem. U.S. Dept. Def. Adv. Group on Electronic Devices, Washington, 1977—, group C chmn., 1988-94; mem. Japan/U.S. Tech. Assessment Team, Washington, 1984; mem. Army Rsch. Labs. Adv. Bd., 1993-95; bd. dirs. 3D Tech. labs., Inc., IMEC, Inc., ARIES Tech., Inc.; chmn. Nat. Rsch. Coun. FAA Security, 1997—. Contbr. articles to profl. jours.; inventor FAR Infrared Laser, 1975. Mem. Am. Phys. Soc., Optical Soc. Am., (com. mem. 1976-79), Am. Def. Preparedness Assn. (dep. chmn. West Coast seminar 1987-88), mem. Nat. Res. Coun. Comm. Optical Sci and Engring., 1995—. Avocations: piano, sports.

HARVEGO, EDWIN ALLAN, mechanical engineer; b. Vallejo, Calif., June 5, 1943; s. Edwin Simon and Bette Jean (Owens) H.; m. Lisa Ann Actis; children: Jessica Marie, Joshua Michael, Erin Alane, Deidre Denise. BSME, U. Calif., Berkeley, 1966, MSME, 1967. Registered profl. engr., Calif., Idaho. Sr. preliminary design engr. AiResearch Mfg. Co., L.A., 1967-72; sr. engr. Gen. Atomic, San Diego, 1972-76; sci. and engring. supr. EG&G Idaho, Inc., Idaho Falls, Idaho, 1976-80, br. mgr., 1980-84, sr. engring. specialist, 1984-91, tech. unit mgr., 1991-94; consulting engr., group leader Lockheed Martin Idaho Techs. Co., Idaho Falls, 1994—; course developer, tchr. internat. workshop, 1997. Author: (tech. publ.) Topics in Two-Phase Heat Transfer and Flow, 1978, (book chpt.) Nuclear Space Power Systems, 1987. Fellow ASME (chmn. nuclear heat exch. com. 1986-88, chmn. Idaho sect. 1989-90, chmn. nuclear engring. divsn. 1992-93, mem. energy conversion bd. 1993—, v.p. energy conversion group 1998—, rep. U.S. Nat. Com. World Energy Coun., 1998—). Achievements include development of

Nuclear Regulatory Commission severe accident and fuel behavior codes at Idaho National Engineering Lab; development of advanced reactor concept for space and terrestrial applications, lead planning and analysis for loss-of-fluid test international test program; development of analysis methods for high-temperature gas-cooled reactor. Avocations: golf, rafting, skiing. Office: Lockheed Martin Idaho Techs Co 2525 N Fremont Idaho Falls ID 83415

HARVELL, TONY, librarian; b. St. Louis, Oct. 19, 1952; s. George T. and Thelma Harvell. BA, S.E. Mo. State U., 1973; MLS, La. State U., 1975; MA, U. Miami, 1989. Assoc. libr. U. Fla., Gainesville, 1981-83; Latin Am. bibliographer U. Miami, Coral Gables, Fla., 1983-91; prof. U. San Diego, 1991—. Mem. ALA, SALALM-L.Am. Office: Univ San Diego Copley Libr 5998 Alcala Pk San Diego CA 92111

HARVEY, DONALD, artist, educator; b. Walthamston, Eng., June 14, 1930; s. Henry and Annie Dorothy (Sawell) H.; m. Elizabeth Clark, Aug. 9, 1952; children—Shan Mary, David Jonathan. Art tchrs. diploma, Brighton Coll. Art, 1951. Art master Ardwyn Grammar Sch., Wales, 1952-56; mem. faculty dept. art U. Victoria, B.C., Can., 1961-95; now prof. emeritus painting U. Victoria. One man exhbns. include, Albert White Gallery, Toronto, 1968, retrospective, Art Gallery of Victoria, 1968; represented in permanent collections, Nat. Gallery Can., Montreal Mus., Albright-Knox Mus., Seattle Art Mus. Mem. accessions com. Art Gallery of Victoria, 1969-72. Can. Council fellow, 1966. Mem. Royal Can. Acad. of Arts (full academician), Can. Group Painters, Can. Painters and Etchers. Home: 1025 Joan Crescent, Victoria, BC Canada V8S 3L3*

HARVEY, ELLEN MAE, county official; b. Chewy, Okla., Mar. 4, 1926; d. William P. and Rose M. (Phelps) Patterson; m. Leonard V. Owens, Mar. 11, 1942 (div. Aug. 1953); children: Mary E., Nellie R., Leonard J., Patrick E.; m. James V. Jones, 1953 (div. 1962); 1 child, Russell V. Jones. Provider adult foster home Jackson County Mental Health, Medford, Oreg., 1965—. Mem. Eagles, Moose. Home: 1801 Poco Way Las Vegas NV 89102-3868

HARVEY, G. CAMERON, drama educator, artistic director; b. Pasadena, Calif., Jan. 6, 1948; s. Charles Cameron and Rose Marie (Wood) H.; m. Mandy Elizabeth Banks, Mar. 23, 1995; 1 child, Brenda Lynn. BA in Drama, U. Calif., Irvine, 1969, MFA in Drama, 1971. Prof. drama U. Calif., Irvine, 1983—, head design dept. drama, 1982—, chair drama, 1995—; producing artistic dir. Utah Shakespearean Festival, Cedar City, Utah, 1990—; theatre cons. The Harvey Co., Laguna Beach, Calif., 1980—; vol. con. Artists Theatre, Laguna Beach, 1996-97. Recipient lighting design awards Hollywood Dramalogue Critics award, L.A., 1983, 85, 92, L.A. Drama Critics Circle, 1983. Mem. United Scenic Artists, Univ. Resident Theatre Assn. (pres. 1996—). Avocation: scuba diving. Home: 830 La Mirada St Laguna Beach CA 92651-3753

HARVEY, GREGORY ALAN, microcomputer technology educator, consultant; b. Harvey, Ill., Feb. 15, 1949; s. Kenneth Herman and Mildred Faye (Pounds) H. BA, U. Ill., 1970; teaching credential, San Francisco State U., 1982. Mem. drafting and design staff Bechtel Engring., San Francisco, 1973-81; computer cons., prin. Harvey & Assocs., San Francisco, 1981-96; prin. Media of the Minds, 1993-96; pres. Mind Over Media, Inc., 1995—; computer cons. PCTeach, Inverness, Calif., 1984-91; profl. lectr. Golden Gate U., 1992. Author: Communication in Writing, 1984, Mastering SuperCalc 3, 1985, Mastering Q&A, 1986, Lotus 1-2-3 Desktop Companion, 1987, WordPerfect Desktop Companion, 1987, Mastering WordStar, 1987, Lotus 1-2-3 Instant Reference, 1988, DOS Instant Reference, 1988, Understanding HyperCard, 1988, HyperTalk Instant Reference, 1988, The Complete Lotus 1-2-3 Handbook, 1989, Mastering PageMaker on the MacIntosh, 1990, Encyclopedia WordPerfect, 1990, Que's WordPerfect Windows QuickStart, 1991, Que's Lotus 1-2-3 Window QuickStart, 1991, PC World's WordPerfect Windows, 1991, Greg Harvey's Excel 4 Handbook Windows, 1992, Greg Harvey's Excel 4 Handbook MacIntosh, 1992, IDG's 1-2-3 for Dummies, 1992, IDG's DOS for Dummies Command Reference, 1993, Windows for Dummies Command Reference, 1993, WordPerfect for Dummies Command Reference, 1993, WordPerfect 6 DOS Handbook, 1993, More Excel for Dummies, 1994, Excel 5 for Mac for Dummies, 1994, Windows 95 for Dummies Quick Reference, 1995, Dummies 101: Excel 5 for Windows 95, 1995, Shockwave for Director for Dummies, 1996, Que's Net Savvy Office, 1997, IDG's Director Studio Secrets, 1997, Internet Explorer 4 for Dummies, Quick Reference, 1997, Windows 98 Dummies Quick Reference, 1998, Active Desktop for Windows for Dummies, 1998. Mem. Internat. Interactive Comm. Soc. Democrat. Zen Buddhist. Avocations: Tai Chi, classical flute, raising Shetland Sheepdogs, hiking, mountain biking. Home: 60 Kyleswood Pl Inverness CA 94937-9717 Office: Mind Over Media Inc PO Box 1175 Point Reyes Station CA 94956-1175

HARVEY, JAMES GERALD, educational counselor, consultant, researcher; b. California, Mo., July 15, 1934; s. William Walter and Exie Marie (Lindley) H. BA Amherst Coll., 1956; MAT (fellow), Harvard U., 1958, MEd, 1962. Asst. to dean grad. sch. edn. Harvard U., Cambridge, Mass., 1962-66, dir. admissions, fin. aid, 1966-69; dir. counseling service U. Calif., Irvine, 1970-72; ednl. cons., Los Angeles, 1972—. Author: (ednl. materials) HARVOCAB Vocabulary Program, 1985—. 1st lt. USAF, 1958-61. Amherst Mayo-Smith grantee, 1956-57; UCLA Adminstrv. fellow, 1969-70. Mem. Am. Ednl. Research Assn., Nat. Council Measurement in Edn. Address: 1845 Glendon Ave Los Angeles CA 90025-4653

HARVEY, JOSEPH EMMETT, construction executive; b. L.A., Dec. 4, 1951; s. Emmett Allan and Mary Summerall (Anderson) H. BA in Psychology with distinction, U. Hawaii, 1974; postgrad., U.S. Internat. U., 1975-76, San Diego State U., 1976-77. Program coord. Crisis House, El Cajon, Calif., 1975-79; ops. mgr. C.S. Goodale Co., San Diego, 1977-84; sales mgr. Dunn & Co., San Diego, 1985-89; constrn. mgr. Comml. Shelving, Inc., Honolulu, 1989-92; constrn. exec. Skylights of Hawaii, Honolulu, 1992-97; pres. Harvey Bldg. Specialties, Inc., Kamuela, Hawaii, 1998—. Mem. Bldg Industry Assn., Constrn. Specifications Inst. (dir. 1994-96, asst. chair western region tech. com. 1994-95, awards chair 1995-97, Constrn. Document Technician cert. 1995, merit award 1993, Pacesetter award 1994), Hawaii Island Contractors Assn., Rotary (Svc. award 1993), Phi Beta Kappa. Avocations: yachting, skiing.

HARVEY, MARC SEAN, lawyer, consultant; b. N.Y.C., May 4, 1960; s. M. Eugene and Coleen (Jones) H. BA with honors, So. Ill. U., 1980; JD, Southwestern U., 1983; postgrad., Loyola Marymount U., L.A., 1984-86. lectr. Loyola Marymount U., 1986; judge pro tem Culver (Calif.) Mcpl. Ct., 1991—. Counsel U.S. SBA, L.A., 1982-83; counsel enforcement div. U.S. SEC, L.A., 1983-84; counsel State Farm Ins. Co., L.A., 1984-85, 20th Century Ins. Co., Woodland Hills, Calif., 1985-86; pvt. practice Encino, Calif., 1986—; lectr. Loyola Marymount U., 1986; judge pro tem Culver (Calif.) Mcpl. Ct., 1991—. Charter mem., trustee Rep. Presdl. Task Force, Washington, 1981—; mem. Nat. Rep. Senatorial Com., Washington, 1983—, Rep. Congl. Leadership Coun., Washington, 1987—, Rep. Senatorial Inner Cir., Washington, 1988—; victory fund sponsor Nat. Rep. Congl. Com., Washington, 1984—; judge pro tem Culver Mcpl. Ct., 1991— (Judge Pro Tem of Yr. award 1991). Recipient 1st Pl. Essay award VFW, 1976, So. Ill. U. scholarship, 1979-81. Mem. ABA, AFTRA, SAG, Am. Trial Lawyers Assn., Calif. Trial Lawyers Assn., L.A. Bar Assn., L.A. Trial Laywers Assn., Themis Soc., Nat. Honor Soc.

HARVEY, NANCY MELISSA, media specialist, art teacher; b. Atlanta, Mar. 31, 1934; d. Alfred Alonzo and Helen Rosella (Puntney) Ettinger; m. Dale Gene Harvey, Aug. 23, 1957; children: Howard Russell, Andrew Dale, Renee Jeannine. BA, U. Mont., 1957; M in Human Svcs., Coll. of Gt. Falls, Mont., 1987. Cert. tchr., Mont. Media specialist, libr. Flathead H.S., Kalispell, Mont., 1971-79; libr., art tchr. Cut Bank (Mont.) H.S., 1979-94. Contbr. poetry to Arts in Mont., Mont. Arts mag., Poetry Today quar., Today's Poets anthology. Recipient Mary Brennan Clapp Poetry awrd Mont. Arts Found., 1973, grantee Mont. Com. for the Humanities, 1985, 8[illegible] (dir.), Mont. Genealogy Soc. (treas. Tangled Roots chpt. 1990—), Delta Kappa Gamma (chpt. pres. 1994-96), Phi Kappa Phi. Democrat. Presbyterian. Avocations: music, painting, creative writing, photography.

HARVEY, O.J., retired psychology educator; b. Corinne, Okla., Aug. 27, 1927; s. Joseph Marion and Nina Inez (Little) H.; m. Mary Christine Minton, Nov. 17, 1950. BA, U. Okla., 1950, MA, 1951, PhD, 1954. Fellow Yale U., New Haven, Conn., 1954-55; asst. prof. psychology Vanderbilt U., Nashville, 1955-58; asst. prof. U. Colo., Boulder, 1958-60; assoc. prof. U. Colo., 1960-62, prof., 1964-91, prof. emeritus, 1991—. Co-author: Conceptual Systems and Personality Organization, 1961, Robbers Cave Experiment, 1988; editor 2 books; contbr. over 100 articles to profl. jours. With USN, 1946-47. Fellow Ctr. for Advanced Study, Palo Alto, Calif., 1964-65; recipient Career Devel. award NIMH, Washington, 1965-70. Avocations: travel, writing, fishing. Home: 435 S 68th St Boulder CO 80303-4308

HARVEY, RAYMOND CURTIS, conductor; b. N.Y.C., Dec. 9, 1950; s. Shirley Nathaniel and Doris Louise (Walwin) H. BMus, MMus, Oberlin Coll., 1973; M. in Musical Arts, Yale U., 1978, D in Musical Arts, 1984. Choral dir. Northfield (Mass.) Mt. Hermon Sch., 1973-76; asst. conductor Des Moines Metro Opera, Indianola, Iowa, 1977-80; music dir. Tex. Opera Theater, Houston, 1978-80; Exxon/arts endowment conductor Indpls. Symphony, 1980-83; assoc. conductor Buffalo Philharmonic, 1983-86; music dir. Marion (Ind.) Philharmonic, 1982-86, Springfield (Mass.) Symphony, 1986-94, Fresno Philharm. Orch., 1993—; guest conductor Minn. Orch., 1991, 92, Detroit Symphony, 1990, 92, N.Y. Philharmonic, 1987, Atlanta Symphony, 1992, Louisville Orch., 1990, 93, Utah Symphony, 1993. Democrat. Methodist. Avocations: running, fitness. Office: Fresno Philharm Orch 2610 W Shaw Ave Ste 103 Fresno CA 93711-2767*

HARVEY, RICHARD BLAKE, political science educator; b. Los Angeles, Nov. 28, 1930; s. George Blackstone and Clara Ethel (Conway) H.; m. Patricia Jean Clougher, Aug. 29, 1965; 1 child: Timothy Harvey. BA, Occidental Coll., 1952; MA, UCLA, 1954, PhD, 1959. Prof. polit. sci. Whittier (Calif.) Coll., 1960—, acad. dean, 1970-80, chmn. polit. sci. dept., 1984-87. Author: Earl Warren, Governor of California, 1970, Dynamics-California Government and Politics, 1996; contbr. articles and book revs. to profl. jours. Grantee Haynes Found., 1961, 68. Mem. Am. Polit. Sci. Assn., Western Polit. Sci. Assn., So. Calif. Polit. Sci. Assn., Newcomen Soc., Pi Sigma Alpha. Democrat. Presbyterian. Club: University. Avocations: reading, racquetball, avocado growing. Home: 424 E Avocado Crest Rd La Habra Hgts CA 90631-8128 Office: Whittier Coll Whittier CA 90608

HARVEY, ROBERT BALLENGEE, retired music educator, administrator; b. Gering, Nebr., Sept. 27, 1924; s. Edward Wayland and Helen Virginia (Ballengee) H.; m. Margaret Barbara Sekora, Nov. 27, 1947 (dec. Jan., 1967); children: Barbara Fox, Patricia Hirsch; m. Nancy Carroll Dye, Apr. 12, 1969; children: Edward Robert, Jennie Elizabeth. BA, Kearney State Tchrs. Coll., 1949; MEd, U. S.D., 1957; EdD, Utah State U., 1975. Cert. chief adminstr. C.Cs., Calif. Band dir., English and bus. instr. Campbell (Nebr.) H.S., 1949-51; band dir., English and bus. instr., principal Bloomfield (Nebr.) H.S., 1952-59; ins. agt. Fremont, Nebr., 1959-64; band dir., English instr. LeGrand (Calif.) H.S., 1964-65; band dir., chmn. arts divsn. Merced (Calif.) C.C., 1964-97; mem. acad. senate Merced (Calif.) C.C.; fellow Nat. Inst. for Staff and Organizational Devel., U. Tex., 1996-97. Tech. sgt. USMC, 1951-52. Mem. NEA, AFM, KC, Calif. Tchrs. Assn., Music Assn. Calif. C.C., Merced Breakfast Lions' Club (2d v.p. 1998-99). Republican. Roman Catholic. Avocations: reading, music (performance and conducting), fishing. Home: 1674 Knoll Ct Merced CA 95340-8627

HARVEY, RUFUS WILLIAM, nonprofit administrator; b. Los Angeles, Aug. 4, 1947; s. Rufus Watson and Edith May (Osborne) H.; m. Sherliane Claudette Raab, Sept. 1, 1974; children: Rufus Brandon, Wendy Jean, Joshua Paul. BA, UCLA, 1972. Freelance musician Canyon Country, Calif., 1965—, tax preparer, 1983—; faculty assoc. The Master's Sem., Sun Valley, Calif., 1994—; dir. pub. rels. TransWorld Missions, L.A., 1977-79; bookkeeper Glendale, Calif., 1979-84; dir. acctg. Insight for Living, Fullerton, Calif., 1984-88; admins. Grace Cmty. Ch., Sun Valley, 1988—; enrolled agent IRS, Washington, 1990—. Mem. Nat. Assn. Ch. Bus. Adminstrn., Christian Mgmt. Assn., Nat. Assn. Enrolled Agents, Nat. Soc. Accts., Inst. of Mgmt. Accts., Assn. of Cert. Fraud Examiners, Calif. Soc. Enrolled Agents, Calif. Soc. of Acct. & Tax Profls. Republican. Protestant. Avocations: musician, trumpet player. Office: Grace Cmty Ch 13248 Roscoe Blvd Sun Valley CA 91352-3798

HARVIE, J. JASON, administrative aide, private secretary; b. Seattle, Wash., Dec. 12, 1937; s. James Joseph Harvie and Betty Clair (Walton) Krussow; m. Maureen W.Y. Johnson, June 12, 1970 (div. Sept. 1980). Cert. Law Enforcement, U. Guam, Agana, 1973, Grad. Basic Police Acad., 1973, Advanced Police Technology, 1974; Diploma, San Francisco Police Acad., 1980. Police officer II Gov. of Guam/Dept. Pub. Safety, Agana, 1972-77; chief dept. safety and security U. Calif. Hastings/Coll. of Law, San Francisco, 1978-82; chief patrol officer San Francisco Parking Authority, 1982-84; aide H.E. Sheik Abdullah O. Mahdi, Pebble Beach, Calif., 1984-96. Decorated Navy Achievement medal USN; named Knight Chevalier, Grand Knight/Police Hall of Fame, Miami, 1989; recipient Legion of Honor award Am. Police Hall of Fame, Miami, 1990. Mem. Am. Fedn. Police, Calif. Peace Officers Assn., Marine's Meml. Club, Am. Police Hall of Fame. Republican. Episcopalian. Avocations: bicycling, swimming, stamp collecting, reading. Home and Office: PO Box 1018 Pebble Beach CA 93953-1018

HARWICH, DAVID CURTIS, video design and production specialist; b. Hollywood, Calif., Sept. 1, 1955. Student, Chaffey Coll., Rancho Cucomonga, Calif. Various positions The Photographer, Upland, Calif., 1969-90, dir. videography, 1982-91; with Video Design & Prodn., Upland, Calif., 1991—. Dir.: (video) What is the Carden Method?, 1990, This Old House Restored, 1991; cinematographer: (motion pictures) True Dedication, 1988, Erosion, 1987, The Making of 17th, 1981; photographer: Family Life in Mexico, 1985 (Bronze medal 1986). Office: Video Design & Prodn 1714 N Vallejo Way Upland CA 91784-1964

HARWICK, BETTY CORINNE BURNS, sociology educator; b. L.A., Jan. 22, 1926; d. Henry Wayne Burns and Dorothy Elizabeth (Menzies) Routhier; m. Burton Thomas Harwick, June 20, 1947; children: Wayne Thomas, Burton Terence, Bonnie Christine Foster, Beverly Anne Carroll. Student, Biola, 1942-45, Summer Inst. Linguistics, 1945, U. Calif., Berkeley, 1945-52; BA, Calif. State U., Northridge, 1961, MA, 1965; postgrad., MIT, 1991. Prof. sociology Pierce Coll., Woodland Hills, Calif., 1966-95, pres. acad. senate, 1976-77, pres. faculty assn., 1990-91, chmn. dept. for philosophy and sociology, 1990-95, co-creator, faculty advisor interdisciplinary program religious studies, 1988-95; chmn. for sociology L.A. C.C. Dist., 1993-95. Author: (with others) Introducing Sociology, 1977; author: Workbook for Introducing Sociology, 1978. faculty rep. Calif. C.C. Assn., 1977-80. Alt. fellow NEH, 1978. Mem. Am. Acad. Religion, Soc. Bibl. Lit., Am. Sociol. Assn. Presbyterian. Home: 19044 Superior St Northridge CA 91324-1845

HARWICK, MAURICE, lawyer; b. L.A., Feb. 6, 1933. AA, L.A. City Coll., 1954; JD, Southwestern U., 1957. Bar: Calif., 1958; U.S. Supreme Ct., 1962. Dep. dist. atty. County of Los Angeles, 1958-60; pvt. practice law, Santa Monica, Calif., 1960—; judge pro tem Municipal Ct., 1966-67, 80-81, 85—; past advisor to dist. atty. Los Angeles County. Chmn. bd. rev. Los Angeles Community Colls. and City Schs.; mem. Project Safer Calif. gov.'s com., 1974-75. Mem. Calif. Bar Assn., Los Angeles County Bar Assn., Dist. Attys. Assn. L.A., Criminal Cts. Bar Assn. (pres. 1972, bd. govs.), Assn. Trial Lawyers Am., Los Angeles County Dist. Attys. Assn., Vikings. Office: 7401 Laurel Canyon Blvd Ste 22 North Hollywood CA 91605-3161

HARWICK, WAYNE THOMAS, economist; b. Oakland, Calif., Feb. 29, 1948; s. Burton Thomas and Betty Corinne (Burns) H. BA in Econs., Calif. State Univ., Northridge, 1970, MA in Econs., 1975; BA in Math., Calif. State Univ., L.A., 1983. Planner Ventura (Calif.) County Schs., 1975-76; labor market economist Calif. Employment Data Rsch., L.A., 1976-83; cost analyst TRW, Redondo Beach, Calif., 1983-88; engring. specialist Northrop-Grumman, Pico Rivera, Calif., 1988-92, 96—; cost economist Aerojet, Azusa, Calif., 1992-94; sr. assoc. Mgmt. Consulting Rsch., Thousand Oaks, Calif., 1994-95; instr. Oxnard (Calif.) Coll., 1975-78; owner Industry Metrics, Torrance, Calif., 1995—; rep. Space Systems Cost Analysis Group for Northrop Grumman Corp.; spkr. in field. Bd. dirs. Homeowners Assn., Torrance, 1993-95, 97—. Mem. Soc. Cost Estimating Analysis (cert. cost analyst), Internat. Soc. Parametric Analysts (So. Calif. bd. dirs. 1997), World Affairs Coun. Lutheran. Avocations: weightlifting, swimming, applied mathematics, religious studies, astronomy. E-mail: tharwick@atdc.northtram.com. Home: 4404 Spencer St Torrance CA 90503-2434 Office: Northrop Grumman Corp 8900 Washington Blvd Pico Rivera CA 90660-3765

HASAN, RAFIQ, management consultant; b. Fatehpur, India, Sept. 25, 1945; came to U.S., 1969; s. Siddeeq and Summa H.; m. Yasmeen Hasan, June 10, 1975; 1 child, Zeeshan. BA in Econs., Karachi U., Pakistan, 1968; MBA in Fin., Pepperdine U., 1971. Corporate fin. cons. Johnson Assocs., West Los Angeles, Calif., 1971-73; sr. fin. analyst U.S. Borax, L.A., 1973-76; mgr. fin. planning Hughes Aircraft, 1976-81; pres. CFD, Mission Viejo, Calif., 1981—. Mem. Assn. Corporate Growth, Instrument Soc. Am., Planning Exec. Inst. Republican. Avocations: tennis, badminton, outdoors. Office: CFD 26321 Marsala Way Mission Viejo CA 92692-5231

HASHIMOTO, LLOYD KEN, communications executive; b. Cheyenne, Wyo., Sept. 21, 1944; s. Harry H. and Bettie M. (Kadota) H. Student in chemistry, 1963-65, student in elec. engring., 1969-72, student in edn., 1979; BSin Vocat. Edn., U. Wyo., 1992. Prin. Teltron Electronics, Laramie, Wyo., 1972—; audio visual technician U. Wyo., Laramie, 1972—; mem. internat. panel Electronics Mag., 1974, 76; instr. workshops and seminars High Tech to a Lay Person, 1978; instr. workshop radio direction finding, 1988—; mem. edn. steering com. U. Wyo. Grad. Mountain Folk Sch., 1993-94. Contbr. articles to profl. jours. Program chmn., unit and dist. commr. Snowy Range dist. Boy Scouts Am., Laramie, 1985—, instr. Longs Peak Coun. With U.S. Army, 1965-69. Recipient award of merit Boy Scouts Am., 1991, Silver Beaver award Boy Scouts Am., 1993, Disting. Commr. award Boy Scouts Am., 1994. Mem. IEEE, Assn. Ednl. Comms. Tech. (assoc. audio visual technician S.E. Wyo. chpt.), Soc. Internat. Devel., Assn. for Field Svc. Mgrs. Internat., Am. Legion, Masons (cryptic Masons youth leadership award for Wyo. 1994), Shriners. Avocations: amateur radio, electronic constrn., camping, fishing, media prodn. Home: 504 S 26th St Laramie WY 82070-4932 Office: Teltron Electronics PO Box 1049 Laramie WY 82073-1049

HASKETT, JAMES ALBERT, university program administrator; b. Franklin, Ind., Mar. 2, 1942; s. John Wendell and Helen Elizabeth (Buscher) H.; m. Martha Brooks Vandivort, Apr. 4, 1970. BS, Ind. U., 1964, PhD, 1970. Systems programmer Ind. U., Bloomington, 1970-82, mgr. distributor processing systems, 1982-84, mgr. performance analysis and capacity planning, 1984-88; dir. computer svcs. Ctrl. Wash. U., Ellensburg, 1988-91, dir. info. resources, 1991-93, dir. computing and telecomm. svcs., 1993-97; dir. office info. tech. Boise State U., 1997—; mem. adj. faculty Ind. U., 1980-81. Creator hist. exhibit Acad. Computing in Retrospect: From CSB to BACS, 1986; contbr. articles to profl. jours. Vol. programmer Monroe County Libr., Bloomington, 1977, Yakima County Substance Abuse Coalition, 1994, Ellensburg (Wash.) Elec. Cmty., 1995. Mem. Assn. Computing Machinery (presenter, track chmn. 1989-90), Geographic Info. coun. (higher edn. rep. 1990-94, vice chair/chair elect 1991-92, chair 1993-94). Avocations: running, cooking Asian food, woodworking. E-mail: jhasket@micron.net. Office: Boise State U Office Info Tech Boise ID 83725

HASSELTINE, ERIC HERMON, government relations consultant; b. Ticonderoga, N.Y., Sept. 14, 1937; s. Wilson Hermon and Helene Elizabeth (Mason) H.; m. Syma Jo Reynolds, Sept. 5, 1967 (div. Feb. 1979); children: Sallie Renee, Eric Wilson. AB, Hamilton Coll., 1959; BS, MIT, 1959, MS, 1961; PhD, U. Calif., Berkeley, 1967. Rsch. engr. Boeing Co., Seattle, 1967-69; mem. tech. staff Sandia Labs., Livermore, Calif., 1969-77; supr. Contra Costa County, Martinez, Calif., 1977-81; dir. advance planning Hofmann Co., Concord, Calif., 1981-87; cons. Hasseltine Best, Lafayette, Calif., 1987-97, Hasseltine Cons., Lafayette, 1997—; mem. Cal-Fed Bay/Delta Adv. Coun., Sacramento, Calif., 1993—. Bd. dirs. Local Agy. Formation Commn., Martinez, 1977-81, Bay Area Air Quality Mgmt. Dist., San Francisco, 1979-80; regent John F. Kennedy U., Orinda, Calif., 1994—; pres., bd. dirs. Family Stress Ctr., Concord, 1978-94, Contra Costa Coun., Walnut Creek, Calif., 1982—. Avocations: sports and art collecting, golf. Office: Hasseltine Cons 3182 Old Tunnel Rd Ste E Lafayette CA 94549-4152

HASTEY, SHARI ROSE, nonprofit foundation administrator; b. New Westminster, B.C., Jan. 5, 1946; d. Gilbert Charles and Norma Gertrude (Booth) Clark; m. Allen Barbour, Sept. 3, 1966 (dec. Jan. 1969); m. Kenneth Gerald Hastey, Sept. 21, 1972 (dec.); children: Timothy, Stephen, Cynthia, Karen. Postgrad. in counseling, Fuller Sem.; tng. programs in violence prevention, tng. programs in cultural diversity, tng. in gang awareness. Head counselor, regional co-dir. Young Life Urban Camps, 1976-83; exec. dir. Cmty. Partnership for Youth, Monterey, Calif., 1993—; ptnr. D&H Assocs., co-owner M.E.S. Ragz, 1991-92; owner Consider It Done, 1990-94; wedding cons. Mem. adv. bd. Salvation Army, 1987-94; chair basic needs com., cmty. rels. com.; mem. Monterey County Homeless Coalition, 1988-92; mem. adv. com. Fort Ord Task Force, 1991-92; bd. dirs. Healthy Start, 1992—, Jim Tunney Youth Found., 1994—. Recipient Outstanding Cmty. Svc. award Sun St. Cts., Inc. 1994, Outstanding Vol. Svc. award Monterey County Vol. Ctr., 1991, Vol. of Yr., 1992; named Woman of Achivement, Seaside Bus. and Profl. Women's Club, Woman of Distinction, Soroptimists Internat., 1990. Office: Cmty Ptnrshp Youth PO Box 42 Monterey CA 93942

HASTINGS, DOC, congressman; b. Spokane, Wash., Feb. 7, 1941; m. Claire Hastings; 3 children. Student, Columbia Basin Coll., Ctrl. Wash. U. Mem. Wash. State Ho. of Reps., 1979-87; pres. Columbia Basin Paper & Supply, 1983-94; mem. 104th and 105th Congress from 4th Wash. dist., 1994—; mem. ways and means com., rules com., energy and utilities com., agriculture com., judiciary com., constitution and elections com.; bd. dirs. Yakima Fed. Savings & Loan; chmn. Franklin County Republican Com., 1974-78. Office: US House Reps 1323 Longworth Bldg Ofc Bldg Washington DC 20515-4704

HASTINGS, ELISA KIPP, English language educator; b. L.A., May 14, 1956; d. Charles F. and Margaret Heaney) Kipp; m. Robert Allan Hastings Jr., July 18, 1987; 1 child, Trevor Carlyle. BA in Theatre Arts, Calif. State U., Northridge, 1978; postgrad., Calif. State U., Dominguez Hills, 1996—. Cert. single subject credential English, English lang. devel. Tchr. Horace Mann Jr. H.S., L.A., 1983-88, Bell Gardens (Calif.) H.S., 1988-92; tchr. Bellflower (Calif.) H.S., 1993—, sch. site coun., 1994-96; festival judge Drama and Shakespeare Festivals, L.A., 1990-92; judge regional speech competition, Cyrpess, Calif., 1995; mem. curriculum devel. com. Bellflower Sch. Dist., 1996—; advisor Calif. Scholarship Fedn., 1994-96. Prodr., dir.: (video prodn.) Tartuffe, 1991; dir. sch. plays and festivals, 198-96. Sponsor Christian Children's Fund, 1984-96; mem. Klanwatch-So. Poverty Law Ctr., 1990-96; guild mem. Shakespeare Festival, L.A., 1995-96; mem. Copiii Lumii Children's World. Recipient Cert. of Appreciation Sch. Site Coun., Bellflower H.S., 1996. Mem. Drama Tchrs. Assn. So. Calif., RESOLVE Nat. Avocations: literature-reading and writing, attending theatre and movies, travel. Home: 6115 John Ave Long Beach CA 90805-3633 Office: Bellflower HS 15301 Mcnab Ave Bellflower CA 90706-4101

HASTINGS, JOHN JACOB, writer, lyricist, consultant; b. Walla Walla, Wash., Oct. 7, 1953; s. Frederic William and Margaret Mary (McElligott) H. *Hastings, the great, great grandson of John Kingport and Mary U., was born in 1953, one-hundred years after his great grandfather, and namesake, John Jacob, who traveled the Oregon Trail in 1864 with his parents. Both John Kingport and John Jacob established homesteads through the United States government. Having passed through four generations, the present Hastings continues to live in the original homestead dwelling. John Jacob and Cynthia passed the homestead down to Vernon Jacob and Delia. The Hastings brothers, Francis Dale, Delbert Gerad and Claude Milburn, worked the land before its present representation, Vern Hastings Farm.* AA, Walla Walla C.C., 1976; BFA, Ea. Wash. U., 1979. Mgr. Monroe Cigar Co., Chgo., 1980-83; prof. Harry Truman C.C., Chgo., 1981; farmer Touchet, Wash., 1986—. *John Jacob Hastings' professional accomplishments are primarily centered around his uncanny ability to take any given topic and express it through the use of poetic reasoning. He uses an "A,B,C,D" rhyme scheme most often [illegible]. The unique style of Hastings' artistry allows the work to stand alone as poetry. However, because of his technique, it is easily adaptable to music as a lyric. Hastings won his first poetic competition at the age of eight-years-old. Currently, he is a finalist in a Poetry Guild of America competition with Public*

Broadcasting System. Author: Four Score Seven, 1995; (poetry) Playing Possum, 1995, Back on the Stack, 1998, Linda's Lullaby in Heaven, 1998, Penultimate Glory, 1998, Excellent annus, 1998; lyricist: Hilltop Records, Hollywood, Calif., 1997-98. Cons. Nat. Orgn. Dems., 1975—; precinct com. mem. Walla Walla (Wash.) County Dem. Ctrl. Com., 1992—, mem. Dem. Nat. Com., 1998, Dem. Senatorial campaign, 1998; activist Peace Movement, Walla Walla, Wash., 1977-86; mem. MADD, ACLU. Mem. Nat. Geographic Soc., Nat. Trust for Hist. Preservation, Walla Walla Pioneers Hist. Soc. (faculty mem.), Nat. Assn. Women in Arts (assoc.), Smithsonian Instn., Libr. Congress (assoc.), Ea. Wash. U. Alumni, Nat. Parks and Conservation Assn. Wilson Ctr., Handyman's Club Am., Nature Conservancy, Hastings Art Soc. (pres, C.L.O.). Episcopalian. Avocations: letter writing, conservationist, tree planter. Home and Office: 504 Locher Rd Touchet WA 99360-9648

HASTINGS, L(OIS) JANE, architect, educator; b. Seattle, Mar. 3, 1928; d. Harry and Camille (Pugh) H.; m. Norman John Johnston, Nov. 22, 1969. B.Arch., U. Wash., Seattle, 1952, postgrad. in Urban Planning, 1958. Architect Boeing Airplane Co., Seattle, 1951-54; recreational dir. Germany, 1954-56; architect (various firms), Seattle, 1956-59, pvt. practice architecture, 1959-74; instr. archtl. drafting Seattle Community Coll., part-time 1969-80; owner/founder The Hastings Group Architects, Seattle, 1974—; lectr. design Coll. Architecture, U. Wash., 1975; incorporating mem. Architecta (P.S.), Seattle, 1980; pres. Architecta (P.S.), from 1980; mem. adv. bd. U. Wash. YWCA, 1967-69; mem. Mayor's Com. on Archtl. Barriers for Handicapped, 1974-75; chmn. regional public adv. panel on archtl. and engring. services GSA, 1976; mem. citizens adv. com. Seattle Land Use Adminstrn. Task Force, from 1979; AWIU guest of Soviet Women's Con., 1983; speaker Pacific Rim Forum, Hong Kong, 1987; guest China Internat. Conf. Ctr. for Sci. and Tech. of the China Assn. for Sci. and Tech., 1989; mem. adv. com. Coll. architecture and urban planning U. Wash., 1993; mem. accreditation team U. Oreg. Coll. Architecture, 1991, N.J. Inst. Tech. Sch. Architecture, 1992; jurur Home of the Yr. ann. award AIA/Seattle Times, 1996. Design juror for nat. and local competitions, including Red Cedar Shingle/AIA awards, 1977, Current Use Honor awards, AIA, 1980, Exhibit of Sch. Architecture award, 1981; Contbr. to: also spl. features newspapers, articles in profl. jours. Sunset mag. Mem. bd. Am. Women for Internat. Understanding, del. to, Egypt, Israel, USSR, 1971, Japan and Korea, 1979, USSR, 1983; mem. Landmarks Preservation Bd. City of Seattle, 1981-83; mem. Design Constrn. Rev. Bd. Seattle Sch. Dist., 1985-87; mem. mus. con. Mus. History and Industry, 1987—; leader People to People del. women architects to China, 1990. Recipient AIA/The Seattle Times Home of Month Ann. award, 1968; Exhbn. award Seattle chpt. AIA, 1970; Environ. award Seattle-King County Bd. Realtors, 1970, 77,; AIA/House and Home/The American Home Merit award, 1971, Sp. Honor award Wash. Aggregates and Concrete Assn., 1993, Prize bridge Am. Inst. Steel Contrn., 1993; Honor award Seattle chpt. AIA, 1977, 83; Women Achievement award Past Pres. Assembly, 1983, Washington Women and Trading Cards, 1983; Nat. Endowment for Arts grantee, 1977; others; named to West Seattle High Sch. Hall of Fame, 1989, Woman of Achievement Matrix Table, 1994; named Woman of Distinction, Columbia River Girl Scout Coun., 1994. Fellow AIA (pres. Seattle chpt. 1975, pres. sr. coun. 1980, state exec. bd. 1975, N.W. regional dir. 1982-87, Seattle chpt. found. bd. 1985-87, Bursar Coll. Fellows 1989-90, Coll. of Fellows historian 1994—, internat. rels. com. 1988-92, vice chancellor 1991, chancellor 1992, Seattle chpt. medal 1995), Internat. Union Women Architects (v.p. 1969-79, sec. gen. 1985-89, del. UIA Congress, Montreal 1990), Am. Arbitration Assn. (arbitrator 1981—), Coun. of Design Professions, Assn. Women Contrs., Suppliers and Design Cons., Allied Arts Seattle, Fashion Group, Tau Sigma Delta, Alpha Rho Chi (medal). Office: The Hastings Group-Architects 603 Stewart St Ste 915 Seattle WA 98101-1264

HATAI, THOMAS HENRY, international marketing professional; b. Tokyo, Dec. 27, 1937; came to U.S., 1951; s. Isamu Herbert and Kiyoko (Kume) H.; m. Geraldine Hatai, Jan. 19, 1970 (div. 1978); children: Dickson Y.V.P., Keio Gijuku Yochisha. BS, Woodbury Univ., 1965. Supr. internat. dept. Union Bank, L.A., 1964-66; with mgmt. United Airlines, L.A., 1966-69; v.p. far east Travel Systems Internat., Oakbrook, Ill., 1969-75; pres. Hatai Internat., L.A., 1975-78; pres., chief exec. officer Pace Mktg., Inc., La Habra, Calif., 1978—; founder, pres. Pace Products, Inc., 1983-91, DBH Global Ltd., 1983—; founder, vice chmn. bd. dirs., CEO Yamamo Cosmetics Inc., 1991—; pres., CEO Yamamo Products Inc. (dba AVEC), 1992—; bd. dirs. Gradn Five Corp., Bangkok, Thailand. Illustrators: The Marty Story, 1954, The St. Meinrad Story, 1954. Mem. United Internat. Club (bd. dirs. 1969 Japan), U.S. C. of C. Republican. Home: 8544 Buena Tierra Pl Buena Park CA 90621-1002 Office: DBH Global Ltd 278 W Imperial Hwy Ste V La Habra CA 90631

HATAY, FERHAT FEVZI, computational scientist, mechanical engineer; b. Antakya, Hatay, Turkey, Sept. 23, 1965; came to the U.S., 1987; s. Necat and Gulsen Hatay. BS in Mech. Engring. summa cum laude, Bogazici U., Istanbul, Turkey, 1987; MS in Mech. Engring., U. Miami, 1989; PhD in Aerospace Engring., U. Colo., 1994. Mech. engring. intern SABANCI Holding, Adana, Turkey, 1985; design engr. UNIPROJECT, Prague, Czechoslovakia, 1986; rsch. engr. U. Miami, Coral Gables, Fla., 1987-89; rsch. fellow Nat. Oceanic amd Atmosperic Assn/Atlantic Oceanographic and Meteorological Labs., Key Biscayne, Fla., 1989-90; univ. fellow Yale U., New Haven, 1990-91; rsch. scientist U. Colo., Boulder, 1991-96; supercomputing cons. Nippon Elec. Co. Sys. Labs., Houston, 1996-97; computation rsch. scientist NASA Ames Rsch. Ctr., Moffett Field, Calif., 1996-97; market devel. engr. Hal/Fujitsu Computer Sys., Campbell, Calif., 1997—; presenter in field. Contbr. articles to profl. jours. Scholar Turkish Nat. Sci. Found., Ankara, Turkey, 1979-87, Uni-lever scholar, Istanbul, 1990. Mem. AIAA, ASME, Assn. for Computing Machinery, Tau Beta Pi. Avocations: mountain biking, bridge, swimming, hiking, basketball. Home: 200 E Dana St #d87 Mountain View CA 94041 Office: HAL Computer Sys A Fujitsu Co 1315 Dell Ave Campbell CA 95008

HATCH, GEORGE CLINTON, television executive; b. Erie, Pa., Dec. 16, 1919; s. Charles Milton and Blanche (Beecher) H.; m. Wilda Gene Glasmann, Dec. 24, 1940; children: Michael Gene Zbar, Diane Glasmann Orr, Jeffrey Beecher, Randall Clinton, Deepika Hatch Avanti. AB, Occidental Coll., 1940; MA in Econs., Claremont Coll., 1941; HHD (hon.), So. Utah U., 1988. Pres. Comms. Investment Corp., Salt Lake City, 1945-95; chmn. Double G Comm. Corp., Salt Lake City, 1956—; dir. Republic Pictures Corp., Los Angeles, 1971-94; pres. Sta. KVEL, Inc., 1978-94; pres. Standard Corp., Ogden, 1993—; past mem. Salt Lake adv. bd. First Security Bank Utah; past chmn. Rocky Mountain Pub. Broadcasting Corp.; past chmn. bd. govs. Am. Info. Radio Network; past bd. govs. NBC-TV Affiliates. *George Hatch commenced his broadcast career as manager of KLO-AM in Ogden, Utah, in 1941. He served as chairman of Intermountain Radio Network, 1941-87, and constructed KALL-AM in Salt Lake City, Utah, in 1945, and KALL-FM, in 1968. He operated radio stations: KGHL-AM and KIDX-FM, Billings, KYSS-AM-FM, Missoula, KMON-AM, Great Falls, KOPR-AM, Butte, Montana; KGEM-AM and KJOT-FM, Boise, KUPI-AM and KQPI-FM, Idaho Falls, KLIX-AM, Twin Falls, Idaho; KULA-AM, Honolulu, Hawaii; WISH-AM-FM, Indianapilis, and WTHI-AM, Terre Haute, Indiana. He also operated television stations KUTV-TV, Salt Lake City, Utah; KARD-TV, Wichita, KSNT-TV, Topeka, Kansas; KTVJ-TV, Joplin, Missouri; and KGMB-TV, Honolulu, Hawaii. He co-founded Telecommunications, Inc., in 1968, and served as Vice-Chairman until 1980.* Past pres. Salt Lake Com. on Fgn. Relations; past mem. Utah Symphony Bd., Salt Lake City; mem., past chmn. and mem. Utah State Bd. Regents, 1964-85. Recipient Svc. to Journalism award U. Utah, 1966, silver medal Salt Lake Advt. Club, 1969, Disting. Svc. award Utah Tech. U., 1984, Disting. Utahan Centennial Yr. award Margaret Thatcher U.K., Utah Festival, 1996. Mem. Nat. Assn. Broadcasters (past pres., radio bd. dirs., ambassador to Inter-Am. mtgs. in Latin Am. 1962), Utah Broadcasters Assn. (past pres., Mgmt. award 1964, Hall of Fame award 1981), Salt Lake City Advt. Club (silver medal 1969), Phi Beta Kappa, Phi Rho Pi (life). Democrat. Avocations: hiking, rock art. Office: The Std Corp 1537 Chandler Dr Salt Lake City UT 84103-4220

HATCH, LYNDA SYLVIA, education educator; b. Portland, Oreg., Feb. 19, 1950; d. Marley Elmo and Undine Sylvia (Crockard) Sims. BA, Wash. State U., 1972; MS, Portland State U., 1975; EdD, Oreg. State U., 1984. Cert. tchr., Oreg. Tchr. 5th grade, outdoor sch. specialist Clover Park Sch. Dist. 400, Tacoma, 1971-72; tchr. 6th grade, outdoor sch. specialist Hillsboro (Oreg.) elem. Dist. 7, 1972-78; tchr. 6th grade, outdoor sch. specialist Bend (Oreg.)-La Pine Sch. Dist., 1978-82, elem. curriculum specialist, 1983-85, tchr. 4th grade gifted and talented, 1985-90; grad. teaching asst. Oreg. State U., Corvallis, 1982-84; asst. prof. No. Ariz. U., 1991—, chair instnl. leadership, 1997-98; ednl. cons., tchr. workshops, 1973—; presenter workshop Soviet-Am. Joint Conf., Moscow State U., 1991, Meeting of Children's Culture Promoters, Guadalajara, Mex., 1994; faculty Ariz. Journey Schs. for Math. and Sci. Tchg. Improvement; coord. Odyssey of the Mind, Bend, 1985-89, tchr.-mentor program for 1st-yr. tchrs., Beaverton, Oreg., 1982-83; presenter Social Edn. Assn. of Australia, 1997. Author: Pathways of America: Lewis and Clark, 1993, Pathways of America: The Oregon Trail, 1993, Pathways of America: The California Gold Rush Trail, 1994, Pathways of America: The Santa Fe Trail, 1995, Fifty States, 1997, U.S. Presidents, 1997, U.S. Map Skills, 1997, Human body, 1998, National Parks and Other Park Service Sites, 1999, Our National Parks; contbr. articles to profl. jours. Vol., leader, bd. dirs. Girl Scouts U.S., 1957—; elder First Presbyn. Ch., Bend, 1980—; vol. hist. interpretation High Desert Mus., Bend, 1987-91; docent Mus. No. Ariz.; pres. bd. dirs. The Arboretum at Flagstaff. Recipient Excellence in Teaching award Bend Found., 1985-86, 86-87; named Tchr. of Yr. Oreg. Dept. Edn., 1982; Celebration Teaching grantee Geraldine Rockefeller Dodge Found., 1989, 90, 91, 92, 93, 94, 95, EPA grantee, 1997-99, Eisenhower Math and Sci. Edn. Act grantee, 1997. Mem. NEA, Nat. Coun. Tchrs. Math., Nat. Sci. Tchrs. Assn., Nat. State Tchrs. of Yr. (nat. pres. 1988-90), Oreg. Coun. Tchrs. Math. (bd. dirs. 1981-82), Oreg. Coun. Tchrs. English (bd. dirs. 1981-82), Ariz. Reading Assn., Ariz. Sci. Tchrs. Assn., No. Ariz. Reading Coun. (exec. bd. 1991-92, 92-93), Ariz. State Early Childhood Adv. Couns. Nat. Coun. for Social Studies, Assn. Tchr. Educators, Coun. for Elem. Sci. Internat. (bd. dirs. 1995-98), Internat. Reading Assn., Oreg.-Calif. Trails Assn., S.W. Oreg.-Calif. Trails Assn., Delta Kappa Gamma (1st v.p.), Phi Delta Kappa (found. rep. 1991-92, v.p. programs 1992-93, historian 1993-94, v.p. membership 1994-95), Golden Key Hon., Kappa Delta Pi (past chpt. counselor), others. Avocations: cross-country skiing, photography, hiking, crafts, gardening. Home: 1480 W University Heights Dr N Flagstaff AZ 86001-8970

HATCH, ORRIN GRANT, senator; b. Homestead Park, Pa., Mar. 22, 1934; s. Jesse and Helen (Kamm) H.; m. Elaine Hansen, Aug. 28, 1957; children: Brent, Marcia, Scott, Kimberly, Alysa, Jess. B.S., Brigham Young U., 1959; J.D., U. Pitts., 1962; LLD (hon.), U. Md., 1981; MS (hon.), Def. Intelligence Coll., 1982; LLD (hon.), Pepperdine U., 1990, So. Utah State U., 1990. Bar: Pa. 1962, Utah 1962. Ptnr. firm Thomson, Rhodes & Grigsby, Pitts., 1962-69, Hatch & Plumb, Salt Lake City, 1976; mem. U.S. Senate from Utah, 1977—, past chmn. labor and human resources com., chmn. Senate judiciary com., joint com. on taxation, fin. com., senate Rep. policy com., com. on Indian affairs, fin. com. Author ERA Myths and Realities, 1983; contbr. articles to newspapers and profl. jours. Recipient Outstanding Legislator award Nat. Assn. Rehab. Facilities, Legislator of Yr. award Am. Assn. Univ. Affiliated Programs, Legis. Leadership award Health Profl. Assn., many others. Mem. Am., Nat., Utah, Pa. bar assns., Am. Judicature Soc. Republican. Mormon. Avocations: golf, poetry, piano playing, composer lyrics.

HATCH, STEVEN GRAHAM, publishing company executive; b. Idaho Falls, Idaho, Mar. 27, 1951; s. Charles Steven and Margery Jane (Doxey) H.; BA, Brigham Young U., 1976; postgrad. mgmt. devel. program U. Utah, 1981; m. Rhonda Kay Frasier, Feb. 13, 1982; children: Steven Graham, Kristen Leone, Cameron Michael, Landon Frasier, McKell Margery. Founder, pres. Graham Maughan Enterprises, Provo, Utah, 1975—, Internat. Mktg. Co., 1980—, Mcht. Acct. Svcs., 1996—; bd. dirs. Goldbrickers Internat., Inc., Net Solutions Internat. Inc. Sec., treas. Zions Estates, Inc., Salt Lake City, Kansas City, Mo. Eagle Scout Boy Scouts Am., 1970; trustee Villages of Quail Valley, 1984-88. Recipient Duty to God award, 1970; missionary France Mission, Paris 1970-72, pub. rels. dir. 1972. Mem. Provo Jaycees, Internat. Entrepreneurs Assn., Mormon Booksellers Assn., Samuel Hall Soc. (exec. v.p. 1979), U.S. C. of C., Provo C. of C. (chmn. legis. action com. 1981-82, mem. job svc. employer com.), Rotary (pres. Provo 1995-96, area rep. 1996-97). Republican. Mem. LDS Ch. Office: Graham Maughan Pub Co 50 E 500 S Provo UT 84606-4809

HATCHER, HERBERT JOHN, biochemist, microbiologist; b. Mpls., Dec. 18, 1926; s. Herbert Edmond and Florence Elizabeth (Larson) H.; m. Beverly J. Johnson, Mar. 28, 1953 (dec. July 1985); children: Dennis Michael, Steven Craig, Roger Dean, Mark Alan, Susan Diane, Laura Jean; m. Louise Fritsche Nelson, May 24, 1986; children: Carlos Howard Nelson, Kent Robert Nelson, Carolyn Louise Tyler. BA, U. Minn., 1953, MS, 1964, PhD, 1965. Bacteriologist VA Hosp., Wilmington, Del., 1956-57; microbiologist Smith, Kline, French, Phila., 1957-60, Clinton (Iowa) Corn Processing, 1966-67; microbiologist, biochemist Econs. Lab. Inc., St. Paul, 1967-84; biochemist EG&G Idaho Inc., Idaho Falls, 1984-90; co-owner B/CG Cons. Svcs., Idaho Falls, 1990—. Chmn. bd. edn. Cross of Christ Luth. Ch., Coon Rapids, Minn., 1974-76; pres. chpt. Aid Assn. Luths., Idaho Falls, 1986; pres.-elect St. Johns Luth. Ch., 1988, pres., 1989. With USNR, 1945-46. Avocations: skiing, hiking, camping, hunting, fishing.

HATFIELD, CHARLES DONALD, newspaper executive; b. Huntington, W.Va., June 15, 1935; s. Howard Donald and LaUna (Wilson) H.; m. Sandra Gail Soto, June 11, 1955; children: John Christopher, Lisa, Joel Thomas. BA, Marshall Coll., 1977. Mem. sports staff Huntington Advertiser, 1953-60, asst. news editor, 1960-67, mng. editor, 1972-79; news editor Herald-Advertiser, Huntington, 1967-69, mng. editor, 1969-72; exec. editor Herald-Dispatch, Huntington, 1979-82, pub., editor, 1982-85; regional v.p. Gannett Co., Inc. E., Huntington, 1985-86; pub., editor Tucson Citizen and Gannett West, 1986—. Author: Don Hatfield Cleans Out His Attic, 1986. Bd. dirs. United Way, Tucson, 1987-95, Greater Tucson Econs. Coun., 1988—, Tucson Mus. Art, 1989—. Mem. AP Mng. Editors Assn. (treas. 1986-88), Am. Soc. Newspaper Editors, Am. Newspapers Pubs. (pres.), Ariz. Newspaper Assn., La Paloma Club, Tucson Country Club. Avocations: writing, reading, tennis, golf. Office: Tucson Citizen PO Box 26767 Tucson AZ 85726-6767*

HATFIELD, ELAINE CATHERINE, psychology educator; b. Detroit, Oct. 22, 1937; d. Charles E. and Eileen (Kalahar) H.; m. Richard L. Rapson, June 15, 1982. BA, U. Mich., 1959; PhD, Stanford U., 1963. Asst. prof. U. Minn., Mpls., 1963-64, assoc. prof., 1964-66; assoc. prof. U. Rochester, 1966-68, U. Wis., Madison, 1968-69; prof. U. Wis., 1969-81; now prof. U. Hawaii, Honolulu; chmn. dept. psychology U. Hawaii, 1981-83. Author: Equity: Theory and Research, 1978, Mirror, Mirror: The Importance of Looks in Everyday Life, 1986, Psychology of Emotions, 1991, Love, Sex and Intimacy, 1993, Emotional Contagion, 1994, Love and Sex: Cross-cultural Perspectives, 1996; contbr. articles to profl. jours. Recipient Disting. Scientist award Soc. Exptl. Social Psychology, 1993. Fellow APA; mem. Soc. Sci. Study of Sex (pres., Disting. Scientist award 1996, Alfred Kinsey award 1998). Home: 3334 Anoai Pl Honolulu HI 96822-1418 Office: U Hawaii 2430 Campus Rd Honolulu HI 96822-2216

HATFIELD, MARK ODEM, former senator; b. Dallas, Oreg., July 12, 1922; s. Charles Dolen and Dovie (Odom) H.; m. Antoinette Kuzmanich, July 8, 1958; children: Mark, Elizabeth, Theresa, Charles. AB, Willamette U., 1943; AM, Stanford U., 1948. Instr. Willamette U., 1949, dean students, assoc. prof. polit. sci., 1950-56; mem. Oreg. Ho. of Reps., 1951-55, Oreg. Senate, 1955-57; sec. State of Oreg., 1957-59, gov., 1959-67; U.S. senator from Oreg., 1967-97; chmn. appropriations com., energy and natural resources com., rules and adminstrn. com., joint printing com., joint libr. com., select com. Indian Affairs, Republican Policy Com.; chmn. Appropriations subcom. on transp. & related agencies. Author: Not Quite So Simple, 1967, Conflict and Conscience, 1971, Between A Rock and A Hard Place, 1976; co-author: Amnesty: The Unsettled Question of Vietnam, 1976, Freeze! How You Can Help Prevent Nuclear War, 1982, The Causes of World Hunger, 1982; co-author: What About the Russians, 1984, Vice Presidents of the United States 1789-1993, 1997. Lt. (j.g.) USN, 1943-45, PTO. Recipient numerous hon. degrees. Republican. Baptist. Office: PO Box 8639 Portland OR 97207-8639

HATFIELD, PAUL GERHART, federal judge, lawyer; b. Great Falls, Mont., Apr. 29, 1928; s. Trueman LeRoy and Grace Lenore (Gerhart) H.; m. Dorothy Ann Allen, Feb. 1, 1958 (dec. Aug. 1992); children: Kathleen Helen, Susan Ann, Paul Allen. Student, Coll. of Great Falls, 1947-50; LL.B., U. Mont., 1955. Bar: Mont. bar 1955. Asso. firm Hoffman & Cure, Gt. Falls, Mont., 1955-56, Jardine, Stephenson, Blewett & Weaver, Gt. Falls, 1956-58, Hatfield & Hatfield, Gt. Falls, 1959-60; chief dep. county atty. Cascade County, Mont., 1959-60; dist. ct. judge 8th Jud. Dist., Mont., 1961-76; chief justice Supreme Ct. Mont., Helena, 1977-78; U.S. Senator from Mont., 1978-79; U.S. dist. judge for Dist. of Mont., Gt. Falls, 1979-96; chief judge, 1990-96, sr. judge, 1996—; Vice chmn. Pres.'s Council Coll. of Great Falls. Author standards for criminal justice, Mont. cts. Served with U.S. Army, 1951-53. Korea. Mem. Am., Mont. bar assns., Am. Judicature Soc. Roman Catholic. Office: US Dist Ct PO Box 1529 Great Falls MT 59403-1529

HATHAWAY, LOLINE, zoo and botanic park curator; b. Whittier, Calif., June 27, 1937; d. Richard Franklin and F. Nadine (Applegate) H.; 1 child, Patrick Paul Kundtz. BA, Reed Coll., Portland, Oreg., 1959; PhD, Washington U., St. Louis, 1969. Instr. St. Louis U., 1966-68; curator of edn. Chgo. Zool. Soc., Brookfield, Ill., 1968-71; cons. on terrestrial biology Ryckman, Edgerly, Tomlinson & Assocs., St. Louis, 1972-75; marina mgr. Lake Piru (Calif.) Recreation Area, 1976-77; curator, dir. Navajo Nation Zool. and Botanical Park, Window Rock, Ariz., 1983—. Vice chmn., chmn. City of Santa Fe Springs (Calif.) Traffic Commn., 1979-83; mem. Navajo Estates Vol. Fire Dept., Yah-ta-hey, N.Mex., 1984-85; bd. dirs. Hathaway Ranch Mus., Santa Fe Springs, 1986-93, Gallup Cmty. Concerts Assn., 1994—; leader 4-H Club, 1989—; master gardener, 1997—. Mem. AAAS (vice chmn. S.W.-Rocky Mountain div. sci. edn. sect. 1983-84, chmn. 1984-85), AAUW (scholarship com. Gallup 1992—, bd. govs. 1997—), Am. Assn. Zool. Parks and Aquariums, Am. Assn. Bot. Gardens and and Arboretums, Assn. Living. Hist. Farms and Agr. Mus., Am. Inst. Biol. Scis., Sierra Club (Ozarks chpt. founder, bd. dirs., sec. Gt. Lakes chpt. 1963-72). Democrat. Home: 27 S LaChee PO Box 4172 Yatahey NM 87375-4172 Office: Navajo Nat Zool and Bot Pk PO Box 9000 Window Rock AZ 86515-9000

HATHAWAY, STANLEY KNAPP, lawyer; b. Osceola, Nebr., July 19, 1924; s. Franklin E. and Velma Clara (Holbrook) H.; m. Roberta Louise Harley, Nov. 26, 1948; children—Susan Garrett, Sandra D'Amico. A.B., U. Nebr., 1948, LL.B., 1950; LL.D., U. Wyo., 1975. Bar: Nebr. 1950, Wyo., 1950, U.S. Dist. Ct. Wyo., Nebr., Mont. 1950, U.S. Supreme Ct. 1964. Sole practice, Torrington, Wyo., 1950-66; gov. Wyo., 1967-75; assoc. Hathaway, Speight & Kunz, Cheyenne, Wyo., 1975—; dir. Apache Corp., Houston; county atty. Goshen County (Wyo.), 1955-62; gov. State of Wyo., 1967-75; sec. U.S. Dept. Interior, 1975. Served with USAAF, 1943-45. Decorated Air medals with 5 clusters. Mem. ABA, Wyo. State Bar Assn. Republican. United Episcopalian. Clubs: Masons (Cheyenne); Shriners (Rawlins, Wyo.). Office: Hathaway Speight & Kunz 2515 Warren Ave Cheyenne WY 82001-3113

HATTAR, MICHAEL MIZYED, mathematics educator; b. El-Salt, Jordan, Mar. 17, 1934; came to U.S., 1954; s. Mizyed Zedan and Rif'a (Naber) H.; m. Helen Jean Sharbrough, June 30, 1962; children: Mai Michelle, Amiel Michael, Khalid Mikhail, Muna Michelle. BA, Greenville (Ill.) Coll., 1958; MS, Western Wash. State U., 1968; postgrad., Oxford U., 1989. Tchr. Don Bosco Tech. Inst., Rosemead, Calif., 1962-76, 95—, chmn., 1968-76; part-time tchr. Rio Hondo Coll., 1983—; tchr. Mt. Sac Coll., 1969—, Ontario (Calif.) High Sch., 1976-92, Rancho Cucamonga (Calif.) High Sch., 1992-95; with Don Bosco Tech. Inst., Rosemead, Calif., 1995—; speaker math. confs. Participant U.S./Russian Joint Conf. on Math. Edn., Moscow, 1993. Recipient Tchr. of Yr. award Industry Edn. Coun. San Gabriel Valley, 1970, Award of Excellence, U.S. Orgn. Med. and Edn. Needs South Bay chpt., 1975, Citation, Assn. Arab-Am. Univ. Grads., 1977, Man of Yr. award Am. Arab Soc., 1978, Commendation, Olympic Neighbor Program, 1984, Tchr. of Yr. award Ontario H.S., 1987-88, Award of Excellence, U.S. Orgn. Med. and Edn.; named Tchr. of Yr. Inland Valley, Calif., 1991, 95. Mem. ASCD, Nat. Coun. Tchrs. of Math., Calif. Math. Coun., San Bernardino County Math. Coun. (Tchr. of Yr. award 1991, pres. 1992-93). Home: 1247 E Dore St West Covina CA 91792-1313 Office: Don Bosco Tech Inst 1151 San Gabriel Blvd Rosemead CA 91770-4251

HATTER, TERRY JULIUS, JR., federal judge; b. Chgo., Mar. 11, 1933. A.B., Wesleyan U., 1954; J.D., U. Chgo., 1960. Bar: Ill. 1960, Calif. 1965, U.S. Dist. Ct. 1960, U.S. Ct. Appeals 1960. Adjudicator Chgo., 1960-61; assoc. Harold M. Calhoun, Chgo., 1961-62; asst. pub. defender Cook County Chgo., 1961-62; asst. U.S. atty. No. Dist. Calif., San Francisco, 1962-66; chief counsel San Francisco Neighborhood Legal Assistance Found., 1966-67; regional legal svcs. dir. Exec. Office Pres. OEO, San Francisco, 1967-70; exec. dir. Western Ctr. Law and Poverty, L.A., 1970-73; exec. asst. to mayor, dir. criminal justice planning L.A., 1974-75; spl. asst. to mayor, dir. urban devel., 1975-77; judge Superior Ct. Calif., L.A., 1977-80; judge U.S. Dist. Ct. (cen. dist.) Calif., L.A., 1979-98, chief judge, 1998—; lectr. Police Acad., San Francisco Police Dept., 1963-66, U. Calif., San Diego, 1970-71, Colo. Jud. Conf., 1973; assoc. clin. prof. law U. So. Calif. Law Ctr., L.A., 1970-74, mem. bd. councilors; prof. law Loyola U. Sch. Law, L.A., 1973-75; mem. faculty Nat. Coll. State Judiciary, Reno, 1974. V.p. Northbay Halfway House, 1964-65; vice chmn. Los Angeles Regional Criminal Justice Planning Bd., 1975-76; mem. Los Angeles Mayor's Cabinet Com. Econ. Devel., 1976-77, Mayor's Policy Com., 1973-77, chmn. housing econ. and community devel. com., City Los Angeles, 1975-77, chmn. housing and community devel. tech. com., 1975-77; vice chmn. Young Dems. Cook County, 1961-62; chmn. bd. Real Estate Coop; bd. dirs. Bay Area Social Planning Coun., Contra Costa, Black Law Center L.A., Nat. Fedn. Settlements & Neighborhood Ctrs., Edn. Fin. & Governance Reform Project, Mexican Am. Legal Def. & Ednl. Fund, Nat. Health Law Program, Nat. Sr. Citizens Law Ctr., Calif. Law Ctr., L.A. Regional Criminal Justice Planning Bd.; mem. exec. com. bd. dirs. Constl. Rights Found; trustee Wesleyan Univ. Meth. Ch.; mem. bd. visitors U. Chgo. Law Sch. Mem. NAACP (exec. com., bd. dirs. Richmond chpt.), Nat. Legal Aid & Defender Assn. (dir., vice chmn.), L.A. County Bar Assn. (exec. com.), Am. Judicature Soc., Charles Houston Law Club, Phi Delta Phi, Order Coif. Office: US Dist Ct 312 N Spring St Los Angeles CA 90012-4703*

HATTERSLEY, JOSEPH GILMORE, research analyst; b. Moulmein, Burma, Jan. 24, 1922; came to U.S., 1925; s. Linn W. and Ruth (Gilmore) H.; m. Elsie Lothras, Feb. 1, 1949; children: William J., Lynn Mary. BA in Econs., U. Calif., Berkeley, 1948, MA in Econs., 1953. Stockbroker Dean Witter & Co., San Marino, Calif., 1953-63; agrl. economist Wash. State U., Pullman, 1968-70; rsch. analyst Wash. State Govt., Olympia, 1974-87. Contbr. articles on health matters to profl. jours. With Signal Corps U.S. Army, 1942-46. Mem. Western Wash. Writers. Avocations: Olympic Trailblazers. Home: 7031 Glen Terra Ct SE Olympia WA 98503-7119

HAUENSTEIN, DONALD HERBERT, JR., computer company executive; b. Canton, Ohio, Dec. 29, 1942; s. Donald Herbert and Mary Alice (Andrichs) H.; m. Maria Del Socorro Moreno, June 5, 1965 (div. Apr. 1979); children: Carlos Ian, Marissa Renee; m. Carol King, May 28, 1988. B in Indsl. Engring., Ohio State U., 1970, MS in Indsl. Engring., 1970; MBA, U. Houston, 1977; exec. mgmt. program, UCLA, L.A., 1986. Indsl. engr. Schlumberger Well Svcs., Houston, 1970-72, supr. of methods, 1972-75; mgr. engring. svcs. Dresser Atlas, Houston, 1975-80; mgr. mfg. engring. VETCO Offshore, Ventura, Calif., 1980-83; dir. mfg. engring. HR Textron, Valencia, Calif., 1983-88; dir. spl. projects HR Textron, Valencia, 1988-90; owner, retail Abacus Computer Svcs., Saugus, 1990—. Pres. St. Christopher's Sch. Bd., Houston, 1976-79, bd. dirs. Orchard Ln. Condominium Assn., Oxnard, Calif., 1986, Arbor Park Condominium Assn., 1987. With USAF, 1961-65. Mem. Tau Beta Pi, Alpha Pi Mu. Republican. Roman Catholic. Avocations: photography, philately. Home: 28025 Tupelo Ridge Dr Santa Clarita CA 91354-1326 Office: Abacus Computer Svcs 23001 Soledad Canyon Rd Saugus CA 91350-2635

HAUER, JAMES ALBERT, lawyer; b. Fond du Lac, Wis., Apr. 3, 1924; s. Albert A. and Hazel M. (Corcoran) H.; children: Stephen, John, Paul, Christopher, Patrick. BCE, Marquette U., 1948, LLB, 1949; bank mgmt. cert., Columbia U., 1957, U. Wis., 1959. Bar: Wis., U.S. Dist. Ct. (ea. dist.), U.S. Ct. Appeals (9th cir.), U.S. Dist. Ct. (fed. dist.) 1958. Patent counsel Ira Milton Jones, Milw., 1949; chief counsel Wauwatosa Realty, Milw., 1950-57; v.p. Wauwatosa (Wis.) State Bank, 1957-67; pres. Milw. We. Bank, 1967-69, Prem Constrn. Co., Milw., 1969-73; pvt. practice Elm Grove, Wis.,

1973-86, Sun City, Ariz., 1986—. Pres., bd. dirs. Sunshine Svc., Sun City, Meals on Wheels, Sun City. With USMCR, 1942-45. Mem. Wis. Bar Assn., Ariz. Patent Law Assn. (charter). Roman Catholic. Office: 9915 W Royal Oak Rd # Gh1078 Sun City AZ 85351-3163

HAUGER, ELEANOR PRAPION KALLEJIAN, pianist, singer; b. Fresno, Calif., July 15, 1920; d. Robert Muggerdich and Prapion R. (Barsamian) Kallejian; m. Harry Hoyt Hauger, Jr., Apr. 17, 1943 (dec. July 1975); children: Philip Hoyt, Steven Harry. Student, UCLA, 1939-41; BA in Music, San Fernando State Coll., 1964. pvt. piano tchr., L.A., Dayton, Ohio. Debut San Fernando State Coll., Northridge, Calif., 1964; performed for symphonies and orchs., chs., L.A., Dayton, Ohio. Mem. AAUW, Westshore Musicians, Phi Beta. Congregationalist. Avocation: bridge.

HAUGHEY, JAMES MCCREA, lawyer, artist; b. Courtland, Kans., July 8, 1914; s. Leo Eugene and Elizabeth (Stephens) H.; m. Katherine Hurd, Sept. 8, 1938; children: Katherine (Mrs. Lester B. Loo), Bruce Stephens, John Caldwell. Student, Deep Springs Coll., 1930-31; LLB, U. Kans., 1939. Bar: Kans. 1939, Mont. 1943. Landman Carter Oil Co., 1939-43; practice in Billings, Mont., 1943-98; ptnr. Crowley, Haughey, Hanson, Toole & Dietrich, 1950-86, counsel, 1986-98; ret. dir. Mont.-Dakota Resources Group Inc. One-man shows include, U. Kans., U. Mont., Mont. State U., Concordia Coll., C.M. Russell Mus., Great Falls, Mont., Boise Mus. Art, Mont. State Mus., Helena, Sandzen Gallery, Bethany Coll., Luidsborg, Kans., Yellowstone Art Ctr., Billings, Mont., also numerous group shows. Pres. Rocky Mountain Mineral Law Found., 1957-58, trustee, 1955—; pres. Mont. Inst. Arts Found., 1965-67; pres. Yellowstone Art Center Found., 1969-71, trustee, 1964-81; mem. Mont. Ho. of Reps., 1960-64, Mont. Senate, 1966-70, senate minority leader, 1969-70. Recipient Gov.'s award for Arts, 1981. Fellow Mont. Inst. Arts (Permanent Collection award 1960); mem. ABA, Am. Coll. Real Estate Lawyers, Yellowstone County Bar Assn. (pres. 1960-61), U. Kans. Law Soc. (bd. govs. 1989-92), Am. Watercolor Soc. (Midwest v.p. 1978-82), N.W. Watercolor Soc. (life), Midwest Watercolor Soc., Kans. Watercolor Soc. (hon.), Mont. Watercolor Soc. (hon.), Am. Artists Profl. League, Phi Delta Theta, Phi Delta Phi. Republican. Episcopalian. Home: 2205 Tree Ln Billings MT 59102-2560 Office: Crowley Haughey Hanson Toole & Dietrich TransWestern Pla II 490 N 31st St Billings MT 59101-1256

HAUGO, DALE GORDON, scenic artist, art director; b. Mason City, Iowa, Sept. 9, 1950; s. Theodore Anfin and Eunice Vera (Brunsvold) H.; m. Demarest Lindsay Campbell, April 7, 1978. BFA in Scenic Design, U. Kans., 1974. Chargeman scenic artist Am. Conservatory Theatre, San Francisco, 1976-90; scenic artist, model maker Indsl. Light and Magic, San Rafael, Calif., 1983-85; ptnr. Campbell and Haugo Design Cons., San Francisco, 1983—; cons. over 200 prodns. for theater, ballet, opera, commercials, videos, 1974—. Supervising scenic artist (motion pictures) The Right Stuff, 1983, Birdy, 1983, Howard the Duck, 1986, Come See the Paradise, 1989, JFK, 1991, Made in America, 1992, Heaven and Earth, 1992, Natural Born Killers, 1993, Interview With The Vampire, 1993, Casino, 1994, The Ghost and the Darkness, 1995, Flubber, 1996, What Dreams May Come, 1997, Instinct, 1998, Any Given Sunday, 1999. Mem. United Scenic Artists, Internat. Alliance Theatrical Stage Employees (San Francisco chpt., exec. bd. 1982-88). Democrat. Avocations: sailing, woodworking, travel. Office: Campbell and Haugo Design Consultants 3751 23rd St San Francisco CA 94114-3416

HAUKLAND, JOANNE MARIE, school system administrator; b. Brainerd, Minn., Feb. 11, 1944; d. Floyd E. and Evelyn (Lindberg) Maxfield; m. Dale E. Haukland, Dec. 29, 1969; children: Karen, Dawn, Linda. BA, Concordia U., Moorehead, Minn., 1966; MA, U. No. Colo., 1975; PhD, U. So. Calif., 1991. Tchr. math. and English various locations, 1966-76; English tchr. Huntington Beach (Calif.) Union High Sch. Dist., 1976-80, dir. spl. projects, 1980-81, rep. liaison, 1981-82, regional occupational prog. liaison, 1983-84, dean, 1983-84, vice prin., 1984-88; prin. Mt. Diablo Unified Sch. Dist., Concord, Calif., 1989-94; asst. supt. Acalanes Union H.S. Dist., Lafayette, Calif., 1994-98, assoc. supt., 1998—. Author manual: ESL/Writing Manual, 1981; co-author: Laboratory Workshop Editing Skills Manual, 1976-80. Mem. humanities bd. City of Huntington Beach, 1984-88; mem. Community Against Substance Abuse, City of Walnut Creek, Calif., 1989—; block capt. March of Dimes, Diabetes Assn., Danville, Calif., 1988—; mem. Drug Task Force, Walnut Creek, 1988—, Acalanes Attendance area, 1996—. Mem. AAUW, ASCD, Mt. Diablo Edn. Assn., Nat. Assn. Secondary Sch. Prins., Assn. Secondary Adminstrs. (state rep. 1995—), Kappan. Democrat. Lutheran. Avocations: snow skiing, writing, reading, Hobie Cat sailing. Home: 148 Santiago Dr Danville CA 94526-1941 Office: Acalanes Union HS Dist 1212 Pleasant Hill Rd Lafayette CA 94549-2623

HAULENBEEK, ROBERT BOGLE, JR., government official; b. Cleve., Feb. 24, 1941; s. Robert Bogle and Priscilla Valerie (Burch) H.; BS, Okla. State U., 1970; m. Rebecca Marie Talley, Mar. 1, 1965; children—Kimberly Kaye, Robert Bogle, III. Micro paleon. photographer Pan Am. Rsch. Co., Tulsa, 1966-67; flight instr. Okla. State U., 1970; air traffic control specialist FAA, Albuquerque, 1970-73, Farmington, N.Mex., 1973-78, flight svc. specialist, Dalhart, Tex., 1978-80, Albuquerque, 1980—; staff officer CAP, Albuquerque, 1970-73, Farmington, 1974-78, advanced through grades to col., 1988, dir. ops. for hdqrs., 1981-86, 98—, N.Mex. Wing dep. commdr., 1986-88, N.Mex. Wing comdr., 1988-91, N.Mex. Wing dir. sr. programs, 1993-95, N.Mex. Wing. Ops. Staff, 1995—; mem. faculty Nat. Staff Coll., Gunter Air Force Sta., Montgomery, Ala., 1981-82; dir. South West Region Staff Coll., Albuquerque, 1986; mem. 1995 Nat. Air Traffic Control Facility of Yr. With U.S. Army, 1964-65. Recipient Meritorious Svc. award CAP, 1978, 81, 82, Lifesaving award, 1982, 95, Exceptional Svc. award, 1981, Distng. Svc. award, 1991. Mem. Exptl. Aircraft Assn., Nat. Assn. Air Traffic Specialists (facility rep. 1978-86), Nat. Assn. Flight Instrs., Aircraft Owners and Pilots Assn., Girl Scouts of Am. (life mem. 1966—), Republican. Presbyterian. Home: 5229 Carlsbad Ct NW Albuquerque NM 87120-2322

HAUN, GREGORY COSMO, artist; b. Atlanta, GA, June 30, 1967; s. Cosmo L. and Lynn Esslinger (Wilcox) H.; m. Jennifer Martin Davis, Aug. 20, 1995. BA, Reed Coll., Portland, Oreg., 1990; MS in Visual Studies, MIT, Cambridge, 1992. Instr. continuing edn. Pacific Northwest Coll. Art, Portland, 1994-98; instr. Mt. Hood C.C., Portland, 1996-97; sr. programmer analyst Mattel, Inc., 1998-99. Exhibited in group show at Portland Art Mus., 1995; author: Photoshop Collage Techniques, 1997, (CD Rom Based Interactive) Personal Dictionaries, 1995; artist: (series of digital photos) Archaeological Collage I, 1993 (purchase award City of Portland Visual Chronicle 1994). Project grantee Archaeological Collage II, Regional Arts & Culture Coun., Portland, 1996. Mem. Creston-Kenilworth Neighborhood Assn. (land-use chair 1997). Office: PrintPaks 513 NW 13th Ave Ste 202 Portland OR 97209-3017

HAUNSCHILD, BRENDALEE C., human resources specialist; b. Oregon City, Oreg., Dec. 29, 1966. BA, Oreg. State U., 1990. Dir. human resources Cranston Machinery Co., Inc., Oak Grove, Oreg., 1993—. Office: Cranston Machinery Co Inc PO Box 68207 Oak Grove OR 97268-0207

HAUSDORFER, GARY LEE, management consultant; b. Indpls., Mar. 26, 1946; s. Walter Edward and Virginia Lee (Bender) H.; AA, Glendale Coll., 1966; BS, Calif. State U.-L.A., 1968; children: Lisa Ann, Janet Lee. Rsch. officer Security Pacific Bank, L.A., 1968-73; v.p., mgr. W. Ross Campbell Co., Irvine, Calif., 1973-81; sr. v.p. Weyerhaeuser Mortgage Co., Irvine, 1982-87; exec. v.p., ptnr. L.J. Melody & Co. of Calif., 1987-89; pres. Hausdorfer Co., 1989—. pres. The Diamond Group, 1994—; Councilman, City of San Juan Capistrano, 1978-94, mayor, 1980-81, 84-85, 88-90; chmn. Capistrano Valley Water Dist., 1980-81, San Juan Capistrano Redevel. Agy., 1983-84, 85-86, South Orange County Leadership Conf.; bd. dirs. Orange County Trans. Corridor Agy., Orange County Transit Dist.; chmn. Orange County Transp. Authority, Newtrac Corp. Recipient cert. of commendation Orange County Bd. Suprs., 1981, congl. commendation, 1985, Theodore Roosevelt Conservation award Pres. Bush, 1990. Republican.

HAUSEL, WILLIAM DAN, economic geologist, martial artist; b. Salt Lake City, July 24, 1949; s. Maynard Romain and Dorthy (Clark) H.; children: Jessica Siddhartha, Eric Jason. BS in Geology, U. Utah, 1972, MS in Geology, 1974. Astronomy lectr., Hansen Planetarium, Salt Lake City, 1968-72; rsch. asst. U. Utah, 1972-74; teaching asst. U. N.Mex., Albuquerque, 1974-75; project geologist Warnock Cons., Albuquerque, 1975; geologist U.S. Geol. Survey, Casper, Wyo., 1976-77; staff geologist Geol. Survey of Wyo., Laramie, 1977-81, dep. dir., 1981-91, sr. econ. geologist, 1991—; cons. Western Gold Exploration and Mining, Anchorage, 1988, 89, Chevron Resources, Georgetown, Mont., 1990, Fowler Resources, Phillipsburg, Mont., 1992, Bald Mountain Mining, U.S., 1993, A and E Diamond Exploration, Calif., 1993, Echo Bay Exploration, Diamond Exploration, U.S., 1994; assoc. curator mineralogy Wyo. State Mus., Cheyenne, 1983-90; state rep. JUKO-KAI Internat., Wyo., 1994; U.S. dir. open divsn. Shorin-Ryu Karate, 1996, open divsn. head, Shorin-Ryu Karate and Kobudo (Juko-Kai Internat), 1997—; instr. martial arts dept. phys. edn. U. Wyo. 1995—, Campus Shorin-Ryu Karate & Kobudo Club. Author: Partial Pressures of Some Lunar Lavas, 1972, Petrogenesis of Some Representative Lavas, Southwestern Utah, 1975, Exploration for Diamondiferous Kimberlite, 1979, Gold Districts of Wyoming, 1980, Ore Deposits of Wyoming, 1982, Geology of Southeastern Wyoming, 1984, Minerals and Rocks of Wyoming, 1986, The Geology of Wyoming's Precious Metal Lode and Placer Deposits, 1989, Economic Geology of the South Pass Greenstone Belt, 1991, Economic Geology of the Cooper Hill Mining District, 1992, Mining History and Geology of Wyoming's Metal and Gemstone Districts, 1993, Geology, Mining Districts, and Ghost Towns of the Medicine Bow Mountains, 1993, Diamonds, Kimberlite and Lamproite in the United States, 1994, Pacific Coast Diamonds-An Unconventional Source Terrane, 1995, Economic Geology of the Seminoe Mountains Greenstone Belt, 1994, The Great Diamond Hoax of 1872, 1995, Geology and Gold Mineralization of the Rattlesnake Hills, Granite Mountains, Wyoming, 1996, Copper, Lead, Zinc, Molybdenum, and Associated Metal Deposits of Wyoming, 1997, Diamond Exploration Targets in the Wyoming Craton Western United States, 1997, Diamonds and Mantle Source Rocks in the U.S., with Special Emphasis on the Wyoming Craton, 1998, Water Training Techniques for Martial Artists, 1998, Gemstones, Semi-Precious Stones, Lapidary Materials and Ornamental Stones of Wyoming, 1998, The Rattlesnake Hills-Wyoming's Little Known Gold District, 1998; contbr. over 350 articles to profl. jours. and 5 books. Grantee NASA, 1981, Office of Surface Mining, 1979, U. Wyo., 1981-92, U.S. Geol. Survey Coop. Geologic Mapping Initiative, 1985-88, 98, Union Pacific Resources, 1991, 92, 93, 94, Diamond Rsch. Grant State of Wyoming, 1998—; recipient Pres.'s cert. excellence in presentation Am. Assn. Petroleum Geologists, 1992; named to World Karate Union Hall of Fame, 1998, Millennium Hall of Fame, 1998. Mem. Wyo. Geol. Assn., Wyo. Profl. Geologists, Soc. Econ. Geologists, U. Utah Geology Club (pres. 1969-71), Laramie Bushido Dojo Karate (pres. 1985-88), U. Wyo. Campus Shotokan Karate Club (instr. 1988-93), Shorin-Ryu Karate and Kobudo Club (U. Wyo. Campus headmaster 1993—), Juko-Kai Internat., Okinawan Karate Fedn. Avocations: karate (7th degree black belt/Dai-shihan), jujutsu and other martial arts (7 black belts including Juko-Kai Internat. Samurai and Juko-Kai Internat. Prof. Martial Arts), sketching. Home: 4238 Grays Gable Rd Laramie WY 82072-6911 Office: Geol Survey of Wyo PO Box 3008 Laramie WY 82071-3008 also: Shorin-Ryn Karate & Kobudo Club Univ Wyoming Box 3625 Wyoming Union Laramie WY 82071

HAUSNER, JERRY, electronic engineer, consultant; b. Bklyn., Jan. 17, 1938; s. Irving and Lee (Schneider) H.; m. Helene B. Hausner, Apr. 14, 1962; children: Joyce Fawn, Jeffrey Mitchell. BSEE, CCNY, 1960. Engr. Polarad Electronics Corp., Long Island City, N.Y., 1960-66; chief engr./product line mgr. Narda Microwave Corp., Hauppauge, N.Y., 1966-84; sr. rsch. specialist Logicon R & D Assocs., Albuquerque, 1984-96; v.p., scientific cons. Electro Sci. Applications, Albuquerque, 1996—; pres. Microwave Theory & Technique Chpt., L.I., N.Y., 1981-82, Albuquerque, 1986, gen. chmn. symposium, Albuquerque, 1992. Patentee in field; contbr. articles to Microwaves, 1977-79. Amb., City of Albuquerque, 1996. Recipient Rsch. Publs. award U.S. Navy Rsch. Lab., Washington, 1994. Mem. IEEE (sr.), N.Mex. Entrepreneurs Assn. (bd. dirs. 1995—, pres. 1998—). Achievements include design of specialized radar equipment for military and commercial applications; development of microwave integrated circuit technology and product line. Home: 12925 Manitoba Dr NE Albuquerque NM 87111-2947 Office: Electro Science Applications 2601 Wyoming Blvd NE Albuquerque NM 87112-1031

HAUTALUOMA, JACOB EDWARD, psychology educator, college associate dean; b. Chatham, Mich., June 28, 1933; s. Toivo Jack and Irja Aurora (Nikkinen) H.; m. Betty Lou Johnson, Mar. 24, 1956; children: Jodi, Grey. BA, U. Minn., Duluth, 1955; MS, PhD, U. Colo., 1967; postgrad., Yale U., 1971-72. Indsl. engr. Am. Steel & Wire, Duluth, Minn., 1955-60; assoc. dean Coll. Natural Scis. and prof. psychology Colo. State U., Ft. Collins, 1965—, dept. assoc. chair, 1998—; vis. prof. U. Minn., Duluth, 1972, U. Hawaii, 1973, Oreg. State U., 1977; lectr. Helsinki Sch. Econs., Finland, 1980, U. Iceland, Reykjavik, 1977, 81, U. Rijeka, Croatia, 1998; prog. assoc. NSF, Washington, 1986-87; cons. in field. Contbr. articles to profl. jours. Mem. com. Indian Hills Community Assn., Ft. Collins, 1988-90; ch. councilman Trinity Luth. Ch., Ft. Collins, 1981-83, 89-90; bd. dirs. Colo. Luth. Family Svcs. and Diabetes Assn.; mem. exec. County Dem., 1969. With USAFR, 1957. Fulbright fellow, 1977, 80, 98, NIMH fellow, 1960-61, 63-64, others. Mem. Am. Psychol. Assn., Soc. for Psychol. Study of Social Issues, Acad. Mgmt., Rocky Mt. Psychology Assn., Colo. Wyo. Assn. Indsl./Orgnl. Psychology. Democrat. Lutheran. Avocations: travel, reading, sports. Home: 701 Dartmouth Trl Fort Collins CO 80525-1522 Office: Colo State U Dept Psychology Fort Collins CO 80523

HAVIS, ALLAN STUART, playwright, theatre educator; b. N.Y.C., Sept. 26, 1951; s. Mickey and Esther H.; m. Julia Fulton. BA, CCNY, 1973; MA, Hunter Coll., 1976; MFA, Yale U., 1980. Film animation tchr. Guggenheim Mus., N.Y.C., 1974-76; playwriting tchr. Dramatist Guild, N.Y.C., 1985-87, Ulster County C.C., Stoneridge, N.Y., 1985-88; prof. theatre, head playwriting program U. Calif.-San Diego, La Jolla, 1988—. Author: (novel) Albert the Astronomer, 1979, (plays) Morocco, 1986 (HBO award), Lilith, 1991, The Gift, 1998, (anthology) Plays by Allan Havis, 1989, A Daring Bridge, 1997, Ladies of Fisher Cove, 1997, Sainte Simone, 1997, (play) A Vow of Silence, 1996, (anthology) Plays by Allan Havis, 1997; editor, contbr.: American Political Plays of 1990's, 1998—. Dramaturg Young Playwrights Festival, N.Y.C., 1984, juror, 1993; juror N.J. Arts Coun., Trenton, 1987; panelist Theatre Communications Group, N.Y.C., 1987; juror McKnight Playwriting Fellowship, 1995; v.p. Literary Mgrs. and Dramaturgs of Am., So. Calif. region, 1995—. Playwriting fellow Nat. Endowment for the Arts, 1986, Rockefeller Found., 1987, Guggenheim Found., 1987-88; recipient New American Plays award Kennedy Ctr./Am. Express, Washington, 1988, Dramatists Guild/CBS award, 1995, HBO award, 1996. Democrat. Jewish. Avocations: tennis, motorcycles, racquetball, swimming, horseback riding. Office: Dept of Theatre Univ Calif-San Diego La Jolla CA 92093

HAWE, DAVID LEE, consultant; b. Columbus, Ohio, Feb. 19, 1938; s. William Doyle and Carolyn Mary (Hassig) H.; m. Margret J. Hoover, Apr. 15, 1962; children: Darrin Lee, Kelly Lynn. Project mgr. ground antenna systems W.D.L. Labs., Philco Corp., 1960-65; credit mgr. for Western U.S., Am. Hosp. Supply Corp., Burbank, Calif., 1965-74; owner, mgr. Hoover Profl. Equipment Co., contract health equipment co., Guasti, Calif., 1974-75; pres. Baslor Care Services, owner convalescent homes, Santa Ana, Calif., 1975-80; pres. Application Assocs., 1980—; bd. dirs., chmn. bd. dirs. Xiron, Inc., 1984—; dir. Medisco Co., Casa Pacifica, Broadway Assocs. Bd. dirs. Santa Ana Community Convalescent Hosp., 1974-79, pres., 1975-79. With USN, 1954-56. Lic. real estate broker, Calif. Mem. Am. Vacuum Soc. Republican. Roman Catholic. Home: 18082 Hallsworth Cir Villa Park CA 92861-4503

HAWES, SUE, lawyer; b. Washington, Mar. 30, 1937; d. Alexander Boyd and Elizabeth (Armstrong) H.; m. James E. Brodhead, June 21, 1963; children: William James Pusey Brodhead, Daniel Alexander Hawes Brodhead. BA, Sarah Lawrence Coll., 1959, MA, 1963; JD, Whittier (Calif.) Sch. of Law, 1983. Bar: Calif. 1988, U.S. Dist. Ct. (cen. dist.) Calif. 1990. Dancer and choreographer N.Y.C., Washington, Latin Am., Europe, 1959-62; instr., dir. dance program dept. theatre and phys. edn. Smith Coll., Northampton, Mass., 1963-65; [illegible] script supr. L.A., 1976-80; prin. Law Office of Sue Hawes, L.A., 1988-96; ptnr., mem. RESULTS. Articles editor Whittier Law Rev., 1982-83. Active Santa Barbara Symphony League. Mem. AAUW, Results, State Bar Calif., Actors' Equity Assn. Democrat. Avocations: music, gardening, politics.

HAWK, NORMAN RAY, academic administrator, retired; b. Butte Falls, Oreg., Apr. 14, 1918; s. Norman Lee and Inez (Pullen) H.; m. Phyllis Virginia Porter, July 1, 1939; children: Kenneth Alan, William Lee, Ronald Dean. BS in History, U. Oreg., 1947, MS in History, 1948, EdD, 1949. Dir. tchr. tng. So. Oreg. Coll., Ashland, 1949; dean of men U. Oreg., Eugene, 1950-57, 59-63; asst. to pres. U. Oreg., 1963-69, acting pres., 1969, v.p. adminstrn. and fin., 1969-82; Carnegie Postdoctoral Fellow U. Mich., Ann Arbor, 1958-59. Col. USAF, 1942-46, Africa, France. Mem. Eugene Town Club. Avocations: travel, photography, gardening, fishing, reading. Home: 1899 Longview St Eugene OR 97403-2601

HAWKES, GLENN ROGERS, psychology educator; b. Preston, Idaho, Apr. 29, 1919; s. William and Rae (Rogers) H.; m. Yvonne Merrill, Dec. 18, 1941; children—Kristen, William Ray, Gregory Merrill, Laura. B.S. in Psychology, Utah State U., 1946, M.S. in Psychology, 1947; Ph.D. in Psychology, Cornell U., 1950. From asst. prof. to prof. child devel. and psychology Iowa State U., Ames, 1950-66, chmn. dept. child devel., 1954-66; prof. human devel., rsch. psychologist U. Calif., Davis, 1966-89, prof. emeritus, 1990—, acad. coord. Hubert Humphrey fellowship program, 1990-97, assoc. dean applied econs. and behavioral scis., 1966-83, chmn. dept. applied behavioral scis., 1982-86, chmn. teaching div., 1970-72, prof. behavioral scis. dept. family practice, Sch. Medicine; acting dir. Internat. Programs, U. Calif., Davis, 1994-97; vis. scholar U. Hawaii, 1972-73, U. London, 1970, 80, 86; bd. dirs. Creative Playthings Inc., 1962-66. Author: (with Pease) Behavior and Development from 5 to 12, 1962; (with Frost) The Disadvantaged Child: Issues and Innovations, 1966, 2d edit., 1970; (with Schutz and Baird) Lifestyles and Consumer Behavior of Older Americans, 1979; (with Nicola and Fish) Young Marrieds: The Dual Career Approach, 1984. Contbr. numerous articles to profl. and sci. jours. Served with AUS, 1941-45. Recipient numerous research grants from pvt. founds. and govtl. bodies; recipient Iowa State U. faculty citation, 1965, Outstanding Service citation Iowa Soc. Crippled Children and adults, 1965, citation Dept. Child Devel., 1980, Coll. Agrl. and Environ. Scis., 1983; named hon. lt. gov. Okla., 1966. Home: 1114 Purdue Dr Davis CA 95616-1736 Office: U Calif Internat House 10 College Park Davis CA 95616-3607

HAWKINS, DAVID RAMON, psychiatrist, writer, researcher; b. Milw., June 3, 1927; s. Ramon Nelson and Alice-Mary (McCutcheon) H.; children: Lynn Ashley, Barbara Catherine. BS, Marquette U., 1950; MD, Med. Coll. Wis., Milw., 1953; PhD, Columbia Pacific U., 1995. Med. dir. North Nassau Mental Health Ctr., Manhasset, N.Y., 1956-80; dir. rsch. Brunswick Hosp., L.I., N.Y., 1968-79; pres. Acad. Orthomolecular Psychiatry, N.Y.C., 1970-80; dir. Inst. Spiritual Rsch., Sedona, Ariz., 1979-88, The Rsch. Inst., Sedona, 1988—; pres. Attractor Rsch., Sedona, 1989—, Veritas Pub., Sedona, 1995—; chmn. Inst. Advaned Theoretical Rsch., 1993—; guest lectr. U. Notre Dame, Harvard U., U. Mich., 1970-88, U. Calif., San Francisco, 1997; Landsberg lectr. U. Calif. San Francisco Med. Sch., 1997; guest on TV news and interview shows including McNeal-Lehrer, Barbara Walters, Today, 1972-76; chief of staff Mingus Mountain RTC, 1995; cons. psychiatrist MJL Hosp., Cottonwood, Ariz., 1995; cons. USN, Dept. Health Edn. Welfare, Congress. Author: (with Linus Pauling) Orthomolecular Psychiatry, 1973, Force vs. Power, 1995; contbr. articles to profl. jours. With U.S. Navy, 1945-46, PTO. Decorated knight Sovereign Order St. John of Jerusalem, Danish Crown; Rsch. grantee N.Y. State Dept. Mental Hygiene, annually, N.Y. State Legis., 1967-87; recipient Mosby Book award, 1953. Mem. AMA, APA, Ariz. Med. Soc., Ariz. Psychiat. Soc., Alpha Omega Alpha. Avocations: inventing, designing, woodcraft, dance, architecture. Office: Rsch Inst 151 Keller Ln Sedona AZ 86336-9748

HAWKINS, HAROLD STANLEY, pastor, police chaplain, school director; b. Santa Ana, Calif., Oct. 16, 1927; s. Henry Jesse and Susan Brown (Young) H.; m. Paula Juanita Paeschke, Feb. 19, 1949; children: Bert Stanley, Harold Paul, Kathleen Faith Mummert. Grad., L.I.F.E. Bible Coll., 1950; cert., So. Bay Regional Police Acad., 1978; DD, Hawthorne Christian Sch./Coll., 1978. Pastor Internat. Ch. of the Foursquare Gospel, Redondo Beach, Calif., 1949-58, 69-97, Reseda, Calif., 1958-66; staff mem. Oral Roberts U., Tulsa, 1966-67; pastor Internat. Ch. of the Foursquare Gospel, Bell, Calif., 1967-69; chaplain Redondo Beach Police, 1978-98, res. police officer, 1978-88; master police chaplain L.A. Police Dept., 1988-92; dir. Camp Cedar Crest, Running Springs, Calif., 1961-81, Wings of Mercy, Santa Ana, 1966-70, Hawthorne (Calif.) Christian Schs., 1973-96. Mem. Redondo Beach Round Table, 1974—, pres. 1991-92; commr. Harbor Commn., Redondo Beach, 1982-92, planning commn., 1996—. With USN, 1944-46, World War II. Rotary (pres. 1982-83). Republican. Office: Internat Ch Foursquare Gospel 324 N Catalina Ave Apt 7 Redondo Beach CA 90277-2810

HAWKINS, ROBERT LEE, health facility administrator; b. Denver, Feb. 18, 1938; s. Isom and Bessie M. (Hugley) H.; m. Ann Sharon Hoy, Apr. 28, 1973; children: Robert, Jeanne, Julia, Rose. AA, Pueblo Jr. Coll., 1958; BS, So. Colo. State Coll., 1965; MSW, U. Denver, 1967. Psychiat. technician Colo. State Hosp., Pueblo, 1956-58, 1962-63, occupl. therapist asst., 1964-65, clin. adminstr. psychiat. team, 1969-75, dir. cmty. svcs., 1975-92, supr. vol. services, 1975—, mem. budget com., 1975—; asst. supt. clin. svcs., 1992—; supt. Colo. Mental Health Inst., Pueblo, 1996—; counselor (part-time) Family Svc. Agy., Pueblo, 1968-69, exec. dir., 1969-70; mem. faculty U. So. Colo., 1968-75; ptnr. Human Resource Devel., Inc., 1970-75; mem. Nat. Adv. Com. on Instnl. Quality and Integrity, U.S. Dept. Edn., Washington, 1993—. Mem. Pueblo Positive Action Com., 1970; chmn. adv. bd. Pueblo Sangre de Cristo Day Care Center, 1969-72; chmn. Gov.'s So. Area Adv. Council of Employment Service, 1975-76, chmn. Pueblo's City CSC, 1976-77, Pueblo Cmty. Corrections, 1985-87, Pueblo Civil Svc. Commn., 1988—; commr. Pueblo Housing Authority, 1986—, Colo. Commn. Higher Edn., 1987—, USED Commn. for Ednl. Quality & Integrity, 1993—; mem. gov's. adv. com. Mental Health Stds., 1981—; mem. Colo. Juvenile Parole Bd., 1977; bd. dirs. Pueblo United Fund, 1969-74, pres., 1973; bd. dirs. Pueblo Community Orgn., 1974-76, Spanish Peaks Mental Health Center, 1976—, Neighborhood Health Center, 1977-79, Pueblo Community Corrections, 1983—, Pueblo Legal Svcs., 1983—, Girl Scouts USA, 1996—; mem. Pueblo Colo. 2010 Commn., 1994—, adv. com. YWCA, 1994—, Healthy Pueblo 2000 Task Force, 1993—. Bd. dirs. Posada Shelter for Homeless, 1990—, Boys Girls club, 1991—, ARC, 1994—, pres., 1994—, Colo. Common Cause, 1998—. With U.S. Army 1958-62. Mem. Nat. Assn. Social Workers (nominating com. 1973-76), ACLU (dir. Pueblo chpt. 1980—), NAACP, Broadway Theatre Guild. Democrat. Methodist. Mem. Kiwanis. Home: 220 Melrose Ave Pueblo CO 81004-1053 Office: Colo State Hosp 1600 W 24th St Pueblo CO 81003-1411

HAWKINS, RONALD E., academic administrator, counselor; b. Portland, Oreg.; m. Peg Hawkins. D in Ministry; EdD, Va. Poly. Inst. and State U. Cert. counselor. Pres. We. Sem., Portland, Oreg., 1995—; provost Liberty U. Author: Strengthening Marital Intimacy, 1991. Fax: (503) 239-4216. Office: Western Seminary 5511 SE Hawthorne Blvd Portland OR 97215-3367

HAWKINS, TRIP, electronics company executive. Chmn. bd. dirs., CEO 3DO, Redwood City, Calif. Office: 3DO 600 Galveston Dr Redwood City CA 94063-4721*

HAWLEY, KIMRA, software company executive. BS in Psychology, Pitts. State U. Prin. MarketBound Assocs.; various mktg. mgmt. positions Amdahl Corp.; imaging mktg. dir. Input Software (formerly Cornerstone Imaging), 1992-96, gen. mgr. software divsn., 1996, now pres., CEO. Office: Input Software 1299 Parkmoor Ave San Jose CA 95126-3448*

HAWLEY, NANCI ELIZABETH, social services administrator; b. Detroit, Mar. 18, 1942; d. Arthur Theodore and Elizabeth Agnes (Fylling) Smisek; m. Joseph Michael Hawley, Aug. 28, 1958; children: Michael, Ronald, Patrick (dec.), Julie Anne. Pres. Tempo 21 Nursing Svcs., Inc., Covina, Calif., 1973-75; v.p. Profl. Nurses Bur., Inc., L.A., 1975-83; cons. Hawley & Assocs., Covina, 1983-87; exec. v.p. Glendora (Calif.) C. of C., 1984-85; dir. membership West Covina (Calif.) C. of C., 1985-87; exec. dir. San Dimas (Calif.) C. of C., 1987-88; mgr. pub. rels. Soc. for Advancement of Material and Process [illegible] Dist., 1992-94; bus. counselor Commerce and Trade Agy., Small Bus. Devel. Ctr., 1994; exec. v.p. Ontario (Calif.) C. of C., 1994-97; CEO, RMH Elec. Contractors, Colorado Springs, Colo., 1997-98; exec. v.p. Teen Resources, Inc., Colorado Springs, 1998; owner/CEO Hawley and Assoc. V.p. San-

gabriel valley chpt. Women in Mgmt. Recipient Youth Motivation award Foothill Edn. Com., Glendora, 1987. Mem. NAFE, Colo. Assn. Nonprofit Orgns., Pub. Rels. Soc. Am., Soc. Nat. Assn. Publs., Am. Soc. Assn. Execs., Nat. Assn. Membership Dirs., Profl. Communicators Assn. So. Calif., West End Bus. Assn. (pres. 1997—), Western Assn. Chamber Execs. (Spl. merit award for mag. pub. 1995), Kiwanis Internat. (sec. 1989-90, pres. West Covina 1990-91, Kiwanian of Yr. 1989), Rotary Internat. Avocations: reading, walking, painting, gardening. Fax: 719-596-2573. E-mail: nanmick58@AOL.com. Office: Hawley and Assoc. PO Box 25461 Colorado Springs CO 80936-5903

HAWLEY, PHILIP METSCHAN, retired retail executive, consultant; b. Portland, Oreg., July 29, 1925; s. Willard P. and Dorothy (Metschan) H.; m. Mary Catherine Follen, May 31, 1947; children: Diane (Mrs. Robert Bruce Johnson), Willard, Philip Metschan Jr., John, Victor, Edward, Erin (Mrs. Kevin Przybocki), George. BS, U. Calif., Berkeley, 1946; grad. advanced mgmt. program, Harvard U., 1967. With Carter Hawley Hale Stores, Inc., L.A., 1958-93, pres., 1972-83, chief exec. officer, 1977-93, chmn., 1983-93; bd. dirs. Weyerhaeuser Co. Trustee Calif. Inst. Tech., U. Notre Dame; chmn. L.A. Energy Conservation Com., 1973-74. Decorated hon. comdr. Order Brit. Empire, knight comdr. Star Solidarity Republic Italy; recipient Award of Merit L.A. Jr. C. of C., 1974, Coro Pub. Affairs award, 1978, Medallion award Coll. William and Mary, 1983, Award of Excellence Sch. Bus. Adminstrn. U. So. Calif., 1987, Bus. Statesman of Yr. award Harvard Bus. Sch., 1989, 15th ann. Whitney M. Young Jr. award L.S. Urban League, 1988; named Calif. Industrialist of Yr. Calif. Mus. Sci. and Industry, 1975. Mem. Calif. Retailers Assn. (chmn. 1993-95, dir.), Beach Club, Calif. Club, L.A. Country Club, Bohemian Club, Pacific-Union Club, Newport Harbor Yacht Club, Multnomah Club, Links Club, Phi Beta Kappa, Beta Alpha Psi, Beta Gamma Sigma. Office: 400 S Hope St Ste 1900 Los Angeles CA 90071-2801

HAWRANEK, JOSEPH PAUL, computer company executive, consultant; b. N.Y.C., Dec. 21, 1937; s. Joseph and Tina Woodsinger H.; m. Joanne Arlene Vinson, Mar. 21, 1959 (dec. 1992); children: David Paul, Daniel Strauss, Scott Joseph. BS in EE, U. Va., Charlottesville, 1960; MBA, U. Va., 1962; PhD, U. Pa., Phila., 1970. Mgr. IBM, Raleigh, N.C., 1966-76; dir. Nat. Semi-Conductor, Santa Clara, Calif., 1976-80, Honeywell, Phoenix, Ariz., 1980-83, Aydin Corp.-Aydin Controls, Ft. Washington, Pa., 1983; pres. Teneron Corp., Beaverton, Oreg., 1983-86, Raven Communications Inc., Phoenix, 1987-88, 89-93; v.p. ops. Telxon Corp., Akron, Ohio, 1988-89; pres. wireless divsn. Calif. Microwave, 1993; pres. Raven Communications Inc., Phoenix, 1994—. Office: Raven Communications 8724 N 67th St Paradise Valley AZ 85253-2701

HAWTHORNE, GREGORY THOMAS, painter, sculptor, gallery owner; b. Detroit, Aug. 13, 1951; s. Herbert Lenard and Barbara Ann (Van Bibber) H.; m. Susan Jane Taylor, Sept. 8, 1973; children: Taylor Justin, Shelby Rae. BS, Wayne State U., 1973. Owner Hawthorne Gallery, Big Sur, Calif., 1995—. One-man shows include Edward Blais Gallery, Palm Springs, Calif., 1982, Northwood Inst. Gallery, Midland, Mich., 1984, Barclay Simpson Gallery, Lafayette, Calif., 1985, Sher Gallery, North Miami Beach, Fla., 1985, 90, 95, Atelier Galerie, Carmel, Calif., 1985, 87, Norman F. Feldheym Libr. Galleries, San Bernardino, Calif., 1986, Art Zen Musee Chair, Chuo-Ku Osaka, Japan, 1989, Cassandra Kersting Gallery, Oakland, Calif., 1990, J. Richards Gallery, Englewood, N.J., 1990; exhibited in group shows at Amb. Gallery, N.Y.C., 1995—, Masterpiece Gallery, Boca Raton, Fla., 1995—, Sher Gallery, 1995—, Gallery Fair, Mendocino, Calif., 1995, Auberge du Soleil, Rutherford, Calif., 1995, Rosen Fine Art, N.J., 1993, numerous others; represented in numerous pub. and pvt. collections. Mem. U.S. Ski Assn. (bd. dirs. Far West Masters 1990-97). Avocations: running, softball, roller hockey, downhill ski racing. Home: Hawthorne Studio Hawthorne Gallery Mule Canyon Big Sur CA 93920 Office: Hawthorne Gallery 48485 Highway 1 Big Sur CA 93920-9694

HAWTHORNE, NAN LOUISE, internet resources consultant, web designer; b. Hawthorne, Nev., Jan. 3, 1952; d. Louis Frederick Haas and Merle Forrest (Ohlhausen) Ritter; m. James Denver Tedford, Dec. 20, 1981. BS, No. Mich. U., 1981. Mng. dir. CyberVPM.com, Seattle, 1997—; pres., dir. Vols. in Agys. of King County, 1997-98; mgr. vols. Seattle Commns., 1993-94; co-host TV program on TCI Pub. Access: Volunteer!; webmaster Purrfect Pals, 1997—, Gov-VPM, POLF, 1997—. Author: Loving the Goddess Within, 1991, Building Better Relationships with Volunteers, 1997, Managing Volunteers in Record Time, 1997, Recognizing Volunteers Right From the Start, 1998. Mem. Wash. State Coun. on Volunteerism and Citizen Svcs., 1992-94; trainer United Way of King County Vol. Ctr., 1993—; bd. dirs. Dovia of King County, 1992, 96—; mem. adv. bd. Retired Sr. Vol. Program, 1995-98; bd. dirs. Cmty. Vol. Svcs.; pres., bd. dirs. Cmty. Vol. Svcs., 1996-97; forum advt. coord. Charity Channel. Mem. Assn. Vol. Adminstrs. (tech. com. 1998—). E-mail: hawthorne@cybervpm.com. Office: CyberVPM.com 9594 1st Ave NE Ste 413 Seattle WA 98115-2012

HAY, ANDREW MACKENZIE, merchant banking and commodities company executive; b. London, Apr. 9, 1928; came to U.S., 1954, naturalized, 1959; s. Ewen Mackenzie and Bertine (Buxton) H.; MA in Econs., St. John's Coll., Cambridge U., 1950; m. Catherine Newman, July 30, 1977. Commodities trader, London and Ceylon, 1950-53; v.p. Calvert Vavasseur & Co. Inc., N.Y.C., 1954-61, pres., 1962-78, pres. Calvert-Peat Inc., N.Y.C., 1978—, Andrew M. Hay, Inc.; chmn. Barretto Peat Inc., N.Y.C., 1974-88; Pacific NW cons. Am. Assn. Exporters and Importers, 1982—; radio and TV appearances. Author: A Century of Coconuts, 1972, Confessions of an Honorary Consul, 1998; Mem. adv. com. on tech. innovation Nat. Acad. Scis., 1978; bd. dirs. Winston Churchill Found.; treas., trustee World Affairs Coun. Oreg., 1986—; apptd. Her Majesty's hon. Brit. consul., 1987; dean Oreg. Counsular Corps, 1991. Capt. Brit. Army. Decorated comdr. Order Brit. Empire. Recipient World Affair Coun. Willard de Weese award, 1992. Mem. Am. Importer Assn. (pres. 1977-79), Pacific N.W. Internat. Trade Assn. (exec. dir. 1986—), Brit. Am. C. of C. (pres. 1966-68), Philippine Am. C. of C. (pres. 1977-79), An. Friends of Cambridge U. (bd. dirs. 1997), St. George's Soc. (bd. dir.), St. Andrew's Soc. (bd. dir.), Recess Club, Downtown Assn. (N.Y.C.), U. Club, Arlington Club. Episcopalian. Home and Office: 3515 SW Council Crest Dr Portland OR 97201-1403

HAY, JOHN LEONARD, lawyer; b. Lawrence, Mass., Oct. 6, 1940; s. Charles Cable and Henrietta Dudley (Wise) H.; m. Ruth Murphy, Mar. 16, 1997; 1 child, Ian. AB with distinction, Stanford U., 1961; JD, U. Colo., 1964. Bar: Colo. 1964, Ariz. 1965, D.C. 1971. Assoc. Lewis and Roca, Phoenix, 1964-69, ptnr., 1969-82; ptnr. Fannin, Terry & Hay, Phoenix, 1982-87, Allen, Kimerer & LaVelle, Phoenix, 1987-94, Gust Rosenfeld, Phoenix, 1994—; judge pro tem Ariz. Ct. Appeals, 1999—; bd. dirs. Ariz. Life and Disability Ins. Guaranty Fund, 1984-95, chmn., 1993-95. Co-author: Arizona Corporate Practice, 1996, Representing Franchisees, 1996. Mem. Dem. Precinct Com., 1966-78, Ariz. State Dem. Com., 1968-78; chmn. Dem. Legis. Dist., 1971-74; mem. Maricopa County Dem. Cen. Com., 1971-74; bd. dirs. ACLU, 1973-78; bd. dirs. Community Legal Svcs., 1983-89, pres., 1987-88; bd. dirs. Ariz. Club, 1994-96; judge pro tempore Ariz. Ct. Appeals, 1999—. Mem. ABA, Ariz. Bar Assn., Maricopa County Bar Assn. (bd. dirs. 1972-85), Assn. Life Ins. Counsel, Ariz. Licensors and Franchisors Assn. (bd. dirs. 1985—, pres. 1988-89), Ariz. Civil Liberties Union (bd. dirs. 1967-84, 95—, pres. 1973-77, 97—, Disting. Citizen award 1979), Phoenix C. of C. (chmn. arts and culture task force 1997—). Home: 201 E Hayward Ave Phoenix AZ 85020-4037 Office: Gust Rosenfeld 201 N Central Ave Ste 3300 Phoenix AZ 85073-3300

HAY, RICHARD LAURENCE, theater scenic designer; b. Wichita, Kans., May 28, 1929; s. Laurence Charles and Ruth Mary (Rhoades) H. BA, Stanford U., 1952, MA, 1955. Tech. dir., designer Oreg. Shakespeare Festival, Ashland, 1953-55, prin. scenic designer, 1970—; instr. drama Stanford U., Palo Alto, Calif., 1957-62, assoc. prof., 1965-69; assoc. artistic dir. for design Denver Ctr. Theater Co., 1984-91; freelance scenic designer Guthrie Theater, Mpls., Am. Conservatory Theater, San Francisco, Mo. Repertory Theater, Kansas City, Mark Taper Forum, Los Angeles, Old Globe Theater, San Diego, Berkekey (Calif.) Repertory Theater, Eisenhower Theatre, others; theatre designer: Source and Space Theatres, Denver Ctr. Theatre Co., New Old Globe Theatre and Festival Stage, Old Globe Theatre, San Diego, Intiman Theatre, Seattle, Black Swan, Angus Bowmer Theatre, Elizabethan Stage, Oreg. Shakespeare Festival. Author: (with others) A Space for Magic: Stage Settings by Richard L. Hay, 1979; exhibitor Prague Quadriennial, 1987, 99, U.S. Inst. Theatre Tech. Biennial Scenography Expn., 1984, 88, 90. Recipient Critics award Hollywood (Calif.) Drama-Logue, 1982, 85, 86, 89, Gov's. award for the Arts State of Oreg., 1989; Fulbright grantee, 1955. Mem. United Scenic Artists, U.S. Inst. Theatre Tech. (bd. dirs. 1994-97, Disting. Achievement award in scenic design 1998), League Hist. Am. Theaters. Democrat. Congregationalist. Avocation: book collecting. Home: 707 Liberty St Ashland OR 97520-3140 Office: Oreg Shakespeare Festival PO Box 158 Ashland OR 97520-0158

HAY, WILLIAM CHARLES, professional hockey team executive; b. Saskatoon, Sask., Can., Dec. 9, 1935; s. Charles and Florence (Miller) H.; m. Nancy Ann Woodman, Aug. 24, 1957; children: Pam, Penny, Donald. B.S. in Geology, Colo. Coll., 1958. Profl. hockey player Chgo. Black Hawks, 1958-67; mgr. Sedco Drilling Co., Calgary, Alta., 1967-70, gen. mgr., from 1970; gen. mgr. Hi-Tower Drilling Co., Calgary, Alta., from 1970; formerly pres., chief operating officer Hockey Can.; pres. Calgary Flames Hockey Club, NHL, 1991—; also alternate governor Calgary Flames; now planning advisor Canadian Hockey Association; exec. dir. Champions in Hockey Endowment Fund; chmn., CEO Hockey Hall of Fame, Toronto. Office: Canadian Hockey Asso, 2424 Univ Dr, Calgary, AB Canada T2N 3Y9

HAYASHI, ARTHUR, prosecutor; b. Spokane, Wash., Aug. 18, 1955; s. Kaoru and Mary I. (Ogata) H.; m. Lynda C. Egger, Mar. 31, 1984. BA in Polit. Sci., Gonzaga U., 1977; JD, U. Wash., 1980. Bar: Wash. 1981, U.S. Dist. Ct. (ea. and we. dists.) Wash. 1981, U.S. Ct. Appeals (9th cir.) 1981. Assoc. McKanna, Herman & Toreson, Spokane, 1980-83, Salter, McKeehen, Gudger & Rabine, Seattle, 1983-84; pvt. practice Spokane, 1984-87; dep. prosecutor Spokane County, 1987—; chmn. bd. dirs. Spokane Fed. Credit Union, 1994—; exec. mem. Wash. State Family Support Coun., Seattle, 1987-94; exec. mem. legal sec.'s adv. com. Spokane C.C., 1992—. Co-contbr.: Best Practices for State Family Law Cases, 1996. Mem. nominating com. Inland Empire coun. Girl Scouts U.S.A., Spokane, 1994—; trustee St. Paul's United Meth. Ch., Spokane, 1994—. Mem. Inns of Ct. (Charles Powell chpt.). Avocations: tennis, basketball, softball. Office: Spokane County Prosecutors Office 1124 W Riverside Ave # LL2 Spokane WA 99201-1132

HAYASHIDA, LARRY W., minister; b. Alamosa, Colo., Feb. 12, 1944; s. Charles T. and Sadako (Katekaru) H.; m. Bette N. Miyake, June 18, 1967; children: Charles Mark, John David. BA, Chapman Coll., 1968, MA, 1874; EdD, U. No. Colo., 1978. Cert. pub. instr., Calif. Adminstr. Faith Ministries World Outreach, Greeley, Colo., 1978-85; prin. Faith Ministries Acad., Greeley, 1982-84; founder, pastor Spectrum Christian Ctr., Sacramento, Calif., 1985—; founder, chmn. Divorce Prevention Task Force, Sacramento, 1987—; founder, pres. Spectrum Inst. Ministry, Sacramento, 1989—; Bd. dris. FACE to FACE ministries, Anaheim, Calif.; publisher Betlar Publishing Co., Rancho Murieta, Calif., 1989—; leadership coun. Integrity Leadership Ministries, Dallas, 1990—. Author: Where Do We Go From Here, 1989; producer, host: (TV prodn.) Aloha 7000, 1983-84, Divorce Prevention, 1988. Advisor Crisis Pregnancy Ctr., Sacramento, 1987. Mem. Internat. Conv. Faith Ministries, Charismatic Bible Ministries, Rotary (Spl. Svc. award 1977). Home: 1167 La Rochelle Ter # C Sunnyvale CA 94089-1754 Office: Spectrum Christian Ctr 11415 Folsom Blvd Rancho Cordova CA 95742-6207

HAYDEN, CEDRIC L., state legislator, dentist; b. Eugene, Oreg., Aug. 4, 1934; s. Jesse and Gwendolen (Lampshire) H.; m. Marilyn Adele Jaekel, Dec. 27, 1961; children: Jonathan, Christopher, Matthew, Cedric Ross, Kaminda. BS, U. Oreg., 1957; DMD, Washington U., St. Louis, 1960; MPH, Loma Linda U., 1979. Dentist Antioch (Calif.) Dental Group, 1963-65; missionary Seventh Day Adventist Ch., Port of Spain, Trinidad, 1965-69; dentist Hayden Family Dentistry Group, Eugene, Oreg., 1970—; legislator Oreg. Ho. of Reps., Salem, 1985-97, chmn. house com. on transp., house com. on gen. govt., 1991-95, asst. majority leader, asst. caucus leader, 1991-95. Lt. (s.g.) USN, 1960-63. Fellow Am. Dental Soc. Anesthesiology. Avocations: skiing, hiking, camping, horseback riding, travel. Home: 2645 Woodstone Pl Eugene OR 97405-1257

HAYDEN, RON L., library director; b. San Pedro, Calif., Dec. 24, 1948; s. Larnie Alphonsis and Myrtie Louise (Pilcher) H.; m. Marilee Ann Brubaker, May 30, 1971 (dec. June 1978); m. Susan Ann Huffman, Jan. 1, 1982. AA, Golden West Coll., 1969; BA, Long Beach State U., 1972; MLS, Fullerton U., 1974. Reference sr. libr. Huntington Beach (Calif.) Libr., 1975-79, pub. svc. libr., 1979-86, libr. dir., 1986—; liason Libr. Patrons Assn., Huntington Beach, 1986—. Author: Collection Development Library Journal, 1979. Recipient Award of Excellence Calif. S.W. Recreation Park Conf., 1990. Mem. ALA (Libr. in Media award, Best of Show award 1990), Calif. Libr. Assn., Friends Libr., So. Calif. Tennis Assn., Rotary (bd. dirs., vocat. chmn. 1988—). Avocations: tennis, running, reading. Office: Huntington Beach Libr 7111 Talbert Ave Huntington Beach CA 92648-1232

HAYES, BONNIE CLARE, writer; b. Watsonville, Calif., Feb. 14, 1934; d. ALfred Leo and Mildred Eileen (Kirkland) Rooney. Head training program Franciscan Cmty., Santa Cruz County, Calif., head of cmty.; nat. councelor Fedn. of Nuns; pvt. practice in home and family support svcs., 1985—. Contbr. articles to profl. jours. Recipient Reg. Winner Egyptian Mau Cat, Cat Fed., 1987-88. Mem. Mt. Tamalpais Intreperative Assn., State Park Support Group. Avocations: hiking, study of art and collectible antiques, rescue work with animals. Office: PO Box 2393 Mill Valley CA 99941

HAYES, BYRON JACKSON, JR., retired lawyer; b. L.A., July 9, 1934; s. Byron Jackson and Caroline Violet (Scott) H.; m. DeAnne Saliba, June 30, 1962; children: Kenneth Byron, Patricia DeAnne. Student, Pomona Coll., 1952-56; BA magna cum laude, Harvard U., LLB cum laude, 1959. Bar: Calif. 1960, U.S. Supreme Ct. 1963. Assoc., McCutchen, Black, Verleger & Shea, L.A., 1960-68, ptnr., 1968-89; ptnr. Baker & Hostetler, 1990-97, ret., 1998. Trustee L.A. Urban Found., 1996—, CFO, 1998—; trustee L.A. Ch. Extension Soc. United Meth. Ch., 1967-77, pres., 1974-77, chancellor ann. conf. Pacific and S.W., 1979-86, dir. 1010 devel. corp., 1993—, v.p., 1995—; Dir., pres. Pacific and S.W. United Meth. Found., 1978-84. Named Layperson of yr. Pacific and S.W. Ann. Conf., United Meth. Ch., 1981, recipient Bishop's award, 1992. Mem. ABA, Am. Coll. Mortgage Attys. (regent 1984-93, pres. 1993-94), Calif. Bar Assn., Los Angeles County Bar Assn. (chmn. real property sect. 1982-83), Toluca Lake Property Owners Assn. (sec. 1990-94), Pomona Coll. Alumni Assn. (pres. 1984-85), Lakeside Golf Club. Office: Baker & Hostetler 600 Wilshire Blvd Fl 12 Los Angeles CA 90017-3212

HAYES, CLAUDE QUINTEN CHRISTOPHER, research scientist; b. N.Y.C., Nov. 15, 1945; s. Claude and Celestine (Stanley) H. BA in Chemistry and Geol. Sci., Columbia U., 1971, postgrad., 1972-73; postgrad., N.Y. Law Sch., 1973-75; JD, Western State Law Sch., 1978. Cert. community coll. tchr. earth scis., phys. sci., law, Calif. Tech. writer Burroughs Corp., San Diego, 1978-79; instr. phys. scis. Nat. U., San Diego, 1980-81; instr. bus. law, earth scis. Miramar Coll., 1978-82; sr. systems analyst Gen. Dynamics Convair, 1979-80, advanced mfg. technologist, sr. engr., 1980-81; pvt. practice sci. and tech. cons. Calif., 1979—; instr. phys. scis., phys. geography, bus. law San Diego Community Coll. Dist., 1976-82, 85-90; U.S. Dept. Def. contractor Def. Nuclear Agy., Strategic Def. Initiative Agy., USAF, Def. Advance Rsch. Projects Agy., 1986—, U.S. Army, 1991—; adj. prof. phys. chemistry San Diego State U., 1986-87; bus. and computer sci. def. rsch. contractor to Maxwell Labs., Naval Ocean Sys. Ctr.; tech. cons. Pizza Hut, Inc., Carts of Colo., Smiths Industries. Contbr. articles to profl. jours.; patentee in field. Mem. Am. Chem. Soc., N.Y. Acad. Sci., Am. Inst. Aero. and Astronautics, Princeton Columbia Barnard Club. Avocations: travel, technical, ancient history, art, people. Home and office: 3737 3rd Ave Apt 308 San Diego CA 92103-4133

HAYES, CYNTHIA ANN, administrative assistant, writer; b. L.A., Sept. 11, 1954; d. Lafayette and Verna (O'Gee) H.; 1 child, LaLaunie Charisse. Student, U. Calif., L.A., 1972-75. Clerk underwriting unit Great Am. Insurance Co., L.A., 1978-79; administrv. asst. Bill Dodd Real Estate Co., L.A., 1979-80, L.A. Dept. Water and Power, 1980—; v.p. Images By Haze, Laguna Niguel, Calif., 1990-91. Author: That Lovely Piece of Art, 1997, The Death of Lillie Maroe, 1998. Donor The Brotherhood Crusade, The Donor's Welfare Plan. Mem. U. Calif. L.A., The Duvall Found. Democrat. Baptist. Avocations: sewing, creating graphic designs, sailing, cycling, attending concerts and theater.

HAYES, DELBERT J., athletic company executive; b. 1935. BA, Wash. State U., 1957. CPA, Wash. Acct. Price, Waterhouse & Co., 1961-69, Linn-Pacific, 1969-70; ptnr. Hayes, Nyman & Co., 1972-75; treas. Nike, Inc., Beaverton, Oreg., 1975-80, exec. v.p., 1980—, also bd. dirs. Office: Nike Inc One Bowerman Dr Beaverton OR 97005-2319*

HAYES, ELIZABETH ROTHS, retired dance educator; b. Ithaca, N.Y., July 3, 1911; d. Leslie David and Emilie Christine (Roths) H. AB, W.Va. U., 1932; MS, U. Wis., 1935; EdD, Stanford U., 1949. Instr. various colls., W.Va. and Ill., 1936-40; asst. prof. U. Wis., 1945; asst. prof. dept. modern dance U. Utah, Salt Lake City, 1941-44, 46-49, assoc. prof., 1954-88, prof. emerita, 1988—; tchrs. summers Chico (Calif.) Tchrs. Coll., 1951, West Va. U., 1952, U. Mich., 1957, U. Iowa, 1965; founder Modern Dance Maj. Program, U. Utah; spkr. in field; cons. univs. dancer, choreographer over 40 dances; dir. over 35 dance concerts and prodns.; contbg. editor Design for Arts In Edn., 1980-85; contbr. numerous articles to profl. publs.; author: Introduction to the Teaching of Dance, 1964, Dance Composition and Production, 2d edit., 1993. Recipient Hon. Disting. Alumnus award, U. Utah, 1993, Sch. Edn. Alumni Achievement award, U. Wis., 1993; univ. faculty rsch. grantee U. Utah, 1986-87. Mem. Nat. Dance Assn. (mem. various coms., chair 1969-71, Dance Heritage award 1977, Honor award 1981), Am. Dance Guild, Am. Acad. Phys. Edn., Congress on Rsch. in Dance, Coun. Dance Adminstrs. (founder). Home: 130 S 13th E # 801 Salt Lake City UT 84102

HAYES, MARY ESHBAUGH, newspaper editor; b. Rochester, N.Y., Sept. 27, 1928; d. William Paul and Eleanor Maude (Seivert) Eshbaugh; m. James Leon Hayes, Apr. 18, 1953; children: Pauli, Eli, Lauri Le June, Clayton, Merri Jess Bates. BA in English and journalism, Syracuse U., 1950. With Livingston County Republican, Geneseo, N.Y., summers, 1947-50, mng. editor, 1949-50; reporter Aurora Advocate, Colo., 1950-52; reporter-photographer Aspen Times, Colo., 1952-53, columnist, 1956—, reporter, 1972-77, assoc. editor, 1977-89, editor in chief, 1989-92, contbg. editor, 1992—; tchr. Colo. Mountain Coll., 1979, Aspen corr. Reuters, 1997—. *At age 8, Mary Eshbaugh and her brother, John Paul, were photographed for a third-grade textbook, Adventures in Science, published by Allyn and Bacon. Fascinated with the book project, Mary decided to follow that formula and become a writer, using real people in photographs. She followed her dream of becoming a writer and today her award-winning feature stories and profiles appear in newspapers and magazines. She has written a cookbook, Aspen Potpourri, featuring residents and their recipes and photographs. Her history book, The Story of Aspen, features photographs of Aspen residents with their stories.* Author, editor: The Story of Aspen, 1996; contbg. editor: Destinations Mag., 1994-97, Aspen Mag., 1996—; editor: Aspen Potpurri, 1968, rev. edit., 1990. Mem. Nat. Fedn. Press Women (1st prizes in writing and editing 1976-80, 1st prize in adv. photography 1998), Colo. Press Women's Assn. (writing award, 1974, 75, 78-85, sweepstakes award for writing 1977, 78, 84, 85, 91-93, 2d place award 1976, 79, 82, 83, 94, 95, Woman of Achivement 1986), Aspen Cmty. Ch. Photographer. Home: PO Box 497 Aspen CO 81612-0497 Office: Box E Aspen CO 81612

HAYES, RAY, JR., lawyer; b. Kansas City, Mo., Feb. 27, 1925; s. Ray and Kathryn L. (O'Hara) H.; m. Millifred Ann Schultz, Jan. 22, 1948; children: Leslie, Rick Lynn, Pat. B.S., U. Denver, 1947, J.D., 1949. Bar: Wash., U.S. Dist. Ct. (we. dist.) Wash., U.S. Supreme Ct., Ariz. 1996, U.S. Dist. Ct. Ariz. 1996. Assoc. Stinson & Hayes, Chehalis, Wash., 1950-53; dep. pros. atty. Lewis County (Wash.), 1953-58, sole practice, Chehalis, 1953-69; of counsel Davies, Pearson, P.C., and predecessor, Tacoma, 1969—. Served to capt. USMC, 1942, 1956. Mem. Wash. State Bar Assn., ABA, Fed. Bar Assn., Assn. Trial Lawyers Am., Wash. State Trial Lawyers Assn., Nat. Transp. Safety Bd. Bar Assn. (founding mem.). Office: Hayes Jefferson PLC 12425 W Bell Rd Ste 202 Surprise AZ 85374-9002

HAYES, ROBERT BRUCE, musician; b. L.A., Sept. 27, 1953; s. Edward Bruce and Dorothy Francis H.; m. (div. Apr. 1986). AA, Grossmart Jr. Coll., El Cajon, Calif., 1976. Bass player R&R band, Hollywood, Calif., 1979; lead guitarist Raw Pain band, Santa Cruz, Calif., 1988-89, The disappear band, San Acacio, Colo., 1998—. Libertarian. Roman Catholic. Avocation: skiing. Home: PO Box 681 La Jara CO 81140-0681

HAYES, ROGER MATTHEW, deputy sheriff; b. Youngstown, Ohio, May 27, 1943; s. Roger and Edith (Wellendorff) H.; m. Carolyn Starr; children: Troy, Trent, Todd. BA, Columbia Coll., 1992; postgrad., U. Colo.; MA, Regis U., 1996. Dep. sheriff Arapahoe County (Colo.) Sheriff Dept., 1986—. Past pres. Arapahoe County Rep. Men's Club; pres. Fraternal Order of Police, Arapahoe County, Colo., West Metro Found.; mem. mil. acad. selection com. U.S. Senator William Armstrong, Denver, 1982, White House Adv. Team, Reagan/Bush, Denver, 1982; pres. West Metro Fire Found. Sgt. USMC, 1963-66, Vietnam. Recipient medal of Merit Air Force Assn., Washington, 1984. Mem. Am. Soc. Pub. Adminstrs., Am. Sociol. Assn. Avocation: golf. Home: 9883 W Progress Pl Littleton CO 80123-2177

HAYFORD, JACK W., minister; m. Anna Marie Smith, 1954; children: Rebecca Hayford Bauer, Jack, Mark, Christa Hayford Andersen. Grad. with honors, LIFE Bible Coll., 1956, DD (hon.), 1977; grad., Azusa Pacific U., 1970; DD (hon.), Oral Roberts U., 1984; D of Lit. (hon.), Calif. Grad. Sch. Theology, 1985. Min. Foursquare Ch., Ft. Wayne, Ind., 1956-60; nat. youth dir. Internat. Ch. of the Foursquare Gospel, L.A., 1960-65; mem. faculty LIFE Bible Coll., L.A., 1965-73, dean students, 1965-70, pres., 1977-82; sr. pastor 1st Foursquare Ch. On The Way, Van Nuys, Calif., 1969—; bd. dirs. Every Home for Christ, Ch. Growth Internat.; speaker in field; guest TV programs including The Merv Griffin Show, Ted Koppel's Prime Time Spl.; tchr. Living Way radio broadcast. Author: Taking Hold of Tomorrow, Rebuilding the Real You, Worship His Majesty, A Passion for Fullness, 12 other books; gen. editor: Spirit Filled Life Bible. Trustee LIFE Bible Coll., L.A.; mem. internat. com. Lausanne Com. for World Evangelization. Recipient Clergyman of Yr. award Religion in Media, 1985, Calif. Community award Religious Heritage of Am., 1988, numerous others. Office: The Ch On The Way 14300 Sherman Way Van Nuys CA 91405-2403

HAYNES, DUANE E., recreation coordinator; b. Denver, Aug. 19, 1954; s. Elmer D. and Jimmiee (Kelly) H. BA in English, Met. State Coll., 1979. lectr. U. So. Colo., Pueblo, Adams State Coll., Colo. Author: (book) Think About It and You, 1973. Recipient awards World of Poetry, Calif., 1991, Editor's Choice, Calif., 1995-96, Internat. Poetry Hall of Fame, 1997. Mem. Internat. Platform Assn., Internat. Soc. Poets. Avocations: dir. of plays and films, tchg. karate, speaker. Home: 2859 Garfield St Denver CO 80205-5067

HAYNES, JANICE JAQUES ELIZABETH, educator, editor; b. Casper, Wyo., May 31, 1924; d. George Havelock and Grace Mary (O'Keefe) Jaques; m. David Clark Haynes, Dec. 16, 1951; children: Judith J., David C. AB, Stanford Univ., 1945; MA, Claremont Grad. Sch., 1947. Tchr. Girls Collegiate Sch., Claremont, Calif., 1945-47, Fullerton (Calif.) Jr. Coll. H.S., 1947-48, Stanley Clark Sch., South Bend, Ind., 1963-69, Wis. Sch. for Deaf, Delavan, 1971-73; editor Gila Bend Herald, Gila Bend, Ariz., 1974-79; migrant coord. La Polama (Ariz.) Elem.; mid. sch. tchr. Humboldt (Ariz.) Jr. High., 1984-87; coord. Yavapai Indian Reservation, Prescott, Ariz., 1988-92. Editor: Prescott Symphony Guild, 1997-98. Mem. Alpha Delta Kappa (pres. 1985-86), Philanthropic Ednl. Orgn. Avocations: short story writing. Home: 831 Bertrand Ave Prescott AZ 86303-4011

HAYNES, MICHAEL SCOTT, SR., resource specialist; b. Hancock, Mich., Feb. 16, 1948; s. Russell L. and Hildegard Eleanor (Habel) H.; m. Joan Loree Donaldson, July 25, 1968; children: Michael Jr., Andrew Lloyd, Gregory Alan. BA in History, Calif. Luth. U., 1970; MS in Spl. Edn., Learning Disabled, Calif. State U., Long Beach, 1993. Cert. tchr. elem. edn., Calif., cert. resource specialist tchr., handicapped specialist, Calif. Tchr. elem. edn. Rio Lindo Sch., El Rio, Calif., 1970-71, Trinity Luth. Day Sch., Hawthorne, Calif., 1973-82; tchr. elem. edn. L.A. Unified Sch. Dist., 1982—, learning handicapped specialist, 1988-90, resource specialist tchr., 1990—;

tchr. chair Am. Luth. Edn. Assn., 1979-82; trustee L.A. Edn. Alliance Restructuring, 1992—; sec. sch. site United Tchrs. L.A., 1991-94; chpt. chair, 1998—. Scoutmaster Boy Scouts Am., 1983-90. With USCG, 1975-85. Recipient Wood badge Boy Scouts Am., 1983. Mem. Calif. Assn. Resource Specialists (univ. liaison 1991-92), So. Calif. Chihuahua Club, Inc. (sec. 1992-94, 96-98, v.p., 1995), Orange Empire Dog Club, Kappa Delta Pi, Phi Delta Kappa. Avocations: baroque recorder, hiking.

HAYNES, OLIVE DURHAM, clergywoman, artist; b. Balt., Oct. 2, 1930; d. John Mills and Mary Matilda (Durham) H. BA in Broadcasting, Ohio State U., 1952, MA in Broadcasting, 1954; MDiv, Princeton Theol. Sem., 1973; DMin, Louisville Presbyn. Theol. Sem, 1980. Ordained to ministry, Presbyn. Ch., 1973. Asst. libr. Columbus (Ohio) Libr. System, 1948-58; continuity writer, artist Cy Landy Advt., Columbus, 1958-59; writer, producer, on-air talent WOSU Radio, TV, Columbus, 1959-70; pastor First Presbyn. Ch., St. Marys, Ohio, 1973-80, Spenceville (Ohio) Presbyn. Ch., 1973-80, Prebyn. Ch., Marion, Ill., 1980-88; assoc. pastor missions and outreach Solano Beach (Calif.) Presbyn. Ch., 1988-95; trustee Med. Benevolence Found. Presbyn. Ch. U.S.a., 1981-86; v.p. ministerial alliance, Merion, Ill., 1981; moderator Maumee Valley Presbytery, St. Mary, Ohio, 1987-88, team leader Med. Mission team to Africa, 1990; writer, presenter AIDS paper Chinese Med. Assn., People to People Project, Beijing, 1990. Artist: creator of note cards now being sold locally, makes and sells woodcraft, doll houses, etc. Initiator, developer Agape Pantry, N.w. Ohio, Latchkey children program, Marion, literacy program, Marion; helped to establish Rainbow House home and resource ctr. for children and women with HIV and AIDS; instrumental in initiation of Church Trucking Ministry to feed the hungry and respond to crisis situations across the nation. Recipient Ohio Ho. Reps. award, 1979, State of Ill. award, 1983, CDC award, 1982, Quality of Life cert. Ill. Hospice, 1983, Disting. Alumni award Louisville Presbyn. Theol. Sem., 1993; Named Woman of Yr. St. Mary's Bus. and Profl. Women's Club, 1979, Regional Woman of Distinction, Women's Hist. Week, Carbondale, Ill., 1986. Mem. Presbyn. AIDS Network: Health, Edn., Welfare (S.W. rep. 1992—), Presbyn. Mission Pastors Network (S.W. rep.), Urban Ministries Com. Presbytery of San Diego. Avocations: art, gardening, reading, travel, theatre. Office: Solano Beach Presbyn Ch 120 Stevens Ave Solana Beach CA 92075-2039 Address: care Cress 3555 Kenlawn St Columbus OH 43224-3451

HAY-ROE, VICTOR, plastic surgeon; b. Edmonton, Alta., Can., Dec. 23, 1930; s. Edmund Archer and Ruth Mildred (Maddison) Hay-Roe; m. Elizabeth Mae Davison, May 8, 1953 (div. 1978); children: Glenn Cameron, Elizabeth Diane, Scott Richard; m. Lynn Siu, Apr. 19, 1980. BSc, U. Alta., 1953, MD, 1955. Resident in surgery Queen's Hosp., Honolulu, 1956-59; resident in plastic surgery U. Pitts. Sch. Medicine, 1963-66; chief of plastic surgery Honolulu Med. Group, Inc., 1967—; clin. assoc. prof. plastic surgery, U. Hawaii, Honolulu, 1973—; trip leader, Interplast plastic surgery team to Samoa, 1978, Jamaica, 1988, 90. Mem. Hawaii Plastic Surgery Soc. (pres. 1986-88), Northwest Soc. Plastic Surgeons, Am. Soc. Plastic and reconstructive Surgeons. Republican. Avocations: chess, needlepoint, cross-stitch, tennis, philately. Home: 2277 Halekoa Dr Honolulu HI 96821-1056 Office: Honolulu Med Group Inc 550 S Beretania St Honolulu HI 96813-2405

HAYS, E. EARL, youth organization administrator; b. Uniontown, Kans.; s. Earl Loren and Avis Marie (Mccollum) H.; m. Betty Ann Frigo, Nov. 21, 1966. BA, Whittier Coll., 1962; MA, Ottawa U., 1993; PhD, Pacific Western U., 1993. Dir. pub. rels., fin., dist. exec. Boy Scouts Am. L.A. Area Coun., 1962-71; asst. dir. exploring Boy Scouts Am. Nat. Coun., North Brunswick, N.J., 1971-73; dir. fin. svcs. Boy Scouts Am. Golden Empire Coun., Sacramento, 1973-75; dir. field svc. Boy Scouts Am. Santa Clara County, San Jose, Calif., 1975-77; scout exec., CEO Boy Scouts Am. Clinton Valley Coun., Pontiac, Mich., 1977-82, Boy Scouts Am. Grand Canyon Coun., Phoenix, 1982—. *E. Earl Hays has more than 36 years progressively responsible experience as a professional Scouting Executive. While Chief Executive Officer in Phoenix, Arizona, youth membership has grown by 84%, ranking among the top 12 out of 328 local councils nationwide. Honored as a member of the Chief Scout Executive's Winners' Circle for Balanced Youth Membership Growth (54,080 youth members), Sound Fiscal Operations, Quality Program, and as a National Quality Council. In 1996-1997, he received the Ansel Adams Mountain Portrait Award for Endowment Development, and the Excellence in Marketing the Scouting Program award from the Western Region Boy Scouts of America.* Bd. dirs. Pontiac Oakland Symphony, 1980-82; pres. United Way Exec. Dirs. Assn., Phoenix, 1984-85. Fellowship honor Boy Scouts Am., 1991, James E. West fellow, 1994. Mem. Ottawa U. Alumni Assn. (bd. dirs. 1995-98), Nat. Eagle Scout Assn. (life, Disting. Eagle Scout 1998), Rotary (pres. Pontiac 1982, bd. dirs., sec.) Phoenix 100 Club (Paul H. Harris fellow). Democrat. Lutheran. Avocations: travel, music, reading, scuba, golf. Office: Grand Canyon Coun 2969 N Greenfield Rd Phoenix AZ 85016-7715

HAYS, RONALD JACKSON, career officer; b. Urania, La., Aug. 19, 1928; s. George Henry and Fannie Elizabeth (McCartney) H.; m. Jane M. Hughes, Jan. 29, 1951; children: Dennis, Michael, Jacquelyn. Student, Northwestern U., 1945-46; B.S., U.S. Naval Acad., 1950. Commd. ensign U.S. Navy, 1950, advanced through grades to adm., 1983; destroyer officer Atlantic Fleet, 1950-51; attack pilot Pacific Fleet, 1953-56; exptl. test pilot Patuxent River, Md., 1956-59; exec. officer Attack Squadron 106, 1961-63; tng. officer Carrier Air Wing 4, 1963-65; comdr. All Weather Attack Squadron, Atlantic Fleet, 1965-67; air warfare officer 7th Fleet Staff, 1967-68; tactical aircraft plans officer Office Chief Naval Ops., 1969-71; comdg. officer Naval Sta., Roosevelt Roads, P.R., 1971-72; dir. Navy Planning and Programming, 1973-74; comdr. Carrier Group 4, Norfolk, Va., 1974-75; dir. Office of Program Appraisal, Sec. of Navy, Washington, 1975-78; dep. and chief staff, comdr. in chief U.S. Atlantic Fleet, Norfolk, Va., 1978-80; comdr. in chief U.S. Naval Force Europe, London, 1980-83; vice chief naval ops. Dept. Navy, Washington, 1983-85; comdr. in chief U.S. Pacific Command, Camp H.M. Smith, Hawaii, 1985-88; pres., chief exec. officer Pacific Internat. Ctr. for High Tech. Rsch., Honolulu, Hawaii, 1988-92; tech. cons., 1992—. Decorated D.S.M. with 3 gold stars, Silver Star with 2 gold stars, D.F.C. with silver star and gold star, Legion of Merit, Bronze Star with combat V, Air Medal with numeral 14 and gold numeral 3, Navy Commendation medal with gold star and combat V. Baptist. Home and Office: 869 Kamoi Pl Honolulu HI 96825-1318

HAYTIN, HAROLD ALEXANDER, venture capital company executive; b. Denver, Aug. 17, 1918; s. Alexander and Bess H.; m. Lois A. Lasker, Sept. 4, 1940; children: Daniel, Jane. BA, UCLA, 1940, grad. exec. program, 1961. Exec. v.p. Telecor Inc., Beverly Hills, Calif., 1970-72, chmn. bd., pres., chief exec. officer, 1972-80; pres. Newcraft Inc., 1966-72; chmn. Bancorp Capital Group, L.A., 1980—; cons. Matsushita Electric Corp. Am., 1980-85; moderator, lectr. Grad. Sch. Mgmt., UCLA extension; arbitrator NYSE, NASD, PSE, 1991—. Pres. L.A. Bd. City Civil Svc. Commn., 1974-84; trustee City of Hope, 1972—; pres. bd. trustees UCLA Found., 1982-86; bd. advs. UCLA Hosp. and Clinics, 1978—; mem. chancellor's assocs. UCLA, 1966—; patron L.A. County Mus. Art, 1965—. Recipient Svc. award UCLA Univ., 1990; named to Legion of Honor Jewish Nat. Fund. Mem. Riviera Country Club, Executive Svc. Corps. Office: 11661 San Vicente Blvd Los Angeles CA 90049-5103

HAYWARD, FREDRIC MARK, social reformer; b. N.Y.C., July 10, 1946; s. Irving Michael and Mildred (Feingold) H.; m. Ingeborg Beck, Aug. 18, 1971 (div. 1974); 1 child, KJ. BA, Brandeis U., Waltham, Mass., 1967; MA, Fletcher Sch. Law & Diplomacy, Medford, Mass., 1968, MALD, 1969. Exec. dir. Men's Rights, Inc., Boston, 1977—; vis. lectr. Tufts U., Medford, Mass., 1979; lectr. in field; conductor workshops in field; mem. adv. bd. Ctr. for Men's Studies, 1988-93; host, prodr. The SacraMENshow; founder Nat. Coalition Just Draft; co-founder Free Men Boston, children's Rights Coun. Sacramento. Author 3 published anthologies; contbg. editor. The Liberator, Forest Lake, Minn., 1988-89; contbg. writer Spectator, Berkeley, Calif., 1988—; contbr. articles to profl. jours. Farrell fellowship on Men, 1989; Fletcher Sch. Law and Diplomacy fellow, 1967-69; recipient award of Excellence Nat. Coalition of Free Men, 1993. Mem. Nat. Congress for-Men (bd. dirs. 1981-90), Am. Fedn. TV and Radio Artists, Men. Internat. (bd. dirs. 1982-86), Children's Rights Coun. of Sacramento. Office: Mr Inc PO Box 163180 Sacramento CA 95816-9180

HAYWORTH, JOHN DAVID, JR., congressman, sportscaster, commentator, broadcaster; b. High Point, N.C., July 12, 1958; s. John David and Gladys Ethel (Hall) H.; m. Mary Denise Yancey, Feb. 25, 1989; children: Nicole Irene, Hannah Lynne, John Micah. BA in Speech and Polit. Sci., N.C. State U., 1980. Sports anchor, reporter Sta. WPTF-TV, Raleigh, N.C., 1980-81, Sta. WLWT-TV, Cin., 1986-87; sports anchor Sta. WYFF-TV (formerly Sta. WFBC-TV), Greenville, S.C., 1981-86, Sta. KTSP-TV, Phoenix, 1987-94; congressman, Ariz. U.S. House Reps., Washington, D.C., 1995—, mem. ways and means com., mem. budget com.; radio commentator; play-by-play broadcaster. Dist. committeeman Ariz. Rep. Com., Scottsdale, 1988-89; bd. dirs. Am. Humanics Found., Ariz. State U., Tempe, 1991-92; chmn. Scout-A-Rama, Theodore Roosevelt coun. Boy Scouts Am., 1991-92. Recipient honor roll award Atlantic Coast Conf., 1977, Young Am. award Unharrie coun. Boy Scouts Am., 1979, Friend of Edn. award Sch. Dist. Greenville County, 1985, Sch. Bell/Friend of Edn. award S.C. Dept. Edn., 1985. Mem. Rotary (bd. dirs. Phoenix 1989-90). Baptist. Avocations: reading, distance running, Bible study, public speaking, television trivia. Office: US House Reps 1023 Longworth Bldg Ofc Bldg Washington DC 20515-0306*

HAZEKAMP, PHYLLIS WANDA ALBERTS, library director; b. Chgo.; d. John Edward and Mary Ann (Demski) Wojciechowski. BA, De Paul U., 1947; MSLS, La. State U., 1959; postgrad., Santa Clara U., U. Chgo. Cert. tchr., Calif., Ariz. Libr. Agrl. Experiment Sta., U. Calif., Riverside, 1959-61; tech. libr. Lockheed Tech. Libr., Palo Alto, Calif., 1962-63; asst. law libr. Santa Clara (Calif.) U. Law Sch., 1963-72; libr. dir. Carmelite Seminary, San Jose, Calif., 1973-78; reference libr. San Jose State U., 1978-79; libr. dir. SAI Engrs., Santa Clara, 1980-81, Palmer Coll. Chiropractic, San Jose, 1981-90; libr. dir. Camp Verde (Ariz.) Community Libr., 1990-98, retired, 1998—; mem. Cultural Commn., Santa Clara, 1968-72; pres. Santa Clara Art Assn., 1973-74; cons. various librs.; lectr. in field. Bd. dirs. Camp Verde Art Coun., 1994—; bd. dirs., spkr. House of Ruth, 1995-98; bd. elders Montezuma Chapel, 1995-98. Mem. Kiwanis Internat., Ladies Guild Montezuma Chapel. Avocations: writing articles, painting, teaching, giving talks to groups.

HAZELTON, PENNY ANN, law librarian, educator; b. Yakima, Wash., Sept. 24, 1947; d. Fred Robert and Margaret (McLeod) Pease; m. Norris J. Hazelton, Sept. 12, 1971; 1 dau., Victoria MacLeod. BA cum laude, Linfield Coll., 1969; JD, Lewis and Clark Law Sch., 1975; M in Law Librarianship, U. Wash., 1976. Bar: Wash. 1976; U.S. Supreme Ct. 1982. assoc. law libr., assoc. prof. U. Maine, 1976-78, law libr., assoc. prof., 1978-81; asst. libr. for rsch. svcs. U.S. Supreme Ct., Washington, 1981-85, law libr., 1985; law librarian U. Wash., Seattle, 1985—, prof. law, 1985—; tchr. legal rsch., law librarianship, Indian law; cons. Maine Adv. Com. on County Law Librs., Nat. U. Sch. Law, San Diego, 1985-88, Lawyers Cooperative Pub., 1993-94. Author: Computer Assisted Legal Research: The Basics, 1993; contbr. articles to legal jours. Recipient Disting. Alumni award U. Wash., 1992. Mem. ABA (sect. legal edn. & admissions to bar, chair com. on librs. 1993-94, vice chair 1992-93, 94-95), Am. Assn. Law Schs. (com. law librs. 1991-94), Law Librs. New Eng. (sec. 1977-79, pres. 1979-81), Am. Assn. Law Librs. (cert., program chmn. ann. meeting 1984, exec. bd. 1984-87, v.p., pres.-elect 1989-90, pres. 1990-91, program co-chair Insts. 1983, 95), Law Librs' Soc. Washington (exec. bd. 1983-84, v.p., pres.-elect 1985-86), Law Librs. Puget Sound, Wash. State Bar Assn. (chair editl. adv. bd. 1990-91), Wash. Adv. Coun. on Librs., Westpac. Office: U Wash Marian Gould Gallagher Law Libr 1100 NE Campus Pkwy Seattle WA 98105-6605

HAZEN, PAUL MANDEVILLE, banker; b. Lansing, Mich., 1941; married. BA, U. Ariz., 1963; MBA, U. Calif., Berkeley, 1964. Asst. mgr Security Pacific Bank, 1964-66; v.p. Union Bank, 1966-70; chmn. Wells Fargo Realty Advisors, 1970-76; with Wells Fargo Realty Advisors, San Francisco, 1979—, exec. v.p., mgr. Real Estate Industries Group, 1979-80, mem. exec. office Real Estate Industry Group, 1980, vice-chmn. Real Estate Industries Group, 1980-84, pres., chief oper. officer Real Estate Industries Group, 1984—, also dir. Real Estate Industries Group, 1984—; pres., treas. Wells Fargo Mortgage & Equity Trust, San Francisco, 1977-84; with Wells Fargo & Co., San Francisco, 1978—, from exec. v.p. to vice-chmn., pres., chief operating officer, 1978-95, chmn, CEO, 1995—, chmn. bd. dirs.; trustee Wells Fargo Mortgage & Equity Trust; bd. dirs. Pacific Telesis Group. Office: Wells Fargo Bank NA 420 Montgomery St San Francisco CA 94104-1298*

HAZEWINKEL, VAN, manufacturing executive; b. L.A., Oct. 2, 1943; s. Ben J. and Betty J. (Bishop) H.; m. Linda Bennett, Sept. 11, 1965; children: Van, Karey. BS, Calif. State U., Long Beach, 1967. With Daily Indsl. Tools Inc., Costa Mesa, Calif., 1959—, v.p., 1966-78, pres., 1978—. Founding mem. bd. dirs. Greater Irvine (Calif.) Indsl. League, 1970-73. Mem. Soc. Mfg. Engrs. Office: 3197 Airport Loop Dr Ste D Costa Mesa CA 92626-3424

HAZLETT, MARK A., lawyer; b. N.Y.C., Aug. 18, 1948. BA, Stanford U., 1970, JD, 1973. Bar: Hawaii 1973. Ptnr. Cades, Schutte, Fleming & Wright, Honolulu; mem. adv. com. to Commr. of Fin. Insts., 1984-86; adj. prof. of law U. Hawaii Law Sch., 1995—. Co-editor: Hawaii Commercial Real Estate Manual, 1988; co-editor, co-author: Hawaii Real Estate Financing Manual, 1990, Hawaii Real Estate Law Manual, 1997. Mem. ABA, Hawaii State Bar Assn. (dir. fin. svcs. divsn. 1982-83, chmn. real property and fin. svcs. sect. 1984, bd. dirs. 1982-98). Office: Cades Schutte Fleming & Wright PO Box 939 1000 Bishop St Honolulu HI 96808

HE, XUZHENG, artist, scenic designer; b. Guangzhou, China, Sept. 21, 1947; came to U.S., 1987; s. Minshi He and Fushang Mai; m. Wenxiu Chen, Mar. 1974; 1 child, Xi. Grad., Zhongshan U., Guangzhou, 1987; BFA, U. Ariz., 1991. Scenic designer Shaoguan Chinese Opera Theatre, 1970-80; artist Guangdong Province Stage Decor Soc., Guangzhou, 1980—; scenic designer Guangdong Province Dance Drama Theatre, Guangzhou, 1980-87; artist Guangdong Province Fine Artists Assn., Guangzhou, 1982-87, Guangzhou (Canton) City Art Festival, 1984; scenic designer Nat. Cultural Troup Peoples Republic China to Australia, Guangzhou, 1986; artist China-Japan Fine Art Exch. Assn., Tokyo, 1988-91; scenic designer Music Theatre Wichita, Kans., 1991-95. Recipient 2d place prize Guangdong Province Art and Lit. Jury Com., 1983, 1st place prize Nat. Juvenile Dance Competition Com., China, 1989. Mem. Oil Painters Am. (assoc.), China-Japan Fine Art Exch. Assn. Home: 5931 E 26th St Tucson AZ 85711-6016

HEADDING, LILLIAN SUSAN (SALLY HEADDING), writer, forensic clairvoyant; b. Milw., Jan. 1, 1944; d. David Morton and Mary Davis (Berry) Coleman; m. James K. Hill (div. 1976); children: Amy Denise; m. John Murray Headding (div. 1987). BA, U. Nev., 1975; MA, U. Pacific, 1976; PhD in Parapsychology, Am. Internat. U., 1997. With Gimbels, Milw., 1963-65; spl. assignment G2 USAPIC U.S. Womens Army Corp., 1963; retail mgr. Frandisco Corp., N.Y.C., 1965-66; dist. mgr. Anita Shops, Los Angeles, 1966-68; store mgr. Clothes Closet, Sunnyvale, Calif., 1969-70; owner Lillian Headding Interiors & Comml. Design, Pittsburg, Calif., 1976-88; mfrs. rep. and assoc. J.G. West, San Francisco, 1989-91; Karate instr. Sch. of the Tiger, Pleasant Hill, Calif., 1988-94, 1st degree black belt, 1973; clairvoyant, psychic cons. on numerous crime and missing persons cases, U.S., Can., Eng. and France, 1972—. Author short stories, poetry. Bd. dirs. and co-founder Cmty. Action Against Rape, Las Vegas, 1972-75; self-def. expert Las Vegas Met. Police Dept., 1972-75, North Las Vegas (Nev.) Police Dept.; co-supr. Family & Children's Svcs., Contra Costa County, Calif., 1985-86. Mem. AAUW, People for Ethical Treatment of Animals, Sister's in Crime Nat. Writers Assn., Philippine Hawaiian Black Belters Assn., Humane Farming Assn., Am. Assn. Profl. Psychics. Democrat. Jewish. Avocations: antiques, gourmet cooking, classical music. Address: Townhouse 33 5333 Park Highlands Blvd Concord CA 94521-3704

HEADLEE, ROLLAND DOCKERAY, professional society administrator; b. Los Angeles, Aug. 27, 1916; s. Jesse W. and Cleora (Dockeray) H.; m. Alzora D. Burgett, May 13, 1939; 1 dau., Linda Ann (Mrs. Walter Pohl). Student, UCLA, 1939. Asst. mgr. Par Assocs., Los Angeles, 1935-43, Finance Assocs., 1946-58; financial cons., lectr., 1958-63; account exec. Walter E. Heller & Co., Los Angeles, 1963-66; exec. dir. emeritus Town Hall Calif., Los Angeles, 1966—; dir. Am. Internat. Bank, Mfrs. Assocs., R.H. Investment Corp. Mem. adv. bd., bd. dirs., Los Angeles council Boy Scouts Am. Served to 1st lt. AUS, 1943-46. Mem. Mensa, L.A. World Affaris Coun., Commonwealth Club of Calif., Econ. Club of Detroit. Methodist. Home: 8064 El Manor Ave Los Angeles CA 90045-1434

HEADLEY, NATHAN LEROY, laboratory executive; b. Phila., Jan. 1, 1936; s. Russell A. and Mary Ellen (Miller) H.; m. Barbara Pinkney, Dec. 28, 1957 (div. Feb. 1986); children: Kimberly, Robert; m. Dolly Day Lopshire, Dec. 18, 1987. AB, MS in Econs., Bucknell U., 1958. Exptl. test pilot Boeing Co., Phila., 1962-70; pres. Med. Diagnostic Ctrs. Inc., Norristown, Pa., 1971-75; various exec. positions to exec. v.p. Nat. Health Labs., Inc., La Jolla, Calif., 1976-85; COO Merris Lab., San Jose, Calif., 1986-89; pres., CEO, bd. dirs. Physicians Clin. Lab. Inc., Sacramento, 1989—. Capt. USMCR, 1958-62. Republican. Methodist. Avocations: golf, horses, sailing. Office: Physicians Clin Lab Inc 3301 C St Ste 100E Sacramento CA 95816-3300

HEADY, FERREL, retired political science educator; b. Ferrelview, Mo., Feb. 14, 1916; s. Chester Ferrel and Loren (Wightman) H.; m. Charlotte Audrey McDougall, Feb. 12, 1942; children—Judith Lillian, Richard Ferrel, Margaret Loren, Thomas McDougall. A.B., Washington U., St. Louis, 1937, A.M., 1938, Ph.D., 1940; hon. degrees, Park Coll., 1973, John F. Kennedy U., 1974, U. N.Mex., 1993. Jr. adminstrv. technician, also adminstrv. asst. Office Dir. Personnel, Dept. Agr., 1941-42; vis. lectr. polit. sci. U. Kansas City, 1946; faculty U. Mich., 1946-67, prof. polit. sci., 1957-67; dir. Inst. Pub. Adminstrn., 1960-67; acad. v.p. U. N.Mex., Albuquerque, 1967-68; pres. U. N.Mex., 1968-75, prof. pub. adminstrn. and polit. sci., 1975-81, prof. emeritus, 1981—; Asst. to commr. Com. Orgn. Exec. Br. of Govt., 1947-49; dir., chief adviser Inst. Pub. Adminstrn., U. Philippines, 1953-54; mem. U.S. del. Internat. Congress Adminstrn. Scis., Spain, 1956, 80, Germany, 1959, Austria, 1962, Poland, 1964, Mexico, 1974; exec. bd. Inter-Univ. Case Program, 1956-67; sr. specialist in residence East-West Center, U. Hawaii, 1965; mem. Conf. on Pub. Service, 1965-70; chmn. bd. Assoc. Western Univs., 1970-71; commr. Western Interstate Commn. Higher Edn., 1972-77; mem. commns. on bus. professions and water resources, mem. exec. com. Nat. Assn. State Univs. and Land Grant Colls., 1968-75. Author: Administrative Procedure Legislation in the States, 1952, (with Robert H. Pealy) The Michigan Department of Administration, 1956, (with Sybil L. Stokes) Comparative Public Administration: A Selective Annotated Bibliography, 1960, Papers in Comparative Public Administration, 1962, State Constitutions: The Structure of Administration, 1961, Public Administration: A Comparative Perspective, 1966, rev. edit., 1979, 5th edit., 1995, One Time Around, 1999; contbr. profl. jours. Chmn. state affairs com. Ann Arbor Citizens Coun., Mich., 1949-52; mem. exec. com. Mich. Meml.-Phoenix Project and Inst. Social Rsch., 1960-66; mem. Gov. Mich. Constl. Revision Study Commn., 1960-62; schs. and univs. adv. bd. Citizens Com. for Hoover Report, 1949-52, 54-58; cons. to Ford Found., 1962; chmn. Coun. on Grad. Edn. in Pub. Adminstrn., 1966; mem., vice chmn. N.Mex. Gov.'s Com. on Reorgn. of State Govt., 1967-70; mem. N.Mex. Am. Revolution Bicentennial Commn., 1970-73, N.Mex. Gov.'s Com. on Tech. Excellence, 1969-75, Nat. Acad. Pub. Adminstrn.; mem., vice chmn. N.Mex. Constl. Revision Commn., 1994-95. Served to lt. USNR, 1942-46. Recipient Faculty Disting. Achievement award U. Mich., 1964, N.Mex. Disting. Pub. service award, 1973, award of distinction U. N.Mex. Alumni Assn., 1975, Outstanding Grad. Tchr. award U. N.Mex., 1981-82, Fulbright sr. lectureship, Colombia, 1992, Waldo award for career contbns. to lit. and leadership of pub. adminstrn., 1994. Mem. Am. Polit. Sci. Assn., Am. Soc. Pub. Adminstrn. (pres. 1969-70), AAUP (chmn. com. T 1957-61), Am. Council Edn. (mem. commn. on fed. relations 1969-72), Phi Beta Kappa, Phi Kappa Phi. Presbyterian. Home: 2901 Cutler Ave NE Albuquerque NM 87106-1714

HEALY, ANNE, sculptor; b. N.Y.C., Oct. 1, 1939; d. Robert Timothy and Mary Rita (Essig) H.; m. Richard Alois Synek, Feb. 28, 1960 (div. 1962); 1 child, Deirdre Leigh. BA, Queens Coll., 1961. One-woman exhbns. include U.S. Theatre Technicians Symposium, 1971, Solow Bldg., N.Y.C., 1971, A.I.R. Gallery, N.Y.C., 1972, 74, 78, 81, 83, CUNY Grad. Ctr., 1974, Hammarskjold Pla. Sculpture Garden, N.Y.C., 1974, 88 Pine St., N.Y.C., 1974-75, Zabriskie Gallery, N.Y.C., 1975, 78, Contemporary Art Ctr., Cin., 1976, Am.'s Cup Ave., Newport Art Assn., Susie Schochet Gallery, R.I., 1976, U. Mass., Amherst, 1976, A.I.R., N.Y.C., 1978, U. of South, Tex., 1979, San Francisco M.O.M.A. Rental Gallery, 1989, Terrain Gallery, San Francisco, 1998; group exhbns. include Outdoor Installations, Basel, Switzerland, 1976, Paris, 1976; represented in permanent collections Mus. Contemporary Crafts, N.Y.C., Mich. State U., Allen Art Mus., Oberlin, Ohio, CUNY Grad. Ctr.; commns. include Wayne State U. Health Care Inst., Detroit, 1979, Springfield Mus. Fine Art, Mass., 1979, City of Pitts., 1981, Prudential Life Ins., Newark, N.J., 1984, State of Wash., 1985, City of Oakland, Calif., 1986, Litton Industries, Los Colinas, Tex., 1986, Stanford U., 1990, Wash. State Art Coun., 1996; instr. sculpture St. Ann's Sch., Bklyn., 1973-79; adj. asst. prof. Baruch Coll., CUNY, 1976-81; guest lectr. Mich. State U., 1973; vis. artist Mich. State U., 1973; guest lectr. U. Cin., 1974, 76, Smith Coll., Northampton, Mass., 1975, U. R.I., Kingston, 1975; vis. prof. U. Iowa, Iowa City, 1979; asst. prof. U. Calif. Berkeley, 1981-85, assoc. prof., 1985-94, prof. 1994—. Arts commr. for sculpture City of San Francisco, 1989-96, pres. arts commn., 1992-95. Featured in numerous popular mags. and profl. jours.; contbr. articles to profl. jours. Office: U Calif Dept Art Kroeber Hall Berkeley CA 94720

HEALY, BARBARA ANNE, insurance company executive, financial planner; b. Chgo., May 21, 1951; d. William James Healy and Eileen Mary (Dooley) Dashiell; m. Joel Feldman, June 25, 1991. BA, No. Ill. U., 1973; MBA, DePaul U., 1976. Cert. fin. planner. Dept. head, instr. St. Benedict High Sch., Chgo., 1973-76; account rep. Xerox Corp., Chgo., 1976-78, mktg. specialist, 1978-79, high volume sr. sales exec., 1979-81; western dist. mgr. McGraw Hill, N.Y.C., 1981-82; fin. planner United Resources Ins. Service, Torrance, Calif., 1982-83, sales mgr., 1983-85, exec. v.p., 1985-86; regional v.p. United Resources Ins. Service, Foster City, Calif., 1986-89; v.p., nat. mktg. dir. Met. Life Resources (formerly United Resources Ins. Svcs.), Phoenix, 1990—; Tempe, Ariz.; instr. Trenton Coll., Riverside, Ill., City Coll. Chgo., Northeastern Ill. U., Chgo., Prairie State Coll., Chicago Heights, 1976-81. Author: Financial Planning for Educators, 1987; contbr. articles to prof. jours.; speaker in field. Mem. Internat. Assn. Fin. Planners, Inst. Cert. Fin. Planners, Registry Fin. Planning Practitioners, Nat. Council Fin. Edn. Republican. Roman Catholic. Avocations: flying, skiing, scuba diving, horse back riding. Home: 20791 W Chartwell Dr Lake Zurich IL 60047-8542 Office: Met Life Resources 426 N 44th St Phoenix AZ 85008-6508

HEALY, JAMES BRUCE, cooking school administrator, writer; b. Paterson, N.J., Apr. 15, 1947; s. James Burn and Margaret Mercy (Patterson) H.; m. Alice Fenvessy, May 9, 1970; 1 child, Charlotte Alexandra. BA, Williams Coll., 1968; PhD, The Rockefeller U., 1973. Mem. faculty Inst. Advanced Study, Princeton, N.J., 1973-75; J.W. Gibbs instr. physics Yale U., New Haven, Conn., 1975-77, research affiliate, 1977-80; dir. Healy-Lucullus Sch. French Cooking, New Haven, 1978-80, Boulder, Colo., 1980—; cons. Claudine's, Denver, 1985-86; vis. instr. Salem (Mass.) State Coll., 1984, and various culinary schs. Author: Mastering the Art of French Pastry, 1984, The French Cookie Book, 1994; contbr. articles and revs. on restaurants and cooking to mags. and profl. jours. Mem. Internat. Assn. Cooking Profls. (cert.), Confederation Nationale des Patissiers, Glaciers, et Confiseurs de France. Methodist. Home and Office: Healy-Lucullus Sch French Cooking 840 Cypress Dr Boulder CO 80303-2820

HEALY, KIERAN JOHN PATRICK, lighting designer, consultant; b. London, June 6, 1957; came to U.S., 1980; citizen of Ireland.; s. Denis Finbarr and Dawn Josephine (O'Hannigan) H.; m. Debra Leslie Liebling, Jan. 6, 1990; children: Conor Thomas, Tighe Joseph. Student, Isleworth Polytechnic, Middlesex, Eng., 1975-76. Lighting designer The Who, 1976-80, The Rolling Stones, 1980; v.p. Showlites, L.A., 1980-81; freelance lighting designer various TV prodns., 1982-89; dir. photography Design Ptnrs., Inc., Hollywood, Calif., 1989-97; lighting designer, owner Spotlight Design Inc., Agoura Hills, Calif., 1997—. Lighting designer for TV programs including Live Aid, ESPY Awards, Arsenio Hall, Gracelands in Africa, The Tonight Show, Whose Line Is It Anyway, other spls. Mem. Nat. Acad. Cable Programming (ACE nomination 1988), Acad. TV Arts and Scis. (Emmy nominations 1984, 87, 89, 92, 94), BECTU (British Film Union). Roman Catholic. Avocations: collecting antiques, fine art and books, films,

sailing, Irish history and genealogy, reading. Office: Spotlight Design Inc 2775 Triunfo Canyon Rd Agoura Hills CA 91301-3425

HEALY, SONYA AINSLIE, health facility administrator; b. Sudbury, Ont., Can., Apr. 7, 1937; came to U.S., 1949; d. Walter B. and Wilma A. Scott; m. Richard C. Healy, Jr., Dec. 16, 1961. Diploma, Good Samaritan Hosp., West Palm Beach, Fla., 1958; student, U. Mass., 1963-64, NYU, 1964-66; BS, Boston U., 1969, MS in Med.-Surg. Nursing, 1974. Various staff nursing, charge nurse positions, suprs., med.-surg. and obstet. nursing, 1958-69; chmn. jr.-sr. teaching team Sch. of Nursing Melrose (Mass.) Wakefield Hosp., 1969-73; asst. dir. nurses Boston State Hosp., 1973-74; asst. dir., DON Mt. Zion Hosp. and Med. Ctr., 1974-75; asst. dir. patient care svcs., DON St. Elizabeth's Hosp., Boston, 1975-80, St. Joseph's Hosp., Nashua, N.H., 1980-82; adminstr. U. Calif. Med. Ctr., San Diego, 1982-91, corp. chief nursing officer, 1991, assoc. dir. hosp. and clinics, dir. patient care svcs., 1982-93; cons. health care Noyes & Assocs. Ltd., Bainbridge Island, Wash., 1993—; mem. acad. affairs com., bd. trustees U. San Diego; clin. assoc. Ul. San Diego, 1984—; mem. adj. faculty San Diego State U.; mem. clin. faculty UCLA Sch. of Nursing; presenter in field. Author: The 12-hour Shift: Is It Viable?-Nursing Outlook, 1984, (handbook) Human Resource Management Handbook, 1987, Human Resources Management Handbook, 1987, Nursing Economics, 1989; mem. editl. adv. bd. dirs. OR Nurse Today, 1989-96; editl. rev. Nursing Economics; contbr. articles to profl. jours. Mem. ASNSA (nominations com. 1978, cert.), Am. Orgn. of Nurse Execs. (bd. dirs. 1990-92, by laws com. 1990-92), Mass. Soc. of Nursing Svcs. Adminstrs. (pres. pres. 1977), Calif. Soc. of Nursing Svc. Adminstrs. (task force on orgns. program com. 1984-85, bd. dirs. 1985-87, mem. com. 1987-88, long range planning com.), San Diego Dirs. of Nurses (sec. 1982-83, pres. 1988-89), Sigma Theta Tau (Zeta Mu chpt.). Avocations: reading, golfing. *

HEALY, THOMAS E., accountant; b. Niagara Falls, N.Y., Sept. 10, 1942; s. George W. and Trudy (Besag) H.; m. Erin S. Colcannon, June 12, 1968; children: Ian T., Kristin M. BA, Willams Coll., 1964; PhD, U. Colo., 1969; M in Acctg., U. Denver, 1978. CPA, Colo. Asst. prof. Westminster Coll., Salt Lake City, 1969-73; lab. tech. Burgess Analytical Lab., North Adams, Mass., 1973-75; auditor Arthur Young & Co., Denver, 1978-79; pvt. practice Boulder, Colo., 1979—; adj. instr. Regis U., Denver, 1980-94. Mem. AICPA, Colo. Soc. CPAs (Silver medalist 1977), Soc. Cert. Sr. Advisors. Democrat. Unitarian-Universalist. Avocations: cross-country Skiing, hiking, biking, jigsaw puzzles. E-mail: THealyCPA@aol.com. Office: 1015 Pine St Boulder CO 80302-4022

HEAPHY, JANIS D., newspaper executive; b. Kalamazoo, Oct. 10, 1951; d. Elvin Julius and Margaret Louise (Throndike) Olson; m. Douglas R. Dern, Aug. 15, 1980 (div. Nov. 1985); m. Robert Thomas Heaphy, Feb. 11, 1989; 1 child, Tanner. BS, Miami U., 1973, MEd, 1976. Tchr. Edgewood Jr. High Sch., Seven Mile, Ohio, 1973-75; acct. exec. L.A. Times, 1976-79, L.A. Mag., 1979-82; mgr. L.A. Omni Mag., 1982-86; sr. acct. exec. L.A. Times, 1986-87, ea. mag. mgr., 1987-89, nat. advt. mgr., 1989-92, retail advt. mgr., 1992—; sr. v.p., advt./mktg. L.A. Times, L.A.; now pub. Sacremento Bee. Co-editor: Secrets of the Master Sellers, 1987. Mem. Advt. Club L.A. Avocations: home decorating, reading, swimming, music. Office: Sacramento Bee McClatchy Newspapers 2100 Q St Sacramento CA 95852*

HEARST, ROSALIE, philanthropist, foundation executive; b. Oklahoma City, Mar. 7; d. Mathis O. and Audell Bertha (Clary) Wynn; m. George Randolph Hearst, Sr., July 16, 1958. Student, Oklahoma City Coll., UCLA. Hearst rep. U.S. Senate Youth Program; pres. George Randolph Hearst Meml. Found. for Diabetic Edn.; pres. Rosalie Hearst Ednl. Found.; bd. dirs. Elvirita Lewis Found; life mem. Eisenhower Med. Ctr., Pathfinders, Tiempo de Los Ninos, Desert Hosp. Aux., Desert Press Club, Coll. of the Desert Aux., Internat. Orphans; bd. dirs. Pathfinder's Ranch Boys' Club; past bd. dirs. numerous charitable orgns.; trustee emeritus The Bob Hope Cultural Ctr.; coord. Officers' Wives Vol. Svcs. Dibble Gen. Hosp., Palo Alto; coord. Am. Women's Vol. Svcs. Sawtelle Hosp. L.A.; created Rosalie and George Hearst Fellowship in Ophthalmology U. Calif Berkeley. Named Woman of Yr. City of Hope, 1971, Disting. Woman Northwood Inst. Midland, Mich., 1988; recipient award for Lifetime Achievement in Community Service Palm Springs Women's Press Club. Home: 550 Camino Del Sur Palm Springs CA 92262-6010

HEARST, WILLIAM RANDOLPH, III, newspaper publisher; b. Washington, June 18, 1949; s. William Randolph and Austine (McDonnell) H.; m. Margaret Kerr Crawford, Sept. 23, 1990; children: William, Adelaide, Caroline. A.B., Harvard U., 1972. Reporter, asst. city editor San Francisco Examiner, 1972-76, publisher, 1984-96; editor Outside Mag., 1976-78; asst. mng. editor Los Angeles Herald Examiner, 1978-80; mgr. devel. Hearst Corp., 1980-82; v.p. Hearst Cable Communications Div., 1982-84; now ptnr. Perkins, Coffield & Buyers, Menlo Park, Calif. Bd. dirs. Sun Microsystems; trustee Carnegie Inst. Washington. Office: Perkins Coffield & Buyers 2750 Sand Hill Rd Menlo Park CA 94025*

HEART, SANDY See **HORNER, SANDRA MARIE GROCE**

HEATH, DONALD WAYNE, securities wholesale executive, financial planner; b. Wendover, Utah, July 2, 1942; s. Earl Charles and Violet (Susich) H.; m. Barbara Lyn Beesley, Aug. 11, 1963 (div. Nov. 1979); children: Jeffrey Earl, Christian Edward, Jill Elena; m. Laurie Jean Lichter, Feb. 28, 1981; children: Michele Samuel, Adam Ryan, Jason Charles. BBA, U. Nev., 1964, postgrad., 1980-81. CLU, chartered fin. cons. Agt., tng. supr., sales mgr. N.Y. Life Ins. Co., Reno, 1969-79; sales mgr. N.Y. Life Ins. Co., Stockton, Calif., 1981-83; commr. of ins. State of Nev., Carson City, 1979-81; field v.p. Integrated Resources, N.Y., 1983-84; securities wholesaler Angeles Corp., L.A., 1984-85; v.p. sales Ins. Office of Am., El Torro, Calif., 1985-87; regional v.p. Capstone Fin. Svcs., Inc., Houston, 1987-88; regional mktg. dir. Ameritas Variable Life Ins. Co., Lincoln, Nebr., 1988—; estate planning and bus. ins. specialist Merrill Lynch Life Agy., Inc., San Diego, 1992—; pres. Heath Fin. Dynamics Corp., Stockton, 1985-92; instr. U. Nev., 1974-80, U. of the Pacific Sch. of Bus. and Pub. Adminstrn., 1986-87. Recipient Paul Hammel Meml. Trophy Nev. Assn. Life Underwriters, 1972; fellow Life Underwriter Tng. Coun. Mem. Internat. Assn. Fin. Planning, Nat. Assn. Security Dealers, Nat. Assn. Ins. Commrs. (chmn. 1979-81, western zone exec. com. 1979-81), Am. Soc. CLU's and Charter Fin. Cons. (Stockton chpt., exec. com. 1979-81), U. Nev. Alumni Assn. (pres. 1976), No. Nev. Assn. Life Underwriters (pres. 1975), Calif. Assn. of Life Underwriters (chmn. ethics com. 1987-88), Masons, Mornging Star, Shriners, Passé Club, Million Dollar Round Table. Avocations: fishing, traveling. Home: 18252 Smokesignal Dr San Diego CA 92127-3123

HEATH, GARY BRIAN, manufacturing firm executive, engineer; b. Pueblo, Colo., Nov. 5, 1954; s. William Sidney Heath and Eleanor Aileen (Mortimer) Svedman, (stepfather) Donald Svedman; m. Francine Marie Tamburelli, Apr. 28, 1990. BSME, U. So. Colo., 1979; MBA, U. Phoenix, 1984. Engr. ADR Ultrasound Corp., Tempe, Ariz., 1979-81; sr. engr. Technicare Ultrasound, Englewood, Colo., 1981-83; engring. mgr. COBE Labs., Inc., Lakewood, Colo., 1983-89; dir. mfg. COBE BCT, Inc., Lakewood, 1989-96, v.p. mfg., 1996—; Patentee fluid flow transfer device, pressure diaphragm for fluid flow device. Mem. Soc. Mfg. Engrs., Soc. Plastics Engrs. Avocations: skiing, fishing, reading, weight training. Home: 7 Mule Deer Trl Littleton CO 80127-5790 Office: COBE BCT INC 1201 Oak St Lakewood CO 80215-4409

HEATON, DEBBIE ANN, mental health services worker; b. El Paso, Tex., Jan. 28, 1959; d. Joe Harrison and Patricia Ann (Major) Williams; m. Donald Esplin Heaton, Aug. 10, 1978 (div. Aug. 1981); 1 child, Marsha Camille. BSBA, Chadwick U., 1993; BS, La Salle U., 1995, M Health Svcs. Mgmt., 1997. Cert. substance abuse counselor, Ariz., behavioral therapist, domestic violence therapist. Receptionist Gallup (N.Mex.) Animal Hosp., 1980-82; clk. Allsup's, Gallup, 1983-85; security guard Giant Refinery, Gallup, 1985-86; asst. mgr. Circle K, Thatcher, Ariz., 1986-87; asst. house mgr. Graham/Greenlee Counseling, Safford, Ariz., 1987-89; adult case mgr. Southeastern Behavioral Health Svcs., Willcox, Ariz., 1989-96; adult mental health case mgr. Ariz. Physicians IPA, Safford, 1996—. Recipient Case Mgmt. Svc. award U. Ariz. Divsn. Rehab. Svcs., 1995. Mem. Assn. Social Work Mgrs., Nat. Assn. Case Mgmt. (conf. workshop presenter 1996). Avocations: horseback riding, writing, animal assisted therapy, raising dogs, collecting classical movies. Home: 3405 S Sage Trl Thatcher AZ 85552-5176

HECHTER, MARC STEVEN, management consultant; b. N.Y.C., May 25, 1952; s. Leon Hechter and Rebecca Naomi Hall Hoge; div. 1985; children: Brandon Christopher, Whitney Marie; m. Mamie May Chinn, Dec. 20, 1987. BA, U. Nev., Las Vegas, 1975, MPA, 1979. Mgmt. analyst Regional Transp. Commn., Las Vegas, 1978-79; prin. planner Clark County Dept. Comprehensive Planning, Las Vegas, 1979-83; adminstr. Nev. Housing Div., Carson City, 1983-86; v.p. Donaldson, Lufkin and Jenrette Securities Corp., N.Y.C. and L.A., 1986-87; sr. mgmt. analyst Clark County Dept. Fin., Las Vegas, 1987-88; exec. asst. to gov. State of Nev., Carson City, 1988-89; contract lobbyist, polit. cons. Wadhams and Assocs., Inc., Las Vegas and Carson City, 1989, 90-91; v.p. Zions First Nat. Bank, Las Vegas, 1989-90; asst. gen. mgr. State Indsl. Ins. System, Carson City, 1991-93; prin., CEO Jayne, Hechter and Co., Inc., Las Vegas, 1993-95; sr. v.p. fin. Saxton Inc., Las Vegas, Nev., 1995—; adj. instr. polit. sci. and history We. Nev. C.C. Past bd. dirs. Nev. Opera Assn.; head coach Silver State Girls Soccer League U-19. Mem. Pi Kappa Phi, Pi Sigma Alpha. Republican. Episcopalian. Avocations: opera, theatre, golf, hiking, soccer. Home: 3456 Distinction Ct Las Vegas NV 89129-6728

HECK, GARY L., security management company executive; b. Great Lakes, Ill., Oct. 31, 1952; s. Walter John and Alice Edna (Vogan) H.; children: Tera Lee, Breyana Marie. AAS, Delta Coll., 1972; BS, Mich. State U., 1974. Cert. protection profl. Police officer Ludington (Mich.) Police Dept., 1974-75; undercover narcotics investigator Thumb Intelligence Group, Cass City, Mich., 1975-77, Jefferson County Sheriffs Dept., Madras, Oreg., 1977-78; police patrolman Lansing Police Dept., 1978-86; chief of security Trammell Crow Co., Dallas, 1986-88; security mgr. Am. Patrol and Guard, Denver, 1988-90; dir. life safety and security Trammell Crow Co., Denver, 1990-95, Vector Property Svcs., Denver, 1995—; cons. emergency response task force Bldg. Owners and Mgrs. Assn., Denver, 1992—. Contbr. North Shore Animal League, Chgo., 1992—; walker March of Dimes, Denver, 1993. Mem. Am. Soc. for Indsl. Security, Downtown Denver Security Assn. (bd. dirs.), Nat. Fire Protection Assn., Nat. Parks and Conservation Assn., Sierra Club, World Wildlife Fund, Planetary Soc. Avocations: environmental and wildlife preservation. Home: PO Box 18429 Denver CO 80218-0429 Office: Vector Property Svcs 1200 17th St Ste 1130 Denver CO 80202-5835

HECKATHORN, I. JAMES, lawyer; b. Wolf Creek, Mont., Sept. 4, 1923; s. Lee and Wilhelmina (Sacht) H.; m. Vera Jean Hensrud; children: James (dec.), Martha. LLB, U. Mont., 1950. Bar: Mont. 1950, U.S. Dist. Ct. Mont., 1950, U.S. Ct. Appeals (9th cir.), Tribal Ct. of Confederated Salish and Kootenai Tribes; cert. civil trial specialist, Nat. Bd. Trial Advocacy. Atty. VA, Helena, Mont., 1952-54; ptnr. Haswell & Heckathorn, Whitefish, Mont., 1954-58, Murphy, Robinson, Heckathorn & Phillips, PC, Kalispell, Mont., 1958-97, Murphy, Robinson, Heckathorn & Phillips (merged with Crowley, Haughey, Toole & Dietrich, 1997—; former mem. Com. for Civil Justice Expense and Delay Reduction Plan, U.S. Dist. Cts. for Dist. of Mont.; standing com. for rev. of discovery practices and litigation conduct of U.S. Dist. Cts. for Mont.; civil rules com. Supreme Ct. of Mont., com. on uniform dist. ct. rules; chmn. settlement masters com. 11th Jud. Dist. With AUS, 1943-46, lt. col. USAR. Mem. ABA, ATLA, Am. Bd. Trial Advocacy (charter mem. Mont. chpt.), N.W. Mont. Bar, State Bar of Mont., Mont. Def. Trial Lawyers Assn. (pres.). Home: PO Box 516 Whitefish MT 59937-0516 Office: Crowley Haughey Hansen Toole & Dietrich LLP 431 1st Ave W Kalispell MT 59901-4835

HECKLER, MARK ALAN, dean; b. Windber, Pa., Oct. 14, 1955; s. Donald Eugene and Cecelia Marie (Kanas) H.; m. Veronica Makuch, May 20, 1978; children: Zachary Adam, Jocelyn Amanda, Miranda Aileen, Susanne Amelia. BA in Comm., Elizabethtown Coll., 1977; MFA in Directing, Cath. U., 1979. Narrator talking books program Libr. of Congress, Washington, 1978-79; dir. theatre, prof. Siena Coll., Albany, N.Y., 1979-95; dir. Sch. of the Arts U. Colo., Denver, 1995-98, dean Coll. Arts and Media, 1998—; governing bd. mem. Cohoes (N.Y.) Music Hall, 1989, Colo. Alliance for Arts Edn., Denver, 1996—, Anne Frank Art and Writing Competition, Denver, 1997—; nat. com. mem. Kennedy Ctr./Am. Coll. Theatre Festival, 1993, 98; resident dir. Park Playhouse, Albany, 1994—; U.S. coord. Internat. Coll. Beijing, 1996-98. Dir., lighting designer and actor various theatre prodns. Recipient Outstanding Alumni award Elizabethtown Coll., 1989, Regional Festival award Kennedy Ctr./Am. Coll. Theatre Festival, 1995. Mem. Assn. for Theatre in Higher Edn. (forum chair 1989-90, v.p. for confs. 1990-91, pres. 1995-97). Lutheran. Avocations: travel, gardening, church service, music. Office: Univ Colo Denver Coll Arts and Media Campus Box 162 PO 173364 Denver CO 80217

HECKMAN, RICHARD AINSWORTH, chemical engineer; b. Phoenix, July 15, 1929; s. Hiram and Anne (Sells) H.; m. Olive Ann Biddle, Dec. 17, 1950; children: Mark, Bruce. BS, U. Calif., Berkeley, 1950, cert. hazardous mgmt. U. Calif., Davis, 1985, int. solid waste mgmt., U. Calif., Berkeley. Registered profl. engr., Calif. With radiation lab. U. Calif., Berkeley, 1950-51; chem. engr. Calif. Rsch. & Devel. Co., Livermore, 1951-53; assoc. div. leader Lawrence Livermore Nat. Lab., 1953-77, project leader, 1977-78, program leader, 1978-79, energy policy analyst, 1979-83, toxic waste group staff engr., 1984-86, waste minimization project leader, 1986-90; div. dir. hazardous waste mgmt. Nationwide Technologies, Inc., Oakland, 1990-91; mng. dir. Heckman & Assocs., 1991-92; v.p. environ. scis. Pan Am Resources Inc., Pleasanton, Calif., 1992—, also bd. dirs.. Mem. Calif. Radioactive Materials Forum. Co-author: Nuclear Waste Management Abstracts, 1983; patentee in field. Bd. dirs. Calif. Industries for Blind, 1977-80, Here and Now Disabled Svcs. for Tri-Valley, Inc., 1980. Calif. Fellow Am. Inst. Chemists, Acad. Hazardous Materials Mgmt.; mem. AAAS, Am. Acad. Environ. Engrs. (diplomate), Am. Chemistry Soc., Am. Inst. Chem. Engrs., Am. Nuclear Soc., Soc. Environ. Mgmt. & Tech., Solid Waste Assn. N.Am., Soc. Profl. Engrs., Water Environ. Fedn., Air and Waste Mgmt. Assn., Internat. Union Pure and Applied Chemistry (assoc.), Nat. Hist. Soc., N.Y. Acad. Scis., Internat. Oceanographic Soc., Environ. Assessment Assn., World Trade Club, San Francisco, Commonwealth Club San Francisco, Richmond Yacht Club, Island Yacht Club (commodore 1971), Midget Ocean Racing Club (sta. 3 commodore 1982-83), U.S. Sailing Assn., Midget Ocean Racing Assn. No. Calif. (commodore 1972). Home and Office: Pan Am Resources Environ Scis Dept 5683 Greenridge Rd Castro Valley CA 94552-2625

HEDBERG, JOHN CHARLES, investor; b. St. Paul, Minn., June 27, 1933; s. William Rueben and Esther Mathilda (Jenson) H.; m. Sarah Cornelia McLouth, Sept. 10, 1954 (div. Sept. 1981); children: John, Theodore, Lisa, Benjamin; m. Carrie Ann Walker, Sept. 19, 1986; children: Patrick, Holly, Emily. BS with distinction, U. Minn., 1955, JD, 1960. Sec.-treas. Chateau Co-Op Restaurant, 1951-54; acctg. intern Gen. Mills, Kankakee, Ill., 1955-56; law clk. Judge Laurens L. Henderson, Phoenix, 1960-61; law ptnr. Cox & Hedberg, Phoenix, 1961-71; pvt. practice Phoenix, 1971-73; ptr. Hedberg & Kirschbaum, Phoenix, 1973-78; legal counsel Sea Ray Boats, Phoenix, 1970-78, v.p., legal counsel, 1978-87; pres. Sea Ray Credit Corp., 1980-87; dir. Sea Ray Boats, Inc., 1982-89, pres., 1988-89; pres. Sea Ray Boats Europe BV, 1988-89; bd. dirs. Healthwaves Corp., Phoenix; trustee Ray Employees' Stock Ownership Trust and Ray Employees Retirement Plan, 1979-89; advocate before Ariz. and appellate cts., U.S. Dist. Ct., Ariz., 9th Cir. Fed. Ct. Appeals. Chmn. U. Minn. Rep. Club, Mpls., 1954-55; chancellor's assoc. U. Tenn., Knoxville, 1987-89; treas./dir. Esperanza, 1989—. Mem. Beta Gamma Sigma. Avocations: tennis, reading. Home: 12636 S Honah Lee Ct Phoenix AZ 85044-3510

HEDGER, CECIL RAYMOND, lawyer; b. Tracy, Minn., Feb. 28, 1947; s. Raymond O. and Willie (Weems) H.; m. Jane E. Scott, June 6, 1970 (div. 1987); 1 child, Anne Kathryn. BA, U. S.D., 1969; JD, U. Nebr., 1972. Bar: Calif. 1972, U.S. Ct. Appeals (9th cir.) 1972, Nebr. 1973, U.S. Ct. Appeals (8th cir.) 1973, U.S. Ct. Appeals (5th cir.) 1973, Utah 1978, U.S. Dist. Ct. Utah 1978, U.S. Ct. Appeals (10th cir.) 1978, Colo. 1981, U.S. Dist. Ct. Colo. 1981. Assoc. Nelson & Harding, Lincoln, Nebr., 1972-74, ptnr., 1974-77; ptnr. Nelson & Harding, Salt Lake City, 1977-79, Denver, 1979-81, 84-88; ptnr. Musick, Peeler & Garnett, L.A. and Denver, 1981-84, Harding & Ogborn (successor firm of Nelson & Harding), Denver, 1990-98; of counsel VanCott, Bagely, Cornwall & McCarthy, Salt Lake City, 1998—; Contbr. chpts. to legal book. Mem. ABA (practice and procedure under the nat. labor rels. act, labor law sect.). Avocations: golf, rocketry, hiking, reading. Office: VanCott Bagely Cornwall & McCarthy PO Box 45340 Salt Lake City UT 84145*

HEDLUND, PAUL JAMES, lawyer; b. Abington, Pa., June 26, 1946; s. Frank Xavier and Eva Ruth (Hoffman) H.; m. Marta Louise Brewer, Dec. 7, 1985; children: Annemarie Kirsten, Brooke Ashley, Tess Kara. BSME, U. Mich., 1968; JD, UCLA, 1973. Bar: Calif. 1973, D.C. 1994, U.S. Dist. Ct. (ctrl. dist.) Calif. 1977, U.S. Dist. Ct. (ea. dist.) Calif. 1991, U.S. Dist. Ct. (no. dist.) N.Y. 1994, U.S. Patent and Trademark Office 1978, U.S. Ct. Appeals (9th cir.) 1994, U.S. Supreme Ct. 1997. Staff engr. So. Calif. Edison, L.A., 1968-70; ptnr. Hedlund & Samuels, L.A., 1974-88, Kananack, Murgatroyd Baum & Hedlund (and predecessor firms), L.A., 1988-92; shareholder Baum, Hedlund, Aristei, Guilford & Downey (and predecessor firms), L.A., 1993—; lectr. in field. *Paul Hedlund has spent the last 26 years fighting for individual's rights as a plaintiffs' lawyer. With involvement in complex issues of multi-district litigation and choice of law analysis, he aggressively sued huge corporations in protecting victims' rights in general and commerical aviation, tractor-trailer, bus and train accident litigation. His extensive academic and work background in mechanical and nuclear engineering formed the foundation for his licensing as a patent attorney which led to concentrating in mass transportation accident litigation. His most recent achievement is arguing a case of a highspeed police pursuit (Lewis v. Sacramento County) before the U.S. Supreme Court.* Mem. Bar. Assn. D.C., Consumer Attys. Calif., L.A. County Bar Assn. Office: Baum Hedlund Aristei Guilford & Downey 12100 Wilshire Blvd Ste 950 Los Angeles CA 90025-7114

HEDRICK, BASIL CALVIN, state agency administrator, ethnohistorian, educator, museum and multicultural institutions consultant; b. Lewistown, Mo., Mar. 17, 1932; s. Truman Bloice and M. LaVeta (Stice) H.; m. Anne Kehoe, Jan. 19, 1957 (div. 1979); 1 dau., Anne Lanier Hedrick Caraker; m. Susan Elizabeth Pickel, Oct. 2, 1980. A.B., Augustana Coll., Rock Island, Ill., 1956; MA, U. Fla., 1957; PhD, Inter-Am. U., Mex., 1965; cert., U. Vienna, Strobl, Austria, 1956. Asst. prof., assoc. prof., prof. So. Ill. U., Carbondale, 1967-74, asst. dir. Univ. Mus., 1967-70, dir. Univ. Mus. and Art Galleries, 1970-77, dean internat. edn., 1972-74; asst. dir. Ill. Div. Mus., Springfield, 1977-80; prof. history U. Alaska, Fairbanks, 1980-88, dir. U. Alaska Mus., 1980-88, founder, dir. internat. affairs, 1985-87; founder, dir. Div. Mus., Archaeology and Publs. State of Mich., Lansing, 1988-91; multicultural cons., 1991—; dir. mktg., cons. Rosalie Whyel Mus. Doll Art, Bellevue, Wash., 1991—; Fulbright sr. lectr., Brazil, 1972; mem. nat. register adv. panel, Ill., 1977-80; mem. Alaska Coun. on Arts, Anchorage, 1983-85; chmn. Fairbanks Hist. Preservation Commn., 1982-88; mem. Alaska Land Use Coun.; bd. dirs. Alaska Hist. Preservation Found., 1986-88; mem. Gov.'s Revitalization Task Force, Lansing, Mich., mem. ethnic coun., Mich., 1988-89; bd. dirs. East King County Visitors Bur., 1993—, officer, 1997—; officer, bd. dirs. Wash. Mus. Assn., 1993—. Author: (with others) A Bibliography of Nepal, 1973, (with Carroll L. Riley) The Journey of the Vaca Party, 1974, Documents Ancillary to the Vaca Journey, 1976, (with C.A. Letson) Once Was A Time, a Wery Good Time: An Inquiry into the Folklore of the Bahamas, 1975, (with J.E. Stephens) In the Days of Yesterday and in the Days of Today: An Overview of Bahamian Folkmusic, 1976, It's A Natural Fact: Obeah in the Bahamas, 1977, Contemporary Practices in Obeah in the Bahamas, 1981; compilations and collections, 1959-69; editor: (with J. Charles Kelley and Riley) The Classic Southwest: Readings in Archaeology, Ethnohistory and Ethnography, 1973, (with J. Charles Kelley and Riley) The Mesoamerican Southwest: Readings in Archaeology, Ethnohistory and Ethnology, 1974, (with Riley) Across the Chichimec Sea, 1978, (with others) New Frontiers in the Archaeology and Ethnohistory of the Greater Southwest, 1980, Trans. of Ill. Acad. Sci., 1979-81, (with Susan Pickel-Hedrick) Ethel Washington: The Life and Times of an Eskimo Dollmaker, The Role of the Steamboat in the Founding and Development of Fairbanks, Alaska, 1986, (with Susan Savage) Steamboats on the Chena, 1988; co-editor: Led Zeppelin live, 1993, 94, 97, Beautiful Children, 1996; author and editor of various other publications; contbr. articles to profl. jours. Chmn. Goals for Carbondale, 1972; active various local state, nat. polit. campaigns. Mem. NMA (bd. dirs. 1989-91), Am. Assn. Mus. (leader accreditation teams 1977—, sr. examiner), Ill. Archaeol. Soc. (pres. 1973-74), Mus. Alaska, Assn. Sci. Mus. Dirs., Midwest Mus. Conf. (treas. 1977-80), Western Mus. Assn., Wash. Mus. Assn. (bd. dirs. 1994—, v.p. 1995-97, pres. 1997—), BD Arts (bd. dirs. 1995-96), Phi Kappa Phi.

HEDRICK, SUSAN ELIZABETH PICKEL, curator; b. Kansas City, Kans., May 28, 1952; d. Roy Darnell and Bera Mozelle (Brookshire) Pickel; m. Basil C. Hedrick, Oct. 2, 1980. BFA in Art History, U. Kans., 1974, MA in Art History, 1977. Curatorial asst. Spencer Mus. Art, Lawrence, Kans., 1976-77; curator decorative art Ill. State Mus., Springfield, 1977-80; pvt. practice appraiser Fairbanks, Alaska, 1980-88; owner, retailer Susan's Doll Shop, Fairbanks, Alaska, 1982-88; curator of collections Rosalie Whyel Mus. Doll Art, Bellevue, Wash., 1989—; cons. Fossil Sta. Mus., Russell, Kans., 1977. Co-author: Ethel Washington: The Life & Times of an Eskimo Doll Maker, 1982, World Colors: Dolls & Dress, 1997, The Rose Unfolds, 1997; contbr. articles to profl. jours. Bd. dirs. Fairbanks Arts Assn., 1986-88, Encore Playhouse, Bellevue, Wash., 1997—. Rsch. grant Alaska State Hist. Commn., 1982-83. Mem. Am. Assn. Mus., Appraisers Assn. Am., Wash. Mus. Assn., United Fedn. Doll Clubs, Costume Soc. Am. Avocations: collecting dolls, collecting rock 'n roll memorabilia, writing, music, computers. Office: Rosalie Whyel Mus Doll Art 1116 108th Ave NE Bellevue WA 98004-4321

HEDRICK, WALLACE EDWARD, business executive; b. Malad, Idaho, Nov. 11, 1947; s. Clarence Franklin and Beth S. Hedrick; BS, U. Nev., Reno, 1970; MA, U. No. Colo., Greeley, 1974; m. Jerrie S. Deffenbaugh, Nov. 20, 1980; children: Ann Elizabeth, Ryan Wallace, Hallie Sue. Regional dir. No. Idaho, Idaho Planning and Cmty. Affairs Agy., Moscow, 1970-73, assoc. chief, Boise, 1973-75; project dir. Pacific N.W. Regional Commn., Boise, 1975-76; pres. Resources N.W., Inc., Boise, 1976-88; dir. Idaho State Lottery, 1988-95; pres. Tri West Lotto Bd., 1993-95; pres. Resources Northwest, Boise, 1995—. Sec.-treas. Idaho Citizens for Responsible Govt., 1978-80; trustee, chmn. Joint Sch. Dist. 2, 1985—; trustee Meridian Sch. Bd.; bd. dirs. Boise Family YMCA, 1994—; exec. com. North Am. Assn. State and Provincial Lotteries. Served with USAR, 1971. Mem. Multi State Lottery Assn. (pres. 1994-95), N.Am. Assn. of State and Provincial Lotteries (regional dir.). Democrat. Home: 9413 Knottingham Dr Boise ID 83704-2234 Office: Resources Northwest PO Box 578 Boise ID 83701-0578

HEE, TIFFANY MALIA, marketing specialist, sales administrator; b. Honolulu, Oct. 10, 1973; d. Calvin Kit Hing and Marie Ichiko (Fujiyama) Hee. Cert., Flinders U., 1994; BA, Mt. Holyoke Coll., 1995. Mgr. Enterprise Rent-A-Car, Honolulu, 1995-97; mktg./sales mgr. GTE Directories, Honolulu, 1997—. Mem. NOW, Image de Hawaii, Keiki Aloha (liaison 1998—). Office: GTE Directories St Address Directories 711 Kapiolani Blvd Ste 670 Honolulu HI 96813-5249

HEEKIN, VALERIE ANNE, telecommunications technician; b. Santa Monica, Calif., Nov. 7, 1953; d. Edward Raphael and Jane Eileen (Potter) H. AA, L.A. Valley Coll., 1980; BS magna cum laude, Calif. Baptist Coll., 1987. Telecommunications technician Pacific Bell Co., N. Hollywood, Calif., 1971—; pres. Odyssey Adventures, Inc., Stevenson Ranch, Calif., 1987—, Countryside Properties, Inc., Stevenson Ranch, 1995—. Pres. Parkwood Sylmar Homeowners Assn., 1981-89; activist civil rights. Republican. Roman Catholic. Avocations: flying, boating, water skiing, hiking, photography, travel. Office: Odyssey Adventures PO Box 221477 Newhall CA 91322-1477

HEEN, WALTER MEHEULA, retired judge, political party executive; b. Honolulu, Apr. 17, 1928; s. Norma K. Tada; 1 child, Cameron K. BA in Econs., U. Hawaii, 1953; JD, Georgetown U., 1955. Bar: Hawaii 1955, U.S. Dist. Ct. Hawaii 1955. Dep. corp. counsel Honolulu, 1957-58; territorial ho. of reps., 1958-59; mem. State Ho. Reps., 1959-64; state senator, 1966-68; mem. Honolulu City Coun., 1969-72, chair, 1972-74; state dist. ct. judge, 1972-74, state cir. ct. judge, 1974-78; U.S. atty. U.S. Dist. Hawaii, 1978-80, U.S. dist. ct. judge, 1981; assoc. judge State Intermediate Ct. Appeals, 1982-94; ret., 1994. Past pres. Honolulu Hawaiian Civic Club; precinct club pres. Dem. Party, 1956-72; vice chmn. Oahu Dem. County Com., 1956-62, chmn., 1962-64; del. State Dem. Party Conv., 1956-70. Recipient Lei Hulu Mamo

award, 1992; named Outstanding Young Man of the Yr., 1962. Mem. Native Hawaiian Bar Assn. (dir. 1994—). Avocations: photography, fishing, surfing, golf, family activities. Office: 777 Kapiolani Blvd Honolulu HI 96813-5211*

HEFFLINGER, LEROY ARTHUR, agricultural manager; b. Omaha, Feb. 14, 1935; s. Leroy William and Myrtle Irene (Lampe) H.; m. Carole June Wickman, Dec. 23, 1956; children: Dean Alan, Andrew Karl, Roger Glenn, Dale Gorden. BS in Fin., U. Colo., 1957. Mgr. Hefflinger Ranches, Inc., Toppenish, Wash., 1963-97; pres. Hefflinger Ranches, Inc., 1973—; bd. dirs. Hop Adminstrv. Com., Portland, Oreg., 1980-86; trustee Agr. and Forestry Edn. Found., Spokane, Wash., 1988-94, vice chmn., 1993-94; mem. adv. bd. Ctrl. Bank, Toppenish, Wash., 1995—. Vestryman, bd. dirs. St. Michael's Ch., Yakima, Wash., 1969-74; mem. capital campaign com. Heritage Coll., Toppenish, 1990-91; bd. dirs. Am. Hop Mus., 1997—. Capt. USAF, 1958-63. Mem. Hop Growers Am. (past pres. 1982-95, bd. dirs.), Hop Growers Wash. (past treas. 1978-83, bd. dirs.), Beta Theta Pi. Republican. Episcopalian. Avocations: scuba diving, cross-country skiing, golf, photography, antique guns. Office: Hefflinger Ranches Inc PO Box 47 Toppenish WA 98948-0047

HEFFNER, DANIEL JASON, film producer; b. N.Y.C., Mar. 30, 1956; s. Richard Douglas and Elaine Peggy (Segal) H.; m. Beth Klein, May 26, 1991; children: Jeremy Aaron, Zachary David. BS in Comm., Ithaca Coll., 1978. Prodn. exec. Columbia Pictures, L.A., 1982-85; prodn. exec., prodr. Walt Disney Pictures, L.A., 1985-88; v.p. prodn. Buena Vista Pictures Distbn. divsn. Walt Disney Co., L.A., 1988-91; pres. Poo Bear Prodns. Inc., 1991—. Asst. dir. (film) The Big Chill, 1982; co-producer (film) Cocktail, 1988; exec. prodr. (film) The Good Mother, 1988; co-exec. prodr. (film) Holy Matrimony, 1993. Mem. Dirs. Guild Am. Democrat. Jewish. Home: 4119 Woodman Ave Sherman Oaks CA 91423-4331 Office: Poo Bear Prodns Inc 13601 Ventura Blvd Ste 154 Sherman Oaks CA 91423-3701

HEFFRON, MICHAEL EDWARD, software engineer, computer scientist; b. Battle Creek, Mich., Dec. 18, 1949; s. Michael Richard and Maxine Beverly (Piper) H.; m. Louella Mae Thompson, Apr. 12, 1969; children: Karen, Jennifer. BS in Computer Sci., Ariz. State U., 1986; MS in Computer Sci., Colo. Tech. U., 1998. Engring. asst. Motorola, Inc., Scottsdale, Ariz., 1977-81; calibration lab. supr. ADR Ultrasound, Tempe, Ariz., 1982-83; engring. aide Motorola, Inc., Scottsdale, 1983-86; v.p. CyberSoft, Inc., Tempe, Ariz., 1986-90; engr. Injection Rsch. Specialists, Inc., Colorado Springs, Colo., 1990-91; software devel. mgr. Injection Rsch. Specialists Co. div. Pacer Industries, Colorado Springs, 1991-92; sr. systems engr. Computer Data Systems Inc., Rockville, Md., 1992-93; software engr. Coergon, Inc., Boulder, Colo., 1993-95, Loral Comm. Systems (purchased by Lockheed Martin 1996), Colorado Springs, Colo., 1995-96, Lockheed Martin, Colorado Springs, 1996-97; sr. software engr. L-3 Comms. Corp. (formerly Lockheed Martin Wideband Sys.), Colo. Springs, 1997—. Patentee in field. Served with USAF, 1970-77. Mem. IEEE, Assn. Computing Machinery, Soc. Reliability Engrs. Republican. Pentecostal Ch. Office: L-3 Comms Corp 1150 Academy Park Loop Ste 240 Colorado Springs CO 80910-3716

HEFLEY, JOEL M., congressman; b. Ardmore, Okla.; s. J. Maurice and Etta A. (Anderson) H.; m. Lynn Christian, Aug. 25, 1961; children: jana, Lori, Juli. BA, Okla. Baptist U., 1957; MS, Okla. State U., 1963. Exec. dir. Community Planning and Research, Colorado Springs, Colo., 1966-86; mem. Colo. Ho. of Reps., 1977-78, Colo. Senate, 1979-86, 100th-104th Congresses from 5th Colo. dist., 1987—; mem. armed svcs. com., mem. natural resources com., mem. small bus.-SBA com., mem. nat. security com., mem. stds. of offcl. conduct. Republican. Baptist. Clubs: Rotary, Colorado Springs Country. Office: Ho of Reps 2230 Rayburn Bldg Washington DC 20515-0605

HEGARTY, GEORGE JOHN, university president, English educator; b. Cape May, N.J., July 20, 1948; s. John Joseph and Gloria Anna (Bonelli) H.; m. Joy Elizabeth Schiller, June 9, 1979. Student, U. Fribourg, Switzerland, 1968-69; BA in English, LaSalle U., Phila., 1970; Cert., Coll. de la Pocatiere, Que., Can., 1970; postgrad., U. Dakar, Senegal, 1970, Case Western Res. U., 1973-74, U. N.H., 1976; MA in English, Drake U., 1977; cert., U. Iowa, 1977; DA, Drake U., 1978; Cert., UCLA, 1979, U. Pa., 1981. Tchr. English, Peace Corps vol. College d'Enseignment General de Sedhiou, Senegal, 1970-71; tchr. English Belmore Boys' and Westfields High Schs., Sydney, Australia, 1972-73; teaching fellow in English Drake U., Des Moines, 1974-76; mem. faculty English Des Moines Area Community Coll., 1976-80; assoc. prof. Am. lit. U. Yaounde, Cameroon, 1980-83; prof. Am. lit. and civilization Nat. U. Cote D'Ivoire, Abidjan, 1986-88; dir. ctr. for internat. programs and svcs. Drake U., Des Moines, 1983-91; prof. grad. program intercultural mgmt. Sch. for Internat. Tng., The Experiment in Internat. Living, Brattleboro, Vt., 1991-93; provost, prof. English Teikyo Loretto Heights U., Denver, 1992-94; pres., prof. English, Teikyo Westmar U., Le Mars, Iowa, 1994-95; program dir. Am. degree program Taylor's Coll., Malaysia, 1996-97; v.p. academic affairs, prof. English Teikyo Loretto Heights U., Denver, 1997—; acad. specialist USIA, 1983-84; workshop organizer/speaker Am. Field Svcs., 1986; cons. Coun. Internat. Ednl. Exch., 1986; evaluator Assn. des Univ. Partiellment Entierément de Langue Francais, 1987, Iowa Humanities Bd., 1990-91, USAID's Ctr. for Univ. Coop. and Devel., 1991; cons. in field. Book reviewer African Book Pub. Record, Oxford, Eng., 1981—, African Studies Rev., 1990—; host, creator TV show Global Perspectives, 1989-91; exhibitor of African art, 1989—; contbr. articles to profl. jours. Commr. Des Moines Sister City Commn., 1984-87, 91; bd. dirs. Iowa Sister State Com., 1988-91; pres. Chautauqua Park Nat. Hist. Dist. Neighborhood Assn., 1991; bd. dirs. Melton Found., 1994-95. Drake U. fellow, 1971-72, 74-76; Nat. Endowment for Humanities grantee, 1981; Fulbright grantee, USIA, 1980-83, 86-88. Mem. Am. Assn. Pres. Ind. Colls. and Univs., NAFSA: Assn. Internat. Educators (sectional chmn. region VI 1986-87, Vt. rep. 1992), Assn. Internat. Edn. Adminstrs., Inst. Internat. Edn. Avocations: collecting non-western art, travel, swimming, writing.

HEIDEN, WILLIAM MARK, entrepreneur; b. Chandler, Ariz., Oct. 26, 1952; s. William Lee and Marion Janet (Robertson) H.; m. Melinda Cuno, July 7, 1973 (div. 1977); m. Patricia Toberman, Nov. 21, 1980; children: Geoffrey, Chase, Devin, Micaela, Buckley. BA, Calif. State U., Fullerton, 1974; MBA, U. So. Calif., 1975. Fin. analyst Pacific Gas & Electric Co., San Francisco, 1975-77; v.p., mgr. Security Pacific Bank, L.A., 1977-80; regional v.p. Union Bank, L.A., 1980-84; mng. dir. Madsen and Co., Inc., L.A., 1985-87; pres. Amcil Holdings, Irvine, Calif., 1987-89; chief exec. officer Incetek, San Marcos, Calif., 1990—. Bd. dirs. Am. Lung Assn., L.A., Emphysema Found. Mem. Am. Gas Assn., No. Electric Power Assn., Ind. Petroleum Assn. Am., Monarch Bay Club. Republican. Lutheran. Home: 25461 Spindlewood Laguna Niguel CA 92677-1901

HEIDMANN, PAUL SCOTT, software engineer; b. Mankato, Minn., Mar. 3, 1967; s. Fred William and Patricia Nan (Patterson) H.; m. Annette Marie Holston, Apr. 5, 1967; children: Laurent Victoria, Megan Olivia, Geneva Melody. BSEE, BS in Math., N.D. State U., 1990, MS in Math., 1992. Software engr. Computing Devices Internat., Bloomington, Minn., 1992-97; staff software engr. Ensco, Scottsdale, Ariz., 1997—; object-oriented cons. Computing Devices Internat., Bloomington, 1996; real-time scheduling theory cons. McDonnell-Douglas, St. Louis, 1997. Local officer Rep. Party, South St. Paul, Minn., 1995-97, state del., Duluth, Minn., 1996. Recipient 1st pl. award KN Rao Meml. Math. Competition, N.D. State U., 1991. Mem. Assn. Computing Machinery, Phi Kappa Phi. Presbyterian. Avocation: automotive work. Office: QRP 11811 N Tatum Blvd Ste 3031 Phoenix AZ 85028

HEIDT, HORACE HAMILTON, JR., music director, conductor, business executive; b. Los Angeles, Oct. 7, 1946. BA in Polit. Sci., Stanford U., 1969; student, UCLA, 1967-68; JD, Southwestern U., 1977. Leader, musician various bands The Satellites, The Tradewinds, Santa Monica, Calif.; music dir. Drake Hotel, Chgo., 1970; producer mus. show featuring artists Helen Forrest, Johnny Desmond and the Modernaires, 1985; leader, musician Mus. Knights; mus. dir. Los Angeles Raiders, current; producer TV pilot. Rec. [illegible] Ball; also numerous theater, radio, TV and club appearances; music dir. Rep. Nat. Conv., 1996. Polit. activist; hon. mayor Toluca Lake. Mem. San Fernando Valley Bus. and Profl. Assn. (pres.), Valley Industry and Commerce Assn. (bd. dirs. new directions for youth).

HEIDT, RAYMOND JOSEPH, insurance company executive; b. Bismarck, N.D., Feb. 28, 1933; s. Stephen Ralph and Elizabeth Ann (Hirschkorn) H.; BA, Calif. State U., San Jose, 1963, MA, 1968; PhD, U. Utah, 1977; m. Joyce Ann Aston, Jan. 14, 1956; children: Ruth Marie, Elizabeth Ann, Stephen Christian, Joseph Aston. Claims supr. Allstate Ins. Co., San Jose, Calif., 1963-65; claims mgr. Gen. Accident Group, San Francisco, 1965-69; owner, mgr. Ray Heidt & Assocs., Logan, Utah, 1969-76; v.p. claims Utah Home Fire Ins. Co., Salt Lake City, 1976—; with Utah State U., 1970-76; dir. Inst. for Study of Pacifism and Militarism; vice-chmn. Benton County Parks and Recreation Bd., 1987-90. Active Kennewick Hist. Preservation Commn., 1989-90, 1st chmn., 1989-90, Magna Area Coun., 1992, pres. 1993-94; bd. trustees, sec. treas. Utah Ethnic and Mining Mus., 1994—. With U.S. Army, 1952-57. Decorated Bronze Star. Mem. Southeastern Wash. Adjusters' Assn. (pres. 1988-90), Utah Claims Assn. (pres. 1977-78), Lions, Am. Legion. Mormon. Republican. Home: 1715 W Flamingo Ave Apt #50 Nampa ID 83651-1669

HEIFETS, LEONID, microbiologist, researcher; b. Russia, Jan. 5, 1926; came to U.S., 1979; s. Boris and Luba Heifets; m. Seraphima Apsit, Jan. 1955 (div. July 1978); children: Michael, Herman. MD, Med. Inst., Moscow, 1947, PhD, 1953; DSc, Acad. Med. Scis., Moscow. Asst. prof. Med. Inst., Arkhangelsk, Russia, 1950-54, assoc. prof., 1954-57; lab. dir. Mechnikov Rsch. Inst., Moscow, 1957-69; sr. rschr. Inst. for Tb, Moscow, 1969-78; rsch. fellow Nat. Jewish Hosp., Denver, 1979-80; lab. dir. Nat. Jewish Ctr., Denver, 1980—; asst. prof. Colo. U., Denver, 1980-86, assoc. prof., 1986-92, prof. microbiology, 1992—; mem. com. on bacteriology Internat. Union Against Tb, Paris, 1986—. Author: Effectiveness of Vaccination, 1968, Clinical Mycobaceriology (Clinics in Laboratory Medicine), 1996; author, editor: Drug Susceptibility, 1991; assoc. editor Internat. Jour. Tuberculosis; contbr. articles to profl. jours. Mem. Am. Soc. Microbiology. Avocations: hiking, snowshoeing, photography, history. Office: Nat Jewish Med Rsch Ctr 1400 Jackson St Denver CO 80206-2761

HEILMAN, MARLIN GRANT, photographer; b. Tarentum, Pa., Sept. 29, 1919; s. Marlin Webster and Martha (Grant) H.; widowed; 1 child, Hans. BA in Econs., Swarthmore Coll., 1941. Prin. Grant Heilman Photography, Inc., Lititz, Pa., 1948—. Author and photographer: Farm Town, 1974, Wheat Country, 1977, FARM, 1988; photographer: Psalms Around us, 1970. Capt. U.S. Army, 1941-45. Decorated Bronze Star, Croix de Guerre, French Army, 1945, Hon Legionaire Firs Clas, French Fgn. Legion, 1943. Avocation: environmental studies.

HEIMANN, JANET BARBARA, volunteer trail consultant; b. Santa Cruz, Calif., Dec. 18, 1931; d. John Louis and Charlotte Lucina (Burns) Grinnell; m. Richard Frank Gustav, July 10, 1953; children: David Robert, Gary Alan, Kathleen Janet. BS, U. Calif., Berkeley, 1954. Vol. trail rschr. Monterey County Pks. Dept.; appointee Carmel Valley Trail Adv. Com., 1993—. Pres. Folsom Freedom Trails, Placer County, Calif., 1980-83; chmn. Adopt-a-Trail, Folsom Lake Trail Patrol, Placer County, 1986-88; bd. dirs. Loomis Basin Horseman Assn., Placer County, 1986-87. Mem. AAUW. Republican. Home: 11565 Mccarthy Rd Carmel Valley CA 93924-9239

HEIMANN, JURGEN STEFFEN, special make-up effects artist, director, writer; b. Mahlberg, Fed. Republic Germany, Apr. 28, 1965; s. Peter Alfonse and Rosemarie (Holland) H. BA, Brooks Inst., 1987. Owner Monster Mecanix SPFX Co., Sherman Oaks, Calif., 1988—, Brillig Prodns., Sherman Oaks, Calif., 1997; owner Monster Mecanix SPFX Co., Sherman Oaks, Calif., 1988—; owner Brillig Prodns., Sherman Oaks, Calif., 1997—. Producer, writer (short films) The Maytag Man, 1984, Blood Red, 1986, Psycho Killer, 1986, Fractions, 1987; spl. effects artist (feature) Robot Jox, 1987, Honey, I Shrunk the Kids, 1988, Leviathan, 1988, The Abyss, 1988, Gremlins 2, 1989, Arachnophobia, 1990, Beethoven, 1991, Lorenzo's Oil, 1991, Baby's Day Out, 1993, Batman Forever, 1995, The Nutty Professor, 1995, Men in Black, 1996, Mighty Joe Young, 1998; prodr., writer, dir. (film) Clambaked, 1998—. Named one of Outstanding Young Men Am., 1987. Democrat. Avocations: watching movies, listening to music, writing scripts, sculpting, art. Home and Office: 13958 Huston St Sherman Oaks CA 91423-1903

HEIMANN-HAST, SYBIL DOROTHEA, language arts and literature educator; b. Shanghai, May 8, 1924; came to U.S., 1941; d. Paul Heinrich and Elisabeth (Halle) Heimann; m. David G. Hast, Jan. 11, 1948 (div. 1959); children: Thomas David Hast, Dorothea Elizabeth Hast-Scott. BA in French, Smith Coll., 1946; MA in French Lang. and Lit., U. Pitts., 1963; MA in German Lang. and Lit., UCLA, 1966; diploma in Spanish, U. Barcelona, Spain, 1972. Cert. German, French and Spanish tchr., Calif. Assoc. in German lang. UCLA, 1966-70; asst. prof. German Calif. State U., L.A., 1970-71; lectr. German Mt. St. Mary's Coll., Brentwood, Calif., 1974-75; instr. French and German, diction coach Calif. Inst. of Arts, Valencia, 1977-78; coach lang. and diction UCLA Opera Theater, 1973-93, ret., 1993, lectr. dept. music, 1973-93; interviewer, researcher oral history program UCLA, 1986-93; dir., founder ISTMO, Santa Monica, Calif., 1975—; cons. interpreter/translator L.A. Music Ctr., U.S. Supreme Ct., L.A., J. Paul Getty Mus., Malibu, Calif., Warner New Media, Panorama Internat. Prodn., Sony Records, 1986—; voice-over artist; founder, artistic dir. Westside Opera Workshop, 1986-94. Author of poems. Mem. KCET Founder Soc. UCLA grantee, 1990-91. Mem. AAUP, MLA, SAG, AFTRA, KCET Founder Soc., Sunset Succulent Soc. (v.p., bd. dirs., reporter, annual show chmn.), German Am. C. of C., L.A. Avocations: performing arts, literature, history, plants, designing and knitting sweaters. Home and Office: 1022 17th St Apt 7 Santa Monica CA 90403-4339

HEIMLER, JAMES LEONARD, architect, consultant; b. L.A., Sept. 17, 1956; s. Charles and Clair (Siebenberg) H.; m. Cynthia Ann Bolander, June 22, 1980; children: Laura Allison, Kevin Johnathan. Student, Calif. State U., Northridge, 1974-76; BS in Environ. Design Architecture, Calif. State Poly. U., 1985. Registered arch., Calif., Wash. Apprentice, jr. draftsman Robert B. Marks Arch., L.A., 1974-83; job capt., sr. draftsman Robert B. Marks ARch., Santa Monica, Calif., 1983; job capt., sr. draftsman & project coordination Choate Assocs., L.A., 1983-85; prin. James Heimler Arch. Inc., Tarzana, Calif., 1985—; mem. Ocean Pk. Cmty. Orgn, Santa Monica, Calif., 1983, L.A. City Ad Hoc Com., 1988. Second place Engring. Design Nat. Competition, 1976. Active Natural Resources Def. Coun., 1982—; Mem. Ocean Park Cmty. Orgn., Santa Monica, Calif., 1983; ad hoc commem. Transitional Height Moratorium Ordinances, L.A., 1987-88; mem. ad hoc com. L.A. City, 1988; mem. L.A. Eco-City Coun.,1992—; oodland Hills-Streetscope Com. Ventura Blvd. Specific Plan, 1993—; Beautification Prlject Com. MTA Right-of-Way, 1996—. AIA mem. San Fernando Valley Chpt.; mem. Archs., Designers, Planners for Social onsibility, Sierra Club, Ocean Park Cmty. Orgn, Santa Monica, Calif., Encino Chamber Commerce, corp. officer Santa Maria Trails Parks Assn. Democrat. Jewish. Avocations. tennis, backpacking, hiking, politics, chess. Office: 19510 Ventura Blvd Ste 210 Tarzana CA 91356-2947

HEINBERG, RICHARD WILLIAM, science educator; b. Kirksville, Mo., Oct. 21, 1950; s. William Henry and Evelyn Lenore (Taylor) H.; m. Janet Lynn Barocco. Student, U. Iowa, 1968-70. Lectr. New Coll. of Calif., Santa Rosa, 1998—; pub./editor Museletter, Santa Rosa, 1992—; contbg. editor Intuition Mag., San Francisco, 1993—. Author: Memories and Visions of Paradise, 1989, 95, Celebrate the Solstice, 1993, A New Covenant with Nature, 1996 (Books to Live By award, 1997), Cloning the Buddha, 1999. Mem. Alliance for Democracy, Santa Rosa, 1996—. Mem. Internat. Soc. for the Comparative Study of Civilizations. Avocations: playing violin, gardening. Office: New Coll of Calif 99 6th St Santa Rosa CA 95401-6200

HEINDL, CLIFFORD JOSEPH, physicist; b. Chgo., Feb. 4, 1926; s. Anton Thomas and Louise (Fiala) H. B.S., Northwestern U., 1947, M.S., 1948, A.M., Columbia U., 1950, Ph.D., 1959. Sr. physicist Bendix Aviation Corp., Detroit, 1953-54; orsort student Oak Ridge Nat. Lab., 1954-55; asst. sect. chief Babcock & Wilcox Co., Lynchburg, Va., 1956-58; research group supr. Jet Propulsion Lab., Pasadena, Calif., 1959-65, mgr. research and space sci., 1965—. Served with AUS, 1944-46. Mem. AIAA, Am. Nuclear Soc., Health Physics Soc., Planetary Soc., Am. Phys. Soc. Home: 179 Mockingbird Ln South Pasadena CA 91030-2047 Office: 4800 Oak Grove Dr Pasadena CA 91109-8001

HEINEMANN, KAKI See MAY, KATHERINE

HEINER, DOUGLAS CRAGUN, pediatrician, educator; b. Salt Lake City, July 27, 1925; s. Spencer and Eva Lillian (Cragun) H.; m. Joy Luana Wiest, Jan. 8, 1946; children: Susan, Craig, Joseph, Marianne, James, David, Andrew, Carolee, Pauli. BS, Idaho State Coll., 1946; MD, U. Pa., 1950; PhD, McGill U., 1969. Intern Hosp. U. Pa., Phila., 1950-51; resident, fellow Children's Med. Ctr., Boston, 1953-56; asst. prof. pediatrics U. Ark. Med. Ctr., Little Rock, 1956-60; assoc. prof. pediatrics U. Utah Med. Ctr., Salt Lake City, 1960-66; fellow in immunology McGill U., Montreal, 1966-69; prof. of pediatrics Harbor-UCLA Med. Ctr., Torrance, 1969-94; disting. prof. of pediatrics UCLA Sch. Medicine, 1985-94, prof. emeritus, 1994—; med. specialist Russia Latter Day Sts. Missions, 1997-99. Author: Allergies to Milk, 1980; mem. editl. bd. Jour. Allergy and Clin. Immunology, 1975-79, Allergy, 1981-88, Jour. Clin. Immunology, 1981-87, Pediat. Asthma, Allergy and Immunology, 1986-94; contbr. over 150 original articles to profl. jours. and chpts. to books. Scoutmaster Boy Scouts Am., Salt Lake City, 1963; com. chmn. Rancho Palos Verdes, 1979-81; high coun. mem. Mormon Ch., Rancho Paos Verdes, 1983-86. 1st lt. med. corps U.S. Army, 1952-53, Korea. Recipient Disting. Alumni award Idaho State U., 1987. Fellow Am. Pediatric Soc., Am. Acad. Allergy and Clin. Immunology (food allergy com. 1981—), Am. Coll. Allergy and Immunology; mem. Soc. for Pediatric Rsch., Western Soc. for Pediatric Rsch. (Ross award 1961), Am. Assn. Immunologists, Clin. Immunology Soc., Am. Acad. Pediatrics. Republican. Avocations: gardening, tennis.

HEINS, MARILYN, college dean, pediatrics educator, author; b. Boston, Sept. 7, 1930; d. Harold and Esther (Berow) H.; m. Milton P. Lipson, 1958; children: Rachel, Jonathan. A.B., Radcliffe Coll., 1951; M.D., Columbia U., 1955. Diplomate Am. Bd. Pediatrics. Intern, N.Y. Hosp., N.Y.C., 1955-56; resident in pediatrics Babies Hosp., N.Y.C., 1956-58; asst. pediatrician Children's Hosp. Mich., Detroit, 1959-78; dir. pediatrics Detroit Receiving Hosp., 1965-71; asst., assoc. dean student affairs Wayne State U. Med. Sch., Detroit, 1971-79; assoc. dean acad. affairs U. Ariz. Med. Coll., Tucson, 1979-83, vice dean, 1983-88, prof. pediatrics, 1985-88. Author: (with Anne M. Seiden) Child Care/Parent Care, 1987; mem. editorial bd. Jour. AMA, 1981-91; contbr. articles to profl. jours. Bd. dirs. Planned Parenthood So. Ariz., 1983, pres., 1988-89, Ariz. Ctr. for Clin. Mgmt.,1991—, Nat. Bd. Med. Examiners, 1983-88; mem. adv. bd. So. Ariz. Women's Fund, 1992—, Ariz. State Hosp., 1985-88. Recipient Alumni Faculty Service award Wayne State U., 1972, Recognition award, 1977, Women on the Move Achievement award YWCA Tucson, 1983, Tuscon women of Vision award Weizmann Inst., 1997, pres.'s disting. svc. award Ariz. Med. Assn., 1997; mem. Ariz. Ctr. Clin. Mgmt. 1990—. Home: 6530 N Longfellow Dr Tucson AZ 85718-2416

HEINZ, RONEY ALLEN, civil engineering consultant; b. Shawano, Wis., Dec. 29, 1946; s. Orville Willard and Elva Ida (Allen) H.; m. Judy Evonne Olney, Oct. 30, 1965. BSCE, Mont. State U., 1973. Surveyor U.S. Army Corps Engrs., Seattle, 1966-73; civil engr. Hoffman, Fiske, & Wyatt, Lewiston, Idaho, 1973-74, Tippetts-Abbott-McCarthy-Stratton, Seattle, 1977-79; asst. editor Civil Engring. Mag. ASCE, N.Y.C., 1974-77; constrn. mgr. Boeing Co., Seattle, 1979-83; owner, gen. mgr. Armwavers Ltd., South Bend, Wash., 1983—; pres. Great Walls Internat. Inc., Elma, Wash., 1993-95, Heinz Internat., Inc., 1995—, Interocean Mgmt. Svcs., Inc., Republic of Panama, 1998—; mem. dams and tunnels del. to China, People to People Internat., Spokane, 1987; mem. U.S. com. on Large Dams. Asst. editor Commemorative Book Internat. Congress on Large Dams, 1987; contbr. articles to profl. publs., including Civil Engring. Mag., Excavator Mag., Internat. Assn. for Bridge and Structural Engring., Japan Concrete Inst., others. Dir. Canaan Christians Fund, Aberdeen, 1993—; bd. dirs. Seaman's Ctr., Aberdeen, Wash., 1990—. Recipient First Quality award Asphalt Paving Assn. Wash., 1991. Mem. ASCE (sec. met. sect. 1975-76, assoc. mem. forum), ASTM (Student award 1973)., USCOLD. Republican. Lutheran. Achievements include management of first commercial installation worldwide of sediment control by water jets, of development of first private harbor and container terminal in Panama in Manzanillo Bay, Colon. Office: Armwavers Ltd PO Box 782 South Bend WA 98586-0782

HEITMAN, GREGORY ERWIN, state official; b. Lewiston, Idaho, June 7, 1947; s. Elmer William and Carmelita Rose Ann (Kinzer) H.; m. Phyllis Ann Pryor, Sept. 25, 1982. BS in Math., U. Idaho, 1969, MBA, 1971; student, Wash. State U., 1965-67. Student communications dir. Assoc. Students U. Idaho, Moscow, 1970-72, advisor, apt. mgr. dept. housing, 1971-72; traffic fatality analyst Idaho Dept. Transp., Boise, 1973-74; ops. mgr. Region IV Health & Welfare State of Idaho, Boise, 1974-78, supr. computer svcs., div. environ. in health and welfare, 1978-85; coord. field svcs., program dir. Idaho Ctr. for Vital Stats. and Health Policy, Boise, 1985—; acting dir. Idaho Ctr. for Health Statistics, Boise, 1988-89, spl. asst. program and policy devel., 1989—; mem. med. records adv. com. Boise State U., 1987—, cons., lectr. 1987—. Active various charitable orgns.; precinct committeeman Dem. of Latah County, 1972; election day coord. Ada County, 1986; vol. Am. Cancer Soc., 1990, Easter Seals, 1992, Arthritis Found., 1996. Mem. Idaho Pub. Health Assn., Assn. Vital Records and Health Statistics, Idaho Pub. Employees Assn., Assn. Govt. Employees. Roman Catholic. Avocations: bowling, card collecting. Home: 1762 E Summerridge Dr Meridian ID 83642-5586 Office: Idaho Vital Stats PO Box 83720 Boise ID 83720-3720

HELD, FRED, management consultant; b. Bklyn., Oct. 17, 1937; s. Sampson and Anna (Purisch) H.; m. Karen Lee Bratton, Dec. 17, 1966; children: Heidi Ann, Krystal Dawn Held Roark. BS in Indsl. Engring., U. So. Calif., 1961, MS in Indsl. Engring., 1964. V.p. ops. Matell Toys Inc., Hawthorne, Calif., 1962-76; v.p. distbn. Bercor, La Mirada, Calif., 1987-89; sr. v.p. Simon Mktg., Beverly Hills, Calif., 1989-92; sr. v.p. ops. Equity Mktg., N.Y.C., 1992-93; owner Fred Held Assocs., Palos Verdes, Calif., 1993-96; sr. v.p., founder HomeGate, Torrance, Calif., 1996-97. Regent Woodbury U., Burbank, Calif., 1985-95; bd. dirs. Calif. State U., L.A., 1985-97, Calif. State U., Long Beach, 1998—; mem. Palos Verdes Ednl. Found., 1997—, Palos Verdes Jr. Achievement, 198—. Mem. Kiwanis. Republican. Avocations: tennis, skiing, rollerblading, fitness, internet. Home: 1320 Via Gabriel Palos Verdes Estates CA 90274

HELD, JAY ALLEN, pastor; b. Canton, Ohio, Dec. 15, 1961; s. Earl E. and E. Jean (Robinson) H.; m. Laureen Elizabeth Allen, Mar. 19, 1988. BS in Theology, Bapt. U. Am., 1985, postgrad.; MA in Counseling, Western Sem., 1990, MDiv, 1994; MA in Missions, Grace Theol. Sem., 1990. Ordained to ministry Canton Baptist Temple, 1990. Inner-city missionary Forest Hills Bapt. Ch., Decatur, Ga., 1980-84; asst. to pastor Allgood Rd. Bapt. Ch., Marietta, Ga., 1984-85, Eastland Bapt. Ch., Orlando, Fla., 1985; tchr. high sch. Eastland Christian Sch., Orlando, 1985; inner-city missionary North Portland Bible Fellowship, Portland, 1989-91, Mt. Sinai Community Bapt. Ch., Portland, 1991-94; urban pastor North Bapt. Ch., 1994—; camp counselor Camp C.H.O.F., Dalton, Ohio, summer, 1981, 82; adolescent counselor Youth Guidance Assn., Portland, 1986-88; program dir. Youth Outreach, Vancouver, Wash., 1988-89; tchr. North Portland Bible Clubs, 1989; instr. North Portland Bible Coll., 1991—, Western Bapt. Coll., 1994—. Mem. Oreg. Gang Task Force, Portland, 1989; tchr., counselor Bridge Bible Club, Mt. Sinai Cmty. Bapt. Ch., 1990-94; coord. Bridge Gang Transition, 1993-94. Grad. fellow Western Sem., 1996. Mem. Oreg. Mediation Assn., Portland Urban League. Home: 836 N Holland St Portland OR 97217-1334

HELD, JOHN, JR., artist, curator; b. Bklyn., Apr. 2, 1947; s. Lawrence and Selma Held; children: Amanda, Nathaniel. BA, Syracuse U., 1969, MLA, 1971. Cert. libr., N.Y. Libr. Mid-York Libr. Sys., Utica, N.Y., 1975-80; art libr. Dallas Pub. Libr., 1981-95; curator Stamp Art Gallery, San Francisco, 1996-97, Modern Realism, San Francisco, 1997—; curator mail art Fine Arts Mus., Havana, Cuba, 1995; curator Bay Area Dada, San Francisco Pub. Libr., 1998. Author: Mail Art: An Annotated Bibliography, 1991, Rubber Stamp Art, 1999; artist stamps Nat. Postal Mus., Paris, 1996. Recipient Cuba travel commn. Stanley Marsh 3, 1995; travel grantee Estonia Art Soc., 1993. Avocations: mail art, performance art, writing. Office: Modern Realism PO Box 410837 San Francisco CA 94141-0837

HELDER, DAVID ERNEST, artist, educator; b. Seattle, Feb. 4, 1947; s. Reinard Wright and Maxine Edda (Spiva) H.; m. Sallye Ann Giles, Aug. 7, 1976; 1 child, Julian Oliver. AA, Yuba Coll., Marysville, Calif., 1966; BA in

Sculpture, Calif. Coll. Arts and Crafts, Oakland, 1969, MFA, 1971; MA in Aesthetic Edn., Stanford U., 1975. Aesthetic edn. and art direction cons. U. Mpls. Super Computer Inst., 1988—. San Francisco Arts Festival, 1980, Stamford (Conn.) Art Assn., 1988, Exhibited in solo shows at Wake Gallery, Cape Town, South Africa, 1972, Margaret Jensen Gallery, San Francisco, 1976, Park Gallery, San Francisco, 1977, Lyle Tuttle Gallery, San Francisco, 1979, Jaymark Gallery, San Francisco, 1981, Kristi Phippen Gallery, Modesto, Calif., 1999, Running Wild Gallery, Murphys, Calif., 1998, Lynne White Running Wild Gallery, Kristi Phippen Gallery, Modesto, Calif., 1999; group shows include San Diego Art Inst., 1988, Alligator Gallery, San Francisco, 1988, Helio Gallery, N.Y.C., 1991, Rayco Gallery, San Francisco, 1991, North East Juried Exposition, Mass., 1993, Running Wild Gallery, Murphys, Calif., 1995, 98. Address: PO Box 54 Hanalei HI 96714 Also: Lynne White Running Wild Gallery 466A Main St Murphys CA 95247

HELFER, DORIS SMALL, librarian; b. L.A., Mar. 14, 1953; d. Eddie and F. Toni (Nierenberg) Small; m. Joseph Helfer, Aug. 28, 1982; children: Alexander, Shana Beth. BA, Calif. State U., 1974; MSL, Western Mich. U., 1975. Head cataloger U. So. Calif. Law Ctr. Libr., L.A., 1975-78; from head cataloger to head tech. svc. RAND Corp., Santa Monica, Calif., 1978-92; libr. dir. AT&T Global Info. Solutions, El Segundo, Calif., 1992-96; sci. libr. Calif. State U., Northridge, 1996—. Fellow Spl. Librs. Assn. Avocations: bicycling, skiing, reading.

HELFERT, ERICH ANTON, management consultant, author, educator; b. Aussig/Elbe, Sudetenland, May 29, 1931; came to U.S., 1950; s. Julius and Anna Maria (Wilde) H.; m. Anne Langley, Jan. 1, 1983; children: Claire L., Amanda L. BS, U. Nev., 1954; MBA with distinction, Harvard U., 1956, DBA, 1958. Newspaper reporter, corr., Neuburg, Fed. Republic of Germany, 1948-52; rsch. asst. Harvard U., 1956-57; asst. prof. bus. policy San Francisco State U., 1958-59; asst. prof. fin. and control Grad. Sch. Bus. Adminstrn., Harvard U., 1959-65; internal cons., then asst. to pres., dir. corp. planning Crown Zellerbach Corp., San Francisco, 1965-78, asst. to chmn., dir. corp. planning, 1978-82, v.p. corp. planning, 1982-85; mgmt. cons., San Francisco, 1985—; co-founding dir., chmn. Modernsoft, Inc.; mem. Dean's adv. coun. San Francisco State Bus. Sch., sch. fin. Golden Gate U.; bd. dirs., past chmn. and pres. Harvard U. Bus. Sch. No. Calif.; trustee Saybrook Inst. Author: Techniques of Financial Analysis, 1963, 10th ed. 2000, Valley of the Shadow, 1997, Valuation, 1966, (with others) Case Book on Finance, 1963, Controllership, 1965; contbr. articles to profl. jours. Exch. student fellow U.S. Inst. Internat. Edn., 1950; Ford Found. doctoral fellow, 1956. Mem. Assn. Corp. Growth (past pres., bd. dirs. San Francisco chpt.), Inst. Mgmt. Cons., Commonwealth Club, Phi Kappa Phi. Roman Catholic. Home: 111 W 3rd Ave Apt 401 San Mateo CA 94402-1521 Office: 1777 Borel Pl Ste 508 San Mateo CA 94402-3514

HELFFERICH, MERRITT RANDOLPH, industry and education consultant; b. Hartford, Conn., Aug. 10, 1935; s. Reginald Humphrey and Virginia (Merritt) H.; m. Carla Anne Ostergren, July 11, 1959 (div. 1977); children: Deirdre Alida, Tryntje Bronwyn; m. April Evalyn Crosby, Aug. 24, 1985. BA, U. Alaska, 1966; MPA, Harvard U., 1990. Surveyor Golden Valley Electric Assn., Fairbanks, Alaska, 1965-66; engring. technician Geophys. Inst., U. Alaska, Fairbanks, 1966-69, field technician, rocket flight meteorologist Poker Flat Rsch. Range, 1969-76, head tech. svcs., 1976-83, asst. dir., 1986-88, assoc. dir., 1988-93; ice technician Humble Oil Co./U. Alaska, S.S. Manhattan, Northwest Passage Voyage, 1969; assoc. v.p. human resource devel. U. Alaska, Fairbanks, 1983, asst. to chancellor, 1983-86, assoc. v.p. human resource devel., 1983, dir. Elvey addition/Internat. Arctic Rsch. Ctr. project, 1994-95; exec. v.p. U. Alaska Tech. Devel. Corp., Fairbanks, 1994-97; sr. cons. Innovation Consulting, Inc., 1997—; legis. liaison U. Alaska, Fairbanks, 1983-86; adv. bd. NSF Polar Ice Coring Office, Fairbanks, 1989-94; bd. dirs. Internat. Small Satellite Orgn., Washington, Snedden Parks Found., Northern Alaska Environ. Ctr., 1994-95. Mem. editl. bd. U. Alaska Press, Fairbanks, 1986-94. Commr. Alaska Women's Commn., Juneau, 1988-89; mem., co-chair Main St. Fairbanks, 1990-94; mem. Fairbanks Native Cultural Ctr. Com., 1991-93; chair Fairbanks North Star Borough Riverfront Commn., 1992-95, mem., 1995—, vice chair, 1997—; bd. dirs. Suedden Parks Found., 1993—, Festival Fairbanks, Inc.; pres. Interior Alaska Land Trust; bd. dirs. Northern Alaska Environ. Ctr., 1994-95, 97-96, mem., 1996—, Alaska High-Tech Bus. Coun., 1995-98. Helfferich Glacier named in his honor U.S. Bd. Geographic Names, 1971; recipient Antarctic Svc. medal NSF, 1971, Nick Begich Scholarship Fund awrad, 1989, Alumni Achievement award U. Alaska Alumni Assn., 1993; elected mem. Coll. of Fellows, U. Alaska Fairbanks, 1997. Fellow Explorers Club (chair exploration com. Alaska Yukon chpt. 1991-92, chair 1995-98); mem. AAAS, Soc. Rsch. Adminstrs., Assn. Univ. Tech. Mgrs., Rotary Club of Fairbanks. Democrat. Avocations: collecting antiquarian Arctic books, hot air ballooning, sailing, hiking. Home: PO Box 80769 Fairbanks AK 99708-0769 Office: Innovation Cons Inc General Delivery Barrow AK 99723-9999

HELFORD, PAUL QUINN, communications educator, academic administrator; b. Chgo., June 27, 1947; s. Norman and Eleanor (Kwin) H.; m. Leslie Gale Weinstein, July 11, 1971; children: Ross Michael, Benjamin Keith. BA, U. Ill., 1969; MA, Northeastern Ill. U., 1977. Cert. tchr., Ill., Oreg., Ariz. Tchr. John Hersey H.S., Arlington Heights, Ill., 1969-73; freelance writer Mill Valley, Calif., 1973-75; mgr., program dir. Sta. KOZY-TV, Eugene, Oreg., 1976-88, mktg., sales, and program dir. Group W Cable, 1984-88; prodr., with mktg. Northland Broadcasting, Flagstaff, Ariz., 1989-91; lectr. cinema and broadcasting No. Ariz. U., Flagstaff, 1989—, acad. coord. for instrnl. TV, 1995-97; dir. Office for Tchg. and Learning Effectiveness, 1997—; dir. Native Am. Video Workshops, 1991—, Flagstaff Festival of the Arts Film Festival, 1992, No. Ariz. U. Instrnl. TV Programming, 1994—; writer New Times, Phoenix, 1992, Flagstaff Live!, 1996—. Writer, prodr. Paul Helford's Hollywood Oldies, 1976-81, In Review, 1981, Live from the Fair, 1981-85, Group W Cable Minutes, 1984-85, Bad Horror and Sci. Fiction, 1985 (Award for Cable Excellence 1986), KOZY movie promotional spots 1976-88 (Award for Cable Excellence 1984, 88, CLIO award nomination 1988, 1989); contbr. articles to profl. jours. Recipient CLIO award 1984, 86, Cable Mktg. Grand award, 1981, 85. Mem. Nat. Assn. Cable Programmers. Avocations: hiking, camping, biking, movies. Office: No Ariz Univ Sch Comm Box 4131 Flagstaff AZ 86011

HELGESON, DUANE MARCELLUS, retired librarian; b. Rothsay, Minn., July 2, 1930; s. Oscar Herbert and Selma Olivia (Sateren) H.; B.S., U. Minn., 1952. Librarian, Chance-Vought Co., Dallas, 1956-59, System Devel. Corp., Santa Monica, Calif., 1959-62, Lockheed Aircraft, Burbank, Calif., 1962-63, C.F. Braun Co., Alhambra, Calif., 1963-74; chief librarian Ralph M. Parsons Co., Pasadena, Calif., 1974-79; pres. Mark-Allen/Brokers-in-Info., Los Angeles, 1976-80; phys. scis. librarian Calif. Inst. Tech., Pasadena, 1980-84; corp. librarian Montgomery Watson, Pasadena, 1985-94, ret. 1994. mem. adv. bd. Los Angeles Trade Tech. Coll., 1974-79, U. So. Calif. Library Sch., 1974-79. Served with USAF, 1952-54. Mem. Spl. Libraries Assn. (chmn. nominating com. 1974). Co-editor: (with Joe Ann Clifton) Computers in Library and Information Centers, 1973. Home: 2706 Ivan Hill Ter Los Angeles CA 90039-2717

HELLEBUST, KARSTEN GENE, writer, retired business economist; b. Mohall, N.D., May 23, 1921; s. Lars M. and Anna (Drivdal) H.; m. Marjory Mae Haughton, Nov. 27, 1949; children: Ann Kristin Lueken, Kent Anders. BS, N.D. State Coll., 1943; postgrad., U. Chgo., 1946, Denver U., 1959. Purchasing agt. Hallack & Howard Lumber Co., Denver, 1948-54; sales promotion mgr. Metron Instrument Co., Denver, 1954-60; mktg. rsch. dir., pricing chief C.A. Norgren Co., Denver, 1960-69; dir. mktg. rsch. Dorr-Oliver Inc., Stamford, Conn., 1969-74; mgr. mktg. planning Berwind Corp., Phila., 1974-83; writer, rschr. Boulder, Colo., 1983—. Co-author: Book Computer (A Replacement for Logarithms), 1960, Strategic Planning Workbook, 1989, 2d edit., 1993, Spanish edit., 1991. Mem. Nat. Assn. Bus. Economists, Phi Kappa Phi, Pi Gamma Mu. Democrat. Unitarian. Avocations: mathematics, traveling, gardening.

HELLENTHAL, S. RONALD, finance company executive; b. Santa Cruz, Calif., Oct. 26, 1949. BA in Bus., Baylor U., 1969, MBA, 1975; BA in Bus., U. Air Force, Colorado Springs, Colo., 1973; postgrad., Portland State U., 1980—. Investigator, dept. def. fed. govt., 1970-73; with law enforcement county govt., 1973-75; transp. cons., 1975-78; owner Rohn Mgmt. Co., Portland, 1978-80; pres. Rohn Mgmt. Corp., Portland, 1980—, Northwest Tours, Inc., Portland, Seattle, 1984—; pres., treas. Monty D. Moore & Co., Portland, 1984—; pres. Rohn Marine Svcs., Seattle, 1986—; chmn. bd. dirs. Rohn Mgmt. Corp., Portland, Northwest Tours, Inc., Seattle; pres. N.W. Tours, Inc. Executours, Rohn Mgmt. Corp., Rohn Marine Svcs., Bar H Ranches & Cattle Co., Hellenthal & Assocs. Staff sgt., U.S. Army, 1966-70, Vietnam, USAFR ret. Mem. Nat. Tour Assn., Portland/Oreg. Visitors Assn., Seattle/King County Visitors Assn., Griffith Park Club. Democrat. Roman Catholic. Avocations: work, scuba diving, boating, sailing, flying. Office: Rohn Mgmt Corp PO Box 8637 Portland OR 97207-8637 also: 3025 SW 1st Ave Portland OR 97201-4707

HELLER, DEAN, state official; b. Castro Vly., Calif., May 10, 1960; m. Lynne Brombach, children: Hilary Anne, Harrison Clark, Andrew Dean. BS with honors, USC. Former mem. Ways & Means & Carson City Rep. Cent. Committee; former Rep. Assembly Caucus, former Nev. St. Assembly; former sr. cons. Bank of Amer.; former stockbroker, broker, trader Pac Stock Exchange; chief dep. Ofc. of St. Tex.; sec. of state State of Nev., Carson City, 1995—; Bd. dirs. Western Nev. Community Coll. Found, Boys & Girls Club. Natl. Assn. Sec. Dealers, Boy Scouts, Natl. Assn. Sec. of State. Home: 110 Plantation Dr Carson City NV 89703-5410 Office: Sec of State 101 N Carson St Ste 3 Carson City NV 89701-4786*

HELLER, JULES, artist, writer, educator; b. N.Y.C., Nov. 16, 1919; s. Jacob Kenneth and Goldie (Lassar) H.; m. Gloria Spiegel, June 11, 1947; children: Nancy Gale, Jill Kay. AB, Ariz. State Coll., 1939; AM, Columbia U., 1940; PhD, U. So. Calif., 1948; DLitt, York U., 1985. Spl. art instr. 8th St. Sch., Tempe, Ariz., 1938-39; dir. art and music Union Neighborhood House, Auburn, N.Y., 1940-41; prof. fine arts, head dept. U. So. Calif., 1946-61; vis. asso. prof. fine arts Pa. State U., summers 1955, 57; dir. Pa. State U. (Sch. Arts), 1961-63; founding dean Pa. State U. (Coll. Arts and Architecture), 1963-68; founding dean Faculty Fine Arts York U., Toronto, 1968-73; prof. fine arts Faculty of Fine Arts, York U., 1973-76; dean Coll. Fine Arts, Ariz. State U., Tempe, 1976-85; prof. art Coll. Fine Arts, Ariz. State U., 1985-90; prof. emeritus, dean emeritus, 1990—; vis. prof. Silpakorn U., Bangkok, Thailand, 1974, Coll. Fine Arts, Colombo, Sri Lanka, 1974, U. Nacional de Tucumán, Argentina, 1990, U. Nacional de Cuyo, Mendoza, Argentina, 1990; lectr., art juror; Cons. Open Studio, 1975-76; mem. vis. com. on fine arts Fisk U., Nashville, 1974; co-curator Leopoldo Méndez exhbn. Ariz. State U., Tempe, 1999. Printmaker; exhibited one man shows, Gallery Pascal, Toronto, U. Alaska, Fairbanks, Alaskaland Bear Gallery, Visual Arts Center, Anchorage, Ariz. State U., Lisa Sette Gallery, 1990, Centro Cultural de Tucumán, San Miguel de Tucumán, 1990; retrospective exhbn. Ariz. State U., Tempe, 1999; exhibited numerous group shows including Canadian Printmaker's Showcase, Pollack Gallery, Toronto, Mazelow Gallery, Toronto, Santa Monica Art Gallery, L.A. County Mus., Phila. Print Club, Seattle Art Mus., Landau Gallery, Kennedy & Co. Gallery, Bklyn. Mus., Cin. Art Mus., Dallas Mus. Fine Arts, Butler Art Inst., Oakland Art Mus., Pa. Acad. Fine Arts, Santa Barbara Mus. Art, San Diego Gallery Fine Arts, Martha Jackson Gallery, N.Y.C., Yuma Fine Arts Assn., Ariz., Toronto Dominion Centre, Amerika Haus, Hannover, Fed. Rep. Germany, U. Md., Smith-Andersen Galleries, Palo Alto, Calif., Grunewald Ctr. Graphic Arts, L.A., Univ. So. Fla., Tampa, Sheldon Meml. Gallery, Lincoln, Nebr., Santa Cruz (Calif.) Mus., Drake U., Iowa, Bradley U., Ill., Del Bello Gallery, Toronto, Honolulu Acad. Fine Arts; represented in permanent collections, Nat. Mus. Am. Art Smithsonian Instn., Washington, Long Beach Mus. Art, Library of Congress, York U., Allan R. Hite Inst. of U. Louisville, Ariz. State U., Tamarind Inst., U. N.Mex., Zimmerli Mus. Rutgers U., N.J., Can. Council Visual Arts Bank, also pvt. collections; author: Problems in Art Judgment, 1946, Printmaking Today, 1958, revised, 1972, Papermaking, 1978, 79, co-editor: North American Women Artists of the Twentieth Century, 1995, Codex Méndez, 1999; contbg. artist: Prints by California Artists, 1954, Estampas de la Revolución Mexicana, 1948; illustrator: Canciónes de Mexico, 1948; author numerous articles. Adv. bd. Continental affairs com. Americas Soc., 1983-86. With USAAF, 1941-45. Can. Coun. grantee; Landsdowne scholar U. Victoria; Fulbright scholar, Argentina, 1990. Mem. Coll. Art Assn. (Disting. Teaching of Art award 1995), Authors Guild, Internat. Assn. Hand Papermakers (steering com. 1986—), Nat. Found. Advancement in the Arts (visual arts panelist 1986-90, panel chmn. 1989, 90), Internat. Assn. Paper Historians, Internat. Coun. Fine Arts Deans (pres. 1968-69). Home: 6838 E Cheney Dr Paradise Valley AZ 85253-3525

HELLER, RONALD IAN, lawyer; b. Cleve., Sept. 4, 1956; s. Grant L. and Audrey P. (Lecht) H.; m. Shirley Ann Stringer, Mar. 23, 1986; 1 child, David Grant. AB with high honors, Univ Mich., 1976, MBA, 1979, JD, 1980. Bar: Hawaii 1980, U.S. Ct. Claims 1982, U.S. Tax Ct. 1981, U.S. Ct. Appeals (9th cir.) 1981, U.S. Supreme Ct. 1992; Trust Ter. of Pacific Islands 1982, Republic of Marshall Islands 1982; CPA, Hawaii. Assoc. Hoddick, Reinwald, O'Connor & Marrack, Honolulu, 1980-84; ptnr. Reinwald, O'Connor & Marrack, 1984-87; stockholder, bd. dirs. Torkildson, Katz, Fonseca, Jaffe & Moore, Honolulu, 1988—; adj. prof. U. Hawaii Sch. Law, 1981; arbitrator ct.-annexed arbitration program First Cir. Ct., State of Hawaii; author, instr. Hawaii Taxes. Bd. dirs. Hawaii Women Lawyers Found., Honolulu, 1984-86, Hawaii Performing Arts Co., Honolulu, 1984-93; mem. panel. of arbitrators Am. Arbitration Assn.; named NFIB Hawaii Oustanding Sml. Bus. Vol. of 1998. Actor, stage mgr. Honolulu Community Theatre, 1983-87, Hawaii Performing Arts Co., Honolulu, 1982-87. Fellow Am. Coll. Tax Counsel; mem. AICPA (mem. coun. 1994-96), ABA, Hawaii State Bar Assn. (chair tax sect. 1997-98, chair state and local tax com. 1994-95), Hawaii Soc. CPAs (chmn tax com. 1985-86, legis. com. 1987-88, bd. dirs. 1988-98, pres. 1994-95), Hawaii Women Lawyers. Office: Torkildson Katz 700 Bishop St Fl 15 Honolulu HI 96813-4187

HELLMAN, EMANUEL SCHOLEM, physician; b. N.Y.C., July 8, 1931; s. Abraham and Selma Sarah (Scholem) H.; m. Dorothea Waeder, June 8, 1956 (div. Apr. 1980); children: Deborah Hellman-Harris, Steven Emanuel; m. Sandra Younker, Apr. 2, 1983. BA in Engring. Scis. and Applied Physics summa cum laude, Harvard U., 1953, MD cum laude, 1957. Commdr. USPHS, 1959; advanced through grades to sr. asst. surgeon USPHS, Bethesda, Md.; asst. clin. prof. medicine Med. Sch. Harvard U., 1968-72; pres. Alban Med. Assocs., Tucson, Ariz., 1972—. Contbr. articles to profl. jours. Bd. dirs. Coun. Tech. and The Individual, L.A., 1985—, African Christian Relief, Tucson, 1997. Republican. Avocations: art, skiing, windsurfing. Office: Alban Med Assocs 6280 E Pima St Tucson AZ 85712-3074

HELLMAN, F(REDERICK) WARREN, investment advisor; b. N.Y.C., July 25, 1934; s. Marco F. and Ruth (Koshl) H.; m. Patricia Christina Sander, Oct. 5, 1955; children: Frances, Patricia H., Marco Warren, Judith. BA, U. Calif., Berkeley, 1955; MBA, Harvard U., 1959. With Lehman Bros., N.Y.C., 1959-84, ptnr., 1963-84; exec. mng. dir. Lehman Bros., Inc., N.Y.C., 1970-73; pres. Lehman Bros., Inc., 1973-75; ptnr. Hellman Ferri Investment Assocs., 1981-89, Matrix Ptnrs., 1981—; chmn. Hellman & Friedman LLC, San Francisco; bd. dirs. DN & E Walter, Levi Strauss & Co., Il Fornaio (Am.) Corp., Franklin Resources, Inc., Sugar Bowl Corp., PowerBar, Inc., Young & Rubicam Holdings, Inc., VIVRA Splty. Ptnrs.; chmn. com. on jobs; chmn. Hellman & Friedman, LLC; hon. trustee The Brookings Inst. Chmn. bd. trustees The San Francisco Found. Mem. Bond Club, Piping Rock Club, Century Country Club, Pacific Union Club. Office: Hellman & Friedman LLC 1 Maritime Plz Fl 12 San Francisco CA 94111-3404

HELLON, MICHAEL THOMAS, tax consultant; b. Camden, N.J., June 24, 1942; s. James Bernard and Dena Louise (Blackburn) H.; BS, Ariz. State U., 1972; m. Toni L. Carson; 3 children. Ins. investigator Equifax, Phoenix, 1968-69; exec. v.p. Phoenix Met. C. of C., 1969-76; ins. co. exec. Londen Ins. Group, 1976-78; pres. Hellon and Assocs., Inc., 1978—; small claims hearing officer Pima County Justice Ct., 1990—; mem. Pima County Bd. Adjustments, 1993—; nat. def. exec. res. U.S. Dept. of Commerce, 1986—; with Inst. Property Taxation, 1988—; bd. dirs. Equity Benefit Life Ins. Co., Modern Income Life Ins. Co. of Mo., First Equity Security Life Ins. Co., Tucson Classics. Mem. Ariz. Occupational Safety and Health Adv. Council, 1972-76, mem. Speaker's Select Com. Auto Emissions, 1976; Phoenix Urban League, 1972-73, Area Manpower Planning Council, 1971-72, Phoenix Civic Plaza Dedication Com., 1972, Phoenix Air Quality Maintenance Task Force, 1976. Pres. Vis. Nurse Service, 1978-79; Rep. precinct capt., 1973—; state campaign dir. Arizonans for Reagan Com., 1980; alt. del. Rep. Nat. Conv., 1980, 84, 88; mem. staff Reagan-Bush Nat. Conv., 1984. campaign mgr. for various candidates, 1972-82; mem. Rep. state exec. com., 1989—; mem. Rep. Nat. Com., 1992—. Bd. dirs. ATMA Tng. Found., 1981-84. Served with USAF, 1964-68. Decorated Bronze Star medal, Purple Heart. Recipient George Washington Honor medal Freedom's Found., 1964; commendation Fed. Bar Assn., 1973. Mem. U.S. C. of C. (pub. affairs com. western div. 1974-76), Inst. of Property Taxation, Internat. Assn. Assessing Officers, U.S. Dept. Commerce Exec. Res., Ariz. C. of C. Mgrs. Assn. (bd. mem. 1974-76), Tucson C. of C. Club: Trunk 'N Tusk; Catalina Soccer (bd. dirs. 1984-88). Home: 5775 N Camino Real Tucson AZ 85718-4213 Office: PO Box 65405 Tucson AZ 85728-5405*

HELLYER, CONSTANCE ANNE (CONNIE ANNE HELLYER), writer, musician; b. Puyallup, Wash., Apr. 22, 1937; d. David Tirrell and Constance (Hopkins) H.; m. Peter A. Corning, Dec. 30, 1963 (div. 1977); children: Anne Arundel, Stephanie Deak; m. Don W. Conway, Oct. 12, 1980. BA with honors, Mills Coll., 1959. Grader, rschr. Harvard U., Cambridge, Mass., 1959-60; rschr. Newsweek mag., N.Y.C., 1960-63; author's asst. Theodore H. White and others, N.Y.C., 1964-69; freelance writer, editor Colo., Calif., 1969-75; writer, editor Stanford (Calif.) U. Med. Ctr., 1975-79; comm. dir. No. Calif. Cancer Program, Palo Alto, 1979-82, Stanford Law Sch., Palo Alto, 1982-97; mgr., vocalist String of Pearls Band, 1991—. Founding editor (newsletters) Insight, 1978-80, Synergy, 1980-82, Stanford Law Alum, 1992-95; editor (mag.) Stanford Lawyer, 1982-98; contbr. articles to profl. jours. and mags. Recipient silver medal Coun. for Advancement and Support Edn., 1985, 89, award of distinction dist. VII, 1994. Mem. No. Calif. Sci. Writers Assn. (co-founder, bd. dirs. 1979-93), Phi Beta Kappa. Democrat. Avocations: singing, piano. Home: 2080 Louis Rd Palo Alto CA 94303-3451

HELM, GEORGE NEVILLE, III, limousine company executive; b. Union City, Tenn., Nov. 4, 1954; s. George Neville and Nancy Lee (Stokes) H.; m. Lana A.; children: Nicholas Aaron, Jonathan Grant. BS in Bus., Ark. State U., 1976. Cert. fin. planner; registered investment advisor; profl. pub. speaker. Mktg. rep. Equitable Life Assurance Soc.of U.S., Lowell, Ark., 1976-77; dist. asst. Equitable Life Assurance Soc.of U.S., 1977-80; sales mgr. John Hancock Fin. Svcs., Little Rock, 1980-82; reg. mgr. John Hancock Fin. Svcs., 1982-84; dir. agencies John Hancock Fin. Svcs., Boston, 1984-86; pres., mortgage banking and real estate fin. specialist Helm & Assocs, Las Vegas, Nev., 1986-96; pres. Elite Limousine & Bodyguardsman Svcs. Inc., Las Vegas, Nev., 1995—. Contbr. articles to profl. jours. Mem. Internat. Assn. Fin. Planners, Internat. Bd. Stds. & Practices for Cert. Fin. Planners, Greater Boston Soc. of Inst. Cert. Fin. Planners. Mem. Ch. of Christ. Office: 3100 Sirius Ave Las Vegas NV 89102-0401

HELMER, M(ARTHA) CHRISTIE, lawyer; b. Portland, Oreg., Oct. 8, 1949; d. Marvin Curtis and Inez Bahl (Corwin) H.; m. Joe D. Bailey, June 23, 1979; children: Tim Bailey, Bill Bailey, Kim Easton. BA in English magna cum laude, Wash. State U., 1970; JD cum laude, Lewis & Clark Coll., 1974; LLM in Internat. Law, Columbia U., 1998. Bar: Oreg. 1974, U.S. Supreme Ct. 1975, U.S. Ct. Appeals (9th cir.) 1975. Assoc. Miller Nash, Portland, 1974-81, ptnr., 1981—; mem. Oreg. Bd. Bar Examiners, Portland, 1978-81; del. 9th Cir. Jud. Conf., 1984-87, mem. exec. com., 1987-90. Author: Arrest of Ships, 1985. Mem. ABA, Oreg. Bar (mem. bd. govs. 1981-84, treas. 1983-84), Maritime Law Assn., Internat. Bar Assn., Pacific N.W. Internat. Trade Assn. (bd. dirs., mem. exec. com.), Multnomah Athletic Club, Phi Beta Kappa. Avocations: antiques, travel, fashion. Office: Miller Nash 111 SW 5th Ave Ste 3500 Portland OR 97204-3699

HELMUTH, PHILIP ALAN, tax consultant; b. Alhambra, Calif., Dec. 29, 1965; s. Melvin I. and Elsie (Borkholder) H. Student, MiraCosta Coll., 1985-89, Palomar Coll., 1989-90. Data entry operator Melco Bus. Svc., Vista, Calif., 1980-83, bookkeeper, 1983-91, ptnr., tax cons., 1992-95, owner, 1995—; bookkeeper Underwater Schs. of Am., Oceanside, 1985-86; owner, notary pub. Vista, 1987—; owner Melco Bus. Svcs., Vista, 1995—; registered rep. H.D. Vest Fin. Svcs. Mem. Nat. Notary Assn. (com. mem. editl. adv. com. 1990-93, pub. image com. 1990-93), Nat. Assn. Enrolled Agts., Calif. Soc. Enrolled Agts. (Palomar chpt. dir. 1995-96, 2d v.p. 1996-98), Escondido Grad. Spokesman Club (sec. 1991-92, pres. 1992-93, treas. 1993-95). Avocations: singing, collecting compact discs, reading history, science fiction. Office: Melco Bus Svc Ste 102 410 S Santa Fe Ave Vista CA 92084-6163

HELWING, GERALDINE MARLENE, psychologist, psychoanalyst, psychoneuroimmunologist; b. Milw., Apr. 5, 1947; d. William Frederick and Olga Wilhelmina (Syring) Helwig; m. Ian Robinson, June 23, 1969; children: Rya (dec.), Chelsea Siobhán Antoinette, Krystal Georgiana Victoria, Lisa Ralet. BA in Psychology, U. Wis.-Stout, 1970, MSE in Sch. Psychology, 1975. Lic. psychologist, Minn. Research assoc., psychotherapist N.W. Psychiat. Clinic, Eau Claire, Wis., 1974-77; pvt. practice psychology and psychotherapy Eau Claire, 1977-79; ptnr. Inst. Psychol. Therapies, Mpls., 1980-84; owner psychol. practice Robinson and Assoc., Mpls., 1984-88; cons., writer Seattle, 1988—; adj. asst. prof. counseling and psychol. services St. Mary's Coll. Grad. Ctr., Mpls., 1987-88; psychoanalytic preceptorship Interpersonal/Sullivanian Analysis with J.M. Tobin, M.D., Eau Claire, 1970-77; cons.; expert witness; pub. speaker, guest on TV and radio shows; allied profl. staff mem. St. Joseph's Hosp., Chippewa Falls, Wis., 1978-80; mem. med. research staff Sacred Heart Hosp., Eau Claire, 1974-77; co-owner, v.p. computer software mfg. co. Interactive Analytic Node, 1985-87. Contbr. articles to profl. jours.; author research papers presented to various profl. orgns. Co-founder, official spokesperson, chmn. tng. com., vol. Disaster Stress Team, Twin Cities ARC and Minn. Network for Disaster Stress Intervention MNDSI, 1985-88; vol. instr. and moderator ARC North Star Disaster Tng. Inst., 1987-88; organizer Minn. Assn. Mental Health Infants; organizer, v.p. pregnancy and drug prevention, intervention and edn. Concerned, Inc., Menomonie, Wis., 1971-73; bd. dirs. Geriatric Day Care Ctr., Luth. Hosp., Eau Claire, 1975-77; vol., organizer, chairperson mentoring program Partnership Edn. and South Whidbey Island Schs., Washington. Mem. Group-Without-A-Name (GWAN) Internat. Psychiat. Research Soc., Inst. Noetic Scis., Internat. Soc. Human Ethology, Internat. Assn. Infant Mental Health (bd. dir. 1988—), Wis. Assn. Infant Devel. (steering com. 1977-79), Minn. Women Psychologists, Minn. Assn. Mental Health of Infants, Midwest Assn. Comatose Care (v.p. 1984-85, pres. 1985-88), Minn. Inst. Noctoric Scis., Clan Gunn Soc. N.Am., Zonta Internat. (corp., gallery fund-raising coms. 1983-84; chair svc. com. 1984-85, co-chair 1985-86, co-chair corp. collection com. 1985-86, status of women com. 1987—, initiated orgn. with high sch. women, mentoring program for local chpt.). Lodge: Zonta (corp., gallery fund-raising coms. 1983-84; chair service com. 1984-85, co-chair 1985-86; co-chair corp. collection com. 1985-86, status of women com. 1987—, initiated orgn. with high sch. women, mentoring program for local chpt.). Avocations: Tae Kwondo Karate (Red Belt), painting, music, geneaology, writing. Home and Office: PO Box 1087 Freeland WA 98249-1087

HELZER, RICHARD BRIAN, artist, educator; b. Hastings, Nebr., Aug. 27, 1943; s. Donald H. and Kathryn (Korslund) H.; m. Kathryn Ann Drown, June 19, 1965; 1 child, Joel Richard. B.A., Kearney Sate Coll., 1965; M.F.A., U. Kans., 1969. Tchr., Topeka Pub. Schs., Kans., 1965-68; mem. faculty Mont. State U., Bozeman, 1970—, prof., 1982—, dir. Sch. Art, 1982—. One-man shows include: Synopsis Gallery, Chgo., C.M. Russell Mus., Great Falls, Mont., Am. Crafts Mus., 1984, Yellowstone Art Ctr., 1984; group shows Schmuck Mus., Pfortzheim, Fed. Republic Germany, 1979, Pyramid Gallery, Rochester, N.Y., 1983, Radford (Va.) Coll., 1986; represented in permanent collections C.M. Russell Mus. Nat. Endowment Arts fellow, 1976; Western States Arts fellow, 1978. Mem. Soc. N.Am. Goldsmiths (founding; bd. dirs.) Home: 52 Hitching Post Rd Bozeman MT 59715-9241 Office: Mont State U Sch of Art Bozeman MT 59717

HEMANN, RAYMOND GLENN, research company executive; b. Cleve., Jan 24, 1933; s. Walter Harold Marsha Mae (Colbert) H.; BS, Fla. State U., 1957; postgrad. U.S. Naval Postgrad. Sch., 1963-64, U. Calif. at Los Angeles, 1960-62; MS in Systems Engring., Calif. State U., Fullerton, 1970, MA in Econs., 1972, cert. in tech. mgmt. Calif. Inst. Tech., 1990; m. Lucile Tinnin Turnage, Feb. 1, 1958; children: James Edward, Carolyn Frances; m. Pamela Lehr, Dec. 18, 1987. Aero. engring. aide U.S. Navy, David Taylor Model Basin, Carderock, Md., 1956; analyst Fairchild Aerial Surveys, Tal-

lahassee, 1957; research analyst Fla. Rd. Dept., Tallahassee, 1957-59; chief Autonetics div. N.Am. Rockwell Corp., Anaheim, Calif., 1959-69; v.p., dir. R. E. Manns Co., Wilmington, Calif., 1969-70; mgr. Avionics Design and Analysis Dept. Lockheed-Calif. Co., Burbank, 1970-72, mgr. Advanced Concepts div., 1976-82; gen. mgr. Western div. Arinc Research Corp., Santa Ana, 1972-76; dir. Future Requirements Rockwell Internat., 1982-85; dir. Threat Analysis, Corp. Offices, Rockwell Internat., 1985-89; pres., chief exec. officer Advanced Systems Rsch., Inc., 1989—; adj. sr. fellow Ctr. Strategic and Internat. Studies, Washington, 1987—; bd. dirs. Fla. State U. Rsch. Found., 1995—, bd. dirs. Assn. Mgmt. Svc. Inc.; bd. dirs., pres. Associated Aviation, Inc., 1980-96; chmn. adv. coun. Coll Engring. Fla State U./Fla. A&M U., 1995—; cons. to dir. Ctrl. Intelligence, Nat. Intelligence Coun., Nat. Air Intelligence Ctr., Inst. Def. Analyses, Battelle Meml. Inst., Ctr. Strategic and Internat. Studies; sec., bd. dirs. Calif. State U., Fullerton, Econs. Found.; mem. naval studies bd. panels NAS, 1985—, Arms Control Working Group; chmn. indsl. panel Nat. Labs. Infrastructure Study, Office Sec. Def., 1995; chmn. indsl. panel Future Dirs. Mil. Aeronautics Study, 1996; asst. prof. ops. analysis dept. U.S. Naval Postgrad. Sch., Monterey, Calif., 1963-64, Monterey Peninsula Coll., 1963; instr. ops. analysis Calif. State U., Fullerton, 1963, instr. quantitative methods, 1969-72; program developer, instr. systems engring. indsl. rels. ctr. Calif. Inst. Tech., 1992-96; lectr. Brazilian Navy, 1980, U. Calif., Santa Barbara, 1980, Yale U., 1985, Princeton U., 1986, U.S. Naval Postgrad. Sch., 1986, Ministry of Def., Taiwan, Republic of China, 1990; Calif. Inst. Tech. Assocs., 1992—; mem. exec. forum Calif. Inst. Tech., 1991—; Chmn. comdr.'s adv. bd. CAP, Calif. Wing; reader Recording for the Blind, 1989—. With AUS, 1950-53. Syde P. Deeb scholar, 1956; recipient honor awards Nat. Assn. Remotely Piloted Vehicles, 1975, 76; named to Hon. Order Ky. Cols., 1985. Comml., glider and pvt. pilot. Fellow AAAS, AIAA (assoc.); mem. IEEE, Ops. Rsch. Soc. Am., Air Force Assn., N.Y. Acad. Scis., Assn. Old Crows, L.A. World Affairs Coun., Phi Kappa Tau (past pres.). Episcopalian. Contbr. articles to profl. jours. and news media. Office: Advanced Sys Rsch Inc 33 S Catalina Ave Ste 202 Pasadena CA 91106-2426

HEMION, DWIGHT ARLINGTON, television producer, director; b. New Haven, Mar. 14, 1926; s. Dwight Arlington and Bernice Ruby (Berquist) H.; m. Katherine Bridget Morrissy, Sept. 1, 1973; children—Katherine, Dwight Gustav. Student pub. schs., Verona, N.J. Asso. dir. ABC-TV, N.Y.C., 1946-49; TV dir. Tonight Show, NBC-TV, N.Y.C., 1950-60; dir. Perry Como TV show, N.Y.C., 1960-67; producer/dir. Yorkshire Prodns., N.Y.C., 1967-70; producer/dir. TV spls. in assn. with ATV, London; producer/dir. Smith-Hemion Prodns., Los Angeles, 1976-90, v.p., 1990—. Dir.: Frank Sinatra: A Man and His Music, 1965 (Emmy award TV Acad. Arts and Scis.); The Sound of Burt Bacharach, 1969, Singer Presents Burt Bacharach, 1970, Barbra Streisand and Other Musical Instruments, 1973, Steve and Eydie-Our Love is Here to Stay, 1975, America Salutes Richard Rodgers: The Sound of His Music, 1976, Bette Midler-Ol' Red Hair is Back, 1977, Ben Vereen ... His Roots, 1977, Steve and Eydie Celebrate Irving Berlind, 1978, IBM Presents Baryshinikov on Broadway, 1979 (Emmy award), Goldie and Kids ... Listen to Us!, 1982 (Emmy award), Sheena Easton...Act I, 1983 (Emmy award), Anne Murray's Winter Carnival...From Quebec, 1984, 4 Emmy Award Shows, 15 Christmas in Wasington shows, 6 TV Acad. Hall of Fame shows, Neil Diamond Hello Again, opening cermemonies Liberty Weekend, Barbra Streisand One Voice, We The People Contitutional Gala, Julie Andrews the Sound of Christmas, All Star Salute to Our Troops, Barbra Streisand...The Concert, Disney's Young Musicians Symphony Orchestra, Disney's American Teachers Awards, 50th, 51st Presdl. Inaugural Galas, numerous other tv spls., events. Served in AC U.S. Army, 1944-46. Named Dir. of Year in TV Dirs. Guild Am., 1965. Mem. Purcival Country Club. Office: Smith-Hemion Prodns Inc Box 15 1438 N Gower St Los Angeles CA 90028-8383*

HEMMERDINGER, WILLIAM JOHN, artist; b. Burbank, Calif., July 7, 1951; s. William John Jr. and Eileen Patricia (Fitzmaurice) H.; m. Catherine Lee Cooper, Aug. 8, 1981. Student Art Ctr. Coll. Design, 1967-69, Nat. Palace Mus., Taiwan, 1973; AA, Coll. of Desert, 1971; BA, U. Calif.-Riverside, 1973; MFA, Claremont Grad. Sch., 1975, PhD, 1979; postgrad. Harvard U., 1977. Curator Calif. Mus. Photography, 1973-74; instr. Coll. of Desert, 1974-79, 80-84, Calif. State U., Long Beach, 1979-80, Otis Art Inst. Parsons Sch. Design, 1979-80, U. Calif., Riverside, 1981-82; vis. artist, lectr. sculpture and environ. design Calif. State Summer Sch. for Arts, Calif. Inst. for Arts, Valencia, 1989; vis. prof. of art Pomona Coll., Claremont, Calif., 1990-92; co-owner Hemmerdinger Fine Art and Appraisal, Palm Desert, Calif. One-man shows include Cirrus Editions, Ltd., 1982, 84, Brand Libr. and Art Ctr., Glendale, Calif., 1991, Old Selectmen's Bldg. Gallery, West Barnstable, Mass., 1995, 96, 97, 98; group shows include NAD, N.Y.C., Whitney Mus. Am. Art, N.Y.C., UNESCO Mus., Paris, Am. Watercolor Soc., N.Y.C., L.A. County Mus. Art, Boyusan Citizens Hall, Internat. Contemporary Art Fair, Olympic Arts Festival, L.A., 1984, Seoul Korea, 1988; works in permanent collections Mus. Contemporary Art, L.A., Tate Gallery, London, Smithsonian Instn., Washington, Mobil Oil Co., N.Y.C., Fed. Reserve Bank, San Francisco, Cape Internet, Osterville, Mass. Recipient Calif. Nat. Watercolor Soc. award, 1974, 1979, Lifetime Achievement award La Quinta Arts Found., 1991; Ford Found. grantee, 1979; NEA grantee, 1979, NEH grantee, 1980. Mem. Nat. Watercolor Soc. (v.p. 1981-82, 83). Contbr. articles to profl. jours. Home: 43-409A Martini Ct Palm Desert CA 92260

HEMMINGS, PETER WILLIAM, orchestra and opera administrator; b. London, Apr. 10, 1934; s. William and Rosalind (Jones) H.; m. Jane Frances Kearnes, May 19, 1962; children—William, Lucy, Emma, Rupert, Sophie. Grad. Gonville and Caius Coll., Cambridge, 1957; LL.D. (hon.), Strathclyde U., Glasgow, 1978. Clk., Harold Holt Ltd., London, 1958-59; planning mgr. Sadlers Wells Opera, London, 1959-65; gen. adminstr. Scottish Opera, Glasgow, 1962-77; gen. mgr. Australian Opera, Sydney, 1977-79; mng. dir. London Symphony Orch., 1980-84; gen. dir. Los Angeles Music Ctr. Opera Assn., 1984—; gen. mgr. New Opera Co., London, 1956-65, dir. Royal Acad. Music; gen cons. Compton Verney Opera Project. Served to lt. Brit. Signal Corps, 1952-54. Decorated Order Brit. Empire. Fellow Royal Scottish Acad. Music, Royal Acad. Music (hon.); mem. Am. Friends of Sadlers Wells (pres. 1994—), Internat. Assn. Opera Dirs., 1977-79, Opera Am. (vice chmn.), Garrick Club (London). Anglican. Home: 775 S Madison Ave Pasadena CA 91106-3831 Office: LA Music Ctr Opera 135 N Grand Ave Los Angeles CA 90012-3013

HEMP, WILLIAM (BILL) HENRY, writer, artist; b. St. Louis, May 3, 1928; s. Norman William and Mary Katherine (Wendler) H.; m. Margaret Missett Collins, Sept. 10, 1960; children: William, Brendan, Joseph, Christopher. BS in Bus. Adminstrn., St. Joseph's U., 1950. Mem. plans and merchandising staff N. W. Ayer & Son, Inc., Phila., 1954-58; mem. mktg. promotion staff Young & Rubicam, N.Y.C., 1960-65; idea cons. Stanley Arnold & Assocs., N.Y.C., 1965-78; creative dir. Burson-Marsteller, N.Y.C., 1978-92; pub. rels. dir. Exceptional Books, Ltd., Los Alamos, N. Mex., 1996-97; program dir. Taos (N. Mex.) County Hist. Soc., 1997—; free lance writer Burston-Marsteller Pub. Rels., N.Y.C., 1993-98; host (public television show) Let's Talk About Taos. Author, illustrator: (books) New York Enclaves, 1975, If Ever You Go to Dublin Town, 1976, Taos Landmarks and Legends, 1996. With USN, 1950-54. Mem. Taos County Hist. Soc. (program dir. 1996-98), Taos Lions Club (pub. rels. dir. 1997-98). Roman Catholic. Avocations: swimming, biking, hiking, kayaking, travel. Home: 121 Hewlett Ave Point Lookout NY 11569 also: PO Box 2665 Taos NM 87571

HEMPHILL, WILLIAM ALFRED, III, marketing executive; b. Pitts., Mar. 3, 1949; s. William Alfred II and Virgie Mae (Fisher) H.; m. Sandra Lynn von Lohen, Feb. 17, 1973; 1 child, Michelle Elise. BS, USAF Acad., 1972; postgrad., Air Force Squadron Officer's Sch., 1977, Ariz. State U., 1981-85; Exec. Masters in Bus. Admin., Claremont Grad. U., 1992; postgrad., Air Force Command and Staff Coll., 1997. Commd. 2d lt. USAF, 1972, advanced through grades to capt., 1976; radar navigator SAC USAF, Blytheville AFB, Ark., 1974-77; B-52 radar navigator SAC USAF, Rapid City, S.D., 1977-79; resigned regular USAF, 1979; maj. USAFR, 1988, area res. liaison officer, 1988-96; wings res. coord., 1996-97; retired USAFR, 1998; mktg. rep. Sperry Def. Systems, Phoenix, 1979-82, Sperry Space Div., Phoenix, 1982-83; product devel. mgr. Motorola Govt. Electronics Group, Tempe, Ariz., 1983-84; mktg. dir. Conrac SCD Div., Duarte, Calif., 1984-88; cons. Upland, Calif., 1988; nat. sales mgr. TEAC Am., Inc., Montebello, Calif., 1989-92; mktg. mgr. Mekel Engring, Walnut, Calif., 1992-94; venture devel. mgr. Thermo Tech. Ventures, Idaho Falls, 1994-96; deputy program mgr. TTV, Idaho Falls, 1996—. Author: (with other); A Programmable Display Generator System, 1982. Position paper writer Rep. Nat. Com., 1980; pres. bd., performer Concert Dance Theater, 1988-92; mem. West End Rep. Club, Ontario, Calif.; vestry mem. St. Mark's Episc. Ch., Upland, Calif., 1988-91, dir. Homeless Shelter, 1988-91. Mem. Am. Mgmt. Assn., Tech. Mktg. Soc. Am., Air Force Assn., USAF Acad. Grad. Assn. Episcopalian. Lodge: Elks. Avocations: golf, tennis, jogging.

HEMRY, LARRY HAROLD, former federal agency official, writer; b. Seattle, Jan. 4, 1941; s. Harold Bernard and Florence Usborne (Achilles) H.; m. Nancy Kay Ballantyne, July 10, 1964 (div. Apr. 1976); children: Rachel Dalayne, Aaron Harold, Andrew LeRoy. BA, Seattle Pacific Coll., 1963; postgrad., Western Evang. Sem., Portland, Oreg., 1969, 70. Ordained to ministry Free Meth. Ch., 1968. Clergyman Free Meth. Ch., Vancouver, B.C., Can., 1963-64, Mt. Vernon, Wash., 1968-69; clergyman Colton (Oreg.) Community Ch., 1969-71; edit clk. Moody Bible Inst., Chgo., 1964-66; pres., founder Bethel Enterprises, Colton, 1969-71; immigration insp. U.S. Immigration and Naturalization Svc., Sumas, Wash., 1972-96. Author, historian: Some Northwest Pioneer Families, 1969, The Hemry Family History Book, 1985; author: An Earnest Plea to Earnest Christians, 1969. chmn. com. to establish and endow the James A. Hemry meml. scholarship fund Seattle Pacific U., 1975. Fellow Seattle Pacific U. (Centurians Club); mem. The Nature Conservancy, The Sierra Club, The Audubon Soc. Avocations: camping, nature study, woodcarving. Home: PO Box 532 Sumas WA 98295-0532

HENAGER, CHARLES HENRY, civil engineer; b. Spokane, Wash., July 11, 1927; s. William Franklin and Mary Agnes (Henry) H.; m. Dorothy Ruth Parker, May 6, 1950; children: Charles Henry, Jr., Donald E., Roberta R. BS in Civil Engring., Wash. State U., 1950. Registered profl. engr., Wash. Instrumentman Wash. State Dept. Hwys., Yakima, 1950-52; engr. Gen. Electric Co., Richland, Wash., 1952-62; shift supr., reactor GE, Richland, Wash., 1962-63, sr. engr., 1963-65; sr. devel. engr. Battelle Pacific N.W. Labs., Richland, 1965-68, sr. rsch. engr., 1968-90, ret., 1990. Contbr. articles to profl. jours.; patentee in field. With USN, 1945-46. Fellow Am. Concrete Inst. (tech. activities com. 1987-89, Del Bloem award 1986), ASTM (subcom. 1980-92), ASCE (pres. Columbia sect. 1961-62); mem. Kennewick Swim Club (pres. 1962-63), Village at Canyon Lakes Assn. (v.p. 1998, bd. dirs. and mem. archtl. control com. 1996-98), Sigma Tau, Tau Beta Pi, Phi Kappa Phi. Republican. Methodist. Avocations: stamp and coin collecting, calligraphy, genealogy. Home: 3413 S Huntington Loop Kennewick WA 99337-2572

HENCH, PHILIP KAHLER, physician; b. Rochester, Minn., Sept. 19, 1930; s. Philip Showalter and Mary Genevieve (Kahler) H.; m. Barbara Joan Kent, July 10, 1954; children: Philip Gordon, John Kahler, Amanda Kent. BA, Lafayette Coll., 1952; MD, U. Pitts., 1958; MSc in Medicine, U. Minn., 1965. Dir. emeritus staff & alumni affairs Scirpps Clinic Med. Group; intern U. Colo. Med. Ctr., 1958-59; fellow in medicine and rheumatology Mayo Graduate Sch., Rochester, Minn., 1959-63; with Inst. for Arthritis and Metabolic Diseases, NIH, Bethesda, Md., 1963-64; asst. div. rheumatology Scripps Clinic and Rsch. Found., La Jolla, Calif., 1965-66, assoc., 1966-70, assoc. mem., 1970-74, mem., head, 1974-82, sr. cons., 1982—, adj. asst. mem. dept. neuropharmacology, mem. dept. acad. affairs; asst. clin. prof. U. Calif. Sch. Medicine, San Diego; cons. to pharm. cos.; mem. People to People Mission to China on study of Aging. Contbr. articles on rheumatic diseases, pain and sleep disorders to profl. jours.; mem. editorial com. Rheumatism Revs., 1974-84; editorial reviewer Arthritis and Rheumatism, Jour. Rheumatology, 1985—; bd. spl. cons. Patient Care mag., 1987—. Mem. bd. advisors San Diego Opera; mem. U. Calif. San Diego Police Dept. Sr. Vol. Program. Recipient Arthritis Found. award (6), San Diego chpt., 1971-80; Philip S. Hench scholar Mayo Grad. Sch. Medicine, 1965. Fellow ACP, Am. Coll. Rheumatology (chmn. nonarticular rheumatism study group 1975-82, com. on preventive and rehab. medicine 1984-85, com. on rheumatologic practice 1975-77); mem. AMA, Nat. Soc. Clin. Rheumatologists (pres. 1997-99), Am. Pain Soc., Calif. Med. Assn., Internat. Assn. for Study Pain, La Jolla Acad. Medicine (pres. 1994-96), Arthritis Found (bd. govs. San Diego chpt., Best Doctors in Am. award 1992-93, 94-95, 96-97), San Diego Hist. Soc., San Diego Mus. Fine Arts, San Diego Opera (bd. advisors). Republican. Avocations: music, swimming, hiking, biking, skiing. Fax: 619-453-0113. Home and Office: 7856 La Jolla Vista Dr La Jolla CA 92037-3530

HENDERSON, ALFY, computer technician, writer; b. Lockhart, Tex., Dec. 8, 1936; s. Walter Henry and Reathy (Breelove) H.; children: Michael Anthony, Meshon Annette. TV technician Bruno's TV, San Antonio, 1963-68, MBC Cable & TV, San Francisco, 1968-69, TV Lab, San Francisco, 1970-75; owner A&J TV, San Francisco, 1975-76; TV technician Renta-Color TV, Carson, Calif., 1979-81; technician Edwards Co., Burbank, Calif., 1986-88. Author: Man-Time and the Universe, 1996. Baptist. Avocations: golf, bowling, science books. Home: 323 W 4th St Apt 408 Long Beach CA 90802-2866 OFFICE: PO Box 1471 Long Beach CA 90801-1471

HENDERSON, CHRISTOPHER LEE, electrical engineer; b. Long Beach, Calif., May 6, 1963; s. James Taylor and Grace Jean (Stringer) H.; m. Teri Lynette Mock, Feb. 21, 1987; 1 child, Jeremy Taylor. BS in Physics, N.Mex. Tech. U., 1985; MSEE, U. N.Mex., 1990. Reliability engr. Honeywell Corp., Albuquerque, 1985-88; prin. mem. tech. staff Sandia Nat. Labs., Albuquerque, 1988—; mem. com. JEDEC EIA, Washington, 1993-97. Contbr. articles to profl. jours. Recipient R & D award I R & D Mag., Chgo., 1995, Tech. Transfer award of Excellence, Fed. Lab. Consortium, Atlanta, 1995; finalist Software Author of Yr. award N.Mex. Entrepreneur's Assn., Albuquerque, 1998. Avocations: skiing, weather. Office: Sandia Nat Labs PO Box 5800 Albuquerque NM 87185-0100

HENDERSON, JAI, museum director. Exec. dir. Calif. Afro-Am. Mus., L.A. Office: Calif Afro-Am Mus Expedition Park 600 State Dr Los Angeles CA 90037-1267*

HENDERSON, JAMES, JR., former senator; b. Ganado, Ariz., May 16, 1942; m. Deborah Henderson; children: Valencia, Clarissa, Jaime Jamesina, Marcus. Cert. in career counseling, Utah State U., 1962. Employment svcs. mgr. Ariz. Dept. Econ. Security-Employment Svcs., Phoenix, 1968-74; vocat. devel. specialist Bur. Indian Affairs, Ft. Defiance, Ariz., 1974-77; dir. divsn. resources The Navajo Tribe, 1977-84, dir. office legis. affairs, 1986-90; senator State of Ariz., 1990-98. With U.S. Army, 1966-68. Decorated Purple Heart; recipient Feed My People Internat. award, 1990, Outstanding Svc. award Navajo Nat. Coun. Resolution, 1990, Chief Manuelito Appreciation award Navajo Tribal Coun. Democrat. Presbyterian. Avocations: boxing, football, wildlife, travel. Office: PO Box 3899 Window Rock AZ 86515-3348*

HENDERSON, JOE H., lawyer, mediator, arbitrator, college dean; b. Pangburn, Ark., Apr. 14, 1936; s. John H. and Nancy L. (Johnston) H.; m. Marian Jones, July 31, 1965 (div. Feb. 1978); 1 child, James H.; m. Linda Gaye Bertucelli, Mar. 21, 1981; stepchildren: Jason, Daniel. BA in Pub. Adminstrn., Calif. State U., Sacramento, 1960; JD, Lincoln U., 1968. Bar: Calif. 1971. Budget and mgmt. analyst Sacramento County, 1960-64; asst. dir. pub. works Marin County, San Rafael, Calif., 1964-66; asst. city mgr. City of Santa Rosa (Calif.), 1966-71; dean sch. of law Empire Coll., Santa Rosa, 1989-97; pvt. practice Santa Rosa, 1971-97; arbitrator, mediator, 1997—. Recipient 1 of 7200 Best Attys. in U.S. award Steven Naifeh & Gregory White Smith, 1987. Mem. Nat. Acad. Arbitrators. Avocation: fishing. E-mail: joehh@sonic.net. Office: PO Box 463 Santa Rosa CA 95402-0463

HENDERSON, KAREN SUE, psychologist; b. Bloomington, Ill., Mar. 25, 1946; d. Charles Lewis and Faye Lanore (Wantland) Henderson; m. David Thomas Biggs, Dec. 2, 1967 (div. 1972); m. Dean Eugene Dixon Jr., Jan. 13, 1973 (div. 1995); children: Christopher, Matthew; m. William Wayne Riggs, May 19, 1998. BA, U. Calif., Berkeley, 1966; MS, San Jose (Calif.) State Coll., 1971; PhD, Union Inst., 1991. Lic. clin. psychol., Alaska; cert. C.C. tchr.; registered play therapist and supr. Pvt. practice clin. psychology, pvt. practice, Anchorage, 1980—; adj. prof. U. Alaska, Anchorage, 1994-95; cons. Alaska Youth and Parent Found., Anchorage, 1989—, Kenai Peninsula Counseling Svcs., 1995—, Parents United, Anchorage, 1989; mental health cons. Rural Alaska Community Action Program, Anchorage, 1988; cons., mem. adolescent treatment team Charter North Hosp., Anchorage, 1985-88; cons. Infant Impaired Hearing Program, Anchorage, 1984-85, Parent Tng. Ctr., Anchorage, 1980-82; psychiat. social worker Langdon Psychiat. Clinic, Anchorage, 1976-80; instr. in psychology U. Alaska Community Coll., Anchorage, 1974-81; parole agt. narcotic outpatient program State Dept. Corrections, Oakland, Calif., 1972-74; group counselor II, caseworker Alameda County Probation Dept., Oakland, Calif., 1971-72; adj. prof. U. Alaska, Anchorage, 1999—; cons. psychologist Alviso (Calif.) Econ. Devel. Program, 1971-72; instr. psychology Coll. of Alameda, 1973; faculty adv. for coop. edn. U. Alaska C.C., 1975-76. Sec., liaison to bd. Susitna Sch. PTA, Anchorage, 1983-84; co-chmn. optional bd. Susitna Sch., 1984-85, chmn., 1985-86, vol. coord., 1988-89; mem. adv. bd. Steller Alt. Sch., 1992-95. Mem. APA, Alaska Psychol. Assn. Democrat. Avocations: running, reading, camping, travel, bridge. Office: 912 W 6th Ave Anchorage AK 99501-2024

HENDERSON, MARK GORDY, lawyer; b. Berkeley, Calif., Feb. 21, 1954; s. John Nelson and Shirley Belle (Queen) H.; m. Elizabeth Andrea Fulmer, June 24, 1978; children: Emily MacCaughey, James Ellis. BA, U. of the Pacific, 1976, JD, 1981, LLM in Bus. and Tax, 1985. Bar: Calif. 1981, U.S. Ct. Appeals (9th cir.) 1985, U.S. Dist. Ct. (ctrl. dist.) Calif. 1988, U.S. Dist. Ct. (ea. dist.) Calif. 1992; cert. specialist in estate planning, trust and probate law. Ptnr. Hiroshima, Jacobs & Roth, Sacramento, 1981-91; pvt. practice law Davis, Calif., 1991—. Exec. dir. Citizens Who Care, Inc., Davis. Mem. Calif. State Bar Assn. (estate planning, trust and probate law sect.), Yolo County Bar Assn., Order of the Coif. Office: Ste 9 429 F St Davis CA 95616-4150

HENDERSON, MARSHA ROSLYN THAW, clinical social worker; b. San Antonio, Dec. 31, 1946; d. Eugene and Ann (Pokloff) Thaw; m. Thomas Jay Henderson, July 14, 1976; 1 child, Ashley Erin. BA, U. Houston, 1968, MSW, 1973. Lic. clin. social worker, Calif.; diplomate Am. Bd. Examiners in Clin. Social Work. Intake worker St. Joseph's Mid Houston Community Mental Health Ctr., 1968-69; caseworker II, Tex. Rsch. Inst. Mental Scis., Houston, 1969-71; pvt. practice, Houston, 1971-73; psychiat. social worker Intercommunity Child Guidance Ctr., Hawaiian Gardens, Calif., 1974-75; clin. social worker Family Guidance Ctr., Buena Park, Calif., 1975-77; pvt. practice, Laguna Hills, Calif., 1976—; exec. dir. Adoption Info. and Resource Ctr., 1997; art therapy workshops Calif. State U., L.A., 1977, U. Calif., Irvine, 1980; ct. apptd. 730-731 child custody evaluator; adj. prof. Grad. Sch. Social WorkU. So. Calif. (Irvine)., 1998—. Med. social work Mission Hosp. Regional Med. Ctr., Mission Viejo, Calif., 1998—. Mem. NASW, Acad. Cert. Social Workers, Calif. Soc. for Clin. Social Worker, Am. Adoption Congress, Calif. Forensic Mental Health Assn., Child Sexual Abuse Network. Avocations: art, music, sailing, bicycling, travel. Office: 25301 Cabot Rd #116 Laguna Hills CA 92653

HENDERSON, SHARLENE OTTESEN, special education educator; b. Salt Lake City, Sept. 9, 1954; d. Elmo Earl and Shirley Dean (Langdorf) Ottesen; m. Kim E. Henderson, Sept. 11, 1975; children: Arlo Patrick, Patience Ann. BS in Spl. Edn., U. Utah, 1986, MEd in Spl. Edn., 1993. Cert. moderate to severe disabilities, hearing impairments, and mild to moderate disabilities. Tchr. East H.S., Salt Lake City, 1985—, Children's Behavior Therapy Unit, Salt Lake City, 1989—; asst. and family support trainer Project TURN-Autism Tchg. Home, Salt Lake City, 1984-88; cons. Autism and behavioral cons. Residential Svcs. Inc., Salt Lake City, 1989-94; cons. Autism secondary curriculum Edn. Svc. Ctr., Richardson, Tex., 1994—; cons., tutor, Salt Lake City, 1989—; pvt. tutor for hearing impaired students, 1993—. United Way coord. East H.S., 1989-94; assn. rep. Salt Lake Tchr.'s Assn., East H.S., 1994-95; mem. East H.S. Improvement Coun., 1994-95, East H.S. Comty. Coun., 1994-95. Mem. Coun. for Exceptional Children, Salt Lake Sch. Dist. Spl. Edn. Improvement Coun., Salt Lake Sch. Dist. Spl. Edn. Comty. Coun. (chair 1992—), Autism Soc. Utah. Avocations: raising and riding horses, making porcelain dolls, gardening, sewing, reading. Office: East H S 840 S 1300 E Salt Lake City UT 84102-3716

HENDERSON, THELTON EUGENE, federal judge; b. Shreveport, La., Nov. 28, 1933; s. Eugene M. and Wanzie (Roberts) H.; 1 son, Geoffrey A. B.A., U. Calif.-, Berkeley, 1956, J.D., 1962. Bar: Calif. 1962. Atty. U.S. Dept. Justice, 1962-63; assoc. firm FitzSimmons & Petris, 1964, assoc., 1964-66; directing atty. San Mateo County (Calif.) Legal Aid Soc., 1966-69; asst. dean Stanford (Calif.) U. Law Sch., 1968-76; ptnr. firm Rosen, Remcho & Henderson, San Francisco, 1977-80; judge U.S. Dist. Ct. (no. dist.) Calif., San Francisco, 1980-90, chief judge, 1990-97; asso. prof. Sch. Law, Golden Gate U., San Francisco, 1978-80. Served with U.S. Army, 1956-58. Mem. ABA, Nat. Bar Assn., Charles Houston Law Assn. Office: US Dist Ct US Courthouse PO Box 36060 San Francisco CA 94102

HENDREN, MERLYN CHURCHILL, investment company executive; b. Gooding, Idaho, Oct. 16, 1926; d. Herbert Winston and Annie Averett Churchill; student U. Idaho, 1944-47; B.A. with honors, Coll. of Idaho, 1986. m. Robert Lee Hendren, June 14, 1947; children—Robert Lee, Anne Aleen. With Hendren's Furniture Co., Boise, 1947-69; co-owner, v.p. Hendren's Inc., Boise, 1969-87, pres. 1987—. Bd. dirs. Idaho Law Found., 1978-84; chmn. Coll. of Idaho Symposium, 1977-78, mem. adv. bd., 1981—; bd. dirs. SW Idaho Pvt. Industry Council, 1984-87; pres. Boise Council on Aging, 1959-60, mem. adv. bd., 1986—; mem. Gov.'s Commn. on Aging, 1960, Idaho del. to White House Conf. Aging, 1961; trustee St. Luke's Regional Hosp., 1981-92; mem. adv. bd. dirs. Boise Philharm. Assn., Inc., 1981—, Ballet Idaho; bd. dirs. Children's Home Soc. Idaho, 1988; founding pres. Idaho Congl. Award Program, 1993—; sustaining mem. Boise Jr. League. Mem. Boise C. of C. (bd. dirs. 1984-87), Gamma Phi Beta. Episcopalian. Home: 3504 Hillcrest Dr Boise ID 83705-4503 Office: PO Box 9077 Boise ID 83707-3077

HENDREN, ROBERT LEE, JR., academic administrator; b. Reno, Oct. 10, 1925; s. Robert Lee and Aleen (Hill) H.; m. Merlyn Churchill, June 14, 1947; children: Robert Lee IV, Anne Aleen. BA magna cum laude, Coll. Idaho, LLD (hon.); postgrad., Army Univ. Ctr., Oahu, Hawaii. Owner, pres. Hendren's Inc., 1947—; pres. Albertson Coll. Idaho, Caldwell, 1987—; bd. dirs. 1st Interstate Bank Idaho. Trustee Boise (Idaho) Ind. Sch. Dist., chmn. bd. trustees, 1966; chmn. bd. trustees Coll. Idaho, 1980-84; bd. dirs. Mountain View coun. Boy Scouts Am., Boise Retail Merchants, Boise Valley Indsl. Found., Boise Redevel. Agy., Ada County Marriage Counseling, Ada County Planning and Zoning Com.; chmn. bd. Blue Cross Idaho. Recipient Silver and Gold award U. Idaho, Nat. award Sigma Chi. Mem. Boise C. of C. (pres., bd. dirs.), Idaho Sch. Trustees Assn., Masons, KT, Shriners, Rotary (Paul Harris fellow). Home: 3504 Hillcrest Dr Boise ID 83705-4503 Office: Albertson Coll Idaho 2112 Cleveland Blvd Caldwell ID 83605-4432

HENDRICK, JAMES T., lawyer; b. Fostoria, Ohio, Mar. 21, 1942. BA with honors and distinction in econs., U. Ill., 1963; JD, Harvard U., 1967. Bar: Ill. 1967, Calif. 1970. Ptnr. Thelen, Marrin, Johnson & Bridges, San Francisco, 1978—. Mem. Ill. Bar Assn. Office: Thelen Marrin Johnson & Bridges Two Embarcadero Ctr San Francisco CA 94111*

HENDRICK, R. EDWARD, medical physicist, researcher, educator; b. Ft. Worth, Sept. 11, 1946; s. Max Hendrick and Enid (Kimes) Thurston; m. Jean R. Paquelet, Oct. 5, 1996; children: Erin G. Hendrick, Laura Shaffer, Dean Shaffer. BA, Hendrix Coll., BS, Columbia U., 1969; PhD, Rockefeller U., 1975. Diplomate Am. Bd. Radiology. Rsch. physicist Carnegie-Mellon U., Pitts., 1975-78; asst. prof. St. Bonaventure (N.Y.) U., 1978-81, assoc. prof., 1981-82; postdoctoral fellow U. Colo. Health Scis. Ctr., Denver, 1982-84, asst. prof., 1984-89, assoc. prof., chief radiol. scis., 1989-97, prof., chief radiol. scis., 1997—; co-chair panel on quality determinants in mammography Agy. for Health Care Policy and Rsch., Bethesda, Md., 1992-94; mem. nat. mammography quality assurance adv. com. FDA, Rockville, Md., 1994-98. Author: ACR Mammography Quality Control Manuals, 1990, 92, 94, 99, Clinical Practice Guideline # 13: Quality Determinants in Mammography, 1994; editor: MRI Principles and Artifacts, 1993. Fellow Soc. for Magnetic Resonance Imaging (treas. 1986-88, pres. 1990-91), Soc. Breast Imaging, Am. Coll. Radiology, Am. Assoc. of Physicists in Medicine. Achievements include early rsch. on clin. applications of magnetic resonance imaging and digital mammography; developed the Am. Coll. of Radiology's

mammography, stereotactic biopsy, and MRI accreditation programs; performed research and education and developed quality assurance techniques that have improved the quality of MRI and mammography in the U.S. Office: U Colo Hlth Scis C278 4200 E 9th Ave Denver CO 80220-3706

HENDRICKS, ALBERT J., national park service executive. Supt. Crater Lake (Oreg.) Nat. Park. Office: Crater Lake Nat Park PO Box 7 Crater Lake OR 97604-0007*

HENDRICKS, JON ALBERT, college dean, educator; b. Kellogg, Idaho, Jan. 18, 1943; s. Grover A. and Wilma Irene (Davenport) H.; m. Hazel O'Rear Reeves, Dec. 27, 1988. BA, U. Wash., 1966; MA, U. Nev., 1968; PhD, Pa. State U., 1971. Prof. U. Ky., Lexington, 1971-88; dept. chair Oreg. State U., Corvallis, 1988-95, dean, 1995—. Author: Aging in Mass Society, 1977, 81, 87, Reminiscence and Life Review, 1995, Ties of Later Life, 1996; editor: Society and Aging, 1988-98. Chair Cmty. Alliance for Diversity, City County Univ., Corvallis, 1993-96; bd. dirs. Non-profit Svc., Corvallis, 1994-95. Recipient Disting. Career Contrbn. award Gerontol. Soc. Am., 1994, Rschr. of Yr. award Sci. Rsch. Soc., Corvallis, 1994, Kalish Innovative Pub. award Gerontol. Soc. Am., 1998. Mem. Assn. for Gerontology in Higher Edn. (pres. 1996—), Sigma Xi. Office: Oregon State U 229 Strand Corvallis OR 97331-2221

HENDRIX, LOUISE BUTTS, retired educator, author; b. Portland, Tenn., June 16, 1911; d. Luther Edward and Johnny Henrietta (McNeill) B.; m. Edwin Alonzo Hendrix, Aug. 1, 1934 (dec. May 1991); children: Lynette Louise, Edwin Alonzo Jr. AB, Chico (Calif.) State Coll., 1932; postgrad., Sacramento State U., 1934-62, Coll. Pacific, 1934-62; Diploma of merit, U Delle Arti, Parma, Italy, 1982. Tchr. jr. high sch. Rio Vista, Calif., 1932-34; newspaper worker Chico Enterprise, 1930-32; tchr. jr. high sch. Alpaugh, Calif., 1944-45; newspaper corr. Sacramento Bee, Marysville Appeal Dem., Live Oak, Calif., 1945-52, Oroville Mercury Register Marysville Appeal Dem., Biggs, Calif., 1935-40; tchr. jr. high sch. Live Oak, 1952-69; ret., 1969. Author: Better Reading and Writing with Journalism, 1974, Sutter Buttes-Land of Histum Yani, 1980, 6th edit., 1992, Petals and Blossoms, 1983, Squaw Man, 1987; contbr. poetry to profl. jours. Mem. Sutter County Parks and Recreation Commn., Yuba City, 1977-80; founder Save Sutter Buttes Assn., Inc., Yuba City, 1978, sec., treas., 1978-90. Recipient Poet of Yr. award World Congress Poets, Orlando, Fla., 1986, Gold Poet award World of Poetry Conv., Anaheim, Calif., 1988. Fellow Internat. Poetry Soc.; mem. AAUW, Calif. Retired Tchrs. Assn., Sierra Club (Conservationist of Yr. 1974), Woman's Club (pres. Yuba City chpt. 1978-79). Democrat. Roman Catholic. Avocations: golf, bicycling, travel, bridge. Home: Covell Gardens 1111 Alvarado Ave #249 Davis CA 95616

HENKEL, CATHY, newspaper sports editor. Office: The Seattle Times 1120 John St Seattle WA 98109-5321

HENLEY, ERNEST MARK, physics educator, university dean emeritus; b. Frankfurt, Germany, June 10, 1924; came to U.S., 1939, naturalized, 1944; s. Fred S. and Josy (Dreyfuss) H.; m. Elaine Dimitman, Aug. 21, 1948; children: M. Bradford, Karen M. B.E.E., CCNY, 1944; Ph.D., U. Calif. at Berkeley, 1952. Physicist Lawrence Radiation Lab., 1950-51; research assoc. physics dept. Stanford U., 1951-52; lectr. physics Columbia U., 1952-54; mem. faculty U. Wash., Seattle, 1954—; prof. physics U. Wash., 1961-95; prof. emeritus, 1995—; chmn. dept. U. Wash., 1973-76, dean Coll. Arts and Scis., 1979-87, dir. Inst. for Nuclear Theory, 1990-91; assoc. dir. Inst. for Nuclear Theory U. Wash., 1991—; rschr., author numerous publs. on symmetries, nuclear reactions, weak interactions and high energy particle interactions; chmn. Nuclear Sci. Adv. Com., 1986-89. Author: (with W. Thirring) Elementary Quantum Field Theory, 1962, (with H. Frauenfelder) Subatomic Physics, 1974, 2nd edit. 1991, Nuclear and Particle Physics, 1975. Bd. dirs. Pacific Sci. Ctr., 1984-87, Wash. Tech. Ctr., 1983-87; trustee Associated Univs., Inc., 1989—, chmn. bd., 1993-96. Recipient sr. Alexander von Humboldt award, 1984, T.W. Bonner prize Am. Physics Soc., 1989, Townsend Harris medal CCNY, 1989; F.B. Jewett fellow, 1952-53, NSF sr. fellow, 1958-59, Guggenheim fellow, 1967-68, NATO sr. fellow, 1976-77. Fellow AAAS (chmn. physics sect. 1989-90), Am. Phys. Soc. (chmn. div. nuclear physics 1979-80, pres. 1992), Am. Acad. Arts and Scis.; mem. NAS, Sigma Xi. Office: Univ Wash Physics Dept PO Box 351560 Seattle WA 98195-1560

HENLEY, JEFFREY O., computer software company executive; b. Phoenix, Nov. 6, 1948; s. Justin Oniel and Jane Ellen (Rice) H.; children: Amy, Julie, Todd. B.A., U. Calif.-Santa Barbara, 1966; M.B.A., UCLA, 1967. Cost acctg. supr. Hughes Aircraft Co., Culver City, CA, 1967-70; div. controller Tridair Industries, Redondo Beach, Calif., 1970-72, Fairchild Camera & Instrument, Mountain View, Calif., 1972-75; dir. fin. Memorex Corp., Santa Clara, Calif., 1975-79; v.p., controller Saga Corp, Menlo Park, Calif., 1979-86; exec. v.p., CFO Saga Corp, Menlo Park, 1986-91, Pacific Holding Co., Menlo Park, Calif., 1986—; pres. Fast Service Restaurant Group, Menlo Park, Calif., from 1985; exec. v.p., CFO Oracle Corp., Redwood City, Calif. Bd. dirs. Herbert Hoover Boys' & Girls' Club, Menlo Park, Calif., 1983, pres., 1984—. Mem. Fin. Exec. Inst., Sigma Phi Epsilon. Republican. Presbyterian. Avocations: golf, running. Home: 51 Monte Vista Ave Atherton CA 94027-5430 Office: Oracle Corp 500 Oracle Pkwy # 5 OP 6 Redwood City CA 94065-1675

HENLEY, RICHARD MERLE, business developer, marketing executive, producer, director; b. Portland, Oreg., Mar. 15, 1952; s. Roy Flanders and Grayce (Roatch) H. AA, Barstow (Calif.) Jr. Coll.; BA, Calif. State U., Long Beach, 1974, postgrad., 1975. Cert. Level V water treatment specialist. Adminstr., drug counselor, supr. Narconon U.S., L.A., 1974-75, nat. adminstr., 1976-77; founder Northland Purewater Inc. (and predecessors), Hollywood and Los Feliz, Calif., 1975-81; exec. dir., then chief exec. officer, chmn. bd. dirs. Northland Purewater Inc. div. Northland Environ. Inc., Burbank, Calif., 1981-88, founder Northland Mfg. Purewater div., 1985; pres., founder RMH Internat. Trading Co., Burbank, 1988—; founder Water Fresh Purity Systems, Inc., Burbank, 1989-91, RMH TV Prodns., Burbank, 1990—; chmn. nat. dealer bd. Sunland Industries, Phoenix, 1983-84; advisor, bd. dirs. Narconon Internat., 1986—. Inventor water processing and treatment systems. Chmn. pub. rels. com. Solar Energy Industries Assn., Washington, 1984-85; mem. Crusade for Religious Freedom, 1985—, Way to Happiness Found., 1985—, Narconon Get Am. Off Drugs, L.A, 1983—. Mem. Nat. Fed. Ind. Businesses, Calif. Assn. Lic. Contractors, Concerned Businessmen Assn., Water Quality Assn., W.I.S.E., Hollywood C. of C., Founders Circle Inc. 500 Coun. of Growing Companies. Republican. Avocations: skiing, writing, lecturing, flying, video and film work. Office: RMH Prodn & Broadcasting 1317 N San Fernando Blvd # 267 Burbank CA 91504-4236

HENNE, ANDREA RUDNITSKY, business educator; b. Phila., Sept. 11, 1952; d. Isadore and Florence (Sanders) Rudnitsky; m. Lawrence Michael Henne, May 27, 1984; children: Laura Joy, Michael Andrew. BS, Temple U., 1974; MA in Edn., UCLA, 1975, EdD, 1983. Prof. L.A. City Coll., 1975-90; dir. curriculum devel. Bridges Learning Ctr., Solana Beach, Calif., 1992-94; instr. San Diego Mesa Coll., 1995-98; web mgr./on-line edn. coord. Calif. Sch. Profl. Psychology, 1999—; bus. cons., San Diego, 1994—. Author: Intensive Records Management, 4th edit., 1998. Vol. Solana Beach Elem. Sch., San Diego, 1990—, Girl Scouts U.S.A., San Diego, 1995—. Edn. Professions Devel. Act fellow UCLA, 1975; named Outstanding Young Careerist, Bus. and Profl. Women, L.A., 1979. Mem. ASCD, Assn. Records Mgmt. and Adminstrn., Inc., Nat. Bus. Edn. Assn., Calif. Bus. Edn. Assn. (sec., v.p. and pres. 1976-79), Delta Pi Epsilon. Avocations: studying piano, computers, aerobics.

HENNEMAN, STEPHEN CHARLES, counselor; b. Chgo., June 17, 1949; s. Charles Philip Jr. and Marion Louise (Eichberger) H.; m. Patrica Ann York, Feb. 14, 1975 (div. Sept. 1980); 1 child Charles Philip III; m. Marion Jean McDermand, Oct. 4, 1980; stepchildren: Ervin F. Schrock Jr., Lisa Ann Schrock, Thomas M. Schrock. BA in Journalism, Colo. State U., 1971; MA in Counseling, U. N.D., 1987. Commd. 2d lt. USAF, 1971, advanced through grades to maj., 1984; missile launch officer 570th Strategic Missile Squadron, Davis Monthan AFB, Ariz., 1972-76; info. officer 321st Strategic Missile Wing, Grand Forks AFB, N.D., 1976-79; missile combat crew flight comdr. 446th Strategic Missile Squadron, Grand Forks AFB, 1980-82; missile combat crew comdr. evaluator 321st Strategic Missile Wing, Grand Forks AFB, 1982, wing nuclear surety officer, 1982-83, chief weapon safety branch, 1983-85; asst. ops. officer 320th Strategic Missile Squadron, F E Warren AFB, Wyo., 1985-86; dep. wing inspector 90th Strategic Missile Wing, F E Warren AFB, 1986-88; ops. officer 319th Strategic Missile Squadron, F E Warren AFB, 1988-89; dep. chief war res. materiel div. Hdqrs. U.S. Air Forces in Europe, Ramstein Air Base, Fed. Republic Germany, 1989-92; vol. and outreach coord. Safe House/Sexual Assault Svcs., Inc., Cheyenne, Wyo., 1992-93; quality control investigator Dept. Employment State of Wyoming, Cheyenne, 1993-95; counselor Wyo. State Penitentiary, Rawlins, 1995-96, counseling team leader, 1996-97; residential counselor Aurora (Colo.) Cmty. Mental Health Ctr., 1997—. Advocate, counselor Safehouse/Sexual Assault Svcs., Inc., Cheyenne, 1985-89; sec., bd. dirs. Carbon County Citizens Organized to See Violence Ended, 1996-97. Mem. ACA, Am. Mental Health Counselors Assn., Colo. Counselors Assn. Avocations: photography, popular music recordings collecting, reading.

HENNESSEY, ALICE ELIZABETH, forest products company executive; b. Haverhill, Mass., May 24, 1936; d. H. Nelson and Elizabeth E. (Johnson) Pingree; A.B. with honors, U. Colo., 1957; cert. with distinction Harvard-Radcliffe Program in Bus. Adminstrn., 1958; m. Thomas M. Hennessey, June 13, 1959; children—Shannon, Sheila, Thomas N. With Boise Cascade Corp. (Idaho), 1958—, sec. to pres., 1958-60, adminstrv. asst. to pres., 1960-61, 65-71, corp. sec., 1971—, v.p., 1974-82, sr. v.p., 1982-96; pres., CEO Idaho Cmty. Found., 1996—. Bd. dirs. Boise Pub. Libr. Found., U. Idaho Found.; sustaining mem. Boise Jr. League; mem. Phi Beta Kappa, Alpha Chi Omega. Office: Boise Cascade Corp PO Box 50 Boise ID 83728-0050

HENRY, DAVID ALLEN, advertising executive; b. Cedar Rapids, Iowa, Apr. 16, 1950; s. Don Albert and Anna Mae (Manwiller) H.; m. Elise Marie Cohen, June 7, 1981 (div. Apr. 1988); children: Lauren, Erica, Sylvia. BBA, U. Iowa, 1972. V.p. mktg. Movie Systems, Inc., Denver, 1975-77; chmn., chief exec. officer Henry Gill Advt., Denver, 1977—; mem. bd. advisors Entrepreneurial Inst. Denver, 1989. Bd. dirs. Direction 2,000 Found., Littleton, Colo., 1990-93, Littleton Pub. Schs. Found., 1993—; nat. advisor White House Conf. for Drug-Free Am., Washington, 1988. Recipient Award of Merit, United Way Mile High Child Care, Denver, 1988, Cert. of Appreciation, Communities for Drug-Free Colo., 1989, Sch. Restructuring Program, Gov. of Colo., 1990, Cert. of Merit, Keep Denver Beautiful, 1990. Mem. Am. Mktg. Assn., Am. Assn. Advt. Agys. (mem. western bd. govs. 1988-92, chmn. bd. dirs. Rocky Mountain Coun. 1988), Denver Advt. Fedn. (bd. dirs. 1987-91), Denver Press Club, Greater Denver C. of C. (mem. bd. advisors 1990, Cert. of Appreciation 1989). Avocations: reading, skiing, scuba diving, golf, travel. Office: Henry Gill Advt 1225 17th St Ste 2500 Denver CO 80202-5525

HENRY, ERNESTYNE ETHEL THATCH, educational administrator; b. St. Louis, July 19, 1917; d. Clarence Hardwill and Evelena (Thompson) Thatch; m. Horace McKinley Henry, Sept. 1, 1942; children: John Harvey McKinley, Joan Marcille Vernadette. U. Ark., 1938, 1936; BS, 1940; MS, U. Ill., 1950; postgrad. various colls. including, U. N.Mex., U. Colo., Colo. State U., U. Santa Clara, U. Denver, 1954-84. Tchr. Ft. Smith (Ark.) pub. schs., 1940-42; with Civil Svc., Denver, 1942-43; tchr. East St. Louis (Ill.) pub. schs., 1947-52; diagnostic and prescriptive coordinator Denver pub. schs., 1952-84; ret.; asst. prin. Fairview Elem. Sch., Denver, 1961-62; founder, dir. Thatch Enterprises, Denver, 1989—; lectr. U. Colo., summer 1959. Contbr. articles to profl. jours. Precinct com. Dem. Party, Denver, 1953-78, voter registration staff, 1952—. Mem. U. Ark. Pine Bluffs Alumni Assn. (bd. dirs. 1978—, Outstanding Alumni), AAUW (v.p. 1986-87), Nat. Coun. Negro Women (v.p.), United Teaching Profession (bldg. rep. 1980-84), Internat. Rels. Club (treas. 1970-89), Opera Colo., Top Ladies of Distinction (charter pres. 1989—), U. Ill. Alumni Assn., Lioness Club (treas. 1990), Phi Delta Kappa, Sigma Gamma Rho (bd. dirs. 1963-65, 69-75). Democrat. Methodist. Avocations: travel, drama, bridge. Office: Thatch Enterprises 1044 Downing St Apt 207 Denver CO 80218-2959

HENRY, FRANCES ANN, journalist, educator; b. Denver, July 23, 1939; d. Lewis Byford and Betsy Mae (Lancaster) Patten; m. Charles Larry, June 28, 1963 (div. May 1981); children: Charles Kevin, Tracy Diane. BA in English, Carleton Coll., 1960; MA in Social Sci., U. Colo., Denver, 1988; MA in Journalism, Memphis State U., 1989. Cert. tchr. Lang. arts tchr. Rolla (Mo.) Pub. Schs., 1963-66; journalism tchr. Douglas County Pub. Schs., Castle Rock, Colo., 1976—, chmn. English dept., 1992-97; mng. editor Douglas County News-Press, Castle Rock, 1986-87; editor Fourth World Bulletin, 1988; exec. editor Daily Helmsman Memphis State U., 1988-89, gen. mgr. Daily Helmsman, 1991-92. Contbr. articles to profl. jours. Recipient Gov.'s award for excellence in edn. Colo. Endowment for Humanities, 1997. Mem. ACLU, Colo. Lang. Arts Soc., Colo. H.S. Press Assn. (sec. 1981-83, pres. 1983-91, bd. dirs., named Colo. Journalism Tchr. of Yr. 1985), Mensa, Kappa Tau Alpha. Democrat. Episcopalian. Office: Douglas County II S 2842 Front St Castle Rock CO 80104-9496

HENRY, JOSEPH, orchestra director; b. Toledo, Ohio, Oct. 10, 1930; s. Thomas and Kathleen (Whyte) H.; m. Evelyn H. (Hipona), Jan. 1, 1995. MusB, Eastman Sch. of Music, 1952, MusM, 1953, D Musical Arts, 1965. Condr. Hillel Little Symphony, Rochester, NY, 1948-53; instr. in music U. Wis., Stevens Point, 1955-57; condr., music dir. Utica (N.Y.) Symphony, 1962-66; condr., prof. SUNY, Oswego, 1967-79; condr., prof., dir. orchs. Ohio U., Athens, 1979-83; music dir. Bay View Festival Chamber Orch., summers 1981, 82, 83; condr., prof. East N.Mex. U., Portales, 1983-85; music dir. Southwest Symphony, 1984-94; music. Missoula (Mont.) Symphony Orch., 1985; music dir. Philharmonia NM, Carlsbad, N.Mex., 1994—; prof. music U. Mont., Missoula; music theory clinician Am. Symphony Orch. League, Mpls., 1990. Composer orchestral work Chromophon, 1970. Sgt. U.S. Army, 1953-55. Fulbright grantee U.S. Inst. Edn., Vienna, Austria, 1957-59. Mem. Condrs.' Guild (bd. dirs. 1992—, chair awards com. 1997—). Avocations: gardening. Office: U Mont Music Dept Missoula MT 59812

HENRY, KAREN HAWLEY, lawyer; b. Whittier, Calif., Nov. 5, 1943; d. Ralph Hawley and Dorothy Ellen (Carr) Hawley; m. John Dunlap, 1968; m. Charles Gibbons Henry, Mar. 15, 1975; children: Scott, Alexander, Joshua; m. Don H. Phemister, June 21, 1991; children: Justin Phemister, Jonathan Phemister, Keith Phemister. BS in Social Scis., So. Oreg. Coll., 1965; MS in Labor Econs., Iowa State U., 1967; JD, U. Calif., Hastings, 1976. Instr., Medford (Oreg.) Sch. Dist., 1965-66; rsch. asst. dept. econs. Iowa State U., Ames, 1966-67; dir. rsch. program Calif. Nurses Assn., San Francisco, 1967-72; labor rels. coord. Affiliated Hosps. of San Francisco, 1972-79; labor coun. Affiliated Hosps. of San Francisco,1976-88; ptnr. Littler, Mendelson, Fastiff & Tichy, San Francisco, 1979-86; labor counsel Affiliated Hosps. of San Francisco, 1979-88; mng. ptnr. labor and employment law Weissburg and Aronson, Inc., San Francisco, 1986-89; prin. Karen H. Henry, Inc., Auburn, Calif., 1991—. Author: Health Care Supervisor's Legal Guide, 1984, Nursing Administration Law Manual, 1986, ADA: Ten Steps to Compliance, 1992, 4th edit., 1998; editl. bd. Health Care Supervisor; contbr. articles on employment law issues to profl. jours. Mem. Calif. Soc. Health-care Attys. (bd. dirs. 1986-87, pres. 1987-88), Am. Hosp. Assn. (ad hoc labor atty. com.), State Bar of Calif. (labor law sect.), Thurston Soc., Order of Coif. (law jour.). Office: Karen H Henry Inc 1141 High St Auburn CA 95603-5132

HENRY, KEITH DOUGLAS, architect; b. Winnipeg, Man., Can., Oct. 25, 1957; s. Charles Eric and Ruth Elva (McDonald) H.; m. Elizabeth Anne McNulty, June 19, 1993. B of Environ. Studies, U. Man., Winnipeg, 1978, MArch, 1982. Design architect Ferguson Folstad Friggstad Architects, Saskatoon, Regina, Sask., Can., 1982-86; assoc. ptnr. Folstad & Friggstad Architects, Saskatoon, 1986-92; ptnr. Friggstad Downing Henry Architects-Wilson Bailey Tech., Saskatoon, 1992—. Prin. works include John Paul II Collegiate (Award of Merit Sask. Assn. Architects 1991), Bedford Rd. Collegiate (City of Sask. Heritage award 1996), Can. Nat. Inst. Blind Svc. Ctr. (Award of Excellence Sask. Masonry Inst. 1993). Recipient Marion M. Graham Collegiate award Am. Assn. Sch. Adminstrs./AIA, 1985, Heritage award City of Saskatoon, 1996. Mem. Royal Archtl. Inst. Can., Sask. Assn. Architects (registered, mem. coun. 1993—, pres. 1995-96), North Saskatoon Bus. Assn., Aurum Club. Avocation: travel. Office: Friggstad Architects, 2233 Avenue C North, Saskatoon, SK Canada S7L 5Z2

HENRY, MICHAEL FITZROY, psychotherapist; b. Port of Spain, Trinidad, Sept. 14, 1949; came to U.S., 1970; s. Francis and Vilma R. (Haynes) H.; m. Margaret J. Baker, May 30, 1976; 1 child, Anthony. AA, Walla Walla (Wash.) C.C., 1972; BA, Whitman Coll., 1975, Whitworth Coll., 1983; PhD, Pacific Western U., 1994. Diplomate Am. Acad. Forensic Counseling; nat. cert. group psychotherapist. Counselor Carondelet Psychiat. Ctr., Richland, Wash., 1976-78, Luth. Family Svcs., Kennewick, Wash., 1989—; pvt. practice Richland, 1989—; cons. Juvenile Justice Ctr., Kennewick, 1983—; tchr. Leadership Inst. Seattle, 1991-92. Mem. NAACP, Tri Cities, Wash., 1984—. Mem. Am. Assn. Marriage and Family Therapy, Am. Counseling Assn., Nat. Assn. of Drug and Alcohol Counseling, Assn. for the Treatment of Sex Abusers, Exch. Club Am. (Mem. of Yr. award 1993). Office: PO Box 429 Richland WA 99352-0429

HENRY, NEIL R., data communications product manager; b. Manchester, Conn., Aug. 25, 1962; s. John James and Patricia Scully Henry; m. Diana Santoro, Sept. 20, 1993; children: Amelia Santoro, Eliza Catherine. BS, Northeastern U., Boston, 1985. Investment analyst First Stage/Zero Stage Capital, Cambridge, Mass., 1983-87; bus. devel. mgr. Octocom Systems, Inc., Wilmington, Mass., 1987-88; product mgr. Octocom Systems, INc., Wilmington, 1990-92; gen. mgr. GEM Tech. Inc., Melbourne, Fla., 1988-90; product mktg. mgr. Telebit, Sunnyvale, Calif., 1993; product mgr. 3Com Corp., Santa Clara, Calif., 1994—; mem. Churchill Group, Palo Alto, Calif., 1993-98. Avocations: running, bicycling. Office: 3Com Corp 5400 Bayfront Plz Santa Clara CA 95054-3600

HENRY, PAUL, political organization administrator. Chmn. Nev. Dem. Party, Las Vegas. Fax: (702) 765-7109. Office: Nev Dem Party 3790 South Paradise Rd Ste 130 Las Vegas NV 89109*

HENRY, PHILIP LAWRENCE, marketing professional; b. Los Angeles, Dec. 1, 1940; s. Lawrence Langworthy and Ella Hanna (Martens) H.; m. Claudia Antonia Huff, Aug. 9, 1965 (div. 1980); children: Carolyn Marie, Susan Michelle; m. Carrie Katherine Hoover, Aug. 23, 1985. BS in Marine Engring., Calif. Maritime Acad., 1961. Design engr. Pacific Telephone Co., San Diego, 1963-73; service engr. Worthington Service Corp., San Diego, 1973-78; pres. Realmart Corp., San Diego, 1978-81; dir. mktg. Orbit Inn Hotel and Casino, Las Vegas, 1981-84; pres. Comml. Consultants, Las Vegas, 1984—, Gray Electronics Co., Las Vegas, 1986—; chmn. bd. dirs. Las Vegas Accomodations Unltd., 1997—; mng. mem. G/Tracker Techs., LLC, 1998, Strobe Detector Techs., LLC, 1998; bd. dirs. Silver State Classic Challenge, Inc. Inventor electronic detection devices, 1986—. Served to lt. (j.g.) USNR, 1961-67. Republican. Avocation: amateur radio, open road auto racing, storm chasing. Home: 1843 Somersby Way Henderson NV 89014-3876

HENRY-JOHN, EMMANUEL SYLVESTER, preacher, counselor; b. Ootacamund, Madras, India, Dec. 15, 1949; came to U.S., 1980; s. Isaac and Sama Thanam (Asirvatham) Henry-J.; m. Laura Elia Garza, Feb. 4, 1984; children: Sarai Samathanam, Isaac Max, Shalani Esther, Arnold Samuel. AS, Schs. for Officers Tng.; BA in Econs., U. Madras, 1970; A.C.P., Assoc. Coll. of Preceptors, 1975; postgrad., U. La Verne, 1988-89; MA, Fuller Theology Sem., 1990. Sales rep. Baba's Ice Cream Factory, Bangalore, India, 1972; tchr. Woizero Comprehensive Higher Dessie Secondary Sch., Ethiopia, 1973-77, Mopa Secondary Sch., Illorin, Kwara, Nigeria, 1977-80; fin. planner John Hancock, Cerritos, Calif., 1982; respiratory therapy technician Burbank (Calif.) Community Hosp., 1983-84; counselor The Salvation Army Rehab. Ctr., Canoga Park, Calif., 1985-86; pastor The Savlation Army, Bakersfield, Calif., 1988-89; comdg. officer The Savlation Army, Gilroy, Calif., 1989—; spiritual counselor Adult Rehab. Ctr., The Salvation Army, Canoga Park, 1980, youth minister ch. for homeless, Bakersfield, 1983, mem. adv. bd., 1988. Vol. food for homeless The Salvation Army, Pakersfield, 1988, spiritual and social work to the needy. Named Best Tchr., Wollo Province, 1974. Mem. Coun. Chs. Greater Bakersfield, Jay Strack Evangelistic Com., Soc. Internat. Missionaries, Christian Ministries Mgmt. Assn., Lions, Masons, Kiwanis. Republican. Avocations: model trains, tennis, videos, photography, play houses. Home: 14401 Bailey Ct Victorville CA 92394-3207

HENSEN, STEPHEN JEROME, lawyer; b. Durango, Colo., Nov. 8, 1961; s. Ronald Jerome and Sandra Lucille (Monroe) H.; m. Janice Lynn Lamunyon; children: Amanda, Stephanie, Cory. BS in Econs., Colo. State U., 1984; JD, Gonzaga U., 1987. Bar: Colo. 1987, U.S. Dist. Ct. Colo. 1987, U.S. Ct. Appeals (10th cir.) 1988, U.S. Supreme Ct. 1994. Atty. Cortez Friedman, P.C., Denver, 1987-93; atty. McKenna & Cuneo, Denver, 1993-95; ptnr. Richman & Hensen, P.C., Denver, 1995—. Mem. Colo. Bar Assn., Denver Bar Assn., Colo. Supreme Ct. Bar Com. Republican. Office: Richman & Hensen PC 1775 Sherman St Ste 1717 Denver CO 80203-4318

HENTZ, MARIE EVA, real estate investor and developer; b. Detroit, Sept. 27, 1920; d. Charles and Eva (Follman) Hentz. Student Detroit Bus. U., Wayne State U. Draftsman, Cadillac Motor Co., Detroit, 1941-44; stenographer Great Lakes Steel Co., River Rouge, Mich., 1945-46, Can. Nat. R.R., Detroit, 1946-49; sec. UNOCAL, L.A., 1950-72; real estate investor, mgr., developer, Thousand Oaks, South El Monte, and Coto de Caza, Calif., 1950—; gen. ptnr. Hentz & Christensen, Ltd., South El Monte, Calif., 1953-86, Hentz Properties, Ltd., Burbank, 1971—. Mem. Union Oil Alumni, Coto Valley Country Club, Women's League of Coto de Caza. Republican. Avocations: gardening, reading, travel.

HENTZ, VINCENT R., surgeon; b. Jacksonville, Fla., Aug. 29, 1942. MD, U. Fla., 1968. Intern Stanford (Calif.) Hosp., 1968-69, resident in plastic surgery, 1969-74, now hand surgeon; fellow in hand surgery Roosevelt Hosp., N.Y.C., 1974-75; prof. functional restoration Stanford (Calif.) U. Office: Stanford Univ 900 Welsh Rd # 15 Stanford CA 94305-5343

HEPLER, KENNETH RUSSEL, manufacturing executive; b. Canton, Ohio, Mar. 31, 1926; s. Clifton R. and Mary A. (Sample) H.; m. Beverly Best, June 9, 1945; 1 child, Bradford R. Student, Cleve. Art Inst., 1946-47, Case Western Res. U., 1948-50. V.p., adminstr. A. Carlisle and Co., San Francisco, 1954-67; pres. K.R. Hepler and Co., Menlo Park, Calif., 1968-73, Paramount Press., Jacksonville, Fla., 1974-75; pvt. practice printing broker, 1976-80; chmn. Hickey and Hepler Graphics Inc., San Francisco, 1981—; instr. printing prodn., San Francisco City Coll. With USAAC, 1943-45. Mem. San Francisco Litho Club (pres. 1972), Phila. Litho Club (sec. 1975-76), Newtown Exchange Club (pres. 1976), Elks. Republican. Presbyterian. Office: Hickey & Hepler Graphics Inc 1633 Bayshore Hwy Ste 222 Burlingame CA 94010-1515

HEPLER, MERLIN JUDSON, JR., real estate broker; b. Hot Springs, Va., May 13, 1929; s. Merlin Judson and Margaret Belle (Vines) H.; m. Lanova Helen Roberts, July 25, 1952; children: Nancy Andora, Douglas Stanley. BS in Bus., U. Idaho, 1977; grad., Realtors Inst., 1979. Cert. residential specialist. Enlisted USAF, 1947, advanced through grades to sgt., 1960, ret., 1967; service mgr. Lanier Bus. Products, Gulfport, Miss., 1967-74; sales assoc. Century 21 Singler and Assn., Troy, Idaho, 1977-79; broker B&M Realty, Troy, 1979—. Mem. Nat. Assn. Realtors, Am. Legion, U. Idaho Alumni Assn., Air Force Sgts. Assn. Republican. Lodge: Lions. Avocations: hunting, fishing. E-mail: mhepler@idaho.tds.net. Home: 1081 Driscoll Ridge Rd Troy ID 83871-9605 Office: B&M Realty W 102 A St PO Box 187 Troy ID 83871-0187

HERB, EDMUND MICHAEL, optometrist, educator; b. Zanesville, Ohio, Oct. 9, 1942; s. Edmund G. and Barbara R. (Michael) H.; divorced; children—Sara, Andrew; m. Jeri Herb. O.D., Ohio State U., 1966. Pvt. practice optometry, Buena Vista, Colo., 1966—; past prof. Timberline campus Colo. Mountain Coll.; past clin. instr. Ohio State U. Sch. Optometry. Mem. Am. Optometric Assn., Colo. Optometric Assn. Home: 16395 Mt Princeton Rd Buena Vista CO 81211-9505 Office: 115 N Tabor St Buena Vista CO 81211 also: Leadville Colorado Med Ctr Leadville CO 80461

HERBAUGH, ROGER DUANE, computer and software company executive; b. Mt. Vernon, Wash., May 20, 1957; s. Donald Lloyd and Kathleen Joyce (Anderson) H.; m. Anne Louise Finlayson, May 8, 1993; children: Andrew David Miller, Celeste Jane Miller, Trevor Allan Miller, Vanessa

Anne Herbaugh, Deirdre Rose Herbaugh. AA, Skagit Valley Coll., 1984; BA, Western Wash. U., 1986. Cert. Microsoft profl. Computer programmer Stockmar Northwestern, Mt. Vernon, 1986-87; CEO, computer cons. Herbaugh & Assocs., Inc. Computer Support Group, Mt. Vernon, 1987—; also pres. bd. dirs. Herbaugh & Assocs., Inc., Mt. Vernon; cons. Shell Oil Co., Anacortes, Wash., 1986-98, BP Oil Co., Ferndale, Wash., 1986-93, ARCO, Blaine, Wash., 1989—, Tosco, Ferndale, Wash., 1993-97, Tosco, Seattle, 1993-97, Tesoro, Anacortes, Wash., 1998—; Microsoft Solutions provider; bd. dirs., pres. Software Plus, Inc., Mt. Vernon, 1991—; mem. adv. coun. Emerson H.S.; mem. tech. adv. coun. Mt. Vernon H.S.; trainer Kiwanis. Sgt. U.S. Army, 1975-81. Mem. Burlington C. of C., Mt. Vernon C. of C., Kiwanis (dist. chmn., immediate past lt. gov., past pres. Mt. Vernon chpt.). Republican. Mem. LDS Ch. Avocations: boating, fishing, travel. Office: Herbaugh & Assocs Inc Computer Support Group 1754 S Burlington Blvd Burlington WA 98233-3224

HERBEL, CAROLENE CAL, apparel designer, retailer; b. Matfield Green, Kans., June 29, 1930; d. Leo John and Bessie B. (Gordon) Callahan; m. Carlton H. Herbel, Oct. 4, 1952 (dec.); children: Kurt C., Belinda Ann Fiedler. BS, Kans. State U., 1952. Owner, designer Carolene Collection Inc., Mesilla, N.Mex., 1977—. Avocation: painting. Home: 1804 Halfmoon Dr Las Cruces NM 88005-3311 Office: Carolene Collection Inc 2010 Calle de Parian Mesilla NM 88046

HERBERT, CHRISTOPHER JAY, marketing professional, management consultant; b. Flint, Mich., May 8, 1953; s. Clarence LaVern and Doris Julia (Potter) H.; m. Nancy Ellen Welch, Dec. 19, 1987. BA, Lewis and Clark Coll., 1975; MBA, Ariz. State U., 1984. Cert. neurolinguistic programming master practitioner, cert. LAB profile, cons./trainer. Planner Maricopa Employment and Tng. Adminstrn., Phoenix, 1977-78; asst. dir. for planning and program devel. Maricopa County Human Resources Dept., Phoenix, 1978-81, CETA adminstr., 1981; v.p. Cons. Assocs., Inc., Phoenix, 1981-82; pres. C.J. Herbert & Co. Inc., Scottsdale, Ariz., 1982-85; v.p. Behavior Rsch. Ctr., Inc., Phoenix, 1985-89; pres. The Insight Group Inc., Tempe, Ariz., 1989—; mem. mktg. com. Phoenix Symphony, 1988-90. Bd. dirs. Grand Canyon Assn., 1992-98, pres., 1994-96, chair governance com., 1996-97, chair strategic planning com., 1997-98; bd. dirs. Grand Canyon Nat. Park Found., 1995—, v.p., 1995—; bd. dirs. The Phoenicians, 1994, Grand Canyon Music Festival, 1998—. Mem. Qualitative Rsch. Cons. Assn. (chair professionalism com. 1992-95, conv. spkr. 1993, 94, 95, treas. bd. dirs. 1995), Am. Assn. Polit. Cons., Am. Assn. Pub. Opinion Rsch., Am. Inst. Wine and Food (chmn. Ariz. chpt. 1993, mem. nat. membership com. 1994), Brotherhood of Knights of the Vine (Master Knight, bd. dirs. Phoenix chpt. 1991-95), Phoenix C. of C. (bd. dirs. 1987-89, chmn. small bus. coun. 1986-87, mem. health coun. 1993-97). Avocations: music, travel, gastronomy, book collecting, bicycling. Office: The Insight Group Inc 2105 E Vaughn St Tempe AZ 85283-3343

HERBERT, GAVIN SHEARER, health care products company executive; b. L.A., Mar. 26, 1932; s. Gavin and Josephine (D'Vitha) H.; children by previous marriage Cynthia, Lauri, Gavin, Pam; 2d. m. Ninetta Flanagan, Sept. 6, 1986. B.S., U. So. Calif., 1954. With Allergan, Inc., Irvine, Calif., 1950—, v.p., 1956-61, exec. v.p., pres., 1961-77, chmn. bd., CEO, 1977-91, chmn. bd., 1992-95, chmn. emeritus; pres. Eye and Skin Care Products Group Smith Kline Beckman Corp., 1981-89; exec. v.p. Smith Kline Beckman Corp., 1986-89; bd. dirs. Beckman Instruments, Inc., Calif. Healthcare Inst. Mem. Rsch. to Prevent Blindness (bd. dirs.), Big Canyon Country Club, Newport Harbor Yacht Club, Pacific Club, Beta Theta Pi. Republican. Office: Allergan Inc PO Box 19534 2525 Dupont Dr Irvine CA 92612-1599

HERBERT, GUY, hockey player; b. Troy, N.Y., Jan. 7, 1967. Goalie Mighty Ducks, Anaheim, Calif. Office: c/o Mighty Ducks 2695 E Katella Ave PO Box 61077 Anaheim CA 92803-6177

HERBST, DAVID W., lawyer; b. Pomona, Calif., June 17, 1952. BA magna cum laude, Pomona Coll., 1974; JD, Stanford U., 1977. Bar: Calif. 1977, U.S. Tax Ct. 1979. Mem. Wise & Shepard, Palo Alto, Calif., 1983—. Mem. ABA, State Bar Calif., Santa Clara County Bar Assn., Palo Alto Bar Assn. Office: Holtzmann Wise & Shepard 3030 Hansen Way Ste 100 Palo Alto CA 94304-1006*

HERCH, FRANK ALAN, lawyer, law librarian; b. Chgo., May 5, 1949; s. Robert Gilbert and Shirley (Berman) H.; m. Ruth Blackwell, Dec. 29, 1971; children: Nathaniel, Rachmiel. BA in Sociology and History, U. Calif., Davis, 1971; MLS, U. Calif., Berkeley, 1972; JD, U. Calif., Davis, 1975. Bar: Calif. 1981, U.S. Dist. Ct. (no. dist.) Calif. 1981. Reference libr. Alameda County Law Libr., Oakland, Calif., 1975-78; asst. law libr. Georgetown U. Law Ctr., Washington, 1978-81; atty. Blackwell, Herch & Herch, Oakland, 1981-87; libr. Cityline Info. Svc. Oakland Pub. Libr., 1984-87; dir. Clark County Law Libr., Las Vegas, Nev., 1987—; lectr. John F. Kennedy U. Sch. of Law, 1977-78, St. Mary's Coll. Paralegal Program, Moraga, Calif., 1981-87; law libr. and rsch. cons. Nev. Civil Jury Instructions Com. Monterey Coll. of Law, Alameda County Bar Assn., Oakland, 1981-87. Editor U. Calif. Davis Law Rev., 1974-75, writer, 1973-74; editor Jazz Rag mag., 1975-85, book revs. Legal Pub. Rev., Legal Information Alert, Business Information Alert, 1989—. Steering com. Second Start: Adult Literacy Program, Oakland, 1984-87; mem. exec. bd. East Bay Info. and Referral Network, Berkeley, 1984-87; mem. Clark County Merit Ins. Task Force, 1992. Recipient Cert. of Leadership Nat. U., Oakland, 1987, Leadership award City of Oakland, 1987. Mem. Am. Assn. Law Librs. (cert. 1978, v.p. West Pacific chpt. 1991-92, pres. 1992-93, sec. and treas. state, city and county law librs. spl. interest sect. 1989-92, chmn. regional meeting com., key issues forums, gov.'s conf. on future of librs. 1990, v.p., pres. elect, 1994—, legal info to the pub. special interest sect.), Nev. Libr. Assn. (chmn., bd. rep. so. dist. 1989). Avocations: writing fiction, playing guitar and keyboards, tennis, videotaping jazz performances. Office: Clark County Law Libr 304 Carson Ave Las Vegas NV 89101-5903

HERDEG, HOWARD BRIAN, physician; b. Buffalo, Oct. 14, 1929; s. Howard Bryan and Martha Jean (Williams) H.; m. Beryl Ann Fredricks, July 21, 1955; children: Howard Brian III, Erin Ann Kociela. Student Paul Smith's Coll., 1947-48, U. Buffalo, 1948-50, Canisius Coll., 1949; DO, Phila. Coll. Osteopathic Medicine, 1954; MD, U. Calif.-Irvine Coll. Medicine, 1962. Diplomate Am. Acad. Pain Mgmt. Intern, Burbank (Calif.) Hosp., 1954-55; practice medicine specializing in gen. medicine, surgery and pain mgmt., Woodland Hills, Calif., 1956—; chief med. staff West Park Hosp., Canoga Park, Calif., 1971-72, trustee, 1971-73; chief family practice dept. West Hills Regional Med. Center (formerly Humana Hosp. West Hills, 1982-83, 84-85, 88-89), mem. exec. com., 1984-85, 88-89, Mem. Hidden Hills (Calif.) Pub. Safety Commn., 1978-82; bd. dirs. Hidden Hills Community Assn., 1971-73, pres., 1972; bd. dirs. Hidden Hills Homeowners Assn., 1973-75, pres., 1976-77; bd. dirs. Woodland Hills Freedom Season, 1961-67, pres., 1962; mem. Hidden Hills City Council, 1984—, mayor pro tem, 1987-90, mayor, 1990-92. Recipient disting. service award Woodland Hills Jr C. of C., 1966. Mem. Woodland Hills C. of C. (dir. 1959-68, pres. 1967), Theta Chi, Gamma Pi. Republican. Home: 24530 Deep Well Rd Hidden Hills CA 91302-1210 Office: 22600 Ventura Blvd Woodland Hills CA 91364-1414

HERDRICH, M. SUSAN, educator, writer; b. Spokane, Wash., July 24, 1945; d. James W. and Mary M. (Miller) Webb; m. Norman W. Herdrich, Aug. 16, 1975; children: Megan Marie, Heidi Susan, Kristin Ruth Maureen. BA in English, Wash. State U., 1967, MA in English, 1969. Cert. tchr., Wash. Prof. Spokane (Wash.) C.C., 1969—; adj. faculty Gonzaga U., 1991—; instr. in field. Author: A Study of Medea in Western Literature, 1969; editor 3 textbooks; editor Eviron. Impact Statement Bureau Land Mgmt., 1984-85. Adult Edn. commn. Spokane (Wash.) Valley United Meth. Ch., 1988—. Fellow Wash. State U., 1967-68. Mem. Philanthropic Ednl. Orgn. Sisterhood, Phi Beta Kappa, Delta Kappa Gamma, Pi Lambda Theta, Phi Kappa Phi. Avocations: creative writing, art, reading. Home: E 12711 Saltese Rd Spokane WA 99213 Office: Spokane C C N 1810 Greene St Spokane WA 99207 also: Gonzaga Univ E 502 Boone Spokane WA 99258-0001

HERENDA, WILLIAM A., executive; b. Jersey City, N.J., Dec. 30, 1965; s. Anthony G. and Grace H.; m. Mary Elen O'Brien, Feb. 16, 1992; children: Bridget, Clare, Devin. BS in Mktg., U. Mass., 1988. Sales rep. Garden State Office Suste,s, Piscataway, N.J., 1988-91; exec. rep. Fujisawa USA, Inc., Sacramento, 1991—. Avocations: running, reading, sports.

HERGER, WALLY W., congressman; b. Yuba City, Calif., May 20, 1945. Formerly mem. Calif. State Assembly; mem. 100th-102d Congresses from 2d Calif. dist., 1987—; mem. agr., mcht. marine and fisheries coms. 100th-103rd Congresses from 2d Calif. dist.; mem. budget com., mem. ways and means com.; owner Herger Gas, Inc. Office: US Ho of Reps 2433 Rayburn Bldg Washington DC 20515-0502*

HERING, WILLIAM MARSHALL, medical organization executive; b. Indpls., Dec. 26, 1940; s. William Marshall and Mary Agnes (Clark) H.; m. Suzanne Wolfe, Aug. 10, 1963. BS, Ind. U., 1961, MS, 1962; PhD, U. Ill., Urbana, 1973. Tchr. Indpls. pub. schs., 1962-66; asst. dir. sociol. resources project Am. Sociol. Assn., 1966-70; dir. social sci. curriculum Biomed. Interdisciplinary Project, Berkeley, Calif., 1973-76; staff assoc. Tchrs. Ctrs. Exchange, San Francisco, 1976-82; dir. research Far West Lab. Ednl. Research and Devel., San Francisco, 1979-82, sr. research assoc., 1982-85; mgr. human resource devel. Bank Am., San Francisco, 1985-94; dir. programs Am. Acad. Ophthalmology, San Francisco, 1994—; mem. Nat. Adv. Bd. Educ. Resource Info. Ctr.; cons. U.S. Dept. Edn.; pres. Social Sci. Educ. Consortium, 1981-82, bd. dirs., 1979-81; bd. dirs. San Francisco Chamber Orch., 1986-94. Nat. Inst. Educ. grantee, 1979-82. Mem. Am. Soc. Tng. and Devel. (v.p. 1986), Alliance Continuing Med. Edn., Alpha Tau Omega, Phi Delta Kappa. Republican. Episcopalian. Contbr. over 100 articles, book chpts. Home: 731 Duboce Ave San Francisco CA 94117-3214 Office: 655 Beach St San Francisco CA 94109-1342

HERMAN, ANDREA MAXINE, newspaper editor; b. Chgo., Oct. 22, 1938; d. Maurice H. and Mae (Baron) H.; m. Joseph Schmidt, Oct. 28, 1962. BJ, U. Mo., 1960. Feature writer Chgo.'s Am., 1960-63; daily columnist News Am., Balt., 1963-67; feature writer Mainichi Daily News, Tokyo, 1967-69; columnist Iowa City Press-Citizen, 1969-76; music and dance critic San Diego Tribune, 1976-84; asst. mng. editor features UPI, Washington, 1984-86, asst. mng. editor news devel., 1986-87; mng. editor features L.A. Herald Examiner, 1987-91; editor/culture We/Mbl Newspaper, Washington, 1991—. Recipient 1st and 2d prizes for features in arts James S. Copley Ring of Truth Awards, 1982, 1st prize for journalism Press Club San Diego, 1983. Mem. Soc. Profl. Journalists, Am. Soc. Newspaper Editors, AP Mng. Editors, Women in Communications. Avocations: music, art. Office: We/Mbl Newspaper 1350 Connecticut Ave NW Washington DC 20036-1722

HERMAN, ELVIN E., retired consulting electronic engineer; b. Mar. 17, 1921; s. John Lawrence and Martha Elizabeth (Conner) H.; m. Grace Winifred Eklund, Sept. 29, 1945; 1 child, Jane Ann Herman Fischer. BSEE, State U. Iowa, 1942. Engr., sect. head Naval Rsch. Lab., Washington, 1942-51; sect. head Corona (Calif.) Labs., Nat. Bur. Stds., 1951-53; sect. head, lab. mgr., tech. dir. radar sys. group Hughes Aircraft Co., El Segundo, Calif., 1953-83; cons. electronic engr., Pacific Palisades, Calif., 1983-88; ret., 1988. Recipient Meritorious Civilian Svc. award Naval Rsch. Lab., 1946. Fellow IEEE. Achievements include 24 patents in field. Home: 1200 Lachman Ln Pacific Palisades CA 90272-2228

HERMAN, GEORGE ADAM, writer; b. Norfolk, Va., Apr. 12, 1928; s. George Adam and Minerva Nevada (Thompson) H.; m. Patricia Lee Glazer, May 26, 1955 (div. 1989); children: Kurt, Erik, Karl, Lisa, Katherine, Christopher, Jena, Amanda; m. Patricia Jane Piper Dubay, Aug. 25, 1989; children: Lizette, Paul, Kirk, Victoria. PhB, Loyola Coll., 1950; MFA, Cath. U., 1954; cert. fine arts, Boston Coll., 1951,52,53. Asst. prof. Clarke Coll., Dubuque, Iowa, 1955-60, Villanova (Pa.) U., 1960-63; asst. prof., playwright in residence Coll. St. Benedict, St. Joseph, Minn., 1963-65; chmn. theatre dept. Coll. Great Falls, Mont., 1965-67; media specialist Hawaii State Dept. Edn., Honolulu, 1967-75, staff specialist, 1975-83; sr. drama critic Honolulu Advertiser, 1975-80; artistic dir. Commedia Repertory Theatre, Honolulu, 1978-80; freelance writer, lectr., composer Portland, Oreg., 1983—. Author: (plays) Company of Wayward Saints, 1963 (McKnight Humanities award 1964), Mr. Highpockets, 1968, A Stone for Either Hand, 1969, Tenebrae, 1984, (novels) Carnival of Saints, 1994 (finalist Oreg. Book Awards 1994), A Comedy of Murders, 1994, Tears of the Madonna, 1995; composer (ballets) The Dancing Princesses, Fraidy Cat. Pres. local chpt. Nat. Sch. Pub. Rels. Assn., Honolulu, 1981-83; bd. dirs. Honolulu Community Theatre, 1981-82, Hawaii State Theatre Coun., Honolulu, 1981. With U.S. Army, 1950-52. Recipient Hartke Playwrighting award Cath. U., 1954, Excellence award Am. Security Coun., 1967. Avocations: directing theatre, lecturing.

HERMAN-DUNN, RUTH ANN, psychologist; b. Salem, Oreg., Jan. 18, 1963; d. Peter Shaw and Theresa Eileen (Little) H. BA, U. Calif., Santa Barbara, 1987; MA, Ohio State U., 1990; PhD in Counseling Psychology, U. Fla., 1993. Fellow in substance abuse Seattle VA, 1993-94, psychotherapist, cons., 1992—; clin. supr. U. Wash., 1995—; ind. rschr. U.Fla., Gainesville, 1989-92. Author and presenter in field. Mem. APA, Wash. Stae Psychol. Assn., Phi Beta Kappa. Democrat. Unitarian Universalist. Avocations: music, gardening, sports spectatorship, reading, home improvement. Office: 4850 California Ave SW Ste 102 Seattle WA 98116-4400

HERMANSON, PAUL DOUGLAS, investor; b. Rapid City, S.D.; s. Melvin B. and Marthaleen H. (Horton) H.; m. Ann L. Alderson (div. May 1991); children: Michele, Edward, Austin. BA in Bus., U. S.D., 1970. CPA, Ariz. Ptnr. Deloitte & Touche, Phoenix, Ariz., 1970-89; with Twin Star Prodns., Scottsdale, Ariz., 1989-91; self-employed investor Phoenix, 1991—; bd. dirs. chmn. pres. Rapid Bowl Inc., Rapid City, S.D.; bd. dirs. Meadowood Lounge Inc., Rapid City. Bd. dirs., treas. Contemporary Forum of Phoenix Art Mus., 1983-89, 94-97 (dirs. circle mem., 1982—, dirs. circle adv. com., 1987-88). Mem. Phoenix Country Club.

HERMSEN, JAMES R., lawyer; b. Orange, Calif., Oct. 2, 1945. BA, U. Wash., 1967, JD, 1970. Bar: Wash. 1971. Mem. Bogle & Gates, PLLC, Seattle; mem. Bur. of Competition Fed. Trade Commn., 1971-73. Mem. ABA, Seattle-King County Bar Assn., Wash. State Bar Assn., Am. Bar Assn., Phi Beta Kappa, Omicron Delta Epsilon, Phi Delta Phi. Office: Bogle & Gates PLLC Two Union Sq 601 Union St Ste 4400 Seattle WA 98101-2341

HERNANDEZ, ARTHUR, college administrator, labor arbitrator, artist; b. Hayden, Ariz., Feb. 23, 1930; s. Sylvestre and Jesus (Benitez) H.; m. Eleanor Cardona, Sept. 29, 1951 (div. 1956); m. Margaret E. Knape, Dec. 15, 1956; children—Maria Adelita, Michele Ann, Maureen Christina, Elizabeth Rose, Antoinette. AA, Los Angeles Valley Coll., 1957; BA, UCLA, 1959, EdD, 1977, BA in Fine Arts. Asst. to area supt. Los Angeles Unified Pub. Schs., 1972-74; coordinator East Los Angeles Coll., Monterey Park, Calif., 1974-76, v.p., 1980—; dean Los Angeles Mission Coll., San Fernando, Calif., 1977-78, acting pres., 1978-80; owner Canyonwood Fine Art Studio; cons. U.S. Office Edn., Washington, A.B.C. Unified Schs.; labor arbitrator Los Angeles County, 1980—, Los Angeles County Schs., Downey, Calif., 1972—. Pres. Latin Am. Civic Assn., San Fernando, 1968, Youth Services Bur., San Fernando, 1969, Headstart Bd. Dirs., 1968-72; chmn. Los Angeles United Way Hispanic Vol. Council, 1982-83. Served with U.S. Army, 1952-57. Fulbright scholar, 1966. Mem. AAUP, Phi Delta Kappa. Democrat. Roman Catholic. Office: Los Angeles Pierce Coll 6201 Winnetka Ave Woodland Hills CA 91371-0001

HERNANDEZ, JEFFREY SCOTT, SR., counselor, administrator; b. N.Y.C., July 17, 1946; s. Theodore and Digna (Riquelmes) H.; m. Rachel Ann Christensen, July 14, 1967 (div. Apr. 1972); 1 child, Jeffrey Scott Jr.; m. Brenda Kay Osborne, July 14, 1995; stepchildren: Caroline Rickels, Brandy Hackney. Cert. in Alcohol and Drug Studies, Saddleback Coll., 1995. Cert. addictions treatment specialist, Calif. Assn. Alcohol and Drug Educators. Adminstrv. case mgr. Gold Coast Counseling, Costa Mesa, Calif., 1991—; [illegible] First Step House of Orange County, Costa Mesa, 1988-90; panel leader Orange County Narcotics Anonymous Hosps. and Instns., 1988—, chairperson, 1996. Cmty. vol. Orange County Sheriff's Dept., 1988—; vol. in probation Orange County Probation Dept., 1989—. Avocations: cycle riding, spiritual development. Office: Gold Coast Counseling Inc 2950 Airway Ave Ste B3 Costa Mesa CA 92626-6004

HERNANDEZ, JO FARB, museum curator, consultant; b. Chgo., Nov. 20, 1952. BA in Polit. Sci. & French with honors, U. Wis., 1974; MA in Folklore and mythology, UCLA, 1975; postgrad., U. Calif., Davis, 1978, U. Calif., Berkeley, 1978-79, 81. Registration Mus. Cultural History UCLA, 1974-75; Rockefeller fellow Dallas Mus. Fine Arts, 1976-77; asst. to dir. Triton Mus. Art, Santa Clara, Calif., 1977-78, dir., 1978-85; adj. prof. mus. studies John F. Kennedy U., San Francisco, 1978; grad. advisor arts adminstrn. San Jose (Calif.) State U., 1979-80; dir. Monterey (Calif.) Peninsula Mus. Art, 1985-93, cons. curator, 1994—; prin. Curatorial and Mus. Mgmt. Svcs., Watsonville, Calif., 1993—; lectr., panelist, juror, panelist in field USIA, Calif. Arts Coun., Calif. Confedn. for Arts, Am. Assn. Mus., Western Mus. Assn., Am. Folklore Soc., Calif. Folklore Soc., others; vis. lectr. U. Wis., 1980, Northwestern U., 1981, San Jose State U., 1985, UCLA, 1986, Am. Cultural Ctr., Jerusalem, 1989, Tel Aviv, 1989, Binat. Ctr., Lima, Peru, 1988, Daytona Beach Mus. Art, 1983, UCLA, 1986, Israel Mus., 1989, U. Chgo., 1981, Mont. State U., 1991, Oakland Mus., 1996, High Mus. Art, Atlanta, 1997, Mus. Am. Folk Art, N.Y., 1998, San Francisco Mus. Modern Art, 1998, U. Calif., 1998, Calif. Arts Coun., 1997, 99; guest curator San Diego Mus. Art, 1995-98; guest on various TV and radio programs. Contbr. articles to profl. publs.; author: (mus. catalogs) The Day of the Dead: Tradition and Change in Contemporary Mexico, 1979, Three from the Northern Island: Contemporary Sculpture from Hokkaido, 1984, Crime and Punishment: Reflections of Violence in Contemporary Art, 1984, The Quiet Eye: Pottery of Shoji Hamada and Bernard Leach, 1990, Alan Shepp: The Language of Stone, 1991, Wonderful Colors: The Paintings of August Francois Gay, 1993, Jeannette Maxfield Lewis: A Centennial Celebration, 1994, Armin Hansen, 1994, Jeremy Anderson: The Critical Link/A Quiet Revolution, 1995, A.G. Rizzoli: Architect of Magnificent Visions, 1997, Misch Kohn: Beyond the Tradition, 1998, Fire and Flux: An Undaunted Vision/the art of Charles Strong, 1998. Bd. dirs. Bobbie Wynn and Co. of San Jose, 1981-85, Santa Clara Arts and Hist. Consortium, 1985, Non-Profit Gallery Assn., 1979-83, v.p., 1979-80; mem. nat. adv. bd. The Fund for Folk Culture, Santa Fe, 1995-98. Recipient Golden Eagle award Coun. Internat. Non-theatrical Events, 1992, Leader of Decade award Arts Leadership Monterey Peninsula, 1992. Mem. Am. Assn. Mus. (mus. assessment program surveyor 1990, 94, lectr. 1986, nat. program com. 1992-93), Calif. Assn. Mus. (chair ann. meeting 1990, chair nominating com. 1988, 90, 93, bd. dirs. 1985-94, v.p. 1987-91, pres. 1991-92), Art Table, Am. Folklore Soc., Western Mus. Conf. (bd. dirs., exec. com. 1989-91, program chair 1990), Nat. Coun. for Edn. in Ceramic Arts, Alliance for Calif. Traditional Arts, Phi Beta Kappa. Office: Curatorial and Mus Mgmt Svcs 345 White Rd Watsonville CA 95076-0429

HERNANDEZ, LILLIAN A., health facility administrator; b. Inglewood, Calif., May 12, 1959; d. John Erling and Lillian Alice (Hastings) Johnson; m. David Robert Hernandez, Aug. 11, 1979; children: Linda Marie, Amber Michelle, Christine Lee. AA, Cerritos Jr. Coll., 1981; BS in Bus., Calif. State U., Long Beach, 1986. Cert. quality circle facilitator. Note teller Bank of Am., Bellflower, Calif., 1978-79; computer operator Piping Products West, Vernon, Calif., 1981; counselor/asst. mgr. Zoe Employment Agy., Los Alamitos, Calif., 1981-82; pers. asst./quality circle facilitator Hazel of Calif. Inc., Santa Fe Springs, 1982-86; employment coord. PARTNERS Nat. Health Plans, San Bernardino, Calif., 1987-89; owner Cream Whippeeze, Riverside, Calif., 1989-91; Riverside County media coord. William Dannemeyer for U.S. Senate, 1991-92; human resources dir. Manor Care Health Svcs., Hemet, Calif., 1993—; Interview panalist City of Riverside, Calif., 1990. Chmn. Citizens' Adv. Affirmative Action Com., Riverside, Calif., 1990; founding mem. Riverside Citizens for Responsible Behavior, 1990—; bd. dirs. Greater Riverside Hispanic Chamber, 1989-91; mem. Community Rels. Commn., 87-94; chmn. recreation and culture, 1989-90, parliamentarian, 1988-90; assoc. mem. Calif. Rep. State Cen. Com., 1989-92; mem. Calif. Rep. State Com., Riverside County Ctrl. Com.; vice-chair 2d supervisoral dist.; adv. com. law enforcement policy, Calif. Rep. State Party, 1989-92, del., 1992—; founding mem. v.p. Riverside Citizens for Responsible Behavior, 1990—, assoc. mem., 1989-92, del., 1992—, sec. health and human svcs. commn., 1995—; mem. Cmty Rels. Commn., 1987-89. Mem. Personnel and Indsl. Rels. Assn., Profls. in Human Resources Assn., Soc. Human Resource Mgmt. Republican. Avocations: snow skiing, water skiing, health spa workouts, collecting antique books, bicycling. Office: Manor Care Health Svcs 1717 W Stetson Ave Hemet CA 92545-6800

HERNANDEZ, ROBERT JOSE, film and video producer, multimedia marketing; b. L.A., Apr. 5, 1960; s. Robert and Kay Diana (Jensen) H.; m. Daphna Levy, Dec. 14, 1956; 1 child, Damian. H.s. grad., San Diego. Owner, operator Spirit Enterprizes, Glendale, Calif., 1990-92; owner, mgr. Millennium Prodns., Pasadena, Calif., 1987—; owner The Loft Performing Arts Ctr., Pasadena, 1996—. Author: Truth about Drugs: A Handbook for Parents, 1995; author, producer (film) The Truth About Drugs, 1995; (comml.) Narconon, 1994 (Nat. finalist Visionaward 1994. Vol. Friends of Narconon, Pasadena, 1987—, pres. 1995—. Named Vol. of Yr. Assn. Better Living Edn. Internat. L.A., 1994. Avocations: photography, scuba diving, music, antique auto collecting. Home: 622 E Villa St Pasadena CA 91101-1120 Office: Golden Millennium Prodns Inc 622 E Villa St # A Pasadena CA 91101-1120

HERNANDEZ-FUJIGAKI, JULIO, urologist; b. Pahuattan, Puebla, Mexico, Sept. 21, 1951; came to U.S., 1989; s. Jose Hernandez-Bernal and Gloria (Fujigaki) Hernandez; m. Johanne Blouin, Oct. 3, 1987; children: Jose-Julio, Valerie. MD in Gen. Surgery, U. Nat. Auanomade Mexico, 1981. Urologist pvt. practice Chula Vista, Calif., 1989—. Author: Tradicion sin tiempo, 1997. Mem. Am. Urol. Assn., Royal Coll. Physicians and Surgeons (Canada), San Diego County Med. Soc. Avocations: reading, writing, music. Office: 480 4th Ave Ste 504 Chula Vista CA 91910-4414

HERNÁNDEZ HERRERO, ISAAC, editor, photojournalist; b. Madrid, Oct. 9, 1967; came to U.S., 1985; s. Enrique Hernández Muñoz and Maria Herrero Novoa; m. Nancy Elaine Black, May 1, 1993; 1 child, Diego Antonio Hernández Black. BA, Brooks Inst. Photography, 1990. Sales clk. Circulo Bookshop, Madrid, 1980-85; location video prodr. Teleimagen, Madrid, 1985-87; pub. rels. Brooks Inst. Photography, Santa Barbara, Calif., 1987-89; art dir. In Focus Mag., Santa Barbara, Calif., 1989-90; color printer Color Svcs., Santa Barbara, Calif., 1990-91; editor-in-chief Mercury Press Internat., Santa Barbara, Calif., 1991—; U.S. editor Automóvil Panamericans Mag., Mexico D.F., 1995—. Photographer numerous mags. and books, 1986—; contbr. articles to profl. jours. Recipient 2d prize photo contest Santa Barbara County Fair, 1989. Mem. Motor Press Guild. Avocations: mountain biking, painting, gardening. Office: Mercury Press Internat 405 Santa Anita Rd Santa Barbara CA 93105-3718

HERNING-SWAIM, SHIRLEY RUTH, general earthworks and utilities contractor; b. Fairbanks, Alaska, Jan. 31, 1954; d. Carl Roland and Mattie Lee (Clay) Herning; m. John Edward Brainerd, Aug. 28, 1972 (div. Sept. 1979); m. Kelvin Eugene Swaim, Apr. 15, 1989; children: Stephanie Michelle, Veronica Renee. AA in Gen. Sci., U. Alaska, Fairbanks, 1975, BS in Home Econs., 1975; cert. in adminstrv. law/fair hearing, Nat. Jud. Coll., Reno, Nev., 1983, 88. Substitute tchr. North Star Borough Sch. Dist., Fairbanks, 1976; driver lic. examiner State of Alaska, Dept. Motor Vehicles, Fairbanks, 1976; carrier U.S. Govt. contract, Fairbanks, 1976-77; employment security specialist Alaska Dept. Labor, Fairbanks, 1977-82; hearing officer, employment security divsn. Alaska Dept. Labor, Anchorage, 1982-83, 85-92; investigator Alaska Dept. Revenue, Alcohol Beverage Control Bd., Fairbanks, 1983-84, Alaska Health & Social Svcs., Fraud Unit, Fairbanks, 1984-85; corporate officer, shareholder Swaim Enterprises, Fairbanks, 1992—; northern regional negotiator Alaska Pub. Employees Assn., Juneau, 1979-81, employee rep., 1977-7. Judge, author: Employment Security Divsn. Unemployment Ins., Appeal Tribunal Case Decisions, 1985-92. Nutrition instr. North Star Coun. on Aging, Fairbanks, 1974. Recipient Appreciation award [illegible] munity Svc. Vol. Assn., Fairbanks, 1993. Mem. Alaska Peace Officers Assn., Nat. Assn. Adminstrv. Law Judges. Democrat. Baptist. Avocations: genealogy, history, sewing, antiques, travel, cake decorating. Office: Swaim Enterprises Inc 2279 Franklin St Fairbanks AK 99709-6236

HEROLD, RALPH ELLIOTT, motion picture arts educator; b. L.A., Dec. 5, 1919; s. Henry Danelle and Isabelle (Baker) H. BS, St. Andrews Coll., 1951; PhD in Mgmt. Sci., Clayton U., 1978. Instr. media sci. L.A. City Schs., 1949-56; staff asst. flight ops. Hughes Aircraft Co., Culver City, Calif., 1955-57; mgr. logistics & program control N.Am. Aviation, L.A., Canoga Park, Downey, Calif., 1957-67; mgr. quality assurance McDonnell Douglas Astronautics, Huntington Beach, Calif., 1967-70; dir. motivational sci. Systematix, Fullerton, Calif., 1970-74; pers. dir. Chapman U., Orange, Calif., 1974-75; instr. Am. film heritage Rancho Coll., Santa Ana, Calif., 1976—. Contbr. numerous articles to profl. jours.; prodr. film-to-video Objective Kobe, own color footage of Kobe, Japan in WWII. Lt. col. U.S. Army Signal Corps, 1940-63. Mem. Theater Hist. Soc. Am., Ret. Officers Assn., Cinecon, Hollywood Stuntman's Assn. Home: 161 Avenida Majorca Laguna Hills CA 92653-4112

HERRANEN, KATHY, artist, graphic designer; b. Zelienople, Pa., Dec. 22, 1943; d. John and Helen Elizabeth (Sayti) D'Biagio; m. John Warma Herranen, Dec. 31, 1974 (div. Feb. 1994); 1 child, Michael John. Student, Scottsdale (Ariz.) C.C., 1990—. Cert. tchr. art, State Bd. Dirs. for Cmty. Coll. of Ariz. Horseback riding instr. Black Saddle Riding Acad., Lancaster, Calif., early 1960's; tel. company supr. Bell Tel., Bishop, Calif., 1965; reporter, part-time photographer Ellwood City (Pa.) Ledger, 1967-70; backcountry guide and cook Mammoth Lakes (Calif.) Pack Outfit, 1970; motel mgr. Mountain Property Mgmt., Mammoth Lakes, 1970-72; reporter, bookkeeper Hungry Horse (Mont.) News, 1973-74; pig farmer Columbia Falls, Mont., 1973-75; fine artist, illustrator, graphic designer Mont., Calif., and Ariz., 1980—; fine arts cons. Collector's Gallery, Galleri II, Yuma, Ariz., 1983-84; wind chime designer, creator Phoenix, 1995—; represented by Marcella's Ariz. Collection, Phoenix, 1995—, Backstreet Furniture and Art, Phoenix, 1995—, Hohn Gallery Fine Arts, Ltd., Scottsdale, 1997—; guest lectr. Paradise Valley Tchrs Acad., Phoenix, 1993, Sr. Adult Edn. Program, Scottsdale (Ariz.) Cmty. Coll., 1994, pastel painting instr., 1996; guest demonstrator Binder's Art Ctr., Scottsdale, 1995, Backstreet Furniture and Art, Phoenix, 1995-96; guest lectr., demonstrator Summer Edn. Program Paradise Valley Sch. Dist. Solo shows include Pinnacle, Phoenix, 1993, Villas of Sedona, Ariz., 1995. Sec. Young Dems., Ellwood City, late 1960's, Vistas Home Owners Assn., Phoenix, 1995—; troubleshooter Maricopa County Elections Dept., Phoenix, 1994-96. Recipient 1st place award Potpourri Artists, Yuma, Ariz., 1981, Subscriber award Butte (Mont.) Arts Coun., 1981, 2nd place award Desert Artists, Yuma, 1982, honorable mention Yuma County Fair, Yuma, 1983, Wildlife Painting Exhibit, Scottsdale, 1993, honorable mention Scottsdale Studio 13, 1991, 92, Special award, 1993, Merit award, 1993, 94 (2). Mem. Nat. Assn. Sr. Friends Fine Artists (chair 1995—, honorable mention 1993, People's Choice award 1996), Nat. and Ariz. chpts. of Women's Caucus for Art, Phoenix Artists Guild, Ariz. Pastel Artists Assn. (charter mem., membership chair 1995-96, 2d v.p., show chair 1996, guest demonstrator 1995, guest lectr. 1998, Merit award 1995), Artists and Craftsmen of Flathead Valley (founder, charter mem., pres. 1981-82), Phi Theta Kappa. Republican. Lutheran. Avocations: public speaking and acting, dancing, stamp collecting, photography, interior decorating. Office: 4114 E Union Hills Dr Unit 1011 Phoenix AZ 85050-3355

HERREN, REBECCA ANN, editor; b. Terre Haute, Ind., May 14, 1955; d. James and Anna (Burgess) Scarbrough; m. Kelly K., June 12, 1977 (div. Mar. 1982); 1 child, Matthew Patrick. Student, U. Nev., Las Vegas, C.C. So. Nev. Graphic layout artist Las Vegas Rev. Jour., 1974-84; coord., mgr. Graphic Typesetting Svcs., Commerce, Calif., 1984-92; pub. rels./mktg. designer MyDAS Mktg., Boulder City, Nev., 1993-94; editor, pub. rels. writer Congregation New Tamid, Las Vegas, 1994-95; reporter Jewish Fedn. Las Vegas, 1995—. Mem. Am. Jewish Press Assn. Avocations: writing, painting, photography, skiing. Office: The Jewish Fedn 3909 S Maryland Pkwy Las Vegas NV 89119-7500

HERRERA, JOHN, professional football team executive; married; 8 children. BA in History, U. Calif., Davis. Tng. camp asst. Oakland Raiders, 1963-68, pub. rels. asst., 1968, dir. pub. rels., 1978-80, sr. exec., 1985—; dir. player pers. B.C. Lions, 1981-82; gen. mgr. Sask. Roughriders, 1983-84; with scouting depts. Tampa Bay Buccaneers, 1975-76, Washington Redskins, 1977. Office: Oakland Raiders 1220 Harbor Bay Pkwy Alameda CA 94502-6570

HERRERA, ROBERT BENNETT, retired mathematics educator; b. L.A., July 24, 1913; s. Royal Robert and Rachel (Mix) H.; AA, L.A. City Coll., 1934; AB, UCLA, 1937, MA, 1939; m. Agnes Mary MacDougall, May 18, 1941; children: Leonard B., Mary Margaret, William R. Tchr. high sch., Long Beach, Calif., 1939-41; statistician U.S. Forest Survey, Berkeley, Calif., 1941-45; faculty L.A. City Coll., 1946-79, prof. math., 1966-79, chmn. math. dept., 1975-79, ret., 1979; lectr. math. UCLA, 1952-75; cons. Ednl. Testing Svc., Princeton, 1965-68, Addison Wesley Pub. Co., 1966-68, Goodyear Pub. Co., 1970-76. Mem. AAAS, Math. Assn. Am. (past sec. So. Calif. sect., past gov.), Am. Math. Soc., Internat. Oceanic Soc., Phi Beta Kappa, Pi Mu Epsilon. Democrat. Author: (with C. Bell, C. Hammond) Fundamentals of Arithmetic for Teachers, 1962. Home: 2737 S Kihei Rd # 159 Kihei HI 96753-9609 Office: PO Box 134 Kihei HI 96753-0134

HERRERA, SHIRLEY MAE, personnel and security executive; b. Lynn, Mass., Apr. 5, 1942; d. John Baptiste and Edith Mae Lagasse; m. Christian Yanez Herrera, Apr. 30, 1975; children: Karen, Gary, Ivan, Iwonne. AS in Bus., Burdette Bus. Coll., Lynn, 1960; student, Wright State U., 1975-78. Cert. facility security officer, med. asst. in pediatrics. Med. asst. Christian Y. Herrera, M.D., Stoneham, Mass., 1972-74; human resource adminstr. MTL Systems, Inc., Dayton, Ohio, 1976-79; dir. pers. and security Tracor GIE, Inc., Provo, Utah, 1979-95; cons. on family dynamics family enrichment program Hill AFB, Utah, 1980-82; cons. on health care memt. Guam 7th Day Adventist Clinic, 1983; cons. on basic life support and CPR, Projecto Corazon, Monterrey, Mex., 1987—; faculty mem. Inst. for Reality Therapy, 1991—. Contbg. editor Inside Tractor, 1991—. Chmn. women's aux. YMCA Counselling Svcs., Woburn, Mass., 1970; chmn. youth vols. ARC, Wright-Patterson AFB, Dayton, 1974-76; trustee Quail Valley Homeowner's Assn., Provo, 1988-89; rep. A Spl. Wish Found., Provo, 1989. Recipient James S. Cogswell award Def. Investigative Svc., Dept. Def., 1987. Mem. Inst. for Realty Therapy (cert.), Pers. Assn. Ctrl. Utah, Women in Mgmt. (coun. mem. 1991-95), Nat. Classification Mgmt. Soc. (chairperson Intermountain chpt. 1992-94). Republican. Avocations: writing, skiing, reading. Home: 3824 Little Rock Dr Provo UT 84604-5234

HERRICK, SYLVIA ANNE, health service administrator; b. Minot, N.D., Oct. 5, 1945; d. Sylvester P. and Ethelina (Harren) Theis; m. Michael M. Herrick, Nov. 8, 1989; children: Leo J., Mark A. BSN, U. N.D., 1967; MS in Pub. Health Nursing, U. Colo., Denver, 1970; sch. nurse credential, San Jose State U., 1991; postgrad., Golden Gate U. RN, Calif.; cert. pub. health nursing, health svc. Pub. health nurse Dept. Pub. Health City of Mpls.; instr. nursing San Francisco State U., 1967-69; cons. exec. search Med-Power Resources, Alameda, 1974-88; coord. health svcs. Alameda Unified Sch. Dist., 1977-91; team mgr. home care nursing and program devel. coord. Vis. Nurse Assn. and Hospice of No. Calif., 1991—; spkr. in field. Mem. Nat. Nurses Bus. Assn., Calif. Sch. Nurses Orgn. (bd. dirs., chair edn Bay Coast sect.), Delta Kappa Gamma. Home: 1711 Encinal Ave Alameda CA 94501-4020

HERRICK, TRACY GRANT, fiduciary; b. Cleve., Dec. 30, 1933; s. Stanford Avery and Elizabeth Grant (Smith) H.; B.A., Columbia U., 1956, M.A., 1958; postgrad. Yale U., 1956-57; M.A., Oxford U. (Eng.), 1960; m. Maie Kaarsoo, Oct. 12, 1963; children: Sylvi Anne, Alan Kalev. economist, Fed. Res. Bank, Cleve., 1960-70; sr. economist Stanford Research Inst., Menlo Park, Calif., 1970-73; v.p., sr. analyst Shuman, Agnew & Co., Inc., San Francisco, 1973-75; v.p. Bank of Am., San Francisco, 1975-81; pres. Tracy G. Herrick, Inc., 1981—; lectr. Stonier Grad. Sch. Banking, Am. Bankers Assn., 1967-76; commencement speaker Memphis Banking Sch., 1974; bd. dirs. Jefferies Group, Inc. (chmn. bd. audit com. 1989-96, chmn. bd. compensation com. 1991-96, dir. 1996), Jefferies & Co., Inc., Anderson Capital Mgmt., Inc. Mem. adv. bd. San Xavier Found. Monterey, Calif. Fellow Fin. Analysts Fedn.; mem. Assn. Investment Mgmt. Rsch., San Francisco Soc. Security Analysts, dir. Com. for Monetary Rsch. and Edn., Inc. Republican. Congregationalist. Author: Bank Analyst's Handbook, 1978; Timing, 1981; Power and Wealth, 1988; contbr. articles to profl. jours. Home: 1150 University Ave Palo Alto CA 94301-2238

HERRIN, STEPHANIE ANN, retired aerospace engineer; b. Oakland, Calif., May 13, 1950; d. Thomas Edgar Herrin and Mary Teresa Silva; m. Este Stovall, May 20, 1989. BSc, U. Pacific, 1976; MSc, Columbia Pacific U., 1978; PhD in Engring. & Applied Scis., U. Bradford, West Yorkshire, U.K., 1994. Reliability engr. Applied Tech. Litton Industries, Sunnyvale, Calif., 1979-80; sr. reliability engr., reliability project mgr. ESL, Inc., Sunnyvale, 1980-84; sr. reliability & quality assurance engr. Martin Marietta, Balt., 1984-85; lead, sr. reliability engr. Los Alamos Tech. Assn., Albuquerque, 1985-86; sr. reliability engr. Boeing, Houston, 1987-89; sr. sys. engr., knowledge capture engr. Astrobiology Inst. NASA-Ames Rsch. Ctr., Moffett Field, Calif., 1988-99; cons. Lawrence Livermore Labs., Livermore, Calif., 1985-87; failure analysis radiographer Ford Aerospace & Comm. Corp., Palo Alto, Calif., 1973-79; owner, analyst Fail Safe Radiography, Palo Alto, 1975-81. Contbr. articles to profl. jours. Recipient U.S. govt. Manned Flight Awareness award, 1994; NASA grantee, 1987-89, 90-93, 94-95; named to Outstanding Scientists of 20th Century, Internat. Biog. Ctr., Cambridge, Eng., 1999. Mem. IEEE (reliability & maintainability soc., engring. in medicine & biology computer soc., info. theory, sys., man & cybernetics, oceanic engring. soc.), AAUW, Soc. Naval Architects & Marine Engrs. Achievements include patent for real-time automated diagnosis and intelligent utility for maintainability. Home: 343 Center St Redwood City CA 94061-3883

HERRINGER, FRANK CASPER, diversified financial services company executive; b. N.Y.C., Nov. 12, 1942; s. Casper Frank and Alice Virginia (McMullen) H.; m. Maryellen B. Cattani; children: William, Sarah, Julia. AB magna cum laude, Dartmouth, 1964, MBA with highest distinction, 1965. Prin. Cresap, McCormick & Paget, Inc. (mgmt. cons.), N.Y.C., 1965-71; staff asst. to Pres., Washington, 1971-73; adminstr. U.S. Urban Mass Transp. Adminstrn., Washington, 1973-75; gen. mgr., chief exec. officer San Francisco Bay Area Rapid Transit Dist., 1975-78; exec. v.p., dir. Transam. Corp., San Francisco, 1979-86, pres., 1986—, CEO, 1991—, chmn., 1996—; bd. dirs. Unocal Corp., Charles Schwab & Co. Trustee Calif. Pacific Med. Ctr. Mem. Cypress Point Club, San Francisco Golf Club, Olympic Club, Pacific Union Club, Phi Beta Kappa. Office: Transam Corp 600 Montgomery St San Francisco CA 94111-2702

HERRINGTON, STEVE EUGENE, writer, illustrator, publishing executive; b. Aloha, Oreg., Aug. 31, 1972; s. Kevin Stephen and Linda May (LeBrun) H. Grad. h.s., Aloha, 1991. Asst. artist Cartoonists Across Am., Lompoc, Calif., 1993; artist, rschr. Software Dept., Santa Cruz, Calif., 1993; CEO, writer Golden Talon Pub./Studios, Aloha, 1994—. Author, illustrator: Angels of Love, Hope and Beauty: An Angel Coloring Book, 1997. Mem. Pacific Rim Martial Arts (student). Avocations: martial arts, meditation, vegetarianism, environmentalism, religious studies. Office: Golden Talon Pub Box 135 17675 SW Farmington Rd Aloha OR 97007-3208

HERRMAN, MARCIA KUTZ, child development specialist; b. Boston, June 16, 1927; d. Cecil and Sonia (Schneider) Kutz; m. Bayard F. Berman, July 23, 1949 (div. 1960); m. William H. Herrman, June 23, 1961; 1 child, Fred. BA, Smith Coll., 1949; MA, Pacific Oaks Coll., 1974. Credentialed tchr., Calif. NIMH intern Cedars-Sinai Med. Ctr., L.A., 1966-67; ednl. therpist L.A. Child Guidance Clinic, 1967-69, Child and Family Study Ctr., Cedars-Sinai Med. Ctr., 1969-71; dir. tng., asst. project dir. handicapped early edn. program Dubnoff Ctr., North Hollywood, Calif., 1972-76; child devel. cons. schs., agys. and families Studio City, Calif., 1969—; cons. L.A. Child Guidance Clinic, Head Start, Child Care and Devel. Svcs., 1969-73; cons. child and parenting program St. Joseph's Ctr., Venice, Calif., 1992—; profl. expert L.A. Unified Sch. Dist., 1976-80; vis. faculty Pacific Oaks Coll., Pasadena, Calif., 1970-76. Vol. Alliance for Children's Rights, 1992-94, Child Advocate's Office, Superior Ct., L.A., 1983—; mem. Dependency Ct. Com., 1988-92, Task Force on Rep. of Children in Dependency Ct., Superior Ct., L.A. County, 1994; mem. oversight and resource coms. Placement Project, joint com. of PPAC and Cmty. Adv. Coun., 1995-98; mem. steering com. Cmty. Based Placement Project, Joint Effort of Youth Law Ctr., L.A. Dept. Children. & Family Svcs. and Calif. Dept. Social Svcs., 1995; mem. L.A. Foster Care Network, 1987-94, L.A. County MacLaren Children's Ctr. Task Force, 1990-95, cmty. mem., 1996—; mem. cmty. adv. com. St. Joseph's Ctr., 1992-96, mem. policy and implementation coms., community of care integration project, 1998—, LA County bd. suprs., mem. policy and implementation coms.; bd. chairperson Keeping Families Together, L.A., 1987-88; trustee Ruth Pearce Fund for Therapeutic Companions, 1994—. Recipient Vol. of Yr. award L.A. County Bd. Suprs., 1986, Commendation for Dedicated Svc. to Community, 1991, Recognition award for Outstanding Svc. to Children L.A. County Inter-Agy. Coun. on Child Abuse, 1991; Sophia Smith scholar, 1949. Fellow Am. Orthopsychiat. Assn. (life); mem. N.Y. Acad. Scis., Assn. Child Devel. Specialists, Nat. Ct. Appointed Spl. Advocate Assn. Democrat. Jewish. Avocations: music, theater, hiking, travel. Home and Office: 3919 Ethel Ave Studio City CA 91604-2204

HERROLD, REBECCA MUNN, music educator, writer; b. Warren, Pa., Sept. 29, 1938; d. Gordon Clifford and Edith Esther (Lind) Munn; m. Stephen Herrold, 1959. MusB, U. Miami, 1960; MA, San Jose State U., 1968; D Mus. Arts, Stanford U., 1974. Asst. prof. Youngstown (Ohio) State U., 1974-75, Oreg. State U., Corvallis, 1975-80; assoc. prof. music San Jose State U., 1980-84, prof. music, 1984—. Author: (textbook) New Approaches to Elementary Classroom Music, 1984, 3d edit., 1999, Mastering the Fundamentals of Music, 1997, Children's Songs from Southeast Asia, 1997; Computer Programs for Music Instruction, Tutor Software, Inc., arranger Shawnee Press Inc., 1974—, pianist in Santa Clara Trio, 1987—, Ruggieri Chamber Players, 1998—. Grantee Apple Computer Co., 1981, Atari Computer Co., 1982, Bell and Howell. Mem. Coll. Music Soc., Am. Assoc. for Gifted Children, Calif. Coun. on Computers in Music, Calif. Coun. Music Tchr. Educators (se.c 1985-86), Stanford Alumni, Music Educators Nat. Conf., League of Am. Pen Women. Democrat. Office: San Jose State U Sch Music and Dance 1 Washington Sq San Jose CA 95192-0001

HERRON, CAROL CHRISTINE, financial planner, home economist; b. Lebanon, Oreg., Dec. 17, 1944; d. Ralph Elwood and Mary Mabel (Morris) H. BS, Oreg. State U., 1967, MS, 1971. Cert. home economist; CFP. Home economist W.F. West H.S., Chehalis, Wash., 1968-69; extension agt. Wash. State U., Bellingham, 1971; extension specialist Wash. State U., Pullman, 1972-74; coord., instr. Portland (Oreg.) C.C., 1974-83; energy cons. Energy Counselors, Beaverton, Oreg., 1983-86; dir. devel. Coll. Home Econs. Oreg. State U., Corvallis, 1986-88; registered rep. Waddell and Reed Fin. Svcs., Beaverton, Oreg., 1988—. Mem. adminstrv. coun. St. Anthony's Ch., 1994—. Mem. Internat. Assn. for Fin. Planning, Am. Assn. Family and Consumer Scis. (nominating com. 1988-90, BSN sect. 1996-98, cert. chair 1992-95, sewing fair facilities chair 1990, 92, 94, ex-officio fin. com. 1993—), Oreg. Home Econs. Assn. (bd. dirs., pres. 1986-89), Oreg. State U. Coll. Home Econs. Alumni Assn. (bd. dirs. 1984-87), Oreg. Consumer League (bd. dirs., pres.). Democrat. Roman Catholic. Avocations: bicycling, gardening. Office: Waddell and Reed Fin Svcs 8625 SW Cascade Ave Ste 290 Beaverton OR 97008-7152

HERRON, ELLEN PATRICIA, retired judge; b. Auburn, N.Y., July 30, 1927; d. David Martin and Grace Josephine (Berner) Herron; A.B. Trinity Coll., 1949; M.A., Cath. U. Am., 1954; J.D., U. Calif.-Berkeley, 1964. Asst. dean Cath. U. Am., 1952-54; instr. East High Sch., Auburn, 1955-57; asst. dean Wells Coll., Aurora, N.Y., 1957-58; instr. psychology and history Contra Costa Coll., 1958-60; dir. row Stanford, 1960-61; assoc. Knox & Kretzmer, Richmond, Calif., 1964-65. Bar: Calif., 1965. Ptnr. Knox & Herron, 1965-74, Knox, Herron and Masterson, 1974-77 (both Richmond, Calif.); judge Superior Ct. State of Calif., 1977-87; pvt. judge, 1987-90; pvt. judge Jud. Arbitration and Mediation Svc., Inc. (JAMS- Endispute), 1990—; ptnr. Real Estate Syndicates, Calif., 1967-77; owner, mgr. The Barricia Vineyards, 1978—. Active numerous civic orgns. Home: 51 Western Dr Richmond CA 94801-4011 also: 15700 Sonoma HGW Sonoma CA 95476

HERRON, MARGARET CATHERINE, nursing administrator; b. Aberdeen Proving Grounds, Md., Mar. 27, 1954; d. Thomas James and Virginia (Owen) Herron. BS in Nursing, San Diego State U., 1977. RN, Calif. Nurse Tri-City Hosp. Mental Health Unit, Oceanside, Calif., 1983-86; admission coord. Vis. Nurse Assn. San Diego, 1986-91; nurse cons. individual case mgmt. Aetna Life & Casualty, San Diego, 1991-93; dir. health care svcs. Interim Health Care, Escondido, Calif., 1993—; bd. dirs. Fraternity House and Michaelle House, residential care facility for people with AIDS, Escondido, Vista; mem. adv. bd. Maric Coll., San Marcos, Calif., 1994—; chair Pediatric Continuity of Care Coalition, 1996-98.. Capt. USAF, 1978-83. Democrat. Avocations: reading, photography, travel. Office: Interim Health Care 1875 S Centre City Pkwy Ste 5J Escondido CA 92025-6525

HERSHMAN, JEROME MARSHALL, endocrinologist; b. Chgo., July 20, 1932; s. Maurice and Gertrude (Zemel) H.; m. Fleurette Kram, Dec. 22, 1957; children: Daniel, Michael, Jeffrey. BS, Northwestern U., 1952; MS, Calif. Inst. Technology, 1953; MD, U. Ill., 1957. Diplomate Am. Bd. Internal Medicine, Endocrinology & Metabolism. Fellow in endocrinology New England Ctr. Hosp., Boston, 1961-63; clin. investigator Northwestern U. Med. Sch., Chgo., 1964-67; chief clin. nuclear medicine Birmingham (Ala.) VA Hosp., 1967-71, chief endocrine sect., 1971-72; prof. Sch. Medicine U. Ala., Birmingham, 1967-72, UCLA, 1972—; chief endocrinology and metabolism West L.A. VA Med. Ctr., 1972—. Editor: Thyroid, 1991—; mem. editorial bd. Am. Jour. of Medicine 1989-95; editor: Practical Endocrinology, 1981, Endocrine Pathophysiology, 2d edit., 1982, 3d edit., 1988, Syllabus of 38th Annual Postgraduate Assembly of the Endocrine Soc., 1986. Capt. USAF, 1959-61, col. USAR, 1985-91. Mem. Am. Thyroid Assn. (dir. 1989-92, pres. 1992-93). Jewish. Achievements include demonstration of thyrotropin-releasing hormone for diagnosis of pituitary and thyroid disease in 1969; discovered thyroid-stimulating activity of human chorionic gonadotropin. Home: 15970 Meadowcrest Rd Sherman Oaks CA 91403-4714 Office: West LA VA Med Ctr 11301 Wilshire Blvd Los Angeles CA 90073-1003

HERSHMAN, LYNN LESTER, artist; b. Cleve.; 1 dau., Dawn. B.S., Case-Western Res. U., 1963; M.A., San Francisco State U., 1972. Prof. U. Calif., Davis, 1984—; Vis. prof. art U. Calif., Berkeley, Calif. Coll. Arts and Crafts, San Jose State U., 1974-78; assoc. project dir. Christo's Running Fence, 1973-76; founder, dir. Floating Mus., 1975-79; ind. film/video producer and cons., 1979—. Author works in field; one-man shows include Santa Barbara Mus. Art, 1970, Univ. Art Mus., Berkeley, Calif., 1972, Mills Coll., Oakland, Calif., 1973, William Sawyer Gallery, 1974, Nat. Galleries, Melbourne, Australia, 1976, Mandeville Art Gallery, U. Calif., San Diego, 1976, M.H. de Young Art Mus., 1978, Pallazo dei Diamonte, Ferrara, Italy, 1978, San Francisco Art Acad., 1980, Portland Center Visual Arts, 1980, New Mus., New Sch., N.Y.C., 1981, Inst. Contemporary Art, Phila., 1981, Anina Nosai Gallery, N.Y.C., 1981, Contemporary Art Center, Cin., 1982, Toronto, Los Angeles Contemporary Exhibits, 1986, Univ. Art Mus. Berkeley, 1987, Madison (Wis.) Art Ctr., 1987, Intersesction for the Arts, San Francisco, Pacific Film Archive, A. Space, "Guerilla Tactics" Toronto, Can., Venice Bienalle Global Village; group exhbns. include Cleve. Art Mus., 1968, St. Paul Art Ctr., 1969, Richmond (Calif.) Art Ctr., 1970, 73, Galeria del Sol, Santa Barbara, Calif., 1971, San Francisco Art Inst., 1972, Richard Demarco Art Gallery, Edinburgh, Scotland, 1973, Laguna Beach (Calif.) Art Mus., 1973, Univ. Art Mus., Univ. Calif., Berkeley, 1974, Bronx (N.Y.) Mus., 1975, Linda Ferris Gallery, Seattle, 1975, Madenville Art Gallery, San Diego, Contemporary Arts Mus., Houston, 1977, New Orleans, 1977, Ga. Mus. Art, Athens, 1977, New Mus., N.Y., 1981, Calif. Coll. Arts and Crafts, 1981, San Francisco Mus. Modern Art, 1979, 80, 90, Art-Beaubourg, Paris, 1980, Ars Electronica, 1989, Am. Film Inst., 1989, Mus. Moving Image Internat. Ctr. for Photography, 1989, Kitchen Ctr. for Video-Music, N.Y., 1990, Robert Koch Gallery, San Francsico, 1990, Inst. Contemporary Art, London, 1990, Frankfurt (Germany) Art Fair, 1990, Inst. Conteporary Art, Boston, 1991, Oakland (Calif.) Mus., 1991, La Cite des Arts et des Nouvelles Technologies, Montreal, 1991, Richard F. Brush Art Gallery, Canton, N.Y., 1992, Jack Tilton Gallery, N.Y., 1992, Southeastern Ctr. for Contemporary Art, Winston-Salem, N.C., 1992, Bonner Kunstverein, Bonn, Germany, 1992, Chgo. Ave. Armory, 1992, Retrospective, Tribute, 1994, Nelson Gallery, Paris, 1994, Hess Collection, 1994. Bd. dirs. San Francisco Art Acad., Spectrum Found., Motion a Performance Collective. Western States Regional fellow (film/video), 1990; grantee Nat. Endowment for the Arts, (2) Art Matters Inc., San Francisco Found., N.Y. State Coun. for the Arts, Zellerbach Family Fund, Inter Arts of Marin, Gerbode Found., The Women's Project, recipient Dirs. Choice award San Francisco Internat. Film Festival, 1987, tribute 1987 Mill Valley Video Festial, Exptl. Video award 1988, 1st prize Montbelliard, France, 1990, 2d prize, Vigo, Spain, 1992, 1993 Ars Electronica, Austria, WRO Poland, Nat. Film Theatre, London, Gerber award Seattle Art Mus., 1994, ZKM/Siemans award, 1995. Mem. Assn. Art Pubs. (dir., Annie Gerber award 1995). Office: 1935 Filbert St San Francisco CA 94123-3503*

HERSLEY, DENNIS CHARLES, environmentalist, software systems consultant; b. Idaho Falls, Idaho, July 11, 1947; s. Cyril R. and Bardella (Webb) H.; m. Jane Anne Lilly, Jan. 16, 1993; children: Cary Connolly, Laura Lilly, Claire Lilly. Student, U. So. Calif., 1964-65; electronics tech. cert., Idaho State U., 1970; postgrad., U. Santa Clara, 1979. Cert. FCC 1st class radio engr. with TV and radar endorsements.;. Ptnr. Intensive Care Tech. Svcs., Pocatello, Idaho, 1972-74; test engring. mgr. Nat. Semiconductor, Sunnyvale, Calif., 1975-76; test ops. mgr. Amdahl Ireland, Ltd., Dublin, 1978; engr., planner, analyst Amdahl Corp., Sunnyvale, 1979-85; CFO, chmn. Provista Software Internat., San Jose, Calif., 1985-86; pres. Almaden Consulting, Santa Cruz, Calif., 1985—; co-founder, pres., dir. non profit sci. rsch. Citizens United for Responsible Environmentalism, Inc., Santa Cruz, Calif., 1994—; CFO Rsch. Consultation, Inc., Santa Cruz, Calif., 1998—; planner, sponsor Fusewest Regional Tech. Conf., Scottsdale, Ariz., 1988-89; tech. curriculum advisor Idaho State U., 1970-75; participant 3d Internat. Conf. on bioaerosols, Fungi and Mycotoxins, 1998. Inventor calculator design, 1975; featured on BBC documentary, 1998. Recipient Outstanding Alumnus award Idaho State U., 1975, Honored Donor award Monterey Bay Aquarium, 1996. Mem. Calif. Assn. Non-Profits, No. Calif. Focus Users Group (asst. editor 1988-90), Santa Cruz Tech. Alliance. Office: CURE 2375 Benson Ave Santa Cruz CA 95065-1674

HERSMAN, MARION FRANK, professional administrator, lawyer; b. Huntington, W.Va., Nov. 12, 1932; s. Marion Rockefeller and Frances Mae (Peabody) H.; m. Carole Anne Birthright, Oct. 1960 (div.); 1 child, Frank Eric Birthright; m. Nina Claire Mohay, Dec. 24, 1976 (div.); 1 child, Alicia Claire; m. Eleonora Georgi Hivrina, April 11, 1995; children: Elizabeth Anne, Diana Frances. B.S. in Chemistry, Physics and Math, Ohio State U., 1953; Ph.D. in Chemistry (Victor Chem. fellow, Colgate Palmolive-Peet fellow, Univ. fellow), U. Ill., 1956; J.D., George Washington U., 1958, LL.M., 1960; M.A., New Sch. for Social Research, 1964. Bar: Va. 1958, N.Y. 1959, D.C. 1960, U.S. Supreme Ct. 1960, U.S. Ct. Appeals (D.C. cir.) 1960. Teaching fellow U. Ill.; patent examiner U.S. Patent Office, Washington, 1956-57; assoc. firm Burns Doane, Benedict & Irons, Washington, 1957-59, Arthur, Dry & Dole, N.Y.C., 1959-60, Fish, Richardson & Neave, N.Y.C., 1960-64; staff assoc. office sci. resources planning NSF, Washington, 1964-67; office of planning and policy studies NSF, 1967-69, head office intergovtl. sci. programs, 1969-72, dir. office intergovtl. sci. and research utilization, 1972-75; exec. dir. Colo. Planning Coordinating Council, 1976; spl. asst., sci. and tech. advisor to Gov. Colo., 1976; sci. and tech. advisor Fedn. Rocky Mountain States, Denver, 1977; dir. Rocky Mountain Tech. Sharing Task Force, 1977; dir. Div. Water Resources Hillsborough County, Tampa, Fla., 1977, dir. Div. Pub. Utilities, 1977-78; dir. Office of Planning and Intergovtl. Relations Hillsborough County, Tampa, 1978-79; asst. county adminstr. Hillsborough County (Fla.) Div. Pub. Utilities, 1978-79; vice chmn. Hillsborough Intergovtl. Resource Recovery Mgmt. Com.; mem. Fla. Community Conservation Com., 1978-80, Urban Consortium, 1978-80; spl. asst. to pres. U. South Fla., 1979-80; atty. NSF, 1980-82; dir. com. on hazardous materials Fed. Emergency Mgmt. Agy., 1981-83; vis. disting. prof. Nova U., 1982, spl. asst. to pres. for program devel., 1982; asst. city mgr. for health and human services City of Austin, (Tex.), 1982-84; exec. v.p. Lawyers Title of Ky., 1983-85; ptnr. LTK Enterprises, 1983-85; exec. v.p., chief operating officer Automation Telecommunications and Management Inc., Austin, Tex., 1984-85; dir. research and state services The Council of State Govts., Lexington, Ky., 1985-87; town mgr. Town of Snow Hill, Md., 1988; county mgr. Nye County, Nev., 1988-90; pres. RH Mgmt. Assocs., 1990—; dir. social svcs. Louis Berger Internat. Cons., Sasatov Oblast, Russia, 1996—; spkr. in field; tchg. assoc. George Washington U., 1957-59; chmn., exec. dir. com. on intergovtl. sci. rels. Fed. Coun. Sci. and Tech., Exec. Office

of Pres., 1979-83; mem. Agrl. Yearbook adv. bd. USDA, 1979, mem. tech. adv. bd. nat. rural cmtys. facilities assessment, 1978; chmn. com. on policy mgmt. and assistance U.S. Office Mgmt. and Budget, Washington, 1974-75; mem. com. on tech. sharing President's Office Sci. and Tech., 1972-74; chmn. So. Nev. Rural Health Fair, 1991; prof. urban engring. nat. U. Mex., Mexico City, 1975; vis. faculty CSC, Kings Point, N.Y., 1975, Fed. Exec. Inst., Charlottesville, Va., 1977, Golden Gate U., 1979-80; vis. prof. U. Colo. Grad. Sch. Pub. Affairs, 1976-77, U. South Fla., 1978, Marin Sch., U. Ky., 1986-88; spl. asst. to dir. NSF, 1976-80; cons. Office Sci. and Tech., Exec. Office of Pres., 1976-80, Western Govs.' Task Force on Regional Policy Mgmt., 1976-77; cons. USDA, 1978; mem. Subcom. on Rsch. Itilization Transp. Rsch. Bd./NRC/NAS, 1981-82; administr. Pahrump Valley Med. Ctr., 1991-92; pres. Nev. Health and Med. Found., 1991-92; U.S. exec. advisor mayor and city coun. City of Narva, Estonia, 1994-96; U.S. exec. advisor City of Tartu, Estonia, 1994, Internat. Exec. Svcs. Corps, 1994; U.S. trade rep. City of Narva, Estonia, 1994; exec. advisor Internat. Exec. Svc. Corps, City of Vladimir, Russia, 1995-96; dir. social svcs. Louis Berger Internat., Inc., 1996-98; exec. advisor Saratov, Russia, 1996-98. Contbg. author: Science and Technology Policies, 1973; bd. editors and consultants: Scholar and Educator, 1977; mem. editorial bd.: Jour. Edn. and Scholar, 1977-87; contbr. articles to profl. jours. Bd. dirs. Warwick Assn., 1980-81; chmn. consumers and bus. affairs com. D.C. Area Neighborhood Council; mem. Washington Mayor's Planning and Budget Adv. Com., 1980-82; vol. exec. Internat. Exec. Svcs. Corps., 1994—; Pahrump Arts Coun., 1994-96. Recipient Pub. Service award states of Ga., La., Ala., Pa., Okla., N.C. Pub. Service award So. Interstate Nuclear Bd., Pub. Service award Nat. Conf. State Legislatures; Picatinny Arsenal fellow, Victor Chem. fellow, Colgate Palmolive-Peet fellow, Ohio State Univ. fellow; U.S. Govt. grantee. Mem. Va., D.C., Fed. bar assns., Am. Chem. Soc., Am. Soc. Pub. Adminstrn. (chmn. sect. on intergovtl. adminstrn. and mgmt. 1977-79, Public Service award), AAAS, Sigma Xi, Phi Lambda Upsilon, Delta Theta Phi (chmn scholarships), Alpha Chi Sigma, Kappa Sigma. Home and Office: PO Box 3434 2070 S Page St Pahrump NV 89041

HERSON, GENE, computer company executive. Pres. Emcon, San Jose, Calif. Office: Emcon 1921 Ringwood Ave San Jose CA 95131-1788*

HERTEL, HOWARD JAY, photographer; b. Oakland, Calif., Apr. 25, 1924; s. Elmer Joseph and Lillian Ruth (Hultberg) H.; m. Laverne Wilson, June 1949 (div. June 1965); children: Douglas Jay (dec.), Kenneth Bruce. Grad. H.S., Lafayette, Calif. Comml. photographer Waters and Hainlin Studio, Oakland, 1942-43; photographer, photo lab. tech. Army Air Forces, 1943-45; photographer Stanford Rsch. Inst., Menlo Park, Calif., 1950-53; freelance photographer San Francisco; faculty mem. Stanford (Calif.) U., 1950-53; market rsch. interviewer Field Rsch. Corp., San Francisco, 1994. Pres. Young Reps., Sacramento. Staff sgt. USAFR, 1964; active Sr. Ctr.-Aquatic Park San Francisco, 1994. Named assoc. Royal Photographic Soc., Bath, Eng., 1955. Mem. Air Force Assn. (life). Avocations: collecting model cars, gourmet cooking.

HERTLEIN, FRED, III, industrial hygiene laboratory executive; b. San Francisco, Oct. 17, 1933; s. Fred and Herta (Komning) H.; m. Clara Kam Fung Tse, Apr. 1958 (div. Apr. 1982); children: Fritz, Hans Wernher, Lisa Marie, Gretel Marga. BS in Chemistry, U. Nev., Reno, 1956; postgrad., U. Hawaii, Manoa, 1956-58. Cert. profl. chemist, indsl. hygienist, safety profl., hazard control mgr.; bldg. insp. and mgmt. planner, biol. safety profl. Grad. teaching ast. in chemistry U. Hawaii, Honolulu, 1956-58; air pollution sampling sta. operator Truesdail Labs., Honolulu, 1957; chemist oceanographical research vessels Dept. Interior, 1957-59; with Bechtel-Hawaiian Dredging, 1959; co-owner marine survey co. Honolulu, 1959-60; radiochemist Pearl Harbor (Hawaii) Naval Shipyard, 1959-62, indsl. hygienist med. dept., 1962-69, head indsl.hygiene br., 1969-72; indsl. hygiene program mgr. Naval Regional Med. Clinic, Pearl Harbor Naval Sta., 1972-78; pres., dir. lab. and indsl. hygiene, co-owner Indsl. Analytical Lab., Inc., Honolulu, 1978-97; pres. F. Hertlein & Assocs., 1970-78; asst. clin. prof. U. Hawaii Sch. Pub. Health, 1973—; tchr. Asbestos and Lead Abatement U.S. Mil. Bases Japan, Okinawa, 1995-97. Contbr. articles to profl. jours. Coord. Merry TubaChristmas, Honolulu, 1992—. Named Outstanding Male Fed. Employee, Honolulu Fed. Exec. Council, 1967, Citizen of Day citation Sta. KGU76, Honolulu, 1972, cert. of achievement Toastmasters Internat., 1974, expression of appreciation U. Hawaii Sch. Pub. Health, 1985. Fellow Am. Inst. Chemists (life); mem. Am. Acad. Indsl. Hygiene, Am. Chem. Soc., Am. Indsl. Hygiene Assn., Profl. Assn. Diving Instrs. (instr. emeritus), Tubists Universal Brotherhood Assn. (life). Home: 1493 Kaweloka St Pearl City HI 96782-1513

HERTNEKY, RANDY LEE, optometrist; b. Burlington, Colo., Jan. 9, 1955; s. Harry Francis and Darleen Mae (Walters) H.; m. Laura Ann Cicaccio, Nov. 28, 1981; children: Lisa Kay, Erin Elizabeth. BA, U. Colo., 1977; OD, So. Calif. Coll. Optometry, Fullerton, 1981. Pvt. practice optometry Yuma and Wray, Colo., 1982—. Precinct committeeman Yuma County Rep. Com., 1986—; mem. bd. rev. Boy Scouts Am., Yuma, 1982—; chmn. bldg. com. Yuma H.S., 1987-89; bd. dirs. Yuma Hosp. Found., 1990-97, vice chmn., 1994-97; chmn. Yuma Sch. Curriculum Com., 1993. Mem. APHA, KC (sec. 1990-95, dep. grand knight 1995-96, grand knight 1996-98), Am. Optometric Assn. (coord. Colo. Polit. Action Com. 1995—), Colo. Optometric Assn. (trustee 1989-90, vice chmn. legis. com. 1994—, nominee Optometrist of Yr. 1996), Coll. Optometrists in Vision Devel. (assoc.), Yuma C. of C. (Bus. of Yr. 1996), Wray C. of C., Lions (treas. 1987-88, pres. 1991-92, Lion of Yr. award 1992). Roman Catholic. Avocations: golf, coin collecting, skiing. Office: 107 S Main St Yuma CO 80759-1913

HERTWECK, ALMA LOUISE, sociology and child development educator; b. Moline, Ill., Feb. 6, 1937; d. Jacob Ray and Sylvia Ethel (Whitt) Street; m. E. Romayne Hertweck, Dec. 16, 1955; 1 child, William Scott. A.A., Mira Costa Coll., 1969; B.A. in Sociology summa cum laude, U. Calif.-San Diego, 1975, M.A., 1977, Ph.D., 1982. Cert. sociology instr., multiple subjects teaching credential grades kindergarten-12, Calif. Staff research assoc. U. Calif.-San Diego, 1978-81; instr. sociology Chapman Coll., Orange, Calif., 1982-87; instr. child devel. MiraCosta Coll., Oceanside, Calif., 1983-87, 88-89; instr. sociology U.S. Internat. U., San Diego, 1985-88 ; exec. dir., v.p. El Camino Preschools, Inc., Oceanside, 1985—. Author: Constructing the Truth and Consequences: Educators' Attributions of Perceived Failure in School, 1982; co-author: Handicapping the Handicapped, 1985. Mem. Am. Sociol. Assn., Am. Ednl. Research Assn., Nat. Council Family Relations, Nat. Assn. Edn. Young Children, Alpha Gamma Sigma (life). Avocations: foreign travel; sailing; bicycling. Home: 2024 Oceanview Rd Oceanside CA 92056-3104 Office: El Camino Preschs Inc 2002 California St Oceanside CA 92054-5693

HERTWECK, E. ROMAYNE, psychology educator; b. Springfield, Mo., July 24, 1928; s. Garnett Perry and Nova Gladys (Chowning) H.; m. Alma Louise Street, Dec. 16, 1955; 1 child, William Scott. BA, Augustana Coll., 1962; MA, Pepperdine U., 1963; EdD, Ariz. State U., 1966; PhD, U.S. Internat. U., 1978. Cert. sch. psychologist, Calif. Night editor Rock Island (Ill.) Argus Newspaper, 1961; grad. asst. psychology dept. Pepperdine Coll., L.A., 1962; counselor VA, Ariz. State U., Tempe, 1963; assoc. dir. Conciliation Ct., Phoenix, 1964; instr. Phoenix Coll., Phoenix, 1965; prof. Mira Costa Coll., Oceanside, Calif., 1966—, mem. senate coun., 1968-70, 85-87, 89-91, chmn. psychology-counseling dept., 1973-75, chmn. dept. behavioral sci., 1976-82, 87-88, 90-91; part-time lectr. dept. bus. adminstrn. San Diego State U., 1980-84, Sch. Human Behavior U.S. Internat. U., 1984-89; prof. psychology Chapman Coll. Mem. World Campus Afloat, 1970; pres. El Camino Preschs., Inc., Oceanside, Calif., 1985—; CEO Nutri-Cal, Inc., Oceanside, Calif., 1996—. Bd. dirs. Lifeline, 1969, Christian Counseling Center, Oceanside, 1970-82; mem. City of Oceanside Childcare Task Force, 1991—; mem. City of Oceanside Community Rels. Commn., 1991-96, vice chair, 1994; mem. steering com. Healthy Cities Project City of Oceanside, Calif., 1993-95. Mem. Am., Western, North San Diego County (v.p. 1974-75) psychol. assns., Am. Assn. for Counseling and Devel., Nat. Educators Fellowship (v.p. El Camino chpt. 1985-90), Mira Costa Full-Time Faculty Assn. (pres. 1990-92), Phi Delta Kappa, Kappa Delta Pi, Psi Chi, Kiwanis (charter mem. Carlsbad club, dir. 1975-77). Home: 2024 Oceanview Rd Oceanside CA 92056-3104 Office: Mira Costa Coll PO Box 586312 Oceanside CA 92058-6312 also: El Camino Preschs Inc 2002 California St Oceanside CA 92054-5673

HERTWECK, GALEN FREDRIC, minister; b. St. Louis, May 31, 1946; s. Vernon L. and Erma G. (Giger) H.; m. Bronte L. McGuire, July 8, 1967; children: John L., Jill R. AA, Mesa (Ariz.) Community Coll., 1967; BA, So. Calif. Coll., 1968; MDiv, Fuller Theol. Sem., Pasadena, Calif., 1972; D of Ministry, Fuller Theol. Sem., 1977. Ordained to ministry Assemblies of God Ch., 1973. Assoc. pastor Harbor Assembly of God, Costa Mesa, Calif., 1972-75, Faith Assembly Ch., Monterey Park, Calif., 1975-76; asst. min. Christian Life Ch., LaCrescenta, Calif., 1976-77; dir. adult ministries Evang. Temple Christian Ctr., Springfield, Mo., 1977-79; pastor King's Chapel Christian Ctr., Springfield, 1979-93; adj. faculty So. Calif. Coll., 1972-75, 97—; pastor Family Christian Ctr., Lake Forest, Calif., 1994—; vis. lectr. Continental Bible Coll., Brussels, 1983, Asia Pacific Theol. Sem. Baguio City, The Philippines, 1988, Asia Theol. Ctr. for Evangelism and Missions, 1984; pres. Springfield Ministerial Alliance, 1984-85; adj. faculty Assemblies of God Theol. Sem., Springfield, 1986-90. Contbr. articles to pubs. Pres. Child Advocacy Coun., Springfield, 1989-91. Mem. Lake Forest C. of C. (v.p. 1997—). Republican. Office: Family Christian Ctr 25422 Trabuco Rd # 105/219 Lake Forest CA 92630-2791

HERTZOG, ELWOOD W., III, directory and advertising consultant; b. Seattle, Jan. 8, 1971; s. Elwood Wesley and Ilene Joyce (Wetta) H. Student, U. Wash., 1989-93. Sr. sales rep. Local Touch Directories, Kirkland, WA, 1994-96; yellow pages cons. USWest Dex, Seattle, 1996—; internet cons. Travel Web Internat. Vol. King County elections Wash. State Rep. Party, Seattle, 1996. Lutheran. Avocations: skiing, swimming. Home: 19525 SE 24th Way Issaquah WA 98029 Office: USWest Dex 13920 SE Eastgate Way Bellevue WA 98009

HERTZOG, EUGENE EDWARD, video producer, editor; b. Oak Park, Ill., Jan. 30, 1932; s. Charles Demetrius and Julia (McKelvey) H.; m. Magdalene Delores Tafoya, Nov. 16, 1957 (dec. Oct. 1997); 1 child, Wayne Alan. Grad., Winona Sch. Profl. Photography, Ind., 1976. Enlisted U.S. Army, 1949, sgt., photographer Signal Corps, 1949-58; project photographer Bur. Reclamation, Ephrata, Wash., 1958-63; regional photographer Bur. Reclamation, Boulder City, Nev., 1963-80, visual info. officer, 1980-94; ind. video prodr. Gene Hertzog Video Prodns., Henderson, Nev., 1994—. Recipient Citation for Meritorious Svc. Sec. of the Interior, 1989, Outstanding Achievement award Assn. Multi-Image Internat., 1986, Indsl. Photo Dept. of Yr. award Profl. Photographer's Assn. Eastman Kodak, 1979. Mem. Profl. Photographers Am., Internat. TV Assn. (merit award 1987), Lake Mead Boat Owners Assn. (past pres.), Colo. River Water Users Assn. (photographer), Las Vegas Jaycees (newspaper editor 1964-70). Democrat. Roman Catholic. Avocations: videography, photography, boating. Home: 1047 Armillaria St Henderson NV 89015-3107 Office: PO Box 61092 Boulder City NV 89006-1092

HERZ, MICHAEL JOSEPH, marine environmental scientist; b. St. Paul, Aug. 12, 1936; s. Malvin E. and Josephine (Daneman) H.; m. Joan Klein Levy, Feb. 3, 1962 (div. 1982); children: David M., Daniel J., Ann K.; m. Naomi Brodie Schalit, Aug. 21, 1984 (div. 1996); children: Nathaniel B., Hallie R.; m. Kate Pearson Josephs, Sept. 27, 1998. BA, Reed Coll., 1958; MA, San Francisco State U., 1962; PhD, U. So. Calif., 1966. Program coord. postdoctoral tng. program U. Calif., San Francisco, 1969-73, asst. prof., 1969-73, assoc. prof. in residence, 1973-74; exec. dir., dir. water quality tng. program San Francisco Bay. chpt. Oceanic Soc., 1974-77; exec. v.p., co-dir. rsch. and policy Oceanic Soc., San Francisco, 1977-84; sr. rsch. scientist San Francisco State U., 1984-88; exec. dir. and baykeeper San Francisco BayKeeper, 1989-95; pvt. cons. Alna, Maine, 1995—; chmn. bd. govs. Tiburon Ctr. Environ. Studies, San Francisco State U., 1985-86; NRC com. mem. Effectiveness of Oil Spill Disperants, Washington, 1985-87, Risk Assessment Mgmt. Marine Systems, Washington, 1996-98; mem. com. on ocean disposal of radwaste Calif. Dept. Health, Sacramento, 1985-92; mem. tech. adv. com. Calif. Office of Oil Spill Prevention and Response, 1992-95; bd. dirs. Friends of the Earth, Washington, 1989—, chmn. bd. dirs., 1997—; bd. dirs. Oceanic Soc., 1984-89; chmn. bd. dirs. Aquatic Habitat Inst.; mem. Alaska Oil Spill Commn., 1989-90; mem. NRC com. Risk Assessment and Mgmt. of Marine Systems, Washington, 1996—. Author, co-editor: (books) Memory Consolidation, 1972, Habituation I & II, 1973; contbr. reports to profl. pubs. Chmn. community adv. bd. Sta. KQED (Pub. Broadcast System affiliate), 1979-85, San Francisco, citizens adv. com. San Francisco Bay Conservation and Devel. Commn., 1979—, chmn. 1984; mem. tech. adv. com. San Francisco Bay Regional Water Quality Control Bd., Oakland, Calif., 1979-82, Assn. Bay Area Govts., Oakland, 1983-84; mem. bay area adv. com. Sea Grant Marine Adv. Program, San Francisco, 1983-89; mem. com. Bur. Land Mgmt., Pacific States Regional Tech. Working Group, 1979-83; bd. dirs. Maine Initiatives, 1996—, Sheepscot Valley Conservation Area, 1995—, Citizens for a Better Environ., 1986-94, Oceanic Soc., 1984-89. Served with U.S. Army, 1958-59. Predoctoral fellow NIMH, U. So. Calif., 1963-64; postdoctoral fellow NIMH, UCLA Brain Research Inst, 1966-68. Mem. AAAS, Calif. Acad. Scis., San Francisco Bay and Estuarine Assn.

HERZBERG, DOROTHY CREWS, secondary education educator; b. N.Y.C., July 8, 1935; d. Floyd Houston and Julia (Lesser) Crews; m. Hershel Zelig Herzberg, May 22, 1962 (div. Apr. 1988); children: Samuel Floyd, Laura Jill, Daniel Crews. *Son Samuel, BA, MA, works for San Mateo Department of Planning, San Mateo, California. He has a wife, Leslie, and a daughter Aliza. Daughter Laura, MD in Pediatrics, works at the Westchester Medical Center, Valhalla, New York. Son Daniel has a BA at the University of California at Berkeley, a BS from the University of Oregon, and an MSW from the University of Michigan.* AB, Brown U., 1957; MA, Stanford U., 1964; JD, San Francisco Law Sch., 1976. Legal sec. various law firms, San Francisco, 1976-78; tchr. Mission Adult Sch., San Francisco, 1965-66; tchr. secondary and univ. levels Peace Corps, Nigeria, 1961-63; investigator Office of Dist. Atty., San Francisco, 1978-80; sr. administr. Dean Witter Reynolds Co., San Francisco, 1980-83; registered rep. Waddell and Reed, 1983-84; fin. services rep. United Resourceds, Hayward, Calif., 1984-86; tax preparer H&R Block, 1987; revenue officer IRS, 1987-89; now tchr. ESL West Contra Costa Sch. Dist., El Cerrito, Calif., 1989—. *Dorothy Herzberg is chairperson of the Social Justice Council of the Unitarian-Universalist Church of Berkeley, California.* Editor: (newsletters) Coop. Nursery Sch. Council, 1969-71, Miraloma Life, 1976-82, Dem. Women's, 1980-81, Stanford Luncheon Club, 1984-85. Bd. dirs. LWV, San Francisco, 1967-69, mem. speakers bur., 1967-80; pres. Council Coop. Nursery Schs., San Francisco, 1969-71; bd. dirs. Miraloma (Calif.) Improvement Club, 1977-88, pres., 1980-81; alt. for supr. San Francisco Mayor's Commn. on Criminal Justice, 1978. Democrat. Unitarian. Home: 1006 Richmond St El Cerrito CA 94530-2616

HERZING, ALFRED ROY, computer executive; b. Kitchener, Ont., Can., June 23, 1958; naturalized, 1982; s. Alfred Georg and Kaethe (Binder) H.; m. Marjorie, Aug. 20, 1983; 1 child, Adam. BSEE, Calif. Poly. Inst., 1981. Telecom. engr. Union Oil Co., L.A., 1982-84; computer planning analyst Union Oil-UNOCAL, 1984-86; supr. facilities mgmt. UNOCAL Corp. Info. Svcs., Anaheim, Calif., 1986-89, bus analyst, 1989, mgr. planning and analysis, 1989-91, mgr. tech. & bus. assessment, 1991-96, exec. dir. Year 2000 Project Office, 1997—; speaker ENTELEC, Dallas, San Antonio, 1983, 85. Host athletic tournament Alfred Roy Herzing Invitational Frisbee Golf Tournament, 1986—. Mem. Toastmasters (L.A. chpt. pres. 1986-87, gov. area 12 1987-88, armnstrv. lt. gov. dist. 52 1988-89, ednl. lt. gov. dist. 52 1989-90, dist. gov. 1990-91, Toastmaster of Yr. 1990, region II conf. edn. presenter 1992, 93, chmn. dist. 52 1992-93, 93-94, pres. speakers forum club 1993-94, CTM/ATY.DTM chmn. founder's dist. 1993-94, 94-95, internat. dir. 1995-97, 3rd v.p. 1998-99), Yorba Linda Achievers Club (charter mem., pres. 1993-94). Republican. Avocations: frisbees, computer simulations. Home: 20365 Via La Vieja Yorba Linda CA 92887-3211 Office: UNOCAL 2929 E Imperial Hwy Ste 200 Brea CA 92821-6731

HESKETH, THOMAS A.E., lawyer, arbitrator, educator; b. Toronto, July 22, 1951; s. Thomas William Hesketh and Mary Patricia Bell Kindermann. BA, Claremont Men's Coll., 1975; JD, U. Calif., San Francisco, 1979. Bar: Calif. 1980, U.S. Supreme Ct. 1989. Tchr. Peace Corps, Morocco, 1973; faculty & paralegal, instr. U. Calif., San Francisco, 1978; legal rsch. and writing Hastings Coll. of the Law, U. Calif., San Francisco, 1985-88; atty., arbitrator Chickering & Gregory, San Francisco, 1990-94; Law Offices of Thomas A.E. Hesketh, San Francisco, 1995—; judge pro tem, arbitrator San Francisco Mcpl. Ct., 1988—; settlement judge pro tem, arbitrator San Francisco Superior Ct., 1992—; tchr. San Francisco Unified Sch. Dist., 1996-98; arbitrator Nat. Assn. Securities Dealers, 1988—; Pacific Stock Exch., 1990—. Sr. articles editor Hastings Constnl. Law Quar., 1978-79. Mem. Civil Grand Jury, San Francisco, 1991-92. Calif. State scholar, 1969-73. Mem. Bar Assn. San Francisco (vol. legal svcs. program). Democrat. Avocations: chess, baseball, international affairs. Office: Law Offices of Thomas AE Hesketh 303 31st Ave San Francisco CA 94121-1706

HESS, HELEN ELIZABETH, retired secondary school educator, musician; b. Elkader, Iowa, Feb. 22, 1930; d. James Dale and Helen Louise (Wahl) Welsch; m. Roger Merle Hess, Dec. 18, 1966. BA, U. So. Miss., 1952, MA, 1955. Tchr. Natchez (Miss.) Pub. Schs., 1952-54; tchr. Bakersfield (Calif.) City Schs., 1955-89, ret., 1989; staff mem. Bakersfield Symphony Orch., 1989—. Life mem. Washington Jr. H.S. PTA; mem. Assistance League Bakersfield, 1990—; bd. dirs. Bakersfield Masterworks Chorale. Named Outstanding Classroom Tchr., Bakersfield Rotary Club, 1970. Mem. Local and State Ret. Tchrs. Assn. Republican. Presbyterian. Avocations: vocal performance, ballroom dancing. Office: Bakersfield Symphony Orch 1401 19th St Ste 130 Bakersfield CA 93301-4451

HESS, RICHARD NEAL, plastic surgeon; b. Phila., June 16, 1957. MD, U. Ariz., 1983. Chmn. plastic surgery Northwest Hosp., Tucson. Office: Aesthetic Surg of Tucson 5585 N Oracle Rd Tucson AZ 85704-3821

HESS, STANLEY WILLIAM, curator, retired fine arts librarian; b. Bremerton, Wash., July 9, 1939; s. Ray Myron and Kathryn Elaine (Joehnke) H. Student, Olympic Coll., Bremerton, 1958-60; BA, U. Wash., 1964; MS of Libr. Scis., Case Western Res. U., 1976. Photographs and slides profl. Seattle Art Mus., 1964-73; assoc. libr. for photographs and slides Cleve. Mus. of Art, 1973-80; head libr. Nelson-Atkins Mus. of Art, Kansas City, Mo., 1980-91; pvt. rschr. Silverdale, Wash., 1992—; curator Evergreen Children's Theatre Puppet Mus., Bremerton, 1998—; lectr. on art librs. and visual resource collections in N.Am., U. Melbourne, Sydney, Australia, 1978; seminar leader on art and visual resource leadership, Australia and New Zealand, 1978, U. Melbourne, U. Auckland, Nat. U. Australia, Emporia (Kans.) State U., 1990, others. Author: Art Galleries Museums in North America; reviewer: Grant Development for Large and Small Libraries; contbg. author: Visual Resource: A Survey of Pictorial Material on Americana Available for Study and Purchase in Institutions in the United States; compiler: An Annotated Bibliography of Slide Library Literature. Mem. Kitsap County Hist. Soc., bd. dirs. 1995-96. Mem. Art Librs. Soc. N.Am., ARLIN/NA (N.W. chpt.), Beta Phi Mu. Episcopalian. Avocations: photography, genealogy, research on life, work of American silversmith Clara Barck Welles. Home: 14841 Olympic Vw Lp Rd NW Silverdale WA 98383

HESS, SUZANNE HARRIET, newspaper administrator, photographer; b. Steubenville, Ohio, Nov. 8, 1941; d. Roswell J. and Ruth R. (Feuer) Caulk; m. Richard Robert Hess, Aug. 28, 1960 (div. Oct. 1989); children: Richard, Rebecca. Student, Lane C.C., 1961. Cert. radiologist, Oreg.; cert. ofcl. USA Track and Field, 1992-97. Med. asst. Dr. John Burket, Medford, Oreg., 1970-72; sec. receptionist Dr. Paul Saarinen, Eugene, Oreg., 1982-84; office mgr. Europcar Internat., Sicily, Italy, 1989-91; visitor svcs. mgr. Conv. and Visitors Assn. Lane County, Eugene, Oreg., 1991-94; office mgr. Nat. Masters News, Eugene, Oreg., 1994-97; adminstrv. editor Nat. Masters News, Eugene, 1998—; bd. dirs. U.S. Amateur Track and Field, Oreg., Photographer Nat. Masters News; nat. sec. USA Track and Field-Masters Com., 1997-98. Sec. Oreg. Track Club, Eugene, 1993-96, com. person for preservation of Prefontaine Rock, 1995; protester Preservation of Old Growth Timber, Eugene, 1994; elected nat. sec. USA Track and Field Masters Com., 1996. Recipient Appreciation award Oreg. Track Club, 1995, 2 Nat. Championship awards U.S. Amateur Track and Field, 1995, Silver medal 16# and 25# weight throw U.S. Amateur Track and Field Nat. Masters Indoor Championship, 1995, Bronze medal discus and hammer U.S. Amateur Track and Field Nat. Masters Outdoor Championships, 1995, Gold medal 16# weight throw and 25# superweight throw U.S. Amateur Track and Field Nat. Masters Weight and Superweight Championships, 1995, Gold medal U.S. Amateur Track and Field Nat. Masters Weight Pentathlon, 1995, Bronze medal 16# weight throw, Silver medal 25# super weight throw U.S. Amateur Track & Field Indoor Nat. Championships, Boston, 1997, Gold medals 16# and 25# superweight U.S. Amateur Track and Field Indoor Nat. Championships, Boston, 1998; named All Am. U.S. Amateur Track and Field, 1995, 97, 98. Democrat. Avocations: track and field, bicycling, travel. Office: Nat Masters News 1675 Willamette St Eugene OR 97401-4013

HESSE, CHRISTIAN AUGUST, mining and underground construction consultant; b. Chemnitz, Germany, June 20, 1925; s. William Albert and Anna Gunhilda (Baumann) H.; B. Applied Sci. with honors, U. Toronto (Ont., Can.), 1948; m. Brenda Nora Rigby, Nov. 4, 1964; children: Rob Christian, Bruce William. Registered profl. engr., Can.; chartered engr., U.K. In various mining and constrn. positions, Can., 1944-61; jr. shift boss N.J. Zinc Co., Gilman, Colo., 1949; asst. layout engr. Internat. Nickel Co., Sudbury, Ont., 1949-52; shaft and tunnel engr. Perini-Walsh Joint Venture, Niagara Falls, Ont., 1952-54; constrn. project engr. B. Perini & Sons (Can.) Ltd., Toronto, Ottawa, and New Brunswick, 1954-55; field engr. Aries Copper Mines Ltd., No. Ont., 1955-56; instr. in mining engring. U. Toronto, 1956-57; planning engr. Stanleigh Uranium Mining Co. Ltd., Elliot Lake, Ont., 1957-58, chief engr., 1959-60; subway field engr. Johnson-Perini-Kiewit Joint Venture, Toronto, 1960-61; del. Commonwealth Mining Congress, Africa, 1961; with U.S. Borax & Chem. Corp., 1961-90; mng. dir. Yorkshire Potash, Ltd., London, 1970-71, gen. mgr., pres. Allan Potash Mines Ltd., Allan, Sask., Can., 1974, chief engr. U.S. Borax & Chem. Corp., L.A., 1974-77, v.p. engring., 1978-81, 87-90, v.p. and project mgr. Quartz Hill molybdenum project, 1981-90; v.p. Pacific Coast Molybdenum Co., 1981-90, v.p. mining devel., 1984-90. Co-author pubs. on submarine tailings disposal. Sault Daily Star scholar, Sault Sainte Marie, Ont., Can., 1944. Fellow Inst. Mining and Metallurgy; mem. SME/AIME (chmn. So. Calif. mining sect. 1994-95), Can. Inst. Mining and Metallurgy (life), Assn. Profl. Engrs. Ont., Prospectors and Developers Assn., N.W. Mining Assn., Alaska Miners Assn., L.A. Tennis Club. Lutheran.

HESSLER, THOMAS JOHN, community activist; b. Cin., Apr. 25, 1937; s. Carl Bernard and Marcella Christina (Hoffmeier) H.; m. Nancy Ann Eshman, Sept. 21, 1963; children: Susan, Cara Snyder, Thomas, Angela Daddario. BSEE, U. Dayton, 1959; MSEE, Ga. Inst. Tech., 1968. Commd. 2d lt. U.S. Army, 1959, advanced through grades to col., 1980, ret., 1985; sr. engr. Planning Rsch. Corp., Sierra Vista, Ariz., 1985-88, TechDyn Corp., Sierra Vista, 1988-93, EDSI, Sierra Vista, 1993-95. Columnist, The Western Forum, 1996—. Vice mayor City of Sierra Vista, 1994-95, mem. coun., 1992-94; mem Sierra Vista Planning and Zoning Commn., 1995—. Mem. Joint Svc. Clubs of Greater Sierra Vista (founder, pres. 1995—),Rotary Club of Sierra Vista (pres. 1998—), Assn. U.S. Army (adv. dir. 1997—), Ret. Officers Assn. (pres.), Armed Forces Comms. and Electronics Assn. (pres.) Republican. Roman Catholic. Avocations: downhill skiing, travel. Home: 2000 Golflinks Rd Sierra Vista AZ 85635-4837

HESTER, GAIL, receptionist, writer; b. Stevens, Ark., Oct. 20, 1950; d. Clifton and Ruby Jewel H.; 1 child, Kim. Grad. H.S., Ogden, Utah, 1968. Mail clk. IRS, Ogden, 1985-87; receptionist Merisel Computer Products, L.A., 1987-92, Levola Home Fashions, L.A., 1993-96, R.T.V. Video, L.A., 1997, Career Strategies, L.A., 1998—; Contbr. poetry to various publs. Avocations: vol. work with abused children, writing, basketball. Home and Office: 1601 Venice Blvd Apt 102 Venice CA 90291-5904

HESTER, PERRIETTA BURKE, artist, educator; b. El Centro, Calif., Mar. 8, 1925; d. Perry Alexander and Agnes M. (Pedersen) Burke; m. Henry Hartwell Hester, Aug. 23, 1947 (div. May 1967); children: Henry Hester Jr., Loraine Hester Dyson, Heather Hester Duckett. BA in Fine Art, San Diego State U., 1947, MA in Fine Art, 1967. Cert. tchr., Calif. Art educator L.A. Unified Schs., 1948-51, La Jolla (Calif.) Mus. Art, 1967-68, U. Calif., San Diego, 1968-70, San Diego Cmty. Coll., 1969—, U. Calif., Irvine, 1985, San Diego (Calif.) Zoological Inst., 1970-95; lectr. in field. One- woman shows include Fine Art Gallery, 1970, The Art Garden, Del Mar, 1980, San Vicente, Ramona, Calif., 1982, Knowles Gallery, La Jolla, 1990. Vol., counselor San Diego Artists, 1985—. Mem. San Diego Portrait Soc. (co-founder, chmn.), The Artist's Gallery. Republican. Presby. Avocations:

travel, painting, walking, golf. Home: 2600 Torrey Pines Rd La Jolla CA 92037

HESTER WILLIAMS, KIM DEATRA, English educator; b. Boston; d. Mary Lee (Taiste) H.; m. Henry Williams III, Aug. 4, 1990; 1 child, Mattea Anisi Oleavia Williams. BA in English Lit., U. Calif., Santa Cruz, 1989; MA in English Lit., U. Calif., San Diego, 1997, postgrad. in lit., 1993—. Tcht. asst. U. Calif., Santa Cruz, 1991; instr. U. Calif., San Diego, 1994-95, Vista C.C., 1997—, Sonoma State U., 1997—. Contbr. articles to publs.; editl. bd. Revista Mujeres Spl. Issue: African American and Chicana/Latina Voices, U. Calif., Santa Cruz, 1993. Office: Sonoma State U Dept English 1801 E Cotati Ave Rohnert Park CA 94928-3609

HETEBRINK, DARROW, pastor; b. Alhambra, Calif., Aug. 19, 1952; s. Harold and Eleanor Hetebrink. AA in Music and BA in Preaching, Pacific Christian Coll., 1987, postgrad. in ministry, 1987—. Ordained to ministry Christian Ch., 1988. Asst. chaplain Chino (Calif.) State Prison Calif. Dept. of Corrections, 1987; chaplain, counselor L.A. County Jail Christian Chaplain Svcs., 1989—; pastor of evangelism Cardiff Ave Christian Ch., L.A., 1988—. Cpl. USMC, 1971-73, Vietnam. Recipient Ch. Growth award Evang. Ch., 1987, Merit awards, 1987, Cert. of Merit Cardiff Ave. Christian Ch., 1991; named one of Outstanding Young Men in Am. Hollywood Street Ministry, 1987. Avocations: camping, fishing, reading, guitar, blues. Address: 2414 Knowlwood Dr Hanford CA 93230-7253

HETLAND, JOHN ROBERT, lawyer, educator; b. Mpls., Mar. 12, 1930; s. James L. and Evelyn (Lundgren) H.; m. Mildred Woodruff, Dec. 1951 (div.); children: Lynda Lee Catlin, Robert John, Debra Ann Allen; m. Anne Kneeland, Dec. 1972; children: Robin T. Willcox, Elizabeth J. Pickett. B.S.L., U. Minn., 1952, J.D., 1956. Bar: Minn. 1956, Calif. 1962, U.S. Supreme Ct. 1981. Practice law Mpls., 1956-59; prof. law U. Calif., Berkeley, 1959-91; prof. emeritus, 1991—; prin. Hetland & Kneeland, PC, Berkeley, 1959—; vis. prof. law Stanford U., 1971, 80, U. Singapore, 1972, U. Cologne, Fed. Republic Germany, 1988. Author: California Real Property Secured Transactions, 1970, Commercial Real Estate Transactions, 1972, Secured Real Estate Transactions, 1974, 1977; co-author: California Cases on Security Transactions in Land, 2d edit., 1975, 3d edit., 1984, 4th edit., 1992; contbr. articles to legal, real estate and fin. jours. Served to lt. comdr. USNR, 1953-55. Fellow Am. Coll. Real Estate Lawyers, Am. Coll. Mortgage Attys., Am. Bar Found.; mem. ABA, State Bar Calif., State Bar Minn., Order of Coif, Phi Delta Phi. Home: 20 Red Coach Ln Orinda CA 94563-1112 Office: 2600 Warring St Berkeley CA 94704-3415

HETRICK, VIRGINIA R., technology architect; b. Port Townsend, Wash., July 8, 1942; d. Donald B. and Zelma R. (Barrie) H. AB, George Washington U., 1964, MA, 1968; PhD, U. Wash., 1974. Prof. U. Fla., Gainesville, 1973-81, rsch. scientist, 1981-83, image process scientist, 1984-86, coord. num intensive comp and vis, 1986-90; mgr. supercomputer svcs. group UCLA, 1990-91, sci. computer mgr., 1991-97, technologist, 1997-98, tech. arch., 1998—; fellow Share Inc., Chgo., 1988-92, dir. vol. resources, 1994-97. Author: Visual Representation of Information, 1989, Application of Supercomputing for the 1990s, 1989, Digital Image Processing Cookbook, 1991, Logical and Visual Organization of Websites, 1997. Mem. Race for the Cure, L.A. and Orange County, 1992—; patient instr. City of Hope, Duarte, Calif., 1993; pres. You Are Not Alone, L.A., 1996—; mem. breast cancer review panel Dept. of Def., 1997-98. Recipient Isaac Davis award George Washington U., 1964, Gilbert Grosvenor fellowship George Washington U., 1964-65, NASA Faculty fellow NASA-AMES RC, 1977. Mem. SIGGRAPH, Assn. Internet Profls., POSSI.

HETT, JOAN MARGARET, civic administrator; b. Trail, B.C., Can., Sept. 8, 1936; s. Gordon Stanley and Violet Thora (Thors) Hett; B.Sc., U. Victoria (B.C., Can.), 1964; M.S., U. Wis., Madison, 1967, Ph.D., 1969. Ecologist, Eastern Deciduous Forest Biome, Oak Ridge Nat. Lab., 1969-72; coor. sites dir. Coniferous Forest Biome, Oreg. State U., Corvallis and U. Wash., Seattle, 1972-77; ecol. cons., Seattle, 1978-84; plant ecologist Seattle City Light, 1984-86; supr. Rights-of-Way, Seattle City Light, 1986-91, vegetation mgmt. mgr., Seattle City Light, 1991—. Mem. Ecol. Soc. Am., Brit. Ecol. Soc., Am. Inst. Biol. Scis., Am. Forestry Assn., Sigma Xi. Contbr. articles to profl. jours.; research in plant population dynamics, land use planning, forest succession.

HETTICH, KAY L., wilderness advocate, mountaineer; b. Denver, Apr. 16, 1956; d. Bedrich V. and Charlotte L. (Quick) H. BA, Princeton (N.J.) U., 1989; MA, U. Calif., 1993. Cert. search mgr. Wilderness patrol U.S. Forest Svc., Trinity Alps Wilderness, Weaverville, Calif., 1995—; dir. The Ayres Recorder Ensemble, Weaverville, 1995—; mem. glacier and crevasse rescue North Cascades Mountaineering Sch., Seattle, 1997. Performer Trinity County Arts Coun., Weaverville, 1995—. Mem. Trinity County Search and Rescue, Nat. Assn. Search and Rescue. Avocations: mountaineering, botanical study, animals and birds, recorder playing, mountain biking. Home: PO Box 2644 Weaverville CA 96093 Office: USFS Weaverville RD PO Box 1190 Weaverville CA 96093

HEUMAN, DONNA RENA, lawyer; b. Seattle, May 27, 1949; d. Russell George and Edna Inez (Armstrong) H. BA in Psychology, UCLA, 1972; JD, U. Calif., San Francisco, 1985. Cert. shorthand reporter, 1978—; owner, Heuman & Assocs., San Francisco, 1978-86; real estate broker, Calif., 1990—; co-founder, chair, CFO Atherton Park Foods, Inc., 1996—. Mem. Hastings Internat. and Comparative Law Rev., 1984-85; bd. dirs. Saddleback, 1987-89. Jessup Internat. Moot Ct. Competition, 1985, N. Fair Oaks Mcpl. Adv. Coun., vice chair, sec., 1993-95. Mem. ABA, NAFE, ATLA, AOPA, Nat. Shorthand Reporters Assn., Women Entrepreneurs, Mensa, Calif. State Bar Assn., Nat. Mus. of Women in the Arts, Calif. Lawyers for the Arts, San Francisco Bar Assn., Commonwealth Club, World Affairs Coun., Zonta (bd. dirs.). Home: 750 18th Ave Menlo Park CA 94025-2018 Office: Superior Ct Calif Hall Of Justice Redwood City CA 94063

HEUSCHELE, WERNER PAUL, veterinary researcher; b. Ludwigsburg, Federal Republic of Germany, Aug. 28, 1929; came to U.S., 1932, naturalized, 1951; s. Karl August and Margarete Anna (Wagner) H.; m. Carolyn Rene Bredeson, Jan. 1, 1983; children: Eric W.K., Mark R. (dec.), Jennifer M. Student, San Diego State Coll., 1947-50; BA in Zoology, U. Calif., Davis, 1952, DVM, 1956; student, NIH, Bethesda, Md., 1966; PhD in Med. Microbiology, Virology, Immunology, U. Wis., 1969. Diplomate Am. Coll. Vet. Microbiologists, Am. Coll. Zoological Medicine. Mgr. veterinary hosp. Zool. Soc. San Diego, 1956-61, head, microbiology/virology, 1981-86, dir. research, 1986—; research veterinarian Plum Island Animal Disease Lab., Orient Point, N.Y., 1961-70; tng. resident in vet. pathology Armed Forces Inst. Pathology, Washington, 1965-66; assoc. prof. infectious disease Kansas State U., Manhattan, 1970-71; head, virology, research and devel. Jensen-Salsbery Labs., Kansas City, Kans., 1971-76; prof. vet. preventive medicine Ohio State U., Columbus, 1976-81; cons. Syntro Corp., San Diego, 1985-88, SIBIA, San Diego, 1983-90, UN-FAO-UNDP, Maracay, Venezuela, 1979, 80; grant rev. panelist USDA, Washington; mem. com. on bovine tuberculosis eradication, com. on animal health and vet. medicine, bd. on agrl. NRC, 1992-96. Contbr. articles to profl. jours. Recipient U. Calif.-Davis Sch. of Vet. Medicine Alumni Achievement award, 1991. Mem. USDA (VS adv. blue-ribbon panel 1987-91), Am. Assn. Zool. Pks. and Aquariums (profl. fellow), Am. Assn. Zoo Veterinarians (pres. 1958-59, sec., treas. 1959-62, Life Mem. award 1993), Am. Vet. Med. Assn., Wildlife Disease Assn. (v.p. 1985-87, Disting. Svc. award 1995), Internat. Union for Conservation of Nature and Natural Resources Vet. Specialist Group, Captive Breeding Specialist Group (species survival com.), Columbus Zoo Assn. (bd. dirs. 1977-81), Am. Coll. Vet. Microbiologists (bd. govs. 1984-87), U.S. Animal Health Assn., Sigma Xi, Phi Zeta. Home: 4690 59th St San Diego CA 92115-3830 Office: Zool Soc San Diego PO Box 551 San Diego CA 92112-0551

HEWITT, CONRAD W., state superintendant of banks. Supt. of banks State of Calif.; commr. Calif. State Dept. Financial Inst. Office: 111 Pine St Ste 1100 San Francisco CA 94111-5613

HEWITT, WILLIAM JAMES, municipal official; b. Apr. 29, 1944; m. Sharon Hewitt; 3 children. BS, Brandon (Can.) U.; cert. in adult edn., Red River C.C., Winnipeg, Can.; cert. in pub. adminstrn., Assiniboine Coll., Brandon; cert. in fire svc. mgmt., Internat. City Mgmt. Assn. cert. fire fighter, fire prevention officer, fire svc. instr., Can. Vol. fire fighter Virden Vol. Fire Dept., 1964-68; fire fighter City of Brandon Fire Dept., 1968-73; asst. fire commr. Office Manitoba Fire Commr., 1973-78, mgr. field svcs. sect., 1978-86; fire chief City of Saskatoon, Can., 1986—; developer Manitoba Fire Coll., apptd. prin., 1978; past chair Manitoba Fire Svcs. Mobile Radio Comm. Com., Manitoba Fire Coll. Protection Tech. Adv. Com., Manitoba Pub. Fire Safety Edn. Com. Contbr. articles to profl. jours.; presenter confs. in Boston, Memphis, Cin., Toronto, Regina, Yellowknife, Winnipeg, Ottawa, others; speaker in field. Mem. Internat. Soc. Fire Svc. Instrs. (bd. dirs. 1976-92), Internat. City Mgmt. Assn. (instr. firesvc. adminstrn. program), Internat. Fire Svcs. Tng. Assn. (fire svc. instr. textbook and fire dept. ops. textbook coms. 1976-81), Internat. Assn. Fire Chiefs (1st v.p. Can. divsn.), Nat. Fire Protection Assn., Can. Fire Chief's Assn. (pres.), Sask. Fire Chief's Assn. (past pres.), Sask. Profl. Qualifications and Standards Bd. (chmn.), Sask. C. of C., N.D. State Fireman's Assn. (hon. life). Office: Fire Dept, 125 Idylwyld Dr S, Saskatoon, SK Canada S7M 1L4*

HEYCK, THEODORE DALY, lawyer; b. Houston, Apr. 17, 1941; s. Theodore Richard and Gertrude Paine (Daly) H. BA, Brown U., 1963; postgrad. Georgetown. U., 1963-65, 71-72; JD, N.Y. Law Sch., 1979. Bar: N.Y. 1980, Calif. 1984, U.S. Ct. Appeals (2nd cir.) 1984, U.S. Supreme Ct. 1984, U.S. Dist. Ct. (so. and ea. dists.) N.Y. 1980, U.S. Dist. Ct. (we. and no. dists.) N.Y. 1984, U.S. Dist. Ct. (cen. and so. dists.) Calif. 1984, U.S. Ct. Appeals (9th cir.) 1986. Paralegal dist. atty. Bklyn., 1975-79; asst. dist. atty. Bklyn. dist., Kings County, N.Y., 1979-85; dep. city atty., L.A., 1985—; bd. dirs. Screen Actors Guild, N.Y.C., 1977-78. Mem. ABA, AFTRA, NATAS, SAG, Bklyn. Bar Assn., Assn. Trial Lawyers Am., N.Y. Trial Lawyers Assn., N.Y. State Bar Assn., Calif. Bar Assn., Fed. Bar Council, L.A. County Bar Assn., Actors Equity Assn. Home: 2106 E Live Oak Dr Los Angeles CA 90068-3639 Office: Office City Atty City Hall E 200 N Main St Los Angeles CA 90012-4110

HEYDET, SHARON LEE FORD, English language educator; b. Seattle, Apr. 26, 1940; d. Ralph Walker and Ethel Ford; m. Richart George Heydet, Jan. 17, 1970; children: Richard, Robert. BA, Ft. Wright Coll., 1962. Tchr. Hoquiam (Wash.) Jr. H.S., 1962-64, Hanau Am. H.S., Germany, 1964-66; English tchr. Burlington Twp. H.S., N.J., 1966-67; tchr. English Mark Keppel H.S., Alhambra, Calif., 1967-70; v.p. R&S Stores, Deer Park, Wash., 1980-82; tchr. English Deer Park H.S., 1987—. Mem. NEA, Nat. Coun. Tchrs. English, Washington Journalism Edn. Assn. (ea. Wash. rep. 1991, sec. 1994-96, chair summer session 1992, 93), Wash. Edn. Assn., Deer Park Women's Golf Club. Roman Catholic. Avocations: walking, traveling, reading, cooking, gardening. Office: Deer Park HS S 800 Weber Deer Park WA 99006

HEYER, CAROL ANN, illustrator; b. Cuero, Tex., Feb. 2, 1950; d. William Jerome and Merlyn Mary (Hutson) H. BA, Calif. Lutheran U., 1974. Freelance artist various cos., Thousand Oaks, Calif., 1974-79; computer artist Image Resource, Westlake Village, Calif., 1979-81; staff writer, artist Lynn-Davis Prodns., Westlake Village, Calif., 1981-87; art dir. Northwind Studios Internat., Camarillo, Calif., 1988-89; illustrator Touchmark, Thousand Oaks, 1989—; cons. art dir., writer Lynn-Wenger Prodns., 1987-89; guest spkr. Thousand Oaks Libr., Author's Faire, Calif. Luth. U., Soc. Children's Book Writers and Illustrators, Illustrators Day, Ventura County Reading Assn.'s Author's Faire; guest artist/spkr. Oxnard Libr.; booksignings/appearances Anaheim Conv. Ctr., L.A. Conv. Ctr., Am. Booksellers Assn.; guest 1996 Readout, grand opening Barnes and Noble, Thousand Oaks; represented by Art Works, N.Y.C.; invited artist Ann. Art Show, Chemers Gallery. Illustrator (children's books) A Star in the Pasture, 1988, The Dream Stealer, 1989, The Golden Easter Egg, 1989, All Things Bright and Beautiful, 1992, Rapunzel, 1992, The Christmas Carol, 1995, Prancer, Gift of the Magi, Dinosaurs Strange and Wonderful, Down the Great Unknown, 1999, Flame and Clay (teachers' big book) 1998, Here Come the Brides, (adult book) The Artist's Market, also L.A. Times, Daily News, The Artist's Mag., News Chronicle; also cover art for Troll Assoc., Top Secret, The Loveless Cafe (cookbook), Ellery Queen's Mystery Mag., Frontispiece Collectors Leather Bound Edition, Crippen and Landru Mystery Covers, Dragon mag., Dungeon mag., Aboriginal Sci. Fiction mag., Wizards of the Coast, (game covers) F.X. Schmid - Puzzle Wizards of the Coast (fantasy collector cards, Dune and Hobbit) and various novels, books and games; illustrator Bugs Bunny Coloring Book, Candyland Work Book, The Dragon Sleeps Step Ahead Workbook, City of Sorcers, CD-ROM cover for Memorex/Roaring Mouse Prodns.; interior art for various publs. including (mags.) Amazing Stories two covers, Interzone, Aboriginal Sci. Fiction Mag., Alfred Hitchcocks Myster Mag., Ideals mag., Realms of Fantasy mag., Sci. Fiction Age mag., Tomorrow mag., (book) Tome of Magic, (book) Top Secret, (book) Loveless Cafe, (book, interiors) Star Trek Next Generation, (also art for game cards), (repeat covers) Crippen and Landru, (game book cover) Wizards of the Coast; writer (screenplay) Thunder Run, 1986; illustrator, writer (children's books) Beauty and the Beast, 1989, The Easter Story, 1989, Excalibur, Robin Hood, 1993, Sleeping Beauty in the Wood, 1996, The Christmas Story, 1996, Down the Great Unknown, 1999, Flame and Clay, 1998; paintings for line of Fantasy Art Prints, Scafa/Tornabene, religious art prints; rep. by Every Picture Tells a Story Gallery, Worlds of Wonder; 2 covers for young adults Hyperion/Disney Press; one-woman show Adventures for Kids Gallery; illustrator poster for motion picture and TV fund; writer Disney ednl. prodns., others; freelance artist Disney Interactive. Recipient Lit. award City of Oxnard Cultural Arts Commn. and Carnegie Art Inst., 1992, Best Cover Art Boomerang award, 1989, Cert. of Merit, Career Achievement award Calif. Luth. U., 1993, Cert. of Excellence Alumni Career Achievement award, 1993, Print's Regional Design Ann. award, 1992, Best Paper Backs award Internat. Reading Assn./Children s Book Coun. Joint Com., 1994, Spectrum Internat. Competition for Best in Contemporary Fantastic Art. Mem. Soc. Children's Book Writers (judge 1990, Mag. Merit award 1988, Keynote spkr.), Assn. Sci. Fiction and Fantasy Artists, Soc. Illustrators (Cert. of Merit 1990-92, winner Ann. Illustration West show). Featured in articles. Home and Office: Touchmark 925 Ave Arboles Thousand Oaks CA 91360

HEYL, ALLEN VAN, JR., geologist; b. Allentown, Pa., Apr. 10, 1918; s. Allen Van and Emma (Kleppinger) H.; student Muhlenberg Coll., 1936-37; BS in Geology, Pa. State U., 1941; PhD in Geology, Princeton U., 1950; m. Maxine LaVon Hawke, July 12, 1945; children: Nancy Caroline, Allen David Van. Field asst. major regional exploration, govt. geologist Nfld. Geol. Survey, summers 1937-40, 42; jr. geologist U.S. Geol. Survey, Wis., 1943-45, asst. geologist, 1945-47, assoc. geologist, 1947-50, geologist, Washington and Beltsville, Md., 1950-67; staff geologist, Denver, 1968-90; cons. geologist 1990—; disting. lectr. grad. coll. Beijing, China and Nat. Acad. Sci., 1988; disting. invited lectr. Internat. Assn. Genesis Ore Deposits 9th Symposium, Beijing, 1994; chmn. Internat. Commn. Tectonics of Ore Deposits. Fellow Instn. Mining and Metallurgy (Gt. Brit.), Geol. Soc. Am., Am. Mineral. Soc., Soc. Econ. Geologists; mem. Inst. Genesis of Ore Deposits, Geol. Soc. Wash., Colo. Sci. Soc., Rocky Mountain Geol. Soc., Friends of Mineralogy (hon. life), Evergreen Naturalist Audubon Soc., Sigma Xi, Alpha Chi Sigma. Lutheran. Contbr. numerous articles to profl. jours., chpts. to books. Home: PO Box 1052 Evergreen CO 80437-1052

HEYMAN, MATTHEW DAVID, entertainment executive; b. Orange, Calif., Nov. 1, 1961; s. Harris B. and Esther (Podvin) H. BS in Econs. cum laude, NYU, 1983; MBA, Harvard U., 1993. Lic. real estate broker, Calif., N.Y., Mass. Teaching asst. econs. dept. NYU, N.Y.C., spring 1983; econ. analyst Chase Manhattan Bank, N.A., N.Y.C., 1984; real estate analyst Community Devel. Commn., Commerce, Calif., 1985-86; dir. real estate Cineplex Odeon Corp., L.A. and N.Y.C., 1986-88; prin. The Heyman Group, L.A. and N.Y.C., 1988-89; v.p. bus. affairs Cineplex Odeon Corp., Toronto, Ont., Can., 1990-91; mng. dir. Grupo Cinemex, Mexico City, Mex. Helbein scholar, 1983. Mem. Internat. Coun. Shopping Ctrs., Beta Gamma Sigma, Omicron Delta Epsilon. Home: 311 Bora Bora Way Apt 215 Marina Del Rey CA 90292 Office: Grupo Cinemax, Blvd MA Camacho 40-16, Mexico DF 11000, Mexico

HIAPO, PATRICIA KAMAKA, lay worker; b. Honolulu, May 18, 1943; d. Ward Charles and Violet Kaopua (Nicholas) McKeown; m. Bernard Joseph Hiapo, July 9, 1960; children: Bernard Jr., Beatrice, Jacqueline, Mary-Louise. Grad. high sch., Honolulu. Cert. catechist, 1988. Area del. St. John Apostle and Evangelist, Mililani, Hawaii, 1981-84; eucharistic min. St. John Apostle and Evangelist, Mililani, 1981-88; hospice and bereavement ministry St. Francis Hosp., Honolulu, 1983, eucharistic min., 1983-88; religious edn. coord. Resurrection of The Lord, Waipahu, Hawaii, 1984-88; dir. religious edn. St. Jude, Ewa Beach, Hawaii, 1988-91; home visitor Hana Like, Honolulu, 1990-98; with Alu Lke Pulama I Na Keiki/Lee Town Ctr., Waipahu, Hawaii, 1998—; mem. marriage encounter team Cath. Ch., Honolulu, 1981-83. Recipient award Our Lady of Peace, 1991. Office: Lee Town Ctr B2-305 94-216 Farrington Hwy Waipahu HI 96797 also: Parents and Children Together-Hana Like 45-955 Kamehameha Hwy Ste 404 Kaneohe HI 96744-3222

HIATT, PETER, retired librarian studies educator; b. N.Y.C., Oct. 19, 1930; s. Amos and Elizabeth Hope (Derry) H.; m. Linda Rae Smith, Aug. 16, 1968; 1 child, Holly Virginia. B.A., Colgate U., 1952; M.L.S., Rutgers U., 1957, Ph.D., 1963. Head Elmora Br. Library, Elizabeth, N.J., 1957-59; instr. Grad. Sch. Library Service Sci. Rutgers U., 1960-62; library cons. Ind. State Library, Indpls., 1963-70; asst. prof. Grad. Library Sch., Ind. U., 1963-66, assoc. prof., 1966-70; dir. Ind. Library Studies, Bloomington, 1967-70; dir. continuing edn. program for library personnel Western Interstate Commn. for Higher Edn., Boulder, Colo., 1970-74; dir. Grad. Sch. Library and Info. Sci., U. Wash., Seattle, 1974-81, prof., 1974-98; prin. investigator Career Devel. and Assessment Center for Librarians, 1979-83, 90-93; dir. library insts. at various colls. and univs.; adv. project U.S. Office Edn.-ALA, 1977-80; prof. emeritus U. Wash., 1998—; bd. dirs. King County Libr. Sys., 1989-97, pres., 1991, 95, sec., 1993, 94; prin. investigator Career Devel. and Assessment Ctrs. for Libr.: Phase II, 1990-93. Author: (with Donald Thompson) Monroe County Public Library: Planning for the Future, 1966, The Public Library Needs of Delaware County, 1967, (with Henry Drennan) Public Library Services for the functionally Illiterate, 1967 (with Robert E. Lee and Lawrence A. Allen) A Plan for Developing a Regional Program of Continuing Education for Library Personnel, 1969, Public Library Branch Services for Adults of Low Education, 1964; dir., gen. editor: The Indiana Library Studies, 1970; author: Assessment Centers for Professional Library Leadership, 1993; mem. editorial bd. Coll. and Rsch. Librs., 1969-73; co-editor Leads: A Continuing Education Newsletter for Library Trustees, 1973-75, Octavio Noda; author chpts., articles on library continuing edn., staff devel. and libr. adult svcs. Mem. ALA (officer), Pacific N.W. Libr. Assn., Assn. Libr. and Info. Sci. Educators (officer, Outstanding Svc. award 1979), ACLU. E-mail: phiatt@waypt.com. Home: 111 E Rhododendron Dr Port Townsend WA 98368-9414

HIBBARD, CHARLES GUSTIN, historian; b. Climax, Mich., May 14, 1925; s. Byron C. Hibbard and B. Todd; m. Shirley Van Drunen, Nov. 29, 1952 (div. Mar. 1976); children: Elizabeth, Catherine, Rebecca, Robert; m. Mavis Hardy, Dec. 22, 1979. BS, U. Utah, 1960, PhD, 1980; MA, U. So. Calif., 1969. Cert. secondary tchr., Utah. Enlisted USAF, 1949, advanced to chief master sgt., air traffic contr., air traffic contr., 1949-70; historian USAF, various locations, 1982-89; postal clk. U.S. Postal Svc., Salt Lake City, 1972-77; pres. Ft. Douglas (Utah) Mil. Mus. Assn., 1993—; bd. dirs. Hill AFB (Utah) Mus., 1986-89. Author: 509th Composite Group Trains at Wendover, 1995 Fall Air Power History; editor, contbr. to book History of Hill AFB, Utah, 1988; contbr. to Ency. of Am. West, 1994, Hist. Dictionary of USAF, 1992. Decorated Bronze Star. Mem. Utah Hist. Soc., Wasatch Westerners (pres. 1991-92), Oreg.-Calif. Trails Assn., Western History Assn. Avocations: photography, fishing. Home: 5100 S 1050 W Trlr 220A Ogden UT 84405-3771 Office: Ft Douglas Mus Assn 32 Potter St Salt Lake City UT 84113-5046

HIBBARD, JUDITH HOFFMAN, health services researcher; b. L.A., Nov. 30, 1948; d. Arnold Mandel and Marian (Carob) Hoffman; m. Michael John Hibbard, Aug. 1, 1968; 1 child, Johanna. BS, Calif. State U., Northridge, 1974; MPH, UCLA, 1975; DrPH, U. Calif., Berkeley, 1982. Asst. prof. U. Oreg., Eugene, 1982-88, assoc. prof., 1988-94; prof., 1994—; adj. investigator Ctr. Health Rsch., Portland, 1982—; clin. prof. pub. health & preventive medicine Oreg. Health Scis. U., Portland, 1995—. Contbr. articles to profl. jours. Recipient New Investigator Rsch. award Nat. Inst. Aging, 1983-86, Dissertation Rch. award Nat. Ctr. Health Svcs. Rsch., 1981-82; grantee NIA, 1988-91, Robert Wood Johnson Found., 1995—. Mem. Agy. for Health Care Policy and Rsch. (grantee 1994—). Avocations: horseback riding, bicycling. Office: U Oregon 119 Hendricks Hall Eugene OR 97403-1209

HIBBARD, RICHARD PAUL, industrial ventilation consultant, lecturer; b. Defiance, Ohio, Nov. 1, 1923; s. Richard T. and Doris E. (Walkup) H.; BS in Mech. Indsl. Engring., U. Toledo, 1949; m. Phyllis Ann Kirchoffer, Sept. 7, 1948; children: Barbara Rae, Marcia Kae, Rebecca Ann, Patricia Jan, John Ross. Mech. engr. Oldsmobile div. Gen. Motors Corp., Lansing, Mich., 1950-56; design and sales engr. McConnell Sheet Metal, Inc., Lansing, 1956-60; chief heat and ventilation engr. Fansteel Metall. Corp., North Chicago, Ill., 1960-62; sr. facilities and ventilation engr. The Boeing Co., Seattle, 1962-63; ventilation engr. environ. health div. dept. preventive medicine U. Wash., 1964-70, lectr. dept. environ. health, 1970-82, lectr. emeritus, 1983—; prin. Indsl. Ventilation Cons. Svcs., 1983—; chmn. Western Indsl. Ventilation Conf., 1962; mem. com. indsl. ventilation Am. Conf. Govtl. Indsl. Hygienists, 1966—; mem. staff Indsl. Ventilation Conf., Mich. State U., 1955—. With USAAF, 1943-45, USAR, 1946-72. Recipient Disting. Svc. award Indsl. Ventilation Conf., Mich. State U., 1975, 93. Mem. Am. Soc. Safety Engrs. (R.M. Gillmore Meml. award Puget Sound chpt.), ASHRAE, Am. Inst. Plant Engrs., Am. Indsl. Hygiene Assn. (J.M. Dallevalle award 1977), Am. Foundryman's Soc. Lodges: Elks, Masons. Contbr. articles on indsl. hygiene and ventilation to profl. jours. Home: 41 165th Ave SE Bellevue WA 98008-4721

HIBBS, JOHN DAVID, software executive, engineer, business owner; b. Del Norte, Colo., Jan. 26, 1948; s. Alva Bernard and Frances Ava (Cathcart) H.; m. Ruthanne Johnson, Feb. 28, 1976. BSEE, Denver U., 1970. Elec. engr. Merrick and Co., Denver, 1972-73; lighting engr. Holophane div. Johns Manville, Denver, 1973-79; lighting products mgr. Computer Sharing Svcs., Inc., Denver, 1979-83; pres., owner Computer Aided Lighting Analysis, Boulder, Colo., 1983-86, Hibbs Sci. Software, Boulder, Colo., 1986—; chmn. bd. Sport Sail Inc., 1996-97; co-founder Sport Sail, Inc. Author CALA, CALA/Pro and PreCALA (WWWeb-Estimator) lighting programs; patentee in field. With USNR, 1970-72. Recipient 1st prize San Luise Valley Sci. Fair, 1963. Mem. IEEE, Illuminating Engring. Soc. North Am. (chmn. computer com. 1988-91), Computer Soc. IEEE (chmn. computer problem set com. 1991-95). Avocations: woodworking, bicycling, sailing. Home and Office: PO Box 400 Fraser CO 80442-0400

HIBLER, JUDE ANN, photojournalist; b. Portland, Oreg., Apr. 6, 1943; d. William Eliot and Myrtle Winifred (Johnson) Henderson; m. Jeffrey Charles Hibler, Jan. 27, 1962; 1 child, Beth Karen. Student, Portland State Coll., 1960-61, Pima C.C., 1980, U. Colo., Boulder, 1982, Antioch U. West, 1981-82. Alcohol counselor Whole Person Health Ctr., Boulder, 1984; adminstrv. mgr. Nordstrom, San Diego, 1985-88; publ., editor, owner Jazz Link Mag., San Diego, 1988-91; co-owner, photojournalist Jazz Link Enterprises, Longmont, Colo., 1991—; cons. El Cajon (Calif.) Jr. High Sch., 1989, Long Beach (Calif.) High Sch., 1990. Co-author: Joe Pass: Improvising Ideas, 1994; contbg. writer: Encyclopedia of Jazz, 1995, The Dale Bruning Jazz Guitar Series Vol. 1: Phrasing & Articulation, 1997; co-prodr. Longmont Jazz Festival, 1997; co-prodr. CD: Dale Bruning Quartet's Tomorrow's Reflections, 1995, Dale Bruning/Michael Moore: Conference Call, 1998; co-prodr., leader, author: Jazz Music & Media Clinic Book, 1996; publ./editor: Jazz Link Mag., 1988 (best jazz pub. 1988); editor The Gift of Jazz mag., 1995-96; photographer: (book covers) Joe Pass Note by Note, 1994, Improvising Ideas, 1994; photojournalist Jazzscene of Oreg., JazzNow Mag., 1992-94, Concord Jazz. Named Outstanding Svc. Nat. Assn. Jazz Educators, 1989, First Friend of Jazz Dr. Billy Taylor's Soundpost, 1991. Mem. San Diego Musicians Union (hon. mem.). Democrat. Avocations: reading, nature walks, knitting, basketball, songwriting. Home and Office: 3721 Columbia Dr Longmont CO 80503-2117

HICE, MICHAEL, editor, marketing professional; b. Carlsbad, N.Mex., June 8, 1946; s. William Elmer and Jewell Irene (Holcomb) H. BA, Tulane U., 1968. Asst. dir. ESL Lang. Ctrs., Houston, 1970-77; program dir. St. Marys Coll., Moraga, Calif., 1977-78; with Savin Corp., San Francisco, 1978-82; gen. sales mgr. Radio Sta. KLSK, Santa Fe, N.Mex., 1983-90; ptnr., v.p. Mountain Time Tours, Santa Fe, N.Mex., 1987-88; ptnr., v.p. sales mktg. cons. Nightingale Hice Inc., Santa Fe, N.Mex., 1990-96; ptnr., editor Indian Artist, Inc., Santa Fe, N.Mex., 1994—; co-founder, arts dir., promoter Homogenesis, San Francisco, 1981-82; freelance writer. Editor Indian Artist, 1994—; co-author: (play) Song of Myself, 1984. Co-founder AID and Comfort, Santa Fe, 1989, Bus. for Social Responsibility, 1993. Recipient Best of Show award N.Mex. Advt. Fedn., 1990, Best Multi-Media Pub. Svc. Campaign award, 1993, Cowles Media award, 1998, Folio Editorial Excellence award, 1998. Mem. Nat. Mktg. Assn. Avocations: hiking, snow skiing, gardening, swimming, yoga. Home: 48A Ojo De La Vaca Rd Santa Fe NM 87505-1457 Office: Indian Artist Inc 1807 2nd St Ste 61 Santa Fe NM 87505-3510

HICK, KENNETH WILLIAM, business executive; b. New Westminster, B.C., Can., Oct. 17, 1946; s. Les Walter and Mary Isabelle (Warner) H. BA in Bus., Eastern Wash. State Coll., 1971; MBA (fellow), U. Wash., 1973, PhD, 1975. Regional sales mgr. Hilti, Inc., San Leandro, Calif., 1976-79; gen. sales mgr. Moore Internat., Inc., Portland, 1979-80; v.p. sales and mktg. Phillips Corp., Anaheim, Calif., 1980-81; owner, pres., chief exec. officer K.C. Metals, San Jose, Calif., 1981-87; owner, pres., chief exec. officer Losli Internat. Inc., Portland, Oreg., 1987-89; pres. Resources N.W. Inc., 1989—; communications cons. Asso. Pub. Safety Communication Officers, Inc., State of Oreg., 1975-93; numerous cons. assignments, also seminars, 1976-98. Contbr. articles to numerous publs. Mem. Oreg. Gov.'s Tax Bd., 1975-76; pres. Portland chpt. Oreg. Jaycees, 1976; bd. fellows U. Santa Clara, 1983-90. Served with USAF, 1966-69. Decorated Commendation medal. Mem. Am. Mgmt. Assn., Am. Mktg. Assn., Assn. M.B.A. Execs., Assn. Gen. Contractors, Soc. Advancement Mgmt., Home Builders Assn. Roman Catholic. Home: 25659 Cheryl Dr West Linn OR 97068-4589 Office: Resources N/W Inc 19727 Highway 99E Hubbard OR 97032-9716

HICKCOX, LESLIE KAY, health educator, consultant, counselor; b. Berkeley, Calif., May 12, 1951; d. Ralph Thomas and Marilyn Irene (Stump) H. BA, U. Redlands, 1973; MA in Exercise Physiology, U. of the Pacific, 1975; MEd, Columbia U., 1979; MEd in Health Edn., Oreg. State U., 1987, MEd in Guidance & Counseling, 1988, EdD in Edn., 1991. Cert. state C.C. instr. (life), Calif. Phys. edn. instr., dir. intramurals SUNY, Stony Brook, 1981-83; instr. health edn. Linn-Benton C.C., Oreg., 1985-94; health and phys. edn. instr. Portland C.C., 1994-95; instr. health edn. Linn-Benton C.C., Oreg., 1985-94; edn. supr., instr. Oreg. State U., Corvallis, 1988-90; instr. human studies and comm. Marylhurst Coll., Portland, Oreg., 1987-96; instr. health edn. U. (New Zealand) Auckland, 1991; phys. edn. instr., dir intramurals Health Edn. Inst. U. (New Zealand) Auckland, Oreg., 1991; instr. health curriculum and supervision Concordia Coll., Portland, Oreg., 1992; health and phys. edn. instr. Portland C.C., 1994-95; instr., coord. dept. health, phys. edn. and recreation Rogue C.C., Grants Pass, Oreg., 1995-97; assoc. prof., coord. health and phys. edn. Western Mont. Coll., Dillon, 1997—; founder Experiential Learning Inst., 1992—, Lilly N.W. High Edn. Tchg. Conf., 1996; founding v.p. Home Health Diagnostics, Portland, Oreg., 1996. Contbr. articles to profl. jours. Mem. ASCD, Nat. Ctr. for Health Edn., Assn. for Advancement of Health Edn., Higher Edn. R & D Soc. Australasia, Coun. for Adult and Exptl. Learning, Kappa Delta Phi, Phi Delta Kappa. Home: 923 1/2 S Washington St Dillon MT 59725-3507

HICKEL, WALTER JOSEPH, investment firm executive, forum administrator; b. nr. Claflin, Kans., Aug. 18, 1919; s. Robert A. and Emma (Zecha) H.; m. Janice Cannon, Sept. 22, 1941 (dec. Aug. 1943); 1 child, Theodore; m. Ermalee Strutz, Nov. 22, 1945; children: Robert, Walter Jr., Jack, Joseph, Karl. Student pub. schs., Claflin; D.Eng. (hon.), Stevens Inst. Tech., 1970, Mich. Tech. U., 1973; LL.D. (hon.), St. Mary of Plains Coll., St. Martin's Coll., U. Md., Adelphi U., U. San Diego, Rensselaer Poly. Inst., 1973, U. Alaska, 1976, Alaska Pacific U., 1991; D.Pub. Adminstrn. (hon.), Willamette U. Founder Hickel Investment Co., Anchorage, 1947—; gov. State of Alaska, 1966-69, 90-94; sec. U.S. Dept. Interior, 1969-70; sec. gen. The Northern Forum, 1994—; former mem. world adv. council Internat. Design Sci. Inst.; former mem. com. on sci. freedom and responsibility AAAS; nominated for pres. at 1968 Republican Nat. Convention; co-founder Yukon Pacific Corp.; founder Inst. of the North, 1996—. Author: Who Owns America?, 1971; contbr. articles to newspapers. Mem. Republican Nat. Com., 1954-64; bd. regents Gonzaga U.; bd. dirs. Salk Inst., 1972-79, NASA Adv. Coun. Exploration Task Force, 1989-91; mem. Governor's Econ. Com. on North Slope Natural Gas, Alaska, 1982. Named Alaskan of Year, 1969, Man of Yr. Ripon Soc., 1970; recipient DeSmet medal Gonzaga U., 1969, Horatio Alger award, 1972, Grand Cordon of the Order of Sacred Treasure award His Imperial Majesty the Emperor of Japan, 1988. Mem. Pioneers of Alaska, Alaska C. of C. (former chmn. econ. devel. com.), Equestrian Order Holy Sepulchre, Knights Malta, KC. Leader of the first Alaska Chamber economic trade mission to Japan. Home: 1905 Loussac Dr Anchorage AK 99517-1225 Office: PO Box 101700 Anchorage AK 99510-1700

HICKEY, MICHELLE ANN, filmmaker, screenwriter; b. Walnut Creek, Calif., Nov. 26, 1964; d. Michael Donald Andrew and Paula Ann (Negherbon) H. BA cum laude, San Francisco State U., 1988; postgrad., U. So. Calif., 1998, UCLA, 1999. Ops. coord. Sta. KRON/NBC-TV, San Francisco, 1988-90; assoc. prodr. Sta. HPTV, Palo Alto, Calif., 1990-92; prodn. mgr. JMP, San Francisco, 1992-94; freelance prodr. San Francisco, Seattle, 1994—; freelance screenwriter L.A., Seattle, 1996—. Screenwriter Leo Rising, 1998, Shadow Boxing, 1998, Women Who Snort, 1997, Last I Recall, 1997. Supporter Habitat for Humanity, 1998. mem. Women in Film, Bay Area Broadcast Skills Bank, Sierra Club, Ctr. for Wooden Boats, Wiggley World, Ind. Feature Project West. Avocations: sailing, snowboarding, tennis, travel, painting. E-mail: mh4cinema@aol.com. Fax: 206-285-1801. Office: Ste 104 3400 Ben Lomond Pl Los Angeles CA 90027

HICKEY, PAUL JOSEPH, lawyer; b. Cheyenne, Wyo., May 20, 1950; s. John Joseph and Winifred (Espy) H.; m. Jeanne M. Mrak, Dec. 29, 1973; children: Mary Bridget, Patrick, Joseph. BA, U. Wyo., 1972, JD, 1975. Bar: Wyo. 1975, U.S. Ct. Appeals (10th cir.) 1976, U.S. Supreme Ct. 1988, Colo. 1990. Law clk. to judge U.S. Ct. Appeals for 10th Cir., Cheyenne, 1975-76; ptnr. Rooney, Horiskey, Bagley, Hickey, Cheyenne, 1976-78, Horiskey, Bagley & Hickey, Cheyenne, 1978-82, Bagley, Hickey, Evans & Statkus, Cheyenne, 1982-88, Hickey & Evans, Cheyenne, 1988-94; Hickey, Mackey, Evans, Walker & Stewart, 1995—; atty. Laramie County Sch. Dist. 1, Cheyenne, 1979—; atty., mem. Wyo. Natural Gas Pipeline Authority, Cheyenne, 1989-94. Mem. Wyo. Water Devel. Com., Cheyenne, 1987-95; bd. dirs. Goodwill Industries, Cheyenne, 1988, United Way, Cheyenne, 1990; pres. Old West Mus., Cheyenne, 1987. Mem. ABA, Nat. Sch. Bds. Assn., Coun. Sch. Attys., Internat. Soc. Barristers, Wyo. State Bar (pres. 1997), Wyo. State Bar Found. (pres. 1993), Laramie County Bar Assn. (pres. 1985), Rotary (bd. dirs. Cheyenne 1988, pres. 1993). Democrat. Roman Catholic. Home: 4000 Bent Ave Cheyenne WY 82001-1133 Office: 1712 Carey Ave Cheyenne WY 82001-4420

HICKEY, WINIFRED E(SPY), former state senator, social worker; b. Rawlins, Wyo.; d. David P. and Eugenia (Blake) Espy; children: John David, Paul Joseph. BA, Loretto Heights Coll., 1933; postgrad. U. Utah, 1934, Sch. Social Service, U. Chgo., 1936; LLD (hon.) U. Wyo., 1991. Dir. Carbon County Welfare Dept., 1935-36; field rep. Wyo. Dept. Welfare, 1937-38; dir. Red Cross Club, Europe, 1942-45; commr. Laramie County, Wyo., 1973-80; mem. Wyo. Senate, 1980-90; dir. United Savs. & Loan, Cheyenne; active Joint Powers Bd. Laramie County and City of Cheyenne. Pub. Where the Deer and the Antelope Play, 1967. Pres., bd. dirs. U. Wyo. Found., 1986-87; pres. Meml. Hosp. of Laramie County, 1986-88, Wyo. Transp. Mus., 1990-92, chmn. adv. council div. community programs Wyo. Dept. Health and Social Services; pres. county and state mental health assn., 1959-63; trustee, U. Wyo., 1967-71, St. Mary's Cathedral, 1986—; active Nat. Council Cath. Women Gov. Residence Found., 1991-93, Wyo. Transp. Mus., 1993—; chair Am. Heritage Assocs. of U. Wyo., 1992-96, hon. chair Citizen of the Century State of Wyo., Am. Heritage Ctr., 1966—. Named Outstanding Alumna, Loretto Heights Coll., 1959, Woman of Yr. Commn. for Women, 1988, United Med. Ctr., Cheyenne, 1998, Legislator of Yr. Wyo. Psychologists Assn., 1988, Family of the Yr. U. Wyo., 1995, Person of Yr., United Med. Ctr., Cheyenne, Wyo., 1998. Mem. Altrusa Club (Cheyenne).

HICKLIN, RONALD LEE, music production company executive; b. Burlington, Wash., Dec. 4, 1937; s. Wendell C. and Theodora (Van Voorhis) H.; children: Jennifer Lynn, Mark Allan; m. Trudi Takamatsu, Oct. 23, 1994. Student, U. Wash., 1956-57. Pres. S.A.T.B. Inc., L.A., 1979-98, Killer Music, Inc., San Marino, Calif., 1982—, T.T. B.B., Inc., Hollywood, 1989-97; ptnr. Killer Tracks, Primat Am., Hollywood, 1990-96. Lead tenor The Eligibles, 1958-62; vocal dir., singer Piece of Cake Inc., 1968-81; arranger, producer Calif. Raisin Adv. Bd., 1982 (recipient 2 Clios 1983); producer/co-writer Wheaties, 1983 (Clio award); producer/composer Gatorade, 1983; producer/performer Levi's 501 Blues, 1984. With USAF, 1959-65. Mem. NARAS (MVP award 1973, 75), AFTRA (nat. bd. dirs. 1970-85, local bd. dirs. 1968-85), Screen Actors Guild (nat. bd. dirs. 1975), Am. Fedn. Musicians, Hollywood C. of C. Avocations: golf, tennis, basketball. Home and Office: 30 Kewen Pl San Marino CA 91108-1104

HICKMAN, CRAIG RONALD, author; b. Borger, Tex., Dec. 5, 1949; s. Winston Whitehead and Verla (Bingham) H.; m. Pamela Lewis, Nov. 17, 1972; children: Jared Winston, Kimberly Michelle, Leigh Megan. BA in Econs. cum laude, Brigham Young U., 1974; MBA with honors, Harvard U., 1976. Cons. Ernst & Ernst (now Ernst & Young), L.A., 1976-77; sr. planning analyst Dart Industries, L.A., 1977-79; campaign mgr. Wright for Gov., Salt Lake City, 1980; mgr. cons. svcs. Arthur Young & Co. (now Ernst & Young), 1980-83; pres. Bennett Info. Group, Salt Lake City, 1983-85; chmn., pres. Mgmt. Perspectives Group, Provo, Utah, 1985-91; author, cons. Provo, 1985—; cons. Frito-Lay, Dallas, 1985, Procter & Gamble, Cin., 1986, AT&T, ea. U.S., 1986, Fla. Power & Light, 1987, Systematic Mgmt. Svcs., Phila., 1988, Geneva Steel, Vineyard, Utah, 1989, Found. Health Corp., Sacramento, 1990, Centex, Dallas, Am. Express, N.Y.C., 1994; keynote speaker numerous corp. confs., U. Md., Notre Dame, Head Start Program, Dalhousie U., numerous assns. and USIA, India, Israel, Egypt, Saudi Arabia, 1985-94; bd. dirs. Am. Parts sys. Co-author: Creating Excellence, 1984 (nat. bestseller paperback 1986), The Future 500, 1987; author: Mind of a Manager, Soul of a Leader, 1990 (internat. bestseller paperback 1992), Practical Business Genius, 1991, The Strategy Game, 1993, The Oz Principle, The Organization Game, 1994, The Productivity Game, 1995; contbr. articles and commentaries to profl. jours. Mem. ASTD. Republican. Mem. LDS Ch. Avocations: reading, fiction writing, skiing, travel. Home: 1007 E 150 S Springville UT 84663-4100

HICKMAN, MAXINE VIOLA, social services administrator; b. Louisville, Miss., Dec. 24, 1943; d. Everett and Ozella (Eichelberger) H.; m. William L. Malone, Sept. 5, 1965 (div. 1969); 1 child, Gwendolyn. BA, San Francisco State U., 1966; MS, Nova U., 1991; postgrad., Calif. Coast U., 1991—. Lic. State of Calif. Dept. Social Svcs. IBM profl. mechanic operator Wells Fargo Bank, San Francisco, 1961-65; dept. mgr. Sears Roebuck & Co., San Bruno, Calif., 1966-77; adminstr. Pine St. Guest House, San Francisco, 1969-88; fin. planner John Hancock Fin. Svcs., San Mateo, Calif., 1977-81; chief exec. officer Hickman Homes, Inc., San Francisco, 1981—; cons. BeeBe Meml. Endowment Found., Oakland, Calif., 1990—, Calif. Assn. Children's Home-Mems., Sacramento, 1989—. Mem. NAACP, San Francisco. Named Foster Mother of Yr., Children's Home Soc. Calif., 1985, Woman of Yr., Gamma Nu chpt. Iota Phi Lambda, 1991. Mem. Foster Parents United, Calif. Assn. Children's Homes, Nat. Bus. League, Order of Ea. Star, Masons (worthy matron), Alpha Kappa Alpha. Democrat. Baptist. Avocations: singing, walking, interior design, real estate. Office: Hickman Homes Inc 67 Harold Ave San Francisco CA 94112-2331

HICKMAN, RUTH VIRGINIA, Bible educator; b. Sac City, Iowa, Oct. 15, 1931; d. Ronald Minor and Ida E. (Willcutt) Wilson; m. Charles Ray Hickman, Aug. 25, 1962; children: Ronald Everett, Lisa Michelle. BS in Home Econs., Morningside Coll., 1953. Ordained to ministry Christian Ch., 1985. Instr. Nat. Ednl. TV, 1964-76; staff coord., tchr. Life for Layman, Denver, 1974-77; founder, tchr. Abundant Word Ministries, Lakewood, Colo., 1980—; tchr. Bible Calvary Temple, Denver, 1980—; sales/trainer Hillestad Internat., Woodruff, Wis., 1978—; Women's com. Billy Graham Assn., Denver, 1986-87. Author: (book) Hope for Hurting People, 1987; speaker, instr. audio and video tape series, 1980—. Leader pilgrimages to Israel, 1984, 87, 94, 96, 98. Mem. Rocky Mountain Fellowship Christian Leaders. Republican. Home: 3043 S Holly Pl Denver CO 80222-7010 Office: Abundant Word Ministries 6900 W Alameda Ave Ste 106 Lakewood CO 80226-3312

HICKS, BETHANY GRIBBEN, lawyer, commissioner; b. N.Y., Sept. 8, 1951; d. Robert and DeSales Gribben; m. William A. Hicks III, May 21, 1982; children: Alexandra Elizabeth, Samantha Katherine. AB, Vassar Coll., 1973; MEd, Boston U., 1975; JD, Ariz. State U., 1984. Bar: Ariz. 1984. Pvt. practice Scottsdale and Paradise Valley, Ariz., 1984-91; law clk. to Hon. Kenneth L. Fields Maricopa County Superior Ct. S.E. dist., Mesa, 1991-93; commr., judge pro tem, domestic rels. and juvenile divsns. Maricopa County Superior Ct. Ctrl. and S.E. Dists., Phoenix and Mesa, 1993—; magistrate Town of Paradise Valley, Ariz., 1993-94. Mem. Jr. League of Phoenix, 1984-91; bd. dirs. Phoenix Children's Theatre, 1988-90; parliamentarian Girls Club of Scottsdale, Ariz., 1985-87, 89-90, bd. dirs., 1988-91; exec. bd., sec. All Saints' Episcopal Day Sch. Parents Assn., 1991-92, pres., 1993-94; active Nat. Charity League, 1995—, Valley Leadership Class XIX, 1997-98. Mem. ABA, State Bar Ariz., Maricopa County Bar Assn., Ariz. Women Lawyers' Assn. (steering com. 1998—). Republican. Episcopalian. Club: Paradise Valley Country. Office: 1810 S Lewis St Mesa AZ 85210-6234

HICKS, DAVID EARL, author, inventor; b. Indpls., Jan. 1, 1931; s. John Arthur and Marguerite (Barnes) H.; m. Shirlene Lavan Barlow, Jan. 22, 1958 (div. June 1973); children: Sharon Lynn, Brenda Kay; m. Margaret Leigh Payne, Feb. 17, 1977; children: David Bradley, Leslie Ann, Brian Patrick. Grad., Nat. Radio Inst., 1953; student, Purdue U., 1959-60, Miami-Dade Community Coll., 1971-72. Cert. advanced paramedic. Tech. writer, editor Howard W. Sams, Inc., Indpls., 1958-64; tech. writer Systems Engring. Labs, Inc., Ft. Lauderdale, Fla., 1964-67; publs. mgr. Novatronics, Inc., Pompano Beach, Fla., 1967-69; pres. Datatek, Inc., Ft. Lauderdale, 1969-71; tech. writer Systems Devel. Corp., Colorado Springs, Colo., 1973-74, Ford Aerospace Corp., Colorado Springs, 1974-76; pres. Nutronics Corp., Colorado Springs, 1982-87; tech. writer Digital Equipment Corp., Colorado Springs, 1978-88; pres. Innovation USA Mag., Colorado Springs, 1989; tech. cons., inventor pvt. practice, Colo. Springs, 1964-65, 75-92; novelist Colo. Springs, 1992—; tech. cons. Japan Electronics, Tokyo, 1962-63, Nutronics Corp., Longmont, Colo., 1987. Author of eight tech. books (two made best seller list) including: Citizens Band Radio Handbook, 1961, Amateur Radio-VHF and Above, 1965, CB Radio Operating Procedures, 1976; contbr. articles to electronics jours.; inventor of new electric charging system, 1978, awarded U.S. patent, 1981; lectr. numerous sci. and invention seminars, 1978—. Communications officer CD, Indpls., 1962-63; judge sci. fair Pub. Sch. System, Colorado Springs, 1986-87. Served with USN, 1948. Recipient Red Cross Hall of Fame, Indpls., 1963; grantee U.S. Dept. of Energy, 1984; recipient Nat. Energy Resources Tech. Innovation award, 1989, Disting. Leadership award Am. Biog. Inst. 1990, cert. of merit Internat. Biog. Ctr., 1990. Mem. Soc. of Am. Inventors (bd. dirs., Pres. award 1989), Am. Radio Relay League, Author's Guild, Author's League of Am. Republican. Avocations: traveling, camping, hiking, photography. Office: PO Box 25053 Colorado Springs CO 80936-5053

HICKS, DOLORES KATHLEEN (DE DE HICKS), association executive; b. Mount Vernon, Iowa, Sept. 22, 1932; d. Edward M. and Olga Marie (Hekl) Staskal; m. Roswell Allen Hicks, Sept. 5, 1952; children: Thomas, Gregory, Bryan, Kevin. Student, Colo. Coll., 1950-52. Exec. women's wardrobe cons. Bullock's, Torrance, Calif., 1985-86; exec. dir. The Vol. Ctr., Torrance, 1986—; pres. Vol. Ctrs. So. Calif., 1988; coord. First Lady of Calif. Outstanding Vol. Awards, Sacramento, 1993; nat. bd. dirs. Vol. Ctrs.-Points of Light Found., Washington, 1993-96. Pres. LWV, Palos Verdes Peninsula, Calif., 1981-83; chair Year of the Coast, Calif. LWV, Sacramento, 1984; active in state and local [illegible] YWCA, Woman of the Yr., YWCA, Torrance, 1986, Woman of Distinction, Soroptomist, Torrance, 1988. Mem. Pvt. Industry Coun. (bd. mem. 1994-97), Cmty. Assn. of the Peninsula (life, pres. 1984-87, Palos Verdes Peninsula Citizen of Yr. 1987, Outstanding Vol. award 1988), So. Bay Prodrs. Guild (Outstanding Interviewer 1995), Vol. Ctrs. of Calif. (bd. mem. 1988—, Founders award 1991), Gamma Phi Beta (alumni mem., Internat. Carnation award 1992, Achievement award 1993). Democrat. Roman Catholic. Avocations: gourmet cooking, home decorating, entertaining, reading, traveling.

HICKS, NORM, airport operations executive; b. 1941. BBA, Golden Gate U., 1964; postgrad., U.S. Naval Postgrad. Sch., 1971. Exec. dir., COO Mohave County Airport Authority, Bullhead City, Ariz. Office: Mohave County Airport Auth 600 Highway 95 Bullhead City AZ 86429-5007*

HICKSON, ERNEST CHARLES, financial executive; b. L.A., July 14, 1931; s. Russell Arthur and Marilyn Louise (Mambert) H.; m. Janice Beleal, Sept. 5, 1959; children: Arthur, Jennifer, Barton. BS, U. So. Calif., 1961; postgrad., UCLA Grad. Sch. of Bus. Admin., 1961-63. Lic. real estate broker, Calif., 1986. Credit supr. ARCO (Richfield Oil), L.A., 1955-60; asst. v.p. Union Bank L.A., 1960-64; v.p. County Nat. Bank (now Wells Fargo), Orange, Calif., 1964-67; v.p., sr. loan ofcr. City Bank, Honolulu, 1967-70; pres., CEO Shelter Corp., 1968-72; exec. v.p., dir. U.S. Fin., Inc., San Diego, 1970-73; pres., CEO USF Investors, 1971-73; exec. v.p. Sonnenblick Goldman, L.A., 1973-76; pres., CEO First Hawaiian Devel., Honolulu, 1976-82; CEO TMH Resources, Laguna Niguel, Calif., 1982—; cons. and expert witness in fin. Author: (novel) The Developers, 1978; editor: (monthly newsletter) Financial Marketing, 1978-83. Staff sgt. USAF, 1950-53. Recipient Exec. award Grad. Sch. of Credit and Fin. Mgmt., Stanford U., 1964, Assocs. award The Nat. Inst. of Credit, UCLA, 1959. Mem. U. So. Calif. Assocs., U. So. Calif. Pres.'s Circle, Urban Land Inst., Town Hall, Salt Creek Club (charter), Pacific Club (Honolulu), Outrigger Canoe Club (Honolulu), Phi Gamma Delta. Avocations: tennis, walking, writing.

HIDALGO, MIGUEL, transportation company executive; b. Detroit, Nov. 10, 1958; s. Manuel and Ann (Molina) H.; m. Rausdha Nelly Cachoa, Nov. 14, 1992; children: Jesahel, Monica Natasha, Samuel. BA in Communications, Pepperdine U., 1981; MS in Aero. Mgmt., Nat. U., 1992, MBA in Internat. Bus. Mktg., 1999. Owner Pacific Trans Service, L.A., 1981-83, Disneyland, Anaheim, Calif., 1984; legal adminstr. Hidalgo & Assocs., L.A., 1985-90; ops. and customs Aero Calif. Airlines, San Diego, 1990-91; pres. AeroCargo, San Diego, 1992-96; owner AeroCargo, Inc., Baja AirWest Express, Nelly's Pilot/Aircraft Supply, Brown Field Rental Car Svc., Nelly's Airport Sta.; mgr. U.S. Airways, 1997—. Author: Baja Nelly's Flightguide to Mexico, 1994; contbr. articles to profl. jours. Active S.W. Rep. Project; advisor Polit. Edn. Project. With USN, mem. Res., ret., 1985-91. Mem. Pepperdine Assocs., San Marino Alumni Assn., Huntington Libr. Republican. Roman Catholic.

HIDDLESTON, RONAL EUGENE, drilling and pump company executive; b. Bristow, Okla., Mar. 21, 1939; s. C.L. and Iona D. (Martin) H.; m. Marvelene L. Hammond, Apr. 26, 1959; children: Michael Scott, Mark Shawn, Matthew Shane. Student, Idaho State U., 1957-58. With Roper's Clothing and Bishop Redi-Mix, Rupert, Idaho, 1960-61; pres., chmn. bd., gen. mgr. Hiddleston Drilling, Rupert, 1961-66, Mountain Home, Idaho, 1966—; bd. dirs. Baker Mfg. Mem. Mountain Home Airport Adv. Bd., 1968—; hon. mem. Idaho Search and Rescue. Mem. Nat. Ground Water Assn. (past pres.), Idaho Ground Water Assn. (hon. life, past pres.), Pacific N.W. Water Well Assn., N.W. Mining Assn., Nat. Fedn. Ind. Businessmen, Ground Water Inst. (bd. dirs.), Aircraft Owners and Pilots Assn., Ducks Unltd., Nat. 210 Owners Club, Nat. Sporting Clays Assn., Masons, Royal Arch, Scottish Rites, El Korzh Shrine. Home: 105 Goodall St Mountain Home ID 83647-1629 Office: RR 3 Box 610D Mountain Home ID 83647-9206

HIDELSON, MARK J., art history educator; b. San Gabriel, Calif., Feb. 17, 1964; s. Joseph William and Evelyn Dolores (Valencia) H.; m. Kelli Ann Mosser, July 2, 1994. BA, U. Calif., Irvine, 1987; MA, San Diego State U., 1992. Instr. art history Brooks Coll., Long Beach, Calif., 1994-97, Rio Hondo Coll., Whittier, Calif., 1995, Cerritos Coll., Norwalk, Calif., 1993—, Santa Monica (Calif.) Coll., 1995—, Orange Coast Coll., Costa Mesa, Calif., 1996—, Saddleback Coll., Mission Jiejo, Calif., 1997—. Mem. Coll. Art Assn., Faculty Assn. Calif. C.C., Santa Monica Coll. Faculty Assn., Kappa Sigma.

HIETT, MALCOLM DOUGLAS, software engineer, non-profit company executive; b. Delano, Calif., 1961; sd. Robert Ernest and Vivian Hiett. BS in Edn., Biola U., 1984; PhD in Instrnl. Tech., U. So. Calif., 1989. Instrnl. designer Perceptronics, Inc., L.A., 1989-90, sr. instrnl. designer, 1990-91, mgr. multimedia systems, 1991-93; advisory software engr. multimedia divsn. IBM Corp., San Jose, Calif., 1993—; instrnl. designer, multimedia cons. Xerox, L.A., 1985-89, U. So. Calif., L.A., 1985-89, Perceptronics, L.A., 1985-89; Internet cons., webmaster SVCC, San Jose, 1996—. Photographer (multimedia CD-Rom) Walk in the Foot Steps, 1996, Multimedia Life Application Bible, 1997, IBM Worldbook Multimedia Encyclopedia, 1998; Webmaster, designer (www.mustardseed.net) The Biblelands Project, 1997—. Pres. Mustardseed Media, 1997—. Mem. IEEE (tutorial coors. 1990), Soc. Applied Learning Tech., Soc. Tech. Comm., Human Factors Soc., Nat. Soc. Performance and Instrn. Avocations: animation, video, multimedia, basketball, running. E-mail: hiett@mustardseed.net. Office: IBM 5600 Cottle Rd 051/M94 San Jose CA 95193

HIGDON, BERNICE COWAN, retired elementary education educator; b. Sylva, N.C., Feb. 26, 1918; d. Royston Duffield and Margaret Cordelia (Hall) Cowan; m. Roscoe John Higdon, Aug. 12, 1945; children: Ronald Keith, Rodrick Knox, Krista Dean. BS, Western Carolina U., 1941; cert. tchr., So. Oreg. Coll., 1967; student, Chapman Coll., 1971. Cert. tchr., Calif. Prin., tchr. Dorsey Sch., Bryson City, N.C., 1941-42; expeditor Glenn L. Martin Aircraft Co., Balt., 1942-45; tchr. elem. sch. Seneca, S.C., 1945-46, Piedmont, S.C., 1946-47; tchr. elem. sch. Columbia, S.C., 1950-51, Manteca, Calif., 1967-68; kindergarten tchr. 1st Bapt. Ch., Medford, Oreg., 1965-67; tchr. elem. sch. Marysville (Calif.) Unified Sch. Dist., 1968-83; tchr. Headstart, Manteca, 1968. Past counselor Youth Svc. Bur., Yuba City, Calif.; troop leader Girl Scouts U.S.A., Medford, 1962-63; past Sunday sch. tchr. 1st Bapt. Ch., Medford; bd. dirs. Christian Assistance Network, Yuba City, 1984-85; deaconess Evang. Free Ch., Yuba City, 1991-93. Recipient cert. of appreciation Marysville Unified Sch. Dist., 1983, Christian Assistance Network, 1985; cert. of recognition Ella Elem. Sch., Marysville, 1983. Mem. Calif. Ret. Tchrs. Assn., Nat. Ret. Tchrs. Assn., Sutter Hist. Soc., AAUW, Am. Assn. Ret. Persons. Avocations: foreign traveling, photography, volunteer work, tole painting. Home: 1264 Charlotte Ave Yuba City CA 95991-2804

HIGGINBOTHAM, LLOYD WILLIAM, mechanical engineer; b. Haydentown, Pa., Nov. 24, 1934; s. Clarence John and Nannie Mae (Piper) H.; m. Genevieve Law, Oct. 17, 1953 (div.); 1 child, Mark William; m. Mary Bannaian, July 23, 1966; 1 child, Samuel Lloyd. With rsch. and devel. TRW Inc., Cleve., 1953-57; pres. Higginbotham Rsch., Cleve., 1957-64, Higginbotham Assocs., Woodland Hills, Calif., 1964—; founder, CEO Engrs. of World, Woodland Hills, Calif., 1993—; founder, pres., CEO Enhance Engring. Edn. Found., Inc., Woodland Hills, 1993—; pres., CEO Engrs. Coun., 1993—; cons. grad. engring. programs UCLA, Calif. State U., L.A., U. So. Calif.; pres. adv. com. Pierce Coll., L.A.; adv. com. So. Calif. Productivity Ctr.; cons. various Calif. legislators. Mem. Town Hall Calif. Recipient Community Svc. award City of Downey, Calif, 1974, Archimedes award NSPE, Outstanding Contbr. Recognition, 1986, Outstanding Leadership Recognition, 1987, William B. Johnson Meml. Internat. Interprofl. award, 1992. Fellow Inst. Advancement Engring. (class of 1982, exec. dir., exec. mgr. 1984-93); mem. Soc. Carbide and Tool Engrs. (chmn., 1974-76), Soc. Mfg. Engrs. (chmn. San Fernando Valley chpt. 1977-79, numerous awards), San Fernando Valley Joint Coun. Engrs. (now Engrs. Coun., Inc., advisor, pres. 1981-82, 92-94), San Fernando Valley engrs. Coun. (pres., CEO 1992—), Profl. Salesmen's Assn., Am. Soc. Assn. Execs., L.A. Coun. Engrs. and Scientists (exec. mgr. 1984-93), N.Y. Acad. Scis., L.A. Area C. of C., Toastmasters, Masons. Republican. Avocations: golf, spectator sports. Office: Higginbotham Assocs 24310 Calvert St Woodland Hills CA 91367-1113

HIGGINS, ISABELLE JEANETTE, librarian; b. Evanston, Ill., Dec. 13, 1919; d. Frank LeRoy and Ada Louise (Wilcox) Heck; m. George Alfred

Higgins, Jan. 23, 1945 (dec. Sept. 1994); children: Alfred Clinton, Donald Quentin, Heather Higgins Aanes, Laura Higgins Palmer, Carol Higgins. BS, Northwestern U., 1940; MLS, U. Md., 1971. Cert. libr., Md. With Liebermann Waelchli Co., Tokyo, 1940-41, Shanghai Evening Post, 1941-42; editl. asst. Newsweek mag., N.Y.C., 1944; wire editor FBIS/FCC, Washington, 1944-46; rsch. and analysis China desk CIA, Washington, 1946-49; supr. library vols. Westbrook Sch., Bethesda, Md., 1965-69; reference libr. Montgomery County Pub. Librs., Bethesda, 1969-83; libr. Brooks Inst. Photography, Santa Barbara, Calif., 1984-96, ret., 1996; treas. Friends of Santa Barbara Pub. Libr., 1987-88. Mem. AAUW (bd. dirs. Santa Barbara br. 1988-94, del. nat. conv. 1989), Spl. Librs. Assn., Calif. Libr. Assn., Santa Barbara Little Gardens Club (pres. 1987-89), Floriade Garden Club (pres. 1990-91). Congregationalist. Avocations: reading, swimming, gardening. Home: 1128 Garcia Rd Santa Barbara CA 93103-2128

HIGGINS, JAMES BRADLEY, dentist; b. Richmond, Ind., July 3, 1941; s. James Randall and Mildred Ethel (White) H.; m. Dorothy Campbell, Dec. 29, 1964; children: Kimberly, Amy, Michaelle Ann, James. DDS, Ind. U., Bloomington, 1966. Resident dentist Ind. State Mental Hosp., Richmond, 1966; pvt. practice dentistry San Jose, Calif., 1968—; lectr. hypnosis Calif. Dental Assts. Assn., 1974-88; cons. Calif. State Bd. Dental Examiners, 1978-80; co-chmn. Santa Clara County Dentist Peer Rev. Com., 1982-84; dental lectr. San Jose Unified Sch. Dist. Bd. dirs. Santa Clara County Health Dept., San Jose, 1986-90, Noble Sch. Parent Tchr. Adv. Bd., San Jose. Capt. Dental Corp, USAF, 1966-68. Mem. ADA, NAACP (life), Nat. Dental Assn., Calif. Dental Assn., Santa Clara County Dental Soc., 100 Black Men of San Jose Assn. (charter). Democrat. Office: 4600 Alum Rock Ave San Jose CA 95127-2463

HIGGINS, MICHAEL LEO, multimedia developer, educator, webmaster; b. San Jose, Calif., Oct. 19, 1958; s. John R. and Jill M. (Macpherson) H. BS in Computer Sci. summa cum laude, Western Internat. U., 1990. Engr., technician Govt. Divsn. Motorola, Scottsdale, Ariz., 1979-90; owner, cons. Ultramedia, Phoenix, 1982—; trainer macromedia products Ariz. Macintosh User's Group, Phoenix, 1994—; bd. dirs. Rite-on-the-Button, Santa Clarita, Calif. Author, developer (CD-ROM) Multimedia Presenter, 1995, Ariz. in Nov., 1995; co-designer/programmer (CD-ROM) Solutions, 1996; programmer, author: (e-mail encoder/decoder) ED, 1998. Mem. Nat. Fedn. Ind. Bus. Avocations: flying planes, singing, music. E-mail: michael@umedia.com.

HIGGINS, RUTH ANN, social worker, family therapist; b. Rock Valley, Iowa, Sept. 23, 1944; d. Neal and Tillie (Feekes) Vonk; m. 1972 (div. Sept. 1986); children: Ashlie Kay, Steven Grant. BA, Northwestern Coll., 1966; MA, U. Colo., 1978; LCSW, U. Denver, 1983. Cert. profl. tchr., Colo., social worker, Colo. Tchr. Adams County Dist. 12, Northglenn, Colo., 1967-69, Dept. Def., Clark AFB, The Philippines, 1969-70, Jefferson County Schs., Lakewood, Colo., 1970-75; social worker Boulder (Colo.) County Mental Health Ctr., 1977, Boulder Community Counseling Ctr., 1979-81, Columbine Counseling Ctr., Broomfield, Colo., 1981—; sch. social worker Adams County Sch. Dist. 12, Northglenn, Colo., 1985—; part time social worker Hospice of Metro Denver, 1984-85, Boulder Valley Pub. Schs., 1985, Lutheran Hospice Care, Wheatridge, Colo., 1985. Author, editor: Nothing Could Stop the Rain, 1976. Counselor trainer for Up With People (Worldsmart), 1998-99. Recipient Hon. Mention Counselor of Yr. award Colo. Sch. Counselors Assn., 1994; named finalist Alteria M. Bryant award Met. Denver Baha'i Ctr., 1996. Mem. Nat. Assn. Social Workers. Democrat. Avocations: stained glass, hiking, reading, music.

HIGHLAND, FREDERICK, writer, humanities educator; b. Audobon, N.J., Feb. 13, 1945; s. Frederick William Sr. and Emily Barbara H.; 1 child, Sophia Angela. BA in English, Suffolk U., 1967; MA in English, U. Wis., Milw., 1971, PhD in Lit., 1983. Vol. Peace Corps, Washington, 1967-69; teaching asst. U. Wis., Milw., 1969-75; instr. Upward Bound Program, Milw., 1970-73; instr. English Bir Zeit U., West Bank, Israel, 1975-76; Pace prof. Chapman Coll., Orange, Calif., 1977-79; edn. specialist Dept. U.S. Navy, Cubi Point, Philippines, 1979-85; dir. Pace Hawaii City Colls. Chgo., Pearl Harbor, 1985-87; writer, rschr. Highland Wordsmith, Washington, 1996—. Author: The Mystery Box, 1998. Mem. Am. Philatelic Soc., Am. Topical Soc., Mystery Writers Am. E-mail: fwh@earthlink.net. Home and Office: Highland Wordsmith PO Box 5961 Bellingham WA 98227-5961

HIGHLANDER, RICHARD WILLIAM, communications executive; b. Beckley, W.Va., Feb. 17, 1940; s. Ronald William and Lucille Bernice (Bland) H.; m. Ida Mae Canterbury, June 26, 1965; one child, Alison Renee. BA, Rutgers U., 1963; MA, U. Ga., 1972. Commd. 2d lt. U.S. Army, 1963, advanced through grades to lt. col., 1979, ret., 1984; dir. communications, def. systems group FMC Corp., Santa Clara, Calif., 1984-94; v.p. comm. United Def. LP, Santa Clara, 1994—. Contbr. articles to profl. jours., Freedom Found. award 1966, 81. Trustee San Jose Repertory Co., 1985. Decorated Legion of Merit with bronze oak leaf cluster, Bronze Star with two bronze oak leaf clusters, Purple Heart. Mem. PRSA (accredited), Assn. U.S. Army, Internat. Assn. Bus. Communicators, Calif. Mfrs. Assn. (bd. dirs. 1985, chmn. bd. 1993), Aerospace Industries Assn. (comm. coun.), Rotary, San Jose Met. C. of C. (bd. dirs.), Chi Psi. Republican. Methodist. Avocations: racquetball, golf. Home: 5906 Gleneagles Cir San Jose CA 95138-2370

HIGHT, HAROLD PHILIP, retired security company executive; b. Crescent City, Calif., Apr. 17, 1924; s. Vernon Austin and Mary Jane (Gontau) H.; m. Margaret Rose Edelman, Nov. 19, 1945 (div. 1949); children: Linda Marie, Beverly Sue; m. Doris Louise Dunn, June 20, 1982 (dec. 1998). Student police sci., Coll. of Redwoods, 1969. With Pan Am. World Airways, South San Francisco, Calif., 1945-51, 52; officer Richmond (Calif.) Police Dept., 1952-54; aircraft electrician Internat. Atlas Svc., Oakland, Calif., 1954-56; security officer radiation lab. AEC, Livermore, Calif., 1956-58; chief police Port Orford (Oreg.) Police Dept., 1958-61; dep. sheriff, sgt., evidence technician Del Notre County Sheriff's Dept., Crescent City, 1961-85; ret., 1985; security officer, sgt. Del Notre Security Svc., Crescent City, 1985. With USN, 1941-45, 51-52. Mem. Internat. Footprint Assn. (sec., treas. bd. dirs. Crescent City 1985—), Navy League U.S. (2d v.p. Crescent City 1984—), Tin Can Sailors, Masons, Scottish Rite (32d degree), Elks, Grange. Republican. Roman Catholic. Avocations: model railroads, walking. Home: 110 Lafayette Way Crescent City CA 95531-8351

HIGHT, MARY KATHRYN (KAY), art historian; b. Iowa City, Iowa, Apr. 25, 1940; d. Donald B. and Kathryn (Hallman) Sweeney; m. B. Boyd Hight, Mar. 31, 1962; children: Kathryn, Kevin. BA, Duke U., 1962; MA, UCLA, 1978, PhD, 1986. Tchr. Va. Beach (Va.) Schs., 1962-63; assoc. Girl Scouts Am., New Haven, 1963-66; assoc. prof. Pomona Coll., Claremont, Calif., 1988-89; lectr. art history UCLA, Irvin, Calif., 1990-96; landmarks commr. City of Santa Monica, Calif., 1996—; lectr. Norton Simon Mus. Art, 1991—. Bd. dirs. L.A. Conservancy, 1981-89, pres. bd. dirs., 1988-89, bd. L.A. master chorale, 1988-92, bd. L.A. Opera League, 1993-95. Grantee Rockefeller Found., 1978. Fellow Huntington Libr.; mem. Coll. Art Assn., L.A. Country Club, Bel-Air Bay Club. Avocations: golfing, traveling. Home: 334 10th St Santa Monica CA 90402-2018

HILBERT, ROBERT S(AUL), optical engineer; b. Washington, Apr. 29, 1941; s. Philip G. and Bessie (Friend) H.; m. Angela Cinel Ferreira, June 19, 1966; children: David M., Daniel S. BS in Optics, U. Rochester, 1962, MS in Optics, 1964. Optical design engr. Itek Corp., Lexington, Mass., 1963-65, supr. lens design sect., 1965-67, asst. mgr. optical engr. dept., 1967-69, mgr. optical engring. dept., 1969-74, dir. optics, 1974-75; v.p. engring. Optical Rsch. Assocs., Pasadena, Calif., 1975-84, sr. v.p., 1985-91, pres., COO, 1991—, also bd. dirs.; lectr. Northeastern U., Burlington, Mass., 1967-69; mem. trustees vis. com. Sch. Engring. and Applied Sci., U. Rochester, 1995-97. Patentee in lens systems. Recipient Future Scientist of Am. award, 1957; Am. Optical Co. fellow U. Rochester, 1962. Fellow Soc. Photo-Optical Instrumentation Engrs.; mem. Optical Soc. Am. (engring. coun. 1990-92), Lens Design Tech. Group (chmn. 1975-77). Jewish. Avocations: reading, the cinema. Home: 5055 Indianola Way La Canada Flintridge CA 91011-2657 Office: Optical Rsch Assocs 3280 E Foothill Blvd Pasadena CA 91107-3103

HILBRECHT, NORMAN TY, lawyer; b. San Diego, Feb. 11, 1933; s. Norman Titus and Elizabeth (Lair) H.; m. Mercedes L. Sharratt, Oct. 24, 1980. B.A., Northwestern U., 1956; J.D., Yale U., 1959. Bar: Nev. 1959, U.S. Supreme Ct. 1963. Assoc. counsel Union Pacific R.R., Las Vegas, 1962; ptnr. Hilbrecht & Jones, Las Vegas, 1962-69; pres. Hilbrecht, Jones, Schreck & Bernhard, 1969-83, Hilbrecht & Assocs, 1983—, Mobil Transport Corp., 1970-72; gen. counsel Bell United Ins. Co., 1986-94; mem. Nev. Assembly, 1966-72, minority leader, 1971-72; mem. Nev. Senate, 1974-78; legis. commn., 1977-78; asst. lectr. bus. law U. Nev., Las Vegas.; oper. mem. Corp. Svcs. Group, 1998—; pres. Corp. Svcs. Co., 1998—, Nev. Incorporating Co., 1998—. Author: Nevada Motor Carrier Compendium, 1990. Mem. labor mgmt. com. NCCJ, 1963; mem. Clark County (Nev.) Dem. Ctrl. Com., 1959-80, 1st vice chmn., 1965-66; del. Western Regional Assembly on Ombudsman; chmn. Clark County Dem. Conv., 1966, Nev. Dem. Conv., 1966; pres. Clark County Legal Aid Soc., 1964, Nev. Legal Aid and Defender Assn., 1965-83; assoc. for justice Nat. Jud. Coll., 1993, 94, 95, 96. Capt. AUS, 1952-67. Named Outstanding State Legislator Eagleton Inst. Politics, Rutgers U., 1969, Best Lawyers in Am., Bar of Nev., 1993. Mem. ABA, ATLA, Am. Judicature Soc., Am. Acad. Polit. and Social Sci., State Bar Nev. (chmn. adminstrv. law 1991-94, chmn. sect. on adminstrv. law 1996), Nev. Trial Lawyers (state v.p. 1966), Am. Assn. Ret. Persons (state legis. com. 1991-94), Rotary, Elks, Phi Beta Kappa, Delta Phi Epsilon, Theta Chi, Phi Delta Phi. Lutheran. Office: 723 S Casino Center Blvd Las Vegas NV 89101-6716

HILDEBRAND, CAROL ILENE, librarian; b. Presho, S.D., Feb. 15, 1943; d. Arnum Vance and Ethel Grace (Cole) Stoops; m. Duane D. Hildebrand, Mar. 21, 1970. BA, Dakota Wesleyan U., Mitchell, S.D., 1965; M in Librarianship, U. Wash., 1968. Tchr. Watertown (S.D.) H.S., 1965-67; libr. dir. Chippewa County Libr., Montevideo, Minn., 1968-70, The Dalles (Oreg.)-Wasco County Libr., 1970-72; libr. Salem (Oreg.) Pub. Libr., 1972-73; libr. dir. Lake Oswego (Oreg.) Pub. Libr., 1973-82; asst. city libr. Eugene (Oreg.) Pub. Libr., 1982-91, acting city libr., 1991-92, libr. dir., 1993—; cons., condr. workshops in field. Vice-chair LWV, Lane County, 1987; bd. dirs. People for Oreg. Librs. Polit. Action Com., 1986—; sec. Citizens for Lane County Libr., 1985-88. Named Woman of Yr., Lane County Coun. of Orgns., 1995, Oreg. Libr. of Yr., 1993. Mem. ALA (chpt. councilor 1990-94), AAUW (bd. dirs. 1986, sec. 1995-96), Pacific N.W. Libr. Assn. (pres. 1989-90), Oreg. Libr. Assn. (pres. 1976-77), Rotary, Phi Kappa Phi. Methodist. Avocations: reading murder mysteries, baking. Office: Eugene Public Libr 100 W 13th Ave Eugene OR 97401-3433

HILDEBRAND, JOHN G(RANT), neurobiologist, educator; b. Boston, Mar. 26, 1942; s. John G. and Helen S. Hildebrand; m. Gail Deerin Burd, July 24, 1982. AB, Harvard U., 1964; PhD, Rockefeller U., 1969. Instr. neurobiology Harvard U. Med. Sch., Boston, 1970-72, asst. prof., 1972-77, assoc. prof., 1977-80, vis. prof., 1980-81; prof. biol. scis. Columbia U., N.Y.C., 1980-85; prof. neurobiol., biochemistry, molecular and cell biology, entomology U. Ariz., Tucson, 1985—, Regents prof., 1989—, dir. div. neurobiology, 1985—; assoc. behavioral biology Harvard U. Mus. Comparative Zoology, Cambridge, Mass., 1980-97; trustee Marine Biol. Lab., Woods Hole, Mass., 1981-89, mem. exec. com., 1981-88; Jan de Wilde lectr. U. Wageningen, The Netherlands, 1992; King Solomon lectr., Hebrew U., Jerusalem, 1995; K.D. Roeder lectr. Tufts U., 1995; Felix Santschi lectr. U. Zurich, Switzerland, 1995. Co-editor: Chemistry of Synaptic Transmission, 1974, Receptors for Neurotransmitters, Hormones, and Pheromones in Insects, 1980, Molecular Insect Science, 1990; devel. neurosci. sect. editor Jour. Neurosci., 1983-88; co-editor Jour. Comparative Physiology A, 1990—; mem. editorial bd. various other jours. Trustee Rockefeller U., N.Y.C., 1970-73. Recipient Javits Neurosci. award Nat. Inst. Neurol. and Communicative Disorders and Stroke, NIH, 1986-94, Merit award Nat. Inst. Allergy and Infections Diseases, NIH, 1986-97, R.H. Wright award Simon Fraser U., B.C., Can., 1990, Max Planck Rsch. award Max Planck Gesellschaft and Alexander von Humboldt-Stiftung of Germany, 1990, Founder's Meml. award Entomol. Soc. Am., 1997, Humboldt rsch. award, 1997; Helen Hay Whitney Found. fellow, 1969-72, A.P. Sloan Found. fellow, 1973-77. Fellow AAAS, Royal Entomol. Soc. U.K.; mem. Am. Soc. Biochemistry and Molecular Biology, Assn. for Chemoreception Scis. (IFF Innovation Rsch. award 1997), Soc. for Neurosci. (treas. 1993-94), Internat. Soc. Neuroethology (pres. 1995-98), Soc. Integrative and Comparative Biology, Internat. Soc. Chem. Ecology (pres. 1998-99), Deutsch Akademic Naturforscher Leopoldina. Avocations: music, lower brass instruments. Home: 629 N Olsen Ave Tucson AZ 85719-5136 Office: U Ariz ARL Div Neurobiology PO Box 210077 Tucson AZ 85721-0077

HILDEBRAND, MARY-ELIZABETH, journal editor; b. N.Y.C., Feb. 23, 1918; d. John and Katherine (Georges) Sorlingas; m. John Perry, June 25, 1939 (dec. Nov. 1973); children: Philip, David, Susan, John. BS (Magna Cum Laude), Columbia U., 1967; MA, Columbia U. Tchrs. Coll., 1970. Cert. English, Spanish tchr., N.Y. Tchr. N.Y. Archdiocese, N.Y.C., 1967-80; editor, pub. Pegasus Pub., Boulder City, Nev., 1986 . Author numerous poems. Life mem. AAUW, Nat. League Am. Pen Women (treas. 1993—, poetry editor Pen Woman mag. 1997—). Episcopalian. Avocation: writing poetry. Office: Pegasus Publishing 525 Avenue B Boulder City NV 89005-2731

HILDEBRANT, ANDY MCCLELLAN, retired electrical engineer; b. Nescopeck, Pa., May 12, 1929; s. Andrew Harmon and Margaret C. (Knorr) H.; m. Rita Mae Yarnold, June 20, 1959; children: James Matthew, David Michael, Andrea Marie. Student, State Tchrs. Coll., Bloomsburg, Pa., 1947-48, Bucknell U., 1952-54, UCLA, 1955-57, Utica Coll., 1965-70. Rsch. analyst Douglas Aircraft Co., Santa Monica, Calif., 1954-57; specialist engring. GE, Johnson City, N.Y., 1957-58, Ithaca, N.Y., 1958-64; elec. engr. GE, Utica, N.Y., 1964-70, Sylvania Electro Systems, Mountain View, Calif., 1970-71, Dalmo-Victor Co., Belmont, Calif., 1971-72, Odetics/Infodetics, Anaheim, Calif., 1972-75, Lear Siegler, Inc., Anaheim, 1975-78, Ford Aerospace, Newport Beach, Calif., 1978-79, THUMS Long Beach Co., Long Beach, Calif., 1979-94; ret., 1994; elec. engring. cons. Perkin-Elmer, Auto Info. Retrieval, Pi-Gem Assn., Pasadena, Calif., Palo Alto, Calif., 1971-73. Patentee AC power modulator for a non-linear load. Juror West Orange County Mpcl. Ct., Westminster, Calif., 1979, U.S. Dist. Ct., L.A., 1991-92. With USN, 1948-52. Recipient Cert. Award in Indsl. Controls Tech., Calif. State U., Fullerton, 1991-92. Mem. Orange County Chpt. Charities (sec. 1988), KC (past grand knight 1987-88). Republican. Roman Catholic. Avocations: woodworking, camping, hiking. Home: 20392 Bluffwater Cir Huntington Beach CA 92646-4723

HILDEN, PATRICIA PENN, history educator; b. Burbank, Calif., May 31, 1944; d. William Swain and Elizabeth Elnore (Hall) Penn; m. Timothy James Reiss, Aug. 17, 1988; stepchildren: Matthew, Suzanna. BA in English/History, U. Calif., Berkeley, 1965; MA in History, U. Calif., Davis, 1977, U. Cambridge, Eng., 1980; PhD in History, U. Cambridge, 1981. Tchr. English various schs., Calif., 1965-73; coord. minority students' spl. action program U. Calif., Davis, 1974-76; fellow Trinity Hall, Cambridge, Eng., 1980-82; vis. fellow Nuffield Coll., Oxford, Eng., 1983-84; asst. prof. history Emory U., Atlanta, 1982—; assoc. prof. history Emory U., 1987—; prof. ethnic studies U. Calif., Berkeley, 1995—; manuscript cons. Cambridge U. Press, 1981—; article cons. Author: Working Women and socialist Politics in France, 1986, Women, Work and Politics: Belgium 1830-1914, 1993, When Nickels Were Indians, 1995; contbr. articles to profl. jours. Eileen Power Meml. Studentship, London Sch. Econs., 1978-79; AAUW fellow, 1979-80; Brit. Acad. fellow, 1980, Social Sci. Rsch. Coun. (U.K.) fellow, 1981, Centre national de la recherche scientifique fellow, Paris, 1982-83, Fulbright fellow, 1983-84. Mem. Am. Hist. Assn., Cambridge Hist. Soc. (rsch. grantee 1981—), Internat. Women's Studies Assn., Indigenous Women's Network, Native Am. Rights Fund, Amnesty Internat., Woodcraft Circle of Native Am. Winter's and Storytellers. Avocation: poetry.

HILGENBERG, MICHAEL CHARLES, real estate agent; b. Shawano, Wis., Dec. 5, 1948; s. Neil Clemence and LaVera Ann (Schroeder) H.; married Dec. 1970 (div. Jan. 1975); 1 child, Heath Michael Hilgenberg-Siegel. BS, U. Wis., 1971; MEd, U. Tex., 1973. Sales mgr., realtor Coldwell Banker Hilgenberg, Green Bay, Wis., 1973-86; broker assoc. ReMax of Desert, Palm Desert, Calif., 1986—. Bd. dirs. Family Svc. of Desert, Indio, Calif., 1997-98. With U.S. Army, 1971-73. Mem. Nat. Assn. Realtors (Broker Mgr. of Yr. mgmt. coun. 1996), Calif. Assn. Realtors (state bd. dirs. 1992—, chmn. profl. stds. 1998, chmn. region 28 1994), Calif. Desert Assn. Realtors (pres. 1993, Realtor of Yr. 1996). Presbyterian. Home: 72551 Sundown Ln Palm Desert CA 92260-6533 Office: ReMax of the Desert 72608 El Paseo Ste 4 Palm Desert CA 92260-3373

HILL, ANNA MARIE, manufacturing executive; b. Great Falls, Mont., Nov. 6, 1938; d. Paul Joseph and Alexina Rose (Doyon) Ghekiere. AA, Oakland Jr. Coll., 1959; student, U. Calif., Berkeley, 1960-62. Mgr. ops. OSM, Soquel, Calif., 1963-81; purchasing agt. Arrow Huss, Scotts Valley, Calif., 1981-82; sr. buyer Fairchild Test Systems, San Jose, Calif., 1982-83; materials mgr. Basic Test Systems, San Jose, 1983-86; purchasing mgr. Beta Tech., Santa Cruz, Calif., 1986-87; mgr. purchasing ICON Rev., Carmel, Calif., 1987-88; materials mgr. Integrated Components Test System, Sunnyvale, Calif., 1988-89; mfg. mgr. Forte Comm., Sunnyvale, 1989-94; new products mgr. Cisco Sys., San Jose, 1994—; cons., No. Calif., 1976—. Counselor Teens Against Drugs, San Jose, 1970, 1/2 Orgn., Santa Cruz, 1975-76. Mem. Am. Prodn. Invention Control, Nat. Assn. Female Execs., Nat. Assn. Purchasing Mgmt., Am. Radio Relay League. Democrat. Avocations: amateur radio operator, music, gardening. Home: 733 Rosedale Ave # 4 Capitola CA 95010-2248 Office: Cisco Systems 110 W Tasman Dr San Jose CA 95134-1700

HILL, BRENDA BARHAM, academic administrator; b. Oakland, Calif.; m. John D. Hill. AB, Occidental Coll., 1971; MA, Claremont Grad. U., 1972, PhD, 1979. Activities advisor Calif. State U., Bakersfield, 1972-74; asst. to v.p. grad. studies U. La Verne, Calif., 1974-79; assoc. provost Claremont U. Ctr., 1979-83; sr. devel. officer Claremont (Calif.) Grad. U., 1983-86; v.p. planning and rsch. Scripps Coll., Claremont, 1986—, sec. bd. trustees, 1996—. Active vol. Claremont Pub. Schs., 1987—. Mem. AAUW, AAHE, SCUP, Cmty. Friends Internat. (bd. mem., pres. 1995-96, 97-98). Office: Scripps Coll 1030 Columbia Ave Claremont CA 91711-3986

HILL, CRAIG A., English educator; b. Ithaca, N.Y., Aug. 25, 1957; s. Charles Stanley and Doris Rae (Manypenny) H.; m. Laurie Beth Schneider, Jan. 1, 1983; 1 child, Liam Orion. BA, San Francisco State U., 1990. Cert. tchr., Idaho. English tchr. Berkeley (Calif.) High Sch., 1991-94, Jenifer Jr. High, Lewiston, Idaho, 1994-96, Moscow (Idaho) High Sch., 1996—; bd. dirs. Inland N.W. Council Tchrs. English, Moscow, Idaho, Inland Mag., Nampa, Idaho. Author: Dict, 1989, Yes James, Yes Joyce, 1994, Another Switch, 1994. Mem. Inland N.W. Coun. Tchrs. English, Nat. Coun. Tchrs. English. Democrat. Avocations: writing, gardening, baseball.

HILL, DALE RICHARD, career officer; b. Charleston, W.Va., Dec. 20, 1939; s. Cecil Thomas Jr. and Frances Eileen (Gillespie) H.; m. Linda Lee Ergeson, Apr. 20, 1962 (dec. 1971); m. Debbie Kay Hildebrant, Feb. 19, 1972 (div. Jan. 1999); children: Mark, Bret, Lara, Dale, Adam. BS, W.Va. State Coll., 1967; MA, Cen. Mich. U., 1977; grad., USA Command and Gen. Staff Coll., 1982. Commd. 2d lt. U.S. Army, Ft. Benning, Ga., 1968; advanced through grades to lt. col. U.S. Army, 1984; aide-de-camp USA Operational Test and Evaluation Agy., Falls Church, Va., 1976-80; ops. officer Hdqrs. 3 Bde, 2 Infantry divsn., Camp Howze, Republic of Korea, 1980-81; emergency action officer Hdqr. Readiness Command, MacDill AFB, Fla., 1981-82; plans tng. officer Hdqrs. Multinat. Force & Observers Sinai, El Gorah, 1982-83; chief current ops. Hdqr. I Corps., Ft. Lewis, Wash., 1983-86; commdr. Yakima (Wash.) Firing Ctr., 1986-89. Democrat. Avocations: gardening, individual athletics. Home: 1616 S 67th Ave Yakima WA 98908

HILL, DEBORA ELIZABETH, author, journalist, screenwriter; b. San Francisco, July 10, 1961; d. Henry Peter and Madge Lillian (Ridgeway-Aarons) H. BA, Sonoma State U., 1983. Talk show host Rock Jour. Viacom, San Francisco, 1980-81; interviewer, biographer Harrap Ltd., London, 1986-87; editor North Bay Mag., Cotati, Calif., 1988; guest feature writer Argus Courier, Petaluma, Calif., 1993-95; concept developer BiblioBytes, Hoboken, N.J., 1994-95, White Tiger Films, San Francisco, 1995—; feature writer The Econs. Press, 1996-97; literary agt. The Thornton Agy., Portland, Oreg., 1997—; assoc. prodr. White Tiger Films, 1995—; concept developer Star Trek: Voyager and Star Trek: Deep Space Nine, 1997-98; mem. Writers Net The Online Wordbiz Directory, Writers for Hire, The Hollywood Direct Access Directory. Author: The San Francisco Rock Experience, 1979, CUTS from a San Francisco Rock Journal, 1982, Punk Retro, 1988, Gale Research-Resourceful Woman, 1994, St. James Guide to Fantasy Writers, 1996, A Ghost Among Us, 1996, St. James Guide to Famous Gays and Lesbians, 1997, Jerome's Quest, 1997, SuperGirls: The Co-Ed Murders, 1999; co-author: Rumour Has a Memory, 1999; co-writer, cons. producer The Danger Club, Danger Club II; contbr. stories and articles to profl. jours. Democrat. Avocations: clothing design, cooking, internet, reading, interior design. E-mail: debora.h111@mailcity.com. Home: 110 Grant Ave Petaluma CA 94952-4809 Address: Thronton Lit Agy 1431 SE Knight St Portland OR 97202

HILL, EARL MCCOLL, lawyer; b. Bisbee, Ariz., June 12, 1926; s. Earl George and Jeanette (McColl) H.; m. Bea Dolan, Nov. 22, 1968 (dec. Aug. 1998); children: Arthur Charles, John Earl, Darlene Stern, Tamara Fegert. BA, U. Wash., 1960, JD, 1961. Bar: Nev. 1962, U.S. Ct. Clms. 1978, U.S. Ct. Apls. (9th cir.) 1971, U.S. Sup. Ct. 1978. Law clk. Nev. sup. ct., Carson City, 1962; assoc. Gray, Horton & Hill, Reno, 1962-65, ptnr. 1965-73; ptnr. Marshall Hill Cassas & de Lipkau (and predecessors), Reno, 1974—, Sherman & Howard, Denver, 1982-91; judge pro tem Reno mcpl. ct., 1964-70; lectr. continuing legal edn.; mem. Nev. Commn. on Jud. Selection 1977-84; trustee Rocky Mountain Mineral Law Found. 1976-95, sec. 1987-88. Contbr. articles to profl. jours. Mem. ABA, ATLA, State Bar Nev. (chmn. com. on jud. adminstrn. 1971-77), Washoe County Bar Assn., Am. Judicature Soc., Lawyer Pilots Bar Assn., Soc. Mining Antiquarians (sec.-treas. 1975—), Prospectors Club. Office: Holcomb Profl Ctr 333 Holcomb Ave Ste 300 Reno NV 89502-1648

HILL, GARY D., lawyer; b. Eugene, Oreg., Apr. 7, 1952; s. Virgil R. and Doris H.; m. Patricia L. Hill, July 10, 1976. BA, Linfield Coll., McMinnville, Oreg., 1974; JD, Northwestern Sch. of Law, Portland, 1981. Bar: Oreg. 1982. News anchor KPTV, Portland, Oreg., 1976-92; pvt. practice Portland, Oreg., 1981-84, 88-92; atty. Hergert & Assocs., Oregon City, Oreg., 1992—. Vol. Oreg. Rep. Party, Portland, 1996, Oregon Dole-Kemp presdl. campaign, 1996. Recipient Am. Juris Prudence award, Lawyers Coop. Pub. Co., 1981; recognized for participation in CLE Oreg. State Bar, 1985, 91. Mem. Oreg. State Bar Assn. (law related edn. com. 1996—, chair-elect small firm and sole practitioner sect. 1997-98, Juvenile and Family Law Sect. 1992—, chair 1998-99), Oreg. Assn. of Family Law Practitioners. Avocations: golf, sailing, fishing. Office: Hergert & Assocs 1001 Molalla Ave Ste 201 Oregon City OR 97045-3768

HILL, GERRY A., special education educator, consultant; b. Vallejo, Calif., Aug. 8, 1940; d. Earl Martin and Mildred (Bogart) H. AA, San Diego City Coll., 1963; BA, San Diego State Coll., 1965; MA, U.S. Internat. U., 1970; EdD, Pacific Western U., 1981. Sec. Am. Meth. Work Team, Great Britain, 1961; trust dept. sec. 1st Nat. Bank, San Diego, 1961-63; classroom tchr. South Bay Union Sch. Dist., Imperial Beach, Calif., 1965-95, spl. edn. tchr., 1975-95; owner Serendipity Learning Ctr., San Diego, 1991—. Vol. Muscular Dystrophy Assn., San Diego, 1975—, Habitat for Humanity, Tijuana, Mex. and San Diego, 1990, San Diego Rescue Mission, 1994—, Rolando Meth. Ch., San Diego, 1994—. Mem. Nat. Tchr. Edn., Orton Soc., San Diego Reading Assn. Republican. Methodist. Avocations: reading, travel. Office: 6161 El Cajon Blvd Ste 290 San Diego CA 92115-3922

HILL, GREG, newspaper bureau chief. San Francisco bur. chief Wall St. Jour. Office: Wall St Jour 201 California St Ste 1350 San Francisco CA 94111-5015*

HILL, HARRY DAVID, city official, human resources professional; b. Whittier, Calif., Oct. 29, 1944; s. Harry Boreman and Winifred Nell (Purvis) Hill; m. Linda Mae Price, Nov. 8, 1969; 1 child, Jon Ryan. AA, Los Angeles Harbor Coll., Wilmington, Calif., 1964; BA in Polit. Sci., UCLA, 1966; M of Pub. Adminstrn. in Human Resources, U. So. Calif., 1972. Personnel aide City of Anaheim, Calif., 1966-67, personnel analyst, 1967-71, sr. personnel analyst, 1971-75, personnel services mgr., 1975-83, asst. human

resources dir., 1983-88, asst. labor rels. dir., 1988-94, dir. human resources, 1994—; chmn. supervisory com. Anaheim Area Credit Union, 1981-89, bd. dirs., 1989-95. Mem. So. Calif. Pub. Labor Coun. (treas. 1986-87, pres. 1988), Internat. Pers. Mgmt. Assn. (pres. western region 1983-84), So. Calif. Pers. Mgmt. Assn. (pres. 1978-79), Coop. Pers. Svcs. (bd. dirs. 1987—). Democrat. Office: City of Anaheim 200 S Anaheim Blvd Fl 3 Anaheim CA 92805-3820

HILL, HARRY RAYMOND, medical educator; b. Salt Lake City, Dec. 18, 1941; s. Harry Leighton and Doris Eleanor (Wax) H.; m. Sandra Elizabeth Champion, Aug. 20, 1966; children: Angela Elizabeth, Wendy Doris, Keely Champion. Student, La. State U., 1960-62; MD, Baylor Coll., 1966. Internship Grady Meml. Hosp. Emory U., Atlanta, 1966-67; with epidemic intelligence svc. Ctr. for Disease Control USPHS, Fort Collins, Colo., 1967-69; resident in pediats., fellow in immunology U. Wash., Seattle, 1969-71; fellow in infectious disease and lab. medicine U. Minn., Mpls., 1971-73, instr. dept. pediats. and lab medicine, 1973-74; asst. prof. pathology and pediats. U. Utah, Salt Lake City, 1974-76; assoc. prof. U. Utah, 1976-81, prof., 1981—; mem. bacteriology, mycology study sect. NIH, Bethesda, Md., 1978-82. Contbr. 270 articles to profl. jours. Recipient Investigator award Howard Hughes Med. Inst., 1978-81. Fellow Infectious Disease Soc. Am.; mem. Soc. Pediat. Rsch., Am. Soc. Clin. Pathology (mem. coun. microbiology 1982-88), Am. Assn. Immunologists, Am. Assn. Pathologists, Western Soc. Pediat. Rsch. (Ross outstanding investigator award 1980, pres. 1993-94), Lancefield Soc. (pres. 1987-88). Democrat. Roman Catholic. Office: U Utah Dept Pathology 50 N Medical Dr Salt Lake City UT 84132

HILL, JAMES HOWARD, public relations executive; b. Toledo, Ohio, Aug. 11, 1947; s. James Howard and Cassie (Clarke) H.; m. Cynthia Diane Carter, Mar. 5, 1988; 1 child, Jasmine Diana. BS in Journalism, Ohio Univ., 1969. Internal communications editor Owens-Corning Fiberglas, Toledo, 1970-73, merchandising supr., 1973-75; dir. pub. info. WGTE-TV/FM, Toledo, 1975-78; producer, writer WGTE/TV, Toledo, 1978-80; mgr. pub. rels. S.C. Johnson & Son, Racine, Wis., 1980-82; dir. pub. rels. Sara Lee Corp., Chgo., 1982-84, dir. pub. rels. and comms., 1984-86; pres., COO Burrell pub. rels., 1986-88; pres., ceo Burrell Pub. Rels. Inc., Chgo., 1988-91; chmn. Hill & Flowers Pub. Rels. Inc., Chgo., 1991-93; v.p. comm. Kaiser Found. Health Plan (Kaiser Permanente); bd. dirs. East Bay Cmty. Found., Marcus Foster Ednl. Inst., Oakland C. of C. Bd. dirs. Travelers and Immigrants Aid, Chgo., 1990-94, Children's and Adolescents Forum, Chog., 1984-94, Mid-Am. chpt. ARC, 1993-94; mktg. adv. com. United Negro Coll. Fund, N.Y., 1991—; adv. bd. E.W. Scripps Sch. Journalism, Ohio U. Recipient Silver Anvils Pub. Rels. Soc. Am., 1986, Gold Quill award Internat. Assn. Bus. Communications, Gold and Silver Trumpets Publicity Club Chgo. Mem. Pub. Rels. Soc. Am., Pub. Rels. Seminar, Alpha Phi Alpha. Avocation: tennis. Office: Kaiser Found Health Plan 1 Kaiser Plz Oakland CA 94612-3610

HILL, JIM, state official; 1 child, Jennifer. BA in Econs., Mich. State U., 1969; MBA, Indiana U., 1971, JD, 1974. Asst. atty. gen. Oreg. Dept. of Justice, 1974-77; hearing referee Oreg. Dept. of Revenue, 1977-81; personnel specialist and cons. State Farm Ins., 1984-86; elected mem. Oreg. House of Reps., 1983-87, Oreg. State Sen., 1987-93; dir. mktg. PEN-NOR, Inc., Portland Gen. Contractors, 1986-88; corp. accts. mgr. for Latin Am. Mentor Graphics, 1988-93; state treas. State of Oreg., Salem, 1994—. Office: Oreg State Treasury 159 State Capitol Salem OR 97310-0840*

HILL, JOHN EARL, mechanical engineer; b. Ely, Nev., July 18, 1953; s. Earl M. and Florence (Lagos) H.; m. Terry Lynn Biederman, Oct. 3, 1981; 1 child, Felicia Biederman. BA in Social Psychology, U. Nev., 1974, BSME, 1981. Cert. engr. in tng. Machinist B&J Machine and Tool, Sparks, Nev., 1977-78; designer, machinist Screen Printing Systems, Sparks, Nev., 1978, Machine Svcs., Sparks, 1978-81; computer programmer U. Nev., Reno, 1980-81; design engr. Ford Aerospace and Communications Corp., Palo Alto, Calif., 1981-82, 86-88; contract design engr. Westinghouse Electric Corp., Sunnyvale, Calif., 1982-83; contract project engr. Adcotech Corp., Milpitas, Calif., 1983-84; sr. engr. Domain Tech., Milpitas, 1984-85; project engr. Exclusive Design Co., San Mateo, Calif., 1985-86; automation mgr. Akashic Memories Corp., San Jose, Calif., 1988-94; ptnr. Automated Bus. Svcs., San Jose; dir. automation engring. Seagate Rec. Media, Fremont, Calif., 1994-97; mgr., equipment engr. FormFactor, Inc., Livermore, Calif., 1997—. Mem. Robotics Internat. of Soc. Mfg. Engrs., Tau Beta Pi, Pi Mu Epsilon, Phi Kappa Phi. Avocations: music, art, hang gliding. Home: 147 Wildwood Ave San Carlos CA 94070-4516 Office: Form Factor Inc 5666 La Ribera St Livermore CA 94550-9275

HILL, JUDITH DEEGAN, lawyer; b. Chgo., Dec. 13, 1939; d. William James and Ida May (Scott) Deegan; children: Colette M., Cristina M. BA, Western Mich. U., 1960; JD, Marquette U., 1971; cert. U. Paris, Sorbonne, 1962; postgrad. Harvard U., 1984. Bar: Wis. 1971, Ill. 1973, Nev. 1976, D.C. 1979. Tchr., Kalamazoo (Mich.) Bd. Edn., 1960-62, Maple Heights (Ohio), 1963-64, Shorewood (Wis.) Bd. Edn., 1964-68; corp. atty. Fort Howard Paper Co., Green Bay, Wis., 1971-72; sr. trust adminstr. Continental Ill. Nat. Bank & Trust, Chgo., 1972-76; atty. Morse, Foley & Wadsworth Law Firm, Las Vegas, 1976-77; dep. dist. atty., criminal prosecutor Clark County Atty., Las Vegas, 1977-83; atty. civil and criminal law Edward S. Coleman Profl. Law Corp., Las Vegas, 1983-84; pvt. practice law, 1984-85; atty. criminal div. Office of City Atty., City of Las Vegas, 1985-89, pvt. practice law, 1989-99, retired. Bd. dirs. Nev. Legal Svcs., Carson City, 1980-87, state chmn., 1984-87; bd. dirs. Clark County Legal Svcs., Las Vegas, 1980-87; mem. Star Aux. for Handicapped Children, Las Vegas, 1986-96; Greater Las Vegas Women's League, 1987-88; jud. candidate Las Vegas Mcpl. Ct. 1987, Nev. Symphony Guild, Variety Club Internat., 1992-93, Las Vegas Preservation Group. Recipient Scholarship, Auto Specialties, St. Joseph, Mich., 1957-60, St. Thomas More Scholarship, Marquette U. Law Sch., Milw., 1968-69; juvenile law internship grantee Marquette U. Law Sch., 1970. Mem. Nev. Bar Assn., So. Nev. Assn. Women Attys., Ill. Bar Assn., Children's Village Club (pres. 1980) (Las Vegas, Nev.). Home: 521 Sweeney Ave Las Vegas NV 89104-1436

HILL, KATHLEEN LOIS, performing art school executive; b. Denver, Sept. 11, 1955; d. James Jenkins and Elaine (Marcella) Hill; 1 child Terrence Drake. BA, Colo. Women's Coll., 1977. Choreographer Fashion Bar TV Comml., Denver, 1981, Pure Gold Cheerleaders USFL, Denver, 1985, Kenny Rodgers Western Wear, Denver, 1990; exec., art dir. Hill Acad. of Dance and Dramatics, Denver, 1976—; bd. dirs. Colo. Dance Alliance, Denver, 1986-89; guest judge I Love Dance, Portland, Oreg., 1991—. Performer Met. Troupers Charity Entertainers, Colo., 1970-76. Named Young Careerist, Bus. and Profl. Women of Am., 1978; recipient Scholastic scholarships Colo. Women's Coll., 1973-77. Mem. Colo. Dance Alliance (bd. dirs. 1986-89), Colo. Dance Festival, Internat. Tap Assn. Democrat. Roman Catholic. Avocations: avid reader, performing arts advocate, travel. Office: Hill Dance Acad/Dramatics 6265 E Evans Ave Ste 14 Denver CO 80222-5822

HILL, LAWRENCE SIDNEY, management educator; b. Gary, Ind., Nov. 10, 1923; m. Evelyn Honig, Mar. 22, 1964; 1 child, Robert J. BSE, Purdue U., 1947; MBA, U. So. Calif., L.A., 1960; MSIE, U. So. Calif., 1962, Engr. I.E., 1965, PhD, 1968. Registered profl. engr., Calif. Asst. indsl. engr. USX Corp., Gary, Ind., 1947; indsl. hygiene engr. Ill. Dept. Pub. Health, Chgo., 1948-51; indsl. engr. USX Corp., Gary, 1951-52; sr. engr. Nat. Safety Coun., Chgo., 1953; sr. indsl. engr. Martin Marietta Co., Balt., 1953-55; group head McDonnell Douglas Co., Santa Monica, Calif., 1955-57; sr. mem. staff The Rand Corp., Santa Monica, 1957-71; prof. mgmt. Calif. State U., L.A., 1969—; cons., prin. engr. Ralph M. Parsons Co., Pasadena, 1973-82; cons., sr. mem. tech. staff TRW Inc., Redondo Beach, Calif., 1982-90; cons., environ. mgr. USN, Long Beach, Calif., 1991-94; vis. lectr. Ops. Rsch. Soc. Am./Inst. Mgmt. Scis., 1973-95, expert witness in safety, mgmt., 1986—. Contbr. articles to profl. jours., books. Mem. Alpha Pi Mu, Alpha Iota Delta. Avocations: profl. and coll. sports. Home: 3653 Oceanhill Way Malibu CA 90265-5637

HILL, MORRIS GERARD, lawyer; b. New Orleans, Sept. 2, 1948; s. Morris Richard and Eunice (Pecot) H.; children: Emily Grayson, Morgan Spencer. JD, Tulane U., 1976. Bar: La. 1976, Calif. 1981. Assoc. Knutson, Tobin et al, La Mesa, Calif., 1981-82, Minyard & Minyard, Orange, Calif., 1982-87; dep. county counsel County of San Diego, 1987—. Office: County of San Diego 1600 Pacific Hwy Ste 355 San Diego CA 92101-2437

HILL, NATHAN SCOTT, educator, writer; b. Fremont, Calif., Jan. 6, 1962; s. N. Eugene and Patricia (Yeager) H.; m. Laura S. Weir, Aug. 19, 1984. BA in Polit. Sci., George Washington U., 1985; MA in Govt., U. Va., 1988; postgrad., U. Calif.-Davis. Co-dir. Calif. Art Rsch., Dixon, 1991—; sr. rsch. and policy analyst Calif. Sch. Bds. Assn., West Sacramento, 1993-96; dir. comm. George Lucas Ednl. Found., Nicasio, CA, 1996-97; exec. dir. Calif. Acad. Standards Commn., Sacramento, 1997—. Author, editor, presenter articles, chpts., papers on art history, cultural policy and planning, polit. sci., and edn. Commr. City of Davis Peace & Justice Commn. 1990-92, chmn., 1991-92; commr. City of Davis Civic Arts Commn., 1992-93; bd. dirs. Napa County Legal Assistance Agy., Napa, Calif., 1995-96; mem. policy adv. bd. U. Calif. Calif. Alliance for Math. and Sci., Oakland, 1995-97. World Affairs Coun. scholar U. Calif.-Davis, 1983; du Pont fellow U. Va., 1985-86; adminstrn. fellow Nat. Endowment for Arts, Washington, 1991; rsch. fellow U. Calif. Washington Ctr., 1992-93. Home: 1545 Ingrid Dr Dixon CA 95620-4210 Office: Acad Standards Commn 801 K St Ste 912 Sacramento CA 95814-3518

HILL, NED CROMAR, finance educator, consultant; b. Salt Lake City, Dec. 18, 1945; s. Richard G. Sharp and Bettie (Cromar) Hill; m. Claralyn Martin, Nov. 26, 1968; children: Evan M., Jonathan C., Aaron R., Joseph B., Alison. Student, Brigham Young U., 1967; BS, U. Utah, 1969; MS, Cornell U., Ithaca, N.Y., 1971; PhD, Cornell U., 1976. Cert. cash mgr. Asst. prof. fin. Cornell U., 1976-77; asst. prof. fin. Ind. U., Bloomington, 1977-81, assoc. prof. fin., 1981-87; Joel C. Peterson prof. fin. Brigham Young U., Provo, Utah, 1987-96, asst. to pres., 1996-98, dean Marriott Sch. Mgmt., 1998—; cons. Hill Fin. Assocs., Bloomington, 1978—. Author: Essentials in Cash Management, 1984, Short-Term Financial Management, 1987; co-founder Jour. Cash Mgmt., 1981, EDI Forum, Jour. Electronic Commerce, 1987. Mem. Utah Info. Tech. Commn., 1993-97; stake pres. Ch. Jesus Christ of the Latter Day Saints, 1982-87; fin. v.p. Boy Scouts Hoosier Trails Council, Bloomington, 1980-86. With U.S. Army, 1971-72. Mem. Nat. Corp. Cash Mgmt., Fin. Mgmt. Assn. (bd. dirs. 1986-88), Phi Beta Kappa, Phi Kappa Phi. Republican. Avocations: vocal music, birding, camping, photography. Office: Brigham Young U Marriott Sch of Mgmt 730 TNRB Provo UT 84602

HILL, RICHARD, executive. CEO, chmn. Novellus Systems, Inc., San Jose, Calif. Office: 3970 N 1st St San Jose CA 95134-1501*

HILL, RICK ALLAN, congressman; b. Grand Rapids, Minn., Dec. 30, 1946; m. Betti Christie, June 10, 1983; children: Todd, Corey, Mike. BA in Econs. and Polit. Sci., St. Cloud State U., 1968. Surety bonding businessman, owner InsureWest, 1968-90; real estate and investment ptnr., 1983—; committeeman State Rep. Party, 1990-94; legis. liaison to Gov. Marc Racicot, Mont., 1993; mem. 105th Congress from Mont dist., 1997—, mem. banking and fin. svcs. com., mem. resources com., mem. small bus. com.; fin. chair State Rep. Party, 1989-91, state chair, 1991-92. Bd. dirs. Mont. Sci. and Tech. Alliance, 1992. Office: 1037 Longworth Bldg Washington DC 20515-2601*

HILL, ROBERT MARTIN, police detective, forensic document examiner, consultant, lecturer; b. Hammond, Ind., Dec. 10, 1949; s. Donald Edwin and Norma Jeanne (Beal) H.; m. Connie Carolina Nordquist, Dec. 19, 1970. BA, U. Minn., 1974; postgrad., U. Phoenix; cert. in fin. fraud, IRS, Glynco, Ga., 1984; cert. in questioned documents, U.S. Secret Service, Glynco, Ga., 1986. Cert. police officer, Ill., Minn., Ariz.; cert. fraud examiner. Police officer Rolling Meadows (Ill.) Police Dept., 1970-72, St. Paul Police Dept., 1972-79; police officer Scottsdale (Ariz.) Police Dept., 1980-81, police fraud detective, 1981—; com. mem. Fraud Ariz. Banker's Assn., 1985-86; lectr. various colls. and orgns.; pres. Assoc. Document Labs., Inc.; forensic document examiner. Recipient Dirs. Commendation U.S. Secret Svc., Washington, 1986, Commendation, Dept. Defense, 1993; named Investigator of Yr. Econ. Crime Investigators, 1991. em. Internat. Assn. Credit Card Investigators (v.p. 1985-86, pres., bd. dirs. 1 986-88, Internat. Law Enforcement Officer of the Yr. award 1986, Ariz. chpt. Police Officer of the Yr. 1984, 86, 93), Internat. Assn. Auto Theft Investigators, Am. Acad. Forensic Scis., Internat. Police Assn., Assn. Cert. Fraud Examiners, Southwest Assn. Forensic Document Examiners, Internat. Assn. for Identification. Republican. Baptist. Avocations: travel, photography, weightlifting. Office: 9065 E Via Linda Scottsdale AZ 85258-5400

HILL, THOMAS QUINTON, communication specialist, graphic designer; b. Talladega, Ala., June 27, 1959; s. Sandy and Maude Verdell (Griggs) H. Student, San Francisco Art Inst., 1978-79, Acad. of Art, San Francisco, 1993-94; BS in Bus. Mgmt., U. Phoenix, 1997. Comms. coord. Sedgwick, San Francisco, 1990-92; comm. cons. Sedgwick Noble Lowndes, San Francisco, 1992-97; prin. Graphic Details Design, San Francisco, 1993—; sr. comm. analyst Kaiser Permanente, Oakland, Calif., 1997—; creative cons. Sedgwick Proposal Com., San Francisco, 1996-97; design cons. Francisco Med. Soc., San Francisco, 1993—; part-time instr. Graphic Arts Inst., San Francisco, 1998. Vol. Alzheimer's Svcs. Orgn., Berkeley, Calif., 1994, Leukemia Soc. Am., San Francisco, 1994, United Way, San Francisco, 1994—. Recipient Award of Appreciation, Leukemia Soc. Am., 1994, Pinnacle of Success award Am. Assn. Med. Soc. Execs., 1995. Mem. Internat. Assn. Bus. Communicators (chpt. pres. 1992—, judge blue ribbon panel 1998, Cert. Appreciation 1997), Am. Inst. Graphic Arts (outreach com. 1993—), Commonwealth Club of Calif., Coun. Comm. Mgmt., 1998—. Avocations: health and fitness, music, theater, films. Office: Kaiser Permanente One Kaiser Plz 20th Fl Oakland CA 94612

HILL, TRIANA JACKIE, global networking specialist, psychic; b. L.A., Dec. 10; d. Benjamin Donee and Margaret Barsam Firestone; 2 children. Founder Interlink Unltd., Kihei, Hawaii, 1987—; psychic cons.; lectr. and breakthrough empowerment workshop tchr. Author/Screenwriter: (books) Nicht von dieser Welt, 1996, Lovers in Two Dimensions, 1999, I Will Always Be With You, An Angel Called Mabel; contbr. articles to profl. jours.; host: (radio) Ask Triana; also TV appearances. Author: Beyond Conception, 1996. Mem. ASTAR, Media Inc., World Coalition Orgn. Avocations: service to humanity and planet, media performances. E-mail: link@mauigateway.com. Home and Office: Interlink Unltd PO Box 1988 Kihei HI 96753

HILL, VALERIE CHARLOTTE, nurse; b. Shaftsbury, Vt., Dec. 2, 1932; d. William Henry Harrison and Angeline Margaret Stella (Fuller) Hill; m. Edward Joseph Klanit (dec. July 1984); 1 child, Joyce Ellen Klanit Artadi. Grad., Mt. Sinai Hosp. Sch. Nursing, 1955. RN, N.Y. Nurse The Jack Martin Respiratory Ctr. of The Mt. Sinai Hosp., N.Y.C., 1955-57; v.p. Chauffeurs Unlimited, Inc., N.Y.C., 1957-77; nurse Rusk Inst., N.Y.C., 1957-58, Beth Israel Med. Ctr., N.Y.C., 1978-79; owner, mgr. Powers Fish Market, Inc., N.Y.C., 1977-84; tchr. Techs. for Creating, Albany, N.Y., 1983-97, Snohomish, Wash., 1997—; nurse Doctors Hosp., N.Y.C., 1984-86; pvt. duty nurse Personal Health Care Svcs., Albany, N.Y., 1987-88; nurse Albany Med. Ctr. Hosp., 1987-95; real estate sales assoc. Century 21-Stanley Major Ltd., West Sand Lake, N.Y., 1988, Century-21 Home Towne Properties, Albany, 1989-92. Author numerous poems. Recipient Outstanding Service to Community award Mayor Koch City of N.Y., 1983. Mem. Alumnae Assn. Mt. Sinai Hosp. Sch. Nursing (bd. dirs. 1968). Democrat. Avocations: reading, writing poetry, dancing, home videos, piano, walking. Home: 7618 129 Dr SE Snohomish WA 98290-6248

HILL, WILLIAM ELMER, III, producer; b. Sterling, Ill., Nov. 3, 1947; s. William Elmer, Jr. and Elizabeth Jane (Ward) H.; m. Susanna Esther Villa, June 17, 1967 (div. 1971); children: William Cassidy, Amanda Jane, Larissa Suzanne. Grad. high sch., Sterling, 1965. CEO Hill Theatres, Santa Fe, [illegible] tech. dir. Taos (N.Mex.) Talking Pictures Fest., 1995—, Internat. Film Fest., Albuquerque, 1997—; projection mgr. Sundance Film Fest., Park City, Utah, 1998; asst. tech. dir. Toronto Internat. Film Festival, 1998. Episcopalian. Avocations: golfing, music, reading.

HILL, WILLIAM U., state supreme court justice. Atty. gen. Cheyenne, Wyo., 1995-98; justice Wyo. Supreme Ct., Cheyenne, 1998—. Office: Wyoming Supreme Court 2301 Capitol Ave Cheyenne WY 82001-3644*

HILLER, JOAN VITEK, sociologist; b. Mpls., Apr. 4, 1960; d. Thomas Mark and Louanne (Howard) Vitek; m. James G. Hiller, Aug. 28, 1987; children: Thomas, John. BA, Coll. St. Catherine, 1982; MS, Tex. A&M U., 1985; PhD, Northwestern U., 1996. Lic. independent social worker, Minn. Statistician Ctr. Health Studies and Policy Rsch./Northwestern U., Evanston, Ill., 1985-87; sr. program evaluation specialist Minn. Dept. Human Svcs., St. Paul, 1987-89; dir. nonprofit svcs. Willowbrooke Orgn. Devel., Burnsville, Minn., 1990-97; v.p. nonprofit and govt. svcs. Social Rsch. Assocs., Colorado Springs, Colo., 1997—; adj. instr. U. St. Thomas, St. Paul, 1989-95, Hamline U., St. Paul, 1988-91, Coll. St. Catherine, 1994-95, Inver Hills C.C., 1988-97; rep. Gov.'s Com. Drug-Free Schs., 1987-89; ex-officio Minn. Juvenile Justice Adv. Com., St. Paul, 1986-87. Bd. dirs. Open Your Heart to the Hungry and Homeless, St. Paul, 1989-94, v.p., 1991-93; bd. dirs. Suicide Awareness Coun., 1996-97, v.p., 1997, Discovery Job Network, 1998—. Mem. NAFE, Nat. Soc. Fund Raising Execs., Am. Sociol. Assn. (mem. com. on pub. affairs 1992-93), Mensa (v.p. Minn. chpt. 1992-94, pres. chpt. 1994-96), Sociologists Minn. (bd. dirs. 1991-93), Plainspeaking (editor So. Colo. chpt. 1998—). Roman Catholic.

HILLIARD, CHARLES STANLEY, investment banker; b. L.A., Aug. 3, 1963; s. Michael Gary and Sharon Gwen Baldwin (Stanley) H. BS, U. So. Calif., 1985; MBA with honors, U. Mich., 1990. CPA, Calif. mem. adv. bd. Calif. Commr. Corps., Sacramento, 1998. Mem. U. So. Calif. Jr. Assocs., L.A., 1994—. Mem. Beta Gamma Sigma, Glendora Country Club. Republican. Presbyterian. Avocations: golf, scuba diving, skiing. Office: Morgan Stanley & Co Inc Ste 2400 1999 Avenue Of The Stars Los Angeles CA 90067-4611

HILLIARD, WILLIAM KENT, chiropractor; b. Prtalys, N. Mex., Aug. 20, 1947; s. John Kent and Jane Elizabeth (Mawk) H.; m. Donna Kay Wilkins, June 5, 1968; children: Charles Collin, William Lee. BA, Eastern N. Mex. U., 1970; D in Chiropractic, Palmer Chiropractic, 1973. Licensed chiropractor. Pvt. practice Portales, N. Mex.; chmn. peer review N. Mex. Chiropractic Assocs., Albuquerque, 1996. Mem. N. Mex. Chiropractic Assn., Masonic Lodge. Republican. Methodist. Avocations: classic cars, fly fishing, scuba diving, hunting. Office: Hilliard Chiropractic Clinic 112 E 4th St Portales NM 88130-6305

HILLICKSON, MICHELE, national parks service official. CEO, supt. Petrified Forest Nat. Park, Ariz. Office: PO Box 2217 Petrified Forest Natl Park AZ 86028*

HILLINGER, CHARLES, journalist, writer; b. Evanston, Ill., Apr. 1, 1926; s. William Agidious H. and Caroline Bruning; m. Arliene Otis, June 22, 1948; children: Brad, Tori. BS in Polit. Sci., UCLA, 1951. Circulation mgr., columnist Park Ridge (Ill.) Advocate, 1938-41; copy boy, libr., feature writer Chgo. Tribune, 1941-43; reporter, feature writer, syndicated columnist L.A. Times, 1946-92, ret., 1992. Author: California Islands, 1957, Bel-Air Country Club, A Living Legend, 1993, Charles Hillinger's America, 1996, Charles Hillinger's Channel Islands, 1998, Hillinger's California, 1997. Mem. adv. bd. Sant Cruz Is. Found., Santa Barbara, Calif., 1992—; treas. 8-Ball Welfare Found. Greater L.A. Press Club, 1992—. With USN, 1943-46. Mem. Greater L.A. Press Club (sec. 1978-88, v.p. 1988-90, pres. 1990-92), Dutch Treat Club W. Avocations: tennis, golf, hearts. Home: 3131 Dianora Dr Rancho Palos Verdes CA 90275-6200

HILLMANN, LEO CHARLES, real estate company executive; b. White Plains, N.Y., Nov. 11, 1946; s. David Augustine and Mary Isabel (Healy) H.; m. Irene Marie May, Feb. 14, 1986; children: Evan Carter, Raegan Lynn, Christine Marie. BCE, Villanova U., 1969; MS in Ops. Rsch., George Washington U., 1978; grad., Naval War Coll., 1989; AS in Real Estate, Cuyamaca Coll, 1990; MA in History, San Diego State U., 1993. Commd. ensign USN, 1969, advanced through grades to comdr., 1983, active submarine svc., 1969-89; pres., CEO Shilo Enterprises, Spring Valley, Calif., 1989—; mem. fac. history dept Mesa Coll., San Diego, Calif., 1995—. Author: Naval Engineering, 1976, The Public at the Creation, 1993. Staff Rep. Conv. Orgn., San Diego, 1996. Mem. Navy League U.S., U.S. Naval Inst., Ret. Officer's Assn., Am. Legion, Calif. Assn. Realtors, San Diego County Assn. Realtors, San Diego State U. Alumnae Assn., U.S. Navy Meml. Assn., USS Constitution Mus., San Diego Zool. Soc., Phi Alpha Theta. Roman Catholic. Avocation: learning. Home: 9787 Avenida Colino Spring Valley CA 91977-5269 Office: 10174 Austin Dr Ste 2693 Spring Valley CA 91977-9998

HILLMER, MARY JANE, interior designer; b. Toronto, Ont., Can., June 28, 1949; d. Robert Wilson and Anna Noreen H. Diploma in Interior Design, Ont. Coll. of Art, Toronto, 1974-78. Interior designer ASID, Phoeniz, 1987—; bd. dirs. Scottsdale C. of C., Ariz.; docent Scottsdale Ctr. for Arts, 1992-98. Com. head Compass, Phoeniz, 1998, Scottsdale Ctr. for Arts, 1998. Mem. ASID (bd. dirs. 1992). Episcopalian. Home: 4542 N 73rd St Apt 3 Scottsdale AZ 85251-1421

HILLS, LINDA LAUNEY, advisory systems engineer; b. New Orleans, June 21, 1947; d. Edgar Sebastien and Isabel (James) Launey; m. Marvin Allen Hills Sr. Jan. 29, 1977 (div. July 1982); 8 stepchildren. Student, Navy Avionics Schs., Memphis and San Diego, 1979-89; certs. in tech. tng., IBM, Chgo. and Kingston, N.Y., Sys. Mgmt. Schs., Chgo. and Dallas. Cert. disaster recovery planner. Sec. Calhoun and Barnes Inc. Co., New Orleans, 1965; clk.-typist, stenographer, med. transcriptionist, teletypist Social Security Adminstrn., New Orleans, 1965-67; dep. U.S. marshal U.S. Marshal's Office, New Orleans, 1967-69; supr. U.S. Atty.'s Office, New Orleans, 1969; with clk.'s office, dep. U.S. clk., courtrom dep. U.S. clk. U.S. Dist. Ct. (ea. dist.) La., New Orleans, 1969-73; steno, sr. sec. Kelly Girl and Norrell Temp Services, New Orleans, 1974; customer engr. trainee IBM, Dallas, 1979; customer engr., sys. mgmt. specialist IBM, San Diego, 1979-84; sys. ctr. rep. NSD Washington System Ctr. IBM, Gaithersburg, Md., 1984-87; ops. specialist mktg. dept. IBM, San Diego, 1987—, adv. sys. engr., 1988-91; lectr., cons. in field. Author 3 workbooks on recovery mgmt., also presentation guide for execs. with cost evaluation, presentation guide for company coms. Vol. Touro Infirmary, Dialysis Unit, New Orleans, 1965-67, New Orleans Recreation Dept. 1964-68, PALS-Montgomery County Mental Health Orgn., Bethesda, Md., 1984-87, various polit. candidates, 1963—; mem. Calif. Gov.'s Subcom. on Disaster Preparedness. Petty officer USN, 1974-78. Mem. NAFE, ACP, DAV, Info. System Security Assn., Women Computer Profls. San Diego, Data Processing Mgmt. Assn., San Diego Zoolog. Soc., Assn. System Mgmt., Smithsonian Instn. (resident assoc.), Nat. Trust Hist. Preservation. Avocations: travel, piano, crocheting, carpentry, woodworking. Office: PO Box 261806 San Diego CA 92196-1806

HILLS, REGINA J., journalist; b. Sault Sainte Marie, Mich., Dec. 24, 1953; d. Marvin Dan and Ardithanne (Tilly) H.; m. Vincent C. Stricherz, Feb. 25, 1984. B.A., U. Nebr., 1976. Reporter UPI, Lincoln, Nebr., 1976-80, state editor, bur. mgr., 1981-82; state editor, bur. mgr. UPI, New Orleans, 1982-84, Indpls., 1985-87; asst. city editor Seattle Post-Intelligencer, 1987—; panelist TV interview show Face Nebr., 1978-81; vis. lectr. U. Nebr., Lincoln, 1978, 79, 80; columnist weekly feature Capitol News, Nebr. Press Assn., 1981-82. Recipient Outstanding Coverage awards UPI, 1980, 82. Mem. U. Nebr. Alumni Assn., Zeta Tau Alpha. Office: Seattle Post-Intelligencer 101 Elliott Ave W Ste 200 Seattle WA 98119-4295

HILLYARD, LYLE WILLIAM, lawyer; b. Logan, Utah, Sept. 25, 1940; s. Alma Lowell and Lucille (Rosenbaum) H.; m. Alice Thorpe, June 24, 1964; children: Carrie, Lisa, Holly, Todd, Matthew. BS, Utah State U., 1965; JD, U. Utah, 1967. Bar: Utah 1967, U.S. Supreme Ct. 1977. Pres. Hillyard, Anderson & Olsen, Logan, 1967—; senator State of Utah, Salt Lake City, 1985—. Rep. chmn. Cache County, Logan, 1970-76; Utah State Rep., 1981-84; pres. Cache County C. of C., 1977. Named one of Outstanding Young Men of Am., Utah Jaycees, 1972; [illegible] Jaycees, 1972, Merit award Cache Valley coun. Boy Scouts Am., 1981. Mem. ABA, Utah State Bar Assn., Cache County Bar Assn., Assn. Trial Lawyers Am., Am. Bd. Trial Advocates. Mormon. Club: Big Blue (Logan).

Lodge: Kiwanis. Office: Hillyard Anderson & Olsen 175 E 1st N Logan UT 84321-4601

HILSON, PHOENIX, writer; b. San Francisco, Apr. 22, 1954; d. David Ridgeway and Virginia Belle (Ely) Geddes; m. Robert Lynn Beach, Apr. 22, 1972 (div. May 1975); 1 child, Dianne Renee; m. Steven Vale Hilson, June 3, 1978; 1 child, Heather Ashley. Bookstore owner Merlyn's Magic Crystal, Dublin, Calif., 1988-92; real estate agent Mason McDuffie, Danville, Calif., 1992-93, Security Pacific, Danville, 1993-94; writer Dublin, 1994—. Author: Wizard's War, 1998, T-Zaddhe, 1998. Mem. Traditional Martinist Order, Rosicrucian. Avocations: reading, research.

HILTON, BARRON, hotel executive; b. Dallas, 1927; s. Conrad Hilton. Founder, pres. San Diego Chargers, Am. Football League, until 1966; v.p. Hilton Hotels Corp., Beverly Hills, Calif., 1954; pres., chief exec. officer Hilton Hotels Corp., Beverly Hills, 1966—, chmn., 1979—, also dir.; chmn., pres., dir. Hilton Equipment Corp, Beverly Hills, Calif; mem. gen. adminstrv. bd. Mfrs. Hanover Trust Co., N.Y.C. Office: Hilton Hotels Corp 9336 Civic Center Dr Beverly Hills CA 90210-3604

HILTON, STANLEY GOUMAS, lawyer, educator, writer; b. San Francisco, June 16, 1949; s. Loucas Stylianos and Effie (Glafkides) Goumas; m. Raquel Estrella Villalba, Feb. 25, 1996. BA with honors, U. Chgo., 1971; JD, Duke U., 1975; MBA, Harvard U., 1979. Bar: Calif. 1975, U.S. Dist. Ct. Calif., U.S. Ct. Appeals (9th cir.), U.S. Supreme Ct. Libr. asst. Duke U. Libr., Durham, N.C., 1972-75, Harvard U. Libr., Cambridge, Mass., 1977-79; minority counsel U.S. Senator Bob Dole, Washington, 1979-80; adminstrv. asst. Calif. State Senate, Sacramento, 1980-81; pvt. practice San Francisco, 1981—; adj. assoc. prof. Golden Gate U., San Francisco, 1991—. Author: Bob Dole: American Political Phoenix, 1988, Senator for Sale, 1995, Glass Houses, 1998 (best writer 1998). Pres. Com. to Stick With Candlestick Park, San Francisco, 1992-96, Value Added Tax Now, San Francisco, 1994—, Save the 4th Amendment, San Francisco, 1995—. Mem. Calif. State Bar, Hellenic Law Soc., Bechtel Toastmasters Club (pres.). Democrat. Avocations: philately, photography, classical music, ancient Greek and Roman history. Office: 580 California St Ste 500 San Francisco CA 94104-1000

HILTS, RUTH, artist; b. Sparks, Nev., Dec. 4, 1923; d. William and Nellie Elisa (DeGoosh) Gonzales; m. Robert Norton Hilts, Sept. 28, 1942; children: Robert Norton, Jr., Deirdre Lynne. BA, U. Nev., 1962. Grad. teaching asst. dept. English U. Nev., Reno, 1962-63, editor-interviewer dept. oral history, 1967-74; profl. artist Reno, 1975—. One-woman shows include Sierra Nev. Mus. Art, 1987-88, Nev. Gallery, Reno, 1990, River Gallery, Reno, 1995, 98, Red Mountain Gallery at Truckee Meadows C.C., Reno, 1995, Nevada Leg. Bldg., Carson City, Nev., 1997; exhibited in group shows at Watercolor West XIV, Riverside, Calif., 1982, Nev. Mus. Art Biennial, Reno, Las Vegas, 1990, 96, Sierra Nev. Coll., Tahoe, 1992-93, Stremmel Gallery, Reno, 1992-94, River Gallery, 1993-94, Sierra Arts Found. Gallery, Reno, 1994-95; represented in permanent collections including Nev. Mus. Art, Kafoury, Armstrong & Co., Reno, Helms Constrn. Co., Reno, Dean Witter, Reynolds, Inc., Reno, Tournament Players Club Summerlin, Las Vegas, Comstock Bank, Reno; contbr. art to publs. Nev. Mag., 1988, Encore, 1995, 98, Neon, 1995, 97. Mem. Comstock Arts Coun., Reno-Sparks Theater Coalition. Mem. Nat. Mus. Women in the Arts, Nev. Mus. Art, Sierra Arts Found. (grantee for excellence 1995), Phi Kappa Phi. Avocations: reading, hiking, mountain and desert camping. Home and Office: 1895 Wren St Reno NV 89509-2334

HILYARD, DAVID FRANKLIN, optician; b. Hartland, Maine, Mar. 16, 1949; s. Clarence Emery and Glenda Irene (Doughty) H.; m. Darrie Jean Young, Sept. 28, 1984; children: Lisa, Chad, Wyatt, Spenser. Student, Norwalk Tech. Inst., 1968-69. Optical technician Laser Optics, Inc., Danbury, Conn., 1966-69, 71-76; radio team chief, sgt. U.S. Army, 1969-71; master optician, supr. Zygo Corp., Middlefield, Conn., 1976-85; specialist, chief optician UCO/Lick Observatory, U. Calif., Santa Cruz, 1985—. Author: (manual) Conventional Optical Polishing Procedures, 1982, Keck Telescope High Resolution Spectograph Optical Components, 1993; co-author: (technical report) University of California Tech. Report #49 Mosaic Project, 1988, Keck Telescope High Resolution Spectograph Design Review, 1990, UCO/Lick Tech. Report #75, 1994. Mem. Am. Inst. of Physics, Optical Soc. of Am., Soc. of Photo-Optical Instrumentation Engrs. Avocations: guitar, fly fishing, gardening. Home: 255 Cottini Way Santa Cruz CA 95060-9467 Office: Univ of California Lick Observatory 1156 High St Santa Cruz CA 95064-0001

HIMELSTEIN, SUSAN, psychologist; b. Norwalk, Ohio, Feb. 27, 1951; d. Warren and Frances (Jenkins) Holzhauser. BS, Miami U., Oxford, Ohi, 1973; MA, UCLA, 1981, PhD with honors, 1987. Lic. psychologist, sch. psychologist, counselor, tchr., Calif. Staff psychologist Verdugo Psychotherapy Inst., Glendale, Calif., 1987-88; counselor, psychologist Beverly Hills (Calif.) Unified Schs., 1988-98; pvt. practice Beverly Hills, 1989—; psychologist, cons., sr. faculty mem. Reiss-Davis Child Study Ctr., 1987-96; adj. prof. Pepperdine U., Culver City, 1989—, vis. prof., 1996—; supr. interns for various univs.; spkr. UCLA Ext. Confs., 1994—. Acad. scholar Calif. State Fellowship, 1981-83. Mem. APA, L.A. County Psychol. Assn., Calif. Psychol. Assn. Office: 9107 Wilshire Blvd Ste 215 Beverly Hills CA 90210-5522

HIMES, DIANE ADELE, buyer, fundraiser, actress; b. San Francisco, Aug. 11, 1943; d. L. John and Mary Louise (Young) H. BA, San Francisco State U., 1964. Rep. west coast home furnishings Allied Stores, nationwide; gift buyer Jordan Marsh, Miami; west coast sales mgr. Xmas catalogue Vicent-Lippe, L.A.; midwest sales mgr. Vicent-Lippe, Chgo.; bd. dirs. L.A. Womens' Shakespeare Group. Actress Nine 'O Clock Players, 1995, short film The Traveling Companion, 1998. Co-chair Californians Against Initiative No On # 64, 1998, M.E.C.L.A., 1997; founding co-chair Life AIDS Lobby, 1994; Beverly Hills rent control bd., 1984. Named Woman of Yr. ACLU, 1987, Christopher Street West, 1988. Avocations: acting, appearing in short films.

HINCHEY, BRUCE ALAN, environmental engineering company executive; b. Kansas City, Mo., Jan. 24, 1949; s. Charles Emmet and Eddie Lee (Scott) H.; m. Karen Adele McLaughlin, Nov. 27, 1969 (div. Nov. 1983); children: Scott Alan, Traci Denise, Amanda Lee, Richard Austin; m. Karen Robitaille, Apr. 10, 1993. Student, U. Mo., Rolla, 1967-71. Source testing crew chief Ecology Audits, Inc., Dallas, 1971-76; lab. mgr. Ecology Audits, Inc., Casper, Wyo., 1976-78; mgr. ops. Ecology Audits, Inc., Dallas, 1978-79; v.p. Kumpe & Assoc. Engrs., Casper, 1979-81; pres. Western Environ. Svcs. and Testing, Inc., Casper, 1981—, Hawk Industries, Inc., 1993—; pres. Mining Assocs. Wyo., Cheyenne, 1986-87. Mem. Wyo. State Ho. of Reps., Cheyenne, 1989—, spkr. of house, mgmt. coun., rules com., energy coun., select water com., sel. edn. com., active Natrona County Rep. precinct, Casper, 1986—, Am. Legis. Exch. Coun., 1989; chair Natrona County Rep. Party, 1988-89. Mem. Am. Inst. Mining Engrs., Nat. Fedn. Ind. Bus. (Guardian award), Air Pollution Control Assn., Casper C. of C., Rotary, Shriners, Masons. Methodist. Office: Western Environ Svcs and Testing Inc 913 N Foster Rd Casper WY 82601-1640

HINCKLEY, GORDON B., church official; s. Bryant S. and Ada (Bitner) H.; m. Marjorie Pay, Apr. 29, 1937; children: Kathleen Hinckley Barnes, Richard G., Virginia Hinckley Pearce, Clark B., Jane Hinckley Dudley. Asst. to Council of Twelve Apostles, Church of Jesus Christ Latter Day Saints, 1958-61, mem. council, 1961-81, Counselor in the First Presidency, 1981-82, Second Counselor in the First Presidency, 1982-85, First Counselor in the First Presidency, 1985-95; pres. of ch., 1995—. Office: First Presidency LDS Ch 47 E South Temple Salt Lake City UT 84150-1005

HINERFELD, SUSAN HOPE SLOCUM, writer, editor; b. N.Y.C., Aug. 6, 1936; d. Milton Jonathan and Belle Esther (Gibralter) Slocum; m. Robert Elliot Hinerfeld, June 27, 1957; children: Daniel Slocum, Matthew Ben. BA, Wellesley Coll., 1957. Co-author: Manhattan Country Doctor, 1986; editor: Wellesley After-Images, 1974; contbr. book revs. to various publs. Mem. Authors Guild, Nat. Book Critics Cir. Democrat. Avocations: reading, collecting antiques. Home: 371 24th St Santa Monica CA 90402-2517

HINES, HORACE H., JR., physicist; b. Jackson, Miss., Oct. 9, 1947; s. Horace H., Sr. and Vineta H.; m. Lynn, June 17, 1973; children: Kenneth, Eric. MS, U. Calif., Davis, 1972, PhD, 1977. Hosp. physicist U. Calif., Davis, 1977-82; sr. physicist ADAC Labs., Sunnyvale, Calif., 1982-86; mgr. engring. ADAC Labs., San Jose, Calif., 1986-90; mgr. advanced mktg. ADAC Labs., Milpitas, Calif., 1990-94; chief tech. officer ADAC Labs., Milpitas, 1994—. Patentee in field. Mem. Am. Assn. Physicist Medicine, Soc. Nuclear Med., Nat. Elec. Mfg. Assn. (chmn. nuclear standards 1994—). Office: ADAC Labs 540 Alder Dr Milpitas CA 95035

HINES, WILLIAM EVERETT, publisher, producer, cinematographer, writer; b. San Bernardino, Calif., Apr. 2, 1923; s. Everett Ellsworth and Etta Elvira (Gillard) H. Student, UCLA, 1941-43, 46; BA, U. So. Calif., L.A., 1950, MA, 1951. Cameraman, film editor N.Am. Aviation, Inc., L.A. and Downey, Calif., 1951-53; founder, pres. Ed-Venture Films, L.A., 1954—; sec., treas. Sampson Prodns., S.A., Panama, 1956-60; v.p. Intro-Media Prodns., Inc., L.A., 1971-75; pres., pub. Ed-Venture Films/Books, L.A., 1985—; cons., expert witness, L.A., 1965—; lectr., instr., L.A., 1958—. Author: Job Descriptions For Film, Video & CGI, 5 edits., 1961-98, Operating Cinematography for Film and Video, 1997; writer Operating Tips column for Internat. Photographer mag., 1987—; contbr. numerous features to profl. jours.; producer: (ednl. film) Running For Sheriff, 1954 (Merit award 1955, 56); producer films., commls. Mem. profl. adv. bd. Calif. State U., Long Beach, 1973—, Northridge, 1974—; chmn. bd. trustees Producers and Film Craftsmen Pension and Health Plans, L.A., 1965-79. Sgt. USAAF, 1943-46. Recipient Spl. citation City of L.A., 1966. Mem. Nat. Assn. Broadcast Employees and Technicians, Internat. Cinematographers Guild, Internat. Alliance Theatrical Stage Employees (nat. exec. bd. dirs. 1989—, dir. tng. 1992—), Soc. Oper. Cameramen (charter, sec. 1978—, corp. liaison 1991—), recipient President's award for Lifetime Achievement Soc. Operating Cameramen, 1995, Am. Film Inst., Publishers Mktg. Assn., Nat. Geog. Soc., Assn. Film Craftsmen (pres., mem. exec. bd. 1957-79), Masons, Shriners, Ephebian Soc., Sigma Nu (Epsilon Pi chpt.). Avocations: tennis, fishing, travel, reading. Office: Ed-Venture Films/Books 1122 Calada St Los Angeles CA 90023-3115

HINKLE, JILL ELAINE, religion educator, counselor; b. Santa Rosa, Calif., Dec. 30, 1956; d. Edward Ben and Rosalie Bertha (Jacoby) H. BA in Psychology, Westmont Coll., 1978; MA in Marriage and Family Ministry, Biola U., 1986, postgrad., 1990—; MA in Coll. Student Affairs, Azusa Pacific U., 1987; cert. in theology, The Julian (Calif.) Ctr., 1988. Cert. secondary tchr., Calif. Tchr., coach Calvary and South Bay Christian high schs., Mountain View, Calif., 1979-82; career and personal alumni counselor Azusa (Calif.) Pacific U., 1984-87; counselor, speaker Ministry Assocs., Orange County, Calif., 1985-86; vocat. dir. Julian Ctr., 1988-89; mem. faculty Biola U., La Mirada, Calif., 1991—; mem. adv. bd., dir. seminars Summit Expeditions, West Covina, Calif., 1987-88; dir. mktg. and personality, career cons. Personality Devel. Inst., Anaheim, Calif., 1989—. Author: (study guide) Holy Sweat, 1987. Counselor Girls Club, Santa Barbara Area YMCA, 1976-77; facilitator City of Long Beach Adminstrs., Dana Point, Calif., 1988; instr. Probation Dept., L.A., 1989-91. Coll. Scholarship Program, Biola U. grantee and fellow, 1990-91. Mem. Assn. Christians in Student Devel., Christian Assn. for Psychol. Studies. Republican. Home: 2689 Santa Ana Ave Costa Mesa CA 92627-4638

HINSHAW, HORTON CORWIN, physician; b. Iowa Falls, Iowa, 1902; s. Milas Clark and Ida (Bushong) H.; m. Dorothy Youmans, Aug. 6, 1924; children: Horton Corwin Jr., Barbara (Mrs. Barbara Baird) (dec.), Dorothy (Mrs. Gregory Patent), William (dec.). A.B., Coll. Idaho, 1923, D.Sc., 1947; A.M., U. Calif., 1926, Ph.D., 1927; M.D., U. Pa., 1933. Diplomate Am. Bd. Internal Medicine, Nat. Bd. Med. Examiners. Asst. prof. zoology U. Calif., 1927-28; adj. prof. parasitology and bacteriology Am. U., Beirut, Lebanon, 1928-31; instr. bacteriology U. Pa. Sch. Medicine, 1931-33; fellow, 1st asst. medicine. Mayo Found., U. Minn., 1933-35, asst. prof., 1937-46, assoc. prof., 1946-49; cons. medicine Mayo clinic, 1935-49, head sec. medicine, 1947-49; clin. prof. medicine, head divsn. chest diseases Stanford Med. Sch., 1949-59; clin. prof. medicine U. Calif. Med. Sch., 1959-79, emeritus prof., 1979—; chief thoracic disease svc. So. Pacific Meml. Hosp., 1958-69; dir. med. svcs.and chief staff Harkness Community Hosp. and Med. Ctr., San Francisco, 1968-75; Dir. med. ops. Health Maintenance No. Calif., Inc.; mem. Calif. Com. Regional Med. Programs, 1969-75. Author: Diseases of the Chest, rev. edit., 1980; co-author: Streptomycin in Tuberculosis, 1949; contbr. over 215 articles to med. publs.; co-discoverer antiTB chemotherapy, exptl. and clin., with several drugs. Del. various internat. confs., 1928-59. Recipient Disting. Alumnus award Mayo Found., 1990. Fellow A.C.P., Am. Coll. Chest Physicians; hon. mem. Miss. Valley Med. Assn.; mem. AMA, Nat. Tb Assn. (bd. dirs., chmn. com. therapy, v.p. 1946- 47, 67-68, rsch. com.), Am. Thoracic Soc. (pres. 1948-49, hon. life 1979), Am. Clin. and Climatol. Soc., Minn. Med. Assn., Am. Bronchoesophalogical Assn., Am. Soc. Clin. Investigation, Cen. Soc. Clin. Rsch., Soc. Exptl. Biology and Medicine, Aero-Med. Assn., Am. Lung Assn. (hon., Hall of Fame 1980), Minn. Soc. Internal Medicine, Sigma Xi, Phi Sigma, Gamma Alpha. Mem. Soc. of Friends. Home: 400 Deer Valley Rd Apt 4L San Rafael CA 94903-5520

HINSON, RONALD W., information services executive; b. Newark, Aug. 6, 1936; s. James Wesley Hinson and Clementine (Smith) Ward; m. Alice Clark Mays, Mar. 16, 1961; 1 child, Sean; m. Earmond L. Williams, May 21, 1988; children: Sean Hinson, Jonathan Doris, Jackie. BA, St. Leo Coll., 1989; MA, Webster U., 1994. Enlisted USAF, 1965, advanced through grades to chief master sgt., ret., 1985; adminstrv. asst. St. Leo Coll., Hampton, Va., 1985-87; mgmt. analyst Army Transport, New Port News, Va., 1987-88; office mgr. VA, Albuquerque, 1988-90; data mgr. U.S. Census Bur., Albuquerque, 1990; health educator Sickle Cell Coun., Albuquerque, 1990-94; mgr. document mgmt. info. svcs. Intel Corp., Rio Rancho, N.Mex., 1994—. Author: U.S. Air Force Maintenance Analysis Guide, 1980; peer reviewer: Sickle Guidelines, 1992, Care of Newborns with Sickle Cell Disease, 1992. Bd. dirs. cmty. affairs 1st Security Bank, Albuquerque, 1990-94, Planned Parenthood, 1996—; mem. gov.'s coun. Phys. Fitness/Health, N.Mex., 1991. Mem. Masons, Kappa Gamma Pi, Delta Epsilon Sigma. Home: 224 Glorieta St NE Albuquerque NM 87123-2716

HINSVARK, DON GEORGE, social services agency professional; b. Helena, Mont., Mar. 27, 1934; s. Almer Burton and Carmen Christine Hinsvark; m. Jacqueline Rica Sarfati, July 10, 1958; children: Jon Felix, Timothy Joel, Michael David, Symone Hinsvark Sass. BA, U. So. Calif., 1956; MA in Tchg. and Counseling, San Diego State U., 1967; postgrad., sch. adminstrn. cert., U. La Verne, 1984-86; Cert. Career Counseling/Legal Asst., U. Calif.-San Diego, 1994. Cert. tchr. gen. elem. and jr. high edn., sch. adminstrn., sch. counselor, Calif. Tchr. San Diego (Calif.) City Schs., 1962-65, dist. counselor, 1965-85, dist. counselor team leader, 1985-91, chmn. sch. attendance rev. bd., 1992; career counselor Dyasayd Consultation, San Diego, 1993; program supr. Voices for Children, San Diego, 1994—; mem. San Diego Commn. on Children, Youth and Families, 1994—, adv. bd. San Diego State U. Sch. Social Work, 1993-95; adv. bd., instr. U. La Verne (Calif.), Edn. Dept., 1984-88; presenter in field. Joint author: Crisis Team Handbook, 1988; contbr. articles to profl. jours. Coach Age Group Swim Team, Coronado, Calif., 1962, Pop Warner Football, Coronado, 1970-71; coach and mgr. Little League Baseball, Coronado, 1970-75, Sr. Little League Baseball, Coronado, 1976-77. Lt. USN, 1956-61, Atlantic and Pacific; capt. USNR; commdg. officer Res. Naval Spl. Warfare Staff unit, 1980-82, 84-86. Recipient NROTC scholarship USN, 1952-56; scholar Nat. Def. Edn. Inst., U.S. Govt. 1966, 68. Mem. Calif. Sch. Social Workers Assn. (pres. San Diego chpt. 1972, state area rep. 1979), San Diego City Student Svcs. Assn. (pres. 1983-84, 86-87), Calif. Sch. Counselors Assn. (area rep. 1982-83, 92-93, Area Counselor of Yr. 1992), Calif. Assn. for Counseling and Devel. (pres. San Diego chpt. 1992-93), Kiwanis (v.p., sec. San Diego chpt. 1987, Educator of Yr. 1991), Am. Counseling Assn. Avocations: swimming, nordic skiing, reading, travel. Home: 720 Country Club Ln Coronado CA 92118-2038 Office: Voices for Children 2851 Meadow Lark Dr San Diego CA 92123-2709

HINZ, SHIRLEY SORENSEN, administrative secretary; b. Denver, Sept. 28, 1942; m. Dale Edward Hinz, Sept. 3, 1966; children: Andrew Christian, Tammy Lynn Dahl. Student, Ft. Lewis Coll., 1961, Barnes Bus. Coll., 1982; diploma in spl. pub., Inst. Children's Lit., 1994. Adminstrv. asst. USDA, Ft. Collins, Colo., 1989; divsn. sec. U.S. Dept. Energy, Golden, Colo., 1991; sect. sec. U.S. Dept. Interior, Ft. Collins, 1992—; mem. labor mgmt. partnership coun. U.S. Dept. Interior, 1994-95. Author numerous poems; writer/songwriter. Active Ault (Colo.) Sr. Ctr., 1989—. Recipient Editor's Choice award Nat. Libr. Congress, Nat. Libr. Poetry, 1995-96, Accomplishment of Merit award Creative Arts & Sci. Enterprises, 1996, Nat. Merit Award cert. Larimer County Fed. Exec. Assn., 1996, awards Poetry Guild, 1996-97; named to Internat. Poetry Hall of Fame, Nat. Libr. Congress, 1997. Mem. Internat. Soc. Poets (disting.), Famous Poets Soc. (Diamond Homer award 1996), Acad. of Am. Poets. Lutheran. Avocations: gardening, studying and working in bonsai, song writing. Home: PO Box 1063 304 Cherry Ln Ault CO 80610 Office: US Dept of Interior 4512 Mcmurry Ave Fort Collins CO 80525-3400

HIPSCHMAN, DAVID, editor; b. Long Branch, N.J., Oct. 13, 1952; s. Leonard and Olga (Weiss) H.; m. Dorrie Dale, Dec. 2, 1987; children: Robert William, Katie. BA in English, Anthropology, Trenton State Coll., 1976. Reporter Delaware Valley News, Frenchtown, N.J., 1977-98; reporter, bur. chief Easton (Pa.) Express, 1978-80; internat. editor San Francisco Chronical, 1980-90; editor, publisher Kinesis, Whitefish, Mont., 1991-95; editor-in-chief Casper (Wyo.) Star-Tribune, 1995—. Author: Flying Sounds, 1978. Mem. Wyo. Press Assn. (bd. dirs. 1997-98). Avocations: aviation, fly-fishing. Office: Casper Star Tribune 170 Star Ln Casper WY 82604-2883

HIRAHARA, PATTI, public relations executive; b. Lynwood, Calif., May 10, 1955; d. Frank C. and Mary K. Hirahara; m. Terry K. Takeda, Sept. 1995. AA, Cypress Coll., 1975; BA, Calif. State U.-Fullerton, 1977. Pub. affairs dir. United Television, Los Angeles, 1977-80; v.p. Asian Internat. Broadcasting Co., Los Angeles, 1980-81; mktg. cons. Disneyland, Anaheim, Calif., 1982; pub. relations agt. Japan External Trade Orgn., Los Angeles, 1982-86, 87-92; owner, pres. Prodns. By Hirahara, Anaheim, 1982—; comml. photographer Hirahara Photography, Anaheim, 1977-83; publicist Tokyo Met. Govt., 1981, World Trade Week Southern Calif., 1997, 98, 99; advisor State Colo. Trade Mission to Japan, 1986, State Ariz. Trade/Investment Mission to Japan, 1987, County Riverside, Calif. for Japanese trade, investment, tourism, 1986-88; coord. JETRO's Bus. Study Series, Los Angeles, 1988; advisor Japan External Trade Ordgn., 1987-88, TV Producer/Host: Images, 1980, Expressions, 1994. Bd. dirs. Nisei Week Japanese Festival, Los Angeles, 1980-81; Anaheim High Sch. 20 Yr. Reunion Com., 1993. Nat. scholar Seventeen Mag. Youth Adv. Coun., 1973; named Orange County Nisei Queen, Suburban Optimist Club, Buena Park, Calif., 1975, nat. semi-finalist Outstanding Young Working Women Competititon Glamour mag., 1983-84; recipient service award Suburban Optimist Club of Buena Park, 1975. Mem. NAFE, Soc. Profl. Journalists (bd. dirs. 1980-81), World Trade Ctr. Assn. Orange County, Japanese Am. Citizens League, Am. Women in Radio and TV (bd. dirs. So. Calif. chpt. 1980-82, vice-chair western area conf. 1981), So. Calif. golf Assn., No. Calif. Golf Assn., Pub. Rels. Soc. Am. (Orange County chpt. 1990), Adelaide Price Elementary Sch., (30 yr reunion chair 1997), Suburban Optimist Club of Buena Park (bd. dirs. 1993-96, chairperson 30th Anniversary Celebration 1996, Optimist of Yr. 1995-96), L.A. Dept. Water and Power Golf Club, Hunter Ranch Golf Club, mem. reader panel, Golf for Women Magazine, Alpha Gamma Sigma.

HIRATSUKA, YUJI, artist, educator; b. Osaka, Japan, Sept. 7, 1954; came to U.S., 1985; s. Toshio and Kameyo (Tsumura) H.; m. Priscilla L. Hiratsuka, Dec. 30, 1989; children: Hana Gabriella, Toshio Alan. BS, Tokyo Gakngei U., 1978; MA, N.Mex. State U., 1987; MFA, Ind. U., 1990. Vis. asst. prof. Colo. Coll., Colorado Springs, 1990-92; assoc. prof. art Oreg. State U., Corvallis, 1992—; vis. instr. Pacific N.W. Coll. of Art, Portland, Oreg., 1994—; instr. summer workshops Sitka Ctr. Art & Ecology, Otis, Oreg., 1997—; printmaker, lectr. Mem. adv. bd. Corvallis (Oreg.) Art Ctr., 1995—, N.W. Print Coun., 1993—. Recipient numerous art competition awards. Mem. Calif. Soc. Printmakers. Home: 1215 NW Kline Pl Corvallis OR 97330 Office: Oreg State U Dept Art Corvallis OR 97331-3702

HIRE, JAMES WILLIAM, hospitality consultant; b. Ligonier, Ind., Sept. 12, 1948; s. Merrill J. and Olive S. (Smith) H.; m. Linda F. Rex, Dec. 24, 1969 (dec. Mar. 1991); m. Nan J. Gonzales, May 5, 1996. BSBA, Tri-State U., 1970; BSBA in Hotel and Restaurant Mgmt., U. Denver, 1973. Gen. mgr. Topeka Inn Mgmt., 1971-77, The Yarrow Hotel, Park City, Utah, 1977-79; sr. prin. Pannell Kerr Forster, Denver, 1979-88; prin. Hire & Assocs., Evergreen, Colo., 1988—; adj. prof. U. Denver, 1997—; bd. trustees Icon Mut. Funds, Englewood, Colo., 1996—; bd. dirs. Aircoa Hotel Ptnrs., Englewood. Mem. adv. bd. of travel and tourism adminstrn. Denver Pub. Schs., 1996—. Mem. Internat. Soc. Hospitality Cons. (cert., charter mem.). Office: Hire and Assocs 1383 Solitude Ln Evergreen CO 80439

HIROHATA, DEREK KAZUYOSHI, career officer; b. Dos Palos, Calif., June 26, 1963; s. Vincent Yoshinobu and Gertrude Sumiko (Kimura) H. BA in Polit. Sci., Calif. State U., Fresno, 1987; grad., Italian Mil. Jump Sch., 1989, USAFE Command & Control Sch., 1990, Brit. Army Jump Sch., 1990; MA in Aerospace Sci., Embry riddle U., Carbondale, 1992; JD, So. Ill. U., Carbondale, 1996. Bar: Calif. 1997, U.S. Ct. Appeals (armed forces) 1997, U.S. Ct. Criminal Appeals (air force) 1997. Commd. 2d lt. U.S. Air Force, advanced through grades to capt., 1991; ground launched cruise missile launch control officer Italy and U.K., 1988-90; emergency actions officer 501 Tactical Missile Wing, RAF Greenham Common, U.K., 1989-90; chief force mgmt. 513 Svcs. Squadron, RAF Mildenhall, U.K., 1990-92; billeting & food svc. coord., laison officer Air Fete, Eng.; treaty inspector escort Conventional Forces Europe; USAFR, 1993—, 932 SVS ops. officer, 1993-97; dept. judge advocate gen. USAF, 1997—. Contbr. to poetry anthologies Am. Poetry Soc., 1993, Poets Pen Quarterly, 1993, Memories Anthology, 1994, Delta. Coord. peer support network Sch. Law So. Ill. U., Carbondale, founder, capt. trial advocacy competition team, 1994-95; mem. Jessup Internat. Moot Ct. team. Mem. ABA, ATLA (founder So. Ill. U.-Carbondale chpt.), Calif. State Bar Assn. Am. Psychology and Law Soc., Christian Legal Soc., Internat. Law Soc., So. Ill. U.-Carbondale Student Bar Assn., So. Ill. U.-Carbondale Law & Medicine Soc., Air and Space Smithsonian, Officers' Christian Fellowship, Airforce Assn., Air Force Edn. Soc., U.S. Capitol Hist. Soc., Calif. State U.-Fresno Alumni Orgn., West Coast Karate Assn., Assn. Air Force Missileers (assoc.), Sigma Nu (alumni advisor So. Ill. U.-Carbondale chpt., dist. commdr., dist. commdr. Far West), Ill. State Bar Assn., State Bar Calif., Lawyer-Pilots Bar Assn., Ground Launched Cruise Missile Hist. Found. Republican. Methodist. Avocations: karate, flying, scuba diving, sky diving, photography. Home: PO Box 243 South Dos Palos CA 93665-0243

HIRONDELLE, ANNE ELIZABETH, ceramic artist; b. Vancouver, Wash., July 8, 1944; d. John Wayne and Alice G. (Tokola) Harvey; m. Robert Lee Schwiesow, Aug. 26, 1967. BA in English, U. Puget Sound, 1966; MA in Counseling Psychology, Stanford U., 1967; postgrad. Sch. Law, U. Wash., 1972-73; student ceramics program, Factory of Visual Art, Seattle, 1973-74; postgrad., U. Wash., 1974-76. Assoc. dir. U. Wash. YMCA, Seattle, 1967-69, dir., 1969-72; lectr., artist-in-residence, workshop leader Pacific Luth. U., Tacoma, 1980, Multnomah Art Ctr., Portland, 1982, Brookhaven Coll., Farmers Branch, Tex., 1988, Internat. Clay Seminar, Calgary, Alta., Can., 1989, Sonoma State Coll., Santa Rosa, Calif., 1990, Emily Carr Sch. Art and Design, Vancouver, B.C., Can., 1990, Tulane U., New Orleans, 1991, Santa Rosa Jr. Coll., 1991, Newport H. S., Bellevue, 1992, Arrowmont Sch. Arts and Crafts, Gatlinburg, Tenn., 1993, Boise State U., 1993, Craft Students League, N.Y.C., 1994. One person shows include Pacific Luth. U., Tacoma, Wash., 1980, Seattle Ctr., 1985, Lawrence Gallery, Portland, Oreg., 1986, 88, Foster/White Gallery at Frederick & Nelson, Seattle, 1986, Martha Schneider Gallery, Highland Park, Ill., 1987, Franklin House Gallery, Port Townsend, Wash., 1985, 87, 90, Garth Clark Gallery, Kansas City, Mo., 1990, Maveety Gallery, Salishan, Oreg., 1991, Schneider-Bluhm-Loeb Gallery, Chgo., 1992, Joanne Rapp Gallery, Scottsdale, Ariz., 1991, 93, The Works Gallery, Phila., 1991, 94, Garth Clark Gallery, N.Y.C., 1992, 94, Garth Clark Gallery, L.A., 1987, 89, 90, 93, 95; exhibited in group shows Oreg. Sch. Arts and Crafts, Portland, 1979, Sussler Gallery, U. Mich., Ann Arbor, 1980, Henry Gallery, U. Wash., Seattle, 1981, Lawrence Salishan Gallery, Gleneden Beach, Oreg., 1982, Hockaday Ctr. for Arts, Kalispel, Mo., 1983, Bellevue (Wash.) Art Mus., 1984, Tacoma Art Mus., 1984, Foster/White Gallery, Seattle, 1985, 87, 93, Gallery Eight, La Jolla, Calif., 1986, 87, 93, Martha Schneider Gallery, Chgo., 1986, 90, Safeco Plaza, Seattle, 1986, Garth Clark Gallery, N.Y.C., 1986, 87, 88, 89, 91, 92, Susan

Cummings Gallery, Walnut Creek, Calif., 1987, Pewabic Pottery, Detroit, 1987, Athenaem Mus., Alexandria, Va., 1988, Lawrence Gallery, Portland, 1988, Faith Nightingale Gallery, San Diego, 1988, 91, Nora Eccles Harrison Mus. Art, Utah State U., Logan, 1989, Cedar Creek Gallery, Creedmore, N.C., 1989, Sonoma State U. Art Gallery, Rohnert, Calif., 1990, Moira-James Gallery, Green Valley, Nev., 1990, 91, Swidler Gallery, Royal Oak, Mich., 1989, 90, 91, The Works Gallery, Phila., Pa., 1990, Am. Craft Mus., N.Y.C., 1991, Conterprary Crafts gallery, Portland, 1991, Pro Art Gallery, St. Louis, 1992, 93, Kirkland (Wash.) Arts Ctr., 1992, MacKenzie Fine Arts Ctr, Dearborn, Mich., 1993, The 1004 Gallery, Port Townsend, Wash., 1993, Craft Alliance, St. Louis, 1993, 94, Ferrin Gallery, Northampton, Mass., 1993, Art Ctr. Gallery Seattle Pacific U., 1993, Schmidt-Bingham Gallery, N.Y.C., 1994, Galleries of Dept. Art Tex. Tech. U., 1994, Artworks Gallery, Seattle, 1994; represented in numerous pub. and pvt. permanent collections including Am. Craft Mus., Ariz. State U. Art Mus., Boise State U., Gateway Tower, Newark Mus., Nora Eccles Harrison Mus. Art, Pacific Lut. U., Oreg. Arts Commn., U. Iowa Mus. Art, The White House, Charles A. Wustum Mus. Fine Arts, others; featured in numerous profl. jours., art. mags., mags. and newspapers. Recipient 1st pl. awards, 1989; Nat. Endowment for Arts visual artist fellow, 1988. Avocation: gardening. Office: Foster/White Gallery 2255 S Hinds St Seattle WA 98144-6720

HIRONO, MAZIE KEIKO, state official; b. Fukushima, Japan, Nov. 3, 1947; came to U.S., 1955, naturalized, 1957; d. Laura Chie (Sato) H. B.A., U. Hawaii, 1970; J.D., Georgetown U., 1978. Dep. atty. gen., Honolulu, 1978-80; Shim, Tam, Kirimitsu & Naito, 1984-88; mem. Hawaii Ho. of Reps., Honolulu, 1980-94; elected lt. gov., 1994. Bd. dirs. Nuuanu YMCA, Honolulu, 1982-84, Moiliili Cmty. Ctr., Honolulu, 1984; dep. chair Dem. Nat. Com., 1997. Mem. U.S. Supreme Ct. Bar, Hawaii Bar Assn., Phi Beta Kappa. Democrat. Office: State Capitol Lt Governor's Office PO Box 3226 Honolulu HI 96801-3226

HIRSCH, ANTHONY T., physician; b. N.Y.C., Jan. 29, 1940; s. Robert S. and Minna Hirsch; m. Barbara Hershan, July 8, 1961; children: Deborah, Kenneth, Steven. BS cum laude, Tufts U., 1961, MD, 1965. Diplomate Am. Bd. Pediatrics, Am. Bd. Allergy-Immunology. Pvt. practice pediatrics Children's Med. Group, L.A., 1973-84; chair dept. pediatrics, dir. residency tng. program in pediatrics White Meml. Med. Ctr., L.A., 1984—. Capt. USAF, 1969-71. Fellow Am. Acad. Pediatrics (chair access task force Calif. br., mem. nat. access task force, chair coun. on pediatric practice), Am. Acad. Allergy-Immunology. Avocation: sailing. Office: White Meml Med Ctr Dept Pediatrics 1701 Cesar Chavez Ave #456 Los Angeles CA 90033-2410

HIRSCH, GILAH YELIN, artist, writer; b. Montreal, Quebec, Can., Aug. 24, 1944; came to U.S., 1963; d. Ezra and Shulamis (Borodensky) Y. BA, U. Calif., Berkeley, 1967; MFA, UCLA, 1970. Prof. of art Calif. State U., Dominguez Hills, L.A., 1973—; adj. prof. Internat. Coll., Guild of Tutors, L.A., 1980-87, Union Grad. Sch., Cin., 1990. Founding mem. Santa Monica (Calif.) Art Bank, 1983-85; bd. dirs. Dorland Mountain Colony, Temecula, Calif., 1984-88. Recipient Disting. Artist award Calif. State U., 1985, Found. Rsch. award, 1988, 89, 97, 98; grantee Nat. Endowment for the Arts, 1985; Dorland Mountain Colony fellow, 1981-84, MacDowell Colony fellow, N.H., 1987, Banff Ctr. for the Arts fellow, Can., 1985; named artist-in-residence RIM Inst., Payson, Ariz., 1989-90, Tamarind Inst. of Lithography, Albuquerque, 1973, Rockefeller Bellagio Ctr., Italy, 1992, Tyrone Guthrie Ctr. for Arts, Annamahkerrig, Ireland, 1993, creative rsch. award Sally Canova Rsch. Scholarship and Creative Activities awards program, 1997, 98. Office: Calif State Univ Dominguez Hills 1000 E Victoria St Carson CA 90747-0001

HIRSCH, JUDD, actor; b. N.Y.C., Mar. 15, 1935; s. Joseph Sidney and Sally (Kitzis) H.; m. Bonni Chalkin, Dec. 24, 1992. BS in Physics, CCNY, 1960. Broadway appearances in Barefoot in the Park, 1966, Knock Knock, 1976 (Drama Desk award for best featured actor), Chapter Two, 1977-78, Talley's Folly, 1980, I'm Not Rappaport, 1985-86 (Tony award for best actor in play 1986, Outer Critics Circle award, 1986), Conversations with My Father, 1992 (Tony award for best actor in play 1992, Outer Critics Circle award, 1992), A Thousand Clowns, 1996; off-Broadway appearances in On the Necessity of Being Polygamous, 1963, Scuba Duba, 1967-69, King of the United States, 1972, Mystery Play, 1972, Hot L Baltimore, 1973, Prodigal, 1973, Knock Knock, 1975, Talley's Folly, 1979 (Obie award), The Seagull, 1983, I'm Not Rappaport, 1985, Below the Belt, 1996; regional appearences include Theater for Living Arts, Phila., 1969-70, Line of Least Existence, Harry Noon and Night, The Recruiting Officer, Annenberg Ctr., Phila., 1971, Hough in Blazes, Conversations with My Father, Seattle Repertory, 1991, L.A., 1993, Scarborough, Eng., 1994, London, 1995, Death of a Salesman, Chapel Hill, N.C., 1994, Robbers, Long Wharf Theater, 1995, Death of a Salesman Manitoba Theatre Ctr., Winnipeg and Royal Alexandra Theatre, Toronto, 1997; stock and tour appearances in A Thousand Clowns, Threepenny Opera, Fantastiks, Woodstock, N.Y., 1964, Peterpat, Houston and Ft. Worth, 1970, Harvey, Chgo., 1971, And Miss Reardon Drinks a Little, Palm Beach, Fla., 1972, I'm Not Rappaport, nat. tour, 1987; TV appearances include The Keegans, 1975, Medical Story, 1975, Delvecchio series, 1976-77, Rhoda, 1977, Taxi series, 1978-83 (Emmy award for best actor in a comedy series, 1981, 1983), Noel Edmunds Saturday Road Show, 1990 (Eng.), Dear John series (Golden Globe award 1988), 1988-92, George and Leo, 1997; TV movies include The Law, 1974, Fear on Trial, 1975, The Legend of Valentino, 1975, The Halloween That Almost Wasn't, 1979, Sooner or Later, 1979, Marriage Is Alive and Well, 1980, First Steps, 1985, Brotherly Love, 1985, The Great Escape-Untold Story, 1988, She Said No, 1990, Betrayal of Trust, 1993, Color of Justice, 1997, Rocky Marciano and Man on the Moon, 1999; films include King of the Gypsies, 1978, Ordinary People (nominated Acad. Award), 1980, Without a Trace, 1983, Teachers, 1984, The Goodbye People, 1984, Running on Empty, 1988, Independence Day, 1996. Mem. Acad. Motion Picture Arts and Scis., Acad. TV Arts and Scis., Screen Actors Guild, Actors Equity Assn., AFTRA. Office: care J Wolfe Provident Fin Mgmt 10345 W Olympic Blvd Los Angeles CA 90064-2548

HIRSCH, KATHLEEN L., realtor; b. St. Louis, Apr. 8, 1944; d. Lawrence William and Lucille Ann (Swanson) Loptien; m. Peter Leander Hirsch, July 14, 1968 (div. June 1981). Student, U. Chgo., 1962-63, No. Ill. U., 1963-64; BA in Biology magna cum laude, Lone Mountain Coll., 1975. Reservation agt. Ea. Airlines, Chgo., 1964-66, Pan Am. Airways, Chgo., 1966-68; traffic clk. Heublein Inc., San Francisco, 1970-72; circulation libr. Lone Mountain Coll., San Francisco, 1974-77; supr. Blue Shield, San Francisco, 1977-80; mktg. rep. Cetus Corp., Emeryville, Calif., 1980-84; realtor Mason McDuffie R.E., Alameda, Calif., 1985-88, Harbor Bay Realty, Alameda, 1988—. Mem. Calif. Assn. Realtors (grad. Realtor Inst. 1995, bd. dirs. 1990, 91), Alameda Assn. Realtors (past pres. 1991, bd. dirs. 1988-92, chair, membership v.p. 1988), Realtor Inst., Women's Coun. Realtors (relocation and referral cert. 1992). Democrat. Unitarian. Avocations: interior design collector, modern art, reading, travel. Office: Harbor Bay Realty 885 Island Dr Ste 200 Alameda CA 94502-6743

HIRSCH, STEVEN A., lawyer; b. Ariz., 1955. BA with distinction, U. Ariz., 1977, JD with high distinction, 1980. Bar: Ariz. 1980; cert. real estate specialist State Bar Ariz. Law clerk to Hon. James D. Hathaway Ariz. Ct. Appeals Divsn. 2, 1980-81; ptnr. Bryan Cave, Phoenix, Ariz. Editorial bd. Ariz. Bar Jour., 1986-89. Fellow Ariz. Bar Found. (bd. dirs. 1989-97, pres. 1995); mem. ABA (del. and dist. rep. young lawyers divsn. assembly 1990-92), Maricopa County Bar Assn. (bd. dirs. 1987-88), Order of Coif. Office: Bryan Cave 2 N Central Ave Ste 2200 Phoenix AZ 85004-1007*

HIRSCH, WALTER, economist, researcher; b. Phila., Apr. 21, 1917; s. Arnold Harry and Ann Belle (Feldstein) H.; m. Leanore Brod, Feb. 12, 1939 (dec. 1985); stepchild, Stephen M. Gold; children: Jeffrey A., Robert A.; m. June Freedman Gold Clark, Dec. 16, 1986. BS in Econs., U. Pa., 1938; LLD (hons.), Chapman Coll., 1968. Economist U.S. Bur. Stats., Washington and N.Y.C, 1946-50, Dept. USAF, Washington, 1950-51, Nat. Prodn. Auth., Washington, 1952-53; dir. indsl. mobilization Bur. Ordnance Dept. USN, [illegible] 1954-56; ops. rsch. analyst Bur. Supplies and Accts. Dept. USN, Arlington, Va., 1956-58; economist, ops. rsch. analyst Internat. Security Affairs Office Sec. of Def., Arlington, 1958-61; chief ops., rsch. analyst Gen. Svcs. Adminstrn., Washington, 1961-63; ops. rsch. analyst Spl. Projects Office [illegible] U.S. Office

Edn., San Francisco, 1967-72; cons. on loan to Office of Dean Acad. Planning San Jose (Calif.) State U., 1972-74. Author: Unit Man-Hour Dynamics for Peace or War, 1957, Internal Study for Office Secretary of Defense: Sharing the Cost of International Security, 1961. Vol. De Young Mus., San Francisco, 1981-84, Calif. Palce of Legion of Honor, Phila. Mus. Art, 1984-86; pres. Met. Area Reform Temples, Washington, Nat. Fedn. Temple Brotherhoods; supporter Phila. Orch., San Francisco Symphony, San Francisco Conservatory Music, Curtis Inst. With USAAF, 1942-46. Recipient Meritorious Civilian Svc. award Navy Dept., 1956. Mem. Pa. Athletic Club, Commonwealth Club of Calif., World Affairs Council, Press Club of San Francisco, Phi Delta Kappa. Avocations: collecting art, music, chess, poetry.

HIRSCHFELD, GERALD JOSEPH, cinematographer; b. N.Y.C., Apr. 25, 1921; s. Ralph and Kate (Zirker) H.; m. Sarnell Ogus, June 5, 1945 (div. June 1972); children—Alec, Marc, Eric, Burt; m. Julia Warren Tucker, July 28, 1981. Student, Columbia U., 1938-40. Cinematic instr. New Inst. for Film, Bklyn., 1947-49; freelance dir. photography for TV and Film N.Y.C., 1949-54; dir. photography, v.p. MPO Videotronics, Inc., N.Y.C., 1954-72; free-lance dir. and cameraman, cinematographer, N.Y.C. and Hollywood, Calif., 1972—; cinema instr. Am. Film Inst., L.A., 1980, Tahoe Film and Video Workshop, Lake Tahoe, Nev., 1984, Washington Film and Video Assn., 1987; staff mem. Internat. Film and Video Workshops, Rockport, Maine, 1996-99, cinema instr. So. Oreg. U., 1998—. Cinematographer for films including: Young Frankenstein, My Favorite Year, Diary of a Mad Housewife, The Neon Empire (ACE award nomination 1990); author: Image Control, 1992 (Kraszna-Krausz Internat. Book Award 1994). With Signal Corps, U.S. Army, 1941-45. Recipient Billy Bitzer award Internat. Photographers of the Motion Picture Industry, 1994. Mem. Internat. Photographer's Union, IATSE, Am. Soc. Cinematographers, Acad. Motion Picture Arts and Scis. Avocations: woodworker, miniaturist. Fax: 541-488-8742. E-mail: gjhfilms@mind.net. Home and Office: 425 Ashland St Ashland OR 97520-3104

HIRSCHFIELD, ALAN JAMES, entrepreneur. BS, U. Okla.; MBA, Harvard U. V.p. Allen & Co., Inc., 1959-67; v.p. fin., dir. Warner Bros. Seven Arts, Inc., 1967-68; with Am. Diversified Enterprises, Inc., 1968-73; pres., CEO Columbia Pictures Industries, N.Y.C., 1973-78; vice chmn., COO 20th Century-Fox Film Corp., L.A., 1979-81, chmn. bd., CEO, 1981-85; cons., investor entertainment industries, L.A., 1985-89; mng. dir. Wertheim Schroder & Co., L.A., 1990-92; co-CEO Data Broadcasting Corp., 1990—; bd. dirs. Cantel Internat., Inc., Chyron Inc. Bd. dirs. Cure for Lymphoma Found., 1998, Nat. Mus. Am. Indian George Gustav Heye Ctr., 1997—; trustee Grand Teton Music Festival, 1998—. Office: PO Box 7443 Jackson WY 83002-7443

HIRSCHMANN, FRANZ GOTTFRIED, aerospace executive; b. Kempten, Germany, Oct. 4, 1945; came to U.S., 1973; s. Kurt Rudolf G. and Linda (Krieger) H.; m. Cindy Villarica, Nov. 27, 1992; children: Dillon G., Michael A. BS, FWG Coll., Cologne, Fed. Republic Germany, 1965; MA, U. Bonn, Fed. Republic Germany, 1973; MBA, Pepperdine U., 1981. Mktg. mgr. Western U.S. and S. Am. regions United Techs./Ambac, L.A., 1978-80; mktg. mgr. Western U.S. and Pacific regions Buehler Inc., L.A. and N.C., 1981-83; mgr. internat. mktg. Gen. Dynamics, Pomona, Calif., 1983-84, mgr. info. svcs., 1984-88, mgr. spl. projects, 1988-89; mgr. competitor analyses Hughes Aircraft Co., Canoga Park, Calif., 1989-91; mgr. bus. devel. and market rsch. Hughes Aircraft Co., Canoga park, Calif., 1991-93, mgr. strategic planning, 1993—; owner cons. bus., 1992—. Author: Mandaic Inscription, 1970; inventor deciphering lang. computer. Vol. Lincoln Club, L.A., 1981; co-founder Retinitis Pigmentosa Found. Mem. Nat. Mgmt. Assn., Pepperdine U. Alumni Assn., Sierra Club (leader, vice chmn. coun. 1990-93). Democrat. Lutheran. Avocations: photography, hiking, sailing, yoga, ancient languages. Home: 406 Las Riendas Dr Fullerton CA 92835-1308 Office: Hughes Aircraft Co 8433 Fallbrook Ave # 26146N Canoga Park CA 91304-3226

HIRSHBERG, JERILYN BURDETTE, biologist, naturalist; b. Berkeley, Calif., Feb. 19, 1942; d. Lee and Burdette Ann (Winkler) H. BA in Zoology, U. Calif., Davis, 1965; MS in Ecology, San Diego State U., 1980. Owner JBH Biol. Surveys, Julian, Calif., 1985—. Discovered Arabis hirshbergiae at Cuyamaca Lake; contbr. articles to profl. publs. Office: JBH Biol Surveys PO Box 2 Julian CA 92036-0002

HIRST, ROBERT H., curator, English educator; b. N.Y.C., Aug. 11, 1941; s. George Keble and Charlotte (Hart) H.; m. Margaret Wade, Mar. 3, 1978; children: Thomas W., Emma C. BA in English, Harvard U., 1963; MA in English, U. Calif., Berkeley, 1965, PhD in English, 1976. Tchg. asst. dept. English U. Calif., Berkeley, 1964-66, prin. editor, Mark Twain project, 1966-76, gen. editor, Mark Twain project head, curator papers, 1980—; asst. prof. dept. English UCLA, 1976-79; instr. U. Calif., Berkeley, 1970-71; presenter and lectr. in field. contbr. articles to profl. jours. Regents Jr. Faculty fellow UCLA, 1978-79, Regents Grad. fellow, 1969-70, Woodrow Wilson fellow, 1963-64; grantee NEH, 1988-97, UCLA, 1977-79; recipient Disting. Achievement award Mark Twain Cir. Am., 1994. Mem. MLA (chmn. com. on scholarly editions 1996-98, Disting. Scholarly Edition award 1993-94). Fax: (510) 642-6349. E-mail: rhirst@library.berkeley.edu. Home: 3550 Robinson Dr Oakland CA 94602-4140 Office: Univ Calif 480 Doe Library # 6000 Berkeley CA 94720-6021

HIRST, WILMA ELIZABETH, retired psychologist; b. Shenandoah, Iowa; d. James H. and Lena (Donahue) Ellis; m. Clyde Henry Hirst (dec. Nov. 1969); 1 child, Donna Jean (Mrs. Alan Robert Goss). AB in Elementary Edn., Colo. State Coll., 1948, EdD in Ednl. Psychology, 1954; MA in Psychology, U. Wyo., 1951. Lic. psychologist, Wyo. Elem. tchr., Cheyenne, Wyo., 1945-49, remedial reading instr., 1949-54; assoc. prof. edn., dir. campus sch. Nebr. State Tchrs. Coll., Kearney, 1954-56; sch. psychologist, head dept. spl. edn. Cheyenne (Wyo.) pub. schs., 1956-57, sch. psychologist, guidance coordinator, 1957-66, dir. rsch. and spl. projects, 1966-76, also pupil personnel, 1973-84; pvt. cons., 1984-98, ret., 1998; vis. asst. prof. U. So. Calif., summer 1957, Omaha U., summer 1958, U. Okla., summers 1959, 60; vis. assoc. prof. U. Nebr., 1961, U. Wyo., summer 1962, 64, extension divsn., Kabul, Afghanistan, 1970, Cath. U., Goias, Brazil, 1974; investigator HEW, 1965-69; prin. investigator effectiveness of spl. edn., 1983-84; participant seminar Russian Press Women and Am. Fedn. Press Women, Moscow and Leningrad, 1973. Sec.-treas. Laramie County Coun. Community Svcs., 1962; mem. speakers bur., mental health orgn.; active Little Theatre, 1936-60, Girl Scout Leaders Assn., 1943-50; mem. Adv. Coun. on Retardation to Gov.'s Commn.; mem., sec. Wyo. Bd. Psychologist Examiners, 1965-71 vice chmn., 1971-74; chmn. Mayor's Model Cities Program, 1969; mem. Gov.'s Com. Jud. Reform, 1972; adv. council Div. Exceptional Children, Wyo. Dept. Edn., 1974; mem. transit adv. group City of Cheyenne, 1974; bd. dirs. Wyo. Children's Home Soc., 1968, treas., 1978-84; rsch. on women's prisons State of Wyo., 1989; bd. dirs. Goodwill Industries Wyo., chmn., 1981-83; mem. Wyo. exec. com. Partners of Americas, 1970-86; del. Internat. Conv. Ptnrs. of Ams., Jamaica, 1987; del., moderator pers. com. Presbytery of Wyo., 1987-90, mem. mission program com., 1991-95, spl. gifts com. 1994—; bd. dirs. workforce opportunities adv. com. AARP, 1992-94; Friendship Force ambassador to Honduras, 1979; chmn. bd. SE Wyo. Mental Health Center, 1969; elder 1st Presbyn. Ch., Cheyenne, 1978—, also bd. deacons; chmn. adv. assessment com. Wyo. State Office Handicapped Children, 1980, 81; mem. allocations com. United Way of Laramie County, active People to People Internat., Child Welfare Project, 1992; participant People to People Internat. Citizen Amb. Program, child welfare project assist Lithuania, Latvia, Estonia, 1992. Named Woman of Year, Cheyenne Bus. and Profl. Women, 1974. Diplomate Am. Bd. Profl. Psychology. Fellow Am. Acad. Sch. Psychology; mem. APA, ASCD, Internat. Council Psychologists (chmn. Wyo. div. 1980-85), AAUP, Am. Assn. State Psychology Bds. (sec.-treas. 1970-73), Wyo. Psychol. Assn. (pres. 1962-63), Laramie County Mental Health Assn. (bd. mem., corr. sec. 1963-69, pres.), Wyo. Mental Health Assn. (bd. mem.), Internat. Platform Assn., Am. Ednl. Research Assn., Assn. for Gifted (Wyo. pres. 1964-65), Am. Personnel and Guidance Assn., Am. Assn. Sch. Adminstrs., NEA (life, participant seminar to China 1978), AAUW, Cheyenne [illegible] 1964-66, mem. exec. bd. 1972-76), Nat. Fedn. Press Women (dir. 1979-85), DAR (vice regent Cheyenne chpt. 1975-77), AARP (state coordinator 1988—, preretirement planning specialist 1986-88, state coord. work force program, 1992—, leadership coun., state del. nat. conv. 1990, pilot project Wyo. state delivery for retirement planning 1990—, AARP Works, op. project state govt. edn. assn. and AARP work force vols. video for retirement planning statewide 1993, master trainer retirement planning 1993—, employment planning master trainer, 1994—, planning com. Area 8 Conf., leadership meeting 1994, mem. adv. coun. Laramie County Widowed Persons Svcs. 1995—, bd. dirs. 1996—), Psi Chi, Kappa Delta Pi, Pi Lambda Theta, Alpha Delta Kappa (pres. Wyo. Alpha 1965-66). Presbyn. Lodge Soc. Colonial Dames XVII Century, Order Eastern Star, Daus. of Nile. Clubs: Wyo. Press Women, Zonta (pres. Cheyenne 1965-66, treas. dist. 12 1974). Author: Know Your School Psychologist, 1963; Effective School Psychology for School Administrators, 1980. Home and Office: 3458 Green Valley Rd Cheyenne WY 82001-6124

HIRT, CYRIL WILLIAM, physicist; b. Flushing, N.Y., Dec. 20, 1936; s. Cyril W. and Margret E. (Plumb) H.; m. Virginia L. Warren, June 22, 1968; children: Heather, Amber. BS, U. Mich., 1958, MS, 1959, PhD, 1963. Staff scientist Los Alamos (N.Mex.) Nat. lab., 1963-72, group leader, 1973-80; chief scientist Sci. Applications Inc., La Jolla, Calif., 1972-73; founder, pres. Flow Sci. Inc., Los Alamos, 1980—. Contbr. numerous articles to profl. jours. Avocations: cooking, reading, hiking, skiing. Office: Flow Sci Inc 1257 40th St Los Alamos NM 87544-1906

HIRZEL, ROBIN LYNN, editor; b. Wenatchee, Wash., Nov. 17, 1970; d. Donald Dwayne and Carolyn Joan (Walker) H. BA in Bus. Adminstrn., English Lit., Williams Woods U., 1994. Circulation mgr. Appaloosa Jour., Moscow, Idaho, 1994-95, asst. editor, 1995-97, editor, 1997—. Avocation: skydiving. Office: Appaloosa Jour 5070 Highway 8 W Moscow ID 83843-4000

HISAKA, ERIC TORU, plastic surgeon; b. Stockton, Calif., 1951. MD, U. Calif., Davis, 1977. Plastic surgeon Valley Care Hosp., Pleasanton, Calif.; also with Tri Valley Surgical Ctr., Pleasanton, Calif. Fax: 925-463-0748. Office: 5720 Stoneridge Mall Rd # 13 Pleasanton CA 94588-2828

HISE, MARK ALLEN, dentist; b. Chgo., Jan. 17, 1950; s. Clyde and Rose T. (Partipilo) H. AA, Mt. San Antonio Coll., Walnut, Calif., 1972; BA with highest honors, U. Calif., Riverside, 1974; MS, U. Utah, 1978; DDS, UCLA, 1983. Instr. sci. NW Acad., Houston, 1978-79; chmn. curriculum med. coll. prep program UCLA, 1980-85; instr. dentistry Coll. of Redwoods, Eureka, Calif., 1983; practice dentistry Arcata, Calif., 1983—; participant numerous radio and TV appearances. Editor: Preparing for the MCAT, 1983-85; contbr. articles to profl. jours.; speaker in field. Recipient awards for underwater photography; Henry Carter scholar U. Calif., 1973, Calif. State scholar 1973, 74, Regents scholar U. Calif., 1973; Calif. State fellow, 1975, NIH fellow, 1975-79. Mem. AAAS, ADA, Calif. Dental Assn., Acad. Gen. Dentistry, Nat. Soc. for Med. Rsch., North Coast Scuba Club. Roman Catholic. Avocation: underwater photography. Home and Office: 1225 B St Arcata CA 95521-5936

HISERT, GEORGE A., lawyer; b. Schenectady, N.Y., Sept. 18, 1944. BS summa cum laude, Brown U., 1966, MS, 1966; JD cum laude, U. Chgo., 1970. Bar: Calif. 1971. Law clk. to Hon. Sterry R. Waterman U.S. Ct. Appeals (2nd cir.), 1970-71; ptnr. McCutchen, Doyle, Brown & Enersen, San Francisco, 1977-93; now ptnr. Brobeck, Phleger & Harrison. Mem. editl. bd. Chgo. Law Rev., 1969-70; ABA sect. on bus. law liaison to UCC Permanent Editl. Bd. Mem. ABA (subcom. letter of credit, subcom. secured trans. of uniform comml. code com. bus. law sect., subcom. on syndications and loan participations of comml fin. svc. com., bus. law sect.), Internat. Bar Assn. (banking law com., bus. law sect.), State Bar Calif. (uniform comml. code com. bus. law sect., vice-chair 1992-93, chair 1993-94), Am. Coll.Comml. Fin. Lawyers, Order of Coif, Sigma Xi. Office: Brobeck Phleger & Harrison Spear St Tower One Market Plz San Francisco CA 94105

HISKES, DOLORES G., educator; b. Chgo.; d. Leslie R. and Dagmar (Brown) Grant; m. John R. Hiskes; children: Robin Caproni, Grant. Student, U. Ill., Chgo. Presenter workshops in devel. and implementation of tutoring programs and ednl. materials. *Dolores has tutored reading for over 30 years, collected classic old reading and spelling texts from all over the world, and developed a special teaching technique ("eyerobics") that helps prevent or correct reversals. She has simplified and incorporated the best of all this information into one comprehensive reading and spelling text. Phonics Pathways is the result of that effort. She continues to write new educational material and publish articles in professional journals such as The California Reader, Winter 1997; Reading Matters, Association of American Educators, October/November 1997; and the National Right To Read Report, February 1998.* Author/illustrator: Phonics Pathways, Pyramid, The Dorbooks, The Short-Vowel Dictionary; developer ednl. games: The Train Game, Blendit!, Wordwatch. Mem. Assn. Am. Educators, Assn. Ednl. Therapists, Calif. Assn. of Res. Specialists, Orton Dyslexia Soc., Learning Disabilities Assn., Nat. Right to Read Found., The Calif. Reading Assn., Pubs. Mktg. Assn., Pacific Ednl. Mktg. Assn., Calif. Watercolor Soc., Commonwealth Club of Calif., Bay Area Ind. Pubs. Assn., Calif. Assn. Resource Specialists. Avocations: watercolors, travel, reading, exercise. E-mail: dolores@dorbooks.com. Office: Dorbooks PO Box 2588 Livermore CA 94551-2588

HITCHCOCK, VERNON THOMAS, farmer, lawyer; b. Selma, Ind., Feb. 21, 1919; s. Lucian Elmer and Loda Alice (King) H.; m. Betty Kathryn Orr, May 24, 1949; children: Brenda, Linda, Nancy, Debra, Randolph. BS in Agr., Purdue U., 1940; JD, Stanford U., 1953. Bar: Calif. 1954, U.S. Supreme Ct. 1961. Pilot Southwest Airways, San Francisco, 1946, TWA, Kansas City, Mo., 1947-51; pvt. practice Healdsburg, Calif., 1954-55; dep. atty. gen. State of Calif., Sacramento, 1956; dep. county counsel Sonoma County, Santa Rosa, Calif., 1957-65; exec. dir. Libyan Aviation Co., Tripoli, 1966-67; legal counsel Sonoma County Schs., 1967-82; farm mgr. Selma, Ind., 1975—; originator Freedom Under Law program. Author: The Airline to Infinity. Active Am. Security Council, 1965—. Served to comdr. USNR, 1941-79. Mem. Res. Officers Assn., Naval Order U.S., Commonwealth Club San Francisco, Quiet Birdmen, Odd Fellows. Republican. Episcopalian. Avocations: music, amateur radio.

HIX, PHYLLIS MARIE, lawyer; b. Bloomfield, Iowa, Mar. 28, 1936. Student, U. Iowa, 1954-56; BS in Occupational Therapy cum laude, U. So. Calif., 1959, JD, 1962. Bar: Calif. 1963. Assoc. Lawler, Felix & Hall, 1963, Overton, Lyman & Prince, 1963-66, Dryden, Harrington & Swartz, 1967-74; pvt. practice, Kernville, Calif., 1974-76, 88—; ptnr. Kurlander & Hix, San Marino, Calif., 1976-88; mem. commn. on jud. nominees evaluation State of Calif., 1979-81, arbitration panel Los Angeles County Superior Ct.; Mcpl. Judge Pro Tem; Superior Ct. Settlement Officer, arbitrator. Co-author (column) Strange As It Seems. Bd. dirs. Pasadena Tournament of Roses Found., 1994-97, treas., 1997. Mem. Calif. Bar Assn. (chmn. resolutions com. 1977, state bar ct., asst. presiding referee, exec. com. 1976-80, bd. govs. 1981-84), L.A. County Bar Assn. (exec. com. 1969-72, chmn. legal med. com. 1974-75, adv. com.), Assn. So. Calif. Def. Counsel (bd. dirs. 1973-75, 77-79), Am. Bd. Trial Advs. (mem. exec. com. 1975-76), Def. Rsch. Inst., Calif. Women Lawyers (founding mem.), Am. Arbitration Assn. (nat. bd. dirs. 1976-80), Am. Indian Bar Assn., Internat. Assn. Def. Counsel, Back Country Horsemen of Calif. (v.p. 1988-90), U.S. Marshals Posse, Kern County Sheriff's Mounted Posse. Fax: 760-376-3764. Office: 112 Buena Vista PO Bin DD Kernville CA 93238

HJELMSTAD, WILLIAM DAVID, lawyer; b. Casper, Wyo., Apr. 4, 1954; s. Alvin Gordon and A. Thecla (Walz) H.; m. Jenny M. Dubé, Nov. 27, 1993; children: Jennifer Ashley, Allison Caitlin. AA in Social Sci., Casper Coll., 1974; BS in Psychology, U. Wyo., 1976, JD, 1979. Bar: Wyo. 1979, U.S. Dist. Ct. Wyo. 1979. Dept. county pros. atty. Hot Springs County, Thermopolis, Wyo., 1979-80; asst. pub. defender Natrona County, Casper, Wyo., 1980-82; sole practice, Casper, 1981— Mem. ATLA, ABA (mem. family law com. 1983-84, adoption com. 1983-84), Wyo. State Bar Assn. (mem. alcohol and substance abuse com., lawyers assistance com. 1988-95), Natrona County Bar Assn., Wyo. Trial Lawyers Assn., Am. Judicature Soc., Acad. Family Mediators, U. Wyo. Alumni Assn., Casper Coll. [illegible] Assn., Wyo. Cowboy Shootout Com., Elks, Kiwanis. Home: PO Box 90001 Casper WY 82609 1001

HJORTSBERG, WILLIAM REINHOLD, author; b. N.Y.C., Feb. 23, 1941; s. Helge Reinhold and Anna Ida (Welti) H.; m. Marian Souidee Renken, June 2, 1962 (div. 1982); children—Lorca Isabel, Max William.; m. Sharon Leroy, July 21, 1982 (div. 1985). BA, Dartmouth Coll., 1962; post-grad., Yale U., 1962-63, Stanford U., 1967-68. Ind. author, screenwriter, 1969—; adj. prof. media and theatre arts Mont. State U., 1991—. Author: Alp, 1969, Gray Matters, 1971, Symbiography, 1973, Toro! Toro! Toro!, 1974, Falling Angel, 1978, Tales & Fables, 1985, Nevermore, 1994, films: Thunder and Lightning, 1977, Legend, 1986; co-author TV film: Georgia Peaches, 1980; contbg. editor Rocky Mountain Mag., 1979; contbr. fiction to Realist, Playboy, Cornell Rev., Penthouse, Oui, Sports Illustrated; contbr. criticism to N.Y. Times Book Rev. Recipient Playboy Editorial award, 1971, 78; Wallace Stegner fellow, 1967-68; Nat. Endowment Arts grantee, 1976. Mem. Authors Guild, Writers Guild Am. Avocations: fly fishing, skiing, collecting modern first editions, art, antique toys. Home and Office: Main Boulder RT Mc Leod MT 59052

HO, APRIL AHULANI, sales professional, choreographer; b. Harbor City, Calif., Nov. 29, 1973; d. Richard Sheu Tim and Hazel Lani Ho. BA, U. Hawaii-Manoa, 1995. Choreographer, co-prodr. Boys and Girls Club Honolulu, 1995; choreographer Dance Ctrl.-Ctrl. YMCA, Honolulu, 1995—; telecom. mgr. Jani-King Hawaii, Honolulu, 1997; asst. supr. sales GTE Hawaiian Tel., Honolulu, 1998—; asst. promotions dir. Hawaii Dance Alliance, Pearl City, 1997-98. Asst. dir. (documentary) Sukeroku, 1995 (Student Video/Film Assn. award 1996); asst. to prodr. (documentary) For All of Us, 1995; screenwriter Umi, 1997; actress Byrds of Paradise-Steven Bochco Prodn., Honolulu, 1994; contbr. articles to mags. Acad. scholar Bernice Pauahi Bishop Estate/Kamehameha Schs., Honolulu, 1993-95, Kua'ana Student Svcs., Honolulu, 1994-95. Mem. Internat. Brotherhood Elec. Workers, Am. Lung Assn. (guest spokesperson/entertainer 1997-98), Maui Writers Conf., U. Hawaii-Hilo Japanese Club (v.p. 1991-92). Avocations: choreography, dance, film, writing.

HO, IWAN, research plant pathologist; b. Souzhou, Jiangsu, China, Apr. 15, 1925; came to U.S., 1956; m. Mei-Chun Chang, Nov. 29, 1975; 1 child, Tomur M. BS, Nat. Shanghai U., 1946; MS, La. State U., 1958; PhD, Oreg. State U., 1984. Microbiologist Seattle Pub. Health Dept., 1962-66; research plant physiologist Forestry Scis. Lab., Corvallis, Oreg., 1970—; courtesy asst. prof. Coll. Forestry, Oreg. State U. Mem. Mycol. Soc. Am., Am. Soc. Plant Physiologists, Internat. Soc. Plant Molecular Biology, Sigma Xi. Democrat. Episcopalian. Avocations: painting, violin, stamp collecting. Home: 1686 SW Bullevard St Philomath OR 97370-9538 Office: Forestry Sci Lab Pacific NW Rsch Sta 3200 SW Jefferson Way Corvallis OR 97331-8550

HO, PIN, artist, consultant; b. Taipei, Taiwan, May 13, 1971; s. Sung Ming and Chin Yu (Wu) H. BA, Art Ctr. Coll. of Design, Pasadena, 1996. Designer, art dir. LTC & C Inc., Gardena, Calif., 1991-94; free-lance illustrator, designer Gardena, 1994—; key asst. DreamWork SKG, Glendale, Calif., 1997—. Avocations: sketching, painting, sculpting, music, bugs. Home: 3216 W 155th St Gardena CA 90249-4404 Office: DreamWork SKG 1000 Flower St Glendale CA 91201-3007

HOADLEY, WALTER EVANS, economist, financial executive, lay worker; b. San Francisco, Aug. 16, 1916; s. Walter Evans Sr. and Marie Howland (Preece) H.; m. Virginia Alm, May 20, 1939; children: Richard Alm, Jean Elizabeth (Mrs. Donald A. Peterson). AB, U. Calif., 1938, MA, 1940, PhD, 1946; D in Comml. Sci., Franklin and Marshall Coll., 1963; LLD (hon.), Golden Gate U., 1968, U. Pacific, 1979; hon. degree, El Instituto Technologico Autonomo de Mexico, 1974. Collaborator U.S. Bur. Agrl. Econs., 1938-39; rsch. economist Calif. Gov.'s Reemployment Commn., 1939, Calif. Gov.'s State Planning Bd., 1941; rsch. economist, teaching fellow U. Calif., 1938-41, supr. indsl. mgmt. war tng. office, 1941-42; econ. adviser U. Chgo. Civil Affairs Tng. Sch., 1945; sr. economist Fed. Res. Bank Chgo., 1942-49; economist Armstrong World Industries, Lancaster, Pa., 1949-54, treas., 1954-60, v.p., treas., 1960-66, dir., 1962-87; sr. v.p., chief economist, mem. mng. com. Bank of Am. NT & SA, San Francisco, 1966-68, exec. v.p., chief economist, mem. mng. com., mem. mgmt. adv. council, chmn. subs., 1968-81; ret., 1981; sr. research fellow Hoover Inst., Stanford U., 1981—; dep. chmn. Fed. Res. Bank, Phila., 1960-61, chmn., 1962-66; chmn. Conf. Fed. Res. Chmn., 1966; faculty Sch. Banking U. Wis., 1945-49, 55, 58-66; adviser various U.S. Govt. Agys.; Wright Internat. Bd. Econ and Investment Advisors, 1987—; spl. adviser U.S. Congl. Budget Office, 1975-87; mem. pub. adv. bd. U.S. Dept. Commerce, 1970-74; mem. White House Rev. Com. for Balance Payment Stats., 1963-65, Presdl. Task Force on Growth, 1969-70, Presdl. Task Force on Land Utilization, Presdl. Conf. on Inflation, 1974; gov. Com. on Developing Am. Capitalism, 1977—, chmn., 1987-88; dir. PLM Internat., 1989-97, Transisco Industries, Inc., 1981-95, Davis/Selected/Venture Advisors, 1981-96. Mem. Meth. Ch. Commn. on World Svc. and Fin. Phila. conf., 1957-64, chmn. investment com., 1964-66; bd. dirs., exec. com. Internat. Mgmt. and Devel. Inst., 1976-97; trustee Pacific Sch. Religion, 1968-89; adviser Nat. Commn. to Study Nursing and Nursing Edn., 1968-73; trustee Duke U., 1968-73, pres.'s assoc., 1973-80; trustee Golden Gate U., 1974-94, chmn. investment com., 1977-93; trustee World Wildlife U.S. Fund The Conservation Found., 1987-90; mem. periodic chmn. adminstrv. bd. Trinity United Meth. Ch., Berkeley, Calif., 1966-84; mem. adminstrv. bd., advisor Lafayette (Calif.) United Meth. Ch., 1984—; mem. bd. overseers vis. com. Harvard Coll. Econs., 1969-74; chmn. investment com. Calif.-Nev. Meth. Found., 1968-75, mem., 1976-91; mem. Calif. Gov.'s Coun. Econ. and Bus. Devel., 1978-82, chmn., 1980-82; trustee Hudson Inst., 1979-84; co-chmn. San Francisco Mayor's Fiscal Adv. Com., 1978-81, mem. 1981-96; chmn. Bay Area Econ. Advisers, 1982—; spl . adviser Presdl. Cabinet Com. Innovation, 1978-79; mem. Calif. State Internat. Adv. Com., 1986-94; regent U. Calif., 1990-91; mem. adv. coun. Calif. Environ. Tech. Ptnrshp., 1993-94; mem. econ. adv. coun. Calif. Inst. Fed. Policy Rsch., 1994—; trustee Internat. Ho. U. Calif. Devel. Com., 1994—, chmn., 1995-97. Fellow Am. Statis. Assn. (v.p., bd. dirs. 1952-54, pres. 1958), Nat. Assn. Bus. Economists (San Francisco chpt. exec. com. 1989—); mem. Am. Fin. Assn. (bd. dirs. 1955-56, pres. 1969), Conf. Bus. Economists (chmn. 1962), Atlantic Coun. of U.S. (bd. dirs. 1985—), Internat. Acad. Mgmt., U.S. Coun. for Internat. Bus. (sr. trustee 1992—), Commonwealth Club of Calif. (pres. 1987, chmn. pub. affairs-comm. com. 1995-98), Am. Econ. Assn., Am. Mktg. Assn., Am. Bankers Assn. (chmn. urban and cmty. affairs com. 1972-73, mem. econ. adv. coun. 1976-78), Nat. Bur. Econ. Rsch. (bd. dirs. 1965-81), Western Econ. Assn. (bd. dirs., mem. steering com. 1966-94), U. Calif. Alumni Assn. (pres. 1989-91, chmn. investment com. 1983-89, 94-96, Alumnus of Yr. 1993), U.S. Nat. Com. on Pacific Econ. Coop. (vice chmn. 1984-89, mem. exec. com. 1989-94), Caux Internat. Roundtable (chmn. steering com. 1993-97), St. Francis Yacht Club, Commonwealth Club, Pacific Union Club, Bankers Club, Silverado Country Club, Phi Beta Kappa Assocs. (bd. dirs. 1986-95), Kappa Alpha. Office: Bank of Am Dept 3001-B 11th Fl 555 California St San Francisco CA 94104-1502

HOAG, JOHN ARTHUR, retired bank executive; b. Freeport, N.Y., Sept. 29, 1932; s. John Hoag and Viola (Babcock) Hobson; m. Jeanette Makaio, Dec. 5, 1959; children: Steve, Vanessa, Kanani. BS, U. Mo., 1955; grad., Pacific Coast Banking Sch., Wash., 1970; MBA, U. Hawaii, 1977. Account exec. Walston & Co., N.Y.C., 1960; mgmt. trainee 1st Hawaiian Bank, Honolulu, 1960, br. mgr., Hilo, 1968, Island v.p., 1970-76, sr. v.p., mgr., 1976, exec. v.p. loan group, 1979, pres., 1989-94, also bd. dirs.; vice chmn. bd. dirs., 1994; retired 1st Hawaiian Bank, 1995; pres. 1st Hawaiian Inc., Honolulu, 1991-95, also bd. dirs.; vice chm. 1st Interstate Bank Hawaii, Honolulu, 1991—; vice chmn. of bd., 1994—, ret., 1995; chmn. bd. Hawaii Reserves, Inc.; vice chmn. Pioneer Fed. Savs. Bank; bd. dirs. Castle Med. Ctr., BancWest Corp. Bd. regents Tokai Internat. Coll., 1992-95, U. Hawaii, 1995—; bd. dirs. Hawaii Med. Svc. Assn., 1981-93, Honolulu Polynesian Cultural Ctr, 1990-93, Kapiolani Med. Ctr. for Women and Children, Honolulu, 1989-95. Capt. USMC, 1955-60. Mem. Pres.' Club U. Hawaii, C. of C. Hawaii (chmn. bd. 1992-93). Mem. LDS Ch. Office: PO Box 3200 999 Bishop St Honolulu HI 96847 also: 1st Hawaiian Bank PO Box 3200 Honolulu HI 96847-0001*

HOAG, WILLIAM HERBERT, construction contractor; b. St. Paul, Jan. 29, 1934; s. Herbert S. and Mildred Hoag; m. Susan Bower, Mar 16, 1956 (div. 1995); children: William R., Robert T., Cynthia E. Student, Cerritos Coll., 1967-69. Roofer Okerstrom Roofing, Livonia, Mich., 1955-59; roofer L.A., 1959-70, Medford, Oreg., 1970-71; contractor Hoag Roofing Inc., Medford, Oreg., 1971-98. Mem. planning commn. Phoenix, 1996-97. With USN, 1951-54. Mem. Nat. Roofing Contractors Assn., Home Builders Assn., Medford C. of C. Republican. Protestant. Avocations: private pilot, volunteer search and rescue, amateur boxing coach.

HOAGLAND, PAMELA REDINGTON, educational consultant, administrator; b. Phoenix, June 2, 1937; d. George Appleton and Margaret Tweed (Rae) H. B.A., U. Ariz., 1959; MEd in Reading Edn., 1965, EdD in Reading and Psychology, 1973. Tchr. Tucson Unified Sch. Dist., 1959-73, asst. dir. instruction, reading, lang. arts, library svcs., 1980-89; co-founder, co-dir. Learning Devel. Ctr., Tucson, 1970-74; profl. devel. assoc. Internat. Reading Assn., 1973—; curriculum specialist and supr. Pima County Spl. Edn. Coop., Tucson, 1973-76; ednl. cons. Redington Cons. Corp., Tucson, 1970—; founder, pres. Redinton Cons. Corp.; lectr. in field; bd. dirs. Behavior Assocs. Chmn. Ariz. Right to Read Council, 1978-80; bd. dirs. Tucson Westside Coalition, 1979-80, bd. dirs. Friends of Tucson Pub. Library, v.p., 1984-92, pres. 1986-88; edn. supr. Grace Episcopal Ch., 1965-67; pres. Tucson Area Reading Council, 1968; mem. alumni bd. U. Ariz. Coll. Edn., 1984—, pres. 1986-88, 90-92. Mem. Nat. Council Tchrs. English, Internat. Reading Assn., Ariz. State Reading Council (pres. 1969), Assn. Supervision and Curriculum Devel., Tucson Adminstrs., Inc. (v.p. 1987-88, pres. 1988-89), Alpha Delta Kappa, Pi Delta Kappa (Disting. lecture series award 1978, Disting. Citizen award U. Ariz., 1995), Pi Beta Phi. Democrat. Contbr. articles to profl. publs.

HOANG, DUC VAN, theoretical pathologist, educator; b. Hanoi, Vietnam, Feb. 17, 1926; came to U.S. 1975, naturalized 1981; s. Duoc Van and Nguyen Thi (Tham) H.; m. Mau-Ngo Thi Vu, 7 children. M.D., Hanoi U. Sch. Medicine, Vietnam, 1952; DSc, Open Internat. U., Sri Lanka, 1989. Dean Sch. Medicine Army of the Republic of Vietnam, Saigon, 1959-63; dean Minh-Duc U. Sch. Medicine, Saigon, 1970-71; clin. prof. theoretical pathology U. So. Calif. Sch. Medicine, L.A., 1978—; adj. prof. Emperor's Coll. Traditional Oriental Medicine, Santa Monica, Calif., 1988-91; initiator of attitudinal immunology. Author: Towards an Integrated Humanization of Medicine, 1957; The Man Who Weights the Soul, 1959; Eastern Medicine, A New Direction?, 1970; also short stories; author introdn. to work of Marie Noël, Vietnamese transl. of La Rose Rouge; translator: Pestis, introduction to the work of Albert Camus, Vietnamese translation of La Peste; editor: The East (co-founder); jour. Les Cahiers de l'Asie du Sud-Est. Founder, past pres. Movement for Fedn. Countries S.E. Asia; co-founder, past v.p. Movement for Restoration Cultures and Religions of Orient; active Vo-Vi Meditation Assn. Am.; mem. The Noetic Inst., 1988—, Internat. Found. for Homeopathy, 1987; founder, pres. Intercontinental Found. for Electro-Magnetic Resonance Rsch., 1989—; coord. Unity and Diversity World Health Coun., 1992—. Named hon. dean The Open Internat. U. of Complementary Medicines, Sri Lanka, 1989; Unity-and-Diversity World Coun. fellow, 1990—. Mem. AAUP, Assn. Clin. Scientists, Am. Com. for Integration Eastern and Western Medicine (founder), Assn. Unitive Medicine (founder, pres.), U. So. Calif. Faculty Member Club (L.A.). Republican. Roman Catholic. Home: 3630 Barry Ave Los Angeles CA 90066-3202

HOANG, LOC BAO, electrical engineer; b. Saigon, Vietnam, Feb. 26, 1964; came to U.S., 1980; s. Chau Van Hoang and Quy Thi Bui; m. Tracy Phuong-Nga Doan, Dec. 7, 1990; children: Kimberly Bao, Christopher Dang-Khoa. BSEE, U. Calif., Berkeley, 1988; MSEE, San Jose State U., 1993. Design engr. Xicor, Inc., Milpitas, Calif., 1989-90; sr. design engr. Nat. Semiconductor Corp., Santa Clara, Calif., 1991-93, Silicon Storage Tech., Inc., Sunnyvale, Calif., 1993-94; design mgr. Winbond Memory Lab., San Jose, Calif., 1994-97, dir. design, 1997—; presenter Internat. Symposium on VLSI Tech., 1993. Mem. IEEE. Achievements include patent for Row Decoder and Driver with Switched-Bias Bulk Regions; semiconductor mem. device with dataline undershoot detection and reduced read access time, electrically byte selectable and byte alterable mem. arrays, flash cell having self-timed progamming and other patents; patent pending for notable findings of methods and design techniques to improve performance and/or reliability of non-volatile semiconductor memories. Avocations: music, movies, swimming, table tennis. Office: Winbond Electronics Corp Am 2727 N 1st St San Jose CA 95134-2029

HOBART, JAMES, sales and marketing executive; b. Panama City, Panama, Aug. 2, 1944; s. Donald and Anna (Posse) H.; m. Alicia Randazzo, Aug. 15, 1990. BBA, U. Okla., 1977. Cert. hypnotherapist, L.A. Regional mgr. Redken Labs., Inc., L.A., 1981-86; v.p. sales/edn. Matrix Essentials, Solon, Ohio, 1986-89; from v.p. sales to gen. mgr. Rusk, Inc., L.A.; gen. mgr. Notare' Internat., Gardena, Calif., 1991-93; v.p. sales, mktg. Tacnica/Hayashi, Northridge, Calif., 1994—. Served in U.S. Navy, 1962-72. Home: 821 Traction Ave Ste 108 Los Angeles CA 90013-1857

HOBBS, GREGORY JAMES, JR., state supreme court justice; b. Gainesville, Fla., Dec. 15, 1944; s. Gregory J. Hobbs and Mary Ann (Rhodes) Frakes; m. Barbara Louise Hay, June 17, 1967; children: Daniel Gregory, Emily Mary Hobbs Wright. BA, U. Notre Dame, 1966; JD, U. Calif., Berkeley, 1971. Bar: Colo. 1971, Calif. 1972. Law clk. to Judge William E. Doyle 10th U.S. Cir. Ct. Appeals, Denver, 1971-72; assoc. Cooper, White & Cooper, San Francisco, 1972-73; enforcement atty. U.S. EPA, Denver, 1973-75; asst. atty. gen. State of Colo. Atty. Gen.'s Office, Denver, 1975-79; ptnr. Davis, Graham & Stubbs, Denver, 1979-92; shareholder Hobbs, Trout & Raley, P.C., Denver, 1992-96; justice Colo. Supreme Ct., Denver, 1996—; counsel No. Colo. Water Conservancy, Loveland, Colo., 1979-96. Contbr. articles to profl. jours. vol. Peace Corps-S.Am., Colombia, 1967-68; vice chair Colo. Air Quality Control Com., Denver, 1982-87; mem. ranch com. Philmont Scout Ranch, Boy Scouts Am., Cimarron, N.Mex., 1988-98; co-chair Eating Disorder Family Support Group, Denver, 1992—. Recipient award of merit Denver Area Coun. Boy Scouts, 1993, Pres. award Nat. Water Resources Assn., Washington, 1995. Fellow Am. Bar Found.; mem. ABA, Colo. Bar Assn., Denver Bar Assn. Avocations: backpacking, fishing, writing poetry. Office: Colo Supreme Ct 2 E 14th Ave Denver CO 80203-2115

HOBBS, GUY STEPHEN, financial executive; b. Lynwood, Calif., Feb. 23, 1955; s. Franklin Dean and Bette Jane (Little) H.; m. Laura Elena Lopez, Jan. 6, 1984; 1 child, Mariah Amanda. BA, U. Calif., Santa Barbara, 1976; MBA, U. Nev., 1978. Sr. rsch. assoc. Ctr. for Bus. and Econ. Rsch., Las Vegas, Nev., 1978-80; pvt. practice mgmt. cons. Las Vegas, 1979-82; mgmt. analyst Clark County, Las Vegas, 1980-81, sr. mgmt. analyst, 1981-82, dir. budget and fin. planning, 1982-84, comptroller, dir. fin., chief fin. officer, 1984-96; pres. Hobbs, Ong & Assocs., Inc., 1996—; lectr. in mgmt. Coll. Bus. and Econs., U. Nev., Las Vegas, 1977-88; pres. Pacific Blue Ent., 1991—; mem. Interim Legis. Com. Infrastructure Fin., 1993-94; mem. Interim Legis. Com. Studying Laws Relating to the Distbn. of Taxes in Nev., 1995-96, 97—. Author publs. in field. Mem. exec. bd. Miss Nevada USA and Miss NEVADA Teen USA, 1996—; instr. Las Vegas Baseball Acad., 1998—. Mem. Am. Soc. Pub. Adminstrn. (Pub. Adminstr. of Yr. 1987), Govt. Fin. Officers Assn. (Fin. Reporting Achievement award 1984-95, Disting. Budget Presentation, award 1993-96), Nev. Taxpayers Assn. Republican. Avocations: sports, photography, travel. Office: Hobbs Ong & Assocs Inc 3900 Paradise Rd Ste 152 Las Vegas NV 89109-0928

HOBERECHT, REYNOTTA, school system administrator; b. Mattoon, Wis., Mar. 26, 1938; d. Laurence Herman and Magdalena Evelina (Waidelich) Jahnke; m. Hal G. Hoberecht, Sept. 19, 1970; 1 child, Marc. BS, U. Wis., 1961; MA, U. San Francisco, 1978. Tchr. Travis (Calif.) Unified Schs., 1971-95, adminstrv. asst., 1995—; participant Unidad de Paleontologia Expdn., Las Hoyas, Spain, 1992. Ecosystems project award Travis Sch. Bd., 1993. Mem. Calif. Tchrs. Assn. (treas. 1994-96, sec. 1967-68).

HOBERG, JANET LEE, controller; b. Grosse Pointe Farms, Mich., Aug. 1, 1954; d. Hobart Ronald and Naomi Lee (Bean) Freeman; m. Michael D. Hoberg, Mar. 5, 1995. Assocs. in Tech., No. Mich. U., 1976; BBA, Calif. State U., Long Beach, 1983; MBA, U. Calif., L.A., 1993. Acct. Gould Electronics, Inc., El Monte, Calif., 1984-85; accounts payable mgr. Gould Electronics, Inc., El Monte, 1985-86, gen. acctg. unit mgr., 1986-87; contr. western ops. Peerless Pump, Montebello, Calif., 1987-88; owner, CEO The Basket Boutique, Arcadia, Calif., 1988-89; plant contr. Goulds Pumps Inc., Vertical Products Divsn., City of Industry, Calif., 1989-91; contr. Goulds Pumps Inc., Vertical Products Divsn., City of Industry, 1991-92, divsn. contr., 1992-93; divsn. contr. Robertshaw (a Siebe Co.), Grayson Divsn., Long Beach, 1994; founder, pres. Feed My Sheep Ministries, Stockton, Calif., 1995—. Mem. NAFE, UCLA Alumni, Mensa, Beta Gamma Sigma, Phi Kappa Phi. Baptist. Avocations: music, playing the flute, reading, puzzles. Office: Feed My Sheep Ministries PO Box 77946 Stockton CA 95267-1246

HOCH, ORION LINDEL, corporate executive; b. Canonsburg, Pa., Dec. 21, 1928; s. Orion L.F. and Ann Marie (McNulty) H.; m. Jane Lee Ogan, June 12, 1952 (dec. 1978); children: Andrea, Brenda, John; m. Catherine Nan Richardson, Sept. 12, 1980. BS, Carnegie Mellon U., 1952; MS, UCLA, 1954; PhD, Stanford U., 1957. With Hughes Aircraft Co., Culver City, Calif., 1952-54; with Stanford Electronics Labs., 1954-57; sr. engr., dept. mgr., divsn. v.p., divsn. pres. Litton Electron Devices div., San Carlos, Calif., 1957-68; group exec. Litton Components divsn., 1968-70; v.p. Litton Industries, Inc., Beverly Hills, Calif., 1970, sr. v.p., 1971-74, pres., 1982-88, chief exec. officer, 1986-93, chmn., 1988-94, chmn. emeritus, 1994—, also dir.; pres. Intersil, Inc., Cupertino, Calif., 1974-82; chmn. exec. com. Western Atlas, Inc., Beverly Hills, Calif., 1994-98; bd. dirs. Litton Industries, Inc., Bessemer Trust Corp., Unova, Inc. Trustee Carnegie-Mellon U. Served with AUS, 1946-48. Mem. IEEE, Sigma Xi, Tau Beta Pi, Phi Kappa Phi. Office: Unova Inc 360 N Crescent Dr Beverly Hills CA 90210-4802

HOCHSCHILD, CARROLL SHEPHERD, medical equipment and computer company executive, educator; b. Whittier, Calif., Mar. 31, 1935; d. Vernon Vero and Effie Corinne (Hollingsworth) Shepherd; m. Richard Hochschild, July 25, 1959; children: Christopher Paul, Stephen Shepherd. BA in Internat. Rels., Pomona Coll., 1956; Teaching credential U. Calif., Berkeley, 1957; MBA, Pepperdine U., 1985; cert. in fitness instrn., U. Calif., Irvine, 1988. Cert. elem. tchr., Calif. elem. tchr. Oakland (Calif.) Pub. Schs., 1957-58, San Lorenzo (Calif.) Pub. Schs., 1958-59, Pasadena (Calif.) Pub. Schs., 1959-60, Huntington Beach (Calif.) Pub. Schs., 1961-63, 67-68; adminstrv. asst. Microwave Instruments, Corona del Mar, Calif., 1968-74; co-owner Hoch Co., Corona del Mar, 1978—. Rep. Calif. Tchrs. Assn., Huntington Beach, 1962-63. Mem. AAUW, P.E.O. (projects chmn. 1990-92, corr. sec. 1992-94, 98-99, chpt. pres. 1994-95), Internat. Dance-Exercise Assn., NAFE, ASTD (Orange County chpt.), Assistance League Newport-Mesa, Toastmistress (corr. sec. 1983), Jr. Ebell Club (fine arts chmn. Newport Beach 1966-67). Republican. Presbyterian.

HOCKENSMITH, ROBERT FRANKLIN, JR., accountant, consultant, financial planner; b. Ft. Knox, Ky., Feb. 8, 1955; s. Robert Franklin Sr. and Shirley Mae (Martin) H. BSBA, U. Ariz., 1981; grad., Coll. Fin. Planning, 1987; MBA, Keller Grad. Sch. Mgmt., 1993. CPA, Ariz. Analyst, acct. Fox & Co., CPAs, Tucson, 1978-80, Ernst & Whinney, CPA, Tucson, 1980-82; computer analyst Arthur Andersen & Co., CPAs, Phoenix, 1982-84; prof. Glendale (Ariz.) Community Coll., 1986-92; pres. Robert F. Hockensmith, P.C., 1984—; speaker nat. tax seminars; newscaster and guest on local TV and radio stas., 1992—. Maj. U.S. Army, 1972—. Mem. AICPAs, Nat. Soc. Pub. Accts., Ariz. Soc. CPAs, Internat. Assn. Fin. Planners, Assn. Quartermaster Officers. Republican. Avocations: body building, swimming. Office: 3233 W Peoria Ave Ste 202 Phoenix AZ 85029-4619

HOCKMUTH, JOSEPH FRANK, physicist, psychotherapist; b. Buffalo, N.Y., Mar. 6, 1942; s. Joseph Frank and Gertrude Marie (Merkley) H.; m. Sharon Louise Van Deusen Tiernan, June 30, 1965 (div.); children: Joseph Fess, Catherine Marie; m. Katherine Nancy Genco, June 1, 1991 (div.). BS in Physics, Calif. State U., 1965; MA in Psychology, Norwich U., 1992. Cert. substance abuse counselor, Ariz. Bd. Behavioral Health Examiners; cert. coll. instr., Ariz. State Bd.; cert. profl. counselor. Rsch. engr. Westinghouse Astroelectronics, Newbury Park, Calif., 1965-66; rsch. engr. Lockheed Missile & Space Co., Sunnyvale, Calif., 1966-69, sr. rsch. engr., 1972-78; radiation effects engr. IRT Corp., San Diego, 1969-72, staff scientist, 1984-87; addictions counselor Charter Hosp., Glendale, Ariz., 1992-93; prin. staff engr. Motorola Govt. Sys. & Tech. Group, Scottsdale, Ariz., 1978-84; tech. staff engr. Motorola GSTG, Scottsdale, Ariz., 1987—, divsn. cons. for radiation effects, 1987—; psychotherapist Fountain Hills, Ariz., 1992—. Contbr. Awakenings mag., 1992—. Funds coord. United Way, Scottsdale, 1988-90; class sponsor Wounded Knee (Wyo.) Tribal Elem. Sch., 1992—. Sgt. Calif. NG, 1960-68. Fellow Am. Counseling Assn., Ariz. Counselors Assn., Noetic Scis. Inst.; mem. ASTM (com. 1985—), IEEE (ofcl. tech. paper reviewer 1993). Roman Catholic. Avocations: guitar, piano, fishing, camping, American Indian culture studies. Home: 15024 E Windyhill Rd Fountain Hls AZ 85268-1323 Office: Motorola GSTG 8201 E Mcdowell Rd # H2550 Scottsdale AZ 85257-3893

HODGE, KATHLEEN O'CONNELL, academic administrator; b. Balt., Dec. 26, 1948; d. William Walsh and Loretto Marie (Wittek) O'Connell; m. Vern Milton Hodge, Apr. 8, 1972; children: Shea, Ryan. BS, Calif. State U., Fullerton, 1971, MS, 1975; postgrad., U. So. Calif., 1974, U. Calif., Irvine, 1977-84. Cert. marriage and family therapist. Counselor Saddleback Coll., Mission Viejo, Calif., 1975-87, prof. of psychology, speech, 1975-87, dean of continuing edn., cmty. svcs., dean emeritus inst., 1987-95, vice chancellor, 1995—; accreditation liaison officer Saddleback Coll., 1986; mem. adv. bd. Nat. Issues Forum, Calif., 1985, 87, Saddleback Coll. Community Services, 1984, Access and Aspirations U. Calif., Irvine, 1979. Author: (workbook) Assessment of Life Learning, 1978; editor emeritus: Flavors in Time Anthology of Literature, 1992. Mem. Calif. Community Coll. Counselors Assn. (region coord. 1987), Calif. Tchrs. Assn., Am. Assn. Women Community and Jr. Colls., Assn. Marriage Family Therapists, C.C. Educators of Older Adults (pres. 1990-92). Democrat. Roman Catholic. Avocations: skiing, reading, political advocacy. Home: 4011 Calle Juno San Clemente CA 92673-2616 Office: Saddleback Coll 28000 Marguerite Pky Mission Viejo CA 92692-3635

HODGEN, LAURIE DEE, geologist, editor; b. Portland, Oreg., July 28, 1949; d. Charles Donald and Verla Lucille (Walker) H.; m. Malcolm Mallory Clark, Sept. 1, 1979; 1 child, Kelly Donald. BA, U. of the Pacific, 1971; cert. continuous improvement/qual. mgmt., U. Calif., Santa Cruz, 1994. Geologic field asst. U.S. Geol. Survey, Menlo Park, Calif., 1972, geologist, 1972-75, geologic map editor, 1975-85, supervisory geologist, 1985-91, asst. br. chief, 1991-95, geologic map editor, 1995—. Arch., builder personal residence, 1981-88. Asst. handicapped riders Westwind 4H, Los Altos Hills, Calif., 1987—. Recipient Blue Pencil award Nat. Assn. Govt. Communicators, 1991, Cert. Recognition Br. Western Tech. Reports, 1995; alumni fellow U. of the Pacific, 1983. Mem. Assn. Earth Sci. Editors. Avocations: backpacking, hiking, horseback riding, drawing, painting. Home: 26135 Altadena Dr Los Altos Hills CA 94022-2009 Office: US Geol Survey 345 Middlefield Rd Menlo Park CA 94025-3591

HODGES, JOSEPH GILLULY, JR., lawyer; b. Denver, Dec. 7, 1942; s. Joseph Gilluly Sr. and Elaine (Chanute) H.; m. Jean Todd Creamer, Aug. 7, 1971; children: Ashley E., Wendy C., Elaine V. BA, Lake Forest Coll., 1965; JD, U. Colo., 1968. Bar: Colo. 1968, U.S. Dist. Ct. Colo. 1969, U.S. Ct. Mil. Appeals 1969. Assoc. Hodges, Kerwin, Otten & Weeks, Denver, 1969-73; assoc. Davis, Graham & Stubbs, Denver, 1973-76, ptnr., 1976-86; pvt. practice, Denver, 1986—. Bd. dirs. Arapahoe Colo. Nat. Bank, Littleton, Colo., 1971-90, Cherry Creek Improvement Assn., Denver, 1979-91; bd. trustees Lake Forest (Ill.) Coll., 1977-87; pres. Colo. Arlberg Club, Winter Park, Colo., 1984-85; treas. St. Johns Episcopal Cathedral, Denver, 1981-96; chmn. bd. Spalding Cmty. Found., 1995—. Capt. USAR, 1969-74. Named Best Lawyers in Am., Woodward/White, N.Y.C., 1994-95. Fellow Am. Coll. Trust and Estate Counsel (state chmn. 1991-96); mem. ABA (chmn. probate divsn. G-2 Tech. 1990-95, coun. mem. real property, probate and trust law sect. 1996—), Am. Judicature Soc., Colo. Bar Assn. (chair probate coun. 1981-82), Denver Bar Assn., Denver Estate Planning Coun., Colo. Planned Giving Roundtable (bd. 1991-94), Rotary Club Denver, Kappa Sigma, Phi Alpha Delta. Republican. Avocations: skiing, hiking, fishing, photography, computers. Office: 3300 E 1st Ave Ste 600 Denver CO 80206-5809

HODGSON, GREGORY BERNARD, software systems architect; b. Chgo., July 17, 1946; s. John George and Lucille (Nass) H.; m. Kathleen Patricia, Aug. 11, 1972 (div. July 1974); m. Kathryn Marie Maytum, Feb. 14, 1976. BS in Computer Engring., U. Ill., 1972. Computer programmer specialist Lockheed Missiles and Space Co., Sunnyvale, Calif., 1972-81, software systems engr., 1981-89; software sys. cons. Lockheed Missiles and

Space Co., Sunnyvale, 1989-95; engr./scientist Hewlett-Packard Co., Sunnyvale, Calif., 1995; software system architect Lockheed Martin Missile and Space Ctr., Sunnyvale, Calif., 1995—; cons. in field. Served with U.S. Army, 1966-69. State of Ill. VA scholar, 1970-72. Mem. Ill. VA Assn. (coord. fed. and state affairs 1970-72). Roman Catholic. Avocations: boating, camping, bowling, softball, volleyball. Home: 469 1/2 Curie Dr San Jose CA 95123-4925

HODGSON, JOHN FREDERICK, II, information systems specialist, photographer; b. Chgo., Sept. 22, 1917; s. John Frederick Hodgson and Lucille Amelia (Blanchard) Horn; m. Connie (Macias) Davis, May 30, 1979 (div. Apr., 1984). AB, U. Chgo., 1956. Computer programmer Northrup Corp., Hawthorne, Calif., 1966-68; systems programmer N. Am. Rockwell, Downey, Calif., 1968-69, Ctrl. Data Corp., L.A., 1969-70, Fed. Elec. Co., Vandenburg, Calif., 1970-72, Informatics, L.A., 1972-74; sr. systems analyst Blue Cross of Calif., Woodland Hills, Calif., 1974-84; photographic artist Escondido, Calif, 1984—; systems programmer System Devel. Corp., Santa Monica, Calif., 1959-66. With USNR, 1941-45, Alaska. Mem. North County Artists Coop. (bd. dirs. 1993-94). Avocations: photography, tennis. Home: 1811 E Grand Ave Unit 99 Escondido CA 92027-3230

HOEFFLIN, STEVEN M., plastic surgeon; b. Seattle, Wash., 1946. MD, UCLA, 1972. Plastic surgeon Santa Monica (Calif.) Hosp.; assoc. clin. prof. UCLA. Office: 1530 Arizona Ave Santa Monica CA 90404-1208

HOEHN, ROBERT J., plastic surgeon, educator; b. East St. Louis, Ill., 1929; children: Robert Anthony Till, Margaret Eve, David Ivan, Daniel Vincent; m. Nancy Ruth Vincent. MD, Washington U., St. Louis, 1956. Diplomate Am. Bd. Plastic Surgery. Intern Vancouver (B.C., Can.) Gen. Hosp., 1956-57; resident in internal medicine, 1957-58; resident McGill U., Montreal, Que., Can., 1960-61; resident in gen. surgery Boston City Hosp., 1961-62; fellow in orthopaedic surgery, 1962; fellow in transplantation immunology Westminster Hosp., London, 1962-63; resident in plastic surgery N.Y. Hosp.-Cornell, 1963-65; clin. prof. plastic surgery U. Colo., 1978—; with Aurora Presbyn. Hosp., 1978—, Aurora Regional Med. Ctr., 1978—, Denver Children's Hosp., 1978—, Porter Meml. Hosp., 1982—, Swedish Hosp., 1982—; pvt. practice. Fellow ACS; mem. AAPS, Am. Soc. Plastic and Reconstructive Surgeons, Plastic Surgery Rsch. Coun. Home: 2601 S Quebec St Villa 3 Denver CO 80231-6039 Office: # 306 3535 Cherry Cr N Dr Denver CO 80209

HOFERT, JACK, consulting company executive, lawyer; b. Phila., Apr. 6, 1930; s. David and Beatrice (Schatz) H.; m. Marilyn Tukeman, Sept. 4, 1960; children: Dina, Bruce. BS, UCLA, 1952, MBA, 1954, JD, 1957. Bar: Calif. 1957; CPA, Calif. Tax supr. Peat, Marwick Mitchell & Co., L.A., 1959-62, tax mgr., 1974-77; v.p. fin. Pacific Theaters Corp., L.A., 1962-68; freelance cons. L.A., 1969-74; tax mgr. Lewis Homes, Upland, Calif., 1977-80; pres. Di-Bru, Inc., L.A., 1981-87, Scolyn, Inc., L.A., 1988-95; bus. cons., 1995—; dir. Valley Fed. Savs. and Loan Assn., 1989-92. Mem. UCLA Law Rev., 1956-57; contbr. articles to tax, fin. mags. Served with USN, 1948-49. Avocation: tennis. Home and Office: 2479 Roscomare Rd Los Angeles CA 90077-1812

HOFFENBLUM, ALLAN ERNEST, political consultant; b. Vallejo, Calif., Aug. 10, 1940; s. Albert A. and Pearl Estelle (Clarke) H. BA, U. So. Calif., 1962. Mem. staff L.A. County Rep. Com., 1967-71; staff dir. Rep. Assembly Caucus Calif. legislature, Sacramento, 1973-75; polit. dir. Rep. Party of Calif., L.A., 1977-78; owner Allan Hoffenblum & Assocs., L.A., 1979—; publ. Calif. Target Book, 1994. Pub. Calif. Target Book, 1994—. Capt. USAF, 1962-67, Vietnam. Decorated Bronze Star medal. Mem. Internat. Assn. Polit. Cons., Am. Assn. Polit. Cons. Jewish. Office: 9000 W Sunset Blvd Ste 707 West Hollywood CA 90069-5807

HOFFLUND, PAUL, lawyer; b. San Diego, Mar. 27, 1928; s. John Leslie and Ethel Frances (Cline) H.; m. Anne Marie Thalman, Feb. 15, 1958; children: Mark, Sylvia. BA, Princeton (N.J.) U., 1950; JD, George Washington U., 1956. Bar: D.C. 1956, U.S. Dist. Ct. D.C. 1956, U.S. Ct. Appeals (D.C. cir.) 1956, Calif. 1957, U.S. Dist. Ct. (so. dist.) Calif. 1957, U.S. Ct. Mil. Appeals 1957, U.S. Ct. Claims 1958, U.S. Ct. Appeals (9th cir.) 1960, U.S. Supreme Ct. 1964, U.S. Tax Ct. 1989. Assoc. Wencke, Carlson & Kuykendall, San Diego, 1961-62; ptnr. Carlson, Kuykendall & Hofflund, San Diego, 1963-65, Carlson & Hofflund, San Diego, 1965-72; Christian Sci. practitioner San Diego, 1972-84; arbitrator Mcpl. Cts. and Superior Ct. of Calif., San Diego, 1984—; pvt. practice San Diego, 1985—; adj. prof. law Nat. U. Sch. Law, San Diego, 1985-94; judge pro tem Mcpl. Ct. South Bay Jud. Dist., 1990—; disciplinary counsel to U.S. Tax Ct., 1989—; asst. U.S. atty. U.S. Dept. of Justice, L.A., 1959-60, asst. U.S. atty. in charge, San Diego, 1960-61, spl. hearing officer, San Diego, 1962-68; asst. corp. counsel Govt. of D.C., 1957-59. Author: (chpt. in book) Handbook on Criminal Procedure in the U.S. District Court, 1967; contbr. articles to profl. jours. Treas. Princeton Club of San Diego; v.p. Community Concert Assn., San Diego; pres. Sunland Home Found., San Diego, Trust for Christian Sci. Orgn., San Diego; chmn. bd. 8th Ch. of Christ, Scientist, San Diego. With USN, 1950-53, comdr. JAGC, USNR, 1953-72, ret. Mem. ABA, San Diego County Bar Assn., Inst. Global Ethics, World Affairs Coun., Phi Delta Phi. Democrat. Avocations: theater, classical music, bridge, fine art, biblical study. Home and Office: 6146 Syracuse Ln San Diego CA 92122-3301

HOFFMAN, CHARLES FENNO, III, architect; b. Greenwich, Conn., May 28, 1958; s. Harrison Baldwin Wright and Louise Elkins (Sinkler) H.; m. Pia Christina Ossorio, Dec. 27, 1980; children: Wilhelmina C. L., Frederic W. S., Henry F., C. Fenno IV. BA in Environ. Design, U. Pa., 1983; MArch, U. Colo., 1986. Designer Fenno Hoffman & Assocs., Boulder, Colo., 1983—; pvt. practice designer Boulder, 1985; assoc. William Zmistowski Assoc. Architects, 1987—, Pellecchia-Olson Architects, Boulder, 1989—; prin. Fenno Hoffman Architects PC, Boulder, Colo., 1991—; cons. Summit Habitats, Inc., 1984—; design cons. The Denver Partnership, 1985, Downtown Denver, Inc., 1985; guest critic U. Colo., 1990—, guest lectr., 1991-92, 94, 95, 96, 97, design instr., 1995—; comml. cons. and design, comm. and software facilities, shopping malls, large scale, mixed use devel., urban renewal projects, 1997—. Prin. works include Ca'Venier Mus. for Venice Bienalle, 1985, Cleveland Pl. Connection, Denver, 1985 (1st prize 1985), hist. renovated house Boulder, 1986, 3 Gates 3 Squares, Denver, 1986, Geneva Ave. House, 1992, Jarrow Sch. master plan, 1994; numerous residential and multi-family projects, 1991—, Northeast Classroom, 1995, US Navy and Marine Corps. Facilities Assessments, 1996; author: Urban Transit Facility, A Monorail for Downtown Denver, 1985. Bd. dirs. Jarrow Sch. Mem. Am. Inst. Architects, Architects & Planners ofBoulder. Democrat. Episcopalian. Avocation: drawing, skiing, bicycling, computers. Office: 505 Geneva Ave Boulder CO 80302-7139

HOFFMAN, DONALD DAVID, cognitive and computer science educator; b. San Antonio, Dec. 29, 1955; s. David Pollock and Loretta Virginia (Shoemaker) H.; m. Geralyn Mary Souza, Dec. 13, 1986; 1 child from previous marriage, Melissa Louise. BA, UCLA, 1978; PhD, MIT, 1983. MTS and project engr. Hughes Aircraft Co., El Segundo, Calif., 1978-83; rsch. scientist MIT Artificial Intelligence Lab, Cambridge, Mass., 1983; asst. prof. U. Calif., Irvine, 1983-86, assoc. prof., 1986-90, prof., 1990-97; cons. Fairchild Lab. for Artificial Intelligence, Palo Alto, Calif., 1984; panelist MIT Corp. vis. com., Cambridge, 1985, NSF, Washington, 1988; conf. host IEEE Conf. on Visual Motion, Irvine, 1989; conf. host Office of Naval Rsch. Conf. on Vision, Laguna Beach, Calif., 1992; vis. prof. Zentrum für Interdisziplinäre Forschung, Bielefeld, Germany, 1995-96. Author: Visual Intelligence, 1998; co-author: Observer Mechanics, 1989; mem. editl. bd. Cognition, 1991—, Psychol. Rev., 1995-96; contbr. articles to profl. jours. Vol. tchr. Turtle Rock Elem. Sch., Irvine, 1988-90. Recipient Distinguished Scientific award, Am. Psychol. Assn., 1989, Troland Rsch. award U.S. Nat. Acad. Scis., 1994; grantee NSF, 1984, 87. Mem. Am. Psychol. Soc. Avocations: running, swimming, racket sports, ice skating. Office: U Calif Dept Cognitive Sci Irvine CA 92697

HOFFMAN, GEORGE ALAN, consulting company executive; b. Albany, N.Y., May 16, 1937; s. Irving Marshall and Margaret (Coyne) H.; m. Kim Thi Nguyen, Oct. 10, 1971; children: Caroline, Christine. AB, U. Calif., Berkeley, 1980, MBA, 1982. Mgmt. analyst Am. Can Co., N.Y.C., 1966-69; cons. Vietnamese Air Force, Bien Hoa, Vietnam, 1970-74, Puslitbang, Jakarta, Indonesia, 1974-75; v.p. Union Bank, Oakland, Calif., 1987—. Author: Indonesian Production-sharing Oil Contracts, 1982, The Guns of T.E. Lawrence, 1996. Mem. Mensa. Club: Commonwealth (San Francisco). Avocation: mountaineering. Office: 460 Hegenberger Rd Oakland CA 94621-1404

HOFFMAN, GEORGE BERNARD, estate planner; b. St. Louis, Dec. 11, 1942; s. George Bernard and Ethel Eva (Drobina) H.; m. Suzanne Carol Johnson, May 9, 1970 (div. Feb. 1992); m. Peggy Ke Bei, Apr. 25, 1997. AA, Mt. San Antonio Coll., Walnut, Calif., 1966; BA, Calif. State Coll., L.A., 1971; MBA, Calif. State U., L.A., 1974; JD, Western State U., 1998. Cert. estate planner; cert. paralegal. Pers. specialist Alpha Beta Mkts., La Habra, Calif., 1965-69, mgr., 1969-79; dir. mktg. Auburn Cord Dusenberg of Calif., L.A., 1979-81; prin. Bertcourt Securities Corp., Upland, Calif., 1981-88; gen. mgr. Penita Investment Ltd., Hong Kong, 1988-92; owner George B. Hoffman Estate Planning, Whittier, Calif., 1992—. With U.S. Army, 1966-68; Vietnam. Decorated Army Commendation medal, Air medal. Mem. VFW, Am. Legion, Calif. Advs. for Nursing Home Reform. Democrat. Roman Catholic. Avocations: golf, sailing, travel. Office: 5000 Birch St Newport Beach CA 92660-2127

HOFFMAN, MAVIS WANDA, business official; b. New Hampton, Iowa, Apr. 8, 1929; d. Sjur Getinus and Bertha (Njus) Saanderson; m. Donald Nordness Hoffman, Dec. 30, 1960; children: Keith Donald, Robert Craig. BA, U. Calif., Berkeley, 1951; MA, San Francisco State U., 1958. Tchr. LaVista Sch. Dist., Hayward, Calif., Irvington (Calif.) Sch. Dist., 1951-52, LaVista Sch. Dist., Hayward, Calif., 1952-54, Richmond (Calif.) Sch. Dist., 1954-55, U.S. Mil. Schs., Erlangen, Germany, 1955-56, San Leandro (Calif.) Sch. Dist., 1956-61; adminstr. San Ramon Engrs., Dublin, Calif., 1975—. Membership chmn. Eugene O'Neill Found., Danville, Calif., 1996—; mem. Dublin Ptnrs. in Edn., 1995-96; mem. Nightowls Aux., Mt. Diablo Rehab. Ctr., 1991—; chmn. workshop monitors Math.-Sci. Conf. for Girls, Tri-Valley Area, 1993-95. Mem. AAUW (life, various offices), World Affairs Coun., U. Calif. Alumni Assn., Dublin C. of C., San Francisco Mus., Oakland Mus., Blackhawk Mus., St. Mary's Mus., Diablo Country Club. Avocations: duplicate bridge, travel, reading non-fiction.

HOFFMAN, TREVOR WILLIAM, professional baseball player; b. Bellflower, Calif., Oct. 13, 1967. Student, U. Ariz. Pitcher San Diego Padres, 1993—. Office: San Diego Padres PO Box 2000 San Diego CA 92112-2000

HOFFMANN, JON ARNOLD, aeronautical engineer, educator; b. Wausau, Wis., Jan. 13, 1942; s. Arnold D. and Rita J. (Haas) H.; m. Carol R. Frye. BSME, U. Wis., 1964, MSME, 1966. Register profl. engr., Calif. Research engr. Trane Co., 1966-68; prof. aeronautical engring. Calif. Poly. State U., San Luis Obispo, 1968—; research engr. Stanford U. NSF Program, 1970; research fellow Ames Research Ctr. Ctr. NASA/ASEE, 1974-75; tech. cons. NASA/AMES Research Ctr., 1977; design engr. Cal/ Poly ERDA contract, 1976-77; prin. investigator NASA-ARC Cooperative Agreement, 1983. Contbr. articles to profl. jours. Grantee NASA, NSF. Mem. ASME. Home: 1044 Via Chula Robles Arroyo Grande CA 93420-4915 Office: Calif Poly State U Dept Aero Enging San Luis Obispo CA 93407

HOFFMANN, KATHRYN ANN, humanities educator; b. Rockville Centre, N.Y., Oct. 26, 1954; d. Manfred and Catherine (Nanko) H.; m. Brook Ellis, Nov. 25, 1987. BA summa cum laude, SUNY Buffalo, 1975; MA, The Johns Hopkins U., 1979, PhD, 1981. Asst. prof. French lit. and lang. U. Wis., Madison, 1981-88; asst. prof. French lit. and lang. U. Hawaii-Manoa, Honolulu, 1992-97, assoc. prof., 1997—; mng. ptnr. Yuval Design Partnership, Chgo., 1988-92. Author: Society of Pleasures: Interdisciplinary Readings in Pleasure in Power during the Reign of Louis XIV, 1997; assoc. editor Substance, 1982-87; contbr. articles to profl. jours.; designer clothing accessories. Grantee NEH, 1993, 95; fellow Inst. Rsch. in Humanities, 1984-85, Am. Coun. Learned Socs., 1984-85, Camargo Found., 1998. Mem. MLA, Internat. Soc. for the Study of European Ideas, Am. Soc. for 18th Century Studies, Hawaii Assn. Lang. Tchrs., N.Am. Soc. for 17th Century French Lit., Soc. for Interdisciplinary French 17th Century Studies (exec. com. 1994-96), Soc. for Interdisciplinary Study Social Imagery, Phi Beta Kappa. Home: 548 Woodland Dr S Hempstead NY 11550-7820 Office: U Hawaii Manoa Dept European Languages & Lit 1890 East West Rd Rm 483 Honolulu HI 96822-2318

HOFFMANN-SNODGRASS, LYNDA LOUISE, artist, watercolorist; b. Beloit, Wis., Mar. 11, 1954; d. Carl Rudolph and Elaine Janet (Patterson) Hoffman; m. Mato Gregory Lamonte Snodgrass, Apr. 19, 1980. BS in Art, So. Oreg. Coll., Ashland, 1978. Artist self employed, 1980—; critique artist and juror Siskiyou Art Assn., Yreka, Calif., 1993-98; artist presenter for auction KSYS-TV, Medford, Oreg., 1996; donating artist for various auctions. Exhibited in solo show at Bentley's Gallery, Ashland, 1989, Solano C.C., Suisan City, Calif., 1990, Exclusive Accents Gallery, Jacksonville, Oreg., 1992, 5th Dimension Nature Gallery, Ashland, 1993, 94, Lakewood Ctr. for the Arts, Lake Oswego, Oreg., 1997; group shows include Rose Show/Oreg. Soc. Artists, Portland, 1993, 95, The Adirondacks 14th Annual Nat. Exhbn. Am. Watercolors, Old Forge, N.Y., 1995, N.W. Watercolor Soc., Kirkland, Wash., 1996. Recipient numerous awards for art. Mem. Watercolor Soc. Oreg. (2d Pl. award 1992). Christian. Avocations: spiritual and native American studies, gourmet cooking, gardening. Home and Studio: 6932 Coleman Creek Rd Medford OR 97501-9673

HOFMANN, ALAN FREDERICK, biomedical educator, researcher; b. Balt., May 17, 1931; s. Joseph Enoch and Nelda Rosina (Durr) H.; m. Marta Gertrud Pettersson, Aug. 15, 1969 (div. 1976); children: Anthea Karin, Cecilia Rae; m. Helga Katharina Aicher, Nov. 3, 1978. BA with honors, Johns Hopkins U., 1951, MD with honors, 1955; PhD, U. Lund, Sweden, 1965; MD honoris causis, U. Bologna, Italy, 1988; hon. fellow, Royal Coll. Physicians, 1996. Intern, then resident dept. medicine Columbia Presbyn. Med. Ctr., N.Y.C., 1955-57; clin. assoc. clin. ctr. Nat. Heart Inst., NIH, Bethesda, Md., 1957-59; postdoctoral fellow, dept. physiol. chemistry U. Lund, Sweden, 1959-62; asst. physician Hosp. of the Rockefeller U., N.Y.C., 1962-64; outpatient physician N.Y. Hosp., N.Y.C., 1963-64; assoc. physician Hosp. of the Rockefeller U., N.Y.C., 1964-66; cons. in medicine, assoc. dir. gastroenterology unit Mayo Clinic, Rochester, Minn., 1966-77; attending physician Med. Ctr. U. Calif.-San Diego, 1977—; asst. prof. dept. medicine Rockefeller U., N.Y.C., 1964-66; assoc. prof. medicine and biochemistry U. Minn. Mayo Grad. Sch., 1966-69, assoc. prof. medicine and physiology, 1969-70, prof. medicine and physiology, 1970-73; prof. medicine and physiology Mayo Med. Sch., 1973-77; cons. physiology Mayo Clinic, Rochester, 1975-77; prof. medicine U. Calif., San Diego, 1977—, adj. prof. pharmacy, U. Calif., San Francisco, 1986—; vis. prof. pharmacy U. Mich., Ann Arbor, 1980-85. Patentee solvent for direct dissolution of cholesterol gallstones, breath test for pancreatic exocrine function, bile acid replacement therapy; contbr. numerous articles to profl. jours., books, films. Recipient Travel award Wellcome Trust, 1961-63, Travel award NSF, 1964, Sr. Scientist award Humboldt Found., Fed. Republic of Germany, 1976, 91 (shared prize) Eppinger Prize, Falk Found., 1976, Disting. Achievement award Modern Medicine mag., 1978 Chancellor's Rsch. Excellence award U. Calif., 1986; Nat. Fedn. fellow, 1959-61, USPHS fellow, 1962-63, Fogarty Internat. Sr. fellow NIH, 1986; Rockefeller Found. scholar, Bellagio, Italy, 1980. Fellow AAAS, Royal Soc. Medicine; mem. Am. Assn. Study of Liver Disease (numerous coms., pres. 1984, Disting. Achievement award 1997), Swedish Soc. for Gastroenterology (hon.), Soc. for Gastrointestinal Radiology (hon.), Gastroent. Soc. Australia (hon.), Chilean Soc. Gastroenterology (hon.), Brit. Soc. Gastroenterology (hon.), Royal Flemish Acad. for Medicine (hon., fgn. corr. mem.), German Soc. for Digestive and Metabolic Disease (hon. mem., Siegfried Thannhauser medal 1996), Serbian Soc. Medicine (hon.), Am. Soc. Clin. Investigation, Assn. Am. Physicians, Am. Liver Found. (chmn. sci. adv. bd. 1986-91), Am. Physiol. Soc. (Horace Davenport medal 1996), Am. Gastroent. Assn. (chmn. biliary diseases coun. 1991-92, Disting. Achievement award 1970, co-winner Beaumont prize 1979, Friedenwald medal 1994), Phi Beta Kappa, Sigma Xi, Alpha Omega Alpha, Omicron Delta Kappa. Home: 5870 Cactus Way La Jolla CA 92037-7069

HOFMANN, PAUL BERNARD, healthcare consultant; b. Portland, Oreg., July 6, 1941; s. Max and Consuelo Theresa (Bley) H.; m. Lois Bernstein, June 28, 1969; children: Julie, Jason. BS, U. Calif., Berkeley, 1963, MPH, 1965, DPH, 1994. Research assoc. in hosp. adminstrn. Lab. of Computer Sci., Mass. Gen. Hosp., Boston, 1966-68; asst. dir. Lab. of Computer Sci., Mass. Gen. Hosp., 1968-69; asst. adminstr. San Antonio Community Hosp., Upland, Calif., 1969-70; assoc. adminstr. San Antonio Community Hosp., 1970-72; dep. dir. Stanford (Calif.) U. Hosp., 1972-74, dir., 1974-77; exec. dir. Emory U. Hosp., Atlanta, 1978-87; exec. v.p., chief ops. officer Alta Bates Corp., Emeryville, Calif., 1987-91; cons. Alta Bates Corp., Emeryville, 1991-92, Alexander & Alexander, San Francisco, 1992-94; disting. vis. scholar Stanford (Calif.) U. Ctr. for Biomed. Ethics, 1993-97; sr. fellow Stanford (Calif.) U. Hosp., 1993-94; sr. cons. strategic healthcare practice Alexander & Alexander Cons. Group, San Francisco, Calif., 1994-97; sr. v.p. strategic healthcare practice Aon Cons., San Francisco, 1997—; instr. computer applications Harvard U., 1968-69; lectr. hosp. adminstrn. UCLA, 1970-72, Stanford U. Med. Sch., 1972-77; assoc. prof. Emory U. Sch. Medicine, Atlanta, 1978-87. Author: The Development and Application of Ethical Criteria for Use in Making Programmatic Resource Allocation Decisions in Hospitals, 1994; contbr. articles to profl. jours. Served with U.S. Army, 1959. Fellow Am. Coll. Hosp. Adminstrs. (recipient Robert S. Hudgens meml. award 1976); mem. Am. Hosp. Assn., U. Calif. Alumni Assn.

HOFMANN, PETER LUDWIG, engineering executive, retired; b. Vienna, Austria, Jan. 25, 1925; s. Arthur Oliver and Louise Mary (Kamhuber) H.; m. Garda Steiner, May 27, 1950; children: Mark Eric, Monica Louise. BEE, Cooper Union, 1950; MS, Union Coll., Schenectady, N.Y., 1954; D. Engring. Sci., Rensselaer Poly. Inst., 1960. Mgr. nuclear design Knolls Atomic Power Lab GE, Schenectady, 1950-61; mgr. engring. physics Hanford Lab. GE, Richland, Wash., 1961-65; mgr. nuclear analysis Battelle N.W. Lab., Richland, 1965-70; mgr. systems analysis Westinghouse Hanford Co., Richland, 1970-74; assoc. dir. planning and analysis Battelle Meml. Inst., Columbus, Ohio, 1974-79, mgr. tech., project mgmt. div., 1979-85, sr. tech. advisor project mgmt. div., 1985-91; ret.; adj. prof. U. Wash., Richland, 1970s; pst mem. adv. com. on reactor physics U.S. Dept. Energy. Editor: Nuclear Waste Management Series; contbr. articles to profl. jours. With U.S. Army, 1943-46, ETO. Mem. Am. Nuclear Soc., Inst. Nuclear Materials Mgmt. (sr.), Sigma Xi, Tau Beta Pi. Home: 11301 NE 7th St Apt X-4 Vancouver WA 98684-4986

HOGAN, CLARENCE LESTER, retired electronics executive; b. Great Falls, Mont., Feb. 8, 1920; s. Clarence Lester and Bessie (Young) H.; m. Audrey Biery Peters, Oct. 13, 1946; 1 child, Cheryl Lea. BSChemE, Mont. State U., 1942, Dr. Engring. (hon.), 1967; MS in Physics, Lehigh U., 1947, PhD in Physics, 1950, D in Engring. (hon.), 1971; AM (hon.), Harvard U., 1954; D in Sci. (hon.), Worcester Poly. U., 1969. Rsch. chem. engr. Anaconda Copper Mining Co., 1942-43; instr. physics Lehigh U., 1946-50; mem. tech. staff Bell Labs., Murray Hill, N.J., 1950-51, sub-dept. head, 1951-53; assoc. prof. Harvard U., Cambridge, Mass., 1953-57, Gordon McKay prof., 1957-58; gen. mgr. semi-conductor products divsn. Motorola, Inc., Phoenix, 1958-60, v.p., 1960-66, exec. v.p., dir., 1966-68; pres., chief exec. officer Fairchild Inst., Mt. View, Calif., 1968-74, vice chmn. bd. dirs., 1974-85; gen. chmn. Internat. Conf. on Magnetism and Magnetic Materials, 1959, 60; mem. materials adv. bd. Dept. Def., 1957-59; mem. adv. coun. dept. electrical engring. Princeton U.; mem. adv. bd. sch. engring. U. Calif., Berkeley, 1974—, adv. bd. dept. chem. engring. Mont. State U., 1988—; mem. nat. adv. bd. Desert Rsch. Inst., 1976-80; mem. vis. com. dept. electric engring. and computer sci. MIT, 1975-85; mem. adv. coun. div. electrical engring. Stanford U., 1976-86; mem. sci. and ednl. adv. com. Lawrence Berkeley Lab., 1978-84; mem. Pres.'s Export Coun., 1976-80; mem. adv. panel to tech. adv. bd. U.S. Congress, 1976-80. Patentee in field; inventor microwave gyrator, circulator, isolator. Chmn. Commn. Found. Santa Clara County, Calif., 1983-85; mem. vis. com. Lehigh U., 1966-71, trustee, 1971-80, also life trustee; trustee Western Electronic Edn. Fund; mem. governing bd. Maricopa County Jr. Coll.; bd. regents U. Santa Clara. Lt. (j.g.) USNR, 1942-46. Recipient Community Svc. award NCCJ, 1978, Medal of Merit Am. Electronics Assn., 1978, Berkeley Citation U. Calif., 1980; named Bay Area Bus. Man of Yr. San Jose State U., 1978, One of 10 Greatest Innovators in Past 50 Yrs. Electronics Mag., 1980. Fellow AAAS, IEEE (Frederick Philips gold medal 1976, Edison silver medal Cleve. Soc. 1978, Pioneering medal for microwave theory and tech. 1993), Inst. Elec. Engrs. (hon.); mem. NAE, Am. Phys. Soc., Menlo Country Club, Masons, Sigma Xi, Tau Beta Pi, Phi Kappa Phi, Kappa Sigma. Democrat. Baptist. Avocations: woodworking, computer programming. Home: 36 Barry Ln Atherton CA 94027-4023

HOGAN, MICHAEL R(OBERT), judge; b. Oregon City, Oreg., Sept. 24, 1946; married; 3 children. A.B., U. Oreg. Honors Coll., 1968; J.D., Georgetown U., 1971. Bar: Oreg. 1971, U.S. Ct. Appeals (9th cir.) 1971. Law clk. to chief judge U.S. Dist. Ct. Oreg., Portland, 1971-72; assoc. Miller, Anderson, Nash, Yerke and Wiener, Portland, 1972-73; magistrate judge U.S. Dist. Ct. Oreg., Eugene, 1973-91, dist. judge, 1991—, chief judge, 1995—; bankruptcy judge U.S. Dist. Oreg., Eugene, 1973-80. Mem. ABA, Oreg. State Bar Assn. Office: US Courthouse 211 E 7th Ave Eugene OR 97401-2722

HOGAN, NANCY KAY, elementary education educator; b. Auburn, Wash., Oct. 5, 1947; d. Henry Grant and Medora Ione (Elder) Kessner; m. David Allan Hogan, June 27, 1970; children: Jeffrey Allan, Jason Patrick, Jennifer Ann. BA in Edn., Western Wash. U., 1969; postgrad., U. Wash., 1973; M Ednl. Tech., City U., 1996. Cert. K-12 tchr., Wash. Tchr. kindergarten Kent (Wash.) Sch. Dist., 1970; elem. tchr. North Thurston Sch. Dist., Lacey, Wash., 1970-73; tchr. McLane Elem. Sch., Olympia, Wash., 1986-93, McKenny Elem. Sch., Olympia, 1993-94; tchr. Hansen Elem. Sch., Olympia, 1994—, also mem. tchr. support team. Mem. NEA, Internat. Reading Assn., Whole Lang. Umbrella, Wash. Edn. Assn., Olympia Edn. Assn., Dist. Inclusion Forum, Hansen Title I Team, Nat. Coun. Tchrs. English. Avocations: reading, boating, walking. Home: 3030 Aspinwall Rd NW Olympia WA 98502-1531 Office: Hansen Elem Sch 1919 Rd Sixty Five Olympia WA 98502

HOHN, HAZEL MARJORIE, author; b. Bklyn.; d. Hamilton Alan Stamper and Hazel P. (Walker) Sprague; m. Werner Aloysius Hohn, July 26, 1960 (div. 1984); children: Carol, Susan; children from previous marriage: James, John. AA, Western Nev. C.C., 1981. Aircraft welder Piper Aircraft, Lock Haven, 1942-43; freelance writer, 1950—; sec. Nat. Air Transport Coord. Com., N.Y.C., 1959; spkr. on aviation history, 1984—. Author: The King Who Could Not Smile; contbr. story to textbook: The New Tall Tales 4th Grade Reader; contbr. articles to newspapers, stories to textbooks, juvenile mags., including Child Life, Scholastic mag., Highlights for Children. Active People for the Ethical Treatment of Animals, Reno, Nev., 1996—. Pilot Women Air Force Svc. Pilot, 1943-45. Mem. Exptl. Air Force Assn. (bd. dirs. 1972—), Air Force Assn. (mem. coun. 1988—), Women Airforce Svc. Pilots WWII, Women Mil. Aviators, Women in Mil. Svc. to Am. (charter mem., recruiter), Ninety Nines, B-26 Marauder Club, B-24 Club (liberator). Democrat. Christian Scientist. Avocations: music, reading, pets, community activities, sports. Home: 2750 Dickerson Rd Apt D Reno NV 89503-4912

HOHNER, KENNETH DWAYNE, retired fodder company executive; b. St. John, Kans., June 24, 1934; s. Courtney Clinton and Mildred Lucile (Forrester) H.; m. Sherry Eloi Anice Edens, Feb. 14, 1961; children: Katrina, Melissa, Steven, Michael. BS in Geol. Engring., U. Kans., 1957. Geophysicist Mobil Oil Corp., New Orleans, Anchorage, Denver, 1957-72; sr. geophysicist Amerada Hess Corp., Houston, 1972-75, ARAMCO, London, 1975-79; far east area geophysicist Hamilton Bros., Denver, 1979-83; owner Hohner Poultry Farm, Erie, Colo., 1979-94; pres. Hohner Custom Feed, Inc., Erie, Colo., 1982-94. Mem. Soc. Exploration Geophysicists. Home: 1201 W Thornton Pkwy Denver CO 80221-5458

HOHNHORST, JOHN CHARLES, lawyer; b. Jerome, Idaho, Dec. 25, 1952; m. Raelene Casper; children: Jennifer, Rachel, John. BS in Polit. Sci./Pub. Adminstrn., U. Idaho, 1975, JD cum laude, 1978. Bar: Idaho 1978, U.S. Dist. Ct. Idaho 1978, U.S. Ct. Appeals (9th cir.) 1980, U.S. Ct. Claims 1983; U.S. Supreme Ct. 1987. Adminstrv. asst. to Sen. John M. Barker Idaho State Senate, 1975; ptnr. Hepworth, Lezamiz & Hohnhorst, Twin Falls, Idaho, 1978—. Contbr. articles to profl. jours. Mem. planning & zoning commn. City of Twin Falls, 1987-90. Mem. ABA, ATLA, Idaho State Bar (commr. 1990-93, pres. 1993), Idaho Trial Lawyers Assn. (regional

dir. 1985-86), 5th Dist. Bar Assn. (treas. 1987-88, v.p. 1988-89, pres. 1989-90), Am. Acad. Appellate Lawyers, Greater Twin Falls C. of C. (chmn. magic valley leadership program 1988-89, bd. dirs. 1989-92), Phi Kappa Tau (Beta Gamma chpt., Phi award 1988). Office: Hepworth Lezamiz & Hohnhorst PO Box 389 133 Shoshone St N Twin Falls ID 83301-6150

HOIVIK, THOMAS HARRY, military educator, international consultant; b. Mpls., June 6, 1941; s. Tony Horace and Helen Lenea (Carlsen) H.; m. Judith Lisa Kohn; children: Todd, Gregory. BA, U. Minn., 1963; grad. with distinction, Naval Test Pilot Sch., 1969; MS with distinction, Naval Postgrad. Sch., 1973; grad. with distinction, Naval War Coll., 1976; MA, Salve Regina U., 1988. Cert. exptl. test pilot, air transport pilot, jet aircraft, helicopter, glider single and multi-engine. Commd. ensign USN, 1963, advanced through grades to capt., 1963-91; test pilot Naval Air Test Ctr., Patuxent River, Md., 1968-71; program mgr. H-53 aircraft Naval Air Systems Command, Washington, 1976-78; comdg. officer Helicopter Mine Countermeasure Squadron 14, Norfolk, Va., 1978-80; dir. U.S. Naval Test Pilot Sch., Patuxent River, 1980-82; fed. exec. fellow Ctr. for Strategic and Internat. Studies, Washington, 1982-83; chair tactical analysis Naval Postgrad. Sch., Monterey, Calif., 1983-85; comdg. officer Naval Air Sta., Willow Grove, Pa., 1985-87; chair applied systems analysis Naval Postgrad. Sch., Monterey, 1987-91, prof. acquisition mgmt. and ops. rsch., 1991—; ret. capt. USN, 1991; dir. test and evaluation sr. level curriculum Defense Acquisition U., 1993—; mem. U.S. Congrl. Study Group on Nat. Strategy, Washington, 1982-83, World Economy, 1982-83; cons. U.S., Internat. Govt. Orgns., 1990—; founder, pres. Lysonics Rsch. Internat., 1993, Inst. for In-Flight Rsch., 1996; flight demonstration pilot Paris Internat. Air Show, 1967. Contbr. articles to profl. jours. Bd. dirs. Vocat. Edn. Bd., Montgomery County, Pa., 1985-87, Congrl. Svc. Acad. Appointment Bd., Phila., 1985-87; youth leader, counselor YMCA, St. Paul, 1955-61. Recipient Legion of Merit Pres. of U.S., 1987, Outstanding Youth Leadership award YMCA, 1960; established U.S. Helicopter Speed Record, 1966. Mem. AIAA, Soc. of Exptl. Test Pilots, Internat. Test and Evaluation Assn. (Internat. Test and Evaluation Cross award 1997), Nat. Contract Mgmt. Assn., Ops. Rsch. Soc. Am., Mil. Ops. Rsch. Soc., U. Minn. "M" Club, Disable Am. Vets, Sigma Alpha Epsilon. Avocation: tennis, music composition. Office: Naval Postgrad Sch Monterey CA 93943

HOKANA, GREGORY HOWARD, engineering executive; b. Burbank, Calif., 1944; s. Howard Leslie and Helen Lorraine H.; m. Eileen Marie Youell, 1967; children: Kristen Marie, Kenneth Gregory. BS in Physics, UCLA, 1966. Design engr. Raytheon Co., Oxnard, Calif., 1967-74; staff engr. Bunker Ramo Corp., Westlake Village, Calif., 1974-84; mgr. analog engring. AIL Systems, Inc., Westlake Village, 1984-91; mgr. product devel. Am. Nucleonics Corp., Westlake Village, 1991-93; tech. mgr. Litton Data Sys., Agoura Hills, Calif., 1994—. Mem. IEEE, Assn. Old Crows. Democrat. Methodist. Avocations: golf, swimming, photography. Home: 3485 Farrell Cir Newbury Park CA 91320-4333 Office: Litton Data Systems PO Box 6008 Agoura Hills CA 91376-6008

HOKANSON, RANDOLPH, concert pianist, educator; b. Bellingham, Wash.; s. Eric and Bina Sofia (Jönsson) H.; m. Dorothy Forrest Cadzow, Jan. 18, 1952. Studied with Harold Samuel, London, 1936-37, studied with Howard Ferguson, 1936-39, studied with Dame Myra Hess, 1937-39; studied with Wilhelm Kempff, Positano, 1962. Concert pianist Columbia Artists, throughout U.S., Can., 1940-49; prof. in piano U. Wash., Seattle, 1949-84. Recordings include At Home With Beethoven, 1985,, Keyboard Works of The Masters, Vol. I, 1998. Sgt. Signal Corps., 1942-46. Mem. Music Tchrs. Nat. Assn.

HOKIN, JEANNE, education educator; b. N.Y.C.; d. Louis and Sophie (Gittleson) Winer; m. Elliott Hokin, May 27, 1966; children: Peggy Willoughby, Debra Linn, Jamie McQueen. BA summa cum laude, U. Calif., Santa Barbara, 1981, PhD, 1989. Prof., lectr. art history Ariz. State U., Tempe, 1988—; v.p. Friends of European Art, Phoenix Art Mus., 1998; vis. prof. in art history, Sch. of Art, Ariz. State U., Tempe, 1986; vis. lectr. ASU Main, 1989, others; lectr. in field. Author: (book) Pinnacles and Pyramids: The Art of Marsden Hartley, 1993; contbr. articles to profl. jours. Lectr. Phoenix Art Mus. Recipient Disting. Tchr. award Sch. of Art, Ariz. State U., 1993; grantee U. Calif., Santa Barbara, 1980-81, 81-82, 1987, Vidda Found., 1988-89; recipient Samuel H. Kress Found. fellowship, 1986, others. Mem. Coll. Art Assn. Home: 13708 E Geronimo Rd Scottsdale AZ 85259

HOLBROOK, DAVID KROESCHER, general manager packaging manufacturer; b. Salt Lake City, Jan. 18, 1951; s. Robert Benson and Marjorie Ruth (Kroescher) H.; m. Arline Johnson, Sept. 7, 1976; children: Jeffrey David, Bradley David, Stanley David, Nicole. BS in Finance, U. Utah, 1975, BS in Mgmt., 1975. From customer svc. mgr. to gen. mgr. Tenneco Packaging, Salt Lake City, 1975-91, gen. mgr., 1991—; bd. dirs. Utah Mfg. Assn., Salt Lake City. Mem. Salt Lake City Rotary Club (student scholarship com. 1991—). Republican. Mem. LDS Ch. Avocations: referee, glass blowing, golf. Home: 2415 Lynwood Dr Salt Lake City UT 84109-1213 Office: Tenneco Packaging 4654 W 1525 S Salt Lake City UT 84104-5322

HOLBROOK, JAMES RUSSELL, lawyer; b. Kansas City, Mo., Sept. 24, 1944; s. Newell James and Martha Inez (Russell) H.; m. Meghan Zanolli, Feb. 12, 1983. Student, MIT, 1962-63; BA, Grinnell (Iowa) Coll., 1966; MA, Ind. U., 1968; JD, U. Utah, 1974. Bar: Utah 1974, U.S. Dist. Ct. Utah 1974, U.S. Ct. Appeals (10th cir.) 1977, U.S. Supreme Ct. 1980. Law clk. to chief judge U.S. Dist. Ct. Utah, Salt Lake City, 1973-75; pvt. practice Salt Lake City, 1975-78, asst. U.S. Atty. of Utah, 1978-80; ptnr. Giauque & Williams, Salt Lake City, 1980-82; gen. counsel Intermountain Power Agy., Murray, Utah, 1982-83; ptnr. Callister Nebeker & McCullough, Salt Lake City, 1983—; mem. adv. com. on revisions to local rules of practice U.S. Dist. Ct. Utah, 1989—, mem. alt. dispute resolution subcom., 1991—, mem. conduct com., 1997—; mem. alt. dispute resolution com. Utah Jud. Coun., 1993—; adj. assoc. prof. alt. dispute resolution U. Utah Coll. Law, Salt Lake City, 1993—. Articles editor Jour. Contemporary Law, 1973-74; contbr. articles to profl. jours. Bd. dirs. Internat. Visitors Utah Coun., Salt Lake City, 1984-96, pres., 1992-93; mem. exhbns. coun. Utah Mus. Fine Arts, Salt Lake City, 1986-92, 94-97, pres., 1988-90; bd. govs. Salt Lake Found., Salt Lake City, 1987-92; bd. dirs. Hansen Planetarium, Salt Lake City, 1997—, pres., 1998—; bd. dirs. Utah Mus. Natural History, Salt Lake City, 1996—, v.p., 1997—. With U.S. Army, 1968-70, Vietnam. Decorated Bronze Star, Army Commendation medal; NSF fellow, 1966-68, Woodrow Wilson Found. fellow, 1966. Mem. ABA, Utah Bar Assn. (commr. 1988-90), Fed. Bar Assn. (pres. Utah chpt. 1984-85, Disting. Svc. award 1995), Am. Arbitration Assn. (bd. dirs. N.Y.C. 1996—), Sutherland Inn of Ct. (master of the bench 1984-95), Alta Club, Phi Beta Kappa, Sigma Phi Epsilon. Democrat. Avocations: fine arts, natural history, skiing, bicycling. Home: 775 Hilltop Rd Salt Lake City UT 84103-3311 Office: Callister Nebeker & McCullough 10 E South Temple Ste 900 Salt Lake City UT 84133-1186

HOLBROOK, MEGHAN ZANOLLI, fundraiser, public relations specialist, state pol. BS in English and Edn., U. Tenn., 1971, postgrad., 1978-83. Dir. ancillary svcs. Ridgeview Psychiat. Hosp., Oak Ridge, Tenn., 1971-83; therapist The Children's Ctr., Salt Lake City, 1985-86; mgr. corp. contbns. Sundance Inst. and Film Festival, Salt Lake City, 1989-91; fund raising and pub. rels. cons. Salt Lake City, 1992—. Fundraiser congl. campaign Wayne Owens, 1986, bus. liaison, 1986-88; fin. dir. gubernatorial campaign Ted Wilson, 1988, mayoral campaign Deedee Corradini, 1991; campaign mgr. gubernatorial campaign Stewart Hanson, 1991-92; del. Dem. Nat. Conv., 1996; chair Utah State Dem. Party, 1996—; mem. bd. dirs. Sundance Inst., 1989—, Inst. at Deer Valley, 1995—; mem. Utah Air Travel Commn., 1996—; mem. pres.'s adv. com. on arts Kennedy Ctr., Washington, 1996—. Mem. Assn. State Dem. Chairs (exec. com. 1998—). Home: 775 Hilltop Rd Salt Lake City UT 84103-3311 Office: 455 S 300 E Ste 102 Salt Lake City UT 84111-3222*

HOLBROOK, WILLIAM FRANCIS, marketing executive; b. Keene, N.H., July 10, 1944; s. Sidney Wallace and Edith (Place) H.; m. Celia Carroll Simon, Sept. 18, 1971; 1 son, William Franklin. BA, Denison U., 1966; Cert. Inst. Modern Lang., Washington, 1968; MBA, Columbia U., 1971. Planning dir. Supermarkets Gen., Woodbridge, N.J., 1971-75; mktg. mgr. Pepsi-Cola Co., Purchase, N.Y., 1975-80; home market mgr. Coca Cola Co., Atlanta, 1980-82; dir. merchandising and sales promotion E & J Gallo Winery, Modesto, Calif., 1982-87; dir. mktg. services Adolph Coors Co., Golden, Colo.; v.p. mktg. Hinckley & Schmitt, Inc., Englewood, Colo., 1994-96; v.p. strategic planning Hinckley & Schmitt, Inc., Englewood, 1997—; pres. W.F. Holbrook & Assocs., Inc., 1997; bd. dirs. Calvary Golf., Inc. Capt., USMC, 1966-69. Mem. Res. Officers Assn., Am. Logistics Assn. (chmn. speakers com. 1979), Mensa, Pepsico Runners Club (founder, pres. 1978-79), Denver Advt. Fedn., Marine Corps Assn., Navy League (life), Marine Corps League, Sigma Chi. Republican. Congregationalist. Home: PO Box 7540 Boulder CO 80306-7540

HOLCK, RICHARD WILLIAM, association executive; b. Denver, May 31, 1947; s. Charles Frederick and Ruby Faye (Bell) H.; m. Carynn Sue Lamb, Aug. 10, 1964; children: Erik, Cheri, Skott. AS in Fire Sci., Red Rocks C.C., Denver, 1976; BSBA, Regis U., 1990. Assembler, repairman IBM, Boulder, Colo., 1966-70; fire fighter, lt. Aurora (Colo.) Fire Dept., 1970-88; dep. exec. dir. Fire & Police Pension Assn., Englewood, Colo., 1988—. Bd. dirs. Fire & Police Pension, Denver, 1980-88; chmn. bd. dirs. FPPA, Denver, 1980-81; coun. mem. Kaiser Permanente Health Adv. Coun., Denver, 1989—, chmn. edn. com., 1990—. Mem. Internat. Found. Employee Benefit Plans, Soc. Human Resource Mgrs., Regis U. Alumni Assn. (class rep. 1990—). Democrat. Roman Catholic. Avocations: skiing, bowling, walking, running. Office: Fire & Police Pension Assn 5290 Dtc Pky # 100 Englewood CO 80111-2721

HOLCOMB, ARTHUR LOY, writer, financial consultant; b. Denver, Dec. 31, 1955; s. Donald Ray and Mary Carole (Moore) H.; m. Barbra Jean Wallace, Aug. 27, 1995; children from previous marriage: Christopher, Terrence. BA in Polit. Sci., U. Calif., Riverside, 1981. Title examiner Safeco Title, Riverside, 1984-86, maj. accts. rep., 1986-88; pvt. practice fin. planning cons. Riverside, 1989-91; advisor Dameron Comms., Riverside, 1988-90. Author: (screenplay) Shades, 1993, (graphic series) Eternal Warrior: Wings of Justice, 1997 (VFW Ann. Outstanding Story), Eternal Warriors, 1998. Gemco Corp. scholar, 1974; rsch. grantee U. Calif., Riverside, 1979; recipient Young Playwright's award Am. Conservatory Theatre, 1969. Mem. Nat. Writer's Union, Sci. Fiction and Fantasy Writer's of Am. Episcopalian. Avocations: painting, golf, travel. Home: 2857 Don Goodwin Dr Riverside CA 92507-7009

HOLDCROFT, LESLIE THOMAS, clergyman, educator; b. Man., Can., Sept. 28, 1922; s. Oswald Thomas and Florence (Waterfield) H.; student Western Bible Coll., 1941-44; BA, San Francisco State Coll., 1950; MA, San Jose State Coll., 1955; postgrad. Stanford, 1960, 63, U. Cal., 1965-67; DDiv., Bethany Bible Coll., 1968; m. Ruth Sorensen, July 2, 1948; children: Cynthia Ruth, Althea Lois, Sylvia Bernice. Instr. Western Bible Coll., 1944-47; instr. Bethany Bible Coll., 1947-55, dean edn., 1955-68, v.p., 1967-68; pres. Western Pentecostal Bible Coll., 1968-87; acad. cons., researcher, Abbotsford, B.C., 1991—; pastor Craig Chapel, 1959-68; dir. Can. Pentecostal Corr. Coll., Abbotsford, 1985-90, 95—. Pres., Assn. Canadian Bible Colls., 1972-76. Author: The Historical Books, 1960, The Synoptic Gospels, 1962, The Holy Spirit, 1962, The Pentateuch, 1951, 96, Divine Healing, 1967, The Doctrine of God, 1978, The Four Gospels, 1988, 94, Anthropology: A Biblical View, 1990, Soteriology: Good News in Review, 1990, Ecclesiology: Christ's Treasure on Earth, 1992. Home: 34623 Ascott Ave, Abbotsford, BC Canada V2S 5A3 Office: Box 466, Abbotsford, BC Canada V2S 5Z5

HOLDEN, DAVID POWELL, minister; b. Chgo., Dec. 23, 1927; s. David Powell and Ann Mary (Walker) H.; m. Gwendolyn Joy Huff, Oct. 23, 1948; children: David III, Daniel, Dorcas, Dennis, Donald, Douglas. BA, William Jewell Coll., Liberty, Mo., 1954; BD, Cen. Bapt. Sem., Kansas City, Kans., 1957, MDiv, 1969; DMin, Golden Gate Bapt. Sem., Mill Valley, Calif., 1983. Ordained to ministry, So. Bapt. Conv., 1951. Pastor Spanish Lake Bapt. Ch., St. Louis, 1956-65, First Bapt. Ch., St. Clair, Mo., 1966-68, Calvary Bapt. Ch., Clinton, Iowa, 1968-76; dir. missions Iowa So. Bapt. Fellowship, Des Moines, 1976-80; dir. Puget Sound Bapt. Assn., Seattle, 1980—; Chmn. Mo. Bapt. Exec. Bd. Missions Co., 1978-80; pres. N.W. Conv. DOM, 1985-86. Bible tchr. YMCA, Clinton, Iowa, 1972-76; mem. Mayor's Blue Ribbon Com., City of Clinton, Iowa, 1972-76. Home: PO Box 1832 Rowlett TX 75030-1832 Office: Puget Sound Bapt Assn 32924 Pacific Hwy S Federal Way WA 98003-6481

HOLDEN, GEORGE FREDRIC, brewing company executive, public policy specialist, author; b. Lander, Wyo., Aug. 29, 1937; s. George Thiel Holden and Rita (Meyer) Zulpo; m. Dorothy Carol Capper, July 5, 1959; children: Lorilyn, Sherilyn, Tamilyn. BSChemE, U. Colo., 1959, MBA in Mktg., 1974. Adminstr. plastics lab. EDP, indsl chems. plant, prodn. process engring., tool control supervision, aerospace (Minuteman, Polaris, Sparrow), Parlin, N.J., Salt Lake City, Cumberland, Md., 1959-70; by-product sales, new market and new product devel., resource planning and devel. and pub. rels. Adolph Coors Co., Golden, Colo., 1971-76; dir. econ. affairs corp. pub. affairs dept., 1979-84, dir. pub. affairs rsch., 1984-86; owner Phoenix Enterprises, Arvada, 1986—; mgr. facilities engring. Coors Container Co., 1976-79; instr. brewing, by-products utilization and waste mgmt. U. Wis.; cons., speaker in field. Mem. bd. economists Rocky Mountain News, 1990—; mem. Heritage Found. Ann. Guide to Pub. Policy Expert, 1987—, Speakers Bur., Commn. on the Bicentennial U.S. Constitution, 1991-93; del. Colo. Rep. Conv., 1976—; adv. Cost of Govt. Day; bd. dirs. Colo. Pub. Expenditures Coun., 1983-86, Nat. Speakers Assn., Colo. Speakers Assn. (bd. dirs. 1987-90, 91-93), Nat. Assn. Bus. Economists, Colo. Assn. Commerce and Industry Execs. Ednl. Found. Sr. fellow budget policy Independence Inst. Colo. "ThinkTank". Mem. U.S. Brewers Assn. (chmn. by-products com. 1983-86, ednl. found. 1984-85, Hon. Gavel, 1975), Am. Inst. Indsl. Engrs. (dir. 1974-78), Washingtons Am. for Tax Reform Found. Co-author: Secrets of Job Hunting, 1972; The Phoenix Phenomenon, 1984; author: Total Power of One in America, 1991; contbr. articles to Chem. Engring. mag., 1968-76, over 400 published articles, white papers in field; over 900 speeches, 560 appearances on radio talk shows nationwide. Home: 6463 Owens St Arvada CO 80004-2732 Office: Phoenix Enterprises PO Box 1900 Arvada CO 80001-1900

HOLDEN, MICHAEL JOHN, lawyer; b. Sheboygan, Wis., Sept. 29, 1955; s. John Robert and Hilda H.; m. Mary Louise Turkovich, Apr. 9, 1983; children: John, Anne. AB, U. Mich., 1977; JD, Duke U., 1980. Bar: Ariz. 1980, U.S. Dist. Ct. Ariz. 1980, U.S. Ct. Appeals (9th cir.) 1980. Assoc. Lewis and Roca, Phoenix, Ariz., 1980-85; ptnr. Lewis and Roca, Phoenix, 1985—. Mem. ABA, Am. Subcontractors Assn. Ariz. (bd. dirs. 1993), Associated Gen. Contractors Ariz. (assoc.), Ariz. State Bar (chmn. constrn. law sect. 1987-89). Office: Lewis and Roca 40 N Central Ave Ste 1900 Phoenix AZ 85004-4429

HOLDEN, WILLIAM WILLARD, insurance executive; b. Akron, Ohio, Oct. 5, 1958; s. Joseph McCullem and Lettitia (Roderick) H.; m. Kim Homan, Aug. 31, 1985; 1 child, Jennifer Catharine. BA, Colgate U., 1981. Crime ins. trainee Chubb & Son, Inc., N.Y.C., 1981-82; exec. protection dept. mgr. Chubb & Son, Inc., San Jose, Calif., 1982-85, Woodland Hills, Calif., 1986-91; sr. v.p., mgr. Fin. Svcs. Group, Inc., Rollins, Hudig, Hall, Aon Fin. Svcs. Group, L.A., 1991—; tng. analyst Chubb & Son, Inc., Warren, N.J., 1985-86. Co-author manual: Chubb Claims Made Training, 1985; contbr. articles to Colgate alumni mag. Mgr., coach Campbell (Calif.) Little League, 1983-85; pres. Le Parc Homeowners Assn., Simi Valley, Calif., 1987-89; mem. Community Assn. Inst., L.A., 1986—; dir. Friends of the Vols. for L.A. Unified Sch. dist. Mem. Profl. Liability Underwriting Soc. (L.A. steering com.), Forum for Corp. Dirs. Republican. Avocations: golf, reading, running, swimming, skiing. Office: Aon Fin Svcs Group Inc 707 Wilshire Blvd Los Angeles CA 90017-3501

HOLDSWORTH, JANET NOTT, women's health nurse; b. Evanston, Ill., Dec. 25, 1941; d. William Alfred and Elizabeth Inez (Kelly) Nott; children: James William, Kelly Elizabeth, John David. BSN with high distinction, U. Iowa, 1963; M of Nursing, U. Wash., 1966. RN, Colo. Staff nurse U. Colo. Hosp., Denver, 1963-64, Presbyn. Hosp., Denver, 1964-65, Grand Canyon Hosp., Ariz., 1965; asst. prof. U. Colo. Sch. Nursing, Denver, 1966-71; counseling nurse Boulder PolyDrug Treatment Ctr., Boulder, 1971-77; pvt. duty nurse Nurses' Official Registry, Denver, 1973-82; cons. nurse, tchr. parenting and child devel. Teenage Parent Program, Boulder Valley Schs., Boulder, 1980-88; bd. dirs., treas. Nott's Travel, Aurora, Colo., 1980—; nurse Rocky Mountain Surgery Ctr., 1996—; instr., nursing coord. ARC, Boulder, 1979-90, instr., nursing tng. specialist, 1980-82. Mem. adv. bd. Boulder County Lamaze Inc., 1980-88 ; mem. adv. com. Child Find and Parent-Family, Boulder, 1981-89; del. Rep. County State Congl. Convs., 1972-96, sec. 17th Dist. Senatorial Com., Boulder, 1982-92; vol. Mile High ARC, 1980; vol. chmn. Mesa Sch. PTO, Boulder, 1982-92, bd. dirs., 1982-95, v.p., 1983-95; elder Presbyn. ch. Mem. ANA, Colo. Nurses Assn. (bd. dirs. 1975-76, human rights com. 1981-83, dist. pres. 1974-76), Coun. Intracultural Nurses, Sigma Theta Tau, Alpha Lambda Delta. Republican. Home: 1550 Findlay Way Boulder CO 80303-6922 Office: Rocky Mountain Surgery Ctr 1630 30th St # 153 Boulder CO 80301-1014

HOLDT, TERRY, computer company executive. CEO, pres., chmn. S3, Santa Clara, Calif. Office: S3 PO Box 58058 2841 Mission College Blvd Santa Clara CA 95052-8058*

HOLFELD, KARL BRADFORD, accountant; b. Alberta, Can., Oct. 31, 1958; s. Karl Bernard and Barbara Anne (Morrow) H.; m. Daphne A. Koropp, Aug. 19, 1989; children: Callie, Taylor. Student, U. Hawaii, 1976-81; BBA in Acctg., U. Alaska, 1989. CFP, CMA. Acct. Anchorage Sand & Gravel Co., Inc., Anchorage, 1986-89, Providence Hosp., Anchorage, 1989-90; gen. acctg. supr. Anchorage Water & Wastewater Utility, 1990-98; asst. contr. Municipality of Anchorage, 1998—; cons. in field. Fin. dir. Anchorage Area Spl. Olympics, Anchorage, 1993—; coach Anchorage West Little League, 1996—. Mem. Internat. Assn. CFPs, Govt. Fin. Officers Assn., Inst. Mgmt. Accts. (cert.), Alaska Karate Assn. (treas. 1998). Avocations: scuba diving, karate, fishing, motorcycles. Fax: (907) 243-6798. E-mail: kholfeld@alaska.net. Office: Municipality of Anchorage PO Box 196650 Anchorage AK 99519

HOLIEN, DAVID L., engineering executive; b. Postville, Iowa, Nov. 7, 1953; s. Willard R. and Arletta A. H.; m. Vicky Ann Boswell; 1 child, Kendra. B in Engring., DeVry Inst. Technology, Chgo., 1976. Sr. design engr. Wescom, Downers Grove, Ill., 1977-83; engring. mgr. Telebit, Lombard, Ill., 1983-86, Telco Sys., Fremont, Calif., 1986-87, XEL Comms., Aurora, Colo., 1987—. Internat. and U.S. patentee in field. Mem. IEEE. Avocation: tennis. Office: XEL Comms Inc 17101 E Ohio Dr Aurora CO 80017-3878

HOLL, WALTER JOHN, architect, interior designer; b. Richardton, N.D., May 14, 1922; s. John and Rose Mary Holl; m. Eleanor Mary Triervieler, Jan. 23, 1943; children: Mark Walter, Michael John, Randolph Gregory, Linda Michelle, Timothy James, John Walter. Student in architecture Internat. Corr. Schs., 1946-47, structural engring., 1959; student in interior design U. Nebr., 1976; student in photography Clarke Coll., 1981. Licensed architect, Calif, interior designer, Ill.; cert. Nat. Coun. for Interior Design Qualifications. Steel detailer, estimator E.J. Voggenthaler Co., Dubuque, Iowa, 1941-42; engr., also methods developer Marinship Corp. Sausalito, Calif., 1942-44; ptnr. Holl & Everly, Dubuque, 1946-47; prin. Holl Designing Co., also W. Holl & Assocs., Dubuque and San Francisco, 1947-87; prin. Walter J. Holl, Architect, Burlingame, Calif, 1987, 89, San Diego, 1989—; mem. convoy USCG Ofcl. Presdl. Security Patrol, 1979; cons. Clarke Coll. Art Students, Dubuque, 1953-61; mem., AIA San Diego Chpt., Bldg. Codes and Standards Com., 1998-99; commd. architect, interior designer and constructor renovations and hist. preservation Dubuque County Courthouse, 1978-85; oral exam commr. Calif. Bd. Archtl. Examiners, 1994—; cert. mem. Calif. State Office Emergency Svc.; participant The Brit. Coun.-Archs. Study Tour, Belfast, No. Ireland, 1995; juror Nat. Coun. for Interior Design Qualification, 1996, 98. Patentee castered pallet. Chmn. Dubuque Housing Rehab. Commn., 1976-77. Served with AUS, 1944-46, ETO. Decorated 2 bronze stars; recipient Nat. Bldg. Design awards, 1968, 69, 73, 94. Mem. AIA (bd. dirs. 1993—, pres.-elect north county sect. San Diego chpt. 1995, pres. 1996, bldg. codes & stds. com., 1998-99), USCG Aux. (comdr. 1975-78), Am. Soc. Interior Designers (profl.), Am. Arbitration Assn. (panel arbitrators), Inst. Bus. Designers (profl. Chgo. chpt.). Roman Catholic. Clubs: Dubuque Golf and Country (bldg. commn. 1953-54), Julien Dubuque Yacht (commodore 1974-75), Mchts. and Mfrs. (Chgo.). Home and Office: Walter J Holl Architect 11255 Tierrasanta Blvd Apt 126 San Diego CA 92124-2890

HOLLAND, GAY WILLMAN, art educator; b. Urbana, Ill., Jan. 30, 1941; d. Harold Bowen and Martha Evangeline (Righter) Willman; m. Morris K. Holland, Feb. 1, 1962 (div. 1969); 1 child, Laura Gay Holland. BFA, Calif. State U., 1974; MFA, U. Ariz., 1984. Asst. prof. Frostburg (Md.) State U., 1984-89; assoc. prof. So. Utah State Coll., Cedar City, 1990—. Illustrator Macmillan Pub. Co., N.Y.C., 1984—, McDougal, Littell & Co., Evanston, Ill., 1989, Addison-Wesley Pub., San Francisco, 1989, numerous illustrations for children's books, 1984-90; work included in annual Best Am. Illustration, Am. Illustration, Inc., N.Y.C., 1984, 85; works exhibited at Soc. Illustrators Student Exhbn., N.Y.C., 1984. Mem. Coll. Art Assn., Met. Mus. Art N.Y. Home: 425 Chicago Ave SE Apt C Bandon OR 97411-9454

HOLLAND, H. RUSSEL, federal judge; b. 1936, m. Diane Holland; 3 children. BBA, U. Mich., 1958, LLB, 1961. With Alaska Ct. System, Anchorage, 1961, U.S. Atty.'s Office, Dept. Justice, Anchorage, 1963-65; assoc. Stevens & Savage, Anchorage, 1965-66; ptnr. Stevens, Savage, Holland, Erwin & Edwards, Anchorage, 1967-68; sole practice Anchorage, 1968-70; ptnr. Holland & Thornton, Anchorage, 1970-78, Holland, Thornton & Trefry, Anchorage, 1978, Holland & Trefry, Anchorage, 1978-84, Trefry & Brecht, Anchorage, 1984; judge U.S. Dist. Ct. Alaska, Anchorage, 1984—. Mem. ABA, Alaska Bar Assn., Anchorage Bar Assn. Office: US Dist Ct 222 W 7th Ave #54 Anchorage AK 99513-7501*

HOLLAND, HENRY NORMAN, marketing consultant; b. Norfolk, Va., Oct. 13, 1947; s. Henry Norman and Edith Leigh (O'Bryan) H.; m. Linda Diane Eggerking, June 1, 1968 (div. 1983); 1 child, Steven Frederick; m. Jane Elizabeth Bond, Dec. 27, 1983. BA, Chaminade Coll., 1972; MBA, U. Hawaii, 1977. Lic. ins. broker, Calif. Mgr. Chevron USA, Honolulu, 1965-75; dealer Dillingham Chevron, Honolulu, 1975-82; gen. mgr. Barcat Enterprises, San Francisco, 1982-85; counselor E.K. Williams of San Francisco, 1985; gen. mgr. Woodside (Calif.) Oil Co., 1985-88; cons. Holland Bus. Mgmt., San Francisco, 1989—; dir. Chevron Fed. Credit Union, Honolulu, 1971-75. Author: Make Yours Service, tng. seminars, newsletter, safety programs; contbr. articles to profl. jours. Loaned mgr. United Way, Honolulu, 1972; nation chief YMCA Indian Guides, Kailua, Hawaii, 1976-79. With U.S. Army, 1967-69, Vietnam. Mem. English Speaking Union, Met. League San Francisco Symphony, Golden Gate Nat. Parks Assn., Nat. Trust for Historic Preservation, San Francisco Mus. Soc., Chevron Adv. Coun., Nat. Assn. Enrolled Agts., Calif. Assn. Enrolled Agts., Sovereign Order of Saint John of Jerusalem Knights Hospitaller, VFW. Republican. Presbyterian. Avocations: travel, sports, bridge, cooking, reading.

HOLLAND, JAMES DANIEL, columnist; b. Alameda, Calif., Feb. 19, 1913; s. James Clinton and Marian Eleanor (O'Connell) H.; m. Vendel Clara Neilsen, Sept. 9, 1934 (dec. 1960); children: James E., Christine E., Patricia C.; m. Kathryn Atheldon Wyatt, Feb. 10, 1962; 1 stepchild, Victor O. Warren. Diploma in Mil. Sci., U.S. Army Command and Gen. Staff Coll., 1952; student, Indsl. Coll., 1954, Heidelberg U., 1955, San Jose State U., 1957; BS in Bus. Mgmt., Calif. Coast U., 1991, MBA, 1995. Various positions Alameda County, Oakland, Calif., 1932-39; commd. 2d lt. U.S. Army, 1939, advanced through grades to col., ret., 1967; exec. v.p. pub. relations Fairhurst Internat., San Francisco, 1967; spl. asst. U.S. Dept. State, Vietnam, 1967-72; gen. mgr. Renaissance II, Los Angeles, 1972-74; dir., mgr. Vinnell Corp., Saudi Arabia, 1975-79; assoc. editor, writer, columnist The Asia Mail, Alexandria, Va., 1979-83, Travelog Mag., Houston, 1984-86; writer, cons. San Francisco, 1986—; advisor, bd. dirs. Vacation Internat., Seattle, 1987-94; bd. govs. Far East Soc., 1985-87, emeritus, 1987. Author: (with others) Burma, The Untold Story, 1986; contbr. numerous articles to Modern Asia, Copley News Service, The Philippines Mail, Asian Voice, 1982—; columnist Far East Soc., 1995—. Bd. dirs. Am. Vietnamese Found., San Francisco, 1988—. Decorated Silver Star with oak leaf cluster, Legion of Merit, Bronze Star with 2 oak leaf clusters, Purple Heart with 1 oak leaf cluster, Joint Commendation Medal U.S. Dept. Def.-Thailand. Mem. Ret. Officers Assn., Pacific-Asia Travel Assn., Korean-Am. C. of C., Hong Kong Fgn. Correspondents Club, Mchts. Exch. Club, Burma Star Assn.

HOLLAND, KATHRYN MARIE, archaeologist, anthropologist; b. Rogers City, Mich., Dec. 24, 1920; d. Otto Frederich and Nina Marie (Caulkett)

Ferdelman; m. John Herschel Holland, Oct. 22, 1942; children: John David, Kay Marie Carlson, William Mark, Linda Ann Wiacek. BA, U. Alaska, 1976; MA in Anthropology, Ariz. State U., 1982, PhD in Anthropology, 1992. Adminstrv. sec. FAA, Anchorage, 1963-75; archaeologist Ariz. State U., Tempe, 1978-92, prof.'s asst., 1984-92; cons., author Anchorage, 1992—; lectr. in field. Author: (books) Rethinking Aleutian Prehistory, 1992, Chulka Bone Tools, 1982; contbg. author: Alaska Anthropological Association Monograph Series, 1988; contbr. articles to profl. jours. With Women's Air Svc. Pilots, WWII, 1942-43. Mem. AAAS, Soc. for Am. Archaeology, Alaska Anthropol. Assn., Alaska Hist. Soc., Pioneers of Alaska, Sigma Xi. Democrat. Presbyterian. Avocations: swimming, gardening, genealogy, mus., travel. Home: 3208 Doris St Anchorage AK 99517-2028

HOLLAND, MICHAEL JAMES, computer services administrator; b. N.Y.C., Nov. 20, 1950; s. Robert Frederick and Virginia June (Wilcox) H.; m. Anita Garay, Jan. 5, 1981 (Aug. 1989); 1 child, Melanie. BA in Comparative Lit., Bklyn. Coll., 1972. Enlisted USN, 1975, advanced to CPO, 1989; field med. technician 3rd Marine Divsn., Okinawa, Japan, 1976-77, 1st Marine Divsn., Camp Pendleton, Calif., 1978-79; clin. supr. Naval Hosp. Subic Bay, Philippines, 1979-81; dept. head Tng. Ctr. USMCR, Johnson City, Tenn., 1981-84; clin. supr. No. Tng. Area, Okinawa, 1984-85, 3rd Marine Air Wing, Camp Pendleton, 1985-88; cons. Naval Regional Med. Command, San Diego, 1988-90; system analyst Naval Med. Info. Mgmt. Ctr. Detachment, San Diego, 1990-92; computer svcs. adminstr. U.S. Naval Hosp., Guam, 1993-95; ret., 1995; svc. rep. Pacific Bell, 1997—. Mem. Fleet Res. Assn., Comm. Workers Am., Nat. City C. of C. (com. 1989-91), Assn. for Computing Machinery.

HOLLAND, ROBIN JEAN, personnel company executive; b. Chgo., June 22, 1952; d. Robert Benjamin and Dolores (Levy) Shaeffer; 1 child, Robert Gene. BA in Pub. Rels. magna cum laude, U. So. Calif., 1977. Account exec., pub. rels. firm, 1977-79, Mgmt. Recruiters, 1979; owner, operator Holland Exec. Search, Marina Del Rey, Calif., 1979—; pres. Bus. Communications, 1983—; cons. on outplacement to bus.; condr. seminars on exec. search; guest lectr. Active Ahead with Horses, Audubon Soc., conservation orgns. Recipient numerous local honors. Mem. Am. Coaster Enthusiasts, LK.A. Can., Mensa, Peruvian Paso Horse Owners and Breeders N.Am. Office: Holland Exec Search 4766 Admiralty Way Ste 9774 Marina Del Rey CA 90292

HOLLENBECK, DOROTHY ROSE, special education educator; b. Yakima, Wash., May 8, 1941; d. George Milford and Blance Mary (McCarthy) Hollenbeck; BS in Speech and Lang. Therapy, Marquette U., 1964; MA in Spl. Edn., San Francisco State U., 1969; m. Thomas M. Chambers, Aug. 14, 1971; adopted children—David, Monique, Christopher, George, Elizabeth. Speech pathologist Mpls. Pub. Schs., 1964-65, Milbrae (Calif.) Sch. Dist., 1965-68; reading specialist Dept. Def., Landstuhl, Germany, 1970-71; tchr. children with extreme learning problems Portland (Oreg.) Public Schs., 1971-80, dept. chmn. spl. edn., 1980-84, program specialist program devel., 1984-86, diagnostic specialist assessment program spl. edn., 1986-94, speech and lang. pathologist, 1994-95; spch. and lang. pathologist, spl. edn. tchr., Chinacum, Washington Sch. Dist. 1995 —; cert. instr. develop. therapy U. Ga., 1982; instr. Portland State U., D.C.E., 1982, 83. HEW Dept. Rehab. fellow, 1969. Mem. Am. Speech and Hearing Assn. (cert. in clin. competence), Common Cause, Cousteau Soc., NEA, Oreg. Edn. Assn., Nat. Council Exceptional Children (presenter nat. conv. 1984). Democrat. Roman Catholic. Author: PEACHES (Pre-Sch. Ednl. Adaptation for Children Who Are Handicapped), 1978. Home: 505 Garfield St Port Townsend WA 98368-4405 Office: Chinacum Pub Schs PO Box 278 Chimacum WA 98325-0278

HOLLENDER, LARS GÖSTA, dental educator; b. Veinge, Sweden, Oct. 22, 1933; came to U.S., 1984; s. Gunnar Yngve and Astrid Margareta (Andersson) H.; m. Gunnel Charlotta Bergdahl, May 19, 1956 (div. 1975); children: Peter, Marie, Lena, Stefan; m. Sheridan Ellen Houston, Apr. 8, 1989; 1 child, Ashley Ellen. DDS, Sch. Dentistry, Malmö, Sweden, 1958, PhD, 1964. Diplomate Am. Bd. Oral and Maxillofacial Radiology. Assoc. prof. Sch. Dentistry, Malmö, 1964-68; prof., chair Sch. Dentistry, Göteborg, Sweden, 1969-87; prof., dir. U. Wash. Sch. Dentistry, Seattle, 1988—; sec. gen. Internat. Assn. Dentomaxillofacial Radiology, 1974-85; vis. prof. UCLA Sch. Dentistry, 1980-82, U. Wash. Sch. Dentistry, 1984-87; sec./treas. Am. Bd. Oral and Maxillofacial Radiology, 1992-94, pres., 1995. Editor-in-chief Odontologist Revy, 1964-69; contbr. over 100 chpts. to books and articles to profl. jours. Recipient Rsch. prize South Swedish Dental Soc., 1964, Rsch. prize Swedish Dental Assn., 1965, Elander Rsch. prize Gothenburg Dental Soc., 1976. Mem. ADA, Am. Acad. Oral and Maxillofacial Radiology (pres. 1997-98), Internat. Assn. Dental and Maxillofacial Radiology (hon.), Australian Maxillofacial Radiology Soc. (hon.), Wash. State Dental Assn., King County Dental Assn. Avocations: reading, golf, cooking, travel, music. Office: Univ Wash Sch Dentistry PO Box 356370 Seattle WA 98195-6370

HOLLOWAY, CINDY, mortgage company executive; b. Queens, N.Y., Aug. 8, 1960; d. Richard Stephen and Beverly Bunny (Harris) Tannenbaum; m. David Milton Holloway (div. Mar. 1986); 1 child, Benjamin Jerome; m. Michael William Douglas, Mar. 21, 1998. BA, Calif. State U., Fullerton, 1981. Lic. real estate broker. Waitress Bob's Big Boy, San Bernardino, Calif., 1984-85; receptionist RNG Mortgage Co., San Bernardino, 1985; loan processor Quality Mortgage Co., Colton, Calif., 1985-88, loan officer, 1988-91; loan officer RNG Mortgage, 1991-92; v.p., br. mgr. Mountain West Fin., 1992-97; prodn. and mktg. mgr. South Pacific Fin., 1997-97; real estate loan mgr. Arrowhead Credit Union, 1998—. Mem. San Bernardino Bd. Realtors (spl. events com. 1988—, comm. com. 1990—), Nat. Trust for Hist. Preservation, San Bernardino Execs. Assn., Assn. Profl. Mortgage Women (bd. dirs. 1989-90, v.p. 1992-93, Affiliate of Yr. award 1990), San Bernardino Execs. Group (bd. dirs. 1994—). Home: PO Box 3187 Crestline CA 92325-3187

HOLLOWAY, ROBERT WESTER, radiochemist; b. Morrilton, Ark., Jan. 3, 1945; s. Otho and Bessie Vance (Woolverton) H.; m. Mary Ella Hamel, Dec. 31, 1970; children: David, Jason. BS, Harding Coll., 1967; postgrad., U. Okla., 1968; PhD, U. Ark., 1977. Asst. prof. U. Ark., Pine Bluff, 1976-79; research chemist DuPont Corp., Aiken, S.C., 1979-81; supervisory chemist EPA, Las Vegas, 1981-94; pres. Nev. Tech. Assocs., Inc., 1994—. Contbr. articles to profl. jours. Served to capt. USAF, 1967-72. Mem. Am. Chem. Soc., Health Physics Soc., Toastmasters, Optimists. Republican. Avocation: sailing. Home: 311 E Desert Rose Dr Henderson NV 89015-8107 Office: Nev Tech Assocs Inc PO Box 90748 Henderson NV 89009-0748

HOLM, MORGAN THOMAS, director news, public affairs; b. Klamath Falls, Oreg., June 15, 1968; s. Thomas Roland and Carol Ann (Seifert) H.; m. Robin Rachelle Truax, Sept. 2, 1989. BA in Comm., So. Oreg. State Coll., 1989. Assignment editor, weekend producer KOBI-TV, Medford, Oreg., 1987-90; from radio reporter to dir. news and pub. affairs Oreg. Pub. Broadcasting, Portland, 1990-97, dir. news and pub. affairs, 1997—. Editor (news broadcast) Doctor-Assisted Suicide, 1995 (First Place award Oreg. Assoc. Press Broadcasters Assn., 1996); exec. producer pub. affairs TV program Seven Days, 1994— (Emmy nominee, 1997). Minister Jehovah's Witnesses, Salem, Oreg., 1981—. U.S. Presidential scholar U.S. Dept. Edn., Washington, 1986, National Merit scholar, 1986. Mem. Nat. Acad. TV Arts and Scis. (Seattle chpt.), Radio-TV News Dir. Assn. E-mail: morganúholm@opb.org. Fax: 503-293-1919. Home: 3225 Starr Ct NE Salem OR 97303-1537 Office: Oregon Public Broadcasting 7140 SW Macadam Ave Portland OR 97219-3013

HOLMAN, ARTHUR STEARNS, artist; b. Bartlesville, Okla., Oct. 25, 1926; s. Newton Davis and Barbara (Hendry) H. BFA, U. N.Mex., 1951; postgrad., Hans Hofmann Sch., 1951, Calif. Sch. Fine Arts, San Francisco, 1953. One-man shows include Esther Robles Gallery, L.A., 1960, David Cole Gallery, San Francisco, 1962, 80, De Young Mus., San Francisco, 1963, San Francisco Mus., 1963, Gumps Gallery, San Francisco, 1964, 65, 66, 69, 87, Marin Civic Ctr. Gallery, 1970, 95, William Sawyer Gallery, San Francisco, 1971, 73, 74, 76, John Bolles Gallery, Santa Rosa, Calif., 1982, Braunstein, Quay Gallery, San Francisco, 1992, group exhbns. include San Francisco Mus., 1960-76, Downey Mus., L.A., 1961, 50 Calif. Artists, Whitney Mus., N.Y.C., Walker Art Ctr., Albright-Knox Gallery, Des Moines Art Ctr., 1962, U. N.C. Annual, 1965, Smithsonian Instn., Washington, 1977, Coll. of Marin, 1983, Hall of Flowers, San Francisco, 1985, 86, 20th Century Landscape Drawings, De Young Mus., San Francisco, 1989, Jan Holloway Gallery, San Francisco, 1989, Bolinas (Calif.) Mus., 1997; represented in permanent collections, San Francisco Mus., Oakland Mus., Mills Coll., Stanford U., Eureka Coll., Achenbach Found., San Francisco. Served with USAAF, 1945-46. Address: PO Box 72 Lagunitas CA 94938-0072

HOLMAN, DAVID CALVIN, television production executive; b. Mercedes, Tex., May 22, 1937; s. Cecil C. and Carolyn (Young) H. Student, Pan Am. Coll., 1955-57, U. Tex., 1957-60, 62-64. Dir. Sta. KTBC-TV, Austin, Tex., 1962-64; producer Norman, Craig, Kummel, Inc., N.Y.C., 1964-67; unit mgr. ABC, N.Y.C., 1968-71, prodn. exec., 1971-74; prodn. exec. sports/1984 Olympics Hollywood, Calif., 1982-84; assoc. producer The Muppet Show Henson Assocs., N.Y.C., 1975-79, producer The Muppets, 1977-79; assoc. producer Ira Barmak Prodns., Hollywood, 1980-81; unit mgr. Trans-Am. Video, Inc., Hollywood, 1981-82; dir. tape prodn. Columbia Pictures TV, Hollywood, 1984-88; v.p. ops. Columbia Pictures TV, Hollywood, Calif., 1988—; v.p. prodn. ops. Columbia Tristar TV, Culver City, Calif., 1994—; guest lectr. U. Tex., Austin, 1987, So. Ill. U., Carbondale, 1987, ex-students assn. of U. Tex., L.A., 1987, 90. Contbr. City to City column Boston Sunday Urbanite, 1969; singer, dancer (off-Broadway prodn.) Ernest In Love, 1965. Served with U.S. Army, 1960-62. Recipient Merit award Tex. Soc. Profl. Engrs., 1963; named one of Outstanding Young Men in Am. U.S. Jaycees, 1970. Mem. Nat. Acad. TV Arts and Scis. (Emmy award 1985), Ex-Students Assn. U. Tex. at Austin (life). Republican. Methodist. Avocations: singing, ballroom dancing, creative writing. Home: 517 Valentine Dr Glendale CA 91202-1143 Office: Columbia Tristar TV 9050 Washington Blvd Culver City CA 90232-2518

HOLMAN, JOHN FOSTER, investment banker; b. Chgo., Dec. 11, 1946; s. William Judson and Evelyn Mae (Foster) H.; m. Paula Susan Anderson, Aug. 1, 1970 (div. Oct. 1978). BS, Ariz. State U., 1969, MBA, 1971, JD, 1975; Cert. Fin. Planner, Coll. for Fin. Planning, 1991. Bar: Ariz. 1975; cert. fin. planner; registered investment advisor; lic. fed. securities. Congl. legis. intern, 1971; trial atty. Johnson, Tucker, Jessen & Dake, Phoenix, 1975-78, Holman, Meador and Hergott, Phoenix, 1978-80; nat. mktg. dir. Franchise Fin. Corp. Am., Phoenix, 1980-87; mng. dir. Fin. Resource Group, Sausalito, Calif., 1987-89; pres. Holman Internat. Group, Phoenix, 1990—; CEO, Internat. Salvage Corp., 1992—; pres. Fin. Freedom Assocs., Ltd., Phoenix, 1992—; v.p. retail and instnl. mktg. McKee Securities, 1993-94; mktg. dir. McKinley Capital Mktg., 1994—; mng. dir. Systematic Fin. Mgmt., 1996—; prin. John F. Holman, P.C., 1981—. Founder Am. Wellness Assn., 1989—; mem. camp com. YMCA, Phoenix, 1968—; life mem. Rep. Senatorial Inner Circle, 1984—, Senatorial Commn., 1991; mem. Rep. Presdl. Task Force, 1989—; elder Presbyn. Ch., 1970—; mem. Ariz. Acad. Town Halls, 1969—. Capt. U.S. Army, 1968-76. Recipient Presdl. Order of Merit, 1991. Mem. Fed. Bar Assn., State Bar Ariz., Sales and Mktg. Execs. Phoenix, Ariz. State U. Alumni Assn. (bd. dirs. 1975-81), Internat. Platform Assn., World Record Setting Am. Transcontinental Relay Team, Mt. Kenya Safari Club, Capitol Hill Club, Delta Sigma Pi, Pi Sigma Epsilon. Address: 124 Washington Ave # A3 Point Richmond CA 94801-3979

HOLMAN, J(OHN) LEONARD, retired manufacturing corporation executive; b. Moose Jaw, Sask., Can., Aug. 30, 1929; s. Charles Claude and Lillian Kathleen (Haw) H.; m. Julia Pauline Benfield, July 18, 1953; children: Nancy Jane, Sally Joan. B.S. in Civil Engring., U. Alta., 1953. Pres. Consolidated Concrete Ltd., Calgary, Alta., Can., 1969-72; dir., pres. BACM Industries Ltd., Calgary, 1972-76; exec. v.p. Genstar Corp., Calgary, 1976-79, San Francisco, 1980-87; dir. several subs. cos. Genstar Corp.; pres., chief exec. officer CBR Cement Corp., San Mateo, Calif., 1986-88, chmn. bd., 1988-89, ret., 1990; bd. dirs., officer several nat. trade assns. Mem. Assn. Profl. Engr. Alta., Calgary Exhbn. and Stampede (hon. life., dir.), Calgary Golf and Country Club, Bernardo Heights Country Club. Home: 111 Country Club Estates, 111-5555 Elbow Dr SW, Calgary, AB Canada T2V 1H7

HOLMAN, PAUL DAVID, plastic surgeon; b. Waynesboro, Va., Mar. 13, 1943; s. Wallace D. and Rosalie S. Holman. BA, U. Va., 1965; MD, Jefferson Med. Coll., 1968. Intern, George Washington U. Hosp., Washington, 1968-69, resident in gen. surgery, 1969-70, 72-74; resident in plastic surgery Phoenix Plastic Surgery Residency, 1974-76; practice medicine specializing in plastic surgery, Phoenix, 1977—; mem. staff Good Samaritan Hosp., Phoenix, St. Joseph's Hosp., Phoenix, Phoenix Children's Hosp. Served to lt. comdr. USNR, 1970-72. Diplomate Am. Bd. Surgery, Am. Bd. Plastic Surgery. Mem. AMA, ACS, Am. Soc. Plastic and Reconstructive Surgeons, Phi Beta Kappa. Office: 2111 E Highland Ave Ste 105 Phoenix AZ 85016-4755

HOLMES, BARBARAANN KRAJKOSKI, secondary education educator; b. Evansville, Ind., Mar. 21, 1946; d. Frank Joseph and Estella Marie (DeWeese) Krajkoski; m. David Leo Holmes, Aug. 21, 1971; 1 child, Susan Ann Sky. BS, Ind. State U., 1968, MS, 1969, specialist cert., 1976; postgrad. U. Nev., 1976-78. Acad. counselor Ind. State U., 1968-69, halls dir., 1969-73; dir. residence halls U. Utah, 1973-76; sales assoc. Fidelity Realty, Las Vegas, Nev., 1977-82. cert. analyst Nev. Dept. Edn., 1981-82; tchr. Clark County Sch. Dist., 1982-87, computer cons., adminstrv. specialist instructional mgmt. systems, 1987-91, chair computer conf., 1990-92, adminstrv. specialist K-6, 1990-93, dean of students summer sch. site adminstr. Eldorado H.S., 1991-96; asst. prin. Garrett Middle Sch., Boulder City, Nev., 1997—; mem. leadership design team Clark County Sch. Dist., 1996-98. Named Outstanding Sr. Class Woman, Ind. State U., 1969; recipient Dir's. award U. Utah Residence Halls, 1973, Outstanding Sales Assoc., 1977; Tchr. of Month award, 1983, Dist. Outstanding Tchr. award, 1984, Dist. Excellence in Edn. award, 1984, 86, 87, 88. Mem. AAUW, Am. Assn. Women Deans, Adminstrs. and Counselors, Am. Personnel and Guidance Assn., Am. Coll. Personnel Assn., Alumnae Assn. Chi Omega (treas. Terre Haute chpt. 1971-73, pres., bd. officer Las Vegas 1977-81), Clark County Panhellenic Alumnae Assn. (pres. 1978-79), Computer Using Educators So. Nev. (sec. 1983-86, pres.-elect 1986-87, pres. 1987-88, state chmn. 1988-89, conf. chmn. 1989-92, sec. 94-96, Hall of Fame 1995), Job's Daus. Club (guardian sec. 1995—), Order Ea. Star, Phi Delta Kappa (Action award 1990-96, newspaper editor 1992-93). Developed personal awareness program U. Utah, 1973-76. Home: 1227 Kover Ct Henderson NV 89015-9017 Office: Garrett Middle Sch 1200 Avenue G Boulder City NV 89005-2921

HOLMES, DAVID M., physician; b. Portland, Oreg., Dec. 4, 1925; s. Paul Harold and Lucile M. (Marsh) Holmes; widowed; children: Patti Narasimhn, David Holmes. BA, Willamette U., 1948; MD, U. Oreg., 1957. Gen. practitioner Molalla (Oreg.) Med. Clin., 1958-65; resident in anesthesiology OHSU, Portland, 1965-67; staff anesthesiologist Emanuel Hosp., Portland, 1967-73, Merideth Park Hosp., Tualatin, Oreg.; med. examiner FAA, Aurora, Oreg.; comml. pilot, Aurora. Lt. (j.g.) USNR, 1943-46. Mem. Columbia Aviation Assn., Exptl. Aviation Assn. Unitarian. Avocations: flying exptl. plane, downhill skiing. Home: 32525 SW Lake Point Ct Wilsonville OR 97070-6441

HOLMES, HENRY W., lawyer; b. Malden, Mass., Apr. 1, 1943; s. Henry W. Holmes. BA, U. Calif., 1966, JD, 1969. Bar: Calif. 1970, U.S. Dist. Ct. (cen. dist.) Calif. 1970, U.S. Ct. Appeals (9th cir.) 1970. Lawyer Pacht, Ross, Warne, Bernhard & Sears, L.A., 1972-78; prin. Schiff, Hirsch & Schreiber, Beverly Hills, Calif., 1978-79; ptnr. Butler, Davidson & Holmes, Beverly Hills, Calif., 1979-84; counsel Cooper, Epstein & Hurewitz, Beverly Hills, Calif., 1984-94; counsel, sports and entertainment law Weissman, Wolff, Bergman, Coleman & Silverman, Beverly Hills, Calif., 1994—; spkr. in field; adj. prof. sports UCLA; adj. prof. sports law Pepperdine U. Law Sch. Contbr. articles to profl. jours. Trustee U.S. Womens Sports Found., N.Y., 1984-97. Named one of Top 20 Sports Lawyers Daily Jour., 1993; Ford Found. fellowship, New Delhi, India, 1969-70. Mem. SAG, Beverly Hills Bar Assn., L.A. Bar Assn., Calif. Bar Assn., Am. Somoa Bar Assn., Explorer's Club. Roman Catholic. Avocations: surfing, acting, art appreciation, scuba diving. Home: 21096 Pacific Coast Hwy Malibu CA 90265-5242 Office: Weissman Wolff Bergman Coleman & Silverman 9665 Wilshire Blvd Fl 9 Beverly Hills CA 90212-2316

HOLMES, PAUL LUTHER, political scientist, educational consultant; b. Rock Island, Ill., Mar. 7, 1919; s. Bernt Gunnar and Amanda Sophia (Swenson) H.; m. Ardis Ann Grunditz, Nov. 1, 1946; children: Mary Ann, David Stephen. BA, U. Minn., 1940; MA, Stanford U., 1949, EdD, 1968; MA, George Washington U., 1964. Career officer U.S. Navy, 1941-64, ret. as capt., adminstr. Laney Coll., Oakland, Calif., 1965-70; dean Contra Costa Coll., San Pablo, Calif., 1970-71; pres. Coll. of Alameda (Calif.), 1971-75, prof. polit. sci., 1975-80; dir. doctoral studies program No. Calif., Nova U., 1975-80; cons. in higher edn., Gig Harbor, Wash., 1981—; regent Calif. Luth. U., 1973-76. Mem. Stanford Univ. Alumni Assn., Rotary, Phi Delta Kappa. Lutheran.

HOLMES, RICHARD ALBERT, software engineer, consultant; b. Santa Barbara, Calif., May 7, 1958; m. Janet M. Dunbar; children: Brian D., Kevin M. AA in Music summa cum laude, City Coll. San Francisco, 1987; BS in Computer Sci. summa cum laude, Nat. U., 1991; postgrad., Stanford U., 1993—. Ind. software cons. San Francisco, 1986-88; software quality assurance contractor Oxford & Assocs., Mountain View, Calif., 1988-89; microkernel diagnostics engr. Apple Computer, Cupertino, Calif., 1990-93, file system engr., 1994-96; operating sys. engr. Hewlett Packard, Cupertino, Calif., 1996-99; staff engr. Veritas, Mountain View, Calif., 1999—. CCSF tchr. & faculty scholar, 1986, 87, Alpha Gamma Sigma scholar, 1987. Mem. IEEE, Assn. for Computing Machinery, Alpha Gamma Sigma (treas. 1986-87). Avocations: playing classical guitar, gem & mineral collecting, computer music and sound generation, music improvisation and composition. Office: Hewlett-Packard Co MS 47LA1 19447 Pruneridge Ave Cupertino CA 95014-0683

HOLMES, RICHARD BROOKS, mathematical physicist; b. Milw., Jan. 7, 1959; s. Emerson Brooks Holmes and Nancy Anne Schaffter; m. Sandra Lynn Wong, June 27, 1998. BS, Calif. Inst. Tech., 1981; MS, Stanford (Calif.) U., 1983. Sr. sys. analyst Comptek Rsch., Vallejo, Calif., 1982-83; staff scientist Western Rsch., Arlington, Va., 1983-85; sr. scientist AVCO Everett (Mass.) Rsch. Lab., 1985-88; prin. rsch. scientist North East Rsch. Assocs., Woburn, Mass., 1988-90; sr. mem. tech. staff Rocketdyne divsn. Rockwell Internat., Canoga Park, Calif., 1990-95; sr. staff scientist Lockheed Martin Rsch. Labs., Palo Alto, Calif., 1995-98; pres. Nutronics, Inc., Carson City, Nev., 1998—; cons. North East Rsch. Assocs., 1990. Contbr. Matched Asymptotic Expansions, 1988; contbr. articles to Phys. Rev. Letters, Phys. Rev., Jour. of the Optical Soc. Am. and IEEE Jour. of Quantum Electronics. Mem. No. Calif. Scholarship Founds., Oakland, 1977; mem. Wilderness Soc., Washington, 1989. Stanford fellow Stanford U., 1982; fellow MIT, 1990; recipient Presdl. Medal of Merit, 1992. Mem. AAAS, SPIE (conf. organizer 1995—), Am. Phys. Soc., Optical Soc. Am. Achievements include patents for means for photonic communication, computation, and distortion compensation; discovery of spin-two phonons. Office: Nutronics Inc 1668 E Clearview Dr Carson City NV 89701-6572

HOLMES, ROBERT EUGENE, state legislative consultant, journalist; b. Shelbyville, Ind., June 5, 1928; s. Eugene Lowell and Sarah Lucinda (Hughes) H.; m. Retha Carolyn Richey, June 27, 1955 (div. Sept. 1966); children: Enid Adair Offley, William Houstoun (dec.), Holly Ann Holmes. *Robert's brother, Maurice Holmes of Shelbyville, Indiana, is a recognized genealogist who has devoted more than 35 years to tracing hundreds of family lines and family history with links to Central Indiana. Maurice has researched more than 50 books and monographs on family and early-day historical data, primarily nineteenth century material. All of his materials are available in theLatter Day Saints Library in Salt Lake City; many are available in major public libraries throughout the U.S., as well as in the Library of Congress. He has also provided free assistance to several thousand families by mail and as a volunteer genealogist for the Shelbyville Public Library. He is a member of the Indiana Society of Mayflower Descendants.* BA in Polit. Sci., DePauw U., 1950; MA in Journalism, Ind. U., 1953; MA in Communs. and Urban Affairs, Stanford U., 1976. Staff reporter Elkhart, Ind. Truth, 1954-57; city editor, investigative editor Press-Enterprise, Riverside, Calif., 1957-70; sr. cons. Calif. State Senate Dem. Caucus, Sacramento, 1971-74, dep. dir., 1978-79; press sec. Lt. Gov. of Calif., Sacramento, 1975-77; project dir. Border Area Devel. Study, U.S. Econ. Devel. Adminstrn., Sacramento, 1978; staff dep. dir. Calif. Senator Robert Presley, Sacramento, 1979-83; chief cons. Joint Legis. Ethics Com., Calif. Legislature, Sacramento, 1981-82; staff dir. Joint Com. on Prison Constrn. and Ops., Calif. Legislature, Sacramento, 1983-94; rsch. cons. Calif. Rsch. Bur., Calif. State Libr., Sacramento, 1991-92; cons. Calif. Hist. State Capitol Commn., 1995-96. *Robert's work in the California Senate Democratic Caucus included organizing and directing a volunteer student group known as Project Loophole, which, from 1970-74, researched and focused public attention on scores of tax inequities and tax breaks for business and other special interests under California law. Its efforts helped reduce or eliminate several. His 1993 research publication, the Criminal Alien, issued through the California Legislature, at that time was considered the most complete study available up to that time of the social, economic and criminal justice burdens upon California from serious criminal acts committed by thousands of illegal immigrant felons in the state. It received the Jack Anderson Excellence in Journalism Award in 1993.* Author, editor rschr. legis. reports; contbg. editor creative writing quar. Noah's Hotel, Inverness, Calif., 1991-98; editor/pub. sports newsletter weekly Big Red Ramblings, 1997—; contbr. articles to mags., short stories, 1961—. Pres., Golden Bear Dem. Club, Sacramento, 1972-74; media dir. Lt. Gov. Campaign, Sacramento and L.A., 1974. Sgt. USMC, 1951-53. Recipient Silver Gavel award ABA, 1969, 1st Place media award Calif. State Bar Assn., 1968, 1st Place award Calif. Newspaper Pubs. Best Series, 1969, 70, 71; Am. Polit. Sci. Assn. Ford Found. fellow Stanford U., 1970. Mem. NAACP, ACLU, Calif. Writers Club, Common Cause. Democrat. Avocations: bicycling, racquetball, world travel, short story writing. Home: 416 Florin Rd Sacramento CA 95831-2007

HOLMES, TIM, sculptor; b. Rapid City, S.D., May 8, 1955; s. Robert M and Polly (Mudge) H.; m. Claudia S. Crase, June 25, 1994; children: Tanner, Kyle, Logan. Apprenticeship with Lyndon Pomeroy, Billings, Mont., 1975-76; BA, Rocky Mtn. Coll., Billings, Mont., 1976; MA, Sir John Cass Sch. of Art, London, 1981. counsellor Sen. High Meth. Camp, Rollins, Mont., 1980-97; teacher St. Paul's Meth. Church, Helena, Mont., 1986-95, U. of Mont, 1996-97; workshop leader Am Soc. Clin. Social Workers, Seattle, 1995. One-man shows include Frye Art Museum, Seattle, 1987, 91; Paxson Gallery, U. of Mont., 1995; Sierra Nev. Mus. Art, Reno, 1995; Hermitage Mus., St. Petersburg, Russia, 1993; Holter Mus. of Art, Helena, Mont., 1996; represented in numerous pub. and pvt. collections. Methodist. Avocations: painting, cartography, dance, mythology; first American artist ever to exhibit at the Hermitage, St. Petersburg, Russia. Home: 422 8th Ave Helena MT 59601

HOLMGREN, JANET L, college president; b. Chgo., Dec. 1, 1948; d. Kenneth William and Virginia Ann (Rensink) H.; m. Gordon A. McKay, Sept. 7, 1968 (div. 1990); children: Elizabeth Jane, Ellen Katherine. BA in English summa cum laude, Oakland U., Rochester, Mich., 1968; MA in Linguistics, Princeton U., 1971, PhD in Linguistics, 1974. Asst. prof. English studies Federal City Coll. (now U. D.C.), Washington, 1972-76; asst. prof. English U. Md., College Park, 1976-82, asst. to chancellor, 1982-88; assoc. provost Princeton (N.J.) U., 1988-90, vice-provost, 1990-91; pres. Mills Coll., Oakland, Calif., 1991—; mem. external adv. bd. English dept. Princeton U. Bay Area Biosci. Ctr. Author: (with Spencer Cosmos) The Story of English: Study Guide and Reader, 1986, Narration and Discourse in American Realistic Fiction, 1982; contbr. articles to profl. jours. Faculty rsch. grantee U. Md., 1978; fellow NEH, 1978, Princeton U., 1968-69, 70-72, NSF, 1969-70; recipient summer study aid Linguistic Soc. Am., Ohio State U., 1970. Mem. Assn. Ind. Caif. Colls. and Univs. (exec. com.), Nat. Assn. Ind. Colls. and Univs., Am. Coun. on Education (chair office of women in higher edn.), Calif. Acad. Sci. (coun.). Democrat. Episcopal. Avocations: traveling, swimming, reading. Office: Mills Coll Office Pres 5000 Macarthur Blvd Oakland CA 94613-1301*

HOLMGREN, MIKE, professional football coach; b. San Francisco, June 15, 1948; m. Kathy Holmgren; children: Gretchen, Emily, Jenny and Calla (twins). BS in Bus. Fin., U. So. Calif., 1970. Coach Lincoln High Sch., San Francisco, 1971-72, Sacred Heart High Sch., 1972-74, Oakgrove High Sch., 1975-80; quarterbacks coach [illegible] State U., 1981-82; quarterbacks coach Brigham Young U., 1982-85; quarterbacks coach San Francisco 49ers, 1985-89, offensive coord., 1989-92; head coach Green Bay

Packers, 1992-98, Seattle Seahawks, 1999—. Office: Seattle Seahawks Kingdome 11220 NE 53rd St Kirkland WA 98033-7595*

HOLMSTROM, DAVID EDWIN ARTHUR, mortgage banking executive, consultant; b. Seattle, Sept. 3, 1943; s. Earl A. and Linnea Sanders (Bystedt) H.; m. Pamela Waite, Sept. 11, 1965 (div. Dec. 1974); m. Elaine Monfils, Feb. 18, 1977; children: Todd Gunnar, Brett David. BSBA, U. Wash., 1966. Asst. v.p. Rainier Nat. Bank, Seattle, 1966-77; pres. Am. Money Investments, Lynnwood, Wash., 1977-80; v.p. Rainier Credit Co., Seattle, 1980-84; v.p., mgr. Nat. Bank of Can. (Laurentide), Seattle, 1984-88, Bank of Calif., Seattle, 1988-91; mng. ptnr. HRM Capital, Inc., Mill Creek, Wash., 1991—. With USAR, 1961-64. Named Jaycee of Yr., 1970. Mem. Mill Creek Country Club (men's chmn. 1989). Office: HRM Capital Inc Ste 100 16000 Bothell Everett Hwy Mill Creek WA 98012-1513

HOLO, SELMA REUBEN, museum director, educator; b. Chgo., May 21, 1943; d. Samuel and Ghita (Hurwitz) Reuben; children from previous marriage: Robert, Joshua; m. Fred Croton, June 18, 1989. BA, Northwestern U., 1965; MA, Hunter Coll., 1972; PhD, U. Calif., Santa Barbara, 1980; postgrad., Mus. Mgmt. Inst., 1985. Lectr. Art Ctr. Coll. of Design, Pasadena, Calif., 1973-77; curator of acquisitions Norton Simon Mus., Pasadena, 1977-81; dir. Fisher Gallery and mus. MA art history/mus. studies program U. So. Calif., L.A., 1981—; guest curator, cons. Getty Mus., Malibu, Calif., 1975-76, 81; guest curator Isetan Mus., Tokyo, 1982, cons. Nat. Mus. for Women in Arts, Washington, 1984; reviewer grants Inst. Mus. Svcs., Washington, 1986-87, Getty Grant Program, 1988-90; panel chmn. Internat. Com. on Exhbn. Exch., Washington, 1984; panelist NEA, Washington, 1985, 91-93, Idaho Commn. on the Arts; admission panel mem. Mus. Mgmt. Inst., 1990; hon. curator Tokyo Fuji Mus.; lectr. museology IVAM, Valencia, Spain, 1994, Complutense U. Masters in Museology, 1994, U. Castilla La Mancha in Museology, 1995; presenter Museo/Mus. Conf., Barcelona, Spain, 1996, Bilbao (Spain) Mus. Fine Arts Conf. on Mus. Edn., 1996; co-author survey com. mus. studies programs, 1986. Author: (catalogues) Goya: Los Disparates, 1976; co-author: La Tauromaquia: Goya, Picasso and the Bullfight, 1986; editor: Keepers of the Flame, The Unofficial Artists of Leningrad, 1990; guest editor New Observations, 1990; contbr. articles to profl. jours. and mag. Fellow La Napoule Art Found., 1988, Fulbright Found., 1994; Kress Found. grantee, N.Y., 1979, Internationes Fed. Republic of Germany grantee, 1985, 92; recipient Fuj Fine Art award, 1990, Sr. Rsch. Fulbright fellowship to Spain, 1994, award from program for cooperation between the program for the Ministry of Culture of Spain and N.Am. Univ. Mem. Am. Assn. Mus., Art Table. Office: U So Calif Fisher Gallery 823 Exposition Blvd Los Angeles CA 90007-4005

HOLSENBACK, J. DANIEL, lawyer, actor; b. Augusta, Ga., Apr. 29, 1964; s. John Alfred H. and Kathleen Elaine Hanley. BA in Politics and Govt., U. Puget Sound, 1986; JD, U. Calif., Davis, 1989. Bar: Calif., 1989. Assoc. Gray, Cary, Ames & Frye, San Diego, 1989-92; ptnr. Tremblay & Holsenback, La Jolla, Calif., 1992—. Contbr. article to U. Calif. Davis Law Rev.; performances include 15 plays, 1992—, 5 films and tv shows, 1992—. Mem. Calif. State Bar Assn., Screen Actors Guild, San Diego County Bar Assn. Democrat. Avocation: surfing. Office: Tremblay & Holsenback 9404 Genesee Ave Ste 300 La Jolla CA 92037-1355

HOLT, DENNIS F., media buying company executive. Student, U. So. Calif. Salesman RKO, L.A.; founder, pres., CEO, chmn. Western Internat. Media Corp., L.A. Office: Western Internat Media Corp 8544 W Sunset Blvd West Hollywood CA 90069-2310

HOLT, JESSICA DICKINSON, artist; b. Lake Geneva, Wis., Oct. 22, 1934; d. Albert Boyd and Byrnice Beatrice (Latimer) Dickinson; m. Edward Brewster Holt, Oct. 8, 1960 (dec. Feb. 1985); children: Douglas Brewster, Melissa Anne Holt Moore, Nancy Louise, Cynthia Ruth. BS, U. Colo., 1957; MFA, U. Ill., Chgo., 1988; postgrad. in Philosophy, Colo. State U., 1997—. 2-D design instr. U. Ill., 1988; artist, tchr. MFA low residency program Vt. Coll. Norwich, Montpelier, 1995-96; artist in edn. resident Wyo. Girls Sch., Sheridan, 1996; initiator, coord. Pass Creek Salon, Parkman, Wyo., 1991-96; editor, workshop dir. Opine, Wyo., 1992-93; lectr. in field. Exhibited in group shows at Rockford Art Mus., 1984, 85, 88, 91, 97, Burpee Art Mus., Rockford, 1985, Nat. Art Coop., Rockford, 1985, 86, Wright Mus. Art, Beloit, Wis., 1986, Chgo. Gallery, 1986, Coll. Ctr. for Arts, Allentown, Pa., 1986, Limelight, Chgo., 1986, U. Ill., 1987, Montgomery Ward Gallery, Chgo., 1987, Betsy Rosenfield Gallery, Chgo., 1987, Gallery 400, Chgo., 1988, ARC Gallery, Chgo., 1988, New Works Gallery, Chgo., 1988, Clark Arts Gallery, Rockford, 1988, 90, Beverly Art Ctr., Chgo., 1988, Randolph St. Gallery, Chgo., 1988, Abel Joseph Gallery, Chgo., 1989, 91, No. Ind. Arts Assn., Munster, 1990, Ucross Found., Clearmont, Wyo., 1991, NAME Gallery, Chgo., 1991, Little Gallery, Calgary, Can., 1991, Laramie County C.C., Cheyenne, Wyo., 1992, 93, Wyo. Arts Coun. Gallery, Cheyenne, 1992, 95, Cmty. Visual Arts Assn. Gallery, Jackson, Wyo., 1992, Banff Ctr. Arts, 1993, Crux Gallery, Chgo., 1993, Wyo. State Mus., Cheyenne, 1993, Ward-Nasse Gallery, N.Y.C., 1994, Nicolaysen Art Mus., Casper, Wyo., 1995, 96, 97, Vt. Coll., Montpelier, 1996, Straumur Art Commune, Harnarfordur, Iceland, 1996, Western Wyo. Coll., Rock Springs, 1997, Side St. Projects, Santa Monica, Calif., 1997; represented in numerous permanent collections; contbr. articles to profl. jours. Pres. Jr. League, Rockford, Ill., 1970; elected county bd. mem. Winnebago County Bd., Rockford, 1976-80; mem. Sheridan Area Resource Coun., 1992-98; visual arts coord. Sherida Arts Coun., 1993-96. Artist-in-residence Banff Centre for Arts, Can., 1993, Straumur Art Commune, Reykjavik, Iceland, 1996. Mem. Coll. Art Assn. (panelist 1995), Wyo. Arts Coun. (grant 1992, fellowship 1993), Chgo. Artist's Coalition, Nicolaysen Art Mus., Yellowstone Art Mus., U. Wyo. Art Mus. Avocations: reading, skiing, hiking, birds, dogs. Home: 1162 Pass Creek Rd Parkman WY 82838

HOLT, MAVIS MURIAL, parents group executive; b. Sturgis, S.D., Apr. 30, 1932; d. Walter Raleigh and Mabel Henrietta (Krauser) Egnew; m. Howard Ray, Dec. 7, 1951; children: David Ray, Roberta Grace, Timothy Mark, Elizabeth Linda. Cert. in counseling, family issues, Multnomah Sch. of Bible, Portland, Oreg.; cert. youth at risk program, Portland State Coll.; student, North Portland Bible Coll. Mgr. The Press, Portland, 1970-71; with McDonald's Corp., Portland, 1970s; exec. dir., founder PAPYAC-Peers and Parents, Inc., Portland, 1991-97. Chairperson Neighbor Watch, Portland; block home chmn., Portland; neighborhood treas., vice chair Mill Park Neighborhood Assn., Portland, land use chair, 1993-98; vice chairperson adv. bd. David Douglas H.S., Portland; activist Neighborhood Involvement, Mill Park, City of Portland, 1985—; mem. Mid County Caring Cmty., David Douglas H.S., 1998; worker various polit. campaigns, 1995-98. Named Neighbor of Yr., Mid County Memo, Portland, 1994, Citizen of Month, 1997; recipient Neighborhood Plan award Mill Park Neighborhood Assn., 1995. Avocations: gardening, hiking, walking, local park development. Home and Office: 1235 SE 115th Ave Portland OR 97216

HOLT, WILLIAM E., lawyer; b. Phila., Aug. 31, 1945. BBA, U. Iowa, 1967, JD with distinction, 1970. Bar: Iowa 1970, Wash. 1971. Law clk. to Hon. William T. Beeks U.S. Dist. Ct. (we. dist.) Wash., 1970-71; ptnr. Gordon, Thomas, Honeywell, Malanca, Peterson & Daheim, Tacoma; adj. prof. U. Puget Sound Law Sch., 1974-75. Note editor Iowa Law Rev., 1969-70. Mem. ABA, Wash. State Bar Assn. (exec. com. real property, probate and trust sect. 1987-89), Phi Delta Phi. E-mail: holtw@gth-law.com. Office: Gordon Thomas Honeywell Malanca Peterson & Daheim PO Box 1157 Ste 2200 Tacoma WA 98401-1157

HOLTAN, RAMER B., JR., lawyer; b. Wilmington, Del., Oct. 20, 1944. AB, Harvard U., 1966; JD cum laude, U. Ill., 1972; postgrad., U. Freiburg, West Germany. Bar: Wash. 1973. Mem. Perkins Coie, Seattle. Articles editor U. Ill. Law Rev., 1971-72. Mem. Order of the Coif. Office: Perkins Coie 1201 3rd Ave Fl 40 Seattle WA 98101-3000

HOLTON, WILLIAM CHESTER, engineer, consultant; b. Caldwell, Idaho, May 2, 1939; s. Chester Clayton and Margaret Ann (MacLaren) H.; m. Rhoberta Phaigh Romo, June 1, 1958 (div. Sept. 1976); children: William Lee, Robert Charles, Ronald Clayton. AS, Regents Coll., 1986. lic. FCC. Electronic technician Litton Industries, L.A., 1963-66; applications engr. 3M Co., Camarillo, Calif., 1966-74; program analyst USN, Port Magu, Calif., 1974-75; video supr. U. Calif., Santa Barbara, 1975-77; cons. Great Am. Tech. Services, L.A., 1977—. Creator digitally controlled screenings theater for Steven Spielberg at Universal Studios, first high speed sound-on-film editing suite in People's Republic of China, variable speed projection control system for Eddie Murphy. Mem. IEEE Computer Soc.

HOLTZ, JOSEPH NORMAN, marketing executive; b. Matawan, N.J., Oct. 11, 1930; s. Joseph Antone and Catherine Martina (Crosby) H.; m. Irene Strano, July 15, 1951; children: Joseph Jr., Karl, Gary, Robert, Eric. AA, De Vry Tech. Inst., 1954; student, Monmouth Coll., 1955-56; BBA, Nat. U., 1988, MBA, 1989; grad., Realtor Inst. Lic. real estate broker Calif., Cert. Factoring Specialist designation Internat. Factoring Inst., Cert. Mortgage Investor designation Nat. Mortgage Investors Inst. Engr. Bendix Aviation, Red Bank, N.J., 1952-56, Hughes Aircraft Co., L.A., 1956-73; pres. Jo-Rene Assocs., Orange, Calif., 1973-86; asst. v.p. Builders Sales Corp., Santa Ana, Calif., 1986-87; exec. v.p. The Lehnert Group, Irvine, Calif., 1987-88; pres. J.N. Holtz Assocs., Orange, 1988—; CEO Holtz Funding Group, Orange, 1994—; v.p., corp. broker Mortgage Outlet Corp., 1992-94; corp. broker Shancie Real Estate Corp., 1992-94. Com. mem. United Way, Santa Ana, 1987-97. Mem. IEEE, Inst. Residential Mktg., Sales and Mktg. Coun., Nat. Assn. Factoring Profls., Nat. Real Estate and Mortgage Investors Assn., Phoenix Club, Am. Soc. for Quality Control. Republican. Avocations: computer programming, travel. Home: 5045-2 E Almond Ave Orange CA 92869-4245 Office: J N Holtz Assocs PO Box 10014 Santa Ana CA 92711-0014

HOLVE, LESLIE MARTIN, pediatrician; b. Santa Ana, Calif., Sept. 26, 1926; s. Alfred A. and Susanna (Winkler) H.; m. Eleanore L. Holve, Aug. 20, 1950; children: Richard L., Stephen A., Kurt Martin. BS, Occidental Coll., L.A., 1947; MD, U. So. Calif., L.A., 1952. Diplomate Am. Bd. Pediatrics. Intern L.A. County Gen. Hosp., 1951-52, resident, 1952; resident UCLA Med. Ctr., Westwood, Calif., 1954-56; pvt. practice L.A., 1956-78, Santa Monica, Calif., 1978-90; cons., med. dir. St. Johns Hosp., Cleft Palate and Craniofacial Ctr., Santa Monica, Calif., 1964—; med. dir. March of Dimes 99th Birth Defects Ctr., Santa Monica.; assoc. clin. prof. UCLA Med. Ctr., 1960—; chief pediatrics St. John's Hosp., Santa Monica, 1964-70; mem. staff UCLA Med. Ctr., St. John's Hosp., Santa Monica Hosp.; mem. Clin. Faculty Review Com. UCLA, 1991—. Contbr. articles to profl. jours. Mem. Rep. Nat. Conv., Washington, 1977-90. Lt. (j.g.) USN, 1952-54. Named Physician of Yr., St. John's Hosp. and Health Ctr., Santa Monica, 1990. Fellow Am. Acad. Pediatrics; mem. L.A. Pediatric Soc. (pres. 1964-65), Am. Cleft Palate Assn. (pres. 1984-85), Calif. Coalition Cleft Palate and Cranio-Facial Teams (chair 1995—), AMA, Calif. Med. Assn., L.A. County Med. Assn., Native Sons Golden West, Salerni Collegium, Westwood Rotary. Republican. Avocations: golf, photography, travel, gardening. Office: St Johns Hosp & Health Ctr Cleft Palate Ctr 1328 22nd St Santa Monica CA 90404-2032

HOLVICK, PATRICIA VALERIE JEAN, property manager, financial planner; b. Seattle, Nov. 10, 1921; d. Henry Carlos Houck and Peggy Dorothy Jacobsen (Houck) Hardwick; m. Carl Andrew Holvick; children: Valerie Ann, Christine Lynn, Debra Jean. BA, U. Washington, Seattle, 1944. Mem. bd. dirs. San Mateo Indsl. Corp., 1950-60, Peninsula Associated Real Estate Devel., 1960-78; v.p. Bay Area Indsl. Corp. Co., Palo Alto, Calif., 1978—; pilot Women Flyers of Am., 1948-54; fin. adv. Ventures Unlimited, 1949-55; pre-sch. tchr. Menlo Park Presbyn. Ch., 1980—. Established and funded 7 endowments for fellowships at Fuller, Gordon-Conwell, Princeton and Luth. Sems., 1961—, endowment Am. Fellowship for Juvenile Diabetes & Immunology AAUW, 1994, funded endowments and fellowship for Alpha Gamma Delta, U. Wash., 1997; pres. Peninsula Alpha Gamma Delta Sorority Alumnae Club, San Mateo County, Calif., 1948-50; mens' program com. Internat. Fedn. Univ. Women, Stanford, Calif., 1992. Mem. AAUW (pres. Menlo-Atherton br. 1989-91, 96-98, citizen amb. Soviet Union 1991, Japan 1995, interbr. coun. chair 1991-92), DAR (chair good citizens com. 1981-96, regent Gaspar De Portola chpt. 1998—), Mortar Board Alumni/Tolo Assn., Toastmasters Internat. (pres. 1998), Presbyn. Women. Democrat. Presbyterian. Avocations: bridge, line dancing, needlepoint, swimming, travel. Home: 34 Barry Ln Atherton CA 94027-4023

HOM, RICHARD YEE, research engineer; b. Phoenix, July 26, 1950; s. Tommy Look and Betty (Mah) H.; m. Kathleen Chien; 1 child, Matthew Richard Chien. BS in Engring. Sci. and Aero. and Aerospace Tech., Ariz. State U., 1973. Asst. engr. Sperry Flight System, Phoenix, 1973; sr. engr., composite tool engring. Boeing Comml. Airplane Co., Seattle, 1973-84; specialist engr. 1984-88, sr. specialist engr. R & D, metall. processing and advanced projects Boeing Aerospace Co., 1984-90, also automation tech.; with customer svcs. and airline support Boeing Comml. Airplane Group, 1990-91; prin. rsch. engr. metallics rsch. and devel. Boeing Def. and Space Group, 1991—. Mem. AIAA, SMA, Air Force Assn., Soc. Mfg. Engrs., Aircraft Owners and Pilots Assn., ASM Internat. Home: 28704 15th Ave S Federal Way WA 98003-3161 Office: Boeing Def and Space Group M/S 8J-74 PO Box 3999 Seattle WA 98124-2499

HOMAN, RALPH WILLIAM, finance company executive; b. Wilkes-Barre, Pa., June 7, 1951; s. Norman Ryan and Adelaide Bernice (Sandy) H.; m. Donna Marie Webb, Jan. 25, 1975. BS in Acctg., Wheeling Coll., 1977; MBA in Mktg., Nat. U., 1986. Paymaster Dravo Corp., Pitts., 1974-75; tax preparer H&R Block, Wheeling, W.Va., 1977; fin. services exec. NCR Credit Corp., Sacramento, 1977-84; leasing exec. CSB Leasing, Sacramento, 1984-85; pres. Convergent Fin. Svcs., Colorado Springs, Colo., 1985—; bd. dirs. Concord Coalition, Colorado Springs. cons. Jr. Achievement, 1990—. Co-winner Name the Plane Contest Pacific Southwest Airlines, 1984; recipient Businessperson of Yr. award, Colo. Springs chpt. Future Bus. Leaders Am., 1995. Mem. The 30/40 Something Social Club (founder, pres. Sedona chpt.), Am. Assn. Boomers (pres. Pikes Peak chpt. 1992-93), Toastmasters (treas. Oak Creek chpt. 1988-89), Kiwanis (sec. 1988-89, founder, chmn. adult soccer league), Concord Coalition (bd. dirs., pres. Colorado Springs chpt.). Avocations: photography, camping, off-road motorcycling, woodworking. Home and Office: Convergent Fin Svcs 5720 Escapardo Way Colorado Springs CO 80917-3340

HONAKER, CHARLES RAY, health facility administrator; b. Charleston, W.Va., Jan. 13, 1947; s. Charles Frederick and Avis Linda (McCarthy) H.; m. Sarah Powers, Aug. 30, 1969; children: Charles Erik, Cara Powers, Katherine Powers, Erin Powers. BA, U. Del., 1977; M in Health Sci., Johns Hopkins U., 1981. Cert. nursing home adminstr., healthcare exec.; diplomate Am. Coll. Healthcare Execs. Dir. residential treatment Gov. Bacon Health Ctr.-State of Del., Delaware City, 1975-80; sr. health planner State of W.Va., Charleston, 1980-83; assoc. hosp. adminstr. Pinecrest State Hosp., Beckley, W.Va., 1983-84; nursing home adminstr. Arthur B. Hodges Ctr., Charleston, W.Va., 1984-86, Carondelet Holy Family Ctr., Tucson, 1986-89; hosp. adminstr. Carondelet Holy Cross Hosp., Nogales, Ariz., 1989-96; CEO St. Thomas More Health Sys., Canon City, Colo., 1996—; bd. mem., v.p. So. Ariz., Am. Cancer Soc., 1989-94; chair, bd. mem. Office of Rural Health, U. Ariz., Tucson, 1990—; chmn. bd. Ariz. Rural Health Assn., Phoenix. Bd. dirs. Sahuarita (Ariz.) Unified Sch. Dist., 1987-91, C. of C., Nogales, 1995, St. Scholastica Acad., Canon City, 1998—, Fremont County, Colo. Econ. Devel. Coun., 1998—. Fellow Am. Acad. Med. Adminstrs., Am. Coll. Health Care Adminstrs.; mem. U.S.-Mex. Border Health Assn., Ariz.-Mex. Commn. (pub. health coms.). Republican. Roman Catholic. Avocations: dog breeding and showing, Arabian horse breeding, shooting, hunting. Home: PO Box 2136 Canon City CO 81215-2136 Office: St Thomas More Health Sys 1338 Phay Ave Canon City CO 81212-2302

HONAKER, STEVIE LEE, career counselor, consultant; b. Wewoka, Okla., Mar. 23, 1945; d. Joe Jack and Ruby Lee (Bowen) H.; 1 child, Charles Byron Howell. BA in Sociology, Colo. State U., 1994, BA in Social Sci., 1994, MEd, 1997, postgrad, 1997—. Lic. practicing counselor. Prin., owner Union Colony Shops, Greeley, Colo., 1970-79, Union Colony Interior Design, Greeley, Colo., 1980-83; career counselor Colo. State U. Career Ctr., Ft. Collins, Colo., 1996—; trainer Colo. Sch. Counselors Assn., Denver, 1998; Myers-Briggs type indicato qualified, 1998; Strong interest inventory qualified, 1998; state rep. 1999. Co-author: Career Video Review, 1996-98. Active Commn. Status Women, Ft. Collins, 1993-95. Mem. Colo. Career Devel. Assn. (newsletter editor 1997-98, pres. 1998—, state rep. 1998), Alpha Kappa Delta. Avocations: scuba diving, mountain jeeping, gardening. E-mail: shonaker@lamar.colostate.edu. Fax: (970) 491-1134. Home: 2060 Stoney Hill Ct # 3 Fort Collins CO 80525-1293 Office: Colorado State U Career Ctr 711 Oval Dr Fort Collins CO 80523

HONG, KI CHOONG, oil recovery expert; b. Seoul, Korea, May 1, 1936; came to U.S., 1956; s. Kwang Hee and Cheung Nim (Park) H.; m. Koon Ja Pang, May 3, 1963; children—Caroline, Marjorie, Sandra, Deborah. B.S., Iowa State U., 1959, M.S., 1961, Ph.D., 1962. Research asst. Iowa Engring. Inst., Ames, 1959-62; research engr. Calif. Research Corp., La Habra, 1962-78; sr. research engr. Chevron Research Co., La Habra., 1978-84; sr. engring. assoc. Chveron Oil Field Research Co., La Habra, 1984-92; sr. tech. advisor Chevron USA Prodn. Co., Bakersfield, Calif., 1992-96; sr. engring. advisor Chevron Petroleum Tech. Co., La Hanbra, 1996-97; pres. KCH Cons., Inc., Irvine Calif., 1997—; lectr. U. Calif.-Irvine, 1973-75, Calif. State U.-Fullerton, 1983-86. Author: Steamflood Resevoir Management, 1994; contbr. over 100 articles to profl. jours. Patentee in field. Assn. Land-Grant Colls. centennial scholar 1962. Mem. Am. Inst. Chem. Engrs., Soc. Petroleum Engrs. Republican. Presbyterian. Clubs: Kyunggi Assn. (pres. 1966), Korean Assn. (Los Angeles) (dir. 1968-71). Office: KCH Cons Inc 7 Glenhaven Ln Irvine CA 92620-1206

HONIGSBERG, PETER JAN, law educator, writer; b. N.Y.C., June 29, 1943; s. Fred and Frida Honigsberg; m. Mary Louise Zernicke; children: Christopher, Liam, Colleen. BA, CCNY, 1965; JD, NYU, 1968. Bar: N.Y. 1968, Calif. 1982. Writer, 1968—; prof. law U. San Francisco Sch. Law, 1987—; cons. legal writing Hastings Coll. Law, San Francisco, Santa Clara (Calif.) U. Sch. Law; lectr. legal writing Continuing Edn. of Bar, Berkeley, Calif.; lectr. bar review Bar Bri Bar Review, L.A. Author: Unemployment Benefits Book, 1981, California Bar Performance Test Skills, 1994, Legal Research, Writing, and Analysis, 1999, Crossing Border Street, 1999. Mem. Friends of Legal Edn. Opportunity Program, San Francisco, 1991; dir. Ctr. for Cmty. Legal Edn., San Francisco, 1998. Recipient grants U. San Francisco, 1990-97, grant Apple Computer, 1992. Home: PO Box 5458 Berkeley CA 94705-0458 Office: Univ San Francisco Sch Law 2199 Fulton St San Francisco CA 94117-1004

HOOKER, JO, interior designer; b. Evanston, Ill., Dec. 13, 1932; d. Armand Francis and Josephine Margaret (Daus) Conto; m. Donald E. Hooker, Feb. 11, 1956 (div. 1975); children: Elizabeth Ann Hooker Gilbertson, Kathryn Maura Hooker. BFA, U. Ill., 1955; postgrad., Ariz. State U., 1972-76. Cert. Nat. Coun. for Interior Design Qualification, 1980; ASID. Interior designer Barrows Design Studio, Phoenix, 1976-94; interior designer, owner Jo Hooker Interior Design, Scottsdale, Ariz., 1994—. Designer showcases for Phoenix Home and Garden, 1986-87, 91. Mem. Am. Soc. Interior Designers (cert. profl., bd. dirs. Ariz. North chpt. 1996—, ethics chair 1994-98, hist. com. 1996-97, Design Excellence award Ariz. North chpt. 1985), Soc. Illustrators, U. Ill. Scholastic Honorary. Office: Jo Hooker Interior Design 6615 N Scottsdale Rd Scottsdale AZ 85250-4421

HOOLEY, DARLENE, congresswoman, county commissioner; b. Williston, N.D., Apr. 4, 1939; d. Clarence Alvin and Alyce (Rogers) Olsen; m. John Hooley; children: Chad, Erin. BS in Edn., Oreg. State U., 1961, postgrad., 1963-65; postgrad., Portland State U., 1966-67. Tchr. Woodburn (Oreg.) & Gervais Sch., 1962-65, David Douglas Sch. Dist., Portland, Oreg., 1965-67, St. Mary's Acad., Portland, 1967-69; mem. West Linn (Oreg.) City Coun., 1976-80; state rep. Oreg. State Ho. of Reps., 1980-87; county commr. Clakamas County (Oreg.) Bd., 1987-96; mem. 105th U.S. Congress from 5th dist. Oreg., 1996—. Vice-chair Oreg. Tourism Alliance, Portland, 1991—. bd. dirs. Pub. Employees Ret. Bd., Portland, 1989—, Cmty. Corrections Bd., Oregon City, 1990—, Providence Med. Ctr., Portland, 1989—; acting chair Oreg. Trail Found. Bd., Oregon City, 1991—; mem. Urban Growth Policy Adv. Com., Portland, 1991—. Named Legislator of the Year Oreg. Libr. Assn., 1985-86, Oreg. Solar Energy Assn., 1985; recipient Spl. Svc. award Clackamas City Coun. for Child Abuse Prevention, 1989. Mem. LWV, Oreg. Women's Polit. Caucus (Women of the Yr. 1988). Democrat. Office: 1419 Longworth Bldg Washington DC 20515-3705*

HOOPER, CATHERINE EVELYN, senior development engineer; b. Bklyn., Nov. 10, 1939; d. Frederick Charles Jr. and Catherine Veronica (Heaney) Podeyn; m. Melvyn Robert Lowney, Nov. 30, 1957 (div. 1970); children: Denise Lowney Andrade, Michele Lowney Budris; m. William White Hooper, Sept. 21, 1974. Student, San Jose (Calif.) City Coll., 1969, De Anza Coll., 1980. Insp. Amelco Semiconductor, Mountain View, Calif., 1966-68; lab. technician Fairchild R & D, Palo Alto, Calif., 1968-73; sr. lab. technician Varian Cen. Rsch., Palo Alto, 1973-84; sr. devel. engr. Hughes Rsch. Labs., Malibu, 1984—. Contbr. articles to profl. jours. Pres. Conejo Valley chpt. Nat. Women's Polit. Caucus., 1994. Mem. Am. Vacuum Soc., Materials Rsch. Soc., Grad. Women in Sci. (L.A. pres. 1990-92), Internat. Soc. Optical Engrs., Sigma Xi (sec. 1987-90, 94). Office: HRL Labs LLC 3011 Malibu Canyon Rd Malibu CA 90265-4797

HOOPER, EDWIN BICKFORD, physicist; b. Bremerton, Wash., June 18, 1937; s. E.B. and Elizabeth (Patrick) H.; m. Virginia Hooper, Dec. 28, 1963; children: Edwin, Sarah, William. SB, MIT, 1959, PhD, 1965. Asst. prof. applied sci. Yale U., New Haven, 1966-70; physicist, asst. dep. assoc. dir. Lawrence Livermore (Calif.) Nat. Lab., 1970—. Contbr. articles to profl. jours. Pres. Danville (Calif.) Assn., 1982-84; pres. Friends Iron Horse Trail, 1984-86; v.p. San Ramon Valley Edn. Found., 1989-90; dir. Leadership, San Ramon Valley, 1990-92. Fellow Am. Phys. Soc. (bd. dirs. div. Plasma Physics 1990-91); mem. AIAA, Am. Assn. for Advancement Sci. Office: Lawrence Livermore Nat Lab L-637 Livermore CA 94550-4436

HOOPER, LINDA IRENE, art educator; b. Salt Lake City, June 4, 1945; d. Richard Wells and Alleen Myrtle (Mikesell) Bleak; m. Preston Doyle Hooper, Aug. 8, 1976; children: Linda Robin, Richard Preston. Bookkeeper various small businesses, Calif., 1963-74; truck driver Calif., 1974-76, paint tchr., 1984—. Mem. Nat. Soc. Decorative Painters (1st v.p., sec.). Republican. Avocations: painting, camping. Home: 19800 Cross Way Tehachapi CA 93561-8907

HOOPER, ROBERT ALEXANDER, producer, communications educator; b. Annapolis, Md., Apr. 13, 1947; s. P. Alexander and Louise (Hickey) H. BA in Econs., U. Calif., San Diego, 1969; JD, U. Calif., Davis, 1974; MFA in Motion Picture and TV, UCLA, 1982. Bar: Calif. 1975. Film prodr. Scripps Inst. of Oceanography, La Jolla, Calif., 1978-79, EPA, Washington, 1979-81; ind. film prodr. with ABC-TV and CBC, Del Mar, Calif., 1981-84; tv prodr. Sta. KUAC-TV, Fairbanks, Alaska, 1984-86; asst. prof. comm. Boston U., 1986-87; assoc. prof. comm. Loyola Marymount U., L.A., 1987-98; exec. prodr. KPBS-TV, San Diego, 1997—; vis. assoc. prof. U. Calif., San Diego, 1999; cons. CBC, Toronto, 1982-83, Radio-TV Malaysia, 1998, Asia-Pacific inst. for Broadcasting Devel., 1998-99, Fiji TV, 1996; Fulbright sr. scholar comm. program U. Sains Malaysia, Penang, 1989-90, U. South Pacific, Fiji, 1994; tng. adviser Am. Samoa Govt.-Sta. KVZK-TV, 1992—; acad. specialist U. Papua New Guinea, 1995; Eisenhower fellow, Malaysia, 1996, course dir., Asia-Pacific Inst. for Broadcasting Devel., Malaysia, 1998—, cons., Radio, TV Malaysia, 1998—. Prodr., dir. (documentaries) Voices From Love Canal, 1978, Decisions at 1000 Fathoms, 1981, Battle at Webber Creek, 1985 (Press Club award), Alaska's Killer Whales, 1989 (Cine Golden Eagle and Silver Apple award); segment prodr. (ABC 20/20) The Deep, 1983; exec. prodr. Nature's Classic, 1998 (Press Club award), Afoot and Afield, 1998, The Impossible Railroad, 1999. Eisenhower fellow, Malaysia, 1996; recipient Hennessy trophy Internat. Environ. Film Festival, Paris, 1983. Mem. Calif. Bar Assn., Eisenhower Fellows Assn., Sigma Delta Chi. Democrat. Avocation: underwater photography. Office: KPBS-TV 5200 Campanile Dr San Diego CA 92182-5400

HOOPER, ROGER FELLOWES, architect, retired; b. Southampton, N.Y., Aug. 18, 1917; s. Roger Fellowes and Justine Van Rensselaer (Barber) H.; m. Patricia Bentley, Aug. 10, 1946; children: Judith Bayard Teresi, Rachel Bentley Zingg, Roger Fellowes III. AB, Harvard U., 1939, MArch, 1948. Ptnr. Malone & Hooper, San Francisco, 1949-60; ptnr., pres. Hooper Olmsted & Emmons, San Francisco, 1964-79; chmn. Hooper Olmsted & Hrovat, San Francisco, 1980-94, retired, 1994. Bd. mgr. Marin YMCA, San Rafael, Calif.; bd. dirs., pres. Marin Conservation League, San Rafael. Lt. comdr. USNR, 1941-45, WWII. Mem. AIA. *

HOOPES, SIDNEY LOU, marketing consultant, educational association administrator; b. Monterey, Calif., Oct. 24, 1944; d. Jack Sidney Wayne Combs and Alta Virginia (Lane) Combs-Snow; m. Dan Fredrick Hoopes, Oct. 11, 1969; children: Rachel Virginia, Sarah Elizabeth. BSBA in Mktg., U. Ark., 1964. Market rschr. Procter & Gamble, Cin., 1964-65; asst. press sec. U.S. Senator J. W. Fulbright, Washington, 1966-68; adminstr. regional office Tex. Chapparal Basketball Team, Lubbock, 1970-71; office adminstr., sec. Tex. Tech. U., Lubbock, 1971-72; office adminstr. Hoopes Law Office, Idaho Falls, Idaho, 1973-82; cons. mktg. and advt. Idaho Falls, 1983—; field rep. to Richard H. Stallings U.S. Congressman; exec. dir. Edn. Found., Idaho Falls, 1994-95; dir. mktg., co-exec. dir. Idaho Falls Opera Thatre, 1995—. Environ. educator Sch. Dist. #91, Idaho Falls, 1982-86; treas. Bonneville County Dem. Party, 1975-76, sec., 1988—; chief fund raiser Yellowstone Nat. Park Inst., 1983-84; bd. dirs. Idaho Falls Opera Theatre, 1984—; dist. field. mgr. U.S. Ho. of Reps. in 2d Congl. Dist. of Idaho. Named One of Outstanding Young Women Dems. in Idaho, 1975; proclaimed Sidney Hoopes Appreciation Day, Idaho Falls Opera Theatre, 1989. Mem. Greater Yellowstone Coalition (charter). Episcopalian. Avocations: grizzly bear research, singing, photography. Home: 2775 W 17th S Idaho Falls ID 83402-5517

HOOPS, WILLIAM JAMES, clergyman; b. Welch, Okla., June 10, 1957; s. Paul Raymond and Bertha Lue (Stillwell) H.; m. Susan Denise Towers, May 12, 1983; 1 child, Robert Paul. BA, Okla. Bapt. U., 1983; MDiv, Golden Gate Sem., 1987. Ordained to ministry So. Bapt. Ch., 1987. Ministerial intern 1st Bapt. Ch., Concord, Calif., 1984-87; pastor 1st Bapt. Ch., Marina, Calif., 1987-91; chaplain USAFR, Travis AFB, Calif., 1975—; instl. min. Fed. Bur. Prisons, Fed. Correctional Instn., Lompoc, Calif., 1991—, Intensive Confinement Ctr., Lompoc, 1996—. Producer TV documentary Insights, 1986-87. Bible tchr. 1st So. Bapt. Ch., Lompoc, 1991—. Capt. USAFR, 1975—. Mem. Air Force Assn., Res. Officers Assn., Calif. So. Bapt. Conv. (revival steering com. 1988-90), Ctrl. Coast Bapt. Assn. (vice moderator 1987-88, dir. evangelism 1988-91), Pacific Coast Bapt. Assn., Lompoc Fed. Correctional Instn. Employees Club (sec. 1991-92), Ctrl. Coast Ministrial Alliance (pres. 1988-89), Calif. Campers on Mission (pres. 1995-98, v.p. 1998—). Avocation: recreational vehicle camping.

HOOVER, GARY LYNN, banker; b. Tipton, Ind., Oct. 20, 1937; s. Carmel Wayne and Virginia Ruth (Mitchell) H.; m. Virginia Maxine james, May 8, 1965 (div. Apr. 1976); m. Laura E. Grigg, June 25, 1988; children: Devin Page, Melissa Virginia. BS, Purdue U., 1959. Nat. bank examiner Internat. Comptroller of the Currency, Washington, 1962-71; v.p. Am. Fletcher Nat. Bank, Indpls., 1971-81; credit examiner Internat. Farm Credit Adminstrn., Washington, 1981-84; v.p. Nat. Bank for Cooperations, Englewood, Colo., 1984-95; chmn. Hoover Farms, Inc., Tipton, Ind.; pres. Hoover Fin. Assn., LLC, Highlands Ranch, Colo., 1995—. With U.S. Army, 1961-66. Republican. Avocations: reading, travel. Home: 9057 S Bear Mountain Dr Highlands Ranch CO 80126-2269

HOOVER, JEANNE KATHRYN, marketing and brand management executive; b. Pontiac, Mich., Jan. 6, 1947; d. Henry John and Mildred Rose (Asher) H. Student, Mich. State U., 1965-69. Cert. profl. direct marketeer. Sr. writer E.F. MacDonald Travel, Southfield, Mich., 1969-71, Flair Merchandising, Detroit, 1971-72; sr. writer, project mgr. S&H Motivation & Travel, Southfield, 1972-76; sr. writer, mktg. supt. Cheshire Prodns., Phoenix, 1976-77; merchandising adminstr. Toyota Motor Sales, U.S.A., Torrance, Calif., 1977-79; v.p., account supr. Campbell Edwald Advt., Hollywood, Calif., 1979-82; mgr. sales promotion Mitsubishi Motor Sales of Am., Cypress, Calif., 1982-97, mgr. market planing, 1998—. Mem. Direct Mktg. Assn., Am. Mgmt. Assn., Direct Mktg. Club So. Calif., Prof. Direct Marketer Alumnus Leadership Calif. Roman Catholic. Avocations: hiking, camping, native American Indian studies, travel, horseback riding. Home: 1 Windstar Aliso Viejo CA 92656-1918 Office: Mitsubishi Motor Sales Am 6400 Katella Ave Cypress CA 90630-5208

HOOVER, ROBERT ALLAN, university president; b. Des Moines, May 9, 1941; s. Claude Edward and Anna Doris H.; m. Jeanne Mary Hoover, Feb. 22, 1968; children: Jennifer Jill Jacobs, Suzanne Elizabeth. BS, Ariz. State U., 1967, MA, 1969; PhD, U. Calif., Santa Barbara, 1973. Instr. polit. sci. Utah State U., Logan, 1971-73, asst. prof. polit. sci., 1973-79, assoc. prof. polit. sci., chair polit. sci. dept., 1979-84, prof. polit. sci., 1984-91, dean Coll. Humanities, Arts and Social Scis., 1984-91; v.p. for acad. affairs U. Nev., Reno, 1991-96; pres. U. Idaho, Moscow, 1996—. Author: The Politics of MX: A New Direction in Weapons Procurement?, 1982, The MX Controversy: A Guide to Issues and References, 1982, Arms Control: The Interwar Naval Limitation Agreements, 1980. Bd. dirs. United Way, Reno, 1994-96, Channel 5, Reno, 1991-95, St. Scholastica Acad., Canon City, Colo., 1991-96. Avocations: skiing, jogging, camping. Office: Univ Idaho Adminstrn Bldg Rm 105 Moscow ID 83844-3151

HOOVER, ROBERT CLEARY, retired bank executive; b. Highland Park, Ill., July 26, 1928; s. Howard Earl and Dorothy (Higgs) H.; m. Beatrice Leona Borroughs, June 21, 1949 (div.); children: Catherine, Robert C. II, Holly; m. Nancy Ellen Pitman, July 25, 1959 (div.); children: John, Elizabeth, Courtney; m. Cecilia Susan Flournoy, July 3, 1981; 1 child, Whitney Suzanne. BA, U. Calif., Berkeley, 1950. Asst. advt. mgr. Hoover Co., North Canton, Ohio, 1951-54; v.p., asst. gen. mgr. Golden State Linen Svc., Oakland, Calif., 1954-61; asst. mgr. Wells Fargo Bank, San Francisco, 1961-66; v.p. Bank Calif. Assn., San Francisco, 1966-84, v.p., spl. asst. to chmn. bd. and chief exec. officer, 1984-94; ret. Bd. mem. Providence Hosp., Oakland, 1985-91, Bay Area Tumor Inst., 1975—. Mem. Am. Inst. Banking, Naval War Coll. Found. (life), Navy League United States (life), Naval Order U.S. (life), Bohemian Club, Claremont Country Club, Pacific Union Club. Republican. Episcopalian. Avocations: swimming, antique collecting, travel, art, skeet and trap. Home: 46 Sotelo Ave Piedmont CA 94611-3535

HOPE, GERRI DANETTE, telecommunications management executive; b. Sacramento, Feb. 28, 1956; d. Albert Gerald and Beulah Rae (Bane) Hope. AS, Sierra Coll., 1977; postgrad. Okla. State U., 1977-79. Instructional asst. II San Juan Sch. Dist., Carmichael, Calif., 1979-82; telecomm. supr. Delta Dental Svc. of Calif., San Francisco, 1982-85; telecomm. coordinator Farmers Savs. Bank, Davis, Calif., 1985-87; telecomm. officer Sacramento Savs. Bank, 1987-95; owner GDH Enterprises, 1993-97; telecomm. analyst II contractor dept. ins. State Calif., 1995—; sr. telecomms. engr. Access Health, Inc., Rancho Cordova, Calif., 1996-97, Any Time Access, Sacramento, 1997-98, GDH Enterprises, North Highlands, 1993-97; employment devel. dept. assoc., info. systems analyst specialist State of Calif., 1998—; founder Custom Label Designer, Sacramento, 1993-96; mem. telecomm. adv. panel Golden Gate U., Sacramento; lectr. in toll fraud prevention and network security. Mem. Telecomm. Assn. (v.p. membership com. Sacramento Valley chpt., 1993, v.p. dir. programs 1997-98, corp. conf. com. programs bd. 1997-99, v.p. pub. rels. bd.), Am. Philatelic Soc., Sacramento Philatelic Assn., Errors, Freaks and Oddities Club, Philatelic Collectors. Republican. Avocations: writing, computers, philately, animal behavior, participating in Christian ministry. Home: 3025 U St Antelope CA 95843-2513 Office: GDH Enterprises Telecom Unit Project Mgmt PO Box 512 North Highlands CA 95660-0512

HOPKINS, ARLENE MARIE, insurance company executive; b. Redwing, Minn., Feb. 22, 1945; d. Arnold Clarence and Margaret (Hammarstrand) Budenski; m. Ernest Richard Hopkins, Sept. 14, 1974. Student, Mpls. Bus. Coll., 1965, Ins. Inst. Am., 1973. Clk. typist Northwestern Nat. Ins. Co., Mpls., 1965-66; file clk. typist Crum and Forster, Mpls., 1966-67, jr. claims examiner, 1967; office adminstr. Crum and Forster, Rochester, Minn., 1967-70; loss coding specialist Crum and Forster, San Francisco, 1970; multiline claim rep. Crum and Forster, Sacramento, 1970-72; workers compensation claims rep. Crum and Forster Indsl. Indemnity, Stockton, Calif., 1972-77; examiner workers compensation div. Crum and Forster Indsl. Indemnity, Sacramento, 1977-82; workers compensation claims supr. Kemper, Sacramento, [illegible] 1987-88; sr. claims supr. Kemper, City of Industry, Calif., 1989, Sacramento, Calif., 1989-90; with div. claims exam. Kemper, Folsom, Calif., 1990—. Mem. VFW (pres. ladies aux. 1983-84). Democrat. Lutheran. Home: 162 Hopfield Dr Folsom CA 95630-8064

HOPKINS, CECILIA ANN, business educator; b. Havre, Mont., Feb. 17, 1922; d. Kost L. and Mary (Manaras) Sofos; B.S., Mont. State Coll., 1944; M.A., San Francisco State Coll., 1958, M.A., 1967; postgrad Stanford U.; Ph.D., Calif. Western U., 1977; m. Henry E. Hopkins, Sept. 7, 1944. Bus. tchr. Havre (Mont.) High Sch., Mateo, Calif., 1942-44; sec. George P. Gorham, Realtor, San Mateo, 1944-45; escrow sec. Fox & Cars 1945-50; escrow officer Calif. Pacific Title Ins. Co., 1950-57; bus. tchr. Westmoor High Sch., Daly City, Calif., 1958-59; bus. tchr. Coll. of San Mateo, 1959-63, chmn. real estate-ins. dept., 1963-76, dir. div. bus., 1976-86, coord. real estate dept., 1986-91; cons. to commr. Calif. Div. Real Estate, 1963-91, mem. periodic rev. exam. com.; chmn. C.C. Adv. Com., 1971-72, mem. com., 1975-91; projector direction Calif. State Chancellor's Career Awareness Consortium, mem. endowment fund adv. com., c.c. real estate edn. com., state c.c. adv. com.; mem. No. Calif. adv. bd. to Glendale Fed. Savs. and Loan Assn.; mem. bd. advisors San Mateo County Bd. Suprs., 1981-82; mem. real estate edn. and rsch. com. to Calif. Commr. Real Estate, 1983-90; mem. edn., membership, and profl. exchange coms. Am. chpt. Internat. Real Estate Fedn., 1985-92. Recipient Citizen of Day award KABL, Outstanding Contbns. award Redwood City-San Carlos-Belmont Bd. Realtors, Nat. Real Estate Educators Assn. award emeritus, 1993; named Woman of Achievement, San Mateo-Burlingame br. Soroptimist Internat., 1979. Mem. AAUW, Calif. Assn. Real Estate Tchrs. (state pres. 1964-65, life hon. dir. 1962—, Outstanding Real Estate Educator of Yr. 1978-79), Real Estate Cert. Inst. (Disting. Merit award 1982), Calif. Bus. Edn. Assn. (certificate of commendation 1979), San Francisco State Coll., Guidance and Counseling Alumni, Calif. Real Estate Educators' Assn. (dir. emeritus, hon. dir. 1990), Real Estate Nat. Educators Assn. (award emeritus for outstanding contributions, 1993), San Mateo-Burlingame Bd. Realtors (award emeritus Outstanding Contbrs. to Membership), Alpha Delta, Pi Lambda Theta, Delta Pi Epsilon (nat. dir. interchpt. rels. 1962-65, nat. historian 1966-67, nat. sec. 1968-69), Alpha Gamma Delta. Co-author: California Real Estate Principles; contbr. articles to profl. jours. Home: 504 Colgate Way San Mateo CA 94402-3206

HOPKINS, HENRY TYLER, museum director, art educator; b. Idaho Falls, Idaho, Aug. 14, 1928; s. Talcott Thompson and Zoe (Erbe) H.; children—Victoria Anne, John Thomas, Christopher Tyler. BA, Sch. of Art Inst., Chgo., 1952, MA, 1955; postgrad., UCLA, 1957-60; PhD (hon.), Calif. Coll. Arts and Crafts, 1984, San Francisco Art Inst., 1986. Curator exhbns., publs. Los Angeles County Mus. of Art, 1960-68; dir. Fort Worth Art Mus., 1968-74, San Francisco Mus. of Modern Art, 1974-86; chmn. art dept. UCLA, 1991-94, dir. F.S. Wight Gallery, 1991-95, dir. Armand Hammer Mus. Art and Cultural Ctr., 1994-99, prof. art, 1999—; lectr. art history UCLA Ext., 1994-99; instr. Tex. Christian U., Ft. Worth, 1968-74; dir. U.S. representation Venice (Italy) Bienniel, 1970; dir. art presentation Festival of Two Worlds, Spoleto, Italy, 1970; co-commr. U.S. representation XVI Sao Paulo (Brazil) Biennale, 1981; cons. NEA, mem. mus. panel, 1979-84, chmn., 1981; cons., mem. mus. panel NEH, 1976. Contbr. numerous articles to profl. jours., also numerous mus. publs. Served with AUS, 1952-54. Decorated knight Order Leopold II, Belgium); recipient special internat. award, Art L.A., 1992. Mem. Assn. Art Mus. Dirs. (pres. 1985-86), Coll. Art Assn., Am. Assn. Museums, Western Assn. Art Museums (pres. 1977-78). Home: 939 1/2 Hilgard Ave Los Angeles CA 90024-3032 Office: UCLA Art Dept 405 Hilgard Ave Los Angeles CA 90024

HOPKINS, PAMELA JENÉ, producer; b. San Francisco, May 1, 1961. Student, U. Calif., Davis, 1979-84. Account coord. J. Walter Thompson, San Francisco, 1989-91, asst. account exec., 1991-92, prodn. coord., 1992-93, asst. prodr., 1993-96, assoc. prodr., 1996—. Office: J Walter Thompson 4 Embarcadero Ctr San Francisco CA 94111-4106

HOPKINS, PHILIP JOSEPH, journalist, editor; b. Orange, Calif., Dec. 10, 1954; s. Philip Joseph and Marie Elizabeth H.; m. Susan Lisa Ingman Hopkins, Oct. 5, 1991; 1 child, Robin Genevieve Hopkins. BA in Journalism, San Diego State U., 1977. Cert. tissue therapist Center for Decubitis Ulcer Research, 1981. Reporter, La Jolla Light & Journal (Calif.), 1973; editorial cons. San Diego Union, 1974; asst. producer Southwestern Cable TV, San Diego, 1974; corr. Mission Cable TV, San Diego, 1975; photojournalist United Press Internat., San Diego, 1976; editor Rx Home Care mag., L.A., 1981, Hosp. Info. Mgmt. mag., 1981; editor, assoc. pub. Arcade mag., 1982; mng. editor Personal Computer Age, L.A., 1983-84; bur. chief Newsbytes syndicated column, 1985-86; v.p. Humbird Hopkins Inc., L.A., 1978-88; personal fin. writer Hume Pub. Co., 1987-89; writer, editor and researcher Ind. Rsch. and Info. Svc., 1988-90; writer, analyst Geneva Bus. Rsch., 1990; sci. writer, The Cousteau Soc., 1990; pub. cons. U. So. Calif., 1989; mgr. KP-IT, Kaiser Permanente, 1991—. Recipient 1st and 4th place awards Nikon, Inc., Photo Contest, 1974; 3rd prize Minolta Camera Co. Creative Photography awards, 1975; Best Feature Photo award Sigma Delta Chi Mark of Excellence contest, 1977. Pres. Ind. Writers of So. Calif., 1988. Mem. Healthcare Info. and Mgmt. Sys. Soc., Computer Press Assn. (life, hon.). Co-author: The Students' Survival Guide, 1977, 78; photographs have appeared in Time and Omni mags., The Mythology of Middle Earth, Parenting Your Aging Parents, Beginners Guide to the SLR, NBC-TV's Saturday Night Live. Office: Kaiser Permanente 393 E Walnut ITSD/992 Pasadena CA 91188

HOPKINS, ROBERT ARTHUR, retired industrial engineer; b. Youngstown, Ohio, Dec. 14, 1920; s. Arthur George and Margaret Viola (Brush) H.; m. Mary Madelaine Bailey, Apr. 6, 1946; 1 child, Marlaine Hopkins Kaiser. BBA, Case Western Reserve U., 1949; cert. loss control engr., U. Calif., Berkeley, 1969. Ins. agt. Nat. Life and Accident Ins. Co., Lorain, Akron, Ohio, 1951-56, San Mateo, Calif., 1951-56; ins. agt., engr. Am. Hardware Mt. Ins. Co., San Jose, Fresno, Calif., 1956-60; loss control engr. Manhattan Guarantee-Continental Ins. Co., Calif., 1967-77. Organizer Operation Alert DC, Lorain, 1951-52; prin. spkr. DC, Fresno, 1957; active Pleasant Hill (Calif.) Civil Action Com., 1981-83; civilian coord. Office Emergency Svcs., Pleasant Hill, 1983-85; advisor, coord. airshows and warbird aircraft, 1980—; chmn. bd. Western Aerospace Mus., Oakland, Calif., 1988; ops. asst. for tower and ops. 50th Anniversary Golden Gate Bridge, San Francisco, 1987; advisor, coord. Travis AFB Air Expo '90, 1990; advisor Air Expo '96, NAS Alameda (Calif.) 50th Anniversary, 1990; advisor NAS Moffett Field Air Show, 1990, 92, Calif. Coast Air Show, Half Moon Bay, 1993-94, Dixon May Fair honoring WWII 50th anniversary, 1995; warbird coord. Port of Oakland Airshow, 1987; warbird advisor/coord. Beale AFB, 1993—; mem. Smithsonian Mus, Smithsonian Air & Space Mus; charter mem. Nat. Mus. of Am. Indian, Am. Air Mus. Britain; life mem. Western Aerospace Mus. Served with USAAC, 1942-46. Recipient Letter of Appreciation Fresno DC, 1957, cert. of appreciation City of Pleasant Hill, 1986, cert. of recognition and spl. citizenship award Calif. State Senate, 1995. Mem. No. Calif. Safety Engrs. Assn. (v.p., pres., chmn. 1974-77), Confederate Air Force (mem. staff, leader Pacific wing 1980—), Nat. Aero. Assn., Aero. Club No. Calif., Hamilton Field Assn. (dir. ops. Wings of Victory Air Show 1987, coord. 1988, 89—, asst. to pres. 1989—, advisor contr. 1990—), VFW (life, state civil disaster chmn. Area 5 Calif. 1991), Air Force Assn., Kiwanis (chpt. sec.-treas.), Am. Air Mus. in Britain. Republican. Roman Catholic. Avocations: fishing, reading, writing, aircraft restoration. Home: 48 Mazie Dr Pleasant Hill CA 94523-3310

HOPKINSON, SHIRLEY LOIS, library and information science educator; b. Boone, Iowa, Aug 25, 1924; d. Arthur Perry and Zora (Smith) Hopkinson; student Coe Coll., 1942-43; AB cum laude (Phi Beta Kappa scholar 1944), U. Colo., 1945; BLS, U. Calif., 1949; MA (Honnold Honor scholar 1945-46), Claremont Grad. Sch., 1951; EdM, U. Okla., 1952, EdD, 1957 Tchr. pub. sch. Stigler, Okla., 1946-47, Palo Verde High Sch., Jr. Coll., Blythe, Calif., 1947-48; asst. librarian Modesto (Calif.) Jr. Coll., 1949-51; tchr., librarian Fresno, Calif., 1951-52, La Mesa, Cal., 1953-55; asst. prof. librarianship, instructional materials dir. Chaffey Coll., Ontario, Calif., 1955-59; asst. prof. librarian ship, San Jose (Calif.) State Coll., 1959-64; assoc. prof., 1964-69, prof., 1969—; bd. dirs. NDEA Inst. Sch. Librs., summer 1966; mem. Santa Clara County Civil Service Bd. Examiners. Recipient Master Gardner cert. Oreg. State U. Extension Svc. Book reviewer for jours. Mem. ALA, Calif. Library Assn., Audio-Visual Assn. Calif., NEA, AAUP, AAUW (dir. 1957-58), Bus. Profl. Women's Club, Sch. Librs. Assn. Calif. (com. mem., treas. No. sect. 1951-52), San Diego County [illegible]), Calif. Tchrs. Assn., LWV (bd. dirs. 1950-51, publs. chmn.), Phi Beta Kappa, Alpha Lambda Delta, Alpha Beta Alpha, Kappa Delta Pi, Phi Kappa Phi (disting. acad. achievement award 1981), Delta Kappa Gamma (sec. 1994-96, legis. liaison, 1996—). Author: Descriptive Cataloging of Library Materials; Instructional Materials for Teaching the Use of the Library. Contbr. to profl. publs. Editor: Calif. Sch. Libraries, 1963-64; asst. editor: Sch. Library Assn. of Calif. Bull., 1961-63; book reviewer profl. jours. Office: 1340 Pomeroy Ave Apt 408 Santa Clara CA 95051-3658

HOPP, RICHARD A., lawyer; b. Seattle, Dec. 11, 1946. BA, San Luis Rey Coll., 1969; JD, U. Wash., 1976. Bar: Wash. 1976. Mem. Stoel, Rives, Boley, Jones & Grey, Seattle; chmn. Seattle Pension Roundtable, 1987—. Articles editor Washington Law Review, 1975-76. Mem. ABA, Wash. State Bar Assn. (bd. dirs. Seattle chpt., western pension conf. 1985-87, tax coun., taxation sect.), Seattle-King County. Office: Stoel Rives Boley Jones & Grey 600 University St Ste 3600 Seattle WA 98101-2070*

HOPPING, WILLIAM RUSSELL, hospitality industry consultant and appraiser; b. Balt., May 3, 1947; s. Russell Leroy and Janet Louise (Cloud) H.; m. Catherine Wilson; 1 child, William Alexander. BS in Hotel Adminstrn., Cornell U., 1969; MBA, U. Denver, 1978. Mgr. Sylvania (Ohio) Country Club, 1972-77; sr. cons. Pannell Kerr Forster, Denver, 1978-82; cons. Ginther Wycoff Grp., Denver, 1982-85; pres. W.R. Hopping & Co., Inc., Denver, 1985—; mem. adv. bd. travel and tourism dept. Arapahoe C.C., 1998. Vol., Big Bros., Inc., Denver, 1990—; chmn. adv. bd. U. Denver Profl. Career Devel. Prog., 1987-88, chmn. task force, Career and Placement Ctr., 1989. 1st lt. U.S. Army, 1970-72. Mem. Appraisal Inst., Internat. Soc. Hospitality Cons. (pres. 1990-91, chmn. 1991-93, chmn. emeritus, 1993—), Cornell Soc. Hotelmen (pres. Rocky Mountain chpt. 1984-85), Counselors of Real Estate. Avocations: bicycling, skiing. Office: W R Hopping & Co Inc 6334 S Yates Ct Littleton CO 80123-6738

HOPSON, ANDY, public relations executive. Pres. Evans Group, Salt Lake City. Office: Evans Group 110 Social Hall Ave Salt Lake City UT 84111-1504*

HORAN, ADEL EDWARD, sociology and psychology educator; b. Salt, Jordan, Sept. 17, 1943; s. Awad and Martha (Neshweiwat) H.; m. Samira A., March 11, 1966; 1 child, Marsha. BFA, Da Vinci Art Acad., 1964; MA in Humanities and Arts, Sussex Coll., 1981; MA in Psychology and Counseling, Liberty U., 1991; PhD in Human Svcs., Social Indsl. Psych, Walden/Ind. U., 1994. Art dir. Nesco Advt., Jordan, 1960-65, Kuwait Oil Co., 1965-70, Samira Advt., Toronto, Can., 1971-75, Readers Digest, Pleasantville, N.Y., 1976-79, Yonkers (N.Y.) Gazette, 1979-82; fine artist Horan Art Studio, Phoenix, 1982-85; instr. Rio Salado Coll., Phoenix, 1985-89, Horan Art Sch., Phoenix, 1989-94; counselor St. John of the Desert, Phoenix, 1989-93; prof. sociology and psychology Ariz. Inst. Bus. and Tech., 1994-96; prof. psychology, sociology, counseling, English, art Maricopa County Colls.-Rio Salado Colls., 1985-89, 96—; adj. prof. Maricopa C.C., Rio Salado Coll., Al Collins Coll., Chapman U., Luke Air Force Base, Ariz., 1996—, Gateway Coll. Author: Origins and Early Egyptian Art, 1982, Art in the Middle East, 1982, Arab-Americans Acculturation into the American Society, 1995, Suicide in the Elderly, 1995, Parental Influence and Student's Drug Use, 1995, Israeli-Arab Conflict 1917-2000, 1996,; publisher (mag.) The Immigrant, 1978, The Arab World, 1978. Recipient proclamations and recognitions for cmty. svcs. and achievements Gov. N.Y., City of Yonkerss, Mayor of Yonkers, City of Scottsdale, Mayor of Scottsdale, Scottsdale Bd. Edn., Rio Saldo Collss., Ariz. Inst. Bus. and Tech., Emir of Kuwait, Chief of Staff-Jordan, Princess Basma of Jordan, Prince Hassan of Jordan, Prince Abdulla of Jordan, Royal Palace of Jordan, Royal Cultural Ctr. Jordan. Mem. Am. Assn. Counseling Devel., Am. Assn. Christian Counseling, Am. Assn. Family Therapists, Am. Assn. of the Aged, Am. Multicultural Assn., Am. Portrait Soc., Phoenix Guild, Calif. Reference, Scottsdale Artists League, Paradise Valley (Ariz.) C. of C., Gibran Khalil Scholar Found. N. Am. Republican. Roman Catholic. Avocations: art, music, travel, helping others.

HORAN, MARY ANN THERESA, nurse; b. Denver, July 4, 1936; d. John Paul and Lucille (Somma) Perito; m. Stephen F. Horan, Sr., Dec. 28, 1957; children: Seanna, Dana, Michelle, Annette, Stephen Jr., Christine, David. BSN, Loretto Heights Coll., Denver, 1958; postgrad, Pima Community Coll., 1982. RN, Ala. Staff nurse Med. Ctr. Hosp., Huntsville, Ala., 1978-79, Crestwood Hosp., Huntsville, 1980-81, St. Joseph Hosp. Eye Surgery, Tucson, 1981—; v.p. Success Achievement Ctr., Tucson, 1987—; Shaklee distbr., 1996—. Contbr. articles to nursing jours., poetry to lit. jours. Republican. Roman Catholic. Home: 8311 E 3rd St Tucson AZ 85710-2550

HORLOR, IAN THOMAS, state official; b. London, Apr. 29, 1953; s. William Thomas and Edna (Barrie) H.; m. Carolyn B. Horlor, Aug. 12, 1978; 1 child, Brian Thomas. BA in History and Polit. Sci., San Diego State U., 1975. Eligibility supr. San Diego County Dept. Social Svcs., San Diego, 1989-93; fin. svc. specialist Wash. State Dept. Social and Health Svcs., Tacoma, 1993-94, fin. spl. supr., 1994-98; program mgr. Wash. State Dept. Social and Health Svcs., Lacey, 1998—. Bd. dirs. Children in Need, San Diego, 1989-93; pres. Carefree East Homeowners Assn., Santee, Calif., 1988-92; troop com. chair Boy Scouts Am., Enumclaw, Wash., 1995—, asst. scoutmaster, 1993-95. Democrat. Avocations: music, woodworking. Home: 445 Victor St Enumclaw WA 98022-8445

HORN, CHRISTIAN FRIEDRICH, venture capital company executive; b. Dresden, Germany, Dec. 23, 1927; came to U.S., 1954, naturalized, 1959; s. Otto Hugo and Elsa H.; m. Christa Winkler, Feb. 13, 1954; 1 child, Sabrina. MS, Technische Hochschule, Dresden, 1951; PhD, Technische Hochschule, Aachen, Germany, 1958. Rsch. scientist German Acad. Sci., Berlin, 1951-53, Farbwerke Hoechst, Germany, 1953-54; rsch. mgr. Union Carbide, N.Y.C., 1954-65; pres. Polymer Tech. Inc., N.Y.C., 1965-74; v.p. W.R. Grace & Co., N.Y.C., 1974-81, sr. v.p., 1981-95, also bd. dirs.; pres. Horn Venture Ptnrs. (formerly Grace Horn Ventures), Cupertino, Calif., 1983—, mng. ptnr., 1987—; pres. Horn Investment Corp., Cupertino, 1996—; bd. dirs. Cardiopulmonary, Timothy's Coffees of the World, Rosti Inc. Patentee in field. With German Army, 1944-45. Decorated Iron Cross. Lutheran. Office: Horn Venture Ptnrs 20300 Stevens Creek Blvd Cupertino CA 95014-2240

HORN, JOHN HAROLD, lawyer; b. Eugene, Oreg., Mar. 4, 1927; s. Harold William and Mildred A. (Truesdale) H.; m. Deloris Eileen Davis, Aug. 22, 1948; children: Lorraine, Deborah, Lisa, Darren. BS, U. Oreg., 1949, JD, 1951. Bar: Oreg. 1951, U.S. Dist. Ct. Oreg. 1957. Ptnr. Horn & Slocum, Roseburg, Oreg., 1951-65, Riddlesbarger, Pederson, Young & Horn, Eugene, 1970-74, Young, Horn, Cass & Scott, Eugene, 1974-82; pvt. practice Roseburg, 1965-70; pvt. practice, Eugene, 1982—. Chmn. fund raising Douglas County unit ARC, 1966, county chmn., 1968; exec. bd., legal advisor Eugene Mission, 1979—; pres. bd. dirs. Jubilee Ministries, Eugene, 1980—; v.p., bd. dirs. His Word Broadcasting, 1989-91, pres. bd. dirs., 1991—. Recipient Outstanding Svc. award ARC, 1968. Mem. ABA, Oreg. Bar Assn., Douglas County Bar Assn. (pres. 1960, chmn. grievance com. 1961-62), Lake County Bar Assn., Lions. Republican. Avocations: aviation, golf, skiing. Home: 640 Elwood Ct Eugene OR 97401-2235 Office: 875 Country Club Rd Eugene OR 97401-2255

HORN, PAUL ERVIN, minister; b. Grinnell, Iowa, Mar. 24, 1919; s. Harry Edgar and Florence Henrietta (Bump) H.; m. Elvis Devlin, Dec. 21, 1940; children: Sandra, Larry, Cynthia. BA, San Jose State U., 1942; MDiv, Berkeley Bapt. Div. Sch., 1945; PhD, Calif. Grad. Sch. Theology, 1973. Ordained to ministry Conservative Bapt. Assn. Am., 1945. Pastor Elmhurst Bapt. Ch., Oakland, Calif., 1945-55, Bell Bapt. Ch., Cudahy, Calif., 1955-66, 1st Bapt. Ch., Montclair, Calif., 1966-77, Calvary Bapt. Ch., Hemet, Calif., 1977-83, 1st Bapt. Ch., Wrightwood, Calif., 1984-90; bd. dirs. Conservative Bapt. Assn. So. Calif., Anaheim, 1956-88, pres., 1959-60, min. at large, 1990—; bd. dirs. Conservative Bapt. Home Mission Soc., Wheaton, Ill., 1960-66; parliamentarian Conservative Bapt. Assn. Am., Wheaton, 1950-85, v.p. western chpt., 1967-74. Mem. Conservative Bapt. Fgn. Mission Soc. (sec. 1988-91). Republican. Avocation: photography. Address: PO Box 1422 Yucaipa CA 92399-1422

HORN, STEPHEN, congressman, political science educator; b. San Juan Bautista, Calif., May 31, 1931; s. John Stephen and Isabelle (McCaffrey) H.;

m. Nini Moore, Sept. 4, 1954; children: Marcia Karen, John Stephen. AB with great distinction, Stanford, 1953, postgrad., 1953-54, 55-56, PhD in Polit. Sci, 1958; M in Pub Adminstrn., Harvard, 1955. Congl. fellow, 1958-59; adminstrv. asst. to sec. labor Washington, 1959-60; legislative asst. to U.S. Senator Thomas H. Kuchel, 1960-66; sr. fellow The Brookings Instn., 1966-69; dean grad. studies and research Am. U., 1969-70; pres. Calif. State U., Long Beach, 1970-88, Trustee prof. polit. sci., 1988-93; mem. 103rd-105th Congress from 38th Calif. dist., 1993—, mem. govt. reform & oversight, transp. & infrastructure com.; sr. cons., host The Govt. Story on TV, The Election Game (radio series), 1967-69, vice chmn. U.S. Commn. on Civil Rights, 1969-80 (commr. 1980-82); chmn. Urban Studies Fellow Adv. Com., U.S. Dept. HUD, 1969-70; mem. Law Enforcement Ednl. Prog. Adv. Com., U.S. Dept Justice, 1969-70; adv. bd. Nat. Inst. Corrections, 1972-88 (chmn. 1984-87),. Author: The Cabinet and Congress, 1960, Unused Power: The Work of the Senate Committee on Appropriations, 1970, (with Edmund Beard) Congressional Ethics: The View from the House, 1975. Active Pres.-elect Nixon's Task Force on Orgn. Exec. Br., 1968, Kutak Found.; vice chmn. Long Beach Area C. of C., 1984-88; co-founder Western U.S. Com. Arts and Scis. for Eisenhower, 1956; chmn. Am. Assn. State Colls. and Univs., 1985-86; mem. Calif. Ednl. Facilities Authority, 1984-93. USAR, 1954-62. Fellow John F. Kennedy Inst. Politics Harvard U., 1966-67. Fellow Nat. Acad. Pub. Adminstrn.; mem. Stanford Assocs., Stanford Alumni Assn. (pres. 1976-77), Phi Beta Kappa, Pi Sigma Alpha. Republican. Office: US Ho of Reps 2331 Rayburn Ho Office Bldg Washington DC 20515-3501*

HORNADAY, ALINE GRANDIER, publisher, independent scholar; b. San Diego, Sept. 14, 1923; d. Frank and Lydia Landon (Weir) Grandier; m. Quinn Hornaday, Oct. 9, 1965. BA, Union of Experimenting Colls., San Diego, 1977; PhD, U. Calif., San Diego, 1984. Pub. San Diego Daily Transcript, 1952-72, columnist, 1972-74; dir. San Diego Ind. Scholars, 1985-87, 94-95; co-pub. Jour. Unconventional History, Cardiff, Calif., 1989—; vis. scholar U. Calif., San Diego, 1984—; speaker at profl. confs. Co-author: The Hornadays, Root and Branch; contbr. articles to profl. jours. and books. Commr. San Diego City Libr. Commn., 1964-70. Mem. San Diego Ind. Scholars, Nat. Coalition Ind. Scholars, Med. Assn. of Pacific, Am. Hist. Assn., Medieval Acad. Am., Nat. Soc. Colonial Dames of Am., Wed. Club (pres. 1964-65). Home and Office: 6435 Avenida Cresta La Jolla CA 92037-6514

HORNBUCKLE, MICHAEL, instructional technology consultant, writer; b. Chia-Yi, Taiwan, June 20, 1961; s. Donald Ray and Chao Tzu (lin) H. BA in Computer Sci., San Francisco State U., 1989. Info. technologist Coll. Ethnic Studies, San Francisco State U., 1984—. Founder (jour.) A Thousand Voices, 1984-88; editor The Yellow Jour., 1984-88. Prodn. mgr. Rainbow Theater Co., San Francisco, 1990-92, Asian Am. Theater Co., San Francisco, 1992-94. Mem. 18 Mighty Mountain Warriors (founder, writer, actor). Home: 950 Rivera St San Francisco CA 94116-1813 Office: Coll Ethnic Studies 1600 Holloway Ave San Francisco CA 94132-1722

HORNDESKI, GREGORY WALTER, artist; b. Cleve., May 14, 1948; s. Walter and Cecile Maria H.; m. Sharon Jo Winklhofer, Apr. 20, 1990. BSc, Washington U., St. Louis, 1970; M in Math, U. Waterloo, Ont., Can., 1971, PhD, 1973. Cert. Mathematician, U. Waterloo. Asst. prof. math. U. Waterloo, Ontario, 1973-78, assoc. prof. math., 1978-82. One-man shows include 20th Century Gallery, Phila., 1988, Alternate Gallery, Dallas, 1984, 86, 88, Cade Gallery, Detroit, 1985, Toni Jones Gallery, Houston, 1985, Gallery 10, Washington, 1985, McIntosh Gallery, Atlanta, 1986, 91, U. Dallas, 1987, Eugene Binder Gallery, 1990, Hooks-Epstein Gallery, Houston, 1991, Dutch Phillips & Co., Dallas, 1994, Harris Gallery, Houston, 1995, Whelan Gallery, Santa Fe, N.Mex., 1998; two-man shows include Alternate Gallery, Dallas, 1985, Plus-Kern Gallerie, Brussels, 1989, Gallery Annext, N.Y.C., 1994, Mulcahy Modern Gallery, Dallas, 1997, Select Art Gallery, Sedona, Ariz., 1997; exhibited in group shows at Groninger (Holland) Mus., 1988, Arlington (Tex.) Mus. Art, 1991; represented in permanent collection Groninger Mus., Dallas Mus. Art. Home: 2819 Don Quixote Santa Fe NM 87505-6493

HORNER, ALTHEA JANE, psychologist; b. Hartford, Conn., Jan. 13, 1926; d. Louis and Celia (Newmark) Greenwald; children: Martha Horner Hartley, Anne Horner Benck, David, Kenneth. BS in Psychology, U. Chgo., 1952; PhD in Clin. Psychology, U. So. Calif., 1965. Lic. psychologist, N.Y., Calif. Tchr. Pasadena (Calif.) City Coll., 1965-67; from asst. to assoc. prof. Los Angeles Coll. Optometry, 1967-70; supr. Psychology interns Pasadena Child Guidance Clinic, 1969-70; pvt. practice specializing in psychoanalysis and psychoanalytic psychotherapy. N.Y.C., 1970-83; supervising psychologist dept. psychiatry Beth Israel Med. Ctr., N.Y.C., 1972-83, coordinator group therapy tng., 1976-82, clinician in charge Brief Adaptation-Oriented Psychotherapy Research Group, 1982-83; assoc. clin. prof. Mt. Sinai Sch. Medicine, N.Y.C., 1977-91, adj. assoc. prof., 1991—; mem. faculty Nat. Psychol. Assn. for Psychoanalysis, N.Y.C., 1982-83; sr. mem. faculty Wright Inst. Los Angeles Postgrad. Inst., 1983-85; pvt. practice L.A., 1983—; clin. prof. dept. Psychology UCLA, 1985-95. Author: (with others) Treating the Neurotic Patient in Brief Psychotherapy, 1985, Object Relations and the Developing Ego in Therapy, 1979, rev. edit., 1984, Little Big Girl, 1982, Being and Loving, 1978, 3d edit. 1990, Psychology for Living (with G. Forehand), 4th edit., 1977, The Wish for Power and the Fear of Having It, 1989, The Primacy of Structure, 1990, Psychoanalytic Object Relations Therapy, 1991, Working With the Core Relationship Problem in Psychotherapy, 1998, Chrysalis, 1999; mem. editorial bd. Jour. of Humanistic Psychology, 1986—, Jour. of the Am. Acad. of Psychoanalysis; contbr. articles to profl. jours. Mem. AAAS, APA, Calif. State Psychol. Assn., Am. Acad. Psychoanalysis (sci. assoc.), So. Calif. Psychoanalytic Soc. and Inst. (hon.). Office: 3579 E Foothill Blvd # 256 Pasadena CA 91107-3119

HORNER, ANTHONY ADAM, pediatrician, educator; b. N.Y.C., May 24, 1960; s. Harry and Joan Ruth (Frankel) H. BA in Biochemistry, U. Calif. San Diego, 1983; MD, St. Louis U., 1987. Diplomate Am. Bd. Pediatrics, Am. Bd. Allergy and Immunology. Resident in pediatrics UCLA Med. Ctr., 1990; fellow in pediatric immunology Boston Children's Hosp., 1994; asst. prof. pediatrics med. sch. U. Calif. San Diego, San Diego, 1994—; dir. pediatric allergy and immunology med. ctr. U. Calif. San Diego, 1994—; co-principle investigator Children's Asthma Mgmt. Program, San Diego, 1994—. Fellow Am. Acad. Pediatrics, Am. Acad. Allergy and Immunology. Avocations: skiing, music, entemology. Office: U Calif San Diego Med Sch 9500 Gilman Dr # Mc663 La Jolla CA 92093-5003

HORNER, HARRY CHARLES, JR., sales executive, theatrical and film consultant; b. Pitts., Oct. 30, 1937; s. Harry Charles and Sara Marie (Hysong) H.; m. Patricia Ann Hagarty, June 15, 1965 (div. 1981); m. Sharon Kae Wyatt, Dec. 30, 1983; children: Jeffrey Brian, Jennifer Leigh, Mark Gregory. BFA, U. Cin., 1963; postgrad., Xavier U., Cin., 1963-64. Mgr. Retail Credit Co., Atlanta, 1964-68; ops. mgr. Firestone Tire and Rubber Co., L.A., 1968-80; exec. v.p. Romney/Ford Enterprises Inc., Scottsdale, Ariz., 1980-85; sales mgr. Environ. Care Inc., Calabassas, Calif., 1985-93; ops. v.p. Albuquerque (N.Mex.) Grounds Maintenance, Inc., 1993—; pres., chief exec. officer The Cons. Group Cos. Ltd., Palm Desert, Calif., 1984—; pres. E. Valley Theatre Co., Chandler, Ariz., 1984-86. Cons. Ariz. Commn. on Arts, Phoenix, 1983-84. Republican. Mem. LDS Ch. Avocations: flying, model railroads. Office: Albuquerque Grounds Maintenance Inc 8442 Washington Pl NE Albuquerque NM 87113-1671

HORNER, MICHELLE, elementary school educator, principal; b. Burbank, Calif., Aug. 9, 1954; d. George Albert Phillips and Geraldine Lou (Anderson) Notman; m. Daniel Kenton Horner, Dec. 1979; children: Jesse Daniel, Molly Anne. BA in Liberal Studies, Calif. State U., Fresno, 1976; M in Adminstrn., adminstrv. svcs. credential, Fresno Pacific Coll., 1993. Tchr. Coarsegold (Calif.) Sch., 1977-81; tchg. prin. Wawona (Calif.) Sch., 1981—; mem. Calif. State Multiage Task Force, Sacramento, 1994-95; mem. info. literacy task force Calif. Tech. Assistance Program, Fresno, Calif., 1996-98. Contbr. unit to: Teachers Make A Difference (Susan Kovalik), 1986. Mgr. Wawona Sch. Recycling Ctr., 1988-98. Recipient Cmty. Svc. award Nat. Pk. Svc., Yosemite, Calif., 1993; named Disting. Sch. Prin., Calif. Dept. Edn., Anaheim, 1995. Mem. ASCD, AAUW, Assn. for Calif. Sch. Adminstrs., Calif. Alliance for Elem. Edn. (founding, mem. planning com. for conf. 1995). Avocations: doll collecting, reading, bird watching, travel. Home: PO Box 806 Yosemite National Park CA 95389-0806 Office: Wawona Sch PO Box 2068 Wawona CA 95389-2068

HORNER, SANDRA MARIE GROCE (SANDY HEART), educator, poet, songwriter, lyricist; b. Dallas; d. Larnell and Lee Ella (Lacy) Groce; divorced; 1 child, Danielle Marie. BA in Sociol./Philosophy with honors, Calif. State U., Dominguez Hills, 1980; postgrad., UCLA, 1978, 82-83, Consumnes River Coll., 1987, Nat. U., 1991, So. Utah U., 1993. Cert. elem. edn. K-8, Nev., K-A Occ. Std.: Bus. and Office Occupations; cert. instr. credential Calif.; cert. lifetime tchg. credential bus., Calif. Prodn. asst., sec. Paramount Pictures Corp., Hollywood, Calif., 1968-74; instr. L.A. C.C. Dist., 1976-78; tchr. Verbum Dei H.S., L.A., 1977-79; tchr., dept. chair L.A. Unified Sch. Dist., 1975-83; tchr. Sacramento (Calif.) City Unified Sch. Dist., 1985-87; editor, pub. Multi-Family Publs., Sacramento, 1986-89; tchr. Clark County Sch. Dist., Las Vegas, Nev., 1991-98; adj. instr. C.C. So. Nev., Las Vegas, 1988-95; radio broadcast interview Poetry Today with Ken Lerch WRTN 93.5 FM, N.Y.C., 1997. Editor: (books/newsletters) Groce Family Newsletter, 1986; recording contracts Hilltop Records, 1996, 97, AME Record Recording Co., 1997, Hollywood Artists Record Co., 1997; author numerous poems; albums include America, Hill Top Country, Star Route USA, Music of America. Recipient Nat. History recognition award Soc. History Rsch. and Preservation, 1989, Editor's Choice awards Nat. Libr. of Poetry, 1996; inducted into Internat. Poetry Hall of Fame, 1996. Mem. AAUW, AAUP, NEA, Internat. Soc. Poets (Disting. Mem.), Am. Bus. Women's Assn., Nev. State Edn. Assn., Internat. Platform Assn. Democrat. Avocations: literature, music, history, art, antiques. Office: PO Box 56392 Sherman Oaks CA 91413-1392

HORNING, JAMES JAY, computer science researcher; b. Chattanooga, July 24, 1942; s. James June and Irma Lee (Burden) H.; m. Jane Elizabeth Olsen. BA, Pacific Union Coll., 1963; MS, UCLA, 1965; PhD, Stanford U., 1969. MTS/masters fellow Hughes Aircraft, Culver City, Calif., 1964-65; computing ctr. dir. Loma Linda (Calif.) U., 1965-66; asst. prof. U. Toronto, Ont., Can., 1969-72, assoc. prof., 1972-77; MRS Xerox Palo Alto (Calif.) Rsch. Ctr., 1977-78, prin. scientist, 1978-82, rsch. fellow, 1982-84; sr. cons. Digital Equip. Corp./Sys. Rsch. Ctr., Palo Alto, 1984-96; rsch. fellow InterTrust Techs. Corp./STAR Lab., Sunnyvale, Calif., 1996-97, dir., 1997—; mem. editl. bd. Springer-Verlag Texts and Monographs in Computer Sci., N.Y.C., 1977-85. Patentee in field; co-author: A Compiler Generator, 1970, Larch: Languages and Tools for Formal Specification, 1993. Fellow Assn. for Computing Machinery (programming lang. editor Comms. of ACM, mem. numerous coms.); mem. IEEE, Internat. Fedn. Info. Processing (chmn. working group, tech. com., Silver core award), Sigma Pi Sigma. Avocations: videography, photography, West Highland White Terriers, fuchsias. Fax: (408) 222-6136. E-mail: @horningintertrust.com. Office: InterTrust Techs Corp 460 Oakmead Pkwy Sunnyvale CA 94086

HOROWITZ, BEN, medical center executive; b. Bklyn., Mar. 19, 1914; s. Saul and Sonia (Meringoff) H.; m. Beverly Lichtman, Feb. 14, 1952; children: Zachary, Jody. BA, Bklyn. Coll., 1940; LLB, St. Lawrence U., 1940; postgrad. New Sch. Social Rsch., 1942. Bar: N.Y. 1941. Dir. N.Y. Fedn. Jewish Philanthropies, 1940-45; assoc., ea. regional dir. City of Hope, 1945-50, nat. exec. sec., 1950-53, exec. dir., 1953-85, gen. v.p., bd. dirs., 1985—, bd. dirs. nat. med. ctr., 1980—; bd. dirs. Beckman Rsch. Inst., 1980—. Mem. Gov.'s Task Force on Flood Relief, 1969-74. Bd. dirs., v.p. Hope for Hearing Found., UCLA, 1972-96; bd. dirs. Forte Found., 1987-92, Ch. Temple Housing Corp., 1988-93, Leo Baeck Temple, 1964-67, 86-89, Westwood Property Owners Assn., 1991—. Recipient Spirit of Life award, 1970, Gallery of Achievement award, 1974, Profl. of Yr. award So. Calif. chpt. Nat. Soc. Fundraisers, 1977; Ben Horowitz chair in rsch. established at City of Hope, 1981. City street named in his honor, 1986. Jewish. Formulated the role of City of Hope as pilot ctr. in medicine, sci., and humanitarianism, 1959. Home: 221 Conway Ave Los Angeles CA 90024-2601 Office: City of Hope 208 W 8th St Los Angeles CA 90014-3208

HOROWITZ, ZACHARY I., entertainment company executive; b. N.Y.C., Apr. 27, 1953; s. Ben and Beverly (Lichtman) H.; m. Barbara J. Natterson; 1 child, Jennifer Lily. BA summa cum laude, Claremont Mens Coll., 1975; JD, Stanford U., 1978. Bar: Calif. 1978. Assoc. Kaplan, Livingston, Goodwin, Berkowitz & Selvin, Beverly Hills, Calif., 1978; from sr. atty. to dir. bus. affairs West Coast CBS Records, L.A., 1978-83; v.p. bus. and legal affairs MCA Records, Universal City, Calif., 1983-84, sr. v.p. bus. and legal affairs, 1984-88; from sr. v.p. bus. and legal affairs to COO Universal Music Group, Universal City, 1986-95, pres., 1995-98, pres., COO, 1999—; bd. dirs. Universal Victor Japan; mem. op. com. Motown Recording Co., L.A., 1988-93. Mem. bd. editors Stanford Law Rev., 1977-78. Nat. bd. dirs. City of Hope, 1989—, vice chmn. Music Industry chpt., 1985-86, chmn. maj. gifts com., 1986-90, nat. campaign co-chmn., 1990-91, pres., 1991-92, chmn., 1993-94, endowment chair, 1995-97, major gifts choir, 1997—, adv. bd. Nashville Celebrity Baseball Game, 1995—. Mem. NARAS (presdl. adv. com. 1996—), Record Industry Assn. Am. (bd. dirs. 1990—, fin. com. 1993—). Office: Universal Music Group 70 Universal City Plz North Hollywood CA 91608-1011

HORST, RANDY, museum director. Dir. Western Mont. Coll. Gallery Mus., Dillion. Office: Western Mont Coll Mus 710 S Atlantic St Dillon MT 59725-3511*

HORTON, BARBARA MARION DEADY, fund developer; b. Oswego, NY, Dec. 14, 1930; d. Harold Eugene and Marion Cecilia (Irwin) Deady; m. Charles Laurence, June 21, 1952; children: Deborah Christine Hovatter, Elizabeth Caroline Michael, Walter Arnold, Patrick Joseph. BS, Northwestern U., Evanston, Ill., 1952. Profl. Reg. Parliamentarian. Exec. dir. Contact Cape Atlantic, Somers Point, N.J., 1993-97. Mem. P.E.O. (chpt. pres. 1986-88), Holly Shores Girl Scout Coun., Frontier Girl Scout Coun. (Thanks Badge 1973, 87), Atlantic Coun. Women's Chamber, Pub. Rels. Coun. (v.p. fin. 1991-92), Alpha Chi Omega (nat. treas. 1980-85). Republican. Roman Catholic. Avocations: reading, swimming, electronics, computer. Home: 12802 W Flagstone Dr Sun City West AZ 85375-3220

HORTON, JULIE, music company executive; b. Washington, Mo., Feb. 15, 1950; d. Richard Wayne and Jeryl Dean (Yates) Vaught; children: Adam, Rachel. BA in Edn., U. Mo., 1971. Prodn. mgr. Papazian Prodns., L.A., 1976-78; music pub. Chappell Intersong Music, Hollywood, Calif., 1978-80; sr. dir. ASCAP Western Region, L.A., 1980-95; music coord., supr. Seque Music, L.A., 1996-97; sr. project mgr. MusiCares, Santa Monica, Calif., 1997—. Mem. NARAS, ASCAP, Calif. Copyright Coun. (former bd. mem.), Country Music Assn, Gospel Music Assn. Democrat. Avocation: building dollhouses.

HORTON, KENNETH, investor; b. Newport, Nebr., May 11, 1921; s. Fred and Clara E. (Cottrel) H.; m. Evelyn H. Shafer, Dec. 29, 1939 (div. 1961); children: Kenneth Eugene, Helen Clara Catherine; m. Arlene J. Mitchell, July 23, 1962. AA, Valley Coll., San Bernardino, Calif., 1951; grad., Law Enforcement Officers Tng. Sch., San Bernardino, Calif., 1957. Crew leader 1st suppression fire crew Civilian Conservation Corp, Glendora, Calif., 1937-39; journeyman R.R. Car Shop/Santa Fe R.R., San Bernardino, 1940-44; boy's counselor San Bernardino County Juvenile Hall, 1948-53; supr. state champion drill team Calif. Youth Authority, Whittier, 1954; layout carpenter Bectal Constrn. Co., Oro grande, Calif., 1954-55; patrolman, vice officer Police Dept., San Bernardino, 1956-66; ind. investor Thousand Oaks, Calif., 1950—. Sustaining mem. Rep. Nat. Com., Washington, 1978—. With U.S. Army, 1944-45. Decorated Combat Infantryman medal, Bronze Star medal; recipient Letter of Appreciation for apprehending holdup man Security Pacific Bank, 1974. Lutheran. Avocations: maker of fine furniture, 1st edition book collection, antique automobiles. Address: PO Box 1432 Thousand Oaks CA 91358

HORTON, LAWRENCE STANLEY, electrical engineer, apartment developer; b. Hanston, Kans., July 25, 1926; s. Gene Leigh and Retta Florene (Abbott) H.; m. Margaret Ann Cowles, Nov. 26, 1946 (dec. 1964); children: Craig, Lawrence Stanley, Steven J.; m. Julia Ann Butler Wirkkula, Aug. 15, 1965; stepchildren: Charles Wirkkula Horton, Jerry Higginbotham Horton. BSEE, Oreg. State U., 1949. Elec. engr. Mountain States Power Co., Calif. Oreg. Power Co., Pacific Power and Light Co., 1948-66; mgr. Ramic Corp., 1966-69; cons. elec. engr. Marquess and Assocs., Medford, Oreg., 1969-85, sec., bd. dirs.; pres., owner Medford Better Housing Assn., 1985—; ptnr. Terpening Terrace, T'Morrow Apts., Johnson Manor, Champion Pk.; bd. dirs. People's Bank of Commerce; former bd. dirs. Valley of Rogue Bank, developer various apt. complexes and retirment communities, 1969—, Northwood Apts., Horton Plz., Fountain Plz., Anna Maria Creekside, Terpening Ter.; bd. dirs. Medford Hist. Commn. Active Medford Planning Commn., Archtl. Review Commn., Housing Authority, Peoples Bank Commerce; bd. govs. State of Oreg. Citizens Utility; pres. United Fund, 1963-64. With USN, 1945-46. Named Rogue Valley Profl. Engr. of Yr., 1969. Mem. IEEE, Nat. Soc. Profl. Engrs., Profl. Engrs. of Oreg., So. Oreg. Rental Owners Assn. (pres.), Rogue Valley Geneol. Soc. (pres.), Medford C. of C. (dir.), Rogue Valley Yacht Club (commodore 1974-75, dir., local fleet capt., champion), Rogue Valley Knife and Fork (past pres.), San Juan 21 Fleet Assn. (western vice commodore, Top Ten San Juan Sailor West Coast, 1980), Jackson Toastmasters (founder 1957), Medford Rotary, Kiwanis (life, pres. Crater Golden 1990-91). Republican. Methodist. Grad. instr. Dale Carnegie course, 1955, 56; contbr. elec. articles to profl. assns., 1956-61. Office: Medford Better Housing Assn 1118 Spring St Medford OR 97504-6272

HORTON, MICHAEL L., mortgage company executive, publishing executive; b. Pasadena, Calif., Oct. 19, 1961; s. Jerry S. and Mary L. Horton. BA in Bus. Econs., Claremont McKenna Coll., 1983. Lic. real estate broker. Gen. mgr. I.W.S., Pasadena, 1976-80; proprietor NBB Svcs. Orgn., Upland, Calif., 1980-85; regional mgr. Sycamore Fin. Group Inc., Rancho Cucamonga, Calif., 1984-87; CEO, pres. Boulder Fin. Corp., Rancho Cucamonga, 1987—, M.C.M. Pub. Corp., Rancho Cucamonga, 1992—; pres., CEO Sandstone Realty Group, Inc., 1995—; chm. C.H.A.M.P. Inc., 1996—; chmn. Champeon Inc., 1996—. Author: A Real Estate Professional's Guide to Mortgage Finance, 1985; author Mortgage Fin. Newsletter, 1984—; author fin. workshop. Mem. Rep. State Ctrl. Com., Calif., 1980—, Bldg. and Industry Assn., Rancho Cucamonga, 1988—, Res Publica Soc., Claremont, Calif., 1986—; donor mem. L.A. World Affairs Coun., 1988—. Claremont McKenna Coll. scholar, 1981-83; recipient Dons D. Lepper Meml. award Exec. Women Internat., 1981, So. Calif. Edison Bus. Competition award, 1979, 81. Mem. Nat. Assn. Realtors, Inland Empire West Bd. Realtors. Avocations: basketball, racquet sports, water sports. Office: Boulder Fin Corp 9121 Haven Ave Ste 180 Rancho Cucamonga CA 91730-5453

HORTON, NADINE ROSE, school system administrator; b. Kauai, Hawaii, Nov. 10, 1944; d. Alfred and Myrtle (Silva) Fernandes; m. Michael G. Sigman, Jan. 5, 1991; children: Debra J., Benjamin J. BA, Coll. Idaho, 1966, MA, 1972; postgrad., U. Idaho, 1990. Tchr. elem. sch. Parma (Idaho) Sch. Dist., 1966-70, Nampa (Idaho) Sch. Dist., 1970-72, Pinedale (Wyo.) Sch. Dist., 1972-73; tchr. elem. sch. New Plymouth (IDaho) Sch. Dist., 1974-75, prin. elem. sch., 1975—; coord. Joint Coun. Econ. Edn., Boise, 1988; mem. goals and testing commn. State Dept. Edn., Boise, 1991-94. Named Celebrity of Yr. Am. Legion Aux., New Plymouth, 1986, Admisntr. of Yr. Idaho Assn. Ednl. Officer Pers., Boise, 1988, Outstanding Elem. Tchr. Am., 1975, Exec. Educator 100, 1986, Prins. of Leadership, 1987. Mem. ASCD (assocs.), Nat. Sch. Pub. Rels. Assn., Nat. Assn. Elem. Sch. Prins. (state rep. 1988-89, fed. rels. coord. 1989—, folio reviewer 1991—, nominating com. rep. 1990, Nat. Disting. Prin. 1989), Idaho Assn. Elem. Sch. Prins. (state pres. 1986), Internat. Reading Assn. (presenter), Phi Delta Kappa. Roman Catholic. Avocations: travel, reading, bowling. Home: 819 S Plymouth Ave # 193 New Plymouth ID 83655-5289

HORTON, PATRICIA MATHEWS, artist, violist and violinist; b. Bklyn., Mar. 6, 1932; d. Edward Joseph and Margaret (Briggs) Mathews; m. Ernest H. Horton Jr., Mar. 6, 1982; 1 stepchild, Carol Horton Tremblay. Student in viola, William Primrose Master Class, 1980; student, Glendale (Calif.) C.C., 1981-90, 93, Art Ctr. Coll. Design, Pasadena, Calif., 1988-93; student in painting composition, Peter Liashkov, L.A., 1993-97. Profl. musician on violin and viola, 1951-86; musician on tour U.S., Can., Cuba, 1952-57. Played with New Orleans Philharm., 1959-61, U.S. Tour of San Francisco Ballet, 1965, L.A. Civic Light Opera, 1974-80; played L.A. engagements of Bolshoi Ballet Co., 1975, Am. Ballet Theatre, 1974-80, N.Y.C. Opera, 1974-80, Royal Ballet of London, 1978, Alicia Alonzo's Cuban Ballet, 1979, Harlem Ballet, 1984, Deutsche Oper Berlin, 1985; played on motion picture and TV soundtrack recs., through 1986; one-woman shows include Claremont (Calif.) Sch. Theology, 1997, Pasadena First United Meth. Ch., 1997. Active Dem. Nat. Com., Women's Caucus for Art. Mem. Am. Fedn. Musicians (life), Alpha Gamma Sigma. Avocation: hiking local mountains, desert and beaches.

HORVATH, IMRE GABOR, television producer and director; b. Constanza, Romania, Oct. 13, 1940; came to U.S., 1947; s. Emory Zoltan and Gabriella H.; children: Adam Zoltan, Gillian Leslie. AB, Columbia U., 1961; MA, NYU, 1963. Supr. research Grolier Pub. Co., N.Y.C., 1962-64; editor, writer Crowell-Collier Pub. Co., N.Y.C., 1964-66; film editor CBS News, other cos., N.Y.C., 1966-68; asst. producer, film editor 60 Minutes CBS News, N.Y.C., 1968-75, producer, writer 60 Minutes, 1975-80; pres., exec. producer Rainbow Broadcasting Co. (Rainbow Media, Inc.), Los Angeles and N.Y.C., 1980—; adj. assoc. prof. journalism Columbia U., N.Y.C., 1976-78. Producer, dir. numerous segments of 60 Minutes including Noah, 1979 (Emmy award 1979), (documentaries) Murder: No Apparent Motive, 1984, Acts of Violence, 1985 (Ace award nominations 1984, 85), Cops: Behind the Badge, 1986 (Gold plaque Chgo. Internat. Film Festival 1986); producer, writer Walk Through the 20th Century with Bill Moyers (Emmy award nomination 1985); exec. producer Crimes of Passion, ABC-TV, 1988-89 (Emmy award nomination 1989), Too Good To Be True, NBC-TV, 1994-95; dir. Unsolved Mysteries, Atlantis, other programs, 1990—. Recipient Journalism award Robert F. Kennedy Found., 1982, Howard Blakeslee award for Med. Journalism Am. Heart Assn., 1976. Mem. Acad. TV Arts & Scis., Dirs. Guild Am., Writers Guild Am.

HORWIN, LEONARD, lawyer; b. Chgo., Jan. 2, 1913; s. Joseph and Jennie (Fuhrmann) H.; m. Ursula Helene Donig, Oct. 15, 1939; children—Noel Samuel, Leonora Marie. LLD cum laude, Yale U., 1936. Bar: Calif. 1936, U.S. Dist. Ct. (cen. dist.) Calif. 1937, U.S. Ct. Appeals (9th cir.) 1939, U.S. Supreme Ct. 1940. Assoc., Lawler, Felix & Hall, 1936-39; ptnr. Hardy & Horwin, Los Angeles, 1939-42; counsel Bd. Econ. Warfare, Washington, 1942-43; mem. program adjustment com. U.S. War Prodn. Bd., 1942-43; attache, legal advisor U.S. Embassy, Madrid, Spain, 1943-47; sole practice, Beverly Hills, Calif., 1948—; dir., lectr. Witkin-Horwin Rev. Course on Calif. Law, 1939-42; judge pro tempore Los Angeles Superior Ct., 1940-42; instr. labor law U. So. Calif., 1939-42. U.S. rep. Allied Control Council for Ger., 1945-47; councilman City of Beverly Hills, 1962-66, mayor, 1964-65; chmn. transp. Los Angeles Goals Council, 1968; bd. dirs. So. Calif. Rapid Transit Dist., 1964-66; chmn. Rent Stabilization Com., Beverly Hills, 1980. Fellow Am. Acad. Matrimonial Lawyers; mem. ABA, State Bar Calif., Order Coif, Balboa Bay Club, Aspen Inst., La Costa Country Club. Author: Insight and Foresight, 1990, Plain Talk, 1931—; contbr. articles to profl. jours. E-Mail address: lhorwin@mindspring.com. Office: 121 S Beverly Dr Beverly Hills CA 90212-3002

HOSPY, PATRICIA L., chiropractor, property management executive; b. Chgo.; d. Joseph F. and Verna M. H. DC cum laude, Life Chiropractic Coll. West, 1992. Ins. agt. Automobile Club So. Calif., Torrance, 1981-87; regional sales mgr. Sebastian No. Calif., Walnut Creek, 1993-94; chiropractor pvt. practice, San Mateo and Hayward, Calif., 1992—; asst. prof. Life Chiropractic Coll. West, San Lorenzo, Calif., 1995—; owner Pat Hospy Enterprises, property mgmt., 1980—. Columnist Modern Salon Mag., Lincolnshire, Ill., 1995—. Mem. Foster City (Calif.) Fitness Resource Group, 1995-98. Mem. Sigma Chi Psi, Pi Tau Delta. Office: 22455 Maple Ct Ste 301 Hayward CA 94541-4031

HOSSLER, DAVID JOSEPH, lawyer, law educator; b. Mesa, Ariz., Oct. 18, 1940; s. Carl Joseph and Elizabeth Ruth (Bills) H.; m. Gretchen Anne, Mar. 2, 1945; 1 child, Devon Annagret. BA, U. Ariz., 1969; JD, 1972. Bar: Ariz. 1972, U.S. dist. ct. Ariz. 1972, U.S. Supreme Ct. 1977. Legal intern to chmn. FCC, summer 1971; law clk. to chief justice Ariz. Supreme Ct., 1972-73; chief dep. county atty. Yuma County (Ariz.), 1973-74; ptnr. Hunt and Hossler, Yuma, Ariz., 1974—; instr. in law and banking, law and real estate

Ariz. Western Coll.; instr. in bus. law, mktg., ethics Webster U; co-chmn. fee arbitration com. Ariz. State Bar, 1990—; instr. agrl. law U. Ariz. Mem. precinct com., Yuma County Rep. Cen. Com., 1974-98, vice chmn., 1982; chmn. region II Acad. Decathalon competition, 1989; bd. dirs. Yuma County Ednl. Found., Yuma County Assn. Behavior Health Svcs., also pres., 1981; coach Yuma High Sch. mock ct. team, 1987—; bd. dirs. Friends of U. Med. Ctr. With USN. Recipient Man and Boy award Boys Clubs Am., 1979, Freedoms Found. award Yuma Chpt., 1988, Demolay Legion of Honor, 1991; named Vol. of Yr., Yuma County, 1981-82. Mem. Assn. Trial Lawyers Am., Am. Judicature Soc., Yuma County Bar Assn. (pres. 1975-76), Navy League, VFW, Am. Legion, U. Ariz. Alumni Assn. (nat. bd. dirs., past pres., hon. bobcat 1996, Disting. Citizen award, 1997, Rotary (pres. Yuma club 1987-88, dist. gov. rep. 1989, dist. gov. 1992-93, findings com. 1996, dist. found. chair 1996—, Van Houton award 1996, Rotary Found. citation for Meritorious svc.). Editor-in-chief Ariz. Adv., 1971-72. Episcopalian (vestry 1978-82). Home: 2802 S Fern Dr Yuma AZ 85364-7909 Office: Hunt and Hossler 330 W 24th St Yuma AZ 85364-6455 also: PO Box 2919 Yuma AZ 85366-2919

HOSTLER, CHARLES WARREN, international affairs consultant; b. Chgo., Dec. 12, 1919; s. Sidney Marvin and Catherine (Marshall) H.; 1 son, Charles Warren, Jr. B.A., U. Calif. at Los Angeles, 1942; M.A., Am. U., Beirut, Lebanon, 1955, Georgetown U., 1950; Ph.D., Georgetown U., 1956. Commd. 2d lt. U.S. Air Force, 1942, advanced through grades to col., 1963; ret., 1963; dir. internat. ops. McDonnell Douglas Corp., Middle East, N.Africa, Beirut, 1965-67; mgr. internat. ops. McDonnell Douglas Corp., Paris, 1963-65; mgr. internat. mktg., missiles and space McDonnell Douglas Corp., 1967-69; pres. Hostler Investment Co., Newport Beach, Calif., 1969-74; chmn. bd. Irvine (Calif.) Nat. Bank, 1972-74; dir. Wynn's Internat., Inc., Fullerton, Calif., 1971-74; dep. asst. sec. for internat. commerce, dir. Bur. Internat. Commerce, U.S. Dept. Commerce, Washington, 1974-76; regional v.p. Mid-East and Africa, E-Systems Inc., Cairo, Egypt, 1976-77; pres. Pacific SW Capital Corp., San Diego, 1977-89; ambassador U.S. Govt., Bahrain, 1989-93; hon. consul gen. State of Bahrain, 1993—; adj. prof. Sch. Internat. Svc., Am. U., Washington, 1955-63; pres. San Diego Consular Corps. Author: Turkism and the Soviets, 1957, The Turks of Central Asia, 1993; contbr. articles to econ., comml. and mil. jours. Chmn. Calif. Contractors State Lic. Bd., 1973-79, San Diego County Local Agy. Formation Commn., 1979-89; chmn. Calif. State Park and Recreation Commn., 1983-89; pres. San Diego Consular Corps, 1996-98. Decorated Legion of Merit; recipient Fgn. Affairs award for pub. svc. U.S. State Dept. Mem. Am. Polit. Sci. Assn., Am. Ordnance Assn., Middle East Inst. (bd. govs. 1962-80, 93—). Office: # 302 1101 First St Coronado CA 92118-1474

HOTCHKIES, BARRY, financial executive; b. York, Eng., June 1, 1945; came to U.S., 1977; s. Livingstone R. and Margaret (Dodsworth) H.; m. Eleanor D. Caldwell, Aug. 1968; children: Blair L., Lindsey E. BS, U. Glasgow, Scotland, 1968; MBA, Dartmouth Coll., 1973. Fin. analyst Royal Trust, Montreal, Can., 1968-71, W.R. Grace & Co., Lausanne, Switzerland, 1973-77; mgr. W.R. Grace & Co., Balt., 1977-81; v.p. W.R. Grace & Co., N.Y.C., 1981-87; chief fin. officer Jacques Borel Enterprises, Inc., N.Y.C., 1987-89; v.p., chief fin. officer rsch. div. W.R. Grace & Co., Columbia, Md., 1989-97; CFO Berkeley (Calif.) Nat. Lab., 1997—. Office: Berkeley Nat Lab 1 Cyclotron Rd Berkeley CA 94720

HOTCHKISS, BILL, author, educator; b. New London, Conn., Oct. 17, 1936; s. William H. and Merle B. (Stambaugh) H. BA in English, U. Calif., Berkeley, 1959; MA in English, San Francisco State U., 1960; MFA in Creative Writing, U. Oreg., 1964, DA in English, 1971, PhD in English, 1974. Tchr. English Colfax H.S., 1960-62; instr. English Sierra Coll., Rocklin, Calif., 1963-79, 84-85; prof. English Sierra Coll., Rocklin, 1988—; instr. English Shasta Coll., 1980-81, Rogue C.C., 1985-88, 90. Author: (grammar and composition textbook) Tilting at Windmills, 1966, (novels) The Medicine Calf, 1981, reissue, 1987, Crow Warriors, 1981, Soldier Wolf, 1982, Ammahabas, 1983, Spirit Mountain, 1984, Mountain Lamb, 1985, People of the Sacred Oak, 1986, Fire Woman, 1987, Dance of the Coyote, To Fell the Giants, 1991, Sierra Santa Cruz, 1992, Yosemite, 1995, (vols. of poetry) Steephollow Poems, 1966, The Graces of Fire, 1974, Fever in the Earth, 1977, Middle Fork Canyon, 1979, Gret Upheaval, 1990, others, (criticism) Jeffers: The Sivaistic Vision, 1975, Poet from the San Joaquin, 1978, poems, forewords and afterwords to numerous publs.; co-author: Shoshone Thunder, 1983, Pawnee Medicine, 1983, McLaffertys, 1986, Desert Moon, 1987, (handbook) Sancho's Guide to Uncommon Literacy, 1990, 93, 95; editor: Sierra Jour., 1965-78, 88-90, 95-96; editor, book designer, printer, publ. Blue Oak Press; book designer, text editor Castle Peak Edits., 1966—; co-editor: Perspectives on William Everson, 1992, Jeffers, The Double Axe, 1977; contbr. work to anthologies including Elegies for Robinson Jeffers, Perspectives on William Everson, Range of Light, California Childhood, others, poems to mags. including Poetry, Beloit, Cambridge, Texas Q, Cardinal, Hard Pressed, Sierra Heritage, Bitterroot, Pudding, numerous others; typesetter, book design advisor Dustbooks, Quintessence, Story Line, others; contbr. to programmed instructional software, filmstrips. Home: 3460 Cedar Flat Rd Williams OR 97544-9605 Office: Sierra Coll NCC 250 Sierra College Dr Grass Valley CA 95945-5726

HOTCHKISS, VIVIAN EVELYN, employment agency executive; b. Fulda, Germany, May 5, 1956; came to U.S., 1957; d. Fred Roy and Rosemary Krug. Student, Pierce Coll., 1974-75, Calif. State U., Northridge, 1976, UCLA, 1991—. Adminstrv. sec. Taurus Fin. Corp., Hollywood, Calif., 1976-79; adminstrv. asst. Peoples Fin. Corp., Encino, Calif., 1979-81, Thor Employment Agy., L.A., 1981-83, Creative Capital Corp., L.A., 1983—; owner, pres. Bus. Systems Staffing & Assocs., L.A., 1985—; exec. dir. Edn., Counseling & Placement Program, L.A., 1990-95. Author: (newsletter) The Leader; contbr. articles to newspaper, 1996-97. Mem. Execs. Assn. L.A. (membership dir. 1989-96, Member of Yr. 1990), Exec. LeTip of West L.A. (membership inspector 1996—, program dir., 1998—). Avocations: wine enthusiast, photography, travel, computers, animals. Office: Bus Sys Staffing & Assocs Inc 10680 W Pico Blvd Ste 210 Los Angeles CA 90064-2223

HOTZ, HENRY PALMER, physicist; b. Fayetteville, Ark., Oct. 17, 1925; s. Henry Gustav and Stella (Palmer) H.; m. Marie Brase, Aug. 22, 1952; children: Henry Brase, Mary Palmer, Martha Marie. B.S., U. Ark., 1948; Ph.D., Washington U., St. Louis, 1953. Asst. prof. physics Auburn U., Ala., 1953-58, Okla. State U., Stillwater, 1958-64; assoc. prof. Marietta Coll., Ohio, 1964-66; physicist, scientist-in-residence U.S. Naval Radiol. Def. Lab., San Francisco, 1966-67; assoc. prof. U. Mo., Rolla, 1967-71; physicist Qanta Metrix div. Finnigan Corp., Sunnyvale, Calif., 1971-74; sr. scientist Nuclear Equipment Corp., San Carlos, Calif., 1974-79, Envirotech Measurement Systems, Palo Alto, Calif., 1979-82, Dohrmann div. Xertex Corp., Santa Clara, Calif., 1982-86; sr. scientist Rosemount Analytical Div. Dohrmann, 1983-91; cons. Burlingame, Calif., 1991—; cons. USAF, 1958-62; mem. lectr. selection com. for Hartman Hotz Lectrs. in law, liberal arts U. Ark. Served with USNR, 1944-46. Mem. Am. Phys. Soc., Am. Assn. Physics Tchrs., AAAS, Phi Beta Kappa, Sigma Xi, Sigma Pi Sigma, Pi Mu Epsilon, Sigma Nu. Methodist. Lodge: Masons. Home: 290 Stilt Ct Foster City CA 94404-1323 Office: Hotz Assocs 525 Almer Rd Apt 201 Burlingame CA 94010-3955

HOUBRICK, MICHAEL PHILIP, talent manager; b. Renton, Wash., May 23, 1960; s. Robert Jacob and Beverly Jane H. Grad. high sch., Spokane, Wash. V.p. mktg. MVA Television Entertainment, Universal City, Calif., 1982-90; talent agt. Kern Agy., Beverly Hills, Calif., 1990-92, Brooke - Dunn - Oliver, L.A., 1992-94; v.p. creative devel. Kragen & Co., West Hollywood, Calif., 1994-97; pres., CEO MR Brick & Co., Hollywood, Calif., 1997—. Co-author: (screenplay) Unforgotten Love, 1997; writer song ARt You Ready for Eddie, 1994. Bd. dirs. Family Assistance Program, Hollywood, 1997—; campaign mgr. Eddie Haskell for Pres., Studio City, Calif., 1994. Mem. Nat. Spkrs. Assn., Nat. Assn. Recording Arts & Scis., Gospel Music Assn., Assn. Country Music, Country Music Assn. Avocations: cartoonist, collecting casino chips. Office: MR Brick & Co 7200 Franklin Ave Apt 218 Los Angeles CA 90046-3083

HOUDE, JOHN MICHAEL, television engineer; b. Falmouth, Mass., Mar. 14, 1959; s. Hervé C. and Bernice E. (Sylvia) H. AAS, Grahm Jr. Coll., Boston, 1979; BS, Emerson Coll., 1981. Lic. 1st class radiotelephone operator. Service technician Falmouth Radio, Inc., 1976-79; maintenance and shift supr. Stas. WERS-FM/CCTV, Boston, 1979-81; news prodn. asst. Sta. WNAC-TV, Boston, 1980-81; engr. Sta. WSBE-TV, Providence, 1982-92; producer, CEO Otter Prodns., 1993—; lighting designer Gateway Players, Wareham, Mass., 1980-85; advisor to tech. dir. Boston Community Services Adminstrn., 1981—; mem. Sta. WSBE-TV Affirmative Action com., 1987-92; producer, chief exec. officer Videoscope Prodns., Providence, 1990-92. Producer, writer (first-aid video) Lifesavers, 1981. Mem., instr. Falmouth Civil Def. Agy., 1976-84; announcer Falmouth Road Race, 1979-83; tech. asst. Muscular Dystrophy Assn. funding events, Barnstable County, Mass., 1980, Tukwila, 1998; mem. Tukwila Cmty. Police Commn., govt. affairs com. Southwest King County C. of C. Recipient cert. of Honor Chi Sigma Beta Soc., 1978, award of Merit Mass. Muscular Dystrophy Assn., 1980, Sml. Bus. of Yr. award Tukwila/Southwest King County, Washington C. of C., Outstanding Sml. Bus. of Yr. award 1998, Making a Difference award Hwy. 99 Action Com., 1998. Mem. Soc. Motion Picture and TV Engrs., Internat. Brotherhood of Elec. Workers (trustee 1987—), Soc. Broadcast Engrs. (cert.), Internat. TV Assn. Avocations: skiing, boating, music, racquetball. Home: PO Box 368 Renton WA 98057-0368 Office: Otter Prodns 14227 Pacific Hwy S Tukwila WA 98168-4179

HOUGHTON, ROBERT CHARLES, secondary education educator; b. Dover, N.H., Apr. 12, 1958; s. Raymond David and Barbara Jean (Lyle) H. Student, USCG Acad., New London, Conn., 1976-77; BA with honors, U. Calif., Riverside, 1987, postgrad., 1987-89. Teaching credential, Calif. Various teaching positions, 1977-80; pharmacy technician Anaheim (Calif.) Meml./Brea (Calif.) Cmty., 1980-85; teaching asst. U. Calif., Riverside, 1988-90; instr. Mt. San Jacinto (Calif.) Coll., 1989-90; tchr. Desert Sands Unified, Indio, Calif., 1990—, interim asst. prin., 1997-98; counselor Chem. Awareness Network, Indio, Calif., 1990—; computer cons. Desert Sands Unified Sch. Dist., Indio, 1994—; resident tchr. Calif. State U., San Bernardino, 1994-95; asst. tour dir. Lakeland Tours, Washington, 1991-98. Mem. NEA, Nat. Coun. Social Studies, Nat. Geographic Soc., Calif. Tchrs. Assn., Nat. Trust Historic Preservation, Civil War Trust. Republican. Avocations: travel, photography, reading, hiking, camping. Home: 79320 Port Royal Ave Indio CA 92201-1262 Office: 81195 Miles Ave Indio CA 92201-2807

HOULGATE, DEKE, public relations consultant, writer; b. L.A., Aug. 8, 1930; s. Carroll Everard (Deke) and Dorothy (Dottie) (Penry) H.; m. Olga Katsigeanis, Jan. 29, 1955; children: Deke (dec.), John, David, Gregory. BA in Journalism, U. So. Calif., L.A., 1954. Sports deskman L.A. Times, 1952-54, reporter, 1956-59, mgmt. trainee, 1959-60, asst. dir. special events, 1960-63; reporter, editor Las Vegas (Nevada) Sun, 1954-56; prin., owner Deke Houlgate Pub. Rels., L.A., 1963-67, Deke Houlgate Enterprises, various, Calif., 1967—; contbr. columns to 15 newspapers. Author: Fastest Men..., 1971, Complete Book of Motorcycles, 1974, Handbook of High Performance Driving, 1976; motor sports writer L.A. Herald-Examiner, 1968-81; radio show producer, 4 stations, L.A., 1963-74. Lobbyist, Sacramento, Calif., 1973, 75. Corp. U.S. Army, 1950-52. Nominated for Pulitzer and SDX awards for coverage of search for downed airliner, 1957. Mem. Soc. Profl. Journalists, Am. Auto Racing Writers & Broadcasters Assn. (gen. vice pres. 1970-79, recipient various writing and radio awards 1969-80), OFS (Old-timer Times editl. employees), Delta Tau Delta. Republican. Methodist. Avocations: running, tennis, classical and jazz music appreciation. Office: Deke Houlgate Enterprises PO Box 4011 Carlsbad CA 92018-4011

HOURIEH, HOUSSIN ALI, electrical engineer; b. Bloudan, Syria, Nov. 15, 1960; came to U.S., 1983; s. Ali M. and Sadieh A. (Zitone) H.; m. Aug. 4, 1984; 1 child, Sami H. AAS, No. Okla. Coll., Tonkawa, 1984; BSEE, Okla. State U., 1987. Staff elec. engr. City of Lamar (Colo.) Utilities, 1988—. Chmn. safety com. City of Lamar, 1993—. Mem. IEEE, Assn. of Energy Engrs. Republican. Islam. Avocations: weight lifting, swimming, camping, tennis, hiking. Home: 700 E Oak St Lamar CO 81052-2933 Office: City of Lamar 100 N 2nd St Lamar CO 81052-2599

HOURIZADEH, ARASH, espresso manufacturing company executive, physician; b. Hackensack, N.J., May 29, 1972; s. Richard and Vida (Monify) H. BS, UCLA, 1994, BA, 1994; postgrad., U. Calif., San Diego, 1994-98. Archtl. fabricator Perspective Models, Van Nuys, Calif., 1991-92; realtor Jon Douglas Co., Encino, Calif., 1990-94; export dir. Astra Mfg. Co., Canoga Park, Calif., 1993—; rschr. depts. immunology and econs. UCLA, 1992-94; mem. bioethics com. U. Calif. San Diego Med. Ctr., 1994-98. Mng. editor Jour. Molecular Investigations, 1992-94, Cancer Update, 1992-94. Outreach dir. Career Network, L.A., 1992; mem. mktg. and promotions com. UCLA Mardi Gras, 1991-93. UCLA Alumni scholar, 1990, Alumni Achievement award, 1994. Mem. UCLA Alumni Assn., UCLA Alumni Scholars, Phi Beta Kappa, Phi Eta Sigma. Avocations: philosophy, ancient Greek civilization, tennis, basketball. Home: 15221 Antelo Pl Los Angeles CA 90077-1602

HOUSE, DAVID L., electronics components company executive; b. 1943. With Raytheon, 1965-69, Honeywell, 1969-72, Microdata, 1972-74; v.p., gen. mgr. Intel Corp., 1974-96; chmn., pres., CEO Bay Network Computers, Santa Clara, 1996; now sr. v.p. Intel Corp., 1996—. Address: Bay Network Computers 4401 Great America Pkwy Santa Clara CA 95052-8185

HOUSE-HENDRICK, KAREN SUE, nursing consultant; b. San Francisco, July 16, 1958; d. Mathas Dean and Marilyn Frances (Weigand) House. Casa Loma Coll., 1985; AS in Nursing, SUNY at Albany, 1987. Psychiat. charge nurse Woodview Calabasas (Calif.) Hosp., 1985-87, Treatment Ctrs. Am., Van Nuys, Calif., 1987-88; cons., RN Valley Village Devel. Ctr., Reseda, Calif., 1988; plastic surg. nurse George Sanders, M.D., Encino, Calif., 1986—; nurse New Image Found., 1989—, Mid Valley Youth Ctr., 1991—; dir. nursing Encino Surgicenter (Sanders), 1992—; dir. nursing Devel. Tng. Svcs. for Devel. Disabled, 1988—; nurse cons. New Horizons for Developmentally Disabled, 1993. Instr., vol. ARC. Recipient Simi Valley Free Clinic Scholarship. Mem. Encino C. of C. Home: 2526 Gayle Pl Simi Valley CA 93065-2338 Office: 16633 Ventura Blvd Ste 110 Encino CA 91436-1834

HOUSEWORTH, RICHARD COURT, state agency administrator; b. Harveyville, Kans., Jan. 18, 1928; s. Court Henry and Mabel (Lynch) H.; m. Laura Louise Jennings, Nov. 1, 1952; children: Louise, Lucile, Court. B.S., U. Kans., 1950. Mgmt. trainee Lawrence Nat. Bank, Kans., 1951-52; pres. 1st Nat. Bank, Harveyville, 1952-55; exec. v.p. Ariz. Bank, Phoenix, 1955-87, cons., 1987-88; dir. Export-Import Bank of the US, Washington, 1988-91; alt. U.S. exec. dir. The Inter-American Devel. Bank, Washington, 1991-93; supt. of banks, Banking Dept. State of Ariz., 1993—; chmn.-elect Conf. of State and Bank Supervisors, Washington. Past pres. Better Bus. Bur., Tucson; past chmn. bd. Pacific Coast Banking Sch. U. Wash.; past pres. Barrow Neurol. Inst. of St. Joseph's Hosp.; past chmn. Valley of the Sun Visitors and Conv. Bur. Served with U.S. Army, 1946-48. Recipient 1st Disting. Service award Scottsdale Jaycees, 1962. Mem. Ariz. C. of C. (1st pres., dir.), Tucson C. of C. (past pres.), Am. Inst. Banking (past pres. Maricopa chpt.), Ariz. Bankers Assn. (past pres.), Urban League of Phoenix (past chmn.), Paradise Valley Club, Met. Club, Phi Delta Theta. Republican. Episcopalian. Home: 83 Colonia Miramonte Paradise Valley AZ 85253 Office: Supt of Banks 2910 N 44th St Ste 310 Phoenix AZ 85018-7256

HOUSNER, JEANETTE ANN, artist, jeweler; b. Richland Center, Wis., Oct. 9, 1940; d. Richard Edward and Ardyce Evelyn (Kotvis) H.; m. Christos John Papadopoulos, Oct. 12, 1964 (div. Aug. 1988); children: Rachel, Sarah. BA, Milw.-Downer Coll., 1962; MFA, Cranbrook Acad. Art, 1964. Instr., office clk. Indian Arts and Crafts Bd., Sitka, Alaska, 1965-66; instr. jewelry Cen. Wash. U., Ellensburg, Wash., 1967-78; bus. mgr. Laughing Horse Summer Theatre, Ellensburg, 1992-93; owner, artist Jewelry, Metalsmithing, Ellensburg, 1966—. Jewelry represented on slides in permanent collection Cranbrook Acad. Art; evening bag Art to Wear, Larson Gallery, Yakima, Wash., 1990 (Best of Accessories award), pendant 21st Kittitas County Show, Gallery One, Ellensburg, 1991 (Outstanding 3-Dimensional award), pin 40th Cen. Wash. Exhbn., Larson Gallery, Yakima, 1996 (hon. mention), pendant 26th Kittitas County Show, Gallery One, Ellensburg, 1997 (hon. mention); exhibited in numerous group shows, 1962—. Office worker Habitat for Humanity, Ellensburg, 1994-96. Mem. AAUW, NOW, LWV, Soc. N.Am. Goldsmiths, Coll. Art Assn., Am. Craft Coun., Larson Gallery Guild. Home and Office: PO Box 636 Ellensburg WA 98926-0636

HOUSTON, ELIZABETH REECE MANASCO, correctional education consultant; b. Birmingham, Ala., June 19, 1935; d. Reuben Cleveland and Beulah Elizabeth (Reece) Manasco; m. Joseph Brantley Houston; 1 child, Joseph Brantley Houston III. BS, U. Tex., 1956, MEd, Boston Coll., 1969. Cert. elem. tchr., Calif., cert. spl. edn. tchr., Calif., cert. community coll. instr., Calif.; cert. adminstr., Calif. Tchr., elem. Ridgefield (Conn.) Schs., 1962-63; staff, spl. edn. Sudbury (Mass.) Schs., 1965-68; staff intern Wayland (Mass.) High Sch., 1972; tchr., home bound Northampton (Mass.) Schs., 1972-73; program dir. Jack Douglas Ctr., San Jose, Calif., 1974-76; tchr. specialist spl. edn., coord. classroom svcs., dir. alternative schs. Santa Clara County Office Edn., San Jose, Calif., 1986-94; instr. San Jose State U., 1980-86, U. Calif., Santa Cruz, 1982-85, Santa Clara U., 1991-94; cons. Houston Rsch. Assocs., Saratoga, Calif., 1981—. Author: (manual) Behavior Management for School Bus Drivers, 1980, Classroom Management, 1984, Synergistic Learning, 1986, Learning Disabilities in Psychology for Correctional Education, 1992. Recipient President's award Soc. Photo-Optical Instrumentation Engrs., 1979, Classroom Mgmt. Program award Sch. Bds. Assn., 1984, Svc. to Youth award, Juvenile Ct. Sch. Adminstrs. of Calif., 1989-94; grantee Santa Clara County Office Edn. Tchr. Advisor Program U.S. Sec. Edn., 1983-84. Home: 12150 Country Squire Ln Saratoga CA 95070-3444

HOUSTON, GAIL TURLEY, English language educator; b. Santa Cruz, Calif., Sept. 29, 1950; d. Eugene Tolton and Inez (Udall) T.; m. Douglas Lee Houston, Apr. 21, 1977 (dec. Apr. 1986); 1 child, Melissa Louise; m. Michael Thomas Amundsen, Feb. 14, 1986; 1 child, Katherine Margaret. BA, Brigham Young U., 1973; MA in Humanities, Ariz. State U., 1978; MA in English, Brigham Young U., 1981; PhD in English, UCLA, 1990. Tchr. Carl Hayden H.S., Phoenix, Ariz., 1974-75; tchg. asst. humanities and English Brigham Young U., Provo, Utah, 1979-81; tchg. asst., assoc. UCLA, 1984-88; asst. prof. Brigham Young U., Provo, 1990-96, U. N.Mex., Albuquerque, 1996—; dir. grad. studies Univ. N.Mex., 1999—. Author: (book) Consuming Fictions, 1994, also book chpt.; contbr. articles to jours. including Comitatus, Philol. Quar., Studies in English Lit., Royalties; Queen Victoria and the Writer, 1999. Faculty adviser BYU VOICE, Brigham Young U., 1995-96, BYU Rhizobia, 1994-96. Mem. AAUP, MLA,. Democrat. Mormon. Avocations: traveling, embroidery. Office: U N Mex English Dept Humanities 356 Albuquerque NM 87131

HOUSTON, JAMES D., writer; b. San Francisco, Nov. 10, 1933; s. Albert Dudley and Alice Loretta (Wilson) H.; m. Jeanne Wakatsuki, Mar. 27, 1957; children: Corinne, Joshua, Gabrielle. BA in Drama, San Jose (Calif.) State U., 1956; MA in Lit., Stanford U., 1962. Lectr. in writing Stanford U., 1968-69; lectr. in writing U. Calif., Santa Cruz, 1969-83, vis. prof., 1987-93; disting. vis. writer U. Hawaii, Honolulu, 1983-84; Allen T. Gilliland chair in telecomm. San Jose State U., 1985-86; vis. writer U. Mich., Ann Arbor, fall 1985, U. Oreg., Eugene, 1994; mem. adv. bd. Squaw Valley Cmty. of Writers, Calif., 1990—, Tandy Beal Dance Co., Santa Cruz, 1985—, Santa Cruz Actors Theatre. Author: (novels) Between Battles, 1968, Gig, 1969 (Joseph Henry Jackson award 1967), Continental Drift, 1978, Love Life, 1985, The Last Paradise, 1998, others; (non-fiction) Californians: Searching for the Golden State, 1982 (Am. Book award 1983), In the Ring of Fire: A Pacific Basin Journey, 1997, others; co-author: (with Jeanne Wakatsuki Houston) Farewell to Manzanar, 1973, (with John R. Brodie) Open Field, 1975; films include Li'a, The Legacy of a Hawaiian Man, 1988, Listen to the Forest, 1991, The Hawaiian Way: The Art and Family Tradition of Slack Key, 1993, Words, Earth and Aloha: The Sources of Hawaiian Music, 1995 (Silver Maile award 1995), (with Jeanne Wakatsuki Houston and John Korty) Farewell to Manzanar, 1976 (NBC World Premiere movie 1976, Humanitas prize 1976); contbr. numerous articles to popular jours. Mem. Calif. Coun. for Humanities, San Francisco, 1983-87, cons., 1988—; mem. steering com. Pacific Rim Film Festival, Santa Cruz, 1988—. Wallace Stegner Writing fellow Stanford U., 1966-67, rsch. fellow East-West Ctr., Honolulu, 1984, Resident fellow Rockefeller Found., Bellagio, Italy, 1995. Mem. PEN West, Western Am. Lit. Assn. (Disting. Achievement award 1999), Calif. Studies Assn. Avocations: bluegrass music, ragtime piano, hatha yoga. Home and Office: 2-1130 E Cliff Dr Santa Cruz CA 95062

HOUSTON, JAMES RUSSELL (RUSS), retired minister; b. Gloversville, N.Y., Oct. 15, 1922; s. Cyril Wyshart and Anna Belle (Wilson) H.; m. Shirley Joan Walters, July 29, 1952; children: Jeffrey, Shawn, Kurt, Kim, Traci. BA, Ky. Christian Coll., 1945, Butler U., 1947; MDiv, Christian Theol. Sem., 1957. Ordained minister Christian Ch. (Disciples of Christ), Aug. 12, 1945. Pastor First Christian Ch., Cayuga, Ind., 1948-54, Park Christian Ch., Dennison, Ohio, 1954-60, Bethany Christian Ch., Evansville, Ind., 1960-64; pastor Ctrl. Christian Ch., Pocatello, Idaho, 1964-86, ret. min. emeritus, 1987—; morning devotions pastor KSEI Radio, Pocatello, 1966-81; asst. chaplain VA, Pocatello, 1994—; bd. dirs. N.W. Region Christian Ch., Beaverton, Oreg., 1970-75. Chaplain Greater Cleve. BSA Res., Clendening, Ohio, 1957-59; rep. ecumenical ministry Idaho State U., Pocatello, 1964-68; pres. Pocatello Ministerial Assn., 1966-67, 69-70; bd. dirs. Idaho-Oreg. Sight Conservation Found., Boise, 1965, ARC, Pocatello, 1970-77; chaplain, lt. col. Civil Air Patrol, Pocatello, 1968-78; instnl. rev. rep. Bannock Regional Med. Ctr., Pocatello, 1990-95, Pocatello Regional Med. Ctr, 1990-95. Named Lion of Yr., Lions Club Internat., 1963, Lifetime Hon. Tail Twister, Pocatello Lions Club, 1987; recipient Svc. award Bannock Regional Med. Ctr., 1986. Avocations: lyric writing, hunting, fishing, RV travel, spectator sports. Home: 1771 N Honeysuckle Ln Inkom ID 83245-1612

HOUSTON, JANE HUNT, retired educator; b. Upper Montclair, N.J., Dec. 22, 1919; d. MacLean and Mary Hunt (Young) H. BA, Duke U., 1941; MEd, U. Wyo., 1960. Cert. tchr., Wyo. Field worker Glendale (Calif.) coun. Girl Scouts U.S., 1941-45; exec. dir. Sacramento coun. Girl Scouts U.S., 1945-46, Cheyenne (Wyo.) coun. Girl Scouts U.S., 1946-56; tchr. Laramie County Sch. Dist. # 1, Cheyenne, 1956-79; ret., 1979. Co-author: Centennial, Wyoming 1876-1976-the Real Centennial. Bd. dirs. Carbon Power and Light Inc., Saratoga, Wyo., 1983-97, Centennial Water and Sewer Dist., 1988—. Mem. LWV, Centennial Valley Hist. Assn. (sec. 1975—), Wyo. State Hist. Soc. (charter), Laramie County Ret. Tchrs. (com. chmn. 1980-95). Republican. Episcopalian. Avocations: outdoor activities, photography, history, reading, community service. Office: Centennial Valley Hist Assn PO Box 200 Centennial WY 82055

HOUSTON, JOHN ALBERT, political science educator; b. Spokane, Dec. 24, 1914; s. John Alexander and Ethel (Robinson) H.; m. Marjorie Anne Robinson, Aug. 14, 1939 (dec. Sept. 1968); children: Alexandra Louise (Mrs. Lee Benham), John Alexander II (dec. Aug. 1979), Ann Celeste; m. Pollyanna Turner, Nov. 1, 1969. A.B. in Econs, Stanford, 1936, M.A. in Internat. Relations, 1947; Ph.D. in polit. sci, U. Mich., 1951. Ins. broker Johnson & Higgins, San Francisco, 1936-37; case aide Calif. Relief Adminstrn., 1938-40; asst., then asso. prof. polit. sci. U. Miss., 1949-54; faculty Knox Coll., Galesburg, Ill., 1954—; prof. polit. sci. Knox Coll., 1957-80, prof. emeritus, 1980—, Philip Sydney Post disting. prof., 1961-80; sec.-treas. Midwest Collegiate Athletic Conf., 1961-67. Author: Latin America in the United Nations, 1956, Book; rev. editor: Midwest Jour. Polit. Sci, 1962-65. Mem. Galesburg Planning Commn., 1956-57. Served to lt. comdr. USNR, 1941-45. Social Sci. Research Council fellow, 1956. Mem. Am. Polit. Sci. Assn., Midwest Conf. Polit. Scientists, Omicron Delta Kappa, Pi Sigma Alpha, Scabbard and Blade, Sigma Alpha Epsilon. Home: 565 Henley Way Ashland OR 97520-3119

HOUTSMA, PETER C., lawyer; b. Denver, 1951. BA in Polit. Sci. and Econs. magna cum laude, U. Colo., 1973; JD magna cum laude, Cornell U., 1976. Bar: Colo. 1976. Mem. Holland & Hart, Denver, 1976—. Mem. Am. Arbitration Assn. (panel arbitrators), Order of Coif, Phi Beta Kappa. Office: Holland & Hart PO Box 8749 Denver CO 80201-8749*

HOUZE, HERBERT GEORGE, writer; b. Brockville, Ont., Can., Apr. 18, 1947; s. McLean and Grace Lynham (Sayce) H.; m. Carolyn Pierce Johnson, July 8, 1972 (div. May 1990); children: Jennifer E., Alexander I M., Andrew W.; m. Christine Mary Reinhard, Sept. 13, 1996. BA, McMaster U., Hamilton, Ont., 1969; MA, Vanderbilt U., 1972. Curator of mil. history Chgo. Hist. Soc., 1973-76; curator Winchester Mus. Buffalo Bill Hist. Ctr., Cody, Wyo., 1983-91; advisor Royal Mil. Coll. Can. Mus., Kingston, Ont., 1979—; dir. John McLaren & Sons Distillers Ltd., London and Perth, 1990—. Author: (books) The Sumptuous Flaske, 1989, To the Dreams of

Youth, 1992, Winchester History, 1994, Colt Rifles & Muskets, 1996, Winchester Model 52, 1997, Winchester Bolt Action Rifles, 1998. Mem. Arms and Armour Soc. London, Armor & Arms Club N.Y., Les Amis du Musee de Liege.

HOVEL, ESTHER HARRISON, art educator; b. San Antonio, Tex., Jan. 12, 1917; d. Randolph Williamson and Carrie Esther (Clements) Harrison; m. Elliott Logan Hovel, Sept. 30, 1935; children: Richard Elliott, Dorothy Auverne. BA, Incarnate Word Coll., 1935; postgrad., Oxford U., 1979, British Inst. Art, Florence, Italy, 1980. Civil svc. auditor U.S. Govt. Office of Price Adminstrn., San Antonio, 1942-44; interior decorator Parkway Interior Design Studio, El Paso, Tex., 1968-72; instr. stained glass and sculpture El Paso Mus. Art, 1972-78; tchr. sculpture Albuquerque Sr. Ctrs., 1983-85; docent El Paso Mus. Art, 1972-82. Exhibited sculpture Museo De Artes, Juarez, Mexico, 1981 (1st place 1981). Bd. dirs. YMCA, Albuquerque, 1963-64 (plaque 1964); charter mem. and bd. dirs. Contact Lifeline Internat., Albuquerque, 1982-92 (2 plaques 1986, 90); mem. Com. on Bicentennial of U.S. Constitution, Washington and N.M., 1987-89. Recipient 2 medals Exxon Corp., 1986, 89, Medal of Merit Pres. Ronald Reagan, 1987; grantee Exxon Corp., 1986, 90. Mem. Jr. League Internat. (various offices 1948-97), Rotary "Anns" (various offices). Republican. Mem. Christian Ch. Avocations: sculpture, stained glass, oil painting, travel, volunteerism. Home: 7524 Bear Canyon Rd NE Albuquerque NM 87109-3847

HOVERSTAD, RONALD ALAN, marketing educator; b. Rochester, Minn., July 27, 1951; s. Norval Andreason and Juanita (Benson) H.; m. Annella Kay Bernard, June 25, 1977; children: Anna, Sara. BA, Augsburg Coll., 1974; MBA, St Cloud State U., 1981; PhD, U. Minn., 1986. Asst. prof. Tex. Christian U., Ft. Worth, 1985-90; asst. prof. U. Pacific, Stockton, Calif., 1990-92, assoc. prof., dir. MBA Program, 1992—. Contbr. articles to profl. jours. Recipient Rsch. fellowship, U. Minn., Mpls., 1984-85. Mem. Am. Mktg. Assn., Assn. for Consumer Rsch., Southern Mktg. Assn. (best paper promotion and pricing 1987), Southwestern Mkgt. Assn., Am. Assn. for Advances in Health Care, Beta Gamma Sigma, Phi Kappa Phi. Democrat. Roman Catholic. Avocations: skiing, hiking, camping. Home: 2112 Piccardo Ct Stockton CA 95207-7870 Office: U Pacific 3601 Pacific Cir Stockton CA 95211-0110

HOVIND, DAVID J., manufacturing company executive; b. 1940. BA, U. Wash., 1964; postgrad., Stanford U., 1984. With PACCAR Inc., Bellevue, Wash., 1964—, sr. v.p., 1986-87, exec. v.p., 1987-93; now pres. PACCAR Inc., 1993—. Office: PACCAR Inc PO Box 1518 777 106th Ave NE Ste B Bellevue WA 98004-5017

HOVIOUS, GREGORY PAUL, municipal contract officer, contract consultant; b. Tripoli, Libya, June 26, 1956; came to U.S., 1959; s. Charles Raymond and Thelma Kathryn (Arnett) H.; m. Kimberly Ann Steed, Dec. 21, 1985; children: Christopher Gregory, Kathryn Ann. BA in Psychology, Calif. State U., Sacramento, 1981; JD, U. of the Pacific, 1984. Staff atty. Allen, Farley and Welch, Sacramento, 1981-84; v.p. Constrn. Contract Mgmt. Svcs., Sacramento, 1984-87; owner Hovious Consulting, Sacramento, 1987-88; gen. mgr. Yancey Co., Sacramento, 1988-90; contract officer City of Sacramento, 1990—; staff cons. Mayor's Minority Bus. Enterprise/Women Bus. Enterprise Adv. Com., Sacramento, 1994—; chmn. City Contracting Policy Com., Sacramento, 1994—. Author: Standard Specifications City of Sacramento, 1991. Bd. dirs. St. Johns the Evangelist Sch., Sacramento, 1996. With U.S. Army, 1975-76. Named Trainee of the Cycle, Assn. of U.S. Army, 1975; named to Outstanding Minority Program, Minority Enterprise Devel. Conf., 1993; recipient Best Program/Outstanding and Dedicated Svc. award Bay Area Contract Compliance Assn., 1996. Mem. Nat. Contract Mgmt. Assn., Project Mgmt. Inst., Constrn. Specification Inst., Constrn. Mgmt. Assn. Am., Am. Pub. Works Assn. Republican. Roman Catholic. Avocation: golf. Office: City of Sacramento 927 10th St Rm 100 Sacramento CA 95814-2702

HOWARD, BRADFORD REUEL, travel company executive; b. Honolulu, Aug. 6, 1957; s. Joseph DeSylva and Marguerite Evangeline (Barker) H.; m. Marcia Andresen, June 23, 1985; children: Evan DeSilva Andresen, Blair Marguerite. BS in Bus., U. Calif., Berkeley, 1979. Owner, operator Howard Janitorial Svcs., Oakland, Calif., 1970-80; prodn. mgr. Oakland Symphony Orch., 1976-80; brand mgr. The Clorox Co., Oakland, 1980-85; gen. mgr., corp. sec. Howard Tours, Inc./Howard Enterprises, Oakland, 1985—; co-owner Howard Mktg. Cons., Oakland, 1985—; cons. Marcus Foster Found., Oakland, 1984-85; pres., gen. mgr. Piedmont (Calif.) Community Theater, 1976-92. Mem. Calif. Alumni Assn. (bd. dirs. 1991-95), U. Calif. Bus. Alumni Assn. (v.p. 1986-88, pres. 1988-89, Bay Area chpt. 1983-84), U. Calif. Devel. Coun., Oakland-Sunrise Rotary (sec. 1985-87, pres. 1987-88), Lake Merrit Breakfast Club. Avocations: theater, athletics, wine appreciation. Office: Howard Tours Inc 526 Grand Ave Oakland CA 94610-3598

HOWARD, CHRISTOPHER PHILIP, business consultant; b. N.Y.C., Aug. 6, 1947; s. Murray and Hope (McGurn) H.; m. Danina Mary Hill, June 29, 1987; children: Sean, Stephen, Coby, Katherine, Sara. BA in Econs., Stanford U., 1968; MBA, Santa Clara U., 1970. Cert. mgmt. cons.; cert. profl. cons. to mgmt; cert. mgmt. acct.; cert. bus. counselor. Cons. Ernst & Ernst, CPAs, Phoenix, 1972-74; ops. mgr. Jensen Tools & Alloys Inc., Phoenix, 1974-77; CFO Pioneer Industries, Inc., Phoenix, 1977-80; sr. v.p. Health-Tech Mgmt., Inc., Phoenix, 1980-84; mng. prin. Howard and Assocs., Inc., Phoenix, 1984-87; consulting mgr. Grant Thornton, CPAs, Reno, 1987-89; mng. dir. Howard Consulting Group, Inc., Reno, 1989—; faculty mem. U. Nev., Reno, 1991—. 1st lt. USAF, 1970-72. Mem. Inst. Cert. Mgmt. Accts., Nat. Bur. Cert. Cons., Inst. Cert. Mgmt. Cons., Inst. Bus. Appraisers, Inst. Mgmt. Cons., Inst. Cert. Bus. Counselors, Stanford U. Alumni Assn. Episcopalian. Office: Howard Consulting Group 6880 S Mccarran Blvd # A-11 Reno NV 89509-6122

HOWARD, GEORGE HARMON, management consultant; b. St. John, Wash., Nov. 14, 1934; s. George Philip and Corrinne Cadwallader (Rippeteau) H.; m. Elizabeth Ann Ogden, Dec. 22, 1956 (dec. July 1991); children: Debra Ann Woodham, Keith Philip, Corrie Lou Govostis, Stacia Elizabeth. BA, Wash. State U., 1957; MBA, Harvard U., 1967. Sales rep. Burroughs Corp., Spokane, Wash., 1957; various positions USAF, Kirtland AFB, 1958-77; vice commdr. AF Contract Mgmt. Div., Kirkland AFB, N.Mex., 1978; mgr. corp. devel. Leisure Dynamics, Evergreen, Colo., 1978-80; pres. HBK Assocs., Inc., Evergreen, 1981-87; dir. ops. ILX Lightwave Corp., Bozeman, Mont., 1988-89; sr. cons. Matrix Mgmt. Group, Seattle, 1990-94; pres. HBK Assocs. Inc., Auburn, Wash., 1994—; pres. Howard Farms, Inc., St. John, Wash., 1986—. Co-author: TFX Acquisition, 1966. Instr. Red Rocks Community Coll., Denver, 1986-87; del. Colo. Rep. Conv., Denver, 1984. Recipient Outstanding Sr. award Wash. State U., 1957, Legion of Merit award USAF, 1978, Bronze star USAF, 1968. Mem. Shrine, York Rite Bodies, Masonic Lodge, Order of Eastern Star, Wheatland Grange, Air Force Assn., The Ret. Officers Assn. Republican. Episcopalian. Avocations: computers, boating, fishing. Home: 6358 S 298th Pl Auburn WA 98001-3040 Office: HBK Assocs 6358 S 298th Pl Auburn WA 98001-3040

HOWARD, JAMES WEBB, investment banker, lawyer, engineer; b. Evansville, Ind., Sept. 17, 1925; s. Joseph R. and Velma (Cobb) H.; m. Phyllis Jean Brandt, Dec. 27, 1948; children: Sheila Rae, Sharon Kae. BS in Mech. Engring, Purdue U., 1949; postgrad., Akron (Ohio) Law Sch., 1950-51, Cleve. Marshall Law Sch., 1951-52; MBA, Case Western Res. U., 1962; J.D., Western State Coll. Law, 1976. Registered profl. engr., Ind., Ohio. Jr. project engr. Firestone Tire & Rubber Co., Akron, 1949-50; gen. foreman Cadillac Motor Car div. GM, 1950-53; mgmt. cons. M.K. Sheppard & Co., Cleve., 1953-56; plant mgr. Lewis Welding & Engring. Corp., Ohio, 1956-58; underwriter The Ohio Co., Columbus, 1959; chmn. Growth Capital, Inc., Chgo., 1960-98; pvt. practice law San Diego, 1979-85; pres. Meister Brau, Inc., Chgo., 1965-73, The Home Mart, San Diego, 1974-82; mng. agt., fin. instn. specialist FDIC/RTC, 1985-90; specialist in charge Office of FDIC-DOL, Portland, Oreg., 1986-87. Developer of "Lite" beer. Co-chmn. Chgo. com. Ill. Sesquicentennial Com., 1968. Served with AUS, 1943-46. Decorated Bronze Star, Parachutist badge, Combat Inf. badge. Mem. ASME, Nat. Assn. Small Bus. Investment Cos. (past pres.), State Bar Calif., Grad. Bus. Alumni Assn. Western Res. U. (past gov.), Masons, Tau Kappa Epsilon, Pi Tau Sigma, Beta Gamma Sigma. Methodist.

HOWARD, JANE OSBURN, educator; b. Morris, Ill., Aug. 12, 1926; d. Everett Hooker and Bernice Otilda (Olson) Osburn; BA, U. Ariz., 1948; MA, U. N.Mex., 1966, PhD, 1969; m. Rollins Stanley Howard, June 5, 1948; children: Ellen Elizabeth, Susan Nuttall. Instr. U. N.Mex. Sch. Medicine, Albuquerque, 1968-70, mem. staff pediatrics, deaf blind children's program, Albuquerque, 1971-72, asst. dir. N.Mex. programs for deaf blind children, 1972-74, instr. psychiatry, instr. pediatrics, coordinator deaf-blind children's program, 1972-76, edn. cons., 1976—, publicity and pub. relations cons., 1983—; Cons. Mountain-Plains Regional Ctr. for Services to Deaf-Blind Children, Denver, 1971-74, Bur. Indian Affairs, 1974. Active Cystic Fibrosis, Mother's March, Heart Fund, Easter Seal-Crippled Children. Recipient fellowships U. N.M., 1965-68, U. So. Calif. John Tracy Clinic, 1973. Fellow Royal Soc. Health; mem. Council Exceptional Children, Am. Assn. Mental Deficiency, Nat. Assn. Retarded Children, AAUW, Pi Lambda Theta, Zeta Phi Eta, Alpha Epsilon Rho. Republican. Methodist. Home: 615 Valencia Dr SE Albuquerque NM 87108-3742

HOWARD, JO ANN, business owner; b. L.A., Nov. 22, 1937; d. John George and Lucile Anne (Farish) Heinzman; m. William Harold Howard, Dec. 2, 1958; children: Teri Lynn Wilson, Tracey Ann Currie, Randall William, Richard John. Student, Mt. San Antonio Coll., 1957. Escrow officer, mgr. So. Cities Escrow, Hemet, Calif., 1970-75; escrow officer Hemet Escrow, 1975-76; ptnr. Ramona Escrow, Hemet, 1976-79; pres., supr. Howard Escrow, Hemet, 1979—; pres. Recon Enterprises, Inc., Hemet, 1976—, Chaparral Accomodators, Inc., Hemet, 1990-96; retired, 1996. Pres. Sorpotimists Internat., San Jacinto-Hemet Valley, Calif., 1979. Named one of Disting. Pres.'s, Soroptimists, 1978-80; recipient Woman of Distinction award Soroptimist Internat. (San Jacinto-Hemet Valley 1990). Mem. Women's Coun. Bd. Realtors (affiliate, treas.), Hemet-San Jacinto Bd. Realtors (affiliate), San Jacinto C. of C., Hemet C. of C., Calif. Escrow Assn. (pres. Calif. chpt. 1991), Riverside County Escrow Assn. (bd. dirs. 1985—), Escrow Inst. of Calif. (bd. dirs. 1992—). Republican. Presbyterian. Avocations: travel, reading, golf. Office: Howard Escrow 166 E Main St Ste 8 San Jacinto CA 92583-4200

HOWARD, MURRAY, manufacturing, real estate and property management executive, farmer, rancher; b. Los Angeles, July 25, 1914; s. George A. J. and Mabel (Murray) H. B.S., UCLA, 1939. C.P.A., Calif. Mgr. budget control dept. Lockheed Aircraft, 1939-45; pres., chmn. bd. Stanley Foundries, Inc., 1945-59, Howard Machine Products, Inc., 1959—, Murray Howard Realty, Inc., 1959—, Murray Howard Devel., Inc., 1969—, Howard Oceanography, Inc., 1967—, Ranch Sales, Inc., 1968—, Murray Howard Investment Corp., 1961—; owner, gen. mgr. Greenhorn Ranch Co., Greenhorn Creek Guest Ranch, Spring Garden, Calif.; pres., chmn. bd. Murray Howard Cattle Co., Prineville, Oreg.; dir. Airshippers Publ. Corp., LaBrea Realty & Devel. Co., Shur-Lok Corp. Served as mem. Gov. Calif. Minority Com. Mem. Nat. Assn. Cost Accts. (dir., v.p.), NAM (dir.). Home: 3771 Lockland Dr Los Angeles CA 90008-3510

HOWARD, NANCY E., lawyer; b. Ft. Wayne, Ind., Aug. 13, 1951. BA, Stanford U., 1973, JD, 1977. Bar: Calif. 1977. Mem. Tuttle & Taylor, L.A., 1977—. Contbr. articles to profl. jours. Mem. Order of Coif., Phi Beta Kappa. Office: Tuttle & Taylor 355 S Grand Ave 40th Fl Los Angeles CA 90071-3176*

HOWARD, VICTOR, management consultant; b. Montreal, Que., Can., Aug. 12, 1923; s. Thomas and Jean (Malkinson) H.; BA, Sir George Williams U., 1947; BSc, 1948; PhD, Mich. State U., 1954; m. Dorothy Bode, Dec. 25, 1953. Mech. design engr. Canadian Vickers Ltd., Montreal, 1942-46; with Aluminum Co. Can., 1946-48, E.B. Badger Co., Boston, 1948-50; asst. prof. Mich. State U., 1952-56; social scientist Rand Corp., 1956-58; staff exec., personnel dir. System Devel. Corp., Santa Monica, Calif., 1958-66; staff cons. Rohrer, Hibler & Replogle, San Francisco, 1966-69; mng. dir. Rohrer, Hibler & Replogle Internat., London and Brussels, 1969-74, ptnr. 1974, mgr. San Francisco, 1974-88, dir., 1979-88; pres. V. Howard and Assocs., 1988—, The Inst. on Stress and Health in the Work Place, 1988—; vice chair State Bd. Psychology, 1989-93. Fellow Brit. Inst. Dirs.; mem. Am. Psychol. Assn., Western Psychol.Assn., U.S. Power Squadrons (comdr. Sequoia Squadron 1981, dist. comdr. 1987), Calif. State Mil. Res. (col. 1984), Reform Club, Hurlingham (London) Club, Thames Motor Yacht Club (Molesey, Eng.), Order of St. John of Jerusalem (chevalier)Sovereign Mil. Order of the Temple (prior Priory of St Francis, Grand Cross), Masons (33 degree), Shriners, Sigma Xi. Home and Office: 530 Los Altos Ct Santa Rosa CA 95403-1329

HOWARTH, SUSAN TEER, management executive, consultant, association executive; b. Amityville, N.Y., Mar. 28, 1951; d. Louis Peter and Nettie Sue (Chavers) Teer. BA magna cum laude, Fairfield U., 1973; MA, SUNY, Albany, 1974. Mgr. tng. employment programs non-profit orgs., 1975-80; dir. employment, tng. and tech. assistance Boston YWCA, 1980-84; v.p. Drake Beam Morin Inc., Boston, 1984-87; sr. v.p. Drake Beam Morin Inc., N.Y.C., 1987-90, group v.p., 1990-92; internat. mgmt. cons., spkr., pers. and bus. coach San Francisco, 1992—; NGO rep. to the UN; internat. devel. cons. Mem. Nat. Bd. YWCA of the U.S.A., N.Y.C., 1992—. Lehman fellow SUNY. Avocations: travel, piano and jogging. Home: 2210 Jackson St Apt 701 San Francisco CA 94115-1309

HOWATT, SISTER HELEN CLARE, human services director, former college library director; b. San Francisco, Apr. 5, 1927; d. Edward Bell and Helen Margaret (Kenney) H. BA, Holy Names Coll., 1949; MS in Libr. Sci., U. So. Calif., 1972; cert. advanced studies Our Lady of Lake U., 1966. Joined Order Sisters of the Holy Names, Roman Cath. Ch., 1945. Life teaching credential, life spl. svcs. credential, prin. St. Monica Sch., Santa Monica, Calif., 1957-60, St. Mary Sch., L.A., 1960-63; tchr. jr. high sch. St. Augustine Sch., Oakland, Calif., 1964-69; tchr. jr. high math St. Monica Sch., San Francisco, 1969-71, St. Cecilia Sch., San Francisco, 1971-77; libr. dir. Holy Names Coll., Oakland, Calif., 1977-94; Spanish instr. Collins Ctr. Sr. Svcs., 1994—. Contbr. math. curriculum San Francisco Unified Sch. Dist., Cum Notis Variorum, publ. Music Libr., U. Calif., Berkeley. Contbr. articles to profl. jours. NSF grantee, 1966, NDEA grantee, 1966. Mem. Cath. Libr. Assn. (chmn. No. Calif. elem. schs. 1971-72). Home and Office: 2550 18th Ave San Francisco CA 94116-3005

HOWE, ART (ARTHUR HENRY HOWE, JR.), professional baseball manager; b. Pitts., Dec. 15, 1946; m. Elizabeth Louise Falconio, Aug. 16, 1969; children: Stephanie Lynn, Gretchen Leigh, Matthew Louis. BS, BA, U. Wyoming, 1969. Computer programmer Westinghouse Corp., 1969-70; player Carolina League, Salem, 1971, International League, Charleston, WV, 1972-75, Pittsburg Pirates, Pittsburg, PA, 1974, 75, International League, Memphis, TN, 1976, Houston Astros, Houston, TX, 1976-83, St. Louis Cardinals, St. Louis, MO, 1984-85; coach Texas Rangers, Arlington, TX, 1985-88; mgr. Houston Astros, Houston, TX, 1988-93; mgr. Puerto Rican League, Bayamon, PR, winters 1979, 80, 82, Ponce, PR, winter 1985; mgr. Oakland Athletics, 1996—; hitting coach Colo. Rockies, 1995. Named Mgr. of Yr. P.R. League, 1980, Dominican Rep. La Romana, 1994-95. Office: Oakland Athletics 7677 Oakport St Ste 200 2d Fl Oakland CA 94621-1933*

HOWE, DRAYTON FORD, JR., lawyer; b. Seattle, Nov. 17, 1931; s. Drayton Ford and Virginia (Wester) H.; m. Joyce Arnold, June 21, 1952; 1 son, James Drayton. A.B., U. Calif.-Berkeley, 1953; LL.B., Hastings Coll. Law, 1957. Bar: Calif. 1958. CPA Calif. Atty. IRS, 1958-61; tax dept. supr. Ernst & Ernst, San Francisco, 1962-67; ptnr. Bishop, Barry, Howe, Haney & Ryder, San Francisco, 1968—; lectr. on tax matters U. Calif. extension, 1966-76. Mem. Calif. Bar Assn., San Francisco Bar Assn. (chmn. client relations com. 1977), Calif. Soc. CPA's. Office: Bishop Barry Howe Haney & Ryder Watergate Tower III 44 Montgomery St Ste 1300 San Francisco CA 94111

HOWE, LINDA ARLENE, nursing educator, writer; b. Pitts., Dec. 12, 1948; d. Alfred Robert and Zella Jane (Lintner) Somerhalder; m. John Joseph Howe, Dec. 7, 1968; 1 child, Thomas Patrick. Diploma in nursing, Columbia Hosp., 1969; Assoc. in English, Richland Coll., 1981; BSN, U. Tex., Arlington, 1982; MS in Nursing, Tex. Woman's U., 1988; MAE in English, The Citadel, 1992; PhD in Higher Edn. Adminstrn., U. S.C., 1997. RN, Pa., S.C.; cert. BCLS. Staff nurse Columbia Hosp., Pitts., 1969-70; staff nurse ICU Brownsville (Pa.) Hosp., 1970-72; charge nurse ICU Kennestone Hosp., Marietta, Ga., 1972-73; staff devel. dir. Autumn Breeze N.H., Austell, Ga., 1973-74; dir. nursing Hideaway Hills N.H., Austell, 1974-76; mgmt. cons. Unicare Svcs., Dallas, 1976-79; supr. ICU Meml. Hosp. of Garland, Tex., 1979-84; dir. edn. Montgomery Gen. Hosp., Olney, Md., 1984-89; dir. Roper Hosp. Sch. Nursing, Charleston, S.C., 1989-95; nurse Richland Meml. Hosp, Columbia, S.C., 1995-96; dir. Olsten Home Health Svcs., Eugene, Oreg., 1996-98; dir. critical care Valley Hosp., Santa Maria, Calif., 1998—; instr. U. Md., College Park, 1985-89; instr. English Trident Tech. Coll., Charleston, 1992-95; speaker and presenter in field. Author: Passion and Persistance: A Biography of Mary Adelaide Nutting, 1997. Leader Girl Scouts USA, Marietta, 1974-76; cub scout den mother Boy Scouts Am., Dallas, 1977-80, counselor, Dallas and Olney, 1981-88; Sunday sch. tchr. Holy Comforter Luth. Ch., 1994-96, congregational coun. sec., 1994-96. Named Instr. of Yr. Nat. Fedn. LPNs, 1990, 92. Mem. ANA, NAFE, Nat. League for Nursing (program com.), S.C. Nurse Educators (treas. 1991-93), Am. Assn. Nurse Historians, Am. Assn. Critical Care Nurses. Avocations: needlecraft, gardening, music, writing. Home: 620 Halton Rd Apt 11107 Greenville SC 29607-3489

HOWE, RICHARD CUDDY, state supreme court chief justice; b. South Cottonwood, Utah, Jan. 20, 1924; s. Edward E. and Mildred (Cuddy) H.; m. Juanita Lyon, Aug. 30, 1949; children: Christine Howe Schultz, Andrea Howe Reynolds, Bryant, Valerie Howe Winegar, Jeffrey, Craig. B.S., U. Utah, 1945, J.D., 1948. Bar: Utah. Law clk. to Justice James H. Wolfe, Utah Supreme Ct., 1949-50; judge city ct. Murray, Utah, 1951; individual practice law Murray, 1952-80; assoc. justice Utah Supreme Ct., 1980—, justice; mem. Utah Constnl. Revision Commn., 1976-85. Chmn., original mem. Salt Lake County Merit Coun.; mem. Utah Ho. of Reps., 1951-58, 69-72, Utah Senate, 1973-78. Named Outstanding Legislator Citizens' Conf. State Legislatures, 1972. Mem. ABA, Utah Bar Assn., Sons of Utah Pioneers. Mem. LDS Ch. Office: Utah Supreme Ct 450 S State St PO Box 140210 Salt Lake City UT 84114-0210

HOWE, RONALD EVANS, minister; b. Charles City, Iowa, Feb. 17, 1945; s. Evans R. and Elizabeth (Atchison) H.; m. M. Kristin Petersmith, Aug. 16, 1970; children: Sarah Elizabeth, Rachel Ellen, Michael Evans. Cert., Moody Bible Inst., 1966, AB, 1969; AB, U. Iowa, 1968, JD, 1972; ThM, Dallas Theol. Sem., 1975. Lic. to ministry Ind. Mission Ch., 1966, ordained Evang. Free Ch. Am., 1990. Bar: Iowa 1972, Tex. 1973, U.S. Tax Ct. 1974. Atty. Lawn Offices of Gordon Macdowell, Dallas, 1972-75; sr. min. Elim Chapel, Winnipeg, Man., Can., 1975-85, Evang. Free Ch., Fresno, Calif., 1985—; broadcaster weekly radio program Free to Live, 1985—; owner, pres. Elim Place, Inc.; adj. prof. Winnipeg Theol. Sem., 1975-85, Briercrest Grad. Sch., Caronport, Sask, Can., 1985-87; bd. dirs. Haggai Inst., Winnipeg, 1977-85, Link Care Ctr., Fresno, 1985—; bd. govs. Winnipeg Bible Coll. and Sem., 1982-85; mem. exec. com. Fresno Christian Sch., 1985—; lectr. in field. Author: (booklet) Breakfast of Champions, 1984. Recipient Commendation for 10 yrs. of contbn. in leadership Mayor City of Fresno, 1995, Outstanding Bus. award for leadership in edn. Compact Fresno, 1998. Mem. North Fresno Rotary. Republican. Home: 889 E Portland Ave Fresno CA 93720-2133 Office: Evang Free Ch 3438 E Ashlan Ave Fresno CA 93726-3506

HOWE, WINONA RUTH, English language educator; b. Modesto, Calif., Apr. 22, 1943; d. Ira Ralph and Bertha Belle (Booth) Scott; m. Vernon Howe, July 25, 1965; children: Andrew, Stephanie. BA, Pacific Union Coll., 1965; MA, Loma Linda U., 1986; PhD, U. Calif., Riverside, 1992. Assoc. prof. La Sierra U., Riverside, 1991—. Contbr. articles to profl. jours. Avocations: travel, Eskimo art. Home: 11238 Rogers St Riverside CA 92505-2628 Office: La Sierra Univ Dept English and Comm 4700 Pierce St Riverside CA 92505-3332

HOWELL, DONALD JAMES, vocational school administrator; b. Bonners Ferry, Idaho, Aug. 14, 1955; s. Leslie Anthony and Roberta Jean (Baker) H.; m. Pamela Yvonne Bryant, Oct. 19, 1973 (div. 1995); children: Cynthia Marie, Anthony Daun. AA in Liberal Arts, Craven C.C., Newbern, N.C., 1983, AA in Pre Edn., 1983; BA in Theology, Twin Cities U., 1984, MA in Edn. Adminstrn., 1986. Cert. tchr., Wash.; cert. state vocat. dir. Enlisted USMC, 1972, advanced through grades to staff sgt., 1978, resigned, 1980; electronics technician Howell Electronics, Jackson, Tenn., 1980-87; vocat. instr. Lake Washington Tech. Coll., Kirkland, Wash., 1987-92; tchr. Juanita H.S., Kirkland, 1991-92; adminstr. Lake Washington Tech. Coll., Kirkland, 1992-93; asst. dir. Tri-Tech Skills Ctr., Kennewick, Wash., 1993—; apptd. mem. new coll. planning com. State Bd. Cmty. and Tech. Colls., 1991; apptd. Gov. Blue Ribbon Com. on Assoc. in Tech. Arts, 1992. Mem. ASCD, Wash. Vocat. Assn. (exec. bd. dirs. 1992—, sec. 1993-95, Instr. of Yr. 1991), Am. Vocat. Assn., Electronics Technicians Assn. (dir. certification 1991—, vice chmn. 1989-90, chmn. 1990-91, Technician of Yr. 1992, Pres.'s award 1990), Kennewick C. of C., Lions Club (treas. 1994-95), Rotary (Columbia Ctr.). Republican. Avocations: running, hiking, mountain biking, dancing, theatre. Office: c/o Spokane Skills Ctr 4141 N Regal St Spokane WA 99207-5878

HOWELLS, R. TIM, professional sports team executive; m. Patty Howells; four children. Grad., U. Utah, 1968. With Howells, Inc., Salt Lake City, 1968-82; v.p., co-owner, pvt. investor Howells, Inc., from 1982; gen. mgr. Utah Jazz NBA, 1989—. Office: Utah Jazz 301 W South Temple Salt Lake City UT 84101-1216*

HOWLAND, JOYCE ELIZABETH, college administrator; b. Corvallis, Oreg., Sept. 13, 1946; d. James Chase and Ruth Louise (Meisenhelder) H.; m. Roosevelt Lucio Adolfo Fernandes, Dec. 29, 1972; children: Benjamin James, Von Patricio. AB, Wellesley Coll., 1968; PhD, Vanderbilt U., 1972. Research asst. GASCO, Santiago, Chile, 1967; instr. Vanderbilt U., Nashville, 1972; asst. prof., coordinator SUNY, Oswego, 1972-78; asst. prof. Onondaga Community Coll., Syracuse, N.Y., 1979; mentor Empire State Coll., Syracuse, 1979; dir. Columbia Coll., Hancock Field, N.Y., 1979-89; mem. community outreach dept. City of Chino, Calif., 1989-90; evaluator Calif. State Poly. U., Pomona, 1990-91; assoc. dir. Coll. Environ. Design Coll. Environ. Design, Pomona, 1991, dir. Office Student Affairs, 1992—; tutor Empire State Coll., Syracuse, 1979-89. Contbr. articles to profl. jours. Den leader Cub Scouts Am., 1985-89, com. chmn., 1989-91; mem. Calif. Poly. Credit Union Bd., 1991-94. Fellow NDEA Title IV, 1968-70. Mem. N.Y. St. Latin Americanists (pres. 1979-80), Am. Econs. Assn., L.Am. Studies Assn., Nat. Acad. Adv. Assn. Home: 3472 Alder Pl Chino CA 91709-2005 Office: Calif State Poly U Coll Environ Design 3801 W Temple Ave Pomona CA 91768-2557

HOWLAND, PETER MCKINNON, academic administrator; b. Corvallis, Oreg., Apr. 2, 1956; s. James Chase and Ruth Louise (Meisenhelder) H. BA, Linfield Coll., 1978; postgrad., Boise State U., 1981-82; MA in Interdisciplinary Studies, Oreg. State U., 1985. Travel agt. Sather Tours and Travel, Salem, Oreg., 1979-81; office asst. then devel. asst. Linfield Coll., McMinnville, Oreg., 1985-90, devel. asst. for rsch., 1990-94, dir. of rsch. and records, 1994—. Mem. Pi Sigma Alpha. Republican. Mormon. Avocations: reading, travel, stamp collecting. Office: Linfield Coll Office Coll Rels 900 SE Baker St Mcminnville OR 97128-6808

HOWLETT, JOHN DAVID, government relations; b. Akron, Colo., July 16, 1952; s. John Butler and Reavis Lavina (Smith) H. BA, U. Nebr., 1975, M in Cmty. and Regional Planning, 1977. Urban and regional planner Oblinger-McCaleb, Denver, 1979-80; staff project mgr. Greater Denver C. of C., 1980-83; dir. econ. devel. City of Littleton, Colo., 1983-87; dir. civic and econ. devel., interim pres. The Denver Partnership, Denver, 1987-91; mng. assoc. Linton, Mields, Reisler & Cottone, Inc., Denver, 1991-95; prin., owner Price Howlett, Inc., Denver, 1995—; mem. Arapahoe/Douglas Pvt. Industry Coun., Englewood, Colo., 1984-87; mem. steering com. New Bus. and Industry Coun., Denver, 1985-87; mem. exec. com. Met. Denver Network, 1987-91. Mem. profl. adv. coun. Coll. Arch. U. Nebr., Lincoln, 1980—; vice chmn. C-470 Inter-Camber Task Force, Denver, 1984-87; trustee AMC Cancer Rsch. Ctr., Lakewood, Colo., 1985-87; mem. exec. bd. Friends Auraria Libr., Denver, 1989-90; mem. vocat. adv. com. Mental Health Corp., 1990-94. Mem. Am. Planning Assn. (pres. Colo. chpt. 1985-87, Karen Smith

Chpt. award 1987), City Club Denver (pres. 1984-85). Democrat. Presbyterian. Avocations: exercise, skiing, travel, reading. Home: 3026 W Prentice Ave Littleton CO 80123-7719 Office: Price Howlett Inc 2547 W 32nd Ave Denver CO 80211-3323

HOWORTH, DAVID, producer, director; b. N.Y.C., Aug. 30, 1941; s. Marion Beckett and Dorothy Huldah (Cowing) H.; m. Bea Borges, May 6, 1967. AA, Santa Barbara (Calif.) C.C., 1970; student, UCLA, 1977, Am. Film Inst., L.A., 1982. V.p., co-owner Golden Coast Films, Santa Barbara, 1971-82, owner, prodr., dir., 1982—. Software developer, prodr.: (CD-ROM/Internet series) Career Link, 1996, Wildlife/Nature series, 1993; prodr., dir.: Careers: Nursing, 1993; co-prodr., co-writer: (ednl. picture) Just Beer, 1983. With USMCR, 1960-65. Recipient awards Columbus Internat. Film/Video Festival, 1993, Nat. Mental Health Assn., 1981, Excellence-Suitable for Family Viewing, No. Calif. Motion Picture and TV Coun., 1975. Mem. NATAS, AMA (acad. med. films), Internat. Interactive Comms. Soc., Greater Santa Barbara Advt. Club (pres. 1972). Avocations: historical films, records, swimming, boating. E-mail: gcf@silcom.com. Office: Golden Coast Films 2020 Alameda Padre Serra Santa Barbara CA 93103-1756

HOWRY, JOE, newspaper editor. Mng. editor Ventura (Calif.) County Star, 1992—. Address: 5250 Ralston St Ventura CA 93003-7318*

HOWSLEY, RICHARD THORNTON, lawyer, regional government administrator; b. Medford, Oreg., Jan. 31, 1948; s. Calvin Nevil and Arvilla Constance (Romine) H.; m. Susan Erma Johnson, Oct. 23, 1971; children: James Denver, Kelly Ann. BA, Willamette U., 1970; MS, Va. Poly. Inst. and State U., 1974; JD, Lewis and Clark Law Sch., 1984. Bar: Oreg. 1984, Wash. 1985, U.S. Dist. Ct. (we. dist.) Wash., 1985. Tech. editor U.S. Bur. Mines, Arlington, Va., 1971-72; program mgr., sr. planner KRS Assos., Inc., Reston, Va., 1972-74; exec. dir. Rogue Valley Council Govts., Medford, 1974-78; exec. dir. Regional Planning Council of Clark County, Vancouver, Wash., 1978-84; pres. Landerholm, Memovich, Lansverk & Whitesides, Vancouver, 1985-92; pvt. practice, Vancouver, 1992—; vice chmn. Oreg. Council of Govts. Dirs. Assn., 1976-77, chmn., 1977-78; mem. regional adv. com. So. Oreg. State Coll., 1975-78. Mem. Medford-Ashland Air Quality Adv. Com., 1977-78. Carpenter Found. scholar, 1966-70, Leonard B. Mayfield Meml. scholar, 1966-67, Albina Page Found. scholar, 1966-70. Mem. ABA, Oreg. State Bar Assn., Wash. State Bar Assn., Am. Planning Assn., Am. Inst. Cert. Planners, Internat. City Mgmt. Assn. (10-yr. service award), Nat. Assn. Regional Councils (10-yr. service award). Democrat. Methodist. Home: PO Box 61448 Vancouver WA 98666-1448 Office: Richard T Howsley PS 314 E Mcloughlin Blvd Vancouver WA 98663-3371

HOYE, WALTER BRISCO, retired college administrator; b. Lena, Miss., May 19, 1930; s. William H. and LouBertha (Stewart) H.; m. Vida M. Pickens, Aug. 28, 1954; children—Walter B. II, JoAnn M. B.A., Wayne State U., 1953. Sports/auto editor Detroit Tribune, 1958-65; sports editor Mich. Chronicle, 1965-68; assoc. dir. pub. relations San Diego Chargers Football Co., 1968-76; media liason NFL, 1972-75; community services officer San Diego Coll. Dist., 1976-78; placement officer Ednl. Cultural Complex, San Diego, 1978-80, info. officer, 1980-82, placement officer, adminstrv. asst., 1982-83, placement/program support supr., 1983-91, supr. program support svcs., 1989—; cons. in field. Bd. dirs. San Diego County ARC; active San Diego Conv. and Tourist Bur., Joint Ctr. Polit. Studies, Am. Cancer Soc., San Diego Urban League, Neighborhood Housing Assn., Public Access TV. Named San Diego County Citizen of Month, May, 1979; recipient United Way Award of Merit, 1974. Mem. Internat. Assn. Auditorium Mgrs., Am. Personnel and Guidance Assn., San Diego Career Guidance Assn., Nat. Mgmt. Assn., Assn. Calif. Community Coll. Adminstrs., Calif. Community Coll. Placement Assn., Rocky Mountain Assn. Student Fin. Aid Adminstrs. Home: 6959 Ridge Manor Ave San Diego CA 92120-3146

HOYEM, ANDREW LEWISON, publisher; b. Sioux Falls, S.D., Dec. 1, 1935; s. Albert Gustav and Ellen Anne (Lewison) H.; m. Sally Cameron Heimann, June 24, 1961 (div. 1964); m. Judith Bordin, Dec. 31, 1970 (div. 1985). B.A., Pomona Coll., 1957. Ptnr. Auerhahn Press, San Francisco, 1961-64; owner Andrew Hoyem Printer, San Francisco, 1965-66; ptnr. Grabhorn-Hoyem, San Francisco, 1966-73; owner Arion Press, San Francisco, 1973-79; pres. Arion Press, 1979—, M & H Type, 1989—. Author: book of poetry Articles, 1969, What If, 1987; artist: book illustrations Flatland, 1980; designer: Moby Dick, 1979, Ulysses, 1988, The Physiology of Taste, 1994. Lt. (j.g.) USN, 1957-60. Clubs: Bohemian, Grolier. Office: Arion Press 460 Bryant St San Francisco CA 94107-1303

HOYT, DIANA VAUGHN, fundraising consultant, small business owner; b. Denver, Jan. 26, 1945; d. Michael and Virginia Rose (Barnes) Grega; m. Michael Lee, Dec. 1967 (div. Dec. 1973); m. Roy Alan Flegenheimer, July 28, 1974 (div. Jan. 1992); m. Robert L. Hoyt, Jan. 9, 1994; children: Elon Michael, Rachel Anne. AA, Hutchinson (Kans.) Jr. Coll., 1965; BS, Kans. U., 1967; MA, Ariz. State U., 1972. Cert. high sch. tchr., Ariz., cert. fundraising, Nat. Soc. of Fund Raising Exec. Math tchr. various high schs., Ariz. and Mo., 1967-75; devel. officer Ariz. Mus. Sci. and Tech., Phoenix, 1986-88, Desert Bot. Garden, Phoenix, 1988-89, Actors Theatre, Phoenix, 1989-91, TERROS Behavioral Health Svcs., Phoenix, 1991-95, Ariz. Cactus Pine Girl Scout Coun., Phoenix, 1995-97. Mem. Samaritans, 1987-96; women's campaign chmn. United Jewish Appeal, 1984-86; mem. Valley Leadership, 1986-87. Recipient Lee Amada Young Leadership award Jewish Fedn. Greater Phoenix, 1981, Golda Meir award, 1990. Mem. Nat. Soc. Fund Raising Execs. (bd. dirs. Greater Ariz. chpt., pres. 1995), Jewish Bus. and Profl. Women's Nat. Coun., Coun. for Jews with Special Needs (pres.), Rotary Internat., Beta Gamma Sigma, Phi Lambda Theta, Phi Theta Kappa. Democrat. Jewish. Home: 4929 E Laurel Ln Scottsdale AZ 85254-4640 Office: Heritage Designs LLC PO Box 10779 Phoenix AZ 85064-0779

HOYT, JAMES EDWARD, church administrator; b. Chgo., Aug. 6, 1955; s. William Francis and Anna Marie (Hynes) H.; m. Patricia Marguerite Therese O'Mahony, Jan. 31, 1981; children: Christopher, Melissa, Michael, Rebecca. BA, Loyola U., Chgo., 1977; MA, Regis U., 1992. Summer coord. St. Mary of the Lake Ch., Chgo., 1974-76; educator Sts. Peter and Paul Sch., Chgo., 1977-78; vol. Jesuit Community, Arequipa, Peru, 1978-79; parish adminstr. Christ the King Ch., Mesa, Ariz., 1985-95; deacon Our Lady of Perpetual Help Ch., Scottsdale, Ariz., 1995—. Mem. Nat. Assn. Ch. Bus. Adminstrs., Nat. Assn. Ch. Pers. Adminstrs., Adminstrs. Diocese of Phoenix (co-founder 1986). Roman Catholic. Office: Our Lady of Perpetual Help Ch 7655 E Main St Scottsdale AZ 85251-4606

HOYT, MARY G., artist, educator; b. Oct. 7, 1929; d. Alvin Chase and Genevive Therese (Cahill) H.; children: Jill Marie, Patricia Anne Eckert, John, Diane Marie, Jill Marie, Patricia Anne Frederick, Mary Elizabeth. BA in Art, Coll. St. Francis, 1950. Art instr. Malta Pub. High Sch., Dekalb, Ill., 1958; tchr. Lock Port (Ill.) Pub. Grade Sch., 1959; art tchr. Yauapai Coll., Prescott, Ariz., 1974-78, Allan Hancock Coll., Santa Maria, Calif., 1978-95; lectr. in field. Author: the Spirit Masters' Guide Book to Enlightenment, 1995. Avocations: camping, fishing, reading, travel. Home: 1411 Via Asueto Santa Maria CA 93454-2623

HOYT, ROBERT PREIS, astronautical engineer, glass artist; b. Boston, Sept. 15, 1968; s. Robert Stevens and Marilyn Jane (Preis) H. BA, Williams Coll., 1990; MS in Astronautical Engring., U. Wash., 1992, PhD, 1994. Rsch. asst. Los Alamos (N.Mex.) Nat. Lab., 1992-94; ptnr., chief engr. Tethers Unltd., Seattle, 1994-97, pres., CEO, chief engr., 1997—. Patentee in field of survivable space tether, terminator tether. Recipient Fellowship award Planetary Soc., 1988. Mem. AIAA. Avocation: glass art. Office: Tethers Unltd Inc 1917 NE 143d St Seattle WA 98125

HRCEK, MARGARET N., writer; b. Houston, Dec. 29, 1947; d. John [illegible] and Pat Annie (Cushman) [illegible]; m. Leon C. H[illegible], June 29, 1979; children: Jason, Jennifer. Payroll/record clk. Houston Fire Dept. Author: (book) Romeo and Juliet, The Birds, 1995, poetry. Avocations: writing, reading, hiking, crocheting. Home: 31552 Black Widow Dr Conifer CO [illegible]

HRONEK, DAVID EDWARD, architect; b. Cleve., Dec. 28, 1960; s. Edward Frank and Norma Anne (Biltz) H. BArch, U. Detroit, 1983. Assoc., project mgr. Fletcher, Valentl, Chillura & Pugliski, Inc., Tampa, Fla., 1982 85, Hellmuth Obatay Kassabaum, Inc., Tampa, Fla., 1985-90; asst. mgr., cons. Eral Walls Assocs., San Diego, 1990—. Author (newsletter) Laboratory, 1996—. Vol. Big Bros./Big Sisters, Tampa, 1984-86, United Way Am., Tampa, 1986-90. Mem. AIA, Nat. Fire Protection Assn., Soc. Coll. & Univ. Planning. Republican. Roman Catholic. Avocations: travel, swimming, dogs, reading, biking. Home: 2802 El Rastro Ln Carlsbad CA 92009-9214 Office: Earl Walls Assocs 5348 Carroll Canyon Rd San Diego CA 92121-1733

HRUDEY, KELLY, hockey player; b. Edmonton, Alberta, Can., Jan. 13, 1961. Goalie San Jose Sharks. Office: c/o San Jose Sharks 525 W Santa Clara St San Jose CA 95113-1520

HRUT, CHRISTOPHER BOLESLAW, sales and marketing executive; b. Szczecin, Poland, Apr. 18, 1958; came to U.S. 1986; s. Zdzislaw and Halina (Maj) H. MSc, Gdansk U., Poland, 1982; Dipl.Eng., Tech. U. Gdansk, 1983; MSc, MIT, 1987; MBA, Harvard U., 1989. Sr. supr. Gdansk Shipyard, 1983-86; exec. asst. Fuji-Xerox, Tokyo, 1988; mng. exec. Network Equip. Technologies, 1989-90; dir. Trimble Navigation & Navigation Techs., Sunnyvale, Calif., 1991—; gen. ptnr. Renaissance Capital, Boston, 1993—; gen. ptnr. European Renaissance Ptnrs.; cons. in field. Contbr. articles to profl. jours. MIT grantee, Harvard Bus. Sch. fellow, Kosciuszko Found. grantee. Mem. Harvard Bus. Sch. Club No. Calif., MIT Club No. Calif., Commonwealth Club of Calif., Harvard U. Club No. Calif., Churchill Club, Kosciuszko Found., Harvard U. Club of Poland (founding chmn. 1991—), Harvard U. Club of Hungary (founding chmn. 1990—), Harvard U. Club of Czechoslovakia (founding chmn. 1990—). Avocations: skiing, windsurfing, piano, art. Home: 445 Encinal Ave Apt H Menlo Park CA 94025-3144 Office: Oracle Corp 500 Oracle Pkwy PO Box 659106 Redwood City CA 94065-0106 also: Zaruskiego 26, PL-80-299 Gdansk-Osowa Poland

HSIAO, CHIE-FANG, neuroscientist; b. Chi-Yei, Taiwan, Jan. 15, 1945; came to U.S., 1983; s. Zu-Chin and Chiao (Ching) H.; m. Shu-Lan Lin, Jan. 29, 1976; children: Kathryne, Amy. BS in Pharmacology, Taipei (Taiwan) Med. Coll., 1976; PhD in Med. Sci., Osaka (Japan) U., 1983. Rsch. assoc. SUNY, Stony Brook, 1983-85, U. Colo., Boulder, 1985-89; rsch. instr. U. Mo., Kansas City, 1989-92; neuroscientist U. Calif., L.A., 1992—; lectr. U. Mo., Kansas City, 1988-89; rsch. instr. Osaka U. Med. Sch., 1981-83, U. Calif., L.A., 1992—. Advisor Taipei Med. Sch. Alumni, Calif., 1993, Taiwanese Assn., Colo., 1985. Recipient Nat. Rsch. Svc. award NIH, 1992, fellowship Fight for Sight Inc., 1984, scholarship Japan Rotary, 1982. Mem. AAAS, Soc. for Neurosci., Naturalistic Soc. USA. Avocations: reading, singing, swimming, yoga, tennis. Home: 1835 Camden Ave Apt 102 Los Angeles CA 90025-4470 Office: Univ Calif 405 Hilgard Ave Los Angeles CA 90095-9000

HSIEH, STEWART, lawyer; b. L.A., Apr. 5, 1953; s. Donald and Eva (Moe) H.; m. Victoria Parrott, Mar. 29, 1979 (div. 1996); children: Joshua, Christine. BS, Calif. State U., L.A., 1975; JD, Southwestern U., 1978. Atty., ptnr. Frye & Hsieh, L.A., 1988—; bd. dirs. Med. Bd. Calif., v.p., 1992—, pres., 1997; mem. low income housing adv. com. Calif. State Treas., 1995-97, chmn., 1996. Mem. com. Boy Scouts Am., 1994, vice chmn.; asst. treas., statewide co-fin. chair Matt Fong for State Treas., 1993-94, Matt Fong for State Contr., 1989-90, Matt Fong for U.S. Senate, 1998, asst. treas.; mem. ctrl. com. Calif. Rep. Party, 1991—, regional co-chair Asian Outreach Project, 1989-90; bd. dirs. RIMPAC, 1990-94; mem. Asian adv. com. Natural Mus. History, County of L.A., 1990-94. Mem. Calif. Soc. Healthcare Attys., State Bar of Calif., L.A. County Bar Assn. (co-chmn. sr. citizen outreach com. 1992-93), L.A. Athletic Club (chmn. bd. 1996, 99). Republican. Office: Frye and Hsieh LLP 626 Wilshire Blvd Ste 800 Los Angeles CA 90017-2921

HSIEH, VICTOR C., artist; b. San Diego, Dec. 29, 1975; s. San C. and Lina S. (Japardi) H. Assoc., Calif. State U., Long Beach, 1994-95. Pvt. practice Calif., 1987—; adv. ArtQuest, Inc., St. Louis, 1996-97. Editor Art in San Diego, 1995-98 (best critic award 1998); contbr. articles to profl. jours.; exhibited in group shows at ArtQuest, 1996-98. Recipient Gold medal Art Inst., San Diego, 1996, Award of Excellence Manhattan Arts, N.Y., 1997, Hunter Mus. Am. Art, Tenn., 1998, Flash Art Mus., Italy, 1998, Mus. Iternat. Contemporary Art, Brazil, 1998. Fellow L.A. Artcore, Municipal Art Gallery; mem. N.Y. Cultural Ctr., L.A. Mus. Art, Art Inst. San Diego, Art in San Diego (founder), Alliance for Arts, Epilepsy Found. Avocations: ice skating, miniature golf, ping pong, mountain climbing. E-mail: vh8@yahoo.com. Home and Office: 9651 Blackgold Rd La Jolla CA 92037-1112

HSIEH, WILLIAM SHEN-CHU, statistician, educator; b. Meizhou, China, Sept. 19, 1920; came to U.S., 1980; s. Lin-Sun and Dai-Mu (Lee) H.; m. Ho Song Hsu, Nov. 22, 1947; children: Henry Y-Ming, James C-Ming, Annie C-Ming. BA, Nat. U. Amoy, Fukien Province, China, 1944, Nat. Polit. U., Nanking, China, 1947. Asst. prof. Fungih U., Taiwan, 1959-60, Tsainkiang U., Taiwan, 1960-62; cons. Taiwan Provincial Govt., 1960-62; sr. specialist Fin. Ministry, China, 1962-68; sr. rschr. First Comml. Bank, Taiwan, 1960-68; statistician Asian Devel. Bank, Manila, 1968-80; editl. writer Internat. Daily News, L.A., 1982-84, China Times, L.A., 1984, Chung Pao (China Daily News), L.A., 1983-86; vis. prof. Kia Yin U., Meizhou, China, 1990—, Gi Nan U., Canton, China, 1992; rschr. U. Mich., IMF Inst. Home: 224 N Moore Ave Apt E Monterey Park CA 91754-1532

HSU, GERALD C., electrical company executive. Chmn., pres., CEO Avanti, Freemont, Calif. Office: Avanti 46871 Bayside Pkwy Fremont CA 94538*

HSU, SHEAUYU, molecular physiologist; b. Taipei, China, Oct. 31, 1961; s. Chiao-Fong and HsiuYin (Chen) H.; m. Shinwin Ma, Aug. 22, 1992; 1 child, Eeway E. BS, Ocean Univ., Keelung, Taiwan, 1983; MS, Univ. S. Miss., 1988; PhD, Univ. Notre Dame, 1993. Rsch. assoc. Stanford Univ., Stanford, 1998—. Author: Handbook in Physiology, 1998; Recent Progress in Hormone Research, 1996; contbr. articles to profl. jours. Recipient Young Investigator award Soc. Study of Reproduction, 1995. Mem. Soc. Study of Reproduction. Avocation: fishing. Office: Stanford Univ Detp Gyn/Ob Stanford CA 94305

HSU, SHU-DEAN, hematologist, oncologist; b. Chiba, Japan, Feb. 21, 1943; came to U.S., 1972; s. Tetzu and Takako (Koo) Minoyama; m. San-San Hsu, Mar. 3, 1973; children: Deborah Te-Lan, Peter Jie-Te. MD, Taipei (Taiwan) Med. Coll., 1968. Diplomate Am. Bd. Internal Medicine, Am. Bd. Hematology, Am. Bd. Med. Oncology. Asst. in medicine Mt. Sinai Sch. Medicine, N.Y.C., 1975-77; asst. instr. medicine U. Tex., Galveston, 1977-78; lectr. in medicine Tex. A&M U., Temple, 1978-80; asst. prof. medicine U. Ark., Little Rock, 1980-83; practice medicine specializing in hematology-oncology Visalia (Calif.) Med. Clinic, 1983—; chief hematology and oncology VA Med. Ctr., Temple, Tex., 1978-80. Contbr. articles to profl. jours. Fellow ACP; mem. N.Y. Acad. Scis., Am. Soc. Clin. Oncology, Am. Soc. Hematology, Calif. Med. Assn., Tulare County Med. Soc. Club: Visalia Racquet. Home: 3500 W Hyde Ave Visalia CA 93291-5620 Office: Visalia Med Clinic PO Box 3347 Olympic Valley CA 96146

HU, CHI-AN, international law educator; b. Zhejiang, China, Nov. 11, 1925; s. Yung-gao and Shou-ning (Zhu) Hu; m. Zhenfen Sophia Liu, Sept. 12, 1957; children: Keli, Qiaoli. BA, Wuhan (China) U., 1946; LLM, U. London, 1950. Assoc. prof. Fudan U., Shanghai, 1951-59, People's U., Beijing, 1960-64; editor World Affairs mag., Beijing, 1965-79; legal advisor Chinese Fgn. Ministry, Beijing, 1980-89; prof. internat. law Peking U., Beijing, 1982—; chancellor, legal advisor permanent mission to UN, Vienna, 1984-86; vis. scholar Inst. of East Asian Studies, U. Calif., Fulton, 1991—. Author: Current Problems of the United Nations, 1956, The Co-existence of Two Social Systems, 1957, Hand Book of Diplomacy, 1979, Legal Status of the Antarctica, 1982. Mem. Internat. Polit. Sci. Assn. (v.p. [illegible]). Avocations: jogging, swimming. Home: Redwood Gardens 2951 Derby St #234 Berkeley CA 94705-1354 Office: U Calif Inst of East Asian Studies 2223 F[illegible] St Berkeley CA 94720

HU, JOHN CHIH-AN, retired chemist, research engineer; b. Nanzhang, Hubei, China, July 12, 1922; came to U.S., 1954, naturalized, 1965; s. Qi-Qing and Zhao-Xian (Zeng) H.; *Mr. Hu, the eldest of seven children, was born in the city of Nanzhang, a city where fourteen generations of his family lived for almost 400 years. He and his wife, Betty, a chemist, also have seven children, six sons and one daughter. Four of his sons received their degrees from MIT while his three other children received their degrees from Stanford University. Although each of his seven children chose engineering as their careers, they are all musically talented and each plays violin as a hobby* BA in Chemistry, Nat. Central U., Nanjing, China, 1946; MS in Organic Chemistry, U. So. Calif., 1957, postgrad., 1957-61; PhD (hon.) Marquis Giuseppe Scicluna Internat. Univ. Foundation, 1985; m. Betty Siao-Yung Ho, Oct. 26, 1957; children: Arthur, Benjamin, Carl, David, Eileen, Franklin, George. Dir. rsch. dept. Plant 1, Taiwan Fertilizer Mfg. Co., Chilung, 1947-54; rsch. assoc. chemistry dept. U. So. Calif., L.A., 1957-61; rsch. chemist Chem Seal Corp. Am., Los Angeles, 1961-62; rsch. chemist Products Rsch. & Chem. Corp., Glendale, Calif., 1962-66; sr. rsch. engr., materials and tech. unit, Boeing Co., Seattle, 1966-71, specialist engr. Quality Assurance Labs., 1971-90, ret., 1990; cons. UN; lectr., China, profl. confs. Fellow Am. Inst. Chemists; mem. Am. Chem. Soc. (chmn. Puget Sound sect. 1988, councilor 1989-92), Royal Soc. Chemistry (London), N.Y. Acad. Sci., Phi Lambda Upsilon. Patentee Chromatopyrography; contbg. author: Analytical Approach, 1983, Advances in Chromotography, vol. 23, 1984; contbr. articles on analytical pyrolysis, gas chromatography, mass spectrometry, polymer characterization, chemistry and tech. of sealants and adhesives to profl. publs. in Chinese and English; editor Puget Sound Chemist, 1984-92; referee profl. jours. Analytical Chemistry, Analytica Chimica Acta, Am. Chem. Soc., short courses. *Mr. Hu is a Certified Professional Chemist, inventor and author. He was a Boeing engineer for 24 years, until his retirement in 1990. His professional interests lie in the fields of organic chemistry, polymeric materials technology, liquid and gas chromatography, mass spectrometry, and analytical pyrolysis. His career history has made him an expert in adhesion science and polymer technology. He was also engaged in the development of new analytical methods for chemical characterization of polymeric materials. Mr. Hu also developed the method of pyrolysis-mass spectrometry, which is the procedure for rapid analysis of high polymers* Home: 2813 Whitworth Ave S Renton WA 98055-5008

HU, LINCOLN, media technology executive, computer scientist; b. Taipei, Taiwan. BS in Computer Sci., Columbia U., 1982, MS in Computer Sci., 1985. Rsch. staff assoc. Columbia U., N.Y.C., 1982-85; dir. tech. devel. Indsl Light & Magic, Lucasfilm Ltd., San Rafael, Calif., 1986-96; chief tech. officer Sony Pictures/Imageworks, Culver City, Calif., 1996—. Mem. Acad. Motion Picture Arts and Scis. (digital imaging tech. awards com. 1995—, sci. engring. award 1995, Tech. Achievement award 1996), Assn. for Computing Machinery. Office: Sony Pictures/Imageworks 9050 Washington Blvd Culver City CA 90232-2518

HUANG, CHIEN CHANG, electrical engineer; b. Nanking, Peoples Republic of China, Feb. 16, 1931; came to U.S., 1957; s. Ling-Kuo Huang and Yi-Ching Liu; m. Li-May Tsai, June 2, 1962; children: Frederick G., Lewis G. BSEE, Taiwan Coll. Engring., Tainan, 1954; MSEE, U. Ill., 1959; postgrad., U. Pa., 1960-62. Engr. Burrough Corp., Paoli, Pa., 1960-64; sr. staff engr. Unisys Corp., San Diego, 1974—; sr. engr. Philco Ford Corp., Blue Bell, Pa., 1965-69; staff engr. Fairchild Semiconductor, Mountain View, Calif., 1969-71; sr. staff engr. Am. Micro Systems, Santa Clara, Calif., 1971-74. Contbr. articles to profl. jours. Home: 14481 Maplewood St Poway CA 92064-6446 Office: Unisys Corp 10850 Via Frontera San Diego CA 92127-1788

HUANG, FRANCIS FU-TSE, mechanical engineering educator; b. Hong Kong, Aug. 27, 1922; came to U.S., 1945, naturalized, 1960; s. Kwong Set and Chen-Ho (Yee) H.; m. Fung-Yuen Fung, Apr. 10, 1954; children: Raymond, Stanley. BS, San Jose State Coll., 1951; MS, Stanford U., 1952; Profl. M.E., Columbia U., 1964; Cultural Doctorate in Energy Sci. (hon.), World U., Ariz., 1990. Design engr. M.W. Kellogg Co., N.Y.C., 1952-58; faculty San Jose (Calif.) State U., 1958—, assoc. prof. mech. engring., 1962-67, prof., 1967-91, prof. emeritus, 1991, chmn. dept., 1973-81; hon. prof. heat power engring. Taiyuan (People's Republic of China) U. Tech., 1981—. Author: Engineering Thermodynamics—Fundamentals and Applications, 1976, 2d edit., 1988. Capt. Chinese Army, 1943-45. Recipient Disting. Teaching award Calif. State Coll. System, 1968-69; named Outstanding Prof. of Yr., Tau Beta Pi, 1967, 76, Prof. of Yr., Pi Tau Sigma, 1985; NSF faculty fellow, 1962-64. Mem. AAAS, ASME, AIAA, AAUP, Am. Soc. Engring. Edn., N.Y. Acad. Scis., Sigma Xi. Home: 1259 Sierra Mar Dr San Jose CA 95118-1235 Office: San Jose State U Dept Mech Engring San Jose CA 95192

HUANG, KAI-LOO, religion educator emeritus; b. Indonesia, 1909; came to U.S., 1935 and 1964; BA, Tsinghua, Beijing, 1934; MA, U. Wis., 1936, PhD, 1938. Vis. prof. emeritus Moravian Coll., Bethlehem, Pa., 1965-84, Univ. Wisc.; lectr. comparative religions, Chinese religions. Contbr. articles to profl. jours. Home: PO Box 55788 Riverside CA 92517-0788

HUANG, KUN LIEN, software engineer, scientist; b. Nantou, Taiwan, Jan. 20, 1953; came to U.S., 1984; s. Chai-Chang and Fei-Chei (Chi) H.; m. Sue Hui Lee, Mar. 24, 1981; 1 child, Wayne. BS, Nat. Taipei Inst. Tech., Taiwan, 1973, N.D. State U., 1986; MS, U. Mo., 1988. Mech. engr. Ta Tung Aluminum Co., Taipei, 1975-76; rsch. mgr. Ta Tung Aluminum Co., Tapei, 1976-77, prodn. tech. mgr., 1977-79, quality control mgr., 1979-84; computer programmer U. Mo., Columbia, 1988; systems analyst, programmer NCR Corp., San Diego, 1989-92; database cons. Gamma-Metrics, 1992-93; software engr. Sci. Applications Internat. Corp., 1993-95; Unix adminstr. Gen. Instrument Corp., 1995-98; sr. database mgr. Indusoft, Inc., 1998—; cons. Computing Ctr., U. Mo., Columbia, 1987-88. Recipient Nat. scholarship Republic China Jaycees, Taipei, 1972. Mem. AAAS, San Diego Taiwanese Cultural Assn. Republican. Avocation: fishing. Home: 8939 Adobe Bluffs Dr San Diego CA 92129-4400

HUANG, LINDA CHEN, plastic surgeon; b. Ithaca, N.Y., July 24, 1952. MD, Stanford U., 1979. Chmn. plastic surgery St. Joseph Hosp., Denver. Office: 1578 Humboldt St Denver CO 80218-1638

HUBBARD, DONALD, marine artist, writer; b. Bronx, N.Y., Jan. 15, 1926; s. Ernest Fortesque and Lilly Violet (Beck) H.; student Brown U., 1944-45; A.A., George Washington U., 1959, B.A., 1958; student Naval War Coll., 1965-66; divorced; children: Leslie Carol, Christopher Eric, Lauren Ivy, Carmeron C. McNall; m. Kay Frances Boldt, Oct. 1998. Commd. ensign U.S. Navy, 1944, advanced through grades to comdr., 1965; served naval aviator, ret., 1967; founder Ocean Ventures Industries, Inc., Coronado, Calif., 1969, operator, 1969-77; marine artist; founder, operator Sea Eagle Pubs., Coronado, 1988; lectr. on marine art; SCUBA instr. Author: Ships-in-Bottles, 2d edition, 1988, A How to Guide to a Venerable Nautical Craft, 1971; Buddelschiffe: Wie Macht Man Sie, 1972; The Complete Book of Inflatable Boats, 1979; Where to Paddle in San Diego County and Nearby Mexico, 1992, Days of Yore: Rhymes & Other Writings, 1995, Neptunes Table: Cooking the Sea Food Exotics, 1997; editor: The Bottle Shipwright; works featured in Am. Artist of the Bookplate, 1970-90, Cambridge Bookplate Press, 1990; contbr. articles in field to publs.; featured on House and Garden TV/What's My Hobby? Decorated Air Medal. Mem. Ships-in-Bottles Assn. (pres. N.Am. div. 1982—), Nature Printing Soc., Am. Soc. Bookplate Collectors adn Designers, San Diego Watercolor Soc. (bd. dirs. 1981-82), San Diego Maritime Assn. Home and Office: 1022 Park Pl Coronado CA 92118-2822

HUBBARD, GREGORY SCOTT, physicist; b. Lexington, Ky., Dec. 27, 1948; s. Robert Nicholas and Nancy Clay (Brown) H.; m. Susan Artimissa Ruggeri, Aug. 1, 1982. BA, Vanderbilt U., 1970; postgrad., U. Calif., Berkeley, 1975-77. Lab. engr. physics dept. Vanderbilt U., Nashville, 1970-73; staff scientist Lawrence Berkeley Lab. Dept. Instrument Techs., Berkeley, Calif., 1974-80; dir. rsch. & devel. Canberra Industries, Inc., Detector Products Divsn., Novato, Calif., 1980-82; v.p., gen. mgr. Canberra Semiconductor, Novato, Calif., 1982-85; cons., owner Hubbard Cons. Svcs., [illegible] Calif., 1979-86, sr. rsch. physicist, 1986-87; divsn. staff scientist space exploration projects office Ames Rsch. Ctr., NASA, Moffett Field, Calif., 1987-90, chief space instrumentation and studies br., 1990-92; dep. chief space projects divsn., 1992-96, assoc. dir.

space directorate, 1996-97, dep. dir. space directorate, 1997—; mem. fed. Sr. Exec. Svc., 1997—; study mgr. Mars Pathfinder Mission, 1990-91; mission mgr. Lunar Prospector Mission, 1994-98; lectr. in field. Founders scholar Vanderbilt U., 1966; recipient Exceptional Achievement medal NASA, 1994, Outstanding Leadership medal, 1998. Mem. AIAA, IEEE, Nuclear Sci. Soc., Am. Phys. Soc., Commonwealth Club Calif., Hon Order Ky. Cols.

HUBBELL, ROBERT NEWELL, psychologist; b. Neenah, Wis., Oct. 23, 1931; s. Ralph Newell and Ruth Elizabeth (Lindsey) H.; m. Joann Marguerite Jansen, Aug. 14, 1954; children: Scott David, Brian Jansen. BS, Northwestern U., 1954; MA, U. Wis., 1961, PhD, 1964. Dean of men, asst. prof. U. Iowa, 1964-67; Am. Coun. on Edn. intern U. Calif., Santa Barbara, 1967-68; assoc. prof., staff psychologist Colo. State U., Ft. Collins, 1968-72; founder, coord. Community Counseling Ctr., Granby, Colo., 1972-76; lic. psychologist, 1976—; pvt. practice clin. psychology Canon City, 1977—; behavioral sci. intern Nat. Tng. Labs., Bethel, Maine, summer 1968; cons. Pomona Coll., summer 1969, Luth. Ch. Am., 1969-70, Higher Edn. Assocs., 1970-72; adj. prof. Walden U., Naples, Fla., 1971-85, Colo. State Penitentiary, 1977-79. Lt. (j.g.) USNR, 1954-57. Contbr. articles to profl. jours. Mem. APA, Biofeedback Soc. Am. (cert.), Am. Soc. Clin. Hypnosis, Nat. Register Health Svcs. Providers in Psychology, Colo. Psychol. Assn. Methodist. Home: 2317 Greenway Cir Canon City CO 81212-2036 Office: PO Box 687 Canon City CO 81215-0687

HUBBS, DONALD HARVEY, foundation executive; b. Kingman, Ariz., Jan. 3, 1918; s. Wayne and Grace Lillian (Hoose) H.; m. Flora Vincent, June 14, 1945; children: Donald Jr., Susan Tyner, Diane Schultz, Wayne, David, Adrienne Busk. BA in Edn., Ariz. State U., 1940; JD, Southwestern U., 1956. Bar: Calif., 1956; CPA. Acct. Wright and Hubbs, L.A., 1945-67; pvt. practice atty. L.A., 1956-81; pres., dir. Conrad N. Hilton Found., L.A., 1981-98, chmn. bd., CEO, 1998—; bd. dirs. Trans World Airlines, 1977; regent Mt. St. Mary's Coll., 1983-98; bd. councilors U. So. Calif. Law Sch., 1992—. Hon. chief of the tribes, Oku Ghana, West Africa. 1st lt. (inf.) U.S. Army. Decorated Purple Heart. Mem. State Bar of Calif., So. Calif. Assn. for Philanthropy (pres. 1985-86), Riviera Country Club, L.A. Country Club. Avocations: cattle ranching, hunting, fishing, golfing. Home: 1658 San Onofre Dr Pacific Palisades CA 90272-2735 Office: Conrad N Hilton Found 10100 Santa Monica Blvd Ste 740 Los Angeles CA 90067-4100

HUBER, COLLEEN ADLENE, artist; b. Concordia, Kans., Mar. 30, 1927; d. Claude Irve and Freda (Trow) Baker; m. Wallace Charles Huber, Oct. 18, 1945 (dec.); children: Wallace Charles II (dec.), Shawn Dale, Devron Kelly (dec.), Candace Lynette, Melody Ann. Student, UCLA, 1974-78; BA cum laude, Calif. Poly. U., 1983. Co-owner, artist The Rocket (community newspaper), Garden Grove, Calif., 1955-58; quick sketch artist Walt Disney Prodn. Co., Burbank, Calif., 1958-59; v.p., art dir. Gray Pub. Co., Fullerton, Calif., 1968-76; tchr. North Orange County Sch. Dist., La Palma, Calif., 1974-76; art dir. Shoppers Guide, Upland, Calif., 1979-81; pub., owner Community Woman/Huber Ad Agy., Anaheim, Calif., 1976-79; artist Bargain Bulletin Pub., Fallbrook, Calif., 1979-82; graphic artist, designer Van Zyen Pub., Fallbrook, 1982-83; cons. sales East San Diego Mag./Baker Graphics, Rancho San Diego, Calif., 1978-88; owner, artist Coco Bien Objet d'Art, Laguna Beach, Calif., 1986-92; instr. Camp Fire Inc., 1990-92; instr. Coco Bien Objet d'Art, Temecula, Calif., 1992-93, Sun City, Calif., 1993—, Castle Rock, Wash., 1993—; dir. edn. Art Acad., Orange County, 1992-94; instr. Lake Elsinore Community Ctr., 1992—, San Jacinto C.C., 1997-98; 2nd v.p. Fine Art Inst., San Bernadina Mus., San Bernardino, Calif. Author: Gail, 1980 (1st Pl. award 1981, 2d Pl. award 1981); artist: Yearlings (2d Pl. award 1985), Penning (1st Pl. award 1987). Participant Art-A-Fair, Laguna Beach Festival Show. Recipient certs. North Orange County ROP, 1976-77, 2d pl. San Bernardino Art Show, 1995, Hon. Mention Nat. Orange Show, 1996, City of Lake Elsinore, 1997, 1st pl. award FAI San Bernardino Mus., 1999. Fellow Zonta (2d v.p. 1990-91), Laguna Beach C. of C. (docent gallery night 1988); mem. Exec. Women, Calif. Press Women Assn. (chmn. jr. journalism contest Orange County chpt. 1985-86, pres. 1986-87; yearly chair Taste of Valley art show 1997), Wildlife Art Assn. Republican. Roman Catholic. Avocations: baseball fan, golf, swimming, dancing, theatre.

HUBER, LINDA RUTH, non-commissioned officer; b. Stafford Springs, Conn., Aug. 3, 1955; d. Joseph Lawrence and Edith Viola (Plante) Young; m. Vernon R. Huber Jr., Dec. 26, 1981; children: James R., Brian D., Chad T., Nicole L., Christopher A. AA, C.C. of Air Force, 1986; student pre-edn. program, Ariz. U. Admission clk. St. Anthony Hosp., St. Petersburg, Fla., 1974-76; customer svc. rep. Zayre Dept. Stores, St. Petersburg, 1976-77; jet engine technician Fighter Interceptor Squadron, Griffiss AFB, N.Y., 1977-79, Logistics Support Squadron, Okinawa, Japan, 1979-81; asst. NCOIC outbound assignments Combat Support Group, McConnell AFB, Kans., 1981-82; jet engine specialist Consolidated Aircraft Maintenance Squadron, Altus AFB, Okla., 1982-84; NCOIC quick engine changes sect. 81 Component Repair Squadron, RAF Bentwaters, UK, 1984-88, NCOIC tech. adminstrn. 355 Component Repair Squadron, Davis-Monthan AFB, Tucson, 1988-92; NCOIC orderly room 355 Ops. Support Squadron, Davis-Monthan AFB, Tucson, 1992—; USAF disaster preparedness support team Combat Support Group, RAF Bentwaters, 1984-88; mem. Desert Shield/Desert Storm support Component Repair Squadron, Davis-Monthan AFB, 1990-91; tutor for AHDH and ADD diagnosed children, 1993—. Coach Pop Warner Mitey Mite Football, Tucson, 1989, Apache Little League Baseball, Tucson, 1988-92; coach (asst.) Pantano Soccer League, Tucson, 1989-92; fundraiser rep. Pop Warner Football, Tucson, 1990-92, U. Ariz. Soccer program, 1993—. Democrat. Lutheran. Avocations: coaching Little League sports, swimming, computer programming, reading, teaching bilingual classes. Office: 355 Ops Support Squadron Davis Monthan AFB Tucson AZ 85707

HUCK, LARRY RALPH, manufacturers representative, sales consultant; b. Yakima, Wash., Aug. 10, 1942; s. Frank Joseph and Helen Barbara (Swalley) H.; 1 child, Larry Ralph II. Student Wash. Tech. Inst., 1965-66, Seattle Community Coll., 1966-68, Edmonds Community Coll., 1969-70. Salesman Kirby Co., Seattle, 1964-68, sales mgr., 1968-69; saleman Sanico Chem. Co., Seattle, 1968-69; salesman Synkoloid Co., Seattle, 1970-71; tech. sales rep. Vis Queen div. Ethyl Corp., Seattle, 1971-75; Western sales mgr. B & K Films, Inc., Belmont, Calif., 1975-77; pres. N.W. Mfrs. Assocs., Inc., Bellevue, Wash., 1977-86; pres. combined sales group, 1984 ; nat. sales mgr. Gazelle, Inc., Tomah, Wis., 1979-81; dir. sales J.M.J. Mktg. E.Z. Frame div., 1984-85; pres. Combined Sales Group, Seattle, 1984; nat. accounts mgr. Upnorth Plastics, St. Paul, 1984-87; pres. Combined Sales Group, Inc., Redmond, Wash., 1987-96; gen. mgr. Otool Co., 1996-98. V.p. Bellevue Nat. Little League; basketball coord. Cath. Youth Orgn., Sacred Heart Ch.; head baseball coach Pierce Coll., Tacoma. With USMC, 1959-66. Mem. Nat. Coun. Salesmen's Orgns., Mfrs. Agts. Nat. Assn., Am. Hardware Mfrs. Assn., Northwest Mfrs. Assn. (pres.), Hardware Affiliated Reps., Inc., Door and Hardware Inst., Internal Conf. Bldg. Ofcls., Am. Baseball Coaches Assn., Marine Corps Assn., 1st Marine Div. Assn., 3d Marine Div. Assn. (life, v.p.). Roman Catholic. Office: 600 Baldwin Park Blvd City Industry CA 91746-1501

HUCKEBY, KAREN MARIE, graphic arts executive; b. San Diego, June 4, 1957; d. Floyd Riley and Georgette Laura (Wegimont) H. Student Coll. of Alameda, 1976; student 3-M dealer tng. program, St. Paul, 1975. Staff Huck's Press Service, Inc., Emeryville, Calif., 1968—, v.p., 1975—. Mem. Rep. Nat. Task Force, 1984—; bd. dirs. CitiArts Benefactors, Concord, Calif., 1990-93, v.p., treas., 1991-93. Recipient service award ARC, 1977. Mem. East Bay Club of Printing House Craftsman (treas. 1977-78), Oakland Mus. Soc., Nat. Trust Historic Preservation, Smithsonian Inst., San Francisco Mus. Soc., Internat. Platform Assn., Am. Film Inst., Commonwealth Club. Home: 1054 Hera Ct Hercules CA 94547 Office: Staff Huck's Press Svc Inc 691 S 31st St Richmond CA 94804-4022

HUDGENS, SANDRA LAWLER, retired state official; b. New Orleans, Feb. 15, 1944; d. Avril Lawler and Peggy V. (Crager) Kelly; m. Adolfo DiGennaro, Oct. 20, 1967 (div. 1970); 1 child, Daniel Darryn DiGennaro; m. Stanley Dalton Hudgens, Feb. 17, 1973; children: Stephanie Hudgens Cap, Richard Stanley, Michael Shane. Student, U. Nev., 1962-64, U. Grenoble, France, 1964-65, U. Aix-Marseille, Nice, France, 1965, U. Nev., Las Vegas, 1980—. Traffic ct. clk. III Clark County Juvenile Ct. Svcs., Las Vegas, 1965-71; planning commr. City of Las Vegas, 1988-92, chmn. planning commn., 1991-92; br. mgr. registration divsn. Dept. Motor Vehicles and Pub. Safety, State of Nev., Las Vegas, 1971-96; rep. Weststar FCU, Las Vegas, 1988-96; advocate State of Nev. Employees Assn., Las Vegas, 1971-96; coord. State of Nev. team City of Las Vegas Corp. Challenge, 1987-90; dir. so. chpt. Am. Fedn. State, County and Mcpl. Employees/State Nev. Employees Assn. retirees AFL/CIO. Past treas., sec. Las Vegas Civic Ballet Assn., Las Vegas, 1987-93; treas. Women's Dem. Club Clark County, Las Vegas, 1996-97, pres., 1998; chmn., vice-chmn. United Blood Svcs. Adv. Coun., Las Vegas, 1993-96; chmn. 1st Ann. Flood Awareness Week, mem. adv. coun. Clark County Regional Flood Dist., Las Vegas, 1987-88; treas., sec., badge and advancement counselor Boy Scouts Am., Las Vegas, 1976-90. Mem. Am. Bus. Women's Assn. (chmn. souvenir program Western Regional Conf. 1997). Democrat. Episcopalian. Avocations: hunting, knitting, photography, RVing, biking. Home: 3840 Russet Falls St Las Vegas NV 89129-7644

HUDSON, CHRISTOPHER JOHN, publisher; b. Watford, Eng., June 8, 1948; s. Joseph Edward and Gladys Jenny Patricia (Madgwick); m. Lois Jeanne Lyons, June 16, 1979; children: Thomas, Ellen, Ronald, Timothy. BA with honors, Cambridge U., Eng., 1969, MA with honors, 1972. Promotion mgr. Prentice-Hall Internat., Eng., 1969-70; area mgr. Prentice-Hall Internat., Eng., France, 1970-71; mktg. mgr. Prentice-Hall Internat., Englewood Cliffs, N.J., 1971-74, dir. mktg., 1974-76, asst. v.p., 1976; group internat. dir. I.T.T. Pub., N.Y.C., 1976-77; pres. Focal Press, Inc., N.Y.C., 1977-82; v.p., pub. Aperture Found. Inc., N.Y.C., 1983-86; head publs. J. Paul Getty Trust, L.A., 1986—. Author: Guide to International Book Fairs, 1976; pub. Aperture, 1983-86, J. Paul Getty Mus. Jour., 1986—. Mem. adv. coun. Nat. Heritage Village, Kioni, Greece; mem. trade with eastern Europe com. Assn. Am. Pubs., N.Y., 1976-79, internat. fairs com., 1986-88. Mem. Internat. Assn. Mus. Publs. (Frankfurt, Fed. Republic Germany, chmn. 1992-95), U.S. Mus. Publ. Group (chmn. 1989—), Internat. Pubs. Assn., Hellenic Soc. (London), Oxford & Cambridge Club (London), Internat. Assn. Scholarly Pubs. (sec.-gen. 1994-97, chmn. internat. contracts com.). Avocation: rural preservation projects in England, Greece and California. Office: J Paul Getty Mus 1200 Getty Ctr Dr Ste 1000 Los Angeles CA 90049-1687

HUDSON, EDWARD VOYLE, linen supply company executive; b. Seymour, Mo., Apr. 3, 1915; s. Marion A. and Alma (Von Gonten) H.; student Bellingham (Wash.) Normal Coll., 1933-36, also U. Wash.; m. Margaret Carolyn Greely, Dec. 24, 1939; children—Edward G., Carolyn K. Asst. to mgr. Natural Hard Metal Co., Bellingham, 1935-37; partner Met. Laundry Co., Tacoma, 1938-39; propr., mgr. Peerless Laundry & Linen Supply Co., Tacoma, 1939—; propr. Independent Laundry & Everett Linen Supply Co., 1946-74, 99 Cleaners and Launderers Co., Tacoma, 1957-79; chmn. Tacoma Public Utilities, 1959-60; trustee United Mut. Savs. Bank; bd. dirs. Tacoma Better Bus. Bur., 1977—. Pres., Wash. Conf. on Unemployment Compensation, 1975-76; pres. Tacoma Boys' Club, 1970; v.p. Puget Sound USO, 1972-91; elder Emmanuel Presbyn. Ch., 1974—; past campaign mgr., pres. Tacoma-Pierce County United Good Neighbors. Recipient Distinguished Citizen's cert. U.S. Air Force Mil. Airlift Com., 1977; U.S. Dept. Def. medal for outstanding public service, 1978. Mem. Tacoma Sales and Mktg. Execs. (pres. 1957-58), Pacific NW Laundry, Dry Cleaning and Linen Supply Assn. (pres. 1959, treas. 1965-75), Internat. Fabricare Inst. (dir. dist. 7 treas. 1979, pres. 1982), Am. Security Council Bd., Tacoma C. of C. (pres. 1965), Air Force Assn. (pres. Tacoma chpt. 1976-77, v.p. Wash. state 1983-84, pres. 1985-86), Navy League, Puget Sound Indsl. Devel. Council (chmn. 1967), Tacoma-Ft. Lewis-Olympia Army Assn. (past pres.) Republican. Clubs: Elks (vice chmn. bd. trustees 1984, chmn. 1985-86), Shriners (potentate 1979), Masons, Scottish Rite, Tacoma, Tacoma Country and Golf, Jesters, Rotary (pres. Tacoma chpt. 1967-68), Tacoma Knife and Fork (pres. 1964). Home: 3901 N 37th St Tacoma WA 98407-5636 Office: Peerless Laundry & Linen Supply Co 2902 S 12th St Tacoma WA 98405-2598

HUDSON, JERRY E., foundation administrator; b. Chattanooga, Mar. 3, 1938; s. Clarence E. and Laura (Campbell) H.; m. Myra Ann Jared, June 11, 1957; children: Judith, Laura, Janet, Angela. B.A., David Lipscomb Coll., 1959; M.A., Tulane U., 1961, Ph.D., 1965; LL.D. (hon.), Pepperdine U., 1983; D of Comm. (hon.), Tokyo Internat. U., 1997; LHD (hon.), U. Portland, 1997, Willamette U., 1997. Systems engr. IBM, Atlanta, 1961; prof. Coll. Arts and Scis., Pepperdine U., 1962-75; provost, dean Coll. Arts and Scis., Malibu Campus, Pepperdine U., 1971-75; pres. Hamline U., St. Paul, 1975-80, Willamette U., Salem, Oreg., 1980-97; exec. v.p. Collins Found., Portland, Oreg., 1997—; dir. Portland Gen. Co., E.I.I.A. Mem. Nat. Assn. Ind. Colls. (bd. dirs.), Phi Alpha Theta. Office: Collins Found 1618 SW 1st Ave Portland OR 97201-5752

HUDSON, JOHN IRVIN, retired career officer; b. Louisville, Oct. 12, 1932; s. Irvin Hudson and Elizabeth (Reid) Hudson Hornbeck; m. Zetta Ann Yates, June 27, 1954; children: Reid Irvin, Lori Ann, John Yates, Clark Ray. BS in Bus. Mgmt., Murray State U., 1971. Commd. 2nd lt. USMC, 1954, advanced through grades to lt. gen., 1987; comdg. officer Marine Fighter Attack Squadron 115, Vietnam, 1968, Marine Corps Air Sta., Yuma, Ariz., 1977-80; asst. wing comdr. 2nd Marine Air Wing, Cherry Point, N.C., 1980-81; comdg. gen. Landing Force Tng. Command/At.,4th Marine Amphibious Brigade, Norfolk, Va., 1981-83, 3rd Marine Aircraft Wing, El Toro, Calif., 1985-87, First Marine Amphibious Force, Campen, Calif., 1986-87; dep. chief staff for manpower Hdqrs. USMC, Washington, 1987-89; dir. U.S. Marine Corps Edn. Ctr., Quantico, Va., 1983-85; ret. active duty Hdqrs. USMC, Washington, 1989. Apptd. to Ariz. State Transp. Bd., 1994—, chmn. 1999. Decorated DFC, DSM, Bronze Star, Air medals, Silver Hawk; flew 308 combat missions in Vietnam in F-4 Phantom. Mem. VFW, Golden Eagles, Marine Corps Aviation Assn. (life), Marine Corps Assn., Marine Corps Hist. Soc., Order of Daedalians (life). Avocations: sports; sailing; hunting; fishing. Home: 12439 E Del Rico Yuma AZ 85367-7366

HUDSON, PATRICK A., plastic surgeon; b. Blickling, Eng., July 4, 1948; came to U.S., 1974; MD, London U., 1972. Diplomate Am. Bd. Plastic Surgery. Intern St. Stephens-Hillingdon, London, 1972-73; resident Danbury Hosp., 1973-74; resident U. N.Mex. Hosp., Albuquerque, 1974-78, fellow in hand surgery, 1978; with Presbyn. Hosp., St. Joseph Hosp., Albuquerque; pvt. practice; preceptor U. N.Mex. Author: Esthetics: Comprehensive Online Information About Cosmetic Plastic Surgery, 1996. Fellow ACS; mem. BMA, NMMS, Am. Assn. Hand Surgery, Am. Soc. Plastic and Reconstructive Surgeons. Office: # 100E 4273 Montgomery Blvd NE Albuquerque NM 87109-6746

HUDSON, SCOTT CAMERON, web technologist; b. Raton, New Mex., Aug. 30, 1972; s. John Eldridge and Sherron Marguerite (Mason) H.; m. Dawn Leah Dunfee, March 10, 1996; 1 child, Connor Cameron. BA in Tech. Journalism, Colo. State U., 1994. Tech. writer, editor Baker Instrument Co., Ft. Collins, Colo., 1994; pvt. practice Colo. Springs, Colo., 1994; book publishing asst. Focus On The Family, Colo. Springs, Colo., 1994-95; tech. writer Sun Microsys., Inc., Broomfield, Colo., 1995-97, web tech., 1997—. Author: 50 Years: Partners in Conservation, 1994. Active Colo. Skywarn, Colo. Springs, Boulder, 1997—, Pikes Peak Amateur Radio Emergency Svc., Colo. Springs, 1997. Mem. Amateur Radio Relay League. Republican. E-mail: hudson310@pcisys.net. Fax: (303) 272-7655. Home: 1637 Reliance Cir Superior CO 80027-4401 Office: Sun Microsystems Inc 303B S Technology Ct Broomfield CO 80021-3411

HUEBNER, ALBERT LOUIS CHARLES, physics educator, writer; b. Bklyn., Feb. 4, 1931; s. Albert Louis and Gladys Mildred (Kraft) H.; m. Mildred Elnick, July 29, 1950; children: Susan Linda, Paul Bertrand, Laura Ann. AB, Bklyn. Coll., 1955; MA, UCLA, 1962. Prin. scientist Rocketdyne Divsn. Rockwell Internat., Canoga Park, Calif., 1957-73; freelance writer, commentator, 1973—; asst. prof. Calif. State U., Northside, 1976—. Author: Mathematical Physics, 1968; contbg. editor Toward Freedom Mag., Burlington, Vt., 1996—, Worldview Mag., N.Y.C., 1984-86; environ. adv. bd. Let's Live Mag., L.A., 1991-96; contbr. articles to profl. jours. Mem. AAAS, Am. Inst. Biomed. Climatology, Phi Beta Kappa, Sigma Pi Sigma, Pi Mu Epsilon. Home: 20331 Mobile St Canoga Park CA 91306-4242 Office: Physics Dept 18111 Nordhoff St Northridge CA 91330-0001

HUENERGARDT, MYRNA LOUISE, college administrator, nurse practitioner; b. Medford, Oreg., Aug. 5, 1928; d. Henry and Matie Daisy (Vroman) H. BS, Columbia Union Coll., Takoma Park, Md., 1961; MA, Columbia U., 1963. RN, Calif.; cert. nurse practitioner. Charge nurse Glendale (Calif.) Adventist Hosp., 1954-57, 61-63; sch. nurse L.A. City Schs., 1957-60; instr. nursing Columbia Union Coll., Takoma Park, Md., 1964-68; dir. sch. nursing Branson Hosp. Sch. Nursing, Toronto, Ont., Can., 1968-71; chair paramed. dept. Southwestern C.C., Chula Vista, Calif., 1971-74; assoc. prof. nursing Loma Linda (Calif.) U., 1974-80; nurse rschr. U. So. Calif., L.A., 1981-83; nurse practitioner Community Health Projects, Covina, Calif., 1983-86; dir. student health svcs. Chaffey C.C., Rancho Cucamonga, Calif., 1986-94; med. edn. cons. Merck, Sharp & Dohme, West Point, Pa., 1991-96; nurse practitioner New Horizon Care Corp., Loma Linda, 1987-95; nurse cons., med. claims reviewer Aetna Ins., Loma Linda, 1994-97. Bd. dirs. ARC, Inland Empire, Calif., 1986-91; cons. Master Plan Com., Substance Abuse, San Bernardino County, Calif., 1990-95. Recipient Sameas award Outstanding Educators of Am., 1972, Disting. Leadership award Am. Biog. Inst., 1989; Fed. Govt. traineeship awards, 1961, 63, 64. Mem. Assn. of Calif. C.C. Adminstrs., Calif. Coalition of Nurse Practitioners, C.C. Health Svcs. Assn. of Calif. (pres. 1992-93), Sigma Theta Tau, Kappa Delta Pi. Republican. Avocations: travel, biking, gardening, concerts, singing. Home: 10636 Amapolas St Redlands CA 92373-8401

HUFF, DALE EUGENE, retired environmental services executive; b. Windsor, Colo., Nov. 1, 1930; s. Floyd Eugene and Katherine Oleva (Parsons) H.; m. Flossie Leone Moses, Nov. 18, 1951; children: Clifford Allen, Herbert Eugene, Dalene Faye, Linda Reneé. BA, Pacific Union Coll., 1963, MA, 1968. Tchr. Pleasant Hill (Calif.) Jr. Acad., 1963-66; prin. Ukiah (Calif.) Jr. Acad., 1966-71; tchr. Paradise (Calif.) Adventist Acad., 1971-80; acct. Loma Linda (Calif.) U., 1980-86, environ. svcs. exec., 1986-96; ret., 1996. With U.S. Army, 1946-49. Mem. Nat. Exec. Housekeeping Assn. (exec. bd. 1987-90). Republican. Avocation: camping. Home: 10961 Desert Lawn Dr # 145 Calimesa CA 92320-2242 Office: Loma Linda U Dept Environ Svcs Loma Linda CA 92350

HUFF, DAVID HERBERT KIMO, lawyer; b. Honolulu, Dec. 12, 1960; s. Donald Charles and Marion (Irons) H.; m. Melinda Munoz, Oct. 28, 1995; 1 child, David Rafael Kalani. BA, U. Hawaii, 1984; JD, Western State U., 1992. Bar: Calif. 1995. Atty. Law Office of Richard Jones, Brea, Calif., 1995-97; dep. county counsel, spl. dep. dist. atty. Office of County Counsel, Riverside, Calif., 1997—. Bd. dirs. Gary Ctr., La Habra, Calif., 1997-98; bd. dirs., v.p. Corona Ranch Properties Homeowners Assn., Corona, Calif., 1998—. With U.S. Army, 1981. Mem. Riverside County Bar Assn., Riverside County Barrister's Assn. Avocations: beach volleyball, bicycling, hiking, wine tasting. E-mail: dhuff@co.riverside.ca.us. Fax: 909-955-6363. Office: Office County Counsel 3535 10th St Ste 300 Riverside CA 92501

HUFF, DENNIS LYLE, marketing professional; b. Chgo., Oct. 8, 1955; s. Barry Sanders Huff and Janada Jean (Patterson) Montgomery; 1 child, Alicia Jean; m. LouAnn Fae Gorder, Nov. 8, 1992. AS in Marine Tech., Coll. Oceaneering, 1984. Diver instr. Comml. Dive Ctr., Long Beach, Calif., 1984-87; owner Flight Shop, California City, 1987-90, Houston Export Co., 1990-92; exec. v.p. AMS, Inc., Oklahoma City, 1992—. With USMC, 1975-81. Avocations: skydiving, deep sea diving, camping, poetry, archaeology. Home: 1136 Birch Cir Alpine UT 84004-1212 Office: AMS Inc 147 Santa Louisa Irvine CA 92606-8854

HUFF, GARY D., lawyer; b. Seattle, May 9, 1950. BA cum laude, U. Wash., 1972, JD, 1975. Bar: Wash. 1975. Lawyer Karr Tuttle Campbell, Seattle, 1986—. Mem. ABA, Wash. State Bar Assn., Seattle-King County Bar Assn., Phi Beta Kappa. Office: Karr Tuttle & Campbell 1201 3rd Ave Ste 2900 Seattle WA 98101-3028

HUFF, MARILYN L., federal judge; b. 1951. BA, Calvin Coll., Grand Rapids, Mich., 1972; JD, U. Mich., 1976. Assoc. Gray, Cary, Ames & Frye, 1976-83, ptnr., 1983-91; judge U.S. Dist. Ct. (so. dist.) Calif., San Diego, 1991-98, chief judge, 1998—. Contbr. articles to profl. jours. Mem. adv. coun. Calif. LWV, 1987—, Am. Lung Assn.; bd. dirs. San Diego and Imperial Counties, 1989—; mem. LaJolla Presbyn. Ch. Named Legal Profl. of Yr. San Diego City Club and Jr. C. of C., 1990; recipient Superior Ct. Valuable Svc. award, 1982. Mem. ABA, San Diego Bar Found., San Diego Bar Assn. (bd. dirs. 1986-88, v.p. 1988, chmn. profl. edn. com. 1990, Svc. award to legal profession, 1989, Lawyer of Yr. 1990), Calif. State Bar Assn., Calif. Women Lawyers, Am. Bd. Trial Advs., Libel Def. Resource Ctr., Am. Inns of Ct. (master 1987—, exec. com. 1989—), Lawyers' Club San Diego (adv. bd. 1989-90, Belva Lockwood Svc. award 1987), Univ. Club, Aardvarks Lt. Office: US Dist Ct Courtroom 1 940 Front St San Diego CA 92101-8994*

HUFFEY, VINTON EARL, clergyman; b. Luana, Iowa, July 7, 1915; s. Walter Angus and Tilda Boleta (Olson) H.; m. Lillian Bertha Crouse, June 22, 1942; children: Naomi, Rhoda, Stephen, Deborah. Student, Ctrl. Bible Coll., Springfield, Mo., 1936-38, North Ctrl. Bible Coll., Mpls., 1938-40. Ordained to ministry Assemblies of God, 1942. Pastor Assemblies of God, Oelwein, Iowa, 1940-43, LeMars, Iowa, 1943-47; evangelist Assemblies of God, Iowa and Mo., 1947-48; pres. youth Assemblies of God, Iowa and North Mo., 1948-52, editor News of West Ctrl., 1948-52; pastor Assemblies of God, Ames, Iowa, 1952-58, Monrovia, Calif., 1958-78; crusader inner-city evangelism Assemblies of God, 1978-93; pastor Assemblies of God, South Pasadena, Calif., 1993-96; motivation lectr. Assemblies of God, 1980-92; originator inner-city revolving loan fund, mem. urban task force So. Calif. Dist. Assemblies of God, Irvine, Calif., Springfield, Mo., Gen. Counsel of the Assemblies of God, 1982. Author: (pamphlet) The Church and America's Inner-cities, 1981; author of poems. Mem. Think Am. Com. City Coun., Duarte, Calif., 1962, lit. rev. com., 1965; chmn. What About Duarte? L.A. County Dept. Human Rels. City of Hope, Duarte, 1963. Recipient Decade of Harvest award So. Calif. Dist. Coun. Assemblies of God, Irvine, Calif., 1994. Republican. Avocations: travel, deep sea fishing. Home and Office: 161 N Mayflower Ave Monrovia CA 91016-2000

HUFFMAN, DONALD GERALD, special education educator; b. Woodman, Wis., Oct. 2, 1938; s. William Henry and Winifred Ruby (Coleman) H.; married; children: Jaki Ann, Sun Re, Wil Don. BS, Columbia County Tchrs. Coll., 1963, U. Wis., 1969; MS Guidance Counseling, U. Wis., 1978; Cert. Spl. Edn., U. Eau Claire, 1973. Cert. (life) tchr. spl. edn., elem. edn. adult basic edn., GED, EMR, TMR, ED/BD, Wis. Prin. Warrens (Wis.) Elem. Sch., 1963-64, Danbury (Wis.) Elem. Sch., 1964-65, Yahara Valley Elem. Sch., Edgerton, Wis., 1965-66, Barneveld (Wis.) Elem. Sch., 1966-69; dir. Edn. Assn. Retarded Citizens, Dubuque, Iowa, 1969-70; prin. DeSoto (Wis.) Elem. Sch., 1970-73; tchr. trainable mentally retarded Independence, Wis., 1973-74; tchr. EMR-ED/BD Iowa-Grant High Sch., Livingston, Wis., 1974-85; tchr. LD 29 Palms (Calif.) High Sch., 1985—; wrestling coach Barneveld High Sch., 1966-69; tchr. ABE/GED Southwest Wis. Vocat. Tech. Coll., Fennimore, Wis., 1986-87; counselor Copper Mountain Coll., Joshua Tree, Calif., 1987-88; leader/tchr. You and Your World contest for good citizens, Middletown, Conn.; mentor tchr. Calif. Dept. Edn., 1990, Calif. New Tchrs. Project, 1991. Leader Boy Scouts Am., Warrens, 1963-64; lay person United Meth. Ch., Montfort, Wis., 1975-85. With USAF, 1957-61, Okinawa. Grantee San Bernardino County Solid Waste Mgmt. Dept., 1994; named Mr. Twentynine Palms, 1989; pub. recognition/commendation City Coun. of Twentynine Palms, 1993, 94. Mem. NEA, Coun. Execptional Children, Learning Disabilities Assn. Calif., Masons, Phi Delta Kappa. Avocations: helping students get jobs, fishing, speaking, family time, travel. Home: 72739 Two Mile Rd Twentynine Palms CA 92277-1535 Office: Morongo Unified Sch Dist 5717 Utah Trail Twentynine Palms CA 92277

HUFFMAN, JOHN ABRAM, JR., minister; b. Boston, May 24, 1940; s. John A. and Dorothy (Bricker) H.; m. Anne Mortenson, June 19, 1964; children: Suzanne Marie (dec.), Carla Lynne, Janet Leigh. BA, Wheaton (Ill.) Coll., 1962; MDiv, Princeton Theol. Sem., 1965, DMin, 1983; MA, U. Tulsa, 1969. Ordained to ministry Presbyn. Ch. (U.S.A.), 1965. Sr. pastor Key Biscayne (Fla.) Presbyn. Ch., 1968-73, 1st Presbyn. Ch., Pitts., 1973-78, St. Andrew's Presbyn. Ch., Newport Beach, Calif., 1978—; moderator Everglades Presbytery, Presbyn. Ch., Fla., 1972, Presbytery of Los Ranchos, 1988; bd. dirs. Gordon-Conwell Theol. Sem., S. Hamilton, Mass., 1969—, Christianity Today, Inc., Carol Stream, Ill., 1976—, World Vision Internat., Inc., Monrovia, Calif., 1986—; chmn. World Vision U.S. Federal, Wash-

ington. Author: "Joshua" vol. of The Communicator's Commentary, 1986. Named Man of the Yr. in Religion, Jr. C. of C., 1977. Office: St Andrew's Presbyn Ch 600 St Andrews Rd Newport Beach CA 92663-5325

HUFFMAN, NONA GAY, financial consultant, retirement planning specialist; b. Albuquerque, June 22, 1942; d. William Abraham and Opal Irene (Leaton) Crisp; m. Donald Clyde Williams, Oct. 20, 1961; children: Debra Gaylene, James Donald. Student pub. schs. Lawndale, Calif. Lic. ins., securities dealer, N.Mex. Sec. City of L.A., 1960, L.A. City Schs. 1960-62, Aerospace Corp., El Segundo, Calif., 1962-64, Albuquerque Pub. Schs., 1972-73, Pub. Service Co. N.Mex., Albuquerque, 1973; rep., fin. planner Waddell & Reed, Inc., Albuquerque, 1979-84; broker Rauscher Pierce Refsnes, Inc., 1984-85; rep., investment and retirement specialist Fin. Network Investment Corp., 1985-89, John Hancock Fin. Svcs., 1989-90; account exec. Eppler, Guerin & Turner, Inc., 1990-91, Fin. Network Investment Corp., Albuquerque, 1991—, fin. cons. retirement and estate planning Nat. Planning Corp., 1998—; instr. on-site corp. training of fin. strategies for retirement Philips Semi Conductors, Honeywell & Gulton Industries Office: Fin Network Investment Corp 6749 Academy NE Ste A Albuquerque NM 87109

HUFFMAN, SHERRI DIANE, advertising and marketing consultant; b. Tulsa, June 14, 1962; children: Alexis Ann, Alexis Alan. Student, Colo. Inst. Art. Lic. series 7 securities SEC; lic. pvt. pilot FAA; lic. life ins., Colo. Fin. planner E.F. Hutton, Inc., Denver, 1983; securities broker Integrated Equities Realty Corp., Denver, 1983; fin. advisor Sears Fin. Network, Denver, 1984; owner Normad, Inc., Denver, 1994—; mktg. dir. I.L.S.A., Denver, 1995; nat. distbr. Nikken, Denver, 1995. Contbr. poetry to mags. Campaign vol. Crider Campaign, Denver, 1995, Bradley Campaign, Denver, 1996; mem. Libr. of Congress, Dem. Nat. Com. Mem. Nat. Assn. Underwater Instrn. (cert diving open I), Nat. Hist. Soc., N.Am. Hunting Club, Denver Press Club. Avocations: scuba diving, aviation piloting, drawing, painting, writing. Address: 4425 Elizabeth St Denver CO 80216-3933

HUFSTEDLER, SHIRLEY MOUNT (MRS. SETH M. HUFSTEDLER), lawyer, former federal judge; b. Denver, Aug. 24, 1925; d. Earl Stanley and Eva (Von Behren) Mount; m. Seth Martin Hufstedler, Aug. 16, 1949; 1 son, Steven Mark. BBA, U. N.Mex., 1945, LLD (hon.), 1972; LLB, Stanford U., 1949; LLD (hon.), U. Wyo., 1970, Gonzaga U., 1970, Occidental Coll., 1971, Tufts U., 1974, U. So. Calif., 1976, Georgetown U., 1976, U. Pa., 1976, Columbia U., 1977, U. Mich., 1979, Yale U., 1981, Rutgers U., 1981, Claremont U. Ctr., 1981, Smith Coll., 1982, Syracuse U., 1983, Mt. Holyoke Coll., 1985; PHH (hon.), Hood Coll., 1981, Hebrew Union Coll., 1986, Tulane U., 1988. Bar: Calif. 1950. Mem. firm Beardsley, Hufstedler & Kemble, L.A., 1951-61; practiced in L.A., 1961; judge Superior Ct., County L.A., 1961-66; justice Ct. Appeals 2d dist., 1966-68; circuit judge U.S. Ct. Appeals 9th cir., 1968-79; sec. U.S. Dept. Edn., 1979-81; ptnr. Hufstedler & Kaus, L.A., 1981-95; sr. of counsel Morrison & Foerster, L.A., 1995—; emeritus dir. Hewlett Packard Co., US West, Inc.; bd. dirs. Harman Internat. Industries. Mem. staff Stanford Law Rev, 1947-49; articles and book rev. editor, 1948-49. Trustee Calif. Inst. Tech., Occidental Coll., 1972-89, Aspen Inst., Colonial Williamsburg Found., 1976-93, Constl. Rights Found., 1978-80, Nat. Resources Def. Coun., 1983-85, Carnegie Endowment for Internat. Peace, 1983-94; bd. dirs. John T. and Catherine MacArthur Found., 1983—; chair U.S. Commn. on Immigration Reform, 1996-97. Named Woman of Yr. Ladies Home Jour., 1976; recipient UCLA medal, 1981. Fellow Am. Acad. Arts and Scis.; mem. ABA (medal 1995), L.A. Bar Assn., Town Hall, Am. Law Inst. (coun. 1974-84), Am. Bar Found., Women Lawyers Assn. (pres. 1957-58), Am. Judicature Soc., Assn. of the Bar of City of N.Y., Coun. on Fgn. Rels., Order of Coif. Office: Morrison & Foerster 555 W 5th St Ste 3500 Los Angeles CA 90013-1024

HUG, PROCTER RALPH, JR., federal judge; b. Reno, Mar. 11, 1931; s. Procter Ralph and Margaret (Beverly) H.; m. Barbara Van Meter, Apr. 4, 1954; children: Cheryl Ann, Procter James, Elyse Marie. B.S., U. Nev., 1953; LL.B., J.D., Stanford U., 1958. Bar: Nev. 1958. With firm Springer, McKissick & Hug, 1958-63, Woodburn, Wedge, Blakey, Folsom & Hug, Reno, 1963-77; U.S. judge 9th Circuit Ct. Appeals, Reno, 1977—; U.S. chief judge 9th Circuit Ct. Appeals, 1996—; dep. atty. gen. State of Nev.; v.p. dir. Nev. Tel. & Tel. Co., 1958-77. Mem. bd. regents U. Nev., 1962-71, chmn., 1969-71; bd. visitors Stanford Law Sch.; mem. Nev. Humanities Commn., 1988-94; vol. civilian aid sect. U.S. Army, 1977. Lt. USNR, 1953-55. Recipient Outstanding Alumnus award U. Nev., 1967, Disting. Nevadan citation, 1982; named Alumnus of Yr. U. Nev., 1988. Mem. ABA (bd. govs. 1976-78), Am. Judicare Soc. (bd. dirs. 1975-77), Nat. Judicial Coll. (bd. dirs. 1977-78), Nat. Assn. Coll. and Univ. Attys. (past mem. exec. bd.), U. Nev. Alumni Assn. (past pres.), Stanford Law Soc. Nev. (pres.). Office: US Ct Appeals 9th Cir US Courthouse Fed Bldg 400 S Virginia St Ste 708 Reno NV 89501-2181

HUGGETT, MONICA, performing company executive. Artistic dir. Portland Baroque Orch., Oreg. Office: Portland Baroque Orch 1425 SW 20th Ave Ste 105 Portland OR 97201*

HUGGINS, EARL MCCLURE, English language educator; b. Phila., Jan. 25, 1939; s. Horace Greely and Helen Marie (Keimer) H.; m. Alice Elizabeth Malia, June 23, 1962; children: Alice Lynn, Donna Marie. BS, So. Ill. U., 1979; MS, Nat. Univ., 1990. Cert. adult sch. tchr., Calif. Aviation electronics technician USN, 1957-81; tchr. San Diego C.C., 1981-84, Chula Vista (Calif.) Adult Sch., 1984—. Ret. sr. vol. San Diego Police Dept., 1991—. Recipient USN Expeditionary award, 1980, Humanitarian Svc. medal, 1980. Mem. Fleet Res. Assn. (parade coord.), Nat. Univ. Alumni Assn. (life), Phi Kappa Phi. Democrat. Avocations: camping, hiking, family activities. Home and Office: 2549 Caulfield Dr San Diego CA 92154-2106

HUGHES, AMBER LYNN, parcel service company administrator; b. L.A., Aug. 27, 1956; d. Raymond Hughes and Darlene Grace (Noe) Preziosi. AA, Golden West Coll., 1976; BA, San Diego State U., 1979. Package car driver United Parcel Svc., Gardena, Calif., 1979-81; human resource supr. United Parcel Svc., Anaheim, Calif., 1981-82; on road supr. United Parcel Svc., Westlake, Gardena, Calif., 1982-85; indsl. engring. supr. United Parcel Svc., Westlake, Ventura, Calif., 1985-86; ctr. mgr. United Parcel Svc., Gardena, Ventura, 1986-90; hub mgr. United Parcel Svc., San Fernando, Calif., 1990-91; div. mgr. United Parcel Svc., Gardena, 1991—; facilitator United Parcel Svc., Kansas City, Mo., 1994, instr., La Miranda, Calif., 1990, Orange, Calif., 1986. Coord. Harvesters, Kansas City, 1994. Recipient Medal of Excellence, Women at Work, 1992. Mem. Brown Betty Club (v.p. 1993—). Democrat. Roman Catholic. Avocations: reading, power walking, camping, racquetball, softball. Office: United Parcel Svc 17115 S Western Ave Gardena CA 90247-5223

HUGHES, ANDREW SCOTT, lawyer; b. L.A., Aug. 19, 1965; s. Richard J. and Linda E. (Levine) H.; m. Anita L. Henningsgaard, Aug. 7, 1987. BA, UCLA, 1987; JD, Santa Clara U., 1990, MBA, 1990. Bar: Calif. 1990, U.S. Dist. Ct. (cen. dist.) Calif. 1991. Assoc. atty. England, Whitfield, Schroeder & Tredway, Oxnard, Calif., 1990-95, ptnr., 1996-98, divsn. counsel, 1998—. Office: Harris Corp 809 Calle Plano Camarillo CA 93012-8516

HUGHES, BRADLEY RICHARD, business executive; b. Detroit, Oct. 8, 1954; s. John Arthur and Nancy Irene (Middleton) H.; m. Linda McCants, Feb. 14, 1977; children: Bradley Richard Jr., Brian Jeffrey. AA, Oakland Coll., 1974; BS in Journalism, U. Colo., 1979, BJ, 1979, MBA in Fin. and Mktg., 1981, MS in Telecommunications, 1990. Cert. office automation profl., cert. systems profl. Buyer Joslins Co., Denver, 1979; mktg. adminstr. Mountain Bell, Denver, 1980-82; ch. cons. AT&T Info. Systems, mktg. exec. AT&T, Denver, 1983-86, acct. exec., 1986-87; mktg. mgr. U.S. West, Denver, 1987-95; dir. U. Colo. Coll. Engring., Denver, 1995—; exec.-on-loan U. Colo. Coll. Engring. Contbr. articles to bus. publs. Bd. dirs. Brandychase Assn.; state del., committeeman Republican Party Colo.; dir. Inst. for Govt. Innovation, bd. dirs. Olmsted Pavillion, dir. Colo. Chess Acad. Mem. IEEE, Assn. MBA Execs., U.S. Chess Fedn., Internat. Platform Assn., Mensa, Intertel, Assn. Telecommunications Profls., Am. Mgmt. Assn., Am. Mktg. Assn., Info. Industry Assn., Office Automation Soc. Internat., World Future Soc., Triple Nine Soc., Internat. Soc. Philos. Inquiry, Assn. Computing Machinery. Republican. American Baptist. Home: 5759 S Jericho Way Aurora CO 80015-3653 Office: U Colo Coll Engring PO Box 104 Denver CO 80201-0104

HUGHES, EDWARD JOHN, artist; b. North Vancouver, B.C., Feb. 17, 1913; s. Edward Samuel Daniell and Katherine Mary (McLean) H.; m. Fern Rosabell Irvine Smith, Feb. 10, 1940 (dec. 1974). Grad., Vancouver Sch. Art, 1933; D Fine Art (hon.), U. Victoria, 1995; DLL (hon.), Emily Carr Inst. Art & Design, Vancouver, B.C., 1997. Exhbns. include retrospective, Vancouver Art Gallery, 1967, Surrey Art Gallery, Art Gallery of Greater Victoria, Edmonton Art Gallery, Calgary Glenbow Gallery, 1983-85, Nat. Gallery Can., Beaverbrook Gallery, Fredericton, 1983-85; represented in permanent collections, Nat. Gallery Can., Ottawa, Art Gallery Ont., Toronto, Vancouver Art Gallery, Montreal Mus. Fine Art, Greater Victoria Art Gallery; ofcl. Army war artist, 1942-46. Served with Can. Army, 1939-46. Recipient Can. Council grants, 1958, 63, 67, 70. Mem. Royal Can. Acad. Arts. Presbyterian. Address: 2449 Heather St, Duncan, BC Canada V9L 2Z6

HUGHES, EDWIN STRODE, public relations executive; b. Austin, Tex., Oct. 6, 1936; s. Frank Miller and Lorine (Mitchell) H.; m. Linda Lee Bennett, June 24, 1961; children: Frank Mitchell, Lee Gordon. B of Journalism, U. Tex., Austin, 1960. Writer, photographer Dallas Morning News, 1958-65; info. supr. Southwestern Bell Telephone, Dallas, 1965-68; gen. info. mgr. Southwestern Bell Telephone, St. Louis, 1968-72; divsn. mgr. external rels. Southwestern Bell Telephone, San Antonio, 1974-86; divsn. mgr. advt. and pub. rels. Southwestern Bell Telephone, Dallas, 1986-90; head employee com. Bell Telephone Labs., Murray Hill, N.J., 1972-74; owner Ed Hughes & Assocs., Tijeras, N.Mex., 1991-95, Laramie, Wyo., 1996-98; pub. rels. counsel Loveland, Colo., 1999—. Pres. East Mountain C. of C., 1994; bd. dirs. Alamo area coun. Boy Scouts Am., San Antonio, 1985-86; pres. San Antonio Bus. Com. for the Arts, 1985. Master sgt. U.S. Army NG, 1954-66. Recipient Award of Excellence Internat. Conf. of Indsl. Editors, 1966. Mem. Pub. Rels. Soc. of Am. (accredited), N.Mex. Pub. Rels. Soc. Am. (pres. 1995, 1st place award of excellence 1995), Tex. Pub. Rels. Assn. (pres. 1983, Best of Tex. award 1980), No. Plains Pub. Rels. Soc. Am. (pres. 1997-98). Republican. Methodist. Home and Office: 2195 Kennington Ct Loveland CO 80538

HUGHES, EMLYN WILLARD, physics educator; b. New Haven, Conn., Feb. 27, 1960; s. Vernon Willard and Inge (Michelson) H.; m. Miriam Feldblu, Jan. 22, 1984; children: Ariel, Isaac, Noah. BS, Stanford U., 1982; PhD, Columbia U., 1987. Poste rouge Ecole Normale, Paris, 1988; postdoctoral Stanford (Calif.) U., 1989-92, Panofsky fellow, 1992-95; prof. Calif. Tech. Inst., Pasadena, 1995-97. Sloan fellow NSF, 1997. Mem. Altadena Country Club. Democrat. Avocations: tennis, soccer, skiing, sailing, hiking. Office: Calif Tech Inst Kellogg Radiation Lab Pasadena CA 91125

HUGHES, EUGENE MORGAN, university president; b. Scottsbluff, Nebr., Apr. 3, 1934; s. Ruby Melvin and Hazel Marie (Griffith) H.; m. Margaret Ann Romeo; children: Deborah Kaye, Greg Eugene, Lisa Ann, Jeff, Mark, Christi. Diploma, Neb. Western Coll., 1954; BS in Math. magna cum laude, Chadron State Coll., 1956; MS in Math., Kans. State U., 1958; PhD in Math., George Peabody Coll. for Tchrs., Vanderbilt U., 1968; DHL, No. Ariz. U., 1998, LLD (hon.), 1998. Grad. asst. dept. math. Kans. State U., Manhattan, 1956-57; instr. math. Nebr. State Tchrs. Coll. at Chadron, 1957-58; asst. prof. math., head dept. Chadron State Coll., 1958-66, assoc. prof., 1966-69, prof. math., 1969-70, dir. rsch., 1965-66, asst. to the pres., 1966-68, dean adminstrn., 1968-70; grad. asst. dept. math. George Peabody Coll. for Tchrs., Nashville, 1962-63, 64-65; asst. to undergrad. dean George Peabody Coll. for Tchrs., 1964, asst. to pres., 1964-65; instr. Peabody Demonstration Sch., 1963-64; prof. math. No. Ariz. U., Flagstaff, 1970-93; dean No. Ariz. U. (Coll. Arts and Scis.), 1970-71, provost univ. arts and sci. edn., 1971-72, acad. v.p., 1972-79, pres., 1979-93, pres. emeritus, 1993—; pres. Wichita State U., 1993—; cons. Nebr. Dept. Edn., 1966-70; mem. adv. bd. United Bank Ariz., 1980-82; mem. nat. adv. bd. Ctr. for Study of Sport in Society, 1990; bd. dirs. Ariz. Bank; mem. adv. bd. Bank IV, 1993-97; bd. dirs. NationsBank N.A. (Midwest), mem. adv. bd., 1997—. Mem. staff bd. trustees Nebr. State Colls., Lincoln, 1969-70; co-dir. workshop tchr. edn. North Cen. Assn. U. Minn., 1968-70; officer fed. ednl. programs, Nebr., Ariz., 1966-93; mem. Ariz. Commn. Postsecondary Edn.; bd. fellows Am. Grad. Sch. Internat. Mgmt., 1980-93; mem. Gov.'s Com. Quality Edn., Chadron Housing Authority, 1968-70, Pres.' Commn. NCAA; pres. bd. dirs. Ariz. State Bd. Edn., 1991, Flagstaff Summer Festival, Ariz. Coun. Humanities and Pub. Policy, Mus. No. Ariz., Grand Canyon coun, Boy Scouts Am.; chair Ariz. Leadership Adv. Coun., 1990-93; mem. Ariz. Town Hall, 1991; commr. Western Interstate Commn. for Higher Edn., 1992-93; mem. Gov.'s Strategic Partnership for Econ. Devel., 1992; mem. Christopher Columbus Quincentenary Commn., 1990—; sec., mem. Wichita/Sedgwick Partnership for Growth, 1993-97, Wichita/Sedgwick County Employment Tng. Bd., 1993-96; bd. dirs. Kids Voting Kans., 1997—; trustee Assn. Western Univs. Inc., 1997—. Ariz. Acad. NSF fellow, 1963, 64; recipient Chief Manuelito award Navajo Tribe, 1976, Disting. Svc. award Chadron State Coll., 1982, Flagstaff Citizen of Yr., 1988, Disting. Math. Grad. award Kans. State U., 1990, Cmty. Svc. award, 1994; named Hon. Chmn. black Bd. Dirs., 1989, Outstanding Citizen, Wichita Soc. of Profl. Engrs., 1998, Kans. Soc. Profl. Engrs., 1998. Mem. NEA, Am. Assn. State Colls.and Univs. (past chmn. & mem. com. on grad. studies 1979—, bd. dirs., mem. com. on accreditation, 1980—), Math. Assn. Am. (vis. lectr. secondary schs. Western Nebr. 1962), Ariz. Edn. Assn., North Cen. Assn. Colls. and Secondary Schs. (coord. 1968-72, cons./evaluator 1977—), Nat. Coun. Tchrs. of Math., Wichita Area C. of C., Flagstaff C. of C., Blue Key, Golden Key, Masons, Elks, Rotary (past pres.), Pi Mu Epsilon, Phi Delta Kappa, Kappa Mu Epsilon, Phi Kappa Phi.

HUGHES, GETHIN B., bishop. Bishop Episcopal Diocese of San Diego, 1992—. Office: Episcopal Diocese of San Diego 2728 6th Ave San Diego CA 92103-6301*

HUGHES, JAMES ARTHUR, electrical engineer; b. Wayne, Nebr., Feb. 15, 1939; s. James Wallace and Ruth Genevieve H.; m. Judy Lorraine Gaskins, July 18, 1967; children: Robert Linn, Benjamin Reed, Barnaby James. BSEE, U. Nebr., 1967. Electronic technician, space tech. labs. TRW, Redondo Beach, Calif., 1963-67, mem. tech. staff systems group, 1967-80, sect. mgr. electronics and def. div., 1980-82, systems engr. space and electronics group, 1982-93, sub-project mgr., 1993—. Designer solid state thermostat, pn generator. Deacon First Bapt. Ch. Lakewood, Long Beach, Calif., 1975-76, 78-80, 87-89; mem. exec. bd. parent-tchr. fellowship, Grace Sch., Rossmoor, Calif., 1981-87. With USN, 1959-63. Mem. AAAS, IEEE, Nat. Soc. Profl. Engrs. Republican. Avocations: sailing, youth sports, photography, personal computing. Office: Space and Electronics Group One Space Park S/1869 Redondo Beach CA 90278-1001

HUGHES, JEFFREY JOHN, lawyer, small business owner; b. Santa Monica, Calif., Sept. 16, 1965; s. Richard Milton and Beverly Elaine (Assay) H. BA, UCLA, 1988; JD, Loyola-Marymount Law Sch., 1992. Bar: Calif., Colo., 1992. Bus. banking officer Wells Fargo Bank, Anaheim, Calif., 1988-89; lawyer Law Offices Jeffrey J. Hughes, Santa Monica, Calif., 1992—; owner Legal Grind, Coffee & Counsel, Santa Monica and Tarzana, Calif., 1996—, Legal Grind's Lawyer Referral & Info. Svc., Santa Monica, Calif., 1998—; adv. bd. Legal Grind, Coffee & Counsel, Paris, 1998; group study exch. mem. Rotary Internat., Paris, 1998. City Coun. candidate, Santa Monica, 1996; active Cath. Big Brother program, Santa Monica, 1996-97; employer Santa Monica- Malibu Unified Sch. Dist. Internship program, Santa Monica H.S., 1998. Mem. Specialty Coffee Assn. Am. Avocations: travelling, water skiing, surfing, running, playing golf. Office: Legal Grind's Lawyer Referral Service 2640 Lincoln Blvd Santa Monica CA 90405-4620

HUGHES, (ROBERT) JOHN, journalist, educator; b. Neath, Wales, Apr. 28, 1930; came to U.S., 1954; s. Evan John and Dellis May (Williams) H.; m. Vera Elizabeth Pockman (div. 1987); children: Wendy Elizabeth, Mark Evan; m. Peggy Janeane Jordan, 1988; 1 child, Evan Jordan. LLD (hon.), Colby Coll., 1978; HHD (hon.), So. Utah U., 1994. Africa corr. Christian Sci. Monitor, 1955-61, Far East corr., 1964-70; editor Christian Sci. Monitor, Boston, 1970-79, columnist, 1985—, dir. radio broadcasting, 1987-89; pres. Hughes Newspapers, Orleans, Mass., 1977-85; assoc. dir. USIA, Washington, 1981-82; dir. Voice of Am., Washington, 1982; asst. sec. of state Dept. State, Washington, 1982-85; asst. sec.-gen. UN, N.Y.C., 1995; editor Deseret News, Salt Lake City, 1997—; pres., pub., editor Concord Comm., Rockland, Maine, 1989-91; prof., dir. internat. media studies program Brigham Young U., Provo, Utah, 1991-96; chmn. Pres. Bush Commn. on U.S. Govt. Internat. Broadcasting, 1991, Presdl./Congressional Commn. Broadcasting to People's Republic China, 1992. Author: The New Face of Africa, 1961, Indonesian Upheaval, 1967. Nieman fellow, Harvard U., 1961-62; recipient Pulitzer prize, 1967, Yankee = quill Sigma Delta Chi, 1977. Mem. Am. Soc. Newspaper Editors (past pres.), Coun. Fgn. Rels., Overseas Press Club (Best Reporting from Overseas 1970). Office: Deseret News PO Box 1257 Salt Lake City UT 84110-1257

HUGHES, LINDA J., newspaper publisher; b. Princeton, B.C., Can., Sept. 27, 1950; d. Edward Rees and Madge Preston (Bryan) H.; m. George Fredrick Ward, Dec. 16, 1978; children: Sean Ward, Kate Ward. BA, U. Victoria (B.C.), 1972. With Edmonton Jour., Alta., Can., 1976—, from reporter to asst. mng. editor, 1984-87, editor, 1987-92, pub., 1992—. Southam fellow U. Toronto, Ont., Can., 1977-78. Office: Edmonton Journal, 10006 101st St PO Box 2421, Edmonton, AB Canada T5J 2S6

HUGHES, MARY KATHERINE, lawyer; b. Kodiak, Alaska, July 16, 1949; d. John Chamberlain and Marjorie (Anstey) H.; m. Andrew H. Eker, July 7, 1982. BBA cum laude, U. Alaska, 1971; JD, Willamette U., 1974; postgrad. Heriot-Watt U., Edinburgh, Scotland, 1971. Bar: Alaska 1975. Ptnr., Hughes, Thorsness, Gantz, Powell & Brundin, Anchorage, 1974-95, mem. mgmt. com., 1991-92; mcpl. atty. Municipality of Anchorage, 1995—. trustee Alaska Bar Found., pres., 1984-98; bd. visitors Coll. of Law, 1980—; trustee Willamette U., 1997—; bd. dirs. Alaska Repertory Theatre, 1986-88, pres., 1987-88; commr. Alaska Code Revision Commn., 1987-94; mem. U. Alaska Found., 1985—, trustee, 1990—; bd. vis. U. Alaska Fairbanks, 1994—; bd. dirs. Anchorage Econ. Devel. Corp., 1989—, chmn. 1994; mem. adv. bd. Providence Health Sys., 1993—; bd. dirs. Providence Alaska Found., 1998—; lawyer rep. 9th Cir. Judicial Conf., 1995—. Fellow Am. Bar Found.; mem. Alaska Bar Assn. (bd. govs. 1981-84, pres. 1983-84), Anchorage Assn. Women Lawyers (pres. 1976-77), Internat. Lawyers Assn. (state chair 1995-97, regional v.p. 1997—), AAUW, Delta Theta Phi. Republican. Roman Catholic. Club: Soroptimists (v.p. 1986-87, pres. 1986-87). Home: 1592 Coffey Ln Anchorage AK 99501-4977 Office: Municipality Anchorage PO Box 196650 Anchorage AK 99519-6650

HUGHES, MICHAEL PATRICK, artist; b. Chgo., Dec. 25, 1950; s. William George and Patricia Ann (Guilfoil) H.; m. Dorothea Sofia Savage, May 11, 1977 (div. June 1987); 1 stepchild, Stefani Savage; m. Deborah Kay Horewitz, Aug. 5, 1991 (div. June 1997). AA in Fine Arts, L.A. Valley Coll., 1975; BFA in Painting, Otis Art Inst., 1977; MFA in Art & Design, Calif. Inst. Arts, 1980. One-man shows include Calif. Inst. Arts, 1979, 80, West Colo. Gallery, Pasadena, Calif., 1980, The Art Dock, L.A., 1985, Orlando Gallery, Sherman Oaks, Calif., 1986, 87, Jose Drudis-Biada Art Gallery, L.A., 1990; group shows include Calif. Inst. Arts, 1980, 81, Lehigh U. Art Gallery, Bethlehem, Pa., 1983, Calif. State U. Art Gallery, San Bernardino, 1982, Future Perfect Gallery, L.A., 1984, Tortue Gallery, Santa Monica, Calif., 1987, Downey Mus. Art, 1988, The Tanzmann Assocs., L.A., 1989, Boritzer/Gray Gallery, Santa Monica, 1991, 98, Touchstone Ctr. Arts, Pitts., 1992, Brand Libr. Art Galleries, Glendale, Calif., 1992, Mt. San Antonio Coll. Art Gallery, Walnut, Calif., 1993, Downtown Arts Devel. Assn., L.A., 1994, 93, others; represented in permanent collections at Lee & Paulette Arnone, Culver City, Calif., Steve Sharpe, Somis, Calif., Joseph A. Hardy Sr., Farmington, Pa., Ellie Blankfort, L.A., Chaim Ben Basat, Sepulveda, Calif., Mr. & Mrs. Murray Horewitz, Connellsville, Pa., Downey Mus. Art, Rudy & Chris Andl, Thousand Oaks, Calif., Miki Warner, Malibu, Calif., Carl Schlossberg, Encino, Calif., Jack Sullivan, San Gabriel, Calif., Mr. & Mrs. Robert Taylor, L.A., Ben Tunnel, L.A., William Bingham, Encino, Calif., Richard Godfrey, L.A., others. Avocations: cooking, golf.

HUGHES, ROBERT MERRILL, control system engineer; b. Glendale, Calif., Sept. 11, 1936; s. Fred P. and Gertrude G. (Merrill) H.; AA, Pasadena City Coll., 1957; 1 child, Tammie Lynn Cobble. Engr. Aerojet Gen. Corp., Azusa, Calif., 1957-64, 66-74; pres. Automatic Electronics Corp., Sacramento, 1964-66; specialist Perkin Elmer Corp., Pomona, Calif., 1974-75; gen. mgr. Hughes Mining Inc., Covina, Calif., 1975-76; project mgr. L&A Water Treatment, City of Industry, Calif., 1976-79; dir. Hughes Industries Inc., Alta Loma, Calif., 1979—; pres. Hughes Devel. Corp., Carson City, Nev.; chmn. bd. Hughes Mining Inc., Hughes Video Corp. Registered profl. engr., Calif., Nev.; lic. gen. bld. contractor. Mem. AIME, Nat. Soc. Profl. Engrs., Instrument Soc. Am., Am. Inst. Plant Engrs. Republican. Patentee in field. Office: PO Box 915 Carson City NV 89702-0915

HUGHES, W. JAMES, optometrist; b. Shawnee, Okla., Oct. 15, 1944; s. Willis J. and Elizabeth Alice (Nimohoyah) H. B.A. in Anthropology, U. Okla., 1966, M.A. in Anthropology, 1972; O.D., U. Houston, 1976; M.P.H., U. Tex., 1977. Lic. Optometrist, Okla., Tex., W. Va. commd. med. officer USPHS, 1966; advanced through the grades to capt./optometrist, USPHS, 1993; physician's asst., Houston, Dallas, 1969-70; teaching asst. in clin. optics U. Houston, 1973-74, contact lens research asst., 1974; Wesley Jessen Contact Lens Rep., 1974-76; extern eye clinic Tuba City Indian Hosp., 1975; teaching fellow pub. health optometry U. Houston, 1975-76; Indian Health Service optometrist, Eagle Butte, S.D., 1976; optometrist vision care project Crockett Ind. Sch. Dist., 1977; vision care program dir. Bemidji Area Indian Health Service, 1977-78; optometrist Navajo Area Indian Health Service, Chinle Health Ctr., 1978-79; adj. prof. So. Calif. Coll. of Optometry, Los Angeles, U. Houston Coll. of Optometry, 1978—, So. Coll. Optometry, Memphis, 1980—; optometrist Shiprock USPHS Indian Hosp., 1979—; chief vision care program Northern Navajo Med. Ctr., 1994—; dir. eye clinic USPHS Northern Navajo Med. Ctr., Shiprock, N.Mex.; Navajo area Indian Health Service rep. to optometry career devel. com. USPHS. Sgt. U.S. Army, 1966-69, Capt. USPHS 1993—. Decorated Bronze Star, Purple Heart. Recipient House of Vision award 1974; Community Health Optometry award 1976; Better Vision scholar, 1973-76. Mem. Am. Pub. Health Assn., Am. Optometric Assn., Tex. Optometric Assn. Commd. Officers Soc., Assn. Am. Indian Physicians, Beta Sigma Kappa. Democrat. Roman Catholic. Contbr. articles to profl. jours.

HUGHS, MARY GERALDINE, accountant, social service specialist; b. Marshalltown, Iowa, Nov. 28, 1929; d. Don Harold, Sr., and Alice Dorothy (Keister) Shaw; A.A., Highline Community Coll., 1970; B.A., U. Wash., 1972; m. Charles G. Hughs, Jan. 31, 1949; children: Mark George, Deborah Kay, Juli Ann, Grant Wesley. Asst. controller Moduline Internat., Inc., Chehalis, Wash., 1972-73; controller Data Recall Corp., El Segundo, Calif., 1973-74; fin. adminstr., acct. Saturn Mfg. Corp., Torrance, Calif., 1974-77; sr. acct., adminstrv. asst. Van Camp Ins., San Pedro, Calif., 1977-78; asst. adminstr. Harbor Regional Ctr., Torrance, Calif., 1979-87; active bookkeeping svc., 1978—; instr. math. and acctg. South Bay Bus. Coll., 1976-77. Sec. Pacific N.W. Mycol. Soc., 1966-67; treas., bd. dirs. Harbor Employees Fed. Credit Union; mem. YMCA Club. Recipient award Am. Mgmt. Assn., 1979. Mem. Beta Alpha Psi. Republican. United Ch. of Christ. Author: Iowa Auto Dealers Assn. Title System, 1955; Harbor Regional Center Affirmative Action Plan, 1980; Harbor Regional Center - Financial Format, 1978—; Provider Audit System, 1979; Handling Client Funds, 1983. Home and Office: 32724 Coastsite Dr Unit 107 Palos Verdes Estates CA 90275-5860

HUIGENS, DANIEL DEAN, dentist; b. Osmond, Nebr., May 16, 1953; s. Mickey Helen (White) H.; m. Linda Sue Wilbourn, May 19, 1982 (div. 1991); 1 child, Matthew Blake. BA, U. LaVerne, 1975; BS, U. Okla., 1979, DDS with honors, 1986. EMT Community Ambulance Svc., San Dimas, Calif., 1971-74; emergency room technician San Dimas Community Hosp., San Dimas, Calif., 1974-77; physician assoc. Muskogee Bone and Joint Clinic, 1979-82; dentist Drs. Huigens and Hanawalt, LaVerne, Calif., 1986-94; pvt. practice LaVerne, 1994—; mem. part time staff UCLA Coll. Dentistry. Mem. ADA, Acad. Gen. Dentistry, Calif. Dental Assn., Tri County Dental Soc., Pomona Valley Amateur Astronomers Assn., LaVerne C. of C., Assn. Flying Dentists, Aircraft Owners and Pilots Assn., Omicron Kappa Upsilon. Avocation: flying. Office: 2187 Foothill Blvd Ste E La Verne CA 91750-2943

HULBURT, LUCILLE HALL, artist, educator; b. Portland, Oreg., Oct. 31, 1924; d. Allen Bergen and Agnes Edna (Davis) Hall; m. Frank Theodore Hulburt, Nov. 28, 1943; children: Robert, Carol Davalos, Clarke. Grad. h.s., Whitefish, Mont. Asst. milliner, illustrator Hat Co., N.Y.C., 1944; cafe owner, operator San Diego, 1950-52; profl. artist Vancouver, Wash., 1978—; resident artist Artist's Gallery 21, Vancouver, 1988—; tchr. children and adult art clases, schs. and home studio, Vancouver, 1978—; artist in residence Wash. State Arts Commn., 1987-88; co-founder, coop. Artists Gallery 21, Vancouver, 1988—; cons. nat. Western Art Show and Auction, Trails West, Vancouver; organizer, com. mem. ann. Summer Art at the Ctr., Vancouver, 1986; judge/jurist art exhibits at county fairs, western art shows various locations in Wash. and Oreg., 1980—. Founder, pres. Boundary Assn. Retarded Children, Bonners Ferry, Idaho, 1964-65; com. mem. 1st Bldg. Com., Columbia Arts Ctr., Vancouver, 1980-81; bd. mem. Local Arts Promotion, Vancouver, 1992, 93. Recipient Best of Show award Western Art Show and Auction, Chinook, Mont., 1983, 84, Community Svc. award Arts Coun., Clark County, Wash., 1988, Windsor-Newton award Watercolor 91, 1991. Mem. S.W. Wash. Watercolor Soc. (co-founder, pres. 1979, 80, 84), Soc. Washington Artists (Grumbacher Silver medal 1990), Am. Artists Profl. League, Order Ea. Star (life), N.W. Watercolor Soc. Avocations: gardening, sewing, swimming. Office: Hulburt Studio 5515 NE 58th St Vancouver WA 98661-2146

HULL, JANE DEE, governor, former state legislator; b. Kansas City, Mo., Aug. 8, 1935; d. Justin D. and Mildred (Swenson) Bowersock; m. Terrance Ward Hull, Feb. 12, 1954; children: Jeannette Shipley, Robin Hillebrand, Jeff, Mike. BS, U. Kans., 1957; postgrad., U. Ariz., 1972-78. Spkr. pro tem Ariz. Ho. of Reps., Phoenix, 1993, chmn. ethics com., chmn. econ. devel., 1993, mem. legis. coun., 1993, mem. gov.'s internat. trade and tourism adv. bd., 1993, mem. gov.'s strategic partnership for econ. devel., 1993, mem. gov.'s office of employement implementation task force, 1993, spkr. of house, 1989-93, house majority whip, 1987-88; secretary of state State of Arizona, Phoenix; gov. State of Ariz., Phoenix, 1997—. Bd. dirs. Morrison Inst. for Pub. Policy, Beatitudes D.O.A.R., 1992, Ariz. Town Hall, Ariz. Econs. Coun.; mem. dean's coun. Ariz. State U., 1989-92; assoc. mem. Heard Mus. Guild, Cactus Wren Rep. Women, ; mem. Maricopa Med. Aux., Ariz. State Med. Aux., Freedom Found., Valley Citizens League, Charter 100, North Phoenix Rep. Women, 1970, Trunk 'N Tusk Legis. Liaison Ariz. Rep. Party, 1993; Rep. candidate sec. of state, 1994. Recipient Econ. Devel. award Ariz. Innovation Network, 1993. Mem. Nat. Orgn. of Women Legislators, Am. Legis. Exch. Coun., Nat. Rep. Legislators Assn. (Nat. Legislator of Yr. award 1989), Soroptimists (hon.). Republican. Roman Catholic. Address: Office of Gov State Capitol 1700 W Washington Ave Phoenix AZ 85007-2812*

HULL, JOSEPH L., state senator; b. Ogden, Utah, Dec. 18, 1945; m. Sandra Glanville. BA, Weber State Coll.; MEd, Utah State U. Educator Utah State U.; mem. Utah State Senate, 1992—, asst. minority whip, 1995-96; mem. Utah Ho. of Reps., 1986-92; educator Sanders Jr. High Sch.; mem. various coms. including edn. and human svcs. Democrat. Office: 5250 W 4000 S Hooper UT 84315-9613*

HULL, LANCE ROLAND, real estate appraiser; b. Pocatello, Idaho, June 18, 1962; s. Roland Eugene and Lila (Atkinson) H. Degree in bus. and fin., Idaho State U., 1994. Supr. processing dept. Kraft Foods, Pocatello, 1980-90; real estate appraiser, cons. Appraisal Svc., Pocatello, 1987—; appraiser HUD, Boise, Idaho, 1992—; panel appraiser Dept. Vet. Affairs, Boise, 1998—. Mem. NRA, Nat. Assn. Realtors, Idaho Assn. Realtors, Greater Pocatello Assn. Realtors, N.Am. Hunting Club. Avocations: kite flying, motorcycling, boating, hunting, stock car racing. Home: 1620 Beth St Pocatello ID 83201-2501 Office: Appraisal Svc PO Box 2061 Pocatello ID 83206-2061

HULL, MICHAEL, estate planner; b. Abilene, Tex., Oct. 17, 1961; s. William Carroll Hull and Sandra Jane (Hull) Butcher; m. Evelyn Bigornia, Aug. 8, 1992; 1 child, Jordan Cordell. AA, Merlo Coll., 1982; Willamette U., 1984. Cert. estate planner; cert. philanthropic developer; cert. paralegal. Estate planner Liberty Estate Planning, Elk Grove, Calif., 1983—; pres., founder The Libr. Found., Elk Grove, 1997-98; regional mgr., dir., Liberty Estate Planning, Chgo., 1998—; bd. mem. Nat. coun. Cert. Estate Planners. Pres., founder Power Plus Team, Elk Grove, 1992-95; football coach Elk Grove H.S., 1995-97; Sunday sch. tchr. Harvest Ch., Elk Grove, 1997—. Republican. Assembly of God. Avocations: coaching football, power lifting. Home: 9212 Cerrolinda Cir Elk Grove CA 95758-5449 Office: Liberty Estate Planning 4827 Laguna Park Dr Ste 1D Elk Grove CA 95758-5159

HULLET, MICHAEL CRAIG, industrial designer, artist, educator; b. Fort Worth, Tex., Oct. 13, 1953; s. Robert and Donna H.; m. Stephanie Richardson, Sept. 21, 1991; children: Gray Lawrence, Jack Vincent. BFA, U. Utah, 1981; student, R.I. Sch. Design, 1983-84; MFA, U. Utah, 1988. Prin., owner Hullet Studios, Salt Lake City, 1989—; asst. prof. U. Utah, Salt Lake City, 1990—; cons. Willets J. Hole & Frederick Hastings Rindge Estate, L.A., 1993—, others; lectr. in field. Design credit N.Y. Times, 1997 (James Beard award), (book) Calif. Impressionism, 1998, James Beard 5th Anniversary Regiment Design Awards. Mem. Salt Lake Arts Council, Gateway Project 2002 Olympic Plan, Salt Lake Neighborhood Activist, District 3, 1995-97. Recipient Commn. award State of Utah, 1996, Hadvar-Hazy Commn. award Steve-Christine Hazy for Installed Works, L.A. 1997. Avocations: cycling, travel, archeology. Home: 778 S 300 W Salt Lake City UT 84101-2603 Office: Univ Utah AAC 161 Art Dept Salt Lake City UT 84112

HULSE, RALPH ROBERT, management consultant; b. St. Joseph, Mo., Jan. 14, 1935; s. Ralph Raymond and Eva Laduska (Hatfield) H.; m. Gwen Lea Bartosh, May 21, 1956 (div. 1959); m. Jutta-Beaujean, Jan. 14, 1961. AB, Cen. Meth. Coll., 1957; MEd, U. Mo., 1965. Continuing edn. programmer U. Mo., Columbia, 1969-71; dir. edn. tng. North Kansas City (Mo.) Meml. Hosp., 1971-74; mgmt. cons. Lawrence-Leiter, Kansas City, 1974-77; adminstr. U.S. Congress, 6th dist., Mo., 1977-78; bus. cons. Hulse & Assocs., Kansas City, 1978-88; adminstr. Sales Tng. Inst. div. Mile Hi Bus. Coll., Denver, 1988-89; bus. cons., pres. Crystal Devel. Systems, Inc, Denver, 1989-95; agent Bankers Life & Casualty Ins., 1994-96; ins. broker Hulse Health/Life Programs, 1996—; founder, bd. dirs. Opportunity Industry Inc., St. Joseph, 1965-71; pres. State Adult Edn. Assn., Mo., 1978-79. Contbr. articles to profl. jours. (Nat. Pub. award 1974, 75). Served with U.S. Army, 1959-61. Mem. Colo. Cons. Assn. (founder, pres. 1985-87). Republican. Methodist. Home and Office: 5282 Union Ct #4 Arvada CO 80002-1946

HUME, WYATT, university administrator. Exec. vice chmn. UCLA. Office: UCLA Care Mail Svcs PO Box 951361 Los Angeles CA 90095-1361*

HUMES, CHARLES WARREN, counselor, educator; b. Cambridge, Mass.; s. Charles W. and Alice E. Humes; m. Marilyn A. Harper, Aug. 7, 1965; children: Rebecca Ellyn Gelber, Malinda Maye. MA, NYU, 1952; EdM, Springfield Coll., 1956; EdD, U. Mass., 1968. Lic. profl. counselor, Va.; cert. profl. counselor, Ariz. Sch. psychologist Westfield Pub. Schs. (Mass.), 1955-62; dir. guidance Westfield Pub. Schs. (Mass.), 1962-70; assoc. prof. Springfield Coll. (Mass.), 1968-70; dir. pupil svc. and spl. edn. Greenwich Pub. Schs. (Conn.), 1970-80; assoc. prof. No. Va. Grad. Ctr., Va. Tech. U., Falls Church, 1980-88, prof. 1988-93, prof. emeritus, 1993—; pvt. practice, Vienna, Va. and Phoenix, 1985—. V.p. Westfield Area Child Guidance Clinic, 1963-65, pres., 1965-66; mem. Greenwich Hosp. Nursing Coun., 1970-75. Mem. APA, ACA (cons.), SAR (registrar, genealogist Palo Verde chpt. 1997—), Conn. Assn. Counselor Edn. & Supervision (pres. 1979-80), Ariz. Counselors Assn., Nat. Geneal. Soc., Phi Delta Kappa (v.p. Va. Tech. 1982-83), Phi Kappa Phi. Author: Pupil Services: Development, Coordination, Administration, 1984; Contemporary Counseling: Services, Applications, Issues, 1987. Book rev. editor Sch. Counselor, 1984-93. Contbr. over 60 articles on counseling to profl. jours. Home and Office: 15038 E Palomino Blvd Fountain Hills AZ 85268-4813

HUMES, LINDA JOYCE, religious organization executive, editor; b. Mountain View, Calif., July 21, 1950; d. Bobby A. Mitchell and Audrey A. (Paddock) Mitchell-Crowell-O'Brien; m. Robert W. Koch, June 2, 1972 (div. July 1986); 1 child, Paul; m. Thomas W. Humes, July 28, 1992; children: Derik, John. AA in Dramatic Arts, Mesa (Ariz.) C.C., 1971; student, Foothill Jr. Coll., Los Altos, Calif., 1968-69, Mesa (Ariz.) C.C., 1969-71. Fraud investigator State Farm Ins. Co., Tempe, Ariz., 1982-90; tchr. River of Life Christian Acad., Phoenix, 1994—; adminstr. River of Life Tabernacle, Phoenix, 1994—; pres., founder Shiloh Spiritual Growth Ministries, Phoenix, 1997—. Author: Moments with the Master, 1997; editor: More than a Conqueror, 1997. Sec. Ariz. Adv. Com. on Arson Prevention, Phoenix, 1982-86; pres. Chandler (Ariz.) Hist. Soc., 1985. Mem. Internat. Assn. Arson Investigators (life, editor Ariz. chpt. 1982-94, internat. assn. 1988-94, bd. dirs. Ariz. chpt. 1986-94). Republican. Avocations: writing, music, photography, Christian activities. Office: River of Life Tabernacle Inc 4039 E Raymond St Phoenix AZ 85040-1930

HUMMEL, JOSEPH WILLIAM, hospital administrator; b. Vinton, Iowa, Dec. 7, 1940; married. BA, Calif. State U., 1965; M Health Adminstrn., U Calif., 1966. Adminstrv. instr. Merrithew Meml. Hosp., Martinez, Calif., 1965; adminstrv. res. Mt. Zion Hosp. and Med. Ctr., San Francisco, 1966-67, adminstrv. pat. care, 1967-68, adminstrv. asst., 1968-70; assoc. adminstr. Valley Med. Ctr., Fresno, Calif., 1970-74; CEO Kern Med. Ctr., Bakersfield, Calif., 1974-86; adminstr. Kaiser Found. Hosp., L.A., 1987—, sr. v.p. area mng. Mem. Calif. Hosp. Assn. (bd. dirs. 1983-89). Home: 2050 Maginn St Glendale CA 91202-1128 Office: Kaiser Found Hosp 4747 W Sunset Blvd Los Angeles CA 90027-6021

HUMPHREY, CAMILLA MARIE, retired special education educator; b. Devils Lake, N.D., July 3, 1928; d. George O. and Annette Sophia (Monson) Loftness; m. Thomas Milton Humphrey, Dec. 26, 1950 (dec. Nov. 1992); children: Ana Oliva Johns, Marlena Marie Hensley. AA, Coll. Marin, 1948; attended, U. Calif., Berkeley, 1948-49; BA in Edn., Pacific Luth. U., 1950; grad., U. Oreg., 1951-53, U. Nev., 1968. Cert. spl. edn., Oreg., boating skills. Tchr. Albany (Oreg.) Elem. Sch., 1950-51; spl. edn. tchr. Children's Hosp. Sch., Eugene, Oreg., 1951-53, Eugene Jr. H.S., 1953-54, Clark County Sch. Dist., Las Vegas, 1968-71. Contbr. articles to profl. jours. Vol. English tchr. Luth. Mission, 1955-56; pres. Oil Wive's Club, Bogota, Colombia, 1956-57, Assistance League Las Vegas, 1980-81; nurse's aid Red Cross, Tripoli, Libya, 1958; fgn. rels. chmn. LVW, Carson City, Nev., 1963; fin. sec. Gen. Fedn. Women's Clubs, Las Vegas, 1983-84; adv. bd. mem. Salvation Army, Las Vegas, 1983-86; vol. R.S.V.P., 1993-95, Thrift Store and Food Bank, McKinleyville, Calif., Patricks Point State Park Bookstore, Trinidad, Calif.; adv. for world concerns, children's issues, preservation natural beauty; bd. dirs. Adult Day Health Care, Mckinleyville, Calif., 1994-95. Recipient 1st and 2d place photography award Gen. Fedn. Women's Clubs, 1982, Nev. short story award, 1984, vol. svc. plaque Help Ctr., Las Vegas, 1986; Silver Platter award Evang. Luth. Ch. in Am. Mission, Bogota, 1956. Mem. AAUW, DAV Aux., Nat. Assistance League (at-large), Pacific Luth. U. Alumni Assn. Lutheran. Avocations: photography, reading, world travel, art and sculpture, interior decorating. Home: 113 Maple Park Ave SE Olympia WA 98501-8701

HUMPHREY, JOHN JULIUS, university program director, historian, writer; b. Booneville, Miss., Jan. 22, 1926; s. George Duke and Josephine (Robertson) H.; m. Mary Margaret Ryan, Jan. 19, 1949 (dec. June 1996); children: George Duke II, Laurie Ann. BS, Miss. State U., 1945; BA, U. Wyo., 1946, MA, 1964, postgrad., 1964-68; postgrad., U. Ariz., 1969-71. Pres. J.J. Humphrey Co. Inc., Laramie, Wyo., 1947-68; lectr. History U. Ariz., Tucson, 1969-71, asst. dir. placement, 1969-70, dir. scholarships, awards, 1970-72, dir. office of scholarships and fin. aid, 1972-84, dir. scholarship devel., 1970-91; asst. to pres. western area Cumberland Coll., Williamsburg, Ky., 1991; v.p. bus. affairs Tucson Coll. Arts and Scis., 1992. Sec. Baird Found., Tucson, 1970—; bd. dirs. Bendalin Fund, Phoenix, 1976—, Cacioppo Found., Tucson, 1986—; cons. DeMund Found., St. Louis, 1970—; mem. Pres. Club U. Ariz. Found.; mem. Ariz. Assn. Fin. Aid Officers, 1970-91, pres., 1973-74; pres. Ariz. Coll. & Univ. Faculty Assn., 1972-73. Ivinson Meml. Hosp. Bd., Laramie, 1964-68. Recipient Spl. award U. Ariz. Black Student Govt., 1983, Black Alumni, 1990; study grantee U. Ariz., 1993—. Mem. Am. Indian Alumni Assn. (Spl. Appreciation for Svc. in Scholarships Native Ams. award 1982), Mormon History Assn., Masons (32 degree, Knight York Cross of Honor), Shriners. Methodist. Home: 6901 E Potawatami Dr Tucson AZ 85715-3246

HUMPHREY, NANCY ADELE, employment and training specialist, consultant; b. Vallejo, Calif., Sept. 28, 1950; d. Avery Edward and Alice Margurete (Norvell) H. BA in History, Calif. Bapt. Coll., 1972. Planning aide Contra Costa County PIC, Concord, Calif., 1976-80, youth programs analyst, 1980-82, employment analyst III, 1982-86; cons. Washington, 1986—; planning analyst III PIC of Solano County, Suisan, Calif., 1997—. Author: The Magnificent Journey, Designing Basic Skills Programs: A Step by Step Process. Democrat. Unitarian. Avocations: reading, enjoying nature, finding creative solutions to social problems. Home: 244 American Canyon Rd Spc 21 American Cyn CA 94589-3030 Office: PIC of Solano County 320 Campus Ln Suisun City CA 94585-1400

HUMPHREY, PHYLLIS A., writer; b. Oak Park, Ill., July 22, 1929; d. Richard William and Antoinette (Chalupa) Ashworth; m. Herbert A. Pihl, Sept. 13, 1946 (div. 1957); children: Christine Pihl Gibson, Gary Fraizer Pihl; m. Curtis H. Humphrey, June 21, 1965; 1 child, Marc. AA, Coll. San Mateo, Calif., 1972; postgrad., Northwestern U., 1945-47. Ptnr. Criterion House, Oceanside, Calif., 1972—. Author: Wall Street on $20 a Month, 1986, Golden Fire, 1986, Sweet Folly, 1990, Flying High, 1995, Once More With Feeling, 1998; author radio scripts Am. Radio Theatre, 1983-84; contbr. short stories and articles to popular mags. Mem. Mensa. Republican. Christian Sci. Ch. Avocations: reading, travel. Office: Criterion House PO Box 586295 Oceanside CA 92058-6295

HUMPHRIES, SANDRA LEE FORGER, artist, teacher; b. Norwalk, Conn., Dec. 1, 1946; d. Edmund Ernest and Grace Muriel (Seale) Forger; m. Stanley Humphries Jr., Aug. 10, 1968 (div. July 1992); children: Colin, Courtney; m. Corby Knight, June 2, 1998. BFA, R.I. Sch. Design, 1968; MA, U. N.Mex., 1994. Studio artist Albuquerque, 1980—; instr. watercolor Sandra Humphries Fine Art, Albuquerque, 1992—; dir. Shows Gallery, Albuquerque, 1994-96, Sandra Humphries Gallery, Albuquerque, 1997—. Exhibited in group shows at Rocky Mountain Watermedia Exhbn., 1983, 86, 89, 90, 91, Western Fedn. Watercolor Socs., 1984, 86, 87, 90, Am. Watercolor Soc. Exhbn., 1985, Nat. Watercolor Soc. Exhbn., 1989, Artists of the West Invitational, 1993, 94, 95, 96. Mem. Nat. Watercolor Soc. (signature), Rocky Mountain Watermedia Soc. (signature), N.Mex. Watercolor Soc. (signature). Home: 3503 Berkeley Pl NE Albuquerque NM 87106-1349

HUMPHRIES, STEPHEN EDWARD, writer; b. Camden, N.J., Oct. 14, 1950; s. Edward W. and Dolores (Weaver) H.; m. Elsa Schroeder, Oct. 30, 1977 (div. Oct. 1983); m. Ruth Ivy Frishman, Sept. 27, 1992. AA with honors, Broward Community Coll., 1970; student, U. Colo., 1972-74, Colo. Sch. Mines, 1981-84, Met. State Coll., 1986-88. Engring. tech., tech. writer Enviro-Test Ltd., Denver, 1975-77; asst. editor Am. Water Works Assn., Denver, 1977; assoc. project scientist TRC Environ. Cons., Denver, 1978-82; geol. asst., writer Colo. Sch. Mines, Golden, 1983-84; reporter, editor High Timber Times, Conifer, Colo., 1984-88, reporter Aspen (Colo.) Times/Times Daily, 1988-89; copy editor The Leader Newspapers, Houston, 1989; mng. editor S. Coast Community Newspapers, Santa Barbara, Calif., 1989-90; freelance writer Houston, 1989-91; editor Tahoe World, Tahoe City, Calif., 1991-93; freelance writer Truckee, Calif., 1993—. Trustee Tahoe Forest Hosp. Found., Truckee Donner Land Trust; vol. U.S. Geol. Survey; adv. bd. Tahoe Truckee Housing Devel. Corp. Recipient 2d place feature photography for weeklies award Colo. Press Assn., 1985, hon. mention news stories for weeklies, 1987, sweepstakes winner feature stories for weeklies, 1989; hon. mention serious columnist for weekly Nat. Newspaper Assn., 1987, hon. mention editorial pages for weeklies, 1989; award Met. Water Providers, 1987, Meritorious Svc. award VFW, 1988. Mem. Internat. Soc. Weekly Newspaper Editors, Soc. Profl. Journalists. Avocations: outdoor sports, photography, reading, computers, gourmet cooking.

HUMPHRY, DEREK, association executive, writer; b. Bath, Somerset, Eng., Apr. 29, 1930; came to U.S., 1978; s. Royston Martin and Bettine (Duggan) H.; m. Jean Edna Crane, May 5, 1953 (dec. Mar. 1975); children: Edgar, Clive, Stephen; m. Ann Wickett Kooman, Feb. 16, 1976 (div. 1990); m. Gretchen Crocker, 1991. Student pub. schs. Reporter, Evening News, Manchester, Eng., 1951-55, Daily Mail, London, 1955-63; editor Havering Recorder, Essex, Eng., 1963-67; sr. reporter Sunday Times, London, 1967-78; spl. writer L.A. Times, 1978-79; founder, exec. dir. Hemlock Soc. N.Am., L.A., 1980-92, pres. 1988-90. Author: Because They're Black, 1971 (M.L. King award 1972), Police Power and Black People, 1972; Jean's Way, 1978, Let Me Die Before I Wake, 1982, The Right to Die, 1986, Final Exit, 1991, Dying With Dignity, 1992, Lawful Exit, 1993, Freedom to Die, 1998. With Brit. Army, 1948-50. Recipient Socrates award for right-to-die activism, 1997. Mem. World Fedn. Right-to-Die Socs. (newsletter editor 1979-84, 1992-94, sec.-treas. 1983-84, pres. 1988-90), Ams. Death with Dignity (v.p. 1993), Hemlock Soc. No. Calif. (v.p. 1994), Euthanasia Rsch. and Guidance Orgn. (pres. 1993—). Home and Office: 24829 Norris Ln Junction City OR 97448-9559

HUNING, DEVON GRAY, actress, dancer, audiologist, photographer, video producer and editor; b. Evanston, Ill., Aug. 23, 1950; d. Hans Karl Otto and Angenette Dudley (Willard) H.; divorced; 1 child, Bree Alyeska. BS, No. Ill. U., 1981, MA, 1983. Actress, soloist, dancer, dir. various univ. and community theater depts., Bklyn., Chgo. and Cranbrook, B.C., Can., 1967—; ski instr. Winter Park (Colo.) Recreation Assn., 1975-79; house photographer C Lazy U Ranch, Granby, Colo., 1979; audiologist, ednl. programming cons. East Kootenay Ministry of Health, Cranbrook, 1985-89; ind. video prodn./asst., 1991—; owner Maxaroma Espresso and Incredible Edibles, 1993-95; pres. Sound Comms., 1989—; writer, prodr., editor Sta. KTVZ, Bend, Oreg., 1996-97; master of ceremonies East Kootenay Talent Showcase, EXPO '86, Vancouver B.C., Can., 1986; creator, workshop leader: A Hearing Impaired Child in the Classroom, 1986. Producer, writer, dir., editor (video) Down With Decibels, 1992; author: Living Well With Hearing Loss: A Guide for the Hearing-Impaired and Their Families, 1992. Sec., treas. Women for Wildlife, Cranbrook, 1985-86; assoc. mem. adv. bd. Grand County Community Coll., Winter Park, Colo., 1975-77; assoc. mem. bd. dirs. Boys and Girls Club of Can., Cranbrook, 1985. Mem. Internat. Marine Animal Trainers Assn. Avocations: snow and water skiing, scuba diving, dancing, marine animals, studying animal behavior.

HUNKER, KURT CHRISTIAN, architect; b. Columbus, Ohio, Dec. 28, 1956; s. Henry Louis and M. Beth (Sterner) H.; m. Julia Cousins, Dec. 18, 1981. BS in Arch., Ohio State U., 1979; MArch, Harvard U., Cambridge, Mass., 1982. Registered architect, Calif. and Nev.; cert. Nat. Counc. of Arch. Reg. Bds. Designer/arch. various firms, 1982-93; project mngr. Cass & Pinnell Arch., Washington, D.C., 1986-87; assoc. prof. New Schl. of Arch., San Diego, 1989—; prin. Kurt Hunker Arch., San Diego, 1994—; lectr. San Diego Mus. of Art, 1990, Friends of Arch., San Diego, 1995; advisor Cartouche Journal, San Diego, 1992-96; organizer AIA Spark Forum, San Diego, 1990; coord. Mid-City Design Charrette. Prin. works include NBC Bank Boerne, Tex., 1985-86, Jackson Aud., Tex., E.W. Scripps Hall, Ohio, 1982-83 (AIA award), designed numerous high schools. Merit award Masonry Assoc., Del Mar, Calif., citation award Am. Schl. & U. magazine, Carlsbad, Calif., 1990. Mem. AIA, Am. Inst. of Arch. Avocations: tennis, fencing, sketching, travel.

HUNKINS, RAYMOND BREEDLOVE, lawyer, rancher; b. Culver City, Calif., Mar. 19, 1939; s. Charles F. and Louise (Breedlove) H.; m. Mary Deborah McBride, Dec. 12, 1968; children: Amanda, Blake, Ashley. BA, U. Wyo., 1966, JD, 1968. Ptnr. Jones, Jones, Vines & Hunkins, Wheatland, Wyo., 1968—; mem. local rules com. U.S. Dist. Ct., 1990—; spl. counsel U. Wyo., Laramie, State of Wyo., Cheyenne; mem. faculty Western Trial Adv. Inst., 1993—, Wyo. Supreme Ct. Commn. Jud. Salary and Benefits, 1996—; owner Thunderhead Ranches, Albany and Platte Counties, Wyo., gen. ptnr. Split Rock Land & Cattle Co.; spl. asst. atty. gen., Wyo. Chmn. Platte County Reps., Wheatland, 1972-74, chmn. adv. coun. Coll. of Commerce and Industry, U. Wyo., 1978-79; bd. dirs. U. Wyo. Found., 1996—, Am. Heritage Ctr., 1995—; mem. Gov.'s Crime Commn., 1970-78; pres. Wyo. U. Alumni Assn., 1973-74, commr. Wyo. Aeronautics Commn., 1987—; moderator United Ch. Christ. With USMC, 1955-57. Fellow Am. Coll. Trial Lawyers (Wyo. state chmn.), Internat. Soc. Barristers, Am. Bd. Trial Advs.; mem. ABA (aviation com. 1980-86, forum com. on constrn. industry litigation sect.), Wyo. Bar Assn. (chmn. grievance com. 1980-86, mem. com. on civil pattern jury instrns.), Wyo. Trial Lawyers Assn. (past pres.), Lions, Elks. Office: Jones Jones Vines & Hunkins PO Drawer 189 9th and Maple Wheatland WY 82201

HUNNICUTT, ROBERT WILLIAM, engineer; b. Pauls Valley, Okla., Aug. 12, 1954; s. James Warren Hunnicutt. BS, N.Mex. State U., 1980; postgrad., U. Ariz., 1996—. Sr. assoc. engr. IBM, Tucson, 1980-94. Mem. Nat. Assn. of Deaf, Ariz. Assn. of Deaf. Avocations: photography, astronomy, skiing, reading, philately. Home: 8383 S Pistol Hill Rd Vail AZ 85641-6146

HUNSAKER, FLOYD B., accountant; b. Collinston, Utah, Sept. 6, 1915; s. Allen G. and Mary Ann (Bowcutt) H.; grad. high sch.; m. Zella D. Hepworth, Mar. 3, 1943; children: Marcia (Mrs. Marvin Bahr), Charlene (Mrs. Abelino Ancira), Sonia (Mrs. Val Fisher), Rhonda (Mrs. Kim Veigel), Tamara (Mrs. Randy Beardall), Shelia (dec. 1945). Lic. ins. salesman, security dealer, notary pub., Lincoln County, Wyo. Owner, operator dairy farm, Bedford, Wyo., 1946-70; acct., Afton, Wyo., 1959—; owner Credit Bur. Star Valley, Afton, 1967-87; mcpl. judge Town of Afton, 1967-77; local office claimstaker Wyo. Unemployment Compensation Dept., 1975-85. Pres., Holdaway Sch. PTA, 1960; active Boy Scouts Am., 1946-49, 58-67; chmn. Cub Scouts com., 1987-95; bd. dirs. Star Valley Sr. Citizens, 1981-83, 84-88; pres. Lower Valley 4-H council, 1961-62, leader, 1959-63; chmn. Star Valley chpt. Am. Revolution Bicentennial Adminstrn., 1975-76, Star Valley chpt. ARC, 1976-96; hon. bd. dirs. Lincoln County Chpt. ARC; ward pres. Sunday Sch., 1985-87; mem. Wyo. Centennial Com., 1990; subdivider Fertile Acres 1981-88; archtl. designer Star Valley Vets. Meml. Monument, 1990; mem. Lincoln County Selective Svc. Bd., 1984-96. Pub. Star Valley Bus. Directory, 1990—. Recipient 50 Yr. Vol. award ARC, 1992, First Place award Farm Bur. Talent Contest; Floyd B. Hunsaker Day named in his honor, 1995. Served with Devils Brigade, 1941-45; ETO. Mem. Farm Bur. (exec. sec. Lincoln County 1961-66), Internat. Platform Assn., Afton C. of C. (dir. 1973-74), Star Valley C. of C. (dir. 1988—, exec. sec. 1989-90, treas. 1991—, Outstanding Cmty. Svc. award 1994), VFW (post svc. officer 1949—, post quartermaster 1959—, dist. comdr. Wyo. 1974-75, 77-78, state dept. jr. vice comdr. 1978-79, sr. vice comdr. 1979-80, state comdr. 1980-81, dist. comdr. 1982-83, 86-88, chmn. state audit com. 1985-94), Am. Legion (post svc. officer, adj. treas. 1975—). Mem. Ch. of Jesus Christ of Latter-day Saints. Home: PO Box 516 323 Adams St Afton WY 83110 Office: 498 Washington St Afton WY 83110

HUNSBERGER, CHARLES WESLEY, library director; b. Elkhart, Ind., Sept. 25, 1929; s. Charles August and Emma Edna (Zimmerman) H.; m. Hilda Carol Showalter, July 3, 1949 (div.); children: Jonathan Wesley, Jerald Wayne, Jane Wannette. BA, Bethel Coll., Mishawaka, Ind., 1952; MLS, Ind. U., 1967. Mem. Ft. Wayne (Ind.) Libr. Staff, 1960-62; dir. Columbia (Ind.) City Libr., 1962-64, Monroe County Libr., Bloomington, Ind., 1964-71, Clark County Libr. Dist., Las Vegas, Nev., 1971-93; owner Las Vegas Libr. Cons. Svcs., 1993—, Las Vegas, Nev. cons. sch., pub. librs., 1968-70; lectr. libr. schs. Ind. U., 1970-71, U. Ariz., 1974, U. Nev., Reno, 1976; mem. Nev. Coun. on Librs., 1973-81, chmn., 1980-81. Mem. Calif. Libr. Assn., ALA, Nev. Libr. Assn. (named Libr. of Yr. 1988), Internat. Assn. of Met. City Librs. (sec./treas., 1992-95), Rotary (pres. 1979-80, Las Vegas-Paradise chpt.). Democrat. Home: 52 Crestview Dr Las Vegas NV 89124-9155

HUNT, ALLEN GERHARD, physicist, geologist; b. N.Y.C., Dec. 22, 1954; s. Albert Charles and Katherine Rebecca (Wollan) H.; m. Beatrix Karthaus, Aug. 7, 1987. MS in Physics, U. Calif. (Riverside), 1980, PhD in Physics, 1983; MA in Geology, Duke U., 1996. Vis. prof. Philipps U., Marburg, Germany, 1985-87; lectr. in physics U. Calif. (Irvine), 1988-90, 97, Calif. State U., Fullerton, 1990-92; post-doctoral rsch. sci. U. Calif. (Riverside), 1992-94; lectr. in physics Calif. State U., San Bernardino, 1994-95; instr. in phys. sci Riverside (Calif.) C.C., 1997—; guest spkr. numerous Sci. confs., nat. and internat., 1981—. Author: On the Market: The Academic Job Search, 1997, numerous poems; contbr. over 50 articles to sci. and tech. mags. Recipient Fulbright Commn. Rsch. fellow, Germany, 1985-87; named Tchr. of Distinction, LDS Student Assn., 1998. Mem. Am. Geophys. Union. Avocations: archeology, climatology.

HUNT, BARNABAS JOHN, priest, religious order administrator; b. Sayre, Pa., Jan. 6, 1937; s. Clarence Elmer and Margarite Frances (Bennett) H. BS in Edn., Pa. State U., 1958, postgrad., Elmira Coll., 1960-61, Portland (Oreg.) State U., 1969-70, Clackamas C.C., 1970-71, Mt. Hood Community Coll., 1973-74. Joined Soc. St. Paul, 1961, ordained priest Episcopal Ch. 1984. H.s. tchr. Pub. Schs., Candor, N.Y., 1958-61; headmaster St. Luke's Sch., Soc. St. Paul, Gresham, Oreg., 1961-64; lic. adminstr. St. Jude's Nursing Home, Inc., Portland and Sandy, Oreg., 1964-73; assoc. rector Soc. St. Paul, Palm Desert, Calif., 1975-89, rector, 1989—; brother in charge St. Paul's Press, Sandy, Oreg., 1969-76; vice chmn. The Resource Devel. Fund Bd. of Carlotta, 1993-97; treas. Desert Samaritans for the Elderly, 1997—. Pres. adv. bd. The Carlotta, 1985-92. Mem. Tri-County Bd., Oreg. Agy. on Aging, 1971-76; pres. Sandy C. of C., 1972; mem. Sandy City Coun., 1975-76, candidate for City Coun., City of Palm Desert, 1986; pres. St. Jude's Home, Inc., Palm Desert, 1989—. Fellow Am. Coll. Health Care Adminstrs. (pres. Coll. Found. 1984-87); mem. Nat. Guild Churchmen (pres. 1982—), Conf. on Religious Life in Anglican Communion (v.p. 1992-97, archivist 1982—). Episcopalian. Home and Office: PO Box 14350 Palm Desert CA 92255-4350

HUNT, DENNIS, public relations executive. BA in English, Notre Dame U.; MA in Edn. Adv. mgr., contbg. editor San Francisco Bus. Mag.; exec. v.p., gen. mgr. Deaver & Hannaford; mng. ptnr. Hunt/Marmillion Assocs., 1983-88; exec. v.p., gen. mgr. Ogilvy Adams &Rinehart, 1988-92; pres. Stoorza, Ziegaus, Metzger & Hunt, Sacramento, 1992—; adj. instr. Santa Monica (Calif.) Coll. Office: Stoorza Ziegaus Metzger & Hunt 555 Capitol Mall Ste 600 Sacramento CA 95814-4502

HUNT, GORDON, lawyer; b. L.A., Oct. 26, 1934; s. Howard Wilson and Esther Nita (Dempsey) H. BA in Polit. Sci, UCLA, 1956; JD, U. So. Calif., 1959. Bar: Calif. 1960. Law clk. Appellate Dept., Superior Ct. L.A. County, 1959-60; mem. firm Behymer & Hoffman, Los Angeles, 1960-65; partner firm Behymer, Hoffman & Hunt, Los Angeles, 1965-68; ptnr. firm Munns, Kofford, Hoffman, Hunt & Throckmorton, Pasadena, 1969-90, Hunt, Ortman, Blasco, Palffy & Rossell, Pasadena, 1990-95; mem. Hunt, Ortman, Blasco, Palffy & Rossell Inc., 1995—; lectr. UCLA, various yrs.; chmn. legal adv. com. Assoc. Gen. Contractors Calif., 1985; arbitrator L.A. Superior Ct., State of Calif. Author: Construction Surety and Bonding Handbook; co-author: California Construction Law, 15th edit.; contbr. numerous articles to legal jours. Mem. ABA, Calif. Bar Assn. (del. Conv. 1964-69), L.A. County Bar Assn. (real property com. 1965-66, exec. com. 1970-72, sec. 1972-73, vice chmn. 1972-75, chmn. real property sect. 1975-76, co-chmn. continuing edn. bar com. 1969-71), Am. Arbitration Assn. (arbitrator, mediator). Office: 301 N Lake Ave Fl 7 Pasadena CA 91101-4108

HUNT, JAMES L., lawyer; b. Chgo., Oct. 20, 1942. BA magna cum laude, DePauw U., 1964; JD, Northwestern U., 1967. Bar: Calif. 1967. Atty. McCuthe, Doyle, Brown & Enersen, San Francisco; atty. rep. 9th Cir. Jud. Conf., 1991-94; bd. dirs. The Lurie Co.; trustee The Lurie Found. Assoc. editor: Northwestern U. Law Rev., 1966-67. Bd. dirs. San Francisco Giants; bd. visitors Northwestern U. Law Sch., 1989—. Mem. Am. Coll. Trial Lawyers, Phi Beta Kappa, Order of the Coif. Office: McCutchen Doyle Brown & Enersen 3 Embarcadero Ctr San Francisco CA 94111-4003

HUNT, LEO, public relations executive. Sr. exec. v.p. Wilson McHenry Co., San Mateo, Calif. Office: Wilson McHenry Co 393 Vintage Park Dr Ste 140 Foster City CA 94404-1172*

HUNT, LORRAINE T., state official; m. Charles Hunt; 3 children. Former pres., CEO Perri Inc.; founder, also bd. dirs. Continental Nat. Bank; lt. gov. State of Nev., 1999—; bd. dirs. First Security Bank Nev.; chmn. bd. trustees Las Vegas Convention and Visitors Authority; former commr. and vice chair Nev. Commn. on Tourism; dir. Nev. Hotel/Motel Assn.; vice chmn. Nev. Motion Picture Found., Nev. Motion Picture Commn. Commr. Clark county Commn., 1995-99. Office: 101 N Carson St Ste 2 Carson City NV 89701*

HUNT, PETER ROGER, film director, writer, editor; b. London, Mar. 11, 1925; came to U.S., 1975; s. Arthur George and Elizabeth H.; widowed; 1 child, Nicholas Constantine. Student, London Sch. Music. Actor English Repertory Theater, London. Camera asst., asst. editor various documentaries; asst. editor various feature films. London Film Co.; scriptor various films Hill in Korea, Admirable Crichton, Next to No Time, Paradise Lagoon, Cry From the Streets, Greengage Summer (Am. title: Loss of Innocence), Ferry to Hong Kong, H.M.S. Defiant (Am. title: Damn the Defiant), Sink the Bismarck, Operation Snaffu; supervising editor, 2d unit dir.: Dr. No, Call Me Bwana, From Russia with Love, Goldfinger, Ibcress File, Thunderball, You Only Live Twice, Jigsaw Man, Desperate Hours; assoc. producer: Chitty Chitty Bang Bang; dir.: On Her Majesty's Secret Service, Gullivers Travels (film and animated), Gold, Shout at the Devil, Death Hunt, Wild Geese II, Assassination, Hyper Sapien, Marlowe, Shirley's World, Persuaders, (NBC-TV movie) Beasts in the Streets, (ABC-TV mini-series) Last Days of Pompeii, (CBS-TV spl.) Eyes of a Witness. Mem. Assn. Cinematic Technicians Great Britain, Broadcasting Entertainment Cinematograph Theatre Union, Dirs. Guild of Am., Motion Picture Acad. Arts, Acad. TV, Broadcasting, Entertainment, Cinematograph, Theatre Union. Office: 2337 Roscomare Rd Ste 2-145 Los Angeles CA 90077-1851

HUNT, ROBERT GARY, medical consultant, oral and maxillofacial surgeon; b. San Diego, July 10, 1945; s. Harvey E. and Pauline A. (Nazarovic) H.; m. Diane G. Hunt, Apr. 26, 1975; 1 child, Christine G. AA, Mesa Coll., San Diego, 1971; BS in Medicine, U. nebr., 1979, MD, 1979; DDS, U. So. Calif., 1976. Diplomate Am. Bd. Oral and Maxillofacial Surgery, Nat. Bd. Med. Examiners; lic. physician, Calif., Nebr.; lic. dentist, Calif., Nebr. Oral and maxillofacial surgeon in pvt. practice San Diego, 1981—. With USAF, 1965-70. Fellow Am. Assn. Oral and Maxillofacial Surgeons, Am. Coll. Oral and Maxillofacial Surgeons, Internat. Coll. Surgeons, Internat. Soc. Plastic, Aesthetic and Reconstructive Surgery, Am. Coll. Oral Implantology; mem. AMA, ADA, So. Calif. Acad. Oral Pathology, Mensa, Omicron Kappa Upsilon, Phi Kappa Phi, Alpha Tau Epsilon, Delta Sigma Delta, others. Home: 2240 Sunset Blvd San Diego CA 92103-1120

HUNT, ROBERT WILLIAM, theatrical producer, data processing consultant; b. Seattle, June 8, 1947; s. William Roland and Margaret Anderson (Crowe) H.; m. Marcie Loomis, Aug. 24, 1968 (div. Dec. 1975); 1 child, Megan; m. Susan Moyer, June 17, 1989 (div. Oct. 1997); children: Donovan, Jillian. BA, U. Wash., 1969. CPA, Wash. Data processing cons Arthur Andersen & Co., Seattle, 1968-78; owner, cons. Robert W. Hunt & Assocs., Seattle, 1978—; exec. producer Village Theatre, Issaquah, Wash., 1979—; developer Francis J. Gaudette Theatre, Issaquah, Wash., 1994; cons. San Francisco Mus. Modern Art, 1981-90, Mus. of Flight, Seattle, 1983-90, Met. Mus. N.Y.C., 1984-85; contracted for acquired mgmt. Everett (Wash.) Performing Arts Ctr., 1998—. Creator arts computer software; prodr. (mus.) Eleanor, 1987, Heidi, 1989, Charlie and the Chocolate Factory, 1989, Book of James, 1990, Funny Pages, 1991, Jungle Queen Debutante, 1991, Glimmerglass, 1995, City Kid, 1995, Bootlegger, 1996, 4:00 AM Boogie Blues, 1998; creator, writer (pop group music and video) The Shrimps, 1984. Chmn. com. Seattle Arts Commn., 1975-78; treas. Arts Resource Svcs., Seattle, 1976-78; gen. mgr. Musicomedy Northwest, Seattle, 1977-79; bd. dirs. Theatre Puget Sound. Grantee Seattle Arts Commn., 1978-79, Wash. State Arts Commn., 1980—, King County Arts Commn., 1980—, Nat. Endowment for the Arts, 1992—. Mem. Wash. Soc. CPAs., Nat. Alliance of Mus. Theatre Producers (treas., bd. dirs.), Seattle Rotary. Office: Village Theatre 303 Front St N Issaquah WA 98027-2917

HUNT, ROGER LEE, judge; b. Overton, Nev., Apr. 29, 1942; s. Ferlin Hansen and Verda (Peterson) H.; m. Mauna Sue Hawkes, July 20, 1965; children: Roger Todd (dec.), Rachelle, Kristina, Tyler, Melanee, Ryan. Student, Coll. So. Utah; BA, Brigham Young U., 1966; JD, George Washington U., 1970. Bar: Nev. 1970, U.S. Dist. Ct. Nev. 1970, U.S. Supreme Ct. [illegible] Dep. dist. atty. Clark County Dist. Atty.'s Office, Las Vegas, Nev., 1971; assoc. Rose & Norwood, Las Vegas, 1971-73; sr. ptnr. Edwards, Hunt, Hale & Hansen, Las Vegas, 1973-92; U.S. magistrate judge U.S. Dist. Ct. Nev., Las Vegas, 1992—. Office: US Dist Ct Foley Fed Bldg #2300 300 Las Vegas Blvd Ste 2300 Las Vegas NV 89101-5883*

HUNT, VANESSA ANN, civilian military employee; b. Dayton, Ohio, Sept. 12, 1956; d. Wade Thomas and Peggie Ann (Allen) H. BA in Polit. Sci., Wright State U., 1979; MA in Edn., Tuskegee Inst., 1983; postgrad., Def. Systems Mgmt. Coll., L.A., 1985-86. Res. tchr. Dayton Bd. Edn., 1980-81, 85; grad. asst., asst. dir. profl. edn. Tuskegee (Ala.) Inst., 1981-83; logistics mgmt. specialist L.A. AFB, 1985—. Mem. Internat. Leadership Conf., Bahamas Faith Ministry and 700 Club, Jerusalem, 1993. Recipient performance award Dept. Air Force, 1991, 92. Mem. NAFE, Air Force Assn., Soc. Logistics Engrs., Phi Delta Kappa, Kappa Delta Pi. Avocations: photography, foreign travel, health and fitness. Office: Hdqrs Space & Missile Sys Ctr 2420 Vela Way Ste 1467 A8 El Segundo CA 90245

HUNT, WILLIAM E., SR., state supreme court justice; b. 1923. BA, LLB, U. Mont., JD, 1955. Bar: 1955. Judge State Workers' Compensation Ct., 1975-81; justice Mont. Supreme Ct., Helena, 1984—. Office: Mont Supreme Ct Justice Bldg Rm 315 215 N Sanders St Helena MT 59620-4522*

HUNTER, DIANA LYNN, real estate consultant; b. Northampton, Mass., Aug. 28, 1963; d. Samuel Joseph and Ilda Cecile (Lindley) H. AB in Econs., Bryn Mawr Coll., 1985; MBA in Fin. and Real Estate, UCLA, 1991, MA in Urban Planning, 1991. Banking industry sr. analyst BEI Golembe Assocs., Washington, 1985-88; fin. analyst Heitman Fin. Svcs. Ltd., Beverly Hills, Calif., 1989; site location analyst First Interstate Bank, L.A., 1990-91; sr. cons. E & Y Kenneth Leventhal Real Estate Group, L.A., 1991-94, Arthur Andersen & Co. LLP, L.A., 1995-96; fin. mgr. Newhall Land and Farming Co., Valencia, Calif., 1996-98, Playa Capital Co., LLC, Playa Vista, Calif., 1998—. Mem. Urban Land Inst. Avocations: tennis, golf, cooking, travel, architecture. Office: Playa Capital Co LLC 12555 W Jefferson Blvd Los Angeles CA 90066-7036

HUNTER, DUNCAN LEE, congressman; b. Riverside, Calif., May 31, 1948; m. Lynne Layh, 1973; children: Robert Samuel, Duncan Duane. J.D., Western State U., 1976. Bar: Calif. 1976. Practiced in San Diego; mem. 97th Congress from 42d Dist. Calif., 98th-105th Congresses from 45th Dist. Calif., 103d-105th Congress from 52d Calif. dist.; mem. nat. security com., subcom. mil. installations and facilities, chmn. subcom. on mil. procurement, subcom. on mil. pers. Served with U.S. Army, 1969-71, Vietnam. Decorated Air medal, Bronze Star. Mem. Navy League. Republican. Baptist. *

HUNTER, KATHLEEN, writer, educator; b. Portland, Oreg., Apr. 11, 1944; d. Harold Wayne and Ruthann (Breitmayer) McKenzie; m. Duncan Bert (Lillywhite) Hunter, July 13, 1963; children: Mindy Lynn, Dana Brad. Student, La. State U., Baton Rouge, 1962, Portland State U., 1963; BA in Journalism, U. Alaska, Fairbanks, 1984. Bookkeeper Consol. Freightways Ltd., others, 1964-72; advt. sales, feature writer Kodiak (Alaska) Fishwrapper, others, 1975-85; mag. editor U. Alaska, Fairbanks, 1983-84; freelance writer and editor Palmer, Alaska, 1984-88; English tchr. Mat-Su C.C., Palmer, 1989-93; life stories tchr. and writer Enterprise, Oreg., 1997—. Author, pub.: Tracking the "Bear," 1986, Alaska Nicknames, 1988; editor mag. Alaska Today, 1984. Bd. dirs., sec. Kids Are People, Palmer, 1993-97; mem., v.p. Valley Performing Arts, Palmer, 1991-97; v.p. 4-H Horse Leaders Coun., 1987; mem., sec. Palmer Hist. Soc., 1985-88. Recipient Joe and Claire Fejes Book Writing award U. Alaska, 1982, James Gordon Bennett award, 1984, various awards Alaska Press Women, 1984, 86, 3d Pl. award nat. Fedn. Presswomen, 1986; Natural Resource grantee Alaska N.W. Pub. Co., 1982, Lola Tilly scholar, 1982. Mem. AAUW, Phi Kappa Phi. Avocations: stained glass art, reading, genealogical research, gardening, acting. Home and Office: PO Box 553 Enterprise OR 97828

HUNTER, PATRICIA RAE (TRICIA), state official; b. Appleton, Minn., June 15, 1952; d. Harlan Ottowa and Clara Elizabeth (Tryhus) H.; m. Clark Waldon Crabbe, May 28, 1978 (div. July 1994); 1 child, Samantha Marcantonio. AS in Nursing, Good Samaritan Hosp., Phoenix, 1974; BS in Nursing, U. San Diego, San Diego, 1981; M Nursing, UCLA, 1985. RN. Oper. rm. supr. Alexian Bros., San Jose, Calif., 1985-86; dir. surg. svcs. Cmty. Hosp. Chula Vista, Calif., 1986-89; assemblywoman State Calif., San Diego, 1989-92; spl. asst. Gov. Wilson Office Statewide Health Planning & Devel., Sacramento, Calif., 1993-94; v.p. The Flannery Group, San Diego, 1997—; commr. Calif. Med. Assistance Commn., Sacramento, 1994—; bd. mem. Premier Home & Health, Phoenix, 1994-95; cons. Summit Schs., Ontario, Calif., 1992-93, hosp., Monterey, Calif., 1984—; mem. adv. bd. Alheimers Assn., San Diego, 1990-92, Arthritis Found., 1990-92. Pres. Calif. Rep. League, 1995-97. Named Rockie Legislator of Yr., Calif. Psychol. Assn., 1990, Legislator of Yr. Calif. Nurse Practitioners Assn., 1992; recipient Alice Pauly award Nat. Women Polit. Caucus, San Diego, 1991. Mem. ANA (v.p. 1982-85), Assn. Oper. Rm. Nurses, NWPC, Bus. and Profl. Orgn., Rotary (bd. mem. 1993-94), Sand Diego Red Cross (bd. mem.), Sigma Theta Tau (leadership award 1991). Republican. Lutheran. Home: 3260 E Fox Run Way San Diego CA 92111-7723 Office: The Flannery Group Ste 501 1121 L St Sacramento CA 95814

HUNTLEY, MARK EDWARD, biological oceanographer; b. Seattle, May 7, 1950; s. James Robert Huntley and Patricia Mary (Barricklow) Kissel; m. Patricia Darlene McFarlane, June 21, 1973 (div. 1980); children: Seth, Timothy; m. Kimberly Batcheller Brown, Sept. 19, 1981 (div. 1992); children: Swan Fairchild, Flannery Elizabeth, Zara Edith, Fletcher Wells. BSC with honors, U. Victoria, B.C., Can., 1976; PhD, Dalhousie U., Halifax, N.S., Can., 1980. Postdoctoral fellow Inst. Marine Resources, Scripps Instn. Oceanography, U. Calif. San Diego, La Jolla, Calif., 1980-82, asst. rsch. biologist, 1982-84; adj. lecturer Scripps Instn. Oceanography, U. Calif. San Diego, La Jolla, 1984—; asst. rsch. biologist marine biology rsch. div. Scripps Instn. Oceanography, La Jolla, 1984-87, assoc. rsch. biologist, 1987—; pres. Aquasearch, Inc., San Diego, 1984-88, chief oper. officer, 1988-93, CEO, 1993—, also chmn. bd. dirs., 1988—; deputy coord. water rsch. project U. Calif. San Diego, La Jolla, 1988-90; chmn. bd. dirs. Aquasearch, Inc., San Diego, 1984—; chief scientist Rsch. Antarctic Coastal Ecosystem Rates, La Jolla, 1986-87, 89, 91-92; exec. and steering com. mem. Global Ocean Ecosystem Dynamics, Washington, 1989—. Editor: Biological Treatment of Agricultural Wastewater, 1989; inventor Aquasearch Growth Module, 1989. Grantee Nat. Sci. Found. Office Naval Rsch., 1980—. Mem. Am. Soc. Limnology and Oceanography, Oceangraphy Soc. Avocations: tennis, gardening, music, body surfing. Office: 0202 Scripps Instn Oceanography La Jolla CA 92093

HUNTSMAN, EDWARD LOYD, business consultant, marketing executive; b. Farmington, N.Mex., Dec. 19, 1951; s. Arral B and Ann McFarland (Viles) H.; m. Debbie J. Komadina, Aug. 21, 1976; 1 child, Steven Christopher. Student, U. N.Mex., 1973-75; BS in Bus. Adminstrn., Pacific Western U., L.A., 1991, MBA in Mgmt., 1993. Staff instr. U. N.Mex., Gallup, 1976-78; sta. mgr., staff mgr. Frontier Airlines, Denver and Durango, Colo., 1977-85; corp. sales mgr. Tamarron Inn and Country Club, Durango, 1985-86; dir. mktg. Royal West Airlines, Las Vegas, 1986-88; mgr. sales and svc. Am. West Vacations, Tempe, Ariz., 1988-91; bus. and mktg. cons. Total Resource Network, Tempe, 1991—; mktg. cons. Huntsman Graphic Design, Phoenix, 1988—; call ctr. dir. Maxserv, Inc., Scottsdale, Ariz., 1993-97. Photographer: Graphic Art Collateral, 1983. Bd. dirs. McKinley County United Way, Gallup, 1976-78; mem. exec. bd. Boy Scouts Am., Las Vegas, 1986-87; staff instr. Police Athletic League, Albuquerque, 1978-80; mem. Durango Area Mktg. Group, 1985-86; elder Presbyn. Ch. U.S.A., Durango, 1985; master instr. USCG Aux., 1996, coxswain, 1996, flotilla comdr., 1997-98, divsn. vice capt., 1999—. Sgt. U.S. Army, 1969-73, Viet Nam and Germany. Decorated Army Commendation medal; recipient Outstanding Leadership award Albuquerque Police Athletic League, 1976, Cert. of Merit for stopping a hijacking attempt Air Transp. Assn. Am./FAA, 1983; col., aide-de-camp to Gov. of N.Mex., 1976; named to Outstanding Young Men of Am., 1987. Avocations: golf, sailing, skiing, fishing, photography. Office: Total Resource Network 2850 S Roosevelt St Tempe AZ 85282-2019

HUNTSMAN, JON MEADE, chemical company executive; b. 1937. BS, U. Pa., 1959, MBA, U. So. Calif., 1970. With Olson Bros. Inc., North Hollywood, Calif., from 1961; assoc. adminstr. HEW, spl. asst. to the pres., 1971-72; with Huntsman Container Corp., Salt Lake City, 1972-83, Huntsman Chem. Corp., Salt Lake City, 1982—; chmn. bd. dirs., CEO Huntsman Corp., Salt Lake City, 1996—. Pres. mission LDS Ch., Washington, 1980-83. Office: Huntsman Corp 500 Huntsman Way Salt Lake City UT 84108 1235

HUNTSMAN, LEE, university provost, academic administrator. Provost, v.p. acad. affairs U. Wash., Seattle. Office: U Wash PO Box 351237 Seattle WA 98195-1237*

HUPP, HARRY L., federal judge; b. L.A., Apr. 5, 1929; s. Earl L. and Dorothy (Goodspeed) H.; m. Patricia Hupp, Sept. 13, 1953; children: Virginia, Karen, Keith, Brian. AB, Stanford U., 1953, LLB, 1955. Bar: Calif. 1956, U.S. Dist. Ct. (cen. dist.) Calif. 1956, U.S. Supreme Ct. Pvt. practice law Beardsley, Hufstedler and Kemble, L.A., 1955-72; judge Superior Ct. of Los Angeles, 1972-84; appointed fed. dist. judge U.S. Dist. Ct. (cen. dist.) Calif., L.A., 1984-97, sr. judge, 1997—. Served with U.S. Army, 1950-52. Mem. Calif. Bar Assn., Los Angeles County Bar Assn. (Trial Judge of Yr. 1983), Order of Coif, Phi Alpha Delta. Office: US Dist Ct 312 N Spring St Ste 218P Los Angeles CA 90012-4704*

HUPPERT, MERLE CECIL, mechanical engineer; b. Dysart, Iowa, June 29, 1917; s. Edwin Alvertis and Rosa (Gulick) H.; m. Leslie Barbara Little, June 17, 1942; children: Judith, Daniel, Frederick. BSME, Iowa State U., 1942; postgrad., Case Inst. Tech., 1944-47, UCLA, 1957, 62. Mech. engr. NASA Lewis Rsch. Ctr., Cleve., 1942-56, Rocketdyne divsn. Rockwell Internat., Caonga Park, Calif., 1956-70; mgr. turbopump analysis sect. Aerojet Nuclear Sys. Co., Sacramento, 1970-72; surface effects ship performance supr. Aerojet Gen. Corp., Tacoma, 1972-74; mem. R&D staff, mech. engr. Aerojet-Gen. Corp., Liquid Rocket Co., Sacramento, 1974-83; pvt. practice cons. El Dorado Hills, Calif., 1984—. Patentee in field; contbr. articles to profl. publs. Recipient Apollo Achievement award NASA, 1969. ASME (sr.), AIAA, Sons in Retirement. Avocations: bowling, golf. Home: 3535 Mesa Verdes Dr El Dorado Hills CA 95762-4552

HURABIELL, JOHN PHILIP, SR., lawyer; b. San Francisco, June 2, 1947; s. Emile John and Anna Beatrice (Blumenauer) H.; m. Judith Marie Hurabiell, June 7, 1969; children—Marie Louise, Michele, Heather, John Philip Jr. J.D., San Francisco Law Sch., 1976. Bar: Calif. 1977. Sole practice, San Francisco, 1977-86; ptnr. Huppert & Hurabiell, San Francisco, 1985—; pres. San Francisco S.A.F.E., Inc., 1983-88, pres. emeritus 1988—. Treas. Rep. election coms.; 1st v.p. Bling Babies Found., 1989-91, bd. dir., sec., 1995-97, 98—; bd. dirs. Calif. State Mining and Mineral Mus., 1990-93. With USN, Vietnam. Decorated Navy Commendation Medal. Mem. Calif. Bar Assn., Assn. Trial Lawyers Am., San Francisco Trial Lawyers Assn., Lawyers Club San Francisco, St. Thomas More Soc., St. Francis Hook & Ladder Soc. (trustee). Roman Catholic. Clubs: The Family, Ferrari Club Am. (pres., chmn. Pacific region 1997-98, regional dir., 1998—), Golden Gate Breakfast Club. Lodge: KC, Alhambra (organizing regional dir. 1983-85). Editor, primary author: C.A.L.U. Business Practices Guidelines, rev. edit., 1980. Avocation: racing vintage automobiles. Office: Huppert & Hurabiell 1390 Market St Ste 1201 San Francisco CA 94102-5306

HURD, GALE ANNE, film producer; b. L.A., Oct. 25, 1955; d. Frank E. and Lolita (Espiau) H. Degree in econs. and communications, Stanford U., 1977. Dir. mktg. and publicity, co-producer New World Pictures, L.A., 1977-82; pres., producer Pacific Western Prodns., L.A., 1982—. Producer: (films) The Terminator, 1984 (Grand Prix Avoiriaz Film Festival award), Aliens 1986 (nominated for 7 Acad. awards, recipient Best Sound Effects Editing award, Best Visual Effects award Acad. Picture Arts & Scis.), Alien Nation (Saturn award for best sci. fiction film), The Abyss, 1989 (nominated for 4 Acad. awards, Best Visual Effects award), The Waterdance, 1991 (2 IFP Spirit awards, 2 Sundance Film Festival awards), Cast a Deadly Spell, 1991 (Emmy award), Raising Cain, 1992, No Escape, 1994, Safe Passage (Beatrice Wood award for Creative Achievement), 1994, The Ghost and the Darkness, 1996, The Relic, 1996, Going West in America, 1996, Dante's Peak, 1997, Virus, 1997, Dead Man on Campus, 1997, Armageddon, 1998, Dick, 1998; exec. producer: (films) Switchback, 1997, Tremors, 1990, Downtown, 1990, Terminator 2, 1991 (winner 3 Acad. awards), Witch Hunt, 1994, Sugartime, 1995; creative cons. (TV program) Alien Nation, 1989-90. Juror Focus Student Film Awards, 1989, 90, Nicholl Fellowship Acad. Motion Picture Arts & Scis., 1989—; mem. Show Coalition, 1988—; mem. Hollywood (Calif.) Women's Polit. Com., 1987—; mem. U.S. Film Festival Juror; bd. dirs. IFP/West, Artists Rights Found.; trustee Am. Film Inst.; bd. dirs. L.A. Internat. Film Festival, Coral Reef Rsch. Found., Ams. for a Safe Future; mentor Peter Stark Motion Picture Producing Program, Sch. of Cinema-TV, U. of So. Calif., Women in Film Mentor Program. Recipient Spl. Merit award Nat. Assn. Theater Owners, 1986, Stanford-La Entrepreneur of Yr. award Bus. Sch. Alumni L.A., 1990, Fla. Film Festival award, 1994. Mem. AMPAS (producer's br. exec. com. 1990—), Am. Film Inst. (trustee 1989—), Americans for a Safe Future (bd. dirs. 1993—), Women in Film (bd. dirs. 1989-90), Inst. for Rsch. on Women and Gender (nat. adv. panel 1997—), Feminist Majority, Phi Beta Kappa. Avocations: scuba diving, Paso Fino horses. Office: Pacific Western Prodns 270 N Canon Dr # 1195 Beverly Hills CA 90210-5323

HURLEY, BRUCE PALMER, artist; b. Tacoma, May 9, 1944; s. Gerald Baynton and Donna Ray (Whealey) H.; m. Ivy Jane Partridge; 1 child, Paul George. BS in Edn., Oreg. Coll. Edn., 1968. Cert. secondary edn. tchr. One-man shows include Goldberg's, 1966, Hillsboro Pub. Libr., 1969, 71, Valley Art Assn., Forest Grove, 1971, 74; group shows include Portland Art Mus., 1970, Northwest Artist Workshop, 1979, Sun Bird Gallery, 1986, Sunriver Juried Show, 1986, 92, Beaverton Arts Showcase, 1990, 91, 92, 93, 94, 96, 97, 98 (1st Place watercolor); represented in permanent collections Oreg. Coll., Oriental Medicine, David Wheeler, D.C., Libr. of Am. Psychiat. Assn., D.C., Schools Med. Plz., Tigard, Oreg., Atty. Mark Olson, N.Y.C., Nicholas S. Law, Cambridge, Eng., others; author: Planet Ploob Vacation, 1992, Divine Soliloquy, 1994; inventor: numerous paintings, drawings and sculptures. Mem. Portland Art Mus. Recipient Cmty. Svc. award Beaverton Arts Commn., 1993, Royal Patronage award Hutt River, Australia, 1995. Mem. Theosophical Soc. Avocations: musicology, camping, cooking, naturopathy, mysticism. Home: 251 NW Bailey St Hillsboro OR 97124-2903

HURLEY, FRANCIS T., archbishop; b. San Francisco, Jan. 12, 1927. Ed., St. Patrick Sem., Menlo Park, Calif., Catholic U. Am. Ordained priest Roman Cath. Ch., 1951; with Nat. Cath. Welfare Conf., Washington, asst. sec., 1958-68; assoc. sec. Nat. Cath. Welfare Conf., now U.S. Cath. Conf., 1968-70; consecrated bishop, 1970; titular bishop Daimlaig and aux. bishop Diocese of Juneau, Alaska, 1970-71; bishop of Juneau, 1971-76, archbishop of Anchorage, 1976—. Office: Archdiocese of Anchorage Chancery Office 225 Cordova St Anchorage AK 99501-2409*

HURLEY, MARK JOSEPH, bishop; b. San Francisco, Dec. 13, 1919; s. Mark J. and Josephine (Keohane) H. Student, St. Joseph's Coll., Mountain VIew, Calif., 1939, St. Patrick's Sem., Menlo Park, Calif., 1944; postgrad., U. Calif., Berkeley, 1943-45; PhD, Cath. U. Am., 1947; JCB, Lateran U., Rome, 1963; LLD, U. Portland, 1971. Ordained to priest Roman Cath. Ch., 1944. Asst. supt. schs. Archdiocese, San Francisco, 1944-51; tchr. Serra High Sch., San Mateo, Calif., 1944; prin. Bishop O'Dowd High Sch., Oakland, Calif., 1951-58, Marin Cath. High Sch., Marin County, Calif., 1959-61; supt. schs. Diocese, Stockton, Calif., 1962-65; chancellor, diocesan counsultor Diocese, 1962-65; asst. chancellor Arcdiocese, San Francisco, 1965-67; vicar gen. Arcdiocese, 1967-69; titular bishop Thunusuda; aux. bishop Thunusuda, San Francisco, 1967-69; bishop Santa Rosa, Cal., 1969—; pastor St. Francis Assisi Ch., San Francisco, 1967—; prof. grad. schs. Loyola U., Balt., 1946, U. San Francisco, 1948, San Francisco Coll. Women, 1949, Dominican Coll., San Rafael, Calif., 1949, Cath. U. Am., 1954; prof. theology Beda Coll. Rome, 1987—, Angelicum U., Rome, 1989—; Del. Conf. Psychiatry and Religion, San Francisco, 1957; mem. bd. Calif. Com. on Study Edn., 1955-60; cons. Congregation for Cath. Edn., 1986—; del.-at-large Cal., White House Conf. on Youth, 1960; Cath. del., observer Nat. Council Chs., Columbus, Ohio, 1964; del. edn. conf. German and Am. educators, Nat. Cath. Edn. Assn., Munich, Germany, 1960; mem. commns. sems., univs. and schs. II Vatican Council, Rome, 1962-65; mem. commn. Christian formation U.S. Cath. Conf. Bishops, 1968; asst. archdiocesan coordinator Campaign on Taxation Schs. Calif., 1958, Rosary Crusade, 1961; adminstr. Cath. Sch. Purchasing Div., 1948-51, St. Eugene's Ch., Santa Rosa, Calif., 1959, St.

John's Ch., San Francisco, 1961; mem. U.S. Bishops' Press Panel, Vatican Council, 1964-65, U.S. Bishops' Com. on Laity, 1964, U.S. Bishops' Com. Cath.-Jewish Relationships, 1965—, U.S. Bishops' Com. on Ecumenical and Interreligious Affairs, 1970, Conf. Maj. Superiors of Men, 1970; chmn. citizens Com. for San Francisco State Coll., 1968—; mem. adminstrn. bd. Nat. Council Cath. Bishops, 1970, mem. nominating com., 1971; mem. Internat. Secretariat for Non-Believers, Vatican, 1973; chmn. Secretariat for Human Values, Nat. Conf. Cath. Bishops, Washington, 1975; mem. Secretariat for Non-Believers, Vatican, 1986—; Vatican del. World Intellectual Properties Orgn., Washington, 1990; adj. prof. philosophy Grad. Theol. Union, Berkeley, Calif., 1994. Syndicated columnist San Francisco Monitor, Sacramento Herald, Oakland Voice, Yakima (Wash.) Our Times, Guam Diocesan Press, 1949-66, TV speaker and panelist, 1956-67; author: Church State Relationships in Education in California, 1948, Commentary on Declaration on Christian Education in Vatican II, 1966, Report on Education in Peru, 1965, The Church and Science, 1982, Blood on the Shamrock, 1989, The Unholy Ghost, 1992, Vatican Star, Star of David, 1996. Trustee N.Am. Coll., Rome, 1970, Cath. U. Am., 1978—, Cath. Relief Services, 1979; cons. Congregation for Edn.; mem. Secretariat for Non-Belief, Vatican City; bd. dirs. Overseas Blind Found., Ctr. for Theology and Natural Sci., Berkeley, FlaxTrust Corp., Belfast, Christians and Israel, Berkeley. Address: 273 Ulloa St San Francisco CA 94127-1226

HURT, CHARLIE DEUEL, III, dean, educator; b. Charlottesville, Va., Sept. 20, 1950; s. Charlie Deuel Jr. and Timie Oletta (Young) H.; m. Susan Edith Scudamore, May 15, 1981. BA, U. Va., 1971; MLS, U. Ky., 1975; PhD, U. Wis., 1981. Engring. librarian U. Va., Charlottesville, 1975-78, automation librarian, 1977-78; asst. prof. McGill U., Montreal, Que., Can., 1981-84, assoc. prof., 1984-86; assoc. prof. Simmons Coll., Boston, 1984-86; dir., prof. lib. sch. U. Ariz., Tucson, 1986-98, assoc. dean social and behavioral sci., 1998—; prin. Info. Prime, Montreal, 1984—; cons. Scudamore & Assocs. Montreal, 1984-85. Author: Information Sources in Science and Technology, 1998; co-author: Scientific and Technical Literature, 1990; contbr. articles to profl. jours. Hollowell grantee Simmons Coll., 1984. Mem. IEEE, Am. Soc. Info. Sci., Am. Mgmt. Assn., N.Y. Acad. Sci. Avocations: statistics, computing. Home: 1820 W Wimbledon Way Tucson AZ 85737-9070 Office: U Ariz Coll Social & Behavioral Sci 200 W Douglass Tucson AZ 85721

HURTADO, TRACY ELLEN, accountant; b. Roseville, Calif., Aug. 4, 1968; d. Corydon Dicks and Nancy (Trott) H. BS in Acctg. cum laude, Calif. State U., Sacramento, 1991. CPA, Nev. Audit mgr. Deloitte & Touche LLP, Reno, Nev., 1991—. Mem. Nev. Soc. CPAs, Inst. Mgmt. Accts. (sec. 1994-96), Delta Sigma Pi (dist. dir. U. Nev.-Reno chpt. 1991-93). Avocations: skiing, tennis, bike riding, volleyball, softball. Office: Deloitte & Touche LLP 50 W Liberty St Ste 900 Reno NV 89501-1949

HUSHEK, JOSEPH CHARLES, chemistry educator; b. Milw., Feb. 1, 1954; s. Charles Joseph and Patricia Louise (Zimmerman) H.; m. Kathleen Louise McFall, July 22, 1983. BA, Occidental Coll., 1976; MA, Fresno Pacific U., 1991. Sci. educator Selma (Calif.) Unified Sch. Dist., 1977—. Recipient yearbook dedication, 1988; fellow GIFT, 1991. Mem. NSTA, NEA, ASCD, Calif. Sci. Tchrs. Assn. Democrat. Roman Catholic. Avocations: golf, travel, scuba diving, snorkeling. Home: 1366 W Sample Ave Fresno CA 93711-2031 Office: Selma High 3125 Wright St Selma CA 93662-2499

HUSKEY, HARRY DOUGLAS, information and computer science educator; b. Whittier, N.C., Jan. 19, 1916; s. Cornelius and Myrtle (Cunningham) H.; m. Velma Elizabeth Roeth, Jan. 2, 1939 (dec. Jan. 1991); children: Carolyn, Roxanne, Harry Douglas, Linda; m. Nancy Grindstaff, Sept. 10, 1994. BS, U. Idaho, 1937; student, Ohio U., 1937-38; MA, Ohio State U., 1940, PhD, 1943. Temp. prin. sci. officer Nat. Phys. Labs., Eng., 1947; head machine devel. lab. Nat. Bur. Standards, 1948; asst. dir. Inst. Numerical Analysis, 1948-54; asso. dir. computation lab. Wayne U., Detroit, 1952-53; asso. prof. U. Calif., Berkeley, 1954-58, prof., 1958-68, vice chmn. elec. engring., 1965-66; prof. info. and computer sci. U. Calif., Santa Cruz, 1968-85, prof. emeritus, 1985—; dir. Computer Center, 1968-77, chmn. bd. info. sci., 1976-79, 82-83; vis. prof. Indian Inst. Tech., Kanpur (Indo-Am. program), 1963-64, 71, Delhi U., 1971; cons. computer div. Bendix, 1954-63; vis. prof. M.I.T., 1966; mem. computer sci. panel NSF, Naval Research Adv. Com.; cons. on computers for developing countries UN, 1969-71; chmn. com. to advise Brazil on computer sci. edn. NAS, 1970-72; project coord. UNESCO/Burma contract, 1973-79; mem. adv. com. on use microcomputers in developing countries NRC, 1983-85. Co-editor: Computer Handbook, 1962. Recipient Disting. Alumni award Idaho State U., 1978, Pioneer award Nat. Computer Conf., 1978, IEEE Computer Soc., 1982; U.S. sr.scientist awardee Fulbright-Alexander von Humboldt Found., Mathematisches Institut der Tech. U. Munich, 1974-75, 25th Ann. medal ENIAC; inducted into U. Idaho Alumni Hall of Fame, 1989. Fellow AAAS, ACM, IEEE (edit. bd., editor-in-chief computer group 1965-71, Centennial award 1984), Brit. Computer Soc.; mem. Am. Math. Soc., Math. Assn. Am., Assn. Computing Machinery (pres. 1960-62), Am. Fedn. Info. Processing Socs. (governing bd. 1961-63), Sigma Xi. Designed SWAC computer, Bendix G-15 and G-20 computers. Home: 10 Devant Ln Bluffton SC 29910-4534 Office: U Calif Computer & Info Sci Santa Cruz CA 95064

HUSSEY, WILLIAM BERTRAND, retired foreign service officer; b. Bellingham, Wash., Oct. 23, 1915; s. Bertrand Brokaw and Ruth (Axtell) H.; m. Fredricka Boone, Dec. 31, 1940 (div. 1957); children: Christina, Pamela, Eva, William Bertrand, Peter; m. Piyachart Bunnag, May 20, 1959. B.S., Boston U., 1938; postgrad., UCLA, 1939-40, Naval War Coll., 1953-54. Asst. housing mgmt. supr. U.S. Housing Authority, 1941-42; chmn. London (Eng.) Liaison Group, also State Dept. rep., 1948-52; spl. State Dept. rep., Rome, 1949, Paris, 1950; chmn. regional conf., Dhahran, Saudi Arabia, 1949, chief civil-mil. relations sect., Munich, Germany, 1952-53, adminstrv. officer, Frankfurt, Germany, 1953-55, attache, Rangoon, Burma, 1955-56, consul, Chiengmai, Thailand, 1957-59; acting dep. chief plans and devel. staff Bur. Ednl. and Cultural Affairs, Dept. State, 1959-60, dep. chief cultural presentations div., 1960-61; mem. del. regional confs. in, Beirut, Lebanon and Kampala, Uganda, 1960; group leader Nat. Strategy Seminar, Asilomar, Calif., 1960; counselor of embassy, Lome, Republic of Togo, 1961-65, Blantyre, Malawi, 1965-66; chargé d'affaires Am. embassys, Maseru, Lesotho, and Tananarive, Madgascar, 1966-67, Port Louis, Mauritius, 1967-68; UN rep., Western Pacific, Apia, Western Samoa, 1969-74, fgn. affairs cons., 1974—; del. UN Law of Sea Conf., 1975-80; assoc. v.p. Los Angeles Olympic Organizing Com., 1982-84; dir. govt. relations Statue of Liberty Centennial, Liberty Weekend, 1986. Served with U.S. Mcht. Marine, 1930-33; served to lt. comdr. USN, 1942-48, ETO; PTO; capt. Res. Recipient Superior Service award Sec. of State, 1968. Address: 5563B Via Portora Laguna Hills CA 92653-6902

HUSTON, HARRIETTE IRENE OTWELL (REE HUSTON), retired county official; d. Harry C. Otwell and Fannie (Mitchell) Otwell Geffert; m. Dan E. Huston, Jan. 21, 1951; children: Terry Dane, Dale Curtis, Ronald William, Randall Philip. BS, Kans. State Coll., 1951. Cert. life & health ins. agt., Wash.; cert. wastewater operator in tng., Wash. Tchr. Kans., Ill., 1955-68; assoc. home economist McCall's Patterns Co., N.Y.C., 1959-62; counselor, owner Dunhill of Seattle Personnel, 1968-75; enrollment officer, trainer, adminstrv. sec. Teller Tng. Insts., Seattle, 1975-76; life and health ins. agt. Lincoln Nat. Sales, Seattle, 1976-77; office mgr., adminstrv. sec. ARA Transp. Group, Seattle, 1977-78; asst. to the pres. Pryde Corp., Bellevue, Wash., 1978-80; sr. sec. Municipality of Met. Seattle, 1980-92, project asst., 1992-93; adminstrv. specialist II King County Dept. Met. Svcs. (formerly Municipality of Met. Seattle, 1993-95; primary and secondary substitute tchr. Sequim (Wash.) Pub. Schs., 1996—. Co-author: Homemaking textbook, 1956; contbr. articles to profl. jours.. Sec. exec., mem. gen. bd. Bellevue Christian Ch., Disciples of Christ, 1976-77, 86-87, chmn. flowers com., 1978-83, elder, 1978, deacon, 1987; bd. dirs., sec. Surrey Downs Cmty. Club, Bellevue, 1983-85; mem. choir Sequim Presbyn. Ch., 1994—, elder, 1996-99, chair congl. life com., 1996-99; vol. leader, coord. Linking Home and Sch. Through the Workplace, 1992-93. Recipient Clothing award check McCall's Patterns Co., N.Y.C., 1962, Certs. of Merit Metro Hdqrs., Seattle, 1981, 82, 83, 86, 89. Mem. Bellevue Bridge Club. Avocations: flower gardening and arranging, interior decorating, home remodeling. Home: 1783 E Sequim Bay Rd Sequim WA 98382-7657

HUSTON, JIMMY, screenwriter, film director; b. Dalton, Ga., Sept. 14, 1947; m. Lynn Mills; children: Georgia, Veronica. BA, U. Ga., 1969. Writer, dir. Viscount Prodns., Atlanta, 1969-71, Peter Barton Prodns., Tallahasse, Fla., 1971-73; dir. EO Prodns., Shelby, N.C., 1974-77; freelance writer, dir. Hollywood, Calif., 1978-83; writer, dir. Motion Picture Mktg., Marina Del Rey, Calif., 1981; screenwriter Metro Goldwyn Mayer/United Artists, Culver City, Calif., 1983-87; dir. Kings Road Entertainment, Los Angeles, 1986-87; screenwriter Universal Pictures, Universal City, Calif., 1987—, Paramount Pictures, Hollywood, 1988—; adj. prof. art U. Tex., Arlington, 1978-86. Screenwriter: Running Scared, 1986, K-9, 1988, Double Whammy, 1988; dir. (films) Death Driver, 1975, Dark Sunday, 1976, Buckstone County Prison, 1977, My Best Friend Is A Vampire, 1987; screenwriter, dir.: Final Exam, 1982, The Wharf Rat (Showtime), 1995; dir. (TV series) High Tide, 1996-97. Mem. Writers Guild Am. Avocations: vintage auto racing, bicycling. Home and Office: 3722 Woodcliff Rd Sherman Oaks CA 91403-5050

HUSTON, MARK LOUIS, economics educator; b. San Francisco, Dec. 5, 1951; s. Arthur Robert and Doris June (Crouch) H.; m. Anne Beyer (div. 1980); 1 child, Lauren Suzanne; m. Edel Corla Savage, Sept. 30, 1982 (div. Feb. 1996); 1 child, Mardel Leyland. BA in Bus., U. San Francisco, 1977; MA in Econs., U. Pitts., 1979; MBA in Bus. Adminstrn., Calif. Coast U., 1987, PhD in Bus. Adminstrn., 1994. Med. adminstrn. specialist USAF, 1970-74; supr. data processing Pacific Mut. Ins. Co., Corte Madera, Calif., 1974-77; asst. fellow U. Pitts., 1977-79; sr. forecast analyst General Tire & Rubber, Akron, Ohio, 1979-81; supr., mgmt. cons. Arabian Bechtel, Jubail, Saudi Arabia, 1981-83; sr. cons., pres. Bus. and Econ. Svcs., San Rafael, Calif., 1983-89; regional v.p. IMPAC, Litchfield, Conn., 1989-90; prof. econs. San Diego-Mesa Coll., San Diego, 1990—. Author: Executive Computer Literacy, 1986, Drug Abuse-Clinet-Pay Programs; Insurance Billing Intake and Billing Handbook, 1986, Economic Principles and Course Notes, 1st edit., 1992, 2d edit., 1993, 3d edit., 1996; producer World War II Film series, 1993. Sgt. USAF, 1970-74. Mem. Am. Fedn. Tchr. Republican. Avocations: swimming, camping, political analysis, film (WWII), hand gunning. E-mail: dramrk@cts.com. Home: 6202 Friars Rd Unit 123 San Diego CA 92108-1099 Office: Mesa Coll 7520 Mesa College Dr San Diego CA 92111-5000

HUTCHERSON, CHRISTOPHER ALFRED, marketing, recruiting and educational fundraising executive; b. Memphis, June 13, 1950; s. Alfred Wayne Hutcherson and Loretta (Morris) Kindsfather; m. Glenda Ann Champ, May 22, 1971 (dec. 1995); m. Barbara A. Haralson, Sept. 27, 1998. *Mr. Hutcherson credits his success to a combination of traits he learned from several extraordinary people. Loretta Kindsfather, mother/business professional (tunnelvision, persistence, fearlessness). Glenda Hutcherson, deceased first wife (how to love and never give up). Barbara Hutcherson, 2nd wife (how to appreciate love, happiness, and life). Vince Ray, marine/executive (dedication/loyalty). Dan Hillard and Mark Elstad, executives (teamwork and commitment), Wayne Hutcherson, father/farmer (work ethic). Brunetta Morris, grandmother/elementary school principal (love of education). Clarence Morris, grandfather/cotton gin manager (serve others with unselfishness). Henry Kindsfather, stepfather/cowboy (consistency/respect for others). Ben Gollehon, band teacher (competitiveness).* BS, U. Houston, 1972, MA in Adminstrn., 1977, postgrad., 1977-79. Cert. tchr. and adminstr., Tex. Pvt. music instr. Spring Br. and Pasadena Ind. Sch. Dists., Tex., 1968-75; jr. high and high sch. band dir. Deer Park (Tex.) Ind. Schs., 1972-80; recruiter M. David Lowe Personnel, Houston, 1981; sales dir. Instl. Financing Svcs., Benicia, Calif., 1982-85; sales mgr. Instl. Financing Svcs., Benicia, 1985-87; nat. tng. dir. Champion Products and Svcs., San Diego, 1987-88, west coast and midwest sales mgr., 1988-89; pres. Camelot, Inc., Auburn, Calif., 1989-91; pres., CEO Camelot Telephone Assistance Program, Inc., Folsom, Calif., 1991-92; nat. dir. sales and mktg. edn. and devel. Nat. Scrip Ctr., Inc., Santa Rosa, Calif., 1992-95; exec. v.p. Scrip Plus Inc., Fresno, Calif., 1995-96; chmn., pres., CEO Children's Heros, Inc., Auburn, 1996—; fund raising cons. non-profit orgns., 1982—; speaker in field. *Mr. Hutcherson is one of the nation's preeminent cause related marketing experts. His career achievements have placed him in "Who's Who" sixteen times in six categories. He is acknowledged as a leader who can bring vision to reality. As a speaker, he delivers an address reflective of commitment to improve children's educational opportunities. He has written an entire methodology and curriculum for national voluntarism. He is dedicated to children with an enthusiasm that motivates people to action. He has raised over 178 million dollars for schools. His life is devoted to developing a permanent source of funding for this nation's schools.* Judge Tex. jr. high and high sch. bands, 1974-81, regional band chmn., 1973-77; choir dir. St. Hyacinth Ch., Deer Park, 1979-81; vice chmn. Ch. Coun. St. Hyacinth Ch., 1980; founder Tex. Region XIX Jr. High Band Competition, 1973 (Spl. Achievement award 1979); 1st chair clarinet Tex. All-State Band, 1968; founder, pres. Glenda Hutcherson Heros Found., 1996—; creator Heroes Reward Card Program, 1996—; founder, pres. Childrens Heros Fund. Mem. Kappa Kappa Psi (v.p. Outstanding Mem. award 1970). Republican. Roman Catholic. Avocations: golf, reading, movies. Home: 14105 Lodestar Dr Grass Valley CA 95949-8362

HUTCHESON, JERRY DEE, manufacturing company executive; b. Hammon, Okla., Oct. 31, 1932; s. Radford Andrew and Ethel Mae (Boulware) H.; B.S. in Physics, Eastern N. Mex. U., 1959; postgrad. Temple U., 1961-62, U. N.Mex., 1964-65; m. Lynda Lou Weber, Mar. 6, 1953; children—Gerald Dan, Lisa Marie, Vicki Lynn. Research engr. RCA, 1959-62; sect. head Motorola, 1962-63; research physicist Dikewood Corp., 1963-66; sr. mem. tech. staff Signetics Corp., 1966-69; engring. mgr. Litton Systems, Sunnyvale, Calif., 1969-70; engring. mgr. Fairchild Semiconductor, Mountain View, Calif., 1971; equipment engr., group mgr. Teledyne Semiconductor, Mountain View, 1971-74; dir. engring. DCA Reliability Labs., Sunnyvale, 1974-75; founder, prin. Tech. Ventures, San Jose, Calif., 1975—; chief exec. officer VLSI Research, Inc., 1981—. Democratic precinct committeeman, Albuquerque, 1964-66. Served with USAF, 1951-55. Registered profl. engr., Calif. Mem. Nat. Soc. Profl. Engrs., Profl. Engrs. Pvt. Practice, Calif. Soc. Profl. Engrs., Semiconductor Equipment and Materials Inst., Soc. Photo-Optical Instrumentation Engrs., Am. Soc. Test Engrs., Presbyterian. Club: Masons. Contbr. articles to profl. jours. Home: 5950 Vista Loop San Jose CA 95124-6562 Office: VSLI Rsch 1754 Technology Dr Ste 117 San Jose CA 95110-1308

HUTCHINSON, DONALD WILSON, state commissioner of financial institutions; b. Seattle, Dec. 29, 1936. BS in Bus. and Edn., Mont. State U., 1960; Grad. Degree in Banking, Pacific Coast Banking Sch., Seattle, 1979. With First Nat. Bank, Bozeman, Mont., 1963-69, Owatonna, Minn., 1969-71; with First Security Bank, Livingston, Mont., 1971-82; v.p. Bank of Sheridan, Mont., 1983-84; gen. mgr., cons. Pryor Creek Devel. Co., Billings, Mont., 1984-85; chief lending officer Valley Bank of Belgrade, Mont., 1986-90; commr. State of Mont. Divsn. Banking and Fin. Instns., Helena, 1990—. Dir. Livingston (Mont.) Meml. Hosp., Livingston Alcohol & Drug Abuse Ctr., Gallatin County (Mont.) Big Bros. and Big Sisters; mem. Belgrade City/County Planning Bd.; treas., bd. trustees, Paul Clark Home/McDonald's Family Place, Butte, Mont. Mem. Livingston Rotary Club (past pres.). Office: Divsn Banking & Fin Instns PO Box 200546 Helena MT 59620-0546

HUTCHINSON, EDWARD PAUL, city official; b. Tucson, May 19, 1961; s. Willard Lafayette and Dorothy Jean (Ellis) H. AAS in Security Adminstrn., C.C. of the Air Force, Montgomery, Ala., 1989; AAS in Electronic Sys. Tech., C.C. of the Air Force, 1994. Cert. peace officer, Ariz.; emergency med. technician; cert. field tng. officer. Enlisted U.S. Air Force, 1978, served in U.S., Europe, Asia, Africa, 1978-95; Elite Guard flight chief 7001st Spl. Security Squadron, Ramstein Air Base, West Germany, 1983-86; non-commd. officer in charge secure communication 53d Combat Communications Squadron, Robins AFB, Ga., 1987-90; aircraft security flight chief 836th Security Police Squadron, Davis-Monthan AFB, Ariz., 1990-91, non-commd. officer in charge, confinement, 1991; shift comdr. 355th Security Police Squadron, Davis-Monthan AFB, 1991-95; ret. USAF, 1995; quality advisor, 1992-95; adult probation surveillance officer Pima County, Tucson, 1996-97; res. officer Tucson Police Dept., 1991-94, South Tucson Police Dept., 1996—; mil. customs insp. U.S. Customs Svc., Nogales, Ariz., 1991-95. Troop com. mem. Boy Scouts Am., Robins AFB, 1988-89; vol. emergency med. technician USAF Clinic, Spangdahlem Air Base, West Germany, 1982-83. Decorated Air Force Commendation medal, two Air Force Achievement medals, Air Force Meritorious Svc. medal; named to Outstanding Young Men in Am., 1987. Christian. Avocations: hunting, fishing, camping, motorcycles, community service. Office: Pima County Adult Probation 2695 E Ajo Way Tucson AZ 85713-6213

HUTCHINSON, JOSEPH CANDLER, retired foreign language educator; b. Hazelhurst, Ga., Jan. 10, 1920; s. George Washington and Lillie Arizona (Rowan) H.; m. June Cruce O'Shields, Aug. 12, 1950 (div. 1980); children: Junie O'Shields, Joseph Candler. BA, Emory U., 1940, MA, 1941; PhD, U. N.C., 1950; postgrad. U. Paris, summers 1951, 53. Tchr., Tech. High Sch., Atlanta, 1941-42; instr. French, German, Italian, Emory U., Atlanta, 1946-47; instr. U. N.C., Chapel Hill, 1947-50, asst. prof., 1954, assoc. prof., to 1957; asst. prof. Sweet Briar (Va.) Coll., 1950-51, 53-54; assoc. prof. Tulane U., New Orleans, 1957-59; fgn. lang. specialist U.S. Office Edn., Washington, 1959-64; acad. adv. hdqrs. Def. Lang. Inst., Washington, 1964-74, Monterey, 1974-77, dir. tng. devel. Def. Lang. Inst. Fgn. Lang. Ctr., Monterey, Calif., 1977-82, asst. acad. dean, 1982-85; dean of policy, from 1985-88; vis. prof. U. Va., Charlottesville, 1966, Arlington, 1970, Georgetown U., 1968, Am. U., 1971; cons. Council of Chief State Sch. Officers, 1960, U. Del., 1966, U. Colo., 1968, U. Ill., 1968; U.S. del. Bur. Internat. Lang. Coordination, NATO, 1964-79, 81-82, 86-87. Author: Using the Language Laboratory Effectively: School Executive's Guide, 1964, The Language Laboratory: Equipment and Utilization in Trends in Language Teaching, 1966, others; editor Dialog on Language Instruction, 1986-88; contbr. articles to profl. jours. Served with U.S. Army (spl. agent, Counter Intellegence Corps), 1942-46, 51-53. Decorated Bronze Star, 5 Battle Stars-Europe, battlefield commission. Mem. Am. Council on Edn. (task force on internat. edn. 1973), NEA (sec. dept. fgn. langs. 1961-64), AARP/VOTE (17th Congl. dist. team), Higher Edn. Assn. Monterey Peninsula, Am. Council on Teaching of Fgn. Lang., MLA, Am. Mgmt. Assn., Am. Soc. Tng. and Devel., Nat. Assn. Ret. Fed. Employees (v.p. Monterey chpt. 1990, pres. 1991-92), Monterey Choral Soc., Camerata Singers, Washington Linguistics Club (v.p. 1970-72). Episcopalian.

HUTCHINSON, WILLIAM KINSEY, III, broadcast executive; b. Carlisle, Pa., Apr. 27, 1953; s. William Kinsey II and Lois Ann (Lackey) H. Student, St. Mary's Internat., Tokyo, 1960-61, Volkshochschule, Karlsruhe, Germany, 1973; BFA, Calif. Inst. of the Arts, Velencia, 1977; MBA, Pepperdine U., 1988. Travel cons. AAA, Washington, 1973-74; park attraction ops. Disneyland, Anaheim, Calif., 1975-78; sales rep. United Airlines, L.A., 1978-84; exec. prodr., mgr. media svcs. The Boeing Co., Long Beach, Calif., 1984—; mem. bd. advisors-rsch. Am. Biog. Inst., 1990—. Editor: New Students Handbook, 1976, Flight Test Progress Report, 1991-94. Mem. Am. Film Inst., S.W. Informational Nomad User's Group (v.p. 1992-93, editor newsletter 1992-93), The Boeing Co. Mgmt. Club. Democrat. Anglican. Avocations: genealogy, photography, travel, cycling. Home: 2071 Crescent Dr Long Beach CA 90804-5620 Office: The Boeing Co D036-0099 3855 N Lakewood Blvd Long Beach CA 90846-0003 also: Boeing 2071 Crescent Dr Signal Hill CA 90804-5620

HUTCHISON, LOYAL DWAYNE, pharmacist; b. Stockton, Calif., Jan. 3, 1933; s. Lester and Muriel (Van Nortwick) H.; m. Jean E. McColl, Jan. 26, 1961; children: Michael, Donald. BS in Pharmacy, U. Pacific, 1966. Pharmacist Fifth St. Pharmacy, Stockton, 1966-76, prin., 1976—; prin. Hutchison Pharmacies Inc., Stockton, 1976—, McKinley Pharmacy, Stockton, 1976—, Lathrop (Calif.) Pharmacy, 1976—. Served with U.S. Army, 1957-59. Fellow Am. Coll. Apothecary; mem. Calif. Pharmacists Assn. (Pac Silver Circle), Am. Pharmacists Assn. Avocations: nordic skiing, backpacking, fishing, theatre. Home: PO Box 1737 Stockton CA 95201-1737 Office: Hutchison Pharmacies Inc 1839 S El Dorado St Stockton CA 95206-2025

HUTNER, HERBERT L., financial consultant, lawyer; b. N.Y.C.; s. Nathan M. and Ethel (Helhor) H.; m. Juli Reding, Nov. 28, 1969; children by previous marriage: Jeffrey J., Lynn M. Colwell; 1 stepson, Christopher D. Taylor. B.A., Columbia U., 1928, J.D., 1931. Bar: N.Y. 1932. Ptnr., Osterman & Hutner, mem. N.Y. Stock Exch., N.Y.C., 1945-57; successively pres. N.E. Life Insurance Co., N.Y.C.; chmn. bd. Sleight & Hellmuth Inc., N.Y.C.; chmn. bd. Pressed Metals of Am., Port Huron, Mich.; chmn. bd. Struthers Wells Corp., Warren, Pa., Plateau Mining Co. Inc., Oak Ridge, Tenn.; investor, cons., L.A., 1963—; dir. United Artists Communications, Inc., 1965-87, Todd AO-Glen Glen, 1987—, L.A. Rams, 1972-75, mem. adv. bd., 1991—; chmn. bd. Cellvent, Inc., 1991—. Chmn. pres.'s adv. com. on arts, Kennedy Ctr., 1982-90; founder L.A. Music Ctr.; chmn. profl. sports com. United Way; corporator Schepens Eye Rsch. Inst., Boston; mem. internat. adv. com. Up With People. Decorated title DATO, Sultan of Johore, Malaysia, Highest Order of the Crown, 1981. Mem. ASCAP, Deepdale Golf Club (Manhasset, N.Y.). Composer: The Super Bowl Song, Go Rams Go, others.

HUTTER, JOHN JOSEPH, JR., pediatric hematologist and oncologist, educator; b. Queens, N.Y., Jan. 26, 1943; s. John Joseph and Dorothy (Bey) H.; m. Maureen J. Lynch, June 17, 1967; children: Catherine, Carolyn. BS in Biology with honors, Manhattan Coll., Riverdale, N.Y., 1963; MD magna cum laude, SUNY, Bklyn., 1967. Diplomate Am. Bd. Pediatrics, sub-bds. hematology and oncology; lic. physician, Calif., Colo., Ariz. Intern, resident in pediatrics Stanford U. Med. Ctr., Palo Alto, Calif., 1967-69; resident in pediatrics U. Colo. Med. Ctr., Denver, 1969-70, NIH trainee in pediatric hematology, 1972-73, instr. pediatrics, 1973-76; assoc. dir. oncology ctr. Children's Hosp., Denver, 1973-76; from asst. prof. to prof. pediatrics U. Ariz. Health Scis. Ctr., Tucson, 1976—, dir. pediatric clin. oncology, 1976—, chief sect. pediatric hematology/oncology, 1991—, dir. Mountain States Regional Hemophilia Ctr., 1990—. Contbr. chpts. to textbooks, articles to profl. jours.; author revs. Trustee Ronald McDonald House, 1979-87, v.p., 1981-83; mem. Tucson Emergency Svcs. Coordinating Coun., 1982-85; trustee Am. Cancer Soc., 1984-85; mem. Angel Charity for Children, 1984—; mem. adv. bd. Children-to-Children, 1991—. Fellow Am. Acad. Pediatrics; mem. Am. Soc. Hematology, Am. Soc. Clin. Oncology, Am. Soc. Pediatric Hematology/Oncology, Am. Acad. Home Care Physicians, Hemophilia Rsch. Soc., We. Soc. for Pediatric Rsch., Alpha Omega Alpha. Avocations: hiking, bird watching. Home: 5770 N Camino Real Tucson AZ 85718-4214 Office: U Ariz Dept Pediatrics 1501 N Campbell Ave Tucson AZ 85724-0001

HUXLEY, MARY ATSUKO, artist; b. Stockton, Calif., Mar. 5, 1930; d. Henry K. and Kiku H. (Kisanuki) Taniguchi; m. Harold Daniels Huxley, 1957. Student, San Francisco Art Inst., 1968; studied with, Thomas C. Leighton, 1970-75. art show judge regional art clubs, corps., pvt. orgns., and county fairs, 1972-98. Solo shows include Artists' Coop., San Francisco, 1973, 75, 76, The Univ. Club, San Francisco, 1976, I. Magnin, San Mateo, 1976, Palo Alto Med. Found., 1992, Galerie Genese, San Mateo, 1993; exhibited in group shows at Catharine Lorillard Wolf Art Club, N.Y.C., 1979, Knickerbocker Artists of Am., N.Y.C., 1979, Salmagundi Club Ann., N.Y.C., 1981, Butler Inst. Am. Art, Youngstown, Ohio, 1982, Am. Artists Profl. League, N.Y.C., 1982, 83, 86, 87, 88, Oil Painters of Am. Ann. Nat. Juried Shows, Gallery at Long Grove, Ill., 1993, 94, Taos, N.Mex., 1997, Oil Painters of Am. Ann. Pacific Coast Regional Juried Show, Jones & Terwilliger Gallery, Carmel, Calif., 1997, San Francisco Ann. Art Festival, 1970-74, Renaissance Gallery, Santa Rosa, Calif., 1973, Paramount Theater, Oakland, Calif., 1974, Met. Club Invitational, San Francisco, Marin Soc. Artists Ann., Ross, Calif., 1976, 97, Soc. Western Artists Ann., San Francisco, 1976, 78, 80, Peninsula Art Assn. Ann., Belmont, Calif., 1980, Fresno (Calif.) Fashion Fair Ann., 1981, 84, De Saisset Gallery, U. Santa Clara, Calif., 1979, Lodi (Calif.) Ann. Grape and Art Festival, 1970, 71, 72, 73, 74, 75, 76, 77, 78, 79, 81, San Mateo County Ann. Floral Fiesta, 1975, 76, 77, 78, 79, 81, Charles & Emma Frye Mus. Gallery, Seattle, 1975, Redwood City Women's Club Ann. Flower Show, 1978, Fremont Art Assn. Anns., 1987, 88, 89, numerous others; represented in numerous pvt. and corp. collections in U.S., Europe and the Far East. Recipient Marjorie Walter Spl. award San Mateo County Exhbn., 1975, Gold medallion and 1st award San Mateo County Fair Fine Arts Exhbn., 1976, Best of Show award Cultural Arts of Palo Alto and Palo Alto Art Club, 1979, Best of Show and 1st award U. Art Ctr. and Palo Alto Art Club Ann., 1981, Spl. Merit award Oakland Art Assn., John Muir Med. Ctr. Ann., 1989, 1st award Burlingame Art Soc. Anns., 1976, 77, 1st award Redwood City Women's Club Ann. Flower Show, 1978, 1st award Soc. Western Artists Palo Alto Med. Ctr. Ann., 1983, 1st award Soc. Soc. Western Artists John Muir Med. Ctr. Ann., 1986, 1st award Fremont Art Assn.

Ann., 1989, numerous others. Mem. Am. Artists Profl. League, Soc. Western Artists (signature, trustee 1986-97, bd. dirs. 1972-75, 98, chmn. juried exhbns. 1998), Am. Soc. Classical Realism, Oil Painters Am. (signature), Allied Artists Am., Marin Soc. Artists (signature), Palo Alto Cultural Ctr. Studio: PO Box 5467 San Mateo CA 94402-0467

HWANG, ALICE YA-PING, architect; b. Honolulu, Aug. 18, 1973; d. Ho Wan and Bessie Chu-Mei (Liu) H. BArch, Tulane U., 1996. Architect AM Ptnrs. Inc., Honolulu, 1996—. Mem. AIA. Avocations: travel, photography. Office: AM Ptnrs Inc 1164 Bishop St Ste 1000 Honolulu HI 96813-2815

HWANG, CORDELIA JONG, chemist; b. N.Y.C., July 14, 1942; d. Goddard and Lily (Fung) Jong; m. Warren C. Hwang, Mar. 29, 1969; 1 child, Kevin. Student Alfred U., 1960-62; BA, Barnard Coll., 1964; M.S., SUNY-Stony Brook, 1969. Rsch. asst. Columbia U., N.Y.C., 1964-66; analytical chemist Veritron West Inc., Chatsworth, Calif., 1969-70; asst. lab. dir., chief chemist Pomeroy, Johnston & Bailey Environ. Engrs., Pasadena, Calif., 1970-76; chemist Met. Water Dist. So. Calif., Los Angeles, 1976-79, rsch. chemist 1980-91, sr. chemist 1992—; mem. Joint Task Group on Instrumental Identification of Taste and Odor Compounds, 1983-85, instr. Citrus Coll., 1974-76; chair Joint Task Group on Disinfection by-products: chlorine, 1990. Mem. Am. Chem. Soc., Am. Water Works Assn. (cert. water quality analyst level 3, Calif.-Nev.), Am. Soc. for Mass Spectometry. Office: Met Water Dist So Calif 700 Moreno Ave La Verne CA 91750-3303

HWANG, KOU MAU, pharmaceutical executive; b. Kaoshiung, Taiwan, Sept. 5, 1940; came to U.S., 1966; s. Tien C. and Zui C. (Yu) H.; m. Sue H. Cheng, Sept. 5, 1969; children: Sandy, Carol, Nancy. BS, Kaohsiung Med. Coll., 1964; MS, Ohio State U., 1969, PhD, 1972; postgrad., Yale U., 1974. Teaching asst. Duquesne U., Pitts., 1965-66, Ohio State U., Columbus, Ohio, 1967-71; rsch. fellow Yale Med. Sch., New Haven, 1972-76; asst. prof. M.D. Anderson Hosp./Univ. Tex., Houston, 1976-77, U. So. Calif., L.A., 1977-79; sr. investigator Nat. Cancer Inst., Frederick, Md., 1980-83; sr. scientist Cetus Inc., San Francisco, 1984; sr. dir. Genelabs Inc., Redwood City, Calif., 1985-93; pres. Sintong Pharm. U.S. Inc., Hayward, Calif., 1993—; vis. prof. Rutger U., Piscataway, N.J., 1985-88; educator Internat. AIDS Confs., U.S., China, 1989; cons., lectr. Kaushiung Med. Coll., Taiwan, 1991-92. Patentee AIDS Therapy, 1989, New Therapy for Herpes Simplex, 1992; inventor in field; contbr. numerous articles to profl. jours. Cultural exch. person Taiwanese Prof. Assn., 1990—. 2nd lt. Taiwanese Army, 1964-65. Rsch. grantee Welch Found., Houston, 1977, Am. Cancer Soc., L.A., 1977-80; sml. bus. grantee U.S. Govt., San Carlo, Calif., 1987-88; recipient Nat. Drug Discovery grants NIAID, Redwood City, 1988-91. Mem. Am. Assn. Cancer Rsch., Am. Chem. Soc., AAAS, Rho Chi. Avocations: sports, gardening, music, sailing, home scientific experiments. Home: 220 Stanbridge Ct Danville CA 94526-2630 Office: Sintong Pharm US Inc 3401 Investment Blvd Hayward CA 94545-3801

HWANG, TZU-YANG, minister; b. Kaohsiung, Taiwan, Republic of China, Sept. 21, 1953; came to U.S., 1985; d. Chi-Chou and Iu-Chih (Tsai) Huang; m. Wei-Chih Shih Hwang, Sept. 6, 1980. MD, Tainan Theol. Sem., 1980; ThD, Princeton (N.J.) Theol. Sem., 1986; PhD, Chinese for Christ Theol. Sem., Rosemead, Calif., 1990. Ordained to ministry Presbyn. Ch. Chairperson, min. Presbytery's Zrhlin Dists. Ch., Champhua, Taiwan, 1981-83; min., lectr., sr. editor Tainan Theol. Sem., 1983-85; founder, min. The Youth Fellowship of Kingston Presbyn. Ch., Princeton, 1985-86; head of religion edn., lectr. Good Shepherd Formosan Presbyn. Ch., Monterey Park, Calif., 1987-88; head of religion edn., lectr. Chinese for Christ Theol. Sem., 1987-88, dir. theology and philosophy, dean students, sr. editor, 1990-98; founder., pres., prof., CEO Am. Chi Chou Theo-Philosophical Inst., 1998—; Vis. Scholar, Harvard U. Div. Sch., Duke U. Div. Sch., Emory U. Candler Sch. Theol., 1991-92; sr. pastor, pres. Light Christ Ch.; chmn., pres., incorporator, bd. dirs., Light Christ Found. Contbr. articles to profl. jours. With Chinese Def., 1972-74. mem. Am. Acad. Religion, Soc. Biblical Literature, ABIRA (internat. and continental gov., internat. Order of Ambassadors), Internat. Biog. Ctr. (dir. gen. honors list), Assn. IBC, Internat. Order of Merit (bd. mem.), Leading Intellectuals of World (founding charter mem.), others. Home: 11768 E Roseglen St El Monte CA 91732-1446 Office: Am Chi Chou Theo-Phil Inst PO Box 4163 11804 Hemlock St El Monte CA 91732-1413

HWANG, VICTOR W., lawyer; b. Baton Rouge, La., May 27, 1971; s. C.J. and Betty W. Hwang. AB with honors, Harvard U., 1993; JD, U. Chgo., 1996. Staff Clinton Presdl. Campaign and Inauguration, Washington, 1995-97; law clk. U.S. AID, Washington, 1997; atty. Mayer, Brown & Platt, L.A., 1997—. Bd. dirs. San Gabriel Valley Habitat for Humanity, San Gabriel, Calif., 1998. Office: Mayer Brown & Platt 3 Embarcadero Ctr San Francisco CA 94111-4003

HWU, RUEY-JEN JENNIFER, electrical engineering educator, researcher; b. Taipei, Taiwan, Mar. 10, 1960; came to U.S., 1984; d. Tze-Hwa and Mien-Ying (Huang) H.; m. Laurence Phillip Sadwick, Apr. 22, 1990; 1 child, Aaron Elliott. BS, Nat. Taiwan Normal U., Taipei, 1982; MS, UCLA, 1986, PhD, 1991. Tchr. physics and chemistry Da-Li Jr. H.S., Taipei, 1982-84; mem. tech. staff elec. sys. group TRW, Redondo Beach, Calif., 1989-90; asst. prof. elec. engring. U. Utah, Salt Lake City, 1990-95, dir. Ctr. Excellence for Electronic Sys. Tech., 1994—, assoc. prof. elec. engring., 1996—. Contbr. articles to IEEE Trans. on Electron Devices, IEEE Trans. on Microwave Theory and Techniques, Jour. Applied Physics, Rev. Sci. Inst., Applied Physics Letters, IEEE Electron Device Letters, Microwave Jour., IEEE Microwave and Guided Wave Letters, Jour. Vacuum Sci. and Tech., Internat. Jour. Infrared and Millimeter Waves. Recipient career advancement award NSF, 1993, young investigator award Office Naval Rsch., 1995, Career award NSF, 1995; grantee TRW Electronic Sys. Group, 1990-91, U. Utah, 1991-95, Utah Ctr. for Inverse Problems, Imaging and Tomography, 1991-94, Utah Ctr. of Excellence Program, 1994—, NSF, 1991-95, Engring. Found., 1991-92, U. Utah Rsch. Found., 1994—, Hercules Aerospace Co., 1994-95, Loral Comms., 1995—. Mem. IEEE (sr. mem., vice chmn. Utah sect. 1991-92, chmn. 1993—). Achievements include patent for integrated modular millimeter-wave antenna/mixer array with minimal inter-antenna coupling, patent pending for advanced microminiature vacuum tube array for high frequency and harsh environments, for high temperature GaAs MESFET electronics, for millimeter-wave waveguide balun, for high frequency sensor using the magnetroresistance of semiconductor materials. Avocations: writing, hiking, badminton, volleyball, playing peepa (Chinese string instrument). Home: 3767 Brockbank Dr Salt Lake City UT 84124-3955 Office: U Utah Dept Elec Engring 3280 Merrill Engring Bldg Salt Lake City UT 84112

HYATT, JAMES ARMSTRONG, university administrator; b. Chilliwack, B.C., Can., May 28, 1949; s. Delbert Harold and Agnes (Barr) H.; m. Sandra Allard, May 23, 1981; children: Kathryn Barr, John Allard. BA, U. Wash., 1972, MBA, 1976. Mgmt. analyst Dept. Social and Health Svcs., Olympia, Wash., 1976-77; planning analyst U. Wash., Seattle, 1977-79; dir. fin. mgmt. ctr. Nat. Assn. Coll. and Univ. Bus. Officers, Washington, 1979-86, exec. v.p., 1986-87; asst. vice chancellor U. Md., College Park, 1987-91; assoc. chancellor U. Calif., Berkeley, 1991-98, vice chancellor, 1998—; bd. dirs., mem. exec. com. Nat. Ctr. for Higher Edn. Mgmt. Sys., Bolder, Colo., 1984-86; cons. U. Mass., Amherst, 1982, Am. U., Washington, 1988-89, U. Md. Sys., College Park, 1994; primary rep. Coun. on Govtl. Rels., 1994—; mem. nat. higher edn. adv. panel Nat. Ctr. on Ednl. Stats., 1983-86; mem. nat. planning com. project to develop Integrated Post-Secondary Edn. Data Sys., U.S. Dept. Edn., 1983-86; mem. nat. task force econs. of rsch. librs. project Coun. on Libr. Resources, 1983-86. Author: Reallocation: Strategies for Effective Resource Management, 1984, University Libraries in Transition, 1986, Financial Management of Colleges and Universities, 1986, Presentation and Analysis of Financial Management Information, 1989. Avocations: writing, sketching, bicycling. Office: Univ Calif 200 California Hall Berkeley CA 94720-1510

HYBL, WILLIAM JOSEPH, lawyer, foundation executive; b. Des Moines, July 16, 1942; s. Joseph A. and Geraldine (Evans) H.; m. Kathleen Horrigan, June 6, 1967; children: William J. Jr., Kyle Horrigan; BA, Colo. Coll., 1964; JD, U. Colo., 1967. Bar: Colo. 1967. Asst. dist. atty. 4th Jud. Dist., El Paso and Teller Counties, 1970-72; pres., dir. Garden City Co., 1973—; dir. Broadmoor Hotel, Inc., 1973—, also vice-chmn., 1987—; chmn., CEO, trustee El Pomar Found, Colorado Springs, Colo., 1973 ; pres. U.S. Olympic Com. 1991-92, 96—; vice chair USAA, San Antonio; dir. KN Energy Inc., Lakewood, Colo., FirstBank Holding Co. of Colo., Lakewood; mem. Colo. Ho. Reps., 1972-73; spl. counsel The White House, Washington, 1981. Pres., trustee Air Force Acad. Found.; sec., dir. Nat. Jr. Achievement; vice chmn. bd. U.S. Adv. Commn. on Pub. Diplomacy, 1990-97; civilian aide to sec. of army, 1986—. Capt. U.S. Army, 1967-69. Republican.

HYDE, ELINOR GODFREY, writer; b. Clarkston, Utah, 1935; d. H. Elbert and Abbie (Scholes) Godfrey; m. Alan A. Hyde, June 3, 1955; children: Kathryn Hyde Kelly, Margaret Hyde Jenkins, Linda Hyde Read, Gordon, Michael, Jim. Student, Brigham Young U., 1953-55. Sec., bookkeeper Firestone Co., Provo, Salt Lake City, 1955; pub. rels., sales Fernwood Candy, Salt Lake City, 1970-86; freelance writer Salt Lake City, 1980—; adminstrv. sec. U. Utah, Salt Lake City, 1983-84; bookkeeper, data processing Callister, Duncan & Nebeker, Salt Lake City, 1988; office aide Collier Heinz Property Mgmt. Co., Salt Lake City, 1991-93. Contbr.: John Godfrey, Descendants, 1981, Cardston and District, 1982, Bingham County, 100 Years, 1986, Canadian Windsong, 1987, Frederick and Abbie Scholes Family 1st Generation, 1990, 25 Years of Company for Dinner, 1992, Frederick and Abbie Scholes Family 2nd Generation Part I, 1995; compiler, editor: East Millcreek 10th Ward, 20 Years 1962-82, 1983; contbr. poems Utah Sings, vol. 5, 1985, vol. 6, 1995, to anthology Seeds-Ke-Dec, 1998; contbr. articles to mags. and newspapers. Leader Boy Scouts Am.; mem. PTA Granite Sch. Dist., Salt Lake City. Mem. League Utah Writers (pres. Salt Lake City chpt., Manuscript of the Yr. 1980, 1st place published article 1980, 3d place published book of the yr. 1987), Nat. League Am. Pen Women (publicity chair Salt Lake City br., treas. Utah and Salt Lake City br. 1990, treas. Salt Lake City br. 1998), Utah State Poetry Soc. Mem. LDS Ch. Avocations: quilts, genealogy, writing.

HYDE, GERALDINE VEOLA, retired secondary education educator; b. Berkeley, Calif., Nov. 26, 1926; d. William Benjamin and Veola (Walker) H.; m. Paul Hyde Graves, Jr., Nov. 12, 1949 (div. Dec. 1960); children: Christine M. Graves Klykken, Catherine A. Graves Hackney, Geraldine J. Graves Hansen. BA in English, U. Wash., 1948; BA in Edn., Ea. Wash. U., 1960, MA in Edn., 1962. Cert. tchr. K-16, Wash.; life cert. specialist in secondary edn., Calif. English educator Sprague (Wash.) Consol. Schs., 1960-62, Bremerton (Wash.) Sch. Dist., 1962-63, Federal Way (Wash.) Sch. Dist., 1963-66; English, journalism and Polynesian humanities educator Hayward (Calif.) Unified Sch. Dist., 1966-86. Charter mem. Hist. Hawai'i Found., Honolulu, 1977—; founding mem. The Cousteau Soc., Inc., Norfolk, Va., 1973—; life mem. Hawai'ian Hist. Soc., Honolulu, 1978—; mem. Moloka'i Mus. and Cultural Ctr., Kaunakaka'i, 1986—, Bishop Mus. Assn., Honolulu, 1973—, Mission House Mus., Honolulu, 1994, Bklyn. Hist. Assn., N.Y., 1994, Berkshire Family History Assn., Pittsfield, Mass., 1994—, Richville (N.Y.) Hist. Assn., 1994—, Swanton (Vt.) Hist. Soc., 1998—, N.Y. Geneal. and Biog. Soc., 1999—, New Eng. Hist. Genealogic Soc., 1998—, Gouverneur Hist. Assn., 1998—, New Wing Luke Asian Mus., Seattle, 1994. Mem. Libr. Congress Assocs. (charter), Nature Conservancy of Hawai'i, Smithsonian Inst. (contbg.), Nat. Geog. Soc., Nat. Trust Historic Preservation, Jr. League Spokane, U. Wash. Alumni Assn. (life), Ea. Wash. U. Alumni Assn. (life). Episcopalian. Avocations: historic and ecologic preservation, genealogy, shell collecting, needlework, crafts. Home: 5051 El Don Dr Apt 1301 Rocklin CA 95677-4470

HYDE, WILLIAM, automotive executive; b. Twin Falls, Idaho, Jan. 19, 1946; s. Cecil Lee and Nona Ida (Daley) H.; m. Betty Sue Thompson, Apr. 26, 1963 (div. 1984); children: Becky Ann, Gerry. BSME, Gen Motors Inst., Detroit, 1968; BSEE, UCLA, 1971. Engr. NASA, Houston, 1971-74; engring mgr. Dept. of Def., Dept. Transp., Midland, Tex., 1979-82; mgr. adv. rsch. engring. div. Automotive Rsch. Corp., Idaho Falls, 1982—; cons. Contbr. articles to profl. jours.; patentee in field.; author: Hydrogen Propulsion and HIgh Energy Physics, 1981. Mem. SAE, AAPS, IEEE, Sun Valley Country Club. Republican. Avocations: flying, scuba diving, snow and water skiing. Office: Automotive Rsch Corp 1685 Whitney St Idaho Falls ID 83402-1768

HYLAND, LAURIE ZOE, financial planner; b. Denver, Nov. 18, 1939; d. Donald John and Marjorie (Bloedorn) Burch; children: Stephen Hyland, Karen Zoe Hyland. BA, U. Denver, 1962. CFP. Adminstr. Boulder C. of C., 1982-83; CFP Fin. Planning and Mgmt., Boulder, 1985-88, v.p., 1989-91; sr. v.p. Premier Planning Assocs., Inc., Boulder, 1991—; seminar designer and facilitator U. Colo. Continuing Edn., Color. State Extension Agy., Boulder Community Schs., Boulder Community Hosp., Boulder County Mental Health Ctr., Boulder. Editor (newsletter) Women Wealth & Power, 1987-90, editor seminar materials, 1985—. Pres. Older Women's League, Boulder, 1989-90; chairperson Boulder Bus. Womens' Leadership Taskforce, 1988-90. Mem. Inst. of CFP, Internat. Assn. of Fin. Planners, Boulder C. of C. (chairperson 1988-90). Avocations: gardening, hiking, reading, skiing. Office: Premier Planning Assocs Inc 4730 Walnut St Ste 208 Boulder CO 80301-2558

HYLKO, JAMES MARK, health physicist, certified quality auditor; b. Detroit, Sept. 11, 1961; s. James John and Frances Rose (Gorski) H. BS in Biochemistry, Ea. Mich. U., 1984; MPH in Health Physics, U. Mich., 1986. Lab. tech. dept. chemistry Ea. Mich. U., Ypsilanti, 1980-84; environ. radiochemist Argonne (Ill.) Nat. Lab., 1984; radiochemist U. Mich., Ann Arbor, 1984-86; health physics tech. Monticello (Minn.) Nuclear Sta., 1985; rsch. scientist/grad. asst. U. Va., Charlottesville, 1986-88; health physicist Fluor Daniel Inc., Chgo., 1988-92, Roy F. Weston, Inc., Albuquerque, 1992—; instr. dept. chem. and nuclear engring. U. N.Mex., 1993-98; guest lectr. Purdue U., 1991; invited spkr. Inst. Atomic Energy, Swierk-Otwock, Poland, 1991. Contbr. over 80 articles to various jours.; tech. reviewer, contbg. editor Jour. Radiation Protection Mgmt., RSO Mag., Power Mag.; book reviewer Jour. Health Physics, and Sci. Books and Films; tech. reviewer Jour. Nuc. Tech. Judge N.Mex. Regional and State Sci. and Engring. Fair, 1993-97. Fellow Inst. Nuclear Power Ops., 1986. Mem. Health Physics Soc. (history com., Rio Grande chpt. exec. bd., treas., co-chair 1999 Midyear Symposium, pres. 1998-99), Am. Nuc. Soc., Am. Soc. Quality Control (cert.), Toastmasters (pres. Fluor Daniel chpt. 1990). Home: 10800 Lowe St NE Albuquerque NM 87111-1837 Office: Roy F Weston Inc 6501 Americas Pkwy NE Ste 800 Albuquerque NM 87110-8146

HYMAN, JACKIE DIAMOND, novelist; b. Menard, Tex., Apr. 3, 1949; d. Maurice Schwartz and Sylvia (Risman) H.; m. Kurt Loren Wilson, Oct. 8, 1978; children: Ari Wilson, Hunter Wilson. BA, Brandeis U., 1971. Staff writer Orange Coast Daily Pilot, Costa Mesa, Calif., 1974-80; part-time copy editor Orange County Register, 1985-87; staff writer, supr. AP, L.A., 1980-83, freelance theatre writer, 1983—; weekly TV columnist AP, 1993-94. Author (as Jacqueline Diamond, Jacqueline Topaz, Jacqueline Jade, or Jackie Hyman): Lady in Disguise, 1982, Song for a Lady, 1983, A Lady of Letters, 1983, The Forgetful Lady, 1984, The Day-Dreaming Lady, 1985, The Dream Never Dies, 1984, Deeper Than Desire, 1984, Swept Away, 1985, Rites of Passion, 1985, Lucky in Love, 1985, Golden Girl, 1986, A Lucky Star, 1986, An Unexpected Man, 1987, Unlikely Partners, 1987, The Eyes of a Stranger, 1987, A Warm December, 1988, The Cinderella Dare, 1988, Capers and Rainbows, 1988, A Ghost of a Chance, 1989, A Lady's Point of View, 1989, Flight of Magic, 1989, Shadowlight, 1989, By Leaps and Bounds, 1990, Echoes, 1990, Old Dreams, New Dreams, 1991, The Trouble With Terry, 1992, A Dangerous Guy, 1993, The Runaway Bride, 1995, Yours, Mine and Ours, 1996, The Cowboy and the Heiress, 1996, One Husband Too Many, 1996, Dear Lonely in L.A..., 1996, Punchline, 1997, Million-Dollar Mommy, 1997, Daddy Warlock, 1997, And The Bride Vanishes, 1997, Sandra and the Scoundrel, 1997, How to Marry a Real, Live Sheikh, 1998, The Cowboy and the Shotgun Bride, 1998, others; ghost writer Kiss and Make Up, for Seniors series of young adult books. Thomas Watson Found. fellow for playwriting in Europe, 1971-72; honoree for achievements as novelist Brea (Calif.) City Coun., 1990. Mem. Romance Writers Am. (nat. bd. dirs. 1984-85, workshop presenter 1998, Bronze medallion 1985, finalist Golden medallion 1986), Fictionnaires (pres. 1986). Avocations: [illegible]. Office: PO Box 1315 Brea CA 92822-1315

HYMERS, ROBERT LESLIE, JR., pastor; b. Glendale, Calif., Apr. 12, 1941; s. Robert Leslie Hymers Sr. and Cecelia Juanita (Flowers) McDonell; m. Ileana Patricia Cuellar, Sept. 27, 1982; children: Robert Leslie Hymers III, John Wesley Hymers (twins). BA, Calif. State U., L.A., 1970; MDiv, Golden Gate Bapt. Theol. Sem., 1973; DMin, San Francisco Theol. Sem., 1981; ThD, La. Bapt. Theol. Sem., 1989. Ordained to ministry Bapt. Ch., 1972. Pastor Ch. of the Open Door, San Rafael, Calif., 1973-75, Fundamentalist Bapt. Tabernacle, L.A., 1975—; guest TV programs. Author: Holocaust II, 1978, The Ruckman Conspiracy, 1989, Inside the Southern Baptist Convention, 1990, Dicisionism and the Death of America, 1999; contbr. articles to profl. jours. Republican. Office: Fundamentalist Bapt PO Box 15308 Los Angeles CA 90015-0308

HYNEK, FREDERICK JAMES, architect; b. Minot, N.D., May 24, 1944; s. Frederick Frank and Esther Irene (Hermanson) H.; m. Jane Rebecca Lowitz, June 9, 1966; children: Tyler James, Scott Anthony. BArch, N.D. State U., 1967. Intern archtl. firms in Bismarck, N.D., 1967-72; architect Gerald W. Deines, Architect, Casper and Cody, Wyo., 1972-73; v.p. Gerald Deines and Assos., 1973-77; propr. Fred J. Hynek, AIA/Architect, Cody, 1977-80; pres. Design Group, P.C., Architects/Planners, Cody, 1980-86; pres. CHD Architects, Cody, 1986-94; CEO Cathexes, Inc., Reno, 1994-95; project mgr. Merrick and Co., Denver, 1995-97, coordinating architect Jefferson County Sch. Dist., Lakewood; adj. faculty archtl. tech. dept., Arapahoe C.C., Littleton, Colo.; mem. cert. of need rev. bd. State of Wyo., 1984-87, selection com. for archtl. students for Western Interstate Commn. for Higher Edn. Profl. Student Exchange Program, U. Wyo., 1979-94; chmn. archtl. adv. commn. City of Cody. Bd. dirs. Cody Stampede, Inc., 1977-82, Cody Nordic Ski Found., Park County Libr. Found.; chmn. Cody Econ. Devel. Council, 1982-84; coach Absaroka Ski Assn., Bill Koch Youth Ski League, 1990-94; mem. Planning Commn., Town of Parker, 1997-98. Served with USAR, 1967-68. Mem. AIA (dir. Wyo. chpt. 1976-83, pres. 1980, 81, sec./treas., 1990-91; conf. chmn. Western Mountain region 1977, mem. awards jury 1981, 92, treas. 1982-86; chmn. design awards jury N.D. 1981, 97, 2 awards for Excellence in Archtl. Design Wyo. chpt.), U.S. Ski Assn., U.S. Ski Coaches Assn., Profl. Ski Instrs. of Am., Cody County C. of C. (dir., pres. 1982). Republican. Presbyterian. Clubs: Cody Country Amb. (Amb. of Yr. 1990). Mem. editorial adv. bd. Symposia mag., 1981-82. Home: 17614 Peyton Dr Parker CO 80134-7554 Office: 809 Quail St Bldg 4 Lakewood CO 80215-5509

IACONO, ROBERT PAUL, neurosurgeon, medical educator; b. L.A., Apr. 7, 1952; s. Paul Edward I. and Rose Marie Barker; m. Young Grace Oh, July 24, 1993; 1 child, Robert Hunter. BS in Biology, U. So. Calif., 1974, MD, 1978. Diplomate Am. Bd. Neurol. Surgery. Intern in straight surgery U. So. Calif. Med. Ctr., L.A. County, 1978-79, resident in neurosurgery, 1979-80; resident in neurosurgery Duke U. Med. Ctr., 1980-84; asst. prof. sect. neurosurgery Health Scis. Ctr. U. Ariz., 1984-90, dir. U. Pain Clinic Health Scis. Ctr., 1985-90; assoc. prof. neurosurgery and anesthesiology Med. Ctr. Loma Linda U., 1991—; chief neurosurgery VA Hosp., Tucson, 1984-90; lectr. in field. Contbr. numerous articles to profl. jours. Fellow ACS; mem. AMA, AAAS, Am. Assn. Neurol. Surgeons (sect. on pain), Am. Assn. Study of Pain, Am. Acad. Pain Medicine, Am. Acad. Pain Mgmt., Am. Epilepsy Soc., Am. Assn. U. Physicians, Japanese Cong. Neurol. Surgeons, Internat. Assn. Study of Pain, Soc. Internat. Neurosurg. Edn., N.Y. Acad. Scis., Soc. Functional and Sterotactic Neurosurgery, Undersea Med. Soc., We. Neurosurg. Soc. Avocations: flying, fishing, hunting.

IAFRATE, GERALD CARL, motion picture company executive, lawyer; b. Denver, Aug. 17, 1951; s. Vincenzo and Anita M. (Iacobelli) I.; m. Linda S. Hartzell, June 26, 1980 (div. Jan. 1983); 1 child, Mario J.; m. Jennine Saltzman, Dec. 10, 1992 (dec. May 1994). BS in Anthropology, NYU, 1971; DC, Cleve. Chiropractic Coll., Kansas City, Mo., 1975; JD, U. San Francisco, 1988. Bar: Calif., 1988, N.Y., 1988; diplomate Nat. Bd. Chiropractic Examiners, 1975; lic. chiropractor Mo., 1975. Pvt. practice, ptnr. Midwest Chiropractic Clinics, Inc., Cameron, Mo., 1976-83; legal affairs commnr. USPHS, Washington, 1989-94; dep. insp. gen., Atlantic Maritime Adminstrn., Washington and London, 1991-92; admiralty law counsel U.S. Naval Inst., Annapolis, Md., 1992-98; pres. Ilex-Ryder Entertainment, Inc., L.A., 1995—; of counsel for admiralty and maritime affairs Mass. Heavy Industries, Inc., Quincy, Mass., 1998—. Contbr. treatise Columbia Internat. Law Rev., 1988. Mem. Emissary Assembly World Jewish Congress, N.Y.C., 1991—. Rear admiral USPHS, 1989-94. Diplomate Command Staff Coll., Ft. Leavenworth, Kans., 1990. Mem. ABA, Res. Officers Assn., Am. Legion (Honor award 1996), Brit. Royal Anthropol. Soc., Beverly Hills Rotary Club. Republican. Jewish. Avocations: building computers, fly fishing, camping. Office: Ilex-Ryder Entertainment 1901 Ave Of The Stars Los Angeles CA 90067-6004 also: Ilex-Ryder Prodns Kaufman Astoria Studios 34-12 36th St Astoria NY 11106

IAMELE, RICHARD THOMAS, law librarian; b. Newark, Jan. 29, 1942; s. Armando Anthony and Evelyn Iamele; m. Marilyn Ann Berutto, Aug. 21, 1965; children: Thomas, Ann Marie. BA, Loyola U., L.A., 1963; MSLS, U. So. Calif., 1967; JD, Southwestern U., L.A., 1976. Bar: Calif. 1977. Cataloger U. So. Calif., L.A., 1967-71; asst. cataloger L.A. County Law Libr., 1971-77, asst. ref. libr., 1977-78, asst. libr., 1978-80, libr. dir., 1980—. Mem. ABA, Am. Assn. Law Librs., Calif. Libr. Assn., So. Calif. Assn. Law Librs., Coun. Calif. County Law Librs. (pres. 1981-82, 88-90). Office: LA County Law Libr 301 W 1st St Los Angeles CA 90012-3140

IBANEZ, ARMANDO P(EREZ), film maker, poet; b. San Diego, Tex., June 26, 1949; s. Geronimo H. and Vicenta (Perez) I. MDiv, Grad. Theol. U., Berkeley, Calif., 1993, MA in Theology, 1993; MFA in Film, Am. Film Inst., L.A., 1998. TV writer Sonrisas, Austin, Tex., 1977-79; reporter Alice (Tex.) Echo-News, 1979-81; staff writer Corpus Christi (Tex.) Caller-Times, 1981-88; campus min. Tulane Cath. Ctr., New Orleans, 1993-95, Stanford (Calif.) Cath. Cmty., 1995-96; chaplain Monastery of the Angeles, Hollywood, Calif., 1996—; co-founder, chairperson Dominican Inst. for the Arts, L.A., 1996; dir., prodr. Pluma Prodns., L.A.; co-founder Power of Poetry-A Celebration, 1990, Aciendo Harte, Corpus Christi, 1985. Author: (book of poetry) Midday Shadows, 1980, Wrestling with the Angel, 1997; prodr., dir. (video documentary) Creating Sacred Space - Reaching Out to the Artist, 1995, (video-poem) Mesquites Never Die, 1992; prodr., writer: (video drama) A Moment of Silence, 1998. Recipient Sweepstakes award for writing contest Harte-Hanks Newspapers, 1985-86, first place Harte-Hanks Comm., Inc., 1985-86, first place Corpus Christi Club, 1986, Colin Higgins Screenplay Prodn. award Colin Higgins Found., L.A., 1997-98. Mem. Poetry Soc. Am. Roman Catholic. E-mail: pluma@earthlink.net. Fax: 323-463-4709. Office: Monastery of the Angels 1977 Carmen Ave Los Angeles CA 90068

IBARRA, JOSE, city council. BA in Mexican-Am. studies, U. Ariz., 1994. Campaign mgr. Mayor George Miller, 1991; with Border Vol. Corps., 1991-94; aide County Supv. Raul Grijalva, 1994; city coun. Tucson, 1995—, vice-mayor. Office: 940 W Alameda St Tucson AZ 85745-2932*

ICE, RICHARD EUGENE, retired minister, retirement housing company executive; b. Ft. Lewis, Wash., Sept. 25, 1930; s. Shirley and Nellie Rebecca (Pedersen) I.; m. Pearl Lucille Daniels, July 17, 1955 (dec. June 7, 1992); children: Lorinda Susan, Diana Laurene, Julianne Adele. AA, Centralia Coll., 1950; BA, Linfield Coll., 1952, LHD (hon.), 1978; MA, Berkeley Bapt. Div. Sch., 1959, DD (hon.), 1995; grad. advanced mgmt. program Harvard U., 1971. Ordained to ministry Am. Bapt. Ch., 1954; pastor Ridgecrest Community Bapt. Ch., Seattle, 1955-59; dir. ch. extension Wash. Bapt. Conv., 1959-61; dir. loans Am. Bapt. Extension Corp., Valley Forge, Pa., 1961-64; assoc. exec. minister Am. Bapt. Chs. of West, Oakland, Calif., 1964-67; dep. exec. sec., treas. Am. Bapt. Home Mission Socs., Valley Forge, 1967-72; pres. Am. Bapt. Homes of the West, Oakland, 1972-95, pres. emeritus, 1995—; dir. Minister's Life Ins. Co., Mpls., 1975-87, chmn. bd. dirs. 1986-87; bd. dir. Bapt. Life Assn., Buffalo, 1988—; pres. Am. Bapt. Homes and Hosps. Assn., 1978-81. v.p. Am. Bapt. Chs. U.S.A., 1990-91; Ministers and Missionaries Benefit Bd., 1982-89; mem. Bapt. Joint Com. on Pub. Affairs; trustee Linfield Coll., 1972—, chmn. bd. trustees, 1994—; trustee Calif./Nev. Methodist Homes, 1975—, Bacone Coll., 1968-77, Grad. Theol. Union, Berkeley, Calif., 1982—; trustee Am. Bapt. Sem. of West, Berkeley, 1979—, chmn. bd. trustees, 1987-93, exec. bd. adv. Sch. of Econ. and Bus. St. Mary's Coll. Calif. Recipient Disting. Baconian award Bacone Coll., 1977, Disting. Alumnus award Centralia Coll., 1981, Meritorious Service award Am. Assn. Homes for Aging, 1982, Merit citation Am. Bapt. Homes and Hosp. Assn., 1985, Award of Honor Calif. Assn. Homes for the Aging,

1988. Mem. U.S. Assn. for UN, Am. Assn. Homes and Svcs. for Aging (Award of Honor 1994), Calif. Assn. Homes for Aging, The Oakland 100, Pi Gamma Mu. Democrat. Clubs: Harvard of San Francisco. Office: Am Baptist Homes of West Stone Ridge Corp Plz V 6120 Stoneridge Mall Rd Pleasanton CA 94588-3211

ICO, LYDIA MALICDEM, English language educator; b. San Carlos City, Pangasinan, The Philippines, Mar. 29, 1939; d. Dionisio and Faustina (Cabansag) Malicdem; m. Orlando Monderin Ico, Nov. 5, 1961; children: Christopher, Lilibeth Grace. BA, Lyceum Coll., 1965, BS in Edn., 1968, MEd, 1973; PhD, U. Philippines, 1981. English instr. Lyceum Coll., Dagupan City, Philippines, 1965-69; asst. prof. English U. Pangasinan, Dagupan City, 1969-77; assoc. prof. English U. Philippines, Laguna, 1981-89; English instr. Chapman U., Vallejo, Fairfield, Calif., 1989-93, Tacoma (Wash.) C.C., 1994-97; assoc. prof. English Pierce Coll., Lakewood, Wash., 1993—. Named outstanding coll. tchr. Dept. Edn., Culture and Sports Philippines, 1977. Mem. Nat. Coun. Tchrs. English, Am. Fedn. Tchrs., Wash. Fedn. Tchrs. Avocations: reading, walking, traveling, listening to music.

IGLITZIN, LARA, foundation administrator; b. Mpls., Apr. 28, 1959; d. Alan and Lynne (Bresler) Iglitzin; m. Vladimir Raskin, Apr. 6, 1997. BA in Russian studies, U. Washington, 1982; MA in Russian studies, Georgetown U., 1985; MA in Russian history, U. Pa., 1991. Publs. officer Inst. for East-West Security Studies, N.Y.C., 1989; project dir. Congl. Roundtable on U.S.-Soviet Rels., Washington, 1983-85; program officer Henry M. Jackson Found., Seattle, 1992-95; exec. dir. Henry M. Jackson Found., 1995—; exec. com. Grantmaker Forum of Cmty. & Nat. Svc., chmn. funder outreach, San Francisco, 1997—; gov. Internat. Human Rights Funders Group, Seattle, 1995—. Bd. dirs. Olympic Music Festival, Seattle, 1992-98, pres., 1996-98; mem. Leadership Tomorrow, Seattle, 1994; vis. com. Seattle U., 1997-99. Office: Henry M Jackson Found 1001 4th Ave Ste 3317 Seattle WA 98154-1101

II, JACK MORITO, aerospace engineer; b. Tokyo, Mar. 20, 1926; s. Iwao and Kiku Ii; came to U.S., 1954, naturalized, 1966; BS, Tohoku U., 1949; MS, U. Washington, 1956; M in Aero. Engring., Cornell U., 1959; PhD in Aero. and Astronautics, U. Wash., 1964; PhD in Engring., U. Tokyo, 1979; children: Keiko, Yoshiko, Mutsuya. Reporter, Asahi Newspaper Press, Tokyo, 1951-54; aircraft designer Fuji Heavy Industries Ltd. Co., Tokyo, Japan, 1956-58; mem. staff structures rsch. Boeing Co., Seattle, 1962—. Mem. AIAA, Japan Shumy and Culture Soc. (pres. 1976-96), Sigma Xi. Mem. Congregational Ch. Contbr. numerous articles on aerodyns. to profl. jours. Office: The Boeing Co M S 67-HC Seattle WA 98124

IKEDA, CLYDE JUNICHI, plastic and reconstructive surgeon; b. Kobe, Japan, 1951; s. Paul Tamotsu and Kazu Ikeda. BA, SUNY, Binghamton, 1973; MD, N.Y. Med. Coll., Valhalla, 1979. Med. dir. Burn Ctr., St. Francis Meml. Hosp., San Francisco, 1992—, med. examiner, 1993—, med. dir. Wound Healing Ctr., 1994—. Fellow Am. Coll. Surgeons. Office: 1199 Bush St Ste 640 San Francisco CA 94109-5977

IKEDA, MOSS MARCUS MASANOBU, retired state education official, lecturer, consultant; b. L.A., Sept. 11, 1931; s. Masao Eugene and Masako (Yamashina) I.; m. Shirley Yaeko Okimoto; children: Cynthia Cecile Ikeda Tamashiro, Mark Eugene, Matthew Albert. BE, U. Hawaii, 1960, MEd, 1962; postgrad. Stanford U., 1961-62; M in Mil. Art and Sci., U.S. Army Command and Gen. Staff Coll., 1975; grad. U.S. Army War Coll., 1976; EdD, U. Hawaii, 1986. Tchr., Farrington H.S., Honolulu, 1962-64; vice-prin. Kailua Intermediate Sch. 1964-65; adminstrv. intern Central Intermediate Sch., Honolulu, 1965-66; vice-prin. Kaimuki H.S., Honolulu, 1966-67; prin. Kawananakoa Intermediate Sch., Honolulu, 1967-68, Kailua H.S., 1969-71, Kalaheo H.S., Kailua, 1972-77; ednl. specialist Hawaii Dept. Edn., Honolulu, 1977-79, ednl. adminstr., 1979-95, ret., 1995; frequent spkr. on edn.; lectr. U. Hawaii, 1987—. Served with AUS, 1951-57, 68-69, col. U.S. Army ret. Decorated Legion of Merit, Army Commendation medal. Mem. Nat. Assn. Secondary Sch. Prins., Western Assn. Schs. and Colls. (past bd. dirs., pres., chair), Accrediting Commn. for Schs. (chair, commr. 1992-94), Network for Outcome-Based Schs., Commonwealth Coun. for Ednl. Adminstrn., Assn. U.S. Army, Res. Officers Assn., Go For Broke Assn., Army War Coll. Alumni Assn., Hawaii Govt. Employees Assn., Hawaii Assn. Ind. Schs. (bd. dirs. emeritus), Phi Delta Kappa, Phi Kappa Phi. Home and Office: 47-494 Apoalewa Pl Kaneohe HI 96744-4565

IKEDA, TSUGUO (IKE IKEDA), social services center administrator, consultant; b. Portland, Oreg., Aug. 15, 1924; s. Tom Minoru and Tomoe Ikeda; m. Sumiko Hara, Sept. 2, 1951; children: Wanda Amy, Helen Mari, Julie Ann, Patricia Kiyo. BA, Lewis & Clark Coll., 1949; MSW, U. Wash., 1951. Social group worker Neighborhood House, Seattle, 1951-53; exec. dir. Atlantic St. Ctr., Seattle, 1953-86; pres. Urban Partnerships, Seattle, 1986-88, Tsuguo "Ike" Ikeda and Assoc., Seattle, 1988—; cons. Seattle, 1988—, cons. Commn. on Religion and Race, Washington, 1973, North Northeast Mental Health Ctr., Portland, 1985; affirmative action cons. NASW, Washington, 1977; cons./trainer various other orgns.; conf. coord. Beyond the Mask of Denial Wash. State Conf. on Drug/Alcohol/Substance Abuse in the Asian/Pacific Islander Cmtys., 1993; coord. Minority Mental Health Colloquium in Wash., 1994-95; coord. Asian Pacific Islander Coming Home Together Summit-95, Tacoma, Asian Pacific Bi-Ann. Leadership Conf., 1995-96, craftsmanship trainer, 1996, 97, 98; Tsuguo "Ike" Ikeda, Pub. Svc. ann. award established in 1987; trainer region II Dept. Children and Family Svcs., Yakima, Wash., 1997, API Cons. and Tng. Project, 1998. Mem. Nat. Task Force to develop standards and goals for juv. delinquency, 1976; mem. Gov.'s Select Panel for social and health svcs., Olympia, Wash., 1977; chmn. Asian Am. Task Force, Community Coll., Seattle dist., 1982, King County Coordinated Health Care Initiative Client Edn., Mktg. Subcom., 1993; div. chmn. social agys. Seattle United Way campaign, 1985; vice-chmn. Wash. State Com. on Vocat. Edn., Olympia, 1985-86, chmn. 1986-87; chmn. regional adv. com. Dept. Social and Health Svcs., 1990-91; mem. Gov. Mike Lawry's Commn. on Ethics Govt., Campaign Practices, 1993—; mem. exec. task force King County Dept. Youth Svcs., 1996-97. With Mil. Intelligence Lang. Sch., 1945-46. Recipient cert. appreciation U.S. Dept. Justice, Washington, 1975-76, Am. Dream award Cmty. Coll. Dist., Seattle, 1984, Asian Counseling & Referral Svc., 1991, 95, Wing Lake Mus., 1991-92, Atlantic St. Ctr., 1992, Seattle Chinese Post, 1992, Bishop's award PNW Conf., U. Meth. Ch., Tacoma, Wash., 1984, cmty. svc. award Seattle Rotary Club, 1985, Outstanding Citizen award Mcpl. League, Seattle and King County, 1986, Outstanding Leadership award Dept. Social and Health Svcs., 1993, cmty. award South Pacific Islander Program Seattle Pub. Schs., 1993, Pasasalmat award Filipino Youth Activities, 1993, Brass Ring award Asian Am. Polit. Alliance, 1993, Cmty. award South Pacific Islander, 1993, Comm. Svc. award Asian Counseling and Referral Svc., 1994, Disting. Alumnus award Multicultural Alumni Partnership U. Wash. Alumni Assn., 1996; award Gen. Bd. Global Ministies, United Meth. Ch., 1995; recognized as Community Treasure, United Way of King County, 1996. Mem. NASW (chpt. pres., Social Worker of Yr. 1971, Social Work Pioneer 1995), Vol. Agy. Exec. Coalition (pres., Outstanding Cmty. Svc. award 1979), Ethnic Minority Mental Health Consortium (chmn., Outstanding Leader 1992, David E. "Ned" Skinner Cmty. Svc. award 1990), Minority Exec. Dirs. Coalition (organizer, mem. chmn. 1980-86). Democrat. Methodist. Avocations: collecting mint Am. stamps and memorabilia about Japanese Am. incarceration during World War II.

ILAO, TOM JAVATE, religious organization official, deacon; b. Cabanatuan, Nueva Ecija, The Philippines, Mar. 7, 1941; came to U.S., 1971; s. Agapito De Guzman and Feliza (Javate) I.; m. Lolita Reyes, Aug. 12, 1972; children: Francis Thomas R., Margaret Mary R., Jeremiah R. BSBA, Far Ea. U., Manila, 1963. Ordained deacon Roman Cath. Ch., 1990; lic. ins. agt., Calif. Lector, eucharistic min. St. Finn Barr Ch., San Francisco, 1974-89; deacon, homilist, coord. baptism, spiritual dir. St. Vincent de Paul Soc., Corpus Christi Ch., San Francisco, 1990—; instr. Confraternity Christian Doctrine, San Francisco, 1984-87; guest homilist Immaculate Conception Ch., San Francisco, 1990—; guest speaker San Francisco Bus. League, San Francisco Press Club, Tenn. Mental and Health Depts., Chattanooga, others. Author: America Under Siege: The Drug Invasion, 1989 (Benjamin Franklin award Pubs. Mktg. Assn. 1990). Workshop leader Calif. Pro-Life Orgn., Oakland, 1974; speaker San Francisco Right to Life, 1975. Recipient Dist. Speech Champion award Livermore (Calif.) Jaycees, 1977; named one of the Most Outstanding Asians of Calif., Asian Voice/Victor Roberts Publs., 1990. Mem. Nat. Writers Club, Nat. Press Club-U.S.A. (cert. of achievement Philippine chpt. 1990), Pubs. Mktg. Assn., Com. Small Mag. Editors and Pubs., Calif. Lawyers for Arts, KC (past grand knight), Toastmasters (past pres. West Portal, Calif. club, Internat. Area Speech champion (2) 1976). Home: 634 Joost Ave San Francisco CA 94127-2341

ILLK, SERENA PEARL, accountant; b. San Angelo, Tex., July 26, 1951; d. Paul Jacob and Goldie Alberta (Crippen) I.; m. Harry Daniel McCormack, June 20, 1984 (dec. Jan., 1990). BA in Acctg., Albertson's Coll. of Idaho, 1973. CPA, Alaska, Wash. From asst. supr. to supr. spl. funds. acctg. dept. Multnomah Sch. Dist., Portland, Oreg., 1974-75; payroll dept. acct. Alyeska pipeline Fluer Alaska, Inc., Valdez, Alaska, 1976-77; various temporary positions in acctg. Seattle, 1978-80; staff acct. Peasley, Tugby & Co., CPAs, Seattle, 1981-83; sr. acct. Boyle & Assocs., CPAs, Anchorage, Alaska, 1984-86; sr. acct. Minkemann & Assocs., CPAs, Anchorage, 1987-90, ptnr., 1991—. Vol. panel mem. KTVA Channel 11, Alaska TV answering tax questions for Alaskan taxpayers, Anchorage, 1991. Mem. AICPA, Alaska Soc. CPAs, Wash. Soc. CPAs. Avocations: golf, mt. bike riding. Office: Minkemann & Assocs CPAs 4300 B St Ste 308 Anchorage AK 99503-5933

IMAMURA, EUGENE HACHIRO, osteopathic physician, surgeon; b. Waipahu, Hawaii. BS, U. Hawaii, 1943; DO, Kansas City Coll. Osteopath, 1953. Intern Waldo Gen. Hosp., Seattle, 1953-54; pvt. practice Seattle, 1955-86, Terrace, 1986—; pres. of staff Waldo Gen. Hosp., Seattle, 1957-58. Author: My Most Unusual Cases, 1997, Vol. II, 1998, BII-More Unusual Cases, 1998; contbr. articles to profl. jours. Life patron Edmonds Art Festival. With U.S. Army, 1944-46. Mem. Am. Osteo Assn. (life mem.), UHS Coll. of Osteo. Med., Am. Coll. Gen. Practitioners, Am. Coll. Osteo. Family Physicians, Wash. Osteop. Med. Assn. (life), Seattle Writers Assn. Avocations: painting, golf, bowling, writing, computer designs. Home: 16024 75th Pl W Edmonds WA 98026-4524 Office: 5707 244th St SW Mountlake Terrace WA 98043-5449

IMANA, JORGE GARRON, artist; b. Sucre, Bolivia, Sept. 20, 1930; s. Juan S. and Lola (Garron) I.; grad. Fine Arts Acad., U. San Francisco Xavier, 1950; cert. Nat. Sch. for Tchrs., Bolivia, 1952; came to U.S., 1964, naturalized, 1974; m. Cristina Imana; children—George, Ivan. Prof. art Nat. Sch. Tchrs., Sucre, 1954-56; prof. biology Padilla Coll., Sucre, 1956-60; head dept. art Inst. Normal Simon Bolivar, La Paz, Bolivia, 1961-62; propr., mgr. The Artists Showroom, San Diego, 1973—. Over 90 one-man shows of paintings in U.S., S. Am. and Europe, 1952—, including: Gallery Banet, La Paz, 1965, Artists Showroom, San Diego, 1964, 66, 68, 74, 76, 77, San Diego Art Inst., 1966, 68, 72, 73, Contrast Gallery, Chula Vista, Calif., 1966, Central Public Library, San Diego, 1969, Universidad de Zulia, Maracaibo, Venezuela, 1969, Spanish Village Art Center, San Diego, 1974, 75, 76, La Jolla Art Assn. Gallery, 1969, 72-93, Internat. Gallery, Washington, 1976, Galeria de Arte L'Atelier, La Paz, 1977, Museo Nacional, La Paz, 1987, Casa del Arte, La Jolla, Calif., 1987, Museo Nacional, La Paz, Bolivia, 1988, Simon Patino Found., Bolivia, 1994; numerous group shows including: Fine Arts Gallery, San Diego, 1964, Mus. of Modern Art, Paris, 1973, exhibits in galleries of Budapest (Hungary), 1975, Moscow (USSR), 1975, Warsaw (Poland), 1976; represented in permanent collections: Museo Nacional, La Paz, Bolivia, Museo de la Universidad de Potosi, Bolivia, Muse Nacional de Bogota, Colombia, S. Am., Ministerio de Edn., Managua, Nicaragua, Bolivian embassy, Moscow and Washington, also pvt. collections in U.S., Europe and Latin Am.; executed many murals including: Colegio Padilla, Sucre, Bolivia, 1958, Colegio Junin, Sucre, Bolivia, 1959, Sindicato de Construccion Civil, Lima, Peru, 1960. Hon. consul of Bolivia, So. Calif., 1969-73. Served to lt. Bolivian Army, 1953. Recipient Mcpl. award Sucre, Bolivia, 1958. Mem. San Diego Art Inst., San Diego Watercolor Soc., Internat. Fine Arts Guild, La Jolla Art Assn. Home: 2510 Torrey Pines Rd La Jolla CA 92037-3424

IMBROGNO, CYNTHIA, magistrate judge; b. 1948. BA, Indiana U. Pa., 1970; JD cum laude, Gonzaga U., 1979. Law clk. to Hon. Justin L. Quackenbush U.S. Dist. Ct. (Wash. ea. dist.), 9th circuit, 1980-83; law clk. Wash. State Ct. of Appeals, 1984; civil rights staff atty. Ea. Dist. of Wash., 1984-85, complex litigation staff atty., 1986-88; with Preston, Thorgrimson, Shidler, Gates & Ellis, 1988-90, Perkins Coie, 1990-91; magistrate judge U.S. Dist. Ct. (Wash. ea. dist.), 9th circuit, Spokane, 1991—. Office: 856 US Courthouse 920 W Riverside Ave Spokane WA 99201-1010

IMHOFF, JUDITH LAMMERS, civic volunteer; b. Peoria, Ill., June 22, 1950; d. Paul David and Virginia (Rose) Lammers; m. Earl John Imhoff, Dec. 1, 1973; children: Elisabeth, Ben, Julia. BA, St. Mary's Coll., 1972. V.p., cons., dir. Lammers, Inc., Ohio, 1972-77; cmty. vol. L.A., 1986-98. Pres. bd. dirs. Kidspace Mus., Pasadena, Calif., 1996—. Home: 744 Fairfield Cir Pasadena CA 91106-3904

IMIG, WILLIAM GRAFF, lawyer, lobbyist; b. Omaha, Aug. 13, 1941; s. Jacob H. and Gretchen (Kirk) I.; m. Joyce Stevens, Dec. 18, 1976; children: Scott, Kari, Steven. BA, Cornell U., 1963, LLB, 1965. Bar: Colo. 1965, U.S. Ct. Appeals (10th cir.) 1965, U.S. Supreme Ct. 1969. Assoc. Sherman & Howard, Denver, 1965-66; v.p., shareholder Ireland, Stapleton, Pryor & Pascoe, Denver, 1970-92; pvt. practice, Denver, 1992—; Colo. counsel Nat. Assn. Ind. Insurers, Des Plaines, Ill., 1971—; Colo. legis. counsel Allstate Ins. Cos., 1982—. Bd. editors Cornell Law rev., 1964-65. Vice chmn., chmn. Colo. Gov.'s Adv. Com. on Ins. and Econ. Devel., 1987-90; trustee Colo. chpt. Nat. Multiple Sclerosis Soc., 1995—; exec. bd. Colo. Assn. of Continue Entities, 1994-96; mem. Working Com. on Risk Based Solvency, Denver, 1991-93, Colo. Bicycle Adv. Bd., Denver, 1992-97, counsel Save the Pavilion, 1989-94. Capt. JAGC, U.S. Army, 1966-70. Mem. Colo. Bar Assn. (bd. govs. 1974-77, pro bono award 1985), Federalist Soc., Am. Arbitration Assn. (arbitrator), City Club of Denver, Denver Law Club, Phi Kappa Phi. Republican. Episcopalian. Home and Office: 1795 Monaco Pky Denver CO 80220-1644

IMLAY, GORDON LAKE, development consultant; b. Fairmont, W.Va., Oct. 12, 1937; s. Julian Mortimer and Fredricka Jane (Harveycutter) I.; m. Margaret Julia Rodina, Aug. 31, 1958; children: Jane Ellen Imlay Skeen, James Elliot. BA, Mo. Valley Coll., 1959; MS, San Jose State U., 1977; EdD, U. Pacific, 1980. Registered recreator; cert. fund raising exec. Dist. scout exec. Boy Scouts Am., Bloomington, Ind., 1959-63; dist. scout exec. Boy Scouts Am., Detroit, 1963-68, field dir., 1968-72; exec. dir. Am. Humanics, Marshall, Mo., 1972-74, Stockton, Calif., 1974-81; v.p. YMCA of Metro Los Angeles, 1981-84; exec. dir. East Valley Family YMCA, No. Hollywood, Calif., 1984-87; exec. v.p. Netzel Assocs., Culver City, Calif., 1987—; cons. Western Wash. U., Bellingham, 1995-97, Idaho Commn. Arts, Boise, 1982; faculty mem. YMCA Nat. Staff Tng., Foster City, Calif., 1982-84; nat. cons. Boy Scouts Am., Dallas, 1974-81; chmn. nat. teen task force YMCA U.S.A., Chgo., 1981-85. Author: Identifying the Community Power Structure, 1977; editor: YMCA Leadership Development with Teens, 1983; contbr. articles to profl. jours. Mem. Nat. Soc. Fundraising Execs. (bd. dirs. Wash. chpt. 1995—, pres. 1998), YMCA Assn. Profl. Dirs. (acad. cert. 1986), Wing PT Country Club (Bainbridge Island, Wash.), Rancho Las Palmas Country Club (Rancho Mirage, Calif.), Rotary (program chmn. No. Hollywood chpt. 1987; sec. Redford Twp., Mich. chpt. 1965), Liona (key mem. Martinsville, Ind. chpt. 1960). Republican. Presbyterian. Avocations: golf, camping, walking, travel, photography. Home: Ste 3A 470 Wood Ave SW Apt 3A Bainbridge Is WA 98110-2749 Office: Netzel Assocs 9696 Culver Blvd Ste 204 Culver City CA 90232-2753

IMLE, JOHN F., JR., oil company executive; b. San Antonio. Degrees in mech. and petroleum engring., Tex. A&M, 1963. Registered petroleum engr., Calif. and Alaska. Engr. trainee Unocal, Houston, 1963-65; various positions Unocal, Alaska, 1968-72; with divsn. internat. oil and gas Unocal, West Africa and N. Sea, 1972-77; project mgr. Heather field Unocal, Eng., 1974; dist. mgr. ops. Unocal, Aberdeen, Scotland, 1977; resident mgr. Netherland's ops. Unocal, 1980, pres. internat. divsn. internat. oil and gas, 1983, sr. v.p. energy resources, 1988; also bd. dirs. Unocal Corp., exec. v.p. energy resources, 1992, pres., 1994—. Served mil., 1965-68. Mem. Am. Assn., Petroleum Geologists, Independent Petroleum Assn., Soc. Petroleum Engrs. Office: Unocal Corp 2141 Rosecrans Ave Ste 4000 El Segundo CA 90245*

INDIEK, VICTOR HENRY, finance corporation executive; b. Spearville, Kans., Nov. 15, 1937; s. Ben W. and Helen Ann (Schreck) I.; m. Marlene Gould, June 2, 1962; children: Kathy, Kevin. Student, U. Nebr., 1955-57; BS in Bus., U. Kans., 1959; postgrad., U. Nebr., 1955-57. CPA, Kans. Audit mgr. Arthur Andersen & Co., Kansas City, Mo., 1961-70; pres., chief exec. officer Fed. Home Loan Mortgage Corp., Washington, 1970-77; pres., dir. Builders Capital Corp., Los Angeles, 1977-84; chief fin. officer, exec. v.p. Fin. Corp. of Am., Irvine, Calif., 1984-88; pres., chief exec. officer FarWest Savs. and Loan Assn., Newport Beach, Calif., 1988—; with Kennedy Wilson, 1989-98; pvt. practice in real estate, 1998—; v.p. and pres. regional Assn. Small Businesses Investment Cos., 1979-81, bd. govs. nat. assn., 1982. Mem. Selective Service Bd., Santa Monica, Calif., 1978; capt. United Fund, Kansas City, 1968. Served with USN, 1959-61. Republican. Roman Catholic. Avocations: boating, skiing. Office: Kennedy Wilson 50 Hillsdale Dr Newport Beach CA 92660*

ING, GRACE SACHIKO NAKAMURA, elementary education educator; b. Honolulu, Aug. 30, 1935; d. Masaichi and Hatsue (Akamine) Nakamura; m. Rudolph K. Y. Ing (div. 1979); children: Darcy, Tracy, Jon Randall. BS in Elem. Edn., U. Hawaii, 1957, cert. in 5th yr., 1958. Tchr. 6th grade Waimanalo (Hawaii) Elem. Sch., Dept. Edn., State Hawaii, 1958-60, tchr. 2d grade, 1960, tchr. remedial reading, 1961, coord. Chpt. I Reading program, 1963-69; HEP installation tchr. Windward Dist. Office, Kaneohe, Hawaii, 1969-73, tchr. lang. arts resource, 1973-74; team tchr. grades 4-6 Blanche Pope Elem. Sch., Waimanalo, 1974; tchr. first grade Ahuimanu Elem. Sch., Kaneohe, 1974, tchr. spl. projects incl. writing, gifted/talented, remedial, 1975—; chmn. NEA mastery in learning project Ahuimanu Elem. Sch., Kaneone, 1985—. Mem. ASCD, NEA, AAUW, Internat. Reading Assn., Hawaii Assn. Supervision and Curriculum Devel., Hawaii State Tchrs. Assn. (bd. dirs. 1982-86, 88-90), Windward Hawaii State Tchrs. Assn. (pres.), Ahuimani Sch. Ohana, Ka Hu Helu Helu, HAwaii State Tchrs. Assn. (chpt. pres., bd. dirs., standing and spl. coms.), Nat. Sci. Tchrs. Assn. Democrat. Methodist. Avocations: reading, travel, collecting recipes, theater. Office: Ahuimanu Elem Sch 47-470 Hui Aeko Pl Kaneohe HI 96744-4599

INGALLS, JEREMY, poet, educator; b. Gloucester, Mass., Apr. 2, 1911; d. Charles A. and May E. (Dodge) Ingalls. AB, Tufts Coll., 1932, AM, 1933; student, U. Chgo., 1938-39; LHD, Rockford Coll., 1960; LittD, Tufts U., 1965. Asst. prof. English Lit. Western Coll., Oxford, Ohio, 1941-43; resident poet, asst. prof. English lit. Rockford (Ill.) Coll., 1948-50, successively assoc. prof. English and Asian studies, prof., chmn. div. arts, chmn. English dept., 1950-60; Fulbright prof. Am. lit., Japan, 1957; Rockefeller Found. lectr. Kyoto Am. Studies seminar, 1958. Author: A Book of Legends, 1941, The Metaphysical Sword, 1941, Tahl, 1945, The Galilean Way, 1953, The Woman from the Island, 1958, These Islands Also, 1959, This Stubborn Quantum, 1983, Summer Liturgy, 1985, The Epic Tradition and Related Essays, 1989; translator (from Chinese) A Political History of China, 1840-1928 (Li Chien-Nung), 1956, The Malice of Empire (Yao Hsin-Nung), 1970, (from Japanese) Tenno Yugao (Nakagawa), 1975. Recipient Yale Series of Younger Poets prize, 1941, Shelley Meml. award, 1950, Lola Ridge Mem. award 1952, 53, and other awards for poetry; apptd. hon. epic poet laureate United Poets Laureate Internat., 1965; Guggenheim fellow, 1943, Chinese classics rsch. fellow Republic of China, 1945, 46, Am. Acad. Arts and Letters grantee, 1944, Ford Found. fellow Asian studies, 1952, 53. Fellow Internat. Inst. Arts and Letters; mem. MLA (chmn. Oriental-western lit. rels. conf.), Assn. Asian Studies (life), Authors Guild, Poetry Soc. Am., New Eng. Poetry Soc., Dante Soc. Am. (life), Phi Beta Kappa, Chi Omega. Episcopalian. Home: 6269 E Rosewood St Tucson AZ 85711-1638

INGALLS-COX, PAMELA LYNN, artist, educator; b. Spokane, Wash., June 10, 1957; d. Richard David and Marjorie Denise (Barry) Ingalls; m. William Charles Cox, Apr. 26, 1980. Student, Accademia Delle Belle Arte, Florence, Italy, 1977-78; BA in Art, Gonzaga U., 1979. Resident artist, chore supr. Jesuit Vol. Corps, Seattle, 1980-81; graphic artist Tourmap Co., Spokane, 1982-86; painter Vashon Island, Wash., 1986—; apprentice Ron Lukas' Painting Studio, Seattle, 1992-95; art instr. Blue Heron Ctr. for Arts, Vashon Island, 1994—; juror art exhbn. Western Wash. State Fair, Puyallup, 1997, Canterbury Faire, Kent, Wash., 1998; exhbn. advisor Blue Heron Ctr. for Arts, Vashon Island, 1997. Exhibited in over 125 including group shows Tacoma (Wash.) Art Mus., 1997 (Hon. Mention 1997), North Valley Art League Ann., Redding, Calif., 1998 (Best of Show 1998), Am. Women Artists Ann., 1998 (3d pl. 1998), Okla. Art Workshops, 1997 (Pres.'s award 1997). Creator after sch. art classes Blue Heron Ctr. for Arts, Vashon Island, 1992-98; art tchr. inner-city kids Readiness to Learn Grant, Seattle, 1994-98; participant Bethlehem Peace Pilgrimage, 1982-83. Recipient over 60 awards including Merit award Batavia Soc. Artists, 1997, Merit award Nat. Oil and Acrylic Painters Soc., 1995, 97, 1st prize Juan de Fuca Internat. Juried Show, 1997. Mem. Nat. Oil and Acrylic Painters Soc., Am. Artists Profl. League, Allied Artists of am., Oil Painters of Am., Women Painters of Wash. (exhbn. coord. 1992-98, 3d pl. award 1997, 1st pl. award 1998). Home: PO Box 263 Vashon WA 98070-0263

INGERMAN, MICHAEL LEIGH, development director; b. N.Y.C., Nov. 30, 1937; s. Charles Stryker and Ernestine (Leigh) I.; m. Madeleine Edison Sloane; Nov. 24, 1984; children by previous marriage: Shawn Marie, Jenifer Lyn. BS, George Washington U., 1963. Health planner, Marin County, Calif., 1969-72; regional cons. Bay Area Comprehensive Health Coun., San Francisco, 1972-73; hosp. cons. Booz, Allen & Hamilton, San Francisco, 1974; health planning coord. Peralta Hosp., Oakland, Calif., 1975-76; pres. Discern, Inc., mgmt. cons., Nicasio, Calif., 1976-93; prin. Human Resources Mgmt. Group, San Francisco, 1991-93; broker assoc. Frank Howard Allen Realtors, Greenbrae, Calif., 1993-98; broker assoc. Alaska Pacific Realty, Sitka, 1995-97; instr. Golden Gate U., 1981-88; dir. of devel. Friends Assn. Svc. for Elderly, Santa Rosa, Calif., 1998—. Bd. dirs. Nicasio Land Owners Assn., 1989-91, pres., 1990; coord. Nicasio Disaster Com., 1988-89; nat. bd. dirs. Am. Friends Svc. Com., 1980-81, bd. dirs. John Woolman Sch., 1980-87, 90-94, bd. chmn., 1991; bd. dirs. Hospice of Marin, 1983-89, pres. bd. dirs., 1988-89; bd. dirs. Vol. Ctr. Marin, 1991-97; bd. dirs. Friends Assn. Svc. for Elderly, 1984-89, pres. 1988-89, mem. fin. com., 1989-98; mem. Marin County Civil Grand Jury, 1977-78, Nicasio Design Rev. Com., 1979-83; mem. allocation com. Marin County United Way, 1993-96, campaign com., 1994-96. Mem. San Rafael Sunrise Lions Club (pres. 1998-99). Office: Friends Assn for Svcs for the Elderly 684 Benicia Dr Santa Rosa CA 95409-3058

INGERSOLL, JOHN GREGORY, physicist, energy specialist, educator; b. Athens, Greece, July 25, 1948; came to U.S., 1971; s. Gregory and Catherine (Asteris) I.; m. Sally Lynn Roberts, Apr. 7, 1984. BS, Nat. Tech. U., Athens, 1970; MS, Syracuse U., 1973; PhD, U. Calif., Berkeley, 1978. Instr. physics U. Calif., 1974-75, research asst. Lawrence Berkeley Lab., 1975-77, from asst. research prof. to assoc. research prof. Lawrence Berkeley Lab., 1978-82; sr. staff scientist Hughes Aircraft Co., Los Angeles, 1983—; staff mem., advisor USN Energy Office, Washington, 1988—; founder, pres. Helios Internat., 1991—; cons. Calif. Energy Commn., Sacramento, 1981-82, U.S. Dept. Energy, Washington, 1981-83, Bldg. Industry, N.Y. and Calif., 1982—, local govts. on alternative fuels; prin. investigator Energy Tech. Group UCLA, 1983-93; mem. tech. team for devel. of a comml. passenger electric vehicle GM, 1990-93; adj. assoc. prof. dept. indsl. and sys. engring U. So. Calif., 1996—. Author: Natural Gas Vehicles, 1996; contbr. over 100 articles on nuclear sci., renewable energy sources, indoor air quality, efficient utilization of energy in bldgs., passive solar systems, solar elec. energy, alternative fuel veh. to profl. jours.; author one book on natural gas vehicles and contbg. author to three books on energy mgmt. in bldgs.; patentee heat pipe devels., non-freon low power air conditioner for electric vehicles and buses. Mem. Rep. Presdl. Task Force, Calif., 1981-83. Served as lt. USNR, 1982—. Recipient 2d Pl. award Edison Electric Inst., Gen. Motors, and Dept. Energy, 1993, 1st Pl. award Smithsonian Inst., AIA, 1996, 1st Pl. award Smithsonian Inst./AIA/Nat. Renewable Energy Lab.-Dept. Energy, 1996; fellow Democritus Nuclear Research Ctr., Athens, 1970, Syracuse U., 1972, Rockefeller Found., 1974. Mem. Gen. Motors team (tasked with development, production, mktg. of passenger electric vehicle). Presbyterian. Avocations: walking, hiking, studying archaeology and history of Greece and Egypt. Home: 21315 Lighthill Dr Topanga CA 90290-4442 Office: Helios Internat Inc 3360 E Foothill Blvd Ste 111 Pasadena CA 91107-6025

INGIBERGSSON, ASGEIR, minister, librarian; b. Alafoss, Iceland, Jan. 17, 1928; arrived in Can., 1968; s. Ingibergur and Sigridur Olga (Kristjansdottir) Runolfsson; m. Janet Smiley, June 27, 1959 (dec. 1989); children: David, Ragnar, Elisabet, Margret; m. Akiko Hayami, Oct. 12, 1991. Candidatus theologiae, U. Iceland, 1957, teaching diploma, 1967; postgrad., Trinity Coll., Ireland, 1958; MLS, U. Alta., Can., 1980. Ordained to ministry Evang. Luth. Ch. Iceland, 1958. Pastor Hvamms Parish, Iceland, 1958-66; chaplain, youth dir. Keflavik, Iceland, 1966-68; pastor Grace Luth. Ch., Man., Can., 1968-71, Bawlf Luth. Ch., Alta., 1971-78; head libr. Camrose (Alta.) Luth. Coll., 1978—. Chmn. bd. trustees Stadarfell Home Econs. Sch., Iceland, 1958-66, Bethany Aux. Hosp., Camrose, 1974-82. Mem. ALA, Can. Libr. Assn., Assn. Coll. Librs. Alta., Libr. Assn. Alta. Home: 6213 42nd Ave, Camrose, AB Canada T4V 2W8 Office: Camrose Luth Coll, Camrose, AB Canada T4V 2R3

INGLE, ROBERT D., newspaper editor, newspaper executive; b. Sioux City, Iowa, Apr. 29, 1939; s. Walter J. and Thelma L (McCoy) I.; m. Martha N. Nelson, Sept. 12, 1964 (div. 1984); 1 child, Julia L.; m. Sandra R. Reed, Mar. 2, 1985. B.A. in Journalism and Polit. Sci., U. Iowa, 1962. Various positions Miami Herald, 1962-75, asst. mng. editor, 1975-77, mng. editor, 1977-81; exec. editor San Jose (Calif.) Mercury News, 1981-93, pres., exec. editor, 1993-95; v.p. Knight-Ridder Inc., San Jose, Calif., 1995—; pres. Knight-Ridder New Media, San Jose, Calif. Pres. Calif. First Amendment Coalition, 1990-92. Mem. AP Mng. Editors Assn., Am. Soc. Newspaper Editors. Office: Knight Ridder New Media 50 W San Fernando St Ste 700 San Jose CA 95113-2413

INGRAM, ARTONYON S., adult basic skills educator; b. Fremont, N.C., Dec. 2, 1962; s. Gliffie and Doris Ingram. BS, Atlantic Christian Coll., 1985; cert. in drugs and alcohol abuse, Pierce Coll., Steilacoom, Wash., 1993, AA, 1993; MEd, City U., Bellevue, Wash., 1995; cert. parent educator, Clover Pk. Tech. Coll., 1995. Teaching parent Onslow Mental Health Ctr., Jacksonville, N.C., 1987-89; social svcs. asst. Rainer Vista Health Care, Puyallup, Wash., 1990-91, Lakewood Health Care, Tacoma, Wash., 1990-91; group life counselor Jessie Dyslin Boys Ranch, Tacoma, Wash., 1991-92; case mgr. Puget Sound Ctr., Tacoma, Wash., 1991; counselor intern Dotters Counseling Ctr., Puyallup, Wash., 1992-93, Cross Rd. Treatment Ctr., Tacoma, 1993; instr. Clover Pk. Tech. Coll., Tacoma, 1993—. Counselor First Bapt. Ch., Jacksonville, N.C. With USNG, 1981-88. Army Nat. Guard scholar, 1978-81, L.N. Forbes scholar, Boeing Engring. scholar, 1993. Mem. Nat. Assn. Alcoholism and Drug Abuse Counselors, Chem. Dependency Profls. Home: 3202 S Mason Ave Apt L106 Tacoma WA 98409-8506 Office: Tacoma Washington Dept Correction Tacoma WA 98408-6745 also: Pierce County Jail Detention Correctional Ctr 910 Tacoma Ave S Tacoma WA 98402-2104

INGRAM, JUDITH ELIZABETH, counselor; b. Alameda, Calif., May 6, 1951; d. William Ralph and Elizabeth (Lelis) Madler; m. Frank David Ingram, Sept. 4, 1971; 1 child, Melanie Anne. AA, Chabot Coll., Hayward, Calif., 1972; BS in Biology summa cum laude, Calif. State U., Hayward, 1978; MA in Counseling, St. Mary's Coll. of Calif., Moraga, 1996. Tech. writer Tech. Writing Svcs., Dublin, Calif., 1990-93; counselor trainee Valley Christian Counseling, Dublin, 1995-96, counselor, dir. devel., 1996-97. Mem. ACA, Am. Med. Writers Assn., Western Assn. for Counselor Edn. and Supervision (bd. officer, newsletter editor), Am. Assn. Christian Counselors, Assn. for Spiritual, Ethical and Religious Values in Counseling, Soc. Tech. Comm. Presbyterian. Avocations: writing fiction and nonfiction, desktop publishing and computer graphic design, reading psychology, philosophy and women's issues. Home: 8724 Augusta Ct Dublin CA 94568-1063

INLOW, RUSH OSBORNE, chemist; b. Seattle, July 10, 1944; s. Edgar Burke and Marigale (Osborne) I.; BS, U. Wash., 1966; PhD, Vanderbilt U., 1975; m. Gloria Elisa Duran, June 7, 1980. Chemist, sect. chief U.S. Dept. Energy, New Brunswick Lab., Argonne, Ill., 1975-78, chief nuclear safeguards br. Albuquerque ops., 1978-82, sr. program engr. Cruise missile systems, 1983-84, program mgr. Navy Strategic Systems, 1984-85, dir. weapon programs div., 1985-88, dir. prodn. ops. div., 1988-90, asst. mgr. safeguards and security, 1990-94, asst. mgr. nat. def. programs, 1994-96, deputy mgr. 1996—; apptd. Fed. Sr. Exec. Svc., 1985. Served with USN, 1966-71. Tenn. Eastman fellow, 1974-75; recipient Pres. Meritorious Exec. award The White House, Pres. Clinton, 1994. Mem. Am. Chem. Soc., Sigma Xi. Republican. Episcopalian. Contbr. articles to profl. jours.

INMAN, ANA M. JIMENEZ, secondary education educator; b. Rio Piedras, P.R., Jan. 5, 1962; d. Antonio Jiménez del Toro and Ana E. Colon Fontan. BA, U. P.R., 1985, postgrad. Cert. secondary Spanish tchr., P.R., profl. edn. cert. continuing tchr. English 4-12, Spanish K-12, Wash., DSHS Med. and Social Svcs. interpreter/translator in Spanish, Wash., notary public, Wash.; cert. cmty. first aid and safety instr. ARC. Tutor La Mansion, Rio Piedras; tchr. Colegio Mater Salvatoris, Cupey, P.R., Colegio Nuestra Senora de Altagracia, Rio Piedras, Colegio San Jose, Rio Piedras; Am. Sch., Bayamón, P.R., Escuela Superior Católica de Bayamón; clk. I-II, interpreter Seafirst Bank-Trust Vault, Seattle; office mgr., adminstrv. asst. El Centro de la Raza, Seattle; adminstrv. team leader, mgr. Las Brisas housing program Consejo Counseling and Referral Svc., Seattle, vocat. rehab. program mgr.; instr. Spanish Rites Of Passage Experience program Ctrl. Area Motivation Program; pvt. tutor in Spanish and all subject matters; acad.-vocat. counselor/tchr. Sea Mar, Seattle. Vol., cert. instr. ARC. Mem. ASCD, Nat. Notary Assn., Wash. State Ct. Interpreters & Translators Soc., Phi Delta Kappa. Avocations: music, reading, literature, painting, crafts. Home: 21808 55th Ave W Mountlake Terrace WA 98043-3210

INMAN, JAMES RUSSELL, claims consultant; b. Tucson, May 24, 1936; s. Claude Colbert and Myra Eugenia (Langdon) I.; m. Charleen M. Bowman, Feb. 22, 1964 (div. 1977); m. Margaret Williams Kendrick, Apr. 26, 1996. Student, Pomona Coll., Claremont, Calif., 1954-60. Supr. res. dept. Honnold Libr. Claremont Coll., 1959-60; supr. casualty claims CNA Ins., L.A., 1961-70; asst. mgr., asbestos specialist, head entertainment claims Firemen's Fund, L.A., Beverly Hills, 1970-83; pres. Wilnor Corp., L.A., 1982—; claims auditor dirs. and officers claims Harbor/Continental Ins., L.A., 1984-86; claims mgr. Advent Mgmt., L.A., 1987, Completion Bond Co., Century City, Calif., 1988; asst. to pres., claims specialist Am. Multiline Corp., L.A., 1988-92; sr. claims specialist Reliance Ins. Co., Glendale, Calif., 1992-94; expert witness in field. Mem. First Century Families: Calif.; mem. com. Baldwin Hills Dam Disaster, 1968-72; pres. Alcohol Info. Ctr., L.A., 1983-85. Mem. L.A. Athletic Club, Wilshire Country Club. Republican. Avocations: classic cars, American and English silver. Home: 623 S Arden Blvd Los Angeles CA 90005-3814

INOUYE, DANIEL KEN, senator; b. Honolulu, Sept. 7, 1924; s. Hyotaro I. and Kame Imanaga; m. Margaret Shinobu Awamura, June 12, 1949; 1 child, Daniel Ken. A.B., U. Hawaii, 1950; J.D., George Washington U., 1952. Bar: Hawaii 1953. Asst. pub. prosecutor Honolulu, 1953-54, pvt. practice, 1954—; majority leader Territorial Ho. of Reps., 1954-58, Senate, 1958-59; mem. 86th-87th U.S. Congresses from Hawaii, U.S. Senate from Hawaii (now 106th Congress), 1962—; sec. Senate Dem. Conf., 1978-88; chmn. Dem. Steering Com., Senate Com. on Appropriations; chmn. subcom. def., mem. Commerce Com.; chmn. subcom. on communications Select Com. on Intelligence, 1976-77, ranking mem. subcom. budget authorizations, 1979-84; former chmn. Select Com. Indian Affairs; mem. Select Com. on Presdl. Campaign Activities, 1973-74; chmn. Sen. select com. Secret Mil. Assistance to Iran and Nicaraguan Opposition, 1987; ranking minority mem. Appropriations subcom. on defense, Commerce, Sci., & Transp. subcom on surface transp. & merchant marine; mem. Indian Affairs Com., Rules & Adminstrn. Com. Joint Com. on the Libr. & Congl. Intern Program, Dem. Steering & Coordination Com., Joint Com. on Printing. Author: Journey to Washington. Active YMCA, Boy Scouts Am. Keynoter; temporary chmn. Dem. Nat. Conv., 1968, rules com. chmn., 1980, co-chmn. conv., 1984. Pvt. to capt. AUS, 1943-47. Decorated D.S.C., Bronze Star, Purple Heart with cluster; named 1 of 10 Outstanding Young Men of Yr. U.S. Jr. C. of C., 1960; recipient Splendid Am. award Thomas A. Dooley Found., 1967 Golden Plate award Am. Acad. Achievement, 1968. Mem. DAV (past comdr. Hawaii), Honolulu C. of C., Am. Legion (Nat. Comdr.'s award 1973). Methodist. Clubs: Lion. (Hawaii), 442d Veterans (Hawaii). Home: 469 Ena Rd Honolulu HI 96815-1749 Office: US Senate 722 Hart Senate Bldg Washington DC 20510-1102*

INTRIERE, ANTHONY DONALD, physician; b. Greenwich, Conn., May 9, 1920; s. Rocco and Angelina (Belcastro) I.; m. Carol A. Yarmey, Aug. 1, 1945; children: Sherry Shoemaker, Michael, Nancy M., Lisa A. MD, U. Mich., 1944. Intern, New Rochelle (N.Y.) Hosp., 1944-45; pvt. practice, Greenwich, Conn., 1947-53, Olney, Ill., 1956-61, Granite City, Ill., 1961-74, San Diego, 1975—; fellow in internal medicine Cleve. Clinic, 1953-55; fellow in gastroenterology Lahey Clinic, Boston, 1955-56. Capt. M.C., AUS, 1945-47. Fellow Am. Coll. Gastroenterology (assoc.); mem. AMA, ACP (assoc.), Am. Soc. Internal Medicine, Fifty Yr. Club Ill. State Med. Soc. Home: 9981 Caminito Chirimolla San Diego CA 92131-2001

INTRILIGATOR, DEVRIE SHAPIRO, physicist; b. N.Y.C.; d. Carl and Lillian Shapiro; m. Michael Intriligator; children: Kenneth, James, William, Robert. BS in Physics, MIT, 1962, MS, 1964; PhD in Planetary and Space Physics, UCLA, 1967. NRC-NASA rsch. assoc. NASA, Ames, Calif., 1967-69; rsch. fellow in physics Calif. Inst. Tech., Pasadena, 1969-72, vis. assoc., 1972-73; asst. prof. U. So. Calif., 1972-80; mem. Space Scis. Ctr., 1978-83; sr. rsch. physicist Carmel Rsch. Ctr., Santa Monica, Calif., 1979—; dir. Space Plasma Lab., 1980—; cons. NASA, NOAA, Jet Propulsion Lab.; chmn. NAS-NRC com. on solar-terrestrial rsch., 1983-86, exec. com. bd. atmospheric sci. and climate, 1983-86, geophysics study com., 1983-86; U.S. nat. rep. Sci. Com. on Solar-Terrestrial Physics, 1983-86; mem. adv. com. NSF Divsn. Atmospheric Sci. Co-editor: Exploration of the Outer Solar System, 1976; contbr. articles to profl. jours. Recipient 3 Achievement awards NASA, Calif. Resolution of Commendation, 1982. Mem. AAAS, Am. Phys. Soc., Am. Geophys. Union, Cosmos Club. Achievements include being a participant Pioneer 10/11 missions to outer planets; Pioneer Venus Orbiter, Pioneers 6, 7, 8 and 9 heliocentric missions. Home: 140 Foxtail Dr Santa Monica CA 90402-2048 Office: Carmel Rsch Ctr PO Box 1732 Santa Monica CA 90406-1732

INVERSO, MARLENE JOY, optometrist; b. Los Angeles, May 10, 1942; d. Elmer Encel Wood and Sally Marie (Sample) Hirons; m. John S. Inverso, Dec. 16, 1962; 1 child, Christopher Edward. BA, Calif. State U., Northridge, 1964; MS, SUNY, Potsdam, 1975; OD, Pacific U., 1981. Cert. doctor optometry, Wash., Oreg. English tchr. Chatsworth (Calif.) High Sch., 1964-68, Nelson A. Boylen Second Sch., Toronto, Ont., Can., 1968-70, Gouverneur (N.Y.) Jr.-Sr. High Sch., 1970-74, 76-77; reading resource room tchr. Parishville (N.Y.) Hopkinton Sch., 1974-75; optometrist and vision therapist Am. Family Vision Clinics, Olympia, Wash., 1982—; coord. Lng. Disability Clin. SUNY, summers, 1975-77; mem. adv. com. Sunshine House St. Peter Hosp., Olympia, 1984-86, Pacific U. Coll. Optometry, Forest Grove, Oreg. 1986. Contbr. articles to profl. jours. Mem. Altrusa Svc. Club, Olympia, 1982-86; tchr. Ch. Living Water, Olympia, 1983-88, Olympia-Lacey Ch. of God, 1989—, sec. women's bd., 1990; bd. advisors Crisis Pregnancy Ctr., Olympia, 1987-89; den mother Cub Scouts Am. Pack 202, Lacey, Wash., 1987-88; vol. World Vision Countertop ptnr., 1986-97. Fellow Coll. Optometrists in Optometric Devel.; mem. Am. Optometric Assn. (sec. 1983-84), Assn. Children and Adults with Learning Disabilities, Optometric Extension Program, Sigma Xi, Beta Sigma Kappa. Avocations: bible study, professional speaking, training, and teaching. Home: 4336 Libby Rd NE Olympia WA 98506-2555

IPSEN, GRANT RUEL, insurance and investments professional; b. Malad, Idaho, Nov. 6, 1932; s. Nephi Ruel and Ada (Hughes) I.; m. Edna Wayne Hughes, July 27, 1956; children: Edna Gaye, LeAnn, Garin Grant, Shawna Lee, Wayne Ruel. BA, Brigham Young U., 1961. CPA, CLU, ChFC. Acct. Ernst & Ernst, Boise, Idaho, 1961-64; with sales dept. Mut. of N.Y., Boise, 1964—; mem. Idaho State Senate, 1992—. Active Boy Scouts Am., 1945—; co-convener Boise Religious Freedom Com., 1991-94. With U.S. Army, 1956-58. Named Agt. of Yr., Boise Assn. Life Underwriters, 1978, Man of Yr., Mut. of N.Y., 1982. Mem. Million Dollar Round Table (life), Brigham Young Univ. Alumni (bd. dirs. 1987-93). Republican. LDS. Avocations: reading, outdoor recreation, hiking, travel.

IRANI, RAY R., oil and gas and chemical company executive; b. Beirut, Lebanon, Jan. 15, 1935; came to U.S., 1953, naturalized, 1956; s. Rida and Naz I.; children: Glenn R., Lillian M., Martin R. BS in Chemistry, Am. U. Beirut, 1953; PhD in Phys. Chemistry, U. So. Calif., 1957. Rsch. scientist, then sr. rsch. scientist Monsanto Co., 1957-67; assoc. dir. new products, then dir. research Diamond Shamrock Corp., 1967-73; with Olin Corp., 1973-83, pres. chems. group, 1978-80; corp. pres., dir. Olin Corp., Stamford, Conn., 1980-83, COO, 1981-83; chmn. Occidental Petroleum Corp. subs. Occidental Chem. Corp., Dallas, 1983-94; CEO Occidental Petroleum Corp., subs. Occidental Chem. Corp., Dallas, 1983-91; chmn. Can. Occidental Petroleum Corp. Ltd., Calgary, 1987—; exec. v.p. Occidental Petroleum Corp., L.A., 1983-84, pres., COO, 1984-91, pres., 1991-96, chmn., CEO, 1991—, also bd. dirs.; bd. dirs. Am. Petroleum Inst., Oxy Oil and Gas USA Inc., Occidental Oil and Gas Corp., Occidental Petroleum Investment Corp., Cedars Bank, Kaufman and Broad Home Corp., Jonsson Cancer Ctr. Found./UCLA. Author: Particle Size; also author papers in field; numerous patents in field. Vice chmn. Am. U. Beirut; trustee U. So. Calif., St. John's Hosp. and Health Ctr. Found., Natural History Mus. Los Angeles County; bd. govs. Los Angeles Town Hall, Los Angeles World Affairs Coun. Mem. Nat. Petroleum Coun., Am. Inst. Chemists, Am. Chem. Soc., Sci. Rsch. Soc. Am., Indsl. Rsch. Inst., The Conf. Bd., The CEO Roundtable, Nat. Assn. Mfrs. (bd. dirs.), Am. Petroleum Inst. (bd. dirs.), U.S.-Russia Bus. Coun. Office: 10889 Wilshire Blvd Los Angeles CA 90024-4201

IRELAND, FAITH, judge; b. Seattle, 1942; d. Carl and Janice Enyeart; m. Chuck Norem. BA, U. Wash.; JD, Willamette U., 1969; M in Taxation with honors, Golden Gate U. Past assoc. McCune, Godfrey and Emerick, Seattle; pvt. practice Pioneer Square, Wash., 1974; judge King County Superior Ct., 1984-98, 1998; past dean Washington Jud. Coll., past mem. Bd. Ct. Edn. Served on numerous civic and charitable bds.; past pro-bono atty. Georgetown Dental Clin.; past bd. dirs. Puget Sound Big Sisters, Inc.; founding mem. Wing Luke Asian Mus., 1967—, past pres., past bd. dirs.; bd. dirs. Youth and Fitness Found., 1998. Recipient Disting. Svc. award Nat. Leadership Inst. Jud. Edn., 1998; named Judge of Yr. Washington State Trial Lawyer's Assn., Man of Yr. for efforts in founding Wing Luke Asian Mus. Mem. Washington Women Lawyer's (founding mem., Pres.'s award, Vanguard award), Wash. State Trial Lawyer's Assn. (past chair bd. dirs), Superior Ct. Judges Assn. (past bd. dirs., pres. 1996-97, vice chair bd. dirs. jud. adminstrn. 1996-98), Rainer Valley Hist. Soc. (founding mem., life), Rotary (bd. dirs. Seattle No. 4 1998). Office: Washington Supreme Ct Temple Justice PO Box 40929 Olympia WA 98504-0929*

IRELAND, LEWIS RAYMOND, management consultant, educator; b. West Branch, Mich., Dec. 14, 1937; s. Clyde Newton and Arma Fotilla (Albright) I.; m. Ouida Frances Hill, Nov. 14, 1937; children: Dee Ann, Mona Gay Parry, Sandra Kay. BS in Bus. Adminstrn., Benedictine Coll., 1972; MS in Sys. Mgmt., Fla. Inst. Tech., 1973; PhD in Bus. Adminstrn., Columbia Pacific U., 1981. Enlisted U.S. Army, 1956, commd. 2d Lt., 1959; advanced through grades to lt. col., 1977, ret., 1979; sect. mgr. SWL Inc., McLean, Va., 1979-89; project mgr. GTE Telecom, Colorado Springs, Colo., 1989-90; pres. L.R. Ireland Assocs., Reston, Va., 1990-95, Project Techs., Monument, Colo., 1995—; pres., chair Project Mgmt. Inst. Author: Quality Management, 1991; contbr. articles to profl. jours. Fellow Project Mgmt. Inst. (Person of the Yr. 1985, Disting. Contbn. 1986, Pres.'s award 1991). Republican. Avocations: chess, reading, photography, hiking. Home and Office: 20290 Doewood Dr Monument CO 80132-8050

IRISH, TERRY LEE, minister; b. Nampa, Idaho, Oct. 18, 1951; s. Carl Orville and Miriam Ivis (Eastly) I.; m. Carol Frances Helliwell, June 21, 1974; children: Jeremy Ryan, Jonathan Kyle, Jennifer Erin Frances. BA, N.W. Nazarene Coll., Nampa, Idaho, 1970-74; MDiv, Nazarene Theol. Sem., Kansas City, 1978. Ordained elder Ch. of Nazarene, 1981. Assoc. pastor First Ch. of Nazarene, Roseburg, Oreg., 1978-80; pastor Ch. of the Nazarene, Cle Elum, Wash., 1980-84; sr. pastor Crestline Ch. of Nazarene, Spokane, Wash., 1984-86; assoc. pastor First Ch. of Nazarene, Baker, Oreg., 1986-88; pastor Ch. of the Nazarene, Crescent City, Calif., 1988—; del. Gen. Christian Life Conv., Anaheim, Calif., 1985. Contbr. articles to profl. jours.; author original drama: He's Alive, 1980; drama script author, producer: King of Love, 1979. Chmn. Spokane County Sexual Abuse Team, Spokane, 1985-86; chmn. Year Round Edn. Task Force, Crescent City, 1991—. Mem. Del Notre Evang. Ministerial Assn. (pres. 1990—), Kiwanis (spiritual aims chmn. 1985-86, 87-88, 89-90). Republican. Home: 177 7th St Crescent City CA 95531-3950 Office: Crescent City Ch Nazarene 224 F St Crescent City CA 95531-4220

IRISH, THOMAS JUDSON, plastic surgeon; b. Forest City, Iowa, May 23, 1936; m. Sandra Rudolph. BS, Iowa State Coll., 1958; MD, State U. of Iowa, 1962. Intern King County Hosp. (now Harborview Hosp.), Seattle, 1962-63; pvt. practice Forest City, Iowa, 1963-66; resident in gen. surgery U. Colo. Med. Ctr., Denver, 1966-70; resident in plastic surgery Norfolk Gen. Hosp. & Kings Daughters Children's Hosp., Va., 1970-72; pvt. practice Plastic Surgeons NW, Tacoma, Wash., 1972—; med. dir. Franciscan Wound Care Ctr.; fellow in plastic surgery Canniesburn Hosp., Glasgow, Scotland, 1971. Fellow ACS; mem. Am. Soc. Plastic and Reconstructive Surgery, Alpha Omega Alpha. Office: 1802 S Yakima Ave Ste 200 Tacoma WA 98405-5304

IRVINE, VERNON BRUCE, accounting educator, administrator; b. Regina, Sask., Can., May 31, 1943; s. Joseph Vern and Anna Francis (Phillip) I.; m. Marilyn Ann Craik, Apr. 29, 1967; children: Lee-Ann, Cameron, Sandra. B. Commerce, U. Sask., 1965; MBA, U. Chgo., 1967; PhD, U. Minn., 1977. Cert. mgmt. acct. Researcher, Sask. Royal Commn. on Taxation, Regina, 1964; lectr. acctg. Coll. Commerce, U. Sask., Saskatoon, 1967-69, asst. prof., 1969-74, assoc. prof., 1974-79, prof., 1979—, head dept. acctg., 1981-84; profl. program lectr. Inst. Chartered Accts., Regina, 1982-84, Soc. Mgmt. Accts., Saskatoon, 1982-84, 94-95. Co-author: A Practical Approach to the Appraisal of Capital Expenditures, 1981; Intermediate Accounting: Canadian Edition, 1982, 5th edit., 1998; contbr. articles to acctg. jours. Grantee John Wiley & Sons, Ltd., 1981, 85, 87, 88, 92, 93, 96, Soc. Mgmt. Accts. Can., 1979, Pres.'s Fund, U. Sask., 1978, Nelson Can. grantee, 1990. Bd. dirs. Big Sisters of Sask., 1987-90. Fellow Soc. Mgmt. Accts. Can. (bd. dirs. 1979-82, 85-87, 89-92, chmn. Nat. Edn. Svcs. com.); mem. Can. Acad. Acctg. Assn. (pres. 1994-95, pres.- elect 1993-94, sec. 1992-93, exec. com., chmn. mem. com. 1989-91), Internat. Acctg. Stds. Com. (Can. rep. 1984-87, 96-97), Internat. Fedn. Accts. Coun. (tech. advisor 1988-90), Soc. of Mgmt. Accts. of Sask. (pres. 1980-81), Sutherland Curling Club (treas. 1979-83), Saskatoon Golf and Country Club (bd. dirs. 1988-90). Home: 45 Cantlon Crescent, Saskatoon, SK Canada S7J 2T2 Office: U Sask, Commerce Bldg 25 Campus Dr, Saskatoon, SK Canada S7N 5A7

IRWIN, ANNA MAE, English language educator; b. Petrolia, Kans., Aug. 19; d. Clarence Newton and Elsie Mildred (Stump) Williams; m. Everett Irwin, Sept. 1, 1938; children: Stanley, Pamela, Steven. BS, Northeastern State U., Tahlequah, Okla., 1940; postgrad., Denver U. and Colo. U., 1960-80. Bookkeeper, typist Fed. Bur. Pub. Rds., Denver, 1942-45; tchr. Denver Pub. Schs., 1945-46; typist State Dept. Employment, Denver, 1958-60; tchr. Aurora (Colo.) Pub. Schs., 1960-84; tutor ESL for refugees State Dept. Edn., Denver, 1988-91. Mem. adv. bd., bd. dirs. Unity Ch., Denver, 1986—; mem. and pres. aux. Goodwill Industries, Denver, 1996—, 2d v.p., 1st v.p. 1992-96, pres. 1993-96; state del., county del., congl. del., precinct com. woman Rep. Party, Denver, 1970-84. Recipient Mary Venable Svc. award for vol. work Goodwill Industries, 1996. Mem. Book Review Club (v.p., program chmn. 1990-93), Cherry Creek Womens Club. Avocations: bridge, travel, book review, ceramics.

IRWIN, MILDRED LORINE WARRICK, library consultant, civic worker; b. Kellerton, Iowa, June 21, 1917; d. Webie Arthur and Bonnie Lorine (Hyatt) DeVries; m. Carl Wesley Warrick, Feb. 11, 1937 (dec. June 1983); children: Carl Dwayne, Arthur Will; m. John B. Irwin, Feb. 1, 1994 (dec. Apr. 10, 1997). BS in Edn., Drake U., 1959; M of Librarianship, Kans. State Tchrs. Coll., 1970. Cert. tchr., libr., Iowa. Elem. tchr. Monroe Ctr. Rural Sch., Kellerton, Iowa, 1935-37, Denham Rural Sch., Grand River, Iowa, 1945-48, Grand River Ind. Sch., 1948-52, Woodmansee Rural Sch., Decatur, Iowa, 1952-55, Centennial Rural Sch., Decatur, 1955-56; elem. tchr., acting libr. Cen. Decatur Sch., Leon, Iowa, 1956-71, media libr. jr. and sr. high sch., 1971-79; libr. Northminster Presbyn. Ch., Tucson, 1984-93, advisor, 1994—; media resource instr. Graceland Coll., Lamoni, Iowa, 1971-72; lit. dir. S.W. Iowa Assn. Classroom Tchrs., 1965-69. Editor (media packet) Mini History and Quilt Blocks, 1976, Grandma Lori's Nourishing Nuggets for Body and Soul, 1985, As I Recall (Loren Drake), 1989, Foland Family Supplement III, 1983; author: (with Quentin Oiler) Van Der Vlugt Family Record, 1976; compiler, editor Abigail Specials, 1991, Abigail Assemblage, 1996; compiler Tribute to Ferm Mills 1911-1992, 1992; co-editor: (with Dorothy Heitlinger) Milestones and Touchstones, 1993; contbr. articles to publs. Leader Grand River 4-H Club for Girls, 1954-58; sec. South Ctrl. Iowa Quarter Horse Assn., Chariton, 1967-68; chmn. Decatur County Dems., 1981-83, del., 1970-83; pianist Salvation Army Amphi League of Mercy Rhythm Notes, 1984-90; pianist, dir. Joymakers, 1990—; Sunday Sch. tchr. Decatur United Meth. Ch., 1945-54, 80-83, lay speaker, 1981-83, dir. vacation Bible sch., 1982, 83. Named Classroom Tchr. of Iowa Classrom Tchrs. Assn., 1962, Woman of Yr., Leon Bus. and Profl. Women, 1978, Northminster Presbyn. Ch. Women, 1990; named to Internat. Profl. and Bus. Women Hall of Fame for outstanding achievements in field of edn. and libr. sci., 1995; English and reading grantee Nat. Dept. Edn., 1966. Mem. NEA (life), AAUW (chmn. Tucson creative writing/cultural interests 1986-87, 89-93, historian, 1994—, Honoree award for ednl. found. programs Tucson br., Svc. award 1991), Internat. Reading Assn. (pres. Clarke-Ring-gold-Decatur chpts. 1967-68), Cen. Cmty. Tchrs. Assn. (pres. 1961-62), Pima County Ret. Tchrs. Assn. (pres. 1989-90), Decatur County Assn. (pres. 1961-63), Decatur County Ret. Tchrs. Assn. (historian 1980-83), Iowa Edn. Assn. (life), Presbyn. Women (hon. life 1990—), Luth. Ch. Libr. Assn. (historian Tucson area chpt. 1991-92, v.p. 1993-94, pres. 1994-95), Delta Kappa Gamma (pres. Iowa Beta XI chpt. 1974-76, sec. 1984-85, historian Ariz. Alpha Gamma chpt. 1986-89). Democrat. Presbyterian. Avocations: walking, hiking, horseback riding, reading, writing. Home: 2879 E Presidio Rd Tucson AZ 85716-1539

IRWIN, R. ROBERT, lawyer; b. Denver, July 27, 1933; s. Royal Robert and Mildred Mary (Wilson) I.; m. Sue Ann Scott, Dec. 16, 1956; children—Lori, Stacy, Kristi, Amy. Student U. Colo., 1951-54, B.S.L., U. Denver, 1955, LL.B., 1957. Bar: Colo. 1957, Wyo. 1967. Asst. atty. gen. State of Colo., 1958-66; asst. div. atty. Mobil Oil Corp., Casper, Wyo. 1966-70; prin. atty. No. Natural Gas Co., Omaha 1970-72; sr. atty. Coastal Oil & Gas Corp., Denver 1972-83, asst. sec. 1972-83; ptnr. Baker & Hostetler, 1983-87; pvt. practice 1987—. Mem. Colo. Bar Assn., Arapahoe County Bar Assn., Rocky Mountain Oil and Gas Assn. Republican. Clubs: Los Verdes Golf, Petroleum, Denver Law (Denver). Office: 650 S Alton Way Apt 4D Denver CO 80231-1669

ISAAC NASH, EVA MAE, educator; b. Natchitoches Parish, La., July 24, 1936; d. Earfus Will Nash and Dollie Mae (Edward) Johnson; m. Will Isaac Jr., July 1, 1961 (dec. May 1970). BA, San Francisco State U., 1974, MS in Edn., 1979, MS in Counseling, 1979; PhD, Walden U., 1985; diploma (hon.), St. Labre Indian Sch., 1990. Nurse's aide Protestant Episcopal Home, San Francisco, 1957-61; desk clk. Fort Ord (Calif.) Post Exchange, 1961-63; practical nurse Monterey (Calif.) Hosp., 1963-64; tchr. San Francisco Unified Schs., 1974; counselor, instr. City Coll. San Francisco, 1978-79; tchr. Oakland (Calif.) Unified Sch. Dist., 1974—; pres. sch. adv. coun., Oakland, 1977-78, faculty adv. coun., 1992-93; advt. writer City Coll., San Francisco, 1978; instr. vocat. skill tng., Garfield Sch., Oakland, 1980-81; pub. speaker various ednl. insts. and chs., Oakland, San Francisco, 1982—; lectr. San Jose State U., 1993; creator Language Arts-Step By Step program E. Morris Cox Elem. Sch., Oakland, 1995, 96; author, presenter material in field. Author video tape Hunger: An Assassin in the Classroom, 1993-94. Recipient Community Svc. award Black Caucus of Calif. Assn. Counseling and Devel., 1988, Cert. of Recognition, 1990; named Citizen of the Day, Sta. KABL, 1988. Mem. ASCD, Internat. Reading Assn., Nat. Assn. Female Execs., Am. Personnel and Guidance Assn., Calif. Personnel and Guidance Assn., Internat. Platform Assn. (Hall Fame 1989, Profl. Speaking cert. 1993), Phi Delta Kappa. Democrat. Avocations: travel, hiking, tennis, music, dancing. Office: Oakland Unified Sch Dist 1025 2nd Ave Oakland CA 94606 2296

ISAACS, JONATHAN WILLIAM, oil company executive; b. Chgo., Apr. 9, 1957; s. Kenneth Sidney and Ruth Elizabeth (Johnson) I. BA, Lake

Forest Coll., 1980. Prin. Kenisa Oil Co., Northbrook, Ill., 1980—, Kenisa Drilling Co., Denver, 1986—. First to utilize Diamonium Phosphate Drilling Mud in Denver Julesburg Basin biodegradable into fertilizer, (HN4) 2 HPO 4; inventor downhole non-metalic oil well tubing system. Mem. NRA, Nat. Skeet Shooting Assn., Ind. Petroleum Assn., Denver Assn. Petroleum Landmen, Rep. Mens Club, Exmoor Country Club, Alpha Nu Chi Psi. Republican. Avocations: dressage, shooting. Office: Kenisa Drilling Co 518 17th St Denver CO 80202-4130

ISAACSON, ROBERT LOUIS, investment company executive; b. Chgo., Apr. 21, 1944; s. Abe B. and Laverne (Skolka) I. BS, Mich. State U., 1966. Mktg. mgr. Florasynth, Inc., San Francisco, 1966-69; br. mgr. Florasynth, Inc., Lincolnwood and Palo Alto, Calif., 1969-72; br. office mgr. Geldermann, Palo Alto, 1972-76; founder, pres. Commodity Investment Cons., Los Altos, Calif., 1976—, Future Funding Cons., Menlo Park, Calif., 1976—; co-founder, co-chmn. Nat. Assn. Futures Trading Advisors; bd. dirs. Futures Industry Assn. Edn. and Tng., Williams & Clarissa, Inc.; bd. dirs., exec. com., membership com. Nat. Futures Assn.; membership Nat. Futures Assn. Regional Bus. Conduct Com.; v.p. Lind-Waldock Co., Chgo.; pres. Interalliance U.S.A. Contbr. articles to mags and profl. jours. Founder Fun for Lunch Bunch. With U.S. Mil., 1966-72. Recipient Doncheon award Managed Accounts Report, 1984. Mem. San Francisco Futures Soc., Managed Futures Assn. (past co-chmn., bd. dirs.), Asian Pacific Managed Futures Assn. (bd. dirs., founding mem.), World Trading Day CARE (exec. com.), Peninsula Commodities Club, Elks, Kiwanis. Avocations: jogging, biking, horseback riding, flying, sailing. Home: 380 La Questa Way Woodside CA 94062-2428 Office: Commodity Investment Cons Future Funding Cons 380 La Questa Way Woodside CA 94062-2428

ISAUTIER, BERNARD FRANÇOIS, business executive; b. Tours, France, Sept. 19, 1942; s. Francois and Genevieve (Roy) I. Grad., Ecole Polytechnique, Paris, 1963, Ecole des Mines, Paris, 1966, Institut d'Etudes Politiques, Paris, 1968. Uranium advisor Rep. of Niger, 1968-70; energy and minerals advisor to min. industry and energy Govt. of France, Paris, 1970-75; gen. mgr. ops. Elf-Aquitaine Group, Tunis, Tunisia, 1976-78; pres., CEO Aquitaine Co. of Can. Ltd., Calgary, Alta., Can., 1978-81, Canterra Energy, Calgary, 1981-85, Polysar Energy & Chem. Corp., Toronto, Ont., Can., 1986-88; chmn., CEO Thomson Consumer Electronics, Paris, 1990-92; CEO, Can. Occidental Petroleum, Calgary, 1993-95; pres., CEO, Chauvco Resources Internat., Calgary, 1997—, also bd. dirs.; bd. dirs. Archer Resources, Calgary, Can. Credit Lyonnais, Montreal, Firan Corp., Toronto, Hurricane Hydrocarbons, Calgary, Lafarge, Paris, Wilan Co.; chn. bd. FracMaster, Ltd., Calgary. Served to lt. Res. Army of France, 1961-64. Decorated Order of Nat. Merite. Avocations: skiing, sailing, scuba diving. Office: 530 8th Ave SW Ste 1310, Calgary, AB Canada T2P 3S8

ISBELL, HAROLD M(AX), writer, investor; b. Maquoketa, Iowa, Sept. 20, 1936; s. H. Max and Marcella E. I.; BA cum laude (scholar), Loras Coll., 1959; MA (fellow), U. Notre Dame, 1962; grad. U. Mich. Grad. Sch. Bank Mgmt., 1982; m. Mary Carolyn Cosgriff, June 15, 1963; children: Walter Harold, Susan Elizabeth, David Harold, Alice Kathleen. Instr., U. Notre Dame, South Bend, Ind., 1963-64; assoc. prof. St. Mary's Coll., 1969-72; asst. prof. San Francisco Coll. for Women, 1964-69; with Continental Bank & Trust Co., Salt Lake City, 1972-83, v.p., 1977-83, comml. credit officer, 1978-83, also dir. Trustee Judge Meml. Cath. High Sch., Salt Lake City, 1977-84; mem. Utah Coun. for Handicapped and Developmentally Disabled Persons, 1980-81; bd. dirs. Ballet West, 1983-90, emeritus, 1990—, Story Line Press, 1994—, Smuin Ballets, San Francisco, 1994—; founder Cath. Found. Utah, pres. 1984-86, trustee, 1984-89. Mem. MLA, Mediaeval Acad. Am., Am. Assn. for the Advancement of Sci. Democrat. Roman Catholic. Club: Alta. Editor and translator: The Last Poets of Imperial Rome, 1971, Ovid: Heroides, 1990; contbr. to publs. in field of classical Latin lit. and contemporary Am. Lit.

ISELY, HENRY PHILIP, association executive, integrative engineer, writer, educator; b. Montezuma, Kans., Oct. 16, 1915; s. James Walter and Jessie M. (Owen) I; m. Margaret Ann Sheesley, June 12, 1948; children: Zephyr, LaRock, Lark, Rodin, Kemper, Heather Capri. Student, South Oreg. Jr. Coll., Ashland, 1934-35, Antioch Coll., 1935-37. Organizer Action for World Fedn., 1946-50, N.Am. Coun. for People's World Conv., 1954-58; Organizer World Com. for World Constl. Conv., 1958, sec. gen., 1959-66; sec. gen. World Constn. and Parliment Assn., Lakewood, Colo., 1966—; organizer worldwide prep. confs. World Constn. and Parliment Assn., 1963, 66, 67, 1st session People's World Parliament and World Constl. Conv., Switzerland, 1968; editor assn, jour. Across Frontiers, 1959—; co-organizer Emergency Coun. World Trustees, 1971; co-organizer World Constituent Assembly, Innsbruck, Austria, 1977, Columbo, Sri Lanka, 1978-79, Troia, Portugal, 1991; organizer Provisional World Parliament 1st session, Brighton, Eng., 1982, 2nd Session, New Delhi, India, 1985, 3d Session, Miami Beach, Fla., 1987; mem. parliament, 1982—; sec. Working Commn. to Draft World Constn., 1971-77, pres. World Svc. Trust, 1972-78, ptnr. Builder Found., Vitamin Cottages, 1955—, (chmn. bd. dirs., 1985—), pres. Earth Rescue Corps., 1984-90, sec.-treas. Grad. Sch. World Problems, 1984— (prof. world problems, 1990—), cabinet mem. Provisional World Govt., 1987—, pres. World Govt. Funding Corp., 1986—, Emergency Earth Rescue Adminstrn., 1995—, co-organizer Global Ratification and Elections Network, 1991— (sec. 1992—), prin. organizer 4th session Provisional World Parliament, Barcelona, 1996, organizer first More Oxygen for the World conf., San Antonio, 1998, now organizing 5th session of Provisional World Parliament, Baghdad, Irag. *Mr. Isley is very active in the Global Ratification and Elections Network, which campaigns for the ratification and implemenation of the Constitution for the Federation of Earth. He writes letters to the organization's members in over 120 countries and he has spoken in 45 countries during his lifework for peace and equity under federal world government.* Author: The People Must Write the Peace, 1950, A Call to All Peoples and All National Governments of the Earth, 1961, Outline for the Debate and Drafting of a World Constitution, 1967, Strategy for Reclaiming Earth for Humanity, 1969, Call to a World Constituent Assembly, 1974, Proposal for Immediate Action by an Emergency Council of World Trustees, 1971, Call to A Provisional World Parliament, 1981, People Who Want Peace Must Take Charge of World Affairs, 1982, Plan for Emergency Earth Rescue Administration, 1985, Plan for Earth Finance Credit Corporation, 1987, Climate Crisis, 1989, Technological Breakthroughs for A Global Energy Network, 1991, Bill of Particulars: Why the U.N. Must Be Replaced, 1994, Manifesto for the Inauguration of World Government, 1994, Call to the Fourth Session of the Provisional World Parliament, 1995, Fifth Session, 1997, Critique of the Report of the Commission on Global Governance, 1995, Using Credit Cards and Electronic Accounting to Initiate New Global Finance System, 1996, Double Jeopardy and the Phytoplankton Project, 1997, The Fallacy of Treating Labor as a Commodity, 1998; co-author, editor: A Constitution for the Federation of Earth, 1974, rev. edit., 1991, also author several other world legis. measures adopted at Provisional World Parliament, 1968-96; co-author: Plan for Collaboration in World Constituent Assembly, 1991, Creator treatment for screen drama History Hangs by a Thread, 1993; designer: prefab modular panel system of constrn., master plan for Guacamaya project in Costa Rica. Candidate for U.S. Congress, 1958, organizer first conv. More Oxygen for the World, San Antonio, 1998. Recipient hon. rsch. doctorate in edn., 1989, Honor award Internat Assn. Educators for World Peace, 1975, Ghandi medal, 1977, Honor award Internat Soc. Universalism, 1993. Mem. ACLU, Am. Acad. Polit. Sci., Fellowship of Reconciliation, World Union, World Federalist Assn., World Future Soc., Earth Island Inst., Populatin Reference Bur., Earth Action, People's Congress, Life Ext. Found., Interfaith Alliance, Internat. Assn. for Hydrogen Energy, Friends of Earth, Wilderness Soc., Solar Energy Soc., Sierra Club, Amnesty Internat., World Resources Inst., Human Rights Watch, Nat. Nutritional Foods Assn., Environ. Def. Fund, Greenpeace, Ctr. for Study of Democratic Instns., War Resistors League, Audubon Soc., Worldwatch Inst., Internat. Assn. Constl. Law, Earth Regeneration Soc., Zero Population Growth, Caner Control Soc., Mt. Vernon Country Club. Socialist. Fax: 303-237-7685. E-mail: wcpagren@aol.com. Home: Lookout Mountain 241 Zephyr Ave Golden CO 80401-9589 Office: 8800 W 14th Ave Lakewood CO 80215-4817

ISERSON, KENNETH VICTOR, emergency medicine educator, bioethicist; b. Washington, Apr. 8, 1949; s. Isadore I. and Edith (Swedlow) I.; m. Mary Lou Sherk, June 16, 1973. BS, U. Md., 1971, MD, 1975; MBA, U. Phoenix, 1987. Diplomate Am. Bd. Emergency Medicine, Nat. Bd. Med. Examiners. Intern surgery Mayo Clinic, Rochester, Minn., 1975; resident emergency medicine Cin. Gen. Hosp., 1976-78; chmn. emergency dept. Tex. A&M Coll. Medicine, Temple, 1980-81; asst. prof. surgery U. Ariz. Coll. Medicine, Tucson, Ariz., 1981-84; residency dir. emergency medicine U. Ariz. Coll. Medicine, Tucson, 1981-91, assoc. prof. surgery, 1984-92; dir. Ariz. Bioethics Program U. Ariz., Tucson, 1991—, prof. surgery, 1992—; pres. Iserson Assocs. Ltd., Tucson, 1984—; vis. scholar Ctr. Clin. Med. Ethics U. Chgo., Pritzker Sch. Medicine, 1990-91. Author: Getting Into a Residency: A Guide for Medical Students, 1988, 4th edit., 1996, Death to Dust: What Happens to Dead Bodies?, 1994, Non-Standard Medical Electives in the U.S. and Canada, 1997, 2d edit., 1998, Get Into Medical School! A Guide for the Perplexed, 1997; sr. editor: Ethics in Emergency Medicine, 1986, 2d edit., 1995, Grave Words: Notifying Survivors About Sudden Unexpected Death, 1999; mem. editorial bd. HEC Forum, Jour. Emergency Medicine, 1985—; contbr. sci. articles to profl. jours. Med. dir. So. Ariz. Rescue Assn., Pima County, 1983—. Capt. USAF, 1978-80. Fellow Am. Coll. Emergency Physicians: mem. AMA, Soc. Acad. Emergency Medicine (pres. 1984-85, chmn. AMA rels. com. 1989—), Wilderness Med. Soc. (bd. dirs. 1987-91).

ISHII, CLYDE HIDEO, plastic surgeon; b. Lihue, Hawaii, Mar. 29, 1952. MD, Jefferson Med. Coll., 1978. Diplomate Am. Bd. Surgery, Am. Bd. Plastic Surgery. Past chief plastic surgery Queens Med. Ctr., Honolulu, asst. chief of surgery; chief plastic surgery Shriners Hosp., Honolulu, 1993—. Office: 1329 Lusitana St Ste 502 Honolulu HI 96813-2412

ISIDORO, EDITH ANNETTE, horticulturist; b. Albuquerque, Oct. 14, 1957; d. Robert Joseph and Marion Elizabeth (Miller) I. BS in Horticulture, N.Mex. State U., 1981, MS in Horticulture, 1984; postgrad., U. Nev., Reno, 1992—. Range conservationist Soil Conservation Service, Estancia, Grants, N.Mex., 1980-82; lab. aide N.Mex. State U. Dept. Horticulture, Las Cruces, 1982, 83-84; technician N.Mex. State U. Coop. Extension Service, Las Cruces, 1983-84, county agrl. extension agt., 1985; area extension agr. U. Nev., Reno, Fallon, 1985—; hay tester Nev. Agrl. Services, Fallon, 1988-92; owner wholesale greenhouse Garden of Edith, 1996—. Mem. AAUW, Am. Soc. Hort. Sci., Am. Horticulture Soc., Am. Botany Soc., Am. Horticulture Therapy Assn., Alpha Zeta, Pi Alpha Psi. Avocations: flute, ch. choir, hiking, gardening, macrame. Home: 3900 Sheckler Rd Fallon NV 89406-8202 Office: Churchill County Coop Extension 1450 Mclean Rd Fallon NV 89406-8880

ISLAM, NAHEED, writer, researcher; b. Bryan, Tex., Jan. 20, 1965; s. Nazrul and Nahar (Chowdhury) I.; m. S. Raihan Zamil, Dec. 30, 1992. BA cum laude, Ohio Wesleyan U., 1988; MA, U. Calif., Berkeley, 1990, postgrad. editl. assoc. South Asian Mag. Action and Reflection, N.Y.C., 1995—; reviewer Signs: Jour. Women and Culture, Seattle, 1996, 97. Contbr. chpts. to books. Grad. Rsch. fellow U. Calif., Berkeley, 1988. Mem. Am. Sociol. Assn., Assn. Asian Am. Studies, Omicron Delta Kappa, Alpha Kappa Delta. Avocations: travel, listening to music, reading, film. E-mail: nislam@socrates.berkeley.edu. Home: 1 Kelton Ct Apt 10H Oakland CA 94611-4861

ISLAMBOULY, HAGAR ABDEL-HAMID, consul general; b. Cairo, Jan. 5, 1947; d. Abdel Hamid and Souad (ElSherif) I.; m. Mohamed Adel Ezzat, Jan. 22, 1970. Diploma, Am. Coll. Girls, Cairo, 1964; BSc in Polit. Sci., Cairo U., 1969. With state info. svc. Ministry Information, Cario, 1970-74; with the cabinet of the ofcl. spokesman Ministry Fgn. Affairs Diplomatic Inst., Cairo, 1974; mem. internal. orgn. dept. Ministry Fgn. Affairs, Cairo, 1975-76; second sec. Embassy of Egypt, Madrid, 1976-80; with cabinet of the asst. minister of fgn. affairs for legal internat. orgns. affairs Ministry Fgn. Affairs, Cairo, 1980-81, mem. cabinet of the head of Egyptian mechanism for negotiation with Israel, 1981-84; counselor Egyptian Embassy, Bonn, Germany, 1984-88; dep. dir. Israeli affairs dept. Ministry Fgn. Affairs, Cairo, 1988-90, dep. dir. internat. orgns. dept., 1990-91, dir. environ. affairs dept., 1991-93, dir. internat. environ. affairs dept., 1991-95, dir. internat. economic affairs dept., 1993-95; consul gen., chief of mission Egyptian Consulate, San Francisco, 1995—; attended UN Conf. for Environ. and Devel., Rio De Janeiro, 1992, Middle East/North Africa Economic Summit, UN Gen. Assembly, UN Agencies and UN Environ. Programs, UN Conf. Trade and Devel., UN Conf. on Population and Devel., 1991-95; attended Morocco Conf. Internat. Trade for Gen. Agreements of Tarrifs and Trade, Uruguay, 1994; mem. Egyptian Gen. Com. assigned to prepare for the Peace Conf. in the Middle East, Ministry Fgn. Affairs, 1990-95; head of the Egyptian delegation to the working group of environ.-multi lateral track of the Peace Conf. in the Middle East, Ministry Fgn. Affairs, 1991-95. Contbr. articles to profl. jours. Active environ. groups in Egypt; mem. regional organization and related com., summits Islamic Conf. Orgn., Arab League, Orgn. African Unity, 1993-95. Recipient The Order of Civil Merit, King of Spain, 1980, Order of Civil Merit, Pres. Germany, 1988. Mem. World State Forum (coord. Middle East affairs 1996—), World Trade Club, UN, San Francisco Consular Corps., World Affairs Coun., San Francisco Ladies of Consular Corps, Commonwealth Club. Islamic. Avocations: reading, classical music, jogging. Fax: 415-346-9480. Office: Egyptian Consulate 3001 Pacific Ave San Francisco CA 94115-1099

ISRAEL, JOAN, social worker; b. Bklyn., July 19, 1943; d. Joseph Israel and Irene (Solon) Kansey; m. Ronald Jerome Janesh, June 28, 1980 (div. Feb. 1985); 1 child, Ariel Naomi. BA, Bklyn. Coll., 1965; MSW, U. Mich., 1974. Lic. clin. social worker, Nev. Social worker Alameda County Welfare Dept., Oakland, Calif., 1965-72; group therapist Pacific Ctr. for Human Growth, Berkeley, Calif., 1975-77; individual and group therapist, bd. dir. Bi-Ctr., San Francisco, 1976-78; clin. social worker, supr. Audrey L. Smith Devel. Ctr., San Francisco, 1977-78; psychiat. social worker South Nev. Adult Mental Health Dept., Las Vegas, 1978-84, part-time clin. social worker, 1988—; pvt. practice clin. social worker Las Vegas, 1984—. Contbr. articles to profl. publs. Organizer Drug/Alcohol Abuse Task Force, Las Vegas, 1983-84, Task Force on AIDS, Las Vegas, 1985-86. Mem. NASW (chair nominating com. 1978-80, 82-84, sec. 1984-86, chair com. on inquiry 1988—, legis. chair 1982-84, diplomate clin. social work), Sierra Club. Democrat. Jewish. Avocations: hiking, singing, opera, science fiction, dance. Office: 3180 W Sahara Ave Ste 25C Las Vegas NV 89102-6073

ISRAEL, MICHAEL L., art gallery manager; b. N.Y.C., Sept. 18, 1957; s. Oscar Harold and Sheila Barbara (Cole) I.; m. Beth Ellen Kjome, Oct. 23, 1994. BFA, U. Hartford, 1980. Mgr. Barney's Place, Greenwich, Conn., 1980-83; session musician N.Y.C., 1983-94; sales cons. Wayne Cross Ford, San Rafael, Calif., 1994-95; mgr. Gold's Gym, Corte Madera, Calif., 1995-97, Michael Thompson Gallery, San Francisco, 1997—; cons. Corp Framing Systems, Stamford, Conn., 1983. Avocations: reading books, painting, sports, cooking. Home: 664 Sierra Point Rd Brisbane CA 94005-1622 Office: Michael Thompson Gallery 1 Sutter St Ste 200 San Francisco CA 94104-4907

ISRAEL, PAUL NEAL, computer design engineer, author; b. Balt., Apr. 22, 1959; s. Sheldon Leonard and Sheila Lee (Goldmacher) I. BS in EECS, U. Calif., Berkeley, 1981. Project mgr. computer sci. dept. U. Calif., Berkeley, 1981-82; design engr. Electronic Signature Lock Corp., Berkeley, 1983; staff engr. Qantel Bus. Systems, Hayward, Calif., 1983-89; sr. hardware design engr. SBE, Inc., Concord, Calif., 1989-90; engring. contractor Renegade Systems, Sunnyvale, Calif., 1990-92; prin. engr. Unisys Corp., San Jose, Calif., 1992-95; sr. design engr. Network Virtual Systems, Inc., San Jose, 1995—. Awarded U.S. patent June, 1997, for Avoiding Instability in Computer Logic, awarded U.S. patent Oct., 1998, for method for cycle request with quick termination without waiting for the cycle to reach the destination by storing information in queue. Mem. IEEE, Assn. Computing Machinery, Bay Area Sci. Fiction Assn. Avocations: model railroading, writing, sports, science fiction. Office: Network Virtual Systems Inc 2077 Gateway Pl Ste 220 San Jose CA 95110-1016

ISRAEL, RICHARD STANLEY, investment banker; b. Oakland, Calif., Sept. 27, 1931; s. Sybil Noble, July 29, 1962; children: Richard Lee, Lynne, Lawrence. BA, U. Calif., Berkeley, 1953, MA, 1953. Copy editor San Francisco Chronicle, 1953-59; publicist CBS TV Network, L.A., 1959-62; sr. v.p. Rogers & Cowan, Beverly Hills, Calif., 1962-69; v.p. Cantor, Fitzgerald, Beverly Hills, 1969-73; pres. Sponsored Cons. Svcs., L.A., 1973—; bd. dirs. Hurst Labeling Systems. Pres. North Beverly Dr. Homeowners Assn., Beverly Hills, 1986-88; v.p. Temple Emanuel, Beverly Hills, 1988-93, L.A. chpt. Juvenile Diabetes Found. Internat, 1987—. With U.S. Army, 1956-58. Recipient Alumni citation U. Calif. Alumni Assn., Berkeley, 1984. Mem. L.A. Venture Assn. (pres. 1987), Assn. for Corp. Growth (pres. bd. dirs. L.A. chpt.). Democrat. Avocations: volleyball, travel. Office: Sponsored Cons Svcs 8929 Wilshire Blvd Ste 214 Beverly Hills CA 90211-1951

ISSARI, M(OHAMMAD) ALI, film producer, writer, consultant; b. Esfahan, Iran, Oct. 3, 1921; s. Abbas Bek and Qamar (Soltan) I.; m. Joan Gura Aamodt, 1958; children: Scheherezade, Katayoun, Roxana. BA, U. Tehran, Iran, 1963; MA, U. So. Calif., 1968; PhD, 1979. Films officer Brit. Embassy, Brit. Council Joint Film Div., Tehran, 1944-50; asst. motion picture officer USIS, Tehran, 1950-65; cons. to various Iranian Govt. ministries on film and TV devels., 1950-77; liaison officer Am. and Iranian govt. ofcls., 1950-65; prof. cinema Coll. Communication Arts and Scis. Mich. State U., East Lansing, 1969-81; also dir. instructional film and multimedia prodn. Mich. State U., 1969-78; mass media cons., 1981—; pres. Multimedia Prodn. Svcs., Thousand Oaks, Calif., 1989—; film, public relations adviser to Iranian Oil Operating Cos. in, Iran, 1963-65; spl. cons. on edn. and instructional TV Saudi Arabian Ministry of Info., 1972; tchr. Persian lang. Iran-Am. Soc., Tehran, 1949-59; introduced audio-visual edn. in Iran, 1951; established first film festivals in Iran. Producer, dir. over 1000 ednl., instructional and documentary films, 1956-78; freelance film reporter: Telenews, UPI, Iran, 1959-61, others; project dir., exec. producer: Ancient Iran Film Series, 1974-78; dir. film prodn. workshops, Cranbrook Inst., Detroit, 1973-74; author: (with Doris A. Paul) A Picture of Persia, 1977, What is Cinema Vérité?, 1979, Cinema in Iran, 1900-1979, 1989; contbr. articles on ednl. communication and audio-visual instruction to periodicals and profl. jours. Founder, exec. sec. Youth Orgn. of Iran, 1951-52; v.p. Rugby Football Fedn., Iran, 1952-53, pres., 1954-55. Decorated Order of Magnum Cap Ord: S.F. Danaie M. Sigillum (Denmark), Order of Cavalieres (Italy), Order of Oranje Nassau (The Netherlands), 1959, Orders of Kooshesh and Pas (Iran), Order of Esteghlal (Jordan), Order of Ordinis Sancti Silvestri Papae (The Vatican); recipient Meritorious Honor award USIA, 1965, Golden Eagle award Coun. for Internat. Non-Theatrical Events, 1975. Mem. Anglo-Iranian Dramatic Soc. (bd. dirs. 1943-50), Mich. Film Assn. (co-founder 1972, bd. dirs. 1972-73), Mid. East Studies Assn., N.Am. Soc. Motion Picture and TV Engrs. (life), Ancient Studies Inst. Inc. (co-founder, pres. 1991, 97-98), House of Iran, Inc. (co-founder, pres. 1990—), Assn. Ednl. Comm. and Tech., Delta Kappa Alpha (v.p. 1967).

ITTNER, PERRY MARTIN, sales and marketing consultant; b. Anaheim, Calif., June 14, 1961; s. Franklin Glenn and Delina (Martin) I.; m. Sylvia Marie Garcia, May 16, 1987; children: Kristina Nicole, Amber Delayne. Student, Cerritos Coll., 1979-82. Purchasing agt. Shield Healthcare, Inc., Van Nuys, Calif., 1979-85; gen. mgr. Propak div. of Devco Med. Co., Santa Fe Springs, Calif., 1985-86; materials mgr. Reliable Med. Supply, Brea, Calif., 1986-87; dir. sales and mktg. Telesis Rsch. Group, La Crescenta, Calif., 1985-90; mktg. product specialist Interhealth Corp., Whittier, Calif., 1988-89; pres. PSI Healthcare Assocs., Inc., Hacienda Heights, Calif., 1990—. Mem. The Planetary Soc., Nat. Assn. Self Employed, Nat. Fedn. Ind. Bus. Avocations: karate, kick boxing, muay thai. Office: PSI Healthcare Assocs Inc 16360 Kennard St Hacienda Heights CA 91745-3603

IVANI, KRISTEN ANN, embryologist; b. San Francisco, Jan. 4, 1960; d. Roger Charles and Marguerite Diana (Rhodes) I.; m. Robert B. Addis, Sept. 25, 1993. BS, U. Calif., Davis, 1982; MS, U. Idaho, 1984; PhD, Colo. State U., 1990. Dir. Ctr. for Reproductive Medicine San Ramon (Calif.) Regional Med. Ctr., 1990—. Contbr. chpt. to book and articles to profl. jours. Recipient Young Investigator award Soc. for Study of Reproduction, 1984; named Outstanding Young Women of Am., 1983. Mem. AAUW (pres. 1995-96), No. Calif. Assn. Reproductive Biologists (pres. 1995—), Am. Soc. Reproductive Medicine, Internat. Embryo Transfer Soc., Gamma Sigma Delta, Phi Sigma, Sigma Xi. Avocations: backpacking, cycling, scuba diving, cross country skiing, hiking. Office: San Ramon Reg Med Ctr 6001 Norris Canyon Rd San Ramon CA 94583-5400

IVERSEN, KRISTEN D., English language educator, editor, writer; b. Des Moines, Mar. 5, 1958; d. Richard Arnold and Marilyn Elaine (Iversen) Anderson; children: Sean Christopher, Nathan Kieran. BA in English, U. Colo., 1981; MA in English, U. Denver, 1991, PhD in English, 1996. Mng. editor MDM Publs., San Jose, Calif., 1982-84; sr. editor Continental Comm., Denver, 1984-86; freelance journalist based in Europe, 1986-89; teaching fellow U. Denver, 1989-96; prof. English Metro State Coll., Denver, 1996-98, Naropa Inst., Boulder, Colo., 1996—; mng. editor Westcliffe Pub., Englewood, Colo., 1998—. Author: Molly Brown: Unraveling the Myth, 1999; contbr. articles and short stories to mags. Named assoc. Rocky Mountain Women's Inst., 1992. Mem. MLA (Rocky Mountain chpt.), Am. Studies Assn., Women Writing the West, Denver Fortnightly Club, Colo. Hist. Soc. Democrat. Avocations: skiing, hiking, travel. Home: 1003 Golden Park Dr Apt A Golden CO 80403-2436

IVINS, ORVILLE RUSH, marketing executive; b. Chadron, Nebr., Feb. 10, 1950; s. James Rush and Gloria Ruth (Leetch) I.; m. Kathy Anne Hawkins, Dec. 19, 1969 (div. 1978); 1 child, Cynthia Anne; m. Beverly Kay Weitl, July 18, 1978. BS Bus. Adminstrn., U. N.C., 1974. Store mgr. Am. Stores, La Habra, Calif., 1974-79; merchandising cons. Alta Loma, Calif., 1979-82; sales rep. Lanier Bus. Products, Atlanta, 1982-83; sales mgr. NBI, Inc., Boulder, Colo., 1983-87; sr. account rep. Itek Graphix Inc., Rochester, N.Y., 1987-90; dist. sales mgr. Data Gen., Westboro, Mass., 1990—; mem. Data Gen. Steering Com. (sales tng. 1990-92, new bus. 1991-92), Westboro; guest lectr. Calif. Poly. U., Pomona, 1984-87. Dir. Longmont (Colo.) Jaycees, 1973, treas., 1974, state chmn. Colo. Jaycees, 1975 (exhausted Rooster); apptd. mem. Denver Regional Coun. Govs., 1974. Recipient Nat. project of Yr. for Sr. Citizen Home Energy Renovation project, 1974. Mem. Tri-County Urban and Regional Info. Systems. Republican. Episcopalian. Avocations: scuba diving, back-packing, climbing. Home: 1702 N White Ave Pomona CA 91768-1900 Office: Anixter Fed Sys 14509 E 33rd Pl Ste A Aurora CO 80011-1221

IVY, BENJAMIN FRANKLIN, III, financial and real estate investment advisor; b. Bremerton, Wash., May 18, 1936; s. Edward Byron Ivy and Ada Josephine (Anderson) Steele; m. Karen Yvonne Thompson, July 14, 1961 (div. June 1979); children: Britt Annemarie Ivy, Zenah Blair; m. Emily Cecile Rawlins, Apr. 18, 1982 (div. June 1992). BME, Cornell U., 1959; MBA, Stanford U., 1961. CFP. Purchasing agent U. Calif., Berkeley, 1960-62; contract adminstr. Lockheed Missiles and Space div., Sunnyvale, Calif., 1962-64; asst. to pres. Tridea subsidiary McDonnell Douglas, Pasadena, Calif., 1964-68; v.p. Mitchum, Jones & Templeton, Inc., Palo Alto, Calif., 1968-74, Paine Webber, Palo Alto, 1974; pres. Morgan Investment Svcs., Inc., Palo Alto, 1974-84; v.p. Morgan, Olmstead, Kennedy & Gardner, Inc., 1974-84; pres., chmn. Ivy Fin. Enterprises, Inc., Palo Alto, 1984—; pres. Ivy Fin. Svcs., Palo Alto; v.p. and registered prin. Assoc. Group, Inc., L.A., 1984—, dir., 1994-98, Cert. Fin. Planner, 1989—. Founder Found. to Eliminate the Nat. Debt, Palo Alto, 1992. Mem. Internat. Assn. Fin. Planners (charter, cert., bd. dirs. 1972-73), Pacific Exch. (assoc.), Cornell U. Alumni Assn., Stanford Alumni Assn. (life), Stanford Bus. Sch. Alumni Assn. (life), Sharon Heights Golf and Country Club, Masons, Elks, Kappa Sigma. Avocations: golf, tennis, poetry, opera, international travel. Office: Ivy Fin Enterprises Inc 525 University Ave Fl 6 Palo Alto CA 94301-1903

IWASAKI, KOUICHI, molecular geneticist; b. Yokosuka, Kanagawa, Japan, Jan. 10, 1961; came to U.S., 1986; s. Yukio and Mayako Iwasaki. BS, Kyoto (Japan) U., 1984, MS, 1986; PhD, U. Wis., 1991. Rsch. assoc. Washington U., St. Louis, 1991-94, U. Wash., Seattle, 1994—. Contbr. articles to profl. jours. Recipient Keck award W. Keck Found., 1992. Mem. AAAS, Soc. for Neurosci. Office: U Wash Dept Genetics PO Box 357360 Seattle WA 98195-7360

IZZO, MARY ALICE, real estate broker; b. Mesa, Ariz., Aug. 5, 1953; d. Edward Lee and Evangeline Lauda (Gorraiz) Meeker; m. Michael David Izzo, Dec. 26, 1971; children: Michael Wade, Clinton Jarred, Antoinette Marie. Student, Pioneer Coll., 1977, Yavapai Coll., 1984-93, 98—. Cert. broker, realtor, Ariz. Sales agt. Babbit Bros., Flagstaff, Ariz., 1970-76; owner Cottonwood (Ariz.) Tees, 1978-84; realtor Weston Realty, Cottonwood, 1985-86, Coldwell Banker Mabery Real Estate, Cottonwood, 1986-89; sales agent, assoc. broker The Glenarm Land Co., Cottonwood, 1989-97;

office mgr., sec. Izzo & Sons Contracting, 1985—, Wilhoit Water Co., 1991-93; sales assoc. Walmart, 1995-96, asst. regional commr., 1996-97; broker, owner ISO Realty, 1997—; office mgr., sec. Gonzales & Sons Electric, 1996-97; para educator Mingus Union H.S., Cottonwood, 1997—. Author: Current Customer Cook Book, 1984. Bd. dirs. cub scouts Boy Scouts Am., 1984, 87; bd. dirs. AYSO Soccer, Verde Valley, Ariz., 1984-87, 92—, soccer coach tournament all girls' traveling team, 1993-95, 97, 98, also pub. dir., asst. regional commn., purchaser, 1996—; leader youth group, Cottonwood. Democrat. Roman Catholic. Avocations: soccer, horseback riding, hiking, sewing, swimming. Fax: 520-634-2548. E-mail: mmizzo@cybertrails.com. Home: 649 E Elm St Cottonwood AZ 86326-4456

JABARA, MICHAEL DEAN, investment banker, entrepreneur; b. Sioux Falls, S.D., Oct. 26, 1952; s. James M. and Jean Marie (Swiden) J.; m. Gundula Beate Dietz, Aug. 26, 1984; children: James Michael, Jenna Mariel. Student, Mich. Tech. U., 1970-72; BSBA, U. Calif., Berkeley, 1974; MBA, Pepperdine U., 1979. Mgr. original Sprint project team So. Pacific Communications Corp., 1976-78; network product mgr. ROLM Corp., 1978-81; cons. McGraw Hill Co., Hamburg (Fed. Republic of Germany) and London, 1982-83; founder, chief exec. officer Friend Techs. Inc. (merger VoiceCom Systems, Inc., acquired by Premiere Techs., Inc. 1997), San Francisco, 1984-88; pres. VoiceCom Ventures, San Francisco, 1988-93; mng. dir. Telecom, EMS Group Ltd., London, 1993-95; owner Jabara & Co. LLC, Glenbrook, Nev., 1993—, TOIR LLC, Glenbrook, 1998—; chmn. bd., COO Bingo Card Minder Corp., Stateline, Nev., 1996. Patentee in field. Bd. dirs. Tahoe-Douglas C. of C.; chmn. Tahoe Citizens Com., 1995—. Mem. Infor. Industry Assn. (conf. program chair 1995), Assn. for Corp. Growth, Caribbean Cable TV Assn., Satellite Broadcasters & Comms. Assn., Pepperdine Bus. Alumni, U. Calif. Berkeley Bus. Alumni, Mich. Tech Alumni Assn., The Classic Cars of the Candy Store, Reno Jaguar Club, Tahoe-Douglas Rotary, Lighting W Ranch Golf Club. Avocations: classic cars, private pilot, golf. Fax: 702-749-5002. E-mail: jabaraco@sierra.net. Office: Jabara & Co PO Box 568 Glenbrook NV 89413-0568

JABBAR, ABDUL, English language educator; b. Delhi, India; came to U.S., 1965; s. Jalal-ud-Deen and Hajira Jalal; m. Talat Jabbar, Aug. 9, 1978; children: Huriya, Talib, Iram. MA in English, U. Punjab, Lahore, Pakistan, 1963, Case Western Res. U., 1967; PhD in English, Case Western Res. U., 1969. Life tchg. credential, Calif. Prof. English City Coll. San Francisco, 1968—, chair dept. interdisciplinary studies, 1995—; faculty mentor profl. devel., San Francisco, 1992, 97; dir. Keats Bicentennial Conf., San Francisco, 1995; guest lectr. Profl. Devel., San Francisco, 1992, 95, 96; vis. prof. English U. Calif., Berkeley, 1988. Contbr. articles to profl. jours. Dir. Assn. South Asian Students, City Coll., 1993-95, Union Arab Students, City Coll. San Francisco, Muslim Students Assn., 1990—. Recipient Fulbright scholarship U.S. Ednl. Found., 1965-66; univ. fellowship Case Western Res. U., Cleve., 1966-68, Nat. Endowment for Humanities awards U. Calif., Berkeley, 1990, U. Hawaii East-West Ctr., 1997. Mem. Nat. Coun. Tchrs. English, Keats-Shelley Assn., D.H. Lawrence Soc. N.Am., South Asian Lit. Assn. (mem. exec. bd. 1984), Calif. Humanities Assn. (mem. exec. bd. 1989), Victorian Alliance, Intercultural Resources (v.p. 1984). Avocations: tennis, nature walks. Home: 221 Cresta Vista Dr San Francisco CA 94127-1636 Office: City Coll San Francisco 50 Phelan Ave San Francisco CA 94112-1821

JACINTO, RICHARD JOHN, retired lawyer, arbitrator; b. Sacramento, Calif., Nov. 28, 1918; s. John and Margaret (DaRoza) J.; m. Ellen M. Welch, May 24, 1947; children: Kathleen, Patricia, Carol, Richard Jr. BA, U. Calif., Berkeley, 1941; JD, McGeorge Coll. Law, 1968. Bar: Calif. 1954. Ptnr. Jacinto & Hubbert, Sacramento, 1952-81; arbitrator Superior Ct. Sacramento County, Calif. Conciliation Panel, Calif. Agrl. Panel. Exec. v.p. Sacramento Valley Employers Coun., 1952-81. Sgt. USAF, 1942-46, World War II, PTO. Home: 1040 El Sur Way Sacramento CA 95864-5269

JACKA, ROBERT EMMETT, printmaker; b. Loma Linda, Calif., Mar. 30, 1961; s. George Washington and Doris Margaret (Reed) J. BA, Calif. State U., Fullerton, 1983. Tchr. Yucaipa High Sch.; graphic designer Johnson Controls, Norton AFB. Recipient J. Carter Brown Chic Chic a Boom award. Mem. Masons, Elks, Scottish Rite. Democrat. Methodist. Avocation: collecting Czech pottery-glass. Home: 1295 E 34th St San Bernardino CA 92404-2606 Office: Yucaipa High Sch 33000 Yucaipa Blvd #666 Yucaipa CA 92399

JACKMAN, JAY M., psychiatrist; b. Bklyn., June 4, 1939; s. James Jeremiah and Dora (Emmer) J.; m. Judith Gail Meisels, Nov. 23, 1963 (div. Sept. 1987); children: Tenaya, Rashi, Jason Scott; m. Myra Hoffenberg Strober, Oct. 21, 1990. BA, Columbia U., 1960; MD, Harvard U., 1964; postgrad., U. Calif., San Francisco, 1966—. Diplomate Am. Bd. Psychiatry and Neurology; subsplty. cert. forensic psychiatry . Rotating intern San Francisco County Gen. Hosp., 1965; psychiat. resident Stanford U., 1969; asst. dir. community psychiatry Mt. Zion Hosp., San Francisco, 1969-70; dir. drug treatment programs Westside Community Mental Health Ctr., San Francisco, 1970-74; pvt. practice San Francisco, 1969-74; dir. Lanakila Clinic Kalihi-Palama Community Mental Health Ctr., Honolulu, 1974-75; pvt. practice specializing in forensic psychiatry, Honolulu, 1975-90, Stanford, Calif., 1990—; cons. Salvation Army Addiction Treatment Facility, Honolulu, 1974-81; chmn. Task Force on Drugs, Nat. Coun. Community Mental Health Ctrs., 1971-75; chmn. no. sect. Calif. Assn. Methodone Programs, 1973-74. Contbr. articles on substance abuse to profl. jours. Trustee Foothill-DeAnza C.C. Bd., 1993—; active Mayor's Adv. Com. on Drug Abuse, Honolulu, 1975-77. Mem. Am. Psychiat. Assn. (commn. on drugs 1973-77), Am. Acad. Psychiatry and Law, Am. Coll. Forensic Psychiatrists, No. Calif. Psychiat. Soc., Santa Clara County Bar Assn. (vol., lay mem. fee arbitration com. 1992), Calif. Attys. for Criminal Justice. Democrat. Jewish. Avocations: backpacking, hiking, dancing, scuba diving, beach walking.

JACKSON, ALLEN KEITH, museum administrator; b. Rocky Ford, Colo., July 22, 1932; s. Monford L. and Leliah Jean (Hipp) J.; m. Barbara May Hollard, June 13, 1954; children: Cary Vincent, Deborah Kay and Edward Keith (twins), Fredrick James. B.A., U. Denver, 1954; postgrad., Cambridge (Eng.) U., 1955; Th.M. (Elizabeth Iliff Warren fellow), Iliff Sch. Theology, 1958; Ph.D., Emory U., 1960. Meth. student minister Erie, Colo., 1955-58; ordained elder Meth. Ch., 1958; instr. sociology Emory U., 1958-60; chaplain, asst. prof. religion and sociology Morningside Coll., Sioux City, Iowa, 1960-62; dean coll. Morningside Coll., 1962-67; pres. Huntingdon Coll., Montgomery, Ala., 1968-93; exec. dir. natural heritage Idaho Mus. Natural History, Idaho State U., Pocatello, 1993—. Contbr. articles to profl. jours. Past pres. Montgomery Area United Appeal. Fulbright scholar Cambridge U., 1955; honor fellow Emory U., 1960. Mem. Ala. Assn. Ind. Colls. and Univs. (pres. 1969-71), Ala. Council Advancement Pvt. Colls. (pres. 1975-81), Phi Beta Kappa, Omicron Delta Kappa, Beta Theta Pi. Club: Rotarian. Home: 6353 Old Ranch Rd Pocatello ID 83204-3841 Office: Mus Natural History Idaho State U Pocatello ID 83204

JACKSON, BEVERLEY JOY JACOBSON, columnist, lecturer; b. L.A., Nov. 20, 1928; d. Phillip and Dorothy Jacobson; student U. So. Calif., UCLA; m. Robert David Jackson (div. Aug. 1964); 1 child, Tracey Dee. Daily columnist Santa Barbara (Calif.) News Press, 1968-92, Santa Barbara Independent, 1992-94; nat. lectr. Santa Barbara History, History of China Recreated, Chinese Footbinding, Shoes for Bound Feet, China Today; free lance writer, fgn. corr. Bd. dirs. Santa Barbara br. Am. Cancer Soc., 1963-92; mem. art mus. coun. L.A. Mus. Art, 1959-96, mem. costume coun., 1983-92; docent L.A. Mus. Art, 1962-64; mem. exec. bd. Channel City Club (formerly Channel City Women's Forum), 1969-97; mem. adv. bd. Santa Barbara Mus. Natural History, Coun. of Christmas Cheer, Women's Shelter Bldg., Direct Relief Internat., Nat. Coun. Drug and Alcohol Abuse, Am. Oceans Campaign; mem adv. bd. Hospice of Santa Barbara, 1981-92, Stop AIDS Coun., Arthritis Found.; bd. dirs. So. Calif. Com. for Shakespear's Globe Theatre, Friends of UCSB Libr.; chmn. Santa Barbara Com. for Visit Queen Elizabeth II, 1982—; founder costume guild Santa Barbara Hist. Soc.; curator Chinese collections Santa Barbara Hist. Mus.; adv. bd. Santa Barbara Choral Soc.; hon. bd. Santa Barbara Salvation Army, Ensemble Theatre Santa Barbara; adv. bd. Storyteller Sch. Homeless Children. Author: Dolls and Doll Houses of Spain, 1970, (with others) I'm Just Wild About Harry, 1979, Spendid Slippers: A Thousand Years of an Erotic Tradition, 1997, Intrigues and Traditions of Chinese Rank, 1999. Mem. Commanderie Bordeaux de San Francisco. Home: PO Box 5118 Santa Barbara CA 93150-5118

JACKSON, CYNTHIA L., lawyer; b. Houston, May 6, 1954. BA, Stanford U., 1976; JD, U. Tex., 1979. Bar: Tex. 1979, Calif. 1980. Mem. Heller, Ehrman, White & McAuliffe, Palo Alto, Calif., 1983—. Mem. ABA. Office: Heller Ehrman White & McAuliffe 525 University Ave Ste 900 Palo Alto CA 94301-1908*

JACKSON, DAVID ROBERT, school system administrator; b. Long Beach, Calif., Jan. 15, 1945; s. Harlan Leroy and Helen Louise (Worthen) J.; m. Stacey Ann Bryan, Nov. 13, 1971; children: David, Daniel, Chad, Loren, Darcy. Student, Fullerton Coll., 1963-64, Brigham Young U., 1965-67, Santa Ana Coll., 1977, Orange Coast Coll., 1977-78. Mgr. trainee Carl Karcher Enterprizes, Fullerton, Calif., 1964; asst. mgr. Household Fin. Co., Santa Ana., Calif., 1964-65; mgr. Chateau Apres Lodge, Park City, Utah, 1965-69; pres. Aero Wash Co., Santa Ana., Calif., 1970-79; exec. dir. Fairmont Schs. Inc., Anaheim, Calif., 1979—. Former leader Boy Scouts Am.; bishop LDS Ch., Corona, 1990-96; chmn. Orange County 2000, Calif., 1991-93, also bd. dirs. Mem. Nat. Ind. Pvt. Sch. Assn. (bd. dirs. 1981—, founding mem., pres. 1993-98), Calif. Assn. Nationally Recognized Schs. (founder, pres. 1992-93), Orange County Pvt. Sch. Assn. (pres. 1990-93, founder). Republican. Avocations: snow skiing, geneology, private pilot. Office: Fairmont Sch 100 S Anaheim Blvd Anaheim CA 92805-3848

JACKSON, DILLON EDWARD, lawyer; b. Washington, Apr. 18, 1945; s. Paul David and Virginia (Dillon) J.; children: David I., Anne E.; m. Misha Halvarsson, Aug. 19, 1989. BA, Middlebury (Vt.) Coll., 1967; JD, U. Wash., 1970. Bar: Wash. 1970, U.S. Dist. Ct. (we. and ea. dists.) Wash. 1970, U.S. Ct. Appeals (9th cir.) 1970, U.S. Dist. Ct. Ariz. 1991. Assoc. Kleist & Helmick, Seattle, 1971-73, Powell Livengood & Silvernale, Kirkland, Wash., 1973-75; ptnr. Keller Jacobsen Jackson & Snodgrass, Bellevue, Wash., 1975-85, Hatch & Leslie, Seattle, 1985-91, Foster Pepper & Shefelman, Seattle, 1991—; chairperson creditor rights and bankruptcy dept. Am. Bankruptcy Bd. Cert.; mem. adv. bd. Applied Environ. Tech., Seattle, 1992—; bd. mem. Consumer Credit Counseling, Seattle, 1975-79; chmn. publs. com. Am. Bankruptcy Inst. Co-author: Commercial Law Desk Book, 1995; contbg. author: Advance Chapter 11 Bankruptcy Practice, 1989-95. Pres. Dox Coop., Seattle, 1989-91. Fellow Am. Coll. Bankruptcy, 1990. Mem. ABA, Wash. State Trial Lawyers Assn., Wash. State Bar Assn. (creditor-debtitor sect., chairperson 1984-88), Continuing Legal Edn. Bd. (chairperson 1991-92). Office: Foster Pepper & Shefelman PLLC 1111 3rd Ave Ste 3400 Seattle WA 98101-3299*

JACKSON, DOUGLAS LEON, airline pilot; b. San Jose, Calif., Oct. 29, 1944; s. Cleveland Grady and Elizabeth Marie (Deaver) J.; m. Marti Michele De Franco, Dec. 21, 1966 (dec. Nov. 1996); 1 child, Brian Douglas; m. Mary Anne Jackson, July 25, 1998. AA, San Jose City Coll., 1965; BA, San Jose State Coll., 1967, MA, 1968. Commd. ensign USN, 1969, advanced through grades to lt., 1972, resigned, 1975; pilot N.W. Airlines, St. Paul, 1976—. Patentee in field. Avocations: inventing, motorcycling, snow skiing, hiking. Home: 745 Casterwood Ct San Jose CA 95120

JACKSON, FRANK, pastor; b. Chgo., Mar. 11, 1941; s. Frank Raymond and Dorothy (Swoul) J.; m. Jimmye Wilkes, Sept. 30, 1967; 1 child, Rachel. B in Humanities, Simpson Coll., 1972; MDiv, Fuller Theol. Sem., 1976; M in Non-Profit Adminstrn., U. San Francisco, 1990. Interim pastor Light House Full Gospel Ch., Pasadena, Calif., 1974-75, Faith United Presbyn. Ch., L.A., 1976-79; assoc. pastor Menlo Park (Calif.) Presbyn. Ch., 1979-83; pastor Faith Presbyn. Ch., Oakland, Calif., 1983—; mem. mission team Faith Equador Missions, Haiti and Jamaica, 1968-69, Kenya, 1975; bd. dirs. Women's Refuge of Oakland/Berkeley, Calif., 1986-89, Harbor House, Oakland, 1990—; trainer, seminar leader San Quentin (Calif.) State Penitentiary, 1987. Voter registrar Interdenominational Ministrial Alliance of L.A., 1976; bd. dirs. Black Leadership Coalition, L.A., 1976-77. Sgt. U.S. Army, Korea. Recipient Community Svc. award Exch. Club of Pasadena, Calif., 1974, Exch. Club of Daly City, Calif., 1983. Mem. Interdenominational Ministrial Alliance of Oakland (fin. sec. 1987-90), Black Presbyn. Caucus of No. Calif. (fin. sec. 1990—). Avocation: judo (black belt). Home: 4142 Maynard Ave Oakland CA 94605-3120 Office: Faith Presbyn Ch 430 49th St Oakland CA 94609-2146

JACKSON, HARRY ANDREW, artist; b. Chgo., Apr. 18, 1924; s. Harry and Ellen Grace J.; m. Theodora Rehard DuBois, 1946 (div.); m. Grace Hartigan, 1948 (div.); m. Claire Rodgers, 1950 (div.); m. Joan Hunt, 1951 (div.); m. Sarah Mason, Sept. 10, 1962 (div.); children: Matthew, Molly; m. Tina Lear, Aug. 11, 1973 (div.); children: Jesse, Luke, Chloe. Diploma, H.S., 1945; LLD (hon.), U. Wyo., 1986. Founder fine art foundry Camaiore, Italy, 1964—, Wyo. Foundry Studios di Harry Jackson, Italy, 1965—; CEO Harry Jackson Studios (formerly Wyo. Foundry Studios, Inc.), Cody, Wyo., 1971—; founder Western Arts Found., 1974—; foundry ptnr. Jackson-Mariani Fine Art Foundry, Camaiore, Italy, 1985—; founder Harry Jackson Art Mus., Cody, Wyo., 1994. Author: Lost Wax Bronze Casting, 1972; one man exhbns. include Ninth St. Show, N.Y.C., 1951, Tibor de Nagy Gallery, N.Y.C., 1952, 53, Martha Jackson Gallery, N.Y.C., 1956, M. Knoedler & Co., N.Y.C., 1960, Amon Carter Mus., Fort Worth, 1961, 68, Kennedy Galleries, N.Y.C., 1964, 68, Smithsonian Instn., Washington, 1964, Whitney Gallery Western Art, Cody, 1964, 81, Mont. Hist. Soc., 1964, NAD, 1965, 68, Nat. Cowboy Hall of Fame, Oklahoma City, 1966, XVII Mostra Internazionale d'Arte, Premio del Fiorino, Florence, Italy, 1966, Pennational Artists Ann., Pa., 1967, Mostra de Arte Moderna, Convento di S. Lazzaro, Camaiore, 1968, Am. Artists Profl. League, N.Y., 1968, Cowboy Artists Am., 1971-76, S.W. Mus., L.A., 1979, Smith Gallery, N.Y.C., 1981, 85; major retrospective exhbns. include Buffalo Bill Hist. Ctr., 1981, Palm Springs Desert Mus., 1981, Mpls. Inst. Art, 1982, Camaiore, Italy, 1985, Met. Mus. Art, N.Y.C., 1987; represented in permanent collections Met. Mus. Art, NAD, Nat. Mus. Am. Art, Nat. Portrait Gallery, Washington, Her Majesty Queen Elizabeth II, Sandringam Castle, Eng., Am. Mus. of Gt. Britain, Bath, Eng., U.S. State Dept., Washington, Lyndon Baines Johnson Meml. Libr., Austin, Tex., Ronald Reagan Meml. Libr., Santa Barbara, Calif., Whitney Gallery Western Art, Plains Indian Mus., Buffalo Bill Hist. Ctr., Cody, Wyo., Wadsworth Atheneum, Hartford, Conn., Alberta Glenbow Mus., Calgary, Can., Univ. So. Calif., Stanford (Calif.) Univ., Love Libr. Univ. Nebr., Lincoln, Portsmouth (R.I.) Abbey, S.W. Mus., Gene Autrey Mus., L.A., Nat. Cowboy Hall of Fame, Oklahoma City, Gilcrease Mus., Tulsa, Fort Pitts Mus., Pitts., Amon Carter Mus., Pro Rodeo Cowboy Hall of Fame, Colorado Springs, Colo., Eiteljorg Mus., Indpls., Shelburne (Vt.) Mus., Columbus (Ga.) Mus. Arts & Scis., Oreg. Hist. Soc., Portland, Salt Lake City Art Ctr., Norfolk (Nebr.) Arts Ctr., Aspen (Colo.) Art Mus., Woolaroc Mus., Bartlesville, Okla., U. Wyo. Art Mus., Laramie, Mont. Hist. Soc., Helena, Norton Mus., Shreveport, La., Columbia U., N.Y.C., Trout Gallery Dickinson Coll., Carlisle, Pa., Ctrl. Wyo. Coll., Riverton, N.W. C.C., Powell, Wyo., Baylor Sch., Chattanooga, Orme Sch., Mayer, Ariz., others; commd. works include (sculpture) William R. Coe Commn., 1959, 60, Fort Pitt Mus., 1964, 73, Plains Indian Mus., Cody, Wyo., Ctrl. Wyo. Coll., Riverton, 1978, 81, Piazza della Chiesa, Capezzano, Pianore, Italy, 1985, Great Western Savs. & Loan, Santa Barbara, Calif., 1985, John Wayne monumental sculpture Beverly Hills, Calif, 1981, 84, (portrait busts) Met. Mus. Trustees, C. Douglas Dillon, 1985, 87, (portrait) "John Wayne" TIME cover, Aug. 8, 1969 (Nat. Best Cover Art award Am. Inst. Graphic Arts 1969), (paintings) Whitney Gallery Western Art, Cody, 1960, 66, (mural) R.K. Mellon. Served with USMC, 1942-45. Decorated Purple Heart with gold star; recipient Gold medal NAD, 1968; grantee Fulbright, 1954, Italian Govt., 1956, 57. Fellow NAD (academician), RISD, Nat. Acad. Western Art, Nat. Sculpture Soc., Am. Artists League; mem. Bohemian Club (San Francisco). Office: PO Box 2836 Cody WY 82414-2836 also: Via Montegiori, 55040 Camaiore Lucca, Italy

JACKSON, ISAIAH, conductor; b. Richmond, Va., Jan. 22, 1945; s. Isaiah Allen and Alma Alverta (Norris) J.; m. Helen Tuntland, Aug. 6, 1977; children: Benjamin, Katharine, Caroline. BA cum laude, Harvard U., 1966; MA, Stanford U., 1967; MS, Juilliard Sch. Music, 1969, DMA, 1973. Founder, condr. Juilliard String Ensemble, N.Y.C., 1970-71; asst. condr. Am. Symphony Orch., N.Y.C., 1970-71, Balt. Symphony Orch., 1971-73; assoc. condr. Rochester (N.Y.) Philharmonic Orch., 1973-87; music dir. Dayton (Ohio) Philharm. Orch., 1987-95, 1987-95; prin. condr. Royal Ballet, Covent Garden, London, 1986, music dir., 1987-90; prin. guest condr. Queensland (Australia) Symphony Orch., 1993-96; music dir. Youngstown (Ohio) Symphony, 1996—; prin. guest condr. Canberra (Australia) Symphony Orch., 1996—; guest condr. N.Y. Philharm. Orch., 1978, Boston Pops Orch., 1983, 90-94, Detroit Symphony Orch., 1983, 85, San Francisco Symphony, 1984, Toronto Symphony, 1984, 90, Orch. de la Suisse Romande, 1985, 88, BBC Concert Orch., 1987, Berlin Symp hony, 1989-95, Dallas Symphony, 1993, Royal Liverpool Philharm., 1995, Houston Symphony, 1995; numerous recordings for Koch, Australian Broadcasting Corp. Recipient First Gov.'s award for arts in Va., Commonwealth Va., 1979, Signet Soc. medal for the arts Harvard U., 1991. Office: care United Arts 3906 Sunbeam Dr Los Angeles CA 90065-3551 Office: Schofer/Gold 50 Riverside Dr New York NY 10024-6555*

JACKSON, JACK, analyst programmer, fine art photographer; b. Indpls., Sept. 26, 1946; s. Milton Lovelace and Anna Elizabeth (Robinson) J.; m. Elizabeth Anne Marshall, Sept. 26, 1981. BFA, Acad. Art Coll., San Francisco, 1983. Analyst programmer Crocker Bank, San Francisco, 1974-78; sr. analyst programmer Genasys Systems, San Francisco, 1978-79; pvt. practice, cons., 1979-83; sr. systems engr. Integral Systems, Walnut Creek, Calif., 1983-86; cons. GTE Govt. Systems, Mountain View, Calif., 1987-88; sr. cons. Deltam Systems, San Mateo, Calif., 1988—. With USN, 1965-69. Democrat. Roman Catholic. Home: 3256 Wyman St Oakland CA 94619-3434 Office: Pacific Bell 2600 Camino Ramon # 2500we San Ramon CA 94583-5099

JACKSON, JANE W., interior designer; b. Asheville, N.C., Aug. 5, 1944; d. James and Willie Mae (Stoner) Harris; m. Bruce G. Jackson; children: Yvette, Scott. Student, Boston U., 1964; BA, Leslie Coll., 1967; postgrad., Artisan Sch. Interior Design, 1980-82. Tchr. Montessori, Brookline, Mass., 1969-72; interior designer, owner Nettle Creek Shop, Honolulu, 1980-88; owner Wellesley Interiors, Honolulu, 1988—. Active Mayor's Com. for Small Bus., Honolulu, 1984. Mem. Honolulu Club. Democrat. Office: Wellesley Interiors PO Box 1622 Kaneohe HI 96744-1622

JACKSON, JEWEL, retired state youth authority executive; b. Shreveport, La., June 3, 1942; d. Willie Burghardt and Bernice Jewel (Mayberry) Norton; children: Steven, June Kelly, Michael, Anthony. With Calif. Youth Authority, 1965-91, group supr., San Andreas and Santa Rosa, 1965-67, youth counselor, Ventura, 1967-78, sr. youth counselor, Stockton, 1978-81, parole agt., 1986, treatment team supr., program mgr., Whittier and Ione, 1981-91; retired, 1991; pres. Valley Paralegal Svc., Stockton. Avocations: reading, horseback riding, interior design, fabric painting, stamp collecting. Home and Office: 2416 Hall Ave Stockton CA 95205-8422

JACKSON, JOHN JAY, clergyman; b. Chula Vista, Calif., July 13, 1961; s. E. Marvin and Mildred L. Jackson; m. Pamela Harrison, Aug. 18, 1979; children: Jennifer, Dena, Rachel, Joshua. BA in Religion, Chapman U., 1981; MA in Theology, Fuller Theol. Sem., 1983; MA in Ednl. Adminstrn., U. Calif., Santa Barbara, 1984, PhD in Ednl. Adminstrn., 1986. Youth dir. First Bapt. Ch., Buena Park, Calif., 1979-81; min. of youth Oxnard (Calif.) First Bapt., 1981-83, min. of edn., 1983-84, assoc. pastor, 1984-87, sr. pastor, 1988-92; exec. min. Am.-Bapt. Chs. Pacific S.W., Covina, Calif., 1993-97; pastor Carson Valley Christian Ctr., Minden, Nev., 1997—. Bd. dirs. Am. Bapt. Homes of the West, Oakland, Calif., 1993-97, Atherton Bapt. Homes, 1993-97; chair integration adv. com. Oxnard Sch. Dist., 1990-92. Recipient Disting. Svc. award Oxnard Sch. Dist., 1992. Mem. Christian Mgmt. Assn., Oxnard C. of C. (leadership com. 1991, chair edn. com. 1988-90). Office: Carson Valley Christian Ctr PO Box 892 Minden NV 89423-0892*

JACKSON, OLIVER L., artist, art educator; b. St. Louis, June 23, 1935; s. Oliver and Mae Nell J. BFA, Ill. Wesleyan U., 1958; MFA, U. Iowa, 1963. Instr. art St. Louis C.C., 1964-67; asst. prof. art Washington U., St. Louis, 1967-69; curriculum specialist, lectr. So. Ill. U., East St. Louis, 1967-69; asst. prof. Afro-Am. studies Oberlin (Ohio) Coll., 1969-70; prof. art Calif. State U., Sacramento, 1971—; vis. artist Sch. of Art Inst., Chgo., 1979, S.E. Ctr. for Contemporary Art, Winston-Salem, N.C., 1980, U. Wash., Seattle, 1985, U. Calif., Santa Barbara, 1985, U. Ill., Champaign, 1988. One-man shows include Seattle Art Mus., 1982, Univ. Art Mus., Berkeley, Calif., 1985, St. Louis Art Mus., 1990, Newport Harbor Art Mus., Newport Beach, Calif., 1993; commd. painting State Office Bldg, San Francisco, 1986; marble sculpture Gen. Svcs. Adminstrn.-Fed. Courthouse, Oakland, Calif., 1986, 93. With U.S. Army, 1961. Fellow in Painting, NEA, Washington, 1980-81, Nettie Marie Jones fellow in Visual Arts, Lake Placid, N.Y., 1984, fellow in Painting, Fleishhacker Found., San Francisco, 1993. Office: c/o Anne Kohs & Assocs 115 Stonegate Rd Portola Vally CA 94028-7648

JACKSON, PATRICK JOSEPH, insurance executive; b. Minn., Mar. 31, 1942; s. Paul Arthur and Lucille Margaret (Cummings) J.; m. Barbara Ann Simpson, July 19, 1964 (div. Apr. 1980); m. Shirley Ann Wellman, Sept. 12, 1982 (div. Sept. 1998); children: Laura Kathleen, Katherine Lucille. BS, Portland State U., 1968. Bank loan officer First Nat. Bank of Oreg., Portland, 1964-68; credit mgr. Meier & Frank Corp., Portland, 1968-70; agt., mgr. Aetna Life, San Jose, Calif., 1970-75; dist. mgr. Calif. Casualty, San Jose, 1975-78; gen. agt. Great So. Life, San Jose, 1978-82; account agt., agy. mgr. Allstate Ins., San Jose, 1982—; instr. Santa Clara (Calif.) U., 1974-76. Author: (monograph) The Affairs of, 1978; newspaper columnist, 1978-82. Mem. ins. subcom. Calif. State Senate, 1978; officer Los Gatos (Calif.) Police Res., 1970-78, treas., 1974-78; mem. Sch. Site Coun., Saratoga, Calif., 1978-80; mem. City Coun., Discovery Bay, Calif., 1991-95, mayor, 1993-94. Named Man of Yr., Los Gatos Youth Unltd., 1978. Mem. San Jose Life Underwriters (bd. dirs. 1974-76), No. Calif. Tollycraft Assn. (sec. 1995-97), Discovery Bay Yacht Club. Republican. Lutheran. Avocations: boating, fishing, shooting, reading. Office: Allstate Ins Co 2923 The Villages Pky San Jose CA 95135-1442

JACKSON, PETER VORIOUS, III, retired association executive; b. Butte, Mont., May 18, 1927; s. Peter V. and Besse Portia (McLean) J.; m. Johnneta Pierce, Apr. 29, 1949; children: Ward, Michelle (Mrs. Jerry Vanhour), Johnathan. Wheat and cattle rancher, 1949—; mem. Mont. Ho. of Reps., 1971-72; chief Grass Conservation bur. Mont. Dept. Natural Resources, Helena, 1972-74; supr. Conservation Dist. Madison County, Ennis, Mont., from 1957; past exec. dir. Western Environ. Trade Assn., Helena.; exec. v.p. Soc. for Range Mgmt., Denver, 1983-92; ret., 1992; vol. to develop and implement grazing lands conservation initiative Soil Conservation Soc. USDA, 1992—; mem. Nat. Steering Com. of Grazing Land Conservation Initiative, 1993-98; nat. sec. grazing lands conservation initiative NRCS-USDA. Author: Montana Rangeland Resources Program, 1970. Mem. Madison County Fair Bd.; pres. Grazing Lands Forum, 1988. Recipient Renner award Soc. Range Mgmt., 1971, Conservation award Mont. Wildlife Fedn., 1966. Mem. Nat. Assn. Conservation Dists. (bd. dirs.), Mont. Assn. Conservation Dists. (exec. v.p. 1974), Soc. for Range Mgmt. (nat. pres., spl. award for outstanding achievement 1992), Masons, Elks, Shriners. Home and Office: PO Box 86 Harrison MT 59735-0086

JACKSON, ROBBI JO, non-hazardous agricultural products company executive, lawyer; b. Nampa, Idaho, Apr. 12, 1959; d. William R. Jackson and Marilyn K. Samp Jackson Nunez. BS in Fin., U. Colo., Boulder and Denver, 1981; JD, U. Denver, 1987, LLM in Taxation, 1990. Bar: Colo. Asst. office mgr. Jerome Karsh & Co., Denver, 1982; office mgr. Almirall & Assocs., Englewood, Colo., 1983-84; assoc. Moye, Giles, O'Keefe, Vermeire & Gorrell, Denver, 1989-90, Holme Roberts & Owen, Denver, 1990-92; in-house gen. counsel Cmty. Corrections Svcs., Denver, 1992-96; CEO Enviro Cons. Svc., LLC, Evergreen and Lakewood, Colo., 1996—. Mem. staff Adminstrv. Law Rev., Denver, 1985, editor, 1985, mng. editor, 1986-87; co-author course of study materials; presenter in field. Mem. fin. com. Mile-High chpt. ARC, Denver, 1990-92; food delivery person Vols. of Am., Meals-on-Wheels, Denver, 1990-92. Recipient scholarships. Mem. ABA, Colo. Bar Assn. (ethics com.). Republican. Avocations: running marathons and other races, bike riding, hiking, swimming, piano and organ playing.

JACKSON, RONALD, bank examiner; b. N.Y.C., Dec. 9, 1969; s. Ronald Clarence Jackson and Brenda (Nunnally) Thomas; 1 child, Ronald II. BA in Econs., San Francisco State U., 1997. Bank examiner Fed. Res. Bank of San Francisco. With USN, 1987-89. Policy and internat. affairs fellow Woodrow Wilson Found., 1996. Avocations: reading, weightlifting, bi-

cycling, sports. Home: 214 Grand Ave Apt 46 Oakland CA 94610-4543 Office: Fed Res Bank San Francisco 101 Market St Ste 4 San Francisco CA 94105-1579

JACKSON, SAMUEL JOHN, scuba diving industry executive; b. Toronto, Ont., Can., Dec. 30, 1947; s. Walter James and Joyce (Thomson) J.; m. Mary Ann Edwards, Sep. 14, 1974; xhildren: Daniel Edwards, David Samuel. BA, York U., Toronto, 1983; MBA, Claremont Grad. Sch., 1997. Mgr. advt. and promotion Prentice-Hall, Scarborough, Ont., 1971-75; dir. comm. Seneca Coll., North York, Ont., 1975-83; dir. mktg. AES Data, Mississanga, Ont., 1983-87; exec. dir. Nat. Assn. Underwater Instructions, Montclair, Calif., 1987-95, Diving Equipment & Mktg. Assn., Anaheim, Calif., 1995—; mem. supervisory com. San Bernardino Cmty. Credit Union, 1988—. Columnist Sources, 1987-95. Bd. dirs. Outdoor Recreation Coalition of Am., Boulder, Colo., 1989-96. Presbyterian. Office: DEMA 2050 S Santa Cruz St Anaheim CA 92805-6820

JACKSON, SHARON JUANITA, management consultant; b. Modesto, Calif., Sept. 21, 1938; d. H. Edward and Beatrice C. (Wright) Melin; m. John L. George, Apr. 27, 1956 (div. 1974); children: Terri A., Tami L., Timothy J., Tobin E. BS in Edn. magna cum laude, Calif. State U., Hayward, 1965; MEd Guidance and Counseling, Hardin-Simmons U., 1976; MBA in Mgmt., Golden Gate U., 1984. Cert. elem. edn., Calif., elem., secondary counseling, Tex. Tchr. elem. Hayward (Calif) Unified Sch. Dist., 1965-73; tchr. diagnostics, group therapist Tex. Youth Coun., Brownwood, 1974-75; assoc. dir. New Directions Psychiat. Half Way House, Abilene, Tex., 1975-77; exec. dir. Mental Health Assn., Abilene, 1977-78, San Francisco, 1979-84; pres. Health Mktg. & Mgmt., San Francisco, 1983—; exec. dir., cons. Vision of Am. At Peace, Berkeley, Calif., 1984, Oakes Children's Ctr., San Francisco, 1985-87; mktg. dir. Mental Health Providers of Calif., 1987-90; prin., v.p. health care devel. Sakhalin region, Russia Health Marketing and Mgmt., 1990-92; instr. managed care U. San Francisco, 1994; sr. assoc. Behavioral Health Alliance dir. nat. practice 1991-92; founding exec. dir., v.p. adminstrn. Planet Live Earthbeat TV, Inc.; bd. dirs. PL Enterprises, Inc.; vis. lectr. McMurry Coll., Abilene, 1976-78; cons. Dyess AFB, Abilene, 1976-78, Abilene Youth Ctr., 1976-78; founder, pres. Health Mktg. & Mgmt.; speaker in field, 1979—. Chair Commn. on Status of Women of Marin County, Calif., 1985—; mem. adv. com. Displaced Homemaker Project, Sacramento, 1985-90; founder, Children's Mental Health Policy Bd., 1984-90; pres. Artisans Gallery, Mill Valley, Calif., 1984—. Grantee Fed. Dept. Justice, Brownwood, 1975, pvt. community founds., Calif., 1979-87. Mem. NAFE, Council of Calif. Mental Health Contractors, Am. Soc. Profl. Exec. Women. Avocations: travel, gourmet cooking, hiking, public speaking. Home and Office: PO Box 2392 Mill Valley CA 94942-2392

JACKSON, STU, professional sports team executive, former university basketball coach; b. Reading, Pa., Dec. 11, 1955; m. Dr. Janet Taylor; four daughters. BA, business administration and management, Seattle U., 1978. Grad. asst. coach U. Oregon, 1981-82, asst. coach, 1982-83; asst. coach Wash. State U., 1983-85; assoc. coach Providence Coll., 1985-87; asst. coach N.Y. Knicks, 1987-89, head coach, 1989-91; dir. basketball ops. NBA, N.Y.C., 1991-92; head coach Univ. Wisc., Madison, 1992-94; pres., gen. mgr. basketball ops. NBA Vancouver expansion team, B.C., Canada, 1994—. NBA Coach of the Month for December, 1989. Office: Vancouver Grizzlies, 800 Griffiths Way, Vancouver, BC Canada V6B 6G1*

JACKSON, SUZANNE ELISE, health education coordinator; b. Webster, Mass., Mar. 1, 1942; d. John Edward and Marguerite Emmaline (Plante) Baczek; m. Dale Lynne Bagby, Sept. 28, 1968 (div. July 1975); m. Stephen Harvey Jackson, July 12, 1975; 1 child, Gabrielle Benette. Diploma, Henry Heywood Hosp., 1963, BA, U. Redlands, 1975. RN Calif. Clin. instr. surgery Henry Heywood Hosp., Gardner, Mass., 1963-64; asst. head nurse Los Gatos Cmty. Hosp., San Jose, Calif., 1964-68; head nurse oper. rm. Good Samaritan Hosp., San Jose, Calif., 1970-76; corp. officer SHJ Corp., San Jose, Calif., 1976-96; health edn. coord. Ac. Medicine Symposium, Monte Sereno, Calif., 1980—; design cons. Suzanne Jackson Designs, Monte Sereno, Calif., 1986—; pres. Calif. Med. Assn. Alliance, 1994-95, bd. dirs., 1986—. Bd. dirs. Calif. Rep. League, Santa Clara County Med. Assn. Aux., San Jose, 1980—, pres. 1985-86; leader, sch. coord. Girl Scouts U.S., Los Gatos, 1983-89; fundraiser Hillbrook Sch., Los Gatos, 1983-90; bd. dirs LWV, Los Gatos, 1986-90; mem. Monte Sereno City Coun., 1994—, vice mayor, 1996, mayor, 1997-98; mem., vice-chmn. Rep. Cen. Com., Santa Clara County, 1998, del. Calif. Rep. Party; commr. Santa County Domestic Violence Coun., 1996—; bd. dirs. Calif. Rep. League, 1996—. Recipient Gilbert & Sullivan Soc. Gypsy Robe, 1984. Mem. Brandeis U. Women, Capitol Club Silicon Valley. Republican. Avocations: tennis, snow skiing, creative arts. Office: 15984 Grandview Ave Monte Sereno CA 95030-3118

JACKSON, THIRSTON HENRY, JR., retired adult education educator; b. Camden, N.J., Mar. 28, 1913; s. Thirston Henry and Elizabeth Loraine (Keck) J.; m. Grace Roberta Ballard, Sept. 26, 1934 (dec. Dec. 1993); 1 child, Diane Jackson Bove. BSEE, Duke U., 1934; MA in Edn., Calif. Luth. U., 1984. Registered profl. engr., Calif.; registered tchr., Calif. Physicist Hughes Aircraft, Hawthorne, Calif., 1932-40; radio engr. Northrop Aviation, Hawthorne, 1940-50; electronic engr. N.Am. Aviation, Inglewood, Calif., 1950-60; sr. design engr. N.Am. Aviation, Downey, Calif., 1960-72; asst. chief engr. Marquardt Aircraft, Van Nuys, Calif., 1972-79; exec. v.p. 21st Century Tech., L.A., 1979-82; tchr. electronics Simi Adult Sch., Simi Valley, Calif., 1982-90; ret., 1990. Patentee automatic navigation device; developer missile navigation heat seeker. Scoutmaster Boy Scouts Am., N.J., 1929-32, N.C., 1932-33, L.A., 1933-54. Mem. Nat. Eagle Scout Assn. (sr.). Avocation: model railroading. Home: 6694 Tremont Cir Simi Valley CA 93063-3945

JACKSON, WILLIAM CHARLES, spacecraft systems engineer; b. Coral Gables, Fla., July 28, 1960; s. Charles Kenneth and Leta Mae (Jennings) J.; m. Sheree Joy Tietz, Jan. 19, 1985; children: Robert Randall, Leta Mae Jackson. BSEE, Northwestern U., 1982, BS in Computer Sci., 1982; MSEE, Air Force Inst. Tech., 1986; ME Space Ops., U. Colo., 1996. Commd. 2d lt. USAF, 1982, advanced through grades to capt.; intelligence analyst USAF, Dayton, Ohio, 1982-85; chief advanced tech. br. Sec. Air Force Office Spl. Projects USAF, L.A., 1986-90; resigned USAF, 1990; instr. computer sci. dept. Chapman Coll., Orange, Calif., 1990; prin. engr. Ball Aerospace, Boulder, 1990—. Author tech. papers in field. Sunday sch. tchr., 1997—. Karate instr. for handicapped children, Niwot, Colo., 1994—. Mem. IEEE, AIAA, Mensa. Republican. Achievements include set-up and operation of a PC-based satellite ground station; development of set of astrodynamics analysis and data reduction software tools for a small satellite program, of proprietary software for performing satellite link budget analysis of innovative mathematical model of a complex spacecraft power subsystem; discovery of a more efficient algorithm for performing non-linear optimization using simulated annealing; designing, building and flying a high-altitude research balloon payload; development of software tools for analyzing performance of spacecraft elec. propulsion system; development of system concept for electro-optical remote sensing of sea ice from space; invention of new class of remote sensing satellite constellation; development of softwave tool to model slewing of a synthetic aperture radar beam; development of advanced remote sensing concepts using nanosatellites; developmet of genetic algorithms to solve complex optimization problems. Home: 7124 Pine Cone Ct Longmont CO 80503-8508 Office: Ball Aerospace & Tech Corp 1600 Commerce St # Tt5 Boulder CO 80301-2734

JACKSON, WILLIAM RICHARD, entrepreneur; b. Nampa, Idaho, Aug. 23, 1936; s. Richard W. and Josie P. (Mulder) J.; m. Marilyn Kay Samp, June 10, 1956 (div. 1975); children: James Lee, Robbi Jo, Jolynn Kay. BA in Secondary Edn., N.W. Nazarene Coll., Nampa, 1957; MA in Secondary Edn. Adminstrn., U. No. Colo., 1961; EdM, U. Denver, 1964, PhD in Higher Edn. Adminstrn. and Rsch., 1991; PhD in, Stanford U., 1991. Owner, operator Janitorial Svc., Walla Walla, Wash., 1950-54; account mgr., collection contractor Montgomery Ward, Walla Walla, Wash., 1953-57; exec. ins. dir. edn. svcs. Idaho Sch. Employment, Boise, 1957-58; sch. tchr., football coach Humanities, Speech & Art, Caldwell, Idaho, 1958-60; tchr. psychology and econs. Englewood (Colo.) Sch. Dist., 1961-64; dir. student coun. Brook Forest Leadership Inst., Evergreen, Colo., 1961-64; co-owner, operator Jackson Bros. Investments, Englewood, 1970-84; co-owner, pres. Internat. Bell Mus., Inc., Evergreen, 1978-86; pres. Jackson Bros. Industries, Evergreen, 1984—, Jackson Internat., Inc., Evergreen, 1984—; chmn. bd. Petro Silver, Inc., Denver, 1979-83; rsch. cons. in agr., toxic waste remediation and hyperbaric oxygenation medicine; sr. cons. Envrion. Health Found., San Francisco; mem. staff Southwest Rsch. Inst., San Antonio, Tex. Co-author: Brook Forest Leadership Curriculum, 1964, Disciplining Curriculum, 1978; author: Hyperbaric Oxygenation Effects on the Cognitive Function of Memory, Barter, The History, Mystery and Mastery of Mutual Exchange, Humic, Fulvic and Micorbial Balance: Organic Soil Conditioning, Environmental Care & Share, 1995, The Arthritis, Osteoporosis and Silica Link, The Calcium Deception, Fabulous Fulvic Electrolyte, 1995. Co-founder Benevolent Brotherhood Found., Denver, 1971—; bd. dirs. Ch. of the Nazarene, past chmn. bd. edn. Grantee Denver Presbyn. Med. Ctr., 1991, Hyperbaric Oxygen Therapy System, San Diego, 1991, Denver, 1991; recipient 1st Pl. Nat. Self-Publishing award Writer's Digest, 1993. Mem. Internat. Found. Hyperbaric Medicine, Undersea and Hyperbaric Med. Soc. (rsch. cons. 1990—), Stanford U. Alumni Assn., Phi Delta Kappa. Republican. Avocation: bartering. Office: Jackson Internat Rsch Ctr PO Box 1749 Evergreen CO 80437-1749

JACOB, TED MANAS, biomedical and forensic photographer; b. Manila, Philippines, July 10, 1960; s. Doroteo Benitez and Teresa Afring (Manas) J.; m. Maria Teresa Frades Escarcha, Oct. 26, 1991; 1 child, Sarah Marie. Diploma, Brooks Inst., 1984; student, TV broadcasting and rec. scis., L.A. City Coll., 1996. With Brooks Photo Ctr., Santa Barbara, Calif., 1985-88; biomed. photographer Childrens Hosp. L.A., 1989-93, audio-visual comms. specialist, 1993-97; freelance biomed./forensic photographer Milpitas, Calif., 1997—; owner Jacob Comm., Milpitas; humanitarian awards com. Childrens Hosp., L.A. Biblical instr. Logos Christian Fellowship Childrens Hosp., 1996-97. Recipient Humanitarian award Children Hosp. L.A., 1996. Mem. Profl. Photographers Am., Health Scis. Comm. Assn., Ophthalmic Photographes Soc., Internat. Indsl. Photographers Assn. Avocations: reading, swimming, sketching, drawing.

JACOBS, ARTHUR DIETRICH, educator, researcher, health services executive; b. Bklyn., Feb. 4, 1933; s. Lambert Dietrich and Paula Sophia (Knissel) J.; m. Viva Jane Sims, Mar. 24, 1952; children: Archie (dec.), David L., Dwayne C., Dianna K. Hatfield. BBA, Ariz. State U., 1962, MBA, 1966. Enlisted USAF, 1951, commd. 2d lt., 1962, advanced through grades to maj., 1972, ret., 1973; indsl. engr. Motorola, Phoenix, 1973-74; mgmt. cons. state of Ariz., 1974-76; mgmt. cons. Productivity Internat., Tempe, Ariz., 1976-79; faculty assoc. Coll. Bus. Adminstrn., Ariz. State U., Tempe, 1977-94, sr. lectr., 1995, ret. 1996; productivity advisor Scottsdale (Ariz.) Meml. Health Services Co., 1979-84; researcher U.S. internment of European-Am. aliens and citizens of European ancestry during World War II. Bd. dirs. United Way of Tempe, 1979-85. Editor, pub. Freedom of Information Times; co-editor: The World War Two Experience—The Internment of German-Americans: Documents, vol. IV; contbr. articles to profl. jours. Mem. Am. Soc. Quality Control, Ariz. State U. Alumni Assn. (bd. dirs. 1973-79, pres. 1978-79), Inst. Indsl. Engrs. (pres. Central Ariz. chpt. 1984-85), Ops. Research Soc. Am., Sigma Iota Epsilon, Beta Gamma Sigma, Delta Sigma Pi. Club: Optimist (life) (Tempe).

JACOBS, JUDITH ANN, freelance writer; b. St. Louis, Apr. 2, 1952; d. Charles C. and Lois Louise (Long) J.; m. Mihaly Kun, Feb. 1, 1982; children: Joshua, Jeremy. BA in Asian Studies, DePauw U., 1974; student Japanese history and lang., Jochi Daigaku, Tokyo. Import traffic agt. Nisho-Iwai, San Francisco, 1974-75; import traffic agt. C. Itoh & Co., San Francisco, 1976-77, E.F. Clements, San Francisco, 1977-78; fgn. corres., S.E. Asia various, 1979-81; editor Cathay Pacific Discovery, Hong Kong, 1982-83; sr. editor/Asia Pacific OAG Travel mags., San Francisco, 1984-92; freelance writer San Francisco, 1992—; Asia-Pacific/West Coast corres. Bus. Travel News, San Francisco, 1996—. Author: Indonesia: A Nation of Islands, 1990; update author: Hidden San Francisco & Northern California, 1997, Hidden Oahu, 1997, Hidden Hawaii, 1997; contbr. to books International Travel, the Nature Company, 1996, Travelers Tales, a Woman's World, 1995, Hong Kong Here Be Dragons, 1992, The Bed & Breakfast Cookbook, 1985; contbr. more than 1,000 articles to various publs. Avocations: cooking, hiking, travel. Home and Office: 99 Valley Hill Dr Moraga CA 94556-0111

JACOBS, KENT FREDERICK, dermatologist; b. El Paso, Tex., Feb. 13, 1938; s. Carl Frederick and Mercedes D. (Johns) J.; m. Sallie Ritter, Apr. 13, 1971. BS, N.Mex. State U., 1960; MD, Northwestern U., 1964; postgrad., U. Colo., 1967-70. Dir. service unit USPHS, Laguna, N.Mex., 1966-67; pvt. practice specializing in dermatology Las Cruces, N.Mex., 1970—; cons. U.S. Army, San Francisco, 1968-70, cons. NIH, Washington, 1983, Holloman AFB, 1972-77; research assoc. VA Hosp., Denver, 1969-70; preceptor U. Tex., Galveston, 1976-77; mem. clin. staff Tex. Tech U., Lubbock, 1977—; asst. clin. prof. U. N.Mex., Albuquerque, 1972—; bd. dirs. First Security Corp. of N.Mex. Author: Breckkan, 1996; contbr. articles to profl. jours. and popular mags. Trustee Mus. N.Mex. Found., 1987—, mem. bd. regents, 1987—, pres., 1989-91, 95—; bd. dirs. Dona Ana Arts Coun., 1992-93, Border Book Festival, 1996—, N.Mex. State U. Found., 1993—. Invitational scholar Oreg. Primate Ctr., 1968; Acad. Dermatology Found. fellow, 1969; named Disting. Alumnus N.Mex. State U., 1985. Fellow Am. Acad. Dermatology, Royal Soc. Medicine, Soc. Investigative Dermatology; mem. AMA, Fedn. State Med. Bds. (bd. dirs. 1984-86), N.Mex. Med. Soc., N.Mex. Bd. Med. Examiners (pres. 1983-84, N.Mex. State U. Alumni Assn. (bd. dirs. 1975-79), Mil Gracias Club (pres. 1972-74) Pres.'s Assocs., Univ. Ambs., Rotary, Phi Beta Kappa, Beta Beta Beta. Democrat. Presbyterian. Home: 3610 Southwind Rd Las Cruces NM 88005-5556 Office: 2525 S Telshor Blvd # 15-106 Las Cruces NM 88011-9148 also: Mus NM PO Box 2087 Santa Fe NM 87504-2087

JACOBS, RALPH, JR., artist; b. El Centro, Calif., May 22, 1940; s. Ralph and Julia Vahe (Kirkorian) J. Paintings appeared in: Prize Winning Art (3 awards), 1964, 65, 66, and New Woman Mag., 1975; one man shows and exhbns. Villa Montalvo, Calif., Stanford Rsch. Inst., Calif., Fresno Art Ctr., Calif., de Young Meml. Mus., Calif., Rosicrucian Mus., Calif., Cunningham Meml. Gallery, Calif., 40th Ann. Nat. Art Exhibit, Utah, Nat. Exhbn. Coun. of Am. Artists Socs., N.Y.C., Am. Artists Profl. League Show, Armenian Allied Arts, Calif., Monterey Peninsula Mus. Art, Calif. Recipient 1st place award Statewide Annual Santa Cruz Art League Gallery, 1963, 64; 2nd place award Soc. Western Artists Ann. M.H. de Young Mus., 1964; A.E. Klumpkey Meml. award, 1965. Address: PO Box 5906 Carmel CA 93921-5906

JACOBS, RANDALL BRIAN, lawyer; b. N.Y.C., July 8, 1951; s. John and Evelyn Jacobs; 1 child, Jillian. BA, Coll. of Idaho, 1972; JD, U. West L.A., 1978. Bar: Calif., D.C., Wis. Lawyer B. Randall Jacobs Law Corp., Brentwood, Calif., 1978—; real estate broker Morgan Reed & Co., Brentwood, 1979—; pvt. investigator Randy Brian Assocs., Brentwood, 1976—. Reserve deputy sheriff, L.A. County Sheriff, L.A., 1979—. Mem. Shom Rim Soc., Nat. Rifle Assn., Masons, Shriners. Office: 522 S Sepulveda Blvd Ste 110 Los Angeles CA 90049-3538

JACOBS, ROBERT COOPER, political scientist, consultant; b. N.Y.C., Jan. 23, 1939; s. Max and Paula (Glotzer) J.; m. Barbara Linda Lax (div.); children: Michael, Deborah; m. Mollie Jenks Edson (div.); children: Elliot, Madeleine, Eleanor. AB, CCNY, 1959; AM, Columbia U., 1961, PhD, 1970. Instr. Colby Coll., Waterville, Maine, 1965-68, asst. prof., 1968-70; from asst. prof. to prof. Cen. Wash. U., Ellensburg, 1970—, dir. law and justice, 1974-88, prof., 1982—; vis. prof. criminal justice Temple U., 1988-89. Contbr. articles to profl. jours. and encyclopedias. Mem. Kittitas County Juvenile Accountability Bd., Ellensburg, 1975-79; trustee Ellensburg Pub. Libr., 1994—, chmn., 1996. N.Y. State Regents scholar, 1955-59; State of N.Y. teaching fellow, 1962-63. Mem. Am. Polit. Sci. Assn., Wash. Assn. Criminal Justice Educators (past pres.), Supreme Ct. Hist. Soc. Democrat. Avocations: computers, hiking, target shooting. Home: 707 E 7th Ave Ellensburg WA 98926 Office: Cen Wash U Dept Polit Sci Ellensburg WA 98926

JACOBS, WILBUR RIPLEY, writer, history educator; b. Chgo.; s. Walter Ripley and Nona Isabel (Deutsch) J.; divorced; children: Elizabeth Shirley Jacobs Hayden, Catherine Elaine,; m. Priscilla Beth Dehmel, Dec. 20, 1982; children: William Ripley, Emily Marilyn. BA with honors, UCLA, MA with honors, PhD; postgrad., Johns Hopkins U. Prof. history U. Calif., Santa Barbara, 1965-88, chmn., dean of students; apt. rsch. scholar Huntington Libr., San Marino, Calif., 1989—; vis. prof. U. Calif., Berkeley, Claremont Grad. Sch., UCLA, Ind. U., U. Mich.; Fulbright prof. Australian Nat. U., Canberra; Am. studies lectr. U. Sidney, Melbourne U., U. Papua New Guinea, U. Queensland; lectr. U. Calif. Alumni Camps; U.S. Dept. State Cultural Exch. Program Yugoslavia, rep. for vis. historians from USSR; lectr. Gene Autry Mus. Western Heritage, 1997. Author: Wilderness Politics and Indian Gifts, 1968 (Pacific Coast Am.-Hist. Assn. prize), The Historical World of Frederick Jackson Turner, 1968, Dispossessing the American Indian, 1985, Francis Parkman, The Historian As Hero, 1991, On the Trail of Turner, 100 Years of Writing Western History, 1994, The Fatal Confrontation, Historical Studies on Indians and the Environment, 1996; co-author: Turner Bolton and Webb, Three Historians of The Frontier, 1965, Survey of American History, 1949; editor: The Paxton Riots and the Frontier Theory, 1958, Letters of Francis Parkman, 1960 (runner up Pulitzer prize in history 1961), Indians of the Southern Colonial Frontier, 1969, Benjamin Franklin, Philosopher-Statesman of Materialist, 1972, Frederick Jackson Turner's Legacy, 1965; writer, narrator A&E TV Biography Series, 1995—; contbr. numerous articles, essays to profl. jours., newspapers, Ency. Brit. Mem. exec. bd. dirs. Econ. Roundtable of So. Calif., Get Oil Out, Santa Barbara, Throop Unitarian Ch. Recipient award of merit Western History Assn., 1997; grantee Stanford U., Rockefeller Found., Ford Found., Am. Philos. Soc., Huntington Libr. Mem. Am. Hist. Assn. (Pacific coast br., pres.), Am. Soc. Ethnohistory (pres.), Am. Soc. Environ. History (pres.), Am. Studies Assn. (pres. Calif. br.), Humane Soc. U.S. (nat. bd.), Assocs. Calif. Inst. Tech., Mass. Hist. Soc., Soc. of Fellows Huntington Libr. Avocations: research, population-environmental history.

JACOBSEN, ERIC KASNER, consulting engineer; b. N.Y.C., July 21, 1932; s. Henry and Caroline (Kasner) J.; BSCE, U. Iowa, 1956; m. Dorothy H. Caldwell, Mar. 30, 1957; 1 son, Steven. Registered profl. engr., Ill., N.Y., Iowa, Mo., Wis. Structural engr. Stanley Engrng. Co., Muscatine, Iowa, 1956-59; asso. dept. mgr. R. W. Booker & Assos., St. Louis, 1959-63; plant mgr. Tri-Cities Terminal div. Nat. Marine Service, Inc., Granite City, Ill., 1963-65; sr. engr. Monsanto Co., 1965-69; chief structural engr. Weitz-Hettalsater Engrs., Kansas City, 1969-72; supr. structural and archtl. engring. Austin Co., Cleve., 1972-78; mgr. Engring. Mining and Metals div., 1978-87, chief structural engr. western dist., 1987-94; cons. structural engr., 1994—; cons. engr. structural and archtl. engring., 1960—; owner/mgr. Jacobsen Farms. Mem. ASCE, ASME, Chgo. Farmers, Chi Epsilon. Presbyterian. Office: 27 Technology Dr Irvine CA 92618-2364

JACOBSEN, FRANK, museum official. Pres., CEO Scottsdale (Ariz.) Ctr. for the Arts Mus. Office: Scottsdale Ctr for the Arts Mus 7380 E 2d St Scottsdale AZ 85251*

JACOBSEN, LAREN, programmer, analyst; b. Salt Lake City, June 15, 1937; s. Joseph Smith and Marian (Thomas) J.; B.S., U. Utah, 1963; m. Audrey Bartlett, July 29, 1970 (div.); children—Andrea, Cecily, Julian. Programmer, IBM Corp., 1963-70; systems programmer Xerox Computer Services, 1970-79; pres. Prescient Investments Co., 1975-82; sr. systems analyst Quotron Systems, Los Angeles, 1979-86; programmer/analyst Great Western Bank, 1987-92. Served with USAR, 1961. Mem. Am. Guild Organists (dean San Jose chpt. 1967), Mensa. Home: PO Box 91174 Los Angeles CA 90009-1174

JACOBSMEYER, JAY MICHAEL, electrical engineer; b. Okaloosa County, Fla., Mar. 13, 1959; s. John Henry and Patricia Ann (McDonough) J.; m. Joyce Ann Deem, June 20, 1981; children: Abigail Ann, Brian James. BS magna cum laude, Va. Poly. Inst. & State U., 1981; MS, Cornell U., 1987. Registered profl. engr., Colo. Commd. 2nd lt. USAF, 1981-90, advanced through grades to capt., 1985; elec. engr. 3397 Tech. Tng. Squadron, Biloxi, Miss., 1981-82; comm. engr. 1st Combat Comm. Group, Wiesbaden, Germany, 1982-85; communications engr. HQ Air Force Space Command, Colorado Springs, 1987-90; resigned USAF, 1990; staff engr. ENSCO, Inc., Colorado Springs, 1990-91, sr. staff engr., 1991-93; co-founder, chief tech. officer Pericle Comm. Co., 1992—. Patent pending wireless data modem; contbr. articles to profl. publs. Maj. USAFR. Decorated Meritorious Svc. medal, Air Force Commendation medal; named Man of Yr., Va. Poly. Inst. and State U., 1981; rsch. grantee, NSF, USN. Mem. IEEE (sr.), Armed Forces Comm. and Electronics Assn. (v.p. 1989-90), Air Force Assn., Omicron Delta Kappa, Eta Kappa Nu. Avocations: road racing, mountain climbing. Home: 2475 Edenderry Dr Colorado Springs CO 80919-3876

JACOBSON, EDWIN JAMES, medical educator; b. Chgo., June 27, 1947; s. Edwin Julius and Rose Josephine (Jirinec) J.; m. Martha Shanks; 1 child, Emily. BA, U. So. Calif., 1969; MD, UCLA, 1976. Diplomate Nat. Bd. Med. Examiners, Am. Bd. Internal Medicine; lic. physician, Calif. Intern in medicine UCLA Hosp., 1976-77, resident in medicine, 1977-79, fellow in nephrology, 1979-81, chief resident in medicine, 1979-81; asst. clin. prof. of medicine UCLA, 1981-88, assoc. clin. prof. medicine, 1988-94, clin. prof. medicine, 1994—; adj. asst. prof. medicine, UCLA, 1980-81; mem. med. sch. admissions com. UCLA, 1981—, med. staff credentials com., 1984—, med.staff exec. com., 1990-94, med. staff/hosp. adminstrn. liaison com. 1991-94, hosp./med. sch. faculty rels. com., 1991—, nat. kidney found., 1991—, med. adv. bd., 1991—; prin. investigator A/M Group Grant, UCLA Med. Ctr., 1993, Peter Langer Meml. Fund Award, 1993; lectr. in field. Author: Medical Diagnosis: An Algorithmic Approach, 1989; co-author: (with P. Healy) Il Proceso Decisionale nella Diagnosi Medica, 1992; manuscript rev. bd.: Bone Marrow Transplantation, 1988—, Jour. Am. Geriatrics Soc., 1989—; editor for symposia in field; contbr. articles to profl. jours.; editor book chpts. Recipient Upjohn Achievement award, 1977. Mem. ACP, Alpha Omega Alpha. Office: UCLA 100 Ucla Medical Plz Ste 690 Los Angeles CA 90024-6992

JACOBSON, JACK, television executive; b. Rochester, N.Y., Apr. 2, 1921; s. Max and Lillain Jacobson; m. Doris Mae Erhard (dec.); 1 child, Steven J. V.p. Ultra Tone Broadcasting, Inc., Dallas, 1945-48; prodr. talent Sta. WHIO-TV, Dayton, Ohio, 1949-62; program/promotion mgr. Sta. KGUN-TV, Tucson, 1962-79; sta. mgr. Sta. KTVK-TV, Phoenix, Ariz., 1979-86; TV cons. Sta. KDTU-TV, Tucson, 1986-93; gen. mgr. Sta. KTTU-TV, Tucson, 1993—; mem. promotion adv. bd. ABC TV Network, 1976-78; pres. Met. Phoenix Broadcasters, 1984-85. Mem. adv. bd. Salvation Army, Tucson, 1967—; mem. exec. bd. Muscular Dystrophy Assn., Tucson, 1969—; active Casa de los Niños, Tucson, 1987—. Sgt. U.S. Army Air Corps, 1942-45, ETO. Decorated Bronze Star medal; recipient Silver Medal award Tucson Advt. Club, 1988. Mem. Ariz. Broadcasters Assn. (bd. dirs. 1985-86). Avocations: fishing, writing. Home: 8661 E 29th St Tucson AZ 85710-7917

JACOBSON, LOWELL STEVEN (JAKE JACOBSON), railroad executive; b. Riley, Kans., Sept. 17, 1940; s. Myron A. and Irene (Anderson) J.; m. Patricia L. Boyce, Feb. 2, 1963; children: Michael W., Jacqulin D. Steel bridge worker Union Pacific R.R., Frankfort, Kans., 1958-64; indsl. foreman Union Pacific R.R., Salina, Kans., 1964-69; indsl. supt. Union Pacific R.R., Kansas City, Mo., 1969-73; trainmaster Union Pacific R.R., Topeka, 1973-85; supt. Union Pacific R.R., Kans., Nebr., Mo., Colo., 1985; railroad cons. S.W. U.S., 1986-87; gen. supt., gen. mgr., v.p. Copper Basin Rlwy., Hayden, Ariz., 1987—. Sgt. USAF, 1963-66. Named Railroader of the Yr., Rlwy. Age Mag., 1994. Avocations: auto restoration, railroad equipment. Office: Copper Basin Ry Highway 177 Hayden AZ 85235

JACOBSON, RAYMOND EARL, electronics company entrepreneur and executive; b. St. Paul, May 25, 1922; s. Albert H. and Gertrude W. (Anderson) J.; BE with high honors, prize for excellence in mech. engrg., Yale U., 1944; MBA with distinction, Harvard U., 1948; B.A. (Rhodes scholar), Oxford U., 1950, M.A., 1954; m. Margaret Maxine Meadows, Dec. 22, 1959 (div. 1986); children: Michael David, Karl Raymond, Christopher Eric. Asst. to gen. mgr. PRD Electronics, Inc., Bklyn., 1951-55; sales mgr. Curtiss-Wright Electronics Div., Carlstadt, N.J., 1955-57; dir. mktg. TRW Computers Co., Los Angeles, 1957-60; v.p. ops. Electro-Sci. Investors, Dallas, 1960-63; pres. Whitehall Electronics, Inc., Dallas, 1961-63, dir., 1961-63; chmn. bd. Gen. Electronic Control, Inc., Mpls., 1961-63, Staco, Inc., Dayton, Ohio, 1961-63; pres. Maxson Electronics Corp., Gt. River, N.Y., 1963-64, Jacobson Assocs., San Jose, Calif., 1964-67; co-founder, pres.,

chmn., chief exec. officer Anderson Jacobson, Inc., San Jose, 1967-88; chmn. Anderson Jacobson, SA, Paris, 1974-88; chmn. Anderson Jacobson, Ltd., London, 1975-85; chmn. Anderson Jacobson Can., Ltd./Ltée, Toronto, 1975-85, Anderson Jacobson, GmbH, Cologne, 1978-83, CXR Corp., San Jose, 1988-94; bd. dirs. Tamar Electronics, Inc., L.A., Rawco Instruments, Inc., Dallas, 1960-63, Micro Radionics, Inc., L.A., 1964-67, Computerman U.S.A., Inc., Reno, 1997—; lectr. engring., UCLA, 1958-60 lectr. bus. admin., UC Berkeley, 1965-66; mem. underwriting Lloyd's London, 1975-96. Eagle Scout Boy Scouts Am., 1935, committeeman 1968-80. Lt. (j.g.) USNR, 1943-46. Mem. Assn. Am. Rhodes Scholars, Harvard Bus. Sch. Assn., Oxford Soc., Yale Club, Brasenose Soc., Sigma Xi, Tau Beta Pi. Republican. Lutheran. Clubs: Courtside Tennis, Seascape Swim and Racquet. Home: 1247 Montcourse Ln San Jose CA 95131-2420

JACOBSON, SVERRE THEODORE, retired minister; b. Loreburn, Sask., Can., Sept. 20, 1922; s. Sverre and Aline Tomina (Joel) J.; m. Phyllis Lorraine Sylte, Sept. 14, 1948; children—Katherine Ann, Paul Theodore. BA, U. Sask., 1946; BD, Luther Theol. Sem., Sask., 1947; postgrad., Luther Theol. Sem., St. Paul, Minn., 1952-53; ThD, Princeton Theol. Sem., 1959. Ordained to ministry Evang. Luth. Ch., 1947. Pastor Lomond, Alta., 1947-53; lectr. Luther Theol. Sem., Saskatoon, Sask., 1956-57; pastor Torquay, Sask., 1958-63; asst. to pres. Evang. Luth. Ch. Can., Saskatoon, 1963-70; pres. Evang. Luth. Ch. Can., 1970-85; interim parish pastor Calgary, Alta., Saskatoon, Weyburn, Elbow and Loreburn, Sask., 1987-98; lectr. Luth. Theol. Sem., Saskatoon, 1987-98. Home: 53 Moxon Crescent, Saskatoon, SK Canada S7H 3B8

JACOBY, SANFORD MARK, management educator, historian; b. N.Y.C., May 13, 1953; s. Arthur and Doris (Alexander) J.; m. Susan Bartholomew, Sept. 9, 1984; children: Alexander, Margaret. AB magna cum laude, U. Pa., 1973; PhD in Econs., U. Calif., Berkeley, 1981. Prof mgmt., history and policy studies UCLA, 1980—; rsch. assoc. UCLA Inst. Indsl. Rels., 1980-90, assoc. dir., 1990-97; vis. scholar Cornell U., Ithaca, N.Y., 1989-90, Meiji U., Tokyo, 1997. Author: Employing Bureaucracy, 1985 (Terry prize 1986), Modern Manors, 1997 (Taft Hist. Prize 1998); editor: Masters to Managers, 1991, Workers of Nations, 1995; mem. editl. bd. Calif. Mgmt. Rev., 1983—, Indsl. Rels. Jour., 1985—, Labor History, 1991—; co-editor Comparative Law and Policy Jour. Rsch. fellow NEH, 1989; recipient Nevins prize Econ. History Assn., 1982, Yardley prize U. Pa., 1974. Mem. Am. Soc. Assn., Indsl. Rels. Rsch. Assn. (chair nominating com. 1987), Am. Econ. Assn., Orgn. Am. Historians, Soc. for the Advancement of Socioecons. Office: UCLA Grad Sch Mgmt 405 Hilgard Ave Los Angeles CA 90095-9000

JADALLAH, CHARLES I., sales executive; b. San Francisco, Nov. 18, 1959; s. Issa Charles Jadallah and Alice Ackall; m. Janine Anne Jadallah, Nov. 3, 1985; children: Jessica, Christopher, Matthew. BS, Calif. State U., San Diego, 1981; MBA, Notre Dame, 1986. Stockbroker First Jersey Securities, San Mateo, Calif., 1981; mgr. Visa Internat., San Mateo, Calif., 1982-85, planner, 1985-88, strategic planning, 1988-90, dir., 1990-94; bd. dirs. Mentor Venture Ptnrs., Pantana Group, Sports I.D., Security. Bd. dirs. U.S. Orgn. Med. Ednl. Needs, San Francisco, 1992—. Avocation: gardening, inventing. Home: 1742 Los Altos Dr San Mateo CA 94402-3603

JAEGER, ELLEN LOUISE, small business owner; b. Spokane, Wash., Nov. 11, 1949; d. L. Walter and Patricia E. (Kelly) Matson; m. Jerald J. Jaeger, Mar. 24, 1948; children: Jennifer Ann, Jason Joseph. BS in Bus. Mgmt., Lewis-Clark State Coll., 1993; MA in Counseling and Human Svcs., U. Idaho, 1993. Owner, operator, buyer Reflections Gift Shop, Coeur d'Alene, Idaho, 1986—; cons. Eagle Springs Gift Shop, Bonners Ferry, Idaho, 1987-90; sch. counselor Sovensen Elem. Sch.; appointee N.W. Retail Adv. Bd., Seattle, 1991-95. mem. bd., fundraiser Cancer Cmty. Charities, 1971-91, hon. mem. bd., 1991—; bd. mem. PTA-Lakes Jr. H.S., 1980-84, pres. bd., 1983-85; vol. office support staff Coeur d'Alene H.S., 1985-86; fundraiser United Way Kootenia County, 1988; bd. dirs. Kootenai Med. Ctr. Found., sec. bd. dirs.; bd. dirs. Coeur d'Alene, 1996, Coeur d'Alene Pub. Libr. Found., 1996. Mem. Rotary Internat. (chmn. group study exch. com. 1992—, bd. dirs.), Coeur d'Alene C. of C. (bd. mem.). Home: 1125 Stanley Hill Rd Coeur D Alene ID 83814-6077

JAFFE, CHARLES J., allergist; b. Phila., Feb. 3, 1946. MD, Duke U., 1971, PhD, 1972. Allergist Scripps Meml. Hosp., Encinitas, Calif.; prof. allergy and immunology U. Calif., San Diego. Mem. Am. Coll. Allergy Asthma and Immunology (chair computer sect.), Am. Acad. Allergy Asthma and Immunology (chair med. informatics), Am. Med. Informatics Assn. (chmn. clin. info. syss.). Office: 477 N El Camino Real Ste A308 Encinitas CA 92024-1329

JAFFE, EDWARD A., lawyer; b. Chgo., Sept. 17, 1945; s. Julius C. and Esther R. (Cohen) J.; m. Marlene E. Epstein, June 16, 1968; children: Kimberly A., Jonathan S. BA, Drake Univ., 1967; JD cum laude, Northwestern Univ., 1970. Bar: Ill. 1970, Hawaii 1971, U.s. Dist. Ct. Hawaii 1971, U.S. Ct. Appeals (9th cir.) 1972, (2d cir.) 1979, U.S. Supreme Ct. 1984. Assoc. Cades, Schutte, Fleming & Wright, Honolulu, 1970-75, ptnr., 1976-88; sr. ptnr. Torkildson, Katz, Fonseca, Jaffe, Moore & Hetherington, Honolulu, 1988—; facualty Nat. Inst. Trail Advocacy, Honolulu, 1985—, Univ. Hawaii Col. Continuing Edn., Honolulu, 1973—; arbitrator Am. Arbitration Assn., Honolulu, 1973—, Ct. Annexed Arbitration Program, Honolulu, 1987—. pres. Temple Emanu-El, Honolulu, 1989-91, bd. trustees, 1980-93. Office: Torkildson Katz Fonseca Jaffe Moore Hetherington Amfac Bldg Flr 15 700 Bishop St Honolulu HI 96813-4124*

JAFFE, IRA SHELDON, film critic, educator; b. N.Y.C., Aug. 19, 1943; s. Samuel and Lillian (Kupietz) J. BA, Columbia Coll., 1964; MFA, Columbia U., 1967; PhD, U. So. Calif., 1975. Advt. copywriter Young & Rubicam, Los Angeles, 1967-68, Cooke & Levitt, Los Angeles, 1970-71; lectr. U. So. Calif. Cinema, Los Angeles, 1970-72; lectr. U. N.Mex. Coll. Fine Arts, Albuquerque, 1972-75, asst. prof., 1975-79, assoc. prof., 1979-88, prof., 1988—, head media arts program, 1989—, Presdl. lectr., 1984-86; bd. dirs. Rodey Film Festival, U. Mex., 1977-87, Internat. Cinema Lecture Series, 1988—; bd. dirs. Sta. KNME-TV, 1990-92; v.p. S.W. Film Ctr., 1988—, Albuquerque Film Soc. Co-editor Women Filmmakers and the Politics of Gender in Third Cinema (spl. issue) Frontiers-A Jour. of Women Studies. Office: U NMex Media Arts Program Albuquerque NM 87131

JAFFE, JAN PAYNTER, advertising and marketing consultant; b. Chgo., Sept. 23, 1944; d. Gilman Caldwell and Helen Jean (Hepner) Paynter; m. Harris S. Jaffe, June 21, 1965 (div. Aug. 1969). B.A., U. Chgo., 1964, M.B.A., 1966; MA, New Sch. Social Research, 1987. Staff exec. devel. program Tatham-Laird & Kudner, Inc., Chgo., 1966-67; v.p. N.Y.C., 1968-73; v.p., mktg. dir. Smith/Greenland Co., Inc., N.Y.C., 1973; v.p., assoc. research dir. McCann-Erickson, Inc., N.Y.C., 1973-79; group product dir. Airwick Consumer Products div. Ciba-Geigy, Teterboro, N.J., 1979; sr. v.p. Backer & Spielvogel, N.Y.C., 1979-85, Chgo., 1986-87; exec. v.p. Bayer Bess Vanderwarker, 1987-88; pres. Jan Jaffe & Assocs., Inc., Aptos, Calif., 1988—; cons. Vol. Urban Cons. Group, 1973-85. Bd. dirs. League Sch., 1976-79, N.Y. Jazz Mus., 1976, Off-Off Broadway Alliance, 1976, Cultural Coun. Santa Cruz, 1990-97, Santa Cruz Baroque Festival, 1990-94; chmn. bd. Encompass Theatre, 1976-79. Mem. Advt. Research Found., Am. Mktg. Assn. Office: 900 Day Valley Rd Aptos CA 95003-9725

JAFFE, ROBERT STANLEY, lawyer; b. Walla Walla, Wash., May 16, 1946. BA, U. Wash., 1968, JD, 1972. Bar: Wash. 1972. Ptnr. Preston Gates & Ellis, L.L.P., Seattle, 1986—. Mem. ABA (mem. corp., banking and bus. law sect., mem. small bus. com. 1982-92), Order of Coif. Office: Preston Gates & Ellis LLP 5000 Columbia Seafirst Ctr 701 5th Ave Ste 5400 Seattle WA 98104-7078

JAFFE, SHERRIL ANN, writer, educator; b. Walla Walla, Wash., Sept. 12, 1945; d. Sam and Vera (Berger) J.; m. David Bromige, Sept. 5, 1969 (div. Dec. 1979); m. Alan Jeffry Lew, Dec. 23, 1979; children: Hannah, Malka. BA, U. Calif., Berkeley, 1967; MA, San Francisco State U., 1970. Lectr. New Sch. for Social Rsch., N.Y.C., 1969-70, U. Calif. Berkeley [illegible] 1990-92, San Francisco State U., 1993-94, Sonoma State U., Rohnert Park, Calif., 1996—. Author: This Flower Only Blooms Every Hundred Years, 1979, The Unexamined Wife, 1983, The Faces Reappear, 1988, Scars Make Your Body More Interesting and Other Stories, 1989, House Tours, 1991, Interior Designs, 1996, Ground Rules: What I Learned My Daughter's Fifteenth Year, 1997. Jewish. Office: Sonoma State U Dept English 1801 E Cotati Ave Rohnert Park CA 94928-3609

JAFFER, ADRIAN MICHAEL, physician; b. Cape Town, S. Africa, Aug. 24, 1943; came to U.S., 1969; s. George Daniel Jaffer and Theresa (Kourie) Binsted; children: Brendan, Terence. MBchB, U. Cape Town Med. Sch., 1966. Diplomate Am. Coll. Physicians. Intern Loyola Univ. Hosp., Maywood, Ill., 1969-70; resident Northwestern U., Chgo., 1970-72; fellow Harvard U., Boston, 1972-73, Scapps Clinic & Rsch., LaJolla, Calif., 1973-75, Northwestern U., Chgo., 1975-76; pvt. practice LaJolla, 1976—; assoc. clin. prof. U. Calif. San Diego, LaJolla, 1976—. Contbr. articles to profl. jours. Mem. AMA, Am. Coll. Rheumotology, Am. Acad. Allergy. Office: 9850 Genesee Ave Ste 860 La Jolla CA 92037-1233

JAGER, MERLE LEROY, aerospace engineer; b. Eugene, Oreg., Sept. 22, 1942; s. Earl Christian and Alma Marie (Jensen) J.; m. Shannon Kay Jacobsen, Mar. 18, 1967; children: Holly, Peter, Melanie, Marissa,. BS in Mech. Engring., Oreg. State U., 1965; MS in Aeronautical Engring., U. So. Calif., 1967. Aerodynamicist Lockheed-Calif. Co., Burbank, 1965-68; rsch. engr. The Boeing Co., Seattle, 1968-70; aerodynamics engr. Gates Learjet Corp., Torrance, Calif., 1970; project engr. Irvin Industries, Inc., Gardena, Calif., 1971-73; aerodynamics mgr. Northrop Corp., Hawthorne, Calif., 1973-91; mgr. flight mechanics Northrop Corp., Pico Rivera, Calif., 1991-95; aerodynamics mgr. McDonnell Douglas Corp., Long Beach, Calif., 1995—. Patentee in field. Treas. Goldenwest Assn., Westminster, Calif., 1976-78; tribal chief YMCA Indian Princesses Program, Huntington Beach, Calif., 1986-87; bishopric counselor Mormon Ch., Westminster, 1986-95. Mem. AIAA, Tau Beta Pi, Pi Tau Sigma, Sigma Tau. Republican. Home: 6771 Findley Cir Huntington Beach CA 92648-3075 Office: McDonnell Douglas Corp Long Beach CA 90810

JAGNOW, DAVID HENRY, petroleum geologist; b. Dubuque, Iowa, Nov. 24, 1947; s. Albert August and Ardath Helen (Goettsch) J.; divorced; children: Daniel David, Robert Carl, Beth Laura. BA in Geology, U. Iowa, 1970; MS in Geology, U. N.Mex., 1977. Exploration geologist Shell Oil Co., Houston, 1973-77; staff geologist Energy Reserves Group, Denver, 1977-78; exploration mgr. Donald C. Slawson Oil Prodr., Oklahoma City, 1978-82; cons. geologist pvt. practice, Edmond, Okla., 1982-87, Los Alamos, N.Mex., 1987—; venture capitalist Venture Capital Info., Edmond, 1986-87, Venture Calital Info., Los Alamos, 1987—; conservation chair Nat. Speleological Soc., 1995—; dir. Project Underground VA, 1995—; mem. caves and karst task force Bur. Land Mgmt., Carlsbad, N.Mex., 1991-93, Guadalupe caverns geology panel Nat. Park Svc., Carlsbad, 1993. Author: Cavern Development in the Guadalupe Mountains, 1979, Stories From Stones, 1992; mem. adv. bd. Jour. Cave and Karst Studies, 1998—. Conservation chair, chair Pajarito Grotto, Los Alamos, 1998—. Recipient Gov.'s Dist. Svc. award Gov. Iowa, 1970, W.A. Tarr award Sigma Gamma Epsilon, 1970, Lowden prize Geology U. Iowa, 1970. Fellow Nat. Speleological Soc. (Conservation award 1995); mem. Am. Assn. Petroleum Geologists, N.Mex. Entrepreneurs Assn. (bd. dirs. 1988-89), Cave Rsch. Found. (chief scientist 1988-89), Omicron Delta Kappa. Lutheran. Avocations: caving, hiking, rock collecting, cave sci., reading. Home: 1300 Iris St Apt 103 Los Alamos NM 87544-3140 Office: Venture Capital Info Inc 901 18th St # 11300 Los Alamos NM 87544-3009

JAGODOWSKI, RICHARD BEN, elementary school educator; b. N.Y.C., Jan. 27, 1950; s. John C. and Mildred (Paulich) J.; m. Theresa Mary Sauer, Nov. 15, 1970; children: Jesse D., Andrew James. BA in Edn., U. Ariz., 1980. Cert. tchr., Ariz. Tchr. Amphitheater Schs., Tucson, 1981—; wage-policy negotiator Amphitheater Schs., 1995-97, mem. employee adv. coun., 1995—, mem. budget adv. coun., 1996—. Youth coach YMCA, Tucson, 1994—. Mem. Planetary Soc. Democrat. Avocations: astronomy, basketball, travel, reading. Home: 3231 E Hardy Pl Tucson AZ 85716-1323 Office: Amphitheater Schs. 701 W Wetmore Rd Tucson AZ 85705-1547

JAKUBCZYK, JOHN JOSEPH, lawyer; b. New Britain, Conn., Dec. 21, 1953; s. Stanley Walter and Madeline Regina (Hinchliffe) J.; m. Petra Kunigunda Mead, Jan. 8, 1983; children: Kristan Marie, John Joseph II, Jamie Nicole, Joseph Michael, Michael Thomas, Stanley Walter, Peter Anthony, Samuel Francis, Justin Peter. BA in Bus. Adminstrn. and Polit. Sci., U. San Diego, 1976; JD, U. Ariz., 1979. Bar: Ariz. 1979, U.S. Dist. Ct. Ariz. 1979, U.S. Ct. Appeals (9th cir.) 1992, U.S. Supreme Ct. 1989. Pvt. practice, Phoenix, 1979—; gen. counsel, Ariz. Right to Life, 1990—; spkr. in field. Author pro-life articles; radio commentator and host. Catechist St. Paul's Cath. Ch., 1982-92; bd. dirs., cons. Ariz. Youth for Life, Phoenix, 1979-82; trustee Ville de Marie Acad., 1991—, pres. 1995—; chmn. polit. action com. Arizonans for Life, 1980-81; pres. Ariz. Right to Life, Phoenix, 1983-85, bd. dirs. 1983-92, v.p. 1988-89; bd. dirs. Life Ednl. Corp., 1984-90, sec.; founder, pres. S.W. Life and Law Ctr.; bd. advisers Free Speech Advs.; precinct committeeman Rep. Com., Phoenix, 1982-96. Actor in cmty. theater prodns. Recipient Pro-Life Action League Protector award, 1987, Wallace McWhirter award, 1989. Mem. ATLA, Ariz. State Bar Assn., Nat. Lawyers Assn. (bd. dirs. 1994—), Maricopa County Bar Assn., St. Thomas More Soc., KC (pro-life comm. 1982-83), Phi Delta Phi. Office: 2711 N 24th St Ste 200 Phoenix AZ 85008-1052

JAKUBOWSKY, FRANK RAYMOND, author; b. Belfield, N.D., Oct. 11, 1931; s. William and Catherine (O'bach) J. Student, U. N.D., 1950-52. Chemist Sherwin-Williams Paint Co., Emeryville, Calif., 1958-85; pres. Jesus Books, Oakland, Calif., 1978—; editor Spiritfest, Berkeley, Calif., 1997—. Author: Creation, 1978, Jesus Was a Leo, 1979, Caldecott, 1985, Frank on a Farm, 1988, The Psychological Patterns of Jesus Christ, 1982, The Creative Theory of the Universe, 1983, Lake Merritt, 1988, Thank God, I Am Alive, 1989, Whitman Revisited, 1989, Spiritual Symbols for the Astrology of the Soul, 1990, This New World; Birth: Sept. 8, 1958, 1990, Perceptive Types, 1993, Father Figure Frank's Stories, 1996, Inspiration Stories, 1998, Universal Mind, 1998. Pfc. U.S. Army, 1952-54. Mem. Urantia Fellowship, Inst. Noetic Scis., Nat. Coun. Geocosmic Rsch. Roman Catholic. Avocations: writing songs for children on fraimba. Home: 1565 Madison St Apt 308 Oakland CA 94612-4511

JALLINS, RICHARD DAVID, lawyer; b. L.A., Mar. 21, 1957; s. Walter Joshua and Elaine Beatrice (Youngerman) J.; m. Katherine Sue Pfeiffer, June 12, 1982; children: Stephen David, Rachel Marie. BA, U. Calif., Santa Barbara, 1978; JD, Calif. Western Sch. Law, 1981. Bar: Calif. 1988, U.S. Dist. Ct. (so. dist.) Calif. 1988. Panel atty. Bd. Prison Terms, Sacramento, 1989-96, Appellate Defenders, Inc., San Diego, 1989-91, Calif. Dept. Corrections, Parole Hearings Divsn., Sacramento, 1992-94; dep. commr. Bd. Prison Terms, 1996—. Mem. ABA, San Diego County Bar Assn., Phi Alpha Delta.

JAMES, BRUCE RICHARD, investor; b. Cleve., Oct. 19, 1942; s. George R. and Dorothy B. (Watson) J.; m. Jo Ann Osborn, Feb. 5, 1966 (div. Feb. 1982); children: Michael, Jeffrey, Stephen; m. Nora Ellen Thomas, May 11, 1985. BS, Rochester (N.Y.) Inst. Tech., 1964. V.p. Keller-Crescent Co., Evansville, Ind., 1964-70; v.p. Cardinal Co., San Francisco, 1970-73; pres., CEO Uniplan Corp., San Francisco, 1973-83, Electrographic Corp., San Francisco, 1983-93; chmn., CEO Barclays Law Pubs., San Francisco, 1986-94; pres., CEO Nev. New-Tech, Inc., Incline Village, Nev., 1993—; bd. dirs. Whittier Trust Co. of Nev., Reno, 1995—, Keystone Corp., Las Vegas, 1998—, Advanced Electronic Pub., San Francisco, 1990-93; chmn. bd. dirs. Polish-Am. Print Co., Warsaw, 1990-93; pres. Printing Industries of Calif., 1989-91. Candidate U.S. Senate, 1997-98; vice chmn. bd. trustees Rochester Inst. Tech., 1993—; chair bd. trustee Sierra Nev. Coll., Incline Village, 1997—; mem. Bd. of Equalization, Reno, 1995-97; trustee U. Nev. Desert Rsch. Inst., 1999—; dir. Nev. Policy Rsch. Inst., 1998—. Commencement spkr. Rochester Inst. Tech., 1998, Alumnus of Yr., 1997; recipient Silver Beaver award Boys Scouts Am., 1992. Mem. NMA, Printing Industries of Am. (chair congl. roundtable), Las Vegas C. of C., Nat. Fedn. Independent [illegible] Confrerie de la Chaine des Rotisseurs, Alexis de Tocqueville Soc. (Nev. state chmn. 1999—). Republican. Episcopalian. Office: Nev New Tech Inc PO Box 9167 Incline Village NV 89452-9167

JAMES, CHARLES E., JR., lawyer; b. Pontiac, Mich., Sept. 19, 1948. BA, Occidental Coll., 1970; JD with highest distinction, U. Ariz. Bar: Ariz. 1973. Ptnr. Snell & Wilmer, Phoenix, 1990. Mem. ABA, Nat. Assn. Bond Lawyers. Office: Snell & Wilmer 1 Arizona Ctr 400 E Van Buren Phoenix AZ 85004-0001*

JAMES, DARYL NORMAN, environmental engineer; b. Culver City, Calif., Feb. 2, 1946; s. Warren and Alayne (Meistral) Smith; m. June Alice McClow, June 24, 1978; children: Matthew Dwayne, Andrew David. A of Engring., El Camino Coll., 1966; BSME, Calif. State U., Long Beach, 1969. Registered profl. engr., Nev., Calif. Structural design engr. Northrup Corp., Hawthorne, Calif., 1969-70; mech. engr. Long Beach (Calif.) Naval Shipyard, 1970-73; recreation supr. City of Manhattan Beach, Calif., 1975-79; engring. technician Spink Corp., Reno, 1979-80; civil engr. Nev. Dept. Transp., Carson City, 1980-86, prin. engr., 1986-92, chief environ. svcs., 1992—. Appointed mem. Parks & Recreation Commn., Carson City, Nev., 1993-94. Avocations: volleyball, skiing, high school coaching, baseball coaching, sailing. Home: 3782 Prospect Dr Carson City NV 89703-7529 Office: Nev Dept Transp 1263 S Stewart St Carson City NV 89701-5229

JAMES, FRANKLIN JOSEPH, JR., public policy educator; b. Tampa, Fla., Nov. 11, 1946; s. Franklin Joseph Sr. and Eve (Keene) J.; m. Melanie Anne Lee, Sept. 9, 1967 (dec. Dec. 1987); children: Charles, Philip. BA in Econs. with honors, U. Ga., 1967; MPhil in Econs., Columbia U., 1976, PhD in Econs., 1976. Rsch. asst. Nat. Bur. Econ. Rsch., N.Y.C., 1969-71; sr. rsch. economist Rutgers U., Ctr. for Urban Policy, New Brunswick, N.J., 1971-74; rsch. assoc. The Urban Inst., Washington, 1974-77; dir. urban policy staff U.S. Dept. Housing and Urban Devel., Washington, 1977-81; prof. pub. policy U. Colo., Denver, 1981—; dir. doctoral studies U. Colo. Grad. Sch. Pub. Affairs, Denver, 1992-96; mem. rsch. adv. com. Fed. Nat. Mortgage Assn., Washington; mem. adv. com. Ctr. Cmty. Devel., N.Y.C. Co-author: President's National Urban Policy Report, 1980, Minorities in the Sunbelt, 1984; co-editor: Future of National Urban Policy, 1990. Staff dir. Colo. Pub. Pvt. Housing State Task Force, Denver; rsch. Gov.'s Task Force on the Homeless, Denver; mem. Mayor's Disbursement Com. for Ryan White Fund, Denver. Mem. Phi Beta Kappa. Democrat. Episcopalian. Avocations: mountain climbing, skiing, hiking, running. Home: 10715 E Pinewood Dr Parker CO 80138

JAMES, GEORGE BARKER, II, apparel industry executive; b. Haverhill, Mass., May 25, 1937; s. Paul Withington and Ruth (Burns) J.; m. Beverly A. Burch, Sept. 22, 1962; children: Alexander, Christopher, Geoffrey, Matthew. AB, Harvard U., 1959; MBA, Stanford U., 1962. Fiscal dir. E.G. & G. Inc., Bedford, Mass., 1963-67; fin. exec. Am. Brands Inc., N.Y.C., 1967-69; v.p. Pepsico, Inc., N.Y.C., 1969-72; sr. v.p., chief fin. officer Arcata Corp., Menlo Park, Calif., 1972-82; exec. v.p. Crown Zellerbach Corp., San Francisco, 1982-85; sr. v.p., chief fin. officer Levi Strauss & Co., San Francisco, 1985-98; bd. dirs. Pacific States Industries, Inc., Basic Vegetable Products, Inc., Clayton Group Inc., Crown Vantage Corp (chmn.), Redem Corp. Author: Industrial Development in the Ohio Valley, 1962. Mem. Andover (Mass.) Town Com., 1965-67; mem. Select Congl. Com. on World Hunger; mem. adv. coun. Calif. State Employees Pension Fund; chmn. bd. dirs. Towle Trust Fund; trustee Nat. Corp. Fund for the Dance, Cate Sch., Levi Strauss Found., Stern Grove Festival Assn., Zellerbach Family Fund, San Francisco Ballet Assn., Com. for Econ. Devel.; bd. dirs. Stanford U. Hosp., Calif. Pacific Med. Ctr. KQED; vice-chmn. World Affairs Coun.; mem. San Francisco Com. on Fgn. Rels. With AUS, 1960-61. Mem. Pacific Union Club, Bohemian Club, Menlo Circus Club, Harvard Club, N.Y. Athletic Club. Home: 207 Walnut St San Francisco CA 94118-2012

JAMES, HELEN ANN, plastic surgeon; b. Palmerston North, New Zealand, May 5, 1940; came to U.S., 1977; d. George Headley and Betty Beatrice (McDonald) J.; married (dec. Apr. 1993). MB, ChB, U. Otago, Dunedin, New Zealand, 1964; Fellow, Royal Coll. Surgeons, London, England, 1972. Diplomate Am. Bd. Plastic Surgery. Internship Palmerston North Hosp., New Zealand, 1965-66; residency plastic surgery Brdg Earn Hosp., Perthshire, England, 1973-74, St. Lukes Hosp., Bradford, England, 1975-77; fellow plastic surgery Mount Sinai Med. Ctr., Miami Beach, 1977-79; residency plastic surgery N.C. Meml. Med. Ctr., Chapel Hill, 1979-81; St. Joseph Hosp., Bellingham, Wash.; pvt. practice Bellingham, Wash. Mem. AMA, Am. Soc. Plastic and Reconstructive Surgeons, Wash. State Med. Assn. Avocations: tennis, birding, cycling. Office: 3001 Squalicum Pky Ste 5 Bellingham WA 98225-1932

JAMES, HERB MARK (JAY JAMES), foundation and insurance executive, free trade consultant; b. Trail, B.C., Can., Jan. 30, 1936; s. George William and Violet Ethyl (Corbin) J. Student, bus. adminstrn. Simon Fraser U., 1965-69; m. Patricia Helen Boyd, Nov. 1, 1958; 1 child, Brad Mark. Founder Internat. Sound Found., Ottawa, Can., 1967—, Blaine, Wash., 1975—; cons. Fed. Bus. Dev. Bank; mem. bus. adv. bd. U.S. Senate, 1981—; pres. Bus. Navigator Svcs.; cons. Can. Internat. Devel. Agy.; founder Better Hearing Better Life projects, Fiji, Kenya, Cayman Islands, Nepal, Costa Rica, Pakistan, Guatemala, Mex., Canassist Mazatlan, Mex., 1995—. Musician B. Pops Orch., South Pacific N.G.O. Group, Ctrl. European Enterprise Devel. Group, North-South Free Trade Adjustment Group; pres. N.W. NAFTA Trade Assn. Govt. of Can. grantee, 1973-83. Mem. Christian Bus. Men's Assn., Can.-Philippines Soc. (co-founder), Conbrio Soc. (hon. dir.), Blaine C. of C., Masons, Shriners, Demolay. Office: Am Bldg PO Box 1587 Blaine WA 98231-1587 also: Ste 970, 104 1015 Columbia St, New Westminster, BC Canada V3M 6V3

JAMES, JOHN SULLIVAN, film and radio producer, director; b. Phoenix, Oct. 24, 1957; s. David Charles and Patricia (Sullivan) J. BS in Broadcasting, Ariz. State U., 1981. Engr. Sta. KAET-TV, Tempe, Ariz., 1976; engr. Sta. KTVK-TV, Phoenix, 1977-84, dir., cinematographer, 1984-85, engr., producer, 1985-87; owner, producer, dir. Creative Illusions, Scottsdale, Ariz., 1986—; owner, pres. J. S. James Enterprises, Inc., Scottsdale, 1984—; tech. dir. Phoenix Boat People-Performance Art Troup, 1984-86/. Dir., prodr.: (short film) Shooter, 1977 (Nat. Student Film Competition award 1978), (radio drama) Black Cat Bone, 1987; creative dir.: (video) The Engulfed Cathedral, 1982; cinematographer: (documentary) Christian Consciousness and Military Service, 1987, Esteban Music Infomercial (Telly award 1996); sr. colorist: (cable TV show) Hey Dude, 1989-90, (video) Summer Olympics-Omni Volleyball-Atlanta, 1996. Mem. Ariz. Prodn. Assn. Avocations: skin diving, horseback riding, mountain hiking, photography, stereo enthusiast. Office: Creative Illusions PO Box 9201 Scottsdale AZ 85252-9201

JAMES, MARION RAY, magazine founder, editor; b. Bellmont, Ill., Dec. 6, 1940; s. Francis Miller and Lorraine A. (Wylie) J.; m. Janet Sue Tennis, June 16, 1960; children: Jeffrey Glenn, David Ray, Daniel Scott, Cheryl Lynne. BS, Oakland City Coll., Ind., 1964; MS, St. Francis Coll., Fort Wayne, Ind., 1978. Sports and city editor Daily Clarion, Princeton, Ind., 1963-65; English tchr. Jac-Cen-Del High Sch., Osgood, Ind., 1965-66; indsl. editor Whirlpool Corp., Evansville and LaPorte, Ind., 1966-68, Magnavox Govt. and Indsl. Electronics Co., Fort Wayne, 1968-79; editor, pub., founder Bowhunter mag., Fort Wayne, Ind., 1971-88; editor-in-chief Bowhunter mag., Kalispell, Mont., 1989—; instr. Ind.-Purdue U., Ft. Wayne, 1980-88. Author: Bowhunting for Whitetail and Mule Deer, 1975, Successful Bowhunting, 1985, My Place, 1991, The Bowhunter's Handbook, 1997; editor: Pope and Young Book of Bowhunting Records, 1975, 93, 99, Bowhunting Adventures, 1977. Recipient Best Editorial award United Community Svc. Pubs., 1970-72; named Alumnus of Yr., Oakland City Coll., 1982, to Hall of Fame, Mt. Carmel High Sch., Ill., 1983. Mem. Outdoor Writers Assn. Am., Fort Wayne Assn. Bus. Editors (Fort Wayne Bus. Editor of Yr. 1969, pres. 1975-76), Toastmasters (Able Toastmaster award), Alpha Phi Gamma, Alpha Psi Omega, Mu Tau Kappa. Home: 2325 Wolftail Pines Whitefish MT 59937-8099

JAMES, MARY SPENCER, nursing administrator; b. London, Ont., Can., July 10, 1949; d. Richard Spencer and Helen Frances (Winterbottom) James; m. Robert Peter Owler, Oct. 4, 1969 (div. June 25, 1975). AA, Norwich U., 1968; Nursing Diploma, Toronto (Ont.) Gen. Hosp., 1973; BA in Psychology, U. Vt., 1975. RN, Calif. Staff nurse Toronto Gen. Hosp., 1973-77, Stanford (Calif.) U. Hosp., 1977-81, B.C. Children's Hosp., Vancouver, 1981-83; sr. staff nurse King Abdul Aziz Mil. Hosp., Tabuk,

Saudi Arabia, 1983-84, Charter Med. Ltd./Tawam Hosp., Al Ain, Abu Dhabi, UAE, 1984-87; nurse Dubai Petroleum Co., UAE, 1987-88; nursing dir. Ygia Polyclinic, Limassol, Cyprus, 1988-89; nurse Stat Travelers, Inc., L.A., 1990-91; staff nurse Lucile Salter Packard Children's Hosp. at Stanford, Palo Alto, Calif., 1991-92; case mgr. H.S.S.I. Home Care and Olsten Healthcare, Milbrae and San Francisco, 1992-93; nursing dir. CHS Home Health Agy., San Francisco, 1993-94; liaison nurse coord., pvt. duty supr. United Nursing Internat., San Francisco, 1994-95; nursing supr. Staff Builders Home Care Svcs., Santa Rosa, Calif., 1995; home health coord. Sun Plus Home Health Svcs., Petaluma, Calif., 1995—. Avocations: aerobics, weight training, hiking, reading. Home: 250 C Douglas St Petaluma CA 94952-2577

JAMES, WAYNE EDWARD, electrical engineer; b. Racine, Wis., Apr. 2, 1950; s. Ronald Dean James and Arlene Joyce (Mickelsen) Dawson; m. Edith Yvonne Cone, Apr. 6, 1997; children: Terry Scott, Kevin Arthur. BS in Electronic Engring. Tech., U. So. Colo., 1976; MS in Computer Sci., Colo. U., 1996. Electronic technician Lawrence Livermore (Calif.) Nat. Lab., 1976-80; electronic technician Inmos Corp., Colorado Springs, Colo., 1980-86, CAD engr., 1986-87; CAD engr. United Techs. Microelectronics Ctr., Colorado Springs, 1988-97, ASIC engr., 1997—. Sec.-treas. Stratmoor Hills Vol. Fire Dept., Colorado Springs, 1983, 84, lt., 1985, capt., 1986. Served with USN, 1968-72. Named Fireman of Yr., Stratmoor Hills Vol. Fire Dept., 1983. Lutheran. Office: UTMC Microelectronic Systems 4350 Centennial Blvd Colorado Springs CO 80907-3701

JAMES, WILLIAM EARL, academic administrator, medical educator; b. Burlington, Colo., May 21, 1933; s. William Earl and Josephine (Nohr) J.; m. Charlne Rae Anderson, Jan. 8, 1936; children: Saundra, Bradley, Melinda, Shelley. AS, La Junta (Colo.) Jr. Coll., 1953; BS, U. Colo., 1955, PhD, 1973. Jr. engr. Motorola Inc., Phoenix, 1957-60; group engr. Martin Marietta, Denver, 1960-69; rsch. fellow Med. Sch. U. Colo., Denver, 1969-73; co-founder, v.p. Internat. Med. Corp., Denver, 1973-79; founder, chmn. bd. Postgrad. Inst. Medicine, Englewood, Colo., 1979—; pres. Postgrad. Inst. Medicine, Englewood, 1979-91. Author, editor books, videos, cassettes. Bd. dirs. Christian Chaplain Svcs., Denver, 1991—, Set Free Prison Ministries, Denver, 1994—. Spl. rsch. fellow NIH, 1969-73. Mem. Alliance for Cont. Med. Edn., Colo. Alliance for Continuing Med. Edn. Republican. Avocation: wild life photography. Office: Postgrad Inst Medicine 304 Inverness Way S Englewood CO 80112-5828

JAMES, WILLIAM LANGFORD, aerospace engineer; b. Southampton, Va., Jan. 13, 1939; s. Leroy and Worthie (Murphy) J.; m. Elaine Cecilia Reed; children: William Jr., Terri Lynne. Student, Va. State Coll., 1956, Hampton Inst., 1958; BS, Calif. State U., Los Angeles, 1962, MS, 1964; postgrad., U. Nev., Reno, 1984; spl. engring. studies, UCLA, 1970-82. Rsch. engr. non-metallic materials lab. N.Am. Aviation, L.A., 1960-67; rsch. analyst tech. staff The Aerospace Corp., El Segundo, 1967-75, materials engr., 1975-85; project engr. program mgmt. office space launch ops. The Aerospace Corp., El Segundo, Calif., 1985-96. Contbr. numerous articles and reports to profl. publs.; patentee in field. Recipient numerous awards for USAF space contributions. Mem. AAAS, Soc. Advancement Material and Process Engring. (vice-chmn. 1987-89). Avocations: traveling, water sports, big game fishing. Home: PO Box 19735 Los Angeles CA 90019-0735 Office: Aerospace Corp M5 712 Los Angeles CA 90009

JAMIESON, JAMES BRADSHAW, foundation administrator; b. L.A., June 10, 1931; s. Charles Cameron and Ruth (Bradshaw) J.; m. Perry McNaughton, Dec. 27, 1959; children: Jeffrey McNaughton, Dalton Charles. AA, Citrus Coll., 1950; BA, Claremont Men's Coll., 1955; MA, Claremont Grad. Sch., 1958; PhD, Brown U., 1966. Assoc. prof. polit. studies Pitzer Coll. and Claremont Grad. Sch., 1968-75; rsch. polit. scientist UCLA, 1972-73; v.p. for devel. Pitzer Coll., 1968-72, v.p., 1973-78, prof. polit. studies, 1975-83, exec. v.p., 1979-83, acting pres., 1978-79; prof. govt. Claremont Grad. Sch., 1975-87; v.p. for rsch. Claremont McKenna Coll., 1983-87; exec. dir. Found. for Performing Art Ctr., San Luis Obispo, Calif., 1987-96; commr. Calif. Postsecondary Edn. Commn., Sacramento, 1987-92; dir. Global Village, Seattle, 1989-95. Contbr. articles to profl. jours. Staff, sec. Ctrl. Coast Performing Arts Ctr. Commn., San Luis Obispo, 1993-95. Sgt. USAF, 1950-52. Fellow Brown U., 1960, 63, tchg. fellow, 1962, fellow Resources for the Future, 1964; rsch. grantee U.S. Dept. Interior, 1972-73; recipient Cal. Poly U. Pres.' Arts award, 1999. Mem. Santa Lucia Flyfishers (bd. dirs. 1988—), Trout Unltd. (bd. dirs. Calif. coun. 1989-94, bd. dirs. nat. bd. 1986-90), Marine's Meml. Club. Avocations: flyfishing, tennis, restoring vintage automobiles. Office: Jamieson Consulting PO 12843 San Luis Obispo CA 93406-2843

JAMIN, MATTHEW DANIEL, lawyer, magistrate judge; b. New Brunswick, N.J., Nov. 29, 1947; s. Matthew Bernard and Frances Marie (Newburg) J.; m. Christine Frances Bjorkman, June 28, 1969; children: Rebecca, Erica. BA, Colgate U., 1969; JD, Harvard U., 1974. Bar: Alaska 1974, U.S. Dist. Ct. Alaska 1974, U.S. Ct. Appeals (9th cir.) 1980. Staff atty. Alaska Legal Svcs., Anchorage, 1974-75; supervising atty. Alaska Legal Svcs., Kodiak, Alaska, 1975-81; contract atty. Pub. Defender's Office State of Alaska, Kodiak, 1976-82; prin. Matthew D. Jamin, Atty., Kodiak, 1982; ptnr. Jamin & Bolger, Kodiak, 1982-85, Jamin, Ebell, Bolger & Gentry, Kodiak, 1985-97; part-time magistrate judge U.S. Cts., Kodiak, 1984—; shareholder Jamin, Ebell, Schmitt & Mason, Kodiak, 1998—. Part-time instr. U. Alaska Kodiak Coll., 1975—; active Theshold Svcs., Inc., Kodiak, 1985—, pres., 1985-92, 95-96. Mem. Alaska Bar Assn. (Professionalism award 1988), Kodiak Bar Assn. Office: US Dist Ct 323 Carolyn Ave Kodiak AK 99615-6348

JAMISON, DEAN TECUMSEH, economist; b. Springfield, Mo., Oct. 10, 1943; s. Marshall Verdine and Mary Dell (Temple) J.; m. Joanne Leslie, Sept. 14, 1971 (div. 1995); children: Julian C., Eliot A., Leslie S.; m. Kin Bing Wu, Jan. 19, 1997. AB in Philosophy, Stanford U., 1966, MS in Engring. Sci., 1967; PhD in Econs., Harvard U., 1970. Asst. prof. grad. sch. bus. Stanford U., Palo Alto, Calif., 1970-73; economist World Bank, Washington, 1976-88, dir., 1992-93, advisor, 1993-98; dir. Ctr. for Pacific Rim Studies UCLA, 1993—, prof. Sch. Pub. Health, Grad. Sch. Edn. and Info. Studies, 1988—; dir. econs. adv. svc. World Health Orgn., Geneva, 1998—; chmn. ad hoc com. on health R&D for developing countries WHO, Geneva, 1996-97, dir. econs. adv. svcs., 1998—; bd. trustees Drug Strategies, 1994—. Author (with L. J. Lau): Farmer Education and Farm Efficiency, 1982, Disease Control Priorities in Developing Countries, 1993, World Development Report 1993: Investing in Health, 1993; cons. editor AERA Ency. Rsch., 6th edit., 1992. Fellow Woodrow Wilson Found., 1967, NSF, 1968. Mem. Inst. Medicine Nat. Acad. Scis. Avocation: tennis. Fax: (310) 206-4018. E-mail: jamisond@who.ch. Office: UCLA Ctr for Pacific Rim Studies 11-292 Bunche Hall Los Angeles CA 90095-1487

JAMISON, LARRY WILLIAM, photographer; b. Glendale, Calif., June 17, 1942; s. William Smith Jamison and Winifred (Verna) Enger; m,. Vicki Lynn Walker, June 27, 1987 (div. June, 1989); 1 stepchild, Elizabeth. BA, San Jose State U., 1969. Photographer Kent (Washington) News Jour., 1969-70, Telegram Tribune Newspaper, San Luis, Calif., 1970-75; owner, photographer Larry Jamison Photography, San Luis, Calif., 1975—; Gold Coast Profl. Photographers, San Luis, v.p., 1979-80, dir. 1980-81, sec. 1982-83. Author: Editorial and Photographs Columns, 1970-75. Deacon 1st Presbyn. Ch., San Luis Obispo, Calif. 1986--, elder. 1970--. With the U.S. Army, 1960-63. Recipient Achievement awards Profl. Photographers of Am., 1978, 1980; Fellowship Merit awards Profl. Photographers of Calif., 1979, 1985, 1986. Mem. Profl. Photographers of Calif. Democrat. Avocations: square dancing, long distance running. Home and Office: 762 Higuera St Apt 1 San Luis Obispo CA 93401-3529

JAMPLIS, ROBERT WARREN, surgeon, medical foundation executive; b. Chgo., Apr. 1, 1920; s. Mark and Janet (McKenna) J.; m. Roberta Cecelia Prior, Sept. 5, 1947; children: Mark Prior, Elizabeth Ann Jamplis Bluestone. BS, U. Chgo., 1941, MD, 1944; MS, U. Minn., 1951. Diplomate Am. Bd. Surgery, Am. Bd. Thoracic Surgery. Asst. resident in surgery U. Chgo., 1946-47; fellow in thoracic surgery Mayo Clinic, Rochester, Minn., 1947-52; chief thoracic surgery Palo Alto (Calif.) Med. Clinic, 1958-81, exec. dir., 1965-81; clin. prof. surgery Stanford U. Sch. Medicine, 1958—; mem. coun. SRI Internat.; chmn. bd. TakeCare Corp.; charter mem., bd. regents Am. Coll. Physician Execs.; mem. staff Stanford Univ. Hosp., Santa Clara Valley Med. Ctr., San Jose, VA Hosp., Palo Alto, Sequoia Hosp., Redwood City, Calif., El Camino Hosp., Mountain View, Calif., Harold D. Chope Cmty. Hosp., San Mateo, Calif.; pres., CEO Palo Alto Med. Found., 1965—; past chmn. Fedn. Am. Clinics; dir. Blue Cross Calif.; varsity football team physician Stanford U. Author: (with G.A. Lillington) A Diagnostic Approach to Chest Diseases, 1965, 2d edit., 1979; contbr. numerous articles to profl. jours. Trustee Santa Barbara Med. Found. Clinic; past pres. Calif. div. Am. Cancer Soc.; past chmn. bd. Group Practice Polit. Action Com.; past mem. athletic bd. Stanford U.; past mem. cabinet U. Chgo.; bd. dirs. Herbert Hoover Boys' Club; past trustee No. Calif. Cancer Program; past bd. dirs. Core Communications in Health, Community Blood Res., others. Served to lt. USNR, 1944-46, 52-54. Recipient Alumni citation U. Chgo., 1968, Nat. Divsn. award Am. Cancer Soc., 1979, Med. Exec. award Am. Coll. Med. Group Adminstrs., 1981, Russel V. Lee award lectr. Am. Group Practice Assn., 1982, Mayo Disting. Alumnus award, 1991. Mem. Inst. Medicine of Nat. Acad. Scis., ACS, Am. Assn. Thoracic Surgery, Am. Surg. Assn., Soc. Thoracic Surgeons (past pres.), Western Thoracic Surg. Assn. (past pres.), Western Surg. Assn., Pacific Coast Surg. Assn., San Francisco Surg. Soc. (past pres.), Portland Surg. Soc. (hon.), Doctors Mayo Soc., Am. Coll. Chest Physicians (bd. govs.), Calif. Acad. Medicine, Am. Fedn. Clin. Research, Am. Group Practice Assn. (past pres.), AMA, Calif. Med. Assn., Santa Clara County Med. Assn., Sigma Xi. Republican. Roman Catholic. Clubs: Bohemian, Pacific Union, Commonwealth of California (San Francisco); Menlo Country (Woodside, (Calif.); Menlo Circus (Atherton, Calif.); Stanford (Calif.) Golf; Rancheros Visitadores (Santa Barbara, Calif.). Office: Palo Alto Med Foundation 300 Homer Ave Palo Alto CA 94301-2726*

JAMPOL, JEFFREY, music industry executive; b. L.A., Sept. 16, 1958; s. Richard Alan and Sylvia X. (Levine) J. Student, Sonoma State U., 1974-76; BA, San Francisco State U., 1978. Retail mgmt. CBS, Inc., San Francisco, 1976-78; local promotion CBS, Inc. Epic Records, San Francisco, 1978-79, WEA, Inc. Atlantic Records, San Francisco, 1979-81; exec. producer Polymedia, Inc., Beverly Hills, Calif., 1981-83; nat. advt./promotion mgr. Music Connection Mag., Hollywood, Calif., 1983-84; nat. advt. dir. Gold Trade Publ., Inc., Encino, Calif., 1984-89; v.p., assoc. publisher Coast Media, Inc., Culver City, Calif., 1990-94; sr. v.p., ptnr. Brentwood News Group, Inc., Westwood, Calif., 1990; pres. Jampol Artist Mgmt., Inc., L.A., 1993—. Mem. Nat. Acad. Rec. Arts and Scis. (bd. dirs. L.A. chpt. 1983-85, voting mem. 1985—), Westchester/LAX C. of C. (bd. dirs. 1992-93), Culver City Jaycees, Santa Monica Jaycees. Democrat. Avocations: sailing, motorcycling, high end audio, contemporary art. Office: 8638 Franklin Ave Los Angeles CA 90069-1408

JAMRA, ELLEN G., college programs director; b. Toledo, May 24, 1949; d. Jamille George and Betty Gene (Chapman) J.; m. Michael Janser, July 20, 1973 (div. June 1983); 1 child, Brooke Elaine. BA, U. Colo., 1971. Devel. dir. Med. Coll. of Ohio, Toledo, 1979-88, dir. ann. giving, 1988-96, alumni dir., 1990-97; alumni dir. U. Colo. HSC, Denver, 1997—. Mem. Coun. for Advancement and Support of Edn., UT-MCO Fed. Credit Union (chmn., dir. 1993-96), Assn. Am. Med. Colls., Josina Lott Found. Developmentally Disabled Children (bd. dirs. 1994-96). Avocations: photography, travel, home improvements. Home: 5747 Xenon Ct Arvada CO 80002-1313

JANCSO, SUSAN ZSUZSA, newspaper editor, translator; b. Budapest, Hungary, Sept. 27, 1941; came to U.S., 1976; d. Bela and Anna (Finger) Vajda; m. Julius Jancso, Nov. 6, 1965; children: Susan, Katalin. AA, L.A. City Coll., 1986; B degree, UCLA, 1989, M degree, 1992; postgrad., Sorbonne U., Paris, France, 1983, Laval U., Que., Can., 1984, Salamanca (Spain) U., 1986. Hostess, cashier Airport Marina Hotel, L.A., 1976-79; office asst. EDD, L.A., 1979-80; sec. Cal/OSHA, L.A., 1980-82; sec. Calif. State Dept. Edn., L.A., 1982-90, mem. ins. fund, 1991-93; English page editor Am. Hungarian Jour., L.A., 1990-93, editor, 1994—. Author: (in Hungarian) Landing in Paris, 1996, Little Joys of Life, 1994, (in English) Little Joys of Life, 1998; translator: (from French) Le Temps d'un Soupir, 1991. Activist for ethnic orgn. Rep. Heritage Groups, Calif., 1980—. Mem. Am. Translators Assn., Hungarian Journalists Assn., UCLA Alumni Assn., Pi Mu Iota. Avocations: literature, music, translation, travel, aviation. Home and Office: Am Hungarian Jour 333 N Rossmore Ave # 1 Los Angeles CA 90004-2439

JANES, ROBERT ROY, museum executive, archaeologist; b. Rochester, Minn., Apr. 23, 1948; m. Priscilla Bickel; children: Erica Helen, Peter Bickel. Student, Lawrence U., 1966-68, BA in Anthropology cum laude, 1970; student, U. of the Ams., Mexico City, 1968, U. Calif., Berkeley, 1968-69; PhD in Archaeology, U. Calgary, Alta., Can., 1976. Postdoctoral fellow Arctic Inst. N.Am., U. Calgary, 1981-82; adj. prof. archaeology U. Calgary, 1990—; founding dir. Prince of Wales No. Heritage Centre, Yellowknife, N.W.T., 1976-86, project dir. Dealy Island Archaeol. and Conservation Project, 1977-82; founding exec. dir. Sci. Inst. of N.W.T.; sci. advisor Govt. of N.W.T., Yellowknife, 1986-89; exec. dir., pres., CEO Glenbow Mus. Art Gallery Libr. and Archives, Calgary, 1989—; adj. prof. archaeology U. Calgary, 1990—. Author books, manuscripts, monographs, book chpts.; ontbr. articles to profl. jours. mem. First Nations/CMA Task Force on Mus. and First Peoples, 1989-92; bd. dirs. Yoho Burgess Shale Found.; mem. nat. adv. bd. Ctr. for Cultural Mgmt., U. Waterloo. Recipient Nat. Parks Centennial award Environ. Can., 1985, Can. Studies Writing award Assn. Can. Studies, 1989, Disting. Alumni award Alumni Assn. of U. Calgary, 1989, L.R. Briggs Disting. Achievement award Lawrence U., 1991, ACE award for Can. cultural mgmt. Assn. Cultural Execs., 1998; Can. Coun. doctoral fellow, 1973-76; rsch. grantee Govt. of Can., 1974, Social Scis. and Humanities Rsch. Coun. Can., 1988-89. Fellow Arctic Inst. N.Am. (bd. dirs. 1983-90, vice chmn. bd. 1985-89, hon. rsch. assoc. 1983-84, chmn. priorities and planning com. 1983-84, exec. com. 1984-86, assoc. editor Arctic jour. 1987—), Am. Anthrop. Assn. (fgn. fellow); mem. Soc. for Am. Archaeology, Can. Archaeol. Assn. (v.p. 1980-82, pres. 1984-86, co-chmn. fed. heritage policy com. 1986-88), Current Anthropology (assoc.), Can. Mus. Assn. (hon. life mem., cert accreditation 1982, Outstanding award in Mus. Mgmt., Outstanding Achievement award for publ. 1996), Internat. Coun. Mus., Can. Art Mus. Dirs. Orgn. (mem.-at-large bd. dirs.), Mus. West (bd. dirs.), Can. Mus. Assn. (bd. dirs.), Alta.Mus. Assn. (moderator seminars 1990, Merit award 1992, Merit award for Museums and the Paradox of Change 1996), Ranchmens Club, Calgary Philharmonic Soc., Sigma Xi. Home: Box 32 Site 32, RR 12, Calgary, AB Canada T3E 6W3 Office: Glenbow Mus-AB Inst, 130 9 Ave SE, Calgary, AB Canada T2G 0P3

JANN, DONN GERARD, minister; b. Eau Claire, Wis., July 17, 1929; s. August William and Dorothy Olive (Nuesse) J.; m. Alice Joan Hartwell, Aug. 29, 1949 (div. 1974); children: Patricia, Scott, Lucinda, Susanna, Todd, Gregg; m. Nancy Ruth Hearn, June 22, 1985. Student, U. Minn., Duluth, 1947-48; BA, Whitworth Coll., 1951; MDiv, Theol. Sem., Princeton, N.J., 1955. Ordained to ministry Presbyn. Ch. (U.S.A.), 1955. Assoc. pastor 1st Presbyn. Ch., Bartlesville, Okla., 1955-59; pastor 1st Presbyn. Ch., Lexington, Nebr., 1960-67, Santa Rosa, Calif., 1967-73; v.p. Presbyn. Ch. Found., N.Y.C., 1973-88; pastor New Hempstead Presbyn. Ch., New City, N.Y., 1988-93; moderator Platte Presbytery, Hastings, Nebr., 1965-66; commr. Presbyn. Gen. Assembly, Portland, Oreg., 1967; chairperson presbytery Christian edn. com. Presbyn. Ch. (U.S.A.), Nebr., 1965-66, presbytery stewardship com., Nebr., 1966-67, synod ch. world interaction com., Calif., 1969-70, presbytery com. on minority candidates, Calif., 1970-71, synod regional budget com., Calif., 1971-72, presbytery com. on spl. gifts, 1989—; chairperson Community Ministries Corp., Lexington, 1966, Profl. Counseling Svcs., Lexington, 1966, County Protestant Community Svcs., Calif., 1969-70; area rep. Ch. Nat. Emergency Convocation on War, Washington, 1968; adj. prof. San Francisco Theol. Sem., San Anselmo, Calif., 1971-72; lectr. Santa Rosa Community Coll., 1972; mem. commn. on stewardship Nat. Coun. Chs., N.Y.C., 1975-88, v.p., chairperson commn. on stewardship, 1984-87, chairperson theol. resource ctr., N.Y., 1986-87. Pres. Coun. Social Svcs., Santa Rosa, 1971. Bd. dirs. Sonoma County (Calif.) chpt. People for Econ. Opportunity, 1968-70; mem. adv. coun. Santa Rosa Sch. Bd.; pres. Coun. Social Svcs., Santa Rosa, 1971; chairperson Interfaith Week of Christian Unity, Calif., 1971-72; active No. Am. Conf. on Christian Philanthropy, N.Y., 1974-87, chair, 1987-88. Mem. Presbytery of Grand Canyon (pres. 1990-93), Area Clergy Assn. (pres. 1990-93). Democrat. Home: 6350 E Kathleen Rd Scottsdale AZ 85254-1980

JANOWICZ, FRANK DOMINIC, correctional educator; b. L.A., Dec. 26, 1943; s. Frank Francis and Kathern Mary (La Blanc) J.; m. Beatrice Louise Janowicz, 1975 (div. Aug. 1983); married, Aug. 27, 1983. AA, Harbor C.C., 1969; BS in Criminal Justice, Calif. State U., L.A., 1977; MS in Instrnl. Tech., Nat. U., 1995. Traffic sch. instr. Alhambra (Calif.) Adult Sch. Dist., 1976-86; policeman L.A. Police Dept., 1970-86; tchr. Calif. Youth Authority, Whittier, 1987-91, L.A. County Office of Edn., Downey, 1992—; assoc. prof. Nat. U., Inglewood, Calif., 1995—; owner J&J Legal Support, Santa Fe Springs, Calif., 1996—. Author: (book/program) Legal Education Awareness Program (LEAP); prodr.: (TV cable show) Law Education, 1997—. Drug grantee L.A. County Office of Edn., 1993. Democrat. Roman Catholic. Avocations: writing, physical fitness, traveling. Home: 9904 Aspen Cir Santa Fe Springs CA 90670-3563

JANSEN, ALLAN W., lawyer; b. Oak Park, Ill., July 22, 1948. BS in Aerospace Engring., U. Ill., 1971; JD, John Marshall Law Sch., 1978. Bar: Calif. 1978, U.S. Dist. Ct. (cen. dist.) Calif. 1978, U.S. Ct. Appeals (9th cir.) 1978, U.S. Patent Office, U.S. Ct. Appeals (fed. cir.) 1986. Ptnr. Lyon & Lyon, L.A., 1986—. Mem. editorial bd. John Marshall Jour. Practice & Procedure, 1977-78. Mem. ABA, Am. Intellectual Property Law Assn., State Bar Calif., L.A. County Bar Assn., L.A. Intellectual Property Law Assn., Phi Delta Phi. Office: Lyon & Lyon 34th Fl 3200 Park Center Dr Ste1200 Costa Mesa CA 92626-7163*

JANSEN, EVAN LEE, pharmaceutical company manager; b. Ft. Worth, Tex., July 23, 1971; s. Robert Leo and Betty Jean (Rothenfluch) J. BA, UCLA, 1993. Territory rep. Forest Pharms., Redlands, Calif., 1993-94, profl. rep., 1994-95; med. rep. Forest Pharms., Palm Desert, Calif., 1995-96; specialty rep. Forest Pharms., Riverside, Calif., 1996-97; divisional sales mgr. Forest Pharms., Denver, 1997—; profl. advisor So. Calif. Cancer Pain Initiative, Loma Linda, 1994-96. Named Outstanding Citizen of Yr., Riverside C.C., 1989. Mem. KC, NRA, Aicraft Owners and Pilots Assn., Phi Delta Theta. Republican. Roman Catholic. Avocation: private pilot. Office: Forest Pharms Inc 13622 Lakefront Dr Saint Louis MO 63045

JANSON, RICHARD ANTHONY, plastic surgeon; b. Passaic, N.J., Nov. 30, 1945; m. Mary Ann Janson, 1971; children: Sarah, Matthew. BA, Rice U., 1967; MD, Med. Coll. Wis., 1971. Diplomate Am. Bd. Plastic Surgery. Intern St. Joseph Hosp., Denver, 1971-72, resident in gen. surgery, 1972-76; resident in plastic surgery U. Tex. Med. Branch, Galveston, 1976-79; pvt. practice Grand Junction, Colo., 1979—. Fellow ACS, Am. Soc. Plastic & Reconstructive Surgeons; mem. Colo. Soc. Plastic & Reconstructive Surgeons. Office: 1120 Wellington Ave Grand Junction CO 81501-6129

JANSSEN, JAMES ROBERT, consulting software engineer; b. Frederick, Md., June 14, 1959; s. Robert James and Kathryn Doris (Randolph) J.; m. Deborah Jane Dellwo, Mar. 15, 1986 (div. Sept. 20, 1988). BSEE, Stanford U., 1981, MSEE, 1982. Simulation technician Varian Assocs., Palo Alto, Calif., 1981; hardware design engr. Fairchild Test Systems, San Jose, Calif., 1982-86, Factron Test Systems, Latham, N.Y., 1986-87; software, sys. designer Schlumberger Technologies Labs., Palo Alto, 1988; software engr. Photon Dynamics, Inc., San Jose, 1989-90, ADAC Labs., Milpitas, Calif., 1990-92; software, system designer ADAC Labs., Aalborg, Denmark, 1992, Milpitas, 1992-94; consulting software engr. self-employed, Sunnyvale, Calif., 1994-96; mem. tech. staff Netscape Comms. Corp., Mountain View, Calif., 1996—; pres., founder Digital Studio Systems, Inc., Sunnyvale, 1990-93. Patentee multiple timing signal generator. Civic vol. City of Sunnyvale, 1993. Mem. Tau Beta Pi. Avocations: motocross racing, guitar playing, auto race driving, auto race spectating. Home and Office: 2028 Lockhart Gulch Rd Scotts Valley CA 95066-2923

JANSSEN-PELLATZ, EUNICE CHARLENE, healthcare facility administrator; b. Urania, La., Mar. 23, 1948; d. Luther Clarence and Eunice Bobby (Pendarvis) Smith. BS in Nursing, Humboldt State U., 1970; MS in Nursing, Calif. State U., Fresno, 1980. Dir. nurses, asst. adminstr., coord. patient care svcs. Mad River Community Hosp., Arcata, Calif.; nursing supr. Fresno (Calif.) Community Hosp. Mem. Am. Soc. Healthcare Risk Mgmt. Home: 824 Diamond Dr Arcata CA 95521-8212

JANTZEN, J(OHN) MARC, retired education educator; b. Hillsboro, Kans., July 30, 1908; s. John D. and Louise (Janzen) J.; m. Ruth Patton, June 9, 1935; children: John Marc, Myron Patton, Karen Louise. A.B., Bethel Coll., Newton, Kans., 1934; A.M., U. Kans., 1937, Ph.D., 1940. Elementary sch. tchr. Marion County, Kans., 1927-30, Hillsboro, Kan., 1930-31; high sch. tchr., 1934-36; instr. sch. edn. U. Kans., 1936-40; asst. prof. Sch. Edn., U. of Pacific, Stockton, Calif., 1940-42; assoc. prof. Sch. Edn., U. of Pacific, 1942-44, prof., 1944-78, prof. emeritus, 1978—, also dean sch. edn., 1944-74, emeritus, 1974—, dir. summer sessions, 1940-72; condr. overseas seminars; mem., chmn. commn. equal opportunities in edn. Calif. Dept. Edn., 1959-69; mem., chmn. Commn. Tchr. Edn. Calif. Tchrs. Assn., 1956-62; mem. Nat. Coun. for Accreditation Tchr. Edn., 1969-72. Bd. dirs. Ednl. Travel Inst., 1965-89. Recipient hon. svd. award Calif. Congress Parents and Tchrs., 1982, McCaffrey disting. Svc. award in recognition of leadership in higher edn., cmty. relationships and internat. svc. San Joaquin Delta Coll., 1996. Mem. NEA, Am. Edn. Rsch. Assn., Calif. Edn. Rsch. Assn. (past pres. 1954-55), Calif. Coun. for Edn. Tchrs., Calif. Assn. of Colls. for Tchr. Edn. (sec., treas. 1975-85), Rotary (Outstanding Rotarian of Yr. award North Stockton 1990, Paul Harris fellow 1980), Stockton Coun. PTA Found., Phi Delta Kappa. Methodist. Home: 117 W Euclid Ave Stockton CA 95204-3122

JANTZER-WHITE, MARILEE JOAN, art history educator; b. Erie, Pa., Nov. 10, 1942; d. Oliver and Marilyn (Andrews) Dumbravo; m. Richard W. Jantzer, Sr., Aug. 2, 1962 (div. 1966); 1 child, Richard; m. Joel E. White, Feb. 12, 1974. BA, Calif. State U., Northridge, 1988; MA, U. Calif., L.A., 1991, PhD, 1998. Cert. Soc. Diagnostic Med. Sonographers; cert. art historian. Radiologic tech. Hamot Hosp., Erie, 1960-63; coronary angiographer White Meml. Med. Ctr., L.A., 1967-75, diagnostic ultrasonographer, 1975-84; adj. prof. L.A. City Coll., 1994-96; adj. prof. art history Ft. Lewis Coll., Durango, Colo., 1998—. Bd. dirs. Durango Art Ctr., 1999—. Mem. Am. Registry Diagnostic Med. Sonographers, Coll. Art Assn., Durango Friends of the Arts, Animas Mus. (bd. mem. 1998), Golden Key Nat. Honor Soc. Avocation: skiing. Home: 70 Animosa Cir Durango CO 81301 Office: Ft Lewis Coll 1000 Rim Dr Durango CO 81301

JANULAITIS, M. VICTOR, consulting company executive; b. Augsberg, Ger., Sept. 25, 1945; came to U.S., 1948, naturalized, 1953; s. Vytautas P. Janulaitis; m. Carol L. George, Nov. 23, 1968; children: Victoria C., Michael G. BS, Loyola U., Chgo., 1967; MBA, U. Chgo., 1971. CPA, Ill.; cert. mgmt. cons.; cert. data processor. With IBM, Chgo., 1967-71, Touche Ross & Co., Chgo., 1971-78; v.p. Damon Corp., Boston, 1978-79; part-time instr. Harvard U. Grad. Sch., 1979-80, ind. cons., 1979-80; v.p. Western ops. Index Systems, L.A. and Boston, 1979-82; founder, chief exec. officer Positive Support Rev., Inc., L.A., 1982—; chmn. UCLA Grad. Sch. Mgmt. Assocs. Program, 1986-88, mem. adv. bd.; vis. prof. U. So. Calif. Grad. Sch. Bus., 1996. Author: (with others) Managing the System Development Process, 1980, Information System Position Description Handguide, 1995, Metrics Handguide for the Internet and Information Technology, 1996, PC Policies and Procedures Managment Handguide, 1995, Client Server Management Handguide, 1994. Treas. adv. bd. Malibu Sch., Calif., 1982, 84. Mem. Am. Inst. CPAs, Ill. Soc. CPAs, Am. Prodn. and Inventory Control Soc. (bd. dirs.), Soc. Mgmt. Info. Systems (So. Calif. chpt., chmn.), Inst. Mgmt. Cons. (L.A. chpt.). Office: Positive Support Rev Inc 2500 Broadway Ste 320 Santa Monica CA 90404-3076

JAOUEN, RICHARD MATTHIE, plastic surgeon. MD, U. Autonoma de Guadalajara, Jalisco, Mexico, 1975. Intern St. Joseph Hosp., Denver, 1976-77, surgeon, 1977-81; plastic surgeon Ind. U. Med. Sch., Indpls., 1981-83, North Colo. Med. Ctr., Greeley, Colo., 1983—. Office: 1640 25th Ave Greeley CO 80631-4957

JAQUITH, GEORGE OAKES, opthalmologist; b. Caldwell, Idaho, July 29, 1916; s. Gail Belmont and Myrtle (Burch) J., m. Pearl Elizabeth Taylor, Nov. 30, 1939; children: Patricia Ann Jaquith Mueller, George, Michele Eugenie Jaquith Smith. *His wife, Pearl Jaquith, is an orthoptics technician*

and former office manager for an opthalmology practice. She is also an avid ladies' championship golfer. His daughter, Patricia Mueller, a CPA, is an office manager for her husband, Donald Muller, an architect. Patricia also has her own accounting and business service in Laguna Niguel, California. His son, George Jaquith who resides in Niceville, Florida, earned his MBA at Stanford and has Wind Canyon Publishing, Inc. for books on aviation. His daughter Michele Smith, wife of David Smith, teaches computer and dyslexia classes in Aurora, Illinois. Michele's husband, David, is a division director of office management and sales for the Caterpillar Company. BA, Coll. Idaho, 1938; MB, Northwestern U., 1942, MD, 1943. Intern Wesley Meml. Hosp., Chgo., 1942-43; resident opthalmology U.S. Naval Hosp., San Diego, 1946-48; pvt. practice medicine, specializing in opthalmology Brawley, Calif., 1948—; pres. Pioneers Meml. Hosp. staff, Brawley, 1953, dir. exec. com. Calif. Med. Eye Coun., 1960—, v.p. Calif. Med. Eye Found., 1976—. Sponsor Anza coun. Boy Scouts Am., 1966—, Gold card holder Rep. Assocs., Imperial County, Calif., 1967-68, PTO. Served with USMC, USN, 1943-47. Mem. Imperial County (pres. 1961), Calif. Med. Assn. (del. 1961—), Nat., So. Calif. (dir. 1966—, chmn. med. adv. com. 1968-69), Soc. Prevention Blindness, Calif. Assn. Opthalmology (treas. 1976—), San Diego, L.A. Opthal. Socs., L.A. Rsch. Study Club, Nathan Smith Daivs Soc., Coll. Idaho Assocs., Am. Legion, VFW, Res. Officers Assn., Basenji Assn., Nat. Geneal. Soc., Cuyamaca Club (San Diego), Elks, Phi Beta Phi, Lambda Chi Alpha (Hall of Fame). Presbyterian (elder). Office: PO Box 511 Brawley CA 92227-0511

JARIABKA, ANDREW JOHN, financial consultant; b. Chgo., Sept. 9, 1955; s. Ivan and Elena J.; m. Penny Kay Crawford, Apr. 23, 1983; 1 child, Justin Andrew. AA in Acctg., Oakton C.C., Niles, Ill., 1976; BS in Bus. Adminstrn., U. Redlands, 1982. Mgr. gen. acctg. Riddell Sporting Goods, Chgo., 1976-79; asst. corp. controller Wynns internat., Fullerton, Calif., 1979-80; corp. controller Bell Helmets Internat., San Marino, Calif., 1980-84, Van De Kamps Bakers, San Marino, 1984-86; pvt. practice San Marino, 1986—. Mem. bd. dirs. Pacific Clinics, Pasadena, 1997—. Office: 2600 Mission St Ste 200 San Marino CA 91108-1676

JARMAN, DONALD RAY, retired public relations professional, minister; b. Benton Harbor, Mich., May 6, 1928; s. Ray Charles and Grace Marie (Timanus) J.; m. Bo Dee Foster, July 7, 1950 (div. 1985); children: Mark, Katharine Law, Luanne Miller; m. Sharon Lee Becker, Feb. 16, 1991. BA, Chapman U., 1950; MDiv, Lexington Theol. Sem., 1953; DMin, Sch. of Theology, Claremont, 1970. Ordained min. Disciples of Christ, 1950; cert. fundraising exec. Nat. Soc. Fundraising Execs., 1980-89. Pastor Sharpsberg (Ky.) Christian, 1950-53, First Christian Ch., Santa Maria, Calif., 1953-58, St. Claire St. Ch. of Christ, Kirkcaldy, Scotland, 1958-61, So. Bay Christian, Redondo Beach, Calif., 1961-71; dir. human value in health care Eskaton, Charmichael, Calif., 1971-73; exec. dir. Northwestern NBA Svc., Portland, Oreg., 1973-85; dir. pub. relations and mktg. Retirement Housing Found., Long Beach, Calif., 1985-89; part time minister Pico Rivera Christian Ch., 1986-87; dir. community rels. Coscan Davidson Homes, Signal Hill, Calif., 1989-96; interim min. Southgate First Christian Ch., 1994-95; pres. So. Calif. Mins., 1967; chmn. Pacific S.W. Region Christian Ch., 1968; mem. gen. bd. Disciples of Christ, 1969-70; exec. dir. Signal Hill Econ. Devel. Bd., 1992-96. Editor: Reachout, 1973-84, Hill Street News, 1992-95; editor-in-chief: December Rose, 1985-89; columnist NW Senior News, 1980-84. Pres. Signal Hill C. of C., 1992-93; treas. Hist. Soc., Signal Hill, 1990-94; commr. L.A. County Commn. on Aging, 1994— (Link award for svc., 1998), Signal Hill Commn. Pks. and Recreation, 1996—; bd. dirs. Bethany Towers, Hollywood, Calif., 1997—. Recipient Master Make-up Technician award Portland Opera, 1983, Outstanding Older American award City of Signal Hill, Calif., 1993. Mem. Rotary (pres. Progress, Oreg. 1983-84, pres. Signal Hill 1993-94, Paul Harris fellow), Chapman U. Alumni Assn. (pres. 1994-95, trustee 1994-96), Los Alamitos Cmty. Art League, So. Calif. Pastel Soc., Lakewood Artist Guild, Masons. Democrat. Avocations: make-up artistry, bread baking, photography, water color, oils and pastels. Home: 1923 Molino Ave Unit 101 Signal Hill CA 90804-1028

JARMEL, MARCIA J., documentary filmmaker; b. N.Y.C., June 25, 1958; d. Eli Jarmel and Roberta (Becker) Jarmel-Estin; m. Ken Schneider, Apr. 30, 1995; 1 child, Mica Jarmel-Schneider. BA in Philosophy, U. Colo., 1980, MA in Journalism and Mass Comm., 1987. Co-editor, assoc. prodr. For Better Or For Worse, 1993; prodr., co-dir., co-editor The F Word, 1994; prodr., dir., writer The Return of Sarah's Daughters, 1997; postprodn. coord., asst. editor End of a Legend, 1997; script cons. Liewella, 1998; freelance feature writer for Metro-Denver publs., and nonprofit orgsn., 1983-87. Grantee Calif. Humanities Coun., 1992, Ind. TV Svc. (ITVS), 1998.

JARMON, LAWRENCE, developmental communications educator; b. L.A., Nov. 7, 1946; s. Robert and Movella (Young) J. BA, Calif. State U., 1969, MA in Adminstrn. Health and Safety, 1988; MS, U. Wash., 1972; EdD in Edn. Adminstrn., Wash. State U., 1975; MA, Calif. State U., L.A., 1988. Cert. alcohol and drug problems specialist. Athletic dir., instr. dept. phys. edn. L.A. SW Coll., 1975-85, agy. dir. summer programfor disadvantaged youth, 1975-94, asst. dean instruction, 1976, project adminstr. NCAA, 1977-79; instr. health edn. Golden West Coll., Huntington Beach, Calif., 1978; instr. dept. English Calif. State U., L.A., 1986; instr. dept. edn. Nat. U., L.A., 1986-88; prof. devel. comm. L.A. S.W. Coll., 1988—, staff devel. coord., dir. nat. youth sports program, 1992-96, dir. coll. recruitment, adminstr. evening divsn., 1997—, supr. Learning Resource Ctr., 1997—. Author numerous booklets, manuscripts and manuals on sports programs and edn. qualifications and policies. Bd. advisors Scholastic Placement Orgn. for Student Athlete, Mount Laurel, N.J.; bd. dirs. Black Edn. Commn., L.A. Unified Sch. Dist., Calif. State U., L.A. Alumni Assn., Involvement for Young Achievers, L.A., L.A. Police Dept. Football Centurions, Paradise Ch. Found., Inc., L.A., Pop Warner Little Scholars, Inc., Phila.; employee assistance program liaison officer L.A. Cmty. Dist. Named one of Outstanding Young Men of Am., 1980, 81. Mem. AHHPERD, Am. Alliance Health Edn., Am. Assn. Sch. Adminstrs., Calif. State U. Alumni Assn., U. Wash. Alumni Assn., Wash. State Alumni Assn., Calif. Assn. Health, Phys. Edn. and Recreation, Calif. State Athletic Dirs. Assn., L.A. Jr. C. of C., Nat. Interscholastic Athletic Adminstrs. Assn., Phi Delta Kappa, Kappa Alpha Psi. Office: LA SW Coll 1600 W Imperial Hwy Los Angeles CA 90047-4810

JARNAGIN, DONALD EDWARD, optometrist; b. Phoenix, Feb. 7, 1945; s. Woodrow Hanchey and Dorothea (Woolard) J.; m. Cheryl Ann Koiser, Aug. 30, 1965 (div. May 1990); children: Pamela, Matthew, Joshua, Rebecca; m. Shawn Lawson, June 25, 1995 (div. Aug. 1998). Student, Ariz. State U., 1963-66; BS, So. Calif. Coll. Optometry, 1968, OD cum laude, 1970. dir. Ariz. Vision Svcs. Plan; chair Ariz. Eye Care Assocs.; bd. chair Omni Eye Svcs. Phoenix; cmty. adv. bd. Charter Hosp. Glendale. Chair bd. adjustment City of Glendale (Calif.), chair bd. commrs. Glendale Housing Authority, chair review com.; active Boy Scouts Am., Youth soccer, baseball and basketball; sect. chair Am. Cancer Soc.; venture fund panel United Way; adv. com. Ctrl. Ariz. Health Sys. Agy.; charter dir. Ariz. Rep. Caucus; steering com., panel recorder Ariz. Rep. Town Hall; dir., treas. West Valley Alliance; founders com. Ariz. State U. West Campus. Capt. U.S. Army Med. Svc. Corp., 1971-73. Mem. Am. Optometric Assn. (trustee, sec./treas., v.p., pres., various coms.), Ariz. Optometric Assn. (pres., O.D. of Yr.), Ctrl. Ariz. Optometry Soc. (pres., O.D of Yr.), Glendale C. of C. (chair state govt. com., chair govt. affairs com.), Rotary (pres., dir., Paul Harris fellow). Avocation: golf. Home: 11236 N 11th Pl Phoenix AZ 85020-5829 Office: 5334 W Northern Ave Ste 106 Glendale AZ 85301-1441

JARRETT, RONALD DOUGLAS, lawyer, nurse; b. Oceanside, Calif., Oct. 31, 1952; s. W. Douglas and Francia Elizabeth (Ladd) J.; m. Lois Ellen Shurmaster, Dec. 26, 1984; 1 child, Emily Rose. AA, AS in Nursing, Cabrillo Coll., Aptos, Calif., 1981; student Nursing Sci., NYU, 1982-89; JD, Lincoln Law Sch., Sacramento, Calif., 1993. Bar: Calif. 1993, U.S. Dist. Ct. (ea. dist.) Calif. 1993, U.S. Dist. Ct. (no. dist.) Calif. 1994. Law clk. CIGNA Counsel, Sacramento, 1992-94; sole practitioner Sacramento, 1994—; med., legal record rev.; pvt. practice, Sacramento, 1992—, computer cons. for lawyers, 1994—. With USN, 1970-73. Mem. ABA, ATLA, Consumer Lawyers Calif., Sacramento County Bar Assn. Avocations: family, computers, Go, flying, history. Office: PO Box 277682 Sacramento CA 95827-7682

JARVIK, GAIL PAIRITZ, medical geneticist; b. Evanston, Ill., Feb. 8, 1959; d. Lawrence Alan and Lenore Mae P.; m. Jeffrey Gil Jarvik, Aug. 22, 1992. PhD in Human Genetics, U. Mich., 1986; MD, U. Iowa, 1987. Sr. rsch. fellow U. Wash., Seattle, 1992-95, asst. prof. medicine, divsn. med. genetics, 1995—; affiliate mem. Fred Hutchinson Cancer Rsch. Ctr., Seattle, 1994—. Contbr. to profl. jours. Howard Hughes Rsch. fellow, 1992-95. Mem. Am. Soc. Human Genetics, Internat. Genetic Epidemiology Soc. *

JARVIS, DONALD BERTRAM, judge; b. Newark, N.J., Dec. 14, 1928; s. Benjamin and Esther (Golden) J.; BA, Rutgers U., 1949; JD, Stanford U., 1952; m. Rosalind C. Chodorcove, June 13, 1954; children: Nancie, Brian, Joanne. Bar: Calif. 1953. Law clk. Justice John W. Shenk, Calif. Supreme Ct., 1953-54; assoc. Erskine, Erskine & Tulley, 1955; assoc. Aaron N. Cohen, 1955-56; law clk. Dist. Ct. Appeal, 1956; assoc. Carl Hoppe, 1956-57; adminstrv. law judge Calif. Pub. Utilities Commn., San Francisco, 1957-91, U.S. Dept. of Labor, 1992—; mem. exec. com. Nat. Conf. Adminstrv. Law Judges, 1986-88, sec. 1988-89, vice-chair, 1990-91, chair-elect, 1991-92, chair 1992-93; pres. Calif. Adminstrv. Law Judges Coun., 1978-84; mem. faculty Nat. Jud. Coll., U. Nev., 1977, 78, 80. Chmn. pack Boy Scouts Am., 1967-69, chmn. troop, 1972; class chmn. Stanford Law Sch. Fund, 1959, mem. nat. com., 1963-65; dir. Forest Hill Assn., 1970-71. Served to col. USAF Res., 1949-79. Decorated Legion of Merit. Mem. ABA (mem. ho. of dels. 1993—, vice chair jud. divsn. 1997-98, chair elect 1998-99), State Bar Calif., Bar Assn. San Francisco, Calif. Conf. Pub. Utility Counsel (pres. 1980-81), Air Force Assn., Res. Officers Assn., Ret. Officers Assn., De Young Museum Soc. and Patrons Art and Music, San Francisco Gem and Mineral Soc., Stanford Alumni Assn., Rutgers Alumni Assn., Phi Beta Kappa (pres. No. Calif. 1973-74), Tau Kappa Alpha, Phi Alpha Theta, Phi Alpha Delta. Home: 530 Dewey Blvd San Francisco CA 94116-1427 Office: 50 Fremont St San Francisco CA 94105-2230

JARVIS, JAMES REES, artist; b. Highland Park, Mich., June 19, 1926; s. Emory Harold J. and Ruth Florence (Knouff) Jordan; m. Esther Mary Hendy, Jan. 10, 1948 (div. Sept. 1984); children: Diana Lynn Curry, Patricia Ann Parker, Jean Marie Bentley; m. Cheryl Eileen Randall, Nov. 13, 1984; 1 child, Linda Ray Cooley. BSME, USAF Program, 1964; MS, U. So. Calif., 1989. Comml. pilot Macomb Flyers, Fraser, Mich., 1948-52; design engr. Northrup Aircraft, Hawthorne, Calif., 1966-89. Scoutmaster Boy Scouts Am., 1953-57. Sr. master sgt. USAF, 1944-66, WWII, Korea, Vietnam. Mem. VFW, Am. Legion, L.A. Mountainability Assn. Republican. Lutheran. Avocations: flying, racing cars, writing. Home and Studio: 691 S Ann Ln PO Box 507 Ash Fork AZ 86320-0507

JARVIS, PETER R., lawyer; b. N.Y.C., July 19, 1950. BA in Econs. magna cum laude, Harvard U., 1972; MA in Econs., Yale U., 1976, JD, 1976. Bar: Oreg. 1976, U.S. Dist. Ct. Oreg. 1976, U.S. Ct. Appeals (9th cir.) 1977, Wash. 1983, U.S. Dist. Ct. (we. dist.) Wash. 1983, U.S. Dist. Ct. (ea. dist.) Wash. 1985, U.S. Tax Ct. 1991. Mem. Stoel Rives LLP, Portland, Oreg. Author: (with others) Oregon Rules of Professional Responsibility (updated annually); editor, author: (with others) The Ethical Oregon Lawyer, 1991, 98; ethics columnists: The Multnomah Lawyer; spkr. on legal ethics issues. Mem. ALI (Harrison Tweed Spl. Merit award 1993), Oreg. State Bar (former mem. legal ethics com., Pres.'s Membership Svcs. award 1991), Wash. State Bar (mem. profl. conduct com.), Phi Beta Kappa. Office: Stoel Rives LLP 900 SW 5th Ave Ste 2600 Portland OR 97204-1232

JARVIS, RICHARD S., academic administrator; b. Nottingham, Eng., Feb. 13, 1949; came to U.S., 1974; s. John Leslie and Mary Margaret (Dodman) J.; m. Marilou Thompson, Nov. 7, 1986; stepchildren: Kimberly Nipko, Christopher Healey. BA in Geography, Cambridge (Eng.) U., 1970, MA, 1974, PhD in Geography, 1975. Lectr. Durham (Eng.) U., 1973-74; assoc. prof. SUNY, Buffalo, 1975-87, asst. to pres., 1986-87; v.p. acad. SUNY, Fredonia, 1987-90, prof. geoscis., 1987-90; vice provost SUNY Sys., Albany, 1990-94; chancellor Univ. and C.C. Sys. Nev., Reno and Las Vegas, 1994—; mem. adv. bd. Bechtel Nev., Las Vegas, 1995-97, NTS Devel. Corp., Las Vegas, 1997, INC, Las Vegas, 1997. Editor: River Networks, 1983; contbr. articles to profl. jours. Trustee United Way, Reno, 1996—, EDAWN, Reno, 1996—. Office: Univ and CC Sys Nev Syss Adminstrn N 2601 Enterprise Rd Reno NV 89512-1666 also: Syss Adminstrn S 5550 W Flamingo Rd Ste Cl Las Vegas NV 89103*

JASON, SONYA, writer; b. Jefferson, Pa.; d. Michael and Sophia (Kovac) Negra; m. John J. Jason; children: John Jr., Gary. BA in Journalism, Calif. State U.-Northridge, L.A., 1963. Social worker Dept. Pub. Social Svcs., L.A., 1964-66; probation officer L.A. Probation, 1966-76; West Coast editor Ethnic Am. News, L.A., 1977-78; freelance writer, 1978—. Author: Concomitant Soldier, 1974, Icon of Spring, 1993, Helper, 1994; contbr. articles to profl. jours. Pres. Am. Citizens Together, L.A., 1986-90. Recipient award Freedom Found. Valley Forge, Pa., 1987. Avocations: travel, historical research, golf, bridge. Home: 21165 Escondido St Woodland Hills CA 91364-5904

JAVAN, JOSEPH, art educator; s. Ghassim and May J. AA, U. Fla., 1981, B of Design, 1983; MFA, Howard U., 1994. Tchr. Santa Fe C.C., Gainesville, Fla., 1983; teaching asst. Howard U., Washington, 1993-94; sr. lectr. Calif. State U., Chico, 1996—; adj. prof. Frostburg (Md.) State U., 1994-96. Author, artist: The Azure Jar, 1989; contbr. articles to profl. jours. Pres. Students Human Rights, U. Fla., 1981-83. Mem. Assn. Historians of 19th Century, Coll. Art Assn. Avocations: sports, travel, photography. Office: Calif State U Dept Art & Art History Chico CA 95928-0820

JAWAD, SAID TAYEB (SAID TAYEB DJAWAD), political commentator, writer; b. Kandahr, Afghanistan, Feb. 27, 1958; came to U.S., 1986; s. Mir Hussain and zakia Shah; m. Shamin Rahman, Nov. 16, 1986. Student, Kabul (Afghanistan) U., 1976-80, Wilhelms U., Muenster, Germany, 1984-86, Long Island U., 1986. Paralegal Lehnardt & Bauman, N.Y.C., 1988-89, Steefel, Levitt & Weiss, San Francisco, 1989—; polit. commentator various newspapers, radio and TV stas. including BBC. Editor weekly newspaper OMAID, 1992-95; pub. Substratum of Human Rights Violations in Afghanistan, Modern Dictatorship, The United States and the Afghan Resistance, Soviets Expansionto the South, Fundamentalism in Central Asia; contbr. articles to BBC World Reports (London) and to profl. jours. throughout world. Bd. dirs. Afghanistan Cultural Soc., San Francisco, 1990-92; mem. Internat. Soc. for Human Rights, Frankfort, Germany, 1983-86; mem. nat. adv. bd. Info. Am., Atlanta, 1991-94; active Amnesty Internat., N.Y.C., 1987—. Mem. World Affairs Coun. Home: One St Francis Pl # 3506 San Francisco CA 94107

JAY, DAVID JAKUBOWICZ, management consultant; b. Danzig, Poland, Dec. 7, 1925; s. Mendel and Gladys Gitta (Zalc) Jakubowicz; came to U.S., 1938, naturalized, 1944; BS, Wayne State U., 1948; MS, U. Mich., 1949, postgrad., 1956-57; postgrad. U. Cin., 1951-53, MIT, 1957; m. Shirley Anne Shapiro, Sept. 7, 1947; children: Melvin Maurice, Evelyn Deborah. Supr. man-made diamonds GE Corp., Detroit, 1951-56; instr. U. Detroit, 1948-51; asst. to v.p. engring. Ford Motor Co., Dearborn, Mich., 1956-63; project mgr. Apollo environ. control radiators N.Am. Rockwell, Downey, Calif., 1963-68; staff to v.p. corporate planning Aerospace Corp., El Segundo, Calif., 1968-70; founder, pres. PBM Systems Inc., 1970-83; pres. Cal-Best Hydrofarms Coop., Los Alamitos, 1972-77, pres. Inkmarks Corp., 1989—; cons. in field, 1983—. Pres., Community Design Corp., Los Alamitos, 1971-75; life master Am. Contract Bridge League. Served with USNR, 1944-46. Registered profl. engr., Calif., Mich., Ohio. Fellow Inst. Advancement Engring.; mem. Art Stamp and Stencil Dealers Assn. (pres. 1993—), Inst. Mgmt. Sci. (chmn. 1961-62), Western Greenhouse Vegetable Growers Assn. (sec.-treas. 1972-75), Tau Beta Pi. Jewish. Patentee in air supported ground vehicle, others. Home: 13441 Roane Santa Ana CA 92705-2271 Office: 13882 Newport Ave Ste E Tustin CA 92780-4666

JAYASUMANA, ANURA PADMANANDA, electrical engineering educator; b. Colombo, Sri Lanka, Dec. 29, 1956; came to U.S., 1980; s. D. Sugathananda and D. Susima (Seneviratne) J.; m. Geetha Gunamalee Polwatte, Sept. 3, 1988; children: Sanah Thusitha, Ruwan Sujith. BSEE, U. Sri Lanka, Moratuwa, Sri Lanka, 1978; MSEE, Mich. State U., 1982, PhD in Elec. Engring., 1984. Electronic engr. Nat. Engring. Rsch. and Devel. Ctr., Jaela, Sri Lanka, 1978-79; asst. lectr. U. Moratuwa, Sri Lanka, 1979-80; asst. prof. elec. engring. Colo. State U., Ft. Collins, 1985-89, assoc. prof. elec. engring., 1989-97, prof. elec. engring. and computer sci., 1997—. Contbr. articles to profl. jours. Named Outstanding Prof., Am. Electronics Assn., 1990, Best Student in Elec. Engring., U. Sri Lanka, 1978; recipient Outstanding Acad. Achievement award Mich. State U., 1983, 82, HSP award for Acad. Excellence, Mich. State U., 1984. Mem. IEEE, Phi Kappa Phi. Achievements include research in digital communication networks and protocols and VLSI testing; findings which include analytical models for timed-token protocols, robust WDM network protocols and testable designs for CMIS and BiCMOS. Office: Colorado State U Dept of Elec Engring Fort Collins CO 80523

JEFFERSON, MYRA LAVERNE TULL, sales executive; b. Chester, Pa.; d. Clarence Ernest and Mary Marie (Gaines) Tull; m. Bernard Carr Jefferson III, Mar. 11, 1983. BS in Computer Sci., Roosevelt U., 1987; postgrad., Chaminade U., 1986-87. Computer programmer Integrated Computer Techs., Phila., 1979-83; cons. Honolulu, 1983-88; data base mgr. E.S.R.D. Network Coordinating Council, Honolulu, 1984-88; comptr. Static Control Products, Phoenix, 1989-93; pres. Lion-S Sales & Svc., Mesa, Ariz., 1991—; cons. NCC #1 Med. Rev. Bd., Honolulu, 1985, Thrifty Constrn. Co., Honolulu, 1986-87, Computer Support, 1985. Apptd. by mayor to the city of Mesa Economic Devel. adv. bd.; apptd. to Industrial Devel. Authority Commn. of Maricopa County; apptd. by gov. Econ. Security Adv. Bd.; treas. bd. Mesa Cmty. Action Network, 1992-95, 2d vice chair, 1995-96; bd. dirs. WOW Project; alumnae Mesa Leadership Tng. Program, Valley Leadership Program, black bd. dirs. project; bd. dirs., co-chair Black Women's Task Force, 1994-95, bd. dirs. the Family Svc. Agy.; treas. Pol. Dist. 29. Recipient award for Outstanding Contbns. to Data Processing, Am. Inst., 1987, Profl. and Scholastic Achievement award Am. Inst., 1986, Outstanding Achievement in Data Processing Profession, Am. Inst., 1986; fellow Ariz. Edn. Policy Fellowship Program. Mem. AAUW, Math. Assn. Am., Am. Math. Soc., Women in Computing, Am. Assn. Ind. Investors, Am. Express Com. Diversity Bd., Coalition for Tomorrow, U.S. Congressman Matt Salmon's Small Bus. Adv. Group, captain Precinct 54 Committeemen. Avocations: reading, crosswords, chess, computers. Office: PO Box 3149 Tempe AZ 85280-3149

JEFFERSON, PAUL, police chief. AA in Edn., L.A. City Coll., 1976; BS in Pub. Mgmt., Pepperdine U., 1979; MA, John F. Kennedy U., 1990. cert. tchr. Calif., 1977. Police officer L.A. Police Dept., 1968-73, detective of police, 1973-77, sgt. of police, 1977-80, police lt., 1981-90, capt. of police, 1990-92; chief of police Modesto Police Dept., Calif., 1992—; chair Com. of Bar Examiners of the State Bar of Calif. Author: Rock Cocaine, 1985. Bd. dirs. Modesto YMCA, Region IV United Way, Gould Med. Found., Modesto Doctors Med. Ctr., The Haven, Modesto Police Activities League, Modesto Salvation Army; chair com. of bar examiners State Bar Calif. Mem. Internat. Assn. Chiefs of Police, Calif. Police Chiefs Assn., Nat. Orgn. Black Law Enforcement Execs., Calif. Police Officers Assn., Stanislaus County Chief's, Sheriff's and Dist. Atty's Assn., FBI Nat. Acad. Associates, Black on Black Crime Inst., Assn. Black Law Enforcement Execs. (past pres.), Oscar Joel Bryant Assn., Black Police Officer Assn., Calif. Peace Officers Standards and Training (mem. adv. com. on cmty. based policing, cultural awareness training and sexual harassment), Modesto Downtown Rotary. Office: 801 11th St Modesto CA 95353 also: PO Box 642 Modesto CA 95353*

JEFFERY, JAMES NELS, protective services official; b. Torrance, Calif., May 16, 1944; s. Daryl Fredrick and Mildred Evelyn (Sogard) J. AA, Long Beach City Coll., 1964; student, Calif. State U., Long Beach, 1964-65, Calif. State U., Sacramento, 1979-80. Capt., firefighter L.A. Fire Dept., 1965-87; dir. Long Beach (Calif.) Search & Rescue Unit, 1968—; asst. chief fire divsn. Calif. Office Emergency Svcs., Riverside, 1987-97; rep. Firescope Communications, Riverside, 1979—. Co-author emergency plans. Chmn. svc. com. Boy Scouts Am., Long Beach, 1979-81, tng. com., 1982—; bd. dirs. Long Beach Community Episepsy Clinic, 1971-72. Recipient Disting. Svc. award Long Beach Jaycees, 1977, Community Svc. award Long Beach Fire Dept., 1978, Silver Beaver award Boy Scouts Am., 1983, Commendation Mayor City of L.A., 1985. Mem. Calif. State Firemen's Assn., Calif. Fire Chiefs Assn., Nat. Coord. Coun. on Emergency Mgmt., Nat. Eagle Scout Assn., So. Calif. Assn. Foresters and Fire Wardens, Lions, Elks. Republican. Lutheran. Avocations: vol. work, camping, hunting. Home: 3916 Cerritos Ave Long Beach CA 90807-3608 Office: PO Box 92257 Long Beach CA 90809-2257

JEFFREDO, JOHN VICTOR, aerospace engineer, manufacturing company executive, inventor; b. Los Angeles, Nov. 5, 1927; s. John Edward and Pauline Matilda (Whitten) J., m. Elma Jean Nesmith (div. 1958); children: Joyce Jean Jeffredo Ryder, Michael John; m. Doris Louise Hinz, (div. 1980); children: John Victor, Louise Victoria Jeffredo-Warden; m. Gerda Adelheid Pillich, 1980. *John Jeffredo's Great Grandfather Francis Jeffredo left Brittany in 1861, landing in Mexico with Napoleon III's French troops, then heading to California in 1863. He married Great Grandmother Jeffredo, A Native American Santa Catalina Islander, in 1865. His Great Grandfather Juan Matias Sanchez, born of an English mother and Spanish father in Spain during Wellington's Peninsula Campaign against Napoleon, left England in 1835. He reached California in 1836, acquiring large tracts of land in the Los Angeles, California area. John's Great Grandfather Thomas Hunter arrived in California with the Mormon Battalion in 1847. He married John's Great Grandmother, Paulina Wala, a Native American San Clemente Islander, in 1851.* Grad. in aeronautical engring., Cal-Aero Tech. Inst., 1948; AA machine design, Pasadena City Coll., 1951; grad. in electronics, The Ordnance Sch. U.S. Army, 1951; postgrad, U. So. Calif., 1955-58, Palomar Coll., 1977-96; MBA, La Jolla U., 1980, PhD in human rels., 1984. Design engr. Douglas Aircraft Co., Long Beach and Santa Monica, Calif., 1955-58; devel. engr. Honeywell Ordnance Corp., Duarte, Calif., 1958-62; cons. Honeywell Devel. Labs, Seattle, 1962-65; supr. mech. engring. dept. aerospace divsn. Control Data Corp., Pasadena, Calif., 1965-68; project engr. Cubic Corp., San Diego, 1968-70; supr. mech. engring. dept. Babcock Electronics Co., Costa Mesa, Calif., 1970-72; owner, operator Jeffredo Gunsight Co., Fallbrook, Calif., 1971-81; chief engr. Western Designs, Inc., Fallbrook, Calif., 1972-81, exec. dir., 1981-88, CEO, 1988-96, owner, operator, 1981-87; owner, operator Western Design Concepts, Inc., 1987-94; exec. dir. JXJ, Inc., San Marcos, Calif., 1981-88, CEO, 1988—; mgr. Jeffredo Gunsight divsn., 1981-94, chief engr. JXJ, Inc., 1987-92 (merger JXJ, Inc. and Western Design Concepts, Fallbrook, Calif.), prin. 1992—, owner, mgr., Energy Assocs., San Diego, 1982-86, pres. Jeffredo Internat., 1984-88, founder, CEO John-Victor Internat., San Marcos, Calif., Frankfurt, Fed. Rep. Germany, 1988—, The Jeffredo Solution, Fallbrook, 1996—, engring. cons. Action Instruments Co., Inc., Gen. Dynamics, Alcyon Corp., Systems Exploration, Inc. (all San Diego), Hughes Aircraft Co., El Segundo, Allied-Bendix, San Marcos, bd. dirs.Indian World Corp., JXJ, Inc., John-Victor Internat. Author: Gabrieleño, New Perspective on the Island Gabrielino, The Ocean People, Wildcatting; contbr. articles to trade jours. and mags.; guest editl. writer Town Hall, San Diego Union; narrator: (film) The Sacred Desert, 1994; spkr. in field; patentee agrl. frost control, vehicle off-road drive system, recoil absorbing system for firearms, telescope sight mounting system for firearms, breech mech. sporting firearm, elec. switch activating system, 37 others, others pending. Mem. San Diego County Border Tsk Force on Undocumented Aliens, 1979-80, 81-82, mgr., rep. Island Gabrieleno Group, NAGPRA repatriation project, 1995—, historian Maritime Shoshone, 1995—, spokesman Island Shoshone, 1995—, chmn. Native Californian Coalition, 1982—, bd. dirs. Nat. Geographic Soc., 1968. With U.S. Army, 1951-53. Recipient Superior Svc. Commendation award U.S. Naval Ordnance Test Station, Pasadena, 1959. Mem. AIAA (sr.), NRA (life), Soc. Automotive Engrs., San Diego Zool. Soc., Sierra Club (life), The Wilderness Soc., Pechanga Band of Luiseno Indians (life), Cova, Catalina Island Mus. Soc., The Planetary Soc., North County Scots. Avocations: chess, music, archaeology, conservation, sculpture. Home: 1629 Via Monserate Fallbrook CA 92028-9305 Office: PO Box 669 San Marcos CA 92079-0669

JEFFREY, FRANCIS, software developer, forecaster; b. Calif., 1950. BA in Computational Neurophysiology, U. Calif., Berkeley, 1972. Research assoc. U. Calif., San Diego, 1972-73; cons. Sci. Applications, Inc., La Jolla, Calif., 1973-75; entrepreneur Big Sur, Calif., 1975-77; cons. Alive Systems Info. Scis., San Francisco, 1978-87; founder, pres., chief exec. officer Alive Systems, Inc. and Elfnet, Inc., Malibu, Calif., 1987—; cons. Inst. for Advanced Computation, Sunnyvale, Calif., 1973-75, Human-Dolphin Found., 1980-82, 87-89, Esalen Inst., 1982-83. *ELFNET embodies his*

Patent Cooperation Treaty International Publication WO97/24663 (1997), a system providing for programming and communication of programs as an integral part of cultural transmission and human communication, based on teleportable packages of relationship, "clumplets," that are swatches of virtual brain tissue transplantable between neuronal environments called "clumps" hosted on conventional computers--So we have a robust cultural medium that can also form the basis for programming in the 21st Century, with its emphasis on network communication as interactive multipersonal environment. After the "2000 Bug" debacle, ELPHIN will replace the opacity of current technology with a lucid humanistic paradigm. Author: (with others) Handbook of States of Consciousness, 1986, John Lilly So Far, 1990, (with others) Voices from The Edge, 1995, Patent Cooperation Treaty International Publication WO 97/24663, 1997, Japanese edit., 1998 ; originator Malibu civic dolphin protection resolution, 1992, whales as living cultural resources resolution, 1994; designer com. co-piloting; creator symposium Radical Connectionsim and the Visualization of Networkk Programs, 1999—. Co-founder New Forum, Monterey, Calif., 1984, Gt. Whales Found., San Francisco, 1986, chmn., CEO; co-founder Big Sur chpt. L5 Nat. Space Soc. Mem. AAAS, IEEE, Assn. for Computing Machinery, Am. Soc. for Cybernetics (founding, control sys. group), Amnesty Internat. (leadership group), Cousteau Soc. (life mem.), Raoul Wallenberg Inst. Ethics (adv. bd.). Achievements include invention of conscious networks system and "adverteasing". E-mail: francis@elfi.com. Home and Office: PO Box 6844 Malibu CA 90264-6844

JEFFREY, JOHN ORVAL, lawyer; b. Portsmouth, Va., Aug. 6, 1963; s. Orval L. and Mary L. (Coakley) J. BA, U. Dayton (Ohio), 1985; diploma internat. legal studies, U. San Diego, Paris, 1987; JD, Southwestern U., L.A., 1988. Bar: Calif. 1988, U.S. Dist. Ct. (cen. dist.) Calif. 1988. Assoc. Shield & Smith, L.A., 1989-90, Hewitt, Kaldor & Prout, L.A., 1990-93; mgr. bus. and legal affairs fx subs. Fox TV. Campaign worker John Glenn Campaign for Pres., N.H., 1984; vol. Amnesty Internat. Mem. ABA (internat. law sect., litigation sect., entertainment/sports law sect.), Internat. Bar Assn., Los Angeles County Bar Assn. (mem. evaluation profl. standards com., mem. legis. activity com., mem. artists and the law com.), Phi Alpha Delta, Alpha Nu Omega. Democrat. Avocations: tennis, long distance running, French reading proficiency.

JEFFRIES, RUSSELL MORDEN, communications company official; b. Carmel, Calif., July 15, 1935; s. Herman M. and Louise (Morden) J.; m. Barbara Jean Borcovich, Nov. 24, 1962; 1 child, Lynne Louise. AA, Hartnell Coll., 1971. Sr. communications technician AT&T, Salinas, Calif., 1955-91; mayor City of Salinas, 1987-91. Pres. El Gabilan Sch. PTA, Salinas, 1971-74, Salinas Valley Council PTA, 1975-76; mem. Salinas City Sch. Bd., 1975-81; mem. Salinas City Council, 1981-87; bd. dirs. Community Hosp. Salinas Found., 1987—, Salinas-Kushikino Sister City, 1987—, pres. 1992-93, John Steinbeck Ctr. Found., 1987-96, Food Bank for Monterey County, 1992-96; hon. bd. dirs. Monterey Film Festival, 1987-96, Calif. Rodeo Assn., 1987; mem. ctrl. bd. Calif. Regional Water Quality, 1992—; commr. Moss Landing Harbor, 1996. Recipient hon. service award PTA, Salinas, 1976; cert. of appreciation Calif. Dept. Edn., 1980, Salinas City Sch. Dist., 1981, Calif. Sch. Bds. Assn., 1981, Steinbeck Kiwanis, Salinas, 1987; named hon. mem. Filipino community Salinas Valley, 1988. Mem. Salinas C. of C., Native Sons Golden West, K.C., Rotary, Moose. Republican. Roman Catholic. Avocations: fishing, hunting, bowling, golf. Home: 204 E Curtis St Salinas CA 93906-2804

JEKOWSKY, BARRY, conductor, music director. MusB and MusM, Juilliard Sch. Founder, music dir. Calif. Symphony Orch.; assoc. condr. Nat. Symphony Orch., Washington, 1994—. Numerous orch. appearances throughout N.Am. and Europe including London Phila. Orch., Halle Orch. Recipient Leopold Stokowski Conducting prize. Achievements include creation of the Young American Composer-in-Residence Program, 1991, unique in its orchestra-laboratory forum. Office: Calif Symphony Orch 1407 Oakland Blvd Ste 103 Walnut Creek CA 94596*

JELLINEK, ROGER, editor; b. Mexico City, Jan. 16, 1938; came to U.S., 1961; s. Frank Louis Mark and Marguerite Lilla Donne (Lewis) J.; m. Margherita DiCenzo, Dec. 22, 1963 (div. 1984); children: Andrew Mark, Claire; m. Eden-Lee Murray, 1984; 1 child, Everett Peter Murray. Student, Bryanston Sch., Dorset, Eng., 1951-56; MA, Cambridge U., Eng., 1961. Assoc. editor Random House, 1963-64; editor Walker & Co., 1964-65; editor N.Y. Times Book Rev., 1966-70, dep. editor, 1970-73; editor in chief Times Books, Quadrangle/N.Y. Times Book Co., 1974-78, sr. editor, 1978-81, editor Lamont newsletter and yearbook, 1981-91; pres. Clairemark, Ltd., 1981—, Jellinek & Murray Literary Agy. Editor Atlantic Realm Project, 1983-93; publisher Hawaii map series. Pres. ArtMaps Ltd., 1996—. With Royal Marines, 1956-57; 2d lt. Brit. Intelligence Corps, 1957-58. Mellon fellow Yale U., 1961-63. Home and Office: 109 Nawiliwili St Honolulu HI 96825-2041

JENES, THEODORE GEORGE, JR., retired career officer; b. Portland, Oreg., Feb. 21, 1930; s. Theodore George and Mabel Marie (Moon) J.; m. Beverly Lorraine Knutson, Jan. 29, 1953; children—Ted, Mark. BS, U. Ga., 1956; MS, Auburn U., 1969; grad., Army Command and Gen. Staff Coll., Armed Forces Staff Coll., Air War Coll.; LLD (hon.), U. Akron, 1986. Enlisted U.S. Army, 1951, commd. 2d lt., 1953, advanced through grades to lt. gen., 1984, various assignments, 1953-75; comdr. 3d Brigade, 2d Inf. Div., Republic of Korea, 1975-76, 172d Inf. Brigade, Ft. Richardson, Alaska, 1978-81; dep. commdg. gen. U.S. Army Tng. Ctr., Ft. Dix, N.J., 1976-78; comdr. 4th Inf. Div., Ft. Carson, Colo., 1982-84; dep. commdg. gen. U.S. Army Combined Arms Combat Devel. Activity, Ft. Leavenworth, Kans., 1981-82; comdg. gen. 3d U.S. Army, Ft. McPherson, Ga., 1984-87; commander U.S. Army Forces Ctrl. Command, Ft. McPherson, Ga., 1984-87; dep. comdg. gen. hdqrs. U.S. Army Forces Command, Ft. McPherson, Ga., 1984-87, ret., 1987; cons. Burdeshaw and Assocs., 1987-88; gen. mgr. Seattle Tennis Club, 1988-94. Decorated D.S.M., Legion of Merit, Bronze Star, Meritorious Service medal, Air medal, Army Commendation medal, Vietnamese Cross of Gallantry with Silver Star. Mem. Assn. of U.S. Army, Rotary. United Methodist. Fax: 425-745-8068. Avocations: reading military history; cycling; skiing, golf. Home: 809 169th Pl SW Lynnwood WA 98037-3307*

JENKINS, BRUCE, sportswriter; b. Oct. 4, 1948; s. Gordon Jenkins; m. Martha Jane Stanton; 2 children. Degree in Journalism, U. Calif., Berkeley, 1971. With San Francisco Chronicle, 1973—, sports columnist, 1989—. Author: Life After Saberhagen, 1986, North Shore Chronicles, 1990. Recipient nat. awards AP, UPI, Basketball Writers Assn.; nominated Pulitzer Prize for columns Barcelona Olympics, 1992. Office: San Francisco Chronicle 901 Mission St San Francisco CA 94103-2905*

JENKINS, BRUCE STERLING, federal judge; b. Salt Lake City, Utah, May 27, 1927; s. Joseph and Bessie Pearl (Iverson) J.; m. Margaret Watkins, Sept. 19, 1952; children—Judith Margaret, David Bruce, Michael Glen, Carol Alice. BA with high honors, U. Utah, 1949, LLB, 1952, JD, 1952. Bar: Utah 1952, U.S. Dist. Ct. 1952, U.S. Supreme Ct. 1962, U.S. Circuit Ct. Appeals 1962. Pvt. practice Salt Lake City, 1952-59; assoc. firm George McMillan, 1959-65; asst. atty. gen. State of Utah, 1952; dep. county atty. Salt Lake County, 1954-58; bankruptcy judge U.S. Dist. Ct., Utah, 1965-78, judge, 1978—, chief judge, 1984-93; adj. prof. U. Utah, 1987-88, 96—. Research, publs. in field; contbr. essays to Law jours.; bd. editors: Utah Law Rev., 1951-52. Mem. Utah Senate, 1959-65, minority leader, 1963, pres. senate, 1965, vice chmn. commn. on orgn. exec. br. of Utah Govt., 1965-66; Mem. adv. com. Utah Tech. Coll., 1967-72; mem. instl. council Utah State U., 1976. Served with USN, 1945-46. Named Alumnus of Yr. award Coll. Law Univ. Utah, 1985; recipient Admiration and Appreciation award Utah State Bar, 1995, Emeritus Merit of Honor award U. Utah Alumni Assn., 1997. Fellow Am. Bar Found.; mem. ABA, Am. Inn Ct., Utah State Bar Assn. (Judge of Yr. 1993), Salt Lake County Bar Assn., Fed. Bar Assn. (Disting. Jud. Svc. awrd Utah chpt. 1993), Order of Coif, Phi Beta Kappa, Phi Kappa Phi, Phi Eta Sigma, Phi Sigma Alpha, Tau Kappa Alpha. Democrat. Mormon. Office: US Dist Ct 462 US Courthouse 350 S Main St Ste 150 Salt Lake City UT 84101-2180

JENKINS, KEVIN J., technology and industrial company executive; b. Edmonton, Alta., Can.; m. Helen Jenkins; 3 children. Law degree, U. Alta.; MBA, Harvard U. Ptnr. law firm Can Airlines, Edmonton, Alta., 1980s; with fin. dept. Can. Airlines, Calgary, Alta., 1985, various positions including CFO; pres. Wardair, 1986-91; pres., CEO Can. Airlines, Calgary, Alta., 1991-96, Westaim Corp., Calgary, Alta., 1996—; also bd. dirs.; pres., CEO Westaim Corp., Calgary, 1996—; bd. dirs. Candian Occidental Petroleum Ltd., mem. Corp. of World Vision Canada. Mem. bus. adv. coun. Faculty of Bus., U. Alta.; mem. Young Pres.'s Orgn.; bd. dirs. Young Life of Can. Office: Westaim Corp, 144 4th Ave SW Ste 1010, Calgary, AB Canada T2P 3N4

JENKINS, SPEIGHT, opera company executive, writer; b. Dallas, Jan. 31, 1937; s. Speight and Sara (Baird) J.; m. Linda Ann Sands, Sept. 6, 1966; children: Linda Leonie, Speight. B.A., U. Tex.-Austin, 1957; LL.B., Columbia U., 1961; DMus (hon.), U. Puget Sound, 1992; HHD, Seattle U., 1992. News and reports editor Opera News, N.Y.C., 1967-73; music critic N.Y. Post, N.Y.C., 1973-81; TV host Live from the Met, Met. Opera, N.Y.C., 1981-83; gen. dir. Seattle Opera, 1983—; classical music editor Record World, N.Y.C., 1973-81; contbg. editor Ovation Mag., N.Y.C., 1980—, Opera Quar., Los Angeles, 1982—. Served to capt. U.S. Army, 1961-66. Recipient Emmy award for Met. Opera telecast La Boheme TV Acad. Arts and Scis., 1982. Mem. Phi Beta Kappa Assocs. Presbyterian. Home: 903 Harvard Ave E Seattle WA 98102-4561 Office: Seattle Opera Assn PO Box 9248 Seattle WA 98109-0248

JENKINSON, EDWARD LEROY, poet; b. Seattle, Nov. 1, 1968; s. Robert Thomas and Alice Carol (Collier) J. AA, Green River C.C., Auburn, Wash., 1994; BA in English/Classical Studies, U. Wash., 1999. Adminstrv. asst. III Thomas Burke Meml. Mus. Natural History, Seattle, 1995—; poetry editor Bricolage Mag., Seattle, 1996-97; poetry event coord. English Undergrad. Assn., U. Wash., Seattle, 1997—; asst. editor, adminstrv. asst. Seattle Rev., 1999—. Asst. dir. Auburn H.S., 1987-90, Bathhouse Theater, Seattle, 1995-96; asst. dir., dir. Green River C.C., Auburn, 1988-91; organizer, dir. Michael McClure/Ray Manzarek, Seattle, 1997, Pandora's Box-Reading Series, 1996-97; prodr. CD Biology Tentative, 1998; editl. asst., asst. editor Seattle Rev. Mag., 1999—. Mem. Archaeol. Inst. Am., King County Arts Commn., Seattle Arts Commn. Democrat. Avocations: painting, bibliophile, amateur archaeology, amateur astronomy, writing. Office: Burke Meml Mus U Wash Seattle WA 98195

JENKINSON, JUDITH ELLEN, librarian; b. Monroe, Mich., Apr. 9, 1943; d. Robert Henry Williams and Caroline (Pardee) Stephenson; m. Arnold Apsey, July 1, 1962 (div. 1977); 1 child, Amy Lou; m. Leif Jenkinson, May 21, 1977, 1 stepchild, Karl J. A.A., Alpena Community Coll., 1964; B.A., Mich. State U., 1966; Arts M.L.S., U. Mich., 1969. Elem. tchr., Lincoln, Mich., 1966-68, high sch. librarian, 1969-72; elem. librarian, Ketchikan, Alaska, 1972-75, 90-95, elem. libr. supr., 1995-98 (ret.), high sch. librarian, 1975-90; mem. City Coun., Ketchikan City, Alaska, 1993—, vice mayor, 1996-97. Mem. Ketchikan Community Coll. Council, 1980-84, pres., 1984-85; del. Alaska Democratic Conv., 1982, 88, 92; dir., producer, actress, mem. stage crew First City Players, 1972—; mem. Ketchikan Greater Dem. Precinct's Com., 1988—, vice chair, 1992-96; ctrl. com. woman State Dem. Party, 1996-98; commr. Ketchikan Gateway Borough Planning Commn., 1989-93, vice-chair, 1992-93. Mem. ALA, NEA, Ketchikan Edn. Assn., NEA-Alaska, Women's Internat. League for Peace and Freedom, Alaska Library Assn. VFW Aux., Swinging Kings Square Dancers (pres. 1985-86), Eagles, Women of the Moose, Delta Kappa Gama. Home: PO Box 5342 Ketchikan AK 99901-0342 Office: 1900 1st Ave Ketchikan AK 99901-6027

JENNER, MIKE, newspaper editor. Reporter, photographer Hattiesburg (Miss.) Am.; editing positions The Phila. Inquirer, Columbia (Mo.) Tribune, Coffeyville (Kans.) Jour.; asst. mng. editor Hartford (Conn.) Courant, mng. editor; ind. newspaper cons.; mng. editor The Bakersfield Californian, 1993-98, exec. editor, 1998—. Office: The Bakersfield Californian 1707 Eye St Bakersfield CA 93301-5299*

JENNETT, SHIRLEY SHIMMICK, home care management executive, nurse; b. Jennings, Kans., May 1, 1937; d. William and Mabel C. (Mowry) Shimmick; m. Nelson K. Jennett, Aug. 20, 1960 (div. 1972); children: Jon W., Cheryl L.; m. Albert J. Kukral, Apr. 16, 1977 (div. 1990). Diploma, Rsch. Hosp. Sch. Nursing, Kansas City, Mo., 1958. RN, Mo., Colo., Tex., Ill. Staff nurse, head nurse Rsch. Hosp., 1958-60; head nurse Penrose Hosp., Colorado Springs, Colo., 1960-62, Hotel Dieu Hosp., El Paso, Tex., 1962-63; staff nurse Oak Park (Ill.) Hosp., 1963-64, NcNeal Hosp., Berwyn, Ill., 1964-65, St. Anthony Hosp., Denver, 1968-69; staff nurse, head nurse, nurse recruiter Luth. Hosp., Wheat Ridge, Colo., 1969-79; owner, mgr. Med. Placement Svcs., Lakewood, Colo., 1980-84; vol., primary care nurse, admissions coord., team mgr. Hospice of Metro Denver, 1984-88, dir. patient and family svcs., 1988, exec. dir., 1988-94; pres. Care Mgmt. & Resources, Inc., Denver, 1996—. Mem. NAFE, Nat. Women Bus. Owners Assn., Nat. Hospice Orgn. (bd. dirs. 1992-95, coun. former bd. mems. 1995—), Nat. Orgn. Profl. Geriatric Care Mgrs., Denver Bus. Women's Network. Mem. Ch. of Religious Sci. Avocations: reading, walking, golf. Office: Care Mgmt & Resources Inc 820 S Monaco Pkwy # 250 Denver CO 80224-1569

JENNINGS, MARCELLA GRADY, rancher, investor; b. Springfield, Ill., Mar. 4, 1920; d. William Francis and Magdalene Mary (Spies) Grady; student pub. schs.; m. Leo J. Jennings, Dec. 16, 1950 (dec.). Pub. relations Econolite Corp., Los Angeles, 1958-61; v.p., asst. mgr. LJ Quarter Circle Ranch, Inc., Polson, Mont., 1961-73, pres., gen. mgr., owner, 1973—; dir. Giselle's Travel Inc., Sacramento; fin. advisor to Allentown, Inc., Charlo, Mont.; sales cons. to Amie's Jumpin' Jacks and Jills, Garland, Tex. Investor. Mem. Internat. Charolais Assn., Los Angeles County Apt. Assn. Republican. Roman Catholic. Home and Office: 509 Mount Holyoke Ave Pacific Palisades CA 90272-4328

JENNINGS, PAUL CHRISTIAN, civil engineering educator, academic administrator; b. Brigham City, Utah, May 21, 1936; s. Robert Webb and Elva S. (Simonsen) J.; m. Millicent Marie Bachman, Aug. 28, 1981; m. Barbara Elaine Morgan, Sept. 3, 1960 (div. 1981); children: Kathryn Diane, Margaret Ann. BSCE, Colo. State U., 1958; MSCE, Calif. Inst. Tech., 1960, PhD, 1963. Prof. civil engring., applied mechanics Calif. Inst. Tech., Pasadena, 1966—; chmn. divsn. engring. Calif. Tech. Inst., Pasadena, 1985-89, v.p., provost, 1989-95, acting v.p. for bus. and fin., 1995, 98-99; mem. faculty bd. Calif. Tech. Inst., 1974-76, steering com., 1974-76, chmn. nominating com., 1975, grad. studies com., 1978-80; cons. in field. Author: (with others) Earthquake Design Criteria. Contbr. numerous articles to profl. jours. 1st lt. USAF, 1965-66. Recipient Honor Alumnus award Colo. State U., 1992, Achievement in Academia award Coll. Engring., 1992; Erskine fellow U. Canterbury, New Zealand, 1970, 85. Fellow AAAS, New Zealand Soc. Earthquake Engring.; mem. ASCE (Walter Huber award 1973, Newmark medal 1992), Seismol. Soc. Am. (pres. 1980), Earthquake Engring. Rsch. Inst. (pres. 1981-83), Athenaeum Club. Avocations: fly fishing; running. Home: 640 S Grand Ave Pasadena CA 91105-2423 Office: Calif Inst Tech Mail Code 212-31 Pasadena CA 91125

JENNISON, BRIAN L., environmental specialist; b. Chelsea, Mass., June 13, 1950; s. Lewis L. and Myra S. (Piper) J. BA, U. N.H., 1972; PhD, U. Calif., Berkeley, 1977; cert. hazardous materials mgr., U. Calif., Davis, 1986. Teaching, rsch. asst. U. Calif., Berkeley, 1972-77; staff rsch. assoc. Dept. of Molecular Biology, Berkeley, 1978-80; instr. dept. biology Calif. State U., Hayward, 1977; sr. biologist San Francisco Bay Marine Rsch. Ctr., Emeryville, Calif., 1980-81; inspector I Bay Area Air Quality Mgmt.Dist., San Francisco, 1981-83, inspector II, 1983-88; enforcement program specialist Bay Area Air Quality Mgmt. Dist., San Francisco, 1988-92; dir. air quality mgmt. div. Washoe County Dist. Health Dept., Reno, Nev., 1992—; cons. U.S. Army Corps of Engrs., L.A., 1980, San Francisco, 1981; instr. U. Calif., Berkeley ext., 1990-93, Assoc. Bay Area Govs., 1990-92; adj. prof. U. Nev., Reno, 1994—. Contbr. articles to profl. jours. Postdoctoral fellow, Harbor Br. Found., 1977-78. Mem. AAAS, Air and Waste Mgmt. Assn. (chmn. Ea. Sierra chpt. 1994-96), Navy League of U.S. (life), Phi Beta Kappa. Avocations: railroad history, photography. Office: Washoe County Dist Health Dept PO Box 11130 Reno NV 89520-0027

JENSEN, BARBARA WOOD, interior design business owner; b. Salt Lake City, Apr. 30, 1927; d. John Howard and Loretta (Sparks) Wood; m. Lowell N. Jensen, June 26, 1947; children: Brent Lowell, Robyn Lynn, Todd Wood. Interior decorator paint and wall paper co., 1947-49; cons., interior designer, 1950-60; pres., treas. Barbara Jensen Interiors, Inc., Salt Lake City, 1960-79; interior designer, 1979—; owner Barbara Jensen Designs, St. George, Utah and Las Vegas; lectr. in field; dir. 1st Women's Bancorp, Utah. Chmn. Utah Legis. Rep. Ball, 1970, Utah Symphony Ball, 1979. Fellow Inst. Profl. Designers (London); mem. Assistance League, Com. Fgn. Affairs, Interior Design Soc. (assoc.), Ft. Douglas Country Club, Knife and Fork Club, Hi-Steppers Dance Club, Ladies Lit. Club, Pres.'s Club of Utah, Bloomington Country Club, Elks. Mormon.

JENSEN, CLAY E., JR., artist, educator; b. Salt Lake City, Mar. 14, 1952. BFA, U. Utah, 1975; MA, U. Calif., Berkeley, 1977, MFA, 1979. Assoc. instr. U. Utah, Salt Lake City, 1975-76; tech. asst. Peter Voulkos, Berkeley, 1977-80; guest instr. Calif. Coll. Arts and Crafts, Oakland, 1980-82, U. Calif., Berkeley, 1984, San Jose (Calif.) State U., 1984, 89-90; assoc. prof. Calif. Coll. of Arts and Crafts, Oakland, 1987—; vis. artist U. Mont., Missoula, 1993; guest instr. Oakland Tech. Shop Internat. Sculpture Ctr., 1993; guest artist Winona (Minn.) State U., 1987; lectr. Internat. Sculpture Ctr., San Jose, 1983. One-man shows include U. Mont., 1993, San Francisco Museum of Modern ARt, 1983. Grantee NEA, 1978. Home and Studio: 951 62d St Studio F Oakland CA 94608

JENSEN, CYNTHIA ANN, marketing professional; b. Phoenix, Sept. 24, 1953; d. Harold Emery and Jacqueline A. (Funk) Canterbury; m. Paul Eldredge Jensen, Jan. 25, 1975; children: Elizabeth Ann, Natalie Marie. Student, Ariz. State U., 1971-72; BS, U. Ariz., 1974. From exec. trainee to asst. buyer May Co. Dept. Stores, Los Angeles, 1975-77; dept. mgr. Bullocks Dept. Stores, Phoenix, 1977-78; real estate sales assoc. Jim Daniel & Assocs. Realtors, Phoenix, 1978-79; asst. buyer Broadway Southwest, Mesa, Ariz., 1979-82; mgr. Peat, Marwick, Mitchell & Co. (name now KPMG Peat Marwick), Phoenix, 1982-87, Lewis & Roca Lawyers, 1987-92; dir. media and cmty. rels. State Bar Ariz., 1992-93; pvt. practice as mktg. cons., 1992-93; dir. client svcs. Jennings Strouss & Salmon, Phoenix, 1993—; cons. Lannan & Cleverly Property Mgmt. Inc., Tempe, Ariz., 1985-86. Mem. long range planning com. Cactus Pine council Girl Scouts U.S., 1984, new dimensions foundations com. Phoenix Symphony Orch., 1983-84, religious edn. bd. Encanto Community Ch., 1980-82, 87-89, 94—, hospitality com., 1984-87. Mem. Internat. Assn. Bus. Communicators (profl. devel. com. 1984-85, v.p. profl. devel., bd. dirs. 1985-86, treas. 1986-87, Service award 1985), Pub. Relations Soc. Am. (awards com. 1989, Copper Quill award 1990), Meeting Planners Internat. (program com. 1984-85, mem. membership com. 1985-86, chmn. 1986-87, bd. mem. 1987-88, sec. 1988-89, awards com. 1987-88, fundraising com. chair 1987-88, by law revision com. 1988-89, Meeting Planner of Yr. Ariz. Sunbelt chpt. 1989), Nat. Assn. Law Firm Mktg. Aminstrs. (NALFMA) (nat. awards com. 1987-88, nat. awards com. chair 1988-89, sec. bd. dirs. 1989-90, mem. membership com. 1991-92, 1st place award for firm newsletter, 1988), Phoenix Met. C. of C. (communications coun. 87-88). Republican. Avocations: gardening, needlework, interior design. Address: 9728 E Sheena Dr Scottsdale AZ 85260-3860

JENSEN, D. LOWELL, federal judge, lawyer, government official; b. Brigham, Utah, June 3, 1928; s. Wendell and Elnora (Hatch) J.; m. Barbara Cowin, Apr. 20, 1951; children: Peter, Marcia, Thomas. A.B. in Econs, U. Calif.-Berkeley, 1949, LL.B., 1952. Bar: Calif. 1952. Dep. dist. atty. Alameda County, 1955-66, asst. dist. atty., 1966-69, dist. atty., 1969-81; asst. atty. gen. criminal div. Dept. Justice, Washington, 1981-83, assoc. atty. gen., 1983-85, dep. atty. gen., 1985-86; judge U.S. Dist. Ct. (no. dist.) Calif., Oakland, 1986—; mem. Calif. Council on Criminal Justice, 1974-81; past pres. Calif. Dist. Atty.'s Assn. Served with U.S. Army, 1952-54. Fellow Am. Coll. Trial Lawyers; mem. Nat. Dist. Atty.'s Assn. (victim/witness commn. 1974-81), Boalt Hall Alumni Assn. (past pres.). Office: US Dist Ct 1301 Clay St Rm 490C Oakland CA 94612-5217*

JENSEN, DENNIS MICHAEL, medical educator, researcher; b. N.Y.C., Mar. 6, 1944; s. Walter Frederick and Grace (Smyth) J.; m. Mary Ellen Brady, Mar. 29, 1971; children: Signe, Kirsten, Evan. BS, U. Wash., 1966, MD, 1970. Diplomate Nat. Bd. Med. Examiners, Am. Bd. Internal Medicine, Am. Bd. Gastroenterology. Resident U. Oreg., Portland, 1970-72, Wadsworth VA Hosp., L.A., 1974-75; fellow UCLA, 1975-77; asst. prof. medicine UCLA Sch. of Medicine, 1977-82, assoc. prof., 1983-88, prof. medicine, 1988—; mem. found. adv. bd., dir. human studies and hemostasis group Ctr. Ulcer Rsch. & Edn., L.A., 1990—; mem rsch. policy com. Am. Digestive Health Found., Bethesda, Md., 1997—. Editor: Therapeutic Laser Endoscopy in GI Disease, 1983, Medical Laser Endoscopy, 1990, Severe Nonvarical UGI Hemorhage, 1991; contbr. articles to profl. jours. Maj. U.S. Army, 1972-74. Grantee NIH-NIDDK, 1984—. Mem. Am. Soc. Gastrointestinal Endoscopy (rsch. com. 1994—), Am. Gastroenterol. Assn. Roman Catholic. Avocations: tennis, jogging, cycling. Office: UCLA Sch of Medicine 44-133 CHS GI Divsn 10833 Le Conte Ave Los Angeles CA 90095-3075

JENSEN, EDMUND PAUL, retired bank holding company executive; b. Oakland, Calif., Apr. 13, 1937; s. Edmund and Olive E. (Kessell) J.; m. Marilyn Norris, Nov. 14, 1959; children: Juliana L., Annika M. BA, U. Wash., 1959; postgrad., U. Santa Clara, Stanford U., 1981. Lic. real estate broker, Oreg., Calif. Mgr. fin. plan and evaluation Technicolor, Inc., Los Angeles, 1967-69; group v.p. Nat. Industries & Subs, Louisville, 1969-72; v.p. fin. Wedgewood Homes, Portland, 1972-74; various mgmt. positions U.S. Bancorp, Portland, 1974-83; pres., COO U.S. Bancorp, Inc., Portland, 1983-93; vice chmn., COO U.S. Bancorp, Inc., Portland, 1993-94; pres., CEO Visa Internat., 1994-98; ret., 1998; bd. dirs. U.S. Nat. Bank of Oreg., U.S. Bank Washington. Chmn. United Way, 1986, N.W. Bus. Coalition, 1987; bd. dirs. Saturday Acad., Portland, 1984—, Visa U.S.A., Visa Internat., Marylhurst Coll., Oreg. Bus. Coun., Oreg. Downtown Devel. Assn., Oreg. Ind. Coll. Found., 1983—, treas., 1986—, chmn., 1988—; bd. dirs. Portland Art Mus., 1983—, vice chmn., 1989—. Mem. Portland C. of C. (bd. dirs. 1981—, chmn. 1987), Assn. Res. City Bankers, Assn. for Portland Progress (pres. 1988), Waverly Country Club, Multnomah Athletic Club, Arlington Club. Office: US Bancorp PO Box 8837 Portland OR 97208-8837

JENSEN, GERALD RANDOLPH, editor, graphics designer; b. Kalispell, Mont., Aug. 12, 1924; s. Hans Clemen and Mabel (Everson) J.; m. Helen Jeanne Levine, Dec. 11, 1943; 1 child, Marjorie Jeanne. MA, Union U., 1976, PhD, 1978; LittD, Internat. Acad. World Frat. of Scholars, London. Regional and nat. dir. Youth & Christian Edn. Internat., Four Square Los Angeles, 1946-54; dir. San Francisco Youth for Christ, San Francisco, 1955-60; v.p. Sacred Records, Whittier, Calif., 1960-63; dir. pub. Full Gospel Bus. Men's Fellowship, Los Angeles, 1962-69; pres. Triangle Prodns., Burbank, Calif., 1970-79, Claiborne-Jensen Advt., Arcadia, Calif., 1980-82, Jerry Jensen & Assoc., Santa Fe Springs, Calif., 1982-85; editor Full Gospel Bus. Men's Fellowship, Costa Mesa, Calif., 1985—; bd. dirs. High Adventure Ministries, Van Nuys, Calif., 1970-94, Found. for Airborne Relief, Long Beach, Calif., 1986-89, Ambassadors of Aid, Vancouver, British Columbia, 1978-94, Friends in the West, Seattle, 1969-94, Internat. Bible Inst., Santa Fe Springs, Calif., 1982-94. Bd. regens Golden State U., Los Angeles, 1979-89; advt. & pub. relations Orange County Jesus Rally, Anaheim, Calif., 1980-81. Recipient Award of Merit Golden State U., 1986. Mem. Evang. Press Assn., Am. Mgmt. Assn. Republican. Avocations: golf, stamp collecting. Home: 5772 Garden Grove Blvd Spc 482 Westminster CA 92683-1859 Office: 3rd Fl 20 Corporate Park Irvine CA 92606-5139

JENSEN, HELEN, musical artists management company executive; b. Seattle, June 30, 1919; d. Frank and Sophia (Kantosky) Leponis; student pub. schs., Seattle; m. Ernest Jensen, Dec. 2, 1939; children: Ernest, Ronald Lee. Co-chmn., Seattle Community Concert Assn., 1957-62; sec. family concerts Seattle Symphony Orch., 1959-61; hostess radio program Timely Topics, 1959-60; gen. mgr. Western Opera Co., Seattle, 1962-64, pres. 1963-64; v.p., dir., mgr. pub. rels. Seattle Opera Assn., 1964-83, preview artists coord., 1981-84; bus. mgr. Portland (Oreg.) Opera Co., 1968, cons., 1967-69; owner, mgr. Helen Jensen Artists Mgmt., Seattle, 1970-92. First v.p. Music and Art Found., 1981-84, pres. 1984-85. Recipient Cert., Women in Bus in the Field of Art, 1973, award Seattle Opera Assn., 1974, Outstanding Svc. award Music and Art Found., 1984, Women of Achievement award Women in Communications, 1992, Gold medal in 100 Meter sprint USA Track and Field Nat. Masters Championships, 1994. Mem. Am. Guild Mus. Artists, Music and Art Found. (life), Seattle Opera Guild (life, bd. dirs. 1988-92,

pres., award of distinction 1983, parliamentarian 1987-89), Ballard Symphony League (sec.), Portland Opera Assn., Portland Opera Guild, Seattle Civic Opera Assn. (pres. 1981—), 200 Plus One, Aria Preview, Lyric Preview Group (chmn. 1988-92), Past Pres. Assembly (pres. 1977-79, parliamentarian 1987-89), Pres.'s Forum (1st v.p. 1990-91, program vice chmn. 1987-88, pres. 1991-92), North Shore Performing Arts Assn. (pres. 1981), Women of Achievement (past pres.'s assembly, chmn.), Pres.'s Forum (pres. 1991-92), Woman's Century Club (chmn. art, drama, music dept. 1992-93, 92-97, 97-98), Helen Jensen Hiking Club. Home: 19029 56th Ln NE Kenmore WA 98028-3156

JENSEN, LAWRENCE ROBERT, lawyer; b. Oakland, Calif., Apr. 7, 1959; s. Robert Johan and Dolores Fawn (Freeland) J.; m. Susan Kim McShane, Aug. 23, 1983 (div. 1986); m. Terry Ann Hutson, July 29, 1989 (div. 1993). BA in Psychology with honors, U. Calif., Santa Cruz, 1984; JD cum laude, Santa Clara U., 1987. Bar: Calif. 1987, U.S. Dist. Ct. (no. dist.) Calif. 1987, U.S. Ct. Appeals (9th cir.) 1991. Assoc. Howell & Hallgrimson, San Jose, 1987-89, Law Offices of Joseph DiCiuccio, San Jose, 1989-90, Hallgrimson, McNichols, McCann & Inderbitzen, San Jose, 1990-92, Liccardo, Rossi, Sturges & McNeil, San Jose, 1992-94; pvt. practice San Jose, 1994—. Bd. dirs. ACLU, No. Calif. Affiliate, 1987-89, 92-94, 97—, Santa Clara Valley chpt., 1986-89, 92-95, 97—, chair, 1993-95; bd. dirs. San Jose Northside Neighborhood Assn., 1992-95, v.p., 1993-95. Recipient Cert. of Recognition State Bar Bd. Govs., 1989. Mem. Santa Clara County Bar Assn. Avocations: sailing, backpacking, art collecting. Office: 95 S Market St Fl 3 San Jose CA 95113-2301

JENSEN, PAUL EDWARD TYSON, business educator, consultant; b. New Orleans, Apr. 27, 1926; s. Paul Christian and Nena Laura (Robertson) J.; m. Jule Valerie Geisenhofer, Jan. 10, 1953; children: Christian, Elena, Constance. BS in Physics, Tulane U., 1947, BBA, 1949; MBA, Golden Gate U., 1976. Asst. mgr. Cuban Atlantic Sugar Co., Lugareño, Cuba, 1952-55; sr. engring. specialist GTE, Mountain View, Calif., 1955-82; sr. staff engr. TRW, Inc., Sunnyvale, Calif., 1982-92; dean Sch. of Bus., Northwestern Poly. U., Fremont, Calif., 1988—, also bd. trustees; cons. geog. info. sys. TRW, Inc., Sunnyvale, 1993-94. Capt. USMCR, 1945-61, WWII, Korea. Fellow Soc. Tech. Comm. (assoc.); mem. IEEE (life, sr. mem.), Am. Phys. Soc., Soc. Computer Simulation, World Future Soc., Assn. Old Crows. Presbyterian. Avocations: amateur radio, jogging, photography, travel. Home: 8033 Regency Dr Pleasanton CA 94588-3131 Office: Northwestern Poly U 117 Fourier Ave Fremont CA 94539-7482

JENSEN, PAUL ROLF, lawyer, real estate investor; b. San Francisco, Nov. 12, 1958; s. Rolf Levald and Ouida (Moore) J.; m. Pamela Balogh, Apr. 3, 1993; children: Peter John, David Christian Rolf. AB, U. Calif., Berkeley, 1981; JD, Whittier Coll., 1990. Bar: Calif. 1991; lic. real estate broker Calif. Dept. Real Estate. Legis. dir. Am. Def. Inst., Washington, 1983-84; campaign advisor U.S. Senator Jeremiah Denton, Washington, 1984-86; assoc. atty. Elhai & McIntosh, Hacienda Heights, Calif., 1991; prin. atty. Jensen & Assocs., Newport Beach, Calif., 1992-95; ptnr. Jensen & McIntosh, Hacienda Heights, 1995—; gen. counsel Jensen Properties, LLC, Newport Beach, 1997—. Mem. Consumer Attys. Calif., Federalist Soc. (pres. Duke Law Sch. chpt. 1990-91), Consumer Attys. L.A., Bahia Corinthian Yacht Club. Republican. Presbyterian. Avocations: sailing, antiquarian book collecting, travel, wine collecting, fishing. Home: 10343 Strong Ave Whittier CA 90601 Office: Jensen and McIntosh 1201 S Hacienda Blvd Hacienda Heights CA 91745

JENSEN, TAMILA CHRIS, lawyer; b. Sanger, Calif., May 5, 1947; d. Vernal August and Mary Patricia (Johnsey) J.; m. Timothy Michael Shanklin, Oct. 15, 1983; 1 child, Berkeley Thorne Shanklin. AB, U. Calif., Berkeley, 1969; JD, U. Calif., Davis, 1973. Bar: Calif. 1973. Assoc. Thomas, Snell, Jamison, Williamson & Asperger, Fresno, Calif., 1973-75; sole practitioner Santa Barbara, Calif., 1975-76; asst. prof. Ind. U., Bloomington, 1976-79; ptnr. Boren, Elperin, Howard & Sloan, L.A., 1979-83; sole practitioner Tamila C. Jensen, Granada Hills, Calif., 1983—. Editor U. Calif. Davis Law Rev., 1973, Bus. Law Jour., 1978-79; contbr. articles to profl. jours. Chair City of Bloomington (Ind.) Energy Task Force, 1977-78; mem. Mayor's Com. on the Charter, Santa Barbara, 1974-75. Mem. San Fernando Valley Bar Assn. (chair women lawyers sect. 1997—), Calif. Women Lawyers, State Bar Calif., Order of Coif, Phi Beta Kappa, Phi Kappa Phi. Democrat. Avocations: reading, cooking, camping, skiing, piano. Office: 10324 Balboa Blvd Ste 200 Granada Hills CA 91344-7349

JERMINI, ELLEN, educational administrator, philosopher; b. Krefeld, Germany, Aug. 25, 1939; came to U.S., 1986.; d. Maximilian and Mathilde (Wachtberger) Wilms; m. Helios Jermini, 1961 (div. June 1989); children: Mariella Arnoldi, Diego Jermini. PhB, U. Healing, 1984, M in Healing Sci., 1985, PhD, 1986; PhB, U. Philosophy, 1992. Sec. Germany, Switzerland, 1962; pub. translator, 1984—; seminar organizer Europe, 1983—; dir. U. Philosophy/European Found., 1986—; pres. U. Healing, Campo, Calif., 1986-99, U. Philosophy, Campo, 1986—; abbot Absolute Monastery, Campo, 1986—; assoc. chmn. bd. Regent. Editor: (newsletter in Italian) Absolute, (newsletter in German) Absolute. Spkr. various univs. and orgns. in Calif. and N.Y., 1989-92, St. Petersburg, Moscow, 1991, Africa, 1994, Egypt, 1995, various seminars and workshops, Ghana, Nigeria. Mem. Toastmasters Internat. (Able Toastmaster). Avocations: writing, skiing, swimming, playing tennis, flying. Home and Office: Univ of Healing 1101 Far Valley Rd Campo CA 91906-3213

JERNIGAN, EARL WESLEY, archaeologist, museum director; b. Alhambra, Calif., June 1, 1940; s. Harvey Richard and Jeanne Jernigan; m. Gisela Evelyn Brashear, June 8, 1968; children: Marcus, Kevin, Thomas, Alan. BA, U. Ariz., 1968, MA, 1970, PhD, 1973. Asst. prof. anthropology U. Ariz., Tucson, 1978-86; sign designer various Tucson firms, 1986-89; dir. mus. Ea. Ariz. Coll., Thatcher, 1989—. Author: Jewelry of the Prehistoric Southwest, 1978, White Metal Universe, 1980; illustrator: (children's) One Green Mesquite Tree (Best Juvenile Book of Yr. 1988), Agave Blooms Just Once (co-recipient Author of Yr. 1990). Avocation: tennis. Office: Ea Ariz Coll Mus Anthropology Thatcher AZ 85552-0769*

JERRYTONE, SAMUEL JOSEPH, trade school executive; b. Pittston, Pa., Mar. 21, 1947; s. Sebastian and Susan Teresa (Chiampi) J.; children: Sandra, Cheryl, Samuel, Sebastian. Assoc. in Bus., Scranton (Pa.) Lackawanna Jr. Coll., 1966. Mgr. House of Jerrytone Beauty Salon, West Pittston, Pa., 1967-68; regional sales dir. United Republic Life Ins., Harrisburg, Pa., 1970-76; night instr. Wilkes-Barre (Pa.) Vo-Tech High Sch., 1976-78; spl. sales agt. Franklin Life Ins. Co., Wilkes-Barre, 1978-80; instr. Jerrytone Beauty Sch., Pittston, Pa., 1968-69, supr., 1969-95; prof. sch. evaluator Nat. Accrediting Com. Arts and Scis., 1974-95; mem. adv. craft com. Wiles-Barre Vo-Tech H.S., 1988—. Mem. com. Rep. Presdl. Task Force, Washington, 1984, mem. parish coun. Guardian Angel Cathedral, Las Vegas, 1997. Mem. Pa. Hairdressers Assn., Nat. Accrediting Com. Cosmetology, Am. Coun. Cosmetology Educators, Masons (3d degree award 1983, 32d degree award Lodge Coun. chpt. consistory 1984), Shriners (Irem temple). Roman Catholic. Avocations: reading, golf, bowling, music, video filming.

JERVIS, JANE LISE, college official, science historian; b. Newark, N.J., June 14, 1938; d. Ernest Robert and Helen Jenny (Roland) J.; m. Kenneth Albert Pruett, June 20, 1959 (div. 1974); children: Holly Jane Pruett, Cynthia Lorraine Pruett; m. Norman Joseph Chonacky, Dec. 26, 1981; children: Philip Joseph Chonacky, Joseph Norman Chonacky. AB, Radcliffe Coll., 1959; MA, Yale U., 1974, MPhil, 1975, PhD in History of Sci., 1978. Freelance sci. editor and writer, 1962-72; lectr. in history Rensselaer Poly. Inst., 1977-78; dean Davenport Coll., lectr. in history of sci. Yale U., 1978-82; dean students., assoc. prof. history Hamilton Coll., 1982-87; dean coll., lectr. in history Bowdoin Coll., 1988-92; pres. Evergreen State Coll., Olympia, Wash., 1992—. Author: Cometary Theory in 15th Century Europe; contbr. articles to profl. jours.; book reviewer; presenter in field. [illegible] St. Peter's Hosp., 1997—; chair Maine selection com. Rhodes Scholarship Trust, 1990-92, chair N.W. selection com., 1992-93; commr. N.W. Assn. Schs. and Colls. Commn. on Colls., 1994—. Office: Evergreen State Coll Office of President Olympia WA 98505

JESKE, KEITH WILLIAM, real estate and mortgage executive; b. Milw., June 16, 1950; s. Gilbert F. and Betty A. (Langdon) J.; children: KC William, Camie Sloan; m. Christy Sue Bynum, Feb. 12, 1993. AA, San Bernardino Valley Coll., 1971; BA, Point Loma, San Diego, 1973; JD, U. West Los Angeles, 1976. Chmn. bd., CEO Keith Jeske Realty, Las Vegas, Nev., 1976—; CEO Levin Mortgage, Las Vegas, 1991—; pres., CEO Echelon Group, 1994—; pres. Fred Sands Las Vegas Properties, 1995—, Sovereign Fin. Corp., 1998—; CEO Nat. Home Funding Corp., 1996; cons. Consumer Credit Counselors, L.A., 1974-78, Culver City (Calif.) Planning Commn., 1975-77. Author: Goal Mind, 1988; contbr. articles to profl. jours. Mediator Community Mediation of San Diego, 1990; educator, arbitrator Alternative Dispute Resolutions, Las Vegas, 1992. Named Sales Person of Yr., Beverly Hills, 1973, Mgr. of Yr., Bd. of Realtors, L.A., 1979. Mem. Nat. Assn. Realtors, Calif. Assn. Realtors, L.A. Bd. Realtors, Culver City Bd. Realtors, Las Vegas Bd. Realtors, Mortgage Brokers Assn., Mortgage Bankers Assn. Home: 135 S Sierra Ave Unit 5 Solana Beach CA 92075-1815

JESSE, SANDRA ELIZABETH, special education educator; b. Green Bay, Wis., Nov. 22, 1960; d. Albert Henry and Janice Elizabeth (Schroeder) J. BA in Edn., Ariz. State U., 1983; MA, No. Ariz. U., 1990. Cert. spl. edn. tchr., adminstr. Special edn. educator Peoria (Ariz.) Unifed Sch. Dist. # 11, 1983—. Religious edn. tchr. St. Helens Ch., Glendale, Ariz., 1989—, mem. religious edn. bd., 1994—. Mem. NEA, Am. Fedn. Tchrs., Learning Disabilities Assn. Roman Catholic. Avocations: music, swimming, spectator sports. Office: Sky View Sch 8624 W Sweetwater Ave Peoria AZ 85381-8101

JESSOP, DOUGLAS WAYNE, lawyer; b. Westpoint, N.Y., July 9, 1951; s. Gordon Lincoln and Rita Marie (Seifert) J.; m. Andrea Beth Margulies, Mar. 31, 1979; children: Elena Naomi, Noah Solomon. BA, U. Colo., 1973, MA, 1975; JD magna cum laude, Boston Coll., 1983. Bar: Colo. 1983, U.S. Dist. Ct. Colo. 1983. Assoc. Sherman & Howard, Denver, 1983-86; asst. prof. law S. Tex. Coll.. Law, Houston, 1986-87; assoc. Davis Graham & Stubbs, Denver, 1987-91; pres. Jessop & Co. PC, 1991—. Contbr. articles to profl. jours. Mem. ABA, Colo. Bar Assn., Denver Bar Assn., Order of the Coif. Avocations: guitar, travel. Home: 803 S Mountain View Rd Castle Rock CO 80104-9553 Office: Jessop & Co PC #930 303 E 17th Ave Ste 930 Denver CO 80203-1262

JESSUP, W. EDGAR, JR., lawyer; b. L.A., Sept. 9, 1922; s. Walter E. and Marian (Moses) J.; m. Audrey B. Vail; children: Bryn W., Holden D. ScB in Engring. magna cum laude, Brown U., 1943; JD, U. So. Calif., L.A., 1949. Bar: Calif. 1950, U.S. Dist. Ct. (cen. dist.) Calif. 1950, U.S. Claims Ct. 1976, U.S. Tax Ct., 1952. Founding ptnr. Ervin, Cohen & Jessup, Beverly Hills, Calif., 1953—; lectr. Sch. Engring. U. So. Calif., 1950-58, Sch. Law, 1965-76; bd. dirs. Logicon, Inc., L.A., Magnetika, Inc., L.A., Software Techs. Corp., L.A. Author: Law & Specifications for Engineers & Scientists, 1963; contbr. articles to profl. jours. Bd. dirs. Assn. Alumni Brown U., Providence, 1985-89; chmn. bd. dirs. Westside Family YMCA, West Los Angeles, Calif., 1988-93, chmn. 1988-93; bd. dirs. Brentwood (Calif.) Westwood Symphony, 1953-93; bd. mgrs. L.A. Metro YMCA, 1984-93. Lt. USNR, 1943-46, ETO, PTO. Mem. ABA, State Bar Calif., L.A. Bar Assn., Beverly Hills Bar Assn., Brown U. Club So. Calif. (pres. 1984-91), Calif. Yacht Club (former flag officer), Order of Coif, Tau Beta Pi, Phi Kappa Phi, Phi Alpha Delta. Office: Ervin Cohen & Jessup 9401 Wilshire Blvd Ste 900 Beverly Hills CA 90212-2974

JETT, JAMES, football player; b. Charlestown, W.Va., Dec. 28, 1970. Wide reciever Oakland (Calif.) Raiders. Office: Oakland Raiders 1220 Harbor Bay Pkwy Alameda CA 94502-6570

JETTMAR, EVA, research scientist, consultant; b. Graz, Austria, Mar. 7, 1968; came to U.S., 1993; d. Ernst and Elfriede (Deutsch) J.; m. Dav Coleman, June 1, 1998. MA, U. Vienna, Austria, 1993; MS, San Diego State U., 1995. Radio sta. dir. Fed. Austrian Radio, Vienna, 1991-92; pub. rels., mktg. Apple Computers, Vienna, 1993-96; jr. rschr. Stanford (Calif.) U., 1997—; sr. rschr. MIT Media Lab., Boston, 1998—; rschr. Austrian Ministry Edn., Vienna, 1994. Contbr. articles to profl. jours. Recipient Fulbright scholar, 1993-95; Fulbright Profl. grantee, 1994, Rsch. grantee Austrian Ministry Sci., Vienna, 1995, Rsch. grantee Austrian Nat. Bank, Vienna, 1996. Mem. Internat. Comm. Assn., Assn. Computing Machinery, Computer Human Interaction. Avocations: usability testing, product design, interface design, graphic design, travelling. Home: 329 Niagra St San Francisco CA 94112-3340 Office: Stanford University PO Box 3230 Stanford CA 94309-3230

JEZINA, CAROL SUSAN, secretary; b. Torrance, Calif., July 16, 1946; d. William Goldy and Helen Aileen (Leake) Gleghorn; m. Milan Josip Jezina, Nov. 4, 1967; children: Steve, Ana, Ive. Student, Harbor Coll., 1965-66. Corr. sec. Croatian Hall, San Pedro, Calif. Bd. dirs. Bustop mag., 1977-80. Active in Rep. politics; fundraiser for congresswoman Bobbi Fiedler; communications chairperson L.A. Cultural Affairs Dept., 1989. Am. Croatian Kolo dancers grantee, 1988-90. Mem. Am. Croatian Club (publicity chairwoman 1989). Roman Catholic. Home: 2124 S Alma St San Pedro CA 90731-5731 Office: Croatian Hall 631 W 9th St San Pedro CA 90731-3107

JILER, LINDA CERISE, fire emergency dispatcher, consultant, researcher, writer; b. Santa Monica, Calif., Dec. 30, 1956; d. Milton John "Jack" Jiler and Peggy Jean Williams. AA, Lassen Coll., 1979, Cert. Forestry Technician, 1980. Cert. Calif. Dept. Forestry and Fire Protection Fire Acad., 1990. Fire clk./firefighter-wildland Lassen Coll. Contract Crew, Susanville, Calif., 1976-77; forestry technician (fire) U.S. Forest Svc. Lassen Nat. Forest/Eagle Lake Ranger Dist./Bogard Ranger Sta., Susanville, Calif., 1977-80; dist. personnel technician U.S. Dept. Interior-Bur. Land Mgmt., Susanville Dist., Calif., 1981-86; pub. contact rep. U.S. Dept. Interior Bur. Land Mgmt. Susanville Dist., Susanville, Calif., 1986; wildland firefighter/dispatcher Lassen Coll. Contract Fire Crew, Susanville, Calif., 1986-87; fire and aviation program asst., lightning detection specialist U.S. Dept. Interior Bur. Land Mgmt., Calif. State Office, Sacramento, 1988-93; 9-1-1 interagy. fire dispatcher Calif. Dept. Forestry and Fire Protection, Camino, 1988-93; 9-1-1 interagency emergency commd. ctr. operator Calif. Dept. Forestry and Fire Protection, Camino Interagency Emergency Command Ctr., 1988-93; cons. info. svcs. Sacramento, 1993—; speaker in field; pub. info. officer USDA-FS, U.S. Dept. Interior-Bur. Land Mgmt., CDF, 1983-93. Author: How to Get A Job with the Federal Government, 1983, rev. edit., 1985, 86, Injury and Claim Processing Manual, 1985, Demobilization Training Guide, 1985, Train-the Trainer Wildland Fire Timekeeping Procedures, 1985, (manual) California State Office SOP for Intelligence Gathering, 1987-88; co-author: (manual) California Interagency Mobilization Guide, 1988, Bur. of Land Management's State Policy for Handling of Burn Victims, 1988. Recipient Cert. of Appreciation, Lassen County Bd. Suprs., 1986, 87, Cert. of Appreciation and Cert. of Recognition for Outstanding Performance, U.S. Forest Svc. Pacific S.W. Region, 1987, Nat. Wildland Coord. Group award for Outstanding Performance, U.S. Forest Svc. Pacific N.W. Region and Wallow Whitman Nat. Forest, 1986, Superior Achievement and Profl. Contbns. award U.S. Dept. Agriculture Forest Svc. and U.S. Dept. Interior Bur. Land Mgmt., 1990; cert. Appreciation Eldorado Bd. Suprs. U.S. Forest Svc., 1992, Recognition award Oakland Athletics Baseball Club, 1987, Recognition award San Diego Padres Baseball Club, 1988. Mem. Calif. State Employees Assn. (classification rep. 1989-93), Calif. Profl. Firefighters, Chronic Fatigue Immune Dysfunction Syndrome Support Groups, Nat. Wildlife Fedn., Nat. Trust for Hist. Preservation, Nat. Audubon Soc., Nat. Conf. Incident Command System Fin. Officers, Nat. Australian Shepherd Club Am., Sigma Kappa (alumni past pres.). Democrat. Avocations: Australian shepherds, calligraphy, sociology studies, child support issues, commercial radio (voice overs).

JIM, EDWARD L.S., surgeon; b. Wailuku, Maui, Hawaii, Sept. 26, 1929; s. A.K. and Ethel (Tam) J.; m. Mardie C. Sughrue, Oct. 8, 1966; children: Edward E., Gregory R. MD, U. Chgo., 1955. Diplomate Am. Bd. Surgery. Intern Kings County Hosp., Bklyn., 1955-56; resident in surgery St. [illegible] Hosp., N.Y.C., 1962-63; clin. instr. surgery NYU, N.Y.C., 1961-62; asst. clin. prof. surgery U. Hawaii Sch. Medicine, Honolulu, 1967-80, assoc. prof., 1981-93, clin. prof., 1994—; pvt. practice Honolulu, 1963—; mem. staff, chief oncology svc. Queen's Med. Ctr., 1969-70. Capt. USAFMC, 1958-60. Fellow ACS; mem. AMA, Soc. Head and Neck Surgeons, Am. Soc. for Head and Neck Surgery, Hawaii Med. Assn., Hawaiian Surg. Assn. (past pres.), Honolulu Rose Soc. Roman Catholic. Avocations: gardening, carpentry, travel. Office: 1488 Ihiloa Loop Honolulu HI 96821-1347

JIMENEZ, JOSEPHINE SANTOS, portfolio manager; b. Lucena, Quezon, Philippines, June 6, 1954; came to U.S., 1972; d. Jose Hirang and Virginia Villapando (Santos) J. BS, NYU, 1979; MS, MIT, 1981. Securities analyst Mass. Mut. Life Ins. Co., Springfield, 1982-83; investment officer One Fed. Asset Mgmt., Boston, 1984-87; sr. analyst, portfolio mgr. Emerging Markets Investors Corp., Washington, 1988-91; mng. dir., portfolio mgr. Montgomery Asset Mgmt., San Francisco, 1991—; founding ptnr. Montgomery Emerging Markets Fund; trustee M.I.T. Corp. Mem. Inst. Chartered Fin. Analysts. Office: Montgomery Asset Mgmt 101 California St San Francisco CA 94111-5802

JIMENEZ, TESSIE CASIANO, realtor; b. Manila, May 13, 1936; came to U.S., 1960, naturalized, 1970; d. Andrew Manglicmot and Irene (Paranada) Casiano; m. Rodolfo Jimenez, May 29, 1960; 1 child, Jonathan Casiano. AA, U. of East, Manila, 1956, student, 1956-60; grad. med. technologist, de Paul Hosp., Va., 1962; cert. profl. achievement, U. Calif., Irvine, 1993. Real estate salesman Better Homes Realty, Union City, Calif., 1975-80, Property Profls., Fremont, Calif., 1981-90, Trout Real Estate, Newark, Calif., 1991-92, Security West Realty, Fremont, 1993—. Mem. Nat. Assn. Realtors, Calif. Assn. Realtors, South Alameda Assn. Realtors (Multi-Million Dollar Club 1977-92, Master Achievement award 1989), No. Calif. Filipino Assn. Roman Catholic. Avocations: attending real estate seminars, continuing education, dancing. Home: 2117 Arapaho Pl Fremont CA 94539-6562 Office: Security West Realty 39111 Paseo Padre Pkwy Ste 121 Fremont CA 94538-1615

JIMENEZ, WALTER ANTHONY, career officer; b. Long Beach, Calif., Oct. 1, 1970; s. Minor Manuel and Ruth Anna (Hohl) J. BS in Aviation Bus. Adminstrn., Embry-Riddle Aerospace U., 1992; M of Criminal Justice Adminstrn., U. Great Falls, 1996. Commd. 2d lt. USAF, 1992, advanced through grades to 1st lt., 1994; capt., 1996—. Sustaining mem. Rep. Nat. Com., Washington, 1996. Recipient Nat. Defense medal, Combat Readiness medal. Mem. NRA, N.Am. Hunting Club. Roman Catholic. Avocations: weight lifting, water skiing, hunting, fishing, reading. Home: 3408 Coyote Ln Great Falls MT 59404-3832 Office: 12 Missile Squadron 341 Missile Wing Bldg 500 Malmstrom AFB Great Falls MT 59402

JIMMINK, GLENDA LEE, retired elementary school educator; b. Lamar, Colo., Feb. 13, 1935; d. Harold Dale and Ruth Grace (Ellenberger) Fasnacht; m. Gary Jimmink, Oct. 24, 1964 (div. 1984); 1 child, Erik Gerard. BA, U. LaVerne, Calif., 1955. Tchr. elem. grades Pomona (Calif.) Unified Sch. Dist., 1955-61, Palo Alto (Calif.) Unified Sch. Dist., 1961-65, San Rafael (Calif.) Sch. Dist., 1966-95; ret.; mem. curriculum coun. San Rafael Sch. Dist., 1983-90, 94-95, mentor tchr., 1989-90, mem. social studies steering com., 1990-95; charter mem. Marin County Curriculum Connection, 1991-95. Artist, pub. (calendar) Dry Creek Valley, 1987; author: World Geography Resource Handbook for Tchrs., 1990, others. Mem. Marin Arts Coun., San Rafael, 1988-95, Big Bros.-Big Sisters, San Rafael, 1986-93, Earthwatch, 1990—. Mem. Colored Pencil Soc. Am., Mendocino Art Assn., Nat. Wildlife Soc., Richmond Art Ctr., Sierra Club, Gualala Arts Assn., Berkeley Art Ctr/. Avocations: art, reading, horticulture, travel.

JIRAUCH, CHARLES W., lawyer; b. St. Louis, Apr. 27, 1944; s. Mary K. (Horan) J.; m. Sally J. Costello, June 1, 1968 (div. Mar. 1977); m. Dana K. Bowen; children: Melissa, Mathew, Kathleen. BSEE, Washington U., 1966; JD, Georgetown U., 1970. Bar: Ill. 1971, Ariz. 1975, Nev. 1991, , Calif. 1993, Colo. 1993, U.S. Patent Office 1970, U.S. Supreme Ct. 1978. Atty. Leydig, Voit & Mayer, Chgo., 1970-71, McDermott, Will & Emery, Chgo., 1971-75, Streich Lang, Phoenix, 1975—. Bd. dirs. Valley Big Bros./Big Susters, 1980-86, pres. bd. dirs., 1985-86, pres., 1988-92; bd. advisors to dean Ariz. State U. Sch. Engring., 1988—. Mem. ABA, Ariz. Bar Found., Maricopa County Bar Found., Am. Judicature Soc., Am. Intellectual Property Law Assn., Ariz. Dem. Coun., Ariz. Civil Liberties Union, Az. chap. Am. Electronic Assn., 1998—; bd. advs. Sch. Engring. Az. State U., 1998—, bd. dirs. Valley Big Brothers/Sisters, 1980-86 (pres. 1985-86, 88-92). Democrat. Roman Catholic. Office: Streich Lang 2 N Central Ave Fl 2 Phoenix AZ 85004-2391

JO, HOJE, finance educator; b. Seoul, Korea, Jan. 23, 1954; came to U.S., 1980; s. Yong Chun and Kyung Hee (Lee) Cho; m. Sahie Kang, May 25, 1981; children: Hellen, Haesue. BA in Chinese Lit., Seoul Nat. U., 1977; MBA in Fin., SUNY, Buffalo, 1982; PhD in Fin., U. Fla., 1986. Asst. prof. U. N.Mex., Albuquerque, 1986-89; asst. prof. fin. Santa Clara (Calif.) U., 1990-96, assoc. prof. fin., 1996—. Contbr. articles to profl. jours. Vice-chmn. exec. bd. Silicon Valley Korean Sch., 1996-98. Recipient Competitive Rsch. award Chgo. Bd. Options Exchange, 1993, Outstanding Paper award Global Fin. Assn., 1994, Best Paper award, 1996, Iddo Sarnat award Jour. Banking and Fin., 1996. Mem. Korean Am. Fin. Assn. (regional dir. 1992-96, exec. bd. dirs. 1996—), Silicon Valley Korean C. of C. (presenter 1992, Profl. Man of Yr. 1992). Methodist. Avocations: singing, swimming. Fax: (408) 554-4029. E-mail: hjo@mailer.scu.edu. Office: Santa Clara Univ 500 El Camino Real Santa Clara CA 95053

JOAQUIM, RICHARD RALPH, hotel executive; b. Cambridge, Mass., July 28, 1936; s. Manuel and Mary (Marrano) J.; m. Nancy Phyllis Reis, Oct. 22, 1960; 1 child, Vanessa Reis. BFA, Boston U., 1955, MusB, 1959. Social dir., coord. summer resort, Wolfeboro, N.H., 1957-59; concert soloist N.H. Symphony Orch., Vt. Choral Soc., Choral Arts Soc., Schenectady Chamber Orch., 1957-60; coord. performance functions, mgr. theatre Boston U., 1959-60, asst. program dir., 1963-64, dir. univ. programs, 1964-70; gen. mgr. Harrison House of Glen Cove; dir. Conf. Svc. Corp., Glen Cove, N.Y., 1970-74, sr. v.p., dir. design and devel.; v.p. Arltec, also mng. dir. Sheraton Internat. Conf. Ctr., 1975-76; v.p., mng. dir. Scottsdale (Ariz.) Conf. Ctr. and Resort Hotel, 1976—; pres. Internat. Conf. Resorts, Inc., 1977, chmn. bd., 1977—; pres. Western Conf. Resorts; concert solist U.S. Army Field Band, Washington, 1960-62. Creative arts cons., editorial cons., concert mgr. Commr. recreation Watertown, Mass., 1967—; mem. Spl. Study Com. Watertown, 1967—, Glen Cove Mayor's Urban Renewal Com., Nat. Com. for Performing Arts Ctr. at Boston U., Jacob K. Javits Fellows Program Fellowship Bd. Bd. dirs. Nat. Entertainment Conf.; trustee Boston U., 1983—, Hotel and Food Adminstrn. Program Adv. Bd., Boston U., 1986—, Ariz. Opera Co. With AUS, 1960-62. Recipient Disting. Alumni award Boston U., 1991. Mem. Assn. Coll. and Univ. Concert Mgrs., Am. Symphonic League, Am. Fedn. Film Socs., Assn. Am. Artists, Am. Pers. and Guidance Assn., La Chaine des Rotisseurs, Knights of the Vine, Order of St. John, Nat. Alumni Council Boston U. Clubs: The Lotos (N.Y.). Office: Scottsdale Conf Ctr & Resort Hotel 7700 E Mccormick Pky Scottsdale AZ 85258-3431 Office: Scottsdale Conf Ctr & Resort Hotel 7700 E Mccormick Pky Scottsdale AZ 85258-3431

JOBE SMITH, JOAN ELAINE, writer, editor; b. Paris, Tex., Jan. 25, 1940; d. Avner Ray and Margaret Fay (Smith) Jobe; m. Jerry Horgan, Mar. 15, 1958 (div. 1962); children: Holly, Dan; m. Edward Gentry, Feb. 14, 1964 (div. 1966); 1 child, Elaine Gentry King; m. John Smith, Nov. 19, 1967 (div. 1990); m. Fred Voss, June 16, 1990. BA, Calif. State U., Long Beach, 1975; MFA, U. Calif., Irvine, 1979. Go-go girl various nightclubs, So. Calif., 1965-72; editor, pub. Pearl Mag., Long Beach, Calif., 1986—. Author: (poetry) The Pow Wow Café, 1998, Bukowski Boulevard, 1998. Recipient Pushcart award 1979, Chiron Prize 1990, 96, Mary Scheirman Poetry award, 1996; recipient numerous grants. Mem. PEN. Buddhist. Avocations: cinema, cooking, poetry. Home: 1044 E 2nd St Apt 8 Long Beach CA 90802-5580

JOEL, J. BRANDT, agent; b. N.Y.C., Dec. 12, 1964; s. Donald G. and Lynda (Peck) J. BA in French Lit., Duke U., 1987. Talent agt. asst. United Talent Agy., Beverly Hills, Calif., 1991-97; talent agt. Creative Artists Agy., Beverly Hills, 1997—. Lt. USN, 1987-91. Democrat. Avocations: college football, golf, reading. Home: 1315 Idaho Ave Apt 1 Santa Monica CA 90403-3009

JOFFE, BARBARA LYNNE, computer applications systems manager, computer artist, project management professional; b. Bklyn., Apr. 12, 1951; d. Lester L. and Julia (Schuelke) J.; m. James K. Whitney, Aug. 25, 1990; 1 child, Nichole. BA, U. Oreg., 1975; MFA, U. Mont., 1982. Cert. project mgr. IBM; cert. project mgmt. profl. Project Mgmt. Inst. Applications engr., software developer So. Pacific Transp., San Francisco, 1986-93; computer fine artist Barbara Joffe Assocs., San Francisco, Englewood, Colo., 1988—; instr. computer graphics Ohlone Coll., Fremont, Calif., 1990-91; adv. programmer, project mgr.-client/server Integrated Sys. Solutions Corp./IBM Global Svcs. So. Pacific/Union Pacific Railroads, Denver, 1994-97; applications sys. mgr. IBM Global Svcs./CoBank, Greenwood Village, Colo., 1997—. Artwork included in exhibits at Calif. Crafts XIII, Crocker Art Mus., Sacramento, 1983, Rara Avis Gallery, Sacramento, 1984, Redding (Calif.) Mus. and Art Ctr., 1985, Euphrat Gallery, Cupertino, Calif., 1988, Computer Mus., Boston, 1989, Siggraph Traveling Art Shown, Europe and Australia, 1990, 91, 4th and 7th Nat. Computer Art Invitational, Cheney, Wash., 1991, 94, Visual Arts Mus., N.Y.C., 1994, 96, IBM Golden Circle, 1996. Mem. Assn. Computing Machinery, Project Mgmt. Inst. (cert.). Avocations: art, gardening, hiking. Home: 7271 S Jersey Ct Englewood CO 80112-1512

JOHANOS, DONALD, orchestra conductor; b. Cedar Rapids, Iowa, Feb. 10, 1928; s. Gregory Hedges and Doris (Nelson) J.; m. Thelma Trimble, Aug. 27, 1950; children—Jennifer Claire, Thea Christine, Gregory Bruce (dec.), Andrew Mark, Eve Marie; m. Corinne Rutledge, Sept. 28, 1985. Mus.B., Eastman Sch. Music, 1950, Mus.M., 1952; D.F.A. (hon.), Coe Coll., 1962. Tchr. Pa. State U., 1953-55, So. Meth. U., 1958-62, Hockaday Sch., 1962-65; now condr. laureate Honolulu Symphony Orch. Mus. dir., Altoona (Pa.) Symphony, 1953-56, Johnstown (Pa.) Symphony, 1955-56, asso. condr., Dallas Symphony Orch., 1957-61, resident condr., 1961-62, mus. dir., 1962-70, assoc. condr., Pitts. Symphony, 1970-79, mus. dir., Honolulu Symphony Orch., 1979—, artistic dir., Hawaii Opera Theater, 1979-83, guest condr., Phila. Orch., Amsterdam Concertgebouw Orch., Pitts. Symphony, Rochester Philharm., New Orleans Philharm., Denver Symphony, Vancouver Symphony, Chgo. Symphony, San Francisco Symphony, Netherlands Radio Philharm., Swiss Radio Orch., Mpls. Symphony, Paris Opera, Boston Symphony, San Antonio Symphony, Orchestre Nat. de Lyon, others; recordings for Marco Polo, Naxos, Turnabout, Candide, others. Advanced study grantee Am. Symphony Orch. League and Rockefeller Found., 1955-58. Mem. Am. Fedn. Musicians Internat. Congress of Strings (dir.). Office: Schofer/Gold 50 Riverside Dr New York NY 10024-6555*

JOHANSEN, RICKY LEE, JR., paralegal investigator; b. Toledo, Oreg., July 13, 1957; s. Richard Lee Johansen and Janet Ann (McKenna) Anspach; m. Ursula Maureen Anderson, Nov. 3, 1979 (div. Sept. 1995); m. Kathleen Jo Childress, Apr., 1998. Student, OVTI/OTCC, Olympia Vocat.-Tech. Inst., Wash., 1976-77; student, Centralia (Wash.) C.C., 1977, U. Alaska, 1977-80, Tanana Valley C.C., Fairbanks, Alaska, 1978; Cert. of Completion in Pharmacy Sci., Acad. Health Sci., U.S. Army, Ft. Sam Houston, Tex., 1991-92; Assoc. Engring. Tech., Cert. Nat. Inst. Cert. Engring. Pvt. practice Fairbanks, Alaska, 1976-90; civil engring. tech. City of Fairbanks Pub. Works, 1977-80; civil/archtl. engring. tech., draftsperson ADEH/ERMB 172d INF BDE, Ft. Wainwright, Alaska, 1983-85; engring. tech., cmty. planning and zoning dept. Fairbanks North Star Borough, 1985-90; pharmacy techologist Madigan Army Med. Ctr., Ft. Lewis, Wash., 1991-93; title examiner First Am. Title Ins. Co., Tacoma, Wash., 1993-95; paralegal investigator Brungardt & Assocs., Shelton, Wash., 1995-97; bus. owner, No. Tier Alaska Internat., Fairbanks, 1983-91; paralegal investigator pvt. practice, Shelton, Wash., 1997-98. Contbr. 2 articles to profl. jours. Campaign worker Congressman Don Young's Campaign, Fairbanks, 1988; commr. Animal Control Commn., Fairbanks, 1988-90. Mr. Future Bus. Leaders of Am. 3rd Place Tumwater Sch. Dist. Supt. of Pub. Instruction, 1976, Winner Law Day Speech Wash. State Bar Assn./Superior Ct. Judges of Thurston County, 1976. Avocations: cartoonist, illustrator, U.S. Mint stamp collecting, history, computers. Home: 321 N 7th St Apt 7 Shelton WA 98584-2506

JOHN, JOSEPH ROBERT, international business consultant, film producer; b. Central Falls, R.I., Mar. 31, 1939; s. Michael Saffer and Hannah (Herniz) J.; m. Patricia Louise Hall, Nov. 21, 1964; children: Jennifer P., Jessica R. BS, U.S. Naval Acad., 1962; MS, U.S. Internat. U., San Diego, 1970; MBA, Harvard U., 1972. Commd. ensign USN, 1962, advanced through grades to capt., 1980; pres., CEO Seafood Galley, Inc., Central Falls, R.I., 1971-85; sr. v.p. internat. Univ. Mech. Contractors, San Diego, 1976-77; pres., mng. dir. Saudi Arabian Trading and Contracting, Riyadh, 1977-79; chmn. Crown Summit Fin. Corp., San Diego, 1981-92; pres., CEO JRJ and Assocs., Inc., Beverly Hills, Calif., 1977—; founder U.S. Naval Cadet Unit C.S. Sperry, Pawtucket, R.I., 1966; assoc. prof. Nat. U., 1976-85, U. LaVerne, 1993-95; moderator staff Nat. Def. U., 1981; adj. faculty U.S. Naval War Coll., 1985, 89-92; mem. leadership com. U.S. Olympic Tng. Ctr., Otay Mesa, Calif, 1988-90. Co-author: Navigation and Operations, 1972, Naval War College Review, 1990; tech. adv. (films) Under Siege; assoc. prodr. Run If You Can, Gun Bus; co-prodr. The Married Man and the Virgin and others. Senator R.I. Model Legis., Providence, 1956; co-founder, pres. Blackstone Valley Youth Coun., 1957; mem. campaign staff/advance staff Pres. Ronald Reagan, Washington, 1976-88, Pres. George Bush, Washington, 1988-90; adv. on trade policy matters Sec. of Commerce, Washington, 1986-90. Decorated Commendation medal, 4 Meritorious Svc. medals, combat action ribbon, 21 additional medals for service in Vietnam, Desert Storm and Anti-Terrorist Campaigns; named one of Outstanding Young Men of Am., 1971. Mem. Naval Acad. Athletic Assn., Naval Acad. Alumni Assn. (bd. dirs.), Navy League of U.S. (bd. dirs.), Surface Navy Assn. (bd. dirs.), I Storm Inc. (advisory bd.), Telalink (advisory bd.), Masons, Benchmark Equity Gp. Republican. Episcopalian. Office: JRJ and Assocs Inc Ste 186 264 S La Cienega Blvd Beverly Hills CA 90211

JOHN, YVONNE MAREE, artist, designer; b. Leeton, N.S.W., Australia, Sept. 8, 1944; came to U.S., 1966; d. Percy Edward and Gladys May (Markham) T.; m. Michael Peter John, Aug. 20, 1966; children: Michael Christian, Stephen Edwin. Artist: selected exhibits of work include: Royal Mus., Sydney, Australia, 1994, Ventura (Calif.) County Courthouse, Wash. Women in Art, Olympia, 1990, Timberland Libr., OLympia, 1990, Maska Internat. Gallery, Seattle, 1991 (cert. of excellence painting), Michael Stone Collection, Washington, D.C., 1992, Nat. Hdqtrs. Am. Soc. Interior Decorators, Washington, 1992, The Funding Ctr., Alexandria, Va., 1992, New Eng. Fine Arts Inst. Nat. Invitational Exhbn., Woburn, Mass., 1993, Mus. d'Art Moderne, Bordeaux, France, 1993, Abney Galleries, N.Y., 1993, Mus. Modern Art, Miami, Coral Gables, Fla., 1993, Hargus Unique Gallery, Pomona, Calif., UN Fourth World Conf. on Women, Beijing, China with Nat. Mus. of Women in Art, Washington, 1995, with Ariz. State U., World's Women on Line, 1995, on World Wide Web http://www.scultura com/maree html, 1996, Gallery Brindabella, Oakville, Ontario, Can., 1996, Art Comm. Internat., Phila., 1996, V.I.P. Lobbies World Bank, Washington, 1996-97, World Fine Art, N.Y.C., 1997; permanent collections include Royal Mus. Sydney, Australia, O'Toole Collection, Melbourne, Victoria, Australia, Ronald Reagan Collection, Calif., Nat. Mus. Women in Arts, Washington, Patterson Collection, Mich., Witherow Collection, Washington, Samaniego Colllection, Calif. Recipient cash and cert. awards, Sydney, Australia, 1950s, ribbon awards Australian County Fairs, 1950s; 1st round winner Hathaway Competition, Ventura, Calif., 1970s. Republican. Roman Catholic. Avocations: tennis, golf, swimming, reading, gardening. Office: Yvonne Maree Designs PO Box 2143 Olympia WA 98507-2143

JOHNS, ROY (BUD JOHNS), publisher, author; b. Detroit, July 9, 1929; s. Roy and Isabel Johns; m. Judith Spector Clancy, 1971 (dec. 1990); m. Frances Moreland, 1992. BA in English and Econs., Albion (Mich.) Coll., 1951. Various editorial positions Mich. and Calif. daily newspapers, 1942-60; bur. chief Fairchild Pubs., 1960-69; dir. corp. communications Levi Strauss & Co., 1969-81, corp. v.p., 1979-81; pres. Synergistic Press, Inc., San Francisco, 1968—; bd. dirs. Applewood Books, Bedford, Mass.; founder, ptnr. Apple Tree Press, Flint, Mich., 1954-55; cons. on comms., pub., and related areas. Author: The Ombibulous Mr. Mencken, 1968, What is This Madness?, 1985; co-editor, author: Bastard in the Ragged Suit, 1977; scriptwriter, exec. producer: What is This Madness?, 1976; exec. producer: The Best You Can Be, 1979 (CINE Golden Eagle award 1980); editor: Old Dogs Remembered, 1993; free-lance writer numerous mag. articles. Mem. Nat. Coun. of Mus. of Am. Indian, N.Y.C., 1980-90; dir. The San Francisco Contemporary Music Players, 1981—, Greenbelt Alliance, San Francisco, 1982—, pres., 1990-95; dir. Save San Francisco Bay Assn., 1996-97, San Francisco Performing Arts Libr. and Mus., 1998—. Inventor sport of ride and tie racing, 1971. Home and Office: 3965 Sacramento St San Francisco CA 94118-1627

JOHNS, TIMOTHY ANDREW, software engineer; b. Abilene, Tex., Feb. 21, 1971; s. Gary Earl and Mary Alice J.; m. Kathryn Daniels, Feb. 7, 1972. BS, Stephen F. Austin State U., 1994. Software engr. MSR Devel., Inc., Nacogdoches, Tex., 1994-96; software engr. Iomega Corp., Nacogdoches, 1996, Blue Water Systems, Inc., Edmonds, Wash., 1996—. Program mgr. WinRT 3.0, 1998, WinOK 2.6, 1998. Com. mem. Holy Rosary Young Adults, Edmonds, 1998. With Tex. N.G., 1989-95. Republican. Roman Catholic. Avocations: music, hiking, ham radio. Office: Blue Water Systems Inc PO Box 776 Edmonds WA 98020-0776

JOHNSON, ALAN BOND, federal judge; b. 1939. BA, Vanderbilt U., 1961; JD, U. Wyo., 1964. Pvt. practice law Cheyenne, Wyo., 1968-71; assoc. Hanes, Carmichael, Johnson, Gage & Speight P.C., Cheyenne, 1971-74; judge Wyo. Dist. Ct., 1974-85; judge U.S. Dist. Ct. Wyo., 1986-92, chief judge, 1992—; part-time fed. magistrate U.S. Dist. Ct. Wyo., 1971-74; substitute judge Mcpl. Ct., Cheyenne, 1973-74. Served to capt. USAF, 1964-67, to col. Wyo. Air N.G., 1973-90. Mem. ABA, Wyo. State Bar, Laramie County Bar Assn. (sec.-treas. 1968-70), Wyo. Jud. Conf. (sec. 1977-78, chmn. 1979), Wyo. Jud. Council. Office: US Dist Ct O'Mahoney Fed Ctr 2120 Capitol Ave Ste 2242 Cheyenne WY 82001-3666*

JOHNSON, ALICE ELAINE, retired academic administrator; b. Janesville, Wis., Oct. 9, 1929; d. Floyd C. and Alma M. (Walthers) Chester; m. Richard C. Johnson, Sept. 25, 1948 (div. 1974); children: Randall S., Nile C., Linnea E. BA, U. Colo., 1968. Pres., administrator Pikes Peak Inst. Med. Tech., Colorado Springs, Colo., 1968-88; mem. adv. com. to Colo. Commn. on Higher Edn., 1979-80, State Adv. Coun. on Pvt. Occupational Schs., Denver, 1978-86; mem. tech. adv. com. State Health Occupations, 1986-88; bd. dirs. All Souls Unitarian Ch., Colorado Springs, 1990—, mem. celebration team, 1990-91, pres. bd. trustees, 1991-93. Mem. Colo. Pvt. Sch. Assn. (pres. 1981-82, bd. dirs. 1976-88, Outstanding Mem. 1978, 80), Phi Beta Kappa. Democrat. Unitarian. Avocations: writing, travel, reading.

JOHNSON, ANNETTE M., arts administrator; b. Sacramento, Calif., June 3, 1960. AA, Chaffey Coll., 1988; BA, Calif. State U., Fullerton, 1991; MPA, Calif. State U., San Bernardino, 1998. Office mgr. L.D. Johnson Co., Glendale, Calif., 1980-84; graphic designer Quality Instant Printing, San Dimas, Calif., 1984-86; asst. to dir. Wignall Mus. Gallery, Rancho Cucamonga, Calif., 1987-89, curator, 1990-98; owner, cons. EM Prodns., Rancho Cucamonga, 1992—; cons. Inland Empire Edn. Found., San Bernardino, Calif., 1994. Vol., sch. site coun. mem. Ctrl. Sch., Rancho Cucamonga, 1998—; mgr. recreation and cmty. svcs. City of Pico Rivera. Mem. Am. Assn. Mus., Assoc. Coll. & Univ. Mus. & Galleries, Calif. Assn. Mus., Wstn. Assn. Mus.

JOHNSON, ARNOLD HJALMER, minister; b. Simrishamn, Sweden, Feb. 29, 1920; came to U.S., 1920; s. John Anton and Anna (Trozell) J.; m. Gertrude Warner (dec.); m. Doris Johnson, June 30, 1972; children: Betty Johnson Tomlinson, Ruth Johnson Coburn, Arnold Hjalmer Jr. AA, North Park Sem., 1941; grad., North Cark Sem., 1945; BA, East Tenn. State U., 1964. Ordained to ministry Evang. Covenant Ch. Am., 1947. Missionary Covenant Mountain Mission, Jonesville, Va., 1945-54; tchr. Hancock County Pub. Schs., Sneedville, Tenn., 1962-72; pres., Ministrial Assn., South Chgo. Area, 1974-77; leader, enabling disabled project, Evang. Covenant Ch., Chgo., 1986-89. Pastor, exec. sec. Jonesville C. of C., 1954-56. Address: 325 Kempton St # 414 Spring Valley CA 91977-5810

JOHNSON, ARTHUR WILLIAM, JR., planetarium executive; b. Steubenville, Ohio, Jan. 8, 1949; s. Arthur William and Carol (Gilcrest) J.; B.Mus., U. So. Calif., 1973. Lectr., Griffith Obs. and Planetarium, 1969-73; planetarium writer, lectr. Mt. San Antonio Coll. Planetarium, Walnut, Calif., 1970-73; dir. Fleischmann Planetarium, U. Nev., Reno, 1973—. Organist, choirmaster Trinity Episcopal Ch., Reno, 1980—; bd. dirs. Reno Chamber Orch. Assn., 1981-87 , 1st v.p., 1984-85. Nev. Humanities Com., Inc. grantee, 1979-83; apptd. Nev. state coord. N.S.T.A./NASA Space Sci. Student Involvement Program, 1994. Mem. Am. Guild Organists (dean No. Nev. chpt. 1984-85, 96—), Internat. Planetarium Soc., Cinema 360 (treas. 1985-90, pres. 1990-98), Pacific Planetarium Assn. (pres. 1980), Lions (pres. Reno Host Club 1991-92), Large Format Cinema Assn. (v.p. 1996—). Republican. Episcopalian. Writer, producer films: (with Donald G. Potter) Beautiful Nevada, 1978, Riches: The Story of Nevada Mining, 1984. Office: Fleischmann Plantarium U Nev 1650 N Virginia St Reno NV 89503-1738

JOHNSON, AUSTON G., auditor; m. Mary Johnson; 3 children. BS, Utah State U. CPA, Utah. Auditor State of Utah, Salt Lake City, 1976—; acctg. adv. bd. U. Utah Sch. Acctg., 1993; sch. accountancy adv. coun. Utah State U., 1994—. With USN, 1969-73. Mem. AICPA (Outstanding Discussion Leader 1993), Utah Assn. CPAs (vice-chmn. state and local govt. com. 1987-88). Office: Office Utah State Auditor 211 State Capitol Bldg Salt Lake City UT 84114-1202*

JOHNSON, BEN E., English language educator; b. Storm Lake, Iowa, Aug. 16, 1940; s. Jonas Birger and Bernice Minnie (Brown) J.; m. Elsa Jean Johnson; children: Steven, Susan, Shelley. BRE, William Tyndale Coll., Detroit, 1962; MA, Ea. Mich. U., Ypsilanti, 1967, MA in Edn., 1964; PhD, U. South Fla., Tampa, 1994. Cert. secondary tchr., social studies, English, Mich. Instr. William Tyndale Coll., Detroit, 1964-68; asst. prof. Trinity Coll., Deerfield, Ill., 1969-76; ednl. cons. AGP, Inc., Santa Barbara, Calif., 1976-84; instr. Lake County C.C., Leesburg, Fla., 1985-86, Manatee C.C., Bradenton, Fla., 1986-87; adj. prof. St. Petersburg (Fla.) Jr. Coll., 1991-92, U. South Fla., Sarasota, 1988—; Selby chair acad. enrichment Sarasota (Fla.) County Pub. Schs., 1992—; edn. cons. AGP, Inc., Santa Barbara, 1976-84. Author 17 books including The Lottery Book, 1991, Doing It Right: Improving College Learning Skills, 1992, Winning the Lottery, 1993, Getting Lucky: Answers to Nearly Every Question About Playing and Winning the Lottery, 1994, CLAST Preparation Guide, 4th edit., 1994, The Reading Edge: Thirteen Ways to Build Reading Comprehension, 2nd edit., 1994, Learn to Rapid Write in Six Days: Speeding Things Up by Writing Less, 1994, Stirring Up Thinking: Experiences in Critical Thinking, 1995. Recipient Golden Gavel award Sarasota Herald, 1994. Mem. Internat. Reading Assn., Nat. Coun. Tchrs. English, Fla. Coun. Tchrs. English. Avocations: painting, cooking, reading.

JOHNSON, BLANCHE THERESE, small business owner; b. St. Louis, June 3, 1943; d. Bertrand D. and Barbara Rose (Temm) Coughlin; m. Charles Henry Johnson, July 17, 1965; children: Tracy, Jennifer Johnson Szluk. BA in Polit. Sci., Trinity Coll., Washington, 1965. Owner Ins. Mgmt. Agy., Canfield, Ohio, 1976-92, Wilderness Adventures, Inc., Gallatin Gateway, Mont., 1992—; co-pub. books on hunting and fishing Wilderness Adventures Press, 1994—. Avocations: wingshooting, fly fishing, photography, cooking. Office: Wilderness Adventures Inc PO Box 627 Gallatin Gateway MT 59730-0627

JOHNSON, BRENDA FAYE, career officer; b. Ft. Leavenworth, Kans., Jan. 13, 1953; d. Hugh Dorsey and Marguerite Elizabeth (Achilles) Johnson; children: Beth Louise, Barbra Marie; life ptnr. Bill Lasarzig. Cert. in lang. and humanities, Scripps Coll., 1970; cert. in fine arts, U.S. Internat. U., San Diego, 1972; AA in Liberal Arts, Fresno City Coll., 1973; BA in Psychology/Sociology, Calif. State U.-Fresno, 1975; MA in German, Antioch Internat. U., Yellow Springs, Ohio, 1986; postgrad. in linguistics, Union Coll., Cin., 1986-87. Cert. educator, counselor, instr. U.S. Army. Commd. 1st lt. U.S. Army, 1976, advanced through grades to capt., 1980; adjutant/test officer U.S. Army Armed Forces Entrance and Examining Sta., Mpls., 1978-80; asst. area club mgr. U.S. Army Command, Grafenwoehr, Fed. Republic Germany, 1982-83; contbg. editor U.S. Army-Trojan, Ft. Leavenworth, 1983; spl. edn. instr. U.S. Army-Acad. div., 1983-84; ops. & quality control supr. U.S. Army-Vocat. Tng., 1984-85; behavioral sci. rsch. analyst U.S. Army-Dept. Mental Health, 1985-86; fire inspector Fresno (Calif.) Fire Dept., 1987-91, U. Calif.-Santa Barbara, 1991—; lang. instr., cons. German-Am. rels., 1983-86; lectr. St. Mary's Cath. Ch. Author: Men in Power, 1986; co-author: The Trial, 1986; co-editor: (mag.) Stray Shots-Book of Poems, 1983. Cultural arts dir., phys. edn. dir. Mormon Ch., Mpls., 1978-79; mgr. Tonemaster Calif., 1988-89; campaign coord. elections Fresno City Coun., 1985; bd. dirs. Burn Aware Bd. Decorated Army Commendation Medal; Calif. Gov.'s scholar, 1969-75. Mem. NAFE, NOW, Assn. U.S. Army, Jr. C. of C. (speech cons. 1983), Calif. Scholarship Fedn., Cen. Calif. Psychol. Assn., Fire Prevention Officers Assn., Soroptimist Internat. (chairperson ways and means), Mensa, Phi Beta Kappa, Phi Kappa Phi, Alpha Gamma Sigma, Phi Theta Kappa. Avocations: swimming, sailing, skating, dance, tennis.

JOHNSON, CHARLES BARTLETT, mutual fund executive; b. Montclair, N.J., Jan. 6, 1933; s. Rupert Harris and Florence (Endler) J.; m. Ann Demarest Lutes, Mar. 26, 1955; children: Charles E., Holly, Sarah, Gregory, William, Jennifer, Mary (dec.). BA, Yale U., 1954. With R.H. Johnson & Co., N.Y.C., 1954-55; pres. Franklin Distbrs., Inc., 1957—; pres., CEO Franklin Resources, Inc., 1969—; bd. dirs. various Franklin and Templeton Mut. Funds; bd. govs. Investment Co. Inst., 1973-88. Trustee Crystal Springs Uplands Sch., 1984-92; bd. dirs. Peninsula Cmty. Found., 1986-96, San Francisco Symphony, 1984—; bd. overseers Hoover Instn., 1993—. Mem. Nat. Assn. Securities Dirs. (bd. govs. 1990-92, 96-98, chmn. 1992), Burlingame Country Club, Pacific Union Club (San Francisco), Commonwealth Club of Calif. (bd. dirs. 1995-97). Office: Franklin Resources Inc PO Box 7777 San Mateo CA 94403-7777

JOHNSON, CHARLES WILLIAM, state supreme court justice; b. Tacoma, Wash., Mar. 16, 1951. BA in Econs., U. Wash., 1973; JD, U. Puget Sound, 1976. Bar: Wash. 1977. Justice Wash. Supreme Ct., 1991—; mem. Wash. State Minority and Justice Commn. Bd. dirs. Wash. Assn. Children and Parents; mem. vis. com. U. Wash. Sch. Social Work; bd. visitors Seattle U. Sch. Law, mem. Washington State Courthouse Sec. Task Force. Mem. Wash. State Bar Assn., Tacoma-Pierce County Bar Assn. (Liberty Bell award young lawyers sect. 1994). Avocations: sailing, downhill skiing, cycling. Office: Wash State Supreme Ct Temple of Justice PO Box 40929 Olympia WA 98504-0929*

JOHNSON, CHRISTINE, educational administrator; b. Antelope Wells, N.Mex., Feb. 6, 1953; d. Charles and Rosa (Vera) J.; m. Ronald D. Sherbon, June 30, 1978 (div. Aug. 1984); m. Carlyle F. Griffin, July 7, 1989. BS in Secondary Edn., N.Mex. State U., 1975; MA in Edn. Adminstrn., Colo. U., 1977, PhD in Edn. Adminstrn., 1984. Tchr. Thomas Jefferson H.S., Denver, 1975-80; spl. asst. Ctrl. Adminstrn., Denver, 1980-81; asst. prin. Abraham Lincoln H.S., Denver, 1981-83, prin., 1986-91; prin. Horace Mann Mid. Sch., Denver, 1984-85; rsch. fellow Colo. Dept. Edn., Denver, 1985-86; exec. dir. K-12 edn. Littleton (Colo.) Pub. Schs., 1991-93; urban policy dir. Edn. Commn. of States, Denver, 1993—; chair com. Nat. Assessment for Edn. Progress, Washington, 1990-94; mem. governing bd. Cross City Campaign, Chgo., 1993—, Prins. Ctr., 1988-90; mem. adv. bd. Nat. Sch. Based Health, Washington, 1993—. Contbr. articles to profl. publs. Chair State Higher Edn. Bd., Denver, 1994—; v.p. Prevention Ctr., Denver, 1992; mem., chair com. Colo. Achievement Commn., Denver, 1993; mem., chair prins. adv. bd. Colo. Gen. Assembly, Denver, 1991-93. Kellogg Found. fellow, 1993, Danforth fellow, 1987. Mem. ASCD, Colo. Commn. on Higher Edn. (chair 1991—), Am. Assn. Sch. Adminstrs., Denver C. of C. (mem. Leadership Denver 1990, award 1990), Phi Delta Kappa. Avocations: jogging, skiing, hiking. Office: Edn Commn of States 707 17th St Ste 2700 Denver CO 80202-3427

JOHNSON, CLINT NEVEL, marketing executive; b. Oakland, Calif., Feb. 1, 1964; s. Wayne Charles and Virginia Lee (Hartzie) J.; m. Eden Jennifer Le Cheminat, Oct. 20, 1969; 1 child, Samantha Jean. Student, U. Nev., Las Vegas, 1988-89; grad. in Gaming Mgmt., U. Nev., 1992-98. Owner Pro-Vend, Reno, Nev., 1988-90; gen. sales mgr. Kick FM Radio, Reno, Nev., 1990-91; v.p., dir. mktg. Baldini's Sports Casino, Sparks, Nev., 1991—. Home: 3815 Corvallis Dr Reno NV 89511-6058 Office: Baldinis Sports Casino 865 S Rock Blvd Sparks NV 89431-5921

JOHNSON, CRANE, writer, lawyer; b. Bayard, Nebr., June 30, 1921; s. Carl Arthur and Pearl (Haskins) J. MA, U. So. Calif., 1948; postgrad., Stanford U., 1949; PhD, Case We. Res. U., 1960; LLB, N.Y. Law Sch., 1962; LLM, NYU, 1968. Vol. legal aid lawyer. Author: Past Sixty, 1953, The Wither'd Garland, 1956, Thirty-Five One Act Plays, 1965, Dracula, 1976, Presque Isle Village, 1995, Three Jacumba Tales, 1998. U.S. rep. at ednl. confs. in London and Vienna. Served with AUS, WWII. Mem. N.Y. Bar Assn. Address: Box 158 Jacumba CA 91934

JOHNSON, DANIEL LEON, aeronautical engineer; b. Manistee, Mich., Jan. 24, 1936; s. Malcolm Storer and Viola Johanna (Hinkle) J.; m. Dorothy Gwynn Chandler, Sept. 22, 1963; children: Romer D., Olin M., Daniela D., Wenona B., Conrad C., Garrett H. *Daniel Johnson participated in the New Mexico senior games and placed third in horseshoes, fourth in the 400 meter run, and his basketball team placed third. Daughter Daniela was Miss New Mexico in 1993, and in the Bob Hope Christmas Pageant. She is married and lives in Logan, Utah. Son Conrad in 1998 placed fourth in the Nation for Division II wrestling at 177 pounds. Daughter Wenona lives in Denver with three children, son Romer lives in Tucson with three children, and son Olin lives in Utah with two children. Son Garrett lives at home.* BS, U.S. Mil. Acad., West Point, N.Y., 1958; MS in Aero. Engring., U. Mich., 1960, MS in Instrumentation Engring., 1960; PhD in Aero. Engring., U. Colo., 1971. Comd. 2d lt. USAF, 1958, advanced through grades to col., 1978; engr. Material Command, Beale AFB, Calif., 1960-62; engr., chief missle test Logistics Command, Hill AFB, Utah, 1963-67; engr., liason Logsitics Command, Vietnam, 1967-68; engr. Aerospace Med. Rsch. Lab., Wright-Patterson AFB, Ohio, 1971-78, chief tech. svcs. divsn., 1978-84; chief scientist Larson-Davis Labs., Provo, Utah, 1984-89; dir. biophysics ops. EG&G MSI, Kirtland AFB, N.Mex., 1989-97; pres. Interactive Acoustics Inc., 1998—; mem. phys. agts. TLV com. Am. Conf. Govtl. Indsl. Hygienists, 1992—; mem. com. on hearing, bioacoustics and biomechanics steering com. NRC, 1990-93. Contbr. over 90 articles to profl. jours., chpts. to books. Decorated Bronze Star, Legion of Merit; recipient Harry G. Armstrong award Aerospace Med. Rsch. Lab., 1977. Fellow Acoustical Soc. Am. (chmn. noise com. 1992-94, vice chmn. com. on stds. 1993-97, dir. com. on stds. 1997—, chmn. ANSI S1 and S12 coms. 1984-96); mem. Soc. Automotive Engrs., Nat. Hearing Conservation Assn., Inst. Noise Control Engring., Am. Indsl. Hygiene Assn. Achievements include development of the analysis that is used by the current International Standard that relates noise exposure to noise induced hearing loss; development (with others) of the measurement metric for environmental noise; determination of the safety limits of low frequency sound; determination in part of the safety limits of some types of impulsive sounds. Office: Interactive Acoustics Inc 4719 Mile High Dr Provo UT 84604-6305

JOHNSON, DAVEY (DAVID ALLEN JOHNSON), baseball team manager; b. Orlando, Fla., Jan. 30, 1943; children: Dave Jr., Dawn, Andrea. Student, Johns Hopkins U.; B.S., Trinity U. Baseball player Balt. Orioles, 1965-72; baseball player Atlanta Braves, 1973-75, Phila. Phillies, 1977-78, Chgo. Cubs, 1978; mgr. Inter-Am. League, Miami, 1979, Jackson League, Tex., 1981, Tidewater, Internat. League, 1983, N.Y. Mets, N.Y.C., 1984-90, Cin. Reds, 1993-96, Balt. Orioles, 1996-97, L.A. Dodgers, 1999—. Recipient Am. Gold Glove, 1969-71; mem. Am. League All-Star Team, 1968, 70, Nat. League All-Star Team, 1973; mgr. Nat. League All-Star Team, 1986, World Series championship team, 1986. Co-holder single season record most home runs by second baseman (42), 1973. Office: Los Angeles Dodgers 1000 Elysian Park Ave Los Angeles CA 90012-1199*

JOHNSON, DAVID SELLIE, civil engineer; b. Mpls., Apr. 10, 1935; s. Milton Edward and Helen M. (Sellie) J. BS, Mont. Coll. Mineral Sci. Tech., 1958. Registered profl. engr., Mont. Trainee Mont. Dept. Hwys., Helena, 1958-59, designer, 1959-66, asst. preconstrn. engr., 1966-68, regional engr., 1968-72, engring. specialities supr., 1972-89, preconstrn. chief, 1989-93, forensic engr., 1965—, traffic accident reconstructionist, 1978—; dir. mktg. Sverdrup Civil, Inc., Helena, 1994—; consulting engr., 1985—. Contbr. articles on hwy. safety to profl. jours. Adv. bd. mem. Helena Vocat.-Tech.

Edn., 1972-73. Fellow Inst. Transp. Engrs. (expert witness coun.); mem. NSPE, Nat. Acad. Forensic Engrs. (diplomate), Mont. Soc. Profl. Engrs., Transp. Rsch. Bd. (geometric design com., tort liability com.), Wash. Assn. Tech. Accident Investigators, Corvette Club, Treasure State Club (pres. Helena 1972-78, sec. 1979-82), Shriners. Avocations: photography, sports car racing. Home and Office: 1921 E 6th Ave Helena MT 59601-4766

JOHNSON, DEE STRICKLAND, poet, musician, retired educator; b. Flagstaff, Ariz., Apr. 18, 1931; d. Troy James and Anna Beth (Hoovler) Strickland; m. John Cavanaugh Johnson, Jan. 10, 1927; children: Daniel Scott, Timothy Wayne, Rebecca Lynn. BS, No. Ariz. U., 1956; MA, U. Ariz., 1961. Tchr. Ariz. Schs., Avondale and Tucson, 1956-59; writer The Mountain View (Ark.) Newspaper, 1973-74; singer Ozark Folk Ctr., Mountain View, 1973-77; tchr. Shirley (Ark.) Pub. Schs., Shirley, 1975-77, pub. schs., Phoenix and Payson, Ariz., 1977-94; freelance writer, entertainer, 1994—. Author, illustrator, editor: Cowman's Wife, 1996, First Roundup, 1997; singer, reciter, (video) Buckshot Dot Live at Pioneer, 1998. Mem. Acad. Western Artists (Female Cowboy Poet of Yr. 1997), Nat. League Am. Pen Women, Western Music Assn. Avocations: writing, singing, drawing. E-mail: buckshotdot@netzone.com. Home: HC3 Box 593F Payson AZ 85541

JOHNSON, DELLENA SHARON, poet, educator; b. Arlington, Va., July 25, 1954; d. Delbert Orville and Dorothy Lena (Kidd) Carberry; m. William Frederick Johnson, Jan. 13, 1984; children: Christopher Kyle, Kristina Nicole, Kimberly Michelle. Student, U. Md. (Munich campus), Germany, 1989. Adminstrv. asst. Nat. Wildlife Fedn., Vienna, Va., 1975-85; asst. editor U.S. Army Cmty. Svc., Munich, 1989; vol. Berlin Sch. Sys., 1990-93; adminstrv. asst. M.I.L., Bowie, Md., 1994; vol. Cochise County Sch. Sys. Sierra Vista, Ariz., 1995—. Contbr. poetry to Am. Poetry Ann., 1994, 96; poet: An Eternity of Beauty, 1998 (semi-finalist 1998), Pathways of Poetry, 1995. Recipient Poetic Achievement award The Amherst Soc., 1996. Mem. Taking Off Pounds Sensibly (weight recorder 1998). Democrat. Methodist. Avocations: crafts, painting, walking in the Ariz. mountains, writing poetry. Home: 1921 Chateau Ln Sierra Vista AZ 85635-4805

JOHNSON, DENNIS KARL, graphic designer; b. Louisville, Nov. 2, 1946; s. Karl Henry and Elizabeth Belle (Singelton) J.; children: Elise Rene, Tea Pirkka; m. Joan G. Black, July 26, 1997. BA, U. South Fla., 1968, MFA, 1972. Asst. prof. Washington U., St. Louis, 1972-75; prof. Lahden Art Sch., Lahti, Finland, 1975-76; sr. graphic designer Ferntiger Assocs., Oakland, Calif., 1978-96; owner Dennis Johnson Design, Oakland, 1996—; art dir. Children Now, Oakland, 1996—; adj. prof. Ohlone Coll., Fremont, Calif., 1996—, Hayward State U., Calif., 1997—. With USN, 1970-71. Grad. fellow U. South Fla., Tampa, 1969-70, 71-72; recipient Graphic award Oraphica Creativa, Jyvaskyla, Finland, 1975, Merit award Pub. Rels. Soc., No. Calif., 1994, 95. Home and Office: 5901 Leona St Oakland CA 94605-1222

JOHNSON, DORIS ANN, educational administrator; b. Marinette, Wis., Dec. 4, 1950; d. Jerome Louis and Jean Fern (Henry) La Plant; m. Daniel Lee Leonard, June 10, 1972 (div. June 1987); children: Jeremiah Daniel, Erica Leigh, Wesley Cyril; m. Paul Robert Johnson, Oct. 21, 1989; stepchildren: Kindra Michelle, Tanya Mari. Student, U. Wis., Oshkosh, 1969-70; BA in Edn., U. Wis., Eau Claire, 1973; MS in Edn., U. Wis., Whitewater, 1975; postgrad., Oreg. State U., 1988—. Reading specialist Brookfield (Wis.) Cen. High Sch., 1975-79; lead instr. N.E. Wis. Tech. Coll., Marinette, 1979-87; dir. adult basic edn. Umpqua C.C., Roseburg, Oreg., 1987-95, dir. developmental edn., 1995—; founding bd. dirs. Project Literacy, Umpqua Region, Roseburg, 1989-98; mem. adv. bd. Umpqua Cmty. Action Network, Roseburg, 1987-94; mem. State Dirs. of Adult Edn., Oreg., 1987—, vice chair, 1992-93, chair, 1993-94; mem. Adminstrn. Assn., Roseburg, 1989—, chair, 1993-94, 94-95; bd. dirs. Greater Douglas United Way, 1994—; adv. bd. Oreg. Litaracy Line, 1994-96. Co-author literacy module Communication Skills, 1988; author ednl. curriculum. Founding mem., bd. dirs. St. Joseph Maternity Home, Roseburg, 1987-90; mem. Literacy Theater, Roseburg, 1988-95; bd. dirs. Greater Douglas United Way, 1994—; mem. Project Leadership, Roseburg, 1988-89; mem. adv. bd. Oreg. Literacy Line, 1994-96; mem. Roseburg Valley Rep. Women, 1994-96. State legalizatoin assistance grantee Fed. Govt., 1988-93, homeless literacy grantee Fed. Govt., 1990-91, family literacy grantee Fed. Govt., 1991-93, intergenerational literacy grantee State of Oreg., 1991, literacy expansion grantee Fed. Govt., 1992-95, literacy outreach grantee Fed. Govt., 1992—, staff devel. spl. projects grantee Fed. Govt., 1992-93. Fellow TESOL, Inst. Inst. Leadership Devel., Am. Assn. Adult and Continuing Edn., Oreg. Assn. Disabled Students, Oreg. Developmental Edn. Studies, Oreg. Assn. for Children with Learning Disabilities, Western Coll. Reading and Learning Assn., Am. Assn. Women in Coll. and Jr. Coll., Roseburg Valley Rep. Women, Altrusa Internat. Club of Roseburg (chair literacy com. 1993-97), Rep. Women. Republican. Lutheran. Avocations: peer counseling, reading, hiking, cooking, running support groups. Home: 761 Garden Grove Dr Roseburg OR 97470-9670 Office: Umpqua CC PO Box 967 Roseburg OR 97470-0226

JOHNSON, E. ERIC, insurance executive; b. Chgo., Feb. 7, 1927; s. Edwin Eric and Xenia Alice (Waisanen) J.; m. Elizabeth Dewar Brass, Sept. 3, 1949; children: Christal L. Johnson Neal, Craig R. BA, Stanford U., 1948. Dir. group annuities Equitable Life Assurance Soc., San Francisco, 1950-54; div. mgr. Equitable Life Assurance Soc., L.A., 1955-59; v.p. Johnson & Higgins of Calif., L.A., 1960-67, dir., 1968-87, chmn., 1986-87; chmn. TBG Fin., L.A., 1988—; bd. dirs. Am. Mutual Fund; exec. v.p. Johnson & Higgins, N.Y.C., 1984-87. Bd. dirs. Sta. KCET, pub. TV, L.A., 1977-95, chmn., 1992-94; mem. adv. bd. UCLA Med. Ctr., 1983—, chmn. 1995-97; bd. dirs. Jonsson Comprehensive Cancer Ctr., UCLA, 1985—, Stanford U. Grad Sch. Bus., 1986-91; trustee Nuclear Decommissioning Trust, Rosemead, Calif., 1986-94. Mem. Calif. Club, L.A. Country Club, Vintage Club, Riviera Tennis Club, Links Club N.Y.C., Beach Club, So. Calif. Tennis Assn. (treas.). Avocations: golf, tennis, contemporary art, spectator sports. Office: TBG Fin 2029 Century Park E Los Angeles CA 90067-2901

JOHNSON, EARVIN (MAGIC JOHNSON), professional sports team executive, former professional basketball coach; b. Lansing, Mich., Aug. 14, 1959; s. Earvin and Christine Johnson; m. Cookie Kelly; 1 son, Earvin. Student, Mich. State U., 1976-79. Basketball player L.A. Lakers, 1979-91, 95-96; sportscaster NBC-TV, 1993-94; head coach L.A. Lakers, 1994, v.p., co-owner, 1994—; talk show host The Magic Hour, 1998—; gold medalist, U.S. Olympic Basketball Team, 1992. Author: (autobiography) Magic, 1983; (autobiography, with Roy S. Johnson) Magic's Touch, 1989; What You Can Do to Avoid AIDS, 1992; My Life, 1992. Recipient Citizenship award, 1992, All-Around Contbns. to Team Success award IBM, 1984; mem. NCAA Championship Team, 1979, NBA All-Star Team, 1980, 82-92, MVP NBA All-Star Game, 1990, 92, NBA Championship Team, 1980, 82, 85, 87, 88; named MVP NBA Playoffs, 1980, 82, 87, NBA, 1987, 89, 90, All-Star Game, 1990, 92, Player of the Year, Sporting News, 1987; recipient Schick Pivotal Player award, 1984; named to All-NBA first team, 1983-91, second team, 1982, NBA All-Rookie Team, 1980. Holder NBA playoff record most assists (2320); NBA Finals single-series record highest assists-per-game avg. (14), 1985, highest assists per game, rookie (8.7), 1980, NBA Finals single game record most points by rookie (42), 1980, NBA Finals single game record most assists one quarter (8), NBA single game record most assists (22). Office: LA Lakers PO Box 10 3900 W Manchester Blvd Inglewood CA 90306 also: Fox News Channel Concourse Level 1211 Avenue Of The Americas New York NY 10036-8701 also: FX Networks Inc 1440 S Sepulveda Blvd Los Angeles CA 90025-3458

JOHNSON, EDITH CURTICE, art education administrator; b. Auburn, N.Y., May 21, 1932; d. Charles Wellman and Michaleine Neilsen (Hansen) Witherell; m. Claude Lee Curtice, Dec. 7, 1958 (dec. Jan. 1968); children: Christian Lee, Alison Ann, Brian Wellman; m. Homer Martin Johnson, Apr. 7, 1977 (div. Jan. 1992). BS in Elem. Edn., SUNY, Potsdam, 1954; MS in Art Edn., Ind. U., 1970, EdD in Art Edn., 1976; MA in Counseling, Calif. State U., Fresno, 1984. Cert. tchr., C.C. tchr., supr., instr., counselor, Calif. [illegible] music tchr. Wrangell (Alaska) Inst., 1955-57, 2d grade music tchr. Tokota (Japan) AFB, 1957-58; visual arts tchr., libr. Tulsa Pub. Schs., 1958-59; 4th grade tchr. North Little Rock (Ark.) Schs., 1961-62; 5th grade tchr. Kirkwood (Mo.) Sch. Dist., 1963; visual arts specialist Clayton (Mo.) Sch. Dist., 1964-69; evaluation specialist CEMREL, Inc. Edn. Lab., St. Louis, 1972-73; supr. art K-12 University City (Mo.) Sch. Dist., 1973-74; profl. assoc. Homer Johnson Assocs., Monterey, Calif., 1977-78; instr. art edn. and phys. edn. Calif. State U., Fresno, 1980-82, 84, 85; curriculum writer art edn. Migrant Edn. PASS Program, Calif. County, Calif., 1985, 91; dir. edn. Fresno Met. Mus., 1986-88; media arts cons. Fresno County Office Edn., Fresno, 1989-90; adminstrv. dir. Calif. Consortium Visual Arts Edn., Fresno, 1988—; lectr. in art edn. Pacific Cultural Found., Taiwan, 1980; mem. edn. com. Fresno Art Mus., 1988-94, Fresno Met. Mus., 1993-94; visual arts cons. Improving Visual Arts Edn., Washington, 1988-91; dir. summer Insts. in Discipline Based Art Edn., Ctrl. Calif. Hawaii, 1994. Author aesthetics cards Not Just A Bunch of Grapes, 1990. Bd. dirs. Pacific Grove (Calif.) Art Ctr., 1974-77, Fresno (Calif.)-Madera Counties ARC, 1990-94. Recipient numerous awards from Calif. Art Edn. Assn., including Douc Langur award, 1981, Outstanding Mus. Educator, 1988, Ruth Jansen award, 1989, award of merit, 1990, 94, also Outstanding Svc. award Nat. Art Assn., 1994. Mem. Nat. Art Edn. Assn. (v.p. Pacific region 1991-93, contbr. column to Nat. Art Edn. News 1992-94), Calif. Art Edn. Assn. (bd. dirs. 1983-91, pres. 1987-89, contbr. column to newsletter 1987-89), Calif. Alliance for Arts Edn., Phi Delta Kappa. Avocations: music, piano, opera, ice skating, art, travel. Home: 3035 E Buckingham Way Fresno CA 93726-4229 Office: Calif Consortium Visual Arts 1111 Van Ness Ave Fresno CA 93721-2002

JOHNSON, ELISSA SARAH, speech pathologist, writer; b. Bklyn., Nov. 3, 1932; d. Frank Wilford and Doris Antonia (Licorish) Ward; m. Edward Paul Johnson, Dec. 31, 1957 (div. July 1962); 1 child, Paul. BA in Edn. Speech, Bklyn. Coll., 1954, MA in Speech Pathology, 1955; postgrad, Howard U., 1968-70. Speech tchr. therapist N.Y.C. Sch. Sys., Bklyn., 1954-67; speech pathologist Bklyn. Coll. Speech Clinic, 1955-57; instr. speech dept. Howard U., Washington, 1968-70; cons. Health Edn. Welfare, Washington, 1969-70; diagnostician speech pathology Tucson Unifed Sch. Dist., 1977-79, speech clinician spl. edn., 1979-86; writer poet Columbia, Md., 1970-77; freelance writer Tucson, 1986—; mem. Harlem Writer's Guild, Bklyn., 1962-68. Author: (book of poetry) Soul of Wit, 1978; contbr. poetry and articles to profl. publs. and mags. Pres. Bunche House, Bklyn. Coll., 1954; mem. steering com. Dem. Nat. Com., 1995—. Recipient Fire Prevention Theme medal Mayor's Office, 1942; scholar Bklyn. Coll., 1950-54. Mem. AAUW, NOW, NEA. Avocations: playing organ, movies, plays, painting. Home: 500 S Placita Quince Tucson AZ 85748-6834

JOHNSON, ELIZABETH HILL, foundation administrator; b. Ft. Wayne, Ind., Aug. 21, 1913; d. Harry W. and Lydia (Buechner) Hill; m. Samuel Spencer Johnson, Oct. 7, 1944 (dec. 1984); children: Elizabeth Katharine, Patricia Caroline. BS summa cum laude, Miami U., Oxford, Ohio, 1935; MA in English Lit., Wellesley Coll., 1937; postgrad., U. Chgo., 1936. Cert. tchr., Ohio. Pres., co-founder S.S. Johnson Found., Calif. Corp., San Francisco, 1947—. Mem. Oreg. State Bd. Higher Edn., Eugene, 1962-75, Oreg. State Edn. Coord. Com., Salem, 1975-82, Assn. Governing Bds., Washington, 1970-80, chairperson, 1975-76; mem. Oreg. State Tchr. Standards and Practices Commn., Salem, 1982-89; bd. dirs. Lewis and Clark Coll., Portland, Oreg., 1985—, Pacific U., Forest Grove, Oreg., 1972-75, 1982-89, 1993-97, Sunriver Prep. Sch., 1983-92, Oreg. Hist. Soc., Portland, 1985-97, Cen. Oreg. Dist. Hosp., Redmond, 1982—, Oreg. High Desert Mus., 1984-87, Bend, Oreg., Health Decisions, 1986-92, Ctrl. Oreg. Coun. Aging, 1991-97; Deschutes County Hist. Soc., 1996—; bd. dirs. Mus. at Warm Springs, Oreg., 1999—. Lt. USNR, 1943-46. Named Honoree March of Dimes White Rose Luncheon, 1984; recipient Aubrey Watzek award Lewis and Clark Coll., 1984, Cen. Oreg. 1st Citizen award, Abrams award Emanuel Hosp., 1982, Pres. award Marylhurst Coll., 1991, Thomas Jefferson award Oregon Historical Soc., 1993, Glenn L. Jackson medallion, 1998, Pres.'s award Redmond C. of C., 1996. Mem. Am. Assn. Higher Edn., Am. Assn. Jr. Colls., ASCD, Soroptimists (hon.), Francisca Club, Town Club, Univ. Club, Waverley Club, Beta Sigma Phi, Phi Beta Kappa, Phi Delta Kappa, Delta Gamma. Republican. Lutheran. Home: 415 SW Canyon Dr Redmond OR 97756-2028 Office: S S Johnson Found 441 SW Canyon Dr Redmond OR 97756-2028

JOHNSON, ELIZABETH MISNER, communications executive; b. Lewiston, Idaho, May 16, 1939; d. Gervase Arthur and Blenda N. (Westerlund) Misner; m. Dohn Robert Johnson, Oct. 13, 1962; children: Dohn Robert Jr., Kevin Arthur. BS in Acctg., U. Idaho, 1961. CPA, Calif., Wash. Audit staff Randall, Emery, Campbell & Parker (now Coopers & Lybrand), Spokane, Wash., 1961-62; audit staff, sr. Price Waterhouse, L.A., 1962-65; CPA L.A., 1966-73; CFO KLP, Inc. dba Call-America, Mesa, Ariz., 1995—; treas., pres., hon. life mem. Arts Coun. Calif. State U., Northridge, 1975—; internat. dir. alumnae devel. Alpha Gamma Delta (recipient unusually outstanding svc. award, 1993), U.S. and Can., 1988-98, com. mem. 2004 Internat. Com. (restructure internat. orgn.), 1994—; chmn. bd. trustees Alpha Gamma Delta Found., 1998—. Pres. Soroptimist Internat., Coeur d'Alene, Idaho, 1991-92, regional nominating com., 1993-94. Mem. Ariz. Soc. of CPAs. Home: 14839 S 47th Way Phoenix AZ 85044-6881

JOHNSON, FANNIE MIRIAM HARRIS, performing company executive; b. Birmingham, Ala., Sept. 11, 1938; d. Moses and Fannie (Williams) Harris; m. Edward L. Johnson, Feb. 13, 1960; children: Angela Fanita, Danielle Nicole. BA, Johnson C. Smith U., Charlotte, N.C., 1958; MA, UCLA, 1967. Cert. tchr., N.C., Ala., Calif. Tchr. Spanish Dunbar High Sch., Bessemer, Ala., 1959-61; tchr. English/drama Simi Valley (Calif.) Unified Sch. Dist., 1979-82; chief exec. officer Miriam & Co. Performing Arts, Moreno Valley, Calif., 1981—; cons. Boy's Club, San Fernando, Calif., 1975-76; cons., leader YWCA, Girl's Club, Moreno Valley, Calif., 1990—; tutor lit. program Riverside County Libr., Moreno Valley, 1990—. Writer, dir. plays: Family Reunion, 1981, Easterlude, 1982; writer, producer play: Worship Experience in the Arts, 1986; author: You Are Mine, 1970. Asst. sec. Fair Housing Coun., Simi Valley, Calif., 1972; pres. Community Devel., Pacoima, Calif., 1976-77; 2nd v.p. NAACP, Moreno Valley, Calif., 1994—. Recipient Outstanding Svc. award NAACP, San Fernando, 1975, Achievement award City Coun., L.A., 1976, Leadership award Ebony Women, Thousand Oaks, Calif., 1980. Mem. Nat. Pen Women, Writer's Guild Am., Optimist Interant., Delta Sigma Theta (sec. 1970-73, svc. award 1972). Democrat. Methodist. Avocations: music, theater, writing. Office: Miriam & Co Performing Arts PO Box 7751 Moreno Valley CA 92552-7751

JOHNSON, FRANK, retired state official, educator; b. Ogden, Utah, Mar. 12, 1928; s. Clarence Budd and Arline (Parry) J.; m. Maralyn Brewer, Aug. 15, 1950; children: Scott, Arline, Laurie, Kelly, Edward. BS, U. Utah, 1955; MS, U. Ill., 1958, PhD, 1960. Instr. U. N.D., Grand Forks, 1955-56; teaching asst. U. Ill., Urbana, 1956-59; rsch. asst. prof. U. Del., Newark, 1959-60; prof. U. Utah, Salt Lake City, 1960-93, assoc. dean, 1970-77; dir. divsn. pub. utilities State of Utah, Salt Lake City, 1989-95; cons. Gen. Foods, Sears, Magnavox, Albertsons, Zion Bank, Nat. Food Brokers Assn., others; owner, part-owner Old Post Office Bldg., Ogden, Utah, Seventeenth St. Storage. Legis. Utah House of Reps., Salt Lake City, 1982-88. Republican. Avocations: mountains, boating, travel, reading, public service. Home: 2373 Dayspring Ln Salt Lake City UT 84124-1887

JOHNSON, FRANK ARTHUR, minister; b. Salmon Arm, B.C., Can., Oct. 29, 1938; s. Frank Alba and Ada Florence (Astleford) J.; m. Muriel Yvonne Critchley, June 27, 1960; children: Richard Frank Alfred, Rosalie-Ann Blize. BS in Edn., Atlantic Union Coll., 1970. Ordained to ministry Seventh-day Adventists, 1978. Tchr., prin. Seventh-day Adventist Ch. Schs., various locations, Can., 1960-74; pastor Seventh-day Adventist Ch., Bonavista, Nfld., Can., 1969-73; ship missionary, B.C. Coast Seventh-day Adventist Ch., 1974-75; pastor, evangelist Seventh-day Adventist Ch., B.C., Alta., Can., 1975-84, Edson, Alta., 1982-85, Edmonton, Alta., 1985—; operator, announcer Voice of Adventist Radio, St. John's, Nfld., 1961-63; dir., speaker TV program Profiles of Faith, Revelstoke, B.C., 1980-82; speaker radio program Sounds of Praise, Edson, 1984-85; contract chaplain [illegible] 74; bd. dirs. Sherwood Park (Alta.) Nursing Home, Coralwood Jr. Acad., Edmonton, 1985—. Mem. Ministerial Assn. Home: 13 Hillcrest Dr, Edmonton, AB Canada T6P 1J1 Office: Seventh day Adventist Ch, 2018 [illegible]

JOHNSON, GARY EARL, governor; b. Minot, N.D., Jan. 1, 1953; s. Earl W. and Lorraine B. (Bostow) J.; m. Dee Simms, Nov. 27, 1976; children: Seah, Erik. BA in Polit. Sch., U. N.Mex., 1975. Pres., CEO Big J Enterprises, Albuquerque, 1976—; gov. State of N.Mex., 1995-98, 98—. Bd. dirs. Entrepreneurship Studies at U. N.Mex., 1993-95. Named to list of Big 50 Remodelers in the USA, 1987; named Entrepreneur of Yr., 1995. Mem. LWV, C. of C. Albuquerque (bd. dirs. 1993-95). Republican. Lutheran. Avocations: rock-climbing, mountain climbing, skiing, pilot, triathlete. Office: Office of Gov Rm 400 State Capitol Santa Fe NM 87503

JOHNSON, GARY KENT, management education company executive; b. Provo, Utah, Apr. 16, 1936; s. Clyde LeRoy and Ruth Laie (Taylor) J.; m. Mary Joyce Crowther, Aug. 26, 1955; children: Mary Ann Johnson Harvey, Gary Kent, Brent James, Jeremy Clyde. Student Brigham Young U., 1954-55, U. Utah, 1955-58, 60-61, U. Calif.-Berkeley, 1962. Sales rep. Roche Labs., Salt Lake City, 1958-61, sales trainer, Denver, 1962, sales trainer, Oakland, Calif., 1962, div. mgr., Seattle, 1962-69; sec.-treas. Western Mgmt. Inst., Seattle, 1969-71; pres. WMI Corp., Bellevue, Wash., 1971-96, pres. GKJ Corp., 1996—, Provisor Corp., 1983-86; speaker, cons. various nat. orgns. Bd. dirs. Big Bros.; del. King County Republican Com. Served with U.S. N.G., 1953-61. Walgreen scholar, 1955-58; Bristol scholar, 1958. Mem. Am. Soc. Tng. and Devel., Internat. Platform Assn., Bellevue Athletic Club. Phi Sigma Epsilon. Mem. LDS Ch. Author: Select the Best, 1976; Antitrust Untangled, 1977; The Utilities Management Series, 1979; Performance Appraisal, A Program for Improving Productivity, 1981, QSE Quality Service Everytime, 1990, Continuous Performance Improvement, 1993. Office: GKJ Corp 1416 W Lake Sammamish Pkwy SE Bellevue WA 98008-5218

JOHNSON, GLENN ALLISTER, communications educator, announcer; b. Turlock, Calif., Jan. 10, 1944; s. Joseph Laurentius and Edithe Evelyn Johnson; m. Kathryn Joyce Willems, June 24, 1967; children: Karen Michelle (dec.), Eric Daniel. BA, Calif. State U., 1966; MS, UCLA, 1967; PhD, U. Iowa, 1970. FCC lic. 1st class. Announcer/reporter KGMS Radio, Sacramento, 1964-65; reporter/news announcer KFBK Radio, Sacramento, 1965-66; reporter/editor City News Svc., L.A., 1966-67; asst. news dir. WSUI/KSUI, U. Iowa, Iowa City, 1967-70; reporter/ops. mgr., news dir. KGMS Radio, Sacramento, 1970-75; sta. mgr. KGMS-KSFM Radio Stas., Sacramento, 1975-79; prof. comm. Wash. State U., Pullman, 1979—; mem. pres.'s adv. bd. Sacramento City Coll., 1979; pub. address announcer Wash. State U., 1980—; mem. adv. bd. Daily News Pullman/Moscow (Idaho), 1991-92; commr. Pullman Meml. Hosp., Pub. Hosp. Dist., 1998—. Columnist (weekly) Daily News Pullman/Moscow, 1983-87; narrator (TV) Growing Crisis, 1986 (UPI 1st place award 1987); prodr./narrator (video program) for Wash. law enforcement on crime reporting, 1992, (video program) Shifting the Balance, 1993. Bd. commrs. Pullman Meml. Hosp., pub. hosp. dist., 1998—. Inducted in to Silver Cir., Nat. Acad. TV Arts and Scis., 1993; Glenn A. Johnson endowment created by students at Wash. State U., 1993—. Mem. Radio-TV News Dirs. Assn., Pullman C. of C. (bd. dirs. 1997—, Mem. of Yr. 1997), Kiwanis Club Pullman. Avocations: motivational/inspirational speaking, gardening, sports, cooking. Home: 225 SW Kimball Ct Pullman WA 99163-2176 Office: Wash State Univ Sch Comm Murrow Ctr # 205 Pullman WA 99164-2520

JOHNSON, GOODYEAR See O'CONNOR, KARL WILLIAM

JOHNSON, GORDON GILBERT, religion educator, minister; b. St. Paul, Nov. 19, 1919; s. Gilbert Oliver and Myrtle Isabel (Bjorklund) J.; m. Alta Fern Borden, May 21, 1945; children: Gregg A., Gayle E. Johnson Boyd. Cert., Moody Bible Inst., 1941; AA, Bethel Coll., St. Paul, 1943; student, Harvard U., 1944, 45; BA, U. Minn., 1945; BD, Bethel Theol. Sem., 1946; ThM, Princeton Theol. Sem., 1950; ThD, No. Bapt. Theol. Sem., 1960. Ordained to ministry Bapt. Gen. Conf., 1946. Pastor 1st Bapt. Ch., Milltown, Wis., 1946-48, Bethel Bapt. Ch., Montclaire, N.J., 1948-51, Central Ave. Bapt. Ch., Chgo., 1951-59; v.p., dean, prof. preaching Bethel Theol. Sem., St. Paul, 1959-84; interim sr. pastor Trinity Bapt. Ch., St. Paul, 1972-73; assoc. pastor, intrim sr. pastor College Ave. Bapt. Ch., San Diego, 1984-89; interim dean Bethel Sem. West, San Diego, 1990-91; interim sr. pastor Clairemont Emmanuel Bapt. Ch., San Diego, 1990-91, First Bapt. Ch., Lakewood, Long Beach, Calif., 1991-92, New Life Ch., Woodbury, Minn., 1993, Elim Bapt. Ch., Mpls., 1995-96; chmn. bd. publ. Bapt. Gen. Conf., Chgo., 1948-53, pres. bd. trustees, 1953-55, chmn. world mission bd., 1955-60, moderator, 1957-58, 85-86; mem. gen. coun. Bapt. World Alliance, Washington, 1965-85; lectr. in field; del. to World Congress on Evangelism, Berlin, 1965; educator for elderhostels for Bethel Coll., Minn., 1992-98; vis. prof. Regent Coll., Vancouver, 1976; pres. Minn. Sem. Consortium, 1979-81. Author: My Church; contbr. articles to profl. jours. With USN, 1944-45. Rsch. scholar Yale U. Div. Sch., 1969. Mem. Acad. Homileticians, Religious Speech Assn.

JOHNSON, GORDON JAMES, artistic director, conductor; b. St. Paul, 1949. BS, Bemidji State U., 1971; MS, Northwestern U., 1977; D in Mus. Arts, U. Oreg.; studied with Leonard Bernstein, Erich Leinsdorf, Herbert Blomstedt. Music dir., condr. Great Falls (Mont.) Symphony Assn., 1981—, Glacier Orch. and Chorale, Mont., 1982-97; artistic dir., condr. Flathead Music Festival, Mont., 1987-96; music dir., condr. Mesa (Ariz.) Symphony Orch., 1997—; grad. teaching fellow U. Oreg., 1979-81; artist in residence Condr's Guild Inst., W.Va. U., condr. orch., 1984; condr. Spokane Symphony at The Festival at Sandpoint; guest condr. St. Paul Chamber Orch., 1971, Spokane Symphony, 1983, 86, Dubuque (Iowa) Symphony, 1985, Charlotte (N.C.) Symphony, 1985, Lethbridge (Alberta, Can.) Symphony, 1986, Cheyenne (Wyo.) Symphony, 1986, West Shore (Mich.) Symphony, 1988, Bozeman (Mont.) Symphony, 1989, Kumamoto Symphony (Kyshu, Japan), 1991, Kankakee (Ill.) Symphony, 1993, Toulon (France) Symphonies, 1994, Guam Symphony, 1995, Tokyo Lumiere Orch., 1995, Fort Collins (Colo.) Symphony, 1995, Wilmslow (Eng.) Symphony Orch., 1997; guest ballet condr. Alberta Ballet, 1986, Oakland (Calif.) Ballet, 1988, Eugene (Oreg.) Ballet, 1993, David Taylor Ballet, Colo., 1994, St. Petersburg (Russia) Ballet, 1995, Western Ballet Theater, Oreg., 1996; spkr. regional conf. Am. Symphony Orch. League, 1987, nat. conf., 1988; mem. adj. faculty U. Great Falls, 1981—, U. Mont., 1996—; lectr. U. Guam, 1995; condr. seminars L.A. Philharmonic Inst., 1983, Condr.'s Guild Inst., 1984, Festival at Sandpoint, Condr.'s Program, 1986, Am. Symphony Orch. League's Am. Condr.'s Program, N.Y. Philharmonic, 1987, Condr.'s Guild "Bruckner Seminar", Chgo. Symphony Orch., 1989, Carnegie Hall Tng. Program for Condrs., Cleve. Orch., 1993. Philharmonic Condr.'s scholar St. Paul Chamber Orch., 1971; L.A. Philharmonic Inst. fellow, 1983; named to Highland Park High Sch. Hall of Fame, St. Paul, 1997. Mem. ASCAP. Office: Great Falls Symphony Assn PO Box 1078 Great Falls MT 59403-1078

JOHNSON, GWENAVERE ANELISA, artist; b. Newark, S.D., Oct. 16, 1909; d. Arthur E. and Susie Ellen (King) Nelson; m. John Wendell Johnson, Dec. 17, 1937; 1 child, John Forrest. Student, Mpsl. Sch. Art, 1930; BA, U. Minn., 1937; MA, San Jose State U., 1957. Cert. gen. elem., secondary, art tchr., Calif. Art tchr., supr. Austin (Minn.) Schs., 1937-38; art tchr. Hillbrook Sch., Los Gatos, Calif., 1947-52; art tchr., supr. Santa Clara (Calif.) Pub. Schs., 1952-55; art tchr., dept. chmn. San Jose (Calif.) Unified Schs., 1955-75; owner Tree Tops studio, San Jose, 1975—. Juried shows: Los Gatos Art Assn., 1976-79, 85-88, Artist of Yr., 1988 (1st and 2d awards), 83, 84 (Best of Show awards), Treeside gallery, 1991, Los Gatos, 1980, 81 (1st awards); Livermore Art Assn., 1977 (2d award), Los Gatos Art Mus., 1981 (1st award), 82 (2d award), 91 (best of show award), Rosicrucean Mus., 1983, Centre d'Art Contemporian, Paris, 1983; creator Overfelt portrait Alexian Bros. Hosp., San Jose, Calif., 1977; exhibited in group shows ann. Garden Art Show, 1981-95, Triton Art Mus., 1983-95. Named People's Choice, Triton Art Mus., 1975; recipient Golden Centaur award Acad. Italia, 1982, Golden Album of prize winning Artists, 1984, Golden Flame award Academia Italia, 1986, others. Mem. San Jose Art League, Santa Clara Art Assn., Los Gatos Art Assn. (Artist of Yr. 1988, 2d, 3d awards), Santa Clara [illegible] achiever's exhbn. 1992, 3 First awards in merit achiever's exhbn. 1993), Soc. Western Artists, Nat. League Am. Penwomen (corr. sec., Merit Achiever award), Los gatos Art Assn., Santa Clara Art Assn., San Jose Art League. [illegible]

JOHNSON, HEDY BONDER, real estate investor; b. Pressig, Germany, Jan. 12, 1945; came to U.S., 1949; d. Michal and Zofia (Czak) Bonder; m. Don L. Johnson, Feb. 28, 1970; children: Dustin Lewis, Geneva Zofia. BS, Fitchburg State Coll., 1966. RN, Calif.; cert. pub. health nurse, Calif. Staff nurse Mt. Auburn Hosp., Cambridge, Mass., 1966-67, Leahi Hosp., Honolulu, 1967-68, Scripps Meml. Hosp., La Jolla, Calif., 1968-69; pub. health nurse San Diego Pub. Health Dept., 1970-73; pvt. investor real estate San Diego County, 1978—. Contbr. poems to various anthologies. Mem. Magee Pk. Poets, Calif. Fedn. Chaparral Poets, New Horizons Poetry Club. Republican. Roman Catholic. Avocations: travel, reading, gardening. Home: PO Box 786 Del Mar CA 92014-0786

JOHNSON, HEIDI SMITH, science educator; b. Mpls., June 1, 1946; d. Russell Ward and Eva Ninette (Holmquist) Smith; m. Alan C. Sweeney, Dec. 21, 1968 (div. 1977); m. Robert Allen Johnson, July 17, 1981. BA, U. Calif., Riverside, 1969; MA, No. Ariz. U., 1992. Park ranger U.S. Nat. Parks Svc., Pinnacles Nat. Monument, 1972-73; aide Petrified Forest Mus. Assn., Ariz., 1973-75; dispatcher police dept. U. Ariz., Tucson, 1975-76; communications operator II dept. ops. City of Tucson, 1976-78; dispatcher Tucson Police Dept., 1978-82, communications supr., 1982-85, communications coord., 1985; substitute tchr. Bisbee (Ariz.) Pub. Schs., 1985-91; instr. English Cochise Community Coll., Douglas, Ariz., 1990-92; tchr. English/creative writing Bisbee H.S., 1992-93; tchr. earth sci. and hist. geology Lowell Mid. Sch., Bisbee, 1993—; GEd tchr. Cochise County Jail, 1988-89; owner Johnson's Antiques and Books, Bisbee, 1990—. Trustee Bisbee Coun. on Arts and Humanities, 1986-88; pres. Cooper Queen Libr. Bd., Bisbee, 1988-91; book sales chmn. Shattuck Libr., Bisbee Mining Mus., 1987-92; founder Riverside (Calif.) chpt. Zero Population Growth, 1968. Mem. Mid-Am. Paleontol. Soc., Paleontol. Soc., So. Calif. Paleontol. Soc., Sierra Club (mem. nat. wilderness study com. 1969-72, wilderness survey leader 1969-72), Paleontol. Soc., Nat. Ctr. Sci. Edn., The Nature Conservancy. Roman Catholic. Avocations: paleontology, flower gardening, book collecting. Home: PO Box 1221 Bisbee AZ 85603-2221

JOHNSON, HIROKO, art history educator; b. Osaka, Japan. Postgrad., U. Tokyo, 1987-89, 91-93; PhD, U So. Calif., 1994. Adj. prof. Occidental Coll., L.A., 1990-95, Pepperdine U., Malibu, Calif., 1989-97, Calif. Poly. U., Pomona, 1996—, Calif. State U., Long Beach, 1994—. Contbr. articles to profl. jours. Recipient Kajima Art Found. award, 1998; Japan Soc for Promotion of Scis. fellow, 1997-98. Mem. Coll. Art Assn., Assn. for Asian Study, Japan Art History Soc., Asiatic Soc. Japan. Avocation: painting.

JOHNSON, JAMES GIBSON, JR., community recycling specialist; b. Flagstaff, Ariz., Feb. 26, 1938; s. James Gibson and Inga Anette J.; m. Faye Bodian, Aug. 23, 1973; children: Jill Johnson, Ginger Johnson, Jonathan Johnson. BA, U. Colo., 1960. Editor, pub. Town and Country Rev., Boulder, Colo., 1963-78; owner James G. Johnson and Assocs., Boulder, Colo., 1978-87; exec. dir. Eco Cycle Recycling, Boulder, Colo., 1987-89; community recycling specialist Office of Energy Conservation, State of Colo., Denver, 1989-97; recycling cons. James G. Johnson Assoc., Boulder, 1997—; Colo. mgr. Southwestern Pub. Recycling Assn., Tuscon, 1999—. Mem. Open Space Bd. Trustees, Boulder, 1980-85, chmn., 1984-85; mem. Boulder County Pks. and Open Space Bd., 1985-93; chmn., 1987-89; mem. Boulder County Planning Commn., 1993—. Democrat. Avocations: running, skiing. Home: 630 Northstar Ct Boulder CO 80304-1021 Office: 630 Northstar Ct Denver CO 80304

JOHNSON, JAMES R. II, multimedia developer; b. San Diego, Calif., Aug. 27, 1961; s. James R. and Nancy J. J.; 1 child, Niles Stuart Johnson. AS, Chaffey Coll., Rancho Cucamonga, Calif., 1982. Sr. vet. tech. Valley Vet. Med. Ctrs., Rancho Cucamonga, 1984-87; instrnl. asst. IV Chaffey Coll., Rancho Cucamonga, 1987-90; cons., owner 2d Story, Inc., San Diego, Calif., 1990-95; dir. prodn. High Text Interactive, San Diego, 1995-. Prodr. (multimedia title) Petware, 1993; developer, programmer: (multimedia title) Digital Video Review, 1994, Rain: A Multimedia Adventure, 1994 (Invision Gold award 1995); sr. developer, prodr.: (multimedia title) Algebra I, 1996. Avocations: camping, fishing, 3-D rendering, digital video. Address: Hightext 10717 Camino Ruiz Ste 216 San Diego CA 92126-2364

JOHNSON, JANE OLIVER, artist; b. Fresno, Calif., Jan. 3, 1929; d. Evan Donaca Oliver and Adaline Dorinda (Nelson) Edwards; m. Vernon Reddinger Allen, Aug. 11, 1946 (div. 1963); children: Lue Elizabeth, Mark Laroy, Stuart Vernon; m. Loren Theodore Johnson, Mar. 8, 1981. Student, Fresno City Coll., 1952-55, Fresno State, 1955-60, Hayward State Coll., 1965-70. Tech. artist Hughes, Northrup, Lockheed, Magnavox, L.A., 1972-84; artist Neighborhood Gallery, L.A., 1976-80. Works exhibited at Beyond Baroque, San Jose Mission, Tribal Treas., Calico Gallery. Mem. state ctrl. com. Calif. Dem. Party, 1993—; active 34th Assembly Dist. Exec. Bd., 1993—, sec. 1997; elected San Bernardino County Dem. Ctrl. Com., 1994—, re-elected, 1996; mem. First Congl. Ch. L.A., 1973—. Mem. ACLU, High Desert Cultural Arts, So. Poverty Law Ctr., Mus. of Tolerance, L.A. County Mus. Art, Stockford Dem. Club (mem. environ. women's caucus 1993—, pres. 1995—). Avocations: writing philosophy, hiking. Home: PO Box 1323 Lucerne Valley CA 92356-1323

JOHNSON, JEROME JOHN, JR. (JAY JOHNSON), producer, photographer; b. New Orleans, Oct. 31, 1952; s. Jerome John and Alveretta Elise (Hewitt) J.; m. Pamela Louise Backstrom, Nov. 7, 1993. B of Gen. Studies, U. Nebr., 1976; postgrad., U. Mo., 1978. Reporter, photographer KMTV, Omaha, 1975-77; reporter, photographer, producer KOMU-TV, Columbia, Mo., 1977-78; documentary producer, photographer Telepress Internat. News Agy., N.Y.C., 1979-80; reporter, photographer KHQ-TV, Spokane, 1980-82; capitol bur. chief KIRO-TV, Seattle, 1991-96, state capitol producer, photographer, 1982—. Prin. photographer (documentary) From Summit to Sea: Nisqually River, 1991 (Emmy award 1991); photographer, producer (documentary) Son of Heaven: Art of Imperial China, 1987 (Emmy award 1987), (news series) Rwandan Civil War Refugees, 1995. Bd. dirs. Regional Water Quality Adv. Bd., Olympia, Wash., 1986; broadcst liaison Inaugural Activities Com., Olympia, 1979. Sgt. USAF, 1972-76. Mem. Nat. Press Photographers Assn., Capitol Corr. Assn (v.p. 1991—), Internat. Alliance Theatrical Stage Employers, Internat. Brotherhood Elec. Workers. Avocations: sailing, backpacking. Home: 4609 31st Ave SE Lacey WA 98503-3632 Office: KIRO-TV Olympia Bur PO Box 6 Olympia WA 98507-0006

JOHNSON, JEROME LINNÉ, cardiologist; b. Rockford, Ill., June 19, 1929; s. Thomas Arthur and Myrtle Elizabeth (Swanson) J.; m. Molly Ann Rideout, June 27, 1953; children: Susan Johnson Nowels, William Rideout. BA, U. Chgo., 1951; BS, Northwestern U., 1952, MD, 1955. Diplomate Nat. Bd. Med. Examiners. Intern U. Chgo. Clinics, 1955-56; resident Northwestern U., Chgo., 1958-61; chief resident Chgo. Wesley Meml. Hosp., 1960-61; mem., v.p. Hauch Med. Clinic, Pomona, Calif., 1961-88; pvt. practice cardiology and internal medicine Pomona, 1988—; clin. assoc. prof. medicine, U. So. Calif., L.A., 1961—; mem. staff Pomona Valley Hosp. Med. Ctr., chmn. coronary care com. 1967-77; mem. staff L.A. County Hosp. Citizen ambassador, People to People; mem. Town Hall of Calif., L.A. World Affairs Coun. Lt. USNR, 1956-58; bd. dirs. Claremont chpt. ARC, 1993—; bd. dirs., health com. Mt. San Antonio Gardens Retirement Home, 1993—. Fellow Am. Coll. Cardiology, Am. Geriatrics Soc., Royal Soc. Health; mem. Galileo Soc., Am. Heart Assn. (bd. dirs. L.A. County div. 1967-84, San Gabriel div. 1963-89), Am. Soc. Internal Medicine, Inland Soc. Internal Medicine, Pomona Host Lions. Avocations: photography, swimming, bicycling, medical and surgical antiques, travel. Home: 648 Delaware Dr Claremont CA 91711-3457

JOHNSON, JOHN HENRY, film director, producer, photographer, educator; b. Pueblo, Colo., Oct. 31, 1951; s. William Admiral "Buddy" and Matilda Marie (Trabucco) J.; m. Nadine Sue Milosavich, Aug. 24, 1974; children: Rebecca Sue, Thomas William. Student, U. So. Colo., 1970-73; Assoc. in Fine Arts, Rochester Inst. Tech., 1973, BFA summa cum laude, 1975; MFA, Cranbook Acad. Art, 1977. Photographer Colo. Hwy. Dept., Eisenhower Tunnel, 1971; cinematographer, prodn. asst., writer various prodn. cos., Colo., 1979-80; prodn. asst. Metro-Goldwyn-Mayer, Canon City, Colo., 1983; studio cameraman, flr. dir. Sta. KOAA-TV, Pueblo, 1970, 97—; dir., cinematographer, editor Humanities div. film series, U. So. Colo., Pueblo, 1971-72; photographer Pueblo Chieftain & Star Journal, 1975; pres., founder Tamarack Prodns., Inc., Pueblo, 1982—; grad. teaching asst. Cranbrook Acad. Art, Bloomfield Hills, Mich., 1977; instr. photography Arapahoe Community Coll., Littleton, Colo., 1978, Community Coll. Denver, 1979; instr. filmmaking and photography Colo. Inst. Art, Denver, 1978-79, U. So. Colo., 1980-81; instr. filmmaking Learning Tree U., Chatsworth, Calif., 1992; instr. photography, filmmaking and screen writing Pueblo C.C., 1994—. Dir., cinematographer, co-writer, co-editor (documentary film) Damon Runyon's Pueblo, 1981 (Golden Eagle award Council on Internat. Nontheatrical Events 1983); dir., writer, producer, cinematographer, editor: (documentary film) Zebulon Pike & The Blue Mountain, 1984 (Golden Eagle award Council on Internat. Nontheatrical Events 1985, Commendation cert. Am. Assn. for State and Local History 1986); dir., writer, producer, cinematographer, editor (feature film) Blue Lights, 1988 (invited feature at the Internat. Sci. Fiction and Fantasy Film Festival, Rome, 1990); photographer represented in books including Visual Concepts for Photographers, 1980, Photographic Materials & Processes, 1986, View Camera Technique, 5th edit., 1986, 6th edit., 1993, 7th edit., 1998, Orlin Helgoe-Shaman of the Prairie, 1986, Southwest Fine Arts Biennial Catalogue, 1976; contbg. editor: Focal Encyclopedia of Photography, 3d edit., 1993. Grantee Thatcher Found., 1973-77, Profl. Photographers Am., 1974, Cranbrook/Ford Found., 1977, NEH, 1979, Colo. Endowment for the Humanities, 1979, U. So. Colo., 1979. Avocations: skiing, music, genealogy, movies.

JOHNSON, JOHN PHILIP, geneticist, researcher; b. Wabash, Ind., June 6, 1949; s. Melvin Leroy and Cleo Pauline (Aldrich) J.; m. Sheryl Kay Kennedy, June 3, 1978; children: Craig Eric, Lindsay Sara. BS, U. Mich., 1971, MD, 1975. Diplomate Am. Bd. Pediatrics, Am. Bd. Med. Genetics. Intern, 2d-yr. resident Children's Hosp. Los Angeles, 1975-77; 3d yr. resident in pediatrics U. Utah, Salt Lake City, 1977-78, fellow in genetics, 1980-82, asst. prof. pediatrics, 1982-85; pediatrician Family Health Program, Salt Lake City, 1978-80; assoc. dir. med. genetics, attending/active staff physician Children's Hosp. Oakland, Calif., 1985-92; dir. med. genetics, attending/active staff physician Children's Hosp., Oakland, 1992-94; dir. med. genetics Shodair Children's Hosp., Helena, Mont., 1994—, active mem. staff, 1995—; clinic physician Utah State Tng. Sch., American Fork, 1982-85; attending and staff physician Primary Children's Med. Ctr., Salt Lake City, 1978-80. Assoc. editor Am. Jour. Med. Genetics, 1995-97; contbr. articles to med. jours. Recipient William J. Branstrom award U. Mich., 1967. Fellow Am. Acad. Pediatrics; mem. Am. Soc. Human Genetics, Soc. for Pediatric Rsch., Alpha Omega Alpha. Avocations: skiing, hiking, camping, piano, jazz. Home: 2604 Gold Rush Ave Helena MT 59601-5625 Office: Shodair Children's Hosp PO Box 5539 Helena MT 59604-5539

JOHNSON, JOHN RICHARD, health facility administrator, consultant; b. Edmonton, Alta., Can., July 6, 1942; came to U.S., 1988; s. John Albert and Agnes Kathleen (Tomlinson) J.; m. Carell Brown, Nov. 25, 1967; children: Richard, Lisa. BS, U. B.C., Vancouver, Can., 1967, MS, 1970, PhD, 1973. Rsch. officer Chalk River (Ont.) Nuc. Lab., 1973-81, mgr., 1981-88; mgr. Health Physics Dept./Pacific Northwest Lab., Richland, Wash., 1988-93; chief scientist Health Physics Dept./Pacific Northwest Lab., Richland, 1993-96, scientist emeritus, 1996—; pres. Internal Dosimetry Instruments and Svcs., Richland, 1996—; adj. prof. McMaster U., 1986-90, Wash. State U., Richland, 1990—. Contbr. over 100 articles to profl. jours. Mem. Nat. Coun. on Radiation Protection (chair sci. com. 1957-75), Canadian Radiation Protection Assn. (pres. 1984-85, Disting. Achievement award 1989), Internat. Radiation Protection Assn. (councillor 1984-88, Outstanding Svc. award 1992), Health Physics Soc. (Disting. Scientific Achievement award 1997). Home: 2629 Harris Ave Richland WA 99352-1639 Office: Pacific NW Nat Lab PO Box 999 MS K3 53 Richland WA 99352 0999

JOHNSON, JON L., advertising executive. Chmn., CEO, dir. Publicis, Salt Lake City. Office: Publicis 110 Social Hall Ave Salt Lake City UT 84111-1504*

JOHNSON, KATHARINE DECKER, artist; b. Piqua, Ohio, Apr. 24, 1951; d. Richard Patrick and Joan Decker; m. Gary William Johnson, May 21, 1994. BA, Xavier U., 1974; masters cert. scientific illustration, U. Calif., Santa Cruz, 1996. Graphic artist G&S Typesetters, Austin, 1985-86; tech. illustrator Tektronix, Inc., Beaverton, Oreg., 1987-90; illustrator Holt, Reinhart & Winston, Austin, 1990-91; tech. illustrator Nat. Instruments Corp., Austin, 1991-94; artist, illustrator EE Design, Livermore, Calif., 1994—; scientific illustrator Livermore Area Recreation and Park Dist., 1995—. Illustrator LabView Graphical Programming, 1994, 2d edit., 1997, LabView Power Programming, 1998, Modern Physics, 1991, World Geography Today, 1991, Biology 2000, 1991; exhibited in group shows Buffalo Mus. of Sci., 1997, Chgo. Bot. Garden, 1997, Mus. of Art and History, 1997, Smithsonian Instn., 1996, No. Ariz. U., 1995, Washington State Conv. Ctr., 1993, 94, 95, 96. Mem. Guild of Nat. Sci. Illustrators, Am. Soc. of Botanical Artists. Office: EE Design 4086 Compton Ct Livermore CA 94550-3453

JOHNSON, KENNETH F., lawyer; b. Ft. Bragg, Calif., June 10, 1938; s. Frank W. and Gertrude Johnson; m. Jane Perry Drennan, June 11, 1961; children: Erik Allan, Mark. BSCE, U. Calif., Berkeley, 1962; JD, U. Calif., Hastings, 1969. Bar: Calif. 1970. V.p., shareholder Crosby, Heafey, Roach & May, Oakland, Calif., 1969—. Note and comment editor: Hastings Law Jour., 1968-69. With USNR, 1962-66. Scholar U. Calif. Hastings, 1967-68, 68-69. Mem. ABA, ATLA, Calif. Bar Assn., Alameda County Bar Assn., Contra Costa County Bar Assn., Bar Assn. San Francisco, Calif. Bus. Trial Lawyers Assn., Assn. Def. Counsel, Order of Coif. Office: Crosby Heafey Roach & May 1999 Harrison St Fl 26 Oakland CA 94612-3572*

JOHNSON, KEVIN MAURICE, professional basketball player; b. Sacramento, Mar. 4, 1966. Student, U. Calif., 1987. Basketball player Cleveland Cavaliers, 1987-88, Phoenix Suns, 1988—. Named to Dream Team II, 1994, NBA Most Improved Player, 1989, All-NBA Second Team, 1989-91, 94, All-NBA Third Team, 1992. Office: care Phoenix Suns 201 E Jefferson St Phoenix AZ 85004-2412*

JOHNSON, KIRSTEN DENISE, elementary education educator; b. L.A., Sept. 21, 1968; d. Daniel Webster Johnson and Marinella Venesia (Ishem) Johnson Miller; 1 child, Khari Malik Manning-Johnson. BBA in Ins., Howard U., 1990; student, Southwestern Sch. Law, L.A., 1991-92, Calif. State U., Dominguez Hills, 1994-97. Asst. Ctr. for Ins. Edn. Howard U., Washington, 1988-89; intern Cigna Ins. Co., L.A., 1989; agt. asst. McLaughlin Co., Washington, 1989-90; legal sec. Harris & Baird, L.A., 1990-92; legal asst. Hamrick & Garrotto, L.A., 1992-94; tchr. 5th grade L.A. Unified Sch. Dist., 1993—; intern Travelers Cos., 1987—; free-lance writer Calif. Mus. Sci., L.A., 1994—; workshop presenter in field. Participant UCLA/CSP Sci. Project; tutor Delinquent Teenage Group Home Residents, 1998—. Nat. Dean;s List, 1987, 88, All Am. scholar, 1989, John Schumacher scholar, 1991, Martin Luther King Jr. scholar, 1996. Mem. UTLA, CTA, Internat. Soc. Poets. Democrat. Avocations: reading, traveling, movies, weight lifting.

JOHNSON, LAWRENCE M., banker; b. 1940. Student, U. Hawaii. With Bank of Hawaii, Honolulu, 1963—, exec. v.p., 1980-84, vice chmn., 1984-89, pres., 1989—, now chmn. bd., CEO; pres. Pacific Century Fin. Corp. Office: Bancorp Hawaii Inc 130 Merchant St PO Box 2900 Honolulu HI 96846-0001 Office: Pacific Century Fin Corp Financial Plz of the Pacific 130 Merchant St Honolulu HI 96813-4450

JOHNSON, LEAYN HUTCHINSON, nursing educator, mental health nurse; b. Elizabeth, Pa., June 3, 1936; d. Ernest Eba and Edna (Caley) Hutchinson; m. Donald E. Johnson, Mar. 10, 1959; children: Donna Lynn, Donald E. Diploma, McKeesport Hosp. Sch. Nursing, 1957; BSN cum laude, Wright State U., 1975; MS, Ohio State U., 1977; PhD in Psychology, U.S. Internat. U., 1987. RN, Calif. From lectr. to asst. prof. U. Hawaii, Honolulu; prin. Ourself Counseling Ctr., Newport Beach, Calif.; asst. prof. Calif. State U., Long Beach; assoc. prof. Mem. ANA, Calif. Nurses Assn., Sigma Theta Tau. Home: 16932 Edgewater Ln Huntington Beach CA 92649-4206 Office: 1400 Quail St Ste 235 Newport Beach CA 92660-2714

JOHNSON, LEONIDAS ALEXANDER, optometrist, minister; b. Chgo., Jan. 16, 1959; s. Leon and Dolores J.; m. Crystal Dwaun Ellington, June 23, 1990. BA in Biology, Ill. Wesleyan U., 1981; BS in Visual Sci., So. Calif. Coll. of Optometry, Fullerton, 1983, OD, 1985; student, Grace Theol. Sem., Long Beach, Calif., 1986-89; MA in Practical Theology, Biola U., La Mirada, Calif., 1997. Optometrist Larry Gotlieb, O.D., Redondo Beach, Calif., 1985-86, James Moses, O.D., Inglewood, Calif., 1986-87, Eyecare U.S.A., Montclair, Calif., 1987-89, Pearle Visioncare, Brea, Calif., 1989-94, Montebello Med. Eye Ctr., Calif., 1994-95; optometrist WATTSHealth Found., Inc., L.A., 1994—, chief vision care svcs., 1996—; mem. quality assurance com. Eyecare U.S.A., 1988-89, medicine com. UHP Healthcare, 1996—; investigator Ocular Hypertension Treatment Study; founder, pres. Crystal Fountain Ministries, Inc., 1997; clin. adj. prof. So. Calif. Coll. Optometry, 1998—. Co-author: What Is This Thing Called Preaching? An Authentic Collection of Sermons by Rev. Leon Johnson, Vol. One, 1996, Vol. Two, 1998; author: Bread of Heaven Songs of Praise: Daily Biblical Devotional Guide Featuring Old Meter Hymns, 1997, The Foolishness of the Message Preached-An Original Collection of Soul Food Filled Sermons, Vol.1, 1999; contbr. articles to profl. jours. Min., deacon Friendship Bapt. Ch., Yorba Linda, Calif. Fellow Am. Acad. Optometry. Home: PO Box 4434 Diamond Bar CA 91765-0434 Office: Watts Health Ctr 10300 Compton Ave Los Angeles CA 90002-3628

JOHNSON, MAGIC See **JOHNSON, EARVIN**

JOHNSON, MARIAN ILENE, education educator; b. Hawarden, Iowa, Oct. 3, 1929; d. Henry Richard and Wilhelmina Anna (Schmidt) Stoltenberg; m. Paul Irving Jones, June 14, 1958 (dec. Feb. 1985); m. William Andrew Johnson, Oct. 3, 1991. BA, U. La Verne, 1959; MA, Claremont Grad. Sch., 1962; PhD, Ariz. State U., 1971. Cert. tchr., Iowa, Calif. Elem. tchr. Cherokee (Iowa) Sch. Dist., 1949-52, Sioux City (Iowa) Sch. Dist., 1952-56, Ontario (Calif.) Pub. Schs., 1956-61, Reed Union Sch. Dist., Belvedere-Tiburon, Calif., 1962-65, Columbia (Calif.) Union Sch. Dist., 1965-68; prof. edn. Calif. State U., Chico, 1972-91. Avocation: travel. Home: 26437 S Lakewood Dr Sun Lakes AZ 85248-7246

JOHNSON, MARY CADY, artist; b. Chgo., Oct. 6, 1914; d. Gilbert Haven and Marian Adelia (Denmark) Cady; m. Elmer Ferdinand Johnson, Oct. 7, 1939 (dec. Jan. 1973); children: Cady Leonard, Derek Herbert. BFA, U. Ill., 1936; BFA, MFA, Art Inst. Chgo., 1945. Supr. art Urbana (Ill.) Pub. Schs., 1938-39; bd. dirs., chmn. art gallery Chile-Am. Cultural Inst., Santiago, 1946-48, Brazilian-Am. Inst., Rio de Janeiro, 1948-55; lectr. art history U. Nev., Las Vegas, 1961-65, 1st dir. art gallery, 1961-65; mem. Nev. State Coun. on the Arts, 1964-71; co-founder, 1st pres. Allied Arts Coun., Las Vegas, 1961. Permanent collections include painting and prints C.C. of So. Nev., Las Vegas, Achenbach Found. for Graphic Arts, San Francisco, Calif. Palace of Legion of Honor, San Francisco, Grunwald Ctr. for Graphic Arts/UCLA, Illini Union/U. Ill., Joiner Ctr./U. Mass., Boston, Krannert Art Mus./U. Ill., U. Ariz. Art Mus., Tucson.

JOHNSON, MORGAN BURTON, artist, writer; b. Santa Monica, Calif., Nov. 25, 1952; s. Arnold and Roma (Burton) J. BA in Psychology, U. Calif., San Diego, 1974; Cert. Fgn. Studies, Lycee du Universite, Dijon, France, 1968. Mgr. Coronet Stores, Las Vegas, Nev., 1975; mgr., chef Diver's Cove Restaurant, Long Beach, Calif., 1977-80; prodn. control asst. Century Plastics, Compton, Calif., 1980; prodn. supr. Analytichem Internat., Harbor City, Calif., 1980-81; sr. planner Sci. Mfg./Am. Hosp., Emeryville, Calif., 1982-85; materials mgr. Applied Biosys. (Perkin-Elmer), Foster City, Calif., 1985-90; owner, pres. Two Bears Restoration, 1990—. Exhibited in group shows at Medford (Oreg.) Ctr., 1993, Mills House Art Gallery, Garden Grove, Calif., 1979, San Bernardino Mus. Art, 1980-81, Calif. Poly State U., San Luis Obispo, 1985, West Coast Biennial, Pacific Grove Art Ctr., 1985, Cunningham Meml. Art Show, Bakersfield, Calif., 1985, The Rogue Gallery, Medford, 1984, 85, 90, 91, C. Erickson Gallery, Half Moon Bay, Calif., 1986-90, Britt Music Festival, Jacksonville, Oreg., 1994; solo shows include Daleo Farms, Sams Valley, Oreg., 1995, Cache Salon, Walnut Creek, 1996, First Congl. Ch., Long Beach, 1996; included in pvt. collections; author: Trees of Other Colors, 1994, Condemned to a Life of Painting Pretty Pictures, 1994, Circle of the White Buffalo, 1996; published in Nat. Libr. Poetry Anthology, 1997, 98. Mem. So. Oreg. Arts Coun., Medford, 1990—, San Francisco Artist's Coop, 1980-83; fin. sec. Long Beach Art Assn., 1978-79; hanging com. mem. San Diego Art Inst., 1974-76. Recipient 1st prize Recreation and Parks Dept., L.A., 1965, 66, Long Beach Art Assn., 1977, 3d pl. award Downey Mus. Art, 1977, 78, So. Oreg. Lambda Excellence award for art, 1998. Avocations: hiking, skiing, gardening. Home and Office: 2130 Capital Ave Medford OR 97504-6944

JOHNSON, MYRNA ELLEN, government relations executive; b. Wagner, S.D., Jan. 17, 1960; d. Wesley Eugene and Erma Harriet (Stephenson) J. BA magna cum laude, Wartburg Coll., 1982. Organizer Clean Water Action/Md. League Conservation Voters, Balt., 1982-83; membership recruiter Cope Energy Svcs., Balt., 1983-84, co-dir., 1984-85; govt. rels. asst. Bicycle USA, Balt., 1985-86, dir. govt. rels., 1986-87; govt. rels. assoc. Nat. Pub. Radio, Washington, 1987-95; dir. govt. affairs Outdoor Recreation Coalition of Am., Boulder, Colo., 1995—; mem. Outward Bound Land Mgmt. Adv. Coun., Golden, Colo., 1996-97. Bd. mem., newsletter editor Greater Balt. Environ. Ctr., 1984-89; bd. mem. Balt. Clergy and Laity Concerned, 1985-86, Gwynn Oak Improvement Assn., Balt., 1989-90; mem. nat. steering com., chair long range planning com. Luth. Vol. Corps, Washington, 1990-94; mem. Cmty. Leadership Coun., Balt., 1990-94; founding mem. Watershed Alliance, Balt., 1990; vol. McGuire for Congress, Sioux City, Iowa, 1994, Indian Peaks Working Group, 1996-97; participant Colo. Outdoor Recreation Resource Project, 1995-96; gardener Boulder Cmty. Garden, 1996-97. State of Iowa scholar, 1978; Regents scholar Wartburg Bd. Regents, 1978, Vera B. Will scholar Wartburg Coll., 1981. Democrat. Avocations: hiking, gardening, reading, dancing, community projects. Office: Outdoor Recreation Coalition Am 2475 Broadway St Boulder CO 80304-4108

JOHNSON, PAM, newspaper editor. Mng. editor Ariz. Republic, Phoenix, 1993-96, v.p. news, exec. editor, 1996—. Office: Ariz Republic PO Box 1950 Phoenix AZ 85001-1950

JOHNSON, PATRICIA DIANE, psychotherapist, consultant; b. L.A., June 16, 1958; d. Frederick Alexander and Mary Jane (Andel) J.; m. John Joseph Casey, June 22, 1995. BA in Psychology, Calif. State U., Domiguez Hills, 1981; MA in Clin. Psychology, Antioch U., Marina del Rey, Calif., 1990. Psychotherapist, marriage and family therapist, cons., L.A., 1991—; head spl. treatment track for HIV clients Matrix Inst. on Addictions, Beverly Hills, Calif., 1991-93; project dir., case mgr. L.A. C.C. dist. L.A. Trade Tech. Coll., 1992—, instr. psychology, 1995; instr. psychology East L.A. Coll., Monterey Park, Calif., 1996—; cons. Motown Records, L.A., 1994; appearances as profl. expert include Montel Williams Show, Leeza Gibbons Show; condr. workshops and class on interracial and biracial issues; mem. gender equity planning com. Calif. Chancellor's Office, Sacramento, 1995-96; staff writer, cons. Biracial Child and Interrace mags., advice col. Metisse Mag. on Internet, Metisse.com adv. com.; cons. on conflict resolution and orgnl. mgmt. to pub. and pvt. sector cos.; presenter in field. Contbr. articles to mags. Bd. dirs. for Women In Non-Traditional Employment Roles (WINTER), Long Beach, Calif., 1996; mem. Dem. Nat. Com., Washington, 1995—. Mem. NOW, Am. Assn. Marriage and Family Therapists (clin.), Calif. Assn. Marriage and Family Therapists (clin.). Home: PO Box 291567 Los Angeles CA 90029-9567 Office: PDJ Psychotherapy & Consulting 9107 Wilshire Blvd Ste 215 Beverly Hills CA 90210-5522

JOHNSON, PETER NEILS, motion picture producer, educator; b. Caldwell, Idaho; s. Clifford Lewis and Afton (Thueson) J.; m. Ann Lee Johnson, Aug. 15, 1981; children: Emily Ann, Daniel Peter, Aaron Clifford. BA, Brigham Young U., 1968, MA, 1972. Dialogue dir. Quinn Martin Prodns.-NBC, San Francisco, 1974-78, Lorimar Prodns.-NBC, L.A., 1979; pvt. practice producing, directing L.A., 1980-83; exec. prodr. motion picture studio Studio Brigham Young U., Provo, Utah, 1983—; chmn. Fresco Pictures, LLC. Author: Thanksgiving Promise, Double Exposure, 1986, Joseph Smith, 1996; dialogue dir. The Streets of San Francisco, 1974; dir. The Restoration, 1982, Man's Search for Happiness, 1986, A More Perfect Union, 1988, The Mountain of the Lord, 1992; producer Encyclopedia Brown: The Case of the Missing Time Capsule (HBO), The Witching of Ben Wagner. With U.S. Army, 1968-70. Recipient regional Emmy award, Cine Golden Eagle U.S. Indsl. Film Festival, Washington,

Gold Camera award U.S. Indsl. Film Festival, Chgo., Gold award Internat. Film and TV Festival of N.Y., N.Y.C., award Chgo. Internat. Film Festival; nominee (nat.) Emmy award. Mem. Dirs. Guild Am., Phi Kappa Phi. Democrat. Mormon. Avocation: skiing.

JOHNSON, QULAN ADRIAN, software engineer; b. Great Falls, Mont., Sept. 17, 1942; s. Raymond Eugene and Bertha Marie (Nagengast) J.; m. Helen Louise Pocha, July 24, 1965; children—Brenda Marie, Douglas Paul, Scot Paul, Mathew James. B.A. in Psychology, Coll. Gt. Falls, 1964. Lead operator 1st Computer Corp., Helena, Mont., 1966-67; v.p., sec.-treas. Computer Corp. of Mt., Great Falls, 1967-76, dir., 1971-76; sr. systems analyst Mont. Dept. Revenue, Helena, 1976-78; software engr. Mont. Systems Devel. Co., Helena, 1978-80; programmer/analyst III info. systems div. Mont. Dept. Adminstrn., Helena, 1980-82; systems analyst centralized services Dept. Social and Rehab. Services State of Mont., 1982-87, systems and programming mgr. info systems, Blue Cross and Blue Shield of Montana, Helena, 1987-98, project coord., 1998—. Mem. Mensa, Assn. Info. Tech. Profls. Home: 2231 8th Ave Helena MT 59601-4841 Office: Blue Cross & Blue Shield Info Systems 404 Fuller Ave Helena MT 59601-5006

JOHNSON, RALPH THEODORE, JR., physicist; b. Salina, Kans., Apr. 29, 1935; s. Ralph Theodore and Mary Alice (Wallerius) J.; m. Ruth Elaine Rohrer, Jan. 25, 1958; children: Barbara A., Thomas T., Gregory E., Janet E. MS in Physics, Kans. State U., 1959, PhD, 1964. Staff mem. GE, Cin., 1957-58; rsch. and teaching asst. Kans. State U., 1958-63; from rsch. scientist to mgr. Sandia Nat. Lab., Albuquerque, 1965-97; mem. N.Mex. Govs. Energy Task Force, 1974; mem. assessment panel Nat. Rsch. Panel, 1978-90; mem. Am. Nat. Std. Writing Com., 1990-97. Contbr. articles to profl. jours. Pres., bd. dirs. Marriage Enrichment Nonprofit Corp. 1st lt. USAF, 1963-65. Achievements include patent for neutron radiation detector; memory phenomenon in amorphous semiconductors; ionic conduction in solid electrolytes; radiation effects in semiconductors and electronics; metrology program development; marriage program development. Home: 6601 Arroyo Del Oso Ave NE Albuquerque NM 87109-2733

JOHNSON, RANDALL DAVID (RANDY JOHNSON), professional baseball player; b. Walnut Creek, Calif., Sept. 10, 1963. Student, U. So. Calif. With Montreal (Can.) Expos, 1985-89; pitcher Seattle Mariners, 1989—. Named to All-Star Team, 1990, 93-95; recipient Cy Young award, 1995; named Pitcher of Yr. Sporting News, 1995; Am. League strikeout leader, 1995. Leader in Am. League Strikeouts., 1992. Office: Seattle Mariners/The Kingdome PO Box 4100 83 King St Seattle WA 98104-0100

JOHNSON, RAY MAURICE, writer; b. Fullerton, Calif., May 11, 1935; s. Ray M. and Maxine T. Johnson; m. Laura O. Johnson, Jan. 13, 1975; children: Ray, Brad, Jeff, Ricky, Beverly, Tess. BA, Fresno State U. Author: The In Vitro Madonna, 1995, Spanish Moss, 1989, Appomattox Bypass, 1995, Rum, 1997, Taxi, 1998, Last Name, Please, 1998, Afrakati, 1998. 1st lt. U.S. Army, 1957-60. Baptist. Home: 1246 Adler Dr Clovis CA 93612-2373

JOHNSON, RICHARD KARL, hospitality company executive; b. Gaylord, Minn., May 27, 1947; s. Karl S. and Mildred (Tollefson) J.; m. Eva Margaret Wick, Oct. 12, 1973; children: Michelle, Richard, Ryan. BA, Gustavus Adolphus U., St. Peter, Minn., 1969. Gen. mgr. Green Giant Restaurants, Inc., Mpls., 1969-71, Mpls. Elks Club, Mpls., 1971-73; dir. concept devel. Internat. Multifoods, Mpls., 1972-75; v.p. concept devel. A&WFood Svcs. Can., North Vancouver, B.C., 1975-81; dir. food and beverages Ramada, Reno, 1981-82; pres., owner R.K. Johnson & Assoc., Reno, 1981—; owner D.J. Mgmt., 1990—; asst. gen. mgr. Gold Dust West Casino, Reno, 1983-85; gen. mgr. P&M Corp., Reno, 1985-86; v.p. ops. C.P.S.W. Inc., Reno and Tempe, Ariz., 1986-87, Lincoln Fairview, Reno, 1987-89; v.p. corp. affairs Myers Realty, 1991—. Mem. Aircraft Owners and Pilots Assn., Nat. Restaurant Assn., Nev. Realtor, Elks Club. Lutheran. Avocations: flying, scuba diving. Home and Office: RK Johnson & Assoc 825 Meadow Springs Dr Reno NV 89509-5913

JOHNSON, RICHARD VERNON, artist, educator; b. Glenwood, Minn., Sept. 21, 1905; s. Benjamin and Ida Josephine (Thompson) J.; m. Bertha Maude Abel, Sept. 6, 1930 (dec. Mar. 1970); m. Dorothy Alice Baldwin, Apr. 18, 1987. Student, Univ. Mont., 1927; cert. in Aircraft Engring., Calif. Tech., Douglas Aircraft, Long Beach, Calif., 1945. Cert. tchr., Calif.; lic. pvt. pilot. Advt. illustrator Foster and Klieser, Long Beach, 1930-40, pictorial painter, 1946-52; art tchr. Orange Coast Coll., Costa Mesa, 1951-76; founding faculty Costa Mesa (Calif.) C.C., 1976-82; retired, 1982; freelance advt. illustrator, N.Y.C., 1940-41; ptnr., art supr. Assoc. Outdoor, Long Beach, 1952-60; artist, tchr. Traditional Artists' Guild, Paramount, Calif. Exhibited one-man and group shows; works represented in permanent collection Long Beach Naval Sta., Superstition Mt. Hist. Mus., Apache Junction, Ariz., Sanctuary Grace United Meth. Ch., Long Beach.; patentee in field. With USAF, 1942-45. Recipient Best of Show, Crescent City Hall Dedication, others. Mem. Laguna Beach Art Assn. (life), Am. Water Color Assn., Pelican Bay Art Assn. Republican. Avocations: music, travel, fishing, sports. Home: 851 Brookhaven Dr Brookings OR 97415-7113

JOHNSON, ROBERT HERSEL, journalist; b. Colorado City, Tex., May 28, 1923; s. Robert Hersel and Leah (Sikes) J.; m. Luise Putcamp, Jr., Feb. 24, 1945; children: Robert Hersel, III, Luise Robin, Jan Leah, Stephanie Neale, Jennifer Anne, Ann Tapia. B.S. in Journalism, So. Methodist U., 1947. Reporter Phoenix Gazette, 1940-42; asst. sports editor Ariz. Republic, Phoenix, 1942-43; newscast writer Sta. KOY, Phoenix, 1943; reporter Dallas Times-Herald, 1946; with AP, 1946-88, Utah-Idaho bur. chief, 1954-59, Ind. bur. chief, 1959-62, Tex. bur. chief, 1962-69, gen. sports editor, 1969-73, mng. editor, 1973-77, asst. gen. mgr., spl. asst. to pres., 1977-84, N.Mex. bureau chief, 1984-88; prof. journalism N.Mex. State U., Las Cruces, 1988, U. N.Mex., Albuquerque, 1989; exec. dir. N.Mex. Found. for Open Govt., Albuquerque, 1989—; mem. Newspaper Readership Coun., 1977-82. Mem. N. Mex. Hist. Records Adv. Bd., 1993—. Capt. USMCR, 1943-46, 51-52. Home: 2740 Tramway Cir NE Albuquerque NM 87122-1205

JOHNSON, RODNEY DALE, law enforcement officer, photographer; b. Montebello, Calif., May 14, 1944; s. Albert Gottfreid and Maxine Elliot (Rogers) J.; m. Karen Rae Van Antwerp, May 18, 1968; 1 child, Tiffany Nicole. AA, Ela Community Coll., 1973; postgrad. Law Enforcement Spl., FBI, Acad., 1976; BA, U. of La Verne, 1978. Cert. tchr. police sci., Calif. Dep., Los Angeles County Sheriff, 1969-75, dep. IV, 1976-78, sgt., 1978—; fire arms inst., Hacienda Heights, Calif., 1975-94; photographer Weddings and Portraits, 1983-94; photography instr., Hacienda Heights, 1983-94; pres. Wheelhouse Enterprises, Inc., Whittier, 1971-86; instr. State Sheriff's Civil Procedural Sch. Los Medanos Coll., Concord, Calif., 1985-88. Creator and actor, Cap'n Andy, 1973-80; song writer for Cap'n Andy theme, 1972. Sgt. USMC, 1965-69, Vietnam, master gunnery sgt. Res., 1969-94, ret.; intelligence chief, Persian Gulf. Recipient Service award Trinity Broadcasting Network, 1979. Mem. Profl. Peace Officers Assn., Sheriff's Relief Assn., Assoc. Photographers Internat., Marine Corps. Intelligence Assn., Inc. Republican. Mem. Assembly of God. Club: Faithbuilders (pres. 1981-87), (Pomona).

JOHNSON, RONALD DOUGLAS, business executive; b. Klamath Falls, Oreg., Sept. 16, 1949; s. Clifford Douglas and Anna Elizabeth (Fine) J.; m. Wendi Susan Brown, Aug. 20, 1972; children: Bryan Douglas, Timothy Christopher, Michael Casey. BA in Polit. Sci., Wash. State U., 1975, MA in Pub. Adminstrn., 1976, MA in Agrl. Econs., 1981. Rsch. asst. Wash. Water Rsch. Ctr., Pullman, 1974-75; mgmt. trainee Potlatch Corp., 1971-74; intern Gov. Daniel J. Evans, Olympia, Wash., 1975; rsch. asst. Wash. State U., Pullman, 1976-79; asst. mgr. Reardan Grain Gowers Assn., Wash., 1980-82; gen. mgr. Bean Growers Warehouse Assn., Twin Falls, Idaho, 1982-84; dry bean group mgr. Rogers NK Seed Co., Boise, Idaho, 1984-95; owner Agraplus, Inc., 1996— [illegible] Rogers Seed Co., Basic Am. Foods, Sunspiced [illegible] Twin Falls. With U.S. Army, 1968-70, Viet Nam. Commn. Econ. Assistance grantee Oreg. State U., 1978, Washington Water Rsch. grantee, Wash. State U., 1976. Home: 4190 N Jones Ave Boise ID 83704-2700 Office: Rogers Seed Co 600 N Armstrong Pl Boise ID 83704-0825

JOHNSON, RUPERT HARRIS, JR., finance company executive. BA, Washington and Lee U., 1962. With Franklin Resources, Inc., San Mateo, Calif., 1965—, exec. v.p., chief investment officer, dir.; sr. v.p., asst. sec. Franklin Templeton Distbrs., Inc.; pres. Franklin Advisers, Inc.; mem. exec. com., bd. govs. Investment Co. Inst.; trustee Santa Clara U., Washington and Lee U.; chmn. bd. dirs. Franklin Mgmt., Inc.; exec. v.p., sr. investment officer Franklin Trust Co.; dir. various Franklin Templeton funds; portfolio mgr. Franklin DynaTech Fund. With USMC, 1962-65. Mem. Nat. Assn. Securities Dealers (dist. conduct com.). Office: Franklin Resources Inc Templeton Group 777 Mariners Island Blvd San Mateo CA 94404-1585*

JOHNSON, RUTH FLOYD, university educator, consultant; b. Plateau, Ala., Apr. 19, 1935; d. Nathan Daniel and Ora Anna (Ellis) Floyd; children: Anthony, Walter, Camille, Quinitta, Annette. Student, Tuskegee Inst., 1951-53; BS in History, Bowie (Md.) State U., 1970; MEd in Counseling, U. Md., 1977; PhD in Human Svcs. Adminstrn., Univ. for Humanistic Studies, San Diego, 1982. Cert. tchr., counselor. Radio personality Sta. WMOZ, 1953-56; owner, dir. Azalea Sch. Dance, 1954-56; numerous posts for fed. govt., 1957-69; tchr., adminstr. Pub. Schs. of Prince George's County, Md., 1970-78; tchr.-counselor Dunbar S.T.A.Y. Sch., Washington, 1974-75; instr. child and youth study divsn. U. Md., 1977-78; CEO Diametron Corp., 1979-81; tchr. L.A. Unified Sch. Dist., 1980-82, Pasadena (Calif.) Unified Sch. Dist., 1982-83, Rialto (Calif.) Unified Sch. Dist., 1984—; profl. devel. coord. Calif. State Polytech. U., 1995—. Author: Remediating Mass Poverty: Development of a Model Program, 1982, Pep Squad handbook, 1991, (with others: Government/Contemporary Issues: A Curriculum Guide, 1976. Active PTAs; mem. organizing com. Peppermill Village Civic Assn., 1966; vol. Boy Scouts Am., 1968-72, Sr. Citizens of Prince George's County, 1974-76; bd. dirs.Mill Point Improvement Assn., 1975-78, Combined Communities in Action, 1976-78; mem. Prince George's County Hosp. Commn., 1978; mem. Altadena Town Coun., 1983; founder Rialto Freedom and Cultural Soc., 1988; mem. Calif. 36th Dist. Bicentennial Adv. Com., 1989; mem. exec. com. Rialto Police/Community Rels. Team, 1993. Recipient Outstanding Svc. to Children and Yourh award Md. Congress PTA, 1969, Services to Boy Scouts Am. award, 1969, Svcs. to Sr. Citizens award, 1975, Community Svc. award Rialto Freedom and Cultural Soc., 1993, others. Mem. NEA, NAACP, Nat. Assn. Univ. Women, Nat. Coun. Negro Women, Zeta Phi Beta, Gamma Phi Delta. Avocations: world travel, theatre, tennis, spectator sports, outdoor activities. Home: PO Box 1946 Rialto CA 92377-1946

JOHNSON, STEPHEN C., electric executive. Pres., CEO Komag, San Jose. Office: Kmoag 1704 Automation Pkwy San Jose CA 95131-1873*

JOHNSON, STEPHEN RANDALL, minister; b. Lansing, Mich., May 17, 1957; s. James Theodore and Juanita Elizabeth (Wall) J.; m. Zane Elizabeth Alkhas, June 20, 1987; children: Stephen James, Faith Elizabeth. BTh, Berean Bible Coll., San Diego, 1984; MST, Bethel Bible Coll., Riverside, Calif., 1985, ThD, 1989. Ordained to ministry Shield of Faith Ministries, 1984, Living Word Internat., 1985. Assoc. pastor Shield of Faith Ministries, Escondido, Calif., 1983-85; founder, sr. pastor His Ch. Christian Fellowship, Escondido, 1985—; instr. Berean Bible Coll., San Diego, 1985-89; pres. north campus Berean Bible Coll., Escondido, 1989-91; founder, pres. Word Bible Coll. and Grad. Sch. Theology, 1991—; conv. speaker His Internat. Ministries, Escondido; founder, missionary statesman His Ch. Christian Fellowship; founder several local chs. Broadcaster KPRZ Radio, 1986—; writer Times Advocate, Times Mirror, Good News Pub., 1984-87; guest TV programs. Office: His Ch Christian Fellowship 600 S Andreasen Dr Ste A Escondido CA 92029-1917

JOHNSON, STEWART WILLARD, civil engineer; b. Mitchell, S.D., Aug. 17, 1933; s. James Elmer Johnson and Grace Mahala (Erwin) Johnson Parsons; m. Mary Anis Giddings, June 24, 1956; children: Janelle Chiemi, Gregory Stewart, Eric Willard. BSCE, S.D. State U., 1956; BA in Bus. Adminstrn. and Polit. Sci., U. Md., 1960; MSCE, PhD, U. Ill., 1964. Registered profl. engr., Ohio. Commd. 2d lt. USAF, 1956, advanced through grades to lt. col.; prof. mechs. and civil engring. Air Force Inst. Tech. USAF, Dayton, Ohio, 1964-75; dir. civil engring. USAF, Seoul, Republic of Korea, 1976-77; chief civil engring. research div. USAF, Kirtland AFB, N.Mex., 1977-80; ret. USAF, 1980; prin. engr. BDM Corp., Albuquerque, 1980-94, Johnson and Assocs., Albuquerque, 1994—; cons. in site surveys, found. design, constrn. of ground stas. for satellite comm. sys., 1992-96; cons. space sci. and lunar basing NASA, U. N.Mex., N.Mex. State U., Los Alamos Nat. Labs., 1986—; adj. prof. civil engring. U. N.Mex., 1987—; prin. investigator devel. concepts for lunar astron. obs. U. N.Mex., N.Mex. State U., NASA, 1987-94; tech. chmn. Space '88, Space '90, Space '94 and Space '96 Internat. Confs., Albuquerque; vis. lectr. Internat. Space U., Japan, 1992, Huntsville, Ala., 1993, Barcelona, Spain, 1994, Stockholm, 1995; mem. panel on siting lunar base European Space Agy., 1994; gen. chair Space 96 and RCEII Conf., Albuquerque, 1996; gen. chmn. Space Conf., Albuquerque, 1998, Robotics Conf., Albuquerque, 1998. Editor Engineering, Construction, and Operations in Space, I, 1988. II, 90, V, 96; contbr. articles to profl. jours. Pres. ch. coun. Ch. of Good Shepherd United Ch. of Christ, Albuquerque, 1983-85, chmn. bd. deacons, 1991-93, moderator, 1996-97; S.W. Conf. (United Ch. Christ) del. to Gen. Synod XIX, St. Louis, 1993, Gen. Synod XX, Oakland, Calif., 1995, Gen. Synod XXI, Columbus, Ohio, 1997; trustee Lunar Geotech. Inst., 1990—; mem. adv. bd. Lab. for Extraterrestrial Structures Rsch., Rutgers U., 1990—. Fellow Nat. Acad. Scis. NRC, 1970-71; recipient World Bar Assn. Space Humanitarian award, 1996. Mem. AIAA (space logistics com., Engr. of Yr. region IV 1990), ASCE (chmn. exec. com. aerospace divsn. 1979, tech. activities com. 1984, chmn. com space engring. and constrn. 1987—, mem. nat. space policy com. 1988—, chmn. 1990—, Outstanding News Corr. award 1981, Aerospace Scis. and Tech. Applications award 1985, 90, Edmund Friedman Profl. Recognition award 1989), Soc. Am. Mil. Engrs., Am. Geophys. Union, Soc. Am. Milit. Engrs., Sigma Xi, Pi Sigma Alpha. Republican. Mem. United Ch. of Christ. Avocations: photography, swimming, walking, gardening, hiking.

JOHNSON, SYLVIA SUE, university administrator, educator; b. Abiline, Tex., Aug. 10, 1940; d. SE Boyd and Margaret MacGillivray (Withington) Smith; m. William Ruel Johnson; children: Margaret Ruth, Laura Jane, Catherine Withington. BA, U. Calif., Riverside, 1962; postgrad., U. Hawaii, 1963. Elem. edn. credential, 1962. Mem. bd. regents U. Calif.; mem. steering com. Citizens Univ. Com., chmn., 1978-79; bd. dirs., charter mem. U. Calif.-Riverside Found., chmn. nominating com., 1983—; pres., bd. dirs. Friends of the Mission Inn, 1969-72, 73-76, Mission Inn Found., 1977—, Calif. Bapt. Coll. Citiznes Com., 1980—; bd. dirs. Riverside Comty. Hosp., 1980—, Riverside Jr. League, 1976-77, Nat. Charity League, 1984-85; mem. chancellors blue ribbon com., devel. com. Calif. Mus. Photography. Named Woman of Yr., State of Calif. Legislature, 1989, 91, Citizen of Yr., C. of C., 1989. Mem. U. Calif.-Riverside Alumni Assn. (bd. dirs. 1966-68, v.p. 1968-70).

JOHNSON, WALTER EARL, geophysicist; b. Denver, Dec. 16, 1942; s. Earl S. and Helen F. (Llewellyn) J.; Geophys. Engr., Colo. Sch. Mines, 1966; m. Ramey Kandice Kayes, Aug. 6, 1967; children—Gretchen, Roger, Aniela. Geophysicist, Pan. Am. Petroleum Corp., 1966-73; seismic processing supr. Amoco Prodn. Co., Denver, 1973-74, marine tech. supr., 1974-76, div. processing cons., 1976-79, geophys. supr. No. Thrust Belt, 1979-80; chief geophysicist Husky Oil Co., 1981-82, exploration mgr. Rocky Mountain and Gulf Coast div., 1982-84; geophys. mgr. ANR Prodn. Co., 1985—; pres. Sch. Lateral Ditch Co.; cons. engr. Bd. dirs. Rocky Mountain Residence, nursing home. Registered profl. engr., cert. geologist, Colo. Mem. Denver Geophys. Soc., Soc. Exploration Geophysicists. Republican. Baptist. Office: 600 17th St Ste 800 Denver CO 80202-5402

JOHNSON, WAYNE EATON, writer, editor, former drama critic; b. Phoenix, May 9, 1930; s. Roscoe and Marion (Eaton) J.; children: Katherine, Jeffrey. BA, U. Colo., 1952; postgrad., Duke U., 1952-53; postgrad. (KLM polit. reporting fellow 1957), U. Vienna, Austria, 1955-56; MA, UCLA, 1957. Reporter Internat. News Service, Des Moines, 1958, Wheat Ridge (Colo.) Advocate, 1957, Pueblo (Colo.) Chieftain, 1959, reporter Denver Post, 1960, contr. writer, music critic, 1961-65, arts and entertainment editor Seattle Times, 1965-82, drama critic, 1980-92; instr. journalism Colo. Woman's Coll., 1962. Author: Show: A Concert Program for Actor and Orchestra, 1971, America! A Concert of American Images, Words and Music, 1973, From Where the Sun Now Stands: The Indian Experience, 1973, Let's Go On: Pacific Northwest Ballet at 25, 1997; editor, co-pub.: Secrets of Warmth, 1992, Footprints on the Peaks, 1995, The Burgess Book of Lies, 1995. With CIC AUS, 1953-55, Korea. Home: 11303 Durland Pl NE Seattle WA 98125-5926

JOHNSON, WAYNE HAROLD, librarian, county official; b. El Paso, Tex., May 2, 1942; s. Earl Harold and Cathryn Louise (Greeno) J.; m. Patricia Ann Froedge, June 15, 1973; children: Meredith Jessica (dec.), Alexandra Noëlle Victoria. BS, Utah State U., 1968; MPA, U. Colo., 1970; MLS, U. Okla., 1972. Circulation libr. Utah State U., Logan, 1968, adminstrv. asst. libr., 1969; with rsch. dept. Okla. Mgmt. and Engring. Cons., Norman, 1972; chief adminstrv. svcs. Wyo. State Libr., Cheyenne, 1973-76, chief bus. officer libr. archives and hist. dept., 1976-78, state libr., 1978-89; county grants mgr. Laramie County, Wyo., 1989—. Trustee Bibliog. Ctr. for Rsch., Denver, pres., 1983, 84; mem. Cheyenne dist. Longs Park coun. Boy Scouts Am., 1982-86; active Cheyenne Frontier Days, 1975—; mem. admissions and allocation com. United Way, 1991-94; mem. Ho. of Reps., Wyo. Legislature, 1993—; chmn. Transp. Hwys. Com., 1999—. Served with USCG, 1960-64. Mem. Aircraft Owners and Pilots Assn., Cheyenne C. of C. (chmn. transp. com. 1982, 83, military affairs com. 1994—), Am. Legion. Republican. Presbyterian. Club: No. Colo. Yacht. Lodges: Masons, Kiwanis (bd. dirs. 1986, 87). Office: 309 W 20th St Cheyenne WY 82001-3601

JOHNSON, WILLIAM HARRY, international management consultant; b. Ridley Park, Pa., Oct. 1, 1941; s. Harry Brown and Florence Lydia (Round) J.; m. Anna Marie Castellanos, Oct. 19, 1984. BS, Drexel U., Phila., 1963; MBA, Drexel U., 1967. Mgmt. exec. DuPont Co., Wilmington, Del., 1963-69; bus. analysis mgr. Imperial Chem. Ind., Wilmington, 1970-76; mgr. analysis and acquisitions Fluor Daniel Corp., Irvine, Calif., 1976-78; fin. analysis mgr. Alexander Proudfoot, Chgo., 1978-79; exec. v.p., chief fin. officer Sego Internat., Niagara Falls, Ont., Can., 1980-82; exec. v.p., gen. mgr. Sci. Mgmt. Corp., Basking Ridge, N.J., 1982-87; exec. mgr. Boeing, Long Beach, Calif., 1987—; bd. dirs. A.M.T. Inc., Pierrefonds, Que., Can., CRA, Inc., Clariton, Pa., Madden Assocs., Buffalo Grove, Ill., KABB Inc., El Segundo, Calif., Sego Internat., Productivity Cons., Inc., Montreal, Commonwealth Cos., London. Author: Explosives Distributors, 1967, Maintenance Productivity - It Can Be Achieved, 1988, Facilities Work Order Guide, 1989, Participative Management in Facilities Operations, 1991; contbr. articles to profl. jours. Mem. Rep. Nat. Com., Washington, El Segundo Residents Assn. Recipient Presdl. Achievement award, Rep. Nat. Com., 1988, Outstanding Achievement award, Sego Internat., 1981. Mem. Inst. Indsl. Engrs., Am. Mgmt. Assn., Nat. Productivity Assn. of Can. (dir. 1980-95), Nat. Assn. Accts., Nat. Petroleum Refinery Assn., Am. Mktg. Assn., Internat. Productivity Orgn., Drexel U. Alumni Assn. (bd. dirs.), Highlander Clan, Lions (Kowloon, Hong Kong), K & C Clans Assn. (Hong Kong), Internat. Bus. Assocs. (Sydney, Australia). Republican. Presbyterian. Avocations: dogs, international traveling, tennis, swimming. Home: 807 Hillcrest St El Segundo CA 90245-2025 Office: Boeing Airlift & Tankers Program Mail Code C078-0317 2401 E Wardlow Rd Long Beach CA 90807-5309

JOHNSON, WILLIAM HUGH, JR., state official, hospital administrator; b. N.Y.C., Oct. 29, 1935; s. William H. and Florence P. (Seinsoth) J.; m. Gloria C. Stube., Jan. 23, 1960; children: Karen A., William H. III. BA, Hofstra U., 1957; MEd, U. Hawaii, 1969. Commd. 2d lt. U.S. Army, 1957, advanced through grades to lt. col., 1972, health adminstr., world wide, 1957-77, health adminstr., world wide, ret., 1977; CEO U. N. Mex. Hosp., Albuquerque, 1977-97; asst. prof. U.S. Mil. Acad., West Point, N.Y., 1962-65; mem. clin. faculty U. Minn., Mpls., 1980-83; preceptor Ariz. State U., Tempe, 1982-83; pres. Albuquerque Area Hosp. Coun., 1980; v.p. strategic alliances U. N.Mex. Health Scis. Ctr.; adminstr. Horizon Splty. Hosp., Albuquerque, 1997—; adj. prof. cabinet sec. N. Mex. Dept Human Svcs., Santa Fe, 1997-99; bd. dirs. Bank Am. of N.Mex., Tri West, Inc.; sec. human svcs. State N.Mex., 1997; adj. prof. U. N.Mex., 1999. Mem. exec. bd. Albuquerque Com. on Devel.; v.p. Vis. Nurse Svc., Albuquerque, 1979; pres. Magnifico Arts Fiesta; bd. dirs. ACCION (Microlender), 1999, Goodwill N.Mex., bd. dirs. Albuqueque Conv. and Visitors Bur., mem. exec. com., 1994—, chmn., 1997-98. Decorated Army Commendation Medal with 2 oak leaf clusters, Order of Merit (Rep. of Vietnam), Legion of Merit. Mem. Am. Hosp. Assn. (governing bd. met. hosp. sect. 1982-86, chmn. com. AIDS, mem. regional policy bd. 1982-86, 88—), Am. Coll. Hosp. Adminstrs., Coun. Tchg. Hosps. (bd. dirs.), N.Mex. Hosp. Assn. (bd. dirs. 1983, chmn. 1995—), Nat. Assn. Pub. Hosps. (bd. dirs. Tri West Inc., Vita S.W.), Greater Albuquerque C. of C. (bd. dirs., econ. planning coun., v.p.), N.Mex. Assn. Commerce and Industry (treas.). Roman Catholic. Home: 7920 Sartan Way NE Albuquerque NM 87109-3128 Office: NMex Dept Human Svcs Bolton Plz 2009 S Pacheco St Santa Fe NM 87505-5473

JOHNSON, WILLIAM POTTER, newspaper publisher; b. Peoria, Ill., May 4, 1935; s. William Zweigle and Helen Marr (Potter) J.; m. Pauline Ruth Rowe, May 18, 1968; children: Darragh Elizabeth, William Potter. AB, U. Mich., 1957. Gen. mgr. Bureau County Rep., Inc., Princeton, Ill., 1961-72; pres. Johnson Newspapers, Inc., Sebastopol, Calif., 1972-75, Evergreen, Colo., 1974-86, Canyon Commons Investment, Evergreen, 1974—; pres. Johnson Media, Inc., Granby, Colo., 1987—. Author: How the Michigan Betas Built a $1,000,000 Chapter House in the '80s. Alt. del. Rep. Nat. Conv., 1968. Lt. USNR, 1958-61. Mem. Colo. Press Assn., Nat. Newspaper Assn., Maple Bluff Country Club, Madison Club, Bishops Bay Country Club, Bal Harbour Club, Beta Theta Pi. Home: 5302 Lighthouse Bay Dr Madison WI 53704-1114 Office: PO Box 409 Granby CO 80446-0409

JOHNSON, WILLIAM R., JR., minister; b. Quincy, Fla., July 4, 1935; s. William R. Sr. and Mable Elaine (Robinson) J.; m. Eleanor Finch, April 4, 1943; children: Raymond Patrice, Malcolm Maurice.; BA, Lane Coll., 1957; MA, Columbia U., 1960; MDiv, Interdenominational Theol. Cert., Atlanta, 1968; MST, Princeton Theol. Sem., 1970; D of Ministry, Vanderbilt U., 1977; DD (hon.), Miles Coll., 1975. Pub. rels. rep. N.Y.C. Housing Auth., 1959-60; dir. youth and student activities Gen. Bd. Christian Edn. Christian Meth. Episcopal Ch., Chgo., 1960-62; adminstrv. and editl. asst. Gen. Bd. Christian Edn. Christian Meth. Episcopal Ch., Memphis, 1962-64, dir. div. higher edn., 1971-74, gen. sec., 1974-86; instr. and dorm counselor Clark Coll., Atlanta, 1964-65; pastor (while student) St. Mark Christian Meth. Episcopal, Birmingham, Ala., 1966-68, Mount Olive Christian Meth. Episcopal Ch., Camden, N.J., 1969-71; pastor Washington Chapel Christian Meth. Episcopal Ch., Memphis, 1980-83, Curry Temple Christian Meth. Episcopal Ch., Compton, Calif., 1986—. Author: Developing the Educational Ministry of Local Church, 1977, Beliefs that Make a Difference, 1984, Discipling Children and Youth the Mandate of the Church, 1995. Pres. Urban League, Memphis, 1975-78; pres. NAACP, Memphis, 1980-81; bd. dirs. Memphis O.I.C., 1977-83, mem. Comm. on Race Rels., Memphis, 1972-75; Founder: Cmty. Dev. Corp. Mem. Lane Coll. Alumni Orgn., Masons (Prince Hall Affiliate), Mystic Order of the Shrine, Alpha Phi Alpha Fraternity. Home: 16615 Estella Ave Cerritos CA 90703-1515 Office: Curry Temple PO Box 5509 Compton CA 90224-5509

JOHNSON, WILLIAM THEODORE, school system administrator; b. Detroit, Jan. 12, 1951; s. Theodore Hamilton and Gloria May (Remy) J.; m. Debra Shoshana Lipner, Nov. 27, 1982; children: Amanda, Emily, Alex. BS in Natural Resources Mgmt., Calif. Poly. State U., San Luis Obispo, 1974; MA in Counseling Psychology, U. Calif., Santa Barbara, 1984; MA in Edn. Adminstrn., Calif. State U., L.A., 1990. Nat. cert. sch. psychologist Nat. Crisis Prevention Inst., Inc. Cons. environ. edn. San Luis Obispo (Calif.) County Office Edn., 1974-77; tchr. Paso Robles (Calif.) Union Sch. Dist., 1978-82; sch. psychologist Baldwin Park (Calif.) Unified Sch. Dist., 1985-96; coord. spl. edn. Santa Barbara County Edn., 1996—; assoc. instr. Nat. Crisis Prevention Inst., Baldwin Park, 1995—. Coach Ctrl. Altadena (Calif.) Little League, 1994, 96. Mem. ASCD, Assn. Calif. Sch. Adminstrs., Baldwin Park Orgn. Suprs. and Adminstrs. (v.p. membership 1993-94, v.p. programs 1994-95, pres. 1995-96). Avocations: fishing, scuba diving, backpacking, gardening.

JOHNSON-HADDAD, BARBARA LUCILLE, writer, artist; b. Huntington Beach, Calif., Oct. 31, 1957; d. Ronald Edward and Jo Anne (O'Hanlon) Johnson; m. Carl E. Nelson, June 24, 1979 (div. May 1981); m. George N. Haddad III, June 11, 1986. AA, Golden West Jr. Coll., Huntington Beach, 1977. Libr. page Santa Ana (Calif.) Pub. Libr., 1979-86; tech.

support Biggernet ISP, San Jose, Calif., 1997; freelance writer, 1982—. Author: Blood Kin, 1995, (short stories) Galaxy, 1997. Mem. Sci. Fiction & Fantasy Writers Assn., Bay Area Sci. Fiction Assn. (sec. 1992—), San Francisco in 2002 Worldcon Bid, San Francisco Writers Assn. Republican. Presbyterian. Avocations: jewelry-making, role-playing games, painting, poetry, cooking. Home and Office: 903 Apricot Ave Apt B Campbell CA 95008-3211

JOHNSTON, BERNARD FOX, author, foundation executive; b. Taft, Calif., Nov. 19, 1934; s. Bernard Lowe and Georgia Victoria (Fox) J.; m. Audrey Rhoades, June 9, 1956 (div. Sept. 1963); 1 child, Sheldon Bernard. BA in Creative Arts, San Francisco State U., 1957, MA in World Lit., 1958. Lectr. philosophy Coll. of Marin, Kentfield, Calif., 1957-58; lectr. humanities San Francisco State U., 1957-58, 67-68; instr. English Contra Costa Coll., San Pablo, Calif., 1958-63; Knowles Found. philosophy fellow, 1962; fellow Syracuse (N.Y.) U., 1964-66; freelance writer Piedmont, Calif., 1968-77; pres. Cinema Repertory, Inc., Point Richmond, Calif., 1978-89; pres., exec. dir. Athena Found., Tiburon-Truckee, Calif., 1990—; exec. prodr. (TV series) The Heroes of Time, (TV documentary) The Shudder of Awe; CEO The Athena Found., Inc., 1997, Mahler Festival, U. Colo., Boulder, 1998. Author: (screenplay) Point Exeter, 1979, Ascent Allowed, 1988 (award); author, editor: Issues in Education: An Anthology of Controversy, 1964, The Literature of Learning, 1971; festival pianist Lake Tahoe Internat. Film Festival, 1998; resident pianist Tahoe-Chrysler Corp., 1998. Arts grantee Silicon Valley Community Found., 1998. Mem. Dirs. Guild Am., Writers Guild Am., Coun. for Basic Edn., Wilson Ctr. Assocs., Assn. Lit. Scholars and Critics, Smithsonian Instn., Donner Land Trust, Nat. Assn. Scholars, Calif. Assn. Scholars, San Francisco State Alumni Assn., Commonwealth Club of Calif. Avocations: classical piano, backpacking, softball. Office: Athena Found 11679 Mougle Ln Truckee CA 96161-6117

JOHNSTON, CHARLES, protective services official. BA in Law Enforcement Adminstrn., San Jose State U.; MPA, U. No. Colo.; grad., Nat. Acad. FBI; attended, Harvard U., Northwestern U., U. Denver, U. Colo. Police officer Salinas (Calif.) Police Dept.; police officer Lakewood (Calif.) Police Dept., 1970-80, acting chief of police, 1980-81, chief of police, 1981—; active Colo. Peace Officer Stds. and Tng. Bd., Justice Assistance Act Adv. Bd. Mem. Jefferson County coun. ARC; chmn. steering com. Law Enforcement Torch Run; active Colo. Spl. Olympics. Decorated Bronze star (4), Purple Heart, Army Air medal; recipient Man of Yr. award Lakewood Sentinel, 1984, Hall of Fame award Lakewood/South Jefferson County C. of C., 1989; named Vol. of Yr., Colo. Spl. Olympics Hall of Fame, 1990. Office: Lakewood Police Dept 445 S Allison Pkwy Lakewood CO 80226-3106*

JOHNSTON, DAVID RITCHEY, construction company executive; b. Highland Park, Ill., Nov. 7, 1950; Sherman and Vivian (Ritchey) J. BS, So. Ill. U., 1976. Owner Survival Systems Constrn., Bath, Maine, 1976-77; cons. Nat. Rec. and Parks Assn., Rosslyn, Va., 1977-78, Planning Research Corp., McLean, Va., 1978-79; v.p. Potomac Energy Group, Alexandria, Va., 1979-83; pres. Passive Solar Industries Council, Alexandria, Va., 1981-83, Lightworks Constrn., Inc., Bethesda, Md., 1983-91, What's Working, Boulder, Colo., 1991—; bd. dirs. Whole Systems Design, Inc., Lorton, Va., Potomac Energy Group, Inc., Bus. Crafters, New Alternative in Pub., Retailing & Advt., Big Horn Builders, Boulder Energy Conservation Ctr., Boulder C. of C., Sustainable Futures Soc., Boulder Energy Conservation Ctr., Boulder County Healthy Cmtys., Internat. Sustainable Tech. Bus. Ctr. Author: Technical Solar Field Guide, 1979; exec. producer (film) Sunbuilders, 1980; pub. Environ. Bldg. News Product Catalog. Pres. Cabin John (Md.) Citizens Assn., 1986; bd. dirs. Renewable Energy Inst., 1982-83, STAR Found., Portland, Maine, 1979-89. Named to Remodeling Industry Hall of Fame, 1989. Mem. Nat. Assn. Remodeling Industry (bd. dirs.), Entrepreneurs Group of Washington, D.C. (pres.), Excellence Group, Bus. Crafters (bd. dirs. 1991—), New Age Pubs. and Retailers Assn., Home Builders Assn. Avocations: computers, scuba diving, backpacking, photography, sustainable design research. Home: 57 Acorn Ln Boulder CO 80304-0490

JOHNSTON, LYLE WAYNE, minister; b. Sioux City, Iowa, Nov. 4, 1948; s. Lester and Vivian (Varner) J.; m. Barbara Paulette Harty, Apr. 22, 1972; children: Milton, Celesta. BA, Morningside Coll., 1978; MDiv, U. Dubuque, 1981. Ordained to ministry United Meth. Ch.: deacon 1983, elder 1985. Min. United Meth. Ch., Randalia-Maynard-Westgate, Iowa, 1979-83, Moulton, Iowa, 1983-85, Schaller-Arthur, Iowa, 1985-89, Kellogg-Pleasant View, Iowa, 1989-90, Holbrook-Heber, Ariz., 1990-95, Bullhead City, Ariz., 1995-97, Williams, Ariz., 1997—; mem., chair archives and history commn. Iowa Conf. United Meth. Ch., 1982-90, Desert S.W. Conf., 1991—, mem., sec. Western ...isdiction, 1992—. Author: Holbrook Arizona—A History, 1993, Frank Wattron, 1996. Mem. Randalia (Iowa) City Coun., 1982-83. With USAF, 1968-69, Vietnam. Mem. Kiwanis. Avocations: reading, travel, writing. Office: United Meth Ch 127 W Sherman Ave Williams AZ 86046-2546

JOHNSTON, OLIVER MARTIN, JR., animator; b. Palo Alto, Calif., Oct. 31, 1912; s. Oliver Martin and Arclissa Florence (Boggs) J.; m. Marie Estelle Worthey, Nov. 10, 1917; children: Richard Oliver, Kenneth Andrew. Student, Stanford U., 1931-34, U. Calif., Berkeley, 1932, Chouinard Art Inst., 1934-35. Directing animator Walt Disney Co., Burbank, Calif., 1935-78; lectr., spkr. in field. Asst. animator Snow White and the Seven Dwarfs, 1937; animation supr. Fantasia, 1940, Bambi, 1942; animator Pinnochio, 1940, The Fox and the Hound, 1981, Victory Through Air Power, 1943, The Three Caballeros, 1945, Make Mine Music, 1946; directing animator Song of the South, 1946, Melody Time, 1948, The Adventures of Ichabod and Mr. Toad, 1949, Cinderella, 1950, Alice in Wonderland, 1951, Peter Pan, 1953, Lady and the Tramp, 1955, Sleeping Beauty, 1959, 101 Dalmatians, 1961, Sword in the Stone, 1963, Mary Poppins, 1964, The Jungle Book, 1967, The Aristocats, 1970, Robin Hood, 1973, Rescuers, 1977, also shorts and TV cartoons; author: Disney Animation -- The Illusion of Life, 1981, Too Funny For Words, 1987, Bambi-the Story and the Film, 1990, Jungle Book Portfolio, 1992, The Disney Villain, English edit., 1993, French edit., 1995; contbg. editor sketch book series; subject of documentary Frank and Ollie; drawings exhibited in Whitney Mus., N.Y.C., 1981. Guest spkr. Russian Govt. and Soyuzmultifilm, 1976, other East European Countries, U.S. Info. Agy. Cultural Exch. Program, 1986. Recipient Pioneer in Film award Delta Kappa Allpha, 1978, honor award Mus. Modern Art, 1978, Annie award Internat. Animated Film Soc., 1980, Disney Legend award, 1989, Grand Prix of the Ams., 1995. Avocations: trains, reading, studying, sports. Address: 748 Flintridge Ave Flintridge CA 91011

JOHNSTON, RICHARD C., newspaper editor. BS, Portland State U., 1965. Reporter The Oregonian, Portland, 1965-66, asst. city editor, 1966-79, Washington corr., 1979-82, asst. mng. editor, 1982-94, asst. to the editor, 1994—. Office: The Oregonian 1320 SW Broadway Portland OR 97201-3499

JOHNSTON, ROBERT JAKE, federal magistrate judge; b. Denver, Sept. 30, 1947; m. Julie Ann Black; children: Jennifer, Robert, Jr., Michelle. BS, Brigham Young U., 1973; JD, U. Pacific, 1977. Bar: Nev. 1977, U.S. Dist. Ct. Nev. 1978, U.S. Ct. Appeals (9th cir.) 1984. Law clk. to Hon. Merlyn Hoyt Nev. 7th Judicial Dist., Ely, 1977-78; dist. atty. White Pine County, Ely, 1979-82; pvt. practice Johnston & Fairman, Ely, 1979-82; deputy dist. atty. Office Clark County Dist. Atty., Las Vegas, Nev., 1983-84; asst. U.S. atty. Office U.S. Atty., Las Vegas, 1984-87; chief civil div. Office U.S. Atty., 1986-87; U.S. magistrate judge U.S. Dist. Ct., Las Vegas, 1987—. Dir. Boy Scouts Am. Boulder Dam Area Coun., Las Vegas. With U.S. Army, 1967-70. Mem. Nev. Bar Assn., Clark County Bar Assn., Fed. Magistrate Judicial Assn. (dir. 1990-92), Las Vegas Track Club, 9th Jud. Cir. Hist. Soc., Southwest Oral History Soc., 9th Cir. Conf. Exec. Com. Office: US Dist Ct 300 Las Vegas Blvd S Ste 4650 Las Vegas NV 89101-5883

JOHNSTON, TONI ANNETTE SOPHIA, interior designer, educator; b. East Chicago, Ind., Aug. 10, 1949; d. Anthony Thomas and Eugenia (Giannaris) Karas; m. June 14, 1976 (div. Apr. 1992ú; children: Christina Shepard, Michael Shepard. Student, Ind. U., 1967-68; BS in Interior Design, Ind. State U., 1973. Free-lance interior designer Colo., Ark., 1975-92; interior designer Garrett's, Santa Barbara, Calif., 1992-93, Thomasville, Agoura Hill, Calif., 1993-94, Ethan Allen Interiors, Thousand Oaks, Calif., 1994-98, Plantation Shutters, Camarillo, Calif., 1998—; instr. decorative textiles Moorpark (Calif.) Coll. Mem. Am. Soc. Interior Designers (allied). Greek Orthodox. Avocations: biking, silk-painting, portraits. Office: Plantation Shutter Co 4820 Adohr Ln Camarillo CA 93012-8580

JOHNSTON, VIRGINIA EVELYN, editor; b. Spokane, Wash., Apr. 26, 1933; d. Edwin and Emma Lucile (Munroe) Rowe; student Portland C.C., 1964, Portland State U., 1966, 78-79; m. Alan Paul Beckley, Dec. 26, 1974; children: Chris, Denise, Rex. Proofreader, The Oregonian, Portland, 1960-62, teletypesetter operator, 1962-66, operator Photon 200, 1966-68, copy editor, asst. women's editor, 1968-80; spl. sects. editor (UPDATE), 1981-83, 88-95; editor FOODday, 1982—; pres. Matrix Assos., Inc., Portland, 1975—, chmn. bd., 1979—; pres. Bones & Brew Inc.; bd. dir. Computer Tools Inc. Cons. Dem. Party Oreg., 1969, Portland Sch. Dist. No. 1, 1978. Mem. Eating and Drinking Soc. Oreg. (past pres.), We. Culinary Inst. (mem. adv. bd.), Internat. Food Media Conf. (past mem. adv. bd.). Democrat. Editor Principles of Computer Systems for Newspaper Mgmt., 1975-76. Home: 4140 NE 137th Ave Portland OR 97230-2624 Office: Oregonian Pub Co 1320 SW Broadway Portland OR 97201-3499

JOHNSTONE, KENNETH ERNEST, electronics and business consultant; b. L.A., Sept. 13, 1929; s. John Ernest and Lorena Hayes (Patterson) J.; m. Edna Mae Iverson, Aug. 20, 1950; children: Bruce, Kent, Anita, Christian, Daniel, Carol, Karen. BSEE, U. Wash., 1966. Registered profl. engr., Wash. Electronics technician The Boeing Co., Seattle, 1955-66, engr., 1966-75; engring. mgr. Boeing Aerosystems Internat., Seattle, 1975-85; ptnr. North Creek Engring., Lynnwood, Wash., 1985-87; pres. SensorLink Corp., Lynnwood, 1987-90; electronics and bus. cons. Bellingham, Wash., 1991—; internat. cons., lectr. in field. Mem. IEEE (sr.), Tau Beta Pi. Avocations: sailing, amateur radio, languages. Home and Office: 3765 E Smith Rd Bellingham WA 98226-9573

JOLIVET, ANNA MARY, retired school system administrator, association executive; b. Tucson, Nov. 24, 1928; d. Joe Turner and Sadie Osborne; m. Clarence Warner Jolivet, June 7, 1952; children: Clarence Michael, Leslie Cecilia. BA in Elem. Edn., U. Ariz., 1950, MEd in Elem. Edn., 1965, EdS in Ednl. Adminstrn., 1972, EdD, 1976. Cer. tchr., prin., supt., Ariz. Tchr. Spring/Dunbar Elem.-Jr. High Sch. Tucson Pub. Schs. Dist. # 1, 1950-59, helping tchr. music dept., tchr. Booth Elem. Sch., 1961-67, prin. Richey Elem. Sch., 1967-70, prin. Cragin Elem. Sch., 1970-75; lectr. Coll. Edn. U. Ariz., Tucson, 1976; adminstrv. asst. learning and staff devel. Tucson Unified Sch. Dist. # 1, 1976-80, dir. planning svcs., 1980-89, asst. supt. high sch. region, 1989; cons. ednl. adminstrn., curriculum devel., 1989—; organizing dir. Tucson Assn. for Child Care, 1970; mem. adv. bd. U. Ariz. Cultural Affairs; speaker AAUW, Nat. Assn. Sch. Pers., Rocky Mountain Ednl. Rsch. Assn. Conf., Nat. Coun. Adminstrv. Women Edn., Ariz. Black Town Hall, Baha'i Faith/ UN Assn. So. Ariz. Pres. Camp Fire Tucson, Inc., 1969-71, adv. bd.; pres. Downtown Devel. Corp., Tucson, 1988-90, Tucson Partnership, Inc., 1990-92, pres., 1998—; allocations divsn. chmn. United Way Tucson, 1982-84, exec. bd., bd. dirs.; v.p. Am.-Israel Friendship League, Tucson, 1989-98, coord. high sch. youth exch., 1990-96, pres., 1998—; exec. com. Tucson Community Found., 1990-96, chair discretionary grants, 1993, pres. bd. dirs., 1996-98; vice chmn. Tucson Pima County Community Profile, 1991-93; chair Sahuaro Coun. Girl Scouts, nominating com.; chair Older Adults Svc. and Info. Sys., 1992-94, Tucson Fund Raising Rev. Bd.; chmn. bd. dirs. Tucson Urban League, 1988-89, guild pres., 1983-84; exec. bd. Tucson Tomorrow; active Ariz. Adv. Health Coun., Tucson Bicentennial Com., Health Systems Agy. Screening com., Goals for Tucson; block grant com. Ariz. Dept. Health, chair proposal revs. 1981, 82; chmn. subcom. Crippled Children's Svc.; trustee Mt. Calvary Bapt. Ch., Tucson Mus. Art, 1988-92, 94—, supt. Sunday Sch., 1994—; bd. dirs. Ariz. Acad. Phoenix, 1983-86, 96—, YWCA, N.Y.C., 1982-94; active Tucson/Pima Libr.; nat. bd. dirs. YWCA of U.S.A., N.Y.C., 1982-94, past mem. nat. nominating com.; past bd. dirs. YWCA Tucson, past chmn. pers. Recipient Women on Move award, YWCA Tucson, 1982, Tucson Met. C. of C., 1996, Woman of Yr., Alumni Achievement award U. Ariz., 1983, Phenomenal Woman award U. Ariz. Black Alumni, 1990, Ptnrs. Democracy award Am.-Israel Friendship League, 1997, U. Ariz. Alumni Centennial award, 1998. Mem. NEA, ASTD, ASCD (state sec. 1981-82, state pres. 1982-83, nat. bd. dirs. 1982-83, exec. coun. 1984-87), Coun. Ednl. Facility Planners Internat. (interface project), Nat. Assn. Elem. Sch. Prins., Nat. Coun. Adminstrv. Women in Edn., Am. Ednl. Rsch. Assn., Am. Assn. Sch. Adminstrs., Ariz. Edn. Assn., Ariz. Sch. Adminstrs., Inc. (region 5 legis. rep.), NAACP (life), Exec. Women's Coun. (v.p. 1992-93), Pi Lambda Theta (past v.p. Alpha Alpha chpt.), Delta Kappa Gamma, Phi Delta Kappa, Alpha Delta Kappa, Alpha Kappa Alpha (past mem. nat. constn. com., past far western region parliamentarian, chair far west regional conf. com. 1986, past pres. Tucson chpt., past treas., undergrad. acad. scholarship). Democrat. Avocations: travel, reading, walking, cooking. Home: 8818 E Harborage Dr Tucson AZ 85710-6225

JOLLES, BERNARD, lawyer; b. N.Y.C., Oct. 5, 1928; s. Harry and Dora (Hirschorn) J.; m. Lenore Madison Jolles, Oct. 11, 1953 (div. Jan. 1984); children: Abbe, Jacqueline, Caroline. BA, N.Y.U., 1951; LLB, Lewis & Clark Coll., 1961. Bar: Oreg. 1963, U.S. Dist. Ct. Oreg. 1964, U.S. Dist. Ct. (no. dist.) Miss. 1968, U.S. Ct. Appeals (9th cir.) 1965, U.S. Supreme Ct. 1979. Assoc. Anderson Franklin Jones & Olsen, Portland, Oreg., 1963-68; ptnr. Franklin Olsen Bennett & Desbarsay, Portland, Oreg., 1968-79, Jolles Bernstein & Garone and predecessor firms Jolles Sokol & Bernstein, Portland, Oreg., 1979—. Editor: Damages, 1974. Bd. dirs. ACLU, Portland, Oreg., 1975—. Fellow Am. Coll. Trial Lawyers; mem. Oreg. State Bar Assn. (pres. 1986-87), Am. Inns of Ct. (sr. barrister 1985—). Avocations: cooking, reading. Office: Jolles Bernstein & Garone 721 SW Oak St Portland OR 97205-3712

JOLLY, MICHAEL JOHN, college administrator; b. Oct. 24, 1960; s. John T. and Lois E. (Sumpter) J. BS, Adams State Coll., 1984, MA, 1985. Dir. housing and residence life Adams State Coll., Alamosa, Colo.; student counselor, lab. instr. Adams State Coll. Mem. Am. Coll. Pers. Assn., Am. Mental Health Counseling Assn., Colo. Counseling Assn., Colo. Coll. Student Devel. Assn., Colo. Volleyball Officials Assn., Colo. State Knowlege Bowl (co-chmn.), Elks (past exalted ruler), Phi Delta Kappa. Office: Adams State Coll Office of Housing Alamosa CO 81102

JOLLY, STEVEN JON, brokerage house executive; b. Madera, Calif., June 18, 1965; s. James Dee and Jere Lynn (Kennedy) J.; m. Tracy J. Vane, Apr. 24, 1991; children: Tanner, Trenton. BS, Calif. State U., Fresno, 1988. Stockbroker Paine Webber, Fresno, 1989-95; 1st v.p. investments Prudential Securities, Fresno, 1995—. V.p. income devel. Am. Cancer Soc. Mem. Sunnyside C.C. (membership com.). Republican. Baptist. Avocations: skiing, jogging, golf. Office: Prudential Securities 7102 N Fresno St Fresno CA 93720-2905

JOLOVICH-MOTES, SONDRA LEA, principal; b. Wheatridge, Colo., July 3, 1965; d. Donald Joseph and Judith Anne (Baker) Jolovich; m. Brian William Motes, Aug. 5, 1989; children: Brian William Jr., Xena Diana. BS, Weber State U., 1989; M. in Edn. Adminstrn., U. Utah, 1992. Cert. tchr. math., sci.; cert. adminstr. Utah. Phys. sci./math. tchr. Salt Lake City Sch. Dist., 1989-91; adminstrv. intern Granite Sch. Dist., Salt Lake City, 1991-92, asst. prin. jr. high, 1992-94; asst. prin. mid. sch. Ogden (Utah) Sch. Dist., 1994-96; prin. Mountain View Elem. Sch., Ogden, 1996—; co-chmn. sch. cmty. coun. Ogden Sch. Dist., 1995-96, mem. dist. site-based decision-making com., 1994-95, mem. dist. testing com., 1995-96. Vol. fundraiser Big Bros./Big Sisters, Jr. League, Ogden, 1996; coach AYSO Soccer, 1997. Mem. Utah Edn. Assn., Nat. Assn. Secondary Sch. Prins., Nat. Assn. Elem. Sch. Prins., Phi Delta Kappa. Democrat. Roman Catholic. Avocations: biking, golf, reading, designing and making wreaths, rose gardening. Office: Mountain View Elem Sch 170 15th St Ogden UT 84404-5661

JONAITIS, ALDONA CLAIRE, museum administrator, art historian; b. N.Y.C., Nov. 27, 1948; d. Thomas and Demie (Genaitis) J. BA, SUNY, Stony Brook, 1969; MA, Columbia U., 1972, PhD, 1977. Chair art dept. SUNY, Stony Brook, 1983-85, assoc. provost, 1985-86, vice provost undergrad. studies, 1986-89; v.p. for pub. programs Am. Mus. Natural History, N.Y.C., 1989-93; dir. U. Alaska Mus., Fairbanks, 1993—. Author: From the Land of the Totem Poles, 1988; editor, author: Chiefly Feasts: The Enduring Kwakiutl Potlatch, 1991; editor: A Wealth of Thought: Franz Boas on Native American Art History, 1995, Looking North: Art from the University of Alaska Museum, 1998. Mem. Native Am. Art Studies Assn. (bd. dirs. 1985-95). Office: U Alaska Mus 907 Yukon Dr Fairbanks AK 99775

JONES, A. DURAND, park administrator. CEO Rocky Mountain Nat. Park, Estes Park, Colo. Office: Rocky Mountain Nat Park Estes Park CO 80517*

JONES, BILL, state official, rancher; b. Coalinga, Calif., Dec. 20, 1949; s. C.W. and Cora Jones; m. Maurine Abramson, Aug. 29, 1971; children: Wendy, Andrea. BS in Agribus. and Plant Sci., Calif. State U., Fresno, 1971. Ptnr. ranch, nr. Firebaugh, Calif.; mem. Calif. Assembly, Sacramento, 1983—, Rep. leader, 1991—; Sec. of State State of California, 1994—. Former chmn. Fresno County Rep. Cen. Com. Named Outstanding Young Farmer, Fresno C. of C. Mem. Fresno County and City C. of C. (past bd. dirs.). Methodist. Avocations: horseback riding, golf, flying, travel. Home: 2254 W Dovewood Ln Fresno CA 93711-2810 Office: Office Sec State 1500 11th St Sacramento CA 95814-5701*

JONES, CARY DENNIS, broadcast executive; b. Los Angeles, July 20, 1950; s. Edward Douglas J. and Alice (Stanton) Serrao; m. Gail Blanchard, Nov. 22, 1980; children: Christina Peyton, Cameron Blair, Tyler Stanton. BA, Washington U., St. Louis, 1972. Account exec. TeleRep Inc., Los Angeles, 1973-75; group sales mgr. Harrington, Righter & Parsons, Los Angeles, Chgo., 1975-80; gen. sales mgr. Eastman CableRep, New York, 1980-81; sr. v.p., gen. mgr. Idaho Ind. TV Inc. and Sta. KTRV-TV, Nampa, Idaho, 1981-86; v.p. Fox Television, Chgo., 1987-92, First Media Television, Portland, 1993-97; v.p., group gen. mgr. Meredith Corp., Portland, 1997—; v.p. Mohawk Broadcasting Ltd., Sta. WPMT-TV, York, Pa. Episcopalian. Club: Oswego Lakes Country Club. Office: KPDX 910 NE Mlk Blvd Portland OR 97232-2774

JONES, CHARLES E., state supreme court justice. BA, Brigham Young U., 1959; JD, Stanford U., 1962. Bar: Calif. 1962, U.S. Dist. Ct. Ariz. 1963, U.S. Ct. Appeals (9th cir.) 1963, Ariz. 1964, U.S. Ct. Appeals (10th cir.) 1974, U.S. Supreme Ct. 1979. Law clk. to Hon. Richard H. Chambers U.S. Ct. Appeals (9th cir.), 1962-63; assoc., ptnr. Jennings, Strouss & Salmon, Phoenix, Ariz., 1963-96; apptd. justice Ariz. Supreme Ct., Phoenix, 1996, vice chief justice, 1997—. Bd. visitors Brigham Young U. Law Sch., 1973-81, chmn., 1978-81. Named Avocat du Consulat-Gen. de France, 1981—; Alumni Dist. Svc. award Brigham Young U., 1982; recipient Aaron Feuerstein award U. Ariz., 1998. Mem. ABA, State Bar Ariz., Fed. Bar Assn. (pres. Ariz. chpt. 1971-73), J. Reuben Clark Law Soc. (nat. chmn. 1994-97), Maricopa County Bar Assn., Pi Sigma Alpha. Office: Ariz Supreme Court 1501 W Washington St Phoenix AZ 85007-3231

JONES, CHARLES IRVING, bishop; b. El Paso, Tex., Sept. 13, 1943; s. Charles I. Jr. and Helen A. (Heyward) J.; m. Ashby MacArthur, June 18, 1966; children: Charles I. IV, Courtney M., Frederic M., Keith A. BS, The Citadel, 1965; MBA, U. N.C., 1966; MDiv, U. of the South, 1977, DD, 1989. CPA. Pub. acctg. D.E. Gatewood and Co., Winston-Salem, N.C., 1966-72; dir. devel. Chatham (Va.) Hall, 1972-74; instr. acctg. U. of the South, Sewanee, Tenn., 1974-77; coll. chaplain Western Ky. U., Bowling Green, 1977-81; vicar Trinity Episcopal Ch., Russelville, Ky., 1977-85; archdeacon Diocese of Ky., Louisville, 1981-86; bishop Episcopal Diocese of Mont., Helena, 1986—; bd. dirs. New Directions Ministries, Inc., N.Y.C.; mem. standing com. Joint Commn. on Chs. in Small Communities, 1988-91, Program, Budget and Fin., 1991-94; v.p. province VI Episcopal Ch., 1991-94, mem. Presiding Bishop's Coun. Advice, 1991-94. Author: Mission Strategy in the 21st Century, 1989, Total Ministry: A Practical Approach, 1993; bd. editors Grass Roots, Luling, Tex., 1985-90; contbr. articles to profl. jours. Founder Concerned Citizens for Children, Russelville, 1981; bd. dirs. St. Peter's Hosp., Helena, 1986—; bd. dirs. Christian Ministry in Nat. Parks, 1992—. With USMCR, 1961-65. Mem. Aircraft Owners and Pilots Assn. Avocations: running, flying, writing, skiing. Office: Diocese Mont 515 N Park Ave Helena MT 59601-2703

JONES, CHARLES J., transportation executive, firefighter; b. Marshfield, Oreg., Jan. 29, 1940; s. Charles J. Cotter and Lois C. (Smith) Meltebeke; m. Sharon S. Madsen, Mar. 29, 1969; children: Mary E., Judith A., Kari C., April M., Autumn C. AS in Fire Sci. Tech., Portland Community Coll., 1974; BS in Fire Adminstrn., Eastern Oreg. State Coll., 1983; diploma, Nat. Fire Acad., 1983, 85; MPA, Lewis and Clark Coll., 1989. Cert. class VI fire officer, Oreg., hazardous materials instr., fire instr. I; lic. real estate agt., Oreg. From firefighter to capt. Washington County Fire Dist., Aloha, Oreg., 1964-74, battalion chief, 1974-81, dir. comms., dir. research and devel., 1981-85, dir. strategic planning, 1986-88; cons. Tualatin Valley Fire & Rescue, Aloha, 1989-90; pres., CEO Jones Transp., 1989—; basic and advanced 1st aid instr. ARC, 1965-80; cons. Washington County Consol. Communications Agy., 1983-86, chmn. 9-1-1 mgmt. bd., 1982-83; mem. adv. bd. Washington County Emergency Med. Svcs., 1981-83; owner/instr. Internat. Vocat. Inst. and Family Tree Learning Ctrs. Jones Internat., Ltd., 1990-95. Editor local newsletter Internat. Assn. Firefighters, 1970; contbr. articles on fire dept. mgmt. to jours. Active Community Planning Orgn., Washington County, 1979-90, chmn. 1988-89. With USAF, 1957-59. Mem. Oreg. Fire Chiefs Assn. (chmn. seminar com. 1982-83, 89, co-chmn. 1981, 84, 86, 87, 88). Republican. Mem. Infinity Universal Ch. Avocations: photography, genealogy, antique auto restoration, traveling, writing. Office: Jones Transp PO Box 7206 Aloha OR 97007-7206

JONES, CLEON BOYD, research engineer; b. Norwalk, Calif., Nov. 9, 1961; s. Cleon Earl and Marjorie Helen (McDade) J. BS in Math., Biola U., 1983. Rsch. libr. Christian Rsch. Inst., San Juan Capistrano, Calif., 1981-84; flight control engr. Leading Systems, Inc., Irvine, Calif., 1984-90; sr. staff engr. Dynamic Rsch., Inc., Torrance, Calif., 1990-98; sr. flight dynamics engr. Frontier Systems, Inc., Irvine, Calif., 1998—. Recipient NASA Group Achievement award Pilot Project Team, 1994. Republican. Avocations: reading, soccer, music, theology, aviation. Home: 5222 Huntswood Cir La Palma CA 90623-1714

JONES, CLYDE WILLIAM, anesthesiologist; b. Barbados, West Indies, Sept. 29, 1929; came to U.S., 1947; s. Lewis F. and Albertha B. (Lewis) J.; m. Norma Anita, Sept. 14, 1963; children: Michael W., Ronald C., Stephen T. BS, City Coll., N.Y.C., 1954; MD, Howard U., 1958. Diplomate Am. Bd. Anesthesiology. Capt. U.S. Navy, 1959-79, med. officer, 1959-63; resident in anesthesiology U.S. Naval Hosp., San Diego, 1963-66; staff anesthesiologist U.S. Naval Hosp., Camp Pendleton, Calif., 1966-67, chief of anesthesiology, 1967-69; chief of anesthesiology 1st Hosp. Co., Danang, Vietman, 1968, U.S. Naval Hosp., Marianas Island, Guam, 1969-71; staff anesthesiologist Naval Regional Med. Ctr., San Diego, 1971-73, chief of anesthesiology, 1973-79; staff anesthesiologist Kaiser Permanente Med. Ctr., San Diego, 1979-81, 87—, chief of anesthesiology, 1981-87. Contbr. articles to profl. jours. Acolyte lay reader, sub Deacon All Sts. Episcopal Ch., San Diego, 1971—; bd. dirs. Bishop's Sch., San Diego, 1980-81, San Diego Civic Light Opera, Inc., 1980-83. Recipient Meritorious Svc. medal, certificate of merit Surgeon Gen. U.S. Navy, 1979. Fellow Am. Coll. Anesthesiologists; mem.Am. Soc. Anesthesiologists (delegate), Assn. Mil. Surgeons of U.S., Am. Soc. Clin. Hypnosis, Internat. Anesthesia Rsch. Soc., Naval Inst., Sigma Pi Phi. Democrat. Avocations: hypnosis, coin collecting, medical volunteer. Home: 5201 Countryside Dr San Diego CA 92115-2136 Office: Kaiser Permanente Med Ctr 4647 Zion Ave San Diego CA 92120-2507

JONES, CURLEY CLEVELAND, librarian; b. Feb. 23, 1941; s. Cleve and Susie J. AA, Sts. Jr. Coll., Lexington, Miss., 1965; BA, Tougaloo (Miss.) Coll., 1969; MLS, SUNY, Geneseo, 1971; MEd, U. Utah, 1975; Cert. of Advanced Study in Librarianship, U. Ill., 1977. Cert. tchr., N.Y. Librarian U. Utah, Salt Lake City, 1972—. Editor Black Bibliography, 1977, supplement, 1981. Adv. to mayor Salt Lake City Cmty. Coun., 1989-96; bd. dirs. Ctrl. City Cmty. Coun., 1998—. Mem. ALA, Assn. Study of Negro Life and History, Mt. Plains Libr. Assn., Utah Libr. Assn., High Marine Lodge.

JONES, D. MICHAEL, banker; b. Tacoma, June 25, 1942; s. Delbert Edward and Marilyn Maurine (Myers) J.; m. Linda R. Lavigne, June 7, 1964; 1 child, Karee Michele. BA in Econs., Wash. State U., 1964. CPA, Wash. Acct. Deloitte Haskins & Sells, Seattle, 1964-68, princ., 1968-72; treas. Old Nat. Bancorp., Spokane, Wash., 1973-76, exec. v.p., 1976-81, pres., 1982-87; pres. Moore Fin. Group Inc. (now West One Bancorp), Boise, ID, 1987-1996; pres., ceo Source Capitol Corp., Spokane, Wa, 1996; bd. dirs. Columbia Paint Co., Spokane. Bd. dirs. Spokane City Libraries, 1974-78, Leadership Spokane, 1982-84; sec. treas., bd. dirs. Spokane Unltd., 1980-86. Recipient Outstanding Alumnus award, Wash. State U., 1986. Mem. Am. Inst. CPA's, Wash. Soc. CPA's, Spokane C. of C. (sec. treas. 1985-86). Episcopalian. Clubs: Spokane (pres. 1984-85); Hayden Lake (Idaho) Country (pres. 1982-83). Office: Source Capitol Corp 1825 N Hutchinson Rd Spokane WA 99212-2444*

JONES, DANIEL LEE, software development company executive; b. Sterling, Colo., Feb. 17, 1954; s. Gerald Dean and Joyce Elaine (Pyle) J.; m. Laurie Elaine Ganong, Sept. 6, 1975; 1 child, Jonathon Alexander. AB cum laude, Dartmouth Coll., 1976; MA in Physics, U. Calif., Davis, 1977, PhD in Physics, 1979. Assoc. in physics U. Calif., Davis, 1976-79; physicist Argonne (Ill.) Nat. Lab., 1979-82; mem. tech. staff TRW, Inc., Redondo Beach, Calif., 1982-84; chief scientist, co-founder Affine Scis. Corp., Newport Beach, Calif., 1984-85; chief scientist Peripheral Systems, Inc., Van Nuys, Calif., 1985-89; dir. info. systems Jones & Jones, Sterling, Colo., 1989—; v.p., co-founder Jones Techs. Inc., Sterling, 1991-92, also bd. dirs.; chief scientist Sykes Enterprises, Inc., Tampa, Fla., 1992—; sec. Jones Techs. Inc., Sterling, 1991-92; cons. Davis Polk & Wardwell, N.Y.C., 1987-91. Author (newspaper column) Your Computer, 1991-93; contbr. articles to profl. jours. Dist. accountability com. RE-1 Valley Schs., Sterling, 1991-94, dist. tech. com., 1991-94; mem. Northwestern Jr. Coll. Found. Bd., 1995—. Recipient Rufus Choate scholar Dartmouth Coll., 1972, Outstanding Contbrn. Inst. of Internal Auditors, 1987-88; tech. transfer grantee TRW, Inc., 1982. Mem. IEEE, IEEE Computer Soc., Assn. for Computing Machinery, Soc. for Indsl. and Applied Math. Republican. Methodist. Avocations: reading, writing, mathematics. Home: 510 Glenora St Sterling CO 80751-4642 Office: Sykes Enterprises Inc 777 N 4th St Sterling CO 80751-3244

JONES, DARCY GLEN ALAN, land use planner, consultant; b. Vancouver, B.C., Can., June 23, 1959; came to U.S., 1962; s. Harry Patrick and Margery Meta (Tierney) J.; m. Amy Lynne Baron, Sept. 30, 1995. BA in Geography, Ctrl. Wash. U., 1982; MS in Regional Planning, Western Wash. U., 1986. Lic. land surveyor, Calif. Land survey technician Jones Assocs., Bellevue, Wash., 1976-85; project planner Stevens Planning Group, San Diego, 1986-87, VTN S.W., San Diego, 1987-88; pres. Jones Engrs. Inc., San Diego, 1988—; legis. adv. County San Diego, 1990—. Den leader Boy Scouts Am., La Mesa, Calif., 1992-94. Mem. Am. Inst. Cert. Planners (cert. land planner), Am. Planning Assn., Calif. Assn. Subdivsn. Cons., Calif. Land Surveyors Assn., Bldg. Industry Assn., Alamo Ct. Homeowners Assn. (pres. 1992—). Avocations: surfing, soccer, fly fishing, piano. Home: 6767 Alamo Ct La Mesa CA 91941-5876

JONES, DONNA MARILYN, real estate broker, legislator; b. Brush, Colo., Jan. 14, 1939; d. Virgil Dale and Margaret Elizabeth (McDaniel) Wolfe; m. Donald Eugene Jones, June 9, 1956; children: Dawn Richter, Lisa Shira, Stuart. Student, Treasure Valley Community Coll., 1981-82; grad., Realtors Inst. Cert. residential specialist. Co-owner Parts, Inc., Payette, Idaho, 1967-79; dept. mgr., buyer Lloyd's Dept. Store, Payette, Idaho, 1979-80; sales assoc. Idaho-Oreg. Realty, Payette, Idaho, 1981-82; mem. dist. 13 Idaho Ho. of Reps., Boise, 1987-90, mem. dist. 10, 1990-94, mem. dist. 9, 1995-98; assoc. broker Classic Properties Inc., Payette, 1983-91; owner, broker ERA Preferred Properities Inc., 1991-98; mem. dist. 9 Idaho Ho. of Reps., 1992-98. Co-chmn. Apple Blossom Parade, 1982; mem. Payette Civic League, 1968-84, pres. 1972; mem. Payette County Planning and Zoning Commn., 1985-88, vice-chmn. 1987; field coordinator Idaho Rep. Party Second Congl. Dist., 1986; mem. Payette County Rep. Cen. Com. 1978—; precinct II com. person, 1978-79, state committeewoman, 1980-84, chmn. 1984-87; outstanding county chmn. region III Idaho Rep. Party Regional Hall of Fame, 1985-86; mem. Payette County Rep. Women's Fedn., 1988—, bd. dirs., 1990-92; mem. Idaho Hispanic Commn., 1989-92, Idaho State Permanent Bldg. Adv. Coun., 1990-98; bd. dirs. Payette Edn. Found., 1993-96, Western Treasure Valley Cultural Ctr., 1993-96; nat. bd. dirs. Am. Legis. Exchange Coun., 1993-98; mem. legis. adv. coun. Idaho Housing Agy., 1992-97; committeeperson Payette County Cen.; chmn. Ways and Means Idaho House of Reps., 1993-97, House Revenue & Taxation Com., 1997-98; mem. Multi-State Tax Compact, 1997-98; Idaho chmn. Am. Legis. Exchange Coun., 1991-95; exec. dir. Idaho Real Estate Commn., 1998—. Recipient White Rose award Idaho March of Dimes, 1988; named Payette/Washington County Realtor of Yr., 1987. Mem. Idaho Assn. Realtors (legis. com. 1984-87, chmn. 1986, realtors active in politics com. 1982—, polit. action com. 1986, polit. affairs com. 1986-88, chmn. 1987, bd. dirs. 1984-88), Payette/Washington County Bd. Realtors (v.p. 1981, state dir. 1984-88, bd. dirs 1983-88, sec. 1983), Bus. and Profl. Women (Woman of Progress award 1988, 90, treas. 1988), Payette C. of C., Fruitland C. of C., Wiesr C. of C.. Republican. Avocations: reading, interior decoration. Home: 1911 1st Ave S Payette ID 83661-3003 Office: ERA Preferred Properties 1610 6th Ave S Payette ID 83661-3348

JONES, DOUGLAS MICHAEL, pastor; b. Omar, W.Va., July 25, 1945; s. Douglas George and Phyllis Lee (Jones) J.; m. Janet Lorraine Spoelstra, Jan. 7, 1967; children: Kimberlee Anne, Michael Paul, Susan Reneé. BA, Biola U., 1972; MA, Internat. Coll., Honolulu, 1984, D in Ministry, 1990. Youth pastor Sunkist Bapt. Ch., Anaheim, Calif., 1970-72; assoc. pastor Ind. Bible Ch., Port Angeles, Wash., 1974-75, sr. pastor, 1975—; bd. dirs. N.W. Ind. Ch. Ext., Tacoma, 1976-86, Western Sem., Seattle, 1994-97; pres. and founder Pac Rim Bible Coll., Port Angeles, 1992-95. Bd. dirs. Clallam County Mental Health, Port Angeles, 1978. Sgt. USAF, 1966-70. Recipient Christian Leadership award The Am. Christian Leadership Coun., 1989. Charter mem. Am. Assn. Christian Counselors. Republican. Avocations: hiking, reading. Home: 1114 W 9th St Port Angeles WA 98363-5626 Office: Ind Bible Ch 112 N Lincoln St Port Angeles WA 98362-2919

JONES, EDDIE, basketball player; b. Oct. 20, 1971. Guard L.A. Lakers. Office: LA Lakers PO Box 10 Inglewood CA 90306

JONES, EDWARD LOUIS, historian, educator; b. Georgetown, Tex., Jan. 15, 1922; s. Henry Horace and Elizabeth (Steen) J.; m. Dorothy M. Showers, Mar. 1, 1952 (div. Sept. 1963); children: Cynthia, Frances, Edward Lawrence; Lynne Ann McGreevy, Oct. 7, 1963; children Christopher Louis, Teresa Lynne. BA in Philosophy, U. Wash., 1952, BA in Far East, 1952, BA in Speech, 1955, postgrad., 1952-54; JD, Gonzaga U., 1967. Social worker Los Angeles Pub. Assistance, 1956-57; producer, dir. Little Theatre, Hollywood, Calif. and Seattle, 1956-60; research analyst, cons. to Office of Atty. Gen., Olympia and Seattle, Wash., 1963-66; coordinator of counseling SOIC, Seattle, 1966-68; lectr., advisor, asst. to dean U. Wash., Seattle, 1968—; instr. Gonzaga U., Spokane, Wash., 1961-62, Seattle Community Coll., 1967-68; dir. drama workshop, Driftwood Players, Edmonds, Wash., 1975-76. Author: The Black Diaspora: Colonization of Colored People, 1988, Tutankhamon: Son of the Sun, King of Upper and Lower Egypt, 1978, Black Orators' Workbook, 1982, Black Zeus, 1972, Profiles in African Heritage, 1972, From Rulers of the World to Slavery, 1990, President Zachary Taylor and Senator Hamlin: Union or Death, 1991, Why Colored Americans Need an Abraham Lincoln in 1992, Forty Acres and a Mule: The Rape of Colored Americans, 1994; editor pub. NACADA Jour. Nat. Acad. Advising Assn., more. V.p. Wash. Com. on Consumer Interests, Seattle, 1966-68. Served to 2d lt. Fr. Army, 1940-45. Recipient Outstanding Teaching award U. Wash., 1986, Tyee Inst. Yr. U. Wash., 1987, appreciation award Office Minority Affairs, 1987, acad. excellence award Nat. Soc. Black Engrs., 1987, Appreciation award Fla. chpt. Nat. Bar Assn., 1990; Frederick Douglass scholar Nat. Coun. Black Studies, 1985, 86. Mem. Nat. Assn. Student [illegible] Social Sci., Nat. Acad. Advising Assn. (bd. dirs. 1979-82, Cert. of Appreciation 1982, editor Jour. 1981—, award for Excellence 1985), Western Polit. Sci. Assn. Democrat. Baptist. Avocations: travel, research, chess. Office: Univ Wash Ethnic Cultural Ctr Seattle WA 98195

JONES, ELIZABETH SELLE, minister; b. L.A., May 15, 1926; d. Raymond Martin Louis and Claire (Holley) Selle; m. James Latimer Jones, Dec. 22, 1945; children: Stephen, Nancy, David, Susan. BA, U. Calif., Santa Barbara, 1970; MDiv, Starr King Sch. for Ministry, Berkeley, Calif., 1980; DMin, San Francisco Theol. Sch., 1994. Ordained to ministry Unitarian Universalist Ch., 1980. Minister Unitarian Universalist Ch. in Livermore (Calif.), 1981-96, minister emerita, 1996—; trustee Starr King Sch. for the Ministry, Berkeley, 1989-97; del. gen. assembly Unitarian Universalist Assn. of Congregations, 1974-91. Pres. Glendale (Calif.) PTA, 1958-60. Mem. Unitarian Universalist Ministers Assn. (exec. com. 1987-89), Amnesty Internat., NOW, Greenpeace, Nat. Peace Inst., LWV, Habitat for Humanity, Neighbor to Neighbor, Planned Parenthood. Democrat.

JONES, GAIL KATHLEEN, educational administrator; b. Oklahoma City, June 28, 1935; d. Lloyd Clifton Jones and Cleo Kathleen (Shackelford) Ahlstedt; m. Jerry Lynn Jones, Aug. 8, 1954; children: Kathleen DeVaughan, Jerry Clifton, Gregory Taylor. BA in English, Cen. Wash. U., 1971. Coordinator outreach program Ellensburg City Library, Wash., 1971-77; dir. alumni affairs and community rels. Cen. Wash. U., Ellensburg, 1977-95, ret., 1995, now disting. emeriti adminstr.; Pub. newsletter Central Today, 1977—. Mem. Wash. Gov.'s com. for Handicapped, 1978-83; officer United Way Bd., Ellensburg, 1982-86; mem. Beautification Commn., Ellensburg, 1980-83, Distributive Edn. Adv. Council, Ellensburg, 1978-82, chair, Ctrl. Wash. U. Centennial, 1990-92. Mem. Council Advancement and Support Edn., AAUW, LWV, Ellensburg C. of C. Presbyterian. Lodge: Soroptimists (charter pres. Kittitas County (Wash.) club 1986-88, dist. dir. 1990-92). Home: 405 N Anderson St Ellensburg WA 98926-3145

JONES, GALEN RAY, physician assistant; b. Salt Lake City, Feb. 1, 1948; s. Leonard Ray and Veda (Whitehead) J.; m. Patricia Ann Poulson, Jan. 21, 1972; children: Brian, Marci, Natalie. Grad., Med. Field Svc. Sch. Ft. Sam Houston, San Antonio, 1971; BS, U. Utah, 1982. Missionary Ch. of Jesus Christ of Latter Day Saints, Alta., Sask., Can., 1967-69; asst. mgr. Cowan's Frostop Hamburger Stand, Salt Lake City, 1969-70; with Safeway Stores, Inc., Salt Lake City, 1970; o.r. tech. Latter Day Saint Hosp., Salt Lake City, 1973-75; physician asst. Lovell Clinic Inc., Lovell, Wyo., 1975-77, Family Health Care, Inc., Tooele, Utah, 1977-86, West Dermatology and Surgery Med. Grp., Redlands, Calif., 1986-95; with blood and marrow transplant program Univ. Hosp. and Primary Childrens Med. Ctr. U. Utah, Salt Lake City, 1996-98; physician asst. D. Edgar Allen Dermatology, Ogden, 1998—; maturation lectr. Tooele Sch. Dist., 1978-86; course dir., instr. EMT, North Big Horn County Search and Rescue, 1976; instr. EMT, Grantsville Ambulance Inc., 1979-85; lectr. on skin care and changes to sr. citizen groups, hosp. auxs., health fairs, 1986—; high sch. sophomore sem. tchr. religion, 1991-96; owner Adventureland and TopHat Video, Magna, Utah, 1982-96. Author: (with others) The P.A. Clinical Practice, 1995. Chmn. County Health Teen Pregnancy Prevention Project, Tooele, 1980-81; adv. bd. State Dept. Health-Rural Health Network, Salt Lake City, 1985-86; health lectr. County Health & Edn. Dept. Progs., Tooele, 1977-86; mormon bishop/pastor Lakeview Ward, Latter Day Saints Ch., Tooele, 1982-86; mem. Utah Acad. Physician Assts. (pres. 1980-81, editor newsletter 1979-80). With U.S. Army, 1971-73. U. Utah grantee, 1966, 67, 69. Fellow Am. Acad. Physician Assts., Utah. Acad. Physicians Assts. Republican. Mem. LDS Ch. Avocations: gardening, hiking, camping, skiing, photography, travel. Home: 2670 Willow Wick Dr Sandy UT 84093-1929 Office: D Edgar Allen Dermatology 3860 Jackson Ave Ogden UT 84403-1956

JONES, GARTH LEWIS, lawyer; b. Seattle, Wash., Aug. 24, 1954; s. Myles C. and Rosetta (Holmes) J.; m. Nyree Rose Cropp, Nov. 19, 1977 (div. 1993); children: Meredyth Elise, Graham Lewis; m. Patricia Dewey, Nov. 11, 1993; 1 child, Randall Dewey. BS in pysch. and sociology, Brigham Young U., 1979, JD, 1984. Legal analyst Washington Supreme Ct. Ofc. of the Admistr. for the Cts., Olympia, Wash., 1984-93; atty. Stritmatter Kessler, Hoquiam, Wash., 1993—. Reporter Supreme Ct. com. on Pattern Jury instructions, Olympia, 1986-93, Supreme Ct. Com. on Pattern Forms, Olympia, 1984-93, Washington Pattern Jury Instructions - Criminal Practice (vol. 11 & 11A), Washington, 1993, Washington Pattern Jury Instructions - Civil Practice (vol. 6 west), Washington, 1989; staff & rep. Superior Ct. Judges' Benchbook Com., Olympia, 1984-93; reporter, author Washington Judges' Benchbook - Civil, 1985. Eagle mem. Washington State Trial Lawyers Assn. Home: 712 Hill Ave Hoquiam WA 98550-1435 Office: Stritmatter Kessler 407 8th St Hoquiam WA 98550-3607

JONES, GEORGIA ANN, publisher; b. Ogden, Utah, July 6, 1946; d. Sam Oliveto and Edythe June Murphy; m. Lowell David Jones; children: Lowell Scott, Curtis Todd. Sculptor, 1964-78, journalist, 1968-80; appraiser real property Profl. Real Estate Appraisal, San Carlos, Calif., 1980-95; online columnist, 1995-97; owner, pub. Ladybug Press, San Carlos, 1996—; leader workshops for writers, 1994—. Author: A Garden of Weedin', 1997, Write What You Know: A Writer's Adventure, 1998; sculptor, 1964-78; patentee Scruples-tag, 1980; editor, pub. Women on a Wire, 1996; author, playwright, A Stitch in Time, 1995, The Usual Suspects, 1995. Mem. Internat. Friends of Lit. and Culture (bd. dirs., U.S. chpt., Pave Peace keynote spkr. internat. congress 1999). Avocations: drawing, designing and building homes, landscape gardening. Office: Ladybug Press 751 Laurel St Ste 223 San Carlos CA 94070-3113

JONES, GILBERT LEED, retired law enforcement officer, coroner, author; b. Inglewood, Calif., Mar. 22, 1947; s. Vernal and Gwendolyn Helen (Leisure) J.; m. JoAnne Lynn Stang-Jones, June 4, 1966; children: Natalie Lynn Jones-Henderson, Dean Leed Jones. AS, Mt. San Antonio Coll., Walnut, Calif., 1978. Advanced cert. for peace officer stds. in tng., Calif. Dep. sheriff Los Angeles County Sheriff's Dept., L.A., 1969-80; dep. sheriff, coroner Mendocino County Sheriff's Dept., Ukiah, Calif., 1980-2000; search and rescue mem. mounted posse Mendocino County Sheriff;s Dept., 1981-96, mounted enforcement officer, 1994-2000, critical incident negotiator, 1995-2000, property mgmt. officer, 1996-2000. Author: (novels) Journey to Horse Heaven, 1997, A Case of Corruption, 1997, Eleven Ninety-Nine! Officer Down!, 1998, In The Company of Their Own Kind, 1998, Legend of the Fall of Pangaea, 1999. Sgt. U.S. Army, 1966-69. Republican. Avocations: wilderness horseback riding, horse training. Office: WordCraft Lit Svcs PO Box 161 Laytonville CA 95454-0161

JONES, GREGORY FAY, publisher, sales professional; b. Monroe, Wis., July 16, 1947; s. Fay Nelson Jones and Lois Mary Fahey; m. Christine Ann Swanson, June 25, 1980 (div. 1990); m. Lisa Louise Wichser, Dec. 6, 1990; children: Casandra M., Julian Wu. BA in Econs., U. Wis., 1969; BA in East Asian Studies, U. Minn., 1978. Sales mgr. China Books & Periodicals, San Francisco, 1980—; pub. Red Mansion Pub., South San Francisco, Calif., 1997—. Editor: Moon Maiden, 1993, Outrageous Chinese, 1994, Ten Years of Madness, 1996, Gate of All Marvelous Things, 1998. Activist McCarthy for Pres. Campaign, Madison, Wis., 1968, Com. to End the War in Vietnam, Madison, 1967-69; mem. adv. bd. U.S.-China People's Friendship Assn., Chgo., 1982-89, Families with Children from China, 1997—. Mem. Pubs. Mktg. Assn., Am. Booksellers Assn., Amnesty Internat., Chinese Lang. Tchrs. Assn., Calif. Chinese Lang. Tcrhs. Assn., San Bruno Mountain Watch. Avocations: music, hiking, reading, travel. Office: China Books & Periodicals Inc 2929 24th St San Francisco CA 94110

JONES, GREGORY TAYLOR, human resources risk manager; b. Fayetteville, Ark., July 21, 1962; s. Jerry Lynn and Gail Kathleen J.; m. Wendes RE Johnson, Apr. 5, 1987 (div. June 1994); children: G. Taylor, Romanda K. Parker L. BSBA, Ctrl. Wash. U., 1983; MPA, Calif. State U., Hayward, 1997. Personnel analyst City of Concord (Calif.), 1990-93, sr. personnel analyst, 1993-95, risk mgr., 1996—; bd. dirs. Contra Costa County Risk Mgmt., Walnut Creek, Calif. Capt. USAF, 1983-90. Mem. Internat. Personnel Mgrs. Assn., Pub. Agy. Risk Mgrs. Assn. Democrat. Avocations: reading, music, writing poetry, painting, travel. Office: City of Concord 1950 Parkside Dr Concord CA 94519-2578

JONES, J. GILBERT, research consultant; b. San Francisco, June 1, 1922; [illegible] Mcht. Marine Acad., 1942-44, San Francisco City Coll., 1942-44, 46-47; AB, U. Calif., Berkeley, 1949, MA, 1952. Lic. pvt. investigator. Ins. insp. Ins. Cos. Insp. Bur., San Francisco, 1959-62; pub. rels. cons., San Francisco, 1962-67; ins. insp. Am. Svc. Bur., San Francisco, 1967-72; propr., mgr. Dawn Universal Internat. San Francisco, 1972—, Dawn Universal Security Svc., San Francisco, 1983—. Mem. SAR, Libr. of Congress Assocs., Sons. Spanish-Am. War Vets. Soc., World Affairs Coun. N. Calif., U. Calif. Alumni Assn., Commonwealth Club of Calif. Republican. Office: PO Box 424057 San Francisco CA 94142-4057

JONES, J. SORTON, lawyer; b. Llandudno, Wales, 1941. BSc, U. St. Andrews, Scotland, 1964; JD, U. Calif., Berkeley, 1973. Bar: Calif. 1973, N.Y. 1975; Registered Civil Engr. Calif. 1969. Mem. Carroll, Burdick & McDonough, San Francisco, 1994—. Fellow Chartered Inst. of Arbitrators London; mem. ABA (internat. law sect.), Corp. Counsel Com., Am. Arbitration Assn., Inst. Civil Engrs. London (assoc.). Office: Carroll Burdick & McDonough 44 Montgomery St Ste 400 San Francisco CA 94104-4606*

JONES, JAMES LITTON, nuclear scientist, research technologist; b. Ridgewood, N.J., July 2, 1956; s. Raymond Bryan and Christa Maria Jones; m. Cynthia Ann Ford, Sept. 6, 1980; children: Nathaniel Dean, Katlyn Maria. BSME, U. Tex., 1979; MS, MIT, 1981; PhD, Idaho State U., 1996. Adv. scientist Idaho Nat. Engring. Lab., Idaho Falls, 1980—; lab. rep. DOE Lab. Adv. Group, Washington, 1991-92; adj. and assoc. prof. Idaho State U. Recipient George Westinghouse Innovation award Westinghouse Electric Co., 1993. Mem. Am. Phys. Soc., Idaho sect. Am. Nuclear Soc. (membership chmn. 1989). Republican. Roman Catholic. Achievements include copatent for device for generating an epithermal neutron beam for boron neutron capture therapy. Home: 1181 Kortnee Dr Idaho Falls ID 83402-5185 Office: Idaho Nat Engring Lab MS-2802 PO Box 1625 Idaho Falls ID 83415-0001

JONES, JAN LAVERTY, mayor. Grad. Stanford Univ. Mayor Mcpl. Govt., Las Vegas, Nev., 1991—. Office: Office of Mayor City Hall 10th Fl 400 E Stewart Ave Las Vegas NV 89101-2927*

JONES, JEAN CORREY, organization administrator; b. Denver, Jan. 12, 1942; d. Robert Magnie and Elizabeth Marie (Harpel) Evans; m. Stewart Hoyt Jones, Aug. 3, 1963; children: Andrew and Correy. BS in History, Social Studies and Secondary Edn., Northwestern U., 1963. Cert. non-profit mgr. History tchr. Glenbrook South H.S., Glenview, Ill., 1963-65; advocacy rsch. dir. Episc. Diocese of Denver, 1977-80; pub. affairs adminstr. United Bank of Denver, 1980-82; exec. dir. Mile Hi coun. Girl Scouts U.S., Denver, 1982—; substitute tchr. Denver Pub. Schs., 1965-80. Active Minoru Yasui Cmty. Vol. Award com., 1979-98, Women's Forum of Colo., 1989-98, Leadership Denver (Member of Yr., 1988), 1988—; pres. Jr. League, Denver, 1979-80, Rotary, Denver, 1995—, pres., 1995-96, commr., chair Colo. Civil Rights commn., Denver, 1987-96, vice chair Health One, Denver, 1996; bd. dirs. Hist. Denver, Inc., 1994—, Samaritan Inst., Denver, 1998; vice chair, trustee Colo. Trust, 1998; pres. Women's Forum of Colo. Inc., 1998—. Named Profl. Woman of Achievement Colo. Women's Leadership Coalition and Colo. Easter Seal Soc., 1995. Mem. Denver Metro C. of C., Univ. Club. Republican. Episcopalian. Avocations: swimming, tennis, reading. Office: Girl Scouts Mile High Coun PO Box 9407 Denver CO 80209-0407

JONES, JERVE MALDWYN, construction company executive; b. L.A., Sept. 21, 1918; s. Oliver Cromwell and Zola (Hill) J.; m. Alice Castle Holcomb, Apr. 12, 1942; children—Jay Gregory, Janey Lee Matt, Joel Kevin. B.S. in Civil Engring., U. So. Calif., 1939. Registered profl. engr., Calif. Stress analyst Northrop Aircraft, L.A., 1940-43; ptnr. Jones Bros. Constrn. Co., Beverly Hills, Calif., 1946-56; pres., chief exec. officer Peck/Jones Constrn. Corp. (formerly Jones Bros. Constrn. Co.), Beverly Hills, Calif., 1956—; cons. Jerve M. Jones Assocs., Beverly Hills, 1970—; chmn. Jones Constrn. Mgmt., Beverly Hills, 1983—. Bd. dirs. Huntington Library, San Marino, Calif., 1984—, Pepperdine U., Malibu, Calif., Boy Scouts Am., L.A., Santa Monica Hosp. Found., YMCA Met. L.A.; chmn. L.A. Music Ctr., United Fund Campaign; life mem. Town Hall Calif., L.A., adv. bd. UCLA Med. Ctr.; mem. State Calif. Strong Motion Instrumentation Program, Dept. Mines and Geology. With USNR, 1943-46, PTO. Recipient Civil Engring. Alumnus of Yr. award U. So. Calif., 1985, Bronze Hat award United Contractors Assn., 1985, Disting. Scout award, 1989. Mem. Constrn. Mgmt. Assn. Am. (nat. pres. 1984, Founders award 1985), Archtl. Guild, Archimedes Circle, Constrn. Industry Commn. (chmn. 1980-84), Assoc. Gen. Contractors Am., Los Angeles Area C. of C. (dir.). Republican. Episcopalian. Clubs: Los Angeles Country, California. Lodge: Rotary (dir. 1962-68). Avocations: yachting; skiing; fly fishing. Office: Peck/Jones Constrn Corp 10866 Wilshire Blvd Fl 7 Los Angeles CA 90024-4300

JONES, JEWEL LOUISE, social services administrator. BA, Langston U., 1962; MA, U. Alaska, 1974. Dir. Social Svcs. Dept., Anchorage, 1970-85, Health and Human Svcs. Dept., Anchorage, 1985-88; mgr. social svcs. divsn. health and human svcs. dept. Muncipality of Anchorage, from 1988; now chair bd. Alaska Housing Fin. Corp., Anchorage. Office: Alaska Housing Fin Corp 4300 Boniface Pkwy PO Box 101020 Anchorage AK 99510-1020

JONES, JOEL MACKEY, academic administrator; b. Millersburg, Ohio, Aug. 11, 1937; s. Theodore R. and Edna Mae (Mackey) Jones; children: Carolyn Mae, Jocelyn Corinne. BA, Yale U., 1960; MA, Miami U., Oxford, Ohio, 1962; PhD, U. N.Mex., 1966. Dir. Am. studies U. Md., Balt., 1966-69; chmn. Am. studies U. N.Mex., Albuquerque, 1969-73, asst. v.p. acad. affairs, 1973-77, dean faculties, assoc. provost, prof. Am. studies, 1977-85, v.p. adminstrn., 1985-88; pres. Ft. Lewis Coll., Durango, Colo., 1988—. Contbr. numerous essays, articles and chpts. to books. Founder Rio Grande Nature Preserve Soc., Albuquerque, 1974—; bd. dirs., mem. exec. com., United Way, Albuquerque, 1980-83; nat. bd. cons. NEH, 1978—; bd. dirs. Mercy Hosp., 1990-94, 1st Nat. Bank; mem. ACE Commn. on Leadership. Farwell scholar Yale U., New Haven, 1960; Sr. fellow NEH, 1972, Adminstrv. fellow Am. Coun. Edn., Washington, 1972-73. Mem. Am. Studies Assn., Am. Assn. Higher Edn., Am. Assn. State Colls. and Univs. (chair com. on cultural diversity, Colo. state rep., 1994—). Home: 150 Eagle Vw Durango CO 81301-6686 Office: Ft Lewis Coll Office of Pres Durango CO 81301-3999

JONES, JOHN HARDING, photographer; b. Pitts., Apr. 28, 1923; s. John F. and Emma Eleanor (West) J.; 1 child, Blair Harding. BFA, Rochester Inst. Tech., 1949; MBA, Pepperdine U., 1978; PhD, U. London, 1983; M in Photography (hon.), Brantridge Forest, Eng.; DLitt (hon.), Ky. Christian U.; EdD, St. John's U. Seaman U.S. Naval Air, 1940, advanced through grades to comdr., 1948; ret., 1963; chief photographer U.S. Steel Corp., Pitts.; mgr. art & photo dept. Magnavox Corp., Urbana, Ill.; chief photographer rehab. medicine sect. U.S. Vet. Adminstrn., L.A.; coord. rehab. medicine domiciliary sect. Wadsworth VA Hosp., L.A.; tchr. Carnegie Mellon Inst., Pitts., Earl Wheeler Schs., Pitts., Seattle U., Art Inst. Pitts.; dir., owner The Little Studio, Panorama City, Calif., 1989—, The Little Studio West, Panorama City, 1994—; owner The Little Studio, Pitts., The Little Studio West. Author: Photography, 1972, The Correspondence Educational Directory, 1976, 79, 84, 94, Correspondence Courses for High School Credit & GED Preparation, 1994. Comdr. USNR, ret. Recipient award Writers Guild, 1977, Merit award Cooking, 1986; elected to Am. Police Hall of Fame, 1996. Mem. Profl. Photographers Am., Masons, Shriners, Order of the Eastern Star (worthy patron 1986). Presbyn. Avocations: bowling, writing, travel, civic activities, stamp collecting. Home: 5320 Zelzah Ave Apt 203 Encino CA 91316-2214

JONES, JOHN WESLEY, entrepreneur; b. Wenatchee, Wash., Nov. 15, 1942; s. Richard F. and Hazel F. (Hendrix) J.; m. Melissa L. Meyer, June 22, 1968 (div. 1982); children: John E., Jennifer L.; m. Deborah G. Matthews, Apr. 24, 1993. BA in Bus./Econs., Western Wash. U., Bellingham, 1966. Trainee Jones Bldg., Seattle, 1967-69; sec. Jones Bldg., 1969-78; owner/mgr. N.W. Inboards, Bellevue, Wash., 1974-78, Jones Bldg., Seattle, 1978-86; pvt. investor Bellevue, 1987—; owner/mgr. J. Jones Enterprises, 1994—; trustee BOMA Health & Welfare Trust, 1982-86, chmn. 1986, mem. Seattle Fire Code Adv. Bd., 1979-86. With USMCR, 1966-72. Mem. Seattle Bldg. Owners and Mgrs. Assn. (trustee 1979-86), Bldg. Owners and Mgrs. In- [illegible] posite Fabricators Assn., Soc. Naval Architects and Marine Engrs., Boat U.S., Seattle Yacht Club, NRA, Internat. Show Car Assn., Nat. Street Rod Assn., Specialty Equipment Mktg. Assn. Republican. Avocations: boating, water skiing, snow skiing, automobiles, photography. Home: 61 Skagit Key

Bellevue WA 98006-1021 Office: 12819 SE 38th St # 288 Bellevue WA 98006-1395

JONES, JOHNPAUL, architect. BArch, U. Oreg., 1967. Registered architect, Wash., Calif., Oreg., Idaho, Hawaii, Ariz., N.Mex., Fla.; nat. cert. architect, NCARB. With Paul Thiry, Architect, Seattle, Oda/McCarty Architects, Hilo, Hawaii; sr. prin. Jones & Jones, Architects and Landscape Architects, Seattle, 1972—; lectr. in field. Prin. works include Cedar River Visitor Facility, Seattle, Dea'ht Tribal Elders Ctr., Neah Bay, Wash., Edn. Pavilion and Children's Zoo, Honolulu, Longhouse Cultural Edn. Ctr., Olympia, Washington, Mercer Slough Nature Ctr., Bellevue, Wash., Overlake Blueberry Farm, Bellevue, Seattle Children's Mus., Stimson Green Hist. Gardens, Seattle, Ctr. Urban Horticulture Bldgs. and Douglas Rsch. Conservatory U. Wash., Seattle, rsch. lab. and support greenhouses U. Alaska, Fairbanks, Tilikum Pl. Urban Pub. Sq., Seattle, Eagle Island State Pk. Bldgs., Boise, Idaho, Gene Coulon Meml. Beach Pk. Bldgs., Renton, Washington (Honor award AIA 1982, 1st Honor award Am. Steel Assn. 1982, Excellence on the Water Honor award Waterfront Ctr. 1987, The Inhabited Landscape award Archtl. League N.Y. Exhbn. 1987), Newcastle Beach Pk. Bldgs., Bellevue (Merit award AIA 1988, Best Design of 1988 Times Mag., Excellence on the Water Honor award Waterfront Ctr. 1988, Honor award regional AIA 1990), Newhalem ranger sta. and campground bldg. North Cascades Nat. Pk., Washington (1st Honor award Am. Wood Coun. 1981), Nat. Pk. Svc. Skagway (Alaska) Maintenance Facility, Hertz Administrn. Maintenance and Regional Facility, SeaTac Airport, Washington, others, (landscape designs) Zool. Soc. San Diego, Woodland Pk. Zoo and Zool. Gardens (Pres.'s Award of Excellence Am. Soc. Landscape Architects 1980), Seattle, City of Honolulu Dept. Pks. and Recreation, N.Mex. State Pks., Carlsbad, Dallas Zoo, Point Defiance Zoo & Aquarium (Merit award Wash. chpt. Am. Soc. Landscape Architects 1981), Tacoma, Ariz.-Sonora Desert Mus., Tucson, San Diego Zoo (Best Exhibit award Am. Assn. Zool. Pks. & Aquariums 1989), others, (historic preservation) Icicle Canyon Arts Ctr., Leavenworth, Washington, Icicle Canyon Guest Lodges, Klondike Goldrush Nat. Hist. Pk. Maintenance Facility, Skagway. Chmn. Pioneer Sq. Hist. Preservation Bd., Seattle; former bd. dirs. King County United Way. Fellow AIA (mem. Seattle chpt.); mem. Nat. Assn. Indian Architects & Engrs. Office: Jones & Jones 105 S Main St Fl 4 Seattle WA 98104-2535*

JONES, JON SYDNEY, writer, educator; b. Britton, S.D., Apr. 6, 1948; s. Edwin O. and Dorothy A. (Paulson) J.; 1 child, Tess Jones. BA in Comms., U. Oreg., 1970. English instr. Cabrillo Coll., Aptos, Calif., 1986—. Author: Bike and Hike: Sixty Tours around Great Britain and Ireland, 1977, Vienna Inside-Out: 16 Walking Tours, 1979, Hitler in Vienna, 1983, Tramping in Europe: A Walking Guide, 1984, Viennawalks: Four Intimate Walking Tours, 1985, Time of the Wolf, 1990, The Hero Game, 1992, Frankie, 1997. Mem. Am. Soc. Journalists and Authors, Authors Guild. Avocations: reading, music, tennis. Home: 210 Martin Dr Aptos CA 95003-4605

JONES, LOUIS WORTH, retired management analyst, journalist; b. St. Louis, Jan. 8, 1908; s. Ed C. and Vida Pearl (Wrather) J.; m. Pauline Marie Ernest, May 24, 1947; children: David Worth, Roger Louis, Ethan Ernest, Faye, Arthur Carlyle. Student, Washington U., St. Louis, 1925-27. Trainee, adminstrv. officer Farm Security Adminstrv., USDA, Washington, 1934-46; mgmt. anaylst War Assets Adminstrn., San Francisco, 1946-48, US AEC, Los Alamos, N.Mex., 1948-50, USN Radiol. Def. Lab., San Francisco, 1950-68; ret., 1968; trustee emeritus The World U., Benson, Ariz.; founder, exec. dir. Intergroup Rels. of No. Calif., 1966-73. Editor, pub. Lou Jones Newsletter, 1959-70; author: (scripts) Meet Mary Wollstonecraft, 1977, Meet Alexander Meiklejohn, 1978. Past v.p. World Univ., Benson, Ariz; vol. alt. coord. Civil Def., San Mateo County, 1957-58; pres. Mid-Peninsula Coun. Civic Unity, 1959-60; mem. Bi-County Commn. Human Rels.; trustee Unitarian-Universalist, 1958. Hon. Soc. scholar, 1925-27; recipient Mem. of Yr. award Unitarian-Universalist, 1977. Mem. AARP, Nat. Assn. Retired Fed. Employees, Intergroup Rels. Assn. No. Calif. (founder), Humanist Cmty. Peninsula (co-founder). Avocations: piano, photography. E-mail: LouisWJ@aol.com. Fax: 650-344-0334. Home: 511 Verano Ct San Mateo CA 94402

JONES, MARGARET LOUISE, supervisory production analyst; b. Roswell, N.Mex., Aug. 12, 1944; d. William Presley and Ida Margaret (Wright) Bratcher; m. Jeffrey Dean Holman, Dec. 19, 1970; 1 child, Sean Eric; m. Don Jones, Dec. 22, 1982. Student, Ea. N.Mex. U., 1962, Red Rocks C.C., Golden, Colo., 1984. Clk. U.S. Geol. Survey, Roswell, N.Mex., 1962-66; resource clk. U.S. Forest Svc., Tallahassee, Fla., 1966-68; apt. mgr. Brinkley Bros., Tallahassee, 1968-69; sec. State of Fla., Tallahassee, 1969-70, 1st Nat. Bank, Roswell, 1970, Bur. Land Mgmt./Soil Conservation Svc./U.S. Geol. Survey, Roswell, 1970-81; supr. clk. BLM, Roswell, 1981-82; fgn. activities asst. Bur. Reclamation, Lakewood, Colo., 1982-84; lead prodn. technician Minerals Mgmt. Svc., Lakewood, Colo., 1984-85, prodn. analyst, 1985-88, staff prodn. analyst, 1988-92, supervisory prodn. analyst, 1992—. Named Outstanding Young Woman of Am., 1980. Mem. Southampton Townhome Assn. (bd. dirs. 1983-85, v.p. 1985-90, pres. 1990—). Democrat. Baptist. Avocations: walking, reading, collectibles, gardening.

JONES, MARGIE RABEN, antiques dealer, educator; b. Scottsbluff, Nebr., Sept. 28, 1933; d. Wells Orville and Lyndall (Hewitt) Raben; m. E. Bruce Jones, May 27, 1956; children: Elizabeth Gwynn Jones, Janet Lee Jones White. BS, U. Wyo., 1955; MS, Pa. State U., 1959; student, Colo. State U., 1970. Home econs. tchr. Cody (Wyo.) High Sch., 1955-56; sci. tchr. Rancier Jr. High Sch., Killeen, Tex., 1956-57; graduate asst. Penn State U., U. Park, Pa., 1957-59; home econs. tchr. Cary Jr. High Sch., Cheyenne, Wyo., 1959-60; instr. consumer scis. Colo. State U., Ft. Collins, 1970-76; antique dealer Old Gray Hare, Cody, Wyo., 1994—. Creator, author private family history books, 1995—; editor: Letters from Home, 1996. V.p., treas., sec. Rabenland, Inc., Huntley, Wyo., 1975-94. Mem. PEO, Am. Assn. U. Women (treas. 1994—), Phi Kappa Phi, Delta Delta Delta. Republican. Presby. Avocations: writing and reasearching family history, gardening, travel, quilting, volunteer work for various church and community organizations.

JONES, MARK ALAN, broadcast technician; b. San Francisco, 1957; m. Stephanie Phillips, 1983. BA in Communication Studies, Calif. State U., 1979. Chief operator Sta. KXPR, Sacramento, 1979-80, with ops./prodn.dept., 1980—. Recipient pub. radio program award for Excellence, Corp. Pub. Broadcasting, 1981. Office: Capital Pub Radio Inc 3416 American River Dr Ste B Sacramento CA 95864-5715

JONES, MARK LOGAN, educational association executive, educator; b. Provo, Utah, Dec. 16, 1950; s. Edward Evans and Doris (Logan) J. BS, Ea. Mont. Coll., 1975; postgrad. in labor rels., Cornell U.; postgrad., SUNY, Buffalo. Narcotics detective Yellowstone County Sheriff's Dept., Billings, Mont., 1972-74; math tchr. Billings (Mont.) Pub. Schs., 1975-87; rep. Nat. Edn. Assn. of N.Y., Buffalo, Jamestown, 1987-91, Nat. Edn. Assn. Alaska, Anchorage, 1991—. Photographs featured in 1991 N.Y. Art Rev. and Am. Artist. Committeeman Yellowstone Dem. Party, Billings, 1984-87; exec. com. Dem. Cen. Com., Billings, 1985-87; bd. dirs. Billings Community Ctr., 1975-87; concert chmn. Billings Community Concert Assn., 1980-87; bd. dirs. Chautauqua County Arts Coun.; bd. dirs. Big Brothers and Big Sisters Anchorage. With U.S. Army, 1970-72. Recipient Distinguished Svc. award, Billings Edn. Assn., 1985, Mont. Edn. Assn., 1987. Mem. Billings Edn. Assn. (bd. dirs. 1980-82, negotiator 1981-87, pres. 1982-87), Mont. Edn. Assn. (bd. dirs. 1982-87), Ea. Mont. Coll. Tchr. Edn. Project, Accreditation Reviewer Team Mont. Office Pub. Edn., Big Sky Orchard, Masonic, Scottish Rite. Avocations: Bonsai, photography, reading, classical and jazz music, hunting, fishing. Home: PO Box 102904 Anchorage AK 99510-2904 Office: Nat Edn Assn Alaska 1840 S Bragaw St Ste 103 Anchorage AK 99508-3463

JONES, NATHANIEL, bishop. Bishop Ch. of God in Christ, Barstow, Calif. Office: Ch of God in Christ 630 Chateau Way Barstow CA 92311-5721

JONES, NEIL FORD, surgeon; b. Merthyr Tydvil, Wales, Nov. 30, 1947; s. John Robert and Kathleen Mary (Ford) J.; m. Barbara Rose Unterman, Feb. 18, 1978; 1 child, Nicholas Huw. B of Medicine, B of Surgery, MA, Oxford (Eng.) U., 1975. Registrar N.E. Thames Regional Plastic Surgery Centre, Billericay, Eng., 1982; fellow in hand surgery and microsurgery Mass. Gen. Hosp. Harvard U., Boston, 1983; asst. prof. surgery U. Pitts., 1984-89, assoc. prof. surgery, 1989-93, dir. hand and microsurgery fellowship, 1987-93; prof., chief of hand surgery UCLA Med. Ctr. dept. orthopedic surgery divsn. plastic and reconstructive surgery, 1993—. Contbr. articles to profl. jours. Fellow Royal Coll. Surgeons Eng., Am. Coll. Surgeons; mem. Am. Soc. Plastic and Reconstructive Surgeons, Am. Soc. Surgery of the Hand, Am. Soc. Reconstructive Microsurgery, Internat. Soc. Reconstructive Microsurgery. Avocation: travel. Home: 532 N Bonhill Rd Los Angeles CA 90049-2326 Office: UCLA Med Ctr 200 UCLA Med Plz # 140 Los Angeles CA 90095-8344

JONES, PETER F., lawyer; b. Hanover, N.H., Jan. 3, 1944; s. J. Franklin Jr. and Elizabeth Anne (Dunning) J.; m. Anne M. Jones, Apr. 17, 1971; children: David, Philip. BA, Ripon Coll., 1967; JD, U. Denver, 1970. Bar: Colo. 1971, U.S. Dist. Ct. Colo. 1971. Assoc. Duane O. Littell, Denver, 1971-76; assoc. Hall & Evans, Denver, 1976-78, ptnr., 1978—. Office: Hall & Evans 1200 17th St Ste 1700 Denver CO 80202-5817

JONES, PETER RONALD, religious studies educator, author, speaker; b. Liverpool, Eng., Nov. 13, 1940; came to U.S., 1991; s. Thomas Ronald and Ellen (Shackleton) J.; m. Rebecca Stuart Clowney, Jan. 30, 1971; children: Eowyn, Gabrielle, Julien, Myriam, Tessa, Zoe, Tobias. BA, U. Wales, Cardiff, 1963; MDiv, Gordon Conwell Theol. Sem., Mass., 1967; MTh, Harvard Divinity Sch., 1969; PhD, Princeton Sem., 1972. Prof. Greek and New Testament Faculte Libre de Theologie Reformée, Aix-en-Provence, France, 1974-91, Westminster Theol. Sem. in Calif., Escondido, 1991—. Author: (commentary) Le Deuxieme Epite aux Corinthiens, 1990; (books), The Gnostic Empire Strikes Back, 1992, Spirit Wars: Pagan Revival in Christian America, 1997. Mem. Am. Acad. of Religions, Soc. of Biblical Lit., Presbyn. Ch. Am. Avocation: golf. Office: Westminster Theol Sem Calif 1725 Bear Valley Pkwy Escondido CA 92027-4128

JONES, RANDY ALLEN, electronic communications technician; b. Spokane, Wash., Mar. 15, 1957; s. Roger Allen Jones and Betty Jean (Wahl) Price; m. Diane Lynn Kenerson, Jan. 26, 1979; children: Michael Allen, Marshal Lynn. Lic. in gen. radiotelephone, FCC. Electronics technician Musonic Svcs., Inc., Spokane, Wash., 1980; radio technician Western Comm., Inc., Spokane, 1981, Switzer Comm., Spokane, 1981-83, Spokane County Comm. Dept., Spokane, 1983-88; electronic comm. sys. field technician Washington State Dept. Natural Resources, Colville, 1988—. Sgt. USMC, 1975-79. Mem. Am. Radio Relay League, Assn. Pub. Safety Comm. Officials Internat. Inc., Panorama Land Amateur Radio Club. (pres. 1992-94, 98—). Avocations: amateur radio, computers, antique radio repair, target shooting. E-mail: rjones@plix.com. Fax: 509-684-7484. Office: Dept Natural Resources PO Box 190 Colville WA 99114-0190

JONES, RICHARD NELSON, clinical laboratory scientist, Arabist; b. Oakland, Calif., Nov. 12, 1950; s. Norman Beecher and Marcia Ruth (Nelson) J.; m. Kathryn Johnson, May 20, 1979; 1 child, Nicholas Richard. BSc, Utah State U., 1976; MA, U. Utah, 1981, PhD, 1991. Registered med. technologist. Scientist dept. trace metals Assoc. Regional and Univ. Pathologists, Inc., Salt Lake City, 1985—; dir. Nr. East Antiquity Cons. Group, Inc., Sandy, Utah, 1991—. Contbr. articles to profl. jours. and dictionaries. Mem. Am. Schs. Oriental Rsch., Soc. Bibl. Lit., Soc. Coptic Archaeology, Paleopath. Soc., Sigma Chi. Home: 9231 Stone Ridge Cir Sandy UT 84093-2698 Office: Assn Regional & U Pathologists Inc 500 Chipeta Way Salt Lake City UT 84108-1221

JONES, ROBERT ALONZO, economist; b. Evanston, Ill., Mar. 15, 1937; s. Robert Vernon and Elsie Pierce (Brown) J.; m. Ina Turner Jones; children: Lindsay Rae, Robert Pierce, Gregory Alan, William Kenneth. AB, Middlebury Coll., 1959; MBA, Northwestern U., 1961, LLD (hon.) Middlebury (Vt.) Coll., 1992. Economist Hahn, Wise & Assoc., San Carlos, Calif., 1966-69; sr. rsch. officer Bank of Am., San Francisco, 1969-74; v.p., dir. fin. forecasting Chase Econometrics, San Francisco, 1974-76; chmn. bd. Money Market Svcs., Inc., Belmont, Calif., 1974-86; chmn. bd. MMS Internat., Redwood City, Calif., 1986-89, chmn. emeritus, 1989—; chmn. bd. dirs. Market News Svc., N.Y.C.; chmn. emeritus Geonomics Inst., Middlebury, 1995—, chmn. bd., 1986-95; chmn. bd. Jones Internat., 1989—; chmn. bd. Market News Svc., Inc., N.Y.C., 1993—; chmn. bd. Jones Fin. Network, Inc., Incline Village, N.Y.; dean coun. Harvard U. Div. Sch., Cambridge, Mass., 1991—; mem. Kellogg Alumni Adv. Bd., Northwestern U., 1993—; instr. money and banking, Am. Inst. Banking, San Francisco, 1971, 72; councilman, City of Belmont (Calif.), 1970-77, mayor, 1971, 72, 75, 76; dir. San Mateo County Transit Dist., 1975-77; chmn. San Mateo County Coun. of Mayors, 1975-76; trustee Incline Village Gen. Improvement Dist., Nev., 1984-85,Carlmont United Meth. Ch., 1978-81, Middleburg Coll., 1997—. Author: U.S. Financial System and the Federal Reserve, 1974, Power of Coinage, 1987. 1st lt. USAR, 1961-68. Named Hon. Life Mem. Calif. PTA, ordo honorum Kappa Delta Rho Nat. Fraternity; recipient Ernst & Young Entrepreneur of the Yr. award, 1986; John Harvard fellow Harvard U., 1996, Stanton Recognition award North Shore Country Day Sch., 1996. Mem. Nat. Assn. Bus. Economists, San Francisco Bond Club. Republican. Methodist. Office: Jones Internat Inc PO Box 7498 Incline Village NV 89452-7498

JONES, ROBERT EDWARD, federal judge; b. Portland, Oreg., July 5, 1927; s. Howard C. and Leita (Hendricks) J.; m. Pearl F. Jensen, May 29, 1948; children—Jeffrey Scott, Julie Lynn. BA, U. Hawaii, 1949; JD, Lewis and Clark Coll., 1953, LHD (hon.), 1995; LLD (hon.), City U., Seattle, 1984, Lewis and Clark Coll., 1995. Bar: Oreg. Trial atty. Portland, Oreg., 1953-63; judge Oreg. Circuit Ct., Portland, 1963-83; justice Oreg. Supreme Ct., Salem, 1983-90; judge U.S. Dist. Ct. Oreg., Portland, 1990—; mem. faculty Nat. Jud. Coll., Am. Acad. Jud. Edn., ABA Appellate Judges Seminars; former mem. Oreg. Evidence Revision Commn., Oreg. Ho. of Reps.; former chmn. Oreg. Commn. Prison Terms and Parole Stds.; adj. prof. Northwestern Sch. Law, Lewis and Clark Coll., 1963—, Willamette Law Sch., 1988—. Author: Rutter Group Practice Guide Federal Civil Trials and Evidence, 1999. Bd. overseers Lewis and Clark Coll. Served to capt. JAGC, USNR. Recipient merit award Multnomah Bar Assn., 1979; Citizen award NCCJ, Legal Citizen of the Yr. award Law Related Edn. Project, 1988; Service to Mankind award Sertoma Club Oreg.; James Madison award Sigma Delta Chi; named Disting. Grad., Northwestern Sch. Law. Mem. Am. Judicature Soc. (bd. dirs. 1997—), State Bar Oreg. (past chmn. Continuing Legal Edn.), Oregon Circuit Judges Assn. (pres. 1967—), Oreg. Trial Lawyers Assn. (pres. 1959, chair 9th cir. edn. com. 1996-97). Office: US Dist Ct House 1000 SW 3rd Ave Rm 1407 Portland OR 97204-2902

JONES, ROGER CLYDE, retired electrical engineering educator; b. Lake Andes, S.D., Aug. 17, 1919; s. Robert Clyde and Martha (Albertson) J.; m. Katherine M. Tucker, June 7, 1952; children: Linda Lee, Vonnie Lynette. B.S., U. Nebr., 1949; M.S., U. Md., 1953; Ph.D. U. Md., 1963. With U.S. Naval Research Lab., Washington, 1949-57; staff sr. engr. to chief engr. Melpar, Inc., Falls Church, Va., 1957-58; cons. project engr. Melpar, Inc., 1958-59, sect. head physics, 1959-64, chief scientist for physics, 1964; prof. dept. elec. engring. U. Ariz., Tucson, 1964-89; dir. quantum electronics lab. U. Ariz., 1968-88, adj. prof. radiology, 1978-86, adj. prof. radiation-oncology, 1986-88, prof. of radiation-oncology, 1988-89, prof. emeritus, 1989—; guest prof. of exptl. oncology Inst. Cancer Research, Aarhus, Denmark, 1982-83; tech. dir. H.S.C. and A., El Paso, 1989-96. Patentee in field. Served with AUS, 1942-45. Mem. Am. Phys. Soc., Optical Soc. Am., Internat. Soc. Optical Engring., Bioelectromagnetics Soc., IEEE, AAAS, NSPE, Am. Congress on Surveying and Mapping, Eta Kappa Nu, Pi Mu Epsilon, N.Mex. Acad. Sci. Home: 5809 E 3rd St Tucson AZ 85711-1519

JONES, ROGER WAYNE, electronics executive; b. Riverside, Calif., Nov. 21, 1939; s. Virgil Elsworth and Beulah (Mills) J.; m. Sherill Lee Bottjer, Dec. 28, 1975; children: Jerrod Wayne, Jordan Anthony. BS in Engring., San Diego State U., 1962. Br. sales mgr. Bourns, Inc., Riverside, 1962-68; sales and mktg. mgr. Spectrol Electronics, Industry, Calif., 1968-77, v.p. mktg., 1979-81; mng. dir. Spectrol Reliance, Ltd., Swindon, England, 1977-79; sr. v.p. S.W. group Kierulff Electronics Corp., L.A., 1981-83; v.p. sales and mktg. worldwide electronic techs. div. Beckman Instruments, Fullerton, Calif., 1983-86; pres., ptnr. Jones & McGeoy Sales, Inc., Newport Beach, Calif., 1986—. Author: The History of Villa Rockledge, A National Treasure in Laguna Beach, 1991. Republican. Office: 5100 Campus Dr Newport Beach CA 92660-2101

JONES, RONALD H., computer information systems executive; b. San Diego, Feb. 11, 1938; s. Henry G. and Geneva H. (Hodges) J.; m. Carol Sue Carmichael, Dec. 9, 1967. BS, San Diego State Coll., 1959, MS, 1961. Project mgr. UNIVAC, San Diego, 1961-67, Computer Scis. Corp., San Diego, 1967-75; v.p. Interactive, Inc., San Diego, 1975-92; owner Consulting Co., San Diego, 1992—; ind. cons., programmer various mfg. & distbg. cos., San Diego, 1992—. Contbr. articles to profl. jours; tech. advisor to Internat. Spectrum Mag. Advisor San Diego State Univ.; Rep. nat. committeeman, 1979—. Mem. AARP, Am. Prodn. and Inventory Control Soc., Assn. for Computing Machinery, Calpirg and Ucan. Presbyterian. Avocations: golf, tennis, fishing, collecting. Home and Office: 2484 Pine St San Diego CA 92103-1042 Office: Ron Jones Cons PO Box 370083 San Diego CA 92137-0083

JONES, STANTON WILLIAM, management consultant; b. New Orleans, May 24, 1939; s. Albert DeWitt and Clara Arimenta (Stanton) J.; m. Helen Marie Trice, May 23, 1964 (div. Aug. 1972); 1 child, Ellen Marie; m. Gladys Marina Caceres, Aug. 21, 1990; children: Hazel Nathalye, Albert Stanton. BS, Embry-Riddle Aero. U., Daytona Beach, Fla., 1973; MBA, Syracuse (N.Y.) U., 1977. Cert. internal auditor. Commd. 2d lt. U.S. Army, 1963, advanced through grades to lt. col., 1979; fixed wing pilot U.S. Army, Ft. Rucker, Ala., 1965-72, rotary wing pilot, 1972; mgmt. cons. Stanton W. Jones & Assocs., San Francisco, 1987—; joint venture ptnr. Budget Analyst to Bd. Suprs., San Francisco, 1988—. Treas. Hunter's Point Boys & Girls Club, San Francisco, 1987-93. Decorated Meritorious Svc. medal. Mem. Alpha Phi Alpha (pres. 1988-90). Roman Catholic. Avocations: chess, reading, jogging. Home: 1948 Cortereal Ave Oakland CA 94611-2632 Office: Stanton W Jones & Assocs 57 Post St Ste 713 San Francisco CA 94104-5025

JONES, THOMAS EVAN, author, researcher, educator; b. Kenosha, Wis., Apr. 3, 1937; s. Ernest Edward and Martha Louise (Hiemke) J. BA, Wheaton (Ill.) Coll., 1958, MA, 1963; MA, Harvard U., 1963; PhD, Johns Hopkins U., 1964; DSSc, New Sch. for Social Rsch., 1975. Jr. instr. Johns Hopkins U., Balt., 1963-64; asst. prof. U. Conn., Storrs, 1964-67; mem. faculty New Sch. for Social Rsch., N.Y.C., 1972-74; adj. assoc. prof. Polytech. Inst. N.Y., 1976-78; cons. Hudson Inst., Croton-on-Hudson, N.Y., 1978-81; sr. sci. advisor, rsch. coord. Vitafort Internat. Corp., Mill Valley, Calif., 1988-93; cons. JoMar Labs., Campbell, Calif., 1993—; seminar leader Futures sect. IBM, White Plains, N.Y., 1973-76; rsch. coord. Goals for Global Soc. Project NSF, 1975-76; rsch. fellow UNITAR, N.Y.C., 1975-76; speaker, author MIT Conf. on Internat. Rels., Boston, 1973; seminar leader U.S. Dept. Agriculture, Washington, 1975; panel organizer, speaker First Global Conf. on the Future, Toronto, 1980. Author: Options for the Future, 1980; contbr. articles to profl. jours., chpts. to books. Aspen Inst. fellow, 1975, Internat. Inst. Applied Systems Analysis fellow, 1975, NSF fellow, 1972-73, Gilman fellow, 1963-64. Mem. World Future Soc. (v.p. N.Y.C. chpt. 1972), Internat. Platform Assn., Inst. of Noetic Scis. Avocations: marathon running, table tennis, world travel, astronomy. Home: 1648 Cottle Ave San Jose CA 95125-3809 Office: JoMar Labs 251 E Hacienda Ave Ste B Campbell CA 95008-6622

JONES, THOMAS ROBERT, social worker; b. Escanaba, Mich., Jan. 3, 1950; s. Gene Milton and Alica Una (Mattson) J.; m. Joy Sedlock. BA, U. Laverne, 1977; MSW, U. Hawaii, 1979. Social work assoc. Continuing Care Svcs., Camarillo, Calif., 1973-78; psychiat. social worker Camarillo State Hosp., 1980-84; psychotherapist Terkensha Child Treatment Ctr., Sacramento, Calif., 1984-86; psychiat. social worker Napa (Calif.) State Hosp., 1986-87; psychiat. social worker Vets. Home Calif., Yountville, 1987-98, chief of social work svc., 1998—. Mem. Nat. Assn. Social Workers, Soc. Clin. Social Work, Acad. Cert. Social Workers. Avocations: creative writing, reading, meditation, classical music. Home: PO Box 1095 Yountville CA 94599-1095 Office: Vets Home Calif Yountville CA 94599

JONES, THORNTON KEITH, research chemist; b. Brawley, Calif., Dec. 17, 1923; s. Alfred George and Madge Jones; m. Evalee Vestal, July 4, 1965; children: Brian Keith, Donna Eileen. BS, U. Calif., Berkeley, 1949, postgrad., 1951-52. Research chemist Griffin Chem. Co., Richmond, Calif., 1949-55; western product devel. and improvement mgr. Nopco Chem. Co., Richmond, Calif., 1955; research chemist Chevron Research Co., Richmond, 1956-65, research chemist in spl. products research and devel., 1965-1982; product quality mgr. Chevron USA, Inc., San Francisco, 1982-87, ret. Patentee in field. Vol. fireman and officer, Terra Linda, Calif., 1957-64; mem. adv. com. Terra Linda Dixie Elem. Sch. Dist., 1960-64. Served with Signal Corps, U.S. Army, 1943-46. Mem. Am. Chem. Soc., Forest Products Research Soc., Am. Wood Preservers Assn., Alpha Chi Sigma. Republican. Presbyterian. Avocations: music, gardening, wine and food.

JONES, VERNON QUENTIN, surveyor; b. Sioux City, Iowa, May 6, 1930; s. Vernon Boyd and Winnifred Rhoda (Bremmer) J.; student UCLA, 1948-50; m. Rebeca Buckovecz, Oct. 1981; children: Steven Vernon, Gregory Richard, Stanley Alan, Lynn Sue. Draftsman III Pasadena (Calif.) city engr., 1950-53; sr. civil engring. asst. L.A. County engr., 1953-55; v.p. Treadwell Engring. Corp., Arcadia, Calif., 1955-61, pres., 1961-64; pres. Hillcrest Engring. Corp., Arcadia, 1961-64; dep. county surveyor, Ventura, Calif., 1964-78; propr. Vernon Jones Land Surveyor, Bullhead City, Ariz., 1978—; city engr. Needles (Calif.), 1980-87; instr. Mohave Community Coll., 1987—. Chmn. graphic tech. com. Ventura Unified Sch. Dist., 1972-78, mem. career adv. com., 1972-74; mem. engring. adv. com. Pierce Coll., 1973; pres. Mgmt. Employees of Ventura County, 1974. V.p. Young Reps. of Ventura County, 1965. Pres., Marina Pacifica Homeowners Assn., 1973. Mem. League Calif. Surveying Orgns. (pres. 1975), Am. Congress on Surveying and Mapping (chmn. So. Calif. sect. 1976), Am. Soc. Photogrammetry, Am. Pub. Works Assn., County Engr. Assn. Calif. Home: PO Box 20761 Bullhead City AZ 86439-0761

JONGEWARD, GEORGE RONALD, retired systems analyst; b. Yakima, Wash., Aug. 9, 1934; s. George Ira and Dorothy Marie (Cronk) J.; m. Janet Jeanne Williams, July 15, 1955; children: Mary Jeanne, Dona Lee, Karen Anne. BA, Whitworth Coll., 1957; postgrad., Utah State U., 1961. Sr. systems analyst Computer Scis. Corp., Honolulu, 1969-71; cons. in field Honolulu, 1972-76; prin. The Hobby Co., Honolulu, 1977-81; sr. systems analyst Computer Systems Internat., Honolulu, 1981-96, asst. v.p., 1994-96; instr. EDP Hawaii Pacific U., Honolulu, 1982-90. Mem. car show com. Easter Seal Soc., Honolulu. 1977-82; active Variety Club, Honolulu, 1978-81. Mem. Mensa (Hawaii pres. 1967-69), Triple-9. Presbyterian. Avocations: piano, community theatre, golf, sports-car rallies. Home: 4108 Avalanche Ave Yakima WA 98908-2915

JONKER, PAMELA LYNN, artist; b. Denver, Apr. 25, 1947; d. William Espy and Geraldine Marie (Plumb) Ingram; m. L. Anton Jonker, Mar. 17, 1968 (div. Feb. 1994); children: Stephanie Lynn, Stacey Marie. BA in Polit. Sci., The Colo. Coll., 1969; postgrad., Calif. State U., Fresno, 1989-92. Artist-sculptor, painter, ceramist, fiber arts Fresno, Calif. and, Espanola, N.Mex., 1979—; devel. coord. Fresno Arts Coun., 1992-93. Fiber artist/quilt hangings, 1980—; wheel-thrown manipulated ceramic bowls, 1992—; author: (exhibit catalog) Calif. State U. Fresno/Phebe Conley Gallery, 1992. Mem. Am. Quilter's Soc., Am. Craft Coun., Fresno Arts Coun., Kappa Alpha Theta. Avocations: gourmet cooking, gardening, interior design. Office: RR 3 Box 1333-9 Espanola NM 87532-9803

JONKER, PETER EMILE, gas company executive; b. The Hague, The Netherlands, Sept. 15, 1948; came to U.S., 1966, naturalized, 1985; s. Jacob and Jurrina (Wories) J.; m. Janet Lynn Gotfredson, Sept. 6, 1974; children: Jeffrey, Annelies. BSChemE cum laude, U. So. Calif., 1971, MSChemE, 1972; JD with honors, Western State U., Fullerton, Calif., 1979. Bar: Calif. 1979. Research engr. Union Oil Co., Los Angeles, 1972-75; regulations coordinator Union Oil Co., L.A., 1975-79, atty., 1979; mgr. govtl. and pub. affairs Western Liquefied Nat. Gas, L.A., 1979-81; mgr. environ. permitting Tosco Corp., L.A., 1981-83; mgr. regional pub. affairs So. Calif. Gas. Co., L.A., 1983-85, mgr. rate design, demand forecast and analysis, 1986-88, mgr. fed. energy affairs, 1988-90, mgr. support svcs., 1990-92; mgr. policy and planning So. Calif. Gas Co., L.A., 1992-94, mgr. external affairs, 1994-95,

dir. govtl. affairs, 1995—; mem. So. Coast Air Quality Mgmt. Dist. Adv. Coun., L.A., 1983-85; mem. Fed. Clean Air Act Adv. Com.; dir. Calif. Coun. for Environ. and Econ. Balance, 1994—. Editor Western State Law Rev., 1976-79; contbr. articles to profl. jours. Trustee, deacon San Marino (Calif.) Presbyn. Community Ch., 1980—; councilman U. So. Calif. Engring. Student Council, Los Angeles, 1971-72, dir. Engring. Alumni Assn., 1971-72; fgn. del. White House Conf., Washington, 1971. Mem. Am. Gas Assn., Air and Waste Mgmt. Assn. (v.p. West Coast chpt. 1984, 85, dir. West Coast sect. 1993—), Fed. Energy Bar Assn., Pacific Coast Gas Assn., Tau Beta Pi (pres., v.p. Calif. Delta chpt. 1970-71). Republican. Avocations: skiing, antiques, piano. Home: 2796 Heritage Dr Pasadena CA 91107-5915 Office: So Calif Gas Co 555 W 5th St Los Angeles CA 90013-1010

JONSEN, ERIC R., lawyer; b. San Francisco, June 5, 1958; s. Richard William and Ann Margaret (Parsons) J.; m. Ida-Marie Thayer, May 8, 1982; children: Kaitlyn, Jeremy, Michelle. BA, Hartwick Coll., 1980; JD, U. Colo., 1985. Bar: Colo., N.Y., U.S. Dist. Ct. Colo., U.S. Ct. Appeals (10th cir.). Assoc. William P. DeMoulin, Denver, 1986-88, Fairfield & Woods, Denver, 1988-90; ptnr. Ciancio, Tasker, Dupree & Jonsen, Denver, 1990—. Mem. ABA, Colo. Bar Assn. Office: Ciancio Dupree & Jonsen 12000 Pecos St Ste 200 Denver CO 80234-2079

JORDAHL, GEIR ARILD, photographer, educator; b. Kristiansund, Norway, Jan. 27, 1957; came to U.S., 1961; s. Sigurd and Solveig Ingvarda (Pedersen) J.; m. Kathleen Patricia O'Grady, Sept. 24, 1983. BA, Calif. State U., Hayward, 1979; MFA, Ohio U., 1983. Life C.C. teaching credential, Calif. Teaching assoc. Ohio U., Athens, 1980-82; instr. photography Chabot Coll., Hayward, Calif., 1983—; owner, mgr. Geir & Kate Jordahl, Photography, Hayward, 1983—; ind. curator, Hayward, 1984—; coord. PhotoCen. Photography Programs, Hayward, 1983—; artist-in-residence Yosemite (Calif.) Nat. Park, 1993; mem. curatorial com. Hayward Forum for Arts/Sun Gallery, 1992. Exhibited in numerous shows including Kansas City (Mo.) Art Inst., 1987, Ohio State Art Gallery, Newark, 1987, Mus. Art U. Oreg., Eugene, 1988, Mus. for Photography, Braunschweig, Germany, 1988, Ansel Adams Gallery, Yosemite, 1989, Mus. Modern Art, Tampere, Finland, 1989, Trenton (N.J.) Mus. Art, 1991, Ansel Adams Ctr. for Photography, San Francisco, 1990, Photo Forum Gallery, Pitts., 1993, Yosemite Nat. Park Mus., 1994, Ansel Adams Gallery, 1995, Yosemite Nat. Park Visitor Ctr., 1996, Fresno Art Mus., 1996, Haggin Art Mus., 1997, Golden State Mus., Sacramento, 1998, Bibliotheque Nat. de France, and other pvt. and pub. collections; author: (book) San Joaquin, River of Spirit, 1997; contbr. to profl. publs.; photographer various catalogues. Precinct capt. Hayward Dem. Com., 1992. Recipient purchase award Hayward Area Forum Arts, 1986, Ohio State U., 1987, Yosemite Nat. Park and Curry Co., 1992, award of excellence Calif. State Fair, 1987, 89, One of Top 100 New Photographers award Maine Photog. Workshops and Kodak Corp., 1987, Innovative New Program award Calif. Parks and Recreation Soc., 1990; scholar Calif. State U., 1975, Ohio U., 1981, Oslo Internat. Summer Sch., 1982, exch. scholar U. Trondheim, Norway, 1983, Peder P. Johnsen scholar Sons of Norway, 1983. Mem. Soc. Photog. Edn., Internat. Assn. Panoramic Photographers, Friends of Photography, San Francisco Camerawork. Avocations: cycling, backpacking, travel. Home and Studio: PO Box 3998 144 Medford Ave Hayward CA 94541-1749

JORDAN, BERNICE BELL, elementary education educator; b. Calvert, Tex.; d. Ocie Wade and Nannie B. (Westbrook) Bell; m. William B. Jordan, Sept. 28, 1956; children: Beverly, Terrence, Keith Jordan. BA, San Jose State Coll., 1959, MA, 1985; student, Prairie View A and M, Tex. Western Coll. Cert. elem. edn., fine arts, multi-cultural. Writer curriculum guide, fine arts Alum Rock Union Elem. Sch. Dist., San Jose, Calif.; writer sch. plan Goss Elem.; tchr. 3rd grade Alum Rock Union Elem. Sch. Dist., San Jose; adv. com., tchr.-cons. San Jose Area Writing Project, San Jose U., 1992—. Mem. Assn. for Supervision and Curriculum Devel., Alum Rock Edn. Assn., Calif. Tchrs. Assn., Calif. Reading Assn., Calif. Elem. Edn. Assn., Santa Clara County Reading Coun., NEA, Alpha Delta Kappa. Home: 3282 Fronda Dr San Jose CA 95148-2015

JORDAN, GLENN, director; b. San Antonio, Apr. 5, 1936. BA, Harvard U., 1957; postgrad., Yale U. Drama Sch., 1957-58. Dir. regional and stock theatre, including Cafe La Mama, late 1950s; N.Y. directorial debut with Another Evening With Harry Stoones, 1961; other plays include A Taste of Honey, 1968; Rosencrantz and Guildenstern Are Dead, 1969, A Streetcar Named Desire at Cin. Playhouse in the Park, 1973, All My Sons at Huntington Hartford Theatre, 1975; founder, N.Y. TV Theater, 1965, dir. various plays, including Paradise Lost and Hogan's Goat; dir. mini-series Benjamin Franklin, CBS, 1974 (Emmy award 1975, Peabody award); Family, ABC-TV series, 1976-77, including segment Rights of Friendship (Dirs. Guild Am. award); numerous TV plays for public TV, including Eccentricities of a Nightingale, 1976; The Displaced Person, 1976; TV movies including Shell Game, 1975, One Of My Wives Is Missing, 1975, Delta County U.S.A, 1977, In The Matter of Karen Ann Quinlan, 1977, Sunshine Christmas, 1977, Les Miserables, 1978, Son-Rise, A Miracle of Love, 1979, The Family Man, 1979, The Women's Room, 1980, Lois Gibbs and the Love Canal, 1982, Heartsounds, 1984 (Peabody award), Toughlove, 1985, Dress Gray, 1986, Something in Common, 1986, Promise, 1986 (2 Emmy awards for producing, directing, Peabody award, Golden Globe award), Echoes in the Darkness, 1987, Jesse, 1988, Home Fires Burning, 1988, Challenger, 1989, The Boys, 1990, Sarah Plain and Tall, 1990, Aftermath, 1990, O Pioneers!, 1991, Barbarians at the Gate, 1992 (Emmy award Outstanding Made for TV Movie, 1993, Golden Globe award, Best Mini-series or movie made for TV, 1994), To Dance with the White Dog, 1994, Jane's House, 1994, My Brother's Keeper, 1994, A Streetcar Named Desire, 1995, Jake's Women (Neil Simon), 1996, After Jimmy, 1996, Mary and Tim, 1996, A Christmas Memory, 1997, The Long Way Home, 1998, Legalese, 1998, Night Ride Home, 1999; dir: feature film Only When I Laugh (Neil Simon), 1981, The Buddy System, 1983, Mass Appeal, 1984. Recipient Emmy awards for N.Y. TV Theater Plays, 1970, Actors Choice, 1970. Office: Creative Artists Agy 9830 Wilshire Blvd Beverly Hills CA 90212-1825 also: 9401 Wilshire Blvd Ste 700 Beverly Hills CA 90212-2920

JORDAN, JEFFREY GUY, marketing and marketing research consultant; b. Oshkosh, Wis., May 21, 1950; s. Berwin Russell and Delores Suzanne (Tomlitz) J. BS, U. Wis., Oshkosh, 1973; postgrad., UCLA, 1978. Analyst corp. planning and rsch. May Co. Dept. Store, L.A., 1973-77; dir. mktg. svcs. DJMC Advt., L.A., 1977-80; dir. mktg. Wienerschnitzel, Internat., Newport Beach, Calif., 1980-84, York Steakhouse Restaurants (Gen. Mills), Columbus, Ohio, 1984-85, Paragon Restaurant Group, San Diego, 1985-87; v.p. mktg. Paragon Steakhouse Restaurants, Inc., San Diego, 1987-94; owner, pres. 1-on-One Mktg. Assocs., 1994—; cons., presenter U.S. Internat. U., San Diego, 1989. Mem. Conv. and Visitors Bur., San Diego; vol. Boys' Club of Am., Oshkosh, 1973-74; fundraising coord. Am. Cancer Soc., L.A., 1976. Mem. Am. Mktg. Assn. (treas., bd. dirs. 1996-97), Multi Unit Foodservice Operators Assn., San Diego Advt. Assn. (creative exec. 1986-88), San Diego C. of C. Republican. Lutheran. Avocations: sports, travel, photography.

JORDAN, JUNE M., poet, English language educator; b. N.Y.C., July 9, 1936; d. Granville I. and Mildred (Fisher) J.; m. Michael Meyer, Apr. 5, 1955 (div. 1966); 1 child, Christopher David. Student, Barnard Coll., 1953-55, 56-57, U. Chgo., 1955-56. Mem. English faculty Sarah Lawrence Coll., CCNY, Conn. Coll., Yale U., New Haven; research assoc. Tech. Housing Dept. Mobilization for Youth; asst. to producer The Cool World, 1964-65; prof. English SUNY, Stony Brook, 1978-89, dir. The Poetry Ctr. and Creative Writing Program, 1986; Chancellor's Disting. lectr. U. Calif., Berkely, 1986, prof. Afro-Am. studies and women's studies, 1989-93; prof. African Am. Studies U. Calif., Berkeley, 1994—, dir. Poetry for the People, 1990—; vis. poet-in-residence MacAlester Coll., 1980, Tchrs. and Writers Collaborative, 1966-68; bd. dirs. The Ctr. for Constnl. Rights, 1984—; bd. govs. N.Y. Found. for Arts, 1986-89; playwright-in-residence New Dramatists, N.Y.C., 1987-88, poet-in-residence, 1988; vis. prof. dept. Afro-Am. studies U. Wis., Madison, summer 1988; poet-in-residence Walt Whitman Birthplace Assn., 1988. Author: Civil Wars, Selected Essays 1963-80, 1981, Things That I Do in the Dark, Selected Poems 1954-77, 1981, Kimako's Story, 1981, Passion, New Poems, 1977-80, 1980, Things That I Do in the Dark, 1977, New Life: New Room, 1975, New Days, Poems of Exile and Return, 1974, Fannie Lou Hamer, 1971, Dry Victories, 1972, His Own Where, 1971, The Voice of the Children, 1980, Who Look at Me, 1969, Living Room, New Poems 1980-84, 1985, On Call, New Political Essays, 1981-85, 1985, Lyrical Campaigns, Selected Poems, 1989, Moving Towards Home, Selected Poems, 1989, Moving Towards Home, Selected Political Essays, 1989, Naming Our Destiny, New and Selected Poems, 1989; editor Soulscript, 1970, Technical Difficulties, New Political Essays, 1992, The Haruko/Love Poetry of June Jordan, 1993, I Was Looking at the Ceiling and Then I Saw the Sky, 1995, Civil Wars (reprint with new introduction), 1995, June Jordan's Blueprint for Poetry for the People, 1996, Kissing God Good Bye, 1997; composer lyrics and libretto Bang Bang Over Alles, Atlanta, 1986; lyricist and libretto for opera I Was Looking at the Ceiling and Then I Saw the Sky, Affirmative Acts, New Political Essays, 1998; contbr. articles, poems to profl. jours.; regular columnist The Progressive mag., 1989—, City Limits. Bd. dirs. Ctr. for Constl. Rights, 1984—. Recipient Achievement award for internat. reporting Nat. Assn. Black Journalists, 1984, M.A.D.R.E. award for Leadership, 1989, Prix de Rome, 1970, Freedom to Write award P.E.N. West, 1991, Lila Wallace Reader's Digest Writers award, 1995; Rockefeller grantee, 1969, CAPS grantee in poetry, 1978; Yaddo fellow, 1979, 80, NEA fellow in creative writing, 1982, N.Y. Found. Arts fellow in poetry, 1985. Mem. Poets and Writers Inc. (dir.), PEN Am. Center (exec. bd.), Am. Writers Congress (exec. bd.). Office: U Calif African Am Studies 660 Barrows Hall # 2572 Berkeley CA 94720-2573

JORDAN, LOIS HEYWOOD, real estate developer; b. Salem, Oreg., Apr. 22, 1913; d. Frank Hall and Winnifred E.(Heywood) Reeves; m. Edmund A. Jordan, Nov. 19, 1936 (dec. Dec. 1982); children: Jolie Mae, E. Andrew Jr., Jennifer Loie. Student, Oreg. State U., 1931-33, N.W. Sch. of Art, Portland, Oreg. Dress designer Portland, 1933-36, real estate developer, 1955—; pres. Jordan Developers, Portland, 1987—. Pres. Alameda Sch. PTA, Portland, 1960; v.p. Ainsworth Sch. PTA, Portland, 1964; pres. Alameda Garden Club, Portland, 1956, Women's Convalescent Home, Portland, 1957; v.p. sec. SW Hills Residential League, Portland, 1968; v.p. Friends Marquam Ravine, Portland, 1976; bd. dirs. Friendly House, Portland, 1986. Mem. Sons and Daus. of Oregon Pioneers (bd. dirs.), Multnomah Athletic Club, Pi Beta Phi (mgr. Oreg. State chpt. 1932-33). Republican. Presbyterian. Avocations: art.

JORDAN, LORNA PAULEY, artist; b. Windsor, Ont., Apr. 21, 1954; came to U.S., 1954; d. Stanely Frank and Dorothy (Ruppel) P.; m. Elverse Morris Jordan, June 25, 1983 (div. May 1986). BA, U. Va., 1976. Artist Lorna Jordan Studio, Seattle, 1979—; artist-in-residence Seattle Pub. Utilities, 1997-98. artist, lead designer Waterworks Gardens, 1996 (Place Design award EDRA/Places 1997); artist, co-designer Justice Garden Path, 1997; exhibited in Paine Webber Gallery, N.Y.C., Boise Art Museum, Ctr. of Contemporary Art, 1994-95. Bd. dirs., pres. On the Boards, Seattle, 1990—; commr. pub. art com., Seattle Arts Commn., 1994, vice-chair, 1995. Recipient Outstanding Local Achievment award ASCE, 1997; fellow N.W. Inst. Architecture and Urban Studies in Italy, Rome, 1998, The MacDowell Colony, Peterborough, N.H., 1994. Mem. Henry Contemporaries of The Henry Gallery, Contemporary Art Coun. of The Seattle Art Mus., The Uncollectors Club of The Seattle Art Mus., Ctr. on Contemporary Art. Fax: 206-634-2715. Home: 4233 Meridian Ave N Seattle WA 98103

JORDAN, MARY ANN, research biologist; b. Mpls., July 31, 1940; d. Richard Charles and Freda (Laudon) J.; m. Paul Warren Lommen, Sept. 25, 1965 (div. 1982); children: Andrea, Kate; m. David Scott Johnson, Jan 14, 1984. Student, Carleton Coll., 1958-60; BA in Math. magna cum laude, U. Minn., 1962; MS, PhD in Cell Biology, U. Rochester, 1968; postgrad., Stanford U., 1963. Postdoctoral fellow in biology Washington U., St. Louis, 1969; rsch. assoc. biology U. Mich., Ann Arbor, 1971-72; rsch. assoc., lectr. Utah State U., Logan, 1974-77; rsch. biologist U. Calif., Santa Barbara, 1978-82, asst. rsch. biologist, lectr., 1982-90, assoc. rsch. biologist, 1991-95, rsch. biologist, 1995—; adj. prof., 1996—; mem. coun. Calif. Breast Cancer Rsch. Program, 1998—; mem. NIH, DOD study sect., 1995, 96, 97. Contbr. articles to profl. jours. Treas. Goleta (Calif.) Civic Ballet, 1984-85. Fellow NSF, USPHS, NIH. Mem. AAAS, Am. Soc. Cell Biology, Am. Assn. Cancer Rsch. Unitarian. Avocations: sports, outdoor recreation, music, painting, gardening. Office: U Calif Dept Molecular Cellular Devel Biol Santa Barbara CA 93106

JORDAN, MICHAEL (RUDY), builder representative; b. Chgo., July 2, 1956; s. Vernon Townsend and Marion (Petersen) J. BS in Psychology, U. Utah, 1986. Acct. exec. Southwestern Bell, Phoenix, 1987-90; builder rep. UDC Homes, Phoenix, 1991-92, Elliott Homes, Phoenix, 1993-95, Richmond Am. Homes, Phoenix, 1995—. Asst. editor (trade mag.) Restrateur, 1990. Mem. World Affairs Coun., Scottsdale, Ariz., 1998, LLCR Republicans, Phoenix, 1998. Mem. Kappa Sigma Fraternity. Republican. Methodist. Avocations: photography, downhill skiing, outdoor hiking.

JORDAN, STEVEN EDWARD, special effects expert; b. Santa Monica, Calif., Sept. 17, 1946; s. Walter E. and Eileen Jordan; m. Penny L. Jordan, Nov. 7,1969; children: Jesse, Tiffany, chris. AS, Mt. San Antonio Coll., 1972; BS, Calif. Poly. Inst., 1974. Spl. effects artist Jaws, Pollution Monster, King Kong, Explorers, Dune, Airplane, Short Circuit, Blade Runner, Dragnet, Friday the 13th part 6, Tango and Cash. Avocations: surfing, photography, woodworking, mechanical devices, computer design and animation. Office: IATSE Local 44 11500 Burbank Blvd North Hollywood CA 91601-2308

JORGENSEN, ERIK HOLGER, lawyer; b. Copenhagen, July 19, 1916; s. Holger and Karla (Andersen) J.; children: Jette Friis, Lone Olesen, John, Jean Ann. JD, San Francisco Law Sch., 1960. Bar: Calif. 1961. Pvt. practice law, 1961-70; ptnr. Hersh, Hadfield, Jorgensen & Fried, San Francisco, 1970-76, Hadfield & Jorgensen, San Francisco, 1976-88 . Pres. Aldersly, Danish Retirement Home, San Rafael, Calif., 1974-77, Rebild Park Soc. Bay Area chpt., 1974-77. Fellow Scandinavian Am. Found. (hon.); mem. ABA, San Francisco Lawyers Club, Bar Assn. of San Francisco, Calif. Assn. Realtors (hon. life bd. dirs.). Author: Master Forms Guide for Successful Real Estate Agreements, Successful Real Estate Sales Agreements, 1991; contbr. articles on law and real estate law to profl. jours.

JORGENSEN, GORDON DAVID, engineering company executive; b. Chgo., Apr. 29, 1921; s. Jacob and Marie (Jensen) J.; BS in Elec. Engring., U. Wash., 1948, postgrad. in bus. and mgmt., 1956-59; m. Nadina Anita Peters, Dec. 17, 1948 (div. Aug. 1971); children: Karen Ann, David William, Susan Marie; m. Barbara Noel, Feb. 10, 1972 (div. July 1976); m. Ruth Barnes Chalmers, June 15, 1990. With R.W. Beck & Assos., Cons. Engrs., Phoenix, 1948—, ptnr., 1954-86; pres. Beck Internat., Phoenix, 1971—. Served to lt. (j.g.) U.S. Maritime Service, 1942-45. Recipient Outstanding Service award Phoenix Tennis Assn., 1967; Commendation, Govt. Honduras, 1970. Registered profl. engr., Alaska, Ariz., Calif., Colo., Nev., N.Mex., N.D., Utah, Wash., Wyo. Mem. IEEE (chmn. Wash.-Alaska sect. 1959-60), Nat. Soc. Profl. Engrs., Am. Soc. Appraisers (sr. mem.), Ariz. Cons. Engrs. Assn., Ariz. Soc. Profl. Engrs., Internat. Assn. Assessing Officers, Southwestern Tennis Assn. (past pres.), U.S. Tennis Assn. (pres. 1987-88, chmn. U.S. Open com.); chmn. U.S. Davis Cup com.; chmn. Internat. Tennis Fed., Davis Cup com. Presbyterian (elder). Project mgr. for mgmt., operation studies and reorgn. study Honduras power system, 1969-70. Home: 74-574 Palo Verde Dr Indian Wells CA 92210-7314 Office: RW Beck & Assocs 3003 N Central Ave Phoenix AZ 85012-2902

JORGENSEN, JUDITH ANN, psychiatrist; b. Parris Island, S.C.; d. George Emil and Margaret Georgia Jorgensen; BA, Stanford U., 1963; MD, U. Calif., 1968; m. Ronald Francis Crown, July 11, 1970 (dec. Oct. 1996). Intern, Meml. Hosp., Long Beach, 1969-70; resident County Mental Health Services, San Diego, 1970-73; staff psychiatrist Children and Adolescent Services, San Diego, 1973-78; practice medicine specializing in psychiatry, La Jolla, Calif., 1973—; staff psychiatrist County Mental Health Services of San Diego, 1973-78, San Diego State U. Health Services, 1985-87; psychiat. cons. San Diego City Coll., 1973-78, 85-86; asst. prof. dept. psychiatry U. Calif., 1978-91, assoc. prof. dept. psychiatry, 1991-96; chmn. med. quality rev. com. Dist. XIV, State of Calif., 1982-83. Mem. Am. Psychiat. Assn., San Diego Psychiat. Soc. (chmn. membership com. 1976-78, v.p. 1978-80, fed. legis. rep. 1985-87, fellowship com. 1989—), Am. Soc. Adolescent Psychiatry, San Diego Soc. Adolescent Psychiatry (pres. 1981-82), Calif. Med. Assn. (former alternate del.), Soc. Sci. Study of Sex, San Diego Soc. Sex Therapy and Edn. (cert. sex therapist), San Diego County Med. Soc. (credentials com. 1982-84). Club: Rowing. Office: 470 Nautilus St Ste 211 La Jolla CA 92037-5970

JORGENSEN, LOU ANN BIRKBECK, social worker; b. Park City, Utah, May 14, 1931; d. Robert John and Lillian Pearl (Langford) Birkbeck; student Westminster Coll., 1949-51; B.S., U. Utah, 1953, M.S.W., 1972, D.S.W., 1979; grad. Harvard Inst. Ednl. Mgmt., 1983; m. Howard Arnold Jorgensen, June 9, 1954; children: Gregory Arnold, Blake John, Paul Clayton. Social work adminstr. nursing home demonstration project, dept. family and community medicine U. Utah Med. Ctr., Salt Lake City, 1972-74; mental health ednl. specialist Grad. Sch. Social Work, U. Utah, 1974-77, 77-80, asst. prof., 1974-80, assoc. prof., 1980-94, prof., 1994-97, prof. emeritus, 1997—, dir. doctoral program, 1984-89, 94-97, assoc. dean, 1986-94; regional mental health cons. Bd. dirs. Info. and Referral Ctr., 1975-82, United Way of Utah, 1976-82, Pioneer Trail Parks, 1977-83, Rowland Hall-St. Marks Sch., 1980-86; Salt Lake County housing commr., 1980-86, Utah State Health Facilities Bd., 1991—, chmn., 1994, 97-98; pres. Human Svcs. Conf. for Utah, 1979-80; bd. dirs. Alzheimer Assn., Utah chpt., 1990-97, Salt Lake County Coalition Bus. and Human Svcs., 1990-94; mem. Valley Mental Health Bd., 1990—. Mem. NASW (pres. Utah chpt. 1978-79), Coun. on Social Work Edn., Commn. Women in High Edn., Adminstrs. of Public Agys. Assn., Human Svcs. Assn. Utah, Jr. League of Salt Lake City, Town Club, Phi Kappa Phi. Republican. Episcopalian. Author: Explorations in Living, 1978, Social Work in Business and Industry, 1979; Handbook of the Social Services, 1981; contbr. articles to profl. jours. Home and Office: 1458 Kristianna Cir Salt Lake City UT 84103-4221

JORGENSEN, PAUL ALFRED, English language educator emeritus; b. Lansing, Mich., Feb. 17, 1916; s. Karl and Rose Josephine (Simmons) J.; m. Virginia Frances Elfrink, Jan. 3, 1942; children: Mary Catherine, Elizabeth Ross Jorgensen Howard. A.B., Santa Barbara State Coll., 1938; M.A., U. Calif. at Berkeley, 1940, Ph.D., 1945. Instr. English Bakersfield (Calif.) Jr. Coll., 1945-46, U. Calif., Berkeley, summer 1946, U. Calif., Davis, 1946-47; mem. faculty UCLA, 1947—, prof. English, 1960-81, prof. emeritus, 1981—; vis. prof. U. Wash., summer 1966; mem. editorial com. U. Calif. Press, 1957-60; mem. Humanities Inst. U. Calif., 1967-69; mem. acad. adv. council Shakespeare Globe Ctr. N.Am. Author: Shakespeare's Military World, 1956, (with Frederick B. Shroyer) A College Treasury, rev. edit, 1967, (with Shroyer) The Informal Essay, 1961, Redeeming Shakespeare's Words, 1962; editor: The Comedy of Errors, 1964, Othello: An Outline- Guide to the Play, 1964, (with Shroyer) The Art of Prose, 1965, Lear's Self-Discovery, 1967, Our Naked Frailties: Sensational Art and Meaning in Macbeth, 1971, William Shakespeare: The Tragedies, 1985; mem. bd. editors Film Quar, 1958-65, Huntington Library Quar, 1965-83, Coll. English, 1966-70; mem. adv. com. Publs. of MLA of Am, 1978-82. Guggenheim fellow, 1956-57; Regents' Faculty fellow in humanities, 1973-74. Mem. Modern Lang. Assn., Shakespeare Assn. Am. (bibliographer 1954-59), Renaissance Soc. Am., Philol. Assn., Pacific Coast (exec. com. 1962-63), Internat. Shakespeare Assn. Episcopalian. Home: 234 Tavistock Ave Los Angeles CA 90049-3229

JORTNER, JULIUS, materials engineer, consultant; b. Cernauti, Rumania, Mar. 3, 1936; came to U.S, 1946; s. Michael Maria (Spielvogel) J.; m. Carolee June Robbins, May 25, 1975. BME, Cooper Union, 1956; MS in Engring., UCLA, 1968. Rsch. engr. Rocketdyne divsn. North Am. Aviation, Canoga Park, Calif., 1956-68, McDonnell Douglas Astronautics Co., Huntington Beach, Calif., 1968-79, Sci. Applications, Inc., Irvine, Calif., 1979-82; pres. Jortner Rsch. and Engring., Inc., Cloverdale, Oreg., 1982—; lectr. in field. Editor: Thermomechanical Behavior of High-Temperature Composites, 1982, Thermostructural Behavior of Carbon-Carbon Composites, 1986; contbr. articles to profl. jours. Mem. ASME (structure and materials com. 1979-91), ASTM (mem. com. D-30 on advanced composites 1969-93), Am. Carbon Soc. (Graffin lectureship 1988, adv. com. 1995—), Nestucca Valley C. of C. (pres. 1996-97). Office: Jortner Rsch & Engring Inc PO Box 219 Cloverdale OR 97112-0219

JOSEPH, EZEKIEL (ED JOSEPH), manufacturing company executive; b. Rangoon, Burma, June 24, 1938; s. Joe E. Joseph and Rachel Levi; m. Sheila G. Rabinovitch, Feb. 17, 1963; children: Renah, Heather, Jerald. Mktg. mgr. Gen. Electric Corp., Waynesboro, Va., 1968-75; dir. Actron div. McDonnell Douglas Corp., Monrovia, Calif., 1975-78; pres. Joseph Machinery Inc., Huntington Beach, Calif., 1978-84, Xtalite Display Systems Inc.), Huntington Beach, 1985-88, Secure Optical Systems Inc., Anaheim, Calif., 1992-98, Peak Machinery Sales, Inc., Irvine, Calif., 1998—; pres. Retract-a-Roof Inc., Huntington Beach. Pres. Temple Beth David, Huntington Beach, 1990-93. Mem. Austin Healey Assoc. Democrat. Avocations: antique cars, sailing. Home: 6245 Greenbrier Dr Huntington Beach CA 92648-5545 Office: Peak Machinery Salse Inc 18011 Sky Park Cir Ste F Irvine CA 92614-6517

JOSEPH, JAMES EDWARD, mechanical engineering technician; b. Napa, Calif., Sept. 24, 1946; s. Wilbur Raymond and Lois Grace (Pouget) J.; m. Deborah Dianne Horvath, June 5, 1971; children: Brian Christopher, Stacy Lynn Joseph Pitts. Diploma, N. Am. Sch. Drafting, 1974, hon. grad. cert., 1977; AA, Napa Valley Coll., 1976; BS, So. Ill. U., 1986. Basic instr. tng. cert., 1993. Naval archtl. aide Mare Island Naval Shipyard, Vallejo, 1967-70; naval archtl. technician Mare Island Naval Shipyard, Vallejo, Calif., 1974-77, 77-89; naval architect tech. supr. Mare Island Naval Shipyard, Vallejo, 1989-91, project leader, 1991-92, material control mgr., 1992-94, engring. technician, 1994—; refinery operator Union Oil Co. Calif., 1971-74; designer, draftsman Morris Guralnick Assocs., Inc., 1974, propulsion technician, 1977; designer, draftsman, owner, operator Joseph's Drafting & Design Svc., 1984-88; mech. engring. technician Puget Sound Naval Shipyard, Bremerton, Wash., 1994—; designer, draftsman Napa Babe Ruth Baseball League, 1986. Author: (material control program) Navyshipydmareinst, 1993, Desk Notes for Ocean Engineering Subsafe Re-Entry Control Group, 1994, Work Control of Critical System Pipe Hangers (Navyshipydmareinst), 1987, Steering & Diving Hydraulic Cylinder Foundation, Inspection, Removal, Repair and Reinstallation (Industrial Process Instruction) 1987. Chair citizen adv. panel Dept. Motor Vehicles, Napa; bd. dirs. Youth Adv. Bd. Oleum Fed. Credit Union, Rodeo, Calif., 1971-74; coach Young Am. Bowling Assn., Napa, 1980-83, 93-94, T-Ball and Babe Ruth Baseball, 1979-80, 85-86; auditor West Park Elem. Sch. PTA, parent vol., outdoor edn. vol. trips; key person for C/124-Puget Sound Naval Shipyard, Combined Fed. Campaign, 1994. With USNR, 1966-72. Mem. AARP, Internat. Platform Assn., Am. Bowling Congress, Olympic Philatelic Soc., Am. Philatelic Soc., Am. Diabetes Assn. Republican. Avocations: golf, bowling, stamp collecting, walking. Home: 12699 Plateau Cir NW Silverdale WA 98383-8006 Office: Puget Sound Naval Shipyard Engring Code 126 Bremerton WA 98314-5000

JOSEPH, JAMES HERZ, author, columnist; b. Terre Haute, Ind., May 12, 1924; s. Lawrence Herz and Lucille (Liberman) J.; m. Marjorie Helen Waterman, Aug. 20, 1950 (div. 1971); children: Nancy Lee, James Jay. Student, Northwestern U., Evanston, Ill., 1942; BA, Stanford U., 1949. Freelance ind. contractor, 1949—; pres. James Joseph Corp., L.A., 1992-96; editor-in-chief Kessler Assocs., L.A., 1986-88; v.p., editl. dir. Am. Automotive Pub. Group, Simi Valley, Calif., 1996; dir. comm. Paisa,Inc., San Dimas, Calif., 1996. Syndicated columnist Quick Stops, 1986-91; author: You Fly It, 1965, Careers Outdoors, 1969, Here is Your Hobby: Snowmobiling, 1970, Annual Snowmobiling Guide, 1972, 73, 74, The Complete Out-of-Doors: Job, Business and Profession Guide, 1974, Beckman's Incredible Flying Circus, 1978, Chilton's Diesel Guide, 1980, The Car-Keeper's Guide, 1982, Chilton's Guide to Auto Detailing, 1993, Ashes, 1994, Driving Emergencies, 1994, Speaking With God, 1997, Road to Discovery in America, 1998, Big Speed: The Quest for Supersonic Speed on Land, 1999, others; co-author: (with William Divale) I Lived Inside the Campus Revoluution, 1970; contbr. articles to major mags. U.S. and abroad, chpts. to books. Fellow Am. Soc. Journalists and Authors (chmn. So. Calif. chpt. 1960—, Dial-a-Writer com. 1997—), Authors Guild Am. Avocations: sailing, fishing, camping. Home and Office: PO Box 24678 Los Angeles CA 90024-0678

JOSEPH, MARK SCOTT, entertainment company executive, television and radio personality; b. Tokyo, Jan. 27, 1968; came to the U.S., 1986; s. Kenneth Phillip and Lila May (Finsaas) J. BA, Biola U., La Mirada, Calif., 1990. Staff writer/columnist Epata Mag., Japan, 1982-89; pres. Pacific Promotions, Tokyo/L.A., 1988-91; reporter FM Yokohama, Tokyo/L.A.,

1990-93; pres. MJM Entertainment Group, L.A., 1991—; reporter Group W CNN, L.A., 1992-94; reporter FM Tokyo, Tokyo/L.A., 1993—; anchor, talk show host NHK TV, Tokyo/L.A., 1994—, anchor/talk show host, 1994—; adj. prof. Biola U., 1995. Author: Out of This World, 1999; contbg. editor RQ mag., 1998—; contbr. articles to various publs. Mem. Japan-Am. Soc., Renaissance Group, BMI (songwriters), Wednesday Morning Club. Avocations: basketball, reading, politics. Office: MJM Entertainment Group Inc PO Box 1731 La Mirada CA 90637-1731

JOSEPHS, ALICE RUTH, retired executive secretary; b. Dvinsk, Latvia, Oct. 19, 1912; came to U.S., 1913; d. Benjamin Solomon and Sarah (Kuritzky) Hodes; m. Ben Gardner, May 10, 1932 (dec. Oct. 1944); 1 child, Steven Robert; m. Fred Josephs, Dec. 8, 1952; children: Susan, Cynthia, David. BA in Journalism, Radio, TV, Film, Calif. State U., Northridge, 1979. Exec. sec. astronomy dept. UCLA, 1965-71; exec. sec. Boy Scouts Am., Van Nuys, Calif., 1988-93. Playwright: Night of Broken Glass. Sec. bd. dirs. Synthaxis Theatre Co., North Hollywood, Calif., 1979-96; bd. dirs. Valley Cities Jewish Comty. Ctr., Van Nuys, 1964, 65, 66, 67-68, pres. women's club, 1967-68; leader Camp Fire Girls, Van Nuys, 1962, 63, 65. Playwright: A Woman's Place, Stars in Her Eyes, Window Panes, Failure Is Impossible—Susan B. Anthony; asst. editor: (mag.) Journalism History, 1977, 78, 79. Mem. AAUW, Am. Assn. Ret. Persons, Nat. Writers Assn., Gold Star Wives Am. (v.p.). Avocations: reading, playing guitar, piano, listening to music, writing. Home: 14341 Chandler Blvd Apt 3 Van Nuys CA 91401-5514

JOSEPHSON, HAROLD ALLAN, real estate developer; b. Montreal, Que., Can., July 21, 1944; s. Joseph and Edith (Marco) J.; m. Sheila Gloria Laing, July 4, 1966 (div. July 1976); children: Daniel, Robert.; MBA with distinction, Harvard U., 1971. V.p. Marcil Mortgage Corp., Montreal, 1976-78; prin. Josephson Properties, Montreal, 1978-83, Los Angeles, 1983—. Mem. Urban Land Inst., Nat. Assn. Indsl. and Office Parks, Internat. Council Shopping Ctrs. Jewish. Avocations: skiing, tennis, flying. Office: 9903 Santa Monica Blvd # 656 Beverly Hills CA 90212-1671

JOSEPHSON, RICHARD CARL, lawyer; b. Washington, Nov. 20, 1947; s. Horace Richard and Margaret Louise (Loeffler) J.; m. Jean Carol Attridge, Aug. 1, 1970; children: Lee Margaret, Amy Dorothy. AB, Case Western Res. U., 1969; JD, Coll. of William and Mary, 1972. Bar: Oreg. 1973. Law clk. Hon. John D. Butzner, Jr., U.S. Ct. Appeals, 4th Cir., Richmond, Va., 1972-73; ptnr. Stoel Rives LLP, Portland, Oreg., 1973—. Bd. dirs. Tucker-Maxon Oral Sch., Portland, 1987—, Vis. Nurse Assn., Portland, 1978-89, Healthlink, Portland, 1984-89, St. Mary's Acad., Portland, 1998—. 1st lt. U.S. Army, 1973-79. Fellow Am. Coll. Bankruptcy, Am. Coll. Comml. Fin. Lawyers; mem. ABA, Am. Bankruptcy Inst., Oreg. Bar Assn. (chmn. debtor-creditor sect. 1980-81). Presbyterian. Avocations: skiing, white water rafting, running, cycling, theatre. Office: Stoel Rives LLP 900 SW 5th Ave Ste 2300 Portland OR 97204-1235

JOSHI-PETERS, KARUNA LAXMIPRASAD, psychologist; b. Patan, Gujerat, India, July 18, 1944; came to U.S., 1971; d. Laxmiprasad Chunilal and Leelvati Laxmiprasad (Shukla) Joshi; m. Ramashanker Misra, May 10, 1965 (div. July 1977); m. Michael Wood Peters, Sept. 8, 1977; children: Adrian Manoj Rohit, Julian Vikram Suhas. BA in English Lit. with honors, Banaras Hindu U., Varanasi, India, 1960, MA in Philosophy, 1962; MA in Psychology, U. Hawaii, 1990, PhD in Psychology, 1992. Lic. clin. psychologist, Hawaii. Jr. rsch. fellow Banaras Hindu U., 1962-64, lectr., 1963; lectr. Patna (India) U., 1964-65; sr. rsch. asst. Indian Inst. Tech., Kanpur, India, 1965-71; teaching asst. dept. philosophy U. Hawaii, Honolulu, 1975-76; psychol. intern Oreg. Health Scis. U., Portland, 1991-92; psychol. examiner spl. svcs. State of Hawaii Dept. Edn., Honolulu, 1992; psychologist State of Hawaii Dept. Health, Kaneohe, 1993; pvt. practice psychology Kaneohe, 1993—; organizer Hawaii Neuropsychology Group, Kaneohe, 1990—. Author rsch. papers in field. East West Ctr. grantee, 1971-75; jr. rsch. fellow Univ. Grants Commn., New Delhi, India, 1962-64. Mem. APA, Hawaii Psychol. Assn., Nat. Acad. Neuropsychology, Internat. Neuropsychol. Soc. Democrat. Avocations: cooking, needlepoint, quilting, hiking, tennis. Office: 46-001 Kamehameha Hwy Ste 419B Kaneohe HI 96744-3749

JOSSELYN, JOHNNY B., artistic director, magazine writer; b. Balt., Mar. 25, 1971; s. Roy Lee Josselyn and Joanne Theresa (Delorenzo) McNealy. BA in Film, Towson State U., 1993; postgrad., UCLA, 1994-97. Creative asst. Balt. Pictures, L.A., 1993-94; visual effects dir. Warner Bros. Pictures, L.A., 1994, art dept. staff, 1994-95; illustrator Paramount Pictures, L.A., 1995-96; art dir. Meridian Entertainment, L.A., 1997, Showtime Films, San Diego, 1998—; prodn. designer L.A., 1998—. Author: various internet websites, 1997-98; contbr. articles to travelling mags. Mem. IATSE. Avocations: travelling, swing dancing, gourmet cooking, jazz. E-mail: johnnyjos@aol.com. Home: 641 N Martel Ave Los Angeles CA 90036-1930

JOURDAN, STEPHANIE CAROL, educator; b. Columbus, Ohio, Aug. 31, 1956; d. Stephen Edgar Junkermann and Marilyn Ann (Hysell) Joseph; m. Raymond Pillault, Mar. 13, 1977 (div. Dec. 1979); m. Raphael Jourdan, June 18, 1989; children: Shanti Delilah, Savannah Rose. Diploma, Hypnosis Motivation Inst., 1988; Bachelor's Degree, Am. Inst. Hypnotherapy, 1996. Cert. hypnoanesthesiologist Nat. Bd. for Hypnotherapy and Hypnotic Anesthesiology. Sr. v.p. Promark, Westwood, Calif., 1981-83; mng. ptnr. Jourdan, Winkler & Tate, North Hollywood, Calif., 1983-87; owner New Focus Profl. Group, Woodland Hills, Calif., 1987—; founder, instr., dir. New Focus Inst. for Clin. Hypnotherapy, Canoga Park, Calif., 1990—; script cons. Sierra Prodns., Irvine, Calif., 1990-91. Author: Psychic Integration: A Workbook of Archetypal Interaction, 1998, Provider Relations: Your Key to Success, 1998; author (audio tapes) Archetypes!, Super Self-Confidence I and II, Inner Peace through Smoking Cessation, 1989-97; contbr. articles to profl. jours. Mem. Am. Assn. Behavioral Therapists, Am. Bd. Hypnotherapy (Spl. Recognition award 1997, 98), Am. Assn. Profl. Hypnotherapists, Nat. Assn. Transpersonal Psychology, Calif. League Med. Hypnotherapists, Inc. (pres. 1996-98). Avocations: collage, quilting, cooking, photography. E-mail: Jourdan1@aol. Fax: 818-340-4099. Office: New Focus Inst 22357 Welby Way Canoga Park CA 91303-2466

JOY, CARLA MARIE, history educator; b. Denver, Sept. 5, 1945; d. Carl P. and Theresa M. (Lotito) J. AB cum laude, Loretto Heights Coll., 1967; MA, U. Denver, 1969, postgrad., 1984-87. Instr. history Community Coll. Denver; prof. history Red Rocks Community Coll., Lakewood, Colo., 1970—; cons. for innovative ednl. programs; reviewer fed. grants, 1983-89; mem. adv. panel Colo. Endowment for Humanities, 1985-89. Contbr. articles to profl. publs. Instr. vocat. edn. Mile High United Way, Jefferson County, 1975; participant Jefferson County Sch. System R-1 Dist., 1983-88; active Red Rocks Community Coll. Speakers Bur., 1972-89, strategic planning com., 1992-97; chair history discipline Colo. Gen. Edn. Core Transfer Consortium, 1986-96, faculty transfer curriculum coun., 1997—; mem. history, geography, civics stds. and geography frameworks adv. com. Colo. Dept. Edn., 1995-96; steering com. Ctr. Teaching Excellence, 1991-92, 1996-97; with North Ctrl. Self-Study Process, 1972-73, 80-81, 86-88, 96-98; with K-16 Linkages Colo. Commn. for Higher Ed., 1997-98. Cert. in vocat. edn. Colo. State Bd. Community Colls. and Occupational Edn., 1975; mem. evaluation team for Colo. Awards, edn. and civic achievement for Widefield Sch. Dist. #3, 1989; mem. Red Rocks Community Coll.-Clear Creek Sch. System Articulation Team, 1990-91; mem. Statue of Liberty-Ellis Island Found. Inc., 1987—, Denver Pub. Libr. Friends Found. Ford Found. fellow, 1969; recipient cert. of appreciation Kiwanis Club, 1981, Cert. of Appreciation Telecommunication Coop. for Colo's. Community Colls., 1990-92; Master Tchr. award U. Tex. at Austin, 1982. Mem. Am. Hist. Assn., Am. Assn. Higher Edn., Nat. Council for Social Studies, Nat. Geog. Soc., Omohundro Inst. Early Am. History and Culture, Nat. Edn. Assn., Colo. Edn. Assn., Colo. Council for Social Studies, The Smithsonian Nat. Assocs., World History Assn., Denver Art Mus., Denver Mus. of Nat. Hist., Community Coll. Humanities Assn., Orgn. Am. Historians, The Colo. Hist. Soc., Colo. Endowment for the Humanities, Colo. Geographic Alliance, Soc. History Edn., Phi Alpha Theta. Home: 1849 S Lee St Apt D Lakewood CO 80232-6252 Office: Red Rocks C C 13300 W 6th Ave Lakewood CO 80228-1213

JOY, JOY JOY, poet; b. Botosani, Romania, Aug. 6, 1927; s. Ioan and Maria (Amariei) Ciobanu. AA, East. L.A. Coll., 1991. Author: A Help for Jesus, 1996, To Be For Jesus, 1997, Christian Poems, 1998. Recipient, Editors Choice award Nat. Libr. Poetry, Accomplishment Merit, Creative Arts & Sci. Enterprises, award cert. Drudry Pub., Cert. Achievement award Am. Poetry Awards. Republican. Home: 7541 Simpson Ave Apt 313 North Hollywood CA 91605-3255

JOYCE, BERNADETTE, producer; b. L.A.; d. Bernard Novey and Columbina Rita (Fina) Stradley; m. Stephen Joyce; children: Natalie, Vanessa. Student, UCLA, Valley Jr. Coll., Sherman Oaks, Calif. Producer: Xena: Warrior Princess, 1996— (Golden Reel award), Hercules the Legendary Journeys, 1993— (Internat. Monitor award 1998), Darkman II and III, 1996-97, Young Hercules, 1997, Amazon High, 1998, Kung Fu: The Legend Continues, The Equalizer, 1987, Bionic Woman movies, 1988, 89,. Avocations: skiing, travel, movies, family. Home: 4724 Barcelona Ct Calabasas CA 91302-1403

JOYCE, PHYLLIS NORMA, educational administrator; b. Bronx, N.Y., June 8, 1955; d. Philip Emmanuel and Dolores (Pizzolanella) Malizio; m. Thomas Patrick Joyce, June 11, 1983; 1 child, Diana. BA, CUNY, 1978; MA, Nova U., 1995. Tchr. St. Raymond's Sch., Bronx, 1980-83; tchr., head English dept. St. Anne Sch., Las Vegas, Nev., 1983-94, prin., 1994—, coord. jr. high Sch., 1988-94. Spl. Olympics vol. KC, Las Vegas, 1983-90; vol. Sons of Erin, Las Vegas, 1990—; pastoral coun. St. Anne Parish, 1996—. Democrat. Roman Catholic. Avocations: tennis, working out, family recreational activities. Office: St Anne Sch 1813 S Maryland Pky Las Vegas NV 89104-3104

JOYCE, ROSEMARY ALEXANDRIA, anthropology educator; b. Lackawanna, N.Y., Apr. 7, 1956; d. Thomas Robert and Joanne Hannah (Poth) J.; m. Russell Nicholas Sheptak, Jan. 7, 1984. BA, Cornell U., 1978; PhD, U. Ill., 1985. Instr. Jackson (Mich.) Community Coll., 1983; lectr. U. Ill., Urbana, 1984-85; asst. curator Peabody Mus., Harvard U., Cambridge, Mass., 1985-86, asst. dir., 1986-89; asst. prof. anthropology Harvard U., Cambridge, Mass., 1989-91, assoc. prof. anthropology, 1991-94; assoc. prof. anthropology U. Calif., Berkeley, 1994—. Author: Cerro Palenque, 1991, Encounters with the Americas, 1995; editor: Maya History, 1993, Women in Prehistory, 1997; contbr. articles to profl. jours. NEH grantee, 1985, 86, NSF grantee, 1989, 98, Famsi grantee, 1996, Heinz Found., Wenner-Gren Found. grantee, 1997; Fulbright fellow, 1981-82. Mem. Soc. for Am. Archaeology, Am. Anthropol. Assn. Office: U Calif Anthropology Dept 232 Kroeber Hall # 3710 Berkeley CA 94720-3710

JOYCE, STEPHEN MICHAEL, lawyer; b. Los Angeles, Mar. 19, 1945; s. John Rowland and Elizabeth Rose (Rahe) J.; m. Bernadette Anne Novey, Aug. 18, 1973; children: Natalie Elizabeth, Vanessa Anne. BS, Calif. State U., Los Angeles, 1970; JD, U. LaVerne, 1976. Bar: Calif. 1976, U.S. Dist. Ct. (cen. dist.) Calif. 1977, U.S. Ct. Claims 1981. Pvt. practice Beverly Hills, Calif., 1976-93; ptnr. Gold & Joyce, Beverly Hills, 1982-84; personal atty. to Stevie Wonder and various other celebrities, 1977—. Contbr. articles to profl. jours. Served to pvt. USAR, 1963-69. Mem. ABA, Calif. Bar Assn., Los Angeles County Bar Assn., Beverly Hills Bar Assn., Los Angeles Trial Lawyers Assn., San Fernando Valley Bar Assn., Calabasas Athletic Club. Democrat. Roman Catholic. Avocation: long distance running. Home: 4724 Barcelona Ct Calabasas CA 91302-1403 Office: 15260 Ventura Blvd Ste 640 Sherman Oaks CA 91403-5340

JOYCE, VICKI MARIE, special education educator; b. Chgo., Sept. 8, 1936; d. Walter and Victoria Juckins; m. Robert Daniel Joyce, Aug., 1956 (div. 1974); children: Jennifer Brining, David. BA, Calif. State U., L.A., 1962; MA, Calif. State U., San Bernadino, 1992. Home econs. tchr. L.A. City Sch. Dist., 1962-65; real estate broker Homes Unltd., Orange County, Calif., 1970-82; tchr. Riverside and San Bernadino County (Calif.) Sch. Dists., 1982-95; resource specialist San Bernadino Unified Sch. Dist., 1995—. Author: A Theoretical Meta-Analysis and Review of Kinesis For Special Education Teachers and Resource Specialists, 1993. Named Outstanding Tchr. Orton Dyslexia Soc., 1993. Mem. Calif. Tchrs. Assn., San Bernadino Tchrs. Assn., Nat. Tchrs. Assn., Nat. Assn. Resource Specialists. Avocations: reading, writing, painting, theater, grandchildren. Home: 1965 Coulston St Apt 37 Loma Linda CA 92354-1733 Office: San Bernardino HS 1850 N E St San Bernardino CA 92405-3918

JUAREZ, CARLOS EDWARD, political scientist, researcher; b. Kansas City, Mo., Dec. 13, 1962; s. Carlos Epitacio and Dolores (Anaya) J.; m. Susan Lai Fah Kam, 1987; children: Julian Kalani, Alexander Keanu. BA, Baylor Univ., 1984; MA, Univ. San Diego, 1986; PhD/MA, UCLA, 1995. Vis. prof. Univ. Andes, Bogota, Colombia, 1991-92; researcher Univ. Calif., San Diego, 1993-97; asst. prof. Hawaii Pacific Univ., Honolulu, 1997—. Contbr. articles to profl. jours. Recipient pres. postdoctoral fellowship U. Calif., 1994-96. Mem. Am. Political Sci. Assn., Latin Am. Studies Assn., Internat. Studies Assn. Democrat. Home: 1552 Saint Louis Dr Honolulu HI 96816-1921 Office: Hawaii Pacific Univ 1188 Fort Street Mall Fl 4th Honolulu HI 96813-2784

JUAREZ, MANUEL J., watercompany executive; b. Mt. View, Calif., Mar. 10, 1970; s. Manuel G. and Paula (Gonzalez) J. BS in computer engring., San Jose State Univ., 1993, MS in elec. engring., 1995. Line crew leader Pacific Gas & Elec. Co., San Jose, Calif., 1989-91; rock plant supr. Kaiser Cement Corp., Cupertino, Calif., 1991-93; software devel. Borland Internat., Inc., Scotts Valcoet, Calif., 1993-95; sr. field engr. Portola Packaging Inc., San Jose, 1995-97; ops. plant mgr. Sierra Spring Water Co., San Jose, 1998—; chmn., CEO Nu Alpha Kappa, Inc., San Jose, 1997—; bd. dirs. Nu Alpha Kappa Fraternity, Inc., 1991-94. Mem. Nu Alpha Kappa (pres. 1992-93). Republican. Roman Catholic. Avocations: comic book collecting. Home: PO Box 520 Alviso CA 95002 Office: Nu Alpha Kappa Inc 1597 Birchmeadow Ct San Jose CA 95131

JUAREZ, MARETTA LIYA CALIMPONG, social worker; b. Gilroy, Calif., Feb. 14, 1958; d. Sulpicio Magsalay and Pelagia Lagotom (Viacrusis) Calimpong; m. Henry Juarez, Mar. 24, 1984. BA, U. Calif., Berkeley, 1979; MSW, San Jose State U., 1983. Lic. clin. social worker; cert. in eye movement desensitization and reprocessing; registered play therapist; cert. alcohol and drug studies. Mgr. Pacific Bell, San Jose, Calif., 1983-84; revenue officer IRS, Salinas, Calif., 1984-85; social worker Santa Cruz (Calif.) County, 1985, Santa Clara County, San Jose, 1985—; co-chair Inter-Agy. Coun. of South Santa Clara County. Recipient award Am. Legion, 1972. Mem. NASW, Nat. Coun. on Alcoholism, Assn. Play Therapists, No. Calif. Sandplay Soc., EMDR Network, Sandplay Therapists Am., Calif. Assn. Play Therapy, South County Multidisciplinary Team (co-founder), Calif. Alumni, U. Calif. Club of Santa Clara County. Democrat. Roman Catholic. Avocations: snow skiing, reading, writing, arts and crafts.

JUBERG, RICHARD KENT, mathematician, educator; b. Cooperstown, N.D., May 14, 1929; s. Palmer and Hattie Noreen (Nelson) J.; m. Janet Elisabeth Witchell, Mar. 17, 1956 (div.); children: Alison K., Kevin A., Hilary N., Ian C.T.; m. Sandra Jean Vakerics, July 8, 1989. BS, U. Minn., 1952, PhD, 1958. Asst. prof. U. Minn., Mpls., 1958-65; sci. faculty fellow Univerista di Pisa, Italy, 1965-66; assoc. prof. U. Calif., Irvine, 1966-72, U. Sussex, Eng., 1972-73; prof. U. Calif., Irvine, 1974-91, prof. emeritus, 1991—; vis. prof. U. Goteborg, Sweden, 1981; mem. Courant Inst. Math. Scis., NYU, 1957-58. Contbr. articles to profl. jours. With USN, 1946-48, Guam. NSF Faculty fellow, Univ. Pisa, Italy, 1965-66. Mem. Am. Math. Soc., Tau Beta Pi. Democrat. Avocation: bird watching. Office: U Calif Math Dept Irvine CA 92717

JUCHEM, ROBERT STANLEY, JR., product development manager, educator; b. Rahway, N.J., Aug. 26, 1951; s. Robert Stanley Sr. and Nancy Ann (Whittian) J.; m. Constance Ann Effertz, Aug. 5, 1972 (div. May, 1992); children Robert, Ben, Bethany, Brittany; m. Jane Ann Butler, Dec. 24, 1993; children Steve Ryan, Michael Ryan, Luke Deforest. Student, Com. College USAF, 1976; BS in Personal and Labor Rels., U. Md., 1978, BS in Bus. and Mgmt., 1978; MBA, Webster Coll., 1980. Missile sys. tech. USAF, 1972-81; aerospace application engr. AMP Inc., Harrisburg, Pa., 1981-82, mgr. new business devel., 1984-90; regional sales mgr. Northern Precision Labs, Morristown, N.J., 1982-83; v.p. bus. devel. Liberty Electronics, Franklin, Pa., 1990-91; v.p. sales and mktg. Pytronnic Industries, Lansdale, Pa., 1991-92; mgr. new product devel. Amphenol Aerospace, Sidney, N.Y., 1992-97; v.p. sales and mktg. Valdor Fiber Optics, Reno, 1997—; mktg. adv. bd. Valdon Fiber Optics, San Jose, Calif., 1996—. Contbr. articles to profl. jour. Mem. Congl. adv. bd. Aberdeen, Md. 1981-85; adv. bd. Catholic Ch., Aberdeen, Md.1982-84. With USAF, 1972-81. Mem. AIAA, IEEE, Tech. Mktg. Assn. Rebuplican. Achievements include contributions to the design and deployment of all air-to-air and air-to-ground missiles introduced into service between August 1972 and February 1981. Avocations: weight lifting, golf, basketball, soccer, fencing. Home: 5404 Tappan Dr Reno NV 89523-2253

JUDAH, JAY STILLSON, historian, educator; b. Leavenworth, Wash., July 7, 1911; s. Stillson and Maude Alice (Cannon) J.; m. Lucile Elaine Baker, Dec. 2, 1935 (dec. Mar. 1987); children: Jay Stillson Jr., Elaine Judah Keller, Diane Judah Moore; m. Helen Janin Nov. 24, 1987. AB, U. Wash., 1934; Libr. cert., U. Calif.-Berkeley, 1941; Litt.D., Chapman Coll., 1955. Head libr. Pacific Sch. Religion, 1941-69, prof. history of religion, 1955-69; libr. dir. Bibliog. Ctr., Grad. Theol. Union, Berkeley, 1966-69; head libr. Common Libr. Grad. Theol. Union, Berkeley, 1969-76; prof. history of religion Grad. Theol. Union, 1969-76; adj. prof. Pacific Sch. Religion, 1974-79; field faculty Vt. Coll., Norwich U., 1984-85; nat. v.p. Alliance for Preservation of Religious Liberty, 1978-79. Author: Jehovah's Witnesses, 1964, History and Philosophy of the Metaphysical Movements in America, 1967, Hare Krishna and the Counterculture, 1974; compiler, editor: Index to Religious Periodical Literature, 1949-52, 1952. Lt. USNR, 1944-46, ETO. Guggenheim fellow, 1934; Sealantic Fund fellow, 1957-58; nat. sr. ranking in tennis doubles of those in the 80s (No. 1 ranking in So. Calif., No. 2 in No. Calif., No. 6 in U.S.). Fellow Internat. Inst. Arts and Letters; mem. Am. Theol. Library Assn. (v.p. 1962-63, pres. 1963-64), Western Theol. Library Assn. (pres. 1954-55), Internat. Assn. Theol. Libraries (sec.-treas. 1955-60). Republican. Mem. Christian Ch. N.Am. Clubs: El Cerrito (Calif.); Tennis (pres. 1958-65); Rossmoor Tennis (pres. 1985-86). Home: 2711 Saklan Indian Dr # 2 Walnut Creek CA 94595-3009

JUDD, BRUCE DIVEN, architect; b. Pasadena, Calif., Sept. 28, 1947; s. David Lockhart and Martha Leah (Brown) J.; m. Diane Reinbolt, Feb. 4, 1976 (div. Oct. 1985); 1 child, Ian David. BArch, U. Calif., Berkeley, 1970, MArch, 1971. Registered arch., Calif., Nev.; cert. Nat. Coun. Archtl. Registration Bds. Designer Ribera and Sue Landscape Archs., Oakland, Calif., 1968-70, Page Clowdsley & Baleix, San Francisco, 1971-75; v.p. Charles Hall Page Assocs., San Francisco, 1975-80; ptnr. Archtl. Resources Group, San Francisco, 1980—; mem. adv. bd. fed. rehab. guidelines program Nat. Inst. Bldg. Scis., HUD, 1979-80; mem. city-wide survey planning com. City of Oakland, Calif., 1979-80; cons. Nat. Main St. Program, Washington. Bd. dirs., co-founder Oakland Heritage Alliance, 1980-85; mem. Calif. Hist. Resources Commn., 1982-86, chmn., 1983-85; bd. dirs. Preservation Action, Washington, 1982-85, 90—, Friends of Terra Cotta, 1981-86, Berkeley Archtl. Heritage Assn., 1993—; mem. bd. advisors Nat. Trust for Hist. Preservation, Washington, 1981-90, advisor emeritus, 1990—; bd. trustees Calif. Preservation Found., San Francisco, 1985—, v.p., 1990-92, trustee, 1990—; active Calif. State Hist. Bldg. Safety Bd., 1991-93, also others. Recipient Excellence Honor award State of Calif., Excellence award in archtl. conservation, Spl. Restoration award Sunset Mag.; named Preservationist of Yr., Calif. Preservation Found., 1993. Fellow AIA (preservation officer No. Calif. chpt. 1978-81, hist. resources com. Calif. coun. 1979-80, nat. hist. resources com. 1981—, chmn. 1981-82); mem. Internat. Assn. for Preservation Tech. (bd. dirs. 1983-85), Park Hills Homes Assn. (chmn. archtl. com. 1992—), U.S./Internat. Coun. Monuments and Sites. Office: Archtl Resources Group Pier 9 The Embarcadero San Francisco CA 94111*

JUDD, THOMAS ELI, electrical engineer; b. Salt Lake City, Apr. 12, 1927; s. Henry Eli Judd and Jennie Meibos; m. Mary Lu Edman, June 21, 1948; children: Shauna, Kirk E., Blake E., Lisa. BSEE, U. Utah. 1950. Registered profl. engr., Utah. Mech. engr. Utah Power & Light Co., Salt Lake City, 1950-55; chief engr. Electronic Motor Car Corp., Salt Lake City, 1955-56, Equi-Tech Corp., Salt Lake City, 1978-79; hydraulic devel. engr. Galigher Co., Salt Lake City, 1956-58; pres. Toran Corp., Salt Lake City, 1958-71, T M Industries, Salt Lake City, 1971-78; chief exec. officer, mgr. Ramos Corp., Salt Lake City, 1979—; project cons. Eimco Corp., Salt Lake City, 1966; design cons. to tech. cos. Patentee in field in U.S. and fgn. countries; contbr. editor U.S. Rail News, 1982—. Cons. Nat. Fedn. Ind. Bus., 1983—. With USNR, 1945-46, PTO. Mem. Tau Beta Pi. Republican. Mormon. Avocation: flying. Office: Ramos Corp 956 Elm Ave Salt Lake City UT 84106-2330

JUDSON, BARBARA MICHAEL, business proposal manager, graphics director; b. Goshen, Ind., Apr. 19, 1938; d. Ernest William and Dorothy Anne (Bartlett) Scully; children: Jennifer Judson Peck, Rebecca Anne. BA, Calif. State U., 1962. Proposal mgr. Rogerson Corp., Irvine, Calif., 1986, Parker Hannifin Corp., Irvine, Calif., 1987—. Home: 34142 Selva Rd Unit 216 Dana Point CA 92629-3780

JUKKOLA, GEORGE DUANE, obstetrician, gynecologist; b. Aliquippa, Pa., Feb. 28, 1945; s. Waino Helmer and Bedelia (Pyle) J.; m. Gretchen Louise Strom, Feb. 14, 1970 (div. 1984); children: David, Jeffrey; m. Wendee Leigh Bookhart, Apr. 23, 1988 (div. 1993). BA in Psychology, U. Calif., Berkeley, 1970; MD, U. Pitts., 1975. Diplomate Am. Bd. Ob-Gyn., Am. Bd. Quality Assurance Utilization Rev. Physicians. Caseworker Pa. Dept. Welfare, Rochester, 1971; resident in ob.-gyn. Akron (Ohio) Med. Ctr., 1975-78; pvt. practice Riverside, Calif., 1978—; co-founder Family Birthing Ctr., Riverside, 1981-87; v.p. Inland Physicians Med. Group, 1987-88; mng. ptnr. Parkview Profl. Ctr., Riveside, 1984-93; chief dept. ob-gyn. Parkview Cmty. Hosp., Riverside, 1986-91, vice-chief of staff, 1992-93, chief of staff, 1994-96; chmn. ob-gyn dept. Moreno Valley Med. Ctr., 1991-93, dir. perinatal svcs., 1992-94, mem.-at-large exec. com., 1996-97, mem. CMA survey team, 1992—; guest lectr. Riverside Cmty. Coll., 1984, 85; health care adv. com. 43d Congl. Dist., Calif., 1994—; mem. Riverside County Fetal-Infant Mortality Com., 1994—; founder, chmn. bd. dirs. Inland Empire OBG IPA, 1996. With USAF, 1965-69. Decorated Air medal with 4 oak leaf clusters. Fellow ACOG; mem. AMA, Am. Coll. Physician Execs., Calif. Med. Assn., Riverside County Med. Assn., Am. Assn. Individual Investors, Victoria Club Riverside, Mensa. Republican. Unitarian-Universalist. Avocations: golf, philately, woodworking, photography. Home: 10252 Victoria Ave Riverside CA 92503-6100 Office: 4294 Orange St Riverside CA 92501-3827

JUMAO-AS, ALEX BARONDA, civil engineer; b. Surigao City, The Philippines, June 12, 1961; came to U.S., 1982; s. Gaudencio Tamosa and Adelaida (Baronda) J.; m. Remedios Panoncillo, Jan. 28, 1981; children: Real James, Rylan Justin. BS in Indsl. Engring. with high honors, U. San Jose Recoletos, Cebu City, Philippines, 1982; grad. mech. and elec. tech. with high honors, U. Alaska, 1988, AAS in Archtl. and Engring. with honors, 1989, BS in Civil Engring. with high hons., 1989. Drafter Dept. Interior Bur. Land Mgmt., Anchorage, 1983-84, Raj Bhargava Assocs., Anchorage, 1984; asst. engr., drafter Unicom, Inc., Anchorage, 1984-93; civil engr. Raytheon Svc. Co., Anchorage, 1993-96, Anchorage Water and Wastewater Utility, Anchorage, 1996—; adj. instr. U. Alaska, 1989-91; v.p. Unicom, Inc. Anchorage Employee Svc. Assn., 1985-86. Mem. Metro Cebu Jaycees, Am. Inst. Design and Drafting, Pundok Bisaya (Cebuano Filipino Assn. Alaska) (v.p.), Bisayans of Alaska (mem. bd. dirs. 1993-94), Filipino-Bisayans of Alaska Inc. (pres. 1996—). Roman Catholic. Avocations: basketball, tennis, volleyball, hiking. Home: 8412 Barnett Dr Anchorage AK 99518-2900 Office: Anchorage Water and Wastewater Utility 3000 Arctic Blvd Anchorage AK 99503-3813

JUMONVILLE, FELIX JOSEPH, JR., physical education educator, realtor; b. Crowley, La., Nov. 20, 1920; s. Felix Joseph and Mabel (Rogers) J.; m. Mary Louise Hoke, Jan. 11, 1952; children: Carol, Susan. BS, La. State U., 1942; MS, U. So. Calif., 1948, EdD, 1952. Assoc. prof. phys. edn. Los Angeles State Coll., 1948-60; prof. phys. edn. Calif. State U., Northridge, 1960-87, emeritus prof. phys. edn., 1987—; owner Felix Jumonville Realty, Northridge, 1974-82, Big Valley Realty, Inc., 1982-83, Century 21 Lamb Realtors, 1983-86, Cardinal Realtors, 1986-87; varsity track and cross-country head coach L.A. State Coll., 1952-60, Calif. State U., Northridge, 1960-71. Served with USCGR, 1942-46. Mem. Assn. Calif. State Univ.

Profs., AAHPER, Pi Tau Pi, Phi Epsilon Kappa. Home: 2001 E Camino Parocela Apt 98N Palm Springs CA 92264-8283

JUNE, DAVID HAROLD, information technology specialist; b. Alameda, Calif., Mar. 26, 1948; s. Harold Burton and Lois (Baugh) J.; m. Leise Palm Purtle; 1 child, Sean Christopher Purtle. BS in Materials Engring., San Jose State U., 1979. Process engr. Fairchild Semiconductor, Mt. View, Calif., 1979-84; process engring. mgr. Intel, Rio Rancho, N.Mex., 1984-85; tech. team mgr. No. Telecom Elec., San Diego, 1985-89; dir. engring. Thesis Group, Dallas, 1989-91; CIM mgr. Read Rite, Milpitas, Calif., 1992-94; dir. engring. and data mgmt. Cell Net Data Sys., San Carlos, Calif., 1994—. Inventor in field; contbr. articles to profl. jours. Office: Cell Net Data Sys 125 Shoreway Rd San Carlos CA 94070-2704

JUNE, ROY ETHIEL, lawyer; b. Forsyth, Mont., Aug. 12, 1922; s. Charles E. and Elizabeth F. (Newnes) J.; m. Laura Brautigam, June 20, 1949; children—Patricia June, Richard Tyler. B.A., U. Mont., 1948, B.A. in Law, 1951, LL.B., 1952. Bar: Mont. 1952, Calif. 1961. Sole practice, Billings, Mont., 1952-57, Sanders and June, 1953-57; real estate developer, Orange County, Calif., 1957-61; ptnr. Dugan, Tobias, Tornay & June, Costa Mesa, Calif., 1961-62; city prosecutor, Costa Mesa, 1962-63, asst. city atty., 1963-67, city atty., 1967-78; sole practice, Costa Mesa, 1962—. Atty., founder, dir. Citizens Bank of Costa Mesa, 1972-92; atty. Costa Mesa Hist. Soc., Costa Mesa Playhouse Patron's Assn., Red Barons Orange County, Costa Mesa Meml. Hosp. Aux., Harbor Key, Child Guidance Ctr. Orange County, Fairview State Hosp. Therapeutic Pool Vols., Inc.; active Eagle Scout evaluation team, Harbor Area Boy Scouts Am., YMCA; atty. United Fund/Community Chest Costa Mesa and Newport Beach; bd. dirs. Boys' Club Harbor Area, bd. dirs. Mardan Ctr. Ednl. Therapy, United Cerebral Palsy Found. Orange County; docent Palm Springs Mus., 1996—. Served with USAF, World War II. Decorated Air medal with oak leaf cluster, D.F.C. Mem. Mont. Bar Assn., Calif. Bar Assn., Orange County Bar Assn., Harbor Bar Assn., Costa Mesa C. of C. (bd. dirs.), Masons, Scottish Rite, Shriners, Santa Ana Country, Amigos Viejos, Los Fiestadores, Palm Springs Calif. Air Mus. (docent).

JUNG, HENRY HUNG, mechanical engineer; b. Hong Kong, Aug. 3, 1957; s. Cheuk-Sun and Siu-Kuen (Ma) J.; m. Mi-Ying Miranda, Mar. 28, 1986. BS MechE, Ariz. State U., 1980; MS MechE, U. Ill., 1983; MBA, Santa Clara U., 1994. Engr. Lockheed Aircraft, Burbank, Calif., 1981-82; researcher U. Ill., Champaign-Urbana, 1982-83; engr. Pratt & Whitney Aircraft, West Palm Beach, Fla., 1983-84; sr. scientist Lockheed Missiles & Space Co., Palo Alto, Calif., 1984-94; sr. mfg. engr. Sun Microsystems Co., Mountain View, Calif., 1994-96; sr. supplies engr. Apple Computer, Cupertino, Calif., 1996-97; sr. mech. project engr. Intel, Santa Clara, Calif., 1997—. Mem. ASME, AIAA, N.Y. Acad. Scis., Sigma Xi, Tau Beta Pi, Pi Tau Sigma. Avocations: tennis, swimming. Home: 21486 Holly Oak Dr Cupertino CA 95014-4928 Office: Intel Corp Mail Stop SC12-201 2200 Mission College Blvd Santa Clara CA 95054-1549

JUNG, SAMSON PANG, computer analyst, investment company executive, astrologer; b. Hong Kong, Sept. 28, 1963; came to U.S. 1978; s. Fook Leung and Mee Yung (Lee) J. AA, City Coll., San Francisco, 1983; BA, San Francisco State U., 1988. Cert. in Chinese and holistic medicine Inst. Acupuncture and Herbal Medicine; cert. Chinese astrologer Ziwei Cultural Rsch. Ctr. Computer cons. Brasswork, San Francisco, 1981-82; dir. Inst. Self Improvement, San Francisco, 1983-88; v.p. Eagle Investment Co., San Francisco, 1985—; computer analyst D.W. Smith & Assoc., Foster City, Calif., 1987—; owner Agatha's Bloomers, San Mateo, Calif., 1989—; bus. cons. Stephen's Book Store, San Francisco, 1991-93; healer, counselor Whole Life Expn., San Francisco, 1981-83; cons. Mind, Body and Spirit Fair, San Francisco, 1982; bus. cons. Stephen's Book Store, San Francisco, 1991—. Author: Holistic Enlightment Learning Process, 1985; inventor acupuncture probe. Counselor Ctr. for Instnl. Change, San Francisco, 1986. Mem. Computer Learning Ctr., Golden Key (life). Avocation: health research. Office: Eagle Investment Co 1887 S Norfolk St San Mateo CA 94403-1155

JUNG, TIMOTHY TAE KUN, otolaryngologist; b. Seoul, Korea, Dec. 1, 1943; came to U.S., 1969; s. Yoon Yong and Helen Chung-Hyuk (Im) J.; m. Lucy Moon Young, Sept. 10, 1972; children: David, Michael, Karen. BS, Seoul Nat. U., 1966, Loma Linda U., 1971; MD, Loma Linda U., 1974; PhD, U. Minn., 1980. Diplomate, Am. Bd. Otolaryngology. Med. intern Loma Linda (Calif.) U. Med. Ctr., 1974-75; resident in surgery U. Minn. Med. Sch., Mpls., 1975-76; resident in otolaryngology U. Minn. Med. Sch., 1976-80, asst. prof. otolaryngology, 1980-84, clin. asst. prof., dir. prostaglandin lab., 1984-85; assoc. prof., dir. otolaryngology rsch. Loma Linda U., 1985-90, prof., dir. otolaryngology rsch., 1990-92, clin. prof., assoc. dir. otolaryngology rsch., 1992—; mem. deafness and communications disorders rev. com. Nat. Inst. Deafness and Communications, NIH, 1989-92. Bd. editors Annals of Otology, Rhinology & Laryngology, 1994—; contbr. numerous chpts. to med. books, over 100 articles and abstracts to med. jours. Sgt. Korean army, 1966-69. Recipient Edmund Price Fowler award. Fellow ACS, Triological Soc., Am. Acad. Otolaryngology (honor award 1990); mem. AMA, Am. Otol. Soc., Am. Neurotol. Soc., Soc. Univ. Otolaryngologists, Assn. Rsch. in Otolaryngology, Centurions, Collegium Otorhinolaryngogicum Amicetiae Sacrum, N.Am. Skull Base Soc., Alpha Omega Alpha. Seventh-day Adventist. Avocations: horticulture, photography, hiking. Home: 11790 Pecan Way Loma Linda CA 92354-3452 Office: 3975 Jackson St Ste 202 Riverside CA 92503-3947

JUNGBLUTH, CONNIE CARLSON, tax manager; b. Cheyenne, Wyo., June 20, 1955; d. Charles Marion and Janice Yvonne (Keldsen) Carlson; m. Kirk E. Jungbluth, Feb. 5, 1977; children: Tyler, Ryan. BS, Colo. State U., 1976. CPA, Colo., Ariz. Sr. acct. Rhode Scripter & Assoc., Boulder, Colo., 1977-81; mng. acct. Arthur Young, Denver, 1981-85; asst. v.p. Dain Bosworth, Denver, 1985-87; v.p. George K. Baum & Co., Denver, 1987-91; acct. Ariz. Luth. Acad., 1994-95; sr. tax acct. Ernst & Young, LLP, Phoenix, 1995-96; nat. tax mgr. McGladrey & Pullen, LLP, 1996—. Active Denver Estate Planning Coun., 1981-85, Ctrl. Ariz. Estate Planning Coun., 1997-98; organizer Little People Am., Rocky Mountain Med. Clinic and Symposium, Denver, 1986; adv. bd. Children's Home Health, Denver, 1986-89; fin. adv. bd. Gail Shoettler for State Treas., Denver, 1986; campaign chmn. Kathi Williams for Colo. State Legislature, 1986; mem. Sch. dist. 12 Colo. Edn. Found. Bd., 1991, Napa Sch. Dist. Elem. Site com., 1992-94; apptd. Ariz. Gov.'s Coun. Develpmental Disabilities, 1998-99, chmn. planning com., 1998-99. Named one of 50 to watch, Denver mag., 1988. Mem. AICPA, Internat. Assn. Fin. Planners, Colo. Soc. CPAs (strategic planning com. 1987-89, instr. bank 1983, trustee 1984-87, pres. bd. trustees 1986-87, bd. dirs. 1987-89, chmn. career edn. com. 1982-83, pub. svc. award 1985-87), Little People of Am., Colo. Mcpl. Bond Dealers, Ariz. Herb Assn., Metro North C. of C. (bd. dirs. 1987-90), Denver City Club (bd. dirs. 1987-88), Phi Beta Phi. Avocations: faith, family, horticulture, philanthropy, gourmet cooking. Office: McGladrey & Pullen LLP 2231 E Camelback Rd Ste 315 Phoenix AZ 85016-3447

JUNGBLUTH, KIRK E., real estate appraiser, mortgage banking executive; b. Lima, Ohio, Apr. 5, 1949; s. Harold A. and Marjorie J. (Brown) J.; m. Connie Carlson, Feb. 5, 1977; children: Tyler, Ryan. Student, Mesa Coll., Grand Junction, Colo., Regis Coll., Denver. Cert. Gen. real estate appraiser, Calif., Ariz. Loan officer, real estate appraiser Home Fed. Savs. & Loan, Ft. Collins, Colo., 1973-76; real estate appraiser Jungbluth & Assocs., Ft. Collins, 1976-83; pres., bd. dirs. Security Diamond Corp., Denver, 1982-90; nat. sales dir. InfoAm. Computers, Denver, 1982-90; chmn. bd. dirs., CEO U.S. Capital Lending Corp., Denver, 1987-91; ct.-appointed receiver Dist. Ct. State of Colo., 1990; mgr. real estate appraisal World Savs. & Loan Assn., Walnut Creek, 1992-93, Pleasanton, Calif., 1993-94. Sgt. USMC, 1969-71. Republican. Avocations: golf, snow skiing, scuba diving.

JUNGKIND, WALTER, design educator, writer, consultant; b. Zurich, Switzerland, Mar. 9, 1923; came to Can., 1968; s. Oskar and Frieda (Leuthold) J.; m. Jenny Voskamp, 1953; children—Christine, Stefan, Brigit. Nat diploma, Kunstgewerbeschule, Zurich, 1943; nat diploma, Regent Street Poly tech., London, 1955. Freelance designer London, 1955-68, lectr. London Coll. Printing and Graphic Arts, 1960-65, sr. lectr., 1965-68; assoc. prof. dept. art and design U. Alta., Edmonton, Can., 1968-72, prof., 1972-90, prof. emeritus, 1990—; Design cons. pub. works Province of Alta., 1972-75; chmn. Canadian Adv. Com. Standards Council Can., 1978—. Initiator and curator internat. exhbn. Graphic Design for Pub. Service, 1972, Language Made Visible, 1973. Recipient Design Can. award Nat. Design Council Can., 1979, 1984; Chmn.'s award Nat. Design Council Can., 1982. Fellow Soc. Chartered Designers Gt. Britain, Soc. Graphic Designers Can. (pres. 1978-82); mem. Internat Coun. Graphic Design Assns. (pres. 1974-76, Design for Edn. award 1972.). Home: 6304-109th Ave, Edmonton, AB Canada T6A 1S2*

JURCZYK, JOANNE MONICA, financial analyst; b. Orange, Calif., Dec. 27, 1958; d. Edward Joseph and Helen Imogene (Shelly) J. BSBA in Econs., Chapman U., 1981. Guest rsch. specialist Disneyland-Walt Disney Co., Anaheim, Calif., 1985-88, guest rsch. coord., 1988-89, guest rsch. survey ops. supr., 1989-91, indsl. engring. tech. analyst, 1991-92; pricing coord. Kirk Paper Corp., Downey, Calif., 1995-96; price analyst Coors Distributing Co., Anaheim, Calif., 1996-97, fin. analyst, 1997—; active Work Exposure Day, Disneyland/U. Disneyland, Anaheim, 1990. Assoc. Met. Mus. Art, 1991—; active youth motivation task force Orange County Unified Sch. Dist., 1992. Mem. Am. Film Inst. Democrat. Roman Catholic. Avocations: literature, music, theatre. Office: Coors Distributing Co 1625 S Lewis St Anaheim CA 92805-6437

JURINSKI, JAMES JOHN, law educator; b. Peekskill, N.Y., Dec. 27, 1949; s. Bernard Anthony Jurinski and Emily Lorenza Hickey; m. Gretchen A. Brevig; children: Hillary Brevig, Alexander Brevig, Reed Brevig, Schuyler Brevig. AB, Hamilton Coll., 1972; MLS, U. B.C., Vancouver, Can., 1976; JD, Lewis and Clark Coll., 1980; MT, Portland State U., 1980. Bar: Oreg., Wash., U.S. Tax Ct., 1981; CPA, Colo., Wash. Prof. Western Wash. U., Bellingham, 1981-84, U. Portland, Oreg., 1986—. Author: (books) Keys to Wills and Probate, 1990, Keys to Personal Insurance, 1991, Credit and Collections, 1992, Keys to Filing for Bankruptcy, 1993, Independent Contractors: Tax and Business Planning, 1994, Buying and Selling a Small Business, 1995, How to File for Bankruptcy, 1996, How to Probate an Estate, 1997, Advising Family Businesses, 1998, Tax Planning for the Elderly, 1998, Religion In The Schools, 1998; editor: Jour. of Legal Studies Edn., 1994-97. Mem. AICPA, Wash. Bar Assn., Oreg. Bar Assn., Acad. Legal Studies in Bus. (mem. exec. com. 1994-97), Multnomah Athletic Club, Family Film Inst. Roman Catholic. Office: U Portland 5000 N Willamette Blvd Portland OR 97203

JUSTESEN, ELAINE TOOMER, genealogist; b. Billings, Mont., June 2, 1929; d. Thomas Henry and Margaret (Stevens) Toomer; m. Glade Clifford Justesen, Aug. 4, 1947; children: Gary, Kirby, Kimball, Thomas, Rick, Brian. Student tech. genealogy, Brigham Young U., Salt Lake City, 1966. Accredited genealogist, Utah. Self-employed profl. genealogist Salt Lake City, 1966-93; editor Geneal. Jour. Utah Geneal. Assn., Salt Lake City, 1994—. Compiler, rschr.: Ancestry of James M. Williams, 1982, 21 family histories, 1982-95. Mem. Nat. Geneal. Soc. (local arrangements chair 1984-85), Assn. Profl. Genealogists, Utah Geneal. Assn. (v.p. 1983-87, bd. dirs. 1974-84). Republican. Mem. Latter-day Saints Ch. Avocations: family, handwork, travel, quilting, reading. Office: Utah Geneal Assn PO Box 1144 Salt Lake City UT 84110-1144

JUVET, RICHARD SPALDING, JR., chemistry educator; b. L.A., Aug. 8, 1930; s. Richard Spalding and Marion Elizabeth (Dalton) J.; m. Martha Joy Myers, Jan. 29, 1955 (div. Nov. 1978); children: Victoria, David, Stephen, Richard P.; m. Evelyn Raeburn Elthon, July 1, 1984. BS, UCLA, 1952, PhD, 1955. Research chemist Dupont, 1955; instr. U. Ill., 1955-57, asst. prof., 1957-61, assoc. prof., 1961-70; prof. analytical chemistry Ariz. State U., Tempe, 1970-95, prof. emeritus, 1995—; vis. prof. UCLA, 1960, U. Cambridge, Eng., 1964-65, Nat. Taiwan U., 1968, Ecole Polytechnique, France, 1976-77, U. Vienna, Austria, 1989-90; mem. air pollution chemistry and physics adv. com. EPA, HEW, 1969-72; mem. adv. panel on advanced chem. alarm tech., devel. and engring. directorate, def. sys. divsn. Edgewood Arsenal, 1975; mem. adv. panel on postdoctoral associateships NAS-NRC, 1991-94; mem. George C. Marshall Inst., 1998—. Author: Gas-Liquid Chromatography, Theory and Practice, 1962, Russian edit., 1966; editl. advisor Jour. Chromatographic Sci., 1969-85, Jour. Gas Chromatography, 1963-68, Analytica Chimica Acta, 1972-74, Analytical Chemistry, 1974-77; biennial reviewer for gas chromatography lit. Analytical Chemistry, 1962-76. Moderator communion com. Valley Presbyn. Ch., Scottsdale, Ariz., 1999—; deacon, 1960—, ruling elder, 1972—, commr. Grand Canyon Presbytery, 1974-76. NSF sr. postdoctoral fellow, 1964-65; recipient Sci. Exch. Agreement award to Czechoslovakia, Hungary, Romania and Yugoslavia, 1977. Fellow Am. Inst. Chemists; mem. AAAS, Am. Chem. Soc. (nat. chmn. divsn. analytical chemistry 1972-73, nat. sec.-treas. 1969-71, divsn. com. on chem. edn., subcom. on grad. edn. 1988—, councilor 1978-89, coun. com. analytical reagents 1985-95, co-author Reagent Chemicals, 7th edit. 1986, 8th edit. 1993, chmn. U. Ill. sect. 1968-69, sec. 1962-63, directorate divsn. officers' caucus 1987-90), Internat. Union Pure and Applied Chemistry, Internat. Platform Assn., Am. Radio Relay League (Amateur-Extra lic.), Sigma Xi, Phi Lambda Upsilon, Alpha Chi Sigma (faculty adv. U. Ill. 1958-64, Ariz. State U. 1975-95, profl. rep.-at-large 1989-94, chmn. expansion com. 1990-92, nat. v.p. grand collegiate alchemist 1994-96). Presbyterian. Rsch. on gas and liquid chromatography, instrumental analysis, computer interfacing, plasma desorption mass spectroscopy. Home: 4821 E Calle Tuberia Phoenix AZ 85018-2932 Office: Ariz State U Dept Chem and Biochem Tempe AZ 85287-1604

KABACK, HOWARD RONALD, scientific research investigator, educator; b. Phila., June 5, 1936; s. Joseph and Evelyn (Bronstein) K.; m. Mollie Schreibman, June 9, 1957; children: Elizabeth, George, Joshua. BA in Biology, Haverford (Pa.) Coll., 1958; MD, Albert Einstein Coll. Med., N.Y.C., 1962. Postgrad. intern Bronx Mcpl. Hosp. Ctr., N.Y.C., 1962-63; postdoctoral fellow Albert Einstein Coll. Med., N.Y.C., 1963-64; staff assoc. Lab. Biochemistry NIH, Bethesda, Md., 1964-66; sr. rsch. investigator Nat. Heart Inst., NIH, Bethesda, 1966-69; assoc. mem. dept. biochemistry Roche Inst. Molecular Biology, Nutley, N.J., 1970-72, mem., 1972-89, head dept., 1983-89, head Lab. Membrane Disorders, 1977-89; prin. investigator Howard Hughes Med. Inst., UCLA, 1989—; adj. prof. Columbia U., N.Y.C., 1985-89, CUNY, 1976-89. Author: Physiology of Membrane Disorders, 1995, Cell Biology in Membrane Organization, 1995; editor, author: Handbook of Biological Physics, 1996. With USPHS, 1964-66. Recipient Life Scis. award 3M, 1993, Disting. Alumnus award Albert Einstein Coll. Med., N.Y.C., 1988, Kenneth Cole award Am. Biophys. Soc., 1988. Mem. Nat. Acad. Scis., Am. Acad. Arts and Scis., Harvey Soc., N.Y. Acad. Scis. Office: Howard Hughes Med Inst UCLA 5-748 MRL Box 951662 Los Angeles CA 90095

KADIS, JONATHAN BRYNN, multimedia and distance learning services director; b. Patuxent River, Md., Sept. 14, 1956; s. Alvin Paul Jr. and Beverly (Jones) K.; m. Tami Louise Stoneking, May 25, 1979; children: Jared Brynn, Justin Brett, Tarissa Lynn, Tasha Lee. AA, AS, Bellevue Community Coll., 1983; Bachelors, Brigham Young U., 1985, Masters, 1986. Service technician Sta. KIRO-TV, Seattle, 1982-83; asst. prodn. mgr., videographer, editor Sta. KBYU-TV, Provo, Utah, 1983-87; producer, dir. Sta. KUID-TV, Moscow, Idaho, 1987-93; mgr. multimedia and distance learning svcs. Utah State U., Logan, 1993-97, supr. Faculty Assistance Ctr. for Tchg., 1993-97, dir. multimedia and distance learning svcs., 1997—, adj. prof. comms.; freelance producer, dir., editor, videographer N.W. Region, 1987—; lectr. U. Idaho, Moscow. Author: Corporate Media Management, 1986. Asst. scoutmaster Boy Scouts Am., Stanwood, 1975-76, chartered orgn. rep., 1990-91, River Heights, Utah, 1996-97, cubmaster, Moscow, 1991-92, scoutmaster and chartered orgn. rep., 1993-97. With Air N.G., 1983—. Recipient Nat. Variety Spl. Emmy award nomination NATAS, IRIS nomination for Outdoor Idaho, Phys. Fitness award. Nat. U. for Continuing Edn. Assn., Emmy nomination for Best of Outdoor Idaho, UPI Documentary Excellence award, Corp. for Pub. Broadcasting-Pub. TV Program award for Bears, Idaho Press Club award, N.Am. film/Video award, 1st pl. All-Media Editorial award Idaho Press Club, award of merit Elkhorn dist. Boy Scouts Am., 1996. Avocations: travel, golf, landscaping, antique video equipment collecting. Home: 180 W 225 N Providence UT 84332-9796 Office: Utah State U Multimedia/Dist Learning 3075 Old Main Hill Logan UT 84332

KADNER, CARL GEORGE, biology educator emeritus; b. Oakland, Calif., May 23, 1911; s. Adolph L. and Otilia (Pecht) K.; m. Mary Elizabeth Moran, June 24, 1939; children: Robert, Grace Wickersham, Carl L. BS, U. San Francisco, 1933; MS, U. Calif., Berkeley, 1936, PhD, 1941. Prof. biology Loyola Marymount U., Los Angeles, 1936-78, prof. emeritus, 1978—; trustee Loyola U., Los Angeles, 1970-73. Served to maj. U.S. Army, 1943-46. Mem. Entomol. Soc. Am. (emeritus), Sigma Xi, Alpha Sigma Nu. Republican. Roman Catholic. Avocation: insect photography. Home: 8100 Loyola Blvd Los Angeles CA 90045-2639

KAEHELE, BETTIE LOUISE, accountant; b. Sherwood, Tenn., Oct. 29, 1950; d. James Henry and Ruby Katherin (Clark) Shetters; divorced; children: Josiah Dean, Dana Marie. AAS, Albuquerque Tech. Vocat. Inst., 1980; BSBA, Nat. Coll., Albuquerque, 1991. Acctg. clk. Am. Auto Assn., Albuquerque, 1980-81, Ryder Truck Rental, Inc., Albuquerque, 1981-82; bookkeeper, sec. Grants Steel Sash & Hardware, Albuquerque, 1986-87; owner Sherwood Svcs., 1982-86; acctg. specialist Burton & Co., Albuquerque, 1987, Neff & Co., Albuquerque, 1987-91; acctg. tech. U. N.Mex. Found., Albuquerque, 1991-92, acct., 1992—; acct. biology dept., acct. II U. N.Mex., Albuquerque, 1997—. Mem. Inst. Mgmt. Accts., NAFE, Nat. Soc. Tax. Profls., N.Mex. Soc. CPAs. Republican. Avocations: reading, dance, theatre, poetry, writing. Home: 4033 Montgomery Blvd NE Apt F2 Albuquerque NM 87109-1120

KAELIN, AL, artist; b. Long Beach, Calif., Sept. 3, 1915; s. Sigisbert Stephen and Benedicta Josefina K.; m. Marion Elizabeth, F. 18, 190; children: Barney, Danny, John, Julie. BEd, UCLA, 1938; MA, Calif. State U., 1964. Syndicated cartoonist Tidings Feature Syndicate, L.A., 1947-69; dir. advt. art Baus and Ross Co., L.A., 1962-70; creative cons. Schick Razors, L.A., 1966-98; art dir. Laser Magic Prodns., Playa Del Rey, Calif., 1981—; free-lance cartoonist Nat. Mags., 1939-70; mag. cover designer Arts & Architecture, L.A., 1955-60. One-man show at Roberts Art Gallery, Santa Monica, Calif., 1967; painter of 2 murals. Sgt. USAF, 1942-46. Roman Catholic. Avocations: photography, writing, architecture. Home: 3119 Chadwick Dr Los Angeles CA 90032-2830

KAEMPEN, CHARLES EDWARD, manufacturing company executive; b. Quincy, Ill., Mar. 10, 1927; s. Charles Herman and Margo (Gochicoa) K.; m. Inger Margareta Nystrom, Aug. 5, 1951; children: Charles Robert, Donald Michael, Annette Earline, Laura Inger. BS in Aeron. Engring., U. Ill., Urbana, 1950; DSc in Astronautics, Internat. Acad. Astronautics, Paris, 1964. Registered profl. engr., Calif., Conn. Sr. designer Saab Aircraft Co., Linköping, Sweden, 1950-52; design analyst Sikorsky Helicopter United Aircraft, Stratford, Conn., 1952-56; space mission analyst Missle div. N.Am. Rockwell, Downey, Calif., 1957-60; staff scientist Hughes Aircraft, Fullerton, Calif., 1961-63; lunar systems analyst Northrop Space Lab., Hawthorne, Calif., 1963-64; pres. Am. Space Transport Co., Tustin, Calif., 1964-66; transport systems analyst Dashaveyor Co., Venice, Calif., 1966-67; pres. Kaempen & Assocs., Orange, Calif., 1967-68; sr. rsch. engr. Baker Oil Tools Inc., L.A., 1968-69; pres. Kaempen Industries, Inc., Santa Ana, Calif., 1969-82, Kaempen & Assocs., 1982—. Author papers on fiberglass composites and filament winding; patentee in field. With U.S. Army, 1944-47. Reciepient Cert. of Merit Pictionary of Internat. Biography, London, 1965,. Fellow AIAA; mem. ASME, ASTM, Soc. Aerospace Materials and Process Engring., Soc. of Plastics Industry, Nat. Soc. Profl. Engrs., Mason. Republican. Lutheran. Home: 3202 E Larkstone Dr Orange CA 92869-5546 Office: Kaempen Composite Products Inc 681 S Tustin St Ste 110 Orange CA 92866-3345

KAGAWA, KATHLEEN HATSUYO, entrepreneur; b. Honolulu, June 9, 1952; d. Shinso and Jane Fumiko (Murata) K.; m. Masamichi Irimajiri (div. 1977). Student, U. Hawaii, Honolulu, 1970-73, Sophia U., Tokyo, 1973; BSBA, U. Beverly Hills, 1977, MBA, 1979, PhD in Internat. Bus., 1982. Mgr. Flipside Record Shop, Honolulu, 1969-70; producer, singer Victor Records, Tokyo, 1973-76; actress Hawaii Five-O, Honolulu, 1976; co-owner Images Internat. of Hawaii, Honolulu, 1976-79; v.p., sec., hostess East-West Connection TV Show, L.A., 1980-81; dir. pub. rels. Fendi, Beverly Hills, 1981-82; pres. Sky Prodns., Inc., Honolulu, 1982-86; v.p., treas. Born Internat., Inc., Honolulu, 1986-89; pres., dir. Mitsumine (USA) Co. Ltd. aka Chapman's Men's Wear aka Alfred Shaheen Stores, 1989—, Hawaii 5-O Properties, Inc., Honolulu, 1990—; adminstrv. exec., corp. sec. new Tokyo-Hawaii Restaurant Co., Ltd., 1981-89; cons. Schlossberg-Cassidy and Assoc., Washington, 1983-86; sponsor State of Hawaii Nat. Aquaculture Assn., Washington, 1983-86; admissions counselor U. Beverly Hills, Honolulu, 1984-86; pres. K & H Devel. Co., Ltd.; realtor Diamond Head Group subs. New Tokyo Restaurant, 1986, bd. dirs; sec.-treas. Azabu Enterprises Ltd., 1989-90, bd. dirs. Pres. GRC Hawaii Co., Ltd., GRC Internat. Co. (dba Park Plaza Waikiki Hotel), 1986—. Named Best in Backstroke, State of Hawaii Swim Competition, 1968. Mem. Gemological Inst. Am. Alumni Assn., Japan-Am. Soc. of Honolulu, Honolulu Bd. Realtors, Mortgage Broker Assn., Pacific and Asian Affairs Coun., Punahou Alumni Assn., Oahu Country Club. Baptist. Club: Oahu Country (Hawaii). Avocations: swimming, reading, songwriting. Home: 3215 Kaohinani Dr Honolulu HI 96817-1042

KÅGE, JONAS, ballet company artistic director; b. Stockholm; m. Deborah Dobson; 1 child, Isabelle. Student, Royal Swedish Ballet Sch. Mem. Royal Swedish Ballet; mem. Am. Ballet Theatre, 1971-75, soloist, 1972-75, prin. dancer, 1973-75; prin. dancer Stuttgart (Germany) Ballet, 1975-76, Geneva (Switzerland) Ballet, 1976-78, Zürich (Switzerland) Ballet, 1978-88; artistic dir. Malmo (Sweden) Opera Ballet, 1988-95; freelance guest artist, master tchr., 1995-97; artistic dir. Ballet West, Salt Lake City, 1997-98; Guest artist Am. Ballet Theatre, 1977—, Frankfort (Germany) Ballet, Basel (Switzerland) Ballet, Royal Swedish Ballet, 1980-81, Deutsche Opera Berlin, 1982, Pitts. Ballet, 1984-85, Nat. Ballet of Can., 1984-85, 85-86, Milw. Ballet, 1984-85, NAPAC Dance Co., 1985-86, Munich Opera Ballet, 1985-86, Nat. Ballet of Portugal, 1986-87, Ariz. Ballet, 1987-88,. Prin. dancer Swan Lake, Coppélia, La Bayadere, Tales of Hoffmann, Lander's Etudes, Shadowplay, Leaves are Fading, Balanchine's Theme and Variations, Gemini, Some Times, Intermezzo, Les Noces, Am. Ballet Theatre, 1971-75, Swan Lake, Don Quixote, Sphinx, Voluntaries, 1977; prin. dancer The Taming of the Shrew, Romeo & Juliet, Onegin, Gemini, La Sacre de Printemps, Greening, Stuttgart Ballet, 1975-76, Apollo, The Four Temperaments, Agon Symphony in C, Who Cares?, Geneva Ballet, 1976-77, Romeo & Juliet, The Sleeping Beauty, Sphinx, Rosalinda, London Festival Ballet (now English Nat. Ballet), 1977, La Sylphide, Cinderella, Swan Lake, Giselle, Romeo & Juliet, 1982-83; prin. dancer Swan Lake, Frankfort Ballet, Giselle, Basel Ballet, Don Quixote, Vienna Ballet, The Taming of the Shrew, Manon, Royal Swedish Ballet, 1980-81, La Sylphide, Deutsche Opera Berlin, 1982, Coppélia, Giselle, Greening, Apollo, Spoleto and Naples, 1982, Swan Lake, Pitts. Ballet Theatre, 1984-85, Romeo & Juliet, Nat. Ballet of Can., 1984-85, Swan Lake, 1985-86; prin. dancer The Merry Widow, Milw. Ballet, 1984-85, Apollo, NAPAC Dance Co., 1985-86, Romeo & Juliet, Munich Opera Ballet, 1985-86, Apollo, Nat. Ballet of Portugal, 1986-87, The Nutcracker, Ariz. Ballet, 1987-88; creator prin. role Chopin Pas de Deux, Malmo Opera Ballet, 1993-94; choreographer Swedish TV, 1983, Simple Symphony, Zurich Ballet, 1984, Baroque Variations, Malmo Opera Ballet, 1988, Swan Lake, 1992-93 (Thalia prize 1993); master of ceremonies dance competition, Swedish TV, 1997. Bd. dirs. Swedish Dance U., Stockholm, Dalhalla amphitheater, Rattvik, Sweden. Recipient Carina Ari medal, 1994. Avocations: photography, skiing, mountain climbing, horseback riding, wilderness guide training. Office: Ballet West Capitol Theatre 50 W 200 S Ste 100 Salt Lake City UT 84101-1663

KAHAN, SHELDON JEREMIAH (CHRISTOPHER REED), musician, singer; b. Honolulu, Mar. 5, 1948; s. Aaron Kahan and Marianne (Royjiczek) Sann. Student, Tel Aviv U., 1967-69, Merritt Coll., 1972-74. Guitarist The Grim Reapers, Miami Beach, Fla., 1965-66; bassist The Electric Stage, Jerusalem, 1969-71; music dir., musician Fanfare, L.A., 1974-75, Jean Paul Vignon & 1st Love, L.A., 1975-76; musician Jenny Jones & Co., L.A., 1976; musician, vocalist Fantasy, L.A., 1977-79; leader, musician, vocalist Fortune, L.A., 1980-83; bassist Johnny Tillotson Show, Nev., 1983; prin. musician, vocalist Heartlight, L.A., 1983-84; leader, musician, vocalist The Boogie Bros., L.A., 1984—; arranger, conductor L.A. Rock Chorus, 1988; musician, vocalist Jeremiah Kahan, L.A., 1988; bass player LIX, L.A., 1990—; solo act Sheldon Kahan, L.A., 1990—; spokesman Moore Old-

smobile & Cadillac, Valencia, Calif., 1987. Compiled musical work copyrighted in Libr. Congress: Sheldon Jeremiah Kahan The Early Years-Vol. I; prodr., disk jockey Kaleidoscope Radio Mag., Am. Radio Ntwork; one-man show El Caapitan, Irvine, Calif., 1990, Sagebrush Cantina, Calabassas, Calif., 1990, Don Jose, Artesia, Calif., Pineapple Hill, Tustin, Calif., 1991, The Fling, Tustin, 1992, Beverly Garland, North Hollywood, Calif., Brian Patch, Garden Grove, Calif., Sugar Suite, Granada Hills, Calif., 1993, The Blarney Stone, Fountain Valley, Calif., 1994, Sunset Lounge, Fullerton, Calif., Rembrandts, Placentia, Calif., 1995, Chez Lynn, Orange, Calif., 1996, Maxwells, Anaheim Hills, Calif., Royal Crown, Fullerton, Calif., 1997, The Oasis, Garden Grove, Calif., 1997, Azar's Red Robin, Newbury Park, Calif., The Stonepiper, Northridge, Calif., Volare, Northridge, 1998, Oh Grady's, Granada Hills, Calif., 1998, Sportspage, Placentia, Calif., 1998. Mem. AFTRA, Am. Fedn. Musicians. Democrat. Jewish. Avocations: chess, aerobics, weight training, comparative religions. Home: 3915 1/2 Fredonia Dr Los Angeles CA 90068-1213

KAHN, EARL LESTER, retired market research executive; b. Kansas City, Mo., May 30, 1919; s. Samuel and Sarah (Kaufman) K. BA, Harvard U., 1940; MA, U. Chgo., 1947. Pres. Social Research, Inc., Chgo., 1946-74; chmn. bd. KPR Assocs., Inc., Scottsdale, Ariz., 1974-88. Contbr. articles to profl. jour. Served to capt. USAF, 1942-46. Mem. Am. Mktg. Assn, Am. Sociol. Assn. Home: 5608 N Scottsdale Rd Paradise Valley AZ 85253

KAHN, EDWIN S., lawyer; b. N.Y.C., Jan. 22, 1938; m. Cynthia Chutter, May 30, 1966; children—David, Jonathan, Jennifer. B.A., U. Colo., 1958; J.D., Harvard U., 1965. Bar: Colo. 1965, U.S. Dist. Ct. (Colo.) 1965, U.S. Ct. Appeals (10th cir.) 1965, U.S. Supreme Ct. 1968. Assoc. Holland & Hart, Denver, 1965-70, ptnr., 1970-77; ptnr., shareholder, Kelly/Haglund/Garnsey & Kahn, LLC, Denver, 1978—. Served as 1st lt. USAF, 1959-62, Eng. Fellow Am. Coll. Trial Lawyers: mem. Denver Bar Assn. (pres. 1984-85). Home: 2345 Leyden St Denver CO 80207-3441 Office: Kelly Haglund Garnsey & Kahn LLC 1441 18th St Ste 300 Denver CO 80202-1250

KAHN, FREDRICK HENRY, internist; b. L.A., Aug. 26, 1925; s. Julius and Josephine Leone (Langdon) K.; m. Barbara Ruth Visscher, Feb. 14, 1952; children: Susan, Kathryn, William. AB, Stanford U., 1947, MD, 1951. Diplomate Am. Bd. Internal Medicine. Rotating intern San Francisco Gen. Hosp., 1950-51, fellow pathology, 1951-52; resident medicine Los Angeles VA Hosp., 1954-57, sr. resident, 1956-57; asst. clin. prof. medicine UCLA Sch. Medicine, 1957-91; attending physician Cedars Sinai Med. Ctr., L.A., 1957-96, attending physician emeritus, 1996—; attending physician UCLA; med. advisor Vis. Nurse Assn., Los Angeles, 1957-87. Contbr. articles to med. jours.; inventor blow-through high altitude chamber; promoter iodine method of personal water disinfection for travelers and hikers. Served with USNR, 1943-46; lt. (M.C.), USNR, 1952-54. Fellow ACP; mem. AMA, Los Angeles County Internal Medicine Soc., Am. Handel Soc., Sierra Club. Avocations: hiking, collecting and listening to baroque music. Home: 3309 Corinth Ave Los Angeles CA 90066-1312

KAHN, IRWIN WILLIAM, industrial engineer; b. N.Y.C., Feb. 3, 1923; s. Milton and Clara (Clark) K.; BS, U. Calif.-Berkeley, 1949; student Cath. U., 1943-44; m. Mildred Cross, May 14, 1946 (dec. May 1966); children: Steven Edward, Michael William, Evelyn Ruth, Joanne Susan; m. 2d, Marajayne Smith, Oct. 9, 1979. Chief indsl. engr. Malsbary Mfg. Co., Oakland, Calif., 1953-57, Yale & Towne Mfg. Co., San Leandro, Calif., 1957-60; sr. indsl. engr. Eitel McCulloch, San Carlos, Calif., 1961-62, Lockheed, Sunnyvale, Calif., 1962-69; v.p. Performance Investors, Inc., Palo Alto, 1969-74; with Kaiser-Permanente Svcs., Oakland, 1974-76; nat. mgr. material handling Cutter Labs., Berkeley, Calif., 1976-83; sr. mgmt. engr. Children's Hosp. Med. Ctr., Oakland, 1983; sr. indsl. engr. Naval Air Rework Facility, Alameda, Calif., 1983-85, Naval Supply Ctr., Oakland, 1985-88; vis. lectr. U. Calif., Berkeley, 1986; tchr. indsl. engring. Laney Coll., Oakland, 1967—, Chabot Coll., Hayward, Calif.; pres. East Bay Table Pad Co., 1990. Chmn. Alameda County Libr. Adv. Commn., 1965—. Served with AUS, 1943-46. Registered profl. engr., Calif. Mem. Am. Inst. Indsl. Engrs. (chpt. pres. 1963-64, chmn. conf. 1967 nat. publ. dir. aerospace div. 1968-69), Calif. Soc. Profl. Engrs. (pres. chpt.). Club: Toastmasters (dist. gov. 1960-61).

KAHN, LINDA MCCLURE, actuary, consultant; b. Jacksonville, Fla.; d. George Calvin and Myrtice Louise (Boggs) McClure; m. Paul Markham Kahn, May 20, 1968. BS with honors, U. Fla.; MS, U. Mich., 1964. Actuarial trainee N.Y. Life Ins. Co., N.Y.C., 1964-66, actuarial asst., 1966-69, asst. actuary, 1969-71; v.p., actuary US Life Ins., Pasadena, Calif., 1972-74; mgr. Coopers & Lybrand, L.A., 1974-76, sr. cons., San Francisco, 1976-82; dir. program mgmt. Pacific Maritime Assn., San Francisco, 1982-97; pres., CEO, P.M. Kahn & Assocs., 1997—. Chmn., CEO, Paul and Linda Kahn Found., 1998—; bd. dirs. Pacific Heights Residents Assn., sec.-treas., 1981; trustee ILWU-PMA Welfare Plan, 1982-97, SIU-PD-PMA Pension and Supplemental Benefits Plans, 1982-90, Seafarers Med. Ctr., 1982-90, others. Fellow Soc. Actuaries (chmn. com. on minority recruiting 1988-91, chmn. actuary of future sect. 1993-95), Conf. Cons. Actuaries; mem. Internat. Actuarial Assn., Internat. Assn. Cons. Actuaries, Actuarial Studies Non-Life Ins., Am. Acad. Actuaries (enrolled actuary), Western Pension and Benefits Conf. (newsletter editor 1983-85, sec. 1985-88, treas. 1989-90), Actuarial Club Pacific States, San Francisco Actuarial Club (pres. 1981), Met. Club, Commonwealth Club, Soroptimists (v.p. 1973-74), Concordia-Argonaut Club, Pacific Club (Honolulu). Home and Office: 2430 Pacific Ave San Francisco CA 94115-1238

KAHN, MARIO SANTAMARIA, international marketing executive; b. Manila, Jan. 16, 1956; came to U.S., 1980; s. Rene L. and Dolores (Santamaria) K.; m. Maria Victoria Legaspi, Dec. 28, 1987; 1 child, Marc Daniel. AB in Mktg. & Comm., De La Salle U., Manila, 1977; MA in Comm. Mgmt. cum laude, U. So. Calif., 1982; postgrad., Stanford U., 1989. Account mgr. McCann-Erickson, Manila, 1977-80; teaching asst. U. So. Calif., L.A., 1980-82; ops. mgr. Dayton-Hudson Corp., Mpls., 1982-85; sr. mgr. Asia Sunkist Growers, Ontario, Calif., 1986—; bd. dirs. Sunkist Soft Drink Internat. Mem. Am. Mktg. Assn., Am. Mgmt. Assn., Stanford Alumni Assn., Annenberg Alumni Assn., De La Salle Alumni Assn. Office: Sunkist Growers Inc 720 E Sunkist St Ontario CA 91761-1861

KAHN, PAUL MARKHAM, actuary; b. San Francisco, May 8, 1935; s. Sigmund Max and Alexandrina K. (Strauch) K.; m. Linda P. McClure, May 20, 1968. BS, Stanford U., 1956; MA, U. Mich., 1957, PhD, 1961. Asst. actuary Equitable Life Assurance Soc., N.Y.C., 1961-71; v.p., life actuary Beneficial Std. Life, L.A., 1971-75; v.p., actuary Am. Express Life Ins. Co., San Rafael, Calif., 1975-77, P.M. Kahn & Assocs., 1977—; adj. prof. actuarial math. San Fransisco State U.; imperial actuary, 1995. Editor Dictionary of Actuarial and Life Ins. Terms, 1972, 2d edit., 1983, Credibility: Theory and Practice, 1975, Computational Probability, 1980. Fellow Soc. Actuaries (Triennial prize 1961-64), Can. Inst. Actuaries, Conf. of Cons. Actuaries; mem. Am. Acad. Actuaries, Internat. Actuarial Assn., Inst. Actuaries (Eng.), Spanish Actuarial Inst., Swiss Actuarial Assn., German Actuarial Assn., Italian Actuarial Inst., Am. Antiquarian Soc., Grolier Club (N.Y.C.) Zamorano Club (L.A.), Roxburghe Club, Concordia-Argonaut Club (San Francisco), Pacific Club (Honolulu). Address: 2430 Pacific Ave San Francisco CA 94115-1238

KAIL, JOSEPH GERARD, communications sales and marketing executive; b. Cin., Dec. 23, 1946; s. Henry Thomas and Cosma (Contadino) K.; m. Patricia Lynne Riedel, June 28, 1969; children: Robert, Daniel, Joseph. BS, Xavier U., Cin., 1969, MEd, 1973. Tchr., athletic coach Alter High Sch., Kettering, Ohio, 1969-77; sales rep. Philips Bus. Systems, Inc., Cin., 1977-78, Hewlett-Packard Co., Dayton, 1978-81; dist. sales mgr. Hewlett-Packard Co., Pitts., 1981-83; sales mgr. Rocky Mountain area Hewlett-Packard Co., Denver, 1983-87, western regional sales mgr. bus. computer systems, 1988-91, western regional mktg. mgr. computer systems, 1991-92, am. mktg. mgr. computer systems organization, 1992-93, nat. sales mgr., home products, 1994-96, nat. sales mgr. comm., 1996—. Com. mem. troop 986, Boy Scouts Am., Denver, 1984-88, Highlands Ranch High Sch. Boosters, Denver, 1988. Republican. Roman Catholic. Avocation: golf. Office: Hewlett-Packard Co 24 Inverness Pl E Englewood CO 80112-5658

KAIN, BARBARA BROWN, communications executive; b. Omaha, Nebr., June 4, 1957; d. Donald Wilbur Brown and Marjorie Ann (Scott) Walker; m. John Christopher Kain, Mar. 28, 1981; children: Matthew, Jessie. B of Journalism, U. Mo., 1979. Reporter Sta. KELO-TV, Sioux Falls, S.D., 1979-81; stockbroker Boettcher & Co., Phoenix, 1981-82; pub. rels. specialist St. Luke's Med. Ctr., Phoenix, 1983-85; comms. dir. Blood Systems, Phoenix, 1985—; chmn. nat. awareness campaign Ams. Blood Ctrs., Washington, 1996—. Writer, dir. (video) Be A Hero, 1996. Bd. dirs. Ams. Blood Ctrs. Found., Washington, 1997—; adv. coun. Scottsdale South YMCA, 1995-97; bd. dirs. Scottsdale Leadership, 1993-97; mem. City of Phoenix Women's Commn., 1984-88. Named Ten Outstanding Young Women Phoenix Jaycees, 1984. Office: Blood Systems 6210 E Oak Scottsdale AZ 85257

KAISCH, KENNETH BURTON, psychologist, priest; b. Detroit, Aug. 29, 1948; s. Kenneth R. Kaisch and Marjorie F. (Howe) Bourke; m. Suzanne Carol LePrevost, Aug. 31, 1969; 1 child, Samuel. BA, San Francisco State U., 1972; MDiv, Ch. Divinity Sch. Pacific, 1976; MS, Utah State U., 1983, PhD in Clin. Psychology, 1986. Ordained deacon Episcopal Ch., 1976, priest, 1977; lic. clin. psychologist, Calif. Intern local parish, 1973-76; ordinand tng. program Ch. of the Good Shepherd, Ogden, Utah, 1976-77; pastor St. Francis' Episc. Ch., Moab, Utah, 1977-80, St. John's Episc. Ch., Logan, Utah, 1980-84; psychol. asst. Peter Ebersole, Ph.D., Fullerton, Calif., 1984-86; intern in clin. psychology Patton State Hosp., Calif., 1985-86; psychol. asst. Ronald Wong Jue, Ph.D., Fullerton and Newport Beach, Calif., 1986-88; pvt. practice clin. psychologist Calif., 1988—; clin. dir. Anxiety Clinic, Fullerton, 1993—; exec. dir. Contemplative Congress, Fullerton, 1988-91, Inner Peace Conf., 1995-97; founder, pres. OneHeart, 1986-98, Contemplative Visions, Fullerton, 1990—; supply priest Episc. Diocese of L.A.; invited lectr. Acad. Sch. Profl. Psychology, Moscow, 1992, 93, Moscow Med. Acad., 1998. Co-author: Fundamentals of Psychotherapy, 1984, Developing Your Feel for Golf, 1998; author: Finding God: A Handbook of Christian Meditation, 1994, The Mental Golf Inventory, 1998; co-editor: God in Russia: The Challange of Freedom, 1999; contbr. numerous articles to profl. jours. Mem. St. Andrew's Episc. Ch., Fullerton. Mem. APA, Calif. Psychol. Assn., Anxiety Disorders Assn. Am., Nat. Register of Health Svc. Providers in Psychology, Phi Kappa Phi, Rotary (past bd. dirs., past officer). Episcopalian. Office: 2555 E Chapman Ave Ste 617 Fullerton CA 92831-3621

KAISER, NINA IRENE, health care consultant; b. San Diego, Nov. 29, 1953; d. Louis Frederick and Mary Elizabeth (Wright) K.; m. N. Klimist, Aug. 27, 1987; children: Kellen Anne Kaiser, Ethan Andrew Kaiser-Klimist. BSN, BA in Women Studies, San Francisco State U., 1980. RN, Calif. RN Calif. Pacific Med. Ctr., San Francisco, 1980-81, Ralph K. Davies Med. Ctr., San Francisco, 1982-85, Planned Parenthood, San Francisco, 1985-86, Visiting Nurses and Hospice, San Francisco, 1986-88; RN supr. St. Mary's Home Care, San Francisco, 1991-93; RN dir. St. Vincent's Homecare and Hospice, Fremont, Calif., 1993-94, Home Health Link, San Leandro, Calif., 1994-98; health care cons. Pres. Daus. of Bilitis, San Francisco, 1977-78; founding mem. Buena Vista Lesbian and Gay Parents Assn., San Francisco, 1985; treas., bd. dirs. Holladay Ave. Homeowners Assn., San Francisco, 1984-96; bd. dirs. Midrasha High Sch., Berkeley, Calif., 1996. With USN, 1971-74.

KAISER, SHARON BURKETT, artist; b. San Raphael, Calif., Sept. 10, 1946; d. John Wesley and Loma Ann (McIntosh) Burkett; m. Michael Charles Kaiser, May 19, 1978; 1 child, Spencer Alexander. BA, San Diego State U., 1970; postgrad studies in painting with Charles Movalli, Apinchapong Yang, Sergei Bongart Sch. of Art, Calif. Art Inst. Artist: one woman shows include: Studio of Long Grove, Ill., 1992, Premier Gallery, Fredricksberg, Va., 1996; group shows: Marco Fine Arts Gallery, Beverly Hills, Calif., 1991, 94, L.A. Art Exposition (featured artist in promotion), 1991, Tokyo Internat. Art Show and Exhbn. (featured artist), 1992, Marco Fine Arts Gallery, Santa Monica, 1992, Carnegie Art Mus., Oxnard, Calif., 1994, Calif. Art Club Gold Medal show, L.A., 1995, 96, 97, 98, The Calif. Heritage Gallery, 1996, Art Expo N.Y.C., 1996, 97, 98, Treasures of the Sierra Nev. Group Show, Nat. History Mus. of L.A. County, 1998; numerous works in galleries and pvt. collections world wide; prints published by Colville Publ., Torrance, Calif., posters by Winn Devon Graphics, Seattle; contbr. articles to Am. Artist Mag., featured in Am. Artist, Vitality Mag. and Calif. Art Club Newsletter. Bd. dirs. Calif. Art Acad. and Mus. Mem. Calif. Art Club (bd. dirs. 1994, signature mem. 1996). Republican. Avocations: reading, skiing, hiking, gardening. Home and Office: 2000 Searidge St Malibu CA 90265-2966

KALB, BENJAMIN STUART, television producer, director; b. L.A., Mar. 17, 1948; s. Marcus and Charlotte K. BS in Journalism, U. Oreg., 1969. Sportswriter, Honolulu Advertiser, 1971-76; traveled with tennis profl. Ilie Nastase; contbr. articles N.Y. Times, Sport Mag. and Tennis U.S.A., 1976; editor Racquetball Illustrated, 1978-82; segment producer PM Mag. and Hollywood Close-Up, 1983-86; exec. producer Ben Kalb Prodns., 1986—; instr. sports in soc. U. Hawaii, 1974-75. Producer (video) The Natural Way to Meet the Right Person, 1987; producer, dir. (video) Casting Call: Director's Choice, 1987, The Natural Way to Meet The Right Person (Best Home Videos of Yr. L.A. Times), (TV pilot and home video) Bizarro, 1988, (infomercial) How To Start Your Own Million Dollar Business, 1990, The Nucelle Promise, 1993-94, Koolatron Companion, 1997; prodr.-dir. (infomercials) Banamex USA Credit Card, 1995, Slimaster Exerciser, 1996, Koolatron Companion, 1997, Yonex Golf, 1998 (short feature film) Against the Ropes, 1996; segment dir. (home video) Movie Magic, 1990, (TV show) Totally Hidden Video; writer-segment dir. (home video) Making of The American Dream Calendar Girl, 1991; producer, host (cable TV show) Delicious Sports, 1987-88; segment dir. Totally Hidden Video (Fox TV Network), 1991-92; prodr., dir. short feature film Love Match, 1995. Served with Hawaii Army N.G., 1970-75. Named Outstanding Male Grad. in Journalism, U. Oreg., 1969. Mem. Sigma Delta Chi (chpt. pres. 1968). Democrat. Jewish. Contbr. articles to mags. and newspapers. Home: 3392 Brookfield Dr Las Vegas NV 89120-1964 Office: 3840 S Jones Blvd Las Vegas NV 89103-2228

KALIHER, MICHAEL DENNIS, librarian, historian; b. Santa Monica, Calif., Nov. 7, 1947; s. Eugene Charles and Phyllis Joan (McCrary) K. BA, U. Ariz., 1990. Pres. Klamath County (Oreg.) Hist. Soc., 1985; founder Native Am. History Week, Klamath County Mus., 1985-86. Contbr. articles to various hist. jours. Mem. Ariz. Libr. Assn., Pi Lambda Theta, Phi Alpha Theta. Roman Catholic. Avocations: backpacking, trout fishing. Home: PO Box 634 Winslow AZ 86047-0634

KALINA, ROBERT EDWARD, physician, educator; b. New Prague, Minn., Nov. 13, 1936; s. Edward Robert and Grace Susan (Hess) K.; m. Janet Jessie Larsen, July 18, 1959; children: Paul Edward, Lynne Janet. B.A. magna cum laude, U. Minn., 1957, B.S., 1960, M.D., 1960. Diplomate Am. Bd. Ophthalmology (dir. 1981-89). Intern U. Oreg. Med. Sch. Hosp., Portland, 1960-61; resident in ophthalmology U. Oreg. Med. Sch. Hosp., 1961-62, 63-66; asst. in retina surgery Children's Hosp., San Francisco, 1966-67; Nat. Inst. Neurol. Diseases and Blindness Spl. fellow Mass. Eye and Ear Infirmary, Boston, 1967; instr. ophthalmology U. Wash., 1967-69, asst. prof., 1969-71, acting chmn. dept. ophthalmology, 1970-71, asso. prof., 1971-72, chmn. dept. ophthalmology, 1971-96, prof., 1972—; mem. staffs Univ. Hosp., Harborview Hosp., Children's Hosp., Seattle; cons. VA Hosp., Seattle, Pacific Med. Ctr., Seattle, Madigan Hosp., Tacoma; assoc. head divsn. ophthalmology dept. surgery Children's Hosp., Seattle, 1975-86; pres. U. Wash. Physicians, 1990-93. Contbr. author: Introduction to Clinical Pediatrics, 1972, Ophthalmology Study Guide for Medical Students, 1975; contbr. numerous articles to profl. publs. Served to capt., M.C. USAF, 1962-63. Fellow ACS, Am. Acad. Ophthalmology (Sr. Honor award 1989); mem. AMA, Assn. Univ. Profs. Ophthalmology (pres. 1983-84, exec. v.p. 1989-94), Assn. Rsch. in Vision and Ophthalmology, Pacific Coast Oto-Ophthalmol. Soc. (councilor 1972-74), King County Med. Soc., Wash. State Acad. Ophthalmology, Phi Beta Kappa. Home: 2627 96th Ave NE Bellevue WA 98004-2107 Office: U Wash Dept Ophthalmology Box 356485 1959 NE Pacific St Seattle WA 98195-0001

KALIS, MURRAY, advertising agency executive, writer; s. Bernard and Bernis Kalis. BS in Comm., U. Ill.; MFA in Printmaking, Drake U., U. Iowa. Former chmn. art dept. Midwestern Coll., Denison, Iowa; creative dir., v.p. Leo Burnett Advt., Chgo.; exec. creative dir., sr. v.p. Young & Rubicam Advt. Joint Ventures, L.A.; pres. Coen/Kalis Advt., L.A., 1989-95; chmn. Kalis & Savage Advt., 1995—. 1st lt. U.S. Army. Recipient cert. of merit N.Y. Art Dirs. One Show; Bronze Lion, Cannes Festival, gold medal Chgo. Film Festival, Clio award, Best in West, Belding, Spl. award UN for Pub. Svc. Advt., intaglio art in permanent collection Phila. Mus. Art. Author: Candida by Amy Voltaire, 1979; Love in Paris, 1980; Are You Experienced? The Jimi Hendrix Story, 1984, (play) Single Scene, 1989. Clubs: Creative, Los Angeles Advt. Office: Kalis & Savage Advt 17383 W Sunset Blvd Ste 450 Pacific Palisades CA 90272-5101

KALISZEK, ANDREW WOJCIECH, mechanical engineer; b. Zlotow, Poland, Apr. 8, 1946; s. Jan Wojciech and Wiera (Labenska) K.; m. Anna D. Makosa, Dec. 26, 1974 (div. Dec. 1979); 1 child, Agata Karina; m. Barbara Nickles, Apr. 16, 1983; 1 stepchild, Mark Robert. MME, Warsaw U. of Tech., 1969, PhD, 1979. Registered profl. engr., Ariz. Rsch. engr. Warsaw U. of Tech., 1972-75, mgr. rsch. lab., 1975-78, acad. lectr., 1978-81; project engr. Universal Rsch. Lab., Elk Grove Village, Ill., 1981-83; sr. project engr. Wico Corp., Niles, Ill., 1983-84; sect. mgr. Zenith Electronics Corp., Glenview, Ill., 1984-87; staff engr. Honeywell Inc., Phoenix, 1987-95; staff rsch. scientist fiber optic sensors Honeywell Technology Ctr., Phoenix, 1995—. Contbr. articles to profl. jours. Mem. Sufact Mount Tech. Assn., Western Chopin Soc. (exec. officer 1989—). Republican. Roman Catholic. Achievements include patents in field. Avocations: bridge, hiking, travels. Home: 1156 E Beverly Ln Phoenix AZ 85022-2668 Office: Honeywell Technology Ctr 21111 N 19th Ave Phoenix AZ 85027-2700

KALKHOVEN, KEVIN N., electronics company executive. Pres., CEO Uniphase, San Jose, Calif. Office: Uniphase 210 Baypointe Pkwy San Jose CA 95134-1621*

KALLAY, MICHAEL FRANK, II, medical devices company official; b. Painesville, Ohio, Aug. 24, 1944; s. Michael Frank and Marie Francis (Sage) K.; BBA, Ohio U., 1967; m. Irma Yolanda Corona, Aug. 30, 1975; 1 son, William Albert. Salesman, Howmedica, Inc., Rutherford, N.J., 1972-75, Biochem. Procedures/Metpath, North Hollywood, Calif., 1975-76; surg. specialist USCI div. C. R. Bard, Inc., Billerica, Mass., 1976-78; western and central regional mgr. ARCO Med. Products Co., Phila., 1978-80; Midwest regional mgr. Intermedics, Inc., Freeport, Tex., 1980-82; Western U.S. mgr. Renal Systems, Inc., Mpls., 1982—; pres. Kall-Med, Inc., Anaheim Hills, Calif., 1982—. Mem. Am. Mgmt. Assn., Phi Kappa Sigma. Home and Office: PO Box 17248 7539 E Bridgewood Dr Anaheim CA 92808-1407

KALLENBERG, JOHN KENNETH, librarian; b. Anderson, Ind., June 10, 1942; s. Herbert A. and Helen S. K.; m. Ruth Barrett, Aug. 19, 1965; children: Jennifer Anne, Gregory John. A.B., Ind. U., 1964, M.L.S., 1969. With Fresno County Library, Fresno, Calif., 1965-70, dir., 1976—; librarian Fig Garden Pub. Library br., 1968-70; asst. dir. Santa Barbara (Calif.) Pub. Library, 1970-76; mem. Calif. Libr. Svcs. bd., 1990—, v.p., 1992-95, pres., 1996-98; Beth Ann Harnish lectr. com., 1988-91, chmn., 1989-90. Mem. Calif. Libr. Assn. (councilor 1976-77, v.p., pres. 1987), Calif. County Librs. Assn. (pres. 1977), Calif. Libr. Authority for Sys. and Svcs. (chmn. authority adv. coun. 1978-80), Kiwanis (pres. Fresno 1981-82, lt. gov. divsn. 5 1991-92, co-editor Cal-Nev-Ha News 1993-94, 95-96). Presbyterian. Office: Fresno County Free Libr 2420 Mariposa St Fresno CA 93721-2204

KALOYÁN, LUIS RIVAS, broadcast executive; b. Armenia, Feb. 28, 1962; s. Jose Luis Rivas and Armenui Kaloyán Agopian; m. Claudia Sanchez, Oct. 1, 1996; children: Luis Armen, Arakel. Grad., CETYS U., Mex.; grad. bus. sch., San Diego State U. Pres., gen. mgr. XHRM FM, National City, Calif., 1989—. Started first alternative rock format in U.S., 1993. Recipient Outstanding Cmty. Svc. to S. Dist. Congress of U.S., 1991, Commendation for Professionalism and Hard Work City Coun. San Diego, 1991, Rep. Presd. award Bd. Govs. Rep. Party, Washington, 1994. Republican. Roman Catholic. Avocation: golf. Office: XHRM-FM 92.5 The Flash/BBC 2434 Southport Way Ste A National City CA 91950-6657

KAM, JAMES TING, scientist, engineer, consultant; b. Hong Kong, July 29, 1945; s. Nai Fai and Big Chun (Au); m. Winna M. Wong, June 9, 1974; children: Kelvin K., Theresa P. PhD, U. Calif., Berkeley, 1974. Registered profl. engr., Calif., Utah, Colo., N.Mex. Project engr. Internat. Engring. Co., San Francisco, 1973-79, sr. hydrologist Sci. Applications Inc., San Leandro, Calif., 1979-81; chief hydrologist Davy McKee Corp., San Ramon, Calif., 1981-85; prin. engr. MK Environ. Svcs., San Francisco, 1985—; cons. in field. U. Calif. scholar, 1972-74. Mem. ASCE, Am. Groundwater Scientists and Engrs., Lions (bd. dirs. San Francisco chpt. 1984-86), Sigma Xi. Avocations: golf, tennis, marathons, triathlon, singing. Home: 2430 35th Ave San Francisco CA 94116-2246

KAM, JIN G., artist, educator; b. Shanghai, China, July 10, 1953; came to U.S., 1989; s. Hong Kam and Xue Yu Li; m. Adeline J. Fu, May 25, 1997. BA, China Nat. Acad. Fine Art, Hangzhou, 1982; postgrad., U.S. Internat. U., San Diego, 1989-91. Instr. Coll. Fine Arts Shanghai U., 1983-87; designer, artist Oh-Ami Inc., Tokyo, 1987-89; artist Symphony Fine Art Inc, San Diego, 1990—. Oil paintings include Roots, 1981, Ballade, 1990. Bd. dirs. Shanghai Tech. Art Inst., 1986-90. Grantee Leonard Berstein Edn. Through the Arts Fund, N.Y.C., 1991, Louis Armstrong Ednl. Found., N.Y.C., 1992, U.S. Post Office, 1995, Miles Davis Estate, N.Y.C., 1995. Avocations: piano, violin, sports, travel. Home: 1324 Elm Ave Apt J San Gabriel CA 91775-3082

KAMADA, MIRA S., art director; b. Summit, N.J., Jan. 14, 1952; d. Robert W. and Viola E. (Rillo) Shallcross; m. Ray F. Kamada, Oct. 27, 1990. BA, Marshall U., 1976, MA, 1980. Art tchr. Wayne (W.Va.) County Bd. Edn., 19779-83; freelance artist Fredericksburg, Va., 1983-85, Monterey, Calif., 1985-88; graphic artist Hampton-Brown Publ. Inc., Carmel, Calif., 1988-90; advt. artist Monterey Herald, 1990-92; prodn. mgr. Smith-Bowan Advt., Monterey, 1992-93; owner, creative dir. Kamada Sci. & Design, Monterey, 1993—; owner Shallcross Gallery, Monterey, 1998—; art dir., organizer Monterey County Artist's Studio Tour, 1994-96; art dir., cons. Somerset Publs. Inc., 1995-98, Monterey Peninsula Visitors & Convention Bur., 1996-98; art dir. Monterey County Travel and Tourism Alliance, Carmel, Calif., 1996-97; publ. Regarding Art jour., 1996-98. Art dir. (mag.) Monterey Peninsula Guide, 1997, Via Monterey County, 1997-98. Mem., art dir. Monterey Peninsula Vis. Convention Bur., 1996—. Mem. Artists Equity (bd. dirs., publs. dir. 1993-97). Democrat. Office: Kamada Sci & Design 499 Calle Principal Ste K Monterey CA 93940-2723

KAMEMOTO, GARETT HIROSHI, reporter; b. Honolulu, Oct. 30, 1966; s. Fred I. and Alice T. (Asayama) K. BA, U. Hawaii, 1989. Reporter Sta. KHVH, Honolulu, 1989-92, 93-94; Sta. KGMB-TV, Honolulu, 1992-93, 94—. Home: 3664 Waaloa Way Honolulu HI 96822-1151 Office: Sta KGMB-TV 1534 Kapiolani Blvd Honolulu HI 96814-3715

KAMILLI, ROBERT JOSEPH, geologist; b. Phila., June 14, 1947; s. Joseph George and Marie Emma (Clauss) K.; m. Diana Ferguson Chapman, June 28, 1969; children: Ann Chapman, Robert Chapman. BA summa cum laude, Rutgers U., 1969; AM, Harvard U., 1971, PhD, 1976. Geologist Climax Molybdenum Co., Empire, Colo., 1976-79, asst. resident geologist, 1979-80; project geologist Climax Molybdenum Co., Golden, Colo., 1980-83; geologist U.S. Geol. Survey, Saudi Arabian Mission, Jeddah, 1983-87, mission chief geologist, 1987-89; rsch. geologist, project chief U.S. Geol. Survey, Tucson, Ariz., 1989-96, scientist-in-charge, 1996—; adj. prof. U. Colo., Boulder, 1981-83, U. Ariz., Tucson, 1997—. Editor: Geologic Highway Map of Arizona; contbr. articles to profl. jours. Henry Rutgers scholar Rutgers U., 1968-69. Fellow Geol. Soc. Am., Soc. Econ. Geologists; mem. Ariz. Geol. Soc. (v.p. 1995-98, pres. 1999), Phi Beta Kappa, Sigma Xi. Avocations: travel, swimming, bicycle riding, music, photography. Home: 5050 N Siesta Dr Tucson AZ 85750-9652 Office: US Geol Survey SW Field Office 520 N Park Ave Ste 355 Tucson AZ 85719-5035

KAMINE, BERNARD SAMUEL, lawyer; m. Marcia Phyllis Haber; children: Jorge Hershel, Benjamin Haber, Tovy Haber. BA, U. Denver, 1965; JD, Harvard U., 1968. Bar: Calif. 1969, Colo. 1969. Dep. atty. gen. Calif. Dept. Justice, L.A., 1969-72; asst. atty. gen. Colo. Dept. Law, Denver, 1972-74; assoc. Shapiro & Maguire, Beverly Hills, Calif., 1974-76; ptnr. Kamine, Steiner & Ungerer (and predecessor firms), L.A., Calif., 1976—; judge pro tem Mcpl. Ct., 1974—, Superior Ct., 1989—; bd. dirs., sec. Pub. Works

Stds., Inc., 1996—; arbitrator Calif. Pub. Works Contract Arbitration Com., 1990—, Am. Arbitration Assn., 1976—; mem. adv. com. legal forms Calif. Jud. Coun., 1978-82. Author: Public Works Construction Manual: A Legal Guide for California, 1996; contbr. chpts. to legal texts, articles to profl. jours. Mem. L.A. County Dem. Cen. Com., 1982-85; mem. Anti-Defamation League, assoc. nat. commr., 1995—, Pacific Southwest Regional Bd., 1982—, pres. bd., 1998—. Col. USAR, 1969—. Mem. ABA, Calif. State Bar Assn. (chair conf. dels. calendar coordinating com. 1991-92), L.A. County Bar Assn. (chair Superior Cts. com. 1977-79, chair constrn. law subsect. of real property sect. 1981-83), Engring. Contractors' Assn. (bd. dirs. 1985—, affiliate chair 1992-93, affiliate DIG award 1996), Assoc. Gen. Contractors Calif. (L.A. dist. bd. dirs. 1995—), Am. Constrn. Insps. Assn. (bd. registered constrn. inspectors 1990-97), Beavers, Res. Officers Assn. (pres. chpt. 1977-78), Omicron Delta Kappa. Office: 350 S Figueroa St Ste 250 Los Angeles CA 90071-1201

KAMINS, PHILIP E., diversified manufacturing company executive; b. 1936. Salesman H. Muehlstein, 1957-62; founder Kamco Plastics Inc., Sun Valley, Calif., 1965-71; pres., CEO PMC Inc., Sun Valley, Calif., also bd. dirs. Office: PMC Inc 12243 Branford St Sun Valley CA 91352-1010*

KAMINSKI, CHARLES ANTHONY, portfolio manager; b. Norwich, Conn.; m. Elizabeth Carbery Wick, Oct. 19, 1985; children: Catherine, Ian, Charles. BEE, MIT, 1970, MEE, 1972; MBA, Harvard U., 1974. Chartered fin. analyst. Assoc. John Barry and Assocs., Newport Beach, Calif., 1974-75; sales mgr. N.Am. Video, Acton, Mass., 1975-79; v.p. mktg. Creare Innovations, Hanover, N.H., 1979-82; pres. Commtech, Cambridge, Mass., 1982-84; group mktg. mgr. Instrumentation Lab. (Allied), Lexington, Mass., 1983-84; dir., portfolio mgr. Baring Am. Asset Mgmt., Boston, 1984-92; chief investment officer GE Fin. Assurance, Seattle, 1992—; bd. dirs. Wash. State Investment Bd. Mem. Inst. CFA, Boston Econ. Club, Sigma Xi, Eta Kappa Nu, Tau Beta Pi. Home: 7224 W Mercer Way Mercer Island WA 98040-5534 Office: GNA Two Union Square Seattle WA 98101

KAMLET, BARBARA LYNN, director of volunteers; b. Denver; d. Sam Henry and Bette Ann (Krim) Kamlet; children: Jennifer S. Silvestain, Lisa M. Silvestain. BA in Secondary Lang. Arts, Colo. State U., 1971; postgrad., Regis U. Dir. of vols. Mercy Med. Ctr., Denver, 1987-96; project dir. InterComm. Caregivers, Denver, 1996-97; regional coord. Bright Beginnings Warm Welcome, Denver, 1997—. Exec. v.p. of community Jr. League of Denver, 1997—, comm. v.p., 1995-97. Home: 7995 E Mississippi Ave Apt D15 Denver CO 80231-6835 Office: Mile High United Way 2505 18th St Denver CO 80211-3939

KAMM, HERBERT, journalist; b. Long Branch, N.J., Apr. 1, 1917; s. Louis and Rose (Cohen) K.; m. Phyllis I. Silberblatt, Dec. 6, 1936; children: Laurence R., Lewis R., Robert H. Reporter, sports editor Asbury Park (N.J.) Press, 1935-42; with AP, 1942-43; with N.Y. World-Telegram and Sun, 1943-66, successively rewrite man, picture editor, asst. city editor, feature editor, mag. editor, 1943-63, asst. mng. editor, 1963, mng. editor, 1963-66; exec. editor N.Y. World Jour. Tribune, 1966-67; editorial cons. Scripps Howard Newspapers, 1967-69; assoc. editor Cleve. Press, 1969-80, editor, 1980-82, editor emeritus, 1982; edit. dir. Sta. WJW-TV, Cleve., 1982-85; instr. journalism Case Western Res. U., 1972-75, Calif. Poly., San Luis Obispo, 1991—. Radio and TV news commentator and panelist, 1950-85, TV talk show host, 1974-85; freelance writer, 1985—; author: A Candle for Popsy, 1953; editor: Junior Illustrated Encyclopedia of Sports, 1960. Bd. overseers Case Western Res. U., 1974-78. Herb Kamm scholarship in journalism established Kent State U., 1983, Calif. Poly., 1995; inducted Cleve. Journalism Hall of Fame, 1986. Mem. AFTRA, Soc. Profl. Journalists (pres. Calif. Missions chpt. 1986-87), Calif. Ambassadors for Higher Edn. Clubs: City of Cleve. (pres. 1982), Silurians. Home: 147 River View Dr Avila Beach CA 93424-2307

KAMSLER, BEN FRANKLIN, literary agent, consultant; b. N.Y.C., Sept. 1, 1905; s. David and Marguerite (Kampf) K.; m. Deltra Eamon, July 25, 1953 (div. Aug. 1971); children: Christopher, Constance; m.Irene Florence Cranz, Aug. 26, 1979. BS in Econs., U. Pa., 1925; postgrad., Columbia U., 1925-26. Broadway prodr. B.F. Kamsler Prodns., N.Y.C., 1932-40; producer B.F. Kamsler Prodns., London, 1962-70; with N.N. Swanson Inc., L.A., 1963-90; lit. agt. B.F. Kamsler Ltd., L.A., 1990—. Broadway prodr. 7 plays, 1932-40, London prodr. 3 plays, 1962-70, Toronto prodr., 1955-58. With inf. U.S. Army, 1942-44. Mem. AFTRA. Democrat. Office: Ben F Kamsler Ltd 5501 Noble Ave Sherman Oaks CA 91411-3521

KANDANES, ANDREW, recording industry executive, percussionist; b. Paterson, N.J., Aug. 6, 1947; s. Anthony and Elmyra Kandanes; m. Denise Kandanes; children: Ace Pothier, Diella, Alexis. Student, USAF Acad., Santa Rosa Jr. Coll.; BA, Coll. of the Redwoods, 1970. Music prodr., pub. Andrew Kandanes & Assocs. Prodr. and arranger (rec.) Firebyrd, 1980; arranger, producer, percussionist (rec.) Not Alone, 1985, This Byrd Has Flown, 1997, 3 Byrds Land in London, 1997; composer: The Rain Song, Rodeo Rider, 1980. Avocations: cooking, gardening, European traveling. Home: PO Box 618 Cobb CA 95426-0618

KANDEL, JOAN ELLEN, osteopath; b. L.A., Apr. 6, 1963; d. William Isadore Kandel and Helen Sylvia (Cutler) Abraham; m. Kristin Graziano, July 13, 1996. BA, U. Calif., 1985; DO, Coll. Osteo. Med. Pacific, 1993. Vol. health educator U.S. Peace Corps, Nuapua, Paraguay, 1986-88; resident, chief resident family practice Cmty. Hosp., Santa Rosa, Calif., 1993-96. Mem. Am. Acad. Family Physicians, Am. Acad. Osteopathy, Physicians for a Violence-Free Soc., Gay and Lesbian Med. Assn. Democrat. Jewish. Avocations: ultimate frisbee, bicycling, gardening, music, dancing.

KANE, BRIAN J., industrial designer; b. Elizabeth, N.J., Apr. 2, 1948; s. James Joseph and Kathleen (Walsh) K.; m. Catherine Elliott Proctor, May 30, 1970; children: Jesse Daniel, Molly Kathleen. BS, U. Bridgeport, 1970. Designer Monte Levin Assocs., N.Y.C., 1970-71, Studio Cappola, Milan, Italy, 1971-72, Atelier Internat., N.Y.C., 1972-77, Met. Furniture, San Francisco, 1977-89; designer, pres. Kane Design Studio, San Francisco, 1989—. Contbr. articles to profl. jours. Office: Kane Design Studio 570 Alabama St San Francisco CA 94110-1301

KANE, KAREN MARIE, public affairs consultant; b. Colorado Springs, Colo., Mar. 7, 1947; d. Bernard Francis and Adeline Marie (Logan) K. Student, Mills Coll., Oakland, Calif., 1965-66; BA, U. Wash., 1970, MA, 1973, PhC, 1977, postgrad. Pub. affairs cons., housing subcom. Seattle Ret. Tchrs. Assn., 1981-84; pub. affairs cons. 1st U.S. Women's Olympic Marathon Trials, 1982-83, Seattle, 1985—. Contbr. articles to newsletters and mags. Vol. various polit. campaigns, Seattle; bd. dirs. Showboat Theatre Found./Bravo (formerly Showboat Theatre Found.), 1984—; chmn. hist. preservation LWV, Seattle, 1989—; mem. Allied Arts of Seattle, trustee, 1987-96, past chmn. hist. preservation com., sec. bd. trustees, mem. exec. com., 1987-96; mem. Mayor's Landmark Theatre Adv. Group, 1991-93; mem. Pike Place Market Hist. Commn., Seattle, 1992-98, chmn., 1997-98; mem. Pike Place Market Com. to Rev. the Hildt Agreement, 1998-99; mem. The Market Constituency, 1999—. Recipient Award of Honor Wash. Trust for Hist. Preservation, 1990, Recognition award Found. for Hist. Preservation and Adaptive Reuse, Seattle, 1991; Am. Found. grantee, 1989, 91. Mem. Am. Assn. Univ. Women, Mills Coll. Alumnae Assn., U. Wash. Alumni Assn., Nat. Trust for Hist. Preservation, Hist. Hawai'i Found., Found. for San Francisco's Archtl. Heritage, Internat. Platform Assn., Wash. Trust for Hist. Preservation, Hist. Seattle Preservation and Devel. Authority. Office: Allied Arts of Seattle 105 S Main St Seattle WA 98104-2535

KANE, MICHAEL JOSEPH, director; b. N.Y.C., July 9, 1922; s. Max and Sophie (Kuznets) Cohen; m. Winifred June Fay, Oct. 1, 1947 (div. 1972); children: Amy Lynn, Jennifer Ann. Student, King-Smith Playhouse and Sch. of Theatre Arts, 1939-41. Actor, stage mgr. in Mister Roberts Leland Hayward Prodns., N.Y.C., 1947-51; stage mgr., assoc. dir. CBS-TV, Hol[illegible] Hollywood, 1953-70; dir., producer various commls., Hollywood, 1957-85; producer, dir. Can You Top This?, Hollywood, 1969-70; lectr. TV/film writing, cable TV prodn., directing for the camera Calif. State U., Fullerton, 1987-92; mem. Radio and TV Dirs. Guild, 1952-58; co-founder The Fullerton Acting Lab., 1992. Dir.: (stage prodn.) Happy Birthday, Wanda June, 1970, (TV prodns.) Gilligan's Island, Hawaiian Eye, The Brady Bunch, Quincy, Hardcastle and McCormick. Served as staff sgt. USAAF, 1942-46. King-Smith Playhouse and Sch. Theatre Arts scholar, 1939-41. Mem. AFTRA, SAG, Soc. Stage Dirs. and Choreographers, Actors Equity Assn., Dirs. Guild Am. (trustee DGA producers pension and health plans).

KANE, PERRY W., publisher, writer; b. N.Y.C., Jan. 24, 1965; s. George Irwin and Susan Jane (Shaver) K. BA in History, Calif. State U., L.A., 1989, MA in History, 1997. Adminstrv. asst. Inst. Cancer and Blood Rsch., Beverly Hills, Calif., 1990-97; pres. Books on Disk Pub., South Pasadena, Calif., 1997—. Author: Gimme Some Truth: The Story of the John Lennon Deportation Case, 1997, Nostradamus & The Millennium, 1998; editor: That's Show Biz: My Life in Vaudeville, 1998. Democrat. Avocations: traveling, playing piano and guitar, hiking, bicycling. Office: Books On Disk Pub PO Box 3246 South Pasadena CA 91031-6246

KANE, THOMAS JAY, III, orthopaedic surgeon, educator; b. Merced, Calif., Sept. 2, 1951; s. Thomas J. Jr. and Kathryn (Hassler) K.; m. Marie Rose Van Emmerik, Oct. 10, 1987; children: Thomas Keola, Travis Reid, Samantha Marie. BA in History, U. Santa Clara, 1973; MD, U. Calif., Davis, 1977. Diplomate Am. Bd. Orthopaedic Surgery. Intern U. Calif. Davis Sacramento Med. Ctr., 1977-78, resident in surgery, 1978-81; resident in orthopaedic surgery U. Hawaii, 1987-91; fellowship adult joint reconstruction Rancho Los Amigos Med. Ctr., 1991-92; ptnr. Orthop. Assocs. of Hawaii, Inc., Honolulu, 1992—; asst. prof. surgery U. Hawaii, Honolulu, 1993—, chief divsn. implant surgery, 1993—. Contbr. articles to profl. jours. Mem. AMA, Am. Assn. Hip and Knee Surgeons, Hawaii Med. Assn., Hawaii Orthop. Assn., Am. Acad. Orthop. Surgery, Western Orthopedic Assn., Alpha Omega Alpha, Phi Kappa Phi. Avocations: tennis, golf, skiing, music, surfing. Office: Orthopaedic Assocs Hawaii 1380 Lusitana St Ste 608 Honolulu HI 96813-2442

KANEHIRO, KENNETH KENJI, insurance educator, risk analyst, consultant; b. Honolulu, May 10, 1934; s. Charles Yutaka and Betty Misako (Hoshino) K.; m. Eiko Asari, June 23, 1962; 1 child, Everett Peter. BA in Counseling Psychology, U. Hawaii, 1956, grad. cert. in Counseling Psychology, 1957; grad. cert. in ins., The Am. Inst., 1971. CPCU; cert. continuing profl. devel. Claims adjustor Cooke Trust Co., Honolulu, 1959-62, underwriter, 1962-66; account supr. Alexander & Baldwin, Honolulu, 1966-68; spl. risk exec. Hawaiian Ins. & Guaranty, Honolulu, 1968-71; br. mgr. Hawaiian Ins. & Guaranty, Hilo, Hawaii, 1971-72, Marsh & McLennan, Inc., Hilo, 1972-78; sr. mktg. rep. Occidental Underwriters, Honolulu, 1978-87; pvt. practice Honolulu, 1987—; coord. Ins. Sch. of Pacific, Honolulu, 1978—; lectr. ins. Hawaii State Cts., 1986—; cons. Dai Tokyo Royal State Ins. Co., 1992—; mem. arbitration panel, ct. observer panel Hawaii State Cts., 1993-96, Hawaii Criminal Ct., 1994—; proctor Hawaii State Bar Exam., 1994—; ins. expert witness, 1995—; instr. ins. agt.'s lic. course, 1995—. Adult leader Boy Scouts Am., Hilo and Honolulu, 1956—, rsch. mgr. Aloha coun., Honolulu, 1980—; edn. chmn. Gen. Ins. Assn., Hawaii, Hilo, 1971-77; ins. cons. Arcadia Retirement Residence, Honolulu, 1987—; cons., Waikole Cmty. Assn.; bd. govs. U. Hawaii Founders Alumni Assn., Honolulu, 1993—, scholarship chmn., 1993—. With U.S. Army, 1957-59. Recipient First Lady's Outstanding Vol. award First Lady/State of Hawaii, 1990; recipient Pres.'s award Boy Scouts Aloha Coun., 1997. Mem. Soc. CPCU (pres. 1986-87, nat. publs. com., 1996—, contbr. jour.), Soc. Ins. Trainers and Educators. Avocations: art, photography, music. Home: 1128 Ala Napunani St Apt 705 Honolulu HI 96818-1606

KANENAKA, REBECCA YAE, microbiologist; b. Wailuku, Hawaii, Jan. 9, 1958; d. Masakazu Robert and Takako (Oka) Fujimoto; m. Brian Ken Kanenaka, Nov. 10, 1989; children: Kent Masakazu, Kym Sachiko. Student, U. Hawaii, Manoa, 1976-77; BS, Colo. State U., 1980. Lab. asst. Colo. State U., Ft. Collins, 1979-80; microbiologist Foster Farms, Livingston, Calif., 1980-81; microbiologist Hawaii Dept. Health, Lihue, 1981-86, Honolulu, 1986—. Mem. Am. Soc. Microbiology (Hawaii chpt.), Nat. Registry of Microbiologists, Am. Soc. Microbiology, Brown Bag Club (Lihue, pres. 1985-86), Golden Ripples (4-H leader), Clover Kids (4-H leader). Avocations: tennis, fishing, golf, jogging. Home: 485 Luakini St Honolulu HI 96817-1449 Office: Hawaii Dept Health Lab 2725 Waimano Home Rd Pearl City HI 96782-1401

KANER, CEM, lawyer, computer software consultant; b. Detroit, July 8, 1953; s. Harry and Wilma Kaner; 1 child, Virginia Rose. Student, U. Windsor (Ont., Can.), 1971-72; BA, Brock U., St. Catharines, Ont., 1974; postgrad., York U., Toronto, Ont., 1975-76; PhD, McMaster U., Hamilton, Ont., 1984; JD, Golden Gate U., 1993. Cert. quality engr.; Bar: Calif., 1993. Asst. mgr. Gallenkamp Shoes, Toronto, 1975; systems analyst Kaners and 1 plus 1, Windsor, 1981-83; lectr. McMaster U., 1981-83; software testing supr. MicroPro (WordStar), San Rafael, Calif., 1983-84; human factors analyst, software engr. Telenova, Los Gatos, Calif., 1984-88; software testing mgr. creativity div. Electronic Arts, San Mateo, Calif., 1988; software devel. mgr., documentation group mgr., dir. of documentation and software testing Power Up Software, San Mateo, 1989-94; pvt. practice Calif., 1994—; sr. assoc. Psylomar Orgn. Devel., San Francisco, 1983-85; lectr. U. Calif., Berkeley Ext., 1995—, U. Calif., Santa Cruz Ext., 1998—; spkr. in field. Author: Testing Computer Software, 1988, (with Jack Falk and Hung Q Nguyen) Testing Computer Software, 2d edit., 1993 (award for excellence No. Calif. Tech. Publ. Competition 1993), (with David Pels) Bad Software: What to do when Software Fails, 1998; (video course) Testing Computer Software, 1995; columnist Software QA; contbr. articles to profl. publs. Cons. Dundas (Ont.) Pub. Library, 1982-83; vol. Santa Clara County Dept. Consumer Affairs, San Jose, 1987-88; alt. mem. San Mateo County Dem. Central Com., 1988-89; chmn. Foster City Dem Club, 1989; vol. dep. dist. atty. County of Santa Clara, Calif., 1994; grievance handler, intellectual property, book contract advisor Nat. Writers Union, San Francisco, Calif., 1994—; bd. dir. No. Calif. Hemophilia Found., Oakland, Calif., 1995-97; participating observer NCCUSL drafting com. for UCC article 2B, NCCUSL com. for uniform electronic transaction act. Scholar, Can. Nat. Rsch. Coun., 1977-78, Can. Natural Scis. and Engring. Rsch. Coun., 1979, Golden Gate U. Tuition scholar, 1989-93. Mem. IEEE (Computer Soc.), ABA, ATLA, APA, ACLU, Assn. for Computing Machinery, Assn. Support Profls., Am. Soc. Quality (sr.), Human Factors and Ergonomics Soc., Soc. for Tech. Comm. (sr.), Software Support Profls. Assn., Software Pubs. Assn. Jewish. Avocation: development of the law of software products liability. Office: PO Box 580 Santa Clara CA 95052-0580

KANG, SUSAN HEESOO, lawyer; b. Seoul, Korea, Sept. 16, 1968; d. Jun Kun Kang and Young Hee (Kim) Lee. BA in Polit. Sci., Journalism, U. So. Calif., 1991; JD, U. San Diego, 1994. Bar: Calif. Dep. comm. dir. Calif. Rep. Party, Burbank, 1994; atty. Fair Elections Found., Costa Mesa, Calif., 1994-95; dep. city atty. City of Anaheim, Calif., 1995—. Mem. Calif. Rep. Party, Burbank, 1995—; alt. del. Rep. Nat. Conv., San Diego, 1996. Mem. Korean Am. Bar Assn., Calif. Rep. Atty.'s Assn. (vice chmn. 1995—), Orange County Bar Assn. Office: City of Anaheim 1275 N Berkeley Ave Fullerton CA 92832-1206

KANIECKI, MICHAEL JOSEPH, bishop; b. Detroit, Apr. 13, 1935; s. Stanley Joseph and Julia Marie (Konjora) K. BA, Gonzaga U., 1958, MA in Philosophy, 1960; MA in Theology, St. Mary's, Halifax, Can., 1966. Ordained priest, 1965; consecrated bishop, 1984. Missionary Alaska, 1960-83; coadjutor bishop Diocese of Fairbanks, Alaska, 1984-85, bishop, 1985—. Address: Bishop of Fairbanks 1316 Peger Rd Fairbanks AK 99709-5199*

KANNER, EDWIN BENJAMIN, electrical manufacturing company executive; b. N.Y.C., July 2, 1922; s. Charles and Grace (Edelson) K.; m. S. Barbara Penenberg, Aug. 3, 1944; children: Jaimie Sue, Richard, Keith. BBA, CCNY, 1943; MBA, Harvard U., 1947. Asst. West Coast mgr. Fairchild Publs., N.Y.C. and L.A., 1948-50; gen. mgr. Dible Enterprises, L.A., 1951-53; sales mgr., gen. mgr., prs. Western Insulated Wire Co. [illegible] Avnet, L.A., 1969-79; exec. v.p., COO Avnet Inc., N.Y.C., 1980-83; pres. Pacific Electricord and Am. Ins. Wire Co., L.A., also Providence, 1948—. Lt. comdr. USNR, 1943-47, PTO. Office: Pacific Electricord 747 W Redondo Beach Blvd Gardena CA 90247-4203

KANODE, CAROLYN KERRIGAN, school nurse, pediatric nurse practitioner; b. Trenton, N.J., July 2, 1937; d. Lawrence Stephen and Louise (Welde) Kerrigan; m. Irwin Kanode, Aug. 26, 1960; children: Cathy, Barbara, Teresa. BS cum laude, Calif. State U., Long Beach, 1976; MS, Pepperdine U., Malibu, Calif., 1984. RN, Calif.; cert. pediatric nurse practitioner. Staff nurse Bellevue Hosp., N.Y.C., 1958-60; charge nurse Westside Hosp., L.A., 1960; office nurse Dr. Lenahan, Fullerton, Calif., 1960-64; sch. nurse Oceanview Sch. Dist., Huntington Beach, Calif., 1977—. Trustee Ocean View Sch. Dist., Huntington Beach, Calif., 1990—; co-founder Huntington Youth Shelter, Huntington Beach, 1987, pres., 1987-90; chair, subcom. Family Resource Ctr., 1995—; mem. HB Children's Task Force. Recipient Humanitarian award Soroptomists, Human Svcs. award City of Huntington Beach, 1995; named Woman of Yr., Calif. Assembly, 1994. Mem. AAUW, Calif. Sch. Nurses Assn. (legis. chair, Calif. Sch. Nurse of Yr. 1990), Orange County Sch. Nurse Orgn. (past pres.), Dream Catchers Guild, Orange County Sch. Bd. Assn. (editor newsletter 1992—, bd. dirs.). Home: 17382 Alta Vista Cir Huntington Beach CA 92647-6130

KANTOR, IGO, film and television producer; b. Vienna, Austria, Aug. 18, 1930; came to U.S., 1947; s. Samuel and Miriam (Sommerfreund) K.; m. Enid Lois Dershewitz, June 24, 1962; children: Loren, Mark, Lisa. AA, UCLA, 1950, BS, 1952, MS in Polit. Sci., 1954. Fgn. corr. Portuguese Mag. Flama, L.A., 1949-57; music supr., editor Screen Gems, Columbia, L.A., 1954-63; post-prodn. supr. various ind. cos. L.A., 1963-64; music supr.-editor Universal-MCA, L.A., 1964-66; pres., film editor Synchrofilm, Inc., L.A., 1966-74; pres., producer Duque Films, Inc., L.A., 1971-78; ind. producer Jerry Lewis Films, Film Ventures, L.A., 1979-84; pres., producer Laurelwood Prodns. Inc., L.A., 1984-87, Major Arts Corp., L.A., 1987—; pres. Jubilee Holding Co., L.A., 1988—. Producer Legends of the West with Jack Palance (TV spl. series), 1992, United We Stand, 1988, Act of Piracy, 1987, The Golden Eagle Awards, 1986, It's A Wonderful World, 1986, The Grand Tour, 1985, Shaker Run, 1984, From Hawaii with Love, 1983, Night Shadows, 1983, Kill and Kill Again, 1981, Hardly Working, 1980, Good Luck, Miss Wyckoff, 1979, Holiday Classic Cartoons, 1994, Mom USA, 1996, many others. Named Emmy nominee, 1967, 68, 69, 70. Mem. Acad. Motion Picture Arts & Scis. (exec. sound bd. 1969-71), Dirs. Guild Am. (assoc. dir.). Democrat. Jewish. Avocations: swimming, chess, ping-pong, philately, collecting movie classics. E-mail: igo.kantor@gte.net. Office: Major Arts Corp 11501 Duque Dr North Hollywood CA 91604-4279 Address: PO Box 1340 Studio City CA 91614-0340

KANTZ, PHILIP C., executive. Dir., pres., CEO Tab Products, Turlock, Calif. Office: 301 S Soderquist Rd Turlock CA 95380-5130*

KAO, ARTHUR MU-SEN, art educator; b. Changhua, Taiwan, Feb. 26, 1942; s. Chung-hsin and Lai-chun (Hsu) K.; m. Angel Ying-ju Hwang, Aug. 16, 1970; children: Samson, Anson, Angela. BA, Nat. Taiwan U., Taipei, 1967; MA, U. Kans., 1975, PhD, 1979. Instr. art Kansas City (Kans.) Art Inst., 1974-76; asst. prof. Chinese U. Hong Kong, 1979-84; asst. prof. Kent (Ohio) State U., 1976-79, assoc. prof., 1985-89; prof. San Jose (Calif.) State U., 1989—; tchr. Chung-Ming Elem. Sch., Taichung, 1960-63; mem. staff Nat. Palace Mus., Taipei, 1970; rsch. asst. Cleve. Mus. Art, 1971; vis. scholar Princeton (N.J.) U., 1984-85. Author: Western Chow Bronze Art, 1985 (Gold Cauldron award 1985), The Thought of Chinese Painting, 1992 (Gold Cauldron award 1992), A Research of Sung Painting, 1994; inventor, author: Easy Input Method for Chinese, 1995, A Research of Yuan Painting, 1998. Mem. exec. bd. Chinese Nat. Devel. Assn., Calif., 1993-95; mem. Asian Art Mus. San Francisco, 1997—. Calif. State U. Rsch. grantee, 1994, 98, Lottery grantee San Jose State U., 1995, 98. Mem. Chinese Art Assn. (mem. exec. bd. 1990—). Home: 1106 Di Napoli Dr San Jose CA 95129-4015 Office: San Jose State Univ Sch Art and Design 1 Washington Sq San Jose CA 95192-0001

KAO, CHENG CHI, electronics executive; b. Taipei, Taiwan, Republic of China, Aug. 3, 1941; s. Chin Wu and Su Chin (Wu) K.; m. Susan Lin, July 4, 1970; children: Antonia Hueilan, Albert Chengwei, Helen Siaolan. BS, Taiwan U., 1963; AM, Harvard U., 1965, PhD, 1969. Research fellow Harvard U., Cambridge, Mass., 1969-70; scientist Xerox Corp., Webster, N.Y., 1970-75; mgr. Internat. Materials Research, Inc., Santa Clara, Calif., 1976-78; exec. v.p. President Enterprises Corp., Tainan, Taiwan, 1979-85; pres. Kolyn Internat., Los Altos, Calif., 1979—. Contbr. articles to profl. jours. Bd. dirs. Taipei Am. Sch., 1980-82. Mem. IEEE, Chinese Inst. Elec. Engring. (bd. dirs. 1982-85), Sigma Xi. Club: Am. in China (Taipei), Palo Alto Hills Golf and Country. Avocations: jogging, golf. Office: Kolyn Internat 4962 El Camino Real Ste 119 Los Altos CA 94022-1410

KAO, FA-TEN, education researcher; b. Hankow, Peoples Republic of China, Apr. 20, 1934; came to U.S., 1956; m. Betty Chia-mai, Dec. 17, 1960; 1 child, Alan. PhD, U. Minn., 1964. Instr. U. Colo. Med. Ctr., Denver, 1965-67, asst. prof., 1967-70, assoc. prof., 1970-81; prof. Health Scis. Ctr, Denver, 1981—; sr. fellow Eleanor Roosevelt Inst. for Cancer Rsch., Denver, 1965—; vis. scientist Oxford U., Eng., 1973-74; rsch. scientist European Molecular Biology Lab., Heidelberg, Fed. Republic of Germany, 1985; World Bank spl. cons. on Chinese Provincial Univs. Devel. Project; hon. prof. Harbin Med. U., 1987, Tongji Med. U., Wuhan, People's Republic of China, 1988. Contbr. articles to profl. jours. Mem. AAAS, Genetics Soc. Am., Am. Soc. Human Genetics, Am. Soc. Cell Biology, Am. Assn. Cancer Rsch. Achievements include research in somatic cell genetics, human molecular genetics, human gene mapping and genome analysis, chromosome microdissection and microcloning. Office: Eleanor Roosevelt Inst Cancer Rsch 1899 Gaylord St Denver CO 80206-1210

KAO, YASUKO WATANABE, retired library administrator; b. Tokyo, Mar. 30, 1930; came to U.S., 1957; d. Kichiji and Sato (Tanaka) Watanabe; m. Shih-Kung Kao, Apr. 1, 1959; children: John Sterling, Stephanie Margaret. BA, Tsuda Coll., 1950; BA in Lit., Waseda U., 1955; MSLS, U. So. Calif., 1960. Instr., Takinogawa High Sch., Tokyo, 1950-57; catalog librarian U. Utah Library, 1960-67, Marriott Library, 1975-77, head catalog div., 1978-90; dir. libr. Teikyo Loretto Heights U., 1991-95. Contbr. articles to profl. jours. Vol., Utah Chinese Am. Community Sch., 1974-80, Asian Assn. Utah, 1981-90. Waseda U. fellow, 1958-59. Mem. ALA, Asian Pacific Librs. Assn., Assn. Coll. and Rsch. Librs., Beta Phi Mu. Home: 2625 Yuba Ave El Cerrito CA 94530-1443

KAPCSANDY, LOUIS ENDRE, building construction and manufacturing executive, chemical engineering consultant; b. Budapest, Hungary, June 5, 1936; came to U.S., 1957; s. Lajos Endre and Margit (Toth) K.; m. Roberta Marie Henson, Jan. 25, 1964; 1 son, Louis. B.S. in Chem. Engring., Tech. U. Hungary, 1956; postgrad. in law, U. San Francisco, 1963-64; M.S. in Petroleum Tech., U. Calif.-Berkeley, 1969. Freedom fighter Hungarian Revolution, Budapest, 1956; profl. football player San Diego Chargers, 1963-65; western regional mgr. Norton Co., San Francisco, 1965-72; product mgr. Koch Industries, Wichita, Kans., 1972-74; v.p., gen. mgr. Flow Systems, Inc., Seattle, 1974-78; pres. Fentron Bldg. Products, Inc., Seattle, 1978-85; CEO Baugh Enterprises Inc., Seattle, 1985—; chem. engring. cons. HK Assocs., Seattle, 1974—. Contbr. articles to profl. jours.; patentee vacuum fraction of crude oil, purification of hydrogen. Bd. dirs. Boy Scouts Chief Seattle, Seattle C. of C., Virginia Mason Med. Ctr.; active United for Wash., Seattle, 1982. With U.S. Army, 1959-62. Fellow AIChE; mem. Constrn. Specifications Inst., TAPPI, Columbia Tower Club, Washington Athletic Club, Rainier Club, Glendale Country Club, Seattle Rotary Lodge, PGA West. Republican. Roman Catholic.

KAPELOVITZ, ABBEY POZE, academic administrator; b. Rochester, N.Y., Nov. 22, 1942; d. Samuel and Marian (Berger) Poze; m. Leonard H. Kapelovitz; children: Mara, Dan. BA, Wellesley Coll. Edn., 1964; MAT, Harvard U., 1965; PhD in English, U. Denver, 1985. Assoc. dean arts, humanities and social scis. U. Denver.

KAPERICK, JOHN ANTHONY, information specialist; b. Tacoma, Wash., July 11, 1964; s. Victor Raymond and Billie Ann (Carlson) K.; m. Dawn [illegible], Aug. 3, [illegible], 1 child, [illegible] Kaperick. Cert., Bates Vocat. Tech. Inst., Tacoma, Wash., 1985; cert., Boeing Computer Svcs., Seattle, 1990. Apprentice cabinetmaker Custom Craft Fixtures, Tacoma, 1986-87; computer operator Vic's Enterprises, Tacoma, 1987-90; info. specialist NOAA (U.S. Dept. Commerce), Seattle, 1990—. Mem. Spl.

Librs. Assn., Environment and Resource Mgmt. Divsn. Avocations: woodworking, gardening, walking, computers. Office: NOAA Hazmat 7600 Sand Point Way NE Seattle WA 98115-6349

KAPLAN, BARRY MARTIN, lawyer; b. N.Y.C., Nov. 9, 1950; s. Stanley Seymour and Lillian (Schner) K.; m. Erica Green, July 26, 1981; children: Matthew Aaron, Elizabeth Rose, Andrew Nathan. BA, Colgate U., 1973; JD cum laude, U. Mich., 1976. Bar: Mich. 1976, Wash., 1978, U.S. Dist. (ea. dist.) Mich. 1976, U.S. Dist. Ct. (we. dist.) Wash. 1978, U.S. Dist. Ct. (ea. dist.) Wash. 1986, U.S. Tax Ct. 1983, U.S. Ct. Appeals (9th cir.) 1990. Law clk. to Hon. Charles W. Joiner U.S. Dist. Ct. (ea. dist.) Mich., Detroit, 1976-78; assoc. Perkins Coie, Seattle, 1978-85, ptnr., 1985—; spkr. in field. Author: Washington Corporation Law and Practice, 1991; contbr. articles to legal jours. and procs. Mem. ABA (litigation sect., securities litigation com., bus. law sect., bus. and corp. litigation com., subcom. chmn. on control transactions 1993), Wash. State Bar Assn. (CLE spkr., bus. law sect., securities com., subcom. chair on dir.'s liability 1993), Wash. Athletic Club. Office: Perkins Coie 1201 3rd Ave Fl 40 Seattle WA 98101-3000

KAPLAN, DIANE SUSAN, foundation executive, consultant; b. Bklyn., Feb. 26, 1957; d. Yehoshua Sharon and Eleanor J. (Wasserman) K.; m. Melvin H. Sather, Sept. 12, 1987; stepchildren: Jay, Jerry, Charles. BA in Communications and Women's Studies summa cum laude, U. Pa., 1977. Dir. pub. affairs Sta. WXPN-FM, U. Pa., Phila., 1975-76, program dir., 1976-77, dir. pub. info., 1977-79; gen. mgr. Sta. KALX-FM, U. Calif., Berkeley, 1979-81; program mgr. Calif. Pub. Broadcasting Commn., Sacramento, 1981-83; exec. dir. Alaska Pub. Radio Network, Anchorage, 1983-90, pres., chief exec. officer, 1990-94; owner Diane Kaplan & Co., 1994—; adminstr. The Rasmuson Found., 1995—. Commr. Anchorage Telephone Commn., 1985; commr. Anchorage Women's Commn.; bd. dirs. United Way, Anchorage, 1988-91, 95—, Anchorage Libr. Found., 1995—, Friends of the Children's Trust, 1996—; mem. Alaska Railroad Adv. Bd., 1997—. Mem. Alaska Press Club (bd. dirs. 1986-89, treas. 1988), Native Comm. Group (co-founder 1991), Alaska Broadcasters Assn. (Disting. Svc. award 1990), Rotary Club, Phi Beta Kappa. Home: PO Box 100108 Anchorage AK 99510-0108 Office: 510 L St Ste 400 Anchorage AK 99501

KAPLAN, DONALD SHELDON, real estate developer and rehabilitator, property management company executive; b. L.A., Aug. 1, 1938; s. Adolph Iven and Ruth Janet (Rose) K.; m. Marsha Lynn Le Van, June 12, 1960 (div. July 1980); children: Lisa Ann, Drew Jason; m. Joanne Natalie Cossu, Apr. 19, 1981; children: Alyson Ilene, Tara Ruth. Student, L.A. City Coll., 1957-58, Pacific State U., 1959-60. Pres. DSK Devel. Co., Inc., 1964--, Assured Maintenance Corp., Inc., 1974--, DSK Mgmt. Co., Inc., 1983--, New Renaissance Investments, Inc., 1986--, Kaplan Enterprises, Inc., L.A., 1986--; pres. Telephony Worldwide Enterprises, 1989—, Voice Telephone Co., 1993—, Fin. Svcs. of Am., 1993—, Western Fin. Investments, 1992—. Home and Office: Kaplan Enterprises Inc 5699 Kanan Rd Apt 234 Agoura Hills CA 91301-3358

KAPLAN, DONNA ELAINE, artist, educator; b. South Amboy, N.J., Dec. 30, 1942; d. Oscar Ivan and Otta Theora (Hamilton) Olsen; m. Barnett Morris Kaplan, Sept. 20, 1975; children: William, Ivan, Benjamin. Diploma in profl. nursing, Chaffey Coll., Alta Loma, Calif., 1964; BS in Occupl. Therapy, U. Puget Sound, Tacoma, 1972; student, Factory of Visual Arts, Seattle, 1977-79. RN, Wash.; cert. psychiat. nurse, Calif.; registered occupl. therapist. Shift charge nurse rsch. unit Langley Porter Neuropsychiat. Inst., San Francisco, 1967-70; supr. nursing Western State Hosp., Steilacoom, Wash., 1972-73; instr. in-svc. edn. Inst. Pa. Hosp., Phila., 1974-75; owner DK Design Studio, North Bend, Wash., 1984—; juror No. Calif. Reg. Fiber Show, Sacramento, Calif., 1993; guest curator Northwest Gallery, 1994; nat. touring guest arts instr. 1987—. Co-author: Beads as Warp and Weft, 1996; contbr. articles to art jours.; exhibitions include: Tacoma Art Mus., Wash., 1980, Window Gallery of Fine Art, Alaska, 1989, Craft Alliance Gallery, St. Louis, 1989, Tohomo Chul Park Gallery, Ariz., 1995, Whatcom Mus. History and Art, Wash., 1995, Bellevue Art Mus., Wash., 1982, 89, 96, Contemporary Crafts Ctr., Seattle, 1996, Raindance Gallery, Oreg., 1996, La. State U., Baton Rouge, 1997. Recipient Best Creative Use of Materials award Absolutely Beads Show/Beads and Beyond, Bellevue, Wash., 1994, Mus. Purchase award Edmonds (Wash.) Art Festival Mus., 1994, 1st pl. award Art Splash, City of Redmond, Wash., 1995. Mem. Seattle Weavers' Guild (corr. sec. 1982-83, Peoples Choice award 1986, Art 3D award 1995), N.W. Designer Craftsmen, N.W. Craft Alliance (v.p., bd. dirs. 1994-96), N.W. Bead Soc., Fiber Art Profls., Friends of Fiber Art Internat. Studio: DK Design Studio 43406 SE 88th St North Bend WA 98045-9455

KAPLAN, EDWARD H., history educator; b. N.Y.C., Jan. 9, 1936; s. Irving and Martha (Kass) K.; m. Alice Susan Blandell, Sept. 6, 1957; children: Joseph T., Samuel A. BS, Georgetown U., 1960; MA, U. Iowa, 1963, PhD, 1970. Instr. history U. Del., Newark, 1964-68; instr. history Western Wash. U., Bellingham, 1968-70, asst. prof., 1971-74, assoc. prof., 1975—, editor Studies on E. Asia/Ctr. Asian Studies, 1994—; dir. Western Wash. U. Ctr. for East Asian Studies, 1976-80, 81-86. Translator: An Economic History of China, 1974; translator/editor: A Monetary History of China, 1994. Mem. exec. bd. Whatcan County Rep. Party, 1985—. With U.S. Army, 1954-57. NEH Translation grantee, 1980. Mem. Assn. for Asian Studies, Am. Oriental Soc. Office: Western Wash Univ Dept History Bellingham WA 98225-9056

KAPLAN, GARY, executive recruiter; b. Phila., Aug. 14, 1939; s. Morris and Minnie (Leve) K.; m. Linda Ann Wilson, May 30, 1968; children: Michael Warren, Marc Jonathan, Jeffrey Russell Wilson. BA in Polit. Sci., Pa. State U., 1961. Tchr. biology N.E. High Sch., Phila., 1962-63; coll. employment rep. Bell Telephone Labs., Murray Hill, N.J., 1966-67; supr. recruitment and placement Unisys, Blue Bell, Pa., 1967-69; pres. Electronic Systems Personnel, Phila., 1969-70; staff selection rep. Booz, Allen & Hamilton, N.Y.C., 1970-72; mgr. exec. recruitment M&T Chems., Rahway, N.J., 1972-74; dir. exec. recruitment IU Internat. Mgmt. Corp., Phila., 1974-78; v.p. personnel Crocker Bank, Los Angeles, 1978-79; mng. v.p. ptnr. western region Korn-Ferry Internat., Los Angeles, 1979-85; pres. Gary Kaplan & Assocs., Pasadena, Calif., 1985—; bd. dirs. Vis. Nurse Found., Home Pharmacy of Calif.; bd. trustees Greater L.A. Zoo Assn.; Pa. State U. Alumni Coun. Mgmt. columnist, Radio and Records newspaper, 1984-85. Chmn. bd. dirs. Vis. Nurse Assn., L.A., 1985-87; former bd. dirs. The Wellness Cmty.-Nat., Pa. State U. Indsl./Orgnl. Psychology Adv. Bd.; Capt. Adj. Gen. Corps., U.S. Army, 1963-66. Alumni fellow Pa. State U., 1998. Mem. Am. Compensation Assn., Soc. Human Resources Mgmt., Big Ten Club of So. Calif. Home: 1735 Fairmount Ave La Canada Flintridge CA 91011-1632 Office: Gary Kaplan & Assocs 201 S Lake Ave Ste 600 Pasadena CA 91101-3018

KAPLAN, JERRY, electronics company executive. CEO Onsale, Menlo Park, Calif. Office: Onsale 1350 Willow Rd # 202 Menlo Park CA 94025-1516*

KAPLAN, MELVIN RAYMOND, physician, medical educator; b. L.A., Dec. 1, 1924; s. Isaac and Rebecca (Harband) K.; m. Harriet Natalie Smith, Feb. 23, 1958; children: Robert Alan, Martin Russell, Roger Jay. MD, U. So. Calif., 1949. Diplomate Am. Bd. Internal Medicine. Rotating intern L.A. County Gen. Hosp., L.A., 1948-50; resident in internal medicine L.A. County Harbor Gen. Hosp./Harbor-UCLA Med. Ctr., Torrance, 1950-53, head physician outpatient dept., 1953-55, chief physician med. sect., 1955-60, vol. faculty; clin. prof. medicine UCLA; pvt. practice physician; pres. Harbor-UCLA Rsch. Edn. Inst., Torrance, 1978-81. Bd. dirs. Harbor UCLA Collegium. Named Silver Knight of Mgmt., Nat. Mgmt. Assn., 1980. Fellow Am. Coll. Physicians; mem. AMA, Calif. Med. Assn., L.A. County Med. Assn. Avocation: trumpet.

KAPLAN, MIKE, film and video producer, director, and distributor, marketing executive; b. Providence, Mar. 16, 1943; s. Julius and Ida (Rabinovitz) k. BA, U. R.I., 1964. Assoc. editor Ind. Film Jour., N.Y.C., 1964-65; publicist MGM, N.Y.C., 1965-68, publicity coord., 1968, nat. publicity dir., 1968-71; v.p. Polaris Prodns. (Stanley Kubrick), London, 1971-73; internat mkgt. exec. Warner Bros., L.A., London, 1973-74; pres. Circle Assocs. Ltd., U.S., London, 1973—, Lion's Gate Distbn., 1975-80; mktg. v.p. Lion's Gate Films (Robert Altman), 1975-80; producer, pres. Circle Assoc. Ltd., L.A., 1978—; v.p. mktg. Northstar Internat., Hal Ashby, L.A., 1981-83; pres. mktg. Alive Films, L.A., 1985-87. Producer: (Film) The Whales of August, 1987; (video) Oak Grove Sch., 1988; assoc. prodr.: (film) Short Cuts, 1992; prodr., dir. (documentary) Luck, Trust and Ketchup: Robert Altman in Carver Country, 1994, (documentary) Ann Sothern: The Sharpest Girl In Town, 1999; actor: Buffalo Bill and The Indians, Welcome To L.A., Choose Me, The Player. Recipient Best Film award Nat. Media Awards, Retirement Rsch. Found., 1987, Key Art award Hollywood Reporter, 1976, 87. Mem. Acad. Motion Picture Arts and Scis., Screen Actors Guild, Publicists Guild. Avocations: songwriting, vintage paper collectibles. Fax: (310) 574-1950. Office: Circle Assocs PO Box 5730 Santa Monica CA 90409-5730

KAPLAN, NADIA, writer; b. Chgo., Feb. 28, 1921; d. Peter and Aniela (Buchynska) Charydchak; m. Norman Kaplan, July 25, 1942 (dec. July 1989); children: Fawn Marie Stom, Norma Jean Martinez. BEd, Pestalozzi Froebel Tchrs. Coll, Chgo., 1948; postgrad., UCLA, 1947, L.A. City Coll., U. Hawaii, Pepperdine U., 1970, Santa Monica Coll., 1981-87. Cert. tchr., Calif. Photographer, mgr. Great Lakes (Ill.) Naval Tng. Sta., 1942-45; primary/kindergarten tchr. L.A. Unified Sch. Dist., 1946-81. Contbr. articles to profl. jours.; creator puzzles various mags. Vol. recreational tchr. Found. for Jr. Blind, L.A., 1956-75, vol. camp counselor Camp Bloomfield, Calif., camp dir., 1956-61, leader cross-country study tour for blind teenagers, 1962; mem. dem. Nat. Com., 1985—. Pestalozzi Froebel Tchrs. Coll. scholar, 1938-41. Mem. AAUW, Women Writers West (membership chair 1982-84), United Tchrs. L.A., Calif. Ret. Tchrs. Assn., Assn. Ret. Tchrs. Ukrainian Orthodox. Avocations: writing, bonsai cultivation, doll collecting, travel, golf. Home: 1827 Fanning St Los Angeles CA 90026-1439

KAPLAN-GILLISPIE, MYLINDA, writer; b. Ft. Worth, Sept. 23, 1955; d. Solomon Kahn and Peggy Michael (McCullough) Kaplan; m. Eric Shachter, 1983 (div. 1983); m. Paul Marshall Gillispie, 1985. BA in Creative Writing, S.W. Mo. State U., Springfield, 1985; BSW, U. Kans., 1991; MSW, U. Mo., 1993. Registered social worker, Kans. Keynote spkr. Western Mo. Mental Health Ctr. State Mental Health Day, Kansas City, 1992. Democrat. Jewish. Avocations: quiltmaking, word study, walking, drawing, singing.

KAPLANSKY, LAURA SHLAFERMAN, non-profit fundraiser, community organizer; b. Springfield, Mass., July 3, 1956; d. Harvey Shlaferman and Julia Rene (Snyder) Fink; m. Steven Nathan Kaplansky, June 8, 1980. BA summa cum laude, U. Louisville, 1977; MA, Balt. Hebrew U., 1980; MSW, U. Md., 1980. Cert. Balt. Inst. Jewish Communal Svc. Campaign assoc., young leadership dir. Jewish Fedn. Cin., 1980-81; women's div. dir. Jewish Fedn. Greater Houston, 1981-85; assoc. dir. San Fernando Valley Region, Jewish Fedn. Coun. Greater L.A., 1985-88; Western asst. region dir. United Jewish Appeal, Western Region, L.A., 1988-93, Western region dir., 1993-95; sr. devel. officer Jewish Fedn. Coun. Greater L.A., 1995-97; exec. dir. Hadassah So. Calif., 1997—; cons. Nat. Congress of the Jewish Deaf, N.Y. and L.A., 1986-92. Nettleroth scholar U. Louisville, 1975, FEREP scholar Coun. Jewish Fedns., N.Y.C., 1978; recipient B'nai B'rith Citizenship award, 1976. Mem. Assn. Jewish Communal Orgn. Pers. (bd. dirs. 1988-92, ann. meeting program co-chair 1991, v.p. 1997-98, 98—), Conf. Jewish Communal Svc. Avocations: camping, skiing, hiking, travel. Office: Hadassah S CA 822 S Robertson Blvd Ste 300 Los Angeles CA 90035-1613

KAPLOWITZ, KAREN (JILL), lawyer; b. New Haven, Nov. 27, 1946; d. Charles Cohen and Estelle (Gerber) K.; m. Alan George Cohen, Aug. 17, 1980; children: Benjamin, Elizabeth. BA cum laude, Barnard Coll., 1968; JD, U. Chgo., 1971. Bar: Calif. 1971, U.S. Dist. Ct. (cen. dist.) Calif. 1971. Assoc. O'Melveny & Myers, L.A., 1971-74; ptnr. Bardeen, Bersch & Kaplowitz, L.A., 1974-80; of counsel Alschuler, Grossman & Pines, L.A., 1980—. Contbr. articles to profl. jours. Mem. vis. com. U. Chgo. Law Sch., 1990-93. Mem. ABA (chmn. employer-employee rels. com. of tors and ins. practice sect.), Assn. Bus. Trial Lawyers (pres.), Calif. Women Lawyers (Fay Stender award 1982), Women Lawyers Assn. L.A. Home: 1 Woodside Ln New Hope PA 18938-9281 Office: Alschuler Grossman & Pines LLP 2049 Century Park E # 39 Los Angeles CA 90067-3101

KAPP, ELEANOR JEANNE, impressionistic artist, writer, researcher; b. Hagerstown, Md., Oct. 16, 1933; d. James Norman and Nellie Belle Weagley; m. Alan Howard Kapp, Sept. 25, 1972. Cert., L.A. Interior Design, 1969; student, U. Utah, 1976-82; studied with Frank Ericson, Salt Lake, 1974; studied with Earl Pierce, Walnut Creek, Calif., 1985-90. Artist Farmers Ins. Group, L.A., 1960-63; interior designer W&J Sloane, Beverly Hills, Calif., 1965-70; ski resort exec. Snowpine Lodge, Alta, Utah, 1970-84; dir. mktg. and pub. rels. Alta Resort Assn., 1979-84; free-lance photographer Alta, 1979—; bus. owner Creative Art Enterprises, Sandy, Utah, 1984-85; artist-resident Collector's Corner Art Gallery, San Ramon, Calif., 1991—; owner E. Jeanne Kapp Fine Arts, Lafayette, Calif., 1985—; artist-resident St. Germain Gallery, Tiburon, Calif., 1993—, Regional Art Ctr. Gift Store, Walnut Creek, Calif., 1994—, Valley Art Ctr., Walnut Creek, 1995—; fine arts curator Contra Costa County Ctrl. Libr., Calif. Author, pub.: The American Connection, 1985, 91; author, prodr. (documentary) A Look at China Today, 1981; photographer: Best of the West, 1983; exhibited in groups shows at Mus. of Fine Art, Salt Lake City, Mus. of Natural History, Salt Lake City, Salt Lake Art Ctr., Canyon Gallery, Alta, Utah, J. Christensen Gallery, Salt Lake City, Cliff Gallery, Snowbird, Utah, Le Salon Des Nation, Paris, Village Framing Gallery, Danville, Calif., 1993, Graphics Gallery, Blackhawk, Calif., 1992-94, Graphics Gallery, Blackhawk, 1992-94, Collectors Corner Gallery, San Ramon, Calif., 1994-95, Calif. Heritage Gallery, San Francisco, 1996, St. Germain Gallery, Tituron, Calif., 1992-97, Danville Fine Art Gallery, 1992-97, Regional Art Ctr. Gift Gallery, Walnut Creek, Calif., 1994-97, Regional Art Ctr. Gift Gallery, Walnut Creek, 1994-97, Gallery Concord, Calif., 1992-97, Arts Benicia, Calif., 1997, Barlett Fine Arts Gallery, Pleasanton, Calif., 1997. Promotion liaison Alta Town Coun., 1980-84; floral decorator Coun. State Govts., Snowbird, Utah, 1976; photographer Utah Dems., Salt Lake City, 1981; mem. Salt Lake County Libr., 1982, founder Alta Br. Libr., 1982; fundraiser Friends of Libr., Alta, 1982; mem. Alta Town-Libr. Adv. Bd., 1983. Recipient Cert. of Appreciation, Salt Lake County Libr. System, 1981, Cert. of Recognition, Gov. Cal Rampton, Salt Lake City, 1972-74, Calendar Cover award Utah Travel Coun., 1981, Internat. Invitational Art Exhibit, Centre Internat. D'Art Contemporain, Paris, 1983. Mem. Internat. Platform Assn., Diablo Art Assn. (pub. rels. chmn. 1987, Hon. Mention award 1989), Concord Art Assn. (qst pl. award 1991), Alamo and Danville Artist's Soc. (cir. leader 1990—, hon. Mention award 1991, chmn. art exhbn. 1993, chmn. art program 1994), Las Junas Artist Assn. (juror's asst. 1992, 2d pl. award 1992, curator art exhbn., vol. Contra Costa County, Calif. Libr.-Main Br., 1995—, Ann. 1st pl. award 1995). Avocations: hiking, biking, tennis, travel, sculpture. Home: 411 Donegal Way Lafayette CA 94549-1707

KAPPY, MICHAEL STEVEN, pediatrics educator; b. Bklyn., Feb. 8, 1940; s. Jack and Lilyan (Banchefsky) K.; m. Peggy Markson; children: Douglas Bruce, Gregory Louis. BA, Johns Hopkins U., 1961; MD, PhD, U. Wis., 1967. Asst. prof. U. Ariz. Med. Sch., Tucson, 1975-78; fellow pediatric endocrinology Johns Hopkins Hosp., Balt., 1978-80; assoc. prof. U. Fla. Med. Sch., Gainesville, 1980-85; clin. prof. U. Ariz. Med. Sch., Tucson, 1985-94; med. dir. Children's Health Ctr., Phoenix, 1985-94; prof. pediatrics U. Colo. Health Sci. Ctr., Denver, 1994—; chief pediatric endocrinology The Children's Hosp., Denver, 1994—. Editor: (jour.) Today's Child, 1985, (book) Wilkins-The Diagnosis and Treatment of Endocrine Disorders in Childhood and Adolescence, 1994. Med. advisor Am. Diabetes Assn., Phoenix, 1985-94; bd. dirs. Ronald McDonald House, Phoenix, 1987-94. Named Tchr. of Yr., St. Joseph's Hosp., Phoenix, 1993. Mem. Assn. Pediatric Program Dirs. (pres. 1992-94), Soc. for Pediatric Rsch., Endocrine Soc., Am. Acad. Pediatrics, Physicians for Social Responsibility, Alpha Omega Alpha. Avocations: photography, cooking, four-wheel drive touring. Office: The Childrens Hosp 1056 E 19th Ave # B-265 Denver CO 80218-1088 Address: 3279 S Pontiac St Denver CO 80224-2765

KARAKEY, SHERRY JOANNE, financial and real estate investment company executive, interior designer; b. Wendall, Idaho, Apr. 16, 1942; d. John Donald and Vera Ella (Frost) Kingery; children: Artist Roxanne, Buddy (George II), Kami JoAnne, Launi JoElla. Student, Ariz. State U., 1960. Corp. sec., treas. Karbel Metals Co., Phoenix, 1963-67; sec. to pub. Scottsdale (Ariz.) Daily Progress, 1969-72; with D-Velco Mfg. of Ariz., Phoenix, 1959-62, dir., exec. v.p., sec., treas., 1972-87; mng. ptnr. Karitage, Ltd., Scottsdale, 1987—.

KARALIS, JOHN PETER, computer company executive, lawyer; b. Mpls., July 6, 1938; s. Peter John and Vivian (Deckas) K.; m. Mary Curtis, Sept. 7, 1963; children: Amy Curtis, Theodore Curtis. BA, U. Minn., 1960, JD, 1963. Bar: Minn. 1963, Mass. 1972, Ariz. 1983, N.Y. 1986, Pa. 1986. Pvt. practice Mpls., 1963-70; assoc. gen. counsel Honeywell Inc., Mpls., 1970-83, v.p., 1982-83; pvt. practice Phoenix, 1983-85; sr. v.p., gen. counsel Sperry Corp., N.Y.C., 1985-87; v.p. gen. counsel Apple Computer Inc., Cupertino, Calif., 1987-89; of counsel Brown and Bain, Phoenix, 1989-92; sr. v.p. corp. devel. Tektronix, Inc., Portland, 1992-98; pres. Corp. Alliance Consulting, LLC, Scottsdale, Ariz., 1998—; mem. bd. advisors Ctr. for Study of Law, Sci. and Tech., Ariz. State U. Coll. Law, Tempe, 1983-89, adj. prof., 1990-91. Author: International Joint Ventures, A Practical Guide, 1992. Recipient Disting. Achievement award Ariz. State U., Tempe, 1985. Mem. Met. Club (N.Y.C.), Gainey Ranch Golf Club.

KARASA, NORMAN LUKAS, home builder, developer, geologist; b. Balt., June 10, 1951; s. Norman and Ona K.; m. Lois J. Hansen, Jan. 4, 1974; children: Andrew, Jane. AB in Geology, Rutgers Coll., 1973; MS in Geophysics, U. Wyo., 1976; MBA in Fin., U. Colo., Colorado Springs, 1990. Systems mgr. Brit. Petroleum, N.Y.C., 1973-74; seismic processing leader Phillips Petroleum, Bartlesville, Okla., 1976-79; geophysicist Phillips Petroleum, Houston, 1979-80; internat. spl. project geophysicist Marathon Oil, Findlay, Ohio, 1980-82; internat. exploration geophysicist Marathon Oil, Houston, 1982-85, internat. reservoir geologist/geophysicist, 1985-86; home builder, designer, owner D'signer Inc., Monument Homes, Colo., 1986—, developer, hydrologist, 1992—; owner Tri-Lakes Montessori Sch.; lic. stock broker, ins. advisor Prin. Group, Colo., 1987—; realtor ReMax. Active Boy Scouts Am., Colo., 1987—. Mem. Home Builder Assocs. Presbyterian. Office: Monument Homes PO Box 1423 Monument CO 80132-1423

KARATZ, BRUCE E., business executive; b. Chgo., Oct. 10, 1945; s. Robert Harry and Naomi Rae (Goldstein) K.; m. Janet Louise Dreisen, July 28, 1968; children: Elizabeth, Matthew, Theodore. BA, Boston U., 1967; JD, U. So. Calif., 1970. Bar: Calif. 1971. Assoc. Keatinge & Sterling, Los Angeles, 1970-72; assoc. corp. counsel Kaufman and Broad, Inc., Los Angeles, 1972-73; dir. forward planning Kaufman and Broad, Inc., Irvine, Calif., 1973-74; pres. Kaufman and Broad Provence, Aix-en-Provence, France, 1974-76, Kaufman and Broad France, Paris, 1976-80, Kaufman and Broad Devel. Group, Los Angeles, 1980-86; chmn., pres., CEO Kaufman and Broad Home Corp., Los Angeles, 1985—, also bd. dirs., also chmn. bd. dirs., 1993; bd. dirs. Nat. Golf Properties, Inc., Honeywell Inc., Fred Meyer, Inc.; trustee Rand Corp. Founder Mus. Contemporary Art, L.A., 1981; trustee Pitzer Coll., Claremont, Calif., 1983—; bd. councilors U. So. Calif. Law Ctr. Mem. Calif. Bus. Roundtable, Coun. on Fgn. Rels., Pacific Coun. on Internat. Policy, L.A. World Affairs Coun. Democrat. Avocations: modern art, skiing, travel, golf. Office: Kaufman & Broad Home Corp 10990 Wilshire Blvd Fl 7 Los Angeles CA 90024-3913

KARAU, JON OLIN, judge; b. Shelby, Mich., Sept. 15, 1918; s. Edward Karl and Pearl Margaret (Ackerman) K.; m. Luella Gay Nichols, Feb. 14, 1945 (dec. 1982); m. Lana Lee Lovelace, Jan. 15, 1983 (div. 1992); 1 child, Larry Jon (dec.); 1 adopted child, John F. Nicholson-Karau; m. Louise Rogers, Sept. 17, 1995; 1 child, Bruce. BSIE, Can. Inst., Windsor, 1947; LLD, Detroit Coll. Law, 1956. Payroll auditor Fisher Body div., Flint, Mich., 1940-47; with Avery Corp., Detroit, 1947-49; supr. blueprint rm. Detroit Arsenal, 1949-59; specs. writer U.S. Govt.-Navy, Port Hueneme, 1959-63; specs. supr. U.S. Govt.-DSA, Detroit/Washington, 1963-68; sr. mgmt. officer USAF, Washington, 1968-73; stockbroker EGT-J.O. Karau Assocs., Sherman, Tex., 1973-78; mcpl. judge City of Pottsboro, Tex., 1978-91; ret., 1991; cons. Grayson C.C., Denison, 1981; with Reiki Wellness Ctr., Denison, 1993-97. Contbr. articles to profl. jours. Bd. dirs. ARC, Sherman, 1974-77, Campfire Denison; chmn. Grayson County Housing Authority, Sherman, 1986-97. With U.S. Army, 1943-45, ETO; lt. col. USAR and Guards, 1947-85. Mem. Internat. Assn. Fin. Planning, Am. Inst. Mgmt., Am. Inst. Fin., Am. Inst. Indsl. Engrs., U.S. Def. Forces Assn., Tex. Mcpl. Cts. Assn., Tex. Judges Assn. (cons.), Mensa, Elks, Lions (regional chmn.), MAsons, Epsilon Delta Chi. Democrat. Avocations: flying, driving, camping, swimming, Reiki healing. Home: 5048 Ridgeview Dr Las Vegas NV 89120-1259

KARDELL, MAXINE G., jewelry and collectibles consultant, marketing executive; b. Bridgeton, N.J., Feb. 28, 1942; d. Louis A. and Bernice L. (Goldberg) Lubow; BS, Temple U., 1962, JD, 1968; m. Sam C. Gould, June 17, 1962 (div. Dec. 1984); children: Jack, Herman, David; m. Allen S. Kardell, Mar., 10, 1991. Head resident dept. student personnel Temple U., 1962-66; dir., treas. Hilltop Interest Program, Inc., Los Angeles, 1973-74; law clk. law firms, L.A., 1975-77; with Buffalo Resources Corp., L.A., 1978-82, corp. sec., 1979-82; corp. sec., securities prin. Buffalo Securities Corp., L.A., 1979-82; corp. sec. LaMaur Devel. Corp., L.A., 1979-82; contracts analyst, land dept. Texaco Inc., L.A., 1982-83; exec. dir. Sinai Temple, West Los Angeles, 1983-85; pres. Cutting Edge, L.A., 1986; adminstr. law firm Robinson, Wolas & Diamant, Century City, 1986, acctg. firm Roth, Bookstein & Zaslow, L.A., 1986-87; project coord. Cipher, 1987; mktg. dir. Am. Bus. Capital, Beverly Hills, Calif., 1988—. Mem. Roscomare Valley Assn. Edn. Com., Bel Air, Calif., 1975-76, beautification com., 1994; subcom. chmn. Roscomare Rd. Sch. Citizens Adv. Coun., Bel Air; active various community drives. Recipient Joseph B. Wagner Oratory award B'nai B'rith, 1959, Voice of Democracy award, 1958-59, award Commentator Club, 1959. Mem. ABA (law office econs. sect.), L.A. County Bar Assn. (assoc., law office econs. sect., fee dispute arbitration panel), Nat. Assn. Legal Adminstrs. (Beverly Hills chpt.), NAFE (network dir.), Nat. Assn. Law Firm Mktg. Adminstrs., Calif. Women Lawyers, Women in Bus. (co-chmn. membership com.), Calif. CPA Soc. (adminstr. com.), Nat. Assn. Synagogue Adminstrs., Am. Assn. Petroleum Landmen, Los Angeles Assn. Petroleum Landmen, Textile Profl. Soc., Comml. Fin. Conf., Phi Alpha Theta, Alpha Lambda Delta. Jewish. Fax: 310-476-3869. Home: 1524 Stone Canon Los Angeles CA 90077 Office: Am Bus Capital 400 S Beverly Dr Ste 208 Beverly Hills CA 90212-4404

KARDINAL, ROYCE ANN, hotel executive; b. Long Beach, Calif., May 17, 1944; d. Roy Perry and Betty Lois (Randolph) Coxwell; m. Glenn Roy Kardinal, Aug. 17, 1965; children: Kimberly, Kristan, Kelsea. AA in Interior Design, Woodbury Coll., L.A., 1966. Cert. hotel adminstrn. Gen. mgr. Great Western Hosts, Wickenburg, Ariz., 1966-79; mng. ptnr. Best Western Rancho Grande, Wickenburg, 1979—. Co-author: The Rightside Up Town on the Upside Down River, 1974. Trustee Ariz. Hotel Found., Phoenix, 1993—; chmn. bd. Desert Caballeros Mus., Wickenburg, 1990-91; pres., bd. trustees Wickenburg Sch. Bd., 1989-96; pres. Las Senoras de Socorro, Wickenburg, 1974, 95; chmn. bd. Wickenburg Film Commn.; co-chmn. Tourism Authority, 1996—; trustee Wickenburg Found. Ednl. Enrichment, 1990-98; adult advisor Internat. Order Rainbow Girls, 1980-95; mem. steering com. Wickenburg Town Forum, 1996; mem. Las Damas, 1968—. Recipient Silver Spur, Desert Caballeros, 1995, Harry T. Needham award Desert Caballeros Western Mus., 1992; named Citizen of the Yr., Wickenburg C. of C., 1991, Woman of the Yr., Bus. and Profl. Women, 1985. Mem. Ariz. Hotel/Motel Assn. (pres. 1992-93), Best Western Internat. (dist. gov. 1992—), Am. Hotel/Motel Assn. (ho. of dels. 1995—). Episcopalian. Avocations: gardening, decorating, reading. Home: One Redbird Hill Wickenburg AZ 85390 Office: Best Western Rancho Grande 293 E Wickenburg Way Wickenburg AZ 85390-1484

KARL, GEORGE, professional basketball coach; b. Penn Hills, Pa., May 12, 1951; m. Cathy Karl; children—Kelci Ryanne, Coby Joseph. Grad., U. N.C., 1973. Guard San Antonio Spurs, NBA, 1973-78, asst. coach, head scout, 1978-80; coach Mont. Golden Nuggets, Continental Basketball Assn., 1980-83; dir. player acquisition Cleve. Cavaliers, 1983-84, coach, 1984-86; head coach Golden State Warriors, Oakland, Calif., from 1986, Albany (N.Y.) Patrons, 1988-89, 90-91, Real Madrid, Spain, 1991-92, Seattle Supersonics, 1992-98, Milwaukee Bucks, 1998—. Named Coach of Yr., Continental Basketball Assn., 1981, 83. Mem. Continental Basketball Assn. *

KARLEN, PETER HURD, lawyer, writer; b. N.Y.C., Feb. 22, 1949; s. S. H. and Jean Karlen; m. Lynette Ann Thwaites, Dec. 22, 1978. BA in History,

U. Calif., Berkeley, 1971; JD, U. Calif., Hastings, 1974; MS in Law and Soc., U. Denver, 1976. Bar: Calif. 1974, Hawaii 1989, Colo. 1991, U.S. Dist. Ct. (so. dist.) Calif. 1976, U.S. Dist. Ct. (no. dist.) Calif. 1983, U.S. Dist. Ct. (Hawaii) 1989, U.S. Supreme Ct. 1990. Assoc. Sankary & Sankary, San Diego, 1976; teaching fellow Coll. of Law U. Denver, 1974-75; lectr. Sch. of Law U. Warwick, United Kingdom, 1976-78; pvt. practice La Jolla, Calif., 1979-86; prin. Peter H. Karlen, P.C., La Jolla, 1986—; adj. prof. U. San Diego Sch. of Law, 1979-84; mem. adj. faculty Western State U. Coll. of Law, San Diego, 1976, 79-80, 88, 92. Contbg. editor Artweek, 1979-95, Art Calendar, 1989-96, Art Cellar Exch. mag., 1989-92; mem. editl. bd. Copyright World, 1988—, IP World, 1997—; contbr. numerous articles to profl. jours. Mem. Am. Soc. for Aesthetics, Brit. Soc. Aesthetics. Office: 1205 Prospect St Ste 400 La Jolla CA 92037-3613

KARLSBERG, PAUL, neurosurgeon; b. Springfield, Mass., July 2, 1933; s. Isador Joseph and Ciel (Robinovitz) K.; m. Helen Fay Pugach, June 23, 1959 (div. Aug. 1995); children: Elizabeth V., Peter L., Sharon D.; m. Norine Carol Dotseth, Sept. 2, 1995. AB, Harvard U., 1954; MD, Boston U., 1958. Diplomate Am. Bd. Neurologic Surgery. Intern New Eng. Med. Ctr., 1958-59; resident U. Calif., San Francisco, 1959-63; chief surgery St. Johns Hosp., Oxnard, Calif., 1978; chief surgery Cmty. Meml. Hosp., Ventura, Calif., 1978-88, ret., 1990; cons. dept. biology and philosophy U. Calif., Santa Barbara, 1993—. Contbr. articles to profl. jours. Pres. Temple Beth Torah, Ventura, Calif., 1976, 78-80. Col. USAR, 1983-93. Fellow Internat. Coll. Surgeons, Am. Bd. Neurological Surgery, Am. Coll. Surgeons; mem. AMA (Calif. chpt.), AAAS, Am. Assn. Neurol. Surgeons, Congress Neurol. Surgeons, N.Y. Acad. Sci. Avocations: music, boating. Office: Neurosurgica Associates 168 N Brent St Ste 408 Ventura CA 93003-2824

KARLSTROM, PAUL JOHNSON, art historian; b. Seattle, Jan. 22, 1941; s. Paul Isadore and Eleanor (Johnson) K.; m. Ann Heath, Dec. 29, 1964; 1 dau., Clea Heath. BA in English Lit, Stanford U., 1964; MA, UCLA, 1969, PhD (Samuel H. Kress fellow), 1973. Asst. curator Grunwald Center for Graphic Arts, UCLA, 1967-70; Samuel H. Kress fellow Nat. Gallery Art, Washington, 1970-71; instr. Calif. State U., Northridge, 1972-73; West Coast regional dir. Archives Am. Art, Smithsonian Instn. at De Young Mus., San Francisco, 1973-91, Huntington Libr., San Marino, Calif., 1991—; guest curator Hirshhorn Mus., Washington, 1977. Author: Louis M. Eilshemius, 1978, Los Angeles in the 1940s Post Modernism and the Visual Arts, 1987, The Visionary Art of James M. Washington, Jr., 1989, Turning the Tide: Early Los Angeles Modernists, 1920-56, 1990; editor: On the Edge of America: California Modernist Art, 1900-1950, 1996, (with others) Diego Rivera: Art and Revolution, 1999; video prodr. David Hockney, 1984, 93, George Tsutakawa in Japan, 1988; contbr. articles to profl. jours. Mem. adv. bd. Humanities West, Jacob Lawrence Catalogue Raisonné Project; bd. dirs. S.W. Art History Coun., Bay Area Video Coalition; sec. Va. Steele Scott Found, Hans and Thordis Burkhardt Found., Noah Purifoy Found. E-mail: pkarlstrom@earthlink.net. Office: Archives Am Art Huntington Libr 1151 Oxford Rd San Marino CA 91108-1218

KARLTON, LAWRENCE K., federal judge; b. Bklyn., May 28, 1935; s. Aaron Katz and Sylvia (Meltzer) K.; m. Mychelle Stiebel, Sept. 7, 1958 (dec.). Student, Washington Sq. Coll., 1952-54; LL.B., Columbia U., 1958. Bar: Fla. 1958, Calif. 1962. Acting legal officer Sacramento Army Depot, Dept. Army, Sacramento, 1958-60; civilian legal officer Sacramento Army Depot, Dept. Army, 1960-62; individual practice law Sacramento, 1962-64; mem. firm Abbott, Karlton & White, 1964, Karlton & Blease, 1964-71, Karlton, Blease & Vanderlaan, 1971-76; judge Calif. Superior Ct. for Sacramento County, 1976-79, U.S. Dist. Ct. (ea. dist.) Calif., Sacramento, 1979-83; formerly chief judge U.S. Dist. Ct., Sacramento, 1983-90, chief judge emeritus, 1990—. Co-chmn. Central Calif. council B'nai B'rith Anit-Defamation League Commn., 1964-65; treas. Sacramento Jewish Community Relations Council, chmn., 1967-68; chmn. Vol. Lawyers Commn. Sun Valley ACLU, 1964-76. Mem. Am. Bar Assn., Sacramento County Bar Assn., Calif. Bar Assn., Fed. Bar Assn., Fed. Judges Assn., 9th Cir. Judges Assn. Club: B'nai B'rith (past pres.). Office: US Dist Ct 501 I St 15th Fl Ste 230 Sacramento CA 95814

KARPELES, DAVID, museum director; b. Santa Barbara, Calif., Jan. 26, 1936; s. Leon and Betty (Friedman) K.; m. Marsha Mirsky, June 29, 1958; children: Mark, Leslie, Cheryl, Jason. BS, U. Minn., 1956, postgrad., 1956-59; MA, San Diego State U., 1962; postgrad., U. Calif., Santa Barbara, 1965-69. Founder Karpeles Manuscript Libr. Mus., Montecito, Calif., 1983—; dir., founder Karpeles Manuscript Libr. Mus., Santa Barbara, Calif., 1988—, N.Y.C., 1990—, Tacoma, Wash., 1991—, Jacksonville, Fla., 1992—, Duluth, Minn., 1993—, Charleston, S.C., 1995—, Buffalo, 1995—; founder, dir. 102 mini-museums throughout U.S. and Can.; established the 1st cultural literacy program, presented to schs. by respective mus. staffs, 1993—. Creator program to provide ownership of homes to low-income families, 1981. Recipient Affordable Housing Competition award Gov. Edmund G. Brown Jr., State of Calif., Dept. Housing and Community Devel., 1981; invited to present Commencement Address to graduating class, U. Minn., Duluth, 1996, also recipient Disting. Alulmni award. Jewish. Home: 465 Hot Springs Rd Santa Barbara CA 93108-2029

KARPENKO, VICTOR NICHOLAS, mechanical engineer; b. Harbin, China, Jan. 23, 1922; s. Nicholas Stephan and Sophia Andrea (Kootas) K.; came to U.S., 1941, naturalized, 1943; student San Francisco State Coll., 1941-42, Oreg. State Coll., 1943; B.S. in Mech. Engring., U. Calif., Berkeley, 1948; m. Lydia Kamotsky, June 23, 1950; children—Victor, Mark, Alexandra. Staff engr. Atomic Products Equipment div. Gen. Electric Co., San Jose, Calif., 1956-57; project engr. nuclear explosives engring. Lawrence Livermore (Calif.) Lab., 1957-65, sect. leader nuclear explosives engring., 1965-66, div. leader Nuclear Test Engring. div., 1966-76, project mgr. Mirror Fusion Test Facility, 1976-85; div. head Magnet System Superconducting Super Collider, Univ. Research Assn., Berkeley, Calif., 1986-87, cons. tech. and mgmt., 1987—; ptnr. devel. cryogenic equipment PHPK Tech. Inc., Westerville, Ohio, 1992—; mem. fusion reactor safety com. Dept. Energy; mem. Containment Evaluation Panel, ERDA. Dist. chmn. U. Calif. Alumni Scholarship Program, 1976-80; com. mem. U. Calif. Alumni Scholarship Program, 1972-76; pres. San Ramon AAU Swim Club, 1964. Served with AUS, 1943-46. Registered profl. mech. and nuclear engr., Calif. Mem. Am. Nuclear Soc., Calif. Alumni Assn. Republican. Greek Orthodox. Home: 613 Bradford Pl Danville CA 94526-2357

KARPILOW, CRAIG, physician; b. San Francisco, Oct. 23, 1947; s. David and Babette (David) K.; BSc, U. Alta. (Can.), 1967; MA, U. So. Calif., 1970; MD, Dalhousie U., 1974. Diplomate Canadian Coll. of Family Practice. Intern, Dalhousie U., Halifax, N.S., Can., 1974-75; resident in family practice medicine Meml. U. Nfld., St. John's, 1975-77; practice medicine specializing in family medicine and occupational medicine, 1978-95; practice occupational medicine, Snohomish, Wash., 1981-83; pres. Internat. Profl. Assocs. Ltd., 1978—; med. dir./clin. N.W. Occupational Health Ctrs., Seattle, 1983-84; ptnr. physician, co-dir. CHEC Med. Ctr., Seattle, 1984-85; head dept. occupational and diagnostic medicine St. Cabrini Hosp., Seattle, 1984-86; med. dir. N.W. Indsl. Health Svcs., 1985-86, Queen Anne Med. Ctr., Seattle, 1985-95, Travel Med. Clinic of Seattle, 1986-94; ptnr. Clin. Assocs., 1990-95. Diplomate Am. Bd. Family Practice; licenciate Med. Coll. Can. Author: Occupational Medicine in The International Workplace, 1991, Handbook of Occupational Medicine, 1994. Fellow Am. Acad. Family Practice, Am. Coll. Occupational & Environmental Medicine, Royal Soc. Tropical Medicine, Am. Coll. Occupational Medicine (recorder Ho. of Dels./bd. dirs. 1990-91); mem. AMA, Am. Soc. Tropical Medicine and Hygiene, Wash. State Med. Assn. King County Med. Soc., Wash. Acad. Family Physicians (rsch. collaborative, Com. on Rsch.), Am. Coll. Occupational and Environ. Medicine (chmn. internat. occupational medicine sect.), N.W. Occupational Med. Assn. (bd. dirs. 1985-92, 95—, pres. 1990-91), Can. Soc. for Internat. Health, Can. Pub. Health Assn., Am. Com. Clin., Tropical and Travel Medicine, Can. Soc. of Northwest, Marimed Found. Pacific N.W. (adv. bd.), Finnish Soc., Corinthian Yacht Club, Nature Conservancy, Rotary (bd. dirs., chmn. internat. rels. com., chmn. Hepatis Project, chmn. Malaria Project), U. So. Calif. Alumni Assn., Kappa Sigma.

KARR, DARYL KELLY PAUL JAMES, film and video service executive; b. Salt Lake City, Oct. 23, 1954; s. Paul Spencer and Dora Ione (Bowman) K.; m. Sarah Irene Bodeman, Feb. 14, 1974 (div. Dec. 1976); 1 child, Spring Charrise; m. Kathy Louise Payne, Apr. 28, 1978 (div. Feb. 1980). Student, Glendale (Ariz.) Community Coll., 1974, Cornell U., 1978. Mgr. Lucky Storers, Inc., Phoenix, 1972-79; prodn. asst. Phoenix Videohlms, 1974-83; owner, mgr. Karr Entertainment World, Orem, Utah, 1979-82, Affiliated Film and Video Svcs., Phoenix, 1982-92; pres. film and video svcs. mktg. divsn., 1989-90; design and installation film transfer system for Gina Mussi, 1991; pres., CEO Phoenix VideoFilms, 1992—; cons. to cinematography students, indsl. orgns., legal firms, advt. agys., ind. film producers, Phoenix, 1982—. Sound designer (film) Fire Brigade, 1984; prodn. supr. (short film) Alley Cats, 1986; post prodn. supr. (indsl. video) Ameed, 1987; producer, dir., writer (video short) Stacey Miller, 1987; producer (sales film) Currency Guard, 1991; producer, dir. cinematographer (promotional video) Forklift Systems, Denver, 1991; editor (film) Summer of the Eagle, Into Paradise, Rockwell, New York Cowboy, Long Walk, Into the Night. Leader Explorer Scouts Am., Phoenix, 1973, cub master Cub Scouts Am., Glendale, 1975; organizer United Way blood drive, Glendale, 1974; vol. Little League Baseball, Phoenix, 1987. Recipient Community Services award United Way, 1974, Rocky Mountain Emmy, 1993, C.I.N.E. Golden Eagle, 1993, GABRIEL, 1993, Angel, 1993, Gold UBEE, 1993; named one of Outstanding Young Men of Am. U.S. Jaycees, 1987, 89. Mem. Soc. Motion Picture and TV Engrs., Classical Film Soc., Am. Film Inst. Republican. Mormon. Avocations: restoring automobiles, camping, racquetball. Office: Phoenix Video Films 2925 W Indian School Rd Phoenix AZ 85017-4162

KARRAS, DONALD GEORGE, tax administrator; b. Sioux City, Iowa, Dec. 23, 1953; s. George D. and Mary T. (Kyriakos) K.; m. Donna Lynn Ciripompa, Mar. 6, 1982; children: Dane Anthony, Dillon James. BA, Augustana Coll., 1977; MBA, U. S.D., 1980, JD, 1981. CPA, S.D. Bar: S.D. 1981. Instr. U. S.D. Sch. Bus., Vermillion, 1980-81; tax sr. acct. Deloitte Haskins & Sells, Denver, 1981-84; tax mgr. The Anschutz Corp., Denver, 1984-87; dir. taxes Kennecott Corp., Salt Lake City, 1988-92; v.p. taxes Newmont Mining Corp., Denver, 1992—. Mem. Colo. Pub. Expenditure Coun. Mem. ABA, S.D. Bar Assn., Tax Execs. Inst., Nat. Mining Assn. (fin. com.), Rocky Mountain Mineral Law Found., Colo. Mining Assn., Internat. Fiscal Assn., Nev. Mining Assn. Republican. Avocations: golf, skiing. Home: 7100 W Princeton Ave Denver CO 80235-3036 Office: Newmont Mining Corp One Norwest Ctr 1700 Lincoln St Denver CO 80203-4500

KARSTAEDT, ARTHUR R., III, lawyer; b. Madison, Wis., Sept. 15, 1951. BA, U. Wis., 1972; JD, U. Denver, 1975. Bar: Colo. 1976. Formerly lawyer Hall & Evans, Denver; ptnr. Harris, Karstaedt, Jamison & Powers, P.C., Englewood, Colo., 1995—. Office: Harris Karstaedt Jamison & Powers PC 5299 Dtc Blvd Ste 1130 Englewood CO 80111-3305*

KARWACKI, ANDRZEJ MICHAEL, landscape architect, artist; b. Brzeg, OP, Poland, Mar. 25, 1967; came to U.S., 1986; s. Tadeusz and Janina (Kaminiecka) K.; m. Jonasz Rice. BFA, Jersey City State U., 1990; M in Landscape Arch., U. Pa., 1994. Landscape architect, designer Hanna-Olin, Phila., 1994, Hargreaves Assocs., San Francisco, 1994-96, SWA Group, Sausalito, Calif., 1996-98; mem., film dir. Film Arts Found., San Francisco, 1995-96; artist Artworks Group, San Francisco, 1995-97; mem. adv. bd. Designed Land Internat. Conf., San Francisco, 1996, art dir. 12/17 Studios, San Francisco, 1997-8. Exhibit author: (gallery exhibits) Berkeley Art Ctr., 1996-97, Somar Gallery, 1996-97, La Jolla Gallery, 1997, U. Calif. Berkeley, 1998. Recipient Landscape Arch. scholarship, U. Pa., 1990-94, Merit award for acad. excellence, Assn. Polish-Am. Engrs., 1993, Van Allen Nomination for travel fellowship, U. Pa., 1994, 1st place in Expo '98 Landscape competition, Lisbon, Portugal, 1995. Avocations: painting, filmmaking, illustration, diving, tennis. Home: 138 Belvedere St San Francisco CA 94117-3916

KASAMA, HIDETO PETER, accountant, business advisor, real estate consultant; b. Tokyo, Nov. 21, 1946; came to U.S., 1969; s. Toshiyoshi and Hamako (Yoshioka) K.; m. Evelyn Patricia Cruz (div. Apr. 1990); children: Jennifer, Nicole, Leona; m. Heidi W. Snare, June 29, 1991; 1 child, Serena. BABA, Seattle U., 1971, MBA, 1973. CPA. Mgmt. trainee Seafirst Bank, Seattle, 1972-74; audit supr. Ernst & Young, Seattle, 1974-79; pres. KASPAC Corp., Seattle, 1979-89; mng. ptnr. Kasama & Co., Seattle, 1980-98; shareholder Von Harten & Co., Seattle, 1998—. Contbr. articles to newspapers. Mem. AICPA, Wash. Soc. CPA's, Columbia Tower Club (founder). Avocations: golf, classical guitar, gardening. Home: 725 9th Ave S Edmonds WA 98020-3311 Office: Von Harten & Co 1809 7th Ave Ste 1400 Seattle WA 98101-1313

KASANIN, MARK OWEN, lawyer; b. Boston, June 28, 1929; s. Jacob Sergei and Elizabeth Owen (Knight) K.; m. Anne Camilla Wimbish, Dec. 18, 1960; children: Marc S., James W. B.A., Stanford U., 1951; LL.B., Yale U., 1954. Bar: Calif. Assoc. McCutchen, Doyle, Brown & Enersen, San Francisco, 1957-62, 63-67; ptnr. McCutchen, Doyle, Brown & Enersen, 1967—. Mem. planning commn. City of Belvedere, Calif., 1974-76. Served with USNR, 1955-57. Named among Best Lawyers in Am., 1997-98. Fellow Am. Coll. Trial Lawyers; mem. Maritime Law Assn. U.S. (exec. com. 1984-87, trustee Product Liability Adv. Coun. Found. 1990—, mem. fed. civil rules adv. com. 1992—). Fax: 415-393-2286. Home: PO Box 698 Belvedere Tiburon CA 94920-0698 Office: McCutchen Doyle Brown & Enersen 3 Embarcadero Ctr San Francisco CA 94111-4003

KASARI, LEONARD SAMUEL, quality control professional, concrete consultant; b. Los Angeles, Sept. 22, 1924; s. Kustaa Adolph and Impi (Sikio) K.; m. Elizabeth P. Keplinger, Aug. 25, 1956; children: Lorraine Carol, Lance Eric. Student, Compton Coll., 1942-43, UCLA, 1964-70. Registered profl. engr., Calif. Gen. construction Los Angeles, 1946-61; supr. inspection service Osborne Labs., Los Angeles, 1961-64; mgr. customer service Lightweight Processing, Los Angeles, 1965-77; dir. tech. service Crestlite Aggregates, San Clemente, Calif., 1977-78; quality control mgr. Standard Concrete, Santa Ana, Calif., 1978-92. Camp dir. Torrance YMCA, High Sierras, Calif., 1969-80, mem. bd. mgrs., 1970—. Served with USN, 1943-46. Recipient Sam Hobbs Svc. award ACI-So. Calif., 1992; named Hon. Life Mem. Calif. PTA, 1983. Mem. Am. Concrete Inst. Democrat. Lutheran. Avocations: skiing, hunting, fishing, backpacking. Office: 2450 W 233rd St Torrance CA 90501-5730

KASE, JOHN D., writer; b. Alma, Mich., June 25, 1960; s. Donald William and Marie Louise (Toepfert) K. Cert., Utah Tech. Coll., 1979, 82; AAS in Gen. Studies, Weber State U., 1993, BA in Comm. and Journalism, 1996. Electronic technician Thiokol Corp., Promontory, Utah, 1982-92; prodn. assoc. Autoliv, Brigham City, Utah, 1993-97; tech. writer Eimco Process Equipment, Salt Lake City, 1997—. Mem. Soc. Tech. Comm. Avocations: photography, hiking, fitness training.

KASHIWA, RUSSELL H., communication executive; b. Honolulu, July 30, 1957; s. George K. and Grace K. (Tanabe) K.; m. Lori K. Marumoto, May 17, 1997. BA in Radio, TV, U. Ariz., 1982. News asst. Sta. KOLD-TV, Tucson, 1982; news photographer Sta. KBIM-TV, Roswell, N.Mex., 1982-83; stringer Sta. KOAT-TV, Albuquerque, 1983-84; founder, producer RHK Prodns., Roswell, 1983-85; producer Honolulu, 1985—; news photographer, editor Sta. KITV-TV, Honolulu, 1988—; cons. City of Roswell, 1984-85. Editor (newsletter) Tropic Topics, 1981; producer (video) Roswell A City That Works, 1984. Bd. dirs. Syracuse (N.Y.) U. Jud. Bd., 1976-77; mem. Leadership Roswell, 1985; producer Chaves County United Way, Roswell; active Boy Scouts Am., 1969-75. Mem. Internat. TV Assn., Jaycees, (Honolulu chpt., Fall bd. 1981). Office: RHK Prodns PO Box 23032 Honolulu HI 96823-3032

KASHNOW, RICHARD A., executive; m. Marcia, 2 children. CEO, pres. Raychem Corp, Menlo Park, Calif. Office: 300 Constitution Dr Menlo Park CA 94025-1140

KASPER, GABRIELE, applied linguistics educator; b. Bochum, Germany, Dec. 27, 1948; came to U.S., 1988; d. Robert and Lore (Heimannsfeld) Giermeroth; 1 child, Jan Simon. MA, U. Bochum, 1975, PhD, 1980. Rschr. U. Bochum, 1976-81; assoc. prof. applied linguistics U. Arhus, Denmark, 1981-89; assoc. prof. U. Hawaii Manoa, Honolulu, 1989-93, prof., 1993—. Editor: Crosscultural Pragmatics, 1989, Interlanguage Pragmatics, 1993, Communication Strategies, 1997; contbr. articles to Studies in 2nd Lang. Acquisition, Applied Linguistics, Jour. Pragmatics. Home: 3349 Anoai Pl Apt A Honolulu HI 96822-1477 Office: Univ Hawaii Manoa ESL 1890 E West Rd Honolulu HI 96822-2318

KASS, JEROME ALLAN, writer; b. Chgo., Apr. 21, 1937; s. Sidney J. and Celia (Gorman) K.; children from previous marriage: Julie, Adam; m. Delia Ephron, May 21, 1982. BA, NYU, 1958, MA, 1959. Playwright: Monopoly, 1965, Saturday Night, 1968, (mus.) Ballroom, 1978 (Tony nomination), (TV) A Brand New Life, 1973, Queen of the Stardust Ballroom, 1975 (Writers Guild Am. award, Emmy nomination), My Old Man, 1979, The Fighter, 1982, Scorned and Swindled, 1984, Crossing to Freedom (aka Pied Piper), 1989, Last Wish, 1991, The Only Way Out, 1993, Secrets, 1995; screenwriter: The Black Stallion Returns, 1981, (miniseries) Evergreen, 1985; author: Four Short Plays by Jerome Kass, 1966, Saturday Night, 1969; adapted to concert form Finian's Rainbow, L.A., 1997, Pajama Game, L.A., 1998; musical version Queen of the Stardust Ballroom, Chgo., 1998. Mem. Dramatists Guild, Writers Guild Am., Phi Beta Kappa.

KASSMAN, ANDREW LANCE, orthodontist; b. N.Y.C., Nov. 14, 1950; s. David and Phyllis Ivy (Einhorn) K.; children: Stacey Arielle, Alexandria Devin; m. Laurie Ann Kassman, July 7, 1997. BS in Engring., Tulane U., 1972; DMD, Tufts U., 1975; cert. orthodontics, Columbia U., 1978. Lab. technician Tufts Med. Ctr., Boston, 1973-75; resident VA Hosp., Northport, N.Y., 1975-76; pvt. practice Astoria, N.Y., 1976-78, Phila., 1978-79, East Pathogue, N.Y., 1979-80; pvt. practice dentistry specializing in orthodontics Tucson, 1980—; chief orthodontia Crippled Children's Ctr., Tucson, 1980—; assoc. staff Tucson Med. Ctr., 1980—. Bd. dirs. Comstock Found., Tucson, 1980—; active Temple Emanu-El, Tucson, 1988, Rancho Vistoso Assn., Oro Valley, Tucson Boys Club, 1988, Jewish Community Ctr., Tucson, 1988. Mem. ADA, Am. Assn. Orthodontists, Pacific Coast Soc. Orthodontists, Tucson Orthodontist Soc., Tucson C. of C. Avocations: baseball, football, tennis, travel. Home: 6501 N Placita Alta Reposa Tucson AZ 85750-4204 Office: 6700 N Oracle Rd Ste 327 Tucson AZ 85704-7740

KASSNER, JAY EDWARD, small business owner; b. San Diego, July 6, 1943; s. Ewald George and Thelma Marie (Ernster) K.; m. Mary Lou Ness, Dec. 10, 1963; 1 child, Adam Wayne; m. Tammy Lynn Peden, Dec. 31, 1982; children: Brittany Michelle, Courtney Marie. BA in Bus. Adminstrn., U. Wash., 1971. Cert. mgmt. specialist, Wash. Acct. Sites & Co., Inc., Seattle, 1971-73; ptnr. Arctic World Ltd., Anchorage, 1972-75; owner Kassner & Assocs., Anchorage, 1976—; pres. Alaska Fishing Charters, Inc., Anchorage, 1990—; v.p. Interior Plant Designs, Inc., Anchorage, 1982—; pres. Norton Sound Constrn., Inc., Anchorage, 1992—; chmn., CEO K & R Enterprises, Inc., Anchorage, 1981—; bd. dirs. Trans-Pacific North, Inc., Kenai, Alaska, TLC Flooring, Inc., Anchorage. Editor: Who's Available, 1969; newspaper editor Jet City News, 1969. 1st lt. inf. U.S. Army, 1966-69; Vietnam. Decorated Bronze Star, Purple Heart; NSF scholar, 1960. Mem. Am. Legion, Elks, Eagles, Moose, Amvets, Mil. Order of Purple Heart. Republican. Lutheran. Avocations: skiing, fishing, hunting, collecting baseball cards and memorbilia.

KASSNER, MICHAEL ERNEST, materials science educator, researcher; b. Osaka, Japan, Nov. 22, 1950; (parents Am. citizens); s. Ernest and Clara (Christa) K.; m. Marcia J. Wright, Aug. 19, 1972 (div. Dec. 1976). BS, Northwestern U., 1972; MS, Stanford U., 1979, PhD, 1981. Metallurgist Sargent and Lundy Engrs., Chgo., 1977; metallurgist Lawrence Livermore (Calif.) Nat. Lab., 1981-90, head phys. metallurgy and joining sect., 1988-90; lectr. San Francisco State U., 1983; prof. Naval Postgrad. Sch., Monterey, Calif., 1984-86; prof., dir. grad. program in materials sci. Oreg. State U., Corvallis, 1990—, Chevron endowed prof., 1996, Northwest Aluminuim prof., 1997—; temporary assignment as project mgr. Office Basic Energy Scis., U.S. Dept. Energy, 1991-96; vis. scholar dept. physics U. Groningen, Netherlands, 1985-87; vis. scholar dept. materials, sci. and engring. Stanford U., 1981-83; vis. prof. U. Calif., San Diego, 1997—. Author over 120 articles; author book on binary phase diagrams; editor various sci. jours. Lt. USN, 1972-76; lt. comdr. USNR, 1976-81. Fulbright scholar, The Netherlands; fellow ASM Internat., 1998. Mem. ASME, Am. Soc. Metals, The Metall. Soc., Materials Research Soc., Sigma Xi. Home: PO Box 269 Otter Rock OR 97369-0269

KASULKA, LARRY HERMAN, management consultant; b. Wagner, S.D., Apr. 5, 1940; s. Alfred E. and Lillian J. (Gasper) K.; m. Susan A. Smart, Sept. 8, 1962; children: Shawn L., Christine A. BS in Electronics, Northrop U., 1961; grad. cert. in bus. adminstrn., UCLA, 1969; grad. cert., Brookings Inst., 1986, Harvard U., 1989; PhD in Bus. Adminstrn., LaSalle U., 1995. Registered profl. engr., Calif. Electronic engr. Douglas Aircraft Co., 1962-77; unit chief avionics McDonnell Douglas Astronautics Co., 1977-81, br. chief avionics, 1981-84; dir. design engr. McDonnell Douglas Electronic Systems Co., 1984-87, dir. program mgmt., 1987-89, dir. new bus., 1989-91; spl. asst. U.S. Dept. Commerce, Office of the Dep. Sec., 1990-91; v.p., dep. gen. mgr. Kennedy Space Ctr. McDonnell Douglas Space Systems Co., 1991-93; v.p., gen. mgr. McDonnell Douglas Aerospace N.Mex. Ops., 1993-94; program mgr. McDonnell Douglas Aerospace, Huntingrton Beach, Calif., 1994-96; mgmt. cons. L.H. Kasulka & Assocs., 1996—; presenter in field. Contbr. articles to profl. jours. Bd. dirs. Brevard Achievement Ctr., Rockledge, Fla., 1991-93; mentor Sci. Engrin. and Rsch. Career Help; mem. Pres. Commn. Exec. Exch. Alumni U. Calif.-L.A. Alumni. Recipient Dir.'s Safety award NASA KSC Ctr., 1992, Group Achievement award NASA JSC Ctr., 1995, Sr. Exec. Svc. award Dept. Commerce, 1990, commendation Inst. Soc. Am., 1983, White House Pres. Bush, 1990; named Outstanding Cadet, CAP-Internat. Aviation Cadet Exch.; named to Hon. Order Ky. Cols. Assoc. fellow AIAA; mem. Armed Forces and Comm. Elec. Assn., Nat. Man. Assn., Assn for Quality Participation, Am. Soc. Quality Control, UCLA Alumni Assn. (mem. Goal/QPC Pres.' Commn. on Exec. Exch. Alumni). Achievements include patent for new low-cost temperature measurement.

KASZNIAK, ALFRED WAYNE, neuropsychologist; b. Chgo., June 2, 1949; s. Alfred H. and Ann Virginia (Simonsen) K.; BS with honors, U. Ill., 1970, M.A., 1973, Ph.D., 1976; m. Mary Ellen Beaurain, Aug. 26, 1973; children: Jesse, Elizabeth. Instr. dept. psychology Rush Med. Coll., Chgo., 1974-76, asst. prof. dept. psychology, 1976-79; from asst. prof. to assoc. prof. dept. psychiatry U. Ariz. Coll. Medicine, Tucson, 1979-82, assoc. prof. dept. psychology and psychiatry, 1982-87, prof. depts. psychology, neurology and psychiatry, 1987—, chmn. U. Ariz. Commn. on Gerontology, 1990-93, acting head U. Ariz. dept. psychology, 1992-93; dir. U. Ariz. Coordinated Clin. Neuropsychology Program, dir. Ctr. Consciousness Studies, 1998—; staff psychologist Presbyn.-St. Luke's Hosp., Chgo., 1976-79, Univ. Hosp., Tucson, 1979—; mem. human devel. and aging study sect. div. research grants NIH, 1981-86. Trustee So. Ariz. chpt. Nat. Multiple Sclerosis Soc., 1980-82; mem. med. and sci. adv. bd. Nat. Alzheimer's Disease and Related Disorders Assn., 1981-84; mem. VA Geriatrics and Gerontology Adv. Com., 1986-89, Ariz. Gov.'s Adv. Com. on Alzheimer's Disease, 1988-92; mem. med. adv. bd. Fan Kane Fund for Brain-Injured Children, Tucson, 1980-92. Grantee Nat. Inst. Aging, 1978-83, 89-94, NIMH, 1984-94, Robert Wood Johnson Found., 1986-89, Fetzer Inst., 1997—, Flinn Found., 1998—. Fellow Am. Psychol. Assn. (Disting. Contbr. award div. 20 1978, pres. clin. geropsychology sect. 1995), Am. Psychol. Soc.; mem. Internat. Neuropsychol. Soc., (bd gov's., 1994-97), Gerontol. Soc. (rsch. fellow 1980). Author 5 books; mem. editorial bd. Psychology and Aging, 1984-87; The Clin. Neuropsychologist, 1986-96, Clin. Geropsychology, 1994—, Jour. Clin. and Exp. Neuropsychol., 1987-90, Jour Gerontology, 1988-92, Neuropsychology, 1992-93; contbr. articles to profl. jours. Home: 2327 E Hawthorne St Tucson AZ 85719-4944 Office: U Ariz Dept Psychology 1503 E University Tucson AZ 85721

KATEMOPOULOS, MILDRED JOSEPHINE, executive secretary; b. Shanghai, China, Apr. 29, 1925; came to the U.S., 1977; d. James Jeremiah and Camille Helmana (Barradas) O'Leary; m. Theodore Demetrius Katemopoulos, Apr. 29, 1946; children: Maureen, Eileen, Kathryn, Paul, Anne-Marie. Grad., Loretto H.S., Shanghai. Pvt. sec. Royal Netherlands Embassy, Shanghai, 1946-49; sec. to mng. dir. Dairy Farm Co., Hong Kong, 1949-58; confidential sec. H.K. Land Co., Hong Kong, 1958-66; writer Children's Page H.K. Sunday Std., Hong Kong, 1966-71; pub. rels. staff Mandarin Hotel, Hong Kong, 1970-73; asst. to CEO Regent Internat. Hotels, Hong Kong, 1974-77; sr. sec. Stanford Rsch. Inst., Menlo Park, Calif., 1977-79; asst. to CEO Cath. Charities, San Jose, Calif., 1981-89, Econ.

and Social Opportunities, San Jose, 1989-94; adminstrv. asst. Christ United Presbyn. Ch., San Jose, 1995—; Author: Loretto School, 1990, Born in Shanghai, 1996, (book of poems) When Silver Turns to Gold, 1996. Chmn. Loretto Internat. in the Far East, Hong Kong, 1966-77; founder, pres. Tuesday Club of Hong Kong, 1970-77; pres. Little Flower Club, Hong Kong, 1972-77. Recipient resolution for decade of svc. to Cath. Charities, Bishop of San Jose, 1989. Roman Catholic. Avocations: writing, editing, gardening, crafts and doll collecting. Home: 6330 Blackberry Ct Gilroy CA 95020

KATHER, GERHARD, retired air force base administrator; b. Allenstein, Germany, Jan. 30, 1939; came to U.S., 1952, naturalized, 1959; s. Ernst and Maria (Kempa) K.; m. Carol Anne Knutsen, Aug. 18, 1962; children: Scott T., Cynthia M., Tracey S., Chris A.; m. Mary Elsie Frank, Oct. 25, 1980. BA in Govt., U. Ariz., 1964; MPA, U. So. Calif., 1971; cert. in personnel adminstrn., U. N.Mex., 1987. Tchr. social studies, Covina, Calif., 1965-67; tng. officer Civil Personnel, Ft. MacArthur, Calif., 1967-70; chief employee tng. and devel. Corps Engrs., L.A., 1970-72; chief employee tng. and devel. Frankfurt Area Army Personnel Office, 1972-73; chief employee rels. and tng. brs. Corps Engrs., L.A., 1973-74; chief employee devel. and tng. Kirtland AFB, N.Mex., 1974-87; labor relations officer, Kirtland AFB and detachments in 13 U.S. cities, 1987-90; project coord., adv. Protection and Advocacy System, 1991-96, ret., 1996. Mem. adv. com. Albuquerque Tech.-Vocat. Inst., 1982-92, U. N.Mex. Valencia Campus, 1985-92; mem. Coalition for Disability Rights, 1988-96; chmn. Comprehensive Accessibility Network, 1990-96; adv. coun. N.Mex. Disability Prevention, 1992-96; recording sec. N.Mex. Commn. Blind State Rehab. Adv. Coun., 1993-96. Served with USAF, 1958-64. Named Prominent Tng. and Devel. Profl., H. Whitney McMillan Co., 1984; Outstanding Handicapped Fed. Employee of Yr., all fed. agys., 1984; recipient Govt. Employees Ins. Co. GEICO Pub. Svc. award for work in phys. rehab., 1988. Mem. Am. Soc. Tng. and Devel. (treas. chpt. 1984-85), Paralyzed Vets. Am. (bd. dirs. 1986-87, pres. local chpt. 1986-87, 1990-92), Toastmasters Internat. (chpt. treas., v.p., pres. 1967-70), Vietnam Vets. of Am., Phi Delta Kappa. Democrat. Roman Catholic. Office: 1720 Louisiana Blvd NE Ste 204 Albuquerque NM 87110-7070

KATHKA, DAVID ARLIN, director educational services; b. Columbus, Nebr.; s. Arlin Arthur and Edith Ferne (Wilcox) K.; m. Anne Condon Butler, Aug. 15, 1965. BA, Wayne (Nebr.) State Coll., 1964, MA, 1966; PhD in History, U. Mo., 1976. Tchr. Ravenna (Nebr.) Pub. Schs., 1964-65; instr. Midwestern Coll., Denison, Iowa, 1966-68; prof. history Western Wyo. Coll., Rock Springs, 1972-87, dean acad. affairs, 1980-84, interim pres., 1984-85, v.p. acad. affairs, 1985-87; dir. State Pks. and Cultural Resources Divsn., State of Wyo., Cheyenne, 1987-94, Sweetwater Bd. Coop. Ednl. Svcs., Wyo., 1994—; adj. prof. U. Wyo., Laramie, 1976—, adj. prof. history Western Wyo. Coll., 1996—; vis. instr. U. Mo., St. Louis, 1971-72; cons. various Wyo. govt. agys.; mem. gov.'s Blue ribbon Task Force on Cultural Resources, Wyo. Trails adv. com. Author hist. papers; contbr. hist. articles to mags. Bd. dirs. Sweetwater Mus. Found., Wyo. Territorial Park, 1987-94, Tracks Across Wyo., Wyo. Hist. Found., Rock Springs Area Cmty. Found.; mem. Wyo. Centennial Commn., 1986-87, Rock Springs Libr. Bd.,1 984-87, Gov.'s Com. on Hist. Preservation, 1982; v.p. Rocky Mountain Region Kidney Found., Denver, 1976-77. Recipient Wyo. Humanities award for exemplary svc., 1990. Mem. Orgn. Am. Historians, Wyo. State Hist. Soc. (pres. 1984-85), Wyo. Assn. Profl. Historians (v.p. 1994-96, pres. 1996-97). Democrat. Office: Sweetwater Bd Coop Ednl Svcs PO Box 428 Rock Springs WY 82902-0428

KATHOL, ANTHONY LOUIS, finance executive; b. San Diego, June 12, 1964; s. Cletus Louis and Regina Antoinette (Ellrott) K.; m. Kathleen Marie Moore, Jan. 23, 1988; children: Nicole Kathleen, Natalie Antoinette, Holly Rose. BS, U. So. Calif., 1986; MBA, U. San Diego, 1988. Fin. aid analyst U. San Diego, 1986-87; bookkeeper Golden Lion Tavern, San Diego, 1987-88; fin. and budget coord. Santa Fe Pacific Realty Corp. (name now Catellus Devel. Corp.), Brea, Calif., 1988-91; mgr. fin. analysis SW U.S. Catellus Devel. Corp., Anaheim, Calif., 1992-93; mgr. leasing Pacific Design Ctr., West Hollywood, Calif., 1994-95, dir. fin. and policy, 1995-96, v.p. asset mgmt., 1996-97; project mgr. Spieker Properties, Orange, Calif., 1997—. Calif. Bldg. Industry Assn. fellow, 1986, U. San Diego fellow, 1987. Mem. U. San Diego Grad. Bus. Students Assn., K.C. (fin. sec. 1990-91), Tau Kappa Epsilon. Republican. Roman Catholic. Avocations: Civil War history, collecting commerative plates and coins, reading, basketball, golf. Home: 3805 Maxon Ln Chino CA 91710-2073 Office: Spieker Properties 1 City Blvd W Ste 102 Orange CA 92868-3692

KATO, BRUCE, curator. Chief curator Alaska State Mus., Juneau, 1987—. Office: Alaska State Mus 395 Whittier St Juneau AK 99801-1718*

KATRAK, KETU, English literature educator. BA in English, U. Bombay, India, 1973; MA in English, Bryn Mawr Coll., 1977, PhD in English, 1982. Lectr./rschr. Afro-Am. studies and English Yale U., New Haven, 1982-84; asst. prof. English Howard U., 1984-86; asst. prof. English U. Mass., Amherst, 1986-89, assoc. prof. English, 1989-93, prof. English, 1993-96; faculty advisor Oxford Summer Program at Trinity Coll. U. Mass., summer 1990; dir. Asian-Am. Studies, prof. English and Comparative Literature U. Calif., Irvine, 1996—; vis. assoc. prof. English, UCLA, 1991; book manuscript reviewer Columbia U. Press, Macmillan, U. Minn. Press, Oxford U. Press, W.W. Norton; lectr. in field. Author: Wole Soyinka and Modern Tragedy: A Study of dramatic Theory and Practice, 1986; co-editor: Wole Soyinka: A Bibliography of Primary and Secondary Sources, 1986; adv. bd. African Am. Rev.; adv. editor Internat. Jour. African Hist. Studies, 1986—; manuscript reviewer Pub. of MLA, Coll. English, Rsch. in African Lit., Genders, African Am. Rev.; contbr. articles to profl. jours. Recipient Chancellor's Award for Multiculturalism, U. Mass., 1993; Bunting fellow, 1988-89; U. Mass. Faculty Rsch. grantee, 1991-92, 92-93, Five-Coll. Asian Am. Studies Com. Faculty Rsch. grantee, summer 1992. Mem. MLA (commn. on status of women in the profession 1988-91, co-chair 1990-91, exec. com. divsn. comparative studies in 20th century lit. 1990-94, com. langs. and literatures of Am. 1998—), African Lit. Assn. (exec. coun. 1991-95). Office: U of CA HIB 207 Asian Am Studies Irvine CA 92697

KATZ, ALAN ROY, public health educator; b. Pitts., Aug. 21, 1954; s. Leon B. and Bernice Sonia (Glass) K.; m. Donna Marie Crandall, Jan. 19, 1986; 1 child, Sarah Elizabeth. BA, U. Calif., San Diego, 1976; MD, U. Calif., Irvine, 1980; MPH, U. Hawaii, 1987; postgrad., U. So. Calif., 1980-81, U. Hawaii, 1982-83. Staff physician emergency medicine L.A. County U. So. Calif. Med. Ctr., 1981-82; staff physician, med. dir. Waikiki Health Ctr., Honolulu, 1983-87; dir. AIDS/STD prevention program Hawaii State Dept. of Health, Honolulu, 1987-88; asst. prof. dept. pub. health scis. U. Hawaii, Honolulu, 1988-94, assoc. prof., 1994—, dir. preventive medicine residency program, 1994—; bd. dirs. Hawaii AIDS Task Group; mem. Chlamydia control workgroup USPHS, 1985-87, sci. adv. bd. Hawaii AIDS Clin. Trials Rsch. Program; staff physician, lab. dir. Diamond Head STD Clinic, Hawaii State Dept. Health, 1998—. Contbr. articles to profl. jours. Me. Leptospirosis ad hoc com. Hawaii State Dept. Health, Honolulu, 1988—, mem. prenatal screening adv. com., 1992—; mem. com. human subjects U. Hawaii, 1989—. USPHS Chlamydia Prevalence Survey grantee, Hawaii, 1986, Tuberculosis Survey grantee U. Hawaii, 1991; recipient presdl. citation for meritorious teaching, U. Hawaii, 1989, regents medal excellence in teaching U. Hawaii, 1992. Fellow Am. Coll. Preventive Medicine; mem. Am. Pub. Health Assn., Soc. Epidemiologic Rsch., Delta Omega. Office: U Hawaii Sch Pub Health Dept Pub Health Sci 1960 E West Rd Honolulu HI 96822-2319

KATZ, BARRY ROBERT, illustrator, graphics designer, urban planner; b. Bklyn., Jan. 13, 1951; s. Louis and Estelle (Lefkowitz) K.; children: Rachel, Jacob. BS in Urban Planning, Calif. Poly. State U., 1971; MA in Architecture and Urban Planning, UCLA, 1978. City planner City of L.A., Manhattan beach, City of West Hollywood, Calif., 1973-85; planning assoc. Engring. Tech., L.A., 1976-79; transp. planner Plantech, L.A., 1979-83; land planner Bohannon-Houston, N.Mex., 1980-83; chief planner Pueblo of Acoma, N.Mex., 1980-83; archtl. planner Archiplan, L.A., 1982-83; transp. cons. Ryan Snyder Assocs., L.A., 1985-86; artist, graphics designer, illustrator Zeroscape Graphics, L.A., 1995—. Co-author: (rsch. book) The Arts in the Economic Life of the City, 1979; animator: (animated short) Digital Reel Estate, 1998, others. Commr. County of L.A. Rent Stabilization Commn., 1979. Mem. SIGGRAPH, ASIFA, Disabled Am. Vets. Democrat. Jewish. Avocations: N-scale model trains, black and white photography, bicycling, ornamental horticulture. Office: Zeroscape Graphics PO Box 480212 Los Angeles CA 90048-1212

KATZ, CHARLES J., JR., lawyer; b. San Antonio, Mar. 25, 1948. AB, Stanford U., 1969; MA, N.Y.U., 1973; JD, U. Tex., 1976. Book review editor Tex. Law Review, 1975-76; mem. Perkins Coie, Seattle, 1982. Mem. Order of the Coif. Office: Perkins Coie 1201 3rd Ave Fl 40 Seattle WA 98101-3099*

KATZ, ILLANA PAULETTE, writer; b. N.Y.C., May 30, 1946; d. Emanuel and Alice (Reich) Schear; m. David Arthur Katz, July 31, 1966; children: Heather, Todd, Ethan, Seth. BA in Anthropology summa cum laude, Calif. State U., 1977, postgrad. Owner, pres., pub. Real Life Storybooks, West Hills, Calif., 1992—; social facilitation cons. Yellen and Assoc., Inc., Granada Hills, Calif., 1996—; mini-course instr. L.A. Unified Sch. Dist., 1985, 93; lectr. State Autism Conv., 1994, Nat. Autism Conv., 1994. Author: Joey and Sam, 1993 (award 1994), Show Me Where It Hurts, 1993, Uncle Jimmy, 1994, Sarah, 1994, Hungry Mind-Hungry Body, 1995; (audiocassette) Was Einstein Autistic?, 1994. Head of Israeli affairs United Synagogue, Beverly Hills, 1988; aliyah councelor Jewish Fedn., L.A., 1991—. Recipient Book Publicists Assn. award for Excellence in Book Publicity, 1997. Mem. Authors and Celebrities Forum (award of excellence 1994), Soc. of Children's Book Writers, Book Publicists Assn. (nominated non-fiction children's book award, 1996), Pub. Mktg. Assn. Avocations: camping, hiking. Home and Office: 8370 Kentland Ave West Hills CA 91304-3329

KATZ, JERRY PAUL, corporate executive; b. L.A., Jan. 24, 1944; s. Samuel and Dorothy Rose (Solovay) K.; m. Judy Simmering, Sept. 10, 1985 (div. 1988); m. Julie Stacey, Aug. 26, 1990; 1 child, Brandon Louis. AA, East L.A. Coll., 1964; BS, BA, Calif. State U., 1970. Registered sanitarian, Calif. Sanitarian L.A. County Health Dept., L.A., 1971-73; dir. Compton (Calif.) Model Cities Vector Control, 1973-74; health officer Lynwood (Calif.) City, 1974-76; pres., chief exec. officer Associated Industries, L.A., 1976—; cons., bd. dirs. All Am. Fire Protection, L.A., 1987—. Founding mem. Moore St. Homeowners Assn., Monterey Park, Calif., 1989—; mem. Nature Conservancy, World Wildlife Fund. Recipient World Record (2) hang gliding Nat. Assn. Aeronautics, 1977; named for Distance-Altitude Gain, Guinness Book of World Records, London, 1977. Mem. Native Am. Rights Fund, Green Peace, Surfrider Found., U.S. Hangliding Assn., Sea Shepard Soc. Avocations: surfing, skiing, flying, mountain bike riding, sailing. Office: Associated Industries 5140 Via Corona St Los Angeles CA 90022-2007

KATZ, JONATHAN DAVID, academic administrator; b. St. Louis, Oct. 19, 1958; s. Berl and Joan Reva (Rosen) K. BA, George Washington U., 1981; MA, U. Chgo., 1986; PhD, Northwestern U., 1995. Mem. faculty gay and lesbian studies City Coll. San Francisco, 1991-95, chair dept. gay and lesbian studies, 1995—. Author: Andy Warhol, 1993, Difference/Indifference, 1997; contbr. numerous articles to profl. jours. Founder Gay/ Lesbian Town Meeting, Chgo., 1987; co-founder Queer Nation, San Francisco, 1990; founder, chmn. bd. Harvey Milk Inst., 1994; bd. mem. Queer Cultural Ctr. Fellow Smithsonian Inst., Washington, 1989-90. Democrat. Jewish. Home: 979 S Van Ness Ave San Francisco CA 94110-2613 Office: City Coll San Francisco Box 469 50 Phelan Ave San Francisco CA 94112-1821

KATZ, LEON, theatre and drama educator; b. Bronx, N.Y., July 10, 1919; s. Bernard and Rachel (Koslow) K.; children: Elia, Fredric. B.S.S., CCNY, 1940; M.A., Columbia U., 1946, Ph.D., 1962. Instr. Cornell U., 1946-47, Hunter Coll., N.Y.C., 1947-49; asst. prof. Vassar Coll., 1949-58; lectr. Columbia, 1958-60; assoc. prof. Manhattanville Coll., Purchase, N.Y., 1960-64; vis. assoc. prof. Stanford, 1964-65; prof. San Francisco State Coll., 1965-68; Andrew Mellon vis. prof. Carnegie-Mellon U., Pitts., 1968-69; prof. drama dept. Carnegie-Mellon U., 1969-77; prof. dept. speech and theater arts U. Pitts., 1977-81; prof. Yale U., 1981-89, prof. emeritus, 1989—; resident dramaturg Mark Taper Forum, L.A., 1990-92; vis. prof. Theater and Film Dept. UCLA, 1991—. drama critic, sta. WQED-TV, San Francisco, 1966-68; film critic syndicated on radio, 1970-72; playwright TV writer; Author: plays Three Cuckolds, 1958, Dracula: Sabbat, 1972, Making of Americans, 1973, Astapovo, 1982, Odyssey, 1986, The Greek Myths, 1987, Midnight Plays, 1992, GBS in Love, 1995, Dear Bosie, 1996, Pinocchio, 1996; TV dramas Confrontation, 1969; Necessity, 1972; co-editor: QED and Other Early Writings by Gertrude Stein, 1970. Co-dir. N.Y. Writers Workshop; curator Am. Theatre Collection. Served to capt. USAAF, 1942-46. Nat. Endowment for Humanities Research grantee, 1972-73; Ford Found. fellow, 1952-53. Mem. AAUP, AFTRA, Actors Equity, Authors Guild, Dramatists Guild. Jewish. Home: 8343 Holy Cross Pl Los Angeles CA 90045-2632

KATZ, LEW, advertising executive. Dir. finance Team One Advertising, El Segundo, Calif. Office: Team One Advertising 1960 E Grand Ave Ste 700 El Segundo CA 90245-5059*

KATZ, ROBERT IRWIN, retired physician; b. Springfield, Mass., Dec. 16, 1924; s. Julius Louis and Florence (Greenburg) K. Student, Tufts Coll., 1942-44; MD, Tufts U., 1948. Diplomate Am. Bd. Surgery, Am. Bd. Thoracic Surgery, Nat. Bd. Med. Examiners. Intern Charity Hosp. of La., New Orleans, 1948-49, resident in pathology, 1949-50; resident in gen. surgery Boston City Hosp., 1953-56; asst. in surgery Boston U. Sch. Medicine, 1955-56; resident in surg. oncology Anderson Cancer Ctr. U. Tex., Houston, 1956-57; resident in thoracic surgery VA Hosp., L.A., 1960-61, Children's Hosp., L.A., 1961; chief thoracic surgery V.A. Hosps., Sepulveda/ San Fernando, Calif., 1962-70; pvt. practice gen. and thoracic surgery L.A., 1970-86; head gen. surgery Naval Hosp., Corpus Christie, Tex., 1987; head dept. surgery Naval Hosp., Cherry Point, N.C., 1988-90; surgeon USS New Jersey WES PAC, 1986, 88; ret., 1990; clin. asst. prof. UCLA Med. Ctr., 1969-89, U. So. Calif., L.A., 1964-96. Contbr. articles to profl. jours. Tournament ofcl. So. Calif. Tennis Umpires Assn., L.A., 1972—; commr. Med. Bd. of Calif., Sacramento, 1980—. With USN, 1944-45, surgeon USMC, 1950-52, US Merchant Marines, 1953. Recipient clin. fellowship Am. Cancer Soc., Houston, 1957-58. Fellow Am. Coll. Chest Physicians; mem. AAAS, AMA, Soc. Thoracic Surgeons (founding), So. Med. Assn., So. Assn. Oncologists, Assn. Mil. Surgeons U.S., Marine Corps Heritage Soc., 2nd Marines Divsn. Assn. (life), Nat. Wildlife Fedn. (life), USTA (life), Naval Res. Assn., M.D. Anderson Assocs. Republican. Jewish. Avocations: tennis, physical fitness. Home and Office: 1733 Centinela Ave Santa Monica CA 90404-4238

KATZ, ROGER, pediatrician, educator; b. Menominee, Mich., Feb. 23, 1938; s. Peter W. and Mae C. (Chudacoff) K.; m. Barbara Morguelan, Feb. 6, 1966; children: Carl, Gary, Robyn. BS, U. Wis., 1960; MD, U. Louisville, 1965. Diplomate Am. Bd. Allergy and Immunology, Am. Bd. Pediatric Allergy, Am. Bd. Pediatrics. Clin. prof. pediatrics UCLA, 1978—; spkr. in field; expert legal evaluator. Author and editor sci. books and manuscripts. Maj. U.S. Army, 1970-72. Named 1 of Best Drs. in Am., 1996, 97. Fellow Am. Acad. Allergy, Asthma and Immunology, Am. Coll. Allergy, Asthma and Immunology (bd. regents 1990-93), Am. Acad. Pediat., Am. Coll. Chest Physicians, Joint Coun. Allergy, Asthma and Immunology (pres. 1986-90). Office: UCLA Med Ctr 100 Ucla Medical Plz Ste 550 Los Angeles CA 90024-6990

KATZ, STEVE ROBERT, novelist, poet, educator; b. N.Y.C., May 14, 1935; s. Alexander and Sally (Goldstein) K.; m. Patricia Oliver Bell, June 2, 1956 (div.); children: Avrum, Nikolai, Rafael. AB, Cornell U., 1956; MA, U. Oreg., 1959. Lectr. fiction U. Iowa, Iowa City, 1969-70; writer in residence Bklyn. Coll., N.Y.C., 1970-71; adj. asst. prof. Queens Coll., N.Y.C., 1971-75; assoc. prof. U. Notre Dame, South Bend, Ind., 1976-78; prof. English and creative writing U. Colo., Boulder, 1978—; adv. bd. Am. Book Rev., Normal, Ill., 1990—. Author: (novel) The Exagggerations of Peter Prince, 1968, SAW, 1972, Wier V Pouce, 1990, Swanny's Ways, 1995 (Am. award 1995); mem. editl. bd. Fiction Collective, 1974-80. Mem. PEN, Writers Guild, Tan Shou You. Avocations: internal martial arts. Home: 669 Washington St Apt 602 Denver CO 80203-3837 Office: U Colo Dept English PO Box 226 Boulder CO 80309-0226

KATZ, TONNIE, newspaper editor. BA, Barnard Coll., 1966; MSc, Columbia U., 1967. Editor, reporter newspapers including The Quincy Patriot Ledger, Boston Herald Am., Boston Globe; Sunday/projects editor Newsday; mng. editor Balt. News Am., 1983-86, The Sun, San Bernardino, Calif., 1986-88; asst. mng. editor for news The Orange County Register, Santa Ana, Calif., 1988-89, mng. editor, 1989-92, editor, v.p., 1992-98, editor, sr. v.p., 1998—. Office: Freedom Newspapers Inc Orange County Register 625 N Grand Ave Santa Ana CA 92701-4347*

KATZ, VERA, mayor, former college administrator, state legislator; b. Dusseldorf, Germany, Aug. 3, 1933; came to U.S., 1940; d. Lazar Pistrak and Raissa Goodman; m. Mel Katz (div. 1985); 1 child, Jesse. BA, Bklyn. Coll., 1955, postgrad., 1955-57. Market research analyst TIMEX, B.T. Babbitt, N.Y.C., 1957-62; mem. Oreg. Ho. of Reps., Salem; former dir. devel. Portland Community Coll., from 1982; mayor City of Portland, Oreg., 1993—; mem. Gov.'s Council on Alcohol and Drug Abuse Programs, Oreg. Legis., Salem, 1985—; mem. adv. com. Gov.'s Council on Health, Fitness and Sports, Oreg. Legis., 1985—; mem. Gov.'s Commn. on Sch. Funding Reform; mem. Carnegie task Force on Teaching as Profession, Washington, 1985-87; vice-chair assembly Nat. Conf. State Legis., Denver, 1986—. Recipient Abigail Scott Duniway award Women in Communications, Inc., Portland, 1985, Jeanette Rankin First Woman award Oreg. Women's Polit. Caucus, Portland, 1985, Leadership award The Neighborhood newspaper Portland, 1985, Woman of Achievement award Commn. for Women, 1985, Outstanding Legis. Advocacy award Oreg. Primary Care Assn., 1985, Service to Portland Pub. Sch. Children award Portland Pub. Schs., 1985. Fellow Am. Leadership Forum (founder Oreg. chpt.); mem. Dem. Legis. Leaders Assn., Nat. Bd. for Profl. Teaching Standards. Democrat. Jewish. Avocations: camping, jogging, dancing. Office: Office of the Mayor City Hall 1220 SW 5th Ave Rm 303 Portland OR 97204-1909*

KATZEN, MOLLIE, writer, artist; b. Rochester, N.Y., Oct. 13, 1950; d. Leon and Betty (Heller) K.; m. Jeffrey David Black, June 26, 1983 (div. Oct. 1985); 1 child, Samuel Katzen Black; m. Carl Shames, Dec. 12, 1986. BFA, San Francisco Art Inst., 1972. Author, illustrator: Mossewood Cookbook, 1977, Enchanted Broccoli Forest, 1982, Still Life with Menu, 1988, Molly Katzen's Still Life Sampler, 1993, Pretend Soup & Other Real Recipes: A Cookbook for Preschoolers & Up, 1994, Enchanted Broccoli Forest, 1995, Moosewood Cookbook Classics: Miniature Edition, 1996. Recipient Graphic Arts award Arnot Art Gallery, 1976, Cert. of Commendation, Calif. State Assembly, 1989. Jewish. Avocations: classical pianist, painter. Office: care Ten Speed Press PO Box 7123 Berkeley CA 94707-0123*

KATZIN, CAROLYN F., nutritionist, consultant; b. London, July 21, 1946; came to U.S., 1983; d. John Mourier and Shelagh B. A. (Tighe) Lade; m. Anthony Arthur Speelman, Mar. 18, 1968 (div. Dec. 1984); 1 child, Zara Jane; m. David Brandeis Katzin. BS with honors, U. London, 1983; MS in Pub. Health, UCLA, 1987. Nutritionist L.A., 1985—; cons. HerbaLife Internat., L.A., 1986—; mem. dean's adv. bd. UCLA Sch. Pub. Health, 1997—; dir. Jonsson Comprehensive Cancer Ctr. Found., UCLA, 1998—; mem. adv. bd. The Wellness Consultancy, L.A.; pres.-elect Am. Cancer Soc., L.A., 1998. Author: (books) The Advanced Energy Guide, 1994, The Good Eating Guide and Cookbook, 1996. Democrat. Jewish. Office: 12011 San Vicente Blvd Ste 402 Los Angeles CA 90049-4946

KATZUNG, BERTRAM GEORGE, pharmacologist; b. Mineola, N.Y., June 11, 1932; m. Alice V. Camp; children: Katharine Blanche, Brian Lee. BA, Syracuse U., 1953; MD, SUNY, Syracuse, 1957; PhD, U. Calif., San Francisco, 1962. Prof. U. Calif., San Francisco, 1958—. Author: Drug Therapy, 1991, Basic and Clinical Pharmacology, 1997, Pharmacology, Examination and Board Review, 1998; contbr. to profl. jours. Markle scholar. Mem. AAAS, AAUP, Am. Soc. Pharmacology and Exptl. Therapeutics, Biophysical Soc., Fed. Am. Scientists, Internat. Soc. Heart Rsch., Soc. Gen. Physiologists, Western Pharmacology Soc., N.Y. Acad. Sci., Phi Beta Kappa, Alpha Omega Alpha, Golden Gate Computer Soc. Office: U Calif San Francisco Dept Cellular/Molec Pharm PO Box 0450 San Francisco CA 94143

KAUFER, SHIRLEY HELEN, artist; b. Bklyn., Oct. 3, 1920; m. Bernard Goldberg, Apr. 18, 1943; children: Alice Jay, Marjorie Vivian. Student, Pratt Inst., 1938-39, Bklyn. Mus., Art Students League, N.Y.C. Art dir. Advt. Agys., N.Y.C., 1938-63; cons. N.Y.C., 1964-73; sculptor Vero Beach, Fla., 1973-77; graphic designer Jewish Fedn. Coun., L.A., 1977-82; with Haystack Mountain Sch., Deer Isle, Maine, summers 1959-65; instr. advt., design, illustration Pels Art Sch., N.Y.C., 1968-71; instr. painting Indian River C.C., Vero Beach, 1973-77. Home: 1029 Via De La Paz Pacific Palisades CA 90272-3536

KAUFMAN, ALBERT I., lawyer; b. N.Y.C., Oct. 2, 1936; s. Israel and Pauline (Pardes) K.; m. Ruth Feldman, Jan. 25, 1959; 1 son, Michael Paul. AA, L.A. City Coll., 1957, BA, U. San Fernando Valley, 1964, JD, 1966. Bar: Calif. 1967, U.S. Ct. Appeals (9th cir.) 1968, U.S. Supreme Ct. 1971, U.S. Dist. Ct. (cen. dist.) Calif. 1967, U.S. Tax Ct. 1971, U.S. Ct. Internat. Trade 1981. Sole practice, Encino, Calif., 1967—; judge pro tem L.A. Mcpl. Ct., 1980—, L.A. Superior Ct., 1991—; family law mediator L.A. Superior Ct., 1980—. Mem. Pacific S.W. regional bd. Anti-Defamation league of B'nai B'rith, 1970-91. Served with USAF, 1959-65, to col. CAP, 1956—. Recipient Disting. Svc. award B'nai B'rith, 1969; Exceptional Svc. award CAP, 1977, 95. Mem. ABA, L.A. County Bar Assn., San Fernando Valley Bar Assn., Consumer Atty. of Calif., Consumer Atty. Assn. L.A. Republican. Clubs: Toastmasters, Westerners 1117 (pres. 1969), B'nai B'rith (pres. 1971-72), Santa Monica Yacht (judge adv.) Office: 17609 Ventura Blvd Ste 201 Encino CA 91316-3825

KAUFMAN, CHARLES DAVID, controller; b. N.Y.C., Apr. 17, 1931; s. M. Laurence and Anna (Goldberg) K.; m. Elvira Sampere Camps, Mar. 1, 1955; children: John, Janet. BS, Northwestern U., 1952; MBA, NYU, 1958. CPA, N.Y. Fin. analyst Nestle Co., Stamford, Conn., 1958-61; area contr. IBM World Trade Corp., Mexico City, 1967-69; dir. fin. controls ITT Corp., Brussels and N.Y.C., 1974-85, controller's dept., 1985-94; ret., 1994. Bd. dirs. Scottsdale League for The Arts, Valley Acad.; vol. cons. Exec. Svc. Corps Ariz., Svc. Corps Ret. Execs. Cpl. U.S. Army, 1952-54. Mem. AICPAs, N.Y. Soc. CPAs, Ariz. Soc. CPAs.

KAUFMAN, CHARLOTTE KING, artist, retired educational administrator; b. Balt., Dec. 5, 1920; d. Ben and Belle (Turow) King; A.B., Goucher Coll., 1969; M.P.H., Johns Hopkins U., 1972, M.Ed., 1976; m. Albert Kaufman, July 22, 1945; children—Matthew King, Ezra King. Dir. public relations Balt. Jewish Community Center, 1962-67; research and editor Johns Hopkins U. Sch. Hygiene and Public Health, Balt., 1969-72, admissions officer, 1972-74, dir. admissions and registrar, 1974-86, dir. study cons. program undergraduates, 1986-89, pub. health acad. adviser, 1989-95. Mem. Am. Pub. Health Assn., Am. Assn. for Higher Edn., Am. Assn. Collegiate Registrars and Admissions Officers, Artists Equity Assn. (v.p. Md. chpt. 1988-90), Md. Printmakers (exec. bd. 1989-94), Palm Springs Desert Mus. Artists Coun. (exec. bd. 1997—), Delta Omega. Democrat. Jewish. Home: Monterey Country Club 159 Las Lomas Palm Desert CA 92260-2153

KAUFMAN, DAVID GRAHAM, construction company executive; b. North Canton, Ohio, Mar. 20, 1937; s. DeVere and Josephine Grace (Graham) K.; student Kent State U., 1956; grad. Internat. Corr. Schs., 1965; grad. N.Y. Inst. Photography, 1983; postgrad. Calif. Coast U.; m. Carol Jean Monzione, Oct. 5, 1957 (div. Aug. 1980); children—Gregory Allan, Christopher Patrick. Cert. constrn. insp.; cert. constrn. project mgr.; cert asbestos insp.; cert. lead insp.; cert. asbestos project designer; cert. lock-out/tag-out. Machinist apprentice Hoover Co., North Canton, Ohio, 1955-57; draftsman-designer Goodyear Aircraft Corp., Akron, Ohio, 1957-60, Boeing Co., Seattle, 1960-61; designer Berger Industries, Seattle, 1961-62, Puget Sound Bridge & Drydock, Seattle, 1963, C.M. Lovsted, Seattle, 1963-64, Tracy, Brunstrom & Dudley, Seattle, 1964, Rubens & Pratt Engrs., Seattle, 1965-66; founder, owner, Profl. Drafting Svcs., Seattle, 1965, Profl. Take-Off Svcs., Seattle, 1966, Profl. Representation Svcs., Seattle, 1967, pres. Kaufman Inc., Seattle, 1967-83, Kaufman-Alaska Inc., Juneau, 1975-83, Kaufman-Alaska Constructors, Inc., Juneau, 1975-83. Trustee, advisor Kaufman Internat., The Kaufman Group, Kaufman Enterprises; constrn. mgr. U. Alaska, 1979-84; constrn. cons. Alaskan native and Eskimo village corps., 1984—; prin.

Kaufman S.W. Assocs., N. Mex., 1984—, Graham Internat., 1992—. Mem. Constrn. Specifications Inst., Assn. Constrn. Insps., Associated Gen. Contractors Seattle Constrn. Coun., Producers Coun. Oreg., Wash., Idaho, Hawaii, Alaska, Portland C. of C., Nat. Eagle Scout Assn., Toastmasters (past gov.), Lions. Republican. Roman Catholic. Home: PO Box 1781 Santa Fe NM 87504-1781 Office: PO Box 458 Haines AK 99827-0458

KAUFMAN, HERBERT MARK, finance educator; b. Bronx, N.Y., Nov. 1, 1946; s. Henry and Betty (Fried) K.; m. Helen Laurie Fox, July 23, 1967; 1 child, Jonathan Hart. BA, SUNY, Binghamton, 1967; PhD, Pa. State U., 1972. Economist Fed. Nat. Mortgage Assn., Washington, 1972-73; asst. prof. Ariz. State U., Tempe, 1973-76; econs. prof. Ariz. State U., 1980-88; fin. prof. Ariz. State U., Tempe, 1988—, chair dept. fin., 1991—; exec. dir. Ctr. for Fin. System Ariz. State U., 1988—; cons. World Bank, Washington, 1985-86, Gen. Acctg. Office, Washington, 1985, Congl. Budget Office, Washington, 1980, N.Y. Stock Exch., 1995—. Author: Financial Markets, Financial Institutions and Money, 1983, (with others) The Political Economy of Policy Making, 1979, Money and Banking, 1991; contbr. articles to profl. jours. Mem. Am. Econ. Assn., Am. Fin. Assn., Nat. Assn. of Bus. Economists. Avocations: tennis, piano. Home: 1847 E Calle De Caballos Tempe AZ 85284-2505 Office: Ariz State U Dept Fin Tempe AZ 85287

KAUFMAN, JEFF, television producer; b. Los Angeles, Aug. 22, 1960; s. Richard and Lois K. BA in History, Journalism, U. So. Calif., 1982. News prodr., writer Sta. KIIS, L.A., 1980-82; news editor, prodr. Sta. KFWB all news radio, L.A., 1980-84; news dir. Sta. K-NEWS all news radio, Anaheim, Calif., 1983; news reporter, anchor Sta. KJCT-TV, Grand Junction, Colo., 1984-86; news prodr. Sta. KCNC-TV, Denver, 1986-89, Sta. KTTV-TV, L.A., 1989, Sta. KCAL-TV, L.A., 1990-94; exec. news prodr. Sta. KNBC-TV, L.A., 1994-95; prodr. Entertainment Tonight, L.A., 1995—; sr. lectr. U. So. Calif. Sch. of Journalism, L.A., 1993-95; mem., bd. dirs. Assoc. Press TV-Radio Assn. of Calif., 1993-95. Recipient 5 Emmy awards L.A., Colo. chpts. of TV Acad., 1987, 88, 92, 93, 96, Golden Mike awards Radio & TV News Assn. of So. Calif., 1992, 93, best newscast awards L.A. Press Club, 1984, 94, AP TV-Radio Assn. of Calif., 1994. Office: Entertainment Tonight 5555 Melrose Ave Los Angeles CA 90038-3112

KAUFMAN, JONATHAN ALLAN (JON), public relations executive; b. N.Y.C., May 31, 1943; s. Stephen Allan (dec.) and Jean (Friedman) K.; m. Jill J. Horowitz, July 17, 1983. BA, Carleton Coll., 1966; MA, Syracuse U., 1967. Vol. VISTA, N.Y.C., 1967-69; rsch. dir. Nat. Welfare Rights Orgn., Washington, 1969-71; polit. campaign mgr. various, San Francisco, 1971-77; exec. dir. Calif. Tax Reform Assn., San Francisco, 1972-77; asst. mgr. Household Fin. Corp., San Francisco, 1977-79; account exec. Solem & Assocs., San Francisco, 1979-84, v.p., 1984-86, exec. v.p., 1986—. Contbr. articles to profl. jours. Bd. dirs. Ann Martin Children's Ctr., Oakland, Calif., Am. Israel Pub. Affairs Com. of No. Calif., San Francisco; chmn. com. mktg. Jewish Fedn. Greater East Bay. Andrew W. Mellon Fellow, Syracuse U., 1966, Max Bondy Citizenship award Windsor Mt. Sch., Lenox, Mass., 1962. Mem. Am. Assn. Polit. Cons., Am. Mktg. Assn. Jewish. Avocations: hiking, travel, food. E-mail: jonúkaufman@solem.com. Home: 107 Alvarado Rd Berkeley CA 94705-1510 Office: Solem & Assocs 550 Kearny St Ste 1010 San Francisco CA 94108-2527

KAUFMAN, JULIAN MORTIMER, broadcasting company executive, consultant; b. Detroit, Apr. 3, 1918; s. Anton and Fannie (Newman) K.; m. Katherine LaVerne Likins, May 6, 1942; children: Nikki, Keith Anthony. Grad. high sch., Newark. Pub. Elizabeth (N.J.) Sunday Sun, Inc., 1937-39; account exec. Tolle Advt. Agy., San Diego, 1947-49; pub. Tucson Shopper, 1948-50; account exec. ABC, San Francisco, 1949-50; mgr. Sta. KPHO-TV, Phoenix, 1950-52; gen. mgr., v.p. Bay City TV Corp., San Diego, 1952-85; v.p. Jai Alai Films, Inc., San Diego, 1961—; TV cons. Julian Kaufman, Inc., San Diego, 1985—; dir. Spanish Internat. Broadcasting, Inc., L.A.; chmn. bd. dirs. Bay City TV Inc. Contbr. articles to profl. jours.; producer (TV show) Pick a Winner. Mem. Gov.'s adv. bd., Mental Health Assn., 1958—; bd. dirs. Francis Parker Sch., San Diego Better Bus. Bur., 1979-84, San Diego Conv. and Visitors Bur., World Affairs Coun., Pala Indian Mission. Served with USAAF, 1942-46. Recipient Peabody award, 1975, Emmy award, 1980. Mem. San Diego C. of C., Advt. and Sales Club, Sigma Delta Chi. Republican. Clubs: San Diego Press, University (San Diego). Home: 3125 Montesano Rd Escondido CA 92029-7302 Office: 7677 Ronson Rd Ste 210 San Diego CA 92111-1538

KAUFMAN, LINDA SCOTT, interior designer; b. Tulsa, Mar. 31, 1942; d. Raymond R. and Wilma L. Scott; m. James Kaufman, June 13, 1981; children: Leslie, Kristen. BS, U. Mo., 1964. Designer Green Baum Bros., N.J., 1976-79; sr. designer Joyce Kwynn Inc., Dallas, 1979-81; mgr., sr. designer Cannell & Chaffin, La Jolla, Calif., 1981-87; owner, lead designer Linda S. Kaufman & Assocs., Coronado, Calif., 1987—. Contbr. articles to Better Homes & Gardens, Bed and Bath, Building Ideas, others. Vol. head of personnel Presbyn. Ch., Coronado, designer for sanctuary. Mem. Am. Soc. Interior Designers (bd. mem. San Deigo chpt., 1st place Design Excellence award 1996, 97, 98, 1st place Designer's Choice award 1995, 1st place People's Choice award 1995). Avocations: yoga, travel, exercise. Home and Office: 920 Adella Ave Coronado CA 92118

KAUFMANN, KAREN A., dance educator; b. Warwick, Va., Nov. 9, 1956; d. Peter J. Kaufmann and Helen F. (Zucker) Oppenheim; m. Steven R. Kalling, June 21, 1997. BA, Hampshire Coll., 1978; MA, Antioch U., 1993. Dance instr. children's dance classes Missoula, Mont., 1978—; artist Mont. Artist in Schs. Program, 1986—; core faculty mem. Creative Pulse grad. program U. Mont., Missoula, 1990—; performer Young Audiences of Mont., 1985—; educator Very Spl. Arts Mont., Missoula, 1989—, bd. dirs., v.p., sec., pres., 1985—; mng. dir. Mont. Transport Co., Missoula, 1993—; cons., panelist Mont. Arts Coun., Helena. Author: The Language of Movement, 1989, A Collection of CM Lesson Plans, 1989; choreographer Dancing Waters, 1995, Moving Words, 1998. Spl. Project grantee Mont. Arts Coun., 1997, grantee Am.-Scandinavian Found., 1997. Office: U Mont Dept Drama/Dance Missoula MT 59812

KAUFMAN-OSBORN, TIMOTHY VANCE, politics and leadership educator; b. Camden, N.J., Feb. 7, 1953; s. Norman Vance and Marjorie (Phipps) Osborn; m. Sharon Anne Kaufman, Sept. 8, 1975; children: Jacob, Tobin. BA, Oberlin Coll., 1976; MA, U. Wis., 1977, Princeton U., 1980; PhD, Princeton U., 1982. Asst. prof. politics Whitman Coll., Walla Walla, Wash., 1982-85; vis. rsch. fellow Princeton (N.J.) U., 1985-86; vis. scholar Doshisha U., Kyoto, Japan, 1990; assoc. prof. politics Whitman Coll., 1985-92, prof. politics, 1992-96, Baker Ferguson prof. politics and leadership, 1996—. Author: Politics/Sense/Experience, 1991; contbr. articles to profl. jours. Mem. Wash. Civil Liberties Union, Seattle, 1991—, bd. dirs. 1993—; bd. dirs. Wash. Coalition to Abolish the Death Penalty, 1994—. Recipient numerous fellowships and grants. Mem. Am. Polit. Sci. Assn., Western Polit. Sci. Assn. (exec. com. 1995-98, Betty Nesvold selection com. 1997, Betty Nesvold Women and Politics award 1992), Pacific N.W. Polit. Sci. Assn. (exec. coun. 1992-95), Soc. for Advancement of Am. Philosophy. Avocations: cello, reading, family. Office: Whitman Coll Dept Politics 345 Boyer Ave Walla Walla WA 99362-2067

KAUL, EMIL WILLIAM (BILL), director of youth development, educator; b. Furstenfeldbruck, Germany; s. Fred Robert and Celeste (Cromley) K.; m. Susan Jurjevich, May 29, 1974; children: Eva, Emily, Emil (dec. 1988), Fred, Elizabeth. BA, Livingston U., 1977; MSc, Troy State U., 1990; D in Arts, U. Miss., 1992. Cert. tchr., N. Mex. Tchr. NCC, Shiprock, N. Mex., 1994, NAPS, Santa Fe, N. Mex., 1994; instr. San Juan Coll., Farmington, N. Mex., 1995—; MI coord. THC/Santa Fe (N. Mex.) H.S., 1994-95; dir. devel. FBGC, Farmington, 1995—; part time tchr. U. N. Mex., Gallup, 1994; p.r. NMTPC/MI Comm. Albuquerque, N. Mex. Author: poetry, essays, various publs., 1992—. Mem. adv. bd. ECE, San Juan Coll., N. Mex., 1997-98, Casa Amigos, Farmington, N. Mex., 1997-98. Mem. Green party. Avocation: music. Home: PO Box 698 Waterflow NM 87421-0698 Office: FBGC PO Box 2491 Farmington NM 87499-2491

[illegible] 1956; s. Alfreds and Skaidrite (Akots) K.; m. Debra Ann Queen, Mar. 27, 1998; 1 child, Amanda. BA, Wartburg Coll., 1979; MBA, U. No. Iowa, 1981; PhD, U. Iowa, 1986. Sr. prof. in human resources. Grad. asst. U. No. Iowa, Cedar Falls, 1979-81; employee rels. asst. Norand Corp., Cedar Rapids, 1983; grad. asst. Univ. Iowa, Iowa City, 1981-86; prof. Boise (Idaho) State U., 1986—; cons. in field. Contbr. articles to profl. jours. Recipient rsch. grants Boise State U., 1987-98, Ponder scholarship U. Iowa, 1983-85; named Adv. of the Yr., Boise State U., 1989. Mem. Soc. for Human Resource Mgmt. (sec., v.p. 1982-83), ASTD (sec. 1989), Assn. of Mgmt., Acad. of Mgmt., Am. Psychol. Assn. Avocations: racewalking, golf, racquetball, tennis, skiing. Home: 1368 E Monterey Dr Boise ID 83706-5077 Office: Boise State U Dept Mgmt Boise ID 83725

KAVIN, REBECCA JEAN, health science executive; b. Dodge, Nebr., June 29, 1946; d. William Wilber Walsh and Dorothy Eleanor (Watson) Williams; m. Paul Babcock, May 15, 1965 (div. Sept. 1976); m. E. Iraj Kavin, Apr. 23, 1977; children: Mark Bijan, Seana Shereen. Cert., Ohio U., 1963. Claims adjuster San Found. for Med. Care, San Diego, 1968-70; adminstrv. asst. Friendly Hills Med. Group, La Habra, Calif., 1971-77; office mgr. Robert M. Peck and Sergio Blesa, MD, Pasadena, Calif., 1978-81; pres. Provider Mgmt. Assocs., La Canada, Calif., 1981—; speaker dept. continuing edn. UCLA, 1985, Hosp. Coun. So. Calif., L.A., 1986, Am. Acad. Med. Preventics, L.A., 1986. Contbr. articles to profl. jours. Mem. Am. Guild Patient Account Mgrs. (lic., speaker L.A. chpt. 1986), U.S. C. of C. Republican. Presbyterian. Avocations: reading, knitting, needlework. Office: Provider Mgmt Assocs 1501 Descanso Dr La Canada CA 91011-3105

KAWACHIKA, JAMES AKIO, lawyer; b. Honolulu, Dec. 5, 1947; s. Shinichi and Tsuyuko (Murashige) K.; m. Karen Keiko Takahashi, Sept. 1, 1973; 1 child, Robyn Mari. BA, U. Hawaii, Honolulu, 1969; JD, U. Calif., Berkeley, 1973. Bar: Hawaii 1973, U.S. Dist. Ct. Hawaii 1973, U.S. Ct. Appeals (9th cir.) 1974, U.S. Supreme Ct. 1992. Dep. atty. gen. Office of Atty. Gen. State of Hawaii, Honolulu, 1973-74; assoc. Padgett, Greeley & Marumoto, Honolulu, 1974-75, Law Office of Frank D. Padgett, Honolulu, 1975-77, Kobayashi, Watanabe, Sugita & Kawashima, Honolulu, 1977-82; ptnr. Carlsmith, Wichman, Case, Mukai & Ichiki, Honolulu, 1982-86, Bays, Deaver, Hiatt, Kawachika & Lezak, Honolulu, 1986-95; propr. Law Offices of James A. Kawachika, Honolulu, 1996-98; ptnr. Kawachika & Ozaki, Honolulu, 1999—; mem. Hawaii Bd. of Bar Examiners, Honolulu; arbitrator Cir. Ct. Arbitration Program State of Hawaii, Honolulu, 1986—. Chmn. Disciplinary Bd. Hawaii Supreme Ct., 1991-97; mem. U.S. dist. Ct. Adv. Com. on the Civil Justice Reform Act of 1990, 1991—. Mem. ABA, ATLA, Hawaii Bar Assn. (bd. dirs. Honolulu chpt. 1975-76, young lawyers sect. 1983-84, 92-93, treas. 1987-88, v.p./pres.-elect 1997-98, pres. 1998-99), 9th Cir. Jud. Conf. (lawyer rep. Honolulu chpt. 1988-90). Avocations: running, tennis, skiing. Office: Grosvenor Ctr Mauka Tower 737 Bishop St Ste 2750 Honolulu HI 96813-3216

KAWAMOTO, HENRY K., plastic surgeon; b. Long Beach, Calif., 1937. Intern U. Calif. Hosp., L.A., 1965; resident gen. surgery Columbia Presbyn. Med. Ctr., N.Y., 1969-71; resident plastic surgery NYU, 1971-73; fellow crano-facial surgery Dr. Paul Tessier, Paris, 1973-74; clin. prof. plastic surgery U. Calif., L.A. Mem. Am. Assn. Plastic Surgery, Am. Soc. Plastic and Reconstructive Surgery, ASMS, AOA. Office: 1301 20th St Ste 460 Santa Monica CA 90404-2054

KAWESKI, SUSAN, plastic surgeon, naval officer; b. Oil City, Pa., Jan. 27, 1955; d. Richard Francis and Lottie Ann (Malek) K.; m. Henry Nicholas Ernecoff, Aug. 7, 1983. BA, Washington and Jefferson Coll., 1976; MA, SUNY, Buffalo, 1979; MD, Pa. State U., 1983. Diplomate Am. Bd. Surgery, Am. Bd. Plastic Surgery. Commd. lt. USN, 1983, advanced through grades to comdr., 1993; intern in gen. surgery Naval Hosp., San Diego, 1983-84; head med. dept. USN, 1984-85; resident in gen. surgery Naval Hosp., San Diego, 1985-89; resident in plastic surgery Pa. State U., Hershey, 1989-91; staff plastic surgeon Naval Med. Ctr., San Diego, 1991-95; head divsn. plastic surgery, surgeon gen. advisor USN, 1994-95; craniofacial fellow Dr. Ian T. Jackson, Mich., 1995-96; head cleft palate/craniofacial team Naval Med. Ctr., 1996-98; resigned, 1998; pvt. practice, San Diego, 1998—; chmn. Cleft Palate/Craniofacial Bd., San Diego; plastic surgery advisor to surgeon gen. USN, 1994-95; presenter in field. Author chpt. to book. Recipient Ernest Witebsky Meml. award for proficiency in microbiology SUNY at Buffalo, 1978. Fellow ACS (assoc., 1st Place Rsch. award 1991); mem. Am. Assn. Plastic and Reconstructive Surgeons, Am. Cleft Palate Assn., Am. Assn. Women Surgeons, Am. Med. Women's Assn., Assn. Mil. Surgeons U.S., Univ. Club. Republican. Roman Catholic. Avocations: skiing, tennis, swimming, oil painting, playing piano. Home: 1158 Barcelona Dr San Diego CA 92107-4151 Office: Craniofacial Reconstructive 3444 Kearny Villa Rd San Diego CA 92123-1959

KAY, ALAN COOKE, federal judge; b. 1932; s. Harold Thomas and Ann (Cooke) K. BA, Princeton U., 1957; LLB, U. Calif., Berkeley, 1960. Assoc. Case, Kay & Lynch, Honolulu, 1960-64, ptnr., 1965-86; judge U.S. Dist. Ct. Hawaii, Honolulu, 1986-92, chief judge, 1992—; bd. regents Internat. Coll. and Grad. Sch., 1994—. Mem. steering com. Fuller Theol. Sem. Hawaii, 1985-86; pres., trustee Hawaii Mission Children's Soc., Honolulu, 1980-86; bd. dirs. Good News Mission, 1980-86, Econ. Devel. Corp. Honolulu, 1985-86, Legal Aid Soc., Honolulu, 1968-71. Mem. ABA, Hawaii Bar Assn. (exec. com. 1972-73, bd. dirs. real estate sect. 1983-86), Fed. Judges Assn. (9th cir. jud. coun. 1994—, 9th cir. Pacific Islands com. 1994—), Am. Inns of Ct. (counselor Aloha Inn 1987—). Republican. Office: US Dist Ct PO Box 50128 Honolulu HI 96850-5000

KAY, HERMA HILL, dean; b. Orangeburg, S.C., Aug. 18, 1934; d. Charles Esdorn and Herma Lee (Crawford) Hill. BA, So. Meth. U., 1956; JD, U. Chgo., 1959. Bar: Calif. 1960, U.S. Supreme Ct. 1978. Law clk. to Justice Roger Traynor, Calif. Supreme Ct., 1959-60; asst. prof. law U. Calif., Berkeley, 1960-62; assoc. prof. U. Calif., 1962, prof., 1963, dir. family law project, 1964-67, Jennings prof., 1987-96, dean, 1992—, Armstrong prof., 1996—; co-reporter uniform marriage and div. act Nat. Conf. Commrs. on Uniform State Laws, 1968-70; vis. prof. U. Manchester, Eng., 1972, Harvard U., 1976; mem. Gov.'s Commn. on Family, 1966. Author: (with Martha S. West) Text Cases and Materials on Sex-based Discrimination, 4th edit., 1996, (with R. Cramton, D. Currie and L. Kramer) Conflict of Laws: Cases, Comments, Questions, 5th edit., 1993; contbr. articles to profl. jours. Trustee Russell Sage Found., N.Y., 1972-87, chmn. bd., 1980-84; trustee, bd. dirs. Equal Rights Advs. Calif., 1976—, chmn., 1976-83; pres. bd. dirs. Rosenberg Found., Calif., 1987-88, bd. dirs. 1978—. Recipient rsch. award Am. Bar Found., 1990, Margaret Brent award ABA Commn. Women in Profession, 1992, Marshall-Wythe medal, 1995; fellow Ctr. Advanced Study in Behavioral Sci., Palo Alto, Calif., 1963. Mem. Calif. Bar Assn., Bar U.S. Supreme Ct., Calif. Women Lawyers (bd. govs. 1975-77), Am. Law Inst. (mem. coun. 1985-), Assn. Am. Law Schs. (exec. com. 1986-87, pres.-elect 1988, pres. 1989, past pres. 1990), Am. Acad. Arts and Scis., Order of Coif (nat. pres. 1983-85). Democrat. Office: U Calif Law Sch Boalt Hall Berkeley CA 94720-7200

KAYE, CAROLE, museum director and curator; b. Somerville, N.J., Apr. 24, 1933; d. Harry and Grace (Schwartz) Golison; m. Paul Littman, June 29, 1952 (dec. Apr. 1960); children: Fern, Alan; m. Barry Kaye; children: Howard. Student, Syracuse U., 1951. With Barry Kaye Assocs., L.A.; owner, curator Carole and Barry Kaye Mus. Miniatures, L.A.; v.p. Barry Kaye Assocs. Mus., 1994—. Past pres. Hadassah, Beverly Hills, Calif.; founder Music Ctr., Cedars-Sinai Hosp., L.A.; mem. Jewish Fedn. Mem. Friends of Ben Gurion U. Office: Carole & Barry Kaye Mus Miniatures 5900 Wilshire Blvd Los Angeles CA 90036-5013*

KAYE, EVELYN PATRICIA (EVELYN PATRICIA SARSON), author, publisher, travel expert; b. London, Oct. 1, 1937; came to U.S., 1963; d. Max and Florence (Wright) K.; m. J. Christopher Sarson, Mar. 25, 1963; children: Katrina May, David Arnold. Advanced level gen. certificate of edn. in English and French, North London Collegiate Sch., Edgware, Middlesex, Eng., 1956, studied in Jerusalem, 1959-60. Sec., publicity asst. Elek Books Ltd., London, 1957-58; gen. reporter Southend Times, Southend-on-Sea, Eng., Willesden Citizen, London, East London News Agy., 1958-61; staff reporter Reuters News Agy., Paris, 1961-62; reporter, feature writer The [illegible] co-founder, pres. Action for Children's TV, 1969-74, 89—; pres. Blue Penguin Publs., 1989-97, Blue Panda Publs., 1997—, spkr. travel and adventurous women's issues. Author: Family Guide to Childrens Television: What To Watch, What To Miss, What To Change and How To Do It, 1974, rev. edit., 1979, The Family Guide to Cape Cod: What to Do When You Don't Want To Do What Everyone Else Is Doing, 1976, Crosscurrents: Children, Families and Religion, 1980, How To Treat TV with TLC: The ACT Guide to Children's Television, 1979; co-author: (textbook) Relationships in Marriage and Family, 1984, Write and Sell Your TV Drama, 1985, 2d edit., 1993, (with A. Loring) The Parents Going-Away Planner, 1987, (with J. Gardner) The Hole in The Sheet, 1987, College Bound: The Students Guide to Getting Ready, Moving In and Succeeding on Campus, (with J. Gardner) Travel and Learn: The New Guide to Educational Travel, 1992, 3rd edit. 1994, Eco-Vacations: Enjoy Yourself and Save the Earth, 1991, Family Travel: Terrific New Vacation Ideas for Today's Families, 1993, Amazing Traveler: Isabella Bird-The Biography of a Victorian Adventurer, 1994, Free Vacations and Bargain Adventures in the U.S.A., 1995, 2d edit. 1998, Active Woman Vacation Guide, 1997; contbr. articles on family, travel, and the arts to nat. mags.; contbr. radio and TV interview on unusual travel incl. CNN TV News, Good Morning Am., ABC-TV, KATU-TV, Portland, Oreg., others. Mem. Am. Soc. Journalists and Authors (exec. coun. 1981-87, pres. 1984-85, v.p. conf. 1990), Pubs. Mktg. Assn. (bd. dirs. 1993-95), Colo. Ind. Pubs. Assn. (founder, pres. 1992-96), Colo. Hunter Jumper Assn. E-mail: ekaye@ibm.net. Home and Office: 3031 5th St Boulder CO 80304-2501

KAYE, PETER FREDERIC, television editor; b. Chgo., Mar. 8, 1928; s. Ralph A. and Sara Corson (Philipson) K.; m. Martha Louise Wood, Mar. 20, 1955; children: Loren, Terry, Adam. BA in Govt., Pomona Coll., 1949. Reporter Alhambra (Calif.) Post-Advocate, 1950-53; reporter, editorial writer, polit. writer The San Diego Union, 1953-68; news and pub. affairs dir. KPBS-TV, San Diego State Coll., 1968-72; corr., producer Nat. Pub. Affairs Ctr. for TV, Washington, 1972-74; comm. dir. So. Calif. First Nat. Bank, San Diego, 1974-75; press sec. The Pres. Ford Com., Washington, 1975-76; mgr. Copley Videotex, San Diego, 1982-84; assoc. editor The San Diego Union, 1976-94; editl. dir. KNSD, San Diego, 1996—; freelance TV producer programs KPBS, PBS, BBC; San Diego corr. Newsweek, 1968-71, McGraw-Hill, 1959-67; lectr. comm. U. Calif., San Diego, 1971; copywriter Washburn-Justice Advt., San Diego, 1959-70. Producer 10 TV programs including including Jacob Bronowski: Life and Legacy, Twenty-Five Years of Presidency, The Presidency, The Press and the People. Press asst. Eisenhower-Nixon Campaign, L.A., 1952; asst. press sec. Richard Nixon Presdl. Campaign, Washington, 1960; dir. Pete Wilson for Mayor Campaign, San Diego, 1971; comm. dir. Flournoy for Gov. Campaign, Beverly Hills, Calif., 1974. With U.S. Mcht. Marines, 1945, U.S. Army, 1950-52. Jefferson fellow East-West Ctr., Honolulu, 1987; recipient Golden Mike awards So. Calif. TV News Dirs. Assn., 1969, 70, 71, Best Pub. Affairs Program award Nat. Ednl. TV, 1970, Best Local TV Series award Radio-TV Mirror, 1971, Nat. Emmy award Spl. Events Reporter, Watergate Coverage, 1973-74, Best Editorial awards Copley Newspapers Ring of Truth, 1979, Sigma Delta Chi, 1985, Calif. Newspaper Pubs. Assn., 1985; San Diego Emmy awards, 1985, 87, 91. Mem. NATAS, State Bar Calif. (bd. govs. 1991-97, v.p. 1993-94, 96-97), Sigma Delta Chi. Republican. Home: 240 Ocean View Ave Del Mar CA 92014-3322

KAYFETZ, VICTOR JOEL, writer, editor, translator; b. N.Y.C., July 20, 1945; s. Daniel Osler and Selma Harriet (Walowitz) K.; BA, Columbia U., 1966; postgrad. U. Stockholm (Sweden), 1966-67; MA in History, U. Calif.-Berkeley, 1969. Teaching asst. in Swedish, U. Calif., Berkeley, 1969-70; tchr., adminstr. Swedish adult edn. programs, 1970-75; corr. Reuters, Stockholm, 1975-78; sub-editor Reuters World Ser., London, 1978; corr. London Fin. Times, Stockholm, 1979-80; free lance translator Swedish, Danish, Norwegian, 1967—; free lance editor Swedish and Am. mags., 1980—. Henry Evans traveling fellow, 1966-67; Nat. Def. Fgn. Lang. fellow, 1967-69; Thord Gray fellow Am.-Scandinavian Found., 1970. Mem. Swedish Am. C. of C., Soc. Advancement Scandinavian Study, Am. Scandinavian Found., Swedish Assn. Profl. Translators, World Affairs Council No. Calif., Sierra Club, Phi Beta Kappa. Author: Sweden in Brief, 1974, 80; Invest in Sweden, 1984, Skanska, the First Century, 1987; editor, translator numerous books, ann. reports, mags. for Swedish govt. agys. interest orgns., univs., indsl. corps., banks.

KAYLAN, HOWARD LAWRENCE, musical entertainer, composer; b. N.Y.C., June 22, 1947; s. Sidney and Sally Joyce (Berlin) K.; m. Mary Melita Pepper, June 10, 1967 (div. Sept. 1971); 1 child, Emily Anne; m. Susan Karen Olsen, Apr. 18, 1982 (div. June 1996); 1 child, Alexandra Leigh. Student, UCLA, Am. Coll. Metaphys. Theology, St. Paul, Minn., 1998. Lead singer and founder rock group The Turtles, Los Angeles, 1965—; lead singer rock group Mothers of Invention, Los Angeles, 1970-72, Flo and Eddie, 1972-83; radio, TV, recording entertainer various broadcast organizations, Los Angeles, 1972—; screenwriter Larry Gelbart, Carl Gotleib prodns., Los Angeles, 1979-85; producer children's records Kidstuff Records, Hollywood, Fla., 1980-83; singer, producer rock band Flo and Eddie, Los Angeles, 1976-83; singer, producer The Turtles (reunion of original band), Los Angeles, 1980—; actor, TV and film Screen Actors Guild, Los Angeles, 1983—; background vocalist various albums for numerous performers; syndicated talk show host Unistar Radio Network, 1989—; radio personality Sta. WXRK-FM, N.Y.C., 1990-91, KLOU, St. Louis, 1993, WGRR, Cin., 1995-97. Author: Hi Bob, 1995, The Energy Pals, 1995; contbr. articles to Creem mag., L.A. Free Press, Rockit mag., Phonograph Record; screenwriter: (film) Death Masque, 1985; actor: (film) 200 Motels, 1971, Get Crazy, 1985, General Hospital; performed at the White House, 1970; exec. producer: (radio) Down Eerie Street, 1998. Recipient 10 Gold and Platinum LP album awards while lead singer, 1965—, Fine Arts award, Bank of Am., L.A., 1965, Spl. Billboard Mag. award, 1992; recorded numerous top ten hit songs with Turtles, Bruce Springstein, The Ramones, Duran Duran, T. Rex, John Lennon and others. Mem. AFTRA, Screen Actors Guild, Am. Fedn. Musicians, AGVA.

KAZMIERSKI, SUSAN HEDWIG, family nurse practitioner, nurse midwife; b. Milw., Oct. 20, 1951; d. Albert Fredrick and Louise (Seimers) K. BSN, U. Wis., Milw., 1975; cert. FNP, Stanford U., 1983, cert. nurse midwife, 1985. RN, N.Mex. Nurse, FNP, nurse midwife ARC, Colombia, 1978-81; nurse Migrant Health, Wild Rose, Wis., 1981-82; nurse midwife Rockridge Health Ctr., Oakland, N.Mex., 1984-86; FNP, Health Care No. N.Mex., Coyote, 1986—; bd. dirs. Health Resources No. N.Mex., Albuquerque, 1990-93. Avocations: canoeing, hiking, cross-country skiing. Home: PO Box 833 Abiquiu NM 87510-0833 Office: Health Care No N Mex 620 Coronado Cordova NM 87523

KEALIINOHOMOKU, JOANN WHEELER, anthropologist, dance ethnologist, educator; b. Kansas City, Mo., May 20, 1930; d. George V. and Leona Lavena (Moore) Wheeler; m. Thomas Samuel Kealiinohomoku, 1952 (div. 1962); 1 child, Halla K. BSS, Northwestern U., 1955; MA, 1965; PhD, Ind. U., 1976. Mem. faculty No. Ariz. U., Flagstaff, 1970-72, 75-87, assoc. prof. anthropology, 1980-87, emeritus prof. anthropology, 1987; sr. rsch. assoc. Ctr. for Colorado Plateau Studies, No. Ariz. U., 1987-92, ind. scholar, 1987—; mem. faculty World Campus Afloat, fall 1972, 73, Semester-at-Sea, 1989; resident scholar Sch. Am. Research, Santa Fe, 1974-75; vis. faculty U. Hawaii, Hilo, spring 1973, summer 1973, 74, U. Hawaii-Manoa, fall 1981, spring, 1991, NYU, summer 1980, 84, U. N.C., Greensboro, summer 1990, Tex. Woman's U., summer 1992, summer Inst. Hawaiian and Polynesian Studies U. Hawaii, Windword C.C., 1993, UCLA, winter 1998. Bd. dirs. Native Ams. for Cmty. Action, Flagstaff Indian Center, 1977-82, sec., 1980-82. Grantee, Am. Philos. Soc., 1966, 69-70, Wenner Gren Found., Ariz. Humanities Coun., 1991; Weatherhead fellow Sch. Am. Research, 1974-75; research fellow East-West Center, 1981; NEH grantee, 1986; recipient Disting. Pub. Scholar award Ariz. Humanities Coun., 1996. Fellow Current Anthropology; mem. Soc. Ethnomusicology (councilor; co-founder Southwestern chpt.), Dance Rsch. Ctr. (charter), Congress on Rsch. in Dance (bd. dirs. 1974-79, award in recognition of outstanding contbn. to dance rsch.), Cross-Cultural Dance Resources (co-founder). Contbr. articles to profl. jours.

KEANE, MELISSA, museum director. Pres., bd. trustees Phoenix Mus. History, mem. bd. trustees. Office: Phoenix Mus History 105 N 5th St [illegible]

KEARNEY, JOSEPH LAURENCE, retired athletic conference administrator; b. Pitts., Apr. 28, 1927; s. Joseph L. and Iva M. (Nikirk) K.; m.

Dorothea Hurst, May 13, 1950; children: Jan Marie, Kevin Robert, Erin Lynn, Shawn Alane, Robin James. B.A., Seattle Pacific U., 1952, LL.D., 1979; M.A., San Jose State U., 1964; Ed.D., U. Wash., 1970. Tchr., coach Paradise (Calif.) High Sch., 1952-53; asst. basketball coach U. Wash., 1953-54; coach, tchr. Sunnyside (Wash.) High Sch., 1954-57; prin. high sch., coach Onalaska (Wash.) High Sch., 1957-61; prin. Tumwater (Wash.) High Sch., 1961-63; asst. dir. Wash. High Sch. Activities Assn., 1963-64; athletic dir., assoc. dir. U. Wash., 1964-76; athletic dir. intercollegiate athletics Mich. State U., East Lansing, 1976-80, Ariz. State U., Tempe, 1980; commr. Western Athletic Conf., Denver, 1980-95; hon. chmn. Holiday Bowl, 1994, commr. emeritus, 1994. Pres. Cmty. Devel. Assn., 1957-61; bd. dirs. U.S. Olympic Com., 1985-94, chmn. games preparation com., 1985—. Recipient Disting. Service award Mich. Assn. Professions, 1979, Citation for Disting. Svc., Colo. Sports Hall of Fame, U.S. Olympic Com. Order of Olympic Shield, 1996. Mem. Nat. Football Found. (ct. of honors com.), Nat. Collegiate Athletic Assn., Nat. Assn. Collegiate Dirs. Athletics (Corbett award 1991, Adminstr. Excellence award), Collegiate Commrs. Assn. (pres., award of Merit 1998), Am. Football Assn. (Commrs. award 1996, Athletic Dir.'s award 1998). Home: 2810 W Magee Rd Tucson AZ 85742-1500

KEARNS, ALBERT OSBORN, minister; b. Shattuck, Okla., Apr. 15, 1920; s. Arthur Alexander and Grace Mae (Booth) K.; m. Maria Metlova, Oct. 18, 1947; 1 child, Alscot. Student, U. Redlands, 1948-52. Ordained to ministry Lighthouse Gospel Fellowship of Mins. and Chs., 1984. Evangelist L.A., 1971-75, Simi Valley, Calif., 1975-84; pastor Somis (Calif.) Christian Ch., 1984-89, Simi Valley, 1989—; advisor, counselor Women's Aglow Fellowship, Thousand Oaks, Calif., 1987—; pub. A.O.K. Books, 1991. Petty officer 2d class USN, 1940-46, PTO. Republican. Home and Office: 1621 Patricia Ave Simi Valley CA 93065-3403

KEARNS, HOMER H., school system administrator. AA in Spanish, West Hills Coll., Coalinga, Calif., 1962; BA in Spanish and Life Sci., Calif. State U., Fresno, 1964, MA in Adminstrn., 1970; PhD in Adminstrn. Higher Edn. and Sociology, Mich. State U., 1971. Tchr., head tchr., prin. Clovis (Calif.) Unified Sch. Dist, 1964-70; asst. prof. edn. dept. curriculum and instrn. coll. edn., assoc. dir. Northwest Cmty. Edn. Devel. Ctr. U. Oreg., Eugene, 1971-72; supt. schs. Sisters (Oreg.) Sch. Dist., 1972-75, Redmond (Oreg.) Sch. Dist., 1975-81; county supt. schs. Deschutes County Edn. Svc. Dist., Bend, Oreg., 1978-81; assoc., dep. supt. Salem-Keizer Pub. Schs., Salem, Oreg., 1981-86, supt. schs., 1986—; mem. exec. com. Coalition for Equitable Sch. Funding, 1988-91; bd. dirs. Marion & Polk Schs. Credit Union, 1992-94, Salem Econ. Devel. corp., Northwest Regional Ednl. Lab., chair bd. equity com. Bd. dirs. Salem Family YMCA, 3rd Century Edn. Found.; past bd. dirs. Oreg. Congl. Awards Coun., Cascade Child Treatment Ctr.; bd. dirs. Salem Sch. Found.; active Oreg. 2000 Com., United Way, County Planning Commn., Econ. Devel. Strategic Planning Group; mem. panel Gannet Found. Named Supt of Yr., Oreg. Counseling Assn., 1988, Outstanding Adminstr. Oreg. Multicultural Edn. Assn., 1994. Mem. Am. Assn. Sch. Adminstrs. (chair suburban supts. adv. com. 1990, exec. com. 1992-94, pres. elect 1994-95, pres. 1995-96, immediate past pres. 1996), Oreg. Assn. Sch. Execs. (bd. dirs., pres. 1990, chair sch. funding coalition 1992, Supt. of Yr. award with Am. Assn. Sch. Adminstrs. 1990), Rotary Internat. Office: Salem/Keizer SD 24J PO Box 12024 Salem OR 97309-0024*

KEARSE, DAVID GRIER, stage and screen writer, journalist; b. Annapolis, Md., June 24, 1937; s. Francis Grier and Esther Carlisle (McCusker) K. BA, U. Miami, 1959; postgrad., Columbia U., 1959-60, NYU, 1988-89. Reporter, editor Capital Gazette Press, Annapolis, 1961-67; critic, copy editor The Balt. Sun, 1967-78; creative dept. Young and Rubicam Advtg., N.Y.C., 1978-83; with pub. rels. dept. Stephen W. Brener Assoc., N.Y.C., 1985-89; ind. screenwriter Hollywood, Calif., 1989—. Author: (musical) Miranda, 1991; author, dir. (play) Once Bitten, 1978; author: (screenplay) Alfredo's Sunset, 1991; dir.: The Winter's Tale, 1978, Playformers, 1989. Co-founder Annapolis Fine Arts Festival, 1963; AIDS vol. Roosevelt Hosp., N.Y.C., 1988-89; mem. Spiritual Adv. Com. AIDS Project L.A.; assoc. Episcopal Order Holy Cross. Mem. The Dramatists Guild, Writers Guild Am. (assoc.), Westwood Village Rotary Club. Democrat.

KEATING, DAVID, photographer; b. Rye, N.Y., Sept. 5, 1962. BA in Philosophy, Yale U., 1985; MA in Studio Art with distinction, U. N.Mex., 1991; student, Calif. Inst. Arts, Santa Clarita, 1992; MFA in Studio Art with distinction, U. N.Mex., 1994. Solo exhbns. include U. N.Mex., 1990 (traveled to Pace U., N.Y.C., Nat. Coun. Alcoholism Conf. of Affiliates, Nashville), 91, Calif. Inst. Arts, 1992, Graham Gallery, Albuquerque, 1994, Univ. Art Mus. Downtown, Albuquerque, 1995, others; group exhbns. include Raw Space Gallery, Albuquerque, 1990, Betty Rymer Gallery, Sch. Art Inst. Chgo., 1991, 92, Randolph St. Gallery, Chgo., 1992, Atlanta Gallery Photography, 1992, San Jose (Calif.) Inst. Contemporary Art, 1992, Univ. Art Mus., Albuquerque, 1993, Ctr. African Am. History and Culture, Smithsonian Instn., Washington, 1994, Mus. Photographic Arts, San Diego, 1996, SF Camera World Gallery, 1999, others; represented in pub. collections, including Univ. Art Mus., Albuquerque; subject of various articles and catalogs, 1992—. NEA Visual Artists fellow in photography, 1994, Van Deren Coke fellow, U. N.Mex., 1991; recipient award Photographers and Friends United Against AIDS/Art Matters Inc., 1992. Home: 1410 Central Ave SW Apt 38 Albuquerque NM 87104-1166

KEATING, NORMA STORRS, professional genealogist, small business owner; b. Newburyport, Mass., June 16, 1943; d. Ernest Nels and Annie Thomas (Brooks) Storrs; m. John Joseph Keating, July 27, 1968; 1 child, Anne Marie. BSN, Ind. U., 1965; cert. profl. genealogist, Salt Lake Inst. Genealogy, 1996. RN, N.J., Calif. Staff nurse Morristown (N.J.) Meml. Hosp., 1965-67; clin. rsch. assoc. Ortho Pharms., Raritan, N.J., 1967-73; owner, CEO, Stained Glass Creations, Yorba Linda, Calif., 1978-88, Your Family Connection, Yorba Linda, 1996—; presenter, leader workshops in genealogy field. Author: (with Nancy Carlberg) Beginning Danish Research, 1992. Bd. dirs., editor newsletter Friends Yorba Linda Pub. Libr., also past pres.; past sec. Friends of Libr. Found.; chmn. Indian Christmas svc. project Orange County coun. Girl Scouts U.S.A., 1990—, publicity chmn., 1987-94, Brownie leader, 1981-82, jr. leader, 1982-85; past pres. Yorba Linda Woman's Club, 2d v.p. membership, 1996—. Recipient Woman of Distinction awad Soroptimists, Placentia-Yorba Linda, 1992, Appreciation pin Orange County coun. Girl Scouts U.S.A., 1992, appreciation plaque Yorba Linda Pub. Libr. Commn., 1993, also others. Mem. DAR (registrar Mojave chpt. 1996—), Assn. Profl. Genealogists (cert.), Nat. Genealogy Soc. (cert.), Orange County Geneal. Soc. (pres. 1980-85), New Eng. Hist. and Geneal. Soc., N.C. Geneal. Soc. Avocations: reading, jigsaw and crossword puzzles, travel. Home and Office: 4653 Avenida Rio Del Oro Yorba Linda CA 92886-3013

KEATS, DONALD HOWARD, composer, educator; b. N.Y.C., May 27, 1929; s. Bernard and Lillian K.; m. Eleanor Steinholz, Dec. 13, 1953; children: Jeremy, Jennifer, Jeffrey, Jocelyn. MusB, Yale U., 1949; MA, Columbia U., 1951; PhD, U. Minn., 1962; student, Staatliche Hochschule fur Musik, Hamburg, Germany, 1954-56. Teaching fellow Yale U. Sch. Music, New Haven, Conn., 1948-49; instr. music theory U.S. Naval Sch. Music, Washington, 1953-54; post music dir. Ft. Dix, N.J., 1956-57; faculty Antioch Coll., Yellow Springs, Ohio, 1957-76; prof. Antioch Coll., 1967-76, chmn. music dept., 1967-71; vis. prof. music U. Wash. Sch. Music, 1969-70, Lamont Sch. Music, U. Denver, 1975-76; composer-in-residence Colo. Music Festival, 1980, Arcosanti, 1986; vis. composer Aspen Music Festival, 1987; prof. music, composer-in-residence Lamont Sch. Music, U. Denver, 1975—, Phipps Prof. in the humanities, 1982-85. Concerts devoted solely to his music often with his participation as pianist, London, 1973, Tel Aviv, 1973, Jerusalem, 1973, N.Y.C., 1975, Denver, 1984, 91; Composer: Divertimento for Winds and Strings, 1949, The Naming of Cats, 1951, The Hollow Men, 1951, String Quartet 1, 1952, Concert Piece for Orchestra, 1952, Variations for Piano, 1955, First Symphony, 1957, Piano Sonata, 1960, An Elegiac Symphony, 1962, Anyone Lived in a Pretty How Town, 1965; ballet New Work, 1966; Polarities for Violin and Piano, 1968-70, String Quartet 2, 1965, A Love Triptych, 1970, Dialogue for Piano and Winds, 1973, Diptych for Cello and Piano, 1975, Upon the Intimation of Love's Mortality, 1975, Branchings for Orch., 1976, Four Puerto Rican Love Songs: Tierras del Alma for soprano, flute and guitar, 1978, Musica Instrumentalis for chamber group, 1980, Concerto for Piano and Orch., 1990, Revisitations for Violin, Cello and Piano, 1992, Elegy for chamber orch., 1993, Scherzo for String Quartet, 1995, Fanfare for Brass, 1996. Served with U.S. Army, 1952-54. Recipient ASCAP awards, 1964—; awards from Ford, Danforth and Lilly founds., Nat. Endowment for Arts; winner Rockefeller Found. Symphonic Competitions, 1965, 66; Guggenheim fellow Europe, 1964-65, 72-73; Nat. Endowment for Arts grantee, fellow, 1975; Fulbright Scholar, 1954-56. Mem. ASCAP, Coll. Music Soc., Am. Music Ctr., Soc. of Composers, Phi Beta Kappa. E-mail: dkeats@du.edu. Home: 9261 E Berry Ave Englewood CO 80111-3507 Office: U Denver Lamont Sch Music Denver CO 80208

KEEBLE, JOHN ROBERT, English writing educator, writer; b. Winnipeg, Man., Can., Nov. 24, 1944; s. Raymond C.W. and Olivia Mae (Wallace) K.; m. Claire Estelle Sheldon, Sept. 4, 1964; children: Jonathan S., Ezekiel J., Carson R.C. BA, U. Redlands, 1966; MFA, U. Iowa, 1969; postgrad., Brown U., 1972-73. Instr. in English Grinnell (Iowa) Coll., 1969-71, writer-in-residence, 1971-72; prof. Eastern Wash. U., Cheney, 1973—; Coal Royalty Trust vis. chair creative writing U. Ala., 1992, 98; vis. prof. U. Ala., 1995, 96. Author: (fiction) Crab Canon, 1971, Mine, 1974, Yellowfish, 1980, Broken Ground, 1987, Red Shirt, 1999, (non-fiction), Out of the Channel, 1991, 2d edit., 1999. Guggenheim fellow, 1982-83; Wash. State Gov.'s Award for Lit., 1992. Mem. Spokane Canoe and Kayak Club (v.p. 1989). Avocations: canoeing, farming, forestry. Office: Eastern Wash U Creative Writing Program 705 W 1st Ave Spokane WA 99204

KEEGAN, JOHN E., lawyer; b. Spokane, Wash., Apr. 29, 1943. BA, Gonzaga U., 1965; LLB, Harvard U., 1968. Bar: Wash. 1968, U.S. Ct. Appeals (9th cir.) 1976, U.S. Supreme Ct. Gen. counsel Dept. Housing and Urban Devel., Washington, 1968-70; instr. in bus. sch. and inst. environ. studies U. Wash., 1973-76, instr. land use and environ. law, 1976-78; now ptnr. Davis, Wright & Tremaine, Seattle. Office: Davis Wright Tremaine 2600 Century Sq 1501 4th Ave Ste 2600 Seattle WA 98101-1688

KEELING, GERALDINE ANN, musicologist, educator; b. Mason City, Iowa, Aug. 10, 1946; d. John Odell and Marie Christine (Birkedal) Field; m. Steven R. Keeling, Aug. 17, 1974. BA cum laude, St. Olaf Coll., 1968; MMus. with high distinction, Ind. U., 1973; postgrad., UCLA, 1982. Assoc. instr. music Ind. U., Bloomington, 1968-70; asst. prof. music Valley City (N.D.) State U., 1970-78; teaching fellow UCLA, 1980-83; pvt. piano tchr. San Gabriel, Calif., 1980—; ch. organist Trinity United Meth. Ch., Pomona, Calif., 1981-90; instr. music. Calif. State U., Fullerton, 1985-86. Contbr. articles to profl. jours. Recipient Gurtha Olin Rodda Disting. Svc. award, 1997; NEH fellow, 1977-78; grantee Internat. Edn. Program Alpha Delta Kappa, 1983-84; recipient John Lennon award, 1982, Atwater Kent award in Musicology, UCLA, 1980. Mem. Music Tchrs. Assn. Calif. (state solo and concerto chmn. 1991-94, br. v.p. 1991-92, br. pres. 1992-94, cert. merit chmn. 1985-88), Am. Musicol. Soc., Am. Liszt Soc. (editorial assoc. 1987-91, bd. dirs. 1988—), The Liszt Soc., Am. Guild Organists (chpt. sec. 1987-90), L.A. Liszt Competition (dir. 1990—), Nat. Fedn. Music Clubs (Pasadena area Jr. Festival chair 1991—), Pi Kappa Lambda. Home: 6318 N Muscatel Ave San Gabriel CA 91775-1844

KEELY, GEORGE CLAYTON, lawyer; b. Denver, Feb. 28, 1926; s. Thomas and Margaret (Clayton) K.; m. Jane Elisabeth Coffey, Nov. 18, 1950; children: Margaret Clayton, George C. (dec.), Mary Anne, Jane Elisabeth, Edward Francis, Kendall Anne. *Wife, Jane Keely, investor, BA Wellesley, MA Columbia University. Daughter, Margaret Stannard, BA, MA, EdD, CCC-SLP, business/education consultant. Husband, Daniel. Residence, Denver, Colorado. Daughter, Mary Keely, BA, MA, CPA. Children: Elisa, Angelo and Lia Marie. Residence, Austin, Texas. Daughter, Elisabeth Wilson, BA, artist and sculptor. Husband, Gregory. Children: Gregory Jr. and Bradley. Residence, Danville, California. Son, Edward Keely, BA, CFA, vice president and a portfolio manager of Janus Funds. Wife, Diane. Daughter, Makenzie. Son, Charles Edward. Residence, Castle Pines, Colorado. Daughter, Kendall Picardi, BA, paralegal/office manager. Husband, Steve. Son, Chris. Residence, Arvada, Colorado.* BS in Bus, U. Colo., 1948; LLB, Columbia U., 1951. Bar: Colo. 1951. Assoc. Fairfield & Woods, Denver, 1951-58, ptnr., 1958-86, sr. dir., 1986-90, of counsel, 1990-91, ret., 1991; v.p. Silver Corp., 1966-86; mem. exec. com. Timpte Industries, Inc., 1970-78, dir., 1980-89. Mem. Colo. Commn. Promotion Uniform State Laws, 1967—; regional planning adv. com. Denver Regional Coun. Govts., 1972-74; bd. dirs. Bow Mar Water and Sanitation Dist., 1970-74; trustee Town of Bow Mar, 1972-74; trustee, v.p. Silver Found., 1970-90, mem. bd., 1983-90; trustee, v.p. Denver Area coun. Boy Scouts Am., 1985-90; bd. dirs. Pub. Broadcasting of Colo., Inc., 1986-90, Sta. KCFR. With USAAF, 1944-47. Fellow Am. Bar Found., Colo. Bar Found.; mem. ABA (ho. of dels. 1977-79), Denver Bar Assn. (award of merit 1980), Colo. Bar Assn., Nat. Conf. Commrs. Uniform State Laws (sec. 1971-75, exec. com. 1971-79 , chmn. exec. com. 1975-77, pres. 1977-79, co-chmn. com. U.S.-Can. Transboundary Pollution Reciprocal Access Act 1979-82, chmn. com. Determination of Death Act 1979-80), Am. Law Inst., Cath. Lawyers Guild of Denver (dir. 1965-67), Denver Estate Planning Coun., U. Club of Denver, (dir. 1966-75, pres. 1973-74), Law Club of Denver (pres. 1966-67, Lifetime Achievement award, 1994), Pinehurst Country Club, Hundred Club, Cactus Club, Rotary, Phi Delta Phi, Beta Theta Pi, Beta Gamma Sigma. Home: 5220 W Longhorn St Littleton CO 80123-1408

KEEN, RONALD LEE, engineer, retired career officer; b. Abilene, Tex., Jan. 28, 1959; s. Larry Lee and Betty Louise (Lesser) K.; Cindy Kaye Smedley, June 17, 1978; children: Cristina, Jordon, Brian. AA in Communication Mgmt., Community Coll. of USAF, 1983; BA in Applied Arts and Sci., Southwest Tex. S. U., 1986; MS in Aero. Sci., Embry Riddle A.U., 1991. Enlisted USAF, 1979, advanced through grades to capt., 1990; sr. group comm. analyst 6920 ESG USAF, Misawa AB, Japan, 1980-83; Intel rsch. analyst HQ electronic securiry CMD USAF, Kelly AFB, Tex., 1983-86; instr. crew ICBM 44 Strategic Missile Wing USAF, Ellsworth AFB, S.D., 1986-88, commdr. crew ICBM 68 Strategic Missile Squad, 1988-89, commdr. alt CMD post ICBM 68 Strategic Missile Squad, 1989-90, evaluator ICBM crew 44 Strategic Missile Wing, 1990-91; officer squad activation HQ Air Force Space Command USAF, Peterson AFB, Colo., 1991-92; officer space ops. evaluator 4 Space Ops. Squad USAF, Falcon AFB, Colo., 1992-94; chief base plans and programs officer 35 Civil Engr. Squadon USAF, Misawa AFB, Japan, 1994-96; chief war plans officer 21 Space Wing USAF, Peterson AFB, Colo., 1996-98; ret.; sr. staff engr. Milstar Automated Comm. Mgmt. Sys., Aero. Radio Inc., Colorado Springs, Colo., 1998—; ops. officer SELM 90-1 44 Strategic Missile Wing, Ellsworth AFB, 1990. Commr. youth baseball and soccer leagues Ellsworth Youth Sports Assn., 1988-91; coach Rapid City (S.D.) Youth Sports Assn., 1989-91, Colorado Springs Youth Sports, 1991-94, 1997—, Colo. Springs Parks and Recreation, 1994, 97; coach Misawa Youth Sports Assn., 1994-96; offensive coach Edgren H.S., Misawa Air Base, Japan, 1996; cubmaster Boy Scouts Am., Ellsworth AFB, 1990-91, Misawa Air Base, Japan, 1996. asst. cubmaster, Colorado Springs, 1991-93, chmn. pack com., 1992-93, scoutmaster, Misawa Air Base, Japan, 1996. Decorated Commendation medal with 2 oak leaf clusters, Meritorious Svc. medal with 2 oak leaf cluster, Air Force Achievement medal with 4 oak leaf clusters. Mem. VFW, Air Force Assn., Nat. Eagle Scout Assn., Air Force Assn. Missilers, Nat. Youth Sports Coaches Assn., Am. Legion. Republican. Avocations: camping, hiking, outdoor sports, raquetball. Home: 8140 Mainsail Ct Colorado Springs CO 80920-4406

KEENAN, ROBERT, architect; b. Rochester, N.Y., Jan. 8, 1950; s. John Lawrence and Frances (Hartigan) K.; m. Marianne Julia Janko, Sept. 9, 1989; 1 child, Robert John. BA, Fordham U., 1971; MArch, Harvard U., 1976. Registered architect, Mass., Calif.; cert. nat. coun. archtl. registration bds. Project architect Archtl. Resources Cambridge Inc., Cambridge, Mass., 1977-79; architect Hoskins, Scott, Taylor & Ptnrs., Boston, 1979-81; project architect Harry Weese & Assocs., Chgo., 1981-89, v.p., 1983-89; sr. resident architect Singapore Mass Rapid Transit Project, 1982-84; chief architect Metro Rail Transit Cons., 1986-89; architect, engring. mgr., urban designer Bechtel Corp., San Francisco, 1989—; chief architect Bay Area Transit Cons., 1989-91, Athens Metro, 1991-94; dir. facility engring. Light Rail Transit, Kuala Lumpur, Malaysia, 1994-95; project architect We. Corridor Ry. Feasibility Study Kowloon-Canton Ry. Corp., Hong Kong, 1995; chief architect West Rail Divsn. Kowloon Canton Ry. Corp., Hong Kong, 1996—; design mgr. Tuen Mun Sect., 1998; speaker, session chmn. Internat. Conf. on Tall Bldgs., Singapore, 1984. Prin. works include Regis Coll. Athletic Facility, Weston, Mass., Singapore Mass Rapid Transit Sys., So. Calif. Red Line Metro Rail, L.A., Bay Area Rapid Transit Sys., San Francisco, Attiko Metro, Athens, Kuala Lumpur (Malaysia) LRT 2, KCRC/West Rail Project, Hong Kong. Mem. AIA. Republican. Roman Catholic. Office: Bechtel Corp PO Box 193965 50 Beale St San Francisco CA 94119-3965

KEENAN, WILLIAM JOHN, writer; b. Phila., Nov. 14, 1934; s. Joseph Edward and Marie (Conners) K.; m. Yolanda Pellettieri Jan. 4, 1959 (div. 1967); 1 child, Jay; m. Carole Tessler, 1967; children: Michael, Patricia. BS, Westchester U., 1956. Writer, producer TV, plays, films; lectr. Lompoc Fed. Penitentiary, Lompoc, Calif., 1987. Author: (play) When We Last Saw Our Hero, (film) King Kong Escapes, 1968, Romantic Adventure, 1987, (TV movie) Little Red, 1981, Peacetime Gunfighter, 1977, (TV series) 6 Million Dollar Man, 1974, Love American Style, 1974, Partridge Family, 1974-75, Laverne and Shirley, 1979, Adam 12, 1975-76, The Blue Knight, 1977, Fantasy Island, 1978, over 200 animated programs including King Kong, 1964, The Jackson 5, The Osmonds, Kid Power, (TV spl.) Year Without Santa Claus, 1974; script editor: (TV series) The Littlest Hobo, 1980-81, Search and Rescue, 1978-79. Mem. Writers Guild Am. West (mem. playwrights com.), Nat. Acad. TV Arts and Scis. Home and Office: 6031 Sadring Ave Woodland Hills CA 91367-1429

KEENE-BURGESS, RUTH FRANCES, army official; b. South Bend, Ind., Oct. 7, 1948; d. Seymour and Sally (Morris) K.; m. Leslie U. Burgess, Jr., Oct. 1, 1983; children: Michael Leslie, David William, Elizabeth Sue, Rachael Lee. BS, Ariz. State U., 1970; MS, Fairleigh Dickinson U., 1978; grad., U.S. Army Command and Gen. Staff Coll., 1986. Inventory mgmt. specialist U.S. Army Electronics Command, Phila., 1970-74, U.S. Army Communications-Electronics Material Readiness Command, Fort Monmouth, N.J., 1974-79; chief inventory mgmt. div. Crane (Ind.) Army Ammunition Activity, 1979-80; supply systems analyst Hdqrs. 60th Ordnance Group, Zweibruecken, Fed. Republic Germany, 1980-83; chief inventory mgmt. div. Crane (Ind.) Army Ammunition Activity, 1983-85, chief control div., 1985; inventory mgmt. specialist 200th Theater Army Material Mgmt. Ctr., Zweibruecken, 1985-88; analyst supply systems U.S. Armament, Munitions and Chem. Command, Rock Island, Ill., 1988-89; specialist logistics mgt. U.S. Army Info. Systems Command, Ft. Huachuca, Ariz., 1989—. Mem. Federally Employed Women (chpt. pres. 1979-80), NAFE, Soc. Logistics Engrs., Assn. Computing Machinery, Am. Soc. Public Adminstrn., Soc. Profl. and Exec. Women, Assn. Info. Systems Profls., AAAS, NOW. Democrat.

KEENEY, EDMUND LUDLOW, physician; b. Shelbyville, Ind., Aug. 11, 1908; s. Bayard G. and Ethel (Adams) K.; m. Esther Cox Loney Wight, Mar. 14, 1950; children: Edmund Ludlow, Eleanor Seymour (Mrs. Cameron Leroy Smith). A.B., Ind. U., 1930; M.D., Johns Hopkins U., 1934. Diplomate Am. Bd. Internal Medicine. Intern Johns Hopkins Hosp., 1934-37, vis. physician, instr. internal medicine, 1940-48; practice medicine, specializing internal medicine San Diego, 1948- 55; dir. Scripps Clinic and Research Found., La Jolla, 1955-67; pres. Scripps Clinic and Research Found., 1967-77, pres. emeritus, 1977—; dir. rsch. on fungus infections OSRD, 1942-46. Author: Practical Medical Mycology, 1955, Medical Advice for International Travel; contbr. articles on allergy, immunology and mycology to med. jours. Bd. dirs. U. San Diego, Allergy Found. Am. Fellow A.C.P.; mem. A.M.A., Am. Soc. Clin. Investigation, Am. Acad. Allergy (pres. 1964), Western Assn. Physicians, Calif. Med. Assn., Western Soc. Clin. Research, Phi Beta Kappa, Alpha Omega Alpha, Beta Theta Pi. Republican. Presbyterian. Home: 338 Via Del Norte La Jolla CA 92037-6539 Office: 10666 N Torrey Pines Rd La Jolla CA 92037-1027

KEEP, JUDITH N., federal judge; b. Omaha, Mar. 24, 1944. B.A., Scripps Coll., 1966; J.D., U. San Diego, 1970. Bar: Calif. 1971. Atty. Defenders Inc., San Diego, 1971-73; pvt. practice law, 1973-76; asst. U.S. atty. U.S. Dept. Justice, 1976; judge Mcpl. Ct., San Diego, 1976-80; judge U.S. Dist. Ct. (so. dist.) Calif., San Diego, 1980—, chief judge, 1991-98; judge U.S. Office: US Dist Ct Ct Rm 16 940 Front St Ste 5190 San Diego CA 92101-8916*

KEFFER, MARIA JEAN, environmental auditor; b. Sacramento, Dec. 10, 1951; d. George Edwin and Genevieve Nellie (Babuska) Scott; m. Gerry Craig Keffer, Nov. 6, 1971; children: Annemarie, Gregory, Margaret. AA in Liberal Arts, San Bernardino Valley Coll., Calif., 1973; BS in Natural Scis., U. Alaska, 1988, MS in Environ. Quality, 1995. Cert. environ. auditor Nat. Registry of Environ. Profls., prin. environ. auditor/EARA - U.K.; registered environ. health specialist, Nat. Environ. Health Assn. and State of Calif. Rsch. lab. assoc. VA/Loma Linda (Calif.) Hosp., 1988-90; environ. health specialist San Bernardino County, Calif., 1990-91, S&S Engring., Eagle River, Alaska, 1991-92; regulatory specialist ENSR Consulting and Engring., Anchorage, 1992-94; quality assurance environ. specialist Alyeska Pipeline Svc. Co., Anchorage, 1994-98; ISO 14001 project mgr. Hoefler Consulting Group, Anchorage, 1998—. Mem. Environ. Auditing Roundtable, Nat. Environ. Health Assn. Office: Hoefler Consulting Group 1205 E International Rd Ste 201 Anchorage AK 99518-1409

KEGLEY, JOSEPH EDWARD, realtor; b. Red Bank, N.J., Dec. 4, 1942; m. Mary F. Blair, Jan. 31, 1942; children: Joseph, Jerry, Kimberley, Laura, Tracey. Grad. h.s. Cert. residential specialist, cert. investment specialist. Franchise owner Southland Corp., N.J., Ariz. and Nev., 1964-85; realtor Century 21 Personal Choice, Mesa, Ariz., 1985—. Mem. Nat. Assn. Realtors, Ariz. Assn. Realtors, Multi-Million Dollar Club. Avocations: traveling, coin collecting, sports. Home: 16533 E Tremaine St Gilbert AZ 85234-5209 Office: Century 21 Personal Choice 2815 S Alma School Rd Ste 115 Mesa AZ 85210-4032

KEHEW, GEORGE MANSIR, artist; b. Harvey, Ill., Aug. 17, 1923; s. George Henry and Blanche Willard (Holt) K.; m. Dolores Smith, Mar. 21, 1947; children: Eric Wayne, Roger Mark, Jai Lynne. Student, Chouinard Art Sch., L.A., Art Ctr. Coll. of Design, L.A. Cert. indsl. edn. tchr. Calif., Calif. C.C. tchr. in art, design and photography. Various positions in field to illustrator Northrop Aircraft Corp., Hawthorne, Calif., 1957-59; lead man, tech. illustrators Cannon & Sullivan, San Diego, 1959-61; art dir. applied oceanog. group Scripps Inst. Oceanography U. Calif., San Diego, 1961-66, illustrator, photographer Office Learning Resources, 1966-67; artist Complete Art Svc., San Diego, Calif., 1966-68; illustrator, tng. visuals Grumman Aerospace, NAS Miramar, Calif., 1972-73; visual info. specialist Naval Edn. and Tng. Support Ctr., San Diego, 1973-85; alt. mem. Equal Employment Opportunity Com., San Diego, 1983. Artist/author: Mac Goes to the Hospital, Best Friends Animal Coloring and Activity Book; creator ofcl. Squadron patch (Red Wolf) for VF-1 Mira Mar Naval Air Sta., logo for Scripps Applied Oceanographic Group, Point Loma, Calif., (game) Bushwacker; syndicated cartoon Hamalot; exhibiting cartoonist 1968 Terre Des Hommes, Man and His World, Pavilion de L'Humor, Montreal; designer, dir. TV show Art Around Us, San Diego Area Instrnl. TV Authority, 1965, others; work exhibited at Kimbell Art Ctr., Park City, Utah, 1998, Prince Gallery, St. George, Utah, 1998, Watchman, Springdale, Utah, 1998, New Garden Cafe Art Gallery, Hurricane, Utah, 1997-98, others; contbr. articles to Desert Mag. Sgt. U.S. Army, 1942-46. Recipient numerous art awards, including Bicentennial First Ann. Best of Show award, 1976, Merit award in publs. San Diego C.C., 1972; grantee in field. Mem. San Diego Watercolor Soc. (pres. 1967-68). Democrat. Avocations: mountain biking, cross country skiing, sailing, classic guitar.

KEHOE, VINCENT JEFFRÉ-ROUX, photographer, author, cosmetic company executive; b. Bklyn., N.Y., Sept. 12, 1921; s. John James and Bertha Florence (Roux) K.; m. Gena Irene Marino, Nov. 2, 1966. Student, MIT, 1940-41, Lowell Technol. Inst., 1941-42, Boston U., 1942; BFA in Motion Picture and TV Prodn., Columbia U., 1957. Dir. make-up dept. CBS-TV, N.Y.C., 1948-49, NBC Hallmark Hall of Fame series, 1951-53; make-up artist in charge of make-up for numerous film, TV and stage prodns., 1942—; dir. make-up Turner Hall Corp., 1959-61, Internat. Beauty Show, 1962-66; pres., dir. research Research Council of Make-up Artists, Inc., 1963—; chief press officer at Spanish Pavilion, N.Y. World's Fair, 1965; free-lance photographer, 1956—. Contbr. photographs to numerous mags. including Time, Life, Sports Illustrated, Argosy, Popular Photography; author: The Technique of Film and Television Make-up for Color, 1970, The Make-up Artist in the Beauty Salon, 1969, We Were There: April 19, 1775, 1974, A Military Guide, 1974, 2d rev. edit., 1993, The Re-Created Officer's

Guide, 1996, The Technique of the Professional Makeup Artist, 1985, 2nd edit., 1995, Special Make-up Effects, 1991; author-photographer bullfighting books: Aficionado! (N.Y. Art Dirs. Club award 1960), Wine, Women and Toros! (N.Y. Art Dirs. award 1962); producer: (documentary color film) Matador de Toros, 1959. Served with inf. U.S. Army, World War II, ETO. Decorated Purple Heart, Bronze Star, CIB; recipient Torch award Council of 13 Original States, 1979. Fellow Co. Mil. Historians; mem. Tenth Foot Royal Lincolnshire Regimental Assn. (life; Hon. Col. 1968), Soc. Motion Picture and TV Engrs. (life), Acad. TV Arts and Scis., Soc. for Army Hist. Research (Eng.) (life), Brit. Officers Club New England (life), 10th Mountain Div. Assn. (life), 70th Inf. Div. (life), DAV (life), Nat. Rifle Assn. (life), Eagle Scout Assn. (life), Naval Club, London. Home and Office: PO Box 850 Somis CA 93066-0850

KEIM, MICHAEL RAY, dentist; b. Sabetha, Kans., June 8, 1951; s. Milton Leroy and Dorothy Juanita (Stover) K.; m. Christine Anne Lorenzen, Nov. 20, 1971; children: Michael Scott, Dawn Marie, Erik Alan. Student, U. Utah, 1969-72; DDS, Creighton U., 1976. Pvt. practice Casper, Wyo., 1976—; vertical math. com. mem. Natrona County Sch. Dist., 1997—. Mem. organizing bd. dirs. Ctrl. Wyo. Soccer Assn., 1976-77; mem. Casper Mountain Ski Patrol, Nat. Ski Patrol Sys., 1980—, avalanche and ski mountaineering advisor No. Divsn. Region III, 1992-96, outdoor emergency care instr. trainer, 1996—; 1st asst. patrol dir. Nat. Ski Patrol Sys., 1996-98, patrol dir., 1998—; bd. dirs., dep. commr. for fast pitch Wyo. Amateur Softball Assn., 1980-84; bd. dirs. Ctrl. Wyo. Softball Assn., 1980-84; pres. Wyo. Spl. Smiles Found., 1995-96; mem. organizing com. Prevent Abuse & Neglect thru Dental Awareness Coalition, Wyo., 1996; mem. adv. com. Natrona County Headstart, 1985—. Recipient Purple Merit Star for Saving a Life, 1992. Mem.. ADA, Fedn. Dentaire Internat., Pierre Fauchard Acad., Wyo. Acad. Gen. Dentristry (sec.-treas. 1980-82, pres. 1982-87), Wyo. Dental Assn. (bd. dirs. 1992-97, chmn. conv. 1993-2000, ADA alt. del. 1994-95, v.p. 1993-94, pres.-elect 1994-95, pres. 1995-96, editor 1997—), Wyo. Dental Polit. Action Com. (sec.-treas. 1985-97), Ctrl. Wyo. Dental Assn. (sec.-treas. 1981-82, pres. 1982-83), Wyo. Dental Hist. Assn. (bd. dirs. 1989-95), Wyo. Donated Dental Svcs. (organizing bd. dirs. 1994, pres. 1995-96), Kiwanis (v.p. Casper club 1988-89, bd. dirs. 1986-96, pres.-elect 1989-90, pres. 1990-91, internat. del. 1989-91, chmn. internat. rels. com. 1992—, Rocky Mountain dist. lt. gov.-elect divsn. 1 1997-98, lt. gov. divsn. 1 1998—), Creighton Club (pres. 1982-84). Methodist. Avocations: hunting, skiing, sports, woodworking, photography. Home: 58 Jonquil St Casper WY 82604-3863 Office: 1749 S Boxelder St Casper WY 82604-3538

KEINER, CHRISTIAN MARK, lawyer; b. Omaha, Mar. 16, 1953; s. John Frederick Keiner and Geraldine Elizabeth (Smith) Eadie; m. Rosemary Monique White, Nov. 21, 1980; 1 child, Colin MacGregor. BA with high honors, U. Calif., Santa Barbara, 1977; JD with distinction, U. of Pacific, 1980. Bar: Calif. 1980, U.S. Ct. Appeals (9th cir.) 1988, U.S. Supreme Ct. 1991. Assoc. Biddle, Walters, Bukey, Sacramento, 1980-82, Biddle and Hamilton, Sacramento, 1982-92; pvt. practice Sacramento, 1992-98; ptnr. Girard and Vinson, 1998—. Contbr. articles to law jours. Bd. dirs. Calif. Found. for Improvement Employer-Employee Rels., Sacramento, 1994—, Calif. Coun. Sch. Attys., Sacramento, 1996—; instr., mem. labor-mgmt. adv. com. U. Calif. Davis Extension, Sacramento, 1986—. Recipient award for adminstrv. law Am. Jurisprudence, 1979. Mem. ABA (pub. law sect.), Sacramento County Bar (adminstv., pub. and employment law sects.), Sacramento Capitol Club, Harry S. Truman Club (pres. 1992), Order of Coif. Democrat. Catholic. Office: 1006 4th St Ste 701 Sacramento CA 95814-3314

KEIPER, MARILYN MORRISON, elementary education educator; b. South Gate, Calif., June 12, 1930; d. David Cline and Matilda Ruth (Pearce) M.; m. Edward E. Keiper, June 18, 1962; children: Becky S. Swickard, Edward M. BA, Calif. State U., L.A., 1954; postgrad., UCLA, 1968. Elem. tchr. Rosemead (Calif.) Sch. Dist., 1954—; recreation leader L.A. County, 1951-62, 2d reader 1st Ch. Christ Scientist, Arcadia, Calif., 1991-94; mem. cons. Janson Adv. Group, Rosemead, 1985—; bd. dirs. Janson PTA, Rosemead, 1985—; participant Sta. KNBC Spirit of Edn., 1990-92. Named Tchr. of the Yr., L.A. County, 1983-84; recipient Recognition award for outstanding service to children, Theta Kappa Chpt. Delta Kappa Gamma, 1996. Fellow Rosemead Tchrs. Assn., Delta Kappa Gamma.

KEIR, GERALD JANES, banker; b. Ludlow, Mass., Aug. 22, 1943; s. Alexander J. and Evelyn M. (Buckley) K.; m. Karen Mary Devine, July 22, 1972; children: Matthew J., Katherine B., Megan E. BA, Mich. State U., 1964, MA, 1966. Reporter Honolulu Advertiser, 1968-74, city editor, 1974-86, mng. editor, 1986-89, editor, 1989-95; sr. v.p. corp. comms. First Hawaiian Bank, Honolulu, 1995—. Co-author text: Advanced Reporting: Beyond News Events, 1985, Advanced Reporting: Discovering Patterns in News Events. Bd. govs. Hawaii Cmty. Found. Recipient Nat. Reporting award Am. Polit. Sci. Assn., 1971, Benjamin Fine Nat. award Am. Assn. Secondary Sch. Prins., 1981; John Ben Snow fellow, 1983, NEH fellow, 1973. Mem. Soc. Profl. Journalists, Asian-Am. Journalists Assn., Social Sci. Assn., Am. Bankers Assn. (comm. coun.), Pacific Club. Office: First Hawaiian Bank PO Box 3200 Honolulu HI 96847-0001

KEIRSEY, DAVID WEST, psychologist, writer; b. Ada, Okla., Aug. 31, 1921; s. Norris Stanley and Jo (Fowler) K.; m. Alice Marie Winterbourne, Dec. 22, 1945; children: Janene, David, Tamara. BA in Psychology, Pomona Coll., 1947; MA in Psychology, Claremont U., 1950, PhD in Psychology, 1967. Clin. lic. psychologist, Calif. Counselor Probation Dept., San Bernardino, Calif., 1950-52; sch. psychologist Rosemead (Calif.) Schs., 1952-55; coord. sch. psychology Covina (Calif.) Schs., 1955-68, Newport Mesa Schs., Newport Beach, Calif., 1968-71; prof. counseling, dept. head Calif. State U., Fullerton, 1971-82; writer Del Mar, Calif., 1982—. Author: Polarization of Intelligence, 1967, Please Understand Me, 1978, Portraits of Temperament, 1987, Please Understand Me II, 1998; co-author: (with Chaniere) Presidential Temperament, 1992. Capt. USMC, 1942-46, PTO. Libertarian. Avocations: tennis, golf, swimming, weight lifting.

KEISLING, PHILLIP ANDREW, state official; b. Portland, Oreg., June 23, 1955; s. Les and Ione Keisling; m. Pam Wiley, Sept. 4, 1988. BA, Yale U., 1977. Speech writer Gov. Tom McCall Campaign, Salem, Oreg., 1978; reporter Willamette Week, Portland, 1978-81; editor Washington Monthly mag., 1982-84; sr. legis asst. Oreg. Speakers of the Ho., Salem, 1985-88; mem. Oreg. Ho. of Reps., Salem, 1989-91; sec. of state State of Oreg., Salem, 1991—; mem. State Land Bd., Salem, 1991—. Chmn. Brooklyn Neighborhood Assn., Portland, 1986-88. Office: Office Sec of State State Capitol Rm 136 Salem OR 97310

KEISTER, JEAN CLARE, lawyer; b. Warren, Ohio, Aug. 28, 1931; d. John R. Keister and Anna Helen Brennan. JD, Southwesten U., 1966. Bar: Calif. 1967, U.S. Supreme Ct. 1972, U.S. Dist. Ct. (so. dist.) Calif. 1988. Legal writer Gilbert Law Summaries, L.A., 1967; instr. Glendale (Calif.) Coll. Law, 1968; pvt. practice Glendale, 1967-70, L.A., Calif., 1970-80, Burbank, Calif., 1987-97, Lancaster, Calif., 1992—, Ventura, Calif, 1997—. Mem. Themis Soc., 1989-97. Recipient Golden Poet award World of Poetry. Mem. Burbank Bar Assn. (sec. 1993), Ventura County Bar Assn., Antelope Valley Bar Assn. Avocations: writing prose and poetry, travel, crochet.

KEITH, BRUCE EDGAR, political analyst, genealogist; b. Curtis, Nebr., Feb. 17, 1918; s. Edgar L. and Corinne E. (Marsteller) K.; m. Evelyn E. Johnston, Oct. 29, 1944; children: Mona Louise, Kent Marsteller, Melanie Ann. AB with high distinction, Nebr. Wesleyan U., 1940; MA, Stanford U., 1952; grad. Command and Staff, Marine Corps Schs., 1958, Sr. Resident Sch., Naval War Coll., 1962; PhD, U. Calif.-Berkeley, 1982. Commd. 2d lt. U.S. Marine Corps, 1942, advanced through grades to col., 1962, ret., 1971, OinC Marine Corps Nat. Media, N.Y.C., 1946-49, support arms coord. 1st Marines, Seoul, Chosin, Korea, 1950, comdg. officer 3d Bn., 11th Marines, 1958-59, ops. officer, Pres. Dwight D. Eisenhower visit to Okinawa, 1960, G-3 ops. officer Fleet Marine Force, Pacific, Cuban Missile Crisis, 1962, mem. U.S. del. SEATO, Planning Conf., Bangkok, Thailand, 1964, G-3, Fleet Marine Force, Pacific, 1964-66, head Strategic Planning Study Dept., Naval War Coll., 1966-68, genealogist, 1967—, exec. officer Hdqrs. Marine Corps programs, Washington, 1968-71; election analyst Inst. Govtl. Studies, U. Calif.-Berkeley, 1974-86, polit. analyst, 1986—; teaching asst. U. Calif.-Berkeley, 1973-74. Bd. dirs., Bay Area Funeral Soc., 1980-83, v.p., 1981-83. Decorated Bronze Star, Navy Commendation medal, Presdl. Unit citation with 3 bronze stars. Recipient Phi Kappa Phi Silver medal Nebr. Wesleyan U., 1940, Alumni award, 1964. Mem. Am. Polit. Sci. Assn., Acad. Polit. Sci., Am. Acad. Polit. and Social Sci., World Affairs Coun. No. Calif., Marine Corps Assn., Ret. Officers Assn. Phi Kappa Phi, Pi Gamma Mu. Republican. Unitarian. Clubs: Commonwealth of Calif. (San Francisco), Marines' Meml. (San Francisco). Lodge: Masons. Contbg. author: The Descendants of Daniel and Elizabeth (Disbrow) Keith, 1979-81; History of Curtis, Nebraska-The First Hundred Years, 1984; author: A Comparison of the House Armed Services Coms. in the 91st and 94th Congresses: How They Differed and Why, 1982; The Johnstons of Morning Sun, 1979; The Marstellers of Arrellton, 1978; The Morris Family of Brookville, 1977; Japan-the Key to America's Future in the Far East, 1962; A United States General Staff: A Must or a Monster?, 1950; co-author: California Votes, 1960-72, 1974; The Myth of the Independent Voter, 1992; Further Evidence on the Partisan Affinities of Independent " Leaners," 1983. Address: PO Box 2368 Walnut Creek CA 94595

KEITH, NORMAN THOMAS, aerospace company administrator; b. Antioch, Calif., Jan. 12, 1936; s. Dean Theodore and Edna Margaret (Doty) K.; m. Marla Mildred Osten, Sept. 9, 1962. B of Tech., Tex. State Tech. Inst. Cert. profl. mgr. Field service engr. Gen. Dynamics Corp., San Diego, 1955-66, supr. Data Ctr., 1966-76, chief data systems, 1976-81, chief property adminstrn., 1981-83, motivational mgr., 1983-86, sr. program adminstr., 1986-90, mgr. total quality mgmt.Convair divsn., 1990—. Contbr. articles to profl. jours. Mem. mil. adv. bd. congressman Ron Packard, 1983-86; sgt. Res. Dep. Sheriff's Office, San Diego County; bd. dirs. San Dieguito Boys/Girls Clubs, Encinitas, 1966-69; loaned exec. United Way, San Diego, 1980-81; security lt. 22nd Dist. AG Assn. State of Calif. Del Mar Fairgrounds, 1992—. Mem. Nat. Mgmt. Assn. (bd. dirs., pres.), Nat. U. Alumni Assn. (life), Woodbury Coll. Alumni Assn., San Diego State U. Alumni Assn., Hon. Dep. Sheriff's Assn. (bd. dirs.). Republican. Lutheran. Lodges: Lions (sec. 1962-63), Elks. Home: 620 Cole Ranch Rd Encinitas CA 92024-6522 Office: Gen Dynamics Convair Div 5001 Kearny Villa Rd San Diego CA 92123-1407

KEITH, PAULINE MARY, artist, illustrator, writer; b. Fairfield, Nebr., July 21, 1924; d. Siebelt Ralph and Pauline Alethia (Garrison) Goldenstein; m. Everett B. Keith, Feb. 14, 1957; 1 child, Nathan Ralph. Student, George Fox Coll., 1947-48, Oreg. State U., 1955. Illustrator Merlin Press, San Jose, Calif., 1980-81; artist, illustrator, watercolorist Corvallis, Oreg., 1980—. Author 5 chapbooks, 1980-85; editor: Four Generations of Verse, 1979; contbr. poems to anthologies and mags. and articles to mags.; one-woman shows include Roger's Meml. Libr., Forest Grove, Oreg., 1959, Corvallis Art Ctr., 1960, 98-99, Human Resources Bldg., Corvallis, 1959-61, Chintimini Sr. Ctr., 1994—, Corvallis Parteral Counseling Ctr., 1992-94, 96, Hall Gallery, Sr. Ctr., 1993, 94, 95-96, 97, 98, Consumer Power, Philomath, Oreg., 1994, Art, Etc., Newburg, Oreg., 1995, 96, 97, 98,; exhibited in group shows at Hewlett-Packard Co., 1984-85, Corvallis Art Ctr., 1992, Chintimini Sr. Ctr., 1992. Co-elder First Christian Ch. (Disciples of Christ), Corvallis, 1988-89, co-deacon, 1980-83, elder, 1991-93; sec. Hostess Club of Chintimini Sr. Ctr., Corvallis, 1987, pres., 1988-89, v.p., 1992-94. Recipient Watercolor 1st price Benton County Fair, 1982, 83, 88, 89, 91, 2d prize, 1987, 91, 3d prize, 1984, 90, 92. Mem. Oreg. Assn. Christian Writers, Internat. Assn. Women Mins., Am. Legion Aux. (elected poet post II Covallis chpt. 1989-90, elected sec. 1991-92, chaplain 1992-93, 94-95, v.p. 1994-95), Chintimine Artists. Republican. Avocations: nature walks, singing in church choir. Office: 304 S College St Newberg OR 97132-3114

KEITH, SUSAN M., fundraiser; b. Oakland, Calif., Aug. 10, 1943; d. John Joseph Jr. and Joyce Julia (Luzi) Moore; m. James Alden Keith, Nov. 14, 1970; children: Christine Marie, Jennifer Moore. BA in English, Calif. State U., Hayward, 1967. Media rels. cons. Calif. Polytech. U., Pomona, 1972-78; dir. of pub. info. Pitzer Coll., Claremont, Calif., 1981-85; dir. of media rels. Claremont U., 1985-87; ptnr. Ring, Robinson & Assocs., Claremont, 1988-90; owner Keith Cons., Claremont, 1988-90; dir. of devel. House of Ruth, Claremont, 1994—. Bd. dirs. Citrus Coll. Found., The Claremont Forum, Claremont C. of C.; adv. bd. St. Ambrose Youth Wellness Program; mem. steering com. Claremont Youth Partnership; past pres. Claremont Bd. of Edn., 1991-92, 94-95, Baldy View Regional Occupation Program Commn., others. Named to Outstanding Young Women of Am., 1978, Grand Marshall, 4th of July Parade, Claremont, 1998; recipient Woman of Achievement, YWCA, Pomona, 1998, Cmty. Hero award L.A. County Fair Assn., 1997. Mem. Pub. Rels. Assn. of So. Calif. Colls. (founding bd. dirs.), Rotary. Avocations: gardening, sailing, friends, family.

KEIZER, SUSAN JANE, artist; b. Montreal, Que., Can., Sept. 26, 1940; d. Roy Laver and Eulalia Frances (Shively) Swank; m. Joel Edward Keizer, Dec. 8, 1964; children: Sidney Jacob, Sarah Rebecca. BA, Reed Coll., 1964; postgrad., U. Calif. Davis, 1973-77, Md. Inst., 1978-79; MA, Calif. State U. Sacramento, 1981. Sci. illustrator Oreg. Health Scis. U., Portland, 1964, Santa Cruz, Davis, Calif., 1967-87; instr. drawing Davis Art Ctr., 1976-78; guest instr. art Calif. State U., Sacramento, 1983; vis. lectr. U. Calif. Davis, 1989; artist Davis, 1976—; guest artist San Jose (Calif.) Mus. Sch., 1986; coord. West Coast Women's Conf., Heceta Head, Oreg., 1983; assoc. dir. Lester Gallery, Inverness, Calif., 1981-82; adj. faculty art Am. River Coll., Sacramento, 1997. Exhibited in numerous one-woman and group shows, 1976—; represented in numerous corp. and pvt. collections. Mem. exec. bd. Nelson ARTfriends U. Calif., Davis, 1992-96, chair benefit exhbn. Nelson Gallery, 1994—. MacDowell Colony fellow, Peterborough, N.H., 1986. Mem. AAUW, Women's Caucus for Art, Artists Equity. Home and Office: 2513 Madrid Ct Davis CA 95616-0141

KELEN, JOYCE ARLENE, social worker; b. N.Y.C., Dec. 5, 1949; d. Samuel and Rebecca (Rochman) Green; m. Leslie George Kelen, Jan. 31, 1971; children: David, Jonathan. BA, Lehman Coll., 1970; MSW, Univ. Utah, 1974, DSW, 1980. Recreation dir. N.Y.C. Housing Authority, Bronx, 1970-72; cottage supr. Kennedy Home, Bronx, 1974; sch. social worker Davis County Sch. Dist., Farmington, Utah, 1976-86; clin. asst. prof. U. Utah., Salt Lake City, 1976—; sch. social worker Salt Lake City Sch. Dist., 1986—; cons. in field, Salt Lake City, 1981—. Editor: To Whom Are We Beautiful As We Go?, 1979; contbr. articles to profl. jours. Utah Coll. of Nursing grantee, 1985. Mem. Nat. Assn. Social Workers (chairperson Gerontology Council, 1983-84, Utah Sch. Social Worker of Yr., 1977), NEA, Utah Edn. Assn., Davis Edn. Assn. Democrat. Jewish. Avocations: tennis, camping, guitar. Home: 128 M St Salt Lake City UT 84103-3854 Office: Franklin Elem Sch 1100 W 400 S Salt Lake City UT 84104-2334

KELLAM, NORMA DAWN, medical, surgical nurse; b. Benton Harbor, Mich., June 13, 1938; d. Edgar Arnold and Bernice (Cronk) K. AA, San Bernardino Valley Coll., 1958; student, Calif. State Coll., Long Beach, 1961-1964, 1965, 1966, 1967; BS, San Diego State Coll., 1961; MS, Calif. State U., Fresno, 1972. Nursing instr. Porterville (Calif.) State Hosp., 1968-69; staff nurse Northside Psychiat. Hosp., Fresno, 1969-72; nursing instr. Pasadena (Calif.) City Coll., 1972-73; night shift lead Fairview Devel. Ctr., Costa Mesa, Calif., 1973-96; freelance writer, 1996—. Contbr. articles to newspapers. Vol. Spanish translator for Interstitial Cystitis Assn. Recipient Cert. of Appreciation for vol. work Interstitial Cystitis Assn. Mem. ANA (Calif. chpt.), Am. Translators Assn. (assoc.), Soc. Urologic Nurses and Assocs., Inc., Phi Kappa Phi.

KELLEHER, RICHARD CORNELIUS, marketing and communications executive; b. Buffalo, Nov. 21, 1949; s. Cornelius and Lucile Norma (White) K.; m. Sherri Fae Anderson, Mar. 17, 1981 (div. 1991); children: Erin Marie, Shawn Michael. BA, U. New Mex., 1975; MBA, U. Phoenix, 1984. Reporter, photographer Daily Lobo, Albuquerque, 1973-75; mgn. editor News Bulletin, Belen, New Mex., 1975-77; various corp. mktg. titles AT&T Mountain Bell, Denver, 1978-84; exec. editor Dairy Mag., Denver, 1984-86; communications dir. Am. Heart Assn., Phoenix, 1987-90; cons. Kelleher Communications & Mktg., Phoenix, 1990—, spl. writer Denver Post, 1977-82, Denver Corr. Billboard Mag., 1977-82. Mem. Gov.'s Roundtable on Employee Productivity, Gov. of Ariz., 1990-91; vol. communications Am. Cancer Soc., 1990-92. Recipient Honor Communications Study award 1986. Mem. Pub. Rels. Soc. Am., Toastmasters.

KELLER, ARTHUR MICHAEL, computer science researcher; s. David and Luba Keller. BS summa cum laude with honors, Bklyn. Coll., 1977, MS, Stanford U., 1979, PhD, 1985. Instr. computer sci. Stanford (Calif.) U., 1979-81, rsch. asst., 1977-85, acting asst. chmn. dept. computer sci., 1982, rsch. assoc., 1985, 89-91, vis. asst. prof., 1987-89, rsch. scientist, 1991-92, sr. rsch. scientist, 1992—; sr. rsch. scientist Advanced Decision Systems, Mountain View, Calif., 1989-92; chief tech. advisor Persistence Software, San Mateo, Calif., 1991—; founder, CFO, COO Epistemics, Inc., Palo Alto, Calif., 1996-99; founder, chief tech. advisor buyermail.com, Mountain View, Calif., 1998—; chief tech. advisor Epistemics, Inc., Palo Alto, Calif., 1999—; sys. analyst Bklyn. Coll. Computer Ctr., 1974-77; summer rsch. asst. IBM, Thomas J. Watson Rsch. Ctr., Yorktown Heights, N.Y., 1980; acad. assoc. IBM San Jose Rsch. Lab., 1981; asst. prof. U. Tex., Austin, 1985-88, adj. asst. prof., 1988-89; mem. program com. Internat. Conf. on Data Engring., L.A., 1986, 87, 89, Internat. Conf. on Very Large Data Bases, Amsterdam, The Netherlands, 1989; mem. program com. Internat. Workshop on Advanced Transaction Models & Architectures, Goa, India, 1996, Internat. Conf. on Info. & Knowledge Mgmt., Rockville, Md., 1996; founder, chief tech. advisor, bd. dirs. Buyermail.com. Corp. Author: A First Course in Computer Programming Using Pascal, 1982. Bd. dirs. Congregation Kol Emeth, Palo Alto. Mem. IEEE (vice chmn. com. database engring. Computer Soc. 1986-87), Assn. Computing Machinery, TeX Users Group (fin. com. 1983-85, internat. coord. 1985-87), Chai Soc. (communications officer 1987-89, v.p. publicity 1989-90). Avocations: singing, travel. Home: 3881 Corina Way Palo Alto CA 94303-4507 Office: Stanford U Dept Computer Sci Gates Bldg 2A Stanford CA 94305-9020

KELLER, J(AMES) WESLEY, credit union executive; b. Jonesboro, Ark., Jan. 6, 1958; s. Norman Grady and Norma Lee (Ridgeway) Patrick; m. Patricia Marie Delavan, July 7, 1979. Student, U. Miss., 1976-78; BS in Bus. and Mgmt., Redlands U., 1991, MBA, 1994. Sr. collector Rodkwell Fed. Credit Union, Downey, Calif., 1978-79; acct. Lucky Fed. Credit Union, Buena Park, Calif., 1979-84; pres., chief exec. officer Long Beach (Calif.) State Employees Credit Union, 1984—. Mem. Credit Union Exec. Soc., Calif. Credit Union League (bd. govs. Long Beach chpt., treas. 1985-86), So. Calif. Credit Union Mgrs. Assn., U. Redlands Whitehead Leadership Soc., Nat. Assn. State Charted Credit Unions (chmn. 1995—), Kiwanis. Republican. Baptist. Avocations: photography, skiing, woodworking, biking. Office: Long Beach State Employees Credit Union 3840 N Long Beach Blvd Long Beach CA 90807-3312

KELLER, KENT EUGENE, advertising and public relations executive; b. Oil City, Pa., Oct. 5, 1941; s. George W. and Lois (Wallace) K.; divorced; children: Eric Trent, Todd Jason. BA, Kent State U., 1963; cert., Chrysler Inst., Detroit, 1968, UCLA, 1973. Editor Oil City (Pa.) Derrick, 1959-60; various mgmt. positions Chrysler Corp., Twinsburg, Ohio, 1960-64, prodn. cont. mgr., 1964-67; group mgr. Chrysler Corp. AMG, Detroit, 1967-69; dir. advt. and pub. rels. Zero Corp., Burbank, Calif., 1969-75; exec. v.p. Basso & Assocs. Inc., Newport Beach, Calif., 1975-80; pres. Jason Trent & Co., Inc., North Tustin, Calif., 1980—; pub. rels. counsel Electronic Convs. Inc., L.A., 1980-85; bd. dirs. Neurosci. Tech. Inc., Tarzana, Calif.; cons. Global Engring., Irvine, Calif., 1989—; co-founder Strategic Concepts, Fountain Valley, Calif., 1990. Editor (industry report) TOLD Report, 1985—, (mag.) Zero Dimensions, 1969-75. Mem. Town Hall of Calif., L.A., 1980—. Mem. Bus. & Profl. Advt. Assn., Pub. Rels. Soc. Am., Back Bay Club. Republican. Presbyterian. Avocations: golf, tennis, collectable art. Home: 18072 Darmel Pl Santa Ana CA 92705-1916 Office: 1440 S State College Blvd Anaheim CA 92806-5724

KELLER, MICHAEL ALAN, librarian, educator, musicologist; b. Sterling, Colo., Apr. 5, 1945; s. Ephraim Richard and Mary Patricia (Warren) K.; m. Constance A. Kyle, Sept. 3, 1967 (div. Aug. 1979); children: Kristen J., Paul B.; m. Carol Lawrence, Oct. 6, 1979; children: Laura W., Martha M. BA, Hamilton Coll., 1967; MA, SUNY, Buffalo, 1970, postgrad., 1970-91; MLS, SUNY, Geneseo, 1972. Asst. libr. for reference and cataloging SUNY Music Libr., Buffalo, 1970-73; acting undergrad. libr. Cornell U., Ithaca, N.Y., 1976; music libr., sr. lectr. Cornell U., Ithaca, 1973-81; head music libr. U. Calif., Berkeley, 1981-86; assoc. univ. libr. for collection devel. Yale U., 1986-93; director Stanford (Calif.) U. Librs., 1993-94, univ. libr., dir. acad. info. resources, 1994—; pub. HighWire Press, Stanford, 1995—; cons. Bates Coll., Lewiston, Maine, 1976, Colgate U., Hamilton, N.Y., 1976, Rutgers U., New Brunswick, N.J., 1982, Brown U., Providence, 1983, U. Alta., Edmonton, Can., 1983, NYU, 1984, L.A. Music Ctr. Opera Co., 1985-89, City of Ferrara, Italy, U. Pitts., Villa I Tatti-Biblioteca Berenson, Florence, Italy, Am. Phys. Soc., Princeton U., Newsweek Mag., Hamilton Coll., Clinton, N.Y., Sierra Nev. Coll., Ind. U., Coun. Australian Univ. Librs., U. Tech., Sydney, Griffith U., Brisbane, Ind. U., Occidental Coll., L.A., U. Melbourne; mem. Nat. Digital Libr. Fedn., 1993—; mem. Bibliog Commn., Repertoire Internat. de la Presse Mus. de XIXe Siecle, 1981-84; chmn. music program com. Rsch. Librs. Group, 1982-86; reviewer NEH, 1982-88, panelist, 1979-95; chmn. Assoc. Music Librs. Group, Joint Com. Retrospecive Conversion in Music, 1989-93; mem. collection mgmt. devel. com. Rsch. Librs. Group, 1986-91, chmn., 1989-91, mem. program adv. com., 1991-93; dir. Berkeley Italian Renaissance Project, 1985-95, Digital Libr. Fedr., 1994—; mem. bd. overseers Stanford U., 1997—; mem. gov. com. Stanford-Japan Ctr. Rsch. Author: MSS on Microfilm in Music Libr. at SUNYAB, 1971, (with Duckles) Music Reference and Rsch. Materials; an annotated bibliography, 1988, 94; contbr. articles to profl. jours. Firefighter, rescue squad mem. Cuyuga Heights Vol. Fire Co., N.Y., 1980-81. Recipient spl. commendation Nat. Music Clubs, 1978, Berkeley Bronze medal U. Calif.-Berkeley, 1983; NDEA Title IV fellow SUNY-Buffalo, 1967-70; Cornell Coll. Arts and Scis. rsch. grantee, 1973-81, U. Calif.-Berkeley humanities rsch. grantee, 1983-84, Coun. on Libr. Resources grantee, 1984, 93-99, Libr. Assn. U. Calif. grantee, 1985-86, NEH grantee, 1986, Deems Taylor award ASCAP., 1988, Stanford U. fellow, 1994-95. Fellow Pierson Coll., Yale U.; mem. ALA, AAUP, Music Libr. Assn. (bd. dirs. 1975-77, mem. fin. com. 1982-83, mem. editl. com. index and bibliography series 1981-85), Internat. Assn. Music Librs., Am. Musicol. Soc. (mem. com. on automated bibliography 1982-83, mem. coun. 1986-88), Conn. Acad. Arts and Scis. (bd. dirs.), Ctr. Rsch. Librs. (mem. adv. com. 1988-90), Conn. Ctr. for Books (bd. dirs.), Book Club of Calif., Roxburghe Club of San Francisco, Bohemian Club, San Francisco. Home: 809 San Francisco Ter Stanford CA 94305-1021 Office: Stanford U Cecil Green Libr Stanford CA 94305-6004

KELLER, RAY B., counselor; b. Big Fork, Mont., Feb. 28, 1934; s. Benjaman Mathew and Mina Amelia (Hanson) K.; m. Barbara Lynn Daly, Dec. 28, 1961; 1 child, Forest Ry. BA, U. Mont., 1964; postgrad., No. Mont. Coll., 1989-91; MEd, Mont. State U., 1996, postgrad., 1996—. Cert. counselor, Mont. Elem. tchr. Pub. Schs. Birch Creek Hutterite Colony, Dupuyer, Mont., 1962-63, Black Feet Indian Reservation, Heart Butte, Mont., 1963-64; youth counselor Mont. State Employment Svc., 1964-67; H.S. counselor Ft. Benton (Mont.) Pub. Schs., 1967-68; counselor for emotionally disturbed, head master Manzanita Ranch Residential Sch., Hyompon, Calif., 1970-82; pvt. practice Bigfork, Mont., 1982-85; edn. tchr. Blackfeet C.C., Browning, Mont., 1987-89; elem. counselor Blackfeet Indian Reservation Pub. Schs., Browning, Mont., 1989-99; pvt. practice diagnosis, instrn. and cons. Reading Essentials, 1999—; cons. in field. Editor Eagle's View Publ., 1989—; co-author: Reading Pals-A Handbook for Volunteers, 1990, Reading Pals-A Teachers Manual, 1990, The Parents Guide-Studying Made Easy, 1991, Gifts of Love and Literacy-A Parents Guide to Raising Children Who Love to Read, 1993, Read With Your Child-Make a Difference, 1994, The Students Guide-Studying Made Easy, 1996. Active Pers. Vol. Svcs., Bigfork, 1970—. With USN, 1955-57. Named Author of Yr., Am. Ednl. Inst., 1993. Mem. Am. Fedn. Tchrs., Lit. Vols. Am., Mont. Counselors Assn., Mont. Counseling Assn. Avocations: reading, hiking, fishing, hunting. Home: PO Box 1814 Browning MT 59417-1814 Office: Eagles View Publ 750 Cascade Ave Bigfork MT 59911-3625

KELLER, ROBERT M., bishop. Bishop Evang. Luth. Ch. in Am., Spokane, Wash., 1987—. Office: Synod of E Washington-Idaho 314 S Spruce St Ste A Spokane WA 99204-1023*

KELLER, SHARON PILLSBURY, speech pathologist; b. L.A., Sept. 28, 1935; d. Edward Gardner and Iris Noriene (Hager) Pillsbury; m. Clarence Stanley Keller (dec. 1982); children: Joan Kathleen, Jennifer Beth, Lauren Elaine. AA, Chaffey Community Coll., Alta Loma, Calif., 1971; BA, U. La

Verne, 1978, MS in Communicative Disorders, 1983. Lic. speech pathologist, sch. audiometrist, calif.; life svc. credential clin. and rehabilitative, Calif. Lang. speech and hearing specialist Chino (Calif.) Unified Schs., 1978-86, Rim of the World Sch. Dist., Lake Arrowhead, Calif., 1986—; speech and lang. pathologist Lake Arrowhead Elem. Sch., 1986-89, Mary P. Henk Mid. Sch., 1986-89, Valley of Enchantment Elem. Sch., Lake Arrowhead, Calif., 1989—; cons. Assn. Speech and Hearing Svcs., Chino, 1984; former cons. infant lang. devel., teenage parent program Buena Vista Continuation H.S., Boys' Republic H.S., Chino; trainer pre-sch. and parent/child interaction Headstart, Chino; active Home program Mountain Cmtys., San Bernardino County Pre-Sch., 1988-89. Anchor Mountain Cmtys. News, Falcon Cable TV. Mem. bd. deacons, moderator Presbyn. Ch., 1991-94, 94—, mem. English handbell choir, 1988-92, children's storyteller, 1994—, pastor nominating com., 1994-95, elder, 1994-97. Mem. AAUW (rec. sec.), Am. Speech-Lang. Hearing Assn. (cert. clin. competence speech-lang. pathologist), Calif. Speech and Hearing Assn., Calif. Tchrs. Assn., Delta Kappa Gamma. Republican. Avocation: interior design. Home: PO Box 1745 Crestline CA 92325-1745 Office: Valley of Enchantment Elem Sch PO Box 430 Lake Arrowhead CA 92352-0430

KELLER, SHELLY B., writer, editor, marketing consultant; b. Ranson, W.Va., Dec. 7, 1948; d. Denzil Eugene Greynolds and Rebecca Jane (Propps) Hayes; m. Howard Lee Keller Jr., Aug. 23, 1969 (div. Sept. 1975); 1 child, Laura Christine; m. Robert Joseph Anselmo, July 15, 1986. BS, U. Md., 1971; postgrad., Boston Coll., 1972-73. Mktg. dir. Tennesse Williams Repertory Co., Key West, Fla., 1977-79; community rels. mgr. The Wis. State Jour. and The Capital Times, Madison, Wis., 1979-81; advt. mgr. The Sacramento Bee's Neighbors, 1981-84; mng. editor Today's Supervisor, Sacramento, 1985-87; mktg. cons. Calif. Dept. Trans., Sacramento, 1984-85. Editor Homegrown Recipes, 1975, Calif. Energy Commn. Biennial Report, 1989, California Association of Homes for Aging Marketing Manual, 1989, Calif. Office Tourism 1991 Ethnic Events Calendar; co-author: 96 Marketing Ideas for Physicians, 1987. Chair Sacramento Rideshare Campaign, 1984-85; mem. adv. com. Sta. KVIE, Sacramento, 1985-87; bd. dirs. Sacramento Community Svcs. Planning Coun., 1989-91; mgr. pub. rels. Calif. State Librs. Partnerships for Change (ethnic outreach) Program, 1989—. Mem. ALA, AAUW, Sacramento Advt. Club (bd. dirs. 1989-90).

KELLER, SHIRLEY INEZ, accountant; b. Ferguson, Iowa, Sept. 15, 1930; d. Adelbert Leslie and Inez Marie (Abbey) Hilsabeck; m. Earl Wilson Keller, Feb. 2, 1957 (dec. 1987); children: Earl William, Cynthia Marie, Eric Walter, Kenneth Paul. Student, U. Iowa, 1949-51; AS, Cameron U., 1971, BS, 1973; postgrad., Arapahoe Community Coll., 1986. High speed radio operator U.S. Army Signal Corps, N.Y.C., Japan, 1951-57; auditor U.S. Dept. Justice, Washington, 1973-76, U.S. Dept. Energy, Oklahoma City, 1976-83, U.S. Dept. Interior, Albuquerque, 1983-86; acct. U.S. Dept. Interior, Denver, 1986-95, ret., 1995; seminar instr. U.S. Dept. Interior, Denver, other cities, 1989-94. Author: Oil and Gas Payor Handbook, 1993. Scorekeeper Boy's Baseball, Lawton, Okla., 1964-72; den mother Boy Scouts Am., Lawton, 1965-66. Sgt. U.S. Army, 1951-57. Decorated Merit Unit Commendation, U.N. Commendation, Korean Svc. medal. Mem. Toastmasters Internat. (sec. Buffalo chpt. 1991, sgt.-at-arms Buffalo chpt. 1992, Competent Toastmaster 1993). Democrat. Roman Catholic. Avocations: family activities, gardening, water aerobics, physical fitness, making chocolate truffles. Home: PO Box 280535 Lakewood CO 80228-0535

KELLER, SUSAN AGNES, insurance executive; b. Moline, Ill., July 12, 1952; d. Kenneth Francis and Ethel Louise (Odendahl) Hulsbrink. Grad. in pub. rels., Patricia Stevens Career Coll., 1971; grad. in gen. ins., Ins. Inst. Am., 1986. CPCU; lic. ins. and real estate agt. Comml. lines rater Bitiminous Casualty Corp., Rock Island, Ill., 1973-78; with Roadway Express, Inc., Rock Island, 1978-81; front line supr. Yellow Freight System, Inc., Denver, 1982-83; supr. plumbing and sheet metal prodn. Bell Plumbing and Heating, Denver, 1983-84; v.p. underwriting farm/ranch dept. Golden Eagle Ins. Co., San Diego, 1985-98; v.p. underwriting Pub. Livery Ins. Svc., 1998—; cons. real estate foreclosure County Records Svc., San Diego, 1986-89, tchr. Ins. Inst. of Am., 1991. Vol. DAV, San Diego, 1985—; tchr. IEA and CPCU courses. Mem. Soc. CPCU (pres., bd. dirs.), Profl. Women in Ins., NAFE. Roman Catholic. Avocations: fishing, reading, boating. Home: 891 Mountainview Rd El Cajon CA 92021-7818 Office: Pub Livery Ins Svc PO Box 1149 Alpine CA 91903-1149

KELLER, WILLIAM D., federal judge; b. 1934. BS, U. Calif., Berkeley, 1956; LLB, UCLA, 1960. Asst. U.S. atty. U.S. Dist. Ct. (so. dist.) Calif., 1961-64; assoc. Dryden, Harrington, Horgan & Swartz, Calif., 1964-72; U.S. atty. U.S. Dist. Ct. (cen. dist.) Calif., Los Angeles, 1972-77; ptnr. Rosenfeld, Meyer & Susman, 1977-78; solo practice, 1978-81; ptnr. Mahm & Cazier, 1981-84; judge U.S. Dist. Ct. (cen. dist.) Calif., Los Angeles, 1984—; ptnr. Rosenfeld, Meyer & Susman, Calif., 1977-78; pvt. practice law Calif., 1978-81; ptnr. Hahn & Cazier, Calif., 1981-84. Office: US Dist Ct 312 N Spring St Ste 1653 Los Angeles CA 90012-4718*

KELLERMAN, FAYE MARDER, novelist, dentist; b. St. Louis, July 31, 1952; d. Oscar and Anne (Steinberg) Marder; m. Jonathan Seth Kellerman, July 23, 1972; children: Jesse Oren, Rachel Diana, Ilana Judith, Aliza Celeste. AB in Math., UCLA, 1974, DDS, 1978. Author: The Ritual Bath, 1986 (Macavity award best 1st novel 1986), Sacred and Profane, 1987, The Quality of Mercy, 1989, Milk and Honey, 1990, Day of Atonement, 1991, False Prophet, 1992, Grievous Sin, 1993, Sanctuary, 1994, Justice, 1995, Prayers for the Dead, 1996, Serpent's Tooth, 1997, Moon Music, 1998, Jupiter's Bone, 1999; contbr. short stories to Sisters in Crime vols. 1 and 3, Ellery Queen Mag., A Woman's Eye, Women of Mystery, the year's 2d finest crime: mystery stories, The Year's 25 Finest Mystery and Crime Stories, A Modern Treasury of Great Detective and Murder Mysteries, Mothers, Murder for Love, Mothers and Daughters. UCLA rsch. fellow, 1978. Mem. Mystery Writers of Am. (So. Calif. bd. dirs.), Womens' Israeli Polit. Action Com., Sisters in Crime. Jewish. Avocations: fencing, gardening, music.

KELLEY, BRUCE DUTTON, pharmacist; b. Hartford, Conn., Jan. 4, 1957; s. Roger Weston and Elizabeth Morrill (Atwood) K.: m. DawnReneé Cinocco, Jan. 19, 1990. Student, U. Hartford, 1975-77; BS in Pharmacy, U. Colo., 1985; diplomas in Russian, Moscow U., Moscow, 1993, 95; BA in Russian, U. Colo., 1995. RPh, Colo. Pharmacist King Soopers, Inc., Boulder, Colo., 1990—; asst. tour leader in Russia U. Tex., El Paso, 1991; Russia asst. guide, U. Ariz., Tucson, 1992 (summer). Vol. Warderburg Student Health Ctr., U. Colo., Boulder, 1981-83, Am. Diabetes Assn. Mem. Elks, Nat. Eagle Scout Assn., Am. Legion. Republican. Avocation: hiking. Home: 6152 Willow Ln Boulder CO 80301-5356 Office: King Soopers Inc 6550 Lookout Rd Boulder CO 80301-3303

KELLEY, JAMES CHARLES, III, dean; b. L.A., Oct. 5, 1940; s. James Charles Jr. and Margaret (Fitzgerrell) K.; m. Susan Cotner, June 7, 1963; children: Jason Fitzgerrell, Megan Amber. BA, Pomona Coll., 1963; PhD, U. Wyo., 1966. Asst. prof. U. Washington, Seattle, 1966-71, assoc. prof., 1971-75; dean San Francisco State U., 1975—; chmn. East Pacific Oceanic Conf., 1986-89. Fulbright prof., Fulbright Commn., Athens, Greece, 1970. Fellow Calif. Acad. Scis. (v.p. 1983-86, pres. 1988-94); mem. Am. Geophysical Union, Oceanography Soc., AAAS, Bohemian Club (San Francisco). Roman Catholic. Avocations: wooden boats, surfing, skiing, backpacking. Home: 380 4th St Montara CA 94037 Office: San Francisco State U Sch Sci San Francisco CA 94132

KELLEY, JOHN DENNIS, architect; b. L.A., Dec. 16, 1945; s. John Richard and Dorothy Anna (Gardett) K; m. Ellen Ann Malkovich, Mar. 30, 1974; children Anne Marie, Sean Nicholas. BA in Econs., U. Calif., Santa Barbara, 1968; postgrad., U. So. Calif., L.A., 1968-69. Lic. arch., Calif. Program control analyst Raytheon, Santa Barbara, Calif., 1969-72; pres. John Kelley Design & Constrn., Santa Barbara, Calif., 1972-84; project arch. Bob Easton Design Assocs., Santa Barbara, Calif., 1984-86, Brian Cearnal Assocs., Santa Barbara, Calif., 1986, Garcia Archs., Santa Barbara, Calif., 1986-87; assoc. arch. James B. Tremaine Arch., Santa Barbara, Calif., 1987-89; prin. John D. Kelley Arch., Santa Barbara, Calif., 1989—; Calif.; dir. Archtl. Found. Santa Barbara, 1991-93; chmn. Hollister Ranch Design com., Calif., 1993-97; chairperson Green Bldg. Now conf., 1996; v.p. substainability Project, Santa Barbara, 1993—. Tchr. built Environ. Edn. Program, Santa Barbara, 1986-88; dir. Summer Solstice Parade, Santa Barbara, 1988-90, Santa Barbara youth basketball, 1994-96; judge, Santa Barbara Beautiful, 1994-95. Recipient Design Award AIA, Santa Barbara, 1994, Santa Barbara Beautiful, 1994, Goleta Beautiful, 1995. Mem. AIA (Santa Barbara chpt. pres. 1993). Office: 1114 State St Ste 235 Santa Barbara CA 93101-2761

KELLEY, KEVIN PATRICK, security, safety, risk management administrator; b. Indpls., Apr. 21, 1954; s. Everett Lee and Emily Louise (Bottoms) K.; m. Kathie Jo Fluegeman, Oct. 13, 1984. BS, Calif. State U., Long Beach, 1984; cert. mgmt. supervision, UCLA, 1984. Mgmt. asst. FBI, Los Angeles, 1973-79; security/safety supr. U. Calif., 1979-82; security/safety adminstr. Micom Systems, Inc., Chatsworth, Calif., 1982-83; loss prevention, safety auditor Joseph Magnin, Inc., San Francisco, 1983-84; loss prevention, safety adminstr. Wherehouse Entertainment, Inc., Gardena, Calif., 1984-86; risk control cons. Indsl. Indemnity Co., Los Angeles, 1986-87, Kemper Group, City of Industry, Calif., 1987-90; account mgr. loss control engring. Tokio Marine Mgmt. Inc., Pasadena, Calif., 1990-97; risk mgmt. cons., 1997—; commr. pub. safety City of Norwalk, Calif., 1984-86. Mem. security com. Los Angeles Olympic Organizing Com., 1984. Mem. Am. Soc. Indsl. Security (cert., Peter Updike Meml. scholar 1985), Am. Soc. Safety Engrs., Chief Spl. Agts. Assn., Risk Ins. Mgmt. Soc., Nat. Safety Mgmt. Soc. (sec. 1985-86), Am. Heart Assn. (governing bd. chmn. 1986-88), Ins. Inst. Am. (cert.). Republican. Roman Catholic. Lodges: Rotary, Kiwanis. Avocations: tennis, swimming, reading, movies, skiing.

KELLEY, LEE, publishing executive. V.p., exec. pub. Motor Trend, L.A. Office: Motor Trend 6420 Wilshire Blvd Los Angeles CA 90048-5502

KELLEY, LOIS ELIZABETH, arts administrator, consultant; b. Peoria, Ill., Jan. 20, 1922; d. Doran A. Dieter and Sylvia Irene Huntington; m. George Thomas Edwards (div. 1949); children: George Thomas Jr., William Clarke; m. Russell Eugene Kelley (dec. June 1981); 1 child, Kathleen Lee. Student, Miss Brown's Bus. Sch., Milw., 1941, U. Ala., Tuscaloosa, 1941; cert. in arts adminstrn., Golden Gate U., 1976. Flight attendant Pan Am. World Airways, 1943-45; legal sec. Helliwell & Clarke, Miami, Fla., 1948; arts adminstr. San Mateo County Fair Arts, San Mateo, Calif., 1972-90; gallery chmn. Foster City (Calif.) Arts and Culture Commn., 1974-93; arts adminstr., pres. Peninsula Art Assn., 1994—. Chmn. Foster City Bicentennial Commn., 1974-78; vice chmn. San Mateo County Arts Coun., 1972-76; pres. Women's Caucus for Art, San Mateo, 1992-93; pres. bd. dirs. San Mateo County Fair and Expn., 1985-86; mem. No. Calif. arts adv. bd. to CAL-EXPO, 1972-94; founder Foster City Art League; jr. leader Girl Scouts U.S.A., Foster City, 1968; initiator, establisher Redwood Grove at San Mateo County Fairgrounds, 1985. Recipient award of appreciation San Mateo County Fair Assn., 1977, 91, Gavel award, 1986; outstanding svc. award dist. IV, Calif. Parks and Recreation Soc., 1992, Outstanding Dedicated Svc. award City of Foster City Arts, 1992.

KELLEY, LOUANNA ELAINE, newspaper columnist, researcher; b. Denver, Oct. 17, 1920; d. John Earl and Violet May (Griffin) Richards; m. George Vanstavoren Kelley, Dec. 1942 (dec. Oct. 1975); children: William Richard, John Henry; stepchild, Joan Fenicle; m. Glen Russell Fenicle, Jan. 1984 (dec. Apr. 1996). Student in Dental Tng., Emily Griffith Sch., 1960-61; Student in Bus., Red Rocks Coll., 1976-77. Dental asst. Colo. Dental, Denver, 1961-70; columnist Front Range Jour., Idaho Springs, Colo., 1975-80; reporter Colo. Transcript, Golden, Colo., 1975-82; columnist, reporter Clear Creek Courant, Idaho Springs, Colo., 1980-88, Mountain Messenger, Idaho Springs, Colo., 1988—; researcher Nat. Mining Hall of Fame, Leadville, Colo. 1987—, lectr. Colo. Sch. Mines, Golden, 1977, Jefferson County Schs., Golden, 1975-84; bd. dirs. Vetco Credit Union, Denver. Author: Take Your Pick And Strike It Rich, 1988; contbr. articles to profl. jours. Historian Clear Creek County and Jefferson County, Colo. Mem. Social Ethics (v.p. 1986—), Colo. Fedn. Women's. Republican. Lutheran. Avocations: social and club activities. Home: 12820 Willow Ln Apt 22 Golden CO 80401-6303 Office: Mountain Messenger PO Box 2090 Idaho Springs CO 80452-2090

KELLEY, MICHAEL JOHN, newspaper editor; b. Kansas City, Mo., July 5, 1942; s. Robert Francis and Grace Lauretta (Schofield) K.; 1 child, Anne Schofield. BA, Rockhurst Coll., 1964. Reporter, polit. writer Kansas City Star & Times, 1960-69; asst. Sen. Thomas F. Eagleton, Washington, 1969-76; pres. Swensen's Midwest, Inc., Kansas City, 1976-80; exec. asst. Cen. States Pension Fund, Chgo., 1981-83, 85-87; asst. mng. editor Kansas City Times, 1984; editor The Daily Southtown, Chgo., 1987-97; mng. editor Las Vegas (Nev.) Sun, 1997—. Office: Las Vegas Sun 800 S Valley View Blvd Las Vegas NV 89107-4411

KELLEY, WILLIAM EUGENE, JR., broadcast executive; b. L.A., Sept. 8, 1947; s. William Eugene and Doris (Wallis) K.; m. Lynne A. Brusaw, Oct. 1967 (div. June 1979); 1 child, Michael W. BA in Cinema/TV, U. So. Calif., L.A., 1973, MA in Humanities, Calif. State U., Dominguez Hills, 1998. Film maker House Ear Inst., L.A., 1970-73; camera operator, dir. Northrop Corp., L.A., 1973-85, prodr., dir., 1985-93; exec. prodr. Northrop Grumman Corp., L.A., 1993-95, TV ctr. mgr., 1995—. Cover photography (jours.) Aviation Week, 1983, 84, Flight Internat., 1984, 85, Soc. Automotive Engrs., 1989. Sgt. USAF, 1966-70. Mem. Soc. Motion Picture and TV Engrs., Internat. TV Assn. (Silver Angel award 1995), Comm. Media Mgrs. Assn., So. Calif. Hist. Aircraft Found. Avocation: classic and vintage motorcycles. Office: MASD KD60/GS One Hornet Way El Segundo CA 90245

KELLOGG, FREDERICK, historian; b. Boston, Dec. 9, 1929; s. Frederick Floyd and Stella Harriet (Plummer) K.; m. Patricia Kay Hanbery, Aug. 21, 1954 (dec. 1975); 1 child, Kristine Marie Calvert. AB, Stanford U., 1952; MA, U. So. Calif., 1958; PhD, Ind. U., 1969. Instr., Boise State U., 1962-64, asst. prof., 1964-65; vis. asst. prof. U. Idaho, 1965; asso. prof. Boise State U., 1966-67; instr. history U. Ariz., 1967-68, asst. prof., 1968-71, asso. prof., 1971—. Founder, chmn. Idaho Hist. Conf., 1964. U.S.-Romania Cultural Exchange Research scholar, 1960-61; Sr. Fulbright-Hays Research scholar, Romania, 1969-70. Named hon. mem. Inst. de istorie "Alexandru D. Xenopol", 1991; recipient cert. recognition Soc. Romanian Studies, 1993, Nicolae Iorga prize Romanian Acad., 1997; ACLS rsch. grantee, 1970-71; Internat. Rsch. and Exchs. Bd. sr. rsch. grantee, 1973-74. Mem. Am. Hist. Assn., S.E. European Studies Assn. Author: A History of Romanian Historical Writing, 1990, The Road to Romanian Independence, 1995, O istorie a istoriografiei romane, 1996; mng. editor Southeastern Europe, 1974—; contbr. articles to academic publs. Office: U Ariz Dept History Tucson AZ 85721

KELLOGG, KENYON P., lawyer; b. Dubuque, Iowa, Aug. 5, 1946; s. Kenyon P. and Maleta (Fleege) K.; m. Carolyn Jo Dick, July 18, 1970; children: Andrew P., Kenyon P., Jonathan P. BSBA summa cum laude, Creighton U., 1968; JD cum laude, U. Mich., 1971. Bar: U.S. Dist. Ct. (we. dist.) Wash. 1971, U.S. Tax Ct. 1980; CPA, Wash. With Arthur Andersen & Co., Omaha and Detroit, 1968-71; assoc. Lane Powell Spears Lubersky, Seattle, 1971-78, ptnr., 1978—. Bd. regents Seattle U., 1989—, dean's coun. Alber's Sch. Bus. and Econs., 1992—; mem. nat. alumni bd. Creighton U., 1995—; trustee Naval Undersea Mus. Found., 1995—; mem. FALES com. USN Acad., 1995—. Capt. USAR, 1968-77. Mem. AICPAs, Wash. Soc. CPAs, Seattle Rotary, Seattle Yacht Club (trustee), Cruising Club of Am., Naval Acad. Sailing Squadron. Avocations: sailing, skiing. Office: Lane Powell Spears Lubersky 1420 5th Ave Ste 4100 Seattle WA 98101-2338

KELLY, BRIAN MATTHEW, industrial hygienist; b. Ogdensburg, N.Y., June 16, 1956; s. Lauris F. and Catherine M. (McEvoy) K. BA, SUNY, Oswego, 1978; BS, Clarkson U., 1981; MS in Indsl. Safety, Cen. Mo. State U., 1990. Cert. indsl. hygienist Am. Bd. Indsl. Hygiene; cert. accident investigator U.S. Dept. Energy, NASA and Nuclear Regulatory Commn. Maintenance engr. Kelly Sales Corp., Madrid, N.Y., 1978-80, carpenter, 1981-82; hygienist indsl. hygiene and toxicology prin. mem. tech. staff ES&H, quality assessments dept. Sandia Nat. Labs., Albuquerque, 1983—; mem. tech. adv. bd. Albuquerque (N.Mex.) Tech. Vocat. Inst., 1989—. Mem. Am. Inst. Chemists, Am. Indsl. Hygienists Assn. (mgmt. com. mem.), N.Y. Acad. Scis., Am. Conf. Govtl. Indls. Hygienists, Am. Soc. Safety Engrs., Am. Acad. Indsl. Hygiene, Gamma Sigma Epsilon, Phi Kappa Phi. Republican. Roman Catholic. Avocations: cycling, fishing, carpentry. Home: 1455 Beall St Bosque Farms NM 87068-9109

KELLY, CAROLYN SUE, newspaper executive; b. Pasco, Wash., Oct. 25, 1952; d. Jerald Davin and Margaret Helen (Nibler) K. BBA, Gonzaga U., 1974; MBA, Seattle U., 1985. CPA, Wash. Acct. Brajcich & Loeffler, Spokane, Wash., 1972-74; auditor Peat, Marwick, Mitchell & Co., Seattle, 1974-77; fin. analyst Seattle Times, 1977-81, asst. circulation mgr., 1981-83, spl. project advt. mgr., 1983-86, dir. mktg. and new bus., 1986-89, v.p., chief fin. officer, 1989-97, sr. v.p. and gen. mgr., 1997—. Bd. dirs. Econ. Devel. Coun., Seattle, 1992, Campfire, Artists Unltd. Mem. Fin. Execs. Avocation: running. Office: Seattle Times PO Box 70 Seattle WA 98111-0070*

KELLY, DENNIS RAY, sales executive; b. Olympia, Wash., Aug. 20, 1948; s. William E. and Irene (Lewis) K.; m. Pamela Jo Kresevich, Mar. 16, 1974. BA, Cen. Wash. U., 1972; postgrad., U. Wash., 1977-78. Sales rep. Bumble Bee Sea Foods, Seattle, 1972-74; retail sales mgr. Pacific Pearl Sea Foods, Seattle, 1974-76; regional sales mgr. Castle & Cooke Foods, Seattle, Phila., and N.Y.C., 1976-80; v.p. sales mktg. Frances Andrew Ltd., Seattle, 1980-82; regional sales mgr. Tenneco West, Seattle, 1982-85; sales and mktg. mgr. for western U.S. David Oppenheimer, Seattle, 1985-96; sales mgr. Rogge Co., 1997—. Alumni advisor Ctrl. Wash. U., Ellensburg, 1979-87, alumni bd. dirs., 1986—, fund drive chmn., 1988—, vendor rels.-mktg. com., 1998—, mem. sch. cmty. group bd.; bd. dirs. Bay Vista Tower Assn., v.p., pres., 1998; mem. Statue of Liberty Ellis Island Found.; chmn. ann. fund drive Ctrl. Wash. U., bd. dirs., 1992; pres. Lake Water Dist., 1998; adv. com. United States Senate Seattle. Mem. New Zealand-Am. Soc., Mfrs. Reps. Club Wash. (bd. dirs.). Republican. Avocations: hiking, backpacking, skiing, snowmobiling. Home: 2821 2nd Ave Apt 1204 Seattle WA 98121-1249 Office: 4123 2nd Ave S Seattle WA 98134-2305

KELLY, J. MICHAEL, lawyer; b. Hattiesburg, Miss., Dec. 5, 1943. BA, Emory U., 1966; LLB, U. Va., 1969. Bar: Ga. 1969, U.S. Supreme Ct. 1978, D.C. 1980, Utah 1982, Calif. 1988. Law clerk to Judge Griffin B. Bell (5th cir.) U.S. Ct. Appeals, Atlanta, 1969-70; ptnr. Alston & Bird (formerly Alston, Miller & Gaines), Atlanta, 1970-77, 81-82; counselor to atty. gen. U.S. Dept. Justice, Washington, 1977-79; counselor to sec. U.S. Dept. Energy, Washington, 1979-81; ptnr., shareholder, dir. Ray, Quinney & Nebeker, Salt Lake City, 1982-87; ptnr. Cooley Godward LLP, San Francisco, 1987—. Mem. Omicron Delta Kappa, Phi Alpha Delta. Office: Cooley Godward LLP 20th Fl 1 Maritime Plz Fl 20 San Francisco CA 94111-3404

KELLY, JEROME BERNARD, insurance company executive; b. Kankakee, Ill., Oct. 4, 1954; s. Joseph B. and Mary J. (Demerly) K.; m. Barbara Fawcett, June 21, 1986; children: Anna, Sarah. BA, Regis Coll., 1980; MBA, U. Phoenix, 1989. V.p. Shearson Hayden Stone, Denver, 1977-83, E.F. Hutton, Denver, 1983-85; portfolio mgr. 17th St. Fin. Mgmt., Denver, 1985-87; stockbroker Dain Bosworth, Denver, 1987-88; owner J.B. Kelly Ins. Agy., Denver, 1988—. Bd. dirs. United Cerebral Palsy Assn. Denver, 1987-90; mem. selection com. Cultural Facilities Tax Dist., Denver, 1995—. Mem. Colo. Bus. Sch. Club (pres. 1988-89), Trout Unltd., Nat. Assn. of Securities Dealers (bd. arbitration 1987—), Am. Arbitration Assn. (panel arbitrators 1990—). Avocations: skiing, fly fishing. Office: JB Kelly Ins Agy 1863 S Pearl St Denver CO 80210-3136

KELLY, JOHN B., state official; b. South Orange, N.J., June 26, 1962; s. Edwin Marshall Jr. and Ruth (Kilpatrick) K.; m. Mary Lynn Vandemeter, Apr. 16, 1988; children: John Alden, Lane Marshall. BA, Lafayette Coll., Easton, Pa., 1984; MPA, Howard U., Cambridge, Mass., 1997. Personal asst. U.S. Rep. Jim Kolbe, Washington, 1985, legis. dir., 1986-90; dir. pub. affairs Ariz. Bd. Regents, Phoenix, 1990-91; policy advisor, state and fed. lobbyist Ariz. Gov. Fife Symington, Phoenix, 1991-95; exec. dir. Gov.'s Office Telecomm. Policy, Phoenix, 1995-96. Office: Office Gov 1700 W Washington St Phoenix AZ 85007-2812

KELLY, JOHN J., prosecutor. U.S. atty. for N.Mex. U.S. Dept. Justice, Albuquerque. Office: US Atty for Dist NMex PO Box 607 Albuquerque NM 87103-0607*

KELLY, JON PEMBROKE, orthopedic surgeon, medical association executive; b. Boston, Oct. 17, 1958; s. Paul Edward and Jane Ruth (Woodman) K., m. Elizabeth Mannino, May 18, 1985; children: Michael, Christopher, Kathleen, Alexandra, Michelle. BA, Notre Dame U., 1980; MD, Tulane U., 1984. Surg. intern San Diego Naval Med. Ctr., 1984-85, orthopedic resident, 1987-91; commd. ensign USN, 1985, advanced through grades to comdr.; intern in gen. surgry Naval Med. Ctr., San Diego, 1984-85, resident in orthopedic surgery, 1987-91; physician emergency room USN, Subic Bay, The Philippines, 1985-87; physician orthops. USN, Guantanomo Bay, Cuba, 1991-92; fellow in hand surgery U. N.Mex., 1992-93; hand surgeon USN, San Diego, 1993-95; gen. orthop. surgeon Palomar Orthop. Specialists, Escondido, Calif., 1995—. Co-author: The Wrist and Its Disorders, 1996. Fellow Am. Acad. Orthop. Surgeons. Avocations: free diving, spear fishing, skiing. Office: Palomar Orthop Specialists 488 E Valley Pkwy Ste 400 Escondido CA 92025-3378

KELLY, KEVIN FRANCIS, lawyer; b. New Orleans, Apr. 27, 1949; s. Frank J. and Dorothy P. (Paige) K.; m. Jean A. Friedhoff, Dec. 27, 1969; children: Bryan F., Eric W. BA, Gonzaga U., 1970; JD, U. Calif. Berkeley, 1973. Bar: Wash. 1973. Law clk. to Hon. Eugene A. Wright U.S. Ct. Appeals, 9th Cir., Seattle, 1973-74; assoc. Davis, Wright, Todd, Riese & Jones, Seattle, 1974-76; ptnr. Wickwire, Goldmark & Schorr, Seattle, 1976-88, Heller, Ehrman, White & McAuliffe, Seattle, 1988—. Bd. dirs. Big Bros. King County, Seattle, 1985-95, v.p., 1991, pres., 1992; bd. trustees Legal Found. Wash., Seattle, 1994-97, pres., 1997. Mem. Wash. Biotechnology and Biomedical Assn. (bd. dirs. 1996—), Wash. Soc. Hosp. Lawyers, Order of Coif. Avocation: cycling. Home: 4040 55th Ave NE Seattle WA 98105-4957*

KELLY, KURT (JOSEPH E. CRONAN), entertainment executive, producer, director; b. Cheboygan, Wis., May 31, 1959; s. William John and Irene Mary (Gardner) Cronan; m. Karen Lynn Neitzel, Apr. 19, 1997. Student in pre-law, liberal arts, No. Mich. U., 1977-78, Oakland U., Royal Oak, Mich., 1979-82. Reporter news, polit. stories various T.V. stas. and radio; mgmt. positions Metromedia, Nationwide Comm., Unistar, AP, others; pres., CEO, Kurt Kelly Entertainment, Inc., Canton, Mich., 1993—; pres., CEO Kurt Kelly Entertainment, Inc., L.A., 1985-92, 97—; creator T.V. series Backstage Pass (All Access). Numerous prodn. credits include Dave Mason, Ford Models, U2, Billy Joel, Phil Collins, The Doors, Lou Gramm, Bruce Springsteen, ZZ Top, Crosby, Stills, Nash & Young, others. Mem. AFTRA, SAG, T.V/Radio Mus., Am. Film Inst., Nat. Assn. T.V. Program Execs. Avocations: philanthropy, sports, travel, arts. Office: Kurt Kelly Entertainment Inc PO Box 241971 Los Angeles CA 90024-9771

KELLY, PAUL JOSEPH, JR., judge; b. Freeport, N.Y., Dec. 6, 1940; s. Paul J. and Jacqueline M. (Nolan) K.; BBA, U. Notre Dame, 1963; JD, Fordham U., 1967; m. Ruth Ellen Dowling, June 27, 1964; children—Johanna, Paul Edwin, Thomas Martin, Christopher Mark, Heather Marie. Bar: N.Mex. 1967. Law clk. Cravath, Swaine & Moore, N.Y.C., 1964-67; assoc. firm Hinkle, Cox, Eaton, Coffied & Hensley, Roswell, N.Mex., 1967-71, ptnr., 1971-92; judge U.S. Ct. Appeals (10th cir.), Santa Fe, 1992—; mem. N.Mex. Bd. Bar Examiners, 1982-85; mem. N.Mex. Ho. of Reps., 1976-81, chmn. consumer and public affairs com., mem. judiciary com. Mem. N.Mex. Pub. Defender Bd.; bd. of visitors, Fordham U. Sch. of Law, 1992—; pres. Oliver Seth Inn of Ct., 1993—; pres. Roswell Drug Abuse Com., 1970-71; mem. Appellate Judges Nominating Commn., 1989-92. Pres. Chaves County Young Reps., 1971-72; vice chmn. N.Mex. Young Reps., 1969-71, treas., 1968-69; mem. bd. dirs. Zia council Girl Scouts Am., Roswell Girls Club, Chaves County Mental Health Assn., 1974-77; bd. dirs. Santa Fe Orch., 1992-93, Roswell Symphony Orch. Soc., 1969-82, treas., 1970-73, pres., 1973-75; mem. Eastern N.Mex. State Fair Bd., 1978-83. Mem. ABA, Fed. Bar Assn., State Bar N.Mex. (v.p. young lawyers sect. 1969, co-chmn. ins. sub-com. 1972-73, mem. continuing legal edn. com. 1970-73). Roman Catholic (pres. parish council 1971-76). K.C. Office: US Court Appeals 10th Circuit Federal Courthouse PO Box 10113 Santa Fe NM 87504-6113

KELLY, ROSEMARY, artist, curator; b. San Francisco, Sept. 26, 1955; d. James Francis and Mary Elizabeth K.; m. Robert Bagnasco Murray, Oct. 16,

1993. BS in Design with honors, U. Calif., Davis, 1973. Owner Tinker Rose, Oakland, Calif., 1984—; master artist, tchr. Nat. Inst. Art and Disabilities Adult Edn., Richmond, Calif., 1991—; artist in residence Calif. Arts Coun. Nat. Inst. Art and Disabilities, Richmond, Calif., 1993-96, curator, 1997—; presenter Internat. Able Arts Forum, Osaka, Japan, 1995—; collaborating artist 20th Century Round Table Dual Lang. Inst., Balatonalmadi, Hungary, 1998. Exhibited at Crocker Art Mus., Sacramento, 1983, Calif. Expo, Sacramento, 1983, 94, Berkeley Repertory Theater, Calif., 1983, Pyramid Art Ctr., Rochester, N.Y., 1984, Gallery Sanchez, San Francisco, 1984, Mendocino Art Ctr., Calif., 1984, Orange County Ctr. Contemporary Art, Santa Ana, Calif., 1985, Vida Gallery, San Francisco, 1985, Altos de Chavon Gallery, La Romana, Dominican Republic, 1985, Southern Exposure Gallery, San Francisco, 1987, Irvine Fine Arts Ctr., Calif., 1988, San Francisco Art Inst., 1991, Prieto Gallery, Oakland, 1992, Cassandra Kersting Gallery, Oakland, 1992, Design Gallery U. Calif., Davis, 1992, DeYoung Mus., San Francisco, 1993, Renwick Gallery Smithsonian Instn., Washington, 1993-94, Florence Katz Gallery, Richmond, 1994-95, 95, Domaine Chandon Winery, Yountville, Calif., 1994-95, Coastal Art Mus., Half Moon Bay, Calif., 1995, Richard L. Nelson Gallery U. Calif., Davis, 1996, 97, 98, Textile Arts Ctr., Chgo., 1996, V. Breier Gallery, San Francisco, 1996, Barbara Anderson Gallery, Berkeley, Calif., 1997, Bumbleshoot Arts Festival, Seattle, 1997, Bedford Gallery Dean Lesher Ctr. for Arts, Walnut Creek, Calif., 1997, Pippin & Leigh Gallery, Redondo Beach, Calif., 1997, Crucible Steel Gallery, San Francisco, 1997, Gallery at Bausch & Lomb Internat. Hdqs., Rochester, N.Y., 1998. Mem. Richmond Art Assns. Group, Textile Arts Coun. De Young Mus. Democrat. Avocation: traveling. Office: Nat Inst Art and Disabilities 551 23rd St Richmond CA 94804-1626

KELLY, THOMAS J., sports association executive; b. Madison, Wis.; m. Carole Duh. BA in Journalism, U. Wis., 1974. Photographer Madison's daily newspapers; sports editor weekly newspaper; pub. rels. dir. midwestern ski resort, 1977; asst. nat. nordic dir. U.S. Ski Assn., 1988-95; dir. comms. U.S. Skiing, 1988—, dir. ops., 1995-96; v.p. pub. rels. U.S. Ski and Snowboard Assn. (formerly U.S. Skiing), 1996—; mem. bd. dirs. Ski Utah. Mem. Rotary. Office: US Ski and Snowboard Assn PO Box 100 Park City UT 84060-0100

KELLY, TIMOTHY DONAHUE, state senator; b. Sacramento, Aug. 15, 1944; m. Lisa B. Nelson, Jan. 1, 1994; children: Ingrid Brose, Theodore Ambrose. Former legis. aide to Calif. and Nev. Legislatures; mortgage banker; mem. Alaska Ho. of Reps., 1976-78, Alaska Senate, 1978—, senate pres., 1989-90. With USMCR, Alaska Air NG. Office: State Capitol Juneau AK 99801-1182

KELLY, WILLIAM BRET, insurance executive; b. Rocky Ford, Colo., Sept. 28, 1922; s. William Andrew and Florence Gail (Yant) K.; m. Patricia Ruth Ducy, Mar. 25, 1944; children: Eric Damian, Kathryn Gail Kelly Schweitzer. BA cum laude, U. Colo., 1947. CPCU. With Steel City Agys., Inc., and predecessor, Pueblo, Colo., 1946—, pres., 1961-76, chmn. bd., 1977—; dir. United Bank Pueblo, 1963-94, chmn. bd., 1983-88; mem. Pub. Expenditure Coun., 1984—; v.p. Colo. Ins. Edn. Found., 1981, pres., 1982. Mem. Pueblo Area Coun. Govts., 1971-73, Colo. Forum 1985—, trustee Pueblo Bd. Water Works, 1966-80, pres., 1970-71; pres. Pueblo Single Fund Plan, 1960-61, Pueblo Heart Coun., 1962, Family Svc. Soc. Pueblo, 1963; mem. 10th Jud. Dist. Nominating Com., 1967-71; pres. U. So. Colo. Found., 1998-99, v.p., 1991, 92, 93, 94, 95, 96, 97, 98; trustee Jackson Found., 1972—, Farley Found., 1979—, Roselawn Cemetery Assn., 1982—, Kelly-Ducy Found., 1983—; hon. parade marshall Colo. State Fair, 1991. With inf. AUS, 1943-45. Decorated Silver Star, Bronze Star with oak leaf cluster, Purple Heart with oak leaf cluster; recipient Disting. Svc. award U. Colo., 1992; honored for cmty. svc. Parkview Episcopal Med. Ctr., 1992; named to Pueblo Hall of Fame, 1995. Mem. Soc. CPCU's, Pueblo C. of C. (past pres.), Pueblo Kiwanis (past pres.), Pueblo Country Club (treas. 1964-66), So. Colo. Press Club (Outstanding Community Svc. award 1991), Phi Beta Kappa. Democrat. Home: 264 S Sifford Ct Pueblo West CO 81007-2843 Office: 1414 W 4th St Pueblo CO 81004-1205

KELSEY, EDITH JEANINE, psychotherapist, consultant; b. Freeport, Ill., Oct. 15, 1937; d. John Melvin and Florence Lucille (Ewald) Anderson; divorced; children: Steven Craig, Kevin John. Student, Pasadena Coll., 1955-58; BA in Psychology, Calif. State U., San Jose, 1980; MA in Counseling Psychology, Santa Clara U., 1984. Lic. marriage, family and child counselor. Counselor, cons., cert. trainer Values Tech., Santa Cruz, Calif., 1981—, dir. research, 1982-84; intern in counseling Sr. Residential Services, San Jose, 1983-84; psychotherapist Process Therapy Inst., Los Gatos, Calif., 1983-86, Sexual Abuse Treatment Ctr., San Jose, 1984-87; cons. in field, Santa Clara Valley, 1982-89; trainer, cons. Omega Assoc., 1987-92; teaching asst. Santa Clara U., 1997—, supr. interns counseling high-risk students, 1997-98; pvt. practice psychotherapy, cons., tng., 1987—. Contbr. articles to profl. jours. Vol. Parental Stress Hotline, Palo Alto, Calif., 1980-85. Mem. Am. Assn. Marriage and Family Therapists, Am. Soc. Aging, Calif. Assn. Marriage and Family Therapists (clin.), Palo Alto C. of C. Democrat. Presbyterian. Avocations: skiing, hiking. Home: 431 Casita Ct Los Altos CA 94022-1774 Office: 153 Forest Ave Palo Alto CA 94301-1615

KELSEY, MICHAEL LOYAL, geography educator; b. Greeley, Colo., Dec. 15, 1953; s. Loyal Lee and Luwanda Marie (Steffens) K. BS, Salisbury State U., 1976; MA in Geography, U. Northern Colo., 1988; PhD in Geography, Kent State U., 1993. Founder, mgr. Salisbury (Md.) State U. Book Co-op., 1975-76; mgmt. trainee J.C. Penney Co., Inc., Salisbury, 1976-77; cost acctg. and time study mgr. W.D. Byron & Sons, Inc., Williamsport, Md., 1978-83; corp. inventory controller Stuart McGuire Co., Inc., Salem, Va., 1983-84; owner, mgr. New Century Ribbon Co., Greeley, Colo., 1984-88; instr., doctoral teaching fellow Kent (Ohio) State U., 1988-91; instr. Montgomery Coll., Rockville, Md., 1991-93; prof., chmn. geography and econs. dept. Aims Coll., Greeley, 1993—; officer, bd. dirs. Seagulf Concepts, Inc., Salisbury, Md., 1975-76; cons. Laserhead Graphics, Greeley, 1993—. Dir. Internat. Ctr. Recipient top bus. student award Rotary Internat., Salisbury, 1975, grad. fellowship U. No. Colo., Greeley, 1986-87, award for tchg. excellence, 1996, Sam W. Walton Free Enterprise fellow and Free Enterprise Educator award, 1996; grantee IBM Corp., Rockville, Md., 1992, NSF Geographic Info. Sys., 1998. Mem. Assn. Am. Geographers, Nat. Coun. for Geographic Edn., Gamma Theta Upsilon (pres. U. No. Colo. 1987-89), Phi Kappa Phi, Omicron Delta Kappa. Home: 4040 W 12th St Apt 6 Greeley CO 80634-2508 Office: Aims CC 5401 20th St Greeley CO 80634-3002

KELTON, ARTHUR MARVIN, JR., real estate developer; b. Bennington, Vt., Sept. 12, 1939; s. Arthur Marvin and Lorraine (Millington) K.; m. Elaine White, Nov. 1, 1986; 1 child, Ashley. BA, Dartmouth Coll., 1961; postgrad., U. Vt., 1963. Ptnr. Kelton and Assocs., Vail, Colo., 1966-77; pres. Kelton, Garton and Assocs. Inc., Vail, 1977-84, Kelton, Garton, Kendall, Vail, 1984-93, Christopher, Denton, Kelton, Kendall, Vail, 1993—. Head agt. Dartmouth Alumni Fund, Hanover, N.H., 1985-90, class pres., 1990-96; Dartmouth Alumni Coun., 1996—; pres. Vail Valley Med. Ctr. Found., 1991—. Republican. Congregationalist. Avocations: skiing, golf, wingshooting. Fax: 970-476-7994. Home: 1034 Homestake Cir Vail CO 81657-5111 Office: Christopher Denton Kelton & Kelton 225 Wall St Ste 210 Vail CO 81657-3615

KELZER, KIMBERLY ANN, artist, furniture designer; b. El PAso, Tex., June 10, 1957; d. Delbert Anthony Kelzer and Ann Juliana (Drews) Tritipo. BA in in painting, San Jose State U., 1983; MFA in furniture design, Southeastern Mass. U., 1990. Seamstress San Jose, Calif., 1976-77; bakery mgr., cake decorator Bay Area, Calif., 1977-87; furniture apprentice Adrience Heritage Collection, South Dartmouth, Mass., 1987-89; artist, 1987—; tchg. asst. Haystack Sch. Craft, Deere Isle, Maine, 1988; lectr. Phila. Coll. Art, 1989; guest artist Murrey (Ky.) State U., 1989, Bucks County C.C., Newtown, Pa., 1990, San Diego State U., 1990; instr. contemporary wood furniture, San Diego Mesa Coll., 1991, instr. beginning and intermediate furniture San Diego State U., 1991, instr. Calif. Coll. Arts Crafts, Oakland, 1991-92, De Anza Coll., Cupertino, Calif., 1991-93, Baulines Crafts Guild, Sausalito, Calif., 1992-94, Haystack Mountain Sch. Crafts, 1993, Penland (N.C.) Sch. Craft, 1993, Calif. Contemporary Crafts Assn., 1994, Anderson Ranch Arts Ctr., Snowmass Village, Colo., 1994, 97, San Diego State U., 1996, Ore. Coll. Arts Craft, Portland, 1997; vis. artist Murrey State U., 1993, Appalachian Ctr. Crafts, Smythville Tenn., 1993; workshop Calif. Contemporary Crafts Assn., 1994, Fairbanks (Alaska) Arts Assn., 1995; symposium presenter Sask. Craft Coun. Saskatoon, Can., 1996, Furniture Soc. Conf., SUNY, Purchase, 1997; tchr. Peters Valley Craft Ctr., Layton, N.J.; bd. mem. Furniture Soc. Exhibited in group shows at Euphrat Gallery, Cupertino, 1987, Jacob K. Javits Convention Ctr., N.Y.C., 1988, Lexena (Kans.) Nat. 3 Dimensional Art Show, 1988, Soc. Arts and Crafts, Boston, 1988, 89, 90, 91, Gallery Nao Faz Mal, Providence, 1988, Views Gallery Phila., 1989, Meredith Gallery, Balt., 1989, 90, 91, 93, The Dairy Barn, Athens, Ohio, 1989, Views Gallery, Manyhunk, Pa, 1989, 90, Design Emphasis 90, Atlanta, 1990, Child and Family Ctr., South Dartmouth, Mass., 1990, Clark Gallery, Gallery Naga, Boston, 1990, Sansar Gallery, Washington, 1991, Franklin Parrasch Gallery, N.Y.C., 1991, Cambridge (Mass.) Art Assn., 1991, Wilder Gallery, Los Gatos, Calif., 1991, Virginia Breir Gallery, San Francisco, 1991, Banaker Gallery, Walnut Creek, Calif., 1992, Tecera Gallery, Los Gatos, 1992, Contract Design Ctr. Gallery, San Francisco, 1992, 93, The Works Gallery, Phila., 1992, 95, Katie Gingrass Gallery, Milw., 1993, Am. Craft Mus., N.Y.C., 1993, Galleria Mesa (Ariz.), 1994, The Soc. Contemporary Crafts, Pitts., 1994, Bellevue (Wash.) Art Mus., 1994, Banaker Gallery, San Francisco, 1996, Clark Gallery, Lincoln, Mass., 1996, Amarillo (Tex.) Mus. Art, 1996, Renwick Gallery, Washington, 1997, Boston Internat. Fine Art Show, 1997, Neuberger Mus. Art, SUNY, Purchase, 1997, Museo Piccolo, Langley, Wash., 1997, John Elder Gallery, N.Y.C., 1998, Corvallis (Ore.) Arts Ctr., 1998, others; one woman shows include Gallery Naga, Clark Gallery, Lincoln, Mass., 1992, Museo, Langley, Wash., 1998; contbr. over 20 articles to profl. jours. Trustee grantee Euphrat Gallery, Cupertino, 1987, WESTAF/NEA Regional Fellowships for Visual Arts grantee, 1993; Merritt sholar Haystack Craft Sch., 1988; recipient Excellence in Design award The Dairy Barn, Athens, 1989, Juror's Recognition award Arrowmont Sch. Arts and Crafts, Gatlinberg, Tenn., 1992. Democrat. Home and Office: PO Box 1372 Freeland WA 98249-1372

KEMERY, WILLIAM ELSWORTH, psychotherapist, hypnotherapist; b. Portland, Oreg., Apr. 16, 1929; s. William Elsworth Jr. and Charlotte Francis (Leydic) K.; m. Norma Mae Ishmael, Nov. 22, 1963 (div. May 1972); children: William M., Robert Z.; m. Marlene Agnes Kwiatkowski, Dec. 15, 1983; children: William E., William M., Robert Z., Bradley E. DD, Episcopal Sem., Balt., 1953; BA, Fresno State U., 1954; PhD (hon.), Hamilton State, 1973; Masters, Newport Internat. U., 1976, PhD, 1979. Cert. psychotherapist, hypnotherapist, sex therapist. Psychotherapist Chula Vista, Calif., 1967—; founding dir. Calif. Hypnotists Examining Coun., L.A., 1974; pres., fellow Acad. Sci. Hypnotherapy, San Diego, 1974—; bishop Holy Episcopal Ch., Chula Vista, 1978—; dir. Assn. of Spiritual Psychology, San Diego, 1968—. Contbr. articles to profl. jours. Named Hon. Mayor, Chula Vist C. of C., 1967, Knight of Grace, Order of St. John of Jerusalem, 1981. Fellow Nutrition and Preventive Medicine Assn.; mem. Internat. Assn. Clin. Hypnotherapy (life), Acad. Orthomolecular Psychiatry, Assn. Huministic Psychology, Internat. New Thought Alliance, Am. Guild Hypnotherapists, Am. Mental Health Counselors Assn., Am. Assn. Sex Educators, Counselors and Therapists. Republican. Avocations: swimming, hiking, jazz, photography. Home and Office: 379 G St Chula Vista CA 91910-4513

KEMMIS, DANIEL ORRA, cultural organization administrator, author; b. Fairview, Mont., Dec. 5, 1945; s. Orra Raymond and Lilly Samantha (Shidler) K.; m. Jeanne Marie Koester, June 9, 1978; children: Abraham, Samuel; children by previous marriage: Deva, John. BA, Harvard U., 1968; JD, U. Mont., 1978. Bar: Mont. 1978. State rep. Mont. Ho. of Reps., Helena, 1975-84, minority leader, 1981-82, Speaker of House, 1983-84; ptnr. Morrison, Jonkel, Kemmis & Rossbach, Missoula, 1978-80, Jonkel & Kemmis, 1981-84; mayor City of Missoula, Mont., 1990-96; dir. ctr. rocky mountain west Univ. Mont., Missoula, 1996—; cons. No. Lights Inst., Missoula, Mont., 1985-89; Kennedy fellow Inst. Politics Harvard U., 1998. Author: Community and the Politics of Place, 1990, The Good City and the Good life, 1995; contbr. articles to profl. jours. Candidate for chief justice Mont. Supreme Ct.; former mem. adv. bd. and bd. dirs. Nat. Civic League; mem. adv. bd. Pew Partnership for Civic Change, 1991-97, Brookings Instn. Ctr. Urban and Met. Policy, Snake River Inst.; chmn. leadership tng. coun. Nat. League Cities, 1992-94; bd. dirs. Charles F. Kettering Found., Inst. for Environ. & Natural Resources U. Wyo., Bolle Ctr. for People and Forests, U. Mont.; fellow Dallas Inst. for Humanities & Culture, 1991-98. presdl. appt. Am. Heritage Rivers Commn., 1998—. Inst. Politics fellow Kennedy Sch. Govt., Harvard LU., 1998; named Disting. Young Alumnus U. Mont., 1981, 100 Visionaries, Utne Reader, 1995; recipient Charles Frankel prize NEH, 1997, Disting. Achievement award, Soc. for Conservation Biology, 1997, Wallace Stegner award, Ctr. Am. West, 1998. Democrat. Home: 521 Hartman St Apt 10 Missoula MT 59802-4771 Office: U Mont Ctr Rocky Mountain West Missoula MT 59812-1158

KEMP, JEANNE FRANCES, office manager; b. L.A., Dec. 8, 1942; d. Damian Thomas and Helen Catherine (Bohin) Hanifee; m. Don H. Kemp, Dec. 16, 1966 (div. 1972). AB, San Francisco State U., 1965. Food svc. technician United Air Lines, San Francisco, 1961-65; clk. N.Y. Life Ins., San Francisco, 1965-66; inventory clk. Ingersoll-Rand, San Francisco, 1966; advt./order clk. Patrick's Stationers, San Francisco, 1966-67; sec. Dartmouth Travel, Hanover, N.H., 1967-68, Olsten Temp. Svcs., N.Y.C., 1968-70; office mgr. Brown U. Devel., N.Y.C., 1970-73; asst. dir. Cen. Opera Svc., N.Y.C., 1974-85; office mgr., sec. Payne, Thompson & Walker, San Francisco, 1986-95; office mgr. Weatherford & Taaffe LLP, San Francisco, 1996—. Editor: Career Guide...Singers, 1985, Operas...for Children, 1985; asst. editor COS Bull., 1976-85; editorial asst.: Who's Who in Opera, 1975. Democrat. Roman Catholic. Avocations: reading, research, writing, theatre, dance. Office: Weatherford & Taaffe LLP Steuart Tower 16th Fl One Market Plz San Francisco CA 94105

KEMPER, TROXEY, magazine editor; b. Granite, Okla., Apr. 29, 1915; s. William Charles and Ona Lee (Dawson) K.; m. Jeanne Doty, May 31, 1954 (div. June 1963); children: Karen Kemper Woolf, Ann. Grad., U. N.Mex., 1951. Civil svc. Dept. of Interior, Denver, 1943; real estate titles Tucumcari (N.Mex.) Abstract Co., 1936-43; reporter News Bureau, Albuquerque, 1949-51; reporter, copy editor Albuquerque Jour., 1951-69; editor Tucumcari Lit. Rev., L.A., 1988—. Author: Lean Into the Wind, 1997, Texas for the Duration, 1998, Shallow Graves, 1998, Comanche Warbonnet, 1991; poetry. With USAF, 1943-46. Mem. Sigma Delta Chi. Democrat. Baptist. Avocations: photography, gardening. Home: 3108 Bellevue Ave Los Angeles CA 90026-3717 Office: Tucumcari Literary Review 3108 Bellevue Ave Los Angeles CA 90026-3717

KEMPF, MARTINE, voice control device manufacturing company executive; b. Strasbourg, France, Dec. 9, 1958; came to U.S., 1985; d. Jean-Pierre and Brigitte Marguerite (Klockenbring) K. Student in Astronomy, Friedrich Wilhelm U., Bonn, Fed. Republic of Germany, 1981-83. Owner, mgr. Kempf, Sunnyvale, Calif., 1985—. Inventor Comeldir Multiplex Handicapped Driving Systems (Goldenes Lenkrad Axel Springer Verlag 1981), Katalavox speech recognition control system (Oscar, World Almanac Inventions 1984, Prix Grand Siecle, Comite Couronne Francaise 1985). Recipient Medal for Service to Humanity Spinal Cord Soc., 1986; street named in honor in Dossenheim-Kochersberg, Alsace, France, 1987; named Citizen of Honor City of Dossenheim-Kochersberg, 1985, Outstanding Businessperson of Yr. City of Sunnyvale, 1990. Avocations: flying, piano, violin, bassoon, studying foreign languages. Office: PO Box 61103 Sunnyvale CA 94088-1103

KEMPTHORNE, DIRK ARTHUR, governor; b. San Diego, Oct. 29, 1951; s. James Henry and Maxine Jesse (Gustason) K.; m. Patricia Jean Merrill, Sept. 18, 1977; children: Heather Patricia, Jeffrey Dirk. BS in Polit. Sci., U. Idaho, 1975. Exec. asst. to dir. Idaho Dept. Lands, Boise, 1975-78; exec. v.p. Idaho Home Builders Assn., Boise, 1978-81; campaign mgr. Batt for Gov., Boise, 1981-82; lic. securities rep. Swanson Investments, Boise, 1983; Idaho pub. affairs mgr. FMC Corp., Boise, 1983-86; mayor Boise, 1986-93; U.S. Senator from Idaho, 1993-98; gov. State of Idaho, 1999—; 1st v.p. Assn. of Idaho Cities, 1990-93; chmn. U.S. Conf. of Mayors Standing Com. on Energy and Environment, 1991-93, mem. adv. bd., 1991-93; sec. Nat. Conf. of Rep. Mayors and Mcpl. Elected Officials, 1991-93; mem. Senate Armed Svcs. Com., 1993—, Senate Small Bus. Com., 1993—, Senate Environ. and Pub. Works Com., 1993—, Nat. Rep. Senatorial Com., 1993—; chmn. Senate Drinking Water, Fisheries and Wildlife Subcommittee, 1995—, mem. advisory commn. on Intergovernmental Rels., 1995-96; chmn. Armed Svcs Personnel Subcommittee, 1996—. Pres. Associated Students U. Idaho, Moscow, 1975; chmn. bd. dirs. Wesleyan Presch., Boise, 1982-85; mem. magistrate commn. 4th Jud. Dist., Boise, 1986-93; mem. task force Nat. League of Cities Election, 1988; bd. dirs. Parents and Youth Against Drug Abuse, 1987—; mem. bd. vis. USAF Acad., 1994—; chmn. Idaho Working Ptnrs. Ltd., 1993—; hon. chmn. Idaho Congressional Award, 1994—. Named Idaho Citizen of Yr. The Idaho Statesman, 1988, Legislator of the Year Nat. Assn. Counties, 1995, State Legislator of the Year Nat. Assn. of Towns and Townships, 1995; recipient U.S. Conference of Mayor's Nat. Legis. Leadership award, 1994, Disting. Svc. award Nat. Conf. State Legislatures, 1995, Disting. Congressional award Nat. League of Cities, 1995, Guardian of Freedom award Council of State Governments, 1995. Republican. Methodist. Office: Office of the Governor PO Box 83720 Boise ID 83720-0034*

KENAGY, JOHN WARNER, surgeon; b. Lincoln, Nebr., May 28, 1945; s. Wyman Black and Sylvia (Adams) K.; m. Barbara Penterman, Feb. 1968 (div. 1975); 1 child, Jennifer; m. Jonell Day, Apr. 21, 1978; children: Susanne, Emma, John Wyman. BS, U. Nebr., 1967, MD, U. Nebr., Omaha, 1971, MPA Harvard U., 1998. Diplomate Am. Bd. Surgery; splty. cert. in gen. vascular surgery. Intern, Hosps. of U. Wash., Seattle, 1971-72, resident in surgery, 1971-76; surgeon Longview Surgical Group, Longview, Wash., 1976—; clin. instr. surgery U. Wash., Seattle, 1979-82, clin. asst. prof. surgery, 1982-89, clin. assoc. prof., 1989—; dir. peripheral vascular svcs. St. Johns Hosp., Longview, 1979-88, chmn. credentials com., 1989-90; dir. trauma svcs. St. Johns Med. Ctr., 1990-92; regional v.p. bus. devel. Lower Columbia Regional Health System; regional v.p. med. divsn. Peace Health, 1995—, regional v.p., med. divsn., 1995-96, regional v.p. bus. devel., 1996—. Editor current concepts in vascular diagnosis St. Johns Vascular Lab., Longview, 1979-88; contbr. articles to profl. jours. Chmn. bd. dirs. Cowlitz Med. Service, Longview, 1985-86. Regents scholar U. Nebr., Lincoln, 1963-67. Fellow ACS, Henry Harkins Surg. Soc. (trustee 1983-84), Seattle Surg. Soc.; mem. Internat. Cardiovascular Soc., Pacific N.W. Vascular Soc. (pres.-elect 1986-87, pres. 1987-88, chmn. com. on standards 1989-91), North Pacific Surg. Soc., Med. Group Mgmt. Assn., Am. Coll. Physician Execs., Alpha Omega Alpha, Theta Nu, Phi Gamma Delta. Republican. Office: Peace Health Regional Office 329 17th Ave Longview WA 98632-1401

KENDALL, HARRY OVID, internist; b. Eugene, Oreg., Nov. 29, 1929; s. Edward Lee and Jessie Avis (Giem) K.; m. Katherine Alexander, June 20, 1951 (div. 1957); 1 child, Jessica Gail Gress; m. Barbara Ann Matt, Jan. 21, 1961 (div. June 1, 1977); children: David Lee, Brian Padraic; m. Wanda Eve Helmer, July 2, 1993. AB, U. Redlands, 1952; MD, Yale U., 1955. Diplomate Am. Bd. Internal Medicine, Am. Bd. Pulmonary Disease. Intern in internal medicine UCLA Med. Ctr., 1955-57; resident in internal medicine West L.A. VA Med. Ctr., 1957-59; staff physician U.S. Naval Regional Med. Ctr., San Diego, 1959-62, Tulare-Kings Counties Hosp., Springville, Calif., 1962-63; staff physician, ptnr. So. Calif. Permanente Med. Group, Fontana, Calif., 1963-67, Kaiser Hosp. and So. Calif. Permanente Med. Group, San Diego, 1967—; dir. respiratory care Kaiser Hosp., San Diego, 1967—; attending physician San Bernardino County Hosp., 1964-67; asst. clin. prof. medicine U. Calif. San Diego Med. Ctr., 1976—; com. mem. numerous hosps. and med. clinics. Mem. NAACP, Amnesty Internat., ACLU. Lt. USNR, 1954-56, lt. comdr. 1961, comdr. 1973. Mem. Am. Thoracic Soc., cAlif. Thoracic Soc., San Diego Pulmonary Soc. Avocations: western history, paleontology, geneology, book collecting.

KENDRICK, BEVERLY ANN, medical-surgical nurse, small business owner; b. Rupert, Idaho, July 17, 1949; d. Robert Alfred and Erna (Plocher) Dockter; m. Sidney Cannon, Aug. 22, 1967 (div.); 1 child, Lisa Ann; m. Budd Leroy Kendrick, Dec. 26, 1978; children: Cassandra Rachelle, Angela Priscilla. Assoc. of Sci., Boise State U., 1989, BS, 1993; grad. bus. program, Idaho Small Bus. Devel. Ctr., Boise, 1997. RN, Idaho; cert. staff devel. continuing edn. nurse; cert. med.-surg. nurse. Coord. infant stimulation program Adult and Child Devel. Ctr., Boise, 1974-78; parent educator St. Alphonsus Regional Med. Ctr., Boise, 1996-97, nurse educator, 1996-97, risk mgr., 1998—; owner Angel Essence, Boise, 1995—. Author: Infant Stimulation Procedure Manual, 1978. Facilitator Women's Network of Entrepreneurial Tng., 1996-97; bd. dirs. Women's Entrepreneurial Mentoring Sys., v.p., 1996-97, pres., 1998—. RN scholar St. Alphonsus Regional Med. Ctr., 1988; named Women in Bus. Adv. of Yr. Idaho SBA, 1998. Mem. AAUW, Angel Collectors' Club Am., Idaho Coalition for Single Moms. Avocations: travel, reading, collecting angel collectibles, angel art. Home: 3125 Maywood Ave Boise ID 83704-5685

KENDRICK, LAURIE LYNN, artist; b. Inglewood, Calif., Apr. 15, 1969; d. R. Davis and Evelyn (Grace) K. BA, Lycee Francais, L.A., 1987. Poet Enright House, County Kerry, Ireland, 1992-95. Contbr. poems to anthologies: Best New Poems, 1995 (award), Amherst Soc. Anthology, 1995 (award), Iliad Press' Anthology, 1996, A Lasting Mirage, 1997. Vol. Beyond Baroque Lit. Ctr., Venice, Calif., 1991-92. Recipient Editor's award for photography Nat. Libr. Photography, 1998. Mem. Nat. Preservation Soc., Wilson Quar., Smithsonian Inst. Avocations: jewelry making, volunteer work, linguistics, travel, reading. Home: 2200 S Coast Hwy Laguna Beach CA 92651-3669 Office: PO Box 34991 Los Angeles CA 90034-0991

KENISON, LYNN T., chemist; b. Provo, Utah, Feb. 20, 1943; s. John Silves and Grace (Thacker) K.; m. Daralyn Wold, June 10, 1969; children: Marlene, Mark, Evan, Guy, Amy, Suzanne. BS in Chemistry, Brigham Young U., 1968, MS in Chemistry, 1971. Tchr. Weber County Sch. Dist., Ogden, Utah, 1968-69; bench chemist (drugs) Salt Lake City/County Health Dept., 1971-74; chemist U.S. Dept. Labor, OSHA Salt Lake Tech. Ctr., 1974—, bench chemist, 1974-77, supr., br. chief, 1977-84, sr. chemist, 1984—; tech. writer OSHA. Editor: Review Methods and Analytical Papers Before Publication, 1984—; tech. writer, 1984—. Councilman West Bountiful City, Utah, 1980-83, 85-89; scouting coord. Boy Scouts Am., cubmaster local pack, 1990-94; full-time missionary LDS Ch., Ark., Mo., Ill., 1962-64; vol. spkr. in local pub. schs., 1988—. Mem. Am. Indsl. Hygiene Assn., Fed. Exec. Assn. (Disting. Svc. award, Jr. Award for Outstanding Fed. and Cmty. Svc. 1980), Toastmasters Internat. (treas. Salt Lake City chpt. 1987-91). Avocations: woodworking, church activities, Boy Scout activities. Home: 1745 N 600 W West Bountiful UT 84087-1150 Office: US Dept of Labor OSHA Salt Lake Tech Ctr 1781 S 300 W Salt Lake City UT 84115-1802

KENNA, LAWRENCE ALLAN, small business owner; b. Tucson, July 1, 1960. BSBA in Fin., No. Ariz. U., 1989; PhD, Walden U., 1994. Owner Kenna Assocs. Appraisal Co., Winslow, Ariz., 1978—; assoc. faculty Northland Pioneer Coll., Winslow, Ariz., 1989—; property mgr. City of Winslow, 1989-93. Mem. ASCD, ICBO, Grad. Spokesman Club. Avocations: fly tieing, fishing, hiking.

KENNARD, JOYCE L., state supreme court justice. Former judge L.A. Mcpl. Ct., Superior Ct., Ct. Appeal, Calif.; assoc. justice Calif. Supreme Ct., San Francisco, 1989—. Office: Calif Supreme Ct 350 McAllister St San Francisco CA 94102-3600

KENNEALLY, TARA D., civil engineer; b. Bronx, N.Y., Feb. 13, 1970; d. William Jerome and Martina Dolores (Feighery) K. BS in Civil Engring., Manhattan Coll., Riverdale, N.Y., 1993. Asst. civil engr. N.J. Dept. Environ. Protection, Trenton, 1993-95; asst. conservation engr. N.Y. Power Authority, N.Y.C., 1995-97; outside plant design engr. NYNEX, Valhalla, N.Y., 1997; sr. acct. rep. PEM, Evans, Inc., Arcadia, Calif., 1998—; sr. acct. mgr. Pasadena (Calif.) Water and Power, 1998. Mem. ASCE, IES. Roman Catholic. Avocations: golf, music, art, interior decorating. E-mail: tkenneally@ci.pasadena.ca.us. Home: 125 N Doheny Dr Apt 304 Los Angeles CA 90048-2862 Office: 150 S Los Robles Ave Ste 200 Pasadena CA 91101-4613

KENNEDY, DEBRA JOYCE, marketing professional; b. Covina, Calif., July 9, 1955; d. John Nathan and Dru Hannah (Lancaster) Ward; m. John [illegible] munications, Calif. State Poly. U., 1977. Pub. rels. coord. Whittier (Calif.) Hosp., 1978-79, pub. relations mgr., 1980; pub. rels. dir. San Clemente (Calif.) Hosp., 1979-80; dir. pub. rels. Garfield Med. Ctr., Monterey Park,

Calif., 1980-82; dir. mktg. and community rels. Charter Oak Hosp., Covina, 1983-85; mktg. dir. CPC Horizon Hosp., Pomona, 1985-89; dir. mktg. Sierra Royale Hosp., Azusa, 1989-90; mktg. rep. PacifiCare, Cypress, 1990-92; regional medicare mgr. Health Net, Woodland Hills, Calif., 1992-95; dist. sales mgr. Kaiser Permante Health Plan, Pasadena, Calif., 1995—. Mem. Am. Soc. Hosp. Pub. Rels., Healthcare Mktg. Assn., Healthcare Pub. Rels. and Mktg. Assn., Covina and Covina West C. of C., West Covina Jaycees. Republican. Methodist. Club: Soroptimists. Contbr. articles to profl. jours.

KENNEDY, DENNIS L., lawyer; b. Tacoma, Oct. 28, 1950. BA, U. Wash., 1972, JD, 1975. Bar: Nev. 1975. Ptnr. Lionel Sawyer & Collins, Las Vegas, Nev., 1979—. Bd. editors Washington Law Review, 1974-75. Fellow Am. Coll. Trial Lawyers; mem. ABA (administrv. law sect., antitrust law sect., forum com. health law 1980—), Am. Acad. Hosp. Attys., Am. Soc. Law and Medicine, Internat. Assn. Gaming Attys., Nat. Health Lawyers Assn., State Bar Nev. (mem. disciplinary comm. 1988—),. Office: Lionel Sawyer & Collins Bank Am Plz 300 S 4th St Ste 1700 Las Vegas NV 89101-6053*

KENNEDY, DONALD, environmental science educator, former academic administrator; b. N.Y.C., Aug. 18, 1931; s. William Dorsey and Barbara (Bean) K.; children: Laura Page, Julia Hale; m. Robin Beth Wiseman, Nov. 27, 1987; stepchildren: Cameron Rachel, Jamie Christopher. AB, Harvard U., 1952, AM, 1954, PhD, 1956; DSc (hon.), Columbia U., Williams Coll., U. Mich., U. Ariz., U. Rochester, Reed Coll., Whitman Coll. Mem. faculty Stanford (Calif.) U., 1960-77, prof. biol. scis., 1965-77, chmn. dept., 1965-72, sr. cons. sci. and tech. policy Exec. Office of Pres., 1976, commr. FDA, 1977-79, provost, 1979-80, pres., 1980-92; prof. emeritus, Bing prof. environ. sci. Stanford U., 1992—; bd. overseers Harvard U., 1970-76; bd. dirs. Health Effects Inst., Nat. Commn. on Pub. Svc., Carnegie Commn. on Sci., Tech. and Govt. Author: Academic Duty, 1997; mem. editorial bd. Jour. Neurophysiology, 1969-75, Science, 1973-77; contbr. articles to profl. jours. Bd. dirs. Carnegie Endowment for Internat. Peace. Fellow AAAS, Am. Acad. Arts and Scis.; mem. NAS, Am. Philos. Soc. Office: Stanford U Inst for Internat Studies Encina Hall 401 Stanford CA 94305-6055

KENNEDY, GWENDOLYN DEBRA, film animator, parapsychologist, artist, play and film writer; b. Daly City, Calif., Nov. 18, 1960; d. Adolphus Brooks and Ella (Robinson) K.; children: Gwendolyn Fincher, Edward James, Jr. Diploma, U. San Francisco, 1987, M in Film and Theater, 1992. Dir. film animation Walt Disney, Buena Vista, Calif., 1994—; pres., owner Black Panther Party Press, 1993—; owner mail order co. La Chateau D'Gwendolyn Kennedy Co., 1991—. Author: Dorothy Dandrige Collection, 1993, Kane Kut Murder Trial, 1993, Poetic Justice, 1994, No Struggle No Progress, 1995, Nyami the Sky God, 1996; (authored two screen plays) Nat Turner, The Pied Piper, 1997; patentee musical boudoir cache. Min. info. Black Panther Party, San Francisco, 1993, leader, comdr., 1993—. Recipient Journalist of Yr. award City News Svc., Mo., 1995. Lutheran. Avocations: ballet, art, track, piano, computers. Home: 285 Bellevue Ave Daly City CA 94014-1305 Office: PO Box 135 Daly City CA 94016-0135

KENNEDY, JOHN EDWARD, art dealer, appraiser, curator; b. Glens Falls, N.Y., Apr. 21, 1930; s. John Edward and Veronica Irene (Young) K.; m. Katherine Joan Donovan, July 14, 1956 (div. June 1973); m. Blake Hale Whitney, Dec. 24, 1995. AB with hons., Boston Coll., 1951; JD, Harvard U., 1956; grad., U.S. Army Command and Gen. Staff Coll., 1964. Bar: Mass. 1956. Asst. counsel New England Mut. Life Ins., Boston, 1956-64; counsel Pa. Life Ins. Co., Beverly Hills, Calif., 1964-68; investment banker Smith Barney and Co., L.A. and N.Y.C., 1968-70; real estate developer Calif. and Hawaii, 1970-80; v.p. Galerie De Tours, Carmel, Calif., 1980-88; curator Gallery Americana, Carmel, 1988-92; patron Monterey Peninsula Mus. of Art., 1988—, Carmel Art Assn., 1985—. Trustee Harrison Meml. Libr., Carmel, 1986-88; commr. Planning commn., Carmel, 1988-94, chmn., 1992-94. With U.S. Army, 1952-53, Korea, Lt. Col., U.S. Army Res., 1969. Decorated Bronze Star for Valor, Purple Heart with cluster; recipient Disting. Mil. Svc. medal Republic of Korea, 1953. Mem. Am. Soc. of Appraisers (cert.), New England Appraisers Assn. (cert.), Am. Planning Assn., Marines Meml. Club. Republican. Episcopalian. Avocation: golf. Home: PO Box 222162 Carmel CA 93922-2162 Office: New Masters Gallery Dolores 7th Carmel CA 93921

KENNEDY, JOHN HARVEY, chemistry educator; b. Oak Park, Ill., Apr. 24, 1933; s. John Harvey and Margaret Helen (Drenthe) K.; m. Joan Corinne Hipsky, June 9, 1956 (div. Mar. 1969); children: Bruce Laurence, Bryan Donald, Brent Peter, Jill Amy.; m. Victoria Jane Matthew, July 2, 1970; 1 child, Karen Anne. BS, UCLA, 1954; AM, Harvard U., 1956, PhD, 1957. Sr. research chemist E.I. du Pont de Nemours, Wilmington, Del., 1957-61; asst. prof. chemistry U. Calif., Santa Barbara, 1961-63, 67-69, assoc. prof., 1969-76, prof., 1976-93, prof. emeritus, 1993—, chmn. dept., 1982-85; assoc. prof. Boston Coll., Chestnut Hill, 1963-64; head inorganic chemistry Gen. Motors, Santa Barbara, 1964-67; cons. Eveready Battery Co., Cleve., 1983—; vis. prof. U. N.C., Chapel Hill, 1980-81, Japan Soc. Promotion of Sci., Nagoya, 1974-75, Leningrad State U., 1989, China Acad. Scis., 1990. Author: Analytical Chemistry, Principles, 1990, Analytical Chemistry, Practice, 1990; contbr. articles to profl. jours.; patentee in field. Mus. dir. Christ the King Episcopal Ch., Santa Barbara, 1982-98. Mem. Am. Chem. Soc., Electrochem. Soc. Democrat. Avocation: music. Home: 5357 Agana Dr Santa Barbara CA 93111-1601 Office: U Calif Dept Chemistry Santa Barbara CA 93106

KENNEDY, KIRBY KENNETH, minister; b. Sidney, Nebr., Mar. 13, 1958; s. Martin Travis and Bessie Louvene (Brittain) K.; m. Debra Susan Klein, Aug. 10, 1985. BA in Religion, Wayland Bapt. U., Plainview, Tex., 1980; MDiv, Southwestern Bapt. Theol. Sem., Ft. Worth, 1984, D Ministry, 1991. Ordained to ministry So. Bapt. Conv., 1982. Min. music and youth Concord Bapt. Ch., Chandler, Tex., 1980-82; pastor 1st Bapt. Ch., Las Lunas, N.Mex., 1982-87, Calvary Bapt. Ch., Roswell, N.Mex., 1987—; pres. Ministerial Fellowship, Cen. Bapt. Assn., Albuquerque, 1984-86, chmn., mem. various coms., 1985-87; mem. associational coun. Pecos Valley Bapt. Assn., Artesia, N.Mex., 1987—, also chmn. stewardship coun., Christian life com.; mem. edn. com. Bapt. Conv. N.Mex., Albuquerque, 1986—, mem., sec. exec. bd., 1986-90, mem. Christian Life Commn., 1990—, convenor Evangelism Conf., 1991; mem. faculty Southeastern N.Mex. Congress on Family Living, Artesia, 1988, 89; chmn. upward 90 campaign Southwestern Bapt. Theol. Sem., N.Mex., 1985-90; nummerous others. Mgr. Valencia County Little League, Los Lunas, 1985; mem. disting. tchr. awards com. Los Lunas Sch. Dist., 1986-87. Mem. Southwestern Bapt. Theol. Sem. Alumni Assn. (pres. N.Mex. 1990-91). Office: Calvary Bapt Ch 1009 W Alameda PO Box 127 Roswell NM 88202-0127

KENNEDY, MICHAEL LEO, biology and chemistry educator; b. Winchester, Mass., Feb. 10, 1956; s, Thomas E. and Margaret L. (Nowell) K.; m. Ann L. Heitkemper, Nov. 10, 1989; 1 child, Evelyn Rose. BS, U. Mass., 1980; MS, Ctrl. Wash. U., 1985; PhD, Ariz. State U., 1994; postdoctoral student, Case Western Reserve U., 1993. Tchg. assoc. math., sci. honors program minority students Ariz. State U., Tempe, 1985-92, rsch. assoc. zoology, 1990-92; adj. faculty Cuyahoga C.C., Parma, Ohio, 1993-94, S. Puget Sound C.C., Olympia, Wash., 1994-95, Evergreen State Coll., Olympia, 1995-96; instr., coord. biology, chemistry, health scis. Pierce Coll., Lakewood, Wash., 1995—; grad. student rep. Phys. Group Dept. Zoology Ariz. State U., Tempe, 1990-91; mem. coun. acad. affairs Pierce Coll., Lakewood, Wash., 1997—. Contbr. articles and abstracts to profl. jours. Vol. instr. Hispanic Mother Daughter Assn., Tempe, Ariz., 1985-92, Math. Sci., Minority Honors Program, Ariz. State U., Tempe, 1985-92; vol. Garfield PTA, Olympia, Wash., 1996-98. With USMC, 1974-76. Grantee: Grad. Student Assn., Ariz. State Coll., 1990, Ariz. State U. Dept. Zoology, 1991, Sigma Xi, 1991. Mem. AAAS, Wash. Native Plant Soc., Am. Soc. Zoologists. Avocation: quality time with daughter. Home: 414 Percival St NW Olympia WA 98502-4856 Office: 9401 Farwest Dr SW Lakewood WA 98498-1919

KENNEDY, ORIN, film company executive; b. N.Y.C., May 24, 1939; s. Solomon Fuchs and Gertrude Krex. BFA, N.Y. Sch. Interior Design, 1963. Prodn. assoc. Fries Entertainment, Los Angeles, 1976-84; exec. location mgr. Metro-Goldwyn-Mayer subs. United Artists Entertainment, Culver City, Calif., 1984-85; exec. location mgr. The Twilight Zone TV series CBS Entertainment, Los Angeles, 1985-86; exec. location mgr. LA Law TV series 20th Century Fox Film Corp., Los Angeles, 1986-94, exec. location mgr. Picket Fences TV series, 1991-96; Chicago Hope TV series, 1994—.

KENNEDY, PEGGY BOOGAARD, artist, writer; b. Longview, Wash., Nov. 12, 1945; d. Johannes Elsworth and Martha Emily (Hill) Boogaard; divorced; children: John Steven, Anjanette M. Kennedy Hage. BA, Seattle Univ., 1967; postgrad., Univ. Juneau (Alaska), Juneau, Alaska, 1982-85. Daycare owner Boogaard's Daycare, Ketchikan, Alaska, 1961-65; tourist info. Ketchikan Visitor's Bureau, Ketchikan, Alaska, 1966; editor Fragments, Seattle, Wash., 1967; tutorial svcs. Saxman, Alaska, 1975-77; sub. tchr. Ketchikan Borough Schs., Ketchikan, 1977-84; tourist info. Josephine's Bazaar, Saxman, 1975; owner Peggy's Daycare, Ketchikan, 1976—. Author short stories and poems. Founder Thespian charter Boogaard's Daycare, Ketchikan, 1973; Sunday sch. dir. Pentecostal Ch., Saxman, 1992-94, 76-95; vol. head cook Salvation Army, 1980-89. With Civil Air Patrol, 1961-63. Recipient Nat. Merit scholarship, 1961, 62, President's award Iliad Press for poetry, 1990. Republican. Avocations: writing, swimming, walking, sewing, reading, art, music. Home: 1200 Woodside Dr Apt F7 Ketchikan AK 99901-6244 Office: 1200 Woodside Dr Apt F7 Ketchikan AK 99901-6244

KENNEDY, R. EVAN, retired structural engineer, executive; b. Worland, Wyo., Mar. 31, 1916; s. Robert Eaker and Addie Miranda (Pritchard) K.; m. Betty Lou Kaser, Feb. 3, 1945; children: Anne Louise, Carter Evan, Robert Gordon. Student, Jamestown (N.D.) Coll., 1934-35; BS in Civil Engring., U. Colo., 1938. Recorder U. S. Geol. Survey, Denver, 1938-39; jr. hydraulic engr. Colo. Water Consv. Bd., Denver, 1939-41; structural draftsman, jr. designer Am. Bridge Co., Trenton, N.J., 1941-42; stress analyst Goodyear Aircraft Corp., Akron, Ohio, 1942-44; liaison engr., group leader, sect. head Goodyear Aircraft Corp., Phoenix, 1944-46; sales rep. Luby-Sonnen Co., Madison, Wis., 1946; project engr. Rentenbach Engring. Co., Knoxville, Tenn., 1946-47; field mgr. Kaser Constrn. Co., West Des Moines, Iowa, 1947; design engr. Moffatt, Nichol & Taylor, Portland, Oreg., 1947-49, Cooper & Rose, Portland, 1949-51; chief structural engr. Barrett & Logan Architects, Portland, 1951-52; chief structural engr. Edmundson, Kochendoerfer & Kennedy A/E, Portland, 1952-53, chief engr., 1954-55, ptnr., 1955-68; mng. ptnr. Edmundson, Kochendoerfer, Kennedy-Daniel, Mann, Johnson, Mendenhall, Portland, 1968-70; chmn. Seismic Design Com., Portland, 1948-50, bd. dirs., treas. Portland Bldg. Code Revisions Com., 1950-53; observer, cons. Effects Nuclear Test U.S. Dept. Commerce, Yucca Flats, Nev., 1955; instr. Oreg. Bd. Higher Edn. Architects Registration Exams., Portland, 1954-58, Engrs. Registration Exams., 1960-63; lectr. Oreg. Dental Sch. Disaster Planning, Portland, 1960-64; mem. A/E Selection Bd. U.S. Gen. Svcs. Adminstrn. NW Divsn., Auburn, Wash., 1973, Nat. Def. Exec. res. U. S. Bur. Pub. Rds., Washington, 1964-71. Contbr. articles to profl. jours. Vice chmn. Fernwood Grade Sch. PTA, Portland, 1952-53, Portland Traffic Safety Commn., 1964-74; chmn. scholarship Grant H.S. Dad's Club, Portland, 1964-67; chmn. engrs. divsn. Portland United Good Neighbors, 1965, chmn. profl. divsn., 1967, 68; chmn. Interfaith Housing Com., Portland, 1969-73, Dulaney Towers Condo Bd., Towson, Md., 1975-78, Dulaney Towers Maintenance Bd., 1976-78, Balt. Energy Coun., 1978, Waterford Condo. Bd., Kensington, Md., 1985-88; pres. Portland Housing Devel. Corp., Portland, 1970-74, Metrohousing, Inc., Portland, 1971-74; mem. Portland Symphonic Choir, 1958-64, Multnomah County Bldg. Code Appeals Bd., Portland, 1964, Nat. Mcpl. League, 1968-79, nat. conv. sect. convenor, 1976, 77, Mayor's Adv. Com., Portland, 1968-69, Congressman Wendell Wyatt Re-election Com., Portland, 1968; treas. Am. Plaza Condo Assn. Bd., Portland, 1991-96; bd. dirs. Chess 4 Success, Portland, 1996-97; mem., elder Towson Presbyn. Ch., 1974-79; bd. dirs. Chess4Success, 1996—; bd. mem. Portland Chess 4 Success. Recipient Meritorious Svc. award City Portland, 1952, Nat. Design Honor award HUD, Washington, 1976, Grand Design award Am. Consulting Engrs. Coun., Washington, 1996. Mem. ASCE (bd. dirs. Oreg. sect. 1953-55, Capital sect. 1980-90, sec. 1983, mem. Md. sect. 1974-90, Oreg. sect. 1990—), AIAA, ASTM (chmn. NW dist. 1970), Am. Concrete Inst., Soc. Am. Mil. Engrs. (Merit award Portland Post 1973), Structural Engrs. Assn. Oreg. (founder, pres. 1949), Profl. Engrs. Oreg. (bd. dirs. 1948-74, chmn. Conv. 100 Yrs. Engring., founder Engr. Yr. award 1964), Prestressed Concrete Inst., Engring. Coun. Rsch. Inst., Consulting Engrs. Coun. Oreg. (treas. 1960, Engring. Excellence Project award 1996), Toastmasters. Republican. Home and Office: 2309 SW 1st Ave Apt 1145 Portland OR 97201-5040

KENNEDY, RICHARD JEROME, writer; b. Jefferson City, Mo., Dec. 23, 1932; s. Donald and Mary Louise (O'Keefe) K.; m. Lillian Elsie Nance, Aug. 3, 1960; children: Joseph Troy, Matthew Cook. BS, Portland State U., 1958. Author: (novel) Amy's Eye, 1985 (Internat. Rattenfanger Lit. prize, Fed. Republic Germany 1988), also 18 children's books including Richard Kennedy: Collected Stories, 1988 and 3 musicals, including adaptation of H.C. Andersen's The Snow Queen; inclusion of stories in: The Oxford Book of Modern Fairy Tales, 1993, The Oxford Book of Children's Stories, 1993. With USAF, 1951-54. Home and Office: 415 W Olive St Newport OR 97365-3716

KENNEDY, THOMAS EDGAR, investment banker; b. Stockton, Calif., Aug. 16, 1958; s. Thomas Jefferson and Evelyn Marie (Bodimer) K.; m. Susan Grace Harris Kennedy, May 4, 1986. BS, U. Pacific, 1980; MBA, Claremont Grad. Sch., 1981. Internal cons. Foster Farms, Livingston, Calif., 1982; acquisitions analyst Cal Gas, Sacramento, Calif., 1982-83, mgr. market planning, 1983-84; turnaround specialist Williams Assocs., Walnut Creek, Calif., 1984-85; chief exec. officer ICSG Info. Systems, Stockton, Calif., 1985-88, Integrative Svcs. Group, Stockton, 1988-89; pres. Kennedy Indsl. Arbitrage Holdings, 1989-92; v.p. fin. svcs. Charles Harris and Assocs., 1992—; mktg. cons. Harris Health Ins. Adminstrn., Stockton, Calif., 1985—. Alt. mem. Rep. Cen. Com., Stockton, Calif., 1985. Outstanding Young Man of Am., 1983. Phi Kappa Phi. Republican. Baptist. Avocations: golfing, championship auto racing teams. Office: Charles Harris & Assoc 2181 Piccardo Cir Stockton CA 95207-8208

KENNEDY, W(ILBERT) KEITH, JR., electronics company executive; b. Phoenix, Ariz., Sept. 19, 1943. BSEE, MS, Cornell U., 1966, PhD, 1968. Researcher microwave solid-state devices Cornell U. and RCA Rsch. Labs., Princeton, N.J., 1964-68; researcher, leader devel. team thin-film fabrication facility Watkins-Johnson Co., Palo Alto, Calif., 1968-71, head R & D devel. dept., 1971-74, solid state div. mgr., 1974-78, also v.p., 1977, devices group v.p., 1978-86, v.p. shareowner rels. and planning coord., 1986-88, co. pres., chief exec. officer, 1988—. Contbr. articles to profl. jours. and procs. Patentee microwave power generator. Bd. dirs. CNF Transp. Inc., Joint Venture Silicon Valley; mem. exec. bd. The Ctr. for Quality Mgmt.-West, Santa Clara Valley Mfg. Group. Mem. IEEE (sr.); mem. Group Electronic Devices of IEEE, Group Microwave Theory and Techs. of IEEE, Calif. C. of C. (bd. dirs.), Phi Eta Sigma, Eta Kappa Nu, Tau Beta Phi, Phi Kappa Phi, Sigma Xi. Office: Watkins-Johnson Co 3333 Hillview Ave Palo Alto CA 94304-1223

KENNERKNECHT, RICHARD EUGENE, marketing executive; b. Glendale, Calif., Apr. 29, 1961; s. Richard and Sharon Mavis (Zane) K. V.p. Def. Tech. Corp. Am., 1993-96; pres. Rocky Mountain divsn. Nat. Telecom. Group, Casper, Wyo., 1996—; mktg. dir. The Uplink-Group, Mills, Wyo., 1996—; nat. sales dir. Bridge21.com, Casper, Wyo., 1998—; pres. FDC Inc., Lost Hills, Calif., 1989-91; profl. sporting clays shooter, exhbn. shooter. Mem. U.S. Sporting Assn. (mem. team U.S.A. 1988, 89, all-Am. team 1988, 89, 90, winner gold medal U.S.-French Profl. Invitational 1990, 91), U.S. Sporting Clays Assn. (mem. rules and ethics com., capt. team Perazzi), Verdugo Hills Ducks Unltd. (founding mem.), Nat. Sporting Clays Assn. (mem. nat. adv. coun. 1991-92), Olin Winchester (adv. coun. 1991-93), Calif. Waterfowl Assn. (shooting sports dir. 1992-93), Western Outdoor News (outdoor columnist 1992-93). Republican. Episcoplian. E-mail: rick@bridge21.net. Home: PO Box 1180 Mills WY 82644-1180 Office: The Uplink-Group PO Box 1180 Mills WY 82644-1180

KENNEY, PATTI MARLENE, sales exeuctive; b. St. Louis, Nov. 6, 1952; d. Herbert Martin and Marlene Marguerite (Short) Foerster; m. Thomas Francis Kenney, June 1, 1968 (div. Aug. 1995); children: Paulette Marlene Potter, Brian Patrick, Thomas Michael. Cert. advt. specialist, master advt. specialist. Customer svc. rep. Hazel, Hazel, So. Calif., 1983; customer svc./salesperson Cubegraphics, Sunnyvale, No. Calif., 1984-86, Mission Laser Works, El Monte, Calif., 1986-88; customer svc. dir. Penn Corp., St. Louis, 1988-89; nat. sales mgr. Ocean Specialty, So. Calif., 1989-94; nat. sales dir. The Newport Connection, Orange County, Calif., 1994-95; regional sales mgr. Vantage Custom Classics, Orange County, 1995-96; customer svc. mgr. Magnet, Inc., Washington, Mo., 1996—; bd. dirs. Specialty Advt. Assn., editor, 1992-94, sec.-treas., 1993-94, v.p., 1994-95, pres., 1995-96. Lutheran. Avocations: golf, meditation, writing, travel. Home: 10215 Larwin Ave Unit 4 Chatsworth CA 91311-0114 Office: Vantage Custom Classics 3111 S Shannon St Santa Ana CA 92704-6350

KENNEY, WILLIAM FITZGERALD, lawyer; b. San Francisco, Nov. 4, 1935; s. Lionel Fitzgerald and Ethel Constance (Brennan) K.; m. Susan Elizabeth Langfitt, May 5, 1962; children: Anne, Carol, James. BA, U. Calif.-Berkeley, 1957, JD, 1960. Bar: Calif. 1961. Assoc. Miller, Osborne Miller & Bartlett, San Mateo, Calif., 1962-64; ptnr. Tormey, Kenney & Cotchett, San Mateo, 1965-67; pres. William F. Kenney, Inc., San Mateo, 1968—; gen. ptnr. All Am. Self Storage, 1985—, Second St. Self Storage, 1990-96, Cochrane Road Self Storage, 1996—. Trustee San Mateo City Sch. Dist., 1971-79, pres., 1972-74; pres. March of Dimes, 1972-73; bd. dirs. Boys Club of San Mateo, 1972-90, Samaritan House, 1989—, Lesley Found., 1992—. With U.S. Army, 1960-62. Mem. State Bar of Calif. (taxation com. 1973-76), San Mateo County Bar Assn. (bd. dir. 1973-75), Calif. Assn. Realtors (legal affairs com. 1978—), San Mateo C. of C. (bd. dirs. 1987-93), Self Storage Assn. (we. region, pres. 1989-90, nat. bd. dirs. 1990-97, nat. v.p. 1994-95, pres. 1996), Rotary (pres. 1978-79, Elks (exalted ruler 1974-75). Republican. Roman Catholic. Home: 221 Clark Dr San Mateo CA 94402-1004 Office: 120 N El Camino Real San Mateo CA 94401-2705

KENSWIL, LAWRENCE, music industry executive; b. Boston, Feb. 9, 1951; s. H. Robert and Josephine S. (Silbert) K.; m. Ann B. Holler, Mar. 28, 1982; children: Jacob, Samuel. BA, Cornell U., 1972; MS, Boston U., 1977; JD, Georgetown U., 1980. Assoc. Mitchell, Silverberg & Knupp, L.A., 1980-83; assoc. dir. legal affairs Universal Music Group (formerly MCA Music Group), Universal City, Calif., 1983-85, dir. legal affairs, 1985-87, sr. dir. legal affairs, 1987-89, v.p. bus. legal affairs, 1989-91, sr. v.p. bus. legal affairs, 1991-95, exec. v.p., 1995—. Mem. Recording Industry Assn. Am. (bd. dirs. 1996—), Internat. Federation Phonographic Industry (bd. dirs. 1996—). Office: Universal Music Group 70 Universal City Plz Universal City CA 91608-1101

KENT, JEFFREY FRANKLIN, baseball player; b. Bellflower, Calif., Mar. 7, 1968. Grad., Edison H.S., Calif. Played 2d base Toronto Blue Jays, 1992; 2d baseman N.Y. Mets, 1992-96, San Francisco Giants, 1996—. Office: San Francisco Giants 3Com Park at Candlestick Pt San Francisco CA 94124*

KENT, STEPHEN SMILEY, lawyer; b. Reno, July 6, 1952; s. Robert Roe and Muriel (Smiley) K.; m. H. Mayla Walcutt, Dec. 19, 1976; children: Kristopher, Kimberly, Alisa. BS (hons.), U. Nev., 1975; JD, U. of the Pacific, 1980. Bar: Nev. 1980. Law clk. to Hon. William N. Forman Reno, 1980-81; assoc. Vargas & Bartlett, Reno, 1981-86; assoc. Beckley, Singleton, Jemison & List, Reno, 1986-89, shareholder, 1989—; mem. exec. coun. Nev. State Bar Young Lawyers Assn., Reno, 1987-89; mem. fee dispute com. Nev. State Bar, Reno, 1985-88, mem. ins. com., 1986-87. Co-author: (manuals/seminars) Nevada Uninsured Motorist Insurance, 1985, Controlling Damages, 1991, Enforcing Judgments, 1989, Pretrial Discovery, 1988. Mem. Neighborhood Adv. Coun., Reno, 1992—. Mem. ABA (litigation sect.), Internat. Assn. Def. Counsel, Nat. Bd. Trial Advocacy (cert. civil trial advocate), Rotary Club Reno. Home: 2815 Columbus Way Reno NV 89503-1848 Office: Beckley Singleton Jemison & List 1575 Delucchi Ln Ste 224 Reno NV 89502-8521

KENT, SUSAN, library director, consultant; b. N.Y.C., Mar. 18, 1944; d. Elias and Minnie (Barnett) Solomon; m. Eric Goldberg, Mar. 27, 1966 (div. Mar. 1991); children: Evan, Jessica, Joanna; m. Rolly Kent, Dec. 20, 1991. BA in English Lit. with honors, SUNY, 1965; MS, Columbia U., 1966. Libr., sr. libr. N.Y. Pub. Libr., 1965-67, br. mgr. Donnell Art Libr., 1967-68; reference libr. Paedergaat br. Bklyn. Pub. Libr., 1971-72; reference libr. Finkelstein Meml. Libr., Spring Valley, N.Y., 1974-76; coord. adult and young adult svcs. Tucson Pub. Libr., 1977-80, acting libr. dir., 1982, dep. libr. dir., 1980-87; mng. dir. Ariz. Theatre Co., Tucson and Phoenix, 1987-89; dir. Mpls. Pub. Libr. and Info. Ctr., 1990-95; city libr. L.A. Pub. Libr., 1995—; tchr. Pima C.C., Tucson, 1978, grad. libr. sch. U. Ariz., Tucson, 1978, 79; panelist Ariz. Commn. Arts, 1981-85; reviewer pub. programs NEH, 1985, 89, panelist challenge grants, 1986-89, panelist state programs, 1988; cons. to librs. and nonprofit instns., 1989-90, 92—; mem. bd. devel. and fundraising Child's Play, Phoenix, 1983; bd. dirs., mem. organizing devel. and fundraising com. Flagstaff (Ariz.) Symphony Orch., 1988; cons., presenter workshops Young Adult Svcs. divsn. ALA, 1986-88; bd. advisors UCLA Grad. Sch. Edn. and Info. Scis., 1998—; presenter in field. Contbr. articles to profl. jours. Chair arts and culture com. Tucson Tomorrow, 1981-85; bd. dirs., v.p. Ariz. Dance Theatre, 1984-86; bd. dirs. women's studies adv. coun. U. Ariz., 1985-90, Arizonans for Cultural Devel., 1987-89, YWCA Mpls., 1991-92; commr. Ariz. Commn. on Arts, 1983-87; participant Leadership Mpls., 1990-91. Fellow Sch. Libr. Sci., Columbia U., 1965-66. Mem. ALA (membership com. S.W. regional chair 1983-86, com. on appts. 1986-87, planning and budget assembly del. 1991-93, gov. coun. 1990-98, chair conf. com. 1996-97), Pub. Libr. Assn. (nominating com. 1980-82, v.p. 1986-87, pres. 1987-88, chair publs. assembly 1988-89, chair nat. conf. 1994, chair legis. com. 1994-95), Calif. Libr. Assn., Urban Librs. Coun. (exec. bd. 1994—, treas. 1996-98, vice chair/chair elect 1998—), Libr. Adminstrn. and Mgmt. Assn. (John Cotton Dana Award com. 1994-95). Office: LA Pub Libr 630 W 5th St Los Angeles CA 90071-2002

KENT, THEODORE CHARLES, psychologist; m. Shirley, June 7, 1948; children: Donald, Susan, Steven. BA, Yale U., 1935, MA, Columbia U., 1940, MA, Mills Coll., 1953, PhD, U. So. Calif., 1951; Dr. Rerum Naturalium, Johannes Gutenberg U., Mainz, Germany, 1960. Diplomate in clin. psychology. Clin. psychologist, behavioral scientist USAF, 1951-65, chief psychologist, Europe, 1956-60; head dept. behavioral sci. U. So. Colo., Pueblo, 1965-78, emeritus, 1978—; staff psychologist Yuma Behavioral Health, Ariz., 1978-82, chief profl. svcs., 1982-83; dir. psychol. svcs. Rio Colo. Health Systems, Yuma, 1983-85; clin. psychologist, dir. mental health Ft. Yuma (Calif.) Indian Health Svc., USPHS, 1985-88; exec. dir. Human Sci. Ctr., San Diego, 1982—. Columnist Yuma Daily Sun, 1982-86. Author (tests) symbol arrangement test, 1952, internat. culture free non-verbal intelligence, 1957, self-other location chart, 1970, test of suffering, 1982; (books) Skills in Living Together, 1983, Conflict Resolution, 1986, A Psychologist Answers Your Questions, 1987, Behind The Therapist's Notes, 1993, Mapping the Human Genome—Reality, Morality and Diety, 1995, Poems For Living, 1995, Genetic Engineering, Yes, No or Maybe--A Look At What's Ahead, 1997; plays and video Three Warriors Against Substance Abuse. Named Outstanding prof. U. So. Colo., 1977. Fellow APA (disting. visitor undergrad. edn. program); mem. AAAS, Deutsche Gesellschaft fur Antropologie, Internat. Assn. Study of Symbols (founder, 1st pres. 1957-61), Japanese Soc. Study KTSA (hon. pres.), Home and Office: Townhouse G-64 4900 Telegraph Rd Ventura CA 93003-4131

KENT, THOMAS EDWARD, lawyer; b. Chgo., Jan. 29, 1957. BA in Sociology, U. Calif., Berkeley, 1979; JD, U. So. Calif., 1982. Bar: Calif. 1982, U.S. Dist. Ct. (cen. dist.) Calif., U.S. Dist. Ct. (no. dist.) Calif., U.S. Dist. Ct. (so. dist.) Calif., U.S. Ct. Appeals (9th cir.), U.S. Supreme Ct. Assoc. Fierstein & Sturman, L.A., 1982-87, Robinson, Diamant, Brill & Klausner, L.A., 1987-91; sole practitioner L.A., 1991—; Arbitrator L.A. County Bar Dispute Resolution Svcs. Mem. L.A. County Bar Assn., San Fernando Valley Bar Assn., Fin. Lawyers Conf., Bankruptcy Forum. FAX: 818-990-6792. Office: 16161 Ventura Blvd # 475 Encino CA 91436-2522

KENYON, CARLETON WELLER, librarian; b. Lafayette, N.Y., Oct. 7, 1923; s. Herbert Abram and Esther Elizabeth (Weller) K.; m. Dora Marie Kallander, May 21, 1948; children: Garnet Eileen, Harmon Clark, Kay Adelle. A.B., Yankton Coll., 1947; M.A., U. S.D., 1950, J.D., 1950; A.M. in L.S, U. Mich., 1951. Bar: S.D. 1950. Asst. law librarian, head catalog librarian U. Nebr., 1951-52; asst. reference librarian Los Angeles County Law Library, 1952-54, head catalog librarian, 1954-60; law librarian State of Calif., Sacramento, 1960-69; became cons. Library of Congress, Washington, 1963; asso. law librarian Library of Congress, 1969-71, law librarian, 1971-

89; cons. county law libraries; lectr. legal bibliography and research. Author: California County Law Library Basic List Handbook and Information of New Materials, 1967; compiler: Calif. Library Laws; assisted in compiling checklists of bars: Am. publs. and subject headings; contbr. articles and book revs. to law revs., library jours. Served with USAAC, 1943-46. Mem. ABA, State Bar S.D., Am. Assn. Law Librarians (chmn. com. on cataloging and classification 1969-71, mem. staff Law Library Inst. 1969, 71), Law Librarians Soc. Washington. Home: 4239 44th Ct NE Salem OR 97305-2117

KENYON, DAVID LLOYD, architect, architectural firm executive; b. Lockport, N.Y., Sept. 9, 1952; s. F. Robert and Betty Jane (Reviere) K.; m. Susan Clair Doyle, Jan. 6, 1990; children: Sean Phillip Kenyon, Colin Doyle Kenyon. A in Civil Tech., SUNY, Utica, 1972; BArch, Syracuse U., 1975. Lic. architect, N.Y., Pa., Ariz., Calif. Oreg., Ill., Washington. Assoc. The Myrus Group, Syracuse, N.Y., 1973-79; assoc. dir. design Chase Archtl. Assocs., Syracuse, N.Y., 1978-80; prin. Kenyon Archtl. Group, Phoenix, Ariz., 1980—; cons. Nat. Trust for Historic Preservation, Washington, 1978; faculty assoc. Ariz. State U. Coll. Architecture, Tempe, Ariz., 1983-89; with nat. solar study USAID, Morocco, 1991; with mission to Malta and Morocco, OPEC, Washington, 1991-92; lectr. Assn. Construction Inspectors, 1993. Author: (textbook) A Hands on Approach to Construction Inspection, 1992. Recipient Energy Innovation award U.S. Dept. Energy, 1988, Environmental Excellence award Crescordia Valley Forward, 1991, Western Regional Design award Am. Inst. Architects, 1991, CAC Honor award, 1992. Fellow Ariz. Acad.; mem. Nat. Trust for Historic Preservation, Soc. Archtl. Historians, Internat. Conference Bldg. Officials. Office: Kenyon Archtl Group LLC 24 W 5th St Tempe AZ 85281-3614

KENYON, DAVID V., federal judge; b. 1930; m. Mary Cramer; children: George Cramer, John Clark. B.A., U. Calif.-Berkeley, 1952; J.D., U. So. Calif., 1957. Law clk. presiding justice U.S. Dist. Ct. (cen. dist.) Calif., 1957-58; house counsel Metro-Goldwyn-Mayer, 1959-60, Nat. Theatres and TV Inc., 1960-61; pvt. practice law, 1961-71; judge Mcpl. Ct. L.A., 1971-72, L.A. Superior Ct., 1972-80; judge U.S. Dist. Ct. (cen. dist.) Calif., L.A., 1980—, sr. judge. Office: US Dist Ct 312 N Spring St Rm 2445 Los Angeles CA 90012-4701

KEOGH, HEIDI HELEN DAKE, advocate; b. Saratoga, N.Y., July 12, 1950; d. Charles Starks and Phyllis Sylvia (Edmunds) Dake; m. Randall Frank Keogh, Nov. 3, 1973; children: Tyler Cameron, Kelly Dake. Student, U. Colo., 1972. Reception, promotions Sta. KLAK, KJAE, Lakewood, Colo., 1972-73; acct. exec. Mixed Media Advt. Agy., Denver, 1973-75; writer, mktg. Jr. League Cookbook Devel., Denver, 1986-88; chmn., coord. Colorado Cache & Creme de Colorado Cookbooks, 1988-90; speakers bur. Mile High Transplant Bank, Denver, 1983-84, Writer's Inst., U. Denver, 1988; bd. dirs. Stewart's Ice Cream Co., Inc., Jr. League, Denver. Contbr. articles to profl. jours. Fiscal officer, bd. dirs. Mile High Transplant Bank; blockworker Heart Fund and Am. Cancer Soc., Littleton, Colo., 1978—, Littleton Rep. Com., 1980-84; fundraising vol. Littleton Pub. Schs., 1980—; vol. Gathering Place, bd. dirs., 1996—, chmn. Brown Bag benefit, 1996; vol. Hearts for Life, 1991—, Oneday, 1992, Denver Ballet Guild, 1992—, Denver Ctr. Alliance, 1993—, Newborn Hope, 1980—, Girls, Inc., 1995—, Girls Hope, VOA Guild, 1996—, Le Bal de Ballet, 1998—; active The Denver Social Register and Record, 1999. Mem. Jr. League Denver (pub. rels. bd., v.p. ways and means 1989-90, planning coun./ad hoc 1990-92, sustainer spl. events 1993-94), Community Emergency Fund (chair 1991-92), Jon D. Williams Cotillion at Columbine (chmn. 1991-93), Columbine Country Club, Gamma Alpha Chi, Pi Beta Phi Alumnae Club (pres. Denver chpt. 1984-85, 93-94, alumnae adv. com. U. Colo. chpt. 1997—), Denver Social Register and Record. Episcopalian. Avocations: traveling, skiing, golf, family activities. Home: 63 Fairway Ln Littleton CO 80123-6648

KEPANI, HERMAN, JR., security officer; b. Honolulu, Mar. 28, 1958; s. Herman Sr. and Rose K. (Paleka) K.; m. Dana Kay Cornelison, Dec. 21; children: Kanoe K. Wong, Mahina M. Armed courier, driver Loomis Armored Car Svc., Kahului, Hawaii, 1985-87; res. law enforcement officer Dept. Land and Natural Resources, State of Hawaii, Kahului, 1987-89; airport security officer Dept. Transp., State of Hawaii, Kahului, 1988-90; security officer, supr. Four Seasons Resort, Wailea, Hawaii, 1990-91; security officer, protection specialist Classic Resorts, Unltd., Kinei, Hawaii, 1991-94; law enforcement officer Wackenhut Corp., Kahului, 1994-96; safety and security officer Kea Lani Hotel Stes. and Villas, Wailea, Hawaii, 1994—; cons. Security Cons. Svcs., Paia, Hawaii, 1987-89; mem. pvt. security coun. Maui County, 1990—. Treas. citizen police acad. Maui Police Dept., 1997—; vol. instr. ARC, Wailuku, 1997—; bd. dirs. affirmative action adv. coun. Officer of Mayor, County of Maui, Wailuku, 1994-98; participant law enforcement torch run Spl. Olympics and Maui Police Dept., 1995-98; mem. Maui squadron USAF Aux. Civil Air Patrol, 2nd lt., 1997—; visitor industry-charity walk security vol. Wailuku, 1991-97; sustaining mem. Rep. Party Hawaii, Honolulu, 1996—. Named Outstanding Grad. in Principles of Pvt. Security, Maui County Hotel and Resort Security Assn., 1995, Security Officer of Yr., 1996. Mem. Protective Svc. Alliance, Internat. Assn. Profl. Protection Agts., Police Marksman Assn. Avocations: family activities, swimming, running, fencing, reading. Home: PO Box 512 Paia HI 96779-0512

KEPNER, JANE ELLEN, psychotherapist, educator, minister; b. Lancaster, Pa., July 13, 1948; d. Richard Darlington and Miriam Kepner; m. Raymond Earl Sparks Jr., July 23, 1969 (div. Apr. 1978); 1 child, Heather Elizabeth. AB, CCNY, 1975; MDiv, Harvard Divinity Sch., 1985. Vol. Vista, Auburn, Ala., 1967-69; creative drama tchr. East Harlem Day Care, N.Y.C., 1972-76; editl. asst. Bantam Books, Inc., N.Y.C., 1976-78; rschr. Theseus Prodns., Greenwich, Conn., 1978-82; homeless advocate Harvard Sq. Chs., Cambridge, Mass., 1984-85; cmty. organizer So. Middlesex Opportunity Coun., Marlboro, Mass., 1985-88; emergency psychiat. clinician Advocates, Inc., Framingham, Mass., 1988-89; assoc. prof. Curry Coll., Milton, Mass., 1989-90; psychologist, mental health advocate Portland (Oreg.) Health Svc., 1991-95, bd. advisors, 1992-94. Organizer emergency food pantry Marlboro City Coun., 1987; tenants rights and housing rights advocates Tenants Action Com., Marlboro, 1985-87. Pfeiffer fellow Harvard U. Div. Sch., 1983. Mem. Am. Counseling Assn., Oreg. Friends of C.G. Jung, Club 53 (bd. dirs. 1992-94), Amnesty Internat., Oreg. Coalition to Abolish the Death Penalty. Avocations: voice, hiking, gardening, biking, running.

KERBS, WAYNE ALLAN, transportation executive; b. Hoisington, Kans., Mar. 21, 1930; s. Emanuel and Mattie (Brack) K.; m. Patricia Ann Aitchison, Dec. 5, 1953; children: Jacqueline Lee Kerbs Kepler, Robert Wayne. BSEE, U. Kans., 1952; MSEE, Ohio State U., 1960; M Engring., UCLA, 1968. Test engr. Mpls.-Honeywell, 1952-54; sr. engr. Booz Allen & Hamilton, Dayton, Ohio, 1957-60; program mgr. Hughes Aircraft Co., L.A., 1960-74; pres., bd. dirs. Kerbs Industries, Inc., Los Alamitos, Calif., 1975—. Developer spacecraft devel. surveyor, 1960's, transit plan, 1996; patentee in field. Vol. PTA, Boy Scouts Am., Meth. Ch., 1952—; organizer Am. Mature Vols., L.a., 1994—; active Orange County Transp. Authority, 1994—. Lt. USN, 1954-57. Fellow Inst. for the Advancement of Engring.; mem. Soc. Automotive Engrs. (sec.), Inst. of Transp. Engrs., Elec. Automobile Assn., Advanced Transit Assn., Transp. Rsch. Bd., Am. Legion, Sigma Tau, Eta Kappa Nu, Kappa Eta Kappa. Republican. Avocations: sports, building, inventing, writing, investing.

KERKLO, NORMA JEAN, publications executive; b. McKeesport, Pa., Dec. 6, 1947; d. John and Edythe (Steiner) Moore; m. John M. Kerklo, Sept. 8, 1964 (div. 1989); children: Mark, Michelle. AA in Journalism, Riverside City Coll.; BA in Tech. Writing, U. Colo. Comm. coord. U. Tex., El Paso; journalist Norco (Calif.) Pony Express; pub. info. asst. State Bd. for C.C. and Occupational Edn., Denver, 1984-85; from assoc. tech. writer to sr. tech. writer McData Corp., Broomfield, Colo., 1986-92; trainer, tech. writer Micro Decisionware, Inc., Boulder, Colo., 1992-94; tech. publ. mgr. EMASS, Englewood, Colo., 1995—. Mem. Soc. for Tech. Comm. (sr. mem., competition mgr. 1990, awards mgr. 1992-94, Achievement award 1991, Excellence award 1994), Soc. for Computing and Informational Processing. Avocations: gardening, travel. Home: Unit C 19692 E Mann Creek Dr Apt C Parker CO 80134-3411 Office: EMASS 10949 E Peakview Ave Englewood CO 80111-0004

KERMAN, BARRY MARTIN, ophthalmologist, educator; b. Chgo., Mar. 31, 1945; s. Harvey Nathan and Evelyn (Bialis) K.; BS, U. Ill., 1967, MD with honors, 1970. Diplomate Am. Bd. Ophthalmology; children: Gregory Jason, Jeremy Adam. Intern Harbor Gen. Hosp., Torrance, Calif., 1970-71; resident in ophthalmology Wadsworth VA Hosp., L.A., 1971-74; fellow in diseases of the retina, vitreous and choroid Jules Stein Eye Inst. UCLA, 1974-75; fellow in ophthalmic ultrasonography Edward S. Harkness Eye Inst., Columbia U., N.Y.C. and U. Iowa Hosps., Iowa City, 1975; asst. prof. ophthalmology UCLA, 1976-78, Harbor Gen. Hosp., 1976-78; asst. clin. prof. ophthalmology UCLA, 1978-83, assoc. clin. prof., 1983-95, clin. prof., 1995—, dir. ophthalmic ultrasonography lab., 1976—; cons. ophthalmologist, L.A., 1976—; chief ophthalmology Century City Hosp., 1995—; exec. bd. Am. Registry Diagnostic Med. Sonographers, 1981-87; jour. reviewer in field. With USAFR, 1971-77. Fellow Am. Acad. Ophthalmology; mem. Am. Soc. Cataract and Refractive Surgery, L.A. Soc. Ophthalmology, Am. Soc. Ophthalmic Ultrasound, Am. Assn. Ophthalmic Standardized Echography, Societas Internat. Pro Diagnostica Ultrasonica in Ophthalmic, Western Retina Study Club. Contbr. articles to profl. jours. Office: 2080 Century Park E Ste 800 Los Angeles CA 90067-2011

KERN, DONALD MICHAEL, internist; b. Belleville, Ill., Nov. 21, 1951; s. Donald Milton and Dolores Olivia (Rust) K. BS in Biology, Tulane U., 1973; MD magna cum laude, U. Brussels, 1983. ECFMG cert.; lic. Calif., Fla. Intern in surgery Berkshire Med. Ctr., Pittsfield, Mass., 1983-84; intern in psychiatry Tufts New England Med. Ctr., Boston, 1984-85; resident in internal medicine Kaiser Found. Hosp., San Francisco, 1985-87; with assoc. staff internal medicine Kaiser Permanente Med. Group, Inc., San Francisco, 1987-89; assoc. investigator AIDS Clin. Trial Unit Kaiser Permanente Med. Ctr., Stanford U., Nat. Inst. Allergy & Infectious Disease, San Francisco, 1988-90; mem. staff internal medicine Kaiser Permanente Med. Group, South San Francisco, 1989-96; mem. staff Desert Med. Group, Palm Springs, Calif., 1996—. Democrat. Roman Catholic. Avocations: theatre, ballet, traveling, 17th and 18th century French antiques.

KERN, PAUL ALFRED, advertising company executive, research consultant, realtor, financial analyst; b. Hackensack, N.J., Mar. 17, 1958; s. Paul Julian and Edith Helen (Colten) K. BS in Commerce, U. Va., 1980; MBA, U. So. Calif., 1983. Sales rep. Procter & Gamble, Cin., 1980-81; rsch. svcs. mgr. Opinion Rsch., Long Beach, Calif., 1984; consumer planning supr. Dentsu, Young & Rubicam, L.A., 1984-85; rsch. exec. DJMC Advt., Inc., L.A., 1986; realtor assoc. Tarbell Realtors, Santa Ana, Calif., 1988-89; corp. pres. Jennskore, Inc., Torrance, Calif., 1989-93, also bd. dirs.; sr. rsch. analyst The Desert Sun, 1997—; bd. dirs. Applicon, Inc., Hillsdale, N.J., Kernokopia, Hillsdale; cons. Venture Six Enterprises, Encino, Calif., 1985-87, DFS/Dorland, Torrance, 1986, IMI Machinery Inc., Charleston, S.C., 1987. Coach, supr. Little League Football, Alexandria, Va., 1981; active Surf and Sun Softball League (1987 champions). Recipient Most Calls Per Day award Procter and Gamble, 1980. Mem. Profl. Research Assn., Am. Mktg. Assn., Am. Film Inst., Internat. Platform Assn., U.S. Tennis Assn. (Michelob Light 4.5 Team Championship 1982), U. Va. Alumni Assn, Nat. Assn. Realtors, Calif. Assn. of Realtors, S. Bay Rd. of Realtors (Torrance-Lomita), Carson Bd. of Realtors. Club: Alta Vista Racquet. Avocations: tennis, chess, softball (S.W.A.T.S. 1987 League Champion), skiing, reading. Home and Office: 48-253 Silver Spur Trl Palm Desert CA 92260-6611

KERN, VALARIE JEAN, medical technologist; b. Newport, R.I., Mar. 29, 1964; d. Lawrence Adam II and Diana Catherine (Gordon) Carpenter; m. Christopher James Fagan, June 14, 1986 (div. Jan. 1992); 1 child, Christopher James Fagan II; m. Ronald Leon Kern, Apr. 11, 1992; children: Aaron Leon, Autumn Marie. AAS in Med. Lab. Tech., Monroe C.C., Rochester, N.Y., 1984. Cert. med. lab. technician, histocompatibility technologist, med. technologist. Blood bank technician ARC, Rochester, 1985-87; quality assurance/quality control technician Ragu Foods, Rochester, 1990; med. lab. technician Nat. Health Labs., Inc., Phoenix, 1990-91; HLA technician Blood Systems, Inc., Scottsdale, Ariz., 1991-92; HLA technologist Genetrix, Inc., Phoenix, 1992-94; med. technologist Lab. Corp. Am., Phoenix, 1994—. Mem. Am. Soc. Clin. Pathologists (assoc.), Landmark Soc. Western N.Y., Blood Bank Assn. N.Y. State (profl.). Republican. Baptist. Avocations: collecting books on history of Rochester, creating and collecting scale miniatures. Home: 505 N Kirchoff Mesa AZ 85203-7313 Office: Lab Corp Am 1225 S 23rd St Phoenix AZ 85034-4804

KERNDT, ARTHUR LORAINE, artist, advertising sales representative; b. Salida, Colo., Jan. 13, 1946. Grad. high sch. Advt. sales rep. High Country Trader. Three-dimensional sculptor: Dinosaurs, Indian Chief, Indian Princess. Hand-crafted display cases. Recipient Blue Ribbon award Chaffee County Fair. Address: 1317 E St Salida CO 81201-2539

KERNER, MICHAEL PHILIP, lawyer; b. N.Y.C., July 21, 1953; s. Arthur and Rosalind (Mehr) K. BA, Antioch Coll., 1976; JD, Lewis & Clark U., 1979; LLM in Taxation with honors, Golden Gate U., 1995. Bar: Calif. 1980 (cert. specialist personal and small bus. bankruptcy law), U.S. Dist. Ct. (no. and ea. dists.) Calif. 1983, U.S. Ct. Appeals (9th cir.) 1983, U.S. Tax Ct., 1996. Staff atty. U.S. EPA, Washington, 1979-80; asst. regional counsel region 9 U.S. EPA, San Francisco, 1980-83; ptnr. Kerner, Weppner & Rosenbaum, San Francisco, 1983-95; prin. Kerner & Assocs., San Francisco, 1996—; bd. dirs. Solano County Legal Assistance, Vallejo, Calif., 1983-86; arbitrator San Francisco Superior Ct., 1991-94. Editor law rev. and law jours. Mem. San Francisco Trial Lawyers Assn., Solano County Bar Assn., Nat. Assn. Consumer Bankruptcy Attys. Democrat. Jewish. Avocations: windsurfing, snowboarding, road and mountain biking. Office: Kerner & Assocs 240 Stockton St Ste 4 San Francisco CA 94108-5306

KERNODLE, UNA MAE, home economics curriculum specialist, retired secondary education educator; b. Jackson, Tenn., Mar. 4, 1947; d. James G. and Mary E. (McLemore) Sikes. B.S. in Home Econs., U. Tenn., 1969; M.Edn., U. Alaska, 1974. Tchr., head dept. vocat. edn. and electives Chugiak High Sch., Anchorage, ret.; home econs. curriculum specialist King Career Ctr., Anchorage; edn. cons. State of Alaska, Anchorage Talent Bank; presenter Gov.'s Conf. on Child Abuse, Alaska Vocat. Edn. Assn. Conf., Alaska Home Econs. Inst., 1989; state officer Alaska Home Econs.; bd. dirs. Kids Are People. Recipient Gruening award, 1989. Mem. NEA, Am. Home Econs. Assn., Am. Vocat. Assn. Democrat. Baptist. Office: Office of Career Tech 2650 E Northern Lights Blvd Anchorage AK 99508-4119

KERPER, MEIKE, family violence, sex abuse and addictions educator, consultant; b. Powell, Wyo., Aug. 13, 1929; d. Wesley George and Hazel (Bowman) K.; m. R.R. Milodragovich, Dec. 25, 1963 (div. 1973); children: Dan, John, Teren, Tina, Stana. BS, U. Mont., 1973; MS, U. Ariz., 1975; postgrad. Ariz. State U., 1976-78, Columbia Pacific U., 1990—. Lic. marriage & family therapist, Oreg.; cert. domestic violence counselor, alcoholism and drug abuse counselor, mental health profl. and investigator. Family therapist Cottonwood Hill, Arvada, Colo., 1981; family program developer Turquoise Lodge, Albuquerque, 1982; co-developer abusers program Albuquerque Shelter Domestic Violence, 1984; family therapist Citizens Coun. Alcoholism and Drug Abuse, Albuquerque, 1984-86; pvt. practice cons. and trainer family violence and treatment, Albuquerque, 1987—; developer sex offender program Union County, Oreg. Co-author: Court Diversion Program, 1985; author Family Treatment, 1982. Lobbyist CCOPE, Santa Fe, 1983-86; bd. dirs. Union County Task Force on Domestic Violence, 1989-91; developer Choices program treatment of sex offenders and victims Union, Wallowa and Baker Counties, Oreg.; mem. Child Abuse Prevention Team, Baker County and Wallowa County, Oreg. Recipient commendation Albuquerque Shelter Domestic Violence, 1984. Mem. Assn. for the Treatment Sexual Abusers (Ea. Oreg. rep.), Nat. Assn. Marriage and Family Therapists, Nat. Assn. Alcoholism Counselors, Delta Delta Delta. Republican. Episcopalian. Club: PEO. Avocations: Art history; reading; Indian culture; swimming; public speaking. Home: 61002 Love Rd Cove OR 97824-8211

KERR, KLEON HARDING, former state senator, educator; b. Plain City, Utah, Apr. 26, 1911; s. William A. and Rosemond (Harding) K.; m. Katherine Abbott, Mar. 15, 1941; children: Kathleen, William A., Rebecca Rae. AS, Weber Coll., 1936; BA, George Washington U., 1939; MS, Utah State U., Logan, 1946. Tchr. Bear River High Sch., Tremonton, Utah, 1940-56, prin. jr. high sch., 1956-60, prin. Bear River High Sch., 1960-71; city justice Tremonton, 1941-46; sec. to Senator Arthur V. Watkins, 1947. Mayor, Tremonton City, 1948-53; mem. Utah Local Govt. Survey Commn., 1954-55; mem. Utah Ho. of Reps., 1953-56; mem. Utah State Senate, 1957-64, chmn. appropriation com., 1959—, majority leader, 1963; mem. Utah Legis. Council. Author: (poetry) Open My Eyes, 1983, We Remember, 1983, Trouble in the Amen Corner, 1985, Past Imperfect, 1988, A Helping Hand, 1990, Sound of Silence, 1991, Power Behind the Throne, 1992, Unreachable Goal?, 1993, The Only Difference, 1994, Please Boss, 1995, Beach Comber, 1995; (history) Those Who Served Box Elder County, 1984, Those Who Served Tremonton City, 1985, Diamond in the Rough, 1987, Facts of Life, 1987, Gettin' and Givin', 1989, Wells Without Water, 1998, Hand in Pocket, 1997, I WAnt to Come Home, 1997. Dist. dir. vocat. edn. Box Elder Sch. Dist. Recipient Alpha Delta Kappa award for outstanding contbn. to edn., 1982, award for outstanding contbrs. to edn. and govt. Theta Chpt. Alpha Beta Kappa, 1982, Excellence Achieved in Promotion of Tourism award, Allied Category award Utah Travel Counc., 1988, Merit award, 1993, Andy Rytting Community Svc. award, 1991; named Tourism Ambassador of Month, 1986. Mem. NEA, Utah, Box Elder edn. assns., Nat., Utah secondary schs. prins. assns., Utah Sheriff's Assn. (hon.), Bear River Valley. C. of C. (sec., mgr. 1955-58), Lions, Kiwanis, Phi Delta Kappa. Mem. Ch. of Jesus Christ of Latter-day Saints. Home: PO Box 246 Tremonton UT 84337-0246

KERR, NANCY KAROLYN, pastor, mental health consultant; b. Ottumwa, Iowa, July 10, 1934; d. Owen W. and Iris Irene (Israel) K. Student Boston U., 1953; AA, U. Bridgeport, 1966; BA, Hofstra U., 1967; postgrad. in clin. psychology Adelphi U. Inst. Advanced Psychol. Studies, 1968-73; MDiv Associated Mennonite Bibl. Sems., 1986; m. Richard Clayton Williams, June 28, 1953 (div.); children: Richard Charles, Donna Louise. Ordained pastor Mennonite Ch., 1987; apptd. pastor Kamloops Presbytery Ch., Can., 1992. Pastoral counselor Nat. Council Chs., Jackson, Miss., 1964; dir. teen program Waterbury (Conn.) YWCA, 1966-67; intern in psychology N.Y. Med. Coll., 1971-72; rsch. cons., 1972-73; coord. home svcs., psychologist City and County of Denver, 1972-75; cons. Mennonite Mental Health Svcs., Denver, 1975-78; asst. prof. psychology Messiah Coll., 1978-79; mental health cons., 1979-81; called to ministry Mennonite Ch., 1981, pastor Cin. Mennonite Fellowship, 1981-83, coord. campus peace evangelism, 1981-83, mem. Gen. Conf. Peace and Justice Reference Council, 1983-85; instr. Associated Mennonite Bibl. Sems., 1985; teaching elder Assembly Mennonite Ch., 1985-86; pastor Pulaski Mennonite Ch., 1986-89; v.p. Davis County Mins.' Assn., 1988-89; exec. dir., pastoral counselor Bethesda Counseling Svcs., Prince George B.C., 1989—; bd. dirs. Tri-County Counselling Clinic, Memphis, Mo., 1980-81; spl. ch. curriculum Nat. Council Chs., 1981; mem. Cen. Dist. Conf. Peace and Justice Com., 1981-89; mem. exec. bd. People for Peace, 1981-83. Mem. Waterbury Planned Parenthood Bd., 1964-67; mem. MW Children's Home Bd., 1974-75; bd. dirs. Boulder (Colo.) ARC, 1977-78, Davis County Mins. Assn. (v.p. 1988-89), Prince George Ministerial Assn. (chmn. edn. and Airport chapel coms. 1990-92), PLURA, B.C. Synod, 1995-98; elder St. Giles Presbyn. Ch., 1996—; mem. Mennonite Disabilities Respite Care Bd., 1981-86; Prince George Children's Svcs. com., 1992-94; bd. dirs. Prince George Neighborlink, 1995—; adv. com. Prince George Planning, 1995, Prince George Cmty. Planning Coun., 1997-98; mem. housing Prince George adv. bd. Mennonite Ctrl. Com., 1998—. Mem. APA (assoc.), Can. Psychol. Assn., Soc. Psychologists for Study of Social Issues, Christian Assn. Psychol. Studies, Soc. Bib. Lit. & Exegesis.

KERRICK, DAVID ELLSWORTH, lawyer; b. Caldwell, Idaho, Jan. 15, 1951; s. Charles Ellsworth and Patria (Olesen) K.; m. Juneal Casper, May 24, 1980; children: Peter Ellsworth, Beth Anne, George Ellis, Katherine Leigh. Student, Coll. of Idaho, 1969-71; BA, U. Wash., 1972; JD, U. Idaho, 1980. Bar: Idaho 1980, U.S. Dist. Ct. Idaho 1980, U.S. Ct. Appeals (9th cir.) 1981. Mem. Idaho Senate, 1990-96, majority caucus chmn., 1992-94, majority leader, 1994-96. Mem. S.W. Idaho Estate Planning Coun. Mem. ABA, Assn. Trial Lawyers Am., Idaho Bar Assn. (3d dist. pres. 1985-86), Idaho Trial Lawyers Assn., Canyon County Lawyers Assn. (pres. 1985). Republican. Presbyterian. Lodge: Elks. Avocations: skiing, photography. Office: PO Box 44 Caldwell ID 83606-0044

KERSBERGEN, JOHN JAY, financial management executive, consultant; b. Hull, Iowa, Sept. 4, 1948; s. John and Elizabeth (Gorzeman) K.; m. Kathleen Kay Van Oort, July 3, 1970; children: Rebecca Ann, Andrew Jay. AAS in Elec. Engring., De Vry Inst., Chgo., 1971; BSBA, Regis U., 1982; student, U. Colo. Elec. engr. tech. specialist Ball Aerospace Systems Group, Boulder, Colo., 1972-82; fin. mgmt. Ball Aerospace Systems Group, Boulder, 1982-92; now with Space Systems Divsn. Hughes Info. Tech. Systems, Aurora, Colo. Mem. Nat. Security Indsl. Assn. (spkr., workshop coord. 1989-91), Performance Mgmt. Assn. (pres. Denver chpt. 1991, 92), Micro-Frame Software Nat. Users Group (pres. 1990, 91), Nat. Contracts Mgmt. Assn., Program Mgmt. Inst. Avocations: quarter horses, classic Chevrolet automobiles. Home: 1830 E 138th Ave Brighton CO 80601-6302

KERSCHNER, LEE R(ONALD), academic administrator, political science educator; b. May 31, 1931; m. Helga Koller, June 22, 1958; children: David, Gabriel, Riza. B.A. in Polit. Sci. (Univ. fellow), Rutgers U., 1953; M.A. in Internat. Relations (Univ. fellow), Johns Hopkins U., 1958; Ph.D. in Polit. Sci. (Univ. fellow), Georgetown U., 1964. From instr. to prof. polit. sci. Calif. State U., Fullerton, 1961-69, prof., 1988—; state univ. dean Calif. State Univs. and Colls. Hdqrs., Long Beach, 1969-71, asst. exec. vice chancellor, 1971-76, vice chancellor for adminstrv. affairs, 1976-77, vice chancellor acad. affairs, 1987-92; exec. dir. Colo. Commn. on Higher Edn., Denver, 1977-83, Nat. Assn. Trade and Tech. Schs., 1983-85, Calif. Commn. on Master Plan for Higher Edn., 1985-87; interim pres. Calif. State U., Stanislaus, 1992-94, spl. asst. to the chancellor, 1994-97; exec. vice chancellor Minn. State Colls. and Univs., St. Paul, 1996-97; vice chancellor emeritus Calif. State U., 1997—; mem. Calif. Student Aid Commn., 1993-96; cons. in field. Mem. exec. com. Am. Jewish Com., Denver, 1978-83; internat. bd. dirs. Amigos de las Americas, 1982-88 (chmn. 1985-87). Served with USAF, 1954-58; col. Res., ret. Home: PO Box 748 Weimar CA 95736-0748

KERSEY, TERRY L(EE), astronautical engineer; b. San Francisco, June 9, 1947; s. Ida Helen (Schmeichel) K. Houseman, orderly Mills Meml. Hosp., San Mateo, Calif., 1965-68; security guard Lawrence Security, San Francisco, 1973-74; electronic engr. and technician engring. research and devel. dept. McCulloch Corp., L.A., 1977; warehouseman C.C.H. Computax Co., Redondo Beach, Calif., 1977-78; with material ops. and planning customer support dept. Allied-Signal Aerospace Co., Torrance, Calif., 1978-91; security guard Guardsmark Inc., L.A., 1993; electronic technician J.W. Griffin, Venice, Calif., 1993-96. Participant 9th Space Simulation conf., Los Angeles, 1977, 31st Internat. Astronautical Fedn. Congress., Tokyo, 1980, Unispace 1982 for the U.N., Vienna. Sgt. USAF, 1968-72, Vietnam. Decorated Vietnam Svc. medal with 2 bronze stars, Republic of Vietnam Campaign medal, Air Force commendation medal for Vietnam campaign Svc. Mem. AAAS, AIAA (sr., mem. space sys. tech. com. 1981—, mem. aerodynamics com. 1980—, mem. Wright Flyer Project Aerodynamics com. 1980—, mem. pub. policy com. 1989—), Nat. Space Inst., Am. Astronautical Soc., The Planetary Soc. (vol. NASA CD-rom project for Cassini mission to planet Saturn 1996-97), Internat. L5 Soc., Ind. Space Rsch. Group, Computer Soc. of IEEE, Space Studies Inst. (sr. assoc.). Zen Buddhist. Avocations: computers, sports, astronomy, science fiction literature.

KERSHAW, DAVID JOSEPH, process engineer; b. San Diego; s. Joseph Edward and Marie Arlene (Yezek) K. BS in Physics, San Diego State U., 1991. Data mgr. Systens Ecology Rsch. Group, San Diego, 1988-90, Naval Ocean Systems Ctr., San Diego, 1990; integration engr. San Diego State U. Found., 1990-91; software and antenna engr. SITCO, Portland, 1991-92; tech. support Computer Assocs., San Jose, Calif., 1992-93; process engr. Intel, Santa Clara, Calif., 1993—. Author: (periodical) World Radio, 1988; editor: (directory) R4D Data Directory, 1989. Mem. Am. Inst. Physics. Achievements include design, development and testing of software for tabel tennis robot to train U.S. Olympic team; engineer manufacturing process that makes it possible to put pentiums in lap top computers. Avocations: amateur radio, computers, physics. Office: Inter MS RN2-18 2200 Mission College Blvd Santa Clara CA 95054-1537

[illegible] May 29, 1946; d. Joe and Ruth (Lazear) K. BSBA in Acctg., San Jose State

U., 1976, MBA, 1977. CPA, Calif., cert. tax profl. Staff acct. Steven Kroff & Co., CPA's, Palo Alto, 1968-71, 73-74; contr. Rand Teleprocessing Corp., San Francisco, 1972; auditor, sr. acct. Ben F. Priest Accountancy Corp., Mountain View, Calif., 1974-83; tchr. San Jose Unified Regional Occupation Program, San Jose, 1977; pvt. practice accounting San Jose, 1977—; lectr. San Jose State U., 1977—. Bd. dirs. San Jose State U. Coll. of Bus. Alumni Assn. Mem. AICPA, Nat. Soc. of Tax Profls., Am. Inst. Tax Studies, Am. Acctg. Assn., Calif. Soc. CPAs, San Jose State U. Coll. Bus. Alumni Assn. (bd. dirs.), Beta Alpha Psi, Beta Gamma Sigma. Democrat. Jewish. Avocations: piano, travel, art history. Home: 4544 Strawberry Park Dr San Jose CA 95129-2213 Office: San Jose State U Acctg & Fin Dept San Jose CA 95192

KERWIN, MARY ANN COLLINS, lawyer; b. Oconomowoc, Wis., Oct. 16, 1931; d. Thomas Patrick and Florence Mary (Morris) Collins; m. Thomas Joseph Kerwin, Dec. 27, 1954; children: Thomas, Edward, Gregory, Mary, Anne, Katherine, John, Michael. BA, Barat Coll., 1953; JD, U. Denver, 1986. Bar: Colo. 1987. Tchr. Country Grade Sch., Wheaton, Ill., 1953-54; travel agt. Chgo. Athletic Club, 1954-55; legal intern City Atty.'s Office, Denver, 1985, Dist. Atty.'s Office, Denver, 1985; atty. Kerwin and Assocs., Denver, 1987-92, Decker, DeVoss & O'Malley, P.C., Denver, 1992-93, King Peterson Brown, LLC, Englewood, Colo., 1993-95; assoc. Daniel F. Lynch, P.C., Denver, 1995—; legal compliance dept. editor United Banks Colo., Inc., Denver, 1988-93. Author: (with others) The Womanly Art of Breastfeeding, 1958, also revised edits., 1963, 81, 87, 91, 97; contbr. articles to profl. jours. Mem. Colo. Breastfeeding Task Force, 1990-93, 96—; adv. bd. St. Luke's Woman's Hosp., Denver, 1986—, Colo. Sudden Infant Death Syndrome Program, 1992-94; sch. bd. Christ the King Sch., Denver, 1970-73; great books leader Jr. and Collegiate Great Books, Denver, 1963-82; marriage spkr. Cath. Archdiocese, Denver, 1965-75; co-founder, bd. dirs. La Leche League Internat., Franklin Park, Ill., 1956—, founder state orgn., 1960—, chmn. bd. 1980-83, sec. 1988-91. Named One of Ten Outstanding Alumnus Barat Coll., 1988. Mem. Colo. Bar Assn., Colo. Women's Bar Assn., Denver Bar Assn., Colo. Alumnae Assn. (pres. 1968-70), Theresians (pres. 1974-76). Avocations: reading, biking, swimming, tennis, singing. Home: 5130 Nassau Cir W Cherry Hills Village CO 80110-5129 Office: Daniel F Lynch PC 1900 Grant St Ste 800 Denver CO 80203-4308

KESEY, KEN, writer; b. La Hunta, Colo., Sept. 17, 1935; s. Fred and Geneva (Smith) K.; m. Norma Faye Haxby, May 20, 1956; children: Shannon, Zane, Jed (dec. 1984) Sunshine. BS, U. Oreg., 1957; postgrad., Stanford U., 1958-60. Pres. Intrepid Trips, Inc., 1964; editor, pub. mag. Spit in the Ocean, 1974—. Author: One Flew Over the Cuckoo's Nest, 1962, Sometimes a Great Notion, 1964, Garage Sale, 1973, Demon Box, 1986, Little Tricker the Squirrel Meets Big Double the Bear, 1988; co-author: Caverns, 1989, The Further Inquiry, 1990, The Sea Lion, 1991, Sailor Song, 1992; (with Ken Babbs) Last Go Round: a Real Western, 1994; author, prodr.: (play) Twister, 1995; (video and script) Twister, 1998. Address: 85829 Ridgeway Rd Pleasant Hill OR 97455-9627

KESLER, ROLAND LINCOLN, JR., English language educator; b. Chgo., July 22, 1949; s. Roland Lincoln and Margaret (Lee) K.; m. Paula Renaud, Apr. 11, 1981. BA, Yale U., 1971; MA, U. Toronto, Ont., Can., 1973, PhD, 1981. Vis. prof. Yangzhou (China) Tchr.'s Coll., 1981-82; asst. prof. Oreg. State U., Corvallis, 1983-91, assoc. prof., 1991—; established Indian Edn. Office, Oreg. State U., 1991, coord. ethnic studies dept., 1993-97. Home: 37041 NW Moss Rock Dr Corvallis OR 97330-9360 Office: Oreg State Univ Dept English 238 Moreland Hall Corvallis OR 97331-8561

KESSLER, A. D., business, financial, investment and real estate advisor, consultant, educator, lecturer, author, broadcaster, producer; b. N.Y.C., May 1, 1923; s. Morris William and Belle Miriam (Pastor) K.; m. Ruth Schwartz, Nov. 20, 1944 (div. 1974); children: Brian Lloyd, Judd Stuart, Earl Vaughn; m. Jaclyn Jeanne Sprague. Student U. Newark, 1940-41, Rutgers U., 1941-42, 46, Albright Coll., 1942, Newark Coll. Engring., 1946; PhD in Pub. Adminstrn. U. Fla., 1972; MBA, Kensington U., 1976, PhD in Mgmt. and Behavioral Psychology, 1977. Sr. cert. rev. appraiser; cert. bus. counselor; cert. exchanger; registered mortgage underwriter; registered investment advisor. Pvt. practice real estate, ins. and bus. brokerage, N.J., Pa., Fla., N.Y., Nev., Calif., Hong Kong, 1946—; pres. Armor Corp., 1947-68; pres. Folding Carton Corp., Am., N.Y.C., 1958-68; exec. v.p. Henry Schindall Assocs., N.Y.C., 1966-67; tax rep. Calif. State Bd. Equalization, 1968-69; aviation cons. transp. div. Calif., Dept. Aeros., also pub. info. officer; 1969-71; FAA Gen. Aviation Safety Counselor; broker, mgr. La Costa (Calif.) Sales Corp., 1971-75; chmn. bd. Profl. Ednl. Found., 1975—, Timeshare Resorts Internat., 1975—, Interex, Leucadia, Calif., 1975-82, The Kessler Orgn., Rancho Santa Fe, Calif., 1975—, The Kessler Fin. Group, Fin. Ind. Inst., 1977—; pres. Ednl. Video Inst., 1978—, Fin. Planning Inst., 1975—, Rancho Santa Fe Real Estate & Land, Inc., 1975—; treas., exec. bd. dirs. Nat. Challenge Com. on Disability, 1983-90; dir. Practice Mgmt. Cons. Abacus Data Systems, 1984—; broker mgr. Rancho Sante Fe Acreage & Homes, Inc., 1987-89; mktg. dir. Commercial Real Estate Services, Rancho Santa Fe, 1987—; cons. broker Glenct. Properties Ptnrs., 1989-90; dir. U.S. Advisors, 1989—; founder Creative Real Estate Movement, 1946—; pub., editor in chief Creative Real Estate Mag., 1975—; pub. Creative Real Estate Mag. of Australia and New Zealand; founder, editor Moderator of Tape of the Month Club; founder, producer, chmn. Internat. Real Estate Expo; chmn. bd. The Brain Trust, Rancho Santa Fe, Calif., 1977—; fin. lectr. for Internat. Cruise Ships, Cunard Line, Norwegian Am. Cruises, P&O, Princess, others; lectr. life enrichment and stress mgmt. Internat. Cruise Ships; Calif. adj. faculty, prof. fin. Clayton U., St. Louis; developer, operator Barnegat Baywood Seaplane Base, Barnegat Bay, N.J.; owner, operator Skyline Airport, Hunterdon County, N.J. Scoutmaster Orange Mountain coun. Boy Scouts Am., 1955-62; harbor master N.J. Marine Patrol, 1958-67; dep. sheriff, Essex County, N.J., 1951-65; mem. pres.' adv. bd. Seton Hall U., 1961-64; chmn. Stop Smoking, 1990, Quick Study, 1990; feature broadcaster/producer Kalaidascope Radio Mag., Am. Radio Network, 1990—. Served with USAF, 1942-45. Decorated D.F.C., Air medal, Purple Heart; named to French Legion of Honor, Order of Lafayette; named a flying col, a.d.c., Gov. of Ga., 1957. Mem. Am. Soc. Editors and Pubs., Author's Guild, Internat. Platform Assn., Nat. Speakers Assn., Nat. Press Photographers Assn., Guild Assn. Airport Execs., Aviation and Space Writers Assn., Nat. Assn. of Real Estate Editors, Internat. Exchangors Assn. (founder), Air Force Assn. (dep. comdr. N.J. chpt. 1955-57). Clubs: Nat. Press, Overseas Press, La Costa Country, Cuyamaca, Rancho Santa Fe Country, Passport. Lodges: Masons, Shriners. Author: A Fortune At Your Feet, 1981, How You Can Get Rich, Stay Rich and Enjoy Being Rich, 1981, Financial Independence, 1987, The Profit, 1987, A Fortune at Your Feet in the '90s, 1994, The Midas Touch, Turning Paper Into Gold, 1994; author, instr. Your Key to Success seminar, 1988, Your Key to Creative Real Estate Success tng. program, 1996; The A to Z of Lease Purchase and 11 Other Options Training Prog.; editor: The Real Estate News Observer, 1975—; fin. editor API, 1978—; fin. columnist Money Matters, 1986—; syndicated columnist, radio and TV host of "Money Making Ideas," 1977—; songwriter: Only You, 1939, If I'm Not Home For Christmas, 1940, Franny, 1940, Flajaloppa, 1940, They've Nothing More Dear Only They've Got It Here, 1941, The Summer of Life, 1956; producer (movies) The Flight of the Cobra, Rena, We Have Your Daughters, Music Row; speaker for radio and TV as The Real Estate Answerman, 1975—; host (radio and TV show) Ask Mr. Money; conceptualist, exec. prodr. (TV show) The Trading Game, 1994; exec. prodr., moderator (TV show) A.D. Kessler's Real Estate Roundtable, 1993—. Inventor swivel seat, siptop, inflatumbrella. Home: PO Box 1144 Rancho Santa Fe CA 92067-1144

KESSLER, RALPH, composer, conductor, educator; b. N.Y.C., Aug. 1, 1919; s. Abraham Julius Kessler and Lillian Eisner; children: Ronny Hormung, Robert Kessler, Rory Bakke. BA, Juilliard Sch., 1948, MA, 1950. Arranger Columbia Broadcast Sys., N.Y.C., 1952-58; creative dir. Music Matters, N.Y.C., 1959-67; prin., owner R.K. Prodns., N.Y.C., L.A., 1967-85, retired, 1985; conductor Pacific Composers Forum, L.A., 1994-98, San Fernando Valley Symphony, L.A., 1996-98. Composer commercials including Yuban Coffee, Sanka, 1968-70 (Clio awards 1968-70), Gershwin Medley-Rodgers Medley, 1997-98, El Alfarero, 1997. Cpl. U.S. Army, 1941-45. Decorated Two Bronze Stars. Mem. Am. Soc. Music Arrangers Composers (bd. mem. 1984-95, v.p. 1996-97), Toastmasters (pres. 1998—), Nature Conservatory, World Wildlife Fedn., Sierra Club. Democrat. Avocations: squash racquets, bridge, swimming. Home: 7036 Keokuk Ave Winnetka CA 91306-3547

KESSLER, ROBERT ALLEN, data processing executive; b. N.Y.C., Feb. 2, 1940; s. Henry and Caroline Catherine (Axinger) K.; m. Marie Therese Anton, Mar. 17, 1967; children: Susanne, Mark. BA in Math., CUNY, 1961; postgrad., UCLA, 1963-64. EDP analyst Boeing Aircraft, Seattle, 1961-62; computer specialist System Devel. Corp., Santa Monica, Calif., 1962-66; mem. tech. staff Computer Scis. Corp., El Segundo, Calif., 1966-67, sr. mem. tech. staff, 1971-72, computer scientist, 1974-81; systems mgr. Xerox Data Systems, L.A., 1967-71; prin. scientist Digital Resources, Algiers, Algeria, 1972-74; sr. systems cons. Atlantic Richfield, L.A., 1981-94; computer cons., 1994—. Mem. Big. Bros. L.A., 1962-66; precinct capt. Goldwater for Pres., Santa Monica, 1964; mem. L.A. Conservacy, 1987. Mem. Assn. Computing Machinery. Avocations: racquetball, theatre, gourmet dining. Home: 6138 W 75th Pl Los Angeles CA 90045-1634 Office: ARCO 515 S Flower St Los Angeles CA 90071-2201

KETCHUM, MILO SMITH, civil engineer; b. Denver, Mar. 8, 1910; s. Milo Smith and Esther (Beatty) K.; m. Gretchen Allenbach, Feb. 28, 1944 (dec. Dec. 21, 1990); children: David Milo, Marcia Anne, Matthew Phillip, Mark Allen. B.S., U. Ill., 1931, M.S., 1932; D.Sc. (hon.), U. Colo., 1976. Asst. prof. Case Sch. Applied Sci., Cleve., 1937-44; engr. F.G. Browne, Marion, Ohio, 1944-45; owner, operator Milo S. Ketchum, Cons. Engrs., Denver, 1945-52; partner, prin. Ketchum, Konkel, Barrett, Nickel & Austin, Cons. Engrs. and predecessor firm, Denver, 1952—; prof. civil engring. U. Conn., Storrs, 1967-78; emeritus U. Conn., 1978—; mem. Progressive Architecture Design Awards Jury, 1958, Am. Inst. Steel Constrn. Design Awards Jury, 1975, James F. Lincoln Arc Welding Found. Design Awards Jury, 1977; Stanton Walker lectr. U. Md., 1966. Author: Handbook of Standard Structural Details for Buildings, 1956; editor-in-chief Structural Engineering Practice, 1981-84; contbr. engring. articles to tech. mags. and jours. Recipient Disting. Alumnus award U. Ill., 1979. Mem. Am. Concrete Inst. (hon., bd. dirs., Turner medal 1966), ASCE (hon., pres. Colo. sect.), Am. Cons. Engrs. Coun., Nat. Acad. Engring., Am. Engring. Edn., Structural Engrs. Assn. Colo. (pres.), Cons. Engrs. Coun. Colo. (pres.), Sigma Xi, Tau Beta Pi, Chi Epsilon, Phi Kappa Phi, Alpha Delta Phi.

KETTEMBOROUGH, CLIFFORD RUSSELL, computer scientist, consultant, manager; b. Pitesti, Arges, Romania, June 8, 1953; came to U.S., 1983; s. Petre and Constanta (Dascalu) I. MS in Math., U. Bucharest, Romania, 1976; MS in Computer Sci., West Coast U., L.A., 1985; MS in Mgmt. Info. System, West Coast U., Los Angeles, 1986; PhD in Computer and Info. Sci., Pacific We. U., 1988; MBA, U. LaVerne, 1992; PhD in Bus. Adminstrn., U. Santa Barbara, 1996; EdD in Computer Tech. in Edn., Nova Southeastern U., 1998. Lic. mathematician. Mathematician, programmer Nat. Dept. Chemistry, Bucharest, 1976-80; sr. programmer, analyst Nat. Dept. Metallurgy, Bucharest, 1980-82; sr. software engr. Xerox Corp., El Segundo, Calif., 1983-88; task mgr. Rockwell Internat., Canoga Park, Calif., 1989-91, cons., 1991-93; mgr. micro devel. Transam. Corp., L.A., 1993-95; MIS dir. Maxicare Health Plans, L.A., 1995-96; computer and info. scientist Jet Propulsion Lab.-NASA, Pasadena, Calif., 1988-89, project mgr., 1996—; adj., asst. prof. W. Coast U., Chapman U., U. Redlands, Nat. U., U. Phoenix, Union Inst., 1991—. Contbr. articles to profl. jours. Sec. Romanian Nat. Body Bldg. Com., Bucharest, 1980-82; pres., chmn. Bucharest Mcpl. Body Bldg. Com., 1978-82. Served to lt. Romanian Army, 1978. Mem. IEEE, Assn. for Computing Machinery. Republican. Avocations: soccer, body building, traveling. Home: 6004 N Walnut Grove Ave San Gabriel CA 91775-2530

KETTERMAN, DIANA PATRICIA, educational psychologist; b. L.A., July 6, 1954; d. Harold P. Ketterman and Mary Lou (Najera) Chavez; m. Lawrence Edward Brockett, Feb. 14, 1976 (div. Apr. 1987); children: Tara, Mark. BA in Psychology with honor, U. Calif., Riverside, 1976; MS in Counseling, Calif. State U., Fullerton, 1979; PhD in Ednl. Psychology, Calif. State U., Riverside, 1989. Lic. ednl. psychologist. Prof.'s asst. Calif. State U., Fullerton, 1979; sch. psychologist Cucamonga (Calif.) Sch. Dist., 1980-82, dir. student svcs., 1982-85; sch. psychologist Walnut (Calif.) Unified Sch. Dist., 1985—; motivational therapist Inst. Motivational Devel., Rancho Cucamonga, Calif., 1984-86; v.p. True Colors Comm. Group, Corona, Calif., 1996-98; dir. Character Champion Leadership, Alta Loma, Calif., 1997—; ednl. cons. in pvt. practice Alta Loma, Calif., 1985—. Author: Success Treasures Map, 1998, Character Champion Vision, 1999. Mem. ASCD, Nat. Assn. Sch. Psychologists, Calif. Assn. Sch. Psychologists, Assn. sychol. Type, Peer Resources Network. Roman Catholic. Fax: 909-980-2758. Office: Character Champion Leadership 6481 Caledon Pl Alta Loma CA 91737

KEY, WILSON BRYAN, author, lecturer; b. Richmond, Calif., Jan. 31, 1925; s. Wilson Bryan and Elizabeth (Jackson) K.; m. Luz N. Baluyot, May 7, 1945 (div. Dec. 1963); children: Leilani, Lotis, Luz; m. Jan Gilman; 1 child, Christina Kathryn. BA, Mexico City Coll., 1951; MA, UCLA, 1953, PhD, Denver U., 1971. Prof. Denver U., 1953-55, Boston U., 1957-61; rsch. dir. Publicidad Badillo, San Juan, P.R., 1961-65; pres. Rsch. and Mktg. Devel., San Juan, 1965-69; prof. U. Western Ont., London, Can., 1969-75; pres., CEO Mediaprobe, Inc., Reno, 1973—. Author: Subliminal Seduction, 1974, Media Sexploitation, 1976, Clam-Plate Orgy, 1981, Age of Manipulation, 1989, Subliminal Ad-Ventures in Erotic Art, 1992. Rsch. dir. Partido Popular, San Juan, 1968. Sgt. USAAF, 1943-47. Mem. AAUP, Author's Guild, Mensa Internat. Avocations: playing jazz piano. Home and Office: Mediaprobe Inc 150 E Laramie Dr Reno NV 89511-7822

KEYLER, ROBERT GORDON, material handling company executive; b. Elgin, Ill., May 9, 1958; s. Robert Dean and Lois Jean (Hobbs) K.; m. Linda Jane Mendes, Sept. 21, 1988 (div. Jan. 1993). Grad., Morris County Vo-Tech., 1980. Mgr. Gardentown Ctr., Rockaway, N.J., 1976-80, Genuine Parts-NAPA, Albuquerque, 1980-88; owner G&B Enterprises, Albuquerque, 1988-91; sales rep. Parts Plus of Albuquerque, 1989-91; v.p. sales and purchasing Material Handling Specialists, Albuquerque, 1991—; cons. in field. Sponsor Youth of Unity, Albuquerque, 1980—; bd. dirs. Unity Ch., Albuquerque, 1986—, pres., 1987. Avocations: youthwork, backpacking, ballooning. Home: 11 Constellation Dr Tijeras NM 87059-8108 Office: Material Handling Specialists 3214 Los Arboles Ave NE Albuquerque NM 87107-1917

KEYSON, MAE, clinical psychologist; b. N.Y.C.; m. George McAuley, Oct. 20, 1979; children: Debra, Lauren, Ronald. BA, Calif. State U., Northridge, 1968; MA, Ariz. State U., 1970, PhD, 1972. Exec. dir. Mental Health Ctr., Woodland Hills, Calif., 1976-82, Northridge Mental Health Ctr., Malibu, Calif., 1982-86; from asst. prof. to assoc. prof. Pepperdine U., Malibu, 1973-86; dir. mind/body Northridge Hosp., 1994-97; clin. psychologist stress reduction program McAuley Med. Corp. Med. Ctr., Woodland Hills, 1997—; cons. in field; adj. prof. Calif. State U., Northridge, 1972-73, Pepperdine U., 1972-73. NIH fellow, 1969-72. Mem. APA, L.A. Psychol. Assn., Calif. State Psychol. Assn. Avocations: art, hiking, writing, films, yoga. Office: McAuley Med Corp 21031 Ventura Blvd Woodland Hills CA 91364-2203

KEYSTON, STEPHANI ANN, small business owner; b. Baytown, Tex., Aug. 6, 1955; d. Herbert Howard and Janice Faye (Stowe) Cruickshank; m. George Keyston III, Oct. 8, 1983; children: Jeremy George, Kristopher Samuel. AA with honors, Merced Coll., Merced, Calif., 1975; BA in Journalism with distinction, San Jose State U., 1976. Reporter, Fresno (Calif.) Bee, 1974-75; reporter, photographer Merced (Calif.) Sun-Star, 1974-77; pub. info. officer Fresno City Coll. (Calif.), 1977-80; dir. comms. Aerojet Tactical Sys. Co., Sacramento, 1980-83; co-owner, v.p. Keyco Landscape Contractor Inc., Loomis, Calif., 1984—. Co-coord. Aerojet United Way Campaign, 1981; Aerojet Tactical Sys. Co. coord. West Coast Nat. Derby Rallies, 1981-83; co-founder, pres. Calif. Lion Awareness. Mem. Internat. Assn. Bus. Communicators (dir. Sacramento chpt. 1983), Citrus Heights C. of C. (v.p. 1983). Republican. Office: Keyco Landscape Contractor Inc 3350 Swetzer Rd Loomis CA 95650-9584 Home: 9700 Burley Dr Weed CA 96094-9747

KEZLARIAN, NANCY KAY, social services administrator, family counselor; b. Royal Oak, Mich., Aug. 26, 1948; d. Barkev A. and Nancy (Israelian) K.; m. Robert S. Vinetz, M.D., Aug. 1995. Student, U. Vienna, Austria, 1969; BA, Albion Coll., 1970; MA in Theatre and TV, U. Mich., 1971; MA in Clin. Psychology, Pepperdine U., 1992. Cert. secondary tchr., Mich., Calif.; lic. Marriage, Family, Child Counselor. Tchr. West Bloomfield Hills (Mich.) High Sch., 1971-76; tchr. ESL, L.A. Pub. Schs., 1976-80; personnel dir. Samuel Goldwyn Co., L.A., 1985-86; dir. adminstrn. and human resources (Norman Lear) Act III Communications, L.A., 1986-90; dir. programs Salvation Army Booth Meml. Ctr., L.A., 1993-94; asst. exec. dir. Florence Crittenton Ctr., L.A., 1994-96, exec. dir., 1996—; owner, mgr. KAZ, hand painted clothing co., L.A., 1980-85; mem. Screen Actors Guild. Actress My Seventeenth Summer, The Big Blue Marble, 1979 (Emmy award for childen's TV programming). Bd. dirs. Calif. Assn. Children's Homes. Named Tchr. of Yr., West Bloomfield Hills High Sch., 1976. Mem. SAG, Pers. and Indsl. Rels. Assn. (legis. rep. dist. 5 1989, 90), Calif. Assn. of Marriage and Family Therapists, L.A. Group psychtherapy Soc., Rotary Internat., Psi Chi. Avocations: writing, world mythologies, theatre, abstract artist, vegetarian chef.

KHABIBULIN, NIKOLAI, hockey player; b. Sverdlovsk, Russia, Jan. 13, 1973. Goaltender Phoenix Suns. Office: c/o Phoenix Suns 9375 E Bell Rd Scottsdale AZ 85260-1500

KHAIAT, LAURENT E., producer, films; b. Tel Aviv, Israel, May 25, 1968; came to U.S., 1983; s. Alain Victor and Anna Michele (Riczker) K.; m. Akemi Nakata, June 2, 1997. Exec. prodr. Los Caminantes en Vivo, L.A., 1989; prodr. The Right Way, L.A., 1990, Death Penalty, L.A., 1994; assoc. prodr. Dark Secret, L.A., 1995, Death Game, Vancouver, B.C., 1996; co-prodr. La Perra de la Frontera, L.A., 1990, Gipsy, L.A., 1990, Killing American Style, L.A., 1991, Samurai Cop, N.Y.C., 1991, Eliminator, L.A., 1992; prodr., dir. Kiss of Steel, 1989; tv prodr. Little Pain, 1995. Recipient Golden Star Halo award So. Calif. Motion Picture Counsel, 1989, Lifetime Membership award, 1989, Jeanie Golden Halo Eagle award, 1989. Mem. Riviera Country Club, Newport Beach Country Club, Sodeguana Country Club, St. Andrews Golf Club. Avocations: golf, horseback riding, snow skiing, swimming, ping-pong. Office: Motion Pictures Internat 421 N Rodeo Dr # 15100 Beverly Hills CA 90210-4500

KHALADJAN, MIKHAIL NIKOLAEVICH, educator, song writer; b. Krasnodar, Russia, Mar. 21, 1961; came to U.S., 1992; s. Nikolai N. and Tamara M. (Doroshenko) K.; 1 child, Gerard. BA in Design, City U. Indsl. Design, Krasnodar, Russia, 1978; M in Pedagogy, Moscow External U. Humanities, 1993, D in Pedagogy, 1994. Sr. designer Voskhod, Moscow, Russia, 1989-90; dir. Intermezzo Firm, Moscow, 1990-91; v.p. Moscow External U. Humanities, 1991-92; pres. Internat. Ctr. Authorized Edn., Inc., Beverly Hills, Calif., 1992—; bd. dirs. Moscow External U. of the Humanities, Zentrum für Internat. Freundschaft und Kultur (Germany). Author: (textbook) Commerical Advertising, 1993; co-author: (with others) Manifesto of the Authorized Revival of Secondary Education, 1996, A Young Man's Book: The Ethical Code of the Authorized Personality, 1997; composer: Seasons, 1994, 95; mem. editl. bd. The MEUH Gerald, Russia. Recipient cert. of acknowledgement World Peace Prayer Soc., 1995, cert. of achievement Hollywood Song Jubilee, 1996. Mem. AAAS, Internat. Acad. Authorized Edn. (academician diploma, Acad. World Star), Am. Assn. Univ. Adminstrs., N.Y. Acad. Scis., Internat. Coun. on Edn. for Tchg. Avocations: music, design, history of edn., cooking. Office: Internat Ctr Autorized Edn PO Box 17211 Beverly Hills CA 90209-3211

KHALAFI, HABIB, architect; b. Tehran, Iran, June 1, 1959; came to U.S., 1977; s. Seyed Mehidi and Parichehis (Khadejnoon) K. BA in Architecture, SUNY, Buffalo, 1985. Project mgr. Kij Warner Amor, Boston, 1983-90, Hoffman Dutz, Phoenix, 1990-91, Sillman Wyman Inc., San Diego, 1991-93; pvt. practice San Diego, 1993—. Avocations: tennis, golf, sailing, running, computer technology. Office: Robertson Khalad & Amor 6195 Cornerstone Ct E Ste 102 San Diego CA 92121-4728

KHALEEL, RAZIUDDIN, groundwater hydrologist; b. Dhaka, Bangladesh, Nov. 10, 1945; came to U.S., 1972; s. Khaliluddin Bhuiyan and Razia (Begum) B.; m. Shaheen Fahmida Islam, Jan. 10, 1975; 1 child, Anisa Jumana. BS, Bangladesh U. Engring., 1966; MS, Asian Inst. Technology, 1970; PhD, Tex. A&M U., 1977. Postdoctoral rsch. fellow N.C. State U., Raleigh, 1977-80; asst. prof. hydrology N.Mex. Inst. Mining & Technology, Socorro, 1980-85; staff engr. Rockwell Hanford Ops., Richland, Wash., 1985-87; from prin. engr. to fellow engr. Westinghouse Hanford Co., Richland, 1987-96; cons. environ. engr. Fluor Daniel N.W., Richland, 1996—; adj. prof. Wash. State U. Tri-Cities, Richland, 1985—; hydrology cons. to UNESCO and govtl. agys., India, Japan, Taiwan, 1985-91; rschr. in groundwater hydrology. Contbr. articles to profl. jours. Pres. exec. coun. Islamic Ctr. Tri-Cities, Richland, 1993-94. Mem. Am. Geophys. Union, Sigma Xi, Phi Kappa Phi, Gamma Sigma Delta, Alpha Epsilon. Home: 2206 Davison Ave Richland WA 99352-1919 Office: Fluor Daniel NW MS B4-43 PO Box 1050 Richland WA 99352

KHALESSI, MOHAMMAD R., structural engineer, researcher; b. Yazd, Iran, Nov. 18, 1952; came to U.S., 1976; s. Mohammad-Ali and Farangis (Bahadorani) K.; m. Fariba Touhidi, Aug. 14, 1977 (div. 1984); 1 child, Ahoo; m. Mercedeh Rusty, Oct. 25, 1986; 1 child, Bobak. BS, Arya Mehr U., Tehran, Iran, 1976; MS, UCLA, 1978, PhD, 1983. Engr. C.F. Braun, Alhambra, Calif., 1980-81; rsch. engr. UCLA, 1981-83; sr. engr. Allied Signal, Torrance, Calif., 1983-87; sr. engring. splst. Boeing N.Am., Downey, Calif., 1987-97; chief technologist Mitratech Probabilistic, Fountain Valley, Calif., 1997—; bd. dirs. Advanced Probabilistic Rsch., Inc.; adv. Unicorp, VanNuys, Calif., 1995—. Contbr. articles to profl. jours. Recipient Outstanding Engring. Merit award Orange County (Calif.) Engring. Coun., 1994. Fellow Inst. Advancement Engring.; mem. AIAA, SAE (chair sub-com. probabilistic method, comm. 1994—, tech. adv. leadership coun. for probabilistic methods 1995—, Disting. Probabilistic Methods Implementations award 1996). Republican. Muslim. Achievements include pioneering work in practical application of probabilistic methods, integration of probabilistic methods with finite element technique, identification of most-probable-failure point in original space. Office: Mitratech Probabilistic LLC 11770 Warner Ave Ste 203 Fountain Valley CA 92708-2661

KHALSA, GURU ROOP KAUR, foundation administrator; b. Oreg., Sept. 16, 1950; d. Sammuel Charles Jr. Phillips and Clara Claudene (Johnson) Ferrenberg. Student, Pearce Women's Coll., 1968-69, U. Oreg., 1969-70, 71, UCLA, 1970. Exec. sec. Sikh Dharma Colo., Denver, 1974-84, Sikh Dharma Ariz., Phoenix, 1984-93; sec. archives, dir. devel. Sikh Dharma Internat., Espanola, N.Mex., 1993—; gen. mgr. Sikh Dharma Internat., Espanola, 1996—; sec. archives, Espanola, 1993—; founder, dir. Amar Infinity Found., Espanola, 1997—. Editor Prosperity Paths, 1993—; dir., prodr.: Heart to Heart, Ave of Participant, New Path to a Great Future. Mem., various positions 3HO Found. Denver, 1975-84, Phoenix, 1984-93, N.Mex., 1993—; bd. dirs. Khalsa Sch., exec. sec., 1988—. Recipient Outstanding Job Settlement and Relocation of Refugees Eucumentical Chs., 1984. Mem. Nat. Soc. Fundraising Execs., Am. Soc. Assn. Execs., Internat. Khalsa Coun. (dev. dir. 1988—, exec. com.), Internat. Kundalini Yoga Tchr. Assn. (OUtstanding Svc. to Devel. Assn. award). Avocations: walking. Home and Office: Amar Infinty Found RR 2 Box 4 Espanola NM 87532-9802

KHAMISA, AZIM NOORDIN, financial consultant; b. Kisumu, Nyanza, Kenya, Feb. 10, 1949; came to U.S., 1974; s. Noordin Hasham and Rahemat (Ahmed) K.; m. Almas B. Hasham, May 8, 1971 (div. Nov. 1980); children: Tasreen, Tariq. Student, Medway Sch. Advanced Tech., Kent, Eng., 1965-66, Loughborough Coll. Advanced Tech., Midland, Eng., 1966-67; BS in Math., U. Nairobi, Kenya, 1968; grad. degree in acctg., Southwest London Coll., 1970. Mng. dir. Rainbow Group Cos., Kenya, 1970-74; v.p. Combined Enterprises, Inc., Can., 1974-78; from v.p. to pres. Readco, San Diego, 1978-81, Islandco, Vancouver, Colo., 1978-81; cons. mergers and acquisitions Atlanta, 1982-87; exec. v.p. Shapery Enterprises, San Diego, 1988-90, Columbia Funding, San Diego, 1988-90, City Suites of Am., San Diego, 1988—; sr. cons., mng. ptnr. Sovereign Capital Markets, 1990—; bd. dirs. Columbia Funding, City Suites of Am., Gaslamp Devel. Comp., Micro-C, Gaslamp Theatre Co.; sr. mng. cons. Sovereign Capital Markets; bd. dirs. Gascamp Devel. Co. Bd. dirs. Esperanza, The Whittier Inst., Internat. Missing Children's Found. Mem. Atlanta Venture Forum, Atlanta C. of C., Aga Kahn Found. (spl. coordinator), Aga Khan Bus. Council, Internat. Bus. Council, M & A Assn., Hospitality Assn., Exec. Com., Brit. Am. Bus.

Group, Nat. Assn. Hotels and Motels, Profl. Cons. Assn. Lodge: Masons. Avocations: skiing, running, racquetball, snorkeling, reading. Office: 8189 Via Mallorca La Jolla CA 92037-2903

KHAN, AHMED MOHIUDDIN, finance, insurance executive; b. Hyderabad, Andhra Pradesh, India, Nov. 14, 1955; s. Mohammad Mominuddin and Mehar-Unnisa Begum Hyderabad; m. Marjorie L. Klein-Khan, Mar. 31, 1983; 1 child, Yosuf F. MBA, U. Palm Beach, 1975; doctoral studies, Calif. Coast U. Inventory auditor RGIS, Inc., Chgo., 1975-78; staff acct. Sommerset, Inc., Chgo., 1979-84; fin. cons. Provident Mutual Fin. Svc., Inc., Phoenix, 1985-91; regional mgr. fin. svcs. US Life/Old Line Life Ins. Co. of Am., Phoenix, 1992—; pres. Khan and Assocs., Fin./Ins. Svcs., Phoenix, 1993—. Named to Execs. Hall of Fame, 1991. Mem. India Assn., U.S.A., Assn. MBA Execs., Nat. Assn. Life Underwriters, Ariz. Assn. Life Underwriters, Millon Dollar Round Table. Democrat. Islam. Avocations: golf, traveling, classical music. Home and Office: 4643 E Grandview Rd Phoenix AZ 85032-3416

KHATRI, SUNIL PAPANCHAND, computer engineer; b. Bombay, India, Apr. 28, 1965; s. Papanchand Vishanji and Gauri Papanchand (Mistry) K.; m. Sangeeta Sunil Kapur, May 24, 1997. B Tech, Indian Inst. Tech., Kanpur, India, 1987; MS, Univ. Tex., 1989. V.p. engring., dir. Envision, Inc., Berkeley, Calif.; microelec. & computer devel. fellow Univ. Tex., Austin, 1987-89; design engr. Motorola, Inc., Austin, 1989-93; univ. fellow Univ. Calif., Berkeley, 1993-94; researcher Univ. Calif., 1994—. Author: Building Client Consultant Relationships on the Internat, 1996; contbr. articles to profl. jours.; patentee in field. Mem. IEEE, ACM, MENSA, Tau Beta Pi, Eta Kappa Nu. Avocations: scultpure, baseball, poetry, sketching. Office: Univ Berkeley Hearst Ave 550B Cory Hall Berkeley CA 96720

KHATTATOV, BORIS, geophysicist; b. Voronej, Russia, Oct. 29, 1968; came to U.S., 1991; s. Vyacheslav and Ella Khattatov; m. Tanya Selezova, June 22, 1993 (div. Aug. 1996). MS, Moscow Inst. Physics and Tech., 1991; PhD, SUNY, Stony Brook, 1995. Sys. adminstr. SUNY, Stony Brook, 1995-96; vis. scientist Nat. Ctr. Atmospheric Rsch., Boulder, Colo., 1996-98; scientist I Nat. Ctr. Atmospheric Rsch., Boulder, 1998—; ski patroller, 1997—. Co-author: Atmospheric Chemistry and Global Change, 1998; contbr. articles to profl. jours. Lt. Russian Army, 1990. Recipient Assimilation and Mapping of Satellite Data award NASA, 1997. Mem. Am. Geophys. Union. Avocations: mountain climbing, biking, skiing.

KHAVARI, MIKE, construction company executive; b. Tehran, Iran, Feb. 20, 1951; came to U.S., 1972; s. Soroosh and Shirin (Khosraviani) Akhtarkhavari; div.; 1 child, Mina. Grad. in Chemistry Engring., Emporia State U., 1975; grad. in Civil Engring., Kans. State U., 1979; cert. in Constrn. Practices, San Diego State U., 1985. Engr. estimator Intercity Excavating Co., Kansas City, Mo., 1980-81; project mgr./estimator Cahill & Assoc., Kansas City, Mo., 1981-83; engr. estimator Engring. Sci. Co., San Diego, 1983-84; project mgr./estimator Hatton Constrn., San Diego, 1984-85; project mgrt. Ferroll Constrn. Mgr., San Diego, 1985-86; pres./owner Khavari Constrn., Inc., San Diego, 1986—. Office: Khavari Constrn Inc 4550 Kearny Villa Rd Ste 118 San Diego CA 92123-1574

KHORMAEI, IRANPOUR (RON KHORMAEI), electronics industry executive, educator. BS in Elec. Engring., Oreg. State U., MS, PhD. Registered profl. engr., Oreg. Rsch. asst. Oreg. State U., 1986-88, 88-89; rsch. scientist Planar Systems, 1988-89; mgr. Planar Systems, Beaverton, Oreg., 1992-95; tech. program mgr. mfg. Hewlett-Packard, Corvallis, Oreg., 1995-96; project mgr. procurement engring. Hewlett-Packard, Vancouver, Wash., 1996-98, product mgr. R&D, 1998—; adj. prof. elec. and computer engring. dept. Oreg. State U., 1995—; mem. adv. bd. material sci. and engring. Oreg. Grad. Inst., 1997—; guest lectr. engring. mgmt. Portland State U., 1998. Contbr. numerous articles to profl. jours.; patentee in field. Mem. IEEE. Home: 16007 NE 15th St Vancouver WA 98684-8793 Office: Hewlett-Packard Co 1115 SE 164th Ave Vancouver WA 98683-9625

KHOSLA, VED MITTER, oral and maxillofacial surgeon, educator; b. Nairobi, Kenya, Jan. 13, 1926; s. Jagdish Rai and Tara V. K.; m. Santosh Ved Chabra, Oct. 11, 1952; children: Ashok M., Siddarth M. Student, U. Cambridge, 1945; L.D.S., Edinburgh Dental Hosp. and Sch., 1950, Coll. Dental Surgeons, Sask., Can., 1962. Prof. oral surgery, dir. postdoctoral studies in oral surgery Sch. Dentistry U. Calif., San Francisco, 1968—; chief oral surgery San Francisco Gen. Hosp.; lectr. oral surgery U. of Pacific, VA Hosp.; vis. cons. Fresno County Hosp. Dental Clinic.; Mem. planning com., exec. med. com. San Francisco Gen. Hosp. Contbr. articles to profl. jours. Examiner in photography and gardening Boy Scouts Am., 1971-73, Guatemala Clinic, 1972. Granted personal coat of arms by H.M. Queen Elizabeth II, 1959. Fellow Royal Coll. Surgeons (Edinburgh), Internat. Assn. Oral Surgeons, Internat. Coll. Applied Nutrition, Internat. Coll. Dentists, Royal Soc. Health, AAAS, Am. Coll. Dentists; mem. Brit. Assn. Oral Surgeons, Am. Soc. Oral Surgeons, Am. Dental Soc. Anesthesiology, Am. Acad. Dental Radiology, Omicron Kappa Upsilon. Club: Masons. Home: 1525 Lakeview Dr Hillsborough CA 94010-7330 Office: U Calif Sch Dentistry Oral Surgery Div 3D Parnassus Ave San Francisco CA 94117-4342

KHUONG-HUU, DIEU DAVID, engineering executive; b. Mytho, Vietnam, Oct. 7, 1931; came to the U.S., 1952; s. Bay and Nhi Thi (Nguyen) Khuong-H.; m. Bich-Chau Thi Dinh, Nov. 22, 1960. BSME, Lafayette Coll., 1956; MSME, MIT, 1957. Registered profl. engr., Calif. Ops. exec. ESSO Standard Oil Co., Saigon, Vietnam, 1958-61; tech. dir. Vietnam Sugar Corp., Saigon, 1961-64; pres., founder Indsl. Devel. Bank, Saigon, 1965-75; dep. min. economy Govt. Vietnam, Saigon, 1966-67, Republic of Vietnam, Saigon, 1968-69; asst. project mgr. Bechtel Inc., San Francisco, 1975-87; prin., v.p. MDA Engring., Inc., Hayward, Calif., 1987—; Chmn. Asian Productivity Orgn., Tokyo, 1972-73. Editor Bus. Mgmt. Monthly, 1960-75. Pres. Am. Univ. Alumni Assn., Saigon, 1968-71, Vietnam Am. Assn., Saigon, 1973-75; founder, pres. Mgmt. Assn. Vietnam, Saigon, 1960-75; founder, sec. gen. Vietnam Flowers & Gardens Assn., Saigon, 1970-75; founder, v.p., Vietnam Fedn. for Edn. Devel., Saigon, 1973-75. MIT fellow, 1957. Avocations: tennis, landscape design, gardening, hiking, camping. Home: 16 Riverton Dr San Francisco CA 94132-1429 Office: MDA Engring Inc 795 Fletcher Ln Hayward CA 94544-1008

KHURSHUDOV, ANDREI, tribologist, researcher; b. Moscow, May 4, 1963; s. George and Eleonora (Budagova) K.; m. Anjella Berlova, Apr. 12, 1991. BS, MS, K.E.T. Inst. Aviation Tech., Moscow, 1985; MS, Inst. Electronic Machines, Moscow, 1991; PhD, Russian Acad. Scis., Moscow, 1992. Engr., Mech. Engring. Rsch. Inst., Russian Acad. Scis., Moscow, 1985-87, rsch. assoc., 1991-93, asst. prof., 1993-94; vis. rschr. Tohoku U., Sendai, Japan, 1993-94, rsch. assoc., 1994-96; vis. rschr. U. Calif., San Diego, 1996-97; adv. engr. IBM Corp., San Jose, Calif., 1997—. Reviewer for jours. ASME Jour. Tribology, 1995-97, WEAR, 1996-98. Recipient awards; Japanese Soc. for Promotion of Sci. scholar, 1993-94. Avocations: music, football. Office: IBM Corp 5600 Cottle Rd # E25501 San Jose CA 95193-0001

KIANG, ASSUMPTA (AMY KIANG), brokerage house executive; b. Beijing, Aug. 15, 1939; came to U.S., 1962; d. Pei-yu and Yu-Jean (Liu) Chao; m. Wan-lin Kiang, Aug. 14, 1965; 1 child, Eliot Y. BA, Nat. Taiwan U., 1960; MS, Marywood Coll., Scranton, Pa., 1964; MBA, Calif. State U., Long Beach, 1977. Data programmer IBM World Trade, N.Y.C., 1963; libr. East Cleve. Pub. Libr., 1964-68; lectr. Nat. Taiwan U., Taipei, 1971-73; with reference dept. U.S. Info. Svc., Taipei, 1971-74; v.p., sr. fin. cons. Merrill Lynch, Santa Ana, Calif., 1977—, Costa Mesa, Calif., 1996—. Author numerous rsch. reports in field. Founder Pan Pacific Performing Arts Inc., Orange County, Calif., 1987; pres. women league Calif. State. U., Long Beach, 1980-82. Mem. AAUW (treas. Newport-Costa Mesa br. 1996—), Chinese Bus. Assn. Soc. Calif. (chmn. 1987—, v.p. 1986-87), Chinese Am. Profl. Women's League (treas. 1993, pres. 1997—), Pacific Rim Investment and trade Assn. (vice-chair 1994-96), U.C.I. Chancellor's Club, Old Ranch Country Club. Democrat. Roman Catholic. Office: Merrill Lynch 650 Town Center Dr Ste 500 Costa Mesa CA 92626-1905

KIBBLE, EDWARD BRUCE, insurance-investment advisory company executive; b. Seattle, May 11, 1940; s. Francis Bruce and Doris Kibble; m. Carol Kibble, July 8, 1961; 3 children. BA, U. Wash., 1972. CLU. Agt. Equitable of Iowa, Seattle, 1962-72; co-founder, co-chmn. Kibble & Prentice, Inc., Seattle, 1972—; bd. dirs. Kibble & Prentice/KPI-Western Ins., Bellevue, Wash., Phoenix Savings Bank, Northwestern Trust. Contbr. articles to profl. jours. Bd. dirs. Sheldon Jackson Coll., N.W. Kidney Found., Seattle Pacific Found. Mem. Assn. for Advanced Life Underwriting, Nat. Assn. Life Underwriters (Seattle Life Underwriter of Yr. award), Million Dollar Round Table, Estate Planning Coun. Seattle (past pres.), Wash. Athletic Club, Columbia Tower Club, Rainier Club, Seattle Yacht Club, Rotary (Seattle). Republican. Avocations: sailing, skiing. Office: 600 Stewart St Ste 1000 Seattle WA 98101-1230

KIBLER, RAY FRANKLIN, III, minister; b. Columbus, Ohio, Sept. 9, 1951; s. Ray F. Jr. and Evelyn B. (Wiehe) K.; m. Victoria Louise Bergstrom, June 30, 1973; children: Jonathan, Joanna. MusB, Calif. State U., Long Beach, 1974; MDiv, Luther Theol. Sem., 1977; ThM, Luther Northwestern Theol. Sem, 1987; D Ministry, Sch. Theology Claremont, 1990; postgrad., Fuller Sem. Ordained to ministry Am. Luth. Ch. (now Evang. Luth. Ch. Am.), 1979. Pastor, interim pastor Calif., 1979—; pastor Theologian program Ctr. Theol. Inquiry, 1998—; mem. faculty Luth. Bible Inst., Anaheim, Calif., 1992; leader in interim ministry and congregational devel., 1986—; dir. oral history project Grad. Theol. Union, 1993-98; paster Ctr. Theol. Inquiry, 1998—. Author: At the Crossroad: A Lutheran Confessional response to the question of what it means to believe in Jesus in today's religiously pluralistic world, 1990; contbr. articles to profl. publs. Developer Regional Archives at Pacific Luth. Theol. Sem., Berkeley, Calif., 1980-92, Oral history project Grad. Theol. Union Faculty, 1993-98. Mem. Am. Soc. Ch. History, Luth. Hist. Conf. (bd. dirs. 1990—, membership sec.). Home: 4249 La Junta Dr Claremont CA 91711-2351

KIDD, HILLERY GENE, educational publisher; b. Cin., May 8, 1945; s. Herbert Kidd and Amber L. (Smith) Reed; m. Sylvia Jean Smith, Dec. 21, 1971 (div. Nov. 1980); 1 child, Shane Thomas; m. Catherine Arnold Dec. 1980 (div. 1989). Student, Austin Peay State Coll., 1963-64. Owner KIDD Contrs., Cin., 1969-72; ptnr., v.p. So. Cemetaries Svcs., Inc., Fayetteville, N.C., 1972-73; state sales dir. Life Safety Inc., Clearwater, Fla., 1975; sales mgr. Jodean Water Conditioning, Lutz, Fla., 1973-78; owner Advanced Water Sys., Largo, Fla., 1978-83; regional v.p., securities broker A.L. Williams Corp., Largo, 1983-86; rep. Uniway of Mid-East Tenn., Knoxville, 1986-92; pres., CEO H.G. KIDD Corp., Boulder City, Nev., 1993—. Author: (textbooks) Human Growth and Development, 1992, Introductory Psychology, 1993, Introductory Sociology, 1993; editor: General Biology: Microbiology, Human Anatomy and Physiology, 1993, English Composition with Essay, American Literature, 1993—, Commonalities in Nursing Care—A, 1993, Commonalities in Nursing Care—B, 1993—, Differences in Nursing Care—A, 1993—, Differences in Nursing Care—B, 1993—, Differences in Nursing Care—C, 1993—, Occupational Strategies in Nursing, 1993—. Lt. col. mil. affairs Tenn. Def. Force, Nashville, 1989-94. 1st lt. 46th Spl. Forces Co. (Airborne), U.S. Army, 1965-68. Mem. Order of DeMolay (counselor 1961-62, life mem.). Republican. Avocations: aircraft piloting, scuba diving, sport parachutist. Office: PO Box 60067 Boulder City NV 89006-0067

KIDD, JASON, professional basketball player; b. San Francisco, Mar. 23, 1973. Guard Dallas Mavericks, 1994-96, Phoenix Suns, 1996—. Active West Dallas Cmty. Ch.; formed Jason Kidd Found., Jason Kidd Basketball Scholarship Fund. Named Pac-10 Player of the Year, 1993-94; named nat. freshman of the yr. by The Sporting News and USA Today, 1993-94; voted Shick Rookie of the Year (with Grant Hill), 1994-95; tied for fourth on all-time NBA rookie impact list, 1994-95. Avocations: R&B music, movies, baseball. Office: Phoenix Suns 201 E Jefferson St Phoenix AZ 85004-2412*

KIDD, JEREMY, artist; b. London, Jan. 4, 1962; s. Michael and Rachel (Nicholson) K. BA in Fine Art and Sculpture with honors, Demontford U., Leicester, Eng. Tchr.; tchr., multi media artist, dir. Fidget Design, London and Calif., 1989-96. Avocations: guitar, song writing, surfing, kickboxing.

KIDD, REUBEN PROCTOR, management engineer; b. Bedford, Va., Feb. 18, 1913; s. Oscar Kibbler and Estelle (Johnson) K.; B.S., Va. Poly. Inst., 1936; m. Margaret Jerome, June 23, 1952. Pres., Frito Corp. of Roanoke (Va.), 1947-49; indsl. engr. USAF, Sacramento, 1956-73; chmn. bd. USDR, Inc., Sacramento, 1961-69, MEN Internat., Inc., Mpls., 1977—; owner The Kidd Cos., operator Precision Tune-Up, Sacramento, 1974—. Served to capt. U.S. Army, 1942-46, to maj., 1949-51. Decorated Silver Star; registered profl. engr., Calif. Republican. Presbyterian. Home: 5413 Valparaiso Cir Sacramento CA 95841-2138 Office: Precision Tune-Up 6241 Spruce Ave Sacramento CA 95841-2052

KIDDER, DAVID MONROE, physician; b. Reed City, Mich., Aug. 28, 1950; s. William Kidder and Eula (Johnson) Kidder Grace; m. Linda Lee Patten, Dec. 23, 1973; children: David William, Kristy Lynn. BS, U. S.C., 1968-74; EMT, paramedic III, Grand Valley State Coll., Grandville, Mich., 1974; DO, Phila. Coll. Osteo., 1978. Diplomate Am. Bd. Family Practice. Family physician Ekalaka (Mont.) Clinic & Hosp., 1979-81, Shelby (Mont.) Clinic, 1981-84, Powder River Clinic, Broadus, Mont., 1984-86, Grand Forks (N.D.) Clinic, 1986—. Co-contbr. aticles to profl. jours. Med.-surg. World Med. Missions, The Phillipines, 1982, Mex., 1991, Bangladesh, 1993; humanatarian relief med. Milk & Honey Ministries, Russia, 1992. Fellow Am. Acad. Family Practice; mem. Am. Acad. Family Physicians, Am. Osteo. Assn., Minn. Med. Bd. (discipline com. 1992, 94, drug diversion com. 1994, pres. bd. 1994). Baptist. Avocations: breeding horses, raising cattle, hunting, fishing. Home: 850 Eastside Rd Deer Lodge MT 59722-9731 Office: Northland Clinic 850 Eastside Rd Deer Lodge MT 59722-9731

KIDWELL, WAYNE L., judge; b. Council, Idaho, 1938; m. Shari Linn; children: Vaughn, Blair. BA, U. Idaho, JD. Bar: Idaho 1964, Hawaii, former U.S. Trust Territories. Prin. law firms, Idaho and Hawaii; past pvt. practice Idaho and Hawaii; past atty. gen. State of Idaho; past majority leader Idaho Ho. of Reps.; past prosecuting atty. Ada County, Idaho; past assoc. dep. atty. gen. Pres. Reagan adminstrn., past liason Dept. Justice U.S. Govt.; past atty. gen. Republic of Marshall Islands; judge Idaho Supreme Ct. Photographer pvt. shows; one-man shows include galleries in Hawaii. Active numerous civic and profl. orgns. Served USMCR, U.S. Army Mil. Police Corps. Office: Idaho Supreme Ct Supreme Ct Bldg PO Box 83720 Boise ID 83720-0101

KIEHN, MOGENS HANS, aviation engineer, consultant; b. Copenhagen, July 30, 1918; came to U.S., 1957; s. Hans-Christian and Lydia-Thea-Constans (Theill) K.; m. Ase Rasmusen, Apr. 28, 1942; children: Marianne, Hans, Lars. BS, ME, PE, Tech. Engring., Copenhagen, 1940; MS, Copenhagen, 1942; degree in Army Intelligence, Def. Indsl. Security Inst., 1972. Registered profl. engr., Ariz. Pres. Hamo Engring., Copenhagen, 1939-47, Evanston, Ill., 1958-78; engr. Sundstrand, Rockford, Ill., 1957-58; pres., owner Kiehn Internat. Engring. Co., Phoenix, 1978—; chmn., pres. ETO Internat. Engring., Phoenix, Ariz., 1978—; tech. engring. cons. Scandinavian Airlines, Sundstrand Engring., McDonnell Douglas, Ford, GM, Chrysler, Honeywell, Motorola, Gen. Electric, Hughes Aircraft; chmn. bd. Internat. Tech. Engring. Recipient 32 patents including rehab. hosp. lighting for highmast, drafting machine, tooling machinery, parts for aircraft, garbage and pollution machine, optical coupler, also others. With Finnish Army, 1939, Danish Underground, 1940-45, Morocco French Fgn. Legion, 1948-53, Vietnam. Mem. AIII, NSPE, Soc. Illuminating Engrs., Nat. Geog. Soc., Am. Fedn. Police, East Africa Wildlife Soc., Interpol Intelligence and Organized Crime Orgn., Adventures Club Denmarkk, Honors Club. Office: Kiehn Internat Tech Engring PO Box 1561 Scottsdale AZ 85252-1561

KIELAROWSKI, HENRY EDWARD, marketing executive; b. Pitts., Dec. 29, 1946; s. Henry Andrew Kielarowski and Evelyn Marie Kline Boileau; m. Lynda Blair Powell, Aug. 1971 (div. 1976); children: Amorette, Blair. BA, Duquesne U., Pitts., 1969; MA, Duquesne U., 1974, PhD, 1974. Pres. Communicators, Inc., Pitts., 1974-76; mktg. specialist McGraw-Hill, Inc., N.Y.C., 1976-81; mktg. dir. Fidelity S.A., Allison Park, Pa., 1981-86; exec. v.p. ARC Systems, Inc., Pitts., 1986-88; v.p. mktg. Providian Financial Corp., San Francisco, 1988-98; pres. La Playa Cons., Inc., San Francisco, 1999—. Author: Microcomputer Consulting in the CPA Environment, 1987; contbr. articles to profl. jours. Mem. Am. Mktg. Assn. (mktg. excellence award 1988), Direct Mktg. Assn. Democrat. Avocations: fiction writing, music, dance, travel, film making. Home: 1496 La Playa San Francisco CA 94122

KIELHORN, RICHARD WERNER, chemist; b. Berlin, Germany, June 17, 1931; s. Richard H. and Auguste (Lammek) K.; m. Anneliese Heinrich, Aug. 9, 1952; children: Anita, Margit. BS, Chem. Tech. Sch., Berlin, 1953. Lab. tech. Zoellner Werke, Berlin, 1950-57, Montrose Chem. Corp., Henderson, Nev., 1957-78; chief chemist Stauffer Chem. Corp., Henderson, 1978-88, Pioneer Chlor Alkali Co., Henderson, 1988-92; tax. cons. H&R Block, Las Vegas, Nev., 1972-96, Exec. Tax Svc., instr., 1978-95. Mem. ASTM, Am. Chem. Soc., Am. Statistical Assn., Nat. Soc. Tax Profls., Nat. Assn. Tax Practitioners. Home: 1047 Westminster Ave Las Vegas NV 89119-1825

KIELSMEIER, CATHERINE JANE, school system administrator; b. San Jose, Calif; d. Frank Delos and Catherine Doris (Sellar) MacGowan; M.S., U. So. Calif., 1964, Ph.D., 1971; m. Milton Kielsmeier; children: Catherine Louise, Barry Delos. Tchr. pub. schs. Maricopa, Calif.; sch. psychologist Campbell (Calif.) Union Sch Dist., 1961-66; asst. prof. edn. and psychology Western Oreg. State Coll., Monmouth, 1966-67, 70; asst. research prof. Oreg. System Higher Edn., Monmouth, 1967-70; dir. spl. services Pub. Schs., Santa Rosa, Calif., 1971-91; cons., 1991—. Mem. Sonoma County Council Community Services, 1974-84, bd. dirs. 1976-82, Sonoma County Orgn. for Retarded/Becoming Independent, 1978-84, bd. dirs. 1978-82; bd. dirs. Gold Ridge Sangha, 1994-97, Hosp. Chaplaincy Svcs., 1996—. Office: 7495 Poplar Dr Forestville CA 95436-9671

KIENHOLZ, LYN SHEARER, international arts projects coordinator; b. Chgo.; d. Mitchell W. and Lucille M. (Hock) Shearer; student Sullins Coll., Md. Coll. Women. Assoc. producer Kurt Simon Prodns., Beverly Hills, Calif., 1963-65; owner, mgr. Vuokko Boutique, Beverly Hills, 1969-75; bd. dirs. L.A. Inst. Contemporary Art, 1976-79, Fellows of Contemporary Art, 1977-79, Internat. Network for Arts, 1979-89, L.A. Contemporary Exhbns., 1980-82; exec. sec., bd. dirs. Beaubourg Found. (now George Pompidou Art and Culture Found.), 1977-81; visual arts adv. Performing Arts Coun., L.A. Music Ctr., 1980-89; bd. govs. Calif. Inst. Tech. Baxter Art Gallery, 1980-85; adv. bd. dirs. Fine Arts Communications, pub. Images & Issues mag., 1981-85; founder, chmn. bd. Calif./Internat. Arts Found., 1981—; bd. dirs., western chmn. ArtTable 1983-89; bd. dirs. Galef Inst., 1992—; exec. bd. Sovereign Fund, 1981-93; exec. bd. dirs. Scandinavia Today, 1982-83, Art L.A., 1987, 88, 89; mem. adv. bd. Otis/Parsons Sch. Design, 1983-85, U. So. Calif. dept. fine arts, 1983-85; bd. dirs. UK/LA Festival of Britain, 1986-88, 92-94; hon. bd. dirs. L'Ensemble des Deux Mondes, Paris, 1986-91; mem. Comité Internat. pour les Museés d'Art Moderne, 1985—, bd. dirs., 1991—; mem. adv. bd. Cyber Studios, 1996—; Bd. dirs. Arts, Inc., 1987-89, Mayacamas Found., 1997—. Mem. Side Street Projects, 1996-98. Co-host nat. pub. radio program ARTS/L.A., 1987-91; contbg. editor Calif. mag., 1984-89. Address: 2737 Outpost Dr Los Angeles CA 90068-2061

KIERSCH, GEORGE ALFRED, geological consultant, retired educator; b. Lodi, Calif., Apr. 15, 1918; s. Adolph Theodore and Viola Elizabeth (Bahmeier) K.; m. Jane J. Keith, Nov. 29, 1942; children—Dana Elizabeth Kiersch Haycock, Mary Annan, George Keith, Nancy McCandless Kiersch Bohnett. Student, Modesto Jr. Coll., 1936-37; BS and Geol. Engr., Colo. Sch. Mines, 1942; Ph.D. in Geology, U. Ariz., 1947. Geologist 79 Mining Co., Ariz., 1946-47; geologist underground explosion tests and Folsom Dam-Reservoir Project U.S. C.E., Calif., 1948-50; supervising geologist Internat. Boundary and Water Commn., U.S.-Mex., 1950-51; asst. prof. geology U. Ariz., Tucson, 1951-55, dir. Mineral Resources Survey Navajo-Hopi Indian Reservation, 1952-55; exploration mgr. resources survey So. Pacific Co., San Francisco, 1955-60; assoc. prof. geol. sci. Cornell U., Ithaca, N.Y., 1960-63, prof., 1963-78, prof. emeritus, 1978—, chmn. dept. geol. scis., 1965-71; geol. cons., Ithaca, 1960-78, Tucson, 1978—; chmn. coordinating com. on environment and natural hazards, Internat. Lithosphere Program, 1986-1991. Author: Engineering Geology, 1955, Mineral Resources of Navajo-Hopi Indian Reservations, 3 vols., 1955, Geothermal Steam-A World Wide Assessment, 1964; author: (with others) Advanced Dam Engineering, 1988; editor/author: Heritage of Engineering Geology--First Hundred Years 1888-1988 (vol. of Geol. Soc. Am.), 1991; editor: Case Histories in Engineering Geology, 4 vols., 1963-69, Engineering GeoSciences and Military Operations, 1998; mem. editorial bd. Engring. Geology/Amsterdam, 1965—. Mem. adv. coun. to bd. trustees Colo. Sch. Mines, 1962-71, pres. coms., 1990—; mem. nine coms. NAE/NAS, 1966-90; reporter coordinating com. 1 CC1 Nat. Hazards U.S. GeoDynamics Com., 1985-90. Capt. C.E., U.S. Army, 1942-45. NSF sr. postdoctoral fellow Tech. U. Vienna, 1963-64; recipient award for best article Indsl. Mktg. Mag., 1964. Fellow ASCE, Geol. Soc. Am. (chmn. div. engring. geology 1960-61, mem. U.S. nat. com. on rock mechanics 1980-86, Disting. Practice award 1986, Burwell award 1992); mem. Soc. Econ. Geologists, U.S. Com. on Large Dams, Internat. Soc. Rock Mechanics, Internat. Assn. Engring. Geologists (U.S. com. 1980-86, chmn. com. 1983-87, v.p. N.Am. 1986-90), Assn. Engring. Geologists (1st receipient Claire P. Holdredge award 1965, 93, hon. mem. 1985), Cornell Club (N.Y.C.), Statler Club, Tower Club (Ithaca), Mining Club of Southwest (Tucson). Republican. Episcopalian. Home and Office: 4750 N Camino Luz Tucson AZ 85718-5819

KIEST, ALAN SCOTT, social services administrator; b. Portland, Oreg., May 14, 1949; s. Roger M. and Ellen Kiest; m. Heather L. Griffin; 1 child, Jennifer S. BA in Polit. Sci., U. Puget Sound, Tacoma, 1970; MPA, U. Wash., 1979. Welfare eligibility examiner Wash. Dept. Social and Health Services, Seattle, 1970-72, caseworker, 1972-76, service delivery coordinator, 1976-82; community svcs. office adminstr. Wash. Dept. Social and Health Svcs., Seattle, 1982—; planning commr. City of Lake Forest Park, 1989, mem. city coun., 1990—, chair city fin. com., 1992-97, vice chmn. city budget com., 1998—; mem. King County Mangaged Health Care Oversight Com., 1993-95; mem. King County Human Svcs. Roundtable, 1995—, vice chair, 1998—. Mem. Eastside Cmty. panel United Way of King County. Mem. Suburban Cities Assn., Met. King County Coun. Reg. Policy Com. Avocations: travel, music. Home: 18810 26th Ave NE Lk Forest Park WA 98155-4146 Office: Wash Dept Social & Health Svcs 14360 SE Eastgate Way Bellevue WA 98007-6462

KILBOURN, LEE FERRIS, architect, specifications writer; b. L.A., Mar. 9, 1936; s. Lewis Whitman and Kathryn Mae (Lee) K.; m. Joan Priscilla Payne, June 11, 1961; children: Laurie Jane, Ellen Mae. BS in Gen. Sci., Oreg. State U., 1963; BS in Architecture, U. Oreg., 1965. Registered architect, Oreg. Specifier Wolff Zimmer Assocs., Portland, Oreg., 1965-75; specifier, assoc. Wolff Zimmer Gunsul Frasca, Portland, 1975-77; specifier, assoc. Zimmer Gunsul Frasca Partnership, Portland, 1977-81, specifier, assoc. ptnr., 1981—. Jr. warden, then sr. warden St. Stephen's Episcopal Parish, Portland. With U.S. Army, 1959-60. Fellow AIA (mem. master spec. rev. com. 1976-78, mem. documents com. 1981-89), Constrn. Specifications Inst. (mem. participating tech. documents com. 1976-78, cert. com. 1980-82, Al Hansen Meml. award Portland chpt. 1987, Frank Stanton Meml. award N.W. region 1987, chpt. pres. 1979-80); mem. Internat. Conf. Bldg. Ofcls. Home: 3178 SW Fairmount Blvd Portland OR 97201-1468 Office: Zimmer Gunsul Frasca Partnership 320 SW Oak St Ste 500 Portland OR 97204-2737*

KILBURN, KAYE HATCH, medical educator; b. Logan, Utah, Sept. 20, 1931; d. H. Parley and Winona (Hatch) K.; m. Gerrie Griffin, June 7, 1954; children: Ann Louise, Scott Kaye, Jean Marie. BS, U. Utah, 1951, MD, 1954. Diplomate Am. Bd. Internal Medicine, Am. Bd. Preventive Medicine. Asst. prof. Med. Sch. Washington U., St. Louis, 1960-62; assoc. prof., chief of medicine Durham (N.C.) VA Hosp., 1962-69; prof., dir. environ. medicine Duke Med. Ctr., Durham, 1969-73; prof. medicine and environ. medicine U. Mo., Columbia, 1973-77; prof. medicine and cmty. medicine CUNY Mt. Siai Med. Sch., 1977-80; Ralph Edgington prof. medicine U. So. Calif. Sch. Medicine, L.A., 1980—; pres. Neurotest Inc., 1988—; pres. Workers Disease Detection Svc. Inc., 1986-95. Author: Chemical Brain Injury, 1997; editor-in-chief Archives of Environ. Health, 1986—; editor jour. Applied Physiology, 1970-80, Environ. Rsch., 1975—, Am. Jour. Indsl. Medicine, 1980—; contbr. more than 200 articles to profl. jours. Capt. M.C., U.S. Army, 1958-60. Avocations: travel, oil painting, swimming, hunting. Home: 3250 Mesaloa Ln Pasadena CA 91107-1129 Office: U So Calif Sch Medicine 2025 Zonal Ave Los Angeles CA 90033-1034

KILCOMMONS, THOMAS MICHAEL, economist; b. Stamford, Conn., Apr. 11, 1966; s. Thomas Joseph and Angela (Forte) Cummings. BSc, U. Calif., Berkeley, 1990. From sales rep. to customer rels. mgr. Citibank, San Lorenzo, Calif., 1990-94, customer rels. mgr., 1994-95; analyst Charles Schwab and Co., San Francisco, 1996—. Avocations: rugby, international travel, sailing, skiing. E-mail: tkilcom1@aol.com. Fax: 415-989-8421. Home: 2115 Castro St San Francisco CA 94131-2224 Office: Charles Schwab & Co 101 Montgomery St # 333-11 San Francisco CA 94104-4122

KILCULLEN, CARMEN SOLARI, retired elementary education educator; b. Healdsburg, Calif., Sept. 5, 1933; d. Ambrose Luca and Teresa Eugenia (Saini) Solari; m. Lawrence Bernard Kilcullen, July 16, 1960; 1 child, Lauren Teresa. BA, San Francisco Coll. for Women, 1955; MA, San Francisco State U., 1963. Cert. tchr., adminstr., supr., Calif. Educator San Francisco Unified Sch. Dist., 1955-94, ret., 1994. Grand pres. Italian Cath. Fedn., San Francisco, 1993-95; mem. Sonoma County Wine Libr. Ass., Healdsburg, Calif., 1993—; pres. Museo Italo Americano Aux., San Francisco, 1996-98. Recipient Apostolic Blessing, Pope John Paul II, Rome, 1995; resolution Carmen Solari Kilcullen Day-Jan. 13, 1996, Calif. State Senate, 1996. Mem. Calif. Ret. Tchrs., Alpha Delta Kappa (scholarship chairperson 1996-98). Avocations: reading, travel.

KILEY, ROBERT RALPH, governmental affairs consultant; b. Honolulu, Apr. 21, 1948; s. Kenneth John and Dorothy Irene (Ambrozich) K.; m. Barbara Lynn Weber, Mar. 1985; children: Tiryn Marie, Kristin Leigh. AA, Fullerton Coll., 1971; BA, U. So. Calif., 1975. Adminstrv. aide Hon. Robert H. Finch for U.S. Senate, Fullerton, 1975-76; field supr. Rep. Nat. Com., Washington, 1976; exec. dir. Rep. Party Orange County, Orange, Calif., 1976-80; pres., cons. Robert Kiley & Assocs., Yorba Linda, Calif., 1980—; lead advancement Pres. and Mrs. Ronald Reagan, Washington, 1984-88. Bd. dirs. Bd. Psychology, Sacramento, 1984-92; chmn. legis. com. Sacramento, 1986-92; co-founder Save Our State-Proposition 1987; pres. Cmty. West Devel. Corp.; exec. dir. Tustin Cmty. Found., 1997—; devel. cons. Costa Mesa Libr. Found., 1998—. Named One of Outstanding Young Men Am., 1977-81; recipient Cert. Appreciation Anaheim Lions Club, 1987, Calif.-Nev. Lions Internat., 1988. Mem. U. So. Calif. Alumni Assn. (life). Office: 5028 Vista Montana Yorba Linda CA 92886-4594

KILEY, THOMAS, rehabilitation counselor; b. Mpls., Aug. 18, 1937; s. Gerald Sidney and Veronica (Kennedy) K.; m. Jane Virginia Butler, Aug. 25, 1989; children: Martin, Truman, Tami, Brian. BA in English, UCLA, 1959; MS in Rehab. Counseling, San Francisco State U., 1989. Cert. rehab counselor, nat. and Hawaii. Former rsch. profl., businessman various S.E. Asian cos.; sr. social worker Episcopal Sanctuary, San Francisco, 1986-88; dir. social svcs. Hamilton Family Ctr., San Francisco, 1988-89; rehab. specialist Intracorp, Honolulu, 1989-91; pres. Heritage Counselling Svc., Honolulu, 1991—; pres. Hunter Employment Svcs., Yuma, Ariz., Brawley and Salinas, Calif., 1995—, Algo Enterprises, Yuma, 1998—. Mem. Am. Counseling Assn., Nat. Assn. Rehab. Profls. in Pvt. Sector, Am. Rehab. Counselors Assn. (profl.), Nat. Rehab. Assn., Rehab. Assn. Hawaii, Rotary, Phi Delta Kappa. Office: Heritage Counselling Svcs PO Box 893098 Mililani HI 96789-0098 also: 2450 S 4th Ave Ste 102A Yuma AZ 85364-8557

KILGORE, L(EROY) WILSON, minister; b. Elmira, N.Y., Feb. 25, 1917; s. Roy Dunning and Bertha Pearl (Bush) K.; m. Ursula Dunbar, June 27, 1940 (wid. 1960); children: Keith, Sharon, Paul, Debra; m. Lois Morse Bell, Feb. 14, 1961; children: Kristie, Richard III, Nancy, Douglas, Cynthia. BA, Colgate U., 1939; MDiv, Colgate-Rochester Div. Sch., 1942; DD (hon.), Colgate U., 1964. Ordained to ministry Presbyn. Ch., 1942. Pastor 1st Presbyn. Ch., Hartford, Conn., 1943-53; sr. pastor Lakewood Presbyn. Ch., Cleve., 1953-64, Cherry Hill Presbyn. Ch., Dearborn, Mich., 1964-72, Valley Presbyn. Ch., Scottsdale, Ariz., 1972-86; interim minister 3d Presbyn. Ch., Rochester, N.Y., 1987-88, 1st Presbyn. Ch., Tulsa, 1990-91, Kirk in the Hills Presbyn. Ch., Bloomfield Hills, Mich., 1995-96; trustee San Francisco Theol. Seminary, San Anselmo, Calif., 1978-90; mem. support agy. Presbyn. Ch. USA, 1978-86; chmn. com. on communication Presbyn. Ch. USA, 1980-82; moderator Grand Canyon Presbytery, 1986-87. Author: What a Way to Live, 1977, When the River Runs Backward 1983, 2d edit. 1989. Mem. Acad. of Parish Clergy, 1976—; trustee, pres. Westminster Village Retirement Ctr., Scottsdale, Ariz., 1990-95. Mem. Rotary. E-mail: lkresort@aol.com. Home and Office: 7800 N 65th St Paradise Vly AZ 85253-3104

KILLACKY, JOHN R., museum administrator, educator, writer, filmmaker. BA, Hunter Coll. Past mng. dir. Trisha Brown Dance Co., Inc.; past dir. Laura Dean Dancers and Musicians; past curator performing arts Walker Art Ctr., Mpls.; exec. dir. Yerba Buena Ctr. Arts., San Francisco, 1996—; gen. mgr. PepsiCo Summerfare, 1986; past program officer Pew Charitable Trusts; adj. prof. U. Minn., 1991-96; cons. in field; lectr. in field. Author, dir. several short films and videos; contbr. articles to profl. jours. Recipient 1st Bank Sally Ordway Irvine award for artistic vision, 1995, William Dawson award for programming excellence Assn. Performing Arts Presenters, 1995. Office: Yerba Buena Ctr Arts 701 Mission St San Francisco CA 94103-3138*

KILLEN, JUDY TIPTON, news editor; b. Billings, Mont., Apr. 12, 1966; d. Jack E. and Barbara M. (Nickelson) Tipton; m. Michael J. Killen, June 22, 1996. BA in Journalism and History, U. Mont., 1988. Reporter Mont. Kaimin, Missoula, 1987-88; reporter Sheridan (Wyo.) Press, 1989-92, news editor, 1993; reporter Powell (Wyo.) Tribune, 1993-94, news editor, 1994—; affiliate Park County Leadership Inst., Cody, Wyo., 1996-98; pres. Wyo. AP, Cheyenne, 1997-98. Recipient Pacemaker award Wyo. Press Assn., 1998. Mem. Jaycees (dir. pub. rels. Sheridan chpt. 1992-93, 1st pl. award state writing contest 1993). Avocations: hunting, fishing, camping. Office: Powell Tribune Inc PO Box 70 128 S Bent St Powell WY 82435-2714

KILLIAN, RICHARD M., library director; b. Buffalo, Jan. 13, 1942; m. Nancy Killian; children from previous marriage: Tessa, Lee Ann. BA, SUNY, Buffalo, 1964; MA, Western Mich. U., 1965; grad. advanced mgmt. library adminstrn., Miami U., Oxford, Ohio, 1981; grad. library adminstrn. devel. program, U. Md., 1985. Various positions Buffalo and Erie County Pub. Libraries, 1963-74, asst. dep. dir., personnel officer, 1979-80; dir. Town of Tonawanda (N.Y.) Pub. Library, 1974-78; asst. city librarian, dir. pub. svcs. Denver Pub. Library, 1978-79; exec. dir. Nioga Library System, Buffalo, 1980-87; library dir. Sacramento (Calif.) Pub. Library, 1987—. Mem. ALA, Calif. Library Assn., Rotary. Home: 3501 H St Sacramento CA 95816-4501 Office: Sacramento Pub Libr Adminstrn Ctr 828 I St Sacramento CA 95814-2589

KILLINGSWORTH, KATHLEEN NOLA, artist, photographer, company executive; b. Eglin AFB, Fla., Sept. 5, 1952; d. Marlin Donald Evans and Winnifred Irene (Pelton) Yow; m. Thomas Marion, Dec. 31, 1973 (div. Feb. 1976). Grad. high sch., Myrtle Point, Oreg. Food svc. Internat. Trade Club, Mobile, Ala., 1970-73; food and beverage Gussies Restaurant and Night Club, Coos Bay, Oreg., 1973-77, Libr. Buttery and Pub, Las Vegas, Nev., 1977-79; beverage dir. Laughlin's (Nev.) Riverside Resort, 1979-80; food and beverage Hyatt Regency Maui, Lahaina, Hawaii, 1980-92; realtor assoc. Wailea (Hawaii) Properties, 1990; sole propr. K N Killingsworth Enterprises, Lahaina, 1990—; assoc. Kona Coast Resort II, 1992—; vol. Lahaina Arts Soc., 1992—; mem. Hui No'eau Visual Arts Ctr., Makawao, Maui, Hawaii, 1992—. Artist numerous watercolor and acrylic paintings; photographer nature greeting cards; pub. Photo Jour. Maui I, 1996. Vol. The Word For Today, Lahaina, 1983-87, Kumalani Chapel, Kapalua, Hawaii, 1983-87, Maui Special Olympics, 1993—; founding mem. & vol. Maui Community Arts & Cultural Ctr.; supporter Teen Challenge, Lahaina, 1987—. Mem. Lahina Arts Soc., 1992—. Republican. Avocations: windsurfing, gemology, arts, creating. Office: K N Killingsworth Enterprises PO Box 5369 Lahaina HI 96761-5369

KILLMASTER, JOHN HENRY, III, artist, educator; b. Allegan, Mich., Dec. 2, 1934; s. John H. and Ora Mae (Backus) K.; m. Rosemary Olson, 1996; children: John Henry IV. BA cum laude, Hope Coll., Holland, Mich., 1968; MFA, Cranbrook Acad. Art, Bloomfield Hills, Mich., 1969. Artist, designer Ambrose Assocs., 1953-56, LaDriere Inc., Detroit, 1957-62; asst. prof. art Ferris State Coll., Big Rapids, Mich., 1966-67, 69-70; prof. art emeritus Boise State U., 1970—; important works include: exterior mural Boise Gallery of Art, 1974; sculpture City of Portland, 1977; lobby mural Morrison Knudsen Corp., Boise, 1982; wall sculpture Idaho First Nat. Bank, 1980; wall relief mural Morrison Performing Arts Ctr., 1984; exhibitions include Denver Art Mus., 1980, Nat. Mus. Am. Art Smithsonian Instn., 1979, 83, San Francisco Mus. Modern Art, 1984, Laval Art Mus., Montreal, 1986, Barcelona (Spain) Art Gallery, 1988, Color and Image , N.Y.C., 1989. Recipient Gov.'s award for excellence in the arts State of Idaho, 1978; Western States Art Found. grantee, 1975. Mem. Nat. Enamelist Soc., N.W. Designers and Craftsmen. Home: 6317 Lion Ave Boise ID 83709-2940

KILMER, MAURICE DOUGLAS, marketing executive; b. Flint, Mich., Sept. 14, 1928; s. John Jennings and Eleanor Minnie (Gerholz) K.; m. Vera May Passino, Mar. 30, 1950; children: Brad Douglas, Mark David, Brian John, David Scott, Karen Sue. B of Indsl. Engring., Gen. Motors Inst., 1951; MBA, U. Minn., 1969. Quality svcs. mgr. ordnance div. Honeywell, Hopkins, Minn., 1964-69; product assurance dir. peripheral ops. Honeywell, San Diego, 1969-71; pres. Convenience Systems, Inc., San Diego, 1972-75; salesman real estate Forest E. Olson Coldwell Banker, La Mesa, Calif., 1976-77; resident mgr. Forest E. Olson Coldwell Banker, Huntington Beach, Calif., 1977-78; mgmt. cons. Century 21 of the Pacific, Santa Ana, Calif., 1978-83; dir. broker svcs. Century 21 of the Pacific, Anaheim, Calif., 1983-85; exec. dir. Century 21 of S.W., Phoenix, 1985-86; sales assoc. Century 21 Rattan Realtors, San Diego, 1986-88; mgr. Rattan Realtors, San Diego, 1988-92, relocation dir., 1993-98; retired, 1998. With U.S. Army, 1951-52. Mem. Am. Soc. for Quality Control, San Diego Bd. Realtors. Republican. Avocation: playing mandolin. Home: 9074 Circle R Oaks Ln Escondido CA 92026-5926

KILMER, NEAL HAROLD, software engineer; b. Orange, Tex., Apr. 24, 1943; s. Harold Norval and Luella Alice (Sharp) K.; m. Jody Geary, Oct. 24, 1998. BS in Chemistry and Math., Northwestern Okla. State U., 1964; MS in Chemistry, Okla. State U., 1971; PhD in Chemistry, Mich. State U., 1979. Rsch. assoc. N.Mex. Petroleum Recovery Rsch. Ctr. N.Mex. Inst. Mining & Tech., Socorro, 1979-81, rsch. chemist, 1981-85, lectr. geol., engring., 1984, asst. prof. mining engring., 1985-86; phys. scientist Phys. Sci. Lab. N.Mex. State U., Las Cruces, 1986-96; software engr. AlliedSignal Tech. Svcs. Corp., Las Cruces, N.Mex., 1996—. Contbr. articles to profl. jours. Mem. Am. Chem. Soc., Am. Inst. Physics, Optical Soc. Am., Sigma Xi, Pi Mu Epsilon, Phi Lambda Upsilon. Presbyterian. Avocation: square dancing. Home: 398 No Problem Dr Las Cruces NM 88005 Office: Software Maintenance & Tng Facility PO Box 9000 Las Cruces NM 88004-9000

KIM, AMMIE YONGMI, interior designer; b. Seoul, Korea, May 19, 1965; arrived in U.S., 1979; d. Robert S. and In Suk Kim; m. Andrew Jung, Oct. 16, 1993; children: Ryan, Elaine. BA, UCLA, 1988, cert., 1993. CAD designer Bif Inc., Pasadena, Calif., 1989-91; project designer Peggy Hahn Interiors, L.A., 1991; owner, designer Ammie Kim Interiors, North Hills, Calif., 1992—. mem. Am. Soc. Interior Designers. Home: 15106 Nordhoff St Unit 28 North Hills CA 91343-2339 Office: Ammie Kim Interiors 8797 Beverly Blvd Ste 319 West Hollywood CA 90048-1832

KIM, DENNIS KYLE, software company executive; b. Glendora, Calif., Aug. 23, 1967; s. Chull Hwan and Kryssa Kija (Kim) K. BA, U. Calif., Irvine, 1994; MBA, U. So. Calif., 1996. Adminstrv. mgr. U. Calif (Irvine) Med. Ctr., 1987-92, sr. adminstrv. mgr., 1992-94; v.p. ops. Holosofx, Inc., L.A., 1994-96, v.p., COO, CFO, 1996—. Mem. Software Coun. So. Calif., L.A. Venture Assn.

KIM, EDWARD WILLIAM, ophthalmic surgeon; b. Seoul, Korea, Nov. 25, 1949; came to U.S., 1957; s. Shoon Kul and Pok Chu (Kim) K.; m. Carole Sachi Takemoto, July 24, 1976; children: Brian, Ashley. BA, Occidental Coll., Los Angeles, 1971; postgrad. Calif. Inst. Tech., 1971; MD, U. Calif.-San Francisco, 1975; MPH, U. Calif.-Berkley, 1975. Diplomate Nat. Bd. Med. Examiners, Am. Bd. Ophthalmology. Intern, San Francisco Gen. Hosp., 1975-76; resident in ophthalmology Harvard U.-Mass. Eye and Ear Infirmary, Boston, 1977-79; clin. fellow in ophthalmology Harvard U., 1977-79; clin. fellow in retina Harvard, 1980; practice medicine in ophthalmic surgery, Laguna Hills and San Clemente, Calif., 1980—; vol. ophthalmologist Eye Care Inc., Ecole St. Vincent's, Haiti, 1980, Liga, Mex., 1989; chief staff, South Coast Med. Ctr., 1988-89; assoc. clin. prof. dept. ophthalmology, U. Calif., Irvine. Founding mem. Orange County Ctr. for Performing Arts, Calif., 1982, dir. at large, 1991; pres. Laguna Beach Summer Music Festival, Calif., 1984. Reinhart scholar U. Calif.-San Francisco, 1972-73; R. Taussig scholar, 1974-75. Fellow ACS, Am. Acad. Ophthalmology, Royal Soc. Medicine, Internat. Coll. Surgeons; mem. Calif. Med. Assn., Keratorefractive Soc., Orange County Med. Assn., Mensa, Expts. in Art and Tech. Office: Harvard Eye Assocs 665 Camino De Los Mares Ste 102 San Clemente CA 92673-2840

KIM, HO GILL, poet; b. Sachon, South Korea, June 22, 1943; s. Jong Soo and Ul Soon (Lee) K.; m. Sherrie Chul Ja Park, Mar. 19, 1970; children: Brian Ki-Man, Eugene Yoo-Jin. BA, Gyeng Sang Univ., Jin-Joo, Korea, 1970; MS in Econs., Kun Kook Univ., Seoul, 1975. Airline pilot Korean Airlines, Seoul, 1972-81; columnist Korean Central Daily News, L.A., 1981-83; pres. Sunflower Farms, L.A., 1984—. Editor: Literary realm, 1987-95, Korean American Literature, 1982-86; author poetry. Capt. Korean Army, 1965-71, Vietnam. Decorated Military Merit Vietnam War Korean Army, 1971; recipient Anti-Communist Poetry award Korea Def. Ministry, 1969, Overseas Korean Literary award Chu Kang Literary Soc., 1997, Modern Si Jo Poetry award Modern SiJo Publ. Co., 1998. Mem. SiJo Soc. Am. (pres. 1995), Korean Literary Soc. Am. (pres. 1982—, adv.), Internat. Pen Club, Acad. Am. Poets. Office: 3065 Mt View Ave Los Angeles CA 90066

KIM, JEAN, academic administrator; b. Seoul, Korea, Jan. 18, 1950; came to U.S., 1962; m. David VandeWater, June 21, 1975; children: Mia, Liana. BA in Sociology, U. Mass., 1973, MA in Sociology, 1976, EdD in Counseling Psychology, 1981. Sr. head of residence U. Mass., Amherst, 1974-78, asst. dir. S.W. residential, 1978-79, asst. dir. student devel., 1979-81; dir. student devel. Western New Eng. Coll., Springfield, Mass., 1981-88; asst. dean student affairs Stanford (Calif.) U., 1988-91; v.p. for student affairs, dean of students U. Hartford, Conn., 1991-95; vice chancellor for student affairs U. Colo., Boulder, 1995—. Recipient Nat. Scholar award Nat. Assn. for Asian and Pacific Am. Edn., 1982. Mem. Nat. Assn. Student Pers. Adminstrs., Nat. Tng. Lab. Inst. for Applied Behavioral Scis. (bd. dirs.). Home: 900 Parkway Dr Boulder CO 80303-2850 Office: U Colo Vice Chancellor Student Affairs PO Box 31 Boulder CO 80309-0031

KIM, JOUNG-IM, communication educator, consultant; b. Taejon, Choongnam, Republic of Korea, May 8, 1947; came to U.S., 1975; d. Yong-Kap Kim and Im-Soon Nam; m. James Andrew Palmore, Jr., Jan. 21, 1989 (div. Nov. 1993). BA in Libr. Sci., Yonsei U., Seoul, Korea, 1970, postgrad., 1974-75; postgrad., U. Hawaii at Manoa, 1975, MA in Sociology, 1978; PhD in Comm., Stanford U., 1986. Rschr. Korean Inst. Family Planning, Seoul, 1974-75; spl. resource person UN/East-West Ctr., Honolulu, 1976; rsch. asst. East-West Ctr., Honolulu, 1977-78; rsch., teaching asst. Stanford U., Calif., 1979-83, instr., 1984; asst. prof. U. Hawaii at Manoa, Honolulu, 1984-95, assoc. prof., 1995—; cons. UN Econ. and Social Commn. for Asia and Pacific, Bangkok, 1979, 84-86, 89, 90-92; cons. UN Devel. Program, Devel. Tng. Comm. Planning, Bangkok, 1984, UN Population Funds, N.Y.C., 1991, 92; mem. faculty communication and info. scis. doctoral program U. Hawaii at Manoa, Honolulu, mem. faculty Ctr. Korean Studies. Contbr. articles to profl. jours., monographs, and chpts. to books. Grantee East-West Ctr., 1972, 75-78; Population Libr. fellow U. N.C., 1973; Stanford U. fellow, 1978-79, 83, 84. Mem. Internat. Comm. Assn., Internat. Network for Social Network Analysis. Avocations: dancing, listening to music, flower arranging, reading, swimming. Office: U Hawaii at Manoa 2560 Campus Rd # 336 Honolulu HI 96822-2217

KIM, KYUN, architect, educator; b. Naju, Chun-Nam, Korea, Nov. 17, 1936; came to U.S., 1956; s. Doo-Chun and Ok-Nang; m. Catherine, June 13, 1964 (div. Nov. 1987); children: Jason, Sonya; m. Sunhee, Jan. 16, 1988; children: Hahn, Jin. BArch, Va. Poly. Inst., 1964; MArch, U. Pa., 1967. Draftsman Ward & Hall, Springfield, Va., 1960-62; designer Perkins & Will, Washington, 1965-66; arch. Stewart, Noble, Class, Phila., 1967-68; arch., ptnr. Lothrop Assocs., White Plains, N.Y., 1968-78; prin. Hershberger & Kim, Tempe, Ariz., 1978-83; Fulbrite prof. Chungbuk U., Cheong-Ju, Chungbuk, Korea, 1983-84; archtl. advisor Junglim A. and E., Seoul, Korea, 1984-86; sr. v.p. Ellerbe Becket, San Francisco, 1987—; instr. design Ariz. State U., Tempe, 1978-83. Contbr. articles to profl. jours. bd. dirs. Croton-on-Hudson planning, 1970s. Avocations: photography, golfing, sailing. Office: Ellerbe Becket 180 Montgomery St Ste 2250 San Francisco CA 94104-4229

KIM, PETER M., physician, internist; b. Sacto., Mar. 12, 1919; s. Daniel and Grace (Aiyun) K.; m. Mary Wesuk Ham, Apr. 9, 1949; children: Peter S., Marilyn S. BA, UCLA, 1941; MD, Med. Coll. of Wis., Milw., 1946. Pvt. practice Kauai, Hawaii. Founder Kauai Med. Group, Island Care HMO; active Am. Lung Assn., Am. Heart Assn., Am. Cancer Soc., Crippled Children's Soc. Col. U.S. Army. Fellow ACP, Am. Coll. Chest Physicians; mem. AMA, Kauai County Med. Soc., Hawaii Med. Assn., Masons, Scottish Rite, Shriners, Rotary. Avocations: golf, gardening. Office: Kauai Med Clin 3420 B Kuhio Hwy Lihue HI 96766

KIM, WAYNE H.S., educational association administrator, consultant. BS in Biology, Yonsei U., Seoul, Republic of Korea, 1978, MPA, 1983; PhD in Pub. Adminstrn., Walden U., 1990; postdoctoral in law, Cambridge (Eng.) U., 1991; JD, Western State U., 1994. Mem. faculty Korea Mil. Acad., Seoul, 1980-83, Calif. State U., Fullerton, 1992-93, Kensington U., Glendale, Calif., 1993-96; v.p., edn. cons. Dr. GAON Inst., Irvine, Calif., 1996—. Contbr. articles to profl. jours. 1st lt. in Korean Army. Mem. Doctorate Assn. N.Y. Educators, NAFSA Assn. Internat. Educators. Office: Dr GAON Inst 4000 Veronica Pkwy Irvine CA 92604

KIM, YONGMIN, electrical engineering educator; b. Cheju, Korea, May 19, 1953, came to U.S., 1976; s. Ki-Whan and Yang-Whi (Kim) K.; m. Eunai Yoo, May 21, 1976; children: Janice, Christine, Daniel. BEE, Seoul Nat. U., Republic of Korea, 1975; MEE, U. Wis., Madison, 1979, PhD, 1982. Asst. prof. U. Wash., Seattle, 1982-86, assoc. prof., 1986-90, prof., 1990—; bd. dirs. Optimedx, Precision Digital Images, Redmond, Wash.; cons. MITRE Corp., McLean, Va., 1990, Lotte-Canon, Seoul, 1991, Seattle Silicon, Bellevue, Wash., 1990-93, U.S. Army, 1989-96, Neopath, Inc., Bellevue, Wash., 1989-90, Trinius Ptnrs., Seattle, 1989-91, Samsung Advanced Inst. Tech., Suwon, Republic of Korea, 1989-92, Daewoo Telecom Co., Seoul, 1989-91, Intel Corp., Santa Clara, 1992, Aptec Systems, Portland, Oreg., 1992-93, Optimedx, Seattle, 1992-96, Precision Digital Images, Redmond, Wash., 1994-96, Micro Vision, Seattle, 1994-96, Hitachi, Tokyo, 1995—, Fujitsu, Tokyo, 1995—; bd. dirs. Image Computing Systems Lab., 1984—, Ctr. for Imaging Systems Optimization, 1991, Optimedx, 1993-96, U. Wash. Image Computing Libr. Consortium, 1995—; program evaluator Accreditation Bd. for Engring. and Tech., 1992—. Contbr. numerous articles to profl. jours., chpts. in books; editor Proceedings of the Annual International Conference of the IEEE EMBS, vol. 11, 1989, Proceedings of the SPIE Medical Imaging Conferences, vol. 1232, 1990, vol. 1444, 1991, vol. 1653, 1992, vol. 1897, 1993, vol. 2164, 1994, vol. 2431, 1995, vol. 2707, 1996, vol. 3031, 1997; mem. numerous editl. bds.; inventor in field. Mem. various nat. coms., chmn. steering com. IEEE TMI; chmn. numerous confs. Recipient Career Devel. award Physio Control Corp., 1982; grantee NIH, 1984—, NSF, 1984—, U.S. Army, 1986—, USN, 1986—; Whitaker Found. biomed. engring. grantee, 1986. Fellow Am. Inst. Med. and Biological Engring., IEEE (Early Career Achievement award 1988, Disting. Speaker 1991); mem. Assn. Computing Machinery, Soc Photo-Optical Instrumentation Engrs., Tau Beta Pi, Eta Kappa Nu. Presbyterian. Subspecialties: computer engring., multimedia, high-performance image computing workstations, image processing, computer graphics, medical imaging, and virtual reality. Home: 4431 NE 189th Pl Seattle WA 98155-2814

KIMBALL, MARK DOUGLAS, lawyer; b. Seattle, May 26, 1959; s. Frederick Burton and Merry Doris (Bredenberg) K. BA, U. Wash., 1979, JD, 1982. Bar: Wash. 1983, U.S. Dist. Ct. (we. dist.) Wash. 1985. Lawyer pvt. practice, Bellevue, Wash., 1983—. Editor: (books) Oregon Revised Statutes Annotated. Mem. Wash. State Bar Assn., Progressive Animal Welfare Soc. Republican. Presbyterian. Office: Mark Douglas Kimball PS 10655 NE 4th St Ste 400 Bellevue WA 98004-5086

KIMBERLEY, A. G., industrial products factory representative, management executive; b. Portland, Oreg., Oct. 29, 1939; s. A. Gurney and Meta (Horgan) K.; m. M. Susan Solie, Sept. 15, 1949 (div.); children: John Langton, Thea Ness; m. Roxanne Johannesen, Mar. 26, 1952. BS, Lewis & Clark Coll., 1959-62; postgrad., U. Oreg., 1963. Mgr. meat and dairy div. Hudson House Co., Portland, 1963-64; pres. Wall-Western Inc., Portland, 1964-92, Kimberley Indsl., Portland, 1982-92; owner Kimberley Boxwood Farm, Wilsonville, Oreg., 1987—, A. G. Kimberley & Co., 1992—; factory rep. to industry including Avery Abrasive, 1980, Tape Master Tool Co., 1980, Tifco Spline Inc., 1983, Nachi Corp., 1983, Midwest Press Brake Dies, 1985, Nordic Saw & Tool Co., 1993, Coast to Coast Indsl., 1993, Taurus Tool & Engring., 1995, Greenleaf Corp., 1995, Dianamic Abrasive, 1995, Electro Abrasives, 1996, C.G.W Grinding Wheel, 1996, Leader Tool & Die, 1997, Bentz Tool, 1998, United Cutting Tool, 1998, Nat. Broach & Machinery, 1998, Cheboygan Tap & Tool, 1998, ABS Imports, 1998, Hayes Abrasives, 1998. Republican. Episcopalian. Home: 16720 SW Wilsonville Rd Wilsonville OR 97070-7544

KIMBRELL, GRADY NED, author, educator; b. Tallant, Okla., Apr. 6, 1933; s. Virgil Leroy Kimbrell and La Veria Dee Underwood; m. Marilyn Louise King, May 30, 1953 (div.); m. Mary Ellen Cunningham, Apr. 11, 1973; children: Mark Leroy, Lisa Christine, Joni Lynne. BA, Southwestern Coll., Winfield, Kans., 1956; MA, Colo. State Coll., 1958. Cert. tchr. (life), Calif., Colo.; cert. adminstr., Calif. Bus. tchr. Peabody (Kans.) High Sch., 1956-58; bus. tchr. Santa Barbara (Calif.) High Sch., 1958-65, coordinator work edn., 1965-75, dir. research and evaluation, 1975-88; cons., textbook researcher and author. Author: Introduction to Business and Office Careers, 1974, The World of Work Career Interest Survey, 1986; co-author: Succeeding in the World of Work, 1970, 6th rev. edit., 1998, Entering the World of Work, 1974, 3rd rev. edit., 1988, The Savvy Consumer, 1984, Marketing Essentials, 1991, 2d edit., 1997, Office Skills, 1998, Advancing in the World of Work, 1992, Exploring Business and Computer Careers, 1992, Employment Skills for Office Careers, 1998. With U.S. Army, 1953-55. Mem. NEA, Calif. Assn. Work Experience Educators (life, v.p. 1968-70), Nat. Work Experience Edn. Assn., Calif. Tchrs. Assn., Coop. Work Experience Assn. Republican. Avocation: breeding and racing quarter horses.

KIMBRIEL-EGUIA, SUSAN, engineering planner; b. San Francisco, July 22, 1949; d. Scott Slaughter and Kathleen (Edens) Smith; m. Floyd Thomas Kimbriel; 1 child, John Thomas; m. Candelario Eguia, Feb. 14, 1991; 1 child, Daniel. Engring. planner, sys. adminstr. various mainframe and PC based sys. Northrop Aircraft, Hawthorne, Calif., 1982-91; owner, operator Susie's Day Care, Palmdale, Calif., 1995—; PC cons. Moselle Ins. Corp., North Hollywood, Calif., 1989-96, Northrop Aircraft, 1991-96; owner, dir. Susie's Family Day Care, 1995—. Avocations: handcrafts, gardening, skating, biking.

KIMBROUGH, LORELEI, elementary education educator; b. Chgo.; d. Paul and Lina (Higgs) Bobbett; children: Denise, Devi, Paul, Jeri Lynn. BS in Edn., Ill. State U., 1947; postgrad., DePaul U., Chgo. U., others. Cert. tchr., Ill. Tchr. of Latin and English Greensboro (N.C.) Pub. Schs.; spl. edn. tchr. Chgo. State Hosp./Reed Zone Ctr., Chgo., Jewish Children's Bur., Chgo.; elem. tchr. Chgo. Bd. of Edn., Pasadena (Calif.) High Sch.; English tchr. Malala H.S., Madang, 1993-94; tchr. jr. h.s. Cathedral Chapel Cath. Sch., 1995-96; tutor to fgn. students. Missionary worker L.A. Archdiocese, Papua New Guinea; vol. ARC, Solheim Luth. Home, Glendale Meml. Hosp. Recipient four-year scholarship State of Ill., Chgo. Musical Coll. award. Mem. Nat. Coun. Tchrs. of English, Ill. Coun. of Social Studies, Nat. Coun. Social Studies.

KIMME, ERNEST GODFREY, communications engineer; b. Long Beach, Calif., June 7, 1929; s. Ernest Godfrey and Lura Elizabeth (Dake) K.; BA cum laude, Pomona Coll., 1952; MA, U. Minn., 1954, PhD, 1955; m. Margaret Jeanne Bolen, Dec. 10, 1978; children by previous marriage: Ernest G., Elizabeth E., Karl Frederick. Mem. grad. faculty Oreg. State U., Corvallis, 1955-57; mem. tech. staff Bell Telephone Labs., Murray Hill, N.J., 1957-65, supr. mobile radio rsch. lab., 1962-65; head applied sci. dept. Collins Radio Co., Newport Beach, Calif., 1965-72; rsch. engr. Northrop Electronics,

Hawthorne, Calif., 1972-74; sr. staff engr. Interstate Electronics Corp., Anaheim, Calif., 1974-79; dir. advanced systems, dir. advanced comm. systems, tech. dir. spl. comm. programs Gould Navcomm Systems, El Monte, Calif., 1979-82; pres. Cobit, Inc, 1982-84; tech. staff Gen. Rsch. Corp., Santa Barbara, 1984-87; v.p. engring. Starfind, Inc., Laguna Niguel, Calif., 1987-88; dir. engring. R&D Unit Instruments, Orange, Calif., 1988-89; staff scientist Brunswick Def. Systems, Costa Mesa, Calif., 1989-90; v.p. engring. Redband Techs., Inc., 1990-96; adj. prof. U. Redlands, Golden Gate Univ., 1989—; adj. faculty math. U. Redlands Whitehead Coll., 1990—, Chapman U., 1997—. Contbr. articles to profl. jours. Mem. AAAS, Aircraft Owners and Pilots Assn., Exptl. Aircraft Assn., Phi Beta Kappa, Sigma Xi. Home: 301 N Starfire St Anaheim CA 92807-2928

KIMMICH, JON BRADFORD, computer science program executive; b. Lancaster, Pa., Aug. 8, 1964; s. John Howard and Alice (Ingram) K. BS in Computer Sci., Ind. U. Pa., 1986; MS in Computer Sci., Ohio State U., 1988; MBA, Seattle U., 1993. Developer Microsoft, Redmond, Wash., 1988-93, lead program mgr., sr. producer, 1993-97, product planner, 1997—; dir. PKT Found. Contbr. articles to profl. jours. Trustee PKT Found. Mem. IEEE (Computer Soc.), Assn. for Computing Machinery, Acad. Interactive Arts and Scis., Internat. Interactive Comms. Soc., Am. Film Inst. Achievements include 7 patents pending. Home: 1442 W Lake Sammamish Pkwy SE Bellevue WA 98008-5218 Office: Microsoft Corp 1 Microsoft Way Redmond WA 98052-8300

KIMPTON, DAVID RAYMOND, natural resource consultant, writer; b. Twin Falls, Idaho, Feb. 19, 1942; s. Lloyd and Retura (Robins) K.; m. Joanna Peak, June 2, 1984; foster children: Donnie, Derrick, Dustin. BS in Forestry, U. Idaho, 1964. Forester U.S. Forest Svc., Panguitch, Utah, 1966-68; with dept. interdisciplinary natural resources U.S. Forest Svc., Ely, Nev., 1968-71; with dept. interdisciplinary natural resources U.S. Forest Svc., Stanley, Idaho, 1971-72, dist. ranger, 1972-78; dist. ranger U.S. Forest Svc., Mountain City, Nev., 1978-84; natural resource cons. Idaho, 1984-92; range conservationist U.S. Forest Svc., Stanley, Idaho, 1992-93; program mgr. natural resources Sawtooth Nat. Recreation Area, Stanley, Idaho, 1993-97; conservationist pvt. practice, 1997—; incident comdr. U.S. Forest Svc., Western States, 1978-86; botanist pvt. and govtl., Idaho, Nev., 1985-92; naturalist schs., pvt., govt., Idaho, Nev., 1988—; bd. dirs. Salmon River Emergency Med. Clinic, Stanley, Idaho, 1984-86, v.p., 1987-92; bd. dirs., v.p. Idaho Mountain Life Health Clinics, Boise, 1985-92. Author Mining Law jour., 1990; author Life Saving Rescue mag., 1989. Pres. Meth. Youth Found., Twin Falls, 1960—; treas., v.p. Chrisman Bd. Dirs., Moscow, Idaho, 1960-63; bd. dirs. Vol. Fire Dept., Ely, 1968-71, Sawtooth Valley Meditation Chapel, 1974-76, Stanley Cmty. Bldg., 1977-78; mem. Sawtooth Valley Assn, Stanley, 1971-72, Vol. Fire Dept. Stanley, 1975-78, Mountain Search and Rescue, Stanley, 1972-78, Coalition of Taxpayers, Stanley, 1990-95. With U.S. Army, 1965-66, Vietnam. Named Outstanding Young Men Am., Bd. Nat. Advs., 1971, Outstanding Mem., White Pine Jaycees, 1969. Mem. Idaho Wildlife, Sawtooth Wildlife Coun. Mem. Christian Ch. Avocations: botany, wildlife, nauturalist, backpacking, hunting. Home: PO Box 32 Stanley ID 83278-0032

KIND, KENNETH WAYNE, lawyer, real estate broker; b. Missoula, Mont., Apr. 1, 1948; s. Joseph Bruce and Elinor Joy (Smith) K.; m. Diane Lucille Jozaitis, Aug. 28, 1971; children: Kirstin Amber, Kenneth Warner. BA, Calif. State U.-Northridge, 1973; JD, Calif. Western U., 1976. Bar: Calif. 1976, U.S. Dist. Ct. (ea., so., no. dists.) Calif., 1976, U.S. Cir. Ct. Appeals (9th cir.); lic. NASCAR driver, 1987. Mem. celebrity security staff Brownstone Am., Beverly Hills, Calif., 1970-76; tchr. Army and Navy Acad., Carlsbad, Calif., 1975-76; real estate broker, Bakersfield, Calif., 1978—; sole practice, Bakersfield, 1976—; lectr. mechanic's lien laws, Calif., 1983—. Staff writer Calif. Western Law Jour., 1975. Sgt. U.S. Army, 1967-70. Mem. ABA, VFW, Nat. Order Barristers, Rancheros Visitadores. Libertarian. Office: 4042 Patton Way Bakersfield CA 93308

KINDER, RALPH EUGENE, environmental engineer, career officer; b. Tulsa, Okla., Apr. 17, 1959; s. Ralph R. Kinder and Mary F. (Green) Milam; m. Petrice Le-Ann Davidson, Dec. 22, 1990; children: Ashleigh Rene, Garrett Ray. BS in Civil Engring., Okla. State U., 1982; MS in Acquisition Mgmt., Fla. Tech., 1994; diploma in environ. engring., Colo. Sch. Mines, Golden, 1996. Commd. 2d lt. U.S. Army, 1982, advanced through grades to maj., 1994; instr. U.S. Army Logistics Mgmt. Coll., 1993-95, environ. engr., advanced degree program, 1996—. Major USMC, 1982—. Decorated Navy Achievement medal, Meritorious Svc. medal. Mem.Tau Beta Pi. Home: 1844 E Alvarado St Fallbrook CA 92028-2505

KINDRED, BRUCE ACTON, computer programmer, graphic artist; b. Riverside, Calif., May 21, 1954; s. Glenn Kindred and Ruby M. Baumbach Johnston; m. Doris K. Horton, May 20, 1977; children: Michelle, Barbara, Robert; 1 foster child, Ricky Edwards. AA in Computer Graphics, Alaska Computer Inst., Anchorage, 1985; PhD in Computer Sci., U. Alaska, Anchorage, 1989; DD (hon.), Am. Fellowship U., San Francisco, 1992. Computer programmer, graphic artist PC Pulse Inc., Bremerton, Wash. Sgt. USMC, 1992-96. Mem. Assn. Shareware Profls., Masons. Office: PC Pulse Inc PO Box 2265 Bremerton WA 98310-0301

KING, ALONZO, artistic director, choreographer. Student, Sch. Am. Ballet, Am. ballet theatre Sch., Harkness House Ballet Arts. Art dir. Lines Contemporary Ballet, San Francisco, 1982—; master tchr. working with Les Ballets de Monte-Carlo, London's Ballet Rambert, Nat. Ballet of Can., N.C. Sch. of Arts, San Francisco Ballet; inaugurator San Francisco Inst. Choreography, 1982; performer Honolulu City Ballet, Santa Barbara Ballet, DTH. Commd. to create and stage ballets for The Joffrey Ballet, Dance Theatre of Harlem; ballets in repertoires of Frankfurt Ballet, Dresden Ballet, BalletMet, Washington Ballet, Hong Kong Ballet; choreographer for Les Ballets de Monte-Carlo; choreogrpaher for prima ballerine Natalia Makarova, Patrick Swazye; original works choreographed include Ocean (3 Isadora Duncan Dance award 1994 for outstanding achievement in choreography, original score and co. performance)), Rock, 1995, Signs and Wonders, Rain Dreaming, Stealing Light, Without Wax, 1990, others. Mem. panels Nat. Endowment for Arts, Calif. Arts Coun., City of Columbus Arts Coun., Lila Wallace-Reader's Digest Arts Ptnrs. Program; former art commr. City and County of San Francisco. Nat. Endowment for Arts Chroeographer's fellow. Office: Lines Contemporary Ballet 50 Oak St Fl 4 San Francisco CA 94102-6011*

KING, CHAROLETTE ELAINE, retired career officer; b. Baker, Oreg., Apr. 10, 1945; d. Melvin Howard and Rella Maxine (Gwilliam) Wright; m. Craig Seldon King, April 14, 1965; children: Andrea Karen, Diana Susan. Clerical positions various firms, Idaho, Va., Conn., 1964-71; nursing sec. VA, San Diego, 1974-77; sec. USN, Agana, Guam, 1972-73; procurement clk. USN, Bremerton, Wash., 1977-80; procurement clk. USN, San Diego, 1980, support svcs. supr., 1980-83, div. dir., 1983-87, program analyst, 1987-93, adminstrv. officer, 1993-96, mgmt. analyst, 1996. Recipient Model Agy. cup USN, San Diego, 1986. Republican. Avocations: reading, camping, sewing, writing, quilting.

KING, ELLEN MCGINTY, lawyer; b. San Francisco, Mar. 1, 1946. AB, U. Calif., Berkeley, 1968; MSJ, Northwestern U., 1971; JD, Stanford U., 1976. Bar: Calif. 1976. Ptnr. Jackson, Tufts, Cole & Black, San Francisco, San Jose, 1976—; mem. faculty fed. practice program U.S. Dist. Ct. (no. dist.) Calif., 1986-89; faculty mem. fed. case mgmt. program U.S. Dist. Ct. (no. dist.) Calif., 1995; panelist Calif. Continuing Edn. for Bar, 1992. Mem. ABA (litigation sect.), Santa Clara County Bar Assn. (panelist 1984, 90), Bar Assn. San Francisco, Phi Beta Kappa. Office: Jackson Tufts Cole & Black LLP 60 S Market St Fl 10 San Jose CA 95113-2351*

KING, FRANK WILLIAM, writer; b. Port Huron, Mich., Oct. 1, 1922; s. William Ernest and Catherine Theresa (Smith) K.; student U. Utah, 1963-65, Santa Monica City Coll., 1941, 48-49; BA, Marylhurst Coll., 1979; MA, U. Portland, 1982; m. Carma Morrison Sellers, Sept. 10, 1981; children: Rosanne, Jeanine Nell, Melanie, Lisa June; one stepson, Michael Sellers. Air traffic contr. FAA, Salt Lake City, Albuquerque and Boise, Idaho; 1949-65, info. officer Western Region, L.A., 1965-68; pub. affairs officer L.A. Dist. C.E., U.S. Army, 1968-69, Walla Walla (Wash.) 1969-77, N. Pacific div. Portland, Oreg., 1977-79, dir. pub. rels. U. Portland, 1979-80; adj. asst. prof. comm. U. Portland, 1982-83; instr. Portland (Oreg.) C.C., 1980-87; freelance writer, 1960—. Exec. asst. L.A. Fed. Exec. Bd., 1965-67; chmn. Walla Walla County Alcoholism Adminstrv. Bd., 1974-75; vice-chmn. Walla Walla County Human Services Adminstrv. Bd., 1976-78, chmn., 1977-78. Served with USMCR, 1942-45. Decorated Air medal; William Randolph Hearst scholar, 1965. Mem. Soc. Profl. Journalists, Pub. Relations Soc. Am. (accredited), Kappa Tau Alpha. Democrat. Roman Catholic. Home and Office: 310 N Fawn Dr Otis OR 97368-9323

KING, GUNDAR JULIAN, retired university dean; b. Riga, Latvia, Apr. 19, 1926; came to U.S., 1950, naturalized, 1954; s. Attis K. and Austra (Dale) Kenins: m. Valda K. Andersons, Sept. 18, 1954; children: John T., Marita A. Student, J.W. Goethe U., Frankfurt, Germany, 1946-48; BBA, U. Oreg., 1956; MBA, Stanford U., 1958, PhD, 1964; DSc (hon.), Riga Tech. U., 1991; D Habil. Oecon., Latvian Sci. Coun., 1992. Asst. field supr. Internat. Refugee Orgn., Frankfurt, 1948-50; br. office mfr. Williams Form Engring. Corp., Portland, Oreg., 1952-54; project mgr. Market Rsch. Assocs., Palo Alto, Calif., 1958-60; asst. prof., assoc. prof. Pacific Luth. U., 1960-66, prof., 1966—, dean Sch. Bus. Adminstrn., 1970-90; vis. prof. mgmt. U.S. Naval Postgrad. Sch., 1971-72, San Francisco State U., 1980, 1987-88; internat. econ. mem. Latvian Acad. Scis., 1990—; regent Estonian Bus. Sch., 1991-99; vis. prof. Riga Tech. U., 1993—. Author: Economic Policies in Occupied Latvia, 1965; contbr. articles to profl. publs. Mem. Gov.'s Com. on Reorgn. Wash. State Govt., 1965-88; mem. study group on pricing U.S. Commn. Govt. Procurement, 1971-72; pres. N.W. Univs. Bus. Adminstrn. Conf., 1965-66. With AUS, 1950-52. Fulbright-Hayes scholar, Thailand, 1988, Fulbright scholar, Latvia, 1993-94. Mem. AAUP (past chpt. pres.), Am. Mktg. Assn. (past chpt. pres.), Assn. Advancement Baltic Studies (pres. 1970), Western Assn. Collegiate Schs. Bus. (pres. 1971), Latvian Acad. Scis., Alpha Kappa Psi, Beta Gamma Sigma. Home: PO Box 44401 Tacoma WA 98444-0401 Office: Pacific Lutheran U Tacoma WA 98447

KING, INDLE GIFFORD, industrial designer, educator; b. Seattle, Oct. 23, 1934; s. Indle Frank and Phyllis (Kenney) K.; m. Rosalie Rosso, Sept. 10, 1960; children: Indle Gifford Jr., Paige Phyllis. BA, U. Wash., 1960, MA, 1968. Indsl. designer Hewlett-Packard, Palo Alto, Calif., 1961-63; mgr. indsl. design Sanborn Co., Boston, 1963-65; mgr. corp. design Fluke Corp., Everett, Wash., 1965-97; prof. indsl. design Western Wash. U., Bellingham, 1985—; pres., CEO Teaque Inc., 1998—; judge nat. and. internat. competitions; cons. in field. Contbr. articles to profl. jours.; designer patents in field. Coach Mercer Island (Wash.) Boys' Soccer Assn., 1972-77; pres. Mercer Island PTA, 1973; advisor Jr. Achievement, Seattle, 1975-78. Recognized as leading one of Am.'s Top 40 Design Driven Cos., ID Jour., 1999. Mem. Idsl. Design Soc. Am. (Alcoa award 1965, v.p. Seattle chpt. 1986-88), Mercer Island Country Club. Office: 14727 NE 87th St Redmond WA 98052-6500

KING, JANE CUDLIP COBLENTZ, volunteer educator; b. Iron Mountain, Mich., May 4, 1922; d. William Stacey and Mary Elva (Martin) Cudlip; m. George Samuel Coblentz, June 8, 1942 (dec. June 1989); children: Bruce Harper, Keith George, Nancy Allison Coblentz Patch; m. James E. King, August 23, 1991 (dec. Jan. 1994). BA, Mills Coll., 1942. Mem. Sch. Resource and Career Guidance Vols., Inc., Atherton, Calif., 1965-69, pres., CEO, 1969—; part-time exec. asst. to dean of admissions Mills Coll., 1994—. Proofreader, contbr., campus liaison Mills Coll. Quarterly mag. Life gov. Royal Children's Hosp., Melbourne, Australia, 1963—; pres. United Menlo Park (Calif.) Homeowner's Assn., 1994—; nat. pres. Mills Coll. Alumnae Assn., 1969-73, bd. trustees, 1975-83; bd. govs. Mills Coll. Alumnae Assn., 1966-73, 75-83, 98—. Named Vol. of Yr., Sequoia Union H.S. Dist., 1988, Disting. Woman Mid-Peninsula (forerunner San Mateo County Women's Hall of Fame), 1975; recipient Golden Acorn award for Outstanding Svc., Menlo Park C. of C., 1991. Mem. AAUW (Menlo-Atherton br. pres. 1994-96, v.p. programs 1996-97, editor Directory and Acorn, 1994—), Atherlons, Palo Alto (Calif.) Area Mills Coll. Club (pres. 1986), Phi Beta Kappa. Episcopalian. Avocations: reading, gardening. Office: Menlo-Atherton HS Resource-Career Guid Vols 555 Middlefield Rd Atherton CA 94027-3400

KING, JANE LOUISE, artist; b. South Bend, Ind., Aug. 9, 1951; d. Bill and Anne Luciel (Hopkins) Berta; m. Gerald William King Jr., July 7, 1973; children: Kelly Anne, Dinah Jolene. Student, Ind. U., South Bend, 1969-70, Ind. U., 1970-71; BFA, Ohio State U., 1973. Ind. artist Colo., 1974—; instr. Sangre de Cristo Art Ctr., Pueblo, Colo., 1982, Art Studio, Longmont, Colo., 1989. Exhibited oil and pastel paintings in numerous group shows including 5th Ann. Internat. Exhibit Kans. Pastel Soc., 10th and 22nd Ann. Pastel Soc. Am., N.Y., Colo. State Fairs, Poudre Valley Art League; prin. works represented in numerous pvt. collections; contbr. poems to At Days End, 1994. Leader 4-H Club, Longmont, 1986—; sec. Longmont Artists Guild Gallery, 1988-89, bd. dirs., 1989; supt. 1st Bapt. Ch., Longmont, 1990-91. Mem. Colo. Artists Assn. (area 1 rep. 1994), Longmont Artists Guild (Grumbacher award 1992), Longmont Arts Coun., Knickerbocker Artists N.Y, Audubon Artists N.Y. Republican. Avocations: gardening, skiing, horseback riding, music, reading. Home: 1508 Kempton Ct Longmont CO 80501-6716

KING, JENNIFER CAROLYN, marketing and promotions entrepreneur; b. N.Y.C., Oct. 8, 1960; d. Robert Eliot and Dorothy Lucine (Jones) K.; m. Timothy C. Fredel, 1989. Student, U. Colo., Boulder, 1978-81; BA in Bus. Mgmt., Simmons Coll., Boston, 1984. Asst. to exec. dir. SRI Internat., Menlo Park, Calif., 1981-82; dir. mktg. Pacific Ventures, Palo Alto, Calif., 1984-85; pres. JCK Enterprises, Menlo Park, 1985—, Synergistic Designs, San Francisco, 1985—, Rugged Elegance, Kennebunkport, Maine, 1989—. Producer promotional campaign (posters) Medical Alley, 1986, 88, (serigraph and lithograph) Ams. Cup Campaign Survival of the Fastest, 1987, N. Calif. campaign Biotech Bay, 1990-91, 92-93, FusionScape Map series promoting world ctrs. of high tech. Recipient Illustration award, Communication Arts, Palo Alto, 1987, Design award, 1987, Graphics Design award, Graphis, Switzerland. Mem. Community Entrepreneurs Orgn., Alumnae Resource Ctr., Simmons Alumnae, Kappa Kappa Gamma. Republican. Presbyterian. Avocations: world-wide travel, skiing, rowing, sailing, family. Office: Synergistic Media Network Inc 594 Howard St Ste 400 San Francisco CA 94105-3006

KING, LEA ANN, community volunteer and leader; b. Elkhart, Ind., July 26, 1941; d. Lloyd Emerson and Mildred Salome (Hostetler) Hartzler; children: Thomas Ellsworth III, Alden Elizabeth. BA in History, DePauw U., 1963. Participant in Intensive Workshop in Intercultural Comm. U. Calif., Irvine, 1993, Study Tour of Ethnic Minorites of China, UCLA Extension, 1990; audited The Ethics of War and Peace, Ethikon Inst., Jerusalem, 1993; attended Three Intercultural Colloquia of Family Life, Cultural Diversity and Human Values, Ethikon Inst., 1989. Producer, hostess Pub. Access cable TV programs; travel writer, photographer. Bd. dirs., chair The Ethikon Inst. for Study of Ethical Diversity and Intercultural Rels.; pres. Vol. Ctr. S. Bay-Harbor-Long Beach, 1993-95; v.p. Comty. Assn. of the Peninsula, chair multicultural com., chair PV 2000; sec. Planned Parenthood L.A., 1991—; past pres. Jr. League; past chair San Pedro Peninsula Hosp. Found.; founding chair Forward-Looking Strategies for Women Coalition, 1985; co-chair United Way Sys. Wide Admissions Com.; mem. Nodrstrom's Com. for Salute to Cultural Diversity, L.A., 1993-95, diversity com. Planned Parenthood Fedn. We. Region, 1996-99; field rep. Congresswoman Jane Harman, Calif. 36th Dist., 1997—. Named Woman of Yr. Nat. Women's Polit. Caucus, San Fernando Valley, 1986, South Bay YWCA; recipient John Anson Ford award L.A. County Commn. on Human Rels., 1992, Spirit of Volunteerism award Jr. League L.A., 1991, Founders award Vol. Ctrs. Calif., 1996, commendations from L.A. Mayor Tom Bradley, L.A. County Bd. Suprs., Calif. State Sen. Robert Beverly, Congressmen Dana Rohrabcher and Howard Berman; mem. Los Angeles County Commn. on Human Rels., 1993, 96, pres., 1997. Home and Office: 229 17th St Manhattan Beach CA 90266-4633

KING, PAULINE URBANO, developer; b. L.A., Mar. 21, 1948; d. Paul DeWitt Urbano and Mary-Louise (Strong) Rhodes; m. George Rangeley King, Jan. 23, 1969 (div. Oct. 1996); children: Anne de Rosset, Phoebe Edmunds, David Raugeley. BA in English Lit., U. Wash., 1971. Project dir. Ariz. Cmty. Found., Phoenix, 1988-94; fundraising cons. Phoenix, 1994-95; dir. devel. Ballet Ariz., Phoenix, 1995-96; v.p. Scottsdale (Ariz.) Healthcare Found., 1996—. Bd. [illegible] 1986-89; mem. founding bd. Maricopa County Ct. Apptd. Spl. Advocates, Phoenix, 1983-84; chmn. task force on children & families Ariz. Supreme Ct., Phoenix, 1987-89; chmn. election bond Phoenix Union H.S., 1994-95. Recipient State Bar Ariz. award of Appreciation, Phoenix, 1990. Mem. Nat. Soc. Fund Raising Execs. Democrat. Episcopalian. Avocations: flyfishing, gardening, children's issues. Office: Scottsdale Healthcare Found Ste 121 10001 N 92nd St Scottsdale AZ 85258

KING, SAMUEL PAILTHORPE, federal judge; b. Hankow, China, Apr. 13, 1916; s. Samuel W. and Pauline (Evans) K.; m. Anne Van Patten Grilk, July 8, 1944; children—Samuel Pailthorpe, Louise Van Patten, Charlotte Lelepoki. B.S., Yale, 1937, LL.B., 1940. Bar: D.C., Hawaii bars 1940. Practiced law Honolulu, 1941-42, 46-61, 70-72, Washington, 1942; atty. King & McGregor, 1947-53, King & Myhre, 1957-61; judge 1st Circuit Ct. Hawaii, 1961-70, Family Ct., 1966-70; sr. judge U.S. Dist. Ct. for Hawaii, 1972—, chief judge, 1974-84; Faculty Nat. Coll. State Judiciary, 1968-73, Nat. Inst. Trial Advocacy, 1976, U. Hawaii Law Sch., 1980-84. Co-translator, co-editor: (O. Korschelt) The Theory and Practice of Go, 1965. Served with USNR, 1941-46; capt. Res. ret. Fellow Am. Bar Found.; mem. ABA, Hawaii Bar Assn. (pres. 1953), Order of Coif. Republican (chmn. Hawaii central com. 1953-55, nat. com. 1971-72). Episcopalian. Home: 1717 Mott-smith Dr Apt 2814 Honolulu HI 96822-2850 Office: US Dist Ct 300 Alamoana Blr Rm C461 Honolulu HI 96813-5000*

KING, SIDSEL ELIZABETH TAYLOR (BETH KING), hotel catering-hospitality professional; b. Edmonton, Alta., Can., July 27, 1932; d. Claude L. and Sadie (Hommy) Taylor; m. Otis A. King, Mar. 21, 1953; children: Ronald R., Lori Beth. AAS in Hotel Mgmt. and Food Svc Industry, U. Alaska, 1989. Sec. Sheriff's Office Courthouse, Edmonton, 1950-51; new accounts clk. First Nat. Bank Anchorage, 1952-53; sec., receptionist rate clk. Alaska Freight Lines, Anchorage, 1954-59; co-owner King's Rentals, Anchorage, 1953—; sec. State of Alaska Dept. Fish and Game, Anchorage, 1959-64, Anchorage Sch. Dist., West High, Wendler and East High, Anchorage, 1964—; exec. sec. Anchorage Daily News, 1969-70; with freight svc. Anchorage Slnd., 1970-71; caterer Clarion Hotel, Anchorage, 1989—; ambassador Clarion Hotel, Anchorage, 1991, Red Cross person, 1990-91. Preservation charter mem. Nat. Soc. Hist. Preservation, 1980's, Nat. Women in the Arts, Washington, 1980's, Nat. Secs. Assn. Anchorage, 1959—. Mem. Alaska Watercolor Soc., U. Alaska-Anchorage Alumni. Avocations: art, reading, knitting, cooking, ice skating. Home: PO Box 244304 Anchorage AK 99524-4304 Office: Regal Alaskan Hotel 4800 Spenard Rd Anchorage AK 99517-3200

KING, VERNA ST. CLAIR, retired school counselor; b. Berwick, La.; d. John Westley and Florence Ellen (Calvin) St. C.; A.B., Wiley Coll., 1937; M.A., San Diego State U., 1977; m. Alonzo Le Roy King, Aug. 27, 1939 (dec.); children—Alonzo Le Roy, Joyce Laraine, Verna Lee Eugenia King Bickerstaff, St. Clair A., Reginald Calvin (dec.). Tchr., Morgan City, La., 1939-40; tchr. San Diego Unified Sch. Dist., 1955-67, parent counselor, 1967-78, counselor grades 1-9, 1978-86; cons. Tucson Sch. Dist., 1977—, dir. compensatory edn., 1983—. Mem. Calif. Democratic State Central Com., 1950—, Dem. County Central Com., 1972—, del. nat. conv., 1976, 84, mem. exec. bd. Dem. State Central Com., 1982—; mem. San Diego County Sander Adv. Commn., 1982; hon. life mem. PTA; bd. dirs. YWCA, 1983—, v.p., 1987-88; chair Dem. County Ctrl. fundraising, 1992—; del. Dem. Nat. Com., 1992. Recipient Key to City, Mayor C. Dail, 1955, cert. United Negro Coll. Fund dr., 1980, Urban League Pvt. Sector award, 1982, 4th Ann. Conf. on Issues in Ethnicity and Mental Health Participants award, 1982 ; named Woman of Dedication, Salvation Army, 1985, Citizen of Yr., City Club and Jaycees, 1985, Woman of Achievement, Pres.' Council, 1983, Henry Auerbach award San Diego Dem. Party Ctrl. Com., 1997; numerous other honors. Mem. NEA (women's council 1980-82), AAUW, Calif. Tchrs. Assn. (state council 1979—, area dir. 1985—), San Diego Tchrs. Assn. (dir. 1958, 64, sec. 1964-67), Nat. Council Negro Women, San Diego County Council Dem. Women (pres. 1986-88), Compensatory Edn. Assn. (area dir. 1982-87), Pres. Women, Inc., Alpha Kappa Alpha (pres. 1978-80), Delta Kappa Gamma. Methodist. Clubs: Women's Inc., Order Eastern Star. Home: 5721 Churchward St San Diego CA 92114-4011

KINGMAN, ELIZABETH YELM, anthropologist; b. Lafayette, Ind., Oct. 15, 1911; d. Charles Walter and Mary Irene (Weakley) Yelm; m. Eugene Kingman, June 10, 1939; children—Mixie Kingman Eddy, Elizabeth Anne Kingman. BA U. Denver, 1933, MA, 1935. Asst. in anthropology U. Denver, 1932-34; mus. asst. Ranger Naturalist Staff, Mesa Verde Nat. Park, Colo., 1934-38; asst. to husband in curatorial work, Indian art exhibits Philbrook Art Ctr., Tulsa, 1939-42, Joslyn Art Mus., Omaha, 1947-69; tutor humanities dept. U. Omaha, 1947-50; chmn. bd. govs. Pi Beta Phi Settlement Sch., Gatlinburg, Tenn., 1969-72; asst. to husband in exhibit design mus. of Tex. Tech. U., 1970-75, bibliographer Internat. Ctr. Arid and Semi-Arid Land Studies, 1974-75; librarian Sch. Am. Research, Santa Fe, 1978-86; research assoc., 1986—; v.p. Santa Fe Corral of the Westerners, 1985-86. Mem. AAUW, LWV, Archeol. Inst. Am. (v.p. Santa Fe chpt. 1981-83), Santa Fe Hist. Soc. (sec. 1981-83). Home: 604 Sunset St Santa Fe NM 87501-1118 Office: Sch Am Rsch 660 Garcia St Santa Fe NM 87501-2858

KINGSTON, TIMOTHY MARK W., reporter, video producer; b. Rustington, Eng.; Came to U.S., 1977.; s. John Whitsed and Pauline Estelle (Tibbett) K. Student in devel. studies, U. Calif., Berkeley, 1984. Staff reporter San Francisco Bay Times, San Francisco, 1986-95; freelance reporter, video producer, news editor San Francisco Frontiers, San Francisco, 1996—. Office: San Francisco Frontiers 2370 Market St San Francisco CA 94117

KINNEY, CAROL NAUS ROBERTS, real estate broker; b. Mpls., May 7, 1923; d. Edward Paul and Esther (Colwell) Naus; m. Thomas R. Roberts, May 2, 1942 (dec. Feb. 1968); children: Thomas Naus, Margaret Elizabeth, Shelley; m. Harry E. Kinney, Aug. 30, 1970 (div. April 1988). BA in Bacteriology magna cum laude, U. Minn., 1946. Mem. staff Los Alamos Scientific Lab., 1964-70; co-owner Harry E. Kinney Gen. Contractor, Albuquerque, 1977-81, 86; real estate broker Christopher Webster, Albuquerque, 1992-94, Kate Southand Real Estate, Albuquerque, 1994-98, Carol Kinney Real Estate, Albuquerque, 1998—. City Councillor Los Alamos, N.Mex., 1968-70; chair 100 Yr. Cmty. Outreach U. N.Mex., Albuquerque, 1986-89; chair bd. of ethics and campaign practices City of Albuquerque, 1990-94; dir. N.Mex. Gov.'s Mansion Found., 1988-92, 96—. Honored as Albuquerque Vol. Jr. League of Albuquerque, 1985; entered into Albuquerque Sr. Hall of Fame, 1989—; named Albuquerque's First Lady, 1974-78, 81-85. Mem. The Nature Conservancy (trustee 1976-90, 92—), N.Mex. Symphony (trustee 1992—), Rio Grande Nature Ctr. (trustee 1984-86, 88—), Beta Sigma Phi (internat. hon. mem.), Phi Beta Kappa. Republican. Unitarian. Avocations: skiing, camping, contractor/foreman for building own home. E-mail: ckinney@albuquerquehomes.com. Fax: 505-343-9554. Home and Office: 2917 Calle del Rio NW Albuquerque NM 87104

KINNEY, JAY MACNEAL, editor, author, illustrator; b. Cleve., July 18, 1950; s. Del Jay and Analee (Lathrop) K.; m. Dixie Leone Tracy, July 8, 1978. Student, Baldwin Wallace Coll., Berea, Ohio, 1968-69, Pratt Inst., Bklyn., 1969-72. Prodn. asst. Whole Earth, Sausalito, Calif., 1980-83; editor Coevolution Quar., Sausalito, Calif., 1983-85; editor-in-chief Gnosis Mag., San Francisco, 1985—; pres. The Lumen Found., San Francisco, 1984—. Contbg. editor Whole Earth Rev., 1985—; editor/author comic art pubs.; contbr. articles to profl. jours.; freelance illustrator. Avocations: music, travel. Office: Gnosis Mag PO Box 14217 San Francisco CA 94114-0217

KINNEY, PAUL WILLIAM, investment company executive; b. Denver, Nov. 3, 1952; s. Thomas Grayson and Margaret Jane Kinney; children: Lauren, Michele, Hope, Elizabeth. AB, Occidental Coll., L.A., 1975; MPA, U. Colo., Denver, 1978. 1st v.p. investments Dean Witter Reynolds Inc., Glendale, Calif., 1978—. Pres. bd. dirs. Glendale (Calif.) Symphony Orch. Assn., 1995—; bd. dirs. Glendale Cmty. Found., 1995—, cfo. Mem. Investment Mgmt. Cons. Assn., Pi Alpha Alpha. Office: Dean Witter 801 N Brand Blvd Ste 908 Glendale CA 91203-3259

KINNEY, RALEIGH EARL, artist; b. Brainerd, Minn., Mar. 11, 1938; s. Earl Martin and Nancy Ann (Wolleat) K., m. Darlene Joyce Fox, Sept. 12, [illegible]. BS, St. Cloud (Minn.) State U., 1965, MA, 1968. Cert. tchr. Art tchr. St. Cloud Jr. High Sch., 1965-70;

art tchr., dept. chmn. St. Cloud Sr. High Sch., 1970-80; ind. instr. watercolor workshop, 1980—. Contbg. artist North Light Pub., 1993, 94. Served with USN, 1957-61. Named Artist of Yr. Phoenix C. of C., 1987. Mem. Ariz. Watercolor Soc. (signature), Midwest Watercolor Soc. (v.p. 1976-77, signature), Plein Air Painters Am. Republican. Avocation: photography. Home: 506 W Pebble Beach Dr Tempe AZ 85282-4827

KINNEY, RAYMOND CHARLES, computer systems administrator; b. Ogden, Utah, Jan. 23, 1955; s. William John and Lily Bernice (Jay) K.; m. Susan Marie Mann, Nov. 6, 1977 (div. April 1994); m. Erin McGrath April 26, 1998; 1 child, Christine AnnMarie. BS in Computer Sci. Magna Cum Laude, Nat. U., Sacremento, Calif., 1992. Astronomy lab. instr. Utah State U., Logan, 1975-77, computer operator, 1976-78; computer field tech. Burroughs, Salt Lake City, Utah, 1978-83; computer sys. adminstr., computer operator supr. Nature's Sunshine Products, American Fork, Utah, 1983-86; computer sys. adminstr. Rosville (Calif.) Telephone Co., 1986—; lectr. in field. Editor Utah Telecommunications Mgmt. Assn., 1985-86. Active Am. Legion, Ogden, 1971-73. Bugler USNR, 1972-73. Recipient Citizenship award DAR, Ogden, 1973, Recognition of Appreciation award Utah Tech. Coll., Salt Lake City, 1984, Recognition of Svc. award Utah Tech. Coll., Provo, 1986; Achievement scholarship Utah State U., Ogden, 1973. Mem. Independent Telephone Pioneer Assn. (certificate appreciation special svc. 1993). Republican. Avocations: music, music dir. E-mail: samkinney@mailexcite.com. Fax: (916) 786-5679. Home: 345 Hemphill Way Roseville CA 95678-5804 Office: Roseville Telephone Co PO Box 969 Roseville CA 95661-0969

KINNIBURGH, HUGH MACKENZIE, digital media specialist, television producer; b. Nyack, N.Y., July 16, 1961; s. Hugh Kinniburgh and Barbara (Friedman) Lee. BFA, NYU, 1984. Stage mgr. Silver Cup Studios, Long Island City, N.Y., 1983-85; mem. R & D staff Internat. Robotics, Inc., N.Y.C., 1985-89; prodr. TCI/Viacom, San Francisco, 1990—; dir. digital media DVP Tech Doc, Campbell, Calif., 1993—; sr. digital video prof. Acad. of Arts, San Francisco, 1994—; prodr., dir. Sunz.com, San Francisco, 1994—. Prodr.: (audio CD) Songs from the Hot Zone, 1997; digital editor: (TV) Thomas Kinkade Art of Travel, 1996, QVC sales shows, 1997-98; prodr., editor: (video) Video Director Zoo, 1997. Contbg. mem. Climate Theater, San Francisco, 1992—. Recipient digital video editing award Avid Tech., Boston, 1994, Best Rock and Roll Video Show award Bay Guardian Newspaper, San Francisco, 1997, Best Music and Entertainment Show award TCI Cablevision, San Francisco, 1997, Cable TV award, San Francisco, 1998. Mem. Soc. Motion Picture and TV Engrs., Internat. TV and Video Assn., Media Alliance, Alliance for Cmty. Media, Bay Area Video Collation. Avocation: restoring vintage muscle cars. Office: DVP Tech Doc 1475 S Bascom Ave Ste 108 Campbell CA 95008-0628

KINNISON, HARRY AUSTIN, transportation engineer; b. Springfield, Ohio, Oct. 2, 1935; s. Errett Lowell and Audrey Muriel (Smith) K. BSEE, U. Wyo., 1964; M. in Transp. Engring., Seattle U., 1983; PhD in Civil Engring., U. Tenn., 1987. Enlisted USAF, 1958, commd. 2d lt. 1964, advanced through grades to capt., 1968, released from active duty, 1968; electronics engr. 1839th Electronics Installation Group, Keesler AFB, Biloxi, Miss., 1972-77; staff engr. Casper (Wyo.) Air Facilities Sector FAA, 1977; test engr. Boeing Aerospace Co., Seattle, 1977-81; grad. rsch. engr. U. Tenn. Transp. Ctr., Knoxville, 1983-87; avionics engr. Boeing Comml. Airplane Co., Seattle, 1981-83, 87-90, maintenance programs engr. customer svcs. div., 1990—. Mem. Inst. Transp. Engrs. (assoc.), Transp. Rsch. Bd. (assoc.). Republican. Mem. Christian Ch. Home: 11630 SE 219th Pl Kent WA 98031-3922 Office: Boeing Comml Airplane Group M/S 2J-21 PO Box 3707 Seattle WA 98124-2207

KINNISON, ROBERT WHEELOCK, retired accountant; b. Des Moines, Sept. 17, 1914; s. Virgil R. and Sopha J. (Jackson) K.; m. Randi Hjelle, Oct. 28, 1971; children—Paul F., Hazel Jo Lewis. B.S. in Acctg., U. Wyo., 1940. C.P.A., Wyo., Colo. Ptnr. 24 hour auto service, Laramie, Wyo., 1945-59; pvt. practice acctg., Laramie, Wyo., 1963-71, Las Vegas, Nev., 1972-74, Westminster, Colo., 1974-76, Ft. Collins, Colo., 1976-97; ret., 1997. Served with U.S. Army, 1941-45; PTO. Mem. Wyo. Soc. C.P.A.s, Am. Legion (past comdr.), Laramie Soc. C.P.A.s (pres. 1966), VFW. Clubs: Laramie Optimist (pres. 1950), Sertoma. Home: PO Box 168 Fort Collins CO 80522-0168

KINSEY, DANIEL L., child and adolescent psychiatrist; b. Bloomington, Ill., Nov. 29, 1961; s. Joseph Edison and Lillian Pearl (Henson) K.; m. Melissa Anne Randolph, Sept. 25, 1987. BA, Ea. Ky. U., 1984; MD, U. Louisville, 1988. Diplomate Am. Bd. Neurology and Psychiatry. Resident U. Ky., Lexington, 1988-93; psychiatrist Harris Hosp., Anderson, S.C., 1993-95, Cleo Wallace Ctrs., Colorado Springs, 1995—; v.p. med. staff Harris Hosp., Anderson, S.C., 1993-95; med. dir. Cleo Wallace Ctr., Colorado Springs, 1998—. Bd. dirs. Opportunity Workshop Ltd., Lexington, 1988-93. Mem. AMA, Colo. Springs Psychiat. Soc. (v.p. 1997—), Am. Psychiat. Assn., Am. Coll. of Physician Execs., Am. Soc. of Clin Psychopharm. Office: Cleo Wallace Ctrs 2525 S Hwy 115 Colorado Springs CO 80906

KINSLER, BRUCE WHITNEY, air traffic controller, consultant, air traffic control engineer, air defense engineer, air traffic control automation specialist; b. Ukiah, Calif., Jan. 11, 1947; s. John Arthur and Mary Helen (Hudson) K.; m. Mickey Kinsler, Apr. 1, 1969 (div. Nov. 1976); 1 child, Arthur Todd; m. Segundina L. Pangilinan, May 27, 1978; 1 stepchild, Stephanie Lizarraga. AA, El Camino Coll., 1979; BA, Calif. State U., Long Beach, 1984. Air traffic controller FAA, various locations, 1971-81; cen. sta. mgr. Times Mirror Security Communications, Irvine, Calif., 1982-84; supr. office services Law Offices Paul, Hastings, Janofsky & Walker, L.A., 1984-85; air traffic control cons. Hughes Aircraft Co., Fullerton, Calif., 1985-88; engr., scientist space sta. div. McDonnell Douglas, Huntington Beach, Calif., 1989-90; ATC/ADGE sr. sys. engr. Hughes Aircraft Co., Fullerton, Calif., 1990-97; air traffic control automation specialist FAA, San Diego, 1997—; mem. citizens adv. com. Calif. Dept. Transp., Sacramento, 1982—. Author air traffic control tng. manuals, air def. manuals. Res. dep. sheriff Orange County, 1991—. With USNR, 1986—. Mem. Nat. Air Traffic Com. (nat. com.), Shelby Am. Auto Club, Human Factors Soc. (pres. Orange County chpt.). Republican. Avocations: sports cars, phys. fitness. Home: 32145 Camino Nunez Temecula CA 92592

KINSLOW, MARGIE ANN, volunteer worker; b. Salt Lake City, Dec. 7, 1931; d. Diamond and Sarah (Chipman) Wendelboe; m. James Ferol Kinslow, Apr. 6, 1954 (dec. July 1982). Student, U. Utah, 1949-53. Jr. vol. chmn. various hosps., Okla., Mont., Colo., 1967-87; pres. Ch. Woman's Orgn., Bartlesville, Okla., 1968; fin. advisor, jr. v.p., vol. chmn. Swedish Med. Ctr., Englewood, 1971-92; pres. Delta Gamma Alumnae, Denver, 1975-76; jr. vol. chair Colo. Assn. Hosp. Aux., Denver, 1977-82, 2d v.p., 1982-84; transp. chair, master class chmn. Rocky Mountain Regional Auditions, Met. Opera, Denver, 1986—; bd. dirs. Hoby Corp. Office vol. Rep. Office, Billings, Mont., 1969-70, Colo. Senator, Denver, 1974-76; vol. various polit. candidates, Denver, 1974-90; various offices Newcomers, Okla., Mont. and Colo., 1967-75. Mem. PEO, Gen. Fedn. of Women's Clubs (bd. dirs. 1994—, corr. sec. We. region), Colo. Fedn. of Women's Clubs (pres. 1994-96, various offices 1986-94), Denver Lyric Opera Guild, Cherry Creek Woman's Club (pres. 1985, Hoby corp. bd. 1997—), Littleton Rep. Women's Club, Delta Gamma Alumnae (pres. 1975-76, Stellar award 1979, Cable award 1991). Episcopalian. Avocations: bridge, travel, people, the arts.

KINSMAN, ROBERT PRESTON, biomedical plastics engineer; b. Cambridge, Mass., July 25, 1949; s. Fred Nelson and Myra Roxanne (Preston) K. BS in Plastics Engring., U. Mass., Lowell, 1971; MBA, Pepperdine U., Malibu, Calif., 1982. Cert. biomed. engr., Calif.; lic. real estate sales person, Calif. Product devel. engr., plastics divsn. Gen. Tire Corp., Lawrence, Mass., 1976-77; mfg. engr. Am. Edwards Labs. divsn. Am. Hosp. Supply Corp., Irvine, Calif., 1978-80, sr. engr., 1981-82; mfg. engring. mgr. Edwards Labs., Inc. subs. Am. Hosp. Supply Corp., Añasco, P.R., 1983; project mgr. Baxter Edwards Critical Care divsn. Baxter Healthcare Corp., Irvine, 1984-87, engring. and prodn. mgr., 1987-93; pres. Kinsman & Assocs., Irvine, Calif., 1993—; expert/auditor Med. Device Certification GmbH, Memmingen, Germany, 1995—; dir. engring. Cardiovascular Dynamics, Inc., Irvine, 1997—; dir. engring. Cardiovascular Dynamics, Inc., 1997—; mem. mgmt. adv. panel Modern Plastics mag., N.Y.C., 1979-80; elected Nat. Hon. Soc., 1967. Vol. worker VA, Bedford, Mass., 1967-71; instr. first aid ARC, N.D., Mass., Calif., 1971-82; pres., bd. dirs. Lakes Homeowners Assn., Irvine, 1985-91; chmn., bd. dirs., newsletter editor Paradise Park Owners Assn., Las Vegas, Nev., 1988—; bd. dirs. Orange County (Calif.) divsn. Am. Heart Assn., 1991—, chmn. devel. com., 1993-95, v.p. bd. dirs., 1993-94, chmn.-elect bd. dirs., 1994-95, chmn. bd. dirs., 1995-96, adv. coun. rep., 1994-96, immediate past chmn. bd. dirs., 1996-97, mem. nominating com., 1995—; mem. steering com. Heart and Sole Classic fundraiser, 1988—, event chmn., 1991-92, mem. devel. com. Calif. affiliate, 1993-95. Capt. USAF, 1971-75, USAFR, 1975-81. Recipient Cert. of Appreciation, VA, 1971, Am. Heart Assn., 1991-95, Outstanding Svc. award., 1996; selected Community Hero Torchbearer 1996 Olympic Games, United Way Am. and Atlanta Com. for Olympic Games. Baxter/Allegiance Found. Community Svc . grantee, Deerfield, Ill., 1992, 93. Mem. Soc. Plastics Engrs. (sr., Mem. of Month So. Calif. sect. 1989), Soc. Mfg. Engrs. (sr.), Am. Mgmt. Assn., Am. Soc. Quality, Arnold Air Soc. (comptr. 1969, pledge tng. officer 1970), Plastics Acad., Demolay, Profl. Ski Instrs. Am., Mensa, Am. Legion, Elks, Phi Gamma Psi. Avocations: skiing, scuba diving, marathon running, golfing, music. Office: Kinsman & Assocs 4790 Irvine Blvd Ste 105-289 Irvine CA 92620-1973

KINT, ARNE TONIS, industrial engineer, mechanical engineer; b. Tallinn, Harjumaa, Estonia, Nov. 2, 1932; came to U.S., 1957; s. Tônis Kint and Salme (Redlich) K.; m. Saima Kärp, Aug. 30, 1964. BS in Mech. Engring., Stockholm Tekniska Inst., 1954; BS in Indsl. Engring., Ga. Tech., 1960; MS in Indsl. Engring., U. Calif., 1963. Registered profl. indsl. engr., Calif.; cert. profl. materials handling and mgmt., Mich. Mech. engr. Philips Neon Co., Stockholm, 1954-57; student indsl. engr. Weirton (W. Va.) Steel Co., 1959; plant, foundry engr. H.C. Macaulay Foundry Co., Inc., Berkeley, Calif., 1960-67; indsl. engring. project leader Matson Navigation Co., San Francisco, 1967-69; area indsl. engr. Interpace Corp., Pitts., 1969-72; cons. indsl. engr. Oakland, Calif., 1972-73; work design, analysis supr. Truck Divsn. Internat. Harvester Co., Inc., San Leandro, Calif., 1973-75; sr. systems project engr. Engineered Sys. & Devel. Corp., Santa Clara and San Jose, Calif., 1975-89; cons. ind. engr. Applied Engring. and Design, Inc., San Jose, Calif., 1989-90; project engr. Jacobs Engring. Group, Martinez, Calif., 1990-92; cons. ind. engr. Indsl. Engring. USA, Oakland, Calif., 1992-98; cons. to pres. Fabricated Metals, Inc., San Leandro, Calif., 1998—. Bd. dirs. Estonian Info. Ctr., Stockholm, 1946-75; pres. Estonian League of Liberation, San Francisco, 1968-73. Decorated Gold Svc. medal Estonian Nat. Found., 1971. Mem. Estonian Soc. San Francisco (pres. 1962, 63), Swedish Am. C. of C., Estonian Ski Club. Avocations: skiing, boating, hunting, travel, fishing. Home: 312 Alta Vista Ave Oakland CA 94610-1941 Office: Fabricated Metals Inc 2401 Merced St San Leandro CA 94577-4286

KINTZER, FREDERICK C., educator, researcher; b. Peoria, Ill., Oct. 7, 1917; s. Arthur LeRoy and Elizabeth Kintzer; m. Ruth E. Lyle, May 1, 1942; children: Frederick C., Janis Coffman. BA, U. Wash., 1941; AM, Stanford U., 1947, EdD, 1952. Tchr. Stevenson (Wash.) Pub. Schs., 1941-42; asst. prof. Earlham Coll., Richmond, Ind., 1947-48; tchr. Centralia (Wash.) Jr. Coll., 1948-54, pres., 1954-58; pres. Olympic Coll., Bremerton, Wash., 1958-60; prof. UCLA, 1960-86; lectr. Nova Southeastern U., Ft. Lauderdale, Fla., 1972—. Author/editor 6 books; contbr. some 150 articles to profl. jours. Served with Signal Corps, U.S. Army, 1942-45. Fulbright sr. rsch. fellow, Ceylon, 1968-69, Kenya, 1986-87. Avocation: swimming. Home: 2050 Binns Ct San Luis Obispo CA 93401-4528

KIPPELEN, BERNARD, physicist, educator; b. Guebwiller, France, Mar. 12, 1963; came to U.S., 1991; s. Joseph and Aurelie (Kaiser) K.; m. Virginie Drujon, Aug. 13, 1994; 1 child, Clara. PhD, U. Pasteur, Strasbourg, France, 1990. Cert. in solid state physics, nonlinear optics. Rsch. asst. Nat. Ctr. Sci. Rsch., Strasbourg, 1990-91; rsch. asst. I Nat. Ctr. Sci. Rsch.-IPCMS, Strasbourg, 1993-94; asst. rsch. scientist U. Ariz., 1991-93, asst. rsch. prof., 1994—. Contbr. numerous articles to profl. jours. and conf. procs. Mem. Am. Phys. Soc., Material Rsch. Soc., Optical Soc. Am. Achievements include the development of highly efficient photorefractive polymers for photonics; research on nonlinear optical materials and optoelectronic devices; patent for photoreactive polymers. Office: Optical Scis Ctr U Ariz Tucson AZ 85721

KIPPUR, MERRIE MARGOLIN, lawyer; b. Denver, July 24, 1962; d. Morton Leonard and Bonnie (Seldin) Margolin; m. Bruce R. Kippur, Sept. 7, 1986. BA, Colo. Coll., 1983; JD, U. Colo., 1986. Bar: Colo. 1986, U.S. Dist. Ct. Colo. 1986, U.S. Ct. Appeals (10th cir.) 1987. Assoc. Sterling & Miller, Denver, 1985-88, McKenna & Cuneo, Denver, 1989-94; sr. v.p., gen. counsel, dir. First United Bank, Denver, 1994-96; prin. Merrie Margolin Kippur Assocs., PC, Denver, 1997—; lectr. in field. Author: Student Improvement in the 1980's, 1984; (with others) Ethical Considerations in Bankruptcy, 1985, Partnership Bankruptcy, 1986, Colorado Methods of Practise, 1988. Contract liaison Jr. League Denver, 1992-94; bd. dirs. Bylaws Parliamentarian, 1994-95, planning coun., 1995-96, nominating com., 1996-97, facilitator, 1996-97, facilitator co-chair, 1997-98, v.p. planning, 1998-99, exec. v.p. membership-tng., 1999—. Mem. ABA, Nat. Network Estate Planning Attys., Colo. Bar Assn., Denver Bar Assn., Gamma Phi Beta, Phi Delta Phi, Pi Gamma Mu. Democrat. Avocations: reading, scuba diving, wine collecting.

KIPROV, DOBRI DOBREV, immunology researcher; b. Sofia, Bulgaria, May 1, 1949; came to U.S., 1977; s. Dobri and Zvetana Kiprov; 1 child, Dobri Kiprov, Jr. MD, Med. Acad., Sofia, 1974. Resident in pathology Sackler Sch. Medicine, Tel Aviv, 1974-77, instr. pathology, 1975-77; resident in pathology Mt. Sinai Hosp., Cleve., 1977-79; clin. and research fellow Mass. Gen. Hosp., Boston, 1979-81; fellow in immunology and plasmapheresis Children's Hosp., San Francisco, 1981-82, dir. plasmapheresis unit, research immunologist, 1982-87; div. immunotherapy chief Calif. Pacific Med. Ctr., 1987—; cons. immunopathology Calif. Pacific Med. Ctr., San Francisco, 1982—; prof. U. Calif., San Francisco, 1984—; med. dir. Bay Area Mobile Apheresis Program; pres. Med. Visual Creations. Contbr. articles to profl. jours. Research grantee Myasthenia Gravis Found., 1982, 83, 84; recipient Tng. and Research award NIH, 1979-81. Mem. AAAS, AMA, Am. Soc. Clin. Pathologists, Am. Soc. Apheresis, Coll. of Am. Pathologists, World Med. Assn., Nat. Inst. Allergy and Infectious Diseases (spl. rev. com. 1985), Am. Soc. Apheresis (bd. dirs., editor newsletter). Avocations: snow and water skiing, windsurfing. Fax: 415-928-4642. Office: 2100 Webster St Ste 220 San Francisco CA 94115-2376

KIRBY, ORVILLE EDWARD, potter, painter, sculptor; b. Wichita, Kans., Jan. 31, 1912; s. Charlie and Elizabeth J. (Sage) K. Student, U. Utah, 1935-36, U. So. Calif., L.A., 1934-35, St. Paul Sch. Fine Art, 1933-34. Owner Orville Kirby Pottery, L.A., 1941-47; owner Sleepy Hollow Pottery, Laguna Beach, Calif., 1948-54, Monroe, Utah, 1955—. Republican. Mormon. Avocation: collecting old coins. Home and Office: 95 W Center St Monroe UT 84754-4159

KIRBY, TERRY, football player; b. Hampton, Va., Jan. 20, 1970. Running back San Francisco 49ers. Office: c/o San Francisco 49ers 4949 Centennial Blvd Santa Clara CA 95054-1229

KIRCH, PATRICK VINTON, anthropology educator, archaeologist; b. Honolulu, July 7, 1950; s. Harold William and Barbara Ver (MacGarvin) K.; m. Debra Connelly, Mar. 3, 1979 (div. 1990); m. Therese Babineau, Feb. 6, 1994. BA, U. Pa., 1971; MPhil, Yale U., 1974, PhD, 1975. Assoc. anthropologist Bishop Mus., Honolulu, 1975-76, anthropologist, 1976-82, head archaeology div., 1982-84, asst. chmn. anthropology, 1983-84; dir., assoc. prof. Burke Mus. U. Wash., Seattle, 1984-87, prof., 1987-89; prof. U. Calif., Berkeley, 1989—, prof. anthropology, endowed chair, 1994—; curator Hearst Mus. Anthropology, 1989—; adj. faculty U. Hawaii, Honolulu, 1979-84; mem. lasting legacy com. Wash. State Centennial Commn., 1986-88; pres. Soc. Hawaiian Archaeology, 1980-81. Author: The Anthropology of History in the Kingdom of Hawaii, 1992, Feathered Gods and Fishhooks, 1985, Evolution of the Polynesian Chiefdoms, 1984, The Wet and the Dry, 1994, The Lapita Peoples, 1996, Legacy of the Landscape, 1996; editor: Island Societies, 1986, Historical Ecology in the Pacific Islands, 1997; contbr. articles to profl. pubs. Recipient J.I. Staley prize in anthropology Sch. Am. Rsch., 1998; grantee NSF, 1974, 76, 77, 82, 87, 88, 89, 93, 96, 98, NEA, 1985, NEH, 1988, Hawaii Com. for Humanities, 1981, rsch. grantee Nat. Geog. Soc., 1986, 89, 96; fellow Ctr. for Advanced Study in Behavioral Scis., 1997-98. Fellow AAAS, NAS (John J. Carty medal for the advancement of sci. 1997), Am. Acad. Arts and Scis., Am. Anthrop. Assn., Am. Philos. Soc., Calif. Acad. Scis.; mem. Assn. Field Archaeology, Polynesian Soc., Sigma Xi. Democrat. Avocation: cross country skiing. Office: U Calif Dept Anthropology 232 Kroeber Hall Berkeley CA 94720-3710

KIRGO, GEORGE, screenwriter; b. Hartford, Conn., Mar. 26, 1926; s. Isadore and Anna (Gordon) K.; m. Carol Newell, 1949 (dec. 1986); children: Julia Gordon, Diana St. Clair, Nicholas Newell; m. Angela Wales, 1989. Student, Wesleyan U., 1943, 46-47. Writer NBC-TV, N.Y.C., 1956-58; ind. screenwriter, 1965—. Author: Hercules, The Big Greek Story, 1958, How to Write Ten Different Best Sellers Now in Your Spare Time and Become the First Author on Your Block Unless There's an Author Already Living on Your Block in Which Case You'll Become the Second Author on Your Block and That's Okay Too and Other Stories, 1960; screenwriter: (films) Red Line 7000, 1965, Spinout, 1966, Don't Make Waves, 1967, Voices, 1973, No Room to Run, 1976, (TV films) Get Christie Love, 1973, Brenda Starr, 1975, Topper, 1979, Angel on My Shoulder, 1980, The Kid With the Broken Halo, 1981, The Kid With the 200 I.Q., 1982, My Palikari, 1982, (with Max Shulman) This Can't Be Love, 1988. Served to tech. sgt. USAAF, 1943-46, PTO. Mem. Writers Guild Am. West (pres. 1987-91), Writers Guild Found. (trustee 1985—, v.p. 1994—), Nat. Acad. Motion Picture Arts and Scis., P.E.N. Ctr. West (Pres.'s award 1988), Nat. Film Preservation Bd. Office: Writers Guild Am W 7000 W 3rd St Los Angeles CA 90048-4329

KIRK, CARMEN ZETLER, data processing executive; b. Altoona, Pa., May 22, 1941; d. Paul Alan and Mary Evelyn (Pearce) Zetler. BA, Pa. State U., 1959-63; MBA, St. Mary's Coll. Calif., 1977. Cert. in data processing. Pub. sch. tchr. State Ga., 1965-66; systems analyst U.S. Govt. Dept. Army, Oakland, Calif., 1967-70; programmer analyst Contra Costa County, Martinez, Calif., 1970-76; applications mgr. Stanford (Calif.) U., 1976-79; pres. Zetler Assocs., Inc., Palo Alto, Calif., 1979—; cons. State Calif., Sacramento, 1985-88. Office: Zetler Assocs Inc PO Box 50395 Palo Alto CA 94303-0395

KIRK, CASSIUS LAMB, JR., lawyer, investor; b. Bozeman, Mont., June 8, 1929; s. Cassius Lamb and Gertrude Violet (McCarthy) K.; AB, Stanford U., 1951; JD, U. Calif., Berkeley, 1954. Bar: Calif. 1955. Assoc. firm Cooley, Godward, Castro, Huddleson & Tatum, San Francisco, 1956-60; staff counsel for bus. affairs Stanford U., 1960-78; chief bus. officer, staff counsel Menlo Sch. and Coll., Atherton, Calif., 1978-81; chmn. Eberli-Kirk Properties, Inc. (doing bus. as Just Closets), Menlo Park, 1981-94; mem. summer faculty Coll. Bus. Adminstrn. U. Calif., Santa Barbara, 1967-73; past mem. adv. bd. Allied Arts Guild, Menlo Park; past nat. vice chmn. Stanford U. Annual Fund; past v.p. Palo Alto C. of C. With U.S. Army, 1954-56. Mem. VFW, Stanford Faculty Club, Order of Coif, Phi Alpha Delta. Republican. Home and Office: 1330 University Dr Apt 52 Menlo Park CA 94025-4241

KIRK, REA HELENE (REA HELENE GLAZER), special education educator; b. N.Y.C., Nov. 17, 1944; d. Benjamin and Lillian (Kellis) Glazer; 3 stepdaughters. BA, UCLA, 1966; MA, Eastern Mont. Coll., 1981; EdD U. So. Calif., 1995. Life cert. spl. edn. tchr., Calif., Mont. Spl. edn. tchr., L.A., 1966-73; clin. sec. speech and lang. clinic, Missoula, Mont., 1973-75; spl. edn. tchr., Missoula and Gt. Falls, Mont., 1975-82; br. mgr. YWCA of L.A., Beverly Hills, Calif., 1989-91; sch. adminstrn., ednl. coord. Adv. Schs. of Calif., 1991-94; dir. Woman's Resource Ctr., Gt. Falls, Mont., 1981-82; dir. Battered Woman's Shelter, Rock Springs, Wyo., 1982-84; dir. Battered Victims Program Sweetwater County, Wyo., 1984-88, Battered Woman's Program, San Gabriel Valley, Calif., 1988, Spl. Edn., Pasadena, 1994-96, prin., 1995; asst. prof. U. Wis., Platteville, 1996—; mem. Wyo. Commn. on Aging, Rock Springs; mem. Community Action Bd. City of L.A. Pres., bd. dirs. battered woman's shelter, Gt. Falls, Woman's Resource Ctr., Gt. Falls; founder, advisor Rape Action Line, Gt. Falls; founder Jewish religious svcs., Missoula; 4-H leader; hostess Friendship Force; Friendship Force ambassador, Wyo., Fed. Republic Germany, Italy; mem. YWCA Mont. and Wyo. Recipient Gladys Byron scholar U. So. Calif., 1993, Dept. Edn. scholar U. So. Calif., 1994, honors Missoula 4-H; recognized as significant Wyo. woman as social justice reformer and peace activist Sweetwater County, Wyo.; nominated Wyo. Woman of the Yr., 1981, 82; honored by L.A. Mayor Bradley for Anti-Poverty work. Mem. Council for Exceptional Children (v.p. Gt. Falls 1981-82, Professionally Recognized Spl. Educator 1998), Assn. for Children with Learning Disabilities (Named Oustanding Mem. 1982), Phi Delta Kappa, Delta Kappa Gamma, Psi Chi, Pi Lamda Theta. Democrat. Jewish.

KIRKBRIDE, MAX VERLYN, retired career officer; b. Ravenwood, Mo., May 15, 1916; s. John Wesley and Grace Elnora (Ross) K.; m. Martha Charlene Beedle, Apr. 20, 1946 (dec. July, 1979); 1 child, Max Verlyn Jr. BS, N.W. Mo. State U., 1940; grad., Command and Gen. Staff Coll., Ft. Leavenworth, Kans., 1946, Armed Forces Staff Coll., Norfolk, Va., 1955, U.S. Army War Coll., Carlisle Barracks, Pa., 1960. Commd. 2d lt. U.S. Army, 1940, advanced through grades to col., 1955, ret., 1971; dir. clerical sch., Armed Forces Sch., Ft. Knox, Ky., 1940-43; dep. G1 and G1 (pers.) Hdqs XX Corps U.S. Army ETO, 1943-46; advisor; U.S. Mil. Mission to Iran, Teheran, 1948-50; battalion and regimental cmmdr. 1st cavalry divsn. U.S. Army, Korea, Japan, 1953-55; chief of staff No. Area Command, Frankfurt, Germany, 1960-63; dir. Standards & Systems Office, Pentagon Washington, D.C., 1963-66; dep. J5 and J5 (long range plans) U.S. Mil. Assistance Command, Saigon, Vietnam, 1966-67; prof. mil. sci. U. Calif., Davis, 1967-71; v.p. Rancho Bernardo Sr. Svcs., San Diego, Calif., 1974—; sec., bd. dirs. Oaks No. Mgmt. Corp. 2, San Diego, 1988—. Co-author (text book) Military Correspondence, 1940; supr. (reference book) Military Personnel, 1965. V.p. Rancho Bernardo Newcomers Club, San Diego, 1973, pres. Rancho Bernardo Newcomers Alumni, Inc. 1975; dir. tax counseling for the elderly, San Diego, 1976-92. Decorated Bronze Star medal, 1945, U.S. Army, Legion of Merit, 1966, 67, 71, Army Commendation medal; recipient U. Calif. medal, 1971. Republican. Home: 13032 Paseo Del Verano San Diego CA 92128

KIRKHOFF, JOHN LOUIS, writer, educator; b. Indpls., July 24, 1923; s. Louis and Ruth Elizabeth (Cunningham) K.; m. Jo Ann Brown, Apr. 9, 1949; children: Kim, Kay. BA, Butler U., 1949; MA, U. So. Calif., 1954. Mgr., supr. Rockwell Internat. Corp., Anaheim, L.A., 1959-81; maj. Northrup Corp., Pico, Rivera, Calif., 1981-89; cons. Douglas Aircraft, Long Beach, Calif., 1989-90; ind. writer San Diego, 1990-97; prof. Ctrl. Tex. Coll., San Diego, 1997—; mgmt. cons. William Black and Assocs., San Diego, 1996-97. Author: A Corner of Time, 1992, (poetry chapbook) Of Time & Flight, 1991, B-2 Bomber, 1993. With U.S. Army, 1942-46. Mem. VFW, Kiwanis (sec., v.p. Los Rancheros br. 1990—). Avocations: tennis, golf, walking. Home: 18211 Verano Dr San Diego CA 92128-1238

KIRKLAND, BERTHA THERESA, project engineer; b. San Francisco; d. Lawrence and Theresa (Kanzler) Schmelzer; m. Thornton C. Kirkland, Jr., Dec. 27, 1937 (dec. July 1971); children: Kathryn Elizabeth, Francis Charles. Ed. pub. schs., Calif. Supr. hosp. ops. Am. Potash & Chem. Corp., Trona, Calif., 1953-54; office mgr., estimator T.C. Kirkland Elect. Contractor, San Bernardino, Calif., 1954-58, estimator, sec./treas., bd. dir., 1958-74; estimator design-installation engr. Add-M Electric, Inc., San Bernardino, 1972-82, v.p., 1974-82; estimator, engr. Corona (Calif.) Indsl. Electric, Inc., 1982-83; project engr. Fischbach & Moore, Inc., L.A., 1984-91; project engr. cons. Fischbach & Moor, Inc., L.A., 1993-94. Mem. Arrowhead Country Club. Episcopalian. Home: 526 Sonora Dr San Bernardino CA 92404-1762

KIRKORIAN, DONALD GEORGE, college official, management consultant; b. San Mateo, Calif., Nov. 30, 1938; s. George and Alice (Sergius) K. BA, San Jose State U., 1961, MA, 1966, postgrad., 1968; postgrad., Stanford U., 1961, U. So. Calif., 1966; PhD, Northwestern U., 1972. Producer Sta. KNTV, San Jose, Calif., 1961; tchr. L.A. City Schs., 1963; instrnl. TV coord. Fremont Union High Sch. Dist., Sunnyvale, Calif., 1963-73; assoc. dean instrn. learning resources Solano C.C., Suisun City, Calif., 1973-85, dean instrnl. services, 1985-89, dean learning resources and staff devel., 1989-99; exec. dir. Learning Resources Assn. of Calif. Cmty. Colls., 1976—; owner, pres. Kirkorian and Assocs., Suisun City; field cons. Nat. Assn. Edn. Broadcasters, 1966-68; adj. faculty San Jose State U., 1968-69, U. Calif., Santa Cruz, 1970-73, U. Calif., Davis, 1973-76; chmn. Bay Area TV

Consortium, 1976-77, 86-87; mem. adv. panel Speech Comm. Assn./Am. Theater Assn. tchr. preparation in speech., comm., theater and media, N.Y.C., 1973-77. Author: Staffing Information Handbook, 1990, National Learning Resources Directory, 1991, 93; editor: Media Memo, 1973-80, Intercom: The Newsletter for Calif. Community Coll. Librs., 1974-75, Update, 1980-90, Exploring the Benicia State Recreation Area, 1977, California History Resource Materials, 1977, Time Management, 1980; contbr. articles to profl. jours. Chmn. Solano County Media Adv. Com., 1974-76; bd. dirs. Napa-Solano United Way, 1980-82; mem. adv. bd. Calif. Youth Authority, 1986-93. Mem. Nat. Assn. Ednl. Broadcasters, Assn. for Edn. Comm. and Tech., Broadcast Edn. Assn., Calif. Assn. Ednl. Media and Tech. (treas.), Western Ednl. Soc. for Telecomm. (bd. dirs. 1973-75, pres. 1976-77, State Chancellor's com. on Telecomm. 1982-86), Learning Resources Assn. Calif. Comm. Colls. (sec.-treas., pres.), Assn. Calif. C.C. Adminstrs. (bd. dirs. 1985-91), Cmty. Coll. Instrnl. Network. Home: 1655 Rockville Rd Suisun City CA 94585-1373 Office: PO Box 298 Fairfield CA 94533-0029

KIRKPATRICK, DAVID PAUL, feature film producer; b. Ohio, June 29, 1951; s. Joseph and Jean (Lude) K. BA, Calif. Inst. Arts, Valencia, 1974. Reader Paramount Pictures, L.A., 1978; pres. prodn. Walt Disney Pictures/Touchstone Pictures, Burbank, Calif., 1987-88; pres. motion picture group Paramount Pictures, 1989-91, prodr., 1991-93; prodr. Rysher Entertainment, Santa Monica, Calif., 1994-97, Original Voices, Santa Monica, 1997—. Supporter Friends of the L.A. Free Clinic. Mem. Acad. Motion Picture Arts & Scis., Prodrs. Guild Am. Roman Catholic. Office: Original Voices 3000 Olympic Blvd Ste 1463 Santa Monica CA 90404-5073

KIRKPATRICK, RICHARD ALAN, internist; b. Rochester, Minn., Jan. 17, 1947; s. Neal R. and Ethel C. (Hull) K.; m. Susan Baxter; children: James N., Ronald S., David B., Mary J., Scott B., Christina Marie. BA in Chemistry with honors, U. Wash., 1968, BS in Psychology, 1968, MD, 1972. Diplomate Am. Bd. Internal Medicine. Intern, resident in internal medicine Mayo Grad. Sch., Rochester, 1972-76, spl. resident in biomed. communications, 1974-75; pvt. practice specializing in internal medicine Longview, Wash., 1976—; founding ptnr. Internal Medicine Clinic of Longview, 1977, Kirkpatrick Family Care, Longview, 1996; mem. clin. faculty U. Wash.; dir. cardiac rehab. program St. John's Hosp.; sec. The Physicians Alliance. Editor: Drug Therapy Abstracts, Wash. Internists; mem. editorial adv. bd. Your Patient and Cancer, Primary Care and Cancer; weekly med. TV talk show host, 1978—; contbr. articles to med. jours. Bd. dirs., v.p. Columbia Theatre for Performing Arts; mem. City Coun., Longview; mem. S.W. Wash. Symphony; bd. dirs. S.W. Wash. Youth Symphony; pres., bd. dirs. Sta. KLTV. Named to Hall of Fame, Lower Columbia Coll., 1996. Fellow ACP (gov.'s coun., sec. Washington chpt.); mem. Wash. State Soc. Internal Medicine (trustee, past pres.), Am. Geriatrics Soc., Am. Soc. Echocardiography, Am. Soc. Internal Medicine, Wash. Med. Assn. (mem. com.), Am. Cancer Soc. (local bd. dirs.), Am. Soc. Clin. Oncology, AMA, Am. Med. Writers Assn. Office: Washington Way at Civic Ctr Longview WA 98632

KIRSCHNER, RICHARD MICHAEL, naturopathic physician, speaker, author; b. Cin., Sept. 27, 1949; s. Alan George and Lois (Dickey) K.; 1 child, Aden Netanya; m. Lindea Bowe. BS in Human Biology, Kans. Newman Coll., 1979; D in Naturopathic Medicine, Nat. Coll. Naturopathic Medicine, 1981. Vice pres. D. Kirschner & Son, Inc., Newport, Ky., 1974-77; co-owner, mgr. Sunshine Ranch Arabian Horses, Melbourne, Ky., 1975-77; pvt. practice Portland, Oreg., 1981-83, Ashland, Oreg., 1983—; seminar leader, trainer Inst. for Meta-Linguistics, Portland, 1981-84; cons. Nat. Elec. Contractors Assn., So. Oreg., 1985-86, United Telephone N.W., 1986; spkr. Ford Motor Co., Blue Cross-Blue Shield, Balfour Corp., NEA, AT&T, Triad Sys., Supercuts, 1986-89, Hewlett-Packard, Pepsi Co., George Bush Co., 1990-91, Goodwill Industries Am., Motorola, 1992, The Homestead T.V.A., Federated Ambulatory Surg. Assn., V.H.A. Satellite Broadcast, 1993, Oreg. Dept. Edn., Anaheim Meml. Hosp., 1994, Inc. 500 Conf., U.S. C. of C., Inst. Indsl. Engrs., 1995, EDS, ASFSA, Safeco Ins., Fairfax County, Va.; spkr., trainer Careertrack Seminars, Boulder, Colo., 1986-93; owner, spkr., trainer R & R Prodns., Ashland, Oreg., 1984—. Co-author: audio tape seminar How to Deal with Difficult People, 1987, video tape seminar, 1988, interactive CD-Rom The Leadership Series: Difficult People, 1997, others; author: (audio tape seminar) How to Find and Keep a Mate, 1988, (videotape seminar) How to Find a Mate, 1990, The Happiness of Pursuit, 1994, (videotape seminar) How to Deal with Difficult People, Vol. II, 1992, (book) Dealing With People You Can't Stand, 1994, Digital Publishing on e World, Discussions of Problem People and Happiness, 1995, (7 vol. video series) Telecare: Exceptional Service on the Phone, 1998. Spokesman Rogue Valley PBS, 1986, 87. Mem. Am. Assn. Naturopathic Physicians (bd. dirs., chmn. pub. affairs 1989-93, bd. dirs. 1995—, Webmaster, 1996-98), Wilderness Soc., Internat. Platform Assn. Republican. Office: R&R Prodns PO Box 896 Ashland OR 97520-0030

KIRSHBAUM, HOWARD M., judge, arbitrator; b. Oberlin, Ohio, Sept. 19, 1938; s. Joseph and Gertrude (Morris) K.; m. Priscilla Joy Parmakian, Aug. 15, 1964; children—Audra Lee, Andrew William. B.A., Yale U., 1960; A.B., Cambridge U., 1962, M.A., 1966; LL.B., Harvard U., 1965. Ptnr. Zarlengo and Kirshbaum, Denver, 1969-75; judge Denver Dist. Ct., Denver, 1975-80, Colo. Ct. Appeals, Denver, 1980-83; justice Colo. Supreme Ct., Denver, 1983-97; arbiter Jud. Arbiter Group, Inc., Denver, 1997—, sr. judge, 1997—; adj. prof. law U. Denver, 1970—; dir. Am. Law Inst. Phila., Am. Judicature Soc., Chgo., Colo. Jud. Inst. Denver, 1979-89; pres. Colo. Legal Care Soc., Denver, 1974-75. Bd. dirs. Young Artists Orch., Denver, 1976-85; pres. Community Arts Symphony, Englewood, Colo., 1972-74; dir. Denver Opportunity, Inc., Denver, 1972-74; vice-chmn. Denver Council on Arts and Humanities, 1969. Mem. ABA (standing com. pub. edn.), Colo. Bar Assn., Denver Bar Assn. (trustee 1981-83), Soc. Profls. in Dispute Resolution. Avocations: music performance; tennis. Office: Jud Arbiter Group Inc 1601 Blake St Ste 400 Denver CO 80202-1328

KIRWIN, ANDREW DEAN, protective services official; b. Albuquerque, Apr. 22, 1964; s. Robert Francis Kirwin and Barbara Jane Cooper; m. Wendy Ann Tomas, Aug. 27, 1988 (div. Dec. 1993); m. Deborah Ellen West, Feb. 14, 1996; 1 child, Daniel Alexander. Student, U. Colo., Denver, 1995—. Cert. paramedic, Colo.; cert. fire officer I, Colo., cert. pub. safety diver, dive rescue specialist Dive Rescue Internat. Firefighter Castlewood Fire Dept., Englewood, Colo., 1987-90; paramedic Castlewood Fire Dept., Englewood, 1990-96, lt., 1996—; chair Metro Dive Team, Denver, 1994—; comdr. Castlewood Dive Rescue Team, Englewood, 1994—; cons. Neighborhood Planning, 1998. Vol. 9 Health Fair, Denver, 1983-90; coll. organizer Perot for Pres. (Colo.), Denver, 1992; active Greater Park Hill Cmty., Inc., Denver, 1995— (co-chair edn. com.); rschr. Norton for Senate Campaign, Denver, 1996; grant reviewer Undergraduate Rsch. Opportunities Program U. Colo. Denver, 1998. Undergrad. Rsch. Opportunities Program grantee, U. Colo., Denver, 1997. Mem. Internat. Assn. Firefighters (sec. 1989—), Internat. Assn. Dive Rescue Specialists, Human Factors and Ergonomics Soc., Divers Alert Network, Golden Key Nat. Honor Soc. Avocations: sailing, SCUBA, photography. E-mail: akirwin@uswest.net. Home: 2572 Eudora St Denver CO 80207 Office: Castlewood Fire Dept 7900 E Berry Pl Englewood CO 80111

KISER, NAGIKO SATO, retired librarian; b. Taipei, Republic of China, Aug. 7, 1923; came to U.S., 1950; d. Takeichi and Kinue (Sōma) Sato; m. Virgil Kiser, Dec. 4, 1979 (dec. Mar. 1981). Secondary teaching credential, Tsuda Coll., Tokyo, 1945; BA in Journalism, Trinity U., 1953; BFA, Ohio State U., 1956, MA in Art History, 1959; MLS, cert. in library media, SUNY, Albany, 1974. Cert. community coll. librarian, Calif., cert. jr. coll. tchr., Calif., cert. secondary edn. tchr., Calif., cert. tchr. library media specialist and art, N.Y. Pub. rels. reporter The Mainichi Newspapers, Osaka, Japan, 1945-50; contract interpreter U.S. Dept. State, Washington, 1956-58, 66-67; resource specialist Richmond (Calif.) Unified Sch. Dist., 1968-69; editing supr. CTB/McGraw-Hill, Monterey, Calif., 1969-71; multimedia specialist Monterey Peninsula Unified Sch. Dist., 1975-77; librarian Nishimachi Internat. Sch., Tokyo, 1979-80, Sacramento City Unified Sch. Dist., 1977-79, 81-85; sr. librarian Camarillo (Calif.) State Hosp. and Devel. Ctr., 1985-93. Author: Short Form Test of Academic Aptitude, 1970, Prescriptive Mathematics Inventory, 1970, Tests of Basic Experience, 1970. Mem. Calif. State Supt.'s Regional Coun. on Asian Pacific Affairs, Sacramento, 1984-91. Library Media Specialist Tng. Program scholar U.S. Office Edn., 1974. Fellow Internat. Biog. Assn. (life); mem. ALA, Am. Biog. Inst. (life, dep. gov. 1988—), Claif. Libr. Assn., Med. Libr. Assn., Asunaro Shogai Kyoiku Kondankai (Lifetime Edn. Promoting Assn., Japan), The Mus. Soc., Internat. House of Japan, Matsuyama Sacramento Sister City Corp., Japanese Am. Citizens League, UN Assn. U.S., Ikenobo Ikebana Soc. Am., L.A. Hototogisu Haiku Assn., Ventura County Archeol. Soc., Internat. Platform Assn., Internat. Soc. Poets. Mem. Christian Science Ch. Avocations: flower arranging, ballroom dance, classical music. Office: Camarillo State Hosp & Devel Ctr Profl Libr PO Box 6022 Camarillo CA 93011-6022

KISER, ROBERTA KATHERINE, medical records administrator, education educator; b. Alton, Ill., Aug. 13, 1938; d. Stephen Robert and Virginia Elizabeth (Lasher) Golden; m. James Robert Crisman, sept. 6, 1958 (div. May 1971); 1 child, Robert Glenn; m. James Earl Kiser, Dec. 19, 1971; 1 child, James Jacob. BEd, So. Ill. U., 1960. Cert. tchr., Ill., Calif. Librarian Oaklawn (Ill.) Elem. Sch., 1960-62, Alsip (Ill.) Elem. Sch., 1966-69; tchr. Desert Sands Unified Sch. Dist., Indio, Calif., 1969-79; prin. Mothercare Infant Sch., Rancho Mirage, Calif., 1980-89; substitute tchr. Greater Coachella Valley Sch., Calif., 1989-91; med. acct. Desert Health Care, Bermuda Dunes, Calif., 1990-92; mentor tchr., computing, typing skills Wilde Woode Children's Ctr., Palm Springs, Calif., 1990-92; chiropractic asst. Rapp Chiropractic Health Ctr, Palm Desert, Calif., 1992-93; sr. med. records clk. Eisenhower Med. Ctr., Rancho Mirage, 1993—. V.p. Palm Desert (Calif.) Community Ch. Montessori Sch. Bd., 1982-85. Republican. Avocation: handbell ensemble musician. Home: 39-575 Keenan Dr Rancho Mirage CA 92270-3610 Office: Eisenhower Med Ctr 39000 Bob Hope Dr Rancho Mirage CA 92270-3221

KISSNER, CHARLES D., electrical company executive. Chmn., pres., CEO Digital Microwave, San Jose, Calif. Office: Digital Microwave 170 Rose Orchard Way San Jose CA 95134-1396*

KITADA, SHINICHI, biochemist; b. Osaka, Japan, Dec. 9, 1948; came to U.S., 1975; s. Koichi and Asako Kitada. MD, Kyoto U., 1973; MS in Biol. Chemistry, UCLA, 1977, PhD, 1979. Intern Kyoto U. Hosp., Japan, 1973-74; resident physician Chest Disease Research Inst., 1974-75; rsch. scholar lab. nuclear medicine and radiation biology UCLA, 1979-87, rsch. scholar Jules Stein Eye Inst., 1988-91; rsch. biochemist La Jolla (Calif.) Cancer Rsch. Found., 1992—. Author papers in field. Japan Soc. Promotion Sci. fellow 1975-76. Mem. Am. Oil Chemists Soc., N.Y. Acad. Scis., Sigma Xi. Home: 920 Kline St Ste 301 La Jolla CA 92037-4320 Office: The Burnham Inst 10901 N Torrey Pines Rd La Jolla CA 92037-1062

KITELEY, BRIAN ALAN, English literature educator, writer; b. Mpls., Minn., Sept. 26, 1956; s. Murray James and Jean (Vette) K.; m. Cynthia Coburn, Aug. 27, 1991. BA, Carleton Coll., 1978; MA, CCNY, 1985. Lectr. Am. U. Cairo, 1987-89; asst. prof. Ohio U., Athens, 1992-94, U. Colo., Denver, 1994—. Author: Still Life with Insects, 1989, I Know Many Songs, But I Cannot Sing, 1996. Recipient Nat. Endowment Arts, 1991, Guggenheim Fellowship, 1992, Whiting Found. Writers award, 1996. Office: U Denver English Dept Pioneer Hall Denver CO 80208

KITTO, FRANKLIN CURTIS, computer systems specialist; b. Salt Lake City, Nov. 18, 1954; s. Curtis Eugene and Margaret (Ipson) K.; m. Collette Madsen, Sept. 16, 1982; children: Melissa Erin, Heather Elise, Stephen Curtis. BA, Brigham Young U., 1978, MA, 1980. Tv sta. operator Sta. KBYU-TV, Provo, Utah, 1973-78; grad. teaching asst. Brigham Young Univ., 1978-80; cable TV system operator Instructional Media U. Utah, Salt Lake City, 1980-82, data processing mgr., 1982-83, media supr., 1983-85, bus. mgr., 1985-87; dir. computer systems tng. MegaWest Systems, Inc., Salt Lake City, 1987-90, dir. new product devel., 1990-91, mgr. tng. and installation, 1991-93, mgr. rsch. and devel., 1993; tng. and installation mgr. Total Solutions, American Fork, Utah, 1993-95, tng., support and installation mgr., 1995; EDI programmer Megawest Systems, Inc., Salt Lake City, 1996; EDI supervisor Megawest Systems, Inc., Midvale, Utah, 1996—. Recipient Kiwanis Freedom Leadership award, Salt Lake City, 1970, Golden Microphone award Brigham Young U., 1978. Mem. Assn. Ednl. Communications and Tech., Utah Pick Users Group (sec. 1983-87, pres. 1987-89, treas. 1989-90), Am. Soc. Tng. and Devel., Assn. for Computer Tng. and Support, Phi Eta Sigma, Kappa Tau Alpha. Mormon. Home: 10931 S Avila Dr Sandy UT 84094-5965 Office: Mega West Sys Inc 6975 Union Park Ctr Ste 500 Midvale UT 84047-6026

KITZHABER, JOHN ALBERT, governor, physician, former state senator; b. Colfax, Wash., Mar. 5, 1947; s. Albert Raymond and Annabel Reed (Wetzel) K. BA, Dartmouth Coll., 1969; MD, U. Oreg., 1973. Intern Gen. Rose Meml. Hosp., Denver, 1976-77; Emergency physician Mercy Hosp., Roseburg, Oreg., 1974-75; mem. Oreg. Ho. of Reps., 1979-81; mem. Oreg. Senate, 1981-95, pres., 1985, 87, 89, 91; gov. State of Oregon, 1995—; assoc. prof. Oreg. Health Sci. U., 1986—. Mem. Am. Coll. Emergency Physicians, Douglas County Med. Soc., Physicians for Social Responsibility, Am. Council Young Polit. Leaders, Oreg. Trout. Democrat. Office: Office of the Gov State Capitol Bldg Rm 254 Salem OR 97310*

KIVELSON, MARGARET GALLAND, physicist; b. N.Y.C., Oct. 21, 1928; d. Walter Isaac and Madeleine (Wiener) Galland; m. Daniel Kivelson, Aug. 15, 1949; children: Steven Allan, Valerie Ann. AB, Radcliffe Coll., 1950, AM, 1951, PhD, 1957. Cons. Rand Corp., Santa Monica, Calif., 1956-69; asst. to geophysicist UCLA, 1967-83, prof., 1983—, also chmn. dept. earth and space scis., 1984-87; prin. investigator of magnetometer, Galileo Mission, Jet Propulsion Lab., Pasadena, Calif., 1977—; overseer Harvard Coll., 1977-83; mem. adv. coun. NASA, 1987-93; chair atmospheric adv. com. NSF, 1986-89, Com. Solar and Space Physics, 1977-86, com. planetary exploration, 1986-87, com. solar terrestial phys., 1989-92; mem. adv. com. geoscis. NSF. Editor: The Solar System: Observations and Interpretations, 1986; co-editor: Introduction to Space Physics, 1995; contbr. articles to profl. jours. Named Woman of Yr., L.A. Mus. Sci. and Industry, 1979, Woman of Sci., UCLA, 1984; recipient Grad. Soc. medal Radcliffe Coll., 1983, 350th Anniversary Alumni medal Harvard U. Fellow AAAS, Am. Geophysics Union, Am. Acad. Arts and Scis.; mem. Am. Phys. Soc., Am. Astron. Soc., Internat. Inst. Astronautics (corr. mem.). Office: UCLA Dept Earth & Space Scis 6847 Slichter Los Angeles CA 90095-1567

KIYOTA, HEIDE P., psychologist; b. Bamberg, Germany, June 6, 1942; came to U.S., 1970; m. Ronald Kiyota; children: Heather, Catherine, Michelle. Student, U. South Africa, 1970-73, NYU, 1973; BS in Psychology, U. Md., 1975; MA, U. Md., Balt., 1979; PhD in Clin. Psychology, U. Hawaii, 1986. Rsch. asst. Dr. H.E. Kaiser, Balt., 1970-76; counselor Regional Inst. for Children and Adolescents, Balt., 1976-77; tchg. asst. dept. psychology U. Md., Balt., 1976-77; supr. multiple offender alcoholism program Balt. City Hosps., 1977-80; rsch. asst. Youth Devel. and Rsch. Ctr. U. Hawaii at Manoa, Honolulu, 1980-83; psychology asst. Kukulu Kumuhana Project, Honolulu, 1981-82; psychologist asst. Dept. Edn./Spl. Edn., Honolulu, 1982; intern in clin. psychology dept. medicine and surgery VA, Honolulu, 1983-84; clin. psychologist Kalihi Palama Counseling Svcs., Honolulu, 1987-89; pvt. practice Mililani, Hawaii, 1988—; presenter convs. in field. Mem. APA, Hawaii Psychol. Assn., Phi Kappa Phi. Home: 1812 Nahenahe Pl Wahiawa HI 96786-2627 Office: 95-390 Kuahelani Ave Ste 2F Mililani HI 96789-1182

KIZZIAR, JANET WRIGHT, psychologist, author, lecturer; b. Independence, Kans.; d. John L. and Thelma (Rooks) Wright; m. Mark Kizziar. BA, U. Tulsa, 1961, MA, 1964, EdD, 1969. Sch. psychologist Tulsa Pub. Schs.; pvt. practice psychology Tulsa, 1969-78, Bartlesville, Okla., 1978-88; lectr. univs., corps., health spas, 1989—. Co-host: Psychologists' Corner program, Sta. KOTV, Tulsa.; author: (with Judy W. Hagedorn) Gemini: The Psychology and Phenomena of Twins, 1975, Search for Acceptance: The Adolescent and Self Esteem, 1979. Sponsor Youth Crisis Intervention Telephone Center, 1972-74; bd. dirs. March of Dimes, Child Protection Team, Women and Children in Crisis, United Fund, YMCA Fund, Mental Health of Washington County, Alternative H.S.; edn. dir. appt. Gov.'s Commn. on Violence Against Women, Pub. Awarness Com., 1990, Women's Found. Fresh Start, 1993. Named Disting. Alumni U. Tulsa, Outstanding Young Woman of Okla. Mem. APA, NOW, Internat. Twins Assn. (pres. 1976-77). Home: 9427 N 87th Way Scottsdale AZ 85258-1913 Office: PO Box 5227 Scottsdale AZ 85261-5227

KLAHR, GARY PETER, lawyer; b. N.Y.C., July 9, 1942; s. Fred and Frieda (Garson) K. Student Ariz. State U., 1958-61; LL.B. with high honors, U. Ariz., 1964. Bar: Ariz. 1967, U.S. Dist. Ct. Ariz. 1967. Assoc., Brazlin & Greene, Phoenix, 1967-68; sr. ptnr. Gary Peter Klahr, P.C., Phoenix, 1968—. Mem. Phoenix City Council, 1974-76; mem. CODAMA, bd. dirs., 1975-89, pres. 1980-81; mem. City Lic. Appeals Bd., 1987-96; vice-chmn, 1988-92, chmn., 1993-96; bd. dirs. 7th Step Found., 1978-84, pres. 1980-82; bd. dirs. Tumbleweed Runaway Center, 1972-76; chmn. Citizens Criminal Justice Comn., 1977-78; co-chmn. delinquency subcom. Phoenix Forward Task Force; vol. Juvenile Ct. referee, 1969; vol. adult probation officer; vol. counselor for Dept. Corrections youth programs, Phoenix; ex-officio mem., spl. cons. Phoenix Youth Commn.; mem. citizen adv. council Phoenix Union H.S. Dist., 1985-90, 95—, co-chmn. 1998—, elected governing bd., 1991-95, v.p., 1992-94; review bd. Phoenix Police Dept., 1985-94; bd. dirs. Metro Youth Ctr., 1986-87; bd. dirs. Svc./Employment/Redevel. (SER) Jobs for Progress, Phoenix, 1985-90, pres., 1986-87, East McDowell Youth Assn., 1992-94; v.p. local chpt. City of Hope, 1985-86; Justice of the Peace Pro Tem Maricopa County Cts., 1985-89; juvenile hearing officer Maricopa County Juvenile Ct., 1985-89; v.p., co-founder Community Leadership for Youth Devel. (CLYDE); co-chmn. Phoenix Union High Sch. Citizens Adv. Com., 1970-72; del. Phoenix Together Town Hall on Youth Crime, 1982. Named 1 of 3 Outstanding Young Men of Phoenix Phoenix Jr. C. of C., 1969; Disting. Citizen award Ariz. chapt. ACLU, 1976. Mem. ABA, ACLU (v.p. cen. chpt. Ariz. 1990-95, pres. 1995—, mem. state bd.), Ariz. State Bar (past sec., bd. dirs. young lawyers sect., co-chmn. unauthorized practice com. 1988-89, mem. other coms.), Maricopa County Bar Assn. (past sec. and bd. dirs. young lawyers sect.), vice-chmn. Junvenile Practice Com., 1998—, Am. Judicature Soc., Jewish Children's and Family Service, Common Cause, NAACP, Ariz. Consumers Council, Phoenix Jaycees, Order of Coif, Phi Alpha Delta. Democrat. Jewish. Contbr. numerous articles to profl. jours.; asst. editor Ariz. Law Rev. 1963-64. Office: 317 E Berridge Ln Phoenix AZ 85012-1223

KLAKEG, CLAYTON HAROLD, cardiologist; b. Big Woods, Minn., Mar. 31, 1920; s. Knute O. and Agnes (Folvik) K.; student Concordia Coll., Moorhead, Minn., 1938-40; BS, N.D. State U., 1942; BS in Medicine, N.D. U., 1943; M.D., Temple U., 1945; MS in Medicine and Physiology, U. Minn.-Mayo Found., 1954; children: Julie Ann, Robert Clayton, Richard Scott. Intern, Med. Ctr., Jersey City, 1945-46; mem. staff VA Hosp., Fargo, N.D., 1948-51; fellow in medicine and cardiology Mayo Found., Rochester, Minn., 1951-55; internist, cardiologist Sansum Med. Clinic Inc., Santa Barbara, Calif., 1955—; mem. staff Cottage Hosp., St. Francis Hosp. Bd. dirs. Sansum Med. Rsch. Found., pres., 1990. Served to capt. M.C., USAF, 1946-48. Diplomate Am. Bd. Internal Medicine. Fellow ACP, Am. Coll. Cardiology, Am. Coll. Chest Physicians, Am. Heart Assn. (mem. council on clin. cardiology); mem. Calif. Heart Assn. (pres. 1971-72, Meritorious Service award 1968, Disting. Service award 1972, Disting. Achievement award 1975), Santa Barbara County Heart Assn. (pres. 1959-60, Disting. Service award 1958, Disting. Achievement award 1971), Calif. Med. Assn., Los Angeles Acad. Medicine, Santa Barbara County Med. Assn., Mayo Clinic Alumni Assn., Santa Barbara Soc. Internal Medicine (pres. 1963), Sigma Xi, Phi Beta Pi. Republican. Lutheran. Club: Channel City. Contbr. articles to profl. jours. Home: 5956 Trudi Dr Santa Barbara CA 93117-2175 Office: Sansum Med Clinic Inc PO Box 1239 Santa Barbara CA 93102-1239

KLAMMER, JOSEPH FRANCIS, management consultant; b. Omaha, Mar. 25, 1925; s. Aloys Arcadius and Sophie (Nadolny) K.; BS, Creighton U., 1948; MBA, Stanford, 1950; cert. in polit. econs. Grad. Inst. Internat. Studies, U. Geneva, 1951. cert. mgmt. cons. Adminstrv. analyst Chevron Corp., San Francisco, 1952-53; staff asst. Enron Corp., Omaha, 1953-57; mgmt. cons. Cresap, McCormick and Paget, Inc., N.Y.C., 1957-75, v.p., mgr. San Francisco region, 1968-75, bd. dirs.; mgmt. cons., prin. J.F. Klammer Assocs., San Francisco, 1975—. CEO, pres. Isabelle Towers Homeowners Assn., 1993-94, bd. dirs., 1993-94, mem. fin. com., 1994-95, mem. rules com., 1995-96, mem. fin. com., 1996—; past bd. dirs. Conard House. Apptd. and attended U.S. Mil. Acad., West Point, N.Y.; served to 1st lt. USAAF, 1943-46; lt. col. USAF (ret.). Rotary Found. fellow, 1950-51; recipient Sovereign Mil. Hospitaller Order of St. John of Jerusalem of Rhodes and of Malta, Alumni Merit award Creighton Coll. Arts & Scis. 1998. Mem. Omaha Club, Knights of Malta, Alpha Sigma Nu. Republican. Roman Catholic. Home: 1998 Broadway San Francisco CA 94109-2281 Office: 1850 Union St San Francisco CA 94123-4309

KLAPER, MICHAEL ANTHONY, physician, nutrition educator; b. Chgo., July 19, 1947; s. David and Jean Ruth (Talendar) K. BS in Zoology magna cum laude, U. Ill., 1969; MD, U. Ill., Chgo., 1972. Diplomate Nat. Bd. Med. Examiners; licentiate Med. Coun. Can. Intern in medicine Vancouver (B.C.) Gen. Hosp., 1972-73; gen. med. practice Surrey (B.C.) Med. Hosp., 1973-77; staff physician Humboldt Med. Ctr.-Hoopa (Calif.) Reservation, 1979-81, Humana Medfirst Clinic, Casselberry, Fla., 1983-86; pvt. med. nutrition practice Santa Cruz and Manhattan Beach, Calif., 1986-93; health dir. Royal Atlantic Health Spa, Pompano Beach, Fla., 1993-95; founding dir. Inst. Nutrition Edn. and Rsch., Manhattan Beach, 1992—; mem. adv. bd. EarthSave Internat., Santa Cruz, 1987—, Earth Comm. Office, L.A., 1988—; nutrition task force mem. Am. Med. Student Assn., Reston, Va., 1992—. Author: Vegan Nutrition: Pure and Simple, 1987, Pregnancy, Children and Vegan Diet, 1987. Recipient Recognition award UN, 1990, Courage of Conscience award Peace Abbey, 1995. Mem. Soc. Nutrition Edn., Am. Acad. Nutrition (faculty 1996—), Phi Beta Kappa, Phi Kappa Phi. Avocations: backpacking, scuba diving, aviation, astronomy, music. Home: PO Box 1055 Makawao HI 96768-1055 Office: Inst Nutrition Edn and Rsch 1601 N Sepulveda Blvd Ste 342 Manhattan Beach CA 90266-5133

KLASING, SUSAN ALLEN, environmental toxicologist, consultant; b. San Antonio, Sept. 10, 1957; d. Jesse Milton and Thelma Ida (Tucker) Allen; m. Kirk Charles Klasing, Mar. 3, 1984; children: Samantha Nicole, Jillian Paige. BS, U. Ill., 1979, MS, 1981, PhD, 1984. Staff scientist Life Scis. Rsch. Office, Fedn. Am. Socs. Exptl. Biology, Bethesda, Md., 1984-85; assoc. dir. Alliance for Food and Fiber, Sacramento, 1986; postgrad. rschr. U. Calif., Davis, 1986-87, 94-96; project dir. Health Officers Assn. Calif., Sacramento, 1987-89; cons. Klasing and Assocs., Davis, Calif., 1989—; mem. expert com. for substances-of-concern San Joaquin Valley Drainage Program, Sacramento, 1987, follow-up task force, 1990-91, drainage oversight com., 1992-94. Author: (chpt.) Consideration of the Public Health Impacts of Agricultural Drainage Water Contamination, 1991. Office: Klasing and Assocs 515 Flicker Ave Davis CA 95616-0178

KLASSEN, PETER JAMES, academic administrator, history educator; b. Crowfoot, Alta., Can., Dec. 18, 1930; came to U.S., 1955; s. John C. and Elizabeth (Martens) K.; m. Nancy Jo Cooprider, Aug. 1, 1959; children: Kenton, Kevin, Bryan. BA, also cert., U. B.C., Can., 1955; MA, U. So. Calif., 1958, PhD, 1962. Cert. secondary tchr. Lectr. U. So. Calif., Los Angeles, 1957-62; prof. history Fresno (Calif.) Pacific Coll., 1962-66; prof. history Calif. State U., Fresno, 1966—, dean sch. social scis., 1979-97, dir. internat. programs, 1992—. Author: The Economics of Anabaptism, 1964, Europe in the Reformation, 1979, Reformation: Change and Stability, 1980, A Homeland for Strangers, 1989; contbr. articles to jours. Pres. West Fresno Home Improvement Assn., 1966-70, Fresno Sister Cities Coun., 1987-90; mem. Calif. Coun. for Humanities, 1987-92. Research grantee Deutscher Akademischer Austauschdienst, 1975. Mem. Am. Hist. Assn., Am. Soc. Ch. History, Fresno City and County Hist. Soc. (pres. 1983-85), Soc. Reformation Rsch., German Studies Assn., Sixteenth Century Studies Assn., Assn. Advancement Slavic Studies, Golden Key, Phi Alpha Theta, Phi Kappa Phi, Phi Beta Delta. Home: 1838 S Bundy Dr Fresno CA 93727-6201 Office: Internat Program Calif State U Fresno CA 93740

KLAUSNER, JACK DANIEL, lawyer; b. N.Y.C., July 31, 1945; s. Burt and Marjory (Brown) K.; m. Dale Arlene Kreis, July 1, 1968; children: Andrew Russell, Mark Raymond. BS in Bus., Miami U., Oxford, Ohio, 1967; JD, U. Fla., 1969. Bar: N.Y. 1971, Ariz. 1975, U.S. Dist. Ct. Ariz. 1975, U.S. Ct. Appeals (9th cir.) 1975, U.S. Supreme Ct. 1975. Assoc. counsel John P. McGuire & Co., Inc., N.Y.C., 1970-71; assoc. atty. Hahn & Hessen, N.Y.C., 1971-72, gen. counsel Equilease Corp., N.Y.C., 1972-74, assoc. Burch & Cracchiolo, Phoenix, 1974-78; ptnr. Burch & Cracchiolo, 1978-98; judge pro tem Maricopa County Superior Ct., 1990—, Ariz. Ct. Appeals, 1992—; ptnr. Warner Angle Roper & Hallam, Phoenix, 1998—. Bd. dirs. Santos Soccer

Club, Phoenix, 1989-90; bd. dirs., pres. south Bank Soccer Club, Tempe, 1987-88. Home: 1390 W Island Cir Chandler AZ 85248-3700 Office: Warner Angel Roper & Hallam 3550 N Central Ave Ste 1500 Phoenix AZ 85012-2105

KLAUSNER, WILLETTE JEAN, theatrical/film producer, marketing consultant; b. Omaha, June 21, 1939; d. William and Gertrude (Jones) Murphy; m. Manuel Stuart Klausner, Feb. 1, 1969. BA in Econs., UCLA, 1961. Rsch. analyst Carnation Co., 1965; project dir. Audience Studies Inc., 1965-68, rsch. unit dir., 1968-72, v.p. rsch., 1972-74; v.p. mktg. rsch. and mktg. Universal Studies Inc., 1974-81; theatre prodr., 1988—; bd. dirs. Constnl. Rights Found., Audrey Skirball-Kenis Theatre, Inc., Ind. Rights Found., Women in Film Found., Am. Cinema Found.; v.p., bd. dirs. L.A. County Music Ctr. Operating Co., 1987—; mem. adv. bd. Pasadena Playhouse. Prodr. Hurlyburly, Westwood Playhouse, 1988-89, The Apprentice, The Richard Pryor Theatre, Hollywood, 1991, Twist George St. Playhouse, 1996 and Walnut St. Theatre, 1993, To Take Arms, Tamarind Theatre, L.A., 1997, The Man in Room 304, Watermark Theatre, N.Y., 1997, Jukebox, Atlas Bar & Grill, 1997, For You, 2100 Square Feet Theater, 1998. Recipient Mehitabel award for outstanding profl. achievement Tobe-Coburn Sch. Fashion Careers, 1978. Mem. Gold Shield UCLA Alumni Assn., The Trusteeship, Am. Inst. Wine and Food (founding mem. 1982—). Avocations: travel, food and wine, theater. Home and Office: Edgework Prodns Inc 5538 Red Oak Dr Los Angeles CA 90068-2551

KLAUSS, KENNETH KARL, composer, educator; b. Parkston, S.D., Apr. 8, 1923; s. Christian and Paulina (Engel) K. *Kenneth Klauss's family has a music tradition. His maternal uncle, violinist Carl Engel, taught at Union College, Lincoln, Nebraska. Engel Hall, on campus, is a music building dedicated to his memory. His sister, pianist Mabel Klauss Anderson, toured in the early 1920s with a Chatauqua group out of Lincoln which was under the leadership of Thurlow Lieurance, an early researcher of the music of Native Americans.* MusB in Composition, U. So. Calif., 1946. Tchr. composition and piano L.A., 1946-50; composer Lester Horton Theater, L.A., 1949-50; tchr. music San Francisco, 1950-61; composer, educator L.A., 1961—; lectr. in music for dance Idyllwild (Calif.) Sch. Music and Arts, 1967-74; lectr. in music history So. Calif. Inst. Architecture, Santa Monica, 1970-76; composer in residence Perry/Mansfield Camp, Steamboat Springs, Colo., 1966; guest performer, composer, lectr. Libr. Congress, Am. U., Washington, 1996. *The Klauss Archive will serve as a reference source for the universities and colleges of southeastern South Dakota. It consists of an extended collection of manuscripts, memorabilia, recordings, scores, and technical and historical books dealing with music and art. The James Art Museum displays an impressive collection of the paintings of Bernard James, a native of Dayton, Tennessee. Both the Archive and the Museum are housed in an historic (1904) building, First and Main Streets, Parkston.* Composer: (opera) Fall of the House of Usher, 1952; author, composer: (poetry/music orchestration) Story of the World Volumes I to VIII, 1952-86, 86-96. Founder, patron Klauss/James Archive and Art Mus., Parkston, 1995—. Recipient hon. mention opera competition Ohio U., Athens, 1954. Democrat. Avocations: history, poetry. Home: 440 Wren Dr Los Angeles CA 90065-5040

KLEBESADEL, LESLIE JOE, research agronomist; b. Troy, Wis., Aug. 18, 1928; s. Arthur Leslie and Ruth Elsie (Hodgson) K.; m. Mary Jane Kleinheinz, Jan. 22, 1955; children: Lani, Daniel, James, William, Thomas. BS, U. Wis., 1954, MS, 1955, PhD, 1958. Rsch. agronomist Joint U. Alaska and USDA, Palmer, 1957-68; supervising agronomist, rsch. leader U. Alaska, Palmer, 1968-84, prof. agronomy, 1984-87, prof. emeritus, 1987—; propr. Kilderkin Prodns., Palmer, 1987—. Author/illustrator: (poetry) Observations by Old Al Aska, 1989; contbr. chpt. to book, articles to profl. jours. Bd. dirs. Matanuska-Susitna Coll., Palmer, 1957-58. Recipient Honor citation Alaska State Legislature, 1988. Fellow AAAS; mem. Soc. for Range Mgmt. (life), Orgn. Profl. Employees of Dept. Agr. (life). Avocations: western history, antique autos and tractors. Home: PO Box 817 Palmer AK 99645-0817 Office: Kilderkin Prodns PO Box 817 Palmer AK 99645-0817

KLEEFELD, CAROLYN MARY, artist, writer, poet; b. Catsford, Eng., May 11, 1935; came to U.S., 1939; d. Sydney Mark and Amelia (Lewis) Taper; m. Travis Kleefeld (div.); children: Carla Ann, Claudia Eve. Student, UCLA, 1955-60. Artist Central Coast, Calif., 1985—; author, poet Malibu, Beverly Hills, Calif., 1960—, Big Sur, 1980—; bd. dirs. Spiritual Emergence Network, Santa Cruz, Calif., Our Ultimate Investment, Hollywood. Author: Climates of the Mind, 1979, Satan Sleeps with the Holy, 1982, Lovers in Evolution, 1983, The Alchemy of Possibility: Reinventing Your Personal Mythology, 1998; included in Mavericks of the Mind: Conversations for the New Millenium, 1993. Supporter Amnesty Internat., N.Y.C., Plowshares, San Francisco, United Way, Ams. for Peace. Recipient 1st prize Bay Area Poets Coalition, San Francisco, 1986, award of Excellence, So. Calif. Poets Pen, San Diego, 1985. Mem. Berkeley Art Assn., Chgo. Artists Coalition. Avocations: swimming, hiking, dancing, gardening, inter-species communication. Office: Atoms Mirror Atoms Inc PO Box 221693 Carmel CA 93922-1693

KLEESE, WILLIAM CARL, genealogy research consultant; b. Williamsport, Pa., Jan. 20, 1940; s. Donald Raymond and Helen Alice (Mulberger) K.; m. Vivian Ann Yeager, June 12, 1958; children: Scott, Jolene, Mark, Troy, Brett, Kecia, Lance. BS in Wildlife Biology, U. Ariz., 1975, MS in Animal Physiology, 1979, PhD in Animal Physiology, 1981. Sales rep. Terminix Co., Tucson, 1971-72; pest control operator, 1973-75; fire fighter Douglas Ranger Dist. Coronado Nat. Forest U.S. Forest Svc., 1975, biol. technician Santa Catalina ranger dist., 1975-76; lab. technician dept. animal scis. U. Ariz., 1977-78, rsch. technician dept. pharmacology and toxicology, 1978, rsch. asst. dept. biochemistry, 1979-81, rsch. specialist muscle biology group, 1981—; genealogy rsch. cons. Tucson, 1988—. Author: Introduction to Genealogy, 1988, Introduction to Genealogical Research, 1989, The Genealogical Researcher, Neophyte to Graduate, 1992, Genealogical Research in the British Isles, 1991; contbr. numerous articles to profl. jours. Chaplain Ariz. State Prisons, Tucson, 1988—. Mem. Ariz. Geneaolgy Adv. Bd. (com. chmn. 1990-92), Herpetologists League, Lycoming County Geneal. Soc., Nat. Geneal. Soc., Nat. Wildlife Fedn., Pa. Geneal. Soc., Soc. for the Study of Amphibians and Reptiles, Soc. of Vertebrate Paleontology, Ariz. State Geneal. Soc. (pres. 1990-93). Republican. Mem. LDS Ch. Avocation: photography. Home: 6521 E Fayette St Tucson AZ 85730-2220 Office: 6061 E Broadway Blvd Ste 128 Tucson AZ 85711-4020

KLEHN, HENRY, JR., engineering company executive; b. 1936. BS in Geol. Enging., U. Calif., MS in Enging. Sci. With Dames & Moore, L.A., 1960-93, v.p. mktg., 1993—. Office: Dames & Moore 911 Wilshire Blvd Ste 700 Los Angeles CA 90017*

KLEIMAN, VIVIAN ABBE, filmmaker; b. Phila., Oct. 11, 1950; d. Philip and Hilda (Kramer) K. BA, U. Calif., 1974. Filmmaker; lectr. Grad. Program in Documentary Film Stanford U., 1995-98; bd. dirs. Cultural Rsch. and Comm., Berkeley, Calif., Catticus Corp., Berkeley; founding dir. Jewish Film Festival, Berkeley, 1981-85, Frameline, San Francisco, 1985—; pres. Signifyin' Works, Berkeley, 1991—; v.p. Film Arts Found., San Francisco, 1983-93; cinematographer Tongues Untied, 1989. Producer, dir. films including Judy Chicago: The Birth Project, 1985, Ein Stehaufmannchen, 1991, My Body's My Business, 1992; producer films including Routes of Exile: A Moroccan Jewish Odyssey, 1982, California Gold, 1984, Color Adjustment, 1992, Roam Sweet Home, 1996, Forgotten Fires, 1998; assoc. producer The Disney Channel, 1982-83; rschr. for various films including A Woman Named Golda, 1982. Recipient George Foster Peabody award Sundance Film Festival, Outstanding Achievement award Internat. Documentary Assn., Nat. Emmy award nominee, The Eric Barnouw awards Orgn. Am. Historians, Red ribbon Am. Film and Video Festival, Best of Festival award Black Maria Festival, Black Internat. Cinema Berlin, Gold Plaque, Social/Polit. Documentary Chgo. Internat. Film Festival, N.C. Silver Juror's prize. Mem. Assn. of Ind. Vdeo and Film, Film Arts Found., Internat. Documentary Assn. Office: 2600 10th St Berkeley CA 94710-2522

KLEIN, ARNOLD WILLIAM, dermatologist; b. Mt. Clemens, Mich., Feb. 27, 1945; s. David Klein; m. Malvina Kraemer. BA, U. Pa., 1967, MD, 1971. Intern Cedars-Sinai Med. Ctr., Los Angeles, 1971-72; resident in dermatology Hosp. U. Pa., Phila., 1972-73, U. Calif., Los Angeles, 1973-75; pvt. practice dermatology Beverly Hills, Calif., 1975—; clin. prof. dermatology/medicine U. Calif. Ctr. for Health Scis; mem. med. staff Cedars-Sinai Med. Ctr.; asst. clin. prof. dermatology Stanford U., 1982-89; asst. clin. prof. to clin. prof. dermatology/medicine, UCLA; mem. Calif. State Adv. Com. on Malpractice, 1983-89; med. adv. bd. Skin Cancer Found., Lupus Found. Am., Collagen Corp., Botox adv. bd., Allergan; presenter seminars in field. Assoc. editor Jour. Dermatologic Surgery and Oncology; reviewer Jour. Sexually Transmitted Diseases, Jour. Am. Acad. Dermatology; mem. editorial bd. Men's Fitness mag., Shape mag., Jour. Dermatologic Surgery and Oncology, Archives of Dermatology; contbr. numerous articles to med. jours. Mem. AMA, Calif. Med. Assn., Am. Soc. Dermatologic Surgery, Internat. Soc. Dermatologic Surgery, Am. Assn. Cosmetic Surgeons, Assn. Sci. Advisors, Los Angeles Med. Assn., Am. Coll. Chemosurgery, Met. Dermatology Soc., Am. Acad. Dermatology, Dermatology Found., Scleroderma Found., Internat. Psoriasis Rsch. Inst., Lupus Found., Discovery Fund for Eye Rsch. (dir.), Hereditary Disease Found. (dir.), Jennifer Jones Simon Found. (trustee), Am. Venereal Disease Assn., Soc. Cosmetic Chemists, AFTRA, Los Angeles Mus. Contemporary Art (founder), Dance Gallery Los Angeles (founder), Am. Found. AIDS Research (founder, dir.), Children's Mus. L.A. (founder), Friars Club, Phi Beta Kappa, Sigma Tau Sigma, Delphos. Office: 435 N Roxbury Dr Ste 204 Beverly Hills CA 90210-5004

KLEIN, EARL H(YMAN), judge; b. Chgo., July 6, 1925; s. Paul J. and Helen (Nathan) Hyman; m. Snira L. Klein, Dec. 25, 1975; children: Paul, Peninna (dec.), Daniel. BA, Yeshiva U., 1947; JD, Loyola Marymount U., L.A., 1957. Bar: Calif. 1957, U.S. Supreme Ct. 1963. Pvt. practice Beverly Hills, Calif., 1957-75; adminstrv. law judge Calif. Unemployment Ins. Appeals Bd., Pasadena, 1975—. Author: Jewish Prayer: Concepts and Customs, 1986. Mem. Calif. Bar Assn., Phi Delta Phi. Office: Calif Unemployment Ins Appeals Bd 433 N Fair Oaks Ave Fl 2D Pasadena CA 91103-3603

KLEIN, EDITH MILLER, lawyer, former state senator; b. Wallace, Idaho, Aug. 4, 1915; d. Fred L.B. and Edith (Gallup) Miller; m. Sandor S. Klein (dec. 1970). BS in Bus., U. Idaho, 1935; tchg. fellowship, Wash. State U., 1935-36; JD, George Washington U., 1946, LLM, 1954; LLD (hon.), U. Idaho, 1998. Bar: D.C. 1946, Idaho 1947, U.S. Supreme Ct. 1954, N.Y. 1955. Pers. spec. Labor and War Depts., Wash., 1942-46; practice law Boise, Idaho, 1947—; judge Mcpl. Ct., Boise, 1947-49; mem. Idaho Ho. Reps., 1948-50, 64-68, Idaho Senate, 1968-82; atty. FCC Wash., 1953-54; FHA N.Y.C., 1955-56. Chmn. Idaho Gov.'s Commn. Status Women, 1964-72, mem., 1965-79, 82-92; mem. Idaho Gov.'s Coun. Comprehensive Health Planning, 1969-76, Idaho Law Enforcement Planning Commn., 1972-82, Nat. Adv. Commn. Regional Med. Programs, 1974-76, Idaho Endowment Investment Bd., 1979-82; trustee Boise State U. Found., Ind., 1973-95; pres. Boise Music Week, 1991-94; bd. dirs. Harry W. Morison Found. Ind., 1978—, St. Alphonsus Regional Med. Ctr. Found., 1982-96; past pres. bd. dirs. Boise Philharm. Assn., Opera Idaho. Named Woman of Yr. Boise Altrusa Club, 1966, Boise C. of C., 1970, Disting. Citizen, Idaho Statesman 1970, Woman of Progress, Idaho Bus. Prof. Women, 1978; recipient Women Helping Women award Soroptomist Club, 1980, Stein Meml. award Y.M.C.A., 1983, Silver and Gold award for Outstanding Svc., U. Idaho, 1985, March of Dimes award to Honor Outstanding Women, 1987, Cert. of Appreciation by Boise Br., AAUW, 1990, Morrison Ctr. Hall of Fame award, 1990, Disting. Cmty. Svc. award Boise Area C. of C., 1995, Lifetime Achievement award Girl Scouts Am., 1996, 50 Yrs. in Law Practice award Idaho State Bar, 1997. Mem. DAR (regent Pioneer chpt. 1991-93). Republican. Congregationalist. Home: 1588 Lenz Lane PO Box 475 Boise ID 83701-0475 Office: 1400 US Bank Plaza PO Box 2527 Boise ID 83701-2527

KLEIN, (MARY) ELEANOR, retired clinical social worker; b. Luzon, Philippines, Dec. 13, 1919; came to U.S., 1921; (parents Am. citizens); d. Roy Edgar and Edith Lillian Hay; m. Edward George Klein, June 24, 1955. BA, Pacific Union Coll., 1946; MSW, U. So. Calif., 1953. Lic. clin. social worker. Social worker White Meml. Hosp., Los Angeles, 1948-56; clin. social worker UCLA Hosp. Clinics, 1956-65, supr. social worker, 1965-67, assoc. dir., 1967-73, dir., 1973-82. Bd. dirs., treas. Los Amigos de la Humanidad, U. So. Calif. Sch. Social Work, hon. life mem. bd. dirs. Calif. div. Am. Cancer Soc., mem. vol. bd. Calif. div., 1964—, del. nat. dir., 1980-84, chmn. residential crusade for Orange County (Calif.) unit, 1985-86; bd. dirs. Vol. Exchange, 1988-97, sec., 1991-96, v.p., 1996-97; v.p. Dem. Club West Orange County, 1996-98, pres., 1998-99. Recipient Disting. Alumni award Los Amigos de la Humanidad, 1984, Outstanding Performance award UCLA Hosp., 1968, various service awards Am. Cancer Soc., 1972-88. Fellow Soc. Clin. Social Work; mem. Nat. Assn. Social Workers (charter), Am. Hosp. Assn., Soc. Social Work Adminstrs. in Health Care (formerly Soc. Hosp. Social Work Dirs.) (nat. pres. 1981, bd. dirs. 1978-82, life mem. local chpt.), Am. Pub. Health Assn., Assn. of Oncology Social Work (charter). Democrat. Unitarian. Avocations: travel, gardening. Home: 1661 Texas Cir Costa Mesa CA 92626-2238

KLEIN, FAY MAGID, health administrator; b. Chgo., Jan. 12, 1929; d. Victor and Rose (Begun) Magid; m. Jerome G. Klein, June 27, 1948 (div. 1970); children: Leslie Susan Janik, Debra Lynne Maslov; m. Manuel Chait, Aug. 28, 1994. BA in English, UCLA, 1961; MA in Pub. Adminstrn., U. So. Calif., 1971. Cert. health adminstrn. Supr. social workers Los Angeles County, 1961-65; program specialist Econ. and Youth Opportunity Agy., L.A., 1965-69; sr. health planner Model Cities, L.A., 1971-72; dir. prepaid health plan Westland Health Svcs., L.A., 1972-74; exec. dir. Coastal Region Health Consortium, L.A., 1974-76; grants and legis. cons. Jewish Fed. Council of L.A., 1976-79; planning coun. Jewish Fed. Couns. of So. Fla., Palm Beach to Miami, 1979-82; adminstrv. dir. program in kidney diseases Dept. Medicine UCLA, 1982-84; exec. dir. west coast Israel Cancer Rsch. Fund, L.A., 1984-94; cons. to non-profit orgns. Santa Monica, 1994—; cons. Arthritis Found., L.A., 1984, Bus. Action Ctr., L.A., 1982, Vis. Nurses Assn., L.A., 1982. Charter mem. Los Angeles County Mus. of Art, Mus. of Contemporary Art, L.A.; cons. L.A. Mcpl. Art Gallery, 1979; mem. UCLA/Armand Hammer Mus. Fellow U.S. Pub. Health, U. So. Calif., 1970-71. Mem. Am. Pub. Health, UCLA Alumni Assn. (life), U. So. Calif. Alumni Assn. (life).

KLEIN, HENRY, architect; b. Cham, Germany, Sept. 6, 1920; came to U.S., 1939; s. Fred and Hedwig (Weiskopf) K.; m. Phyllis Harvey, Dec. 27, 1952; children: Vincent, Paul, David. Student, Inst. Rauch, Lausanne, Switzerland, 1936-38; BArch, Cornell U., 1943. Registered architect, Oreg., Wash. Designer Office of Pietro Belluschi, Architect, Portland, Oreg., 1948-51; architect Henry Klein Partnership, Architects, Mt. Vernon, Wash., 1952—. Bd. dirs. Wash. Pks. Found., Seattle, 1977-92, Mus. N.W. Art, 1988-95. With U.S. Army, 1943-46. Recipient Louis Sullivan award Internat. Union Bricklayers and Allied Craftsmen, 1981; Presdl. Design award Nat. Endowment Arts, 1988; George A. and Eliza Howard Found. fellow. Fellow AIA (Seattle chpt. medal 1995). Jewish. Home: 1957 Little Mountain Rd Mount Vernon WA 98274-8311 Office: Henry Klein Partnership 314 Pine St Mount Vernon WA 98273-3852

KLEIN, HERBERT GEORGE, newspaper editor; b. L.A., Apr. 1, 1918; s. George and Amy (Cordes) K.; m. Marjorie Galbraith, Nov. 1, 1941; children: Joanne L. (Mrs. Robert Mayne), Patricia A. (Mrs. John Root). AB, U. So. Calif., 1940; Hon. Doctorate, U. San Diego, 1989. Reporter Alhambra (Calif.) Post-Advocate, 1940-42, news editor, 1946-50; spl. corr. Copley Newspapers, 1946-50, Washington corr., 1950; with San Diego Union, 1950-68, editl. writer, 1950-52, editl. page editor, 1952-56, assoc. editor, 1956-57, exec. editor, 1957-58, editor, 1959-68; mgr. communications Nixon for Pres. Campaign, 1968-69; dir. comm. Exec. Br., U.S. Govt., 1969-73; v.p. corp. rels. Metromedia, Inc., 1973-77; media cons., 1977-80; editor-in-chief, v.p. Copley Newspapers, San Diego, 1980—; publicity dir. Eisenhower-Nixon campaign in Calif., 1952; asst. press sec. V.P. Nixon campaign, 1956; press sec. Nixon campaign, 1958; spl. asst., press sec. to Nixon, 1959-61; press sec. Nixon Gov. campaign, 1962; dir. comm. Nixon presdl. campaign, 1968; mem. Advt. Coun., N.Y. Author: Making It Perfectly Clear, 1980. Trustee U. So. Calif.; past chmn. Holiday Bowl; bd. dirs. Clair Burgener Found., Greater San Diego Internat. Sports Coun.; mem. com. Super Bowl XXII and XXXII; chair internat. com. Scripps Health and Sci. Found.; active Olympic Tng. Site Com.; bd. dirs. San Diego Econ. Devel. Com. With USNR, 1942-46; comdr. Res. Recipient Fourth Estate award U. So. Calif., 1947, Alumnus of Yr. award U. So. Calif., 1971, Gen. Alumni Merit award, 1977, Spl. Svc. to Journalism award, 1969, Headliner of Yr. award L.A. Press Club, 1971, San Diego State U. First Fourth Estate award, 1986, Golden Man award Boys and Girls Club, 1994, Newspaper Exec. of Yr. award Calif. Press Assn., 1994; named Community Champion, Hall of Champions, 1993. Mem. Am. Soc. Newspaper Editors (past dir.), Calif. Press Assn., Pub. Rels. Seminar, Gen. Alumni U. So. Calif. (past pres.), Alhambra Jr. C. of C. (past pres.), Greater San Diego C. of C. (mem. exec. com.), Bohemian Club, Fairbanks Country Club, Kiwanis, Rotary (hon.), Sigma Delta Chi (chmn. nat. com., chmn. gen. activities nat. conv. 1958), Scripps Inst. (chair internat com.), Delta Chi. Presbyterian. Home: 5110 Saddlery Sq PO Box 8935 Rancho Santa Fe CA 92067-8935 Office: Copley Press Inc 350 Camino De La Reina San Diego CA 92108-3003

KLEIN, JAMES MIKEL, music educator; b. Greenville, S.C., Aug. 27, 1953; s. Rubin Harry Klein and Billie (Mikel) Newton. BM, U. Tex., 1975, MM, 1977; MusD, U. Cincinnati, 1981. Prin. trombone player Austin (Tex.) Symphony Orch., 1973-77; conducting asst. U. Tex., Austin, 1975-77, U. Cin., 1977-78; dir. instrumental music Valparaiso (Ind.) U., 1978-84; prof. music Calif. State U. Stanislaus, Turlock, 1984—, spkr. of faculty, 1997-98, 99-00; mem. faculty Nat. Luth. Music Camp, Lincoln, Nebr., 1985-86, 95-97; guest conductor, clinician, adjudicator various states, internationally, 1978—; trombone player Modesto (Calif.) Symphony Orch., 1984—; conductor Stanislaus Youth Symphony, Modesto, 1985; music dir. Modesto Symphony Youth Orch., 1986—; site adminstr. Nat. Honors Orch., Anaheim, Calif., 1986, Indpls., 1988, Cin., 1992, asst. condr., Kansas City, 1996, Phoenix, 1998; faculty, coord. instrumental music Calif. State Summer Sch. of Arts, 1987-88. Pres. Turlock Arts Fund for Youth, 1986-88; mem. internat. Friendship Com., subcom., City of Modesto, 1990-92; vol. Big Bros. Am. Recipient Meritorious Prof. award Calif. State U., Stanislaus, 1988, Outstanding Young Man of Am. award, 1990. Mem. Music Educators Nat. Assn., Nat. Sch. Orch. Assn. (pub. rels. chair 1994-96), Am. Fedn. Musicians (local 1), Condrs. Guild, Am. Symphony Orch. League, Calif. Orch. Dir.'s Assn. (pres.-elect 1988-90, pres. 1990-92, Orch. Dir. of the Year, 1994). Avocations: sailing, racquetball, reading, skiing. Home: 565 N Daubenberger Rd Turlock CA 95380-9144 Office: Calif State U Dept Music 801 W Monte Vista Ave Turlock CA 95382-0256

KLEIN, MARC S., newspaper editor and publisher; b. Feb. 16, 1949; married; 2 children. BA in Journalism, Pa. State U., 1970. Bur. chief Courier-Post, Camden, N.J., 1970-75; asst. mng. editor Phila. Bull., 1975-81; editor Jewish Exponent, Phila., 1981-83; editor, pub. Jewish Bull. of No. Calif., San Francisco, 1984—; publ. Jewish Cmty. Online. Past pres. Temple Israel, Alameda; former bd. dirs. Oakland-Piedmont Jewish Community Ctr. Recipient 1st place awards Phila. Press Assn., 1973, 1st place award N.J. Press Assn., 1973; Wall St. Jour. Newspaper Fund intern, fellow, 1969. Mem. Am. Jewish Press Assn. (pres.), Soc. Profl. Journalists (past bd. dirs.). Office: 225 Bush St Ste 1480 San Francisco CA 94104-4216*

KLEIN, R. KENT, lawyer; b. Richmond, Mo., Feb. 11, 1944. BA with distinction, U. Ariz., 1965, JD, 1968. Bar: Ariz. 1968. Atty. State Compensation Fund Ariz., 1968-74, Lewis & Roca, Phoenix, 1974—. Mem. State Bar Ariz. Office: Lewis & Roca Renaissance 2 40 N Central Ave Phoenix AZ 85004-4429*

KLEIN, RICHARD MICHAEL, publisher. BFA, Carnegie Mellon Inst., 1988. Graphic designer ANSI, N.Y.C., 1988-89; design mgr. N.Y.C. Sch. Constrn. Authority, N.Y.C., 1989-91; art dir. Macy's Advt., San Francisco, 1991-94; creative dir. Surface Mag., San Francisco, 1994-96, co-pub., 1996—. Art dir. Surf Design, 1997, Print Ann. award 1998. Avocations: tennis, skiing, painting. Home: 2852B Pine St San Francisco CA 94115-2512 Office: Surface Pub 1388 Haight St # 168 San Francisco CA 94117-2909

KLEIN, ROBERT GORDON, state supreme court justice; b. Honolulu, Nov. 11, 1947; s. Gordon Ernest Klein and Clara (Cutter) Elliot; m. Aleta Elizabeth Webb, July 27, 1986; children: Kurt William, Erik Robert. BA, Stanford U., 1969; JD, U. Oreg., 1972. Dep. atty. gen. State of Hawaii, 1973, with state campaign spening commn., 1974, with state dept regulatory agys., 1975-78; judge State Dist. Ct. Hawaii, 1978-84; judge cir. ct. State of Hawaii, 1984-92, supreme ct. justice, 1992—. Office: Supreme Ct 417 S King St Honolulu HI 96813-2902*

KLEIN, SNIRA L(UBOVSKY), Hebrew language and literature educator; came to U.S., 1959, naturalized, 1974; d. Avraham and Devora (Unger) Lubovsky; m. Earl H. Klein, Dec. 25, 1975. Tchr. cert., Tchrs. Seminar, Netanya, Israel, 1956; B. Rel. Edn., U. Judaism, 1961, M in Hebrew Lit., 1963; BA, Calif. State U., Northridge, 1966; MA, UCLA, 1971, PhD, 1983. Tchg. asst. UCLA, 1969-71; instr., continuing edn. U. Judaism, L.A., 1971-76, 94—, instr., 1975-84; vis. lectr. UCLA, 1985-91; adj. asst. prof. U. Judaism, 1984-94. Mem. Assn. for Jewish Studies, Nat. Assn. of Profs. of Hebrew, World Union of Jewish Studies. Jewish. Avocations: gardening, music. Office: U Judaism 15600 Mulholland Dr Los Angeles CA 90077-1519

KLEINBERG, JAMES P., lawyer; b. Pitts., Mar. 28, 1943. BA, U. Pitts., 1964; JD, U. Mich., 1967. Bar: Calif. 1968. Trial atty. antitrust divsn. Dept. Justice, 1967-68; ptnr. McCutchen, Doyle, Brown & Enersen, Palo Alto, Calif.; atty. rep. 9th Cir. Jud. Conf. No. Dist. Calif., 1984-84, mem. exec. com., 1984-87; mem. adv. group No. Dist. Calif., 1990—; mem. civil trial advocacy consulting group Bd. Legal Specialization, 1979-90, mem. com. adminstrn. justice, 1984-87; panelist Ann. Fed. Practice Insts., 1992—. Mem. visitors com. U. Mich. Law Sch., 1985—. Fellow Am. Bar Found. Office: McCutchen Doyle Brown & Enersen 3 Embarcadero Ctr Ste 1500 San Francisco CA 94111-4038

KLEINER, HAROLD J., record company executive; b. Bronx, N.Y.; s. Herman and Fraj Kleimer; m. Vivian Kisinger, Jan. 15, 1970. Assoc. mgr. artists and repertoire Columbia Records, Burbank, Calif., 1972-75, creative dir. Vista Mktg., 1976-86, dir. artists and repertoire, 1986-87; from dir. product devel. to exec. prodr. dir. product devel. Walt Disney Records, Burbank, 1990—; founder Garwin Music Inc., Nashville; chmn. prodr. of yr. com. CBS Records. Recipient 2 Gold Record awards.

KLEINFELD, ANDREW JAY, federal judge; b. 1945. BA magna cum laude, Wesleyan U., 1966; JD cum laude, Harvard U., 1969. Law clk. Alaska Supreme Ct., 1969-71; U.S. magistrate U.S. Dist. Ct. Alaska, Fairbanks, 1971-74; pvt. practice law Fairbanks, 1971-86; judge U.S. Dist. Ct. Alaska, Anchorage, 1986-91, U.S. Ct. Appeals (9th cir.), San Francisco, 1991—. Contbr. articles to profl. jours. Mem. Alaska Bar Assn. (pres. 1982-83, bd. govs. 1981-84), Tanana Valley Bar Assn. (pres. 1974-75), Phi Beta Kappa. Republican. Office: US Ct Appeals 9th Cir Courthouse Sq 250 Cushman St Ste 3-a Fairbanks AK 99701-4665

KLEINFELD, ELIZABETH ANNE, English literature educator, magazine editor; b. Hempstead, N.Y., June 18, 1969; d. Robert J. and Therese (O'Regan) K.; m. Travitt Lee Hamilton, Mar. 16, 1992. BS in History, Bradley U., 1992; MS in English, Ill. State U., 1994. Editor-in-chief Broadside Literary Jour./Acts, Peoria, Ill., 1988-89, 90-91; instr. of English Ill. State U., Normal, 1993-94, Red Rocks C.C., Lakewood, Colo., 1995—; resident instr. English C.C. of Aurora, 1996—; editor-in-chief Inscape Lit. Mag., 1997—. Mem. MLA, Nat. Coun. Tchrs. of English. Home: 2227 E 14th Ave Denver CO 80206-2107 Office: CC of Aurora 1600 E Center Tech Pkwy Aurora CO 80011

KLEINSMITH, BRUCE JOHN See NUTZLE, FUTZIE

KLEPINGER, JOHN WILLIAM, trailer manufacturing company executive; b. Lafayette, Ind., Feb. 7, 1945; s. John Franklin and R. Wanda (North) K.; m. Mary Patricia Duffy, May 1, 1976; 1 child, Nicholas Patrick. BS, Ball State U., 1967, MA, 1968. Sales engr. CTS Corp., Elkhart, Ind., 1969-70; exec. v.p. Woodlawn Products Corp., Elkhart, 1970-78; v.p. Period Ind., Henderson, Ky., 1976-78, Sotebeer Constrn. Co., Inc., Elkhart, 1978-81; gen. mgr. Wells Industries Inc., Ogden, Utah, 1981—, Wells Cargo, Inc., Phoenix,

1995—; regional dir. Zion's First Nat. Bank, Ogden, 1986—. Bd. dirs. St. Benedict's Hosp., Ogden, 1986-94, chmn., 1987-94; bd. dirs. Weber County Indsl. Devel. Corp., Nat. Job Tng. Partnership Inc., 1986-89; mem. Weber-Morgan Pvt. Industry Coun., 1983-96, Utah Job Tng. Coordinating Coun., 1988-96, chmn. 1993-94. Named Ogden Bus. Man of Yr., Weber County Sch. Dist., 1984. Mem. Nat. Assn. Trailer Mfrs. (bd. dirs., vice chmn. 1994-95, chmn. 1995-97, sec., treas. 1998—), Weber County Prodn. Mgrs. Assn. (pres. 1984-85, 92-93), Nat. Assn. Pvt. Industry Couns. (bd. dirs. 1986-96, pres. 1988-92), Nat. Alliance Bus. (bd. dirs. 1987-90), Ogden Area C. of C. (bd. dirs. 1986-96, treas. 1986-89), Phoenix C. of C., Exch. Club (bd. dirs. Ogden 1984-86). Roman Catholic. Avocations: finance, community service, leadership, sports, travel. Home: 5181 Aztec Dr Ogden UT 84403-4606 Office: Wells Industries Inc PO Box 1619 Ogden UT 84402-1619

KLEVAN NEELY, JAN MARIE, communications executive; b. Lodi, Calif., June 22, 1951; d. Stanley Philip and Mary Louise (Canepa) Klevan; divorced; children: Aaron, Jessica. BA in Comm. Arts, U. of the Pacific, 1977, tchg. credential, 1996. News reporter KOVR-TV, Sacramento and Stockton, Calif., 1979-89; exec. dir. Stockton Opera Assn., 1990-91; comm. mgr. San Joaquin Partnership, Stockton, 1991—. Commr. Stockton Arts Commn., 1996, 97, 98; chair arts and crafts Stockton Asparagus Festival, 1996, 97, 98; bd. mem. First Night Stockton, 1998; chair Christian bd. edn. First Congl. Ch., Stockton, 1998. Named Outstanding Reporter, Calif. Sch. Bds. Assn., 1989; alumni fellow U. of the Pacific, Stockton, 1990. Mem. Soc. Profl. Journalists, C. of C. Ind. BBQ (co-chair 1998). Avocations: tap dancing, jazz dancing. Office: San Joaquin Partnership 2800 W March Ln Ste 470 Stockton CA 95219-8218

KLEVIT, ALAN BARRE, publishing executive, motivational speaker, writer; b. Balt., June 25, 1935; s. Robert and Minnie (Goodman) K.; m. Marilyn Rosenthal, Nov. 26, 1955; children: Mindy Faith, Lawrence Michael, Richard Steven. BS in Econs., Georgetown U., 1956, MA in Econs., 1960; MA in Pub. Adminstrn. and Urban Affairs, Am. U., 1970. Asst. mgr. AS Beck Shoe Co., Washington, 1956-57; stat., economist Commerce Dept., Washington, 1957-60; securities analyst, rsch. dir. T.J. McDonald & Co., Washington, 1960-62; mgmt. analyst, div. chief Fed. Aviation Adminstrn., Washington, 1962-73; CEO Art Fair, Inc., Silver Spring, Md., 1974-90; founder, dir. Klevit Fine Art, Internat., Silver Spring and Malibu, Calif., 1987—; founder, exec. officer Robert Klevit Found. for Humanitarianism, Silver Spring and Malibu, Calif., 1987—; dir. Stardust Pub., Malibu, 1990—; co-founder, dir. Charity Editions, Silver Spring and Malibu, 1987; mem. faculty Mgmt. by Objectives Fed. Exec. Sch., Charlottesville, Va., 1969-71; motivational speaker, Malibu, 1988—. Author: Three Days in Sedona, 1990, How to Make Your Dreams Come True, 1991, Follow the Rainbow, 1991, (book and audiocassette) Pass the Pickles, Please and Other Stories, 1995; (video) Journey Within, 1993; host radio show: Today's Art World with Alan Klevit, 1983-84, (TV Show) Off the Beaten Path with Alan Klevit, 1992—; contbr. articles to mags. and newspapers including regular contbns. to Malibu Mag.; writer, prodr., featured performer tv commls., 1994—. Bd. dirs. Summer Opera, Washington, 1987—, Marine & Mountain Wildlife Rescue, Malibu, 1991—; mem. Hammer Mus. Mem. Inst. for Econometric Rsch., World Wildlife Fedn., Inst. for Noetic Scis., Planetary Soc., Malibu C. of C., Masons. Avocations: charity art auctioneer, theater, classical music, travel, karate. Office: Stardust Pub PO Box 6356 Malibu CA 90264-6356

KLIEN, WOLFGANG JOSEF, architect; b. Hollabrunn, Austria, Sept. 29, 1942; s. Josef and Maria (Kainz) K.; Dipl. Ing., Vienna Tech. U., 1967; m. Jean M. Klien; children: Christina Olga, Angelika Maria. Designer, E. Donau, Architect, Vienna, 1968; with C. Nitschke & Assos., Architects, Columbus, Ohio, 1968-71; project architect GSAS Architects, Phoenix, 1971-75, 77-78; prodn. architect Harry Glueck, Vienna, 1976-77; v.p. architecture Am. Indian Engring. Inc., Phoenix, 1978-81; pres. S.W. Estate Group, Inc., real estate devel., San Diego, 1980-82; pres., tech. dir., branch mgr. Ariz. br. office SEG-S.W. Estate Group, Inc., Phoenix, 1982-86; prin. Klien & Assoc., Architecture, Planning, Devel. Cons., Phoenix, 1986—, Atlantic-Pacific Trading Corp., Internat. Trade, Phoenix, 1986-88; pres., gen. mgr. Polybau, Inc., Hayward, Calif., 1988-90; pres. Libra Cons., Inc., Phoenix, 1989—; ptnr. Heart Devel. Co., LLC, dBa Heart Homes, 1993-96; v.p. Sunrise Custom Homes, Inc., 1995—. founder, pres. SOS-Children's Villages of Ariz., Inc., 1998—. Recipient Great Silver Medal of Merit, Republic of Austria, 1993. Mem. AIA, Austro-Am. Coun. West, Austrian Soc. Ariz. (founder 1985, v.p. 1985-86, pres. 1987—). Roman Catholic. Home and Office: 11797 E Casitas Del Rio Dr Scottsdale AZ 85255

KLIEWER, STEPHEN PAUL, educator; b. Lakeview, Oreg., July 14, 1951; s. Paul Gerry and Mavis Shirley (Fairbanks) K.; m. Marilyn Elizabeth, July 1, 1974 (div. Sept. 1995); children: Erin Krista, Bryce Alan; m. Midge Archer, Oct. 7, 1995. BA, Whitman Coll., 1973; MDiv, Princeton Theol. Seminary, 1977; D in Ministry, San Fran Theol. Seminary, 1985. Ordained to ministry of the Presbyn. Ch., cert. profl. fundraiser. Pastor Presbyn. Ch., Reardon, Wash., 1977-82, La Grande, Oreg., 1982-87, Lake Oswago, Oreg., 1987-90; from sr. devel. to dir. rsch. Oreg. Health Sci. U., Portland, 1990-94, dir. rsch. devel. and outreach, 1994—; fundraising cons. Kruse Way Rotary Found., Lake Oswego, Oreg., 1997—, Mt. Hood Cmty. Coll., Gresham, Oreg., 1998—; bd. dirs. Bridges Family Svcs., Portland, Oreg., 1997—, Oreg. Acad. Family Practice Found., Sherwood, Oreg., 1996—. Author: Creative Use of Diversity in the Local Church, 1985. Cross Cultural Edn. grantee Dept. Family Medicine Pub. Health Svc., Bethesda, Md., 1995, Medicine and Spirituality grantee NIH, Washington, 1998. Mem. Nat. Soc. Fundraising Execs., Willamette Valley Devel. Offices, Kruse-Way Rotary (pres. 1997-98), Presbytary of The Cascades, Lake Oswego C. of C. Home: 2434 NE 21st Portland OR 97201 Office: Oregon Health Science U 3181 SW Sam Jackson Park Portland OR 97201

KLIGERMAN, MORTON, pediatrician; b. Phila., Dec. 2, 1958; s. Edward Martin and Lois (Fair) K.; m. Angelica Patricia Lopez, Apr. 4, 1992. BS in Biol. Scis., Carnegie-Mellon U., 1980; MD, Pa. State U., 1984. Diplomate Am. Bd. Pediatrics. Resident in pediatrics U. Calif., San Diego, 1984-87; pediatrician Southbay Pediatrics, Chula Vista, Calif., 1987-91, Pediatric Healthcare, San Diego, 1991-94; urgent care pediatrician Children's Hosp. San Diego, 1987—; pediatrician Children's Primary Care, Chula Vista, 1994—; clin. assoc. U. San Diego, 1995—; asst. prof. pediatrics U. Calif., San Diego, 1995—. Contbr. articles to profl. jours. Fellow Am. Acad. Pediatrics; mem. San Dieo County Med. Soc., Calif. Med. Assn. Democrat. Jewish. Avocations: creative and satiric writing, foreign travel, computers, fitness. Home: 1268 Silverado Dr Chula Vista CA 91915 Office: Children's Primary Care Med Group 480 Fourth Ave Ste 306 Chula Vista CA 91910

KLIMA, ROGER RADIM, physiatrist; b. Prague, Czechoslovakia; came to U.S., 1982, naturalized, 1988; s. Josef and Radka Klima. BA, Zatlanka Coll., Prague, 1971; MD, Charles U., Prague, 1978. Diplomate Am. Bd. Phys. Medicine and Rehab., Am. Bd. Electrodiagnostic Medicine. Resident in surgery Charles U., 1978-79, resident in orthopedic surgery, 1979-81; fellow, clin. clk. Beverly Hills Med. Ctr. and Cedars-Sinai Med. Ctr., L.A., 1984-86; resident in surgery U. Medicine and Dentistry-N.J. Med. Sch., Newark, 1986-87; resident in phys. medicine and rehab. U. Medicine and Dentistry-N.J. Med. Sch./Kessler Inst., Newark and West Orange, 1987-90; mem. phys. medicine and rehab. faculty Stanford (Calif.) U. and affiliated hosps., 1990—; dir. phys. medicine and rehab. outpatient svcs. Palo Alto (Calif.) VA Health Care Sys., 1992—, also co-dir. comprehensive pain mgmt.; clin. instr. in phys. medicine and rehab. U. Medicine and Dentistry-N.J.Med. Sch., 1989-90; clin. instr. in phys., medicine and rehab. Stanford U. Sch. Medicine, 1990-96, asst. prof., 1996—. Contbr. articles to profl. jours. Recipient first ann. Thompson Humanitarian award Stanford U. Phys. Medicine and Rehab., 1994, 97. Mem. Am. Acad. Phys. Medicine and Rehab. (liaison resident physician coun. 1989-90), Assn. Acad. Physiatrists, Am. Assn. Electrodiagnostic Medicine. Office: Stanford U Med Ctr Divsn Phys Medicine and Rehab Rm NC 104 Stanford CA 94305

KLIMAN, SUSAN SCHAEFER, architect; b. Tucson, Dec. 2, 1963; d. John Paul and Helen (Schwarz) Schaefer; m. Douglas Hartley Kliman, Feb. 18, 1989; 1 child, Randall John. BArch, Cornell U., 1986; MArch, U. Ariz., 1994, postgrad., 1996. Registered architect, Ariz. Project mgr. Giuliani Assocs. Architects, Washington, 1986-88; designer Richard Luke Architect, Las Vegas, Nev., 1988-89; project mgr. HSA Architects, Las Vegas, 1989-91, PAA Inc., Tucson, 1991-93; prin. Klimatic Archtl. Design, LLC, Tucson, 1993—; grad. tchg. asst. U. Ariz., spring 1993, grad. rsch. asst., 1994-95. Instr. swimming, lifeguard Montgomery County Recreation Dept., Silver Spring, Md., 1986-88; Brownie leader Girl Scout U.S.A., Las Vegas, 1988-89, 2d v.p. Frontier coun., 1989-91, bd. dirs., Sahuaro coun., 1991-92, 1st v.p., 1992-93. Mem. AIA, AAUW, Alpha Phi (Tucson alumni v.p. 1991-96, sec. 1996—).

KLINE, BRENT P., editor; b. Denver, Feb. 18, 1968; s. Lee M. and Beth V. (Lovenstein) K.; m. Kari L. Hansen, Aug. 18, 1990; 1 child, Kendall Montana. BA in Journalism, BA in Econs., U. No. Colo., 1998. Sports dir. Sta. KTVM-TV, Butte, Mont., 1990-93; editor Telemation Inc., Denver, 1993-96; nonlinear editor Encore Media Group, Denver, 1996-97, mgr. nonlinear post, 1997—; freelance editor, cons. Inkline Post, others, Denver, 1996—. Recipient Silver Teddy award, 1997, hon. mention Acad. Arts and Scis., 1989. Mem. Colo. Film Video Orgn. Office: Encore Media Group 4100 E Dry Creek Rd Littleton CO 80122-3729

KLINE, FRED WALTER, retired communications company executive; b. Oakland, Calif., May 17, 1918; s. Walter E. and Jean M. Kline; m. Verna Marie Taylor, Dec. 27, 1952; children—Kathleen, Nora, Fred Walter. B.A. in Calif. History, U. Calif.-Berkeley, 1940. With Walter E. Kline & Assocs. and successor Fred Kline Agy., Inc., from 1937; chmn. bd., pres. Kline Communications Corp., Los Angeles, 1956-96, ret., 1996; pres. Capitol News Service. Commr. Los Angeles County Fire Services Commn., Calif. Motion Picture Devel. Council; cons., advisor Calif. Film Commn.; former fed. civil def. liaison; developer state-wide paramedic rescue program; Calif. chmn. Office of Asst. Sec. Def.; mem. Calif. Com. for Employer Support of Guard and Res.; mem. Los Angeles Film Com. Served with USAAF, World War II; brig. gen. Calif. Mil. Dept. Recipient Inter-Racial award City of Los Angeles, 1963, named Man of Yr., 1964. Mem. Acad. Motion Picture Arts and Scis., Radio and TV News Assn. So. Calif., Pub. Relations Soc. Am., Calif. Newspaper Pubs. Assn., Cath. Press Council (founding mem.), Pacific Pioneer Broadcasters, Footprinters Internat., Am. Mil. Govt. Assn. (past pres.), Navy League, Calif. State Police Officers Assn., Internat. Assn. Profl. Firefighters (hon. life), Peace Officers Assn. Los Angeles County (life), Internat. Assn. Chiefs of Police, Internat. Assn. Fire Chiefs, Calif. Fire Chiefs Assn., Fire Marshals Assn. N.Am., Nat. Fire Protection Assn., Nat. Fin. Writers Assn., Hollywood C. of C., Nat. Fire Sci. Acad., Calif. State Mil. Forces, Calif. Pubs. Assn., So. Calif. Cable Club. Sigma Delta Chi. Clubs: Greater Los Angeles Press, Media (Los Angeles), Sacramento Press. Columnist Calif. newspapers. Office: 1180 Weber Way Sacramento CA 95822-1840

KLINE, HOWARD JAY, cardiologist, educator; b. White Plains, N.Y., Nov. 5, 1932; s. Raymond Kline and Rose Plane; divorced; children: Michael, Ethan; m. Ellen Sawamura, June 13, 1987; 1 child, Christopher. BS, Dickinson Coll., 1954; MD, N.Y. Med. Coll., 1958. Intern San Francisco Gen. Hosp., 1958-59; resident Mt. Sinai Hosp., N.Y.C., 1959-61; sr. resident U. Calif. Med. Ctr., San Francisco, 1961-62; cardiology fellow Mt. Sinai Hosp., N.Y.C., 1962-64; dir. cardiology training program St. Mary's Hosp., San Francisco, 1970-90, Calif. Pacific Med. Ctr., San Francisco, 1992—; clin. prof. medicine and cardiology U. Calif. Med. Ctr., San Francisco, 1984—; vis. prof. Nihon U., Tokyo, 1986. Editor (jours.) Hosp. Practice, Cardiology, 1992—; contbr. articles to Hosp. Practice. Lt. col. U.S. Med. Corps, 1967-69. Fellow ACP, Am. Heart Assn., Am. Coll. Cardiology, Am. Coll. Chest Physicians; mem. Burkes Tennis Club. Avocations: painting, reading, running, skiing, tennis. Office: 2100 Webster St Ste 516 San Francisco CA 94115-2382

KLINE, RORY R., regional marketing; b. Mt. Pleasant, Tex., Sept. 25, 1951; d. Jimmie Lee and Helen Marguerite (McBrayer) Justiss; m. Hamid Eshragh, Sept. 1, 1978; children: Jennifer Leigh, Natalie Elizabeth, Jessica Christine. Student, Stephen F. Austin State U., 1970-72; Assoc. degree, Massey Bus. Coll., 1974. Adminstrv. asst. to athletic dir./head coach Stephen F. Austin State U., Nacogdoches, Tex., 1971-77; asst. mgr. mgmt. sys. Am. Gen. Capital Mgmt., 1977-78; corp. recruiting, tng. mgr. Tex. Instruments, Inc., 1978-81; corp. mgr., pers. and adminstrn. Oceaneering Internat., Inc., 1981-84; cert. pers. cons. Quest Pers., 1984-86, Steitz and Corbett, 1987; owner, cert. pers. cons. Pers. Resources, 1987-92; human resource mgr. Nat. Contract Staffing, 1992-93; area mktg. mgr. Norrell Svcs., Inc., Las Vegas, Nev., 1993—; cons. Eshragh Pers. Resources, Houston, 1987-89; instr. Harris County C.C., Houston, 1985-89. Mem. Nat. Assn. Pers. Cons. (cert. pers. cons.), Nat. Assn. Temporary Svcs., Soc. Human Resource Mgmt. (sr. profl. human resources, conv. chmn. 1992), So. Nev. Assn. Temporary Svcs., So. Nev. Human Resource Assn. (chmn. publicity 1993, sec. 1994), Toastmasters Internat. Avocations: reading, self-devel., outdoor activities.

KLING, ROBERT WILLIAM, economist; b. Buffalo, N.Y., Nov. 15, 1957; s. William Alexander and Barbara Lorna (Hicks) K.; m. Celeste Holder, Nov. 17, 1979; children: Matthew Moore, John Alexander. AB in Econs., Davidson Coll., 1979; MA in Econs., U. Kans., 1982, PhD in Econs., 1985. Asst. prof. econs. Colo. State U., Fort Collins, 1984-90, assoc. prof. econs., 1990—, chmn. dept. econs., 1996—; vis. prof. U. Montpellier, France, 1991-92, Tech. U. Budapest, Hungary, 1993, U. Naples, Italy, 1993; vis. lectr. U. Pitts., 1998. Contbr. articles to profl. jours. Rsch. grantee Am. Farmland Trust, 1997; recipient Cermak Advising award Colo. State U., 1995. Mem. Am. Econ. Assn., Assn. for Cultural Econs., Assn. for Evolutionary Econs., Omicron Delta Epsilon (v.p. 1992-94). Democrat. Presbyterian. Office: Colo State U Dept Econs Fort Collins CO 80523-1771

KLINGENSMITH, ARTHUR PAUL, business and personal development consultant; b. L.A., May 23, 1949; s. Paul Arthur and Hermine Elinore K.; m. Donna J. Bellucci, Apr. 26, 1976 (div. Jan. 1981). AA in Social Sci., Indian Valley Jr. Coll., 1976; BA in Indsl. Psychology, San Francisco State U., 1979; MA in Indsl. Psychology, Columbia Pacific U., 1980. Enlisted USAF, Biloxi, Miss.; advanced through grades to staff sgt. USAF; instr. radio ops. USAF, Biloxi, 1968-72; air traffic control operator USAF, Hamilton AFB Novato, Calif., 1972-74; resigned USAF, 1974; elec. technician Calif. Dept. Transp., Oakland, 1975-78; right of way agt. Calif. Dept. Transp., San Francisco, 1978-85; sr. right of way agt. Calif. Dept. Transp., Sacramento, 1985-87, computer researcher, 1985-87; v.p., cons. Associated Right of Way Svcs., Inc., 1989-92; pvt. practice relocation and redevel. cons., 1987-96, bus. and pers. devel. cons., 1996—. V.p. bd. dirs. PAST Found. Mem. Inst. Noetic Scis., World Future Soc. Republican. Avocations: automobile restoration, painting, writing. Home and Office: Arthur P Klingensmith & Assocs PO Box 574 Sausalito CA 94966-0574

KLINK, PAUL LEO, business executive; b. Auburn, N.Y., July 28, 1965; s. Charles Lawrence and Regina Joyce (Maniscalco) K. Student, SUNY, Cayuga, 1979-85. Pres., CEO Aloha Direct divsn. of Klink, Inc., Honolulu, 1979—; pres. http://www.hawaiian.com/ Inc., 1995—, Viva Japan, Inc., 1998—; pres. Info. Tech., 1979, Aloha Direct, 1995, Hawaii Visitors Database Bur., 1997, First Class Mailing Svcs., 1997; v.p. PhytoTech U.S.A., 1996; pres., CEO Katana Mktg., 1998. Contbr. and edited articles for profl. jours. Co-chmn. direct mktg. com. Aloha United Way, Honolulu, 1988—, bd. dirs. Student Aloha; mem. Friends of Hawaii State Congressman, Ewa Beach, 1988—, Friends of State of Hawaii Gov., Honolulu, 1988—, Friends of the Mayor of the City of Honolulu, 1988—; bd. dirs. Postal Customer Coun., 1992—, Kids Voting Hawaii, 1997—; founder Rock 'n Vote, Aloha Found.; co-founder Live Aloha: attendee inauguration of U.S. Pres. William J. Clinton and U.S. V.p. Albert Gore, 1993, 97; bd. dirs. First Night Honolulu, Student Aloha/Aloha United Way, 1998—. Mem. Direct Mktg. Assn., Chinese C. of C., Korean C. of C., Filipino C. of C., C. of C. of Hawaii, Ad 2 (pres. 1995-96, chmn. bd. dirs. 1996-97), Japanese C. of C., Am. Mktg. Assn., Honolulu Publs. Assn., Honolulu Advt. Fedn., Pacific Club, Rotary. Avocations: surfing the internet, movies, world travel, Hawaiiana research, photography. Office: Klink Inc Box 8578 330 Saratoga Rd Honolulu HI 96815-1945

KLIPPING, ROBERT SAMUEL, geophysicist; b. Glaston, N.D., Dec. 5, 1928; s. Roy Samuel and Marie (Peterson) K.; m. Gayle Cleone Swanson, Sept. 29, 1951; children: Barbara, Sharon, Joan. BS in Geology, Colo. Coll., Colorado Springs, 1953. Geophys. computer scientist Gen. Geophys. Co., Denver, 1953-57; geophys. supr. Mandrel Indsl. Inc., Denver, 1957-65, area mgr., 1965-69; geophys. Pennzoil Co., Denver, 1969-72, exploration mgr., 1972-78; geophys. cons., owner Klipping & Assocs., Denver, 1978—. Author: American Association of Petroleum Geologists, 1976, Montana Geological Society, 1978. Staff sgt. U.S. Army, 1946-48. Mem. Am. Assn. Petroleum Geologists, Soc. Exploration Geophysicists, Denver Geophys. Soc. (treas. 1972-73, sec. 1973-74). Republican. Methodist. Avocations: woodworking, antique cars, golf, fishing. Home: 14645 Sterling Rd Colorado Springs CO 80921-2618 Office: Klipping & Assocs 518 17th St Denver CO 80202-4130

KLOBE, TOM, art gallery director; b. Mpls., Nov. 26, 1940; s. Charles S. and Lorna (Effertz) K.; m. Delmarie Pauline Motta, June 21, 1975. BFA, U. Hawaii, 1964, MFA, 1968; postgrad., UCLA, 1972-73. Vol. peace corps Alang, Iran, 1964-66; tchr. Calif. State U., Fullerton, 1969-72, Santa Ana (Calif.) Coll., 1972-77, Orange Coast Coll., Costa Mesa, Calif., 1974-77, Golden West Coll., Huntington Beach, Calif., 1976-77; art gallery dir. U. Hawaii, Honolulu, 1977—; acting dir. Downey (Calif.) Mus. Art, 1976; cons. Judiciary History Mus., Honolulu, 1982-96, Maui (Hawaii) Arts and Cultural Ctr., 1984-94, curator Kāia Wai Ola: This Living Water, 1994; exhibit designer Inst. for Astronomy, Honolulu, 1983-86; exhibit design cons. Japanese Cultural Ctr. Hawaii, 1993—; juror Print Casebooks; project coord. Crossings '97, France, Hawaii. Recipient Best in Exhbn. Design award Print Casebooks, 1984, 86, 88, Vol. Svc. award City of Downey, 1977; Exhbn. grantee NEA, 1979—, State Found. Culture and the Arts, 1977—. Mem. Hawaii Mus. Assn., Nat. Assn. Mus. Exhbn. Roman Catholic. Office: U Hawaii Art Gallery 2535 The Mall Honolulu HI 96822-2233

KLOHS, MURLE WILLIAM, chemist, consultant; b. Aberdeen, S.D., Dec. 24, 1920; s. William Henry and Lowell (Lewis) K.; m. Dolores Catherine Borm, June 16, 1946; children: Wendy C., Linda L. Student Westmar Coll., 1938-40; BSc, U. Notre Dame, 1947. Jr. chemist Harrower Lab., Glendale, Calif., 1947, Rexall Drug Co., L.A., 1947-49; sr. chemist Riker Labs., Inc., L.A., 1949-57, dir. medicinal chemistry, Northridge, Calif., 1957-69, mgr. chem. rsch. dept., 1969-72, mgr. pharm. devel. dept., 1972-73, mgr. tech. liaison and comml. devel., 1973-82; cons. chemist, 1982—. Contbr. articles to profl. jours. Served to lt. USNR, 1943-46. Riker fellow Harvard U., 1950. Mem. Am. Chem. Soc., Am. Pharm. Assn., Adventures Club (L.A.). Home and Office: Lake Wildwood 19831 Echo Blue Dr Penn Valley CA 95946-9414

KLOPE, THOMAS MICHAEL, landscape architect; b. Ventura, Calif., Oct. 10, 1957; s. William Taft and Rose Ann (Gowdy) K.; m. Mary Jane Dowd, Mar. 27, 1982; children: Lisa Michelle, Brian Francis, Matthew Thomas. BS in Landscape Architecture, Calif. Polytech State U., 1980; M of Landscape Architecture, Harvard U., 1987. Lic. landscape architect, Calif. Landscape architect pvt. practice, Los Altos, Calif.

KLOSINSKI, LEONARD FRANK, mathematics educator; b. Michigan City, Ind., July 16, 1938; s. Frank and Helen (Podgorna) K.;. BS, U. Santa Clara, 1961; MA, Oreg. State U., 1963. Programmer NASA Ames Rsch. Ctr., Mountain View, Calif., 1963; instr. math. Santa Clara (Calif.) U., 1964-68, asst. prof., 1968-76, assoc. prof., 1976—; dir. Nat. Sci. Found. Insts., 1969-74; mng. editor, treas. Fibonacci Assn., 1975-80; dir. William Lowell Putnam Math. Competition, 1978—. Author: Santa Clara Silver Anniversary Contest Book/ Problems and Solutions of the University of Santa Clara High School Mathematics Contests, 1985, Students' Solutions Manual to Accompany Lynn E. Garner's Calculus and Analytical Geometry, 1988; editor: William Lowell Putnam Mathematical Competition Problems and Solutions , 1965-84, 1985; contbr. articles to profl. jours. Mem. Math. Assn. Am. (coun. on competitions 1992—, Putnam prize com. 1975—, adv. bd. Math. Horizons 1993—, sec.-treas. No. Calif. sect. 1979—, vice-chair No. Calif. sect. 1999, Disting. Tchg. award No. Calif. sect. 1999, award for disting. coll. or univ. tchg. math. 1999). Democrat. Roman Catholic. Avocation: art collecting. Office: Santa Clara U Math Dept Santa Clara CA 95053

KLOTT, DAVID LEE, lawyer; b. Vicksburg, Miss., Dec. 10, 1941; s. Isadore and Dorothy (Lipson) K.; m. Maren J. Randrup, May 25, 1975. BBA summa cum laude, Northwestern U., 1963; JD cum laude, Harvard U., 1966. Bar: Calif. 1966, U.S. Ct. Claims. 1968, U.S. Supreme Ct. 1971, U.S. Tax Ct. 1973, U.S. Ct. Appeals (Fed. cir.) 1982. Ptnr. Pillsbury, Madison & Sutro, San Francisco, 1966—; mem. tax adv. group to sub-chpt. C J and K, Am. Law Inst.; tchr. Calif. Continuing Edn. of Bar, Practising Law Inst., Hastings Law Sch., San Francisco; bd. dirs. and counsel Marin Wine and Food Soc. Commentator Calif. Nonprofit Corp. Law; bd. dirs. Joan Shorenstein Barone Found. for Harvard, The Phyllis J. Shorenstein Fund for the Asian Art Mus. San Francisco; counsel Drum Found. Mem. ABA (tax exempt fin. com.), Calif. State Bar Assn. (tax sect.), San Francisco Bar Assn., Am.-Korean Taekwondo Friendship Assn. (1st dan-black belt), Harvard Club, Northwestern Club, Olympic Club, City Club San Francisco (founding mem.), Bay Club (charter mem.), Harbor Point Racquet and Beach Club, Internat. Wine and Food Soc. (bd. dirs., exec. com., bd. govs. Ams.), Beta Gamma Sigma, Beta Alpha Psi (pres. local chpt.). Office: Pillsbury Madison & Sutro 235 Montgomery St Ste 1616 San Francisco CA 94104-2902

KLUCK, CLARENCE JOSEPH, physician; b. Stevens Point, Wis., June 20, 1929; s. Joseph Bernard and Mildred Lorraine (Helminiak) K.; divorced; children: Paul Bernard, Annette Louise Kluck Winston, David John, Maureen Ellen. BS in Med. Sci., U. Wis., 1951, MD, 1954. Resident San Joaquin Hosp., French Camp, Calif., 1955-56; asst. instr. medicine Ohio State U., Columbus, 1958-60; physician, chief of medicine Redford Med. Ctr., Detroit, 1960-69; practice medicine specializing in internal medicine Denver, 1969-83; med. dir. Atlantic Richfield Co., Denver, 1983-85; corp. med. dir. Cyprus Minerals Co., Englewood, Colo., 1985-92; pres. Kluck Med. Assocs., Englewood, 1992—; bd. dirs. Climbo Catering, Detroit, 1967-69, Met. Labs., Denver, 1970-81, Provost, Inc., Denver, 1985-92; pres., CEO, chmn. bd. Corpcare, Inc., Englewood, 1992-97; CEO, pres. Corpcare Med. Assocs., P.C., 1992-97; pres. Denver Occupational and Aviation Medicine Clinic, P.C., 1995—. Contbr. articles to profl. jours. Served to capt. U.S. Army, 1956-58. Recipient Century Club award Boy Scouts Am., 1972. Fellow Am. Occupational Med. Assn., Am. Coll. Occupational and Environ. Medicine, Am. Coll. Occupational Medicine; mem. Am. Acad. Occupational Medicine, Rocky Mountain Acad. Occupational Medicine (bd. dirs. 1985-88), Arapahoe County Med. Soc., Denver Med. Soc. (bd. dirs. 1973-74, council mem. 1981-87), Colo. Med. Soc. (del. 1973-74, 81-87), Am. Mining Congress Health Commn., Am. Soc. Internal Medicine, Colo. Soc. Internal Medicine. Roman Catholic. Clubs: Flatirons (Boulder, Colo.); Metropolitan. Avocations: fishing, hiking, skiing, flying, golf. Office: 3700 Havana St Ste 200 Denver CO 80239-3242

KLUCK, LINDA ANN, academic administrator; b. Phoenix, Dec. 25, 1960; d. Wilbert Cigle and Dorothy Helen (Pierce) Dyer; 1 child, Amanda Kluck. AA, Santa Fe C.C., 1998; postgrad., Coll. Santa Fe, 1998—. Svc. rep. Mountain Bell, Phoenix, 1978-86; sch. dir. The Children's Workshop, Santa Fe, 1989-91; acct. specialist Sunwest Bank, Santa Fe, 1991-95; adminstrv. coord. Santa Fe C.C., 1995—; adv. bd. Children's Workshop Sch., Santa Fe, 1995—; commr. N.Mex. Commn. on Higher Edn., Santa Fe, 1996-98. Active Las Compadres de Santa Fe, 1991-95; events com. Open Hands, Santa Fe, 1993-96; vol. Habitat for Humanity, Santa Fe, 1990-95. Avocations: community involvement, PTO. Office: Santa Fe CC 6401 S Richards Ave Santa Fe NM 87505-4887

KLUG, JOHN JOSEPH, secondary education educator, director of dramatics; b. Denver, Apr. 27, 1948; s. John Joseph Sr. and Dorthea Virginia (Feely) Carlyle. BA in English, U. N.C., 1974; MA in Theatre, U. Colo., 1984. Tchr. Carmody Jr. High Sch., Lakewood, Colo., 1976-78; tchr. Golden (Colo.) High Sch., 1978—, dir. of dramatics, 1978—; producer, dir. Children's Theatre Tours, 1978—; theatrical cons., 1983—; improvisational workshop leader, 1983—. Playwright, editor: Children's Theatre scripts, 1983—; producer, dir. Denver Theatre Sports, 1993—. Recipient Bravo/TCI Theatre award, 1995. Home: 4565 King St Denver CO 80211-1357 Office: Golden HS 701 24th St Golden CO 80401-2398

KLYCINSKI, FREDERICK ALLEN See ALLEN, RICK

KMET, REBECCA EUGENIA PATTERSON, pharmacist; b. Ellisville, Miss., June 17, 1948; d. Eugene Roberts and Ruth Winn (Pettis) Patterson; m. Joseph Paul Kmet, Mar. 29, 1969. BS in Pharmacy, U. Ariz., 1971; MBA, Nat. U., 1981. Pharmacist Santa Monica (Calif.) Bldg. Profl. Pharmacy, 1972-73, Vets. Hosp., West Los Angeles, Calif., 1973-74, Kaiser Med. Ctr., San Diego, 1979-82, Farmersville Drug Store, Farmersville, Calif., 1991-95; relief pharmacist various locations, 1995—. Community svc. vol; cmty. activist; mem. Eagle Forum, Marine Corps San Diego Recruit Depot Hist. Soc. Lt. USN, 1975-78. Recipient Presdl. Achievement award Rep. Party Nat. Congl. com. Mem. DAR, Navy League, Naval Hist. Found., U.S. English, Eagle Forum, Rho Chi, Kappa Epsilon. Republican. Avocations: theology, reading, writing, antiqueing, gardening. Home: PO Box 42557 Tucson AZ 85733-2557

KNAPP, (MARY) GWEN, columnist; b. Wilmington, Del., Nov. 18, 1961; d. Laurence Bernard and Eleanor (Agnew) K. B, Harvard U., 1983. Copy editor Wilmington News Jour., 1983-85; sports reporter, copy editor Phila. Inquirer, 1985-95; sports columnist San Francisco Examiner, 1995—; dep. press sec. Oreg. Dems., Portland, fall 1992. Vol. constrn. worker Habitat for Humanity, New Orleans, 1993. Recipient 1st pl. event story award AP Sports Editors, 1994. Avocation: swimming. Office: San Francisco Examiner 110 5th St San Francisco CA 94103-2918

KNAPP, LONNIE TROY, elementary education educator; b. Charles City, Iowa, Dec. 2, 1948; s. Troy Leroy and Anna Mildred (Conner) K.; m. Nancy Maureen Godfrey, Aug. 19, 1972; children: Eric Lonnie, Jamie Troy, Dusty Mack. BA, U. No. Iowa, 1972. Elem. tchr. Clear Lake, Iowa, 1972-92, Palm Springs (Calif.) Unified Sch. Dist., 1992—. Contbr. articles to profl. jours. Recipient Outstanding Tchr. award, Conservation Tchr. award, Iowa, North Cen. U.S. Mem. NEA, Iowa Edn. Assn., Calif. Tchrs. Assn., Clear Lake Edn. Assn. (various offices).

KNAUF, JAMES EDWARD, artist; b. Denver, Dec. 2, 1948; s. Robert Joseph and Betty Lou (Quick) K.; m. Elaine Marie Padoll, Nov. 1, 1978; children: Noah, Trevor. BFA, U. Calif., Irvine, 1974. Avocations: surfing, sailing. Office: 15049 N 6th St Phoenix AZ 85022-3615

KNAUFF, HANS GEORG, physician, educator; b. Bad Hersfeld, Germany, July 8, 1927; s. Friedrich and Sophie (Sauer) K.; student U. Erlangen, 1947-49, U. Freiburg, 1949, U. Basel, 1949-51, U. Heidelberg, 1951-52; Dr. Med., U. Heidelberg, 1953; m. Sigrid W. Keppner, Aug. 28, 1956; children—Ursula v. Wrangel, Barbara K. Asst., pharmacology dept. Heidelberg (W. Ger.) U., 1953; with pharmacology dept. Univ. Coll., London, 1953, Royal Coll. Surgeons, London, 1954; with Pathol. Inst., Heidelberg U., 1955, Med. Clinic, U. Munchen, 1955-63; privat dozent for internal medizin München and Marburg, 1961-67; prof. internal medizin, 1967; prof. Med. Clinic, U. Marburg (W. Ger.), 1967-83. Served with German Air Force, 1943-45. Mem. Deutsche Gesellschaft für Innere Medizin. Mem. Luth. Ch. Contbr. articles to sci. jours. Home: 2155 Westhill Wynd, West Vancouver, BC Canada V7S 2Z3

KNECHT, BEN HARROLD, surgeon; b. Rapid City, S.D., May 3, 1938; m. Jane Bowles, Aug. 27, 1961; children: John, Janelle. BA, U. S.D., 1960; MD, U. Iowa, 1964; cert. total quality mgmt., U. Wash., 1998. Diplomate Am. Bd. Surgery. Intern Los Angeles County Gen. Hosp., 1964-65; resident in surgery U. Iowa Sch. Medicine, Iowa City, 1968-72; surgeon Wenatchee (Wash.) Valley Clinic, 1972—; med. dir. Cascade Hosp. and Surgery Ctr., 1997—; chmn. med. informatics Wen Valley Clinic, 1995—, chmn. gen.-vasc. surg. dept., 1996—; dir. emergency rm. Ctrl. Wash. Hosp., Wenatchee, 1972-79, chief surgery, 1983-86; chmn. claims rev. panel Wash. State Med. Assn., Seattle, 1979-82, prof. liability com. risk mgmt., 1985-90; clin. prof. surgery U. Wash.; mem. adv. risk mgmt. com. Wash. State Physicians Ins. Subscribers, 1990-98, regional adv. com. Nat. Libr. Medicine, 1991-93. Fundraiser Cen. Wash. Hosp. Found., 1987; del. Gov.'s Conf. on Librs., 1991. Lt. comdr. USN, 1965-68, Vietnam. Mem. AMA (alt. del. 1985-87, del. 1988-98, surg. caucus exec. com. 1991-94), ACS (bd. dirs. Wash. chpt. 1981-84), Am. Coll. Physician Execs., Am. Soc. Quality, North Pacific Surg. Assn., Wash. State Med. Assn. (trustee 1979-98), Chelan-Douglas County Med. Soc., Am. Soc. Gen. Surgery (founding bd. 1994—, bd. dir.1992—), Rotary (chmn. youth com. 1976-78). Avocations: snow and water skiing, reading, hiking, computing. Office: Wenatchee Valley Clinic 820 N Chelan Ave Wenatchee WA 98801-2028

KNELL, DORA MARIE, publishing executive; b. Sonoma, Calif., Nov. 30, 1922; d. Viggo Riis Sorensen and Inez Frances Bonvecchio; m. Frederick Gerald Knell, June 22, 1947 (dec. June 1986); children: Gregory L., Catherine L., Theodora C., Valerie P., Vivian M., Geoffrey F., Derek P. AA, Santa Rosa Jr. Coll., 1944; AB in Journalism, U. Calif., Berkeley, 1954; credential in Spanish, Univ. Iberoam., Mexico City, 1970; credential in graphic arts, Indian Valley Coll., 1978. CEO Graphic Arts Mgmt. Co., San Rafael, Calif., 1978—. Editor: Manifestations of Thought, 1980, Sahar, 1981, California Controversies, 1986, (newspaper) The Active Democrat, 1988-92; prodr.: (TV show) The Square Table, 1995—. Chmn. bd. dirs. HOPE, Inc., Chgo., 1969-72, housing com. FACSAC, Marin County, San Rafael, 1972-76; bd. dirs. LWV, Marin County, 1974-76, Nat. Women's Polit. Caucus, Marin County, 1994-96; elected mem. Dem. Cen. Com., Marin County, 1974-92; deacon St. Luke Presbyn. Ch., San Rafael, 1989-92; co-owner R-Ranch, R-Wild Horse Ranch. Recipient Cert. of Appreciation, AAUW, 1976, Nat. Women's Polit. Caucus, 1991, Cert. of Recognition, Santa Rosa Jr. Coll., 1987. Mem. San Rafael C. of C. Democrat. Presbyterian. Avocations: pilot, horseback riding, swimming, skeet shooting, canoeing. Home: 11 Peacock Ln San Rafael CA 94901-1507 Office: Graphic Arts Mgmt Co 3140 Kerner Blvd Ste B San Rafael CA 94901-5435

KNIERIM, ROBERT VALENTINE, electrical engineer, consultant; b. Oakland, Calif., Sept. 27, 1916; s. Otto Valentine and Edith May (Bell) K.; m. Esther Perry Bateman, July 10, 1954; children: Kathleen Dianne, David Lyell, Daniel Goddard. BS, U. Calif., Berkeley, 1941; postgrad., U. Pitts., 1942, U. Colo., 1944-45, Raytheon Field Engring Sch, 1945. Registered profl. elec. engr., Calif. Student engr. Westinghouse Corp., East Pittsburgh, Pa., 1942; marine elec. engr. U.S. Maritime Commn., Oakland, 1943-44; elec. engr. U.S. Bur. Reclamation, Denver, 1944-45, Sacramento, 1945-48; field engr. Raytheon Corp., Waltham, Mass., 1945; electronics engr. Sacramento Signal Depot, 1948-49; assoc. elec. engr. Calif. Office Architecture and Constrn., 1949-57, sr. elec. engr., 1957-76; cons. engring., 1976. Mem. Century Club of Golden Empire Coun. Boy Scouts Am., 1969-87, instnl. rep. 1948-54, dist. chmn., camping and activities com. 1951-54; mem. Cascade Pacific Coun. Boy Scouts of Am. 1987—. Recipient James E. West Fellowship award Boy Scouts of Am., 1994. Mem. Sacramento Engrs. Club (charter), IEEE (sr., life), Nat. Rifle Assn. (life), Sierra Club (life, chpt. treas. 1962-65), Nat. Assn. Corrosion Engrs. (life), Calif. Alumni Assn. (life), Eta Kappa Nu, Alpha Phi Omega (life). Republican. Congregationalist. Lodge: Masons. Home and Office: Cons Elec Engring 10325 SW Ashton Circle Wilsonville OR 97070-9532

KNIGHT, CONSTANCE BRACKEN, writer, realtor, corporate executive; b. Detroit, Oct. 30, 1937; d. Thomas Francis and Margaret (Kearney) Bracken; m. James Edwards Knight, June 14, 1958 (div. Feb. 1968); children: Constance Lynne Knight Campbell, James Seaton, Keith Bracken. Student, Barry Coll., 1955-56, Fla. State U., 1958-60; AA, Marymount Coll., 1957. Columnist, feature writer Miami Herald, Ft. Lauderdale, Fla., 1954-55, 79-80; pub. rels. dir. Lauderdale Beach Hotel, 1965-67; columnist, feature writer Ft. Lauderdale News/Sun-Sentinel, 1980-81; owner Connie Knight and Assoc. Pub. Rels., Ft. Lauderdale, 1981-85; editor, pub. Vail (Colo.) Mag., 1986-89, contbg. freelance writer, 1989—; editorial cons. Vail Valley Mag., 1993; pres. Knight Enterprises, Vail, 1994—; instr. Colo. Mountain Coll., Vail, 1979; copywriter Colo. Ski Mus., Vail, 1986-96. Mem. Planning and Environ. Commn., Vail, 1990-92, Vail Licensing Authority, 1995—. Mem. Soc. Profl. Journalists, N.Am. Ski Journalists (treas. 1990-93). E-mail: cknight@vail.net. Fax #: (970) 476-3615. Office: 385 Gore Creek Dr Apt 201 Vail CO 81657-3606

KNIGHT, JANET ANN, elementary education educator; b. Covina, Calif., July 22, 1937; d. Arnold M. and Thelma (Lyle) Ostrum; m. Ronald L. Knight, Sept. 14, 1957; children: Barbara Lynne, Susan Kaye. BA in Edn., Cen. Wash. U., 1979; MA in Edn., Heritage Coll., 1992. Cert. elem, secondary tchr., Wash. 2nd grade tchr. Kennewick (Wash.) Pub. Schs., 1980-81, 1st grade tchr., 1981-85, 3rd grade tchr., 1985-93, 4th grade tchr., 1993—; lang. arts dist. com. Kennewick Sch. Dist., 1985-89, curriculum, instrn. com., 1989-92, dist. curriculum and instruction renewal cycle for learning excellence, 1992-94, dist. assessment com., 1992-95. Mem. Richland (Wash.) Light Opera Co., 1963-75. Mem. NEA, ASCD, Wash. Edn. Assn., Kennewick Edn. Assn., Wash. Orgn. Reading Devel., Benton County Coun. of Internat. Reading Assn., Order of Rainbow for Girls, Sigma Tau Alpha. Episcopalian. Avocations: Petit Basset Griffon Vendeen show dogs, ceramics, golf, photography, reading. Home: 120 Heather Ln Richland WA 99352-9155 Office: Westgate Elem Sch 2514 W 4th Ave Kennewick WA 99336-3115

KNIGHT, JEFFREY RICHARD, small business owner; b. Salt Lake City, Apr. 22, 1962; s. Richard M. and Donna H. (Hallman) K.; m. Carrie Lyn Jackson. BBA, Calif. State Poly. Inst. U., 1984, MBA, 1986. owner KD Enterprises, 1995—; pres. Lockheed Martin Activities Coordinating Com., Camarillo, 1991-93. With Lockheed Martin, Camarillo, Calif., 1985-96; prin. engr. DirecTV, quality assurance mgr., 1996—; owner, KD Enterprises, pres. Co. Activities Coordinating Com., Camarillo, 1991-93. Treas. Hillcrest Park Home Owners Assn., 1990-92, pres., 1992-93; chmn. Calif. State Poly. Inst. U. Rose Float Com., 1984-85. Mem. Thailand Darts Assn., Rose Float Alumni Assn. (treas. 1985-86, bd. dirs. 1987-88, pres. 1991-93, historian/archivist 1994—, chmn. 50th float activities com.), Nat. Employee Svcs. and Recreation Assn. (pres. Gold Coast chpt. 1994-95), Toastmasters Internat. (chpt. treas. 1996, v.p. pub. rels. 1996, Competent Toastmaster award 1996). Republican. Avocations: philately, softball, darts. Home: 2143 Saxe Ct Thousand Oaks CA 91360-3148

KNIGHT, PHILIP H(AMPSON), shoe manufacturing company executive; b. Portland, Oreg., Feb. 24, 1938; s. William W. and Lota (Hatfield) K.; m. Penelope Parks, Sept. 13, 1968; children: Matthew, Travis. B.B.A., U. Oreg.; M.B.A., Stanford U. C.P.A., Oreg. Chmn., chief exec. officer, past pres. Nike, Inc., Beaverton, Oreg., 1967—. Bd. dirs. U.S.-Asian Bus. Coun., Washington, 1st lt. AUS, 1959-60. Named Oreg. Businessman of Yr., 1982, One of 1988's Best Mgrs., Bus. Week Magazine. Mem. AICPA. Republican. Episcopalian. Office: Nike Inc One Bowerman Dr Beaverton OR 97005-6453*

KNIGHT, ROBERT EDWARD, banker; b. Alliance, Nebr., Nov. 27, 1941; s. Edward McKean and Ruth (McDuffee) K.; m. Eva Sophia Youngstom, Aug. 12, 1966. BA, Yale U., 1963; MA, Harvard U., 1965, PhD, 1968. Asst. prof. U.S. Naval Acad., Annapolis, Md., 1966-68; lectr. U. Md., 1967-68; fin. economist Fed. Res. Bank of Kansas City (Mo.), 1968-70, research officer, economist, 1971-76, asst. v.p., sec., 1977, v.p., sec., 1978-79; pres. Alliance (Nebr.) Nat. Bank, 1979-94, also chmn., 1983-94; pres. Robert Knight Assocs., banking and econ. cons., Cheyenne, 1979—; chmn. Eldred Found., 1985—; vis. prof., chair banking and fin. E. Tenn. State U., Johnson City, 1988; mem. faculty Stonier Grad. Sch. Banking, 1972—, Colo. Grad. Sch. Banking, 1975-82, Am. Inst. Banking, U. Mo., Kansas City, 1971-79, Prochnow Grad. Sch. Banking, U. Wis.; mem. extended learning faculty Park Coll., 1996—; mem. Coun. for Excellence for Bur. Bus. Rsch. U. Nebr., Lincoln, 1991-94, mem. Grad. Sch. Arts & Scis Coun., Harvard, 1994—; chmn. Taxable Mcpl. Bondholders Protective Com., 1991-94. Trustee, 1984-85, Knox Presbyn. Ch., Overland Park, Kans., 1965-69; bd. regents Nat. Comml. Lending Sch., 1980-83; mem. Downtown Improvement Com., Alliance, 1981-94; trustee U. Nebr. Found.; bd. dirs. Stonier Grad. Sch. Banking, Box Butte County Devel. Commn., Nebr. Com. for Humanities, 1986-90; mem. fin. com. United Meth. Ch., Alliance, 1982-85, trustee, 1990-93; Box Butte County Indsl. Devel. Bd., 1987-94; mem. Nebr. Com. for the Humanities, 1986-90. Woodrow Wilson fellow, 1963-64. Mem. Am. Econ. Assn., Am. Fin. Assn., So. Econ. Assn., Nebr. Bankers Assn. (com. state legis. 1980-81, com. comml. loans and investments 1986-87), Am. Inst. Banking (state com. for Nebr. 1980-83), Am. Bankers Assn. (econ. adv. com. 1980-83, cmty. bank leadership coun.), Western Econ. Assn., Econometric Soc., Rotary, Masons. Contbr. articles to profl. jours. Home and Office: 429 W 5th Ave Cheyenne WY 82001-1249

KNIGHT, VICK, JR., author, educator, counselor; b. Lakewood, Ohio, Apr. 6, 1928; s. Vick Ralph and Janice (Higgins) K. BS, U. So. Calif., 1952; MA, L.S. State Coll., 1956; postgrad. Whittier Coll., 1959-61, Long Beach State Coll., 1960-61, Calif. State Coll.-Fullerton, 1961-64, Claremont U., 1963-65, UCLA, 1993-98; EdD, Calif. Coast U., 1991, postgrad, UCLA, 1993-98; m. Beverly Joyce McKeighan, Apr. 14, 1949 (div. 1973); children: Stephen Foster, Mary Ann; m. Carolyn Schlee, June 6, 1981; children: Kathy, Meri. Producer-dir. Here Comes Tom Harmon radio series ABC, Hollywood, Calif., 1947-50; tchr., vice-prin. Ranchito Sch. Dist., Pico Rivera, Calif., 1952-59; prin. Kraemer Intermediate Sch., Placentia, Calif., 1959-64; dir. instructional svcs. Placentia Unified Sch. Dist., 1964-65, asst. supt., 1965-71; program dir. World Vista Travel Svcs., 1970-72; dir. grad. extension La Verne Coll., 1971-73; v.p. Nat. Gen. West Investments, 1971-74; bd. dir. community rels. and devel. Childrens Hosp. of Orange County (Calif.), 1974-84; sr. dir. curriculum and edn. svcs. Elsinore Union High Sch. Dist., Lake Elsinore, Calif., 1985-88; exec. dir. Elsinore Valley Community Devel. Corp., 1989-92; dean Sch. Edn. Newport U., Newport Beach, Calif., 1992-96; pres. Aristan Assocs.; bd. dirs. Key Records, Hollywood. Dist. chmn. Valencia Coun. Boy Scouts Am.; chmn. Cancer Soc. Ptnrs. of Ams., also chmn. Sister City Com.; chmn. Community Chest Drives; chmn. adv. com. Esperenza Hosp.; mem. Educare; hon. life mem. Calif. PTA. Bd. dirs. U. Calif.-Irvine Friends of Library, pres., 1975-77; bd. trustees Lake Elsinore Unified Sch. Dist., 1991, pres. 1993-99; bd. dirs. Muckenthaler Cultural Groups Found.; chmn. bd. William Claude Fields Found. Club With USN, 1946-48. Recipient Disting. Citizen award Whittier Coll., 1960; Educator of Yr. award Orange County Press Club, 1971, Author and Book award U. Calif., 1973, Children's Lit. award Calif. State U.-Fullerton, 1979, Bronze Pelican award Boy Scouts Am.; named Canyon Lake Man of the Yr., 1994; mem. NEA, ASCAP, Nat. Sch. Pub. Rels. Assn. (regional v.p.), U.S. Jr. C. of C. (bd. dir., Young Man of Calif. 1959), Calif. Jr. C. of C. (state v.p.), Pico Rivera Jr. C. of C. (pres.), Canyon Lake C. of C. (pres. 1998), Audubon Soc., Western Soc. Naturalists, Calif. Tchrs. Assn., Internat. Platform Assn., Soc. Children's Book Writers, Authors Guild, Authors League Am., Anti-Slubberdegullion Soc., Bank Dicks, Assn. Hosp. Devel., Art Experience, Good Bears of World, Los Compadres con Libros, Blue Key, Skull and Dagger, Les Amis du Vin, Phi Sigma Kappa, Alpha Delta Sigma, E Clampus Vitus, Theta Nu Epsilon, Kiwanian (pres.), Master Mason, Canyon Lake Home Owners Club (pres. 1989-91), West Atwood Yacht (commodore) Club. Writer weekly Nature Notebook newspaper columns, 1957—, wine columnist Riverside Press-Enterprise, 1991—, S. Coast Wines Mag.; fine arts editor Placentia Courier; editor curriculum guides: New Math., Lang. Arts, Social Scis., Pub. Rels., Biol. Sci. Substitute Tchrs; author: (ecology textbooks) It's Our World; It's Our Future; It's Our Choice, Snakes of Hawaii, Earle the Squirrel, Night the Crayons Talked; My Word!; Send for Haym Salomon!, Joby and the Wishing Well; Twilight of the Animal Kingdom; A Tale of Twos, Who's Zoo, A Navel Salute, Friend or Enema?, John Sevier: Citizen Soldier, Toasting Temecula Wines, A Rainforest Adventure, also math. instrn. units; contbr. articles to various jours. Home: 22597 Canyon Lake Dr S Canyon Lake CA 92587-7595

KNITTLE, WILLIAM JOSEPH, JR., media executive, psychologist, religious leader, management and marketing consultant, educator; b. Santa Monica, Calif., June 11, 1945; s. William Joseph Knittle and Lahlee (Duggins) Morrell; m. Linda Catherine Black, Apr. 19, 1969 (div. Aug. 1977); 1 child, Kristen Elizabeth; m. Alexis Carrell Upton, Sept. 30, 1977 (div. Aug. 1996); 1 child, Jonathan Kynan. Student, Inst. for Japanese Culture, 1960, Am. Nat. Theater and Acad., 1962-64; BA in English, Loyola U., L.A., 1966, MA in Comm. Arts, 1970, MA in Counseling Psychology, 1973; PhD in Communication Theory and Social Psychology, Lawrence U., Santa Barbara, Calif., 1976; D of Dharma in Asian Religion and Philosophy, U. Oriental Studies, L.A., 1980; MBA, U. La Verne, 1983; grad., Grantsmanship Ctr., L.A., 1980. Ordained Sramanera, Buddhist monk, 1976; ordained Bikkhu, Vietnamese lineage, 1977, Chinese lineage, 1977; ordained Zen Master and High Tchr. in all Buddhist Traditions, Fo Kuang Shan Monastery, Taiwan, 1977. Assoc. editor Black Belt mag., 1960-65; asst. news dir., pub. affairs/continuity acceptance coord. Sta. KHJ-TV, L.A., 1966-67; news editor Sta. KFWB Radio, L.A., 1967-69; profl. photographer, 1969-80; dir. news and media rels. Loyola Marymount U., L.A., 1969-75; pvt. therapist, hypnotherapist L.A., 1974—; gen. mgr., dir. televised studies Media Five Film and TV Prodns., L.A., 1976-79, v.p., 1981-83; assoc. dir. divsn. of continuing edn. U. La Verne, Calif., 1979-81; pres. Western News Assocs., L.A., 1983—; adj. prof. U. La Verne, Calif., 1980—; chmn. East-West psychology dept. U. Oriental Studies, L.A., 1979-83; asst. to dean UCLA Sch. Medicine, 1985-86; advt./mktg. dir. summer sessions UCLA, 1986-98; prof. Coll. Buddhist Studies, L.A., 1991—; chief instr. martial arts Loyola Marymount U., 1963-74; lectr. L.A. Police Dept., 1978; founder Realization Therapy, 1976; host Campus report, KHJ-AM/KRTH-FM, L.A., 1973-74, At Your Leisure program KXLU-FM, L.A., 1972-76; dir. film segments KCOP-TV, L.A., 1966; tech. dir. Quien Lo Sabe program KMEX-TV, L.A., 1964; instr. systematic theology and sacred scripture L.A. Archdiocese, 1969-72; cons. Yu Shing Corp. Taiwan, 1992, Zhong Shan (Sun Yat Sen) Victory Ship (Nat. Treas.) Mem. Complex, Peoples Republic of China, 1997, CITIC Pharms. Co., Peoples Republic of China, 1998—, Purex Corp., 1980. Author: Survival Strategies for the Classroom Teacher, 1982; syndicated columnist various newspapers, mags., 1970—; Hollywood corr. Columbia mag., 1974-87; contbr. articles to profl. jours.; writer/cinematographer On Campus series KNBC-TV, L.A., 1974; speechwriter Chinese Democracy Advocates, 1996—. Media spokesman Am. Cancer Soc., 1960-62; media teenage coord. Los Angeles County March of Dimes, 1961-68; assoc. dir. Pasadena/San Gabriel Valley Counseling Ctr., Pasadena, 1973-74; assoc. abbot Internat. Buddhist Med. Ctr., L.A., 1976-81; bd. dirs. Dharma Vijaya Buddhist Vihara, L.A., 1985—; founding mem. So. Calif. Buddhist Sangha Coun., L.A. Buddhist Union, So. Calif. Interreligious Coun.; host, announcer 3d Internat. Karate Championship Tournament, 1975, 5th ann. open Am. Tae Kwon Do-Kung Fu Championship Tournament, 1976; host, announcer Dedication of Wat Thai Buddhist Temple, North Hollywood, 1980. Recipient Martial Arts Pioneer award Am. Tae Kwon Do-Kung Fu Assn., 1976, Nat. Headliners award Wash. Press Club, 1968, Internat. Journalism award Sigma Delta Chi, 1968. Mem. AAAS, NATAS, Assn. for Transpersonal Psychology, Inst. for Holistic Edn., Soc. Interdisciplinary Study of Mind, L.A. Film Critics Cir., Internat. Brotherhood of Magicians, Internat. Imagery Assn., Am. Soc. Tng. and Devel., Nat. Book Critics Circle, Investigative Reporters and Editors, Am. Fedn. Police (chaplain 1985—), Nat. Police Acad., Nat. Acad. TV Arts and Scis. Avocations: martial arts, magic, pseudoscience, religious history, qigong. Home and Office: Western News Assocs PO Box 24130 Los Angeles CA 90024-0130

KNOBBE, LOUIS JOSEPH, lawyer; b. Carroll, Iowa, Apr. 6, 1932; s. Louis C. and Elsie M. (Praeger) K.; m. Jeanette M. Sganga, Apr. 3, 1954; children: Louis, Michael, Nancy, John, Catherine. BSEE, Iowa State U., 1953; JD, Loyola U., L.A., 1959. Bar: Calif. 1960, U.S. Supreme Ct. 1963; U.S. Patent and Trademark Office. Tech. staff Bell Telephone Labs., 1953-54; patent engr. GE, Washington, 1955-56, N.Am. Aviation, Downey, Calif., 1956-59; patent lawyer Beckman Instruments, Fullerton, Calif., 1959-62; co-founder, ptnr. Knobbe, Martens, Olson & Bear, Newport Beach, Calif., 1962—; lectr. Am. Intellectual Property Law Assn., Computer Law Assn., Inc., L.A. Intellectual Property Law Assn., San Diego Bar Assn., Orange County Patent Law Assn.; adj. prof. Sch. Law U. San Diego, 1987—. Co-author: Attorney's Guide to Trade Secrets, 1972, 2d edit., 1996, How to Handle Basic Patent, 1992; contbg. author: Using Intellectual Property Rights to Protect Domestic Markets, 1986; contbr. articles to profl. jours. Bd. dirs. Orange County (Calif.) Performing Arts Ctr., 1975-83, Orange County chpt. Assn. Corp. Growth; past pres. Philharmonic Soc. Orange County; bd. mem., past v.p. Opera Pacific, Orange County. Fellow Inst. Advancement Engring.; mem. ABA, IEEE (past chmn. Orange County sect., Centennial medal 1984), Am. Intellectual Property Law Assn., Am. Arbitration Soc. (mem. panel neutrals), State Bar Calif., Orange County Bar Assn. (mem. civil mediation panel), Orange County Patent Law Assn., San Diego Patent Law Assn., Licensing Execs. Soc., Santa Ana North Rotary, First Friday Friars, Pacific Club, Balboa Yacht Club, Phi Kappa Phi, Tau Beta Pi, Eta Kappa Nu. Avocations: boating, still and video photography, travel and exploration in Lake Powell, Death Valley, deserts of Arizona and Baja, California. Office: 620 Newport Center Dr Fl 16 Newport Beach CA 92660-6420

KNOELKER, MICHAEL, science observatory administrator; b. Feb. 9, 1953. Diploma in Physics, U. Göttingen, Germany, 1978; PhD in Physics, U. (Germany) Freiburg, 1983. Asst. prof. U. Göttingen, 1983-87, 88-90; astronomer Kiepenheuer-Instut Sonnenphysik, Freiburg, 1990—; affiliate scientist High Altitude Obs. Nat. Ctr. Atmospheric Rsch., Boulder, Colo., 1994-95, sr. scientist, dir. High Altitude Obs., 1995—; vis. scientist High Altitude Obs. Nat. Ctr. Atmospheric Rsch., Boulder, 1987-88. Office: NCAR High Altitude Observatory 3450 Mitchell Ln Boulder CO 80301*

KNOLL, JAMES LEWIS, lawyer; b. Chgo., Oct. 5, 1942. AB, Brown U., 1964; JD, U. Chgo., 1967. Bar: Ill. 1967, Oreg. 1971, Wash. 1984, Alaska 1993. Mediator, arbitrator Portland, Oreg.; adj. prof. law Northwestern Sc. Law, Lewis and Clark Coll., 1982-91. Mem. ABA (mem. TIPS coun. 1989-92, chair property ins. com. 1984-85, mem. fidelity surety com., chair comml. tort com. 1985-86), Oreg. State Bar (editor 2 vol. text on ins. 1983, 96), Wash. State Bar, Oreg. Assn. Def. Coun. (pres. 1984). Office: 1500 SW Taylor St Portland OR 97205-1819

KNOLL, RAYMOND L., physician, surgeon, consultant; b. Newkirk, Okla., May 11, 1907; s. Daniel L. and Delia Elizabeth (DeMott) K.; m. Victoria A. Tetz, Aug. 8, 1932 (dec. Feb. 1963); children: M. Dean, R. Manley, Vance L.; m. Marie M. Sommers, July 29, 1964. BA, Union Coll., 1929; MD, Loma Linda Sch. Medicine, Loma Linda, Calif., 1944. Pvt. practice Lodi, Calif., 1947-64; cons. Pollock Pines, Calif., 1964—. Author, pub.: How to Live to Be 101 and Be Able to Enjoy It, 1998. Home: 5731 Pony Express Trl Pollock Pines CA 95726-9794

KNOLL, WILLIAM LEE, animation director; b. Long Beach, Calif., July 9, 1948; s. Robert B. aned Virginia M. (Humphrey) K.; m. Susan D. Spafford Johnson, May 28, 1971 (div. Dec. 1976); m. Linda L. Gill, July 18, 1981; 1 child, Tracy Lynn. BA, San Diego State U., 1974. Mem. Motion Picture Screen Cartoonists, North Hollywood, Calif., 1976—; asst. animator DePatie-Freleng, Van Nuys, Calif., 1976-80, Hanna-Barbera, North Hollywood, 1980-86; FX animator Boss Films, Marina del Rey, Calif., 1986; dir. Marvel Prodns., Van Nuys, 1986-87; timing dir. D.I.C., Burbank, Calif., 1988-91, Warner Bros. Animation, Sherman Oaks, Calif., 1991-96, Dreamworks, Inc., Encino, Calif., 1996-97, Walt Disney TV Animation, North Hollywood, Calif., 1998—; mem. adv. com. for animation devel. Mt. San Antonio Coll., 1996—. Animator: (animated program) Ziggy's Gift, 1982 (Emmy award 1982-83); dir.: (animated program) Muppet Babies, 1986 (Emmy award 1986-87); timing dir.: (animated program) Animaniacs, 1995 (Emmy award 1995-96), (children's program) Animaniacs, 1995 (Emmy award 1995-96). Chmn. Animal Control Commn., South Pasadena, 1983-84; v.p. Booster's Club, South Pasadena, 1983-84; pres. Covina (Calif.) Am. Little League, 1989, 90; candidate Covina Unified Sch. Dist. Sch. Bd., 1995. Recipient Certs. of Appreciation, City of South Pasadena, 1984, Covina Firefighters, 1996, Cert. of Recognition City of Covina, 1995. Mem. NATAS, Aztec Athletic Found., Covina Breakfast Lions (pres. 1988—, Lion of Yr. 1995, 96), Lions Internat. Youth Exch. (dist. chmn. 1991-94, govenor 1993), Lambda Chi Alpha Alumni. Avocations: golf, reading, charitable activities. Home: 2412 E Rio Verde Dr West Covina CA 91791-2140 Office: Disney TV Animation 5200 Lankershim Blvd Ste 600 North Hollywood CA 91601-3100

KNOLLER, GUY DAVID, lawyer; b. N.Y.C., July 23, 1946; s. Charles and Odette Knoller; children: Jennifer Judy, Geoffrey David. BA cum laude, Bloomfield (N.J.) Coll., 1968; JD cum laude, Ariz. State U., 1971. Bar: Ariz. 1971, U.S. Dist. Ct. Ariz. 1971, U.S. Sup. Ct. 1976. Trial atty. atty. gen.'s hons. program Dept. Justice, 1971-72; atty., adv., NLRB, 1972-73, field atty. region 28, Phoenix, 1972-74; assoc. Powers, Ehrenreich, Boutell & Kurn, Phoenix, 1974-79; ptnr. Froimson & Knoller, Phoenix, 1979-81; sole practice, Phoenix, 1981-84; ptnr. Fannin, Terry & Hay, P.A., 1984-85; sole practice, Phoenix, 1985—; of counsel Burns & Burns. Mem. bd. visitors Ariz. State U. Coll. Law, 1975-76; pres. Ariz. Theatre Guild, 1990, 91. Fellow Ariz. Bar Found.; mem. ABA, State Bar Ariz. (chmn. labor relations sect. 1977-78), Ariz. State U. Coll. Law Alumni Assn. (pres. 1977). Office: 3550 N Central Ave Ste 1401 Phoenix AZ 85012-2112

KNOOP, VERN THOMAS, civil engineer, consultant; b. Paola, Kans., Nov. 19, 1932; s. Vernon Thomas and Nancy Alice (Christian) K. Student,

Kans. U., 1953-54; BSCE, Kans. State U., 1959. Registered profl. engr., Calif. Surveyor James L. Bell, Surveyors and Engrs., Overland Park, Kans., 1954; engr. asst. to county engr. Miami County Hwy. Dept., Paola, 1955; engr. State of Calif. Dept. Water Resources, L.A., 1959-85, sr. engr., 1986-88; chief, water supply evaluations sect. State of Calif. Dept. Water Resources, L.A., Glendale, 1989—; hydrology tchr. State of Calif. Dept. Water Resources, L.A., 1984; mem. Interagency Drought Task Force, Sacramento, 1988-91. Mem. Jefferson Ednl. Found., Washington, 1988-91, Heritage Found., Washington, 1988—, Nat. Rep. Senatorial Com., Washington, 1990—, Rep. Presdl. Task Force, Washington, 1990-91. With U.S. Army, 1956-57. Decorated Good Conduct medal U.S. Army, Germany, 1957. Mem. ASCE (life, dir. L.A. sect. hydraulics/water resources mgmt. tech. group 1985-86, chmn. 1984-85), Profl. Engrs. Calif. Govt. (dist. suprs. rep. 1986—), Am. Assn. Individual Investors (life), L.A. World Affairs Coun., Singles Internat. Baptist. Home: 116 N Berendo St Los Angeles CA 90004-4711 Office: State of Calif Dept Water Resources 770 Fairmont Ave Glendale CA 91203-1035

KNOPF, KARL GORDON, educator; b. Harrisburg, Pa., Apr. 5, 1952; s. Gordon G. and Edna (Dearth) K.; m. Margaret Knopf; children: Chris, Kevin. BA, San Diego State, 1974; MA, San Jose State, 1978; EdD, Nova Southeast, 1981. Prof. Foothill Coll., Los Altos Hills, Calif., 1976-85, dean, 1985-95; pres. Fitness Edn of Older Adults, Los Altos Hills, Calif., 1985—; prof. Foothill Coll., Los Altos Hills, Calif., 1995—; cons. AARP, Washington, Time Life Medical, N.Y., Dept. of Public Health, Champs, Stanford, Calif. Author: Adaptive PE, 1995, Fitness Over 50, 1989, Wakes Work-out, 1996. Recipient NISOD award League of Innovtion, 1995. Avocations: youth programs, seniors, swimming, fitness. Office: Fitness Educators of Older Adults 759 Chopin Sr Ste 1 Sunnyvale CA 94087

KNORR, MARJORIE S., writer; b. Tulsa, Okla., Mar. 29, 1924; d. Montgomery P. and Beulah E. Stitt; m. Owen A. Knorr, Dec. 22, 1951; children: Christopher A., Andrew P., Julie D. BS, U. Ill., 1945; MA, Calif. State U., Sacramento, 1975. Bacteriologist Abbott Labs., North Chgo., 1945-49, Colo. Found. Rsch. in TB, Denver, 1949-52; cons. Clarr County Health Dept., Las Vegas, Nev., 1976; tchr. U. Nev., Las Vegas, 1981-83; instr. Truckee Meadows C.C., Reno, Nev., 1981-83; freelance writer Reno, Nev., 1985—. Contbr. over 60 articles to profl. jours. Mem. Nat. Writers Club (8th place award). Home: 4535 Lakewood Ct Reno NV 89509-5834

KNOTT, WILLIAM ALAN, library director, library management and building consultant; b. Muscatine, Iowa, Oct. 4, 1942; s. Edward Marlan and Dorothy Mae (Holzhauer) K.; m. Mary Farrell, Aug. 23, 1969; chidren: Andrew Jerome, Sarah Louise. BA in English, U. Iowa, 1967, MA in L.S., 1968. Asst. dir. Ottumwa (Iowa) Pub. Libr., 1968-69; libr. cons. Iowa State Libr., Des Moines, 1968-69; dir. Hutchinson (Kans.) Pub. Libr. and S. Cen. Kans. Libr. System, Hutchinson, 1969-71; dir. Jefferson County Pub. Libr., Lakewood, Colo., 1971—. Served with U.S. Army, 1965-67. Mem. ALA, Colo. Libr. Assn. Author: Books by Mail: A Guide, 1973; co-author: A Phased Approach to Library Automation, 1969; editor: Conservation Catalog, 1982. Office: Jefferson County Pub Libr 10200 W 20th Ave Lakewood CO 80215-1402

KNOWLES, MYLES MIKE, television broadcast engineer; b. Port Huron, Mich., May 10, 1950; s. Myles Henry and Barbara Ann (Beck) Donovan; m. Mary Jane Howarth, Sept. 10, 1983; children: Christina Lynn, Jennifer Michelle. BA, Mich. State Univ., 1972. Owner, trainer, farrier Shooting Star Ranch, Boulder, Colo., 1976-83; sr. tech. Media Systems, Lahaina, Hawaii, 1985-86; owner/tech. KW Sound, Wailuku, Hawaii, 1983-92; master tech. Media Plus, Wailea, Hawaii, 1987-89; editor/videographer Broadcast Prod. Svcs., Lahaina, Hawaii, 1989-91; producer/videographer Millenium Films, Lahaina, Hawaii, 1992—; chief engr. Paradise TV Network, Lahaina, Hawaii, 1991—. Videographer, editor music video, 1996; producer, dir., editor documentary, 1994, 95, 92; exec. producer A Message of Hope TV show. Vol. Maui Cmty. TV, 1995—. Recipient Communicator award of Distinction Communicator Awards, 1996, Aegis awards for Camera and Dir., 1998. Mem. Soc. Motion Picture and TV Engrs., Soc. Broadcast Engrs., Wedding and Event Videographers Assn. Home: 26 Luanaiki Pl Kihei HI 96753-7112 Office: Paradise TV Network 1024 Front St Lahaina HI 96761-1613

KNOWLES, TONY, governor; b. Tulsa, Jan. 1, 1943; m. Susan Morris; children: Devon, Lucas, Sara. BA in Econs., Yale U., 1968. Owner, mgr. The Works, Anchorage, 1968—, Downtown Deli, Anchorage, 1978—; mayor Municipality of Anchorage, 1981-87; now gov. State of Alaska, 1994—. Mem. citizen's com. to develop comprehensive plan for growth and devel., Anchorage, 1972; mem. Borough Assembly, Anchorage, 1975-79; bd. dirs. Fairview Cmty. Ctr., March of Dimes, Pub. TV Sta. KAKM, numerous sports facilities coms. Served with U.S. Army, 1961-65, Vietnam. Mem. Anchorage C. of C. (bd. dirs.). Office: Office of the Governor PO Box 110001 Juneau AK 99811-0001*

KNOWLES, WILLIAM LEROY (BILL KNOWLES), television news producer, journalism educator; b. L.A., June 23, 1935; s. Leroy Edwin and Thelma Mabel (Armstrong) K.; children from previous marriage: Frank, Irene, Daniel, Joseph, Ted; m. Sharon Weaver, Dec. 28, 1990. B.A. in Journalism, San Jose State Coll., 1959; postgrad., U. So. Calif., 1962-63. Reporter, photographer, producer KSL-TV, Salt Lake City, 1963-65; producer, editor, writer WLS-TV, Chgo., 1965-70; news writer ABC News, Washington, 1970-71; asso. producer ABC News, 1971-75, ops. producer, 1975-77; So. bur. chief ABC News, Atlanta, 1977-81; Washington bur. chief ABC News, 1981-82, West Coast bur. chief, 1982-85; prof. U. Mont., Missoula, 1986—; jazz writer and historian; v.p., co-owner Present Past Productions, Inc.; adv. U. Mont. Student Documentary Unit. Served with U.S. Army, 1959-62. Decorated Commendation medal; Gannett fellow Ind. U., 1987; Media Mgmt. fellow Poynter Inst. Media Studies, 1988. Mem. Assn. for Edn. in Journalism (head radio-TV divsn. 1995-96). Office: U Mont Sch Journalism Missoula MT 59812

KNOX, ELIZABETH LOUISE, community volunteer, travel consultant; b. Forest Hills, N.Y.; d. Frederick Conrad and Emma M. Wissel; m. Rudolph T. Haas Jr., Feb. 1944 (div. June 1955); 1 child, Rudolph T. III; m. James Henry Knox, Aug. 22, 1956 (dec. Feb. 1987),; children: Julie Frances, Alice Carrie. Student, Hunter Coll. Ret. co-owner Del Mar (Calif.) Travel Bur. Mem. bd. trustees Salk Inst., La Jolla, 1994—; co-chair Salk Inst. Coun., 1995—; v.p. women's assn., 1969-70, pres., 1970-72, trustee, 1981-82, chmn. Andy Williams golf tournament benefit, 1969-70, chmn. 30th anniversary com., 1990-92; co-chmn. fashion show benefit Bishop's Sch., La Jolla, 1967, chmn., 1968, trustee, devel. chmn., 1971—, v.p., 1980-82, pres., 1982-86, headmaster's adv. coun., 1986—; bd. dirs. women's aux. Scripps Meml. Hosp., La Jolla, 1963-64, co-chmn. candlelight ball, 1963; charter mem. La Jolla unit Children's Hosp., San Diego, 1956, chmn. ways and means La Jolla unit, 1956-59, chmn. 10th annual fair benefit, 1963, pres. La Jolla unit, 1965, bd. dirs. women's auxiliary, 1962-64, chmn. San Diego stadium premiere benefit, 1967; bd. regents Calif. Luth. Univ., 1994—. Recipient Nat. Lane Bryant award, 1966, Woman of Valor award Temple Beth Israel, 1967, Jonas Salk award of Congress Salk Inst., 1972, Pres.'s award Women's Assn./Salk Inst., 1978, Woman of Dedication award San Diego Door of Hope Aux./Salvation Army, 1986. Mem. La Jolla Beach and Tennis Club, Del Mar Turf Club. Home: 2688 Hidden Valley Rd La Jolla CA 92037-4025

KNUDSON, MELVIN ROBERT, management consultant, business executive; b. Libby, Mont., Oct. 27, 1917; s. John and Serina (Bakken) K.; BS in Wood Chemistry, Oreg. State U., 1942; m. Melba Irene Joice, Mar. 5, 1946; children—Mark Bradley, Kevin Marie, Kari Lynne. Mgr. quality control J. Neils Lumber Co., Libby, Mont., 1946-55; mgr. research and devel. St. Regis Paper Co., Libby, 1955-65, div. dir. tech. devel., Tacoma, Wash., 1965-69, div. dir. short and long-range planning, 1969-70; exec. v.p. Property Holding and Devel. Co., Tacoma, 1970-75; exec. v.p. and gen. mgr. U.S. Computers, Inc., Tacoma, 1975-79; corp. mgmt., orgn., univ. governance and adminstrn. cons., 1979—; owner Knudson Travel, Tacoma, 1981—; bd. dirs., special cons., incorporator Larex Internat. Corp.; founder, dir. LAREX, Inc., Mpls., 1994—. Mem. adv. bd. Coll. Engring., Wash. State U., 1967—, chmn., 1971-73; trustee 1st Luth. Ch., Libby, 1948-56, chmn., 1954-56; trustee Sch. Dist. # 4, Libby, 1964-65, trustee Christ Luth. Ch., Tacoma, 1966-71, com. chmn.; trustee Greater Lakes Mental Health Clinic, 1969-73, com. chmn., 1970-73; bd. regents Pacific Luth. U., Tacoma, 1969—, chmn., 1976-81; mem. Steilacoom Improvement Com., 1971-73; chmn. Pacific Luth. U. Pres. Search Com., 1974-75; dir. Wauna Dance Club, 1976-79; dir. Pacific Luth. Univ. "Q" Club, 1976-86; bd. dirs. Tenzler Library, Tacoma, 1980-83, Crime Stoppers, 1981-84, Operation Night Watch, 1989; vol. Baby-Rocker NICU, Tacoma, Wash. Served to lt. col. F.A., Paratroops, U.S. Army, 1941-46. Recipient Disting. Service award Pacific Luth. U., 1986. Mem. Wash. Realtors Assn., Wash. Securities Sales, Am. Governing Bds., Center for Study of Democratic Institutions. Republican. Clubs: Tacoma Country and Golf, Normana Male Chorus (Norwegian Singers Assn. Am.). Patentee high-temperature wood-drying process, patentee Ultrarefined Arabinogalactan product; developer domestic natural gum. Home: 6928 100th St SW Lakewood WA 98499-1819 Office: 1103 A St Ste 200 Tacoma WA 98402-5007

KNUDSON, THOMAS JEFFERY, journalist; b. Manning, Iowa, July 6, 1953; s. Melvin Jake and Coreen Rose (Nickum) K. B.A. in Journalism, Iowa State U., 1980. Reporter/intern Wall Street Jour., Chgo., summer 1979; staff writer Des Moines Register, 1980-99; sr. writer Sacramento (Calif.) Bee, 1999—. Office: Sacramento Bee PO Box 15779 Sacramento CA 95852-0779*

KO, DANIEL, graphic designer; b. Taipei, Taiwan, July 6, 1966; came to U.S., 1976; s. David and Evelyn K. BFA, Art Ctr. Coll. Design, 1990. Designer Landmark Entertainment Group, North Hollywood, Calif., 1991-92, Siegel & Gale, L.A., 1992-93; sr. designer Patrick Soo Hoo Designers, Torrance, Calif., 1993—.

KO, HYUNOK, artist, jeweler; b. Seoul, Korea, Aug. 29, 1962; came to U.S., 1975; d. Inshik and Ohi (Han) K.; m. James Steven Drage, Sept. 14, 1986. MFA, Columbia U., 1989; BA, U. Calif., Berkeley, 1993. Cert. substitute tchr., Calif. Instr. sculpture shop Buck's Rock, New Milford, Conn., summer 1994; translator Korean-English Alameda (Calif.) Sch. Dist., 1994-95; substitute tchr. Spectrum Ctr., San Lorenzo, Calif., 1995, summer 96; jeweler Koko Jewelry, Berkeley, Calif., 1996—. Exhibited in group shows Columbia (Mo.) Coll., 1992, SRW Gallery, Sierra Madre, Calif., 1995. Mem. Calif. Autism Found. (cert. appreciation 1996). Avocations: piano, visiting art galleries, reading biographies of famous people. Home: 34906 Seal Rock Ter Fremont CA 94555-3255

KOART, NELLIE HART, real estate investor and executive; b. San Luis Obispo, Calif., Jan. 3, 1930; d. Will Carleton and Nellie Malchen (Cash) Hart; m. William Harold Koart, Jr., June 16, 1951 (dec. 1976); children: Kristen Marie Kittle, Matthew William. Student Whittier Coll., 1947-49; BA, U. Calif.-Santa Barbara, 1952; MA, Los Angeles State Coll., 1957. Life diploma elem. edn., Calif. Farm worker Hart Farms, Montebello, Calif., 1940-48; play leader Los Angeles County Parks and Recreation, East Los Angeles, Rosemead, Calif., 1948-51; elem. tchr. Potrero Heights Sch. Dist., South San Gabriel, Calif., 1951-55, vice prin., 1955-57; real estate salesman William Koart Real Estate, Goleta, Calif., 1963-76, real estate investor KO-ART Enterprises, Goleta, 1976—, pres. Wm. Koart Constrn. Co., Inc., Goleta, 1975-91; real estate sales person Joseph McGeever Realty Co., Goleta, 1976-91; adv. bd. Bank of Montecito, Santa Barbara, Calif., 1983—. Editor: Reflections, 1972. Charter mem. Calif. Regents program Calif. Fedn. Republican Women, 1989; treas. Santa Barbara County Fedn. Republican Women, Alamar-Hope Ranch, 1981-82, treas. County Bd., 1983-84, auditor, 1985, 96, 97; treas. Com. to Recall Hone, Maschke and Shewczyk, Goleta, 1984; treas. Santa Barbara County Lincoln Club, 1983-87, bd. dirs., 1983-93; assoc. mem. state central com. Calif. Republican Party, 1985-87. Mem. Santa Barbara Apartment Assn., Antique Automobile Club of Am. (sec. treas. Santa Barbara 1980-84), Serena Cove Owners Assn. (sec.-treas, bd. dirs 1990—), Goleta Bus. Roundtable Advisory Group. Clubs: Moderate Republican Majority, Alamar - Hope Ranch republican Women's Club, GALS Republican Women's Club, Santa Barbara Women's Club, Channel City Club, Santa Barbara County Lincoln Club, Santa Barbara County Tax-Payers Assn. Avocations: swimming, numismatics, geneology, college and professional football. Office: KO-ART Enterprises PO Box 310 Goleta CA 93116-0310

KOBZA, DENNIS JEROME, architect; b. Ullysses, Nebr., Sept. 30, 1933; s. Jerry Frank and Agnes Elizabeth (Lavicky) K.; B.S., Healds Archtl. Engring., 1959; m. Doris Mae Riemann, Dec. 26, 1953; children—Dennis Jerome, Diana Jill, David John. Draftsman, designer B.L. Schroder, Palo Alto, Calif., 1959-60; sr. draftsman, designer Ned Abrams, Architect, Sunnyvale, Calif., 1960-61, Kenneth Elvin, Architect, Los Altos, Calif., 1961-62; partner B.L. Schroder, Architect, Palo Alto, 1962-66; pvt. practice architecture, Mountain View, Calif., 1966—. Served with USAF, 1952-56. Recipient Solar PAL award, Palo Alto, 1983, Mountain View Mayoral award, 1979. Mem. C. of C. (dir. 1977-79, Archtl. Excellence award Hayward chpt. 1985, Outstanding Indsl. Devel. award Sacramento chpt., 1980) , AIA (chpt. dir. 1973), Constrn. Specifications Inst. (dir. 1967-68), Am. Inst. Plant Engrs., Nat. Fedn. Ind. Bus. Orgn. Club: Rotary (dir. 1978-79, pres. 1986-87). Home: 38440 May Ct Palo Alto CA 94303-4545 Office: 2083 Old Middlefield Way Mountain View CA 94043-2401

KOCAOGLU, DUNDAR F., engineering management educator, industrial and civil engineer; b. Turkey, June 1, 1939; came to U.S., 1960; s. Irfan and Meliha (Uzay) K.; m. Alev Baysak, Oct. 17, 1968; 1 child, Timur. BSCE, Robert Coll., Istanbul, Turkey, 1960; MSCE, Lehigh U., 1962; MS in Indsl. Engring., U. Pitts., 1972, PhD in Ops. Rsch., 1976. Registered profl. engr., Pa., Oreg. Design engr. Modjeski & Masters, Harrisburg, Pa., 1962-64; ptnr. TEKSER Engring. Co., Istanbul, 1966-69; project engr. United Engrs., Phila., 1964-71; rsch. asst. U. Pitts., 1972-74, vis. asst. prof., 1974-76, assoc. prof. indsl. engring., dir. engring. mgmt., 1976-87; prof., dir. engring. mgmt. program, Portland State U., 1987—; pres. TMA-Tech. Mgmt. Assocs., Portland, Oreg., 1973—, pres. Portland Internat. Conf. Mgmt. Engring. and Tech., 1990—. Co-author: Engineering Management, 1981; editor: Management of R&D and Engineering, 1992, Innovation in Technology Management-The Key to Global Leadership, 1997; co-editor: Technology Management—The New International Language, 1991; series editor Wiley Series in Engring. and Tech. Mgmt., 1984-98; contbr. articles on tech. mgmt. to profl. jours. Lt. C.E., Turkish Army, 1966-68. Fellow IEEE (Centennial medal 1984, editor-in-chief trans. on engring. mgmt. 1986—); mem. Informs (chmn. Coll. Engring. Mgmt. 1979-81), Am. Soc. Engring. Edn. (chmn. engring. mgmt. div. 1982-83), IEEE Engring. Mgmt. Soc. (fellow, publs. dir. 1982-85), ASCE (mem. engring. mgmt. bd. govs. 1988—), Muhendis, Ilim Adamlari ve Mimarlar Dernegi Soc. Turkish Engrs. and Scientists (hon.), Am. Soc. Engring. Mgmt. (dir. 1981-86), Omega Rho (pres. 1984-86). Office: Portland State U Engring Mgmt Program PO Box 751 Portland OR 97207-0751

KOCEN, LORRAINE AYRAL, accountant; b. Levittown, N.Y., July 20, 1956; d. Edward Joseph and Joan Dorothy (Destefanis) Ayral; m. Ross Kocen, Oct. 4, 1981; 1 child, Daniel. BS, Hofstra U., 1978; MBA, U. Minn., 1985. Engr. Sperry Systems Mgmt., Great Neck, N.Y., 1978-81; fin. analyst ITT Consumer Fin. Corp., Mpls., 1981-84; cost acct. Mercy Med. Ctr., Mpls., 1984-85, contr., 1985-86; bus. segments acct. GTE, Thousand Oaks, Calif., 1986-88, Cerritos project acct., 1988-90, Cerritos project adminstr., 1990-92, fin. adminstr., 1992-93, sr. sales adminstr., 1993-94, adminstr. mobile comms., 1994-96; fin. mgr. Blue Cross of Calif., Newbury Park, 1996-97; bus. analyst GTE, Newbury Park, 1997—. Asst. editor newsletter Healthcare Fin. Mgmt. Assn., Mpls., 1985-86. Mem. archtl. com. Foxmoor Hills Homeowners Assn., Westlake, Calif., 1989. Office: GTE 851 Lawrence Dr Newbury Park CA 91320-2200

KOCH, GERD HERMANN, artist, educator; b. Detroit, Jan. 30, 1929; s. Hermann and Margaret (Sondermann) K.; 1 child, Keari. BFA, Wayne State U., 1951; postgrad., UCLA, 1950, 56; MFA, U. Calif., Santa Barbara, 1967. Art instr. self-workshops So. Calif., 1952—; art instr. Santa Barbara C.C. Adult Edn., 1965-68, U. Calif. Ext., Santa Barbara/Ventura, 1966-74; prof. art Ventura Coll., 1960, 66—, mem. orgnl. bd. Calif. State U. Channel Islands Regional Arts Ctr. Info., Camarillo, 1998—. One-person shows include Esther Robles Gallery, L.A., 1959, 61, 63, 65, Santa Barbara Mus. of Art, 1960, Pasadena (Calif.) Art Mus., 1958, Long Beach (Calif.) Mus. Art, 1961, La Jolla (Calif.) Mus. Art, 1961, Esther Bear Gallery, Santa Barbara, 1965, 67, Ventura Chamber Music Festival, 1998; retrospectives include Carnegie Art Mus., Oxnard, Calif., 1988, Ojai Art Ctr., 1998; exhibited in three man travel show Western Assn. of Art Mus., 1960-63; collections include L.A. County Art Mus., U. Mont., U.N.C., State of Va. Art Collection, La Jolla Art Mus., Calif. State U. Long Beach. Mem. Ojai Beautiful, 1957-63. Recipient First Purchase awards L.A. County Mus. Art, 1959, Calif. State Fair (profl. competition), 1963, Nat. Water Color Soc., 1976. Mem. Nat. Water Color Soc. (juror ann. exhibit 1963, 80, 96). Avocation: international tour leader. Home and Office: 444 Aliso St Ventura CA 93001

KOELMEL, LORNA LEE, data processing executive; b. Denver, May 15, 1936; d. George Bannister and Gladys Lee (Henshall) Steuart; m. Herbert Howard Nelson, Sept. 9, 1956 (div. Mar. 1967); children: Karen Dianne, Phillip Dean, Lois Lynn; m. Robert Darrel Koelmel, May 12, 1981; stepchildren: Kim, Cheryl, Dawn, Debbie. BA in English, U. Colo., 1967. Cert. secondary English tchr. Substitute English tchr. Jefferson County Schs., Lakewood, Colo., 1967-68; sec. specialist IBM Corp., Denver, 1968-75, pers. administr., 1975-82, asst. ctr. coord., 1982-85, office systems specialist, 1985-87, backup computer operator, 1987—; computer instr. Barnes Bus. Coll., Denver, 1987-92; owner, mgr. Lorna's Precision Word Processing and Desktop Pub., Denver, 1987-89; computer cons. Denver, 1990—. Editor newsletter Colo. Nat. Campers and Hikers Assn., 1992-94. Organist Christian Sci. Soc., Buena Vista, Colo., 1963-66, 1st Ch. Christ Scientists Thornton-Westminster, Thornton, Colo., 1994—; chmn. bd. dirs., 1979-80. Named to Pres.'s Club, Avon, 1997, 98, 99. Mem. NAFE, Nat. Secs. Assn. (retirement ctr. chair 1977-78, newsletter chair 1979-80, v.p. 1980-81), Am. Guild Organists, U. Colo. Alumni Assn., Avon Ind. Sales Rep and Pres. Club, Alpha Chi Omega (publicity com. 1986-88). Republican. Club: Nat. Writers. Lodge: Job's Daus. (recorder 1953-54). Avocations: needlepoint, piano, bridge, reading, golf.

KOENIG, JOHN M., producer, musician, lawyer; b. L.A., May 9, 1950; s. Lester and Catharine (Heerman) K.; m. Elaine Peterson, Aug. 30, 1980. BA, UCLA, 1972; JD, U. So. Calif., 1987. Bar: Calif. 1987. Record producer, 1968—; co-prin., cellist Jerusalem Symphony Orch., 1976-77; cellist Swedish Radio Symphony Orch., Stockholm, 1977; pres. Contemporary Records, Inc., L.A., 1978-84; assoc. Skadden, Arps, Slate, Meagher & Flom, L.A., 1987-91; asst. lectr. U. So. Calif., L.A., 1985-87; ptnr. May & Koenig, Santa Monica, Calif., 1991-94. Prodr.: (record albums) Joe Henderson, Relaxin' at Camarillo, 1980 (Grand Prix du Disque 1981), Freddie Hubbard, Mistral, 1980, Bobby Hutcherson, Solo/Quartet, 1982, Jimmy Rogers, Blue Bird (W.C. Handy award 1995), Jimmy D. Lane, Long Gone, 1997, Jimmy Rogers All Stars, Blues Blues Blues (featuring Mick Jagger, Eric Clapton, Page & Plant), 1999. Mem. Nat. Acad. Recording Arts and Scis. (producers com., L.A. chpt.). Avocation: chamber music.

KOENIG, MARIE HARRIET KING, public relations director, fund raising executive; b. New Orleans, Feb. 19, 1919; d. Harold Paul and Sadie Louise (Bole) King; m. Walter William Koenig, June 24, 1956; children: Margaret Marie, Susan Patricia. Major in Voice, La. State U., 1937-39; Pre-law, Loyola U., 1942-43; BS in History, U. LaVerne, 1986. Adminstrv. asst. to atty. gen. State of La., New Orleans, 1940-44; contract writer MGM Studios, Culver City, Calif., 1944-46; asst. sec., treas. Found. for Ind., L.A., 1950-56, Found. for Social Rsch., L.A., 1950-56; dir. communications Incentive Rsch. Corp., L.A., 1969-78; rsch. supr., devel. dept. Calif. Inst. Technology, Pasadena, Calif., 1969; dir. funding devel. Rep. Party of L.A. County, South Pasadena, 1989-92. Author: Does the National Council of Churches Speak for You?, 1978; delivered lecture series on U.S. fgn. policy. Named Hon. Citizen Colonial Williamsburg Found., 1987; active Nat. Trust for Historic Preservation, 1986, Friends of the Huntington Libr., 1986, Town Hall of L.A., 1986—, Pasadena City Women's Club, 1982-84, The Masquers Club, Women of L.A.; past mem. Coun. Women's Clubs; charter mem. Nat. Mus. of Women in Arts; bd. mem. Pasadena Opera Guild; contbg. mem. L.A. World Affairs Coun., 1990, L.A. County Mus. Art, 1990; past pres., pub. chmn., Pasadene Rep. Women Federated; charter mem. Freedoms Found. at Valley Forge L.A. County Chpt., Autry Mus. Western Heritage, 1986, Women of L.A.; pres. Greater L.A. Women's Coun., Navy League of the U.S. Recipient Pres.'s award So. Calif. Motion Picture Coun., 1996, Cert. Recognition Calif. State Assembly, 1989, 95, Recognition of Excellence, Achievement and Commitment U.S. Ho. Reps., 1989, Cert. Merit Rep. Presdl. Task Force, 1986, Cert. Appreciation U.S. Def. Com., 1984, Hon. Freedom Fighter award U.S. Def. Com., 1985, Cert. Appreciation Am. Conservative Union, 1983, Cert. Commendation Rep. Cen. Com. L.A. County, 1972, Cert. Appreciation Eisenhower-Nixon So. Calif. Com., 1952; named Disting. Citizen of Yr. L.A. Area Coun. Boy Scouts Am. Mem. Women in Communication, Greater L.A. Press Club, World War II Meml. (charter). Republican. Avocations: reading, music, opera. Home: 205 Madeline Dr Pasadena CA 91105-3311

KOENIG, PIERRE, architecture educator, architect; b. San Francisco, Oct. 17, 1925; s. Harold Rudolph and Blanche Jeanne (Chigé) K.; m. Merry Sue Thompson, July 10, 1954 (div. Sept. 1959); 1 child: Randall Francis; m. Gaile Carson, July 10, 1962 (div. Sept. 1975); 1 child: Jean Pierre; m. Gloria Gladys Kaufman, Oct. 28, 1984. BArch, U. So. Calif., 1952. Registered architect, Calif. Pvt. practice, 1952—; from asst. to prof. architecture Sch. Architecture U. So. Calif., L.A., 1964-97, prof. architecture, 1997—, disting. prof. arch., 1998—, asst. dir. Inst. Building Rsch., 1969-72, dir. Chemehuevi Planning Program, 1972-78; guest lectr. CCNY, 1963, Pratt Inst., N.Y., 1963; vis. instr. and lectr. Yale U., New Haven, Conn., 1963; lectr. Art Ctr. Sch., Pasadena, Calif., 1991-94; guest spkr. San Francisco Mus. Modern Art, 1990, UCLA Design Ctr., Santa Monica, Calif., 1993; spkr. and panelist Mus. Contemporary Art, L.A., 1990; spkr. L.A. County Mus. Art, 1996. Exhibited in group show at the Mus. Modern Art, L.A., 1989-90. Prin. works include Lamel house, Glendale, Calif., 1950, also numerous other exposed steel and glass and prefabricated houses in Calif. Corp. U.S. Army, 1943-46. Recipient Sao Paulo Biennial Exhbn. award, 1957, AIA House and Home Mag. award, 1957, 1960, 1962-63, AIA Sunset Mag. Honor award, 1959, 1961-62, Western Constrn. Honor award, 1959, Am. Inst. of Iron and Steel award, 1963, Best Exhbn. Bldg. award, 1964, L.A. Grand Prix award, 1964, AIA L.A. Fiesta award, 1967, 36 Best Bldgs. in L.A. since 1945 award, 1967, AIA Olympic Arch. award, 1984, L.A. Dept. of Cultural Affairs award, 1989, AIA 100 Archs./100 Yrs. award, 1995, AIA Calif. Council 25 Year award for Excellence in Design, 1996, AIA Calif. Coun. Maybeck award for Outstanding Lifelong Achievement in Archtl. Design, 1996, Lifetime Achievement in Arch. award Pacific Design Ctr., 1998. Fellow AIA. Avocations: photography, running, music, miniatures, computers. Home and Office: 12221 Dorothy St Los Angeles CA 90049-5220

KOEP, LAWRENCE JAMES, surgeon; b. Pasadena, Calif., May 6, 1944; s. Ambrose Urban and Loma Mary (Riordan) K.; m. Jennifer Leigh James, FEb. 4, 1982 (div. Jan. 1992); children: Alexander, Erik, Lauren. BS, Johns Hopkins U., 1966, MD, 1970. Diplomate Am. Bd. Surgery. Intern Johns Hopkins Hosp., Balt., 1970-71, resident, 1971-76; assoc. prof. U. Colo., Denver, 1976-81; pvt. practice Phoenix, 1981—; bd. dirs. Donor Network Ariz. Mem. ACS, Am. Soc. Transplant Surgeons, Western Surg. Assn. Avocations: golf, old Fords. Home: 3729 E Rancho Dr Paradise Valley AZ 85253-5022 Office: 1410 N 3rd St Phoenix AZ 85004-1608

KOEPPEL, GARY MERLE, publisher, art gallery owner, writer ; b. Albany, Oreg., Jan 20, 1938; s. Carl Melvin and Barbara Emma (Adams) K.; m. Emma Katerina Koeppel, May 20, 1984. BA, Portland State U., 1961; MFA, State U. Iowa, 1963. Writing instr. State U. Iowa, Iowa City, 1963-64; guest prof. English, U. P.R. San Juan, 1964-65; assoc. prof. creative writing Portland (Oreg.) State U., 1965-68; owner, operator Coast Gallery, Big Sur, 1971—, Pebble Beach, Calif., 1986—, Maui, Hawaii, 1985—, Hana, Hawaii, 1991—, Lahaina, Hawaii, 1992; owner Coast Pub. Co., Coast Seri Graphics, Coast Pub., Coast Licensing, Coast Odvt., 1991—; editor, pub. Big Sur Gazette, 1978-81; producer, sponsor Maui Marine Art Expo., 1984-95, Calif. Marine Art Expo., Paris Marine Art Expo., Hawaiian Cultural Arts Expo., 1993; founder The Blue Movement, 1994; founder, pres. Global Art Expos, 1994, Planet Big Sur, 1996, Coast Constrn., 1998. Author: Sculptured Sandcast Candles, 1974, Henry Miller, The Paintings, 1991. Mem. Eagle Scouts, 1952, Jr, Asst. Scoutmaster, 1953, master, deMolay, 1955; founder Big Sur Vol. Fire Brigade, 1975; chmn. coordinating com. Big Sur Area Planning, 1972-75; chmn. Big Sur Citizens Adv. Com., 1975-78. Mem. In[illegible] 1971-75, 82-84), Big Sur Grange, Audubon Soc., Cousteau Soc., Phi Gamma

Delta, Alpha Delta Sigma. Address: Coast Gallery PO Box 223519 Carmel CA 93922-3519

KOERBER, JOHN ROBERT, computer programmer; b. L.A., Aug. 17, 1955; s. Thomas Joseph and Betty (Turner) Koerber; m. Kimberly Sue Rider, Mar. 15, 1986. BS, Yale U., 1977. Computer technician Tech Mart, Tarzana, Calif., 1977-79; programmer, ptnr. J&J Computer Svc., Northridge, Calif., 1979-80; sr. programmer Mitec Computer Bus. Systems, Chartsworth, Calif., 1980-87; sr. software engr. Dracon div. Harris Corp., Camarillo, Calif., 1987-88; programmer, cons. SALING Computer Systems, Chatsworth, 1988—. Mem. IEEE (affiliate, Commns. Soc.), Assn. for Computing Machinery. Democrat. Avocation: theatre pipe organ maintenance. Home: 6657 Franrivers Ave West Hills CA 91307-2816 Office: Saling Computer Systems 8466 Melba Ave West Hills CA 91304-3120

KOESTEL, MARK ALFRED, geologist, photographer; b. Cleve., Jan. 1, 1951; s. Alfred and Lucille (Kemeny) K.; children: Jennifer Rose, Bonnie Leigh. BS, U. Ariz., 1978. Registered profl. geologist Wyo., Alaska, Ind.; registered environ. assessor, Calif. Sr. geologist Union Oil Co. of Calif., Tucson and Denver, 1978-86; mgr. geology Harmsworth Assocs., Laguna Hills, Calif., 1986-88; sr. project mgr. Applied GeoSystems, Irvine, Calif., 1988-90; cons. geologist, photographer Adventures in Geology/Outdoor Images, Chino, Calif., 1990—. Contbr. articles and photographs to profl. jours. and mags. N.Mex. state rep. Minerals Exploration Coalition, Tucson and Denver, 1982. Sci. Found. scholarship No. Ariz. U., 1969, Acad. Achievement scholarship, 1970, Disting. Scholastic Achievement scholarship, 1971. Mem. Am. Inst. of Profl. Geologists (cert.), Soc. of Mining Engrs., Aircraft Owners and Pilots Assn., Geol. Soc. of Am., Nat. Geographic Soc. Avocations: woodworking, photography, backpacking, travel, scuba. Home and Office: 13214 Breton Ave Chino CA 91710-5952

KOESTER, BERTHOLD KARL, lawyer, law educator, retired honorary German consul; b. Aachen, Germany, June 30, 1931; s. Wilhelm P. and Margarethe A. (Witteler) K.; m. Hildegard Maria Buettner, June 30, 1961; children: Georg W., Wolfgang J., Reinhard B. JD, U. Muenster, Fed. Republic Germany, 1957. Cert. Real Estate Broker, Ariz. Asst. prof. civil and internat. law U. Muenster, 1957-60; atty. Cts. of Duesseldorf, Fed. Republic Germany, 1960-82; v.p. Bank J. H. Vogeler & Co., Duesseldorf, 1960-64; pres. Bremer Tank-u., Kuehlschiffahrtsges.m.b.H., 1964-72; atty., trustee internat. corps., Duesseldorf and Phoenix, 1973-82, Phoenix, 1983—; of counsel Tancer Law Offices, Phoenix, 1978-86; prof. internat. bus. law Am. Grad. Sch. Internat. Mgmt., Glendale, Ariz., 1978-81; with Applewhite, Laflin & Lewis, Real Estate Investments, Phoenix, 1981-86, ptnr., 1982-86, Beucler Real Estate Investments, 1986-88, Scottsdale, Ariz.; chief exec. officer, chmn. bd. German Consultants in Real Estate Investments, Phoenix, 1989—; hon. consul Fed. Republic of Germany for Ariz., 1982-92; prof. internat. bus. law Western Internat. U., Phoenix, 1996—; chmn., CEO Arimpex, Inc., Phoenix, 1981—; bd. dirs. Ariz. Ptnrship for Air Transp., 1988-92; chmn. Finvest Corp., Phoenix, 1990—. Contbr. articles to profl. jours. Pres. Parents Assn. Humboldt Gymnasium, Duesseldorf, 1971-78; active German Red Cross, from 1977. Mem. Duesseldorf Chamber of Lawyers, Bochum (Fed. Republic Germany) Assn. Tax Lawyers, Bonn German-Saudi Arabian Assn. (pres. 1976-79), Bonn German-Korean Assn., Assn. for German-Korean Econ. Devel. (pres. 1974-78), Ariz. Consular Corps (sec., treas. 1988-89), Nat. Soc. Arts and Letters (Ariz. Valley of Sun chpt.), German-Am. C. of C., Phoenix Met. C. of C., Rotary (Scottsdale, Ariz.). Home: 6201 E Cactus Rd Scottsdale AZ 85254-4409 Office: PO Box 15674 Phoenix AZ 85060-5674

KOETSER, DAVID, export company executive; b. Amsterdam, The Netherlands, July 22, 1906; came to U.S., 1939; s. Joseph and Mathilda Pauline (Hollander) K. Grad., Lyceum, Amsterdam, 1926. Owner Music Pub. Co., Amsterdam, 1935-39; exec. sec. The Netherlands C. of C., 1947-56; owner D.K. Co., Inc., San Francisco, 1957-84. Contbr. articles to profl. jours. Moderator U.S. Small Bus. Adminstrn., Score workshops, San Francisco, 1987—. Staff sgt. CIC, 1942-45, ETO. Mem. Holland Am. Soc. (treas. 1950—), World Trade Club (entertainment com. 1960—), Internat. Exporters Assn. (pres. 1965, recipient Pres. E award). Avocation: travel. Home and Office: PO Box 257 Lafayette CA 94549-0257

KOFRANEK, JAN JAROSLAV, architect; b. Prague, Czech Republic, Oct. 1, 1939; came to U.S., 1969; s. Jan and Marie (Baresova) K.; m. Marcela Zakova, Mar. 27, 1969. MS, Czech Tech. U., Prague, 1962. Registered architect, Wash., 1972. Job capt. Prague Project Inst., Czech Republic, 1963-68, Ceska Architect, Vienna, Austria, 1968-69; project architect Quinton-Budlong, Seattle, 1969-71; project larchitect J. Graham & Assocs., Seattle, 1971-73, WWA, Honolulu, 1973-74; v.p. Campisell Assocs., Seattle, 1974-79; architect pvt. practice, Seattle, 1979—. Mem. AIA, Bellevue Club. Avocations: skiing, tennis, hiking. Office: 116 1/2 S Washington St Seattle WA 98104-2522

KOGA, ROKUTARO, physicist; b. Nagoya, Japan, Aug. 18, 1942; came to U.S., 1961, naturalized, 1966; s. Toyoki and Emiko (Shinra) K.; m. Cordula Rosow, May 5, 1981; children: Evan A., Nicole A. B.A., U. Calif.-Berkeley, 1966; Ph.D., U. Calif.-Riverside, 1974. Research fellow U. Calif.-Riverside, 1974-75; research physicist Case Western Res U., Cleve., 1975-79, asst. prof., 1979-81; physicist Aerospace Corp., L.A., 1981-96, sr. scientis, 1996—. Mem. Am. Phys. Soc., Am. Geophys. Union, IEEE, N.Y. Acad. Scis., Sigma Xi. Contbr. articles to profl. confs.; research on gamma-ray astronomy, solar neutron observation, space scis., charged particles in space and the effect of cosmic rays on microcircuits in space. Home: 7325 Ogelsby Ave Los Angeles CA 90045-1356 Office: Aerospace Corp Space Environ and Tech Ctr Los Angeles CA 90009

KOHAN, BETSY BURNS, lawyer; b. La Mesa, Calif., Jan. 24, 1949; d. William Richard and Winifred Marion Burns; m. Dennis Lynn Kohan, Mar. 8, 1986; children: Toni Kick, Bart, Elyse, David Karowsky. BA, Stanford U., 1971; JD, U. Colo., 1974. Bar: Colo. 1974, Calif. 1985. Ptnr. Karowsky, Witwer & Oldenburg, Greeley, Colo., 1974-82; pvt. practice, Greeley, 1983-84; v.p., assoc. gen. counsel Sun Savs., San Diego, 1985-86; v.p., asst. gen. counsel Imperial Savs. & Loan Assn., San Diego, 1986-88, Am. Real Estate Group, Irvine, Calif., 1988-90, Columbia Savs. & Loan Assn., Irvine, 1990-91; staff atty. FDIC, Irvine, 1991-94; prof. Anhui Inst. Fin. and Trade, Bengbu, China, 1994, Guangzhou (China) Inst. Fgn. Trade, 1995; sr. counsel Nissan Motor Acceptance Corp., Torrance, Calif., 1996—; mem. Commn. on Legal and Jud. Edn., Colo. Supreme Ct., Denver, 1983-84. Contbr. articles to legal publs. Chmn. Colo. Commn. on Women, Denver, 1978-80; vice chmn. bd. trustees U. No. Colo., 1980-84. Named Outstanding Coloradoan, Colo. Jaycees, 1980, Outstanding Young Lawyer, Colo. Bar Assn., 1979. Mem. L.A. Bar Assn. (comml. law com. 1997—). Home: 525 E Seaside Way Unit 204 Long Beach CA 90802-8001 Office: Nissan Motor Acceptance Corp 990 W 190th St Fl 6 Torrance CA 90502-1019

KOHAN, DENNIS LYNN, international trade educator, consultant; b. Kankakee, Ill., Nov. 22, 1945; s. Leon Stanley and Nellie (Foster) K.; m. Julianne Johnson, Feb. 14, 1976 (dec. Sept. 1985); children: Toni, Bart, Elyse; m. Betsy Burns, Mar. 8, 1986; 1 child, David. BA, Ill. Wesleyan U., 1967; MPA, Gov.'s State U., 1975; postgrad., John. Marshall Law Sch., 1971-74. Police officer Kankakee County, 1967-75; loan counselor, security officer Kankakee Fed. Savs. & Loan, Kankakee, 1975-76; mgr. Bank Western, Denver, 1976-85; mgr. real estate lending dept. Cen. Savs., San Diego, 1985-87; maj. loan work-out officer Imperial Savs., San Diego, 1987-88; cons. Equity Assurance Holding Corp., Newport Beach, Calif., 1987-88; compliance officer Am. Real Estate Group and New West Fed. Savs. and Loan, Irvine, Calif., 1988-90; co-founder Consortium-Real Estate Asset Cons., Costa Mesa, Calif., 1990-91; investigator, criminal coord. Resolution Trust Corp., Newport Beach, Calif., 1991-94; instr. Inst. for Internat. Trade Anhui Inst. Fin. and Trade, Bengbu, People's Republic of China, 1994-95; instr. Guangzhou Inst. Fgn. Trade, People's Republic of China, 1995—; owner Kohan Internat. Bus. Forensics, 1995—; instr. U. No. Colo. Coll. Bus., Greeley, 1981-85; chmn. bd. North Colo. Med. Ctr., Greeley, 1983-85; pres. bd. Normedco, Greeley, 1984-85. Vol. cons., chmn. ARC, Colo., 1979-85; campaign mgr. Donley Senatorial campaign, Colo., 1982, Kinkade City Coun. campaign, Colo., 1983; chmn. Weld County Housing Authority, 1981. Staff sgt. U.S. Army, 1969-71, Vietnam. Mem. Nat. Assn. Realtors, Shriners, Kiwanis.

KOHL, ARTHUR L., consulting chemical engineer, writer; b. Orilla, Ont., Can., Aug. 21, 1919; s. Harold and Anne (Finmark) K.; m. Evelyn Dolores Belinsky, Nov. 25, 1943; children: Harold, Martin. BE in Chem. Engring., U. So. Calif., 1943, MS in Chem. Engring., 1947; postgrad., UCLA, 1955. Registered profl. engr., Calif. Rsch. engr. Turco Products, Inc., L.A., 1942-44; chief chem. engr., rsch. Fluor Corp., Ltd., L.A., 1947-60; program mgr. Rockwell Internat., Canoga Park, Calif., 1960-89; cons. engr. in pvt. practice, Woodland Hills, Calif., 1989—. Sr. author: Gas Purification, 5th edit., 1997; contbr. chpt. to book, articles to profl. jours.; holder more than 30 patents. 2d lt. U.S. Army, 1944-46. Recipient Tech. Achievement award Engrs. Joint Coun., L.A., 1967. Mem. AIChE (Outstanding Achievement award 1966). Avocations: watercolor painting, tennis. Home: 22555 Tiara St Woodland Hills CA 91367-3336

KOHL, JOHN PRESTON, management educator; b. Allentown, Pa., Dec. 26, 1942; s. Claude Evan and Edna Lenoir (Woodland) K.; m. Nancy Ann Christensen, Mar. 11, 1967; children—John P. Jr., Mark C. B.A., Moravian Coll., 1964; M.Div., Yale U., 1967; M.S. in Mgmt., Am. Tech. U., 1974. M.S. in Counseling, 1976; Ph.D. in Bus. Adminstrn., Pa. State U., 1982. Ordained to ministry United Ch. of Christ, 1967. Minister, Christ Congl. Ch., New Smyrna Beach, Fla., 1968-71, First Congl. Ch., Hutchinson, Minn., 1971-73; instr. Pa. State U., University Park, 1978-82; asst. prof. mgmt. U. Tex., El Paso, 1982-85; assoc. prof. mgmt. San Jose State U., Calif., 1985-87; prof. mgmt., chmn. dept. mgmt. U. Nev., Las Vegas, 1988—; cons. in field. Co-author: (text) Personnel Management, 1986. Served to capt. U.S. Army, 1973-78; to col. USAR, 1993—. Decorated Nat. Def. Service medal, Meritorious Service medal, Army Commendation medal. Mem. Acad. Mgmt. Contbr. articles to profl. publs. Home: 7545 Tara Ave Las Vegas NV 89117-2922 Office: U Nev Las Vegas Coll Bus Econs Las Vegas NV 89154

KOHLER, DOLORES MARIE, gallery owner; b. Rochester, N.Y., June 26, 1928; d. Thomas Beranda and Kathryn (Held) White; m. Reuel S. Kohler, June 27, 1946; children: Richard, Kathryn Kohler Farnsworth, Linda Kohler Barnes, Pamela Kohler Conners. BMus, U. Utah, 1976. Lic. real estate broker, lic. cert. gen. real estate appraiser. Broker Kohler Investment Realty, Bountiful, Utah, 1962—; registered rep. Frank D. Richards, Salt Lake City, 1986-93, Internmountain Fin. Svcs. Corp., Salt Lake City, 1996—; appraiser FHA/HUD, 1962—; owner Marble House Gallery, Salt Lake City, 1987—; owner Sandcastle Theaters, Bountiful, 1976-98. Composer songs, 1973—. Music chmn. N. Canyon Stake LDS Ch., Bountiful, 1989-93, sec. North Canyon 3d Ward Sunday Sch., 1993-98, music dir. Relief Soc., 1996—. Mem. Inst. Real Estate Mgmt. (pres. 1984), Salt Lake Bd. Realtors, Salt Lake Art Dealers Assn. (v.p. 1988-90, pres. 1990-91), U. Utah Coll. Fine Arts Alumni Assn. (coun. 1995—, sec. 1997), Composers Guild, Mu Phi Epsilon. Avocations: music composing, travel. Home: 2891 S 650 E Bountiful UT 84010-4455 Office: Marble House Gallery 44 Exchange Pl Salt Lake City UT 84111-2713

KOHLER, ERIC DAVE, history educator; b. Cin., Oct. 24, 1943; s. Walter Joseph and Irmgard (Marx) K.; m. Kathryn D. K. Kohler, June 22, 1968. AB, Brown U., 1965; MA, Stanford U., 1967, PhD, 1971. Vis. asst. prof. history Calif. State U., Humboldt, 1970-71; asst. prof. U. Wyo., Laramie, 1971-78, assoc. prof., 1978—, acting head history dept., 1989-90. Chair Ivinson Hosp. La Grande Fleur Charity Ball, 1993. Recipient Deutcher Akademischer Austauchdienst award, 1968, U. Wyo. Faculty Devel. award, 1972. Mem. Am. Cath. Hist. Assn., Am. Hist. Assn., Am. Assn. for History of Medicine, German Studies Assn. (program dir. 1989). Club: Laramie Country. Avocations: golf, elec. wiring, computers. Office: U Wyo Dept History PO Box 3198 Laramie WY 82071-3198

KOHLER, FRED CHRISTOPHER, tax specialist; b. Cleve., Oct. 21, 1946; s. Fred Russell and Ruth Mary (Harris) K.; BS (Austin scholar), Northwestern U., 1968; MBA (Faville fellow), Stanford, 1970. Sr. analyst adminstrv. svcs. div. Arthur Andersen & Co., San Francisco, 1970-75, fin. systems analyst, sr. cost accountant Hewlett Packard Co., Palo Alto, Calif., 1975-77, internat. mktg. systems adminstr., 1977-80, sr. planning and reporting analyst corp. hdqrs., 1980-86, fin. planning and reporting mgr., 1986-90, tax mgr., 1990-92, sr. tax mgr., Hewlett Packard Co., 1992—. Mem. World Affairs Coun. No. Calif., Commonwealth Club, Churchill Club, Northwestern U. Alumni Club No. Calif., Stanford Alumni Assn., Beta Gamma Sigma. Home: 1736 Oak Creek Dr Apt 211 Palo Alto CA 94304-2112 Office: 3000 Hanover St Palo Alto CA 94304-1112

KOHL-WELLES, JEANNE ELIZABETH, state senator, sociologist, educator; b. Madison, Wis., Oct. 19, 1942; d. Lloyd Jr. and Elizabeth Anne (Sinness) K.; m. Kenneth D. Jenkins, Apr. 15, 1973; children: Randall Hill, Brennan Hill, Terra Jenkins, Kyle Jenkins, Devon Jenkins; m. Alexander Sumner Welles, Nov. 10, 1985. BA, Calif. State U., Northridge, 1965, MA, 1970; MA, UCLA, 1973, PhD, 1974. Tchr. L.A. Sch. Dist., 1965-70; lectr. Calif. State U., Long Beach, 1973-85; vis. asst. prof. U. Calif., Irvine, 1974-77; So. Calif. mgr. Project Equity/U.S. Dept. Edn., 1978-84; asst. dean, coord. women's programs U. Calif., Irvine, 1979-82; lectr. Calif. State U., Fullerton, 1982-85, U. Wash., Seattle, 1985—; chair senate higher edn. com., 1998; asst. prof. Pacific Luth. U., Tacoma, Wash., 1986-88; state legislator from 36th dist. Wash. Ho. of Reps., Olympia, 1992-94, majority whip, 1993-94; mem. Wash. Senate, Olympia, 1994—; Wash. State Senate, 1998; chair Senate Higher Edn. COm., 1999—. Author: Growing Up Equal, 1979, Explorations in Social Research, 1993, Student Study Guide-Marriage and the Family, 1993, 94, 95, 97, 98; contbr. articles to profl. jours. Bd. dirs. Com. for Children, Seattle, 1986-91, Queen Anne Cmty. Coun., Seattle, 1988-93, Stop Youth Violence, Wash., 1993—, Queen Anne Helpline, Seattle, 1992—, Youth Care, 1996—; mem. Wash. State Sentencing Guidelines Commn., 1995—, Wash. State Child Care Coord. Com., 1995—; mem. Gov.'s Task Force on Higher Edn., 1995-96. Grantee U.S. Dept. Edn., 1988-89, 90-91. Home: 301 W Kinnear Pl Seattle WA 98119-3732 Office: Wash State Senate PO Box 40436 Olympia WA 98504-0436

KOHN, KARL GEORGE, educator, composer; b. Vienna, Austria, Aug. 1, 1926; came to U.S., 1939, naturalized, 1945; s. Frederick and Margit (Fisch) K.; m. Margaret Case Sherman, June 23, 1950; children: Susanna Margaret, Emily Elizabeth. Cert., N.Y. Coll. Music, 1944; B.A. summa cum laude, Harvard U., 1950, M.A., 1955. Instr. music Pomona Coll., Claremont, Calif., 1950-54; asst. prof. Pomona Coll., 1954-59, assoc. prof., 1959-65, prof., 1965-85, William M. Keck Distinguished Service prof., 1985-94, prof. emeritus, 1994—; teaching fellow Harvard, 1954-55; mem. faculty Berkshire Music Center, Tanglewood, summers 1954, 55, 57. Composer: Castles and Kings, 1958, The Monk From Shu, 1959, Three Scenes For Orchestra, 1960, Serenade For Wind Quintet and Piano, 1961, Capriccios, 1962, Concerto Mutabile, 1962, Interludes, 1964, Sonata da Camera, 1965, Leisure and Other Songs; Cantata for baritone and chamber ensemble, 1965, Encounters for flute- piccolo and piano, 1966, Episodes for Piano and Orchestra, 1966, Introductions and Parodies, 1967, Encounters for Horn and Piano, 1967, Encounters III for Violin and Piano, 1971, Esdras; for flute and piano solo, mixed chorus and orch., 1971, Encounters IV for Oboe and Piano, 1972, Centone per Orchestra, 1973, Innocent Psaltery for symphonic wind orch. and percussion, Prophet Bird for chamber ensemble, Souvenirs II for oboe and harp, Also The Sons; for solo quartet, mixed chorus, organ or piano, four hands, Serenade II for concert band, 1977, Encounters VI for cello and piano, 1977, Paronyms II for saxophones and piano, 1978, Son of Prophet Bird for harp, 1977, Sonatina for marimba, 4 hands, 1977, Third Rhapsody for piano, 1977, Waldmusik, Concerto for clarinet and orch, 1979, Prophet Bird II for piano and chamber ensemble, 1980, Recreations II for two guitars, 1980, Quartet for saxophones, 1981, What Heaven Confers for mixed chorus and piano, 1981, Capriccios II for chamber ensemble, 1982, Time Irretrievable, for orch., 1982, Dream Music for two pianos, 1983, San Gabriel Set for chamber ensemble, 1984, Entr'acte for string quartet, 1985, Cantilena II for violin and marimba, 1985, Senza Sordino for horn and viola, 1985, Concords for violin and guitar, 1985, The Resplendent Air, five songs for high voice and piano, 1985, 2 Pierrot Songs for voice, flute, clarinet, violin, cello and piano, 1986, Choice Wood, Precious Metals for flute, trumpet, marimba and glockenspiel, 1986, An Amiable Piece for two pianos, winds and percussion, 1987, Lions on a Banner-Seven Sufi Texts for soprano solo, chorus of mixed voices and orch., 1988, For Four Flutes, 1989, Soliloquy for guitar, 1989, Before Beethoven for clarinet, cello, and piano, 1989, A Tranquil Piece for piano, 1989, Etude for tuba, 1990, Trace for piano, 1990, Rûckgabe for orch. of brass, percussion and strings, 1990, Cassation for wind quintet, 1990, Neofantasy for organ, 1990, Soliloquy II for Cello, 1991, Ode for String Orch., 1991, Soliloquy II for cello, 1991, Ode for string orch., 1991, Concords II for viola and cello, 1992, Concert music for string orch., 1993, Accords for two guitars, 1993, Ternaries for flute and piano, 1993, Reconnaissance for large chamber ensemble, 1995, Set of three for chamber ensemble, 1993-95, Memory and Hope Essay for Orch., 1996, Sax for 4 Saxophone Quartet, 1997, More Reflections for Clarinet and Piano, 1997, Toccata and Virelais for accordian and harp, 1998, Tripartita for vihuela or guitar, 1998, Four Minims for piano, 1998. Bd. dirs. Monday Evening Concerts, Los Angeles, 1963-85. Served as tech. sgt. U.S. Army, 1944-46, PTO. Faculty Fulbright research scholar Finland, 1955-56; Guggenheim fellow; grantee Howard Found., 1961-62; Mellon Found. grantee, 1974; NEA grantee, 1975-76, 79, 86. Mem. Coll. Music Soc. Avocation: swimming. Home: 674 W 10th St Claremont CA 91711-3716 Office: Pomona Coll Thatcher Bldg College Avenue St Claremont CA 91711

KOHN, ROBERT SAMUEL, JR., real estate investment consultant; b. Denver, Jan. 7, 1949; s. Robert Samuel and Miriam Lackner (Neusteter) K.; m. Eleanor B. Kohn; children: Joseph Robert, Randall Stanton, Andrea Rene. BS, U. Ariz., 1971. Asst. buyer Robinson's Dept. Store, L.A., 1971; agt. Neusteter Realty Co., Denver, 1972-73, exec. v.p., 1973-76; pres. Project Devel. Svcs., Denver, 1976-78, pres., CEO, 1978-83; pres. Kohn and Assocs., Inc., 1979-83; pres. The Burke Co., Inc., Irvine, Calif., 1983-84, ptnr., 1984-91; sr. mktg. assoc. Iliff, Phoenix, 1992-94; owner RSKJ, Inc., 1992-97. Mem. Bldg. Owners and Mgrs. Assn. (pres. 1977-78, dir. 1972-78, dir. S.W. Conf. Bd. 1977-78), Denver Art Mus., Denver U. Libr. Assn., Central City Opera House Assn., Inst. Real Estate Mgmt., Newport Beach Tennis Club. Republican. Jewish.

KOHN, WALTER, educator, physicist; b. Vienna, Austria, Mar. 9, 1923; m. Mara Schiff; children: J. Marilyn , Ingrid E. Kohn Katz, E. Rosalind. BA, U. Toronto, Ont., Can., 1945, MA, 1946, LLD (hon.), 1967; PhD in Physics, Harvard U., 1948; DSc (hon.), U. Paris, 1980; PhD (hon.), Brandeis U., 1981, Hebrew U. Jerusalem, 1981; DSc (hon.), Queens U., Kingston, Can., 1986, Fed. Inst. of Tech., Zurich, 1994, U. Wuerzburg, 1995, Tech. U. Vienna, 1996; PhD (hon.), Weizmann Inst., Israel, 1997. Indsl. physicist Sutton Horsley Co., Can., 1941-43; geophysicist Koulomzine, Que., Can., 1944-46; instr. physics Harvard U., Cambridge, Mass., 1948-50; asst. prof. physics Carnegie Mellon U., Pitts., 1950-60, assoc. prof. physics, 1953-57; prof. physics U. Calif., San Diego, 1960-79, chmn. dept. physics, 1961-63; dir. Inst. for Theoretical Physics, U. Calif., Santa Barbara, 1979-84; prof. dept. physics U. Calif., Santa Barbara, 1984-91, prof. of physics emeritus, rsch. prof. of physics, 1991—; rsch. physicist Ctr. for Quantized Electronic Structures, U. Calif., Santa Barbara, 1991—; vis. scholar U. Pa., U. Mich., U. Wash., U. Paris, U. Copenhagen, U. Jerusalem, Imperial Coll., London, ETH, Zurich, Switzerland; cons. Gen. Atomic, 1960-72, Westinghouse Rsch. Lab., 1953-57, Bell Telephone Labs., 1953-66, IBM, 1978; mem. or chmn. rev. coms. Brookhaven Nat. Labs., Argonne Nat. Labs., Oak Ridge Nat. Labs., Ames Lab., Tel Aviv U. (physics dept.), Brown U., Harvard U., U. Mich., Simon Frazer U., Tulane U., Reactor Divsn. NIST, Gaithersburg, Md.; chmn. S.D. divsn. Acad. Senate, 1968-69; dir. NSF Inst. Theoretical Physics, U. Calif. Santa Barbara, 1979-84; mem. senate rev. com. U. Calif. Management Nat. Labs., 1986-89; adv. bd. Statewide Inst. Global Conflict and Cooperation, 1982-92; mem. bd. govs. Weizmann Inst. of Sci., 1997—. Contbr. over 200 sci. articles and revs. to profl. jours. With inf., Can. Army, 1944-45. Recipient Buckley prize, 1960, Davisson-Germer prize, 1977, Nat. Medal of Sci., 1988, Feenberg medal, 1991, Niels Bohr/UNESCO Gold Medal, 1998, Nobel prize in chemistry, 1998; Lehman fellow Harvard U., 1946-46, fellow Nat. Rsch. Coun., 1950-51, sr. fellow NSF, 1958, Guggenheim fellow, 1963, sr. postdoctoral fellow NSF, 1967. Fellow AAAS, Am. Phys. Soc. (counselor-at-large 1968-72), Am. Acad. Arts and Scis.; mem. NAS, Internat. Acad. Quantum Molecular Scis., Am. Philos. Soc. Achievements include research on electron theory of solids and solid surfaces. Office: U Calif Dept Physics Santa Barbara CA 93106*

KOHRING, VICTOR H., state legislator, construction executive; b. Waukegan, Ill., Aug. 2, 1958; s. Heinz H. and Dolores E. Kohring. *Kohring moved to Alaska with his family in 1963 from Chicago, at the age of four. Driving the Alaska-Canada Highway, three thousand miles later they settled in the community of Chugiak. Nine months thereafter, the Kohring family survived the 1964 Great Alaska Earthquake, the strongest quake ever recorded in North American history. Rep. Kohring was actively involved in athletics in his youth. While at Anthony J. Dimond High School in Anchorage, he won two Most Valuable Player Awards in basketball, was selected to the All-Anchorage All-Star Basketball Team and lead his team to the Alaska High School State Basketball Championship in 1976.* AAS in Bus. Adminstrn., Matanuska-Susitna C.C., Palmer, Alaska, 1985; BA in Mgmt. Sci., Alaska Pacific U., 1987, MBA, 1989. State legislator Ho. of Reps., Dist. 26 Wasilla and Peters Creek/Chugiak, 1994, re-elected 1996, 98—; mem. ho. fin. com. Ho. of Reps., 1994, 96, 98—; chmn. house budget subcom. dept. edn. Ho. of Reps., Wasilla, 1995-96, chmn. adminstrn. com., 1995-96, chmn. environ. conservation com., 1997-98, chmn. cmty. and regional affairs com., 1997-98, chmn. commerce and econ. devel. com., 1997-98, chmn. law com., 1999—, chmn. natural resources com., 1999—; constn. exec., 1978—; real estate developer, 1978-82; owner South Ctrl. Bldg. Maintenance. *Rep. Kohring, BA 1987, MBA 1989, Alaska Pacific University, is currently a third-term state legislator and represents Wasilla and Chugiak in the Alaska State Legislature. He is a memeber of the House Finance Committee, and is Chairman of the Departments of Law and Natural Resources Budget Committees. Rep. Kohring was appointed by Governor Walter J. Hickel to the Alaska Housing Finance Corporation Board of Directors in 1991 and 1993, where he served as vice-chairman. Rep. Kohring is a regular guest columnist in newspapers throughout Alaska, and is currently in the process of publishing a book containing a five-year accumulation of writings.* Bd. dirs. Alaska Housing Fin. Corp., Anchorage, 1991-94; vice chmn., mem. Iditarod Trail Com.; mem. Matanuska-Susitna Borough Econ. Devel. Commn., 1993-94; chmn. Wasilla Planning and Utilities Commn., 1991-94; mem. Alaska del. Rep. Nat. Conv., Dallas, 1984, dist. del. rep., 1984, 86, 90, 92; treas. Rep. Orgn. Alaska, 1990, fin. chmn., 1990-91. Mem. NRA (life), Nat. Fedn. Ind. Bus., Christian Businessman's Assn., Greater Wasilla C. of C., Chugiak-Eagle River C. of C., Anthony J. Dimond H.S. Alumni Assn., Pioneers of Alaska. Republican. Home: PO Box 870515 Wasilla AK 99687-0515 Office: Alaska Ho of Reps State Capitol Bldg Juneau AK 99801

KOHWI-SHIGEMATSU, TERUMI, research scientist; b. Tokyo, Aug. 30, 1949; d. Teruhiko and Futaba (Takamatsu) Shigematsu; m. Yoshinori Kohwi; 1 child, Minoree. BS magna cum laude, Washington Coll., 1971; MA, John Hopkins U., 1973; PhD, U. Tokyo, 1978. Sci. fellow Japan Soc. for Promotion, Tokyo, 1978-79; rsch. scientist Inst. Tuberculosis and Cancer, Sendai, Miyaginken, Japan, 1979-81; postdoctoral fellow Fred Hutchinson Cancer Rsch. Ctr., Seattle, Wash., 1981-84; asst. staff scientist La Jolla (Calif.) Cancer Rsch. Found., 1984-88; staff scientist La Jolla (Calif.) Cancer Rsch. Found., La Jolla, 1988-94; sr. staff scientist La Jolla (Calif.) Cancer Rsch. Found., 1994-96; sr. staff scienist life scis. divsn. Lawrence Berkeley Lab.-U. Calif., Berkeley, 1996—. NIH Fogarty Internat. fellow, 1981-82, Leukemia Soc. Am. spl. fellow, 1983-85. Mem. NIH (chem. pathology study sect. 1992-96), Am. Cancer Soc. (Faculty award 1988-93). Home: 2991 Shasta Rd Berkeley CA 94708-2143 Office: Lawrence Berkeley Lab Univ Calif Berkeley CA 94720

KOKALJ, JAMES EDWARD, retired aerospace administrator; b. Chgo., Oct. 29, 1933; s. John and Antoinette (Zabukovec) K. AA in Engring., El Camino Coll., Torrance, Calif., 1953. Dynomometer lab. technician U.S. Electric Motors, L.A., 1953-54; devel. lab. technician AiResearch divsn. Garrett, L.A., 1956-59; tech. rep. McCulloch, L.A., 1959-65; dist. mgr. Yamaha Internat., Montebello, Calif., 1965-67; salesman Vasek Polak BMW, Manhattan Beach, Calif., 1967-68; sr. svc. rep. Stratos-We. div. Fairchild, Manhattan Beach, 1968-70; asst. regional mgr. we. states J.B.E. Olson div. Grumman, L.A., 1970-71; gen. mgr. Internat. Kart Fedn., Glendora, Calif., 1971-73; logistics support data specialist Mil. Aircraft divsn. Northrop Grumman, Hawthorne, Calif., 1974-95; ret., 1995. Author: Technical Inspection Handbook, 1972; contbr. articles to profl. jours. With USN, 1954-56. Mem. U.S. Naval Inst., Internat. Naval Rsch. Orgn., Nat. Maritime Hist. Soc., So. Calif. Hist. Aircraft Found. Republican. Roman Catholic. Avocations: woodworking, ship modeling, maritime history, auto and aircraft restoration. Home: 805 Bayview Dr Hermosa Beach CA 90254-4147

KOLANOSKI, THOMAS EDWIN, financial company executive; b. San Francisco, Mar. 1, 1937; s. Theodore Thaddeus and Mary J. (Luczynski) K.; m. Sheila O'Brien, Dec. 26, 1960; children: Kenneth John, Thomas Patrick, Michael Sean. BS, U. San Francisco, 1959, MA, 1965. Cert. fin. planner; registered rep. Educator, counselor, administr. San Francisco Unified Sch. Dist.; adminstr. Huntington Beach (Calif.) Union, 1969-79; v.p. fin. svcs. Waddell & Reed, Inc., Ariz., Nev., Utah, So. Calif., 1979-94; retired Waddell & Reed, Inc., 1994; investment cons. Foothill Securities Inc.; personal fin. planner. Fellow NDEA, 1965. Mem. Nat. Assn. Secondary Sch. Prins., Internat. Assn. of Fin. Planners, Nat. Assn. Securities Dealers. Republican. Roman Catholic. Avocation: fly fishing. Fax: 714-434-9425. Home: 1783 Panay Cir Costa Mesa CA 92626-2348

KOLAROV, KRASIMIR DOBROMIROV, computer scientist, researcher; b. Sofia, Bulgaria, Oct. 16, 1961; came to the U.S., 1987; s. Dobromir Krastev and Margarita Georgieva (Kurukafova) K.; m. Janet Louise Barba, July 4, 1990; children: April, Kathryn, Sonia, Elena. BS in Math. with honors, U. Sofia, Bulgaria, 1981, MS in Ops. Rsch. with honors, 1982, MA in English, 1982; MS in Mech. Engring., Stanford U., 1990, PhD in Mech. Engring., 1993. Rschr. Bulgarian Acad. Scis., Sofia, 1982-83; rsch. assoc., vis. prof. Inst. Mechanics and Biomechanics, Bulgarian Acad. Scis., Sofia, 1983-87; tchg. asst. Stanford (Calif.) U., 1988-92; mem. rsch. staff Interval Rsch. Corp., Palo Alto, Calif., 1992—; vis. prof. Inst. for Civil Engring., Sofia, 1983-86; lectr. H.S. U., Sofia, 1985; reviewer Jour. Robotic Sys., Palo Alto, 1991—; others. Contbr. articles to profl. jours. Mem. IEEE, Assn. for Computing Machinery, Soc. for Indsl. and Applied Math. Avocations: bridge, travel, skiing, bicycling, flying. Office: Interval Rsch Corp 1801 Page Mill Rd # C Palo Alto CA 94304-1216

KOLB, DOROTHY GONG, elementary education educator; b. San Jose, Calif.; d. Jack and Lucille (Chinn) Gong; m. William Harris Kolb, Mar. 22, 1970. BA (with highest honors), San Jose State U., 1964; postgrad., U. Hawaii, Calif. State U., L.A.; MA in Ednl. Tech., Pepperdine U., 1992. Cert. life elem. educator, mentally retarded educator K-12, learning handicapped pre-sch., K-12, adult classes. Tchr. Cambrian Sch. Dist., San Jose Calif., 1964-66, Cen. Oahu (Hawaii) Sch. Dist., Wahiawa, 1966-68, Montebello (Calif.) Unified Sch. Dist., 1968—. Named to Pi Lambda Theta, Kappa Delta Pi, Pi Tau Sigma, Tau Beta Pi; recipient Walter Bachrodt Meml. scholar.

KOLB, KEITH ROBERT, architect, educator; b. Billings, Mont., Feb. 9, 1922; s. Percy Fletcher and Josephine (Randolph) K.; m. Jacqueline Cecile Jump, June 18, 1947; children: Brooks Robin, Bliss Richards. Grad. basic engring., US Army Specialized Training Rutgers U., 1944; BArch cum laude, U. Wash., 1947; MArch, Harvard U., 1950. Registered architect, Wash., Mont., Idaho, Calif., Oreg., Nat. Council Archtl. Registration Bds. Draftsman, designer various archtl. firms Seattle, 1946-54; draftsman, designer Walter Gropius and Architects Collaborative, Cambridge, Mass., 1950-52; prin. Keith R. Kolb, Architect, Seattle, 1954-64, Keith R. Kolb Architect & Assocs., Seattle, 1964-66; ptnr. Decker, Kolb & Stansfield, Seattle, 1966-71, Kolb & Stansfield AIA Architects, Seattle, 1971-89; pvt. practice Keith R. Kolb FAIA Architects, Seattle, 1989—; instr. Mont. State Coll., Bozeman, 1947-49; asst. prof. arch. U. Wash., Seattle, 1952-60, assoc. prof., 1960-82, prof., 1982-90, prof. emeritus, 1990—. Design architect Dist. II Hdqrs. and Comm. Ctr., Wash. State Patrol, Bellevue, 1970 (Exhbn. award Seattle chpt. AIA), Hampson residence, 1970 (nat. AIA 1st honor 1973, citation Seattle chpt. AIA 1980), Acute Gen. Stevens Meml. Hosp., 1973, Redmond Pub. Libr., 1975 (jury selection Wash. coun. AIA 1980), Tolstedt residence, Helena, Mont., 1976, Herbert L. Eastlick Biol. Scis. Lab. bldg. Wash. State U., 1977, Redmond Svc. Ctr., Puget Sound Power and Light Co., 1979, Computer and Mgmt. Svcs. Ctr., Paccar Inc., 1981 (curatorial team selection Mus. History and Industry exhbn. 100th anniversary of AIA 1994), Seattle Town House, 1960 (curatorial team selection Mus. History and Industry exhbn. 100th anniversary of AIA 1994), Comm. Tower, Pacific N.W. Bell, 1981 (nat. J.F. Lincoln bronze), Forks br. Seattle 1st Nat. Bank, 1981 (commendation award Seattle chpt. AIA 1981, nat. jury selection Am. Architecture, The State of the Art in the '80's 1985, regional citation Am. Wood Coun. 1981), R.g. ops. control Ctr. Sacramento Dist. Corps Engrs. McChord AFB, Wash., 1982, Puget Sound Blood Ctr., 1983-88, expansion vis./dining/recreation facilities Wash. State Reformatory, Monroe, 1983, Univ. Sta. P.O., US Postal Svc., Seattle, 1983, Guard Towers, McNeil Island Corrections Ctr. Wash., 1983, Magnolia Queen Anne Carrier Annex, U.S. Postal Svc., Seattle, 1986, Tolstedt residence, Seattle, 1987, Maxim residence, Camano Island, Wash., 1991, Carmean residence alterations/additions, Seattle, 1995, 96, 97. Pres. Laurelhurst Community Club, Seattle, 1966. Served with U.S. Army, 1943-45, ETO. Decorated Bronze Star medal ETO; recipient Alpha Rho Chi medal; selected Am. Architects, Facts on File, inc., 1989. Fellow AIA (dir. Seattle chpt. 1970-71, sec. Seattle chpt. 1972, Wash. state coun. 1973, pres. sr. coun. Seattle chpt. 1994-96, trustee Seattle Archtl. Found. 1994-96, Citation award Seattle chpt. for a Seattle 1960 Town House, 1990); mem. U. Wash. Archtl. Alumni Assn. (pres. 1958-59), Phi Beta Kappa, Tau Sigma Delta. Home and Office: 3379 47th Ave NE Seattle WA 98105-5326

KOLB, KEN LLOYD, writer; b. Portland, Oreg., July 14, 1926; s. Frederick Von and Ella May (Bay) K.; m. Emma LaVada Sanford, June 7, 1952; children: Kevin, Lauren, Kimrie. BA in English with honors, U. Calif., Berkeley, 1950; MA with honors, San Francisco State U., 1953. Cert. jr. coll. English tchr. Freelance fiction writer various nat. mags., N.Y.C., 1951-56; freelance screenwriter various film and TV studios, Los Angeles, 1956-81; freelance novelist Chilton, Random House, Playboy Press, N.Y.C., 1967—; instr. creative writing Feather River Coll., Quincy Calif., 1969; minister Universal Life Ch. Author: (teleplay) She Walks in Beauty, 1956 (Writers Guild award 1956), (feature films) Seventh Voyage of Sinbad, 1957, Snow Job, 1972, (novels) Getting Straight, 1967 (made into feature film), The Couch Trip, 1970 (made into feature film), Night Crossing, 1974; contbr. fiction and humor to nat. mags. and anthologies. Foreman Plumas County Grand Jury, Quincy, 1970; chmn. Region C Criminal Justice Planning commn., Oroville, Calif., 1975-77; film commr. Plumas County, 1986-87. Served with USNR, 1944-46. Establishment Ken Kolb Collection (Boston U. Library 1969). Mem. Writers Guild Am. West, Authors Guild, Mensa, Phi Beta Kappa, Theta Chi. Democrat. Club: Plumas Ski (pres. 1977-78). Avocations: skiing, tennis, traveling. Home and Office: PO Box 30022 Cromberg CA 96103-3022

KOLB, WILLIAM HARRIS, computer programmer, analyst; b. St. Paul, Nov. 9, 1943; s. Hart Benjamin Kolb and Seba Ruth (Harris) Tomkins; m. Dorothy Lucille Gong, Mar. 22, 1970. AA, Santa Monica Coll., 1964; BS, Calif. Poly. State U., 1967; cert., Computer Learning Ctr., 1976, 95. Programmer/analyst Star-Kist Foods, Terminal Island, Calif., 1977-80, Gould Def. Sys., El Monte, Calif., 1980-82, Union Bank, L.A. 1982-83, Dynalectron Corp., Norco, Calif., 1983-84, Whittaker Corp., Van Nuys, Calif., 1984-87, ITT Barton Instruments, City of Industry, Calif., 1988-94, Automatic Data Processing, San Dimas, Calif., 1995—. Avocations: piano, barbershop singing, bodybuilding.

KOLBE, JAMES THOMAS, congressman; b. Evanston, Ill., June 28, 1942; s. Walter William and Helen (Reed) K. BA in Polit. Sci., Northwestern U., 1965; MBA in Econs., Stanford U. 1967. Asst. to coordinating architect Ill. Bldg. Authority, Chgo., 1970-72; spl. asst. to Gov. Richard Ogilvie Chgo., 1972-73; v.p. Wood Canyon Corp., Tucson, 1973-80; mem. Ariz. Senate, 1977-83, majority whip, 1979-80; mem. 99th-106th Congresses from 5th dist. Ariz., 1985—; mem. appropriations com. 99th-105th Congresses from 5th dist. Ariz., 1987—, chmn. appropriations subcom. on treasury, postal svc. and ge, 1997—. Trustee Embry-Riddle Aero. U., Daytona Beach, Fla.; bd. dirs. Community Food Bank, Tucson; Republican precinct committeeman, Tucson, 1974—. Served as lt. USNR, 1968-69, Vietnam. Republican. Methodist. Office: US Ho of Reps 2266 Rayburn Washington DC 20515-0305

KOLCH, ZELMA TRUJILLO, elementary education educator; b. Dawson, N.Mex., Apr. 12, 1934; d. Antonio S. and Lily (Avila) Trujillo; children: Camille, Paul, Michael, Lawrence Jeffrey. BA, East Tex. State U., 1982, MA, 1988. Bilingual tchr. Garland (Tex.) Ind. Sch. Dist., 1982-86, Denver Pub. Schs., 1986—. Creator Jamboree! Am. Myths and Legends, 1997. Author: Vecas En Ingles Para Ninos en Escuelas Elementales o Para los

que están aprendiendo inglés, 1998. Mem. NEA, Colo. Bilingual Educators Assn., Colo. Edn. Assn., Denver Classroom Tchrs. Assn. (rep. 1995—, bd. dirs. 1995-97). Democrat. Roman Catholic. Avocations: knitting, dancing, reading, sewing. Home: 1817 Quail St Apt 8 Lakewood CO 80215-2736

KOLDE, BERT, professional basketball team executive. Vice chmn. Portland Trail Blazers. Office: Portland Trail Blazers One Center Ct Ste 200 Portland OR 97227

KOLDEN-RAMSEY, MELANIE ANN, journalist; b. Oak Park, Ill., July 12, 1960; d. John Alden Kolden and Nancy Carolyn (Myers) Robers; m. Thomas Charles Ramsey, May 9, 1992; 1 child, Wesley. BA, Calif. State U., Northridge, 1988; postgrad., Calif. State U., Dominguez Hills, 1992—. Intern L.A. mag., Century City, Calif., 1987; assoc. calendar editor L.A. Weekly, 1987-92; entertainment calendar coord. San Francisco Chronicle, 1992—. Mem. Soc. Profl. Journalists, Northern Calif. Newspaper Guild. Office: San Francisco Chronicle 901 Mission St San Francisco CA 94103-2905

KOLDEWYN, WILLIAM ALMON, aerospace physicist; b. Ogden, Utah, Apr. 23, 1942; s. William John Koldewyn and Mary Emiline (Islaub) Hills; m. Katherine Sandra Trapp, Aug. 7, 1967; children: Kennis, Kami. BS in Physics, Weber State U., 1967; PhD in Physics, Wesleyan U., 1976. Dir. engring. Scientech, Boulder, Colo., 1982-87; staff cons., program mgr. Ball Aerospace, Boulder, 1988—; mem. adv. bd. Laser Inst. Am., 1985-87; cons. Lawrence Livermore Labs., Livermore, Calif., 1985-87. Chair, mem. various school dist. coms., Boulder, 1985-95. Mem. Am. Phys. Soc. Avocations: stock market analysis, system simulation, alternative energy, music, gardening. Home: 933 Columbia Pl Boulder CO 80303-3211

KOLENIAK GIGNOUX, BARBARA DONNA, nurse; b. N.Y.C., Feb. 20, 1950; d. William Zazula and Catherine Sheridan (Quigley) Koleniak; m. James Lee Rold, Dec. 29, 1974 (div. June 1991); children: Christopher, William, Cara; m. John Gordon Gignoux, July 7, 1996. Nursing Diploma, St. Vincent's Sch. Nursing, Richmond, 1971; BA, Marymount Manhattan Coll., N.Y.C., 1973. RN; cert. HIV/AIDS testing and counseling. Staff nurse N.Y. Med. Coll., N.Y.C., 1971-72; pvt. duty nurse N.Y. Nurse Registry, N.Y.C., 1972-73; staff nurse U. Nebr. Med. Ctr., Omaha, 1973-74, Children's Hosp., Omaha, 1975, ENCOR Med. Support Unit, Omaha, 1987-89; nurse mgr. St. Clare's Home A.R.F., Neptune, N.J., 1990; clin. coord. pediat. HIV/AIDS program Jersey Shore Med. Ctr., Neptune, 1990-96; pub. speaker on pediat. HIV/AIDS. Reviewer curriculum manual The Best Parent I Can Be, 1989. Recipient Starfish award Starfish Soc. N.J., 1992. Democrat. Roman Catholic.

KOLKEY, DANIEL MILES, lawyer; b. Chgo., Apr. 21, 1952; s. Eugene Louis and Gilda Penelope (Cowan) K.; m. Donna Lynn Christie, May 15, 1982; children: Eugene, William, Christopher, Jonathan. BA, Stanford U., 1974; JD, Harvard U., 1977. Bar: Calif. 1977, U.S. Dist. Ct. (cen. dist.) Calif. 1979, U.S. Dist. Ct. (no. dist.) Calif. 1980, U.S. Dist. Ct. (ea. dist.) Calif. 1978, U.S. Dist. Ct. (so. dist.) Calif. 1994, U.S. Dist. Ct. Ariz. 1992, U.S. Ct. Appeals (9th cir.) 1979, U.S. Supreme Ct. 1983. Law clk. U.S. Dist. Ct. judge, N.Y.C., 1977-78; assoc. Gibson Dunn & Crutcher, L.A., 1978-84, ptnr., 1985-94; counsel to Gov. and legal affairs sec. to Calif. Gov. Pete Wilson, 1995-98; assoc. justice Calif. Ct. of Appeal, 3rd Appellate Dist., Sacramento, 1998—; arbitrator bi-nat. panel for U.S.-Can. Free Trade Agreement, 1990-94; commr. Calif. Law Revision Commn., 1992-94, vice chair, 1993-94, chair, 1994; mem. Blue Ribbon Commn. on Jury Sys. Improvement, 1996. Contbr. articles to profl. publs. Co-chmn. internat. rels. sect. Town Hall of Calif., L.A., 1981-90; chmn. internat. trade legis. subcom., internat. commerce steering com. L.A. Area C. of C., 1983-91 (mem. law & justice com., 1993-94); mem. adv. coun. and exec. com. Asia Pacific Ctr. for Resolution of Internat. Bus. Disputes, 1991-94; bd. dirs., L.A. Ctr. for Internat. Comml. Arbitration, 1986-94, treas., 1986-88, v.p. 1988-90, pres., 1990-94; assoc. mem. ctrl. com. Calif. Rep. Party, 1983-94, mem. ctrl. com., 1995-98, dep. gen. coun. credentials com., Republican Nat. Convention, 1992, alt. Calif. Delegation, 1992, Calif. del., 1996; mem. L.A. Com. on Fgn. Rels., 1985-95, Pacific Coun. Internat. Policy, 1999—; gen. counsel Citizens Rsch. Found., 1990-94. Master Anthony Kennedy Inns of Ct., 1996—; mem. Am. Arbitration Assn. (panel of arbitrators, arbitrator large complex case dispute resolution program 1993-94), Chartered Inst. Arbitrators, London (assoc. 1986-94), Friends of Wilton Park So. Calif. (chmn. exec. com. 1986-94, exec. com. 1986—). Jewish. Office: Ct of Appeal 3rd Appellate Dist 914 Capitol Mall Sacramento CA 95814-4906

KOLLIGIAN, LEO, lawyer; b. Fresno, Calif., Aug. 25, 1917; s. Sam and Mary (Gigerian) K.; m. Dorothy Ohanian, Mar. 12, 1942; 1 child, Lee Jay. BA, Fresno Calif. State Coll., 1938; JD, U. Calif., Berkeley, 1941. Chmn. war dept. 9th Dt Deferment Com., Sacramento, 1943-45; dep. atty. gen. Sacramento, 1945-46; pvt. practice Fresno, 1946—; regent U. Calif., 1985-96. Trustee emeritus St. Agnes Med. Ctr., Fresno, Profl. Office CB, Met. Mus. Avocations: swimming, water skiing, tennis, reading. Home: 6544 N Van Ness Blvd Fresno CA 93711 Office: 1100 W Shaw Fresno CA 93711

KOLODNY, STEPHEN ARTHUR, lawyer; b. Monticello, N.Y., 1940; s. H. Lewis and Ida K.; children: Jeffery, Lee. BA in Bus. Adminstrn., Boston U., 1963, JD, 1965. Bar: Calif. 1966, U.S. Dist. Ct. (cen. dist.) Calif. 1966; cert. family law specialist. Sole practice L.A., 1966-95; with Kolodny & Anteau, L.A., 1995—; lectr. on family law subjects. Co-author: Divorce Practice Handbook, 1994; author: Evidence ABA Advocate, 1996. Mem. ABA (family law sect., author ABA Advocate), Internat. Acad. Matrimonial Lawyers (bd. govrs., pres. USA chpt.), Calif. State Bar Assn. (cert. family law specialist, lectr. State Bar panel, CEB programs, mem. family law sect.), Los Angeles County Bar Assn. (lectr., mem. and past chmn. family law sect.), Beverly Hills Bar Assn. (lectr., mem. family law sect.).

KOLOVOS, NICHOLAS, writer, highway inspector; b. Sault Saint Marie, Mich., Mar. 21, 1913; s. George A. and Kannela (Pappas K.; m. Katherine Chapekis, Sept. 6, 1940 (dec. Sept. 1988); children: Connie Lee, George Casey. Inspector U.S. Hwy.; prin. writer, humorist, satirist, composer Nicholas G. Kolovos. Democrat. Greek Orthodox. Home: 10200 Chapman Ave Apt 109 Garden Grove CA 92840-2826

KOLSRUD, HENRY GERALD, dentist; b. Minnewaukan, N.D., Aug. 12, 1923; s. Henry G. and Anna Naomi (Moen) K.; m. Loretta Dorothy Cooper, Sept. 3, 1945; children:—Gerald Roger, Charles Cooper. Student Concordia Coll., 1941-44; DDS, U. Minn., 1947. Gen. practice dentistry, Spokane, Wash., 1953—. Bd. dirs. Spokane County Rep. Com., United Crusade, Spokane; at-large-del. Republican Planning Com.; mem. Republican Presdl. Task Force. Capt. USAF, 1950-52. Recipient Employer of the Yr. award Lilac City Bus. and Profl. Women, 1994. Mem. ADA, Wash. State Dental Assn., Spokane Dist. Dental Soc. Lutheran. Clubs: Spokane Country, Spokane, Empire. Lodges: Masons, Shriners. Home: 2107 W Waikiki Rd Spokane WA 99218-2780 Office: 3718 N Monroe St Spokane WA 99205-2850

KOLTAI, STEPHEN MIKLOS, mechanical engineer, consultant, economist, writer, educator; b. Ujpest, Hungary, Nov. 5, 1922; came to U.S., 1963; s. Maximilian and Elisabeth (Rado) K.; m. Franciska Gabor, Sept. 14, 1948; children: Eva, Susy. MS in Mech. Engring., U. Budapest, Hungary, 1948, MS in Econs., MS, BA, 1955. Engr. Hungarian Govt., 1943-49; cons. engr. and diplomatic service various European countries, 1950-62; cons. engr. Pan Bus. Cons. Corp., Switzerland and U.S., 1963-77, Palm Springs, Calif., 1977—. Patentee in field. Charter mem. Rep. Presdl. task force, Washington, 1984—. Avocations: tennis, golf.

KOMDAT, JOHN RAYMOND, data processing consultant; b. Brownsville, Tex., Apr. 29, 1943; s. John William and Sara Grace (Williams) K.; m. Judy Jean Garrette, Aug. 26, 1965 (div.); m. Barbara Milroy O'Cain, Sept. 27, 1986; children: Philip August, John William. Student U. Tex., 1961-65. Sr. systems analyst Mass. Blue Cross, Boston, 1970-74; pvt. practice data processing cons., San Francisco, 1974-80, Denver, 1981; prin. sys. analyst mgmt. info sys. internat. mgmt. firm, Denver, 1980-90; prin. sys. analyst Info. Mgmt. Comm. Staff Dept. Adminstrn. State Colo., 1989-97;

mem. Mus. Modern Art, CODASYL End User Facilities Com., 1974-76, funds distbn. com. Mile High United Way. Served with U.S. Army, 1966-70. Mem. IEEE, AAAS, ACLU, Colo. Info. Mgmt. Assn., Assn. Computing Machinery, Denver Art Mus., Friend of Pub. Radio, Friend of Denver Pub. Libr., Colo. State Mgrs. Assn, Nature Conservancy, Sierra Club, Common Cause, Trout Unlimited. Democrat. Office: 1900 S Lincoln St Denver CO 80210-4010

KOMENICH, KIM, photographer; b. Laramie, Wyo., Oct. 15, 1956; s. Milo and Juanita Mary (Beggs) K. BA in Journalism, San Jose State U., 1979. Reporter/photographer Manteca (Calif.) Bull., 1976-77; staff photographer Contra Costa Times, Walnut Creek, Calif., 1979-82, San Francisco Examiner, 1982—; lectr. San Francisco Acad. Art; vis. lectr. Mo. Sch. Journalism, 1998—. John S. Knight fellow Stanford U., 1993-94; recipient 1st Pl. award UPI, 1982, 85, Nat. Headliner award, 1983, 88, 87 1st Pl. award World Press Photo Awards, 1983, 1st Pl. award AP, 1985, 87, Disting. Svc. award Sigma Delta Xi, 1986, Pulitzer prize, 1987, others. Office: San Francisco Examiner 110 5th St San Francisco CA 94103-2918

KOMISSARCHIK, EDWARD A., computer scientist; b. Moscow, Russia, July 5, 1949; came to U.S., 1990; s. Alexander and Riva (Zilberstein) K.; m. Stella Mnatsakanian, Sept. 5, 1969; 1 child, Julia. M in Math., Lomonosov U., Moscow, 1971; PhD of Computer Sci., Inst. Cybernetics, Russia, 1978. Rsch. scientist Inst. Control Scis., Acad. Scis., Moscow, 1971-77, Inst. Sys. Studies, Acad. Scis., Moscow, 1977-90; assoc. prof. Inst. Radio Electronics and Automation, Moscow, 1978-90; pres., chief tech. officer Accent, Inc., San Francisco, 1993-96; dir./ Aspect Telecomm., San Jose. Contbr. articles to profl. jours. Mem. IEEE, ACM, Internat. Platform Assn., Russian Math. Soc., Scientists Club. Avocations: public speaking, medieval history, tennis. Home: 2452 Melendy Dr San Carlos CA 94070-3623

KOMPALA, DHINAKAR SATHYANATHAN, chemical engineering educator, biochemical engineering researcher; b. Madras, India, Nov. 20, 1958; came to U.S., 1979; s. Sathyanathan and Sulochana Kompala; m. Sushila Viswamurthy Rudramuniappa, Nov. 18, 1983; children: Tejaswi Dina, Chytanya Robby. BTech., Indian Inst. Tech., Madras, 1979; MS, Purdue U., 1982, PhD, 1984. Asst. prof. chem. engring. U. Colo., Boulder, 1985-91, assoc. prof., 1991—; vis. assoc. chem. enging. Calif. Inst. Tech., 1991-92; vis. prof. Internat. Ctr. Biotech., Osaka U., Japan, 1999. Editor Cell Separation Sci. and Tech., 1991; contbr. articles to profl. jours. Recipient NSF Presdl. Young Investigators award, 1988-93; NSF Biotech. Rsch. grantee, 1986-89, 89-92, 95-99; Dept. Commerce rsch. grantee, 1988; The Whitaker Found. grantee, 1990-93. Mem. Am. Inst. Chem. Engrs., Am. Chem. Soc. (program chair biochem. tech. divsn. 1993). Office: U Colo PO Box 424 Boulder CO 80309-0424

KONG, KENNETH SEHKIANG, computer technician; b. K. Terengganu, Terengganu, Malysia, Nov. 6, 1969; came to U.S., 1995; s. Seng Fook and Chiewsia (Ong) K. BSBA in Computer Info. Systems, Hawaii Pacific U., 1997, MBA in Fin., 1998. Asst. EDP adminstr. Schering Plough (m) Sdn Bhd, Kuala Lumpur, Malaysia, 1991; programmer, software support Syntex Computer (m) Sdn Bhd, Petaling Jaya, Malaysia, 1992; asst. sales mgr. Adlycom Sdn Bhd, Petaling Jaya, 1992-93; svc. mktg. exec. Unifloor (m) Sdn Bhd, Petaling Jaya, 1994; computer technician ISLE Computer Consulting, Honolulu, Hawaii, 1996—. Mem. Hawaiian Island Investment Group, Delta Mu Delta, Epsilon Delta Pi. Home: 2068 Saint Louis Dr Honolulu HI 96816-2035 Office: ISLE Computer Consulting 1240 Alamoana Blvd Ste 307 Honolulu HI 96813

KONG, LAURA S. L., geophysicist; b. Honolulu, July 23, 1961; d. Albert T.S. and Cordelia (Seu) K.; m. Kevin T.M. Johnson, Mar. 3, 1990. ScB, Brown U., 1983; PhD, MIT/Woods Hole Oceanog. Instn., 1990. Grad. rschr. Woods Hole (Mass.) Oceanog. Instn., 1984-90; postdoctoral fellow U. Tokyo, 1990-91; geophysicist Pacific Tsunami Warning Ctr., Ewa Beach, Hawaii, 1991-93; seismologist U.S. Geol. Survey Hawaiian Volcano Obs., 1993-95; rschr. U. Hawaii, Honolulu, 1996—; mem. Hawaii State Earthquake adv. bd., 1994—; mem. equal opportunity adv. bd. Nat. Earth Svc. Pacific Region, Honolulu, 1992-93, Asin-Am./Pacific Islander spl. emphasis program mgr., 1992-93; legis. researcher Hawaii State Senate, 1996—. Contbr. articles to profl. jours.; spkr., editl. reviewer in field. Rsch. fellow Japan Govt.-Japan Soc. for Promotion of Sci., 1990; recipient Young Investigator grant Japan Soc. for Promotion of Sci., 1990. Mem. Am. Geophys. Union, Seismol. Soc. Am., Hawaii Ctr. for Volcanology, Assn. Women in Sci., Sigma Xi. Avocation: sports. Office: U Hawaii Hawaii Inst Geophysics 2525 Correa Rd Honolulu HI 96822-2219

KONING, HENDRIK, architect; came to the U.S., 1979; BArch, U. Melbourne, Australia, 1978; MArch II, UCLA, 1981. Lic. architect Calif. 1982, contractor, 1984; registered architect, Australia; cert. Nat. Coun. Archtl. Registration Bds. Prin. in charge of tech., code, and prodn. issues Koning Eizenberg Architecture, 1981—; instr. UCLA, U. B.C., Harvard U., MIT; lectr. in field. Exhbns incl. "House Rules" Wexner Ctr., 1994, "The Architect's Dream Houses for the Next Millenium", The Contemporary Arts Ctr., 1993, " Angels & Franciscans", Gagosian Gallery, 1992, "Conceptual Drawings by Architects", Bannatyne Gallery, 1991, Koning and Eizenberg Projects Grad. Sch. Architecture & Urban Planning UCLA, 1990, others; prin. works include Digital Domain renovation and screening rm., Santa Monica, Lightstorm Entertainment offices and THX theater, Santa Monica, Gilmore Bank addition and remodel, L.A., 1548-1550 Studios, Santa Monica, (with RTA) Materials Rsch. Lab. U. Calif., Santa Barbara, Ken. Edwards Ctr. Cmty. Svcs., Santa Monica, Peck Park Cmty. Ctr. Gymnasium, San Pedro, Calif., Sepulveda Recreation Ctr. Gymnasium, L.A., (Nat. Concrete /Masonry award 1996, AIA Calif. Coun. Honor award 1996, AIA L.A. Chpt. Merit Award, 1997, L.A. Bus. Coun. Beautification awrd 1996, AIA/SFV Design award 1995), PS# 1 Elem. Sch., Santa Monica, Famers Market additions and master plan, L.A. (Westside Urban Forum prize 1991), Stage Deli, L.A., Simone Hotel, L.A. (Nat. Honor award AIA 1994), Boyd Hotel, L.A. Cmty. Corp. Santa Monica Housing Projects, 5th St. Family Housing, Santa Monica, St. John's Hosp. Replacement Housing Program, Santa Monica, Liffman Ho., Santa Monica, (with Glenn Erikson) Electric Artblock, Venice (Beautification award L.A. Bus. Coun. 1993), 6th St. Condominiums, Santa Monica, Hollywood Duplex, Hollywood Hills (Record Houses Archtl. Record 1988), Calif. Ave. Duplex, Santa Monica, Tarzana Ho. (Merit award L.A. chpt. AIA 1991, Merit Award AIA Calif. Coun., 1998, Sunset Western Home awards 1993-94), 909 Ho., Santa Monica (Merit award L.A. chpt. AIA 1991), 31st St. Ho., Santa Monica (Honor award AIACC 1994, Record House 1995, Nat. AIA Honor award 1996), others. Recipient 1st award Progressive Architecture, 1987; named one of Domino's Top 30 Architects, 1989. Fellow AIA (juror San Diego design awards 1992, panelist honor awards 1994, Calif. coun. spl. awards 1997, nat. interior design awards 1997), Royal Australian Inst. Archs.; mem. Nat. Trust for Hist. Preservation, So. Calif. Assn. Non-Profit Housing, L.A. Conservancy. Office: Koning Eizenberg Architecture 1548 18th St Santa Monica CA 90404-3404

KONOVNITZINE, ELENA, secondary school educator; b. Belgrade, Yugoslavia, Aug. 27, 1932; came to U.S. 1949; d. Andrey Podshivalov and Elena (Genet) Bohonos; m. Alex P. Konvnitzine, Sept. 19, 1954; children: Tatiana, Peter, Constantin. AA, L.A. City Coll., 1966. BA, Calif. State U. L.A., 1970, MEd, 1976. Substitute tchr. Pasadena (Calif.) Unified Sch. Dist., 1974-82, South Pasadena (Calif.) Unified Sch. Dist., 1982-83; tchr. 7th and 8th grades Holy Trinity Sch., L.A., 1983-85; substitute tchr. L.A. Unified Sch. Dist., 1985—. Church choir conductor Church-Slavic, 1976-96, conductor early morn. services in English Holy Transfiguration Russian Orthodox Church, Hollywood, CA, 1976-98. Mem. United Tchrs. L.A., Alpha Mu Gamma (2nd v.p. 1963-66). Avocations: singing, church choir. Home: 2021 Driftstane Dr Glendora CA 91740-5309

KONRAD G. GREGORY, protective services official; b. Denver, Sept. 13, 1951; s. George and Beverly K. Student, Met. State Coll., Inst. Pub. Theology. Carrier, clk. U.S. Post Office, Denver, 1972-81; owner, pres. Ivory Publ., Inc., Denver, 1981—; code enforcement staff City and County of Denver, 1995—, cons. in field. Author: Keys to Freedom & Harmony Through Your Numerological Respect, 1983, A Fish Rots From The Head, 1995. Vol. Dominican Sister Havel Health Agy., Denver, 1970—. Avoca-

tions: travel, writing, nature. Office: Ivory Publ Inc PO Box 40595 Denver CO 80204-0595

KONTNY, VINCENT L., rancher, engineering executive; b. Chappell, Nebr., July 19, 1937; s. Edward James and Ruth Regina (Schumann) K.; m. Joan Dashwood FitzGibbon, Feb. 20, 1970; children: Natascha Marie, Michael Christian, Amber Brooke. BSCE, U. Colo., 1958, DSc honoris causa, 1991. Operator heavy equipment, grade foreman Peter Kiewit Son's Co., Denver, 1958-59; project mgr. Utah Constrn. and Mining Co., Western Australia, 1965-69, Fluor Australia, Queensland, Australia, 1969-72; sr. project mgr. Fluor Utah, San Mateo, Calif., 1972-73; sr. v.p. Holmes & Narver, Inc., Orange, Calif., 1973-79; mng. dir. Fluor Australia, Melbourne, 1979-82; group v.p. Fluor Engrs., Inc., Irvine, Calif., 1982-85, pres., chief exec. officer, 1985-87; group pres. Fluor Daniel, Irvine, Calif., 1987-88, pres., 1988-94; pres. Fluor Corp., Irvine, 1990-94, vice chmn., 1994; ret., 1994; purchased Last Dollar Ranch, Ridgway Co. 1989, Centennial Ranch, Colona Co., 1992, owner Double Shoe Cattle Co. Contbr. articles to profl. jours. Mem. engring. devel. coun., U. Colo.; mem. engring. adv. coun., Stanford U. Lt. USN, 1959-65. Republican. Roman Catholic. Club: Cet. (Costa Mesa, Calif.). Avocation: snow skiing.

KOON, RAY HAROLD, management and security consultant; b. Little Mountain, S.C., Nov. 19, 1934; s. Harold Clay and Jessie Rae (Epting) K.; m. Bertha Mae Gardner, Aug. 19, 1958; children: Shari Madilyn Koon Goode, Schyler Michele Koon Richards, Kamela Suzanne Koon Scott. BSBA, Old Dominion U., 1957; postgrad., Columbia (S.C.) Coll., 1957-58. Lic. pvt. pilot. Supr. office svcs. FBI, Norfolk, Va., 1953-61, Las Vegas, Nev., 1961-62; agt. State Gaming Control Bd., Carson City, Nev., 1962-64, coord., 1967-80, chief of investigations, 1980-83; prodn. control mgr. Colite Industries, Inc., West Columbia, S.C., 1964-67; pres. Assoc. Gaming Consultants, Las Vegas, 1983; dir. gaming surveillance Hilton Hotels Corp., Beverly Hills, Calif., 1983-86; pres. JRJ Enterprises, Las Vegas, 1986-88, Assoc. Cons. Enterprises, Las Vegas, 1983—; pres. Assoc. Gaming Cons., Las Vegas, 1983—, CEO, 1990—; past sec. Sta. KNIS-FM. Editor, pub. Ray Koon's Gaming/Gram, 1986—; columnist Casino Gaming Internat., 1990-92. Chief vols. Warren Engine Co. 1, Carson City Fire Dept., 1962-83; mem. Carson City Sheriff's Aero Squadron, 1983—, past comdr.; past mem. exec. bd. Nev. Bapt. Conv. With U.S. Army, 1957-59. Mem. Nev. Arbitration Assn. (bd. dirs. 1986-90), Las Vegas C. of C. (mem. commerce crime prevention and legis. action coms. 1989-90), Zelzah Shrine Aviation Club (past comdr.), Nat. Intelligence and Counterintelligence Assn. (bd. dirs. 1995—), Assn. Former Intelligence Officers, Toastmasters, Masons. Republican. Avocations: flying, do-it-yourself projects. Office: Assoc Cons Enterprises 3271 S Highland Dr Ste 705A Las Vegas NV 89109-1051

KOONCE, GENIO CARDWELL, retired field engineer; b. North Wilkesboro, N.C., Sept. 22, 1928; s. Charles Franklin Koonce and Virginia Lucille (Cardwell) Hemphill; m. Gladys Ellen Dimitripolis, Mar. 3, 1953 (dec. Dec. 1994); children: Charles, Richard, Robert, Kathleen, Rebecca; m. Laris Berggren, Feb. 16, 1997. Assoc. Tech. Arts, Edmonds (Wash.) C.C., 1974. Chief electronic technician U.S. Coast and Geodetic Survey, Seattle, 1961-65; nat. sales mgr. Wesmar (Mfg.), Seattle, 1969-72; field engr. Black Clawson (Mfg.), Everett, Wash., 1974-76, Western Gear Corp., Everett, 1976-81; field svc. supr. Bombardia, Portland, Oreg., 1983-85; ret., 1985. Sonar technician 1st class USN, 1945-60. Mem. K.C. (4th degree). Democrat. Roman Catholic. Avocations: writing, photography. Home: 2605 15th St Apt 513 Everett WA 98201-1759

KOONIN, STEVEN ELLIOT, physicist, educator, academic administrator; b. Bklyn., Dec. 12, 1951. BS, Calif. Inst. Tech., 1972; PhD, MIT, 1975. Asst. prof. Calif. Inst. Tech., Pasadena, Calif., 1975-78; assoc. prof. Calif. Inst. Tech., Pasadena, 1978-81, prof., 1981—; v.p., provost Calif. Inst. Tech., 1995—; cons. Inst. for Def. Analysis, MITRE Corp., Lawrence Livermore Nat. Lab., Oak Ridge Nat. Lab. Author: Computational Physics, 1985, Computational Nuclear Physics, vol. 1, 1991, vol. 2, 1993. Recipient Green Prize for Creative Scholarship, Calif. Inst. Tech., 1972, Assoc. Students Teaching award Calif. Inst. Tech., 1975-76, Sr. U.S. Scientist award Humboldt Found., 1985-86, Fusion Power Assocs. Leadership award, 1994, E.O. Lawrence award U.S. Dept. Energy, 1998; Alfred P. Sloan fellow, 1977-81. Fellow AAAS, Am. Acad. Arts and Scis., Am. Phys. Soc. (chmn. APS divsn. nuclear physics 1988-89, exec. bd. dirs. 1994—). Office: Calif Inst of Tech Office of Provost 206-31 Pasadena CA 91125

KOPEČEK, JINDŘICH, biomedical scientist, biomaterials and pharmaceutics educator; b. Strakonice, Bohemia, Czechoslovakia, Jan. 27, 1940; came to U.S., 1986; s. Jan and Herta Zita (Krombholz) K.; m. Marie Porcari, Aug. 11, 1962 (Div. 1984); 1 child, Jana; m. Pavla Hrušková, Apr. 27, 1985. MS in Polymer Chemistry, Inst. Chem. Tech., Prague, Czechoslovakia, 1961; PhD in Polymer Chemistry, Inst. Macromolecular Chemistry, Prague, 1965; DSc in Chemistry, Czechoslovak Acad. Scis., Prague, 1990. Rsch. sci. officer Inst. Macromolecular Chemistry, Prague, 1965-67, 68-72, head lab. of med. polymers, 1972-80; postdoctoral fellow NRC, Ottawa, Can., 1967-68; head lab. of biodegradable polymers Inst. Macromolecular Chemistry Czechoslovak Acad. of Scis., Prague, 1980-88; co-dir. Ctr. Controlled Chem. Delivery U. Utah, Salt Lake City, 1986—, prof. bioengring., pharmaceutics and phamaceutical chemistry, 1989—; chair dept. pharmaceutics and pharmaceutical chemistry U. Utah, 1999—; vis. prof. Université Paris-Nord, Paris-Villetaneuse, 1983, U. Utah, 1986-88; adj. prof. material sci. U. Utah, 1987—; invited lectr. internat. meetings, univs.; disting. lectr. Nagai Found., Tokyo, 1997. Mem. editl. bd. 12 sci. jours., U.S., U.K., The Netherlands, Poland, 1973—; contbr. over 250 articles to sci. publs. Recipient best sci. papers award Praesidiums of the Czechoslovak and USSR Acads. of Sci., 1977, awards Chem. Sec. of Czechoslovak Acad. Scis., 1972, 75, 77, 78, 85; rsch. grantee NIH, U. Utah, industry, 1986—, Czechoslovak Acad. of Sci., 1970-88; disting. lectureship Nagai Found., Tokyo, 1997. Fellow Am. Assn. Pharm. Sci., Am. Inst. Med. and Biol. Engring.; mem. AAAS, Am. Chem. Soc., Am. Assn. Cancer Rsch., Soc. Biomaterials (Clemson award for basic rsch. 1995), Soc. for Molecular Recognition, Controlled Release Soc. (bd. govs. 1988-91, v.p. 1993-94, pres.-elect 1994-95, pres. 1995-96), Czech Learned Soc. (hon.). Achievements include 37 patents in biomedical field; formulation and development of comprehensive approach to the problems of designing macromolecular carriers to modulate the pharmacokinetics and tissue localization of therapeutic agents; research in the synthesis and physical characterization of hydrogels, in biocompatibility of biomedical polymers. Office: U Utah Dept Pharm and Pharm Chemistry 305 2000 E Rm 301 Salt Lake City UT 84112

KOPLIN, DONALD LEROY, health products executive, consumer advocate; b. Greenleaf, Kans., Dec. 31, 1932; s. Henry G. Koplin and Edith Mary Stevens; m. Patricia Joynes, June 2, 1962 (div. Aug. 1974); children: Marie Claire, Marie Joelle (adopted); m. Joan Freudenthal, June 28, 1997. Student, U. San Diego, 1956-59, 67-68. Electronics test insp. Gen. Dynamics, San Diego, 1956-59; cryptographer Dept. of State, Washington, 1959-67; communications program officer Dept. of State, France, Angola, Madagascar, Qatar, India, Oman, Benin and the Bahamas, 1977-86; tech. writer Ryan Aero. Corp., San Diego, 1967-68; comml. dir., tech. advisor, pub. rels. officer Societe AGM, San Francisco, Athens, Greece, Antananarivo and Morondava, Dem. Republic of Madagascar, 1968-72; founder, dir. Soc. Bells, Cyclone & Akai, Antananarivo, 1972-74; founder, ptnr., assoc. editor Angola Report, Luanda, 1974-75; polit. reporter Angola Report, Reuters, AP, UPI Corr., BBC, Luanda; supr. Tex. Instruments, Lubbock, 1976-77; exec. Dial A Contact Lens, Inc., La Jolla, Calif., 1986-90, Assn. for Retarded Citizens, San Diego, 1991-92, Club Med, Copper Mountain, Colo., 1992-94; CEO Vient Inc., 1994-97, Koplin Kollection Fine Arts Gallery, La Jolla, Calif., 1996-98. Active San Diego Zool. Soc. With USN, 1951-55, Korea. Mem. Am. Fgn. Svc. Assn. Republican. Roman Catholic. Avocation: writing. Home: 6718 Evergreen Ave Oakland CA 94611-1518

KOPP, DAVID EUGENE, manufacturing company executive; b. St. Louis, Apr. 21, 1951; s. Doyle Eugene and Irene Audrey (Gloyeske) K. BA in English, U. South Fla., 1975. Supr. Titleist Golf Co., Escondido, Calif., 1979-80; supr. Imed Corp., San Diego, 1980-82, process engr., 1982-83, sr. process engr., 1983-85; area mgr. Husky Injection Molding Systems Inc., Newport Beach, Calif., 1985-91; dir. sales Tech C.B.I. Inc., Scottsdale, Ariz., 1991-93; exec. v.p. Top-Seal Corp., Phoenix, 1993-97, v.p., gen. mgr., 1997—. Mem. Soc. Plastic Engrs. (affiliate, bd. dirs., student liaison person Canoga Park, 1985-87). Republican. Roman Catholic. Avocations: golf, music, sports, running, tennis. Home: 9980 N 106th St Scottsdale AZ 85258-9203 Office: Top-Seal Corp 2236 E University Dr Phoenix AZ 85034-6805

KOPPENBRINK, JOAN WAISANEN, semiconductor supplier executive; b. St. Paul, Dec. 12, 1950; d. Waino Victor and Carol Anne (Kruse) Waisanen; m. Walter E. Koppenbrink III, May 27, 1972; children: Kristin R., Kimberly D. BA in Chemistry, U. Mo., 1971; MA in Biochemistry, Washington U., St. Louis, 1975; MBA, Ariz. State U., Tempe, 1985. Chemist Sigma Chem., St. Louis, 1973-74; rsch. chemist Monsanto, St. Louis, 1974-76; rsch. chemist Armour-Dial, Phoenix, 1976-81, product mgr., 1981-84; sales and mktg. exec. Rodel, Phoenix, 1984—, v.p. corp. mktg. Contbr. articles to profl. jours.; presenter in field. Bd. dirs., chmn. Greater Phoenix Youth at Risk Found., 1989-96; vol. fundraiser John C. Lincoln Hosp., Phoenix, 1995—. Office: Rodel 3804 E Watkins Phoenix AZ 85034

KOPSCO, CAROL JEAN, social worker, mental health psychotherapist, counselor; b. Amherst, Ohio, Sept. 2, 1947; d. John and Elizabeth G. (Horvath) K. BA, Baldwin-Wallace Coll., 1970; MA, U. Miami, 1973; MSW, Ariz. State U., 1990. Cert. substance abuse counselor. Social worker Fla. State Health and Rehabilitative Svc., Miami, 1974-76, pub. assistance eligibility specialist II, 1976-82; eligibility specialist II Ariz. Dept. Econ. Security, Tucson, 1985-86; crisis counselor supr. Info. and Referral Svc. of Tucson, 1987-90; child and family therapist Ariz. Children's Home Assn., Tucson, 1990—; mental health psychotherapist Ariz. State Dept. Health Svcs., Tucson, 1990-91; med. social worker Samaritan Nursing Svcs., Tucson, 1991—; team leader student group producing quick reference for cmty. crisis orgn. Ariz. State U. Sch. Social Work, Tucson, 1989; med. social worker Olsten-Kimberly Vis. Nurse Svc., 1992-94; Indian health svc. med. social worker and discharge planner area hosps., 1994-95. Vol. Casa San Juan Bosco Shelter, Nogales, Sonora, Mexico, 1985-87, Help-On-Call Crisis Hotline, Tucson, 1987-90. Mem. NASW (student rep. 1989), Phi Kappa Phi. Democrat. Avocation: photography. Home: 5231 N 1st Ave Tucson AZ 85718-4701

KORAN, DENNIS HOWARD, publisher; b. L.A., May 21, 1947; s. Aaron Baer and Shirley Mildred (Kassan) K.; m. Roslynn Ruth Cohen, Apr. 6, 1979; 1 child, Michael; stepchildren: Jeff, Beth, Judy. Student, U. Leeds, Eng., 1966-67, UCLA, 1979-80; BA, U. Calif., Berkeley, 1980; postgrad., Loyola U., L.A., 1982-84, 86-89. Co-founder, co-editor Cloud Marauder Press, Berkeley, 1969-72, Panjandrum/Aris Books, San Francisco, 1973-81; founder, editor Panjandrum Books, San Francisco, 1971—, Panjandrum Press, Inc., San Francisco, 1971—; substitute tchr. L.A. Unified Sch. Dist., 1997—; co-dir. poetry reading series Panjandrum Books, 1972-76. Author: (book of poetry) Vacancies, 1975, After All, 1993; (with Mike Koran) Refrigerator Poems: Variations on 24, 48 & 120 Words, 1997; editor Panjandrum Poetry Jour., 1971—; co-editor Cloud Marauder, 1969-72; author poetry pub. various jours. Liaison between U.S. Govt. and Seminole Indians VISTA, Sasakwa, Okla., 1969-70. Nat. Endowment for Arts Lit. Pub. grantee, 1974, 76, 79, 81, 82, 84, Coord. Coun. for Lit. Mags., 1971-80, grantee Lit. Pub. Calif. Arts Coun., 1985-86, L.A. Cultural Arts Found., 1986. Mem. Lovers of the Stinking Rose, Poets and Writers. Avocations: rare book collecting, travel, athletics, stamp and coin collecting. Office: Panjandrum Books 6156 Wilkinson Ave North Hollywood CA 91606-4518

KORB, LAWRENCE JOHN, metallurgist; b. Warren, Pa., Apr. 28, 1930; s. Stanley Curtis and Dagna (Pedersen) K.; B.Chem.Engring., Rensselaer Poly. Inst., Troy, N.Y., 1952; m. Janet Davis, Mar. 30, 1957; children: James, William, Jeanine. Sales engr. Alcoa, Buffalo, 1955-59; metall. engr. N. Am. Rockwell Co., Downey, Calif., 1959-62; engring. supr. metallurgy Apollo program Rockwell Internat. Co., Downey, 1962-66, engring. supr. advanced materials, 1966-72, engring. supr. metals and ceramics space shuttle program, 1972-88; cons., 1988—; mem. tech. adv. com. metallurgy Cerritos Coll., 1969-74. Served with USNR, 1952-55. Registered profl. engr., Calif. Fellow Am. Soc. Metals (chmn. aerospace activity com. 1971-76, judge materials application competition 1969, handbook com. 1978-83, chmn. handbook com. 1983, chmn. publs. coun. 1984). Republican. Author articles, chpts. in books. Home: 251 S Violet Ln Orange CA 92869-3740

KORB, ROBERT WILLIAM, former materials and processes engineer; b. Warren, Pa., Mar. 12, 1929; s. Dallas Weigand and Evelyn Eleanor (Peterson) K.; m. Diane Marie Anderson, Oct. 14, 1964 (div. 1972); 1 child, Karen; m. Setsu Campbell, Aug. 9, 1980; children: Theresa Campbell, Mark Campbell, Laura Campbell. BS in Chemistry, U. Nev., 1951. Chemist Rezolin, Inc., Santa Monica, Calif., 1956-57; mem. tech. staff Hughes Aircraft Co., Culver City, Calif., 1957-64; mem. tech. staff Hughes Aircraft Co., Fullerton, Calif., 1971-74, group head materials engring., 1974-79, sect. head materials and processes engring., 1979-93; mem. tech. staff TRW Systems, Redondo Beach, Calif., 1964-71; ret., 1993. Contbr. articles to profl. jours.; patentee flexible cable process. 1st lt. USAF, 1951-56. Mem. Inst. for Interconnecting and Packaging Electronic Circuits (co. rep.), Soc. for Advancement Materials and Process Engring. Republican. Avocations: golf, skiing, tennis, photography. Home: 31222 Calle Bolero San Juan Capistrano CA 92675-5392

KOREC, JACEK, corporation executive; b. Warsaw, Poland, Aug. 27, 1951; s. Anatol and Natalia (Galazka) K.; m. Alicja Lawnicka, Nov. 27, 1971; 1 child, Bartosz. MS, Tech. U., Warsaw, 1974, DSc, 1978. Sci. asst. Inst. Tech. Elec. Materials, Warsaw, 1974-81; Alexander von Humboldt fellow Rheinisch Westfalische Tech. Hochschule, Aachen, Germany, 1981-83; asst. Rheinish Westfalische Tech. Hochschule, Aachen, Germany, 1983-86; rschr. Allgemeine Elec. Ges. Rsch. Inst., Frankfurt, Germany, 1986-88; sr. mgr. Daimler-Benz AG Rsch. Inst., Frankfurt, 1988-96; project leader Siliconix, Santa Clara, Calif., 1991-96; mem. adv. bd. Power Semiconductor Rsch. Ctr., N.C. State U., Raleigh, 1991-96; mem. program com. Internat. Conf., Internat. Symposium Power Semiconductor Devices, 1993, 96, 97, publicity chmn., 1997. Contbr. articles to profl. jours.; patentee in field. Avocations: guitar, fishing, sailing.

KORGE, PAAVO, cell physiologist; b. Tartu, Estonia, Sept. 6, 1943; came to U.S., 1989; s. Kuno and Elsa (Ruus) K.; m. Sirje Kipper, Dec. 26, 1964; children: Indrek, Kristjan. PhD in Physiology, Tartu U., 1969, DSc in Physiology, 1974. From jr. scientist to assoc. prof. Tartu U., 1967-76, prof., 1978-89; asst. prof. Washington State U., Pullman, 1989-92, prof., 1992—; vis. scientist Copenhagen U., 1976-78; sci. bd. dirs. Tartu U., 1976-89; chmn. all union conf. on hormonal regulation phys. activity, 1973, 77, 82, 87. Author: Molecular Mechanism of Glucocorticoid Action, 1981, Hormons and Physical Fitness, 1983, Glucocorticoids in the Regulation of Heart Function and Metabolism, 1984; contbr. articles to profl. jours. Grantee USSR Sports Com., 1978-82, Inst. Aviation, Leningrad, USSR, 1983-88; USSR Ministry Higher Edn. scholar, 1976; recipient Young Scientist award Estonian Govt., 1978. Mem. N.Y. Acad. Scis. Avocations: basketball, tennis. Home: 1718 S Ogden Dr Los Angeles CA 90019-5035 Office: UCLA Sch Medicine Cardiovascular Rsch Labs MRL Bldg R3-645 675 Cir Dr So Los Angeles CA 90024-1760

KORITAN, BRUCE (VAN) LEE, entertainer, composer; b. Phila., Feb. 28, 1948; s. Gilbert David and Dorothy Beatrice (Silverman) K.; m. Ruth Flora Dubinbaum, Dec. 18, 1991. Student, Phila. Inst. Music., 1963-64, 66, U. Madrid, 1968-69, Temple U., 1969, Scottsdale Community Coll., 1981-82. Singer, pianist, solo act MGM Grand Hotel, Las Vegas, Nev., 1973; bass-baritone soloist Bach and Madrigal Soc., Phoenix, 1975-76; mus. dir., pianist Ernie Menehune Polynesian Revue, Los Angeles, Hawaii, Lake Tahoe, 1976-77; singer-pianist Princess Cruises, Caribbean and Alaska, 1978; pianist Frankie Carle Orch., Phoenix, 1983, Victor Lombardo Orch., Phoenix, 1984-85; pianist, singer Koritan Trio Ariz. Biltmore Hotel, Phoenix, 1984-86, Scottsdale Princess Hotel, Ariz., 1987-88, Registry Resort, Scottsdale, 1988-90, Phoenician Resort, Scottsdale, 1991—; cantorial soloist Temple Beth Shalom, Sun City, Ariz., 1992—; bd. dirs. Ariz. Composers Forum, Phoenix, 1985-90, pres., 1988-90; composer-in-residence, Temple U. Music Festival, Ambler, Pa., 1969; bd. dirs. Hispanic Dance Inst., Phoenix, v.p., 1991-93; chmn. aux. com. Phoenix Chamber Orch., 1988. Composer, pianist Twentieth Century Pictures at an Exhibition, 1988; composer, singer, pianist Zane, 1986; composer, lyricist: Har Zion in the Desert, 1966, I Pledge My Allegiance to our Glorious Flag, 1964; lyricist: Waking From a Dream, 1989; composer: Treadmill in Oblivion, 1989, Erev Shabbat Service, 1998. Composer, fundraising Esperança 100 Guild, Phoenix, 1981; performer, fundraising Am. Fedn. for the Blind, Littleton, Colo., 1973; composer for video Mental Health Assn. of Maricopa County, Phoenix, 1987; co-producer, pianist-singer Interfaith Concert for Russian-Jewish Resettlement, Phoenix, 1990, 91; artist solo exhbn. fundraising Grace Found., Cave Creek, Ariz., 1990; composer Flagstaff Festival of Arts, Oak Creek, 1991. With USMCR. Fellow, diplomate Internat. Naturopathic Assn., Las Vegas, Nev., 1976; recipient Spl. Merit award Red Cross Internat. Art Exhibition, 1962, Spl. Recognition and Achievement award Lions Internat., North Las Vegas, Nev., 1975. Mem. ASCAP, Am. Fedn. Musicians, Guild Temple Musicians. E-mail: BaruchLK@aol.com.

KORMONDY, EDWARD JOHN, university official, biology educator; b. Beacon, N.Y., June 10, 1926; s. Anthony and Frances (Glover) K.; m. Peggy Virginia Hedrick, June 5, 1950 (div. 1989); children: Lynn Ellen, Eric Paul, Mark Hedrick. BA in Biology summa cum laude, Tusculum Coll., 1950, DSc (hon.), 1997; MS in Zoology, U. Mich., 1951, PhD in Zoology, 1955. Teaching fellow U. Mich., 1952-55; instr. zoology, curator insects Mus. Zoology, 1955-57; asst. prof. Oberlin (Ohio) Coll., 1957-63, assoc. prof., 1963-67, prof., 1967-69, acting assoc. dean, 1966-67; dir. Commn. Undergrad. Edn. in Biol. Scis., Washington, 1968-72; dir. Office Biol. Edn., Am. Inst. Biol. Scis., Washington, 1968-71; mem. faculty Evergreen State Coll., Olympia, Wash., 1971-79, interim acting dean, 1972-73, v.p., provost, 1973-78; sr. profl. assoc., directorate sci. edn. NSF, 1979; provost, prof. biology U. So. Maine, Portland, 1979-82; v.p. acad. affairs, prof. biology Calif. State U., Los Angeles, 1982-86; sr. v.p., chancellor, prof. biology U. Hawaii, Hilo/West Oahu, 1986-93; pres. U. West L.A., 1995-97. Author: Concepts of Ecology, 1969, 76, 83, 96, General Biology: The Integrity and Natural History of Organisms, 1977, Handbook of Contemporary World Developments in Ecology, 1981, International Handbook of Pollution Control, 1989, (textbook) Biology, 1984, 88, Fundamentals of Human Ecology, 1998; contbr. articles to profl. jours. Served with USN, 1944-46. U. Ga. postdoctoral fellow radiation ecology, 1963-64; vis. research fellow Center for Bioethics, Georgetown U., 1978-79; research grantee Nat. Acad. Scis., Am. Philos. Soc., NSF, Sigma Xi. Fellow AAAS; mem. Ecol. Soc. Am. (sec. 1976-78), Nat. Assn. Biology Tchrs. (pres. 1981), N.Am. Assn. Environ. Edn., Soc. Calif. Acad. Scis. (bd. dirs. 1985-86, 93-97, v.p. 1995-96), Sigma Xi, Phi Kappa Phi.

KORNBERG, ARTHUR, biochemist; b. N.Y.C., N.Y., Mar. 3, 1918; s. Joseph and Lena (Katz) K.; m. Sylvy R. Levy, Nov. 21, 1943 (dec. 1986); children: Roger, Thomas Bill, Kenneth Andrew; m. Charlene Walsh Levering, 1988 (dec. 1995). BS, CCNY, 1937, LLD (hon.), 1960; MD, U. Rochester, 1941, DSc (hon.), 1962; DSc (hon.), U. Pa., U. Notre Dame, 1965, Washington U., 1968, Princeton U., 1970, Colby Coll., 1970; LHD (hon.), Yeshiva U., 1963; MD honoris causa, U. Barcelona, Spain, 1970. Intern in medicine Strong Meml. Hosp., Rochester, N.Y., 1941-42; commd. officer USPHS, 1942, advanced through grades to med. dir., 1951; mem. staff NIH, Bethesda, Md., 1942-52, nutrition sect., div. physiology, 1942-45; chief sect. enzymes and metabolism Nat. Inst. Arthritis and Metabolic Diseases, 1947-52; guest research worker depts. chemistry and pharmacology coll. medicine NYU, 1946; dept. biol. chemistry med. sch. Washington U., 1947; dept. plant biochemistry U. Calif., 1951; prof., head dept. microbiology, med. sch. Washington U., St. Louis, 1953-59; prof. biochemistry Stanford U. Sch. Medicine, 1959—, chmn. dept., 1959-69, prof. emeritus dept. biochemistry, 1988—; Mem. sci. adv. bd. Mass. Gen. Hosp., 1964-67; bd. govs. Weizmann Inst., Israel. Author: For the Love of Enzymes, 1989; contbr. sci. articles to profl. jours. Served lt. (j.g.), med. officer USCGR, 1942. Recipient Paul-Lewis award in enzyme chemistry, 1951; co-recipient of Nobel prize in medicine, 1959; recipient Max Berg award prolonging human life, 1968, Sci. Achievement award AMA, 1968, Lucy Wortham James award James Ewing Soc., 1968, Borden award Am. Assn. Med. Colls., 1968, Nat. medal of sci., 1979. Gairdner Foundation International Awards, 1995. Mem. Am. Soc. Biol. Chemists (pres. 1965), Am. Chem. Soc., Harvey Soc., Am. Acad. Arts and Scis., Royal Soc., Nat. Acad. Scis. (mem. council 1963-66), Am. Philos. Soc., Phi Beta Kappa, Sigma Xi, Alpha Omega Alpha. Office: Stanford U Sch of Med Dept Biochemistry Beckman Ctr Rm B400 Stanford CA 94305-5307*

KORN-DAVIS, DOTTIE, artist, educator, consultant; b. L.A.; d. William and Anne Miller. BA, UCLA, 1961; MA, San Diego State U., 1981. Artist-in-residence Laocheng Tchrs. U., Shandong, China, 1996; active Art in the Cmty./Woman's Caucus for Arts, San Diego, 1994-97; open studio artist COVA, 1995. Exhibited in group shows at Multicultural Aarts Inst., San Diego, San diego Artists Guild, Spectrum Gallery, San Diego, Riverside (Calif.) Arts Mus., San diego Art Inst., Orange County Ct. for Contemporary Art, Santa Ana, Calif., L.A. Mcpl. Art Gallery, U. Wis. Ctr., Waukesha, Art Union Gallery, San Diego, Gallery Ten, Rockford, Ill., Next Door Gallery, San Diego, USCD Cross Cultural Ctr. Gallery, San Diego, numerous others. Bd. dirs. Artists Guild/Mus. Art, 1991-92. Recipient 1st Prize award San Diego Artists Guild, 1983. Avocations: travel, hiking, theatre, dance.

KORNS, LEOTA ELSIE, writer, mountain land developer, insurance broker; b. Canton, Okla., Jan. 19, 1916; d. James Abraham and Ida Agnes (Engel) Klopfenstine; m. Richard Francis Korns, July 1, 1943 (wid. Dec. 17, 1988); 1 child, Michael Francis. BS, Pitts. State U. of Kans., 1966. Sec. various firms, Kans. City, Mo., 1937-45; cons. Electrolux Corp., St. Paul, 1946-49; sec. health, safety and waste IAEA, Vienna, Austria, 1959-60; tchr. Montezuma-Cortez H.S., Cortez, Colo., 1966-67; ins. agent Korns Ins. Agy., Durango, Colo., 1968—; owner, pres. Korns Investments, Inc., Durango, Colo., 1970—; bd. dirs. LaPlata County Landowners Assn., Durango, 1981-87; authored and instr. women's history course, U. N.Mex., Albuquerque, Ft. Lewis Coll., Durango, and Mesa (Ariz.) C.C., 1970-75; also spkr. in field. Author: (novel) Yesterday Should Have Been Over, 1965; (play) Angry Young Men, 1957; writer numerous short stories including The Combine, 1960. Convenor, mem. NOW, Durango, 1970—; precinct capt. Curango Rep. Com., 1981—. Mem. Ink Slingers Writing Group, Unity Sch. Christianity, Trimble Hot Springs. Avocations: mountain walking, swimming, piano, cross-country skiing. Home: 556 2d Ave Durango CO 81301-5604

KOROGODSKY, DANILA ZINOVY, theater set and costume designer, educator; b. Kaliningrad, Russia, Oct. 22, 1955; came to U.S., 1989; s. Zinovy Yakovlevich and Liah Danilovna (Kirstein) K.; m. Irina German, June 15, 1995. MFA in Theatre Design and Tech., Inst. Theater, Music and Film, Leningrad, Russia, 1977. Resident designer Leningrad Theater for Youth, 1977-87; guest prof. Ind. U., Bloomington, 1991-92; prof. design DePaul U., Chgo., 1992-94, Calif. State U., Long Beach, 1996—. Office: Calif State Univ 1250 Bellflower Ave Long Beach CA 90840

KOROLEV, NICHOLAS ALEXANDER, writer, artist; b. Elizabeth, N.J., Nov. 27, 1959; s. Dewitt Grant Cottrell and Dorothy Grace Streitz. BA in Fine Art, Thomas Edison State Coll., 1991. Freelance artist, writer, 1981—; owner, mgr. Call of the Wild Gallery & Frame Shop, Burlington, N.J., 1985-91; stage mgr. Actore Reperatory Theatre of Sedona, Ariz., 1998; tchr. Sedona Arts Ctr., 1993-95. Illustrator: (book) What I Saw by Kato the Dog, 1995; contbr. articles to mags. Recipient Best in Show award Burlington Hist. Soc. Art Show, 1988; named one of Top 100, Arts for the Parks, 1991, Top 50, Nat. Forest Art Competition, 1991. E-mail: skywolf@sedona.net.

KORSUNSKY, MORDKO ISAAKOVITCH, mechanical engineer; b. Uman, Ukraine, USSR, Feb. 19, 1935; came to U.S., 1980; s. Itsko and Dvora (Sternherts) K.; m. Tana Zilberman, Mar. 5, 1971; 1 child, Elina. BS, Lvov Electromech. Coll., Ukraine, 1954; MS, Poly. Inst., Lvov, 1959. Mech. engr., mgr. Cathod-Ray Tubes Co., Lvov, 1959-79; sr. mech. engr. Farallon Oceanic, San Leandro, Calif., 1980-81, Eaton Corp., San Jose, Calif., 1981-88, Dade Behring Inc., San Jose, 1988—; projects leader engring. diploma, Poly. Inst., Lvov, 1961-80, referee engring. diploma projects, 1961-80, referee PhD dissertations, 1968-79. Author: Processes Automation in Machine and Instrument Construction, 1968. Recipient Nat. prize USSR Govt. and USSR Acad. Sci., 1968, First prize Semiconductor Internat., 1985. Achievements include invention of Glass Parts Loader, Manipulator of Glass Parts. Home: 1774 Twenty First Ave San Francisco CA 94122 Office: Dade Behring Inc 3403 Yerba Buena Rd San Jose CA 95135-1500

KORTVELESY, J. SCOTT, ophthalmologist, educator; b. N.Y.C., Oct. 7, 1956. AB in Chemistry and Biology cum laude, Dartmouth Coll., 1978; MD, SUNY, Syracuse, 1982. Diplomate Am. Bd. Ophthalmology, Nat. Bd. Med. Examiners; lic. physician, Va., Md., D.C., Pa., Hawaii. Intern in internal medicine George Washington U. Hosp., Washington, 1982-83; resident in ophthalmology Eye and Ear Hosp.-Eye and Ear Inst., Pitts., 1984-87, fellow in ocuplastic surgery, summer 1988; mem. staff, fellow in neuro-opthalmology and orbital surgery Allegheny Gen. Hosp., Pitts., 1987-88; staff ophthalmologist neuro-ophthalmology, orbital surgery Straub Clinic and Hosp., Honolulu, 1988—; mem. cons. staff dept. surgery Kapiolani Med. Ctr. for Women and Children, Honolulu, 1990—; assoc. clin. prof. dept. surgery Sch. Medicine U. Hawaii, Honolulu, 1991—; vis. asst. prof. neuro-ophthalmology and orbital surgery dept. ophthalmology Eye and Ear Inst., 1988; coord. for Hawaii, Ophthalmology Grand Rounds, 1993—; cons. Tripler Army Med. Ctr., Honolulu, 1996—; presenter profl. confs.; participant med.-surg. eye mission work, locations including Saipan, Northern Mariana Islands, 1990, 1993, Samoa and Manua Islands, 1991. Contbr. articles to med. jours. Mem. profl. adv. com. Hawaii chpt. Nat. Multiple Sclerosis Soc., 1995—. Named One of Hawaii's Top Drs., Honolulu Mag., 1996-98. Mem. AMA, Am. Acad. Ophthalmology, Hawaii Med. Assn., Hawaii Ophthalmol. Soc. (sec. 1994-96). Office: Straub Clinic and Hosp Inc Dept Ophthalmology 888 S King St Honolulu HI 96813-3083

KORTZ, DIRK ANDREW, artist; b. Newark, July 3, 1944; s. Frank Joseph and Barbara Jane (Mason) K.; 1 child, Ezra Jack. BA in Creative Writing, San Francisco State U., 1975, postgrad. in Film. Works exhibited at Elaine Horwitch Gallery, Santa Fe, 1985, William Campbell Gallery, Ft. Worth, 1989, Leslie Muth Gallery, Santa Fe, 1992, Rod Goebel Gallery, Taos, N.Mex., 1993, Munson Gallery, Santa Fe, 1993, Edith Lambert Gallery, Santa Fe, 1993, 94, 95, 96, Mus. Fine Arts, Santa Fe, 1993, Gallery at the Rep, Santa Fe, 1993, Owings Dewey Gallery, Santa Fe, 1993, 94, 95, 96, Copeland-Rutherford Gallery, Santa Fe, 1994, 95, Ctr. for Contemporary Arts, Santa Fe, 1995, Hahn Ross Gallery, Santa Fe, 1997, 98, 99; represented in permanent collections U. Ariz. Mus., Tempe, Rising Tide Prodns., Nashville, films exhibited, Atlanta Internatl. Film Fest., (Spec. Jury Awd. Gold Medal), 1970, Monterey Independent Film Maker's Fest., 1970, Sinking Creek Film Fest., 1972, Seattle Fire Film Fest., 1976, Ann Arbor Film Fest., 1978, Athens Internatl. Film Fest., included in collections, The Carnegie Inst. Mus. of Art, Mus. of Sci. and Art, Univ. of Oklahoma, other pvt. collections. Home and Office: 2200 W Alameda #22 Santa Fe NM 87501

KOSA, FRANK, filmmaker; b. Jan. 10, 1968; s. Gyorgy Kramer and Kate (Kennedy) K.; m. July Rusk; children: Matthew, Kate. BA, U. Mass., 1989. Prodr., writer Pie Films, L.A., 1992—. Prodr.: The Revolutionary War, 1995 (Cable Ace award 1996), Ancient Mysteries, 1996; assoc. prodr: Music of Bernard Herrmann, 1993. Mem. Writers Guild Am. Avocations: scuba diving, travel writing. Office: Pie Films 2218 21st St Santa Monica CA 90405-1708

KOSCHÉ, RENÉ, artist, entrepreneur; b. Washington, Nov. 1, 1954; d. Earl Julius Sr. and Marie Catherine Kosché; m. Randal Charles Thomas, July 28, 1979; 1 child, Rayna Cascadas Thomas. Student, U. Md., 1972-75. Freelance artist. Illustr.: Where Have All the Flower Children Gone, 1988; performer theatre, 1997-98; stage mgr. Rainbow Theater, 1995, Last Acre of Memory, 1998. Mgr., bd. dirs. 2d Hand Rose Thrift Shop, Seattle, 1997—; bd. dirs. City of Hope, 1997—; active St. John the Evangelist Ch., 1998—; vol. Las Senoritas Drill Team, Seattle, 1997—, Rainbow Family of Living Light, 1975—; sec., treas. Stilly Falls Water Assn., Granite Falls, Wash., 1998—. Anonymous grantee, Seattle, 1996. Mem. Internat. Brotherhood of Painters and Allied Trades. Democrat. Roman Catholic. Office: 4817 Aurora Ave N Ste 301 Seattle WA 98103

KOSHALEK, RICHARD, museum director, consultant; b. Wausau, Wis., Sept. 20, 1941; s. H. Martin and Ethel A. (Hochtritt) K.; m. Elizabeth J. Briar, July 1, 1967; 1 child, Anne Elizabeth. Student, U. Wis., 1960-61, MA, 1965-67; BA, U. Minn., 1965. Curator Walker Art Ctr., Mpls., 1967-72; asst. dir. NEA, Washington, 1972-74; dir. Ft. Worth Art Mus., 1974-76, Hudson River Mus., Westchester, N.Y., 1976-80, Mus. Contemporary Art, L.A., 1980—; mem. Pres.' Coun. on Arts, Yale U., New Haven, Conn., 1989-94; mem. internat. bd. Biennale di Venezia, Italy, 1992-93; mem. internat. adv. bd. Wexner Ctr., Ohio State U., Columbus, 1990—; mem. com. of assesors The Tate Gallery of Art, London; mem. internat. jury Philip Morris Art award, 1996; commr. Kwangju Biennale, 1997; mem. screening com. Osaka Triennale, 1997; selection com. Museo de Art Contemporaneo de Monterrey prize, 1997-98; panel chair Phila. Exhbns. Initiative, 1998, fed. adv. com. for internat. exhbns. Nat. Endowment for the Arts, 1997; cons. in field. Co-curator (exhibitions and books) Panza Collection, 1986, Ad Reinhardt, 1991, Arata Isozaki, 1991, Louis I. Kahn, 1992, Robert Irwin, 1993, At the End of the Century: One Hundred Years of Architecture, 1998, Richard Serra, 1998. Mem. Chase Manhattan Bank Art Com., N.Y.C., 1986—; chmn. architect selection Walt Disney Concert Hall, L.A., 1988-90; mem. adv. Neighborhood Revitalization Bd. for Pres. Clinton, Little Rock, Ark., 1993; bd. dirs. Am. Ctr. in Paris, 1993—. Recipient Parkinson Spirit of Urbanism award U. So. Calif. Archtl. Guild, 1996; NEA fellow, 1972, Durfee Found. fellow, 1992, Design fellow IBM, 1984. Mem. Am. Assn. Mus. Dirs. Office: Mus Contemporary Art Calif Plz 250 S Grand Ave Los Angeles CA 90012-3021

KOSHT, RANDY MICHAEL, publishing executive; b. L.A., May 4, 1953; s. Norman Lowell and Esther Martha (McAfee) K.; m. Janice Roberta Putney, Dec. 18, 1976; children: Mary Rose, Roberta Jane. AA in Art, El Camino Coll., 1973; student, Calif. State U., Long Beach, 1973-75. Gen. mgr. Fragments West, Long Beach, 1975-77, contbg. editor, 1978-83; prodn. mgr. Yachts & Classics mag., Garden Grove, Calif., 1983-85, Walker's Manual, Garden Grove, 1985-88; publs. coord. PLG, Inc., Newport Beach, Calif., 1988-95; records ctr. mgr. PLG, Inc., Newport Beach, 1996—; editor, mng. editor Galaxy Prodns., Long Beach, 1980-81, 81-84; founder A&Mania, Anaheim, Calif., 1982—; rschr., cons. A&M Records, L.A., 1982, 87; composer, performer Musikah Avodah, Orange, Calif., 1993—; founder, COO RKM Mktg., Anaheim, 1997—. Editor, pub.: A&M Records: Teh Discography, 1986, 93. Jewish. Avocations: collecting A&M records, apartment 3-G and Pogo comic strips, TV guide. Office: RKM Mktg 9778 Katella Ave Ste 204 Anaheim CA 92804-6447

KOSKI, CHARLENE WEBER, social worker; b. Phila., Mar. 2, 1943; d. Walter Gotlieb and Dorothy (Peart) W.; m. Billy Mack Carroll, Oct. 3, 1959 (div. Sept. 1974); children: Dorothy Patricia, Robert Walter, Lydia Baker, Billy Bob, Elizabeth Louise; m. John Edward Thomaston, Sept. 26, 1974 (div. July 1986); m. Stan Koski, Dec. 31, 1994. BSW with honors, Coll. Santa Fe, 1983; MSW, N.Mex. Highlands U., 1988. Client service agt. I Social Svcs. div. Dept. Human Svcs., Albuquerque, 1975-78, client service agt. IV, 1978-83; social worker II Social Svcs. div. Dept. Human Svcs., Bernalillo, N.Mex., 1983, social worker III, 1983—. Mem. Nat. Assn. Social Workers, N.Mex. Council on Crime and Deliquency, Albuquerque Retarded Assn., Child Welfare League. Democrat. Home: 72 Umber Ct NE Albuquerque NM 87124-2454 Office: New Mexico Dept Human Svcs Div Social Svcs PO Box 820 Bernalillo NM 87004-0820

KOST, GERALD JOSEPH, physician, scientist; b. Sacramento, July 12, 1945; s. Edward William and Ora Imogene K.; m. Angela Louise Baldo, Sept. 9, 1972; children: Christopher Murray, Laurie Elizabeth. BS in Engring., Stanford U., 1967, MS in Engring.-Econ. Systems, 1968; PhD in Bioengring., U. Calif., San Diego, 1977; MD, U. Calif., San Francisco, 1978. Diplomate Nat. Bd. Med. Examiners, Am. Bd. Pathology. Resident dept. medicine UCLA, 1978-79, resident dept. neurology, 1979-80; resident dept. lab. medicine U. Wash., Seattle, 1980-81, chief resident dept. lab. medicine, 1981-82, cardiopulmonary-bioengring. and clin. chemistry researcher, 1982-83; asst. prof. pathology U. Calif., Davis, 1983-87, assoc. prof., 1987-93, prof., dir. clin. chemistry, faculty biomed. engring., 1993—; vis. prof. and Lilly scholar, 1990, numerous sci. cons., nat. and internat. speaker, invited lectr. Author: Handbook of Clinical Automation Robotics and Optimization, 1996, Point-of-Care Testing, 1999; contbr. numerous articles to profl. and sci. jours.; editor, author various monographs, video, audio and internet prodns. Recipient awards, honors and rsch. grants including Bank Am. Fine Arts award, 1963, Millberry Art award, 1970, Nat. Rsch. Svc. award Nat. Heart, Lung and Blood Inst., 1972-77, Young Investigator award Acad. Clin. Lab. Physicians and Scientists, 1982, 83, Nuclear Magnetic Resonance award U. Calif., Davis, 1984-88; S.A. Pepper Collegiate scholar, 1963; fellow Stanford U., 1967-68, Internat. scholar MOP, Venezuela, 1967, NIH, 1970, Highest Honor Calif. Scholarship Fedn.; grantee Am. Heart Assn., U. Calif., Davis, Lawrence Livermore Nat. Lab., others. Mem. Sigma Xi, Phi Kappa Phi, Mu Alpha Theta. Avocations: trumpet, photography, art, outdoor sports.

KOSTIC, PETAR JOVAN, physicist; b. Zemun, Serbia, Nov. 20, 1953; s. Jovan Petar and Mira Branko (Sever) K. BS in Elec. Engring., Physics, U. Belgrade, 1980, MS in Elec. Materials, 1985, PhD, 1988. Rschr., asst. scientist Serbian Acad. Sci., Belgrade, 1981-87; vis. scientist Argonne (Ill.) Nat. Lab., 1987-88; asst. scientist U. Belgrade, 1988-91; vis. scientist, asst. scientist Argonne Nat. Lab., 1991-96; vis. rschr. U. Calif., Santa Cruz, 1997—. Mem. Am. Physics Soc., Materials Rsch. Soc. E-mail: petar@physics.ucsc.edu. Office: U Calif Dept Physics Santa Cruz CA 95064

KOSTOULAS, IOANNIS GEORGIOU, physicist; b. Petra, Pierias, Greece, Sept. 12, 1936; came to U.S., 1965, naturalized, 1984; s. Georgios Ioannou and Panagiota (Zarogiannis) K.; m. Katina Sioras Kay, June 23, 1979; 1 child, Alexandra. Diploma in Physics U. Thessoloniki, Greece, 1963; MA, U. Rochester, 1969, PhD, 1972; MS, U. Ala., 1977, Instr. U. Thessaloniki, 1963-65; teaching asst. U. Ala., 1966-67, U. Rochester, 1967-68; guest jr. research assoc. Brookhaven Nat. Lab., Upton, N.Y., 1968-72; research physicist, lectr. UCLA, U. Calif.-San Diego, 1972-76; sr. research assoc. Mich. State U., East Lansing, 1976-78, Fermi Nat. Accelerator Lab., Betavia, Ill., 1976-78; research staff mem. MIT, Cambridge, 1978-80; sr. system engr., physicist Hughes Aircraft Co., El Segundo, Calif., 1980-86; sr. physicist electro-optics and space sensors Rockwell Internat. Corp., Downey, Calif., 1986—. Contbr. articles to profl. jours. Served with Greek Army, 1961-63. Research grantee U. Rochester, 1968-72. Mem. Am. Phys. Soc., Los Alamos Sci. Lab. Exptl. Users Group, Fermi Nat. Accelerator Lab. Users Group, High Energy Discussion Group of Brookhaven Nat. Lab., Pan Macedonian Assn., Save Cyprus Council Los Angeles, Sigma Pi Sigma. Club: Hellenic U. Lodge: Ahepa. Home: 2404 Marshallfield Ln # B Redondo Beach CA 90278-4406 Office: Raytheon Sys Co Mail Code EO/E1/A117 2000 E El Segundo Blvd El Segundo CA 90245-4501

KOSTRIKIN, MARYBETH ELAINE, excavating company executive; b. Clarkston, Wash., Nov. 22, 1954; d. William Bruce and Rachel Ann (Osborn) Hodgson; m. David Kostrikin, Jan. 6, 1983; children: Troy James Pierson, Rachel Anne. Student, U. Idaho, 1972-75, Clackamas C.C., Oregon City, Oreg., 1976, 77. Meter reader, energy specialist Canby (Oreg.) Utility Bd., 1978-84; sec. Kostco Landscape Mgmt., Canby, 1983-91; v.p. KLM Excavating, Inc., Canby, 1991—. Mem. Nat. Fedn. Ind. Bus. Republican. Baptist. Avocations: jet-skiing, ATVs, horses.

KOTADA, KELLY KENICHI, lawyer; b. Honolulu, Nov. 16, 1962; s. Setsuko (Yoshihara) K. BA, U. Hawaii, 1985; JD, Thomas Cooley Law Sch., Lansing, Mich., 1988. Bar: Hawaii 1988, U.S. Dist. Ct. Hawaii 1988, U.S. Ct. Appeals (9th cir.) 1992. Clk. Mich. Ct. Appeals, Lansing, 1986-87; assoc. Cronin, Fried, Sekiya, Kekina & Fairbanks, Honolulu, 1988-89; law clk. Cir. Ct. of the 1st Cir., Honolulu, 1989-90; assoc. Edmunds, Verga & O'Brien, Honolulu, 1990-91, Law Offices of Ian Mattoch, Honolulu, 1992-95; pvt. practice Honolulu, 1995—; arbitrator Cir. Ct. of 1st Cir., 1995—; vol. judge Honolulu Dist. "Teen" Ct., 1996—; barrister Am. Inns of Ct. IV, Honolulu, 1990-92. Legal counsel Hawaii Jaycees, 1994—. Mem. ABA, ATLA, Hawaii State Bar Assn., Consumer Lawyers Hawaii (instr. "People's Law Sch." 1993-95). Office: Law Offices of Kelly Kotada 900 Fort Street Mall Ste 910 Honolulu HI 96813-3716

KOTLER, RICHARD LEE, lawyer; b. L.A., Apr. 13, 1952; s. Allen S. Kotler and Marcella (Fromberg) Swartz; m. Cindy Jasik, Dec. 9, 1990; children: Kelsey Elizabeth, Charles Max. BA, Sonoma State Coll., 1976; JD, Southwestern U., 1979. Bar: Calif. 1980, U.S. Dist. Ct. (cen. dist.) Cal. 1980; cert. family law specialist. Sole practice Newhall, Calif., 1980-83, 88—; sr. ptnr. Kotler & Hann, Newhall, 1983-88; pvt. practice Law Offices of Richard L. Kotler, Newhall, 1984-86; judge pro temp Municipal Ct., 1981-84, Superior Ct., 1985—. Chmn. Santa Clarita Valley Battered Women's Assn., Newhall, 1983-87; bd. dirs. Santa Clarita Valley Hotline, Newhall, 1981-83. Recipient Commendation award L.A. County, 1983; named SCV Paintball champion. Mem. Santa Clarita Valley Bar Assn. (v.p. 1985—), Los Angeles Astronomy Soc., Newhall Astronomy Club. Avocations: astronomy, classic cars, collecting stamps, precious metals, trout fishing. Office: 23942 Lyons Ave Ste 202 Newhall CA 91321-2459*

KOTTKAMP, JOHN HARLAN, lawyer; b. Portland, Oreg., Oct. 19, 1930; s. John Henry and Anna Margaret (Schnell) K.; m. Elizabeth Ann Lawrence, July 10, 1954; children: Elizabeth, Andrew, Molly, Jennifer, Carrie. B.S., U. Oreg., 1952, LL.B., 1957. Bar: Oreg. 1957, U.S. Dist. Ct. Oreg. 1957, U.S. Supreme Ct. 1971. Assoc. Kilkenny & Fabre, Pendleton, Oreg., 1957-59, Fabre, Collins & Kottkamp, Pendleton, 1959-61; pvt. practice, Pendleton, 1961-64; ptnr. Kottkamp & O'Rourke, Pendleton, Oreg., 1964—. Served with U.S. Army, 1952-54. Fellow Am. Bar Found., Am. Coll. Trial Lawyers. Republican. Club: Pendleton Country. Lodge: Elks. Office: Kottkamp & O'Rourke LLP 331 SE 2nd St Pendleton OR 97801-2224

KOTTLOWSKI, FRANK EDWARD, geologist; b. Indpls., Apr. 11, 1921; s. Frank Charles and Adella (Markworth) K.; m. Florence Jean Chriscoe, Sept. 15, 1945; children: Karen, Janet, Diane. Student, Butler U., 1939-42; AB, Ind. U., 1947, MA, 1949, PhD, 1951. Party chief Ind. Geology Survey, Bloomington, summers 1948-50; fellow Ind. U., 1947-51, instr. geology, 1950; adj. prof. N.Mex. Inst. Mining and Tech., Socorro, 1970-95; econ. geologist N.Mex. Bur. Mines and Mineral Resources, 1951-66, asst. dir., 1966-68, 70-74, acting dir., 1968-70, dir., 1974-91, state geologist, 1989-91, dir. emeritus, state geologist emeritus, 1991—; geologic cons. Sandia Corp., 1966-72. Contbr. articles on mineral resources, stratigraphy and areal geology to tech. jours. Mem. Planning Commn. Socorro, 1960-68, 71-78, chmn., 86-90; mem. N.Mex. Energy Resources Bd.; chmn. N.Mex. Coal Surface Mining Commn.; sec. Socorro County Democratic Party, 1964-68. Served to 1st lt. USAAF, 1942-45. Decorated D.F.C., Air medal; recipient Richard Owen Disting. Alumni award in Govt. and Industry, U. Ind., 1987. Fellow AAAS, Geol. Soc. Am. (councilor 1979-82, mem. exec. com. 1981-82, Disting. Svc. award coal geology divsn., Cady Coal Geology award 1996); mem. AIME, Am. Assn. Petroleum Geologists (hon.; dist. rep. 1965-68, editor 1971-75, pres. energy minerals divsn. 1987-88, Disting. Svc. award), Assn. Am. State Geologists (pres. 1985-86), Soc. Econ. Geologists, Am. Inst. Profl. Geologists (Pub. Svc. award 1986), Am. Commn. Statigraphic Nomenclature (past sec., chmn.), Cosmos Club, Rotary Internat. (Paul Harris fellow), Sigma Xi. Home: 703 Sunset St Socorro NM 87801-4657 Office: NMex Bur Mines NMex Tech 801 Leroy Pl Socorro NM 87801-4681

KOUNS, ALAN TERRY, writer, consultant; b. Long Beach, Calif., Dec. 31, 1941; s. Ambert Tullis and Elsa May (Lauritzen) K. MAC, U. Pa. Journalist print, broadcast media, 1961-70; pub. rels. writer U. So. Calif., 1965; health scis. writer, 1970-72, assoc. prodr. ednl. TV, 1973; cons., writer D'Antoni & Assocs., 1974; corr. U.S. Info. Agy., 1975-81, 82-93; med. filmstrip scriptwriter Trainex Corp., 1980-81; lectr. communication arts Calif. State Polytechnic U., Pomona, 1981; writer, publicist City of Hope Nat. Med. Ctr., 1981-82; assoc. editor Creative Age Publs., 1982-88; cons. med. communications, media rels., 1984—; L.A. corr. Physicians Radio Network, 1987. Contbr. articles to jours. including Emergency Med. Svcs., L.A. Times, Ocular Surgery News, Radiology Today, The Russian, others. Mem. Am. Med. Writers Assn., Ivy League Assn. So. Calif. (bd. dirs.), Nat. Assn. Sci. Writers. Democrat. Home: 9936 Ramona St #5 Bellflower CA 90706-6951

KOURLIS, REBECCA LOVE, judge; b. Colorado Springs, Colo., Nov. 11, 1952; d. John Arthur and Ann (Daniels) Love; m. Thomas Aristithis Kourlis, July 13, 1978; children: Stacy Ann, Katherine Love, Aristithis Thomas. BA with distinction in English, Stanford U., 1973, JD, 1976, LLD, U. Denver, 1997. Bar: Colo. 1976, D.C. 1979, U.S. Dist. Ct. Colo. 1976, U.S. Ct. Appeals (10th cir.) 1976, Colo. Supreme Ct., U.S. Ct. Appeals (D.C. cir.), U.S. Claims Ct., U.S. Supreme Ct. Assoc. Davis, Graham & Stubbs, Denver, 1976-78; sole practice, Craig, Colo., 1978-87; assoc. Gibson, Dunn & Crutcher, Denver, part time 1981-87; judge 14th Jud. Dist. Ct., 1987-94; arbiter Jud. Arbiter Group, Inc., 1994-95; justice Colo. Supreme Ct., 1995—; water judge divsn. 6, 1987-94; lectr. to profl. groups. Contbr. articles to profl. jours. Chmn. Moffat County Arts and Humanities, Craig, 1979; mem. Colo. Commn. on Higher Edn., Denver, 1980-81; mem. adv. bd. Colo. Divsn. Youth Svcs., 1988-91; mem. com. civil jury instructions, 1990-95, standing com. gender & justice, 1994-97, chair jud. adv. coun., 1997—, co-chair com. on jury reform, 1996—; co-chair com. on atty. grievance reform, 1997—; mem. long range planning com. Moffat County Sch., 1990; bd. visitors Stanford U., 1989-94, Law Sch. U. Denver, 1997—; bd. dirs. Kent Denver Sch., 1996—. Fellow Am. Bar Found., Colo. Bar Found.; mem. Am. Law Inst., Rocky Mountain Mineral Found., Colo. Bar Assn. (bd. govs. 1983-85, mineral law sect. bd. dirs. 1985, sr. v.p. 1987-88), Dist. Ct. Judges' Assn. (pres. 1993-94), N.W. Colo. Bar Assn. (Cmty. Svc. award 1993-94). Office: State Jud Bldg 2 E 14th Ave Rm 415 Denver CO 80203-2115

KOUYMJIAN, DICKRAN, art historian, Orientalist, educator; b. Tulcea, Romania, June 6, 1934; came to U.S. (parents Am. citizens), 1939; s. Toros S. and Zabelle I. (Calusdian) K.; m. Angèle Kapoïan, Sept. 16, 1967. BS in European Cultural History, U. Wis., 1957; MA in Arab Studies, Am. U., Beirut, 1961; PhD in Near East Lang. and Culture, Columbia U., 1969. Instr. English Columbia U., N.Y.C., 1961-64; dir. Am. Authors, Inc., N.Y.C., 1965-67; asst. prof. and asst. dir. Ctr. for Arabic Studies Am. U., Cairo, 1967-71; assoc. prof. history Am. U. Beirut, 1971-75; prof. art history Am. U., Paris, 1976-77; prof. history and art, dir. Armenian Studies program Calif. State U., Fresno, 1977—; dir. Sarkis and Meline Kalfayan Ctr. for Armenian Studies, Calif. State U., Fresno, 1990—; Fulbright disting. lectr., prof. Armenian and Am. Lit., Yerevan (Armenia, USSR), 1987; cons. archaeology UNESCO, Paris, 1976; prof., chairholder Armenian Sect., Inst. Nat. des Langs. et Civilisations Orientales, U. Paris, 1988-91; 1st incumbent Haig & Isabel Berberian endowed chair Armenian Studies Calif. State U., Fresno, 1989—, 2nd incumbent William Saroyan endowed chair of Armenian studies U. Calif., Berkeley, 1996-97. Author: Index of Armenian Art, part I, 1977, part II, 1979, The Armenian History of Ghazar P'arpetzi, 1986, Arts of Armenia, 1992; co-author: (with A. Kapoïan) The Splendor of Egypt, 1975; author and editor: William Saroyan: An Armenian Trilogy, 1986, William Saroyan: Warsaw Visitor and Tales of the Vienna Streets, 1990; editor: (books) Near Eastern Numistatics, Iconography, Epigraphy and History, 1974, Essays in Armenian Numismatics in Honor of C. Sibilian, 1981, Armenian Studies: In Memoriam Haïg Berbèrian, 1986; editl. bd. Armenian Rev., 1974—, Ararat Lit. mag., 1975—, Revue des Etudes Armèniennes, 1978—, NAASR Jour. Armenian Studies, Jour. of the Soc. for Armenian Studies, 1995—; contbr. articles to profl. jours. Served with U.S. Army, 1957. Recipient St. Sahaq and St. Mesrob medal His Holiness Karekin I, Catholics of All Armenians, 1996, Outstanding Prof. award Am. U., Cairo, 1968-69, 69-70, Outstanding Prof. of Yr. award Calif. State U., 1985-86, Hagop Kevorkian Disting. Lectureship in Near Eastern Art and Civilization, NYU, 1979; Fulbright fellow, USSR, 1986-87; grantee NEH, Paris, 1980-81, 95, Bertha & John Garabedian Charitable Found., 1994-99. Mem. Am. Oriental Soc., Am. Numismatic Soc., Mid. East Studies Assn. (charter), Coll. Arts Assn., Soc. Armenian Studies (charter, pres. 1985-86, 92-94), Société asiatique (Paris), Medieval Acad., Internat. Assn. of Armenian Studies, Mid. East Medievalist, Assn. Paléographique Internat., Phi Kappa Phi (nat. scholar Fresno chpt. 1998). Avocations: music, film, bibliophile. Home: 30 rue Chevert, 75007 Paris France Office: Calif State U Armenian Studies Program 5245 N Backer Ave # Pb4 Fresno CA 93740-8001

KOVACHY, EDWARD MIKLOS, JR., psychiatrist; b. Cleve., Dec. 3, 1946; s. Edward Miklos and Evelyn Amelia (Palenscar) K.; m. Susan Eileen Light, June 21, 1981; children: Timothy Light, Benjamin Light. BA, Harvard U., 1968, JD, 1972, MBA, 1972; MD, Case Western Reserve U., 1977. Diplomate Nat. Bd. Med. Examiners. Resident in psychiatry Stanford U. Med. Ctr., Stanford, Calif., 1977-81; pvt. practice psychiatry mediator mgmt. cons. Menlo Park, Calif., 1981—. Columnist The Peninsula Times Tribune, 1983-85. Trustee Mid-Peninsula H.S., Palo Alto, Calif., 1990—; mem. gift com. Harvard Coll. Class of 1968, 25th reunion chmn. participation, San Francisco, 1993, 30th reunion chmn. participation, West Coast, 1998. Mem. Am. Psychiat. Assn., Physicians for Social Responsibility, Assn. Family and Conciliation Cts., No. Calif. Psychiat. Soc. Presbyterian. Avocations: personal activism, musical comedy, athletics. Office: 1187 University Dr Menlo Park CA 94025-4423

KOVINICK, PHILIP PETER, writer; b. Detroit, July 4, 1924; s. Philip Peter and Christine (Selesan) K.; m. Marian Tsugie Yoshiki, June 17, 1973. AB, Calif. State U., Chico, 1954, MA, 1955. Tchr. social studies, dept. head Lennox (Calif.) H.S., 1957-76; curator art exhibits L.A., 1976-86, prof., rschr., 1977—, lectr., 1976—. Co-author: Contemporary International Problems, 1961, An Encyclopedia of Women Artists of the American West, 1997; author: (catalog) The Woman Artist in the American West, 1860-1960, 1976; co-author (mags.) Art News, 1976, S.W. Art, 1998; contbr. articles to profl. jours., chpts. to books. Mem. L.A. Corral of Westerners, Huntington Corral of Westerners, Archives of Am. Art, Huntington Libr. Reader. Democrat. Avocation: high repetition exercises. Home: 4735 Don Ricardo Dr Los Angeles CA 90008-2812

KOVNER, JOEL WYATT, medical economist, banker; b. N.Y.C., May 19, 1941; s. Sidney J. and Natalie (Lieberman) K.; BA, Cornell U., 1963; MPH, UCLA, 1964, PhD, 1968; postgrad. Harvard U., 1975-79; m. Ronna D. Kovacs, Jan. 28, 1995; children: Chloe, Emily, Noah, Jacob, Alexandra. Mem. faculty UCLA, 1968; economist Kaiser Found. Health Plan, L.A., 1969-72, dir. med. econs., 1972-79, v.p., 1979-81; mgr. planning and support services Kaiser-Permanente Med. Care Program, L.A., 1979-81; chmn., CEO HealthCare Fin. and Cons. Corp., 1996—; chmn., CEO, pres. Mountain Engring., 1997—; chmn., CEO, pres., founder First Profl. Bank, 1982-96; cons. in field. Mem. APHA (chmn. med. care 1980-81), Health Info. Soc. (pres. 1971-72), Ops. Rsch. Soc. Jewish. Contbr. articles to profl. jours. Home: 29665 Harvester Rd Malibu CA 90265-3724 Office: HealthCare Fin and Cons LLC 29665 Harvester Rd Malibu CA 90265-3724 also: Mountain Engring LLC 29665 Harvester Rd Malibu CA 90265-3724

KOVTYNOVICH, DAN, civil engineer; b. Eugene, Oreg., May 17, 1952; s. John and Elva Lano (Robie) K. BCE, Oreg. State U., 1975, BBA, 1976. Registered profl. engr., Calif., Oreg. V.p. Kovtynovich, Inc., Contractors and Engrs., Eugene, 1976-80, pres., chief exec. officer, 1980—. Apptd. to State of Oreg. Bldg. Codes and Structures Bd., 1996—. Fellow ASCE; mem. Am. Arbitration Assn. (arbitrator 1979—), N.W. China Coun., Navy League of U.S., Eugene Asian Coun. Republican. Avocations: flying, skiing, fishing, hunting. Office: Kovtynovich Inc PO Box 898 Lake Oswego OR 97034-0143

KOWALSKI, KAZIMIERZ, computer science educator, researcher; b. Turek, Poland, Nov. 7, 1946; came to U.S., 1986; naturalized, 1994; s. Waclaw and Helena (Wisniewska) K.; m. Eugenia Zajaczkowska, Aug. 5, 1972. MSc, Wroclaw (Poland) U. Tech., 1970, PhD, 1974. Asst. prof. Wroclaw U. Tech., 1970-76, assoc. prof., 1976-86; assoc. prof. Pan Am. U., Edinburg, Tex., 1987-88; prof. computer sci. Calif. State U.-Dominguez Hills, Carson, 1988—, chmn. computer sci. dept., 1998—; lectr. U. Basrah, Iraq, 1981-85; cons. XXCal, Inc., L.A., 1987-91; conf. presenter in field; rsch. fellow Power Inst. Moscow, USSR, 1978; info. sys. tng. UNESCO, Paris, 1978. Co-author: Principles of Computer Science, 1975, Organization and Programming of Computers, 1976; also articles. Recipient Bronze Merit Cross, Govt. of Poland, 1980, Knights' Cross of the Order of Merit Republic of Poland, 1997. Mem. IEEE Computer Soc., The N.Y. Acad. Scis., Assn. for Computing Machinery, Assn. for Advancement of Computing in Edn., Am. Assn. for Artificial Intelligence, Mensa, Sigma Xi. Avocations: travel, puzzles. Home: 3836 Weston Pl Long Beach CA 90807-3317 Office: Calif State U 1000 E Victoria St Carson CA 90747-0001

KOYLE, MARTIN ALLAN, surgeon, educator; b. Winnipeg, Man., Can., May 8, 1952; s. Sydney Alexander and Leatrice Rosalie (Hirt) K.; m. Patricia Ellen Canfield, Feb. 18, 1989; children: Charles Louis, Alexander William, Leah Claire. MD, U. Man., 1976. Diplomate Am. Bd. Urology. Intern in flexible surgery L.A. County-U. So. Calif. Med. Ctr., 1976-77; resident in surgery U. Man., Winnipeg, Can., 1977-78; jr. resident in urology Brigham and Womens Hosp., West Roxbury VA Hosp., 1980-81; fellow in organ transplantation Pacific Med. Ctr. San Francisco and Harvard Program,

Longwood, 1981-82; sr. resident in urology Harvard Program in Urology, Boston, 1982-83, chief resident in urology, 1983-84; fellow in pediat. urology UCLA Med. Ctr., 1984-85; dir. emergency dept. Primecare Corp., Marina del Rey, Calif., 1979-80; asst. prof. surgery and urology UCLA Sch. Medicine, 1985-89; assoc. chief divsn. urology, dir. pediat. urology Harbor/UCLA Med. Ctr., Torrance, Calif., 1985-89; assoc. prof. surgery and urology U. Colo. Sch. Medicine, Denver, 1989-91, chmn. dept. pediat. urology Children's Hosp., 1991—; mem. med. staff U. Hosp., Denver, 1989—, Rose Med. Ctr., Denver, 1990—, Presbyn.-St. Luke's Med. Ctr., Denver, 1990—; cons. Fitzsimons Army Med. Ctr., Denver, 1989-96; mem. staff U. Colo. Cancer Ctr., Denver, 1991—, St. Joseph's Hosp., Denver, 1992—, Luth. Med. Ctr., Wheat Ridge, Colo., 1993—; mem. staff St. Anthony Hosp., Ctrl., Denver, 1993—, North Westminster, Colo., 1993—; mem. staff Aurora (Colo.) Regional Med. Ctr., 1993—, North Suburban Med. Ctr., Thornton, Colo., 1993—; prof. surgery/urology and pediatrics U. Colo., Denver, 1996—; mem. adv. bd. Bayer Pharms., New Haven, Conn.; presenter in field; Pfizer vis. prof. U. Calif., Irvine, Orange, 1994. Mem. editl. bd. Jour. Urology, Pediat. Surgery Internat., Infections in Urology, Urology; contbr. more than 50 articles to profl. jours.; author chpts. in books. Grantee Harbor/UCLA Med. Ctr., 1984-89, 88-89, NIH, 1986-89, Cook Urol., Inc., 1987-89, Sandoz Rsch. Inst., 1987-89, Miles Pharms., 1988-89, U. Colo. Sch. Medicine, 1993-94; recipient 1st prize L.A. Urol. Assn., 1988; Sandoz fellow Am. Soc. Transplant Surgeons, 1989. Fellow ACS, Am. Acad. Pediats.; mem. Urologic Soc. for Transplantation and Vascular Surgery (charter), Western Assn. Transplant Surgeons (charter), Genitourinary Reconstructive Surgeons (charter), Soc. U. Urologists, Am. Urol. Assn. (nominating com. South Ctrl. sect. 1993-94, future meetings com. 1993-95, adv. com. office edn. 1996—, del. health policy coun. 1997—, 1st prize Joseph F. MacCarthy Essay Contest 1987, 1st prize Miley Wesson Resident's Essay Contest 1989, 2d prize Poster award 1989, T. Leon Howard award 1993, 94), Pacific Rim Assn. for Pediat. Urologic Surgery, Soc. for Pediat. Urology, Am. Soc. Transplant Surgeons, Transplantation Soc., Soc. for Young Pediat. Urologists, Am. Assn. Pediat. Urologists (charter), Wee Willies, Am. Lithtripsy Soc., Univ. Urologic Forum, Children's Cancer Group (surg. discipline com. 1991—, germ cell cancer com. 1991—, Wilms' tumor com. 1993—), Colo. Organ Recovery Sys. (med. adv. com. 1994—), Societe Internat. d'Urologie, European Soc. for Pediat. Urology, Brit. Assn. Pediat. Urol. Surgeons, among others. Jewish. Avocations: hockey, skiing, reading, theatre, music. Office: Childrens Hosp Dept Pediats Urology 1056 E 19th Ave Denver CO 80218-1088

KOZINSKI, ALEX, federal judge; b. Bucharest, Romania, July 23, 1950; came to U.S., 1962; s. Moses and Sabine (Zapler) K.; m. Marcy J. Tiffany, July 9, 1977; children: Yale Tiffany, Wyatt Tiffany, Clayton Tiffany. AB in Econs. cum laude, UCLA, 1972, JD, 1975. Bar: Calif. 1975, D.C., 1978. Law clk. to Hon. Anthony M. Kennedy U.S. Ct. Appeals (9th cir.), 1975-76; law clk. to Chief Justice Warren E. Burger U.S. Supreme Ct., 1976-77; assoc. Covington & Burling, Washington, 1979-81; asst. counsel Office of Counsel to Pres., White House, Washington, 1981; spl. counsel Merit Systems Protection Bd., Washington, 1981-82; chief judge U.S. Claims Ct., Washington, 1982-85; judge U.S. Ct. Appeals (9th cir.), 1985—; lectr. law U. So. Calif., 1992. Office: US Ct Appeals PO Box 91510 125 S Grand Ave Ste 200 Pasadena CA 91105-1652

KOZLOW, BEVERLY KAY, physical therapist, clinical psychologist, realtor; b. Detroit, Aug. 10, 1931; d. Samuel and Genevieve Ione (Griffin) K.; m. Roy Carl Gleaves, Apr. 16, 1959 (div. 1975). BS, Eastern Mich. U., 1953; MS, UCLA, 1959; PhD, Sierra U., 1987. Registered physical therapist. Phys. therapist Walter Reed Army Med. Ctr., Washington, 1953-55, Crippled Children's Soc., Rockville, Md., 1955-56, San Bernardino (Calif.) County Hosp., 1957-59; coord. phys. therapy program UCLA, 1959-67; home health phys. therapist Vis. Nurses Assn. L.A., 1967-68; from staff to dir. phys. therapy L.A. County Med. Dept., 1968-73; dir. in-patient/out-patient acute and rehab. svcs. Valley Med. Ctr., Van Nuys, Calif., 1973-81; contract phys. therapist L.A., 1981-89; home health phys. therapist Vis. Nurses Assn., Stuart, Fla., 1992-96; CPS Great River Property, Guerneville, Calif., 1997—; adj. faculty U.S. Army Command and Gen. Staff Coll., Ft. Leavenworth, Kans., 1986-92. Ret. col. U.S. Army. Mem. Am. Physical Therapy Assn., Ret. Officers Assn., Med. Specialists Corps Assn. (past. v.p.). Democrat. Jewish. Avocations: reading, traveling, gardening. Home: 14740 Old Cazadero Rd Guerneville CA 95446-9004

KRAAI, JANICE KAY, adult education educator; b. Holland, Mich., Sept. 30, 1955; d. Vernon Theodore and Dorothy Ruth (Poll) K. BA, U. Mich., 1976; MA, U. Ariz., 1981. Cert. reading tchr., ESL tchr. VISA vol. ACTION, San Juan County, Utah, 1977-79; chpt. 1 reading tchr. Chinle (Ariz.) Jr. H.S., 1981-82, Ganado (Ariz.) H.S., 1985-88; devel. edn., ESL and citizenship instr. Northland Pioneer Coll., Holbrook, Ariz., 1989—; mem. citizenship task force on Ariz. Stds. Project, Ariz. Dept. Edn., Phoenix, 1998. Avocations: log home building, travel, hiking, photography, nature. Office: Northland Pioneer Coll PO Box 610 Holbrook AZ 86025

KRAFT, GEORGE HOWARD, physician, educator; b. Columbus, Ohio, Sept. 27, 1936; s. Glen Homer and Helen Winner (Howard) K.; children: Jonathan Ashbrook, Susannah Mary. AB, Harvard U., 1958; MD, Ohio State U., 1963, MS, 1967. Diplomate Am. Bd. Phys. Medicine and Rehab., Am. Bd. Electrodiagnostic Medicine. Intern U. Calif. Hosp., San Francisco, 1963-64, resident in phys. medicine and rehab., 1964-65; resident in phys. medicine and rehab. Ohio State U., Columbus, 1965-67; assoc. U. Pa. Med. Sch., Phila., 1968-69; asst. prof. U. Wash., Seattle, 1969-72, assoc. prof., 1972-76, prof., 1976—; chief of staff U. Wash. Med. Ctr., Seattle, 1993-95; dir. electrodiagnostic medicine U. Wash. Hosp., 1987—, dir. Multiple Sclerosis Ctr., 1982—; co-dir. Muscular Dystrophy Clinic, 1974—; assoc. dir. rehab. medicine Overlake Hosp., Bellevue, Wash., 1989—; bd. dirs. Am. Bd. Electrodiagnostic Medicine, 1993-96, chmn., 1996—. Co-author: Chronic Disease and Disability, 1994, Living with Multiple Sclerosis: A Wellness Approach, 1996; cons. editor: Phys. Medicine and Rehab. Clinics, 1990—, EEG and Clin. Neurophysiology, 1992-96; assoc. editor Jour. Neurol. Rehab., 1988—, Muscle and Nerve, 1998—; contbr. articles to profl. jours. Sci. peer rev. com. C Nat. Multiple Sclerosis Soc., N.Y.C., 1990-96, chmn., 1993-96, med. adv. bd., 1991—; bd. sponsors Wash. Physicians for Social Responsibility, Seattle, 1986—. Rsch. grantee Rehab. Svcs. Adminstrn., 1976-81, Nat. Inst. Handicapped Rsch., 1984-88, Nat. Multiple Sclerosis Soc., 1990-92, 94-95, Nat. Inst. Disability and REhab. Rsch., 1998—. Fellow Am. Acad. Phys. Medicine and Rehab. (pres. 1984-85, Zeiter award 1991); mem. Am. Assn. Electrodiagnostic Medicine (pres. 1982-83), Assn. Acad. Physiatrists (pres. 1980-81), Am. Acad. Clin. Neurophysiology (pres. 1995-97), Am. Acad. Neurology, Internat. Rehab. Medicine Assn., Alpha Omega Alpha. Episcopalian. Office: U Wash Dept Rehab PO Box 356490 Seattle WA 98195-6490

KRAFT, RICHARD JOE, sales executive; b. Toppenish, Wash., Apr. 20, 1944; s. Joseph Nian and Rose Goldie (Merrick) K.; m. Karolyn Idell Keyes, Oct. 9, 1963 (div. 1982); children: Craig J., Jeffrey Eugene; m. Margaret Celeste Porter, Apr. 9, 1983. Student, Yakima Valley Coll., 1962-63; student, U. Wash., 1964-70. Project engr. Gray & Osborne Consulting Engrs., Seattle, 1965-76; project engr., constrn. cons. Pool Engring., Ketchikan, Alaska, 1976-81; project mgr. Cape Fox Corp., Ketchikan, 1982; project engr. Buno Constrn., Woodinville, Wash., 1983, Straiger Engring. Svcs., Ketchikan, Sitka, Alaska, 1984; owner Kraft Constrn. Svcs., Kirkland, Wash., 1984-85; dir. mcpl. projects ESM, Inc., Renton, Wash., 1985-86; estimator Active Constrn., Inc., Gig Harbor, Wash., 1987; sr. sales engr. Advanced Drainage Systems, Inc., Woodinville, 1987-93; with Ty-Matt, Inc., Ketchikan, 1993-94; owner Kraft Constrn. Svcs., Ketchikan, 1994—; storm sewer/sanitary specification subcom. Am. Pub. Works Assn., Wash. state chpt., 1985-93. Pres. Snohomish (Wash.) Camp, Gideons Internat., 1990-91; pres. exec. com. Maltby (Wash.) Congl. Ch. Mem. Utility Contractors Assn. Wash. (bd. dirs. 1990-92). Mem. Christian Ch. Avocations: old cars, outdoor sports activities. Home and Office: PO Box 1168 Wrangell AK 99929-1168

KRAFT, WILLIAM ARMSTRONG, retired priest; b. Rochester, N.Y., Apr. 13, 1926; s. William Andrew and Elizabeth Ruth (Armstrong) K. BA, St. Bernard Coll., 1947; ThM, Immaculate Heart Theol. Coll., 1951; D of Ministry, Claremont Sch. of Theology, 1981. Ordained priest Roman Cath. Ch., 1951. Dir. and founder of Newman Apostolate Diocese of San Diego, Calif., 1951-63; dir. of pub. rels. Diocese of San Diego, 1956-63, dir. of cemeteries, 1964-70, exec. dir. of devel., 1979-91; founding pastor St. Therese of Child Jesus Parish, San Diego, 1956-70, Good Shepherd Parish, San Diego, 1970-77; pastor St. Charles Borromeo Parish, San Diego, 1977-79; bd. dirs. Cath. Charities, San Diego; bd. of consultors Diocese of San Diego, 1985-91, mem. Presbyteral Coun., 1985-91, mem. bldg. commn., 1977-91. Bd. dirs. Am. Nat. Red Cross, San Diego, 1956-63, Legal Aid Soc., San Diego, 1956-65, Travelers' Aid Soc., San Diego, 1956-65; mem. Presdl. Task Force, Washington, 1984—; spl. dep. San Diego County Sheriff, 1964—. Named Prelate of Honor to Pope, Pope John Paul II, Vatican City, 1985, Knight Comdr. of Equestrian, Order of The Holy Sepulchre, Latin Patriarcii, Jerusalem, 1984, Knights of Columbus 4th degree. Mem. Benevolent and Protective Order of Elks, Univ. Club Atop Symphony Towers, Nat. Cath. Conf. for Total Stewardship (bd. dirs.), Nat. Cath. Devel. Conf., Nat. Soc. Fund Raising Execs. (cert.). Republican. Avocations: music appreciation, swimming. Home: 6910 Cibola Rd San Diego CA 92120-1709

KRAG, OLGA, interior designer; b. St. Louis, Nov. 27, 1937; d. Jovica Todor and Milka (Slijepcevic) Golubovic. AA, U. Mo., 1958; cert. interior design UCLA, 1979. Interior designer William L. Pereira Assocs., L.A., 1977-80; assoc. Reel/Grobman Assocs., L.A., 1980-81; project mgr. Kaneko/Laff Assocs., L.A., 1982; project mgr. Stuart Laff Assocs., L.A., 1983-85; restaurateur The Edge, St. Louis, 1983-84; pvt. practice comml. interior design, L.A., 1981—, pres., R.I., 1989—. Mem. invitation and ticket com. Calif. Chamber Symphony Soc., 1980-81; vol. Westside Rep. Coun., Proposition 1, 1971; asst. inaugural presentation Mus. of Childhood, L.A., 1985. Recipient Carole Eichen design award U. Calif., 1979. Mem. Am. Soc. Interior Designers, Inst. Bus. Designers, Phi Chi Theta, Beta Sigma Phi. Republican. Serbian Orthodox. Home and Office: 700 Levering Ave Apt 10 Los Angeles CA 90024-2797

KRAHMER, DONALD LEROY, JR., lawyer; b. Hillsboro, Oreg., Nov. 11, 1957; s. Donald L. and Joan Elizabeth (Karns) K.; m. Suzanne M. Blanchard, Aug. 16, 1986; children: Hillary, Zachary. BS, Willamette U., 1981, MM, 1987, JD, 1987. Bar: Oreg. 1988. Fin. analyst U.S. Bancorp, Portland, 1977-87; intern U.S. Senator Mark Hatfield, 1978; legis. aide State Sen. Jeannette Hamby, Hillsboro, Oreg., 1981-83, State Rep. Delna Jones, Beaverton, Oreg., 1983; bus. analyst Pacificorp, Portland, 1987; mgr. mergers/acquisitions Pacificorp Fin. Svcs., Portland, 1988-89; dir. Pacificorp Fin. Svcs., 1990; CEO, pres. Atkinson Group, Portland, 1991—; ptnr. Black Helterline, Portland, 1991—; bd. dirs., sec. Marathon Fin. Assocs., Portland, 1989; bd. dirs. Self-Enhancement, Inc.; chmn. Willamette Forum; bd. dirs. Oreg. Entrepreneur Forum, 1993—, editor, 1993, chmn. adv. bd., 1995, chmn. bd., 1998; founder co-chmn. Oreg. Emerging Bus. Initiative, 1997—; bd. dirs. Concordia Univ. Found., 1995-97. Treas. Com. to Re-Elect Jeannette Hamby, 1986; bd. dirs. fin. com./devel. com. Am. Diabetes Assn., Portland, 1990-96; founder Needle Bros., 1994; chmn. Atkinson Grad. Sch. Devel. Com., Salem, 1989-92; Bd. Vis. Coll. Law, Willamette U., 1997—; mem. adv. bd. Ctr. for Law and Entrepreneurship, U. Oreg. Sch. Law, 1997—; founder Conf. of Entrepreneurship, Salem, 1984, chmn. Entrepreneurship Breakfast Forum, Portland, 1993; chmn., founder Oreg. Conf. on Entrepreneurship and Awards Dinner, 1994-99, sr. v.p., 1999—; mem. exec. com., bd. dirs. Cascade Pacific Coun. Boy Scouts Am., 1998—, chmn. cmty. fund. dir., 1997. Recipient Pub.'s award Oreg. Bus. Mag., 1987, Founders award Willamette U., 1987, award Scripps Found., 1980, Bus. Jour. 40 Under 40 award, 1996. Mem. ABA, Oreg. Bar Assn. (chmn. exec. com., fin. instns. com. sec., exec. com., bus. law sect., chmn. 1999, sec. 1998), Multnomah County Bar Assn., Washington County Bar Assn., Assn. for Corp. Growth, Oreg. Biosci. Assn., Portland Soc. Fin. Analysts, Japan-Am. Soc. Oreg., Assn. Investment Mgmt. and Rsch., City Club, Software Assn. of Oreg., Oreg. Biotech. Assn., Multnomah Athletic Club, Arlington Club. Republican. Lutheran. Home: 16230 SW Copper Creek Dr Portland OR 97224-6500 Office: Black Helterline 1200 Bank of Calif Tower 707 SW Washington St Portland OR 97205-3536

KRAM, MARK LENARD, hydrogeologist, environmental geochemist; b. L.A., July 8, 1961; s. Albert and Marjorie (Chudner) K. BA in Chemistry, U. Calif., Santa Barbara, 1983; MS in Geology, San Diego State U., 1988. Cert. ground water profl. Geochemist Marine Sci. Inst. U. Calif., Santa Barbara, 1984; geochronologist San Diego State U. Found., 1985-86; material specialist Decisive Testing, San Diego, 1987; geochemist Naval Ocean Sys. Ctr., San Diego, 1986-88; hydrogeologist Naval Facilities Engring. Svc. Ctr., Pt. Hueneme, Calif., 1989—, site characterization and analysis penetrometer sys. field project mgr., 1991-97, lead internal groundwater cons., 1990-98. Author: We CAN Change the World, 1991; co-author: Practical Handbook of Soil, Vadose Zone, and Ground-Water Contamination: Assessment, Prevention, and Remediation, 1994, Natural Attenuation General Data User's Guide, 1998; editor: (govt. document) United States Air Force Remediation Handbook for POL-Contaminated Sites, 1994; contbr. articles to Applied Organometallic Chemistry, others. Founder, chmn. Student Environ. Action, San Diego State U., 1986, chmn., 1987, vice-chmn., 1988; tech. reviewer Surfrider Found., Santa Barbara, 1991—. Mem. ASTM. Achievements include discovery of method for in-situ delineation of volatile organic contaminant/dense non-aqueous phase liquid contaminant plumes using cone penetrometer deployed laser spectroscopy; invention of high resolution piezocone for determining hydrogeologic parameters controlling fate and transport of contaminants in groundwater. Office: 1734 Castillo St Santa Barbara CA 93101

KRAMARSIC, ROMAN JOSEPH, engineering consultant; b. Mokronog, Slovenia, Feb. 15, 1926; came to U.S., 1957; s. Roman and Josipina (Bucar) K; m. Joanna B. Ruffo, Oct. 29, 1964; children: Joannine M., Roman III. Student, U. Bologna, Italy, 1947-48; B of Applied Sci. in Mech. Engring., U. Toronto, 1954, M of Applied Sci., 1956; PhD, U. So. Calif., 1973. Registered profl. engr., Ont. Rsch. engr. Chrysler Rsch., Detroit, 1957-58; chief design engr. Annin Corp., Montebello, Calif., 1959-60; mgr. Plasmadyne Corp., Santa Ana, Calif., 1960-62; sr. rsch. engr. NESCO, Pasadena, Calif., 1962-64; asst. prof. U. So. Calif., L.A., 1971-77; mgr. engring. div. MERDI, Butte, Mont., 1977-78; sr. rsch. engr. RDA, Albuquerque, 1978-85; sr. staff mem. BDM, Albuquerque, 1985-90; owner Dr. R. J. Kramarsic's Engring. Svcs., Laguna Beach, Calif., 1985—; cons. various tech. cos., So. Calif., 1964—; mem. various govt. coms. evaluating high power lasers. Author tech. presentations; contbr. articles to profl. jours. Violinist Albuquerque Civic Light Opera, 1980-85. Mem. ASME (sr.), AIAA (sr.), ASM Internat., Nat. Ski Patrol (aux. leader 1990-94). Roman Catholic. Avocations: classical music, violin, skiing. Office: Kramarsic's Engring Svcs PO Box 608 Laguna Beach CA 92652-0608

KRAMER, ALEXANDER GOTTLIEB, financial director; b. DesPlaines, Ill., Sept. 21, 1964; s. Gottlieb G. and Norma L. Kramer. BA in Econ. Devel. and Internat. Rels., Lake Forest Coll., 1987; M in Internat. Fin., Am. Grad. Sch. Internat. Mgmt., Glendale, Ariz., 1990. Asst. to dir. parliamentary affairs Spanish Parliament, Madrid, 1985-87; intern to chief polit. consular U.S. Dept. State, Rabat, Morocco, 1987-88; project mgr. H. Shapiro & Assocs., Inc., Chgo., 1988-90; dir. fin. and logistics Pacific Inter-Trade Corp., Westlake Village, Calif., 1990-93; fin. dir. Export SBDC Sr. Counsel Internat., L.A., 1993-95; head trade fin. group Am. Honda Motor Co., Torrance, Calif., 1995—; prof. internat. fin., UCLA, 1991—; mem. adv. bd. Bestone Group, Hong Kong and Shanghai; bd. dirs. Export Mgrs. Assn. Calif. Mem. Fgn. Trade Assn. (bd. dirs.). Avocations: international development, tennis, Latin American art. Office: Honda Motor Co 100-2W-SE 1919 Torrance Blvd Torrance CA 90501-2722

KRAMER, ANNE PEARCE, writer, communications and film executive, educator, psychotherapist, research psychoanalyst; m. Stanley Kramer (div.); children: Larry David, Casey Lise. BA magna cum laude, U. So. Calif., MA, 1965, PhD, 1972. Gen. exec. asst. to producer/dir. Stanley Kramer Prodns., prodn. exec., assoc. producer, story editor, casting dir., dialogue dir.; sr. lectr. cinema and comparative lit. U. So. Calif., L.A.; acting asst. prof. comparative lit. and film Calif. State U., Long Beach; pres. Cathexis 3, L.A.; story editor, v.p. creative affairs Castle Hill Prodns., Inc., L.A., 1978-80; story editor Columbia Pictures, 1981-83, exec. story editor, 1985-88, exec. creative dir., 1983-86, creative cons. to the chmn., 1987—; free-lance cons. film prodn. and editorial pub., 1986—; creative collaborator Clifton Fadiman, Ency. Brit. Films; judge Focus Award for Screenwriting; cons. comm. Sta. KPFK-Radio, govt. Author: (with others) Directors at Work, 1970, Neo-Metamorphoses-A Cyclical Study, Comparative Transformations in Ovidian Myth and Modern Literature, 1972, Interview with Elia Kazan, 1974, Focus on Film and Theatre, Minorities in Media: A Psychoanalytic Focus, 1990. Bd. dirs. Model UN; expert witness on censorship for Los Angeles Dist. Atty.; nurses aide ARC, Children's Hosp.; former pres. Recovery Found. for Disturbed Children; ednl. cons., instr. Camarillo State Mental Hosp.; mem. Psychoanalytic Ctr. Calif. (clin. affiliate). Mem. MLA, AAUP, APA (div. 39 psychoanalysis), Women in Film, Women In Psychoanalysis, Delta Kappa Alpha, Phi Kappa Phi, Pi Beta Phi.

KRAMER, BARRY ALAN, psychiatrist; b. Phila., Sept. 9, 1948; s. Morris and Harriet (Greenberg) K.; m. Paulie Hoffman, June 9, 1974; children—Daniel Mark, Steven Philip. B.A. in Chemistry, NYU, 1970; M.D., Hahnemann Med. Coll., 1974. Resident in psychiatry Montefiore Hosp. and Med. Ctr., Bronx, N.Y., 1974-77; practice medicine specializing in psychiatry, N.Y.C., 1977-82; staff psychiatrist L.I. Jewish-Hillside Med. Ctr., Glen Oaks, N.Y., 1977-82; asst. prof. SUNY, Stony Brook, 1978-82; practice medicine specializing in psychiatry, L.A., 1982—; asst. prof. psychiatry U. So. Calif., 1982-89, assoc. prof. clin. psychiatry, 1989-94, prof. clin. psychiatry U. So. Calif. U. Hosp., 1994-98; ward chief Los Angeles County/U. So. Calif. Med. Ctr., 1982-98; med. dir. ECT, Cedars Sinai Med. Ctr., 1998—; cons. Little Neck Nursing Home (N.Y.), 1979-82, L.I. Nursing Home, 1980-82; dir. ECT U. So. Calif. Sch. Medicine, 1990. Reviewer: Am. Jour. Psychiatry, Hospital and Community Psychiatry; mem. editorial bd. Convulsive Therapy; contbr. articles to profl. jours., papers to sci. meetings. NIMH grantee, 1979-80; fellow UCLA/U. So. Calif. Long-Term Gerontology Ctr., 1985-86. Fellow Am. Psychiat. Assoc.; mem. AMA, Assn. Convulsive Therapy (editorial bd.), Soc. Biol. Psychiatry, Calif. Med. Assn., L.A. Med. Assn., Am. Assn. Geriatric Psychiatry, Gerontol. Soc. Am., So. Calif. Psychiat. Soc. (chair ETC com.). Jewish. Office: Cedars Sinai Med Ctr Thalians 223 W 8730 Alden Dr Los Angeles CA 90048 also: PO Box 5792 Beverly Hills CA 90209-5792

KRAMER, DONOVAN MERSHON, SR., newspaper publisher; b. Galesburg, Ill., Oct. 24, 1925; s. Verle V. and Sybil (Mershon) K.; m. Ruth A. Heins, Apr. 3, 1949; children: Donovan M. Jr., Diana Sue, Kara J. Kramer Cooper, Eric H. BS in Journalism, Pub. Mgmt., U. Ill., 1948. Editor, publisher, ptnr. Fairbury (Ill.) Blade, 1948-63, Forrest (Ill.) News, 1953-63; ptnr. Gibson City (Ill.) Courier, 1952-63; pres., publisher, editor Casa Grande (Ariz.) Valley Newspapers, Inc., 1963—; mng. ptnr. White Mt. Pub. Co., Show Low, Ariz., 1978—. Wrote, edited numerous articles and newspaper stories. Many award-winners including Sweepstakes award in Ill. and Ariz. Mem., chmn. Econ. Planning and Devel. Bd. State of Ariz., Phoenix, 1976-81; pres. Indsl. Devel. Authority of Casa Grande, 1977—; founding pres. Greater Casa Grande Econ. Devel. Found., exec. bd. dirs., 1982-99 (Lifetime Achievement award 1994); gov. apptd. bd. mem. Ariz. Dept. Transp., 1992-97, chmn., 1997; adv. bd. dept. journalism U. Ariz. With USAAF, WWII, PTO. Recipient Econ. Devel. plaque City of Casa Grande, 1982. Mem. Ariz. Newspapers Assn. (pres. 1980, Master Editor-Pub. 1977, Hall of Fame, 1998), Cmty. Newspapers Ariz. (pres. 1970-71), Inland Newspapers Assn., Newspapers Assn. Am., Ctrl. Ariz. Project Assn., Nat. Newspapers Assn., Greater Casa Grande C. of C. (pres. 1981-82, Hall of Fame 1991), Soc. Profl. Journalists. Republican. Lutheran. Avocations: hiking, fishing, nature studies, travel, health awareness, econ. devel., military history. Home: PO Box 15002 1125 E Cottonwood Ln Casa Grande AZ 85222-2950

KRAMER, GORDON, mechanical engineer; b. Bklyn., Aug. 1937; s. Joseph and Etta (Grossberg) K.; m. Ruth Ellen Harter, Mar. 5, 1967 (div. June 1986); children: Samuel Maurice, Leah Marie; m. Eve Burstein, Dec. 17, 1988. BS Cooper Union, 1959; MS, Calif. Inst. Tech., 1960. With Hughes Aircraft Co., Malibu, Calif., 1959-63; sr. scientist Avco Corp., Norman, Okla., 1963-64; asst. div. head Batelle Meml. Inst., Columbus, Ohio, 1964-67; sr. scientist Aerojet Electrosystems, Azusa, Calif., 1967-75; chief engr. Beckman Instrument Co., Fullerton, Calif., 1975-82; prin. scientist McDonnell Douglas Microelectronics Co., 1982-83, Kramer and Assocs., 1983-85; program mgr. Hughes Aircraft Co., 1985-96; ret., 1996; cons. Korea Inst. Tech. NSF fellow, 1959-60. Mem. IEEE. Democrat. Jewish. Home: 153 Lake Shore Dr Rancho Mirage CA 92270-4055

KRAMER, GORDON EDWARD, manufacturing executive; b. San Mateo, Calif., June 22, 1946; s. Roy Charles and Bernice Jeanne (Rones) K.; BS in Aero. Engring., San Jose State Coll., 1970; m. Christina Hodges, Feb. 14, 1970; children: Roy Charles, Charlena. Purchasing agent Am. Racing Equipment, Brisbane, Calif., 1970-71, asst. to v.p. mktg., 1971-72; founder, pres. Safety Direct Inc., hearing protection equipment, Sparks, Nev., 1972—; dir. Hodges Transp., Condor Inc.; mem. adv. bd. to pres. Truckee Meadows Community Coll., 1991—. Named Nev. Small Businessperson of Yr., Nev. Small Bus. Adminstrn., 1987, Bus. Person of Yr. Sparks Community C. of C., 1987. Mem. Am. Soc. Safety Engrs., Safety Equipment Distributors Assn., Indsl. Safety Equipment Assn., Nat. Assn. Sporting Goods Wholesalers, Nat. Sporting Goods Assn., Nev. State Amature Trapshooting Assn. (dir. 1978-79), Pacific Internat. Trapshooting Assn. (Nev. pres. 1979-80, 80-81), Nev. Mfrs. Assn. (dir. 1992—), Advanced Soccer Club (pres.1985-86). Republican. Methodist. Rotary Club (pres. Spark Club 1988-89). Office: Safety Direct Inc 56 Coney Island Dr Sparks NV 89431-6335

KRAMER, LORNE C., protective services official. BA in Pub. Mgmt., U. Redlands, 1977; MPA with honors, U. So. Calif., 1979; Advanced Exec. Cert., Calif. Law Enforcement Coll., 1987; grad., Nat. Exec. Inst., 1993. Comdr. L.A. Police Dept., 1963-91; chief police Colorado Springs (Colo.) Police Dept., 1991—; Cons., instr. drugs and gangs Nat. Inst. Justice, Office Juvenile Justice U.S. Dept. Justice. Active Colo. State DARE Adv. Bd.; bd. dirs. Ctr. Prevention Domestic Violence, Pikes Peak Mental Health. Mem. Colo. Assn. Chiefs Police (bd. dirs., major cities rep.), Internat. Assn. Chiefs Police (juvenile justice com.), Police Exec. Rsch. Forum. Office: PO Box 2169 Colorado Springs CO 80901-2169*

KRAMER, REMI THOMAS, film director; b. L.A., Mar. 7, 1935; s. Justina Magdelene Kramer; m. Agnes Marie Gallagher, Feb. 1, 1969; children: Matthew, Christiana, Timothy, Ian, Vincent, Brigitte, Danika. BA, UCLA, 1956; MA, Calif. State U., L.A., 1963. Art dir. Doyle, Dane, Bernbach Advt., L.A., 1965-66, N.W. Ayer Advt., N.Y.C., 1966-67; dir. John Urie & Assocs. Haboush Co., Hollywood, Calif., 1967-69, Columbia-Screen Gems, Hollywood, 1969-76, 79-81, 1st Asian Films, Hollywood and Manila, 1976-77, Peterson Co., Hollywood, 1977-79; freelance film dir. Hollywood, 1981-85; founder Oz Enterprises, Inc., Sandpoint, Idaho, 1985—. Author: The Legend of Lonestar Bear Series, 1988—, How Lonestar Got His Name, 1988, Soaring with Eagles, 1989, The Mystery of the Walking Cactus, 1990 (The 100 Best Products of the Yr. 1990, Best Illustration: Creativity 90, 1990); author, illustrator: Klondike Ike, 1992; writer, dir. film High Velocity, 1976; patentee children's pacifier toy; designer Lonestar Bear plush animal collection. With U.S. Army, 1958-60. Recipient Clio award, 1971, 1st Internat. Broadcast awards, 1973, Cine Golden Eagle award, 1976, The Golden Teddy award, 1990, 91. Mem. Dirs. Guild Am., Writers Guild Am. Roman Catholic. Avocations: oil painting, inventing. Office: PO Box 637 Sandpoint ID 83864-0637

KRAMER, STEVEN G., ophthalmologist; b. Chgo., Feb. 28, 1941; s. Paul and Maria Kramer; m. Anne Crystal Kramer, Dec. 26, 1961 (div.); children: Janice Lynn, Kenneth David; m. Bernadette E. Coatar, June 30, 1974 (div.); children: Daniel Steven, Susan Mary; m. Susan E. Garrett, Jan. 17, 1997. BA in Biology, U. Chgo., 1967; MD, Case Western Res. U., 1965; PhD, U. Chgo., 1971. Cert. assoc. examiner Am. Bd. Ophthalmology; lic. ophthalmologist, Calif., Wash. Instr. ophthalmology U. Chgo., 1968-71; chief of ophthalmology Madigan Army Med. Ctr., Tacoma, 1971-73; chief of ophathlmology VA Med. Ctr., San Francisco, 1973-75; prof. ophthalmology, chmn. U. Calif., San Francisco, 1975—, dir. Beckman Vision Ctr., 1988—; mem. various coms. VA Hosp., San Francisco, 1973—; mem. exec. med. bd. sch. medicine U. Calif., 1975—, mem./chmn. various coms., 1975—, mem. clin. dept. chmn. group, 1975—, mem. governing bd. continuing med. edn. program, 1984-85, mem. clin. rev. working group, 1985-86, pres.-elect med. staff, 1985, pres., 1986-88, mem. chancellor's governance group, 1986—, mem. adv. group devel. spine svcs., 1992—; v.p. That Man May See, Inc., 1975—, bd. trustees, 1975—, campaign cabinet mem. for Vision Rsch. Ctr., 1983—; sec., bd. govs. Francis Proctor Found. for Rsch. in Opthalmology, 1975—; mem. Rsch. to Prevent Blindness, Inc., N.Y., 1976—, ad hoc adv.

com., 1976-77; NIH mem. vision rsch. program com. NEI, 1978-82, chmn., 1980-82; site visit chmn. U. Wash., Seattle, 1979, Mass. Eye and Ear Infirmary, Boston, 1980, dept. neurobiology Harvard Med. Sch., Boston, 1980; mem. joint program and planning bd. sch. medicine U. Calif./Mt. Zion, 1985-88; mem. courtesy staff San Francisco Gen. Hosp.; lectr. in field. Editor, editl. bd. therapeutics rev. sect. Survey of Ophthalmology, 1977-84, diagnostic and surg. techniques sect., 1984—; sci. referee Am. Jour. Ophthalmology, 1967-81, editl. bd., 1981—; editl. bd. Ophthalmic Soc.; sci. referee Life Scis.; editor CMA Ophthalmology Epitomes, Western Jour. Medicine, 1976-77; med. adv. bd. Nat. Soc. to Prevent Blindness, 1979—; editor sect. cornea and sclera Yearbook of Ophthalmology, 1982. Mem. legis. com. for State of Calif., 1977; bd. dirs. Found. for Glaucoma Rsch., 1980—. Maj. U.S. Army, 1971-73. USPHS Spl. fellow in ophthalmologic rsch., 1970; VA Hosp. Rsch. Program grantee; NIH grantee, That Man May See grantee. Mem. AMA, ACS, Am. Acad. Ophthalmology, Am. Intra-Ocular Implant Soc., Assn. for Rsch. in Vision and Ophthalmology, Pacific Coast Oto-Ophthalmology Soc., Frederick C. Cordes Eye Soc., Calif. Med. Assn. (sci. adv. panel 1974—, adv. panel on ophthalmology subcom. for accreditation 1976-77, 78), Calif. Assn. Ophthalmology (adv. cons.), Assn. Univ. Profs. of Ophthalmology (chmn. resident placement svc. com., mem. ophthalmology resident and fellowship edn. com.), No. Calif. Soc. to Prevent Blindness (med. adv. bd.), Pan Am. Assn. Ophthalmology, Am. Congress, San Francisco Ophthal. Round Table, Rsch. to Prevent Blindness, Inc., Retinitis Pigmentosa Internat. Soc. (founding mem., sci. adv. bd.), Castroviejo Corneal Soc., Internat. Cornea Soc., Internat. Soc. Refractive Keratoplasty, Calif. Cornea Club, Ophthalmologic Hon. Soc. of Am. Ophthal. Soc., Phi Beta Kappa, Alpha Omega Alpha, Sigma Xi. Achievements include patents on surg. instrument tray; multi-compartmentalized bottle; instrument for cataract extraction through small incision; bottle closure; reminder closure; surg. instrument; internally sterile pulsatile irrigator, others. Office: U Calif Beckman Vision Ctr 10 Kirkham St # K-301 San Francisco CA 94122-3815

KRAMLICH, JOHN CHARLES, chemical engineer, educator; b. Spokane, Wash., Mar. 21, 1951; s. Fred and Sydney Jean (Snapp) K.; m. Karen Marie Moore, Dec. 22, 1975. BSChemE, Wash. State U., 1973, MS in Environ. Engring., 1975, PhDME, 1980. Grad. rsch.-tchg. asst. Wash. State U., Pullman, 1975-80; rsch. engr., dir. div. Energy and Environ. Rsch. Corp., Irvine, Calif., 1980-91; assoc. prof. mech. engring. U. Washington, Seattle, 1991-97, prof. mech. engring., 1997—; lectr. U. Calif. Irvine, 1987-89 ; bd. dirs. western states sect. Combustion Inst., Livermore, Calif., 1987—. Contbr. articles to profl. jours. Mem. Sigma Xi. Avocations: collecting rare books, western R.R. history and artifacts, bicycling. Office: U Washington Dept Mech Engring Box 352600 Seattle WA 98195-2600

KRAMNICZ, ROSANNE, freelance writer; b. Binghamton, N.Y., Mar. 26, 1948; d. Peter W. and Helena T. (Piotrowski) K.; m. Colin Douglas Anable, Dec. 10, 1990. BA/BS, Reed Coll., 1970. News columnist The Am., Deer River, Minn., 1976-78, Wester Itasca Rev., Bemidji, Minn., 1977-78; news feature writer Va. Pilot, Virginia Beach, 1979; film script rschr. Warner Bros., Phoenix, 1980-81; feature writer Bangor (Maine) Daily News, 1995; columnist, feature writer Peninsula Daily News, Port Angeles, Wash., 1990-92; freelance writer Nordland, Wash., 1992—; writing tchr. Maine Women in the Arts, Bangor, 1985, Oahu (Hawaii) Arts, 1982. Co-author: (poetry) Stylus, 1984 (Libr. award); contbr. articles and stories to numerous jours., periodicals, and other publs. Mem. Jefferson County Dem. Club, Port Townsend, Wash., 1996—, Marrowstone Island Cmty. Assn., Nordland, 1991—; vol. EMT and CPR instr. Squaw Lake (Minn.) Ambulance, 1978-79, Chimacun (Wash.) Food Bank, 1989-93. Recipient Merit award Famous Poets Soc., 1995; named Select Poetry Reader/Writer, Minn. Arts Coun., 1977. Avocations: animal activism, swimming, organic gardening, dancing, adventure. Home: 281 Nolton Rd Nordland WA 98358-9539

KRASNER, SCOTT ALLAN, physician, health facility administrator; b. Chgo., Mar. 29, 1956; s. Oscar J. and Bella (Kidder) K.; m. Terri Lee Henderson, Aut. 19, 1979; children: Jennifer Alyse, Lauren Michelle, David Andrew. BS with honors, UCLA, 1978; MD, Med. Coll. Wis., 1983; MPH, U. Ariz., 1993. Diplomate Nat. Bd. Med. Examiners, Am. Bd. Preventive Med., Am. Bd. Independent Med. Examiners. Resident Union Meml. Hosp., Balt., 1983-86, U. Ariz., Tucson, 1986-88; med. dir. clin. svcs. Helian Occupl., Tucson, 1988—; asst. med. dir. Planned Parenthood Ariz., Tucson, 1986—; clin. assoc. prof. Univ. Ariz., Tucson., 1989—; profl. adv. com. Judy's Nurses, Tucson, 1992—; chair peer rev. com. Helian Occupl., Tucson, 1995—. Chair fin. com. Stone Ave. Temple Restoration, Tucson, 1995—. Recipient Wagner award Med. Coll. Wis., 1983. Mem. Am. Coll. Occupl. and Environ. Med., Western Occupl. Med. Assn., Pima County Med. Soc., Ariz. Med. Assn. Jewish. Avocations: hiking, traveling, cruising. Home: 5901 W Broom Tail Pl Tucson AZ 85743-9691 Office: Helian Occupl 2545 E Adams St Tucson AZ 85716-3426

KRASNER, STEPHEN DAVID, political science educator; b. N.Y.C., Feb. 15, 1942; s. Jack and Lillian Rhoda (Weiss) K.; m. Joan Beverly Karliner, Sept. 3, 1967 (div. Sept. 1987); children: Daniel J., Rachel L.; m. Patricia L. Brandt, Feb. 13, 1999. BA, Cornell U., 1963; M in Internat. Affairs, Columbia U., 1967; PhD, Harvard U., 1972. Asst. prof. Harvard U., Cambridge, Mass., 1971-75; from asst. to assoc. prof. UCLA, 1976-81; prof. Stanford (Calif.) U., 1981—. Author: Sovereignty: Organized Hypocrisy, 1999. Fellow Am. Acad. Arts and Scis.; mem. Coun. on Fgn. Rels., Am. Polit. Sci. Assn., Am. Econs. Assn. Office: Stanford U Dept Polit Sci Stanford CA 94305-2044

KRAUS, JOHN WALTER, former aerospace engineering company executive; b. N.Y.C., Feb. 5, 1918; s. Walter Max Kraus and Marian Florance (Nathan) Sandor; m. Janice Edna Utter, June 21, 1947 (dec. Feb. 1981); children: Melinda Jean Kraus Peters, Kim Kohl Kraus; m. Jean Curtis, Aug. 27, 1983. BS, MIT, 1941; MBA, U. So. Calif., 1972. Registered indsl. engr., Calif. From indsl. engr. to indsl. engring. mgr. TRW, Inc., Cleve., 1941-61; spl. asst. Atomics Internat., Chatsworth, Calif., 1961-65; br. chief McDonnell Douglas Astronautics Co., Huntington Beach, Calif., 1966-74; sr. mgr. McDonnell Douglas Space Systems Co., Huntington Beach, Calif., 1983-93; pres. Kraus and DuVall, Inc., Santa Ana, Calif., 1975-83; retired, 1993; cons. Tech. Assocs. So. Calif., Santa Ana, 1974-75. Author: (handbook) Handbook of Reliability Engineering and Management, 1988. Mem. Nat. Def. Industries Assn. (formally Am. Def. Preparedness Assn., life, chmn. tech. div. 1954-57), Nat. Soc. Profl. Engrs. (life), Oasis Sailing Club (commodore 1996—). Republican. Avocations: sailing, reading, gardening. Home: 2001 Commodore Rd Newport Beach CA 92660-4307

KRAUS, MITCHELL, financial planner; b. L.A., Jan. 31, 1971; s. Arthur and Rini (Simon) K. BA, U. Pa., 1993. Fin. planner AFP Group, Inc., L.A., 1993-98. Bd. dirs. Optimist Internat. (Brentwood chpt.), 1997-98; guest lectr. L.A. Unified Sch. Dist., 1998; vol. Hugh O'Brien Youth program, L.A. Jr. C. of C. and Venice Family Clinic, L.A., 1997-98; v.p., L.A. Jr. C. of., 1998-99. Mem. Internat. Assn. Fin. Planning, Nat. Assn. Life Underwriters, Gen. Agts. and Mgrs. Assn., Am. Soc. CLU and ChFC, L.A. Jr. C. of C. (Mem. of the Month 1995). Fax: 310-207-1628. E-mail: mkraus@ix.netcom.com. Office: AFG Group Inc 12100 Wilshire Blvd Ste 500 Los Angeles CA 90025

KRAUS, PANSY DAEGLING, gemology consultant, editor, writer; b. Santa Paula, Calif., Sept. 21, 1916; d. Arthur David and Elsie (Pardee) Daegling; m. Charles Frederick Kraus, Mar. 1, 1941 (div. Nov. 1961). AA, San Bernardino Valley Jr. Coll., 1938; student Longmeyer's Bus. Coll., 1940; grad. gemologist diploma Gemological Assn. Gt. Britain, 1960, Gemological Inst. Am., 1966. Clk. Convair, San Diego, 1943-48; clk. San Diego County Schs. Publs., 1948-57; mgr. Rogers and Boblet Art-Craft, San Diego, 1958-64; part-time editorial asst. Lapidary Jour., San Diego, 1963-64, assoc. editor, 1964-69, editor, 1970-94, sr. editor, 1984-85; pvt. practice cons., San Diego, 1985—; lectr. gems, gemology local gem, mineral groups; gem & mineral club bull. editor groups. Mem. San Diego Mineral & Gem Soc., Gemol. Soc. San Diego, Gemol. Assn. Great Britain, Mineral. Soc. Am., Gemological Inst. Am., Epsilon Sigma Alpha. Author: Introduction to Lapidary, 1987; editor, layout dir.: Gem. Cutting Shop Helps, 1964, The Fundamentals of Gemstone Carving, 1967, Appalachian Mineral and Gem Trails, 1968, Practical Gem Knowledge for the Amateur, 1969, Southwest Mineral and Gem Trails, 1972, Introduction to Lapidary, 1987; revision editor Gemcraft (Quick and Leiper), 1977; contbr. articles to Lapidary jour., Keystone Mktg. catalog. Home and Office: PO Box 600908 San Diego CA 92160-0908

KRAUSE, KEITH WINSTON, quality engineer; b. Houston, Aug. 22, 1957; s. Leeland Stanford Jr. and Kay Marjorie (Keller) K.; m. Debbie Ann Richardson, Sept. 4, 1984 (div. Oct. 1988); m. Angeles Arquisola, July 3, 1991; stepchildren: Michelle Economos, Steven Economos. BS in Indsl. Tech., Tex. So. U., 1980. Draftsman B-1 divsn. Rockwell Internat., L.A., 1977-78; draftsman Rocketdyne divsn. Rockwell Internat., Canoga Park, Calif., 1978; draftsman Schlumberger Well Svcs., Houston, 1979; quality mgr. pipe design Hughes Aircraft Co., El Segundo, Calif., 1980-97; quality mgr. Irvin Aerospace Co., Santa Ana, Calif., 1997; sr. quality project engr. Fairchild Aerospace Co., Torrance, Calif., 1997—; mgr. quality engring. Krauswe, Keith, Winston. Author: Electronics Workmanship Criteria Manual, 1996. Indsl. Tech. scholar Tex. So. U., 1977. Mem. C. of C., Phi Beta Sigma (life, v.p. 1978-79). Avocations: karate, sports, landscaping, interior decorating and design, electronics, music.

KRAUSE, MARCELLA ELIZABETH MASON (MRS. EUGENE FITCH KRAUSE), retired secondary education educator; b. Norfolk, Nebr.; d. James Haskell and Elizabeth (Vader) Mason; student Northeast C.C., 1928-30; B.S., U. Neb., 1934; M.A., Columbia, 1938; postgrad. summers U. Calif. at Berkeley, 1950, 51, 65, Stanford, 1964, Creighton U., 1966, Chico (Calif.) State U., 1967; m. Eugene Fitch Krause, June 1, 1945; 1 dau., Kathryn Elizabeth. Tchr., Royal (Nebr.) pub. schs., 1930-32, Hardy (Nebr.) pub. schs., 1933-35, Omaha pub. schs., 1935-37, Lincoln Sch. of Tchrs. Coll., Columbia, 1937-38, Florence (Ala.) State Tchrs. Coll., summer 1938, Tchrs. Coll., U. Nebr., 1938-42, Corpus Christi (Tex.) pub. schs., 1942-45, Oakland (Calif.) pub. schs., 1945-83. Bd. dirs. U. Nebr. Womens Faculty Club, 1940-42; mem. Nebr. State Tchrs. Conv. Panel, 1940—; mem. U. Nebr. Reading Inst., 1940; speaker Iowa State Tchrs. Conv., 1941; reading speaker Nebr. State Tchrs. conv., 1941; lectr. Johnson County Tchrs. Inst., 1942; chmn. Reading Survey Corpus Christi pub. schs., 1943; chmn. Inservice Reading Meetings Oakland pub. schs., 1948-57. Mem. Gov.'s Adv. Commn. on Status Women Conf., San Francisco, 1966; service worker ARC, Am. Cancer Soc., United Crusade, Oakland CD; Republican precinct capt., 1964-70; v.p. Oakland Fedn. Rep. Women. Ford Found. Fund for Advancement Edn. fellow, 1955-56; scholar Stanford, 1964; Calif. Congress PTA scholar U. Calif., 1965, Norfolk (Nebr.) Hall of Success Northeast C.C., 1990; recipient award of Excellence, U. Nebr. Tchrs. Coll., 1998. Mem. Nat. Council Women, AAUW (dir.), Calif. Tchrs. Assn., Oakland Mus. Assn., U. Nebr. Alumni Assn. (Alumni Achievement award 1984), Californians for Nebr., Ladies Grand Army Republic, 1960, 1986-87 Ruth Assn., Martha Assn. (pres. East Bay chpt. 1979), Sierra DAR (regent), Eastbay DAR Regents Assn. (pres.), Nebr. Alumni Assn. (life, alumni achievement award 1984), Grand Lake Bus. and Profl. Women, Internat. Platform Assn., Eastbay Past Matrons Assn., P.E.O., Pi Lambda Theta (pres. No. Calif. chpt.), Alpha Delta Kappa. Methodist. Mem. Order Eastern Star (past matron). Contbr. articles to profl. jours. Home: 5615 Estates Dr Oakland CA 94618-2725

KRAUSE, THOMAS EVANS, record promotion and radio consultant; b. Mpls., Dec. 17, 1951; s. Donald Bernhard and Betty Ann (Nokleby) K.; m. Barbara Ann Kaufman, Aug. 17, 1974 (div. Apr. 1978); m. Nicole Michelle Purkerson, Aug. 13, 1988; children: Andrew Todd Evans, Allison Michelle. Student, Augsburg Coll., 1969-73; BA, Hastings Coll., 1975. Lic. 3d class with broadcast endorsement FCC. Air personality Sta. KHAS Radio, Hastings, Nebr., 1974-75; air personality, news dir. Sta. KWSL Radio, Sioux City, Iowa, 1975-76; asst. program dir. Sta. KISD Radio, Sioux Falls, S.D., 1976-78; music dir. Sta. KVOX Radio, Fargo, N.D., 1978; program dir. Sta. KPRQ Radio, Salt Lake City, 1978-79; air personality Sta. KIOA Radio, Des Moines, 1980; program dir., ops. mgr. Sta. KKSS Radio, Sioux Falls, 1981-83; program dir. Stas. KIYS/KBBK Radio, Boise, Idaho, 1983-87; program dir., ops. mgr. Sta. WSRZ AM/FM Radio, Sarasota, Fla., 1988-90; owner, cons. Tom Evans Mktg., Seattle, 1990—; editor., pub. Northwest Log, Seattle, 1991-96; mgr. neverMAN, 1994—; co-founder Sta. KCMR Radio, Augsburg Coll., Mpls., 1973; TV show coord./host Z-106 Hottraxx, Sarasota, 1988-90; air personality/guest disc jockey various radio stas., Pacific N.W., 1990—; host Am. Music Report. Sta. KIX-106 Radio, Canberra, Australia, 1992; instr. Sta. KGRG-FM and KENU-AM, Green River Coll., Auburn, Wash., 1994—. Contbr. articles to various trade publs., mags. Bd. judges Loyola U. Marconi Awards, Chgo., 1992-93; bd. dirs. Habitat for Humanity, Snohomish County, Wash., 1992-96, Martin Luther King Day Celebration, Sarasota County, Fla., 1989-90, Shoreline/So. County YMCA, 1992-95; dist. coord. Carter for Pres., Nebr. 1st Dist., 1975-76; hon. chairperson March of Dimes Walk Am., Sioux Falls, 1977; media vol., MC or spokesperson M.S. Soc., MDA, Am. Diabetes Assn., Human Soc., others. Mem. Free Methodist Ch. Avocations: sports, films, science fiction, photography, travel. Office: Tom Evans Mktg 16426 65th Ave W Lynnwood WA 98037-2710

KRAUSZ, STEPHEN, social services administrator, physiologist; b. Salford, England, Aug. 4, 1950; arrived in U.S., 1957; s. Ernest and Anna K.; m. Rae Vicki (Sigman) Krausz, Sept. 3, 1972; children: Joseph, Dora, Elisheva, Nili, Raphael, Gavriella. BSc, Bklyn. Coll., 1971; MSc, Hebrew U., Jerusalem, 1973, PhD, 1977. Cert. tchr., Colo. Tchg. asst. Hebrew U., 1971-77; rsch. assoc. UCLA Sch. Medicine, L.A., 1977-78; asst. prof. Howard U. Sch. Medicine, Washington, 1978-83; salesman various cos., Denver, 1983-90; asst. dir. Jewish Children's Adoption Network, Denver, 1990—. Contbr. articles to profl. jours. Mem. Am. Physiol. Soc., North American Coun. Adoptable Children, Adoptive Families Am., Mile-Hi Down Syndrome Soc., Sigma Xi. Democrat. Jewish. Avocations: hiking, nature. Office: Jewish Children's Adoption Network PO Box 16544 Denver CO 80216-0544

KRAVITZ, ELLEN KING, musicologist, educator; b. Fords, N.J., May 25, 1929; d. Walter J. and Frances M. (Prybylowski) Kokowicz; m. Hilard L. Kravitz, Jan. 9, 1972; 1 child, Julie Frances; stepchildren: Kent, Kerry, Jay. BA, Georgian Ct. Coll., 1964; MM, U. So. Calif., 1966, PhD, 1970. Tchr. 7th and 8th grade music Mt. St. Mary Acad., North Plainfield, N.J., 1949-50; cloistered nun Carmelite Monastery, Lafayette, La., 1950-61; instr. Loyola U., L.A., 1967; asst. prof. music Calif. State U., L.A., 1967-71, assoc. prof., 1971-74, prof., 1974—; founder Friends of Music at Calif. State U., L.A., 1976. Author: Music in Our Culture, 1996; Jour. Arnold Schoenberg Inst., L.A.; jour. editor Vol. I, No. 3, 1977, Vol II, No. 3, 1978; author (with others) Catalog of Schoenberg's Paintings, Drawings and Sketches; mem. editl. adv. bd. Jour. Arnold Schoenberg Inst., 1977-87. Mem. Schoenberg Centennial Com., 1974, guest lectr., 1969—. Recipient award for masters thesis U. So. Calif., 1966. Mem. Am. Musicol. Soc., L.A. County Mus. Art, L.A. Music Ctr., Mu Phi Epsilon, Pi Kappa Lambda. Home: PO Box 5360 Beverly Hills CA 90209-5360

KRAVITZ, HILARD L(EONARD), physician; b. Dayton, Ohio, June 26, 1917; s. Philip and Elizabeth (Charek) K.; divorced; children: Kent C., Kerry, Jay; m. Ellen King, Jan. 9, 1972; 1 child, Julie Frances. BA, U. Cin., 1939, MD, 1943. Lic. physician, Calif., Ohio. Resident in internal medicine Miami Valley Hosp., VA Hosp., Dayton, 1946-49; practice medicine specializing in internal medicine Dayton, 1950-54, Beverly Hills and Los Angeles, Calif., 1955—; practice medicine specializing in internal medicine and cardiology Los Angeles, 1955—; attending physician Cedars-Sinai Med. Ctr., 1955—; cons., med. dir. Adolph's Ltd., Los Angeles, 1955-74; mem. exec. com. Reiss-Davis Clinic, Los Angeles, 1966-70; chmn. pharmacy and therapeutic com. Cent City Hosp., Los Angeles, 1974-79; mem. pain commn. service Dept. Health and Human Services, Washington, 1985-86. Patentee sugar substitute, 1959, mineral-based salt, 1978. V.p. Friends of Music Calif. State U., Los Angeles, 1979-81. Served to capt. U.S. Army, 1944-46, ETO. Decorated Bronze Star with oak leaf cluster; Fourragere (France). Mem. AMA, Calif. Med. Assn., Los Angeles County Med. Assn., Am. Soc. Internal Medicine, Calif. Soc. Internal Medicine (del. 1974). Jewish. Office: 436 N Bedford Dr Ste 211 Beverly Hills CA 90210-4312

KRAVITZ, LENNY, singer, guitarist. Albums: Let Love Rule, 1989, Mama Said, 1991, Are You Gonna Go My Way, 1993 (2 Grammy nominations), Circus, 1995. Office: care CAA 9830 Wilshire Blvd Beverly Hills CA 90212-1804 also: Virgin Records 550 Madison Ave New York NY 10022-3211 also: Virgin Records 2100 Columbia Ave Santa Monica CA 90404*

KRAW, GEORGE MARTIN, lawyer, essayist; b. Oakland, Calif., June 17, 1949; s. George and Pauline Dorothy (Herceg) K.; m. Sarah Lee Kenyon, Sept. 3, 1983. BA, U. Calif., Santa Cruz, 1971; student, Lenin Inst., Moscow, 1971; MA, U. Calif., Berkeley, 1974, JD, 1976. Bar: Calif. 1976, U.S. Dist. Ct. (no. dist.) Calif. 1976, U.S. Supreme Ct. 1980, D.C., 1992. Pvt. practice, 1976—; ptnr. Kraw & Kraw, San Jose, 1988—; Mem. ABA, Nat. Assn. Health Lawyers, Inter-Am. Bar Assn., Union Internationale des Avocats. Office: Kraw & Kraw 333 W San Carlos St Ste 1050 San Jose CA 95110-2735

KRAYE, SHERWIN HOWARD, engineering executive; b. Chgo., Apr. 3, 1941; s. Philip Morton and Frances (Binder) K.; m. Saundra Jean Schneier, June 30, 1963 (div. Aug. 1982); children: Tamra Lynn, Kevin Michael; m. Harriet Carol Svirsky, July 9, 1987. BS in Engring. Sci., USAF Acad., 1963; MS in Indsl. Engring., Purdue U., 1965; MBA, Pepperdine U., Malibu, Calif., 1986. Prof. USAF Acad., Colorado Springs, Colo., 1968-69; program mgr. Teledyne Systems, Northridge, Calif., 1969-72; pres. Plast-Alum Mfg. Inc., Burbank, Calif., 1972-82, Conserdyne Corp., Valencia, Calif., 1982-88; gen. mgr. Benhar Mills, L.A., 1988-90; v.p., gen. mgr. Cable Tech. Group, Albuquerque, N.Mex., 1990-92; pres. Santa Fe Techs. Inc., Albuquerque, 1992—; chmn. bd. dirs. Calif. State Energy Bank, Sacramento, 1982-84; mem. adv. bd. Alliance Transp. Rsch., Albuquerque, 1992-96, N.Mex. Congestion Mgmt./Air Quality Bd., 1994-95. Contbr. articles to profl. jours. campaign advisor Fullerton for Gov., Santa Fe, 1998. Capt. USAF, 1963-68. Mem. Intell Transp. Systems. Republican. Jewish. Avocations: white water rafting, skiing, reading, teaching. Home: 1121 Salamanca St NW Albuquerque NM 87107-5625 Office: Santa Fe Techs Inc 2021 Girard Blvd SE Bldg 2 Albuquerque NM 87106-3100

KREBS, EDWIN GERHARD, biochemistry educator; b. Lansing, Iowa, June 6, 1918; s. William Carl and Louise Helena (Stegeman) K.; m. Virginia Frech, Mar. 10, 1945; children: Sally, Robert, Martha. AB in Chemistry, U. Ill., 1940; MD, Washington U., St. Louis, 1943, DSc (hon.), 1995; DSc honoris causa, U. Geneva, 1979; hon. degree, Med. Coll. Ohio, 1993; DSc (hon.), U. Ind., 1993, U. Ill., 1995; D honoris causa, U. Nat. De Cuyo, 1993. Intern, asst. resident Barnes Hosp., St. Louis, 1944-45; rsch. fellow biol. chemistry Wash. U., St. Louis, 1946-48; prof., chmn. dept. biol. chemistry Sch. Medicine U. Calif., Davis, 1968-76; from asst. prof. to prof. biochemistry U. Wash., Seattle, 1948-66, prof., chmn. dept. pharmacology, 1977-83, prof. biochemistry and pharmacology, 1984-91; investigator, sr. investigator Howard Hughes Med. Inst., Seattle, 1983-90, sr. investigator emeritus, 1991—; mem. Phys. Chemistry Study Sect. NIH, 1963-68, Biochemistry Test Com. Nat. Bd. Med. Examiners, 1968-71, rsch. com. Am. Heart Assn., 1970-74, bd. sci. counselors Nat. Inst. Arthritis, Metabolism and Digestive Diseases, NIH, 1979-84, Internat. Bd. Rev., Alberta Heritage Found. for Med. Rsch., 1986, external adv. com. Weis Ctr. for Rsch., 1987-91; mem. subgroup interconvertible enzymes IUB Spl. Interest Group Metabolic Regulation; internat. adv. bd. Advances in Second Messenger Phosphoprotein Rsch.; external adv. com. Cell Therapeutics Inc., Seattle; adv. bd. Kinetek, Vancouver, B.C. Mem. editorial bd. Jour. Biol. Chemistry, 1965-70; mem. editorial adv. bd. Biochemistry, 1971-76; mem. editorial and adv. bd. Molecular Pharmacology, 1972-77; assoc. editor Jour. Biol. Chemistry, 1971-93; mem. internat. adv. bd. Advances in Cyclic Nucleotide Rsch., 1972—; editorial advisor Molecular and Cellular Biochemistry, 1987—. Recipient Nobel Prize in Medicine or Physiology, 1992, Gairdner Found. award, Toronto, 1978, J.J. Berzelius lectureship, Karolinska Institutet, 1982, George W. Thorn award for sci. excellence, 1983, Sir Frederick Hopkins Meml. lectureship, London, 1984, Rsch. Achievement award Am. Heart Assn., Anaheim, Calif., 1987, 3M Life Scis. award FASEB, New Orleans, 1989, Albert Lasker Basic Med. Rsch. award, 1989, CIBA-GEIGY-Drew award Drew U., 1991, Steven C. Beering award, Ind. U., 1991, Welch award in chemistry Welch Found., 1991, Louisa Gross Horwitz award Columbia U., 1989, Alumni Achievement award Coll. Liberal Arts and Scis. U. Ill., 1992, Kaul Found. award for excellence, 1996; John Simon Guggenheim fellow, 1959, 66. Mem. NAS, Am. Soc. Biol. Chemists (pres. 1986, ednl. affairs com. 1965-68, councillor 1975-78), Am. Acad. Arts and Scis., Am. Soc. Pharmacology and Exptl. Therapeutics. Achievements include lifelong study of the protein phosphorylation process. Office: U Wash Dept Pharmacology PO Box 357370 Seattle WA 98195-7370

KREBS, JENNIFER AMANDA, city administrator; b. Ann Arbor, Mich., Nov. 13, 1968; d. Robert David and Judy Ellen (Eldred) Tarte; m. Theodore Wesley Folkerth, Apr. 15, 1990 (div. Dec. 1994); 1 child, Timothy Alexander; m. Sean Krebs, Dec. 21, 1996. BA with honors, UCLA, 1989; MA, McGill U., 1994. Switching supr. Sta. KBLR-TV, Las Vegas, 1994-95; prodn. technician TVW, Olympia, Wash., 1995-96; TV coord. City of Enumclaw, Wash., 1997—; chair subcom. Regional Govt. Access Group, 1997—. Pres., bd. dirs. Kid's Base, Enumclaw, 1997—, mem. Kid's Voting, Enumclaw, 1997—. Grant Dobson Entrepreneurial Group, 1992; Max Bell fellowship McGill U., 1991, Regents fellowship UCLA Regents, 1985-89. Mem. Alliance for Cmty. Media, Phi Beta Kappa. Home: PO Box 1237 Enumclaw WA 98022-1237 Office: City of Enumclaw 1339 Griffin Ave Enumclaw WA 98022-3091

KREDLO, THOMAS ANDREW, real estate appraiser; b. East Chicago, Ind., Jan. 27, 1952; s. Raymond Vincent and Marna Maude (Smith) K. BS, Ind. U., 1977. Loan officer Michigan City (Ind.) Savs. and Loan, 1978-81; assoc. appraiser Meyer & Assocs., Hillsboro, Oreg., 1981-85, Lamb, Hanson, Lamb, Seattle, 1985-93; staff appraiser Strategic Mortgage Svcs., Denver, 1993-96, Alpha Appraisal & Consulting, Renton, Wash., 1997—. Author of short stories. Mem. Ptarmigan Mountaineering Club. Democrat. Roman Catholic. Avocations: mountaineering, bicycling, walking, back packing. Office: Alpha Appraisal & Consulting 16711 163rd Pl SE Renton WA 98058-8273

KREGER, MELVIN JOSEPH, lawyer; b. Buffalo, Feb. 21, 1937; s. Philip and Bernice (Gerstman) K.; m. Patricia Anderson, July 1, 1955 (div. 1963), children: Beth Barbour, Arlene Roux; m. Renate Hochleitner, Aug. 15, 1975. JD, Mid-valley Coll. Law, 1978; LLM in Taxation, U. San Diego, 1988. Bar: Calif. 1978, U.S. Dist. Ct. (cen. dist.) Calif. 1979, U.S. Tax Ct. 1979, U.S. Supreme Ct. 1995; cert. specialist in probate law, trust law and estate planning law, taxation law, Calif. Life underwriter Met. Life Ins. Co., Buffalo, 1958-63; bus. mgr. M. Kreger Bus. Mgmt., Sherman Oaks, Calif., 1963-78, enrolled agt., 1971—; pvt. practice North Hollywood, Calif., 1978—. Mem. Nat. Assn. Enrolled Agts., Calif. Soc. Enrolled Agts., State Bar Calif., L.A. Bar Assn., San Fernando Valley Bar Assn. (probate sect., tax sect.). Jewish. Avocations: computers, travel. Office: 11424 Burbank Blvd North Hollywood CA 91601-2301

KREILKAMP, ANN RENEE, philosopher, magazine editor; b. San Antonio, Dec. 19, 1942; d. Bernard Leo and Renee Marian (Rosenberger) K.; children: Sean Cudmore, Colin Cudmore; m. Jeffrey Scott Joel, Aug. 22, 1947. BA, Cath. U. Am., 1964; PhD, Boston U., 1972. Tchr. New Coll. Calif., Sausalito, 1972-73; cons., tchr., conf. presenter in astrology Idaho, Wyo., Wash., Calif., 1976-96; founder, editor, publ. Crone Chronicles: A Jour. of Conscious Aging, Jackson, Wyo., 1989—; Contbr. over 50 articles to astrol. mags., 1985-95; founder, publ. 2 cmty. mags., 1978-83; editor: What Matters, 1998. Office: Crone Corp PO Box 81 Kelly WY 83011

KREINBERG, PENELOPE PETTIT, counselor; b. N.Y.C., Aug. 3, 1946; d. William Dutton and Carole (Earle) P.; m. Robert Lee Kreinberg, July 4, 1968; children: Joshua Adam, Patricia Dawn, Sarah Lynn. BA in Psychology/Sociology/Anthropology, Cornell U., 1968; MA in Counseling Psychology, Lewis & Clark Coll., 1993. Portland (Oreg.) chair Candlelighters for Children, 1982, 87, Oreg. pres., 1988-90; instr., counselor Clackama C.C., Portland, 1993—; pvt. practice counselor Portland, 1994-96; bd. dirs. Candlelighters for Children, Oreg., 1984-96; bd. dirs. Candlelighters Childhood Cancer Found., Washington, 1990-96. Bd. dirs. Camp Ukandu, Am. Cancer Found., Portland, 1985-89, mem. adv. bd. svc. and rehab. com., 1987-89; mem. local sch. adv. com. Grant H.S. PTA, Portland, 1984-88, 92-96; vol. U.S. Peace Corps, Colombia, 1968-70; vol. facilitator Dougy Ctr. for Grieving Children, Portland, 1994-96; vol. Ronald McDonald House, Portland, 1988-89; People to People Citizen Ambassador to South Africa, 1996; vol. ARC, Portland, 1998— Recipient Cmty. Svc. award J. C. Penney, 1990, Met. Family Svc. award City of Portland, 1988. Mem. Nat. Counseling Assn., Oreg. Counseling Assn., Am. Assn. Mental Health Counselors,

Oreg. Assn. Aging and Devel., Assn. for Psychol. Type, Am. Assn. Women in C.C.s, Oreg. Career Devel. Assn., Phi Beta Kappa, Delta Gamma. Democrat. Episcopalian. Avocations: fine arts, hiking, outdoor activities. Home: 3145 NE 20th Ave Portland OR 97212-2410

KREISSMAN, STARRETT, librarian; b. N.Y.C., Jan. 4, 1946; d. Bernard and Shirley (Relis) K.; m. David Dolan, Apr. 13, 1985; 1 child, Sonya. BA, Grinnell Coll., 1967; MLS, Columbia U., 1968. Asst. circulation libr. Columbia U., N.Y.C., 1968-70; sci. libr. N.Y. Pub. Libr., N.Y.C., 1970-71; outreach libr. Stanislaus County Free Libr., Modesto, Calif., 1971-73, Oakdale libr., 1974-79, acquisitions libr., 1979-85, br. supr., 1985-92, county libr., 1992—. Writer book revs. Stanislaus County Commn. on Women. Mem. ALA, Pub. Libr. Assn., Calif. Libr. Assn. (legis. com. 1993-95), Rotary. Office: Stanislaus County Free Libr 1500 I St Modesto CA 95354-1120

KREITZBERG, FRED CHARLES, construction management company executive; b. Paterson, N.J., June 1, 1934; s. William and Ella (Bohen) K.; m. Barbara Braun, June 9, 1957; children: Kim, Caroline, Allison, Bruce, Catherine. BSCE, Norwich U., 1957, DS in Bus. Adminstrn. (hon.), 1994. Registered profl. engr., Ala., Alaska, Ariz., Ark., Calif., Colo., Del., D.C., Fla., Ga., Idaho, Ill., Ind., Iowa, Kans., Ky., Md., Mass., Minn., Miss., Mo., Nebr., Nev., N.H., N.J., N.Mex., N.Y., Ohio, Okla., Oreg., S.C., S.D., Tenn., Va., Vt., Wash., W.Va., Wis., Wyo. Asst. supt. Turner Constrn. Co., N.Y.C., 1957; project mgr. Project Mercury RCA, N.J., 1958-63; schedule cost mgr. Catalytic Constrn. Co., Pa., 1963-65, 65—; cons. Meridien Engring., 1965-68; prin. MDC Systems Corp., 1968-72; chmn., CEO O'Brien-Kreitzberg Inc., San Francisco, 1972—; lectr. Stanford (Calif.) U., U. Calif., Berkeley. Author: Crit. Path Method Scheduling for Contractor's Mgmt. Handbook, 1971; tech. editor Constrn. Inspection Handbook, 1972; contbr. articles to profl. jours. Bd. dirs. Partridge Soc.; chmn. bd. trustees Norwich U. 2d lt. C.E., U.S. Army, 1957-58. Recipient Disting. Alumnus award Norwich U., 1987, Crystal Vision award Nat. Assn. Women in Constrn., 1997; named Boss of Yr., Nat. Assn. Women in Constrn., 1987; Kreitzberg Amphitheatre named in his honor, 1987, also Kreitzberg Libr. at Norwich U., 1992; Bay Area Discovery Mus.-Birthday Room and Snack Bar named in honor of Kreitzberg family, 1989. Fellow ASCE (Constrn. Mgr. of Yr. 1982); mem. Am. Arbitration Assn., Constrn. Mgmt. Assn. Am. (founding, bd. dirs.), Soc. Am. Value Engrs., Community Field Assn., Ross Hist. Soc., N.J. Soc. Civil Engrs., N.J. Soc. Profl. Planners, Project Mgmt. Inst., Constrn. Industry Pres. Forum. Avocations: running, bicycling, tropical fish. Home: 19 Spring Rd PO Box 1200 Ross CA 94957-1200 Office: O'Brien-Kreitzberg Inc 50 Fremont St Fl 24 San Francisco CA 94105-2230

KREJCI, ROBERT HARRY, non-profit organizations development consultant; b. Chgo., June 4, 1913; s. John and Johanna (Tischer) K.; m. Marian Hallock, Mar. 28, 1941 (dec. Aug. 1986); 1 child, Susan Ann Krejci Stevens. BS in Forestry with honors, Mich. State U., 1940. Dist. exec. Boy Scouts Am., Chgo., 1940-48, asst. scout exec., 1948-50; scout exec. Boy Scouts Am., Herrin, Ill., Huntington, W.Va., 1950-65; devel. cons. The Cumerford Corp., Kansas City, 1965-73; dir. western divsn. The Cumerford Corp., Ft. Lauderdale, Fla., 1974-78; devel. cons. in pvt. practice, San Diego, 1978-90; co-founder, pres. Philanthropy Coun., San Diego, 1987-93; dir. World War II Farm Labor Camp, State of Ill., 1942, 43. Author: How to Succeed in Fund Raising For Your Non-Profit Organization, 1989. Vol. organizer United Way, various cities, Ill., 1955, 56. Recipient George Washington medal Freedoms Found. at Valley Forge, 1953; named Vol. of Yr. Philanthropy Coun., 1996, Exemplar, Rancho Bernardo Rotary Found., 1995. Mem. Rotary Internat. (Paul Harris fellow). Avocations: travel, gardening, writing, collecting humor. Home: 16566 Casero Rd San Diego CA 92128-2743

KREJCI, ROBERT HENRY, aerospace engineer; b. Shenandoah, Iowa, Nov. 15, 1943; s. Henry and Marie Josephine (Kubicek) K.; m. Carolyn R. Meyer, Aug. 21, 1967; children—Christopher S., Ryan D. B.S. with honors in Aerospace Engring., Iowa State U., Ames, 1967, M.Aerospace Engring., 1971. Commd. 2d lt. U.S. Air Force, 1968, advanced through grades to capt., 1978; lt. col. Res.; served with systems command Space Launch Vehicles Systems Program Office, Advanced ICBM program officer; research assoc. U.S. Dept. Energy Lawrence Livermore lab.; dept. mgr. advanced tech. programs Strategic div. Thiokol Corp., 1978-84, mgr. space programs, 1984-85, mgr. Navy advanced programs, 1986—. Decorated A.F. commendation medal, Nat. Def. Service medal, Meritorious Svc. medal. Fellow AIAA. Home: 885 N 300 E Brigham City UT 84302-1310 Office: Thiokol Propulsion PO Box 707 Brigham City UT 84302-0707

KREMPEL, RALF HUGO BERNHARD, author, artist, art gallery owner; b. Groitzsch, Saxony, Germany, June 5, 1935; came to U.S., 1964; s. Curt Bernhard and Liesbeth Anna Margarete (Franz) K.; m. Barbara von Eberhardt, Dec. 21, 1967 (div. 1985); 1 child, Karma. Student, Wood and Steel Constrn. Coll., Leipzig, German Democratic Republic, 1955. Steel constructor worldwide, 1955-73; co-owner San Francisco Pvt. Mint, 1973-81; prin. artist San Francisco Painter Magnate, 1982—; dir. Stadtgalerie Wiprechtsburg Groitzsch, Germany, 1991—, Museumsgalerie am Markt, Groitzsch, 1994—. Exhbns. Centre Internat. d'Art Contemporain, 1985, Art Contemporain Cabinet des Dessins, 1986, Galerie Salammbo-Atlante, 1987 and others, Retrospective Mus.-gallery Borna, 1993; inventor, designer Visual Communication System, utilizing colors instead of letters to depict and transmit messages; 6 Order of the Universe registrations Libr. of Congress, Washington, 1991—. Avocations: art research, photography. Home: 2400 Pacific Ave San Francisco CA 94115-1280 Office: San Francisco Painter Magnate Rincon Ctr San Francisco CA 94119-3368 also: Brühl 2, 04539 Groitzsch Germany

KREMPEL, ROGER ERNEST, public works management consultant; b. Waukesha, Wis., Oct. 8, 1926; s. Henry and Clara K.; m. Shirley Ann Gray, June 16, 1948; children: John, Sara, Peter. Student Ripon Coll., 1944, Stanford U., 1945; BCE, U. Wis.-Madison, 1950. Registered profl. engr., Wis., Colo.; registered land surveyor, Wis. Asst. city engr., Manitowoc, Wis., 1950-51; city engr. dir. pub. works, Janesville, Wis., 1951-75; dir. water utilities, pub. works Ft. Collins, Colo., 1975-84; dir. natural resources, streets and stormwater utilities, Ft. Collins, 1984-88; faculty affiliate Internat. Sch. for Water Resources, Colo. State U.; pub. works mgmt. cons., 1988—; lectr. various univ., coll., nat. confs. and seminars. Contbr. numerous articles to profl. pubs. Past pres. bd. Janesville YMCA. With U.S. Army, 1944-46. Recipient numerous tech. and profl. awards, Distin. Svc. citation U. Wis. Coll. Engring., 1989, Outstanding Leadership and Cmty. Devel. award Janesville C. of C., 1972. Fellow ASCE (life, Gov. Civil Engr. award 1984, Wis. Oustanding Civil Engring. Achievement award 1970); mem. NSPE, ASCE (Mgmt. award 1990), Am. Water Works Assn. (life), Am. Pub. Works Assn. (life mem., past pres. Colo. and Wis. chpts., past mem. rsch. found., Man of Yr. 1971, Nichols award 1984, Swearingen award 1988), Pub. Works Hist. Soc. (pres. 1993-95), Wis. Soc. Profl. Engrs. (past pres.), Am. Acad. Environ. Engrs. (diplomate, 1982-91), Colo. Engrs. Coun. (pres. 1990-91, honor award 1989).

KRENDL, CATHY STRICKLIN, lawyer; b. Paris, Tex., Mar. 14, 1945; d. Louis and Margaret Helen (Young) S.; m. James R. Krendl, July 5, 1969; children: Peggy, Susan, Anne. BA summa cum laude, North Tex. State U., 1967; JD cum laude, Harvard U., 1970. Bar: Alaska 1970, Colo. 1972. Atty. Hughes, Thorsness, Lowe Gantz & Clark, Anchorage, 1970-71; adj. prof. U. Colo. Denver Ctr., 1972-73; from asst. prof. to prof. law, dir. bus planning program U. Denver, 1973-83; ptnr. Krendl, Horowitz & Krendl, Denver, 1983—. Author: Business Organizations, 1997, Colorado Business Corporation Act Deskbook, 1998; editor: Colorado Methods of Practice, vols. 1983-98, Closely Held Corporations in Colorado, vols. 1-3, 1981; contbr. articles to profl jours. Named Disting. Alumna North Tex. State U., 1985. Mem. Colo. Bar Assn. (bd. govs. 1982-86, 88-91, chmn. securities subsect. 1986, bus. law sect. 1988-89, Professionalism award), Denver Bar Assn. (pres. 1989-90). Avocation: reading. Home: 370 17th St Ste 5350 Denver CO 80202-5655

KREPS, DAVID MARC, economist, educator; b. N.Y.C., Oct. 18, 1950; s. Saul Ian and Sarah (Kaskin) Kreps; m. Anat Ruth Admati, Jan. 4, 1984; children: Tamar, Oren, Avner. AB, Dartmouth Coll., 1972; MA, PhD, Stanford U., 1975. Asst. prof. Stanford U., 1975-78, assoc. prof., 1978-80, prof., 1980-84, Holden prof., 1984—; rsch. officer U. Cambridge, Eng., 1978-79, fellow commoner Churchill Coll., Cambridge, 1978-79; vis. prof. Yale U., New Haven, 1982, Harvard U., Cambridge, Mass., 1983, U. Paris, 1985; vis. prof. U. Tel Aviv, 1989-90, sr. prof. by spl. apppintment, 1991—. Author: Notes on the Theory of Choice, 1988, A Course in Microeconomic Theory, 1990, Game Theory and Economic Modelling, 1990; co-editor Econometrica, 1984-88. Alfred P. Sloan Found. fellow, 1983, John S. Guggenheim fellow, 1988. Fellow Econometric Soc.; mem. Am. Econ. Assn. (J.B. Clark medal 1989), Am. Acad. Arts and Scis., Nat. Acad. Scis. Office: Stanford U Grad Sch of Bus Stanford CA 94305-5015

KRESA, KENT, aerospace executive; b. N.Y.C., Mar. 24, 1938; s. Helmy and Marjorie (Boutelle) K.; m. Joyce Anne McBride, Nov. 4, 1961; 1 child, Kiren. BSAA, MIT, 1959, MSAA, 1961, EAA, 1966. Sr. scientist rsch. and advanced devel. divsn. AVCO, Wilmington, Mass., 1959-61; staff mem. MIT Lincoln Lab., Lexington, Mass., 1961-68; dep. dir. strategic tech. office Def. Advanced Rsch. Projects Agy., Washington, 1968-73; dir. tactical tech. office Def. Advanced Rsch. Project Agy., Washington, 1973-75; v.p., mgr. Rsch. & Tech. Ctr. Northrop Corp., Hawthorne, Calif., 1975-76; v.p., gen. mgr. Ventura divsn. Northrop Corp., Newbury Park, Calif., 1976-82; group v.p. Aircraft Group Northrop Corp., L.A., 1982-86, sr. v.p. tech. devel. and planning, 1986-87, pres., COO, 1987-90; chmn. bd., pres., CEO Northrop Grumman Corp., L.A., 1990—; bd. dirs. John Tracy Clinic.; mem. Chief of Naval Ops. exec. panel Washington, Def. Sci. Bd., Washington, DNA New Alternatives Working Group, L.A., Dept. Aeronautics and Astronautics Corp. Vis. Com. MIT. Bd. dirs. John Tracy Clinic for the Hearing-Impaired, W.M. Keck Found., L.A. World Affairs Coun.; bd. govs. L.A. Music Ctr. Recipient Henry Webb Salsbury award MIT, 1959, Arthur D. Flemming award, 1975, Calif. Industrialist of Yr. Calif. Mus. of Sci. and Industry and the Calif. Mus. Found., 1996, Bob Hope Disting. Citizen award Nat. Security Indsl. Assn., 1996; Sec. of Def. Meritorious Civilian Svc. medal, 1975, USN Meritorious Pub. Svc. citation, 1975, Exceptional Civilian Svc. award USAF, 1987. Fellow AIAA; mem. Aerospace Industries Assn. (past bd. govs.), Naval Aviation Mus. Found., Navy League U.S., Soc. Flight Test Engrs., Assn. U.S. Army, Nat. Space Club, Am. Def. Preparedness Assn., L.A. Country Club. Office: Northrop Grumman Corp 1840 Century Park E Los Angeles CA 90067-2101*

KRETZMAR, MARY LYNN, vocational education and sign language interpreter, educator; b. Hawthorne, Calif., Sept. 13, 1957; d. Hugh Leeroy and Joell (Morgan) K. Cert. in sign lang. interpretation, El Camino Coll., Torrance (Calif.) Unified Sch. Dist., 1993. Sec. Casio-PhoneMate, Inc., Torrance, 1991-96; sign lang. interpreter El Camino Coll., 1993—, instrnl. ednl. aide, 1996—; vocat. specialist transition program Manhattan Beach Unified Sch. Dist., Torrance, Manhattan Beach, Calif., 1996—. Poet (collection) Snapshot, 1996; contbr. poetry to lit. publs.; editor newsletter Hands of Friendship, El Camino Coll., 1991-92. Supporter AIDS Project L.A., 1993—, Best Buddies, 1996—, Father Flannagan's Home for Boys, 1996—, Paralyzed Vets. of Am., 1996—. Avocations: gardening, cross-stitch, crocheting, music, church.

KREUTZBERG, DAVID W., lawyer; b. Edwardsville, Ill., May 20, 1953. BA summa cum laude, Ariz. State U., 1975, JD magna cum laude, 1978. Bar: Ariz. 1978, U.S. Dist. Ct. (Ariz. dist.) 1978. Law clk. to Hon. William E. Eubank Ariz. Ct. Appeals, Phoenix, 1978-79; ptnr. Squire, Sanders & Dempsey LLP, Phoenix, 1989. Mem. ABA (mem. bus. law sect.), State Bar Ariz., Maricopa County Bar Assn., Phi Beta Kappa. Office: Squire Sanders & Dempsey LLP Two Renaissance Sq 40 N Central Ave Ste 2700 Phoenix AZ 85004-4424*

KREVANS, JULIUS RICHARD, university administrator, physician; b. N.Y.C., May 1, 1924; s. Sol and Anita (Makovetsky) K.; m. Patricia N. Abrams, May 28, 1950; children: Nita, Julius R., Rachel, Sarah, Nora Kate. B.S. Arts and Scis, N.Y. U., 1943, M.D., 1946. Diplomate: Am. Bd. Internal Med. Intern, then resident Johns Hopkins Med. Sch. Hosp., mem. faculty, until 1970, dean acad. affairs, 1969-70; physician in chief Balt. City Hosp., 1963-69; prof. medicine U. Calif., San Francisco, 1970—, dean Sch. Medicine, 1971-82, chancellor, 1982-93, chancellor emeritus, 1993—. Contbr. articles on hematology, internal med. profl. jours. Served with M.C. AUS, 1948-50. Mem. A.C.P., Assn. Am. Physicians. Office: U Calif San Francisco Sch Medicine San Francisco CA 94143-0296

KRIEG, DOROTHY LINDEN, soprano, performing artist, educator; b. Moline, Ill.; d. Carl Victor Lundin and Maybelle Eugenia (Bohman) Linden; m. Eugene D. Krieg, Nov. 24, 1949; m. John C. Ludke, Feb. 1, 1996. Studied piano, voice, pvt. instrs., from 1932; student, Am. Conservatory, 1938-44; studied, opera and oratorio with numerous Maestri. Tchr. Midwestern Conservatory, Chgo., 1947-49; pvt. practice teaching singing Chgo., 1952-94, L.A., 1994—; past treas. Nat. Assn. Tchrs. Singing Chgo. Began singing career in vaudeville at age 4; later appeared with Midwest Opera Co.; artist Moments of Opera show, Colosimo's and on TV; appearances in Chgo. area include supper clubs Singer's Rendevous, Caruso's, Singing Sorinis, Pucci's, Black Forest in Three Lakes, Wis., Northernaire Showboat in Three Lakes, Wis., ballrooms Drake Hotel, Conrad Hilton Hotel, Blackstone Hotel, others, polit. convs., USO shows; concert artist Chgo. Symphony Orch., from 1950's appearing at Orch. Hall, on tour and on TV with condrs. Fritz Reiner, Rafael Kubelic, George Schick, others; soprano soloist ann. performances Messiah, Marshall Field Choral Soc., 27 yrs., Bryn Mawr Community Ch., Chgo., 17 yrs., Chgo. Temple, 10 yrs., other chs. and temples throughout Chgo.; soloist major oratorio socs. including Swedish Choral Club, Apollo Club, Rockefeller Chapel Choir, Collegium Musicum, St. Louis Bach Soc., Cornell Coll., Calvin Coll., Testor Chorus, Rockford, Ill.; soloist U.S. premieres Vivaldi's Gloria and Handel's Psalm 112, Orch. Hall with Chgo. Symphony; female soloist Chgo. Swedish Glee Club, Chgo. Swedish Male Chorus, Schwaebisher Saengerbund, Chgo. Master Bakers Chorus, Combined German Male Choruses at Civic Opera Ho., others; tchr. voice prodn., phrasing, stage deportment, coach opera, oratorio, English, French and Italian lit., German lieder. 1st pl. winner West Side div. Chicagoland Music Festival Contest, 1939; named Western Springs Music Club scholar. Mem. Seal Watch (Can., Magdalen Islands), Greenpeace, Internat. Fund Animal Welfare, Internat. Soc. Animal Rights, People for Ethical Treatment of Animals, Whale Adoption Project. Avocations: cats, gemology, stero and video recording, Swedish culture. Address: 15459 Celtic St Mission Hills CA 91345-1303

KRIEGER, DAVID MALCOLM, peace foundation executive, lawyer; b. L.A., Mar. 27, 1942; s. Herbert D. and Sybil Krieger; m. Carolee Kehaulani Gamble, Aug. 14, 1967; children: Jeffrey, Jonathon, Mara. BA, Occidental Coll., 1963; MA, U. Hawaii, 1967, PhD, 1968; JD cum laude, valedictorian, Santa Barbara Coll. Law, 1987. Bar: Calif., 1987. Asst. prof. polit. sci. U. Hawaii, Honolulu, 1969-70; asst. prof. internat. rels. San Francisco State U., 1970-72; researcher Ctr. for Study of Dem. Instns., Santa Barbara, 1972-74; project coord. Found. Reshaping the Internat. Order, Rotterdam, The Netherlands, 1980-81; pres. Nuclear Age Peace Found., Santa Barbara, 1982—. Editor: The Tides of Change, Peace, Pollution and Potential of The Oceans, 1974, Disarmament and Development, 1980, Waging Peace in the Nuclear Age, Ideas for Action, 1988, Waging Peace II, Vision and Hope for the 21st Century, 1992, Speaking of Peace, Quotations on War, Peace and the Human Spirit, 1995, Nuclear Age Peace Calendar, Days of Remembrance, Days of Renewal, 1996, Splitting the Atom, A Chronology of the Nuclear Age, 1996; author: The Oceans: A Common Heritage, 1975, Countdown for Survival, 1981, Disarmament and Development: The Challenge of the Control and Management of Dual-Purpose Technologies, 1981, Preventing Accidental Nuclear War, 1984, A Magna Carta for the Nuclear Age, 1995, Peace Is a Path, 1996, Nuclear Weapons and the World Court, 1998; contbr. articles to profl. publs. 2d lt. U.S. Army, 1968-69. Recipient Bronze medal Hungarian Engrs. for Peace, 1995, Peace award War and Peace Found., 1996, Big Canvas award Santa Barbara Mag., 1996, Peace and Culture award Soka Gakkai Internat., 1997, Highest Honor award Soka U., 1997. Office: Nuclear Age Peace Found 1622 Anacapa St Santa Barbara CA 93101-1910

KRIEGER, WILLIAM CARL, English language educator; b. Seattle, Mar. 21, 1946; s. Robert Irving Krieger and Mary (McKibben) Durfee; m. Patricia Kathleen Callow, Aug. 20, 1966; children: Richard William, Robert Irving III, Kathleen Elizabeth. BA in English, Pacific Luth. U., 1968, MA in Humanities, 1973; PhD in Am. Studies, Wash. State U., 1986. Instr. Pierce Coll., Tacoma, 1969-98; ombudsman, 1995-98; chmn. English dept. Pierce Coll., Tacoma, 1973-79, 81-84, 95-98, chmn. humanities divsn., 1979-81, prof. English, 1969—; adj. prof. hist. and English Cen. Wash. State U., 1980; vis. prof. hist. and English So. Ill. U., Carbondale, 1981-84, Pacific Luth. U., Tacoma, 1981-84; head coach Gig Harbor H.S. Wrestling, 1990-95; dean acad. edn. Walla Walla Comm. Coll., 1998—; bd. dirs. Thoreau Cabin Project, Tacoma, 1979—; project dir. Campus Wash. Centennial Project, Tacoma, 1984-89; spl. cons. Clover Park Sch. Dist., Tacoma, 1985; lang. arts cons. Inst. for Citizen Edn. in Law, U. Puget Sound Law Sch., 1990. Author: A Necessary Evil? Sports and Violence, 1998. Apptd. Wash. State Centennial Commn., Constns. Com., Pierce Couny Centennial Com.; mem. bd. dirs. Tacoma Symphony; choir dir. Rosendale Ch.; mem. Peninsula Comty. Chorus, 1993-97, pres., 1995; dir. Peninsula Madrigal Singers, 1995-97. Recipient Disting. Achievement award Wash. State Centennial Commn., 1989, Outstanding Achievement award Pierce County Centennial Commn., 1989, Centennial Alumni recognition Pacific Luth. U., 1990; named Outstanding Tchr. Nat. Inst. Staff and Orgnl. Devel., 1992; NEH rsch. fellow Johns Hopkins U. and Peabody Conservatory of Music, 1994. Mem. Thoreau Soc. (life), Community Coll. Humanities Assn. (standing com. 1982-83), Am. Studies Assn., Wash. Community Coll. Humanities Assn. (bd. dirs. 1982-84, grantee, 1984), Western Wash. Ofcls. Assn. Avocations: officiating high sch. and coll. football, hiking, powerlifting, poetry, vocal music. Home: 4415 68th Street Ct NW Gig Harbor WA 98335-8312 Office: Pierce Coll 9401 Farwest Dr SW Tacoma WA 98498-1919

KRIENKE, CAROL BELLE MANIKOWSKE (MRS. OLIVER KENNETH KRIENKE), realtor; b. Oakland, Calif., June 19, 1917; d. George and Ethel (Purdon) Manikowske; student U. Mo., 1937; BS, U. Minn., 1940; postgrad. UCLA, 1949; m. Oliver Kenneth Krienke, June 4, 1941 (dec. Dec. 1988); children: Diane (Mrs. Robert Denny), Judith (Mrs. Kenneth A. Giss), Debra Louise (Mrs. Ed Paul Davalos). Demonstrator, Gen. Foods Corp., Mpls., 1940; youth leadership State of Minn. Congl. Conf., U. Minn., Mpls. 1940-41; war prodn. worker Airesearch Mfg. Co., Los Angeles, 1944; tchr. L.A. City Schs., 1945-49; realtor DBA Ethel Purdon, Manhattan Beach, Calif., 1949; buyer Purdon Furniture & Appliances, Manhattan Beach, 1950-58; realtor O.K. Krienke Realty, Manhattan Beach, 1958—. Manhattan Beach bd. rep. Community Chest for Girl Scouts U.S., 1957; bd. dirs. South Bay council Girl Scouts U.S.A., 1957-62, mem. Manhattan Beach Coordinating Coun., 1956-68, South Coast Botanic Garden Found., 1989—; v.p. Long Beach Area Childrens Home Soc., 1967-68, pres. 1979; charter mem. Beach Pixies, 1957-93, pres. 1967; chmn. United Way, 1967; sponsor Beach Cities Symphony, 1953—, Little League Umpires, 1981-91. Recipient Long-standing Local Bus. award City of Manhattan Beach, 1993. Mem. DAR (life, citizenship chmn. 1972-73, v.p. 1979, 83—), Calif. Retired Tchrs. Assn. (life), Colonial Dames XVII Century (charter mem. Jared Eliot chpt. 1977, v.p., pres. 1979-81, 83-84), Friends of Library, South Bay Assn. of Realtors, Nat. Soc. New England Women (life, Calif. Poppy Colony), Internat. Platform Assn., Soc. Descs. of Founders of Hartford (life), Friends of Banning Mus., Hist. Soc. of Centinela Valley, Manhattan Beach Hist. Soc., Manhattan Beach C. of C. (Rose and Scroll award 1985), U. Minn. Alumni (life). Republican. Mem. Community Ch. (pres. Women's Fellowship 1970-71). Home: 924 Highview Ave Manhattan Beach CA 90266-5813 Office: OK Krienke Realty 1716 Manhattan Beach Blvd Ste A Manhattan Beach CA 90266-6285

KRINGS, AXEL WERNER, educator. Diploma in Elec. Engring., FH Aachen, Germany, 1982; MS, U. Nebr., Lincoln, 1991; PhD, U. Nebr., 1993. Faculty Tech. U. Claushal, Germany, 1993-94; asst. prof. U. Idaho, Boise, 1995-96; asst. prof. computer sci. and elec. engring. U. Idaho, Moscow, 1996—. E-mail: http://www.cs.uidaho.edu/ krings. Office: Univ Idaho Moscow ID 83844-1010

KRIPPNER, STANLEY CURTIS, psychologist; b. Edgerton, Wis., Oct. 4, 1932; s. Carroll Porter and Ruth Genevieve (Volenberg) K.; m. Lelie Anne Harris, June 25, 1966; stepchildren: Caron, Robert. BS, U. Wis., 1954; MA, Northwestern U., 1957, PhD, 1961; PhD (hon.), U. Humanistic Studies, San Diego, 1982. Diplomate Am. Bd. Sexology. Speech therapist Warren Pub. Schs. (Ill.), 1954-55, Richmond Pub. Schs. (Va.), 1955-56; dir. Child Study Ctr. Kent (Ohio) State U., 1961-64; dir. dream lab. Maimonides Med. Ctr., Bklyn., 1964-73; prof. of psychology Saybrook Grad. Sch., San Francisco, 1973—; adj. prof. psychology Calif. Inst. Human Sci., 1994—; vis. prof. U. P.R., 1972, Sonoma State U., 1972-73, U. Life Scis., Bogota, Colombia, 1974, Inst. for Psychodrama and Humanistic Psychology, Caracas, Venezuela, 1975, West Ga. Coll., 1976, John F. Kennedy U., 1980-82, Inst. for Rsch. in Biopsychophysics, Curitiba, Brazil, 1990; adj. prof. Calif. Inst. Integral Studies, 1991-97; lectr. Acad. Pedagogical Scis., Moscow, 1971, Acad. Scis., Beijing, 1981, Minas Gerais U., Belo Horizonte, Brazil, 1986-87. Author: (with Montague Ullman) Dream Telepathy, 1973, rev. edit., 1989, Song of the Siren: A Parapsychological Odyssey, 1975; (with Alberto Villoldo) The Realms of Healing, 1976, rev. edit., 1987, Human Possibilities, 1980, (with Alberto Villoldo) Healing States, 1987; (with Jerry Solfvin) La Science et les Pouvoirs Psychiques de l'Homme, 1986, (with Joseph Dillard) Dreamworking, 1988, (with David Feinstein) Personal Mythology, 1988, (with Patrick Welch) Spiritual Dimensions of Healing, 1992, (with Dennis Thong and Bruce Carpenter) A Psychiatrist in Paradise, 1993, (with David Feinstein) The Mythic Path, 1997, (with Andre de Carvalhe) Sonhos Exoticos, 1998; editor: Advances in Parapsychological Research, Vol. 1, 1977, Vol. 2, 1978, Vol. 3, 1982, Vol. 4, 1984, Vol. 5, 1987, Vol. 6, 1990, Vol. 7, 1994, Vol. 8, 1997, Psychoenergetic Systems, 1979, Dreamtime and Dreamwork, 1990; co-editor: Galaxies of Life, 1973, The Kirlian Aura, 1974, The Energies of Consciousness, 1975, Future Science, 1977, Broken Images, Broken Selves, 1997; mem. editl. bd. Alternative Therapies in Health and Medicine, Jour. Humanistic Psychology, Jour. Transpersonal Psychology, Jour. Indian Psychology, Dream Network, Humanistic Psychologist; contbr. 500 articles to profl. jours. Bd. dirs., adv. bd. Acad. Religion and Phys. Rsch., Survival Rsch. Found., Hartley Film Found., Inst. for Multilevel Learning, Humanistic Psychology Ctr. N.Y., Joseph Plan Found. Recipient Svc. to Youth award YMCA, 1959, Citation of Merit Nat. Assn. Creative Children and Adults, 1975, Cert. Recognition Office Gifted and Talented, U.S. Office Edn., 1976, Volker medal South Africa Soc. Psychical Rsch., 1980, Bicentennial medal U. Ga., 1985, Charlotte Bühler award, 1992, Dan Overlade Meml. award, 1994, Humanist of Yr. award Ch. of Humanism, 1996, Career Achievement award Parapsychological Assn., 1998. Fellow APA (pres. divsn. 32, 1980), Am. Soc. Clin. Hypnosis, Am. Psychol. Soc., Soc. Sci. Study Religion, Soc. Sci. Study Sexuality, Western Psychol. Assn.; mem. AAAS, Am. Soc. Psychical Rsch., Am. Ednl. Rsch. Assn., Am. Counseling Assn., Internat. Council Psychologists, Assn. for Study of Dreams (pres. 1993-94), Soc. for the Anthropology Consciousness, Com. for Study Anomalistic Rsch., Inter-Am. Psychol. Assn., Assn. Humanistic Psychology (pres. 1974-75), Assn. Transpersonal Psychology, Internat. Soc. Hypnosis, Internat. Soc. for Study of Dissociation, Nat. Assn. for Gifted Children, Sleep Rsch. Soc., Soc. Sci. Exploration, Biofeedback Soc. Am., Coun. Exceptional Children, Soc. Accelerative Learning and Tchg., Soc. Gen. Sys. Rsch., Swedish Soc. Clin. and Exptl. Hypnosis, Western Psychol. Assn., Internat. Soc. Gen. Semantics, Menninger Found., Nat. Soc. Study of Edn., Parapsychol. Assn. (pres. 1983), Soc. Clin. and Exptl. Hypnosis, World Future Soc. E-mail: skrippner@saybrook.edu. Home: 79 Woodland Rd Fairfax CA 94930-2153 Office: Saybrook Grad Sch 450 Pacific Ave Rm 300 San Francisco CA 94133-4611

KRISE, THOMAS WARREN, career officer, English language educator; b. Fort Sam Houston, Tex., Oct. 27, 1961; s. Edward Fisher and Elizabeth Ann (Bradt) K.; m. Patricia Lynn Love, Sept. 5, 1987. BS, USAF Acad., 1983; MSA, Cen. Mich. U., 1986; MA, U. Minn., 1989; PhD, U. Chgo., 1995. Commd. 2d lt. USAF, 1983, advanced through grades to maj.; dep. missile comdr. 742d Strategic Missile Squadron, Minot AFB, N.D., 1983-85, missile crew comdr., 1985-86, ICBM flight comdr., 1986-87; mem. English faculty USAF Acad., Colorado Springs, 1989-92, 97—; sr. mil. fellow Inst. for Nat. Strategic Studies, 1995-97; vice-dir. Nat. Def. U. Press, 1995-97; dir. English major program USAF Acad., 1997—; exec. officer Air Force Humanities Inst., 1997—. Asst. editor War, Literature and the Arts, 1991-92, assoc. editor, 1998—; gen. editor: McNair Papers monograph series, 1995-97; contbr. articles to profl. jours. Adult literacy tutor Coalition for Adult Literacy, Colorado Springs, 1989-91, literacy tutor trainer, Adult Literacy Network, Colorado Springs, 1991-92. Recipient Pres.' Student Leadership award U. Minn., 1989; Summer Inst. grant Nat. Endowment for the Humanities, Johns Hopkins U., 1990, Seiler Rsch. grant F.J. Seiler Rsch.

Lab., A.F. Systems Command, 1991, Rsch. grant USAF Inst. Nat. Security Studies, 1998, CBS Bicentennial Narrators scholarship, 1994. Mem. SAR (Pikes Peak chpt. pres. 1991-92), Toastmasters Internat. (U. Minn. chpt. pres. 1988-89), MLA, Am. Soc. for 18th Century Studies, Soc. for 18th Century Am. Studies (sec.-treas. 1995—), Colorado Springs Adult Literacy Network (pres. 1991-92), Assn. of Grads. USAF Acad. (bd. dirs. 1991-95, Chgo. chapter pres. 1993-95), Army and Navy Club (Washington), Phi Kappa Phi. Episcopalian. Avocations: travel, sailing, writing, hiking. Home: 2635 Edenderry Dr Colorado Springs CO 80919-3868 Office: Dept English 2354 Fairchild Dr Ste 6d45 U S A F Academy CO 80840-6299

KRISHNAMURTHY, V.V., chemist; b. Madras, Tamil Nadu, India, Dec. 11, 1954; came to U.S., 1977; s. E.R. and Seetha (Lakshmi) Vaitheeswaran; m. Sharada Ganapathi, Sept. 9, 1984; children: Kamesh, Umesh. BSc, Madras U., 1974, MSc, 1976; PhD, Kent State U., 1980. Rsch. assoc. U. So. Calif., L.A., 1980-85; specialist NMR, U. Calif., Berkeley, 1985-89; mgr. NMR applications Varian Assocs., Florham Park, N.J., 1989-93; mgr. NMR Gilead Scis., Foster City, Calif., 1993-96; mgr. NMR worldwide applications Varian Assocs., Palo Alto, Calif., 1996—; cons. PTRL, Richmont, Calif., 1987-89, Avery Internat., Pasadena, Calif., 1982-85. Contbr. articles to profl. jours. Mem. Am. Chem. Soc. Avocations: reading, hiking. Home: 3588 Pimlico Dr Pleasanton CA 94588-2915 Office: Varian NMR Instruments 3120 Hansen Way # 298 Palo Alto CA 94304-1030

KRISTIN, KAREN, artist; b. L.A., Aug. 27, 1943; d. Earle Barnard and Ann Maxine (Taylor) Immel; m. Richard Edward Amend, Aug. 21, 1976 (div. Aug. 1981); m. Gary Marchal Lloyd, Oct. 1, 1985 (div. Sept.1989). Student, Art Ctr. Coll. Design, 1961, Valley Jr. Coll., 1962, Pierce Jr. Coll., 1967, 68, UCLA, 1969, 70. Lectr. UCLA Ext. Program, 1973-76; scenic artist Hollywood, Calif., 1978-83; ptnr., designer, lead painter Sky Art Scenic Art Svcs., Hollywood, Calif., 1983-88; owner, pres., lead painter, designer Sky Art Karen Kristin, Inc., Englewood, Colo., 1989—; spkr., lectr. in field. Co-author (under Karen Kristin Amend): Handwriting Analysis: The Complete Basic Book, 1980, Achieving Compatbility with Handwriting-Analysis, vol. I, Understanding Your Emotional Relationships, 1992, vol. II, Exploring Your Sexual Relationships, 1992; prin. murals include The Cirque Du Soleil Theater, Las Vegas, 1993, N.Mex. Mus. Natural History, 1989, 90, Forum Shops at Caesars, Las Vegas, 1992, 97, Kansas City Station Hotel and Casino, Kansas City, Mo., 1996, Sunset Station Hotel and Casino, Las Vegas, 1997, Venetian Hotel and Casino, Las Vegas, 1998; sky art backdrops for numerous movies, comml.s., and TV. Mem. Am. Assn. Handwriting Analysts (spkr. 1991—), Am. Handwriting Analysis Found. (sprk. 1991—), Human Graphics Ctr., Graphex Internat. and Gold NIBS, Universal Soc. of Integral Why (mentor 1994—). Democrat. Avocations: photography, reading, traveling, camping, fishing. Office: Sky Art Karen Kristin Inc 3051 S Broadway Englewood CO 80110-1528

KRITZER, EDDIE, television producer; b. Boston, Nov. 8, 1947; s. George and Betty (Goldman) K.; m. Donna French, Sept. 5, 1964 (div. May 1998); children: Heather, Justin. Grad. high sch., Revere, Mass., 1965. Prodr., creator Global Satellite Network, 1981-98, Sta. NBC-AM, 1989-90, various radio stas., 1992; exec. prodr. Sta. CBS-TV, 1997—; creator, exec. cons. Sta. ABC-TV, 1998—; founder, pres. Global Satellite Network, L.A., 1981. Creator, prodr. Rockline, 1981, 98; creator, exec. cons. Am. Comedy Awards ABC-TV, 1986; prodr. Kids Say the Darndest Things, CBS-TV, ; How Do They Do That, NBC Radio, 1990; exec. prodr. (TV movie) False Witness, NBC-TV, 1989. With U.S. Army, 1962-63. Office: Ekp Productions 8484 Wilshire Blvd Ste 205 Beverly Hills CA 90211

KRIVIS, SCOTT ALAN, accountant, limousine company executive; b. L.A., Sept. 21, 1959; s. Gene Howard and Ruth (Lewinstein) K.; m. Kimberly Louise LaVally, July 17, 1983; children: Shayna, Shelea, Shelby. BSBA, Calif. State U., Northridge, 1982. CPA, Calif. Staff acct. Weber, Lipshie & Co., Beverly Hills, Calif., 1982-87; owner, mgr. Scott Krivis & Co., Tarzana, Calif., 1987—; pres. Straightline Transp. Svcs., Inc., Van Nuys, Calif., 1991—. Treas. Temple Beth Ami, Reseda, Calif., 1992-94, Blue Grass Homeowners Assn., Chatsworth, Calif., 1996—. Mem. Calif. Soc. CPA's, Zeta Beta Tau (trustee Northridge 1984—). Avocations: basketball, golf, softball. Home: 20331 Celtic St Chatsworth CA 91311-1702 Office: 18757 Burbank Blvd Ste 120 Tarzana CA 91356-3345

KROHN, KENNETH ALBERT, radiology educator; b. Stevens Point, Wis., June 19, 1945; s. Albert William and Erma Belle (Cornwell) K.; 1 child, Galen. BA in Chemistry, Andrews U., 1966; PhD in Chemistry, U. Calif., 1971. Acting assoc. prof. U. Wash., Seattle, 1981-84, assoc. prof. radiology, 1984-86, prof. radiology and radiation oncology, 1986—, adj. prof. chemistry, 1986—; guest scientist Donner Lab. Lawrence Berkeley (Calif.) Lab., 1980-81; radiochemist, VA Med. Ctr., Seattle, 1982—; affiliate investigator Fred Hutchinson Cancer Rsch. Ctr., 1997—. Contbr. articles to profl. jours.; patentee in field. NDEA fellow; recipient Aebersold award, 1996. Fellow AAAS; mem. Am. Assn. for Cancer Rsch., Am. Chem. Soc., Radiation Rsch. Soc., Soc. Nuclear Medicine, Acad. Coun., Sigma Xi. Home: 550 NE Lakeridge Dr Belfair WA 98528-8720 Office: U Washington Imaging Rsch Lab PO Box 356004 Seattle WA 98195-6004

KROKEN, PATRICIA ANN, health science association administrator; b. Sturgis, Mich., June 26, 1947; d. Jesse W. and Dorothy Beth (Hollister) Penn; m. Bruce Edward Kroken, Jan. 28, 1967; children: Christina, Jennifer. BS in English cum laude, No. Mich. U., 1970. Reporter Marinette (Wis.) Eagle-Star, 1973-77; account exec. Sta. KGRT/KGRD, Las Cruces, N. Mex., 1977-78, Sta. KRZY, Albuquerque, 1978-80, Sta. KGGM-TV, Albuquerque, 1980-81; v.p., account supr. Rick Johnson & Co., Albuquerque, 1984-87; expansion sales mgr. Bueno Foods, 1987-89; bus. devel. dir. Radiology Assocs., Albuquerque, 1990-93, exec. dir., 1993—; adj. prof. U. N. Mex, Albuquerque, 1983-94. Contbr. articles to various jours. Lectr. N. Mex. Womens Polit. Caucus, Albuquerque, 1986. Fellow Am. Coll. Med. Practice Execs.; mem. Radiology Bus. Mgmt. Assn. (chair publs. com. 1997—, pres.-elect 1998, Calhoun award 1996), N.Mex. Med. Group Mgmt. Assn. (pres. 1995). Avocations: pub. speaking, riding horses, writing. Home: 12501 Oakland Ave NE Albuquerque NM 87122-2274 Office: Radiology Assocs 8307 Constitution NE Albuquerque NM 87110

KROLICKI, BRIAN KEITH, state official; b. Providence, Dec. 31, 1960; s. Thadeus James Krolicki and Gail Carolyn (Gourdeau) Jacus; m. Kelly Lea DiGiusto, May 21, 1994. BA in Polit. Sci., Stanford U., 1983. Cert. gov. fin. mgr.; lic. securities dealer. Assoc. banker Bankers Trust Co., N.Y.C., 1984-85; sr. account exec. First Commodity Boston, Zephyr Cove, Nev., 1985-86; account exec. Smith Barney, San Francisco, 1986-87; investment banker Smith Barney, Manama, Bahrain, 1987-89; pres. Inter Am. Mktg. Corp., Reno, London, 1989-91; chief dep. state treas. and sec. state bd. fin. State Nev., Carson City, 1991—; sec. Nev. Master Lease Corp., Carson City, 1992—. Mem. Rep. State Ctrl. Com., Nev., 1990—; vice chmn. planning commn. Douglas County, Minden, Nev., 1991—; chmn. support svcs. Am. Cancer Soc., Nev., 1993-96; bd. dirs. found. Lake Tahoe (Calif.) C.C., 1996—. Mem. Nev. Govt. Fin. Officer Assn. (pres. 1997—). Avocations: guitar, outdoors. Home: PO Box 7033 Stateline NV 89449-7033 Office: State Treasurers Office Capitol Complex Carson City NV 89710

KROLL, C(HARLES) DOUGLAS, minister; b. Florence, S.C., June 19, 1949; s. Clifford Carl and Martha Kurtain (Gasque) K.; m. Lana Gale Gerling, May 1, 1976; children: Timothy, Matthew. BS, USCG Acad., 1971; MDiv, Luther Theol. Sem., 1980; MA, U. San Diego, 1985. Ordained to ministry Luth. Ch.-Mo. Synod, 1980. Assoc. pastor Faith Luth. Ch., Saginaw, Mich., 1980-81; instr. Luth. High Sch., San Diego, 1984-85; dean of chapel Luth. High Sch., LaVerne, Calif., 1985-86; pastor St. Paul's Luth. Ch., Pomona, Calif., 1986—; chaplain US Naval Reserve, various cities, 1981-96, Old Baldy Coun. Boy Scouts Am., Ontario, Calif., 1986—; chmn. Nat. Luth. Com. on Civic Youth Agys., 1990-93; dir. Scouting in the Luth. Ch. conf., 1991. Author: A History of Navy Chaplains Serving With the Coast Guard, 1983; contbr. articles to profl. jours. Mem. religious relationships com. Boy Scouts Am., 1991—. Recipient Lamb award Luth. Coun. USA, 1987, Silver Beaver award Boy Scouts Am., 1989. Mem. Am. Legion (chaplain 1990-91). Home: 324 W Foxpark Dr Claremont CA 91711-3630 Office: St Paul's Luth Ch 610 N San Antonio Ave Pomona CA 91767-4908

KROMKA, JAMES THOMAS MICHAEL, designer, illustrator; b. Phoenix, Mar. 10, 1954; m. Linda Mae, Oct. 12, 1985. Student, Pasadena Coll. Design, 1972-74. Staff artist Riverside County Libr. System, 1969-72; circulation promotional artist Press Enterprise, Riverside, Calif., 1970-71; artist Lily div. Owens-Ill., Riverside, 1972-73; owner, mgr. Slinky Ink Graphics, Walnut Creek, Calif., 1974-76; co-designer, constrn., mgr. Aesop's Restaurant, Riverside, 1976-78; owner, mgr. Bouhouze Custom Paint, Edgemont, Calif., 1978-79; graphic designer, dir. Robertshaw Controls, Corona, Calif., 1979-82; art dir., illustrator, prodn. artist Tobi's Graphics, Inc., El Monte, Calif., 1982-83; graphic designer, tech. illustrator Graphic Art Svcs., Chino, Calif., 1983—, D. Sign Design Kustoms, 1985—; tchr. animation MTI Coll., 1998-99; art dir., illustrator Interactive Illusions a Tristar Internat. Co., Irvine, Calif., 1999—. Home and Office: 2556 Reservoir Dr Norco CA 91760-2327

KRONENBERG, JACALYN (JACKI KRONENBERG), nurse administrator; b. N.Y.C., July 21, 1949; d. Martin Jerome and Joyce (Weinberg) Jacobs; m. Robert Kronenberg, Jan. 23, 1971 (div.); 1 child, Joshua Louis. BA, William Paterson Coll. of N.J., 1971; ADN, Phoenix Coll., 1977. RN, Calif.; cert. IV nurse, chemo, ACLS, PALS. Asst. charge nurse Phoenix Gen. Hosp.; nurse Ariz. State Crippled Children's Hosp., Tempe; maternal, child nurse Desert Samaritan Hosp., Mesa, Ariz.; nurse mgr. PPS Inc., Phoenix, Med-Pro 2000, Phoenix; clin. nurse II Phoenix Children's Hosp.; nurse mgr. adolescent unit Shriners Hosp., L.A.; nurse mgr. pediatrics, oncology, gynecology, med./surg. Santa Monica (Calif.) Hosp. Med. Ctr., 1993-94; dir. nurses, dir. patient care svcs. NMC Homecare, Anaheim, Calif., 1994; dir. med./surg. svcs. and staffing, nursing office/supr. Midway Hosp. Med. Ctr., L.A., 1995; dir. patient care svcs., dir. nursing edn. Children's Home Care Infusion Svcs. & Pediatrics, Children's Home Care, L.A., 1995—; clin. nurse II UCLA Med. Ctr., 1998—; cons. Kronenberg & Kutches Cons., Redondo Beach, Calif.; mem. joint rsch. project on pediatric cystic fibrosis and human growth factor U. Calif., Irvine; rschr. in field; cons. Kronenberg & Kronenberg Cons. Homecare, 1996—. Mem. Oncology Nursing Soc., IV Nursing Soc., Pediatric Nursing Soc. Home: 332B Calle Miramar Redondo Beach CA 90277-6347

KRONSCHNABEL, ALAN JAMES, musician, real estate agent; b. Dickinson, N.D., Mar. 30, 1923; s. Alphonse Ludwig and Blanche Cecilia (Flanagan) K.; m. Dorothy Deane Garner, Sept. 22, 1944; children: Dahnie, Michael, Bradley. BA, Wash. State U., 1947. Owner, mgr. Valley Furniture Co., Tonasket, Wash., 1948-51; underwriter Allstate Ins. Co., Seattle, 1952-55; dist. mgr. Channel Master Corp., Chgo., 1955-68; regional mgr. Portland, Oreg., 1968-74; ins. agent Occidental Life Ins., Chelan, Wash., 1975-85; real estate agent Johnson's-Better Homes and Gardens, Chelan, 1986—; leader, mgr. North Cen. Wash. Big Band, Wenatchee, 1980—; leader Al Knobel Quartet, 1993; mem. Wash. Assn. Realtors. Pres. Chelan County Property Owners Assn., Wenatchee, 1969; commr. Chelan County, 1977; mem. steering com. Wash. Assn. of Counties, Olympia, 1977-80; chmn. Lake Chelan Sewer Dist., 1983. Served to capt. USAF, 1944-47, ETO. Decorated Air Medal with three oak leaf clusters; recipient Cert. of Merit Allied Arts Council, 1978. Mem. Caterpillar Club, Beta Theta Pi, Phi Mu Alpha Sinfonia. Republican. Roman Catholic. Club: Lake Chelan Boat. Lodge: Eagles. Avocations: golfing, tennis, music, fishing, exploring wilderness. Home: RR 2 Box 12 Chelan WA 98816-9700

KROOTH, RICHARD, editor, sociology and political studies educator; b. Chgo., May 8, 1935; s. Arthur Louis Wolf and Helen Löwenrosen (Feldman/Wasserfogel) K.; m. Ann Baxandall, Aug. 30, 1963; 1 child, Karl William. BS, DePaul U., 1958; JD, U. Wis., 1962; PhD in Sociology, U. Calif., Santa Barbara, 1981. Bar: Ga. 1964. Ptnr. Krooth & Krooth, Atlanta, 1962; editor in chief Harvest Pub., Berkeley, Calif., 1975—; rsch. dir. Harvest Pubs., Berkeley, 1965—; econ. cons. Global Enterprises, Berkeley and San Francisco, 1984—; jury cons. Jury Consulting Svcs., Santa Cruz, Calif., 1989—; assoc. and vis. scholar, prof., rschr. U. Calif., various locations, 1981-96; prof. Calif. Inst. Mgmt., Berkeley, 1990-93; adj. prof. Golden Gate U., San Francisco, 1994—. Author: Japan: Five Stages of Development, 1976, The Great Social Struggle, vols. 1-3, 1978-80, Arms & Empire: Imperial Patterns Before WWII, 1981, Common Destiny: Japan and U.S. in Global Age, 1990, Quest For Freedom: Transformation of Europe, 1993, Race and the Jury: Inequality and Justice, 1993, The Middle East: A Geopolitical Study, 1995, Mexico, NAFTA and Hardships of Progress, 1995, The Great Homestead Strike of 1892, 1999, Ecosystems in Distress, 1999; contbr. articles to profl. jours. Founder Wis. Alliance Party, 1968-73; founder, dir. Law and Labor Rsch. Group, Santa Barbara, Calif., 1978-81; acad. dir. Diversion Team: Criminal Youth, Riverside, Calif., 1980-82; coord. Media's Effect on Children, Riverside, 1982-83. Recipient Outstanding Book award for human rights in N.Am., Gustavus Myers Ctr., 1994; grantee Louis M. Rabinowitz Found., N.Y.C., 1973-80; Faculty Senate grantee U. Calif., Riverside, 1979-83. Mem. Am. Arbitration Assn. (arbitrator and comml. panel 1983—), Ga. Bar Assn., Smithsonian Inst. (assoc.), DePaul Alumni Assn., U. Calif. Alumni Assn., Phi Gamma Mu. Office: Harvest Pub Box 9515 Berkeley CA 94709

KROPOTOFF, GEORGE ALEX, civil engineer; b. Sofia, Bulgaria, Dec. 6, 1921; s. Alex S. and Anna A. (Kurat) K.; came to Brazil, 1948, to U.S., 1952, naturalized, 1958; BS in Engring., Inst. Tech., Sofia, 1941; ext. courses in computer sci. U. Calif., 1968; Registered profl. engr., Calif.; m. Helen P., July 23, 1972. With Std. Eletrica S.A., Rio de Janeiro, 1948-52, Pacific Car & Foundry Co., Seattle, 1952-64, T.G. Atkinson Assocs., Structural Engrs., San Diego, 1960-62, Tucker, Sadler & Bennett A-E, San Diego, 1964-74, Gen. Dynamics-Astronautics, San Diego, 1967-68, Engring. Sci., Inc., Arcadia, Calif., 1975-76, Incomtel, Rio de Janeiro, Brazil, 1976, Bennett Engrs., structural cons., San Diego, 1976-82; project structural engr. Hope Cons. Group, San Diego and Saudi Arabia, 1982-84; cons. structural engr. Pioneered engrng. computer software. Warrant officer U.S. Army, 1945-46. Fellow ASCE; mem. Structural Engrs. Assn. San Diego (assoc.), Soc. Am. Mil. Engrs., Soc. Profl. Engrs. Brazil. Republican. Russian Orthodox. Home: 7430 Park Ridge Blvd Apt E San Diego CA 92120-2252

KROTKI, KAROL JOZEF, sociology educator, demographer; b. Cieszyn, Poland, May 15, 1922; emigrated to Can., 1964; s. Karol Stanislaw and Anna Elzbieta (Skrzywanek) K.; m. Joanna Patkowski, July 12, 1947; children—Karol Peter, Jan Jozef, Filip Karol. BA (hons.), Cambridge (Eng.) U., 1948, MA, 1952; MA, Princeton U., 1959, PhD, 1960. Civil ser. Eng., 1948-49; dep. dir. stats. Sudan, 1949-58; vis. fellow Princeton U., 1958-60; rsch. adviser Pakistan Inst. Devel. Econs., 1960-64; asst. dir. census rsch. Dominion Bur. Stats., Can., 1964-68; prof. sociology U. Alta, 1968-83, prof., 1983-91, prof. emeritus, 1991—; vis. prof. U. Calif., Berkeley, 1967, U. N.C., 1970-73, U. Mich., 1975, U. Costa Rica, 1993; coord. program socio-econ. rsch. Province Alta., 1969-71; cons. in field. Author 14 books; contbr. articles to profl. jours. Served with Polish, French and Brit. Armed Forces, 1939-46. Decorated 9 wartime medals; recipient Achievement award Province of Alta, 1970, Commemorative medal for 125th Ann. of Can., 1992; hon. citizen Gizalki, Poland, 1994; grantee in field. Fellow Am. Statis Assn., Royal Soc. Can. (v.p. 1986-88), Acad. Humanities and Social Scis. (v.p. 1984-86, pres. 1986-88); mem. Fedn. Can. Demographers (v.p. 1977-82, pres. 1982-84), Can. Population Soc., Assn. des Demographes du Que., Soc. Edmonton Demographers (founder, pres. 1990-96), Ctrl. and E. European Studies Soc. (pres. 1986-88), Population Assn. Am., Internat. Union Sci. Study Population, Assn. Internat. des Demographes de Langue Francaise, Internat. Statis. Inst., Royal Statis. Soc. Roman Catholic. Home: 10137 Clifton Pl, Edmonton, AB Canada T5N 3H9 Office: U Alta, Dept Sociology, Edmonton, AB Canada T6G 2H4

KROUT, BOYD MERRILL, psychiatrist; b. Oakland, Calif., Jan. 31, 1931; s. Boyd Merrill and Phoebe Lenore (Colby) K.; m. Helena Luise Keel, Aug. 25, 1965. AB, Stanford U., 1951, MD, 1955. Diplomate Am. Bd. Psychiatry and Neurology. Intern San Francisco Hosp., 1954-55; resident Boston U. Hosps., 1958-60, Boston Va Hosp., 1960-61; asst. to clin. prof. UCLA Sch. Medicine, 1961-95, vis. prof., 1995—; chief physician Harbor/UCLA Med. Ctr., Torrance, 1961-95. Capt. USAF, 1955-58. Fellow Am. Psychiat. Assn., So. Calif. Psychiat. Soc. (councillor 1988-91), Am. Psychiat. Soc.; mem. L.A. County Med. Soc. Republican. Office: Harbor/UCLA Med Ctr PO Box 6 Torrance CA 90507-0006

KROWN, SEYMOUR RICHARD, film production executive; b. L.A., Feb. 17, 1931; s. Samuel F. and Frances Krown; m. Leatrice Krown, Nov. 19, 1955; children: Cheryl, Kenneth, Joel. Student, Calif. Poly. Inst., 1949-52. Engr. NBC, Hollywood, Calif., 1955-59; editor Paramount TV Prodns., Hollywood, 1959-63; prodn. mgr. United Prodns. Am., Burbank, Calif., 1963-75; v.p. prodn. L.A., 1977—; producer, dir. Walt Disney Prodns., Burbank, 1975-77. Dir. (TV show) The Mickey Mouse Club; producer: (films) An Evening with Stephen Leacock, The Gift, Inside the Mountain, Gold!, The First Metal, (TV documentary) Christopher Columbus: The Voyage of Discovery, 1987, I Made It Through The Rain, 1996. Served as cpl. U.S. Army, 1953-55. Recipient Chris award Columbus Film Festival, 1970, Golden Babe award Chgo. Film Festival, 1986. Mem. Dirs. Guild Am., Pacific Pioneer Broadcasters. Office: United Prodrs Am Pictures 14101 Valleyheart Dr Ste 200 Sherman Oaks CA 91423-2864

KRUEGER, KURT DONN, lawyer; b. Worthington, Minn., May 8, 1952; s. Donn Kurt and Lola (Lueck) K.; m. Kim Short, Jan. 2, 1983; children: Krista Marie, Kurt Derrick. BA in Gov., Mont. State U., 1974; JD, George Mason U., 1978. Bar: Va. 1978, U.S. Dist. Ct. (ea. dist.) Va. 1979, U.S. Ct. Appeals (4th and D.C. cirs.) 1979, Mont. 1980, U.S. Dist. Ct. Mont. 1980, U.S. Ct. Appeals (9th cir.) 1985, U.S. Supreme Ct. 1990. Law clk. to superior ct. judge Washington, 1978-80; staff atty. Mont. Legal Svcs. Assn., Butte, 1980-83; pvt. practice Butte, 1984—; bd. dirs Mont. Legal Svcs. Assn., Helena, 1984—, pres., 1988-89. State rep. Mont. State Legis., Helena, 1985-87; bd. dirs. Big Bros. and Big Sisters, Butte, 1985-88, Butte Silver Bow Zoning Bd. Adjustment, 1989-92; adv. bd. vigilante dist. Boy Scouts Am., 1989—. Mem. Va. Bar Assn., Mont. Bar Assn., Butte Silver Bar Assn., Assn. Trial Lawyers Am., Mont. Trial Lawyers Assn., Trout Unlimited, Ducks Unlimited, Skyline Sportsman (bd. dirs. 1997—), Mont. Wildlife Fedn. (bd. dirs. 1998—). Democrat. Methodist. Avocations: hiking, fishing, skiing, hunting. Office: 66 W Park St Ste 211 Butte MT 59701-1714

KRUEGER, VIRGINIA CARMICHAEL, foundation administrator; b. Batavia, N.Y., Feb. 18, 1933; d. Dayton Jay and Gladys Edith (Trietley) C.; m. Robert Blair Krueger, June 2, 1956 (div. Sept. 1985); children: Lisa C., Paula L., Robert B. Jr. BS, SUNY, Buffalo, 1953; MS, U. So. Calif., 1977. Tchr. San Diego Schs., La Jolla, Calif., 1954-56; tchr. So. Pasadena, Calif., 1957-65, Pasadena, Calif., 1985-87; art cons. Contemporary Art Consultants, L.A., 1978-89; cons. Jones, Krueger & Martin, Pasadena, 1991-93; exec. dir. Pasadena Found., 1993—. Mem. Arts Commn., Pasadena, 1993-98, chair, 1995-97; chair Docent Coun., L.A. County Mus. of Art, L.A., 1974-75; chair bd. dirs. Fellows of Contemporary Art, L.A., 1991-92. Recipient Gold Crown award Pasadena Arts Coun., 1997, Rehab. Svc. award PACED, Pasadena, 1990, Honor award So. Calif. Rehab. Assn., L.A., 1984. Mem. Rotary (bd. dirs. Pasadena chpt. 1997-98). Office: Pasadena Found 16 N Marengo Ave Ste 300 Pasadena CA 91105

KRUGER, KENNETH CHARLES, architect; b. Santa Barbara, Calif., Aug. 19, 1930; s. Thomas Albin and Chleople (Gaines) K.; m. Patricia Kathryn Rasey, Aug. 21, 1955; children: David, Eric. B.Arch., U. So. Calif., 1953. Registered architect, Calif. Pres. Kruger Bensen Ziemer, Santa Barbara, 1960-90; part-time instr. architecture dept. Calif. Poly., San Luis Obispo, 1993-95; part-time architect, 1993—; regent Calif. Archtl. Found., 1997—. Bd. dirs. United Boys & Girls Club; bd. trustees, corp. sec. Unitarian Ch. Fellow AIA; mem. Archtl. Found. Santa Barbara (pres. 1987-89). Democrat. Home: 1255 Ferrelo Rd Santa Barbara CA 93103-2101

KRUGER, PAUL ROBERT, insurance broker; b. Ft. Dodge, Iowa, Nov. 16, 1957; s. Robert Wayne and Corinne Maxine (Wierson) K.; m. Lisa Diane Rouselle, June 9, 1990; children: Whitney Katherine, Austin Jacob and Garrett Jackson (twins). BSBA in Fin. and Mktg., Iowa State U., 1980. Claims rep. IMT Ins. Co., Des Moines, 1981-82; sales mgr. JCPenney Fin. Svcs., Plano, Tex., 1982-89, GranTree Furniture Rental, Aurora, Colo., 1989-90; sales rep. Sentry Ins., Denver, 1990—; with Preferred Risk Ins., Englewood, Colo., 1991—; ins. broker The Urman Co., Englewood, 1992—; ednl. cons. Sylvan Learning Ctrs., Littleton, Colo., 1997—. Mem. Life Underwriting Tng. Coun., Boulder C. of C., Apt. Assn. Met. Denver (social com. 1989-90, amb. club 1989-90, trade show com. 1989-90), Boulder Jaycees (bd. dirs. 1983-84), Phi Kappa Tau (song leader 1979-80, pledge trainer 1977-78, asst. treas. 1978-79). Republican. Mem. Ch. of Nazarene. Avocations: outdoor sports, aerobics, running, skiing. Home: 21224 E Belleview Pl Aurora CO 80015-6406

KRUGGEL, JOHN LOUIS, plastic surgeon; b. Lake Mills, Iowa, Jan. 27, 1931; s. August and Elizabeth (Gleitz) K.; m. Kathleen Ann Lawson, June 1958 (div. 1972); children: Deborah, Natalie, Victoria, Pamela, Michael; m. Donna Marie Koerner, Mar. 2, 1978; 1 child, Matthew. AS, Waldorf Coll., 1951; MD, U. Iowa, 1957. Diplomate Am. Bd. Plastic Surgery, Am. Bd. Surgery. Intern Mercy Hosp., San Diego; resident Orange Meml. Hosp., Orlando, Fla., Mercy Hosp., San Diego, U. Calif., San Francisco; pvt. practice in plastic surgery San Diego, 1966—. Capt. USAF, 1959-61. Mem. Am. Soc. Plastic and Reconstructive Surgery, Calif. Soc. Plastic and Reconstructive Surgery, Calif. Med. Soc., San Diego County Med. Soc. (del. to Calif. Med. Assn.). Avocations: snow skiing, water skiing, hiking, pilot. Office: 4060 4th Ave Ste 120 San Diego CA 92103-2120

KRULAK, VICTOR HAROLD, newspaper executive; b. Denver, Jan. 7, 1913; s. Morris and Besse M. (Ball) K.; m. Amy Chandler, June 1, 1936; children: Victor Harold Jr., William Morris, Charles Chandler. B.S., U.S. Naval Acad., 1934; LL.D., U. San Diego. Commd. 2d lt. USMC, 1934; advanced through grades to lt. gen.; service in China, at sea, with USMC (Fleet Marine Forces), 1935-39; staff officer, also bn. regimental and divsn. comdr. World War II, World War II; chief staff (1st Marine Div. Korea); formerly comdg. gen. (Marine Corps Recruit Depot), San Diego; formerly spl asst. to dir., joint staff counterinsurgency and spl. activities (Office Joint Chiefs Staff); comdg. gen. Fleet Marine Force Pacific, Pacific, 1964-68; ret., 1968; v.p. Copley Newspaper Corp., 1968-79; pres. Words Ltd. Corp., San Diego. Trustee Zool. Soc. San Diego. Decorated D.S.M., Navy Cross, Legion of Merit with 3 oak leaf clusters, Bronze Star, Air medal, Purple Heart (2) U.S.; Cross of Gallantry; Medal of Merit Vietnam; Distinguished Service medal (Korea), Order of Cloud and Banner, Republic of China. Mem. U.S. Naval Inst., U.S. Marine Corps Assn., Am. Soc. Newspaper Editors, InterAm. Press Assn., U.S. Strategic Inst. (chmn.). Home: 3665 Carleton St San Diego CA 92106-2163 Office: Words Ltd 3045 Rosecrans St San Diego CA 92110-4827

KRUPP, EDWIN CHARLES, astronomer; b. Chgo., Nov. 18, 1944; s. Edwin Frederick and Florence Ann (Olander) K.; m. Robin Suzanne Rector, Dec. 31, 1968; 1 son, Ethan Hembree. BA, Pomona Coll., 1966; MA, UCLA, 1968, PhD (NDEA fellow, 1970-71), 1972. Astronomer Griffith Obs., Los Angeles Dept. Recreation and Parks, 1972—, dir., 1976—; mem. faculty El Camino Coll., U. So. Calif., extension divs. U. Calif.; cons. in ednl. TV Community Colls. Consortium; host teleseries Project: Universe. Author: Echoes of the Ancient Skies, 1983, The Comet and You, 1986 (Best Sci. Writing award Am. Inst. Physics 1986), The Big Dipper and You, 1989, Beyond the Blue Horizon, 1991, The Moon and You, 1993, Skywatchers, Shamans & Kings, 1996; editor, co-author: In Search of Ancient Astronomies, 1978 (Am. Inst. Physics-U.S. Steel Found. award for Best Sci. Writing 1978), Archaeoastronomy and the Roots of Science; editor-in-chief Griffith Obs., 1984—; contbg. editor Sky & Telescope, 1993—. Mem. Am. Astron. Soc. (past chmn. hist. astronomy divsn.), Astron. Soc. Pacific (past dir., recipient Klumpke-Roberts outstanding contbns. to the public understanding and appreciation of astronomy award 1989, G. Bruce Blair medal for contbns. to Pub. Astronomy 1996), Internat. Astron. Union, Explorers Club, Sigma Xi. Office: Griffith Observatory 2800 E Observatory Ave Los Angeles CA 90027-1255

KRYCZKO, THADDEUS WALTER, record producer; b. Buffalo, N.Y., Oct. 29, 1954; s. Thaddeus Walter and Rita Stephanie (Zbrzezny) K. BA, SUNY, Buffalo, 1976; MFA, U. Calif., Irvine, 1978. Project coord. Snug Harbor Cultural Ctr., S.I., N.Y., 1979-80; sr. cons. The Pacific Rsrc. Group, Irvine, Calif., 1980-82; v.p., dir. product devel. Walt Disney Records, Burbank, Calif., 1982—; theater program dir. Irvine Cultural Ctr., 1980-81; instr. Shakespeare Stella Adler Conservatory West, 1991-94. Lead actor (theatre) Three Penny Opera, 1978; producer over 200 song and story recordings including: (children's series) The Wuzzles, 1986 (Best Children's

Record 1986), (soundtrack story) Indiana Jones and the Temple of Doom, The Black Cauldron, Bambi, Peter Pan, Willow, Who Framed Roger Rabbit, The Little Mermaid, Beauty and The Beast, The Lion King (Grammy award 1994), Goosebumps; author: Follow That Ghost, 1986. V.p. Best Entertainment Softball Teams, L.A., 1986-96. Recipient 36 Gold and 16 Platinum Record awards Rec. Industry Assn. Am.; acting fellow SUNY, 1978-79. Mem. Nat. Acad. Rec. Arts and Scis. (Grammy award nomination 1984, 1989-90, 93-94, 97-98, 4 Parent's Choice awards 1990). Office: Walt Disney Records 500 S Buena Vista St Burbank CA 91521-6231

KUBO, EDWARD HACHIRO, JR., prosecutor; b. Honolulu, July 9, 1953; s. Edward H. and Rose M. (Coltes) K.; children: Diana K., Dawn M., Edward H. III. BA in Polit. Sci., U. Hawaii, 1976; JD, U. San Diego, 1979. Bar: Hawaii 1979. Dep. pros. atty. Honolulu City Prosecutor's Office, 1980-83, 85-90; assoc. Carlsmith & Dwyer, Honolulu, 1983-85; asst. U.S. atty. U.S. Atty.'s Office, Honolulu, 1990—; instr. Honolulu Police Dept. Acad., Waipahu, Hawaii, 1986-89; lectr. U.S. Dept. Justice, Lincoln, Neb., 1997, Pearl Harbor Police Acad., 1995, Western State Vice Investigators Assn. Conf., Houston, 1997, Las Vegas, 1998; spkr. teleconf. U.S. Dept. Justice Violence Against Women Act, 1998, Hawaii Bar Assn. H.S. Mock trial adv., 1996-98. Co-author: Concurrent Jurisdiction for Cilil RICO, 1987. Recipient Nat. Art medal (France), 1992, Cert. of Appreciation, U.S. Immigration and Naturalization Svc., 1992, Drug Enforcement Adminstrn., 1997, Plaque of Appreciation, U.S. Border Patrol, 1995, cert. appreciation bureau Alcohol, Tobacco & Firearms, 1999. Mem. Hawaii Bar Assn., Order of Barristers.

KUBOTA, GAYLORD, museum director. Exec. dir. Alexander & Baldwin Sugar Mus., Puunene, Hawaii. Office: Alexander & Baldwin Sugar Mus PO Box 125 Puunene HI 96784-0125

KUBSCH, CHRISTIAN, film producer; b. West Berlin, Germany; came to the U.S., 1981; Grad., John F. Kennedy Internat. Sch., Berlin, 1981; postgrad., L.I. U. With Universal Studios Hollywood, Universal Studios Florida, 1988; film prodr. Landmark Entertainment; dir. Japan divsn. MCA, 1992; v.p., exec. in charge of prodn. IMAX Corp., 1995, Lucas Digital, 1994-97, Universal Pictures, 1999. Prodn. asst. 2010 Space Odyssey, 1985-86; preprodn. coord. Star Trek Adventure, 1987; project mgr. Back to the Future-The Ride, 1988-90; 1st asst. dir. The Sleeze Beeze-Rock Video, 1990; assoc. prodr. The Golden Swan, 1990; prodr. Dreamsquare @Sanrio Puroland, 1990-91, Kaguya Hime @Harmonyland, 1991, Mars Attacks!, 1996; line prodr. Murderous Vases, 2099, Charlies Angst, 1991; project mgr./design Starquest Adventure, 1992; project dir. Polar Quest, 1992, Terminator 2/3D, 1993, Jurassic Park, 1993; VFX prodr. Industrial Light and Magic, 1994, The Mask, 1994, Titanic, 1996, Digital Domain, 1996, Spawn, 1997, Hulk, 1998; prodr. (feature film) Frankenstein, Universal Pictures, 1998.

KUCHAR, THEODORE, conductor, academic administrator, musician; b. N.Y.C.. Music dir., condr. Boulder (Colo.) Philharm. Orch., 1987—; prin. violist leading orchs. Cleve. and Helsinki, Finland; soloist, chamber musician Australia, Europe, New Zealand, U.S., Russia, festivals including Blossom, Edinburgh, Kuhmo, Tanglewood, others; dir. orchestral studies U. Colo., 1996—; artistic dir., prin. condr. Nat. Symphony Orch. Ukraine; artistic dir. Australian Festival Chamber Music, 1990—; past music dir. Queensland Philharm. Orch., Brisbane, Australia, W. Australian Ballet, Perth. Muscian Penderecki's String Trio, N.Y.C., 1994; music dir., condr. recordings with Nat. Symphony Orch. and Ukrainian Chamber Orch. including Lyatoshynsky's Symphonies Nos. 2 and 3 (Best Internat. Recording of Yr. 1994), others; music dir., condr. worldwide tours. Paul Fromm fellow, 1980; recipient bronze medal for his work in promoting that country's music Finnish Govt., 1989. Office: Boulder Philharm Orch 2590 Walnut St Ste 6 Boulder CO 80302-5700*

KUDENOV, JERRY DAVID, zoology educator; b. Lynwood, Calif., Dec. 19, 1946; s. William and Marion Kudenov; m. Kathryn Anne Brown, May 30, 1969; children: Peter Alexander, Michael William. BA, U. Calif., San Diego, 1968; MS, U. Pacific, 1970; PhD, U. Ariz., 1974. Research scientist Ministry for Conservation, Melbourne, Australia, 1974-79; asst. prof. zoology U. Alaska, Anchorage, 1980-82, assoc. prof., 1982-86, prof., 1987—, chmn. dept. biol. sci., 1986-90, SEM lab. mgr., 1999—; vis. asst. prof. U. So. Calif., Los Angeles, 1979-80. Assoc. editor Am. Geophys. Union Antarctic Rsch. Series, 1994-97. Mem. AAAS, Am. Soc. Zoologists, Sci. Research Soc. N. Am., Biol. Soc. Wash., So. Calif. Acad. Scis. (bd. dirs. 1980), Internat. Polychaete Assn., Microscopical Soc. of Am. Avocation: fishing. Home: 3930 Alitak Bay Cir Anchorage AK 99515-2366 Office: U Alaska Anchorage Dept Biol Scis 3211 Providence Dr Anchorage AK 99508-4614

KUDO, EMIKO IWASHITA, former state official; b. Kona, Hawaii, June 5, 1923; s. Tetsuzo and Kuma (Koga) Iwashita; BS, U. Hawaii, 1944; MS in Vocational Edn., Pa. State U., 1950; postgrad. U. Hawaii, U. Ore., others; m. Thomas Mitsugi Kudo, Aug. 21, 1951; children: Guy J.T., Scott K., Candace F. Tchr. jr. and sr. high sch., Hawaii, 1945-51; instr. home econs. edn. U. Hawaii Tchrs. Coll., Honolulu, 1948-51, Pa. State U., State College, 1949-50; with Hawaii Dept. Edn., Honolulu, 1951-82, supr. sch. lunch svc., 1951-64, home econ. edn., 1951-64, dir. home econ. edn., 1964-68, adminstr. vocat.-tech. edn., 1968-76, asst. supt. instructional svcs., 1976-78, dep. supt. State Dept. Edn., 1978-82; cons. Am. Samoa vocat. edn. state plan devel., 1970-71, vocat. edn. U. Hawaii, 1986, internat. secondary program devel. Ashiya Ednl. Sys., Japan, 1986-91, cons. to atty. gen. mental health svcs. for children and adolescents State of Hawaii, 1994; chief planner devel. State of Hawaii Children and Adolescents Mental Health Svcs. Implementation Plan, 1994-95; state coord. industry-labor-edn., 1972-76; mem. nat. task force edn. and tng. for minority bus. enterprise, 1972-73; mem. steering com. Career Info. Ctr. Project, 1973-78; co-dir. Hawaii Career Devel. Continuum project, 1971-74; mem. Nat Accreditation and Instl. Eligibility Adv. Council, 1974-77, cons., 1977-78; mem. panel Internat. Conf. Vocat. Guidance, 1978, 80, 82, 86, 88; state commr. edn. commn. of the states, 1982-90; mem. Hawaii edn. coun., 1982-90; dir. Dept. Parks and Recreation, City and County of Honolulu, 1982-84; bd. dirs. Honolulu Neighborhood Housing Svcs., 1991—. Exec. bd. Aloha coun. Boy Scouts Am., 1978-88. Japan Found. Cultural grantee, 1977; Pa. State U. Alumni fellow, 1982; bd. trustees St. Louis High Sch., 1988-95; mem. Gov.'s Commn. on Sesquicentennial Observance of Pub. Edn. In Hawaii, 1990-91; mem. Commn. State Rental Housing Trust Fund, 1992-98; mem. steering com. Hawaii Long Term Care Coalition, 1992—. Mem. Am. Assn. Retired Persons (mem. state legis. com. 1990-92), Pa. State U. Disting. Alumni, Western Assn. Schs. and Colls. (accreditation team mem. Ch. Coll. of Hawaii 1972-73), Am. Vocat. Assn., Hawaii Vocat. Assn., NEA, Hawaii Edn. Assn. (trustee 1992—), Hawaii State Ednl. Officers Assn. (Konawaena H.S. Hall of Fame 1997), Am., Hawaii Family Consumer Sci. Assn., Nat., Hawaii ASCD, Am. Tech. Edn. Assn., Hawaii Recreation and Park Assn., Omicron Nu, Pi Lambda Theta, Phi Delta Kappa, Delta Kappa Gamma. Author handbooks and pamphlets in field. Home and Office: 217 Nenue St Honolulu HI 96821-1811

KUECHEL, REBECCA JUNE, elementary education educator; b. Santa Ana, Calif., Nov. 17, 1961; d. George Raymond and Barbara June (DeVault) K. BS, No. Ariz. U., 1983, MEd, 1994. Cert. elem., spl. edn. tchr., adminstr., Ariz. Tchr. C.W. McGraw Elem. Sch., Yuma, Ariz., 1984—. Mem. ASCD, ASA, Las Dedicadas Assistance League of Yuma, No. Ariz. U. Alumni Assn., Phi Kappa Phi. Republican. Lutheran. Home: 2227 E 26th Way Yuma AZ 85365-3261 Office: Yuma Sch Dist One 450 W 6th St Yuma AZ 85364-2973

KUEHN, KLAUS KARL ALBERT, ophthalmologist; b. Breslau, Germany, Apr. 1, 1938; came to U.S., 1956, naturalized, 1971; s. Max and Anneliese (Hecht) K.; m. Eileen L. Nordgaard, June 22, 1961 (div. 1972); children: Stephan Eric, Kristina Annette; m. Lynda O. Hubbs, Oct. 2, 1974. Student, St. Olaf Coll., 1956-57; BA, BS, U. Minn., 1961; MD, 1963. Diplomate Am. Bd. Ophthalmology. Resident in ophthalmology UCLA Affiliated Hosps., 1968-71; practice medicine specializing in ophthalmology, San Bernardino, Calif., 1971—; chief ophthalmology dept. San Bernardino County Med. Ctr., 1979-80; assoc. clin. prof. ophthalmology Jules Stein Eye Inst. and UCLA Med. Ctr., 1978-81. Served to capt. U.S. Army, 1963-64. Fellow Am. Acad. Ophthalmology; mem. AMA, Calif. Med. Assn., Calif. Assn. Ophthalmology (bd. dirs.). Office: 902 E Highland Ave San Bernardino CA 92404-4007

KUENNING, GEOFFREY HOUSTON, computer science educator; b. Great Falls, Mont., June 21, 1951; s. John Horace and Cherie May Abigail (Callison) K.; m. Patricia Jean Crandall, Dec. 5, 1992; 1 child, Alexandra Caitlin Renee. BS, Mich. State U., 1973, MS, 1974; PhD, UCLA, 1997. Programmer Bell Computer Products, Sunnyvale, Calif., 1975-76; computer scientist Digital Equipment Corp., Maynard, Mass., 1976-77; cons., 1978-82; mgr. Callan Data Systems, Westlake Village, Calif., 1983-84; pres. Interrupt Tech. Corp., Granada Hills, Calif., 1984—; asst. prof. Harvey Mudd Coll., Claremont, Calif., 1998—. Spkr. L.A. Opera Spkrs. Bur., 1995—. Mem. IEEE, Assn. for Computing Machinery, 1973—. Office: Harvey Mudd Coll 301 E 12th St Claremont CA 91711-5901

KUETHE, DEAN OTIS, scientist; b. N.Y.C., Sept. 8, 1956; s. James L. Kuethe and Janet L. (Tolbert) De Soto; m. Rebecca D. Gardner, Sept. 16, 1995; 1 child, Isabel Snow Kuethe. BS, SUNY, Syracuse, 1977; PhD, Duke U., 1986. Scientist Duke U., Durham, N.C., 1987-90, MIT, Cambridge, Mass., 1990-94, Lovelace Respiratory Rsch. Inst., Albuquerque, 1994—. Vol. Park Bldr. Sunflower Meadow, Tijeras, N. Mex., 1998. Grantee NIH, 1997-01. Mem. Am. Physical Soc., Am. Physiological Soc. Avocations: woodwork, rock and ice climbing. Office: LRRI 2425 Ridgecrest Dr SE Albuquerque NM 87108-5129

KUHL, RONALD WEBSTER, marketing executive; b. Chgo., Dec. 12, 1938; s. Robert Emerson and Kathleen (Webster) K.; m. Mary Walls, Sept. 28, 1968; children: David Douglas, Kevin Lathrop. BS in Econs., U. Pa., 1960; MBA, Harvard U., 1964. Account exec. Young & Rubicam Advt., N.Y.C., 1964-71; v.p. mgmt. supr. Young & Rubicam Advt., San Francisco, 1988-90; mgr. promotion and design The First Ch. of Christ Scientist, Boston, 1971-75; account exec. BBDO Advt., San Francisco, 1975-77; acct. supr. Ketchum Communications, San Francisco, 1977-80; dir. mktg. ComputerLand Corp., Hayward, Calif., 1985-88; v.p. mktg. communications Ventura Software Inc., San Diego, 1990-92; v.p. mktg. Castelle, Santa Clara, Calif., 1992-94; v.p. advt. and mktg. svcs. Interactive Video Enterprises, San Ramon, Calif., 1994-96; v.p. mktg. and svcs. NetSoft, Irvine, Calif., 1996-98. 1st lt. U.S. Army, 1960-62. Avocations: antique collecting, tennis, swimming, travel. Office: NetSoft Enterprises 31 Technology Dr Irvine CA 92618-2322

KUHLMAN, WALTER EGEL, artist, educator; b. St. Paul, Nov. 16, 1918; s. Peter and Marie (Jensen) K.; m. Nora McCants; 1 son, Christopher; m. Tulip Chestman, April 9, 1979. Student, St. Paul Sch. Art; BS, U. Minn., 1941; postgrad., Tulane U., Academié de la Grand Chaumierè, Paris, Calif. Sch. Fine Arts. mem. faculty U. Calif. Sch. Fine Arts, Stanford, U. Mich., Santa Clara (Calif.) U., U. N.Mex., Sonoma State U., Rohnert Park, Calif., (prof. emeritus, 1988—). One person shows include U. N.Mex., Walker Art Center, Mpls., The Berkshire Museum, Mass., La Jolla Museum of Contemporary Art, Calif., Santa Barbara Mus. of Art, Calif., San Francisco Mus. of Modern Art, 1958, New Arts Gallery, Houston, 1959-61, Roswell Mus. Palace of Legion of Honor, Calif., 1956, 59, 61, 62, 64, San Francisco Mus. Art, De Saisset Mus., Jonson Gallery U. N.Mex., 1963, 64, 65, Charles Campbell Gallery, San Francisco, 1981, 83, 85, Djurovich Gallery, Sacramento, The Carlson Gallery, San Francisco, 1989, Gump's Gallery, San Francisco, 1976, 1992, University Gallery, Sonoma State U., Natsoulis Gallery Davis, Calif., Albuquerque Mus. Fine Arts, 1994, George Krevsky Fine Arts, San Francisco, 1994, 96, Robert Green Gallery, Mill Valley, Calif.; group shows include N.Y. World's Fair, St. Paul Gallery, WPA Exhibition, Lawson Galleries, San Francisco, A 1948 Portfolio: 16 Lithographs (Diebenkorn, Lobdell, Hultberg), All Annual Invitational Exhibitions, San Francisco Mus. Modern Art, 1948-58, Petit Palais Mus., Paris, San Francisco Mus. Modern Art, III Biennial of Sao Paulo, Museo de Arte Moderna, Brazil, L.A. County Mus., Mus. Modern Art, Rio de Janiero, San Francisco Mus. Modern Art, 1955, 57, 66, 76, 96, Graham Found., Chgo, L.A. County Mus., Calif. Palace of the Legion of Honor, Virginia Mus. Fine Arts, Richmond, Stanford U., Gallery, Roswell Mus., 1961, 62, Univ. Art Mus., Austin, Texas Santa Fe Mus. Fine Arts, NM, Ca. Palace of Legion of Honor, Richard L. Nelson Gallery, UC Davis, Natsoulis Gallery, Northern California Figuration Expositions Art USA, 1992, 93, 94, George Krevsky Fine Art, San Francisco, Art Mus. Santa Cruz, Calif., 1993, Pasquale Ianetti Art Galleries, San Francisco, 1994, Robert Green Fine Arts, Mill Valley, Calif. 1994, 95, Acad. Arts and Letters, N.Y. 1995; permanent Collections include: The Phillips Collection, Washington, Nat. Gallery Am. Art, Washington, Walker Art Ctr., Washington, San Francisco Mus. Modern Art, Brit. Mus., Met. Mus. Art, NAD, N.Y., others. Recipient Maestro award Calif. Arts Coun., Outstanding Calif. Working Artist and Tchr. award; fellow Tiffany Found., Graham Found., Cummington Found. Mem. Nat. Acad. Design N.Y. Studio: Indsl Ctr Bldg Studio 335 480 Gate 5 Rd Sausalito CA 94965-1461

KUHN, DONALD MARSHALL, marketing professional; b. Miami, Fla., Nov. 2, 1922; s. Paul Carlton Kuhn and Helen (Merrick) Bond; m. Jane Emma Williams, Dec. 24, 1948 (dec. 1988); children: Marshall Merrick, Richard Williams, Diane Joan, Paul Willard; m. Kay Bardsley, Feb. 25, 1990. BA in Journalism and Drama, U. Miami, 1949. Cert. fundraising executive. Advt. copywriter Sears Roebuck and Co., Chgo., 1949-50; dir. pub. relations Tb Inst. Chgo. and Cook County, 1950-54; dir. fundraising Dade County Tb Assn., Miami, 1955-59, Minn. Tb and Health Assn., St. Paul, 1959-60, Mich. Lung Assn., Lansing, 1960-68, Am. Lung Assn., N.Y.C., 1968-78; nat. founder, dir. regional fin. program Rep. Nat. Com., Washington, 1978-79; exec. v.p., dir. fundraising div. Walter Karl, Inc., Armonk, N.Y., 1979-90, cons., 1990-93; cons. May Devel. Svcs., Greenwich, Conn., 1993—; mem. direct mktg. task force Am. Red Cross, Washington, 1983-84; mem. direct mail task force Am. Heart Assn., Dallas, 1982. Editor: Non-profit Council Info. Exchange, 1987-90; contbr. articles to Fundraising Mgmt. Mag. Bd. dirs. Isadora Duncan Internat. Inst., N.Y.C., 1987—. Mem. Nat. Soc. Fundraising Execs. (bd. dirs. 1978-80), Direct Mktg. Assn. (mem. operating com., non-profit coun. 1987-90, recipient non-profit coun. fundraising achievement award 1991). Republican. Congregational. Avocations: personal computers, croquet. Home and Office: 6305 S Geneva Cir Englewood CO 80111-5437

KUHN, ROBERT LAWRENCE, investment banker, corporate financier, strategist, author, educator; b. N.Y.C., Nov. 6, 1944; s. Louis and Lee (Kahn) K.; m. Dora Elana Serviarian, June 23, 1967; children: Aaron, Adam, Daniella. AB in Human Biology, Johns Hopkins U., 1964; PhD in Brain Sci., UCLA, 1968; MS in Mgmt., MIT, 1980. Investment banker, fin adv. representing various firms, N.Y.C., L.A., Beijing, Tokyo, 1980—; cons. corp. strategy and fin., N.Y.C., L.A., Beijing, Tokyo, 1980—; pres. The Geneva Cos., Irvine, Calif, 1991—; adj. prof. Grad. Sch. Bus. Adminstrn., NYU, 1981-89; exec.-in-residence U. So. Calif., 1990; bd. advisors, U. So. Calif. Sch. Bus., 1992—; internat. adviser in fin. and high tech. to govts. U.S., Israel, Fed. Republic Germany, China, 1984—; vice chmn. bd. dirs. Data Software and Systems; bd. dirs. Tower Semiconductor, N.Y.C.; cons. and lectr. in field. Author: Mid-Sized Firms: Success Strategies and Methodology, 1982, Creativity and Strategy in Mid-Sized Firms, 1988, (with George Geis) The Firm Bond: Linking Meaning and Mission in Business and Religion, 1984, Micromanaging: Transforming Business Leaders with Personal Computers, 1987, To Flourish Among Giants: Creative Management for Mid-Sized Firms, 1985 (Japanese translation, 1986, Macmillan Book Club main selection), (with Arie Lavie) Industrial Research and Development in Israel, 1986, Dealmaker: All the Negotiating Skills and Secrets You Need, 1988, Investment Banking: The Art and Science of High-Stakes Dealmaking, 1989, Japanese translation, 1990, Chinese translation, 1995, (with Don Gamache) The Creativity Infusion, 1989; editor: Commercializing Defense-Related Technology, 1984; (with Raymond Smilor) Corporate Creativity: Robust Companies and the Entrepreneurial Spirit, 1984; (with Margaret Maxey) Regulatory Reform: Private Enterprise and Risk Assessment, 1985; (with Eugene Konecci) Technology Venturing: American Innovation and Risk Taking, 1985; (with Raymond Smilor) Managing Take-Off in Fast Growth Companies, 1985; Frontiers in Creative and Innovative Management, 1985; (with Yuji Ijiri) New Directions in Creative and Innovative Management, 1988; Medical Information Sciences, 1988; Commercializing Strategic Defense Technologies, 1986, Commercializing SDI Technologies (with Stewart Nozette, 1987). Editor-in-chief: Handbook for Creative and Innovative Managers, 1987, Libr. of Investment Banking, 7 vols., 1990; contbg. editor, columnist Jour. Bus. Strategy, 1984-90. Sloan fellow MIT, Cambridge, 1979; sr. research fellow in creative and innovative mgmt. IC2 Inst., U. Tex., Austin, 1983—. Mem. Phi Beta Kappa. Avocations: weight-lifting, table tennis, chess, classical music. Office: The Geneva Coms 5 Park Plz Irvine CA 92614-5995

KUHNS, CRAIG SHAFFER, business educator; b. Spokane, Wash., Apr. 14, 1928; s. Theodore Lewis and Audrey Grace (Shaffer) K. BS, U. Calif., Berkeley, 1950, BA, 1954, MBA, 1955. Analyst Standard Oil Co. of Calif., San Francisco, 1955-57; bus. educator U. Calif./San Jose State U., 1958-63, City Coll. of San Francisco, 1963—; adj. faculty U. San Francisco, 1977-90. 1st lt. U.S. Army, 1951-52, col. Mil. Intelligence USAR, 1953-80, col. AUS, ret. Mem. Calif. Alumni Assn., U.S. Army War Coll. Alumni Assn., Res. Officers Assn., Japan Soc. Republican. Avocation: travel. Home: 8 Locksley Ave Apt 8A San Francisco CA 94122-3850 Office: City Coll of San Francisco 50 Phelan Ave San Francisco CA 94112-1821

KUHNS, DAVID WALLACE, emergency physician; b. Indiana, Pa., May 12, 1958; s. Jack Wallace and Rachel Louise (Stineman) K.; m. Catherine Marie Couch, Sept. 2, 1992 (dec. June 1994). BA in Physics, Indiana U. of Pa., 1980; MD, Temple U., 1985. Diplomate Am. Bd. Emergency Medicine. Resident in emergency medicine Darnell Army Hosp., Ft. Hood, Tex., 1985-88; emergency physician Womack Army Med. Ctr., Ft. Bragg, N.C., 1988-92, dir. pre-hosp. care, 1988-90, dir. emergency svcs., 1990-92; emergency physician Bannock Regional Med. Ctr., Pocatello, Idaho, 1992; emergency physician Boundary County Hosp., Bonners Ferry, Idaho, 1992—, dir. emergency svcs., 1993—, chief of staff, 1995—. Contbr. articles to profl. jours. Maj. U.S. Army, 1985-92. Fellow Am. Coll. Emergency Physicians, Am. Acad. Emergency Medicine. Avocations: outdoor and indoor sports. Home: HC 85 Box 349 Bonners Ferry ID 83805-9625 Office: Boundary County Hosp HC 61 Box 61A Bonners Ferry ID 83805-9500

KUHNS, SALLY NELSON, trumpeter, music ensemble director, educator; b. West Chester, Pa., Oct. 19, 1952; d. Kenneth Nelson and Katharine (Rhodes) Foster; m. Thomas Joseph Kuhns, July 7, 1990. Student, Ithaca Coll., 1970; MusB in Performance, New Sch. Music, Phila., 1974; MusM in Performance, Northwestern U., 1981. Trumpeter Youth Orch. of Greater Phila., 1970-74; asst. prin. trumpeter Ft. Wayne (Ind.) Philharm., 1975-79, Oreg. Symphony, Portland, 1978—; founder, dir. Portland Unlimited Chamber Ensemble, 1979—; trumpeter Oreg. Coast Festival, Sunriver Music Festival, 1979-82; 1st trumpeter Met. Brass Co., Portland, 1981-84, Peter Britt Festival, Jacksonville, Oreg., 1982-86; tchr. trumpet Warner Pacific U., Portland, 1983-84, U. Portland, 1985—. Rec. artist: (with Met. Brass Co.) Made in Oregon, 1986, Christmas Past and Present, 1987; writer, contbr. Woodwind, Brass and Percussion World; soloist Oreg. Symphony, 1984, 96. Recipient Am. Brass Chamber Music award Aspen Music Festival, 1977; scholar New Sch. Music, 1969-74, Berkshire Music Festival, 1975, Aspen Festival 1976-79, Spoleto Festival, 1980. Mem. Internat. Trumpet Guild, Portland Brass Soc., Am. Fedn. Musicians. Home and Office: 7826 SW 5th Ave Portland OR 97219-4630

KUIVINEN, NED ALLAN, pathologist; b. Mt. Vernon, Ohio, May 19, 1936; s. Thomas Oscar and Pauline Ruthella (Pealer) K.; m. Deborah Berle Miller, Feb. 5, 1972; children: David Joseph, Matthew Thomas. BS, Ohio State U., 1958, MD, 1962. Diplomate Am. Bd. Pathology. Pathologist St. Joseph's Hosp., Phoenix, 1969-98; dir. clin. lab. W. O. Boswell Meml. Hosp., Sun City, Ariz., 1970-98; pathologist D. E. Webb Meml. Hosp., Sun City, Ariz., 1988-98; dir. clin. lab. Vencor Hosp. Phoenix, Youngtown, Ariz., 1990-92, ret., 1998. Lt. comdr. U.S. Navy, 1966-68. Fellow Am. Soc. Clin. Pathology, Coll. Am. Pathology; mem. Ariz. Med. Assn., Ariz. Soc. Pathologists (pres. 1993-95). Avocations: musical instruments, windsurfing, skiing. Home: 4757 E Valley Vista Ln Paradise Vly AZ 85253-4068 Office: Pathology Assocs Ltd 49 E Thomas Rd Ste 101 Phoenix AZ 85012-3104

KULKOSKY, PAUL JOSEPH, psychology educator; b. Newark, N.J., Mar. 3, 1949; s. Peter Francis and Rose Mary (Leonetti) K.; m. Tanya Marie Weightman, Sept. 16, 1978. BA, Columbia U., N.Y.C., 1971, MA, 1972; PhD, U. Wash., 1975. Research assoc. Cornell U., White Plains, N.Y., 1980-81, instr. psychiatry, 1981-82; asst. prof. psychology U. So. Colo., Pueblo, 1982-86, assoc. prof., 1986-89, chmn. dept. psychology, 1988-91, prof., 1989—; bd. advisors Pueblo Zool. Soc., 1984-85, 1988-91, bd. dirs., 1985-88; editorial cons. to pubs.; consulting editor Jour. Neurotherapy. Contbr. chpts. to books, articles to profl. jours.; referee psychol. jours. Liaison Rocky Mountain Region Coun. undergrad. psychology programs, 1990-91. Named Hon. Affiliate Prof. Am. U., Washington, 1977; rsch. grantee NIH, 1984-97; staff fellow Nat. Inst. Alcohol Abuse and Alcoholism, 1976-80. Mem. AAAS (vice chmn. psychol. scis. sect. Southwestern and Rocky Mountain divsn. 1990-91, chmn. 1991-92, exec. com. Colo. rep. 1991-94, pres.-elect 1994-95, pres. 1995-96, past pres. 1996—), Consortium Aquariums, Univs. and Zoos, Internat. Soc. Biomed. Rsch. on Alcoholism (charter), Soc. for Study Ingestive Behavior (charter), Colo.-Wyo. Acad. Sci. (exec. com. 1997—), U. So. Colo. Club, Sigma Xi (treas. 1986-96), Phi Kappa Phi. Home: 417 Tyler St Pueblo CO 81004-1405 Office: U So Colo 2200 Bonforte Blvd Pueblo CO 81001-4901

KULONGOSKI, THEODORE RALPH, state supreme court justice; b. Nov. 5, 1940; married; 3 children. BA, U. Mo., 1967, JD, 1970. Bar: Oreg., Mo., U.S. Dist. Ct. Oreg., U.S. Ct. Appeals (9th cir.). Legal counsel Oreg. State Ho. of Reps., 1973-74; founding and sr. ptnr. Kulongoski, Durham, Drummonds & Colombo, Oreg., 1974-87; deputy dist. atty. Mulnomah County, Oreg., 1992—. State rep. Lane County (Oreg.), 1974-77, state senator, 1977-83; chmn. Juvenile Justice Task Force, 1994, Gov.'s Commn. Organized Crime; mem. Criminal Justice Coun.; exec. dir. Met. Family Svc., 1992; dir. Oreg. Dept. Ins. and Fin., 1987-91. Mem. Oreg State Bar Assn., Mo. Bar Assn. Office: Oreg Supreme Ct 1163 State St Salem OR 97310-1331

KUMAR, RAJENDRA, electrical engineering educator; b. Amroha, India, Aug. 22, 1948; came to U.S., 1980; s. Satya Pal Agarwal and Kailash Vati Agarwal; m. Pushpa Agarwal, Feb. 16, 1971; children: Anshu, Shipra. BS in Math. and Sci., Meerut Coll., 1964; BEE, Indian Inst. Tech., Kanpur, 1969, MEE, 1977; PhD in Electrical Engring., U. New Castle, NSW, Australia, 1981. Mem. tech. staff Electronis and Radar Devel., Bangalore, India, 1969-72; rsch. engr. Indian Inst. Tech., Kanpur, 1972-77; asst. prof. Calif. State U., Fullerton, 1981-83, Brown U., Providence, 1980-81; prof. Calif. State U., Long Beach, 1983—; cons. Jet Propulsion Lab., Pasadena, Calif., 1984-91. Contbr. numerous articles to profl. jours.; patentee; efficient detection and signal parameter estimation with applications to high dynamic GPS receivers; multistage estimation of received carrier signal parameters under very high dynamic conditions of the receiver; fast frequency acquisition via adaptive least squares algorithms. Recipient Best Paper award Internat. Telemetering Conf., Las Vegas, 1986, 10 New Technology awards NASA, Washington, 1987-91. Mem. IEEE (sr.), NEA, AAUP, Calif. Faculty Assn., Auto Club So. Calif. (Cerritos), Sigma Xi, Eta Kappa Nu, Tau Beta Pi (eminent mem.). Avocations: gardening, walking, hiking, reading. Home: 13910 Rose St Cerritos CA 90703-9043 Office: Calif State U 1250 N Bellflower Blvd Long Beach CA 90840-0001

KUMMER, GLENN F., manufactured housing executive; b. Park City, Utah, 1933. B.S., U. Utah, 1961. Sr. acct. Ernst & Ernst, 1961-65; trainee Fleetwood Enterprises Inc., Riverside, Calif., 1965-67, purchasing mgr., 1967-68, plant mgr., 1968-70, gen. mgr. recreational vehicle div., 1970-71, asst. v.p. ops., 1971-72, sr. v.p. ops., 1972-77, exec. v.p. ops., 1977-82, pres., 1982-98, dir., 1983—, chmn., CEO, 1998—. Office: Fleetwood Enterprises Inc PO Box 7638 3125 Myers St Riverside CA 92503-5544

KUNG, FRANK F., biotechnology and life sciences venture capital investor; b. 1948. BS, Nat. Tsing Hwa U., Taiwan, 1970; MBA, U. Calif., Berkeley, 1983, PhD in Molecular Biology, 1976. Post doctoral rsch. scientist Univ. Calif., Berkeley, 1976-77; rsch. dir. Clin. Bio-Rsch., Emeryville, Calif., 1977-79; scientist, asst. to pres. Cetus Corp., Berkeley, Calif., 1979-81; dir. Cetus Immune Corp. (subs. of Cetus Corp.), Palo Alto, Calif., 1980-84; pres., CEO Genelabs Techs., Inc., Redwood City, Calif., 1984-95, chmn., 1984-96; chmn. BioAsia Investments, Palo Alto, Calif., 1996—. Office: BioAsia Investments 575 High St Ste 201 Palo Alto CA 94301-1648

KUNKEE, RALPH EDWARD, viticulture and enology educator; b. San Fernando, Calif., July 30, 1927; s. Azor Frederick and Edith Electa (Engle)

K. AB, U. Calif., Berkeley, 1950, PhD, 1955. Research biochemist E.I. Du Pont De Nemours, Wilmington, Del., 1955 60; prof. enology U. Calif., Davis, 1963-91, prof. emeritus, 1991; cons. UNFAO, Bangalore, India, 1986. Co-author: Technology of Winemaking, 1971, Principles and Practices of Winemaking, 1996 (recipient prize in enology Internat. Office of Vines and Wines 1998). Fulbright fellow, Mainz, Fed. Republic Germany, 1970-71, France fellow, Montpellier, France, 1977-78; recipient Prix en Oenologie award l'Office Internat. de la Vigne et du Vin, 1998. Fellow AAAS; mem. Am. Chem. Soc., Am. Soc. Microbiology, Am. Soc. Enology and Viticulture (sec./treas. 1983-85, hon. rsch. lectr. 1997), Soc. Wine Educators. Home: 820 Radcliffe Dr Davis CA 95616-0941 Office: U Calif Dept Viticulture & Enology 1 Shields Ave Dept & Davis CA 95616-5270

KUNTZ, DAVID WILLIAM, multimedia producer; b. Newark, N.J., Feb. 11, 1952; s. William R. and Loretta (Hauke) K.; m. Cynthia L. Becker, Sept. 11, 1976; children: Brian Christopher, Kimberly Diane, David Randall. BA, NYU, 1974; MBA, U. Phoenix, L.A., 1995. Prodn. mgr. Nissan Motor Corp., Gardena, Calif., 1983—; cons., developer Automotive Svc. Excellence, Washington, 1997-98; mem. Svc. Technician's Soc. adv. bd., L.A., 1996-97. Author: Impacts Plus: Guide to Customer Satisfaction, 1988. Mem. Orange City (Calif.) Rep. Party, 1998. Recipient Nat. Grand award Soc. Consumer Affairs Profls., 1988. Mem. Toastmasters (pres. local chpt. 1991-98). Avocations: photography, marathons. Home: 6401 Fallingwater Dr Huntington Beach CA 92647-6506 Office: Nissan Motor Corp PO Box 191 Gardena CA 90248-0191

KUNZ, PHILLIP RAY, sociologist, educator; b. Bern, Idaho, July 19, 1936; s. Parley P. and Hilda Irene (Stoor) K.; m. Joyce Sheffield, Mar. 18, 1960; children: Jay, Jenifer, Jody, Johnathan, Jana. BS, Brigham Young U., 1961, MS cum laude, 1962; PhD (fellow), U. Mich., 1967. Instr. Eastern Mich. U., Ypsilanti, 1964, U. Mich., Ann Arbor, 1965-67; asst. prof. sociology U. Wyo., Laramie, 1967-68; prof. sociology Brigham Young U., Provo, Utah, 1968—; acting dept. chmn. Brigham Young U., 1973; dir. Inst. Geneal. Studies, 1972-74; cons. various ednl. and rsch. instns., 1968—; missionary Ch. Jesus Christ LDS, Ga. and S.C., 1956-58, mem. high coun., 1969-70, bishop; mission pres. La. Baton Rouge Mission, 1990-93. Author: 10 Critical Keys for Highly Effective Families, other books; contbr. articles on social orgn., family rels. and deviant behavior to profl. jours. Housing commr. City of Provo, 1984—. Served with AUS, 1954-56. Recipient Karl G. Maeser rsch. award, 1977. Mem. Am. Sociol. Assn., Rocky Mountain Social Sci. Assn., Am. Coun. Family Rels., Rural Sociol. Soc., Am. Soc. Criminology, Soc. Sci. Study of Religion, Religious Rsch. Assn., Sigma Xi, Phi Kappa Phi, Alpha Kappa Delta (Alcuin award 1997). Democrat. Home: 3040 Navajo Ln Provo UT 84604-4820 Office: Brigham Young Univ Dept Sociology Provo UT 84602

KUO, FRANKLIN F., computer scientist, electrical engineer; b. Apr. 22, 1934; came to U.S., 1950, naturalized, 1961; s. Steven C. and Grace C. (Huang) K.; m. Dora Lee, Aug. 30, 1958; children: Jennifer, Douglas. BS, U. Ill., 1955, MS, 1956, PhD, 1958. Asst. prof. dept. elec. engring. Poly. Inst. Bklyn., 1958-60; mem. tech. staff Bell Telephone Labs., Murray Hill, N.J., 1960-66; prof. elec. engring. U. Hawaii, Honolulu, 1966-82; exec. dir. SRI Internat., Menlo Park, Calif., 1982-94; v.p. Gen. Wireless Comm. Corp., 1994-98; sr. advisor W Channel Sys., 1998—; dir. info. systems Office Sec. of Def., 1976-77; liason scientist U.S. Office Naval Research, London, 1971-72; cons. prof. elec. engring. Stanford U., Calif., 1982—; vis. prof. U. Mannheim, Germany, 1995-96; mem. exec. panel Chief of Naval Ops., 1980-85. Author: Network Analysis and Synthesis, 1962, (2d edit.), 1966, Linear Circuits and Computations, 1973; co-author: System Analysis by Digital Computer, 1966, Computer Oriented Circuit Design, 1969, Computer Communications Networks, 1973, Protocols and Techniques in Data Communication Networks, 1981, Multimedia Communications, 1997; cons. editor, Prentice-Hall Inc., 1967—; mem. editorial bd. Future Generations Computer Systems; contbr. articles to profl. jours.; developer Alohanet packet broadcast radio network. Mem. Pres. coun. U. Ill.; adv. bd. Beckman Inst. Recipient Alexander von Humboldt Found. Rsch. award, 1994. Fellow IEEE; mem. The Internet Soc., Tau Beta Pi, Eta Kappa Nu. Home: 824 La Mesa Dr Portola Valley CA 94028-7421

KUO, PING-CHIA, historian, educator; b. Yangshe, Kiangsu, China, Nov. 27, 1908; s. Chu-sen and Hsiao-kuan (Hsu) K.; m. Anita H. Bradley, Aug. 8, 1946. A.M., Harvard U., 1930, Ph.D., 1933. Prof. modern history and Far Eastern internat. relations Nat. Wuhan U., Wuchang, China, 1933-38; editor China Forum, Hankow and Chungking, 1938-40; counsellor Nat. Mil. Council, Chungking, China, 1940-46, Ministry Fgn. Affairs, 1943-46; participated in Cairo Conf. as spl. polit. asst. to Generalissimo Chiang Kai-shek, 1943; during war yrs. in Chungking, also served Chinese Govt. concurrently in following capacities: mem. fgn. affairs com. Nat. Supreme Def. Council, 1939-46; chief, editorial and pubs. dept. Ministry Information, 1940-42, mem. central planning bd., 1941-45; tech. expert to Chinese delegation San Francisco Conf., 1945; chief trusteeship sect. secretariat UN, London; (exec. com. prep. commn. and gen. assembly), 1945-46; top-ranking dir. Dept. Security Council Affairs, UN, 1946-48; vis. prof. Chinese history San Francisco State Coll., summers 1954, 58; assoc. prof. history So. Ill. U., 1959-63, prof. history, 1963-72, chmn. dept. history, 1967-71, prof. emeritus, 1972—; sr. fellow Nat. Endowment for Humanities, 1973-74; Pres. Midwest Conf. Asian Studies, 1964. Author: A Critical Study of the First Anglo-Chinese War, with Documents, 1935, Modern Far Eastern Diplomatic History (in Chinese), 1937, China: New Age and New Outlook, 1960, China, in the Modern World Series, 1970; Contbr. to Am. hist. pubs. and various mags. in China and Ency. Brit. Decorated Kwang Hua medal A-1 grade Nat. Mil. Council, Chungking, 1941; Auspicious Star medal Nat. Govt., Chungking, 1944; Victory medal, 1945. Mem. Am. Hist. Assn., Assn. Asian Studies. Club: Commonwealth (San Francisco). Home: 8661 Don Carol Dr El Cerrito CA 94530-2752

KURAISHI, AKARI LUKE, real estate company executive; b. Nagano, Japan, July 29, 1959; came to U.S. 1984; s. Atsushi and Kuniko (Tomita) K.; m. Hiromi Lydia Hatae, Oct. 10, 1987; children: Katrina Ayumi, Kristin Kasumi. BA, Nat. Def. Acad., Yokosuka, Japan, 1982; MBA, U. Dallas, 1986. Registered internat. mem. Internat. Real Estate Inst., real estate broker, Calif. Mgr. Gateway Travel & Tours, Dallas, 1985-87; with portfolio investments dept. Mitsui Real Estate Sales USA Co., Ltd., L.A., 1987-90; mgr., 1990-91; asst. v.p. Mitsui Real Estate Sales USA Co., Ltd., L.A., 1991-95, v.p., broker/officer, 1995—; dir. ALKALY Inc., Orange, Calif., 1991—; v.p. Santa Ana (Calif.) Corp., 1992—, Santa Ana Mgmt. Corp., 1992—; sec. MI Ptnrs. LA Co., Ltd., 1993—. Mem. NRA, Colt Collectors Assn., Orange County Japanese Am. Assn. (bd. dirs. 1994—, treas. 1996—), Japanese-Am. Network (charter mem., bd. dirs. 1997—), U. Dallas Alumni Assn., Greater So. Calif. CCIM (L.A. chpt.), Lake Elsinore Sportman Assn. Home: 2348 E Trenton Ave Orange CA 92867-4454 Office: Mitsui Real Estate Sales USA Co Ltd 601 S Figueroa St Fl 4600 Los Angeles CA 90017-5751

KURI, JOHN ANTHONY, film company executive; b. L.A., Feb. 16, 1945; s. Emile and Carrie Lou (Carson) K.; m. Judy Lee Justus, Feb. 20, 1970 (div. Apr. 1988); children: Janiene, John Jr., Jason, Jay; m. Jennifer White, Jan. 3, 1998. Cert. indsl. mgmt., Orange Coast Coll., 1968; cert. bus. adminstrn., U. Calif., Irvine, 1969. Prodr. Major H. Prodns., Inc., Hollywood, 1980-82; CFO Lion Films, Ltd., London, 1983-85; pres. Kurissama Prodn., Inc., Montreal, 1985-87, Sheffield Entertainment, Inc., Encino, Calif., 1988-90, Kuri Prodns., Inc., L.A., 1990—; prodr. Imagine Films, 1990, Disney Television, 1994. Contbr. articles to profl. jours. Recipient Christopher award, 1994, Western Heritage award Cowboy Hall of Fame, 1991, Emmy nomination, 1974, Golden Halo L.A. Film Coun., 1981. Mem. Acad. Motion Picture Arts & Scis. (visual effects award com. 1984-91, fgn. film award com. 1984-95), Writers Guild Am., Dirs. Guild Am., Soc. Motion Picture & TV Art Dirs. Avocations: flying, soaring, jazz guitar.

KURILCHYK, WALTER, real estate consultant, appraiser; b. N.Y.C., Aug. 17, 1921; s. Thomas and Margaret (Grechyla) K.; m. Virginia A. Kurilchyk, Sept. 3, 1949; children: Deborah Ann, Stephen Paul. BS in Police Adminstrn. and Sci., Mich. State U., 1950; lifetime tchg. credential, Calif. State U., Fullerton, 1973. Cert. pilot, FAA. Pvt. practice real estate broker Lansing, Mich., 1952-60; real estate specialist U.S. VA, L.A., 1960-63; real estate specialist, appraiser U.S. HUD, Santa Ana, Calif., 1963-78; chief appraiser U.S. HUD, Fresno, Calif., 1975-76; pvt. practice real estate cons. Santa Ana, 1978—; assoc. prof. Golden West Coll., Huntington Beach, Calif., 1970-80; pub. Aviation History Publishing, 1997. Author Chasing Ghosts, 1997. Pres. USA-USSR Hist. Aviation, Inc., Capistrano Beach, Calif., 1987-96; dir. USA-USSR Hist. Aviation Search in Artic Ocean, Capistrano Beach., 1987—, coord., 1990—; mem. mil. adv. com. Congressman Ron Packard, Carlsbad, Calif., 1982-83. With USN, WWII. Mem. Naval Aviation Grandpa Pettibone Squad (life), DAV (life), VFW (life). Republican. Avocations: flying, reading, history. Home: 34821 Camino Capistrano Capistrano Beach CA 92624

KURSEWICZ, LEE Z., marketing consultant; b. Chgo., Oct. 26, 1916; s. Antoni and Henryka (Sulkowska) K.; ed. Chgo. and Bata ind. schs.; m. Ruth Elizabeth Venzke, Jan. 31, 1940; 1 son, Dennis. With Bata Shoe Co., Inc., 1936-78, plant mgr., Salem, Ind., 1963-65, v.p., mng. dir., Batawa, Ont., Can., 1965-71; v.p., dir. Bata Industries, Batawa, 1965-71, plant mgr., Salem, 1971-76; pres. Bata Shoe Co., Inc., Belcamp, Md., 1976-77, sr. v.p., dir., 1977-79; gen. mgr. Harford Insulated Panel Systems div. Hazleton Industries, 1981-82. City mgr. City of Batawa, 1965-71; vice chmn. Trenton (Ont.) Meml. Hosp., 1970-71; pres. Priestford Hills Community Assn., 1979-80; chmn. adv. bd. Phoenix Festival Theatre, Hartford County Community Coll., 81; vice chmn. Harford County chpt. ARC, 1980-81, chmn., 1982-83; chmn. Harford County Econ. Devel. Adv. Bd., 1983-85; mem. Susquehanna Region Pvt. Industry Council, 1983-85. Mem. Am. Mgmt. Assn. Clubs: Rotary, Bush River Yacht (commodore 1956), Bush River Power Squadron (comdr. 1957), Western Hills Country of Salem (pres. 1975), Trenton Country (pres. 1968-69), Md. Country. Home and Office: 31382 Abanita Way Laguna Niguel CA 92677-2725

KURTH, MATTHIAS C., neurologist; b. Leipzig, Germany, Mar. 16, 1955; m. Janice Hall, May 23, 1987; children: Carol, Susan. BA, Rice U., 1977; PhD, Baylor U., 1986, MD, 1986. Asst. prof. dept. neurology Tex. Tech. U., Lubbock, 1991-93; med. dir. Young Parkinson Referral Ctr., Santa Maria, Calif., 1993-95; asst. clin. dir. Nat. Parkinson Found., Miami, Fla., 1995—; assoc. dir. movement disorders Barrow Neurol. Inst., Phoenix, 1993-96, co-dir. movement disorders, 1996—. Recipient Cohen scholarship, Houston, 1973; grantee Welch Found., 1976; predoctoral fellow NIH, 1977. Avocation: skiing. Office: St Josephs Hosp & Med Ctr Barrow Neurol Inst 222 W Thomas Rd Ste 401 Phoenix AZ 85013-4423

KURTTI, JEFF, writer; b. Seattle, Oct. 20, 1961; s. Robert Alan and Evelyn Anne (Evich) K. Comms. supr. Walt Disney Imagineering, Glendale, Calif., 1989-91; corp. mktg. supr. The Walt Disney Co., Burbank, Calif., 1991-95. Author: (books) The Great Movie Musical Trivia Book, 1996, Since the World Began: Walt Disney World - The First 25 Years, 1996, The Art of The Little Mermaid, 1997, The Art of Mulan, 1998, A Bug's Life: The Making of an Epic of Miniature Proportions, 1998; writer/prodr.: (documentaries) The Making Fun and Fancy Free, 1997, The Making of Sleeping Beauty, 1997, The Making of Mary Poppins, 1997, The Making of the Jungle Book, 1997, The Making of Peter Pan, 1998, The Making of Old Yeller, 1998, The Making of The Little Mermaid, 1998; writer: (laser discs) Pocahontas, 1996, Toy Story, 1996, Sleeping Beauty, 1997, The Hunchback of Notre Dame, 1997. Mem. Am. Soc. Journalists and Authors, Writers Guild of Am. West. Office: 23 Aloha Dr Pacific Palisades CA 90272-4639

KURTZ, TERRY CECIL, secondary education educator, news anchorman; b. O'Neill, Nebr., Oct. 7, 1944; s. Robert Vonn and Myrtle Marie (Brown) K.; children: Marlin Vonn Robert, Terrence Robert Bryan, Jessica Faye Aguiar, Natalie Nicole, Kyle Robert Scott; 1 stepdau., Shelley Marie Owings; m. Rebecca Lynn Cottingim, July 20, 1995; 1 child, Robert Terrance Thomas. BA in Social Sci. and Art, Dakota Wesleyan U., 1967. Lifetime tchg. credential, Calif. Tchr. U.S. History and Cinematography Apple Valley (Calif.) H.S., 1967—; radio announcer Sta. KBRX-AM, O'Neill, 1960-63, Sta. KAVR AM-FM, Apple Valley, 1970-81; sports anchor, dir. Sta. KVVT-TV, Victorville, Calif., 1986-91; news and sports dir., anchorman Hi-Desert Cablevision, Victorville, 1991—. Interviews include Sonny Bono, Roy Rogers, Willie Nelson, Pete Wilson, Keith Olberg, others. Republican. Avocations: playing softball and basketball, baseball, football, music. Office: Hi-Desert Cablevision 12490 Business Center Dr Victorville CA 92392

KURTZIG, SANDRA L., software company executive; b. Chgo., Oct. 21, 1946; d. Barney and Marian (Boruck) Brody; children: Andrew Paul, Kenneth Alan; BS in Math., UCLA, 1968; MS in aeronaut. engring., Stanford U., 1968. Math analyst TRW Systems, 1967-68; mktg. rep., Gen. Electric Co., 1969-72; chmn. bd., CEO, pres. ASK Computer Systems, Mountain View, Calif., 1972-85, chmn. bd., 1986-89; founder The ASK Group, 1972—, chmn., pres., CEO, 1989-93; chmn. emeritus, 1993—, chmn. E-Benefits, 1996—. bd. dirs. Hoover Instn., Harvard Bus. Sch., Stanford Sch. of Engring., UCLA Anderson Grad. Sch. Mgmt. Author: CEO: Building a $400 Million Company from the Ground Up, 1991, 94. Cited one of 50 most influential bus. people in Am., Bus. Week, 1985. Office: 2420 Sand Hill Rd Ste 201 Menlo Park CA 94025-6942

KURTZMAN, RALPH HAROLD, retired biochemist, researcher, consultant; b. Mpls., Feb. 21, 1933; s. Ralph Harold, Sr. and Susie Marie (Elwell) K.; m. Nancy Virginia Leussler, Aug. 27, 1955; children: Steven Paul, Sue. BS, U. Minn., 1955; MS, U. Wis., 1958, PhD, 1959. Asst. prof. U. R.I., Kingston, 1959-62, U. Minn., Morris, 1962-65; biochemist U.S. Dept. Agriculture, Albany, Calif., 1965-97; ret., 1997; instr. U. Calif., Berkeley, 1981-82; cons. Bliss Valley Farms, Twin Falls, Idaho, 1983-84; pres. Santa Clara Valley Tex. Instrument PC Users' Group, 1991-92, editor, 1993-97; cons. in field. Editor Internat. Jour. Mushroom Scis., 1995—; inventor mushroom substrate (compost) preparation, 1982, decaffeination of beverages, 1973; contbr. articles to profl. jours. Chmn. Berkeley YMCA Camp Program Com., 1971-72; official Amateur Athletic Union (swimming), San Francisco, 1973-80; treas. Calif. Native Plant Soc., 1970. Mem. Am. Mushroom Inst., Mycological Soc. Am. (organizer symposium mushroom cultivation in Am. tropics 1998), Mycological Soc. Japan, Sigma Xi. Avocations: computers, wood working, photography. Home and Office: 445 Vassar Ave Berkeley CA 94708-1215

KUSAKA, MARYANNE WINONA, mayor; b. Kamuela, Hawaii, Sept. 11, 1935. BA in Elem. Edn., U. No. Colo. Mayor City of Lihue, Hawaii, 1994—. Office: County of Kauai 4444 Rice St Ste 235 Lihue HI 96766

KUSHNER, TODD ROGER, computer scientist, software engineer; b. Bethesda, Md., June 18, 1956; s. Harvey David and Rose Molly (Rehert) K.; m. Lea Louise Friedman, Nov. 11, 1990; children: Joshua Philip, Daniel Stuart. BS in Life Scis., MIT, 1976; MS in Computer Sci., U. Md., 1980, PhD in Computer Sci., 1982. Rsch. technician NIH, Bethesda, 1976-77; programmer Tech. Mgmt. Inc., Washington, 1977-78, GTE-Telenet, McLean, Va., 1978-79; grad. rsch. asst. U. Md., College Park, 1980-82, mem. rsch. staff, 1985-88; computer scientist SRI Internat., Menlo Park, Calif., 1982-83; sr. software engr. Vicom Sys. Inc., San Jose, Calif., 1983-85; sr. engr. Stanford Telecoms., Reston, Va., 1988-89; adv. programmer IBM Corp., Gaithersburg, Md., 1989-93; sr. scientist CTA Inc., Rockville, Md., 1993-96; mem. sr. software staff Lockheed Martin Fed. Systems, Denver, 1996—; adj. lectr. U. Santa Clara, Calif., 1983, U. Md., Gaithersburg, 1989-90, Johns Hopkins U., Gaithersburg, 1989-93; participant Software Process Interchange Network, McLean, Va., 1993—. Contbr. articles to profl. publs. Grad. fellow Air Force Office Sci. Rsch., 1980. Mem. IEEE Computer Soc., Assn. Computer Machinery. Democrat. Jewish. Avocations: swimming, racquetball, skiing, golf. Home: 6240 S Elmira Cir W Englewood CO 80111-5601 Office: Lockheed Martin Fed Systems PO Box 179 Denver CO 80201-0179

KUSTER, ROBERT KENNETH, scientist; b. Los Angeles, July 11, 1932; s. Arthur Rollo Kuster and Ermine Rosebud (Prittchett) Woodward. AS, Gavilan Coll., 1974, AA in Humanities, 1981; student, San Jose State U., 1955, 1974-76, UCLA, 1977. Installer Western Electric Co., Inc., Corpus Christi, Tex., 1951-53, 1955, San Jose, Calif., 1957-59, 1960-63; ptnr., scientist, cons. WE-Woodward's Enterprises, Morgan Hill, Calif., 1973—, technician AT&T Tech., Inc., San Jose, 1983-85; scientist pvt. practice, Gilroy, 1978—. Served to sgt. U.S. Army Corps Engrs., 1952-54. Mem. AAAS, Astron. Soc. Pacific, Calif. Acad. Scis., N.Y. Acad. Scis., Am. Legion, VFW. Baptist. Lodge: Elks. Avocations: photography, golf, camping, hiking, music. Home: 17506 Hoot Owl Way Morgan Hill CA 95037-6524 Office: Woodward's Enterprises 179 Bender Cir Morgan Hill CA 95037-3533

KUTER, KAY E., writer, actor; b. L.A., Apr. 25, 1925; s. Leo E. and Evelyn Belle (Edler) K. *The first Kuter to emigrate from Germany was Bernhard Kuter, in 1748. His sons were Revolutionary War captains under "Mad" Anthony Wayne. Maternal great-grandparents, Jessie McGill and Giovanni Maggginetti emigrated from Scotland and Switzerland, respectively, marrying and traveling to Salt Lake City by covered wagon in 1868. Jessie McGill Magginetti appeared with Harry Lauder at the Great Salt Lake Theatre, beginning family's theatrical tradition. Mother acted in silent films. Father was a pioneer motion picture art director, 1920-1965, designing over 300 films, and a founder, later president, of the Society of Motion Picture and Television Art Directors.* Student, Pomona Coll., 1943, UCLA, 1944; BFA in Drama, Carnegie Inst. Tech., 1949, BFA, 1949. Radio actor NBC, 1944; actor, 1944—. Actor in 198 musicals, off-Broadway, stock, repertory, touring, and Shakespearean stage prodns.; 45 feature films; more than 400 TV shows, including 7 yrs. as a series regular (Newt Kiley) in Green Acres and Petticoat Junction; voiceover actor for cartoon series Aladdin, The Little Mermaid, The Litte Mermaid on Ice, Prince Valiant, Biker Mice From Mars, Fantastic Four; in cartoon spls. Olympic Mascot Izzy, Annabelle's Wish; in CD-ROMS The Beast Within, Ultima 9, Grim Fandango The Curse of Monkey Island, Heretic II; in radio prodns. Getting Married, Treasure Island, Macbeth, Satanic Verses, Heartbreak House; author: Carmen Incarnate, 1946, Ships That Never Sailed, 1994, Hollywood Houdini, Picture Perfect World, 1995; voiceover spokesman Hershey's Kisses, 1989—; editor: The Jester, 1956-60, The Jester 35th Anniversary, 1960, 50th Anniversary, 1976; contbr. to Nat. Libr. Poetry anthologies, 1995, 96, 97; dir. more than 50 stage prodns. including Steve Allen's The Wake. Bd. dirs. Family Svc. of L.A., 1950-70. Mem. SAG (bd. dirs. 1970-73), ADA, AEA, AFTRA, ACLU, NOW, NARAL, Internat. Platform Assn., Book Publicists of So. Calif., Nat. Soc. Hist. Preservation, Smithsonian, Carnegie Mellon U. Westcoast Drama Alumni Clan (founding mem., officer, bd. dirs. 1968-80), Ephebian Soc., Internat. Soc. Poets (disting. mem.), Albert C. May soc., Acad. Am. Poets, Andrew Carnegie Soc., Pacific Pioneer Broadcasters, Carnegie Mellon U. Alumni Assn. (regional v.p. 1976-79, Svc. award 1979), Masquers Club (bd. dirs. 1953-75, rec. sec. 1956-70, corr. sec. 1957-69, v.p. 1971-75), Actors' Fund of Am. (life mem.), others. Democrat. Avocations: composing, set design, piano. Home: 6207 Satsuma Ave North Hollywood CA 91606-3819

KUTVIRT, DUDA CHYTILOVA (RUZENA), scientific translator; b. Pilsen, Czechoslovakia, Sept. 17, 1919; came to U.S., 1949; d. Frantisek and Ruzena (Vitousek) Chytil; m. Otakar Kutvirt, July 10, 1942 (dec.); children: Thomas (dec.), Daniel. BA, Smith Coll., 1940; MA, Mills Coll., 1942. Rsch. asst. U. Rochester Med. Sch., 1942-44; scientific translator Eastman Kodak Rsch. Labs., Rochester, 1944-45, 61-78. Voter registrar LWV, Albuquerque, 1980—, Rochester, 1955-70; vol. U. N.Mex. Hosp. Svc. League, Albuquerque, 1979—; mem. Albuquerque com. for fgn. affairs. Home: 5 Pool St NW Albuquerque NM 87120-1809

KUWABARA, DENNIS MATSUICHI, optometrist; b. Honolulu, July 20, 1945; s. Robert Tokuichi and Toshiko (Nakashima) K.; m. Judith Naomi Tokumaru, June 28, 1970; children: Jennifer Tomiko, Susan Kazuko. BS, So. Calif. Coll. Optometry, 1968, OD cum laude, 1970. Pvt. practice optometry Waipahu, Honolulu, Hawaii, 1972—; pres. 1st Study Club for Optometrists, Honolulu, 1982-83; chmn. Bd. Examiners in Optometry, Honolulu, 1982-90; state dir. Optometric Extension Found., Honolulu, 1980-88. Served to lt. Med. Service Corps, USN, 1970-72. Named Outstanding Young Person of Hawaii, Hawaii State Jaycees, 1979. Fellow Am. Acad. Optometry (diplomate cornea and contact lens sect. 1991); mem. Hawaii Optometric Assn. (pres. 1979-80, Man of Yr. award 1976, Optometrist of Yr. 1983), Am. Optometric Assn., Armed Forces Optometric Soc. Home: 94-447 Holaniku St Mililani HI 96789-1710 Office: 94-748 Hikimoe St Waipahu HI 96797-3350 also: 1441 Kapiolani Blvd Ste 1520 Honolulu HI 96814-4407

KUWABARA, LORI ANNE, educator, writer, consultant; b. Downey, Calif., Jan. 16, 1961; d. Harry Keiso and Yoriko Janet (Kubo) K. BA in English, U. Calif., Berkeley, 1983; MA in Edn., U. Calif., L.A., 1986; MA in Journalism, U. Calif., Berkeley, 1990. Cert. secondary tchr., Calif. Tchr. Internat. Edn. Svcs., Tokyo, 1984-85, Electronic Language Sch., North Hollywood, Calif., 1985-86, Saugus (Calif.) High Sch., 1986-88; instr., lectr. U. Calif., Berkeley, 1988-92; instr. U. Calif. Extension, Berkeley, 1991-93; english instr. El Camino Coll., Torrance, Calif., 1993-94; English instr. Santa Rosa (Calif.) Jr. Coll., 1994—; cons. Nat. SEED Project, Wellesley, Mass., 1997—; instr. Columbia Review, San Francisco, 1991-92; reader Ednl. Testing Svcs., Oakland, Calif., 1989-97; freelance journalist, 1989-93. Author (short story) Women's Words, 1998; contbr. articles to profl. jours.; lectr. in field. Recipient Excellence in Edn. award Santa Rosa C. of C., 1998. Mem. Nat. Council Teachers of English, Nat. Japanese Am. Historical Soc., Am. Assn. U. Women, Asian Pacific Am. Higher Edn., Pi Lambda Theta. Democrat. Avocations: sports, travel, writing, arts, gardening. Office: Santa Rosa Jr College 1501 Mendocino Ave Santa Rosa CA 95401

KUZMA, GEORGE MARTIN, bishop; b. Windber, Pa., July 24, 1925; s. Ambrose and Anne (Marton) K. Student, Benedictine Coll., Lisle, Ill.; BA, Duquesne U., postgrad.; postgrad., U. Mich.; grad., SS Cyril and Methodius Byzantine Cath. Sem. Ordained priest Byzantine Cath. Ch., 1955. Asst. pastor SS Peter and Paul Ch., Braddock, Pa., 1955-57; pastor Holy Ghost Ch., Charleroi, Pa., 1957-65, St. Michael Ch., Flint, Mich., 1965-70, St. Eugene Ch., Bedford, Ohio, 1970-72, Annunciation Ch., Anaheim, Calif., 1970-86; rev. monsignor Byzantine Cath. Ch., 1984, titular bishop, 1986, consecrated bishop, 1987; aux. bishop Byzantine Cath. Diocese of Passaic, N.J., 1987-90; bishop Van Nuys, Calif., 1991—; judge matrimonial tribunal, mem. religious edn. commn., mem. commn. orthodox rels. Diocese of Pitts., 1955-69; judge matrimonial tribunal, vicar for religious Diocese of Parma, 1969-82; treas., bd. dirs., chmn. liturgical commn., mem. clergy & seminarian rev. bd., liaison to ea. Cath. dirs. religious edn., bd. dirs. diocesan credit union, chmn. diocesan heritage bd., chmn. diocesan ecumenical commn. Diocese of Van Nuys, 1982-86; vicar gen. Diocese of Passaic; episcopal vicar for Ea. Pa.; chmn. Diocesan Retirement Plan Bd.; pres. Father Walter Cizsek Prayer League; chaplain Byzantine Carmelite Monastery, Sugarloaf, Pa. Assoc. editor Byzantine Cath. World; editor The Apostle. With USN, 1943-46, PTO. also: Byzantine Cath Eparchy of Van Nuys 8131 N 16th St Phoenix AZ 85020-3999*

KUZNETSKY, MICHELLE HOPE, recording industry executive, producer; b. L.A., Aug. 29, 1970; d. Richard David and Lynne Faith (Rosenberg) K. BA, U. Calif., Santa Barbara, 1992; JD, Southwestern Law Sch., L.A., 1995. Music supr. Tri-Tone Music, West L.A., 1995—; prodr. Colonial Pictures, L.A. Democrat. Avocations: running, screenwriting, BMI performance nights. Office: Tri-Tone Music 8282 W Sunset Blvd # C Los Angeles CA 90046-2416

KVAMME, MARK D., marketing professional. Programmer Apple Computer; founding mem., then internat. product mgr. in U.S. Apple France; founder, pres., CEO Internat. Solutions; dir. internat. mktg. Wyse Tech.; pres., chmn. CKS Group, Cupertino, Calif. Office: USWEB/CKS 10443 Bandley Dr Cupertino CA 95014-1912*

KWAN, BENJAMIN CHING KEE, ophthalmologist; b. Hong Kong, July 12, 1940; came to U.S., 1959; s. Shun Ming and Lurk Ming (Lai) K.; m. Catherine Ning, Aug. 29, 1964; children: Susan San, David Daiwai. MD, Wash. U., St. Louis, 1967. Diplomate Am. Bd. Ophthalmology. Ptnr. So. Calif. Permanente Med. Ctr., Harbor City, 1976—, chief of svc. ophthalmology, 1976-88; clin. prof. dept. ophthalmology UCLA, 1995—. Chmn. winter blossom ball Chinese Am. Debutante's Guild, 1993. Capt. U.S. Army, 1969-71. Recipient Svc. award Asian Am. Sr. Citizens Svc. Ctr., 1993, Proclamation award Calif. Sec. of State, 1993, Svc. award East L.A. Chinese Everspring Sr. Assn.,, 1994. Fellow Am. Acad. Ophthalmology; mem. Chinese Am. Ophthal. Soc. (pres. elect 1997-99, pres. 1999, Svc. award 1994), Chinese Physician's Soc. So. Calif. (bd. dirs., pres. 1983, svc. award 1983, 89), Orgn. Chinese Ams. (pres. L.A. chpt. 1986-87). Roman Catholic. Avocations: ballroom dancing, singing, snow skiing. Home: 6327 Tarragon Rd Rancho Palos Verdes CA 90275-5834 Office: 1050 Pacific Coast Hwy Harbor City CA 90710-3509

KWON, CHUHEE, physics researcher; b. Seoul, Korea, Dec. 10, 1965; came to U.S., 1990; d. Yonghwan and Dongsuk (Choi) K.; m. Yonggyu Gim, July 7, 1991; 1 child, Albert Genehyuk. BS in Physics, Seoul Nat. U., 1988; MS in Physics, Pohang (Korea) Inst. Sci. and Tech., 1990; PhD in Physics, U. Md., 1995. Tchg. asst. Pohang Inst. Sci. and Tech., 1988, rsch. asst., 1989-90; tchg. asst. U. Md., College Park, 1990-91, rsch. asst., 1991-95, rsch. assoc., 1995-97; postdoctoral fellow Los Alamos (N.Mex.) Nat. Lab., 1997—. Contbr. articles to profl. jours.; inventor in field. Recipient Grad. Student Travel grant U. Md., 1995. Mem. Materials Rsch. Soc. (Grad. Student award 1995), Am. Phys. Soc. Office: Los Alamos Nat Lab MS-K763 Los Alamos NM 87545

KWON, TERESA EUN YOUNG, illustrator; b. Seoul, Korea, July 14, 1972; d. Hyok Yun and He Young Kwon. BFA, Acad. Art, San Francisco, 1995. Photographer Fairmont HOtel/Mark Hopkins, San Francisco, 1993-96; illustrator Mindscape, Novato, Calif., 1996, Proactive Networks, Santa Clara, 1997, Bay Area Display, San Francisco, 1997. One-woman shows include Planetary REnaissance Gallery, Minn., 1996, Fillmore Ctr., San Francisco, 1997, Korean Student Assn., 1998, African Cultural Mus., 1998; illustrator: Signifying Monkey, 1998. Avocations: swimming, tennis, gardening, reading, music.

KWONG, RAYMOND, minister; b. Hong Kong, May 11, 1954; came to U.S., 1969; s. Johnny C. and Kwan (Luke) K.; m. Anne W. Pang, Feb. 14, 1981; 1 child, Caleb. BS, U. Calif., Berkeley, 1976. Ordained to ministry Bapt. Ch., 1981. Min. outreach Bay Area Chinese Bible Ch., San Leandro, Calif., 1979-84; asst. pastor Holy Word Ch., San Francisco, 1984-86; founder, pastor Bible Bapt. Ch., San Francisco, 1986—; guest talk show Chinese Outreach, Millbrae, Calif., 1990—; host weekly radio broadcast Family Voice. Author newsletter Challenger, 1990—; mem. editorial staff newsletter Voice, 1990—. Com. mem. San Franciscans for Common Sense, 1989-90; founder, pres. Chinese Family Alliance, San Francisco, 1990—. Republican. Office: Chinese Family Alliance 450 Taraval St # 246 San Francisco CA 94116-2530

KYL, JON L., senator; b. Oakland, Nebr., Apr. 25, 1942; s. John and Arlene (Griffith) K.; m. Caryll Louise Collins, June 5, 1964; children: Kristine Kyl Gavin, John Jeffry. BA, U. Ariz., 1964, LLB, 1966. Atty. Jennings, Strouss & Salmon, Phoenix, 1966-86; mem. 100th-103rd Congresses from 4th Ariz. dist., 1987-94; senator 106th Congress, Ariz., 1995—; mem. Energy & Natural Resources Com., Jud. Com., select com. on Intelligence. Past chmn. Phoenix C. of C.; founding dir. Crime Victim Found.; Phoenix Econ. Growth Corp.; past bd. dirs. Ariz. Acad.; past chmn. Young Rep.; gen. coun. Ariz. Rep. Party. Mem. Ariz. State Bar Assn. Office: US Senate 724 Hart Senate Bldg Washington DC 20515-0302*

KYTE, LYDIANE, retired botanist; b. L.A., Jan. 6, 1919; d. Aurele and Helen Scott (Douglas) Vermeulen; m. Robert McClung Kyte, June 2, 1939; children: Katherine Liu, Bobbin Cave, William Robert Kyte. BS, U. Wash., 1964. Supt. Weyerhaeuser Co., Rochester, Wash., 1972-77; lab mgr. Briggs Nursery, Olympia, Wash., 1977-80; owner Cedar Valley Nursery, Centralia, Wash., 1980—; cons. Internat. Exec. Service Corps, Brazil, 1987, Egypt, 1990. Author: Plants From Test Tubes: An Introduction to Micropropagation, 1983, 2d rev. edit., 1988, 3d edit., 1996. Mem. Internat. Plant Propagators' Soc., Internat. Assn. Plant Tissue Culture, Am. Assn. for Hort. Sci., Am. Assn. Univ. Women. Avocation: gardening. Home and Office: Cedar Valley Nursery 3833 Mc Elfresh Rd SW Centralia WA 98531-9510

LABA, MARVIN, management consultant; b. Newark, Mar. 17, 1928; s. Joseph Abraham and Jean Cecil (Saunders) L.; m. Sandra Seltzer, Apr. 16, 1961 (div. May 1974); children: Stuart Michael, Jonathan Todd; m. Elizabeth Luger, June 11, 1974 (div. 1979). BBA, Ind. U., 1951. Buyer Bamberger's (Macy's N.J.), Newark, 1951-67; v.p., mdse. adminstr. Macy's N.Y., 1967-73, v.p., gen. mdse. mgr. Howland/Steinback, White Plains, N.Y., 1973-75, Pomeroy's, Levittown, Pa., 1975-76; v.p., gen. mdse. mgr., sr. v.p., exec. v.p. May Co. Calif., North Hollywood, 1976-79; pres., chief exec. officer G. Fox & Co. (div. of the May dept. stores), Hartford, Conn., 1979-82; pres. Richard Theobald & Asocs., L.A., 1983; pres., chief exec. officer Marvin Laba & Assocs., L.A., 1983—. With U.S. Army, 1946-48. Avocations: coins, tennis, theatre, travel. Office: Marvin Laba & Assoc 6255 W Sunset Blvd Ste 617 Los Angeles CA 90028-7407

LABATE, FRANK RICHARD, minister; b. Phillipsburg, N.J., July 11, 1959; s. John Assunto and Constance (Cuva) L.; m. Ruth Anne Mayers, Aug. 22, 1982. BA in Theology, Columbia Union Coll., 1982; MDiv, Andrews U., 1987. Ordained to ministry Seventh-day Adventist Ch., 1989. Minister Seventh-day Adventist Ch., Yale, Va., 1983—; pres., owner Rick Labate Prodns., Yale, 1987—; bd. dirs. J&P Music Ministries, Marcellus, Mich., 1986—. Recording artist and orchestration arranger including (tape) Treasures of Yesteryear, 1988; author (sermon): The God Who Lets Us Begin Again, 1988. Named One of Top Ten Sermons for 1986 Andrews U., 1986. Home: PO Box 1165 Sumas WA 98295-1165

LABBE, ARMAND JOSEPH, museum curator, anthropologist; b. Lawrence, Mass., June 13, 1944; s. Armand Henri and Gertrude Marie (Martineau) L.; m. Denise Marie Scott, Jan. 17, 1969 (div. 1972). BA in Anthropology, Univ. Mass., 1969; MA in Anthropology, Calif. State U., 1986; lifetime instr. credential in anthropology, State Calif. Curator collections Bowers Mus., Santa Ana, Calif., 1978-79, curator anthropology, 1979-86, chief curator, 1986—, dir. rsch. and collections, 1991—; instr. prof. Santa Ana Coll., 1981-86, U. Calif., Irvine, 1983, 87, 91, 93, Chapman U., 1996, Calif. State U., Fullerton, 1982, 83, 88, 97, 98, part-time faculty, appt. rsch. assoc. dept. anthropology, 1997—, Calif. State U., Fullerton, 1997—; trustee Balboa Arts Conservation Ctr., San Diego, 1989—, Ams. Found., Greenfield, Mass., 1985-94, Quintcentenary Festival Discovery, Orange County, Calif., 1990-91, Mingei Internat. Mus., La Jolla, Calif., 1993—, treas. bd. dirs. 1996—; inaugural guest lectr. Friends of Ethnic Art, San Francisco, 1988; hon. bd. dirs., Ethnic Arts Coun., L.A.; mem. Orange County 46th Congressional Dist. Art Bd., 1997—. Author: Man and Cosmos, 1982, Ban Chiang, 1985, Colombia Before Columbus, 1986 (1st prize 1987), Leigh Wiener: Portraits, 1987, Colombia Antes de Colón, 1988 (honored at Gold Mus. Bogotá, Colombia, 1988), Images of Power: Master Works of the Bowers Museum of Cultural Art, 1992; co-author Tribute to The Gods: Treasures of the Museo del Oro, Bogotá, 1992, Guardians of the Life Stream: Shamans, Art and Power In Prehispanic Central Panama, 1995, Shamans, Gods, and Mythic Beasts: Colombian Gold and Ceramics in Antiquity, Am. Found. Arts, 1998. Hon. bd. dirs. Ethnic Arts Coun. L.A.; cons. Orange County Coun. on History and Art, Santa Ana, 1981-85; mem. Task Force on County Cultural Resources, Orange County, 1979; cons., interviewer TV prodn. The Human Journey, Fullerton, 1986-89; treas., bd. trustees Mingei Internat. Mus., San Diego, 1996—; mem. art bd. Orange County 46th Congl. Dist., 1997—. With USAF, 1963-67. Recipient cert. of Recognition Orange County Bd. Suprs., 1982, award for outstanding scholarship Colombian Community, 1987; honored for authorship Friends of Libr., 1987, 88. Fellow Am. Anthrop. Assn.; mem. AAAS, Am. Assn. Mus., N.Y. Acad. Scis., S.W. Anthrop. Assn. Avocations: photography, travel. Home: 2854 Royal Palm Dr Apt C Costa Mesa CA 92626-3828

LABINS, DEBORAH LYNNE, maternal women's health nurse; b. Atlanta, Jan. 5, 1957; d. Harold Whitney and Lois Romaine (Moudy) Hampson; m. Steven Thomas Labins, Mar. 18, 1978; children: Jennifer, Christine, Eric. AA in Nursing, Pierce Coll., Woodland Hills, Calif., 1978. RN, Calif. Nurses' aide Motion Picture and TV Hosp., Woodland Hills; staff nurse labor and delivery room, postpartum, nursery Granada Hills (Calif.) Community Hosp.; nurse labor and delivery room West Hills Regional Med. Ctr. (formerly Humana Hosp.), West Hills, Calif.

LABOVITZ, EARL A., allergist; b. Cleveland, Miss., June 12, 1949. MD, U Miss, 1975. Allergist Desert Samaritan Hosp., Mesa, Ariz. Office: Mesa-Tempe Allergy & Asthma Clinic 2451 E Baseline Rd Ste B-300 Gilbert AZ 85234-2471

LACAYO, OMAR D'LEÓN, artist; b. Managua, Nicaragua, Mar. 5, 1929; s. David and Gullermina (Estrada) L. D in Fine Arts, U. Managua, Nicaragua, 1957. Artist: one man exhibitions include: Museo de Tauroentum, France, 1982, Carnegie Mus., Calif., 1983, Ethinos Gallery, Calif., 1986, Gallery Qualli, Mexico City, 1987, Gallery Costa de Oro, Calif., 1988, Gallery Fernandez, Calif., 1989, Palm Street Gallery, Calif., 1990, Museo Galeria Omar d'León, Managua, Nicaragua, 1990, The Americas Collection, Miami Fla. Bond Gallery, San Francisco, 1993; numerous group exhibitions include: Bienial in Spain, Madrid, 1950, Bienial in France, N.Y. World's Fair, 1950, Bienial de Sao Paulo, Brazil, 1969, Galeria Tagüe, Managua, 1975, Fisherman's Wharf, San Francisco,1980, Moss Gallery, San Francisco, 1980, Segund Bienal, Mexico City, 1980, Presidential Collection, White House, Washington, 1983, Art Inst., Chgo., 1987, Christie's, Manson and Woods, Internat., N.Y.C., 1989, 90, The Armand Hammer Mus., L.A., 1991, William Doyle Galleries, N.Y., 1991, Gallery Los Pipitos, Managua, 1993, Galleries Contil, Josefina, Managua, Christie's, William Doyle, N.Y.C., 1992; permanent collections include: Mus. Modern Art of Latin Am., Washington, 1980, Gallery of Carole R. Korn Asid, Miami, 1982, Carnegie Art Mus., N.Y.C.; his poetry is included in Treasured Poems of America, Cenizas Literature, Poesia Nicaragüense and other anthologies. Recipient Gold medal Managua, Nicaragua, early 1950's, Silver medal Jeugos de Guatemala, Honorable mention, Bogota, Colombia, 3d prize Camarillo Art Ctr., 1900, 1st, 2d and best overall, 1983; special diploma from Consul Gen. Nicaragua, 1994. Avocations: writing, archaeology, classical music, philosophy, botanics. Home: PO Box 3125 Camarillo CA 93011-3125

LACHEMANN, MARCEL, professional baseball manager; b. L.A., June 13, 1941. BSBA, U. So. Calif., 1962. Former player Kansas City A's (moved to Oakland); pitching coach Calif. Angels (now Anaheim Angels), 1983-92, 97—, mgr., head coach, 1994-96; pitching coach Anaheim Angels, 1996—, Fla. Marlins, 1992-94. Office: Anaheim Angels 2000 E Gene Autry Way Anaheim CA 92806-6100

LACKIE, KENNETH WILLIAM, physical scientist; b. Port Chester, N.Y., Dec. 25, 1939; s. Herbert Kenneth and Thelma Elen (Hedman) L.; m. Joanne Virginia White, Dec. 11, 1966 (div. May 8, 1988). BS in Chemistry, Bucknell U., 1961; student, NYU, 1960. Oceanographer Naval Oceanographic Office, Washington, 1961-75; head Washington liaison office Naval Ocean Rsch. and Devel. Act, Arlington, Va., 1976-79; asst. to dir. internat. and spl. programs Office of Naval Rsch., Arlington, Va., 1980-85, dir. ASW environ. acoustic support program, 1986-89, dep. asst. chief naval rsch., 1990-91; sci. staff asst. to dir. Naval Rsch. Lab., Washington, DC, 1992-96; mgr. Washington liaison office applied physics lab. U. Wash., Seattle, 1997—; mem. various bd. USN, Washington, 1986-96, chair low-frequency active acoustics workshop, 1987. Columnist Turning Wheels mag., 1986—. Mem. The Oceanography Soc., Marine Tech. Soc., Mensa, DC Coun. Car Clubs (bd. dirs. 1976—). Avocation: old car restoration. Home: 6629 32nd St NW Washington DC 20015-2309 Office: U Washington Applied Physics Lab 1013 NE 40th St Seattle WA 98105-6698

LACROSSE, PATRICK, museum administrator. CEO, pres. Oreg. Mus. of Sci. & Industry, Portland, Oreg. Office: Oreg Mus Sci and Industry 1945 SE Water Ave Portland OR 97214-3356

LACY, GREGORY LAWRENCE, protective services official; b. Long Beach, Calif., June 12, 1949; s. George Lawrence and Pauline L. (Smith) L.; m. Cheryl Ann Carey, Apr. 16, 1987 (div. May 1990); children: Megan Lee, Tess Jordan; adopted children: Randy J., Jennie A.; m. Suphan Wongruan, June 4, 1991. AS in Forestry, Bottineau (N.D.) Sch. Forestry, 1967; cert. law enforcement, N.D. Police Acad., Bismarck, 1967; AS in Engring., N.D. State Sch. Sci., 1972. Cert. EMT, emergency trauma tech., law enforcement, N.D., Alaska. Law enforcement officer Langdon (N.D.) Police Dept., 1972-77; law enforcement officer, tng. officer Smith Securty - Spl. Divsn., Anchorage, 1977-80; security officer, field tng. officer AHTNA-Am. Guard & Alert Security Co., Anchorage, 1980—; tng. officer Langdon Police Dept., 1973-77. Active Campaign for Sheriff Re-election, Cavalier County, Langdon, 1973-77; pub. fire arms tng. Langdon Police Dept., 1973-77. Mem. NRA (life), Air Couriers Assn., Gold Prospectors Assn. (life). Baptist. Avocations: hunting, fishing, photography, hiking, computers. Home: 3705 Arctic Blvd # 622 Anchorage AK 99503-5774 Office: AHTNA-American Guard & Alert Security Co 1413 Hyder St Anchorage AK 99501-5431

LACY, JOHN R., lawyer; b. Dallas, Dec. 15, 1942. BS, San Diego State U., 1966; MS, U. So. Calif., 1971; JD, U. Calif., 1973. Bar: Calif. 1973, Hawaii 1974. Atty. Goodsill Anderson Quinn & Stifel, Honolulu; arbitrator Ct. Annexed Arbitration Program, 1986—. Comment editor Hastings Law Jour., 1972-73. Mem. ABA, Hawaii Bar Assn., State Bar Calif., Am. Bd. Trial Advs., Maritime Law Assn. U.S., Thurston Soc., Order of Coif. E-mail: jlacy@goodsill.com. Office: Goodsill Anderson Quinn & Stifel PO Box 3196 1800 Alii Pl 1099 Alakea St Honolulu HI 96813-4500

LADEHOFF, ROBERT LOUIS, bishop; b. Feb. 19, 1932; m. Jean Arthur Burcham (dec. Feb. 1992); 1 child, Robert Louis Jr. Grad., Duke U., 1954, Gen. Theol. Sem., 1957, Va. Theol. Sem., 1980. Ordained deacon, priest The Episcopal Ch., 1957;. Priest in charge N.C. parishes, 1957-60; rector St. Christopher's Ch., Charlotte, N.C., 1960-74, St. John's Ch., Fayetteville, 1974-85; bishop, co-adjutor of Oreg., 1985, bishop, 1986—. Office: Diocese of Oreg PO Box 467 Lake Oswego OR 97034-0467

LADEWIG GOODMAN, JEANNE MARGARET, artist; b. Grand Rapids, Mich., June 26, 1923; d. Roland Adolph and Margaret Francis (Palmer) Ladewig; m. Larry Goodman, June 1963 (div. 1966). BEd, Concordia Coll., 1945; MS in Art Edn., Ill. Inst. Tech., 1970; postgrad., Chgo. Art Inst., 1959-68. Tchr. Luth. Schs., Chgo., 1952-62; tchr. art Park Ridge (Ill.) Pub. Sch. Dist. 64, 1962-74, Art coord., 1974-86; workshop presenter NAEA-IAEA; guest lectr. U. Ill., 1971-72; adv. bd. Contemporary Art Workshop, Chgo.; hiring cons. Evanston (Ill.) Schs., 1985. Exhibited in group shows at Ditmar Gallery Northwestern, 1972, Abney Galleries, 1973, Concordia U., 1996, Ariz. State U. Gammage Auditorium, 1998, World Fine Art, N.Y., 1997; contbr. articles to profl. jours. Vol. free meals Luth. Ch., Chgo., 1990-95; vol. Terra Mus. of Art, Chgo., 1989-95. Grantee Helene Wurlitzer Found., 1972; 1st prize water color show Artist Guild of Chgo., 1986. Mem. AAUW, Chgo. Soc. of Artists, Chgo. Artists Coalition, Nat. League Am. Pen Women. Lutheran. Avocation: travel, writing.

LAFONTAINE, THOMAS E., chemical engineer; b. North Adams, Mass., Jan. 2, 1952; s. Omer Charles and Isabella Frances (Luczinski) LaF.; m. Catherine Hackett, July 9, 1981; children: Christina, Colima. Dir. tech. internat. Cameron-Yakima (Wash.), Inc., 1981-87; dir. engring. Agro Industries de Tecuman S.A., Tecuman, Mexico, 1987-88; pres., owner Teltech Engring., Yakima, 1988—; tech. dir., v.p. Intercon Pacific, Inc. (now Teltech Co.), Portland, 1989—; cons. Phillippine Govt. Contbr. articles to profl. jours. Mem. Am. Water Works Assn., Air Pollution Control Assn., Internat. Carbon Soc. Achievements include development of specially treated activated carbons for specific use, conversion of cubi nut shells into activated carbon; design of installation and startup of activated carbon manufacturing plants in Philippines, China, Mexico, Malaysia and U.S. Office: Teltech Co 12005 Summitview Ext Yakima WA 98908-8712

LA FORCE, JAMES CLAYBURN, JR., economist, educator; b. San Diego, Dec. 28, 1928; s. James Clayburn and Beatrice Maureen (Boyd) La F.; m. Barbara Lea Latham, Sept. 23, 1952; children: Jessica, Allison, Joseph. BA, San Diego State Coll., 1951; MA, UCLA, 1958, PhD, 1962. Asst. prof. econs. UCLA, 1962-66, assoc. prof., 1967-70, prof., 1971-93, prof. emeritus, 1993—, chmn. dept. econs., 1969-78, dean Anderson Sch. Mgmt., 1978-93; acting dean Hong Kong U. Sci. & Tech., 1991-93; bd. dirs. Rockwell Internat., Jacobs Engring. Group Inc., The Timken Co., The Black Rock Funds, Imperial Credit Industries, Inc., Payden & Rygel Investment Trust, Providence Investment Coun. Mut. Funds, Motor Cargo Industries; chmn. adv. com. Calif. Workmen's Compensation. Author: The Development of the Spanish Textile Industry 1750-1800, 1965, (with Warren C. Scoville) The Economic Development of Western Europe, vols. 1-5, 1969-70. Bd. dirs. Nat. Bur. Econ. Rsch., 1975-88, Found. Francisco Marroquin, Lynde and Harry Bradley Found., Pacific Legal Found., 1981-86; trustee Found. for Rsch. in Econs. and Edn., 1970—, chmn., 1977—; mem. bd. overseers Hoover Inst. on War, Revolution and Peace, 1979-85, 86-93; mem. nat. coun. on humanities NEH, 1981-88; chmn. Pres.'s Task Force on Food Assistance, 1983-84. Social Sci. Research Council research tng. fellow, 1958-60; Fulbright sr. research grantee, 1965-66; Am. Philos. Soc. grantee, 1965-66. Mem. Econ. History Assn., Mont Pelerin Soc., Phi Beta Kappa. Office: UCLA Anderson Grad Sch Mgmt 405 Hilgard Ave Los Angeles CA 90095-9000

LAFRANCE, REGINALD MICHAEL, JR., television producer and director, videographer; b. L.A., July 28, 1962; s. Reginald Michael and Lena Ruth (Slack) LaF.; m. Rosa Negron Baez, Apr. 21, 1997; children: Jordan, Michael Robison, Taira Lauren. BA in Comms., U. Nev., Las Vegas, 1986. Producer, dir. PBS KLVX TV, Las Vegas, 1984—, ABC KTKA TV, Topeka, 1993-94; freelance videographer A&E TV, N.Y.C., 1996—, Hard Copy TV, 1996—, Showtime TV, 1996—, CNN TV, Atlanta, 1996—, Extra TV, L.A., 1996—. Dir., producer documentary The Water Rules, 1997, The Last of the Medicine Men, 1996. Recipient Emmy award, 1997, NEA award, 1997, Telly award, 1996, Edward R. Murrow award, 1997.

LAGASSE, BRUCE KENNETH, structural engineer; b. Bklyn., Feb. 1, 1940; s. Joseph F. Lagasse and Dora S. Gould. BSME, U. Calif., Berkeley, 1964. Structures engr. Rockwell Internat., Canoga Park, Calif., 1964-69; mem. tech. staff Hughes Aircraft Co., Los Angeles, 1969-70; scientist/engr. Hughes Aircraft Co. (now Raytheon Sys. Co.), El Segundo, Calif., 1972-97; sr. engr. Litton Ship Systems, Los Angeles, 1971-72; scientist, engr. Raytheon Systems Co., El Segundo, 1997—; lectr., tech. edn. class coord. Hughes Aircraft Co., El Segundo, 1980-97; cons. in field, Van Nuys, Calif., 1979—. Libertarian state chmn., L.A., 1977-79, nat. committeeman, Washington, 1979-81; chair Libertarian Judicial Com. (state and national), 1996—. Mem. ASME. Avocations: reading, jogging, hiking, symphonic music, photography. Home: 7247 Balboa Blvd Van Nuys CA 91406-2702

LAGER, DOUGLAS ROY, property tax consultant; b. Eau Claire, Wis., Dec. 10, 1947; m. Barbara Joyce Johnston, Oct. 5, 1985; 1 child, Jeffrey D. BSBA in Acctg., Rockhurst Coll., Kansas City, Mo., 1971. Cert. gen. appraiser, Colo. Head dept. personal property Jackson County Assessor, Kansas City, Mo., 1971-74; property assessment specialist Wis. Dept. Revenue, Madison, 1974-80; property tax cons. Property Tax Svc., Mpls., 1980-84, Denver, 1984-87; property tax cons. Avtax, Inc., Denver, 1987—. Avocations: electronics, personal computers. Home: 9 White Alder Littleton CO 80127-3598 Office: Avtax Inc 5555 Dtc Pkwy Ste C3300 Englewood CO 80111-3072

LAGORIA, GEORGIANNA MARIE, curator, writer, editor, visual art consultant; b. Oakland, Calif., Nov. 3, 1953; d. Charles Wilson and Margaret Claire (Vella) L.; m. David Joseph de la Torre, May 15, 1982; 1 child, Mateo Joseph. BA in Philosophy, Santa Clara U., 1975; MA in Museology, U. San Francisco, 1978. Exhbn. coord. Allrich Gallery, San Francisco, 1977-78; asst. registrar Fine Arts Mus., San Francisco, 1978-79; gallery coord. de Saisset Mus., Santa Clara, Calif., 1979-80, asst. dir., 1980-83, dir., 1983-86; dir. Palo Alto (Calif.) Cultural Ctr., 1986-91; ind. writer, editor and cons. mus. and visual arts orgns., Hawaii, 1991-95; dir. The Contemporary Mus., Honolulu, 1995—; v.p. Non-Profit Gallery Assn., San Francisco, 1980-82; bd. dirs. Fiberworks, Berkeley, Calif., 1981-85; field grant reviewer Inst. Mus. Svcs., Washington, 1984, 85, 97, 98; adv. bd. Hearst Art Gallery, Moraga, Calif., 1986-89, Womens Caucus for Art, San Francisco, 1987—; mem. adv. bd. Weigand Art Gallery, Notre Dame Coll., Belmont, Calif. Curator exhbns. The Candy Store Gallery, 1980, Fiber '81, 1981; curator, author exhbn. catalogue Contemporary Hand Colored Photographs, 1981, Northern Calif. Art of the Sixties, 1982, The Artist and the Machine: 1910-1940, 1986; author catalogue, guide Persis Collection of Contemporary Art at Honolulu Advertiser, 1993; co-author: The Little Hawaiian Cookbook, 1994; coord. exhbn. selections Laila and Thurston Twigg-Smith Collection and Toshiko Takaezu ceramics for Hui No'eau Visual Arts Ctr., Maui, 1993; editor Nuhou (newsletter Hawaii State Mus. Assn.), 1991-94; spl. exhbn. coord. Honolulu Acad. Arts, 1995; dir. The Contemporary Mus., Honolulu, 1995—. Mem. Arts Adv. Alliance, Santa Clara County, 1985-86; grant panelist Santa Clara County Arts Coun., 1987; mem. art adv. bd. Kapiolani C.C., 1994—. Exhbn. grantee Ahmanson Found., 1981, NEA, 1984, Calif. Arts Coun., 1985-89. Mem. Am. Assn. Mus., ArtTable, 1983—, Calif. Assn. Mus. (bd. dirs. 1987-89), Hawaiian Craftsmen (bd. dirs. 1994-95), Honolulu Jr. League, Key Project (bd. dirs. 1993-94). Democrat. Roman Catholic. Avocations: dance, fiction writing. Home and Office: 47-665 Mapele Rd Kaneohe HI 96744-4918

LAI, HIM MARK, writer; b. San Francisco, Nov. 1, 1925; s. Mark Bing and Hing Mui (Dong) L.; m. Laura Jung, June 12, 1953. AA, San Francisco Jr. Coll., 1945; BS in Engring., U. Calif., Berkeley, 1947. Mech. engr. Utilities Engring. Bur., San Francisco, 1948-51, Bechtel Corp., San Francisco, 1953-84; lectr. Chinese Am. history San Francisco State U., 1969, 72-75, U. Calif., Berkeley, 1978-79, 84; researcher, writer on Chinese Am. history San Francisco, 1967—; dir. Chinese of Am. 1785-1980 Exhbn. Chinese Cultural Found. San Francisco, 1979-80; coord. Chinese Am. in Search of Roots Program, 1991—; cons. Asian Am. Studies Program Chinese Materials Rsch. Collection U. Calif., Berkeley, 1986-88, nat. edn. program Ams. All, 1992-96; adj. prof. Asian Am. studies dept. San Francisco State U., 1990—; coord. Chinese Cmty. Hour Cantonese radio program, 1971-84. Co-author: Chinese of America, 1785-1980: Exhibition Catalog, 1980, Island: Poetry and History of Chinese Immigrants on Angel Island, 1910-1940, 1980; author: A History Reclaimed: An Annotated Bibliography and Guide of Chinese Language Materials on the Chinese of America, 1986, From Overseas Chinese to Chinese American: History of Development of Chinese American Society During the Twentieth Century, 1992; assoc. editor: A History of the Chinese in California, A Syllabus, 1969; co-editor: Collected Works of Gilbert Woo, 1991; mem. editl. bd. Amerasia Journal, 1979—, Chinese America: History and Perspectives, 1986—; contbr. articles to profl. jours. Mem. Chinese Hist. Soc. Am. (pres. 1971, 76, 77, bd. dirs. 1972-81, 84, 85-91, 93—), Chinese Culture Found. San Francisco (bd. dirs. 1975-85, 87-94, 96—, pres. 1982, bd. chairperson 1983, 84, 85, 89). Home: 357 Union St San Francisco CA 94133-3519

LAI, LIWEN, molecular geneticist, educator; b. Taipei, Taiwan, 1957; d. Kwan-Long Lai. BS, Nat. Taiwan U., 1980; MS, U. Calif., San Francisco, 1983; PhD, U. Tex., Dallas, 1987. Diplomate Am. Coll. Med. Genetics. Postdoctoral fellow NIH, Bethesda, Md., 1987-89; asst. rsch. sci. U. Ariz., Tuscon, 1990-94, asst. dir. Molecular Diagnostic Lab., 1992—, rsch. asst. prof., 1995-97; rsch. assoc. prof., 1997—. Rsch. grantee Elks, 1994-96, Dialysis Clinic Inc., 1994-96, So. Ariz. Found., 1996—, NIH, 1997—. Mem. Am. Soc. Human Genetics, Am. Soc. Gene Therapy. Office: U Ariz Dept Medicine 1501 N Campbell Ave Tucson AZ 85724-0001

LAI, WAIHANG, art educator; b. Hong Kong, Jan. 7, 1939; s. Sing and Yu-ching L.; came to U.S., 1964; BA, Chinese U. Hong Kong, 1964; MA, Claremont Grad. U., 1967; m. Celia Cheung, Aug. 13, 1966. Asst. prof. art Maunaolu Coll., Maui, Hawaii, 1968-70; prof. art Kauai (Hawaii) Community Coll., 1970—. Vis. prof. art Ariz. State U., Tempe, summer 1967. Recipient Excellence in Teaching award U. Hawaii, 1992, Nat. Inst. Staff and Orgnl. Devel. Excellence award U. Tex., 1993. Mem. Kauai (pres. 1974—) Watercolor Socs., Phila. Watercolor Club, Hawaii Computer Art Soc., Kauai Oriental Art Soc. (pres. 1981—), AM. Watercolor Soc. Author: The Chinese Landscape Paintings of Waihang Lai, 1966, The Watercolors of Waihang Lai, 1967; illustrator: The Tao of Practice Success, 1991, Advertisements for Acupuncturists, 1992. Home: PO Box 363 Lihue HI 96766-0363 Office: Kauai Community Coll Lihue HI 96766

LAIDIG, ELDON LINDLEY, financial planner; b. Oberlin, Kans., Jan. 20, 1932; s. Ira Lawless and Minnie Lorene (Williams) L.; m. Mary Jane Urban, Feb. 13, 1953 (dec. June 1981); 1 child, Larry Wayne; m. Lois Audrey Davey Cameron, Feb. 11, 1983. BS, Ft. Hay Kans. State U., 1954; MS, U. Tex., 1960, PhD, 1967. CFP. Jr. high prin. Jefferson County Pub. Schs., Arvada, Colo., 1963-88; pvt. practice fin. planner Personal Benefit Svcs., Arvada, 1988—. Author: The Influence of Situational Factors on Administrative Behavior, 1967, An Organizational Manual, 1979; editor various local and state newsletters; contbr. fin. column Arvada Cmty. News. Bd. dirs. Highlander's Inc., Denver, 1978-83, Arvada Coun. for the Arts and Humanities, 1982, chmn., 1988-93; pres. Jefferson County Sch. Adminstrs., Lakewood, Colo., 1971-72; elder Arvada Presbyn., 1964—; v.p. Arvada Sister Cities Internat., 1992—. Named as Comdg. Officer of Outstanding Coast Guard Unit, 2d Coast Guard Dist., 1968; recipient Disting. Svc. citation U.S. Dept. of Def., 1974, Unit citation Def. Civil Preparedness Agy., 1974, Don

Kemp award for outstanding fundraising Arvada Ctr. for the Arts & Humanities, 1983. Mem. Arvada Hist. Soc. (v.p. 1983-85), Res. Officers Assn. (pres. Denver chpt. 1974, pres. Dept. of Colo., nat. councilman 1979), Arvada Sentinal and N.W. Metro C. of C. (Arvada Man of Yr. 1990), Rotary (bd. dirs. Arvada chpt. 1989-96), Friendship Force of Greater Denver (pres. 1997). Avocations: traveling, gardening, reading. Home: 7038 Ammons St Arvada CO 80004-1849 Office: Personal Benefit Svcs 5400 Ward Rd Arvada CO 80002-1819

LAIDLAW, HARRY HYDE, JR., entomology educator; b. Houston, Apr. 12, 1907; s. Harry Hyde and Elizabeth Louisa (Quinn) L.; BS, La. State U., 1933, MS, 1934; PhD (Univ. fellow, Genetics fellow, Wis. Dormitory fellow, Wis. Alumni Rsch. Found. fellow), U. Wis., 1939; m. Ruth Grant Collins, Oct. 26, 1946; 1 child, Barbara Scott Laidlaw Murphy. Teaching asst. La. State U., 1933-34, rsch. asst., 1934-35; prof. biol. sci. Oakland City (Ind.) Coll., 1939-41; state apiarist Ala. Dept. Agr. and Industries, Montgomery, 1941-42; entomologist First Army, N.Y.C., 1946-47; asst. prof. entomology, asst. apiculturist U. Calif.-Davis, 1947-53, assoc. prof. entomology, assoc. apiculturist, 1953-59, prof. entomology, apiculturist, 1959-74, asso. dean Coll. Agr., 1960-64, chair agr. faculty, staff, 1965-66, prof. entomology emeritus, apiculturist emeritus, 1974—; coord. U. Calif.-Egypt Agrl. Devel. Program, AID, 1979-83. Rockefeller Found. grantee, Brazil, 1954-55, Sudan, 1967; honored guest Tamagawa U., Tokyo, 1980. Trustee, Yolo County (Calif.) Med. Soc. Scholarship Com., 1965-83. Served to capt. AUS, 1942-46. Recipient Cert. of Merit Am. Bee Jour., 1957, Spl. Merit award U. Calif.-Davis, 1959, Merit award Calif. Central Valley Bee Club, 1974, Merit award Western Apicultural Soc., 1980, Gold Merit award Internat. Fedn. Beekeepers' Assns., 1986; recipient Disting. Svc. award Ariz. Beekeepers Assn., 1988, Cert. of Appreciation Calif. State Beekeepers' Assn., 1987, award Alan Clemson Meml. Found., 1989, Award Distinction Coll. Agrl. and Envrion. Scis., U. Calif. Davis, 1997, Alumni Citation Excellence U. Calif. Davis Alumni Assn., 1997; NIH grantee, 1963-66; NSF grantee, 1966-74. Fellow AAAS, Entomol. Soc. Am. (honoree spl. symposium 1990, C.W. Woodworth award Pacific br. 1981); mem. Am. Inst. Biol. Scis., Am. Soc. Integrative Biology, Nat. Assn. Uniformed Svcs., Ret. Officers Assn. (2d v.p. Sacramento chpt. 1984-86), Scabbard and Blade, Sigma Xi (treas. Davis chpt. 1959-60, v.p. chpt. 1966-67), Alpha Gamma Rho (pres. La. chpt. 1933-34, counsellor Western Province 1960-66). Democrat. Presbyterian. Author: (books) Instrumental Insemination of Honey Bee Queens, 1977, Contemporary Queen Rearing, 1979; (slide set) Instrumental Insemination of Queen Honey Bees, 1976; (with R. E. Page Jr.) Queen Rearing and Bee Breeding, 1998. Achievements include determination of cause of failure of attempts to artificially inseminate queen honey bees; invention of instruments and procedures to consistently accomplish same; elucidation of genetic relationships of individuals of polyandrous honey bee colonies; design of genetic procedures for behavioral study and breeding of honey bees for general and specific uses. Home: 761 Sycamore Ln Davis CA 95616-3432 Office: U Calif Dept Entomology Davis CA 95616

LAING-MALCOLMSON, SALLY ANNE, enrolled tax agent, tax consultant; b. Seattle, Sept. 25, 1957; d. Ian Laing-Malcolmson and Frances Rutherford (Arold) Cook; children: Rhiannon Ethel Quandt, Peter Eugene Stone, Benjamin Elliott Stone. AS in Bus., SUNY, 1989. With accounts payable dept. King County Airport, Seattle, 1984-86; bookkeeper Driftmeir Architects, P.S., Kirkland, Wash., 1986; pvt. practice tax cons. Bellevue, Wash., 1987—; tax specialist Puget Sound Nat. Bank, Tacoma, 1990-92; bookkeeper Papillon, Inc.; tax specialist Barbara Pulley CPA, 1995, Energy Relcon, 1996—; sec. Washington State Tax Cons., Bellevue, 1991—, tax specialist Barbara Pulley, CPA, Missoula, Mont; bookkeeper/sec. Energy Re/con, Inc., Stevensville, Mont. Newsletter editor PTA, 1991-93. Mem. Pentecostal Ch. Avocations: reading, sewing, swimming, tennis, camping. Home and Office: 3170 Kinsler Ln Stevensville MT 59870-6967

LAIRD, FRANK N., political science educator; b. Ashtabula, Ohio, Dec. 12, 1952; s. Frank Earl and Mary Yolanda (Fiori) L.; m. Pamela Walker, June 17, 1989. BA, Middlebury Coll., 1975; postgrad., Edinburgh (Scotland) U., 1975-76; PhD, MIT, 1985. Postdoctoral rsch. fellow Harvard U., Cambridge, Mass., 1985-87; asst. prof. U. Denver, 1987-94; assoc. prof., 1994—; cons. Sigma Xi, New Haven, Conn., 1985. Contbr. articles to profl. jours. Rsch. grantee NSF. Mem. Am. Polit. Sci. Assn., AAAS, Soc. for Risk Analysis, Assn. for Pub. Policy Analysis and Mgmt., Soc. for Social Studies of Sci. Office: U Denver Grad Sch Internat Studies Denver CO 80208

LAIRD, JERE DON, news reporter; b. Topeka, Aug. 8, 1933; s. Gerald Howard and Vivian Gertrude (Webb) L.; m. Alexandra Berezowsky, Aug. 4, 1957; children: Lee, Jennifer, Christopher. BA in Journalism, U. Nev., 1960. Disc jockey Sta. KHBC Radio, Hilo, Hawaii, 1949-50; announcer, chief engr. Sta. KOLO Radio, Reno, Nev., 1951-58; program dir. Sta. KOLO-TV, Reno, 1958-60; news reporter Sta. KCRA Radio and TV, Sacramento, Calif., 1960-61, Sta. KRLA Radio, L.A., 1962-63; news reporter, editor Sta. KNXT-TV, L.A., 1964-68; news reporter, fin. editor Sta. KNX-CBS Radio, L.A., 1968—; fin. reporter Sta. KCBS-TV, L.A., 1990—; lectr. U. So. Calif., L.A., 1984-85; instr. Calif. State U., Northridge, 1978-79. Cpl. U.S. Army, 1953-55. Recipient Emmy award, L.A., 1964, Peabody award, U. Ga., 1984, Best Bus. News award, L.A. Press Club, 1983, 84, 86, 87, 88, 89, Martin K. Gainsburgh award, Fiscal Policy Coun., Fla., 1978. Mem. Radio TV News Assn. (bd. dirs. 1966-68, Golden Mike award 1984), Sigma Delta Chi. Avocation: sailing. Office: Sta KNX-CBS 6121 W Sunset Blvd Los Angeles CA 90028-6423

LAKE, RUTH ELAINE, optics technician; b. San Jose, Calif., June 18, 1954; d. Charles Gregory and Beverly June (Beaudoin) Attarian; children: Michael, Christopher (dec.). Student, Calif. State U., Fresno; cert. with honors, San Joaquin Valley Coll., 1988. Optical lab. technician Peggy's Optical Svc., Fresno; instr. in dispensing optics San Joaquin Valley Coll., Fresno; dispensing optician Frame-N-Lens, Clovis, Calif. Mem. CSCLA, OAA, FNAO, OAA, RSLD. Home: 456 Helm Ave Clovis CA 93612-0713

LAKE, STANLEY JAMES, security consulting company executive, motel chain executive, locksmith; b. Oklahoma City, June 3, 1926; s. Clyde Edward Lake and Helene Frances (Herndon) Hunnicut; m. Lila Marguarite Mosley, Mar 29, 1947 (div. Aug. 1952); children: Katherine, Marilyn, Stanley James II; m. Norma Jean Phelps, Jan. 21, 1960. Student, Mont. State U., 1946-48. Owner, mgr. Lake Oil Co., Glendive, Mont., 1949-53, Lake Mining Co., Salt Lake City, 1954-57, Lake Realty Co., Denver, 1958-63, Stanlake Corp., Denver, 1964—, Stanlake Luxury Budget Motels, Denver, 1979—, Lake's Security and Lock Svc., Englewood, Colo., 1979—; co-owner, instr. Colo. Karate Assn., Denver, 1965-73, 2d degree black belt. Originator modular budget motel concept, 1963. Chmn. bd. for karate Rocky Mountain region AAU, 1972-73. With USAAC, 1945-46. Recipient Presdl. award for teaching karate to disadvantaged and civic orgns., 1972, numerous others. Mem. Assn. Locksmiths Am. (cert. master locksmith), Rocky Mountain Locksmiths Assn., Japan Karate Assn. Rocky Mountain Area (chmn. bd. 1970-73), Masons, Shriners. Republican. Methodist. Avocations: computers, skiing, reading, investing, airplane pilot. Home: 6026 S Elizabeth Way Littleton CO 80121-2816 Office: Lake's Security & Lock Svc 6200 S Syracuse Way Ste 125 Englewood CO 80111-4745

LAKRITZ, BRADLEY WILLIAM, educational director; b. Hanford, Calif., Nov. 15, 1960; s. Simon and Mary Elizabeth (Lyon) L.; m. Miriam Ann Epstein, Mar. 18, 1984 (div. Oct. 1993); 1 child, Emily Sara; m. Dena Meryl Cohen, June 19, 1994; children: Noah Jacob, Mia Rachel. BA in Comm., U. Calif., San Diego, 1983. Prodn. mgr. Video Monitoring Svcs., San Francisco, 1983-86; media coord. Bur. Jewish Edn., San Francisco, 1987-93, tech. coord., 1993-98; dir. ednl. tech. Marin Acad., San Rafael, Calif., 1998—. Exec. prodr. Noah's Multimedia Comm. Network, San Rafael, 1992 [illegible]; exec. prodr. feature length documentary Hanford-Confidence Town U.S.A., 1991; author website Jewish Edn. Online, 1994 (Judaism on the Web award 1998); writer media revs. No. Calif. Jewish Bull., San Rafael, 1995—; curriculum writer family history video project, 1988 (Calif. Student Media Festival [illegible]). Grantee, Jewish Cmty. Endowment Fund, San Francisco, 1989, Bernard Osher Philanthropies Found., San Francisco, 1995, Righteous Persons Found., L.A., 1997. Mem. Coalition for Advancement of Jewish Edn. (coord. media network 1992-98), Computer Using Educators, Inc., Media Alliance, Internat. Soc. for Tech. in Edn., Apple Libr. Users Group, Bay Area Video Coalition. Avocations: hiking, mountain biking, camping, photography, multimedia production. Home: 65 North Ave Apt 2A San Rafael CA 94903-4830 Office: Marin Acad 1600 Mission Ave San Rafael CA 94901-1859

LALL, VIVEK, aerospace engineer, educator; b. Djakarta, Indonesia, Mar. 5, 1969; came to U.S., 1989; s. Vinod Behari and Shashi Kiran (Sinha) L. BS in mech. engring., Carleton U., 1988; MS in aero. engring., Embry-Riddle Aero. U., 1991; PhD in aerospace engring., Wichita State U., 1995. Rsch. engr. Hawker-Siddeley, Ottawa, Ontario, Canada, 1988-89; adj. prof. Embry-Riddle Aero. U., Daytona, Fla., 1989-91; sr. engr. Raytheon Aircraft, Wichita, Kans., 1993-96; splst. engr. Boeing Comml. Airplane Gp., Seattle, 1996—; tchr. USAF personnel, McConnell AFB, Kans., 1993-95. Contbr. articles to profl. jours. Recipient doctoral rsch. fellowship Wichita State U./NASA Ames Rsch. Ctr., 1992-95. Mem. AIAA, Canadian Aeros. and Space Inst., Sigma Gamma Tau Aero. Honor Soc., Pi Mu Epsilon Mathematics Honor Soc. Achievements include research and design of airplane wings, dynamic flight loads, and rotor dynamics for aerospace vehicles, also CFD, structural dynamics, turbulence modeling. Office: Boeing Comml Airplane Gp PO Box 3707 Seattle WA 98124-2207

LALLY, NORMA ROSS, federal agency administrator, retired; b. Crawford, Nebr., Aug. 10, 1932; d. Roy Anderson and Alma Leona (Barber) Lively; m. Robert Edward Lally, Dec. 4, 1953 (div. Mar. 1986); children: Robyn Carol Murch, Jeffrey Alan, Gregory Roy. BA, Boise (Idaho) State U., 1974, MA, 1976; postgrad., Columbia Pacific U., 1988—. With grad. admissions Boise State U., 1971-74; with officer programs USN Recruiting, Boise, 1974; pub. affairs officer IRS, Boise and Las Vegas, 1975-94; ret., 1994; speaker in field, Boise and Las Vegas, 1977—. Contbr. articles to newspapers. Mem. task force Clark County Sch. Dist., Las Vegas. Staff sgt. USAF, 1950-54. Mem. NAFE, Women in Mil. Svc. Am., Mensa, Marine's Meml. Club (life), Am. Legion. Avocations: writing, dancing, music, golf, swimming. Home: 3013 Hawksdale Dr Las Vegas NV 89134-8967

LA LUMIA, FRANK MUNZUETO, artist; b. Chgo., Aug. 9, 1948; s. Frank Sr. and Pearle (Grater) LaL.; m. Sally Jorgenson, Jan. 19, 1981 (div. Sept. 1986). BS, Bradley U., 1970. pvt. tchr. workshops, nationwide. Mem. Nat. Watercolor Soc. (signature), Plein Air Painters Am. (signature). Home: PO Box 3237 Santa Fe NM 87501-0237

LAM, ANDREW QUANG, journalist; b. Saigon, Vietnam, May 23, 1963; came to U.S., 1975; s. Thi Quang and Bich Thi (To) L. BA, U. Calif., Berkeley, 1981-86. Assoc. editor Pacific News Svc., San Francisco, 1989—; contbg. writer San Jose Mercury News, Calif., 1997—, commentator Nat. Pub. Radio, Washington, 1996—; jr. fellow World Acad. of Arts and Scis., Washington, 1996—. Editor: Once Upon A Dream, 1995; essayist: The Nation, 1992, L.A. Times Mag., 1994; contbr. articles to profl. jours. Bd. dirs. Vietnamese Health Orgn., San Francisco, 1992-97. Fellow. Rockefeller Found. (UCLA), 1992; recipient Soc. of Profl. Journalists award, 1993, Asian Am. Journalists Assn. Nat. award, 1993, 1995, Media Alliance Meritorious award, Calif., 1994. Avocations: classical music, travel. Office: Pacific News Service Ste 210 660 Market St San Francisco CA 94104

LAMADRID, ENRIQUE RUSSELL, Spanish language educator, translator; b. Embudo, N.Mex., Dec. 6, 1948; s. Enrique Eufrasio and June Darlington (Darress) L.; m. Jo Carlota Domínguez, Dec. 27, 1973; children: Carlos Andrés, Armando José, Ana Yasmín. BA in English, U. N.Mex., 1970; MA in Spanish, U. So. Calif., 1976, PhD in Spanish, 1978. Cert. fed. ct. interpreter. Asst. prof. U. Oreg., Eugene, 1976-79; instr. No. N.Mex. C.C., Española, 1979-85; assoc. prof. U. N.Mex., Albuquerque, 1985—; cons. Smithsonian Instn., Washington, 1992, 93, 98; Library of Congress, Washington, 1998, US AID, Washington, 1991, Mus. of N.Mex., Santa Fe, 1988, 92. Author: Tesoros del Espíritu: A Portrait in Sound of Hispanic New Mexico, 1994 (Library of Congress award 1994), Pilgrimage to Chimayo: Contemporary Portrait of a Living Tradition, 1999; author, translator An Eye in the Wall: Mexican Poetry 1970-1985, 1986, En Breve: Minimalism in Mexican Poetry 1885-1985, 1988; co-author: Communicating in Spanish, 1983. Folklorist, tchr. Sr. Arts, Albuquerque, 1988—; mem. Spkr.'s Bur., N.Mex. Endowment for Humanities, 1985—; mem. N.Mex. Cuartocentenario Commn., City of Albuquerque, 1998. Recipient Disting. Educator award Pub. Svc. Co. of N.Mex., 1990; Fulbright fellow, Ecuador, 1992, Rockefeller fellow, U. N.Mex., 1993-94. Mem. Am. Assn. Tchg. Spanish and Portuguese, Am. Folklore Soc. Democrat. Avocations: folk music, nature. Office: UNM Dept Spanish Portuguese Albuquerque NM 87131

LAMAY-ABNER, JULIE ANN, English educator; b. Hollywood, Calif.; d. Warren Gerry LaMay and Mildred Louse DuVall; m. Willis Bruce Abner, June 26, 1976 (div.); children: Millie Ann Abner, Willis Warren Abner. AS in Bus., Victor Valley Coll., 1988; BS in English Lit., Calif. State U., 1990, MA in English Composition, 1992, PhD in English Composition, 1998. Lectr. dept. English Calif. State U., San Bernardino, 1992—; pres., founder Four Directions Inst., Wrightwood, Calif., 1998—; dean instrn., co-founder The Native Am. Inst., Wrightwood, 1995-98; instr. dept. English Riverside (Calif.) C.C., 1992—, Victor Valley Coll., Victorville, Calif., 1992—, Chaffey C.C., Rancho Cucamonga, Calif., 1997—, San Bernardino (Calif.) Valley Coll., 1996—, Mt. St. Marys Coll., L.A., 1995—, Park Coll., Barstow, Calif., 1995—, Crafton Hills Coll., Yucaipa, Calif., 1994, Fed. Prison Camp Boron, Calif., 1994; bd. dirs. Nat. Am. Inst.; advisor, founder Nat. Am. Students Assn., 1994—; presenter in field. Mem. editl. bd. Am. Indian Culture and Rsch. Jour., 1997—; book review editor Studies in American Indian Literatures, 1998—; contbr. articles to profl. jours. Mem. MLA, Assn. for the Study Am. Indian Literatures (exec. com. 1995—), Nat. Coun. Tchrs. English, Coll. Composition and Comm., Nat. Assn. for Ethnic Studies, Assn. for Am. Indian Prof., Nat. Indian Edn. Assn. E-mail: fourdir@m-scomm.com. Office: Four Directions Inst PO Box 1117 Wrightwood CA 92397-1117

LAMB, DARLIS CAROL, sculptor; b. Wausa, Nebr.; d. Lindor Soren and June Berniece (Skalberg) Nelson; m. James Robert Lamb; children: Sherry Lamb Sobh, Michael, Mitchell. BA in Fine Arts, Columbia Pacific U., San Rafael, Calif., 1988, MA in Fine Arts, 1989. Exhibited in group shows at Nat. Arts Club, N.Y.C., 1983, 85, 89, 91-93, 95-97 (Catherine Lorillard Wolfe award sculpture 1983, 97, C.L. Wolfe Horse's Head award 1994, Anna Hyatt Huntington cash award 1995, honorable mention 1996, medal of honor, 1998), N.Am. Sculpture Exhibit, Foothills Art Ctr., Golden, Colo., 1983-84, 86-87, 90-91 (Pub. Svc. Co. of Colo. sculpture award 1990), Nat. Acad. of Design, 1986, Nat. Sculpture Soc., 1985, 91, 95, 97, (C. Percival Dietch Sculpture prize 1991), Loveland Mus. and Gallery, 1990-91, Audubon Artists, 1991, Allied Artists Am., 1992, 95, Pen and Brush, 1993, 95-97 (Roman Bronze award 1995), Colorado Springs Fine Arts Mus., 1996, 98; represented in permanent collections Nebr. Hist. Soc., Am. Lung Assn. of Colo., Benson Park Sculpture Garden, Loveland, U.S. Space Found. Mem. Catherine Lorillard Wolfe Art Club, N.Am. Sculpture Soc., Pen & Brush, Colo. Osteopathic Found. Office: PO Box 9043 Englewood CO 80111-0301

LAMB, RONALD ALFRED, editor; b. Seattle, Mar. 17, 1948; s. Lowell Rendall and Esther Irene (Fischer) L.; m. Nancy Sandine, Apr. 20, 1973; children: Braden Daniel, Kirsten Marie. AA, Highline Coll., 1968; BA, U. Wash., 1970. Sports writer Federal Way/Des Moines (Wash.) News, 1972-74; sports writer Skagit Valley Herald, Mt. Vernon, Wash., 1975-77, reporter, 1977-79; reporter Bremerton (Wash.) Sun, 1979-84; editor Microsoft Press, Bellevue and Redmond, Wash., 1984-98. Editor: Command Performance: Microsoft Excel, 1986 (Achievement award Puget Sound chpt. Soc. Tech. Comm. 1986), Computer Lib/Dream Machines, 1987 (Non-fiction Computer Book of Yr. award Computer Press Assn. 1988), Variations in C, 2d edit., 1989 (Merit award Puget Sound chpt. Soc. Tech. Comm. 1989), Inside OLE 2, 1994 (Merit award Puget Sound chpt. Soc. Tech. Comm. 1994), Word 6 for Windows Companion, 1994 (Excellence award Puget Sound chpt. Soc. Tech. Comm. 1994), The Ultimate Windows 95 Book, 1995 (Disting. award Puget Sound Chpt. [illegible] award Internat. Tech. Publs. Competition 1996; Official Microsoft Internet Explorer Book, 1996 (Merit award Puget Sound chpt. Soc. Tech. Comm. 1996-97); contbg. author: Tukwila: Community at the Crossroads, 1991 (1st place non-fiction books history Wash. Press Assn., 1992). Del. to state conv. Wash. State Dem. Party, Tacoma, 1984; sec. South Ctrl. Schs. Adv. Coun., Tukwila, 1987-88; mem. Foster Friends of Libr., Tukwila, 1988—; chmn. South Ctrl. 2000 Com., Tukwila, 1987-89, Foster Annexation Com., Tukwila, 1988-89; bd. dirs. South Ctrl. Sch. Dist., Tukwila, 1989-93, chmn. bd. dirs., 1991-93. Mem. Soc. Profl. Journalists, King County Dirs. Assn. (bd. dirs. 1992-93), Wash. State Sch. Dirs. Assn. (urban schs. com. 1993). Democrat. Avocations: hiking, reading, theater, gardening, genealogy. Home: 4251 S 139th St Tukwila WA 98168-3260

LAMB, WILLIS EUGENE, JR., physicist, educator; b. L.A., July 12, 1913; s. Willis Eugene and Marie Helen (Metcalf) L.; m. Ursula Schaefer, June 5, 1939 (dec. Aug. 1996); m. Bruria Kaufman, Nov. 29, 1996. BS, U. Calif., 1934, PhD, 1938; DSc (hon.), U. Pa., 1953, Gustavus Adolphus Coll., 1975, Columbia U., 1990; MA, Oxford (Eng.) U., 1956; MA (hon.), Yale, 1961; LHD (hon.), Yeshiva U., 1965; Dr.rer.nat (hon.), U. Ulm., Germany, 1997. Mem. faculty Columbia U., 1938-52, prof. physics, 1948-52; prof. physics Stanford U., 1951-56; Wykeham prof. physics and fellow New Coll., Oxford U., 1956-62; Henry Ford 2d prof. physics Yale U., 1962-72, J. Willard Gibbs prof. physics, 1972-74; prof. physics and optical scis. U. Ariz., Tucson, 1974—, Regents prof., 1990—; Morris Loeb lectr. Harvard U., 1953-54; Gordon Shrum lectr. Simon Fraser U., 1972; cons. Philips Labs., Bell Telephone Labs., Perkin-Elmer, NASA; vis. com. Brookhaven Nat. Lab. Recipient (with P. Kusch) Nobel prize in physics, 1955, Rumford premium Am. Acad. Arts and Scis., 1953; award Rsch. Corp., 1954, Yeshiva award, 1962; Guggenheim fellow, 1960-61, sr. Alexander von Humboldt fellow, 1992-94. Fellow Am. Phys. Soc., N.Y. Acad. Scis.; hon. fellow Inst. Physics and Phys. Soc. (Guthrie lectr. 1958), Royal Soc. Edinburgh (fgn. mem.); mem. Nat. Acad. Scis., Phi Beta Kappa, Sigma Xi. Office: U Ariz Optical Scis Ctr PO Box 210094 Tucson AZ 85721-0094

LAMBE, JAMES PATRICK, lawyer; b. Washington, June 4, 1952; s. John Joseph and Patricia Ann (Job) Lambe; m. Marie Barbara Giardino, May 21, 1977; children: Katherine Mary, Joseph Patrick. AB with honors, U. Mich., 1974; JD, U. Ill., 1977. Bar: Calif. 1977, U.S. Dist. Ct. (ea. dist.) Calif. 1977, U.S. Ct. Appeals (9th cir.) 1978, U.S. Supreme Ct. 1981, U.S. Dist. Ct. (ctrl. dist.) 1983, D.C. 1985; cert. specialist in criminal law State Bar Calif. Bd. Legal Specialization; cert. criminal trial advocate Nat. Bd. Trial Advocacy. Assoc. Wagner & Wagner, Fresno, Calif., 1978-79, Parichan, Renberg, Crossman & Harvey, Fresno, 1979; claims atty. CIGNA Corp., Fresno, 1979-85; dep. city atty. City of Fresno, 1985-86; dep. pub. defender County of Fresno, 1986—; cons., author Continuing Edn. of the Bar, U. Calif./State Bar Calif., Berkeley, 1992—. Cons. to books: California Criminal Law Procedure and Practice, update, 1992, 2d edit., 1994, 3d edit., 1996, 4th edit., 1998, California Criminal Law Forms Manual, 1995, update, 1997; co-author: (book chpt.) California Criminal Law Procedure and Practice, 4th edit., 1998. Mem. Vols. in Parole. Mem. Calif. Attys. for Criminal Justice, Calif. Pub. Defenders Assn., D.C. Bar, Fresno County Bar Assn., State Bar Calif. (conf. of dels. 1996—, bd. dirs. 1998—), Phi Alpha Delta. Democrat. Avocation: distance running. Office: Office of Pub Defender 2220 Tulare St Ste 300 Fresno CA 93721-2104

LAMBERT, BILL, city official; b. Abington, Mass., Apr. 21, 1954; s. Robert Errol and Mary-Addison Herrick (Blanchard) L.; m. Maria Socorro Aguilar, Dec. 19, 1986; children: Julissa Sanhueza, Daniel Alejandro Perales, Paul Raymundo Perales. BA, Bowdoin Coll., Brunswick, Maine, 1976; MBA, U. Calif., Berkeley, 1980. Sales rep. Norton Co., Worcester, Mass., 1976-78; devel. offficer HUD, Washington, 1980-81; econ. devel. coord. Spanish Speaking Unity Coun., Oakland, Calif., 1982-86; bus. analyst City of Berkeley, 1986-89, econ. devel. project coord., 1989-94, mgr. econ. devel., 1994—; bd. dirs. No. Calif. Cmty Loan Fund, San Francisco, 1990—. Bd. dirs. Big Bros. East Bay, Oakland, 1985-90; sec. City of Berkeley Loan Adminstrn. Bd., 1986-93. Recipient Calif. Gov.'s award for environ. and econ. leadership 1996; named Outstanding Young Man of Am., Jaycees, 1984. Mem. Calif. Assn. Econ. Devel. (bd. dirs. 1997—), Calif. Assn. Local Econ. Devel. (award for excellence in econ. devel. programs 1995), Nat. Congress Cmty. Econ. Devel., Nat. Coun. Urban Econ. Devel. Avocations: basketball, camping running, cross-country skiing, carpentry. Office: City of Berkeley Office Econ Devel 2118 Milvia St Ste 200 Berkeley CA 94704-1113

LAMBERT, RICHARD THOMAS, philosophy educator; b. Rochester, N.Y., Mar. 28, 1943; s. Gerard Thomas and Dorothy Margaret (Zugelder) L.; m. Barbara Ann Weydert, June 14, 1978; children: Gregory Thomas, Christopher David, Emily Marie. BA, St. Bernard's Coll., 1965; PhD, U. Notre Dame, 1971. Prof. Carroll Coll., Helena, Mont., 1970—; exch. prof. Loras Coll., Dubuque, Iowa, 1976-77. Author (articles series) Helena Ind. Record, 1990; contbr. articles to profl. jours. Lector, catechist Cathedral St. Helena, 1978—; mem. Helena Citizens Coun., 1981-82. Recipient scholarship N.Y. State Bd. Regents, 1961-65, Grad. fellowship U.S. Dept. Edn., 1966-70. Mem. Am. Cath. Philos. Assn., Am. Philos. Assn., Internat. Berkeley Soc., Delta Epsilon Sigma (v.p. 1994-96, pres. 1996-98). Roman Catholic. Avocations: walking, reading. Home: 812 12th Ave Helena MT 59601-3766 Office: Carroll Coll Helena MT 59625

LAMBERT, THOMAS P., lawyer; b. Kankakee, Ill., Oct. 14, 1946. BA, Loyola U., L.A., 1968; JD, UCLA, 1971. Bar: Calif. 1971. Atty. Mitchell, Silberberg & Knupp, L.A., 1971—. Note and comment editor UCLA Law Rev., 1970-71. Mem. ABA (antitrust law sect., litigation sect.), State Bar Calif., Beverly Hills Bar Assn., L.A. County Bar Assn. Office: Mitchell Silberberg & Knupp 11377 W Olympic Blvd Los Angeles CA 90064-1625*

LAMBERTON, LOWELL H., business educator; b. Portland, Oreg., Aug. 6, 1944; s. Forest H. Lamberton and Frances Ruth (Carrier) Love; m. Ruth Althea Lenzen, Dec. 14, 1991; 1 child, L. Heather. BA, Walla Walla Coll., 1966; MA, U. Nebr., Linocln, 1968; MBA, Suffolk U., 1977, advanced profl. cert., 1987. Grad. asst. U. Nebr., Lincoln, 1966-68; instr. English Atlantic Union coll., South Lancaster, Mass., 1968-69; asst. prof. English Cen. N.Eng. Coll., Worcester, Mass., 1969-74; bus. instr. Wenatchee (Wash.) Valley Coll., 1978-81; prof. bus. Cen. Oreg. C.C., Bend, 1981—; cons. U.S. Forestry Svc., 1984-89, various small cos. and corps., 1981—; pres. bd. dirs. Consumer Credit Counseling, 1996-98. Author: Human Relations: Strategies for Success 1995, Working with People: H.R. Guide, 1997. Mem. Faculty Assn. (pres. local chpt. 1997-98). Baptist. Home: 2081 NE Hollowtree Ln Bend OR 97701-6552 Office: Cen Oreg CC 2600 NW College Way Bend OR 97701-5933

LAMBORN, DOUGLAS L., state legislator; b. May 24, 1954; m. Jeanie Lamborn; children: Luke, Eve, Will, Nathan, Mark. Grad., U. Kans., 1978, JD, 1985. Pvt. practice Colo. Springs, 1987—; mem. Colo. Ho. of Reps., 1994-96, Rep. whip, 1997; pres. pro tem Colo. State Senate (Dist. 9); mem. appropriations com., fin. com., state, veterans and mil. affairs com., 1999. Active mem. Antelope Trails Elem. Sch. Prins. Adv. Coun., former mem. Pike's Peak Area Coun. of Govs. Citizen's Adv. Com. Republican. Office: 259 Colo State Capitol Denver CO 80203 also: 200 E Colfax Rm 259 Denver CO 80203*

LAMBREV, GARRETT IVAN, librarian, writer; b. Gt. Falls, Mont., Oct. 11, 1942; s. Dragomir Ivan and Esther Garrett (Benson) L.; m. Yani Herdes, Mar. 27, 1978. BA in History, Pomona Coll., 1964; MA, Stanford (Calif.) U., 1966; MLIS, U. Calif., Berkeley, 1986. Cert. C.C. tchr., Calif. Social worker Mendocino County Welfare Dept., Ukiah, Calif., 1966-68, San Francisco Dept. Social Svcs., 1968-70; libr. Oakland (Calif.) Pub. Libr., 1986—. Author: Life Before the Final Punchline, 1981, Wheatberry Fantasies, 1986, On and Off the Path, 1990. Founder, coord. Bay Area Campaign to Free Mordechai Vanunu, Oakland, 1987-97. Green Party. Roman Catholic. Avocations: reading, running, traveling. Home: 1926 Leimert Blvd Oakland CA 94602 Office: 6833 International Blvd Oakland CA 94621

LAMEIRO, GERARD FRANCIS, research institute director; b. Paterson, N.J., Oct. 3, 1949; s. Frank Raymond and Beatrice Cecilia (Donley) L., BS, Colo. State U., 1971, MS, 1973, PhD, 1977. Sr. scientist Solar Energy Rsch. [illegible] Colo., [illegible]; asst. prof. mgmt. sci. and info. systems Colo. State U., Fort Collins, 1978-83, mem. editorial bd. energy engring., 1978-82, editorial bd. energy econs. policy and mgmt., 1981-82, lectr. dept. computer sci., 1983, lectr. dept. mgmt., 1983; pres. Successful Automated Office Systems, Inc., Fort Collins, 1982-84; product mgr. Hewlett Packard, 1984-88;

computer networking cons., 1988-89, Ft. Collins.; mem. editorial bd. The HP Chronicle, 1986-88, columnist, 1988, mgmt. strategist, 1988-91; dir. Lameiro Rsch. Inst., 1991-97, sr. rsch. fellow, dir., 1993-97; mkt. developer Hewlett-Packard Co., 1996-97, product mktg. mgr. Hewlett-Packard Co.; 1997-98, corp. bus. model strategist Hewlett-Packard Co., 1998—. Author: Campaign Code of Ethics, 1988, Ten Laws for Winning Presidential Elections, 1992, Ten Laws for Creating Wealthy Nations, 1994; mem. editorial bd. Hp Chronicle, 1986-88, Energy Engring., Policy and Mgmt., 1981-82, Energy Engring., 1978-82; developer LRI Presdl. Electoral Outlook Model, 1992, LRI Gold Model for Projecting Presdl. Elections, 1996. Mem. Presdl. Electoral Coll., 1980. Recipient nat. Disting. Svc. award Assn. Energy Engrs., 1981, Honors Prof. award Colo. State U., 1982; Colo. Energy Rsch. Inst. fellow 1976; NSF Postdoctoral fellow 1977. Mem. Assn. for Computing Machinery, Assn. Energy Engrs. (pres. 1980, Nat. Distinguish Service award 1981, internat. bd. dirs. 1980-81), Am. Mgmt. Assn., Am. Soc. for Tng. and Devel., Am. Mktg. Assn. (exec.), Am. Soc. For Quality Control, IEEE Computer Soc., Inst. Indsl. Engrs., U.S. C. of C., Crystal Cathedral Golden Eagles Club, Platinum Eagles Club, The Heritage Found., Sigma Xi, Phi Kappa Phi, Beta Gamma Sigma, Kappa Mu Epsilon. Roman Catholic. Author: Ten Laws for Winning Presidential Elections, 1992, Campaign Code of Ethics, 1988, Ten Laws for Creating Wealthy Nations, 1994; contbr. articles in mgmt. and tech. areas to profl. jours. Home: PO Box 9580 Fort Collins CO 80525-0500 Office: Hewlett-Packard Co Bldg 5U MS-B7 Fort Collins CO 80528

LAMERS, WILLIAM MATTHIAS, JR., psychiatrist; b. Milw., Dec. 24, 1931; s. William Matthias and Mary (McGuire) L.; m. Clara M. Jones, June 8, 1958 (div.); children: William M. III, Mark Laurence, Jennifer Marie; m. Elizabeth P. DuBois, Dec. 31, 1982. MD, Marquette U., 1958; LHD (hon.), Starr-King Theol. Sem., Berkeley, Calif., 1983. Resident in psychiatry U. Cin., 1959-62; NIMH fellow in child psychiatry The Child Guidance Home, Cin., 1961-63; assoc. clin. prof. U. Calif. Med. Ctr., San Francisco, 1967-81; assoc. clin. prof. psychiatry U. Calgary, Alta., Can., 1981-85; med. dir. The Bresler Med. Ctr., Santa Monica, Calif., 1985—, A Touch of Care, L.A., 1989-91, Hospice of the Canyon, Calabasas, Calif., 1991—; mem. bio-ethics com. L.A. County Bar, 1986—; mem. Calif. Acad. of Medicine, San Francisco, 1975-82. Author: (with others) Teenage Pregnancy, 1968, Cancer, Stress and Death, 1982, Fathering; editor Thanatos, The Hospice Jour. 1982—. Lt. comdr. USN, 1963-65. Recipient Outstanding Achievement award Marin Med. Soc., 1978. Mem. AAAS, Assn. of Hospice Physicians, Nat. Hospice Orgn. (chmn. accrediation com. 1978-81), Internat. Work Group, Death Dying, Brumnt (pres. 1980-84). Achievements include first physician to develop a hospice program in the U.S. Home and Office: 9510 Yerba Buena Rd Malibu CA 90265-2233

LAMM, BARBARA HAVILAND, writer, researcher; b. Waynesville, N.C., May 28, 1920; d. Willis Bradley and Mary Lucile (Satterthwaite) Haviland; 1 child, Willis Haviland Lamm. AB, Stanford U., 1942; MEd, U. N.C., 1959. Model John Powers, N.Y.C., 1943, San Francisco, 1947-48; civilian employee Econ. and Fin. Directorates Office of Mil. Govt. U.S., Berlin, 1945-47; civilian employee in cryptography Signal Sect., 6th Army Hdqrs., San Francisco; instr. social studies, counselor N.C. Pub. Schs., 1954-64; instr. history and govt., rehab. counselor spl. svcs. Calif. Pub. Schs., 1964-79; creator REACH Abuse and Rape Ctr., Haywood County, N.C., 1985; instr. adult edn. Haywood C.C., N.C., 1985-88. Author: The American Constitution in Context, 1996; also articles. Mem. Inner Wheel Internat. Avocations: hiking, music, poker, writing. Home: 20 Irwin Way Apt 731 Orinda CA 94563-2586

LAMM, DONALD STEPHEN, publishing company executive; b. N.Y.C., May 31, 1931; s. Lawrence William and Aleen Antonia (Lassner) L.; m. Jean Stewart Nicol, Sept. 27, 1958; children: Douglas William, Robert Lawrence, Wendy Nicol. BA with honors, Yale, 1953; postgrad., Oxford (Eng.) U., 1956. With W.W. Norton & Co., Inc., N.Y.C., 1956-68; from v.p. to pres. W.W. Norton & Co., Inc., 1968-94, chmn., 1984—, also dir.; bd. dirs. W.W. Norton & Co., Ltd., London, Liveright Pub. Corp., Nat. Book Co., Scranton, Pa.; guest fellow Yale U., 1980, 85, Phi Beta Kappa lectr. 1994; Ida Beam disting. vis. prof. U. Iowa, 1987-88; guest fellow Woodrow Wilson Ctr., 1996; regents lectr. U. Calif., Berkeley, 1997—; pres. Yale U. Press; mem. bd. advisors Yale Rev., mem. bd. Control U. Calif. Press; fellow Ctr. for Advanced Study in the Behavioral Scis., 1998—. Author: (with others) The Spread of Economic Ideas, 1989, Beyond Literacy, 1990, Book Publishing in the United States Today, 1997; mem. editl. bd. Logos. Mem. coun. Woodrow Wilson Ctr., Inst. Early Am. History and Culture, Williamsburg, Va.; bd. dirs. Roper Ctr. Pub. Opinion Rsch. With U.S. Army, 1953-55. Fellow Branford Coll., Yale U. Fellow Am. Acad. Arts and Scis.; mem. Manuscript Soc., Coun. Fgn. Rels., Century Assn., Elizabethan Club, Phi Beta Kappa (senator 1990—). Home: 741 Calle Picacho Santa Fe NM 87501-6607 Office: WW Norton & Co Inc 500 5th Ave Fl 6 New York NY 10110-0054

LAMM, WARREN EDGAR, design firm owner, artist, illustrator; b. Walnut Park, Calif., Aug. 7, 1937; s. Melber Ivon and Marjorie Helen (Crandall) L. BA, San Jose (Calif.) State U., 1963. Staff artist KNTV-Channel 11, San Jose, 1963-68, art dir., 1968-76; sr. designer KRON-TV-Channel 4, San Francisco, 1976-93; contract designer KGO-TV-Channel 7, San Francisco, 1993—; owner Lamm Design, San Jose, 1993—; artist, designer stills and animation for broadcast, 1976-93. Recipient award N.Y. Art Dirs., 1986, awards Soc. Illustrators, 1978-83. Mem. NATAS (7 Emmy awards 1976-93). Avocations: art, sports, sports booster groups. Office: Lamm Design 296 Woz Way San Jose CA 95110-2705

LAMONICA, JOHN, food executive; b. Bklyn., Apr. 26, 1954; s. Lou and Alda (Merola) L. BS in Acctg., Bklyn. Coll., 1977. With N.S.L. Enterprises, 1982—; with Aniellos Pizza, 1979—, Lamonicas N.Y. Pizza, 1980—; restaurant cons. Developer of new pizzas. Republican. Mem. Beverly Hills Gun Club, Shelby Am. Club. Office: 1066 Gayley Ave Los Angeles CA 90024-3402

LAMONT, SANDERS HICKEY, journalist; b. Atlanta, Nov. 9, 1940; s. Louis Earnest and Dorothy Rebecca (Strickland) LaM.; m. Patricia Jean Taylor, Aug. 5, 1966; children—Patricia Ruth, Zachary Taylor. A.A., Marion Mil. Inst., Ala., 1960; B.A. in Journalism, U. Ala., 1962; postgrad. U. Mich., 1977-78. Reporter, bur. chief Gannett News Service, various locations, 1961-74; mng. editor Ft. Myers News Press, Fla., 1974-77; exec. editor Marietta Times, Ohio, 1978-80, Modesto Bee, Calif., 1980-98; ombudsman Sacramento Bee, Calif., 1998—; chmn. AP News Execs. Council, Calif., 1984-85. NEH journalism fellow, U. Mich., 1977-78; Pulitzer prize juror, 1984-85. Served to 1st lt. U.S. Army, 1963-65. Mem. Am. Soc. Newspaper Editors, AP Mng. Editors, Soc. Profl. Journalists . Methodist. Office: The Sacramento Bee PO Box 15779 Sacramento CA 95816*

LA MONT, TAWANA FAYE, camera operator, video director; b. Ft. Worth, May 12, 1948; d. Jerry James and Roberta Ann (Wilkinson) La M. AA, Antelope Coll., 1979; BA in Anthropology, UCLA, 1982. Forest technician, trail constrn. supr. Angeles Nat. Forest, Region 9 U.S. Forest Svc., Pear Blossom, Calif., 1974-79; trail constrn. supr., maintenance asst. Calif. State Parks, 1979-81; cable TV installer Sammons Comm., Glendale, Calif., 1981-83, camera operator, 1983-87; video studio and ENG remotes dir., mgr., program mgr. channel 6 Sammons Cable, Glendale, Calif., 1981-97; video dir., prodr. LBW & Assocs. Internat., Ltd., 1988—; pres., CEO Chamblee Found., Ltd., 1995—; mem. ednl. access channel satellite program evaluation com., Glendale and Burbank, 1990-92; mem. Foothill Cmty. TV Network, Glendale and Burbank, 1987-95. Prodr., dir. (homeless video) Bittersweet Streets, 1988; cameraperson Rockin in A Hard Place, 1988-93; dir., editor over 1000 videos. Active Glendale Hist. Soc., 1992-96; bd. dirs. Am. Heart Assn., 1992-96, comms. chair; bd. dirs. ARC, 1993—, mem. disaster svcs. team, cultural diversity chair, 1994-95; mem. mktg. com. Burbank YMCA, 1994-96; bd. dirs. Glendale Rose Float Assn., 1995—, pub. chmn., 1997-98. Recipient award of appreciation LBW and Assocs. Internat., 1988, Bur. Census, 1990, USMC, 1991, Verdugo Disaster Recovery Project, 1995, ARC, 1995, ARC Spl. citation for exceptional vol. svc., 1995, award of outstanding pub. svc. Social Security Adminstrn. HHS, 1989, dedicated svc. award Am. Heart Assn., 1992, cert. of appreciation, 1994, 95. Mem. NAFE, NRA, Internat. Alliance Theatrical Stage Employees, Moving Picture Technicians, Artists and Allied Crafts, Internat. Photographer's Guild (local 600), Am. Women in Radio and TV, Am. Bus. Women Assn., UCLA Alumni Assn. (life), Wildlife Waystation, Alpha Gamma. Democrat. Avocations: photography, animals, flying, sailing, travel. Office: PO Box 142 Lake Hughes CA 93532-0142

LAMOREAUX, LAURA ELÁN, artist; b. Manhattan, N.Y., Nov. 5, 1955; d. Marilyn Jeanne L.; m. Michael Edward Hilleman. AS (with honors), Columbia Greene Coll., 1973; student, UCLA, Westwood, 1983, Otis Palson Sch. Design, L.A., 1984-88. RN, Calif. Design artist (CD cover and 8 record labels) The Message Is in the Music, 1994. Recipient Creative award Internat. Art Show, Paris, 1994. Avocations: gardening, reading, hiking, mediation, writing poetry. Home and Office: 151 Westlake Blvd Malibu CA 90265-2442

LAMOUREUX, CHARLES HARRINGTON, botanist, arboretum administrator; b. West Greenwich, R.I., Sept. 14, 1933; s. Emile and Cora May (Harrington) L.; m. Florence May Kettelle, Aug. 28, 1954; children: Mark Harrington, Anne Maile. BS in Botany, U. R.I., 1953; MS in Botany, U. Hawaii, 1955; PhD in Botany, U. Calif., Davis, 1961. From asst. to assoc. prof. botany U. Hawaii, Honolulu, 1959-71, prof., 1971—, chair dept. botany, 1962-65, 76-78, acting assoc. dean curriculum coll. arts and scis., 1976-77, 83, project coord. instrnl. assistance unit, 1977-79, assoc. dean acad. affairs coll. arts and scis., 1985-91; dir. Harold L. Lyon Arboretum, U. Hawaii, Honolulu, 1992—; rsch. assoc. botany Bernice P. Bishop Mus., Honolulu, 1963—; vis. asst. prof. botany U. B.C., Can., summer 1963; vis. colleague dept. botany Canterbury U., Christchurch, New Zealand, 1965-66; mem. sci. adv. com. Pacific Tropical Bot. Garden (name changed to Nat. Tropical Bot. Garden), 1967-94; dir. summer inst. sci. amd math. tchrs. U.S. children Far East NSF, Chofu, Japan, 1968-71, reviewer, mem. various rev. panels; faculty mem. ctr. Pacific islands studies U. Hawaii, 1971—; guest sci. Nat. Biol. Inst. Indonesia, Bogor, 1972-73, 79-80; mem. adv. com. plants and animals quarantine br. Hawaii State Dept. Agr., 1973-79, 89—; study lectr./leader Smithsonian Assocs. Study Tours S.E. Asia, 1985, 86, 88-97, Melanesia, 1987; rschr. in field; bot. and ecol. cons. to various businesses and agys. including State Hawaii Dept. Bus. and Econ. Devel., UNESCO, UN Devel. Programme. Author: Trailside Plants of Hawaii's National Parks, 1976, (U.S. Nat. Pk. Svc. Dir.'s award 1977, Nat. Pks. Coop. Assn. Award of Excellence 1977-78), rev. edits., 1982, 96; bd. editors Pacific Sci., 1965—, editor-in-chief, 1985-86; manuscript reviewer for various jours. and presses; contbr. articles to profl. jours. Active Hawaii Audubon Soc., 1959—, past pres., 1st v.p., Hawaiian Bot. Gardens Found., 1959-67, 1st v.p.; life mem. Conservation Coun. Hawaii, 1959—, state bd. dirs., mem. com. flora conservation, Hawaiian Bot. Soc., 1959—, trustee endowment fund, past pres., v.p., sec., treas., newsletter editor; bd. dirs. Hawaii Mus. Assn., 1996—, v.p., 1998-99; bd. dirs. Friends Honolulu Bot. Garden, 1992—, trustee Nat. Ctr. for Plant Conservation, 1996—. Mem. Bot. Soc. Am., Am. Assn. Bot. Gardens and Arboreta, Hawaiian Acad. Sci. (councillor 1991-93, pres.-elect 1993, pres. 1994-95), Pacific Sci. Assn. (life, standing com. botany 1971—), Internat. Assn. Plant Taxonomists, Internat. Assn. Wood Anatomists. Avocations: photography, travel, opera. Home: 3426 Oahu Ave Honolulu HI 96822-1254 Office: Harold L Lyon Arboretum 3860 Manoa Rd Honolulu HI 96822-1180

LAMPERT, ELEANOR VERNA, retired human resources specialist; b. Porterville, Calif., Mar. 23; d. Ernest Samuel and Violet Edna (Watkins) Wilson; student in bus., fin. Porterville Jr. Coll., 1977-78; grad. Anthony Real Estate Sch., 1971; student Laguna Sch. of Art, 1972, U. Calif.-Santa Cruz, 1981; m. Robert Mathew Lampert, Aug. 21, 1935; children—Sally Lu Winton, Lary Lampert, Carol R. John. Bookkeeper, Porterville (Calif.) Hosp., 1956-71; real estate sales staff Ray Realty, Porterville, 1973; sec. Employment Devel. Dept., State of Calif., Porterville, 1973-83, orientation and tng. specialist CETA employees, 1976-80. Author: Black Bloomers and Han-Ga-Ber, 1986. Sec., Employer Adv. Group, 1973-80, 81—; mem. U.S. Senatorial Bus. Adv. Bd., 1981-84; charter mem. Presdl. Republican Task Force, 1981—; mem. Rep. Nat. Congl. Com., 1982-88; pres. Sierra View Hosp. Vol. League, 1988-89 ; vol. Calif. Hosp. Assn., 1983-89, Calif. Spl. Olympics Spirit Team. Recipient Merit Cert., Gov. Pat Brown, State of Calif., 1968. Mem. Lindsay Olive Growers, Sunkist Orange Growers, Am. Kennel Club, Internat. Assn. Personnel in Employment Security, Calif. State Employees Assn. (emeritus Nat. Wildlife Fedn., NRA, Friends of Porterville Library, Heritage Found., DAR (Kaweah chpt. rec. sec. 1988—), Internat. Platform Assn., Dist. Fedn. Women's Clubs (recording sec. Calif. chpt. 1988—), Ky. Hist. Soc., Women's Club of Calif. (pres. Porterville chpt. 1988-89, dist. rec. sec. 1987-89), Mo. Rep. Women of Taney County, Internat. Sporting and Leisure Club, Ladies Aux. VFW (No. 5168 Forsyth, Mo.), Ozark Walkers League.

LAMSON, ROBERT WOODROW, retired school system administrator; b. L.A., Dec. 28, 1917; s. Ernest K. and Mabel (Mahoney) L.; m. Jeannette Juett, July 22, 1949; children: Robert Woodrow Jr., Nancy Virginia, Kathleen Patricia. BA, Occidental Coll., 1940; MA, U. So. Calif., 1955. Cert. tchr., prin., supt., Calif. Tchr. El Monte (Calif.) Sch. Dist., 1940-43; tchr. L.A. City Sch. Dist., 1945-49, prin., 1949-55, supr., 1955-57, adminstrv. asst., 1957-59, area supt., 1959-78; ret., 1978; agt. Keilholtz Realtors, La Canada, Calif.; instr. various colls. and univs. so. Calif.; a founder, v.p., bd. dirs. U.S. Acad. Decathlon, Cerritos, Calif., 1981-86. Bd. dirs. 10th Dist. PTA, L.A., 1965-70; chmn. Scout-O-Rama, Gt. Western coun. Boy Scouts Am., 1980. Lt. comdr. USNR, 1943-46, mem. Res. ret. Mem. Am. Assn. Sch. Adminstrs., Assn. Adminstrs. L.A., Alumni Occidental Coll. in Edn. (a founder, past pres., bd. dirs.), Town Hall, Nat. PTA (hon. life), Calif. PTA (hon. life, bd. dirs. 1978-80), 31st Dist. PTA (hon. life, bd. dirs. 1965-78, auditorium named in his honor 1978), Phi Beta Kappa, Alpha Tau Omega. Republican. Avocations: gardening, reading. Home: 4911 Vineta Ave La Canada Flintridge CA 91011-2624 Office: Richard Keilholtz Realtors 727 Foothill Blvd La Canada Flintridge CA 91011-3405

LAMUN, JOANNE, theatre producer, writer, educator, director; b. Casper, Wyo., Apr. 20, 1939; d. Lloyd Kenneth and Anne (Dilso) Blower; m. John R. Lamun, June 17, 1961 (div. 1987); children: Laura Anne, Lisa Christine. BS in Speech, Northwestern U., 1961; MA in Theatre, U. Colo., 1965. Tchr. Boulder Valley Schs., Boulder, Colo., 1962-66, 92—; tchr. Davidson High Sch., Davidson, Mich., 1966-67, Royal Oak Pub. Schs., Royal Oak, Mich., 1968-72, St. Agatha High Sch., Redford, Mich., 1980-91; founder, producer, dir. Lathrop Youtheater, Lathrup Village, Mich., 1973-91, Peanut Butter Players, Lathrup Village and Boulder, Mich. and Colo., 1987—. Author: (children's mus.) Once Upon a Rainbow, 1980 (Playwriting award), There's A Frog..., 1982, Double Dealing With the Devil, 1984, Wild, Wild Quest, 1985, Sandcastles, 1985, Listen to the Children, 1987, Peter Pandemonium, 1990, Snow White 2000, 1996. Active mem. theatre adv. bd. Denver Children's Mus., 1996—. Recipient Best of Boulder (Peanut Butter Players) Boulder Daily Camera, 1993, 94, 97, 98, Boulder Daily Camera Pacesetter, 1999. Avocations: needlepoint, knitting, reading, gardening. Home and Office: Peanut Butter Players 2445 Mapleton Ave Boulder CO 80304-3755

LAMUNIÈRE, CAROLINE PARKER, artist; b. Cleve., Nov. 22, 1942; d. Lorand Victor Johnson and Dorothy (Strom) Ussher; m. Robert Parker, Sept. 7, 1966; children: Robert F. Parker Jr., Juliana Johnson; m. Jean Marie Lamunière, Oct. 23, 1991. BA in Art History, Skidmore Coll., 1965. Exhibited in group shows at Berkshire Mus., Pittsfield, Mass., 1977, Peel Gallery, Danby, Vt., 1980, 83, 85, 87-88, 91, Elain Starkman Gallery, N.Y.C., 1980, 84-86, Brocton (Mass.) Mus., 1982, Hood Coll., Frederick, Md., 1982, Albright Knox Mus., Buffalo, 1984, 87, Nat. Soc. for Painters in Acrylic & Casein, 1984, 86, 88, Franz Bader Gallery, Washington, 1987-89, 91; Gallaudet U., Washington, 1988, Ariel Gallery, N.Y.C., 1990-92, Lois Hodes Gallery, Balt., 1992, XX c. Art Gallery, 1992, 96-98, Hand Artes Gallery, Truchas, N.Mex., 1997, Woman Made Gallery, Chgo., Elaine eckwith Gallery, Jamaica, Vt., 1998. Address: 2953 Plaza Blanca Santa Fe NM 87505-6518

LANAHAN, DANIEL JOSEPH, lawyer; b. Bklyn., Jan. 13, 1940. Attended, L.I. U., Temple U.; JD, San Francisco Law Sch., 1969. Bar: Calif. 1970. Dir. Ropers, Majeski, Kohn & Bentley, P.C., Santa Rosa, Calif., 1970-96; mng. ptnr. Lanahan & Reilley L.L.P., Santa Rosa, 1997—. Mem. State Bar Calif., San Mateo Bar Assn., Internat. Assn. Def. Counsel, Assn. Def. Counsel. Office: Lanahan & Reilley LLP Ste 300 3558 Round Barn Blvd Santa Rosa CA 95403-1780*

LANCE, ALAN GEORGE, state attorney general; b. McComb, Ohio, Apr. 27, 1949; s. Cloyce Lowell and Clara Rose (Wilhelm) L.; m. Sheryl C. Holden, May 31, 1969; children: Lisa, Alan Jr., Luke. BA, S.D. State U., 1971; JD, U. Toledo, 1973. Bar: Ohio 1974, U.S. Dist. Ct. (no. dist.) Ohio 1974, U.S. Ct. Mil. Appeals 1974, Idaho 1978, U.S. Supreme Ct. 1996. Asst. pros. atty. Fulton County, Wauseon, Ohio, 1973-74; ptnr. Foley and Lance, Chartered, Meridian, Idaho, 1978-90; prin. Alan G. Lance, Meridian, Idaho, 1990-94; rep. Idaho Ho. of Reps., Boise, 1990-94, majority caucus chmn., 1992-94; atty. gen. State of Idaho, 1995—. Capt. AUS, 1974-78. Mem. ABA, Nat. Assn. Attys. Gen. (vice chair conf. western attys. gen.), Ohio Bar Assn., Idaho Bar Assn., Idaho Trial Lawyers Assn., Meridian C. of C. (pres. 1983), Am. Legion (judge adv. 1981-90, assoc. judge adv. 1997—, state comdr. 1988-89, alt. nat. exec. com. 1992-94, nat. exec. com. 1994-96, chmn. nat. fgn. rels. commn. 1996-97, ex-officio mem. N.H. POW/MIA com. 1996—), Elks. Republican. Avocation: fishing. Home: 1370 Eggers Pl Meridian ID 83642-6528 Office: PO Box 83720 Boise ID 83720-3720*

LAND, DONALD PAUL, chemistry educator; b. Waukesha, Wis., Aug. 30, 1962; s. Glenn Frederick and Alice Louise (Barnhart) L.; m. Theresa Ann McDonald, Nov. 25, 1989 (div. June 1997); children: Max Thomas, Natalie Alice. BA in Chemistry, Lawrence U., 1984; PhD in Chemistry, U. Calif., Irvine, 1989. Undergrad. rsch. asst. dept. chemistry Lawrence U., Appleton, Wis., 1982-84; rsch. asst. dept. chemistry U. Calif, Irvine, 1984-89, postdoctoral rschr. Inst. Surface and Interface Studies, 1989-90; Alexander von Humboldt postdoctoral fellow Inst. for Surface Rsch. and Vacuum Physics, Rsch. Ctr., Juelich, Germany, 1990-91; asst. prof. chemistry U. Calif., Davis, 1991-97, assoc. prof. chemistry, 1997—. Contbr. articles to profl. jours. Recipient Grad. Rsch. award IBM Corp., 1988; grantee Petroleum Rsch. Found., 1991-93, 95-97, NSF, 1995-98, 96—. Mem. Am. Chem. Soc. (sec. Sacramento sect. 1996), Am. Vacuum Soc. Fax: (530) 752-8995. E-mail: dpland@ucdavis.edu. Home: 1209 Impala Pl Davis CA 95616-5714 Office: U Calif Dept Chemistry Davis CA 95616

LAND, KENNETH DEAN, test and balance agency executive, energy and environmental consultant; b. Central City, Nebr., Oct. 5, 1931; s. Adrew Kenneth Land and Marie Eveline (Weaver) Gehrke. Grad., El Camino Coll., Gardena, Calif., 1954-56; student, Long Beach City Coll., 1958, Calif. State Coll., Long Beach, 1959. Cert. quality assurance inspector for smoke removal and life safety systems. Gen. mgr. Air Heat Engrs., Inc., Santa Fe Springs, Calif., 1956-61; sales and estimating engr. Thermodyne Corp., Los Alamitos, Calif., 1962-64; pres., founder Air Check Co., Inc., Santa Ana, Calif., 1964-69; chief engring. technician Nat. Air Balance Co., Los Angeles, 1969-73; gen. mgr. B&M Air Balance Co., South El Monte, Calif., 1973-78; chief exec. officer, founder Land Air Balance Tech. (LABTECH), Las Vegas, Nev., 1978—; bd. dirs. Energy Resources and Mgmt., Inc., San-I-Pac, Internat., Inc., Energy Equities Group, Inc.; founder, pres. Utility Connection, 1990—. Active Las Vegas Founders Club-Las Vegas Invitational PGA Tournament, 1983—, player, 1992; former trustee Assoc. Air Balance Coun.-Sheet Metal Workers Internat. Apprenticeship Tng. Fund; mem. Citizens Against Govt. Waste, 1990—, YNOT Night for YMCA, 1987—; co-founder The Golf Com., operators charity golf tournament for Am. Cancer Soc., 1990, 91, Am. Diabetes Assn., 1992, Nev. Child Seekers, 1992— . With USN, 1951-54, journalist. Mem. ASHRAE (pres. so. Nev. chpt. 1983-84, editor chpt. bull. 1979-89, Citizen of Yr. 1989), CSI (co-founder Las Vegas chpt., pres. 1989-90, editor, founder chpt. bull. 1987-90, S.W. regional mem. chmn. 1990-91), Assn. Energy Engrs., Am. Soc. Profl. Cons., Associated Air Balance Coun. (cert. test and balance engr. 1966—, internat. pres. 1988-89, bd. dirs. 1982-90, mem. numerous coms.), Sheet Metal Workers Internat. Tng. Fund, Internat. Conf. Bldg. Officials, Internat. Assn. Plumbing and Mech. Officials, Nat. Fedn. Ind. Businessmen, Rotary (So. El Monte Calif. Club 1977-78, Las Vegas S.W. Nev. Club 1978-94, bd. dirs. 1983-85, 88-90, photographer 1987-90, chmn. internat. svc., 4 Paul Harris fellowships, charter mem. Las Vegas West Club, Nev., 1994—), Citizens for Pvt. Enterprise, Nev. Taxpayers Assn., UNLV Golf Found., UNLV Presdl. Assocs. Group, Nev. Devel. Assn., Nev. Nuclear Waste Study Com. adv. coun., Sheet Metal and Air Conditioning Contractors Assn. (nat. and so. Nev. chpt. bd. dirs.), Associated Gen. Contractors (nat. and Las Vegas chpt.), Nat. Energy Mgmt. Inst. (cert., co-chmn. Nev. adv. coun., instr. Energy Mgmt. Tng. 1991), Las Vegas C. of C., Nat. Inst. Bldg. Scis., Nev. Assn. Ind. Businessman, Nat. Fire Protection Assn., Am. Soc. Hosp. Engrs., Nev. Profl. Facility Mgrs. Assn., 1992—, Las Vegas Country Club. Avocations: golf, dancing, racquetball, collecting jazz, swing and big band music.

LANDA, MATTHEW, computer company executive. Pres., CEO CMC Ind., Santa Clara, Calif. Office: CMC Ind 4950 Patrick Henry Dr Santa Clara CA 95054-1822*

LANDAR, HERBERT JAY, linguistics educator, author; b. N.Y.C., Dec. 7, 1927; s. Leo and Mildred (Mann) L.; m. Muriel Anne Epstein; children: Clifford, Nancy, Stephen. BA, Queens Coll., 1949; MA, Yale U., 1955, PhD, 1960. Instr. Reed Coll., Portland, Oreg., 1957-59; prof. linguistics Calif. State U., L.A., 1960-91, prof. emeritus, 1991—; vis. prof. Ind. U., Bloomington, 1976-77, Université Blaise Pascal, Clermont-Ferrand, France, 1987-88. Author: Language and Culture, 1966, (in Japanese) Kotoba-To Bunka, 1977; contbr. numerous articles to profl. jours. Cpl. U.S. Army, 1950-52. Guggenheim Found. fellow, 1967-68; Fulbright Commn. grantee, 1987-88. Home: 220 San Anselmo Ave San Francisco CA 94127-2030

LANDERS, VERNETTE TROSPER, writer, educator, association executive; b. Lawton, Okla., May 3, 1912; d. Fred Gilbert and LaVerne Hamilton (Stevens) Trosper; m. Paul Albert Lum, Aug. 29, 1952 (dec. May 1955); 1 child, William Tappan; m. 2d, Newlin Landers, May 2, 1959 (dec. Apr. 1990); children: Lawrence, Marlin. AB with honors, UCLA, 1933, MA, 1935, EdD, 1953; Cultural doctorate (hon.) Lit. World U., Tucson, 1985. Tchr. secondary schs., Montebello, Calif., 1935-45, 48-50, 51-59; prof. Long Beach City Coll., 1946-47; asst. prof. Los Angeles State Coll., 1950; dean girls Twenty Nine Palms (Calif.) High Sch., 1960-65; dist. counselor Morongo (Calif.) Unified Sch. Dist., 1965-72, coordinator adult edn., 1965-67, guidance project dir., 1967; clk.-in-charge Landers (Calif.) Post Office, 1962-82; ret., 1982. V.p., sec. Landers Assn., 1965—; sec. Landers Vol. Fire Dept., 1972—; life mem. Hi-Desert Playhouse Guild, Hi-Desert Meml. Hosp. Guild; bd. friends Copper Mountain Coll., 1990-91; bd. dirs., sec. Desert Emergency Radio Service; mem. Rep. Senatorial Inner Circle, 1990-92, Regent Nat. Fedn. Rep. Women, 1990-92, Nat. Rep. Congl. Com., 1990-91, Presdsl. Task Force, 1990-92; lifetime mem. Girl Scouts U.S., 1991. Recipient internat. diploma of honor for community service, 1973; Creativity award Internat. Personnel Research Assn., 1972, award Goat Mt. Grange No. 818, 1987; cert. of merit for disting. svc. to edn., 1973; Order of Rose, 1978, Order of Pearl, 1989, Alpha Xi Delta; poet laureate Center of Internat. Studies and Exchanges, 1981; diploma of merit in letters U. Arts, Parma, Italy, 1982; Golden Yr. Bruin UCLA, 1983; World Culture prize Nat. Ctr. for Studies and Research, Italian Acad., 1984; Golden Palm Diploma of Honor in poetry Leonardo Da Vinci Acad., 1984; Diploma of Merit and titular mem. internat. com. Internat. Ctr. Studies and Exchanges, Rome, 1984; Recognition award San Gorgonio council Girl Scouts U.S., 1984—; Cert. of appreciation Morongo Unified Sch. Dist., 1984, 89; plaque for contribution to postal service and community U.S. Postal Service, 1984; Biographee of Yr. award for outstanding achievement in the field of edn. and service to community Hist. Preservations of Am.; named Princess of Poetry of Internat. Ctr. Cultural Studies and Exchange, Italy, 1985; community dinner held in her honor for achievement and service to Community, 1984; Star of Contemporary Poetry Masters of Contemporary Poetry, Internat. Ctr. Cultural Studies and Exchanges, Italy, 1984; named to honor list of leaders of contemporary art and lit. and apptd. titular mem. of Internat. High Com. for World Culture & Arts Leonardo Da Vinci Acad., 1987; named to honor list Foremost Women 20th Century for Outstanding Contbn. to Rsch., IBC, 1987; Presdl. Order of Merit Pres. George Bush-Exec. Coun. of Nat. Rep. Senatorial Com., Congl. cert. of Appreciation U.S. Ho. of Reps.; other awards and certs. Life fellow Internat. Acad. Poets, World Lit. Acad.; mem. Am. Personnel and Guidance Assn., Internat. Platform Assn., Nat. Ret. Tchrs. Assn., Calif. and Nat. Assn. for Counseling and Devel., Am. Assn. for Counseling and Devel. (25 yr. membership pin 1991), Nat. Assn. Women Deans and Adminstrs., Montebello Bus. and

Profl. Women's Club (pres.), Nat. League Am. Pen Women (sec. 1985-86), Leonardo Da Vinci Acad. Internat. Winged Glory diploma of honor in letters 1982), Landers Area C. of C. (sec. 1985-86, Presdl. award for outstanding service, Internat. Honors Cup 1992-93), Desert Nature Mus., Phi Beta Kappa, Pi Lambda Theta (Mortar Bd., Prytanean UCLA, UCLA Golden Yr. Bruin 1983), Sigma Delta Pi, Pi Delta Phi. Clubs: Whittier Toastmistress (Calif.) (pres. 1957); Homestead Valley Women's (Landers). Lodge: Soroptimists (sec. 29 Palms chpt. 1962, life mem. 1983, Soroptimist of Yr. local chpt. 1967, Woman of Distinction local chpt. 1987-88). Author: Impy, 1974, Talkie, 1975, Impy's Children, 1975; Nineteen O Four, 1976, Little Brown Bat, 1976; Slo-Go, 1977; Owls Who and Who Who, 1978; Sandy, The Coydog, 1979; The Kit Fox and the Walking Stick, 1980; contbr. articles to profl. jours., poems to anthologies. Guest of honor ground breaking ceremony Landers Elem. Sch., 1989, dedication ceremony, 1991. Home: PO Box 3839 Landers CA 92285-0839

LANDES, WILLIAM ALAN, publishing executive; b. Bronx, Apr. 27; s. Sidney H. and June Dorothy (Heal-Gordon) L.; m. Sharon, Dec. 14, 1991 (div. Apr. 1995); children: Wendy, Paula. BA & BS, Hunter Lehman Coll., 1968; MS, NYU, 1969; MA, Calif. State U., 1972; PhD, UCLA, 1989. Mgr. Jay's, N.Y.C., 1967-69; assoc. producer New World Prodns., Hollywood, Calif., 1971-72; entertainment editor Showcase Mag., Hollywood, Calif., 1972-75; artistic dir., dir. theatre Players U.S.A., San Gabriel, Calif., 1975-78; artistic dir. Merrick Studios, Hollywood, 1978-79; producer, dir. Empire Entertainment, Studio City, Calif., 1979—; CEO, chmn. Players Press, Inc., Studio City, Calif., 1980—. Capt. USAF, 1962-67. Mem. SAG, AFTRA, AEA, DGA, SSDC, Writers Guild. Avocations: writing, painting.

LANDGRAF, SUSAN I, journalism educator, photographer, poet; b. Painesville, OH, Oct. 23, 1941; d. Edward H. and Rosemary (Mogar) Dermitt; m. Richard C. Landgraf, April 6, 1961; children: Brett C., Theodore T., Jennifer M., Lisa R. AA in Social Sciences, Green River C.C., Auburn, WA, 1977; BA cum laude, U. Wash., 1985, MFA, 1987. Reporter, photographer Valley Pub. Co., Kent, Wash., 1977-79; reporter, editor The Daily Journal-Am., Bellevue, Wash., 1979-83; teaching assoc., asst. U. Wash., Seattle, 1985-88; prof., chmn. dept. journalism Highline C.C., Des Moines, Wash., 1988—; keynote speaker, Nat. Writers Club, Seattle, 1993; curriculum developer, Highline C.C., 1996-97; lectr., NISOD, Austin, 1998. Contbr. articles to prof. jours; exhibited in group shows at Burien Arts Gallery and Renton Library. Vol. Probation Officer, Superior Ct. Wash., 1973-75. Theodore Morrison scholar, Bread Loaf, Vt., 1994; recipient Soc. Profl. Journalists awards, 1977-79, Suburban Newspapers Am. 1st pl. award, 1977-79, Phi Betta Kappa, 1986, Acad. Am. Poets award, U. Wash., Seattle, 1985, Soc. for Humanistic Anthropology award, 1988. Avocations: writing, photography, traveling, gardening. Home: 4828 51st Ave S Seattle WA 98118-1842 Office: Highline CC PO Box 98000 Des Moines WA 98198-9800

LANDIS, RICHARD GORDON, retired food company executive; b. Davenport, Okla., Apr. 5, 1920; s. John William and Venna Marie (Perrin) L.; m. Beth Throne, Nov. 6, 1943; children: Gary Perrin, Dennis, Michael, Kay Ellen. BA, U. LaVerne, 1942; postgrad., Claremont Grad. Sch., 1947; LLD (hon.), U. LaVerne, 1981. Mgmt. Delmonte Corp, San Francisco, 1942-83, pres., 1971-77, pres. & chief exec. officer, 1977-78, chmn. & chief exec. officer, 1978-81; pres. Pacific div. R.J. Reynolds, Inc., San Francisco, 1981-83; former chancellor U. LaVerne, Calif.; bd. dirs. Oregon Steel, Portland, Stanford Rsch. Internat., Menlo Park, Calif. Mem. Commn. of Calif., 1984—; chmn. Pacific Basin Econ. Coun., 1975-83; officer Boy Scouts Am., 1946—, Invest in Am.; Lt. USAF, 1942-46. Mem. Pacific Union Club, Bohemian Club, Peachtree C. of C. Republican. Avocations: golf, edn. activities, youth programs. Office: 120 Montgomery St Ste 1880 San Francisco CA 94104-4321

LANDIS, WILLIAM EMERY, artist, poet; b. Auburn, Calif., July 6, 1929; s. John Bartle and Oneita Sarah (Lampman) L. AB, Oberlin (Ohio) Coll., 1951; DDS, U. St. Louis, 1956. freelance poet, 1976—. One-man shows include Torsiello Gallery, Oakland, Calif., 1985, 86; two-man shows include Sohlman Gallery, Calif., 1976, 78; group exhbns. include Marin Art & Garden Ctr., 1990-91, Mykonos, Greece, 1992; represented in permanent exhibits Witteveen Gallery, Amsterdam, 1992-93. Capt. USAF, 1956-58. Oberlin Coll. Cons. Music scholar, 1948; recipient 2d place Hyde Park Poetry League, Cin., 3d place Berkeley 71st Ann. Poetry Comp. Home: 3225 Grand Ave Oakland CA 94610-2759

LANDOVSKY, JOHN, artistic director; b. Riger, Latvia, Jan. 2, 1935; came to U.S., 1950; s. Jains and Olga (Kalnins) L. Dancer Weïrtterberg Stadiis Opera House, Stuttgart, Fed. Republic Germany, 1965, Internat. Ballet Co., Chgo., 1960-70, Lyric Opera of Chgo., 1960-70; asst. prof. U. Ill., Urbana, 1976-80; director Duluth (Minn.) Ballet Co., 1980-82, Ballet Hawaii, Honolulu, 1982, Hawaii State Ballet, Honolulu, 1982—. Office: Hawaii State Ballet 1418 Kapiolani Blvd Honolulu HI 96814-3603

LANDRE, DEBRA ANN, mathematics educator; b. Quantico, Va., Sept. 15, 1955; d. Thomas F. and Joy L. (Carstens) L. BA in French and Math., Bradley U., 1976, MS in Edn., 1977; MS in Math., Ill. State U., 1979. Math. instr. Bradley U., Peoria, Ill., 1977-79, Ill. Valley Community Coll., Peru, 1980, Ill. Wesleyan U., Bloomington, 1981; computer sci. instr. Lincoln Coll., Bloomington, 1981-85; math. instr. Ill. State U., Normal, 1979-85; pres. Quality Input Inc., Normal, 1983-85; dir. acad. computing San Joaquin Delta Coll., Stockton, Calif., 1985-88; prof. math. San Joaquin Delta Coll., Stockton, 1988—. Author: Explorations in Elementary Algebra, 1992, Explorations in Intermediate Algebra, 1992, Explorations in College Algebra, 1992, Explorations in Statistics and Probability, 1992, Amusements in Algebra, 1994; co-author: Mathematics: Theory into Practice, 1980, Microprocessor-Based Operations: Systems Software, 1985, Data Acquisition, 1985; contbr. articles to profl. jours. Treas. Acad. Senate Calif. C.C., 1996-97; mem. chancellor's consultation com. Calif. C.C., 1997—. Mem. Am. Statis. Assn., Calif. Assn. Dirs. Acad. Computing (pres. 1988-90), Calif. Ednl. Computer Consortium (bd. dirs. 1987-90, editor 1988-90), No. Calif. C.C. Computer Consortium (sec./editor 1986-91), Calif. Math. Coun. C.C. (editor exec. bd. 1990—, pres. elect 1991-93, pres. 1994-95, past pres. 1995-97, mem. found. 1995-97), Am. Math. Assn. of Two Yr. Colls. (del. 1993-97, editor 1994-97), Calif. Tchrs. Assn. (pres.-elect 1994-95, pres. 1995-96), Calif. Assn. Women in Edn. and Rsch., C.C. Assn. (dist. dir. 1995-97, pres. 1997—). Avocations: international travel, horses. Office: San Joaquin Delta Coll 5151 Pacific Ave Stockton CA 95207-6304

LANDRE, RICK THOMAS, police officer; b. Woodstock, Ill., Dec. 21, 1956; s. Thomas F. and Joy Lois (Carstens) L. BA, Bradley U., 1979. Dist. sales mgr. Frantz Mfg., Sterling, Ill., 1979-81, Overhead Door Corp., Dallas, 1981-87; detective Lodi (Calif.) Police Dept., 1987—; cons. in field. Author: Gabgs...The Choice Is Ours, 1991. Bd. dirs. Ptnrs. in Prevention, Lodi, 1990-91, Drug and Alcohol Edn.-County Edn., French Camp, Calif., 1990-91, Inter Agy. Networking Coun., Lodi, 1990-91; organizer Late Night Basketball League, Lodi, 1991; mem. Tri County Gang Task Force, 1990-91. Named Officer of Yr., 1990. Republican. Roman Catholic. Avocations: horses, wine and cheese making, camping. Office: Lodi Police Dept 230 W Elm St Lodi CA 95240-2002

LANDRUM, LARRY JAMES, computer engineer; b. Santa Rita, N.Mex., May 29, 1943; s. Floyd Joseph and Jewel Helen (Andreska) L.; m. Ann Marie Hartman, Aug. 25, 1963 (div.); children: Larry James, David Wayne, Andrei Mikhail, Donal Wymore; m. 2d, Mary Kathleen Turner, July 27, 1980. Student N.Mex. Inst. Mining and Tech., 1961-62, N. Mex. State U., 1963-65; AA in Data Processing, Ea. Ariz. Coll., 1971; BA in Computer Sci., U. Tex., 1978. Tech. svc. rep. Nat. Cash Register, 1966-73; with ASC supercomputer project Tex. Instruments, Austin, 1973-80, computer technician, 1973-75, tech. instr., 1975-76, product engr., 1976-78, operating sys. programmer, 1978-80; computer engr. Ariz. Pub. Svc., Phoenix, 1980-84, sr. computer engr., 1984-87, lead computer engr., 1987-88, sr. computer engr., 1988-90, sr. control sys. engr., 1990-94; software engr. CDI Corp., 1996-98; project engr. Sargent & Lundy, 1998 ; pres., chmn. bd. dirs. Glendale [illegible] software engr. CDI Corp., Phila., 1996-98; project engr. Sargent & Lundy LLC, 1998—; instr. computer fundamentals Ea. Ariz. Coll., 1972-73, Rio Salado C.C., Phoenix, 1985-86; mem. bd. trustees Epworth United Meth. Ch., 1987-89, chmn. 1988; mem. cmty. devel. adv. com. City of Glendale (Ariz.), 1988-90, chmn., 1991-92; local arrangements chmn. Conf. on Software Maintenance, 1988. Mem. IEEE Computer Soc., Assn. Computing Machinery, Mensa, Phi Kappa Phi. Methodist. Home: 6025 W Medlock Dr Glendale AZ 85301-7321

LAND-WEBER, ELLEN, photography educator; b. Rochester, N.Y., Mar. 16, 1943; d. David and Florence Epstein; 1 child, Julia. BA, U. Iowa, 1965, MFA, 1968. Faculty mem. UCLA Extension, 1970-74, Orange Coast Coll., Costa Mesa, Calif., 1973, U. Nebr., Lincoln, 1974; asst. prof. photography Humboldt State U., Arcata, Calif., 1974-79, assoc. prof., 1979-83, prof., 1983—; photographer Seagram's Bicentennial Courthouse Project, 1976-77, Nat. Trust for Hist. Preservation/Soc. Photographic Edn., 1987. Author: The Passionate Collector, 1980, To Save a Life: Stories of Jewish Rescue; contbr. sects. to books; photographs pub. in numerous books and jours. Nat. Endowment for Arts fellow, 1974, 79, 82; Artist's support grantee Unicolor Corp., 1982, Polaroid 20X24 Artist's support grantee, 1990, 91, 93, 94; Fulbright sr. fellow, 1993-94. Mem. Soc. for Photog. Edn. (exec. bd. 1979-82, treas. 1979-81, sec. 1981-83). Avocation: weaving. Office: Humboldt State U Art Dept Arcata CA 95521

LANE, GLORIA JULIAN, foundation administrator; b. Chgo., Oct. 6, 1932; d. Coy Berry and Katherine (McDowell) Julian; m. William Gordon Lane (div. Oct. 1958); 1 child, Julie Kay Rosewood. BS in Edn., Cen. Mo. State U., 1958; MA, Bowling Green State U., 1959; PhD, No. Ill. U., 1972. Cert. tchr. Assoc. prof. William Jewell Coll., Liberty, Mo., 1959-60; chair forensic div. Coral Gables (Fla.) High Sch., 1960-64; assoc. prof. No. Ill. U., DeKalb, 1964-70; prof. Elgin (Ill.) Community Coll., 1970-72; owner, pub. Lane and Assocs, Inc., San Diego, 1972-78; prof. Nat. U., San Diego, 1978-90; pres., chief exec. officer Women's Internat. Ctr., San Diego, 1982—; founder, dir. Living Legacy Awards, San Diego, 1984—. Author: Project Text for Effective Communications, 1972, Project Text for Executive Communication, 1980, Positive Concepts for Success, 1983; editor Who's Who Among San Diego Women, 1984, 85, 86, 90—, Systems and Structure, 1984. Named Woman of Accomplishment, Soroptimist Internat., 1985, Pres.'s Coun. San Diego, 1986, Center City Assn., 1986, Bus. and Profl. Women, San Diego, 1991, Woman of Yr., Girls' Clubs San Diego, 1986, Woman of Vision, Women's Internat. Ctr., 1990, Wonderwoman 2000 Women's Times Newspaper, 1991; recipient Independence award Ctr. for Disabled, 1986, Founder's award Children's Hosp. Internat., Washington, 1986, Making Difference for Women award, Soroptimist Internat., 1998, Women Who Mean Business Courage Award San Diego Bus. Jour., 1998. Avocations: computers, painting, writing. Home and Office: 6202 Friars Rd Apt 311 San Diego CA 92108-1008

LANE, JAMES F., software engineer; b. Jersey City, Nov. 6, 1953; s. Francis Robert and Margaret Ellen Lane. BS in Computer Sci., Worcester Poly. Inst., 1971-75; postgrad., U. Colo., 1978. Software engr. LFE Corp., Waltham, Mass., 1975-76, Martin Maretta, Waterton, Colo., 1976-77; sr. software engr. Digital Group, Denver, 1977; systems analyst Johns-Manville, Littleton, Colo., 1977-78; systems software designer, project leader Microsoft, Redmond, Wash., 1978-85; pres. Elvyn Software, Inc., Redmond, Wash., 1985-87; mgr. PDL group, mgr. software engring. dept. Hanzon Data Inc., Bothell, Wash., 1985-90; owner Novelty Hill Software, Inc., Redmond, 1987—. Vol. Seattle Folklife Fest., 1986-97. Avocations: Lindy Hop, Argentine Tango. Home: 22006 NE 114th St Redmond WA 98053-5701 Office: Novelty Hill Software Inc Redmond WA 98053

LANE, LARRY K., air industry service executive; b. 1948. BS in Social Scis., Oreg. Coll. Edn., 1974. With Evergreen Aviation Ground Logistics, 1967-78, 1984—, now chmn.; regional sales rep. Skyline Mobile Home Mfr., McMinnville, Oreg., 1978-84; pres. Evergreen Internat. Airlines, Inc., 1992—; bd. dirs. Evergreen Internat. Aviation. With USAR, 1969-75. Office: Evergreen Internat Airlines Inc 3850 NE Three Mile Ln Mcminnville OR 97128-9402

LANE, MARGARET ANNA SMITH, property manager developer; b. Aspinwall, Pa., Nov. 26, 1918; d. Max Charles and Mary Ann (Jones) Smith; m. Frank A. Lane Jr., Feb. 7, 1954; 1 child, Alan Michael. AB, UCLA, 1940; MS, U. So. Calif., 1949. Cert. secondary tchr., Calif. Demonstration and tng. tchr. UCLA and U. Calif., Northridge, 1948-74; pvt. practice Cottonwood, Ariz., 1975—; tchr. dept. chmn. L.A. City Schs., 1948-74; sec.-treas. Silver Hoof, Inc., Sedona, Stone Pine Gallery, Ltd., Sedona. Mem. Pi Gamma Mu. Avocations: Native American cultures, art. Home: PO Box 4289 West Sedona AZ 86340-4289

LANE, WILLIAM KENNETH, physician; b. Butte, Mont., Nov. 5, 1922; s. John Patrick and Elizabeth Marie (Murphy) L.; m. Gilda Antoinette Parision, Aug. 21, 1954; children: William S., Francine Deirdre. Student, U. Mont., 1940-41, Mt. St. Charles Coll., 1941-43; MD, Marquette U., 1946; postgrad., Med. Coll. Wis. Intern Queen of Angels Hosp., L.A., 1946-47, resident physician, 1954-56; pvt. practice internal medicine San Francisco, 1947-51; resident in urology VA Hosp., Long Beach, Calif., 1956-58; physician VA Hosp., Long Beach, Oakland and Palo Alto, Calif., 1958—; lectr. on psychology of the elderly Foothill Coll., Los Altos, 1972-74; rschr. in field. Bd. dirs., mem. No. Cheyenne Indian Sch.; mem. Josef Meier's Black Hills Theatrical Group, S.D., 1940. With U.S. Army, 1943-46, ETO, lt. USN, 1951-54, Korea. Mem. AMA, Am. Geriatrics Soc., Nat. Assn. VA Physicians, San Francisco County Med. Soc., Woodrow Wilson Ctr. (assoc.), St. Vincent de Paul Soc., Cupertino Landscape Artists (past pres.), Audubon Soc., Stanford Hist. Soc., San Jose Movie/Video Club, San Jose Camera Club, Sierra Club. Roman Catholic. Avocations: oil and watercolor painting, hiking, mountain climbing, outdoor video camcorder photography. Home: 18926 Sara Park Cir Saratoga CA 95070-4164 Office: Stanford VA Med Ctr 3801 Miranda Ave # 171 Palo Alto CA 94304-1207

LANEY, DAVID SCOTT, video company executive; b. Santa Ana, Calif., Feb. 13, 1971; s. Vern Richard and Catherine Marie (Downs) L.; m. Gail Lynn Wilkendorf, Nov. 11, 1995. BA in communications, Master's Coll., 1993. Production asst. KARM-FM, Visalia, Calif., 1991, KDUV-FM, Visalia, Calif., 1992; program dir. KTMC-AM, Santa Clarita, Calif., 1992-93; media engr. Grace Bapt. Ch., Newhall, Calif., 1990-93; pres., founder Laney 5 Productions, Visalia, Calif., 1993—; media asst. Grace Cmty. Ch., 1993-95. Vol. Bill Glass Prison Ministries, 1989—; leader Awana Club Internat., Visalia, 1996—; notary pub. State of Calif., 1994—. Mem. Assn. Profl. Videographers, Valley Bridal Assn., Inc., Visalia C. of C. Republican. Avocations: photography, nintendo 64, vocal performance. Office: Laney 5 Productions 2348 W Whitendale Ave Ste A Visalia CA 93277-8703

LANEY, LEROY OLAN, economist, banker, educator; b. Atlanta, Mar. 20, 1943; s. Lee Edwin and Paula Izlar (Bishop) L.; m. Sandra Elaine Prescott, Sept. 3, 1966; children: Prescott Edwin, Lee Olan III. B Indsl. Engring., Ga. Inst. Tech., 1965; MBA in Fin., Emory U., 1967; MA in Econs., U. Colo., 1974, PhD in Econs., 1976. Budget analyst Martin-Marietta Corp., Denver, 1971-72; economist Coun. Econ. Advisers, Washington, 1974-75; internat. economist U.S. Treasury Dept., Washington, 1975-78; sr. economist Fed. Res. Bank Dallas, 1978-88; prof. econs., chmn. dept. Butler U., Indpls., 1989-90; sr. v.p. 1st Hawaiian Bank, Honolulu, 1990-98; prof. econs. and fin. Hawaii Pacific U., Honolulu, 1998—; chmn. Fed. Res. Com. on Internat. Rsch., Washington, 1981-83; vis. prof. U. Tex., Arlington and Dallas, 1978-85; adj. prof. So. Meth. U., Dallas, 1982-85. Editor bank periodicals, 1975-88; contbr. articles to profl. jours. Mem. Internat. Fin. Symposium, Dallas, 1982-85; Hawaii Coun. on Revenues. Lt. USN, 1967-71. Scholar Ga. Inst. Tech., 1961; rsch. fellow Emory U., 1965-67, teaching fellow U. Colo., 1972-73; rsch. grantee Butler U., 1989-90. Mem. Am. Econ. Assn., Western Econ. Assn., Indpls. Econ. Forum, Plaza Club, Honolulu Rotary, Omicron Delta Epsilon, Lambda Alpha, Kappa Sigma. Avocations: sailing, skiing, reading, fly-fishing. Office: Sch Bus Adminstrn Hawaii Pacific Univ Honolulu HI 96813

LANG, GEORGE FRANK, insurance executive, consultant, lawyer; b. Orange, N.J., Aug. 21, 1937; s. Frank W. and Hilda I. (Pierson) L.; m. Grace D. Preisler, Jan. 30, 1960; children: Christine, Gregg, Cynthia; m. Valerie J. Hanson, Nov. 24, 1978. BS, Ill. Wesleyan U., 1960; JD, Ill. Inst. Tech., 1968. Account exec. Scarborough & Co., Chgo., 1960-67; dir. fin. inst. George F. Brown & Sons, Chgo., 1967-69; v.p., dir. Fin. Ins. Svc., Schaumburg, Ill., 1969-79; pres. City Ins. Svc., Elizabeth, N.J., 1980-84; mng. dir. Res. Fin. Mgmt., Miami, Fla., 1984-85; v.p. Beneficial Ins. Group, Newport Beach, Calif., 1985-86; v.p. Ask Ins. Svc., Irvine, Calif., 1986-89, cons. product ctr. sales, 1989; cons. Nat. Dealer Ins. Systems, 1989, New Liberty Adminstrn., 1990—, Home Crest Ins., 1991—, Great Western Ins. Agy., 1992—, Dana Harbor Ins. Svcs., Inc., 1995—; cons. in field. Bd. dirs. Woodview Civic Assn., Mt. Prospect, Ill., 1964-70, pres., bd. dirs., 1969; bd. dirs. Chippendale Assn., Barrington, Ill., 1972-76, v.p., bd. dirs., 1976. Avocations: boating, fishing, traveling. Home: 173 Ave del Poniente San Clemente CA 92672-4647 Office: 24921 Dana Point Harbor Dr Dana Point CA 92629-2933

LANG, MARGO TERZIAN, artist; b. Fresno, Calif.; d. Nishan and Araxie (Kazarosian) Terzian; m. Nov. 29, 1942; children: Sandra J. (Mrs. Ronald L. Carr), Roger Mark, Timothy Scott. Student, Fresno State U., 1939-42, Stanford U., 1948-50, Prado Mus., Madrid, 1957-59, Ariz. State U., 1960-61; workshops with, Dong Kingman, Ed Whitney, Rex Brandt, Millard Sheets, George Post. Maj. exhbns. include, Guadalajara, Mex., Brussels, N.Y.C., San Francisco, Chgo., Phoenix, Corcoran Gallery Art, Washington, internat. watercolor exhbn., Los Angeles, Bicentennial shows, Hammer Galleries, N.Y.C., spl. exhbn. aboard, S.S. France, others, over 50 paintings in various Am. embassies throughout world; represented in permanent collections, Nat. Collection Fine Arts Mus., Smithsonian Instn.; lectr., juror art shows; condr. workshops.; interviews and broadcasts on Radio Liberty, Voice of Am. Bd. dirs. Phoenix Symphony Assn., 1965-69, Phoenix Musical Theater, 1965-69. Recipient award for spl. achievements Symphony Assn., 1966, 67, 68, 72, spl. awards State of Ariz., silver medal of excellence Internat. Platform Assn., 1971; honoree U.S. Dept. State celebration of 25 yrs. of exhbn. of paintings in embassies worldwide, 1989. Mem. Internat. Platform Assn., Ariz. Watercolor Assn., Nat. Soc. Arts and Letters (nat. dir. 1971-72, nat. art chmn. 1974-76), Nat. Soc. Lit. and Arts, Phoenix Art Mus., Friends of Mexican Art, Am. Artists Profl. League, English-Speaking Union, Musical Theater Guild, Ariz. Costume Inst., Phoenix Art Mus., Scottsdale Art Ctr., Ariz. Arts Commn. (fine arts panel 1990-91), Friends of Art and Preservation in Embassies. Home: 6127 E Calle Del Paisano Scottsdale AZ 85251-4212

LANG, THOMPSON HUGHES, publishing company executive; b. Albuquerque, Dec. 12, 1946; s. Cornelius Thompson and Margaret Miller (Hughes) L. Student, U. N.Mex., 1965-68, U. Americas, Mexico City, 1968-69. Advt. salesman Albuquerque Pub. Co., 1969-70, pres., treas., gen. mgr., dir., 1971—; pub., pres., treas., dir. Jour. Pub. Co., 1971—; pres., dir. Masthead, Internat., 1971—; pres. Magnum Systems, Inc., 1973—; pres., treas., dir. Jour. Ctr. Corp., 1979—; chmn. bd., dir. Starline Printing, Inc., 1985—; chmn. bd. dirs. Corp. Security and Investigation, Inc., 1986—; pres., bd. dirs. Eagle Systems, Inc., 1986—. Mem. HOW Orgn., Sigma Delta Chi. Home: 8643 Rio Grande Blvd NW Albuquerque NM 87114-1301 Office: Albuquerque Pub Co PO Drawer JT(87103) 7777 Jefferson St NE Albuquerque NM 87109-4343

LANG, WENDY FRANCES, artist, photographer; b. Cleve., Feb. 15, 1938; d. H. Jack and Frances (Wise) L. BA, Antioch Coll., 1961; MA, Stanford U., 1963; student, Colegio de Mex., Mexico City, 1962, Inst. des Hautes Etudes, Paris, 1964-65. Assoc. film producer Richard Kaplan Prodns., Inc., N.Y.C., 1966; human resource specialist Community Devel. Agy., Project Head Start, N.Y.C., 1966-68; adminstrv. assoc. Model Cities Com., Office of Mayor, N.Y.C., 1968; tech. asst. Volt Tech. Corp., N.Y.C., 1968-69; photographer self-employed, N.Y.C., 1969-79; tchr. photography L.A. City Coll. Community Svcs., 1979-82; coord. The Photography Mus., L.A., 1980-81; interpreter Pasadena City Coll. Hearing Impaired Program, 1981-83; freelance interpreter L.A., 1984—; freelance photographer Nonstock, N.Y.C., 1984—; bd. dirs. Cameravision, chair grants com. 1976-77, activities com. (artists' hotseat), 1978-79; bd. dirs. L.A. Ctr. for Photographic Studies, 1979-82; bd. dirs., coord. Internat. Theatre Festival XV World Games for the Deaf, L.A., 1983-85; bd. dirs., 2d v.p. So. Calif. Recreation Assn. of the Deaf, 1983-87; bd. dirs., sec.-treas. Self-Actualization Inst. for the Deaf, 1983—, bd. dirs., treas. Damien Project, L.A., 1990-91. Exhibited works in one-person show at Cleve. Playhouse Gallery; group exhbns. include Soho/ Camerawoks, L.A., Friends of Photography, Carmel, Steps into Space, L.A., Butler Inst. Am. Art, Youngstown, Ohio, Status Gallery, L.A., Clarence Kennedy Gallery, Cambridge, Mss., others; works featured in publs. including Wolf Mag. of Letters, Minolta Contact Sheet, Hispanic Am. Report, Worldmark Ency.; (rec. album) Communication Arts, 1974. Mem. Soc. for Photog. Edn., Friends of Photography, Ctr. for Creative Photography, Internat. Ctr. for Photography (N.Y.C.), Mus. of Photography. Home: 1231 Kipling Ave Los Angeles CA 90041-1616

LANG, WILLIAM EDWARD, mathematics educator; b. Salisbury, Md., Oct. 22, 1952; s. Woodrow Wilson and Clara T. L. BA, Carleton Coll., 1974; MS, Yale U., 1975; PhD, Harvard U., 1978. Vis. mem. Inst. for Advanced Study, Princeton, N.J., 1978-79; exch. prof. Universite de Paris, Orsay, 1980; C.L.E. Moore instr. MIT, Cambridge, 1980-82; asst. prof. U. Minn., Mpls., 1982-83, assoc. prof., 1983-89; vis. assoc. prof. Brigham Young U., Provo, Utah, 1988-89, prof., 1989—. Contbr. articles to profl. jours. Fellow NSF 1974-77, 79-80. Mem. Am. Math. Soc., Math. Assn. Am., Math. Scis. Rsch. Inst., Sigma Xi. Republican. Office: Brigham Young Univ Dept Math Provo UT 84602

LANGE, GARY DAVID, periodontist; b. Mpls., Dec. 13, 1936; s. Emil and Esther Catherine (Schwartzkopf) L.; m. Donna Lynn Hall, Mar. 23, 1969; 1 child: Christian Elizabeth. BA, Augsburg Coll., Mpls., 1959; BS, U. Minn., 1961, DDS, 1963, MSD, 1971. Lic. periodontist. Dental intern U. S. Army Dental Corps, Tacoma, 1963-64; staff dentist and comdg. officer U. S. Army Dental Sect., Fulda, Fed. Republic of Germany, 1964-67; staff dentist U. S. Army Dental Corps, Ft. Bragg, N.C., 1967-69; periodontal resident U. Minn., Mpls., 1969-71; pvt. practice Rochester, Minn., 1971-74; staff periodontist VA, St. Petersburg, Fla., 1974-83, dir. gen. practice residency, 1983-86; chief dental svcs. VA, Columbia, Mo., 1986-92; chief dental svc. VA Med. Ctr., Prescott, Ariz., 1992-98, ret., 1998; asst. prof. Sch. Dentistry U. Minn., 1971-73, Kansas City Dental Sch., divsn. Grad Periodontics, U. Mo., 1987-92. Maj. U.S. Army, 1963-69. Mem. ADA, Am. Acad. Periodontology, Rotary Internat. Independent. Avocations: tennis, hiking, golf, sailing, kayaking, hunting, skiing. Home: 2069 Meadowbrook Rd Prescott AZ 86303-5696

LANGE, VIDIE, artist; b. Dubuque, Iowa, Mar. 24, 1932; d. George Rider and Elizabeth (Adams) Burden; m. Robert Brookings, Dec. 29, 1950; children: Cornelia, Robert, Swasey. Student, Art Inst. Chgo., U. Iowa, Clark Coll., 1955-65. Tchr. summer workshop Lac Ct. Oreilles Indian Reservation, Wis., 1977-84; instr., originator Lumina Workshop, Boulder, 1977-84; instr. The Colo. Mountain Coll., Breckenridge, 1984. One-man shows include Parker Bratton Gallery, N.Y.C., 1984, U. Colo., Boulder, 1987, 93, Payton Rule Gallery, Denver, 1990, BC Space, Laguna Beach, Calif., 1998; group shows include Sangre de Christo Arts Ctr., Pueblo, Colo., 1993, U. Colo., 1993, 96, Denver Art Mus., 1993, 94, Rocky Mountain Coll. Art and Design, 1993, BC Space, 1997; numerous video installations; numerous pub. and pvt. exhbns. Avocations: martial arts, languages. Office: Lumina 3732 Wonderland Hill Boulder CO 80304

LANGENDOEN, DONALD TERENCE, linguistics educator; b. Paterson, N.J., June 7, 1939; s. Gerrit and Wilhelmina (Van Dyk) L.; m. Sally Wicklund, Aug. 16, 1964 (div. Mar. 1982); 1 child, David; m. Nancy Susan Kelly, July 28, 1984. BS, MIT, 1961, PhD, 1964. Asst. prof. Ohio State U., Columbus, 1964-68; vis. assoc. prof. Rockefeller U., N.Y.C., 1968-69; prof. Bklyn. C. and Grad. Ctr., CUNY, N.Y.C., 1969-88, U. Ariz., Tucson, 1988—; exec. officer grad. linguistics program, CUNY, N.Y.C., 1971-78; head dept. linguistics, U. Ariz., Tucson, 1988-97; vis. prof. City U. Hong Kong, 1998; vis. scientist IBM T.J. Watson Research Ctr., Yorktown Heights, N.Y., 1986-87; sr. lectr. Fulbright, Utrecht, Holland, 1977. Author: The London School of Linguistics, 1968; co-author: The Vastness of Natural Languages, 1984; editor: Linguistics Abstracts, 1997—; co-editor: Optimality Theory: An Overview, 1997. Fellow N.Y. Acad. of Scis., N.Y.C., 1977; named Ptnr. in Edn., Bd. of Edn., N.Y.C., 1982. Mem. AAAS (chair sect. Z 1999—), Linguistic Soc. Am. (sec., treas. 1984-88, pres. 1998—), Assn. for Computational Linguistics, Assn. for Linguistic and Lit. Computing. Office: U Ariz Dept Linguistics Box 210028 Tucson AZ 85721-0028

LANGGUTH, A(RTHUR) J(OHN), writer, journalism educator; b. Mpls., July 11, 1933; s. Arthur John and Doris Elizabeth (Turnquist) L. BA cum laude, Harvard U., 1955. Corr. Cowles newsletter, 1959; mem. bur. Look Mag. Bur., Washington, 1959; polit. corr. for Presdl. election Valley Times Cowles Publs., San Fernando Valley, Calif., 1960; corr. Calif. gubernatorial election Cowles Publs., 1962; reporter N.Y. Times, Dallas, 1963, N.C., Miss., Ala., 1963; corr. S.E. Asia N.Y. Times, 1964, bur. chief Saigon (Vietnam), 1965; spl. assignment N.Y. Times Mag., 1968, 70. Author: Jesus Christs, 1968, paperback edit., 1969, reissue with new illustrations, 1993, Wedlock, 1972, paperback edit., 1973, Marksman, 1974, Macumba, White and Black Magic in Brazil, 1975, Hidden Terrors, 1978, paperback edit., 1979, Portuguese edit., 1979, Brazilian book club edit., 1983, Russian edit., 1985, Saki, A Life of Hector Hugh Munro, 1981, paperback edit., 1982, Patriots, The Men Who Started the American Revolution, 1988, paperback edit., 1989, audio version, 1989, A Noise of War: Caesar, Pompey, Octavian and the Struggle for Rome, 1994, audio version, 1995; contbr. articles to profl. jours. including The N.Y. Times Mag., N.Y. Times Book Rev., Washington Post Book World, L.A. Times Book Rev., numerous others. Shaw travelling fellow Harvard Coll., 1955-56, fellow John Simon Guggenheim Meml. Found., 1976-77. Mem. Author's Guild. E-mail: langguth@bcf.usc.edu. Home: 1922 Whitley Ave Los Angeles CA 90068-3233 Office: U So Calif ASC-102C University Park Los Angeles CA 90089-0281

LANGLEY, GARY ALFRED, public relations consultant; b. Livingston, Mont., Oct. 29, 1946; s. Alfred Cameron and Victoria Ann (Ricci) L.; m. Pamela Jane Patrick, Oct. 22, 1972; children: Jefferson Patrick, Kari Jane. BA, U. Mont., 1969. Reporter, Livingston (Mont.) Enterprise, 1964-65; copy editor Spokane (Wash.) Spokesman-Review, 1969; reporter, asst. city editor, asst. editorial page editor Missoula (Mont.) Missoulian, 1969-72; bur. chief Mont. Lee Newspapers State Bur., Helena, 1972-77; dir. communications Mont. Stockgrowers Assn., Helena, 1977-81; owner Langley Public Relations Cons., Helena, 1979—. Editor: The Pick and Shovel Jour., 1980—. Exec. dir. Found. Resource Edn., 1987—; v.p. Mont. Pub. Lands Used Sensibly, 1988—. Mem. Am. Soc. Assn. Execs., Mont. Soc. Assn. Execs. (pres., bd. dirs.), Western Environ. Trade Assn., Mont. Mining Assn. (exec. dir. 1981—, bd. dirs.), Am. Mining Congress (bd. govs.), Western Mining Coordinating Council, Helena C. of C., Montana Club, Last Chance Press Club (bd. dirs., past pres.), Sigma Delta Chi. Republican. Lutheran. Home: 2860 Village Rd Helena MT 59602-9500 Office: 2301 Colonial Dr Helena MT 59601-4995

LANGLEY, JAMES WALLACE, family practice physician, banker; b. Dearborn, Mich., Jan. 27, 1933; s. James Monroe and Mildred Elizabeth (Brite) L.; m. Margaret Lyons, Feb., 1955 (div. Feb. 1979); children: Roseanne, Annette, Jeanette, Barbara, James, Joseph, John, Stephen, Michael, Mark; m. Sheri K. Orr, June 23, 1979. MD, U. Mich., 1957. Diplomate Am. Bd. Family Practice; cert. added qualifications Am. Bd. Geriatrics, Am. Bd. Sports Medicine. Family practice physician, Denver, Colo., 1958—; family practice and geriatrics physician Colo., 1994—, family practice, geriatrics, sports medicine physician, 1997—; owner, bd. dirs. North Valley Bank, Thornton, Colo., 1963—. Mem. AMA, Colo. Med. Soc., Clear Creek Valley Med. Soc. Avocation: airline transport pilot, fixed wing, and helicopter pilot. Office: North Valley Bank 9001 N Washington Thornton CO 80400

LANGONI, RICHARD ALLEN, civil engineer; b. Trinidad, Colo., Aug. 7, 1945; s. Domenic and Josephine (Maria) L.; A of Applied Sci., Trinidad State Jr. Coll., 1966; BSCE Colo. State U., 1968; MA, U. No. Colo., 1978; m. Pamela Jill Stansberry, Aug. 19, 1972; children: Kristi, Kerri. Civil engr. Dow Chem. Co., Golden, Colo., 1968-71; city engr., dir. public works City of Trinidad, 1971-74; civil engr. Clement Bros. Constrn. Co., 1974-75; instr. Trinidad State Jr. Coll., 1975-78; city engr., dir. public works City of Durango (Colo.), 1978-82; traffic engr. Colo. Dept. Transp., Durango, 1982—. Recipient Meritorious Svc. award City of Durango; registered profl. engr. Colo., N.Mex. Mem. Nat. Soc. Profl. Engrs., ASCE, Am. Public Works Assn., Water Pollution Control Fedn., Profl. Engrs. Colo., Durango C. of C., Nat. Ski Patrol (Purgatory and Wolf Creek), Phi Theta Kappa, Chi Epsilon. Home: 30 Moenkopi Dr Durango CO 81301-8599

LANGSLET, CAREEN ANN, occupational therapist; b. Portland, Oreg., Nov. 9, 1944; d. Arlie Carroll and Lorraine Belle (Harper) Carter; m. Robert Carl Marshall, Jan. 1, 1966 (div. June 1988); children: Kelly A., Jason A. BA, U. Okla., 1967; MS, U. Puget Sound, 1981. Cert., Am. Occupl. Therapy Assn. Occupl. therapist Multnomah Edn. Svc. Dist., Portland, 1986—. Home: 208 SW Lane St Portland OR 97201-4300 Office: Multnomah Edn Svc Dist 11611 NE Ainsworth Cir Portland OR 97220-9017

LANIER, WILLIAM JOSEPH, college program director; b. Great Falls, Mont., Dec. 20, 1963; s. Bolder Lanue and Nancy Jo (Kiszczak) L. AS, No. Mont. Coll., 1985, B Tech., 1987, MEd, 1989. Drafting intern Columbus Hosp., Great Falls, 1985-87; grad. asst. No. Mont. Coll., Havre, 1987-89; dir. student life Mont. State U. -No. (formerly No. Mont. Coll.), Havre, 1989-95, 1995—. Bd. dirs. Havre Encourages Long Range Prevention, 1992—, Hill County Crimestoppers, 1991-93; adv. bd. No. Ctrl. Mont. Upward Bound, Harlem, 1992—; mem. Nat. Eagle Scout Assn., Irving, Tex., 1991—. Recipient Golden N award student senate No. Mont. Coll., 1992. Mem. Am. Counseling Assn., Am. Coll. Pers. Assn., Nat. Assn. Student Pers. Adminstrs., No. Mont. Coll. Alumni Assn. (bd. dirs 1990—). Avocations: reading, collecting baseball cards. Home: MacKenzie Hall Havre MT 59501 Office: Mont State U PO Box 7751 Havre MT 59501-7751

LANKFORD, DUANE GAIL, investment banker, mountaineer; b. Ft. Collins, Colo., July 18, 1932; s. William Oliver and Mary Martha (Lago) L.; m. Eleanor Polly, June 18, 1955 (div. 1983); children: Scott, Kurt Edwin, Rebecca Ann; m. Jariyaporn Ekkanasing, Nov. 8, 1991. Student, Colo. State Coll. of Edn., 1950-51, Denver U., 1952-55. Lic. stockbroker over 40 states security commns. and all U.S. exchs. Mgr. Dial Fin., Denver, 1953-59; mgr. investment banking Peters Writer & Christianson, Denver, 1959-60, E.I. DuPont De Nemours, Denver, 1960; mgr. mcpl. investment banking Bache & Co., Denver, L.A., N.Y.C., 1961-68; v.p. sales Fin. Programs, Inc., San Francisco, 1968-69; fin. advisor Lankford & Co., Denver, 1969; mgr. muni bonds W.E. Hutton & Co., Denver, 1969-71; owner/operator Lankford & Co., Denver, 1972—, The Wilderness Inst./Lankford Mountain Guides, Denver, 1978—; chmn. Denver Lenders Exch., 1957-58; cons. advisor numerous cities, towns, states and corps.; expert witness in investment banking and mountaineering; cons. numerous legal firms; cons./advisor numerous fed. agys. Contbr. articles to profl. jours. Worldwide mountaineer numerous maj. peaks. Mem. Am. Alpine Club, Pioneers. Libertarian. Avocations: internat. mountaineering, internat. travel, philosophy, opera, classical music.

L'ANNUNZIATA, MICHAEL FRANK, international official, nuclear scientist; b. Springfield, Mass., Oct. 14, 1943; s. Michael Peter and Irene M. L'Annunziata; m. Maria del Carmen Elena Monge, Mar. 3, 1973; children: Michael O., Helen, Frank E. BS, St. Edward's U., Austin, Tex., 1965; MS, U. Ariz., 1967, PhD, 1970. Rsch. chemist Amchem Products, Inc., Ambler, Pa., 1971-72; rsch. assoc. U. Ariz., Tucson, 1972-73; prof., sect. head U. Chapingo, Mexico, 1973-75; rsch. scientist Nat. Inst. Nuclear Rsch., Mexico City, 1975-77; assoc. officer IAEA, Vienna, Austria, 1977-80, 2d officer, 1980-83, 1st officer, head sci. visits program, 1983-86, sr. officer, head fellowships and tng. sect., 1986-91; mng. dir. LMS Internat. Tech. Svcs., Ltd., Coronado, Calif., 1992-95; dir. WorldTech Internat. Tech. Svcs., Oceanside, Calif., 1995—; bd. dirs. internat. sci. programs Uppsala (Sweden) U.; internat. IAEA cons.; cons., lectr. Forestry Rsch. Inst., Ibadan, Nigeria, 1994, 95, Ministry Edn., Jakarta, Indonesia, 1995, Internat. Sales and Mktg., Packard Instrument Co., Meriden, Conn., 1995-99, Egypt Atomic Energy Authority, Cairo, 1995, 96, Gezira Rsch. Sta., Wad Medani, Sudan, 1995, Ethiopian Sci. and Tech. Commn., Addis Ababa, 1996, Nat. Radiation Commsn., Arusha, Tanzania, 1996; vis. lectr. Advanced Sch. Tropical Agriculture, Cardenas, Mexico, 1973, Atomic Energy Commn. of Ecuador, Quito, Ecuador, 1978, Timiryazev Agrl. Acad., Moscow, 1980, 81, Nuclear Rsch. Inst. in Vet. Medicine, Lalahan, Turkey, 1981, IAEA Seibersdorf Labs., Seibersdorf, Austria, 1978-82, U. Guanajuato, Mex., 1981, Coll. Montecillo, Chapingo, Mex., 1989, Korea Atomic Energy Rsch. Inst., Seoul, 1991, Nat. Atomic Energy Agy., Jakarta, 1991-94, Zhejiang Argl. U., Hangzhou, China, 1992, Centrl Nuc. "La Reina", Santiago, Chile, 1992, Internat. Atomic Energy Agy., Vienna, 1993, Mt. Makulu Ctrl. Rsch. Sta., Lusaka, Zambia, 1994, Office Atomic Energy Peace, Bangkok, 1995, Swedish Radiation Protection Inst., Stockholm, 1996, CIEMAT, Madrid, 1996, Laguna Verde Nuc. Power Plant, Vera Cruz, Mex., 1996, Oak Ridge (Tenn.) Nat. Labs., 1998, Min. Water and Irrigation, Amman, Jordan, 1998, Wyeth-Ayerst, Pearl River, N.Y., 1998, Chem. Industry Inst. Toxicology, Research Triangle Park, N.C., 1998; hon. prof. Zhejiang Agrl. U., 1992. Author: (textbooks) Radiotracers in Agricultural Chemistry, 1979, Radionuclide Tracers, Their Detection and Measurement, 1987; author, editor (with J.O. Legg) Isotopes and Radiation in Agricultural Sciences, Vol. 1, 1984, Vol. 2, 1984, Handbook of Radioactivity Analysis, 1998. Contbr. articles to profl. jours. Recipient hon. teaching diploma, silver plaque Central U. Ecuador, Quito, 1978. Mem. AAAS, N.Y. Acad. Scis., Am. Nuclear Soc., Sigma Xi, Phi Lambda Upsilon, Gamma Sigma Delta. Roman Catholic. Achievements include discovery of molecular D-chiro-inositol phosphate in soil/plant systems; determination of the biochemical mechanism and pathway involved in the formation of soil chiro-inositol phosphate; elucidated mechanisms of soil organic phosphorus fixation; first separation of the radioactive nuclides Sr-90 from soil surfaces after nuclear fallout; execution of over 80 fact-finding, planning, and implementation missions to over 60 countries of Asia, Africa, Europe, Latin America, North America, and the Middle East for the United Nations, International Atomic Energy Agency from 1978 to the present; development of several chemical and instrumental techniques for the analysis of radioactive nuclides. Office: WorldTech Internat Tech Svcs PO Box 1471 Oceanside CA 92051-1471

LANSDOWNE, KAREN MYRTLE, retired English language and literature educator; b. Twin Falls, Idaho, Aug. 11, 1926; d. George and Effie Myrtle (Ayotte) Martin; BA in English with honors, U. Oreg., 1948, MEd, 1958, MA with honors, 1960; m. Paul L. Lansdowne, Sept. 12, 1948; children: Michele Lynn, Larry Alan. Tchr., Newfield (N.Y.) H.S., 1948-50, S. Eugene (Oreg.) H.S., 1952; mem. faculty U. Oreg., Eugene, 1958-65; asst. prof. English, Lane C.C., Eugene, 1965-82, ret., 1982; cons. Oreg. Curriculum Study Center. Rep., Cal Young Neighborhood Assn., 1978—; mem. scholarship com. First Congl. Ch., 1950-70. Mem. MLA, Pacific N.W. Regional Conf. C.C.s, Nat. Council Tchrs. English, U. Oreg. Women, AAUW (sec.), Jaycettes, Pi Lambda Theta (pres.), Phi Beta Patronesses (pres.), Delta Kappa Gamma. Co-author: The Oregon Curriculum: Language/Rhetoric, I, II, III and IV, 1970. Home: 2056 Lincoln St Eugene OR 97405-2604

LANTER, SEAN KEITH, software engineer; b. Los Alamos, N.Mex., May 8, 1953; s. Robert Jackson and Norma Esther (Jonas) L.; m. Lauri Jane Willand, July 16, 1977; children: Tully Erik, Sarah Elizabeth, Rachel Erin. BA in Physics, U. Utah, 1974, MSME, 1977; MS in Computer Sci., LaSalle U., 1998. Registered profl. engr., Wash. Sr. engr. Boeing Comml. Airplane Co., Seattle, 1977-82; systems analyst Internat. Submarine Tech. Ltd., Redmond, Wash., 1982-83; engr. software Advanced Tech. Labs., Bellevue, Wash., 1983-84; engr. contract Rho Co., Redmond, 1984-85; sr. tech. staff Cedar Software Inc., Redmond, 1985-87; pres. Connexions Engrng. and Software, Woodinville, Wash., 1987-88; pres., chief engr. Connexions Engrng., Inc., Woodinville, 1990-95; sys. engr. Microrim Software, Inc., Bellevue, Wash., 1995-96; cons., contract programmer, 1990—. Contbr. articles to profl. jours. Mem. Assn. Computing Machinery, NSPE. Lutheran. Avocations: chamber music, reading, history, baseball. Office: Connexions Engrng PO Box 3007 Woodinville WA 98072-3007

LANTOS, THOMAS PETER, congressman; b. Budapest, Hungary, Feb. 1, 1928; m. Annette Tillemann; children: Annette, Katrina. B.A., U. Washington, 1949, M.A., 1950; Ph.D., U. Calif.-Berkeley, 1953. Mem. faculty U. Wash., San Francisco State U., 1950-83; TV news analyst, commentator, sr. econ. and fgn. policy adviser to several U.S. senators; mem. Presdl. Task Force on Def. and Fgn. Policy, 97th-105th Congresses from 11th (now 12th) Calif dist., 1981—; ranking minority mem., internat. rels. subcom. on internat. ops. and human rels., internat. rels. subcom. on western hemisphere, mem. gov. reform and oversight com.; founder study abroad program Calif. State U. and Coll. System. Mem. Millbrae Bd. Edn., 1950-66. Democrat. Office: US Ho of Reps 2217 Rayburn HOB Washington DC 20515-0512

LANTRIP, IVOLUE MAY, secretary; b. Cherryvale, Kans., Mar. 13, 1929; d. John Franklin Sanders and Treva Jenneve (Rohrbough) McKinnon; m. Truman Leo Lantrip, July 23, 1949; children: Michael Dennis, Richard Oden. Grad. h.s., Benicia, Calif. Sec. Benicia H.S., 1948-54, 62-67, counselors sec., 1961-62; fin. sec., bookkeeper Benicia Unified Sch. Dist., 1967-71, ret. Author: The American Genealogy of the Lantrip Family, 1994. Mem. DAR (Acalanes chpt. historian 1984-86, 88-90, treas. 1986-88), Carquinez Strait Stitchers Quilt Guild (treas.), Ret. Pub. Employees Assn. of Calif. Avocations: oil painting, china painting, quilting/wearable art, genealogy, travel. Home: 22 Alta Loma Benicia CA 94510-2608

LANTZ, ANNA MAE, secondary school educator; b. Canton, Ohio, Mar. 5, 1938; d. Roy Kenneth and Mabel Elmina Shank; m. Lamar Eugene Lantz, Mar. 21, 1959; children: Melody Ann, Thomas Edward, Marla Joy. Student, Goshen Coll., 1957-58; BA in English and Edn., Ind. U., 1990; postgrad., Western N.Mex. U., 1995—. Stenographer Hoover Co., North Canton, Ohio, 1956-57; med. receptionist, sec. Goshen (Ind.) Coll. Health Ctr.; adminstrv. sec. loan processing Salem Bank & Trust Co., Goshen; tchr. lang. arts, English lang. Hot Springs H.S., Truth or Consequences, N.Mex., 1993—; mentor tchr. Hot Springs H.S., 1996-97, 98—, chairperson evaluation com., 1997-98; trainer, chairperson Character Counts! program, Truth or Consequences, 1996—. Mem. NEA (mem. com. sick leave bank 1997—, other coms.), Nat. Coun. Tchrs. of English, Libr. of Congress, Am. Assn. Ret. Persons. Avocations: reading, traveling, walking, boating, family activities.

LANTZ, NORMAN FOSTER, electrical engineer; b. Pekin, Ill., June 8, 1937; s. Norman Gough and Lenore (Elsbury) L.; m. Donnis Maureen Ballinger, Sept. 7, 1958 (div. Aug. 1991); children: Katherine, Deborah, Norman Daniel; m. Judith Eliane Peach, Dec. 7, 1991. BSEE, Purdue U., 1959, MSEE, 1961. System engr. GE Co., Phila., 1961-72; mem. tech. staff The Aerospace Corp., El Segundo, Calif., 1972-75, mgr., 1975-79, dir., 1979-83, prin. dir., 1983-90, sr. project leader, 1991—; dir. Internat. Found. for Telemetering, Woodland Hills, Calif., 1985—. 2d lt. U.S. Army, 1960-61. Mem. AIAA (sr.), IEEE, INCOSE, Am. Mgmt. Assn. Office: The Aerospace Corp Sr Project Engineer El Segundo CA 90245-4691

LAPAN, STEPHEN D., gifted education educator, consultant; b. Aurora, Ill., Oct. 23, 1940; s. Richard James and Gladys Letitia (Dennis) L.; m. Karen Kay roetzoel, Feb. 1, 1964 (div. 1966). BA, Parsons Coll., 1962; MEd, U. Ill., 1966; PhD, U. Conn., 1972. Tchr. Roberts-Thawville (Ill.) Sch. Dist., 1962-64, Elk Grove Sch. Dist., Des Plaines, Ill., 1964-66; asst. dir. Ill. State Dept. Edn., Chgo., 1966-68; program assoc. Coop. Edn. Regional Lab, Northfield, Ill., 1968-69, U. Ill., Urbana, 1969-70; asst. prof. to prof. Northeastern Ill. U., Chgo., 1973-86; assoc. to prof. Northern Ariz. U., Flagstaff, 1986—. Co-author: Survival in the Classroom, 1978; author: (monograph) Meaning of Intelligence, 1989; editor of four monographs on edn., 1991-98; contbr. articles to profl. jours. Edn. advisor Adlai Steverson III Senate campaign, Ill., 1969-70. Recipient Lifetime Achievement award Ariz. Assn. Gifted and Talented, 1991. Avocations: reading, swimming. Home: 3130 Valley Vista Dr Sedona AZ 86351-7235 Office: Ctr Excellence in Edn PO Box 5774 NAU Flagstaff AZ 86011

LAPIROFF, JERRY, secondary school educator; b. Bklyn., Feb. 11, 1947; s. Harry and Betty (Klein) L.; m. Helen Chu, July 24, 1988; children: Harris, Mariah. Tchr. John F. Kennedy High Sch., 1971—; Fulbright exch. tchr., 1992-93; coord. Virtual H.S. Project. Named Spl. Recognition advisor Journalism, 1989, DistING. advisor Dow Jones Newspaper Fund, 1992. Office: 39999 Blacow Rd Fremont CA 94538-1913

LAPOTA, DAVID, oceanographer, marine biologist; b. L.A., June 1, 1949; s. Mathew H. and Jane E. (Cassell) L.; m. Jeannette Harward, June 28, 1975. BS in Zoology, San Diego State U., 1973, MA in Geography, 1982; PhD in Biology, U. Calif., Santa Barbara, 1998. Data analyst San Diego State Found., 1974-79; biologist Naval Ocean Systems Ctr., San Diego, 1979-82, scientist, 1982—. Patentee in field; contbr. articles and abstracts to profl. jours. and chpts. to books. With USAR, 1969-75. Fellow Explorers Club; mem. Am. Geophys. Union, Biol. Soc. Washington, Oceanography Soc. Home: 6678 Hemingway Dr San Diego CA 92120-1616 Office: Space and Naval Warfare Sys Ctr Marine Environ Br Code D362 San Diego CA 92152-5000

LARA, ADAIR, columnist, writer; b. San Francisco, Jan. 3, 1952; d. Eugene Thomas and Lee Louise (Hanley) Daly; m. James Lee Heig, June 18, 1976 (div. 1989); children: Morgan, Patrick; m. William Murdock LeBlond, Nov. 2, 1991. BA in English, San Francisco State U., 1976. Reader Coll. of Marin, Kentfield, Calif., 1976-83; freelance editor, 1983-86; mng. editor San Francisco Focus mag., 1986-89; exec. editor San Francisco mag., 1988-89; columnist San Francisco Chronicle, 1989—. Author: History of Petaluma: A California River Town, 1982, Welcome to Earth, Mom, 1992, Slowing Down in a Speeded-up World, 1994, At Adair's House, More Columns by America's Funniest Formerly Single Man, 1995; contbr. articles to profl. publs. Recipient Best Calif. Columnist award AP, 1990. Democrat. Avocations: reading, photography, travel, softball, biking. Office: San Francisco Chronicle 901 Mission St San Francisco CA 94103-2905

LARA, TONY RICHARD, industrial engineer, consultant; b. Prescott, Ariz., June 9, 1947; s. Brigido S. and Antonio (Abril) L.; m. Marilyn Larson, July 31, 1969; children: Jennifer, Kristen. AA in Tech. Edn., Yavapai C.C., Prescott, 1972; BA in Tech. Edn. cum laude, Ariz. State U., 1974; AA in Supervision, Maricopa Tech. C.C., Phoenix, 1978. Facility engr. Airesearch Mfg. Co., Phoenix, 1973-79; maintenance coord. Garrett Engine divsn. Allied-Signal Aerospace Co., Phoenix, 1979-80; capital/facility engr. Garrett Fluid Systems divsn. Allied-Signal Aerospace Co., Tempe, Ariz., 1980-89, supr. time std., 1989-91, supr. N/C programming, 1991-92, sr. indsl. engr., 1992—. Mem. adv. bd. Maricopa County Skill Ctr., Phoenix, 1981-92. Sgt. USMC, 1966-69, Vietnam. Mem. Soc. Mfg. Engrs., Kappa Delta Pi. Roman Catholic. Avocations: consulting, old cars, woodworking, fishing.

LARCOM, DAVID LOUIS, newspaper pressman, artist, writer, educator; b. Denver, May 31, 1958; s. Louis Edward and Alice Ruth (O'dell) L.; m. Safitri Larcom, May 3, 1972; 1 child, Louis Wartoyo. Grad., Colo. Mountain Coll.; postgrad., Colo. Inst. Art, 1977-80. Pressman Blueprints Inc., Colorado Springs, Colo., 1984-88, Herald Printers, Monterey, Calif., 1988-91; ESL instr. Sch. for Internat. Tng., Jakarta, Indonesia, 1991-95; pressman Mountain Mail, Salida, Colo., 1995—. Author: English is Fun, 1994, 3d edit., 1995; writer Tests of English as a Fgn. Lang. tests, study material, 1990-95. Mem. Art of the Rockies, Salida, 1995—, Chaffee County Coun. Arts, Salida, 1995—. With USN, 1980-84. Avocations: painting, writing, guitar. Home: 1239 D St Salida CO 81201

LARGE, TIMOTHY WALLACE, religious organization administrator; b. Palo Alto, Calif., Feb. 23, 1942; s. Charles Delano Henry and Jean Eleanor (Parker) L.; m. Vickie Lee Olson, Aug. 6, 1978; children: Jonathan Jeffrey, Sarah Jean. BSBA, Menlo Coll., 1964; MBA, U. Santa Clara, 1966; cert., Multnomah Sch. Bible, Portland, Oreg., 1973; M of Div., Talbot Theol. Sem., La Mirada, Calif., 1978. CPA, Calif. Acct. Bramer Accountancy Corp., Santa Fe Springs, Calif., 1974-76; instr. Biola Coll., La Mirada, Calif., 1978; acct. Conservative Bapt. Assn. So. Calif., Anaheim, 1978-83; CPA H. Canaday, P.A., Santa Fe Springs, 1983—; adminstr. Temple Baptist Ch., Perris, Calif., 1985-87; treas. Inst. Evangelico, La Puenta, Calif., 1987—; cons. Exec. Leasing, La Mirada, 1976—. Treas. Founders chpt. Kidney Found. So. Calif., Orange County, 1974-76; chaplain Christian Hosp. Med. Ctr., Perris, 1985—. Served with U.S. Army, 1965-69. Fellow Nat. Assn. Ch. Bus. Adminstrs.; mem. AICPA, Am. Mgt. Assn., Christian Ministries Mgt. Assn. Republican. Baptist. Avocations: bowling, ping pong, travel. Home: 26928 Potomac Dr Sun City CA 92586 3164 Office: 14864 Valley Blvd La Puente CA 91746-3225

LARGENT, REGINA MARY, military science educator; b. Argentia, Newfoundland, Can., June 28, 1953; d. Elton L. and Theresa M. (Biersack) L. AA, Fla. Jr. Coll., Jacksonville, 1973; BS, Fla. State U., 1975; MA, U. Mass., 1986. Commd. 2d lt. U.S. Army, 1977, advanced through grades to lt. col., 1996; Assoc. prof. English U.S. Mil. Acad., West Point, N.Y., 1986-89; chief, Pers. Divsn., 5th Pers. Group U.S. Army, Hanau, Germany, 1989-90; comdr./pers. officer, 11th Armored Cavalry U.S. Army, Fuldan, Germany, 1990-92; chief, strategic plans, I Corps and Ft. Lewis U.S. Army, Ft. Lewis, Wash., 1993-94; dir. Joint Info. Bur., Multinational Forces U.S. Army, Port au Prince, Haiti, 1994-95; dep. pers. officer, Ft. Lewis and I Corps U.S. Army, Ft. Lewis, 1995-96; prof. Mil. Sci. and Composition U. Portland (Oreg.), 1996—. Assoc. editor: (jour.) Mass. Studies in English, 1985-86; editor: (jour.) Dandelion, 1976-77, Fla. Student Assn. Jour., 1975-76. Mem. VFW, MLA, AAUW, Adj. Gen. Corps Regiment (v.p. 1995-96, Horatio Gates Bronze medal 1993, presdl. award 1996), Am. Legion. Democrat. Avocations: hiking, golf. Home: E2 13216 NE Salmon Creek Ave Vancouver WA 98686-2882 Office: U Portland AROTC 5000 N Willamette Blvd Portland OR 97203-5743

LARIZADEH, M(OHAMMED) R(EZA), business educator; b. Tehran, Iran, Apr. 14, 1947; came to U.S., 1966; s. Hassan and Nosrat (Saremi) L.; m. Dianne Ellen Pincus, Mar. 25, 1973; children: Dariush, Darya Anna. BA in Econs., Bus., UCLA, 1972, cert. in acctg., 1974. Cert. colls. teaching credential, Calif. (life); lic. real estate agent, Calif. Auditor Peat, Marwick & Mitchell, L.A., 1972-74; controller Petromain Constrn. Co., Tehran, 1975-77; v.p. fin. Pilary Marine Shipping Co., Tehran, 1977-79; prof. Iranian Inst. Banking, Tehran, 1975-78; pres. Audicount Acctg. and Auditing Group, L.A., 1984—; prof. bus. and acctg. East L.A. Coll., 1980-87, vice-chmn. dept. bus. and acctg., 1987—, chmn. dept. bus. adminstrn., 1988—; prof. acctg. Santa Monica (Calif.) Coll., 1987—; mgmt. cons. L.P. Assocs. Mfg. Co., L.A., 1981—; mng. dir. Barrington Enterprises, L.A.; prof. Santa Monica Coll., 1987. Author/translator: Accounting/Auditing, 1975. Mem. NEA, Internat. Fedn. Bus. Edn., Am. Mgmt. Assn., Am. Acctg. Assn., Faculty Assn. Calif. C.C.s, Am. Fedn. Tchrs., Calif. Tchrs. Assn., Am. Entrepreneur Assn., Nat. Assn. Realtors, Am. Assn. Pub. Accts., Calif. Assn. Bus. Educators, Calif. Assn. Realtors, Nat. Soc. Pub. Accts., Calif. Bus. Edn. Assn., Internat. Fedn. Bus. Edn., Inst. Mgmt. Accts., UCLA Alumni Assn. (life), Alpha Kappa Psi.

LARK, RAYMOND, artist, art scholar; b. Phila., June 16, 1939; s. Thomas and Bertha (Lark) Crawford. Student, Phila. Mus. Sch. Art, 1948-51, L.A. Trade Tech. Coll., 1961-62; BS, Temple U., 1961; LHD, U. Colo., 1985. Ednl. dir. Victor Bus. Sch., L.A., 1969-71; pub. rels. exec. Western States Svc. Co., L.A., 1968-70; owner, mgr. Raymond Lark's House of Fine Foods, L.A., 1962-67; from exec. sec. to v.p. Physicians Drug and Supply Co., Phila., 1957-61; lectr. L.A. Trade Tech. Coll., 1973, Compton (Calif.) Coll., 1972, Nat. Secs. Assn., Hollywood, Calif., UCLA, U. Utah, Salt Lake City, 1993, others. One-man shows include, Dalzell Hatfield Galleries, L.A., 1968-86, Arthur's Gallery Masterpieces and Jewels, Beverly Hills, Calif., 1971, Dorothy Chandler Pavillion Music Center, L.A., 1974, Honolulu Acad. Arts, 1975, UCLA, 1983, U. Colo. Mus., 1984, Albany State Coll. Art Gallery, Albany, Ga., 1988, Utah Mus. Fine Arts, Salt Lake City, 1989, Mind's Art Gallery, Dickinson U., Dickinson, N.D., 1989, Trinton Mus. Art, Santa Clara, Calif., Greenville (N.C.) Mus. of Art, 1993, Springfield (Mo.) Art Mus., 1995, Washington County Museum of Fine Arts, Hagerstown, Md., 1996, The Peninisula Fine Arts Center, Newport News, Va., 1996, N.C. State U., Raleigh, 1998, others; group exhbns. include, Smithsonian Instn., 1971, N.J. State Mus., Trenton, 1971, Guggenheim Mus., N.Y.C., 1975, Met. Mus. Art, 1976, La Galerie Mauffe, Paris, 1977, Portsmouth (Va.) Mus., 1979, Ava Dorog Galleries, Munich, W. Ger., 1979, Accademia Italia, Parma, 1980, Ames Art Galleries and Auctioneers, Beverly Hills, 1980, Le Salon des Nations at Centre International d'Art Contemporain, Paris, 1983, Tivolio Gallery, Salt Lake City, 1991, Hyatt Regency Hotel, Capitol Hill, Washington, 1993, Alexandria Mus. Art, La., 1998, Hill country Arts Found., Ingram, Tex., 1998, others; represented in permanent collections, Library of Congress, Ont. Coll. Art, Toronto, Mus. African and African Am. Art and Antiquities, Buffalo, Carnegie Inst., numerous others; art commns. for TV and film studios include, All in the Family, Carol Burnett Show, Maude, The Young and the Restless, Universal City Studios, Palace of the Living Arts, Movie Land Wax Mus.; author works in field; author and contbr. more than 50 scholarly treatises on art, edn. and the hist. devel. of Black Ams., chpts. to encyclopedias and textbooks, articles to jours., introductions to mus. exhbn. catalogues. Recipient gold medal Acad. Italia, 1980, also numerous gold medals and best of show awards, 3 presdl. proclamations; award Internat. Platform Assn.; Dr. Raymond Lark Day proclaimed by State of Md.,

1994; grantee Nat. Endowment Arts, ARCO Found., Colo. Humanities Program, Adolph Coors Beer Found. Mem. Art West Assn. (pres. 1968-70). Address: PO Box 76169 Los Angeles CA 90076-0169

LARKIN, ERNEST ELDON, priest, consultant, retired educator; b. Chgo., Aug. 19, 1922; s. Clement J. and Helen M. (McKeown) L. PhB, Mt. Carmel Coll., 1943; D of Sacred Theology, St. Thomas U., Rome, 1954. Ordained priest Roman Cath. Ch., 1946. Assoc. prof. The Cath. U. Am., Washington, 1959-71; founder, tchr. Kino Inst., Phoenix, 1972—; dir. retreats and workshops throughout country. Author: Silent Presence, 1981, Christ Within Us, 1984; editor: Spiritual Renewal of American Priesthood, 1973; contbr. articles to profl. jours. Active Carmelite Order, Darien, Ill., 1940—. Home: 1954 N 24th St Phoenix AZ 85008-3556 Office: Kino Inst 1224 E Northern Ave Phoenix AZ 85020-4295

LAROCK, BRUCE EDWARD, civil engineering educator; b. Berkeley, Calif., Dec. 24, 1940; s. Ralph W. and Hazel M. L.; m. Susan E. Gardner, June 17, 1968; children: Lynne M., Jean E. BS in Civil Engring., Stanford U., 1962, MS in Civil Engring., 1963, PhD, 1966. Registered profl. engr., Calif. Asst. prof. U. Calif., Davis, 1966-72, assoc. prof., 1972-79, prof., 1979—; sr. vis. fellow U. Wales, Swansea, 1972-73; U.S. sr. scientist Tech. U., Aachen, Germany, 1986-87. Author: (with D. Newnan) Engineer-in-Training Examination Review, 3d edit., 1991; contbr. over 80 tech. articles to profl. jours. Mem. ASCE, Sigma Xi, Tau Beta Pi. Lutheran. Avocation: duplicate bridge. Office: Dept Civil Environ Engring U Calif Davis CA 95616-5294

LAROCQUE, MARILYN ROSS ONDERDONK, writer, public relations consultant; b. Weehawken, N.J., Oct. 14, 1934; d. Chester Douglas and Marion (Ross) Onderdonk; B.A. cum laude, Mt. Holyoke Coll., 1956; postgrad. N.Y. U., 1956-57; M. Journalism, U. Calif. at Berkeley, 1965; m. Bernard Dean Benz, Oct. 5, 1957 (div. Sept. 1971); children: Mark Douglas, Dean Griffith; m. 2d, Rodney C. LaRocque, Feb. 10, 1973. Jr. exec. Bonwit Teller, N.Y.C., 1956; personnel asst. Warner-Lambert Pharm. Co., Morris Plains, N.J., 1957; editorial asst. Silver Burdett Co., Morristown, 1958; self-employed as pub. rels. cons., Moraga, Calif., 1963-71, 73-77; pub. rels. mgr. Shaklee Corp., Hayward, 1971-73; pub. rels. dir. Fidelity Savs., 1977-78; exec. dir. No. Calif. chpt. Nat. Multiple Sclerosis Soc., 1978-80; v.p. pub. rels. Cambridge Plan Internat., Monterey, Calif., 1980-81; sr. account exec. Hoefer-Amidei Assocs., San Francisco, 1981-82; dir. corp. comms., dir. spl. projects, asst. to chmn. Cambridge Plan Internat., Monterey, Calif., 1982-84; dir. comms. Buena Vista Winery, Sonoma, Calif., 1984-86, asst. v.p. comms. and market support, 1986-87; dir. comms. Rutherford Hill Winery, St. Helena, Calif., 1987-88; pres. LaRocque-Hannaford Pub. Rels. and Pub. Affairs, Napa, Calif., 1988-91; pres. LaRocque Profl. Svcs., Inc., 1991-95; writer, pub. rels. cons., 1995—; instr. pub. rels. U. Calif. Extension, San Francisco, 1977-79.; corr., reviewer Napa Valley Register. Mem. exec. bd., rep-at-large Oakland (Calif.) Symphony Guild, 1968-69 ; co-chmn. pub. rels. com. Oakland Mus. Assn., 1974-75; cabinet mem. Lincoln Child Ctr., Oakland, 1967-71, pres. membership cabinet, 1970-71, 2d v.p. bd. dirs., 1970-71; bd. dirs. Calif. Spring Garden and Home Show, 1971-77, 1st Agrl. Dist., 1971-77, Dunsmuir House and Gardens, 1976-77; mem. Calif. State Rep. Cen. Com., 1964-66; v.p. Piedmont coun. Boy Scouts Am., 1977; mem. vol. coun. Di Rosa Art & Nature Preserve, 1997-98; mem. Theater at the Opera House, Napa Valley. Mem. U. Calif. Alumni Assn., Pub. Rels. Soc. Am. (chpt. dir. 1980-82; accredited), Sonoma Valley Vintners Assn. (dir. 1984-87), Internat. Wine and Food Soc. (Marin chpt.), San Francisco Mus. Soc., San Francisco Asian Arts Mus., Smithsonian Assocs., Libr. Congress Assocs., Nat. Trust Hist. Preservation, Sonoma Valley C. of C. (bd. dirs. 1984-87), Napa County Landmarks Inc. (bd. dirs. 1993-94), Theater at the Opera House, Napa Valley, adv. Junior League of Napa, Am. Assn. Univ. Women (Napa Valley chpt.), Napa Valley Republican Women, Knights of the Vine (master lady 1985-90), Mount Holyoke Coll. Alumnae Club, Silverado Country Club, DAR (vineyard trails chpt.). Office: LaRocque Pub Rels 1800 Soscol Ave # A Napa CA 94559-1345

LARONGE, LAWRENCE STEVEN, health administrator, tax professional; b. East Cleve., Nov. 15, 1943; s. Marc and Irence Catherine (Waggonhoffer) L.; m. Sangaroon See-Kaing, Oct. 18, 1975; 1 child, Lindsey Scott. BS in Bus., Miami U., 1966; MBA in Mgmt., Golden Gate U., 1976. Cert. cmty. coll. instr., Calif., comml. pilot, FAA, tax preparer, Calif. Commd. 2d lt. USAF, 1966, advanced through grades to col., 1974; tax compliance officer Calif. Franchise Tax Bd., Sacramento, 1975-79; instr. Los Rios C.C., Sacramento, 1978-90; spl. agt. USAFR Office of Spl. Inv., Washington, 1979-96; tax cons. Sacramento, 1979—; analyst Calif. Dept. Health Svcs., Sacramento, 1979-88, contract mgr., 1988—. Golf coach Mira Loma H.S., Sacramento, 1996-97. Decorated Air medal, 2 Commendation medal, Meritorious Svc. medal. Mem. Air Force OSI Spl. Agts. Assn., Inland Soc. Tax Consultants, No. Calif. Golf Assn., Granite Bay Golf Club. Avocations: golf, classic Jaguars. Home: 6925 Vera Cruz Ct Citrus Heights CA 95621-4328 Office: Med Managed Care Divsn Dept Health Svcs 714 P St Sacramento CA 95814-6401

LA ROSA, FRANK EDWARD, retired English language and humanities educator; b. Pitts., Oct. 12, 1938; s. Joseph Edward and Rosemary (Caruso) La R.; m. Lois Jean Wilson, 1965 (div. May 1968); 1 child, Charles Edward; m. Evelyn Claire Ballard, July 25, 1969; children: Angela Claire, Andrew Frank, Joseph Salvatore, Marianna Rosalind. BA in English, U. Miami, 1961, MA in English, 1963; PhD in English, U. Ill., 1968. Asst. prof. English U. North Tex., Denton, 1968-70; prof. English and humanities San Diego City Coll., 1970-98; ret., 1998. Lit. editor FaultLine, 1996-98; contbr. poetry and prose to lit. publs. (Cmty. Awards prize 1994). Founding mem. City Works 1994, San Diego City Coll., 1994. Mem. Rudolf Steiner Group. Avocations: sculpture, ceramics, writing. Home: 2381 Recuerdo Cv Del Mar CA 92014-2957

LAROSA, GIANNI, aerospace industry administrator; b. S. Biagio Platani, Italy, Jan. 22, 1937; came to U.S., 1954; s. Alfonso and Santa (Marino) LaR.; m. Maria Cappello, Jan. 6, 1958; children: Alfonso, Sandra, Claudio, Julio. Student, Cass Tech., 1962; diploma in art, Musée de Art Modern, Tonneins, France, 1993. Owner indsl./comml. food svc. equipment mfg. business Detroit, 1970-74; supr. aerospace industry, 1985—; presenter in field. Exhbns. include San Bernardino County (Calif.) Mus., 1992, San Clemente (Calif.) Art Fest, 1992, Paris City Hall, 1993, Modern Art Mus. Unet, Tonneins, France, 1993, Soho Internat. Art Competition, N.Y.C., 1993, Wirtz Gallery, Miami, 1993, Bower Mus., Orange County, Calif., 1995, Discover The Illusion of Flickering Color, Sapporo, Japan, 1997; represented in permanent collection at Modern Art du Unet, Bordeaux, France. Recipient award Fine Arts Inst., 1992, award Soho Internat. Competition, 1993, award Mayor of Paris, Internat. Art Competition, 1993, Gold medal Musee Des D'Beux Arts D'Unet, France, 1996; named Disting. Vis., Mayor of Miami, Fla., 1994. Home: 26641 Domingo Dr Mission Viejo CA 92692-4114

LARSEN, CARTER LAWRENCE, pianist, composer; b. San Francisco, Mar. 23, 1955; s. Carter Lawrence and Caroline (Martin) L.; m. Jane Catherine Coleman, Sept., 1984 (div. Jan. 1991); 1 child, Laurence. MusB, San Francisco Cons. Music, 1979; postgrad., Raperswil, Switzerland, 1980, Dartington Sommerset, Eng., 1981. Prin. Carter Larsen Music, Inc., Malibu, Calif., 1994—, Carter Larsen Mus. Pub., Inc., Malibu, 1995—; taught piano, theory and composition to advanced students of composition and piano performance for more than 25 yrs.; formed and led 2 exptl. rock/classical bands in the late 1960s and early 1970s, performing concerts in N.Y., Mass. and Calif. Performed more than 300 concerts throughout Europe, 1979—, major concerts with the Royal Philharmonic Orch. and the London Symphony Orch. as soloist with TV appearances and broadcasts on BBC-TV and Europe's largest FM stas., original compositions including film music and classics with interviews on the largest radio and TV stas. throughout the U.K.; asst. repititeur to various opera cos. based in and around London, 1979-84; performed and recorded as regular accompanist to mezzo soprano Catherine Coleman in several internat. appearances; judge in various competitions including the 1985 Newport Internat. Pianoforte Competition in presence of HRH Diana, Princess of Wales; recorded works by Saint-Saens, Mendelssohn, Liszt, Granados as well as original compositions; gave world premiere performances and recordings of several undiscovered pieces of significant composers including Saint-Saens and Liszt in major London concert debuts; composed musical scores for Pierced Heart (feature film), Scarecrow (TV film), Impressions (arts video CD-ROM). Avocations: walking, skiing, opera. Office: Carter Larsen Music Inc PO Box 6083 Malibu CA 90264-6083

LARSEN, GWYNNE E., computer information systems educator; b. Omaha, Sept. 10, 1934; d. Melvin and Vernetta (Allen) Bannister; m. John M. Larsen, June 8, 1958; children: Bradley Allen, Blair Kevin, Randall Lawrence. A in Bus. Adminstrn., Denver U., 1956, MBA, 1975, PhD, 1979; BS, Met. State Coll., 1971. Instr. Met. State Coll. Denver, 1979-81, asst. prof., 1981-85, assoc. prof., 1985-88, prof., 1989—, acting chair computer dept., 1991-92; book reviewer McGraw Hill, 1991, Harcourt Brace Jovanovich, 1991, Macmillan Pub. Co., 1993, Southwestern Pub. Co., 1993; presenter Mountain Plains Mgmt. conf., Denver, 1982, Rocky Mountain Bus. Expo, Denver, 1982, Red Rocks C.C., 1984, Colo.-Wyo. Acad. Sci. conf., 1985, Boulder, 1986, Colorado Springs, 1987; local coord. John Wiley & Sons, Denver, 1982, 83; panel chmn. on office automation Assn. for Computing Machinery, Denver, 1985; spkr. ASTD, 1986, Am. Pub. Works Assn., 1986; participant numerous presentations and confs. Author: (with others) Computerized Business Information Systems Workbook, 1983, Collegiate Microcomputer, 1992, (with Verlene Leeberg) Word Processing: Using WordPerfect 5.0, 1989, Word Processing: Using WordPerfect 5.1, 1991, First Look at WordPerfect 5.1, 1991, First Look at DOS, 1991, First Look at NetWare, 1992, Using WordPerfect for Windows, 1993, (with Marold and Shaw) Using Microsoft Works: An Introduction to Computing, 1993, Using Microsoft Works, An Introduction to Computing, 1993, First Look at WordPerfect 6.0 for Windows, 1994, Using WordPerfect 6.0 for Windows, 1994, Using Microsoft Works for Windows, An Introduction to Computing, 1996, Beyond the Internet, 1996, (with Marold) Using Microsoft Works 4.0, 1997; co-author: Microsoft Office 97 Online Course; apptd. editl. bd. Jour. Mgmt. Sys., 1988, Jour. Microcomputer Sys. Mgmt., 1989, Info. Resources Mgmt. Jour., 1991; mem. editl. rev. bd. Jour. Info. Resources Mgmt. Sys., 1985—, Jour. Mgmt. Info. Sys., 1986—, Jour. Database Mgmt. Sys., Jour. Database Mgmt. Sys., 1987—, Jour. End User Computing, 1990—; contbr. articles to profl. jours. Mem. Info. Resources Mgmt. Assn., Colo.-Wyo. Acad. Scis. Avocations: walking, aerobics, reading detective stories. Home: 8083 S Adams Way Littleton CO 80122-3603 Office: Met State Coll Denver Campus Box 45 PO Box 173362 Denver CO 80217-3362

LARSEN, KIMBERT E., journalist; b. Boulder, Colo., June 14, 1941; s. Junius and Dorothy May (Cavanaugh) Larsen. AA, Idaho State U., 1963. Bur. reporter Deseret News, Salt Lake City, 1959-60, Salt Lake Tribune, Salt Lake City, 1960-63; assoc. editor Register Sys. of Newspapers, Denver, 1963-64, Denver, 1966-69; city hall reporter Ind.-Record, Helena, Mont., 1964; editor Western Mont. Register, 1965-66; nat. affairs staff writer Nat. Cath. News Svc., Washington, 1969-70; Billings (Mont.) Gazette, Billings, 1970-90; freelance writer Billings, 1990—. Author: The Case for Rimrocks National Monument, 1970; contbr. Ecotage!, 1972; mem. editl. bd. The Billings Gazette, 1983-85. Pres. Idaho Young Dems., Pocatello, Idaho, 1963; chmn. Diocesan Pastoral Coun., diocese of Great Falls-Billings, 1995—, Parish Pastoral Coun. of Holy Rosary Ch. in Billings, 1994-97; mem. Billings Coalition for Human Rights. Travel grant, Norwegian Royal Ministry of Fgn. Affairs, Oslo, 1980. Mem. Yellowstone Valley Audubon Soc. Democrat. Roman Catholic. Avocations: books, classical music, travel, hiking. Home: 2451 Cascade Ave Billings MT 59102-0535

LARSEN, LOREN JOSEPH, retired pediatric orthopedic surgeon; b. Idaho Falls, Idaho, Oct. 10, 1914; s. Charles Wilford and Marie (Jacobsen) L.; m. June Elmer, Mar. 20, 1943; children: Mary Ann, Loren J. Jr. BA, U. Utah, 1939; MD, U. Chgo., 1941. Intern Alameda County Hosp., 1942; resident orthopedic surgery Samuel Merit Hosp., Oakland, Calif., 1943-44; postgrad. tng. U. Calif., 1944-46, San Francisco Gen. Hosp., 1946-47; clin. prof. orthopedic surgery U. Calif., San Francisco, 1957-60; chmn. emeritus dept. orthopedic surgery Children's Hosp., San Francisco, 1957-88; chief of staff emeritus Shriner's Hosp. Crippled Children, San Francisco, 1968-80; pvt. practice San Francisco; cons. orthopedics U.S. Army Letterman Gen. Hosp., San Francisco, 1959—, U.S. Naval Hosp., Oakland, Calif., 1960-75, King Faisal Hosp., Ridyaah, Saudi Arabia, 1968. Contbr. 37 articles to profl. jours. Mem. Scoliosis Rsch. Soc. (founding), Am. Orthopedic Foot and Ankle Soc. (founding). Republican. Achievements include discovery of reporting syndrome, later named Larsen Syndrome; genetic research to determine the location of the chromosome and genes responsible for inheritance characteristics. Home: 437 Twin Lakes Cir Santa Rosa CA 95409-6448 Office: 3838 California St San Francisco CA 94118-1522

LARSEN, LOWELL DON, retired pathologist; b. Ephraim, Utah, Jan. 7, 1929; s. Rulon J. and Verna Irene (Madsen) L.; m. Roswitha Erika Lentsch, Apr. 3, 1954; children: Rolf E., Myron D., Kristine A. Larsen Parrish, Denise Larsen Tribble. BA, U. Utah, 1952, MD, 1959. Commd. 2d lt. U.S. Army, 1958, advanced through grades to col., 1974; chief pathology U.S. Army, Landstuhl, Germany, 1965-67; chief anatomical pathology U.S. Army, Honolulu, 1968-70; cmdr. 3rd Army Med. Lab. U.S. Army, Atlanta, 1970-73; cmdr. Med. Lab. Pacific U.S. Army, Sagamiono, Japan, 1973-76; chief pathology, comdr. 28th combat support hosp. U.S. Army, Ft. Bragg, N.C., 1976-78; ret. U.S. Army, 1978; dir. anatomic pathology Tex. Tech. U. Sch. Medicine, Lubbock, 1978-89; ret. Tex. Tech. U. Sch. Medicine, 1989. Decorated Legion of Merit. Fellow Coll. Am. Pathologists, Am. Soc. Clin. Pathologists. Avocations: golf, crafts. Home: 2681 Flamingo Dr Salt Lake City UT 84117-6310

LARSEN, MARY ELIZABETH, magazine publisher; b. Mountain View, Calif., Oct. 29, 1962; d. John Arthur and Alicia Conway (Donohue) Larsen. BA, U. Calif., Santa Cruz, 1984; Magistère, U. Paris, Sorbonne, 1985; MA, U. Cin., 1986. Editor, pub. Fiddler Mag., Los Altos, Calif., 1993—. Office: Fiddler Mag PO Box 125 Los Altos CA 94023-0125

LARSEN, MICHAEL F., literary agent, writer; b. N.Y.C., Jan. 8, 1941; s. Frederick and Miriam Viola (Chaims) L.; m. Elizabeth Pomana, Aug. 29, 1992. BA, CCNY, 1964. Pub. rels. asst. William Morrow, N.Y.C., 1965-67, Bantam Books, N.Y.C., 1967-69; pub. rels. dir. Pyramid Books, N.Y.C., 1969-70; ptnr. Larsen-Pomada Literary Agts., San Francisco, 1972—. Author: How To Write With a Collaborator, 1987, Americas Painted Ladies, 1992, How to Write a Book Proposal, 1997, Literary Agents! How They Work and How to Find, 1997. Mem. Nat. Writers Orgn., Woman's Nat. Book Assn. (v.p. 1997—), Calif. Writers Assn., Commonwealth Club. Avocations: yoga, France. Office: Larsen & Pomada Literary Agts 1029 Jones St San Francisco CA 94109-5023

LARSEN, RICHARD LEE, former mayor and city manager, business, municipal and labor relations consultant, arbitrator; b. Jackson, Miss., Apr. 16, 1934; s. Homer Thorsten and Mae Cordelia (Amidon) L.; m. Virginia Fay Alley, June 25, 1955; children: Karla, Daniel, Thomas (dec.), Krista, Lisa. BS in Econs. and Bus. Adminstrn, Westminster Coll., Fulton, Mo., 1959; postgrad., U. Kans., 1959-61. Fin. dir. Village of Northbrook, Ill., 1961-63; city mgr. Munising, Mich., 1963-66, Sault Ste. Marie, Mich., 1966-72, Ogden, Utah, 1972-77, Billings, Mont., 1977-79; mcpl. cons., 1979—, pub./pvt. sector labor rels. cons., arbitrator, 1979—; mayor City of Billings, Mont., 1990-95; dep. gen. chmn. Greater Mich. Found., 1968. Bd. dirs. Ctrl. Weber Sewer Dist., 1972-77; chmn. labor com. Utah League Cities and Towns, 1973-77, Mont. League Cities and Towns, 1977-79; bd. dirs., coach Ogden Hockey Assn., 1972-77, Weber Sheltered Workshop, 1974-77, Billings YMCA, 1980-86, Rimrock Found., 1980-86; chmn. cmty. rels. coun. Weber Basin Job Corps Ctr., 1973-77; bishop LDS Ch. With USCG, 1953-57. Recipient Cmty. Devel. Disting. Achievement awards Munising, 1964, Cmty. Devel. Disting. Achievement awards Sault Ste. Marie, 1966-70, Citizen award Dept. of Interior, 1977, Alumni Achievement award Westminster Coll., 1990, Dist. award of merit Boy Scouts Am., 1993, Silver Beaver award Boy Scouts Am., 1994; named Utah Adminstr. of Yr., 1976. Mem. Internat. City Mgmt. Assn. (L.P. Cookingham career devel. award 1974, Clarence Ridley in-service tng. award 1979), Utah City Mgrs. Assn. (pres. 1972-74), Greater Ogden C. of C. (dir.), Rotary (pres. Billings 1997-98), Phi Gamma Delta. Home and Office: 1733 Parkhill Dr Billings MT 59102-2358

LARSON, BRENT T., broadcasting executive; b. Ogden, Utah, Sept. 23, 1942; s. George Theodore and Doris (Peterson) L.; m. Tracy Ann Taylor; children: Michelle, Brent Todd, Lindsey. Student, pub. schs., Los Angeles; diploma in radio operational engring., Burbank, Calif., 1962. Owner, mgr. Sta. KAIN, Boise, Idaho, 1969-77; owner, operator Sta. KXA Radio, Seattle, 1975-83, Sta. KYYX Radio, Seattle, 1980-83, Sta. KGA Radio, Spokane, Wash., 1978-84, Sta. KUUZ Radio, Boise, 1976-82, Sta. KOOS Radio, North Bend, Oreg., 1980-81, Sta. KODL Radio, The Dalles, Oreg., 1974-80, Sta. KKWZ Radio, Richfield, Utah, 1980-94, Sta. KSVC Radio, Richfield, 1980-94; v.p. Casey Larson Fast Food Co., Oreg. and Idaho, 1976-94, Imperial Broadcasting Corp., Idaho, 1970—, KSOS Am & KLZX FM, 1983—; pres. First Nat. Broadcasting Corp., 1970—; v.p. Larson-Wynn Corp., 1974—, Brentwood Properties, Ogden, 1977—; pres. Sta. KSIT Broadcasting, Rock Springs, Wyo., 1980-90, Gold Coast Communications Corp., Oreg., 1980-81, Sevier Valley Broadcasting Co., Inc., Utah, 1980-94, Brent Larson Group Stas., Western U.S., 1969—; v.p. mktg. Internat. Foods Corp., Boise, 1969-81; ptnr. Larson Tours and Travel, Burley, Idaho, 1977-87; v.p. Harrison Square Inc., 1995—; bd. dirs. Casey-Larson Foods Co., La Grande, Oreg., Studio City Entertainment (Nev. L.C.), 1996—. Bd. dirs. Met. Sch., 1981-93, Children's Aid Soc., 1991-94; chmn. bd. ZLX Limited Libility Co., 1995—. Mem. Am. Advt. Fedn., Nat. Assn. Broadcasters, Nat. Radio Broadcasters Assn., Wash. Broadcasters Assn., Oreg. Broadcasters Assn., Idaho Broadcasters Assn., Utah Broadcasters Assn., Citizens for Responsible Broadcasting (bd. dirs.). Republican. Mem. LDS Ch. Home: 5777 S 3550 W Roy UT 84067-8131 Office: First Nat Broadcasting Corp 4455 S 5500 W Ogden UT 84315-9650

LARSON, DOROTHY ANN, business educator; b. Nekoosa, Wis., Feb. 27, 1934; d. Edwin E. and Ruby E. (Burch) L.; children: Jean Marie Harkey, Kenneth Lee Fitz, Cynthia Ann Anderson. BS with high distinction in Bus. and English, No. Ariz. U., 1969; MA in English, 1971; EdD in Bus., Ariz. State U., 1980. Tchr. English, Cottonwood (Ariz.) Oak Creek Elem. Sch., 1969-70; tchr. bus. and English, Mingus Union High Sch., Cottonwood, 1970-79, dir. vocat. edn., 1976-79; mem. faculty dept. bus. administrn. Yavapai Coll., 1979-94, chairperson bus. divsn., 1981-86, prep. coord. Yavapai Tech., 1994-95; cons. Ariz. Dept. Edn.; curriculum specialist Northern Ariz. U., 1995-98; mem. adv. coun. Gov's. Coun. Practitioners. Mem. Ariz. Bus. Edn. Assn. (pres. 1980-81), Nat. Bus. Edn. Assn., Am. Vocat. Assn., Ariz. Edn. Assn., NEA, Nat. Tech. Prep. Network, Pi Omega Pi, Delta Pi Epsilon, Phi Kappa Phi, Alpha Delta Kappa, Phi Delta Kappa. Republican. Editor Ariz. Bus. Edn. Newsletter, 1972-74. Home: 542 S Marina Dr Gilbert AZ 85233-6610

LARSON, KENNETH GERARD, real estate professional; b. Bklyn., Apr. 6, 1949; s. Lawrence Joseph and Agnes Lucy (Hannon) L.; m. Diane Marie D'Amico, May 24, 1980. BSBA, Pfeiffer Coll., 1971. Lic. real estate broker, Colo. Real estate salesman Van Schaack & Co., Denver, 1979-80; real estate broker Perry & Butler Realty, Denver, 1980-87, Re/Max Internat., Denver, 1987-90; owner, broker Profl. Relocation Assocs. Realty, Broomfield, Colo., 1993—. Contbr. articles to profl. jours. Mem. ethics com. Jeffco Bd. Realtors, Lakewood, Colo., 1985-87; task force mem. Denver Ctr. for Performing Arts, Denver, 1993-94. Mem. Colo. Archaeol. Soc. (v.p. 1993-94, dir. 1995—), Native Am. Rights Fund, Nat. Mus. of the Am. Indian (Cert. of Appreciation 1995). Republican. Avocations: photography, music, Am. indian langs. Office: Profl Relocation Assocs Realty 10557 Garrison St Broomfield CO 80021-3636

LARSON, MARK DEVIN, communications executive; b. Rockford, Ill., Aug. 6, 1955; s. Burdette D. Larson and Inga Mae Sandberg; m. Marcia L. Sutton, Feb. 14, 1976; children: Jeffrey, Brandon, Kristin. Grad. high sch., Rockford, 1973. Announcer WRWC Radio, Rockton, Ill., 1971-72; announcer, asst. prodn. dir. WRRR-AM, Rockford, 1972-73; prodn. dir., afternoon host WROK-AM, Rockford, 1973-76; announcer KFMB-AM, San Diego, 1976-77, asst. program dir., 1977-78, program and ops. mgr., afternoon personality, 1978-94; gen. mgr. KPRZ-AM Radio, San Diego, 1994—; co-founder The Program Group, San Diego, 1984-94; co-owner, cons. KISN AM/FM, Salt Lake City, 1985-95; founder, pres. Mark Larson Media Svcs., El Cajon, Calif., 1985—; nat. program dir./radio Midwest TV, 1988-93. Creator (audio seminar series) Personal Program Power, 1985-93; host (TV show) KTTY-TV, 1993-94 (Emmy award 1993); columnist Daily Californian, 1995—. Chmn., co-founder Family Heritage Found., 1988—, Prison Fellowship, San Diego, 1990-96; comm. chmn. San Diego County Rep., 1995; active San Diego Youth for Christ, 1987-97. Named Citizen of Yr., San Diego City Club and Jaycees, 1995. Mem. Media Fellowship Internat. (chmn. 1998—), San Diego Radio Broadcasters Assn. (pres. 1998—), City Club San Diego, Heart to Heart Internat. Avocations: collecting rare books, collecting political autographs and memorabilia, family activities, internat. relief efforts, travel, writing. Office: Sta KPRZ Salem Comm Ste 9255 9255 Towne Centre Dr SD San Diego CA 92121-3038

LARSON, MAUREEN INEZ, rehabilitation consultant; b. Madison, Minn., Mar. 10, 1955; d. Alvin John and Leona B. (Bornhorst) L.; m. Michael Earl Klemetsrud, July 7, 1979 (div. Sept. 1988); m. Kenneth Bell, Dec., 1993 (div. 1997). BA in Psychology cum laude, U. Minn., 1977; MA in Counseling, U. N.D., 1978. Cert. rehab. counselor, ins. specialist; disability analyst. Employment counselor II, coordinator spl. programs Employment Security div. State of Wyo., Rawlins, 1978-80; employment interviewer Employment Security div. State of Wash., Tacoma, 1980; lead counselor Comprehensive Rehab. Counseling, Tacoma, 1980-81; dir. counseling Cascade Rehab. Counseling, Tacoma, 1981-87, dist. mgr., 1987-90; regional mgr. Rainier Case Mgmt., Tacoma, 1991-92; owner Maureen Larson and Assocs., Gig Harbor, Wash., 1992—; state capt. legis. div. Provisions Project Am. Personnel and Guidance Assn., 1980. Advocate Grand Forks (N.D.) Rape Crisis Ctr., 1977-78; mem. Pierce County YMCA; bd. dirs. Boys and Girls Clubs of Tacoma, 1991-98, chairperson sustaining drive, 1991-98, sec.-treas., 1992-93, pres., 1994, auction com. and spl. events com. State of Minn. scholar, 1973-77; recipient Alice Tweed Tuohy award U. Minn., 1977, Nat. Disting. Svcs. Registry award Libr. of Congress, 1987; named bd. mem. vol. of Yr. Boys and Girls Clubs of Tacoma, 1992. Mem. Nat. Fedn. Bus. and Profl. Women (rec. sec. 1978-80, runner-up Young Careerists' Program 1980), Nat. Rehab. Assn. (bd. dirs. Olympic chpt. 1988-97, pres. 1990-91, chairperson state conf. planning com. 1990, 93, 96), Nat. Rehab. Counseling Assn. (bd. dirs. 1993, State of Wash. Counselor of Yr. 1991, Pacific Region Counselor of Yr. 1992), Nat. Rehab. Adminstrs. Assn. (bd. dirs. 1993), Women in Workers Compensation Orgn., Washington Self-Insured Assn., Pi Gamma Mu. Avocations: dog training, skiing, aerobics, ballet, arts. Office: M Larson & Assocs 13504 82nd Ave NW Gig Harbor WA 98329-8642

LARSON, PAUL MARTIN, lawyer; b. Tacoma, June 8, 1949; s. Charles Philip and Margeret (Kobervig) L.; m. Kristina Simonson, June 19, 1971; children: Kristin Ilene, Paul Philip, Erika Louise. AB, Stanford U., 1971; JD, Gonzaga U., 1974. Bar: Wash. 1975, U.S. Dist. Ct. (we. dist.) Wash. 1975, U.S. Dist. Ct. (ea. dist.) Wash. 1978, U.S. Ct. Appeals (9th cir.) 1981. Assoc. Hoff & Cross, Tacoma, 1975-76; ptnr., prin. Brooks & Larson, P.S., Yakima, Wash., 1976-87; ptnr. Bogle & Gates, Yakima, 1987-93, Larson & Perkins, 1994—. Author: (with others) Commercial Law Deskbook, 1981. Pres. Cardio & Pulmonary Inst., Yakima, 1981; bd. dirs. Yakima YMCA, 1981-98, Yakima Youth Commn., 1989-93, Yakima Valley chpt. ARC, 1990-93; bd. dirs. Sisters of Providence Med. Ctr.-Yakima Found., 1986-96, pres., 1992-93. Fellow ABA (standing com. lawyer's responsibility for client protection 1984-89); mem. Wash. State Bar Assn. (spl. dist. counsel, 1985-96, pres. corp. bus. and banking sect. 1987-88, chmn. unauthorized practice of law task force 1995-96), Yakima Estate Planning Coun. (pres. 1981), Rotary. Avocations: tennis, fishing. Office: Larson & Perkins PO Box 550 Yakima WA 98907-0550

LARSON, WILLIAM, electrical company executive. Pres., chmn. Network Assocs., Santa Clara, Calif. Office: Network Assocs 3965 Freedom Cir Santa Clara CA 95054-1203*

LASAROW, WILLIAM JULIUS, retired federal judge; b. Jacksonville, Fla., June 30, 1922; s. David Herman and Mary (Hollins) L.; m. Marilyn Doris Powell, Feb. 4, 1951; children: Richard M., Elisabeth H. BA, U. Fla., 1943; JD, Stanford U., 1950. Bar: Calif. 1951. Counsel judiciary com. Calif. Assembly, Sacramento, 1951-52; dep. dist. atty. Stanislaus County, Modesto, Calif., 1952-53; pvt. practice law L.A., 1953-73; bankruptcy judge U.S. Cts., L.A., 1973-94; chief judge U.S. Bankruptcy Ct., Central dist., Calif., 1978-90; judge Bankruptcy Appellate Panel 9th Fed. Cir., 1980-82; fed. judge U.S. Bankruptcy Ct., L.A., 1973; faculty Fed. Jud. Ctr. Bankruptcy Seminars,

Washington, 1977-82. Contbg. author, editor legal publs.; staff: Stanford U. Law Review, 1949. Mem. ABA, Am. Coll. Bankruptcy, Am. Bankruptcy Inst., Nat. Conf. Bankruptcy Judges, Los Angeles County Bar Assn., Wilshire Bar Assn., Blue Key, Phi Beta Kappa, Phi Kappa Phi. Home: 11623 Canton Pl Studio City CA 91604-4164

LASCELLES, SUSAN, artist; b. Chgo., Jan. 29, 1958; d. Robert John and Donna Lee (Hjorth) L.; m. David Linn Hekelnkaemper, Apr. 17, 1998; 1 child, Michael Lascelles DiCenzo. Student, Ohio State U., 1984-87; BA, Empire State Coll., 1990. Artist, painter, photographer, stained glass, animator (film) Uncut, 1981; one-person shows include The Little Gallery, Springfield, Ohio, 1981, Millennium, N.Y.C., 1981, Rosenmarkt, Zurich, Switzerland, 1982, Upper Arlington Pub. Libr., Columbus, Ohio, 1987, The Dance Circle, Ithaca, N.Y., 1989, Dodajk Internation, Tucson, 1990, New Doors of the Arts, Tucson, 1993, Orts Theatre of Dance, Tucson, 1995, 96, 97, 98, Urban Picnic and Art Auction, Tucson, 1998, Daturo Studios and Gallery, Tucson, 1999, others; represented in permanent collections Corning Mus. Glass Film Libr., Mus. Post Modern Art, Empire State Coll., Farber Husli, Switzerland, Kip Krane, Mechanicsburg, Ohio. Acad. merit scholar Scarlet and Gray, Ohio State U., Columbus, 1985, 87; grantee Changes Inc., N.Y.C., 1993. Avocations: gardening, pets, horses, music. Home: 7151 S Sandpiper Ave Tucson AZ 85746 Office: Art Studio/Gallery 15 E Toole Ave Tucson AZ 85701

LASKIN, BARBARA VIRGINIA, marketing executive; b. Chgo., July 2, 1939; d. Cyril Krieps and Gertrude Katherine (Kujawa) Szymanski; children: Dawn Katherine Doherty, Amy Lynn Anderson. BA, U. Ill., Chgo., 1967; MA, Am. U. Beirut, 1978, Georgetown U., 1985. Asst. buyer Carson, Pirie, Scott & Co., Chgo., 1967-69; fgn. svc. officer Dept. State, Washington, 1969-79; mgr. gift shops Marriott Hotels, Washington, 1979-81; office mgr. Robt Schwinn & Assoc., Bethesda, Md., 1983-85; exec. dir. Internat. Acad. Trial Lawyers, San Jose, Calif., 1985-97; mktg. mgr. convention and destination mgmt. svcs. San Jose Conv. and Vis. Bur., 1998—. Fellow Rotary Club San Jose; mem. AAUW (v.p. 1987), Am. Soc. Assn. Execs., Meeting Planners Internat., Internat. Spl. Events Soc. (v.p. membership 1996), Internat. Spl. Events Found. (dir.), Profl. Conservation Mgrs. Assn. Roman Catholic. Office: San Jose Conv & Vis Bur 333 W San Carlos St Ste 1000 San Jose CA 95110-2734

LASKO, ALLEN HOWARD, pharmacist; b. Chgo., Oct. 27, 1941; s. Sidney P. and Sara (Hoffman) L.; BS (James scholar), U. Ill., 1964; m. Janice Marilynn Chess, Dec. 24, 1968 (div. Aug. 1993); children: Stephanie Paige, Michael Benjamin. Staff pharmacist Michael Reese Hosp. and Med. Center, Chgo., 1964-68; clin. pharmacist City of Hope Med. Center, Duarte, Calif., 1968-73; chief pharmacist Monrovia (Calif.) Cmty. Hosp., 1973-74, Santa Fe Meml. Hosp., L.A., 1974-77; pvt. investor, 1977-93; clin. pharmacist Foothill Presbyn. Hosp., Glendora, Calif., 1993—. Recipient Roche Hosp. Pharmacy Rsch. award, 1972-73. Mem. Magic Castle, Mensa, Rho Pi Phi. Jewish. Author: Diabetes Study Guide, 1972, A Clinical Approach to Lipid Abnormalities Study Guide, 1973, Jet Injection Tested As An Aid in Physiologic Delivery of Insulin, 1973. Home: 376 Hill St Monrovia CA 91016-2340 Office: Foothill Presbyn Hosp 250 S Grand Ave Glendora CA 91741-4218

LASKUS, JACEK WOJCIECH, photography director; b. Warsaw, Poland, Aug. 29, 1951; came to U.S. 1977; s. Edward and Irena (Wodzinska) L.; m. Marianne Hjertstrad (div.); m. Victoria Westhead (div.). BA, Polish Film Acad., Lodz, Poland, 1976. Dir. photography various orgns. including PBS-TV, Showtime, NBC-TV, CBS-TV, 1982—. Dir. photography various performances including Far from Poland, 1982, Parting Glances, 1985, Heart, 1986, Square Dance, 1986, Penn and Tellers Invisible Thread, 1987 (ACE award 1988), Circus, 1988, Caine Mutiny Court Marshal, 1988 (ASC Outstanding Cinematography, 1989), Incident At Dark River, 1990, Rules Of The Game (feature film), 1993, Garden of Redemption, 1996 (ASC nominee Outstanding Cinematography, 1997), Gold Coast, 1997, Soldiers Sweetheart, 1997, Devil's Arithmetic, 1998. Roman Catholic. Home and Office: 1865 N Curson Ave West Hollywood CA 90046-2205

LASLO, LAURA ELIZABETH, technical librarian, security manager, artist; b. Cleve., June 27, 1953; d. George Edward and Elizabeth Ann Laslo. AA, Grossmont Jr. Coll., El Cajon, Calif., 1974; BA, San Diego State U., 1976, cert. in tchg. Art tchr. Cajon Valley Sch. Dist., El Cajon, 1978-79; San Diego County sr. clk. Registrar of Voters, 1979-82; security mgr. Nat. Advanced Sys., San Diego, 1982-83; tech. libr. IVAC Corp., San Diego, 1983-86; tech. libr., security mgr. Logicon, Inc., San Diego, 1987—. One-women shows include All Media Student Art Exhibit, 1976, Bastille Gallery, 1977, Extra Ordinaire Gallery, 1981, San Diego and Mex. Art Exchange, 1982, The Right Bank Art Gallery, 1983, 1620 Lewis St. Gallery, 1986. Hist. commr. La Mesa (Calif.) City, 1990—; mem. San Diego Mus. of Art. Recipient commendation City of La Mesa, 1991. Mem. San Diego Artist Guild. Avocations: tennis, music, historical preservation.

LASORDA, THOMAS CHARLES (TOMMY LASORDA), professional baseball team manager; b. Norristown, Pa., Sept. 22, 1927; s. Sam and Carmella (Covatto) L.; m. Joan Miller, Apr. 14, 1950; children: Laura, Tom Charles. Student pub. schs., Norristown. Pitcher Bklyn. Dodgers, 1954-55, Kansas City A's, 1956; with L.A. Dodgers, 1956—; mgr. minor league clubs L.A. Dodgers, Pocatello, Idaho, Ogden, Utah, Spokane, Albuquerque, 1965-73; coach L.A. Dodgers, 1973-76, mgr., 1976-96, v.p. fin., 1996-98, gen. mgr., 1998—. Author: (with David Fisher) autobiography The Artful Dodger, 1985. Served with U.S. Army, 1945-47. Named Pitcher of Yr. Internat. League, 1958; L.A. Dodgers winner Nat. League pennant, 1977, 78, 81, 88, winner World Championship, 1981, 88; 2d Nat. League mgr. to win pennant first two yrs. as mgr.; named Nat. League Mgr. Yr. UPI, 1977, AP, 1977, 81, Baseball Writers' Assn. Am., 1988, Sporting News, 1988, Baseball Writers Assn. Am., 1983, 88; recipient Milton Richman Meml. award Assn. Profl. Baseball Players Am.; coach Nat. League All-Star team, 1977, 83-84, 86, 93; elected to the Baseball Hall of Fame, 1997. Mem. Profl. Baseball Players Am. Roman Catholic. Club: Variety of Calif. (v.p.). Office: care Los Angeles Dodgers 1000 Elysian Park Ave Los Angeles CA 90012-1112*

LASORTE, JOSEPH JOHN, rail transportation executive; b. Cut Bank, Mont., Oct. 17, 1950; s. Joseph John and Alice Mae (Maetche) LaS.; m. Cynthia Lois Laas, Nov. 19, 1982; children: Nickolas Joseph, Johanna May. Grad. high sch., Shelby, Mont. Foreman track dept. Burlington No. Santa Fe, Chester, Mont., 1967—. Illustrator: Poems for the Purpose, 1996. Bd. dirs. Liberty Village Arts Ctr. Avocations: drawing/painting, fishing, hunting, gardening. Home: PO Box 232 Chester MT 59522-0232 Office: Burlington No Santa Fe Railroad PO Box 218 Chester MT 59522-0218

LASSEN, BETTY JANE, educator; b. Topeka, Kans., Apr. 19, 1923; d. Harvey Leroy and Anna Elizabeth (Day) Rose; m. Emil Lassen Jr., June 5, 1944 (dec. Sept. 1989); 1 child, Emil III. Instr., guide YMCA-YWCA, Albuquerque, 1975-84, U. N.Mex. Continuing Edn., Albuquerque, 1979—, Ft. Lewis Coll. Continuing Edn., Durango, Colo., 1992-93; liaison, asst. coord. San Juan Coll. Elder Hostel, Farmington, N.Mex., 1993-94; owner, pres. Outdoor Adventure Tours, Inc., Albuquerque, 1982—; mem. curriculum com., human svcs. tng. coun. gerontology divsn. continuing edn. U. N.Mex., 1979-82; spkr. in field. Designer ski equipment; contbr. articles, poetry to profl. publs. Vol. instr., guide for disabled Easter Seals Soc., Albuquerque, 1983; vol. campground host Nat. Park Svc., Chaco Canyon Ruins, N.Mex., 1990; campaign vol. Dem. Party, Albuquerque, 1976. Recipient Appreciation award Easter Seals Soc., 1983. Mem. Puerto Del Sol Ladies Golf Assn. (pres. 1976-77), N.Mex. Outfitters/Guides, N.Mex. Cross-Country Ski Club (sec. 1973-76), N.Mex. Mountain Club. Avocations: cross-country skiing, hiking, bicycling, golf, ballroom dancing. Home: 2916 Santa Clara Ave SE Albuquerque NM 87106-2947

LASSESEN, CATHERINE AVERY CLAY, small business owner, manager, trainer; b. Corte Madera, CA, Nov. 8, 1961; d. Ralph Kindel Boyland Clay and Susan Avery (Kendall) Clay; m. B. Rune Lassesen, Mar. 2, 1991. BA in Hotel Adminstrn., U. Nev., 1985. Promotions asst. Tropicana Hotel, Las Vegas, Nev., 1985; front desk mgr. Marriott Corp., various locations, 1986-88; mgr. Six Ravens Ranch, Boonville, Calif., 1988-96, CEO, 1988-92; owner/mgr. Custom Engraving by Catherine, Boonville, Calif., 1989-96; co-owner, trainer Bridgegate Stables & Tack Barn One, Boonville, 1991-93; owner, instr. Flying Colors An Equine Edn. Svc. Six Ravens Ranch, Boonville, Calif., 1994-96; mgr. Hestehaven, 1996—; coach Mendocino County vaulting team, 1994-96; horse show mgr. Skandifest, Turlock, Calif., 1997. Publicity dir. Mendocino County Fair and Apple Show, 1992-94. Named one of the Women of Yr., Clark County, Las Vegas, Nev., 1986. Mem. Ind. Career Women (historian 1991-92, v.p. 1992-93), U. Nev. Las Vegas Alumni Assn., Delta Zeta (province alumnae dir. 1991-93, nat. alumnae/collegiate rels. chmn. 1995-96, area alumnae dir. great western states 1996-98), Am. Vaulting Assn., Am. Quarter Horse Assn., Am. Paint Horse Assn., N.Am. Horseman Assn., Am. Horse Show Assn., Calif. Gymkhana Assn. (judge 1992—, dist. 37 pres. 1992-93, co-chmn. 1993-94), N.Am. Riding for the Handicapped Assn., Inc., Norwegian Fjord Horse Registry. Office: Hestehaven PO Box 160 Days Creek OR 97429-0160

LAST, DIANNA LINN SCHNEIDER, marketing company executive; b. Canton, Ohio, Dec. 29, 1944; d. Ld Mervyn and Veronica Lee Schneider; m. David D. Last, Nov. 29, 1969; 1 child, Jason Holden. BA in German, Ohio State U., 1966. Rsch. asst., programmer trainee high-energy physics dept. Ohio State U., Columbus, 1964-66; mfg. programmer RANCO, Inc., Columbus, 1966-68; sr. edn. rep. Honeywell Info. Systems, Cleve., 1968-72; dist. mgr. Honeywell Info. Systems, Orlando, Fla., 1972-78, telecommunications cons., 1978-79; mgr. networking edn. Honeywell Info. Systems, Phoenix, 1979-81, mgr. distributed systems, 1981-84; account and tech. mgr. Honeywell Info. Systems, Beijing, People's Republic of China, 1985; resident dir., chief rep. Honeywell Bull (formerly Honeywell Info. Systems), Beijing, People's Republic of China, 1985-87; dir. Integrated Info. Architecture Honeywell Bull, Phoenix, 1987-88; dir. info. mgmt. U.S. mktg. Bull (formerly Honeywell Bull), Phoenix, 1988-90; pres. Last Concepts Internat. Mktg. & Export Mgmt. Co., Phoenix, 1990—; exec. dir. Ctr. Bus. Skills Devel.-China For Thunderbird Am. Grad. Sch. Internat. Mgmt., 1998—; exec. dir. Ctr. Bus. Skills Devel. China: For Thunderbird Am. Grad. Sch. of Internat. Mgmt., 1998—; bd. advisors Internat. Bus. Orgn., Am. Grad. Sch. Internat. Mgmt., 1981-84, 90—; cons., speaker in field; co-founder, past co-chair Ariz. Internat. Trade Orgn., 1992—; co-founder, chmn. Am. High-Tech Forum, Beijing, 1985-87; bd. dirs. Enterprise Network, 1997—, chair mktg. com.; adj. faculty internat. bus. Maricopa Colls., 1994—; mem. governing bd. Internat. Studies Acad. 7-12 Charter Sch.; bd. dirs. Digital Network Access, 1995-97. Chalice bearer, lay reader St. John Baptist Episcopal Ch., Phoenix, 1983—, mem. bishop's com., 1980-83, mem. vestry, 1991-92; adv. bd. Ariz. Assn. Children and Adults with Learning Disabilities, 1983-84; design task force Maricopa C.Cs., 1984; active World Trade Ctr. Ariz., 1992—; mem. internat. adv. coun. Paradise Valley Coll., 1994—; bd. dirs. Ctr. for New Dirs., Phoenix, 1987-90. Mem. IEEE (past vice chmn. programs), Coun. Fgn. Rels. (mem. Phoenix com. 1994—), Ariz. Software Assn. (internat. com. 1990-92). Home: 1274 E Marconi Ave Phoenix AZ 85022-3232

LATHAM, JAMES RICHARD, research scientist; b. Pomona, Calif., July 1, 1946; s. James Richard and Norma Elizabeth (Mills) L.; m. Pamela June Staley Latham, Aug. 31, 1968; 1 child, Joan Elizabeth Latham. Student, U. Calif., Berkeley, U. Calif., Hayward; AS in Electronics & Computer Tech., U. Calif., Livermore, 1999, AS in Electronics and Telecom. Sys., 1999. Technician Coast Mfg./Hexel Co., Livermore, Calif., 1966-69, Crown Zellerbach Co., San Leandro, Calif., 1969-70; sr. rsch. technician Kaiser Aluminum & Chem. Corp., Pleasanton, Calif., 1970-82; sr. technician Clorox Tech. Ctr., Pleasanton, Calif., 1982—. Patentee in field. Named Merit Scholarship Finalist; recipient Naval Res. Officers Training Corp. scholarship. Mem. Am. Chemical Soc. Div. Chemical Technicians (treas. 1993-94), Livermore Amateur Radio Klub (sec. 1997), Alameda County Sheriff's Comms. Team. Mem. LDS Ch. Avocations: sailing, amateur radio (KE6QJV).

LATHI, BHAGAWANDAS PANNALAL, electrical engineering educator; b. Bhokar, Maharashtr, India, Dec. 3, 1933; came to U.S., 1956; s. Pannalal Rupchand and Tapi Pannalal (Indani) L.; m. Rajani Damodardas Mundada, July 27, 1962; children: Anjali, Shishir. BEEE, Poona U., 1955; MSEE, U. Ill., 1957; PhD in Elec. Engring., Stanford U., 1961. Rsch. asst. U. Ill., Urbana, 1956-57, Stanford (Calif.) U., 1957-60; rsch. engr. Gen. Electric Co., Syracuse, N.Y., 1960-61; cons. to semicondr. industry India, 1961-62; assoc. prof. elec. engring. Bradley U., Peoria, Ill., 1962-69, U.S. Naval Acad., Annapolis, Md., 1969-72; prof. elec. engring. Campinas (Brazil) State U., 1972-78, Calif. State U., Sacramento, 1979—; vis. prof. U. Iowa, Owa City, 1979. Author: Signals, Systems and Communication, 1965, Communication Systems, 1968 (transl. into Japanese 1977), Random Signals and Communication Theory, 1968, Teoria Signalow I Ukladow Telekomunikacyjnych, 1970, Sistemy Telekomunikacyjne, 1972, Signals, Systems and Controls, 1974, Sistemas de Comunicacion, 1974, 86, Sistemas de Comunicacao, 1978, Modern Digital and Analog Communication Systems, 1983, 89 (transl. into Japanese 1986, 90), Signals and Systems, 1987, Linear Systems and Signals, 1992, Signal Processing and Linear Systems, 1998; contbr. articles to profl. jours. Fellow IEEE. Office: Calif State U 6000 J St Sacramento CA 95819-2605

LATHROP, F. STEVEN, commercial real estate developer, lawyer; b. L.A., Jan. 15, 1947; s. Charles F. and Elizabeth D. (Shannon) L.; m. Bonnie L. Yates, Sept. 14, 1968; children: Elizabeth A., David C. BS in Fin., U. Wash., 1969; JD, Willamette U., 1973. Lic. real estate broker, Wash., comml. pilot, Wash.; bar: Wash. 1973, U.S. Dist. Ct. (we. dist.) Wash. 1973, U.S. Dist. Ct. (ea. dist.) Wash. 1980, U.S. Supreme Ct. 1997. Assoc. Davis, wright, Todd, Riese & Jones, Seattle, 1973-76; ops. mgr. Anderson Hay & Grain, Ellensburg, Wash., 1976-77; atty. F. Steven Lathrop, P.S./Lathrop Winbauer Harrel & Slothower, Ellensburg, 1977—; mcpl. judge City of Ellensburg, 1980-88; pres. So. Wax Co., Inc., Ellensburg, 1985-89, Lathrop Devel. Co., Ellensburg, 1989—. Pres. Kittitas Valley Cmty. Hosp. Found., Ellensburg, 1991-93, Ctrl. Wash. U. Found., Ellensburg, 1982—, chair, 1994-96; mem. Kittitas County Devel. Coun., 1980-89. With USAR, 1969-75. Mem. Kittitas County Bar Assn. (pres. 1987-88), Ellensburg C. of C. (pres. 1981-82), Columbia Tower Club (charter), Wash. Athletic Club, Yakima Country Club. Avocations: golf, hunting, flying, white water rafting. Office: Lathrop Winbauer Harrel and Slothower PO Box 1088 201 W 7th Ave Ellensburg WA 98926-2816

LATHROP, JACQUELINE PHILLIPS, social sciences educator, writer; b. Milw., Mar. 19, 1934; d. Ralph Frederick and Emily Rose (Mayer) Phillips; m. Donald Branum Lathrop, July 28, 1989; children: Deborah Kneubuhl Durham, Douglas Kneubuhl, Mark Kneubuhl, Stacy Kneubuhl Stewart, Joseph Cantrell, Jennifer Cantrell. BA, Calif. State U., San Jose, 1976, MA, 1978. Cmty. coll. tchg. credential, Calif. Instr. art history Foothill Coll., Los Altos, Calif., 1978—; lectr. Stanford (Calif.) Com. for the Arts, 1994-96. Author: Ancient Mexico: Cultural Traditions in the Land of the Feathered Serpent, 6th edit., 1998, Mexico: Conquest, Revolution, Rebirth, 1996. Mem. The Mex. Mus., San Francisco, lectr., 1992-94; mem. M.H. DeYoung Mus. Fellow in Am. Cultures, U. Calif., Berkeley, 1992. Mem. Am. Inst. Archaeology. Avocations: painting, photography, gardening. E-mail: HappyValy@aol.com. Office: Foothill Coll 12345 El Monte Rd Los Altos Hills CA 94022

LATHROP, MITCHELL LEE, lawyer; b. L.A., Dec. 15, 1937; s. Alfred Lee and Barbara (Mitchell) L.; m. Denice Annette Davis; children: Christin Lorraine Newlon, Alexander Mitchell, Timothy Trewin Mitchell. BSc, U.S. Naval Acad., 1959; JD, U. So. Calif., 1966. Bar: D.C. 1966, Calif. 1966, U.S. Supreme Ct. 1969, N.Y. 1981; registered environ. assessor, Calif. Dep. counsel L.A. County, Calif., 1966-68; with Brill, Hunt, DeBuys and Burby, L.A., 1968-71; ptnr. Macdonald, Halsted & Laybourne, L.A. and San Diego, 1971-80; sr. ptnr. Rogers & Wells, N.Y.C., San Diego, 1980-86; sr. ptnr., exec. com. Adams, Duque & Hazeltine, L.A., San Francisco, N.Y.C., San Diego, 1986-94, firm chmn., 1992-94; sr. ptnr. Luce, Forward, Hamilton & Scripps, San Diego, N.Y.C., San Francisco, L.A., Chgo., 1994—; presiding referee Calif. Bar Ct., 1984-86, mem. exec. com., 1981-88; lectr. law Calif. Judges Assn., Practicing Law Inst. N.Y., Continuing Edn. of Bar, State Bar Calif., ABA, others. Author: State Hazardous Waste Regulation, 1991, Environmental Insurance Coverage, 1991, Insurance Coverage for Environmental Claims, 1992; mem. editl. bd. Def. Counsel Jour., 1997. Western Regional chmn. Met. Opera Nat. Coun., 1971-81, v.p., mem. exec. com., 1971—, now chmn.; trustee Honnold Libr. at Claremont Colls., 1972-80; bd. dirs. Music Ctr. Opera Assn., L.A., sec., 1974-80; bd. dirs. San Diego Opera Assn., 1980—, v.p., 1985-89, pres.-elect, 1993, pres., 1994-96; bd. dirs. Met. Opera Assn., N.Y.C.; mem. nat. steering coun. Nat. Actors Theatre, N.Y. Mem. ABA, N.Y. Bar Assn., Fed. Bar Assn., Fed. Bar Council, Calif. Bar Assn., D.C. Bar Assn., San Diego County Bar Assn. (chmn. ethics com. 1980-82, bd. dirs. 1982-85, v.p. 1985), Assn. Bus. Trial Lawyers, Am. Intellectual Property Law Assn., Assn. So. Calif. Def. Counsel, Los Angeles Opera Assos. (pres. 1970-72), Soc. Colonial Wars in Calif. (gov. 1970-72), Order St. Lazarus of Jerusalem, Friends of Claremont Coll. (dir. 1975-81, pres. 1978-79), Am. Bd. Trial Advocates, Judge Advocates Assn. (dir. Los Angeles chpt. 1974-80, pres. So. Calif. chpt. 1977-78), Internat. Assn. Def. Counsel, Brit. United Services Club (dir. Los Angeles 1973-75), Mensa Internat., Calif. Soc., S.R. (pres. 1977-79), Calif. Club (Los Angeles), Valley Hunt Club (Pasadena, Calif.), Met. Club (N.Y.C.), The Naval Club (London), Phi Delta Phi. Republican. Home: 455 Silver Gate Ave San Diego CA 92106-3327 Office: Luce Forward Hamilton and Scripps 600 W Broadway 26th Fl San Diego CA 92101-3311 also: Citicorp Ctr 153 E 53rd St Frnt 26 New York NY 10022-4611

LATINI, HENRY PETER, real estate management consultant, journalist; b. Portland, Maine; s. Joseph and Mary Rose (Di Santo) L.; m. Betty Shevock, Oct. 20, 1951; children: Mary Celeste, Lisa Ann Kirkendall, Monica Louise King. AB, U. Miami, Coral Gables, Fla., 1951; postgrad., U. Maine, 1980-81, U. Hawaii, 1984. Spl. agt. FBI, Washington, 1951-79; owner, pres. Nat. Bur. Spl. Investigations, Portland, 1979-82; owner, v.p. Data Base Inc., Reston, Va., 1980-84; v.p. Cert. Mgmt. Inc., Honolulu, 1985-94, Latini-Kirkendall: Architecture, Seattle and Honolulu, 1992-97; owner Residential Mgmt. Cons., Seattle, Wash., 1992-97; mng. ptnr. Latini-Kirkendall Architecture, Seattle and Honolulu, 1992-97; co-owner Koapaka Ctr Inc., Honolulu, 1992-95, mgmt. advisor, 1997—; chmn. bd. dirs. A.R. Corp., Honolulu, 1987-92, CMI, 1992-95; mem. Cmty. Assns. Inst., Honolulu; pres. Common Area Maintenance Co., 1991-95. Feature writer real estate Hawaii Newspaper Agy., 1997—. Membership chair Portland Club, 1980-84; mem. Civil Svc. Commn., Cape Elizabeth, Maine, 1981-83; dir. security Mus. of Art, Portland, Maine, 1982-83; vol. Hawaiian Open and Ko'Olina Sr. Invitational Tournament. Mem. Soc. Former Spl. Agts. of the FBI Inc. (Hawaii chpt., sec. 1987-88, v.p. 1988-89, chmn. 1989-90), Inst. Real Estate Mgmt. Am. Soc. for Indsl. Security (Maine chpt., founder 1980, pres. 1980-82), Elks. Republican. Roman Catholic. Avocations: volunteerism, Honolulu Symphony, Honolulu Opera Theater.

LATTANZIO, STEPHEN PAUL, astronomy educator; b. Yonkers, N.Y., June 29, 1949; s. Anthony Raymond and Anella Lattanzio; m. Barbara Regina Knisely, Aug. 14, 1976; children: Gregory Paul, Timothy Paul. BA in Astronomy, U. Calif., Berkeley, 1971; MA in Astronomy, UCLA, 1973, postgrad., 1973-75. Planetarium lectr. Griffith Obs., Los Angeles, 1973-75; instr. astronomy El Camino Coll., Torrance, Calif., 1974-75; planetarium lectr. Valley Coll., Los Angeles, 1975; prof. astronomy Orange Coast Coll., Costa Mesa, Calif., 1975—, planetarium dir., 1975—; mem. adv. commn. Natural History Found. Orange County, Calif., 1988-91; scientific advisor instructional TV series Universe: The Infinite Frontier, 1992—. Co-author: Study Guide for Project: Universe, 1978, 2d rev. edition 1981; textbook reviewer, 1978—; co-screenwriter Project: Universe instructional TV series episode, 1979; contbr. articles to profl. jours. Mem. Astron. Soc. Pacific, The Planetary Soc., Sigma Xi (assoc.), Phi Beta Kappa. Avocation: astronautics. Office: Orange Coast Coll 2701 Fairview Rd Costa Mesa CA 92626-5563

LATTMAN, LAURENCE HAROLD, retired academic administrator; b. N.Y.C., Nov. 30, 1923; s. Jacob and Yetta (Schwartz) L.; m. Hanna Renate Cohn, Apr. 12, 1946; children—Martin Jacob, Barbara Diane. BSChemE, Coll. City N.Y., 1948; MS in Geology, U. Cin., 1951, PhD, 1953. Instr. U. Mich., 1952-53; asst. head photogeology sect. Gulf Oil Corp., Pitts., 1953-57; asst. prof. to prof. geomorphology Pa. State U., 1957-70; prof., head dept. geology U. Cin., 1970-75; dean Coll. of Mines U. Utah, 1975-83, dean Coll. Engring., 1978-83; pres. N.Mex. Tech., Socorro, 1983-93, pres. emeritus, 1993—; bd. dirs. Pub. Svc. Co. of N.Mex.; cons. U.S. Army Engrs., Vicksburg, Miss., 1965-69, also major oil cos. Author: (with R.G. Ray) Aerial Photographs in Field Geology, 1965, (with D. Zillman) Energy Law; Contbr. articles to profl. jours. Mem. N.Mex. Environ. Improvement Bd., 1995—. With AUS, 1943-46. Fenneman fellow U. Cin., 1953. Fellow Geol. Soc. Am.; mem. Am. Assn. Petroleum Geologists, Am. Soc. Photogrammetry (Ford Bartlett award 1968), Soc. Econ. Paleontologists and Mineralogists, AIME (Disting. mem. 1981, Mineral Industries Edn., award 1986—), Assn. Western Univs. (chmn. bd. dirs. 1986-87), Sigma Xi. Home: 11509 Penfield Ln NE Albuquerque NM 87111-6526

LAU, ELIZABETH KWOK-WAH, writer; b. Hong Kong, Jan. 7, 1940; m. Edmond Y. Lau, June 5, 1965; children: Melissa, Ernest. BA, Brigham Young U., 1963; MSW, U. Kans., 1965. Supr. N.E. Community Mental Health Ctr., San Francisco, 1968-73; clin. dir. Chinatown Child Devel. Ctr., San Francisco, 1973-75, program specialist Kai Ming Head Start Program, San Francisco, 1975-77; clin. social worker VA Hosp., Palo Alto, Calif., 1977-86; social work coord. VA Hosp., San Francisco, 1986-95, managed care coord., 1995-97; tour dir. Pacific Delight Co., N.Y.C., 1984—; freelance writer San Francisco, 1980—; host, interviewer Sta. KTSF-TV, San Francisco, 1982-94, Jade Channel, San Francisco, 1994—; bd. dirs. Kai Ming Head Start Program. Author: Innovative Parenting, 1980, How to Love Your Children, 1983, How to Raise a Successfull Child, 1984, How to Train a Bright Child, 1985, Understanding Your Children, 1987, The Art of Child Rearing, 1989, Getting to Know Americans, 1990, Providing Guidance to Teenagers, 1991, The Art of Parenting I & II, 1994, The American Welfare System, 1998, The Social Service for Chinese Americans, 1998, The Tennis Star: Michael Chang, 1998. V.p. Parents-Tchrs. League Zion Luth. Sch., San Francisco, 1981-83; bd. dirs. Christ Found., 1990-96, Kai Ming Head Start Program, 1985—; chairperson bd. deacons Zion Luth. Ch., 1990-91. Recipient Performance award VA Med. Ctr., Palo Alto, 1979, 83, Social Wokr Research award VA Med. Ctr., Palo Alto, 1985, named Fed. Employee of Yr., 1990. Mem. Nat. Assn. Social Workers (cert.). Home: 470 Ortega St San Francisco CA 94122-4622

LAU, FRED H., protective services official. Chief of police San Francisco, 1996—. Office: San Francisco Police Dept 850 Bryant St Ste 525 San Francisco CA 94103-4603*

LAUBE, ROGER GUSTAV, retired trust officer, financial consultant; b. Chgo., Aug. 11, 1921; s. William C. and Elsie (Drews) L.; m. Irene Mary Chadbourne, Mar. 30, 1946; children: David Roger, Philip Russell, Steven Richard. BA, Roosevelt U., 1942; postgrad., John Marshall Law Sch., 1942, 48-50; LLB, Northwestern U., 1960; postgrad., U. Wash., 1962-64. Cert. fin. cons. With Chgo. Title & Trust Co., Chgo., 1938-42, 48-50, Nat. Bank Alaska, Anchorage, 1950-72; mgr. mortgage dept. Nat. Bank Alaska, 1950-56, v.p., trust officer, mgr. trust dept., 1956-72; v.p., trust officer, mktg. dir., mgr. estate and fin. planning div. Bishop Trust Co., Ltd., Honolulu, 1972-82; instr. estate planning U. Hawaii, Honolulu, 1978-82; exec. v.p. Design Capital Planning Group, Inc., Tucson, 1982-83; pres., sr. trust officer, registered investment adviser Advanced Capital Advisory, Inc. of Ariz., Tucson, 1983-89; registered rep., pres. Advanced Capital Investments, Inc. of Ariz., Prescott, 1983-89; pres., chief exec. officer Advanced Capital Devel., Inc. of Ariz., Prescott, 1983-89; mng. exec. Integrated Resources Equity Corp., Prescott, 1983-89; pres. Anchorage Estate Planning Coun., 1960-62, Charter mem., 1960-72, Hawaii Estate Planning Coun., 1972-82, v.p., 1979, pres., 1980, bd. dirs., 1981-82; charter mem. Prescott Estate Planning Coun., 1986-90, pres. 1988. Charter mem. Anchorage Community Chorus, 1946, pres., 1950-53, bd. dirs., 1953-72, Alaska Festival of Music, 1960-72; mem. Anchorage camp Gideons Internat., 1946-72, Honolulu camp, 1972-82, mem. Cen. camp, Tucson, 1982-85, Prescott, 1985-90, Port Angeles-Sequim Camp, 1990—; mem. adv. bd. Faith Hosp., Glenallen, Alaska, 1960-, Cen. Alaska Mission of Far Ea. Gospel Crusade, 1960—; sec., treas. Alaska Bapt. Found., 1955-72; bd. dirs. Anchorage Symphony, 1965-72; bd. dirs. Bapt. Found. of Ariz., 1985-90; bd. dirs., mem. investment com. N.W. Bapt. Found., 1991-97; mem. mainland adv. coun. Hawaii Bapt. Acad., Honolulu, 1982—; pres. Sabinovista Townhouse Assn., 1983-85; bd. advisers Salvation Army, Alaska, 1961-72, chmn., Anchorage, 1969-72, bd. advisers, Honolulu, 1972-82, chmn. bd. advisers, 1976-78; asst. staff judge adv. Alaskan Command, 1946-48; exec. com. Alaska Conv., 1959-61, dir. music Chgo., 1938-42, 48-50, Alaska, 1950-72, Hawaii, 1972-82, Tucson, 1982-85, 1st So. Bapt. Ch., Prescott Valley, Ariz., 1985-90; 1st Bapt. of Sequim, Wash., 1990-98;

chmn. bd. trustees Hawaii, 1972-81, Prescott Valley, 1986-89, Sequim, Wash., 1991 ; worship leader Waikiki Ch., 1979-82. 1st lt., JAGD, U.S. Army, 1942-48. Recipient Others award Salvation Army, 1972. Mem. Am. Inst. Banking (instr. trust div. 1961-72), Am. Bankers Assn. (legis. com., trust div. 1960-72), Nat. Assn. Life Underwriters (nat. com. for Ariz.), Yavapai County-Prescott Life Underwriters Assn. (charter), Anchorage C. of C. (awards com. 1969-71), Internat. Assn. Fin. Planners (treas. Anchorage chpt. 1969-72, exec. com. Honolulu chpt. 1972-82, Ariz. chpt. 1982-90, del. to World Congress Australia and New Zealand 1987), Am. Assn. Handbell Ringers. Baptist. Home: Sunland Country Club 212 Sunset Pl Sequim WA 98382-8515

LAUBER, MIGNON DIANE, food processing company executive; b. Detroit, Dec. 21; d. Charles Edmond and Maud Lillian (Foster) Donaker. Student Kelsey Jenny U., 1958, Brigham Young U., 1959; m. Richard Brian Lauber, Sept. 13, 1963; 1 child, Leslie Viane (dec.). Owner, operator Alaska World Travel, Ketchikan, 1964-67; founder, owner, pres. Oosick Soup Co., Juneau, Alaska, 1969—. Treas., Pioneer Alaska Lobbyists Soc., Juneau, 1977—. Mem. Bus. and Profl. Women, Alaska C. of C. Libertarian, Washington Athletic Club. Author: Down at the Water Works with Jesus, 1982; Failure Through Prayer, 1983, We All Want to Go to Heaven But Nobody Wants to Die, 1988. Home: 321 Highland Dr Juneau AK 99801-1442

LAUCHENGCO, JOSE YUJUICO, JR., lawyer; b. Manila, Philippines, Dec. 6, 1936; came to U.S., 1962; s. José Celis Sr. Lauchengco and Angeles (Yujuico) Sapota; m. Elisabeth Schindler, Feb. 22, 1968; children: Birthe, Martina, Duane, Lance. AB, U. Philippines, Quezon City, 1959; MBA, U. So. Calif., 1964; JD, Loyola U., L.A., 1971. Bar: Calif. 1972, U.S. Dist. Ct. (cen. dist.) Calif. 1972, U.S. Ct. Appeals (9th cir.) 1972, U.S. Supreme Ct. 1975. Banker First Western Bank/United Calif. Bank, L.A., 1964-71; assoc. Demler, Perona, Langer & Bergkvist, Long Beach, Calif., 1972-73; ptnr. Demler, Perona, Langer, Bergkvist, Lauchengco & Manzella, Long Beach, 1973-77; sole practice Long Beach and L.A., 1977-83; ptnr. Lauchengco & Mendoza, L.A., 1983-92; pvt. practice L.A., 1993—; mem. commn. on jud. procedures County of L.A., 1979; tchr. Confraternity of Christian Doctrine, 1972-79; counsel Philippine Presdl. Commn. on Good Govt., L.A., 1986. Chmn. Filipino-Am. Bi-Partisan Polit. Action Group, L.A., 1978. Recipient Degree of Distinction, Nat. Forensic League, 1955. Mem. Criminal Cts. Bar Assn., Calif. Attys. Criminal Justice, Calif. Pub. Defenders Assn., Philippine-Am. Bar Assn., U. Philippines Vanguard Assn. (life), Beta Sigma. Roman Catholic. Lodge: K.C. Avocations: classical music, opera, romantic paintings and sculpture, camping, shooting. Office: 3545 Wilshire Blvd Ste 247 Los Angeles CA 90010-2388

LAUDICINA, SALVATORE ANTHONY, executive; b. Bklyn., Sept. 16, 1960; s. Victor Anthony and Anne (Calabrese) L. BS, Pace U. Film inspector United Artists Corp., N.Y.C., 1981-82; print & publicity mgr. MEM/UA Entertainment Co., N.Y.C., 1982-84, regional sales coord., 1984-85, east coast sales mgr., 1985-86; coll. sales coord. Films, Inc., N.Y.C., 1986, east coast sales mgr., 1986-87; lic. dir. Motion Picture Lic. Corp., Stamford, Conn., 1987-89; v.p. Motion Picture Lic. Corp., L.A., 1989-96, sr. v.p., 1996—. Roman Catholic. Avocation: golf. Office: Motion Picture Lic Corp 5455 S Centinela Ave Los Angeles CA 90066-6942

LAUER, GEORGE, environmental consultant; b. Vienna, Austria, Feb. 18, 1936; came to U.S., 1943; s. Otto and Alice (Denton) L.; m. Sandra Joy Comp, Oct. 1, 1983; children by previous marriage: Julie Anne, Robert L. BS, UCLA, 1961; PhD, Calif. Inst. Tech., 1967. Mem. tech. staff N.Am. Aviation, Canoga Park, Calif., 1966-69; mgr. Rockwell Internat., Thousand Oaks, Calif., 1969-75; div. mgr. ERT, Inc., Westlake Village, Calif., 1975-78; dir. Rockwell Internat., Newbury Park, Calif., 1978-85; dir. Tetra-Tech Inc., Pasadena, Calif., 1985-86; pres. Environ. Monitoring and Services, Inc., 1986-88; sr. cons. Atlantic Richfield, Inc., Los Angeles, 1988—; rsch. prof. Desert Rsch. Inst., U. Nev., Las Vegas, 1998—. Contbr. articles to profl. jours.; patentee in field. Mem. adv. bd. Environment Rsch. and Tech.; mem. adv. coun. Scaqmo, 1996—. Served with U.S. Army, 1957-59. Fellow Assn. for Computing Machinery; mem. Am. Chem. Soc., Am. Statistical Soc., Air Pollution Control Assn. Republican. Jewish. Home: 6009 Maury Ave Woodland Hills CA 91367-1052 Office: Atlantic Richfield Inc 515 S Flower St Ste 3700 Los Angeles CA 90071-2295

LAUGHLIN, EDWARD VINCENT, III, drummer, recording artist, golfer; b. N.Y.C., Feb. 15, 1960; s. Edward V. Jr. and Agnes (Lebednik) L. Drummer, mgr. Menagerie Band, N.Y.C., 1979-86; drummer, rec. artist N.Y.C., 1986-91, Joey Crist Band, Tucson, 1994-98. Drummer, songwriter Pacific Coast Highway, 1986; drummer, rec. artist It Don't Matter, 1994 (Ariz. Best Video Rec. 1995); drummer, prodr. Apollo Project Band, 1998. Vol. Young Reps., N.Y., 1967—. Mem. U.S. Golf Assn., U.S. Tennis Assn. Avocations: golf, tennis. Home: 7887 N LaCholla Tucson AZ 85741

LAURANCE, MARK RODNEY, applications engineer, entrepreneur; b. Seattle, Nov. 27, 1959; s. Sidney Laurance and Patricia Louise Sadlier; m. Brendalynn Legarda. BS in Astronomy, U. Wash., 1984, BS in Physics, 1984, MS in Astronomy, 1992. Computer ops. programmer Seattle Police Dept., Seattle, 1980-85; researcher U. Wash., Seattle, 1984-90; lighting engr. Korry Electronics Co., Seattle, 1990-92; optical engr. Can.-France-Hawaii Telescope Corp., Kamuela, Hawaii, 1992-96; pres. Digitek Hawai'i, Inc., Kamuela, Hawaii, 1995-96; applications engr. Zygo Tech. Instrument Co., Sunnyvale, Calif., 1996—; owner Laurance Design Group, San Francisco, 1996-98; applications engring. mgr. Zygo Advanced Imaging Systems, Sunnyvale, Calif., 1998—. Contbr. articles to profl. jours. Mem. chpt. mgmt. program mgr., exec. bd. dirs. Hawaii State Jaycees, 1995; exec. v.p. Kona Jaycees, 1994, comty. fundraising dir., 1993; cert. prime trainer Jr. Chamber Internat., 1994; mem. nat. nominations com. Outstanding Young Men of Am., 1997, Outstanding Young Women of Am., 1997. Recipient C. William Brownfield Meml. award for outstanding first yr. jaycee Kona Jaycees, 1994, Presdl. Excellence award Hawaii State Jaycees, 1995, First Place Speak-Up Competition award Hawaii State Jaycees, 1995; named to Outstanding Young Men of Am., 1989, Outstanding Exec. V.P. of Quar., Hawaii Jaycees, 1995, Finalist Three Outstanding Young Persons of Hawaii Jaycees, 1995, Outstanding Young Men of Am., 1997, Outstanding Young Ams. Nat. Nominating Com., 1997. Mem. SPIE Internat. Soc. Optical Engring. Avocations: bicycling, photography, guitar playing, hiking. Office: 650 N Mary Ave Sunnyvale CA 94086-2906

LAUTH, HAROLD VINCENT, corporate affairs executive; b. St. Paul, Jan. 10, 1933; s. Harold Vincent and Kerrie M. (Denevan) L.; m. Mildred Ann Hellmann, Aug. 6, 1955; children: Susan M. Foster, Michael L., Karen P., Stephen C., Jennifer A., Nancy L. BS in Bus., U. Md., 1957. Press rep. Milk Industry Found., Washington, 1957-59; pub. rels. and advt. mgr. Volkswagen Am., Washington, 1959-60; dir. corp. affairs Kaiser Industries Corp., Oakland, Calif. and Washington, 1960-76, instr. pub. affairs George Washington U., 1967-68; polit. project mgr., v.p. U.S. Hubert H. Humphrey, 1967-68; dir. corp. affairs Kaiser Resources Ltd., Vancouver, B.C., Can., 1976-78; dir. corp. affairs Kaiser Engrs. Inc., Oakland, 1978-88; pres. Lauth Pacific, Oakland, 1988—. cons. Kaiser Permanente, Bings Golf. Pres., Oakland-Dalian Friendship City Soc., 1986-90; chmn. mayor's smoking ordinance com., Oakland, 1987-88, mem. mayor's com. on internat. trade & fgn. investment; mem. steering com. U. Calif./Oakland Metro Forum; mem. adv. bd. United Way Alameda County, 1974-76; chmn. pub. rels. com. Mercy Retirement and Care Ctr.; bd. dirs. New Oakland Com., v.p. 1983-84; mem. bus. symposia Holy Names Coll., Oakland, St. Mary's Coll., Moraga, Calif., chmn. 1991-93; bd. dirs. Northern Calif. Golf Assn. Mem. Pub. Relations Soc. Am. (pres. Washington chpt. 1968), Nat. Press Club, Soc. Profl. Journalists (sec. Wash. chpt. 1966-68), Commonwealth Club, Claremont Country Club (dir. 1987-89), Golf Course Supts. Assn. Home: 5466 Hilltop Cres Oakland CA 94618-2604

LAUVER, LYDIA MONSERRAT OLLIS, public relations executive; b. Pitts., May 9, 1958; d. Jay Edwin and Ascension (Romero) Ollis; m. Kevin John Lauver, Jan. 20, 1990; 2 children. AA in Media Tech. with honors, Bellevue Community Coll., 1982, AA in Gen. Studies with honors, 1982, BS in Bus., City U., 1983. Graphic illustrator Boeing Co., Seattle, 1978-80; freelance mktg. Kiro Video, City U., Seattle, 1980-83; dir. pub. rels. Vyzis Devel. Co., Bellevue, Wash., 1983-87; pub. rels. account exec. The Rockey Co., Bellevue, 1987-92; prin. Lauver & Co., Bellevue, 1992—. Trustee Bellevue Schs. Found., 1989-92; bd. dirs. Seattle Seafair, 1989-92; advisor pub. rels. com. YMCA Greater Seattle, 1989—; advisor Wash. State March of Dimes, 1988-91; vol. Spl. Olympics, 1976-80; chair Bellevue Chamber Ann. Dinner, 1990. Seattle Women in Advt. scholar, 1982. Mem. Nat. Pub. Rels. Soc. (APR designation 1987). Roman Catholic. Avocations: traveling, reading, sewing, computers. Office: Lauver & Co 12643 NE 2nd St Bellevue WA 98005-3206

LAVALLEE, CHARLES PHILLIP, music educator, musician; b. Williston, Vt., Mar. 23, 1928; s. Arthur Israel and Azilda H. (Roux) L.; m. Rita Poldina Perla; 1 child, Lynn Marie. BA, U. Calif., Los Angeles, 1960; MA, Calif. State U., Los Angeles, 1971; PhD, Columbia Pacific U., 1986. Instr. music I.G. Hook Jr. High Sch., Victorville, Calif., 1960-68, 74-84; instr. music Victor Valley High Sch., Victorville, 1968-70, counselor, 1971-73; counselor, instr. music Hesperia (Calif.) Jr. High Sch., 1973-74; instr. music Hesperia (Calif.) High Sch., 1984-92; instr. Victor Valley Coll., Calif., 1991—. With U.S. Army, 1950-52. Mem. Music Edn. Nat. Conf., NEA, So. Calif. Sch. Band and Orch. Assn., Am. Fedn. Musicians, Internat. Assn. Jazz Educators. Democrat. Roman Catholic. Avocations: photography, composing and arranging music. Home: 18961 Tamarac Rd Apple Valley CA 92307-4920

LAVENTHOL, DAVID, museum official. Chmn. bd. trustees Mus. of Contemporary Art, L.A. Office: Mus of Contemporary Art California Plz 250 S Grand Ave Los Angeles CA 90012-3021*

LAVENTHOL, DAVID ABRAM, newspaper editor; b. Phila., July 15, 1933; s. Jesse and Clare (Horwald) L.; m. Esther Coons, Mar. 8, 1958; children: Peter, Sarah. BA, Yale U., 1957; MA, U. Minn., 1960; LittD (hon.), Dowling Coll., 1979; LLD (hon.), Hofstra U., 1986. Reporter, news editor St. Petersburg (Fla.) Times, 1957-62; asst. editor, city editor N.Y. Herald-Tribune, 1963-66; asst. mng. editor Washington Post, 1966-69; from assoc. editor to pub., CEO Newsday, L.I., N.Y., 1969-86; group v.p. newspapers Times Mirror Co., L.A., 1981-86, sr. v.p., 1987-93, pres., 1987-93; pub., CEO L.A. Times, 1989-93; editor-at-large Times Mirror Co., L.A., 1994-98; cons. editor, 1998—; mem. Pulitzer Prize Bd., 1982-91, chmn., 1988-89; vice-chmn. Internat. Press Inst., 1985-93, chmn., 1993-95. Bd. dirs. United Negro Coll. Fund, 1988, Mus. Contemporary Art, L.A., 1989—, chmn., 1993-97; bd. dirs. Associated Press, 1993-96, Columbia Journalism Sch., 1995—, Nat. Parkinson Found., 1995—, Saratoga Performing Arts Ctr., 1993-96. With Signal Corps AUS, 1953-55. Recipient Columbia Journalism award for Disting. Svc., 1994. Mem. Am. Soc. Newspaper Editors (chmn. writing awards bd. 1980-83), Council Fgn. Relations. Clubs: Century (N.Y.C.), Regency (L.A.). Office: LA Times Times Mirror Sq Los Angeles CA 90053-3816

LAVIN, LAURENCE MICHAEL, lawyer; b. Upper Darby, Pa., Apr. 27, 1940; s. Michael Joseph and Helen Clair (McGonigle) L. BS, St. Joseph's U., Phila., 1962; JD, Villanova (Pa.) U., 1965. Bar: Pa., S.C. Vol. U.S. Peace Corps, Thika, Kenya, 1966-67; atty. Community Legal Svcs., Phila., 1968-70, exec. dir., 1971-79; exec. dir. Palmetto Legal Svcs., Columbia, S.C., 1981-85; dir. Law Coordination Ctr., Harrisburg, Pa., 1985-88, Nat. Health Law Program, L.A., 1988—; chmn. bd. dirs. L.A. Poverty Dept.; bd. dirs., chmn. civil com. Nat. Legal Aid and Defender, Washington, 1976-78. Founding mem. Pa. Coun. to Abolish Death Penalty, Harrisburg, 1986; bd. dirs. L.A. Poverty Dept., 1996—. Mem. ABA, Pa. Bar Assn. (chmn. legal svcs. to pub. com. 1985-88). Democrat. Avocations: reading, arts, acting. Home: 1133 22nd St Santa Monica CA 90403-5721 Office: Nat Health Law Program 2639 S La Cienega Blvd Los Angeles CA 90034-2675

LAVIN, MATTHEW T., horticultural educator. Assoc. prof. biology dept. Mont. State U., Bozeman. Recipient N.Y. Botanical Garden award Botanical Soc. Am., 1993. Office: Montana State U Dept Biology 310 Lewis Hall Bozeman MT 59717-0002

LA VINE, ROBERT L., lawyer; b. San Francisco, Dec. 24, 1929; s. Jack and Fay L.V.; m. Betty Ann La Vine, June 2, 1951; 1 child, Barbara. BS, U. Calif., 1952; JD, U. Calif. (Hastings), 1959. Bar: Calif., 1959; CPA, Calif. V.p., gen. counsel Willig Freight Lines, San Francisco, 1964-97; ptnr. La Vine & Shain, San Francisco, 1961—. Capt. U.S. Army, 1952-54. Mem. San Francisco Bar. Assn., San Francisco Lawyers Club. Fax: 415-777-0222. Office: 5 3rd St Ste 415 San Francisco CA 94103-3205

LAVINE, STEVEN DAVID, academic administrator; b. Sparta, Wis., June 7, 1947; s. Israel Harry and Harriet Hauda (Rosen) L.; m. Janet M. Sternburg, May 29, 1988. BA, Stanford U., 1969; MA, Harvard U., 1970, PhD, 1976. Asst. prof. U. Mich., Ann Arbor, 1974-81; asst. dir. arts and humanities Rockefeller Found., N.Y.C., 1983-86, assoc. dir. arts and humanities, 1986-88; pres. Calif. Inst. Arts, Valencia, 1988—; adj. assoc. prof. NYU Grad. Sch. Bus., 1984-85; cons. Wexner Found., Columbus, Ohio, 1986-87; selection panelist Input TV Screening Conf., Montreal, Can., and Granda, Spain, 1985-86; cons., panelist Nat. Endowment for Humanities, Washington, 1981-85; faculty chair Salzburg Seminar on Mus., 1989; co-dir. Arts and Govt. Program, The Am. Assembly, 1991; mem. arch. selection jury L.A. Cathedral. Editor: The Hopwood Anthology, 1981, Exhibiting Cultures, 1991, Museums and Communities, 1992; editor spl. issue Prooftexts jour., 1984. Bd. dirs. Sta. KCRW-FM (NPR), KCET-Pub. TV, L.A. Philharm. Assn., Endowments, Inc. Recipient Class of 1923 award, 1979, Faculty Recognition award, 1980 U. Mich.; Charles Dexter traveling fellow Harvard U., 1972, Ford fellow, 1969-74, vis. rsch. fellow Rockefeller Found., N.Y.C., 1981-83. Jewish. Office: Calif Inst Arts Office Pres 24700 Mcbean Pkwy Santa Clarita CA 91355-2397

LAVRAKAS, LEFTERIS, educator, researcher, consultant; b. Watertown, Mass., Oct. 18, 1919; s. Apostle and Fotini (Jeanides) L.; m. Billye Jayne Charleville, June 26, 1945; children: Paula, Char-Lee, John, Debra. BS, U.S. Naval Acad., 1942; Master's degree, Calif. State U., Fullerton, 1973; PhD, Claremont (Calif.) Grad. Sch., 1977. Lifetime cmty. coll. tchg. credential, Calif. Commd. ensign USN, 1939, advanced through grades to capt., 1962; served in 3 wars; adj. instr. Orange Coast Coll., Costa Mesa, Calif., 1971-76; instr. elem. sch. Huntington Beach, Calif., 1973-74; cons., adminstr. Saddleback Coll., Mission Viejo, Calif., 1976-84; mem. faculty Columbia Pacific U., 1984—; part-time cons. L.A. cmty. coll. dist., 1977-79; ind. rschr. Calif. cmty. colls., 1984—. Decorated 2 Bronze Stars, Knight's Cross (The Netherlands). Mem. U.S. Naval Acad. Alumni Assn. Republican. Home: 354 Broadway Costa Mesa CA 92627

LAW, FLORA ELIZABETH (LIBBY LAW), retired community health and pediatrics nurse; b. Biddeford, Maine, Sept. 11, 1935; d. Arthur Parker and Flora Alma (Knutti) Butt; m. Robert F. Law, 1961; children : Susan E., Sarah F., Christian A., Martha F.; m. John F. Brown, Jr., 1982. BA, Davis and Elkins (W.Va.) Coll., 1957; postgrad., Cornell U.-N.Y. Hosp., N.Y.C., 1960; BSN, U. Nev., Las Vegas, 1976, MS in Counseling Edn., 1981. RN, Nev.; cert. sch. nurse. Staff nurse So. Nev. Community Hosp. (now Univ. Med. Ctr.), Las Vegas, 1975-76; relief charge nurse Valley Psychiat. Inst., Las Vegas, 1976; pub. health nurse Clark County Dist. Health Dept., Las Vegas, 1977-78; sch. nurse Clark County Sch. Dist., Las Vegas, 1978-94; ret., 1994. Chair task force on sch. nursing Nev.'s Commn. for Profl. Standards in Edn.; mem. nurse practice act revision com. Nev. State Bd. Nursing. Mem. Nat. Assn. Sch. Nurses (past state dir., sch. nurse liaison Clark County Tchrs. Assn.), Clark County Assn. Sch. Nurses (past pres.), Sigma Theta Tau. Home: 3420 Clandara Ave Las Vegas NV 89121-3701

LAW, NANCY ENELL, school system administrator; b. South Gate, Calif., Jan. 12, 1935; d. Frank Ronald Cruickshank and Grace Margaret (Wright) Brotherton; m. George Otto Enell, Aug. 26, 1955; children: George, Grace; m. Alexander Inglis Law, Feb. 1, 1987. BS, U. So. Calif., 1956, MEd, 1961, PhD, 1977. Tchr. El Monte (Calif.) City Schs., 1956-58, Pasadena (Calif.) City Schs., 1958-62; from tchr. to project cons. Fullerton (Calif.) Elem. Sch. Dist., 1966-76; evaluation specialist San Juan Unified Sch. Dist., Carmichael, Calif., 1976-84; from dir. evaluation svcs. to adminstr. accountability Sacramento (Calif.) City Schs., 1984—; officer divsn. H Am. Ednl. Rsch. Assn., 1995—. Mem. Phi Delta Kappa. Avocations: creative handiwork, piano. Home: 9046 Laguna Lake Way Elk Grove CA 95758-4210 Office: Sacramento City Schs 520 Capitol Mall Sacramento CA 95814-4704

LAWRENCE, DAVID NORMAN, broadcasting executive, consultant; b. Kalispell, Mont., June 19, 1941; s. James Lynn and Lola Alameda (Greenfield) L.; children: Robert Lynn, Cary Lee. Student, John Brown U., 1959-62, N.W. Nazarene Coll., 1963-68; BA, Golden State U., 1987. Mgr. Sta. KHAP, Aztec, N.Mex., 1962-65; mgr. sales, program dir. Sta. KCVR, Lodi, Calif., 1968-73; dir. devel. Far East Broadcasting Co., Manila, 1977-78; dir. of media Far East Broadcasting Co., La Mirada, Calif., 1978-84; dir. internat. programming High Adventure, Simi Valley, Calif., 1984-91; media cons. various orgns., L.A.; bd. dirs. Trans World Missions, Glendale, Calif., 1989-98; internat. media cons. Faith Ctr., Glendale, Calif.; rep. many internat. radio/TV stas. Bd. dirs. Lodi Lions Profl. Baseball, 1971-76; pres. Kiwanis Club Greater Lodi, 1975; mem. pers. bd. City of Buena Park, Calif., 1989—, chmn., 1990. Recipient Outstanding Svc. award City of Buena Park, 1991; named Outstanding Club Pres., Kiwanis, 1975. Mem. Nat. Religious Broadcasters (various awards). Mem. Evang. Free Ch. Am. E-mail: dlawrence3@compuserve.com. Home: 17571 Bonner Dr Santa Ana CA 92705-2613

LAWRENCE, DWIGHT TIMOTHY, insurance executive, consultant; b. L.A., May 8, 1959; s. William Jr. and Elizabeth (Johnson) L. BA, Ea. Wash. Univ., 1982; MBA, Nat. Univ., 1982. Sr. cost acct. Coleco Toys Mfg., Tustin, Calif., 1983-86; sr. fin. analyst Toyai Scripto Corp., Fontana, Calif., 1986-90; sr. mgmt. analyst Pharmavite Corp., Mission Hills, Calif., 1990-94; asst. dir. of budgets VANS, Inc., Orange, Calif., 1994-96; dir. of budgets TransAmerica Corp., L.A., 1996—; cons. H.S. and Coll. career day, Fullerton, Calif., 1995—, Bus. Achievers, San Bernardino, Calif., 1995—. Mem. dem. fund raiser, San Bernardino, Calif., 1990—; Capt. U.S. Army Res., 1981-85. Recipient Kaiser Aluminum Acctg. award Kaiser Corp., Wash., 1981. Mem. NAACP, Nat. Assoc. of Accts., Black MBA Assoc., Legion of Valor (assoc.), Urban League. Catholic. Office: TransAmerica 1150 S Olive St Ste 2723 Los Angeles CA 90015-2258

LAWRENCE, FREDERICK D., executive. CEO, chmn., pres. Calif. Microwave, Sunnyvale. Office: 1143 Borregas Ave Sunnyvale CA 94089-1306

LAWRENCE, JEROME, playwright, director, educator; b. Cleve., July 14, 1915; s. Samuel and Sarah (Rogen) L. BA, Ohio State U., 1937, LHD (hon.), 1963; DLitt, Fairleigh Dickinson U., 1968; DFA (hon.), Villanova U., 1969; LittD, Coll. Wooster, 1983. Dir. various summer theaters Pa. and Mass., 1934-37; reporter, telegraph editor Wilmington (Ohio) News Jour., 1937; editor Lexington Daily News, Ohio, 1937; continuity editor radio Sta. KMPC, Beverly Hills, Calif., 1938-39; sr. staff writer CBS, Hollywood, Calif. and N.Y.C., 1939-42; pres., writer, dir. Lawrence & Lee, Hollywood, N.Y.C. and London, 1945—; vis. prof. Ohio State Univ., 1969, Salzburg Seminar in Am. Studies, 1972, Baylor Univ., 1978; prof. playwriting Univ. So. Calif. Grad. Sch., 1984—; co-founder, judge Margo Jones award, N.Y.C., 1958—; co-founder, pres. Am. Playwrights Theatre, Columbus, Ohio, 1970-85; bd. dirs. Am. Conservatory Theatre, San Francisco, 1970-80, Stella Adler Theatre, L.A., 1987—, Plumstead Playhouse, 1986—; keynote speaker Bicentennial of Bill of Rights, Congress Hall, Phila., 1991; hon. mem. Nat. Theatre Conf., 1993; adv. bd. Am. Theatre in Lit. Contemporary Arts Ednl. Project, 1993—; playwright, 1944—. Scenario writer Paramount Studios, 1941; master playwright NYU Inst. Performing Arts, 1967-69; author-dir. for: radio and television UN Broadcasts; Army-Navy programs D-Day, VE-Day, VJ-Day; author: Railroad Hour, Hallmark Playhouse, Columbia Workshop; author: Off Mike, 1944, (biography, later made into PBS-TV spl.) Actor: Life and Times of Paul Muni, 1978 (libretto and lyrics by Lawrence and Lee, music by Billy Goldenberg); co-author, dir.: (album) One God; playwright: Live Spelled Backwards, 1969, Off Mike, (mus. with Robert E. Lee) Look, Ma, I'm Dancin', 1948 (music by Hugh Martin), Shangri-La, 1956 (music by Harry Warren, lyrics by James Hilton, Lawrence and Lee), Mame, 1966 (score by Jerry Herman), Dear World, 1969 (score by Jerry Herman), (non-mus.) Inherit the Wind (translated and performed in 34 langs., named best fgn. play of year London Critics Poll 1960), Auntie Mame, 1956, The Gang's All Here, 1959, Only in America, 1959, A Call on Kuprin, 1961, Diamond Orchid (revised as Sparks Fly Upward, 1966), 1965, The Incomparable Max, 1969, The Crocodile Smile, 1970, The Night Thoreau Spent in Jail, 1970, (play and screenplay) First Monday in October, 1978, (written for opening of Thurber Theatre, Columbus) Jabberwock: Improbablilities Lived and Imagined by James Thurber in the Fictional City of Columbus, Ohio, 1974, (with Robert E. Lee) Whisper in the Mind, 1994, The Angels Weep, 1992, (novel) A Golden Circle: A Tale of the Stage and the Screen and Music of Yesterday and Now and Tomorrow and Maybe the Day After Tomorrow, 1993; Decca Dramatic Albums, Musi-Plays., Selected Plays of Lawrence and Lee, 1996; contbg. editor Dramatics mag., mem. adv. bd., contbr. Writer's Digest; Lawrence and Lee collections at Libr. and Mus. of the Performing Arts, Lincoln Ctr., N.Y., Harvard's Widener Libr., Cambridge, Mass., Jerome Lawrence & Robert E. Lee Theatre Rsch. Inst. at Ohio State U., Columbus, est. 1986. A founder, overseas corr. Armed Forces Radio Service; mem. Am. Theatre Planning Bd.; bd. dirs. Nat. Repertory Theatre, Plumstead Playhouse; mem. adv. bd. USDAN Center for Creative and Performing Arts, East-West Players, Performing Arts Theatre of Handicapped., Inst. Outdoor Drama; mem. State Dept. Cultural Exchange Drama Panel, 1961-69; del. Chinese-Am. Writers Conf., 1982, 86, Soviet-Am. Writers Conf., 1984, 85; Am. Writers rep. to Hiroshima 40th Anniversary Commemorative, Japan, 1985; mem. U.S. Cultural Exchange visit to theatre communities of Beijing and Shanghai, 1985; adv. coun. Calif. Ednl. Theatre Assn., Calif. State U., Calif. Repertory Co., Long Beach, 1984—. Recipient N.Y. Press Club award, 1942, CCNY award, 1948, Radio-TV Life award, 1948, Mirror awards, 1952, 53, Peabody award, 1949, 52, Variety Showmanship award 1954, Variety Critics poll 1955, Outer-Circle Critics award 1955, Donaldson award, 1955, Ohioana award, 1955, Ohio Press Club award, 1959, Brit. Drama Critics award, 1960, Moss Hart Meml. award, 1967, State Dept. medal, 1968, Pegasus award, 1970, Lifetime Achievement award Am. Theatre Assn., 1979, Nat. Thespian Soc. award, 1980, Pioneer Broadcasters award, 1981, 95, Diamond Circle award Pacific Pioneer Broadcasters, 1995, Ohioana Library career medal, Master of Arts award Rocky Mountain Writers Guild, 1982, Centennial Award medal Ohio State U., 1970, William Inge award and lectureship Independence Community Coll., 1983, 86—, Disting. Contbr. award Psychologists for Social Responsibility, 1985, ann. awards San Francisco State U., Pepperdine U., Career award Southeastern Theatre Conf., 1990; named Playwright of Yr. Baldwin-Wallace Coll., 1960; named to Honorable Order of Ky. Colonels, 1965, Tenn. Colonels, 1988; named to Theater Hall of Fame, 1990. Fellow Coll. Am. Theatre, Kennedy Ctr.; mem. Nat. Theatre Conf. (hon.), Acad. Motion Picture Arts and Scis. (nominating com. best fgn. films 1997), Acad. TV Arts and Scis. (2 Emmy award 1988), Authors League (coun.), ANTA (dir., v.p.), Ohio State U. Assn. (dir.), Radio Writers' Guild (founder, pres.), Writers Guild Am. (dir., founding mem. Valentine Davies award), Dramatists Guild (coun.), ASCAP, Calif. Ednl. Theatre Assn. (Profl. Artist award 1992), Century Club N.Y., Phi Beta Kappa, Sigma Delta Chi. Avocations: traveling, photography, swimming. *

LAWRENCE, PAULA DENISE, physical therapist; b. Ft. Worth, May 21, 1959; d. Roddy Paul and Kay Frances (Spivey) Gillis; m. Mark Jayson Lawrence, Apr. 20, 1985. BS, Tex. Women's U., 1982. Lic. phys. therapist, Tex., Calif. Sales mgr. R. and K Camping Ctr., Garland, Tex., 1977-82; staff phys. therapist Longview (Tex.) Regional Hosp., 1982-83, dir. phys. therapy, 1983-87, dir. rehab. svcs., 1987-88; staff phys. therapist MPH Home Health, Longview, Tex., 1983-84; owner, pres. Phys. Rehab. Ctr., Hemet, Calif., 1988—; mem. adv. com. div. health occupations Kilgore (Tex.) Coll., 1985-88; mem. profl. adv. bd. Hospice Longview, 1985-88. Bd. dirs. V.I.P. Tots; active Valle Vista PTA, sec. 1998—. Mem. NAFE, Am. Phys. Therapy Assn., Calif. Phys. Therapy Assn., Am. Bus. Women's Assn. (v.p. 1987, 89, pres. 1990, Woman of Yr. 1988, 91), Assistance League Aux., Soroptomist (corr. sec. 1992, dir. 1993-95, 97-98, sec. 1995-97, v.p. 98-99), Hemet C. of C. (sec. 1998-99, bd. dirs.), Psi Chi, Omega Rho Alpha. Avocation: travel. Home: 43725 Mandarin Dr Hemet CA 92544-8529 Office: 901 S State St Ste 500 Hemet CA 92543-7185

LAWRENCE, RALPH ALAN, minister; b. Wendell, Idaho, Apr. 18, 1931; s. Wayne Harold and Evelyn Frances (McConnell) L.; m. Beverley Jean Miller, June 9, 1957 (div. 1974); children: Alan, Douglas, Kerry Philpot; m. Audrey Stall Shelden, Dec. 28, 1975; children: Wayne Shelden, Mark Sheldon, Sharon Glover, Laurel Bishop, Scott Sheldon. BA in Bus. Adminstrn., Albertson Coll. of Idaho, 1953; MDiv, Boston U., 1956; DD

(hon.), Albertson Coll. of Idaho, 1986. Ordained to ministry Meth. Ch., 1956. Min. youth Christ Ch., Kennebunk, Maine, 1954-56, Shoshone-Richfield (Idaho) Parish, 1956-60, St. Paul's Ch., Idaho Falls, Idaho, 1960-64, Nyssa (Oreg.) Meth. Ch., 1964-68, Pioneer United Meth. Ch., Portland, Oreg., 1968-74, 1st United Meth. Ch., Payette, Idaho, 1974-81; dist. supt. Ea. Dist., Oreg.-Idaho Conf., 1981-87; pastor Meridian (Idaho) United Meth. Ch., 1987-95; retired, 1995; asst. pastor 1st United Meth. Cathedral of Rockies, 1995—; del. World Meth. Conf., 1986, 91, 96, Jurisdictional Conf., 1984; pres. Classic Journeys Internat., 1979—. Mem. SAR, Acad. Model Aeronautics, Denison Soc., Kiwanis, Stephen Ministries. Home: 3335 N Bunchberry Way Boise ID 83704-0717

LAWRENCE, SALLY CLARK, academic administrator; b. San Francisco, Dec. 29, 1930; d. George Dickson and Martha Marie Alice (Smith) Clark; m. Henry Clay Judd, July 1, 1950 (div. Dec. 1972); children: Rebecca, David, Nancy; m. John I. Lawrence, Aug. 12, 1976; stepchildren: Maia, Dylan. Docent Portland Art Mus., Oreg., 1958-68; gallery owner, dir., Sally Judd Gallery, Portland, 1968-75; art ins. appraiser, cons. Portland, 1975-81; interim dir. Mus. Art. Sch., Pacific Northwest Coll. Art, Portland, 1981, asst. dir., 1981-82, acting dir., 1982-84, dir., 1984-94, pres., 1994—; bd. dirs. Art Coll. Exch. Nat. Consortium, 1982-91, pres., 1983-84. Bd. dirs. Portland Arts Alliance, 1987—, Assn. Ind. Colls. of Art and Design, 1991—, pres., 1995-96, sec. 1996—. Mem. Nat. Assn. Schs. Art and Design (bd. dirs. 1984-91, treas. bd. dirs. 1994-96, pres. 1996—), Oreg. Ind. Coll. Assn. (bd. dirs. 1981—, exec. com. 1989-94, pres. 1992-93). Office: Pacific NW Coll of Art 1241 NW Johnson St Portland OR 97209-3023

LAWRENCE, SANFORD HULL, physician, immunochemist; b. Kokomo, Ind., July 10, 1919; s. Walter Scott and Florence Elizabeth (Hull) L. AB, Ind. U., 1941, MD, 1944. Fellow in biochemistry George Washington U., 1941; intern Rochester (N.Y.) Gen. Hosp., 1944-45; resident Halloran Hosp., Staten Island, N.Y., 1946-49; chief med. svce. Ft. Ord Regl. Hosp., 1945-46; dir. biochemistry rsch. lab. San Fernando (Calif.) VA Hosp.; asst. prof. UCLA, 1950—; cons. internal medicine and cardiology U.S. Govt., Los Angeles County; lectr. Faculte de Medicine, Paris, various colls. Eng., France, Belgium, Sweden, USSR, India, Japan; chief med. svc. Ft. Ord Regional Hosp.; chmn. Titus, Inc., 1982—. Author: Zymogram in Clinical Medicine, 1965; contbr. articles to sci. jours.; author: Threshold of Valhalla, Another Way to Fly, My Last Satyr, and other short stories; traveling editor: Relax Mag. Mem. Whitley Heights Civic Assn., 1952—; pres. Halloran Hosp. Employees Assn., 1947-48. Served to maj. U.S. Army, 1945-46. Recipient Rsch. award TB and Health Assn., 1955-58, Los Angeles County Heart Assn., 1957-59, Pres. award, Queen's Blue Book award, Am. Men of Sci. award; named one of 2000 Men of Achievement, Leaders of Am. Sci., Ky. Col., named Hon. Mayor of West Point, Ky. Mem. AAAS, AMA, N.Y. Acad. Scis., Am. Fedn. Clin. Research, Am. Assn. Clin. Investigation, Am. Assn. Clin. Pathology, Am. Assn. Clin. Chemistry, Los Angeles County Med. Assn. Republican. Methodist. Avocations: bridge, comml. pilot, pianist, organist. Home: 2014 Whitley Ave Los Angeles CA 90068-3235 also: 160 rue St Martin, 75003 Paris France

LAWRENCE, WILLIAM, JR., elementary education educator; b. L.A., Mar. 2, 1930; s. Willie and Nellie (January) L.; m. Elizabeth Johnson, Jan. 13, 1951; children: William III, Timothy Dwight, Walter Fitzgerald. BA in Psychology, Columbia Coll., Mo., 1981; LLB, LaSalle U., 1982; MA in Edn., Claremont Coll., 1992; postgrad., Calif. Coast U., 1992—. Enlisted U.S. Army, 1947, advanced through grades to lt., 1957, commd. sgt. maj., 1965; served U.S. Army, Vietnam, 1965-70; instr. U.S. Military Acad., West Point, N.Y., 1970-73; with Berlin Brigade, U.S. Army, Berlin, Germany, 1973-76; dep. sheriff L.A., 1958-65; probation officer San Bernardino County, Calif., 1985-89; own recognizance investigator L.A. County, 1989; tchr. Pomona Unified Sch. Dist., Pomona, Calif., 1989—; sch. site technician, 1996. Decorated U.S. Army Dist. Svc. Cross for Extraordinary Heroism in Combat, Silver Star, 7 Purple Hearts. Mem. Legion of Valor, 555Th Parachute Battalion (pres.). Democrat. Roman Catholic. Avocations: photography, free fall parachuting. Home: 1456 S Lilac Ave Bloomington CA 92316-2130 Office: Pomona Unified Sch Dist 800 N Garey Ave Pomona CA 91767-4616

LAWRIE, LAURA ANNE, editor; b. N.Y.C., May 24, 1958; m. William Charles Edward Lawrie; 1 child, Aurora Zoe. MusB, Boston U., 1978; MusM, Kings Coll., London, 1979. Editl. asst. The New Grove Dictionary of Music and Musicians, London, 1980; music editor Novello & Co. Ltd., London, 1980-84; prodn. editor Harvester Press, Brighton, Eng., 1984-86; gen. mgr. Signal Graphics, Lewes, Eng., 1986-89; editor The New Grove Dictionary of Opera, London, 1989-92, The Macmillan Dictionary of Art, London, 1992-96; mng. editor Am. Behavioral Scientist/Saye Publs., Inc., Mesa, Calif., 1996—; pub. cons. Oxford Univ. Press, Oxford, Eng., and N.Y., 1989—, W.W. Norton, N.Y., 1996—, Gale Rsch., Detroit, 1997—, Microsoft Press, Seattle, 1997—, Prentice Hall, N.J., 1998—, Bloomsbury Pub., London, Eng., 1998—, Blackwell Pubs., Mass., 1998—, Garland, N.Y., 1998—. Contbr.: Encyclopedia of American Industries, 1997, Encyclopedia of Emerging Industries, 1998, Encarta World English Dictionary, 1999—. Mem. Mu Phi Epsilon. Avocations: hiking, reading.

LAWS, JOYCE DAVIS, artist; b. George West, Tex., Dec. 24, 1939; d. Clarence Leslie and Gretchen (Karger) Davis; m. James Woodford Laws, June 6, 1961; children: Pamela Suzanne, Julie Anne Laws Johnson. Cert. of nursing, Lilly Jolly Sch. of Nursing, 1961. RN, Tex. contbr. paintings, People in Watercolor, 1997, Inside East Sacramento, 1998. Mem. No. Calif. Watercolor Assn. Calif., Watercolor Assn. Calif., assoc. mem. Nat. Watercolor Soc. Calif., Am. Watercolor Assn. N.Y. Avocations: boating, gardening.

LAWSON, DENNIS LEE, plant broker, writer; b. Rock Island, Ill., Feb. 19, 1947; s. Kenneth Stewart and Phyllis Marie (Johnson) L. BA in philosophy, Long Beach State Univ., 1973. Combat corpsman U.S. Army, 1966-72; ambulance driver Parker's Ambulance Svc., Los Alamitos, Calif., 1972-74; marine aquarium cons. Tex's Tropicals, Long Beach, Calif., 1972-74; waste water treatment plant mgr. Star-Kist Tune, Inc., Terminal Island, Calif., 1974-76; comml. fisherman Hawaii, 1977; nursery foreman Kamehameha Investment Corp., Hawaii, 1977-88; comml. tropical fish diver Hawaii, 1980-85; nursery mgr. Hyatt Regency Waikoloa, Waikoloa, Hawaii, 1988-90, Royal Waikoloan Hotel, Waikoloa, Hawaii, 1990-91; writer Hawaii, 1991—; garden ctr. mgr. WalMart, Hawaii, 1995-97; writer columnist for local mag., 1996-97. With U.S. Army, 1966-72, Korea. Recipient Nat. Def. Svc. medal U.S. Army, 1968. Avocations: writing, deep sea fishing, unique plant propagation, diving, campanionship, caught 5301/2 lb. Pacific Blue Marlin and 201 lb. Yellowfin Tuna, 1988.

LAWSON, MARGUERITE PAYNE, small business owner; b. Detroit, Apr. 30, 1935; d. LeRoy and Marguerite Lenore (Archambeau) Payne; m. William Allen Stanke, Sept. 4, 1954 (div. Sept. 1962); children: Elizabeth Susan Hankey, Elaine Kathryn Dinwiddie; m. Vernon Arthur Lawson, Aug. 15, 1975. BA in Social Sci., Mich. State U., E. Lansing, 1957. Lic. real estate assoc.; cert. tax preparer. Tchr. El Segundo Unified Sch. Dist., Calif., 1957-58, Las Virgenes Unified Sch. Dist., Calif., 1962-66, Timber Unified Sch. Dist., Thousand Oaks, Calif., 1966-72, Muroc Unified Sch. dist., Edwards, Calif., 1972-78; store owner Margie Lawson's Gourmet Ctr., Lancaster, Calif., 1978—; tour leader Royal Cruise Line voyages, 1987-92; speaker various local clubs, TV sta., Lancaster and Palmdale, Calif., 1977—. Contbr. newspaper articles to Antelope Valley Press, 1975—, also photojournalist; pub. travel writer. Candidate Lancaster (Calif.) City Coun., 1977, Antelope Valley Hosp. Bd., 1982; pres. College Terrace Park Condo Assn., 1987-92; founder, chmn., judge Curtain Call, 1989—; judge Gourmet Products Show, 1992—; patron to 4 local theatrical groups, 1986—. Mem. AAUW, Mensa, Intertel, Am. Booksellers Assn., Asst. League Antelope Valley, Desert Amigas-Domestic Violence (affiliate), Alpha Charter Guild. Republican. Avocations: cruising, world travel, photography, theater, tournament poker. Home: 2849 W Avenue J4 Lancaster CA 93536-6016 Office: Margie Lawson's Gourmet Ctr 906 W Lancaster Blvd Lancaster CA 93534-2306

LAWSON, THOMAS CHENEY, fraud examiner; b. Pasadena, Calif., Sept. 21, 1955; s. William McDonald and Joan Bell (Jaffee) L.; m. Susan Sullivan; children: Christopher, Brittany. Student, Calif. State U., Sacramento, 1973-77. Cert. internat. investigator, fraud examiner. Pres. Tomatron Co., Pasadena, 1970-88, Tom's Tune Up & Detail, Pasadena, 1971-88, Tom's Pool Svc., Sacramento, 1975-78, Tom Supply Co., 1975—; mgmt. trainee Permoid Process Co., L.A., 1970-75; prof. automechanics Calif. State U., Sacramento, 1973-75; regional sales cons. Hoover Co., Burlingame, 1974-76; mktg. exec. River City Prodns., Sacramento, 1977-78; territorial rep. Globe div. Burlington House Furniture Co., 1978; So. Calif. territorial rep. Marge Carson Furniture, Inc., 1978-80; pres. Ted L. Gunderson & Assos., Inc., Westwood, Calif., 1980-81; pres., CEO Apscreen, Newport Beach, Calif., 1980—; founder Crditbase Co., Newport Beach, Calif., 1980-89, Worldata Corp., Newport Beach, 1980-89, Trademark Enforcement Corp., L.A., 1985-86; pres. Carecheck, Inc., Newport Beach, 1990—, CEO Badchex, Inc., Newport Beach, 1992—. Mem. Editl. Rev. bd. The White Paper, Jour. Assn. Cert. Fraud Examiners. Calif. Rehab. scholar, 1974-77. Mem. Christian Businessmen's Com. Internat., Coun. Internat. Investigators, Am. Soc. Indsl. Security (cert., chmn. Orange County chpt. 1990), Nat. Pub. Records Rsch. Assn., Pers. and Indsl. Rels. Assn., World Assn. Detectives, Assn. Cert. Fraud Examiners (editl. rev. bd. 1995—), Soc. Human Resource Mgmt. Office: 2043 Westcliff Dr Ste 300 Newport Beach CA 92660-5511

LAWTON, MICHAEL JAMES, entomologist, pest management specialist; b. Balt., Aug. 6, 1953; s. James William and Mary Eileen (O'Connor) L.; m. Barbara Ann Byron, Dec. 19, 1983. BS, U. Md., 1975. Cert. entomologist. Technician, tech. dir. Atlas Exterminating Co., Towson, Md., 1975-78; asst. tech. dir. Western Exterminator Co., Irvine, Calif., 1978-83, tng. and tech. dir., 1984-95, dir. sales and mktg., 1996, v.p. sales and mktg., 1997—. Democrat. Office: Western Exterminator Co 1732 Kaiser Ave Irvine CA 92614-5739

LAX, KATHLEEN THOMPSON, bankruptcy judge; b. 1945. BA, U. Kans., 1967; JD, U. Calif., L.A., 1980. Law clk. U.S. Bankruptcy Ct., L.A., 1980-82; assoc. Gibson, Dunn & Crutcher, L.A., 1982-88; judge ctrl. dist. U.S. Bankruptcy Ct., L.A., 1988—; bd. dirs. L.A. Bankruptcy Forum, 1988—; bd. govs. Fin. Lawyers Conf., L.A., 1991-92, 94—. Bd. editors: Calif. Bankruptcy Jour., 1988—. Office: US Bankruptcy Court 21041 Burbank Blvd Woodland Hills CA 91367-6606*

LAYCOCK, ANITA SIMON, psychotherapist; b. Cheyenne, Wyo., Dec. 17, 1940; d. James Robert and Dorothy (Dearmin) Simon; m. Maurice Percy Laycock, June 18, 1965(dec. 1976); 1 child, (dec.). BA, U. Wyo., 1962, MA, 1971. Lic. counselor, Wyo., nationally cert. addiction specialist. Grad. student counselor, psychometrist Wyo. State Prison, Rawlins, 1971-73; counselor, trainer Dept. of Insts. State of Colo., Denver, 1973-75; counselor, tchr. supr. Jefferson County Evaluation-Diagnostic Ctr., Rawlins, 1975-78; psychometrist Wyo. State Penitentiary, Rawlins, 1978-79; counselor, therapist Rocky Mountain Arts and Scis., Cheyenne, 1979-81; counselor, therapist supr., dir. SWARA, Rock Springs, Wyo., 1981-85; therapy dir. St. Joseph Residential Treatment, Torrington, Wyo., 1985-88; dir. psychiatric unit Nat. Med. Enterprises Hill-Haven-Pk. Manor, Rawlins, 1988-89; chief exc. officer Simon-Laycock & Assocs., Rawlins, 1989—; cons. Kids in Distressed Situations, Rawlins, 1990-91, Child Devel. Ctr., Rawlins, 1991—; dir. Pub. Offender and Forensic Mental Health Program, Rawlins, 1988-91. Author: (programs) related to sex offenders. Pres. Cheyenne City Panhellenic, 1965-68. Named Miss Wyo.-Miss Universe, 1960; named Miss Wool of Wyo., 1965. Mem. ACA, Nat. Sex Offenders Counselors, Nat. Assn. Drug and Alcohol Counselors, Pub. Offenders Counselors Assn., Western Corrections Assn., Wyo. Assn. Addiction Specialists (pres. 1988—). Avocations: profl. animal trainer, artist. Office: Simon Laycock & Assocs 1716 Old Yellowstone Rd # 124 Cheyenne WY 82009-9183

LAYDEN, FRANCIS PATRICK (FRANK LAYDEN), professional basketball team executive, former coach; b. Bklyn., Jan. 5, 1932; m. Barbara Layden; children: Scott, Michael, Katie. Student, Niagara U. High sch. basketball coach L.I., N.Y.; head coach, athletic dir. Adelphi-Suffolk Coll. (now Dowling Coll.); head basketball coach, athletic dir. Niagara U., Niagara Falls, N.Y., 1968-76; asst. coach Atlanta Hawks, 1976-79; gen. mgr. Utah Jazz, Salt Lake City, 1979-88, head coach, 1981-88, v.p. basketball ops., until 1988, pres., 1989—. Bd. dirs. Utah Soc. Prevention Blindness; bd. dirs. Utah chpt. Multiple Sclerosis Soc., Utah Spl. Olympics. Served to 1st lt. Signal Corps, AUS. Office: Utah Jazz Delta Ctr 301 W South Temple Salt Lake City UT 84101-1216

LAYE, JOHN E(DWARD), contingency planning and business continuity consulting executive; b. Santa Monica, Calif., May 26, 1933; s. Theodore Martin and Evelyn Rosalie (Young) L.; m. Jeanne Tutt Curry, Dec. 23, 1955; children: John Russell, Linda Helen. A.A., Los Angeles Community Coll., 1952; B.A., Naval Postgrad. Sch., 1967; M.S., U. So. Calif., 1975. Cert. emergency mgr. Cert. mgmt. cons. Inst. Mgmt. Cons. Enlisted U.S. Navy, 1951, advanced through grades to lt. comdr., 1965; naval aviator, project mgr., worldwide, 1955-75; ret., 1975; emergency services exec. Marin County, Calif., 1975-76, Solano County, Calif., 1976-82; cons., mng. ptnr. Contingency Mgmt. Cons. (formerly Applied Protection Systems), Moraga, Calif., 1982—; mem. faculty Emergency Mgmt. Inst., Nat. Emergency Tng. Ctr., Emmitsburg, Md., 1982—; mem. faculty U. Calif. Bus. and Mgmt. extenstion, 1993—; instr. George Washington U., 1998—. Dir. Emergency Preparedness Mgrs. Cert. Program, 1993—; pres. Calif. Emergency Services Assn., 1988; chpt. bd. dirs., lectr. internat. contingency planning and disaster recovery, 1976—. Decorated Air medal, Navy Commendation medal, Navy Achievement medal, Viet Nam cross of Gallantry; recipient commendation Gov.'s Office Emergency Svcs., State Fire Marshal, Calif. Emergency Svcs. Assn., City Orinda. Fellow Bus. Continuity Inst.; mem. Nat. Coordinating Council Emergency Mgmt. (chmn. bus. and industry com. 1992-95), Orinda Assn. (bd. dirs. 1988-90, pres. 1989, Vol. Yr. award 1991), U. So. Calif. Alumni (bd. dirs. 1980-87, pres. east bay club 1984), U. So. Calif. Inst. Safety and Systems Mgmt. Triumvirate (founding bd. mem.). Presbyterian. Office: Contingency Mgnt Cons 346 Rheem Blvd Ste 202 Moraga CA 94556-1588

LAYMAN, CHARLES DONALD, plastic surgeon; b. Portland, Mar. 20, 1949. MD, U Oreg. Health Scis. U., 1975. Plastic surgeon St. Vincent Med. Ctr., Portland; clin. assoc. prof. plastic surgery U. Oreg. Health Sci. Ctr. Office: 9155 SW Barnes Rd Ste 220 Portland OR 97225-6629

LAYTON, HARRY CHRISTOPHER, artist, lecturer, consultant; b. Safford, Ariz., Nov. 17, 1938; s. Christopher E. and Eurilda (Welker) L.; LHD, Sussex Coll., Eng., 1969; DFA (hon.), London Inst. Applied Research, 1972, DSc (hon), 1972; DD (hon.), St. Matthew U., Ohio, 1970, PhD (hon.), 1970; m. Karol Barbara Kendall, July 11, 1964 (div. Jan. 1989); children: Deborah, Christopher, Joseph, Elisabeth, Faith, Aaron, Gretchen, Benjamin, Justin, Matthew, Peter. Cert. clin. hypnotherapist. Pres. Poems, Art & Myths; pres., CEO Layton Studio Graphic Design; lectr. ancient art Serra Cath. High Sch., 1963-64, L.A. Dept. Parks and Recreation, summer 1962, 63, 64; interior decorator Cities of Hawthorne, Lawndale, Compton, Gardena and Torrance (Calif.), 1960-68; one-man shows paintings; Nahas Dept. Stores, 1962, 64; group shows include: Gt. Western Savs. & Loan, Lawndale, Calif., 1962, Gardena (Calif.) Adult Sch., 1965, Serra Cath. High Sch., Gardena, 1963, Salon de Nations Paris, 1983; represented in permanent collections: Sussex Coll., Eng., Gardena Masonic Lodge, Culver City-Foshey Masonic Lodge, Gt. Western Savs. & Loan; paintings include: The Fairy Princess, 1975, Nocturnal Covenant, 1963, Blindas Name, 1962, Creation, 1962. Elder Ch. of Jesus Christ of Latter-day Saints, Santa Monica, Calif., 1963—; mgr., Art, Poems & Myth; works pub. in Our World's Favorite Gold and Silver Poems, 1991, Our World's Favorite Poems, 1993, World's Best Poems, 1993, Outstanding Poets of 1994, Best Poems of 1995, others; appt. dep. dir. gen. IBC for the Ams., Cambridge, Eng., 1990. Editor's Choice award Nat. Libr. of Poetry, 1994, 95. Mem. Am. Hypnotherapy Assn., Nat. Notary Assn., Internat. Soc. Artists, Internat. Platform Assn., Am. Security Council, Soc. for Early Historic Archaeology, Am. Councilor's Soc. of Psychol. Counselors, Le Salon Des Nation Paris Geneva, Ctr. Internat. d'Art Contemporain, Internat. Soc. Poets (disting.), Internat. Masonic Poetry Soc., Am. Legion, Masons (32 deg.), Shriners, K.T., Alpha Psi Omega. Republican. Home and Office: Layton Studio Graphic Design Inc 3654 Centinela Ave Apt 10 Los Angeles CA 90066-3147

LAYTON, MARILYN SMITH, English language educator; b. Des Moines, Nov. 29, 1941; d. Sam Solomon and Mollie (Leiserowitz) Hockenberg; m. Charles Kent Smith, July 1, 1962 (div. Nov. 1974); children: Laurence Joseph, Eleanor Gwen; m. Richard Howard Layton, Dec. 14, 1975. BA, Northwestern U., 1963; MA, U. Mich., 1964; postgrad., U. Wash., 1972-74. Instr. part time English and humanities North Seattle Community Coll., 1969-74, tenured instr., 1975—; lectr., cons. on pedagogy. Author: (with others) Let Me Hear Your Voice, 1983 (Gov.'s Writers' award 1984), (with H. Collins) Intercultural Journeys Through Reading and Writing, 1991, Choosing to Emerge As Readers and Writers, 1993; mem. editorial bd. Jour. Basic Writing, 1986-89, Teaching English in the Two-Yr. Coll., 1987-90; contbr. articles to profl. jours. Mem. Conf. on Coll. Composition and Communication (mem. exec. com. 1983-86, editorial bd. 1987-90), Nat. Coun. Tchrs. English (chmn. nat. two-yr. coll. coun. 1985-86), Pacific N.W. Conf. on English in the Two-Yr. Coll. (chmn., 1982-83), Wash. C.C. Humanities Assn. Avocations: photography, nature, beading, painting on silk with dyes and on canvas with oils, travel. Office: North Seattle Community Coll Dept Humanities 9600 College Way N Seattle WA 98103-3514

LAZAR, JOHN EDWARD, administrator non-profit organization; b. Bklyn., Mar. 24, 1950; s. John and Elizabeth (Titch) L. BA, St. John's U., Bklyn., 1971; postgrad., Bklyn. Coll., 1972-73; MDiv, Sem. of Immaculate Conception, 1980. Cert. tchr., N.Y.; ordained clergyman Roman Cath. Ch. 1980. English tchr. N.Y.C. Bd. Edn., Bklyn., 1973-79; clergyman Roman Cath. Diocese of Bklyn., 1980-93; pres. POMOC, Inc., N.Y.C., 1981-84; dir. housing Argus Cmty., Inc., Bronx, N.Y., 1993-96; devel. cons. Met. Cmty. Ch., L.A., 1997—; exec. dir. San Fernando Valley Am. Cancer Soc., Sherman Oaks, Calif., 1998—; exec. dir. Peregrinatio Ad Petri Sedem-U.S. Office of Pilgrimages, Vatican City, 1985-86. Author: Outpouring the Spirit: Gay and Lesbian Spirituality in the Judeo Christian Tradition, 1996; TV show host Polish Profiles, 1989-93. Commr. City of West Hollywood (Calif.) Lesbian and Gay Adv. Bd., 1998—; bd. dirs. City Vol. Corps., N.Y.C, 1990-96, Stonewall Dem. Club, L.A., 1997—; v.p. Polish Am. Congress, N.Y.c., 1989-93; co-prodr. civic celebration Bklyn. Outdoor Mus. of Art, 1993; mem. com. Mayor's Planning Com. L.A. Vol. Festival, 1998; chmn. N.Y.C. Comptr.'s Polish Adv. Com., 1982-89, 94-96. Named Hon. Alumnus, Our Lady of the Lake Sem., 1982; recipient Pres.'s award Stonewall Dem. Club, 1998, Commendation award N.Y.C. Comptr., 1995, Citizen of Yr. award Polish Am. World, 1982. Mem. Polish Inst. Arts and Scis. in Am., Inc., So. Calif. Assn. Non Profit Housing, Inc. Democrat. Avocations: bicycling, reading, prestidigitation, downhill skiing. E-mail: johnweho@ix.netcom.com. Home: 1351 N Curson Ave Ph 1 Los Angeles CA 90046-4092 Office: Am Cancer Soc 4940 Van Nuys Blvd Ste 301 Sherman Oaks CA 91403-1742

LAZAREVICH, EMIL ROBERT, sculptor; b. San Francisco, Apr. 11, 1910; s. Zsivko and Hermine (Lyall) L.; m. Jean E. Kane, Feb. 26, 1938 (dec. July 1962); 1 dau., Ann Jean (Mrs. Harold A. Papazian); m. Virginia Owens Sciaroni, June 28, 1974 (div. Sept. 1979). Student, U. Calif., Berkeley, 1927-29, U. San Francisco, 1935-37. One-man shows, Santa Barbara (Calif.) Mus. Art, 1945, 49, 69, M.H. de Young Meml. Mus., San Francisco, 1946, Jepson Art Inst., Los Angeles, 1949, Ankrum Gallery, Los Angeles, 1961, 63, 66, Ventura (Calif.) Coll., 1970, 82, Santa Barbara City Coll., 1978, Carnegie Cultural Arts Ctr., Oxnard, Calif., 1984, Ankrum Gallery, 1987; exhibited in numerous group shows, including, Palace Legion of Honor, San Francisco, 1960, Long Beach (Calif.) Mus. Art, 1962, La Jolla (Calif.) Art Center, 1962, Cedars-Sinai Fellowship Council, Los Angeles, 1963, Fullerton (Calif.) Jr. Coll., 1964, Fullerton Art League, 1966, Esther Bear Gallery, Santa Barbara, 1966, 67, 68, 69, 70, 71, 74, Ann. Internat. Exhbn. Miniature Art, Toronto, 1994, N.Am. Sculpture Exhbn., Golden, Colo., 1994; represented in permanent collections, Crocker Art Gallery, Sacramento, Denver Mus. Art, Hirshhorn Mus. and Sculpture Garden at Smithsonian Instn., Washington, San Francisco Art, also numerous pvt. collections. (Recipient award Santa Barbara Mus. Art 1944, Am. Sculpture, Met. Mus. Art 1951, Sacramento State Fair 1954, 58, purchase awards San Francisco Art Commn. 1955, San Francisco Art Commn. 1958). Home: 57 N San Marcos Rd # B Santa Barbara CA 93111-1961

LAZARUS, FRANCIS MARTIN, academic administrator; b. Elma, N.Y., Dec. 29, 1944; s. Edward Alois and Olivia Anne (Peters) L.; m. Carol Mary Scheminger, June 29, 1968; children: Catherine M., Julie A., James E. AB, Canisius Coll., 1966; MA, Cornell U., 1968, PhD, 1973. Asst. prof. English U.S. Mil. Acad., West Point, N.Y., 1970-73; asst. prof. Classics Salem Coll., Winston-Salem, N.C., 1973-78; adminstrv. fellow Memphis State U., 1978-79; assoc. acad. dean Salem Coll., Winston-Salem, 1979-80; dean Coll. Arts and Scis. U. Dayton, Ohio, 1980-88; v.p. acad. affairs Marquette U., Milw., 1988-96; v.p., provost U. San Diego, 1996—; chair acad. consortium Gt. Midwest Conf., Chgo., 1992-95. Editor: Faith, Discovery, Service, 1991. Bd. trustees Youth Leadership Acad., Milw., 1993-96. Capt. U.S. Army, 1970-73. Recipient Pres.'s award Wis. Dental Assn., 1994; named Outstanding Young Man Am. U.S. C. of C., 1973. Mem. Am. Coun. Edn. (fellow 1978), Am. Philol. Assn., Classical Soc. Am. Acad. in Rome, Vergilian Soc., Assn. Cath. Colls. and Univs. Avocation: fishing. Office: U San Diego 5998 Alcala Park San Diego CA 92110-2429

LAZORKO, CATHERINE, municipal officer; b. Phila., Aug. 23, 1964; d. Anthony and Marge (Biddle) L.; m. David Brower, May 21, 1995; children: Naveed, Shaan, Nicholas, Benjamin. BA, U. Tex., El Paso, 1986; MA, N.Mex. State U., 1995. Reporter Abilene (Tex.) Reporter-News, 1986-87, El Paso Times, 1988-91; editor, newswriter N.Mex. State U., Las Cruces, 1991-98, coll. instr., 1996-97; pub. info. officer City of Las Cruces, 1998—. Contbr. articles to mags. and newspapers. Publicity coord. Border Book Festival, Las Cruces, 1997. Recipient various awards N.Mex. Press Women, 1991, award for journalistic excellence Soc. Intercoll. Press Assn., 1985, others. Mem. Las Cruces Press Women (v.p.), So. N.Mex. Press Club (awards of excellence 1994, 95, 96), Mesilla Valley Track Club, Las Cruces Soc. Friends. Quaker. Office: City of Las Cruces Las Cruces NM 88004

LAZZI, GIANLUCA, electronics engineer, researcher; b. Rome, Apr. 25, 1970; s. Romano and Annamaria (Pastore) L. D in Electronics Engring., U. La Sapienza, Rome, 1994; PhD in Elec. Engring., U. Utah, 1998. Registered profl. engr., Rome. Vis. rschr. Nat. Italian Bd. for Nuc. and Alternative Energies, Rome, 1994-95; sci. collaborator U. La Sapienza, Rome, 1994-95; rsch. assoc. U. Utah, Salt Lake City, 1995-98, rsch. asst. prof., 1998—; cons. BCD Sistemi, Rome, 1993-94. Co-author: software packages for the Italian Nat. TV Network, 1988; contbr. articles to profl. jours. Recipient Young Scientist award Internat. Union Radio Sci., 1996, Curtis Carl Johnson Meml. award Bioelectromagnetics Soc., 1996. Mem. IEEE, Italian Elec. and Electronic Soc. Office: Univ Utah Dept of Elec Engr 3280 Merrill Engring Bldg Salt Lake City UT 84112

LE, DIANA LYNN, county worker; b. Leon, Iowa, Mar. 21, 1956; d. Charles Edward Watt Sr. and Nora Eunice (Dickerson) W.; m. Hang Le; 1 child, Brian Trung. BSW, Graceland Coll., 1980; student, U. Kans., 1981-83. Social work intern St. Michael's (Ariz.) Sch., 1979, Father Benedict Justice Sch. and Seton Ctr., Kansas City, Mo., 1980, Mattie Rhodes Ctr., Kansas City, Mo., 1982-83; child care worker Gillis Home for Boys, Kansas City, 1980-84; community work experience program worker Social and Rehab. Svcs. State of Kans., Kansas City, 1983-84; contractual assignee Reorganized Ch. of Jesus Christ of Latter-day Saints, San Jose, Calif., 1984-87; counselor II summer youth NOVA/Summer Youth Employment Program, 1987; ESL instr. Wilson Adult Edn. Ctr., 1987-88, Overfelt Adult Edn. Ctr., 1987-98; eligibility worker II East Valley Social Svcs., Santa Clara County, Calif., 1992-94; family support officer Dist. Atty.'s Office Santa Clara County, 1994—. Counselor in tng. for camps and Bible schs. Reorganized Ch. Jesus Christ Latter-day Saints, Iowa, 1969-73, counselor children's camp, San Jose, 1985, mem. ethnic community program com., East San Jose, 1984-87. Honored for Community Outreach in Ethnic Ministries, Reorganized Ch. Jesus Christ Latter-day Saints, 1985-87. Club: Intercultural (Lamoni, Iowa) (activity chmn. 1977-79). Avocations: sewing, crafts, reading, biking.

LE, HUNG DUC, pediatrician; b. Saigon, Vietnam, June 24, 1948; s. Hue Q. and Tuyet T. (Trinh) L.; m. Tu B Le, Mar. 30, 1973; children: Linh M., Lan M., Minh D. MD, Univ. Saigon, 1974. Diplomate Am. Bd. Pediatrics. Medical officer W.W. Hastings Indian Hosp, Tahlequah, Okla., 1978-91, Phoenix Indian Medical Ctr., 1991—. Recipient Physician's Recognition award Am. Medical Assn., 1997-2000, Superior Svc. award Dept. Health & Human Svcs., 1991. Fellow Am. Acad Pediatrics (Prep Edn. award 1994-

96). Home: 4749 E Hearn Rd Phoenix AZ 85032-5568 Office: Phoenix Indian Med Ctr 4212 N 16th St Phoenix AZ 85016 5319

LE, KHANH TUONG, utility executive; b. Saigon, Vietnam, Feb. 25, 1936; parents Huy Bich and Thi Hop; m. Thi Thi Nguyen, Apr. 22, 1961; children: Tuong-Khanh, Tuong-Vi, Khang, Tuong-Van. BS in Mech. Engring., U. Montreal, 1960, MS in Mech. Engring., 1961. Cert. profl. engr. Project mgr. Saigon Met. Water Project Ministry Pub. Works, Saigon, 1961-66; dep. dir. gen. Cen. Logistics Agy. Prime Min. Office, Saigon, 1966-70; asst. dir., chief auditor Nat. Water Supply Agy. Min. Pub. Works, Saigon, 1970-75; mgr. Willows Water Dist., Englewood, Colo., 1975—; dean sch. mgmt. scis., asst. chancellor acad. affairs Hoa-Hao U., Long-Xuyen, Vietnam, 1973-75; chmn. bd. dirs. Asian Pacific Devel. Ctr., 1994-96. Treas. Met. Denver Water Authority, 1989-92; mem. Douglas County Water Authority, 1993—; mem. Front Range Water Forum presided over by Gov. Roy Romer, Colo., 1993—; vol. Water for People, 1994—; mem. bus. adv. com. C.C. of Denver. Recipient Merit medal Pres. Republic Vietnam, 1966, Pub. Health Svc. medal, 1972, Edn. Svc. 1st class medal, 1974, Pub. Works 1st class medal, 1972, Rural Reconstrn. 1st class medal, 1973, Svc. award Asian Edn. Adv. Coun., 1989; co-recipient Engring. Excellence award Am. Cons. Engrs Coun., 1994; named to Top Ten Pub. Works Leaders in Colo., Am. Pub. Works Assn., 1990. Mem. Am. Water Works Assn., Water Environ. Fedn., Colo. Water Congress, Asian C. of C. (bd. dirs. 1993-97), Vietnamese Profl. Engrs. Soc. (founder), Amnesty Inter nat., Friendship Bridge, Asian Culture Inst., Am. Water Resources Assn. (dir.-at-large). Buddhist. Avocations: reading, swimming, tennis, hiking. Office: Willows Water Dist 6970 S Holly Cir Ste 200 Englewood CO 80112-1066

LE, NGUYEN MINH, computer company executive; b. Dong Thap, Vietnam, Mar. 22, 1952; came to U.S., 1975; s. Vinh Phat Le and Banh Thi Nguyen; m. Nuong Thi Liet Huynh, 1973; children: Dan, Long. MS in Tech. Mgmt., Pepperdine U., Malibu, Calif., 1996. Painter Dallas Apartments, 1976-77; machinist N.W. Industries, Oklahoma City, 1978-79; auto mechanic Harbor Auto Sales, Long Beach, Calif., 1980-81; operator L.A. County Sanitation Dist., Carson, 1981-84; pres. Dan Long Landscape, Long Beach, 1982-85, Dolphin Microcomputer Corp., Long Beach, 1985—; chmn. Tinvi Computers, Vietnam, 1991—. Mem. Rep. Senatorial Trust, Washington, 1992—, Bus. Execs. for Nat. Security, 1997—, Progressive Nat. Movement, Saigon, 1969-75, Tan Dai Viet Party, Vietnam, 1969—; pres. Nguyen Ngoc Huy Found., Long Beach, 1991—. Buddhist. Avocations: hiking, swimming, reading. Home: 6466 E Bixby Hill Rd Long Beach CA 90815-4709 Office: Dolphin Microcomputer Corp 1234 E South St Long Beach CA 90805-4321

LEA, SCHMIDT-ROGERS, music educator, musician; b. Louisville, Ky., Sept. 18, 1947; d. Chester A. and June Elizabeth (Long) S.; m. Larry Edward Rogers, May 28, 1976. BS, Ind. U., 1969; MM, U. Hawaii, 1971. Staff pianist U. Hawaii, Honolulu, 1971-72; contract pianist Honolulu Symphony, 1971-76; organist Foothills United Meth. Ch., La Mesa, Calif., 1988—; adj. prof. Southwestern Coll., Chula Vista, Calif., 1987—; lectr. Internat. Coll. Music Soc. Conf., Berlin, 1995; artist in residence San Diego City Schs., 1983. Editor: (four hand piece by Marie Jakll) Valses a quatre mains, 1995, Sonate, 1996; contbr. to anthology. Chmn. H.B. Goodlin Found., San Diego, 1997—. Scholar Indpls. Music Club, 1967; recipient Emily Orr Clifford award Ind. Musician's Assn., 1965. Mem. Am. Guild Organists (bd. dirs. San Diego br. 1992-94), Spreckels Organ Soc. (bd. dirs. 1994-96), Music Tchrs.' Assn. Calif. (pres. San Diego br. 1995-97, bd. dirs. 1993—), Coll. MusicSoc. (lectr. 1995). Avocations: golf, bicycling, reading. Fax: (619) 670-4012. E-mail: pianoL@inetworld.net. Home: 4383 Kansas St Apt 8 San Diego CA 92104-1249 Office: Southwestern Coll 900 Otay Lakes Rd Chula Vista CA 91910-7223

LEACH, JOHN F., newspaper editor, journalism educator; b. Montrose, Colo., Aug. 6, 1952; s. Darrell Willis and Marian Ruth (Hester) L.; m. Deborah C. Ross, Jan. 2, 1982; children: Allison, Jason. BS in Journalism, U. Colo., 1974, MA in Journalism, 1979; MA in Am. Studies, U. Sussex, Falmer, Brighton, Eng., 1983. News reporter Boulder (Colo.) Daily Camera, 1974-79; news reporter The Ariz. Republic, Phoenix, 1979-85, asst. city editor, 1985-93; news editor The Phoenix Gazette, 1993-94; asst. mng. editor Phoenix Gazette, 1994-95, The Ariz. Republic and The Phoenix Gazette, 1995-97; sr. editor The Ariz. Republic, Phoenix, 1997—; faculty assoc. Ariz. State U., Tempe, 1990—; pres., dir. Best of the West, Phoenix. Bd. Regents scholar U. Colo., 1970, Rotary Found. scholar, 1982. Mem. Ariz. Press Club (treas. 1984-86, pres. 1986-87), Soc. Profl. Journalists, Reporter's Com. for Freedom of Press, Soc. News Design, Investigative Reporters and Editors. Home: 4313 E Calle Redonda Phoenix AZ 85018-3733 Office: The Ariz Republic 200 E Van Buren St Phoenix AZ 85004-2238

LEACH, RICHARD MAXWELL, JR. (MAX LEACH, JR.), corporate professional; b. Chillicothe, Tex., June 14, 1934; s. Richard Maxwell and Lelia Booth (Page) L.; m. Wanda Gail Groves, Feb. 4, 1956; children: Richard Clifton, John Christopher, Sandra Gail, Kathy Lynn. BS in Acctg. magna cum laude, Abilene Christian U., 1955. Registered Fin. Planner., CLU. Asst. dir. agys. Am. Founders Ins. Co., Austin, Tex., 1960-62; owner A.F. Ins. Planning Assocs., Temple, Tex., 1962-65; v.p. sales Christian Fidelity Life Ins. Co., Waxahachie, Tex., 1966-67; exec. v.p. Acad. Computer Tech., Inc., Dallas, 1968-69; pres., chief exec. officer Inta-Search Internat., Inc., Dallas, 1969-71; prin., chief exec. officer, fin. cons. Leach and Assocs., Albuquerque, 1971—; pres. The Wright Edge, Inc., 1988-90; pres., CEO Action Mktg. Programs, Inc., 1989-92; CEO Vacation Premiums Internat., Inc., 1990-92; pres., CEO ITM Corp., Albuquerque, 1993-98; founder, chmn., CEO Health Maximization Rsch. Studies Inst. Internat., Albuquerque, 1999—; chmn. bd. United Quest Inc., Albuquerque, Hosanna Inc., Albuquerque; real estate broker; commodity futures broker; exec. dir., bd. dirs. New Heart, Inc., Albuquerque, 1975-85; owner Insta-Copy, Albuquerque, 1973-76, Radio Sta. KYLE-FM, Temple, 1963-64. Editor, author Hosanna newspaper, 1973-74. Gen. dir. Here's Life, New Mexico, Albuquerque, 1976; exec. dir. Christians for Cambodia, Albuquerque, 1979-80. Served with U.S. Army, 1955-57. Home: 3308 June St NE Albuquerque NM 87111-5029 Office: 2801T Eubank Blvd NE # 150 Albuquerque NM 87112-1316

LEACH, SHAWNA, food service director; b. Lehi, Utah, July 9, 1949; d. Lloyd D. and Dawna Mae (Marrott) Boren; m. Micheal Merrell Wiley, Aug. 11, 1967 (div.); children: Shannon Espinoza, Cyndie Keetch Anderson, Michael Shane, Stacie Cooper; m. Calvin Donald Leach, Feb. 18, 1983. Cert. in dietary managing, Ctrl. Ariz. Coll., 1993. Mgr. cafeteria Provo (Utah) Sch. Dist., 1976-86; supply clk. Bur. of Reclamation, Page, Ariz., 1987-88; dir. food svc. Page Unified Sch. Dist., 1988—. Mem. Am. Sch. Food Svc. Assn. (dir., adminstr. I 1992—, instr. 1993—), Am. Sch. Bus. Officials, Ariz. Sch. Bus. Officials, Ariz. Sch. Food Svc. Assn. (chair certification 1992, state v.p. 1995-96, state pres. elect 1996-97, state pres. 1997-98), Dietary Mgrs. Assn., Page Recycles. Democrat. LDS. Avocations: gardening, crocheting, crewel embroidering. Home: PO Box 3618 Page AZ 86040-3618 Office: Page Unified Sch Dist PO Box 1927 Page AZ 86040-1927

LEADER, ALAN HOWARD, college dean emeritus; b. London, Nov. 4, 1927; came to U.S., 1930; s. Morris and Anne (Trachamofsky) L.; m. Louise Ann Bush, June 18, 1950; children: David, Jonathan. BS, U. Rochester, 1952, MS, 1960; DBA, Ind. U., 1963. Asst. purchasing agt. Taylor Instrument Cos., Rochester, N.Y., 1951-60; prof. mgmt. Western Mich. U., Kalamazoo, 1963-77; assoc. dir. Inst. Pub. Affairs, Kalamazoo, 1972-77; prof., dean Coll. Bus. and Pub. Administrn. U. Guam, Mangilao, 1978-85; dean Sch. of Bus. So. Conn. State U., New Haven, 1985-96, dean emeritus, 1996-98; lectr. Seattle U., 1996—; bd. dirs. Kalamazoo-Battle Creek Am. Soc. Tng. and Devel., Kalamazoo, 1975-77, G.U.A.M., Agana, Guam, 1980-82, So. Conn. Ctr. Joint Coun. on Econ. Edn., New Haven, 1986-96; ptnr. Leader Assocs., 1963—; pres. Pacific Area Rsch. Inst., Mangilao, 1979-85; chmn. mgmt. sci. and adminstr. sections Mich. Acad. Sci., Arts and Letters, 1973-77. Editor, dir. New Eng. Bus. Admin. Assn. Bus. Jour., 1987-96; contbr. articles on planning, mgmt. and edn. to profl. jours. Served with [illegible] 1981-85; [illegible] Guam Econ. Devel. Authority, Agana, 1979-82; bd. dirs. Guam Spl. Olympics, 1980-85; mem. Guam Press Club, 1982-85. With AUS, 1944-45. Predoctoral fellow, Ford Found., Ind. U., 1960, 61, 62; recipient Herman B Wells rsch. grant Ind. U., 1962-63; mem. research workshop, Ford Found., 1965, Order of the Chamorri, Govt. Guam, 1985. Mem. AAUP, Acad. of Mgmt., Am. Econs. Assn., Rotary. Avocations: cooking, photography. Home: 9043 Sand Point Way NE Seattle WA 98115-3953 Office: Leader Assocs 9043 Sand Point Way NE Seattle WA 98115-3953

LEAHY, T. LIAM, marketing and management consultant; b. Camp Legeunne, N.C., Apr. 15, 1952; s. Thomas James and Margaret May (Munnelly) L.; m. Shannon Kelly Brooks, Apr. 21, 1990. BS, St. Louis U., 1974, MA, 1975. V.p. sales Cablecom Inc., Chgo., 1976-80, Kaye Advt., N.Y.C., 1980-82; group pubr. Jour. Graphics Pub., N.Y.C., 1983-85; pres., gen. mgr. Generation Dynamics, N.Y.C., 1985-86; pres. Leahy & Assocs., N.Y.C., 1982-86, Tarzana, Calif., 1982—; assoc. Am Coun. of Execs. Assoc., Glendale, 1991-95; bd. dirs. Cons. Assn.; dir. RBAC, 1998—. Contbr. articles to profl. jours. Fellow Success Mgmt. Ctrs. (sr.); mem. Turnaround Mgmt. Assn., L.A. C. of C. Avocations: music, film. Office: Leahy & Assocs 19131 Enadia Way Reseda CA 91335-3828

LEAKE, BRENDA GAIL, enterostomal therapist nurse practitioner; b. Harriman, Tenn., Aug. 5, 1950; d. James Frank and Pauline Ruby (McGuffey) Judd; m. Lee Leake, Aug. 1, 1970 (div. Apr. 1974). AS in Nursing, U. Nev., Las Vegas, 1971, BN, 1986; cert. enterostomal therapist, U. Calif., San Diego, 1975. RN, Nev.; cert. enterostomal therapist, urol. nurse. Staff nurse Humana Hosp. Sunrise, Las Vegas, 1971-73, relief charge nurse, 1973-76, enterostomal therapist, 1976—; speaker Hospice Vol. program, Las Vegas, 1982—, I Can Cope program, Las Vegas, 1984—. Author instructional guide. Vol. Am. Cancer Soc., 1983—, mem. program devel. nurse edn. com. Mem. Internat. Assn. Enterostomal Therapists (cert.), Nat. Assn. Pediatric Pseudobstructure Soc., Am. Nurses Assn., So. Nev. Nurses Assn., World Council Enterostomal Therapists, Am. Urol. Assn. (cert.), So. Nev. Ostomy Assn. (med. advisor 1976—), Crohns & Colitis Assn., Advanced Practitioners Nursing (cert., program chmn. 1986—), Wound Healing Soc., Internat. Assn. Bowel Disfunction, Tourette Syndrome Assn., Inc., Am. Soc. Adults Pseudo Obstruction, Inc., Assn. Advancement of Wound Care, Lupus Found. Republican. Presbyterian. Avocations: hiking, gardening, traveling. Office: Sunrise Hosp 3186 S Maryland Pkwy Las Vegas NV 89109-2306

LEAL, GEORGE D., engineering company executive; b. 1934. B in Civil Engring., MA, Santa Clara U., 1959. With Dames & Moore, Inc., L.A., 1959—, CEO, 1981—, now CEO, pres.; bd. dirs. BW/IP Internat. Inc. Office: Dames & Moore Inc 911 Wilshire Blvd Ste 700 Los Angeles CA 90017*

LEAL, STEVE, city council; married. BA in Polit. Sci., U. Calif. Property mgmt. and devel., 1985—; adminstrv. specialist Pima County, 1993—; city coun., 1989—; cmty. svc. Salvation Army Hospitality House, Tucson-Pima County Hist. Commn., Citizens Adv. Commn. Democrat. Office: 4300 S Park Ave Tucson AZ 85714-1652*

LEALE, OLIVIA MASON, import marketing company executive; b. Boston, May 5, 1944; d. William Mason and Jane Chapin (Prouty) Smith; m. Euan Harvie-Watt, Mar. II, 1967 (div. Aug. 1979); children: Katrina, Jennifer; m. Douglas Marshall Leale, Aug. 29, 1980. BA, Vassar Coll., 1966. Cert. paralegal, beginning yoga instr. Sec. to dir. Met. Opera Guild, N.Y.C., 1966; sec. to pres. Friesons Printers, London, 1974-75; guide, trainer Autoguide, London, 1977-79; ptnr. Inmark Internat. Mktg. Inc., Seattle, 1980—. Social case worker Inner London Ednl. Authority, 1975-76. Democrat. Presbyterian. Avocations: reading, making doll house furniture, painting, knitting, Yoga. Home and Office: 1233 Shenandoah Dr E Seattle WA 98112-3727

LEALI, SHIRLEY ANN, mathematician, educator; b. Adel, Ga.; d. Rufus and Georgia R. (Hall) W.; m. Robert M. Leali Jr., June 18, 1971. BA, U. Denver, 1973; MA, U. Colo., Denver, 1984; PhD, U. Denver, 1992. Instr., adminstr. Denver Pub. Schs., 1974-93; assoc. prof. math. Weber State U., Ogden, Utah, 1993—, U. No. Colo., Greeley, Colo., 1995-96; cons. Ogden Sch. Dist., 1994—; nat. gender equity expert. Contbr. articles to profl. jours. Bd. dirs. State of Utah Black Adv. Coun., 1997. Ednl. Tech. Initiative grantee Weber State U., 1994, Thiokol, 1994. Fellow Nat. Coun. Tchrs. of Math.; mem. Assn. Math. Tchr. Educators, Internat. Study Group on Ethnomath., Utah Sci. Tchrs. Assn. Achievements include work and recognition for advancing gender equity and awareness. Avocation: playing classical guitar. Home: 4566 Monroe Blvd Ogden UT 84403-3022 Office: Weber State U Ogden UT 84403

LEAPHART, W. WILLIAM, state supreme court justice; b. Butte, Mont., Dec. 3, 1946; s. Charles William and Cornelia (Murphy) L.; m. Barbara Berg, Dec. 30, 1977; children: Rebecca, Retta, Ada. Student, Whitman Coll., 1965-66; BA, U. Mont., 1969, JD, 1972. Bar: Mont. 1972, U.S. Dist. Ct., U.S. Ct. Appeals (9th cir.) 1975, U.S. Supreme Ct. Law clk. to Hon. W.D. Murray U.S. Dist. Ct., Butte, 1972-74; ptnr. Leaphart Law Firm, Helena, Mont., 1974-94; justice Mont. Supreme Ct., Helena, 1995—. Home: 510 Dearborn Ave Helena MT 59601-2761 Office: Mont Supreme Ct Justice Bldg 215 N Sanders StRoom 315 Helena MT 59620*

LEARY, G. EDWARD, state finance commisioner; m. Betty Chamberlain; 5 children. BS in Polit. Sci., U. Utah, 1971, MBA, 1981. Cert. Internat. Rels. With collections and lending dept. Draper Bank and Trust, 1974-77; examiner Utah Dept. Fin. Instns., Salt Lake City, 1977-82, industry supr., 1982-87, chief examiner, 1987-92, commr., 1992—; chmn. Bd. Fin. Instns.; mem. Utah Housing Fin. Agy. Bd., Utah Appraiser Registration and Cert. Bd. With USN, 1971-73. Capt. USNR, ret. 1995. Mem. Conf. State Bank Supr. (chmn.-elect). Office: Utah Dept Fin Instns PO Box 89 Salt Lake City UT 84110-0089

LEASE, JANE ETTA, environmental science consultant, retired librarian; b. Kansas City, Kans., Apr. 10, 1924; d. Joy Alva and Emma (Jaggard) Omer; B.S. in Home Econs., U. Ariz., 1957; M.S. in Edn., Ind. U., 1962; M.S. in L.S., U. Denver, 1967; m. Richard J. Lease, Jan. 16, 1960; children—Janet (Mrs. Jacky B. Radifera), Joyce (Mrs. Robert J. Carson), Julia (Mrs. Earle D. Marvin), Cathy (Mrs. Edward F. Warren); stepchildren—Richard Jay II, William Harley. Newspaper reporter Ariz. Daily Star, Tucson, 1937-39; asst. home agt. Dept. Agr., 1957; homemaking tchr., Ft. Huachuca, Ariz., 1957-60; head tchr. Stonebelt Council Retarded Children, Bloomington, Ind., 1960-61; reference clk. Ariz. State U. Library, 1964-66; edn. and psychology librarian N.Mex. State U., 1967-71; Amway distbr., 1973—; cons. solid wastes, distressed land problems reference remedies, 1967; ecology lit. research and cons., 1966—. Ind. observer 1st World Conf. Human Environment, 1972; mem. Las Cruces Community Devel. Priorities Adv. Bd. Mem. ALA, Regional Environ. Edn. Research Info. Orgn., NAFE, P.E.O., D.A.R., Internat. Platform Assn., Las Cruces Antique Car Club, Las Cruces Story League, N.Mex. Library Assn. Methodist (lay leader). Address: 2145 Boise Dr Las Cruces NM 88001-5149

LEASE, RICHARD JAY, police science educator, former police officer; b. Cherokee, Ohio, Dec. 10, 1914; s. Harold and Mabelle (Fullerton) L.; m. Marjorie Faye Stoughton, Sept. 2, 1939 (div. Apr. 1957); children: Richard Jay II, William Harley; m. Jane Etta Omer, Jan. 16, 1960; stepchildren: Janet Radifera, Joyce Carson, Julia Marvin, Catherine Warren; adopted children: Alan Fudge, Stephen V. Graham. Student, Wittenberg U., 1932-33; BA, U. Ariz., 1937, MA, 1961; postgrad., Ind. U., 1950, 60, Ariz. State U., 1956, 63-65, 67—; grad., U. Louisville So. Police Inst., 1955. Grad. asst . U. Ariz., Tucson, 1937-38; with Tucson Police Dept., from 1938; advanced from patrolman to sgt., also served as safety officer Pima County Sheriff's Dept., Tucson, 1953, patrol supr., 1953-55, investigator, 1955-56; tchr. sci. pub. schs. Tucson, 1957-59; lectr. dept. police adminstrn. Ind. U., Bloomington, 1960-65; asst. prof. dept. police sci. N.Mex. State U., Las Cruces, 1965—; cons. law enforcement problems HEW, 1960, Indpls. Police Dept., 1962, Harrisburg Community Coll. Police Sci. Dept., 1967, Phoenix Police Dept., 1968—; advisor police tng. programs several small city police depts., Ind., 1960-63, Indpls., 1962; mem. oral bd. for selection chief in Bateville, Ind., 1962, oral bd. for selection sgts. and lts., Las Cruces Police Dept., 1966—. Author: (with Robert F. Borkenstein) Alcohol and Road Traffic: Problems of Enforcement and Prosecution, 1963, The Dreams, Hopes, Recollections and Thoughts of a Professional Good Samaritan; cons. editor Police, various rsch. publs. on chem. intoxification tests, psychol. errors of witnesses, reading disabilities, delinquency. Participant numerous FBI seminars; active youth work, philanthropy, among Am. Indians in Southwest; founder awards outstanding ROTC cadets N.Mex. State U., 1967—, founder Wiltberger ann. awards Nat. Police Combat Pistol Matches; scoutmaster Yucca council Boy Scouts Am., 1966—. Served to 1st lt. USMCR, 1942-45, PTO. Fellow Am. Acad. Forensic Scis. (sec. gen. sect.); mem. Internat. Assn. Chiefs of Police, Internat. Assn. Police Profs., Brit. Acad. Forensic Scis., Can. Soc. Forensic Sci., Am. Soc. Criminology, Ret. Officers Assn., Assn. U.S. Army (2d v.p. 1969—), NEA, N.Mex. Edn. Assn., N.Mex. Police and Sheriffs Assn., Internat. Crossroads, NRA (benefactor mem.), Marine Corps League (life), Sigma Chi. Lodges: Masons, Elks. Home and Office: 2145 Boise Dr Las Cruces NM 88001-5149

LEASH, R(USSELL) MORONI, medical crisis counselor; b. Sacramento, Calif., Sept. 2, 1958; s. Neil H. and Velma D. (Carraway) L.; m. Moneen Rochelle Rougier, Oct. 10, 1989 (div. Jan. 1997); children: Ryan Neil, Danielle Nicole. BA in Psychology, Calif. State U., Sacramento, 1984, MSW, 1986; MSc in Health Care Adminstrn., Calif. State U., Long Beach, 1988; PhD student, Brigham Young U., 1995—. Licensed clinical social worker, Calif. Psychotraumatologist U. Calif. Davis, Sacramento, 1986-89, psychiatric emergency counselor, 1989-90; case mgr. Sacramento (Calif.) County Mental Health, 1990-91; sch. counselor Del Paso Heights (Calif.) Sch. District, 1991; critical care intensive care couselor Kaiser Found. Hosps., Sacramento, 1991-98, alzhiemer's program counselor, 1998—; cons. Napa (Calif.) State Hosp., 1987-97, Harper Valley Med. Group, Sacramento, 1988-97. Author: Death Notification, 1995, Death Notification: Practical Guidelines for Health Care Professionals, 1996, The Sequential Death Notification Technique, 1997. Missionary LDS Ch., Thailand Bangkok Mission, 1977-79. Recipient Alumnus of Yr. award Calif. State U., Sacramento, 1997. Mem. Nat. Assn. Social Workers. Republican. Mem. LDS Ch. Avocations: spending time with my children, ranching, building, hiking, swimming. E-mail: Lifecare@sprynet.com. Home: PO Box 254441 Sacramento CA 95865-4441 Office: Kaiser Foundation Hospitals 2025 Morse Ave Sacramento CA 95825-2115

LEATON, MARCELLA KAY, insurance representative, business owner; b. Eugene, Oreg., Oct. 9, 1952; d. Robert A. and Wanda Jo (Garner) Boehm; m. Michael G. Schlegel, Aug. 9, 1975; children: Kaellen June, Krystalynn Michele. Grad. high sch., Springfield, Oreg. Sales rep. The Prudential, Novato, Calif., 1973—; bus. owner Marcella Enterprises, Novato, 1983—; owner, operator Meetings Extraordinaire, 1987—; owner Mastermind Escapes, 1990—; ind. travel agt., 1995—. Contbr. articles, poetry to profl. pubs. Mem. Nat. Assn. Life Underwriters (nat. quality award 1978, 80, 84), Marin Life Underwriters, Nat. Assn. Profl. Saleswomen (founder Marin chpt., pres. 1982-85, 91-93, chmn. 1985-87, nat. v.p. 1985-86, awards and recognition chmn. 1985-88, nat. pres. 1987-90, exec. dir. 1988-91, regional v.p. 1991-92, N.W. region conf. chmn. 1993), Leading Life Producers No. Calif., Million Dollar Round Table (qualifying), Marin Rowing Assn. (travel chmn. 1992-93), President's Club, Western Star Club, Headers Club. Fax: 415-897-5347. Office: Marcella Enterprises 1929 Benton Ln Novato CA 94945-1747

LEAVITT, JEROME EDWARD, childhood educator; b. Verona, N.J., Aug. 1, 1916; s. Thomas Edward and Clara Marie (Sonn) L.; m. Florence Elizabeth Wilkins, Aug. 23, 1963. *Jerry Leavitt, BS 1938 Iowa State College, MA 1942 NYU, EdD Northwestern 1952, hasn't lost contact with the needs and interests of young children. In his retirement, he continues to write books for young children. He and his wife Florence E. (Wilkins) Leavitt live in Tucson, Arizona, the place they decided to retire in many years ago. This is where they use as headquarters for their writing and as a base for the cruises that they take each year.* B.S., Newark State Coll., 1938; M.A., N.Y. U., 1942; Ed.D., Northwestern U., 1952. Tchr. pub. schs. Roslyn Heights, N.Y., 1938-42; instr. Sperry Gyroscope, Bklyn., 1942-45; prin., supr. pub. schs. Los Alamos, N.Mex., 1945-49; prof. edn., exec. asst. to dean Portland (Oreg.) State U., 1952-66; prof. edn. U. Ariz., Tucson, 1966-69; prof. elem. edn., coordinator Child Abuse Project, Calif. State U., Fresno, 1969-81; pres. Jerome Leavitt, Inc., 1981—. Author: Nursery-Kindergarten Edn., 1958, Carpentry for Children, 1959, By Land, By Sea, By Air, 1969, The Beginning Kindergarten Teacher, 1971, America and Its Indians, 1971, The Battered Child, 1974, Herbert Sonn: Yosemite's Birdman, 1975, Child Abuse and Neglect: Research and Innovation, 1983, others; contbr. articles to profl. jours. Mem. ASCD (life), NEA (life), Assn. Childhood Edn. Internat. (life), Soc.Profs. Edn., Calif. Tchrs. Assn., Profs. Curriculum, Phi Delta Kappa, Kappa Delta Pi, Epsilon Pi Tau. Home and Office: Villa Campana 6653 E Carondelet Dr Apt 124 Tucson AZ 85710-2138

LEAVITT, MICHAEL OKERLUND, governor, insurance executive; b. Cedar City, Utah, Feb. 11, 1951; s. Dixie and Anne (Okerlund) L.; m. Jacalyn Smith; children: Michael Smith, Taylor Smith, Anne Marie Smith, Chase Smith, Weston Smith. BA, So. Utah U., 1978. CPCU. Sales rep. Leavitt Group, Cedar City, 1972-74, account exec., 1974-76; mgr. underwriting Salt Lake City, 1976-82; chief operating officer, 1982-84, pres., chief exec. officer, 1984-92, gov., state of Utah, 1993—; bd. dirs. Pacificorp, Portland, Oreg., Utah Power and Light Co., Salt Lake City, Great Western Thrift and Loan, Salt Lake City. Utah Bd. Regents, chmn. instl. coun. So. Utah State U., Cedar City, 1985-89; campaign chmn. U.S. Sen. Orrin Hatch, 1982, 88, U.S. Sen. Jake Garn, 1980, 86; cons. campaign Gov. Norman Angerter, 1984; mem. staff Reagan-Bush '84. 2d lt. USNG, 1969-77. Named Disting. Alumni So. Utah State Coll. Sch. Bus., 1986. Mem. Chartered Property Casualty Underwriters. Republican. Mormon. Avocation: golf. Office: Office of the Governor 210 State Capitol Building Salt Lake City UT 84114-1202*

LEAVITT, MYRON E, judge. Justice Nev. Supreme Court, Carson City. Office: Supreme Ct Capitol Complex 201 S Carson St Carson City NV 89710*

LEAVY, EDWARD, judge; m. Eileen Leavy; children: Thomas, Patrick, Mary Kay, Paul. AB, U. Portland, 1950, LLB, U. Notre Dame, 1953. Dist. judge Lane County, Eugene, Oreg., 1957-61, cir. judge, 1961-76; magistrate U.S. Dist. Ct. Oreg., Portland, 1976-84, judge, 1984-87, cir. judge U.S. Ct. Appeals (9th cir.), 1987-97, sr. judge, 1997—. Office: US Ct Appeals Pioneer Courthouse 555 SW Yamhill St Ste 232 Portland OR 97204-1323*

LEBEAU, CHARLES PAUL, lawyer; b. Detroit, Dec. 11, 1944; s. Charles Henry Jr. and Mary Barbara (Moran) L.; m. Victoria Joy (Huchin), May 15, 1970; children: Jeffrey Kevin, Timothy Paul. AA, Macomb County Community Coll., Warren, Mich., 1967; BA, Wayne State U., 1969; JD, U. Detroit, 1972; grad. tax program, NYU Sch. Law, 1972-73. Bar: Mich. 1973, U.S. Tax Ct. 1973, Calif. 1987, U.S. Ct. Internat. Trade. 1988, U.S. Supreme Ct. 1988, U.S. Dist. Ct. (so. dist.) Calif. 1988. Tax atty. Ford Motor Co., Dearborn, Mich., 1973-75; assoc. Hoops & Huff, Detroit, 1975-76, Miller, Canfield, Paddock & Stone, Detroit, 1976-78; tax mgr. Oceaneering Internat., Santa Barbara, Calif., 1978-79; tax counsel Signal Cos. Inc., Beverly Hills and La Jolla, Calif., 1979-83; assoc. Gray, Cary, Ames & Frye, San Diego, 1983-84; of counsel James Watts Esq., La Jolla, 1985, Murfey, Griggs & Frederick, La Jolla, 1986; pvt. practice La Jolla and San Diego, 1987—; lectr. grad. tax program Golden Gate U., San Diego, 1979-87; adj. prof. law U. San Diego, 1982-85, 88-89; mem. Law Rev., U. Detroit, 1971-72; lectr. in taxation. Contbr. articles on internat. tax to profl. jours.; monthly tax case commentator Taxes Internat., London, 1981-85. Campaign coord. United Way, Santa Barbara, 1979. Mem. ABA, Mich. Bar Assn., Calif. Bar Assn., San Diego County Bar Assn., Pi Sigma Alpha. Republican. Roman Catholic. Avocations: sailing, tennis, walking. Home: 1999 Via Segovia La Jolla CA 92037-6441 Office: Law Offices Charles LeBeau Ste 1070 4660 La Jolla Village Dr San Diego CA 92122-4608 also: 400 Renaissance Ctr Ste 500 Detroit MI 48243

LEBER, MIKE, advertising executive. Chief fin. officer Alcone Mktg. Group, Irvine, Calif. Office: Alcone Mktg Co 15 Whatney Irvine CA 92618-2808*

LE BERTHON, ADAM, lawyer; b. L.A., June 12, 1962; s. Edward Lynch and Veronica Rose (Franks) Le B; m. Kelly Elizabeth McKee, Mar. 23, 1996; children: John Thomas. BA cum laude with dept. honors, U. San Diego, 1985; JD, U. So. Calif., L.A., 1989. Bar: Calif. 1989, U.S. Dist. Ct. (ctrl. dist.) Calif. 1989, U.S. Ct. Appeals (9th cir.) 1989, U.S. Dist. Ct. (so.

dist.) Calif. 1990, (no. dist.) Calif. 1990, (ea. dist.) Calif. 1990. Assoc. White & Case, L.A., 1989-91, Straw & Gilmartin, Santa Monica, Calif., 1991-97; ptnr. Gilmartin & Le Berthon LLP, Santa Monica, 1997-99; assoc. Arnold and Porter, L.A., 1999—. Editor So. Calif. Law Rev., 1988-89; contbr. articles to profl. jours. Recipient Am. Jurisprudence award U. So. Calif., 1987. Mem. Calif. State Bar Assn., Order of the Coif, Phi Alpha Delta, Omicron Delta Epsilon, Kappa Gamma Pi. Home: 125 Montana Ave Apt 207 Santa Monica CA 90403-1054 Office: Arnold & Porter 44th Fl 777 S Figueroa St Los Angeles CA 90017-4000

LEBLANC, LAUREEN ALISON, service company administrator; b. Santa Ana, Calif., Feb. 25, 1964; d. Thomas Albert and Kathleen Mary (Thompson) Cox; m. Mark J. LeBlanc, July 17, 1992; children: Katherine Morgan, (from a previous marriage) Robert Daniel, Alicia Michelle. Grad. high sch., Oakland Park, Fla., 1982. Horse trainer, mgr. various show horse stables, U.S. and Europe, 1975-84; office mgr. Land Title Ins. Co., Ft. Lauderdale, Fla., 1979-82; gen. mgr. Boca Travel Trailer Resort, Boca Raton, Fla., 1982-85; asst. mgr. credit Boca Raton Hotel and Country Club, 1985-90; credit and accounts receivable mgr. Callaway Gardens Resort, Pine Mountain, Ga., 1990-94; contr. Holiday Inn Denver Internat. Airport Hotel Trade & Conv. Ctr., 1994—. Mem. NAFE, Internat. Assn. Hospitality Accts., U.S. Dressage Assn., Nat. Assn. Credit Mgrs. Avocations: sailing, fishing, diving, racquetball, tennis.

LEBLANC, MICHELE MARIE, video production consultant, electrical engineer; b. San Francisco, Aug. 26, 1950; d. Charles Louis and Doris Mae (Marlowe) LeBlanc; children: Kimberly Marie, James Francisco, Michael Jonathan. Student, Deanza Coll., 1968-78, L.A. Valley Coll., 1981-82. Electro-mechanical technician Varian Assocs., Palo Alto, Calif., 1979-80; reliability engr. Systron Donner, Van Nuys, Calif., 1980-81; elec. technician Walt Disney Prodns., Glendale, Calif., 1981-82, tech. writer, 1982-83; field engr. Colortran, Inc., Burbank, Calif., 1984-85; tech. editor, cons. Comprehensive Designers, Culver City, Calif., 1985-86; field engr. Minisystems/Honeywell, City of Industry, Calif., 1986-87; sr. engr. Northrop, Inc., Hawthorne, Calif., 1987—; tech. publicist Iwerks Entertainment, Calif., 1995; pres. lighting, sound TV and films Stagelights Ltd., 1998-99; firm; under contract Select Entertainment/Universal Studios, 1997. Video editor (TV) L.A. Nightlife, 1985— (Emmy award 1986); field engr.: L.A. County Art Mus. Show/Anderson Wing, 1986, Olympics-Imax Theater, 1984; camerawoman, video editor (TV) L.A. Nightlife Show Phyllis Diller-Friars Club, 1986; guest spkr. Women's Interguild Caucus, Hollywood, Calif., 1987, Women in Film, Tech. Dir. Acad. Awards Night, Beverly Hills, 1990; tech. writer Walt Disney, 1994; tech. publicist Iwerks Entertainment, Burbank, 1995-96; engring. asst. Illusion, Inc., 1997. Guest speaker Women's Interguild Caucus, Hollywood, Calif., 1987. Named one of Firstline Women Suprs. Am. Mgmt. Assn., 1979. Mem. Behind the Lens (pres. 1988-89, asst. treas. 1987-88), Women in Film, Am. Film Inst., Nat. Forensic League. Office: Stagelights Ltd PO Box 594 Verdugo City CA 91046-0594

LE BLANC, SUZANNE, museum director. Exec. dir. Lied Discovery Children's Mus., Las Vegas, Nev. Office: Lied Discovery Childrens Mus 833 Las Vegas Blvd N Las Vegas NV 89101-2030*

LEBLOW, G. HAGNY, artist; b. June 5, 1924; d. Henry Aaron and Mabel Alice (Warn) Hagny; m. Raymond E. Leblow, Mar. 10, 1950; children: Bonnie, Charles, Colin. Grad., h.s., 1942. Formerly sec. with State of Calif., Oakland. Artist, painting country and farm scenes. Republican. Lutheran. Avocations: painting, sewing, reading. Home: 2691 Oakes Dr Hayward CA 94542-1225

LE BON, DOUGLAS KENT, investment manager; b. Rapid City, S.D., Oct. 27, 1953; s. Stanley and Elodis (Holm) Le B.; m. Eva Marie Dyer; 1 child, Shauna. BSBA, Calif. State U., Dominguez Hills, 1976, MBA, 1979. Valuation cons. Houlihan, Lokey, Howard & Zukin, L.A., 1979-83; v.p., prin. Wilshire Assocs., Inc., Santa Monica, Calif., 1983-90; co-founder, mng. dir. Pathway Capital Mgmt., L.A., 1990—. Vice chmn., chmn. fin. com. L.A. area coun. Boy Scouts Am., 1991-99; mem. corp. bd. Sch. Mgmt., Calif. State U., Dominguez Hills, 1994-98. Avocations: scuba diving, skiing. Office: Pathway Capital Mgmt 5 Park Plz Irvine CA 92614-5995

LE CAIN, LLOYD GEORGE, career officer; b. Glenridge, N.J., Nov. 23, 1947; s. Lloyd George and Dorothy Margret (Hagedorn) Le C.; m. Valentine Nishihara, July 8, 1989. BS, Tex. A&M, 1972. Commd. ensign USN, 1972, advanced through grades to cmmdr.; ships officer Exxon Co. U.S., 1972-91; naval officer naval station Pearl Harbor USN, Honolulu, Hawaii, 1991—. Mem. U.S. Naval Inst. (life), Surface Navy Assn. (life), Nat. Defense Transp. Assn. (life), Naval Reserve Assn. (life). Republican. Roman Catholic. Avocations: hospice vol., ethics instr., computer programming. Home: 1041 Hui St Kailua HI 96734-3856 Office: Naval Sta Pearl Harbor Bldg 150 Rm 308 Code 30 Pearl Harbor HI 96860

LECKMAN, JUDITH ANN, engineering executive; b. Pitts., Aug. 4, 1972; s. Thomas Jay and Patricia Susan (Diederich) L. BS in Mech. Engring., MIT, 1994; MME, Stanford U., 1996. Graduate rotation engr. Intel Corp., Albuquerque, N. Mex., 1994-95; indsl. engr. Intel Corp., Santa Clara, Calif., 1995-96; tool install sys. and bus. requirements mgr. Intel Corp., Phoenix, 1997, FCT fin. bus. process mgr., 1998—; liaison to Pa. State U. quality and mfg. mgmt. program Intel Corp., State Coll., Pa., 1996—, FCT fin. bus. process mgr., 1997—; presenter in field. Mem. Nat. Soc. Profl. Engrs., Soc. Women Engrs., Toastmasters Internat., Sigma Xi. Avocations: running, hiking. Home: 951 W Saragosa St Chandler AZ 85224-6856

LE CLAIR, DOUGLAS MARVIN, lawyer, educator, judge; b. Montreal, Nov. 13, 1955; s. Lawrence M. and Joan B. Le Clair; m. Debra L. Garland, Oct. 12, 1985. BA, Loyola U., 1977; JD, Southwestern U., 1980; peace officer cert., Mesa C.C. Law Enforcement Acad., 1985; cert. theology, min., Kino Religious Inst., 1994; Juris Canonica Licentiae, St. Paul U., 1998; M in Canon Law, U. Ottawa (Can.), 1998; cert. theology, min., Kino Religious Inst., 1994. Bar: Ariz. 1982, U.S. Dist. Ct. Ariz. 1983, U.S. Ct. Appeals (9th cir.) 1983, U.S. Tax. Ct. 1987, U.S. Ct. Claims 1987, U.S. Supreme Ct. 1987; ordained deacon Roman Cath. Ch., 1995. Pvt. practice Mesa, Ariz., 1983—; mem. faculty law & acctg. Sterling Sch., Phoenix, Ariz., 1992-96; judge Tribunal of Diocese, Phoenix, 1998—. Author: Le Clair/Morgan Income Tax Organizer, 1982-83; prodn. editor Computer Law Jour., 1979-80. Res. officer Mesa Police Dept., 1984-92. Named One of Outstanding Young Men Of Am., 1979. Mem. ABA, Ariz. Bar Assn., Maricopa County Bar Assn., Internat. Platform Assn., Southwestern Student Bar Assn. (exec. bd. 1978-79), Southwestern U. Tax Law Soc., Mesa C. of C., Delta Theta Phi, Phi Alpha Theta. Office: 400 E Monroe St Phoenix AZ 85004

LE CLAIR, LAURIE (ISABELLA LAURENCE LE CLAIR), artist; b. Athens, Greece; d. Leopold Joseph and Ellenanne (Marsh) LeC.; m. Kevin R. Wilson, Oct. 25, 1987. Student, Radford Coll., 1967-70; diploma in arts rsch., Corcoran Sch. Art, Washington, 1973. One-person shows include Washington Project for Arts, 1975, Gallery Theatre, Barnsdall Par, L.A., 1979, Collusion Unltd., Seattle, 1994, 98, Kittredge Gallery, U. Puget Sound, Tacoma, Wash., 1995, Battery St. Gallery, Seattle, 1995, Kurt Lidtke Gallery, Seattle, 1997; exhibited in group shows Corcoran Gallery of Art, Washington, 1973, 55 Mercer St. Gallery, N.Y.C., 1973, WPA Inaugural Exhibit, Washington, 1976, So. Calif. Ctr. for Arts, Pasadena, 1980, WPA, Washington, 1982, Vault Gallery, L.A., 1983, Ctr. on Contemporary Art, Seattle, 1995, Kurt Lidtke Gallery, Seattle, 1996, Seattle Art Mus. Rental/Sales Gallery, 1998. Democrat.

LECLERC, MARC GREGORY, insurance agent; b. Yuma, Ariz., Apr. 6, 1959; s. Norman A. and Marie Isoline (Baptiste) LeC. Diploma, Scottsdale (Ariz.) C. C., 1981. Ins. agt. Mass. Mutual, Phoenix, 1988—. Polit. coord. Mass. Mutual Polit. Action Com., Phoenix, 1992—; fundraiser numerous charities, Phoenix, 1985—. Mem. Nat. Assn. Life Underwriters (Nat. Quality award 1991), Phoenix Assn. Life Underwriters (chmn. awards 1993—), Mass. Mutual Agts. Assn. (pres. 1992-93). Republican. Avocations: scuba diving, windsurfing, mountain climbing, cycling, carpentry. Office: Mass Mutual Ins 6900 E Camelback Rd Ste 300 Scottsdale AZ 85251-8043

LECRON, MARY FRAZER See **FOSTER, MARY FRAZER**

LEDDY, THOMAS WINTER, philosophy educator; b. Oakland, Calif., Sept. 30, 1949; s. John Barnes and Jane Anne L.; m. Karen Lee Haas, Aug. 4, 1985. BA in Philosophy, U. Calif., Santa Cruz, 1971; MA in Humanities, San Francisco State U., 1974; PhD in Philosophy, Boston U., 1983. Instr. Chabot Coll., Hayward, Calif., 1974-75, Napa (Calif.) Coll., 1975-77, U. Mass., Boston, 1980-82; asst. prof. Alfred (N.Y.) U., 1982-83; asst. prof. San Jose (Calif.) State U., 1983-89, assoc. prof., 1989-95, prof., 1995—. Author: (chpt.) Philosophy and Architecture, 1994; contbr. articles to profl. jours. Mem. Am. Soc. Aesthetics (bd. trustees 1996—), Am. Philos. Assn., British Soc. Aesthetics, Internat. Assn. Aesthetics. Democrat. Avocations: photography, museums, collage. E-mail: Twleddy@email.sjsv.edu. Office: San Jose State U Dept Philosophy 1 Washington Sq San Jose CA 95192-0001

LEDERER, MARION IRVINE, cultural administrator; b. Brampton, Ont., Can., Feb. 10, 1920; d. Oliver Bateman and Eva Jane (MacMurdo) L.; m. Francis Lederer, July 10, 1941. Student, U. Toronto, 1938, UCLA, 1942-45. Owner Canoga Mission Gallery, Canoga Park, Calif., 1967—; cultural heritage monument Canoga Mission Gallery, 1974—; Vice pres. Screen Smart Set women's aux. Motion Picture and TV Fund, 1973—; founder sister city program Canoga Park-Taxco, Mexico, 1963; Mem. mayor's cultural task force San Fernando Valley, 1973—; mem. Los Angeles Cultural Affairs Commn., 1980-85. Mem. Los Angeles Cultural Affairs Commn., 1980-85. Recipient numerous pub. service awards from mayor, city council, C. of C. Mem. Canoga Park C. of C. (cultural chmn. 1973-75, dir. 1973-75). Presbyn. Home: PO Box 32 Canoga Park CA 91305-0032 Office: Canoga Mission Gallery 23130 Sherman Way Canoga Park CA 91307-1402

LEDFORD, GARY ALAN, real estate developer; b. San Diego, Dec. 30, 1946; s. Loren Oscar and Madge Francis (Condon) L.; m. Winifred Jess Ledford, Nov. 19, 1994; children: Kelly, Jeanne, Robert. BSCE, U.S. Army Engring. Coll., 1967. Pres. Mastercraft Contractors/Mastercraft Diversified Svcs., Inc./Masterplan, Inc., Colo. Springs, 1969-73; v.p. K.L. Redfern, Inc., Orange, Calif., 1973-75; pres. Ledford Industries, Inc./G.A. Ledford & Assocs., 1975-82, Watt Jess Ranch, Inc., Apple Valley, Calif., 1985-94; chmn. Jess Ranch, Apple Valley, 1994—, Jess Ranch Water Co., Apple Valley, 1986—; pres., ceo Jess Ranch Devel. Co., Inc., 1996—; pres. Jess Ranch Security Co., Inc., 1996—; v.p., gen. mgr. Jess Ranch Realty, 1996—; gen. ptnr. GLBT Assocs., 1978-79; chmn. Watt-Jess/Ledford, Apple Valley, 1992-94; pres. LJ&J Investments, Inc., Apple Valley, Ledford-Schaffer/Rogers, Apple Valley. Designer computer software, 1979. Past pres. Cultural Arts Found., 1991-92, Victorville, Calif; bd. trustees Apple Valley Christian Care Ctr., High Desert Questors, Victorville; past pres. Victor Valley Mus. Assn., Baldy View B.I.A. Capt. C.E., U.S. Army, 1967-69, Vietnam. Mem. Internat. Coun. Shopping Ctrs., Nat. Assn. Home Builders', Nat. Planning Assn., NRA (life), High Desert Constrn. Indsutry Assn. (past v.p.), Bldg. Industry Assn., VFW, Sr. Housing Coun. Republican. Avocations: hunting, chess, equestrian. Home: 11401 Apple Valley Rd Apple Valley CA 92308-7503 Office: Jess Ranch 11401 Apple Valley Rd Apple Valley CA 92308-7599

LEE, ALDORA G., social psychologist; b. Schenectady, N.Y.; d. Alois W. and M. Dorothy (Swigert) Graf. AB, Ind. U.; MA, Stanford U.; PhD, U. Colo. Dir. women studies Wash. State U., Pullman, 1976-78, dir. unit on aging, 1976-81; cons. in market research Syva, Palo Alto, Calif., 1982; staff market rsch. analyst Allstate Rsch. and Planning Ctr., Menlo Park, Calif., 1983—; rep. Wash. Assn. Gerontol. Edn., N.W. region rep. Nat. Women's Studies Assn., 1978-81. Contbr. articles to profl. jours. Mem. Menlo Park Libr. Commn., 1984-92, chmn., 1985-87; instr. Career Action Ctr., Palo Alto, 1984-87; Menlo Park rep. system adv. bd. Peninsula Libr. System, 1992-97; mem. Allstate Found. Com., San Francisco Bay area, 1993-94, No. Calif., 1995-97, mem. regional com., 1993-95; libr. reference assoc. vol. Health Libr. Sr. Ctr., Palo Alto, Calif., 1997-98. Recipient Allstate Good Hands award for Cmty. Svc., 1994, 96. Mem. Am. Mktg. Assn., Am. Psychol. Soc., Am. Sociol. Assn., Western Psychol. Assn., SRI Organon Toastmasters (Toastmaster of Yr. 1989, Able Toastmaster, Competent Toastmaster, mentor GeoSpeakers 1994), Phi Beta Kappa, Sigma Xi.

LEE, BEVERLY ING, educational administrator; b. Honolulu, Oct. 10, 1932; d. Tim Sheu and Helen (Heu) Ing; m. Daniel David Lee, June 21, 1962; children: Helen Ann Esq, Terence Daniel, Scott David. BA, Coll. of the Pacific, Stockton, Calif., 1954; MA, Columbia U., 1957. Policewoman Honolulu Police Dept., 1957-61; counselor Ewa Elem., Highlands Intermediate and Waipahu High Schs., 1961-69; adminstr. Dept. Edn. State of Hawaii, Honolulu, 1969-89; contr., v.p., pres. Classic Travel, Honolulu, 1988—; bd. dirs. Hawaii State Employees Credit Union, Honolulu, vice chair, 1994, chair, 1995; bd. dirs. Mahalo Airport Travel Agy.; mem. adv. bd. Travel Univ. Internat. Adv. Bd., 1994—. Mem. Gov.'s Commn. on Child Abuse, Honolulu, 1985-89; bd. dirs. Hawaii Family Stress Ctr., Honolulu, 1983—, Child and Family Svc., 1975-85; mem. Casey Family Program Adv. Com., 1986—, Parents Anonymous, 1988-92, Prevent Child Abuse Hawaii, 1975—. Mem. AAUW (life), Hawaiian Airlines Travel Agy. (adv. bd. 1991-93), Mahalo Airlines Travel Agy. (adv. bd. 1994—), Travel U. Internat. (adv. bd. 1994—), Casey Family (adv. bd. 1986—), Prevent Child Abuse Hawaii (bd. dir. 1975—), Child & Family Svcs. (bd. dir. 1975-85), Delta Kappa Gamma, Tri Delta. Avocations: travel, plants, photography. Office: Classic Travel 1413 S King St Ste 201 Honolulu HI 96814-2505

LEE, BLAINE NELSON, executive consultant, educator, author; b. Olympia, Wash., Apr. 3, 1946; s. Elwyn Earl and Thelma Marie (Woods) Reeder; m. Shawny Christian Lee; children: Blaine, Benjamin, Adam, Michal, Joseph, Joshua, Casey, Abraham, Eliza, Gabriel, Celeste, Isaac. BS in Psychology, Brigham Young U., Provo, Utah, 1969, MS in Ednl. Psychology, 1972; PhD in Ednl. Psychology, U. Tex., 1982. Cert. ednl. specialist, secondary edn., ednl. adminstrn. Dir. instrnl. sys. USAF, San Antonio, 1972-75; assoc. prof. USAF Acad., Colorado Springs, Colo., 1975-78; edn. dir. Heritage Sch., Provo, Utah, 1978-81; asst. prof. Utah Valley State Coll., Orem, Utah, 1981-84; pres. Skills for Living, Salem, Utah, 1984-86; v.p. Covey Leadership Ctr., Provo, Utah, 1986-97, Franklin Covey Co., Provo, 1997—; ednl. cons. in field. Author: Affective Objectives, 1972, Personal Change, 1982, Stress Strategist, 1986, Principle Centered Leadership, 1990, Power Principle: Influence with Honor, 1997; contbr. articles to profl. jours. High councilman LDS Ch., mem. gen. bd., 1970-72; pres. Provo PTO. Named Outstanding Young Man of Am., U.S. C. of C., 1976, 84. Mem. APA, ASTD, Am. Mgmt. Assn., Nat. Spkrs. Assn., Phi Delta Kappa. Avocations: cmty. theatre, choir dir., camping, poetry, soccer coach. Home: 10435 S 600 E Salem UT 84653-9389 Office: Franklin Covey Co 360 W 4800 N Provo UT 84604-5675

LEE, CANDIE CHING WAH, retail executive; b. Hong Kong, British Crown Colony, June 17, 1950; came to U.S., 1973:; d. Willard W. and Yuk Ching (Yau) L. Student, Hong Kong Tech. Coll., Kowloon, 1968-70. Office mgr. Crown Enterprises, Ltd., Hong Kong, 1970-73; buyer, mgr. Hawaii Resort Industries, Inc., Honolulu, 1973-76, v.p., 1976-82; pres. Hawaii Resort Shops, Inc., Honolulu, 1983—. Mem. Am. Mgmt. Assn., Oahu Country Club. Republican. Avocation: reading. Office: Hawaii Resort Shops Inc 468 Ena Rd Honolulu HI 96815-1734

LEE, CHAN-YUN, physicist, process engineer, educator; b. Hwa-Liang, Taiwan, July 19, 1952; came to U.S., 1988; s. Hsiao-Feng and Shu-Yun (Huang) L.; m. Chia-Li Yang, Jan. 13, 1983; children: Yifan E., Ethel Y., Elias Y. BS in Physics, Soochow U., Taipei, Taiwan, 1974; MS, U. So. Calif., 1980; PhD, U. Notre Dame, 1988. Cert. assoc. prof., lectr. Dept. Edn. Asst. prof. physics Tatung Inst. Tech., Taipei, 1982-86, assoc. prof., 1986-88, chmn. physics sect., 1986-88; cons. Tatung Semiconductor Divsn., Taipei, 1985-88; dir. Tatung Natural Sci. Mus., Taipei, 1986-88; lab. instr. U. Notre Dame, Notre Dame, Ind., 1988-94; process engr. Lam Rsch. Co., Fremont, Calif., 1994-96, sr. process engr., 1996—, mgr. metal etch key accounts, 1998—; assoc. prof. physics San Jose City Coll., Calif., 1998—; rsch. asst. U. So. Calif., L.A., 1977-79. *Over twenty years extensive experience in conducting professional research on both IC processing techniques and high temperature super conductivity. While serving as a consultant for a semiconductor company and managing the key accounts for a major plasma etcher manufacture company, Chan-Yun Lee has the responsibility of performing process engineering research, design, development,and evaluation in support of the company's complex semiconductor equipment. He has also initiated and implemented many research projects in the fields of semiconducting thin film growth and applications, the absolute photo ionization cross sections of alkali elements in the VUV region, relativistic corrections to the semi conducting properties of selected materials.* Contbr. numerous articles to profl. jours. 2d lt. Chinese Artillery, 1974-76. Recipient Excellent Rschrs. prize Chinese Nat. Sci. Coun., Taipei, 1986, 87, 88, Outstanding Acad. Pub. prize Hsieh-Tze Indsl. Revival Com., Taipei, 1987, 88, 27th Ann. Sci. & Tech. Pers. Rsch. & Study award Chinese Nat. Sci. Coun., 1989. Mem. Chinese Physics Assn. Achievements include development of model of relativistic corrections to semiconducting properties of selected materials, simulated and calculated the dynamical sysceptibility of square lattice antiferromagnets; successfully developed the first large size SAC process in the world on high density plasma TCP etcher with satisfactory yields; designed and constructed a spectrophotometer to measure the absolute photoabsorption cross section of atomic potassium in VUV region. Avocations: moutain hiking, swimming, computer program design, fishing. Home: 471 Via Vera Cruz Fremont CA 94539-5325 Office: Lam Rsch Co 4400 Cushing Pkwy Fremont CA 94538-6401

LEE, CYNTHIA, television producer, playwright, filmmaker; b. Bklyn.. BA, San Diego State U., 1973. Copywriter, prodr., account exec. Maj. Market Radio, Portland, Oreg., 1975-77; media analyst Walt Disney Prodns., Burbank, Calif., 1978-80; story analyst NBC, Burbank, Calif., 1980-83; dir. broadcast media May Dept. Stores, L.A., 1980-86; CEO CloverLeaf Prodns., Beverly Hills, Calif., 1986—; freelance news prodr., photographer various affiliates, 1996—. Author: (book) Twice Blessed, 1995; (plays) Blavatsky, 1985 (Dramalogue award), Demons and Angels, 1993 (Dramalogue award); prodr: (documentary) The Great Bronze Age of China, 1983, A Hole In The Sky, 1997, A Miracle In Danville, 1997 (winner film grant Am. Film Inst./Nat. Endowment for Arts 1997). Playwriting award Dramalogue, 1986, 93; Recognition award Geisinger Hosp., Danville, Pa., 1997. Mem. Internat. Soc. Panetics, Internat. Documentary Assn., L.A. Playwrights Alliance, Dramatists Guild. E-mail: CLeeOver@aol.com.

LEE, DENNIS TURNER, civil engineer, construction executive; b. Dallas, Jan. 6, 1941; s. Joseph Thomas and Elizabeth Lee; m. Dianna Christine Ricker, Aug. 8, 1964; children: Christopher Scott, Karen Denise, Suzanne Elizabeth. BSCE, So. Meth. U., 1964; MS in Constrn. Mgmt., Stanford U., 1965. Cert. project mgmt. profl., asbestos contr./supr. Constrn. engr. Kaiser Engrs., Oakland, Calif., 1965-66; project engr. Hoffman Constrn. Co., Portland, Oreg., 1969-76, supt., 1977, project ops. mgr., 1978-84; sr. project mgr. Chanen Constrn. Co., Phoenix, 1985-87, Sundt Corp., Phoenix, 1987-93, Linthicum Constructors, Scottsdale, Ariz., 1993; account exec. Water Purge Sys., Scottsdale, 1994; facilities mgr. InteSys Technologies, Inc., Gilbert, Ariz., 1994-97; project mgr. Motorola New Constrn. Team ICF-Kaiser, Chandler, Ariz., 1998—; mem. lawyer ethics discipline com. Ariz. State Bar, 1990-93. 1st lt. C.E. U.S. Army, 1966-69. Decorated Army Commendation medal. Mem. ASCE, Project Mgmt. Inst. (pres. 1990-93), Environ. Info. Assn. (bd. dirs. 1992-93), Toastmasters (pres. 1992). Achievements include pioneered use of time lapse movie technology in construction operations; designed jobsite concrete precasting and steam curing plants; pioneered use of lasers in construction. Avocations: hiking, camping, skiing, in-line skating. Home: 8019 E Voltaire Ave Scottsdale AZ 85260-4933

LEE, DONNA JEAN, retired hospice and respite nurse; b. Huntington Park, Nov. 12, 1931; d. Louis Frederick and Lena Adelaide (Hinson) Munyon, m. Frank Bernard Lee, July 16, 1949; children: Frank, Robert, John. AA in Nursing, Fullerton (Calif.) Jr. Coll., 1966; extension student, U. Calif., Irvine, 1966-74; student, U. N.Mex., 1982. RN, Calif.; cert. Intraventous Therapy Assn. U.S.A. Staff nurse Orange (Calif.) County Med. Ctr., 1966-71, staff and charge nurse relief ICU, CCU, Burn Unit, ER, Communicable Disease, Neo-Natal Care Unit, 1969-71, charge nurse communicable disease unit, 1969-70; staff and charge nurse ICU, emergency rm., CCU, med./surg. units Anaheim (Calif.) Meml. Hosp., 1971-74; charge and staff nurse, relief Staff Builders, Orange, 1974-82; agy. nurse Nursing Svcs. Internat., 1978-89; asst. DON Chapman Convalescent SNF, Orange, 1982; geriatric and pediatrics nurse VNASS, 1985 93; hospice/respite nurse VIA Upjohn Home Healthcare Svcs and VNA Support Svcs. of Orange, 1985-93; ret.; staff relief nurse ICU/CCU various hosps. and labs, including plasmapheresis nurse Med. Lab. of Orange, 1978. Mem. AACN, Harvard Med. Sch. Nurses, Am. Lung Assn., Am. Heart Assn.Arthritis Found. Baptist. Home: 924 S Hampstead St Anaheim CA 92802-1740

LEE, ERIC TOM, apparel business owner, designer; b. San Francisco, Calif., June 5, 1971; married, Dec. 16, 1995. AA, DeAnza College, Cupertino, Calif., 1995. Owner Journees, Cupertino, Calif., 1992—, Remix Clothing, Cupertino, 1997—; designer Silicon valley Chemlabs, Sunnyvale, 1996—; in purchasing Rhythm Music, San Jose, Calif., 1998—; cons. Xotica Power Divsn., Seattle and Full Circle Prod. Performing artist and organizer, Global Dance Network. Avocations: technology, music, inline skating, hiking. Office: Journees PO Box 2531 Cupertino CA 95015

LEE, GERALDINE HOSTETLER, retired elementary education educator, shop owner; b. Bowling Green, Ohio, Mar. 26, 1916; d. Harry Sylvester and Mable Grace (Bushong) Hostetler; m. Robert Eugene Lee, June 24, 1939 (dec. June 1990); children: Jeri Jean, Dinah Anne. BS in Edn., Ashland U., 1956. Tchr. various schs., Ohio, Wyo., Calif.; tchr. East Sch., Sutherlin, Oreg., 1959-76; ret.; owner Blue Unicorn Gift Shop. Author: A History of Sutherlin Oregon, 1990, Up and Down, 1997, Why I Never Reached 2nd Grade, 1997, And BarAbbas Wept, 1997. Mem. Northwest Visions, dis Ability Ctr., Assn. Writers. Avocations: writing, sculpting, painting, crocheting. Home: Apt 111 1800 NW Hughwood Ct Roseburg OR 97470

LEE, GILBERT BROOKS, retired ophthalmology engineer; b. Cohasset, Mass., Sept. 10, 1913; s. John Alden and Charlotte Louise (Brooks) L.; m. Marion Corinne Rapp, Mar. 7, 1943 (div. Jan. 1969); children: Thomas Stearns, Jane Stanton, Frederick Cabot, Gilbert Eliot Frazar. BA, Reed Coll., 1937; MA, New Sch. for Social Rsch., 1949. Asst. psychologist U.S. Naval Submarine Base Civil Svc., Psychophysics of Vision, New London, Conn., 1950-53; rsch. assoc. Project Mich., Vision Rsch. Labs., Willow Run, 1954-57; rsch. assoc. dept. ophthalmology U. Mich., Ann Arbor, 1958-72, sr. rsch. assoc., 1972-75, sr. engring. rsch. assoc. ophthalmology, 1975-82, part-time sr. engr. ophthalmology, 1982—; sec. internat. dept., 23d St. YMCA, N.Y.C.; cons. W.K. Kellogg Eye Ctr., Ann Arbor, 1968—. Local organizer, moderator (TV program) Union of Concerned Scientists' Internat. Satellite Symposium on Nuclear Arms Issues, 1986; producer (TV show) Steps for Peace, 1987; designer, builder portable tristimulus Colorimeter; (videotape) Pomerance Awards, UN.; broken lake ice rescue procedure rsch., by one person in a dry suit, all weather conditions, 1966, 89-93 (videotape). Precinct del. Dem. County Conv., Washtenaw County, 1970, 74; treas. Dem. Club, Ann Arbor, Mich., 1971-72, 74-79; vice chmn. nuclear arms control com., 1979; chmn. Precinct Election Inspectors, 1968-75; scoutmaster Portland (Oreg.) area coun. Boy Scouts Am., 1932-39. Capt. AUS, 1942-46, 61-62. Mem. AAAS, Nat. Resources Def. Coun., Fedn. Am. Scientists, N.Y. Acad. Sci., Nation Assocs., ACLU, Sierra Club, Amnesty Internat. Home: 4131 E Pinchot Ave Phoenix AZ 85018-7115

LEE, GLENN RICHARD, medical administrator, educator; b. Ogden, Utah, May 18, 1932; s. Glenn Edwin and Thelma (Jensen) L.; m. Pamela Marjorie Ridd, July 18, 1969; children—Jennifer, Cynthia. B.S., U. Utah, 1953, M.D., 1956. Intern Boston City Hosp.-Harvard U., 1956-57, resident, 1957-58; clin. asso. Nat. Cancer Inst., NIH, 1958-60; postdoctoral fellow U. Utah, 1960-63; instr. U. Utah Coll. Medicine, 1963-64, asst. prof. internal medicine, 1964-68, assoc. prof., 1968-73, prof., 1973-96, assoc. dean for acad. affairs, 1973-76, dean, 1978-83, prof. emeritus, 1996—; chief of staff Salt Lake VA Med. Ctr., 1985-95. Author: (with others) Clinical Hematology, 10th edit, 1998; Contbr. (with others) numerous articles to profl. jours.; editorial bd.: (with others) Am. Jour. Hematology, 1976-79. Served with USPHS, 1958-60. Markle Found. scholar, 1965-70; Nat. Inst. Arthritis, Metabolic and Digestive Disease grantee, 1977-82. Mem. A.C.P., Am. Soc. Hematology, Am. Soc. Clin. Investigation, Western Assn. Physicians, Am. Inst. Nutrition. Mem. LDS Ch. Home and Office: 3781 Ruth Dr Salt Lake City UT 84124-2331

LEE, GRACE TZE, controller; b. Taipei, Republic of China, Aug. 11, 1953; came to U.S., 1974; d. Tang Chi and Ming (Shu) L. BA, Nat. Taipei U., 1974; BS, U. Nev., 1977; postgrad., UCLA, 1988. Fgn. currency specialist Deak-Perera Co., L.A., 1977-80; asst. mgr. Universal Supply Co., L.A., 1980; contr. AJR Electronics Inc., L.A., 1981-84; western zone asst. mgr. Samsung Electronics Co., L.A., 1984; contr. Gideon Nol Inc., L.A., 1985-87, James G. Wiley Co., L.A., 1987-91, Jetset Tours Inc. (N.Am.), L.A., 1991-95, DER Travel Inc., L.A., 1995-96, F&M Sales, Inc., L.A., 1996—, Entex Info. Svcs., Inc., L.A., 1998—. Home: 23442 Batey Ave Harbor City CA 90710-1204

LEE, HARRISON HON, naval architecture librarian, consultant; b. Stockton, Calif., Sept. 20, 1943; s. Hon Bo and Lulu Joyce Lee; m. Estelle Toby Wlosko, May 11, 1980. AA, Stockton (Calif.) Coll., 1967; BA, Stanislaus State Coll., Turlock, Calif., 1969; MA, Sonoma State U., Cotati, Calif., 1973; MS in Libr. Sci., Simmons Coll., 1978. Lectr. Ecole d'Humanite, Renti, Switzerland, 1973-75; libr. M. Rosenblatt & Son, Inc., N.Y.C., 1978-89; libr. cons. SELF, Stockton, 1989—. Mem. Spl. Libr. Assn., Soc. Naval Archs. and Marine Engrs. Unitarian.

LEE, ISAAC, minister; b. O-Dam-Ri, Hwanghae Do, Korea, Mar. 29, 1945; came to U.S., 1967; s. Chan-Bom and Choon-Bong (Kang) L.; m. Susan Lim, Sept. 18, 1973; children: Christina, Caroline. MDiv, Reformed Presbyn. Sem., L.A., 1982. Assoc. pastor Korean Presbyn. Ch. Phila., L.A., 1979-85; dir., founder Cornerstone Ministries Internat., L.A., 1985-89, Seattle, 1989—. Editor: Love North Korea, 1989. With U.S. Army, 1969-71, Korea. Home: 14532 Willow Ln SE Mill Creek WA 98012-5760 Office: Cornerstone Ministries Internat 3810 196th St SW Ste 2 Lynnwood WA 98036-5746

LEE, JAI JUNG, accountant; b. Seoul, Republic of Korea, Feb. 22, 1949; came to U.S., 1977; s. Sung B. and Young A. (Koo) L.; m. In S. Choi, Aug. 20, 1980; children: Marcus, Michael. LLB, Kyung Hee U., Seoul, 1972; postgrad., USAMMCS, 1973; MBA, Calif. State U., L.A., 1984. Cert. tax preparer, Calif. Staff acct. Pyramid Optical Co., Irvine, Calif., 1978-80; sr. acct. Kim, Kang Yun & Co., CPA's, L.A., 1981-84, Simon, Steemke & Co., CPA's, Rolling Hills Estates, Calif., 1984-91; pvt. practice Lee & Co., Artesia, Calif., 1991—. Referee Am. Youth Soccer Orgn., Torrance, Calif., 1990—. Roman Catholic. Avocations: running, biking, golf. Office: Lee & Co 18021 Norwalk Blvd Ste 201 Artesia CA 90701-4254

LEE, JAMES KING, technology corporation executive; b. Nashville, July 31, 1940; s. James Fitzhugh Lee and Lucille (Charlton) McGivney; m. Victoria Marie Marani, Sept. 4, 1971; children: Gina Victoria, Patrick Fitzhugh. BS, Calif. State U., Pomona, 1964; MBA, U. So. Calif., 1966. Prodn. and methods engring. foreman GM Corp., 1963-65; engring. adminstr. Douglas MSSD, Santa Monica, Calif., 1965-67; gen. mgr. mgmt. systems, computer tech. TRW Systems, Redondo Beach, Calif., 1967-68; v.p. corp. devel. DataStation Corp., L.A., 1968-69; v.p., gen. mgr. Aved Systems Group, L.A., 1969-70; mng. ptnr. Corp. Growth Cons., L.A., 1970-81; chmn., pres., CEO Fail-Safe Tech. Corp., L.A., 1981-93; pres., COO The Flood Group Inc., Torrance, Calif., 1994-96, pres., CEO, CyberSense Sys. Corp., 1996—. Author industry studies, 1973-79. Mem. L.A. Mayor's Cmty. Adv. Com., 1962-72, aerospace conversion task force L.A. County Econ. Devel. Commn., 1990-92; bd. dirs. USO Greater L.A., 1990-99, v.p. personnel 1990-92, exec. v.p., 1992-93, pres. 1993-99; asst. adminstr. SBA, Washington, 1974; vice chmn. Traffic Commn., Rancho Palos Verdes, Calif., 1975-78; chmn. Citizens for Property Tax Relief, Palos Verdes, 1976-80; mem. Town Hall Calif. Recipient Golden Scissors award Calif. Taxpayers' Congress, 1978. Mem. So. Calif. Tech. Execs. Network, Am. Electronics Assn. (chmn. L.A. coun. 1987-88, vice chmn. 1986-87, nat. bd. dirs. 1986-89), Nat. Security Industries Assn. Republican. Baptist. Home: 28874 Crestridge Rd Pls Vrds Est CA 90275-5063 Office: CyberSense Sys Corp 3521 Lomita Blvd Ste 201 Torrance CA 90505-5016

LEE, JERRY CARLTON, university administrator; b. Roanoke, Va., Nov. 21, 1941; m. Joan Marie Leo; 1 child, Zan. BA, W.Va. Wesleyan Coll., 1963; postgrad., W.Va. U. Grad. Sch. Indsl. Relations, 1963-64, U. Balt. Sch. Law, 1967-69; MA, Va. Poly. Inst., 1975, EdD, 1977; LLD (hon.), Gallaudet U., 1986. Mgmt. trainee Gen. Motors Corp., 1964-65; v.p. adminstrn. Comml. Credit Indsl. Corp., Washington, 1965-71; dir. gen. services Gallaudet Coll., Washington, 1971-77, asst. v.p. bus. affairs, 1978-82, v.p. adminstrn. and bus., 1982-84; pres. Gallaudet U. (formerly Gallaudet Coll.), Washington, 1984-88, Nat. U., San Diego, 1989—. Hon. bd. dirs. D.C. Spl. Olympics; commn. in adminstrn. org. Rehab. Internat.; bd. dirs. People to People, Deafness Research Found., Am. Assn. Univ. Adminstrs., Am. Coun. on Edn. Commn. on Women in Higher Edn.; hon. advocacy bd. Nat. Capital Assn. Coop. Edn.; mem. Personnel Policies Forum Bur. Nat. Affairs. Served with USAR, 1966-72. Recipient Nat. Service award, Hon. Pres. award Council for Better Hearing and Speech, 1986, One-of-a-Kind award People-to-People, 1987, Advancement Human Rights & Fundamental Freedoms award UN, U.S.A., Disting. Alumni award Va. Poly. Inst., 1985, Pres.' award Gallaudet Coll. Alumni Assn., Gallaudet Community Relations award, U.S. Steel Found. Cost Reduction Incentive award Nat. Assn. Coll. and Univ. Bus. Officers, award Am. Athletic Assn. Deaf, 1987. Mem. Am. Assn. Univ. Adminstrs. (Eileen Tosney award 1987), Consortium of Univs. Washington Met. Area (exec. com.), Nat. Collegiate Athletic Assn. (pres.' commn.), Nat. Assn. Coll. Aux. Services (jour. adv. bd., journalism award), Alpha Sigma Pi (Man of Yr. award 1983-84). Lodge: Sertoma (life, found. nat. adv. com.). Avocations: tennis, long distance running, weightlifting. Office: Nat Univ 11255 N Torrey Pines Rd La Jolla CA 92037-1011*

LEE, JIMMY S.M., electronic executive. Chmn., pres., CEO Integrated Silicon Solutions, Inc., Santa Clara, Calif. Office: Integrated Silicon Solutions Inc 2231 Lawson Ln Santa Clara CA 95054-3311*

LEE, JOHN JIN, lawyer; b. Chgo., Oct. 20, 1948; s. Jim Soon and Fay Yown (Young) L.; m. Jamie Pearl Eng, Apr. 30, 1983. BA magna cum laude, Rice U., 1971; JD, Stanford U., 1975; MBA, 1975. Bar: Calif. 1976. Assoc. atty. Manatt Phelps & Rothenberg, L.A., 1976-77; asst. counsel Wells Fargo Bank N.A., San Francisco, 1977-79, counsel, 1979-80, v.p., sr. counsel, 1980, v.p., mng. sr. counsel, 1981-98, v.p., asst. gen. counsel, 1998—; mem. governing com. Conf. on Consumer Fin. Law, 1989-93. Bd. dirs. Asian Bus. League of San Francisco, 1981—, gen. counsel, 1981. Fellow Am. Coll. Consumer Fin. Svcs. Attys., Inc., (bd. regents 1995—), mem. ABA (chmn. subcom. on housing fin., com. on consumer fin. svcs., bus. law sect. 1983-90, vice chmn. subcom. on securities products, com. on consumer fin. svcs., bus. law sect. 1993-95, chmn. subcom. on securities products, com. on consumer fin. svcs., bus. law sect. 1995-96, chmn. subcom. on electronic banking, com. on consumer fin. svcs., bus. law sect. 1996—, co-chmn. joint subcom. on electronic fin. svcs., bus. law sect. 1997—, co-chmn. directory com., minority in-house counsel group 1995—), Consumer Bankers Assn. (lawyers com.), Soc. Physics Students, Stanford Asian-Pacific Am. Alumni/ae Club (bd. dirs. 1989-93, v.p. 1989-91). Democrat. Baptist. Office: Wells Fargo Bank NA Law Dept 633 Folsom St 7th Fl San Francisco CA 94107-3600

LEE, JONG HYUK, accountant; b. Seoul, Korea, May 6, 1941; s. Jung Bo and Wol Sun L. BS Han Yang U., Seoul, Korea, 1964, BA, Sonoma State U. Rohnert Park, Calif., 1971; MBA in Taxation, Golden Gate U., San Francisco, 1976. CPA Calif. m. Esther Kim Jan. 24, 1970. Cost Acct., internal auditor Foremost-McKesson Co., San Francisco, 1971-74, sr. acct. Clark, Wong, Foulkes & Barbieri, CPAs. Oakland , Calif., 1974-77, pres. J.H. Lee Accts. Corp., Oakland, 1977-89, 95-97, J. Lee Assocs., 97—. Bay Cities Restaurants, Inc., Wendys Franchise, 1989-94; Instr., Armstrong Coll., Berkeley, Calif., 1977-78; lectr. acctg., dir. sch. of bus., The U.S. Korea Bus. Inst., San Francisco State U.; adv. bd. mem. Ctr. for Korean Studies, Insts. of East Asian Studies U. Calif.,Berkely; dir. United Labor Bank, Oakland bd. dirs. Korean residents Assn., 1974, Multi-svc. Ctr. for Koreans, 1979, BetterBus. Bur., 1984-87; chmn. cacus Calif.-Nev. ann. conf. United Meth Ch., 1977; commr. Calif. State Office Econ. Opportunity, 1982-86; pres. Korean Am. Dem. Network; mem. Dem. Nat. Fin. Coun.; regional chmn. Adv. Coun. on Peaceful Unification Policy, Rep. of Korea; Commr. Asian Art Mus. San Francisco, 1988-91; Commr. Oakland Cmty. and Econ. Devel. 1997; bd., dir., East Bay Asian Local Devel. Corp with Korean Marine Corps, 1961-64; 1st lt. Calif. State Mil. Res. Mem. AICPA, Nat. Assn. Asian Am. CPAs (bd. dir.), Am. Acctg. Assn., Nat. Assn. Accts., Internat Found. Employee Benefit Plans, Calif. Soc. CPAs, Oakland C. of C., Korean Am. C. of C. (pres. Pacific N. Coast Rotary. Democrat. Author tax and bus. column Korea Times, 1980. Home: 180 Firestone Dr Walnut Creek CA 94598-3645 Office: 369 13th St Oakland CA 94612-2636

LEE, JOSELYN C.R., physician, researcher; b. Hong Kong, June 7, 1961; came to U.S., 1979; d. Joseph Mui Hok and Myra Jeannon (Yip) L. BS in Chemistry, Stanford (Calif) U., 1983, MS in Biology, 1984; MD, U. Chgo., 1990. Diplomate Am. Bd. Pediatrics; lic. physician, Calif., S.C. Tchr. asst. dept. chemistry Stanford U., 1983-84; rsch. asst. pharmacology and physiology U. Chgo., 1987-89; intern dept pediatrics Harbor UCLA Hosp., Torrance, Calif., 1990-91, resident in pediatrics, 1991-93; temporary clin. lectr. pediatrics Hong Kong U. Sch. Medicine, 1993-94; pediatric cardiology fellow Med. U. S.C., Charleston, 1994—. Recipient Bristol-Meyres Squibb Affiliate Travel award Am. Coll. Cardiology, 1997, Young Investigator award Am. Acad. Pediatrics, 1995, Grantham scholar, Dr. and Mrs. Charles Yau scholar, Hong Kong Govt. scholar. Mem. Phi Beta Kappa, Phi Lambda Upsilon. Avocations: piano, singing. Office: Stanford U Dept Chem Stanford CA 94305

LEE, KANG S., artist, educator; b. Seoul, Korea, June 5, 1937; came to U.S., 1967; d. Kee Young and Young Sook (Choy) L.; m. Frank James Sheppard (dec. 1990). BFA, Univ. Hong Ik, Seoul, 1963; postgrad., Univ. Colo., 1968-70; MA, Univ. Phoenix, 1989. Cert. tchr. Mgr. advt., presentation J.C. Penney, Colorado Springs, 1970-79; dist. merchandise presentation mgr. J.C. Penney, Denver, 1980-85; prof. Pikes Peak C.C., Colorado Springs, 1991—; prof. Univ. Colo., Colorado Springs, 1992—. Exhibited in group shows Nat. Art Exhibition, Seoul, 1962-66 (Creative Excellence awards); also one-woman shows. Judge mktg. and distributive edn. Colo. and Nat., 1975-86; v.p. Friendship Force Internat., 1990—; coord. Internat. Cultural Celebration, Colorado Springs, 1993-95; mem. Common Ground Arts and Cultural, Colorado Springs, 1994—, sr. adv. com. Colorado Springs, 1995—; deacon First Presbyn. Ch., Colorado Springs. Recipient 6 Corporation awards, 1974-79. Republican. Avocations: nature, birds, animals, plants, gardening. Home: 525 Quebec Cir Colorado Springs CO 80911-2615

LEE, KENNETH, secondary education educator. Elem. tchr. Highlands Intermediate Sch., Pearl City, Hawaii, 1986—. Recipient Tchr. Excellence award Internat. Tech. Edn. Assn., Hawaii, 1992. Office: Highlands Intermediate Sch 1460 Hoolaulea St Pearl City HI 96782-2198*

LEE, LILA JUNE, historical society officer, library director; b. Ukiah, Calif., July 12, 1923; d. Arthur L. and Leila Edna (Rose) Romer; m. Dale R. Laney, May 1, 1944 (div. Sept. 1952); m. Robert James Lee, Apr. 16, 1955; children: Arthur John, Margarett June. Officer Mendocino County Hist. Soc., Ukiah, 1960-95; libr. dir. Held Poage Libr., Ukiah, 1970—. Mem. conf. of Calif. Hist. Soc. (regional v.p. 1980—), Mendocino County Hist. Soc. (v.p., treas., fin. sec.). Republican. Presbyterian. Avocation: California postcards collector. Office: Mendocino County Hist Soc 603 W Perkins St Ukiah CA 95482-4726

LEE, LONG CHI, electrical engineering and chemistry educator; b. Kaohsiung, Taiwan, Oct. 19, 1940; came to U.S., 1965; s. Chin Lai Lee and Wen Wang; m. Laura Meichau Cheng, Dec. 1, 1967 (dec. Dec. 1988); children: Gloria, Thomas; m. Masako Suto, Jan. 6, 1990 (dec. July 1996); m. Linda L. Chang, Apr. 8, 1997. BS in Physics, Taiwan Normal U., Taiwan, 1964; MA in Physics, U. So. Calif., L.A., 1967, PhD in Physics, 1971. Rsch. staff U. So. Calif., L.A., 1971-77; physicist SRI Internat., Menlo Park, Calif., 1977-79, sr. physicist, 1979-81; prof. elec. engring. San Diego State U., 1982—, adj. prof. chemistry, 1986—; adj. asst. prof. U. So. Calif., L.A., 1977; chmn. bd. Fiber Does, Inc., 1994-98, Superior Evaporants, Inc., 1994—; bd. dirs. Genix, Biotech, Inc. Contbr. papers to profl. jours. Pres. Taiwanese Cultural Assn. in San Diego, 1983, 93. Rsch. grantee NSF, 1980-94, NASA, 1979-94, Air Force Office Sci. Rsch., 1980-89, Naval Rsch. Office, 1986-89. Mem. IEEE, Am. Phys. Soc., Am. Geophys. Union, Inter-Am. Photochem. Soc., Formesan Assn. for Pub. Affairs (pres. San Diego chpt. 1990-91), Taiwanese-Am. Investment Club (pres. 1995-96). Office: San Diego State U Dept Elec & Computer Engring San Diego CA 92182

LEE, LORRIN L., marketing executive, architect, designer, author, speaker; b. Honolulu, July 22, 1941; s. Bernard Chong and Betty (Lum) L.; m. Nina Christine Fedoroscko, June 10, 1981. BArch, U. Mich., 1970; MBA, Columbia Pacific U., 1981, PhD in Psychology, 1981. Registered arch., Hawaii. Arch. Clifford Young AIA, Honolulu, 1971-72, Aotani & Oka AIA, Honolulu, 1972-74, Geoffrey Fairfax FAIA, Honolulu, 1974-76; seminar leader Lorrin Lee Program, Honolulu, 1976-81; star grand master coord. Enhance Corp., 1981-83; 5-diamond supr. Herbalife Internat., L.A., 1984-85, mem. global expansion team, 1993—; presdl. dir. Uni-Vite Internat., San Diego, 1989-92; rep. Internat. Pen Friends, 1995—; mgr. Cyber Media Sales, 1996—. Author: Here is Genius, 1980. Editor Honolulu Chinese Jaycees, Honolulu, 1972, v.p., 1983; active Makiki Cmty. Ctr., Honolulu, 1974. 1st lt. U.S. Army, 1967-70, Okinawa. Recipient Braun-Knect-Heimann award, 1959, 1st prize in design Kidjel Cali-Pro Internat., 1975, Kitchen Design award Sub-zero Contest, 1994; named Honolulu Chinese Jaycee of Yr., Honolulu Chinese Jaycees, 1973. Mem. Nature Conservancy, Sierra Club. Avocations: international travel, hiking, desktop publishing, photography, reading. Fax: 808-947-8817. E-mail: lorrin@global-homebiz.com. Office: 758 Kapahulu Ave # 101 Honolulu HI 96816

LEE, MARGARET ANNE, social worker, psychotherapist; b. Scribner, Nebr., Nov. 23, 1930; d. William Christian and Caroline Bertha (Benner) Joens; m. Robert Kelly Lee, May 21, 1950 (div. 1972); children: Lawrence Robert, James Kelly, Daniel Richard. AA, Napa Coll., 1949; student, U. Calif., Berkeley, 1949-50; BA, Calif. State Coll., Sonoma, 1975; MSW, Calif. State U., Sacramento, 1977. Diplomate clin. social worker; lic. clin. social worker, Calif.; lic. marriage and family counselor, Calif.; tchr. Columnist, stringer Napa (Calif.) Register, 1946-50; eligibility worker, supr. Napa County Dept. Social Services, 1968-75; instr. Napa Valley Community Coll., 1978-83; practice psychotherapy Napa, 1977—; oral commr. Calif. Dept. Consumer Affairs, Bd. Behavioral Sci., 1984-90; bd. dirs. Project Access, 1978-79. Trustee Napa Valley C.C., 1983—, v.p. bd., 1984-85, pres. bd., 1986, 90, 95, clk., 1988-89; bd. dirs. Napa County Coun. Econ. Opportunity, 1984-85, Napa chpt. March of Dimes, 1957-71, Mental Health Assn. Napa County, 1983-87; vice chmn. edn. com. Calif. C.C. Trustees, 1987-88, chmn. edn. com., 1988-89, legis. com., 1985-87, bd. dirs., 1989—, 2d v.p., 1991, 1st v.p., 1992, pres., 1993; mem. student equity rev. group Calif. C.C. Chancellors, 1992; bd. dirs. C.C. League Calif., 1992-95, 1st v.p., 1992. Recipient Fresh Start award Self mag., award Congl. Caucus on Women's Issues, 1984; named Woman of distinction, Soroptimist Internat. and Sunrise Clubs of Napa, 1997. Mem. NASW, Calif. Elected Women's Assn. Edn. and Rsch. Democrat. Lutheran. Office: 1100 Trancas St Napa CA 94558-2908

LEE, MARTHA, artist, writer; b. Chehalis, Wash., Aug. 23, 1946; d. William Robert and Phyllis Ann (Herzog) L.; m. Peter Reynolds Lockwood, Jan. 25, 1974 (div. 1982). BA in English Lit., U. Wash., 1968; student, Factory of Visual Art, 1980-82. Reporter Seattle Post-Intelligencer, 1970; personnel counselor Theresa Snow Employment, 1971-72; receptionist Northwest Kidney Ctr., 1972-73; proprietress The Reliquary, 1974-77; travel agt. Cathay Express, 1977-79; artist, 1980—; represented by Mahler Fine Arts, Seattle, Ferrier Gallery, Ocean Park, Wash. Painter various oil paintings; exhibited in numerous one-woman and group shows throught Oreg. and Wash.; author: To The Beach and Other Poems, 1998. Avocations: horseback riding, beachcombing, reading, music. Home and Studio: PO Box 1157 Ocean Park WA 98640-1157

LEE, MEREDITH, German literature and language educator; b. St. Louis, July 11, 1945; m. Anthony Battaglia, Nov. 18, 1977. BA summa cum laude, St. Olaf Coll., Northfield, Minn., 1968; MPhil with distinction, Yale U., 1971, PhD, 1976. Asst. prof. U. Calif., Irvine, 1974-81; assoc. prof. U. Calif., 1981-93; prof. U. Calif., Irvine, 1993—, dean undergrad. studies, 1984-88, assoc. dean humanities, 1982-84, chair dept. German, 1991—; sec., treas., dir. Goethe Soc. N.Am., 1979-94, exec. sec., 1994-98; chair area adv. com. Coun. for Internat. Exch. Scholars, Washington, 1986-88. Author: Studies in Goethe's Lyric Cycles, 1978; co-editor: Interpreting Goethe's Faust Today, 1994, Displacing Authority: Goethe's Poetic Reception of Klopstock, 1999; contbr. articles to profl. jours. Danforth fellow, 1968-74; Fulbright scholar, Göttingen, Fed. Republic Germany, 1972-73. Mem. Am. Assn. Tchrs. German, Am. Soc. for 18th Century Studies, Soc. For Values in High Edn., Modern Lang. Assn., German Studies Assn. (exec. com. 1983-86), Phi Beta Kappa. Lutheran. Office: U Calif Dept German Irvine CA 92697-3150

LEE, MICHAEL CHARLES, landscape architect; b. Renton, Wash., July 27, 1948; s. Charles Edmund and Doris Darlene (Litch) L. BA, U. Wash., 1974. Landscape designer Robert W. Chittock, Seattle, 1973, Jongejan-Gerrard-McNeal Assocs., Bellevue, Wash., 1973-79; owner, mgr. Michael Lee Landscape Architect, Seattle, 1979—; owner Colvos Creek Nursery, Vashon Island, Wash.; instr. horticulture U. Wash. Exptl. Coll., Seattle, 1974-86. Author: Trees of Western Washington, 1975; garden columnist Highline Times, Burien, Wash., 1977-78; contbr. articles to profl. jours; botanical illustrator books and posters. Mem. Arboretum Found. Avocations: gardening, art, music, hiking, writing. Office: 1904 3rd Ave Ste 415 Seattle WA 98101-1150

LEE, MURLIN E., solutions manager; b. Crescent City, Calif., Jan. 4, 1957; s. George Lee and Ida Burl (Wilson) M.; m. Jeanine Marie Metcalfe, Apr. 13, 1985; children: Kimberly, Kristen, Gina. BS in Bus. Adminstrn., Calif. Poly. U., Pomona, 1981; MS in Software Engring., Nat. U., San Jose, Calif., 1988. Mgr. George M. Lee Enterprises Inc., Crescent City, Calif., 1979-80, Wells Aviation, Ontario, Calif., 1980-81, Bard Software, San Jose, Calif., 1982-84; software engr. Litton Applied Techology, San Jose, 1984-89; program mgr. Condor Systems, Inc., San Jose, 1989-95; tech. mgr. Aspect Devel. Inc., Mountain View, Calif., 1995—. Republican. Avocations: computers, gardening, model railroads, bicycling, music. Home: 4081 Will Rogers Dr San Jose CA 95117-2730 Office: Aspect Development Inc 1300 Charleston Rd Mountain View CA 94043-1331

LEE, PALI JAE (POLLY JAE STEAD LEE), retired librarian, writer; b. Nov. 26, 1929; d. Jonathan Everett Wheeler and Ona Katherine (Grunder) Stead; m. Richard H.W. Lee, Apr. 7, 1945 (div. 1978); children: Catherine Lani Honcoop, Karin Lee Robinson, Ona G., Laurie Brett, Robin Louise Lee Halbert; m. John K. Willis, 1979 (dec. 1994). Student, U. Hawaii, 1944-46, Mich. State, 1961-64. Cataloguer and processor U.S. Army Air Force, 1945-46; with U.S. Weather Bur. Film Library, New Orleans, 1948-50, FBI, Wright-Patterson AFB, Dayton, Ohio, 1952, Ohio Wholesale Winedealers, Columbus, Ohio, 1956-58, Civil. Engring., Ohio State U., Columbus, 1959; writer tech. manual Annie Whittenmeyer Home, Davenport, Iowa, 1960; with Grand Rapids (Mich.) Pub. Library, 1961-62; dir. Waterford (Mich.) Twp. Libraries, 1962-64; acquisition librarian Pontiac (Mich.) Pub. Libraries, 1965-71, dir. East Side br., 1971-73; rsch. asst. dept. anthropology Bishop Mus., Honolulu, 1975-83; pub. Night Rainbow Pub., Honolulu, 1984—. Author: Mary Dyer, Child of Light, 1973, Giant: Pictorial History of the Human Colossus, 1973, History of Change: Kaneohe Bay Area, 1976, English edit., 1983, Na Po Makole-Tales of the Night Rainbow, 1981, rev. edit., 1988, Mo'olelo O Na Pohukaina, 1983, Ka Ipu Kukui, 1994; contbr. articles to profl. jours. Chmn. Oakland County br. Multiple Sclerosis Soc., 1972-73, co-chmn. Pontiac com. of Mich. area bd., 1972-73; sec. Ohana o Kokua, 1979-83, Paia-Willis Ohana, 1982-91, Ohana Kame'ekua, 1988-91; bd. dirs. Detroit Multiple Sclerosis Soc., 1971; mem. Mich. area bd. Am. Friends Svc. com., 1961-69; mem. consumer adv. bd. Libr. for Blind and Physically Handicapped, Honolulu, 1991-96, mem. adv. bd., 1997-98; pres. consumer 55 plus bd. Honolulu Ctr. for Ind. Living, 1990-94, pres., 1995-96; pres. Honolulu chpt. Nat. Fedn. of Blind, 1991-94, 1st v.p. #93 state affiliate, 1991-94, editor Na Na Maka Aloha newsletter, 1990-94; 1st v.p. Hawaii chpt. Talking Book Readers Club, 1994-95, pres., 1996. Recipient Mother of the Yr. award Quad City Bus. Men, 1960, Bowl of Light award Hawaiian Community of Hawaii, 1989. Mem. Internat. Platform Assn., Soc. Friends. Office: PO Box 10706 Honolulu HI 96816-0706

LEE, PAMELA ANNE, bank executive, accountant, business analyst; b. San Francisco, May 30, 1960; d. Larry D. and Alice Mary (Reece) L. BBA, San Francisco State U., 1981. CPA, Calif. Typist, bookkeeper, tax acct. James G. Woo, CPA, San Francisco, 1979-85; tutor bus. math. and statistics San Francisco State U., 1979-80; teller to ops. officer Gibraltar Savs. and Loan, San Francisco, 1978-81; sr. acct. Price Waterhouse, San Francisco, 1981-86; corp. acctg. mgr. First Nationwide Bank, Daly City, Calif., 1986-89, v.p., 1989-91, v.p., project mgr., 1991-92, sr. conversion and bus. analyst, 1992-93; sr. bus. analyst, asst. v.p. Bank of Am., 1993-96, sr. bus. analyst, v.p. Bank of Am., 1996-98; mktg. cons., v.p. Bank Am., San Francisco, 1998—; acctg. cons. New Performance Gallery, San Francisco, 1985, San Francisco Chamber Orch., 1986. Founding mem., chair bd. trustees Asian Acctg. Students Career Day, 1988-89; vol. Mickaboo Cockatiel Rescue, 1998—. Mem. NAFE, AICPA, Calif. Soc. CPA's. Republican. Avocations: reading, music, travel, personal computing, crafting. Office: 425 1st St 3d Fl San Francisco CA 94105

LEE, QWIHEE PARK, plant physiologist; b. Republic of Korea, Mar. 1, 1941; came to U.S., 1965; d. Yong-sik and Soon-duk (Paik) Park; m. Ick-whan Lee, May 20, 1965; children: Tina, Amy, Benjamin. MS, Seoul Nat. U., Republic of Korea, 1965; PhD, U. Minn., 1973. Head dept. plant physiology Korea Ginseng and Tobacco Inst., Seoul, 1980-82; instr. Sogang U., Seoul, 1981, Seoul Women's U., 1981; research assoc. U. Wash., Seattle, 1975-79. Exec. dir. Korean Community Counseling Ctr., Seattle, 1983-86. Named one of 20 Prominent Asian Women in Wash. State, Chinese Post Seattle, 1986. Mem. AAAS. Buddhist. Home: 13025 42nd Ave NE Seattle WA 98125-4624 Office: U Wash Dept Pharm SJ-30 1959 NE Pacific St Seattle WA 98195-0001

LEE, RICHARD FRANCIS JAMES, evangelical clergyman, media consultant; b. Yakima, Wash., Sept. 13, 1967; s. Richard Francis and Dorothy Aldean (Blackwell). Diploma, Berean Coll., Springfield, Mo., 1989; BA, U. Wash., Seattle, 1990; postgrad., Gonzaga Sch. Law, 1994-97, Fuller Theol. Seminary, 1997—. Lic. clergyman Gen. Coun. of the Assemblies of God, Seattle, 1989—. Author: Tell Me the Story, 1982, The Crimson Detective Motion Picture, 1996. Named Most Likely to be President, Franklin High Sch., Seattle, 1986. Pentecostal. Avocations: collector, writer, itinerant speaker, filmmaker. Home: 262 N Los Robles Ave Apt 105 Pasadena CA 91101-1534 Office: Evangel Outreach Ministries 2604 E Boone Ave Spokane WA 99202-3718

LEE, SIMI, sportswriter, sports promoter; b. San Francisco, May 3, 1947; d. Edward and Winnie (Loy) L. BA in Polit. Sci., U. Calif., Berkeley, 1969; JD, U. Calif., San Francisco, 1976. Sportswriter San Mateo (Calif.) Times, 1976—. Mem.jr. Olympic softball com. Amateur Softball Assn., San Mateo, 1986—. Mem. Calif. Press Women (Calif. Sportswriter award 1984, 88, 90).

LEE, SUN MYUNG, physician; b. Seoul, Korea, July 9, 1940; d. Jong Suk and Soo Nam Lee; m. Hi Young; children: Sandra Shon, Grace, David. BS, Yonsei U., Seoul, 1961, MD, 1965. Diplomate Am. Acad. Family Practice. Intern Riverside Methodist Hosp., Columbus, Oh., 1967-68; resident Veteran's Adminstrn. Hosp., Dayton, Oh., 1968-69; intern Riverside Meth. Hosp., Columbus, Ohio, 1966-67; resident Ohio State VA Hosp., Dayton, 1967-70; pvt. practice family medicine Drs. Lee & Lee PS, Spokane, Wash., 1974—; mem. med. staff Ea. State Hosp., Medical Lake, Wash., 1972-74; pres. Drs. Lee & Lee P.S., 1974—. Author: Best Poetry of 1997, 1997; columnist Rainier Forum, Korea Post, 1995-96. Pres. Korean Lang. Sch., Spokane, 1974; Guwonsa, Korean Presbyn. Ch. Spokane, 1989—; bd. trustees Korean Assn. Inland Empire, Spokane, 1995. Recipient Editors Choice award Nat. Libr. Poetry, 1996. Fellow Am. Acad. Family Physicians. Avocations: choral music, poetry, gardening. Office: Drs Lee and Lee PS 17 E Empire Ave Spokane WA 99207-1707

LEE, YEU-TSU MARGARET, surgeon, educator; b. Xian, Shensi, China, Mar. 18, 1936; m. Thomas V. Lee, Dec. 29, 1962 (div. 1987); 1 child, Maxwell M. AB in Microbiology, U. S.D., 1957; MD, Harvard U., 1961. Cert. Am. Bd. Surgery. Assoc. prof. surgery Med. Sch., U. So. Calif., L.A., 1973-83; commd. lt. col. U.S. Army Med. Corps, 1983, advanced through grades to col., 1989; chief surg. oncology Tripler Army Med. Ctr., Honolulu, 1983—; assoc. clin. prof. surgery Med. Sch., U. Hawaii, Honolulu, 1984-92, clin. prof. surgery, 1992—. Author: Malignant Lymphoma, 1974; author chpts to books; contbr. articles to profl. jours. Pres. Orgn. Chinese-Am. Women, L.A., 1981, Hawaii chpt., 1988; active U.S.-China Friendship Assn., 1991—. Decorated Nat. Def. Svc. medal, Army Commendation medal, Army Meritorious Svc. medal, Army Humanitarian Svc. medal; recipient

Chinese-Am. Engrs. and Scis. Assn., 1987; named Sci. Woman Warrior, Asian-Pacific Womens Network, 1983. Mem. ACS, Soc. Surg. Oncology, Assn. Women Surgeons. Avocations: classical music, movies, hiking, ballroom dancing. Office: Tripler Army Med Ctr Dept Surgery Honolulu HI 96859

LEE, YOUNG HO (JINWOL), Buddhist monk, educator; b. Uiwang, Kyonggi, Korea, Apr. 28, 1950; came to U.S., 1986; s. Chong Taek and Kyong Bok (Kim) L. BA, Dongguk U., Seoul, 1984, Sogang U., Seoul, Korea, 1986; MA, U. Hawaii, 1990; PhD, U. Calif., Berkeley, 1998; Diploma, Haein Sangha Coll., Korea. Buddhist monk. Pres. Soc. Zen Studies, Seoul, 1982-83; Dharma tchr. Kiwonjong-sa Temple, Seoul, 1984-86; Dharma and Zen tchr. Daewonsa Temple, Honolulu, 1986-92; v.p. Hawaii Assn. Internat. Buddhists, Honolulu, 1992-94; internat. advisor Soc. Buddhist Christian Studies, Pitts., 1994-96; Zen and Dharma tchr. Group in Buddhist Studies U. Calif., Berkeley, 1996—; cons. United Religion, San Francisco, 1996. Contbr. articles to profl. jours. Mem. Am. Acad. Religion, Soc. Buddhist-Christian Studies, Calif. buddhist Assn. (founder, pres., advisor 1992-96). Home: 2810 Lavender Dr Walnut Creek CA 94596-6420 Office: Univ of Calif-Berkeley Group in Buddhist Studies Berkeley CA 94704

LEE, YOUNG MOO, protein chemist; b. Seoul, Jan. 17, 1941; came to U.S., 1968; s. Ki Yung and Ji H. (Han) L.; m. Il Hui Kang, Mar. 27, 1971; 1 child, Robert S. BS in Chemistry, Seoul Nat. U., 1963; PhD in Nutrition, U. Calif., Berkeley, 1973. Asst. rsch. biochemist U. Calif., Davis, 1983-84; rsch. specialist Mich. State U., East Lansing, 1985, assoc. prof., 1986; dir. protein biochem. Applied Immune Scis., Santa Clara, Calif., 1987-93; dir. protein structure lab. U. Calif., Davis, 1994—. Contbr. articles to profl. jours. 1st lt. Korean Air Force, 1963-67. Mem. AAAS, Am. Chem. Soc., The Protein Soc., Assn. of Biomolecular Resource Facility, Sierra Lions Club (pres. 1994-95). Achievements include patent for recombinant bovine conglutinin and fragments. Avocations: white water rafting, backpacking, reading, singing. Office: Protein Structure Lab Univ Calif Davis CA 95616

LEEB, CHARLES SAMUEL, clinical psychologist; b. San Francisco, July 18, 1945; s. Sidney Herbert and Dorothy Barbara (Fishstrom) L.; m. Storme Lynn Gilkey, Apr. 28, 1984; children: Morgan Evan, Spencer Douglas. BA in Psychology, U. Calif.-Davis, 1967; MS in Counseling and Guidance, San Diego State U., 1970; PhD in Edn. and Psychology, Claremont Grad. Sch., 1973. Assoc. So. Regional Dir. Mental Retardation Ctr., Las Vegas, Nev., 1976-79; pvt. practice, Las Vegas, 1978-79; dir. biofeedback and athletics Menninger Found., Topeka, 1979-82, dir. children's div. biofeedback and psychophysiology ctr. The Menninger Found., 1979-82; pvt. practice, Claremont, Calif., 1982—; dir. of psychol. svcs. Horizon Hosp., 1986-88; dir. adolescent chem. dependency and children's program Charter Oak Hosp., Covina, Calif., 1989-91; founder, chief exec. officer Rsch. and Treatment Inst., Claremont, 1991—; lectr. in field. Contbr. articles to profl. jours. Mem. Am. Psychol. Assn., Calif. State Psychol. Assn. Office: 937 W Foothill Blvd Ste D Claremont CA 91711-3358

LEEDS, JEFFREY L., company executive; b. Bklyn., Mar. 8, 1961; s. Howard Myron Leeds and Arlene (Rabinowitz) Singer; m. Maresha Sceats, Feb. 27, 1993. BA, San Diego State U., 1983, MA, 1987; PhD, Ariz. State U., 1991. Prin. rsch. investigator Logicon, Inc., San Diego, 1988-91; dir. tng. BMDP Statis. Software, L.A., 1991-93, Quarterdeck Corp., Santa Monica, Calif., 1993-95, sr. product mgr. Symantec Corp., Santa Monica, 1995-97; group product mgr. Network Assocs., Santa Clara, Calif., 1997—. Patentee color for ATC controls; author numerous govt. reports in field. Mem. APA. Jewish. Avocations: tropical fish, sports, collectibles, music, snow skiing. Home: 4051 Berryman Ave Los Angeles CA 90066-5423

LEEDS, MARGARET ANN, assistant principal; b. Memphis, Tex., Sept. 14, 1934; d. Roy Alvin and Abbie Cordelia (O'Neal) Massey; m. Charles Stanton Leeds, Nov. 3, 1959 (div. 1965). BA, Baylor U., 1956; MLA, U. So. Calif., 1976. Cert. tchr. secondary theatre arts, French, phys. edn., English. Tchr. Rexford Jr. and Sr. H.S., Beverly Hills, Calif., 1958-60; substitute tchr. Beverly Hills Unified Sch. Dist., 1960-66; tchr. phys. edn. Beverly Hills H.S., 1966-89, chair dept. phys. edn., 1981-89, asst. prin., 1989—, coach various sports incl. volleyball, gymnastics, fencing, 1966-89; cons. Calif. Dept. Edn., 1986—, ofcl. volleyball ofcl. Nat. Assn. Girls and Women's Sports, 1975-80; presenter sessions to various confs., 1985—; conductor insvc. tng. workshops. Author: Beverly Hills Unified School District Physical Education Scope and Sequence, 1988, Beverly Hills High School Health Fitness Manual, 1987, Fight Back: A Woman's Guide to Self Defense, 1978; contbr. articles to profl. jours.; prodr. video tapes: Implementing Health Fitness in Schools, 1987, Physical Education is Alive and Well in Beverly Hills, California, 1986. Cons. Calif. Gov.'s Coun. on Phys. Fitness and Sports, 1993—; adv. bd. L.A. UNICEF, 1993—; ham radio operator Beverly Hills Disaster Comm. Sys. Vol., 1994—, L.A. County Disaster Comm. Sys. Vol., 1994—. Recipient Calif. Educator award Calif. Dept. Edn., 1987. Mem. NEA, AAHPERD (reviewer Jour. Health, Phys. Edn., Recreation and Dance 1989—, Calif. phys. best coord. 1988—, pub. rels. coord. 1987-91), Calif. Tchrs. Assn., Beverly Hills Edn. Assn. (pres. 1969-70), Calif. Assn. Health, Phys. Edn., Recreation and Dance (pres. unit 401 1986-88, dir. CORE Project 1987-91, pub. rels. chair 1987—, adminstrn. and supervision chair phys. edn. adv. com. 1994—, Honor award 1993, Outstanding Secondary Phys. Educator 1987, Calif. Phys. Educator of Yr. 1985). Baha'i Faith. Avocations: travel, folk art collecting, marathon running/jogging, backpacking, reading. Home: 1557 S Beverly Glen Blvd Los Angeles CA 90024-6163 Office: Beverly Hills High Sch 241 S Moreno Dr Beverly Hills CA 90212-3698

LEEDS-HORWITZ, SUSAN BETH, school system administrator, speech-language pathology educator; b. L.A., Mar. 14, 1950; d. Henry Herbert and Lee (Weiss) Leeds; m. Stanley Martin Horwitz, Nov. 28, 1975; 1 child, Brian David. BA, Calif. State U., Northridge, 1971; MEd, U. S.C., 1973; adminstrv. credential, U. LaVerne, 1984. Itinerant speech pathologist L.A. City Schs., 1973-74; severe lang. disorders tchr. L.A. County Bd. Edn., Downey, Calif., 1974-88; tchr. on spl. assignment Santa Clarita Valley Spl. Edn. Local Plan Area, Newhall, Calif., 1986-88; coord. spl. programs, testing, evaluation and migrant edn. Castaic (Calif.) Union Sch. Dist., 1988-94, adminstr., 1988-1994; ednl. cons. Richmond, Calif., 1994-95; coord. grants & project devel. Glendale (Calif.) Unified Sch. Dist., 1995—. Author: Project Próspero: A Traditional Bilingual Education Program for Grades 2-8, 1991, Project TEAM: Together Everyone Achieves More Comprehensive School Program, 1995, Hoover-Keppel-Keppel Healthy Start Family Resource Center, 1996, Volunteers for Youth: From the Community for the Community, 1996, FRANKLIN: Focusing on Educational Restructuring and Needs of Kids and Their Families Through Upgraded Learning and Instruction with a Neighborhood Learning Center, 1996, SB1510 School-Based Educational Technology Program, Daily High School, 1996, Project Y.E.S. (Youth Enrichment Services), 1997, Pathway to Teaching, 1997, Glendale High School Healthy Start Family Resource Center, 1998, Opening New Doors to Careers. Grantee student enhancement program Kaiser-Permanente Community Svcs., 1992, Opening Need Doors to Careers, School-to-Career grantee Burbank, Glendale and La Cañada Sch. Dists., 1997, Tobacco Use Prevention Edn. grantee, 1998. Mem. ASCD, Am. Speech Lang and Hearing Assn. (cert.), So. Calif. Assn. Alumnae Panhellenic (pres. 1993-94), Down Syndrome Congress, Assn. Calif. Sch. Adminstrs., San Fernando Valley Panhellenic Assn. (rep. 1976-96, pres. 1993-95), Glendale Schs. Mgmt. Assn., Santa Clarita Valley C. of C. (edn. com., anti-gang com., tchr. tribute com.), Delta Kappa Gamma, Alpha Xi Delta (Edna Epperson Brinkman award 1985), Phi Delta Kappa, Delta Rho Bldg. Corp. of Alpha Xi Delta (pres. 1996—). Office: 223 N Jackson St Glendale CA 91206-4334

LEELAND, STEVEN BRIAN, electronics engineer; b. Tampa, Fla., Dec. 27, 1951; s. N. Stanford and Shirley Mae (Bahner) L.; m. Karen Frances Hayes, Dec. 20, 1980; children: Crystal Mary, April Marie. BSEE, MSEE magna cum laude, U. South Fla., 1976. Registered profl. engr., Ariz. Engr. Bendix Avionics, Ft. Lauderdale, Fla., 1976-77; prin. engr., instr. Sperry Avionics, Phoenix, 1977-84; prin. staff engr. Motorola Govt. Electronics Group, Scottsdale, Ariz., 1984-88; engring. fellow, mgr. dept. software engring. Fairchild Data Corp., Scottsdale, 1988-98; prin. staff engr. Teledesic Sys. Arch., Motorola Space Sys. Tech. Group, 1998—; cons. Motorola Govt. Electronics Group, 1991. Patentee systolic array, 1990; contbr. articles to profl. jours. Mem. IEEE (Phoenix chpt. Computer Soc. treas. 1978-79, sec. 1979-80, chmn. 1980-81, 81-82), Tau Beta Pi, Pi Mu Epsilon, Phi Kappa Phi, Omicron Delta Kappa, Themis. Republican. Adventist. Avocations: chess, computers, biking, exercise, health. Home: 10351 E Sharon Dr Scottsdale AZ 85260-9000 Office: Fairchild Data Corp 5025 E Washington St Phoenix AZ 85034-2015

LEESON, SUSAN M., state judge. Law clerk U.S. 9th Cir. Ct. of Appeals; Tom. C. Clark judicial fellow U.S. Supreme Ct.; prof. polit. sci., assoc. prof. law Willamette U., Salem, Oreg.; judge Oreg. Ct. Appeals, 1993-98, Oreg. Supreme Ct., 1998—. Former mem. Oreg. Criminal Justice Coun., Marion-Polk Local Govt. Boundary Commn. Office: Supreme Ct Bldg 1163 State St Salem OR 97310-0260*

LEETS, PETER J., consulting firm executive; b. London, Mar. 12, 1946; came to U.S., 1948; s. Earl Edward and Doris Eileen L.; m. Anne E. Shahinian, May 15, 1982. BS in Mktg., Ind. U., 1969. Salesman Ortho Pharm. Corp., Raritan, N.J., 1969-74; account mgr. Revlon Inc., Indpls., 1974-76; regional dir. Revlon Inc., Cleve., 1976-79; field sales mgr. Revlon Inc., Bay Village, Ohio, 1979-83; nat. field sales mgr. Binney & Smith, Bethlehem, Pa., 1983-85; v.p., dir. sales Dell Pub. Co., Inc., N.Y.C., 1985-87; exec. v.p. Geneva Corp., Irvine, Calif., 1987-88; pres. Geneva Cos., Costa Mesa, Calif., 1988-90; exec. v.p. Exec. Assets Corp., Irvine, Calif., 1990-91; pres. Exec. Assets Corp., 1992-94; reg. mng. prin. Right Mgmt. Cons., Irvine, Calif., 1994—; bd. dirs. Career Beginnings, Career Transition Ptnrs., Constl. Rights Found., Prof. Coaches Mentors Assn. Chairperson Orange County Econ. Outlook Conf.; bd. dirs. Forum for Corp. Dirs., PIHRA Found. Fellow Outplacement Inst.; mem. Internat. Assn. Career Mgmt. Profls. (bd. dirs.), Ind. U. Alumni (life), Delta Chi. Office: Right Mgmt Cons Inc 3333 Michelson Dr Ste 400 Irvine CA 92612-1684

LEFEBVRE, PEGGY ANDERSON, advertising executive; b. Springfield, Mo., Dec. 2, 1951; d. Paul William and Norma Jean (Turk) Anderson; m. Donald E. Lefebvre, July 25, 1980. BA in Graphic Arts cum laude, U. Ill., 1974; MBA, Pacific Western U., 1993. Coord. advt. and trade show Bell & Howell, Salt Lake City, 1971-74; designer, prodn. asst. Sta. KUTV, Salt Lake City, 1974; art dir. Associated Advt., Salt Lake City, 1977-80; owner, creative dir. Lefebvre Advt., Anaheim, Calif., 1980—; freelance designer various advt. agys., Chgo.; bd. dirs. Delmark Corp.; past guest lectr. advt. copywriting and bus. devel. Nat. U., Inc. Mag., Orange Coast Coll. One woman shows Ward Gallery, Chgo., 1974, Atrium Gallery, Salt Lake City, 1976. Past bd. dirs. MADD, Orange County Sexual Assault Network; mem. Anaheim Area Visitor and Conv. Bd., Western States Advt. Agy. Assn. Recipient Excellence in Creative Direction award, Bus. and Profl. Advt. Assn., 1989, 94, Outstanding Achievement in Advt. award Western Assn. Conv. & Visitor Burs, Award of Merit Bus. Comms. and Mktg. Assn. L.A., 1991, 95, Award of Excellence, 1995, Telly award, 1996, Summit award for outdoor advtg., 1996, Silver Microphone award, 1996. Mem. DAR. Republican. Office: Lefebvre Advt 1547 E La Palma Ave Anaheim CA 92805-1614

LEFEVRE, GREG, broadcast executive; b. Los Angeles, Jan. 28, 1947; s. Robert Bazille and Anna Marie (Violé) L.; m. Mary Deborah Bottoms, July 10, 1971. AA, Valley Coll., 1970; BS, San Diego State U., 1972, postgrad. Asst. news dir. Sta. KDEO, San Diego, 1971-73; reporter Sta. KFMB-TV, San Diego, 1973-75; sr. reporter Sta. KDFW-TV, Dallas, 1976-81; news dir. Sta. KSEE-TV, Fresno, Calif., 1981-83; corr. Cable News Network, San Francisco, 1983-89, bur. chief, 1989—. Mem. AP Broadcasters, Soc. Profl. Journalists, Radio and TV News Dirs. Assn. Club: Dallas Press (v.p. 1978-81). Office: CNN Am Inc 50 California St Ste 950 San Francisco CA 94111-4606

LEFKOWITZ, JERRY BRUCE, pathology educator; b. Richmond, Va., Oct. 27, 1956; s. Meyer Bear and Shirley Lefkowitz. BS in Chemistry, U. Richmond, 1979; MD, Med. Coll. Va., 1983. Diplomate Am. Bd. Pathology. Intern U. Louisville, 1983-84, resident, 1984-88; fellow U. N.C., Chapel Hill, 1988-91; asst. prof. U. Colo. Health Sci. Ctr., Denver, 1991—. Fellow Coll. Am. Pathologists; mem. Am. Soc. Hematology, Colo. Assn. Continuing Med. Edn. (treas., bd. dirs. 1994—). Avocations: photography. Office: U Colo Health Sci Ctr 4200 E 9th Ave Denver CO 80220-3706

LEFRANC, MARGARET (MARGARET SCHOONOVER), artist, illustrator, editor, writer; b. N.Y.C., Mar. 15, 1907; d. Abraham and Sophie (Teplitz) Frankel; m. Raymond Schoonover, 1942 (div. 1945). Student, Art Students League, N.Y.C., Kunstschule des Westerns, Berlin, NYU Grad. Sch., Andre L'Hote, Paris, Acad. Grande Chaumiere, Paris. Tchr. art Adult Edn., Los Alamos, 1946, Miami (Fla.) Mus. Modern Art, 1975-76; mem. Art in the Embassies Program, Paris, 1998—. Exhibited in one-person shows at Mus. N.Mex., Santa Fe, 1948, 51, 53, Philbrook Art Ctr., Tulsa, 1949, 51,, Okla. Art Ctr., 1950, Recorder Workshop, Miami, 1958, St. John's Coll., Santa Fe, 1993, 97, A Lifetime of Imaging (works on paper), 1921-95, Figurative Works, 1920-30, Cline Fine Art Gallery, 1997; group shows include Salon de Tuileries, Paris, 1928, 29, 30, Art Inst. Chgo., 1936, El Paso Mus. Art, 1964, Mus. Modern Art, 1974, North Miami Mus. Contemporary Art, 1984, Miami Collects, 1989, Women's Caucus Invitational, 1990, Gov.'s Gallery, Santa Fe, 1992, Gene Autry Western Heritage Mus, 1995, Gilcrease Mus., Tulsa, 1996, Mus. N.Mex. Santa Fe, 1996, Brigham Young U., Provo, Utah, 1996, Art in the Embassies Program, Paris, 1998—; represented in collections at Beiles Artes, Mexico City, Mus. Fine Arts, Santa Fe. Bd. dirs., pres. Artist Equity of Fla., 1964-68; v.p. Miami Art Assn., 1958-60; founder, bd. dirs. Guild Art Gallery, N.Y.C., 1935-37. Recipient Illustration award Fifty Best Books of Yr., Libr. of Congress, 1948, Hon. Mention award Rodeo Santa Fe, Mus. N.Mex., 1949, others, Gov.'s award for Excellence and Achievement in the Arts, 1996.

LEFTWICH, JAMES STEPHEN, management consultant; b. Stevenage, Eng., Nov. 30, 1956; came to U.S., 1957; s. James Wright and Del Maureen (Thomson) L.; m. Carol Petersen, Nov. 7, 1980 (div. Jan. 1982). AA in Criminal Justice, Butte Coll., Oroville, Calif., 1981; BA, S.W. U., 1993. Lic. internat. accredited safety auditor; cert. hazardous material specialist. Prodn. mgr. Artistic Dyers Inc., El Monte, Calif., 1976-80; mgr. loss control and risk mgmt. Mervyn's Dept. Stores, Hawyard, Calif., 1982-91; dir. risk mgmt. Save Mart Corp., Modesto, Calif., 1991-93; v.p. ops. I.C.S. Corp., San Ramon, Calif., 1993-94; pres. I.C.S. Corp., Irvine, Calif., 1994-95; v.p. Health Systems of Am. Internat., 1995-96; CEO Corp. Health Systems Internat., Walnut Creek, Calif., 1996-99, CHSI of Nev., Las Vegas, 1996—; cons. R.I.M. Assocs., Walnut Creek, Calif., 1989-96; instr. Claims Mgmt. Inst., 1993; bd. dirs. Am. Real Estate Bur., San Ramon, 1996-98. Script-writer, tech. advisor 12 safety videos; contbr. articles on safety and risk mgmt. to profl. publs. Res. police officer Cotati (Calif.) Police Dept., 1983-85; fundraiser United Way, Hayward, 1986, Am. Found. for AIDS Rsch., L.A., 1990; bd. dirs. Bay Area Safety Coun., Oakland, Calif., 1987-88; trustee Calif. Safety Ctr., Sacramento, 1990-91, dir., 1991—. Mem. Am. Soc. for Safety Engrs., Nat. Safety Mgmt. Soc., Nat. Fire Protection Assn., Risk and Ins. Mgmt. Soc., Nat. Assn. Chiefs Police, Nat. Environ. Tng. Assn. Avocations: snow skiing, swimming, running, biking, jet skiing. Office: Corp Health Systems Internat 2121 N California Blvd Ste 290 Walnut Creek CA 94596-7305

LÉGARÉ, HENRI FRANCIS, archbishop; b. Willow-Bunch, Sask., Can., Feb. 20, 1918; s. Phillippe and Amanda (Douville) L. B.A., U. Ottawa, 1940; theol. student, Lebret, Sask., 1940-44; M.A., Laval U., 1946; Dr. Social Sci., Cath. U. Lille, France, 1950; LL.D. (hon.), Carleton U., Ottawa, 1959, Windsor (Ont.) U., 1960, Queens U., Kingston, Ont., 1961, U. Sask., 1963, Waterloo (Ont.) Luth. U., 1965, U. Ottawa, Can., 1984; Doctor of Univ., U. of Ottawa. Ordained priest Roman Cath. Ch., 1943; prof. sociology Laval U., 1947, U. Ottawa, 1951; exec. dir. Cath. Hosp. Assn. Can., 1952-57; dean faculty social scis. U. Ottawa, 1954-58, pres., 1958-64; provincial Oblate Fathers, Winnipeg, Man., 1966-67; bishop of Labrador, 1967-72; archbishop Grouard-McLennan, Alta., 1972-96. Contbr. articles to profl. jours. Chmn. Canadian Univs. Found., 1960- 62. Decorated grand cross merit Order Malta, 1964; order merit French Lang. Assn. Ont., 1965. Mem. Assn. Canadian Univs. (pres. 1960-62), Can. Conf. Cath. Bishops (pres. 1981-83), Internat. Assn. Polit. Sci.

LEGER, RICHARD ROUBINE, public relations executive, writer; b. Schenectady, N.Y., Oct. 27, 1935; s. Roubine Joseph and Catherine Bernice (Waikas) L.; m. Lawrence Lowell Putnam, Sept. 14, 1957 (div. 1971); children: Philip Augustus, William Richard, Catherine Lowell; m. Dianne Lee Williams, May 14, 1978. BA, U. Rochester, 1957. Reporter Wall St. Jour., N.Y.C., 1960-63, 69-70, Atlanta, 1963-69, San Francisco, 1972-76; fgn. corr. Wall St. Jour., London, 1976-78; bur. chief Wall St. Jour., Nairobi, Kenya, 1978-80; econ. editor San Francisco Chronicle, San Francisco, 1982-84; owner/pub. Sebastopol Times, Sebastopol, Calif., 1985-86; pres. Leger Networks, Inc., San Francisco, 1988—. Avocations: sailing, travel, writing.

LEGERE, DIANE J., art association administrator, alpaca breeder; b. Inglewood, Calif., July 18, 1952; d. Charles E. and June L. Brown; m. Richard M. Legere, July 21, 1984. BA, San Jose State U., 1976. Regional mgr. Am. Internat. Grou Subs., Seattle, 1987-92; exec. dir. Western Art Assn., Ellensburg, Wash., 1992—; dir., curator Clymer Mus. Art, Ellensburg, 1996—; bd. dirs., past 2d v.p., past chair human resources The Clymer Mus. of Art, Ellensburg, Wash., 1992-95, dir., curator, 1996—; bd. dirs., chair promotions com. Laughing Horse Summer Theatre, 1995. Author, editor: (newsletter) Brush Strokes, 1993—. Mem. Tourism Task Force, 1992, Tourism C. of C., Ellensburg, Wash., 1995. Theatre Arts scholar Kiwanas, 1970. Mem. Alpaca Breeders of Am., Wash. Athletic Club. Avocations: painting, sculpture, writing, gardening, antique roses. Office: Clymer Mus Art 416 N Pearl St Ellensburg WA 98926-3112

LEGGE, CHARLES ALEXANDER, federal judge; b. San Francisco, Aug. 24, 1930; s. Roy Alexander and Wilda (Rampton) L.; m. Janice Meredith Sleeper, June 27, 1952; children: Jeffrey, Nancy, Laura. AB with distinction, Stanford U., 1952, JD, 1954. Bar: Calif. 1955. Assoc. Bronson, Bronson & McKinnin, San Francisco, 1956-64, ptnr., 1964-84, chmn., 1978-84; judge U.S. Dist. Ct. (no. dist.) Calif., San Francisco, 1984—. Served with U.S. Army, 1954-56. Fellow Am. Coll. Trial Lawyers; mem. Calif. Bar Assn. (past chmn. adminstrn. justice com.). Republican. Clubs: Bohemian, World Trade (San Francisco); Orinda (Calif.) Country. Office: US Dist Ct PO Box 36060 Rm 19-5424 450 Golden Gate Ave Ste 36052 San Francisco CA 94102-3482*

LEGINGTON, GLORIA R., middle school educator. BS, Tex. So. U, Houston, 1967; MS, U. So. Calif., L.A., 1973. Cert. adminstr. (life). Tchr., mentor L.A. Unified Sch. Dist., 1991-93; tchr. insvc. classes for area colloquim, parents, tchrs., faculty shared decision making coun., 1993-94, mem. faculty senate, 1992-93, mem. sch. improvement, 1993-94; del. U.S. Spain Joint Conf. on Edn., Barcelona, 1995. Sponsor 8th grade, 1994-97. Named semi-finalist Nat. Libr. Poetry, 1997, recipient Editor's Choice award, 1997. Mem. NEA, Internat. Reading Assn., United Tchrs. L.A., Calif. League of Mid. Schs. Avocations: painting, writing, collecting black memorabilia, reading, traveling.

LEGRAND, SHAWN PIERRE, computer systems programmer; b. San Diego, Nov. 27, 1960; s. Roger and Violet Louise (Howe) L. Grad. high sch., El Cajon, Calif.; student, U. Calif., San Diego, 1992-95. Cert. computer programmer; cert. in neural networks. Computer operator Grossmont CCD, El Cajon, 1978-79; computer systems programmer ICW, San Diego, 1979—. Recipient Math. Achievement award Bank of Am., 1978. Mem. IEEE Computer Soc., Assn. Computing Machinery. Republican. Office: ICW 11455 El Camino Real San Diego CA 92130-2088

LEGRO, THOMAS RYAN, entertainment industry executive; b. Southgate, Calif., Dec. 7, 1956; s. Donald James and Patsy Ruth (Payne) LeG.; m. Andrea M. Saxon, Apr. 21, 1979 (div. June 1989); children: Kellie, Christopher; m. Helen Louise Riddington, Aug. 4, 1990. BS in Econs., Calif. State U., Pomona, 1988; JD, U. LaVerne, 1997. Technician Pacific Bell, Santa Ana, Calif., 1979-84; mgr. AT&T, Anaheim, Calif., 1984-90; pres. Atlantic City Games, Riverside, Calif., 1990—; sr. ptnr. Ampac, Inc., Ontario, Calif., 1997—. Contbr. articles to profl. jours. Mem. Palm Spring Visitor and Convention Bur., 1996-98. Mem. Inland Empire Internat. Bus. Assn. (bd. dirs. 1996-98, award 1998), Inland Empire Nat. Catering Execs. (bd. dirs. 1991-98, award 1993), World Affair Coun. Inland Counties, Am. Soc. Internat. Law. Republican. Avocations: golf, swimming, hiking. Office: Atlantic City Games 4125 Indus Way Riverside CA 92503-4848

LEHINGER, SUSAN ELIZABETH, school psychologist; b. Grannis, Ark., Dec. 3, 1934; d. Richard Erskine and Rhoda Jane (Barton) Thames; m. Alfred Lee Lehinger, Feb. 3, 1950; children: Debra Lynne, Scott Keith, Sheila Helen, Valerie Jane, Cass Theodore, Katje Jill. BA Sociology, B Social Work with honors, Ea. Wash. U., 1970, MS in Psychology with honors, 1975, BA in Anthropology with honors, 1980, MPA with honors, 1982; PhD with honors, Gonzaga U., 1983. Cert. sch. psychologist, Wash. Social worker Cmty. Action Coun., Spokane, Wash., 1970-71; social worker, counselor Booth Meml. Hosp., Spokane, 1971-72; caseworker II and III Wash. Dept. Social and Health Svcs., Spokane, 1972-75; psychologist III, Lakeland Village Sch. for Devel. Disabled, Medical Lake, Wash., 1975-84; prof., dir. human svcs. dept. Flathead Valley C.C., Kalispell, Mont., 1984-92, faculty rep. to bd., 1990-92; sch. psychologist, behavior specialist Wenatchee (Wash.) Sch. Dist. 246, 1992—. Contbr. articles to profl. jours. and various pubs. Vice chmn. Spokane County Dem. Ctrl. Com., 1963-66; dist. office mgr. Congressman Thomas S. Foley, Spokane, 1965-66; mem. fin. com. Booth Gardiner for Gov. Com., Spokane, 1984; bd. rep. United Way Kalispell, 1985-87; v.p. bd. Columbia Valley Cmty. Health, Wenatchee, 1994-96, pres. bd., 1996-98. Mem. NASP, AAUW, Pi Gamma Mu, Alpha Kappa Delta, Phi Delta Kappa. Roman Catholic. Avocations: writing poetry and articles, research on autism and developmental disabilities, computers, trivia, criminology. Home: 15811 W Pine Bluff Rd Nine Mile Falls WA 99026-9769 Office: Wenatchee Sch Dist 246 112 Elliott Ave S Wenatchee WA 98801-2500

LEHMAN, LARRY L., state supreme court justice. Judge Wyo. County Ct., 1985-88, Wyo. Dist. Ct. (2nd dist.), 1988-94; justice Wyo. Supreme Ct., Cheyenne, 1994-98, chief justice, 1998—. Office: Supreme Court Bldg 2301 Capitol Ave Cheyenne WY 82001-3644

LEHMAN, PATRICIA, adult education educator; b. Denver, Dec. 6, 1944; Bert Earl and Bonnie Asinath (VanSickle) L. BA, Colo. State U., 1966; MFA with honors, U. Kansas, 1972. Designer Hallmark Cards, Kansas City, Mo., 1964; art dir. Computer Image Corp., Denver, 1966-68; flight attendant Am. Airlines, Chgo., 1968-70; adj. prof. U. Kansas, Lawrence, 1970-72; asst. prof. U. So. Miss., Hattiesburg, 1972-73, U. Mass., Boston, 1973-75; prof. C.C. Denver, 1975—; chairperson, design, computer graphics and multimedia C.C. Denver, 1990—, instr. U. Colo., 1987-92, dir. Adv. Bd. Multimedia, 1995—;. Producer computer animated videos, 1975-81; writer, producer, dir. cable tv series, 1996. Chairperson Boulder Arts Commn., 1992-97, bd. mem. Boulder Mus. Contemporary Art, 1995-98. Recipient Award for Teaching Excellence, Nat. Inst. Staff and Org. Devel., 1997;grantee title III rsch. computer graphics U.S. Govt./ CCD, 1986—. Mem. Spl. Interest Group Computer Graphics, Corona Investments, Hist. Boulder. Democrat. Avocations: skiing, mountain biking, hiking. Home: 429 Maxwell Ave Boulder CO 80304-3935 Office: Community College of Denver 1111 W Colfax Ave Denver CO 80204-2097

LEHMKUHL, LYNN, publishing executive. Pres. Teen Magazine, L.A. Office: c/o Teen/Petersen Pub Co LLC 6420 Wilshire Blvd Los Angeles CA 90048-5515*

LEHR, JEFFREY MARVIN, immunologist, allergist; b. N.Y.C., Apr. 29, 1942; s. Arthur and Stella (Smellow) L.; m. Suzanne Kozak, June 10, 1946; children: Elisa, Alexandra, Vanessa, Ryan. BS, City Coll., Bklyn., 1963; MD, NYU, 1967. Intern, resident Beth Israel Hosp., N.Y.C., 1967-69; resident in allergy/immunology, internal medicine Roosevelt Hosp., N.Y.C., 1969-72; chief of allergy/immunology USAF, Wright Patterson AFB, Ohio, 1972-74; allergist, immunologist Monterey, Calif., 1974—. Chmn. Monterey Bay Ari Pollution Hearing Bd., 1982-95; v.p. Lyceum of Monterey, 1977-83. Fellow Am. Acad. Allergy/Immunology, Am. Coll. Allergy/Immunology, Am. Assn. Cert. Allergists; mem. Am. Lung Assn. (v.p. 1989-91), Monterey County Med. Soc. (pres. 1988-89). Avocations: tennis, jogging, golf, hiking,

backpacking. Office: 798 Cass St Monterey CA 93940-2918 also: 262 San Jose St Salinas CA 93901-3901

LEHR, LESTER EUGENE, music educator; b. Alpena, S.D., Mar. 20, 1938; s. Emanuel and Martha Magdalena (Feiok) L.; m. Jacquelyn Beth Blair, June 19, 1958 (div. Aug. 1984); children: Christopher Neal, Brent Jacque; m. Marjorie Roberta Ferguson, Aug. 10, 1984; stepchildren: Michelle Christine Sutera, David Arthur Sutera. BA, Calif. State U., Sacramento, 1960; MA, Eastman Sch. Music, 1961; D of Musical Arts, U. Soc. Calif., 1980. Standard secondary life teaching credential in music. Music tchr. Sacramento (Calif.) Unified Sch. Dist., 1961-66; prof. music Am. River Coll., Sacramento, 1966—; conductor Sacramento (Calif.) Valley Symphonic Band, 1984—, City Unified Honor Band, Sacramento, 1966, North Area High Sch. Honor Band, Sacramento, 1968, 69, 70, San Juan Unified Sch. Dist. High Sch. Honor Band, Sacramento, 1983, Woodland (Calif.) Elem. Honor Band, 1988. Producer, conductor (cassette tape) Is There Any Ragtime on Mars?, 1990. Mem. Nat. Educators Assn., Am. Fed. Tchrs. (founding pres. at Am. River Coll., 1972-73), Calif. Music Educators Assn. (higher edn. rep. 1981-82, Outstanding community svc. award, 1989), Coll. Band Dirs. Nat. Assn., Assn. Community Bands, Kiwanis Club Internat., 3d Degree Free Masons (brother). Avocations: flying, fishing, camping, traveling, reading. Office: The CA Wind Orchestra PO Box 1503 Carmichael CA 95609-1503

LEHRER, WILLIAM PETER, JR., animal scientist; b. Bklyn., Feb. 6, 1916; s. William Peter and Frances Reif (Muser) L.; m. Lois Lee Meister, Sept. 13, 1945; 1 child, Sharon Elizabeth. BS, Pa. State U., 1941; MS in Agr., MS in Range Mgmt., U. Idaho, 1946, 55; PhD in Nutrition and Biochemistry, Wash. State U., 1951; LLB, U. Chgo., 1972, JD, 1974; MBA, Pepperdine U., 1975. Mgmt. trainee Swift & Co., Charleston, W.Va., 1941-42; farm mgr. Maple Springs Farm, Middletown, N.Y., 1944-45; rsch. fellow U. Idaho, Moscow, 1945; asst. prof. to prof. U. Idaho, 1945-60; dir. nutrition Albers Milling Co., L.A., 1960-62; dir. nutrition and rsch. Albers Milling Co., 1962-74, Albers Milling Co. & John W. Eshelman & Sons, L.A., 1974-76, Carnation Co., L.A., 1976-81; ret.; cons. in field; speaker, lectr. more than 40 univs. in U.S. and abroad. Contbr. 115 articles to profl. jours.; co-author: The Livestock Industry, 1950, Dog Nutrition, 1972; author weekly column Desseret News, Salt Lake City. Mem. rsch. adv. co. U.S. Brewers Assn., 1969-81; mem. com. on dog nutrition, com. animal nutrition Nat. Rsch. Coun. NAS, 1970-76. With U.S. Army Air Corps, 1942-43. Named Disting. Alumnus, Pa. State U., 1963, 83, Key Alumnus, 1985; named to U. Idaho Alumni Hall of Fame, 1985; recipient Alumni Achievement award Wash. State U., 1993. Fellow AAAS, Am. Soc. Animal Sci.; mem. Am. Inst. Nutrition, Coun. for Agrl. Sci. & Tech., Am. Registry of Profl. Animal Scientists, Am. Inst. Food Technologists, Animal Nutrition Rsch. Coun., Am. Dairy Sci. Assn., Am. Soc. Agrl. Engrs., Am. Feed Mfrs. Assn. (life, nutrition coun. 1962-81, chmn. 1969-70), Calif. State Poly. U. (adv. coun. 1965-81, Meritorious Svc. award), The Nutrition Today Soc., Am. Soc. Animal Sci., Poultry Sci. Assn., Nat. Block & Bridle Club, Hayden Lake Country Club, Alpha Zeta, Sigma Xi, Gamma Sigma Delta (Alumni Award of Merit), Xi Sigma Pi. Republican. Avocations: river running, hunting, fishing, gardening, restoring furniture. Home: Rocking L Ranch 12180 N Rimrock Rd Hayden Lake ID 83835-9210

LEHTIHALME, LARRY (LAURI) K., financial planner; b. Montreal, Que., Can., Feb. 26, 1937; came to U.S., 1964; s. Lauri Johann and Selma Maire (Piispanen) L.; m. Elizabeth Speed Smith, Sept. 9, 1961; children: Tina Beth, Shauna Lyn. Student, Sir George Williams U., Montreal, 1960-64, Mission Coll., San Fernando, Calif., 1978-80, Pierce Coll., Woodland Hills, Calif., 1990-92. Lic. in variable annuity, life and disability ins., Calif.; lic. securities series 7 SEC, series 63. Acct., customer svc. cons. No. Electric, Montreal, 1957-64; salesman Remington Rand Systems, Wilmington, Del., 1964-67; account exec., comm. cons. Pacific Tel. & Telegraph Co., L.A., 1968-84; tech. customer support specialist AT&T, L.A., 1984-85; fin. adv., registered rep. Am. Express Fin. Advisors, L.A., 1987—; mem. L.A. World Affairs Coun., 1998-99. Mem. ctrl. com. Calif. 39th Assembly Dist. Rep. Com., 1976-81, City of L.A., 12th dist.; pres. North Hills Jaycees, 1969-70; sec.-treas. Com. Ind. Valley City and County Govt., 1978-82; subchmn. allocations United Way, Van Nuys, Calif., 1990; fundraiser North Valley YMCA, 1986—, Kids Safe Edn. Found.; formerly active numerous comty. and polit. orgns. in San Fernando Valley. Named Jaycee of Yr., Newark (Del.) Jaycees, 1966, Granada Hills Jaycees, 1971; recipient cert. of merit U.S. Ho. of Reps., 1973, cert. appreciation City of L.A., 1980, 84, State of Calif., 20th senate dist., 1983, Comty. Spirit award, 1990. Mem. L.A. Olympic Organizing Com. Alumni Assn., Jr. Chamber Internat. (life, senator 1973), U.S. Jaycees (life, Jaycee of Yr. 1965, Outstanding Local Jaycee 1965-66, Presdl. award Honor 1967, Jaycee of Month 1966-67, asst. gen. chmn. 1970-71, state dir. N. Hollywood chpt. 1970-71, Cert. Merit 1971, state gen. chmn., 1971-72, 72-73, Outstanding State Chmn. Calif. dist. 22 1973-74), L.A. World Affairs Coun., Granada Hills C. of C. (bd. dirs. 1976-83, Man of Yr. award 1973), Granada Hills Jr. C. of C. Episcopalian. Avocation: community service. Home: 11408 Haskell Ave Granada Hills CA 91344-3959 Office: Am Express Fin Advisors 11145 Tampa Ave Ste 20A Northridge CA 91326-2270

LEIBERT, RICHARD WILLIAM, special events producer; b. N.Y.C., Nov. 11, 1948; s. Richard William and Rosemarie Martha (Bruns) L. BS, Boston U., 1966-70; student, Northwestern U., 1971. Producer Sta. WBZ AM/FM, Boston, 1968-70; prodn. dir. Sta. WMMR-FM, Phila., 1970; exec. producer Sta. WIND-AM, Chgo., 1970-72; program dir. Sta. KGB AM-FM, San Diego, 1972-80; pres. Events Mktg., Inc., L.A., 1980—; dir. Nat. Fireworks Ensemble, Los Angeles, Calif., 1985—. Creator (mascot, publicity stunts) Sta. KGB Chicken, 1974; creator, producer (radio fireworks show) Sta. KGB Sky Show, 1976; writer, producer (network radio show) New Music News, 1983; creator, dir. (touring co.) Nat. Fireworks Ensemble, 1985. Recipient Emmy award, 1978; named Program Dir. of Yr. Billboard Mag., 1976, Radio Program of Yr. Billboard Mag., 1976. Avocations: sailing, baseball. Office: Events Mktg Inc PO Box 65694 Los Angeles CA 90065-0694

LEIBSLA, MELVIN DONALD, data processing executive; b. Cleve., Mar. 27, 1953; s. Melvin Donald and Marguerite (Scribbner) L.; m. Barbara A. Stasko, July 4, 1981; children: Michael, Jason. BS in Applied Sci., Miami U., 1975; grad., Sch. Bank Mgmt., Madison, Wis., 1990. Programmer/analyst Fed. Res. Bank Cleve., 1975-80; system analyst Olympia Brewing, Tumwater, Wash., 1980-82; system analyst/auditor N.W. Pipeline, Salt Lake City, 1982-84; EDP audit mgr. Zions Bancorp, Salt Lake City, 1984—; speaker in field. Contbr. articles to profl. jours. Active in developing digital signatures on internet for the State of Utah. Active local ch. parish coun., Salt Lake City, 1989—. Mem. EDP Auditors Assn. (pres., v.p. 1989-91, bd. dirs. 1989-94), Data Processing Mgmt. Assn. Republican. Roman Catholic. Avocations: marathons, coaching and refereeing soccer, church activities. Office: Zions Bancorp 2200 S 3270 W West Valley City UT 84119-1112

LEIGH, VINCENTA M., health administrator; b. N.Y.C., June 27, 1947; d. Emanuel and Ines Masciandara; m. Hoyle Leigh, Sept. 16, 1967; 1 child, Alexander. BA, Lehman Coll., 1968; MSN, Yale U., 1973. Psychiat. clinician Jacobi Hosp., Bronx, N.Y., 1971; pediatric nurse Conn. Mental Health Ctr., New Haven, 1971-73; instr. in psychiat. nursing Yale U., New Haven, 1973-77; asst. dir. mental health nursing edn. Conn. Valley Hosp., Middletown, 1980-81; nurse coord. Inst. of Living, Hartford, Conn., 1981-85, asst. dir. nursing, 1985-89; asst. clin. profl. psychiatry U. Calif., San Francisco, 1989—; coord. Intensive outpatient program Kaiser Permanente, Fresno, Calif., 1996—. Contbr. articles to profl. jours. Mem. ANA, Am. Psychosomatic Soc., Internat. Coll. Psychosomatic Medicine, Am. Orthopedic Assn., Jr. League. Avocations: piano, reading, trombone, skiing.

LEIGHNINGER, DAVID SCOTT, cardiovascular surgeon; b. Youngstown, Ohio, Jan. 16, 1920; s. Jesse Harrison and Marjorie (Lightner) L.; m. Margaret Jane Malony, May 24, 1942; children: David Allan, Jenny. BA, Oberlin Coll., 1942; MD, Case Western Res. U., 1945. Intern Univ. Hosps. of Cleve., [illegible]cular surgery rsch. lab. Case Western Res. U. Sch. Medicine, Cleve., 1948-49, 51-55, 57-67, instr. surgery, 1951-55, sr. instr., 1957-64, asst. prof., 1964-68, asst. clin. prof., 1968-70; resident Cin. Gen. Hosp., 1955-57; practice medicine specializing in cardiovascular surgery, Cleve., 1957-70; pvt. practice medicine specializing in cardiovascular and gen. surgery Edgewater Hosp., Chgo., 1970-82, staff surgeon, also dir. emergency surg. services, 1970-82; staff surgeon, also dir. emergency surg. svcs. Mazel Med. Ctr., Chgo., 1970-82; emergency physician, Raton, N.Mex. and Trinidad, Colo., 1982-85; assoc., courtesy, or cons. staff Marymount Hosp., Cleve., Mt. Sinai Hosp., Cleve., Geauga Community Hosp., Chardon, Ohio, Bedford Community Hosp (Ohio), 1957-70. Tchr. tng. courses in CPR for med. personnel, police, fire and vol. rescue workers, numerous cities, 1950-70. Served to capt., M.C., AUS, 1946-48. Recipient Chris award Columbus Internat. Film Festival, 1964, numerous other award for sci. exhibits from various nat. and state med. socs., 1953-70; USPHS grantee, 1949-68. Fellow Am. Coll. Cardiology, Am. Coll. Chest Physicians; mem. AMA, Mont Reid Surg. Soc. (Cinn.). Contbr. numerous articles to med. jours., chpts. to med. texts; spl. pioneer research (with Claude S. Beck) in physiopathology of coronary artery disease and CPR; developed surg. treatment of coronary artery disease; developed vein graft by-pass in late 1940's; achieved 1st successful defibrillation of human heart, 1st successful reversal of fatal heart attack; provided 1st intensive care of coronary patients. Home: HC 68 Box 77 Fort Garland CO 81133-9708

LEIGHTON, HENRY ALEXANDER, physician, consultant; b. Manila, Nov. 12, 1929; (parents U.S. citizens).; s. Raymond Harry and Theola Marie (Alexander) L.; m. Helga Maria Hell, Jan. 17, 1970; children: Alan Raymond, Henry Alexander, Michael Ballinger, John, Marni, Tammy Ballinger. BA in History, U. Calif., Berkeley, 1952, MPH, 1971; MD, U. Calif., San Francisco, 1956. Diplomate Am. Bd. Preventive Medicine. Intern So. Pacific Gen. Hosp., San Francisco, 1956-57; resident in surgery Brooke Gen. Hosp., Ft. Sam Houston, Tex., 1960-62; commd. 2d. lt. U.S. Army, 1957, advanced through grades to col., 1971; div. surgeon 8th Inf. div. U.S. Army, Germany, 1964-66; comdr. 15th Med. Bn. U.S. Army, Vietnam, 1966-67; instr. Med. Field Service Sch. U.S. Army, San Antonio, 1968-70; resident preventive medicine U.S. Army, Ft. Ord, Calif., 1971-72, chief preventive medicine, 1973-76; chief preventive medicine U.S. Army-Europe, 1976-79, ret., 1979; chief occupational health MEDDAC U.S. Army, Ft. Ord, 1981-89; pvt. practice Salinas, Calif., 1990—. Neighborhood commr. Boy Scouts Am., 1964-66; bd. dirs. Am. Lung Assn. of Calif., 1982-84, and of affiliate, 1980-86, The Calif. Acad. Preventive Medicine, 1994-96; pres. The Bluffs Homeowners Assn., 1986. Decorated Air medal with oak leaf cluster, Bronze Star, Legion of Merit, Meritorious Service medal. Fellow Am. Coll. Preventive Medicine; mem. Am. Pub. Health Assn., Am. Coll. Occupational Medicine, Assn. Mil. Surgeons, Ret. Officers Assn., Assn. U.S. Army, Theta Xi. Lodges: Masons, Shriners. Office: 14096 Reservation Rd Salinas CA 93908-9208

LEINEWEBER, PETER ANTHONY, forest products company executive; b. Portland, Oreg., Sept. 28, 1944; s. Peter Cornelius and Isabel (Brown) L.; m. Heidi Milly Baxter, July 14, 1978; children: John James, Joseph Stephen, Thomas Gregory. BS, Portland State U., 1968; MBA, U. Wash., 1970. Loan officer U.S. Nat. Bank Oreg., Portland, 1962-69; mgr. Pacific N.W. Bell, Portland, 1970-76; sr. v.p. Market Transport, Ltd., Portland, 1976-90; v.p. Crown Pacific, Portland, 1990—; pres. Yellowstone Trucking, L.P., Coeur d'Alene, Idaho, 1998—; dir. Market Transport, Ltd., Portland, TOC Mgmt. Svcs., Tigard, Oreg. Dir. Portland State U. Found. Mem. Oreg. Trucking Assns. (Mem. of Yr. 1990), Multnomah Athletic Club, University Club. Democrat. Roman Catholic. Avocation: youth activities. Office: Crown Pacific 121 SW Morrison St Ste 1500 Portland OR 97204-3145

LEINO, DEANNA ROSE, business educator; b. Leadville, Colo., Dec. 15, 1937; d. Arvo Ensio Leino and Edith Mary (Bonan) Leino Malenck; adopted child, Michael Charles Bonan. BSBA, U. Denver, 1959, MS in Bus. Adminstrn., 1967; postgrad. Community Coll. Denver, U. No. Colo., Colo. State U., U. Colo., Met. State Coll. Cert. tchr., vocat. tchr., Colo. Tchr. Jefferson County Adult Edn., Lakewood, Colo., 1963-67; retired tchr. bus., coordinator coop. office edn., Jefferson High Sch., Edgewater, Colo., 1959-93, ret., 1993; sales assoc. Joslins Dept. Store, Denver, 1978—; mem. ea. team, clk. office automation Denver Svc. Ctr. Nat. Park Svc, 1993-94, U.S. Dept. Labor, 1994—, wage hour asst.; instr. Community Coll. Denver, Red Rocks, 1967-81, U. Colo. Denver, 1976-79, Parks Coll. Bus. (name now Parks Jr. Coll.), 1983—, Front Range C.C., 1998—; dist. adviser Future Bus. Leaders Am. Author short story. Active City of Edgewater Sister City Project Student Exchange Com.; pres. Career Women's Symphony Guild; treas. Phantoms of Opera, 1982—; active Opera Colo. Assocs. & Guild, I Pagliacci; ex-officio trustee Denver Symphony Assn., 1980-82. Recipient Disting. Svc. award Jefferson County Sch. Bd. 1980, Tchr. Who Makes A Difference award Sta. KCNC/Rocky Mountain News, 1990, Youth Leader award Lakewood Optimist Club, 1993; inducted into Jefferson High Sch. Wall of Fame 1981 Mem. NEA (life), Colo. Edn. Assn., Jefferson County Edn. Assn., Colo. Vocat. Assn., Am. Vocat. Assn., Colo. Educators for and about Bus., Profl. Secs. Internat., Career Women's Symphony Guild, Profl. Panhellenic Assn., Colo. Congress Fgn. Lang. Tchrs., Wheat Ridge C. of C. (edn. and scholarship com.), Federally Employed Women, Delta Pi Epsilon, Phi Chi Theta, Beta Gamma Sigma, Alpha Lambda Delta. Republican. Roman Catholic. Club: Tyrolean Soc. Denver. Avocations: decorating wedding cakes, crocheting, sewing, music, world travel. Home: 3712 Allison St Wheat Ridge CO 80033-6124

LEISSRING, JOHN COTHER, pathologist; b. Milw., Mar. 29, 1935; s. William Frederick and Alice Jane (Webb) Leissring; m. Judith Lee Lentz, June 1959 (div. 1981); children: Matthew William, Malcolm Arthur. BS, U. Wis., 1957, MS in Anatomy, 1961, MD, 1961. Diplomate Bd. Med. Examiners, Wis., Calif., Am. Bd. Pathology, Am. Bd. Dermatology. Rsch. asst. dept. endocrinology U. Wis., 1955-57, rsch. asst. dept. anatomy, 1957-59; intern U.S. Naval Hosp., Oakland, Calif., 1961-62; resident in pathology Stanford U. Med. Ctr., 1965-69; instr. pathology Stanford (Calif.) Med. Sch., 1968-69; asst. clin. prof. U. Calif. Med. Sch., San Francisco, 1969-74; pathologist Santa Rosa (Calif.) Meml. Hosp., 1969—. Author: Life and Work of Michael Brenner, 1991, Songs My Father Never Sang, 1996; contbr. articles to profl. jours. Lt. comdr. USN, 1959-65. Recipient Borden award in rsch. Borden Inst., Madison, Wis., 1961. Fellow Coll. Am. Pathologists, Am. Soc. Clin. Pathologists; mem. Pacific Derm. Soc., Calif. Soc. Pathologists, Pacific Dermatologic Soc., Press Club of San Francisco, Musicians Union, AFL/CIO, Pho Kappa Phi, Alpha Omega Alpha. Avocations: sculpting, building designing, poetry, writing, music. Home: 1015 Mcdonald Ave Santa Rosa CA 95404-3524 Office: Drs Leissring and DeMeo 1144 Montgomery Dr Santa Rosa CA 95405-4802

LEIST, ANDREW JOHN, artist, musician, composer, producer; b. Canoga Park, Calif., Nov. 22, 1963; s. Charles Doll and Carole Mae (Wellman) L.; m. Judy Cathy Richter, July 7, 1990. AS in Computer Tech., L.A. Pierce Coll., 1984; student, Calif. State U., Northridge, 1988-92. Sr. electronics technician Control Fed. Systems, Marina Del Rey, Calif., 1984-90; project coord. Cedars-Sinai Med. Ctr., L.A., 1990—. Musician (recording) Airplay, 1982; composer, producer (recording) Damned if You Do, 1993. Mem. Nat. Assn. Recording Arts and Scis., Am. Soc. Composers, Authors, Publishers.

LEIVISKA, NANCY LYNN, entertainment production company executive; b. Evanston, Ill., July 19, 1948; d. Laurie and Dorothy June (Sterner) Leiviska; student Wis. State U., La Crosse, 1966-68, UCLA, 1968-70; 1 child, Stefan Kendall Gordy. Sec. to Sammy Davis, Jr., 1968-70; with Motown Records, Hollywood, Calif., 1970-71, editor Motown Newsletter, 1972-75, asst. to chmn. bd., 1976-78, dir. video ops., 1979-82, exec. dir. video prodn. film div., 1982-83; pres. Stefanino Prodns., Hollywood, 1984—; owner Leiviska & Assocs., 1972—; creative assoc. Shelly Berger of Star Direction, Hollywood, Calif., 1990-92; founder Inner-Workout Artist Group. Assoc. dir. (film) The Legend Continues (Michael Jackson), 1987-88; dir., editor Soul to Soul The Temptations, 1990; creative cons. Smokey Robinson Biography, 1990; dir., writer Billy Dee Williams, 1990. Mem. Am. Film Inst., AFTRA, ASCAP, Nat. Acad. Songwriters, Women in Film, Orgn. Women in Music. Office: 15515 W Sunset Blvd Ste 101 Pacific Palisades CA 90272-3528

[illegible] Louis, Apr. 21, 1957; s. John Robert and Helen (Caicuey) L.; m. Bernadette Leiweke; 1 child, Francesa Leiweke. Grad. high sch., St. Louis. Salesperson New Eng. Mut. Life Ins. Co., St. Louis, 1976-79; asst. gen. mgr. St. Louis Steamers/MISL, 1979-80; gen. mgr. Balt. Blast/MISL, 1980-81; v.p., gen. mgr. Kansas City (Mo.) Comets/MISL, 1981-84; v.p. Leiweke and Co., Kansas City, 1984-85; pres. Kansas City Comets/MISL, 1986-88; v.p. sales and mktg. div. Minn. Timberwolves, Mpls., 1988-91; sr. v.p. of bus. ops. Denver Nuggets, Denver, 1991-92; pres. Denver Nuggets, Denver, CO, 1992-96; pres., CEO LA Kings, Los Angeles, 1996—. Bd. dirs. Kidney Found., Minn., 1989—, Spl. Olympics, Minn., 1989—, Timberwolves Community Found., Minn., 1989—; pres. Staples Ctr. Arena. Named Rookie of the Yr., Mo. Life Underwriters, 1976, Kansas Citian of the Yr., Kansas City Press Club, 1983; recipient William Brownfield award U.S. Jaycees, 1978, William Brownfield award Mo. Jaycees, 1978, Excalibur award Am. Cancer Soc., 1987. Mem. Kansas City Mktg. and Sales Execs., Mpls. Club. Avocations: running, golf, cross-country skiing, soccer, basketball. Office: LA Arena Co 865 S Figueroa St Ste 2350 Los Angeles CA 90017-5491

LEM, RICHARD DOUGLAS, painter; b. L.A., Nov. 24, 1933; s. Walter Wing and Betty (Wong) L.; B.A., UCLA, 1958; M.A., Calif. State U.-Los Angeles, 1963; m. Patricia Ann Soohoo, May 10, 1958; 1 son, Stephen Vincent. Exhibited in one-man shows at Gallery 818, Los Angeles, 1965; group shows at Lynn Kottler Galleries, N.Y.C., 1973, Palos Verdes Art Gallery, 1968, Galerie Mouffe, Paris, France, 1976, Le Salon des Nations, Paris, 1984, numerous others; represented in permanent collections; writer, illustrator: Mile's Journey, 1983, 2nd edit., 1995; cover illustrator: The Hermit, 1990, The Hermit's Journey, 1993. Served with AUS, 1958-60. Mem. UCLA Alumni Assn. Address: 1861 Webster Ave Los Angeles CA 90026-1229

LEMBECK, JAMES PETER, nutritionist, writer, consultant; b. Huntington, N.Y., Nov. 21, 1955; s. Gustav William and Eileen Mary (McEnery) L. BS, Buffalo State U., 1980; MS, Westbrook U., 1992; D, Lafayette U., 1994. Cert. herbalist, N.Mex.; microsoft cert. sys. engr. Nutrition/fitness dir. Apple Health and Fitness, N.Y.C., 1978-79; nutrition cons. J.L. Consulting, Watertown, N.Y.C., Mass., 1982-89, Silerhawk Inc., Parker, Colo., 1994-95; pres. Advanced Nutrient Sci., Parker, 1995-97; freelance writer; cons. Nutrition Industry, 1977—, Parker, 1991—, Perkins Sch. for Blind, Watertown, 1982-84; mem. adv. bd. Nat. Body Bldg. mag., 1986—; microsoft cert. sys. engr.; cert. Novell assoc. Contbr. articles to profl. trade and consumer mags. With USAR, 1984-88. Mem. Nat. Nutritional Foods Assn., Herbal Rsch. Found. Roman Catholic. Avocations: camping, weight training, hiking, cycling. Home: 11587 N Hot Springs Dr Parker CO 80138-3840 Office: PO Box 668 Parker CO 80134-0668

LEMERT, JAMES BOLTON, journalist, educator; b. Sangerfield, N.Y., Nov. 5, 1935; s. Jesse Raymond and Caroline Elizabeth (Brown) L.; m. Rosalie Martha Bassett, Mar. 23, 1972. AB, U. Calif., Berkeley, 1957, M in Journalism, 1959; PhD, Mich. State U., 1964. Newspaper reporter Oakland (Calif.) Tribune, 1955-56, Chico (Calif.) Enterprise-Record, 1957, 58-60; asst. prof. journalism So. Ill. U., Carbondale, 1964-67; asst. prof. U. Oreg., Eugene, 1967-69, assoc. prof., 1969-76, prof. sch. journalism/comm., 1976—, dir. divsn. comm. rsch., 1967-94, dir. grad. program Sch. Journalism, 1983-86, 88-93; chairperson task force to revise faculty governance U. Oreg., 1983-84, mem. senate, 1981-83, 86-88, 93-94, mem. pres.'s adv. coun., 1990-91, chairperson pres.'s adv. coun., 1991-92, mem. grad. coun., 1984-86, 89-90, 94-96, chairperson grad. coun., 1993-94, chairperson task force on rsch. and grad. edn., 1990-91. Prodr., on-air host Old Grooves show Sta. KWAX-FM, 1977-80, 82-84; author: Does Mass Communication Change Public Opinion After All? A New Approach to Effects Analysis, 1981, Criticizing the Media: Empirical Approaches, 1989, News Verdicts, The Debates and Presidential Campaigns, 1991, Politics of Disenchantment: Bush, Clinton, Perot and the Press, 1996; editor Daily Californian, 1957; contbr. articles to profl. jours., newspapers and mags., chpts. to books. Mem. Oreg. Alcohol and Drug Edn. Adv. Com., 1968-69; pres. South Hills Neighborhood Assn., 1976-77, bd. dirs., 1982-84, 86-88; bd. dirs. Traditional Jazz Soc. Oreg., 1981-83, 87; v.p. Met. Cable Access Corp., 1983-84; mem. exec. bd. AAUP, 1975-76, 91-94; mem. state exec. com., head chpt. Assn. Oreg. Faculties, 1981-83, 85-87, state v.p., 1987-89, del. to Oreg. Faculties Polit. Action Com., 1986-89. Recipient Outstanding Journalist award Sigma Delta Chi, 1957, Donald M. McGammon Communication Rsch. Ctr. critical rsch. grantee, 1988-89, Allen Family Found. grantee; NSF fellow, 1963, 64; Calif. Newspaper Pubs. fellow, 1957; Butte County Alumni scholar, 1953-54. Mem. Assn. Edn. in Journalism and Mass Comm. (vice chairperson civic journalism interest group 1995-96), Am. Assn. Pub. Opinion Rsch., Am. Polit. Sci. Assn., Phi Beta Kappa (membership chmn. 1985-86, v.p., pres. 1989-91). Home: PO Box 2224 Waldport OR 97394-2224*

LEMIEUX, CLAUDE, professional hockey player; b. Buckingham, Que., July 16, 1965. Right wing Montreal Canadiens, 1983-90, N.J. Devils, 1990-95, Colo. Avalanche, 1995—; mem. Stanley Cup Championship teams, 1986, 95, 96. Named to Que. Major Jr. Hockey League All-Star second team, 1983-83, first team, 1984-85; recipient Guy Lafleur trophy, 1985, Conn Smythe trophy for most valuable player in playoffs, 1995. Office: Colo Avalanche McNichols Arena 1635 Clay St Denver CO 80204-1743*

LEMIRE, DAVID STEPHEN, school psychologist, educator; b. Roswell, N.Mex., May 23, 1949; s. Joseph Armon and Jeanne (Longwill) L.; BA, Linfield Coll., 1972, MEd, 1974; EdS, Idaho State U., 1978; postgrad. U. Wyo.; EdS in Ednl. Adminstrn. and Instructional Leadership, U. Wyo., 1988; postgrad. U. Wyo., PhD in Curriculum and Instruction Kansas State U. Cert. sch. counselor, sch. psychologist, psychotherapist. Student pers. worker, psychology instr., Calif. Sch. counselor, psychol. technician and tchr. Goshen County Sch. Dist. 1, Torrington, Wyo., counselor Aspen High Sch., Aspen, Colo.; sch. counselor Unita County Sch. Dist., Evanston, Wyo., coord. R&D Lifelong Learning Ctr. 1986-87; dir. spl. svcs. and sch. psychologist Bighorn County Sch. Dist. #4, Basin, Wyo., 1989-90; sch. psychologist Sweetwater County Sch. Dist. #2, Green River, Wyo., 1990-91; dir. housing, residence supr. Pratt (Kans.) Community Coll., 1991-92; tchr. Highland C.C. and Cloud County C.C., Kans., pres. David Lemire Software Enterprises, Evanston; dir. Inst. for Advanced Study of Thinkology. Mem. ASCD, Nat. Assn. Sch. Psychologists (cert.), Am. Psychol. Assn. Author: (with Richard Mueller) Instructional Psychology, Fifty or More Ethical Dilemas: Reading/Writing Activities for the Secondary and College Classroom, Twenty Simple and Inexpensive Learning Style/Personal Style/Self Concept Instruments for Professionals and Educators with Research and Supporting Documentation; former editor WACD Jour.; former mng. editor Jour. Humanistic Edn.; contbr. articles to profl. jours. Address: PO Box 1287 Manhattan KS 66505-1287 also: Creative Therapeutics Adminstrv Offices 2390 Riviera St Reno NV 89509-1144

LEMKE, HERMAN ERNEST FREDERICK, JR., retired elementary education educator, consultant; b. Argo, Ill., July 13, 1919; s. Herman and Augusta Victoria (Statt) L.; m. Geneva Octavene Davidson, Sept, 5, 1942; children: Patricia, Herman E.F. III, Gloria, John, Elizabeth. BA, George Peabody Coll., 1949, MA, 1952. Cert. social sci. tchr., Tenn., elem. tchr., Calif. Tchr. Cadd Parish Sch., Shreveport, La., 1950-55, Pacific Sch. Dist., Sacramento, 1956-58, Sacramento Sch. Dist., 1958-89; part-time tchr. Sacramento County Sch., 1974-84. Co-author: Natural History Guide, 1963, (field guide) Outdoor World of Sacramento Region, 1975; contbr. articles to profl. jours. Asst. dist. Commn. Boys Scouts Am., Shreveport, 1954, cubmaster, 1954; leader 4-H Club, Shreveport, 1950-54; elder Faith Luth. Ch., Fair Oaks, Calif., 1981-88. Recipient Scouter award, Boy Scouts Am., Shreveport, 1954, Honorary Svc. award Am. Winn Sch. PTA, 1982, Calif. Life Diploma Elem. Schs., 1961. Mem. Calif. Congress Parents Tchrs. Inc. (life). Democrat. Avocations: backpacking, coin collecting, stamp collecting, antiques, fishing. Home: 7720 Magnolia Ave Fair Oaks CA 95628-7316

LEMKIN, PAMELA AYLEEN, health facility administrator, oncological nurse, consultant; b. Torrance, Calif., Aug. 10, 1953; d. John Andrew and Jane Angela (Seymour) Renke; m. Stephen Richard Lemkin, July 16, 1986; 1 child, Victoria Jane. AA, El Camino Coll., Torrance, 1974; BSN, Calif. State U., Dominguez Hills, 1989. Staff nurse Harbor and UCLA Med. Ctr., Carson, Calif., 1974, Ann Arundel Gen. Hosp., Annapolis, Md., 1975-76; [illegible] Torrance Meml. Med. Ctr., 1976-83, clin. educator, 1979-83; dir. edn. Active Care, Torrance, 1983; v.p. Doctors Home Tech, Inc., Torrance, 1984-93; pres. DHT and Torrance Meml. Home Health and Hospice, 1993—, chmn. adv. bd. DHT and Torrance Meml. Home Health and Hospice, 1983—; mem. adv. bd. Cambrian Home Health, Tor-

rance, 1993—. Author: (with others) Everyone's Guide to Cancer Therapy, 2d ed., 1994, 3d ed., 1997; contbr. articles to various profl. periodicals; host (TV ednl. program) Health Quest, 1993—. Recipient PRO award Pub. Communicators L.A., 1996, PRISM award Pub. Rels. Soc. Am., 1996. Mem. Nat. Assn. Home Care, Nat. Hospice Orgn., Calif. Assn. Health Svc. at Home. Avocation: traveling. Office: DHT Torrance Meml Home Health and Hospice 3330 Lomita Blvd Torrance CA 90505-5002

LEMMON, DIANNE, nursing researcher, nursing administrator; b. Baker City, Oreg., July 15, 1949; d. Seth Beal and Helen Francis (Fenn) Dennis; m. Jack Phillip Lemmon, Nov. 16, 1967; children: Tara Lemmon Schleicher, Kali Lemmon Nelson. BA, Calif. State U., 1973; ADN, Shasta Coll., 1977. Cert. urology RN Am. Bd. Urol. Allied Health Profls. Staff nurse Sacred Heart Hosp., Eugene, Oreg., 1977-79, Grande Ronde (Oreg.) Hosp., 1979-81, St. Vincent Hosp., Portland, Oreg., 1981-89; urology-oncology rsch. nurse Oreg. Health Scis. U., Portland, 1989—; mem. nurses com. S.W. Oncology Group. Dir. ch. choir. Vol. Am. Cancer Soc. (mem. prostate cancer task force 1996—, chairperson patient svcs. com. Oreg. divsn. 1998, Western Pacific divsn. blue ribbon quality of life task force, 1998—); mem. Soc. Urology Nurses and Assocs. (program chair 1994-96). Republican. Avocations: music, cooking, sewing, gardening, family activities. Office: Oreg Health Scis U L588 3181 SW Sam Jackson Park Rd Portland OR 97201

LEMMONS, PHILIP, editor; b. Okla., 1946; married; 2 children. Grad. with honors, Harvard U. Editl. dir. PC World, San Francisco, 1991—. Office: 106 Communications 501 2d St Ste 600 San Francisco CA 94107-1496

LEMON, LESLIE GENE, retired diversified services company executive; b. Davenport, Iowa, June 14, 1940. BS, U. Ill., 1962, LLB, 1964. Bar: Ill. 1964, Ariz. 1972. Asst. gen. counsel Am. Farm Bur. Fedn., Chgo., 1964-69; sr. atty. Armour and Co., Chgo., 1969-71; with Viad Corp (formerly The Dial Corp and The Greyhound Corp.), Phoenix, 1971-99; gen. counsel The Dial Corp (formerly Greyhound Corp.), Phoenix, 1977-96, v.p., 1979-99; ret., 1999. Vestryman All Saints Episcopal Ch., Phoenix, 1975-81; trustee Phoenix Art Mus., 1985-98; bd. dirs. Phoenix Children's Hosp., 1985-98; bd. visitors U. Calif. Med. Sch., Davis, 1983—. Mem. ABA, Nat. Conf. Uniform Law Commrs., Assn. Gen. Counsel, Maricopa County Bar Assn., State Bar Ariz., Phoenix C. of C. (bd. dirs. 1989-95), Am. Arbitration Assn. (bd. dirs. 1996—). Home: 1136 W Butler Dr Phoenix AZ 85021-4428

LENDERMAN, JOANIE, elementary education educator; b. Medford, Oreg., Jan. 20, 1946; d. Jay Lenderman and Vivian Spencer. BS in Edn., So. Oreg. Coll., Ashland, 1969; MS in Edn., Portland State U., 1972; postgrad., U. Va., 1985. Elem. tchr. Beaverton (Oreg.) Schs., 1972-76, Internat. Sch. Svcs., Isfahan, Iran, 1976-78; ESL instr. Lang. Svcs., Tucker, Ga., 1983-84; tchr. Fairfax (Va.) Schs., 1985-86; elem. tchr. Beaverton (Oreg.) Schs., 1990-96. Mem. Nat. Trust for Hist. Preservation, Hist. Preservation League of Oreg., Portland. Mem. AAAS, AAUW, U.S. Hist. Soc., Platform Soc., Smithsonian Instn., Am. Mus. Natural History, Nat. Mus. Women in Arts, U.S. Hist. Soc., The UN, The Colonial Williamsburg Found., Wilson Ctr., N.Y. Acad. Sci., Hist. Preservation League of Oreg., Noetics Soc. Home: 4105 Jefferson Pkwy Lake Oswego OR 97035-1479

LENEAU, THOMAS ERVIN, retired gas company executive; b. Mpls., Aug. 3, 1950; s. Thomas J. and Evelyn F. (Schwantees) LeN. BS in Math., St. Cloud State U., 1972; MEd, U. Minn., 1977; B in Acctg., U. Minn., Duluth, 1979; MBA, Ariz. State U., 1985. CPA, Ariz., Minn. Math. instr. Duluth Pub. Schs., 1972-78; acctg. instr. U. Minn., Duluth, 1978-79; auditor Deloitte, Haskins & Sells, Mpls., 1979-81; v.p. fin. Rio Verde Devel., Scottsdale, Ariz., 1981-86; pres., CEO Black Mountain Gas Co., Cave Creek, Ariz., 1986-98, also bd. dirs.; ret., 1998. Treas. Foothills Community Found., Carefree, Ariz., 1989-94; mem. adv. bd. Desert Foothills Land Trust, Cave Creek, Ariz., 1995—, treas. 1997—; treas. Desert Foothills Land Trust, 1997—. Mem. AICPA. Office: Black Mountain Gas Co PO Box 427 Cave Creek AZ 85327-0427

LENGWIN, EMMA JEAN, small business owner; b. Sharon, Pa., June 7, 1940; d. Peter James and Laura Adeline (McGrath) Rotunno; m. Lawrence Joseph Lengwin, Feb. 29, 1964; children: Ronald Allen, Robert Andrew. With Am. Chain & Cable, Commerce, Calif., 1959-60, So. Calif. Edison, Whittier, 1960-67; salesman Prestige Properties, Brea, Calif., 1976-80; v.p. Park Auto Bake, Inc., L.A., 1967-83, Grants Pass (Oreg.) Ice, 1985—. Contbr. stories to newspapers. Avocations: gardening, books, animals, letter writing. Home: 6150 Donaldson Rd Grants Pass OR 97526-7863 Office: Grants Pass Ice 551 SW G St Grants Pass OR 97526-2472

LENGYEL, CORNEL ADAM (CORNEL ADAM), author; b. Fairfield, Conn., Jan. 1, 1915; s. Elmer Alexander and Mary Elizabeth (Bismarck) L.; m. Teresa Delaney Murphy, July 10, 1933; children: Jerome Benedict, Paul Joel, Michael Sebastian, Cornelia (Mrs. Charles Burke). LittD (hon.), World Acad. of Arts and Culture, Taiwan, 1991. Editor, supr. Fed. Research Project, San Francisco, 1938-41; music critic The Coast, San Francisco, 1937-41; shipwright, personnel officer Kaiser Shipyard, Richmond, Calif., 1942-44; mgr. Forty-Nine Theatre, Georgetown, Calif., 1946-50; editor W.H. Freeman Co., San Francisco, 1952-54; founder, exec. editor Dragon's Teeth Press, Georgetown, 1969—; vis. prof., lectr. English lit. Calif. State U., 1962-63; writer-in-residence Hamline U., St. Paul, 1968-69; guest lectr. MIT, 1969; transl. from Hungarian; editorial cons. HEW; ednl. dir. ILGWU. Author: (history) American Testament: The Story of the Promised Land, 1956, Four Days in July, 1958, I, Benedict Arnold: The Anatomy of Treason, 1960, Presidents of the U.S.A., 1961, Ethan Allen and the Green Mountain Boys, 1961, Jesus the Galilean, 1966, The Declaration of Independence, 1969; (poetry) Thirty Pieces, 1933, First Psalms, 1950, Fifty Poems, 1965, Four Dozen Songs, 1970, The Lookout's Letter, 1971, Late News from Adam's Acres, 1983, El Dorado Forest: Selected Poems, 1986, Advice to a Future Poet: Poems Early and Late, 1996; (plays) The World's My Village, 1935, Jonah Fugitive, 1936, The Giant's Trap, 1938, The Atom Clock, 1951, Eden, Inc., 1954, rev. edit. The Master Plan, 1963, Will of Stratford, 1964, Three Plays, 1964, The Case of Benedict Arnold, 1975, Doctor Franklin, 1976, The Shadow Trap, 1977, The Second Coming, 1985, Mengele's Passover, 1987, A Clockmaker's Boy: Part One, 1987; (novel) Malunkyaputta: His Quest for Edification, 1996; (essay) The Creative Self, 1971, contbr. to anthologies, The Golden Year, 1960, Interpretation for Our Time, 1966, The Britannica Library of Great American Writing, 1961, The Menorah Treasury, 1964, The Courage to Grow Old, 1988, From These Hills, 1990, Blood to Remember, 1991, Anthology of Contemporary Poets, 1992, World Poetry, 1993, We Speak for Peace, 1993, also Poet Lore, The Coast, The Argonaut, Saturday Rev., Menorah Jour., Kayak, Old Crow, Mandrake Rev., Midstream. Served with U.S. Merchant Marine, 1944-45. Recipient Albert M. Bender award in lit., 1945; recipient 1st prize Maritime Poetry Awards, 1945, 1st prize Poetry Soc. Va., 1951, Maxwell Anderson award drama, 1950, Di Castagnola award Poetry Soc. Am., 1971, Internat. Who's Who in Poetry award, 1972; Huntington Hartford Found. resident fellow, 1951, 64; MacDowell Colony resident fellow, 1967; Ossabaw Island Found. fellow, 1968; Nat. Endowment for Arts fellow, 1976-77. Mem. MLA, AAUP, PEN, Poetry Soc. Am., Poetry Soc. Eng., Authors Guild. Address: Adam's Acres Georgetown CA 95634

LENHART, JAMES ROBERT, sales manager, food service administrator; b. Detroit, Apr. 29, 1952; s. Robert Bernard and Harriett Frances (Ebert) L.; m. Lauren Michi Fujimoto, Oct. 1, 1983; children: Amanda Mariko, Samuel James Kai. Student, Naval Schs. of Photography, Pensacola, Fla., 1973, U. Hawaii, 1977-79. Beverage mgr. Bobby McGee's, Honolulu, 1978-79, Marriott Hotels, Maui, Hawaii, 1979-81; bartender various restaurants, Maui, 1981-82; owner Plantation Prime Rib Restaurant, Kauai, Hawaii, 1982-85; account exec. Inter Island Distributors, Kauai, 1985-86; sales mgr. Superior Coffee and Foods, Honolulu, 1986—. With USN, 1973-77, PTO. Mem. VFW, Am. Culinary Assn., Internat. Food Svc. Execs., Hawaii Mfrs. Assn., Chefs de Cuisine/Hawaii, Hawaii Restaurant Assn., Hawaii Hotel Assn. Republican. Methodist. Avocations: kayaking, running, racquetball, outrigger canoe paddling, hunting. Home: 7007 Hawaii Kai Dr Honolulu HI 96825-3134 Office: Superior Coffee and Foods 99-910 Iwaena St Aiea HI 96701-3248

LENNOX, GLORIA (GLORIA DEMEREE), real estate executive; b. Baden, Pa., Feb. 14, 1931; d. Gilbert and Marion (Slosson) Whetson; m. William Lennox, June 19, 1954 (div. 1985); children: Cheryl Lennox Watson, Lynda Lennox Huerta, Jim; m. Philip Demeree, July 4, 1985. BS in Edn., Kent State U., 1954; MA in Spl. Edn., Ariz. State U., 1968; grad., Realtor's Inst. Grad. Realtor Inst.; cert. residential specialist, cert. residential broker state and nat. Tchr. Maple Leaf Sch., Garfield Heights, Ohio, 1954-55, Madison (Ind.) Dist. Elem. Sch., 1958, Scottsdale (Ariz.) Schs., 1961-68, Devereux Sch., 1968-70, Tri-City Mental Health Sch., Mesa, Ariz., 1970-71; br. mgr. M. Leslie Hansen, Scottsdale, 1972-74; v.p., gen. mgr. John D. Noble and Assocs., Scottsdale, 1974-83; pres., broker Gloria Lennox & Assocs., Inc., Scottsdale, 1983-96; sales mgr., v.p. Coldwell Banker Success, Scottsdale, 1996—. Chmn. bd. Interfaith Counseling Svc., 1988, 89; trustee Scottsdale Congl. United Ch. of Christ, 1986-88, 92, 96. Kent State U. scholar, 1950-54; disting. honoree Women's Impact Group, 1998. Mem. Nat. Assn. Realtors, Ariz. Assn. Realtors (Realtor Assoc. of Yr. 1975), Scottsdale Assn. Realtors (life, Hall of Fame award 1992, Disting. Career award 1994), Women's Coun. Realtors, Realtor Nat. Mktg. Inst., Scottsdale Bd. Realtors (pres. 1981-82, Realtor of Yr. 1982), Ariz. Town Halls, Ariz. Country Club. Republican. Avocations: bridge, golf, traveling. Home: 7561 N Via Camello Del Sur Scottsdale AZ 85258-3098 Office: Coldwell Banker Success Office VP 10605 N Hayden Rd # 6102 Scottsdale AZ 85260-5518

LENTZ, CONSTANCE MARCHAND, accountant; b. Tampa, Fla., May 6, 1948; d. George Ray and Allie Mae (Renner) L. BSBA, Calif. State U., Northridge, 1970, MSBA, 1974. CPA, Nev. Staff acct. Laventhol & Horwath CPA, Las Vegas, Nev., 1981-84; sr. mgr., acct. Deloitte, Haskins & Sells, Las Vegas, 1984-90; acct., pres. Constance M. Lentz, CPA, Ltd., Las Vegas, 1990—. Treas., bd. dirs. Warm Springs Res. Homeowners Assn., Henderson, Nev., 1990-94; trustee New Vista Ranch, Las Vegas, 1990-96, treas., 1995-96; treas. bd. trustees Las Vegas Natural History Mus., 1989-94; treas., bd. dirs. Clark County unit/Nev. divsn. Am. Cancer Soc., Las Vegas, 1978-85; bd. dirs., treas. Nev. Pub. Health Found., 1996—. Mem. AICPA, Nev. Soc. CPAs, Las Vegas C. of C. (Leadership Las Vegas grad. 1991), Leadership Las Vegas Alumni Assn. Avocations: reading, running, working out, sailing. Office: 930 S 3d St Ste 100A Las Vegas NV 89101-6843

LENZ, PHILIP JOSEPH, municipal administrator; b. Monterey Park, Calif., Sept. 15, 1940; s. Philip George and Irene Mary (Bowers) L.; m. Mary Lou Antista, July 16, 1966; children: Brian Joseph, Jonathan Thomas. BA, Calif. State U., L.A., 1966; MS, Pepperdine U., 1974; cert. instr. total quality mgmt., Calif. State U., San Bernardino, 1993; cert. participating mgmt., Calif. State U., 1998. Dir. West Valley div. San Bernardino County (Calif.) Probation Dept., 1977-79, dir. juvenile div., 1979-82, dir. adminstrv. services, 1982-88, dir. dist. services, 1988-90; dep. chief probation officer, 1990—; instr. dept. bus. Calif. State U., San Bernardino; instr. dept. social rels. Loma Linda U., 1988. Sec. bd. trustees Upland (Calif.) Sch. Dist., 1986—, pres. sch. bd., 1989-90, 94-96; mgr., coach Upland Am. Little League, 1981-90, bd. dirs., 1982-90; pres. Fontana (Calif.) Family Svc. Agy., 1972-74; mem. adv. com. corrections Chaffey Coll., Alta Loma, Calif., 1977-97; mem. Upland Parks and Recreation Com., 1986-97, chmn., 1989-91; bd. dirs. Highlander Ednl. Found., v.p., 1991-96; mem. Calif. Youth Authority CADRE of Cons.; mem. San Bernardino County Com. on Sch. Dist. Orgn., 1998—. Recipient Tim Fitzharris award Chief Probation Officers of Calif., 1987. Mem. Calif. Probation, Parole and Correctional Assn. (liaison, regional v.p. 1981-83, 2d v.p. 1985-86, 1st v.p. 1986—, pres. 1987—), Probation Bus. Mgr.'s Assn. (regional chmn. 1984-86, v.p. 1987), Western Correctional Assn., Assn. for Criminal Justice Rsch. (bd. dirs.), Probation Adminstrs. Assn. (regional chair 1992-93). Democrat. Roman Catholic. Avocations: baseball, bicycle riding, hiking. Home: 1375 Stanford Ave Upland CA 91786-3147 Office: San Bernardino County Dept Probation 175 W 5th St San Bernardino CA 92401-1401

LEO, MABEL RAE, writer, office manager; b. Sailor Springs, Ill.; d. Bob Maglone; widow, 1988. Author: The Saga of Jack Durant, 1996, America—The Italian Dream, 1998, Yahoody Who?, 1999. Mem. Soc. Southwestern Authors, Ariz. Authors Assn. Republican. Roman Catholic. Avocations: reading, genealogy, antiques. Home: PO Box 17413 Phoenix AZ 85011-0413

LEO, MARY GAYE, school administrator; b. Colorado Springs, Colo., Oct. 19, 1951; d. Bernard Johnston and Mary Ellen (Hardy) Lamar; m. Dominick Louis Leo; children: Dominick Christopher, Rachel Gabreilla. BA, U. Colo., 1973, MA, 1978; PhD in Ednl. Adminstrn. Denver U., 1985. Cert. bicultural/bilingual instr. Communications & group dynamics instr., Denver area, 1972-73; with Denver Pub. Sch. Sys., 1973-94, arts mgmt./theater dir., 1973-87; asst. prin. Lake Mid. Sch., 1987-89, Martin Luther King Mid. Sch., Denver Pub. Schs., 1989-91; asst. prin. West H.S., Denver, 1991-94; prin. Skyview H.S., Denver, 1994-96; with Mapleton Pub. Sch. Sys., 1994-96; prin. Rifle (Colo.) Middle Sch., 1996—; adj. faculty U. Colo., Boulder, Colo.; adj. edn. faculty Met. State Coll., Denver; prof. edn. adminstrn. U. Phoenix. Author: (musical) Celebration, 1979, (children's fantasy) Bob, The Magical Unicorn, 1981, (book) The Raven and I-E Locus of Control as Measures of High Ability; developer Authentic School Project for Drop Out Prevention, Academy Model for Middle Level Education. Lectr., workshop coord. Colo. Arts and Humanities Coun., 1974-75. Gov.'s Creativity grantee, 1990-91, Recipient Colo. Hispanic Bar Assn. Cmty. Svc. award, 1994. Mem. ASCD, NAFE, Nat. Council Tchrs. English, Colo. Assn. Sch. Execs., Colo. Partnership. Home: 4554 S Alton St Englewood CO 80111-1207

LEON, BRUNO, architect, educator; b. Van Houten, N.Mex., Feb. 18, 1924; s. Giovanni and Rose (Cunico) L.; m. Louise Dal-Bo, Sept. 4, 1948 (dec. 1974); m. Bonnie Bertram, Sept. 12, 1976; children: Mark Jon, John Anthony, Lisa Rose. Student, Wayne State U., 1942, U. Detroit, 1945-48; LHD (hon.), U. Detroit, 1984; BArch, N.C. State Univ., 1953. Registered architect, Mich., N.C., Mass., N.Y., N.Mex., Fla. Head design staff Fuller Research Found., Raleigh, N.C., 1954-55; archtl. designer I.M. Pei & Assos., N.Y.C., 1955-56; instr. Mass. Inst. Tech., 1956-59; designer Catalano & Belluschi (architects), Cambridge, Mass., 1958-59; asst. prof. U. Ill. at Urbana, 1959-61; dean Sch. Architecture, U. Detroit, 1961-93, dean emeritus, 1993; pvt. practice architecture, 1956—. Served with USAAF, 1942-45. Fellow AIA (dir. Detroit 1963-64); mem. Alpha Sigma Nu (hon.), Phi Kappa Phi. Home: 9 Redonda Ct Santa Fe NM 87505-8308

LEON, JOAN, development consultant, nonprofit company executive; b. Englewood Cliffs, N.J., July 3, 1938; d. Herman Joseph and Angela Victoria (Swetlock) Schaefer; m. Dennis Leon, Mar. 20, 1965 (div. 1988); children: Ann, Susan; m. Ramon Lauro Jimenez, Nov. 23, 1993; stepchildren: Jonah, Sarah. BA, Ursinus Coll., 1959; postgrad., U. Calif., Berkeley, 1983-84. Editor Welsbach Corp., Phila., 1961-63; with dept. devel. and pub. rels. Phila. Coll. Art, 1963-71; dir. devel. and pub. rels. Thomas A. Dooley Found., San Francisco, 1972-74; devel. dir. Ctr. for Ind. Living, Berkeley, Calif., 1974-77; asst. dir. State Dept. Rehab., Sacramento, Calif., 1977-83; v.p., co-founder World Inst. on Disability, Oakland, Calif., 1983-95, CEO, 1995-97, pres., CEO, 1997-98; adv. bd. U.S. Interagy. Coord. Coun., 1997—; devel. cons. Ed Roberts Campus, Berkeley, 1997—, also bd. dirs.; bd. dirs. World Inst. on Disability, Oakland. Avocations: gardening, ancient history, Shakespeare Oxford Society. E-mail: jleonberk@aol.com. Home and Office: 3143 Eton Ave Berkeley CA 94705

LEON, RICHARD HAYWARD, minister; b. Seattle, Mar. 9, 1935; s. Douglas Hayward and Helen (Hanson) L.; m. Carolyn Vandiver, Sept. 17, 1961; children: Jay Christopher, Catherine Marie, Mary Wynne. BA, U. Wash., 1957; MA, Benares Hindu U., India, 1961; MDiv, Princeton Theol. Sem., 1962; D in Ministry, San Francisco Theol. Sem., 1982. Asst. pastor Hamburg (N.Y.) Presbyn. Ch., 1962-65, sr. pastor, 1965-70; sr. pastor Union Ch. of Manila, Makati, Rizal, Philippines, 1970-76; sr. pastor First Presbyn. Ch., Spokane, Wash., 1976-86, Bellevue, Wash., 1986—. Founder, chmn. Christian Aid Network, Spokane, 1985. Recipient Pastoral Leadership award Whitworth Coll., 1983. Mem. Rotary Club Bellevue. Avocations: tennis, golf. Office: First Presbyn Ch 1717 Bellevue Way NE Bellevue WA 98004-2853

LEONARD, GLEN M., museum administrator; b. Salt Lake City, Nov. 12, 1938; s. Burnham J. and Allene (Green) L.; m. Karen Wright, Mar. 15, 1968; children: Cory, Kyle, Keith. BA, U. Utah, 1964, MA, 1966, PhD, 1970. Mng. editor Utah State Hist. Soc., Salt Lake City, 1970-73; sr. rsch. assoc. history divsn. Ch. of Jesus Christ of Latter-day Saints, Salt Lake City, 1973-78; dir. Mus. Ch. History and Art, Salt Lake City, 1979—; mem. adv. bd. editors Utah Hist. Quarterly, Salt Lake City, 1973-88; assoc. editor Jour. Mormon History, Provo, Utah, 1974-80; bd. dirs. Western Studies Ctr., Brigham Young U., Provo. Co-author: The Story of the Latter-day Saints, 1976; contbr. articles to profl. publs. Mem. Hist. Preservation Commn., Farmington, Utah, 1986-92; mem. adv. coun. Mormon Pioneer Nat. Hist. Trail, Nat. Pk. Svc., 1980-86; mem. Utah Pioneer Sesquicentennial Celebration Coordinating Coun., 1995-97. Recipient Dale Morgan Article award Utah State Hist. Soc., 1973, Mormon History Assn. Article awards, 1990, 96. Mem. Orgn. Am. Historians, Western History Assn., Am. Assn. Mus. (mus. assessment program cons.), Western Mus. Assn., Utah Mus. Assn. (bd. dirs. 1980-83), Am. Assn. State and Local History. Avocations: photography, music, gardening. Office: Mus Ch Hist and Art 45 N West Temple Salt Lake City UT 84150-3810

LEONARD, VICTORIA LEE, ballet instructor; b. Detroit, Nov. 10, 1957; d. Stanly Arnold Nelson and Margaret June (Lyman) Olson; m. David H. Leonard, Nov. 7, 1987 (div. Sept. 1997); children: Clifford B., William H. BFA, Univ. San Diego, 1980; MFA, Univ. Calif., 1983. Dance faculty Mankato State Univ., Mankato, Minn., 1983-84, Allentown Coll., Center Valley, Pa., 1984-86, DeFore Dance Ctr., Costa Mesa, Calif., 1990—, Rancho Santiago Coll., Santa Ana, Calif., 1992—; dir., owner Beau Corps Studio, Tustin, Calif., 1998—; faculty, dancer Ballet Guadalajara, Jalisco, Mexico, Long Beach, Calif., 1981-82; dancer Long Beach Ballet, 1986-87; dancer, choreographer Ballet Pacifica, Costa Mesa, 1987-88, examiner Saddleback Dance Ctr., 1995—; amb. to Russian for Dance Educators, 1998. Mem. Am. Alliance for Health, Recreation and Dance. Avocations: skiing, pilates, water sports, theatre. Home: 10965 Mathews Dr Tustin CA 92782-3304 Office: Rancho Santiago C C 1530 W 17th St Santa Ana CA 92706-3398

LEONG, CAROL JEAN, electrologist; b. Sacramento, Jan. 9, 1942; d. Walter Richard and Edith (Bond) Bloss; m. Oliver Arthur Fisk III, Apr. 12, 1964 (div. 1973); 1 child, Victoria Kay. BA in Sociology, San Jose (Calif.) State Coll., 1963; degree, Western Bus. Coll., 1964; cert. in electrolysis, Bay Area Coll. Electrolysis, 1978; degree in esthetics, Zenzi's Coll., 1998. Registered and cert. clin. profl. electrologist, Calif. Model various orgns., Calif., 1951-64; employment counselor Businessmen's Clearinghouse, Cin., 1966-67; dir. personnel Kroger Food Corp., Cin., 1967-68; prin. Carol Leong Electrolysis, San Mateo, Calif., 1978—; prin. Designs by Carol, San Mateo, 1987—; mem. Profl. Women's Forum, 1988—. Contbr. articles to profl. publs. Pres. Peninsula Aux. Lighthouse for the Blind, 1984-85, 95, 96, 97, 98, 1st v.p., 1993, 94, 95; mem. Civic Garden Club, 1995—, Best Friends Animal Orgn., 1992—, The Nature Conservancy, 1995—, Nat. Fedn. Rep. Women, 1996; vol. Nat. Kidney Found. No. Calif., 1995—. Recipient Cert. of Appreciation San Francisco Lighthouse for the Blind, 1981-82, 83. Mem. Internat. Guild Profl. Electrologists (mem. continuing edn. com.), NAFE, Profl. Women's Forum, Peninsula Humane Soc., San Francisco Zool. Soc., Friends of Filoli, Am. Electrologists Assn., Electrologists Assn. Calif., Internat. Platform Assn, Chi Omega. Republican. Presbyterian. Avocations: golf, tennis, ballet, theater, photography. Home: 1447 Woodberry Ave San Mateo CA 94403-3712 Office: Carol Leong Electrolysis 359 N San Mateo Dr Ste 4 San Mateo CA 94401-2560

LEONG, JAMES CHAN, artist; b. San Francisco, Nov. 27, 1929; s. Tony C. and May (Chung) L.; m. Karen Swensen, 1951 (div. 1961); children: Kim Franklin, Mai Ann Leong Cozzupoli; m. Dean Yee Leong, Nov. 29, 1976; 1 child, James Chan Jr. BFA, Calif. Coll. Arts and Crafts, Oakland, 1951, MFA, 1953; MA in Art Edn., San Francisco State Coll., 1954. One-man shows include Barone Gallery, N.Y., 1955, 56, 57, 60, Am. Gallery, L.A., 1955, Galleria dell'Obelisco, Rome, 1960-61, Feingarten Galleries, N.Y., L.A., 1962, Galleria dell'Ariete, Milan, 1962, Royal Athena Galleries, N.Y., 1963-67, Cerberus Gallery, N.Y., 1969, Gloria Luria Gallery, Miami, 1970, Coll. Arts and Architecture, Pa. State U., 1971, USIS, Istanbul, Izmir, Ankara, Turkey, 1974, Kama Studio, Rome, 1975, Larcada Gallery, N.Y., 1975, Galleria Galtung, Oslo, 1976, Galleri 47, Copenhagen, 1976, Gallerie Oljemark, Helsinki, 1976, Studio Due, Rome, 1976, Can. Cultural Ctr. in Rome, Transamerica, 1988, Lasater Gallery, Seattle, 1994, others; exhibited in group shows at MOMA, N.Y.C., Whitney Mus. Ann, Downtown Gallery, N.Y.C., Contemporary Arts Soc., London, Gimpel Fils Ltd., London, Bklyn. Mus. Biennial, Carnegie Internat., Pitts., Princeton Art Mus., Rome Biennial, Nat. Inst. Arts and Letters, Corcoran Gallery, Am. Acad. Rome, Quadriennale Internat., Rome, USIS Germany, Stuttgart, Frankfurt, Munich, Berlin, Cologne, Hamburg, Am. Fedn. Arts, Gallery 88, Rome, Adele Bednarz Gallery, L.A., Mostra Nazionale, Viterbo, Gallery Dache, N.Y., Galleria Giorgi, Florence, Galleria L'Incontro, Milan, Galleria Nuovo Carpine, Rome, James Willis Gallery, San Francisco, Rome Quadriennale, Accademia Italia (gold medal), Galleria Il Ponte, Rome, Seafirst Gallery, Seattle, Rutgers U. Zimmerli Art Mus., Tapei Gallery, Manhattan, Chgo. Cultural Ctr., Fisher Gallery U. So. Calif.; represented in permanent collections at Princeton Mus., U. Tex., NYU Mus., Harvard U., Rochester Mus., Dallas Mus. Fine Arts, Ga. Mus., Mid. Tenn. State U., Indpls. Mus. Art, Roy Neuberger Mus., Weatherspoon Art Gallery, U. Wash., Tacoma, Harborview Med. Ctr., Seattle; commd. murals Chung Mei Home for Boys, El Cerrito, Calif., Ping Yuen Housing Project, San Francisco, San Francisco State Coll.; contbr. articles to profl. jours. Commr. Seattle Arts Commn. Recipient John Hay Whitney Opportunity fellowship, 1951, Fulbright grant for Norway, 1956, John Simon Guggenheim Found. grant, Rome, 1959. Home and Office: 89 Yesler Way Ste 4 Seattle WA 98104-2545

LEONG, LAM-PO (LANBO LIANG), artist, educator; b. Guangzhou, Guangdong, China, July 3, 1961; came to U.S., 1983; BFA in Chinese Brush Painting, Guangzhou Fine Arts Inst., 1983; MFA in Painting with high distinction, Calif. Coll. Arts & Crafts, 1988. Instr. art Calif. Coll. Arts and Crafts, Oakland, 1986-87, U. Calif. Ext. and ASUC, Berkeley, 1989, 90—, San Jose (Calif.) State U. Ext., 1989-91, Chabot Coll., Hayward, Calif., 1989-94; lectr. San Francisco State U., 1988-95, asst. prof., 1996—; instr. Laney Coll., Oakland, Calif., 1997—, Diablo Valley Coll., Pleasant Hill, Calif., 1998—; artistic dir. Oakland Asian Cultural Ctr., Calif., 1990-92; lectr. and spkr. in field, including TV appearances, Asian Art Mus. San Francisco, 1990, 92, 93, 95, 96, 97, 98, Chinese Cultural Ctr., San Francisco, 1993. One-man shows include Markings Gallery, Berkeley, 1984, Sumitomo Bank, Albany, Calif., 1985, Calif. Coll. Arts & Crafts, 1985, Rosicrucian Egyptian Mus., San Jose, 1986, U. Utah, Salt Lake City, 1986, Patrick Gallery, Regina, Sask., Can., 1986, Mus. Macao Luis De Camoes, Macao, 1986, Kai Ping County Mus., Guangdong, 1987, Chinatown Gallery, San Francisco, 1987, Guangzhou (China) Fine Arts Mus., 1988, The Arlington Gallery, Oakland, 1989, Moy Ying Ming Gallery, Chgo., 1990, Chinese Culture Ctr., San Francisco, 1991, Stanwood Gallery, San Francisco, 1992, Sanuk Fine Asian Collectables, San Francisco, 1992, The Univ. Gallery, San Francisco, 1994, Michael Thompson Gallery, San Francisco, 1995, China Art Expo '95, Guangzhou, China, 1995, MTC Gallery, Oakland, Calif., 1996, Galerie du Monde, Hong Kong, 1997, d.p. Fong Galleries, San Jose, Calif., 1997, Instituto Cultural de Macau, 1998; exhibited in group shows at Hong Kong Arts Ctr., 1980, Chinese Painting Exhibit Guangdong Province, 1981 (3d Prize award 1981), Macao Artists Assn. Exhbn., 1982-96, Mus. Guangzhou Fine Arts Inst., 1983, Nat. Mus. Art, Beijing, 1985, Macao Young Artist Exhbn. (Excellence award, 1st prize), Pacific Art Ctr., Seattle, 1985, Chinese Culture Ctr., 1986, Faculty & MFA Show Calif. Coll. Arts & Crafts, San Francisco Campus, 1986, Chinese-Am. Artist Exhbn., Taipei, Taizhong, Taiwan, 1986, Sullivan Galleries, Salt Lake City, 1987, Oriental Gallery, N.Y., 1987, Santa Cruz Art League (Spl. award 1988, 1st prize 1990), Asian Resource Gallery, Oakland, 1988, Nat. Mus. Fine Arts, Beijing, 1988, 90, Chinese Art Gallery, San Leandro, Calif., 1989, Stanwood Gallery, 1989, Gallery Imago, San Francisco, 1990, Sun Gallery, Hayward, 1990, N.Y. Art Expo, N.Y.C., 1991, Gallery 5, Santa Monica, Calif., 1991, Butterfield & Butterfield Auction, San Francisco, 1992, 95-96, Asian Art Mus., San Francisco, 1992, Ke Shan Art Gallery, Taipei, 1993, Wan Fung Art Gallery, Hong Kong, 1993, Gallery On The Rim, San Francisco, 1994, Resource for Art, 1995, Ginsberg Collection, 1995, Macao Art Expo, 1988-96, Acad. Art Coll., San Francisco, 1996, Shanghai Arts Mus., 1997, Pacific Heritage Mus., San Francisco, 1998, Ethan Cohen Fine Art, N.Y., 1998; work represented in various mus., corp. and pvt. collections including Guangzhou Arts Mus., Macao Camoes Mus., Mus. Guangzhou Fine Arts Inst., Asian Art Mus. San Francisco, United Savs. Bank, Calif., Hotel East

21, Tokyo, The Tokyo Westin Hotel, Comml. Bank, San Francisco, Westin Surabaya, Indonesia; author: Brush Paintings of Lam-Po Leong, 1986, Journey of the Heart, 1994, Lampo Leong: Contemplation.Forces, 1997, The Common Ground of Light and Gravity: Lampo Leong's Contemplation/Forces, 1998; illustrator: Brushstrokes-Styles and Techniques of Chinese Painting, 1993, The Tao of Power, 1986; designer (garden courtyard) New Chinatown Pk., San Francisco, 1993; designer (multi-image projection) Ctr. Arts Yerba Buena Gardens, San Francisco, 1996. Recipient Outstanding Merit award Young Art Now Competition, 1980, Decade of Achievement award Asian/Pacific Heritage Week, 1988, 2d prize Zunyi Internat. Brush Painting Competition, 1989, Gold Medal award 15th Macao Painting and Calligraphy Exhbn., 1998; inductee Pan-Pacific Asian Hall of Fame at San Francisco Internat. Expo., 1987; grantee City of Oakland Cultural Arts Divsn., 1994-96. Mem. Asian Artists Assn. Am., Oriental Art Assn., U.S.A. (v.p.), Macao Soc. Social Scis., Hai-Ri Artists Assn. (China), Nat. Modern Meticulous Painting Soc. (China), Chinese Am. Culture Exch. Assn. (co-founder, dir. 1992—). Avocations: film, ballroom dance, travel, photography. Office: Brushwork Gallery 166 Palisades Dr Daly City CA 94015-4517

LEON-GUERRERO, DAVID MESA, telecommunications company official; b. Honolulu, Apr. 29, 1955; s. Mariano Cepeda and Josefina (Cruz) L-G.; m. Alicia Laurentina Ceja, Nov. 18, 1984; children: Jessica Alicia, Jake David. AS, San Diego City Coll., 1979; BBA cum laude, Nat. U., 1980; MBA in Internat. Bus., George Washington U. Sales assoc. Pacific Telephone, San Diego, 1979-81; sales assoc. AT&T, San Diego, 1981-85, account exec., 1985-87, tech. cons., 1987-88, tech. cons. II, 1988-90; technical mktg. mgr. AT&T, Basking Ridge, N.J., 1990-95; sales mgr. GBM, Bus. Comm. Syss., Lucent Techs., Phoenix, Ariz., 1995—; nat. acct. mgr. Lucent, 1997—; Mem. adv. bd. Ariz. Tech. Incubator, 1996—. mentor HISPA Phoenix chpt. Lucent Techs., 1997. With U.S. Army, 1973-77. Mem. Phoenix C. of C. (electronics comm. task force 1996—, press. tech. roundtable 1997), Execs. Assn. Greater Phoenix. Republican. Roman Catholic. Office: Lucent Tech 4747 N 7th St Ste 314 Phoenix AZ 85014-3656

LEPIE, ALBERT HELMUT, chemist, researcher; b. Malapane, Silesia, Germany, Aug. 6, 1923; came to U.S., 1963; s. Albert and Emilia (Zachlod) L.; m. Claire Kortz, 1956 (div. 1964); 1 child, Karin. Degree in chem. engring., Staatliche Ing. Schule, Essen, Germany, 1953; diploma in chemistry, Tech. Hochschule, Aachen, Germany, 1959; D in Natural Scis., Tech. Hochschule, Munich, Germany, 1961. Chem. engr. Pahl'sche Gummi & Asbest, Düsseldorf, 1953-59; chemist Deutsche Versuchanstalt für Luftfahrt, Munich, 1961-63; rsch. chemist U.S. Naval Propellant Plant, Indian Head, Md., 1963-64; rsch. chemist Naval Weapons Ctr., China Lake, Calif., 1964-95, ret., 1995; chmn. mech. properties panel Joint Army, Navy, NASA, and Air Force Interag. Rocket Propulsion, 1977-84. Inventor air curtain incinerator for energetic materials and fiber peal force measurement device, flywheel high rate tensile tester for viscoelastic materials. Recipient Joint Army, Navy, NASA, and Air Force award, 1984, William B. McLean award Naval Weapons Ctr. Mem. Am. Chem. Soc. (sec. China Lake chpt. 1968, 69), China Lake Astron. Soc., Sigma Xi. Roman Catholic. Avocations: astronomy, computer programming, motorcycling. Home: 121 S Desert Candles St Ridgecrest CA 93555-4218

LEPORIERE, RALPH DENNIS, quality engineer; b. Elizabeth, N.J., Nov. 8, 1932; s. Maximo and Christian (Lello) L.; m. Judith Louise Crowhurst, Nov. 19, 1960; children: Bonnie Ann, David Anthony. BS in Chemistry, Rutgers U., 1954. Registered profl. engr., Calif. Chemist N.Y. Quinine & Chemical Works, Newark, 1954-55; asst. to chief quality control C.D. Smith Pharmacal Co., New Brunswick, N.J., 1955-56; asst. supr. quality control White Labs., Kenilworth, N.J., 1958-60; statistician Calif. and Hawaiian Sugar Co., Crockett, Calif., 1960—; instr., chmn. quality control dept. Laney C.C., Oakland, Calif., 1967-87; asst. prof., chmn. quality control dept. John F. Kennedy U., Martinez, Calif., 1967-72; instr., mem. adv. com. ann. statis. short course U. Calif., Davis, 1969-94. Pres. PTA Napa Junction Elem. Sch., Napa County, Calif., 1971-73; mem. early childhood com., program adv. com. Napa Valley Unified Sch. Dist., Napa County, 1972-76; v.p. Am. Canyon County Water Dist., American Canyon, Calif., 1971-73, pres., 1973-83, gen. mgr., 1981. Recipient Hon. Service award Calif. State PTA, 1973. Fellow Am. Soc. Quality Control (cert. quality engr., chmn. San Francisco sect., founder East Bay Subsect. 1970-71); mem. Soc. Mfg. Engrs. (sr.), Am. Statis. Soc., Am. Chem. Soc. Republican. Roman Catholic. Home: 618 Kilpatrick St Vallejo CA 94589-1305 Office: Calif & Hawaiian Sugar Co 830 Loring Ave Crockett CA 94525-1104

LEPS, ANTS ARVO, mass communication educator, consultant; b. Pärnu, Estonia, Jan. 26, 1936; came to U.S., 1949; parents Erich and Pauline (Elfriede) L.; m. Virve Põld, Sept. 1963. Student, Wesleyan U., Middletown, Conn., 1954-57; BA, U. Ill., 1961, MA, 1965; PhD, UCLA, 1979. Asst. physicist Nuclear Chgo. Corp., Des Plaines, Ill., 1959-60; engring. writer Gen. Dynamics Corp., Pomona, Calif., 1962-65; tech. publs. analyst System Devel. Corp., Santa Monica, Calif., 1965-70; instr. Santa Monica Coll., 1968-70; research assoc. Inst. for Ednl. Devel., El Segundo, Calif., 1970-71; cons. instructional design Northridge, Calif., 1972—; prof. dept. Radio-TV-Film Calif. State U., Northridge, 1979—, coord. MA program in mass communication, 1981-90, prof., 1988—; cons. to various TV, film and edn. agencies, Estonia, 1990-91. Author, editor: (with others) Art of Multi-Image, 1978; author: (with others) Mass Media and the Individual, 1983; contbr. chpt. on ednl. & instrnl. TV to The Encyclopaedia of Educational Media Communications and Technology, 1988; presenter various media confs., 1980—; contbr. articles to profl. jours. Bd. dirs. Build Rehab. Industries, North Hollywood, Calif., 1980-87; mem. Mus. Contemporary Art, L.A.; mem. adv. com. Glendale Community Coll., 1990—. Mem. AAUP, Acad. TV Arts and Scis., Soc. Motion Picture and TV Engrs., Internat. TV Assn., Assn. for Multi-Image (publs. bd, devel. bd., coord., chmn. bd. dirs., 1975-94), Am. Psychol. Assn., Internat. Interactive Communications Soc., Broadcast Edn. Assn., UCLA Alumni Assn. (life), Grad. Sch. Edn. Alumni Assn. (v.p. 1988-90, 91-93, bd. dirs., Teaching of Yr. award of Excellence 1991), Assn. Visual Communicators (exec. com. 1988-90, bd. dirs., pres. L.A. chpt. 1989-90, Pres.'s award 1990), Assoc. for Ednl. Communications and Tech. (life), Assn. Computing Machinery, Internat. Visual Literacy Assn., Internat. Documentary Assn., Spl. Interest Group-Computer Graphics (L.A. chpt.), Spl. Interest Group Human Computer Interface, SIGCHI, L.A. County Mus. Art, Sierra Club (cert. outing hike leader, 1996—), Calif. Faculty Assn., So. Calif. Early Music Soc., Estonian Heritage Soc., Phi Beta Delta (Omega chpt.)., L.A. Macintosh Users Group. E-mail: ants.leps@csun.edu. Office: Calif State U Northridge Dept Radio TV Film Northridge CA 91330

LERAAEN, ALLEN KEITH, financial executive; b. Mason City, Iowa, Dec. 4, 1951; s. Myron O. and Clarice A. (Handeland) L.; m. Mary Elena Partheymuller, Apr. 14, 1978. BBA in Data Processing and Acctg., No. Ariz. U., 1975. CFA. Data processing supr. Stephenson & Co., Denver, 1978-81, contr., 1981-85, arbitrageur, trader, 1985-88, v.p., 1985-90, exec. v.p., 1990—; v.p., sec. bd. dirs. Circle Corp., Denver, 1985—. Mem. Assn. Investment Mgmt. and Rsch., Denver Soc. Security Analysts. Avocation: flying. Home: 5692 S Robb St Littleton CO 80127-1942 Office: 100 Garfield St Fl 4 Denver CO 80206-5597

LERMAN, EILEEN R., lawyer; b. N.Y.C., May 6, 1947; d. Alex and Beatrice (Kline) L. BA, Syracuse U., 1969; JD, Rutgers U., 1972; MBA, U. Denver, 1983. Bar: N.Y. 1973, Colo. 1976. Atty. FTC, N.Y.C., 1972-74; corp. atty. RCA, N.Y.C., 1974-76; corp. atty. Samsonite Corp. and consumer products divsn. Beatrice Foods Co., Denver, 1976-78, assoc. gen. counsel, 1978-85, asst. sec., 1979-85; ptnr. Davis, Lerman, & Weinstein, Denver, 1985-92, Eileen R. Lerman & Assocs., 1993—; bd. dirs. Legal Aid Soc. of Met. Denver, 1979-80. Bd. dirs., vice chmn. Colo. Postsecondary Ednl. Facilities Authority, 1981-89; bd. dirs., pres. Am. Jewish Com., 1989-92; mem. Leadership Denver, 1983. Mem. ABA, Colo. Women's Bar Assn. (bd. dirs. 1980-81), Colo. Bar Assn. (mem. bd. govs.), Denver Bar Assn. (trustee), N.Y. State Bar Assn., Rhone Brackett Inn (pres. 1997-98), Denver Law Club, Rutgers U. Alumni Assn., Univ. Club. Home: 1018 Fillmore St [illegible] Denver CO 80209-2809

LERNER, KATHY MASON, artist, business woman; b. Oakland, Calif., Apr. 2, 1941; d. John Jacob and Katherine (Hughert) Mason; m. Howard Heseman, 1964 (div. 1971); m. Michael Lerner; children: Jude, Thessaly, Zachary. Avocations. gardening, sculpture, interior design. Home: 830 La Playa Way San Rafael CA 94903-2920

LERNER, VLADIMIR SEMION, computer scientist, educator; b. Odessa, Ukraine, Sept. 12, 1931; came to U.S., 1990; s. Semion N. and Manya G. (Grosman) L.; m. Sanna K. Gleyzer, Sept. 28, 1954; children: Alex, Tatyana, Olga. BSEE, Odessa Poly. Inst., 1954; MEE, Inst. Problem's Controls, Moscow, 1959; PhD in Elec. Engring., Moscow Power Inst., 1961; D Sci. in Systems Analysis, Leningrad State U., 1974. Prof. elec. engring. Kishinev (Moldova) State U., 1962-64; prof. elec. engring. and control systems Kishinev Poly. Inst., 1964-79; sr. scientist in applied math. Acad. Sci., Kishinev, 1964-79; dir. math. modeling and computer sci. lab. Rsch. Inst., Odessa, 1979-89; sr. lectr. UCLA, 1991-93, rschr., 1993—; chmn. computer sci. dept. West Coast U., L.A., 1993-97, Nat. U., L.A., 1997—; mem. adv. bds. Acad. Sci., Kishinev, 1964-79, Poly. Inst., Kishinev, 1964-79; vis. prof. Leningrad State U., 1971-73; cons., mem. adv. bd. Poly. Inst., Odessa, 1979-89; mem. hon. editl. adv. bd. Encyclopedia of Life Support Syss., Informational Macrodynamics. Author: Physical Approach to Control Systems, 1969, Superimposing Processes in Control Problems, 1973, Dynamic Models in Decision Making, 1974, Special Course in Optimal and Self Control Systems, 1977, Lectures in Mathematical Modelling and Optimization, 1995, Mathematical Foundations of Informational Macrodynamics, 1996, Lectures in Informational Macrodynamics, 1996, Informational Macrodynamics: Theory, Numerical Insights and Applications, 1999; contbr. numerous articles to sci. jours.; holder 23 patents; founder new sci. discipline Informational Macrodynamics. Recipient Silver medal for rsch. achievements, Moscow, 1961, outstanding achievements in edn., Kishinev, 1975. Avocations: bicycling, travel.

LEROSE, THOMAS M., photographer; b. Kenosha, Wis., May 15, 1954; s. Leonard Dominic LeRose and Arelene E. Kollman; m. Sarah Christine Aldrich. AA with honors, Cabrillo Coll., Aptos, Calif., 1978. Owner, operator LeRose Photography, El Portal, Calif., 1986-94; photo lab. technician Yosemite (Calif.) Pk. and Curry Co., 1987-89; portrait photographer Midwest Mktg., Earth City, Mo., 1994-95; photo lab. technician Kits Cameras Inc., Santa Fe, 1995-96; portrait photographer Am. Studios, Santa Fe, 1996—; owner, operator Golden Heart Photography, Santa Fe, 1996—; operator photo tour LeRose Photography, El Portal, 1990-94; photo cons. Golden Heart Stock Photography, Santa Fe, 1996—. One-man exhbns. include Mariposa Post Office, 1994, Mariposa County Arts Coun. Gallery, 1994; featured photographer Mariposa C. of C. brochure, 1987, RVing Am.'s Back Rds., 1989, U.S. Bur. Land Mgmt. Merced River Canyon Recreational Display and Guide, 1990, Yosemite 18-month calendar, 1991-92, Southern N. Mex. Mag., 1998, N. Mex. Film Commn. Bus. Directory, 1998-99, N. Mex. Mag., 1998-99, Photographer's Forum Best of 97, Alburque Jour., 1998, Names and Numbers Dir., 1997-98. Instr. photography Mariposa County Sch. Dist., 1992; instr. skiing El Portal Elem. Sch., Yosemite, Calif., 1983-89. Mem. Nat. Pks. and Conservation Assn., Environ. Def. Fund, Nat. Wildlife Fedn. Avocations: hiking, camping, skiing, poetry. Office: Golden Heart Photography PO Box 22430 Santa Fe NM 87502-2430

LE ROY, ROBERT POWELL, minister, educator, writer; b. Ellensburg, Wash., Oct. 5, 1923; s. Bernard Rayme Jr. and Sibyl Powell Le Roy; m. Marion Knutson, July 30, 1946 (div. Jan. 1960); children: Marcie Jane Le Roy Root, Sibyl Marie Le Roy Ward; m. Shirley June Passmore, May 25, 1962; children: Kenny, Margaret, Beth, Roberta. BA in Edn., Pacific Luth. U., Tacoma, Wash., 1950; MS in Edn., Chadron (Nebr.) Tchrs. Coll., 1965; postgrad., U. Mo., Independence, 1972-73. Ordained minister Bapt. Ch., 1950. Educator, Bapt. evangelist Tacoma Bible Presbyn. Ch., Langley, Wash., 1945—; founder, editor Alarming Cry newspaper, Pasadena, Calif., 1953—; editor Western Voice News, Englewood, Colo., 1955-57; tchr. Colo. State Reform Sch., Golden, 1958-60; co-founder Minutemen, Independence, Mo., 1962-80; Bapt. evangelist Independence, 1965—; founder Christian Sons of Liberty, Liberty, Mo., 1970—; lectr. in field. Author: Scientific Approach to Creation, 1965, All About UFOs, 1973, From My Foxhole to Tokyo (World War II History of 11th Airborne Division 1943-46), 1990, The Bible and UFOs, 1997, LeRoy Family History (1790-1990), 1987. Founder, pastor All-Am. Bible Bapt. Ch., Langley, 1980—; chaplain, historian Am. Legion, Clinton, Wash., 1993-99; co-founder Wash. State Populist Party, Seattle, 1984—; candidate Gov., Wash., 1984—. With U.S. Army, 1943-46. Recipient Bronze Star, 2 Purple Hearts. Avocations: gardening, farming. Home: 3339 S Le Roy Cir Clinton WA 98236 Office: PO Box 48 Langley WA 98260

LE SAGE, BERNARD E., lawyer; b. Pasadena, CAlif., Mar. 29, 1949. BA, U. Notre Dame, 1971; JD, Loyola U., L.A., 1974. Bar: Calif. 1974. Extern clk. to Hon. William P. Clark Calif. Supreme Ct., 1974; with Buchalter, Nemer, Fields & Younger, L.A., 1979—. Mem. ABA, State Bar Calif., Los Angeles County Bar Assn. (trustee 1982-84), Los Angeles County Bar Barristers (pres. 1983-84), Chancery Club. Office: Buchalter Nemer Fields & Younger Ste 2400 601 S Figueroa St Los Angeles CA 90017-5704*

LESCH, BARRY M., lawyer; b. N.Y.C., Apr. 26, 1945. BA, U. Pa., 1965; MA, Ind. U., 1971; JD, U. Calif., Berkeley, 1975. Bar: Calif. 1975, U.S. Supreme Ct. 1980. With Laughlin, Falbo, Levy & Moresi, Sacramento. Mem. State Bar Calif. (cert. specialist workers compensation law). Office: Laughlin Falbo Levy & Moresi 106 K St Fl 2 Sacramento CA 95814-3218

LESCROART, JOHN THOMAS, writer; b. Houston, Jan. 14, 1948; s. Maurice Eugene and Loretta Therese (Gregory) L.; m. Leslee Ann Miller, 1976 (div. 1978); m. Lisa Sawyer, Sept. 2, 1984; children: John Jack Sawyer Lescroart, Justine Rose Lescroart. BA in English Lit. with honors, U. Calif., Berkeley, 1970. Pvt. practice, 1981—. Author: Sunburn, 1981, Son of Holmes, 1986, Rasputin's Revenge, 1987, Dead Irish, 1989, The Vig, 1990, Hard Evidence, 1993, the 13th Juror, 1994, A Certain Justice, 1995, Son of Holmes & Rasputin's Revenge, 1995, Guilt, 1997, The Mercy Rule, 1998. Recipient Joseph Henry Jackson award San Francisco Found., 1978; N.Y. Times Best Seller list for 13th Juror, 1995 and Guilt, 1998. Mem. El Macero Country Club. Avocations: fishing, baseball, food and wine. Home and Office: 129 C St Ste 3 Davis CA 95616-4632

LESHNE, CARLA, videomaker, videographer, editor; b. Washington, May 18, 1959; d. Stanley and Ann (Blackmarr) Leshne; 1 child, Kai. BA in World and Comparative Lit., San Francisco State U., 1982, MA in Broadcast Comm. Arts, 1992. Videomaker, editor Mission Creek Video, San Francisco, 1989—; freelance videographer San Francisco, 1997—; mem. Paper Tiger/Deep Dish TV Collective, 1989—. Videos include Across From City Hall, 1990, SF Says No. . ., 1991, Lies, 1993; filmmaker Tulum Melody, 1992.

LESKO, RONALD MICHAEL, osteopathic physician; b. Homestead, Pa., Mar. 25, 1948; s. Andrew Paul and Elizabeth Ann (Tarasovic) L.; m. Helena Alexandra Shalayeva, July 29, 1990. BS, U. Pitts., 1970; DO, Coll. Osteo. Medicine & Surgery, Des Moines, 1973; MPH, Loma Linda U., 1985. Diplomate Am. Osteo. Bd. Family Physicians, Am. Osteo. Bd. Preventive Medicine (bd. dirs., chmn. pub. health rep., chmn. bd. exam. com. 1991-97). Family physician pvt. practice Port Richey, Fla., 1974-80; flight surgeon USN, NAS Chase Field Beeville, Tex., 1981-83; resident gen. preventive medicine Loma Linda (Calif.) U. Med. Ctr., 1983-85; pvt. practice family and preventive medicine, pvt. practice, Del Mar, Calif., 1988—; flight surgeon, capt. USNR, NAS Miramar, San Diego, 1988-95; ret. USNR, Loma Linda, Calif., 1996; attending physician ambulatory care svc. J.L. Pettis Meml. VA Hosp., Loma Linda, Calif., 1986-88; staff physician Scripps Meml. Hosp., La Jolla, Calif., 1990—; lectr., 1985—; cons. Jour. Am. Osteo. Assn., Chgo., 1987, phys. rediness div. USN, Washington, 1988; med. advisor blue ribbon adv. com. Nutrition Screening Initiative, Washington, 1991. Contbr. articles to med. jours.; rschr. in nutrition and metabolism in human physiology. Med. adviser March of Dimes Suncoast chpt., New Port Richey, 1977-79; bd. dirs. Fla. Gulf Health Systems Agy., Region IV, 1977-79, Price Pottenger Nutrition Found., San Diego, 1988—. Fellow Am. Osteo. Coll. Occupational and Preventive Medicine (trustee 1989-91, chmn. pub. health divisional com. 1989-91), Am. Coll. Preventive Medicine; mem. APHA, Am. Osteo. Assn., San Diego Osteo. Med. Assn., Osteo. Physicians and Surgeons Calif., Am. Coll. Family Physicians-Osteo., U.S. Naval Flight Surgeons. Avocations: scuba diving, photography, marksmanship, art, music. Office: 13983 Mango Dr Ste 103 Del Mar CA 92014-3146

LESLIE, JACQUES ROBERT, JR., journalist; b. L.A., Mar. 12, 1947; s. Jacques Robert and Aleen (Wetstein) L.; m. Leslie Wernick, June 21, 1980; 1 child, Sarah Alexandra. BA, Yale U., 1968. Tchr. New Asia Coll., Chinese U., Hong Kong, 1968-70; free-lance journalist Washington, 1970-71; fgn. corr. L.A. Times, Saigon, 1972-73, Phnom Penh, 1973, Washington, 1974; chief New Delhi (India) bur. L.A. Times, 1974-75, Madrid, 1975-76; chief Hong Kong bur. L.A. Times, 1976-77; freelance journalist, 1977—; contbg. writer Wired Mag., 1993—; contbg. writer Wired mag., 1993—. Author: The Mark: A War Correspondent's Memoir of Vietnam and Cambodia. Recipient Best Fgn. Corr. award Sigma Delta Chi, 1973, citation for reporting Overseas Press Club, 1973. Home: 124 Reed St Mill Valley CA 94941-3448

LESLIE, MARK, executive. Pres., CEO, co-chmn. Veritas Software, Mountain View, Calif. Office: 1600 Plymouth St Mountain View CA 94043-1232*

LESLIE, ROBERT LORNE, lawyer; b. Adak, Alaska, Feb. 24, 1947; s. J. Lornie and L. Jean (Conelly) L.; children—Lorna Jean, Elizabeth Allen. B.S., U.S. Mil. Acad., 1969; J.D., Hastings Coll. Law, U. Calif.-San Francisco, 1974. Bar: Calif. 1974, D.C. 1979, U.S. Dist. Ct. (no. dist.) Calif. 1974, U.S. Ct. Claims 1975, U.S. Tax Ct. 1975, U.S. Ct. Appeals (9th and D.C. cirs.), U.S. Ct. Mil. Appeals 1980, U.S. Supreme Ct. 1980. Commd. 2d lt. U.S. Army, 1969, advanced through grades to maj., 1980; govt. trial atty. West Coast Field Office, Contract Appeals, Litigation Div. and Regulatory Law Div., Office JAG, Dept. Army, San Francisco, 1974-77; sr. trial atty. and team chief Office of Chief Trial Atty., Dept. Army, Washington, 1977-80; ptnr. McInerney & Dillon, Oakland, Calif., 1980—; lectr. on govt. contracts CSC, Continuing Legal Edn. Program; lectr. in govt. procurement U.S. Army Materiel Command. Col. USAR. Decorated Silver Star, Purple Heart. Mem. ABA, Fed. Bar Assn., Associated Gen. Contractors, The Beavers. Office: Ordway Bldg Fl 18 Oakland CA 94612-3610

LESMEZ, GWENDOLYN BILLINGS, manufacturing company executive; b. Columbus, Ohio, Feb. 24, 1965. BS in Mktg., Calif. State U., L.A., 1988. Asset mgr. Fujita Corp. USA, Santa Monica, Calif., 1989-93; owner, pres. The Planet Sack, L.A., 1994—. Mem. NOW, Nat. Assn. Women Bus. Owners, Nat. Assn. Female Execs.. Office: The Planet Sack 1320 W 12th Pl Los Angeles CA 90015-2015

LESSER, GERSHON MELVIN, physician, lawyer, medical and legal media commentator; b. N.Y.C., Apr. 3, 1933; s. Herman and Dora (Kronfeld) L.; m. Michelle Elyse Lesser; children: Hadrian, Aaron (deceased), Jason. BA, UCLA, 1954; MD, U. So. Calif., 1958; JD, UWLA, 1977. Diplomate Am. Bd. Forensic Medicine, Am. Bd. Psychotherapists, 1998. Atty. in pvt. practice L.A., 1977-82; med. dir. Westside Hosp., Am. Med. Inc., Beverly Hills, 1964-75; pvt. practice cardiology L.A., 1963-92; mem. pres.'s coun. Salk Inst., La Jolla, Calif.; broadcaster KGIL Radio, San Fernando Valley, 1984-92, KCRW-Nat. Pub. Radio, Santa Monica, Calif., 1980-94; med. broadcaster KTTV, Hollywood, Calif., 1984-86; med. dir. CD, L.A., 1978-89; adj. prof. law U. West L.A. Sch. Law, 1980-87; instr. internal medicine and med. malpractice, U. So. Calif. Sch. Medicine, L.A., 1963-85. Author: Growing Younger, 1987, When You Have Chest Pain, 1989; TV commentator Alive and Well, USA Cable, Century Cable, L.A., 1984-95; host TV program Law, Life and Medicine. Fellow Am. Coll. Legal Medicine, Royal Soc. Health, Am. Coll. Angiology, Am. Coll. Geriatrics; mem. ABA, AMA, Calif. Med. Assn., Am. Acad. Preventive Medicine, Am. Coll. Thoracic Medicine, Am. Coll. Cardiology, Am. Soc. Internal Medicine, Calif. Bar Assn., L.A. Bar Assn., L.A. County Med. Assn.Salerni Collegium, Phi Delta Epsilon. Office: Atkins Agy 8484 Wilshire Blvd Ste 205 Beverly Hills CA 90211-3213

LESSER, JULIAN (BUD), film producer, historian; b. San Francisco, Jan. 18, 1915; s. Sol Leonard and Fay (Grunauer) L.; m. Genee Kobacker, 1938 (div. 1952); m. Betsy Bamberger, Jan. 24, 1955 (div. Jan. 1980); children: Stephen, Belinda, David; m. Helene Feinberg, Aug. 8, 1983. BA, Stanford U., 1936; postgrad. Grad. Sch. Bus., Harvard U., 1937. Salesman J.E. Brulatour & Co., Eastman Raw Films, Hollywood, Calif., 1937-39; chair Def. Coun. Film Bur., L.A., 1941-42; v.p. Sol Lesser Prodns., L.A., 1947-58; pres. Royal Prodns., L.A., 1950-80; lectr., slide presentation Hollywood, The Surprises. Journalist/historian niche periodicals, 1985—. Maj. USMCR, 1942-49. Mem. USMC Combat Corrs. (bd. dirs. 1996-98, seminar coord. 1998, Dickson award 1994). Avocations: swimming, walking, photo collecting, family. Office: 1901 S Bentley Ave Los Angeles CA 90025-5615

LESSER, WENDY, literary magazine editor, writer, consultant; b. Santa Monica, Calif., Mar. 20, 1952; d. Murray Leon Lesser and Millicent (Gerson) Dillon; m. Richard Rizzo, Jan. 18, 1985; 1 stepchild, Dov Antonio; 1 child, Nicholas. BA, Harvard U., 1973; MA, Cambridge (Eng.) U., 1975; PhD, U. Calif., Berkeley, 1982. Founding ptnr. Lesser & Ogden Assocs., Berkeley, 1977-81; founding editor The Threepenny Rev., Berkeley, 1980—; Bellagio resident Rockefeller Found, Italy, 1984. Author: The Life Below the Ground, 1987, His Other Half, 1991, Pictures at an Execution, 1994, A Director Calls, 1997, The Amateur, 1999; editor: Hiding in Plain Sight, 1993. Fellow NEH, 1983, 92, Guggenheim fellow, 1988, ACLS, 1996, Open Soc. Inst. fellow, 1998—. Democrat. Office: The Threepenny Rev PO Box 9131 Berkeley CA 94709-0131

LESTER, JOHN JAMES NATHANIEL, II (SEAN LESTER), engineer, environmental analyst, human rights activist; b. Houston, May 7, 1952; s. John James Nathaniel Lester and Margaret Louise (Tisdale) Sharp; m. Elisabeth Bluml., Dec. 31, 1995. Student, U. Tex., 1970, Lee Coll., 1971; AS, Grossmont Coll., 1979; BA in Behavioral Sci., Nat. U., 1987; y. Registered profl. stationary engr., Tex. Nuclear power specialist USN, various, 1971-77; microbiology lab. technician VA, San Diego, 1978; prin. engring. asst. San Diego Gas & Electric, 1979-85, engring. environ. analyst, 1985-88; owner Calif. Triad Gem & Mineral Co.; founder Ctr. for Creative Healing. Dir. logistics, mem. regional bd. Gary Hart Presdl. Campaign, San Diego, 1984; founding mem. Inlet Drug Crisis Ctr., Houston, 1970; vol. dir. Aid for Guatemalan Refugees and Orphans, 1988; vol. for Dali Lama, Tibetan Refugee Rights and Ceremonies, 1989; mem. bldg. com. Tibetan Sch. Medicine, Crestone, Colo.; mem. San Luis Valley Tibetan Project, Crestone; active Clinton Presdl. Campaign, 1992; founder Pema Tashi Ling Found. for Tibetan Studies, 1992—. Mem. ASME, IEEE (interim pres., founding mem. San Diego region Ocean Engring. Soc. 1984-85), Mensa, Assn. Humanistic Psychology, Amnesty Internat., Hunger Project, Earth Stewards, Human Rights Watch, Tibet Watch, Sierra Club. Buddhist. Avocations: scuba diving, freelance photography, photojournalism, back-packing, Tibetan Buddhist ceremonial rites and practice. Home and Office: PO Box 710 Makawao HI 96768-0710

LESTER, WILLIAM ALEXANDER, JR., chemist, educator; b. Chgo., Apr. 24, 1937; s. William Alexander and Elizabeth Frances (Clark) L.; m. Rochelle Diane Reed, Dec. 27, 1959; children: William Alexander III, Allison Kimberleigh. BS, U. Chgo., 1958, MS, 1959; postgrad., Washington U., St. Louis, 1959-60; PhD, Cath. U. Am., 1964. Phys. chemist Nat. Bur. Stds., Washington, 1961-64; asst. dir. Theoretical Chemistry Inst./U. Wis., Madison, 1965-68; rsch. staff IBM Rsch. Lab., San Jose, Calif., 1968-75, mgr., 1976-78; tech. planning staff IBM T.J. Watson Rsch. Ctr., Yorktown Heights, N.Y., 1975-76; dir. Nat. Resource for Computation in Chemistry, Lawrence Berkeley (Calif.) Lab., 1978-81, also assoc. dir., staff sr. scientist, 1978-81, faculty sr. scientist, 1981—; prof. chemistry U. Calif., Berkeley, 1981—, assoc. dean Coll. Chemistry, 1991-95; lectr. chemistry U. Wis., 1966-68; cons. NSF, 1976-77, mem. chem. divsn. adv. panel, 1980-83, adv. com. Office Advanced Sci. Computing program, 1983-87, chmn., 1987, sr. fellow for sci. and engring., asst. to dir. for human resource devel., 1995-96; mem. U.S. nat. com. Internat. Union Pure and Applied Chemistry, 1976-79; mem. com. on recommendations for U.S. Army Basic Sci. Rsch. NRC, 1984-87, mem. steering com., 1987-88; chemistry rsch. evaluation panel AF Office Sci. Rsch., 1974-78; chmn. Gordon Conf. Atomic and Molecular Interactions, 1978; mem. NRC panel on chem. physics Nat. Bur. Stds., 1980-83; mem. com. to survey chem. scis. NRC, 1982-84, Fed. Networking Coun. Adv. Com., 1991-95; mem. blue ribbon panel on high performance computing

NSF, 1993; mem. com. on high performance computing and comm.: status of a major initiative NRC, 1994-95, mem. com. on math. challenges from theoretical computational chemistry, NRC, 1994-95; tech. assessment bd. Army Rsch. Lab. Nat. Rsch. Coun., 1996—; coun. mem. Gordon Rsch. Conf., 1997—; mem. adv. bd. Model Instns. Excellence Spelman Coll., 1997—; mem. external vis. com. Nat. Partnership Advanced Computational Infrastructure, 1999—. Editor: Procs. of Conf. on Potential Energy Surfaces in Chemistry, 1971, Recent Advances in Quantum Monte Carlo Methods, 1997; author: (with Brian L. Hammond and Peter J. Reynolds) Monte Carlo Methods in Ab Initio Quantum Chemistry, 1994; mem. editl. bd. Jour. Phys. Chemistry, 1979-81, Jour. Computational Chemistry, 1980-87, Computer Physics Comm., 1981-86; mem. adv. bd. Sci. Yr., 1989-93, Comms. on Analysis, Geometry and Physics, 1997—. Recipient Alumni award in sci. Cath. U. Am., 1983. Fellow AAAS (com. on nominations 1988-91, nat. bd. dirs. 1993-97), Calif. Acad. Scis., Am. Phys. Soc. (chmn. div. chem. physics 1986); mem. Am. Chem. Soc. (sec.-treas. Wis. sect. 1967-68, chmn. div. phys. chemistry 1979, treas. div. computers in chemistry 1974-77), Nat. Orgn. Black Chemists and Chem. Engrs. (Percy L. Julian award 1979, Outstanding Tchr. award 1986, exec. bd. 1984-87). Home: 4433 Briar Cliff Rd Oakland CA 94605-4624 Office: U Calif Dept Chemistry Berkeley CA 94720

LETA, DAVID EDWARD, lawyer; b. Rochester, N.Y., June 9, 1951; married; 2 children. BA, SUNY, Binghamton, 1973; JD, U. Utah, 1976. Bar: Utah, 1976, U.S. Ct. Appeals (9th and 10th cir.), U.S. Tax Ct., U.S. Supreme Ct. Assoc. Roe & Fowler, 1976-80, ptnr., 1980-82; ptnr. Hansen, Jones, & Leta and predecessor firms Hansen, Jones, Maycock & Leta, Hansen & Anderson, 1982-92, Snell & Wilmer, Salt Lake City, 1992; adj. prof. U. Utah. 1978-80; presenter, lectr. numerous seminars and legal edn. seminars. Contbr. articles to profl. jours. Trustee Ballet West. Mem. ABA (bankruptcy cts., rules and legislation subcoms. bus. bankruptcy section), Utah State Bar (first chmn. bankruptcy sec.), Utah Bankruptcy Lawyers Forum (initial trustee). Office: Snell & Wilmer 111 E Broadway Ste 900 Salt Lake City UT 84111-5235

LETCHER, NAOMI JEWELL, quality engineer, educator, counselor; b. Belle Point, W. Va., Dec. 29, 1924; d. Andrew Glen and Ollie Pearl (Meadows) Presley; m. Frank Philip Johnson, Oct. 5, 1945 (div. Dec. 1953); m. Paul Arthur Letcher, Mar. 6, 1954; children: Frank, Edwin, Richard, David. AA, El Camino Jr. Coll., 1964; BA, Calif. State U., 1971. Inspector N. Am. Aviation, Downey, Calif., 1964-71; substitute tchr. ABC Unified sch. Dist., Artesia, Calif., 1971-72; recurrence control rep. Rockwell Internat., Downey, Calif., 1972-80, quality engr., 1981-86; counselor Forest Lawn Cemeteries, Cerritos, Calif., 1980-81; tech. analyst Northrop, Pico Rivera, Calif., 1986-89; gov. divsn. D-2 area T.M. Internat., Downey, Calif., 1978-79. Author: History of the Letcher Family, 1995. Docent Temecula (Calif.) Valley Mus., 1994—. Mem. AAUW, Nat. Mgmt. Assn., NOW, Srs. Golden Yrs. Club, Alpha Gamma Sigma. Democrat. Baptist. Avocations: genealogy, needlework, stamp collecting, dancing, bowling.

LETOURNEAU, MARK STEPHEN, English language educator, researcher; b. Idaho Falls, Idaho, Apr. 11, 1955; s. Joseph Richard Louis and Janet Marie (Casavant) LeT.; m. Georgette Samuel Faraj, June 5, 1982; children: Annette, Sarah. BA, U. Vt., 1977; MA, Purdue U., 1979, PhD, 1986. Teaching asst. Purdue U., West Lafayette, Ind., 1977-86, instr., 1986-87; asst. prof. English Weber State U., Ogden, Utah, 1987-89, 90-92, assoc. prof., 1992-98, prof., 1998—; vis. prof. Purdue U., summer 1987, U. Khartoum, Sudan, 1989-90. Contbr. articles and papers to profl. jours. Rsch. grantee Purdue U., 1984, 85, Weber State Coll., 1988, 91, Fulbright grantee Coun. for Internat. Exchange of Scholars, Khartoum, 1989-90. Mem. Linguistic Soc. Am., Nat. Coun. Tchrs. of English, Conf. on Coll. Composition and Communication. Democrat. Episcopalian. Avocations: playing guitar, reading. Office: Weber State U 3750 Harrison Blvd Ogden UT 84408-0001

LETTS, J. SPENCER, federal judge; b. 1934. BA, Yale U., 1956; LLB, Harvard U., 1960. Commd. U.S. Army, 1956, advanced through grades to capt., resigned, 1965; pvt. practice law Fulbright & Jaworski, Houston, 1960-66, Troy, Malin, Loveland & Letts, L.A., 1973-74, Hedlund, Hunter & Lynch, L.A., 1978-82, Latham & Watkins, L.A., 1982-85; gen. counsel Teledyne, Inc., 1966-73, 75-78, legal cons., 1978-82; judge U.S. Dist. Ct. (cen. dist.) Calif., L.A., 1986—. Contbr. articles to profl. jours. Mem. ABA, Calif. State Bar, Tex. State Bar, L.A. Bar Assn., Houston Bar Assn. Office: US Dist Ct 312 N Spring St Ste 243J Los Angeles CA 90012-4704*

LEUNG, ALEXANDER KWOK-CHU, pediatrician educator; b. Hong Kong, Oct. 1, 1948; s. Ping and Wai (Tai) L.; children: Albert, Alex Jr., Amy, Alan, Andrew. MB BS, U. Hong Kong, 1973; DCH, Royal Coll. Physicians London, 1977, Royal Coll. Physicians Ireland, 1979. Intern U. Hong Kong, 1973-74; lectr. in child health U. Queensland, Brisbane, Australia, 1977; pediat. cons. Foothills Provincial Hosp., Calgary, Alta., Can., 1980-92; resident in pediat. U. Calgary, 1974-77, fellow in pediat. endocrinology, 1978-80, clin. asst. prof. pediat., 1980-90, cons. Univ. Med. Info. Svc.,, 1988—, clin. assoc. prof. pediat., 1990—; med. dir. Asian Med. Ctr. in affiliation with U. Calgary Med. Clin., 1994—; cons. pediat. Alta. Children's Hosp., Calgary, 1980—; hon. advisor Am. Biog. Inst. of Rsch., Raleigh, N.C., 1987—, Internat. Biog. Ctr., Cambridge, Eng., 1988—. Mem. editl. bd. Advances in Therapy, 1995—, Can.'s Clin. Jour. Medicine, Med. Scope Monthly, 1996—; contbr. numerous sci. articles to profl. pubs., 8 chpts. to books. Recipient Physician Recognition award AMA, 1985, 88, 90, 93, 96, Gold Medal award Am. Biog. Inst., 1987, Golden Acad. award Am. Biog. Inst., 1992. Fellow Royal Coll. Pediats. and Child Health, Royal Coll. Physicians of Can., Royal Coll. Physicians of Edinburgh, Royal Coll. Physicians of Ireland, Royal Acad. Medicine, Royal Coll. Physicians and Surgeons Glasgow, Royal Soc. Health (Eng.), Hong Kong Coll. Paediatricians, Hong Kong Acad. Medicine, Am. Acad. Pediatrics (PREP Fellowship award 1987, 90, 96), Can. Pediat. Soc., Royal Coll. of Pediats. Child Health, Hong Kong Acad. Med., Hong Kong Coll. Pediatricians. Achievements include serving as examiner for Med. Coun. of Can. Qualifying Examination. Office: Alberta Children's Hosp, 1820 Richmond Rd SW, Calgary, AB Canada T2T 5C7

LEUNG, KASON KAI CHING, computer specialist; b. Hong Kong, July 2, 1962; came to U.S., 1963; s. Patrick Kin Man and Esther Mo Chee (Shum) L. BA in Computer Sci., U. Calif., 1984. Microcomputer specialist Coopers & Lybrand, San Francisco, 1985-87; freelance computer specialist San Francisco, 1988-90; computer applications specialist T.Y. Lin Internat., San Francisco, 1990-92; tech. specialist Ziff-Davis Labs., Foster City, Calif., 1993-94; tech. analyst PC Mag., Foster City, Calif., 1995; sr. tech. analyst Ziff-Davis Benchmark Operation, Foster City, Calif., 1996; sr. tech. specialist Ziff-Davis Labs., Foster City, Calif., 1997—. Mem. Assn. for Computing Machinery. Avocations: computers, sports, music, reading. Home: 90 Stanford Heights Ave San Francisco CA 94127-2318

LEUNG, VITUS JOSEPH, computer scientist. BS, Rensselaer Poly. Inst., 1982; MS in Engring., Princeton U., 1983; PhD, U. Calif., Irvine, 1997. Mem. tech. staff Bell Labs., Holmdel, N.J., 1982-90; temp. mem. tech. staff Sandia Nat. Labs., Albuquerque, 1997-98, sr. mem. tech. staff, 1998—. Contbr. articles to profl. pubs. and procs. Mem. IEEE, Assn. for Computing Machinery.

LEUPP, EDYTHE PETERSON, retired education educator, administrator; b. Mpls., Nov. 27, 1921; d. Reynold H. and Lillian (Aldridge) Peterson; m. Thomas A. Leupp, Jan. 29, 1944 (dec.); children: DeEtte (dec.), Patrice, Stacia, Roderick, Braden. BS, U. Oreg., 1947, MS, 1951, EdD, 1972. Tchr. various pub. schs. Idaho, 1941-45, Portland, Oreg., 1945-55; dir. tchr. edn. Northwest Nazarene Coll., Nampa, Idaho, 1955-61; sch. adminstr. Portland Pub. Schs., 1963-84; dir. tchr. edn. George Fox Coll., Newberg, Oreg., 1984-87; ret., 1987; vis. prof. So. Nazarene U., Bethany, Okla., 1988-95, Asia Pacific Nazarene Theol. Sem., 1996; adj. prof. Warner Pacific Coll., Portland, 1996-97; pres. Portland Assn. Pub. Sch. Adminstrs., 1973-75; dir.-at-large Nat. Coun. Adminstrv. Women in Edn., Washington, 1973-76; state chmn. Oreg. Sch. Prins. Spl. Project, 1978-79; chair Confdn. Oreg. Sch. Adminstrs. Ann. Conf.; rschr. 40 tchr. edn. programs in colls. and univs.; designer tchr. edn. program George Fox Coll. Author tchr. edn. materials. Pres. Idaho State Aux. Mcpl. League, 1957, Nampa PTA, 1958, Nampa unit AAUW, 1956; bd. dirs. Portland Fedn. Women's Clubs, 1963. Recipient Golden Gift award, 1982; named Honored Tchr. of Okla., 1993, Hazel Fishwood scholar, 1970; Idea fellow Charles Kettering Found., 1978, 80, 87, 91, 92, 93, 94. Mem. ASCD, Am. Assn. Colls. Tchr. Edn., Delta Kappa Gamma (pres. Alpha Rho 1986-88), Phi Delta Kappa, Pi Lambda Theta. Republican. Nazarene. Avocations: travel, crafts, photography. Home: 8100 SW 2nd Ave Portland OR 97219-4602

LEUSCHEN, RONALD JAMES, county official; b. San Bernardino, Calif., Feb. 6, 1950; s. Robert James and Norma June (Bradford) L.; m. Carolyn Mary Harp; children: James, Kelly, Patrick. AA, San Bernardino Valley Coll., 1970; BA, Calif. State U., San Bernardino, 1974, postgrad., 1975. Cert. govtl. fin. mgr., Calif. Police officer City of Riverside (Calif.), 1973; adminstr. Deutsch Co., Banning, Calif., 1974-76; chief, assessment divsn. County Assessor, San Bernardino, 1976-88; property tax mgr. County Auditor/Controller, San Bernardino, 1988—. Author: Web Site Directory, 1996. Bd. dirs. Ctr. for Individuals with Disabilities, San Bernardino, 1990—; candidate for county assessor, 1994, for San Bernardino C.C. bd., 1990. Mem. Native Sons of Golden West, Assn. of Govtl. Accts., Internat. Inst. Pub. Appraisers. Roman Catholic. Avocations: collecting old cars, coins. Home: 3434 N F St San Bernardino CA 92405-2469

LEUS MCFARLEN, PATRICIA CHERYL, water chemist; b. San Antonio, Mar. 12, 1954; d. Norman W. and Jacqueline S. (Deason) Leus; (div.); 1 child, Kevin Bryant. AA, Highline Community Coll., 1974; BS in Chemistry, Eastern Wash. U., 1980. Cert. operator grade II water treatment and distbn., grade I wastewater and collection operator Ariz. Dept. Environ. Quality; cert. in asbestos identification through microscopy; cert. CPR and first aid. Lab. technician, oil analyst D.A. Lubricant, Vancouver, Wash., 1982-83; plant chemist Navajo Generating Sta., Page, Ariz., 1983-92, chemist, 1992—. Sci. judge Page Schs. Sci. Project Fair, 1985, 91; chemist Navajo Generating Sta./Page Sch. Career Day, 1986, 89, 90; life mem. Girl Scouts Am.; vol., leader AWANA Clubs Internat., 1992-98. Mem. Am. Chem. Soc., Cousteau Soc., Menninger Soc., Sigma Kappa (life mem., treas. 1976-78). Baptist. Avocations: snow skiing, aviation, sewing, crafts, flower gardening. Office: Navajo Generating Sta Lab Svcs Dept PO Box 850 Page AZ 86040-0850

LEUTY, GERALD JOHNSTON, osteopathic physician and surgeon; b. Knoxville, Iowa, July 23, 1919; s. John William and Mable Reichard (Johnston) L.; m. Martha L. Weymouth, Jan. 24, 1940 (div. 1957); children: Maxine Joanne, Robert James, Gerald Johnston Jr., Karl Joseph; m. Norma Jean Hindman, Dec. 30, 1969; children: Barbara Jayne, Patrick Jack. AB, Kemper Mil. Sch., Boonville, Mo., 1939; postgrad., Drake U., Des Moines, 1944-45; DO, Des Moines Coll. Osteopathy, 1949; embalmer, Coll. Mortuary Sci., St. Louis, 1941. Mortician/embalmer Cauldwell-McJihon Funeral Home, Des Moines, 1939-40; aero. engr. Boeing Aircraft Co., Wichita, Kans., 1941-42; osteopathic physician and surgeon Knoxville (Iowa) Osteopathic Clinic, 1949-56; dir. Leuty Osteopathic Clinic, Earlham, Iowa, 1957-77; osteopathic physician and surgeon in pvt. practice Santa Rosa, Calif., 1977—; prof. clin. med. Western U. Health Svcs., Pomona, Calif., 1985—. Mem. Iowa's Gov. Blue Med. Adv. Bd., 1972-77. With U.S. Army, 1942-46. Named Physician of the Yr., 6th Dist. Iowa Ostepathic Soc., 1975, Disting. Leadership award, Am. Biog. Inst., 1988, others. Fellow Internat. Co.. Angiologists; mem. Am. Ostepathic Assn. (ho. of dels., life mem. 1989), Iowa Osteopathic Soc. (pres. 6th dist. 1974), Soc. Osteopathic Physicians, No. Calif. Osteopathic Med. Soc. (pres. 1981), Osteopathic Physicians and Surgeons of Calif. (pres. 1982), Am. Acad. Osteopathy (chmn. component socs. com. 1988, pres. Calif. divsn. 1987, pres. No. Calif. divsn. 1989, 91-93, 95), North Coast Osteopathic Med. Assn. (pres. 1992), Am. Med. Soc. Vienna (life mem.), Am. Legion (6th dist. comdr. 1974-75), Lions (pres. 1946). Republican. Presbyterian. Avocations: photography, travel. Home: 5835 La Cuesta Dr Santa Rosa CA 95409-3914

LEVADA, WILLIAM JOSEPH, archbishop; b. Long Beach, Calif., June 15, 1936; s. Joseph and Lorraine (Nunez) L. B.A., St. John's Coll., Camarillo, Calif., 1958; S.T.L., Gregorian U., Rome, 1962, S.T.D., 1971. Ordained priest Roman Cath. Ch., 1961, consecrated bishop, 1983. Assoc. pastor Archdiocese of L.A., 1962-67; prof. theology St. John's Sem., Camarillo, Calif., 1970-76; ofcl. Doctrinal Congregation, Vatican City, Italy, 1976-82; exec. dir. Calif. Cath. Conf., Sacramento, 1982-84; aux. bishop Archdiocese of L.A., 1983-86; archbishop Archdiocese of Portland, Oreg., 1986-95; coadjuctor archbishop of San Francisco, 1995. Trustee Cath. U. Am.; chmn. bd. dirs. Pope John XXIII Med.-Moral Rsch. and Edn. Ctr. Mem. Nat. Conf. Cath. Bishops (com. on doctrine), U.S. Cath. Conf., Cath. Theol. Soc. Am., Canon Law Soc. Am. Office: Archbishop of San Francisco Pastoral Ctr 445 Church St San Francisco CA 94114-1720*

LE VEQUE, MATTHEW KURT, public affairs and marketing consultant; b. Los Angeles, May 24, 1958; s. Edward Albert and Vera Eleanora (Behne) LeV. BA in Polit. Sci., UCLA, 1981. Reapportionment cons. Calif. State Legislature, Sacramento, 1981; cons. Berman and D'Agostino Campaigns, Inc., L.A., 1982-91; coord. L.A. Olympic com., 1984; spl. asst. Congressmen H. Waxman and H. Berman, Calif., 1982-85; cons. The Helin Orgn., Newport Beach, Calif., 1984-86; sr. cons. Calif. State Senate, L.A. and Sacramento, 1985-92; campaign fin. coord Levine for U.S. Senate, L.A., 1991; sr. assoc. Pacific West Comms. Group, L.A., 1992-93; chief staff L.A. State Assemblyman Terry Friedman, 1993-94; pub. affairs and mktg. exec. Rogers & Assocs., L.A., 1995—. Active numerous local and nat. Dem. polit. campaigns. Avocations: cycling, running. Office: 531 24th St Hermosa Beach CA 90254-2618

LEVEQUE, THOMAS JOSEPH, elementary school educator, writer; b. Burbank, Calif., July 25, 1951; s. Francois Dazincourt and Marquerite June (Brodie) L.; m. Carolyn Jean Bauer, Aug. 26, 1978 (div. Dec., 1991); children: Julie Elaine, Holly Nicole. BA, Loyola U., L.A., 1973; MA, Calif. State U., L.A., 1994; postgrad studies in Edn., UCLA, 1994—. Dir. comedy devel. Comsky/Kander Prodns., L.A., 1974-76; dir. creative affairs Avco Embassy Pictures, L.A., 1976-82, Internat. Cinema Corp., L.A., 1982-85; v.p. creative affairs Frank Capra Prodns., L.A., 1985-87; v.p. acquisitons Trans World Entertainment, L.A., 1987-89; tchr. Nevin Ave. Elem. Sch., L.A., 1989—; rep. instrnl. cabinet L.A. Unified Sch. Dist., 1994; chair Leadership Team Nevin Ave. Elem. Sch., L.A., 1995, mem. sch. mgmt. team, 1996—. Mem. choir St. Jerome's Ch., L.A., 1981, liturgy com. 1991-94. Mem. Computer Use in Edn. Group, United Tchrs. L.A. Democrat. Roman Catholic. Avocations: golf, reading, cooking, travel, music. Office: Nevin Ave Elem Sch 1569 E 32d St Los Angeles CA 90011-2213

LEVETON, IAN SINCLAIR, civil engineer; b. Birmingham, Eng., Nov. 27, 1942; came to U.S., 1953; s. Eric Karl and Zena (Altman) L. BA in Physics and Econs., NYU, 1965; cert. of achievement, Orange Coast Coll., Costa Mesa, Calif., 1990. Computer programmer trainee Bklyn. Union Gas Co., 1969; computer programmer Elizabeth Arden Sales Corp., N.Y.C., 1970; electronics expeditor Bendix Navigation & Controls, Teterboro, N.J., 1971; inventory control supr. Roman Products Inc., South Hackensack, N.J., 1972; nuclear mech. engr. Pub. Svc. N.J., Newark, 1973; mech. engr. Chemplant Designs divsn. DuPont, N.Y.C., 1974-78, Holmes and Narver, Inc., Orange, Calif., 1978-82; tech. writer nuclear safety So. Calif. Edison, Rosemead, Calif., 1983-85; civil engr. tech. City of Santa Ana, Calif., 1985—; cons. Islian Assocs., Teaneck, N.J., 1970-71. Mem. Teaneck Bicentennial Com., 1976; coord. United Way, City Pub. Works Agy., Santa Ana, 1992. Mem. KP (sec. 1974-76). Avocations: tennis, boating, reading, music, traveling. Home: 19302 Steven Ln Huntington Beach CA 92646-2711

LEVI, DAVID F., federal judge; b. 1951. BA, Harvard U., MA, 1973; JD, Stanford U. Bar: Calif. 1983. U.S. atty. ea. dist. State of Calif., Sacramento, 1986-90; judge U.S. Dist. Ct. (ea. dist.) Calif., 1990—; chmn. task force on race, religious and ethnic fairness U.S. Ct. Appeals (9th cir.), 1994-97, mem. jury com., 1993-95. Adv. com. on Civil Rules, 1994—; vis. com. U. Chgo. Law Sch., 1995-98. Mem. Am. Law Inst., Milton L. Schwartz Inn of Ct. (pres. 1992-95). Office: 2504 Fed Bldg 650 Capitol Mall Sacramento CA 95814-4708

LEVI, HERBERT A., deputy city manager, consultant; b. Dunkirk, Ind., May 31, 1931; s. Lawrence Warren and Virginia Roselyn (Avery) L.; m. Virginia Elizabeth Webster, Dec. 7, 1950; children: Victor Herbert, Michael David, Demetrius Titus. BA, Ball State U., Muncie, Ind., 1952; MPA, Calif. State U., Long Beach, 1978. Cert. tchr., Calif. Debit mgr. Mammoth Life Ins. Co., Muncie, 1951-53; chemist City of L.A. Pub. Works, 1954-55, sr. indsl. waste inspector, 1959-66, safety engring. asst., 1967-69, sr. personnel analyst, 1969-71, contract compliance officer, 1971-75; adminstrv. analyst III City of Long Beach (Calif.) City Mgr., 1975-78; personnel analyst III City of Long Beach Personnel, 1978-82; adminstrv. officer Long Beach Pub. Libr., 1982-90; dep. city mgr., exec. dir. police complaint commn. City of Long Beach, 1990-91; ret., 1991—, cons. to bus. and govt., 1993—; mem. policy bd. Ctr. for Pub. Policy and Adminstrn., Calif. State U., 1986-90. Author: Equal Opportunity Compliance for Cities, 1978; co-author: Contract Compliance Manual, 1976. Founder Vet. Stadium Citizen's Com., Long Beach, Calif., 1983; mem. Lakewood (Calif.) High Sch. Community Adv. Coun., 1974; chair Hamilton High Sch. Community Adv. Coun., L.A., 1969; mem. KLON-FM 88 Community Adv. Bd., Long Beach, 1985. Recipient Excellence in Performance award City of L.A. Bd. Pub. Works, 1977, Employee of Yr. award City of Long Beach, Personnel, 1981. Mem. Am. Soc. Pub. Adminstrn., Internat. Personnel Mgmt. Assn., Equal Opportunity Compliance Officers Assn. (pres., co-founder 1971-77), So. Calif. Personnel Mgmt. Assn. (v.p. programs 1983-84), Long Beach Mgmt. Club, Pi Alpha Alpha (v.p. 1989-91). Avocations: do-it-yourselfer, gardening, volleyball, camping, vol. svc. Home and Office: 5153 E Hanbury St Long Beach CA 90808-1845

LEVI, WERNER, political science educator; b. Halberstadt, Germany, Mar. 23, 1912; arrived in U.S., 1940; s. Gustav and Zipora (Petuchowski) L.; widower; children: Antonia J., Matthew D. JD, U. Fribourg, 1934; MA, U. Minn., 1943, PhD, 1944. Asst. instr. to prof. U. Minn., 1943-63; prof. to prof. emeritus U. Hawaii, Honolulu, 1963—; vis. prof. Melbourne U., 1947, Marburg U., 1948, New Delhi U., 1950, Grad. Inst. Internat. Studies, Geneva, 1958-59; Carnegie vis. prof. U. Hawaii, 1961; rschr., lectr. India, Korea, 1964-65, Australia, Tahiti, 1966, Western Europe, 1969, Japan, 1964-65, 86. Author: American Australian Relations, 1947, Fundamentals of World Organization, 1950, Free India in Asia, 1952, Modern China's Foreign Policy, 1953, Australia's Outlook on Asia, 1958, The Challenge of World Politics in South and Southeast Asia, 1968, International Politics: Foundations of the System, 1974, Law and Politics in the International Society, 1976, The Coming End of War, 1981, From Alms to Liberation, 1989, Contemporary International Law, 1991. Fulbright scholar, Australia, 1955, Germany, 1968; Am. Inst. Indian Studies fellow, 1964; recipient Internat. Essay Contest award Com. Econ. Devel., 1958. Home: 2400 Sonoma St Honolulu HI 96822-1915

LEVICH, ROBERT ALAN, geologist; b. Bklyn., Apr. 16, 1941; s. Leonard Walter and Dinah (Cohen) L.; m. Stella Araba Nkrumah, June 10, 1964; children: Alexander Kwamina, Walter Abraham, Leo Augustine. BS in Geology, CUNY, Bklyn., 1963; MA in Geol. Scis., U. Tex., 1973. Cert. profl. geologist. Vol. Peace Corps Ghana 3 Geologists, Kade, Ghana, 1963-65; tchg. asst. in geology U. Tex., Austin, 1965-67, rsch. asst. in chem. engring., 1967-68; geologist Ghana Geol. Survey, Sunyani, 1969-72, U.S. Atomic Energy Commn., Austin,, Tex., Spokane, Wash., 1973-81; regional mgr. Apache Energy & Minerals Co., Spokane, 1981-82; cons. expert East Africa Internat. Atomic Energy Agy., Vienna, Austria, 1982-83; geologist, phys. scientist U.S. Dept. Energy, Argonne, Ill., Las Vegas, Nev., 1984-88; chief tech. analysis br. U.S. Dept. Energy/YMP, Las Vegas, Nev., 1988-89; internat. programs mgr. U.S. Dept. Energy/YMP, Las Vegas, 1989-96; mgr. Yucca Mountain Site Description Document, 1996—; U.S. rep., joint tech. com. Internat. Stripa Project, Stockholm, 1989-92; lead U.S. del. OECD/Nuclear Energy Agy. Site Evaluation and Design Experiments, Paris, 1990—; U.S. Dept. Energy rep., joint tech. com. OECD/NEA Alligator Rivers Analogue Project, Sydney, NSW, Australia, 1990-92; project dir. USDOE/Atomic Energy, Can. Ltd. Subsidiary Agreement, 1991-95; tech. coord. USDOE/Switzerland Nat. Co-op. for Disposal Radioactive Waste Project Agreement, 1991-96; project dir. USDOE/Swedish Nuclear Fuel & Waste Mgmt. Co. Hard Rock Lab. Project Agreement, 1993-96. Author, co-author, editor reports. Fellow Geol. Soc. Am., Soc. Econ. Geologists; mem. Am. Nuclear Soc. (Internat. High Level Radioactive Waste Mgmt. Conf. program com., steering com.), Assn. Geoscientists for Internat. Devel., Am. Inst. Profl. Geologists (v.p. Nev. sect. 1993, 94, mem. nat. screening bd. 1994-96, chmn. nat. screening bd. 1996—), Nat. Peace Corps. Assn. Achievements include development of international radioactive waste natural analogue study, developed and negotiated international bilateral technical cooperative projects in geologic disposal of radioactive waste with Canada, Switzerland, Sweden, Japan, Spain and France; managed development of Yucca Mountain Site Description Document. Office: US Dept Energy YMP 1551 Hillshire Dr Las Vegas NV 89134-6321

LEVIN, ALAN SCOTT, pathologist, allergist, immunologist, lawyer; b. Chgo., Jan. 12, 1938; s. John Bernhard and Betty Ruth (Margulis) L.; m. Vera S. Byers, June 15, 1971. BS in Chemistry, U. Ill., Champaign-Urbana, 1960; MS in Biochemistry, U. Ill., Chgo., 1963, MD, 1964; JD, Golden Gate U., 1995. Diplomate Am. Bd. Allergy and Immunology, Am. Bd. Pathology; bar: Calif. 1995, Tex. 1996. Intern Children's Hosp. Med. Ctr., Boston, 1964-65; adj. instr. pediatrics U. Calif., San Francisco, 1971-72, asst. prof. immunology dept. dermatology, 1972-78, adj. assoc. prof., 1978-88; dir. lab. immunology U. Calif. & Kaiser Found. Rsch. Inst. Joint Program Project, San Francisco, 1971-74; attending physician dept. medicine Mt. Zion/U. Calif. San Francisco Hosps., 1971—; dir. div. immunology Western Labs., Oakland, Calif., 1974-77; med. dir. MML/Solano Labs. Div. Chemed-W.R. Grace, Inc., Berkeley, Calif., 1977-79; med. dir. Levin Clin. Labs., Inc., San Francisco, 1979-81; pvt. practice San Francisco, 1981—. Contbr. articles to profl. jours., chpts. to books. Lt. USN, 1966-69, Vietnam. Decorated Bronze Star, Silver Star, 4 Air medals; Harvard Med. Sch. traineeship grantee, 1964, USPHS hematology tng. grantee U. Calif., San Francisco Med. Ctr., 1969-71; recipient Faculty Rsch. award Am. Cancer Soc., 1970-74. Fellow Coll. Am. Pathologists, Am. Coll. Emergency Physicians, Am. Soc. Clin. Pathologists; mem. AMA, Am. Acad. Allergy and Immunology, Am. Coll. Allergy and Immunology, Am. Assn. Clin. Chemists, Am. Acad. Environ. Medicine, Calif. Med. Assn., San Francisco Med. Soc. Jewish. Office: Immunology Inc 500 Sutter St Ste 512 San Francisco CA 94102-1114

LEVIN, ALVIN IRVING, composer, educator; b. N.Y.C., Dec. 22, 1921; s. David and Frances (Schloss) L.; m. Beatrice Van Loon, June 5, 1976 (div. 1981). BMus in Edn., U. Miami (Fla.), 1941; MA, Calif. State U., L.A., 1955; EdD with honors, UCLA, 1968. Composer, arranger for movies, TV, theater Allied Artists, Eagle-Lion Studios, Los Angeles, 1945-65; tng. and supervising tchr. Los Angeles City Schs., 1957-65, adult edn. instr., 1962-63; research specialist Los Angeles Office Supt. edn., 1965-67; asst. prof. ednl. research Calif. State U., Los Angeles, 1968; asst. prof. elem. edn. Calif. State U., Northridge, 1969-73; self-employed, Northridge, 1973—; founder, pres. Alvin Irving Levin Philanthropic Found., 1973—, ordained to ministry Ch. of Mind Sci., 1975; founder, pres. Divine Love Ch. An Internat. Metaphys. Ch., 1977—, Meet Your New Personality, A Mind Expansion Program, 1975-77. Bd. overseers Calif. Sch. Profl. Psychology, 1974—; gen. chmn., producer Fiftieth Anniversity Pageant of North Hollywood Park, 1977. Author: My Ivory Tower, 1950, Symposium: Values in Kaleidoscope, 1973, (TV series) America, America!, 1978-79, (docudrama) One World, 1980; composer: Symphony for Strings, 1984, Tone Poem for MaleChorus and Brass, 1984, Hymn to the United Nations for chorus and Male Chorus and Brass, 1984, Hymn to the United Nations for chorus and symphonyorch., 1991, Hiawatha Suite for Chorus and Symphony Orch., 1994, My Ivory Tower: Multimedia Extravaganza for orchestra, chorus, ballet, and narrator, 1995-98, We Are Not Alone, Chorus and Symphony Orchestra, 1996, North Hollywood: Metamorphosis, A Symphonic Suite, 1996-97, Introspection for Symphony Orchestra, 1997, Concerto in a Minor for Violin and Orchestra, 1997, (music-drama) Happy Land, 1971, (musical plays) A Tale of Two Planets, 1988, Blueprint for a New World Model, 1991, My Ivory Tower: Multimedia Extravaganza for orchestra, chorus, ballet, and narrarator, 1995-98, Song of Isreal, Symphonic Suite for Orchestra and Chorus, 1999; prodr. UN Festival Calif. State U., Northridge, 1991; compiler, contbr. U.S. Dept. Edn. reports Adult Counseling and Guidance, 1967, Parent Child Preschool Program, 1967, English Classes for Foreign Speaking Adult Professionals, 1967, Blueprint for New World Order, 1991. Recipient plaque State of Calif., 1977, Golden Merit medal. Rep. Presdl. Task Force, 1985; named to Rep. Task Force Presdl. Commn., 1986. Mem. Nat. Soc. for Study Edn., AAUP, Am. Statis Assn., Internat. Coun. Edn. for Tchg., L.A. World Affairs Coun., Internat. Platform Assn., World Federalist Assn. (pres. San Fernando Valley chpt. 1991—), North Hollywood C. of C. (dir. 1976—), Phi

Delta Kappa. Home and Office: 5407 Colfax Ave Apt 223 North Hollywood CA 91601-5209

LEVIN, BARRY RAYMOND, rare book dealer; b. Phila., June 11, 1946; s. Sidney and Bertha (Zwerman) L.; m. Sally Ann Fudge, Aug. 19, 1983. Student, Santa Monica City Coll., 1964-65. Various aerospace positions McDonnell Douglas, AstroPeen, 1967-72; owner Barry R. Levin Sci. Fiction & Fantasy Lit., 1973—; cons. sci. fiction, fantasy and horror films, 1976—. Author: (rare book catalogs) Titles from the Back Room, 1981, Great Works and Rarities of Science Fiction and Fantasy, 1982, One Small Step, 1983, Newsletters, 1980—, others; contbr. articles to profl. jours. With U.S. Army, 1965-67. Mem. Antiquarian Booksellers Assn. Am., Am. Booksellers Assn., Bibliog. Soc. Am., Bibliog. Soc. Great Britain, New Eng. Sci. Fiction Assn., So. Calif. Booksellers Assn., Internat. League Antiquarian Booksellers, Internat. Assn. of the Fantastic in the Arts, Internat. Platform Assn., Sci. Fiction Writers Am., Horror Writers Am., Manuscript Soc., Sci. Fiction Rsch. Assn., Assn. Sci. Fiction and Fantasy Artists, Lewis Carroll Soc., others. Jewish. Office: Barry R Levin Sci Fiction & Fantasy Lit 720 Santa Monica Blvd Santa Monica CA 90401-2602

LEVIN, HAL ALAN, psychiatrist; b. Bklyn., Feb. 13, 1935; s. David and Rose M. (Rosen) L.; children of former marriage: Julie Levin Keith, Susan Levin Davis, Mark D. Levin; m. Sharon Greenleaf, Feb. 9, 1973; children: Anne Levin Warrick, Julie Elizabeth, Alisa M., Kimberly L. Grimes, Christopher Lenk. BS, Roosevelt U., 1958; MD, Tulane Med. Sch., New Orleans, 1967. Diplomate Am. Bd. Psychiatry and Neurology, Am. Bd. Forensic Examiners, Am. Bd. Forensic Medicine. Intern Norfolk (Va.) Gen. Hosp., 1967-68; resident in psychiatry Sheppard & Enoch Pratt Hosp., Towson, Md., 1968-70, Crownsville (Md.) Hosp., 1970-71; fellow in forensic psychiatry U. So. Calif., L.A., 1983-84; staff psychiatrist Atascadero (Calif.) State Hosp., 1971-72; pvt. practice psychiatry San Bernardino, Calif., 1972-85; asst. prof. clin. psychiatry Mich. State U., East Lansing, 1985-86; asst. dir. mental health State of Mich., Lansing, 1985-86; dir. mental health State of Ariz., Phoenix, 1986-87; pvt. practice psychiatry Tempe, Ariz., 1987—; cons. psychiatrist San Bernardino County Hosp., 1972-85, San Bernardino Superior Ct., 1972-85; dir. Desert Valley Clinic, Apple Valley, Calif., 1973-80; med. dir. Big Bear (Calif.) Psychiat. Clinic, 1980-84; med. dir. Ctr. for Behavioral Health, Tempe, 1989—; cons. numerous ins. cos., city, county, state and fed. agencies for occupl., personal injury and med. malpractice cases. cons. Jewish Family Svcs., Tempe, 1990—, Interfaith Counseling, Mesa, Ariz., 1991—. Mem. AMA, Am. Psychiat. Assn., Ariz. Med. Assn., Am. Acad. Psychiatry & the Law, Am. Bd. Forensic Examiners, Friends of Phoenix Symphony. Democrat. Avocations: computers, film, reading, swimming, music. Office: 5410 S Lakeshore Dr # 103 Tempe AZ 85283-2171

LEVIN, LAUREN (LO LEVIN), artist, teacher, designer; b. Framingham, Mass., June 8, 1949; d. Abraham and Ida Rena (Cohen) L. Grad., Art Inst. Boston, 1971; postgrad., Sch. Fashion Design, Boston, 1976, Parsons Sch. Design, N.Y.C., 1979. Owner, creator Struck of Loke (improvisational theater and cafe), Worcester, Mass., 1971-75; designer, 'Lo'Scapes Fashion Art, Honolulu, 1983—; artist portraits and impressions Faces by 'Lo', Honolulu, 1969—, Cape Cod, 1969—, Ibiza, Spain, 1969—; owner, operator, artist Artspace Gallery, Honolulu, 1990-91; tchr. Very Spl. Arts, Hawaii, 1983—. Mem. Pacific Handcrafters Guild (bd. dirs.), Hawaii Handcrafters Ednl. Found. (bd. dirs. 1992—). Avocations: portraits, fabric art and design, teaching art with disabled, costuming. Home: PO Box 61820 Honolulu HI 96839-1820

LEVIN, LINDA ROSE, mental health counselor; b. Des Moines, June 29, 1951; d. Morris Sam and Betty Francis (Burns) Nemirovski; m. Michael Arthur Levin, Feb. 25, 1971; children: David Bradley, Shane Michael. Student, Grandview Jr. Coll., 1969-70; BS in Psychology, Ottawa Univ., 1992, MA in Counseling, 1994. Cert. hypnotherapist, advanced hypnotherapist. Asst. dir. trade practice Better Bus. Bur., Phoenix, 1980-83; program coord. Carnation Health and Nutrition Ctr., Phoenix, 1983-85; v.p. AAA Telephone Answering Svc., Phoenix, 1985-90; past state of Ariz. rep. Toughlove, Phoenix, 1988-90; counselor level II, resident advisor Wayland Family Ctrs., Phoenix, 1990-91; case mgr. for the serious mentally ill Community Care Network, Phoenix, 1991-92; pvt. practice in hypnotherapy Counseling Ctr. for Personal Growth, Phoenix, 1992—. Vol. arbitrator Better Bus. Bur., 1983—. Mem. Am. Arbitration Assn. Democrat. Jewish. Avocations: swimming, reading, karate (brown belt), aerobics. Office: Counseling Ctr for Personal Growth 13231 N 35th Ave # A-2 Phoenix AZ 85029-1233

LEVIN, MORTON D(AVID), artist, printmaker, educator; b. N.Y.C., Oct. 7, 1923; s. Louis and Martha (Berusch) L. B.S. in Art Edn, CCNY, 1948; student in painting, Andre LHote, Paris, 1950; in sculpture, Ossip Zadkine, 1950; etching and engraving, Federico Castellon, N.Y.C., 1948, Stanley W. Hayter, Paris, 1951; student in lithography, Pratt Graphic Art Center, N.Y.C., 1966. Founder, dir., instr. printmaking, painting Morton Levin Graphics Workshop, San Francisco, 1972-91. One-man shows include Galerie Breteau, Paris, 1952, Winston Gallery, San Francisco, 1972, 80, 83, 85-97, 98; exhibited in group shows at Seattle Art Mus., 1946-49, Libr. of Congress, Washington, 1946, 49, Pa. Acad. Fine Arts, 1948, Mus. Modern Art, Paris, 1951, Pallazzo del Academia, Genoa, Italy, 1951; represented in permanent collections at N.Y. Pub. Libr., Libr. of Congress, History of Medicine Divsn. Nat. Libr. Medicine; work featured in Jour. Erotic Arts, Yellow Silk #34, 1990. Served with inf. U.S. Army, 1943-45. Recipient Bryan Meml. prize Villager Travel Exhbn., N.Y.C., 1964, prize Washington Sq. Art Exhbn., 1964.

LEVINE, ARNOLD MILTON, retired electrical engineer, documentary filmmaker; b. Preston, Conn., Aug. 15, 1916; s. Samuel and Florence May (Clark) L.; m. Bernice Eleanor Levich, Aug. 31, 1941; children: Mark Jeffrey, Michael Norman, Kevin Lawrence. BS in Radio Engring., Tri-State U., Angola, Ind., 1939, DSc, 1960; MS, U. Iowa, 1940. Head sound lab. CBS, N.Y.C., 1940-42; asst. engr., div. head ITT, N.Y.C. and Nutley, N.J., 1942-65; lab. head, lab. dir. ITT, San Fernando, Calif., 1965-71; v.p. aerospace, gen. mgr., sr. scientist ITT, Van Nuys, Calif., 1971-86; ret., 1986. Patentee fiber optics, radar, motion picture digital sound, communications and TV fields. Past mem. bd. dirs., v.p., pres. Am. Jewish Congress, L.A. Recipient San Fernando Valley Engr. of Yr. award, 1968; Profl. designation Motion Picture Art & Scis., UCLA, 1983. Fellow IEEE (life), Soc. Motion Picture and TV Engrs., USCG Aux. (vice comdr. 1990-91, flotilla cmdr. 1992-94). Avocations: sailing, amateur radio, filmmaking, swimming. Home: 10828 Fullbright Ave Chatsworth CA 91311-1737

LEVINE, C. BRUCE, lawyer; b. Liberty, N.Y., Aug. 20, 1945. Student, Stanford U.; BA magna cum laude, UCLA, 1967; JD cum laude, Harvard U., 1971. Bar: Calif. 1971. Mem. Greenberg, Glusker, Fields, Claman & Machtinger, L.A., 1971—. Editor Harvard Law Rev., 1970-71. Mem. State Bar Calif., L.A. County Bar Assn. (chmn. income tax com. tax sect. 1979-80), Beverly Hills Bar Assn. (chmn. taxation com. 1977-78), Phi Beta Kappa, Pi Gamma Mu. Office: Greenberg Glusker Fields Claman & Machtinger Ste 2100 1900 Avenue of the Stars Los Angeles CA 90067-4301*

LEVINE, MICHAEL, public relations executive, author; b. N.Y.C., Apr. 17, 1954; s. Arthur and Virginia (Gaylor) L. Student, Rutgers U., 1978. Owner, operator TV News Mag., Los Angeles, 1977-83; owner Levine/Schnieder Pub. Rels., now Levine Comms. Office, Inc., Los Angeles, 1982—; mem. Gov.'s adv. bd. State Calif., Sacramento, 1980-82; pres., owner Aurora Pub., L.A., 1986—; moderator Thought Forum; lectr. in field; founder, moderator L.A. Media Roundtable. Author: The Address Book: How to Reach Anyone Who's Anyone, 1984, The New Address Book, 1986, The Corporate Address Book, 1987, The Music Address Book, 1989, Environmental Address Book, 1991, Kid's Address Book, 1991, Guerrilla P.R., Lessons at Halfway Point, Take It From Me, Selling Goodness, The Princess & The Package, Raise Your Social I.Q., 1998; pub., writer For Consideration [illegible] Mem. Ronald Reagan [illegible] The Actor's [illegible] Charity, 1987, bd. dirs. Felice Found., Micah Ctr.; adv. bd. Dare America; founder, moderator L.A. Media Roundtable; moderator U. Judaism Thought Forum. Mem. TV Acad. Arts and Scis., Entertainment Industries Coun., Musician's Assistance Program, West Hollywood C. of C. (bd. dirs. 1980-82). Jewish. Office: Ste 555 5750 Wilshire Blvd Los Angeles CA 90036-3697

LEVINE, MICHAEL JOSEPH, insurance company executive; b. Boston, Mar. 23, 1945; s. Sam and Helen Alice (Michelman) L.; m. Margaret Mary Gutierrez, Aug. 6, 1983; children: Samuel Jacob, Rebecca Lynn. BA, Boston U., 1967; MBA, N.Mex. State U., 1991. Supr. underwriting Comml. Union. Ins., Boston, 1969-73; mgr. Harris-Murtagh Ins., Boston, 1973-75, Cohen-Goldenberg Ins. Agy., Boston, 1975-77; v.p. Southwest Underwriters Ins., Deming, N.Mex., 1977-83, pres., 1983-86; pres. Consol. Ins. Cons., Deming, N.Mex., 1985—; instr. fin. and ins., N.Mex. State U., Las Cruces; pres., dir. Small Bus. Devel. Ctr., Sul Ross State U., Alpine, Tex., 1992—. V.p. Border Area Mental Health Svcs., So. N.Mex., 1978—; pres. Deming Arts Council, 1979-81; treas. Luna County (N.Mex.) Crimestoppers, Inc., 1979—. Mem. Mensa, Soc. CPCU's (cert.), Soc. Cert. Ins. Counselors (cert.), Ins. Mktg. Assocs., Luna County C. of C. (v.p. 1981-84), Ind. Ins. Agts. N.Mex. (state dir. 1985—), Southwest N.Mex. Ind. Ins. Agts. (treas. 1981-83, pres. 1983-85). Avocations: tennis, model railroads, computers, rock collecting.

LEVINE, PEGGY AYLSWORTH, psychotherapist, writer, poet; b. Newark, May 2, 1921; d. Roscoe Nichols and Helen (Dorsen) Aylsworth; m. Samuel Schultz, Mar. 29, 1950 (div. 1979); children: Christie Romero, Ronald M. Schultz; m. Norman Philip Levine, Sept. 20, 1986. BA in Psychology, Lindenwood Coll., 1977; MA in Psychology, Antioch West Coll., L.A., 1978. Rschr. Carl Byoir & Assocs., N.Y.C., 1941-43; rsch. editor True Mag., Fawcett Pubs., N.Y.C., 1944-45; adminstr. Valley Ctr. of Arts, Encino, Calif., 1966-69; pub. rels. dir. Comsky Gallery, L.A., 1970; pvt. practice psychotherapy Santa Monica, Calif., 1980—. Author: (children's album) The Glooby Game, 1949, (poetry) Letters to the Same Address, 1989, Along These Lines, 1995, (novels) Morning in the Long Night City, 1992, Among These Several, 1996; contbr. poems to various mags., revs. V.p. Valley Ctr. of Arts, 1956-57, publicity dir., 1955-65; publicity dir. Alliance for Survival, Santa Monica, 1979-81. Avocations: art collecting, reading, ephemera and stamp collecting, reading plays, photography; established a Sunday salon, 1998. Home and Office: 606 Raymond Ave Apt 1 Santa Monica CA 90405-4530

LEVINE, PHILIP, poet, retired educator; b. Detroit, Jan. 10, 1928; s. A. Harry and Esther Gertrude (Priscol) L.; m. Frances Artley, July 12, 1954; children: Mark, John, Teddy. B.A., Wayne State U., 1950, A.M., 1955; M.F.A., U. Iowa, 1957, studied with John Berryman, 1954. Instr. U. Iowa, 1955-57; instr. Calif. State U., Fresno, 1958-99 (ret.); prof. English Calif. State U., 1969-92, Tufts U.; tchr. Princeton U., Columbia U., U. Calif., Berkeley.; Elliston lectr. poetry U. Cin.; poet-in-residence Vassar Coll., Nat. U. Australia; chmn. lit. panel Nat. Endowment Arts, 1985; adj. prof. NYU, Spring, 1984, Univ. prof. Brown U., spring 1985; tchr. NYU, U. Iowa, Vanderbilt U., U. Houston; part-time vis. prof. various univs. Author: On the Edge, 1961, Silent in America: Vivas for Those Who Failed, 1965, Not This Pig, 1968, 5 Detroits, 1970, Thistles, 1970, Pili's Wall, 1971, Red Dust, 1971, They Feed They Lion, 1972, 1933, 1974, On The Edge & Over, 1976, The Names of the Lost, 1976 (Lenore Marshall award Best Am. Book Poems 1976), 7 Years from Somewhere, 1979 (Nat. Book Critics Circle prize 1979, Notable Book award Am. Libr. Assn. 1979), Ashes, 1979 (Nat. Book Critics Circle prize 1979, Nat. Book award 1979), Don't Ask, 1979, One for the Rose, 1981, Selected Poems, 1984, Sweet Will, 1985, A Walk with Tom Jefferson, 1988 (Bay Area Book Reviewers award), What Work Is, 1991 (L.A. Times Book Prize 1991, Nat. Book award for poetry, 1991), New Selected Poems, 1991, Earth, Stars, and Writers, 1992, The Bread of Time: Toward an Autobiography, 1994, Simple Truth, 1994 (Pulitzer Prize for poetry 1995); editor: (with Henri Coulette) Character and Crisis, 1966, (with E. Trejo) The Selected Poems of Jaime Sabines, (with Ada Long) Off the Map, The Selected Poems of Gloria Fuertes, 1984, (with D. Wojahn and B. Henderson) The Pushcart Prize XI, 1986, The Essential Keats, 1987, Poetry, 1998. Active anti-Vietnam war movement. Recipient Joseph Henry Jackson award San Francisco Found., 1961, The Chaplebrook Found. award, 1968, Frank O'Hara Meml. prize, 1973; Amer. Academy of Arts and Letters Award of Merit, 1974; Levinson Prize, 1974; Harriet Monroe Meml. prize for poetry, 1976; Golden Rose award New Eng. Poetry Soc., 1985, Ruth Lilly Poetry Prize, Modern Poetry Assn. and Am. Council Arts, 1987, Elmer Bobst award NYU, 1990, Lit. Lion New York Public Library 1993; named outstanding lectr. Calif. State U., Fresno, 1971, outstanding prof. Calif. State U. System, 1972; Stanford U. poetry fellow, 1957, Nat. Inst. Arts and Letters grantee, 1973, Guggenheim fellow, 1973-74, 80; Nat. Endowment for Arts grantee, 1969, 70 (refused), 76, 81, 87. Address: 4549 N Van Ness Blvd Fresno CA 93704*

LEVINE, STEPHEN, journalist; b. L.A., July 7, 1962. BA, U. Calif., Berkeley, 1986. Staff writer Calif. Lawyer Mag., San Francisco, 1989-91; writer-at-large The Washington Post, 1991—; staff writer, reporter The Bus. Times, San Francisco, 1991—, Ctr. for Investigative Journalism, San Francisco, 1993—; investigator U. Calif., Santa Cruz, 1998. Author: (book) Paper Trails, 1997 (award 1997); assoc. prodr.: (documentary) Hot Guns, 1997 (award). Bd. dirs. Calif. Vote Found., Sacramento, 1997—. Recipient Emmy award, 1998, Excellence in Journalism award Soc. Profl. Journalists, 1997, James Madison Freedom of Internation award, 1997, Conjune Journalism award Nat. Press Club, 1989. Office: # 37 48 Shattuck Sq # 37 Berkeley CA 94704-1119

LEVINSON, BETTY ZITMAN, artist; b. Chgo., May 14, 1908; d. Samuel and Ella (Block) Z.; m. Julius Yale Levinson, Aug. 19, 1928 (dec. Dec., 1981); children: Lila Scher, Joyce Levinson, Robin Boushie. Student, U. Chgo., 1966, Art Inst. Chgo., 1972. Exhibitions include N. Shore Art League, Chgo., Spertus Mus., 57th St. Art Festival, Old Town Chamber Art Festival, Oak Park Art Festival; represented in collections at Deer Path Gallery, Lake Forest, Camino Real Gallery, Boca Raton, Fla., Prism Gallery, Evanston, Ill., Fort Wayne (Ind.) Mus. Art Alliance; juried group shows include Palm Springs (Calif.) Mus., Faulkner Libr. Gallery, 1998. Founder, mem. United Cerebral Palsy Assn. N.Y.C., 1949, pres. Stamford, Conn., 1954-58, v.p. Chgo., 1968—; patron Mus. Contemporary Art, Chgo. Historic Soc.; trustee Spertus Mus., Chgo.; active supporter print and drawing club Art Inst. Chgo. Recipient Honor Mother of Yr. Conn. Mother of Yr. Am. Mother's Com., N.Y., 1954, Award of Excellence Chgo. Soc. Artists, 1980, 1st prize David Adler Cultural Ctr., Libertyville, Ill., 1986, award of excellence, 1988, 2d prize Am. Jewish Art Club, Chgo., 1990, award of excellence Deer Path Gallery, Lake Forest, Ill., 1994, award for excellence, Cultural Ctr. for Abstract Painting, 1995, 96, award United Cerebral Palsy Chgo., 1996, award excellence Karpeles Manuscript Mus., Santa Barbara, 1997. Mem. English Speaking Union, Shakespeare Globe Ctr., Chgo. Soc. Artists, United Cerbral Palsy Chgo. (life v.p.), Master Santa Barbara Mus. Avocations: golf, walking, swimming, art. Home: Casa Dorinda 300 Hot Springs Rd Apt 89 Montecito CA 93108-2053

LEVINSON, KENNETH LEE, lawyer; b. Denver, Jan. 18, 1953; s. Julian Charles and Dorothy (Milzer) L.; m. Shauna Titus, Dec. 21, 1986. BA cum laude, U. Colo., 1974; JD, U. Denver, 1978. Bar: Colo. 1978, U.S. Ct. Appeals (10th cir.), 1978. Assoc. atty. Balaban & Lutz, Denver, 1979-83; shareholder Balaban & Levinson, P.C., Denver, 1984—, pres., 1994—. Contbr. articles to profl. jours. Pres., Dahlia House Condominium Assn., 1983-85, bd. dirs., 1991-94; intern Reporters Com. for Freedom of the Press, Waashington, 1977; atty. grievance hearing bd., 1988—; jr. varsity volleyball coach Good Shepherd Cath. Ch., 1992-95. Recipient Am. Jurisprudence award Lawyers Co-op, 1977, 3d Place award Rocky Mountain Fiction Writers Mystery Novel Contest, 1994. Mem. Colo. Bar Assn. (profl. liability com. 1991-94), Denver Bar Assn., Am. Arbitration Assn. (arbitrator), Denver Law Club.

LEVINSON, SHAUNA T., financial services executive; b. Denver, Aug. 1, 1954; d. Charles and Geraldine D. Titus; m. Kenneth L. Levinson, Dec. 21, 1986. BA cum laude, U. Puget Sound, 1976; M Bank Mktg. with honors, U. Colo., 1986. Cert. fin. planner. Fin. planning analyst Swift and Co., Chgo., 1977-79; from credit analyst to asst. v.p. CVC Bank of Denver, 1979-84, v.p. fin. svcs. First Nat. Bank S.E. Denver, 1984-94, dir. mktg. First Nat. Banks, 1991-94; pres., CEO Fin. Directions, Inc., Denver, 1994—, Levinson Resources, Inc., Denver, 1994—; mem. bankers edn. com. Colo. Bankers Assn., Denver, 1992-94. Contbr. articles to profl. jours. Chmn. human resources com., mem. adminstrv. coun. Jr. League of Denver, 1983—; mem. cmty. assistance fund, placement adv. com.; fundraiser Women's Libr. Assn. U. Denver, 1990-94, 96—, Good Shepherd Cath. Sch., 1986-95, Jewish Cmty. Ctr., Denver, 1990-95, St. Mary's Acad., 1995—, Theodor Herzl Day Sch., 1996—. Recipient Gold Peak award Am. Bankers Assn.-Bank Mktg. Assn., 1987; named Businessperson of Week Denver Bus. Jour., 1995. Mem. Jr. League Denver, U. Denver Women's Libr. Assn., U. Denver Pioneer Hockey, St. Andrews Soc. (life), Crestmoor Gardeners (treas. 1994—), Betty Baur Lambert Soc. (life), Kappa Alpha Theta (Chgo. NW alumnae 1977-79, Denver alumae), Phi Kappa Phi, Phi Chi Theta. Office: 1624 Market St Ste 475 Denver CO 80202-1518

LEVINSON, STEVEN HENRY, state supreme court justice; b. Cincinnati, OH, June 8, 1946. BA with distinction, Stanford U., 1968; JD, U. Mich., 1971. Bar: Hawaii 1972, U.S. Dist. Ct. Hawaii 1972, U.S. Ct. Appeals (9th cir.) 1972. Law clk. to Hon. Bernard H. Levinson Hawaii Supreme Ct., 1971-72; pvt. practice Honolulu, 1972-89; judge Hawaii Cir. Ct. (1st cir.), 1989-92; assoc. justice Hawaii Supreme Ct., Honolulu, 1992—. Staff mem. U. Mich. Jour. Law Reform, 1970-71. Active Temple Emanu-El. Mem. ABA (jud. adminstrn. divsn. 1989—), Hawaii State Bar Assn. (dir. young lawyers divsn. 1975-76, dir. 1982-84), Nat. Jud. Coll. (state jud. leader 1991—). Jewish. Office: Supreme Ct of Hawaii Ali Tolani Hale 417 King St Honolulu HI 96813*

LEVITAN, ROGER STANLEY, lawyer; b. Washington, Jan. 31, 1933; s. Simon Wolfe and Bessie (Abramson) L.; m. Maria Anneli Stennius, May 27, 1975 (div. 1980); 1 child, Mark Howard; m. Laurel Lynn Allen, July 9, 1982; 1 child, Brandon Wolfe. BS in Econs., U. Pa., 1954; JD, Columbia U., 1957. Bar: D.C. 1957, U.S. Ct. Appeals (D.C. cir.) 1957, Ariz. 1976. Tax specialist, reorgn. br. IRS, Washington, 1957-62; atty. McClure & Trotter, Washington, 1962-65; assoc. ptnr. Main Lafrentz, Washington and N.Y.C., 1970-72; dir. taxes U.S. Industries, Inc., N.Y.C., 1972-73; asst. tax counsel Am. Home Products Co., N.Y.C., 1973-75; ptnr., Bilby & Shoenhair, P.C., Tucson, 1976-89; ptnr. Snell & Wilmer, Tucson, 1989-90; ptnr. Molloy, Jones & Donohue P.C., Tucson, 1991-92; counsel Hecker, Phillips & Zeeb, 1992—; lectr. Am. Law Inst., State Bar Ariz. Legal counsel Tucson Community Found., 1981—. Contbr. articles to profl. jours. Mem. ABA (chmn. ann. report com. 1965-67, continuing legal edn. com. 1969-70), Ariz. Bar Found., State Bar Ariz. (chmn. sect. taxation 1987-88, mem. tax specialization adv. bd., 1991-93). Home: 727 E Chula Vista Rd Tucson AZ 85718-1028 Office: 405 W Franklin St Tucson AZ 85701-8209

LEVITOW, ROBERTA LYNNE, theater artist, educator; b. L.A., Dec. 1, 1950; d. Abe and Charlotte Winifred (Lewis) L.; m. Michael John Hall, Sept. 9, 1979 (div. Sept. 1983); m. Mitchell Reed Greenhill, Apr. 19, 1995; stepchildren: Matthew, Tejinder. BA in Drama, Stanford U., 1972; grad. Directing Workshop for Women, Am. Film Inst., L.A., 1991. Jr. coll. tchg. credential, Calif. Artist-in-residence Pacific Conservatory of Performing Arts, Santa Maria, Calif., 1974-78; artistic dir. Skid Road Theater, Seattle, 1978-82; staff dir. L.A. Theater Ctr., 1983-88; assoc. artist, dramaturg Mark Taper Forum, L.A., 1987-94; conf. dir. ASK Theater Projects, L.A., 1993-94; free-lance stage dir., dramaturg, 1975—; adj. asst. prof. dept. theater UCLA, 1990-98, adj. assoc. prof., 1998—. Stage dir. Kaspar, Santa Maria, 1977, Grease, Seattle, 1980, Yerma, Juneau, 1987, Etta Jenks, L.A., N.Y.C., 1988, Miriam's Flowers, N.Y.C., 1990, Little Egypt, N.Y.C., 1991, Hedda Gabler, Portland, Maine, 1993, Why Things Burn, San Francisco, 1994, Electra, San Antonio, 1994, Having Our Say: The Delany Sisters First 100 Years, Houston, Berkeley, 1997, The Secret Rapture, Santa Barbara, Calif., 1998, Everybody's Ruby, N.Y.C., 1998, The Faraway Nearby, Washington, 1998, numerous others; asst. to dir. In The Presence of Mine Enemies, Showtime Prodns., 1995; assoc. prodr., story writer Raven's Blood, 1996. Mem. adv. panel NEA, Washington, 1995; mem. selection panel Pew Charitable Trust, Phila., 1996-97, Am. Film Inst., 1997, AT&T Onstage, N.Y.C., 1998. Recipient Alan Schneider award Theater Comm. Group, N.Y.C., 1990; directing fellow NEA, 1982. Mem. Soc. Stage Dirs. and Choreographers (bd. dirs. 1991—), Theater Comm. Group (bd. dirs. 1994—, v.p. bd. dirs. 1998—), Dirs. Guild of Am. (George Schaefer Observership 1999). Avocations: drawing, painting, hiking. Office: UCLA Dept Theater 405 Hilgard Ave Los Angeles CA 90095-9000

LEVITT, IRENE HANSEN, sales associate, writer, artist; b. Berkeley, Calif., Aug. 18, 1953; d. Alvin Kenneth and Bertha (Schiff) Hansen; m. Kim De Wayne, Oct. 22, 1983. BA in Art, Calif. Luth. U., 1976. Bookkeeper, data processor, sec. pvt. contractor, 1984-95; sales assoc. Dayton Hudson Corp., J.C. Penney Co., 1995—. Painter acrylic collage exhibits in art gallery in L.A.; photographer with exhibits of greeting card and prints in numerous art galleries in the Seattle area; exhibited in art show, Oakland, Calif., 1972, L.A., 1986, Seattle, 1994; author: (plays) A Cancer of Proximity, 1987, The Price of the Retreat, 1987, Sacrifices to the Compromise, 1987, In Order to Bury Our Dead, 1987, Foxtrot, 1993, The Loom, 1993, (novel) The Renaissance of the Poppy, 1991, (anthology) Diaries of the Affluent, 1993. Vol., alumni rep. Calif. Luth. U., Thousand Oaks, Calif., 1987; vol. Am. Cancer Soc., Modesto, Calif., 1991-92; vol. Redmond Cmty. Celebration of the Arts, 1995, El Camino Real Playhouse, San Juan Capistrano, Calif., 1998. Recipient award in art Alameda County Art Com., 1972, Mark Van Doren Meml. Poetry prize Calif. Luth. U., 1976; Undergrad. scholar VA, 1972-76, U.S. Civil Svc. Commn., 1972-75. Avocations: reading, hiking, touring museums, tennis.

LEVY, ALAN DAVID, real estate executive; b. St. Louis, July 19, 1938; s. I. Jack and Natalie (Yawitz) L.; grad. Sch. Real Estate, Washington U., 1960; m. Abby Jane Markowitz, May 12, 1968; children: Jennifer Lynn, Jacqueline Claire. Property mgr. Solon Gershman Inc., Realtors, Clayton, Mo., 1958-61; gen. mgr. Kodner Constrn. Co., St. Louis, 1961-63; regional mgr. Tishman Realty & Constrn. Co., Inc., N.Y.C., 1963-69, v.p., Los Angeles, 1969-77; exec. v.p., dir. Tishman West Mgmt. Corp., 1977-88; pres. Tishman West Cos., 1988-92, chmn. Tishman Internat. Cos., 1993—; guest lectr. on real estate mgmt. to various forums. Mem. L.A. County Mus. Art; former chmn. Am. Art Coun.; trustee Archives Am. Art, Harvard-Westlake Sch.; bd. govs. W.L.A. coun. Boy Scouts Am. Mem. Bldg. Owners and Mgrs. Assn. L.A. (dir.), N.J. (co-founder, hon. dir.), Inst. Real Estate Mgmt. (cert. property mgr.), Urban Land Inst., Internat. Council Shopping Centers. Contbr. articles on property mgmt. to trade jours. Office: 10900 Wilshire Blvd Ste 510 Los Angeles CA 90024-6528

LEVY, DAVID, lawyer, insurance company executive; b. Bridgeport, Conn., Aug. 3, 1932; s. Aaron and Rachel (Goldman) L. BS in Econs., U. Pa., 1954; JD, Yale U., 1957. Bar: Conn. 1958, U.S. Supreme Ct. 1963, D.C. 1964, Mass. 1965, N.Y. 1971, Pa. 1972; CPA, Conn. Acct. Arthur Andersen & Co., N.Y.C., 1957-59; sole practice Bridgeport, 1959-60; specialist tax law IRS, Washington, 1960-64; counsel State Mut. Life Ins. Co., Worcester, Mass., 1964-70; assoc. gen. counsel taxation Penn Mut. Life Ins. Co., Phila., 1971-81; sole practice Washington, 1982-87; v.p., tax counsel Pacific Life Ins. Co., Newport Beach, Calif., 1987—. Author: (with others) Life Insurance Company Tax Series, Bureau National Affairs Tax Management Income Tax, 1970-71. Mem. adv. bd. Tax Mgmt., Washington, 1975-90, Hartford Inst. on Ins. Taxation, 1990-97; bd. dirs. Citizens Plan E Orgn., Worcester, 1966-70. With AUS, 1957. Mem. ABA (vice-chmn. employee benefits com. 1980-86, ins. cos. com. 1984-86, torts and ins. practice sect., subcom. chair ins. cos. com. tax sect. 1994—), Assn. Life Ins. Counsel, AICPA, Beta Alpha Psi. Jewish.

LEVY, DAVID HOWARD, astronomer, writer; b. Montreal, Que., Can.; s. Nathaniel Lewis and Edith (Pailet) L.; m. Wendee Esther Wallach, Mar. 23, 1997; 1 child, Nanette, Vigil. BA, Acadia U., Wolfville, N.S., Can., 1972; MA, Queens U., Kingston, Ont., Can., 1979, DS (hon.), 1994, DS (hon.), Acadia U., 1995. Observer Planetary Sci. Inst., Tucson, 1982-92; asst. discipline specialist Internat. Halley Watch, Tucson, 1985-96; observer Palomar (Calif.) Asteroid and Comet Survey, 1989-96; adj. scientist Flandrau Sci. Ctr., Tucson, 1991—; instrnl. specialist U. Ariz., Tucson, 1992-93, sr. instrnl. specialist, 1993-96; shoemaker Levy Cometograph Observing Team, 1996—. Author: The Joy of Gazing, 1982, 2d edit., 1985, The Universe for Children: How Astronomy-minded adults can teach children to love the sky, 1984, (with S.J. Edberg) Observe: Comets, 1985, (with S.J. Edberg) Observe: Meteors, 1986, Observing Variable Stars: A guide for the beginner, 1989, The Sky: A User's Guide, 1991, (Polish translation), 1996, Clyde Tombaugh:

Discoverer of Planet Pluto, 1991, The Man Who Sold the Milky Way: A Biography of Bart Bok, 1993, Astronomy Day: Bringing Astronomy to the People, 4th edit., 1996, (with Steve Edberg) An Observing Guide for Comets, Asteroids, Meteors, and Zodiacal Light, 1994, The Quest for Comets: An explosive trail of beauty and danger, 1994, Skywatching, 1995, (with Tim B. Hunter) Medical Devices, Abbreviations, Acronyms and Eponyms: A Pocket Guide, 1993, Comet Shoemaker-Levy 9 Slide Set, 1994, Impact Jupiter: The Crash of Comet Shoemaker-Levy 9, 1995, Stars and Planets, 1995, More Things in Heaven and Earth: Poets and Astronomers Read the Night Sky, 1997, (with Larry and Nancy Lebofsky) Sharing the Sky: A Parent's and Teacher's Guide to Astronomy, 1997, Comets: Creators and Destoyers, 1998, The Ultimate Universe, 1998; co-author (TV program) Three Minutes to Impact (Emmy 1998), 1998; contbr. over 300 articles to profl. jours.; contbg. editor Sky and Telescope Star Trails Column, 1988—, sci. editor Parade Mag., 1998—. Recipient Chant medal Royal Astron. Soc. Can., 1980; named in his honor asteroid 3673 Levy, 1985, E.E. Barnard award Western Amateur Astronomers, 1988, Leslie C. Peltier award Astron. League, 1988, G. Bruce Blair award Western Amateur Astronomers, 1990, Walter H. Haas award Assn. Lunar and Planetary Observers, 1990, Ruth Northcott Meml. lectr. Can. Astron. Soc. and Royal Astron. Soc. Can., 1995, Tandy Scholars lectr., 1995, Amateur Achievement award Astron. Soc. of Pacific, 1993, Group Achievement award NASA, 1995, Pub. Svc. Group Achievement award NASA, 1996. Mem. Am. Astron. Soc., Royal Astron. Soc. Can., Am. Assn. Variable Star Observers. Jewish. Achievements include 21 comet discoveries which is tied for 3d place in history for largest number of comet finds.

LEVY, DAVID STEVEN, college administrator; b. L.A., Mar. 9, 1955; s. Henry and Gloria Grace (Barouh) L. BA, Occidental Coll., 1977; MA, 1979. Asst. dir. fin. aid Calif. State Coll., San Bernardino, 1978-79; fin. aid counselor Calif. State U.-Northridge, 1979-80; assoc. dir. student fin. aid Calif. State U.-Dominguez Hills, 1980-82; dir. fin. aid Occidental Coll., L.A., 1982-88; dir. fin. aid Calif. Inst. Tech., Pasadena, Calif., 1988—, assoc. dean of students, 1991—; mem. Title IA Adv. Com. Calif., 1977-80; negotiator U.S. Dept Edn. Mem. life-long learning com. Calif. Postsecondary Edn. Commn., 1980—, mem. student fin. aid issues com., 1984—; mem. Sallie Mae Fin. Aid Adv. Bd., 1994—. Recipient Meritorious Svc. award Coll. Bd., 1997; Richter fellow Princeton U., 1976; Calif. State U. adminstrv. fellow, 1981—. Mem. Nat. Assn. Student Fin. Aid. Adminstrs. (Meritorious Achievement award 1988, Distinguised Service Awd., 1997, 98 bd. dirs. 1991-94, commn. dir. 1994-95, Leadership award 1997), Mortar Board Alumni Assn. (pres. 1977—), Calif. Assn. Student Fin. Aid Adminstrs. (life, ind. segmental rep. 1984, sec. 1985, treas. 1986-88, lifetime mem. 1996, Pres.'s award 1986, 93, 97, Meritorious Svc. award 1994, Segmental Leadership award 1992, Creative Leadership award 1990), Western Assn. Student Fin. Aid Adminstrs. (Disting. Svc. award 1990, College Brd. Reg. Dist. Service Awd., 1997, Pres. Disting. Svc. award 1992, 97), Phi Beta Kappa, Delta Phi Epsilon, Psi Chi, Phi Alpha Theta, Sigma Alpha Epsilon. Jewish. Co-editor Calif. Student Aid Commn. Student Aid Workbook, 1977—; co-author, contbr. Playing the Selective College Admissions Game, 1994; contbr. Paying Less for College, 1995, Top Colleges for Science, 1995. Home: 2704 Franklin St La Crescenta CA 91214-2907 Office: CalTech 515 S Wilson Ave Pasadena CA 91106-3212

LEVY, EMANUEL, film and sociology educator, film critic; b. Tel Aviv, Israel, Feb. 4, 1947; came to U.S., 1973; s. Abraham and Motti (Panigel) L. BA, Tel Aviv U., 1971; MA, Columbia U., 1975, PhD, 1978. Asst. prof. CUNY, N.Y.C., 1978-82; assoc. prof. Columbia U., N.Y.C., 1983-86, Wellesley Coll., Boston, 1986-89; prof. film and sociology Ariz. State U., Phoenix, 1990—; film critic Variety, L.A., 1991—. Author: And the Winner Is: The History and Politics of the Oscar Awards, John Wayne and the American Way of Life, 1988, George Cukor, Master of Elegance, 1994, others; film critic Variety, L.A., 1991—. Recipient Nat. Jewish Book award, 1980. Mem. Nat. Soc. Office: Ariz State U Dept Arts and Scis 4701 W Thunderbird Glendale AZ 85305-4900

LEVY, EZRA CESAR, aerospace scientist, real estate broker; b. Havana, Cuba, Sept. 22, 1924; s. Mayer D. and Rachel Levy; m. Gaynor D. Popejoy, 1980; children from previous marriage: Daniel M., Diana M. Levy Friedman, Linda R. Levy Brenden. *Wife AKA Cantor Galit Levy, is a religious leader in Seal Beach, and also lends her vocal talents to the Veteran's Hospital, and at Retirement and Nursing Homes. Son, Daniel, is a school principal. His wife, Sandra, was named California's Teacher of the Year in 1996. Daughter, Diana, a trained dental assistant, works as a receptionist/assistant to a dermatologist. Her husband, Richard, is an actor and hair stylist. Daughter, Linda, is presently Site Manager/Coordinator for the International Homestay Program in Southern California, which locates guest homes for visiting students from overseas. Her husband, William, is a CPA.* MS, UCLA, 1951. Sect. head Douglas Aircraft Co., Santa Monica, Calif., 1951-54; dept. head Lockheed Aircraft Co., Van Nuys, Calif., 1954-56, Librascope, Glendale, Calif., 1956-57, Radioplane, Van Nuys, 1957-58; asst. dept. mgr. Space Tech. Labs., Redondo Beach, Calif., 1958-60; asst. divsn. dir. TRW, Redondo Beach, Calif., 1960-74; now real estate broker, owner Jaunty Real Estate, Glendale, Calif. Author: Laplace Transform Tables, 1958; contbr. articles to profl. jours. Cpl. U.S. Army, 1944-46. Mem. Temple City C. of C. (bd. dirs. 1992-97), Masons (past master and sec.). Democrat. Jewish. Avocations: art, music, philately. Home: 1935 Alpha Rd Apt 102 Glendale CA 91208-2146 Office: Jaunty Real Estate Glendale CA 91208

LEVY, JEROME, dermatologist, retired naval officer; b. Bklyn., Aug. 17, 1926; s. Alexander and Pauline (Wollkof) L.; m. Leona Elsie Eligator, June 6, 1948; children—Andrew B., Eric J., Peter C., David J. Student, Wesleyan U., 1944-45; postgrad., 1952-54; A.B., Yale U., 1947; M.D., Albany Med. Coll., 1958. Diplomate Am. Bd. Dermatology. Commd. ensign M.C., U.S. Navy, 1957, advanced through grades to capt., 1972; intern U.S. Naval Hosp., Newport, R.I., 1958-59; resident U.S. Naval Hosp., Phila., 1960-62, U. Pa. Grad. Sch. Medicine, Phila., 1962-63; chief dept. dermatology U.S. Naval Hosp., Memphis, 1963-67, Yokosuka, Japan, 1967-70, Long Beach, Calif., 1974-75; head outpatient dermatology clinic San Diego Naval Hosp., 1970-72; sr. med. officer Keflavik, Iceland, 1972-74; ret., 1975; med. dir. dermatology Westwood Pharm Co., Buffalo, 1975-82; acting chief dermatology dept. Buffalo Gen. Hosp., 1981-82; cons. Erie County Health Dept., 1979-82; clin. assoc. prof. SUNY, Buffalo Med. Sch., 1980-82; practice medicine specializing in dermatology, Coronado, Calif., 1982-90. Contbr. articles to med. jours. Decorated Navy Commendation medal, Joint Service Commendation medal; Knight's Cross of the Order of Falcon (Iceland). Fellow Am. Acad. Dermatology, ACP; mem. AMA, So. Med. Assn., Assn. Mil. Surgeons, U.S., Navy League, Alpha Omega Alpha. Republican. Jewish. Home: 3352 Lucinda St San Diego CA 92106-2932

LEVY, KENNETH, executive. CEO KLA Tencor, San Jose, Calif. Office: 160 Rio Robles San Jose CA 95134-1813*

LEVY, MARIAN MULLER, transportation executive; b. N.Y.C., Mar. 10, 1942; d. Arthur Russ and Diana Elise (Ornstein) Muller; m. Richard Dennis Levy, Nov. 16, 1962 (dec. Ded. 1995); children: Dawn, Nicole, Jason, Adam. Student, Bklyn. Coll., 1959-61, 68-70. Sec. ASCAP, N.Y.C., 1959-61; tchr. spl. edn Garden Park Sch., Phoenix, 1974-76; v.p. Pac Expediters, Ltd., Scottsdale, Ariz., 1976-98, pres., 1998—. Bd. dirs. Outreach, Phoenix, 1982-92; co-chmn. Council Jews Spl. Needs, Phoenix, 1987-88; chairperson Hospice of the Valley Art Com. Recipient Paul D. Mahoney Outstanding Svc. award Hospice of the Valley, 1991. Mem. Scottsdale Ctr. for Arts, Phoenix Art Mus., The Heard Mus. Avocations: travel, art, theater, music. Home: 7850 E Camelback Rd Unit 602 Scottsdale AZ 85251-2291 Office: Pac Expediters Ltd 3020B N Scottsdale Rd Scottsdale AZ 85251-7210

LEVY, MICHAEL LEE, neurosurgeon; b. San Diego, Calif., Sept. 20, 1960; s. Lee Issaac and Sharline Sheridan (Day) L.; m. Karen Marie Lorman, Jan. 7, 1989; children: Danielle Montana, Dillon Michael. BA, U. Calif. San Diego, 1981; MD, U. Calif. San Francisco, 1986, postgrad. Resident U. So. Calif. Sch. Medicine, L.A., 1986-93; sr. resident Divsn. Neurol. Surgery Children's Hosp. of L.A., 1989, Huntington Meml. Hosp., Pasadena, Calif., 1989, Kenneth E. Norris Cancer Hosp., L.A., 1990; resident supr. U. So. Calif. Sch. Medicine, L.A., 1992; fellow in pediatric neurol. surgery Dept. Neurol. Surgery, L.A., 1993; mem. coms. in field, including chmn./sgt.-at-arms com. Congress of Neurol. Surgeons Ann. Mtg., San Francisco, 1995; dir. surg. epilepsy team, dir. neurotrauma, Children's Hosp., L.A. Mem. editl. bd. Jour. of Health Comms., 1995-99, Neurosurgery, 1995-99; editor: (newsletter) Congress of Neurol. Surgeons, 1996-97; contbr. numerous articles to profl. jours. and publs. Recipient Rudolph Taussig scholarship U. Calif. San Francisco, 1982-84, CHOMP scholarship, 1983-86, Tucker scholarship, 1984-86, numerous awards in field. Mem. Congress of Neurol. Surgeons (exec. com. 1996-99), Am. Assn. Neurol. Surgeons, L.A. County Med. Assn., Calif. Med. Assn., Calif. House Officer Med. Soc., L.A. Acad. Medicine, Alpha Omega Alpha. Achievements include devel. of an endoscopic system for the treatment of hydrocephalus, heads-up virtual displays for microneurosurgery, three dimensional anatomic image reconstruction and stereolithography, specialization in pediatric vascular and midline tumor surgery. Avocations: surfing, diving. Office: Childrens Hosp of LA 1300 N Vermont Ave Ste 906 Los Angeles CA 90027-6005

LEW, RONALD S. W., federal judge; b. L.A., 1941; m. Mamie Wong; 4 children. BA in Polit. Sci., Loyola U., L.A., 1964; JD, Southwestern U., 1971. Bar: Calif. 1972. Dep. city atty. L.A. City Atty's. Office, 1972-74; ptnr. Avans & Lew, L.A., 1974-82; commr. fire and police pension City of L.A., 1976-82; mcpl. ct. judge County of L.A., 1982-84, superior ct. judge, 1984-87; judge U.S. Dist. Ct. (cen. dist.) Calif., L.A., 1987—; Bar: Calif. 1971. Mem. World Affairs Council of L.A., 1976—, Christian Businessmen's Com. of L.A., 1982—; active Com. of 100, Chinese Am. Heart Coun., Friends of the Mus. Chinese Am. History. 1st lt. U.S. Army, 1967-69. Recipient Vol. award United Way of L.A., 1979, cert. of merit L.A. Human Relations Commn., 1977, 82. Mem. Am. Judicature Soc., Calif. Assn. of Judges, So. Calif. Chinese Lawyer's Assn. (charter mem. 1976, pres. 1979), Chinese Am. Citizens Alliance, San Fernando Valley Chinese Cultural Assn., Delta Theta Phi. Office: US Dist Ct 312 N Spring St Los Angeles CA 90012-4701

LEWALLEN, ELINOR KIRBY, organization executive, lay church worker; b. Miltonvale, Kans., May 17, 1919; d. Osbourn Eddy and Grace Dale (Gorrell) Kirby; m. Thomas Monroe Lewallen, Jr., Aug. 14, 1948; children: Janet, Dean, Gary, Kent, Bonnie. AA, Coffeyville Jr. Coll., 1939; BA, Baker U., 1943; postgrad., U. Colo., 1969-70, Iliff Sch. Theology, Denver, 1986, 90, 94. Youth pres. Kans. Conf. United Meth. Youth, Baldwin, Kans., 1940-41; program dir. for young adults YWCA, Rockford, Ill., 1943-46; program dir. Bus. and Profl. Girls Club of YWCA, Denver, 1946-48; program dir. for young adults YWCA, Denver, 1943-48; nat. pres. Fedn. Parents and Friends of Lesbians and Gays, Denver, 1987-88, chmn. Fedn. Parents-FLAG Religious Issues Task Force, 1988-91; chmn. religious issues task force Nat. Parents and Friends of Lesbians and Gays, Denver, 1988-91; rsch. sec. values study The Iliff Sch. of Theology, 1977-84; numerous leadership roles Park Hill United Meth. Ch., Denver, 1953—; del. to ann. conv. Colo., 1979-88; mem. conf. task force on AIDS, Rocky Mt. Conf., 1986-92, com. on sexuality ministries, 1981—; mem. steering com. John Wesley Iliff Group; presenter United Meth. Gen. Conf. Com. to Study Homosexuality, St. Louis, 1991; mem. adm. coun. Park Hill United Meth. Ch., 1993-96, ch. staff parish com., 1998—. Author: Viewpoint. Chmn. impact neighborhood task force Denver Anti-Crime Coun., 1972-80; election judge, Denver 1981-97; mem. Colo. Gov.'s Adv. Coun. on AIDS, 1987-88. Recipient award of recognition Denver Anti-Crime Coun., 1980, Outstanding Leadership award Nat. Parents, Families, and Friends of Lesbians and Gays, 1988, 92, Hall of Honor and Swan award Denver Parents, Families and Friends of Lesbians and Gays, 1994, Civil Rights Awd. A.A.U.W. Trailblazers event (Denver), 1998. Mem. LWV, A.A.U.W., Assn. Group Workers (charter Colo. chpt.). Democrat. Home: 2258 Krameria St Denver CO 80207-3931

LEWIN, LINDA, writer, producer, educator; b. Newark, Feb. 13, 1940; d. William and Ruth Edna (Meyer) L. BS, Rutgers U., New Brunswick, 1961; postgrad., Temple U., 1974-78. Editor UN, N.Y.C., 1964-69; exec. editor Simon & Schuster, N.Y.C., 1970-74, sr. editor, product developer, 1978-80; pub. rels. coord. Alexander Co., N.Y.C., 1981-83; writer, editor, owner Dynamic Comm., N.Y.C., L.A., 1985-90; prodr., owner Spinning Wheel Prodns., San Francisco, Calif., 1991—. Editor, translator: (script) The Wild Child, 1974; author: Fun-to-Read Animal Stories, 1979, Bible Stories for the Very Young, 1985; contbr. Romper Room Activity Book, 1987; contbr. articles to mags.; prodr.: (TV program) A Garden Grows, 1973, Puppet Playhouse, 1973; writer/prodr. Take 12, 1976, Mime Time, 1985, (documentary) The Way It Used to Be, 1989; (video) Story Circle Series, 1992-95, Stories from Africa (Cable Pick of the Month 1993); writer, prodr.: (filmstrips) Growing Up Indian, 1980; writer: (filmstrip) Stress Managment for Classroom Teachers, 1981, Teaching in the Middle School, 1981, Teaching Learning Disabled Students, 1981. N.J. State scholar Rutgers U., 1957; scholar Sagan Found., 1957. Mem. Editl. Freelancer's Assn., Soc. Children's Book Writers & Illustrators. Avocations: camping, hiking, swimming, storytelling, photography. Home: 111 Piccadilly Pl Apt G San Bruno CA Office: Spinning Wheel Prodns PO Box 422242 San Francisco CA 94142

LEWIS, ALVIN THOMAS, minister, missionary; b. Meeteetse, Wyo., Aug. 21, 1912; s. Fred Thomas and Earnie Earl (Knauss) L.; m. Minnie L. Wallace, Apr. 19, 1941; children: Anita, Ruth, Flora, Hilma. AB, Westmont Coll., 1946. Ordained to ministry Evang. Ch., 1942. Missionary The Orinoco River Mission, Venezuela, S.Am., 1939-80; missionary Evang. Alliance Mission (merged with Orinoco River Mission), Wheaton, Ill., 1980-82, ret., 1982. Mem. S.W. Info. Svcs. Home: 2404 N Cactus St Silver City NM 88061-5721

LEWIS, BRIAN A., train station agent; b. Rochester, Minn., Dec. 16, 1949; s. Allan Andrew L. and Beverly Ann (La Port) Heinen; m. Karen Louise Conklin; children: Sarah Ann, Kelsie Claira, Cole Brian. AAA, Spokane C.C., 1974, AAS, 1981. Bridge man Amtrak, Spokane, 1973-74, ticket clk., 1974-75, sta. agt., 1975-79, sta acctg., 1979-84; sta. agt. Amtrak, Belton, Mont., 1984; sta. acctg. Amtrak, Whitefish, Mont., 1984; sta. agt. Amtrak, Klammath Falls, Oreg., 1985—. Inventor in field. With USN, 1968-71. Mem. Sons of Norway, Demolay, Am. Legion. Republican. Lutheran. Avocations: drag racing, ranching, commodity futures trading. Home: 11445 Highway 66 Klamath Falls OR 97601-9257 Office: Amtrak 1600 Oak Ave Klamath Falls OR 97601-3286

LEWIS, CARSON MCLAUGHL, retired plastic surgeon; b. Dallas, 1931. MD, U. Tex., Galveston, 1956. Plastic surgeon Scripps Meml. Hosp., Calif.; dir. Total Body Wellness Inc., La Jolla, Calif.; mem. tchg. staff U. Hosp., San Diego. Mem. Internat. Soc. Aesthetic Plastic Surgeons (dir. ednl. found.). Office: 8236 Caminito Lacayo La Jolla CA 92037-2210

LEWIS, CHARLES JEREMY, congressman; b. Spokane, Wash., Oct. 21, 1934. BA, UCLA, 1956. Former underwriter life ins. underwriter; field rep. for former U.S. Rep. Jerry Pettis; mem. Calif. State Assembly, 1968-78; vice chmn. rules com., chmn. subcom. on air quality; mem. 96th-106th Congresses from 35th (now 40th) Calif. dist., 1979—; chmn. appropriation com. Va.-HUD subscom., mem. defense subcom., select com. on intelligence, chmn. subcom. on human intelligence; co-chair Calif. Congl. Delegation. Presbyterian. Office: US Ho of Reps 2112 Rayburn Bldg Washington DC 20515-0540*

LEWIS, CHARLES S., III, lawyer; b. Baker, Oreg., Aug. 19, 1953. Student, U. So. Calif.; BS magna cum laude, Lewis and Clark Coll., 1975; JD magna cum laude, Willamette U., 1978. Bar: Oreg. 1978, U.S. Tax Ct. 1978. Mem. Stoel Rives, LLP, Portland, Oreg., 1978—. Co-author: The Tax Reform Act of 1986: Analysis and Commentary, 1987. Mem. ABA (taxation and bus. law sects.), Delta Mu Delta. Office: Stoel Rives LLP 900 SW 5th Ave Ste 2300 Portland OR 97204-1268*

LEWIS, EDWARD B., biology educator; b. Wilkes-Barre, Pa., May 20, 1918; s. Edward B. and Laura (Histed) L.; m. Pamela Harrah, Sept. 26, 1946; children: Hugh, Glenn (dec.), Keith. B.A., U. Minn., 1939; Ph.D., Calif. Inst. Tech., 1942; Phil.D., U. Umea, Sweden, 1982; DSc, U. Minn., 1993. Instr. biology Calif. Inst. Tech., Pasadena, 1946-48, asst. prof., 1949-56, prof., 1956-66, Thomas Hunt Morgan prof., 1966-88, prof. emeritus, 1988—; Rockefeller Found. fellow Sch. Botany, Cambridge U., Eng., 1948-49; mem. Nat. Adv. Com. Radiation, 1958-61; vis. prof. U. Copenhagen, 1975-76, 82; researcher in developmental genetics, somatic effects of radiation. Editor: Genetics and Evolution, 1961. Served to capt. USAAF, 1942-46. Recipient Gairdner Found. Internat. award, 1987, Wolf Found. prize in medicine, 1989, Rosenstiel award, 1990, Nat. Medal of Sci. NSF, 1990, Albert Lasker Basic Med. Rsch. award, 1991, Louisa Gross Horowitz prize Columbia U., 1992, Nobel Prize in Medicine, 1995. Fellow AAAS; mem. NAS, Genetics Soc. Am. (sec. 1962-64, pres. 1967-69, Thomas Hunt Morgan medal), Am. Acad. Arts and Scis., Royal Soc. (London) (fgn. mem.), Am. Philos. Soc., Genetical Soc. Great Britain (hon.). Home: 805 Winthrop Rd San Marino CA 91108-1709 Office: Calif Inst Tech Div Biology 1201 E California Blvd Pasadena CA 91125-0001

LEWIS, EDWIN REYNOLDS, biomedical engineering educator; b. Los Angeles, July 14, 1934; s. Edwin McMurtry and Sally Newman (Reynolds) L.; m. Elizabeth Louise McLean, June 11, 1960; children: Edwin McLean, Sarah Elizabeth. AB in Biol. Sci., Stanford U., 1956, MSEE, 1957, Engr., 1959, PhD in Elec. Engring., 1962. With research staff Librascope div. Gen. Precision Inc., Glendale, Calif., 1961-67; mem. faculty dept. elec. engring. and computer sci. U. Calif., Berkeley, 1967—, dir. bioengring. tng. program, 1969-77, prof. elec. engring. and computer sci., 1971-94, prof. grad. sch., 1994—, assoc. dean grad. div., 1977-82, assoc. dean interdisciplinary studies coll. engring., 1988-96; chair joint program bioengring. U. Calif., Berkeley and San Francisco, 1988-91. Author: Network Models in Population Biology, 1977, (with others) Neural Modeling, 1977, The Vertebrate Inner Ear, 1985, Introduction to Bioengineering, 1996; contbr. articles to profl. jours. Grantee NSF, NASA, 1984, 87, Office Naval Rsch., 1990-93, NIH, 1975—; Neurosci. Rsch. Program fellow, 1966, 69; recipient Disting. Tchg. citation U. Calif., 1972, Berkeley citation, 1997; Jacob Javits Neurosci. investigator NIH, 1984-91. Fellow IEEE, Acoustical Soc. Am.; mem. AAAS, Assn. Rsch. in Otolaryngology, Soc. Neurosci., Toastmasters (area lt. gov. 1966-67), Sigma Xi. Office: Dept Elec Engring & Computer Scis U Calif Berkeley CA 94720

LEWIS, FREDERICK THOMAS, insurance company executive; b. Tacoma, Apr. 1, 1941; s. Arthur Thomas and June Louise (Levenhagen) L.; m. Sarah Carolyn Boyette, Apr. 18, 1971; adopted children: Johanna, Elizabeth, Sarah, Jonathan, Matthew. Student, Concordia Coll., Portland, Oreg., 1959-61, Dominican Coll., San Rafael, Calif., 1967-71. Registered health underwriter. Enroute coord. Trans World Airlines, N.Y.C., 1961-62, 64-66; customer svc. rep. Trans World Airlines, Oakland, Calif., 1966-75; dist. rep. Aid Assn. for Luths., Twin Falls, Idaho, 1975-96, dist. mgr., 1984-88. Vocalist Oakland Symphony Chorus, 1972-75; soloist Magic Valley Chorale, Twin Falls, 1979-83. Cantor Immanuel Luth. Ch., Twin Falls, 1984-98; organizer Theos of Magic Valley, Filer, Idaho, 1984; dir. planned giving/major gifts Concordia U. Found., Portland, 1998—. With U.S. Army, 1962-64. Mem. Nat. Assn. Life Underwriters (tng. coun. fellow 1984, Nat. Quality award, Nat. Sales Achievement award, Health Ins. Quality award 1978-96), So. Idaho Life Underwriters (pres. 1980-81, edn. chmn. 1984-86, nat. local com. mem. 1986-89), So. Idaho Health Underwriters (bd. dirs. 1986-88), Idaho State Assn. Life Underwriters (area v.p. 1988-89, sec. 1989-90, pres.-elect 1990-91, pres. 1991-92, state conv. exhibitor chmn. 1992-94, Bill Rankin Life Underwriter of Yr. award 1993), Idaho Fraternal Congress (ins. counselor 1976, bd. dirs. 1976-85, pres. 1981-82), Lions (local v.p. 1979-81, pres. 1982-83, organizer women's aux. 1983, sec. 1986-87, 92-93, treas. 1993-94, sec.-treas. multiple dist. 39 1994-95, vice-dist. gov. 39W 1995-96, dist. gov. 39W 1996-97). Republican. Avocations: ceramics, numismatics, gardening, music. Home and Office: 1612 Targhee Dr Twin Falls ID 83301-3546

LEWIS, GERALD JORGENSEN, judge; b. Perth Amboy, N.J., Sept. 9, 1933; s. Norman Francis and Blanche M. (Jorgensen) L.; m. Laura Susan McDonald, Dec. 15, 1973; children by previous marriage: Michael, Marc. AB magna cum laude, Tufts Coll., 1954; JD, Harvard U., 1957. Bar: D.C. 1957, N.J. 1961, Calif. 1962, U.S. Supreme Ct. 1968. Atty. Gen. Atomic, LaJolla, Calif., 1961-63; ptnr. Haskins, Lewis, Nugent & Newnham, San Diego, 1963-77; judge Mcpl. Ct., El Cajon, Calif., 1977-79; judge Superior Ct., San Diego, 1979-84; assoc. justice, Calif. Ct. of Appeal, San Diego, 1984-87; dir. Fisher Scientific Group, Inc., 1987-98, Bolsa Chica Corp., 1991-93, Gen. Chem. Group, Inc., 1996—; of counsel Latham & Watkins, 1987-97; dir. Wheelabrator Techs., Inc., 1987-93, Henley Mfg., Inc., 1987-89; adj. prof. evidence Western State U. Sch. Law, San Diego, 1977-85, exec. bd., 1977-89; faculty San Diego Inn of Ct., 1979—, Am. Inn of Ct., 1984—. Cons. editor: California Civil Jury Instructions, 1984. City atty. Del Mar, Calif., 1963-74, Coronado, Calif., 1972-77; counsel Comprehensive Planning Orgn., San Diego, 1972-73; trustee San Diego Mus. Art., 1986-89; bd. dirs. Air Pollution Control Dist., San Diego County, 1972-76. Served to lt. comdr. USNR, 1957-61. Named Trial Judge of Yr., San Diego Trial Lawyers Assn., 1984. Mem. Am. Judicature Soc., Soc. Inns of Ct. in Calif., Confrerie des Chevaliers du Tastevin, Order of St. Hubert (knight comdr.), Friendly Sons of St. Patrick, The Irish 50 Aztec Big 50, Bohemian Club, La Jolla Country Club (dir. 1980-83), Prophets, The K Club (County Kildare). Republican. Episcopalian. Home: 6505 Caminito Blythefield La Jolla CA 92037-5806 Office: Latham & Watkins 701 B St Ste 2100 San Diego CA 92101-8197

LEWIS, GREGORY WILLIAMS, scientist; b. Seattle, Mar. 3, 1940; s. Delbert Srofe and Eileen Julianne (Williams) L.; m. Stephanie Marie Schwab, Sept. 18, 1966; children: Jeffrey Williams, Garrick Peterson. BS, Wash. State U., 1962, MA, 1965, PhD, 1970. Tchr., rsch. asst. Wash. State U., Pullman, 1965-69; prin. investigator U.S. Army Med. Rsch. Lab., Ft. Knox, Ky., 1970-74; prin. investigator USN Pers. R & D Ctr., San Diego, 1974—, head neurosci. lab., 1980-95, leader security sys., 1981-83, head neurosci. projects office, 1987-89, divsn. head neuroscis., 1989-95, sr. prin. scientist, 1995—; cons. in field. Contbr. articles to profl. jours. Bd. dirs., pres. Mesa View Homeowners Assn., Calif., 1980-82; bd. dirs. Santa Fe Homeowners Assn., Calif., 1994-96. Capt. U.S. Army, 1967-74. Fellow Internat. Orgn. Psychophysiology; mem. AAAS, Soc. Neurosci., Internat. Brain Rsch. Orgn., N.Y. Acad. Scis., Soc. Psychophysiol. Rsch., Sigma Xi, Alpha Kappa Delta, Delta Chi, Psi Chi. Achievements include research in ophthalmic ultrasonography, neuroelectric research and development of brain activity and variability for improving the evaluation of education and training materials, personnel assessment, and prediction of job performance; physiological correlates of performance; psychophysiology of individual differences; neuromagnetic research directed toward individual differences and personnel performance; neuroelectric and neuromagnetic data acquisition and analysis; patent for development of neuroelectric and neuromagnetic method and system for individual identification and impairment of function using artificial neural network analyses; patent pending for development of neuroelectric and neuromagnetic method and system to objectively evaluate an individual's interest level in education, training, and other materials; developing personnel performance models for use in preliminary design and rapid prototyping of ship systems. Avocations: music, electronics, working on timber land and vacation log home. Home: 410 Santa Cecelia Solana Beach CA 92075-1505 Office: USN Pers R&D Ctr 53335 Ryne Rd San Diego CA 92152-7250

LEWIS, JASON ALVERT, JR., communications executive; b. Clarksville, Tex., Aug. 17, 1941; s. Jason Allen and Mary (Dinwiddie) L. Student, Stockton Coll., 1959-60, San Jose Jr. Coll., 1962-63. Field engr. telephone tech. Pacific Bell, San Francisco, 1983-84; systems technician AT&T, San Francisco, 1984—. Patentee in field. With U.S. Army, 1964-66. Mem. Internat. Platform Assn., Cousteau Soc., Astron. Soc. Pacific, San Francisco Zool. Soc., Planetary Soc., U.S. Naval Inst. Democrat. Avocations: photography, astronomy. Home: 139 Pecks Ln South San Francisco CA 94080-1744

LEWIS, JOHN CHRISTOPHER, allergist; b. Boston, Oct. 15, 1950. MD, Loyola U., Maywood, 1982. Asst. prof. medicine Mayo Med. Sch., Scottsdale, Ariz., Scottsdale Meml. Hosp. North/Mayo Clinic Hosp. Office: Mayo Clinic Scottsdale 13400 E Shea Blvd Scottsdale AZ 85259-5499

LEWIS, JOHN CLARK, JR., manufacturing company executive; b. Livingston, Mont., Oct. 15, 1935; s. John Clark and Louise A. (Anderson) L.; m. Carolyn Jean Keesling, Sept. 4, 1960; children: Robert, Anne, James. BS, Fresno (Calif.) State U., 1957. With Service Bur. Corp., El Segundo, Calif., 1960-70, Computer Scis. Corp., 1970; with Xerox Corp., El Segundo, 1970-77, pres. bus. systems div., 1977; pres. Amdahl Corp., Sunnyvale, Calif., 1983-87, CEO, 1983, chmn., 1987—. Served with USNR, 1957-60. Roman Catholic. Office: Amdahl Corp 1250 E Arques Ave Sunnyvale CA 94086-4730

LEWIS, JOHN WILSON, political science educator; b. King County, Wash., Nov. 16, 1930; s. Albert Lloyd and Clara (Lewis) Seeman; m. Jacquelyn Clark, June 19, 1954; children: Cynthia, Stephen, Amy. Student, Deep Springs Coll., 1947-49; AB with highest honors, UCLA, 1953, MA, 1958, PhD, 1962; hon. degree, Morningside Coll., 1969, Lawrence U., 1986, Russian Acad. Sci., 1996. Asst. prof. govt. Cornell U., 1961-64, assoc. prof., 1964-68, Asst. prof. govt., 1961-64; prof. polit. sci. Stanford U., 1968-97, William Haas prof. Chinese politics, 1972-97, William Haas prof. emeritus, 1997—, co-dir. arms control and disarmament program, 1971-83, co-dir. NE Asia U.S. Forum on Internat. Policy, 1980-90, co-dir. Ctr. for Internat. Security and Arms Control, 1983-91, sr. fellow, 1991—, dir. Project on Peace and Cooperation in the Asian-Pacific Region; chmn. Internat. Strategic Inst., 1983-89; chmn. joint com. on contemporary China Social Sci. Rsch. Coun.-Am. Coun. Learned Socs., 1976-79; mng. dir. Generation Ventures, 1994—; former vice chmn., bd. dirs. Nat. Com. on U.S.-China Rels.; cons. Senate Select Com. on Intelligence, 1977-81, Los Alamos Nat. Lab., 1987-92, Lawrence Livermore Nat. Lab., Dept. of Def., 1994-96; mem. Def. Policy Bd., 1994-96; chmn. com. advanced study in China Com. Scholarly Comm. with People's Republic of China, 1979-82; mem. com. on internat. security and arms control Nat. acad. Scis., 1980-83; organizer first univ. discussion arms control and internat. security matters Chinese People's Inst. Fgn. Affairs, 1978, first academic exch. agreement Dem. People's Repb. of Korea, 1988; negotiator first univ. tng. and exch. agreement People's Rep. of China, 1978. Author: Leadership in Communist China, 1963, Major Doctrines of Communist China, 1964, Policy Networks and the Chinese Policy Process, 1986; co-author: The United States in Vietnam, 1967, Modernization by Design, 1969, China Builds the Bomb, 1988, Uncertain Partners: Stalin, Mao, and the Korean War, 1993, China's Strategic Seapower: The Politics of Force Modernization in the Nuclear Era, 1994; editor: The City in Communist China, 1971, Party Leadership and Revolutionary Power in China, 1970, Peasant Rebellion and Communist Revolution in Asia, 1974; contbr.: Congress and Arms Control, 1978, China's Quest for Independence, 1979, others; mem. editl. bd. Chinese Law and Govt., China Quar., The Pacific Rev. Served with USN, 1954-57. Mem. Assn. Asian Studies, Am. Polit. Sci. Assn., Coun. Fgn. Rels. Home: 541 San Juan St Stanford CA 94305-8432 Office: Stanford U Encina Hall Stanford CA 94305-6105

LEWIS, KEITH ALLEN, artist; b. Bellefonte, Pa., Sept. 1, 1959; s. Donald Allen and Frances Irene (Parnay) L.; life ptnr: Paul Boutin. BS in Chemistry, Dickinson Coll., 1981; MFA in Jewelry/Metals, Kent State U., 1993. Analytical chemist Rhône-Poulenc Rorer, Lewes, Del., 1984-90; lectr. art U. Wash., Seattle, 1993-94; asst. prof. art Ctrl. Wash. U., Ellensburg, 1994—; chair adv. bd. Metalsmith Mag., 1996-99. Works exhibited at Akron (Ohio) Art Mus., 1993-94, Craft Coun., London, 1996, Tacoma Art Mus., 1998; represented by Susan Cummins Gallery, Mill Valley, Calif. Activist Del. Lesbian & Gay Health Advocates, Wilmington, 1984-90; co-founder ACT-UP: Del., 1990. Mem. Soc. N.Am. Goldsmiths, Seattle Metals Guild. Democrat. Office: Ctrl Wash U Dept Art Ellensburg WA 98926

LEWIS, LORENA IONA, elementary guidance counselor, educator; b. Shiprock, N.Mex., Oct. 14, 1954; d. John and Iona (Chiscilly) L.; m. Dennis Martine, Aug. 11, 1976 (div. May 1997); children: Rendessa Martine, Omar Martine. BS in Elem. Edn., Eastern N.Mex. U., 1978, M in Spl. Edn., 1979; MA in Counselor Edn., Western N.Mex. U., 1996. Elem. spl. edn. tchr. Gallup-McKinley County Schs., Ramah, N.Mex., 1980-84, 1st grade tchr., 1984-87; 2d grade tchr. Gallup-McKinley County Schs., Tohatchi, N.Mex., 1989-91, elem. guidance counselor, 1991-98. Drug Free Schs. grantee Gallup-McKinley County Schs., 1993. Mem. N.Mex. Counseling Assn. Democrat. Mem. Native Am. Ch. Avocations: canning fruits, gardening, sewing, baking, hiking. Home: PO Box 1328 Tohatchi NM 87325-1328 Office: Gallup-McKinley County Schs Dist PO Box 1318 Gallup NM 87305-1318

LEWIS, LOUISE MILLER, gallery director, art history educator; b. St. Louis, Dec. 4, 1940; d. Hugh Milton and Jeanne (Vical) Miller; m. Guy R. Lewis, Nov. 26, 1966; 1 child, Kevin. BA with distinction, 1963; cert. practique de la langue Francaise, U. Paris, 1963; MA in French, U. N.Mex., 1966, MA in Art History, 1972. Curator Art Mus. U. N.Mex., Albuquerque, 1966-70, asst. dir., 1970-72, acctg. dir., 1970, 71-72; assoc. dir. Art Gallery Calif. State U., Northridge, 1972-80, dir., 1980—; asst. prof. art history/recent art of internat. origins Calif. State U., 1972-79, assoc. prof., 1979-83, prof., 1983—, v.p. faculty, 1990-92, pres. faculty, 1992-94. Mem. Phi Beta Kappa. Office: Calif State U 18111 Nordhoff St Northridge CA 91330-0001*

LEWIS, MARION ELIZABETH, social worker; b. Los Alamos, Calif., Dec. 7, 1920; d. James Henry and Carolina Sophia (Niemann) Eddy; m. William Ernest Lewis, May 30, 1943 (dec. Oct. 1954); children: Doris Lenita, Paul William. Student, Jr. Coll., Santa Maria, Calif., 1939-40, Bus. Coll., Santa Barbara, Calif., 1940-41, Alan Hancock Coll., 1958-61; BA in Sociology cum laude, Westminster Coll., Salt Lake City, 1964. Office clk. Met. Life Ins. Co., Santa Barbara, 1942-43; sales clk. Sprouse Reitz Co., Laguna Beach, Calif., 1943-44; office clk. U.S. Army, Santa Maria AFB, 1944-45; sch. crossing guard Calif. Hwy. Patrol, Los Alamos, 1956-58; office clk. Holaday Children's Ctr., Salt Lake City, 1964; social worker Sonoma County Social Svc., Santa Rosa, Calif., 1964-78, ret., 1978; sales rep. Avon Products, Los Alamos, 1957-61; sales clk. Gen. Store, Los Alamos, 1957-59; office clk. Sonoma County Pub. Health Dept., 1979-80. Deacon Presbyn. Ch., 1956—, moderator Presbyn. Women, First Presbyn. Ch., Santa Rosa, Calif., 1990-91, vice moderator, 1989-90, sem. rep., 1978-80, 92-94. Mem. AAUW, R.I. Geneal. Soc., Sonoma County Geneal. Soc., Calif. Automobile Assn., Nat. Geographic Soc., Sonoma County Assn. Ret. Employees, Sequoia Club, Westminster Coll. Alumni Assn., Alpha Chi. Democrat. Avocations: hiking, travel, gardening, crafts, genealogical research. Home: 61 Sequoia Cir Santa Rosa CA 95401-4992

LEWIS, MARK EARLDON, city manager; b. Boston, June 27, 1951; s Frederick Cole Lewis and Barbara (Forsyth) Corrigan; m. Kristine Mietzner, May 1, 1983; children: Anna Kristine, Benjamin Mark. BA, Washington State U., 1975; BS, We. State U., 1993, JD, 1995. Bar: Calif. 1996. Adminstrv. asst. City and Borough of Juneau, Alaska, 1975-77; city mgr. City of Valdez, Alaska, 1978-82; commr. State of Alaska Dept. of Community and REgional Affairs, Juneau, 1982-83; dep. city mgr. City of South San Francisco, Calif., 1984-87, city mgr., 1987-88; city mgr. City of Monterey Park, Calif., 1988-91, City of Colton, Calif., 1991-93, Union City, 1995—. Dir. Monterey Park Boys' and Girls' Club, 1990; vice chmn. allocation team United Way, 1990, area group chmn. 1989-90; exec. com. mem. Calif., colo., Ariz. and Nev. Innovation Group, 1987. Mem. State Bar Calif., Calif. City. Mgrs. Assn. (exec. com. 1996). Avocation: sailing. Home: 4350 Coventry Ct Union City CA 94587-5900 Office: 34009 Alvarado Niles Rd Union City CA 94587-4452

LEWIS, MARK RICHARD, aerospace engineer, educator; b. Spokane, Feb. 4, 1962; s. Robert Mead and Patricia Ruby Jane (Gation) L. *One must acknowledge the role of Mark Lewis' parents, Robert Lewis, BA University of Washington 1974, and Patricia Lewis, BA University of Washington 1974. Through their courage and achievement, they inspired Mark and his sister Professor Laurie Lewis, Ph.D., laying an essential foundation for all.* AA, Highline Coll., 1982; BS, U. Wash., 1986, MS, 1991. Performance engr. Boeing Aerospace, Seattle, 1987-88; assoc. U. Wash., Seattle, 1991-92; adj. prof. Bellevue (Wash.) Coll., 1994-95; sr. propulsion engr. Boeing Comml. Airplane Group, 1996—; adj. prof. Shoreline (Wash.) Coll., 1992, Highline (Wash.) Coll., 1993. *Mark Lewis has recently been involved in computational fluid dynamic analysis of axisymetric nozzle configurations for a nacelle aerodynamics group at Boeing. He has also done research that resulted in AIAA paper 96-0850 "Aerodynamic Testing for HSCT: A Shock Tube Design Study". Mark also has an intense interest in teaching, and has taught courses in Dynamics, Mechanics of Materials, and Statics.* Mem. AIAA, Seattle Profl. Engring. Employees Assn., Golden Key, Tau Beta Pi Assn., Phi Theta Kappa. Democrat. Avocations: weight, lifting. Office: Propulsion Sys Divsn BCAG PO Box 3707 Seattle WA 98124-2207

LEWIS, MARY JANE, communication specialist, video producer, writer; b. Kansas City, Mo., July 22, 1950; d. J.W. Jr. and Hilda (Miller) L. BA, Stephens Coll., Columbia, Mo., 1971; MA, NYU, 1984, PhD, 1996. Cert. video prodr. Olelo: The Corp. for Cmty. TV, Honolulu. Office mgr. Crazy Shirts, Inc., Honolulu, 1974-79; creator Exotic Exports, Honolulu, 1979-80; asst. buyer Bloomingdale's, N.Y.C., 1980-82, office mgr., media dir. Andiamo, Inc., N.Y.C., 1982-85; freelance stylist Condé Nast, Inc., N.Y.C., 1985-86; lectr. U. Hawaii, Honolulu, 1988; tchg. fellow NYU, 1989-90, adj. prof., 1990-92; lectr. U. Hawaii, Kapiolani C.C., Honolulu, 1992-97, U. Hawaii, Honolulu C.C., 1994-97; adj. faculty Fashion Inst. Tech., N.Y.C., 1983; lectr. U. Hawaii, adult edn. programs, 1986—; lectr. NYU Sch. Continuing Edn., 1991-94; video stylist, asst. prodr. State of Hawaii Dept. Edn., Honolulu, 1994—, Kapiolani C.C.; creator adult edn. comm. courses; video prodr., dir. Office of the Mayor, City & County of Honolulu, U. Hawaii Svc. Learning Program, 1998. Author: Careers in Fashion Manual, 1994; (TV/movie scripts) The Last Rose of Summer, 1992, The Mustard Seed, 1997. Mem. AAUW, NEA, Women in Comm., Film and Video Assn. Hawaii, The Fashion Group Internat., Inc., U. Hawaii Profl. Assn., Cmty. TV Prodrs. Assn. State of Hawaii, U. Hawaii Women's Campus Club, Honolulu Acad. Arts, NYU Alumni Assn., Kappa Alpha Theta (pres. pledge class 1968—). Avocations: psychic tarot readings, harpsicord, sailing, gardening, cats. E-mail: mary.lewisphd@gte.net. Home: 91-513 B Hapalua St Ewa Beach HI 96706-2929

LEWIS, NANCY PATRICIA, speech and language pathologist; b. Miami, Fla., Sept. 23, 1956; d. James and Sara (Gilman) L. BS, U. Fla., 1978; MS, U. Ariz., 1980. Postgrad. fellow U. Tex. Med. Br., Galveston, 1979-80, speech lang. pathologist, 1980-81; speech lang. pathologist Albuquerque Pub. Schs., 1982-84; child devel. specialist Albuquerque Spl. Presch., 1984—; pvt. practice speech-lang. pathology Albuquerque, 1985—; coord. Project Ta-kos, 1987—; artist Trash Warrior wearable art; instr. Express Ability in movement, 1992—; linguistic cons. Adaptive Learning Tech., Inc., 1997—; spkr. in field. Author (dianostic procedure) Khan-Lewis Phonological Analysis, 1986; (therapeutic materials) Familiar Objects and Actions, 1985. Labor coord. Lama Found., San Cristobal, 1988, fundraiser, 1988-91, speech pathology cons., 1990—, bd. dirs., 1990—; bd. dirs. Vol. for Outdoors, Albuquerque, 1984—; cmty. vol. mediator N.Mex. Ctr. for Dispute Resolution, 1993—; cons. Robert Wood Johnson Found. City of Santa Fe Carino Children's Project, 1993—; developer, instr. Conflict Resolution Curriculum, 1993—. Fellow U. Tex. Med. Br., Galveston, 1981. Mem. Am. Speech Lang. and Hearing Assn., N.Mex. Speech Lang. and Hearing Assn. Democrat. Avocations: swimming, hiking, camping, hot springs, peace.

LEWIS, NORMAN, retired English language educator, writer; b. N.Y.C., Dec. 30, 1912; s. Herman and Deborah (Nevins) L.; m. Mary Goldstein, July 28, 1934; children—Margery, Debra. B.A., CUNY, 1939; M.A., Columbia U., 1941. Instr., lectr CUNY, N.Y.C., 1943-52; assoc. prof. English NYU, N.Y.C., 1955-64; instr. Compton Coll., Calif., summers 1962-64, UCLA, 1962-69; prof. English Rio Hondo Coll., Whittier, Calif., 1964-91, chmn. communications dept., 1964-75. Author: (with others) Journeys Through Wordland, 1941, Lessons in Vocabulary and Spelling, 1941, (with Wilfred Funk) Thirty Days to a More Powerful Vocabulary, 1942, rev. edit., 1970, Power with Words, 1943, How to Read Better and Faster, 1944, rev. edit., 1978, The Lewis English Refresher and Vocabulary Builder, 1945, How to Speak Better English, 1948, Word Power Made Easy, 1949, rev. edit., 1978, The Rapid Vocabulary Builder, 1951, rev. edit., 1980, 3d edit., 1988, How to Get More Out of Your Reading, 1951, Twenty Days to Better Spelling, 1953, The Comprehensive Word Guide, 1958, Dictionary of Correct Spelling, 1962, Correct Spelling Made Easy, 1963, rev. edit. 1987, Dictionary of Modern Pronunciation, 1963, New Guide to Word Power, 1963, The New Power with Words, 1964, Thirty Days to Better English, 1964, The Modern Thesaurus of Synonyms, 1965, RSVP-Reading, Spelling, Vocabulary, Pronunciation (books I-III), 1966, 77, See, Say, and Write! (books I and II), 1973, Instant Spelling Power, 1976, R.S.V.P. for College English Power (books I-III), 1977-79, R.S.V.P. with Etymology (books I and II), 1980-81, Instant Word Power, 1980, New American Dictionary of Good English, 1987; editor: New Roget's Thesaurus of the English Language in Dictionary Form, 1961; also numerous articles in nat. mags.

LEWIS, OLI PAREPA, curator; b. Cleve., Dec. 14, 1958; d. Raymond Joseph and Yarmila Manlet; m. Fred Lewis. BA, U. Las Vegas. Gen. mgr., curator Guinness World Records Mus., Las Vegas, Nev., 1990—; pres. Mus. and Attractions in Nev. Recipient Voluntourism award Nev. Commn. Tourism, 1994. Office: Guinness World Records Mus 2780 Las Vegas Blvd S Las Vegas NV 89109-1102*

LEWIS, R. DAVID, music educator; b. Flint, Mich., Jan. 3, 1943; s. John Grover Lewis and Lucille Rosamund Schippers; m. Mary Victoria Huckelbury, June 20, 1970; children: Mark Edward, John-Paul Tavin. BA, Calif. State U., L.A., 1965, MA, 1967. Cert. C.C. tchr., Calif. Tchr. Montebello (Calif.) Jr. H.S., 1967-70, Alhambra (Calif.) H.S., 1970-76; prof. music Fullerton (Calif.) Coll., 1976—; 1st violinist Peter Britt Festival, Jacksonville, Oreg., 1961-68, San Gabriel (Calif.) Valley Symphony, 1965-72, Fullerton Symphony Piano Quintet, 1995—; mus. dir. Fullerton Symphony, 1979—. Bd. dirs. Pacific Auditorium Found., Fullerton, 1989-95; pres. North Orange County Fine Arts Found., 1996-98. Mem. Am. String Tchrs. Assn., Fullerton Coll. Faculty Assn., Faculty Assn. Calif. C.C.'s, Fullerton Coll. Faculty Senate. Home: PO Box 348 Fullerton CA 92836-0348 Office: Fullerton Coll 321 E Chapman Ave Fullerton CA 92832-2011

LEWIS, RALPH JAY, III, management and human resources educator; b. Balt., Sept. 25, 1942; s. Ralph Jay and Ruth Elizabeth (Schmeltz) L. BS in Engring., Northwestern U., 1966; MS in Adminstrn., U. Calif., Irvine, 1968; PhD in Mgmt., UCLA, 1974. Rsch. analyst Chgo. Area Expressway Surveillance Project, 1963-64, Gen. Am. Transp. Co., Chgo., 1965-66; assoc. prof. mgmt. and human resources mgmt. Calif. State U., Long Beach, 1972—; cons. Rand Corp., Santa Monica, Calif., 1966-74, Air Can., Montreal, Que., 1972-73, Los Angeles Times, 1973;. Co-author: Studies in the Quality of LIfe, 1972; author instructional programs, monographs; co-designer freeway traffic control system. Bd. dirs. Project Quest, Los Angeles, 1969-71. Mem. AAAS, APA, The World Future Soc., Soc. of Mayflower Descendants, SAR (Ill. Soc.), Beta Gamma Sigma. Democrat. Office: Calif State U Dept Human Resources Mgmt Long Beach CA 90840

LEWIS, ROBERT TURNER, retired psychologist; b. Taft, Calif., June 17, 1923; s. D. Arthur and Amy Belle (Turner) L.; m. Jane Badham, Mar. 23, 1946; children: Jane, William, Richard. BA, U. So. Calif., 1947, MA, 1950; PhD, U. Denver, 1952. Chief psychologist Hollywood Presbyn. Hosp., L.A., 1953-58; dir. psychol. svcs. Salvation Army, Pasadena, Calif., 1958-68; dir. Pasadena Psychol. Ctr., 1964-74; successively asst. prof., assoc. prof. and prof., Calif. State U., L.A., 1952-83, prof. emeritus, 1984—; assoc. dir. Cortical Function Lab., L.A., 1972-84; clin. dir. Diagnostic Clinic, West Covina, Calif., 1983-85; dir. Job Stress Clinic, Santa Ana, Calif., 1985-95. Author: Taking Chances, 1979, A New Look at Growing Older, 1995, Money Hangups, 1995; co-author: Money Madness, 1978; Human Behavior, 1974; The Psychology of Abnormal Behavior, 1961. Served to lt. (j.g.) USNR, 1943-46, PTO. Mem. APA, Calif. State Psychol. Assn. Republican.

LEWIS, SHIRLEY JEANE, psychology educator; b. Phoenix, Aug. 23; d. Herman and Leavy (Hutchinson) Smith; AA, Phoenix C.C., 1957; BA, Ariz. State U., 1960; MS, San Diego State U., 1975, MA, 1986; MA, Azusa Pacific U., 1982; PhD, U. So. Calif., 1983. Cert. Tchr., Calif.; m. Edgar Anthony Lewis (div.); children: Edgar Anthony, Roshaun, Lucy Ann Jonathan. Recreation leader Phoenix Parks and Recreation Dept., 1957-62; columnist Ariz. Tribune, Phoenix, 1958-59; tchr. phys. edn. San Diego Unified Schs., 1962—; adult educator San Diego C.Cs., 1973—, instr. psychology, health, Black studies, 1977—, counselor, 1981—; cmty. counselor S.E. Counseling and Cons. Svcs. and Narcotics Prevention and Edn. Systems, Inc., San Diego, 1973-77; counselor educator, counselor edn. dept. San Diego State U., 1974-77; marriage, family, child counselor Counseling and Cons. Ctr., San Diego, 1977—; inservice educator San Diego Unified and San Diego County Sch. Dists., 1973-77; Fulbright Exch. councelor, London, 1994-96, asst. principal Oceanside Unified Sch. Dist., 1997-98; lectr. in field. Girl Scout phys. fitness cons., Phoenix, 1960-62; vol. cmty. tutor for high sch. students, San Diego, 1963; sponsor Tennis Club for Youth, San Diego, 1964-65; troop leader Girl Scouts U.S., Lemon Grove, Calif., 1972-74; vol. counselor USN Alcohol Rehab. Center, San Diego, 1978; mem. sch. coun.'s adv. bd. San Diego State U. Named Woman of Year, Phoenix, 1957, One of Outstanding Women of San Diego, 1980; recipient Phys. Fitness Sch. award and Demonstration Sch. award Pres.'s Coun. on Phys. Fitness, Taft Jr. High Sch., 1975, Excel award Corp. Excellence Edn., 1989; Delta Sigma Theta scholar, 1957-60; Alan Korrick scholar, 1956. Mem. NEA, Calif. Tchrs. Assn., San Diego Tchrs. Assn., Assn. Marriage and Family Counselors, Am. Personnel and Guidance Assn., Calif. Assn. Health, Phys. Edn. and Recreation (v.p. health), Am. Alliance of Health, Phys. Edn. and Recreation, Assn. Black Psychologists (corr. sec. 1993), Assn. African-Am. Educators, Delta Sigma Theta (Delta of Yr. 1987). Democrat. Baptist. Contbr. articles to profl. jours. Home: 1226 Armacost Rd San Diego CA 92114-3307 Office: 2630 B St San Diego CA 92102-1022

LEWIS, WILLIAM JEFFREY, engineering executive; b. Port Hueneme, Calif., Mar. 15, 1962; s. William Sexauer and Patricia (Rogers) L. BS in mech. engring., Okla. State U., 1984; MS in mfg. systems engring., Stanford U., 1987. Cert. engr. in tng., 1984. Hwy. draftsman Okla. Hwy. Dept., Oklahoma City, 1982; summer drilling engr. Exxon Co. USA, Midland, Tex., 1983; weapons/subsystems engr. Gen. Dynamics, Ft. Worth, 1984-87; mfg. engr. Ford Motor Co., Ypsilanti, Mich., 1987; mech. engr., project leader Apple Computers, Inc., Cupertino, Calif., 1988-96; mech. engring. mgr. Cisco Systems, San Jose, Calif., 1996—. Patentee in field. Vol. Big Brothers/Big Sisters, Palo Alto, Calif., 1991-93. Mem. ASME, NSPE. Republican. Roman Catholic. Avocations: swimming, weightlifting, tennis. Home: 707 Continental Cir Apt 1238 Mountain View CA 94040-3382 Office: Cisco Sys 170 W Tasman Dr San Jose CA 95134-1706

LEWIS MILL, BARBARA JEAN, school psychologist, educator; b. Sacramento, Sept. 12, 1959; d. William Vasse and Mary Allene (Bridges) Lewis; m. Thomas Steven Mill, Oct. 17, 1981; 1 child, Thomas William. BA, U. Calif., Davis, 1981; MA, U. Calif., Santa Barbara, 1984. Pupil pers. svcs. credentials; cert. basic and sch. psychologist; cert. behavioral intervention case mgr. Pub. rels. asst. Coll. Agrl. and Environ. Scis., U. Calif., Davis, 1979-81; adminstrv. asst. libr. U. Calif., Santa Barbara, 1981-84; sch. psychologist intern Ventura (Calif.) County Supt. of Schs. Office, 1984-85, sch. psychologist, 1985-91; sch. psychologist Rio Sch. Dist., Oxnard, Calif., 1985, Ojai (Calif.) Sch. Dist., 1991-92, Santa Paula (Calif.) Sch. Dist., 1991—; coord. Primary Intervention Program, Santa Paula (Calif.) Sch. Dist., 1992-94; mem. planning com. Dropout Prevention/Outreach Program, Grace Thille Sch., Santa Paula, 1994. Mem. adv. bd. Pleasant Valley Rainbow Girls, Camarillo, Calif., 1986-89; bd. dirs. Strawberry Patch Presch., Oxnard, 1995-96; v.p. Rose Ave. Sch. PTA, 1997-98; co-pres. Hueneme Swimming Assn., 1998—. Mem. ASCD, Nat. Assn. Sch. Psychologists (nat. cert. sch. psychologist), Internat. Reading Assn., Calif. Assn. Sch. Psychologists (Outstanding Sch. Psychologist region IV 1998), Ventura County Assn. Sch. Psychologists (exec. bd. 1987-91, 93-94, dir. pub. rels. 1991-93, 94-96, pres.-elect 1997-98, pres. 1998—, Outstanding Sch. Psychologist 1989, Meritorious Svc. award 1993), Hueneme Swimming Assn. (co-pres., bd. dirs. 1998—), Order Ea. Star, Rainbow for Girls (life, state officer Grand Scribe 1979). Avocations: parent education and outreach, conservation, creative arts, historical preservation, health and fitness. Home: 935 S L St Oxnard CA 93030-6707

LEWITZKY, BELLA, choreographer; b. Los Angeles, Jan. 13, 1916; d. Joseph and Nina (Ossman) L.; m. Newell Taylor Reynolds, June 22, 1940; 1 child, Nora Elizabeth. Student, San Bernardino Valley (Calif.) Jr. Coll., 1933-34; hon. doctorate, Calif. Inst. Arts, 1981; PhD (hon.), Occidental Coll., 1984, Otis Parsons Coll., 1989, Juilliard Sch., 1993; DFA, Santa Clara U., 1995; DFA (hon.), Calif. State U., Long Beach, 1997. Chmn. dance dept., chmn. adv. panel U. So. Calif., Idyllwild, 1956-74; founder Sch. Dance, Calif. Inst. Arts, 1969, dean, 1969-74; vice chmn. dance adv. panel Nat. Endowment Arts, 1974-77, mem. artists-in-schs. adv. panel, 1974-75; mem. Nat. Adv. Bd. Young Audiences, 1974—, Joint Commn. Dance and Theater Accreditation, 1979; com. mem. Am. chpt. Internat. Dance Coun. of UNESCO, 1974—; trustee Calif. Assn. Dance Cos., 1976—, Idyllwild Sch. Music and Arts, 1986-95, Dance/USA, 1988-95, Calif. State Summer Sch. of Arts, 1988—; cons. the dance project WNET, 1987—. Co-founder, co-dir. Dance Dance Assocs., L.A., 1951-55; founder, 1966; artistic dir. Lewitzky Dance Co., L.A.; choreographer, 1948—; founder, former artistic dir. The Dance Gallery, L.A.; contbr. articles in field; choreographed works include Trio for Saki, 1967, Orrenda, 1969, Kinaesonata, 1971, Pietas, 1971, Ceremony for Three, 1972, Game Plan, 1973, Five, 1974, Spaces Between, 1975, Jigsaw, 1975, Inscape, 1976, Pas de Bach, 1977, Suite Satie, 1980, Changes and Choices, 1981, Confines, 1982, Continuum, 1982, The Song of the Woman, 1983, Nos Duraturi, 1984, 8 Dancers/8 Lights, 1985, Facets, 1986, Impressions #1, 1987, Impressions #3, 1988, Agitime, 1989, Impressions #3, 1989, Episode #1, 1990, Glass Canyons, 1991, Episode #2, 1992, Episode #3, 1992, Episode #4, 1993, Meta 4, 1994, Four Women in Time, 1996. Mem. adv. com. Actors' Fund of Am., 1986—, Women's Bldg. Adv. Council, 1985-91, Calif. Arts Council, 1983-86, City of Los Angeles Task Force on the Arts, 1986—; mem. artistic adv. bd. Interlochen Ctr. for Arts, 1988—. Recipient Mayoral Proclamation, City of L.A., 1976, 1982, ann. award Dance mag., 1978, Dir.'s award Calif. Dance Educators Assn., 1978, Plaudit Award, Nat. Dance Assn., 1979, Labor's Award of Honor for Community Svc., L.A. County AFL-CIO, 1979, L.A. Area Dance Alliance and L.A. Junior C. of C. Honoree, 1980, City of L.A. Resolution, 1980, Distguished Artist Award, City of L.A. and Music Ctr., 1982, Silver Achievement award YWCA, 1982, California State Senate Resolution, 1982, 1984, Award of Recognition, Olympic Black Dance Festival, 1984, Distinguished Women's Award, Northwood Inst., 1984, California State U. Distinguished Artist, 1984, Vesta Award, Woman's Bldg, L.A., 1985, L.A. City Council Honors for Outstanding Contributions, 1985, Woman of the Year, Palm Springs Desert Museum, Women's Committee, 1986, Disting. Svc. award Western Alliance Arts Adminstrs., 1987, Woman of Achievement award, 1988, Am. Dance Guild Ann. award, 1989, So. Calif. Libr. for Social Studies & Rsch. award, 1990, Am. Soc. Journalists & Authors Open Book award, 1990, Internat. Soc. Performing Arts Adminstrs. Tiffany award, 1990, Burning Bush award U. of Judaism, 1991, 1st recipient Calif. Gov.'s award in arts for individual lifetime achievement, 1989; honoree L.A. Arts Coun., 1989, Heritage honoree, Nat. Dance Assn., 1991, Vaslav Nijinsky award, 1991, Hugh M. Hefner First Amendment award, 1991, Artistic Excellence award Ctr. Performing Arts U. Calif., 1992, Lester Horton Lifetime Achievement award Dance Resource Ctr. of L.A., 1992, Occidental Coll. Founders' award, 1992, Dance/USA honor, 1992, Visual Arts Freedom of Expression award Andy Warhol Found., 1993, Artist of Yr. award L.A. County High Sch. Arts, 1993, Freedom of Expression honor Andy Warhol Found. Visual Arts, 1993, Calif. Alliance Edn. award, 1994, Lester Horton Sustained Achievement award, 1995 Dance Resource Ctr. of L.A., Lester Horton award for Restaging and Revival, Dance Resource Ctr. of L.A., 1996, 97, Disting. Artists of 1996, High Sch. of Performing Arts, Houston Tex., Bill of Rights award, Am. Civil Liberties Union of So. Calif., Nat. Medal of Arts, 1996, Gypsy award Profl. Dancers Soc., 1997, Nat. Medal Arts, 1997; grantee Mellon Found., 1975, 81, 86, Guggenheim Found., 1977-78, NEA, 1969-94; honoree Women's Internat. League Peace and Freedom, 1995; presented with Key to the City, Cin., 1997. Mem. Am. Arts Alliance (bd. dirs. 1977), Internat. Dance Alliance (adv. council 1984—), Dance/USA (bd. dirs. 1988), Phi Beta (hon.).

LEY, DAVID CHANPANNHA, secondary education educator; b. Phnom Penh, Cambodia, May 23, 1966; came to U.S., 1988; s. Ley Savun Dom and Samonn Khieu Mao; m. Leakhena Seth Lee, Dec. 25, 1997; 1 child, Kevin Vitou. Cert. in econs., Phnom Penh City Coll., 1987; AA in Math., Lang. Arts, Laney Coll., Oakland, Calif., 1991; BA in Social Welfare, U. Calif., Berkeley, 1993; MA in Edn., Calif. State U., Dominguez Hills Carson, Calif., 1996; postgrad., U. So. Calif. Cert. tchr., Calif. Study group facilitator Laney Coll. Transfer Ctr., Oakland, 1989-93; tchr. Whittier Sch., Long Beach Unified Sch. Dist., Calif., 1993-98; asst. prof. Calif. State U., Dominguez Hills, 1998; ESL instr. San Leandro (Calif.) Unified Sch. Dist., 1998—; math. tchr. Carter Mid. Sch., Oakland (Calif.) Unified Sch. Dist., 1998—; student advisor Laney Coll. Info. Dept., Oakland, 1990; counselor, tutor Nat. Hispanic U., Oakland, 1990. Vol. interpreter Phillippines Refugee Ctr., Bataan, The Phillippines, 1987; vol. tutor Roosevelt Jr. High Sch., Oakland, 1993. Odell Wilson scholar U. Calif., Berkeley, 1991-92, E. Armstrong scholar, 1992-93, J. Wrasse scholar, 1992-93, Title VII scholar Calif. State U., Dominguez Hills, 1994—. Mem. Nat. Assn. Edn. Achievement Cambodian, Loation, Vietnames Ams., Calif. Assn. Asian and Pacific Am. Edn., Khmer Educators Orgn., Univ. Calif. Berkeley Alumni Assn. (life, scholarship, cert.), Phi Kappa Phi (life, cert.), Golden Key Nat. Honor Soc. (life, cert.). Avocations: math, football, basketball, romantic movies and

music, writing. Office: Carter Middle Sch Long Beach Unified Sch Dist 4521 Webster St Oakland CA 94609

LEYDEN, NORMAN, conductor; m. Alice Leyden; children: Robert, Constance. Grad., Yale U., 1938; MA, Columbia U., EdD, 1968. Bass clarinetist New Haven Symphony; arranger Glenn Miller Air Force Band, Eng., France; chief arranger Glenn Miller Orch., 1946-49; freelance arranger N.Y.C.; mus. dir. RCA Victor Records, Arthur Godfrey, 1956-59; with Oreg. Symphony, 1970—, assoc. conductor, 1974—, condr.; music dir. Seattle Symphony Pops, 1975-93; tchr. Columbia U.; guest condr. over 40 Am. symphony orchs. including Boston Pops, Minn. Orch., Pitts. Symphony, St. Louis Symphony, San Diego Symphony, San Francisco Symphony, Nat. Symphony, Utah Symphony; condr. Army Air Force. Office: Oreg Symphony Orch 921 SW Washington Ste 200 Portland OR 97205-3415*

LEYLAND, JAMES RICHARD, professional baseball team manager; b. Toledo, Dec. 15, 1944; m. Katie Leyland. Player various minor league teams Detroit Tigers, 1964-69, coach minor league system, 1970-71, mgr. minor league system, 1971-81; coach Chgo. White Sox, 1981-85; mgr. Pitts. Pirates, 1985-96, Fla. Marlins, Miami, 1997-98, Colo. Rockies, Denver, 1998—. Christmas chmn. Salvation Army, 1990-91. Named Nat. League Mgr. of Yr. Baseball Writers' Assn. Am., 1988, 90, Sporting News, 1990, Man of Yr. Arthritis Found., 1989, Epilepsy Found., 1991. Office: Colorado Rockies 2001 Blake St Denver CO 80205-2000*

LEZHAN, ERLENE, artist; d. Stephen Walter Etherton and Florence Ida (Galbraith) L.; 5 children. Piano tchr. Greeley, Colo., 1981-85, art tchr. for handicapped children, 1981-86. Author: Sinners of the Surf, 1992, (manuscript) A New Day, 1981; exhibited Historic Bi-Centennial paintings U. No. Colo., 1976. Recipient Cert. and Flag Union Pacific R.R., 1976. Mem. Nat. Soc. Lit. and the Arts. Home: 1240 28th Ave Apt 1C Greeley CO 80631-3442

LI, CHIAYANG, environmental engineer; b. Taipei, Taiwan, Rep. of China, May 11, 1963; came to the U.S., 1988; s. Kao-Kon and Chin-Chi (Hsu) L.; m. Yi-Ju Wu, Dec. 24, 1994. BS in Environ. Sci., Feng-Chia U., 1985; MS in Environ. Engring., Ga. Inst. Tech., 1990. Rsch. asst. Ga. Inst. Tech., Atlanta, 1988-90; environ. engr. Holton and Dycus, Inc., Knoxville, Tenn., 1991-93, Indsl. Compliance, Knoxville, 1993—. Contbr. articles to profl. jours. Mem. Am. Chem. Soc., Am. Water Works Assn. Achievements include research in effect of soil organic carbon on sorption of benzene vapor, retardation factors of benzene and jet fuel vapors in unsaturated soil. Home: 25730 SE 41st Pl Issaquah WA 98029-5732 Address: Indsl Compliance 165 S Union Blvd Ste 1000 Lakewood CO 80228-2214

LI, GRACE CHIA-CHIAN, accountant, business planning manager; b. Taipei, Taiwan, Republic of China, Aug. 7, 1963; came to U.S., 1987; d. Chuan-Chun and Yu-Lin (Hsueh) L.; m. Michael H. Chang, Dec. 21, 1993. BA, Nat. Cheng Chi U., Taipei, 1985; MBA, Wash. U., 1989. CPA, Calif. Acct. Cosa Libermann LTD, Taipei, 1985-86; cost acctg. supr. Johnson & Johnson, Taipei, 1988; planning and control specialist IBM Corp., Taipei, 1986-87; fin. analyst Ameritech Cellular, St. Louis, 1989-92; mgr. market planning Ameritech Internat., Hoffman Estates, Ill., 1992-94; internat. mktg. mgr. Pactel Internat., Walnut Creek, Calif., 1994; bus. cons. Decision Consulting, San Ramon, Calif., 1994-95; bus. planning mgr. Mitsubishi Wireless Comms., Inc., Sunnyvale, Calif., 1995—; guest spkr. on China telecom. industry devel. Nat. Comm. Forum, Chgo., 1993. Mem. NAFE, AICPA, Ill. CPA Soc., Chgo. Com. Fgn. Rels. Avocations: reading, traveling, listening to music. Office: Mitsubishi Wireless Comm Inc 1050 E Arques Ave Sunnyvale CA 94086-4651

LI, HUA HARRY, computer scientist, electrical engineer; b. Tianjin, People's Republic of China, Nov. 22, 1956; came to U.S., 1982; s. Hua Sheng and Bao Ai Li; m. Maiying Lu, Nov. 4, 1982; children: Alen Lee, Kevin Lee. BS in Electronics Engring., Tianjin U., 1982; MSECE, U. Iowa, 1984, PhD in ECE, 1989. Lectr. Tianjin U., 1982; asst. prof. computer sci. Tex. Tech U., Lubbock, 1989-95, assoc. prof. computer sci., 1995-96; prin. engr. 53 Inc., Santa Clara, Calif., 1997; sr. computer architect Smedia Corp., San Jose; computer cons., 1990—; inventor 1994 World Congress Neural Network Conf. Indsl. Neural Network Award; assoc. prof. computer engring. San Jose State U., 1997—. Author, editor: Vision Computing with VLSI Circuits, 1994, Fuzzy Logic and Intelligent Systems, 1995, Video Compression, 1996. Mem. IEEE. Avocations: camping, piano, fishing. Office: San Jose State Univ Computer Sci Dept Computer Engring Dept San Jose CA 95192 Address: 37576 Summer Holly Cmn Fremont CA 94536-6569

LI, LILIA HUIYING, journalist; b. Hunan, China, June 14, 1932; d. Chun-chu and Sol-ran (Chang) L.; m. Ma Luk Son, May 18, 1953 (dec. Feb. 1963); 1 child, Blanche; m. George Oakley Totten III, July 1, 1976; children: Vicken Yuriko, Linnea Catherine. BA, Yenching U., China, 1946; MA (equivalent), U. Hong Kong, 1955. Mng. dir. Oriental Evening News, Hong Kong, Midday News, Hong Kong, Tsuwan Daily News, Hong Kong; gen. mgr. Ch. Guest House, Hong Kong, 1962-68; spl. corr. UN, N.Y.C., 1975; dir. L.A. br. The Mirror Monthly, Hong Kong, 1988—; vis. lectr. East Asian Studies Ctr. U. So. Calif., L.A., 1976, fellow, 1976—; leader delegation of Hong Kong Businesswomen to Conf. on Commerce, Beijing, 1956; speaker First Internat. Women's Conf., Mexico City, 1975; organizer Internat. Women's Year Arts Festival, N.Y.c., 1975-77; invited participant Straits Exch. Found., Taiwan, 1993, ceremonies at Hand Over of Hong Kong to People's Republic of China, 1997; founder, pres. China Seminar-forum for peace across the Taiwan straits, 1985—, a forum for good rels. across the Taiwan straits, 1991—. *The China Seminar is a non-profit, non-governmental peace forum. It promotes discussion among intellectuals and at times officials from either or both sides of the Taiwan Straits for the purpose of solving the relationship in a peaceful manner for the mutual benefit of both sides. It holds six or more forums per year in which speakers of various persuasions present their ideas, followed by discussion with the attendees. Proceedings are usually in Mandarin Chinese. The China Seminar is financed by the President, Lilia Li, and does not accept financial contributions from any official from any government. There are no membership dues.* Author: Unforgettable Journey, 1957, Nine Women and Other Writings, 1959, Li Huiying's Writings, 1979, Sidelights on World Affairs, 1985, Expanded Edition of Collected Writings, 1988; contbr. numerous articles to periodicals. Mem. China Soc. People's Friendship Studies, Beijing; mem. St. John's Episcopal Ch., L.A., L.A.-Guangzhou Sister City Assn. Mem. Asian-Am. Journalists Assn., Assn. for Asian Studies. Republican. Avocations: photography, calligraphy, gardening, flower arrangements, interior decorating. Home and Office: 5129 Village Grn Los Angeles CA 90016-5205

LI, MINGFANG, educator; b. Huang Yuan, Qinghai, China, May 11, 1956; s. Yaowen and Yulan (Dong) L.; m. Xiaohui Qian, May 20, 1983; 1 child, Bing. BE in Mgmt., No. U. Tech., Beijing, China, 1982; MBA, Appalachian State U., Boone, N.C., 1985; PhD, Va. Tech., 1990. Assoc. prof. Calif. State U., Northridge, 1990—. Office: Calif State U Northridge 18111 Nordhoff St Northridge CA 91330-0001

LI, YONGHUI ROGER, engineer; b. Hefei, China, July 3, 1963; came to U.S., 1991; s. Fukun Li and Keling Zhang. BS with honors, Tongji U., Shanghai, 1985, M of Engring., 1988; MSc, Syracuse U., 1993; PhD, U. Tex., 1996. Rsch. engr. Tongji U., 1988-89; asst. prof. Anhui (China) Archtl. Engring. Inst., 1989-91; tchg. asst. Syracuse U., 1991-93; rsch. asst. U. Tex., Austin, 1993-96; engr. Englekirk & Sabol, Inc., L.A., 1996—. Contbr. articles to profl. jours. Participant Applied Tech. Coun., Redwood City, Calif., 1997. Mem. ASCE, Earthquake Engring. Rsch. Inst., Structural Engrs. Assn. So. Calif. Avocations: sports, travel. Home: 823 S Chapel Ave Apt 23 Alhambra CA 91801-4427 Office: Englekirk and Sabol Consulting Engrs 2116 Arlington Ave Los Angeles CA 90018-1353

LIANG, LANBO See LEONG, LAM-PO

LIAO, JAMES C., chemical engineering educator; b. Kaoshiung, Taiwan, Sept. 22, 1958; s. Shu-Nan and Pi-cheng (Chen) L.; m. Kelly C. Chen, Sept. 15, 1986; children: Carol, Clara. BSChemE, Nat. Taiwan U., 1980; PhD in Chem. Engring., U. Wis., 1987. Rsch. scientist Eastman Kodak Co., Rochester, N.Y., 1987-89; asst. prof. Tex. A&M U., College Station, 1990-93, assoc. prof., 1993-97; prof. UCLA, 1997—. Named Presdl. Young Investigator, NSF, 1992. Mem. AIChE, Am. Chem. Soc. Office: Dept Chem Engring UCLA Los Angeles CA 90095-1592

LICCARDO, SALVADOR A., lawyer; b. San Francisco, Mar. 15, 1935; s. Samuel and Rosalie (Pizzo) L.; m. Laura Liccardo, Nov. 21, 1959; children—Laura, Kathleen, Paul, Rosalie, Sam. B.A., U. Santa Clara, 1956, J.D., 1961. Bar: Calif. 1962, U.S. Ct. Appeals (9th cir.) 1962, U.S. Supreme Ct. 1966. Sole practice law, San Jose, Calif., 1962-65; ptnr. Caputo & Liccardo, San Jose, 1965-76; pres./officer Caputo, Liccardo, Rossi & Sturges, P.C., San Jose, 1976-82; pres. Caputo, Liccardo, Rossi, Sturges & McNeil, P.C., San Jose, 1982—; mem. Santa Clara County Joint Com. of Bench and Bar on Ct. Reorgn.; lectr. in field. Editor-in-chief Jour. Calif. Trial Lawyers Assn., 1981. Contbr. articles to profl. jours. Founder, bd. dirs., officer Trial Lawyers for Pub. Justice, Washington, 1983—, pres. 1989-90 ; pres. bd. regents Bellermine Prep. Coll., San Jose, 1982—; mem. bd. fellows U. Santa Clara. Served to 1st lt. U.S. Army, 1956-58. Recipient Cert. of Appreciation for Service as Judge Pro Tem Santa Clara County Superior Ct., 1982-84; Michael Shallo award in polit. sci. U. Santa Clara, 1956, Silver medal for outstanding student, 1956. Fellow Internat. Acad. Trial Lawyers; mem. Inner Circle of Advocates, Am. Bd. Trial Advocates, Assn. Trial Lawyers of Am., ABA, Calif. Trial Lawyers Assn. (bd. dirs. 1976-82, 87—), Am. Bd. Profl. Liability Attys. Democrat. Roman Catholic. Club: Civic. Office: Caputo Liccardo Rossi Sturges & McNeil 1960 The Alameda Fl 2D San Jose CA 95126-1441

LICENS, LILA LOUISE, administrative assistant; b. Puyallup, Wash., Feb. 18, 1949; d. C.L. and Joan L. (Rubert) Vormestrand. Cert., Knapp Bus. Coll., 1968. Cert. profl. sec. Adminstrv. asst. Weyerhaeuser Co., Tacoma, 1968-93, adminstrv. asst. bleached paperboard, 1993—. Mem. adv. bd. Bates Tech. Coll., 1994—. Mem. Internat. Assn. Adminstrv. Profls. (pres. Mt. Rainier chpt. 1994—, pres. Wash.-Alaska divsn. 1990-91, pres.-elect 1989-90, sec. 1987-89, pres. Sea-Tac chpt. 1985-87), Fed. Way Women's Network (treas. 1988, sec. 1989, pres. 1995, 96). Avocations: travel, photography, reading. Home: 771 108th St S Tacoma WA 98444-5666

LICHTENBERG, LARRY RAY, chemist, consultant, researcher; b. Marceline, Mo., July 25, 1938; s. Kenneth Ray and Evelyn (Lauck) L.; m. Clarice Elaine Dameron, Dec. 23, 1961; children: Julia-Isabel Dameron. BS in Chemistry, Northeast Mo. State U., 1962. Chemist Bell & Howell, Chgo., 1962-62; jr. chem. engr. Magnavox Corp., Urbana, Ill., 1963-64; process engr. Gen. Electric Co., Bloomington, Ill., 1964-70; mfg. engr. Burr-Brown, Tucson, 1970-72; sr. staff engr. Process Optimization Specialists, Scottsdale, Ariz., 1972—; mem. corp. tech. council Motorola, Scottsdale, 1982-98, process optimization specialists cons. Contbr. articles to profl. jours. Mem. Am. Chem. Soc., Internat. Soc. Hybrid Microelectronics (pres. Phoenix chpt. 1981-82). Republican. Baptist. Avocations: photography, sailing, amateur radio. Office: Process Optimization Specialists 9708 W Chino Dr Peoria AZ 85382

LIDMAN, ROGER WAYNE, museum director; b. June 8, 1956; s. Arthur Arvid and Elna G. (Bernson) L.; m. Cynthia Louise Platt, May 26, 1988. BA in Anthropology, Ariz. State U., 1987, postgrad. studies, 1987-91. Mus. aide Pueblo Grande Mus., Phoenix, 1976-84, exhibit preparator, 1984-86, ops. coord., 1986-89, acting dir., 1989-90, dir., 1990—; chair Ariz. Archaeol. Adv. Commn., 1998. Recipient Outstanding Personal Svc. award Mus. Assn. Ariz., 1998. Mem. Am. Assn. Mus. (officer small mus. adminstr. com. 1993-94, treas. 1994-96), Mus. Assn. Ariz. (v.p. 1994-95, pres. 1995-96), Ctrl. Ariz. Mus. Assn. (v.p. 1992, pres. 1993-94, 95-96), Papago Salado Assn. (treas. 1996-99), Western Mus. Assn. (at-large mem. 1998—). Avocations: scuba diving, golf, natural history. Office: Pueblo Grande Mus 4619 E Washington St Phoenix AZ 85034-1909

LIDSTONE, HERRICK KENLEY, JR., lawyer; b. New Rochelle, N.Y., Sept. 10, 1949; s. Herrick Kenley and Marcia Edith (Drake) L.; m. Mary Lynne O'Toole, Aug. 5, 1978; children: Herrick Kevin, James Patrick, John Francis. AB, Cornell U., 1971; JD, U. Colo., 1978. Bar: Colo. 1978, U.S. Dist. Ct. Colo. 1978. Assoc. Roath & Brega, P.C., Denver, 1978-85, Brenman, Epstein, Raskin & Friedlob, P.C., Denver, 1985-86; shareholder Brenman, Raskin & Friedlob, P.C., Denver, 1986-94; mem. Friedlob Sanderson Raskin Paulson & Tourtilott, LLC, Denver, 1995-98, Norton Lidstone, LLC, Englewood, Colo., 1998—; adj. prof. U. Denver Coll. Law, 1985—; speaker in field various orgns.; fluent in Spanish. Editor U. Colo. Law Rev., 1977-78; co-author: Federal Income Taxation of Corporations, 6th edit.; contbg. author: Legal Opinion Letters Formbook, 1996; contbr. articles to profl. jours. Served with USN, 1971-75, with USNR, 1975-81. Mem. ABA (Am. Law Inst.), Colo. Bar Assn., Denver Bar Assn., Denver Assn. Oil and Gas Title Lawyers. Office: Norton Lidstone LLC 5445 Dtc Pkwy Ste 850 Englewood CO 80111-3076

LIE, YU-CHUN DONALD, electrical engineer; b. Taipei, Taiwan, Apr. 25, 1965; came to U.S., 1989; s. Kuo-Chin and Shu-Ling (Kung) L.; m. Ching-Wen Wendy Yang, Aug. 26, 1995; 1 child, Paul Emmanuel. BSc, Nat. Taiwan U., Taipei, 1987; MSc, Calif. Inst. Tech., 1990, DPhil, 1995. Cert. engr.-in-tng., Calif. Comm., electronics, rsch. officer Taiwanese Army, 1987-89; head tchg. asst. Calif. Inst. Tech., Pasadena, 1990-95; sr. process devel. engr. Rockwell Semiconductor Sys., Newport Beach, Calif., 1995-97, staff engr., 1997—, intern, 1998—; summer intern Motorola Inc., Phoenix, 1994, Jet Propulsion Lab., Pasadena, Calif., 1993. Contbr. over 20 articles to profl. jours., chpts. to books. Rotary Internat. scholar, Evanston, Ill., 1989-90; recipient Grad. Student award Internat. Union Material Rsch. Soc., 1994, various scholarships and contests. Mem. IEEE. Baptist. Achievements include patents and papers on doping and designing semiconductor devices and materials.

LIEBAU, FREDERIC JACK, JR., investment manager; b. Palo Alto, Calif., Sept. 30, 1963; s. Frederic Jack and Charlene (Conrad) L. BA, Stanford U., 1985. Press aide Office of V.P., Washington, 1982; intern L.A. Times, 1983; analyst Capital Rsch. Co., L.A., 1984-86; ptnr., portfolio mgr. Primecap Mgmt. Co., Pasadena, Calif., 1986—; owner Liebau Farms. Home: 1382 Bedford Rd San Marino CA 91108-2001 Office: Primecap Mgmt Co 225 S Lake Ave Ste 400 Pasadena CA 91101-3093

LIEBHABER, MYRON I., allergist; b. Dec. 28, 1943. MD, U. Ariz., 1972. Allergist Coll. Hosp., Santa Barbara, Calif.; assoc. vis. clin. prof. UCLA. Office: Santa Barbara Med Found Clinic 215 Pesetas Ln Santa Barbara CA 93110-1416

LIGGINS, GEORGE LAWSON, microbiologist, diagnostic company executive; b. Roanoke, Va., June 19, 1937; m. Joyce Preston Liggins, Sept. 3, 1966; 1 child, George Lawson Jr. BA, Hampton U., 1962; cert. med. technician, Meharry Med. Sch., 1963; MPH, U. N.C., 1969; PhD, U. Va., Charlottesville, 1975. Med. technician Vets. Hosp., Hampton, Va., 1963-66; rsch. technician U. N.C. Med. Sch., Chapel Hill, 1966-69; postdoctoral fellow Scripps Clinic, La Jolla, Calif., 1975-76, Salk Inst., La Jolla, 1976-77; rsch. mgr. Hyland div. Baxter, Costa Mesa, Calif., 1977-78; R & D dir. diagnostics div. Baxter, Roundlake, Ill., 1978-83; pres., COO Internat. Immunology, Murrieta, Calif., 1983-86; chmn., CEO Bacton Assay Systems, Inc., San Marcos, Calif., 1986—; cons. Beckman Instruments, Inc., Brea, Calif., 1987-90, Paramax divsn. Baxter, Irvine, Calif., 1988-90, Scantibodies Lab., Santee, Calif., 1990-92; presenter in field; mem. virology study Cold Spring Harbor Lab., L.I., N.Y., 1974. Contbr. articles to profl. jours. Bd. dirs. San Diego Cancer Ctr. Found. U. Calif., Palomar Coll. Found., San Marcos. Fellow NIH, 1975, Am. Cancer Soc., 1976. Mem. Am. Soc. Microbiology, Am. Assn. Clin. Chemistry (chmn. San Diego sect. 1998), Van Slyke Soc. of Am. Assn. Clin. Chemistry (chmn. elect 1997. program chmn. San Diego Conf. Nucleic Acids 1996), Nat. Hampton Alumni Assn. (v.p. 1996—), N.Y. Acad. Scis., Omega Psi Phi. Republican. Methodist. Avocations: music, golf, tennis, literature. Office: Bacton Assay Systems Inc 772 N Twin Oaks Valley Rd San Marcos CA 92069-1714

LIGHT, DOTTY JEAN, artist; b. Garnett, Kans., Mar. 31, 1925; d. Eugene August and Anna Caroline (Katger) Stomp; m. Frankl Michael Light, June 2, 1951; children: Amy Jo, Cecily, Jonathan Lise, Seth, Katie, Megan, Jeremy. RN, St Francis Hosp. Sch. Nursing; student, Wichita State U., U. Colo. Clin. instr. St. Francis Hosp., Wichita, KS, 1946-47; nurse VA Hosps., Wichita, Eugene and Springfield, Oreg.; judge art shows Lane County Fair, Eugene, Bohemia Days, Cottage Grove, Oreg., Applegate Art Show, Veneta, Oreg. Mem. Pastel Soc. Oreg., Emerald Empire Art Assn. (pres. 1972-74, 81, 89, bd. dirs.). Republican. Roman Catholic. Avocations: crafts, sewing, antiques. Home: 3515 Valentine Ct Springfield OR 97477-1849

LIGHTFOOT, GRETCHEN GRAHAM, fundraiser; b. Lafayette, Ind., Dec. 16, 1966; d. Howard Eugene and Rebecca Kay (Goins) Graham; m. John Michael Lightfoot, Aug. 30, 1997. BA, Ind. U., 1991; devel. dir. cert., U. San Francisco, 1997. Devel. assoc. San Francisco Sch. Vols., 1994-95; fundraising coord. Women Defenders, Berkeley, Calif., 1995-96; pub. rels. officer Union Bank of Calif., L.A., 1997; asst. dir. devel. & alumni rels. Viewpoint Sch., Calabasas, Calif., 1997—. Mem. Calabasas C. of C. (edn. com. 1997—), Woodland Hills C. of C. (edn. com. 1997—), Devel. Exec. Roundtable, Pub. Communicators of L.A., Calif. Attys. for Criminal Justice. Democrat. Avocations: hiking, dancing, biking, reading, music. Office: Viewpoint Sch 23620 Mulholland Hwy Calabasas CA 91302-2097

LIGHTSTONE, RONALD, lawyer; b. N.Y.C., Oct. 4, 1938; s. Charles and Pearl (Weisberg) L.; m. Nancy Lehrer, May 17, 1973; 1 child, Dana. AB, Columbia U., 1959; JD, NYU, 1962. Atty. CBS, N.Y.C., 1967-69; assoc. dir. bus. affairs CBS News, N.Y.C., 1969-70; atty. NBC, N.Y.C., 1970; assoc. gen. counsel Viacom Internat. Inc., N.Y.C., 1970-75; v.p., gen. counsel, sec. Viacom Internat. Inc., 1976-80; v.p. bus. affairs Viacom Entertainment Group, Viacom Internat., Inc., 1980-82, v.p. corp. affairs, 1982-84, sr. v.p., 1984-87; exec. v.p. Spelling Entertainment Inc., L.A., 1988-91, CEO, 1991-93; chmn. Multimedia Labs. Inc., 1994—; CEO, pres. New Star Media Inc., 1997—. Served to lt. USN, 1962-66. Mem. ABA (chmn. TV, cable and radio com.), Assn. Bar City N.Y., Fed. Communications Bar Assn.

LIKENS, JAMES DEAN, economics educator; b. Bakersfield, Calif., Sept. 12, 1937; s. Ernest LeRoy and Monnie Jewel (Thomas) L.; m. Janet Sue Pelton, Dec. 18, 1965 (div.); m. Karel Carnohan, June 4, 1988 (div.); children: John David, Janet Elizabeth. BA in Econs., U. Calif., Berkeley, 1960, MBA, 1961; PhD in Econs., U. Minn., 1970. Analyst Del Monte Corp., San Francisco, 1963; economist 3M Co., Mpls., 1968-71; asst. prof. econs. Pomona Coll., 1969-75, assoc. prof. econs., 1975-83, prof. econs., 1983-85, Morris B. and Gladys S. Pendleton prof. econs., 1989—, dept. chair, 1998—; vis. asst. prof. econs. U. Minn., 1970, 71, vis. assoc. prof., 1976-77; pres., dean Western CUNA Mgmt. Sch., Pomona Coll., 1975—; chmn. bd. 1st City Savs. Fed. Credit Union, 1978—; coord. So. Calif. Rsch. Coun., L.A., 1980-81, 84-85; mem. adv. coun. Western Corp. Fed. Credit Union, 1993—; cons. in field. Author: (with Joseph LaDou) Medicine and Money, 1976, Mexico and Southern California: Toward A New Partnership, 1981, Financing Quality Education in Southern California, 1985; contbr. articles to profl. jours. Served with USCG, 1961-67. Rsch. grantee HUD-DOT, Haynes Found. Mem. ABA, Am. Econ. Assn., Western Econ. Assn. Home: 725 W 10th St Claremont CA 91711-3719 Office: Pomona Coll Dept Econs Claremont CA 91711

LIKINS, PETER WILLIAM, university administrator; b. Tracy, Calif., July 4, 1936; s. Ennis Blaine and Dorothy Louise (Medlin) L.; m. Patricia Ruth Kitsmiller, Dec. 18, 1955; children: Teresa, Lora, Paul, Linda, Krista, John. BCE, Stanford U., 1957, PhD in Engring. Mechanics, 1965; MCE, MIT, 1958; PhD (hon.), Lafayette Coll., 1983, Moravian Coll., 1984, Med. Coll. Pa., 1990, Lehigh U., 1991, Allentown St. Francis de Sales, 1993, Czech Tech U., 1993. Devel. engr. Jet Propulsion Lab., Pasadena, Calif., 1958-60; asst. prof. engring. UCLA, 1964-69, assoc. prof., 1969-72, prof., 1972-76, asst. dean, 1974-75, asso. dean, 1975-76; dean engring. and applied sci. Columbia U., N.Y.C., 1976-80, provost, 1980-82; pres. Lehigh U., Bethlehem, Pa., 1982-97, U. Ariz., Tucson, 1997—; cons. in field. Author: Elements of Engineering Mechanics, 1973, Spacecraft Dynamics, 1982; Contbr. articles to profl. jours. Mem. U.S. Pres.'s Coun. Advisors Sci. and Tech., 1990-93. Ford Found. fellow, 1970-72; named to Nat. Wrestling Hall of Fame. Fellow AIAA; mem. Nat. Acad. Engring., Phi Beta Kappa, Sigma Xi, Tau Beta Pi. Office: Univ Ariz PO Box 210066 Tucson AZ 85721-0066

LILLA, JAMES A., plastic surgeon; b. Comfrey, Minn., June 12, 1943. MD, Stanford U., 1969. Plastic hand surgeon Sutter Cmty. Hosp., Calif. Office: Hand Surg Assocs 1201 Alhambra Blvd Ste 410 Sacramento CA 95816-5243

LILLEGRAVEN, JASON ARTHUR, paleontologist, educator; b. Mankato, Minn., Oct. 11, 1938; s. Arthur Oscar and Agnes Mae (Eaton) L.; m. Bernice Ann Hines, Sept. 5, 1964 (div. Feb. 1983); children: Brita Anna, Ture Andrew; m. Linda Elizabeth Thompson, June 5, 1983. BA, Long Beach State Coll., 1962; MS, S.D. Sch. Mines and Tech., 1964; PhD, U. Kans., 1968. Professional geologist, Wyo. Postdoctoral fellow Dept. Paleontology U. Calif., Berkeley, 1968-69; from asst. prof. to prof. zoology San Diego State U., 1969-75; from assoc. prof. to prof. geology and zoology U. Wyo., Laramie, 1975—, assoc. dean Coll. Arts and Scis., 1984-85; program dir. NSF Systematic Biology, Washington, 1977-78; assoc. dean U. Wyo. Coll. Arts and Scis., 1984-85, temporary joint appointment Dept. Geography, 1986-87; U.S. sr. scientist Inst. for Paleontology Free U., Berlin, 1988-89; mem. adv. panel geology and paleontology program NSF, 1997—. Author, editor: Mesozoic Mammals the First Two Thirds of Mammalian History, 1979, Vertebrates, Phylogeny and Philosophy, 1986; mem. editl. bds. of Research and Exploration (Nat. Geographic Soc.), Jour. of Mammalian Evolution, Jour. of Vertebrate Paleontology, Cretaceous Rsch.; co-editor, contbr. Geology, Rocky Mountain Geology; contbr. articles to profl. jours. Recipient numerous rsch. grants NSF, 1970-98, George Duke Humphrey Disting. Faculty award, Humboldt prize. Mem. Am. Soc. Mammalogists, Am. Assn. Petroleum Geologists, Paleontol. Soc., Soc. Vertebrate Paleontology (pres. 1985-86), Linnean Soc. London, Soc. Mammalian Evolution, Sigma Xi. Avocations: computer graphics, outdoor activities.

LILLIG, MARGO ANDREA, child development professional; b. Des Moines, Jan. 21, 1957; d. Melvin Andrew and Catherine Patricia (Hoban) L. BA, San Francisco State U., 1981, tchg. credentials. Tchr. Windrush Sch., El Cerrito, Calif., 1986-93; child devel. specialist Discovery Toys, Livermore, Calif., 1993-98; tchr. trainer comty. rels. Early Childhood Resources, Corte Madera, Calif., 1998—. Mem. Nat. Assn. Edn. Young Child, Internat. Reading Assn. Office: Early Childhood Resources 50 El Camino Dr Corte Madera CA 94925-2057

LILLO, JOSEPH LEONARD, osteopath, family practice physician; b. Mt. Gilead, Ohio, Aug. 12, 1954; s. Joseph and Betty Jean (Rogers) L.; m. Barbara Anne Burm, June 25, 1976; children: Marie, Michael, Laura. BS in Zoology, Ariz. State U., 1976; DO, Kirksville Coll. Osteo. Med., 1979. Diplomate, bd. cert. Am. Bd. Family Practice; diplomate Nat. Bd. Examiners in Osteo. Medicine and surgery. Intern Phoenix Gen. Hosp., 1979-80; physician/surgeon Med. Arts P.A., Scottsdale, Ariz., 1980—; mng. ptnr. Granite Reef Devel. Corp., Scottsdale, 1986-88; adminstr. Scottsdale Cmty. Hosp., 1988-89; chmn. dept. family practice Tempe St. Luke's Hosp., 1992-93, chmn. credentials com., 1994-95; med. dir. Scottsdale Convalescent Plaza, 1988-89; family practice com. Scottsdale Meml. Hosp., 1997—; chmn. dept. family practice Scottsdale Healthcare, 1998-2000. Chmn. bd. Am. Cancer Soc., Scottsdale, 1990, bd. dirs., 1987-93; guest faculty Christ the King Cath. Sch., 1987—; vol. physician Mission of Mercy, 1997—. Named Physician of the Yr. Scottsdale Cmty. Hosp., 1986. Mem. Am. Coll. Osteo. Family Physicians, Am. Osteo. Assn., Ariz. Osteo. Med. Assn. Republican. Roman Catholic. Avocations: running, basketball, computers, gardening, reading. Home: 3433 E Contessa Cir Mesa AZ 85213-7038 Office: Med Arts PA 1525 N Granite Reef Rd Ste 16 Scottsdale AZ 85257-3998

LILLY, ELIZABETH GILES, mobile park executive; b. Bozeman, Mont., Aug. 5, 1916; d. Samuel John and Luella Elizabeth (Reed) Abegg; m. William Lilly, July 1, 1976; children: Samuel Colborn Giles, Elizabeth Giles. RN, Good Samaritan Hosp., Portland, Oreg., 1941; student, Walla Walla Coll., Lewis and Clark Coll. Bus., Portland. ARC nurse, tchr. area high schs., Portland; owner Welton Studio Interior Design, Portland; in pub. rels. Chas. Eckelman, Portland, Fairview Farms-Dairy Industry; owner,

builder Mobile Park Plaza, Inc., Portland. Del. platform planning com. Rep. Party; mem. Sunnyside Seventh Day Adventist Ch., deaconess. Recipient Svc. award Multnomah County Commrs., 1984. Mem. Soroptimist Internat. (local bd. dirs., bd. dirs. Women in Transition), Rep. Women's Club (pres.), C. of C., World Affairs Coun., Toastmistress (pres.), Oreg. Lodging Assn. (pres. bd. dirs.), Rep. Inner Circle (life). Address: 19825 SE Stark St Portland OR 97233-6039

LILLY, LUELLA JEAN, academic administrator; b. Newberg, Oreg., Aug. 23, 1937; d. David Hardy and Edith (Coleman) L. BS, Lewis and Clark Coll., 1959; postgrad., Portland State U., 1959-61; MS, U. Oreg., 1961; PhD, Tex. Woman's U., 1971; postgrad., various univs., 1959-72. Tchr. phys. edn. and health, dean girls Cen. Linn Jr.-Sr. High Sch., Halsey, Oreg., 1959-60; tchr. phys. edn. and health, swimming, tennis, golf coach Lake Oswego (Oreg.) High Sch., 1960-63; instr., intramural dir., coach Oreg. State U., Corvallis, 1963-64; instr., intercollegiate coach Am. River Coll., Sacramento, 1964-69; dir. women's phys. edn., athletics U. Nev., Reno, 1969-73, assoc. prof. phys. edn., 1971-76, dir. women's athletics, 1973-75, assoc. dir. athletics, 1975-76; dir. women's intercollegiate athletics U. Calif., Berkeley, 1976-97; organizer, coach Lue's Aquatic Club, 1962-64; v.p. PAC-10 Conf., 1990-91. Author: An Overview of Body Mechanics, 1966, 3d rev. edit., 1969. Vol. instr. ARC, 1951; vol. Heart Fund and Easter Seal, 1974-76, Am. Heart Assn., 1991-95, ofcl. Spl. Olympics, 1975; mem. L.A. Citizens Olympic Com., 1984; bd. dirs. Las Trampas, 1993-98, sec. 1996-98. Recipient Mayor Anne Rudin award Nat. Girls' and Women's Sports, 1993, Lifetime Sports award Bay Area Women's Sports Found., 1994, Golden Bear award Vol. of Yr., 1995; inducted Lewis and Clark Coll. Athletic Hall of Fame, 1988; named to U. Calif. First 125 Yrs. Women of Honor. Mem. AAHPER (life), AAUW, Nat. Soc. Profs., Nat. Assn. Coll. Women Athletic Adminstrs. (divsn. I-A women's steering com. 1991-92), Women's Athletic Caucus, Coun. Collegiate Women Athletics Adminstrs. (membership com. 1989-92), Western Soc. Phys. Edn. Coll. Women (membership com. 1971-74, program adv. com. 1972, exec. bd. 1972-75), Western Assn. Intercollegiate Athletics for Women (exec. bd. dirs. 1973-75, 79-82), Oreg. Girls' Swimming Coaches Assn. (pres. 1960, 63), Ctrl. Calif. Bd. Women Ofcls. (basketball chmn. 1968-69), Calif. Assn. Health, Phys. Edn. and Recreation (chmn.-elect jr. coll. sect. 1970), Nev. Bd. Women Ofcls. (chmn. bd., chmn. volleyball sect., chmn. basketball sect. 1969), No. Calif. Women's Intercollegiate Conf. (sec. 1970-71, basketball coord. 1970-71), No. Calif. Intercollegiate Athletic Conf. (volleyball coord. 1971-72), Nev. Assn. Health Phys. Edn. and Recreation (state chmn. 1974), No. Calif. Athletic Conf. (pres. 1979-82, sec. 1984—), Soroptimists Club (bd. dirs. 1988-98, v.p. 1989, 92-93, sec. 1993-95, 1st v.p. 1996-97, corr. sec. 1997-98, pres. 1998—), Phi Kappa Phi, Theta Kappa. Avocation: Held Am. records in swimming, 1950's. Home and Office: 60 Margrave Ct Walnut Creek CA 94596-2511

LILLY, MICHAEL ALEXANDER, lawyer, author; b. Honolulu, May 21, 1946; s. Percy Anthony Jr. and Virginia (Craig) L.; m. Kathryn I. Collins, Aug. 10, 1991; children: Michael Jr., Cary J., Laura B., Claire F., Winston W. AA, Menlo Coll., Menlo Park, Calif., 1966; BA, U. Calif., Santa Cruz, 1968; JD with honors, U. of Pacific, 1974. Bar: Calif. 1974, U.S. Dist. Ct. (no., so. and ea. dists.) Calif. 1974, U.S. Ct. Appeals (9th cir.) 1974, Hawaii 1975, U.S. Dist. Ct. Hawaii 1975, U.S. Ct. Appeals (D.C. cir.) 1975, U.S. Supreme Ct. 1978, U.S. Ct. Appeals (7th cir.) 1979. Atty. Pacific Legal Found., Sacramento, 1974-75; dep. atty. gen. State of Hawaii, Honolulu, 1975-79, 1st dep. atty. gen., 1981-84, atty. gen., 1984-85; ptnr. Feeley & Lilly, San Jose, Calif., 1979-81, Ning, Lilly & Jones, Honolulu, 1985—. Author: If You Die Tomorrow-A Layman's Guide to Estate Planning. Dir. Diamond Head Theatre; Lt. USN, 1968-71, Vietnam; capt. USNR. Named hon. Ky. col.; decorated Legion of Merit award, 1997. Mem. Nat. Assn. Attys. Gen., Hawaii Law Enforcement Ofcls. Assn., Navy Res. Assn. (pres. 14th dist. 1986-89), Navy League (pres. pacific region, nat. dir., contbg. editor Fore 'N Aft mag., dept. judge adv. to bd. Honolulu coun.), Outrigger Canoe Club. Home: 2769 Laniloa Rd Honolulu HI 96813-1041 Office: Ning Lilly & Jones 707 Richards St Ste 700 Honolulu HI 96813-4623

LILLY-HERSLEY, JANE ANNE FEELEY, nursing researcher; b. Palo Alto, Calif., May 31, 1947; d. Daniel Morris Sr. and Suzanne (Agnew) Feeley; children: Cary Jane, Laura Blachree, Claire Foale; m. Dennis C. Hersley, Jan. 16, 1993. BS, U. Oreg., 1968; student, U. Hawaii, 1970; BSN, RN, Sacramento City Coll., 1975. Cert. ACLS, BCLS. Staff and charge nurse, acute rehab. Santa Clara Valley Med. Ctr., San Jose, Calif., staff nurse, surg. ICU and trauma unit; clin. project leader mycophenolate mofetil program team Syntex Rsch., Palo Alto; pres. Rsch. Consultation Inc., Santa Cruz, Calif. Co-founder, CFO and dir. scientific rsch. Citizens United Responsible Environmentalism, Inc., CURE (internat. non-profit edn./rsch. orgn.); mem. Monterey Bay Aquarium. Mem. AACN, Nature Conservancy, Nat. park and Conservation Assn., World Wildlife Fund., Smithsonian Assn., Nature Plant Soc.

LILLYMAN, WILLIAM JOHN, German language educator, academic administrator; b. Sydney, Australia, Apr. 17, 1937; came to U.S., 1963, naturalized, 1974; s. John and Christina Mary (Munro) L.; m. Ingeborg Wolz, Sept. 14, 1962; children: Gregory, Christina. AB, U. Sydney, 1959; PhD, Stanford U., 1964. Asst. prof. Stanford (Calif.) U., 1964-67; assoc. prof. U. Calif., Santa Cruz, 1967-72; prof. German U. Calif., Irvine, 1972—, dean humanities, 1973-81, vice chancellor acad. affairs, 1981-82, interim exec. vice chancellor, 1982-88, 98—. Author: Otto Ludwig's Zwischen Himmel und Erde, 1967, Otto Ludwig: Romane und Romanstudien, 1977, Reality's Dark Dream The Narrative Fiction of Ludwig Tieck, 1979, Goethe's Narrative Fiction, 1983; co-editor; Probleme der Moderne, 1983, Horizonte Festschrift für H. Lehnert, 1990, Critical Architecture and Contemporary Culture, 1994. Mem. MLA, Am. Assn. Tchrs. German. Office: U Calif Exec Vice Chancellor's Office 509 Administrn Bldg Irvine CA 92697-3150*

LIM, ALAN YOUNG, plastic surgeon; b. St. Louis, Apr. 11, 1953. MD, U. Calif., San Diego, 1979. Plastic surgeon Kaiser-Permanente, Sacramento, Calif.; asst. clin. prof. U. Calif. Davis. Office: Plastic Surg 2025 Morse Ave Sacramento CA 95825-2115

LIM, EDWARD HONG, artist; b. Shanghai, Sept. 1, 1956; s. David D.P. and Linda Q. (Deng) L.; m. Shelley Xiang, June 14, 1989; children: Monica, Jessica. Student, City Coll., San Francisco, 1980-82, Acad. of Art, San Francisco, 1982-84. Art dir. Art Works, San Francisco, 1984-86; freelance artist San Francisco, 1986—. Illustrator story bds. for film Sphere, 1988, other film and TV prodns. Home and Studio: 2696 17th Ave San Francisco CA 94116-3003

LIM, HARRISON BING CHEUNG, social services administrator; b. China, Nov. 30, 1936; came to the U.S., 1970; s. Fook How and Oy Lin Lim; m. Margaret Ma, Nov. 24, 1965; children: Artina, Jackson, Rosana, Samson. M in Lit., Chinese U. Hong Kong, 1963, M in History, 1967. Coll. instr. Royden Coll., Hong Kong, 1963-70; dean Grammar Coll., Hong Kong, 1963-70; coll. instr. Willmington Coll., Hong Kong, 1963-70; sr. counselor Pub. Health Dept./Mental Health Divsn., San Francisco, 1973-82; exec. dir., founder Charity Cultural Svcs. Ctr., San Francisco, 1983—, Crosscultural Cmty. Svcs. Ctr., San Jose, Calif., 1991—; Chinese-Am. del. chair 5th World Congress of Poets, 1981; bd. mem. Ctrl. Chinese H.S., San Francisco, 1985—, supt., 1987-91; supt. Asian Art Inst., San Francisco, 1991-92, Acad. Chinese Art, San Francisco, 1997—; bd. dirs. Nat. Am. Bank. Author: Bai Kuo Man, 1998; co-author: Silent River, 1961, Tong Tai Flower, 1961. Pres. Sino-Am. Cultural Assn., Calif., 1975—; founding bd. mem. Pres. Chiang Edn. Found., Calif., 1978—; presiding pres. Chinese Consol. Benevolent Assn., Calif., 1983; gen. sec. Dr. Sun Yat Sen's Free Prin. Assn., Calif., 1983-89; appointee Ex-Mayor Frank Jordan's Chinatown Econ. Task Force, San Francisco, 1992. Harrison B. Lim Day named in his honor by Sec. of State, San Francisco, 1990; named Unsung Hero/Asian Pacific Heritage, Sta. KQED-TV and San Francisco Examiner, 1995. Mem. Ning Yung Consol. Benevolent Assn., Lim Family Benevolent Assn. (pres. 1978-79). Avocations: writing, reading, teaching, traveling. Office: Charity Cultural Svcs Ctr 827 Stockton St San Francisco CA 94108

LIM, HWA AUN, research geneticist, bioinformaticist, consultant; b. Alor Setar, Kedah, Malaysia, July 29, 1957; came to U.S., 1981; s. Keng Hoon and Beng See (Tan) L. BSc (hons.), Imperial Coll. of Sci.Tech., London, 1981; MA, U. Rochester, 1982, PhD, 1986; MBA, Univ. Phoenix, Univ. Calif. Rsch. asst. Imperial Coll. of Sci. & Tech. & Medicine, London, 1978-81, U. Rochester, Rochester, N.Y., 1981-85; medical asst. Strong Meml. Hosp., Rochester, N.Y., 1985-86; rsch. assoc. Lab. for Laser Energetics, Rochester, N.Y., 1986-87; rsch. assoc. Fla. State U., Tallahassee, 1987-89, univ. faculty, 1989-95; dir. bioinformatics HYSEQ, Sunnyvale, Calif., 1995-96; v.p. sci. & tech. Pangea Systems, Oakland, 1996-97; pres., CEO D'Trends Inc, San Ramon, Calif., 1997—; adj. prof. St. Johns Fisher Coll., Rochester, 1986-87; vis. academician USSR Acad. Scis., Moscow, Kiev, Tbilisi, 1989; prin. investigator Fla. State U., 1989-95; founding adv. Internet Biologists, 1997—. Co-author: Computer Analysis of Genetic Macromolecules: Structure, Function and Evolution, 1994; editor: Electrophoresis, Supercomputing and Genome, 1991, Bioinformatics, Supercomputing and Genome, 1993, Isozymes: Roles in Evolution, Genetics and Physiology, 1994, Bioinformatics and Genome Research, 1994, Gene Families: Structure, Function, Genetics and Evolution, 1996, Molecular Bioinformatics-Sequence Analysis, 1997, Genes, Gene Families and Isozymes, 1998; mng. editor Internat. Jour. Genomic Rsch., 1989—; assoc. editor Internat. Jour. Modern Physics C: Physics and Computers, 1989—; editor Jour. Modelling and Scientific Computing, 1991—; contbr. articles to profl. jours. Mem. rev. panel NSF, Arlington, Va., 1992, Nat. Cancer Inst., Bethesda, Md., 1994; bioinformatics expert UN, Daejon, Korea, Rome, Washington, 1993. Recipient numerous grants. Mem. AAAS, N.Y. Acad. Scis., Internat. Assn. Math. & Computer Modelling, Internat. Human Genome Orgn., Soc. Chinese Bioscientists in Am. (life). Achievement: started subject area of bioinformatics in late 1980s. E-mail: hal@d-trends.com. Fax #: (925) 355-9182.

LIM, LARRY KAY, university official; b. Santa Maria, Calif., July 4, 1948; s. Koonwah and Nancy (Yao) L.; m. Louise A. Simon, Aug. 15, 1988. BA, UCLA, 1970, teaching cert., 1971. Asst. engr. Force Ltd., L.A., 1969; tchg. asst. UCLA, 1970-71; tchr. L.A. Sch. Dist., 1971-82; dir. pre-coll. programs Sch. Engring., U. So. Calif., L.A., 1979—; presenter minority math.-based intervention symposium U. D.C., Washington, 1988; presenter NEMEPA/WEPAN nat. conf., 1997. Newsletter editor, 1981-92. Bd. dirs. Developing Ednl. Studies for Hispanics, L.A., 1983-88. Named Dir. of Yr., Math., Engring., Sci. Achievement Ctr. Adv. Bd., 1986, 91, 92. Mem. Nat. Assn. Pre-Coll. Dirs., Nat. Assn. Minority Engring. Program Adminstr., Lotus/West Club (pres. 1981-92). Avocation: automobile racing. Office: U So Calif Sch Engring OHE 104 Los Angeles CA 90089-1455

LIM, SALLY-JANE (SJ LIM), insurance consultant; b. Manila; came to U.S., 1990; d. Teddy and Sonia (Yii) L.; children: Robin Michael, Rodney Jovin, Romelle Gavin Lim Velasco. BA, BS in Commerce magna cum laude, Coll. of Holy Spirit, Manila. CPA, The Philippines; LUTCF. Treas, contr. Ky. Fried Chicken, Makati, Philippines, 1968-73; ins. rep. Insular Life Assurance Co., Makati, 1972-82; project analyst Pvt. Devel. Corp. of Philippines, Makati, 1972-78; account exec. Genbancor Devel. Corp., Makati, 1978-80; risk mgr. Filcapital Devel. Corp., Makati, 1978-82; pres. and gen. mgr., ins. broker Sally-Jane Multiline Insce., Inc., Makati, 1978-90; real estate broker Sally-Jane Realty, Inc., Manila, 1980-90; ins. rep. and v.p. Macaulay Club Sun Life of Makati, 1982-91; rep. Prudential Ins. & Fin. Svcs., Prudential Property & Casualty Ins. Co., Prudential Healthcare Plan Calif., Inc.; registered rep. Pruco Securities Corp., L.A. Dist., South Pasadena, Calif., 1990-92, Asian Pacific Dist., Calif., 1992—. Recipient Young Achiever award Young Achiever Found., Quezon City, Philippines, 1988, Golden Scroll award Philippine Ednl. Youth Devel., Inc., Quezon City, 1988, Young Famous Celebrity Mother's award Golden Mother/Father Found., Quezon City, 1990, Recognition of Excellence cert. San Gabriel Valley YWCA, 1992, Most Outstanding Ins. Exec. of The Philippines bronze trophy Consumers' Union of the Philippines, Manila, 1983, 88, Ten Outstanding Profl. Svc. award TOPS Nat. Achievement Rsch. Soc., Manila, 1988, Women of Achievement award, internat. quality awards, numerous others. Fellow, Life Underwriters Tng. Coun.; mem. Million Dollar Round Table (Life mem.) Nat. Assn. Life Underwriters, Calif. Assn. Life Underwriters, Arcadia C. of C., Asian Bus. Assn., Filipino-Am. C. of C., Greater Pasadena Assn. Life Underwriters, Chinese C. of C. (bd. dirs. L.A. 1992—). Avocations: Broadway musicals, ballet, fashion shows, concerts, ballroom dancing. Home: 1006 # A Royal Oaks Dr Monrovia CA 91016-3737 Office: Prudential of Am 1255 Corporate Center Dr Ph Steb Monterey Park CA 91754-7609

LIMA, MARILYNNE, foreign language educator, consultant; b. Murray, Utah, Aug. 20, 1938; d. John William and Mary Elsie (Barr) Fitzgerald; m. Marco Antonio Lima, Aug. 22, 1959 (div. 1986); children: Maria Lorraine, Shawn Antonio. BA, Brigham Young U., Provo, Utah, 1962, MA, 1972. Cert. tchr. Utah. Tchr. Spanish/English Jordan Sch. Dist, West Jordan (Utah) Jr. High, 1962-67; supr. student tchrs. Brigham Young U., 1967-68; tchr. Spanish/English Granite Sch. Dist., Evergreen Jr. High, Salt Lake City, 1968-69; tchr. Spanish Brigham Young U., 1978-79, Granite Sch. Dist., Cottonwood High Sch., Salt Lake City, 1969—; sales cons. Scott Foresman Pub., Salt Lake City, 1993-96; presider, presenter numerous adv. placement seminars in Spanish, 1976-86. Mem. Am. Fedn. Tchrs., Utah Fgn. Lang. Assn., Sigma Delta Pi. Mem. Ch. Latter Day Saints. Avocations: traveling and living in Spanish-speaking countries, reading, family events. Office: Cottonwood HS 5717 S 1300 E Salt Lake City UT 84121-1023

LIN, AMY YUH-MEI, industrial engineer, real estate investor; b. Chuang-Hua, Taiwan, Jan. 22, 1948; Came to U.S., 1973; d. Tu-To and Show-Lan (Wu) Tsai; m. Edward Yih-Ling Lin, Dec. 24, 1975; children: Shirley, Kenneth. BSBA, Cheng Kung U., Taiwan, 1971; MS in Indsl. Engring., W.Va. U., 1975. Supr. Yellow Springs (Ohio) Instrument Corp., 1977-78; indsl. engr. MSI Data Corp., Costa Mesa, Calif., 1978-79; sr. programmer, analyst MAI Basic Four Corp., Tustin, Calif., 1979-81; supr., sr. indsl. engr. LH Rsch., Inc., Tustin, 1981-85; sr. indsl. engr. Rockwell Internat., Anaheim, Calif., 1985-90; pres., gen. mgr. Maylyne Creations, Irvine, Calif., 1990—, Fortune Investment & Mgmt., Irvine, 1989—. Sec. Cheng Kung U. Found., 1992, treas. 1994—; v.p., treas. Woodbridge High Sch. Chinese Parent Assn., Irvine, Calif., 1993—. Mem. Cheng Kung U. Alumni Assn. (treas. 1992, v.p. 1994—), Apt. Owners Assn. So. Calif., Internat. Inst. Indsl. Engring. Avocations: tennis, writing, reading, ping pong. Office: PO Box 18404 Irvine CA 92623-8404

LIN, FRANK C., computer company executive. Chmn. bd. dirs., pres., CEO Trident Microsys. Inc., Mountain View, Calif. Office: Trident Microsys Inc 189 Bernardo Ave Mountain View CA 94043-5203*

LIN, HUN-CHI, molecular biologist; b. Yun-Lin, Taiwan, Republic of China, Nov. 8, 1953; came to U.S., 1980; s. Shun-Tau and Yu-Hwa (Tsai) L.; m. Shau-Ping Lei, July 6, 1980; children: Victoria, Benita. BS, Nat. Taiwan U., Taipei, 1976, MS, 1978; PhD, UCLA, 1984. Teaching asst. UCLA, 1983; rsch. scientist Ingene, Santa Monica, Calif., 1984-85, project dir., 1985-87, prin. investigator, 1985-87; rsch. dir. Sinogen, L.A., 1987; pres., dir. rsch. Trigen, Inc./Splty. Lab., Inc., Santa Monica, 1987—, assoc. rsch. dir., 1991-96, dir. clin. trials, 1995—. Contbr. articles to profl. jours. Lt. Chinese Army, 1978-80. Mem. Am. Soc. Microbiology, Drug Info. Assn. Office: Splty Lab Inc 2211 Michigan Ave Santa Monica CA 90404-3905

LIN, LAWRENCE SHUH LIANG, accountant; b. China, July 5, 1938; s. Wan Chow and Inn Chi Lin; came to U.S., 1967, naturalized, 1979; LLB, Soochow U., 1963; MBA, Pepperdine U., 1970; JD, U. West L.A., 1998; m. Grace Yu, July 31, 1966; children: Ray, Lester. Spl. project acctg. supr. Motown Records, Hollywood, Calif., 1975; chief acct. Elektra/Asylum/Nonesuch Records, Beverly Hills, Calif., 1976-77, United Artists Music Pub. Group, Hollywood, 1977-80; contr.-adminstr. Pasadena (Calif.) Guidance Clinics (name now Pacific Clinics, 1980-86; v.p. Stew Kettle Corp., L.A., 1986-87; v.p. LKL Corp., L.A., 1987-89; internat. fin. cons. Pacific Capital Mgmt., Alhambra, Calif., 1990. Mem. Inst. Mgmt. Accts., Nat. Assn. Security Dealers. Baptist. Office: Pacific Capital Mgmt 670 Monterey Pass Rd Monterey Park CA 91754-2419

LIN, TAO, software engineer; b. Shanghai, Aug. 6, 1958; came to U.S., 1986; s. Cheng-hui Lin and Wei-jing Wu; m. Ping Kuo, Aug. 10, 1989; children: Jason, Jessie. BS, East China Normal U., Shanghai, 1982; MS, Tohoku U., Sendai, Japan, 1985; PhD, Tohoku U., 1990. Technician Dongtong Electronics Inc., Shanghai, 1977-78; rsch. asst. Electronics Rsch. Lab U. Calif., Berkeley, 1986-87, postgrad. researcher, 1987-88; applications engr. Integrated Device Technology Inc., Santa Clara, Calif., 1988-90; sr. applications engr. Sierra Semiconductor Corp., San Jose, Calif., 1990-91; applications mgr. Sierra Semicondr. Corp., San Jose, Calif., 1991-92, software engring. mgr., 1992-94; strategic planning and applications engring. mgr. IC Works Inc., San Jose, 1994-95; sr. mem. tech. staff NeoMagic Corp., Santa Clara, 1995—. Contbr. articles to profl. jours. Mem. IEEE. Home: 3552 Rockett Dr Fremont CA 94538-3425 Office: NeoMagic Corp 3260 Jay St Santa Clara CA 95054-3309

LIN, THOMAS WEN-SHYOUNG, accounting educator, researcher, consultant; b. Taichung, Republic of China, June 3, 1944; came to U.S., 1970; s. Ju-chin and Shao-chin (Tseng) L.; m. Angela Kuei-fong Hou, May 19, 1969; children: William Margaret. BA in Bus. Adminstrn., Nat. Taiwan U., Taipei, 1966; MBA, Nat. Chengchi U., Taipei, 1970; MS in Acctg. and Info. Systems, UCLA, 1971; PhD in Acctg., Ohio State U., 1975. Cert. mgmt. acct., Calif. Internal auditor Formosa Plastics Group, Taipei, 1967-69, spl. asst. to the pres., 1969-70; asst. prof. U. So. Calif., L.A., 1975-80, assoc. prof., 1980-86, prof. acctg., 1986-90, acctg. cir. prof., 1990—, dir. doctoral studies acctg., 1982-86; cons. Intex Plastics, Inc., Long Beach, Calif., 1979-81, Peat, Marwick, Mitchell, L.A., 1982, City of Chino, Calif., 1982; bd. dirs., audit com. chmn. FCB Taiwan Calif. Bank, 1997—. Author: Planning and Control for Data Processing, 1984, Use of Mathematical Models, 1986, Advanced Auditing, 1988, Using Accounting Information in Business Planning, Product Costing, and Auditing, 1991, Cost Management: A Strategic Emphasis, 1999; assoc. editor Internat. Jour. Bus., 1997—; mem. editl. bd. Jour. Acctg. Edn., Quarterly Jour. Bus. and Econs., Am. Jour. Math. and Mgmt. Scis., Chinese Acctg. Rev., Hong Kong Jour. Bus. Mgmt., 1988—; contbr. articles to profl. jours. Bd. dirs. U. So. Calif. Acctg. Circle, L.A., 1986-88, 93—, Taiwan Benevolent Assn. Am., Washington, 1986-89; pres. Taiwan Benevolent Assn. Calif., L.A., 1986-88. 2d lt. China Army, 1966-67. Recipient cert. appreciation L.A. City Mayor Tom Bradley, 1988, Congressman Martinez award for outstanding cmty. svc., 1988; Faculty Rsch. scholar U. So. Calif. Bus. Sch., L.A., 1984-87. Mem. Am. Acctg. Assn. (bd. dirs. 1986-88), Chinese Acctg. Profs. N.Am. (founding pres. 1976-80), Inst. Cert. Mgmt. Accts. (cert. of disting. performance 1978), Inst. Mgmt. Accts. (coord. 1984—, Author's trophy 1978, 79, 81, 87), EDP Auditor Assn., Inst. Mgmt. Scis. Republican. Baptist. Avocation: gardening. Home: PO Box 8023 Rowland Hghts CA 91748-0023 Office: U So Calif Leventhal Sch Acctg Univ Park ACC 109 Los Angeles CA 90089-1421

LIN, XI-WEI, electronics engineer; b. Gejiu, Yunnan, China, Dec. 18, 1961; came to U.S., 1987; s. Heqing Lin and Lizhi Shen; m. Jiawen Wang, Nov. 2, 1989. BS, Beijing U., 1982; MS, U. Paris, Orsay, France, 1984, PhD, 1987. Rsch. asst. U. Paris, Orsay, 1984-87; rsch. assoc. Northwestern U., Evanston, Ill., 1987-91; staff scientist Lawrence Berkeley (Calif.) Lab., 1991-95; principle engr. VLSI Tech. Inc., San Jose, Calif., 1995—; vis. scholar ctr. rsch. and energy U. Que. (Can.), 1985; vis. scholar Inst. Physics U. Fed. Rio Grande Do Sul, Porto Alegre, Brazil, 1994. Contbr. articles to profl. jours. Ministry of Rsch. & Tech. fellow, 1984-86, Nat. Inst. Nuclear and Particle Physics fellow, 1986-87. mem. IEEE, Materials Rsch. Soc. Achievements include invention of several techniques in sub-micron integrated circuit technology; first to synthesize Gallium Nitride in Gallium Arsenide via ion beam technique for optical applications; numerous contributions in areas of ion beam-material interaction, interface, defects, electronic device processing. Office: VLSI Tech Inc 1109 McKay Dr # 2 San Jose CA 95131-1797

LINAHON, JAMES JOSEPH, music educator, musician; b. Mason City, Iowa, Sept. 6, 1951; s. Robert Eugene and Teresa Darlene (Mulaney) L.; m. Kathryn Anne Tull, Apr. 12, 1987; children: Michael, Katie, Joseph. BA in Music, U. No. Iowa, 1973; M in Music Edn., North Tex. State U., 1975. Assoc. dir. jazz studies Chaffey Coll., Rancho Cucamonga, Calif., 1975-80; prof. music, dir. jazz studies Fullerton (Calif.) Coll., 1980—; cons. U. No. Colo., U. Alaska, U. Calif., U. Ariz., U. Hawaii, DePaul U., Chgo., U. So. Calif., Wash. State U., S.D. State U., 1978—; cons., artist Playboy Jazz Festival, Reno Internat. Jazz Festival, Queen Mary Jazz Festival, Disneyland, All That Jazz; record producer MCA, Warner Bros, ABC, Columbia; performer for Frank Sinatra, Henry Mancini, Beverly Sills, Ella Fitzgerald, Sarah Vaughan, Tony Bennett, Merv Griffin; U.S. Jazz amb., worldwide, 1996. Artist, producer: (jazz compact disc) Time Tripping, 1984 (Album of Yr. Downbeat Mag., 1987), (classical compact disc) Gradus Ad Parnassum, 1990, (compact disk) Season of Our Lives, 1994; composer: (musical composition) Snow Wisp, 1986 (finalist Columbia Artists search). Performer, producer Theatre Palisades, Pacific Palisades, Calif., 1986, Claremont (Calif.) Community Found., 1992; guest soloist Claremont (Calif.) Symphony Orch., 1991. Recipient Major Landers scholarship Iowa Band Master's Assn., Iowa, 1969; named Dee Bee Album of Yr. (5 awards) Downbeat Mag., 1978-87. Mem. NARAS (Outstanding Recordings 1989), Internat. Assn. Jazz Educators (higher edn. rep. 1992-93), Internat. Trumpet Guild, Internat. Assn. Jazz Edn., Am. Soc. Composers, Authors and Publishers, Nat. Assn. Coll. Wind and Percussion Instrs., Am. Fedn. Musicians. Roman Catholic. Avocations: gourmet cooking, home improvement, travel. Home: 560 W 10th St Claremont CA 91711-3714 Office: Fullerton Coll 321 E Chapman Ave Fullerton CA 92832-2011

LINAWEAVER, WALTER ELLSWORTH, JR., physician; b. San Pedro, Calif., Oct. 16, 1928; s. Walter Ellsworth and Catherine Breathed (Bridges) L.; m. Lydia Anne Whitlock, Oct. 5, 1957; children: Catherine Ann, Nancy Alyn, Walter E. III. BA cum laude, Pomona Coll., 1952; MD, U. Rochester, 1956. Diplomate Am. Bd. Allergy and Immunology, Am. Bd. Pediatrics, Am. Bd. Pediatric Allergy. Intern pediatrics Med. Ctr. U. Rochester, N.Y., 1956-57, resident pediatrics Med. Ctr., 1958-59; asst. resident pediatrics Med. Ctr. UCLA, 1957-58; fellow allergy and immunology Med. Ctr. U. Colo., Denver, 1959-61, instr. pediatrics Sch. Medicine, 1961; pvt. practice Riverside (Calif.) Med. Clinic, 1962—; asst. clin. prof. pediatrics Loma Lida U. Med. Sch., 1965—. Elder Presbyn. Ch. Staff sgt. U.S. Army, 1946-48. Inducted into Athletic Hall of Fame Pomona Coll., Claremont, Calif., 1979. Fellow Am. Acad. Allergy, Asthma & Immunology, Am. Acad. Pediat., Southwestern Pediat. Soc. (emeritus, v.p. 1978), L.A. Acad. Medicine; mem. Riverside County Med. Soc. (councilor 1964-66), Riverside County Heart Assn. Republican. Avocations: gardening, American and British military history. Home: 1296 Tiger Tail Dr Riverside CA 92506-5475 Office: Riverside Med Clinic 3660 Arlington Ave Riverside CA 92506-3912

LINCOLN, ALEXANDER, III, financier, lawyer, private investor; b. Boston, Dec. 1, 1943; s. Alexander Jr. and Elizabeth (Kitchel) L.; m. Isabel Fawcett Ross, Dec. 27, 1969. BA, Denver U., 1967; JD, Boston U., 1971. Bar: Colo. 1972, U.S. Ct. Appeals (10th cir.) 1972, U.S. Supreme Ct. 1979. Atty. Dist. Ct. Denver, 1973-78, Colo. Ct. Appeals, Denver, 1978-80; mng. ptnr. Alexander Lincoln & Co., Denver, 1980—. Mem. Colo. Bar Assn. (fin. com. 1975-76), Colo. Soc. Mayflower Descendants (life, bd. dirs. 1975—), Order of Founders and Patriots (life). Republican. Avocations: skiing, mountain climbing, horticulture. Home and Office: 121 S Dexter St Denver CO 80246-1052

LINCOLN, SANDRA ELEANOR, chemistry educator; b. Holyoke, Mass., Mar. 11, 1939; d. Edwin Stanley and Evelyn Ida (Mackie) L. BA magna cum laude, Smith Coll., 1960; MSChem, Marquette U., 1970; PhD in Inorganic Chemistry, SUNY, Stony Brook, 1982. Tchr., prin. Oak Knoll Sch., Summit, N.J., 1964-74; tchr. Holy Child High Sch., Waukegan, Ill., 1974-76; lectr. chemistry, dir. fin. aid Rosemont (Pa.) Coll., 1976-78; teaching asst. SUNY, Stony Brook, 1978-82; prof. chemistry U. Portland, Oreg., 1982—. Contbr. articles to profl. jours. Cath. sister Soc. Holy Child Jesus, 1963—. Recipient Pres.'s award for Teaching, SUNY, Stony Brook, 1981; Burlington No. Outstanding scholar, 1987. Mem. Am. Chem. Soc., Phi Beta Kappa, Sigma Xi. Democrat. Home: 5431 N Strong St Portland OR 97203-5711 Office: U Portland 5000 N Willamette Blvd Portland OR 97203-5743

LIND, JEFFERY A., academic administrator; b. Lodi, Calif., Jan. 30, 1942; s. Roy A. and Alice I. L.; m. Julieann Medeiros, Apr. 22, 1966; children: Michelle, Kristina, Gregory. D of Common Law, Universal Life U., 1986. Ins. agt. Am. Nat., Stockton, Calif., 1966-73, v.p. U.S. Life Ins. Co., Lodi, 1973-75, dir. agencies Nat. Home Life, Pa., 1975-79, nat. dir. Mass Mut. Life, L.A., 1979-82; pres. Universal Trust, Lodi, 1982-86, Universal Metals, Lodi, 1986-89, Commart Ins. Mkt., Pioneer, Calif., 1989-94, Sch. Law Comartrust, Pine Grove, Calif., 1994—; Author: Contract Trust, 1992. Sgt. U.S. Army, 1964-70. Mem. U.S. Bar Assn., Internat. Bar Assn. Lutheran. Avocations:

hunting, fishing, camping, hiking. Home: 13480 Marko Ln Pine Grove CA 95665-4010 Office: Sch Law Comartrust 12800 Ste D Pine Grove CA 95665

LIND, TERRIE LEE, social services administrator; b. Spokane, Wash., June 5, 1948; d. Clifford and Edna Mae (Allenbach) Presnell; m. Stephen George Lind, Aug. 29, 1970 (div. Mar. 1981); children: Erica Rachel, Reid Christopher. BA cum laude, Wash. State U., 1970, MA, 1971. Cert. tchr., Wash., Ariz.; cert. in Porch Index Communicative Ability. Specialist communication disorders U. Tex., Houston, 1971-73; clin. supr. The Battin Clinic, Houston, 1973-76; specialist communication disorders Spokane Guilds Sch., 1980-82; program coord. Fresno (Calif.) Community Hosp., 1982-87; program adminstr. Advantage 65* sr. access program Health Dimensions, Inc., San Jose, Calif., 1987-90; dir. patient svcs. San Jose Med. Ctr., 1990-92; v.p. comty. svcs. Planned Parenthood Mar Monte, San Jose, 1992—; cons. Adolescent Chem. Dependency Unit, Fresno, 1984-87. Mem. AAUW (officer 1976-82), Am. Speech and Hearing Assn. (cert., Continuing Edn. award 1985-86), Wash. Speech and Hearing Assn. (co-chmn. state conv. program com. 1981-82), Soc. Consumer Affairs Profls. in Bus., Wash. State U. Alumni Assn. Avocations: snow and water skiing, flying, sailing, golf, travel. Home: 1717 Don Ave San Jose CA 95124-1905 Office: Planned Parenthood 1691 The Alameda San Jose CA 95126-2203

LINDE, HANS ARTHUR, state supreme court justice; b. Berlin, Germany, Apr. 15, 1924; came to U.S., 1939, naturalized, 1943; s. Bruno C. and Luise (Rosenhain) L.; m. Helen Tucker, Aug. 13, 1945; children: Lisa, David Tucker. BA, Reed Coll., 1947; JD, U. Calif., Berkeley, 1950. Bar: Oreg. 1951. Law clk. U.S. Supreme Ct. Justice William O. Douglas, 1950-51; atty. Office of Legal Adviser, Dept. State, 1951-53; pvt. practice Portland, Oreg., 1953-54; legis. asst. U.S. Sen. Richard L. Neuberger, 1955-58; from assoc. prof. to prof. U. Oreg. Law Sch., 1959-76; justice Oreg. Supreme Ct., Salem, 1977-90, sr. judge, 1990—; Fulbright lectr. Freiburg U., 1967-68, Hamburg U., 1975-76; cons. U.S. ACDA, Dept. Def., 1962-76; mem. Adminstrv. Conf. U.S., 1978-82, Oreg. Law Commn., 1997—. Author: (with George Bunn) Legislative and Administrative Processes, 1976. Mem. Oreg. Constl. Revision Commn., 1961-62, Oreg. Law Commn., 1997—, Oreg. Commn. on Pub. Broadcasting, 1990-93; bd. dirs. Oreg. Pub. Broadcasting, 1993—. With U.S. Army, 1943-46. Fellow Am. Acad. Arts and Scis.; mem. Am. Law Inst. (council), Order of Coif, Phi Beta Kappa. *

LINDE, LUCILLE MAE (JACOBSON), motor-perceptual specialist; b. Greeley, Colo., May 5, 1919; d. John Alfred and Anna Julia (Anderson) Jacobson; m. Ernest Emil Linde, July 5, 1946 (dec. Jan. 27, 1959). BA, Coll. State Coll. of Edn., 1941, MA, 1947; EdD, U. No. Colo., 1974. Cert. tchr. Calif., Colo., Iowa, N.Y.; cert. ednl. psychologist; guidance counselor. Dean of women, dir. residence C.W. Post Coll. of L.I. Univ., 1965-66; asst. dean of students SUNY, Farmingdale, 1966-67; counselor, tchr. West High Sch., Davenport, Iowa, 1967-68; instr. grad. tchrs. and counselors, univ. counselor, researcher No. Ariz. U., Flagstaff, 1968-69; vocat. edn. and counseling coord. Fed. Exemplary Project, Council Bluffs, Iowa, 1970-71; sch. psychologist, counselor Oakdale Sch. Dist., Calif., 1971-73; sch. psychologist, intern Learning and Counseling Ctr., Stockton, Calif., 1972-74; pvt. practice rsch. in motor-perceptual tng. Greeley, 1975—; rschr. ocumeter survey Lincoln Unified Sch. Dist., Stockton, 1980, 81, 82, Manteca (Calif.) H.S., 1981; spkr. Social Sci. Edn. Consortium, U. Colo., Boulder, 1993; mem. Monday Morning steering com. House Spkr. Newt Gingrich, 1997-98; mem. Friends of Sen. Al D'Amato, 1997-99; mem. Friends of Newt Gingrich, 1998-99; mem. Attention Disorder Advocacy Group, 1997-98; attend seminars for ADD and ADHD, alleviating lag/dysfunctional in neural system noted, 1997-98, 1998-99, presenter seminars in field. *Dr. Lucille M. Linde, a private practice motor-perceptual training specialist, uses developmental learning to alleviate neurological lag/dysfunction on the motor-perceptual-conceptual-social-emotional levels with no age or developmental limits known. Symptoms thus may not be lifelong. After receiving her Ed.D. at the University of Northern Colorado, her doctoral supervisor and the superintendent of schools in Stockton, California, helped her obtain scientifically documented, statistically significant data with large groups. She is the author of five books published in Library of Congress, two U.S. patents, and has received many awards and a Vendorship for Perceptual Training approved by the California State Department of Health.* Author: Psychological Services and Motor Perceptual Training, 1974, Guidebook for Psychological Services and Motor Perceptual Training (How One May Improve in Ten Easy Lessons!), 1992, Manual for the Lucille Linde Ocumeter: Ocular Pursuit Measuring Instrument, 1992, Motor-Perceptual Training and Visual Perceptual Research (How Students Improved in Seven Lessons!), 1992, Effects of Motor Perceptual Training on Academic Achievement and Ocular Pursuit Ability, 1992; inventor ocumeter, instrument for measuring ocular tracking ability, 1989, target for use, 1991; patentee in field. Mem. Rep. Presdl. Task Force, 1989-96, trustee, 1991-92, charter mem., 1994—, life mem., 1994-95; mem. Rep. Nat. Com., 1990, 93-96, 97, 98, Rep. Nat. Com. on Am. Agenda, 1993, Nat. Rep. Congl. Com., 1990, 92, 93, 95, 96, 97, 98, Nat. Fedn. Rep. Women, Greeley Rep. Women, 1996-99; advisor Senator Bob Dole for Pres.; charter mem. Rep. Newt Gingrich's Speaker's Task Force, Senator Phil Gramm's Presdl. Steering Com.; at-large- del. Rep. Platform Planning Com.; team leader Nat. Rep. Rapid Response Network, Campaign America, 1996; active Heritage Found. (certificate as honored mem. leadership adv. bd., 1998), Attention Deficit Disorder Adv. Group, Christian Bus. Men's Assn., Friends U.N.C. Librs., Citizens Against Govt. Waste, 1996-99, Concerns of Police Survivors, 1996-98, Nat. Assn. of Police Orgn., elected to Libr. of Congress Nat. membership, 1997-98. Recipient Presdl. medal of merit and lapel insignia, 1990, Nat. Rep. Senatorial Com., 1991-98, cert. of appreciation Nat. Rep. Congl. Com., 1992, 95, lapel pin Rep. Senatorial Inner Circle, 1990-96, Rep. Presdl. commemorative honor roll, 1993, Rep. Senatorial Freedom medal, 1994, Rep. Legion of Merit award, 1994, 96, Rep. Congl. Order of Freedom award, 1995, Senatorial Inner Cir. Lapel Pin, 1998, Lapel Pin award RNC, 199 6, Leadership citation Rep. Senatorial Inner Cir./ Rep. Nat. Conv., 1996, Legion of Merit Rep. Presdl. exec. com., 1996, Honor cert. House Spkr. Newt Gingrich, 1996; named to Rep. Nat. Hall of Honor, 1992. Mem. AAUP, NAFE, Nat. Assn. Sch. Psychologists and Psychometrists (spkr. conf. 1976), Rep. Senatorial Inner Cir. (name engraved on Ronald Wilson Reagan Eternal Flame of Freedom, 1995, on the Nat. Rep. Victory Monument, Washington, 1996, Rep. Sen. Inner Cir. Conv. Medallion 1996, RNC Mems. Only pin 1996), 20th Century Rep. Leader, Rep. Sen. Inner Cir., 1998, The Smithsonian Assocs., Ronald Reagan Presdl. Libr. and Mus., Bush Presdl. Libr. and Mus., Children and Adults with Attention Deficit Disorder, Nat. Fragile Found., Nat. Trust for Hist. Preservation, Internat. Platform Assn., Friends of Newt Gingrich, 1998-99, Independence Inst., Assn. Children Learning Disabilities (spkr. internat. conv.1976), Linrary of Congress Assn., 1999, CHADD (Chldrn. and Adults with Attention Deficit Disorder), LDA (Learning Disabilities of Colorado), Natl. Fragile Found., Fraxa Rsch. Found., 1999, Greeley Rep. Women's Club, Pi Omega Pi, Pi Lambda Theta. Avocations: music, archtl. design. Home: 1954 18th Ave Greeley CO 80631-5208

LINDE, MAXINE HELEN, lawyer, business executive, private investor; b. Chgo., Sept. 2, 1939; d. Jack and Lottie (Kroll) Stern; B.A. summa cum laude, UCLA, 1961; J.D., Stanford U., 1967; m. Ronald K. Linde, June 12, 1960. Bar: Calif. 1968. Applied mathematician, reseach engr. Jet Propulsion Lab., Pasadena, Calif., 1961-64; law clk. U.S. Dist. Ct. No. Calif., 1967-68; mem. firm Long & Levit, San Francisco, 1968-69, Swerdlow, Glikbarg & Shimer, Beverly Hills, Calif., 1969-72; sec., gen. counsel Envirodyne Industries, Inc., Chgo., 1972-89; pres. The Ronald and Maxine Linde Found., 1989—; vice chmn. bd., gen. counsel Titan Fin. Group, LLC, Chgo., 1994-98. Mem. bd. visitors Stanford Law Sch., 1989-92, law and bus. adv. coun., 1991-94, dean's adv. coun. 1992-94. Mem. Order of Coif, Phi Beta Kappa, Pi Mu Epsilon, Alpha Lambda Delta.

LINDEGREN, JACK KENNETH, elementary and secondary education educator; b. Fresno, Calif., Feb. 9, 1931; s. Henry Jack and Katherine (Metzler) L.; m. Betty Jo Rowland, Dec. 1960 (div. Apr. 1963); m. Elaine Finnegan, Apr. 27, 1963; children: Susan Carol, Karen Ann. BA, Fresno State Coll., 1954; MA, Calif. State U., Fresno, 1976. Educator, adminstr. Fresno County, Firebaugh, Calif., 1954-5; educator Calaveras County Schs., San Andreas, Calif., 1964-66, Kings County Schs., Corcoran, Calif., 1966-80, Kern County Schs., Bakersfield, Calif., 1985-87, L.A. Unified Schs., 1985—; educator L.A. Unified Schs., 1977-92; instr. ARC, Hanford, Calif., 1974-79.; instr. County Sci. Insvc., 1985. Inventor electroanalysis device Chrysler award., 1965. Participant Desert Opera, Palmdale, Calif., 1986-88; bd. mem., chmn. ARC, Hanford, 1973-78. Sgt. U.S. Army, 1955-57. Mem. NAS, AAAS, NEA, Nat. Assn. Legions of Honor, Nat. Space Soc., Tehran Shrine, Fresno East/West Game Corcoran Band Club, Santa Clara U. Alumni Assn., Internat. DeMolay Alumni Assn. (life), Assn. Calif. Sch. Adminstrs., Calif. State U. of Fresno Alumni Assn. (life), Scottish Rite (life), Corcoran/Tulare Masons (life, Bethel guardian 1978-80, Pin 1980), Odd Fellows (30 Yr. Mem. award 1991), Mensa (elder, deacon bushop, 10 v.p. Membership award). Presbyterian. Avocations: reading, science and religious literature (Mensa spl. interest groups in religion).

LINDEMAN, DOUGLAS JAY, film producer; b. N.Y.C., June 1, 1951; s. Benjamin and Georgette L.; m. Lanna Gail Vuyas, Sept. 4, 1974 (div. Oct. 1986); 1 child, Penelope Jane. Student, Denison U., 1969-71. Writer, reporter People Mag., L.A., 1985-88; founder Cottrell & Lindeman, L.A., 1988—, Film Kitchen, L.A., 1994—; mktg. cons. IFP, L.A., 1991—, active West Coast Devel., AIVF, L.A., 1995. Prodr.: (films) Bar Girls, 1995, Shooting Porn, 1996, Shelf Life, 1994, Angels Ladies, 1998, Gentleman B, 1999. Publicity cons. L.A. Regional Food Bank, Calif., 1991-93, Cirque du Soleil, Montreal, 1991. Mem. Ind. Feature Orgn. Avocation: advising young filmmakers. Office: Film Kitchen 7223 Beverly Blvd Los Angeles CA 90036

LINDEMULDER, CAROL ANN, interior designer, artist; b. San Diego, May 2, 1936; d. Franklin Geert and Leone Augusta (Oltman) L. BA in Decorative Arts, U. Calif., Berkeley, 1959; postgrad. in fine arts, San Diego State U., 1965-67. Tchr. interior design and fine arts adult edn. divsn. San Diego City Schs., 1960-67; with Milo of Calif., Inc. subs. Milo Electronics Corp., 1968-73, corp. staff asst., 1972, asst. to dir. mktg., 1972-73; with Frazee Industries, 1975-77; owner, designer-artist Call Carol, San Diego, 1976--; former instr. U. Calif. Extension, San Diego, instr. San Diego landscape painting, 1993—. One-woman show Point Loma Art Assn., 1967, Scandia Interiors, 1977, Cen. Fed. Savs. & Loan, 1978, John Duncan Interiors, 1979, Villa Montezuma Mus., 1981; exhibited in group shows Calif. Western U., 1963, Jewish Community Ctr., 1963-64, So. Calif. Expn., 1964, San Diego Mus. Art, 1966, 71, 75, San Diego State U., 1974, Spectrum Gallery, 1985, A.R.T. Beasley Gallery, 1985, Atrium Gallery, Mich., 1989, San Diego Artist Showcase, 1991, Doug Pratt Gallery, San Diego, 1995—, San Diego Invitational, 1997-98, 99, Howard Mandville Gallery, Kirkland, Wash., 1998, Lanning Gallery, Sedona, Ariz., 1998, Boehm Gallery Palomar Coll., San Marcos, Calif., 1998. Coord. Christmas program San Diego Community Vol. Bur., 1961; a founder, treas., bd. dirs. Save Our Heritage Orgn., 1969-71, pres., 1974-75, 79-81; mem. San Diego Hist. Sites Bd., 1985-93, vice chmn., 1985-92; founder, pres. Save the Coaster Com., 1981-83; co-founder San Diego Hist. Preservation Endowment Fund, 1990; mem. Calif. Preservation Found. Named Vol. of Month, San Diego Community Vol. Bur., 1961; recipient President's commendation Save Our Heritage Orgn., 1984. Mem. Nature Conservancy, Jr. League San Diego. Republican. Avocations: gardening, travel. Fax: 760-728-2622. Office: PO Box 2108 Fallbrook CA 92088-2108

LINDGREN, JENNIFER GOUX, business executive, financial planner, educator; b. L.A., Jan. 10, 1946; d. Warren Goux and Violet (Louis) Goux Knupp; m. Larry E. Lindgren, July 1, 1967; children: Todd E., Kristen E., Kurt W. BA in Psychology, UCLA, 1967. Cert. tchr., Calif.; CFP; gen. securities lec., Calif.; lic. ins. agt., Calif. Elem. tchr. L.A. City Schs., 1968-72; art tchr. Sierra Canyon Day Camp, Newhall, Calif., summer 1975,76; co-owner Lindgren's Jewelry, Porterville, Calif., 1978—; instr. Porterville Adult Sch., 1988-94; investment exec. Baraban Securities/Volker Ins., Woodland Hills, Calif., 1989-94, Fin. West Group, Tarzana, Calif., 1994, Investment Ctrs. of Am., Bank of Sierra, Porterville, 1995—. Troop co-leader Girl Scouts U.S., Porterville, 1984-86; student host family Rotary Internat., Porterville, 1990-91; sec.-treas. Porterville Edn. Found., 1988—. Mem. AAUW (pres., v.p., other offices 1987—, Named Gift honoree 1991), Inst. CFPs, Central Valley Soc. CFPs, UCLA Alumni Assn., Porterville C. of C., Zonta Club. Republican. Avocations: bicycling, boating, skiing, walking, gourmet cooking. Office: 90 N Main St Porterville CA 93257-3712

LINDHOLM, DONALD WAYNE, lawyer; b. Des Moines, Dec. 12, 1937; s. Rudolf William and Hazel Marie (Yoder) L.; m. E. DeAnne Wilson, Feb. 4, 1962; children: Dawn DeRae, Dow William. LLB, U. Ariz., 1966. Bar: Ariz. 1966, U.S. Dist. Ct. Ariz. 1966, U.S. Claims Ct. 1975, U.S. Ct. Appeals (9th cir.) 1988. Asst. city atty. City of Phoenix, 1966-74; ptnr. Flynn, Kimerer, Thinnes, Derrick & Lindholm, Phoenix, 1974-78; shareholder Donald W. Lindholm, P.C., Phoenix, 1978-81; counsel Treon, Warnicke & Roush, Phoenix, 1981; owner Capt. Jack's Landing Channel Island Harbor, Oxnard, Calif., 1982-85; shareholder Burch & Cracchiolo, P.A., Phoenix, 1985—. Fellow Ariz. Bar Found.; mem. ABA (family law section), Assn. Trial Lawyers Am., Nat. Inst. Mcpl. Law Officers (zoning and planning com.), State Bar of Ariz. (family law section, cert. specialist in domestic relations bd. of legal specialization), Ariz. Trial Lawyers Assn., Maricopa County Bar Assn. (family law sect.). Avocations: mountain biking, hiking, skiing, flying. Office: Burch and Cracchiolo PA 702 E Osborn Rd Ste 200 Phoenix AZ 85014-5234

LINDHOLM, DWIGHT HENRY, lawyer; b. Blackduck, Minn., May 27, 1930; s. Henry Nathanial and Viola Eudora (Gummert) L.; m. Loretta Catherine Brown, Aug. 29, 1958; children: Douglas Dwight, Dionne Louise, Jeanne Marie, Philip Clayton, Kathleen Anne. *Dwight cruised the South Pacific 1982-83 for 13 months on a 51' sailboat with his wife, five children (then ages 13-22), and Rottweiler and Pekinese dogs. With no prior boating experience, they did it with only "the sextant, compass, and watch." It was the year of the greatest El Nino of recorded history. They withstood 3 hurricanes, but anchor never dragged and hull never touched the bottom. 26 days at sea going and 40 days returning. In French Polynesia they visited the Marquesas, Tuamotos ("Dangerous Archipelago"), and Society Islands.* Student, Macalester Coll., 1948-49; BBA, U. Minn., 1951, LLB, 1954; postgrad., Mexico City Coll. (now U. of Ams.), 1956-57. Bar: Minn. 1954, Calif. 1958. Sole practice Los Angeles, 1958-65, 72-81, 84—; ptnr. Lindholm & Johnson, Los Angeles, 1965-69, Cotter, Lindholm & Johnson, Los Angeles, 1969-72; sole practice Los Angeles, 1972-81; of counsel Bolton, Dunn & Moore, Los Angeles, 1981-84. Mem. Calif. Republican Central Com., 1962-63, Los Angeles Republican County Central Com., 1962-66; bd. dirs. Family Service Los Angeles, 1964-70, v.p., 1968-70; bd. dirs. Wilshire YMCA, 1976-77; trustee Westlake Girls Sch., 1978-81; hon. presenter Nat. Charity League Coronet Debutante Ball, 1984; bd. dirs. Calif. State U.-Northridge Trust Fund, 1989-93; bd. dirs. Queen of Angeles/Hollywood Presbyn. Med. Ctr., 1990—; chmn., CEO Queen of Angels, Hollywood Presbyn. Found., 1997—. Served as capt. JAG Corps USAF, 1954-56. Recipient Presdl. award Los Angeles Jr. C. of C., 1959. Mem. Calif. Bar Assn., L.A. County Bar Assn., Wilshire Bar Assn. (bd. govs. 1989-91), Internat. Genealogy Fellowship of Rotarians (founding pres. 1979-86), Calif. Club, Ocean Cruising Club Eng. (Newport Harbor port officer), Rotary (dir. 1975-78), Delta Sigma Pi, Delta Sigma Rho, Delta Theta Phi (state chancellor 1972-73). Presbyterian. Avocations: sailing, offshore cruising. Office: 3580 Wilshire Blvd Fl 17 Los Angeles CA 90010-2501

LINDHOLM, RICHARD THEODORE, economics and finance educator; b. Eugene, Oreg., Oct. 5, 1960; s. Richard Wadsworth and Mary Marjorie (Trunko) L. m. Valaya Nivasananda, May 8, 1987. BA, U. Chgo., 1982, MA, 1983, PhD, 1993. Ptnr. Lindholm and Osanka, Eugene, 1986-89, Lindholm Rsch., Eugene, 1989—; guest lectr. Nat. Inst. Devel. Adminstrn., Bangkok, Thailand, 1989; pres. Rubicon Inst., Eugene, 1988—; adj. asst. prof. U. Oreg., Eugene, 1988—. Campaign co-chmn. Lane C.C. Advocates, Eugene, 1988; coord., planner numerous state Rep. Campaigns, Oreg., 1988—; campaign mgr. Jack Roberts for Oreg. State Labor Commn., 1994; mem. staff Oreg. Senate Rep. Office, 1989-90; precinct committeeperson Oreg. Rep. Party, 1987-92, 94—; bd. dirs. Rubicon Soc., Eugene, 1987—, pres., 1993-98. Republican. Lutheran. Home: 3335 Bardell Ave Eugene OR 97401-8021

LINDLEY, F(RANCIS) HAYNES, JR., foundation president emeritus, lawyer; b. L.A., Oct. 15, 1945; s. Francis Haynes and Grace Nelson (McCanne) L.; m. Hollinger McCloud Lindley, Apr. 1, 1977; 1 child, Anne Hollinger Lindley. BA, Claremont (Calif.) Men's Coll., 1967; MFA, Claremont (Calif.) Grad. Sch., 1972; JD, Southwestern U., L.A., 1976. Bar: Calif. 1976, U.S. Supreme Ct. 1980. Deputy pub. defender Office of Pub. Defender, L.A., 1977-79; staff atty., Dept. Trial Counsel The State Bar of Calif., L.A., 1979-81; pvt. practice, 1981-90; pres. John Randolph Haynes and Dora Haynes Found., L.A., 1987-97, pres. emeritus, 1997—; trustee John Randolph Haynes and Dora Haynes Found., L.A., 1978—. Mem. bd. dirs. TreePeople, L.A., 1985-87, So. Calif. Assn. Philanthropy, L.A., 1985-89; mem. bd. fellows Claremont (Calif.) U. Ctr. and Grad. Sch., 1987—; mem. bd. dirs. Marin Agrl. Land Trust, 1995—. Recipient Disting. Svc. award The Claremont (Calif.) Grad. Sch., 1994. Avocation: sailing, art history, banjo. Home: PO Box 1414 Ross CA 94957-1414 Office: John Randolph Haynes and Dora Haynes Found 888 W 6th St Ste 1150 Los Angeles CA 90017-2737

LINDLEY, JEARL RAY, lawyer; b. Abilene, Tex., Mar. 12, 1934; s. Hardie and Hope Clement Mourant; m. Annabelle Sim Yee Lindley, May 22, 1954; children: Katheryn Ann, Michael Andrew, Carolyn Elizabeth. BS in Chemistry, N.Mex. State U., 1960; MD, U. Colo., 1964; MS, U. Ill., 1967; JD, South Tex. Coll. of Law, 1997. Asst. clin. prof. of surgery Rush Med. Coll. of Rush U., Chgo., 1969-71, U. Ill. Sch. of Medicine, Chgo., 1969-71; assoc. clin. prof. of surgery Tex. Tech. U. Sch. of Medicine, El Paso, 1976-80; atty., counselor Las Cruces, N.Mex., 1997—; adj. prof. N.Mex. State U., Las Cruces, 1984-86. Author publs. in field (McNeil Meml. Rsch. award 1967). Bd. dirs. Meml. Gen. Hosp., Las Cruces, 1983, So. N.Mex. Regional Dialysis Ctr., Las Cruces, 1984-89; instr. ACLS, AHA, Las Cruces, 1980-86, ATLS, Am. Coll. Surgeons, Las Cruces, 1980-86; mem. med. svcs. com. Dona Ana Emergency, Las Cruces, 1979, City County Hosp. Bd. Govs., Las Cruces, 1981-83; mem. internat. bd. dirs. N.Mex. State U. Alumni Assn., 1979-81; mem. bd. counselors Citizens Bank, Las Cruces, 1991-93. Named to Outstanding Young Men of Am., 1969, Marine of Yr., Marine Corps League, 1990; commd. Ky. Col., State of Ky., 1989; proclamation of Jearl R. Lindley Day/Mayor of Truth or Consequences, N.Mex., 1990; recipient Disting. Citizen medal Dept. of N.Mex. Marine Corps League, others. Fellow Am. Coll. Surgeons, Internat. Coll. of Surgeons, Southwestern Surg. Congress; mem. Internat. Endovascular Soc., Soc. Clin. Vascular Surgery, Dona Ana County Med. Soc., AHA, Am. Legion, Marine Corps Assn., Marine Corps Heritage Found., Naval Inst., Marine Meml. Club, Air Force Assn., Marine Corps League (Commandant Dept. of N.Mex. 1990-91, Dept. Commandant's medal 1991, medal with bronze star 1988-90). Republican. Mem. Ch. of Christ. Avocations: shooting, photography, travel in an RV, reading. Home: 4566 Mockingbird St Las Cruces NM 88011-9616

LINDLEY, NORMAN DALE, physician; b. Henrietta, Tex., July 18, 1937; s. Hardie Lindley and Hope (Clement) Mourant; m. Luise Ann Moser, May 29, 1964; children: Norman Dale Jr., Roger Paul. BS, N.Mex. Highlands U., 1960; MD, U. Colo., 1964. Diplomate Am. Bd. Ob-Gyn. Rotating intern Kans. City (Mo.) Gen. Hosp., 1964-65; resident in ob-gyn. St. Joseph Hosp., Denver, 1965-68; med. officer USAF, Cheyenne, Wyo., 1968-70; pvt. practice physician Alamogordo, N.M., 1970—; dir. N.Mex. Found. for Med. Care, Albuquerque, 1985-88, N.Mex. Med. Rev. Assn., Albuquerque, 1985-88; physician liaison Am. Assn. Med. Assts., Chgo., 1987-93; physician advisor N.Mex. Soc. Med. Assts., 1984—. Bd. dirs. Otero County Boys and Girls Club, Alamogordo, 1977—, pres., 1979-81; bd. dirs. Otero County Assn. for Retarded Citizens, 1985-91, pres., 1989-90; bd. dirs. Otero County chpt. Am. Cancer Soc., 1970-72. Capt. USAF, 1968-70. Rsch. grantee NSF, 1959, 60. Fellow Am. Coll. Ob-Gyn.; mem. AMA, Am. Fertility Soc., Am. Inst. Ultrasound in Medicine, Am. Soc. Colposcopists and Cervical Pathologists, N.Mex. Med. Soc. (councilor 1985-88), Otero County Med. Soc. (pres. 1972-73, 83-84), Rotary (pres. White Sands chpt. 1981-82, bd. dirs. 1988-89, Svc. Above Self award 1979, Paul Harris fellow 1987). Avocations: watercolor painting, leatherworking, foreign languages. Home: 2323 Union Ave Alamogordo NM 88310-3849 Office: Thunderbird Ob-Gyn 1212 9th St Alamogordo NM 88310-5842

LINDO, EDWIN THESSALONIANS, minister; b. Turlock, Calif., June 25, 1953; s. William Edward and Josephine Mary (Mello) L.; m. Tonja Debralee Herr, Oct. 30, 1971; children: Phillip Paul, Shonna Desiri. Student, Bethany Bible Coll., 1971, Berean Coll., 1973, Intern. Bible Inst. and Sem., 1980, Modesto Jr. Coll., 1982-85. Ordained to ministry Assemblies of God, 1984. Youth and music min. Keyes (Calif.) Assembly of God, 1973-79; sr. pastor, sect. youth dir. Livingston (Calif.) Assembly of God, 1979-80; asst. pastor Northwest Assembly of God, Salida, Calif., 1981-85; warehouseman Gen. Foods Corp., Modesto, Calif., 1982—; sr. pastor Airport Assembly of God Ch., Modesto, 1986—; dist. Bible Quiz coord. Assemblies of God, Santa Cruz, Calif., 1979-80; dir. of meals to the poor, Airport Assembly of God Ch., 1985—. Mem. Stanislaus County Safety Coun., Modesto, 1974-77; representing majority whip 15th Congl. dist., Nat. Prayer Breakfast and Sem., Washington, 1986; bd. dirs. Credit Union for Organized Labor, Modesto, 1991—. Merrell fellow Harvard Theol. Sem., 1986. Democrat. Office: Airport Assembly of God 603 Benson Ave Modesto CA 95354-3833

LINDQUIST, LOUIS WILLIAM, artist, writer; b. Boise, Idaho, June 26, 1944; s. Louis William and Bessie (Newman) L.; divorced; children: Jessica Ann Alexandra, Jason Ryan Louis. BS in Anthropology, U. Oreg., 1968; postgrad., Portland State U., 1974-78. Researcher, co-writer with Asher Lee, Portland, Oreg., 1977-80; freelance artist, painter, sculptor Oreg., 1980-91, 98—; assoc. mem. of Com. for Sci. Investigation of Claims of the Paranormal, Skeptical Inquirer jour. Sgt. U.S. Army, 1968-71, Vietnam. Mem. AAAS, Internat. Platform Assn., Nat. Ctr. for Sci. Edn., Inc., N.Y. Acad. Scis., N.Am. Hunting Club. Democrat. Avocations: reading, beachcombing, listening to classical, jazz and native North American music. Home and Office: PO Box 991 Bandon OR 97411-0991

LINDQUIST, STANLEY ELMER, retired psychology educator; b. Georgetown, Tex., Nov. 9, 1917; s. Elmer H. and Esther (Nyberg) L.; m. Ingrid Walden, June 15, 1940; children: Douglas, Russell, Brent. BA, Calif. State U., 1940; PhD, U. Chgo., 1950; LittD (hon.), Trinity Coll., Chgo., 1975. Prof. Psychology Trinity Coll., Chgo., 1946-53; prof. Psychology Calif. State U., Fresno, 1953-88, prof. emeritus, 1988—; dir. Bakersfield br. Calif. State U. Fresno, 1956-58; pres., founder Link Care Found., Fresno, 1964-91, pres. emeritus, 1991—. Author: Action Helping Skills, 1975, Reach Out: Become an Encourager, 1984. With U.S. Army, 1944-46, ETO. Decorated Purple Heart with three bronze stars. Fellow Am. Scientific Assn. (pres. 1989-90); mem. APA, Christian Assn. Psychologists (pres. 1977-78), Sigma Xi. Republican. Mem. Evang. Free Ch. of Am. Avocations: woodworking, writing, fishing. Home: 5142 N College Ave Fresno CA 93704-2610 Office: Link Care Found 1734 W Shaw Ave Fresno CA 93711-3416

LINDSAY, HELEN MILLS, psychotherapist; b. Cleve., June 2; d. Don Parmenter Mills and Grace Elidia Stroup; m. Harry Anderson Lindsay, July 21, 1991. BA, Case Western Ress. U., 1932; MS of Social Sci., Boston U., 1947. Lic. clin. social worker. Sr. sen. Calif. Sr. Legislature, 1985—; pres. Aux. Laguna Hills Adult Day Health Care, 1993—. Mem. Leisure World Dem. Club (pres. 1984-85, Leisure Worlder of Month 1996). Avocations: playing piano, gardening. Address: 801 Ronda Mendoza Unit A Laguna Hills CA 92653-5902

LINDSAY, KAREN LESLIE, insurance company executive; b. Honolulu, Jan. 20, 1955; d. William Keenum and Betty K.T. (Loo) Taylor; 1 child, Kenneth P. Lindsay. BA, Stephens Coll., 1977. Lic. gen. agt. life/accident/disability NASD. Mktg. asst. Pacific Guardian Life, Honolulu, 1983-84; fin. specialist Travelers Ins., Honolulu, 1984-87, Hamden, Conn., 1987-89; fin. mgr. Abercrombi & McKiernan, Dairen, Conn., 1989; pres. Benefits Internat., Inc., Honolulu, 1990—. Author (monthly newsletter) Legislative Retom, 1993. Mem. Nat. Assn. Life Underwriters, Internat. Assn. Fin. Planners, Hawaii State Underwriters (legal chairperson 1993-94), Gen. Agts. Assn., Japan Am. Soc., Pacific Rim Found., Mid Pacific Country Club (golf com. 1993—). Republican. Avocations: golf, tennis, painting. Home: 1309 McCully St$D Honolulu HI 96822-1362 Office: Benefits Internat Inc 1314 S King St Ste 624 Honolulu HI 96814-1941

LINDSEY, JOANNE M., flight attendant, poet; b. Peoria, Ill., Aug. 27, 1936; d. George Edward and Elsie Rosetta (Mann) L.; m. Aug. 1959 (div. 1961). AA, El Camino Coll., Torrance, Calif., 1958. Exec. adminstrv. sec. Space Tech. Labs. (formerly Ramo-Woolridge), Hawthorne, Calif., 1958-64; flight attendant Am. Airlines, L.A., 1964—. Contbr. poems to anthologies, 1996—. Attended People to People Amb. Program's So. African Tour of

Women Writers, 1998. Mem. AAUW, Acad. Am. Poets, Audie Murphy Rsch. Found., Internat. Soc. Poets, L.A. World Affairs Coun.. Avocations: gardening, writing, skiing, mountain biking, home refurbishing. Home: 846 American Oaks Ave Newbury Park CA 91320-5572

LINDSEY, WILLIAM FUSSELL, retired newspaper association executive; b. Rocky Mount, N.C., Mar. 22, 1923; s. Robert Penn and Wallolah (Fussell) L.; B.A. Westminster Coll., 1948; BS, U. Colo., 1950; m. Gwen R. Caverly, Dec. 28, 1948; children: Charles Penn, Rebecca Ruth. Jr. acct. Redecker, Stanley & Alhberg, Denver, 1950-52; with Colo. Press Service, Denver, 1952-64; sec.-mgr. Colo. Press Assn., Denver, 1964-90, ret., 1990; With USAAF, World War II. Decorated D.F.C., Air medal with six oak leaf clusters; recipient Big Hat award U. Colo. Journalism Sch., 1982. Mem. Newspaper Assn. Mgrs. (pres. 1978), Nat. Newspaper Assn. (dir. 1978), Nat. Editorial Assn., Soc. Profl. Journalists, Advt. Club Denver, Colo. C. of C., Denver Press Club, Kissing Camels Club, Kissing Camels Golf Club, Delta Tau Delta. Home: Kissing Camels Estates 5081 Lyda Ln Colorado Springs CO 80904-1007 Office: Colo Press Assn Press Bldg 1336 Glenarm Pl Denver CO 80204-2115

LINDSKOG, MARJORIE OTILDA, elementary school educator; b. Rochester, Minn., Oct. 13, 1937; d. Miles Emery and Otilda Elvina (Hagre) L. BA, Colo. Coll., 1959, MA in Teaching, 1972. Field advisor/camp dir. Columbine council Girl Scouts U.S., Pueblo, Colo., 1959-65; staff mem. Wyo. Girl Scout Camp, Casper, 1966, dir., 1967; tchr. Sch. Dist. 60, Pueblo, 1966—; asst. dir. camp Pacific Peaks Girl Scouts U.S., Olympia, Wash., 1968, dir., 1969; instr. Jr. Gt. Books Program, 1981—; mem. adv. bd. Newspapers in Edn., 1988—; mem. supervisory com. Pueblo Tchr.'s Credit com.; lectr., instr. edn. U. So. Colo., 1990-96; instr. math. Adams State Coll., 1991; mem. adv. bd. ctr. for advancement teaching sci., math, and tech. U. So. Colo., 1992-94; apptd. by Gov. to Colo. Standards Assessment Devel. and Implementation Coun., 1993—. Author: (series of math. lessons) Bronco Mathmania, 1987, 88, 89, 90, 91, 92, 93, 94, 95, Welcome to Wall Street, 1992, 93, 94, 95, 96, Day to Day Math, 1994, Mental Math, 1995, Everyday Math, vol. 1 and 2, 1996, Word Problems, 1996; area co-chair Channel 8 Pub. TV Auction, Pueblo, 1983-87; contbr. articles to profl. jours. Bd. dirs. Columbine Girl Scout Council, 1983-85, Dist. #60 Blood Bank, 1985—; mem. Pueblo Greenway and Nature Ctr., 1981—. Recipient Thanks badge Girl Scouts U.S., Presdl. award for Outstanding Tchg. in Elem. Math., 1995. Mem. Nat. Council for Tchrs. Math., Colo. Coun. Tchrs. Math. (Outstanding Elem. Math Tchr. of Yr. 1989), Intertel, Mensa, Phi Delta Kappa, Alpha Phi. Lutheran. Club: Pueblo Country. Lodge: Sons of Norway. Home: 2941 Country Club Dr Pueblo CO 81008-1202 Office: Baca Elem Sch 2800 E 17th St Pueblo CO 81001-4741

LINDSTROM, KRIS PETER, environmental consultant; b. Dumont, N.J., Oct. 18, 1948; s. Sven Rune and Moyra Hilda (Coughlan) L.; m. Annette Gail Chaplin, June 25, 1978; 1 child, Karl Pierce. MPH, U. Calif., Berkeley, 1973; MS in Ecology, U. Calif., Davis, 1983. Registered environ. health specialist, Calif. Sr. lab. analyst County Sanitation Dists. Orange County, Fountain Valley, Calif., 1970-72, environ. specialist, 1973-74; environ. specialist J.B. Gilbert and Assocs., Sacramento, 1974-78; prin. K.P. Lindstrom & Assocs., Sacramento, 1978-84; pres. K.P. Lindstrom, Inc., Pacific Grove, Calif., 1985—; mem. rsch. adv. bd. Nat. Water Rsch. Inst., Fountain Valley, 1991—. Author: Design of Municipal Wastewater Treatment Plants, 1992; editor publs., 1989, 90. Chmn. City of Pacific Grove (Calif.) Mus. Bd., 1992-96, City of Seal Beach (Calif.) Environ. Bd., 1970. Mem. Water Environ. Fedn. (chmn. marine water quality com. 1987-90), Calif. Water Pollution Control Assn., Pacific Grove Residents Assn. (bd. dirs., pres., v.p. 1992-98). Office: KP Lindstrom Inc PO Box 51008 Pacific Grove CA 93950-6008

LINEBAUGH, DAVID EUGENE, fire marshal, educator; b. Colorado Springs, Colo., Aug. 26, 1955; s. Gary Eugene and Doris Irene (Llewellyn) Finch; m. Beverly Joan Good, Feb. 14, 1985; children: Christopher Aaron, Quinlan Scott. AAS, Pikes Peak C.C., Colorado Springs, 1992; BS, Colo. Christian U., 1994, MS, 1997. Dispatcher/patrolman Manitou Springs (Colo.) Police Dept., 1975-76, Colo. State Patrol, Colorado Springs, 1976-77; v.p. High Country Heat Pumps and Air Conditioning, Colorado Springs, 1978-84; combination inspector Regional Bldg. Dept., Colorado Springs, 1984-87; chief inspector Colorado Springs Fire Dept., 1987-90, dep. fire marshal, 1990-94, fire marshal, 1994—; prof. fire sci. Pikes Peak C.C., 1994—; prof. mgmt. Colo. Christian U., 1998—. Contbr. articles to profl. jours. Mem. Regional Bldg. Commn., Pikes Peak Regional Bldg. Dept., Colorado Springs, 1983-84; mem. Pikes Peak leadership com. Citizens Goals, Colorado Springs, 1995-96; mem. cmty. action com. City of Colorado Springs, 1996; bd. dirs. Wagon Wheel Coun.-Girl Scouts Am., 1997. Recipient Achievement award Colorado Springs C. of C., 1993, Disting. Achievement award Colo. Christian U., 1994, Pikes Peak Leadership Grad. award Citizens Goals, 1995. Mem. Internat. Fire Code Inst. (chmn. edn. and cert. com. 1995—), Nat. Fire Protection Assn. (inspector qualification com. 1991—), Fire Marshals Assn. N.Am., Internat. Conf. Bldg. Ofcls., Fire Marshals Assn. Colo. (sec. 1993), Colo. Christian Univ. Alumni Assn. (bd. dirs. 1997). Republican. Methodist. Home: 3440 Rio Vista Dr Colorado Springs CO 80917-2783 Office: Colorado Springs Fire Dept Office Fire Marshal 31 S Weber St Colorado Springs CO 80903-1913

LING, DAVID CHANG, international book dealer; b. Shanghai, Feb. 17, 1939; s. H.C. and Katherine (Chang) L.; m. Janine Peters, June 20, 1970 (div. Feb. 1975). BA, U. Ore., 1962; MA, U. Wis., 1964, PhD, 1971. Vis. instr. U. of the South, Sewanee, Tenn., 1964-65; asst. prof. U. Wis., Kenosha, 1969-73; owner Ling's Internat. Books, San Diego, 1974—. Mem. Phi Beta Kappa. Democrat. Home: 5012 Westminster Ter San Diego CA 92116-2103 Office: Ling's Internat Books 7531 Convoy Ct San Diego CA 92111-1113

LING, JIAYI, artist; b. Shanghai, Nov. 5, 1970; came to U.S., 1988; d. Zhike Ling and MingLi Xu. BA magna cum laude, Lawrence U., 1994; MS, Kans. State U., 1997; MFA, Wash. State U., 1998. Rsch. asst. Kans. State U., Manhattan, 1994-97; instr. Wash. State U., Pullman, 1996-98; graphics asst. Physics Edn. group Kans. State U., 1998—; co-founder Young Women/Student Caucus of Art, 1997; mem. Fedn. Internat. Color-Ink Artists, 1997; pres. United Coun. Internat. Orgns., Wash. State U., 1997, pres. Chinese Students and Scholars Friendship Assn., 1997; spkr. in field. One-woman shows include Kans. State U., 1995; exhibited in group shows at Wash. State U. Art Gallery, 1997, U. Idaho, 1997, Woman's Caucus for Art Ann. Conf., 1997, ArtSpace Gallery, Seattle, 1997, Ont. (Can.) Coll. Arts and Design, 1998, Taichung Mcpl. Culture Ctr., Taiwan, 1998; exhibited in traveling shows; represented in numerous pvt. collections. Recipient Ruth Bateman award Lawrence U., 1994, Travel grant Kans. State U., 1995. Mem. Coll. Arts Assn., Women's Caucus Art (bd. dirs. 1998).

LING, MICHAEL JAMES, investment advisor; b. Portland, Maine, Sept. 17, 1959; s. Harmon Ling and Nancy Burnett (Pert) Sherman; m. Kathryn Duane Denton, June 9, 1992. BA in Econs., U. Calif., Berkeley, 1993. Registered investment advisor. Residential advisor Job Corps, Clearfield, Utah, 1983-85; asst. housing mgr. Coll. of the Redwoods, Eureka, Calif., 1986-92; personal fin. advisor Am. Express Fin. Advisors, Boise, Idaho, 1994-96; fin. advisor IFG Network Securities, Boise, 1996; pres. Berkeley, Inc., Boise, 1996—; pres. Treasure Valley Econs. Assn., Boise, 1996-98. Bd. dirs., pres.-elect United Cerebral Palsy Idaho, Boise, 1996-98; bd. dirs. Learning Lab., Boise, 1996-98. With USN, 1977-81. Mem. Calif. Alumni Assn. Idaho (pres. 1995-98). Avocations: golf, tennis, reading. E-mail: berkleyine@uswest.net. Fax: 208 345 8945. Office: Berkeley Inc 2402 W Jefferson St Boise ID 83702-4811

LING, ROBERT MALCOLM, banker, publishing executive; b. Akron, Ohio, July 6, 1931; s. Howard George and Catherine Zola (Smith) L.; m. Lois Claire Fisher Ling, Nov. 1, 1992; children: Shelly, Robert Jr., Amy, Beth, Patricia. BA in Journalism, Mich. State U., 1952. Asst. pres. Dike-O-Seal, Inc., Chgo., 1955-56; gen. mgr. Vollwerth Marquette (Mich.) Co., 1956-58, pres., 1958-75; pres. Vandco Incorp., Marquette, 1975-85, Cable Americal Corp., Rancho Cordova, Calif., 1985-89, Romali Holdings, Inc., Rancho Cordova, Calif., 1989—; chmn. Gold River Bank, Fair Oaks, Calif., 1990-92, Sacramento Safety Ctr., Inc., 1996—; publisher Grapevine-Independent [illegible] of Rancho Cordova, Calif., 1986-87. Capt. U.S. Army, 1952-55. Republican. Home: 6032 Puerto Dr Rncho Murieta CA 95683-9313 Office: Romali Holdings Inc 3338 Mather Field Rd Rancho Cordova CA 95670-5966

LINGLE, CRAIG STANLEY, glaciologist, educator; b. Carlsbad, N.Mex., Sept. 11, 1945; s. Stanley Orland and Margaret Pearl (Ewart) L.; m. Diana Lynn Duncan, Aug. 21, 1972; 1 son, Eric Glenn. BS, U. Wash., 1967; MS, U. Maine, 1978; PhD, U. Wis., 1983. Nat. rsch. coun. resident rsch. assoc. Coop. Inst. for Rsch. in Environ. Scis., U. Colo., Boulder, 1983-84, rsch. assoc., 1984-86; program mgr. polar glaciology divsn. polar programs NSF, Washington, 1986-87; cons. Jet Propulsion Lab., Pasadena, Calif., 1987-88; nat. rsch. coun. resident rsch. assoc. NASA Goddard Space Flight Ctr., Oceans and Ice Branch, Greenbelt, Md., 1988-90; rsch. assoc. prof. Geophys. Inst., U. Alaska, Fairbanks, 1990—, acting dir. Alaska synthetic aperture radar facility, 1997-98. Contbr. articles to profl. jours. Recipient Antarctic Svc. medal of U.S., NSF, 1987, Rsch. Project of Month award Office of Health and Environ. Rsch., U.S. Dept. Energy, 1990, Group Achievement award NASA, 1992. Mem. AAAS, Internat. Glaciological Soc., Am. Geophys. Union, Sigma Xi. Avocations: downhill and cross-country skiing, canoeing, hiking. Office: Geophys Inst Univ Alaska PO Box 757320 Fairbanks AK 99775-7320

LINHART, EDDIE GENE, aerospace executive; b. Leachville, Ark., Mar. 8, 1941; s. Eddie Clifton and Della Inez (Towell) L.; m. Claudia Jean Benninger, May 25, 1962; children: Willian Gene, Bonnie Jean. BA, Calif. State U., Long Beach, 1975, MA, 1977; grad., Claremont Grad. Sch. Registered profl. engr. Calif. V.p. AVCO Aerostructures Divsn., Nashville, 1979-81, Northrop Corp., Hawthorne, Calif., 1981-85; pres. Western Gear Corp., CIty of Industry, Calif., 1985-88; pres., chief exec. officer Precision Aerotech, Inc., La Jolla, Calif., 1988-90, EGL Holdings, Inc., Laguna Hills, Calif., 1990—, Astech/MCI, Inc., Santa Ana, Calif., 1991-93; chmn. Advanced Metal Cos., Inc., Menlo Park, Calif., 1992—; chmn., CEO TFI Acquisition, Inc., 1995—; dir. Calif. State U., L.A., 1983—. Bd. dirs. Boy Scouts Am., L.A., 1984—, dist. chmn., 1983-85. With USN, 1958-62. Recipient Disting. Engring. Achievement award San Fernando Valley Engrs. Coun., 1986; award for Achievement as chmn. Ind. Adv. Bd. Calif. State U., 1986, Frank E. Reeves Internat. Interprofl. award Ins. Mgmt. Engring., 1988. Fellow Soc. Mfg. Engrs. (dir. 1979—), Inst. Advancement of Engring.; mem. Am. Mgmt. Assn. (Silver Knight), Calif. Soc. Profl. Engrs., Soc. Automotive Engrs. (chmn. mfg. com. 1983-85, Achievement award 1985), Navy League. Republican. Lutheran. Avocations: golf, fishing, stamp collecting, coin collecting, restoring antique automobiles. Office: EGL Holdings Inc 27641 Fargo Rd Laguna Hills CA 92653-7809

LINK, JULIA ANNE, urban horticulture educator; b. San Diego, June 8, 1955; d. Charles Dickenson and Alice Mary (Maben) L. AS in Dental Assisting, Pacific Coll., 1973; BA in Fine Arts, San Diego Art Inst., 1978; postgrad., Solano Coll., 1990. Registered dental asst., Calif. Dental asst. Office of Robert Prario, DMD, San Diego, 1981-86; ind. sign designer Fairfield, Calif., 1986-89; greenhouse mgr. Solano Coll., Suisun, Calif., 1986-90; biol. aide U.S. Forest Svc., Berkeley, Calif., 1987-89, pub. rels. specialist, 1988-89; educator, program coord. U. Calif. Coop. Extension, Fairfield, Calif., 1990—; cons. in field; chair adv. com. agr./horticulture Solano Coll., 1996—. Author: Prisms, 1991, Moments & Memories, 1993; contbr. 28 poems to profl. publs. Poetry reading, spkr. in field. Recipient Editor's Choice award Nat. Libr. Poetry, 1993, 94, Pres. award, 1994; Calif. Assn. Nurserymen scholar, 1988. Mem. Internat. Soc. Poets, Am. Forests, Lit. Book Rev. Guild. Avocations: plants, drawing, painting, animation, writing. Office: U Calif Coop Extension 2000 W Texas St Fairfield CA 94533-4443

LINK-JOBE, JANNICE LOUISE, education educator; b. Oregon City, Oreg., Apr. 8, 1947; d. Wilford Martin and Helen Louise (Hart) Link; m. Harvey Richard Jobe, May 31, 1973; 1 child, Tiffany Danielle-Louise. BS in Natural Scis., Oreg. Coll. Edn., Monmouth, Oreg., 1975, MS in Natural Scis. and Edn., 1977; EdD in Secondary Edn., Oreg. State U., Corvallis, 1996. Chemistry tchr. Ctrl. H.S., Independence, Oreg., 1977-89; asst. prin. Central High, 1989-91; prin. Talmadge Mid. Sch., Monmouth, 1991-96; prof. edn. Western Oreg. State U., Monmouth, 1996—, team leader proficiency based tchr. prep. program, 1997-98; prin. Sunrise Elem., Albany, Oreg., 1998—; writer chemistry questions Am. Coll. Testing, Chgo., 1984-88; invited presenter 2d ann. U.S.-China Conf. on Edn., Beijing, 1998, Nat. Conf. Am. Assn. Colls. and Tchr. Edn., New Orleans, 1998, Nat. Stds. Based Tchg. and Learning Conf., Portland, Oreg., 1997; proficiency based evaluation sys. cons., 1998; lead rschr. China-U.S. Cmty. Edn. Project. Contbr. articles to Oreg. Sci. Jour., 1983-86. Bd. mem. Gang Task Force, Monmouth, 1991—; bd. dirs. YMCA, Salem, Oreg., 1995—. U.S. Presdl. finalist for sci. tchg. State of Oreg., 1985, 86., Tchr. of the yr., 1983-84. Fellow NAESP, ASCD, Confedn. Oreg. Sch. Adminstrs., Nat. Assn. Secondary Sch. Prins., Confederation of Sch. Adminstrn, Oregon Middle Level Assn., Phi Delta Kapa (v.p. Willamette Valley chpt., 1996—), Oreg. Counselors Assn. (hon., Adminstr. of Yr. State of Oreg., 1994, proficiency based evaluation sys. cons. 1998), Oreg. Sci. Tchrs. (pres. 1984-85). Avocations: sailing, hiking, reading, gardening, fishing, family activities. Home: 414 Stadium Dr S Monmouth OR 97361-1939 Office: Sunrise Elem Sch Albany OR 97321

LINKLETTER, ARTHUR GORDON, radio and television broadcaster; b. Moose Jaw, Sask., Can., July 17, 1912; s. Fulton John and Mary (Metzler) L.; m. Lois Foerster, Nov. 25, 1935; children: Jack, Dawn, Robert (dec.), Sharon, Diane (dec.). A.B., San Diego State Coll., 1934. Program dir. Sta. KGB, San Diego, 1934; program dir. Calif. Internat. Expn., San Diego, 1935; radio dir. Tex. Centennial Expn., Dallas, 1936; San Francisco World's Fair, 1937-39; pres. Linkletter Prodns.; ptnr., co-owner John Guedel Radio Prodns.; chmn. bd. Linkletter Enterprises; owner Art Linkletter Oil Enterprises. Author: theme spectacle Cavalcade of Golden West, 1940; author and co-producer: theme spectacle Cavalcade of Am, 1941; writer, producer, star in West Coast radio shows, 1940-55; former star, writer: People Are Funny, NBC-TV and radio, Art Linkletter's House Party, CBS-TV and radio; Author: People Are Funny, 1953, Kids Say The Darndest Things, 1957, The Secret World of Kids, 1959, Confessions of a Happy Man, 1961, Kids Still Say The Darndest Things, 1961, A Child's Garden of Misinformation, 1965, I Wish I'd Said That, 1968, Linkletter Down Under, 1969, Oops, 1969, Drugs at My Door Step, 1973, Women Are My Favorite People, 1974, How to be a Super Salesman, 1974, Yes, You Can!, 1979, I Didn't Do It Alone, 1979, Public Speaking for Private People, 1980, Linkletter on Dynamic Selling, 1982, Old Age is not for Sissies, 1988; co-host (with Bill Cosby) series Kids Say the Darnedest Things, 1998—; lectr. convs. and univs. Nat. bd. dirs. Goodwill Industries; commr. gen. to U.S. Exhibit at Brisbane Expo 88, Australia, 1987; amb. to The 200th Anniversary Celebration, Australia, 1987—; bd. regents Pepperdine U.; pres. bd. advisors Ctr. on Aging, UCLA; chmn. bd. French Found. for Alzheimers Rsch. Recipient numerous awards. Address: 8484 Wilshire Blvd Ste 205 Beverly Hills CA 90211-3213

LINN, BRIAN JAMES, lawyer; b. Seattle, July 8, 1947; s. Bruce Hugh and Jeanne De V. (Weidman) L.; m. Renee Diane Mousley; children: Kelly, Kareem, Kari. BA in Econs., U. Wash., 1972; JD, Gonzaga Sch. Law, 1975. Bar: Wash. 1975, U.S. Supreme Ct. 1979. Mng. atty. Legal Svcs. for Northwestern Pa., Franklin, 1975-76; staff atty. The Nat. Ctr. for Law and the Handicapped, 1976-78, U. Notre Dame Law Sch., South Bend, Ind., 1976-78; pvt. practice, Seattle, 1978—; lectr. Seattle U., 1980-85. Chmn. civil and legal rights subcom. Gov.'s Com. on Employment of the Handicapped, 1981-87; arbitrator King County Superior Ct., 1981—, judge pro tem, 1989—. Editor Gonzaga Law Rev., 1974-75. Mem. Wash. State Devel. Disabilities Planning Council, 1980-83; trustee Community Service Ctr. for the Deaf and Hard of Hearing, Seattle, 1982-84; chmn. legal rights task force Epilepsy Found. Am., 1979-81; mem. Witness for Peace Delegation, Nicaraqua, 1993. Served with U.S. Army, 1967-69; Vietnam. Mem. Wash. State Bar Assn. (chair world peace through law sect. 1990-91, spl. dist. counsel 1991-95), Omicron Delta Epsilon. Democrat. Methodist. Hon. editor DePaul Law Rev., 1978; contbr. articles to profl. jours. Home: 9716 S 204th Ct Kent WA 98031-1400 Office: 245 SW 152nd St Seattle WA 98166-2307

LINN, CAROLE ANNE, dietitian; b. Portland, Oreg., Mar. 3, 1945; d. James Leslie and Alice Mae (Thorburn) L. Intern, U. Minn., 1967-68; BS, Oreg. State U., 1963-67. Nutrition cons. licensing and cert. sect. Oreg. State Bd. Health, Portland, 1968-70; chief clin. dietitian Rogue Valley Med. Ctr., Medford, Oreg., 1970—; cons. Hillhaven Health Care Ctr., Medford, 1971-83; lectr. Local Speakers Bur., Medford. Mem. ASPEN, Am. Dietetic Assn., Am. Diabetic Assn., Oreg. Dietetic Assn. (sec. 1973-75, nominating com. 1974-75, Young Dietitian of Yr. 1976), So. Oreg. Dietetic Assn., Alpha Lambda Delta, Omicron Nu. Democrat. Mem. Christ Unity Ch. Avocations: sewing, needlecrafts, cooking, swimming, skiing. Office: Rogue Valley Med Ctr 2825 E Barnett Rd Medford OR 97504-8332

LINN, DIANA PATRICIA, elementary education educator; b. Perth, Australia, Dec. 31, 1943; came to U.S., 1948; d. Evan Andrew and Grace Henrietta (Springhall) Jarboe; m. Jim F. Erlandsen, July 9, 1966 (div. Mar. 1989); children: Rebecca, Tim, Jenny; m. Richard George Linn, Mar. 31, 1990; 1 stepchild, Cristal. AA, Olympic Coll., 1963; BA in Elem. Edn., Western Wash. U., 1965; MEd, U. Ariz., 1969. Cert. tchr., Wash. Tchr. 3d grade Neomi B. Willmore Elem., Westminster, Calif., 1965-66; tchr. English and sci. 7-8th grade Sunnyside Jr. H.S., Tucson, 1966-70; tchr. kindergarten All Seasons, Tucson, 1972-74; tchr. K-1st grade St. Cyril's, Tucson, 1974-77; tchr. 1st grade Grace Christian Sch., Tucson, 1977-80; tchr. K-1st grade, reading K-6th grade Ridgeview Christian Ctr., Spokane, Wash., 1983-85, Spokane Christian Schs., 1985-87; dir. Ridgeview Christian Learning Ctr., Spokane, 1987-88; tchr. kindergarten Arlington Elem., Spokane, 1988—; mem. curriculum study com. Sunnyside Sch. Dist., Tucson, 1967-68; chmn. accreditation and sch. bd. St. Cyril's Sch., Tucson, 1976-77; chair faculty involvement group, chair staff devel., chair wellness com. Arlington Elem., Spokane, 1992-93, sch. reporter, 1994-95; instr. reading readiness Family Learning Fair, Home Schooling Seminar, Spokane Falls C.C., Spokane, 1988; chair, coord. pre-sch. coop. Arlington Elem. with Spokane Falls C. C. of Spokane C.C., 1992-93; chair faculty involvement group, Arlington Elem., Spokane, 1995—, Grant Elem. Sch., 1996-97, also wellness chair, 1996—, strategic plan com., 1998—; chmn. Imagination Celebration, 1994, 95; mem. early childhood com. equity com. Arlington Elem., Spokane, 1995-96. Coord. Christian edn. Valley Foursquare Ch., Spokane, 1982-87; coord. children's ch. Victory Faith Fellowship, Spokane, 1993—; Brownie troop leader Willmore Elem., Westminster, 1965-66; ednl. restructuring rep. for Arlington Elem., Spokane Sch. Dist. # 81, 1992-93; mem. equity com. Early Childhood Com., 1996—, mem. strategic planning com., 1998—, wellness chmn., 1996—. Scholar Naval Officer's Wives Club, 1961-62; recipient Eisenhower grant, 1990, 94, 96-97. Mem. ASCD, NEA, Wash. Edn. Assn., Spokane Edn. Assn. (Arlington Elem. rep. 1991-93), CPA Wives Club (sec., ball chair 1983-84), Alpha Delta Kappa (membership chair 1994-95, corr. sec. 1996—). Republican. Avocations: collecting dolls, plates, swimming, quilt-making. Home: 1324 S Perry St Spokane WA 99202-3572 Office: Grant Elem Sch 1300 E 9th Ave Spokane WA 99202-2499

LINN, MARCIA CYROG, education educator; b. Milw., May 27, 1943; d. George W. and Frances (Vanderhoof) Cyrog; m. Stuart Michael Linn, 1967 (div. 1979); children: Matthew, Allison; m. Curtis Bruce Tarter, 1987. BA in Psychology and Stats., Stanford U., 1965, MA in Ednl. Psychology, 1967, PhD in Ednl. Psychology, 1970. Prin. investigator Lawrence Hall Sci. U. Calif., 1970-87, prin. investigator Sch. Edn., 1985—, asst. dean Sch. Edn., 1983-85, prof., 1989—; Fulbright prof. Weizmann Inst., Israel, 1983; exec. dir. seminars U. Calif., 1985-86, dir. instnl. tech. program, 1988-96, chair cognition and devel., 1996—; cons. Apple Computer, 1983—; mem. adv. com. on sci. edn. NSF, 1978—, Ednl. Testing Svc., 1986—, Smithsonian Instn., 1986—, Fulbright Program, 1983-86, Grad. Record Exam. Bd., 1990-94; chair Cognitive Studes Bd. McDonell Found., 1994-97; mem. computing svcs. adv. bd. Carnegie Mellon U., 1991—; mem. steering com. 3d Internat. Math. and Sci. Study, U.S., 1991—. Author: Education and the Challenge of Technology, 1987; co-author: The Psychology of Gender--Advances Through Meta Analysis, 1986—, Designing Pascal Solutions, 1992—, Designing Pascal Solutions with Data Structures, 1996; contbr. articles to profl. jours. Sci. advisor Parents Club, Lafayette, Calif., 1984-87; mem. Internat. Women's Forum, Women's Forum West, 1992—, membership com., 1995—; bd. dirs. Nat. Ctr. for Sci. Edn., 1997—; mem. bd. on behavioral, cognitive and sensory scis. Nat. Rsch. Coun., 1997—, mem. com. on info. tech. literacy, computer sci. and telecomms., 1997—; mem. nat. adv. bd. Nat. Ctr. for Improving Studnet Learning and Achievement in Math. and Sci., 1997—. Recipient fellow Ctr. for Adv. Study in Behavior. Scis. 1995-96, Excellence Ednl. Rsch. award Coun. Sci. Soc. Pres., 1998. Fellow AAAS (bd. dirs. 1996—), APA, AAUW (mem. commn. tech. and gender 1998—), Am. Psychol. Soc.; mem. Nat. Assn. Rsch. in Sci. and Teaching (bd. dirs. 1983-86, assoc. editor jour., Outstanding Paper award 1978, Outstanding Jour. Article award 1975, 83, Disting. Contbns. to Sci. Edn. Through Rsch. award 1994), Am. Ednl. Rsch. Assn. (chmn. rsch. on women and edn. 1983-85, Women Educators Rsch. award 1982, 88, edn. in sci. and tech. 1989-90, ann. mtg. program com. 1996, Willystine Goodsell award 1991), Nat. Sci. Tchrs. Assn. (mem. rsch. agenda com. 1987-90, task force 1993-94), Soc. for Rsch. in Child Devel. (editl. bd. 1984-89), Soc. Rsch. Adolescence, Sierra Club. Avocations: skiing, hiking. Office: U Calif Sch Edn 4611 Tolman Hall Berkeley CA 94720

LINNAN, JUDITH ANN, psychologist; b. Pasadena, Calif., July 11, 1940; d. Robert Emmet Linnan and Jane Thomas (Shutz) H.; m. Ralph Theodore Comito, Feb. 1, 1964 (div. Mar. 1975); children: Matthew, Andrew, Kristine. BA, U. Portland, 1962; MS, Calif. State U., Long Beach, 1974; PhD, CCI Internat. U., 1982; postgrad., Newport Psychoanalytical Inst., 1984-87, 95—. Lic. marriage family child couns., pupil pers. lifetime, lic. rsch. psychoanalyst. Probation officer L.A. County Probation Dept., 1962-63; social worker L.A. County Dept. Probation and Social Svcs., 1963-69; counselor Huntington Beach (Calif.) Free Clinic, 1970-73, counseling ctr., Calif. State U., Long Beach, 1973-74; psychologist Fullerton (Calif.) Union High Sch. Dist., 1975-80, Psychiat. Med. Group, Orange County, Calif., 1981-82; psychologist, dir. Berkeley Psychol. Svcs., Placentia, Calif., 1982—; pvt. practice psychotherapist Huntington Beach, 1975—; founder, dir. Pacific Acad., Fullerton, 1981-82; dir. human resources So. Calif. Coll. Optometry, Fullerton, 1986—; cons., expert witness Orange County Social Svcs., 1992—; dir. student parent program Placentia Sch. Dist., 1993—. Democrat. Roman Catholic. Avocation: horses. Office: Berkeley Psychol Svcs 101 N Kraemer Blvd Ste 125 Placentia CA 92870-5000

LINSTEADT, STEPHEN MICHAEL, health care executive; b. Ukiah, Calif., Feb. 27, 1956; s. George Franklin and Teresa Jane (Stanley) L.; m. Cynthia Lynn Shaughnessy, Aug. 30, 1980 (div. June 1993); children: Jennifer Sara, Diana Jane; m. Sharon Marie Burlkund, Aug. 14, 1993; children: Rachel Marie Saar, Emma Eloise. AA, Grossmont Coll., 1976; BFA, Calif. State Univ., 1979. Asst. controller Design Profl. Fin. Corp., Monterey, Calif., 1980-83; sr. acct. The Hertz Corp., N.Y., 1983-85; region fleet mgr. The Hertz Corp., Secaucus, N.J., 1985-88; dir., N.Am. fleet ops. The Hertz Corp., Park Ridge, N.J., 1988-91; dir. region fleet ops., yield mgmt. The Hertz Corp., L.A., 1991-98; v.p. Biophysics Rsch. Inst., L.A.; pres. Wholistic Care Group, Inc., L.A.; treas., bd. dirs. Holographic Repatterning Assoc., 1998—. Recipient Merit award for Outstanding Achievement in Painting Grossmont Coll., 1976. Avocations: painting, skiing, hiking. Office: Wholistic Care Group Inc 4339 Agnes Ave Studio City CA 91604-1702

LINSTONE, HAROLD ADRIAN, management and systems science educator; b. Hamburg, Fed. Republic Germany, June 15, 1924; came to U.S., 1936; s. Frederic and Ellen (Seligmann) L.; m. Hedy Schubach, June 16, 1946; children: Fred A., Clark R. BS, CCNY, 1944; MA, Columbia U., 1947; PhD, U. So. Calif., 1954. Sr. scientist Hughes Aircraft Co., Culver City, Calif., 1949-61, The Rand Corp., Santa Monica, Calif., 1961-63; assoc. dir. planning Lockheed Corp., Burbank, Calif., 1963-71; prof. Portland (Oreg.) State U., 1970—; pres. Systems Forecasting, Inc., Santa Monica, 1971-98; cons. 1973—. Author: Multiple Perspectives for Decision Making, 1984; co-author: The Unbounded Mind, 1993, The Challenge of the 21st Century, 1994, Decision Making for Technology Executives, 1999; co-editor The Delphi Method, 1975, Technological Substitution, 1976, Futures Research, 1977; editor-in-chief Technol. Forecasting Social Change, 1969—. NSF grantee, Washington, 1976, 79, 85. Mem. Inst. Mgmt. Scis., Ops. Rsch. Soc., Internat. Soc. Systems Scis. (pres. 1993-94). Avocation: photography. Office: Portland State U PO Box 751 Portland OR 97207-0751

LINTON, LAVONNE EVANGELINE, nurse; b. Meadow Grove, Nebr.; d. Gottfried August Albert and Selma Naemi (Schutt) Schulze; m. Leonard Glen Jones, June 4, 1944 (dec. Nov. 1944); m. Hersell Plant Linton, May 14, 1946; children: Alan Douglas, Ronnie Lee, Suzanne Kay. Diploma in

nursing, Luth. Hosp., St. Louis; BS in Health Arts, St. Francis Coll., Joliet, Ill. RN. Charge nurse obstetrics Colo. Gen. Hosp., Denver, 1945-46; charge nurse Sedgwick County Hosp., Julesburg, Colo., 1953-54, 1967-74; supr. South Eventide Home, Fort Collins, Colo., 1974-78; supr., insvc. dir., infection control nurse, purchasing dir. North Shore Manor, Loveland, Colo., 1978-97. Mem. PEO (rec. sec., chaplain, guard). Republican. Lutheran. Avocations: worldwide traveling, golf, bridge, water aerobics.

LINXWILER, LOUIS MAJOR, JR., retired finance company executive; b. Blackwell, Okla., Mar. 7, 1931; s. Louis Major and Flora Mae (Horton) L.; m. Susan Buchanan, July 27, 1963; children: Louis Major III, Robert William. BS, Okla. State U., 1953. Mgr. credit dept. Valley Nat. Bank, Tucson, 1957-60; sales rep. Vega Industries, Syracuse, N.Y., 1960-62; program dir. Am. Cancer Soc., Phoenix, 1962-67; v.p., mgr. credit dept. United Bank Ariz., Phoenix, 1967-76; dean edn. Am. Inst. Banking, Phoenix, 1976-80; cons. Phoenix, 1980-81, United Student Aid Funds Inc., Phoenix, 1981-82; founder, pres., chief exec. officer Ariz. Student Loan Fin. Corp., Phoenix, 1982-88, also bd. dirs.; founder, chmn., chief exec. officer Western Loan Mktg. Assn., Phoenix, 1984-90, also bd. dirs.; pres. Precision Design and Engring., Inc., Escondido, Calif., 1993—, Circulator Motor Co., Phoenix, 1996—; organizer, mng. ptnr. Energy Transition Products, L.L.C., 1998—. Editor: Money and Banking, 1978. Pres. City Commn. Sister Cities, Phoenix, 1986-87, Am. Inst. Banking, Phoenix, 1973-74, Phoenix YMCA Bd. Dirs., 1974-75; v.p. North Mountain Behavioral Inst., Phoenix, 1975-77. Served to 1st lt. U.S. Army, 1954-56. Mem. Shriners, Hiram Club, Rotary (bd. dirs. 1982-83, 93-94, 96-97), Beta Theta Pi. Republican. Presbyterian. Avocations: restoring automobiles, World War II history, travel. Home: 3311 E Georgia Ave Phoenix AZ 85018-1424

LIONAKIS, GEORGE, architect; b. West Hiawatha, Utah, Sept. 5, 1924; s. Pete and Andriani (Protopapadakis) L.; student Carbon Jr. Coll., 1942-43, 46-47; BArch., U. Oreg., 1951; m. Iva Oree Braddock, Dec. 30, 1951; 1 dau., Deborah Jo. With Corps Engrs., Walla Walla, Wash., 1951-54; architect Liske, Lionakis, Beaumont & Engberg, Sacramento, 1954-86, Lionakis-Beaumont Design Group, 1986—. Mem. Sacramento County Bd. Appeals, 1967—, chmn., 1969, 75, 76; pres. Sacramento Builders Exchange, 1976. Served with USAAF, 1943-46. Mem. AIA (pres. Central Valley chpt., 1972—), Constrn. Specifications Inst. (pres. Sacramento chpt., 1962; nat. awards, 1962, 63, 65), Sacramento C. of C. (code com., 1970—). Club: North Ridge Country (pres. 1987). Lodge: Rotarian (pres. East Sacramento 1978-79). Prin. works include Stockton (Calif.) Telephone Bldg., 1968, Chico (Calif.) Main Telephone Bldg., 1970, Mather AFB Exchange Complex Sacramento, 1970, Base Chapel Mather AFB, Sacramento, 1970, Woodridge Elementary Sch., Sacramento, 1970, Pacific Telephone Co. Operating Center Modesto, Calif., 1968, Sacramento, 1969, Marysville, Calif., 1970, Red Bluff, Calif., 1971, Wells Fargo Banks, Sacramento, 1968, Corning, Calif., 1969, Anderson, 1970, Beale AFB Exchange Complex, Marysville, 1971, Cosumnes River Coll., Sacramento, 1971, base exchanges at Bergstrom AFB, Austin, Tex., Sheppard AFB, Wichita Falls, Tex., Chanute AFB, Rantoul, Ill., McChord AFB, Tacoma, Wash., health center Chico State U., Sacramento County Adminstrn. Center, Sacramento Bee Newspaper Plant. Home: 160 Breckenwood Way Sacramento CA 95864-6968 Office: Lionakis Beaumont Design Group 1919 19th St Sacramento CA 95814-6714

LIPOFSKY, MARVIN BENTLEY, art educator; b. Elgin, Ill., Sept. 1, 1938; s. Henry and Mildred (Hyman) L.; 1 child, Lisa Beth; m. Ruth Okimoto, 1990. BFA in Indsl. Design, U. Ill., 1961; MS, MFA in Sculpture, U. Wis., 1964. Instr. design U. Wis., Madison, 1964; asst. prof. design U. Calif., Berkeley, 1964-72; prof., chmn. glass dept. Calif. Coll. Arts and Crafts, Oakland, 1967-87, pres. faculty assembly, 1984-87; guest instr. Haystack Mountain Sch., Deer Isle, Maine, 1967, 73, 87, San Francisco Art Inst., 1968, Hunterdon Art Ctr., Clinton, N.J., 1973, Pilchuck Sch. Glass, Stanwood, Wash., 1974, 77, 81, 84, 88; vis. prof. Bazalel Acad. Art and Design, Jerusalem, 1971; pres. faculty assembly, 1984-87. One-man shows include Richmond (Calif.) Art Ctr., 1965, Anneberg Gallery, San Francisco, 1966, Crocker Art Gallery, Sacramento, 1967, San Francisco Mus. Art, 1967, Mus. Contemporary Crafts, N.Y.C., 1969, U. Ga., Athens, 1969, Utah Mus. Fine Arts, U. Utah, Salt Lake City, 1969, Calif. Coll. Arts and Crafts, 1970, Stedelijke Mus., Amsterdam, The Netherlands, 1970, Galerie de Enndt, Amsterdam, 1970, Baxter Art Gallery, Calif. Inst. Tech., Pasadena, 1974, Yaw Gallery, Birmingham, Mich., 1976, 78, Gallery Marionie, Kyoto, Japan, 1979, 87, U. Del., Newark, 1979, Greenwood Gallery, Washington, 1980, SM Gallerie, Frankfurt, Fed. Republic Germany, 1981, Galerie L. Hamburg, Fed. Republic Germany, 1981, Betsy Rosenfield Gallery, Chgo., 1982, Robert Kidd Gallery, Birmingham, Mich., 1984, Holsten Galleries, Palm Beach, Fla., Maurine Littleton Gallery, Washington, Union Bulgarian Artists, Sofia, 1991, Marvin Lipofsky: A World of Glass, 1994, Judah L. Magnes Mus., Berkeley, Calif., 1994, Marvin Lipofsky's World of Glass Show: A Hist. Retrospective, 1996, Kennedy Art Ctr. Gallery, 1996, Holy Names Coll., Oakland, Calif., 1996; vis. artist, critic Gerriet Rietveld Academie, Amsterdam; vis. artist Atheneium Sch. Art and Design, Helsinki, Finland, 1970, UCLA, 1973, Sommervail, Battle Mountain Glass Symposium, Vail, Colo., Miasa (Japan) Bunka Ctr., 1987, Internat. Glass Sumposium, Novy Bor, Czech Republic, 1982, 85, 88, 91. Trustee Calif. Coll. Arts and Crafts, Oakland, 1984-87. Named Calif. Living Treasure, 1985, Hon. Mem., Hungarian Glass Art Soc., 1996; named to Coll. Fellows, Am. Craft Coun., 1991; NEA fellow, 1974, 76. Mem. Glass Art Soc. (hon. life, pres. 1978-80, jour. editor 1976-80, advisor 1980—), Am. Craft Coun. (trustee 1986-90, trustee emeritus 1998—), Bay Area Studio Art Glass (pres. 1993—).

LIPOMI, MICHAEL JOSEPH, health facility executive; b. Buffalo, Mar. 9, 1953; s. Dominic Joseph and Betty (Angelo) L.; m. Monica Lipomi; children: Jennifer, Barrett, Ryan, Eric. BA, U. Ottawa, 1976; MS in Health Adminstrn., U. Colo., 1994. Mktg. dir. Am. Med. Internat. El Cajon Valley Hosp., Calif., 1980-83; dir. corp. devel. Med. Surg. Ctrs. Am., Calif., 1983-85; CEO Stanislaus Surgery Ctr., Modesto, Calif., 1985—. Author: Complete Anatomy of Health Care Marketing, 1988; co-host med. TV talk show Health Talk Modesto. Bd. dirs. Am. Heart Assn., Modesto, 1988-89; pres. Modesto Community Hospice, 1987-88; active local govt.; sec.-treas. Modesto Industry and Edn. Council, 1989. Mem. Calif. Ambulatory Surgery Assn. (pres. 1988-89, mem. legis. com. 1994, mem. rsch. and edn. found. bd. 1994—), No. Calif. Assn. Surgery Ctrs. (pres. 1986-88), Federated Ambulatory Surgery Assn. (mem. govt. rels. com. 1988, bd. dirs. 1989—, chmn. govt. rels. com. 1990), Modesto C. of C. (bd. dirs. 1989-92, 97—), Rotary. Avocations: golf, tennis, skiing. Office: Stanislaus Surgery Ctr 1421 Oakdale Rd Modesto CA 95355-3359

LIPPE, PHILIPP MARIA, physician, surgeon, neurosurgeon, educator, administrator; b. Vienna, Austria, May 17, 1929; s. Philipp and Maria (Goth) L.; came to U.S., 1938, naturalized, 1945; m. Virginia M. Wiltgen, 1953 (div. 1977); children: Patricia Ann Marie, Philip Eric Andrew, Laura Lynne Elizabeth, Kenneth Anthony Ernst; m. Gail B. Busch, Nov. 26, 1977. Student Loyola U., Chgo., 1947-50; BS in Medicine, U. Ill. Coll. Medicine, 1952, MD with high honors, 1954. Rotating intern St. Francis Hosp., Evanston, Ill., 1954-55; asst. resident gen. surgery VA Hosp., Hines, Ill., 1955, 58-59; asst. resident neurology and neurol. surgery Neuropsychiat. Inst., U. Ill. Rsch. and Ednl. Hosps., Chgo., 1959-60, chief resident, 1962-63, resident neuropathology, 1962, postgrad. trainee in electroencephalography, 1963; resident neurology and neurol. surgery Presbyn.-St. Luke's Hosp., Chgo., 1960-61; practice medicine, specializing in neurol. surgery, San Jose, Calif., 1963—; instr. neurology and neurol. surgery U. Ill., 1962-63; clin. instr. surgery and neurosurgery Stanford U., 1965-69, clin. asst. prof., 1969-74, clin. assoc. prof., 1974-96, clin. prof. 1996—; staff cons. in neurosurgery O'Connor Hosp., Santa Clara Valley Med. Ctr., San Jose Hosp., Los Gatos Cmty. Hosp., El Camino Hosp. (all San Jose area); chmn. divsn. neurosugery Good Samaritan Hosp, 1989-97, chmn. dept. clin. neuroscis., 1997—; founder, exec. dir. Bay Area Pain Rehab. Center, San Jose, 1979—; clin. adviser to Joint Commn. on Accreditation of Hosps.; mem. dist. med. quality rev. com. Calif. Bd. Med. Quality Assurance, 1976-87, chmn., 1976-77; cons., med. expert Med. Bd. Calif., 1996—. Served to capt. USAF, 1956-58. Diplomate Am. Bd. Neurol. Surgery, Nat. Bd. Med. Examiners, Am. Bd. Pain Medicine. Fellow ACS, Am. Coll. Pain Medicine (bd. dirs. 1991-94, v.p. 1991-92, pres. 1992-93); mem. AMA (Ho. of Dels. 1981—, mem. CPT editl. panel, 1995—, mem. sr. adv. panel Guides to the Evaluation of Permanent Impairment 1997—), Am. Coll. Physician Execs., Calif. Med. Assn. (Ho. of Dels. 1976-80, sci. bd., council 1979-87, sec. 1981-87, Outstanding Svc. award 1987), Santa Clara County Med. Soc. (coun. 1974-81, pres. 1978-79, Outstanding Contbn. award 1984, Benjamin J. Cory award 1987), Chgo. Med. Soc., Congress Neurol. Surgeons, Calif. Assn. Neurol. Surgeons (dir. 1974-82, v.p. 1975-76, pres. 1977-79, Pevehouse disting. svc. award 1997), San Jose Surg. Soc., Am. Assn. Neurol. Surgeons (chmn. sect. on pain 1987-90, dir. 1983-86, 87-90, Disting. Svc. award 1986, 90), Western Neurol. Soc., San Francisco Neurol. Soc., Santa Clara Valley Profl. Standards Rev. Orgn. (dir., v.p., dir. quality assurance 1975-83), Fedn. Western Socs. Neurol. Sci., Internat. Assn. for Study Pain, Am. Pain Soc. (founding mem.), Am. Acad. Pain Medicine (sec. 1983-86, pres. 1987-88, Philipp M. Lippe Disting. Svc. award 1995, exec. med. dir. 1996—), Am. Bd. Pain Medicine (pres. 1992-93, exec. v.p., 1994—), Alpha Omega Alpha, Phi Kappa Phi. Assoc. editor Clin. Jour. of Pain; contbr. articles to profl. jours. Pioneered med. application centrifugal force using flight simulator. Office: PO Box 41217 San Jose CA 95160

LIPPOLD, ROLAND WILL, surgeon; b. Staunton, Ill., May 1, 1916; s. Frank Carl and Ella (Immenroth) L.; m. Margaret Cookson, June 1, 1947; children: Mary Ellen Lippold Elvick, Catherine Anne Lippold Rolf, Carol Sue Lippold Webber. BS, U. Ill., 1940, MD, 1941. Diplomate Am. Bd. Surgery. Intern Grant Hosp., Chgo., 1941-42, resident in surgery, 1942-43, 47-48; resident in surgery St. Francis Hosp., Evanston, Ill., 1946-47; fellow in pathology Cook County Hosp., Chgo., 1947-48, resident in surgery, 1949-50; practice medicine specializing in surgery Chgo., 1950-53; also asst. in anatomy U. Ill., Chgo., 1950-53; practice medicine specializing in surgery Sacramento, 1953-68; chief med. officer No. Reception Ctr.-Clinic, Calif. Youth Authority, Sacramento, 1954-68, chief med. services, 1968-79; cons. in med. care in correctional instns.; cons. Calif. State Personnel Bd. Contbr. articles to med. publs. Chmn. Calif. Expn. Hall of Health, 1971-72. Comdr. M.C., USNR, 1943-73, PTO. Mem. Sacramento Surg. Soc., Sacramento County Med. Soc., Calif. Med. Assn., AMA, Sacramento Hist. Soc. (life). Republican. Lutheran. Home: 1811 Eastern Ave Sacramento CA 95864-1724

LIPSCOMB, ANNA ROSE FEENY, entrepreneur, arts organizer, fundraiser b. Greensboro, N.C., Oct. 29, 1945; d. Nathan and Matilda (Carotenuto) L. Student langs., Alliance Francaise, Paris, 1967-68; BA in English and French summa cum laude, Queens Coll., 1977; diploma advanced Spanish, Forester Instituto Internacional, San Jose, Costa Rica, 1990; postgrad. Inst. Allende San Miguel de Allende, Mex., 1991. Reservations agt. Am. Airlines, St. Louis, 1968-69, ticket agt., 1969-71; coll. rep. CBS, Holt Rinehart Winston, Providence, 1977-79, sr. acquisitions editor Dryden Press, Chgo., 1979-81; owner, mgr. Historic Taos (N.Mex.) Inn, 1981-89, Southwest Moccasin and Drum, Taos; pres., co-owner Southwest Products, Ltd., 1991—; owner, pres. All One Tribe, Inc., 1996—; fundraiser Taos Arts Celebrations, 1989—; bd. dirs. N.Mex. Hotel and Motel Assn., 1986—; sem. leader Taos Women Together, 1989; founder All One Tribe Found., 1994, All One Tribe Drumming Festival, 1991—; mem. adv. bd. Drum Bus. Mag., 1996—. Editor: Intermediate Accounting, 1980; Business Law, 1981. Contbr. articles to profl. jours.; patentee in field. Bd. dirs., 1st v.p. Taos Arts Assn., 1982-85; founder, bd. dirs. Taos Spring Arts Celebration, 1983—; founder, dir. Meet-the-Artist Series, 1983—; bd. dirs. and co-founder Spring Arts N.Mex., 1986; founder Yuletide in Taos, 1988, A Taste of Taos, 1988; bd. dirs. Music from Angel Fire, 1988—; founding mem. Assn. Hist. Hotels, Boulder, 1983—; organizer Internat. Symposium on Arts, 1985; bd. dirs. Arts in Taos, 1983, Taoschool, Inc., 1985—, Roadrunner Recyclers, 1995—, TALKBACK, 1997—; mem. adv. bd. Chamisa Mesa Ednl. Ctr., Taos, 1990—; founder All One Tribe Found., 1994. Recipient Outstanding English Student of Yr. award Queens Coll., 1977; named Single Outstanding Contbr. to the Arts in Taos, 1986. Mem. Millicent Rogers Mus. Assn., Taos Lodgers Assn. (mktg. task force 1989), Taos County C. of C. (1st v.p. 1988-89, bd. dirs. 1987-89, advt. com. 1986-89, chmn. nominating com. 1989), Internat. Platform Assn., Taos Women Bus. Owners, Phi Beta Kappa. Home: Talpa Rte Taos NM 87571 Office: PO Drawer N Taos NM 87571

LIPSCOMB, JEFFREY JON, fund specialist; b. San Diego, May 8, 1946; s. Willis L. and Marjorie (Jones) L.; m. Jo Ann Elaine Nielsen, Oct. 1, 1983; 1 child, Amanda Nielsen. Student, Occidental Coll., 1964-68, Harvard U., 1971, New England Conservatory Music, 1972. Chief cash flow analyst St. Johnsbury Co., Cambridge, Mass., 1970-81; pvt. investor San Diego, 1981-88; registered rep. New England Securities, Sacramento, 1988-97; registered investment specialist Bankam. Investment Svcs., 1997—. Columnist (fin. commentary) The Bus. Jour. Sacramento, 1990-91. Mem. East Sacramento (Calif.) Improvement Assn., 1988-97; pianist celebrity benefit concerts Stanford Children's Home, Sacramento, 1989. Mem. Inst. Cert. Fund Specialists, Internat. Assn. Fin. Planning (practitioner divsn. 1993—), Nat. Assn. Life Underwriters, Sacramento Assn. Life Underwriters, New Eng. Leaders Assn., Sutter Lawn Tennis Club (pres. 1992-93), The Sutter Club, Investment Trust Boston Cornerstone Club. Republican. Presbyterian. Avocations: chamber music, genealogy, tennis, chess. Office: 1551 W Capitol Ave West Sacramento CA 95691-3217

LIPSCOMB, RICHARD HENRY, playwright, former museum administrator; b. St. Louis, Oct. 29, 1918; s. Fred R. and Olive (Clendennen) L.; m. Lois Mae Colwell, July 13, 1956; children—Peter Stephen, Geoffrey Nicholas. B.A., Tulane U., 1941; M.A., Cornell U., 1942. Asst. prof., dir. theater U. Ala., Tuscaloosa, 1946-48; assoc. prof. drama U. Tex., Austin, 1948-49; music and drama reviewer Citizen-News, Hollywood, Calif., 1949-55; casting dir. Wisbar Prodns. Fireside Theater, NBC-TV, 1950-53; screenwriter RKO-Radio Pictures, Hollywood, 1954-55; asst. producer You Are There TV program CBS-TV, Hollywood, 1955-57; chief edn. and music concert producer Natural History Mus., Los Angeles, 1964-84; motion picture researcher Assocs. & Aldrich, Hollywood, 1958-66. Author: play The Other 23 1/2 Hours, with Louise Randall Pierson, 1961, Javelin, 1961, A Faculty for Drama, 1979, Wandervogel's Hearthside, 1979, Keeper of the Garden of Eden, 1984, Coming of Age in New Orleans, 1986; TV script The Verdict is Yours (nominated for Emmy award), 1960; radio concert commentaries broadcast by Sta. KFAC-FM, 1964-84; TV script Bannister Wins the Mile produced by CBS-TV, 1956. Mem. Mayor's Com. on Music, Los Angeles, 1962-64; mem. citizen's music com. Sta. KFAC-FM, Los Angeles, 1968-74. Served with U.S. Army, 1943-46. Mem. Am. Assn. Mus. (com. on edn. 1970-73), Writers Guild of Am. West, AAUP, Dramatists Guild. Republican. Christian Scientist.

LIPSKY, IAN DAVID, mechanical engineering executive; b. Bklyn., May 26, 1957; s. Eugene Herman and Janet Dorothy (Heller) L; m. Cheryl Joy Weinberg. BS in Marine Engring., Maine Maritime Acad., 1979; postgrad., U. San Francisco, 1998—. Registered profl. engr., Calif.; lic. U.S. Coast Guard, Merchant Mariners Document steam & motor vessels, 1979. Third asst. engr. Interlake Steamship Co., Cleve., 1979-81; port engr. Exxon Internat. Co., Florham Park, N.J., 1981-84; prodn. supr. Alfred Conhagen Inc. Calif., Hercules, 1984-87, gen. mgr., 1987-89, v.p., 1989—. Mem. Soc. Naval Architects & Marine Engrs., Marine Port Engrs. N.Y., Inst. Marine Engrs. (London), Port Engrs. San Francisco, Nat. Soc. Profl. Engrs. Democrat. Jewish. Avocations: golfing, running, triathlons. Home: 153 Koch Rd Corte Madera CA 94925-1263 Office: Alfred Conhagen Inc Calif 3900 Oregon St Benicia CA 94510-1102

LIPSON, LESLIE MICHAEL, political science educator; b. London, Nov. 14, 1912; came to U.S., 1947, naturalized, 1953; s. Alexander and Caroline Rachel (Goodman) L.; m. Helen M. Fruchtman, Oct. 2, 1980; 1 son by previous marriage, David Roger. B.A., Oxford U., 1935, M.A., 1945; Ph.D., U. Chgo., 1938. Prof. polit. sci. and dir. Sch. Public Adminstrn., Victoria U., Wellington, N.Z., 1939-46; prof. polit. sci. Swarthmore (Pa.) Coll., 1947-49, U. Calif., Berkeley, 1950-83; chmn. undergrad. program dept. polit. sci. U. Calif., 1977-80, prof. emeritus, 1980—; mem. faculty Fromm Inst. for Lifelong Learning, San Francisco, 1983—, acad. advisor, 1989—; civilian guest lectr. Nat. War Coll., Washington, 1948-75, Air War Coll., Montgomery, Ala., 1954-86; prof. polit. sci. UN program tech. assistance in L.Am., Fundacao Getulio Vargas, Rio de Janeiro, 1953; vis. prof. Columbia U., 1961, Stanford U., 1963, U. Copenhagen, 1970-71, also others; vis. lectr. Oxford U., Inst. Commonwealth Studies, London, U. Inst. Internat. Higher Studies, Geneva, U. Pavia, U. Zagreb, also others; panelist, reporter Brit. Press on PBS program World Press, Sta. KQED-TV, San Francisco, 1963-75; seminar leader Danforth Assocs. Conf., Estes Park, Colo., 1970; panelist weekly radio program World Affairs Coun., 1986-87; cons. in field. Author: The American Governor, 1939, reprinted, 1968, The Politics of Equality, 1948, The Great Issues of Politics, 1954, 10th edit., 1997, The Democratic Civilization, 1964, The Ethical Crises of Civilization, 1993, (with Elizabeth M. Drews) Values and Humanity, 1971, I Do Not Itch to Etch, Views in Verse, 1987, Not Yet the Yeti: Rhymes for the Times, 1997; contbr. articles to profl. jours. and Ency. Brit. Trustee World Affairs Council No. Calif., 1979-87. Served with Home Guard, 1941-44, N.Z. Commonwealth Fund fellow Harkness Found., 1935-38; Rockefeller fellow, 1955-56, 59-60, grantee, 1967. Mem. NOW, UN Assn. (bd. dirs. San Francisco chpt. 1988-92). Democrat. Jewish. Home: 25 Stoddard Way Berkeley CA 94708-1719 Office: U Calif Dept Polit Sci Berkeley CA 94720

LISALDA, SYLVIA ANN, primary education educator; b. San Diego, Oct. 14, 1949; d. Joseph and Irene (Valdez) Lisalda; m. Robert Holguin Marquez, Sept. 1, 1979 (div. 1986). AA, Valley Coll., Van Nuys, Calif., 1964; BA in English, Calif. State U., Northridge, 1971. Tchr. kindergarten L.A. Unified Schs., 1965—. Democrat. Roman Catholic. Avocations: writing children's books, playing guitar and piano. Office: Sylmar Elem Sch 13291 Phillippi Ave Sylmar CA 91342-2899

LISTERUD, MARK BOYD, retired surgeon; b. Wolf Point, Mont., Nov. 19, 1924; s. Morris B. and Grace (Montgomery) L.; m. Sarah C. Mooney, May 26, 1954; children: John, Mathew, Ann, Mark, Sarah, Richard. BA magna cum laude, U. Minn., 1949, BS, 1950, MB, 1952, MD, 1953. Diplomate Am. Bd. Surgery. Intern King County Hosp., Seattle, 1952-53; resident in surgery U. Wash., Seattle, 1953-57; practice medicine specializing in surgery Wolf Point, 1958-93; mem. admission com. U. Wash. Med. Sch., Seattle, 1983-88; instr. Dept. Rural and Community Health, U. N.D. Med. Sch., 1991. Contbr. articles to med. jours. Mem. Mont. State Health Coordinating Council, 1983, chmn. 1986—; bd. dirs. Blue Shield, Mont., 1985-87. Served with USN, 1943-46. Fellow Am. Coll. Surgeons, Royal Soc. Medicine; mem. N.E. Mont. Med. Soc. (pres.), Mont. Med. Assn. (pres. 1968-69), AMA (alt. del., del. 1970-84). Clubs: Montana, Elks. Avocations: fishing, hunting. Home: Rodeo Rd Wolf Point MT 59201 Office: 100 Main St Wolf Point MT 59201-1530

LISTON, ALBERT MORRIS, investor, administrator, educator; b. Carlinville, Ill., Aug. 6, 1940; s. Joseph Bostick and Hazel Marie (Smalley) L.; AB in Econs., U. Calif., Davis, 1963; MA in Govt., Calif. State U., Sacramento, 1970; postgrad., U. Calif., Santa Barbara, 1980—; m. Angela Lynne Carbonatto, Jan. 1998. Rsch. analyst Ombudsman Activities Project polit. sci. dept. U. Calif., Santa Barbara, 1970-72; asst. prof. polit. sci. dept. Calif. State U., Fullerton, 1973-79; investor, 1980—. Lt. Supply Corps, USNR, 1963-66. Mem. Am. Polit. Sci. Assn., Commonwealth Club Calif., Kappa Sigma, Phi Kappa Phi. Democrat. Office: PO Box 8027 Missoula MT 59807-8027

LITMAN, ROBERT BARRY, physician, author, television and radio commentator; b. Phila., Nov. 17, 1947; s. Benjamin Norman and Bette Etta (Saunders) L.; m. Niki Thomas, Apr. 21, 1985; children: Riva Belle, Nadya Beth, Caila Tess, Benjamin David. BS, Yale U., 1967, MD, 1970, MS in Chemistry, 1972, MPhil in Anatomy, 1972, postgrad. (Life Ins. Med. Rsch. Fund fellow) Yale U., Univ. Coll. Hosp., U. London, 1969-70; Am. Cancer Soc. postdoctoral rsch. fellow Yale U., 1970-73. Diplomate Am. Bd. Family Practice. Resident in gen. surgery Bryn Mawr (Pa.) Hosp., 1973-74; USPHS fellow Yale U. Sch. Medicine, 1974-75; pvt. practice medicine and surgery, Ogdensburg, N.Y., 1977-93, San Ramon, Calif., 1993—; mem. med. staff A. Barton Hepburn Hosp., 1977-93, John Muir Med. Ctr., 1993—, San Ramon (Calif.) Regional Med. Ctr., 1993—, also chmn. med. edn., chmn. dept. family practice, 1998—; commentator Family Medicine Stas. WWNY-TV and WTNY-Radio, TCI Cablevision, Contra Costa T.V.; moderator Ask the Doctor; clin. preceptor dept. family medicine State Univ. Health Sci. Ctr., Syracuse, 1978—. Author: Wynnefield and Limer, 1983, The Treblinka Virus, 1991, Allergy Shots, 1993; contbr. articles to numerous sci. publs. Pres. Am. Heart Assn. No. N.Y. chpt., 1980-84. Fellow Am. Coll. Allergy, Asthma, and Immunology, Am. Acad. Family Physicians; mem. AMA (Physicians Recognition award 1970—), Calif. State Med. Assn., Alameda-Contra Costa County Med. Assn., Joint Coun. Allergy and Immunology, Nat. Assn. Physician Broadcasters (charter), Acad. Radio and TV Health Communicators, Book and Snake Soc., Gibbs Soc. of Yale U. (founder), Sigma Xi, Nu Sigma Nu, Alpha Chi Sigma. Home and Office: PO Box 1857 San Ramon CA 94583-6857

LITTLE, CHARLES GORDON, geophysicist; b. Liuyang, Hunan, China, Nov. 4, 1924; s. Charles Deane and Caroline Joan (Crawford) L.; m. Mary Zughaib, Aug. 21, 1954; children: Deane, Joan, Katherine, Margaret, Patricia. BSc with honors in Physics, U. Manchester, Eng., 1948; PhD in Radio Astronomy, U. Manchester, 1952. Jr. engr. Cosmos Mfg. Co. Ltd., Enfield, Middlesex, Eng., 1944-46; jr. physicist Ferranti Ltd., Manchester, Lancashire, Eng., 1946-47; asst. lectr. U. Manchester, 1952-53; prof. dept. geophysics U. Alaska, 1954-58, dep. dir. Geophys. Inst., 1954-58; cons. Ionosphere Radio Propagation Lab. U.S. Dept. Commerce Nat. Bur. Standards, Boulder, Colo., 1958-60, chief Upper Atmosphere and Space Physics divsn., 1960-62, dir. Central Radio Propagation Lab., 1962-65; dir. Inst. Telecommunication Sci. and Aeronomy, Environ. Sci. Services Adminstrn., Boulder, Colo., 1965-67; dir. Wave Propagation Lab. NOAA (formerly Environ. Sci. Services Adminstr.), Boulder, Colo., 1967-86; sr. UCAR fellow Naval Environ. Prediction Research Facility, Monterey, Calif., 1987-89; George J. Haltiner rsch. prof. Naval Postgrad. Sch., Monterey, 1989-90. Author numerous sci. articles. Recipient U.S. Dept. Commerce Gold medal, 1964, mgmt. and sci. research awards NOAA, 1969, 77, Presdl. Meritorious Exec. award, 1980. Fellow IEEE, Am. Meteorol. Soc. (Cleveland Abbe award 1984); mem. NAE, AIAA (R.M. Losey Atmos. Sci. award 1992). Address: 4907 Country Club Way Boulder CO 80301-3656

LITTLE, GLEN GORDON, retired circus clown, educator; b. Genoa, Nebr., Dec. 5, 1925; s. Glenn Arthur and Elsie Viola L.; m. Shirley Mae-Moss, Oct. 12, 1950 (div. Oct. 1970); 1 child, Tawnya René Little Wiseman; m. Patricia Margaret Cosgrove, Oct. 12, 1971; 1 stepchild, Roxanne Kay Cosgrove Webster. Pvt. practice Denver, 1963-67; from circus clown to dir. clowns Ringling Brothers-Barnum and Bailey Circus, Venice, Fla., 1968-80, dir. clowns, 1980-90, ret., 1990. Author: Circus Stories, 1997. With USN, 1943-44. Achieved Master Clown status Irving Feld pres. Ringling Brothers-Barnum and Bailey Circus, Washington, 1983; inducted to Clown Hall of Fame, Delavin, Wis., 1991; face on collector plate Danbury (Conn.) Mint, 1994. Mem. Disabled Am. Veterans. Avocations: building clown gags, reading history books. Home: 222 E 8th St Burley ID 83318

LITTLE, JERRY JAMES, artist; b. Oakland, Calif.; s. James Herman and Helen Janette (Bohannon) L.; m. Alma Jean Obusek, Aug. 29, 1970; children: Tyler, Todd. AA, Stockton (Calif.) Coll., 1950-51; student, Lane Cmty. Coll., Eugene, Oreg., 1963, U. Oreg., Eugene, 1964-65; studied with Millard Sheets, Gerald, Brommer, Alan Haemer, others. Band leader Jerry Little and His Orch., Walnut Creek, Calif., 1948-51; mgmt. rep. AT&T Co., San Francisco, 1955-61; flight instr., comml. pilot Greens Flying Svc., Eugene, 1962-70; sales rep., graphic designer CPC Internat., Inc., Eugene, 1963-88; owner Jerrys Fine Art, Walnut Creek, Calif., 1989—; exhbn. co-chair arts Oreg. Watercolor Assn., Portland, 1982; art demonstrator, lectr., cons. Calif. Watercolor Assn., Orinda, 1995—; juror art show Ann. Napa Waercolor Art Show, Tiburon, Calif., 1996, Acad. Art Coll., 1998, Modesto Art League, 1998, Napa Ann. Art Show, 1998; exhbn. installer Exptl. Watercolor Soc., Alamo, Calif. 1995. Artist design ad formats, 1962-89, graphic design, 1962-89; artist: (art books) Collage Techniques, 1994, Best of Watercolor Places, 1996; featured in Internat. Artist Mag., The Artist Mag., others; exhibited in numerous pvt. collections. With USN, 1951-54. Recipient Best of Show award in visual art Western Oreg. Exposition, 1982, 1st awards in visual art Lane County Fair, Eugene, 1983, Valley Artists Assn., Pleasanton, Calif., 1993. Mem. Nat. Watercolor Soc. (signature mem.), Calif. Watercolor Assn. (signature mem., chmn. steering com. 1995, pres. 1998-99, outstanding achievement membership 1996), Am. Watercolor Assn. (assoc.), Alamo/Danville Watercolor Soc., Pleasanton Art Soc., Diablo Art Assn. (award 1993, 94, 95). Avocations: avid reader, snow skiing, water skiing, golf, travel. Home: 2549 Pine Knoll Dr Apt 4 Walnut Creek CA 94595-2023

LITTLE, LOREN EVERTON, musician, ophthalmologist; b. Sioux Falls, S.D., Oct. 28, 1941; s. Everton A. and Maxine V. (Alcorn) L.; m. Christy Gyles; 1 child, Nicole Moses; children from previous marriage: Laurie, Richard. BA, Macalester Coll., 1963; BS, U. S.D., 1965; MD, U. Wash., 1967. Prin. trumpeter Sioux Falls Mcpl. Band, 1956-65; trumpeter St. Paul Civic Orch., 1960-62; leader, owner Swinging Scots Band, St. Paul, 1960-63; trumpeter Edgewater Inn Show Room, Seattle, 1966-67, Jazztet-Arts Council, Sioux Falls, 1970-71, Lee Maxwell Shows, Washington, 1971-74; residency in ophthalmology Walter Reed Med. Ctr., Washington, 1974; co-leader, trumpeter El Paso (Tex.) All Stars, 1975; freelance trumpeter, soloist various casinos and hotels, Las Vegas, Nev., 1977—. Trumpeter (album) Journey by R. Romero Band, 1983, Sizenter, 1997; soloist for numerous entertainers including Tony Bennett, Burt Bacharach, Jack Jones, Sammy Davis Jr., Henry Mancini, Jerry Lewis Telethon, for video Star Salute to Live Music, 1989; with Stan Mark Band Nat. Pub. Radio Broadcast, 1994, 95; soloist on video Stan Mark Live at the 4 Queens Hotel, Las Vegas; pres. S&L Music, S&L Records; prodr. Carl Saunders Debut Album Out Of the Blue, 1996, Eclecticism, 1999. Trustee Nev. Sch. of the Arts, Las Vegas, 1983—; pres. S&L Music SNL Rec. Served to lt. col. U.S. Army, 1968-76, Vietnam. Decorated Silver Star, Purple Heart, Bronze Star, Air medal; fellow Internat. Eye Found., 1974; Dewitt Wallace scholar Readers Digest, 1963-65. Fellow ACS, Am. Acad. Ophthalmology; mem. Am. Fedn. Musicians, Nat. Bd. Med. Examiners. Presbyterian. Avocations: history, music, medicine, sports, skiing.

LITTLE, MARK DOUGLAS, secondary school educator; b. Boulder, Colo., Feb. 11, 1961; s. John Russell and Joanne Jean (Bartelma) L.; m. Kathleen Little, June 27, 1998. BS, Colo. State U., 1986; MA, U. Denver, 1994. Lic. tchr., Colo. Part-time tchr. Boulder Valley RE2 Schs., Broomfield, Colo., 1987-88, substitute tchr., 1988-90; tchr. sci. Broomfield H.S., 1990—; alt. sta. mgr., cons. Cmty. Radiation Monitoring Program, Broomfield, 1994—. Named Tchr. of the Yr., Mosaic Lodge 184, 1990, 97; Woodrow Wilson fellow, 1996, 97. Mem. NEA, Nat. Sci. Tchrs. Assn., Nat. Assn. Biology Tchrs. Presbyterian. Avocations: golf, fishing, reading, outdoor sports. Home: 1649 Garnet St Broomfield CO 80020-6607 Office: Broomfield H S 1 Eagle Way Broomfield CO 80020-3532

LITTLE, WILLIAM PAUL, small business owner; b. Bradford, Ohio, Apr. 5, 1933; s. Don Forest and Virginia Lou (Alexander) L.; 1 child, William Paul Jr. AA, Oakland City Coll., Calif., 1948; BS, Ohio State U., 1950. Supr. Pac Bell, Oakland, Calif., 1950-80; owner, operator Heavy Equip. Installation, Oakland, 1985-90, Little Splty. Control Circuits, Oakland, 1990—; chm. nom. com. E.B. Fed. Telenedet Union, Oakland, Calif. Bd. mem. Concord Swimming Pool Assn.; bd. mem. St. Chutburt Church; commd. USN, 1950-52, Korea. Avocations: sailing, home restorations. Home: 686 McElroy St Oakland CA 94607

LITTLEBIRD, FORREST DOUGLAS, preventive medicine, tropical medicine physician; b. Liberal, Kans., June 11, 1963; s. Forrest Douglas Littlebird and Priscilla Kay (Farmer) MacFarlane. Student, Tex. A&M U., 1981-84; DO, U. North Tex., 1989; MPH, U. Hawaii, 1995; diploma in tropical medicine & hygiene, Mahidol U., Bangkok, Thailand, 1997. Diplomate Am. Bd. Preventive Medicine, Am. Osteo. Bd. Family Practice. Rotating intern Pacific Hosp., Long Beach, Calif., 1989-90; staff physician Student Health Ctr. U. So. Calif., L.A., 1991-92; resident in internal medicine U. Hawaii, Honolulu, 1992, resident in preventive medicine, 1992-96, clin. faculty, 1995; staff physician Pub. Health Dept., Long Beach, 1993-94; emergency care physician Schofield Emergency Rm., Honolulu, 1994-97; staff physician Tripler Army Med. Ctr./Hosp., Honolulu, Molokai Gen. Hosp., Centinela Med. Ctr., SureCare med. cir., 1997, Hawaii Permanente Med. Group, Occupl. Health Svcs., 1997; lectr. in field; vis. faculty Mahidol U., Bangkok, Chulalongkorn U., Sukhothai Thammathirat Open U., Thailand. Legis. aide Ho. of Reps., Hawaii State Legis., Honolulu, 1996; mem. Nat. Coun. for Internat. Health, 1995-96. Robert A. Welch Found. Rsch. fellow, 1983; Naval ROTC nat. scholar, 1981. Mem. Am. Osteo. Assn., Am. Coll. Osteo. Family Practice, Am. Soc. Tropical Medicine/Hygiene, Am. Coll. Occupl. and Environ. Medcine, Am. Coll. Preventive Medicine. Avocations: skiing, mountaineering, international health volunteering. Home: 747 Amana St Apt 2219 Honolulu HI 96814-5112 also: 107 Treasure Island Laguna Beach CA 92651 Office: Kinkaid Med Registry A Bus Trust 504 N State College Blvd Anaheim CA 92806-2919

LITTLEFIELD, EDMUND WATTIS, mining company executive; b. Ogden, Utah, Apr. 16, 1914; s. Edmund Arthur and Marguerite (Wattis) L.; m. Jeannik Mequet, June 14, 1945; children: Edmund Wattis, Jacques Mequet, Denise Renee. BA with great distinction, Stanford U., 1936, MBA, 1938. With Standard Oil Co. of Calif., 1938-41, Golden State Co., Ltd., 1946-50; v.p., treas. Utah Internat. Inc. (formerly Utah Constrn. & Mining Co.), San Francisco, 1951-56; exec. com., dir. Utah Internat. Inc. (formerly Utah Constrn. & Mining Co.), 1951—, exec. v.p., 1956, gen. mgr., 1958—, pres., 1961—, chmn. bd., 1971—, chief exec. officer, 1971-78, chmn. exec. com., dir., 1978-86; bd. dirs. SRI Internat., FMC Gold. Served as lt. (j.g.) USNR, 1941-43; spl. asst. to dep. adminstr. Petroleum Adminstrn. for War 1943-45. Recipient Ernest C. Arbuckle award Stanford Bus. Sch. Assn., 1970, Golden Beaver award, 1970, Bldg. Industry Achievement award, 1972, Harvard Bus. Statesman award, 1974, Internat. Achievement award World Trade Club, 1986, Lone Sailor award U.S. Naval Found., 1997; named to Nat. Mining Hall of Fame. Mem. San Francisco C. of C. (pres. 1956), Bus. Council (hon. mem., past chmn.), Conf. Bd., Phi Beta Kappa, Chi Psi. Clubs: Burlingame (Calif.) Country; Pacific Union, San Francisco Golf (San Francisco); Augusta National Golf, Eldorado Country; Bohemian, Cypress Point (Pebble Beach, Calif.); Vintage. Office: 550 California St San Francisco CA 94104-1006

LITTLEJOHN, JOHN JOSEPH, petroleum engineer; b. Waco, Tex., Sept. 6, 1948; s. Lacy Welborn and Winfred Rachael (Young) L.; m. Susan Louise Ilse, 1972; children: Hillary, Elizabeth, Neal, Nathan. BS, Baylor U., 1971; MA, Harvard U., 1972, PhD, 1975. Explorationist Shell Oil Co, Houston, 1975-78; cons. various cos., Houston, 1978-81; pres. Rubicon Petroleum Inc., Houston, 1981-91; chmn., pres. Rubicon Petroleum Inc., Colorado Springs, Colo., 1978—; vice-chmn. Advocates Internat., Annandale, Va., 1993—; chmn. Internat. Tchg. Ministry, Dallas, 1994—. Mem. Am. Assn. Petroleum Geologists, Soc. Exploration Geophysics, Soc. Petroleum Engring. Baptist. Office: Rubicon Petroleum Inc 6 Pine Rd Colorado Springs CO 80906-4253

LITVACK, SANFORD MARTIN, lawyer; b. Bklyn., Apr. 29, 1936; s. Murray and Lee M. (Korman) L.; m. Judith E. Goldenson, Dec. 30, 1956; children—Mark, Jonathan, Sharon, Daniel. BA, U. Conn., 1956; LLB, Georgetown U., 1959. Bar: N.Y. 1964, D.C. 1979. Trial atty. antitrust div. Dept. Justice, Washington, 1959-61; asst. atty. gen. Dept. Justice, 1980-81; asso. firm Donovan, Leisure, Newton & Irvine, N.Y.C., 1961-69; ptnr. Donovan, Leisure, Newton & Irvine, 1969-80, 81-86, Dewey, Ballantine, Bushby, Palmer & Wood, N.Y.C., 1987-91; sr. exec. v.p., chief of corp. ops. The Walt Disney Co., Burbank, Calif., 1991—, also bd. dirs. Bd. dirs. Bet Tzedek. Fellow Am. Coll. Trial Lawyers; mem. ABA, Fed. Bar Coun., N.Y. State Bar Assn. (sec. antitrust sect. 1974-77, chmn. antitrust sect. 1985-86), Va. Bar Assn., Calif. Inst. of Arts (bd. dirs.), Am. Arbitration Assn. (bd. dirs.). Office: The Walt Disney Co 500 S Buena Vista St Burbank CA 91521-0004

LIU, DON, ophthalmologist, medical researcher; b. Nanjing, China, July 17, 1947; came to the U.S., 1964; s. Robert Ching Ming and I. Tu Liu; m. Helen Cheng, June 21, 1975; children: David, Grace, Glory, Daniel. BS in Physics, Purdue U., 1969; MS in Physics, U. Mass., 1971; MD, SUNY, Buffalo, 1977. Dir. oculoplastics/orbit. Ford Hosp., Detroit, 1982-90; dir. oculoplastics/orbit. svc. U. So. Calif.-L.A. County Hosp., L.A., 1990—; assoc. dir. tech. transfer U. So. Calif., 1995—; chief oculoplastic and orbital surgery King Khaled Eye Specialist Hosp., Riyadh, Saudi Arabia, 1998—; organizer Internat. Conf. U.S.A., China and Hong Kong, Taiwan, 1985, 87, 89, 92, 93, 95; cons. to med. industries, state govt. and the Chinese govt. on health care; [illegible] Ophthalmology, 1991—, Ophthalmalic, Plastic and Recontructive Surgery, 1991—, Ophthalmic Surgery and Lasers, 1994—; mem. adv. bd. Med. Books for China, Internat., 1985—; vis. prof., lectr. various institutions in U.S., China, Taiwan, Indonesia, England, and Holland. Contbr. numerous book chpts. and articles to textbooks and profl. jours.; mem. editl. bd. numerous jours. Campaign fundraiser Mike Woo for Mayor, L.A., 1993; So. Calif. coord. Bush/Quayle, 1992, L.A.; sponsor San Marino (Calif.) Sch. Dist., 1990—; active Boy Scouts Am., Amnesty Internat., ch. activities. Recipient numerous tchg. awards, hon. degrees and titles from Chinese med. instns. Fellow ACS, Am. Acad. Facial Plastic and Reconstructive Surgery (com. mem. 1992-96), Am. Soc. Ophthalmic, Plastic and Reconstructive Surgery (fellowship dir. 1994—, Outstanding fellow 1981), Am. Acad. Ophthalmology (hon. award 1994), Am. BdOphthalmology (assoc. examiner 1991—); mem. AMA, Chinese Am. Ophthalmologic Soc.(sec.-treas. 1988-92), Internat. Soc. Ocuplastic Surgeons (bd. dirs.), Com. of 100. Office: 1975 Zonal Ave # 516 Los Angeles CA 90033-1039

LIU, GANG KEVIN, engineering executive; b. Taipei, Taiwan, Mar. 28, 1955; s. Shang-Ming and Ie-De (Hsu) L. MS in Mechanics, U. Minn., 1980; PhD in Aeronautics and Astronautics, Stanford U., 1986. Navigation analyst Intermetrics Inc., Warminster, Pa., 1985-88; mem. tech. staff Litton Aero Products, Woodland Hills, Calif., 1988-95; program mgr. SiRF Tech. Inc., L.A., 1995-97; v.p. engring. EverMore Tech. Inc., Hsinchu, Taiwan, 1997—, JK Tech. Inc., Torrance, Calif., 1997—. Lt. Taiwan Army, 1977-79. Mem. AIAA (sr.). Home: 7150 Rainbow Dr Apt 20 San Jose CA 95129-4547 Office: JK Tech Inc 20695 S Western Ave Ste 200 Torrance CA 90501-1834

LIU, KATHERINE CHANG, artist, art educator; b. Kiang-si, China; came to U.S., 1963; d. Ming-fan and Ying (Yuan) Chang; m. Yet-zen Liu; children: Alan S., Laura Y. MS, U. Calif., Berkeley, 1965. Instr. U. Va. Ext., Longwood Coll.; mem. tchg. staff Intensive Studies Seminar, Sanfa Fe, 1995, 96, 97, 98, 99; invited mem. L.A. Artcore Reviewing and Curatorial Bd., 1993; invited juror, lectr. over 75 exhbns. and orgns., Kans., S.C. Watercolor Socs., 1998, Alaska, Ga., Tex. and Okla. Watercolor Soc. Anns., 1997, Adirondacks Nat. Show, N.Y., 1999, Ann. Exhibit Watercolor Ohio, 1999, Watercolor Soc. Oreg., 1999, The Collage Soc. Am., 1999; juror, lectr. Ala. Watercolor Soc. Ann., 1996, Midwest Watercolor Soc. Nat. Exhibit, 1996, Watercolor West Nat. Open, 1996. One-woman shows include Harrison Mus., Utah State U., Riverside (Calif.) Art Mus., Ventura (Calif.) Coll., Fla. A&M U., Gail Harvey Gallery, Santa Monica, 1998, J.J. Brookings Gallery, San Francisco, 1998, Louis Newman Galleries, L.A., L.A. Artcore, Lung-Men Gallery, Taipei, Republic of China, Lew Allen Contemporary, Santa FE Drawing Exhibit, Golden West Collage Gallery, 1999; invitational shows include: Crossing Cultures, Lewallen Contemporary, 1998, State of the Arts International Biennial, Parkland Coll. Ill., 1989, 91, 97, Treasures for the Community: The Chrysler Mus. Collects, 1989-96, 97, Watercolor U.S.A. Hon. Soc. Invitational, 1989, 91, 93, 95, 97, Hunter Mus. Art, Tenn., 1993, Bakersfield Art Mus., 1994, Sandra Walters Gallery, Hong Kong, 1994, Horwitch-Newman Gallery, Scottsdale, Ariz., 1995, Hong Kong U. Sci. and Tech. Libr. Art Gallery, 1996, J.J. Brookings Gallery, San Francisco, 1996, 97, 98, John N Joe Gallery, L.A., 1996, Bill Armstrong Gallery, Springfield, Mo., 1996, Chrysler Mus. Fine Art, Norfolk, Va., 1997, Invitational, U. B.C. Art Gallery, 1992, U. Sydney Art Mus., 1992, Ruhr-West Art Mus., Wise, 1992, Macau Art Mus., 1992, Rosenfeld Gallery, Phila., 1994, Mandarin Oriental Fine Arts, Hong Kong, 1994; contbr. works to 23 books and 41 periodicals. Co-curator Taiwan-USA-Australia Watermedia Survey Exhbn., Nat. Taiwan Art Inst., 1994; sole juror San Diego Watermedia Internat., 1993, Triton Mus. Open Competition, 1994, Northern Nat. Art Competition, 1994, Watercolor West Nat., 1993, Tenn., Utah, Hawaii, N.C. Watercolor Socs., North Am. Open, Midwest Southwest and over 30 state-wide competitions in watermedia or all-media; co-juror Rocky Mountain Nat., San Diego Internat. and West Fedn. Exhibits. Recipient Rex Brandt award San Diego Watercolor Internat., 1985, Purchase Selection award Watercolor USA and Springfield (Mo.) Art Mus., 1981, Gold medal, 1986, Mary Lou Fitzgerald meml. award Allied Arts Am. Nat. Arts Club, N.Y.C., 1987, Achievement award of Artists Painting in Acrylic Am. Artists Mag., 1993; NEA grantee, 1979-80. Mem. Nat. Watercolor Soc. (life, chmn. jury 1985, pres. 1983, Top award 1984, cash awards 1979, 87), Watercolor U.S.A. Honor Soc., Nat. Soc. Painters in Casein and Acrylic (2nd award 1985), Rocky Mountain Nat. Watermedia Soc. (juror 1984, awards 1978, 80, 86).

LIU, ZHONG-PING (PETER LIU), natural medicine specialist, actor; b. Beijing, People's Republic of China, June 5, 1958; came to U.S., 1986; s. De-Rang Liu and Yin-Mei Zhang. BS in Plant Protection, Hunan Agrl. U., Changsha, Hunan, China, 1981; AAS in Data Processing Tech., Del. Tech., Wilmington, 1990; BS in Computer Info. Systems, Goldey-Beacom Coll., Wilmington, 1991; MS in Oriental Medicine, Samra U., L.A., 1996; cert. in ESL, Nanjing Normal U. Cert. in advanced English as a second lang., Del. Tech.; cert. in ornamental hort. Longwood Gardens, Inc.; tng. in Chinese opera, drama, singing, dance and film acting. Gardener Gaotian Econ. Plant Garden, Shaodong, Hunan, China, 1975-78; asst. rschr. Hunan Inst. Plant Protection, Changsha, Hunan, China, 1982-84; curator Jiangsu Inst. Botany/Nanjing Bot. Garden Mem. Sun Yat-Sen, Nanjing, Jiangsu, China, 1984-86; horticulturist Longwood Gardens, Inc., Kennett Square, Pa., 1986-87; computer lab. asst. Goldey-Beacom Coll., Wilmington, Del., 1990-91, sr. asst./computer cons., 1991-94; observer, intern Samra U., L.A., 1995-96. Prin. actor in film, TV, theatre, voice-over and commls.; contbr. rsch. articles to profl. jours. Mem. SAG, AFTRA, Calif. Chinese Medicine Assn. Avocations: Chinese opera, pop and classical music, stamp collecting, basketball, cycling. Home: PO Box 3273 Alhambra CA 91803-0273

LIVELY, RICKY, artist; b. Glenwood Springs, Colo., Feb. 21, 1967; s. Waldo F. and Doris (Wood) L. Grad., Rifle High Sch., Rifle, Colo., 1986. Laborer Davis Lumber Co., Silt, Colo., 1986-88; landscape laborer West Canyon Tree Farm, New Castle, Colo., 1988, 90; laborer Turss Fab. Inc., New Castle, Colo., 1988; artist New Castle, Colo. Art displayed Aviations Access (Internet), 1998—. Founder New Castle Art Guild, 1996, Art Phest ArtShow, 1997—, art tchr., vol. New Castle Riverside Jr. High, 1998—. Fellow Rocky Mountain Elk Found., Mule Deer Found.; mem. Am. Soc. Aviation Artists (assoc.), Nat. Rifle Assn., Mus. of Flight. Republican. Protestant. Avocations: hiking, hunting, fishing, photography, camping, building models. Office: Ricky L Lively Originals PO Box 421 New Castle CO 81647-0421

LIVINGSTON, LOUIS BAYER, lawyer; b. N.Y.C., Dec. 12, 1941; s. Norman and Helen (Bayer) L.; m. Mari Livingston, Apr. 6, 1968; children: Diana, Alex, Ann. BA, Yale U., 1963; LLB, Harvard U., 1966. Bar: N.Y. 1967, Oreg. 1971. Atty. NLRB, Memphis, 1967-68, Poletti, Freidin et al., N.Y.C., 1968-71; ptnr. Miller, Nash, Wiener, Hager & Carlsen, Portland, Oreg., 1971—. Office: Miller Nash Wiener Hager & Carlsen 111 SW 5th Ave Ste 3400 Portland OR 97204-3699*

LIVSEY, HERBERT C., lawyer; b. Salt Lake City, Aug. 20, 1941. BS, U. Utah, 1967, JD, 1969; LLM in Taxation, NYU, 1971. Bar: Utah 1969. Shareholder, fin. dir. Ray, Quinney & Nebeker P.C., Salt Lake City, 1969—. Assoc. editor: Utah Law Review, 1968-69; graduate editor: Tax Law Review, 1970-71. Fellow Am. Coll. Trust and Estate Counsel; mem. Utah State Bar Assn. (chmn. tax sect. 1978-79), Order of the Coif, Phi Kappa Phi, Delta Theta Phi. Office: Ray Quinney & Nebeker PC PO Box 45385 Salt Lake City UT 84145-0385*

LIVZIEY, JAMES GERALD, secondary school educator; b. Buffalo, July 30, 1927; s. James Ephlyn and Helena Charlote (Kiener) L.; m. June Ellen Andersen, July 25, 1955; children: Naomi Lynn, Patricia Ellen. AA, Southwestern Jr. Coll., 1970; BA, San Diego State U., 1972. Enlisted U.S. Navy, 1945, advanced through grades to lt. comdr., 1967, ret., 1969; high sch. instr. SWHS Dist., Chula Vista, Calif., 1972—. Recipient award Freedoms Found., 1991; fellow Taft Inst., 1977, Pacific Acad. Advanced Studies, 1978. Fellow Alpha Gamma Sigma; mem. Naval Inst. USN, Masons, Knight Comdr. Ct. Honor (32d degree). Avocations: golfing, reading, educational reasearch. Home: 675 Mariposa Cir Chula Vista CA 91911-2510

LJUBICIC DROZDOWSKI, MILADIN PETER, consulting engineer; b. Lujecani, Yugoslavia, Sept. 28, 1921; came to U.S., 1959; s. Peter Miladin and Martha Jovan (Viktorovic) Ljubicic; m. Dusica Cile Pavic, Sept. 9, 1948. Diploma in engring., U. Belgrade, Yugoslavia, 1951, 52; ancien éleve, Ecole Nationale Superieure de l'Armement, Paris, 1956; MSME, UCLA, 1964, PhD in Mec. Engring., 1971. Design and test engr. Fed. Mogul Bower, El Monte, Calif., 1959-62; chief advanced armament analytical support Hughes Helicopters, Culver City, Calif., 1962-78; engring. supr. Bechtel Power Corp., Norwalk, Calif., 1978-80; engring. adviser Bechtel Espana, Madrid, 1980-87; v.p. Koach Engring., Sun Valley, Calif., 1987; engring. cons. Mission Viejo, Calif., 1987—; asst. to chmn. continuum mechanics, Belgrade, 1955-56; guest lectr. Sch. Engring. and Applied Sci., UCLA, 1971; prof., Loyola Marymount U., L.A., 1978-80. Contbr. to profl. publs. Mem. Am. Soc. Mech. Engrs., Am. Def. Preparedness Assn., Spanish Nuclear Soc. Avocations: European history, art history, archeology, photography. Home and Office: 26426 Lope De Vega Dr Mission Viejo CA 92691-3316

LLANUSA, STEVEN MICHAEL, elementary education educator; b. Burbank, Calif., Feb. 26, 1960; s. Louis Henry and Margaret Mary (Ferruzza) L.; life ptnr. Glenn Miya; children: Anthony Miya Llanusa. AA, L.A. Valley Coll., Van Nuys, Calif., 1982; BA, UCLA, 1985. Cert. tchr., Calif. Tchr. nursery sch. Child Devel. Ctr., L.A. Valley Coll. Campus, 1979-82; asst. tchr. UCLA Child Devel. Ctr., 1982-85; tchr. L.A. Unified Sch. Dist., Lincoln Heights, Calif., 1987-89, Colton Unified Sch. Dist., Bloomington, Calif., 1989—; curriculum specialist Gerald Smith Sch., Bloomington, 1993—. Chmn. diversity com. UCLA, 1992-94. Recipient cmty. svc. award ARC, 1981; scholar Tau Alpha Epsilon, 1982. Mem. ASCD, San Bernardino Humane Soc., UCLA Alumni Assn. (bd. dirs.-at-large 1992-94, co-chmn. Lambda alumni 1993-94, beginning tchr. support mentor), U. So. Calif. Lambda Alumni Assn. (edn. com. 1993-94), Sigma Phi Epsilon. Roman Catholic. Avocations: computer philanthropy theatre. Home: 2627 San Andres Way Claremont CA 91711-1556 Office: Gerald Smith Sci Magnet Sch 9551 Linden Ave Bloomington CA 92316-1430

LLOYD, IVAN GRAHAM, artist; b. Coventry, Eng., May 1, 1946; s. Harold and Irene Gwyneth (Griffiths) L.; m. Lissa Belle Graham (div. Apr. 1978); 1 child, Sohraq Alladine; m. Lystra Monique Hibbert, Apr. 7, 1994; 1 child, Hashme Amin. Diploma, St. Martins Sch. Art, London, 1964; SO level cert., Hillcroft Comprehensive, London, 1962. Owner, artist Camel Art Gallery, Tangiers, Marocco, 1964-74; set designer, artist in residence Southern Ariz. Light Opera Co., Tucson, Ariz., 1976-84; owner, artist Dayspring Studios, Tucson, Ariz., 1986—. Author, illustrator: Badi The Pride of Martyrs, 1997, Unfurling of the Black Standard, 1998; permanent exhibition of historical Bahai paintings Metro Denver Bahai Ctr., Denver, 1995.

LLOYD, JOSEPH WESLEY, physicist, researcher; b. N.Mex., Jan. 31, 1914; s. William Washington and Mattie May (Barber) L.; m. Lenora Lucille Hopkins, Jan. 24, 1944 (dec. June 1969); 3 children (dec.); m. Ruth Kathryn Newberry, Nov. 19, 1988; children: Kathryn Ruth Jordan, Mary Evelyn Jordan. Student, Pan Am. Coll., 1942. Plumber Pomona, Calif., 1951-57; plumber, pipefitter Marysville, Calif., 1957-79; ret., 1979; ind. researcher in physics and magnetism, Calif., 1944—. With CAP, 1944-45. Mem. Ch. of Christ.

LLOYD, MICHAEL JEFFREY, recording producer; b. N.Y.C., Nov. 3, 1948; s. John and Suzanne (Lloyd) Sutton; m. Patricia Ann Varble, Sept. 6, 1980; children: Michael, Christopher, Jeni, Deborah. Student, U. So. Calif. V.p. artists and repertoire MGM Records, Inc., 1969-73; ind. record producer, 1973—; pres. Heaven Prodns., 1975—, Michael Lloyd Prodns., 1979—, Taines-Lloyd Film Prodns., 1984-85; music dir. TV series Happy Days; music dir. Kidsongs, Living Proof, NBC-TV movie, Kidsongs Videos; prodr. Love Lines, NBC-TV movie Swimsuit; guest lectr. UCLA, Pepperdine U.; judge Am. Song Festival. Composer: (music for feature films) Tough Enough, If You Could See What I Hear, Dirty Dancing, All Dogs Go to Heaven, (music and lyrics) Rudolph the Red Nose Reindeer- The Movie, 1998; composer music for 8 Movies of the Week, 12 TV spls., 28 TV series and 35 feature motion pictures. Recipient 50 Gold Album awards, 24 Platinum Album awards, 26 Gold Single awards, 2 Platinum Single awards, 3 Grammy awards, 41 Chart Album awards, 100 Chart Single awards, 10 Broadcast Music Inc. awards, 1 Am. Music award, 1 Dove award, 2 Nat. Assn. of Record Minets. Mem. ASCAP (12 awards), Am. Fedn. Musicians, Screen Actors Guild, Nat. Assn. Rec. Arts and Scis., AFTRA.

LO, WAITUCK, artist; b. Honolulu, June 9, 1919; s. Wai Tong and Kam T. Lo; m. Agnes Ching, Jan. 4, 1958; children: Edwina, Felix, Lisa Ann. BS, Utopia U., Shanghai, China, 1942; postgrad., Yen Yu Inst. Fine Art, Shanghai, Ind. U. Exhibited in group shows at Assn. Honolulu Artist Jury Art Show, 1956, 57 (Most Decorative award 1956, 57), Assn. Honolulu Artists non-jury show, 1957 (Popular award 1957), Narcissus Festival Art Exhbn., 1960 (Kaiser award 1960, Most Popular award 1960), Maul County Fair Art Exhbn., 1963 (2d prize 1963); commd. silk painting Pepsi-Cola U.S.A., 1987; paintings reproduced by Regency Card Co. Recipient 1st Place Water Color award Assn. Honolulu Artists, 1965, 68, Hayward award Assn. Honolulu Artists, 1968, 1st Place Water Color award Home Builders Assn. Art Show, 1966; Honorable Mention in Oil and Water Color, Assn. Honolulu Artists, 1966, Internat. Assn. Artists, 1979. Club: Toastmasters (Honolulu) (pres. 1986).

LOARIE, THOMAS MERRITT, healthcare executive; b. Deerfield, Ill., June 12, 1946; s. Willard John and Lucile Veronica (Finnegan) L.; m. Stephanie Lane Fitts, Aug. 11, 1968 (div. Nov. 1987); children: Thomas M., Kristin Leigh Soule. BSME, U. Notre Dame, 1968; Student, U. Minn., 1969-70, U. Chgo., 1970-71, Columbia U., 1978. Registered profl. engr., Calif. Prodn. engr. Honeywell, Inc., Evanston, Ill., 1968-70; various positions Am. Hosp. Supply Co., Evanston, Ill., 1970-83, pres. Heyer-Schulte divsn., 1979-83; pres. COO Novacor Med. Corp., Oakland, Calif., 1984-85, also bd. dirs.; pres. ABA Bio Mgmt., Danville, Calif., 1985-87; chmn., CEO Keravision, Inc., Fremont, Calif., 1987—; founder, chmn., med. device CEO Roundtable, 1993—; asst. prof. surgery Creighton U. Med. Sch., Omaha, 1986-94; speaker in field. Contbr. articles on med. tech. and pub. policy to Wall St. Jour., others. Bd. dirs. Marymount Sch. Bd., 1981-84; bd. dirs. United Way Santa Barbara, 1981-84, assoc. chairperson, 1982-83, treas., 1983. Named One of 50 Rising Stars: Exec. Leaders for the 80's Industry Week mag., 1983. Mem. Assn. for Rsch. in Vision and Ophthalmology, Contact Lens Assn. Ophthalmology, Health Industry Mfrs. Assn. (spl. rep. bd. dirs. 1993-96, bd. dirs. 1997—, exec. com. 1997—, treas. 1998—), Am. Entrepreneurs for Econ. Growth, Med. Tech. Leadership Forum, Calif. Healthcare Inst. (bd. dirs. 1998—). Roman Catholic. Avocations: competitive running, snow skiing, backpacking, oil painting, the arts. Office: KeraVision Inc 48630 Milmont Dr Fremont CA 94538-7353

LOBAUGH, LESLIE E., JR., corporate lawyer, holding company executive. AB, Santa Clara U., 1967; JD, Georgetown U., 1970. Bar: Calif. Assoc. Holdberg, Finger, Brown & Abramson, 1971-75; staff atty. Pacific Lighting, 1975-77, sr. counsel, 1977-82, asst. gen. counsel, 1982-85, assoc. gen. counsel, 1985-86; v.p., gen. counsel Pacific Enterprises, 1986—, So. Calif. Gas Co., 1986—. Office: Pacific Enterprises 555 West 5th St Los Angeles CA 90013-1011*

LOBEL, CHARLES IRVING, physician; b. Phila., Nov. 9, 1921; s. Maurice and Dora (Barnett) L.; m. Julia Valentine Skellchock, June 12, 1955; children: Meredith Anne Lobel-Angel. AA, San Jose State U., 1948; student, Stanford U., 1948-49; MD, U. So. Calif., 1954. Physician Permanente Med. Group, Inc., South San Francisco, 1954-65; physician, courtesy staff Chope Cmty. Hosp., San Mateo, Calif., 1965-89, Sequoia Hosp., Redwood City, Calif., 1965-94; physician Permanente Med. Group, Inc., Redwood City, Calif., 1965-95; clin. prof. medicine divsn. rheumatology Stanford U. Sch. Medicine, 1965—; chief profl. edn. Kaiser Found. Hosp., Redwood City, 1968-80, rehab. coord, 1968-80, pres med. staff, 1968-70; mem. Calif. Med. Assn. Staff Survey Com., San Francisco, 1970-90; mem. 4th dist. Bd. Med. Quality Assurance State Calif., 1979-84. 1st Lt. U.S. Army, 1942-46. Decorated Combat Infantry Badge, Bronze Star, Presdl. Unit citation, 3 Battle Stars. Fellow Am. Acad. Family Physicians, Am. Coll. Rheumatology; mem. AMA, AAAS, San Mateo County Med. Soc. (bd. dirs. 1973-78), Calif. Med. Soc. (alt. del. 1979-83), N.Y. Acad. Scis., Am. Heart Assn., Royal Soc. of Med., Med. Friends of Wine, Arthritis Found. No. Calif., Phi Delta Epsilon. Avocations: music, theatre, literature, travel, [illegible] Office: Stanford U Clinic [illegible] Wilbur Dr Palo Alto CA 94304-2201

LOBERT, JÜRGEN MICHAEL, research chemist; b. Tauberbischofsheim, Germany, Mar. 24, 1958; came to U.S., 1991; s. Helmut Wilhelm Heinz and Irmgard Elisabeth (Ochs) L. Diploma, Tech. Hochschule, Darmstadt, Germany, 1985; PhD, Johannes Gutenberg U., Mainz, Germany, 1990. Rsch. asst. Tech. Hochschule, Darmstadt, 1984-85; vis. scientist Hahn Meitner Inst., Berlin, 1986; rsch. chemist Max Planck Inst., Mainz, 1986-91; rsch. assoc. NOAA, CMDL, Boulder, 1991-96; project scientist Scripps Inst. Oceanography, La Jolla, Calif., 1997—. Contbr. articles to profl. jours. Mem. Am. Geophys. Union, European Geophys. Soc. Avocations: skydiving, computer graphics, music, worldwide web publishing, outdoors. Home: PO Box 2226 La Jolla CA 92038-2226 Office: C4/SIO/U Calif San Diego 9500 Gilman Dr # 0239 La Jolla CA 92093-0239

LOBIG, JANIE HOWELL, special education educator; b. Peoria, Ill., June 10, 1945; d. Thomas Edwin and Elizabeth Jane (Higdon) Howell; m. James Frederick Lobig, Aug. 16, 1970; 1 child, Jill Christina. BS in Elem. Edn., So. Ill. U., 1969; MA in Spl. Edn. Severely Handicapped, San Jose State U., 1989. Cert. elem. tchr., Calif., Mo., Ill., handicapped edn., Calif., Mo.; ordained to ministry Presbyn. Ch. as deacon, 1984. Tchr. trainable mentally retarded children Spl. Luth. Sch., St. Louis, 1967-68; tchr. trainable mentally retarded and severly handicapped children Spl. Sch. Dist. St. Louis, 1969-80, head tchr., 1980-83; tchr. severly handicapped children San Jose (calif.) Unifed Sch. Dist., 1983-86; tchr. autistic students Santa Clara County Office Edn., San Jose, 1986—; tchr. Suzanne Dancers, 1991-92. Vol. Am. Cancer Soc., San Jose, 1986-89, 92, St. Louis Reps., 1976-82, Am. Heart Assn., 1985—, Multiple Sclerosis Soc., 1990—; troop leader Camp Fire Girls, San Jose, 1984-85; moderator bd. deacons Evergreen Presbyn. Ch., 1986-89; mem. exec. bd. Norwood Creek Elem. Sch. PTA, 1983-86. Mem. Council for Exceptional Children, Assn. for Severly Handicapped, Nat. Edn. Assn., Calif. Tchrs. Assn. Independent. Avocations: golf, bowling, bridge, needlework. Home: 3131 Creekmore Way San Jose CA 95148-2805 Office: Weller Elem Sch 345 Boulder St Milpitas CA 95035-2899

LOBO, KEITH R., executive. Pres, CEO Quickturn Design, San Jose, Calif. Office: 55 W Trimble Rd San Jose CA 95131-1013

LOBSINGER, THOMAS, bishop; b. Ayton, Ont., Can., Nov. 17, 1927. Ordained priest Roman Cath. Ch., 1954, bishop, 1987. Bishop Whitehorse, Y.T., Can., 1987—. Home: 5119 5th Ave, Whitehorse, YK Canada Y1A 1L5

LOCATELLI, PAUL LEO, academic administrator; b. Santa Cruz, Calif., Sept. 16, 1938; s. Vincent Dino and Marie Josephine (Piccone) L. B.S. in Acctg., Santa Clara U., 1961; MDiv, Jesuit Sch. Theology, 1974; DBA, U. So. Calif., 1971. CPA, Calif. Ordained priest Roman Cath. Ch., 1974. Acct., Lautze & Lautze, San Jose, Calif., 1960-61, 1973-74; prof. acctg. Santa Clara (Calif.) U., 1974-86, assoc. dean Bus. Sch. and acad. v.p., 1978-86, pres., 1988—. bd. dirs. chair, Assn. Jesuit Colls. and Univs., JV:SV Network; bd. trustees Inst. for the Internat. Edn. of Students; exec. com. Ind. Colls. and Univs. of Calif., adv. couns. Parents Helping Parents and Community Found.; past rector Jesuit Comty. at Loyola Marymount U. Past trustee U. San Francisco, Seattle U., St. Louis U. and Loyola Marymount U., Regis U.; past mem. Sr. Commn. of Western Assn. Schs. and Colls., Acctg. Edn. Change Commn. Mem. AICPA, NCCJ (bd. dirs., chair), Calif. Soc. CPAs (Disting. Prof. of the Yr award, 1994), Am. Acctg. Assn., Am. Leadership Forum Silicon Valley (bd. dirs., chair). Democrat. Office: Santa Clara U 500 El Camino Real Santa Clara CA 95053-0015*

LOCH, PATRICIA ANN, software company executive, consultant; b. Omaha, May 2, 1944; d. Frank and Elizabeth (Duffield) Barrick; m. Charles Joseph Loch, Nov. 25, 1967; children: Michelle Kathleen, Justin Randall. BS in Math., Wake Forest U., 1966. Programmer IBM, Raleigh, N.C., 1966-68, Almay Cosmetics, Raleigh, N.C., 1968; contract programmer Kelly Assocs., Mpls., 1969-70, Bre-Mar Systems, N.Y.C., 1971; systems analyst Met. Life Ins. Co., N.Y.C., 1970-71; cons. Bd. Coop. Edn. Svcs., Yorktown, N.Y., 1972-75; pres., cons. P. Loch Assocs., Danville, Calif., 1975—; cons. Target Pub., Pleasanton, Calif., 1976-88. Mem. Assn. Small System Users (dir. membership 1981-82, dir. facilities 1985-87), NAFE, AAUW, Round Hill Country (Alamo, Calif.), Amador Athletic Club (Pleasanton). Avocations: aerobics, bowling, tennis, boating. Home: 8071 E Del Trigo Scottsdale AZ 85258-1751

LOCHEN, ELISABETH YVONNE MARIE-LAURE, director, sound consultant; b. Metz, France, June 24, 1953; came to U.S., 1996; d. Jacques Olaf and Helene Horber; children: Sebastien, Judicaelle. B in Biology, Phdin Louis Pasteur U., Strasbourg, France, 1977, M in Psychology, 1978; M in Psychology, Phdin Louis Pasteur U., Strasbourg, France, 1979, PhD in Psychology and Comm., 1981. Sound engr. Fesjelheu, Paris, 1985-90; chmn., gen. mgr. LC Concept, Paris, 1990-96; dir. Paris and L.A., 1995—; chmn. Merjithur Studios, Paris, 1985-90, French Studio Assn., Paris, 1987-90, Assoc. French Recording Studio, Paris, 1988-90. Digital sound for movie theatres provided for Basic Instinct, Free Willy, Falling Down, Cliffhanger, Back Beat, Silent Tongue, Boiling Point, Heaven and Earth, Cyrano de Bergerac, L'amant-The Lover, L 627, Jusqu'au bout du monde, L'accompagnatrice, IP 5, Tous les matins du monde, Arizona Dream, La belle historie, Lune de Fiel; Inventor digital sound system for movie theaters. Mem. Soc. Motion Picture and TV Engrs. (sound cinema sect.), Tech. French Cinema Comm., Nat. Recording Edition Sydicate. Office: #102 10927 Santa Monica Blvd # 102 Los Angeles CA 90025-4503

LOCHMILLER, KURTIS L., real estate entrepreneur; b. Sacramento, Dec. 30, 1952; s. Rodney Glen and Mary Margaret (Frauen) L.; m. Mariye Susan Mizuki, Nov. 9, 1951; children: Margaux Sian, Chase Jordan. BA in Econs. and Fin., U. Denver, 1975. Dist. sales mgr. Hertz Truck Div., Denver, 1975-76; drilling foreman Shell Oil, Alaska, Mont., Colo., 1976-79; pres., owner Kurtex Mortgage & Devel. Co., Denver, 1979—, Kurtex Properties Inc., Denver, 1980-86; pres., chief exec. officer Kurtex Inc., Denver, 1981—, Bankers Pacific Mortgage, Denver, 1980—, Bankers Fin. Escrow Corp., Denver, 1984—, Northwest Title & Escrow, Denver, 1984—; pres., chief exec. officer Steamboat Title, Steamboat Springs, Colo., 1985—, First Escrow, Denver, 1986—, Fidelity-Commonwealth-Continental Escrow, Denver, 1984—; pres. Colonnade Ltd., Denver, 1981-88; pres., bd. dirs. Breckridge (Colo.) Brewery. V.p., founder Colfax on the Hill, Denver, 1984; mediator, arbitrator Arbitrator/Mediation Assn., Denver, 1986; mem. Police Athletic League, Denver, 1988. Recipient Pres. Spl. Achievement/Founder award Colfax on the Hill, Denver, 1984, Spl. Mayor's award, City & County of Denver, 1985. Mem. Nat. Assn.of Real Estate Appraisers, Internat. Brotherhood of Teamsters, Colo. Mortgage Bankers Assn., Mortgage Banking Assn., Denver C. of C., Phi Beta Kappa, Omicron Delta Epsilon. Clubs: U.S. Karate Assn. (Phoenix) (3d degree Black Belt), Ferrari (Portland). Lodge: Internat. Supreme Council Order of Demolay. Avocations: collecting cars, karate, fishing, art collecting. Home: 1 Carriage Ln Littleton CO 80121-2010 Office: Bankers Fin Escrow Corp 9655 E 25th Ave Ste 101 Aurora CO 80010-1056

LOCHTE, RICHARD SAMUEL, writer; b. New Orleans, Oct. 19, 1946; s. Richard Samuel and Eileen Helen (Carbine) L.; m. Jane Bryson, July, 1989. BA, Tulane U., 1968. Theater critic Los Angeles mag., 1975-95. Screenwriter: Escape to Athena, 1979, Sleeping Dog, 1988; author: Sleeping Dog (Nero Wolfe award 1985), Laughing Dog, 1988, Blue Bayou, 1992, The Neon Smile, 1995; book columnist L.A. Times, 1996—. Served to lt. comdr. USCG, 1976. Recipient spl. award Mystery Writers of Am., 1986. Mem. Writers Guild of Am., L.A. Drama Critics Circle (v.p. 1986), Nat. Book Critics Circle, Authors Guild Am., Mystery Writers Am. (bd. dirs. 1988), Pvt. Eye Writers Am., Internat. Crime Writers. Avocations: tennis, archery. Office: PO Box 5413 Santa Monica CA 90409-5413

LOCKART, BARBETTA, fabric designer, artist, jeweler, art educator; b. Sacramento, Calif., Feb. 28, 1947; d. Bernard Elwood and Naomi Joyce (Wilson) L.; m. Michael Stanley Ray, Dec. 29, 1982 (div. AA in English, Southwestern Coll., Chula Vista, Calif., 1974; BA, San Diego State U., 1975; MA in Edn. Adminstrn., N.Mex. State U., Las Cruces, 1979, MA in Counseling and Guidance, 1981. Sec., interim coord., tchr. Indian Edn. Project, Palm Springs (Calif.) Unified Sch. Dist., 1976-79; outreach counselor Tecumseh House/Boston Indian Coun., 1980-81, asst. dir., 1981; acad. counselor, coord. native Am. affairs Ea. N.Mex. U., Portales, 1981-82; ind. researcher in field of counseling, Albuquerque, 1982-89, Sacramento, Calif., 1989-97; pres., Sacramento, 1989—; owner Dearwater Designs, Albuquerque, 1985-88, Sacramento, 1988-90, Barbetta's Beads & Art, Sacramento, 1990-97, ITSA, 1997—; instr. in fabric design. Rockefeller Found. fellow, 1978-79; Nat. Inst. Edn. fellow, 1979-80. Author: Resolving Discipline Problems for Indian Students: A Preventative Approach, 1981, Auctions and Auction-Going: Make Them Pay Off for You; contbr. articles to profl. jours.

LOCKE, FRANCIS PHILBRICK, retired editorial writer; b. Lincoln, Nebr., May 1, 1912; s. Walter Leonard and Annette Elizabeth (Philbrick) L.; m. Carroll Day, Dec. 31, 1936; children: Margaret Locke Newhouse, Alice Locke Carey, Walter Day. BA cum laude, Harvard Coll., 1933; posgrad., Harvard U., 1946-47. Reporter Miami (Fla.) Daily News, 1934-36, editorial writer, 1936-41; editorial writer St. Louis Post-Dispatch, 1941; editor of editorial page Miami Daily News, 1941-46; Nieman fellow Harvard U., Cambridge, Mass., 1946-47; assoc. editor Dayton (Ohio) Daily News, 1947-63; editorial writer Riverside (Calif.) Press-Enterprise, 1963-72. Author: (chpt.) Public Men In & Out of Office, 1943; contbr. articles to profl. jours. Bd. dirs. Mission Inn Found., Riverside, 1987-95; mem. adv. bd. YWCA, Riverside; trustee Miami U., Oxford, Ohio, 1954-63; divsn. chmn. United Way, Dayton, 1956-57. Recipient aviation writing award TWA, 1956. Mem. Nat. Conf. Editorial Writers, Soc. Profl. Journalists (nat. editorial writing prize 1946), Harvard U. Alumni Assn. (S.W. and Pacific regional dir. 1980-86, Harvard medal 1983), Harvard-Radcliffe Club So. Calif. (bd. dirs. 1975-92), Harvard Club Dayton (pres. 1961-63). Democrat. Congregationalist. Avocations: classical music, Gilbert & Sullivan, Civil War military history, baseball, college football. Home: 7368 Westwood Dr Riverside CA 92504-2729

LOCKE, GARY, governor; b. Jan. 21, 1950; s. James and Julie L.; m. Mona Lee Locke, Oct. 15, 1994. BA in Polit. Sci., Yale U., 1972; JD, Boston U., 1975. Dep. prosecuting atty. State of Wash., King County; with Ho. of Reps., Wash., 1982-93; gov. State of Washington, 1996—; cmty. rels. mgr. U.S. West; chief exec. King County, 1993. Named First in effectiveness among Puget Sound area lawmakers Seattle Times, 1990. Office: Office of the Gov PO Box 40002 Olympia WA 98504-0002*

LOCKLIN, GERALD IVAN, language educator, poet, writer; b. Rochester, N.Y., Feb. 17, 1941; s. Ivan Ward and Esther Adelaide (Kindelen) L. BA, St. John Fisher Coll., 1961; MA, U. Ariz., 1963, PhD, 1964. Instr. Calif. State U., L.A., 1964-65; prof. English Calif. State U., Long Beach, 1965—; Author: (novella) The Case of the Missing Blue Volkswagen, 1984, (short stories) The Gold Rush, 1989, numerous poems; co-editor: A New Geography of Poets, 1992; featured in The Oxford Companion to Twentieth Century Literature in English, 1996; contbr. about 2,000 works to periodicals. Author: Down and Out, 1999, Go West, Young Toad: Selected Writings, 1999. Mem. PEN USA/West, The E.E. Cummings Soc., The Hemingway Soc., Assoc. Writing Programs. Avocations: swimming, jazz, travel, Yankees, Lakers. Office: Calif State U English Dept Long Beach CA 90840

LOCKLIN, PAUL G., executive. Pres., CEO CIDCO, Morgan Hill, Calif. Office: 220 Cochrane Cir Morgan Hill CA 95037-2803*

LOCKTON, DAVID BALLARD, business executive; b. Indpls., Mar. 28, 1937; s. Richard Curtis and Violet (Ballard) L.; m. Mary Shullenberger, Aug. 1961 (div. Dec. 1969); children: Jennifer Anne, Mary Wendell; m. Kathy Austin, Apr. 3, 1971; 1 child, Richard A. BA, Yale U., 1959; JD, U. Va., 1962; postgrad. in bus. sch. ext. program, Stanford U., 1972. Ptnr. Lockton and Scopelitis, Inc., Indpls., 1965-70; founder, pres., chief exec. officer Ontario (Calif.) Motor Speedway, 1968-71; chief exec. off., publisher, owner Calif. Bus. Mag., L.A., 1972-75; pres., chief exec. officer Lola Grand Prix, Ltd., L.A., 1976-79; founder, chief exec. officer Data Broadcasting, Inc., San Mateo, Calif., 1980-85; chmn., founder, CEO Interactive Network, Inc., 1986—; pres. Lockton Ventures, 1996—; co-founder, bd. dirs. A.Z.L. Resources, Inc., 1964-75; creator, developer Internat. Race of Champions TV Racing Series, 1972—, co-founder, chmn. Repair Shop Systems, Inc., 1986; dir. Enseco, Inc., 1986; nationwide lectr. on entrepreneurship and info. tech. Patentee in interactive TV. Recipient Meritorious Svc. award Soc. Automotive Engrs., 1970. Mem. Jonathan Club (L.A.), Crooked Stick Golf Club (co-founder) (Indpls.), Carmel Valley Ranch, Penrod Soc. (co-founder, Indpls.). Republican. Episcopalian. Avocations: jazz piano, golf. Office: Lockton Ventures 405 El Camino Real Ste 423 Menlo Park CA 94025-5240

LOCKWOOD, WILLIAM GODFREY, free lance writer; b. Chgo., June 26, 1940; s. William Hyde and Jean Frances (Rein) L. Lic. gen. contractor, Calif. Foreman Demand Drywall, Santa Anna, Calif., 1968-77, Cal Coast Drywall, Grover City, Calif., 1977-80; investigator Bright & Powell Attys., Santa Barbara, Calif., 1985-87. Inventor: Construction Equipment, 1976 (patented); contbr. articles to various publs. Sponsor Children Internat., 1985-96. With U.S. Army, 1963-65. Recipient 1st place trophy Stockcar drag races, Pomona, Calif., 1961. Mem. Screenwriters Assn. Santa Barbara (2d pl. award 1988), Santa Barbara Maritime Mus. Republican. Avocations: computers, sport parachuting.

LOCKYER, BILL, state attorney general; b. Oakland, Calif., May 8, 1941; 1 child, Lisa. BA in Polit. Sci., U. Calif., Berkeley; cert. in sec. tchg., Calif. State U., Hayward; JD, U. of the Pacific. Past tchr. San Leandro, Calif.; Mem. Calif. State Assembly, 1973; state senator State of Calif., 1982; pres. pro tem, chmn. senate rules com., chmn. senate jud. com. Calif. State Senate, 1994-98; atty. gen. State of Calif., 1999—; active San Leandro Sch. Bd., 1968-73. past chair Alameda County Dem. Ctrl. Com. Named Legislator of Yr. Planning and Conservation League, 1996, Calif. Jour., 1997,. Office: Office of Atty Gen 1300 I St Ste 1740 Sacramento CA 95814*

LODEN, D. JOHN, advertising executive. Pres., CEO FCB Healthcare, San Francisco, Calif. *

LODGE, EDWARD JAMES, federal judge; b. 1933. BS cum laude, Coll. Idaho, 1957; JD, U. Idaho, 1969. With Smith & Miller, 1962-63; probate judge Canyon County, Idaho, 1963-65; judge Idaho State Dist. Ct., 1965-88; U.S. bankruptcy judge State of Idaho, 1988; dist. judge, now chief judge U.S. Dist. Ct. Idaho, 1989—. Recipient Kramer award for excellence in jud. adminstrn.; named three time All-Am., disting. alumnus Coll. Idaho, Boise State U., Professionalism award Idaho State Bar, 1997; named to Hall of Fame Boise State U., Coll. Idaho. Mem. Idaho Trial Lawyer Assn., Idaho State Bar Assn. (Professionalism award 1997), U.S. Fed. Judges Assn., Boise State Athletic Assn., Elks Club. Office: US Dist Ct MSC 040 550 W Fort St Fl 6 Boise ID 83724-0101*

LODWICK, MICHAEL WAYNE, lawyer; b. New Orleans, Sept. 21, 1946; s. Frank Tillman Jr. and Grace Evelyn (Hilty) L.; children: Sarah Peirce, Jane Durborow, Elizabeth Hilty; m. Mary League, June 15, 1991. BA, La. State U., 1968; MA, Tulane U., 1972, PhD, 1976; JD, Loyola U., New Orleans, 1981. Bar: La., U.S. Dist. Ct. (ea. dist.) La. 1981, U.S. Ct. Appeals (5th cir.) 1981, U.S. Ct. Appeals (D.C. cir.) 1982, U.S. Ct. Appeals (11th cir.) 1986, U.S. Ct. Appeals (9th cir.) 1990, U.S. Ct. Appeals (3d cir.) 1996, U.S. Ct. Appeals (4th cir.) 1996, U.S. Supreme Ct., 1987, Calif. 1990. Instr. to asst. prof. Tulane U., New Orleans, 1976-78; assoc. Barham & Churchill, New Orleans, 1981-83, O'Neil, Eichin & Miller, New Orleans, 1983-87, ptnr., 1987-89; ptnr. Fisher & Porter, 1989-97, Porter, Groff & Lodwick, 1997—. Editor, co-founder and pub. Plantation Soc. in Americas jour., 1979-83, 86—; editor-in-chief Loyola Law Rev., 1980-81; contrbr. articles to profl. jours. Mem. New Orleans Symphony Chorus, 1985-89, Pacific Chorale, 1989—. Tulane U. fellow, 1970-72; recipient Loyola U. Law Rev. Honor award, 1981, Loyola Law Alumni award, 1981. Mem. ABA, La. State Bar Assn., State Bar Calif., Fed. Bar Assn., Assn. Transp. Law, Logistics and Policy, Maritime Law Assn. U.S. Home: 20241 Seashell Cir Huntington Beach CA 92646-4436 Office: Porter Groff & Lodwick 110 Pine Ave 11th Fl Long Beach CA 90802

LOEFFLER, GARRY ANTONE, principal, municipal official; b. Lewiston, Idaho, Mar. 12, 1941; s. John Antone and Germaine Agnes (Meyer) L.; m. Bonnie Louise Ferguson, Dec. 28, 1968; children: Stacey Anne, Brian John, Bradley Scott. BS in Edn., U. Idaho, 1963; MS in Sch. Adminstrn., Calif. State U., Hayward, 1983. Tchr. Roosevelt Sch., San Leandro, Calif., 1965-70, vice prin., 1970-74; prin. Wash. Sch., San Leandro, Calif., 1975-80, Wilson Sch., San Leandro, Calif., 1980-85; prin. Garfield Sch., San Leandro, Calif., 1985-97, facilitator conversion to yr.-round edn. Mem. city coun. City of San Leandro, 1994—. Lt. U.S. Army, 1963-65. Mem. ASCD, Am. Assn. Sch. Adminstrs., Assn. Calif. Sch. Adminstrs., San Leandro Adminstrs. Assn. (pres. 1991, Outstanding Sch. Adminstr. award 1992), World Future Soc., Phi Delta Kappa. Democrat. Roman Catholic. Avocations: model railroading, reading, writing, cartooning, traveling. Home: 235 Begier Ave San Leandro CA 94577-2813 Office: City San Leandro 835 E 14th St San Leandro CA 94577-3782

LOEH, CORINNE RACHOW, artist; b. Livingston, Ill., Apr. 6, 1918; d. Tipmer Charles and Mae Leona (Batemon) Rachow; m. Hugo William Loeh (dec.); children: Sandra Mae Blaeser, Danna Clare Koschkee (dec.). Grad., Blackburn Coll., 1937; BS in Edn., Greenville Coll., 1950; MS in Art Edn., So. Ill. U., 1958. Tchr. pub. schs., Ill., 1937-52; art supr. Unit Dist. #1, Carlyle, Ill., 1952-55; tchr. art high sch., supr. K-9 Unit Dist. #2, Greenville, Ill., 1955-65, title one author, dir., 1965-69; prof. art Greenville Coll., 1956-65; art dir. Unit Dist. #46, Elgin, Ill., 1969-77; freelance artist Oro Valley, Ariz., 1982—; art collector CLO Art Gallery, Oro Valley, 1982—; cons. in field. Author: Prescription for Titans, 1971; editor: Ill. Art Edn. Assn. News, 1972, 77; one-woman shows include Judson Coll., Elgin, 1979, Western Gallery, Tucson, Ariz., 1985, 87; represented in permanent collections at Archives of Nat. Mus. Women in Arts, Washington, Tucson Mus. Art. Mem. AAUW, Ill. Art Edn. Assn., Nat. Mus. Women in Arts (charter), Surface Designers, Fibert Arts Internat., Tucson Art Mus., Met. Mus. Art Internat., Nat. Art Edn. Assn. Republican. Home and office: 151 E Carolwood Dr Oro Valley AZ 85737-7939

LOEHWING, RUDI CHARLES, JR., publicist, radio broadcasting executive, journalist; b. Newark, July 26, 1957; s. Rudy Charles Sr. and Joan Marie (Bell) L.; m. Claire Popham, Sept. 4, 1987; children: Aspasia Joyce, Tesia Victoria, Rudi Douglas, Anna Marie, Samantha Diane, Ian Ryan. Student, Biscayne U., 1975, Seton Hall U., 1977, Hubbard U., 1980. Announcer radio sta. WHBI FM, N.Y.C., 1970-72; producer Am. Culture Entertainment, Belleville, N.J., 1973-74; exec. producer Am. Culture Entertainment, Hollywood, Calif., 1988-94; CEO Broadcaster's Network Internat., Hollywood, U.K., Calif., also U.K., 1989—, Broadcaster's Network Internat., Ltd., Hollywood, also U.K.; bd. dirs. First Break, Hollywood, also U.K., 1988—. Author: Growing Pains, 1970; dir. exec. producer TV documentaries and comml. advertisements, 1983; patentee in field. Devel. dir. Tricentennial Found., Washington, 1989-90; bd. dirs. Civic Light Opera of South Bay Cities, 1998—, Tax Edn. Assn., Just Say No to Drugs, L.A., 1989, Hands Across the Atlantic, Internat. Country Top 10, The Rock of Russia, Job Search, Hollywood, U.K. and Russia. Named Youngest Comml. Radio Producer and Announcer for State of N.Y., Broadcaster's Network Internat., 1972. Mem. Nat. Press Club, Broadcasters Network Assn. (bd. dirs. 1977—), Profl. Bus. Comms. Assn. (founder 1989), BNI News Bur. (chmn. 1991—), Civic Light Opera of South Bay Cities (bd. dirs. 1996—). Avocations: flying, music, writing, photography, martial arts (recipient awards). Office: Broadcasters Network Internat Ltd 2624 Medlow Ave Ste B Los Angeles CA 90065-4617

LOETE, STEVEN DONALD, pilot; b. Tacoma, Aug. 21, 1959; s. Donald Kenneth and Ida Lorraine (Buck) L.; 1 child, Samantha; m. Jodi Christine Barnett, 1998; 1 child, Tiffani. BA, Pacific Luth. U., 1984. Pilot contracting office USAF, Williams AFB, Ariz., 1985; flight instr. Clover Park Tech. Coll., Tacoma, 1986; charter pilot Stellar Exec., Chandler, Ariz., 1986-87; pilot, airline capt. Maui Airlines, Guam, 1987; airline capt., checkairman Westair Airlines, Fresno, Calif., 1987-98; airline pilot Air Wis., 1998—; owner Northwestern Properties. Contbr. Save the Children, 1988-90; mem. Angel Flight, U. Puget Sound, 1981-83; bd. dirs. aviation adv. com. Clover Park Tech. Coll., 1991—. 1st lt. USAF, 1983-93. Mem. Airline Pilots Assn. (chmn. organizing com. 1989, chmn. coun. 1989-91). Republican. Methodist. Avocations: racquetball, fishing. Home and Office: PO Box 57 Spanaway WA 98387-0057

LOEWENTHAL, NESSA PARKER, communications educator; b. Chgo., Oct. 13, 1930; d. Abner and Frances (Ness) Parker; m. Martin Moshe Loewenthal, July 7, 1951 (dec. Aug. 1973); children: Dann Marcus, Ronn Carl, Deena Miriam; m. Gerson B. Selk, Apr. 17, 1982 (dec. June 1987). BA in Edn. and Psychology, Stanford U., 1952. Faculty Stanford Inst. for Intercultural Communication, Palo Alto, Calif., 1973-87; dir. Trans Cultural Svcs., San Francisco, 1981-86, Portland, Oreg., 1986—; dir. dependent svcs. and internat. edn. Bechtel Group, San Francisco, 1973-81, internat. edn. cons., 1981-84; mem. adv. com. dept. internat. studies Lesley Coll., Cambridge, Mass., 1986—; mem. Oreg. Ethics Commns., 1990—; mem. Bay Area Ethics Consortium, Berkeley, 1985-90; chmn. ethics com. Sietar Internat., Washington, 1987—, mem. governing bd., 1992-95; mem. faculty Summer Inst. for Internat. Comms., Portland, Oreg., 1987-97; core faculty Oreg. Gov.'s Sch. Svc. Leadership, Salem, 1995-97. Author: Professional Integration, 1987, Update: Federal Republic of Germany, 1990, Update: Great Britain, 1987; author, editor book series Your International Assignment, 1973-81; contbr. articles to profl. jours. Mem. equal opportunity and social justice task force Nat. Jewish Com. on Pub. Affairs; bd. dirs. Kids on the Block, Portland, Portland Jewish Acad., 1996—, Portland Ashkalon Sister City Assn.; bd. dirs., co-chair ethics com. Soc. Humanistic Judaism, 1996—; mem. Lafayette (Calif.) Traffic Commn., 1974-80; bd. dirs. Ctr. for Ethics and Social Policy, 1988-91; mem. exec. bd. and planning com. Temple Isaiah, Lafayette, 1978-82; bd. dirs. Calif. Symphony, Orinda, 1988-90; mem. exec. com. overseas schs. adv. com. U.S. Dept. State, 1976-82; mem. cmty. rels. com. Portland Jewish Fedn.; mem. Nat. Jewish Cmty. Rels. Task Force Social Justice and Econ. Opportunity, 1995—; mem. Task Force on Racism, Ethnicity and Pub. Policy, 1998—. Named Sr. Interculturalist, Sietar Internat., 1986. Mem. ASTD (exec. bd. internat. profl. performance area 1993—), Soc. for Intercultural Edn. Tng. and Rsch. (chmn. 1986-87, nomination com. 1984-86, co-chmn. 1989-90, chmn. ethics com. 1989—, governing bd. 1992-95), World Affairs Coun., Portland City Club. Democrat. Avocations: photography, swimming. Office: TransCultural Svcs 712 NW Westover Ter Portland OR 97210-3136

LOFGREN, ZOE, congresswoman; b. San Mateo, Calif., Dec. 21, 1947; d. Milton R. and Mary Violet L.; m. John Marshall Collins, Oct. 22, 1978; children: Sheila Zoe Lofgren Collins, John Charles Lofgren Collins. BA in Polit. Sci., Stanford U., 1970; JD cum laude, U. Santa Clara, 1975. Bar: Calif., 1975. D.C. Adminstrv. asst. to Congressman Don Edwards, San Jose, Calif., 1970-79; ptnr. Webber and Lofgren, San Jose, 1979-81; mem. Santa Clara County Bd. Suprs., 1981-94; congresswoman 104th-106th U.S. Congress, Calif. 16th Dist., 1995—; part-time prof. Law, U. Santa Clara, 1978-80; jud. com., judiciary subcom. on comml. and adminstrv. law, subcom. on crime, sci. com. subcoms. on basic rsch. & tech.; house com. on sci., subcommittee on tech., basic rsch.; mem. jud. sci. stds. ofcl. conduct 105th Congress. Exec. dir. Community Housing Developers, Inc., 1979-80; trustee San Jose Community Coll. Dist., 1979-81; bd. dirs. Community Legal Svcs., 1978-81, San Jose Housing Svc. Ctr., 1978-79; mem. steering com. sr. citizens housing referendum, 1978; del. Calif. State Bar Conv., 1979-82, Dem. Nat. Conv., 1976; active Assn. Immigration and Nationality Lawyers, 1976-82, Calif. State Dem. Cen. Com., 1975-78, Santa Clara County Dem. Cen. Com., 1974-78, Notre Dame High Sch. Blue Ribbon Com., 1981-84, Victim-Witness Adv. Bd., 1981-94. Recipient Bancroft-Whitney award for Excellence in Criminal Procedure, 1973. Mem. Santa Clara County Bar Assn. (trustee 1979—), Santa Clara County Women Lawyers Com. (exec. bd. 1979-80), Sanata Clara Law Sch. Alumni Assn. (v.p. 1977, pres. 1978), Nat. Women's Polit. Caucus, Assn. of Bay Area Govts. (exec. bd. 1981-86). Office: US House Reps 318 Cannon Bldg Ofc Bldg Washington DC 20515-0516 also: 635 N 1st St Ste B San Jose CA 95112-5110*

LOFLIN, ANDREA, small business owner; b. Columbia, Md., Jan. 22, 1970; d. Marvin Dee and JoJean (Hansen) L.; m. Arild Larsen, May 26, 1989 (div. October 7, 1994); 1 child, Shirsten Kari; m. Gene Anaya, Nov. 30, 1996. BA, Brigham Young U., 1998. CMT, MTCP (medical transcription cert.) , Calif. Med. transcriptionist ExecuMed Inc., Golden, Colo., 1988-96; pres. Career Step, Provo, UT, 1992—. Author: Keyboard Kinetics, 1992, Career Step Medical Transcription Training Program (13 books, 16 tapes), 1992-1997, including Medical/Surgical Wordlist, 1998, Intermediate Transcription, 1998, Advanced Transcription, 1998, Grammar and Style Essen-

tials, 1997, Medical Word Building, 1997, Anatomy and Physiology, 1997, Abbreviations, Medical Plurals, How to Look Up Words, Word-Differentiation and Formatting, 1997, Focus on Medical Specialties, 1997, Drug Reference, 1997, Making Your Career Step, 1996, and Pronunciation Book, 1995. Mem. LDS Ch. Avocations: reading, family, religion. Office: Career Step 224 S 500 W Provo UT 84601

LOFTHOUSE, RUSS WILBERT, school administrator; b. Chgo., Jan. 21, 1945; s. Russell Wilber and Anne Marie (Daker) L.; m. Pamlin I. Axelson, Aug. 7, 1976; one child, James. BA in Elem. Edn., U. Denver, 1971; MA in Elem. Edn., U. Colo., Denver, 1978, PhD in Edn., 1991. Cert. elem tchr., Colo., elem. prin., Colo. Tchr. Cherry Creek Schs., Englewood, Colo., 1971-86, prin., 1986—; mem. adv. bd. Teaching and Computers, N.Y.C., 1986—. Recipient Disting. Tchr. award Cherry Creek Schs., 1985; named Colo. Tchr. of Yr., Colo. Dept. Edn., 1986; runner-up Nat. Tchr. of Yr., 1986. Mem. Assn. Supervision and Curriculum Devel., Am. Acad. and Inst. Human Reason (dir. community leaders and succesful schs.), Fulbrite Tchrs. Alumni Assn., NEA, Nat. State Tchs. of Yr., Phi Delta Kappa. Avocations: outdoor activities, reading, advising and consulting. Home and Office: 8505 E Temple Dr Apt 502 Denver CO 80237-2545

LOFTIN, ORRIN KEITH, retired career officer, poet, actor; b. Fayetteville, N.C., Mar. 16, 1960; s. Leonza and Willie Elizabeth (Adams) L.; m. Sandra Denise Chisholm, Apr. 3, 1985; 1 child, Jauté Desireé, Procasius Darnell. BS in Math., Fayetteville State U., 1984; MA in Space Sys. and Computer Sys., Webster U., 1992. Enlisted USAF, 1985, advanced through grades to capt., 1985—; pres., founder Loftin, Algorithms, Inc., 1993-94. Author: (poetry) Infinity of Blue, The Rent, Am. Poetry Assn. award, 1990. Republican. Presbyterian. Avocations: piano, backgammon, chess, tennis, windsurfing. Home: 3805 7th St NE Trlr 114 Great Falls MT 59404-1155

LOFTIS, JAMES MADISON, sales executive; b. Long Beach, Calif., Mar. 15, 1960; s. James Madison and Gloria E. (Ray) L. BS in Pub. Adminstrn., U. So. Calif., 1985, postgrad. Account exec. Mayor's Bus. Office, City of L.A., 1984-85; supr. Arab Security Studies and Tng. Ctr., Saudi Arabia, 1985-87; outside sales rep. Marshall Electronics, Irvine, Calif., 1988-89; regional sales mgr. Sakata Inx, Torrance, Calif., 1990-97; nat. sales mgr. Matsuo Electronics, Huntington Beach, Calif., 1998; internat. bus. devel. mgr. Technical Electronics Group, ASM Group, Manila, The Philippines, 1998—. Mem. World Trace Ctr. Assn. Orange County, Life Extension Found., Oxford Club, Kappa Alpha. Republican. Avocations: scuba diving, swimming, weight lifting, domestic and foreign investments, international travel. Office: 10330 Pioneer Blvd Ste 270 Santa Fe Springs CA 90670-8283 also: 12/F Citibank Ctr, 8741 Paseo de Roxas, 1226 Makati City The Philippines

LOFTUS, THOMAS DANIEL, lawyer; b. Seattle, Nov. 8, 1930; s. Glendon Francis and Martha Helen (Wall) L. BA, U. Wash., 1952, JD, 1957. Bar: Wash. 1958, U.S. Ct. Appeals (9th cir.) 1958, U.S. Dist. Ct. Wash. 1958, U.S. Ct. Mil. Appeals 1964, U.S. Supreme Ct. 1964. Trial atty. Northwestern Mut. Ins. Co., Seattle, 1958-62; sr. trial atty. Unigard Security Ins. Co., Seattle, 1962-68, asst. gen. counsel, 1969-83, govt. rels. counsel, 1983-89; of counsel Groshong, LeHet & Thornton, 1990-98; mem. Wash. Commn. on Jud. Conduct (formerly Jud. Qualifications Commn.), 1982-88, vice-chmn., 1987-88; judge pro tem Seattle Mcpl. Ct., 1973-81; mem. nat. panel of mediators Arbitration Forums, Inc., 1990—. Sec., treas. Seattle Opera Assn., 1980-91; pres., bd. dirs. Vis. Nurse Svcs., 1979-88; pres., v.p. Salvation Army Adult Rehab. Ctr., 1979-86; nat. committeeman Wash. Young Rep. Fedn., 1961-63, vice chmn., 1963-65; pres. Young Reps. King County, 1962-63; bd. dirs. Seattle Seafair, Inc., 1975; bd. dirs., gen. counsel Wash. Ins. Coun., 1984-86, sec., 1986-88, v.p., 1988-90, Am. Mediation Panel of Mediators, 1990-96; bd. dirs. Arson Alarm Found., 1987-90; bd. visitors law sch. U. Wash., 1993—. 1st lt. U.S. Army, 1952-54, col. Res., 1954-85. Fellow Am. Bar Found.; mem. Am. Arbitration Assn. (nat. panel arbitrators 1965—), Am. Arbitration Forums, Inc (nat. panel arbitrators 1992), Nat. Assn. Security Dealers (bd. arbitrators 1997—), Am. Mediation Panel, Wash. Bar Assn. (gov. 1981-84), Seattle King County Bar Assn. (sec., trustee 1977-82), ABA (ho. of dels. 1984-90), Internat. Assn. Ins. Counsel, U.S. People to People (del. Moscow internat. law-econ. conf. 1990), Def. Rsch. Inst., Wash. Def. Trial Lawyers Assn., Wash. State Trial Lawyers Assn., Am. Judicature Soc., Res. Officers Assn., Judge Advocate General's Assn., Assn. Wash. Gens., U. Wash. Alumni Assn., Coll. Club Seattle, Wash. Athletic Club, Masons, Shriners, Ranier Club, Pi Sigma Alpha, Delta Sigma Rho, Phi Delta Phi, Theta Delta Chi. Republican. Presbyterian. Home: 3515 Magnolia Blvd W Seattle WA 98199-1841 Office: Coll Club Bldg Ste #300 505 Madison St Seattle WA 98104

LOGAN, CAROLYN, English language educator; b. Dover, N.J., Mar. 12, 1942; d. Reginald M. and Rachel Carolyn (Spencer) L.. BA, U. Wyo., 1964, MA, 1967; PhD, The Union Inst., Cin., 1994. Tchr. Lakewood (Calif.) H.S., 1964-66; instr. English and women's studies Casper (Wyo.) Coll., 1967—. Author: (textbook) Counterbalance, 1997. State coord. NOW, Wyo., 1993-98. Recipient Outstanding Tchr. award Burlington No., Casper, 1989. Mem. AAUW, MLA (women's caucus), Nat. Women's Studies Assn., Rocky Mt. MLA. Avocations: fly fishing, golf. Office: Casper Coll 125 College Dr Casper WY 82601-4612

LOGAN, JAMES SCOTT, SR., federal agency administrator; b. Stanford, Ky., June 18, 1948; s. James M.H. and Lillian Elizabeth (Givens) L.; m. Rose Marie Helm, Aug. 31, 1968; children: James Matthew, Tasha Marie. AA, Columbia (Mo.) Coll., 1990, BS/BA cum laude, 1992; postgrad., U. Colo., 1992—. Unit adminstr. USAR, Lakewood, Colo., 1972-82; continuity of govt. planner Fed. Emergency Mgmt. Agy. Region VIII, Lakewood, 1983-90, tech. hazards program specialist, 1991-92, sr. tech. hazards program specialist, 1992-95; team leader state and local programs Fed. Emergency Mgmt. Agy. Region VIII, Lakewood, Colo., 1995—; emergency analyst Office of Regional Dir., Denver, 1995—, dir. preparedness tng. and exercises divsn., 1998—; chmn. bd. dirs. Rocky Mountain Human Svcs. Coalition, 1995—, pres. bd. dirs. 1998-99. Mem. NAACP, Denver, 1992; mem. NCOA NCO Assn., Denver, 1979—; mem. citizen's adv. com. polit. sci. dept. U. Colo., Denver. With U.S. Army, 1968-71, Vietnam, USAR, 1972. Decorated Legion of Merit. Mem. VFW, Am. Legion, Pi Sigma Alpha. Democrat. Baptist. Avocations: reading, computers, political science. Home: 16952 E Bates Ave Aurora CO 80013-2243 Office: FEMA Region VIII PO Box 25267 Bldg 710A Denver CO 80225-0267

LOGAN, LEE ROBERT, orthodontist; b. L.A., June 24, 1932; s. Melvin Duncan and Margaret (Seltzer) L.; m. Maxine Nadler, June 20, 1975; children: Chad, Casey. BS, UCLA, 1952; DDS, Northwestern U., 1956, MS, 1961. Diplomate Am. Bd. Orthodontics. Gen. practice dentistry, Reseda, Calif., 1958-59; practice dentistry specializing in orthodontics, Northridge, Calif., 1961—; pres. Lee R. Logan DDS Profl. Corp.; mem. med. staff Northridge Hosp.; owner Maxine's Prodn. Co.; owner Maxine's Talent Agy.; guest lectr. UCLA, U. So. Calif., dir dental edn. Northridge Med. Ctr. Contbr. articles to profl. jours. Served to lt. USNR, 1956-58. Named (with wife) Couple of Yr. Autistic Children Assn., 1986; recipient Nat. Philanthropy award, 1987, 1st Pl. winner Austistic Jogathon, 1981-98, 1st Pl. Mem. Am., San Fernando Valley Dental Assn. (pres. 1998), Am. Assn. Orthodontists, Pacific Coast Soc. Orthodontists (dir., pres. so. sect. 1974-75, chmn. membership 1981-83), Found. Orthodontic Research (charter mem.), Calif. Soc. Orthodontists (chmn. peer rev. 1982-93), G.V. Black Soc. (charter mem.), Angle Soc. Orthodontists (pres. 1981-82, bd. dirs. 1982-99, nat. pres. 1985-87, dir. 1985-96), U. S.C. Century Club Fraternity, Xi Psi Phi, Chi Phi. Home: 4830 Encino Ave Encino CA 91316-3813 Office: 18250 Roscoe Blvd Northridge CA 91325-4226

LOGAN, PATRICIA JEAN, interior designer; b. Aurora, Ill., Feb. 24, 1926; d. Harley J. and Svea (Andrews) Benjamin; m. Marcel Guillaume, June 21, 1974. BA, MA, UCLA, 1951. Interior designer, 1951—. Author: Maliblue, 1980, (videos) Contemporary American Art, 1993. Bd. dirs. League for Crippled Children. Recipient awards City of Santa Monica, Calif., 1960, City of L.A., 1974, L.A. Times, Chgo. Tribune. Mem. Am. Soc. Interior Designers (historian), Am. Mus. Contemporary Art (pres. 1989—).

LOGAN, RICHARD WALTER, bakery engineering mechanic; b. Harvey, Ill., Apr. 7, 1950; s. Harry Carry Logan and Nancy Jane (Pierce) Graham; m. Catherine Jene Grazier, Dec. 6, 1968 (div. Oct. 1971); 1 child, Richard Wayne; m. Linda Lee Carr, Oct. 16, 1971. AA in Gen. Studies, Scottsdale Community Coll., 1979. Cert. vet. technician, Ariz. Vet. technician Illiana, South Holland, Ill., Shea Animal Hosp., Phoenix; sheet metal mechanic Capitol Engring. Co., Phoenix, 1979-80; owner, mgr. South Park Air Conditioning Co., Phoenix; shop foreman, mechanic Carlton Enterprises, Scottsdale, Ariz.; bakery engring. mechanic Holsum Bakery, Inc., Phoenix, 1982—. With U.S. Army, 1968-71, Vietnam. Winner Best Editorial Communications contest Valley of Sun United Way, 1986; recipient Golden Note award and Barbershopper of Month award Phoenix chpt. Soc. for Preservation and Encouragement Barbershop Quartet Singing in Am., 1978. Mem. Internat. Assn. Machinists (founding editor The Caliper Phoenix 1985-87), Clann Maclennan Assn. (life), Caledonian Soc. Ariz., Scottish-Am. Mil. Soc. Republican. Avocations: woodworking, outdoor activities. Home: PO Box 60762 Phoenix AZ 85082-0762 Office: Holsum Bakery Inc 408 S 23d Ave Phoenix AZ 85009-5852

LOGGINS, PAUL GREGORY, marketing professional; b. Torrance, Calif., Sept. 22, 1968; s. John Frances Loggins. BA, Calif. State U., Chico, 1994. Prin. Loggins Promotion, Harbor City, Calif., 1989—. Republican. Avocations: concerts, camping, boating, music prodn., stock market. Office: Loggins Promotion/Backstage Entertainment 26239 Senator Ave Harbor City CA 90710-3721

LOGSDON, RICHARD M., English language educator, magazine editor; b. Boise, Idaho, June 2, 1948; s. Richard M. and Eula Jane (Randall) L.; m. Juliet Anne de Neufuille, Dec. 27, 1968; children: Tobias, Heather. BA, U. Oreg., 1970, MA, 1972, PhD, 1976. English prof. C.C. So. Nev., Las Vegas, 1975—. Author: (textbooks) Community College Reader, 1984; editor-in-chief Red Rook Rev., 1995-98; author of short stories. Coach boys and girls teams Nev. State Youth Soccer, 1981-93; head soccer coach mens team Las Vegas Premiere Soccer League, 1991-98. Avocations: coaching soccer, writing fiction, fishing, sports. Home: 3090 S El Camino Rd Las Vegas NV 89102 Office: CC So Nev 3200 E Cheyenne Ave Las Vegas NV 89030

LOH, EDITH KWOK-YUEN, oncology nurse, health education specialist; b. Hong Kong, May 1, 1948; came to U.S., 1972; d. Chun Wing and Pui King (Chan) Lee; m. Kevin Kai-Tsu Loh, Mar. 30, 1972; children: Elizabeth, Jennifer, Jeffrey. RN, Hong Kong Govt. Nursing Sch., 1971, Tex. Woman's U., 1976; BSN magna cum laude, Hawaii Loa Coll., 1989; MPH, U. Hawaii, 1990, postgrad., 1994-98. Cert. health edn. specialist; RN, Hawaii, Tex., Hong Kong, Eng. Student gen. nurse Hong Kong Govt. Hosps., 1968-70; pediatric nurse Queen Elizabeth Hosp., Hong Kong, 1971-72; head nurse oncology Ctr. Pavillion Hosp., Houston, 1972-75; oncology nurse Dr. Kevin Loh, Inc., Honolulu, 1978-90; nurse coord., health instr. Hawaii Hematology, Oncology, Inc., Honolulu, 1991-92; vol. rschr. immunol. studies U. Hawaii, 1990, guest lectr. Sch. Pub. Health, 1994—; health educator Baby S.A.F.E., Adminstrv. Office Dept. Health, Honolulu, 1993-94, vol. rsch. asst., 1997; presenter Am. Indian and Alaska Native Caucus 123d ann. meeting APHA, San Diego, 1995, Queen's Hosp., 1998; mem. planning workshop com. Queen's Hosp., Wellness Dept., 1996-98. Vol. recruitor Hawaii Bone Marrow Donor Registry, Honolulu, 1992; chmn. cmty. svc. com., Honolulu, 1992—; dir. Health Svcs. for Sr. Citizens, 1993; bd. dirs. Hawaii Cancer Children Found., 1992-94; chmn. edn. Hawaii Coalition for Continuing Health Edn. and Profl. Devel.; dir. United Chinese Soc., 1998. Recipient Award of Merit, Nat. Dean's List, Nat. Collegiate Nursing award, 1989; named All American Scholar, 1989. Mem. AMA, APHA, Hawaii Pacific U. Nursing Honor Soc., Am. Cancer Soc., Soc. for Pub. Health Edn.-Hawaii (bd. dirs., sec., life), Assoc. Chinese Univ. Women Inc. (chmn. welfare com. 1992, chmn. cmty. svc. com. 1991-95, mem. in parliamentary procedure legis. com. 1992, v.p. 1996, pres.-elect 1997, pres. 1998, bd. dirs. 1999), Soc. Pub. Health Edn. (bd. dirs. 1992-99, sec. 1992-93, program planner 1998), Hawaii Soc. for Health Care Edn. and Tng. (health edn. workshop planner 1996-98, fundraiser and subcom. chmn. 1996, chmn. edn. and v.p. 1997), Nat. Wellness Assn., Chinese Women's Club, Orgn. Chinese Am. Women, U. Hawaii Alumni Assn. (life), Navy League of U.S. (life mem. Honolulu coun.), Sigma Theta Tau. Avocations: swimming, jogging, aerobic dancing, playing Chinese harp and butterfly harp, reading. Home: 1815 Kumakani Pl Honolulu HI 96821-1327

LOHMAN, ARTHUR GROVER, civilian military employee; b. Barksdale AFB, La., Dec. 6, 1950; s. Paul Oswald and Julia Alice (Rider) L.; m. Julie Rae Bohn, July 25, 1975 (div. Dec. 5, 1986; dec. Feb. 1998); children: Arthur G. Jr., Timothy E.; m. Terry Ann Hess, Jan. 10, 1988 (div. Nov. 19, 1990). Student logistics, C.C. of the Air Force, Maxwell AFB, 1974, 77-78; student, Weber State U., 1969, 74, 83-85. Enlisted USAF, 1970, advanced through the grades to sgt., ret., 1982; electronics tech. LN-12 navigation sect. USAF, Hill AFB, Utah, 1984-88, electronics tech. cir. bd. mfg. sect., 1988-92, electronics tech. aim 9 sidewinder missile sect., 1992-95, electronics tech. F16/B1 aircraft microwave sect., 1995—; mail clk., date transcriber IRS, Ogden, Utah, 1983-84; mem. hazardous waste process action team, safety monitor working group Air Craft Avionics Divsn., Hill AFB, Utah, 1989-90; hazardous waste site mgr. Cir. Card Mfg., Hill AFB, Utah, 1988-90, mem. quality com., 1989-90; participant Peace Autograph Project Display, Mus. Peace and Solidarity, Samarkand, Uzbekistan, 1993—. Creator: Cartoon Bug, 1982. Pub. affairs cmty. escort Ogden Air Logistics Ctr., Hill AFB, Utah, 1988-90; judge sci. fair Bonneville H.S., Weber State Univ., Ogden, Utah, 1989, speech contest judge, 12th Annual Health Occupation Students Am. Nat. Leadership Conf., Utah, 1989; master of ceremonies Hill AFB Talent Competition, 1993; jr. olympic bowling coach Young Am. Bowling Alliance, Layton, 1996—. Mem. Utah State Poetry Soc. (affil. Acad. Am. Poets and Nat. Fedn. State Poetry Socs.), Learning Disabilities Assn. Utah, Toastmasters Internat. (gov.'s award 1990), Order of Internat. Fellowship. Avocations: poetry, chess, bowling, acting in community theater, collecting rare books. Office: OO-ALC/LARPJ 7274 Wardleigh Rd Hill Air Force Base UT 84056-5137

LOHMAN, FRANK BOSTWICK, information security administrator; b. San Francisco, Feb. 20, 1949; s. Frank Joseph and Elizabeth Ann (Bostwick) L.; m. Keiko Ikeda, Feb. 1, 1972; children: Kristopher David, Kari Ann. AA, Barston Cmty. Coll., 1976; BA in Marketing, Chapmans Coll., 1980. Commd. ensign USMC, 1969, advanced through grades to Gysgt.; mgr. programming team EMC, Honolulu, 1988-89; project mgr. HMSA, Honolulu, 1989-90, security adminstr., 1990—; mgr. Club Sys., USMC, Viequez, P.R., 1976-77, Marine Corps Exchange, Barston, 1977-80. Mem. ISSA (pres. 1996—), Information Sys. Security Assn. (v.p. 1990-96). Republican. Episcopalian. Avocations: outdoor sports, fast cars, collecting movies, basketball, swimming. Home: 1420 Victoria St Apt 703 Honolulu HI 96822-3504 Office: HMSA PO Box 11629 818 Keeaumoku St Honolulu HI 96814-2365

LOHMAN, LORETTA CECELIA, social scientist, consultant; b. Joliet, Ill., Sept. 25, 1944; d. John Thomas and Marjorie Mary (Brennan) L. BA in Polit. Sci., U. Denver, 1966, PhD in Am. History, 1996; MA in Social Sci., U. No. Colo., 1975. Lectr. Ariz. State U., Tempe, 1966-67; survey researcher Merrill-Werthlin Co., Tempe, 1967-68; edn. asst. Am. Humane Assn., Denver, 1969-70; econ. cons. Lohman & Assocs., Littleton, Colo., 1971-75; rsch. assoc. Denver Rsch. Inst., 1976-86; owner, rsch. scientist Lohman & Assocs., Littleton, 1986—; affiliate Colo. Water Resources Rsch. Inst., Ft. Collins, Colo., 1989-91; tech. adv. com. Denver Potable Wastewater Demo Plant, 1986-90; cons. Constrn. Engring. Rsch. Lab., 1984—; peer reviewer NSF, 1985-86, Univs. Coun. Water Resources, 1989—; WERC consortium reviewer N.Mex. Univs.-U.S. Dept. Energy, 1989—; course cons. Regis Coll., Denver, 1992—. Contbr. articles to profl. jours. Vol. Metro Water Conservation Projects, Denver, 1986-90; vol. handicapped fitness So. Suburban Parks and Recreation. Recipient Huffsmith award Denver Rsch. Inst., 1983; Nat. Ctr. for Edn. in Politics grantee, 1964-65. Mem. ASCE (social and environ. objectives com.), Orgn. Am. Historians, Pub. Hist. Assn., Sigma Xi, Pi Gamma Mu, Phi Alpha Theta. Avocations: vegetable and xeriscape gardening, traveling, miniature boxes. Home and Office: 3375 W Aqueduct Ave Littleton CO 80123-2903

LOHRLI, ANNE, retired English language educator, author; b. Bake Oven, Oreg., Feb. 9, 1906; d. Gottfried and Anna (Hüsser) L. BA, Occidental Coll., L.A., 1927, MA, 1928; MA, Columbia U., 1932; PhD, U. So. Calif., 1937. Tchr. L.A. city schs., 1937-45; prof. English N.Mex. Highlands U., Las Vegas, 1945-65; vis. prof. U. Trieste, 1954. Compiler: Household Words, List of Contributors, etc., 1973; contbr. some 40 articles in Dickensian, Princeton U. Rev., Victorian Studies, Pacific Historian, others, 1963-94. Mem. Phi Beta Kappa, Phi Kappa Phi. Home: 901 Marlene St Apt 3 Ukiah CA 95482-5987

LOKEY, FRANK MARION, JR., broadcast executive, consultant; b. Ft. Worth, Oct. 15, 1924; s. Frank Marion Sr. and Corinne (Whaley) L. Student, Smith-Hughes Evening Coll., 1955-59. Announcer, newscaster, disc jockey, morning personality Radio Stas. WAPI, WBRC and WSGN, Birmingham, Ala., 1941-52; pres. WRDW-TV, Augusta, Ga., 1952-55; asst. gen. mgr., mgr. sales, news anchor Sta. WLW-A TV (now named WXIA-TV), Atlanta, 1955-66; co-owner, gen. mgr. Sta. WAIA, Atlanta, 1960-62; S.E. news corr., talk show host CBS News N.Y., N.Y.C., 1960-66; asst. to owner, gen. mgr. Sta. WBIE-AM-FM, Atlanta, 1962-64; asst. to pres., gen. mgr. Stas. KXAB-TV, KXJB-TV, KXMB-TV, Aberdeen, Fargo, Bismarck, S.D., N.D., 1966-67; exec. v.p., gen. mgr. St. WEMT-TV, Bangor, Maine, 1967-70; pres., gen. mgr. Stas. KMOM-TV, KWAB-TV, Odessa-Midland, Big Spring, Tex., 1970-75; exec. v.p., gen. mgr. Sta. KMUV-TV (now named KRBK-TV), Sacramento, Calif., 1975-77; CEO Lokey Enterprises, Inc., Sacramento, L.A., El Centro, Calif., 1977—, also chmn. bd. dirs.; cons., troubleshooter 16 TV stas. nationwide, 1977—; cons., actor 5 movie prodn. cos., Hollywood, Calif., 1980—; cons., outside dir. Anderson Cons., Manhattan, L.I., N.Y., 1981—; network talk show host/news corr. for 7 news orgns. worldwide, 1984—; bd. dirs. Broadcast Audience Behavior Rsch., Manhattan, 1986—, mem. inner circle, 1986—; owner/franchiser The Party Place. Creator, originator approach to real estate mktg. Hon. mem. Imperial County Bd. Suprs., El Centro, 1986—, El Centro City Coun., 1987—. Mem. Am. Legion. Baptist. Avocations: producer big bands parties, movie acting, ancient history, tracing family tree. Home: 2709 Us Highway 111 Imperial CA 92251-9772 Office: Lokey Enterprises Inc 626 W Main St El Centro CA 92243-2920

LOMBARD, GEORGE, electronics company executive. Pres., CEO Signal Tech., Sunnyvale, Calif. Office: Signal Tech 975 Beneficia Ave Sunnyvale CA 94086*

LOMBARDI, EUGENE PATSY, orchestra conductor, violinist, educator, recording artist; b. North Braddock, Pa., July 7, 1923; s. Nunzio C. and Mary (Roberto) L.; m. Jacqueline Sue Davis, Mar. 1955; children: Robert, Genanne. BA, Westminster Coll., 1948; MA, Columbia U., 1948; Edn. Specialist, George Peabody Coll., 1972; MusD, Westminster Coll., 1981. Band dir. Lincoln H.S., Midland, Pa., 1948-49; orch. dir. Male H.S., Louisville, 1949-50, Phoenix Union H.S., 1950-57; orch. dir., prof. Ariz. State U., Tempe, 1957-89. Condr. Phoenix Symphonette, 1954-61, 70-73, Phoenix Symphony Youth Orch., 1956-66, Phoenix Pops Orch., 1971-83, Fine Arts String Orch., Phoenix, 1995-97. With USAAF, 1943-46. Decorated Bronze Star; recipient Alumni Achievement award Westminster Coll., 1976, gold medal Nat. Soc. Arts and Letters, 1973, Disting. Tchr. award Ariz. State U. Alumni, 1974, Phoenix appreciation award, 1983. Mem. Music Educators Nat. Conf., Am. String Tchrs. Assn. (pres. Ariz. unit 1965-67), Am. Fedn. Musicians, Ariz. Music Educators Assn. (pres. higher edn. sect. 1973-75, Excellence in Teaching Music award 1989), Ind. Order Foresters, Phi Delta Kappa, Phi Mu Alpha, Alpha Sigma Phi. Republican. Methodist. Home: 920 E Manhatton Dr Tempe AZ 85282-5520

LOMELI, MARTA, elementary education educator; b. Tijuana, Baja Calif, Mex., Oct. 28, 1952; came to U.S. 1954; d. Jesus and Guadalupe (Ascencio) Lomeli; m. Rudolph Benitez, 1978 (div. 1982); children: Pascual Lomeli Benitez; m. David E. Miller, Aug. 16, 1991. BA, San Diego State U., 1977. With M & N Tree Nursery, Vista, Calif., 1957-70; libr. Vista Boys Club, 1969-70; vol. tutor MECHA U. Calif. San Diego, La Jolla, 1971-73; tchr. aide San Diego City Schs., 1976-77; bilingual educator National City (Calif.) Schs., 1978—; mem. restructuring com. Lincoln Acres Sch., 1991. Author numerous poems. Mem. Lincoln Acres Com. to Advise the Prin., National City, 1986-88, Com. to Advise the Supt., National City, 1986-88; art editor Lincoln Jr. H.S., Vista, Calif., 1964-65, Third World U. Calif., San Diego, 1970-73; mem. Lincoln Acres Sch. Site Coun., 1988-89, 94-96; mem. high tech. com. Nat. Sch. Dist., 1993-94; vol. tchr. St. Vincent de Paul's Ctr. for Homeless, San Diego, 1991-93, Shaolin Kempo Karate (black belt 2d degree); mem. Paradise Hills Citizens Patrol, 1994—. Mem. Calif. Tchrs. Assn. (site rep. Nat. City 1985), Calif. Assn. Bilingual Edn. (sec. 1986), Nat. Assn. Bilingual Edn., La Raza Club (pres., co-founder 1970). Independent. Avocations: drawing cartoons, karate, writing. Home: Box 113 2939 Alta View Dr Ste O San Diego CA 92139-3394

LOMELÍ, REFUGIO (JESSE LOMELÍ), athletics educator; b. Aguascalientes, Mex., July 23, 1941; came to U.S., 1954, naturalized, 1965; s. J. Jesus and Maria Guadalupe (Ascencio) L.; m. Barbara L. McMinn, Aug. 24, 1968; children: Lorena, Maya, Marc. Assoc., Palomar Coll., 1962; Bachelors degree, U. of the Americas, Mexico City, 1965; Masters degree, San Diego State U., 1972; postgrad., U. Pitts., 1972-74. Firefighter U.S. Forest Service, So. Calif. region, 1962-66; tchr. Santana H.S., Santee, Calif., 1967-73; counselor, tchr., soccer coach Mira Costa Coll., Oceanside, Calif., 1973—. Named Community Coll. Soccer Coach of Yr., Pacific Coast Conf., 1985. Mem. Nat. Assn. Fgn. Student Advisors, Am. G.I. Forum. Lodge: KC. Home: 1250 Vista Colina Dr San Marcos CA 92069-4956 Office: Mira Costa Coll PO Box 586312 Oceanside CA 92058-6312

LOMMATSCH, I. LAVON, retired business administration consultant; b. Denver, June 6, 1940; d. William Theodore and Iro (Watenpaugh) Fisher; m. Lynn Lommatsch, June 1, 1985; children: James Waldorf, Lance Waldorf, Stacy Waldorf, Eric, Keith. Student, U. Colo., 1960-61, Front Range C.C., Denver, 1984, Don Kagy Real Estate Sch., Denver, 1985. Lic. realtor, Colo. With juvenile divsn. Adams County Dist. Atty., Brighton, Colo., 1983-86; with Adams County Parks and Cmty. Resources, Brighton, 1986-95; ret. Charter mem. bd. dirs. Women In Crisis, Adams County, 1983; prodr., dir. walk-a-thons Adams County Trails and Greenway Found.; active fundraising Amaranth Diabetes Found., Alternatives to Domestic Violence, Cmty. Health Svcs., Hearing/Seeing Dogs, Santa's Workshop, Shriner's Burn Ctrs. Recipient Excellence award Nat. Assn. County Info. Officers, 1986, State Recognition award Heart Assn. Mem. Order Ea. Star (worthy matron 1977-78), Order Amaranth, Inc. (grand royal matron 1991-92), White Shrine Jerusalem. Lutheran. Avocations: music, outdoors, wildlife.

LOND, HARLEY WELDON, editor, publisher; b. Chgo., Feb. 5, 1946; s. Henry Sidney and Dorothy (Shaps) L.; m. Marilyn Moss, Aug. 20, 1981; 1 child Elizabeth. BA in Journalism, Calif. State U., L.A., 1972. Adminstrv. dir. Century City Ednl. Arts Project, L.A., 1972-76, hon. dir., 1982—; founder, editor Intermedia mag., L.A., 1974-80; prodn. mgr. FilmRow Publs., L.A., 1981; assoc. editor Box Office mag., Hollywood, Calif., 1981-84, editor, assoc. pub., 1984-94; dir. publs. Entertainment Data, Inc., 1994-95; pres. CyberPod Prodns., 1995—; chief copy editor The Hollywood Reporter, 1995—; syndicated columnist Continental Features, Washington, Tel-Aire Publs., Dallas, 1986—; hon dir. Monterey (Calif.) Film Festival, 1987; mem. media adv. bd. Cinetex Internat. Film Festival, 1988; cons. Take 3 Info. Svc.; web architect-master, OnVideo website, 1995—. Editor: Entertainment Media Electronic Info. Svc.; contbg. editor: (video) Family Style Mag.; contbr. articles to profl. publs. Calif. Arts Council grantee, 1975, Nat. Endowment for Arts grantee, 1976-77. Mem. MLA, Soc. Profl. Journalists, Assn. for Edn. in Journalism and Mass Communication, Speech Communication Assn., Soc. for Cinema Studies. Home and Office: PO Box 17377 Beverly Hills CA 90209-3377

LONDON, ANDREW BARRY, film editor; b. Bronx, N.Y., Jan. 1, 1949; s. Max Edward and Nellie (Steiner) L. BA in Cinema magna cum laude, U. So. Calif., 1970. Represented by Mont. Artists, Santa Monica, Calif. Prin. works include: (features) The Meteor Man, 1993, F/X 2, 1991, Rambo III, 1988, Planes, Trains and Automobiles, 1987, Link, 1986, Cloak & Dagger, 1984, Psycho II, 1983, The True Story of Eskimo Nell, 1975, (TV shows) A Memory in My Heart, 1999, Murder at 75 Birch, 1998, Before He Wakes, [illegible] Evil Has a Face, 1996, Don't Talk to Strangers, 1994, Day of Reckoning, 1993, Mortal Sins, 1992, Running Delilah, 1992, True Tales, 1992, Sweet Poison, 1991, Tales from the Crypt, 1989-90, Beauty and the Beast pilot, 1987, The Christmas Star, 1986; sound editor: Wolfen (MPSE Golden Reel

award 1982), Hammett, Roadgames, Psycho II, I'm Dancing As Fast As I Can, Perfect, Protocol, Coal Miner's Daughter, The Long Riders, others. Mem. Acad. Motion Picture Arts and Scis., Motion Picture Sound Editors (Golden Reel award 1982), Phi Beta Kappa. Office: 2622 Armstrong Ave Los Angeles CA 90039-2613

LONDON, DOUGLAS, English educator; b. N.Y.C., May 30, 1952; s. Robert David and Ellin (Naumburg) L.; m. Kathy Ellin Kilroy, June 19, 1977; children: Kevin, Katie, Lindsay, Charlie. BA, Kenyon Coll., 1974; MA, U. Md., 1984, Johns Hopkins U., 1993. Cert. advanced prof. Md. Prin. Bullis Sch., Potomac, Md., 1975-97, coach varsity soccer team, 1978-97; chair English dept. Dawson Sch., Lafayette, Colo., 1998—, coach varsity soccer, dir. summer programs, 1998—. Home: 228 Wildwood Ln Boulder CO 80304-0400 Office: Alexander Dawson Sch 4801 N 10th St Lafayette CO 80026

LONDON, RAY WILLIAM, clinical and forensic psychologist, consultant, researcher; b. Burley, Idaho, May 29, 1943; s. Loo Richard and Maycelle Jerry (Moore) L. AS, Weber State Coll., 1965, BS, 1967; MSW, U. So. Calif., 1973, PhD, 1976, Exec. MBA, 1989, cert. in Dispute Resolution, Pepperdine U., 1993. Diplomate: Am. Bd. Psychol. Hypnosis (dir. 1984—, pres. 1989—), Am. Acad. Behavioral Medicine, Am. Bd. Med. Psychotherapy, Internat. Acad. Medicine and Psychology., Am. Bd. Profl. Neuropsychology, Am. Bd. Adminstrv. Psychology, Am. Bd. Examiners Clin. Soc. Work, Am. Bd. Clin. Hypnosis in Social Work (pres. 1989-91), Am. Bd. Profl. Psychology, Am. Bd. Family Psychology (dir. 1993—), Am. Bd. Child and Adolescent Psychology (dir. 1992—), NASW Clin. Soc. Work, Am. Bd. Forensic Examiners (cert.); cert. Am. Assn. Sex Therapists, Soc. Med. Analysts; registered internat. cons., cert. mgmt. cons., congl. asst. U.S. Ho. of Reps., 1964-65; rsch. assoc. Bus. Advs., Inc., Ogden, Utah, 1965-67; dir. counseling and consultation svcs. Meaning Found., Riverside, Calif., 1966-69; mental health and mental retardation liaison San Bernardino County (Calif.) Social Svcs., 1968-72; clin. trainee VA Outpatient Clinic, L.A., 1971-72, Children's Hosp., 1972-73, clin. fellow, 1973-74; clin. trainee Reiss Davis Child Study Ctr., L.A., 1973-74, L.A. County-U. So. Calif. Med. Ctr., 1973; psychotherapist Benjamin Rush Neuropsychiat. Ctr., Orange, Calif., 1973-75; clin. psychology postdoctoral intern Orange County (Calif.) Mental Health, 1976-77; postdoctoral fellow U. Caif.-Irvine-Calif. Coll. Medicine, 1978; clin. psychologist Orange Police Dept., 1974-80; pvt. practice consultation and assessment, Santa Ana, Calif., 1974—; chief oper. officer London Assocs. Internat., 1974-80; cons. to public schs., agys., hosps., bus., nationally and internationally, 1973—; presenter nat. and internat. lectures, seminars and workshops; pres. bd. govs. Human Factor Programs, Ltd., 1976—; pres. Internat. Bd. Medicine and Psychology, 1980-84; chief exec. officer Human Studies Ctr., 1987—; pres., chief exec. officer London Assocs. Internat.; Organizational Behavior-Crisis-Devel. Cons., 1980—; research affil. Ctr. for Crisis Mgmt. U. So. Calif. Grad. Sch. Bus. Adminstrn., 1988-90; pres., chief exec. officer Am. Bd. Clin. Hypnosis, Inc.; mem. faculty UCLA, U. So. Calif., Calif. State U., U. Calif., Irvine, Calif. Coll. Medicine, Internat. Cong. of Psychosomatic Medicine, Internat. Coll.; research assoc. Nat. Commn. for Protection of Human Subjects of Biomed. and Behavioral Research, 1976; fellow Inst. for Social Scientists on Neurobiology and Mental Illness, 1978. Editor: Internat. Bull. Medicine and Psychology, 1980—, A.B.C.D. Report, 1988— behavioral medicine Australian Jour., 1980, adv. editor Internat. Jour. Clin. and Exptl. Hypnosis, 1981-92, mng. editor, 1991—, assoc. editor, 1992—; cons. editor Internat. Jour. Psychosomatics, 1984—; Experimentelle und Klinische Hypnose, 1987—, cons. Am. Jour. Forensic Psychology, 1986, Jour. Mgmt. Consulting, 1992—; pub.: London Behavioral Medicine Assessment, 1982, A Behavior-Cris-Development newsletter, ABCD Newsnote; producer: TV series Being Human, 1980; contbg. author World Book Ency. and books; contbr. articles to profl. jours. Recipient Congl. recognition U.S. Ho. of Reps., 1978, Morton Prince award, 1993; named scholar laureate Erickson Advanced Inst., 1980. Fellow Internat. Acad. Medicine and Psychology (dir. 1981—), Soc. Clin. Social Work (dir. 1979-80), Royal Soc. Health, Am. Coll. Forensic Psychology, Soc. Clin and Experimental Hypnosis (bd. dirs. 1985—, treas. 1987-89), Profl. Acad. Custody Evaluators, Acad. Family Psychology; mem. Acad. Psychosomatic Medicine, Am. Psychol. Assn., Am. Group Psychotherapy Assn., Am. Orthopsychiat. Assn., N.Y. Acad. Sci., Soc. Behavioral Medicine, Internat. Psychosomatic Inst., Australian Coll. Pvt. Consulting Psychologists, Australian Psychol. Soc., Internat. Coun. Psychologists, Acad. Mgmt., Assn. Profl. Cons., Inst. Mgmt. Cons., Internat. Forum Corp. Dirs., Nat. Assn. Corp. Dirs., Profl. and Tech. Cons. Assn., Soc. Indsl. and Orgnl. Psychology, So. Calif. Mediation Assn. (mem. law soc.), Acad. Family Mediators, Am. Coll. Forensic Examiners, Am. Soc. Trial Cons., Am. Psychology Law Soc., Nat. Assn. Expert Witnesses, Soc. Profls. in Dispute Resolution, Am. Registry of Arbitrators, Am. Soc. Clin. Hypnosis (approved cons.), Toastmasters, Phi Delta Kappa, Delta Sigma Rho, Tau Kappa Alpha, Pi RhoPhi, Lambda Iota Tau. Office: London Assocs Internat 18062 Irvine Blvd Ste 200 Tustin CA 92780-3328

LONEGAN, THOMAS LEE, retired restaurant corporation executive; b. Kansas City, Mo., July 4, 1932; s. Thomas F. and Edna L. (Payton) L.; m. Donna F. Ednie, Apr. 11, 1958; children: Timothy L., John M. BSME, Gen. Motors Inst., 1955; MS in Mgmt., USN Post Grad Sch., 1963; grad., Indsl. Coll. Armed Forces, Washington, 1970; postgrad., Calif. State U., Long Beach, 1979 83; grad., Coll. for Fin. Planning, Denver, 1984. Registered profl. engr., Mass.; CFP. Commd. ensign USN, 1956, advanced through grades to comdr., 1978; dir. pub. works, officer in charge of constrn. Naval Weapons Sta., Seal Beach, Calif., 1974-78; ret., 1978; dir. cen. staff McAthco Enterprises, Inc., Camarillo, Calif., 1985, exec. v.p., CFO, 1986-90, pres., CEO,, 1991-93, exec. v.p., CFO, 1994-95; ret.; bd. dirs. McAthco Enterprises; exec. v.p. engring. Orange County Engring. Coun., 1977-78. Author: Analysis and Attenuation of Air Borne Noise in Industrial Plants, 1955, Formalized Training of Maintenance Personnel, 1963. Vol. various couns. Boy Scouts Am., 1968-76. Decorated Bronze Star with combat device, Meritorious Svc. medal, Jt. Svcs. Commendation medal, Navy Achievement medal; decorated Order of Chamoro (Guam); named Sr. Engr./ Arch. Yr. Naval Facilities Engr. Command, 1972; recipient Silver medal Boy Scouts Am., 1974. Fellow Soc. Am. Mil. Engrs., Ret. Officers Assn., GM Inst. Robots Honor Soc.; mem. Beta Gamma Sigma. Avocations: reading, theater, music, foreign travel. Home: 8578 Amazon River Cir Fountain Valley CA 92708-5510

LONERGAN, THOMAS FRANCIS, III, criminal justice consultant; b. Bklyn., July 28, 1941; s. Thomas Francis and Katherine Josephine (Roth) L.; m. Irene L. Kaucher, Dec. 14, 1963; 1 son, Thomas F. BA, Calif. State U., Long Beach, 1966, MA, 1973; MPA, Pepperdine U., L.A., 1976; postgrad., U. So. Calif., L.A., 1973-76. Dep. sheriff Los Angeles County Sheriff's Dept., 1963-70; U.S. Govt. program analyst, 1968—; fgn. service officer USIA, Lima, Peru, 1970-71; dep. sheriff to lt. Los Angeles Sheriff's Office, 1971-76, aide lt. to div. chief, 1976-80; dir. Criminal Justice Cons., Downey, Calif., 1977—; cons. Public Adminstrv. Service, Chgo., 1972-75, Nat. Sheriff's Assn., 1978, 79; cons. Nat. Inst. Corrections, Washington, 1977-89, coordinator jail ctr., 1981-82 ; tchr. N. Calif. Regional Criminal Justice Acad., 1977-79; lectr. Nat. Corrections Acad., 1980-83; spl. master Chancery Ct. Davidson County, Tenn., 1980-82, U.S. Dist. Ct. (no. dist.) Ohio, 1984-85, Santa Clara Superior Ct. (Calif.), 1983-89, Calif. Supreme Ct., 1984-87; U.S. Dist. Ct. Ga., Atlanta, 1986-87, U.S. Dist. Ct. (no. dist.) Calif., 1982-93—, U.S. Dist. Ct. (no. dist.) Idaho, 1986, U.S. Dist. Ct. Oreg. 1986, U.S. Dist. Ct. Portland 1987, U.S. Dist. (no. dist.) Calif. 1984-89, 95-97. Author: California-Past, Present & Future, 1968; Training-A Corrections Perspective, 1979; AIMS-Correctional Officer; Liability-A Correctional Perspective; Liability Law for Probation Administrators; Liability Reporter; Probation Liability Reporter; Study Guides by Aims Media. Mem. Am. Correctional Assn., Nat. Sheriff's Assn. Roman Catholic.

LONERGAN, WALLACE GUNN, economics educator, management consultant; b. Potlatch, Idaho, Mar. 18, 1928; s. Willis Gerald and Lois (Gunn) L.; m. Joan Laurie Penoyer, June 1, 1952; children: Steven Mark, Kevin James. BA, Coll. Idaho, 1950; MBA, U. Chgo., 1955, PhD, 1960. Asst. dir., asst. prof. bus. Indsl. Relations Ctr. U. Chgo., 1960-70, assoc. dir., assoc. prof., 1970-74, dir., prof., 1974-84; vis. prof. Rikkyo U., Tokyo, 1985; vis. fellow Merton Coll. Oxford (Eng.) U., 1986; chair, prof. bus., econs. divsn. Albertson Coll. Idaho, Caldwell, 1987—; v.p. Human Resources Research Cons., Chgo., 1980-87. Author: Leadership and Morale, 1960, Group Leadership, 1974, Performance Appriasal, 1978, Leadership and Management, 1979. Chmn. Episcopal Commn. on Higher Edn., Chgo., 1970-80, mgmt. com. United Way Chgo., 1982-85. 1st lt. U.S. Army, 1950-53, Korea. Named Disting. Alumni Coll. Idaho, 1962; vis. scholar Internat. Anglican Exchange, N.Y.C., 1976, Tokyo, 1986. Mem. Internat. House Japan, Internat. Indsl. Relations Research Assn., Acad. Mgmt., Rotary. Avocations: power walking, hiking. Home: 812 E Linden St Caldwell ID 83605-5335 Office: Albertson Coll Idaho Bus Econs Divsn 2112 Cleveland Blvd Caldwell ID 83605-4432

LONG, BARBARA ELLIS, psychologist; b. St. Louis, Mar. 8, 1923; d. Oliver Everett and Melva Augusta (Westcott) Ellis; m. Richard Rodne Long, June 18, 1946 (dec. 1975); children: Susan Long Hood, Roger Ellis. Student, Washington U., St. Louis, 1941-42; BS with honors, U. Ill., Urbana, 1945, MA, 1846; PhD, Union Inst., Cin., 1973. Lic. clin. psychologist, Calif. Clin. psychologist Community Child Guidance Ctr., Yale Child Study Ctr., Portland and New Haven, 1948-49, 51-52, Thurston County Child Guidance Ctr., Olympia, Wash., 1952-56, St. Louis County Child Guidance Clinic, Clayton, Mo., 1958, Richland County Mental Health Clinic, Columbia, S.C., 1959-61; pvt. practice Columbia and St. Louis, 1959-65, 71-73; project dir., methodologist St. Louis County Health Dept., Clayton, Mo., 1965-67; instr., rsch. psychologist Webster Coll., Webster Groves, Mo., 1967-68; clin. and rsch. psychologist St. Louis State Hosp., 1968-71; children's svc. coordinator Dept. Pub. Health and Welfare, San Mateo County, San Mateo, Calif., 1973-75; pvt. practice San Carlos, Calif., 1976—; cons. mental health agys. and schs., U.S.A., Gt. Britain, Denmark, UNESCO, Indonesia, 1970—; mem. adj. faculty U. Calif. Santa Cruz Extension, 1974, U. San Francisco, 1978-79, Palo Alto Sch. of Profl. Psychology, 1982; expert witness San Mateo County (Calif.) Family Ct. Svcs. Author: The Journey to Myself, 1978; editor People Watching, 1969-72, Jour. Clin. and Child Psychology, 1976-77; contbr. articles to profl. jours. Fellow Am. Psychol. Assn., Am. Orthopsychiat. Assn.; mem. San Mateo County Psychol. Assn., Calif. State Psychol. Assn., Soc. Personality Assessment, Bay Area Multiple Personality Soc., Assn. Family and Conciliation Cts., Profl. Acad. Custody Evaluators, Psi Chi, Alpha Kappa Delta. Episcopalian. Avocations: gardening, traveling, watercolors, jewelry making.

LONG, BRUCE ALAN, office automation specialist; b. Dodge City, Kans., Nov. 9, 1946; s. William Levi and Edith (Chasin) L.; m. Irina Alexandrovnova Svistunova, Sept. 5, 1992. Office automation specialist Ariz. State U., Tempe, Ariz., 1985—. Author: William Desmond Taylor: A Dossier, 1991; editor Taylorology, 1993-2000. With U.S. Army, 1966-69. Avocations: silent film.

LONG, JEANINE HUNDLEY, state legislator; b. Provo, Utah, Sept. 21, 1928; d. Ralph Conrad and Hazel Laurine (Snow) Hundley; m. McKay W. Christensen, Oct. 28, 1949 (div. 1967); children: Cathy Schuyler, Julie Schulleri, Kelly M. Christensen, C. Brett Christensen, Harold A. Christensen; m. Kenneth D. Long, Sept. 6, 1968. AA, Shoreline C.C., Seattle, 1975; BA in Psychology, U. Wash., 1977. Mem. Wash. Ho. of Reps., 1983-87, 93-94, chair joint com. pension policy mem. Inst. Pub. Policy; mem. Wash. Senate, 1995—; ranking mem. Human Svcs. and Corr. com., Wash. Senate. Mayor protem, mem. city coun. City of Brier, Wash., 1977-80. Republican. Office: PO Box 40482 Olympia WA 98504-0482

LONG, MARGARET KAREN, art educator; b. Bridgeport, Conn., Mar. 18, 1950; d. Felix Joseph and Clayda Erna (Town) Petko; m. James Ray Long, July 1, 1977 (div. May 1991); children: Mason Douglas, Megan Elizabeth. AA in Photography & Comml. Art, L.A. Harbor Coll., 1973; BFA in Art and Human Svcs., Calif. State U., Fullerton, 1976; MA in Philosophy & Art History, Calif. State U., Dominguez Hills, 1982; MA in Counselor Edn., Calif. State U., San Bernadino, 1993. Cert. secondary tchr. Calif. Photographer, artist pvt. practice, San Pedro, Calif., 1968-73; photographer Blalack Studios, Fullerton, Calif., 1973-76; artist 110 Wilshire Studios, Fullerton, Calif., 1974-77; med. recs. tech. Long Beach (Calif.) Meml. Hosp., 1977-80; instr. photography S.E. L.A. ROP Adult Edn., Cerritos, Calif., 1980; instr. art, social studies ABC Unified Sch. Dist., Cerritos, Calif., 1980-82; educator art, journalism, yearbook Coachella Unified Sch. Dist., Thermal, Calif., 1983—; mentor tchr. Calif. Dept. Edn., 1989-95; counselor to disturbed teens, Insight, Thermal, 1986-94; pres. Faculty Forum, Coachella Valley H.S., 1993-94; dept. chair Visual and Performing Arts Dept., Thermal, 1983-94, coord., site rep., 1988-91; mem. accreditation and steering coms., Calif. Accreditation for Schs., Thermal, 1976-77, 93-94. Exhibited in group shows Malden Gallery Invitational Show, 1975, Laguna All Calif. Show, 1976. Foster parent State Dept. Social Svcs., Rancho Mirage, Calif., 1991-92; mem. Friends of Coachella Libr., 1986-94. Mem. Calif. Art Edn. Assn., Hi-Desert Artists Coop. (exhibitor 1984-85). Avocations: painting, drawing, photography, land investments.

LONG, MARIE KATHERINE, public relations consultant, researcher; b. Cleve., Dec. 8, 1925; d. Mike Kurilich and Katherine (Grasso) Kurilich; m. Elgen Marion Long, May 12, 1946; children: Donna Marie Long Weiner, Harry Elgen. Student, Cleve. Coll., 1943-44, Harbor Jr. Coll., L.A., 1954-55. Lic. real estate agt., Calif. Exec. sec. Fawick Airlfex Co., Cleve., 1943-44, Pillsbury and Globe Mills, L.A., 1944-48; ptnr. Elgen Long, gen. contractor, San Mateo, Calif., 1958-77, Woodside (Calif.) Investment Co., 1964-71; logistics mgr. pub. rels. Crossroads Endeavor, Woodside, 1971—; pub. rels. cons. Elgen Long Enterprises, San Mateo, 1971—; research on Amelia Earhart disappearance, San Mateo, 1972—; adminstrv. coord., project mgr. pub. rels. Internat. Human Potential Orgns., San Francisco, 1977-82; cons. to books and mags., 1971—. Co-author: (book) Solving Amelia Earhart Mystery, 1999. Troop leader Girl Scouts U.S.A., San Mateo, 1954-61; fundraiser Woodside High Sch. Band, 1966-68; Am. Heart Assn., also other orgns., San Mateo, 1973—; v.p. Western Aerospace Mus., Oakland, Calif., 1982—, also life mem.; mem. People to People, Hunger Project; adv. com. USN Meml. Found. Mem. Internat. Platform Soc., Peninsula Press Club. Democrat. Avocations: reading, bowling, music, dancing, aviation history. Home and Office: 11975 Danvers Cir San Diego CA 92128-4343

LONG, MICHAEL ALAN, musician; b. Chgo., Oct. 14, 1945; s. Irving Robert and Libby (Zasser) L.; m. Isola Charlayne Jones, Aug. 3, 1989 (div. Oct. 1995). BA in English, Ariz. State U., 1967; MFA, Phila. Inst. Music, Kharkov Ukraine, 1993; Mus D, State Musical Inst., Kharkov, Ukraine, 1997. Artist in residence Ariz. State U., Tempe, 1968-73; investment banker Bancom Fin. Corp., Phoenix, 1972-83; edn. dir. U.S. Office Econ. Opportunity, Phoenix, 1969-72; dir. artists and repertoire Solaris Classics, Phoenix, 1997; internat. mgr. Russian Fed. Orch., Moscow, 1995-97; artist adv. Ariz. Coun. of the Arts, Phoenix, 1970-75; cons. Ministry of Culture of Republic of Ukraine; cons. concerts in field. Classical recordings include Hovhaness Symphony for Guitar, Music of the Royal Courts, Hovhaness Mystery of the Holy Martyrs; writer, performer Mr. Cobb's Corner, 1978; internat. concerts. Recipient Best Documentary Sound Track, U.S. Coun. of the Arts, 1969, Internat. Gold medal Swedish Arabian Horse Assn., Stockholm, 1982. Jewish. Avocations: weightlifting, collecting books and art, ancient numismatics, breediing horses. Office: 3550 N Central Ave Ste 701 Phoenix AZ 85012-2109

LONG, ROBERT MERRILL, retail drug company executive; b. Oakland, Calif., May 19, 1938; s. Joseph Milton and Vera Mai (Skaggs) L.; m. Eliane Quilloux, Dec. 13, 1969. Student, Brown U., 1956-58; BA, Claremont Men's Coll., 1960. With Longs Drug Stores Inc., Walnut Creek, Calif., 1960—, dist. mgr., 1970-72, exec. v.p., 1972-75, pres., 1975-77, pres., chief exec. officer, 1977-91; chmn., chief exec. officer Longs Drug Stores, Walnut Creek, Calif., 1991—. Mem. Nat. Assn. Chain Drug Stores (dir.). Office: Longs Drug Stores Corp PO Box 5222 141 N Civic Dr Walnut Creek CA 94596-3858

LONG, WILLIAM JOSEPH, software engineer; b. Kokomo, Ind., Feb. 1, 1956; s. George Alexander and Rebecca Bethina (Burgan) L. BA, Harvard U., 1979; cert. in project mgmt., U. Calif., Berkeley, 1994. Cons. Bechtel Corp., San Francisco, 1982-85; assoc. prof. Dalian (Liaoning, China) Inst. Tech., 1985-86; software engr. Bechtel Corp., San Francisco, 1986-92; EDI project mgr. Pacific Gas & Electric Co., San Francisco, 1992-94; software engr. Am. Pres. Lines, Oakland, Calif., 1994-95; mem. adv. bd. Synetics, Inc., San Francisco, 1987—; owner William J. Long and Assocs., Oakland, Calif., 1990—. Vol. English tutor, Oakland, Calif., 1983—. Rsch. grantee Smithsonian Astrophys. Obs., Cambridge, Mass., 1976. Mem. IEEE, Assn. Computing Machinery, Am. Assn. Artificial Intelligence, Math. Assn. Am. Avocations: languages, photography, playing hammer dulcimer, jogging. Home and Office: William J Long and Assocs 2225 7th Ave #33 Oakland CA 94606-1969

LONGENECKER, MARTHA W., museum director. BA in Art, UCLA; MFA, Claremont Grad. Sch.; studied with Millard Sheets, Shoji Hamada, Tatsuzo Shimaoka. Owner ceramics studio Claremont, Calif.; prof. art, now prof. emeritus San Diego State U.; founder, dir. Mingei Internat. Mus., San Diego; coord. editing, design and prodn. of exhbn. documentary publs. Mingei Internat. Mus. World Folk Art.; condr. tours. Contbr. chpts. to books; developer videotapes; exhibited at Dalzell Hatfield Galleries. San Diego State U. Found. grantee, 1967, Calif. State U. Rsch. grantee, 1978; recipient Disting. Alumna award Claremont Grad. Sch., 1980, Essence of Life award ElderHelp of San Diego, 1993, Living Legacy award Women's Internat. Ctr., 1994, Women of Distinction award Soroptimist Internat. of La Jolla, 1994. Office: Mingei Internat Mus Folk Art Balboa Park 1439 El Prado San Diego CA 92101-1617 Address: Mingei Internat Mus PO Box 553 La Jolla CA 92038-0553*

LONSDALE, PETER N., film editor; b. Shipley, Yorkshire, Eng., Dec. 14, 1951; came to U.S., 1959; s. Glyn and Sarah (Lee) L.; m. Marilyn Shenker, July 28, 1985 (div.); m. Gloria DeGeare, Jun. 20, 1992; 1 child, Sarah Rochelle. BA in Motion Picture, UCLA, 1977. Apprentice editor (films) Chu Chu & The Philly Flash, 1981, Doctor Detroit, 1982-83, Gorky Park, 1983-84; asst. editor: The River Rat, 1983-84, Firstborn, 1984, Pretty in Pink, 1985-86, Beverly Hills Cop II, 1986-87, JFK, 1991; first asst. editor: Back to the Future, 1984-85, Ruthless People, 1986; asst. ADR editor: The Color Purple, 1985; assoc. editor: Who Framed Roger Rabbit, 1987-88, Back to the Future II, 1989, Back to the Future III, 1990, This Boy's Life, 1993; visual effects editor: Coneheads, 1993; film editor: Rocketeer, 1991, Blossom Time, 1994, Schemes, 1994, Life Matters, (documentary) 1995, Gabriel Knight Z: The Beast Within (C-D-Rom Game), 1995-96, Lion King II (Simba's Pride), 1996-98. Mem. Motion Picture and Video Tape Editors Guild. Avocations: photography, computers, guitar. E-mail: editor@ecom.net. Home: 14217 Valerio St Van Nuys CA 91405-1452 Office: Walt Disney TV Animation 500 S Buena Vista St Burbank CA 91521-0004

LOO, THOMAS S., lawyer; b. 1943. BS, U. So. Calif., JD. Bar: Calif. 1969. Ptnr. Bryan Cave LLP, Santa Monica, Calif., 1986—. Office: Bryan Cave LLP 120 Broadway Ste 300 Santa Monica CA 90401-2386*

LOOFT, MICHELLE RENEÉ, office manager, consultant; b. Norman, Okla., Oct. 11, 1968; d. Vincent Francis and Janet Patricia (Lopez) L. BA, Eastern Wash. U., 1992. Medical records supr. Pulse Health Svcs., San Leandro, Calif., 1992-93; medical records supr. Health Visions, San Leandro, Calif., 1993-96, office mgr., 1996—; cons. Jan Lin Assocs., San Leandro, 1994-96. Council mem. East Bay Employer Advisory Council, Oakland, Calif., 1997-98; supr. com. Laurel Grove Federal Credit Union, Castro Valley, Calif., 1998; vol. Democratic Party, Spokane, Wash., 1988. Avocations: karate, fiction writing, scuba diving, running, Italian dining.

LOOG, JOHN EARLE, JR., art gallery director; b. Phila., Aug. 21, 1959; s. John Earle and Patricia Ann (Bock) L. Student, Cornell U., 1976; BSBA, U. So. Calif., 1981. Br. mgr. Finlay Fine Jewelry, L.A., 1981-84; mktg. mgr. Sol Bergman Estate Jewelers, Cleve., 1984-85; ptnr. Vizuals, Inc., L.A., 1985-88; dir. Gordon Gallery, Rancho Mirage, Calif., 1988-95, Charles Hecht Galleries, L.A./La Jolla/Palm Desert, Calif., 1995—; antiques/art cons. Comerford's Antiques, Palm Desert, 1991-95, Den of Antiquities, Rancho Mirage, Calif., 1993-95; dir. Enviro Tech. Products, Palm Springs, 1988-97. Mem. La Soc. Honoraria Hispanica. Episcopalian. Home: Monterey Country Club 195 Las Lomas Palm Desert CA 92260-2153 Office: Charles Hecht Galleries 73-375 El Paseo Dr Palm Desert CA 92260

LOOMIS, CHRISTOPHER KNAPP, metallurgical engineer; b. San Francisco, May 6, 1947; s. Richard and Evaline Elsie (Crandal) L.; m. Merril Ellen Purdy, Dec. 8, 1968; 1 child, Nicole Lee; m. Sandra Lee Marsh, Feb. 14, 1993. Profl. Engring. degree, Colo. Sch. Mines, 1969. Process engr. Alcan Aluminum Corp., Riverside, Calif., 1969-73, prodn. supt., 1973-76; process engr. Alcan Aluminum Corp., Oswego, N.Y., 1976-78, maintenance engr., 1978-80; metall. engr. Hazelett Strip-Casting Corp., Colchester, Vt., 1980-81; chief engr. ARCO Metals Co., Chgo., 1981-84; maintenance supt. Cerro Metal Products, Paramount, Calif., 1984-85, mgr. engring. and maintenance, 1985-86; supt. tech. svcs. Golden Aluminum Co., Ft. Lupton, Colo., 1987-88; process devel. engr. Golden Aluminum Co., Lakewood, Colo., 1988-91, corp. environ. and process engr., 1991; engr. IV Coors Brewing Co., Golden, Colo., 1991-93, material engr. V, 1993-96; owner Loomis Engring. and Design, Arvada, Colo., 1996—. Mem. Am. Soc. for Metals, Metall. Soc., Colo. Sch. Mines Alumni Assn., Am. Soc. for Quality Control, Fedn. Fly Fishers (life), Trout Unltd. (life). Episcopalian. Avocations: fishing, camping, mechanics, home repair. Office: Loomis Engring and Design 6572 Owens Ct Arvada CO 80004-2765

LOOMIS, JAMES ARTHUR, broadcast technician, newsletter editor; b. Portland, Oreg., June 10, 1953; s. Frank Clark Jr. and Jacqulyn Hope (Shade) L. AA in Electronics Tech., Shasta Coll., Redding, Calif., 1976. Cert. Microcomputer Tech., Nat. Radio Inst., Washington, 1987, HVAC/ refrigeration, 1990. Computer technician Redding, 1975; electronics technician various TV repair shops, Redding, 1975-77; broadcast maintenance engr. KGO-ABC TV, San Francisco, 1977-79, KATU-Fisher Broadcasting, Portland, Oreg., 1979—. Editor newsletter The Trainmaster, 1995 (Jack Holst award 1996). Mem. Nat. Railway Hist. Soc., Refrigeration Svc. Engrs. Soc. Home: 12440 SE Stephens St Portland OR 97233-1336

LOPATA, MARTIN BARRY, business executive; b. Bronx, N.Y., Apr. 6, 1939; s. Julius A. and Rose (Silverman) L.; m. Sarah G. Lopata, July 4, 1965 (div. 1978; children: Warren A., Lawrence M.; m. Lynette Wyrick, May 6, 1989 (div. 1991). Grad., H.S. Art and Design, N.Y.C.; student, N.Y.C. C.C., Bklyn. Ordained minister Ch. of Divine Sci., 1983. Sales mgr. H. Natoway Co., L.A., 1961-62; contract mgr. A.S. Aloe Co., L.A., 1962-64; merchandise mgr. S.E. Rykoff Co., L.A., 1964-70; v.p. Kirby Sales, L.A., 1970-71; pres. MBL Industries Inc., Santa Ana, Calif., 1971-87, Unicorn Seminars Inc., Huntington Beach, Calif., 1987-88, Unicorn Investments Internat., Huntington Beach, 1988-91; chair Yes Ednl. Sys., Reno, Nev., 1995-97; gen. mgr. retail divsn. Maintex Inc., Industry, Calif., 1998—; chmn. Soviet Am. Internat. Co., 1988-92; joint venture Sovaminco Soviet Am. Internat. Co. #104, Moscow; pres. Coastal-West Industries, 1991-92. Patron Am. Mus. Nat. History, N.Y.C., 1984-91; bus. chmn. Ctr. for Soviet-Am. Dialogue, Washington, 1987-91; chmn. Com. on Bus.-A New Way of Thinking in a New Age, Moscow, 1987; bd. dirs. Three Mountain Found., Lone Pine, Calif., 1987-88, Inside Edge, Irvine, Calif., 1987-94, found. pres., 1993-94; vice chmn. United Ch. Religious Science, Los Angeles, 1986-87, pres. Huntington Beach Ch. Religious Sci., 1985; min. Cmty. Ch. by the Bay, 1983—; chmn. Blissful Wisdom Found., 1996—. Mem. Masons (32d degree), Shriners. Avocation: boating. Home: 16391 Wimbledon Ln Huntington Beach CA 92649-2188

LOPER, JAMES LEADERS, broadcasting executive; b. Phoenix, Sept. 4, 1931; s. John D. and Ellen Helen (Leaders) L.; m. Mary Louise Brion, Sept. 1, 1955; children: Elizabeth Margaret Sehran (Mrs. Michael K. Sehran), James Leaders Jr. BA, Ariz. State U., 1953; MA, U. Denver, 1957; PhD, U. So. Calif., 1967; DHL (hon.), Columbia Coll., 1973; LLD (hon.), Pepperdine U., 1978. Asst. dir. bur. broadcasting Ariz. State U., Tempe, 1953-59; news editor, announcer Sta. KTAR, Phoenix, 1955-56; dir. ednl. TV, Calif. State U., Los Angeles, 1960-64; v.p. Community TV So. Calif., Los Angeles, 1962-63; asst. to pres. Sta. KCET-Pub. TV, Los Angeles, 1963-65, sec., 1965-66, dir. ednl. services, 1964-65, asst. gen. mgr., 1965-66, v.p., gen. mgr., 1966-69, exec. v.p., gen. mgr., 1969-71, pres., gen. mgr., 1971-76, pres., CEO, 1976-82; exec. dir. Acad. TV Arts and Scis., 1983-98; bd. dirs., chmn. audit com. Western Fed. Savs. and Loan Assn., L.A., 1979-93; bd. dirs. Global View, Washington; bd. dirs. Tennessee Ernie Ford Enterprises, 1994—; chmn. bd. Pub. Broadcasting Service, Washington, 1969-72; dir. Calif. Arts Coun., 1991—; adj. prof. Sch. Cinema and TV U. So. Calif., 1984—; sr. lectr. U. So. Calif., Los Angeles, 1969-70; pres. Western Ednl. Network, 1968-70; mem. Gov.'s Ednl. TV and Radio Adv. Com., Calif., 1968-74; U.S. rep. CENTO Conf. Radio and TV, Turkey, 1978, trustee Internat. Council Nat. Acad. TV

Arts and Scis., 1988—. Contbr. articles to profl. jours; contbr. to ETV: The Farther Vision, 1967, Broadcasting and Bargaining: Labor Relations in Radio and Television, 1970. Mem. adv. bd. Jr. League of Los Angeles, 1970-76, Jr. League of Pasadena, 1972-75, Los Angeles Jr. Arts Ctr., 1968-72; exec. v.p. Assocs. of Otis Art Inst., 1971-77, pres., 1975-77; chmn., dir. The Performing Tree, Los Angeles; bd. dirs. Sears-Roebuck Found., 1976-79; chmn. bd. visitors Annenburg Sch. Communications, U. So. Calif., 1975-80; trustee Poly. Sch., Pasadena; mem. Calif. State Arts Commn., 1991. Recipient Disting. Alumnus award Ariz. State U., 1972; Alumni award of Merit, U. So. Calif., 1975; Gov's. award Hollywood chpt. Nat. Acad. TV Arts and Scis., 1975; Alumni Achievement award Phi Sigma Kappa, 1975; named Centennial Alumnus Nat. Assn. of State Univs. and Land Grant Colls., 1988. Named to Hall of Fame Walter Cronkite Sch. Comms., Ariz. State U., 1994 Mem. Acad. TV Arts and Scis. (past gov., v.p. Hollywood chpt., trustee nat. acad.), TV Acad. Found., Hollywood Radio and TV Soc. (treas., dir.), Western Ednl. Soc. Telecommunications (past pres.), Assn. Calif. Pub. TV Stas. (past pres.), Young Pres.'s Orgn., Phi Sigma Kappa, Pi Delta Epsilon, Alpha Delta Sigma, Sigma Delta Chi. Presbyterian (chmn. Mass Media Task Force So. Calif. synod 1969-75). Clubs: Valley Hunt (Pasadena), Bel-Air Bay, California, Los Angeles, 100 of Los Angeles, Calif. (Los Angeles), Twilight Pasadena, Lincoln Club, L.A.

LOPES, JAMES LOUIS, lawyer; b. Watsonville, Calif., Feb. 1, 1947; s. Allen M. and Norma Maxine (McElroy) L.; m. Gail R. Lopes, Mar. 24, 1979; children: Elizabeth, Jane. BS, U.Calif., Davis, 1969; JD, U. Pacific, 1974; LLM, Harvard U., 1975. Bar: Calif. 1974, U.S. Ct. Appeals (9th cir.), U.S. Dist. Ct. (no., ea., ctrl. dists.) Calif. Assoc. Gendel, Raskoff, Shapiro & Quittner, L.A., 1975-78; ptnr. Gordon, Peitzman & Lopes, San Francisco, 1978-81, Howard, Rice & Nemerovski, San Francisco, 1982—; adv. com. bankruptcy/creditors' rights Practicing Law Inst., 1992—. Co-author: Law and Business of Computer Software, 1989; contbr. articles to profl. jours. Mem. ABA (bankruptcy com., 1980—), Calif. Bankruptcy Forum (bd. dirs. 1990-93), Calif. State Bar Assn., Turnaround Mgmt. Assn. (bd. dirs. 1996—). Avocations: flying, contract bridge. Office: Howard Rice & Nemerovski 7th Fl 3 Embarcadero Ctr Ste 7 San Francisco CA 94111-4003

LOPEZ, ANGELO CAYAS, freelance illustrator; b. Norfolk, Va., Mar. 29, 1967; s. Felizardo Pardo and Teresita (Cayas) L. BS in Graphic Design, San Jose State U., 1992. Cashier Marriott's Great Am., Santa Clara, Calif., 1985; page tech. svc. dept. Sunnyvale (Calif.) Pub. Libr., 1985-90, tech. svc. clk., 1993—; intern Palo Alto (Calif.) Fast Stats, 1990-91; framer Aaron Bros., Sunnyvale, 1991-92; cashier Linden Tree Children's Bookstore, Los Altos, Calif., 1992-94; Executed mural Beryessa br. San Jose Pub. Libr., Grace Cmty. Covenant Ch., Los Altos, Calif., 1998. Contbr. illustrations to books including Two Moms A Zark and Me, 1993, Night Travelers, 1994, Cherubic Children's New Classic Storybook, Vol. 2, 1998; contbr. illustrations and cartoons to mags. Vol. Arts Project, Santa Clara, 1990; tutor San Jose (Calif.) Chinese Alliance Ch., 1993-95; active Santa Clara U. Mission Ch., 1992-95; mem. local Svc. Employees Internat. Union of Sunnyvale Pub. Libr., 1995—. Democrat. Avocations: reading, painting, basketball, watching old movies. Home: 231 N 15th St San Jose CA 95112-1839

LOPEZ, CARL A. TAYLOR, lawyer; b. Chgo., Oct. 23, 1948; s. Abraham Nieves and Faye Ellen (Taylor) L.; m. Diana Callahan, May 31, 1980; children: Taylor, Derek, Carlyn. BA, Willamette U., 1972; JD, Georgetown U., 1975. Bar: Wash. 1975, U.S. Dist. Ct. (we. dist.) Wash. 1978, U.S. Ct. Appeals (9th cir.) 1978, U.S. Ct. of Claims 1994, U.S. Dist. Ct. (ea. dist.) Wash. 1997. Prin. Francis, Lopez & LePley, Seattle, 1977-84, Lopez & Fantel, Seattle, 1985—. Mem. ATLA, Wash. State Trial Lawyers Assn. Office: Lopez & Fantel 1510 14th Ave Seattle WA 98122-4024

LOPEZ, DANIEL HERALDO, academic administrator; b. Puerto de Luna, N.Mex., Feb. 14, 1946; s. Julian and Tiofila (Ocaña) L.; m. Linda Vigil, July 12, 1975. BA in Polit. Sci., U. N.Mex., 1970, MA in Polit. Sci., 1972, PhD in Polit. Sci., 1982. Cabinet sec. N.Mex. Dept. Fin. and Adminstrn., Santa Fe, 1984-86; chief of staff for senate fin. and sr. staff analyst House Appropriations and Fin. Com., Santa Fe, 1987-89; assoc. and dep. dir. terminal effects rsch. and analysis N.Mex. Inst. Mining and Tech., Socorro, 1987-89, adj. prof., 1994—; v.p. institutional devel. N.Mex. Inst. Mining and Technology, Socorro, 1989-93, pres., 1993—; exec. dir. N.Mex. Adv. Coun. on Vocat.-Tech. Edn., 1973-82; adj. prof. U. N.Mex., Albuquerque, 1975-82, N.Mex. Inst. Mining and Tech., Socorro, 1994—; cabinet sec. N.Mex. Employment Security Dept., Albuquerque, 1983-84. Mem. League of United Latin Am. Citizens, Albuquerque; mem., past pres. Albuquerque Hispano C. of C. Staff Sgt. USAF, 1968-69, Korea. Mem. N.Mex. Tech. Rsch. Found. (v.p. 1994), N.Mex. First Exec. Com. (v.p. 1994), N.Mex. Children's Found., N.Mex. Industry Network Corp. (exec. com. 1994), N.Mex. Amigos, Rio Grande Tech. Found. Avocations: running, world travel. Home: One Olive Ln Socorro NM 87801 Office: NMex Inst Mining and Tech Office of the Pres Socorro NM 87801*

LOPEZ, FELIX BILGERA, insurance company executive; b. Dagupan, Pangasinan, The Philippines, Aug. 1, 1958; came to U.S., 1991; s. Pedro Carrera and Norma Luz (Bilgera) L.; m. Rosalina Fermin, Jan. 18, 1985; 1 child, Felix Reginald. BA magna cum laude, U. Pangasinan, 1978; LLB, Ateneo de Manila U., 1980; MBA, U. of the East, The Philippines, 1983. Pres., owner F.B. Lopez Ins. Svc., L.A., 1992—, Asia Pacific Reins. Brokers, L.A., 1992—; dir. Am. Inst. Ins., L.A., 1994—; exec. v.p. Bergen Isle Ins. Co., British Virgin Island, 1992-93; sr. v.p. Commonwealth Ins. Co., The Philippines, 1989-90; gen. mgr. Asian Reins. Pool, East Asia, 1983-86; chmn. jour. com. Philippine Ins. Inst., 1988. Author: Basic Reinsurance, 1993; co-author: Intro to MacroEconomics, 1980. Fellow Life Underwriter Tng. Coun.; mem. Internat. Order Demolay (chpt. founder, life), Soc. Trainers and Educators, Young Mens Christian Assn. (life), L.A. Bayanihan Lions (project chmn. 1998). Roman Catholic. Avocations: golf, reading, photography, teaching. Office: FB Lopez Ins Svcs 7847 Florence Ave Ste 128 Downey CA 90240-3783

LOPEZ, JOE JESUS, safety engineer; b. San Francisco, July 28, 1926; s. Miguel Galvan and Julia (Calderon) L.; m. Teresa Bernadino, Nov. 28, 1970; children: Jose Miguel, Silvia, Ann Maria, David. BBA, Tex. Tech. U., 1957, postgrad., 1959-60; postgrad., U. So. Calif., 1978-79. Cert. safety profl. Ground safety officer Reese AFB, Tex., 1953-69; safety mgr. NASA Goddard Space Flight Ctr., Greenbelt, Md., 1969-80; phys. scientist U.S. Dept. Energy, Washington, 1980-83, safety and health mgr., 1983-85; dir. environ., safety and health Zia, Los Alamos, N.Mex., 1985-86; mgr. environ., safety and health Johnson Controls World Svc. Inc., Los Alamos, 1986—. With U.S. Army, 1944-46, staff sgt. USAF, 1951-53. Mem. Am. Soc. Safety Engrs. (sec. N.Mex. sect. 1990-92), K.C., Rotary (treas. Los Alamos club 1988-91). Roman Catholic. Avocations: collecting coins, golf. Home: 1604 Camino Uva Los Alamos NM 87544-2727 Office: Johnson Controls World Svcs Pajarito & W Jemez Rd Los Alamos NM 87544

LOPEZ, JUSTO JOSE, sales executive; b. Mayaguez, P.R., Mar. 15, 1957; s. Justo Lopez-Garcia and Ramonita Rivera Elias; m. Elizabeth Nguyen, Oct. 13, 1991 (div. Sept. 1998); 1 child, Claudia Linh. BSCS in Engring., Ohio State U., 1981. Engr. Gen. Dynamics, Ft. Worth, 1981-84; sr. engr. Northrop Corp., Hawthorne, Calif., 1984-87; pre/post sales engr. Unisys Corp., Camarillo, Calif., 1987-94; system engr. Armon Networking, Santa Barbara, Calif., 1994-95; Latin Am. sales mgr. Tekelec Inc., Calabasas, Calif., 1995-98; regional sales mgr. Latin Am. and Caribbean Netcom Systems, Calabasas, 1999—; sales cons. Informatica, Port Hueneme, Calif., 1993-94. Avocations: homebrew, biking, camping. Home: 2927 Capella Way Thousand Oaks CA 91362-4938

LOPEZ, PETER EDWARD, artist; b. Las Vegas, N.Mex., May 14, 1940; s. Pedro (Pete) Ernest and Maria Emma (Chavez) L.; children: Kathryn Gouveia, Yvette Navarro. BA in Art Edn., U. N.Mex., 1976. Employment rep. N.Mex. Dept. Labor, Santa Fe; instr. Rancho Valmora (N.Mex.) Sch., 1996; spkr. in field. Exhibited in group shows Tri-Cultural Arts Exhibit, Espanola, N.Mex., 1987, Gallinas River Gallery, Las Vegas, 1990, Montez Gallery, Santa Fe, 1993-96, Arrott Art Gallery, N.Mex. Highlands U., Las Vegas, 1994-96, [illegible] Albuquerque, 1991; Spanish Colonial Traditional Arts Market, Santa Fe, 1990—. Bd. dirs. Las Vegas Arts Coun., 1998, Retablo wood relief demonstrator El Rancho de las Golondrinas, N.Mex., 1991. Recipient invitation award Imagenes de la Fe Exhibit, Espanola, 1994, 1st pl. Retablo art Tri-Cultural Arts, 1987, 1st place award N.Mex. State Fair, Retablos, 1998. Mem. Spanish Colonial Arts Soc. (Spanish Market Poster award 1993). Avocations: encouraging art for young people, hiking, camping, gardening, reading. Home: PO Box 183 Montezuma NM 87731-0183

LOPEZ, STEVEN RICHARD, small business owner, consultant; b. Flagstaff, Ariz., Dec. 14, 1944; s. John and Trinidad (Rodriquez) L.; (div. 1983); children: David Allen, Laura Marie, Jonel Christina, Steven Christopher. BFA, U. Ariz., 1968; MBA, U. Phoenix, 1992. Art dir. Curran-Morton Advt., Phoenix, 1968-70; owner Steve Lopez Graphic Design, Phoenix, 1970-73; asst. art dir. Ulrich Studios, Phoenix, 1973-78; artist, illustrator Goodyear (Ariz.) Aerospace/Loral Def. Systems, 1978-90; pres. Z-Boz, Inc., Glendale, Ariz., 1990-92; owner L&A Janitorial/Clean Room Specialists, 1994—; pres. Exigency Alert, Inc., Glendale, 1988-90; owner Lopez & Assocs., Glendale, 1989—, pres., 1991; v.p. South Paw, Inc., Peoria, Ariz., 1990-91; cons. Teddy Bear Factory, Inc., Peoria, 1990-91, Beanies Soft Toy Factory, Phoenix, 1990, Maquiladoras, Mex.; exec. advisor Jr. Achievement, Phoenix, 1979-80; amb. to Mex., U.S. JCI Senate, Tulsa, 1987-88. Patentee eyeglass floatation apparatus. Mem. adv. com. City of Glendale, 1985, City of Glendale Cable TV Task Force, 1987; bd. dirs. All Am. Cities Com., Glendale; bd. trustees Valley of the Sun United Way, Phoenix. Mem. Glendale C. of C., U.S. Jaycees (Excellence award 1977, Upson award 1982), Ariz. Jaycees (life, pres. 1985-86, Excellence award 1986), Glendale Jaycees (pres. 1978-81, Chmn. of the Yr. 1977). Democrat. Roman Catholic. Avocations: computers, running, fishing, travel. Home: 4927 W Mclellan Rd Glendale AZ 85301-4010

LOPEZ-NAVARRO, EDUARDO LUIS, family therapist; b. Santiago de Cuba, Oriente, Cuba, June 29, 1959; came to U.S, 1970; s. Eduardo Regino and Alicia Del Pilar (Navarro) Lopez. BA, UCLA, 1982; MS in Psychology with honors, Calif. State U., L.A., 1991. Counselor L.A. Unified Sch. Dist., 1982-90; family therapist Family Counseling Svcs., San Gabriel, Calif., 1990-93; program coord. El Centro del Pueblo, L.A., 1993—; family therapist Hillsides Home for Children, Pasadena, Calif., 1992—, El Centro Del Pueblo, L.A., 1993—; dir. North Ctrl. L.A. Family Preservation Project; radio talk show host KWKW AM 1330; cons. (counselor) UCLA/Valley Alternative Magnet Sch., Ban Nuys, 1990; rsch. asst. UCLA/Fernald Sch., 1981; lectr. in field; expert presenter and cons. various TV programs including Univision and Telemundo Networks, L.A., 1993—. Author: Voces: Escuchando màs allá de las palabras, 1997, El Arte de la Mala Comunicacion, 1999; contbr. articles to profl. jours.; author video: The World of Perpetual Night: Insights into the Psychology of Street Prostitution, 1990. Counselor Hollywood Sunset Cmty. Clinic, L.A., 1986-89; family counselor St. Matthias Ch.; mem. san Gabriel Valley Child Abuse Coun.; dir. Latino Family Preservation, L.A., 1994. Am. Assn. for Marriage and Family Therapy Minority fellow, 1981; recipient Counseling Dept. Spl. Recognition award Hollywood Sunset Cmty. Clinic, 1988, Exito Internat. award. Mem. Calif. Assn. Marriage and Family Therapists, Am. Assn. Marriage and Family Therapists. Roman Catholic. Avocations: writing poetry, photography, video science. Office: El Centro Del Pueblo 1157 Lemoyne St Los Angeles CA 90026-3206

LOPICCOLO, JOHN, conductor, music director; m. Mary Lopiccolo; children: Sabrina, John Michael. MusB in Music Edn., San Francisco State U.; MusM in Orchestral Conducting, Ea. Washington U. Music dir., conductor Idaho Falls (Idaho) Symphony Soc., Inc.; founder, music dir., conductor Idaho Falls Symphony Chorale; concert programmer ann. POPS concerts, Idaho; guest condr. Charlotte, Dubuque, Spokane, S.D., Bremerton, Great Falls, Lethbridge, Walla Walla, Fla. Festival Symphonies, Mont. All-State Orch.; cover-condr. Boise Philharm., 1995-96. Guest condr. (play) Porgy and Bess, Vancouver, B.C. Judge Idaho State Civic Symphony, Idaho Falls Symphony Young Artist Competition, Idaho Falls Music Club Scholarship Awards. Recipient Outstanding Svc. award Greater Idaho Falls C. of C. Office: Idaho Symphony Soc Inc 498 A St Idaho Falls ID 83402-3576*

LOPP, MICHAEL LAWRENCE, engineering professional, magazine editor; b. Loveland, Calif., Feb. 10, 1970; s. Lawrence John and Nancy Jo (Wallace) L.; m. Rachelle Rands, July 27, 1997. With dept. quality assurance Symantec, Cupertino, Calif., 1988-89; with dept. R&D, Borland, Scotts Valley, Calif., 1989-95, Netscape, Mt. View, Calif., 1995—. Editor-in-chief Bitsifter Digest, 1995—. Avocations: hockey, writing, golf. Home: 24985 Soquel Rd Los Gatos CA 95033-9240

LORANCE, ELMER DONALD, organic chemistry educator; b. Tupelo, Okla., Jan. 18, 1940; s. Elmer Dewey and Imogene (Triplett) L.; m. Phyllis Ilene Miller, Aug. 30, 1969; children: Edward Donald, Jonathan Andrew. BA, Okla. State U., 1962; MS, Kansas State U., 1967; PhD, U. Okla., 1977. NIH research trainee Okla. U., Norman, 1966-70; asst. prof. organic chemistry So. Calif. Coll., Costa Mesa, 1970-73, assoc. prof., 1973-80, prof., 1980—, chmn. div. natural scis. and math., 1985-89, chmn. chemistry dept., 1990-93, chmn. divsn. natural scis. and math., 1993—. Contbr. articles to profl. jours. Mem. AAAS, Am. Chem. Soc., Internat. Union Pure and Applied Chemistry (assoc.), Am. Inst. Chemists, Am. Sci. Affiliation, Phi Lambda Upsilon. Republican. Mem. Ch. Assembly of God. Avocations: reading, gardening, music. Office: So Calif Coll 55 Fair Dr Costa Mesa CA 92626-6520

LORD, HAROLD WILBUR, electrical engineer, electronics consultant; b. Eureka, Calif., Aug. 20, 1905; s. Charles Wilbur and Rossina Camilla (Hansen) L.; B.S., Calif. Inst. Tech., 1926; m. Doris Shirley Huff, July 25, 1928; children—Joann Shirley (Mrs. Carl Cook Disbrow), Alan Wilbur, Nancy Louise (Mrs. Leslie Crandall), Harold Wayne. With GE, Schenectady, 1926-66, electronics engr., 1960-66; pvt. cons. engr., Mill Valley, Calif., 1966-90. Coffin Found. award Gen. Electric Co., 1933, GE Inventors award, 1966. Fellow IEEE (life, tech. v.p. 1962, Centennial medal 1984, IEEE Magnetics Soc. 1984 Achievement award). Contbr. articles to profl. jours. Patentee in field. Home: 1565 Golf Course Dr Rohnert Park CA 94928-5638

LORD, JACKLYNN JEAN, student services representative; b. Sacramento, Feb. 2, 1940; d. Jasper Jackson and Celia (Moreno) Opdyke; m. Roger O'Dell Large Sr., Sept. 30, 1958 (div.); 1 child, Roger O'Dell Jr.; m. Brent Andrew Nielsen, Aug. 6, 1966 (dec. Sept. 1974); 1 child, Taumie Celia; m. Mark William Lord, Mar. 5, 1983; 1 child, Jacklynn Michelle. Student, Sacramento State U., 1958-60, Cabrillo Coll., 1962-66, Sacred Coll. of Jamilian Theology and Div. Sch., Reno, 1976—. Ordained Ch. Internat. Community Christ. Communications cons. Pacific Telephone Co., San Jose, Calif., 1966-74, Nev. Bell Co., Reno, 1974-76; student services rep. for extension program Jamilian U. of Ordained, Reno, 1976—; asst. music dir. Internat. Community Christ, Reno, 1980—; choral instr. Jamilian Parochial Sch., Reno, 1976—; sexton Jamilian Handbell Choir, Reno, 1981—; organist Symphonietta, Reno, 1983—. Composer/performer (albums) Children Love Trumpet, 1993, Lovers Love Trumpet, 1994, Five Suites for Piano and Trumpet, 1995, Sonata for Piano & Flugelhorn, 1997, The Next 1,000 Years (A Ballet), 1998. Mem. Nat. League Concerned Clergywomen. Republican. Avocations: tennis, gardening, pvt. pilot. Home: 1990 Humboldt St Reno NV 89509-3645 Office: Internat Cmty Christ 643 Ralston St Reno NV 89503-4436

LORD, JAMES LORIN, dentist; b. Ellensburg, Wash., Nov. 20, 1937; s. James Roy and LaVerda (Murtol) L.; m. Linda Lord, Dec. 29, 1964 (div. May 1979); children: Steve, Jeff, Eric. BS in Zoology, Wash. State U., 1960; DDS, U. Wash., 1964, MSD in Prosthodontics, 1970, Cert. in Restorative Dentistry, 1970; Cert. in Osseointegrated Implants, U. Goteborg/Inst. Applied Bio., Sweden, 1983. Lic. dentist, Wash. Pvt. practice gen. dentistry Garfield, Wash., 1964-65; pvt. practice gen. dentistry Seattle, 1966-70, pvt. practice part-time limited to prosthodontics, 1970-74, pvt. practice half-time limited to prosthodontics, 1974-76, pvt. practice prosthodontics, 1976—; instr. prosthodontics U. Wash., Seattle, 1965-71, asst. prof., 1971-73, part-time 1973-74, asst. prof. grad. faculty, 1971-74, assoc. prof. prosthodontics, 1974-76, clin. asst., 1976-86, clin. prof., 1986—; attending staff U. Wash. Hosp. [illegible] Providence Med. Ctr., 1991-92. Contbr. numerous articles to profl. jours. Recipient Outstanding Instr. award Class of 1971 U. Wash., 1967-68, Most Outstanding Dental Instr. Class of 1972, 1968-69, Outstanding Instr. award Class of 1976, 1973-74, Instr. of Yr. award Class of 1978, 1975-76; USPHS grantee, 1963. Fellow Am. Coll. Dentists, Internat. Coll. Dentists, Acad. Prosthodontics (exec. coun. 1989—), mem. ADA, Am. Coll. Prosthodontics (bd. dirs. 1992-94), Am. Prosthodontic Soc., Am. Soc. for Geriatric Dentistry, Pacific Coast Soc. Prosthodontics (exec. coun. 1977, 86-90, pres. 1990-91, membership chair 1993-94), Fedn. Prosthodontic Orgns. (chmn. dental practice 1981-83, pres. 1990-91), Wash. State Soc. Prosthodontists (pres. 1985), Wash. Dental Assn. (exec. coun. 1988-92, legis. dir. 1992-93, alt. del. to ADA house 1989-92, del. 1995, rep. to WSDLA critical issues com. 1994-95), U. Wash. Dental Alumni Assn. (pres. 1977), Seattle King County Dental Assn. (pres. 1987-88, del. WSDA house 1990-94, exec. coun. 1982-86, other coms.), Psi Omega, Omicron Kappa Upsilon. Home: 3118 Portage Bay Pl E # F Seattle WA 98102-3833 Office: 10212 5th Ave NE Ste 240 Seattle WA 98125-7452

LORD, JANE ANNE, insurance broker; b. Alton, Ill., Oct. 14, 1932; d. H. L. and Cora LaRue (Reeder) Neudecker; widowed; children: Brian B., Jane Elizabeth. BA, So. Ill. U., 1957; MA, Monticello Coll. for Women, 1962; PhD, UCLA, 1982. Ins. broker, 1957—. Bd. dirs. Am. Heart Assn., Found. for Retarded. Named to Lewis and Clark Hall of Fame. Mem. AAUW, Nat. Assn. Life Underwriters, Palm Springs C. of C., Nat. Assn. Ins. Women, Rotary Internat., Order of Eastern Star, Life Champion Circle, Tempo de los Ninos. Avocations: art, music, ballet. Office: 400 S Farrell Dr Ste B105 Palm Springs CA 92262-7961

LORD, MIA W., world peace and disarmament activist; b. N.Y.C., Dec. 2, 1920; m. Robert P. Lord (dec. Nov. 1977); children: Marcia Louise, Alison Jane. BA in Liberal Arts cum laude, Bklyn. Coll., 1940; postgrad., San Francisco State U., 1984—. Hon. sec. Commonwealth of World Citizens, London; membership sec. Brit. Assn. for World Govt., London; sec. Ams. in Brit. for U.S. Withdrawal from S.E. Asia, Eng.; organizer Vietnam Vigil to End the War, London; pres. Let's Abolish War chpt. World Federalist Assn., San Francisco State U.; appointed hon. sec. Commonwealth of World Citizens, London; officially invited to Vietnam, 1973; organizer Vietnam Vigil to End the War, London. Author: The Practical Way to End Wars and Other World Crises: the case for World Federal Government: listed in World Peace through World Law, 1984, and in Strengthening the United Nations, 1987, War: The Biggest Con Game in the World, 1980. Hon. sec., nat. exec. mem. Assn. of World Federalists-U.K.; founder, bd. dirs. Crusade to Abolish War and Armaments by World Law. Nominated for the Nobel Peace Prize, 1975, 92, 93; recipient four Merit awards Pres. San Francisco State U. Mem. Secretariat of World Citizens USA (life), Assn. of World Federalists USA, Brit. Assn. for World Govt. (membership sec.), Crusade to Abolish War and Armaments by World Law (founder, dir.), World Govt. Orgn. Coord. Com., World Fed. Authority Com., Campaign for UN Reform, Citizens Global Action, World Constitution and Parliament Assn., World Pub. Forum, Internat. Registry of World Citizens. Home: 174 Majestic Ave San Francisco CA 94112-3022

LORENZ, TIMOTHY CARL, real estate agent; b. Glendale, Calif., June 9, 1947; s. Raymond Jerome and Majorie Nadine (Bevis) L.; m. Jeanann Carrington, Apr. 16, 1966 (div. 1982); children: Julianne, Todd; m. Nadyne Claire Buck, Sept. 11, 1982; stepchildren: Ron, Eve, SeAnn, Dray. BA in Psychology, Calif. State U., Los Angeles, 1969, MA in Psychology, 1972. Lic. real estate agt., Calif. Chief investigator L.A. County Dept. Consumer Affairs, 1976-81; co-owner Newport Holistic Health Clinic, Newport Beach, Calif., 1981-83; chief investigator Orange County Office Consumer Affairs, Santa Ana, Calif., 1983-86; agt. Century 21 Niguel, Laguna Niguel, Calif., 1986-94, mgr.; owner The Carousel, San Juan Capistrano, Calif., 1987-93, Depot...Pourri Gift Shop, San Juan Capistrano, 1991-93; v.p. Landingham Composites, Inc., San Clemente, 1994-96; sec. MTD, Inc., Overland, Kans., 1995—; v.p. Century 21 Automated Real Estate Ctr., Laguna Niguel, 1994—; instr. psychology Mt. San Antonio, Walnut, Calif., 1976-83; chmn. bd. dirs. Real Reasons, Laguna Niguel, 1982-90; distbr. Amway, Dana Point, Calif., 1983—; instr. Saddleback Coll., 1992-93; dir., treas.-sec. Landingham Composites, 1994-96. Co-author Renter Rights and Responsibilities, 1978; producer T.V. talk show Coping in Today's World, 1982 (Best of Pub. Access award 1982). Pres. Bur. Electronic and Appliance Repair Bd., Sacramento, Calif., 1980, 86, legis. com., 1979; founding mem. Nat. Automobile Dealers Consumer Action Panel, L.A., 1978-81; bd. dirs. God's Gang, 1996—. Recipient Letter Commendation Atty. Gen., L.A., 1980. Mem. Nat. Assn. Realtors, Assn. Foster Parents North Cen. South Orange County (pres. 1986-88), State Calif. Foster Parent Assn., Nat. Assn. Foster Parents, Dana Point C. of C., Newport Beach C. of C. Republican. Avocations: bldg. miniature doll houses, woodworking, home constrn. Home: 32802 Pointe Stirling Apt F Dana Point CA 92629-3144

LORENZEN, ROBERT FREDERICK, ophthalmologist; b. Toledo, Ohio, Mar. 20, 1924; s. Martin Robert and Pearl Adeline (Bush) L.; m. Lucy Logsdon, Feb. 14, 1970; children: Roberta Jo, Richard Martin, Elizabeth Anne. BS, Duke, 1948, MD, 1948; MS, Tulane U., 1953. Intern, Presbyn. Hosp., Chgo., 1948-49; resident Duke Med. Center, 1949-51, Tulane U. Grad. Sch., 1951-53; practice medicine specializing in ophthalmology, Phoenix, 1953—; mem. staff St. Joseph's Hosp., St. Luke's Hosp., Good Samaritan Hosp., Surg. Eye Ctr. of Ariz. Pres. Ophthalmic Scis. Found., 1970-73; chmn. bd. trustees Rockefeller and Abbe Prentice Eye Inst. of St. Luke's Hosp., 1975—. Recipient Gold Headed Cane award, 1974; named to Honorable Order of Ky. Cols. Fellow ACS, Internat. Coll. Surgeons, Am. Acad. Ophthalmology and Otolaryngology, Pan Am. Assn. Ophthalmology, Soc. Eye Surgeons; mem. Am. Assn. Ophthalmology (sec. of ho. of dels. 1972-73, trustee 1973-76), Ariz. Ophthal. Soc. (pres. 1966-67), Ariz. Med. Assn. (bd. dirs. 1963-66, 69-70), Royal Soc. Medicine, Rotary (pres. Phoenix 1984-85). Republican. Editor in chief Ariz. Medicine, 1963-66, 69-70. Office: 500 W Thomas Rd Phoenix AZ 85013-4224

LORTS, JACK EDWARD, secondary education educator, poet; b. Wichita, Kans., Sept. 4, 1940; s. Kenneth Warren and Doris Maxine (Hedberg) L.; m. Cecilia Ann Kennedy, Nov. 9, 1960; children: Jacqueline, Gerine, Virginia. BA, Calif. State U., Fullerton, 1962; MEd, U. Oreg., 1978. cert. secondary and elem. tchr., Calif., Oreg., supt. and adminstr., Oreg. Tchr. lang. arts El Rancho Sch. Dist., Pico Rivera, Calif., 1962-63, Valle Lindo Sch. Dist., South El Monte, Calif., 1963-68, 69-74, Medford (Oreg.) Sch. Dist., 1968-69, South Umpqua Sch. Dist., Myrtle Creek, Oreg., 1974-88; Instr. lang. arts Umpqua Community Coll., Roseburg, Oreg., 1975-88; supt., prin. Annex Sch. Dist., Ontario, Oreg., 1988-93; supt. Central Howell Sch. Dist., Silverton, Oreg., 1993-97, Fossil Sch. Dist., Fossil, Oreg., 1997—; tchr., cons. Oreg. Writing Project, 1983—, presenter Oreg. writing festival, 1985-88, 93—, Nat. Coun. Tchrs. of English-regional conf., 1997. Contbr. poems, articles to Ariz. Quar., Country Teacher Vis-a-Vis, English Jour., Kans. Quar., Oreg. English, others. NEH fellow Kenyon Coll., 1984. Mem. Nat. Council Tchrs. English, Am. Assn. Sch. Adminstrs., Confederation Oreg. Sch. Adminstrs., Phi Delta Kappa. Democrat. Methodist. Lodge: Masons (master local lodge 1981, 83). Office: Fossil Sch Dist PO Box 206 Fossil OR 97830

LOSH, SAMUEL JOHNSTON, engineering administrator; b. Hershey, Pa., Nov. 11, 1932; s. Charles Seibert and Esther Dora (Johnston) L.; m. Llewellyn Mathews Hall, Sept. 26, 1964 (div. Oct., 1994); children: Elizabeth Mathews, Stephen Johnston. BSME, MIT, 1954; postgrad., Syracuse U., Utica, 1956-57, UCLA, 1968-74, U. So. Calif., 1975-81. Cert. profl. mgr. Inst. Cert. Profl. Mgrs. Engr. RCA, Camden, N.J., 1954-55; instr. Syracuse U., Utica, 1956; mem. tech. staff TRW, L.A., 1957-59; systems engr. Hoffman Electronics, L.A, 1959-62; spacecraft systems engr. Lockheed Calif. Co., Burbank, 1962-64; sr. systems specialist Xerox Spl. Info. Systems, Pasadena, Calif., 1964-87; sr. systems engr. Datametrics Corp., Chatsworth, Calif., 1987-89; pres. Milner Street, Inc., Pasadena, 1980—; sec. Regina Properties, Inc., Pasadena, 1981-92. Chmn. L.A. chpt. MIT Ednl. Coun., 1978—; facilitator Math. Standards Program, L.A. Unified Sch. Dist., 1994. Recipient George Morgan award MIT Ednl.Coun., 1987; named Silver Knight of Mgmt., Nat. Mgmt. Assn., 1980. Mem. IEEE, AIAA, MIT Alumni Assn. (bd. dirs. 1981-83). Republican. Unitarian. Avocations; skiing, travel, apt. mgmt. Home and Office: PO Box 50368 Pasadena CA 91113-0308

LOTT, BRENDA LOUISE, insurance company executive; b. Clinton, Ind., July 20, [illegible] Ralph Rundle, June 16, 1974 (div. July 1985); children: Danielle Marie

Rundle, John Robert Rundle; m. Mark Lee Lott, July 4, 1985. BA in Polit. Sci., Colo. Women's Coll., Denver, 1976; student, Ins. Inst. of Am. Claim adjuster Allstate Ins. Co., Englewood, Colo., 1973-83; field claim adjuster Transamerica Ins. Co., Englewood, 1983-86; claim examiner Colonial Ins. Co., Denver, 1986-87, examiner/supr., 1987-89, regional claim mgr., 1990-92; dir. financial and insurance svcs. Innovative Svcs. Am., Golden, Colo., 1992—; staff speaker Western Ins. Info. Svc., Denver, 1983-85; participant, invited faculty mem. 5-day lecture series Colonial Univ., Anaheim, Calif., 1990. Sponsor Plan Internat. foster parents program, 1989—. Mem. NAFE, LWV, NAACP (mem.-at-large), Ins. Women of Denver, Internat. Customer Svc. Assn., Colo. Claims Assn. (bd. dirs. 1986-88), Claim Mgrs. Coun., Denver Claims Assn., PGA Tours Ptnrs. Avocations: raquetball, co-ed flag football, basketball, tennis, golf. Office: Innovative Svcs of Am 13922 Denver West Pkwy Ste 200 Golden CO 80401-3140

LOTT, DAVIS NEWTON, advertising agency executive, publisher; b. San Antonio, May 8, 1913; s. James and Sissilla (Davis) L.; m. Arlene Marion Peterson, Nov. 1, 1942; children: Vicki Arlene, Christy Sue, Laurie Ann. *Davis's mother, Sissilla Amy Davis, married James Newton Lott, 1911. His sister, Suellen Cummins, mother of Kathy and Debbie with grandson, Ryan. Davis's father-in-law, Andrew Peterson, emigrated from Mosjoen, Norway, 1915, and married Sena Hendrickson 1919, in Mandan, North Dakota. His wife Arlene, listed in Who's Who of American Women, was twice past president of the National Charity League, is mother of Vicki, Christy and Laurie, all Coronet debutantes including Vicki's daughter Kristen Arnett. Vicki married Terry Olson of Richfield, Idaho. Christy was deceased in 1974. Laurie married Joseph Engelhardt of Manhattan Beach, California. Granddaughter Kristen married Sheriff Scott Collins of Sandy, Utah, where they are raising Michael Davis Collins and Kaylee Collins.* B.S., Northwestern U., 1935; post-grad. UCLA. With Better Homes and Gardens and Successful Farming, Des Moines, Iowa, 1935-36; with Abbott, Labs., North Chicago, Ill., 1936-37; copywriter J. Walter Thompson, Chgo., 1938-39; owner and pres. Lott Advt. Agy., L.A., 1939-41, 46—; pres. USA Corp., Marina Del Rey, Calif.; pres. Lott Publs., Santa Monica, Calif.; pub. Am. Carwash Rev., Am. Personal Protection Rev., Candy WORLD, Tobacco and Sundries WORLD, Specialty/Fancifoods WORLD, Chocolate and Nut WORLD, SugarFree WORLD,New Inventions WORLD, Organic WORLD, Teen Scene, Bubble 'n' ChewinGum WORLD, Cracker/Snack WORLD, Surfing Illustrated, Smoker's Digest, Books and Authors WORLD, New Products and Mail Order WORLD, The Cosa News, Tennis Illustrated, Cigar World; dir. spl. projects MicrolertSystems Internat. Past bd. dirs. Los Angeles Library Assn. Comdr. USNR capt., 1941-46, 1951-52, World War II, Korea. Named Assoc. Dean of Candy Industry, Nat. Candy Wholesalers Assn., 1974. Author: Rules of the Road, 1942, Handbook of the Nautical Road; Emergency Shiphandling Manual, 1943, Collision Prevention, 1947, Treasure Trail, 1944, Star Spangled Broadcast, 1950, Mystery of Midnight Springs, 1954, Dodge City Justice, 1957, The Inaugural Addresses of the American Presidents, 1964, The Presidents Speak, 1965, See How They Ran 1972, The Presidents Illustrated, 1976, Jimmy Carter-And How He Won, 1976; co-author: (with Bruce Greenland) musical comedy The Music Room, 1982, The Presidents Speak-The Inaugural Addresses from Washington to Clinton, 1995, 3d edit., 1997; screenplay: Third Coming, 1999. Founder S.O.S. (Save Ourselves Soc.) to Protect Environ. Recipient George Washington medal for lit. excellence Freedoms Found., 1995. Mem. Phi Delta Theta. Home: 13222 Admiral Ave Unit B Marina Del Rey CA 90292-7042 Office: Lott Pub Co Candy World PO Box 9669 Marina Del Rey CA 90295-2069

LOTZ, LINDA A., religious organization administrator; b. Phila., Sept. 12, 1949; d. Joseph Samuel and Charlotte S. (Stambrugh) L.; m. Imad Alduri, Oct. 1994. BA in Govt. Adminstrn., Shippenburg U., 1991. Pub. info. officer Senator Ineeman Hawkins, Harrisburg, 1982-83; dir. of programs Am. Friends Svc. Com., Pasadena, Calif., 1985-96; clergy, interfaith dir. Laity United for Econ. Justice, L.A., 1996—. photographer numerous reports, publs. and pvt. collections, 1985—. Office: 548 S Spring St Los Angeles CA 90013-2307

LOUCKS, THOMAS ALEXANDER, mining industry executive; b. Bronxville, N.Y., Jan. 23, 1949; s. William Dewey Jr. and Carolyn (Bade), L.; m. Dominique MarieSolange Chesneau, Aug. 11, 1973; children: Christopher Stewart, Averil Melissa, Frances Alexandra. BA in Geology, Dartmouth Coll., 1971, MA in Geology, 1973; MBA, Stanford U., 1985. Research geologist Kennecott Copper, Salt Lake City, 1974-76; exploration geologist Bear Creek Mining Co., Tucson, Ariz., 1976-80; project geologist Climax Molybdenum, Golden, Colo., 1980-83; sr. project geologist AMAX Exploration, Golden, 1983; bus. analyst Newmont Mining Corp., N.Y.C., 1985-88; v.p. corp. devel. Royal Gold, Inc., 1988-92; v.p. Denver Mining Fin. Co., 1988—, exec v.p., 1992—. Contbr. articles to profl. jours.; photographer photos in maga. Bd. dirs. Flying Dutchman Homeowner's Assn., Keystone, Colo., 1987-97; trip leader, sec. Boy Scouts Am., New Canaan, Conn., 1986-88. Sigma Xi grantee, 1972. Mem. Geol. Soc. Am. (Penrose Bequest grant, 1972), Soc. Mining Engrs., Am. Inst. Mining Engrs (exec. com. sec.), Dartmouth Club, Club of N.Y. Republican. Avocations: skiing, mountaineering, tennis, photograpy. Home: 5270 S Logan Dr Littleton CO 80121-1240 Office: 1660 Wynkoop St Ste 1000 Denver CO 80202-1115

LOUDEN, SUZANNE LOIS, educational consultant; b. Monroe, Mich., Apr. 3, 1937; d. James Clifford and Pauline Lois (Crumm) Brancheau; m. Roger William Lousen, Sept. 8, 1972; 1 child, Thomas James. BA in Edn./Music, U. Dayton, 1966; MA in Counseling and Guidance, John Carroll U., 1972; MA in Spl. Edn., U. Colo., 1976. Cert. sch. adminstr. Tchr. St. Joseph's (Mo.) Sch., Manteca (Calif.) Schs., St. Anthony's Sch., New Riegel, Ohio; youth dir. Dayton, Ohio; elem. sch. counselor Harrison Sch. Dist., Colorado Springs, Colo.; instr. U. Colo., Colorado Springs; cons. various schs., Colo.; instr. cooking classes, 1985—. Author (lesson plan books) The Sunshine Series, 1980. Mem. govt. team Leave No Child Behind, Denver, 1993. Mem. Am. Sch. Counselors Assn., Colo. Sch. Counselors Assn. (v.p., treas.), Nat. Assn. Mediation in Edn., Nat. Coun. Self-Esteem, Nat. Honor Soc. for Women. Roman Catholic. Avocations: cooking, reading, writing, walking. Home and Office: 14065 Gleneagle Dr Colorado Springs CO 80921-3219

LOUGANIS, GREG E., former Olympic athlete, actor; b. San Diego, Jan. 29, 1960; s. Peter E. and Frances I. (Scott) L. Student, U. Miami, Fla., 1978-80; BA in Drama, U. Calif., Irvine, 1983. Mem. U.S. Nat. Diving Team, 1976—. Author: Breaking The Surface, 1995; prodr. video diary Breaking the Surface; actor (play) Working, Camelot and Carousel, 1978, Equus, 1980, Pippin, 1983, Dance Kaliedescope, 1987, Cinderella, 1989, The Boyfriend, 1990, The Only Thing Worse You Could Have Told Me..., 1995, (TV), Challenge of the Sexes, 1979, 81, The Brain, 1985, NBC Superstars, 1985, Battle of the Network Stars, 1985, Recap of the 1984 Olympics, 1985, color commentary for U.S. Olympic Festival, 1985, U.S. Diving Championships, 1985, Circus of the Stars, 1986, Hollywood Sqs., 1986, 87, collor commentary for Acapulco Cliff Diving, 1989, NBC Jeep Superstars, 1990, color commentary for U.S. Diving Nats., 1990, Coach Hill-Nickleodeon Sport Theater, 1997, Where Are They Now?, 1997, Breaking the Surface, 1996, (film) Dirty Laundry, 1985, 16 Days of Glory, 1985, 89, Object of Desire, 1990, Mighty Ducks II, 1992, It's My Party, 1995, Touch Me, 1997. Recipient Silver medal Olympic Games, 1976, 2 Olympic Gold medals, 1984, 2 Olympic Gold medals, 1988; James E. Sullivan award, Olympic Games, 1984; inducted into Olympic Hall of Fame, 1985; winner 47 U.S. nat. diving titles; 5 World Diving Championships (platform and springboard) 1986, Jesse Owens award, 1987, Pan Am Gold medal, 1979, 83, 87; Gold medalist (platform and springboard) Seoul Olympics, 1988, Maxwell House/U.S. Olympic Com. Spirit award 1988 Olympic Games. Home: PO Box 4130 Malibu CA 90264-4130

LOUGHEED, ARTHUR LAWRENCE, investment advisor, tax and pension consultant; b. Fresno, Calif., Aug. 11, 1944; s. Evan Archabald and Irene Elizabeth (Westby) L.; m. Margaret Ickes, Feb. 19, 1965 (div. Dec. 1983); children: Christopher, Jennifer Lougheed Branaugh, Evan; m. Nancy Lee Sanderson, May 11, 1985. Postgrad., U. So. Calif., 1964-65; MS in Fin. Svcs., Am. Coll., Bryn Mawr, Pa., 1980, MS in Mgmt., 1985. Registered investment advisor; enrolled agt.; CFP, ChFC, CLU, CPCU. Regional v.p. life and mut. fund ops. Farmers Ins. Group New World Life Ins. Co., L.A., 1965-74; mgr. pension and profit sharing plans Aetna Life & Casualty Aetna Fin. Group, Hartford, Conn., 1974-76; nat. dir. mktg. and sales tng. CNA Cos., Chgo., 1976-81; COO Lawrence-Lee, A Calif. Corp., Palm Springs, Calif., 1981—. Assoc. editor: CAL Underwriter Mag., 1975-76; contbr. tech. articles to profl. mags. and jours. Mem. faculty curriculum adv. com. Ext. Sch. Bus. & Mgmt., U. Calif., San Diego, 1986-94; mem. faculty internat. ins. exec. edn. U. Calif., Irvine, 1984; coll. and h.s. sports ofcl. CIF-Calif. Mich H.S. & Coll. Athletic Assn., 1962-74. Recipient Coll. News Photographer 1st pl. AP, 1963. Mem. Internat. Assn. for Fin. Planning (bd., v.p. edn. 1990-92), Am. Soc. CLU and ChFC (various offices), Am. Soc. Pension Actuaries (assoc. profl., fin. com. 1996—), Nat. Assn. Life Underwriters, Internat. Bd. CFS, Nat. Soc. Enrolled Agts., Calif. Assn. Ind. Accounts (pres. 1994), San Diego Assn. Life Underwriters (bd. dirs. 1982-84), Verdugo Hills Assn. Life Underwriters (bd. dirs. 1975-77), San Diego Lodge Masons (master), Al Bahr Temple Shriners (noble). Avocations: golf, photography, literature. Home and Office: 466 S Via Las Palmas Palm Springs CA 92262-4250

LOUGHEED, PETER, lawyer, former Canadian official; b. Calgary, Alta., Can., July 26, 1928; s. Edgar Donald and Edna (Bauld) L.; m. Jeanne Estelle Rogers, June 21, 1952; children—Stephen, Andrea, Pamela, Joseph. B.A., U. Alta., 1950, LL.B., 1952; M.B.A., Harvard U., 1954. Bar: Alta 1955. With firm Fenerty, Fenerty, McGillivray & Robertson, Calgary, 1955-56; sec. Mannix Co., Ltd., 1956-58, gen. counsel, 1958-62, v.p., 1959-62, dir., 1960-62; individual practice law, from 1962; formerly mem. Alta. Legislature for Calgary West; formerly leader Progressive Conservative Party of Alta., 1965-85; premier of Alta., 1971-85; ptnr. Bennett Jones, Calgary, 1986—. Office: Bennett Jones Verchere, 4500 Bankers Hall E 855 2d St SW, Calgary, AB Canada T2P 4K7

LOUGHRIN, JAY RICHARDSON, mass communications educator, consultant; b. Mankato, Minn., Oct. 21, 1943; s. J. Richardson and Jane Aileen (Smith) L.; m. Helen Marie Struyk, Aug. 8, 1964 (div. Sept. 1985); children: Jennifer, Amy; m. Yolanda Christina Ramos, July 17, 1986; children: Tawny, Heather. BA in Drama, Calif. State U., Los Angeles, 1968; postgrad., San Diego State U., 1968-69, UCLA, 1970-71, U. Redlands, Calif., 1983-84, Fla. State U., 1990; MA, Whittier (Calif.) Coll., 1992. Prodn. asst. Andrews-Yagemann Prodns., Hollywood, Calif., 1961-63; with merchandising, sales Sta. KTTV-TV, Hollywood, 1963-64; assoc. producer Born Losers Am. Internat. Pictures, Hollywood, 1964; assoc. producer V.P.I. Prodns., Hollywood, 1964, Ralph Andrews Prodns., North Hollywood, Calif., 1965; producer Stein Erikson Ski Films, North Hollywood, 1965, F.K. Rocket Films, North Hollywood, 1966-68; dir. promotion and publicity Sta. KCST-TV, San Diego, 1968-69; prof. mass communication Rio Hondo Coll., Whittier, 1969—; sales mgr. Warren Miller Films, Hermosa Beach, Calif., 1984-85, cons., 1985-86; exec. producer Echo Prodns., Hollywood, 1985-87; cons. Radio Concepts, Los Angeles, 1978-80, Tom Cole Prodns., Los Angeles, 1985-87, Chuck Richards Whitewater, Lake Isabella, Calif., 1984-86; media relations cons. Police Officers Standards and Training, Sacramento, 1986—; venue mgr. Los Angeles Olympic Organizing Com., Long Beach, Calif., 1984. Winter sports writer Kern Valley Sun; contbr. articles to Review Publs., Orange Coast mag., Jet Am. mag., Ted Randall Report. Pres. Rue Le Charlene Homeowners Assn., Palos Verdes, Calif., 1984, Hilltop Homeowners Assn., Walnut, Calif., 1989-90; v.p. West Walnut Homeowners Assn., 1988-89. Recipient Pub. Service Programming award Advt. Council, N.Y.C., 1982; named Adviser of Yr., U. So. Calif.'s 50th Annual Journalism Awards, Los Angeles, 1985. Mem. Acad. TV Arts and Scis., Rio Hondo Coll. Faculty Assn. (pres. 1978), So. Calif. Broadcasters Assn. (Pub. Service award 1978), N.Am. Snowsport Journalists Assn. Republican. Avocations: sailing, skiing, whitewater rafting, motorcycling, bicycling. Office: Rio Hondo Coll 3600 Workman Mill Rd Whittier CA 90601-1616

LOUIE, DAVID A., television journalist; b. Lakewood, Ohio, June 19, 1950; s. Troy and May (Chan) L. BS in Journalism, Northwestern U., 1972. Reporter KGO-TV, San Francisco, 1972-77, reporter, bur. chief, 1979-95, bus. editor and anchor, 1995—; asst. news dir. WXYZ-TV, Detroit, 1977-79. Contbr. articles to profl. jours. Bd. dirs. United Way of Bay Area, San Francisco, 1980-82, Peninsula Humane Soc., San Mateo, Calif., 1981. Mem. NATAS (exec. com., vice chmn. bd. dirs. 1990-94, chmn. bd. dirs. 1994-96, trustee 1986-90, Emmy award 1980, 88, Silver Circle award 1995), Asian Am. Journalists Assn. (nat. pres. 1990-92, Lifetime Achievement award 1996), Radio TV News Dirs. Assn. (ex-officio bd. dirs.). Office: Sta KGO-TV 900 Front St San Francisco CA 94111-1450

LOUNSBURY, JOHN FREDERICK, geographer, educator; b. Perham, Minn., Oct. 26, 1918; s. Charles Edwin and Maude (Knight) L.; m. Dorothea Frances Eggers, Oct. 3, 1943; children—John Frederick, Craig Lawrence, James Gordon. B.S., U. Ill., 1942, M.S., 1946; Ph.D., Northwestern U., 1951. Asst. dir. rural land classification program Insular Govt., P.R., 1949-52; cons., research analyst Dayton Met. Studies, Inc., Ohio, 1957-60; chmn. dept. earth scis., prof. geography Antioch Coll., 1951-61; prof. geography, head dept. geography and geology Eastern Mich. U., 1961-69; chmn. dept. geography Ariz. State U., 1969-77; dir. Ctr. for Environ. Studies, 1977-80; prof. emeritus Ariz. State U., 1987—; project dir. Geography in Liberal Edn. Project, Assn. Am. Geographers, NSF, 1963-65, project dir. commn. on coll. geography, 1965-74; dir. environment based edn. project US. Office Edn., 1974-75; dir. spatial analysis of land use project NSF, 1975-85. Author articles, workbooks, textbooks. Mem. Yellow Springs Planning Commn., Ohio, dir. research, 1957-60; mem. Ypsilanti Planning Commn., 1961-66; research com. Washtenaw County Planning Commn., 1961-69; mem. cons. Ypsilanti Indsl. Devel. Corp., 1961-63. Served with AUS, 1942-46, ETO. Named Man of Yr., Yellow Springs C. of C., 1956-57. Fellow Ariz.-Nev. Acad. Sci.; mem. Assn. Am. Geographers (chmn. East Lakes div. 1959-61, mem. nat. exec. council 1961-64, chmn. liberal edn. com. 1961-65), Nat. Council Geog. Edn. (chmn. earth sci. com. 1961-68, regional coord. 1961-63, mem. exec. bd. 1968-71, 77-83, v.p. 1977-78, pres. 1979-80, Disting. Svc. award 1988, Disting. Mentor award 1990), Mich. Acad. Sci. Arts and Letters (chmn. pub. relations com. 1964-69, past chmn. geography sect.), Ohio Acad. Sci. (past exec. v.p.), Mich. Acad. Sci., Ariz. Acad. Sci., Am. Geog. Soc., AAAS, Sigma Xi, Delta Kappa Epsilon, Gamma Theta Upsilon. Home: 7850 E Vista Dr Scottsdale AZ 85250-7641 Office: Ariz State U Dept Geography Tempe AZ 85281

LOUNSBURY, STEVEN RICHARD, lawyer; b. Evanston, Ill., July 26, 1950; s. James Richard and Reba Janette (Smith) L.; m. Dianne Louise Daley, Apr. 16, 1983; children: Jimson, Cody, Richard. BA, U. Calif., Santa Barbara, 1973; JD, U. West L.A., 1977. Bar: Calif. 1979, U.S. Dist. Ct. (cen. dist.) Calif. 1979, Oreg. 1997. Pvt. practice L.A., 1979-83; contract atty. FAA, L.A., 1981; trial atty. Hertz Corp., L.A., 1983-86; mng. counsel 20th Century Ins. Co., Woodland Hills, Calif., 1986-94; mng. atty. Lounsbury and Assocs., Brea, Calif., 1986-94; sr. trial atty. Bollington, Lounsbury and Chase, Brea, 1994—; arbitrator Orange County Superior Ct., Santa Ana, Calif., 1992—. Dir. internat. rels. Rotary Internat., Venice-Marina Club, Calif., 1980-81; dir. L.A. Jr. C. of C., 1981-82. Mem. ABA, Calif. Bar Assn., Oreg. Bar Assn., Calif. House Counsel (bd. dirs., chmn. membership 1993-94). Avocations: snow skiing, music, travel. Office: Bollington Lounsbury and Chase 1800 E Imperial Hwy Ste 101 Brea CA 92821-6070

LOURIE, IVEN, editor, writer; b. Long Island, N.Y., Dec. 13, 1946; s. Norman Victor and Betty (Pokrassa) L.; m. Moira Dougherty, May 25, 1975 (div.); children: Bethany, Taramin. BA, Univ. Chgo., 1969; MFA, Univ. Ariz., 1978. Adminstrv. asst. Ctr. for Employment Training, Tucson, Ariz., 1980-82; rsch. asst. Tucson Unified Schs., 1982-83; sr. editor Gateways Books & tapes, Nevada City, Calif., 1988—; adj. prof. Sierra Coll., Rocklin, Calif., 1996—. Author: Miro's Dream, 1988; editor: Chicago Review, 1966-69, Inner Journeys, 1988—. Vol. tchr. Mus. of Ancient & Modern Art, Penn Valley, Calif., 1990—. Avocations: music, hiking.

LOUX, GORDON DALE, organization executive; b. Souderton, Pa., June 21, 1938; s. Curtis L. and Ruth (Derstine) L.; m. Elizabeth Ann Nordland, June 18, 1960; children: Mark, Alan, Jonathan. Diploma, Moody Bible Inst., Chgo., 1960; BA, Gordon Coll., Wenham, Mass., 1962; BD, No. Bapt. Sem., Oak Brook, Ill., 1965, MDiv, 1971; MS, Nat. Coll. Edn., Evanston,Ill., 1984; LHD (hon.), Sioux Falls Coll., 1985. Ordained to ministry, Bapt. Ch., 1965. Assoc. pastor Forest Park (Ill.) Bapt. Ch., 1962-65; alumni field dir. Moody Bible Inst., Chgo., 1965-66, dir. pub. rels., 1972-76; dir. devel. Phila. Coll. Bible, 1966-69; pres. Stewardship Svcs., Wheaton, Ill., 1969-72; exec. v.p. Prison Fellowship Ministries, Washington, 1976-84, pres., CEO, 1984-88; pres., CEO Prison Fellowship Internat., Washington, 1979-87; pres. Internat. Students, Inc., Colorado Springs, Colo., 1988-93, Stewardship Svcs. Group, Colorado Springs, 1994—, Trinity Cmty. Found., 1996—. Author: Uncommon Courage, 1987, You Can Be a Point of Light, 1991; contbg. author: Money for Ministries, 1989, Dictionary of Christianity in America, 1989. Bd. dirs. Evang. Coun. for Fin. Accountability, Washington, 1979-92, vice chmn., 1981-84, 86-87, chmn., 1987-89; vice chmn. Billy Graham Greater Washington Crusade, 1985-85; bd. dirs. Evang. Fellowship of Mission Agys., 1991-94. Named Alumnus of Yr., Gordon Coll., 1986. Mem. Broadmoor Golf Club (Colo. Springs). Republican. Home: 740 Bear Paw Ln Colorado Springs CO 80906 Office: PO Box 38898 Colorado Springs CO 80937-8898

LOUX, JONATHAN DALE, business development consultant; b. Oak Park, Ill., Mar. 23, 1966; s. Gordon Dale and Elizabeth (Nordland) L.; m. Jan Mary Peters, July 22, 1989; children: Kara Leigh, Kurtis Dale, Kenton Stanley, Kourtney Grayce. BS, Eastern Coll., St. Davids, Pa., 1988. CPA, Ill. Acctg. supr. Capin, Crouse, LLP, Wheaton, Ill., 1989-93; supr. internal audit Select Beverages, Ind., Darien, Ill., 1993-94; exec. v.p. Gordon D. Loux & Co., LLC, Colorado Springs, Colo., 1994—; pres. Loux Group, LLC, Colorado Springs, 1996—. Mem. AICPA, Ill. CPA Soc. Republican. Presbyterian. Home and Office: 6335 Moccasin Pass Ct Colorado Springs CO 80919-4452

LOVE, AMY DUNDON, business executive, marketing and sales executive; b. Atlanta, Mar. 6, 1966; d. David Milton and Jo Ann (Pleak) L. BBA in Mktg., BBA in Mgmt., Tex. Tech. U., Lubbock, 1988; MBA, Harvard U., Boston, 1993. Unit mgr. Procter & Gamble, Cin., 1988-91; asst. to pres. SLT Environ. Inc., Conroe, Tex., 1992; sr. assoc. Booz, Allen & Hamilton, San Francisco, 1993-95; v.p. sales and mktg. Navigation Technologies, Sunnyvale, Calif., 1995-96, v.p. mktg. and distbn. N.Am. and Europe, 1996-97; founder, CEO, pub. Real Sports mag. ADL Inc., San Jose, Calif., 1998—; founder/CEO/pub. Amy Love's Real Sports Mag.; mentor, career counselor Career Action Ctr., 1996—. Publ. Real Sports mag. Founder Tex. State Student Govt. Pres. Coun., Austin, Tex., 1987; exec. adv. Jr. Achievement, Houston, 1989; mem. exec. bd. Taft/HBS Partnership, Boston, 1989; vol. The Role Model Project for Girls, 1998. Mem. Stanford Fast Break Club, Harvard Alumni Club. Democrat. Avocations: basketball, biking, hiking, tennis, reading, entrepreneurial activities. Home: 1311 Cherry Ave San Jose CA 95125-3722

LOVE, LAURIE MILLER, science editor; b. Fed. Republic Germany, May 7, 1960; came to U.S., 1961; d. Thomas Walter and Jacquelyn (Jolley) Miller; m. Raymond Lee Love; 1 child, Emily Liesel Love. Student, U. Minn., 1979-80; BA in Psychology, Scripps Coll., 1983; postgrad., UCLA. Programmer specialist Control Data Corp., San Diego, 1982, asst. mgr. software retail store, 1983-84; support technician Ashton-Tate, Torrance, Calif., 1984, editor-in-chief, 1985-87; mgr. tech. pub. Ashton-Tate, Torrance, 1986-87; product mgr. Apple Products, Nantucket Corp., Los Angeles, 1987-88; sr. mktg. cons. Macintosh Market Launch Systems, Rancho Palos Verdes, Calif., 1988; pres. Miller Tech. Pub., Santa Cruz, 1987—; contractor, writer, editor Claris Corp., Santa Clara, Calif., Apple Computer, Cupertino, Calif., Live Picture, Inc., Soquel, Calif., Aladdin Sys., Watsonville, Calif., MetaCreations, Scotts Valley, Calif.; dir. Live Picture, Inc., 1996-97. Tech. and devel. editor Addison-Wesley, Osborne/McGraw Hill, TAB books; author Using ClarisWorks, 1992, Using ClarisWorks for Windows, 1993; contbr. feature articles to monthly mag., 1985—, computer product manuals, 1987—. Recipient Live Picture User Guide Excellence awards (3) The Soc. for Tech. Comm., 1996. Mem. Soc. Tech. Comm. (sr., Silicon Valley chpt., Excellence awards 1996), Women in Tech. Internat., Phi Beta Phi (asst. treas. 1980). Democrat. Methodist. Avocations: classical piano, writing, bicycling, modern dancing.

LOVE, SANDRA RAE, information specialist; b. San Francisco, Feb. 20, 1947; d. Benjamin Raymond and Charlotte C. Martin; B.A. in English, Calif. State U., Hayward, 1968; M.S. in L.S., U. So. Calif., 1969; m. Michael D. Love, Feb. 14, 1971. Tech. info. specialist Lawrence Livermore (Calif.) Nat. Lab., 1969—. Mem. Beta Sigma Phi. Democrat. Episcopalian. Office: Lawrence Livermore Nat Lab PO Box 808 Livermore CA 94551-0808

LOVE, SUSAN DENISE, accountant, consultant, small business owner; b. Portland, Oreg., Aug. 5, 1954; d. Charles Richard and Betty Lou (Reynolds) Beck; m. Daniel G. Oliveros, Dec. 21, 1979 (div. Nov. 1983); m. Michael Dean Love, Aug. 24, 1984 (div. Mar. 1989); m. Michael Eugene Watson, July 28, 1990 (div. Dec. 1994); m. David Phillip Dulaney, Aug. 22, 1998. BA in Graphic Design, Portland State U., 1976. Office mgr. Rogers Machinery Co., Portland, 1972-77; exec. sec. Creighton Shirtmakers, N.Y.C., 1977-80; dir. adminstrn. Henry Grethel div. Manhattan Industries, N.Y.C., 1980-81; exec. asst. S.B. Tanger and Assocs., N.Y.C., 1981-83; exec. asst., bookkeeper M Fin. Corp., Portland, 1983-84; acct. cons., owner Office Assistance, Portland, 1984—; owner WE LOVE KIDS Clothing Store, Portland, 1985—; owner, pres. Oreg. Music and Entertainment, 1989—; sec./treas. Designers' Roundtable, Portland, 1985-88; co-owner, The Tuxedo Club, 1992-95. Mem. Oreg. State Pub. Interest Rsch. Group, Portland, 1985-90, Oreg. Fair Share,Salem, 1987, mem. adv. bd. career and life options program Clackamas Community Coll., 1989-91. Mem. Women Entrepreneurs Oreg. (bd. dirs. 1988-98, pres. 1992-95, Mem. of Yr. award 1991, 95), Brentwood-Darlington Neighborhood Assn. (treas. 1993—), North Clackamas County C. of C., Nat. Fedn. Ind. Bus., Outer S.E. Coalition. Democrat. Avocations: bicycling, aerobics, camping, hiking, music, graphic design. Office: Office Assistance PO Box 1784 Clackamas OR 97015-1784

LOVE, SUSAN MARGARET, surgeon, educator, medical administrator; b. N.J., Feb. 9, 1948; d. James Arthur and Margaret Connick (Schwab) L.; life ptnr. Helen Sperry Cooksey, Sept. 8, 1982; 1 child, Katherine Mary Love-Cooksey. BS, Fordham U., 1970; MD, SUNY, N.Y.C., 1974; DSc (hon.), Northeastern U., 1991; D of Humane Sci. (hon.), Simmons Coll., 1992; LHD (hon.), U. R.I., 1997; DSc (hon.), SUNY, N.Y.C., 1998. Clin. fellow in surgery Harvard Med. Sch., Boston, 1977-78, clin. instr. in surgery, 1980-87; dir. breast clinic Beth Israel Hosp., Boston, 1980-88; clin. assoc. in surg. oncology Dana Farber Cancer Inst., Boston, 1981-92; dir. Faulkner Breast Ctr. Faulkner Hosp., Boston, 1988-92; asst. clin. prof. surgery Harvard Med. Sch., Cambridge, 1987-92; assoc. prof. clin. surgery UCLA Sch. Medicine, 1992-96; dir. UCLA Breast Ctr., 1992-96; adj. prof. surgery UCLA, 1966—; mem. adv. coun. Breast and Cervical Cancer Coun., State of Calif. Dept. Human Svcs., 1994—; mem. NSABP Oversight Com., Pitts., 1994; mem. adv. com. Women's Health Initiative Program, Washington, 1993-95; prin. investigator Nat. Surg. Adjuvant Breast and Bowel Project, 1985-96; mem. Pres.'s Nat. Action Plan on Breast Cancer, DHHS, 1994—; co-chair Biol. Resources Working Group, 1994-98, mem. exec. and steering coms., 1995—. Author: Dr. Susan Love's Breast Book, 1990, 95, Dr. Susan Love's Hormone Book, 1997, Atlas of Techniques in Breast Surgery, 1996; (book chpts.) Breast Disease, 1987, Clinics in Oncology: Breast Cancer, 1989, The Woman's Guide to Good Health, 1991; contbr. articles to profl. jours. Founder, bd. dirs. Nat. Breast Cancer Coalition, 1991—; mem. breast cancer subcom. divsn. cancer treatment Bd. Sci. Counselors, Nat. Cancer Inst., 1992-95; conf. com. co-chair Sec.'s Conf. to Establish Nat. Action Plan on Breast Cancer, 1993. Recipient Rose Kushner award Am. Med. Writers Assn., 1991, Achievement award Am. Assn. Physicians for Human Rights, 1992, Women Making History award U.S. Senator Barbara Boxer, 1993, Woman of Yr. award YWCA, 1994, Frontrunner award Sara Lee Corp., 1994, Spirit of Achievement award Albert Einstein Coll. of Yeshiva U., 1995, Abram L. Sachar medallion Brandeis U., 1996, Bicentennial honoree U. Louisville, 1997, Walker prize Boston Mus. Sci., 1998; prin. investigator grantee Dept. of Def., 1994, 96. Mem. Am. Med. Women's Assn. (pres. br. 39 1987), Soc. for Study of Breast Disease, Am. Soc. Preventive Oncology, Southwestern Oncology Group (women's health and breast com. 1992-96, surg. rep. 1992-96), L.A. Med. Soc., Boston Surg. Soc., N.Am. Menopause Soc., Am. Assn. Cancer Rsch., Am. Coll. Women's Health Physicians, Assn. Women Surgeons. Office: PO Box 846 Pacific Palisades CA 90272-0846

LOVELAND, JACQUELINE JANE, neuroscientist, biologist; b. Point Pleasant Borough, N.J., Feb. 16, 1952; d. George Clark and Virginia Mae (Skimmons) L.; m. Alan Dale Nunes, Aug. 22, 1974 (div. Aug. 1978); 1 child, Emmett Todd Nunes. BA, San Jose State U., 1981, MA, 1987. Rsch.

assoc. NASA-Ames Rsch. Ctr., Mt. View, Calif., 1980-83; supr., sr. case mgr. Cmty. Companions, Inc., San Jose, Calif., 1983-85, cons., 1985; neurosci. biologist Syntex Rsch. Inst. of Pharmacology, San Jose, Calif., 1985-93; safety pharmacology biologist Syntex Rsch. Inst. of Pathology, Toxicology & Metabolism, Palo Alto, 1993-95; clin. rsch. assoc. Roche Global Devel., Palo Alto, 1995—. Contbr. articles to profl. jours.; author abstracts. Mem. AAAS, Soc. Neurosci., Drug Info. Assn., Psi Chi, Phi Theta Kappa. Avocations: camping, dancing, swimming, skiing. Office: Roche Global Devel 3401 Hillview Ave Palo Alto CA 94304-1320

LOVELESS, PEGGY ANN, social work administrator; b. Decatur, Ill., June 9, 1952; d. William Walter and Rose Marie (Sheppard) L. Student, Ill. State U., 1970-72; BA, U. Ill., 1974, MSW, 1976. Cert. lic. clin. social worker; cert. in health care ethics; diplomate Am. Bd. Examiners in Clin. Social Work. Social worker Met.-Police Social Svcs., Urbana, Ill., 1976-80; clin. supr. Ctr. Children's Svcs., Danville, Ill., 1980-84; med. social worker Sarah Bush Lincoln Health Ctr., Mattoon, Ill., 1984-86, Portland (Oreg.) Adventist Med. Ctr., 1986-88; dept. supr., social worker Oreg. Health Scis. U., Portland, 1988-92, interim dir. social work, 1992-93, asst. dir. social work Ctr. Ethics, 1993-96, mem. ethics consulting svc., 1991-96; behavioral health case mgr. PacifiCare Behavioral Health, 1996-98; case mgr. Pacific Gateway Hosp., Portland, Oreg., 1998—. Vol. Goose Hollow Family Homeless Shelter, Portland, 1993-94, vol. supr., 1994-95, bd. dirs., 1996-97. Mem. Soc. Social Work Adminstrs. Health Care (com. nominations 1995-96, chair, pres. meeting planning com. 1994, com. mem. devel. 1997), Oreg. Soc. Social Work Adminstrs. Health Care (pres. elect 1993, pres. 1994, chair/conf. com. 1995). Avocations: reading, walking, skiing, travel. Office: Pacific Gateway Hosp 1345 SE Harney St Portland OR 97202-7196

LOVELL, CAROL, museum director. Dir. Kauai Mus., Lihue, Hawaii. Office: Kauai Mus 4428 Rice St Lihue HI 96766-1338*

LOVELL, CHARLES C., federal judge; b. 1929; m. Ariliah Carter. BS, U. Mont., 1952, JD, 1959. Assoc. Church, Harris, Johnson & Williams, Great Falls, Mont., 1959-85; judge U.S. Dist. Ct. Mont., Helena, 1985—; chief counsel Mont. Atty Gen.'s Office, Helena, 1969-72. Served to capt. USAF, 1952-54. Mem. ABA, Am. Judicature Soc., Assn. Trial Lawyers Am. Office: US Dist Ct PO Drawer 10112 301 S Park Ave Rm 504 Helena MT 59626-6289*

LOVELL, CHARLES MUIR, museum curator, photographer; b. Chgo., Nov. 22, 1952; s. Charles Julian and Dixie (Hefley) L. BS, East Tex. State U., 1980; MFA, Cen. Wash. U., 1984. Registrar Tacoma Art Mus., 1985, curator, 1986-87; dir. Yuma Art Ctr., Ariz., 1987-90, Wellington B. Gray Gallery, E. Carolina U., 1990-94; curator Weatherspoon Art Gallery, 1994-95; dir. U. Art Gallery, N. Mex. State U., 1995-98. Author exhbn. catalogs Northwest Now, 1986, Paul Horiuchi: Master of the Collage, Tacoma Art Mus., 1987, Ten Years After, Yuma Art Ctr., 1989, Minnie Evans, Artist, East Carolina U., 1993, Into the Nineties, Prints from the Tamarind Institute, U.N.C. Greensboro, 1995, Jaune Quick-To-See-Smith, Modern Times, N. Mex. State U., 1997; artist solo exhbn. Idaho State U., 1985. Exhbns. grantee Nat. Endowment for the Arts; spl. exhbns. grant Minnie Evans, Artist, 1993, Stockman Found.; conservation grant N. Mex. State U. Retablo Collection, 1998, U.S. Mex. fund for culture Retablo Lectr. Series Imagenes Sagradas, 1997; Inst. Mus. Services conservation grantee, Tacoma Art Mus., 1985. Mem. Am. Assn. Mus., Coll. Art Assn., N. Mex. Mus. Assn. (v.p. 1997-98). E-mail: artglry@nmsu.edu. Home: PO Box 328 Mesilla NM 88046 Office: NMex State Univ Dept 3572 PO Box 30001 Las Cruces NM 88003-8001

LOVELL, EMILY KALLED, journalist; b. Grand Rapids, Mich., Feb. 25, 1920; d. Abdo Rham and Louise (Claussen) Kalled; student Grand Rapids Jr. Coll., 1937-39; BA, Mich. State U., 1944; MA, U. Ariz., 1971; m. Robert Edmund Lovell, July 4, 1947. Copywriter, asst. traffic mgr. Sta. WOOD, Grand Rapids, 1944-46; traffic mgr. KOPO, Tucson, 1946-47; reporter, city editor Alamogordo (N.Mex.) News, 1948-51; Alamogordo corr., feature writer Internat. News Service, Denver, 1950-54; Alamogordo corr., feature writer El Paso Herald-Post, 1954-65; Alamogordo news dir., feature writer Tularosa (N.Mex.) Basin Times, 1957-59; co-founder, editor, pub. Otero County Star, Alamogordo, 1961-65; newscaster KALG, Alamogordo, 1964-65; free lance feature writer Denver Post, N.Mex. Mag., 1949-69; corr. Electronics News, N.Y.C., 1959-63, 65-69; Sierra Vista (Ariz.) corr. Ariz. Republic, 1966; free lance editor N.Mex. Pioneer Interviews, 1967-69; asst. dir. English skills program Ariz. State U., 1976; free-lance editor, writer, 1977—; part-time tchr., lectr. U. Pacific, 1981-86; part-time interpreter Calif., 1983-91, Interpreters Unlimited, Oakland, 1985-91; sec., dir. Star Pub. Co., Inc., 1961-64, pres., 1964-65. 3d v.p., publicity chmn. Otero County Community Concert Assn., 1950-65; mem. Alamogordo Zoning Commn., 1955-57; mem. founding com. Alamogordo Central Youth Activities Com., 1957; vice chmn. Otero County chpt. Nat. Found. Infantile Paralysis, 1958-61; charter mem. N.M. Citizens Council for Traffic Safety, 1959-61; pres. Sierra Vista Hosp. Aux., 1966; pub. rels. chmn. Ft. Huachuca chpt. ARC, 1966. Mem. nat. bd. Hospitalized Vets. Writing Project, 1972-99; vol. instr. autobiography & creative writing, 1991—. Recipient 1st Pl. awards N.Mex. Press Assn., 1961, 62. Pub. Interest award Nat. Safety Council, 1962. 1st Pl. award Nat. Fedn. Press Women, 1960, 62; named Woman of Year Alamogordo, 1960. Editor of Week Pubs. Aux., 1962, adm. N.Mex. Navy, 1962, col. a.d.c. Staff Gov. N.Mex., 1963, Woman of Yr., Ariz. Press Women, 1973. Mem. N.Mex. (past sec.), Ariz. (past pres.) press women, N.Mex. Fedn. Womens Clubs (past dist. pub. rels. chmn., hon. life Alamogordo), N.Mex. Hist. Soc. (life), N.Mex. Fedn. Bus. and Profl. Womens Clubs (past pres., hon. life Alamogordo), Pan Am. Round Table Alamogordo, Theta Sigma Phi (past nat. 3d v.p.), Phi Kappa Phi. Democrat. Moslem. Author: A Personalized History of Otero County, New Mexico, 1963; Weekend Away, 1964; Lebanese Cooking, Streamlined, 1972; A Reference Handbook for Arabic Grammar, 1974, 77; contbg. author: The Muslim Community in North America, 1983. Home: 3400 Wagner Heights Rd Apt 226 Stockton CA 95209-4855

LOVELL, HOWELL, JR., non profit organization executive; b. San Jose, Calif., Oct. 12, 1938; s. Howell and Rebecca (Oser) L.; m. Donna Lovell, Apr. 21, 1965 (div. Apr. 1994); children: Howell III, Eric, Kathleen. BA, Stanford U., 1960, JD, 1963. Pvt. practice lawyer San Francisco, 1965-92; exec. dir. Pets in Need, Redwood City, Calif., 1992-93, Recording for The Blind & Dyslexic, Palo Alto, Calif., 1995—. Sec. Palo Alto Family YMCA, 1990-91, 93-94, 97-98, vice chair, 1998—, bd. dirs. 1993—. Mem. Nat. Soc. Fund Raising Execs. (bd. dirs., v.p. programs 1998—), Palo Alto C. of C., Ferne Ave. Home Owners Assn. (pres. 1996—), Internat. Domino Assn. (bd. dirs., treas. 1994-98), San Francisco Down Town Garden Club (pres. 1994), Kiwanis (bd. dirs., pres.-elect Palo Alto chpt.), YWCA fin. comm., 1998—. Avocations: genealogy, photography, sports. Home: 124 Ferne Ave Palo Alto CA 94306-4644 Office: Recording for The Blind & Dyslexic 488 W Charleston Rd Palo Alto CA 94306-4103

LOVELL, JOAN ELLEN, mental health professional; b. Alton, Ill., Oct. 24, 1955; d. Lee Roy and Arlou (Brown) Waller; 1 child, Frank. AS, RN, Monticello Coll., Godfrey, Ill., 1974; BA in Social Work, Calif. State U., Northridge, 1977; MA in Psychology, Calif. Grad. Inst., Westwood, 1988, PhD in Psychology, 1996. RN, Calif., psychol. asst., Calif.; registered psychologist Calif. Nurse, asst. head nurse St. Francis Med. Ctr., 1977-80; crisis resolution unit nurse Dept. Mental Health L.A. County, L.A., 1983-85, homeless coord., 1985-87, patient rights advocate, 1987-92, children and youth svc. coord., 1993—; mental health cons. Fed. Project 90044, L.A., 1992-93; owner Medi Fact Rsch., Huntington Beach, Calif., 1992-97; cons. Philippine-Am. Orgn., Long Beach, Calif., 1985-87. Ct. advocate for victims of rape L.A. Commn. Against Assaults on Women, L.A., 1977, rape hotline counselor, 1976-77. Mem. APA (affiliate), Calif. Psychol. Assn.

LOVELL, TERRY JEFFRY, business educator; b. Sacramento, Mar. 26, 1953; s. Charles C. and Maxine (Carter) L.; m. Shannon Lynn Pribble, Mar. 17, 1992; children: Jared Cameron, Terry Jessica. BA in Sociology, U. Mont., 1976; MBA, Ariz. State U., 1985; PhD in Bus., Greenwich U., 1992. Tchr./rsch. asst. Ariz. State U., Tempe, 1983-88; asst. prof. bus. U. Alaska, Anchorage, 1988-90; prof. bus. Yavapai Coll., Prescott, Ariz., 1990—; presenter, rsch. in field. Contbr. articles, rsch. papers in field. Home constrn. vol. Habitat for Humanity, Prescott, 1995—; pres. faculty senate Yavapai Coll., 1995. Mem. APA, Acad. Mgmt., Am. Sociol. Assn. Avocation: woodworking. Fax: (520) 776-2160. E-mail: bcuterry@yavapai.cc.az.us. Office: Yavapai Coll 1100 E Sheldon St Prescott AZ 86301-3220

LOVEN, CHARLES JOHN, human resource executive; b. N.Y.C., Feb. 17, 1937; s. John and June Emma (Custer) Azzaro. BA, Occidental Coll., 1962; MA, Calif. State U., L.A., 1967. Group scheduler Douglas Space Systems, Huntington Beach, Calif., 1963-65; personnel rep. Shell Oil Co., L.A., 1965-71; dir. indsl. rels. Calif. Computer Products, Anaheim, 1971-80; sr. v.p., dir. personnel dept. Thompson Recruitment Advt., L.A., 1980-92; dir. pers. dept. UAW/Labor Employment and Tng. Corp., Bell, Calif., 1994-95; cons., 1995—. With USCG, 1954-58. Mem. Employment Mgrs. Assn., Exec. Human Resources Round Table, PIHRA, SHRM.

LOVENTHAL, MILTON, writer, playwright, lyricist; b. Atlantic City; s. Harry and Clara (Feldman) L.; m. Jennifer McDowell, July 2, 1973. BA, U. Calif., Berkeley, 1950, MLS, 1958; MA in Sociology, San Jose State U., 1969. Researcher Hoover Instn., Stanford, Calif., 1952-53, spl. asst. to Slavic Curator, 1955-57; librarian San Diego Pub. Library, 1957-59; librarian, bibliographer San Jose (Calif.) State U., 1959-92; tchr. writing workshops, poetry readings, 1969-73; co-producer lit. and culture radio show Sta. KALX, Berkeley, 1971-72; editor, pub. Merlin Press, San Jose, 1973—. Author: Books on the USSR, 1951-57, 57, Black Politics, 1971 (featured at Smithsonian Inst. Special Event, 1992), A Bibliography of Material Relating to the Chicano, 1971, Autobiographies of Women, 1946-70, 72, Blacks in America, 1972, The Survivors, 1972, Contemporary Women Poets an Anthology, 1977, Ronnie Goose Rhymes for Grown-Ups, 1984; co-author: (Off-Off-Broadway plays) The Estrogen Party to End War, 1986, Mack the Knife, Your Friendly Dentist, 1986, Betsy & Phyllis, 1986, The Oatmeal Party Comes to Order, 1986, (plays) Betsy Meets the Wacky Iraqi, 1991, Bella and Phyllis, 1994; co-writer (mus. comedy) Russia's Secret Plot to Take Back Alaska, 1988; co-lyricist Intern Girl, 1998. Recipient Bill Casey Award in Letters, 1980; grantee San Jose State U., 1962-63, 84. Mem. Assn. Calif. State Profs., Calif. Alumni Assn., Calif. Theatre Coun., Am. Assn. for Advancement of Slavic Studies, Soc. for Sci. Study of Religion. Office: PO Box 5602 San Jose CA 95150-5602

LOVERIDGE, RONALD O., mayor; b. Antioch, Calif., 1938; m. Marsha Jean Loveridge, 1964; 2 children. BA in Polit. Sci., U. Pacific, 1960; MA Polit. Sci., Stanford U., 1961, PhD in Polit. Sci., 1965. Assoc. prof. polit. sci. U. Calif., Riverside, 1965—, assoc. dean coll. social scis., 1970-72, chair acad. ednl. policy com., 1990-92; mem. Riverside City Coun., 1979-94; mayor City of Riverside, 1994—; chair land use com. Riverside City Coun., 1980-94; exec. com. Western Riverside Coun. of Govts., 1994—. Contbr. articles to profl. jours. Chair Earth Day City of Riverside, 1990; co-chair Citrus Heritage Tourism Task Force, 1991; mem. Californians Against Waste. Mem. Greater Riverside C. of C., Northside Improvement Assn., Urban League, So. Calif. Assn. Govts. (exec. com. 1994—). Office: 3900 N Main St Riverside CA 92522-0001

LOVINS, L. HUNTER, public policy institute executive; b. Middlebury, Vt., Feb. 26, 1950; d. Paul Millard and Farley (Hunter) Sheldon; m. Amory Bloch Lovins, Sept. 6, 1979; 1 child, Nanuq. BA in Sociology, Pitzer Coll., 1972, BA in Polit. Sci., 1972; JD, Loyola U., L.A., 1975; LHD, U. Maine, 1982. Bar: Calif. 1975. Asst. dir. Calif. Conservation Project, L.A., 1973-79; exec. dir., co-founder Rocky Mountain Inst., Snowmass, Colo., 1982—; vis. prof. U. Colo., Boulder, 1982; Henry R. Luce vis. prof. Dartmouth Coll., Hanover, N.H., 1982; pres. Nighthawk Horse Co., 1993, Lovins Group, 1994. Co-author: Brittle Power, 1982, Energy Unbound, 1986, Least-Cost Energy Solving the CO2 Problem, 2d edit., 1989. Bd. dirs. Renew Am., Point Found., Basalt and Rural Fire Protection Dist., E Source, Roaring Fork Polocrosse Assn.; vol. EMT and firefighter. Recipient Mitchell prize Woodlands Inst., 1982, Right Livelihood Found. award, 1983, Best of the New Generation award Esquire Mag., 1984, Nissan prize, 1995. Mem. Calif. Bar Assn., Am. Quarter Horse Assn., Am. Polocrosse Assn. Avocations: rodeo, fire rescue, polocrosse. Office: Rocky Mountain Inst 1739 Snowmass Creek Rd Snowmass CO 81654-9199

LOVVIK, DARYL VAUGHN, consulting geologist; b. Eau Claire, Wis., July 26, 1941; s. Oscar W. and Pearl B. (Johnson) L.; m. Sherly Berog; children: Liezel Bayo, Lenie Bayo, Welanie Bayo. B.S. in Geology, W. Tex. State U., 1975; MBA, U. of Phoenix. Cert. profl. geologist; registered profl. geologist, Alaska, Ariz., Ark. Cons. geologist, Golden, Colo., 1975-77; exploration geologist Cotter Corp., Moab, Utah, 1977-79; pres. Southwestern Geol. Survey, Mesa, Ariz., 1979-86; water resource dir. Tohono O'Odham Nation, Sells, Ariz., 1986-89, Ariz. Dept. Water Resources, 1990-96; pres. Southwestern Geol., Tempe, Ariz., 1986—, Pac-Isle Enterprises, Tacloban, Philippines, 1994—, Philippine Connection, Tempe, 1993—. Contbr. articles to profl. jours. With USAF, 1960-64. Mem. Am. Inst. Profl. Geologists, Geol. Soc. Am., Am. Assn. Petroleum Geologists, Am. C. of C. (The Philippines), Soc. Mining Engrs. Republican. Episcopalian. Home: 8808 N 35th Dr Phoenix AZ 85051-3764

LOW, LEWIS L., physician, medical educator; b. L.A., Oct. 15, 1962. BA in Genetics, U. Calif., Berkeley, 1984; MD, St. Louis U., 1988. Diplomate Am. Bd. Critical Care Medicine and Internal Medicine. Intern Letterman Army Med. Ctr., 1988-89, resident internal medicine, 1989-91; fellow critical care medicine Walter Reed Army Med. Ctr., 1991-93; instr. in medicine Uniformed Svcs. U. Health Scis., Bethesda, Md., 1991-93; chief critical care medicine Madigan Army Med. Ctr., Tacoma, Wash., 1993-95; med. dir. respiratory care sect. Madigan Army Med. Ctr., Tacoma, 1994-95; clin. instr. medicine U. Wash., Seattle, 1994-95; dir. critical care medicine St. Francis Med. Ctr., Honolulu, 1995—; asst. prof. medicine and surgery U. Hawaii, Honolulu, 1995—. Contbr. articles to profl. jours. Maj. U.S. Army, 1988-95. Fellow ACP; mem. Soc. Critical Care Medicine. E-mail: lewis@sfhs-hi.org. Office: St Francis Med Ctr 2230 Liliha St Honolulu HI 96817-1646

LOW, MARISSA E., health care administrator; b. San Francisco; d. Fred and Winifred L. AA, Fashion Inst. of Design and Mdse., 1979; Cert. Corp. Communications, Calif. State U.-Long Beach, 1987; BSBA, U. Redlands, 1992. Assoc. area mgr. Buffums, Glendale, Calif., 1979-80; asst. buyer Buffums, Long Beach, Calif., 1981-83; mdse. control mgr. Buffums, Long Beach, 1983-86, advt. mgr., 1987-89; account rep. CompuMed, Culver City, Calif., 1989-91; physician recruiter Pioneer Ind. Physician Network, Artesia, Calif., 1991-92; provider rels. mgr. Mullikin Ind. Physician Assn., Long Beach, Calif., 1992-93; dir. provider rels. Mullikin Ind. Physician Assn., Daly City, 1993-94; dir., payor, provider rels., regional network mgr. AHI Healthcare Systems, Inc., San Mateo, Calif., 1994-95; regional contracts mgr. Nat. Med., Inc., Modesto, Calif., 1996—. Judge Miss Lakewood Pageant of Beauty, 1987; vol. Long Beach Conv. and Visitors Coun., 1987, Am. Cancer Soc. 1996; pub. rels. chmn. March of Dimes, Calif., 1986; v.p. programs, spl. projects, chmn. bd. dirs., nomination com. chmn. Women's Coun., 1985-91; sec. Women's Bus. Conf., 1985; com. mem. Interval House Le Bal des Papillons. Recipient Cert. Appreciation Orange County Commn. on Status of Women, 1991, Interval House, 1991. Mem. NAFE, Am. Mktg. Assn., Group Health Assn. of Am., Acad. Health Svcs. Mktg. (chmn. managed care com. Health Futures Forum 1992), Healthcare Fin. Mgmt. Assn. Avocations: travel, art, ballet. Office: 1005 W Orangeburg Ave Ste B Modesto CA 95350-4163

LOW, MERRY COOK, civic worker; b. Uniontown, Pa., Sept. 3, 1925; d. Howard Vance and Eleanora (Lynch) Mullan; m. William R. Cook, 1947 (div. 1979); m. John Wayland Low, July 8, 1979; children: Karen, Cindy, Bob, Jan. Diploma in nursing, Allegheny Gen. Hosp., Pitts., 1946; BS summa cum laude, Colo. Women's Coll., 1976. RN, Colo. Dir. patient edn. Med. Care and Rsch. Found., Denver, 1976-78. Contbr. chpt. to Pattern for Distribution of Patient Education, 1981. Bd. dirs. women's libr. assn. U. Denver, 1982—, vice chmn., 1985-86, chair, 1986-87, co-chair spl. event, 1992; bd. dirs. Humanities Inst., 1993—, pres.-elect, 1998, bd. dirs. Rocky Mountain Conservation Ctr., 1999—, co-chair Founder's Day, 1994, chair Culturefest, 1995-96; adv. com. U. Denver Women's Coll., 1995—; mem. DuArt bd. U. Denver, 1998; docent Denver Art Mus., 1979—, vol. exec. bd., 1988-94, nat. docent symposium com., 1991, chair collectors' choice benefits, 1988, pres. vols., trustee 1988-90, mem. alumni assn. bd. U. Denver, 1994—, sec., 1996-98; bd. dirs. Lamont Sch. Music Assocs., 1990-96; search com. for dir. Penrose Libr., 1991-92; trustee ch. coun., chair invitational art show 1st Plymouth Congl. Ch., Englewood, Colo., 1981-84; co-chair art auction Colo. Alliance Bus., 1992-93, com., 1994-97; bd. adv. Rocky Mountain Conservation Ctr., 1999—, chair 1999. Recipient Disting. Svc. award U. Denver Coll. Law, 1988, King Soopers Vol. of Week award, 1989, Citizen of Arts award Fine Arts Found., 1993, Outstanding Vol. Colo. Alliance of Bus., 1994, U. Denver Cmty. Svc. award, 1996. Mem. Am. Assn. Mus. (vol. meeting coord. 1990-91), P.E.O. (pres. Colo. chpt. DX 1982-84), U. Denver Alumni Assn. (bd. dirs., sec. 1996-98). Republican. Congregationalist. Home: 2552 E Alameda Ave Apt 11 Denver CO 80209-3324

LOWDER, ROBERT JACKSON, insurance agent; b. Ogden, Utah, Mar. 18, 1927; s. Milo Howard and Mabel Erma (Jackson) L.; m. HElen Barkdull, Feb. 27, 1953; children: Alyson, Karin, Christine. BA, U. Utah, 1951. chartered life underwriter; chartered fin. cons. Sales Graybar Electric Co., Salt Lake City, 1952-62; mgr. appliance sales Graybar Electric Co., Boise, Idaho, 1962-67; agt. Conn. Mutual Life Ins. Co., Boise, Idaho, 1967—; pres. Boise Estate Planning Coun., 1989, Boise Valley CLU Soc., 1988, Boise Assn. Life Underwriters, 1984. Bd. dirs. St. Luke's Planned Giving Com., Boise,1986-90, Boise State U. Athletic Endowment, 1987-92. Seaman 1st class USN, 1945-47. Mem. Sunrise Rotary, Hillcrest Country Club. Republican. Avocations: tennis, golf, skiing. Office: Conn Mutual Life Ins Co PO Box 7186 Boise ID 83707-1186

LOWE, JAMES ALLEN, lawyer; b. L.A., Apr. 23, 1946; s. Fitzhugh Lee and Dorothy Helen (Van Kirk) L.; m. Francis Elaine Pirnat, June 6, 1967 (div. Aug. 1979); children: David T., Michael D.; m. Sandra Sue Larson, May 31, 1984 (dec. June 1988); children: Tammy Foulke, Robert, Krueger; m. Caroline Margaret Gellrick, June 6, 1992; children: Bryce Otsuka, Cardene Otsuka, Brent Otsuka. BA, U. Colo., 1968, JD, 1970. Bar: Colo. 1971, Ct. Mil. Appeals 1971, U.S. Dist. Ct. (10th cir.) 1988, U.S. Dist. Ct. (fed. cir.) 1989, U.S. Supreme Ct. 1993. Judge adv. USAF, 1971-75; chief deputy dist. atty. Dist. Attys. Office, Pueblo, Colo., 1975-80; atty. Sobol & Sobol, Denver, 1980-82, pvt. practice, Denver, 1982-95; ptnr. Lowe & Meyer, Denver, 1996—. Lt. col. USAF, 1971-95. Republican. Avocations: skiing, hiking.

LOWE, OARIONA, dentist; b. San Francisco, June 17, 1948; d. Van Lowe and Jenny Lowe-Silva; m. Evangelos Rossopoulos, Dec. 18, 1985; children: Thanos G., Jenny Sophia. BS, U. Nev., Las Vegas, 1971; MA, George Washington U., 1977; DDS, Howard U., 1981; pediatric dental cert., UCLA, 1984. Instr. Coll. Allied Health Scis. Howard U., Washington, 1974-76, asst. prof., 1976-77; research asst. Howard U. Dental Sch., Washington, 1977-81; resident gen. practice Eastman Dental Ctr., Rochester, N.Y., 1981-82; dir. dental services City of Hope Med. Ctr., Duarte, Calif., 1984-86; dental staff Whittier (Calif.) Presbyn. Hosp., 1987—, chief dental staff, 1992-94; asst. prof. Loma Linda (Calif.) U., 1991—; vis. lectr. pediatric dentistry UCLA; mem. oral cancer task force Am. Cancer Soc., Pasadena, Calif., 1985—; internat. spkr. Europe, Asia. Contbr. articles to profl. jours. Del. People to People Internat. Mem. ADA, Am. Soc. Dentistry for Children (v.p.), Nat. Soc. Autistic Children, Calif. Dental Assn., Am. Acad. Pediatric Dentistry, San Gabriel Valley Dental Soc. (chmn. 1991—), Sigma Xi, Alpha Omega. Republican. Presbyterian. Avocations: cooking, bicycling, walking, aerobic dancing. Office: 8135 Painter Ave Ste 202 Whittier CA 90602-3175

LOWE, RICHARD GERALD, JR., computer programming manager; b. Travis AFB, Calif., Nov. 8, 1960; s. Richard Gerald and Valerie Jean (Hoefer) L.; m. Claudia Maria Arevalo, 1993; 1 child, Alvaro Arevalo. Student, San Bernardino Valley Coll., 1978-80. Microsoft cert. sys. engr. Tech. specialist Software Techniques Inc., Los Alamitos, Calif., 1980-82, sr. tech. specialist, 1982-84, mgr. tech. services, 1984-85; mgr. cons. services Software Techniques Inc., Cypress, Calif., 1985-86; sr. programmer BIF Accutel, Camarillo, Calif., 1986-87; systems analyst BIF Accutel, Camarillo, 1987-88; mgr. project Beck Computer Systems, Long Beach, Calif., 1986-91, v.p. devel., 1991-93; dir. tech. svcs. Trader Joe's Co., S. Pasadena, Calif., 1994—. Author: The Autobiography of Richard G. Lowe, Jr., 1991, The Lowe Family and Their Relatives, 1992; contbr. articles to profl. jours. Vol. min., field staff mem. L.A. Found. Ch. of Scientology, 1993—; active Concerned Citizens for Human Rights. Mem. Assn. Computing Machinery, Digital Equipment Corp. Users Group, UniData Users Group, Internat. Assn. Scientologists. Avocations: reading and writing science fiction, collecting movies, battlefield simulations, painting fantasy miniatures, collecting stamps. Office: Trader Joe's Co 538 Mission St South Pasadena CA 91030-3036

LOWE, RICHARD R., real estate broker, pianist; b. Woodland, Calif., Nov. 3, 1938; s. Russell James and Alice Meriam (Tucker) L.; m. Lorna Dorothy Whitcome, May 28, 1966; children: Jennifer Lowe McTigue, Vanessa Lowe Beaton, Jonathan Whitcombe Lowe (dec.). BA, U. Calif., Berkeley, 1952; MCP, MIT, 1961. Planner Crocker Land Co., San Francisco, 1961-64, John Carl Warnecke & Assocs., Honolulu, 1964-66, Victoria Ward Ltd., Honolulu, 1966-69, Lemmon, Freeth, Haines et al, Honolulu, 1969-75, Wailea Devel. Co., Maui, Hawaii, 1975-78; v.p. Hugh Menefee Devel. Corp., Honolulu, 1978-81; ind. realtor Honolulu, 1962—. Trustee Friends of Bot. Gardens, Honolulu, 1966-75; bd. dirs. Honolulu Cmty. Assn., 1966-69. Capt. USMCR, 1952-54. Mem. Am. Planning Assn., Outrigger Canoe Club. Avocations: playing piano, music research, literary reading and discussion.

LOWE, ROBERT STANLEY, lawyer; b. Herman, Nebr., Apr. 23, 1923; s. Stanley Robert and Ann Marguerite (Feese) L.; m. Anne Kirtland Selden, Dec. 19, 1959; children: Robert James, Margaret Anne. AB, U. Nebr., 1947, JD, 1949. Bar: Wyo. 1949. Ptnr. McAvoy & Lowe, Newcastle, 1949-51, Hickey & Lowe, Rawlins, 1951-55; county and pros. atty. Rawlins, 1955-59, pvt. practice, 1959-67; assoc. dir. Am. Judicature Soc., Chgo., 1967-74; gen. counsel True Oil Co. and affiliates, 1974-98, of counsel, 1998-99; bd. dirs. Hilltop Nat. Bank, Casper, sec., 1981—; legal adv. divsn. Nat. Ski Patrol Sys., 1975-88; city atty. City of Rawlins, 1963-65; atty., asst. sec. Casper Mountain Ski Patrol, 1988—. Mem. Wyo. Ho. of Reps., 1952-54; bd. dirs. Vols. in Probation, 1969-82; leader lawyer del. to China, People to People, 1986; mem. Wyo. Vets. Affairs Commn., 1994—, chmn., 1996—; mem. legis. com. United Vets. Coun. Wyo., 1993—; trustee Troopers Found., Inc., 1994—, pres., 1994—; chmn. Casper C. of C. Military Affairs Com., 1995—; pres. Casper WWII Commemorative Assn., 1995-96, Navy League Wyo. Coun. (pres. 1997—). Recipient Dedicated Community Worker award Rawlins Jr. C. of C., 1967, Yellow merit star award Nat. Ski Patrol System, 1982, 85, 87, 88, Small Bus. Administrate Vet. Advocate award, 1998, Disting. Svc. award Disabled Am. Vets. Dept., 1994. Fellow Am. Bar Found. (life); mem. VFW (life mem.; post adv. 1991-96, nat. aide-de-camp 1993-94, 99—, judge adv. dist. 3 Dept. Wyo., 1994—, mil. order of cootie grand judge adv. 1994—), ABA (sec. jud. adminstrn. divsn. lawyers conf., exec. com. 1975-76, chmn. 1977-78, chmn. judicial qualification and selection com. 1986-93, coun. jud. adminstrn. divsn. 1977-78, mem. com. to implement jud. adminstrn. stds. 1978-83, Ho. of Dels. state bar del. 1978-80, 86-87, state del. 1987-93, Assembly del. 1980-83, mem. standing com. on the fed. judiciary 1997-99, ad hoc com. state justice initiatives 1997-99), Am. Judicature Soc. (dir. 1961-67, 85-89, bd. editors 1975-77, Herbert Harley award 1974), Wyo. State Bar (chmn. com. on cts. 1961-67, 77-87), Nebr. State Bar Assn., Ill. State Bar Assn., D.C. Bar, Inter-Am. Bar Assn., Selden Soc., Inst. Jud. Adminstrn., Rocky Mountain Oil and Gas Assn. (legal adv. com. 1976-99, chmn. 1979-82, 90-91), Rocky Mountain Mineral Law Found. (trustee 1980-94), Am. Law Inst. (life), Order of Coif, Delta Theta Phi (dist. chancellor 1982-83, chief justice 1983-93, assoc. justice 1993—; Percy J. Power Meml. award 1983, Gold Medallion award 1990), Casper Rotary Club (pres. 1985-86), Casper Rotary Found. (dir., sec. 1990—). Mem. Ch. of Christ, Scientist. Home and Office: 97 Primrose Casper WY 82604-4018 Office: 895 River Cross Rd Casper WY 82601-1758

LOWELL, J(AMES) DAVID, geological consultant, cattle rancher; b. Nogales, Ariz., Feb. 28, 1928; s. Arthur Currier and Lavina (Cumming) L.; m. Edith Walmisly Sykes, Mar. 30, 1948; children—Susan, William, Douglas. B.S. in Mining Engring., U. Ariz., 1949, E.Geol., 1959; M.S. in Geology, Stanford U., 1957; D. Hon. Causa, U. Nat. Mayor de San Marcos, Peru, 1998. Registered profl. engr., Ariz. Mining engr. to mine foreman Asarco, Chihuahua City, Mex., 1949-51; field geologist to dist. geologist AEC, Grand Junction, Colo., 1951-54, chief geologist to v.p. S.W. ventures Ventures Ltd. and subs., Denver and Tucson, 1955-59; dist. geologist Utah Internat., San

Francisco and Tucson, 1959-61; geol. cons. Lowell Mineral Exploration, Tucson, 1961—, pres., Chile, 1985—, pres. Acuarios Mineral, Peru, 1991-96, chmn. Areguipa Resources Ltd., Can., 1993-96, pres. Exploraciones Mineras Lowell SA de CV, Mexico, 1998—, pres. Lowell Mineral Exploration LLC., Ariz., 1998—; mem. bd. dirs. Soc. Econ. Geologists Found., 1986-91. Lindgren disting. lectr. Soc. Econ. Geologists, 1978; cons. to numerous oil and mining cos., U.S. and other countries, 1961—, to nat. govt. orgn., U.S., Dominican Republic, Chile and Taiwan, 1961—; cons. retainer Bechtel Corp., San Francisco, 1976—. Assoc. editor Econ. Geology, New Haven, 1970-75. Recipient Disting. Citizen award U. Ariz., 1974, Soc. Econ. Geol. Thayer Lindsley Dist. Lectr., 1977, Silver Medal Soc. Econ. Geologists, 1983, Medal of Merit Am. Mineral Hall of Fame, 1994. Mem. Ariz. Geol. Soc. (pres. 1965-66), Am. Inst. Mining Engrs. (pres. Yavapai sect. 1957, Daniel Jackling award 1970), Can. Inst. Mining and Metall. Engrs. (disting. lectr. 1972), Internat. Assn. on Gensis of Ore Deposits, Mining and Metallurgy Soc. Republican. Episcopalian. Clubs: Mining of S.W. (Tucson) (dir. 1969-70); Prescott Country (Ariz.). Home: 789 Avenida Beatriz Rio Rico AZ 85648-2200 Office: Lowell Mineral Exploration 789 Avenida Beatriz Rio Rico AZ 85648-2200

LOWELL, LAURETTA JANE, craftsperson, poet; b. Gunnison, Colo., 1946; d. Howard Milton and Linnia Marie Lowell; m. Robert Bruce Campbell, 1994. Assoc. Gen. Studies, Pikes Peak C.C., 1987; student, Mesa State Coll., 1991. Nurses aide St. Francis Hosp., Colorado Springs, Colo., 1978-85; owner Light in Leather, Delta, Colo.; owner house cleaning bus. Colorado Springs, 1977-87; ptnr., co-owner Light in Leather/Green Knight Pub., Delta, Colo., 1996—. Author, pub.: Selected Poems of A Religious Nature, 1996, Sample a Poetry Treat, 1997; included in Best Poems of 1998 and numerous other anthologies (editors awards); lyricist Summer Song, 1998. Organizer reunion 1264th Army Engineer Battalion, Delta, 1991-93; leader 4-H, Colorado Springs and Delta, 1984-90; advocate for mental health issues Colo. Health Networks, Colorado Springs, 1996-98; advocate Columbine Group, 1992—. Phi Theta Kappa scholar, 1985, Colo. State Coll. scholarship, 1965. Fellow United Meth. Women; mem. Internat. Soc. Poets (life mem., Poetry Hall of Fame 1996). Avocations: camping, fishing, sewing, cooking, writing. Office: Light in Leather/Green Knight Pub 263 1575 Rd Delta CO 81416-9794

LOWEN, ROBERT MARSHALL, plastic surgeon; b. Detroit. MD, U. Mich. Med. Sch., 1971. Diplomate Am. Bd. Plastic Surgery, cert. surgery of the hand. Internship Pacific Presbyn., San Francisco, 1971-72; resident general surgery Stanford U. Med. Ctr., 1983-85; resident plastic surgery U. Okla. HSC, Okla. City, 1985-86; fellow hand surgery U. Colo. HSC, Denver, 1986-87, resident plastic surgery, 1987-88; pvt. practice Mountain View, Calif., 1988—; mem. staff El Camino Hosp., Mountain View, Calif., 1988—. Mem. Am. Soc. Plastic and Reconstructive Surgeons, Am. Soc. Lasers in Medicine aSurgery, Calif. Med. Soc., Lipoplasty Soc. North Am., Santa Clara County Med. Assn. E-mail: www.enhanced-you.com. Home and Office: 305 South Dr Ste 1 Mountain View CA 94040-4207

LOWENTROUT, PETER MURRAY, religious studies educator; b. Salinas, Calif., Mar. 14, 1948; m. Christine Ione, Sept. 30, 1980; children: Mary, Brandon. AB, U. Calif., Riverside, 1973; PhD, U. So. Calif., L.A., 1983. Prof. religious studies Calif. State U., Long Beach, 1981—. Contbr. articles to profl. jours. Capt. Orange County Fire Dept., Orange, Calif., 1977-94. Mem. Am. Acad. Religion (regional pres. 1989-90), Ctr. for Theology and Lit. U. Durham (Eng.), Sci. Fi. Rsch. Assoc. (pres. 1991, 92). Office: Calif State U Dept Religious Studies 1250 N Bellflower Blvd Dept Long Beach CA 90840-0001

LOWERY, TRUITT, retired educator, counselor; b. Lisbon, La., May 11, 1936; s. Hermie Davis and Frances L.; m. Eleanor Louise Wayne, Nov. 23, 1961; children: Sheila Denise, Sheuvonda Maria. BSc, Grambling State U., 1958; MSc, U. So. Calif., L.A., 1964; student, U.S. Internat. U. Dept. head bus. edn. and computer depts. Gardena H.S., L.A., 1965-93; tchr. Claiborne Parish Sch. Sys., Homer, La., 1958-60; stenographer State Dept. Edn., L.A., 1959-61; tchr. L.A. Unified Sch. and Cmty. Coll. Districts, 1961-96; with U.S./Internat. U., 1973-74; retired L.A. Unified Sch. Cmty. Coll. Districts, 1997—; Delegate to various profl. conferences. Author: Handbook For Church School Superintendents, 1973, Letterwriting For Business Education Teachers, 1975. Founder Bus. Edn. Dept. Haynesville (La.) High Sch., Computer Dept. Gardenia Sr. High, L.A.; mem. pastor's adv. com., sunday sch. supr., v.p. lay council Lewis Metropolitan Christian Meth. Episcopal Ch. Recipient several commendation awards Mayor L.A. Tom Bradley, Gov. Calif. Ronald Reagan, Congressman Robert E. Ferrell, Congresswoman Maxine Waters; NDEA grantee Alverno Coll., Milw. Mem. Nat. Bus. Edn. Assn. (western, Calif. chpts., state recognition award), United Bus. Edn. Assn., Inter-National Bus. Edn. Assn., Parents Tchrs. Students Assn., L.A. City Unified Schs. Counselors Assn., Delta Pi Epsilon (sec.), Gamma Rho Tau (v.p.), Alpha Kappa Mu. Democrat. Avocations: reading, playing piano. Home: PO Box 43603 Los Angeles CA 90043-0603

LOWI, ALVIN, JR., mechanical engineer, consultant; b. Gadsden, Ala., July 21, 1929; s. Alvin R. and Janice (Haas) L.; m. Guillermina Gerardo Alverez, May 9, 1953; children: David Arthur, Rosamina, Edna Vivian, Alvin III. BME, Ga. Inst. Tech., 1951, MSME, 1955; PhD in Engring., UCLA, 1956-61. Registered prof. engr., Calif. Design engr. Garrett Corp., Los Angeles, 1956-58; mem. tech. staff TRW, El Segundo, Calif., 1958-60, Aerospace Corp., El Segundo, 1960-66; prin. Alvin Lowi and Assocs., San Pedro, 1966—; pres. Terraqua Inc., San Pedro, Calif., 1968-76; v.p. Daeco Fuels and Engring. Co., Wilmington, Calif., 1978—; also bd. dirs. Daeco Fuels and Engring. Co.; pres. Lion Engring., Inc.; vis. research prof. U. Pa., Phila., 1972-74; sr. lectr. Free Enterprise Inst., Monterey Park, Calif., 1961-71; bd. dirs. So. Calif. Tissue Bank; research fellow Heather Found., San Pedro, 1966-. Contbr. articles to profl. jours.; patentee in field. Served to lt. USN, 1951-54, Korea. Fellow Inst. Humane Studies; mem. ASME, NSPE, Soc. Automotive Engrs., Soc. Am. Inventors, So. Bay Chamber Music Soc., Scabbard and Blade, Pi Tau Sigma. Jewish. Avocations: chamber music, jazz, photography, classic automobiles, motor sports, philosophy of science. Home and Office: 2146 W Toscanini Dr Palos Verdes Peninsula CA 90275-1420

LOWITZ, LEZA, writer, editor; b. San Francisco, Dec. 29, 1962; m. Shogo Oketani, Mar. 1995. BA in English Lit., U. Calif., Berkeley, 1984; MA in English, San Francisco State U., 1988. Lectr. San Francisco State U., 1988-89, Rikkyo U., Tokyo, 1990-92, Tokyo U., 1992-93; art critic Art in America, N.Y.C., 1990-94, Asahi Evening News, Tokyo, 1990-93; poetry revs. editor Japan Times, Tokyo, 1990—. Editor: (Japanese translation) Other Side River, Vol. II, 1995, A Long Rainy Season, Vol. I, 1994, Manoa, 1995; co-translator: Japan: Spirit and Form, 1994; translator: The Essence of Japanese, 1994; author poetry: Old Way to Fold New Paper, 1996. Recipient awards Nat. Endowment for the Arts, 1997, Benjamin Franklin award for Editl. Excellence, 1995, Pen Syndicated Fiction award 1989, Browning Soc. award in dramatic monologue, 1986, 87; grantee Calif. Arts Coun., 1997, NEH, 1994-95. Mem. PEN, Marin Arts Coun. (bd. dirs. poetry ctr. 1998—, contbg. editor MANOA 1990—).

LOWMAN, CARL DARRYL, financial executive; b. Phila., Dec. 1, 1962; s. Carl Norman and Delores (Guy) L. BBA, U. Mass., 1984. Budget analyst asst. The Gillette Co., Boston, 1984-85, adminstrv. and controls analyst, 1985-86, budget analyst, 1986-87; fin. analyst Continental Airlines, Inc., Houston, 1987-89, sr. fin. analyst, 1989-91, mgr. budgets and forecasting, 1991-95; treas., dir. fin. svcs. Western Pacific Airlines, Inc., Colorado Springs, 1995-98; treas. Mincom, Inc., Denver, 1998—. Recipient Multicultural Achievers in Bus. and Industry award YMCA of the Pikes Peak Region, 1996. Mem. Treasury Mgmt. Assn. Democrat. Episcopalian. Avocations: golf, skiing, traveling, the arts. Fax: (303) 940-6193. Office: Mincom Inc Ste 900 1675 Broadway Denver CO 80202

LOWNDES, DAVID ALAN, programmer analyst; b. Schenectady, N.Y., Oct. 28, 1947; s. John Henry and Iris Anne (Hepburn) L.; m. Peggy Welco, May 3, 1970; children: Diana Justine, Julie Suzanne. AB, U. Calif., Berkeley, 1969, postgrad., 1972-73. Acct., credit mgr. The Daily Californian, Berkeley, 1973-75; bus. mgr. The Daily Californian, 1975-76; acct. Pacific Union Assurance Co., San Francisco, 1976-77, acctg. mgr., 1977-78; sr. acct. U. Calif., San Francisco, 1978-88, programmer analyst, 1988—. Avocations: genealogy, microcomputing. Home: 1829 Gaspar Dr Oakland CA 94611-2350 Office: U Calif 250 Executive Park Blvd San Francisco CA 94134-3306

LOWRY, LARRY LORN, management consulting company executive; b. Lima, Ohio, Apr. 12, 1947; s. Frank William and Viola Marie L.; m. Jean Carroll Greenbaum, June 23, 1973; 1 child, Alexandra Kristin. BSEE, MIT, 1969, MSEE, 1970; MBA, Harvard U., 1972. Mgr. Boston Consulting Group, Menlo Park, Calif., 1972-80; sr. v.p., mng. ptnr. Booz, Allen & Hamilton Inc, San Francisco, 1980—. Western Electric fellow, 1969, NASA fellow, 1970. Mem. Sigma Xi, Tau Beta Pi, Eta Kappa Nu. Presbyterian. Home: 137 Stockbridge Ave Atherton CA 94027-3942

LOWRY, LINDA ELEANOR, artist, educator; b. Lubbock, Tex., June 30, 1956; d. David Auld and Stella (West) L. BA, Colo. Coll., 1978; postgrad., Sch. Visual Arts, 1978-79, Tyler Sch. Art, 1979-80; MFA, U. Colo., 1983. Instr. U. Colo., Boulder, 1982-91, Colo. State U., Ft. Collins, 1983-84, Rocky Mountain Coll. Art and Design, Denver, 1984-85, Colo. Coll., Colorado Springs, 1989-90, U. Colo., Denver, 1990; chair art dept. Arapahoe Cmty. Coll., Littleton, Colo., 1990-95, coord. painting and drawing, 1990-97; instr. Artreach, Denver, 1983-90; vis. artist Denver Art Mus., 1985, 1999; chair exhibition com. Colo. Gallery of Arts, Littleton, 1993-97; juror The Eleventh Congl. Art Competition, Denver, 1993, Congressman Shaeffer's Nat Scholarship Award, Denver, 1994, U. No. Colo. Student Show, Greeley, 1994. Author, illustrator: (book) Inside Colorado: An Artist's View of Colorado Interiors, 1993; one-person shows include Gallery 44, Boulder, 1993, Martin County Arts Mus., Stuart, Fla., 1994; exhibited in group shows at Indpls. Mus. Art, 1984, Viridian Gallery, N.Y.C., 1988, Denver Art Mus., 1983. Mem. arts adv. bd. Paul Mellon Arts Ctr., Wallingford, Conn., 1997—. Recipient Merit award Henry Hopkins, Artreach '88, Salt Lake City, 1988, Excellence award Artists of Colo., Denver, 1996; artist-in-residence Rocky Mountain Nat. Park, 1990. Mem. Coll. Art Assn., Arapahoe Cmty. Coll. Art Club (advisor 1990-97, Appreciation award 1990-95). Avocations: equestrian, gardener. Office: Arapahoe Cmty Coll Art Dept 2500 W College Dr Littleton CO 80120-1956

LOWRY, MIKE, former governor, former congressman; b. St. John, Wash., Mar. 8, 1939; s. Robert M. and Helen (White) L.; m. Mary Carlson, Apr. 6, 1968; 1 child, Diane. B.A., Wash. State U., Pullman, 1962. Chief fiscal analyst, staff dir. ways and means com. Wash. State Senate, 1969-73; govtl. affairs dir. Group Health Coop. Puget Sound, 1974-75; mem. council King County Govt., 1975-78, chmn., 1977; mem. 96th-100th congresses from 7th dist. Wash., 1979-1989; governor State of Wash., 1993-96. Chmn. King County Housing and Community Devel. Block Grant Program, 1977; pres. Wash. Assn. Counties, 1978. Democrat. Address: PO Box 4246 Seattle WA 98104-0246

LOWRY, WILLIAM PRESCOTT, meteorologist, consultant; b. Colón, Nov. 2, 1927; s. Porter Prescott and Margaret Johanna (Grosse) L.; children: Porter P. II, Samuel C. AB in math., U. Cin., 1950; MS in meteology, U. Wis., 1955; PhD, Oreg. State U., 1962. Physicist U.S. Corps of Engrs., Soda Springs, Calif., 1951-53; meteorologist Oreg. Forestry Dept., Corvallis, 1955-64; cons. USPHS, Cin., 1963; assoc. prof. Oreg. State U., Corvallis, 1964-72, U. Pa., Phila., 1971-72; prof. U. Ill., Urbana, 1972-81; prof. emeritus, 1981—; cons. Applied Meteorology & Climatology, McMinnville, Oreg., 1985—; owner Peavine Pubs., McMinnville, 1987—. Author Weather & Life, 1969, Atmospheric Ecology, 1988, Fundamentals of Biometeorology Vol. 1, 1989, Vol. 2, 1998. 1st lt. USAR, 1950-56. Recipient Achievement in Biometeorology award Am. Meteorol. Soc., 1998. Fellow AAAS.

LOYA, PRAXEDES, social services administrator; b. Riverside, Calif., Nov. 14, 1938; s. Jose Luz and Guadalupe (Arevalo) Loya. AA, Riverside City Coll., 1958; BA, San Jose State U., 1961; MSW, U. Washington, 1971. Adoptions supr. Riverside County, Riverside, 1972-89; social supr. II Riverside County DPSS, Riverside, 1989—; social svc. supr. II Riverside County, Riverside. Sgt. U.S. Army, USAF, 1963-68. Recipient Community Svc. award City of Riverside, 1980, 85. Mem. NASW, CSWO (past pres. and treas.), ERC, OIC (past treas.), CAAA (past nominations com.), LGFR (chmn.), CSSRC (bd. dirs.), CSA. Home: 5510 Magnolia Ave Riverside CA 92506-1819

LOYA, RANALDO, senior physician assistant; b. Whittier, Calif., July 1, 1954; s. Bernard Romero and Nora (Valverde) L. AA in Gen. Edn., Rio Hondo Coll., Whittier, Calif., 1980; BS in Health Sci., Calif. State U., Dominguez Hills, 1982; MHA, U. LaVerne, 1997. Cert. primary care physician asst.; cert. physician's asst.; cert. personal trainer IFPA; cert. sports nutritionist. Emergency med. technician, ambulance driver, attendant Adams Ambulance Co., South Gate, Calif., 1974-75; emergency room technician, clerk Maywood-Bell Cmty. Hosp., Bell, Calif., 1975; sr. physician asst. Physician Asst. Svcs., L.A., 1981-94; physician asst. urgent care Ball-Taft Med. Clinic Ctr., Anaheim, Calif., 1984-85; sr. physician asst., corp. v.p., admin. Signal Med. Mgmt., Long Beach, Calif., 1985-88; sr. physician asst. U. Calif. Irvine Med. Ctr., Orange, Calif., 1988-90, U. So. Calif. Emergency Med. Assoc., L.A., 1989-90, U. Calif. Mt. Zion Med. Ctr., San Francisco, 1990-94, La Clinica Esperanza Mission Neighborhood Health Ctr., San Francisco, 1991-94; fellow: Am. Acad. Physician Assts., Washington, 1982—; Calif. Acad. Physician Assts., Anaheim, 1982—; past mem. instl. review bd., Project Inform, San Francisco, 1991-92. Contbr. New England Journal of Medicine, 1990; mem. editl. bd. Clinician Reviews. Human rights commr., City of Palm Springs, Calif., 1996—; mem. Long Beach Pride, Inc., 1987-90, past v.p.; mem. Human Rights Campaign Fund, Washington, 1996—; mem. Orange County Gay and Lesbian Comm. Svcs. Ctr., Garden Grove, Calif., 1987-88; mem. adv. bd. The Desert Sun Newspaper Cmty.; mem. Dr. Martin Luther King Commemorative Day Com., Amnesty Internat. With USN, 1975-79, Hawaii. Recipient Meritorious Mast, USN, 1978. Fellow Physicians Assts. Latino Heritage; mem. NAACP, Nat. Assn. Mulitcultural Edn., Calif. Acad. Physician Assts. (minority affairs com.), Calif. Assn. Human Rels. Orgns., Nat. Trust for Hist. Preservation, Internat. AIDS Soc., Drew U. Med. Sch. Alumni Assn., Hispanic C. of C. Democrat. Mem. Unity Ch. Avocations: reading, public speaking, weight lifting. Home: 1179 N Calle Rolph Palm Springs CA 92262-4938

LOZITO, CAROL L., artist; b. N.Y.C.; d. Michael and Rita Theresa Lozito. Student, Sch. Visual Arts, N.Y.C., 1968-71, Acad. of Art Coll., San Francisco, 1985-86. Exhibited works at Zantman Art Galleries, Ross Watkins Gallery, Palm Desert, Artexpo L.A., Guide Dogs of the Desert, The Living Desert, Palm Desert, Regal Fine Art, Hollywood, Fla., Casino Art Gallery, Catalina Island, Calif., others. Recipient Best of the West award Southwest Art Mag., 1998, Assistance with Endangered Wildlife Conservation award, 1998. Mem. Palm Springs Desert Mus. (artists coun. 1998). Achievements include bringing the plight of the endangered wildlife to the public's awareness through colorful, unique and distinctly youthful style of art. Avocation: swimming. Studio: Endangered Wildlife Art TM 7660 Fay Ave H-298 La Jolla CA 92037

LU, GUIYANG, electrical engineer; b. Guiyang, China, May 10, 1946; came to U.S., 1982; s. Wen and Yunqiu Deng; m. Jing Du; 1 child, Jia. Degree in elec. engring., Tsing Hua U., Beijing, 1970; postgrad., South China U. Tech., Guangzhou, 1980-81; MA in Math., Calif. State U., Fresno, 1984; MSEE, Poly. U., N.Y.C., 1986. Instr. in elec. engring. South China U. Tech., Guangzhou, 1973-80; v.p. engring. Kawahara Corp., N.Y.C., 1986-88; H.S. math. tchr. N.Y.C. Bd. Edn., 1988-90; sr. R&D engr. Avid Inc., Norco, Calif., 1991—. Mem. IEEE. Home: 1718 Eastgate Ave Upland CA 91784-9210 Office: Avid Inc 3179 Hamner Ave Norco CA 91760-1983

LU, JIAN, computer scientist; b. Beijing, China, Dec. 13, 1962; arrived in U.S., 1988; s. Zhenshan and Rongbin (Guo) L.; m. Chessy Qi Si, Jul. 14, 1988. BE, Zhejiang Univ., Hangzhou, China, 1984; MS, Acad. Scis., 1987; PhD, Dartmouth Coll., 1993. Rsch. engr. Min. of Railway, Beijing, 1984-88; rsch. assoc. Univ. Calif., Davis, 1993-95; rsch. staff mem. Lawrence-Livermore Lab., Livermore, Calif., 1995-96; sr. scientist Apple Computer Inc., Cupertino, Calif., 1996—; cons. Naval Surface Warfare Ctr., Dahlgren, Va., 1993-94, VA Medical Ctr., San Francisco, 1994. Contbr. over 30 articles to profl. jours.; patentee in field. Mem. IEEE (sr., vice chmn. Santa Clara Valley chpt. 1997-99). Home: 979 Azalea Dr Sunnyvale CA 94086-6745 Office: Apple Computer Inc One Infinite Loop MS302 3MT Cupertino CA 95014

LU, MATTHIAS, priest, educator; b. Lu Kia-tun, Pao-ting, Hebei, China, June 2, 1919; came to U.S.; naturalized; s. Paul and Rose (Yang) L. Student, St. Vincent's Maj. Sem., China, 1937-38; PhB, Pontifical Urbaniana U., Rome, 1939, BTh., 1941, Licentiate in Philosophy, 1942, Licentiate in Sacred Theology, 1944, PhD, 1946; postgrad., U. Toronto, Can., 1948-56, Pontifical Inst. Mediaeval Studies, 1948-59, St. Francis Xavier U., Antigonish, Can., 1949-51; PhD (hon.), Scicluna Internat. U., 1987; ThD (hon.), Albert Einstein Internat. Acad. Found., Kansas City, Kans., 1993. Ordained priest Roman Cath. Ch., 1942. Lectr. in philosophy Fujen U., Peiping, China, 1946-48; asst. pastor, chmn. ednl. com. for parish co-ops Thorold, Ont., Can., 1951-56; instr. U. Notre Dame, Ind., 1956-58; asst. prof. St. John's U., Collegeville, Minn., 1959-62; asst. prof. St. Mary's Coll., Moraga, Calif., 1962-72, scholar in residence, 1973—, dir. St. Thomas Aquinas Internat. Ctr. for Everyone, 1974—; prof. U. Ottawa, Can., 1957-59; vis. lectr. St. Bonaventure U., N.Y., 1958-59, Cath. U. Paris, 1960; rsch. assoc. U. Calif., Berkeley, 1962—; chaplain Christian Bros. St. La Salle Schs., 1963—, local br. 11, Italian Cath. Fedn., Oakland, Calif., 1983—, Oakland coun. KC, 1978—; instr. Holy Names Coll., Calif., 1965-69; assoc. prof. John F. Kennedy U., Calif., 1966; vicar for Chinese and East Asian peoples Roman Cath. Ch., 1969-86; mem. Oakland Priests' Senate, 1972-75; vis. prof. Ignatius Inst., U. San Francisco, 1981-82; dir. Chinese transls. Lublin U. Internat. Transl. Ctr., 1984-86; cons. doctoral com. Union Inst. Grad. Coll., Cin., 1997—. Author, translator in field; also articles; producer program Stas. KUSF-FM, KSMC-FM, 1972—. Recipient Pro Ecclesia et Pontefice medal Pope Pius XII, 1939, Gold medal Pope John Paul II and Bishop of Oakland, 1985, Einstein medal Internat. Albert Einstein Acad. Found., 1988. Hon. mem. Mexican Cath. Philos. Soc.; mem. AAAS, Am. Philos. Assn., Am. Cath. Philos. Assn., Am. Oriental Soc., Am. Acad. Polit. and Social Sci., Cath. Theol. Soc. Am., Soc. Internat. pour l'Etude de la Philosophie Médiévale, Chinese Hist. Soc. Am., Internat. Soc. St. Thomas Aquinas, Internat. Jacques Maritain Soc., Internat. Soc. Metaphysics, Internat. Assn. Symbolic Logic, Internat. Soc. Chinese Philosophy, Internat. Assn. for Christian Thought, World Congregation of Bros. Christian Schs., (affiliated bro. 1988—), Internat. Assn. Educators for World Peace (vice chmn. spl. cons.), NGO, UNECOSOC, UNDPI, UNCED, UNESCO. Office: St Thomas Aquinas Internat Ctr St Mary's Coll PO Box 3014 Moraga CA 94575-3014

LU, MING LIANG, software company executive, educator; b. Xinbin, Liaoning, China, May 13, 1960; s. Chun Jiu and Shang Qing (Wu) L.; m. Wei Lin, Nov. 21, 1985; 1 child, Si. B of Engring., Dalian (China) U. Tech., 1982, M of Engring., 1985, D of Engring, 1989. Asst. lectr. Dalian U. Tech., 1985-86, lectr., 1989-91; rschr. Leeds (Eng.) U., 1991-94; sr. rschr. Tokyo Inst. Tech., 1994-95, assoc. prof., 1995-97; v.p. Aigis Sys., Inc., Newark, Calif., 1997—; cons. Japan Energy Corp., Okayama, 1994-97; presenter in field. Contbr. 70 articles to profl. jours., chpts. to books. Mem. Am. Inst. Chem. Engrs., Internat. Soc. Productivity Enhancement. Avocations: music, swimming, mountain hiking. E-mail: mingllu@aol.com.

LU, PAUL HAIHSING, mining engineer, geotechnical consultant; b. Hsinchu, Taiwan, Apr. 6, 1921; came to U.S., 1962; m. Sylvia Chin-Pi Liu, May 5, 1951; children: Emily, Flora. BS in Mining Engring., Hokkaido U., Sapporo, Japan, 1945; PhD in Mining Engring., U. Ill., 1967. Sr. mining engr., br. chief Mining Dept. Taiwan Provincial Govt., Taipei, 1946-56; sr. indsl. specialist mining and geology U.S. State Dept./Agy. for Internat. Devel., Taipei, 1956-62; rsch. mining engr. Denver Rsch. Ctr. Bur. of Mines, U.S. Dept. Interior, 1967-90; geotech. cons. Lakewood, Colo., 1991—. Contbr. over 60 articles to profl. jours. Rsch. fellow Hokkaido U., 1945-46, Ill. Mining Inst., 1966-67. Mem. Internat. Soc. for Rock Mechanics, Am. Rock Mechanics Assn., Mining and Materials Processing Inst. Japan, Chinese Inst. of Mining and Metall. Engrs. (dir., mining com. chair 1960-62, Tech. Achievement award 1962, merit award 1996). Achievements include development of prestressed concrete mine supports; invention of new technologies of rock stress measurement with hydraulic borehole pressure cells and measurement of geomechanical properties of rock masses with borehole pressure cells; invention of integrity factor approach to mine structure design. Home and Office: 1001 S Foothill Dr Lakewood CO 80228-3404

LU, WEI, telecommunications executive; b. Hangzhou, Zhejiang, China, Feb. 17, 1967; came to U.S., 1996; s. Xie Xiu Lu and Cui guan Cai; m. Jianhong Hu, June 6, 1992; 1 child, Dexi. B of Engring., Zhejiang U., 1989, M of Engring., 1991; PhD in Wireless Mobile ATM, U. of Tech., Kuala Lumpur, Malaysia, 1995. Chief designer UNITOP TELECOM, Hangzhou, Zhejiang, 1989-93; invited rschr., project leader wireless-ATM U. of Tech., Kuala Lumpur, 1993-95; guest scientist, project leader mobile-ATM German Nat. Rsch. Ctr. for Info. Tech., Berlin, 1995-96; sr. cons. CDMA-PCS Nortel/Lucent, N.J., 1996-97; dir. UTS Inc., Alameda, Calif., 1997—; sr. cons. ATM sys. Ministry of Sci., Tech. and Environment, Malaysia, 1994-98; sr. cons. ATM and broadband networkd interconnection Ministry of Post and Telecom., China, 1996-98. Prin. editor: (book) WM ATM 98 Proceedings, 1998; inventor and patentee in field; contbr. articles to profl. jours. Recipient 1st prize award China Inst. Sci. and Tech., 1993, Silver medal Nat. Computer Bd., 1996; fellow U. of Tech., 1993-95. Mem. IEEE (sr. mem., reviewer network arch. and switching sys., reviewer wireless ATM sys.), China Inst. Comms. (sr. mem.), Assn. Computing Machinery, Japan Inst. Electronics and Info. Engrs. (sr. mem.), Sigma Xi. Avocations: tennis, traveling, music, games. E-mail: wwlu@ieee.org. Office: UTS Inc 1275 Harbor Bay Pkwy Alameda CA 94502-6553

LUBATTI, HENRY JOSEPH, physicist, educator; b. Oakland, Calif., Mar. 16, 1937; s. John and Pauline (Massimino) L.; m. Catherine Jeanne Berthe Ledoux, June 29, 1968; children: Karen E., Henry J., Stephen J.C. AA, U. Calif., Berkeley, 1957, AB, 1960; PhD, U. Calif., 1966; MS, U. Ill., 1963. Research assoc. Faculty Scis. U. Paris, Orsay, France, 1966-68; asst. prof. physics MIT, 1968-69; assoc. prof., sci. dir. visual techniques lab. U. Wash., 1969-74, prof., sci. dir. visual Techniques lab., 1974-98; vis. lectr. Internat. Sch. Physics, Erice, Sicily, 1968, Herceg-Novi, Yugoslavia Internat. Sch., 1969, XII Cracow Sch. Theoretical Physics, Zapokane, Poland, 1972; vis. scientist CERN, Geneva, 1980-81; vis. staff Los Alamos Nat. Lab., 1983-86; guest scientist SSC Lab., 1991-93; mem. physics editorial adv. com. World Sci. Pub. Co. Ltd., 1982-93. Editor: Physics at Fermilab in the 1990's, 1990; contbr. numerous articles on high energy physics to profl. jours. Alfred P. Sloan research fellow, 1971-75. Fellow AAAS, Am. Phys. Soc.; mem. Sigma Xi, Tau Beta Pi. Office: Elem Particle Experiment Group U Wash PO Box 351560 Seattle WA 98195-1560

LUBECK, MARVIN JAY, ophthalmologist; b. Cleve., Mar. 20, 1929; s. Charles D. and Lillian (Jay) L. A.B., U. Mich., 1951, M.D., 1955, M.S., 1959. Diplomate Am. Bd. Opthamology; m. Arlene Sue Bitman, Dec. 28, 1955; children: David Mark, Daniel Jay, Robert Charles. Intern, U. Mich. Med. Ctr., 1955-56, resident ophthalmology, 1956-58, jr. clin. instr. ophthalmology, 1958-59; pvt. practice medicine, specializing in ophthalmology, Denver, 1961—; mem. staff Rose Hosp., Porter Hosp., Presbyn. Hosp., St. Luke's Hosp.; assoc. clin. prof. U. Colo. Med. Ctr. With U.S. Army, 1959-61. Fellow ACS; mem. Am. Acad. Ophthalmology, Denver Med. Soc., Colo. Ophthalmol. Soc. Home: 590 S Harrison Ln Denver CO 80209-3517 Office: 3600 E Alameda Ave Denver CO 80209-3111

LUCA, MARK, retired art educator; b. San Francisco, Oct. 14, 1918; s. Angelo and Jessey (Dorr) L.; 1 child, Angelo. BA with honors, San Francisco State Coll., 1940; MA, Columbia U., 1948; PhD, U. Calif. Berkeley, 1958. Cert. elem., secondary educator, Calif. Art instr. State Coll., Potsdam, N.Y., 1948-50; supr. edn. U. Calif., Berkeley, 1958-78; ret., 1978; exch. prof. U. London, 1969; art instr. Calif. Coll. Arts and Crafts, Oakland, 1978-88; edn. instr. Hayward State U., 1984-87, 89-90; instr. Columbia Pacific U., 1986—; art supr. (part-time) Castro Valley (Calif.) schs., 1964-65; coord. child art U. Calif. Ext., Berkeley, 1965; asst. dir./curator/edn. dir. Museo Italo-Americano, San Francisco, 1978-81. Artist: (painting and printmaking) exhibits of work in U.S., Mexico, South Am.; co-author: (textbook) Understanding Children's Art, 1967, Art Education, 1968; author: (state guides) Teaching Gifted Children Art Grades 1-12, 1973; contbr. articles to profl. jours. Cons. art and multi-ethnic edn. San Mateo County schs., 1970; radio readings Sta. KPFA-FM, Berkeley, 1970-71; art judge San Francisco pub. schs., 1969, 70, 71; cons. statewide humanities framework, Sacramento, 1970; bd. dirs. Youth-in-Arts, San Rafael, 1987-92,

Rohnert Park Assn. for the Arts 1994-95 (dir. visual arts FTA gallery 1996-97); mem., exhibits coord. North Bay Italian Cultural Found., 1995-97. Recipient mural scholarship Columbia U., 1948, internat. fellowship Mexican govt. Instituto Politecnico Mexico, D.F., 1951, U.S. govt. grants for E.P.O.C.H. project, 1968-72; named Outstanding Art Educator Calif. Art Edn. Assn., 1978. Mem. Calif. Tchrs. Assn. (life), Calif. Soc. Printmakers (founding, sec. 1968-98, historian 1972-73), Calif. Writers Club (pres. Berkeley br.). Democrat. Unitarian. Avocations: art, writing, walking, theater, music. Home: 300 Enterprise Dr #312 Rohnert Park CA 94928-7819

LUCAS, BETH ANNE, television producer; b. Grand Rapids, Mich., Sept. 15, 1960; d. Gordon Patrick and Phyllis (Sablack) Galka; m. Mark Fordham, Mar. 19, 1982 (div. 1985); m. Gus Lucas, June 3, 1991. BA in Psychology, Antioch U., 1995. Segment producer Breakaway, Metromedia TV, Hollywood, Calif., 1983; asst. dir. Anything for Money, Paramount TV, Hollywood, 1984; post prodn. supr. Heathcliff DIC, Hollywood, 1984; post prodn. supr. Beauty and the Beast, Witt-Thomas Prodns., Hollywood, 1986-88; assoc. producer Anything But Love, 20th Century Fox, Hollywood, 1989; assoc. producer Easy Street Viacom Prodns., Hollywood, 1984-85; mgr. post prodn. Matlock, Perry Mason, Father Dowling, Jack and the Fatman, Hollywood, 1990-91; project coord. Teen Dating Violence Prevention Team, Haven Hills, Inc. Vol. Children Are Our Future, Haven Hills Battered Woman's Shelter; mem. AIDS Project, L.A., L.A. Mission, Children Def. Fund. Mem. NASW, APA, NOW, Amnesty Internat., Am. Profl. Soc. on the Abuse of Children, Calif. Profl. Soc. on the Abuse of Children, Nature Conservancy, Nat. Parks and Conservation Assn., Feminist Majority, Nat. Abortion Rights Action League, Greenpeace, Smithsonian Assocs., Mus. Contemporary Art, Los Angeles County Mus., Sta. KCET, UCLA Alumni Assn., Child Help USA, Childreach, Mus. of Tolerance. Avocations: world travel, skiing, writing, wine tasting, cooking.

LUCAS, DONALD LEO, private investor; b. Upland, Calif., Mar. 18, 1930; s. Leo J. and Mary G. (Schwamm) L.; BA, Stanford U., 1951, MBA, 1953; m. Lygia de Soto Harrison, July 15, 1961; children: Nancy Maria Lucas Thibodeau, Alexandra Maria Lucas Ertola, Donald Alexander Lucas. Assoc. corp. fin. dept. Smith, Barney & Co., N.Y.C., 1956-59; gen., ltd. ptnr. Draper, Gaither & Anderson, Palo Alto, Calif., 1959-66; pvt. investor, Menlo Park, Calif., 1966—; bd. dirs. Cadence Design Systems, San Jose, Calif., Coulter Pharm., Inc., Palo Alto, Oracle Corp., Redwood Shores, Calif., Macromedia, San Francisco, TriCord Systems, Inc., Plymouth, Minn., Transcend Svcs., Inc., Atlanta. Mem. bd. regents Bellarmine Coll. Prep., 1977—; regent emeritus U. Santa Clara, 1980—. 1st lt. AUS, 1953-55. Mem. Am. Coun. Capital Formation (dir.), Stanford U. Alumni Assn., Stanford Grad. Sch. Bus. Alumni Assn., Order of Malta, Stanford Buck Club, Vintage Club (Indian Wells, Calif.), Menlo Country Club (Woodside, Calif.), Menlo Circus Club (Atherton, Calif.), Jackson Hole Golf and Tennis Club, Sand Hills Golf Club, Teton Pines Club, Bighorn Country Club, Calif., Zeta Psi. Home: 224 Park Ln Atherton CA 94027-5411 Office: 3000 Sand Hill Rd Ste 3-210 Menlo Park CA 94025-7119

LUCAS, GEORGE W., JR., film director, producer, screenwriter; b. Modesto, Calif., May 14, 1944. Student, Modesto Jr. Coll.; BA, U. So. Calif., 1966. Chmn. Lucasfilm Ltd., San Rafael, Calif. Creator short film THX-1138 (Grand prize Nat. Student Film Festival, 1967); asst. to Francis Ford Coppola on The Rain People; dir. Filmmaker (documentary on making of The Rain People); dir., co-writer THX-1138, 1970, American Graffiti, 1973; dir., author screenplay Star Wars, 1977; exec. producer More American Graffiti, 1979, The Empire Strikes Back, 1980, Raiders of the Lost Ark, 1981, Indiana Jones and the Temple of Doom, 1984, Labyrinth, 1986, Howard the Duck, 1986, Willow, 1988, Tucker, 1988, Radioland Murders, 1994; exec. producer, co-author screenplay Return of the Jedi, 1983; co-exec. producer Mishima, 1985; co-author, co-exec. producer Indiana Jones and the Last Crusade, 1989; exec. producer (TV series) The Young Indiana Jones Chronicles, 1992-93. Office: Lucasfilm Ltd PO Box 2009 San Rafael CA 94912-2009

LUCAS, JAMES BRUNO, public relations consultant; b. Berkeley, Calif., Nov. 15, 1950; s. James M. and Elizabeth A. (Pilorz) L.; m. Liesel C. Friedrich, Dec. 21, 1985; children: Charles M., Benjamin A. BA, Kenyon Coll., 1973; MA, Duke U., 1980. Accredited Pub. Rels. Soc. Am. Staff writer The Raleigh (N.C.) Times, 1978-80; sr. pub. info. rep. Met. Water Dist. So. Calif., L.A., 1981-84; copywriter Corp. Comm. Group, Marina del Rey, Calif., 1984-87; sr. account exec. Burson-Marsteller, L.A., 1987-89; cons. Lucas Corp. PR and Investor Rels., Santa Monica, Calif., 1989-90, 94—; dir. Pub. Rels. Health Net, Woodland Hills, Calif., 1990-94. Recipient 1st place investigative reporting N.C. Press Assn., 1979, Annual Report awards Fin. World Mag., N.Y., 1992, 93. Home and Office: PO Box 1305 Santa Monica CA 90406-1305

LUCAS, LESLEE SUZANNE, artist; b. Eureka, Calif., Mar. 31, 1963; d. Jack Frederick Jr. and Judy Joan (Johnson) Moore; m. Robert Scott Lucas, Feb. 4, 1989; 1 child, Aaron Matthew Lukosh. BS in Drawing with honors, Portland State U., 1986; MFA in Printmaking, U. S.D., 1988. Freelance artist Portland, Oreg., 1988—. Exhibited in show at Baird Purviance exhbn. Sonoma Arts Guild, 1993 (Bronze award). Vol. art tchr. Multnomah County Jail, Portland, 1994—; mem. adv. bd. Liturgical and Sacred Arts Ctr., 1993—, founding mem. Sanctuary for the Arts, 1998—. Named Vol. of Yr., Multnomah County Jail, 1996, Loon color publication award CIVA catalog, 1999. Democrat. Roman Catholic. Office: PO Box 6443 Portland OR 97228-6443

LUCAS, LINDA LUCILLE, dean; b. Stockton, Calif., Apr. 22, 1940; d. Leslie Harold Lucas and Amy Elizabeth (Callow) Farnsworth. BA, San Jose State Coll., 1961, MA, 1969; EdD, U. San Francisco, 1982. Dist. libr. Livermore (Calif.) Elem. Schs., 1962-64; libr. Mission San Jose High Sch., Fremont, Calif., 1964-69; media reference libr. Chabot Coll., Hayward, Calif., 1969-75; asst. dean instrn. Chabot-Las Positas Coll., Livermore, 1975-91; assoc. dean instrn. Las Positas Coll., Livermore, 1991-94, dean acad. svcs., 1994—; participant Nat. Inst. for Leadership Devel., 1991. Bd. dirs. Tri-Valley Community TV, Livermore, 1991-98, Valley Choral Soc., 1993-98, Chabot-Las Positas Colls. Found., Pleasanton, Calif., 1991-94; mem. needs assessment com Performing Arts Coun., Pleasanton. Mem. ALA, Coun. Chief Librs., Assn. Calif. Community Coll. Adminstrs., Calif. Libr. Assn. Avocations: choral music, photography. Office: Las Positas Coll 3033 Collier Canyon Rd Livermore CA 94550-7650

LUCAS, ROBERT ANTHONY, academic consultant, educator; b. Chgo., Aug. 11, 1939; s. John Jerome and Bernice Beatrice (Ludwig) L.; m. Nancy Beissner, Nov. 18, 1966 (div. 1978); children: Michael Steven, Daniel Edward; m. Wendy Carol Wayland, Jan. 15, 1989; children: Rachel Anna, Rebecca Kate. BA, John Carroll U., 1961; MA, U. Ill., 1963, PhD, 1970. Asst. prof. English dept. U. Mich., Ann Arbor, 1968-71, program rep. R & D adminstrn., 1971-75; dir. res. dev. Calif. Poly. State U., San Luis Obispo, 1975-86, assoc. v.p. grad. studies, rsch. and faculty devel., 1986-92; dir. Inst. for Scholarly Productivity, San Luis Obispo, 1992—. Contbr. articles to profl. jours. Mem. Nat. Coun. Univ. Rsch. Adminstrs. (mem. exec. com. 1990-91), Soc. Rsch. Adminstrs. Democrat. Roman Catholic. Avocations: singing, writing.

LUCAS, SUZANNE, statistician, entrepreneur; b. Baxter Springs, Kans., Jan. 16, 1939; d. Ralph Beaver and Marguerite (Sansocie) L.; children: Patricia Sue Jennings Melrose, Neil Patric Jennings. BA in Math., Calif. State U., Fresno, 1967, MA in Ednl. Theory, 1969; MS in Stats., U. So. Calif., 1979. Asst. to dir. NSF Inst., Calif. State U., Fresno, 1968; tchr. secondary math. Fresno city schs., 1968-78; statistician corp. indsl. rels. Hughes Aircraft Co., L.A., 1979-80; personnel adminstr. Hughes Aircraft Co. Space and Comm. Group, L.A., 1981-82, mem. tech. staff in math., 1982-85, staff engr., 1986-87; mem. tech. staff cost analysis The Aerospace Corp., 1987-90; sr. staff engr. Hughes Aircraft Co. Electro Optical Systems, [illegible] scientist engr., [illegible]; scientist engr. Raytheon Sys. Co., El [illegible] Manhattan Beach, Calif., 1989-97; pres. Lucas Enterprises, Manhattan Beach, 1993—; lectr. in biostats. U. So. Calif., 1979. Kiwanis scholar, 1958. Mem. Internat. Soc. Parametric Analysts (pres. So. Calif. chpt. 1991-92), Soc. Cost Estimating and Analysis (cert.), Am. Psychol. Assn., Am. Statis. Assn., U. So. Calif. Alumni Assn. (life), Kappa Mu Epsilon. Office: Lucas Enterprises PO Box 3868 Manhattan Beach CA 90266-1868

LUCAS, THERESA EILEEN, elementary education educator; b. Bellingham, Wash., Jan. 6, 1948; d. John M. and Lillian Sigrid (Westford) Cairns; m. Paul T. Lucas, 1970 (div. June 1987); children: Jeffrey Thomas, Aimee Michelle. BA, U. No. Colo., 1970, MA, 1985. Cert. elem. edn. grades K-6, spl. edn. grades K-12, Colo. Tchr. spl. edn. Baker Elem. Sch. Adams County Sch. Dist. 50, Westminster, Colo., 1970-77, tchr. 1st grade Berkeley Gardens Elem. Sch., 1978-84, tchr. kindergarten Harris Park Elem. Sch., 1984-87, tchr. kindergarten Tennyson Knolls Elem. Sch., 1987—; mem. sch. coms. Baker Elem. Sch., Berkeley Gardens Elem. Sch., Harris Park Elem. Sch., Tennyson Knolls Elem. Sch., Adams County Sch. Dist. 50, Westminster, 1970—; co-author literacy grant Adams County Ednl. Found., 1994, Gov.'s Creativity grant Tennyson Knolls Elem. Sch., 1989-90. Vol. Rainbows for All God's Children, Spirit of Christ Ch., Arvada, Colo., 1988-90, vol. crisis hotline, 1990-91; campaign vol. pro-edn. candidates, Arvada, 1992. Mem. ASCD, NEA, Internat. Reading Assn., Colo. Edn. Assn., Colo. Coun. Internat. Reading Assn., West Adams County Coun. Internat. Reading Assn., Westminster Edn. Assn. (membership rep. Tennyson Knolls Elem. Sch. 1990-95). Democrat. Avocations: reading, biking, dancing, walking, crafts. Home: 8279 Iris St Arvada CO 80005-2136

LUCE, R(OBERT) DUNCAN, psychology educator; b. Scranton, Pa., May 16, 1925; s. Robert Rennselaer and Ruth Lillian (Downer) L.; m. Gay Gaer, June 6, 1950 (div.); m. Cynthia Newby, Oct. 5, 1968 (div.); m. Carolyn A. Scheer, Feb. 27, 1988; 1 child, Aurora Newby. BS, MIT, 1945, PhD, 1950; MA (hon.), Harvard U., 1976. Mem. staff research lab electronics MIT, 1950-53; asst. prof. Columbia U., 1953-57; lectr. social relations Harvard U., 1957-59; prof. psychology U. Pa., Phila., 1959-69; vis. prof. Inst. Advanced Study, Princeton, 1969-72; prof. Sch. Social Scis., U. Calif., Irvine, 1972-75; Alfred North Whitehead prof. psychology Harvard U., Cambridge, Mass., 1976-81, prof., 1981-83, Victor S. Thomas prof. psychology, 1983-88, Victor S. Thomas prof. emeritus, 1988; chmn. Harvard U., 1988-94; disting. prof. cognitive sci. U. Calif., Irvine, 1988-94, dir. Irvine Rsch. Unit in math. behavioral sci., 1988-92, disting. rsch. prof. cognitive sci. and rsch. prof. econs., 1994—; dir. Inst. for Math. Behavioral Sci., 1992-98; chmn. assembly behavioral and social scis. NRC, 1976-79. Author: (with H. Raiffa) Games and Decisions, 1957, Individual Choice Behavior, 1959, (with others) Foundations of Measurement, I, 1971, II, 1989, III, 1990, Response Times, 1986, (with others) Stevens Handbook of Experimental Psychology, I and II, 1988, Sound & Hearing, 1993. Served with USNR, 1943-46. Ctr. Advanced Study in Behavioral Scis. fellow, 1954-55, 66-67, 87-88, NSF Sr. Postdoctoral fellow, 1966-67, Guggenheim fellow, 1980-81; recipient Disting. award for Rsch. U. Calif., Irvine, 1994. Fellow AAAS (chair elect psychology sect. 1998—, chair, 1999), APA (disting. sci. contbn. award 1970, bd. sci. affairs 1993-95), Am. Psychol. Soc. (bd. dirs. 1989-91); mem. Am. Acad. Arts and Scis., Am. Philos. Soc., Nat. Acad. Scis. (chmn. sect. psychology 1980-83, class behavioral and social scis. 1983-86), Am. Math. Soc., Math. assn. Am., Fedn. Behavioral Psychol. and Cognitive Scis. (pres. 1988-90), Psychometric Soc. (pres. 1976-77), Psychonomic Soc., Soc. Math. Psychology (pres. 1979), Sigma Xi, Phi Beta Kappa, Tau Beta Pi. Home: 20 Whitman Ct Irvine CA 92612-4057 Office: U Calif Inst Math Social Sci Plz Irvine CA 92697-5100

LUCENTE, ROSEMARY DOLORES, educational administrator; b. Renton, Wash., Jan. 11, 1935; d. Joseph Anthony and Erminia Antoinette (Argano) Lucente; BA, Mt. St. Mary's Coll., 1956, MS, 1963. Tchr. pub. schs., Los Angeles, 1956-65, supr. tchr., 1958-65, asst. prin., 1965-69, prin. elem. sch., 1969-85, 86—, dir. instrn., 1985-86, 1986—; nat. cons., lectr. Dr. William Glasser's Educator Tng. Ctr., 1968—; nat. workshop leader Nat. Acad. for Sch. Execs.-Am. Assn. Sch. Adminstrs., 1980; L.A. Unified Sch. Dist. rep. for nat. pilot of Getty Inst. for Visual Arts, 1983-85, 92—, site coord., 1983-86, team leader, mem. supt.'s adv. cabinet, 1987—. Recipient Golden Apple award Stanford Ave. Sch. PTA, Faculty and Community Adv. Council, 1976, resolution for outstanding service South Gate City Council, 1976, resolution for commitment to youth L.A. City Coun., 1996; named Woman of Yr., Calif. State Senate, 1997. Mem. Nat. Assn. Elem. Sch. Prins., L.A. Elem. Prins. Orgn. (v.p. 1979-80), Assn. Calif. Sch. Adminstrs. (charter mem.), Assn. Elem. Sch. Adminstrs. (vice-chair chpt. 1972-75, city-wide exec. bd., steering com. 1972-75, 79-80), Asso. Adminstrs. L.A. (charter), Pi Theta Mu, Kappa Delta Pi (v.p. 1982-84, hon. educator award, 1998), Delta Kappa Gamma. Democrat, Pi Delta Kappa. Roman Catholic. Home: 6501 Lindenhurst Ave Los Angeles CA 90048-4733 Office: Figueroa St Sch 510 W 111th St Los Angeles CA 90044-4299

LUCHETTI, CATHY LEE, writer, historian; b. Phoenix, June 10, 1945; d. Myles Anthony and Coralee (Waymire) Colligan; m. Larry Luchetti, July 20, 1970 (div. 1992); children: Zack, Jeremy John, Micah. BA, U. Utah, 1970. writer Hot on the Trail, TNN; cons. Secrets of Gold Rush, PBS. Author: Women of the West, 1982, Under God's Spell: Frontier Evangelists, 1989, Home on the Range: A Culinary History of the American West, 1990, I Do: Courtship. Love & Marriage in the West, 1994, The Hot Flash Cookbook, 1997, Medicine Women: The History of American Women Doctors, 1998. Recipient Literary Excellence award Pacific Northwest Booksellers, 1982, James Beard Best Writing Am. Food award, 1994. Democrat. Avocations: mountaineering, backpacking.

LUCHTERHAND, RALPH EDWARD, financial advisor; b. Portland, Oreg., Feb. 9, 1952; s. Otto Charles II and Evelyn Alice (Isaac) L.; children: Anne Michelle, Eric Alexander, Nicholas Andrew, Mistie Rose Beaudoin; m. Victoria Marie Schiffbauer, Nov. 8, 1997. BS, Portland State U., 1974, MBA, 1986. Registered profl. engr., Oreg.; gen. securities broker NYSE/NASD, CFP. Mech. engr. Hyster Co., Portland, 1971-75, svc. engr., 1975-76; project engr. Lumber Systems Inc., Portland, 1976-79; prin. engr. Moore Internat., Portland, 1979-81, chief product engr., 1981-83; project engr. Irvington-Moore, Portland, 1983, chief engr., 1983-86; ind. cons. engr., 1986; engring. program mgr. Precision Castparts Corp., Portland, 1986-87; personal fin. adv., Am. Express Fin. Advs., Clackamas, Oreg., 1987-94, sr. fin. adv., 1994—; ptnr. Bacon, Luchterhand Wilmot & Assocs. Divsn. of Am. Express Fin. Advisors, Clackamas, Oreg., 1996—; apptd. to Silver Team, 1991, Gold Team, 1994. Treas. Village Bapt. Ch., Beaverton, Oreg., 1988-91; bd. dirs. Carus Community Planning Orgn., Oregon City, Oreg., 1993—; active Rolling Hills Cmty. Ch., Tualatin, Oreg., 1995—. Republican. Home: 24440 S Eldorado Rd Mulino OR 97042-9629 Office: Bacon Luchterhand Wilmot & Assocs Am Express Fin Advisors 8800 SE Sunnyside Rd Ste 114 Clackamas OR 97015-5702

LUCKETT, BYRON EDWARD, JR., chaplain, career officer; b. Mineral Wells, Tex., Feb. 2, 1951; s. Byron Edward and Helen Alma (Hart) L.; m. Kathryn Louise Lambertson, Dec. 30, 1979; children: Florence Louise, Byron Edward III, Barbara Elizabeth, Stephanie Hart. BS, U.S. Mil. Acad., 1973; MDiv, Princeton Theol. Sem., 1982; MA, Claremont Grad. Sch., 1987. Commd. 2d lt. U.S. Army, 1973, advanced through grades to lt. col.; stationed at Camp Edwards E., Korea, 1974-75; bn. supply officer 563rd Engr. Bn., Kornwestheim, Germany, 1975-76; platoon leader, exec. officer 275th Engr. Co., Ludwigsburg, Germany, 1976-77; boy scout project officer Hdqrs., VII Corps, Stuttgart, Germany, 1977-78; student intern Moshannon Valley Larger Parish, Winburne, Penn., 1980-81; Protestant chaplain Philmont Scout Ranch, Cimarron, N.Mex., 1982; asst. pastor Immanuel Presbyn. Ch., Albuquerque, 1982-83, assoc. pastor, 1983-84; tchr. Claremont High Sch., 1985-86; Protestant chaplain 92nd Combat Support Group, Fairchild AFB, Wash., 1986-90; installation staff chaplain Pirinclik Air Station, Turkey, 1990-91; protestant chaplain Davis-Monthan AFB, Ariz., 1991-95; dir. readiness ministries Offutt AFB, Nebr., 1995-96, sr. protestant chaplain, 1996-98; sr. protestant chaplain Elmendorf AFB, AK, 1998—; mem. intern program coun. Claremont (Calif.) Grad. Sch. Contbr. articles to profl. jours. Bd. dirs. Parentcraft, Inc., Albuquerque, 1984, United Campus Ministries, Albuquerque, 1984, Proclaim Liberty, Inc., Spokane, 1987-90; bd. dirs. western region Nat. Assn. Presbyn. Scouters, Irving, Tex., 1986-89, chaplain, 1991-93; mem. N.Mex. Employer Co, in Support of the Guard and Reserve, Albuquerque, 1984, Old Baldy coun. Boy Scouts Am., 1980, chmn. Fairchild [illegible] Coop., Fairchild AFB, 1986-87; pres. Co. Grade Officers Coun., Fairchild AFB, 1987-88. Capt. U.S. Army Reserve; chaplain USAF Res., 1983-86, lt. col. 1998. Recipient Dist. Award of Merit for Disting. Svc. Boy Scouts Am., 1977. Mem. Soc. Cin. Md., Mil. Order Fgn. Wars U.S., Civil Affairs Assn. Presbyterian. Home: 4929 Castle Ct Anchorage AK 99508-4804 Office: 3 WG/HC 9824 L St Ste 101 Elmendorf AFB AK 99506-2630

LUCKMAN, CHARLES, architect; b. Kansas City, Mo., May 16, 1909; m. Harriet McElroy, 1931; children: Charles, James M., Stephen A. Grad. magna cum laude, U. Ill., 1931; LLD, U. Miami, Fla., 1950; AFD (hon.), Calif. Coll. Arts and Crafts, 1958; DFA (hon.), Adelphi U., 1986; LLD (hon.), Pepperdine U., 1989. Lic. architect, 1931 Registered architect, 48 states and D.C. sr. registration Nat. Archtl. Registration Bds. Employed in architect's office for license qualifications, 2 years; joined Colgate- Palmolive-Peet Co. as retail salesman, 1931, Chgo. sales supr., 1933; mgr. Colgate-Palmolive-Peet Co. as retail salesman (Wis. dist.), 1934; divisional mgr. Colgate- Palmolive-Peet Co. as retail salesman (Cin. hdqrs.), 1935; with Pepsodent Co. (later Pepsodent Div. of Lever Bros. Co.), 1935-50, sales promotion mgr., sales mgr., 1935-36, v.p. in charge sales, 1936, in charge sales and advt., 1937, v.p., gen. mgr., 1938, exec. v.p., 1942-43, pres., 1943-46; exec. v.p. Lever Bros., Jan.-July 1946, pres., 1946-50; pres., partner Pereira & Luckman, Los Angeles, 1950-58; founder, ptnr. The Luckman Partnership, Inc., 1958—; chmn. bd., chief exec. officer Ogden Devel. Corp., 1968-74, Luckman Mgmt. Co., 1973—; dir. Hollywood Bowl. Maj. projects include Madison Sq. Garden, N.Y.C., Conv. and Exhbn. Center, Los Angeles, U.S. World's Fair Pavilion, N.Y.C., Los Angeles World Zoo, U. Calif. at Santa Barbara, Civic Plaza, Phoenix, Prudential Center, Boston, State Office Bldg, Madison, Wis., Phoenix Civic Plaza, Los Angeles Internat. Airport, First Nat. Bank of Ariz, Phoenix, Broadway Plaza, Los Angeles, United Calif. Bank, Los Angeles, U. Del. Student Living Center, La Jolla VA Hosp, Aloha Stadium, Honolulu, 9200 Sunset Tower, Los Angeles, Manned Space Craft Center, Houston, VA Hosp, West Los Angeles, Calif., Hoover Library and Linear Accelerator Center, Stanford U., 1st Natl Bank of Oreg, Portland, Forum, Inglewood, Calif., Ralph M. Parsons Co. hdqrs, Pasadena, Calif., Nat. Security and Resources Study Center, Los Alamos, Hyatt Regency Hotels, Dearborn, Mich., The Harriet & Charles Luckman Fine Arts Complex, L.A., The Harriet & Charles Luckman Child Guidance Clin., L.A., Phoenix, City Hall and Police Bldg., Inglewood, Xerox Corp. hdqrs., Stamford, Conn., Warner Bros. Office Bldg., Burbank, Calif., Orange County Conv./Civic Ctr., Orlando, Fla.; also numerous other pub. bldgs; author: (autobiography) Twice in a Lifetime, 1988. Pres., chmn. bd. Los Angeles Orchestral Soc., 1962; v.p., dir. So. Calif. Symphony Assn.; mem. bd. assocs., pres. council George Pepperdine Found., Los Angeles; trustee Calif. State Colls.; chmn. bd. trustees, 1963-65; bd. govs. Library Presdl. Papers; trustee Nat. Art Mus. Sport; mem. U. Ill. Found.; Calif. mem. Ednl. Commn. of States; mem. bd. Am. Nat. Red Cross, YMCA; bd. dirs., past pres. AID-United Givers.; Mem. Pres.'s Commn. on Equality of Treatment and Opportunity in Armed Services and Civil Rights, Gov.'s Commn. Met. Area Problems; dir. Advt. Council; trustee Adelphi U.; chmn. Citizens Food Com., 1947; mem. Commerce and Industry Assn. N.Y.C., Los Angeles World Affairs Council, Com. Econ. Devel., Council U.S. Assocs. of Internat. C. of C.; bd. dirs. Nat. Adv. Council Community Chest, Am. Heritage Found.; bd. assocs. Northwestern U., Calif. Inst. Tech.; chmn. Nat. Council Trustees of Freedoms Found. at Valley Forge, 1986. Decorated Star of Solidarity Republic of Italy; chevalier Nat. Order Legion of Honor France; Order of St. John; recipient Horatio Alger award Am. Schs. and Colls. Assn., George Washington Honor medal Freedom's Found., 1964, 67, 68, Make Am. Beautiful award Nat. Assn. Realty Bds.; named Outstanding Mgmt. Exec. N.Y. Mgmt. Club, Man of Year Constrn. Industries, 1974; Disting. Achievement award U. Ill., 1970; Henry Laurence Gantt medal Am. Mgmt. Assn. and ASMF, 1981. Mem. AIA (Fellowship award 1963), Ill. Soc. Architects, U.S. Jr. C. of C. (One of Outstanding Young Men 1945, dir.), Tau Beta Pi, Theta Tau, Gargoyle. Home and Office: The Luckman Mgmt Co 9220 W Sunset Blvd West Hollywood CA 90069-3501

LUCZO, STEPHEN J., executive. CEO, pres. Seagate Tech., Inc., Scotts Valley, Calif. Office: Seagate Tech Inc 920 Disc Dr Scotts Valley CA 95066-4542*

LUDIN, IRWIN STEVAN, business/information technology consultant; b. Pitts.; s. Louis and Freda Ludin; m. Janet Lee Ludin; children: Melissa, Michael. BS in Indsl. Engring./Ops. Rsch., U. Pitts., 1971, MS in Indsl. Engring./Ops. Rsch., 1972; MBA, City U., Seattle, 1980. Instr. U. Pitts., 1971-72; engr. Westinghouse Bettis Atomic Power Lab., West Mifflin, Pa., 1973-77; mfg. analyst Boeing Co., Seattle, 1978-79, project planner, 1980-82, sr. systems analyst, 1983-89, sr. arch. info. tech., 1990—; v.p. Practical Creative Solutions, Inc., Redmond, Wash., 1995—; review bd. referee IEEE, Piscataway, N.J., 1996. Author: The People Side of Project Management, 1992, The DP Manager's Model Reports and Formats, 1992, The Noah Project: The Secrets of Practical Project Management, 1993, Just in Time Systems for Computing Environments, 1994, Stand and Deliver: The Fine Art of Presentation, 1995, Reducing Project Risk, 1997, Project Management Methodology: A Practical Guide for the Next Millennium, 1997, Project Management Practitioner's Handbook, 1998; asst. editor N.W. Artificial Intelligence Forum, 1994-95. Mem. Help Desk Inst., Software Support Profls. Assn. (exec. adv. coun. 1997-98). Avocations: music, reading, hiking. Office: Practical Creative Solutions Inc 10402 180th Ct NE Redmond WA 98052-7200

LUDIN, ROGER LOUIS, physics educator; b. Jersey City, June 13, 1944; s. Fredric E. and Gwendolyn C. (Rogers) L.; m. Diane E. Wilson, Aug. 26, 1966; children: Stephen L., Joyce E. BS in Physics, Brown U., 1966; MS in Physics, Worcester Polytech. Inst., 1968, PhD in Physics, 1969. Postdoctoral fellow Worcester (Mass.) Polytech. Inst., 1969-70; prof. Burlington County Coll., Pemberton, N.J., 1970-85; lectr. Calif. Poly. State U., San Luis Obispo, 1984—. Author lab. manuals for introductory physics; author computer assisted instrn. for gen. physics. Active Medford Lakes (N.J.) Bd. Edn., 1976-84, pres. 1978-84; bd. dirs. Medford Lakes Athletic Assn., 1974-84; soccer coach Morro Bay (Calif.) High Sch., 1985—. Named Tchr. of Yr. Burlington County Coll., 1982, 83. Mem. Am. Assn. Physics Tchrs. (sec., treas. N.J. sect. 1976-84, named Outstanding Contbr. to Physics Edn. 1984, editor So. Calif. sect. 1985-87, v.p. 1987-89, pres. 1989-92), Am. Phys. Soc., AAAS, Lions, Sigma Xi. Avocations: photography, coaching youth sports, camping, canoeing, acting. Home: 2691 Koa St Morro Bay CA 93442-1709 Office: Calif Poly State U Physics Dept San Luis Obispo CA 93407

LUEDTKE, ROGER A., lawyer; b. Wausau, Wis., Apr. 10, 1942. BS, U. Wis., 1964, MA, 1968, JD, 1974. Bar: Wis. 1974, Oreg. 1974. Atty. Schwabe, Williamson & Wyatt, Portland, Oreg., 1974—. Mem. Oreg. State Bar, Phi Eta Sigma. Address: Schwabe Williamson & Wyatt Stes 1600-1800 Pacwest Ctr 1211 SW 5th Ave Portland OR 97204-3713

LUEHRSEN, SANDRA LEE, former education administrator, artist; b. Chgo., Oct. 1, 1951; d. Kenneth Charles and Joyce Ruth (Schneeberger) L. BA in Art, No. Ill. U., 1973, MA in Art, 1976; MFA, Ariz. State U., 1979. Grad. asst. Sch. Art, Ariz. State U., Tempe, 1977-79, asst. dean Grad. Coll., 1979-98; artist, color designer Tempe, 1998—; juror Regional Women's Exhbn., Ea. N.Mex. State U., Portalis, 1993, Sculpture Commn., Tempe Art Ctr., 1995; awards juror Ceramics and Sculpture Mill Ave Festival of Arts, Tempe, 1997. Featured artist: The Best of Pottery, 1996, The Best of New Ceramic Art, 1997, and in jours.; exhibited in group shows Visual Arts Gallery, Phoenix, 1993, NCECA Conf., San Diego, 1993, Pima Arts Coun., Tucson, 1994, Ea. N.Mex. U., Portales, 1994, Downey (Calif.) Art Mus., 1994, San Angelo (Tex.) Mus. Fine Arts, San Angelo, 1994, 95, Babahatchie Gallery, Tempe, 1995, NCECA, Mpls., 1995, Art Mus. U. Memphis, 1995, Ariz. State U., Tempe, 1995, Auckland (New Zealand) Inst. and Mus., 1995, Shemer Art Ctr., Phoeniz, 1996, Adobe Patio Gallery, Las Cruces, N.Mex., 1996, Lincoln (Calif.) Arts, 1996, 98, Kennedy-Doublass Ctr. for Arts, Florence, Ala., 1996, Los Paisanos Galery, El Paso, Tex., 1997, 98, Guildford (Conn.) Handcraft Ctr., Inc., 1997, Pa. State U., University Park, 1997; featured in numerous publs. Bd. dirs. Tempe Art Ctr., 1997—. Recipient Merit award Feats of Clay Exhbn., Lincoln Arts, 1996, Merit award Ground Exhbn., Las Cruces Potters Guild, 1996, 98; selected Am. Crafts Coun. Libr. Artist Registry, 1997. Mem. Nat. Coun. Edn. Ceramic Arts, Color Mktg. Group, Ariz. Designer Craftsmen, Ariz. Clay. Avoca- [illegible] Home and Office: [illegible] Tempe AZ 85281-6409

LUEPKE, GRETCHEN, geologist; b. Tucson, Nov. 10, 1943; d. Gordon Maas and Janice (Campbell) Luepke; B.S., U. Ariz., 1965, M.S., 1967; U.

Colo., summer, 1962. Geol. field asst. U.S. Geol. Survey, Flagstaff, Ariz., 1964; with U.S. Geol. Survey, Menlo Park, Calif., 1967—, geologist, Pacific Br. of Marine Geology, 1976—. Registered geologist, Ore. Mem. U.S. Congress Office Tech. Assessment Workshop, Mining and Processing Placers of EEZ, 1986. Fellow Geol. Soc. Am. (Interdisciplinary Perspectives on the Hist. Earth Scis., Penrose Conf. 1994, Cordilleran sect. com. on geology and pub. policy 1998—); mem. Soc. Econ. Paleontologists and Mineralogists (chmn. com. libraries in developing countries 1988-91), Ariz. Geol. Soc., Peninsula Geol. Soc., Bay Area Mineralogists (chmn. 1979-80), History of the Earth Scis. Soc., Internat. Assn. Sedimentologists, Internat. Marine Minerals Soc. (charter), Geospeakers Toastmasters Club (charter, Competent Toastmaster 1995), Sigma Xi. Editor: Stability of Heavy Minerals in Sediments; Econ. Analysis of Heavy Minerals in Sediments; editor book rev. Earth Scis. History, 1989—. Contbr. articles on heavy-mineral analysis to profl. jours.; contbr. info. on offshore placer heavy-mineral resources to Circum-Pacific Map Project. Office: 345 Middlefield Rd Menlo Park CA 94025-3561

LUEVANO, FRED, JR., computer systems executive; b. Alamogordo, N.Mex., June 21, 1943; s. Fred Macias and Margaret (Baca) L.; m. Lupe Olmos, July 11, 1964; children: Michael, James Paul. AA in bus., Fullerton Coll., 1975; BA in Mgmt., U. Redlands, 1979, MA in Mgmt., 1985. Cert. data processing mgr., disaster recovery planner. Mgr. computer ops. Hoffman Electronics, El Monte, Calif., 1971-76; mgr. computer ops. and tech. services City of Anaheim, Calif., 1976-79; mgr. data processing Wyle Data Services, Huntington Beach, Calif., 1979-83; mgr. corp. computer ops. Northrop Grumman Corp., Pico Rivera, Calif., 1983, mgr. corp. computing, 1985—, dir. disaster revovery program, 1983—, dir. disaster recovery and security, 1988-90; Northrop Grumman Corp. Pico Rivera, Calif., 1990-92; mgr. data processing Northrop Grumman Corp., Pico Rivera, Calif., 1992—; cons. on info. sys., La Habra, Calif., 1971—; chmn. cert. bd. dirs. Disaster Recovery Inst., spkr., 1991-95. Cub master Boy Scouts Am., La Habra, 1979-84, chmn. com. 1975-79; councilman candidate City of La Habra Heights, Calif., 1982; pres. Red Coach Club, 1979-80, 86-88; pres. La Habra Parents for Swimming Inc., 1986-88; chmn. bd. dirs. Pub. and Pvt. Bus., Inc., 1998. Served with USN, 1961-65. Named Enterprise Sys. Mgr. of Yr., Assn. for Computer Ops. Mgrs.(AFCOM), 1998. Mem. Am. Mgmt. Assn., Telecom. Assn., Assn. Computer Ops. Mgrs. (speaker 1983-94), Northrop Mgmt. Club. Republican. Roman Catholic. Avocations: fishing, basketball. Office: Northrop Grumman Corp MS 770/XC 8900 Washington Blvd Pico Rivera CA 90660-3765

LUEY, BETH EDELMANN, editor, educator; b. Columbus, Ohio, Feb. 23, 1946; d. Abraham and Rita (Duker) Edelmann; m. Michael Laurence Luey, Jan. 28, 1967; 1 child, Anna Eleanor. BA, Radcliffe Coll., 1967; MA, Harvard U., 1968. Rsch. asst. Com. Study Orgn. of Peace, N.Y.C., 1968; mng. editor World Law Fund, N.Y.C., 1969-71; freelance editor Pitts., 1971-73, Tempe, Ariz., 1977-80; asst. then assoc. editor U. Pitts. Press, 1973-77; dir. hist. editing program Ariz. State U., Tempe, 1980-92, dir. scholarly pub. program, 1992—. Author: Handbook for Academic Authors, 1987, 3d edit., 1995, Editing Documents & Texts, 1990; editor Pub. Rsch. Quar., 1988-94, Documentary Editing, 1998—. Bd. dirs. Ariz. Ctr. Book, Phoenix. Mem. Soc. Scholarly Pub. (bd. dirs. 1994-98), Soc. History Authorship, Reading and Pub. (bd. dirs. 1997—). Office: Dept Hist Ariz State U Tempe AZ 85287-2501

LUFT, HERBERT, history educator, former dean; b. Frankfurt, Germany, Aug. 17, 1942; came to U.S., 1961; s. Theodor and Hedwig (Theismann) L.; married; children: Sebastian, Rebecca. BA, Pepperdine U., 1965, MA, 1966; PhD, U. So. Calif., 1976. Mem. faculty Pepperdine U., Malibu, Calif., 1967—, prof. history, 1982—, exec. v.p., 1981-83; dean European programs Pepperdine U., Malibu, London, Heidelberg (Germany) and Florence (Italy), 1983-93. Mem. Kiwanis, Phi Alpha Theta. Mem. Ch. of Christ. Home: 24255 PCH Malibu CA 90263-4225

LUFT, RENE WILFRED, civil engineer; b. Santiago, Chile, Sept. 21, 1943; came to U.S., 1968; s. David and Malwina (Kelmy) L.; m. Monica Acevedo, Aug. 24, 1970; children: Deborah Elaine, Daniel Eduardo; m. Laura J. Gigaute, July 11, 1998. CE, U. Chile, 1967; MS, MIT, 1969, DSc, 1971. Registered profl. engr., Alaska, Calif., Wash., Mass., N.H., R.I., Republic of Chile; registered structural engr., Vt. Asst. prof. civil engring. U. Chile, 1967-68; research asst. MIT, Cambridge, Mass., 1969-71, vis. lectr., 1983-84; staff engr. Simpson, Gumpertz & Heger Inc., Arlington, Mass., 1971-74, sr. staff engr., 1975-78, assoc., 1978-83, sr. assoc., 1984-90; prin. Simpson, Gumpertz & Heger Inc., San Francisco, 1990-91; head design div. Simpson, Gumpertz & Heger Inc., 1991-95; sec. seismic adv. com. Mass. Bldg. Code Commn., 1978-80, chmn., 1981-82; mem. Boston seismic instrumentation com. U.S. Geol. Survey; mem. slabs on ground com. Post-Tensioning Inst., 1994—, also chmn. structural subcom. Contbr. articles to profl. jours. Mem bldg seismic safety coun. Earthquake Hazards Reduction Program, 1983-91, chmn. rsch. com. 1987-88. Mem. ASCE, Boston Soc. Civil Engrs. (chmn. seismic design adv. com. 1981-86, Clemens Herschel award for tech. paper 1980, pres.'s award for leadership in earthquake engring. 1984), Am. Concrete Inst., Earthquake Engring. Research Inst., Structural Engrs. Assn. Calif., NSPE (Young Engr. of Yr., 1979), Sigma Xi, Chi Epsilon. Home: 206 Windsor Dry Petaluma CA 94952-7516 Office: 222 Sutter St Ste 300 San Francisco CA 94108-4445

LUHN, ROBERT KENT, writer, magazine editor; b. Oakland, Calif., Nov. 23, 1953; s. Joel Adrian and Norma Jeanne (Arnold) L.; 1 child, Pudge. Student, U. Calif., Davis, 1972-76. Freelance writer, 1968—; broadcaster, 1979-82; sr. editor PC World mag., San Francisco, 1983-90, contbg. editor, 1990-94; contbg. editor Calif. Republic mag., San Francisco, 1990-94, editor in chief Computer Currents Mag., 1994—. Author: The Swedish Catfish & Other Tales, 1979, Collected Works, Vol. 3, 1985, Going West, 1988, The Wit is Out, 1993; contbr. fiction, features and poetry to numerous pubs., including Harper's, Mother Jones, Omni, Am. Film, Hudson Rev., Nantucket Rev., Christian Sci. Monitor, San Francisco Chronicle, Chgo. Tribune, Phila. Inquirer, PC mag., Computerworld, The Oregonian, Exec. Update, Grapevine Weekly; columnist Computer Currents, 1993—. Adv. bd. mem. Baykeeper, San Francisco, 1994-96. Mem. ACLU, Amnesty Internat., Greenpeace, Environ. Defense Fund. Avocations: tennis, quoits, writing.

LUIS-WELLS, CYNTHIA JO, sports writer; b. San Diego, Dec. 28, 1954; d. Jose Amaro and Iva Pearl (Black) Luis; m. John Turner Wells IV, Aug. 10, 1985; 1 child, Christopher. BA in Comm., UCLA, 1977. Sports writer San Diego Sentinel, 1973, Pacific Daily News, Agana, Guam, 1978; sports editor Pacific Daily News, Agana, 1978-81; sports writer Honolulu Star-Bull., 1981-87, asst. sports editor, 1987-91, acting asst. mng. editor, summer 1989, sportswriter, columnist, 1991—. Voter Hawaii Sports Hall of Fame, 1997—; v.p. Lanikai Canoe Club, 1986-87, Panhellenic of Hawaii, 1987-90. Recipient column writing award Women's Sports Found., N.Y.C., 1988, sports writing award Kalos Kagathos, L.A., 1993; State honoree Nat. Women and Girls in Sport, N.Y., 1998; named Athlete of Month, Honolulu Quarterback Club, 1997. Mem. Soc. Prof. Journalists, Assn. Women in Sports Media, Internat. Surf Mus., Alpha Gamma Delta. Office: Honolulu Star-Bull 605 Kapiolani Blvd Honolulu HI 96813-5129

LUIZZI, RONALD, wholesale distribution executive; b. Neptune, N.J., Apr. 7, 1953; s. Alfredo Luizzi and Mary Kay (Mumford) Figart; m. Kim T. Richardson, May 14, 1994. BA in Psychology, Trenton State Coll., 1975. Pres., chief exec. officer Profl. Divers, Inc., Neptune, 1975-78; nat. dir. projects Nat. Assn. Scuba Diving Schs., Long Beach, Calif., 1978-81; sales mgr. TW Systems, Inc., Honolulu, 1981-85; gen. mgr. TW Systems, Ltd.-Kona, Kailua-Kona, Hawaii, 1985-97, Sobel-Westex, Hawaii, 1998—; East coast regional dir. Nat. Assn. Scuba Diving Schs., Neptune, 1977-78. Contbg. author: (tng. manual) Gold Book, 1977, Safe Scuba, 1977. Scuba advisor YMCA-Kona, Kailua-Kona, 1985—. Mem. Nat. Assn. Instnl. Laundry Mgrs. (cert.), Hawaii Assn. Instnl. Laundry Mgrs. (allied), Nat. Exec. House Keepers Assn. (allied), Hawaii Hotel Assn. (allied), Rotary (sec. 1988-89, v.p. 1989-90, pres. 1990-91), Kona-Kohala C. of C. Avocations: scuba diving, sport fishing, racquetball, jogging, exotic bird collector. Home: 76-6303 Kaheiau St Kailua Kona HI 96740-2275 Office: Sobel-Westex Hawaii 77-6429 Kuakini Hwy Ste C104 Kailua Kona HI 96740-2227

LUKE, DAVID KEVIN, investment company executive; b. Las Vegas, Nev., Dec. 14, 1960; s. Freddie Allen and Janet Anne (Shelton) L.; Lee-Ann Marie Petryshyn, Apr. 22, 1983; children: Krista Lee-Ann, David Nathan, Spencer Matthew, Ruth Alyssa, Zane Louis-Allan. BA, Brigham Young U., 1984; M of Internat. Mgmt., Am. Grad. Sch. of Internat. Mgmt., 1986. cert. investment broker. Cons. Internat. Small Bus. Inst., Denver, 1985; mgmt. trainee GM Can., Oshawa, Ont., 1986-87; supr. GMAC Can., Toronto, Ont., 1987-89; investment broker A.G. Edwards & Sons, Scottsdale, Ariz., 1989-96; portfolio mgr., assoc. v.p. investments Everen Securities, Inc., Scottsdale, 1996—; incorporator Protip, Inc., 1991-93. Instr. Ariz. Coun. on Econ. Edn., Tucson, Ariz., 1990-93; treas. Kyrene Schs. Cmty. Found., Tempe, Ariz., 1993-94, appointee Supt. Fin. Com., Advancement Chmn. 1994-95; scoutmaster troop 540 Boy Scouts of Am., 1996—. Mem. Ch. Jesus Christ Latter Day Saints. Home: 6135 E Gold Dust Ave Paradise Valley AZ 85253-1242 Office: Everen Securities Inc 7150 E Camelback Rd Ste 444 Scottsdale AZ 85251-1260

LUKE, NANCY ANN, lawyer; b. L.A., May 15, 1957; d. Teddy Edward and Coriene (Pfaeffle) L. BA, U. Tenn., 1980; JD, Loyola U., L.A., 1983. Bar: Calif. 1983. Law clk., assoc. Thorpe, Sullivan, Workman & Thorp, L.A., 1981-84; assoc. Parkinson, Wolf, Lazar & Leo, L.A., 1984-86, Sedwick, Detert, Moran & Arnold, L.A., 1986-89; assoc. Kirtland & Packard, Irvine, Calif., 1989-95, ptnr., 1996-97; pvt. practice Irvine, 1997—; cons. Assn. Calif. Cremationists. Mem. So. Calif. Assn. Health-Risk Mgrs. Avocations: working with troubled adolescents, writing and performing music, writing poetry. Office: 2102 Business Center Dr Ste 30 Irvine CA 92612-1001

LUKER, KRISTIN, sociology educator; b. San Francisco, Aug. 5, 1946; d. James Wester and Bess (Littlefield) L. BA, U. Calif., Berkeley, 1968; PhD, Yale U., 1974. Postdoctoral fellow U. Calif., Berkeley, 1974-75, asst. prof. sociology, San Diego, 1975-81, assoc. prof., 1981-85, prof., 1985-86, co-dir. women's studies program, 1984-85, prof. jurisprudence and social policy, sociology, Berkeley, 1986—; Doris Stevens prof. women's studies, prof. sociology Princeton (N.J.) U., 1993-95. Author: Taking Chances: Abortion and the Decision Not to Contracept, 1976 (hon. mention Jessie Bernard award), Abortion and the Politics of Motherhood, 1984 (Charles Horton Cooley award 1985). Bd. dirs. Ctr. for Women's Studies and Services, San Diego, Ctr. for Population Options, Washington. Recipient Disting. Teaching award U. Calif., San Diego, 1984; Guggenheim Found. grantee, 1985. Mem. Am. Sociol. Assn., Sociologists for Women in Soc. Office: U Calif Berkeley Jurisprudence & Social Policy 2240 Piedmont Ave Berkeley CA 94720-2151*

LUKER, LYNN MICHAEL, lawyer; b. Idaho Falls, Idaho, Aug. 30, 1953; s. Nephi Michael Luker and Betty Ruth (Schild) L.; m. Helen Marie Dahlquist, June 19, 1976; children: Daniel Jacob, Jean Marie, Rebecca Jane, David Alexander, Eric Carlyle, Rachel Elizabeth, Andrew Dahlquist, Emily Ruth. AB, U. Calif., Berkeley, 1977; JD, U. Idaho, 1980. Bar: Idaho 1980, U.S. Dist. Ct. Idaho 1981, U.S. Ct. Appeals (9th cir.) 1984, U.S. Supreme Ct. 1985, Utah 1986. Law clk. to presiding justice Idaho Supreme Ct., Boise, 1980-82; sole practice Boise, 1982-83; assoc. Goicoechea Law Office, Boise, 1983-85, ptnr., 1985-97; pvt. practice Boise, 1997—; mem. Idaho Appellate Rules Com., 1986-92; chmn. workers compensation sect. Idaho State Bar, 1993-95, chair, specialist cert. com. worker's compensation, 1995—; mem. Gov.'s Adv. Com. on Worker's Compensation, 1995-98. Editor-in-chief U. Idaho Law Rev., 1979-80. Calif. State scholar, 1974-77, Warren scholar 1979-80. Mem. Assn. Trial Lawyers Am., Idaho Trial Lawyers Assn. Republican. Mormon. Avocations: family, gardening, photography, German language, scouting. Office: Goicoechea Law Office 5400 Franklin Rd Boise ID 83705-1078

LULLI, BONNIE JEAN, medical group administrator; b. Cin., Jan. 1, 1943; d. Richard Roland and Mary Elizabeth (Kinzer) Lang; m. Arden Darryl Allen, Jan. 30, 1972 (div. Jan. 1988); 1 child, John C.; m. Gordon Agusto Lulli, Sept. 2, 1989. BA in Bus., Calif. State U., Northridge, 1965. Office mgr. Dr. Richard Clancy, Glendale, Calif., 1963-68; bus. mgr. Dr. Vivagene Loop, Glendale, 1969-75; bus. and office mgr. Dr. Robert B. Gold, Santa Ana, Calif., 1975-87; gen. mgr. So. Calif. Assoc. Plastic Surgeons-Expert Med. Mgmt. Corp., Anaheim, 1987-89; bus. adminstr. Meml. Cardiology Med. Group, Inc., Long Beach, Calif., 1990—; owner Physicians' Med. Ins. Billing Svc., Huntington Beach, Calif., 1975-90; mem. physicians' office mgrs.' task force Long Beach Meml. Med. Ctr., 1994—. Sec. Fountain Valley (Calif.) Youth Baseball, 1980-86; Stephen min., class instr. Roman Cath. Ch., Huntington Beach. Mem. Med. Group Mgmt. Assn., Profl. Assn. Health Care Office Mgrs. Avocations: snow skiing, working out, reading, travel. Home: 8771 Burlcrest Dr Huntington Beach CA 92646-4618 Office: Meml Cardiol Med Group Inc 2898 Linden Ave Ste 120 Long Beach CA 90806-1627

LUM, JEAN LOUI JIN, nurse educator; b. Honolulu, Sept. 5, 1938; d. Yee Nung and Pui Ki (Young) L. BS, U. Hawaii, Manoa, 1960; MS in Nursing, U. Calif., San Francisco, 1961; MA, U. Wash., 1969, PhD in Sociology, 1972. Registered nurse, Hawaii. From instr. to prof. Sch. Nursing U. Hawaii Manoa, Honolulu, 1961-95, acting dean, 1982, dean, 1982-89, prof. emeritus, 1995—; project coordinator Analysis and Planning Personnel Svcs., Western Interstate Commn. Higher Edn., 1977; extramural assoc. div. Rsch. Grants NIH, 1978-79; mem. mgmt. adv. com. Honolulu County Hosp., 1982-96; mem. exec. bd. Pacific Health Rsch. Inst., 1980-88; mem. health planning com. East Honolulu, 1978-81; mem. rsch. grants adv. coun. Hawaii Med. Svcs. Assn. Found., Nat. Adv. Coun. for Nursing Rsch., 1990-93. Contbr. articles to profl. jours. Trustee Straub Pacific Health Found., Honolulu; bd. dirs. Friends of the Nat. Inst. of Nursing Rsch., 1994-97. Recipient Nurse of Yr. award Hawaii Nurses Assn., 1982; named Disting. Practitioner in Nursing, Nat. Acads. of Practice, 1986; USPHS grantee, 1967-72. Fellow Am. Acad. Nursing; mem. Am. Nurses Assn., Am. Pacific Nursing Leaders Conf. (pres. 1983-87), Council Nurse Researchers, Nat. League for Nursing (bd. rev. 1981-87), Western Council Higher Edn. for Nurses (chmn. 1984-85), Western Soc. for Research in Nursing, Am. Sociol. Assn., Pacific Sociol. Assn., Assn. for Women in Sci., Hawaii Pub. Health Assn., Hawaii Med. Services Assn. (bd. dirs. 1985-92), Western Inst. Nursing, Mortar Bd., Phi Kappa Phi, Sigma Theta Tau, Alpha Kappa Delta, Delta Kappa Gamma. Episcopalian. Home: 3185 Waialae Ave Honolulu HI 96816-1511 Office: U Hawaii-Manoa Sch Nursing Webster Hall 2528 The Mall Honolulu HI 96822

LUM, JODY MAE KAM QUON, real property appraiser; b. Honolulu, Sept. 15, 1961; d. Joseph Tai and Alice Moi (Lau) L. BA, U. Hawaii, 1983. Cert. residential appraiser. Asst. appraiser Hanamura Appraisal Co., Honolulu, 1986-87; real estate staff appraiser Am. Savs. Bank, Honolulu, 1987-89; real property appraiser III City and County of Honolulu, Hawaii, 1989-90; real property appraiser IV City and County of Honolulu, 1990—. Active, profl. young adult co-leader Kalihi Union Ch., 1993-97. Named Outstanding Woman of Yr., 1991. Mem. Honolulu Chinese Jaycees (rec. sec. 1989-90, mem. devel. v.p. 1990-91, community devel. v.p. 1991-92, Woman of Yr. 1989-90, Outstanding Community Devel. v.p. 1991-92). Avocations: aerobics, reading Christian psychology, Christian Hula. Office: City and County Honolulu 842 Bethel St Honolulu HI 96813-4320

LUMAN, ROBERT M., protective services official; b. Long Beach, Calif., Nov. 8, 1934; m. Annette Luman; 2 children. MPA, U. So. Calif.; grad., FBI Nat. Acad., 1991. From patrol officer to dep. chief Long Beach (Calif.) Police Dept., 1968-96, chief of police, 1996—. Bd. dirs. Am. Heart Assn., Long Beach, ARC, Long Beach; active Long Beach Cmty. Partnership, Nat. Conf., St. Marys Bd. Trustees. Mem. Internat. Assn. Chiefs Police, L.A. County Police Chiefs Assn., Calif. Peace Officers Assn. (Law Enforcement Profl. Achievement award 1992), Long Beach Area C. of C. (bd. dirs.), Rotary. Avocations: fishing, boating. Office: Long Beach Police Dept 400 W Broadway Long Beach CA 90802-4401*

LUNA, B. MARTIN, lawyer; b. Waimea, Kauai, Hawaii, July 25, 1938. BA, Emory U., 1960, MA, 1962; LLB, George Washington U., 1967. Bar: Hawaii 1968, U.S. Dist. Ct. Hawaii, U.S. Ct. Appeals (9th cir.), U.S .Supreme Ct. Ptnr. Carlsmith Ball Wichmans Case, Wailuku, Hawaii. Office: Carlsmith Ball Wichman Case Mukai & Ichiki PO Box 1086 2200 Main St Ste 400 Wailuku HI 96793-1691*

LUNA, JAMES ALEXANDER, counselor; b. Orange, Calif., Feb. 9, 1950; s. Alejandro Alejo L. and Adlaide Julia (Osuna) Ramos; 1 child, Micah Alexander Fierro. BFA, U. Calif., Irvine, 1976; MS, San Diego State U., 1983. Instr. art U. Calif., Irvine, Davis, San Diego, 1983-95. Installation, performance and video artist. Recipient Bessie award for performance, 1991, WSAF award for sculpture; Rockefeller video grantee, 1992, Native Am. Pub. Broadcasting Consort video grantee, 1995. Home: Star Rte Box 150 Valley Center CA 92082 Office: Palomar Coll 1140 W Mission Rd San Marcos CA 92069-1415

LUND, JOHN WILLIAM, civil engineering educator, researcher; b. Berkeley, Calif., July 7, 1936; s. John Jørgensen and Lydia Marie (Olsen) L.; m. Jacqueline Lee Urling, June 1962 (div. Mar. 1985); 1 child, John David; m. Eva Odzganova, Nov. 3, 1990; 1 child, Thomas Erik. M of Transp. Engring., U. Calif., Berkeley, 1962; BS in Civil Engring., U. Colo., 1958, PhD in Civil Engring., 1967. Profl. engr., Oreg., Calif. Asst. prof. civil engring. U. Alaska, 1964-65; assoc. prof. civil engring., engring. tech. Oreg. Inst. Tech., Klamath Falls, 1967-97, prof., 1967-97, chmn. dept. civil engring. tech., 1977-80, assoc. dean, divsn. chmn. engring. techs., 1980-82, 83-87, rsch. assoc. Geo-Heat Ctr., 1975-97, dir. Geo-Heat Ctr., 1997—, dean engring. and indsl. techs., 1996-97; mem. Oreg. State Bd. Examiners for Engring. and Surveying, Salem, 1984-93, chmn. com. nat. fundamentals of engring., 1985—; cons. Zbinden Engring., Klamath Falls, 1984—. Author, editor: Geothermal Direct-use Engineering and Design Guidebook, 1998; author: Southern Oregon Cross Country Ski Trails, 1989. Mem. Oreg. Recreational Trails Adv. Com., Salem, 1990—; treas. Ross Ragland Theater Guild, Klamath Falls, 1992-94. 1st lt. U.S. Army, 1959-60. Mitsubishi fellow U. Auckland, New Zealand, 1995. Mem. ASCE, Am. Soc. Engring. Edn., Geothermal Resources Coun. (1st v.p. 1997-98, Geothermal Pioneer award 1997, pres.-elect 1999—), Internat. Geothermal Assn. (treas. 1995-98), Triaxial Inst. Asphalt Pavement Constrn. (hon.), Nat. Coun. Examiners for Engring. and Surveying (Disting Svc. award 1993). Democrat. Avocations: cross-country skiing, hiking, travel. Office: Oreg Inst Tech Geo-Heat Ctr 3201 Campus Dr Klamath Falls OR 97601

LUND, VICTOR L., retail food company executive; b. Salt Lake City, 1947; married. BA, U. Utah, 1969, MBA, 1972. Audit mgr. Ernst and Whinney, Salt Lake City, 1972-77; sr. v.p. Skaggs Cos. Inc., from 1977; v.p., contr. Am. Stores Co., 1980-83, sr. v.p., contr., from 1983, exec. v.p., co-chief exec. officer, vice-chmn., chief fin. and adminstrv. officer, pres., CEO, dir., 1992-95, now chmn., CEO, dir., 1995—. Office: Am Stores Co PO Box 27447 Salt Lake City UT 84127-0447 also: Am Stores Co 709 E South Temple Salt Lake City UT 84102-1205*

LUNDBERG, LARRY THOMAS, business executive; b. Pleasanton, Kans., Mar. 19, 1938; s. William Rex and Lucille Maxine (Rosebrook) L.; m. Sharon Colleen Kirksey, Jan. 26, 1957; children: Julie, John, William. BA, U. Wash., 1965; postgrad., Wash. State U., 1974-80. Cert. secondary tchr. Clerk G.N.Ry., Wenatchee/Seattle, 1957-65; tchr. Grandview (Wash.) Sch. Dist., 1965-66, South Kitsap Sch. Dist., Port Orchard, Wash., 1966-67; acctg. supr. Weyerhaeuser Co., Tacoma, 1967-69; pres., chief exec. officer Commander Bd. Wash., Seattle, 1969-70; asst. exec. dir. Wash. State Sch. Dirs., Olympia, 1970-80; gen. mgr., CEO Trout, Inc., Chelan, Wash., 1980—. Author: Negotiations, 1978. Bd. dirs. Traffic Assn., Wenatchee, Wash., 1987—; commr. Wash. State Apple, 1995. With U.S. Army, 1957-60. Mem. Internat. Apple Inst. (bd. dirs. 1988), Chelan, Wash. C. of C. (bd. dirs. 1989—). Office: Trout-Blue Chelan Inc PO Box 669 Chelan WA 98816-0669

LUNDBLAD, ROGER LAUREN, research director; b. San Francisco, Oct. 31, 1939; s. Lauren Alfred and Doris Ruth (Peterson) L.; m. Susan Hawly Taylor, Oct. 15, 1966 (div. 1985); children: Christina Susan, Cynthia Karin. BSc, Pacific Luth. U., 1961; PhD, U. Wash., 1965. Rsch. assoc. U. Wash., Seattle, 1965-66, Rockefeller U., N.Y.C., 1966-68; asst. prof. U. N.C., Chapel Hill, 1968-71, assoc. prof., 1971-77, prof. pathology and biochemistry, 1977-91; adj. prof., 1991—; dir. sci. tech. devel. Baxter-Hyland/Immuno, Duarte, Calif., 1991—; vis. scientist Hyland div. Baxter Healthcare, Glendale, Calif., 1988-89. Author: Chemical Reagents for Protein Modification, 1984, 2d edit., 1990; editor: Chemistry and Biology of Thrombin, 1977, Chemistry and Biology of Heparin, 1980, Techniques in Protein Modification, 1994; editor-in-chief: Biotechnology and Applied Biochemistry, 1996—; contbr. articles to profl. jours. Recipient Career Achievement award U. N.C., 1986. Mem. Am. Soc. Biochem. Molecular Biology, Am. Soc. Microbiology, Am. Heart Assn., Sigma Xi. Office: Baxter Healthcare 1720 Flower Ave Duarte CA 91010-2923

LUNDE, DOLORES BENITEZ, retired secondary education educator; b. Honolulu, Apr. 12, 1929; d. Frank Molero and Matilda (Francisco) Benitez; m. Nuell Carlton Lunde, July 6, 1957; 1 child, Laurelle. BA, U. Oreg., 1951, postgrad., 1951-52; postgrad., U. So. Calif., L.A., 1953-54, Colo. State U., 1957-58, Calif. State U., Fullerton, 1967-68. Cert. gen. secondary tchr., Calif.; cert. lang. devel. specialist. Tchr. Brawley (Calif.) Union High Sch., 1952-55; tchr. Fullerton (Calif.) Union High Sch. Dist., 1955-73; tchrs. aide Placentia (Calif.) Unified Sch. Dist., 1983-85; tchr. continuing edn. Fullerton Union High Sch. Dist., 1985-91; tchr. Fullerton Sch. Dist., 1988, Fullerton Union H.S. Dist., 1989-94; presenter regional and state convs., so. Calif., 1986-88. Innovator tests, teaching tools, audio-visual aids. Vol. Luth. Social Svcs., Fullerton, 1981-82, Messiah Luth., Yorba Linda, Calif., 1981-88, 91—. Recipient Tchr. of Yr. award Fullerton Union High Sch. Dist., 1989. Mem. NEA, AAUW (life, bull. editor 1979-80, corr. sec. 1981-83, program v.p. 1983-84, gift honoree Fullerton br. 1985), Calif. State Tchrs. Assn., Fullerton Secondary Tchrs. Assn., Internat. Club/Spanish Club (advisor La Habra, Calif. 1965-72), Tchrs. English to Speakers Other Langs., Calif. Assn. Tchrs. English to Speakers Other Langs. Avocations: singing, folk and interpretive dance, guitar, reading, travel. Home: 4872 Ohio St Yorba Linda CA 92886-2713

LUNDE, DONALD THEODORE, physician; b. Milw., Mar. 2, 1937; m. Marilynn Krick; children: Montgomery, Christopher, Glenn, Evan, Bret. BA with distinction, Stanford U., 1958, MA in Psychology, 1964, MD, 1966. Diplomate Nat. Bd. Med. Examiners. Ward psychologist Palo Alto (Calif.) VA Hosp., 1965-66, chief resident in psychiatry, 1969-70, assoc. chief tng. and research sect., 1970-72, acting chief tng. and research sect., 1971-72; intern in internal medicine Palo Alto/Stanford Hosp., 1966-67; resident in psychiatry Stanford (Calif.) U. Sch. Medicine, 1967-69, instr. psychiatry, 1969-70, asst. prof. psychiatry, 1970-75, dir. med. sch. edn. in psychiatry, 1971-74, clin. assoc. prof. psychiatry, 1978-89, clin. prof. psychiatry, 1989—, clin. prof. emeritus, 1997—; lectr. Law Sch. Stanford U., 1971-81; staff physician Atascadero (Calif.) State Hosp., 1968. Author books and articles in field. Served with USN, 1958-61. Fellow Am. Psychiat. Assn., Am. Coll. Forensic Psychiatry; mem. No. Calif. Psychiat. Soc., Phi Beta Kappa, Alpha Omega Alpha. Office: 1111 E Tahquitz Way Ste 121 Palm Springs CA 92262-0102

LUNDEEN, RONALD ARTHUR, theology educator; b. St. Paul, Sept. 17, 1943; s. Arthur Olaf and Marilynn Barbara Lundeen; m. Linda Kalmoe; children: Aaron, Nathan, Joel, Rachel, Margo, Karissa. BA, Luther Coll., Decorah, Iowa, 1965; MDiv, Luther Theol. Sem., St. Paul, 1969; DMin, San Francisco Theol. Sem., 1979. Cert. fund raising exec. ACFRE. Pastor Grace Luth. Ch., Duluth, Minn., 1969-71, Messiah Luth. Ch., Mankato, Minn., 1971-74; dir. planned giving Luther Coll., 1974-77; pastor Advent Luther Ch., Des Moines, 1977-80; dir. devel. Luther Sem., 1980-83; pastor Messiah Luth. Ch., Fargo, N.D., 1983-85; dir. of major gifts L.C.A., N.Y.C., 1983-87; pres. N.W. Devel., St. Paul, 1986-91; v.p. Luth. Social Svcs. of New Eng., Natick, Mass., 1991-96; v.p. for advancement San Francisco Theol. Sem., San Anselmo, Calif., 1996—; Pres. Northwest Devel. Counselors, Inc., St. Paul, 1985-91. Author: Stewardship and Fiscal Responsibility, 1979. Bd. dirs. Planned Parenthood, Minn., 1970-75, Luth. Youth Found., Mpls., 1985—, Fellowship, Inc., Phoenix, 1990-93. Mem. Rotary. Avocations: scuba, amateur radio, Køkwn, flying. Home: 54 Aaron Dr Novato CA 94949-5497 Office: SFTS 2 Kensington San Anselmo CA 94960

LUNDERVILLE, GERALD PAUL, bilingual education educator; b. Springfield, Mass., Feb. 22, 1941; s. Leon Albert and Florence Marion (Jolivette) L.; m. Martha Ann Sumner, Mar. 26, 1966 (div. Aug. 1971); m. Bony Lek, June 30, 1984. BA cum laude, U. N.H., 1963; MA, Middlebury

Coll., 1969, U. Rochester, 1973, Calif. State U., Long Beach, 1994. Instr. Spanish Berwick Acad., South Berwick, Maine, 1963-64; tchr. French, Spanish Barnstable High Sch., Hyannis, Mass., 1967-68; instr. Spanish Cape Cod Community Coll., West Barnstable, Mass., 1968-71; tchr. French, Spanish Stevens High Sch. Annex, Claremont, N.H., 1973-74; tchr. English Centro de Estudios Norteamericanos, Valencia, Spain, 1974-75; dept. head fgn. langs. Merrimack (N.H.) High Sch., 1975-80; tchr. Spanish El Camino Coll., Torrance, Calif., 1980-85; tchr. ESL Wilson High Sch., Long Beach, Calif., 1980—, dept. head ESL, 1987-88, tchr. bilingual social studies/ Spanish, 1992—. Author: 20th Century Baseball Trivia, 1992; contbr. articles to Am. Atheist Mag. Active Long Beach Area Citizens Peace, 1982—, Animal Protection Inst. Am., Sacramento., 1983—; mem. Civil War Round Table of Long Beach. Served with U.S. Army, 1964-67, Vietnam. Mem. NEA, ACLU, NOW, Modern and Classical Lang. Assn. So. Calif., Tchrs. of English as a 2d Lang., Soc. for Preservation of English Lang. and Lit., VERBATIM, Nat. Humane Edn. Soc., Merrimack Tchrs. Assn. (sec. 1977-80), Lambda Pi. Avocations: cooking, tennis, reading, travel, writing. Home: 1740 Washington St Long Beach CA 90805-5535

LUNDGREN, SUSAN ELAINE, counselor, educator; b. Martinez, Calif., May 31, 1949; d. Elmer Alfred and Shirley (Bright) L.; 1 child, Alicia Hadiya. AA, Diablo Valley Coll., 1969; BA in English, San Francisco State U., 1971, MA in Counseling, 1975; EdD, U. San Francisco, 1983; cert. in gen. mgmt., John F. Kennedy U., 1988. Instr., counselor Diablo Valley Coll., Pleasant Hill, Calif., 1976—, coordinator, 1986-90, women's ctr. faculty dir., 1983-85; adj. prof. grad. career devel. John F. Kennedy U., Orinda, Calif., 1982—. Sec., bd. dirs. Rape Crisis Ctr., Concord, Calif., 1985. Named participant in leadership devel. inst. AAUW and Nat. Assn. Community Colls., 1985. Mem. Eureka Consortium (conf. speaker 1984, 86). Avocations: camping, travel, photography. Home: 3738 Victor Ave Oakland CA 94619-1533 Office: Diablo Valley Coll 321 Golf Club Rd Pleasant Hill CA 94523-1529

LUNDIN, DAVID ERIK, lawyer; b. Middletown, Conn., May 8, 1949; s. Irving Erik and Majorie (Walker) L.; 1 child, Erik Stewart. BA, U. Redlands, 1971; JD, UCLA, 1974. Bar: Calif. 1974. Atty. advisor FTC, Washington, 1976-77; ptnr. Fredman, Silverberg & Lewis, San Diego, 1977-85, Sternberg, Eggers, Kidder & Fox, San Diego, 1985-87, Finley Kumble Wagner, San Diego, 1987-88, Lorenz, Alhadeff, Lundin and Oggel, San Diego, 1988-91; prin. David E. Lundin and Assocs., 1992—. Mem. bd. fellows U. Redlands, Calif., 1984-86; trustee San Diego Art Ctr., 1984-86, San Diego Bus. Innovations Ctr., 1992—, pres., 1994—. Mem. ABA (litigation and antitrust sects., pvt. antitrust litigation and antitrust exemptions com.), Western Behavioral Sci. Inst. (counsel 1981-86), Whispering Palms Country Club, Cotillion Club (sec. 1984-85). Mem. United Ch. Christ.

LUNDIN, JOHN E., lawyer; b. Mpls., May 9, 1940. BA, U. Ariz., 1962, JD with distinction, 1967. Bar: Ariz. 1967, U.S. Supreme Ct. 1977. Mem. Gallagher & Kennedy, Phoenix, Ariz., 1987—; judge pro tem Ariz. Ct. Appeals, 1984-85, 91. With U.S. Army, 1963-65. Fellow Ariz. Bar Found.; mem. State Bar Ariz. (v.p. 1991-92), Maricopa County Bar Assn. (bd. dirs. 1977-85, pres. 1984-85), Ariz. Commn. on Judicial Performance Rev., Phi Delta Phi. Office: Gallagher & Kennedy 2600 N Central Ave Ste 1800 Phoenix AZ 85004-3020*

LUNDIN, NORMAN KENT, artist, educator; b. Los Angeles, Dec. 1, 1938; s. John R. and Louise A. (Marland) L.; m. Sylvia Johnson; children: Kelly Jean, Christopher David. B.A., Sch. Art Inst. Chgo., 1961; M.F.A., U. Cin., 1963. Asst. to dir. Cin. Art Mus., 1962-63; instr. art U. Wash., Seattle, 1964-66, asst. prof., 1966-68, assoc. prof., 1968-75, prof., 1976—; vis. artist Hornsey Coll. Art, London, 1969-70; vis. prof. Ohio State U., Columbus, 1975; prof. San Diego State U., 1978; vis. prof. U. Tex.-San Antonio, 1982, Chelsea Coll. Art, London, 1996. Exhibited one-man shows, Francine Seders Gallery, Seattle, Space, L.A., Jack Rasmussen Gallery, Washington, Allen Stone, N.Y.C., Adams Middleton Gallery, Dallas, Allport Gallery, San Francisco, Stephen Haller Fine Art, N.Y.C., 1987-94, Schmidt-Bingham Gallery, N.Y.C., 1997, Koplin Gallery, L.A., 1997; group shows include Mus. Modern Art, N.Y.C., Whitney Mus. Am. Art, N.Y.C., Denver Art Mus., Seattle Art Mus., San Francisco Mus. Modern Art. Nat. Endowment Arts grantee; Fulbright-Hays grantee Norway, 1963-64; Tiffany Found. grantee, 1968; Ford. Found. grantee Soviet Union, Eastern Europe, 1978-79. Office: U Wash Sch Art Seattle WA 98105

LUNDQUIST, PEGGY ANN, editor, publisher; b. Chgo., Dec. 20, 1952; m. Richard C. Lundquist, Oct. 18, 1975. Student, Coll. of DuPage, 1970-71, Western Ill. U., 1971-72, Portland C.C., Rock Creek, Oreg., 1982-84. Draftsman Brighton, Wheaton, Ill., 1972-73; scheduling/project control exec. Brown & Root Engring./Constrn., Lombard, Ill., 1973-80; project control specialist Rust Engring./Constrn., Beaverton, Oreg., 1981-86; part-time libr. asst. St. Helens (Oreg.) Libr., 1987-90; part-time mcpl. clk. City of North Plains, Oreg., 1988-90; editor, pub., owner Black Sheep Press, Scappoose, Oreg., 1989; exec. dir. World Congress on Coloured Sheep, Eugene, 1986-89; coord. Black Sheep Gathering, Eugene, 1990—. Avocations: handspinning, shepherding, reading, weaving, photography. Home and Office: 25455 NW Dixie Mountain Rd Scappoose OR 97056

LUNDSTROM, MARJIE, newspaper editor. Grad., U. Nebr. Columnist, editor, nat. corr. The Denver Post, 1981-89; with The Sacramento Bee, 1989-90, 91—; nat. corr. Gannett News Svc., Washington, 1990-91. Recipient Pulitzer Prize for nat. reporting, 1991. Office: The Sacramento Bee PO Box 15779 Sacramento CA 95852-0779

LUNDY, BARBARA JEAN, training executive; b. Chgo., Feb. 2, 1950. Cert. mediator U. Denver. Tchr., facilitator Red Rocks C.C., Golden, Colo., 1986-90, AMI, St. Lukes Hosp., Denver, 1986-90; tchr. Arapaho C.C., Denver, 1991-95; tng. mgr. Denver Options, 1995—. Author, editor Market Mountain Writers, 1978-81; co-author: You Can Collect Child Support, 1989. Profl. vol. VIDA Vols., Pueblo, Colo., 1971-73; vol. dir. Legal Aid Soc., Denver, 1980-85; bd. mem., editl. bd. Colo. Women's Polit. Caucus, Denver, 1980-81; state commn. mem. Colo. Child Support Commn., Denver, 1984-85; co-founder Kids in Need Support (KINS), Denver, 1986-87; com. mem. Denver Dist. Ct.: Bench, Bar, Cmty. Rels. Com., Denver, 1987-89. Mem. Assn. Persons Supported Employment (spkr. nat. conv. 1998), Hayna Writers. Avocations: science, history and philosophy reading, piano, writing. Office: Denver Options 5250 Leetsdale Dr Ste 200 Denver CO 80246-1451

LUNDY, GILBERT MOULTON, JR., computer science educator; b. New Orleans, Sept. 29, 1954; s. Gilbert Moulton and Loretta Maureen (Taylor) L.; m. Yong Ae Yi, Feb. 18, 1978 (div. 1988); children: Benjamin Lee, Miriam Yong. BA in Math., Tex. A&M U., 1976; MS in Computer Sci., U. Tex., Dallas, 1983; PhD in Computer Sci., Ga. Inst. Tech., 1988. Software engr. E-Systems, Inc., Dallas, 1981-84; rsch. asst. Ga. Inst. Tech., Atlanta, 1984-88; assoc. prof. computer sci. U.S. Naval Postgrad. Sch., Monterey, Calif., 1988—. Contbr. articles on computer and telecom. networks to sci. jours. 1st lt. U.S. Army, 1977-81. Mem. IEEE, Assn. for Computing Machinery. Avocations: running, hiking, camping, various sports, reading. Office: US Naval Postgrad Sch Dept Computer Sci Code CS Monterey CA 93943

LUNDY-SLADE, BETTIE B., retired electronics professional; b. Marinette, Wis., Feb. 16, 1924; d. Adolph Gustav and Bertha Julian (Keller) Limberg; m. George Wesley Lundy II, Nov. 11, 1951 (div. 1956); children: George Wesley III, Genise Wynell, Charles Edward; m. Jim Donovan Slade, July 20, 1973. Lic. vocat. nurse, psychiat. technician, Calif. With Allis Chalmers, Milw., 1942-44, Gen. Dynamics, San Diego, 1959-65, Tetedyne Ryan, San Diego, 1966-76, Cubic, San Diego, 1976-86; ret., 1986. Author: (poetry) Do You Have a Minute, 1991, (biography) Growing Up on a Farm During the Depression, 1995; artist over 100 paintings, 1986—. Den mother Boy Scouts Am., San Diego; Sunday sch. tchr. Luth. Ch., San Diego. With USN Waves, [illegible] Appreciation Mother Teresa, 1992, Gen. Norman Schwarzkoph, 1993, Queen Elizabeth, 1993. Mem. Internat. Soc. Poets (life), Nat. Parks & Conservation, Smithsonian Assocs., Peal Ctr. Christian Living, Nat. Audubon Soc., Nat. Mus. Women in Arts. Republican. Avocations: soft sculpture, crocheting, short stories and poetry, , oil, acrylic and water color painting. Home: 6315 Thorn St San Diego CA 92115-6908

LUNSFORD, MORLAN HOWARD, toxicology laboratory technician; b. Sasebo, Japan, May 3, 1973; arrived in U.S., 1973; s. Dalton William and Mutsuko (Kobayashi) L. Diploma, David Starr Jordan, Long Beach, Calif., 1991. Lab. technician Specialty Labs., Inc., Santa Monica, Calif., 1994—; ptnr. Romantic Nights, Culver City, Calif., 1995-96. Crew chief Long Beach Search & Rescue, Long Beach, Calif., 1989-91. Republican. Avocations: violin, opera, chemistry, travel.

LUO, YIQI, ecologist, researcher; b. Yixin, Jiangsu, China, May 26, 1957; came to U.S., 1985; s. Tongshen and Zhongmei (Yu) L.; m. Aimin Yang, Jan. 16, 1984; children: Jessica, Peter. BS in Agronomy, Yangzhou (China) U., 1982; PhD in Ecology, U. Calif., Davis, 1991. Lectr. Jiangsu Agrl. Coll., 1982-85; vis. scholar U. Calif., Davis, 1985-86, grad. rsch. asst., 1986-91; postdoctoral fellow UCLA, 1991-92, Stanford (Calif.) U., 1992-94; asst. rsch. prof. Desert Rsch. Inst., Reno, 1994-97, assoc. rsch. prof., 1997—; adj. asst. prof. U. Nev., Reno, 1994—. Editor: Carbon Dioxide and Environmental Stress, 1997; contbr. articles to profl. jours. Recipient Oversea Study scholarship Chinese Edn. Commn., 1985, Rsch. grants NSF, U.S. Dept. Energy and USDA, 1994—. Mem. AAAS, Am. Geophysical Union, Ecol. Soc. Am., Am. Assn. Agronomy. Achievements include discovery of a universally invariant function for quantifying global terrestrial carbon flux; developed a global terrestrial ecosystem model which predicts the potential carbon sink is possibly 2.5 times the "missing" sink; identified a mechanism in controlling photosynthetic acclimation to elevated CO_2. Office: Desert Rsch Inst 7010 Dandini Blvd Reno NV 89512-3998

LUONGO, JOHN R., executive. Pres., CEO Vantive Corp., Santa Clara, Calif. Office: 2455 Augustine Dr Santa Clara CA 95054-3002*

LURVEY, IRA HAROLD, lawyer; b. Chgo., Apr. 6, 1935; s. Louis and Faye (Grey) L.; m. Barbara Ann Sirvint, June 24, 1962; children: Nathana, Lawrence, Jennifer, Jonathan, David, Robert. BS, U. Ill., 1956; MS, Northwestern U., 1961; JD, U. Calif., Berkeley, 1965. Bar: Calif. 1965, Nev. 1966, U.S. Dist. Ct. (cen. dist.) Calif. 1966, U.S. Tax Ct. 1966, U.S. Ct. Appeals (9th cir.) 1966, U.S. Supreme Ct. 1975. Law clk. to hon. justices Nev. Supreme Ct., Carson City, 1965-66; from assoc. to ptnr. Pacht, Ross, Warne, Bernhard & Sears, Inc., 1966-84; predecessor firm Shea & Gould, L.A.; founding ptnr. Lurvey & Shapiro, L.A., 1984—; lectr. legal edn. programs; mem. Chief Justice's Commns. on Ct. Reform, Weighted Caseloads; mediator family law L.A. Superior Ct. Editor Community Property Jour., 1979-80, Primary Consultant CFL 2d, 1994; columnist Calif. Family Law Monthly; contbr. articles to profl. jours. Former chmn. L.A. Jr. Arts Ctr.; past pres. Cheviot Hills Homeowners Assn.; exec. v.p., counsel Hillel Acad. Sch., Beverly Hills, Calif., 1977—. With U.S. Army, 1957-58. Fellow Am. Acad. Matrimonial Lawyers (pres. So. Calif. chpt. 1991-92, mem. nat. bd. govs. 1992-94), Internat. Acad. Matrimonial Lawyers; mem. ABA (chair family law sect. 1996-97, liaison family law to sr. lawyers' divsn. 1998—, exec. com. 1991-97, governing coun. 1986—, fin. officer 1991-92, chmn. support com., chmn. CLE, chmn. policy and issues com., vice chmn. com. arbitration and mediation, bd. of editors Family Adv. mag.), Calif. Bar Assn. (editor jour. 1982-85, chmn. family law sect. 1986-87, exec. com. family law sect. 1982-88, specialization adv. bd. family law 1979-82), L.A. County Bar Assn. (chmn. family law sect. 1981-82, exec. com. family law 1989-92), Beverly Hills Bar Assn. (chmn. family law sect. 1976-77). Home: 2729 Motor Ave Los Angeles CA 90064-3441 Office: Lurvey & Shapiro Ste 1550 1333 Beverly Green Drive Los Angeles CA 90035-1018

LUSH, PAMELA GRACE MEINE, international publishing company executive; b. Wellsboro, Pa., Apr. 1, 1961; d. Stanley Gale and Karen (Kohler) L. BA, Colo. State U., 1983. Traffic coord. Leo Burnett Advt., Chgo., 1983-85; sr. account exec. Cardiff Pub., Englewood, Colo., 1985-88; pres. PGL Assocs., Denver, 1988-90; v.p. Interfax-US, Denver, 1991-92; pres. DGL Internat. Pub., Denver, 1990-93, DGL Publs., Denver, 1990-93. Editor, pub.: The Child Care Directory, 1991; pub.: The Family Resource Guide, 1992, The Petroleum Tech. Resource Guide, 1992, The Agricultural Technical Resource Guide, 1992, The Mining/Environmental Technical Resource Guide, 1992. Mem. Soviet Task Force Under Gov. Roy Romer, Denver, 1990-92, Internat. Gateway Com., Denver, 1990-92. Named nominee for Pulitzer Prize for Internat. Reporting, 1991, Pulitzer Prize for Meritorious Pub. Svc., 1991. Presbyterian. Avocations: tennis, skiing.

LUSHECK, CATHERINE, art historian, consultant; b. Cin., July 5, 1965; d. Kenneth A. and Elizabeth Emma (Schmolt) L. Student, U. Strasbourg, France, 1985-86; BA, DePauw U., 1987; MA, U. Calif., Berkeley, 1992, postgrad. Intern Internat. Inst. Human Rights, Coun. Europe, Strasbourg, 1985-86; program coord. Face-to-Face Carnegie Endowment for Internat. Peace, Washington, 1988-90; rsch. asst. history of art U. Calif., Berkeley, 1991-92, 93-94; grad. intern dept. European drawings J. Paul Getty Mus., Malibu, Calif., 1992-93; asst. curator Reliance Group Holdings, Inc., N.Y.C., 1994-97; instr. history of art, writing and visual experience U. Calif., Berkeley, 1998—; grad. intern Nat. Mus. Am. Art, Smithsonian Instn., Washington, 1989-90; grad. student instr. U. Calif., Berkeley, 1992-93; art history lectr. Oxford U. Summer Programs, Paris, 1996; art cons. Roudnice Lobkowicz Found., Prague, Czech Republic, 1998; lectr. in field. Co-editor, contbr. (catalogue) The Saul P. and Gayfred Steinberg Collection, 1997; author (rsch. summary) Mode and Manner in the Drawings of Peter Paul Rubens, 1998. Med. team translator DePauw U. Winter Term in Mission, L'Acul, Haiti, 1985. Chester Dale predoctoral fellow Met. Mus. Art, N.Y.C., 1994-95; predoctoral fellow Belgian-Am. Ednl. Found., Brussels, 1995-96; Robert H. and Clarice Smith predoctoral fellow Ctr. for Advanced Study in the Visual Arts, Washington, 1996-97. Mem. Am. Assn. Mus., Historians Netherlandish Art, Coll. Art Assn., Phi Beta Kappa. Avocations: sailing, travel writing, hiking, yoga. E-mail: klusheck@socrates.berkeley.edu. Home: 1793 Northwood Ct Oakland CA 94611-1167 Office: U Calif Dept History Art 405 Doe Library Berkeley CA 94720-6020

LUSKY, JOHN A., lawyer; b. Louisville, Oct. 30, 1951. BA, Harvard U., 1973; JD, Stanford U., 1977. Bar: Oreg. 1977. Ptnr. Miller, Nash, Wiener, Hager & Carlsen, Portland, Oreg. Mem. Oreg. State Bar. Office: Miller Nash Wiener Hager & Carlsen 111 SW 5th Ave Ste 3500 Portland OR 97204-3699*

LUST, PETER, JR., microwave engineer, consultant; b. Montreal, Que., Can., Apr. 21, 1960; came to U.S., 1975, naturalized, 1987; s. Peter Clark and Evelyn (Heymanson) L.; Gloria Ruth Bingle, Apr. 5, 1985; children: Peter Alexander III, Elizabeth Ann, Matthew Eric. Student, Lowry Tech. Tng. Ctr., Community Coll. A.F., Albuquerque, USAF Acad.; BSEE, Pacific Western U., 1990. Computer meterologist Electro Rent, Burbank, Calif., 1982-84; microwave engr., program mgr. satellite and space shuttle communications systems Transco Products, Camarillo, Calif., 1984-90, internat. tech. mktg. mgr., 1990-93; prin. Electronic Note Co., Port Hueneme, Calif., 1984—; rep. ATeldix, Zeiss, Germany, Bosch Telecom. With USAF, 1979-82. Recipient Technol. award USAF, 1980, Discovery award NASA, 1987, Internat. Leaders in Achievement award, Cambridge. Mem. Assn. Old Crows, Channel Islands Health Club. Avocations: computing programming, hiking, developing spacecraft, swimming, model airplanes. Office: Electronic Note Co 300 E Esplanade Dr Ste 900 Oxnard CA 93030-1275

LUTES, NATALIE K., budget analyst; b. Denver, July 23, 1958; d. Norman Ellsworth Jr. and Mabel Arletta (Caul) Wilmot; m. Joseph Donald Lutes, Nov. 19, 1977; children: Jade, Andrew, Jennifer, Cody, Jessie. BS in Fin. magnu cum laude, Met. State Coll., Denver, 1991; postgrad., U. Colo., Denver. Staff asst. Met. State Coll., 1981-86, asst. budget dir., budget analyst, 1986—. Vol. Colo. SIDS Program, Denver, 1985-93. Mem. Acad. Mgmt. Inst. Office: Met State Coll 1100 Stout St # 1319 Denver CO 80204-2064

[illegible] sonville, Fla., Apr. 23, 1957; s. John James and Julie-Ann (Birchard) L.; m. Amanda Lisa Marsh, June 18, 1994; children: April Wilhelmina, Carly Julietta. AA in Dramatic Arts, Mesa Coll., San Diego, 1983; student, Calif. State U., Northridge, 1983-85. Freelance art dir. N.Y.C., 1985-90, freelance prodn. designer, art dir. L.A., 1991-96; art. dir. Foundation Imaging, Valencia, Calif., 1997—. Prodn. designer: (film) D.A.V.I.D.; (TV) Men Seeking Women, The Monkee's Special, Cheyenne, Dinosaur Valley Girls, I Have a Dream; art dir.: Hypernauts, Ravager, Without Warning, The Home Show. With USN, 1976-79. Mem. Aircraft Owners and Pilots Assn., Exptl. Aircraft Assn. Republican. Lutheran. Avocations: flying and building airplanes, mountain bikes, running.

LUTIN, DAVID LOUIS, real estate development and finance consultant; b. East Hartford, Conn., Apr. 18, 1919; s. Solomon and Esther (Newman) L.; AB, Ohio No. U., 1946; MBA, Syracuse U., 1949; m. Dorothy Marmor, Dec. 3, 1944; children: Gary, Marnie (Mrs. George Wittig). Housing economist and field rep. HHFA, Washington, 1950-57; dir. urban renewal City of Brookline, Mass., 1957-58; cons. on urban renewal and housing Com. for Econ. Devel., N.Y.C., 1958-59; propr. David L. Lutin Assocs., real estate devel. and fin. cons., Rye, N.Y., 1959-73, Phoenix, 75—; v.p. real estate and mortgages Am. Bank and Trust Co., N.Y.C., 1973-75. Assoc. prof. housing econs., M.I.T., 1951-52. Served to capt. AUS, 1942-46. Decorated Purple Heart. Mem. Am. Econ. Assn., Nat. Planning Assn., Mortgage Bankers Assn., Urban Land Inst., Am. Planning Assn., Am. Statis. Assn., Nat. Assn. Home Builders. Contbr. articles and reports on econs., housing and urban devel. to profl. jours. Home and Office: 10330 W El Rancho Dr Sun City AZ 85351-3854

LUTTER, DELORES KAY, environmental engineer; b. Watertown, S.D., Sept. 6, 1946; d. Anton P. and Julia E. (Garner) L. BS, Black Hills State U., 1971. Cert. hazardous materials mgr.; registered environ. assessor; registered hazardous substance profl.; registered environ. health specialist. Environtl. specialist IV State of S.D., Pierre, 1974-83; program mgr. San Mateo County, Redwood City, Calif., 1984-92; sr. environtl. engr. Battelle PNNL, Richland, Wash., 1992—. Recipient Cert. of Appreciation U.S. Dept. Energy, 1997. Mem. Acad. of Cert. Hazardous Materials Mgrs. (local assn. pres. 1997, v.p. 1996, Champion of Excellence 1995, Outstanding Svc. award 1994, special achievement award, 1998), No. Calif. Indsl. Hygiene Assn., Nat. Environtl. Health Assn. Home: PO Box 1246 Richland WA 99352-1246 Office: PO Box 999 Richland WA 99352-0999

LUTZ, JEFFREY CHRISTIAN, aerospace engineer; b. La Mesa, Calif., Nov. 25, 1959; s. Jimme Christian Lutz and Grace Evelyn (Weaver) Durelli; m. Stephanie Pearl Aldrich; children: Jeremiah Christian, Stephan Peter. BS in Aerospace Engring., San Diego State U., 1989. Aircraft assembler Teledyne Ryan Aero., San Diego, 1985-86, design engr., 1989—. Mem. Am. Mensa Ltd. Office: Teledyne Ryan Aero 2701 Harbor Dr Dept 340 San Diego CA 92113-3639

LUTZ, JOHN SHAFROTH, lawyer; b. San Francisco, Sept. 10, 1943; s. Frederick Henry and Helena Morrison (Shafroth) L.; m. Elizabeth Boschen, Dec. 14, 1968; children: John Shafroth, Victoria. BA, Brown U., 1965; JD, U. Denver, 1971. Bar: Colo. 1971, U.S. Dist. Ct. Colo. 1971, U.S. Ct. Appeals (2d cir.) 1975, D.C. 1976, U.S. Supreme Ct. 1976, U.S. Dist. Ct. (so. dist.) N.Y. 1977, U.S. Tax Ct. 1977, U.S. Ct. Appeals (10th cir.) 1979, N.Y. 1984, U.S. Ct. Appeals (9th cir.) 1990, U.S. Dist. Ct. (no. dist.) Calif. 1993. Trial atty. Denver regional office U.S. SEC, 1971-74; spl. atty. organized crime, racketeering sect. U.S. Dept. Justice, So. Dist. N.Y., 1974-77; atty. Kelly, Stansfield and O'Donnell, Denver, 1977-78; gen. counsel Boettcher & Co., Denver, 1978-87, Kelly, Stansfield and O'Donnel, Denver, 1987; spl. counsel, 1987-88, ptnr., 1988-93; of counsel LeBoeuf, Lamb, Greene and Mac Rae, L.L.P., 1993-94, ptnr. 1995—; spkr. on broker, dealer, securities law and arbitration issues to various profl. orgns. Contbr. articles to profl. jours. Bd. dirs. Cherry Creek Improvement Assn., 1980-84, Spalding Rehab. Hosp., 1986-89; chmn., vice-chmn. securities sub sect. Bus. Law Sect. of Colo. Bar, 1990, chmn., 1990-91. Lt. (j.g.), USNR, 1965-67. Mem. ABA, Colo. Bar Assn., Denver Bar Assn., Am. Law Inst., Securities Industry Assn. (state regulations com. 1982-86), Nat. Assn. Securities Dealers, Inc. (nat. arbitration com. 1987-91), St. Nicholas Soc. N.Y.C., Denver Law Club, Denver Country Club, Denver Athletic Club (dir. 1990-93), Rocky Mountain Brown Club (founder, past pres.), Racquet and Tennis Club. Republican. Episcopalian. Office: LeBoeuf Lamb Greene MacRae LLP 633 17th St Ste 2000 Denver CO 80202-3620

LUTZ, WILLIAM LAN, lawyer; b. Chgo., May 18, 1944; s. Raymond Price and Sibyl (McCright) L.; m. Jeanne M. McAlister, Dec. 27, 1969; children: William Lan, David Price. BS, U. Tex., 1965, JD, 1969. Bar: Tex. 1969, N.Mex. 1970. Assoc. Martin, Lutz, Cresswell & Hubert and predecessor firms, Las Cruces, N.Mex., 1969-82; former U.S. atty. dist. N.Mex. U.S. Dept. Justice, Albuquerque, 1982-91; ptnr. Martin, Lutz, Roggow & Brower, P.C., Las Cruces, 1991—. Mem. ABA, N.Mex. Bar Assn. (mem. bd. bar commrs. 1995-97); Aggie Sports Assn. (bd.dirs.) N.Mex. State U. Methodist. Office: Martin Lutz & Brower PO Drawer 1837 2100 N Main St Ste 3 Las Cruces NM 88004-1837

LY, VI KIM, artist, educator; b. Saigon, Vietnam, Jan. 10, 1967; came to U.S., 1980; d. Tai and Muoi (Huynh) L. BFA, U. Cin., 1990; MFA, San Francisco Art Inst., 1992. Asst. art dir. Euphrat Mus. Art, Cupertino, Calif., 1992-94; prof. art Monterey (Calif.) Peninsula Coll., 1994-96, Cabrillo (Calif.) Coll., 1994-95, San Jose (Calif.) City Coll., 1993-96; chair visual arts dept. Learning Tree U., Chatsworth, Calif., 1998—. Represented in permanent collections San Jose Mus. Art, 1996. Recipient Silver award Art of Calif. Mag., 1993, Crocker-Kingsley Merit award Crocker Art Mus., 1993. Mem. Women in Animation, L.S. Siggraph, Coll. Art Assn. Home: 2415 S Santa Fe Ave # 113 Los Angeles CA 90058-1139 Office: Learning Tree U 20920 Knapp St Chatsworth CA 91311-5933

LYASHENKO, NIKOLAI NIKOLAEVICH, mathematician, educator; b. Leningrad, Russia, Jan. 19, 1946; came to U.S., 1990; s. Nikolai Makarovich and Rufina Stepanovna (Poshekhonova) L.; m. Tatiana Vasilievna Giga, June 21, 1969; 1 child, Anna Nikolaevna. BS, Leningrad U., 1966, MS, 1969, PhD in Physics and Math. Scis., 1974, D in Phys. Math. Scis., 1986. Assoc. prof. Leningrad Elec. Engring. Inst., 1975-85; prof. Leningrad Poly. Inst., 1986-88; dir. info. processing lab. Leningrad Inst. Informatics and Automation, 1988-90; vis. prof. George Mason U., Fairfax, Va., 1991—; pres. Knowledge Extraction Tools, Inc., L.A. Contbr. numerous articles to profl. jours.; patentee in field. Avocation: playing piano. Office: 801 S Grand Ave Fl 10 Los Angeles CA 90017-4613

LYBARGER, MARJORIE KATHRYN, nurse; b. Holland, Mich., Apr. 23, 1956; d. Richard Simon and Mary Kathryn (Homan) Denuyl; m. John Steven Lybarger, Aug. 22, 1981; children: Ashley Ann, Ryan Christopher. BA in Psychology, Biola U., Calif., 1979, BS in Nursing, 1984. RN, Calif. Staff nurse Presbyn. Intercommunity Hosp., Whittier, Calif, 1985-86, Healthcare Med. Ctr., Tustin, Calif., 1986-88; staff nurse med.-telemetry unit Friendly Hills Regional Med. Ctr., La Habra, Calif., 1988-90; staff nurse telemetry unit Riverside (Calif.) Community Hosp., 1990-93; staff nurse med. telemetry unit St. Anthony's Ctrl. Hosp., Denver, 1993-94; clin. RN 1 cardiovascular intermediate care unit St. Anthony's Ctr., Denver, 1994-98, staff RN, 1998—. Mem. Gamma Phi Beta. Republican. Avocations: swimming, tennis. Home: 8489 W 95th Dr Broomfield CO 80021-5330

LYBECK, KEVIN LEE, lawyer; b. Havre, Mont., May 23, 1959; s. Harold Lybeck and Marilyn Joanne (Thielman) Willman; m. Susan Clyatt Lybeck, July 3, 1982; children: Erik Christopher, Jason Michael. BA, Mont. State U., 1982; JD, Gonzaga U., 1985. Bar: U.S. Dist. Ct. (we. dist.) Wash. 1986. Atty. The Gaines Law Firm, P.S., Seattle, 1986-96; corp. sec. Contractors Bonding & Ins. Co., Seattle, 1990—, sr. v.p., 1995—; spkr. in field. Contbr. chpts. to books. Mem. ABA (vice-chmn. FSLC 1995—), Wash. State Bar Assn. Avocations: reading, swimming, baseball, basketball. Office: Contractors Bonding & Ins Co 1213 Valley St Seattle WA 98109-4428

LYDON, MARY ELIZABETH, artist, poet; b. Sacramento, Nov. 9, 1954; d. Richard Martin and Mary (Dahimes) L. AA with honors, Sacramento [illegible] Calif. Surgery technician Dr.'s Hosp., Carmichael, Calif., 1972-82; photographer/printer Kodak Films, Sacramento, 1975-87; assembly/ad specialist ABK Enterprises, Sacramento, 1997—; photographer Calif. Arts League, 1993; photo exhibit Crocker Art Mus., 1993. Author: Anthology of

World's Famous Poets, 1982, Anthology of 19th Century Poets, 1985, Book of Am. Folklore, 1987, The Sound of Poetry, 1992; photographer Photographers Forum mag., 1992, The National Libr. of Poetry, 1998. Mem. Philoptochos, Greek Orthodox Annunciation Ch., Sacramento. Democrat. Greek Orthodox. Avocations: music (piano and guitar), songwriting, underwater photography, scuba diving. Home and Office: 806 48th St Sacramento CA 95819-3512

LYE, WILLIAM FRANK, history educator; b. Kimberley, B.C., Can., Feb. 19, 1930; came to U.S., 1955, naturalized, 1981; s. Arthur Percy and Jessie Loretta (Prince) L.; m. Velda Campbell, Oct. 16, 1953; children: William Mark, Matthew Campbell, David Arthur, Victoria, Regina. Student Ricks Coll., 1953-55, Duke U., 1963; BS, Utah State U., 1959; MA, U. Calif.-Berkeley, 1959; PhD, UCLA, 1969. Instr. polit. sci. Ricks Coll., Rexburg, Idaho, 1959-63, 67-68, head dept. polit. sci., 1959-63; teaching asst. dept. history UCLA, 1964-65; asst. prof. Utah State U., Logan, 1968-69, acting head dept. history and geography, 1969-70, assoc. prof., head dept. history and geography, 1970-73, prof., head dept. history and geography, 1973-76, dean Coll. Humanities, Arts and Social Scis., 1976-83, v.p. for univ. relations, prof. dept. history and geography, 1983-91, prof. history, 1991-95, emeritus, 1996—; vis. lectr. dept. history Brigham Young U., Provo, Utah, 1970; temporary lectr. dept. history U. Cape Town, Republic of South Africa, 1974; social cons. for project design teams in land conservation, U.S. Agy. for Internat. Devel. Khartoum, Sudan, 1978, Maseru, Lesotho, 1979; mem. higher edn. taskforce on telecommunications, Utah, 1977-82; chmn. State of Utah Telecommunications Coop., 1987, Regents' Com. on Credit by Exam., Utah, 1976; mem. adv. com. Sta. KULC-TV, State Ednl. Telecommunications Operating Ctr., 1976-80; bd. dirs., exec. com. Children's Aid Soc. Utah, 1985-89, pres., 1990-91; mem. Utah Statehood Centennial Commn., 1989-96, Utah Christopher Columbus Quincentenary Commn., 1990-91. Author: (with Colin Murray) Transformations on the Highveld: The Tswana and Southern Sotho, 1980, paperback edit., 1985; editor: Andrew Smith's Journal of His Expedition into the Interior of South Africa, 1834-36, 1975. Producer (TV series) Out of Africa, 1977, The God Seekers, 1978; contbr. articles and book revs. to profl. publs. Chmn. State Day celebration, Logan, Utah, 1973, univ. drive for new Logan Regional Hosp; bishop LDS Ch., 1993-96; chair bd. Nora Eccles Harrison Mus. of Art, 1996—; pres. Friends of USU Librs., 1997—. Recipient Leadership award Standard of Calif., 1957, Idea of Yr. award Utah State U., 1971, Faculty Service award Associated Students, Utah State U., 1977-78, Nicholas and Mary Kay Leone Leadership award, 1991, Caring for Children award Children's Aid Soc. Utah, 1994, Disting. Svc. award Utah State U., 1999; Woodrow Wilson Nat. fellow 1958, Foreign Area fellow Social Sci. Research Council, Republic of South Africa, England, 1966-67, 67-68; faculty devel. grantee Utah State U., 1972, Human Sci. Research Council of South Africa publ. grantee, 1975, Mauerberger Trust grantee, 1976. Mem. African Studies Assn., Royal African Soc., Western Assn. Africanists (program chmn. 1972-74, pres. 1974-76), Am. Soc. Landscape Architects (accreditation bd. 1976-93), Phi Kappa Phi, Phi Alpha Theta. Home: 60 Raymond Ct Logan UT 84321-4259 Office: Utah State U Dept History 650 N 1100 E Logan UT 84322-0710

LYMAN, JING, social activist; b. Phila., Feb. 23, 1925; d. Bennet Fellows and Marjorie (Page) Schauffler; m. Richard Wall Lyman, Aug. 20, 1947; children: Jennifer P., Holly Lyman Antolini, Christopher M., Timothy R. BA, Swarthmore Coll., 1947. Carpentry tchr. Shady Hill Sch., Cambridge, Mass., 1948-50; founding mem., exec. dir. Midpeninsula Citizens for Fair Housing, Palo Alto, Calif., 1965-66; founding bd. mem., chmn. fair housing task force Stanford (Calif.) Midpeninsula Urban Coalition, 1968-74; founding bd. mem. Women & Philanthropy, N.Y.C., 1975-81; founder, pres. Nat. Coalition for Women's Enterprise, Inc., N.Y.C., 1983-89; trustee Ci-tizen's Trust (formerly Working Assets Common Holdings), San Francisco, 1984-94; pres. HUB Co-Ventures, Palo Alto, 1989—; bd. chmn., CEO Am. Leadership Forum, Stanford, 1991-94; cons. Am. Enterprise Inst., Washington, 1982-83; mem. bd. overseers vis. com. Harvard and Radcliff Colls., 1973-79; bd. dirs. Rosenberg Found., San Francisco, 1973-80. Co-author: (handbook) Women's Economic Development Handbook: A Working Guide to Women's Self-Employment, 1987. Bd. dirs. Career Action Ctr., Palo Alto, 1974-80, Found Ctr., N.Y.C., 1976-82, vice-chmn. 1980-81, chmn. 1981-82,; adv. com. Coun. on Founds., Washington, 1977-82, SRI/HUD, 1978-80, Conf. of Mayors, 1980-81; bd. govs. Stanford Assocs., 1980-86; trustee The Enterprise Found., Columbia, Md., 1983—, Enterprise Sr. Ventures, 1997—; mem. selection com. of John W. Gardner Leadership award, ind. sector, Washington, 1985-88; adv. coun. Global Fund for Women, Palo Alto, Calif., 1987, The Spring Found., 1994-97, Leadership Calif., Pasadena, 1994—, James MacGregor Burns Acad. Leadership U. Md., College Park; bd. dirs. Am. Leadership Forum, 1989-97, hon. trustee, 1997—; numerous other civic activities. Recipient Wider Opportunities for Women award Jane Fleming Women's Employment award Washington, 1984, Uncommon Woman award Stanford U., 1991, WAVE award Alumnae Resources, San Francisco, 1995, Women of Vision award Career Action Ctr., Cupertino, Calif., 1998, Lifetime Achievement award Sr. Coord. Coun., Palo Alto, 1998. Democrat. Avocations: environment, music appreciation, painting, hiking, swimming.

LYMAN, PETER, librarian, educator; b. San Francisco, Sept. 13, 1940; s. George and Pauline (Richey) L.; m. Barrie Thorne, Nov. 23, 1971; children: Andrew Thorne-Lyman, Abigail Thorne-Lyman. BA in Philosophy, Stanford U., 1962, PhD in Polit. Sci., 1972; MA in Polit. Sci., U. Calif., Berkeley, 1963. From asst. prof. to prof. Mich. State U., East Lansing, 1968-87; dir. ctr. for scholarly tech. U. So. Calif., L.A., 1988-91, libr., 1991-94; U. Calif., Berkeley, 1994-98, prof., assoc. dean Sch. Info. Mgmt. and Systems,, 1994—; vis. prof. Stanford U., Palo Alto, Calif., 1978-79, 82-83, U. Calif., Santa Cruz, 1976-77, 81-82; bd. dirs. Sage Publ., Inc., Newbury Park, Calif., Internet Archive, San Francisco; adv. bd. Getty Info. Inst., L.A., 1994—, Next Computer, Inc., 1987-92; presenter and cons. in field. Contbr. articles to profl. jours. Bd. dirs. Coun. on Libr. and Info. Resources, Washington, 1995—, Rsch. Libr. Group, Mountain View, Calif., 1994-96, Educom, Washington, 1993-96; trustee Babbage Inst., Mpls., 1994—. Fax: 510-642-5814. E-mail: plyman@sims.berkeley.edu. Home: 78 El Camino Real Berkeley CA 94705-2424 Office: Univ Calif 102 S Hall Berkeley CA 94720-4600

LYNCH, CHARLES ALLEN, investment executive, corporate director; b. Denver, Sept. 7, 1927; s. Laurence J. and Louanna (Robertson) L.; divorced; children: Charles A., Tara O'Hara, Casey Alexander; m. Justine Bailey, Dec. 27, 1992. BS, Yale U., 1950. With E.I. duPont de Nemours & Co., Inc., Wilmington, Del., 1950-69, dir. mktg., 1965-69; corp. v.p. SCOA Industries, Columbus, Ohio, 1969-72; corp. exec. v.p., also mem. rotating bd. W.R. Grace & Co., N.Y.C., 1972-78; chmn. bd., chief exec. officer Saga Corp., Menlo Park, Calif., 1978-86, also dir.; chmn., chief exec. officer DHL Airways, Inc., Redwood City, Calif., 1986-88; also dir.; pres., chief exec. officer Levolor Corp., 1988-89, also bd. dir., chmn. exec. com. of bd., 1989-90; chmn. Market Value Ptnrs. Co., Menlo Park, Calif., 1990-95; chmn., dir. Fresh Choice, Inc., Santa Clara, Calif., 1995—, chmn., 1995—; also bd. dirs.; bd. dirs. Pacific Mut. Holdings Co., PST Vans, Inc., SRI Internat., Madge Networks N.V., Palo Alto Med. Found., Age Wave, Inc.; chmn. La Salsa Franchise, Inc. Bd. dirs. United Way, 1990-92, past chmn. Bay Area campaign, 1987; chmn., dir. Bay Area Coun.; past chmn. Calif. Bus. Roundtable; mem. adv. bd. U. Calif.-Berkeley Bus. Sch., Governance Bd. Mem. Yale Club (N.Y.C.), Internat. Lawn Tennis Club, Menlo Country Club (Calif.), Pacific Union Club (San Francisco), Coral Beach and Tennis Club (Bermuda), Vintage Club (Indian Wells, Calif.), Menlo Circus Club. Republican. Home: 96 Ridge View Dr Atherton CA 94027-6464 Office: 2901 Tasman Dr Ste 109 Santa Clara CA 95054-1137

LYNCH, LINDA LOU, reading and language arts specialist, educator; b. L.A., Feb. 9, 1941; d. Alexander Alfred and Gizella Mary (Bajus) Laszloffy; m. John Joseph Lynch, June 13, 1964; children: Valerie Ann, Colinda Lee, Lee Anne Ellen. BS, Calif. State U., Northridge, 1964; MEd, Loyola Marymount U., L.A., 1990; EdD, Pepperdine U., 1995. Cert. tchr., Calif. Computer programmer Union Bank, L.A., 1962-64; substitute tchr. various sch. dists. Calif., 1964-68, 79-80; tchr. Richard H. Dana Mid. Sch., Hawthorne, Calif., 1980-88; reading specialist Wiseburn Sch. Dist., Hawthorne, 1988-91, 94—; elem. sch. tchr. Juan de Anza Elem. Sch., Hawthorne, 1991-93; reading specialist Wiseburn Sch. Dist., 1994—; adj. faculty mem. Loyola Marymount U., L.A., 1991—, dir. reading program Grad. Sch., 1992; rsch. asst. Pepperdine U., L.A., 1992-94, teaching asst., 1993, asst. dir. student tchrs., 1993, adj. prof., 1994—; adj. prof. Chapman U., L.A., 1995—. Mem. NEA, AAUW, ASCD, Am. Edn. Rsch. Assn., Internat. Reading Assn., Calif. Reading Assn., Ventura County Reading Assn., Calif. Tchrs. Assn., Wiseburn Faculty Assn., Phi Delta Kappa. Democrat. Roman Catholic.

LYNCH, MARTIN ANDREW, retail company executive; b. Chgo., Oct. 5, 1937; s. George Irwin and Cecilia Veronica (Corley) L.; children: Kathleen Marie, Kevin Michael, Karen Ann, Daniel Patrick, Michelle Eileen. BSc, DePaul U., 1962. CPA, Ill., Calif. Audit mgr. Price Waterhouse & Co., Chgo., 1962-69; asst. to pres. Scot Lad Foods, Chgo., 1969-70; v.p. fin. N.Am. Car Corp., Chgo., 1970-76; sr. v.p. fin. Tiger Internat. Inc., L.A., 1976-83; exec. v.p., chief fin. officer Duty Free Shoppers Group Ltd., San Francisco, 1983-89, Casino USA Inc., Santa Barbara, Calif., 1989—, Smart & Final Inc., Santa Barbara, 1989—. Mem. AICPA, Calif. CPA Soc., Fin. Execs. Inst., Nat. Assn. Whole Grogery, Inst. Food Distbn. Assn., Bel Air Country Club (L.A.). Roman Catholic. Avocations: jogging, swimming, skiing, golf. Office: Smart & Final Inc 600 Citadel Dr Los Angeles CA 90040-1562

LYNCH, NITA MARIE SMITH, vocational curriculum developer; b. Portland, Oreg., Aug. 11, 1952; d. Jay Harvey Jr. and Harriet Smith; m. Paul Michael Lynch (dec.). AAS, C.C. of Air Force, 1987, C.C. of Air Force, 1989; BS with highest honors, U. So. Miss., 1991, MS, 1992, postgrad., 1992—. Cert. tchr., Miss. Enlisted USAF, 1979; tech. tng. instr. USAF, Keesler AFB, Miss., 1985-89; curriculum developer USAF, Keesler AFB, 1989-95; ret. USAF, 1995; ednl. cons., 1995—. *Nita Lynch is an educational consultant with 20 years experience in developing education, training, and awareness products for computer security, information practition, and contingency planning and management professionals. Her work has been enhanced by post-graduate research in "The Contribution of Adult Education to the Professionalization of Information Systems Security".* Contbr. articles to profl. jours. Mem. Fed. Women's Program, 1992-95. Mem. Am. Vocat. Assn., Am. Assn. Adult and Continuing Edn., Fed. Info. Sys. Security Edn. Assn., Soc. Applied Learning Tech., Info. Sys. Security Assn., Phi Kappa Phi. Home and Office: 7815 SE Carlton St Portland OR 97206-6320

LYNCH, PHYLLIS ANNE, stockbroker; b. Lakeville, Minn., Aug. 9, 1944; d. Eugene and Helen mary (Brown) L.; children from previous marriage: Evan Astrowsky, Amy Astrowsky. BS in Mktg., Fairfield U., 1983. Lic. securities broker, N.Y. Account exec. Blythe Eastman Dillon, N.Y.C., 1976-79, Great Western Fin., L.A., 1979-91, Smith Barney, L.A., 1991-92; fin. rep. Fidelity Investments, L.A., 1992-96; investment broker A.G. Edwards & Sons, Inc., Coral Gables, Fla., 1996—. Treas. L.A. Children's Hosp. Aux., Conejo Valley, Calif., 1988-90; bd. mem. L.A. County H.S. for the Arts, L.A., 1989-91. Recipient Parent of the Yr. award L.A. County Bd. Edn., 1991. Mem. Women's Polit. Action, Miami Project to Cure Paralysis. Avocations: tennis, golf.

LYNCH, ROBERT BERGER, lawyer; b. LaCrosse, Wis., June 10, 1931; s. Jan P. and Eve (Berger) L.; m. Iris D. Healy; children: Jan Fredrick, Jerry Wayne Coggins. B.S., U.S. Merchant Marine Acad., 1955; J.D., U. of the Pacific, 1967. Engr. Aerojet Gen. Corp., Sacramento, Calif., 1955-61, proposal mgr., 1961-63, asst. contract adminstrn. mgr., 1963-66, contract adminstrn. mgr., 1967-70; admitted to Calif. bar, 1969, U.S. Supreme Ct. bar, 1972; individual practice law. Rancho Cordova, Calif., 1969—; instr. bus. law Solano Community Coll., 1977-79, San Joaquin Delta Coll., 1978-79; mediator family law panel Sacramento Superior Ct.; mcpl. ct. (traffic) pro tem judge, Sacramento. Active various charity fund-raising campaigns in Sacramento Calif., 1966-68; mem. mission com. St. Clements Episcopal Ch., Rancho Cordova, Calif., 1967-68; trustee Los Rios Community Coll. Dist., Calif., 1971-79. With USCG, 1949-51, USNR 1951-80, Nat. Guard 1988-91, Maj. AUS, ret. Mem. IEEE, Calif. Wildlife Fedn., Internat. Turtle Club, Marines Meml. Assn., Am. Legion, Mensa. Office: 10615 Coloma Rd Rancho Cordova CA 95670-3939

LYNCH, TIMOTHY JEREMIAH-MAHONEY, lawyer, educator, theologian, realtor, writer; b. June 10, 1952; s. Joseph David and Margaret Mary (Mahoney) L.m. on private internat. law U.S. State Dept., Washington; mem. Dead Sea Scrolls Rsch. Project, 1998; mem. author and writers group on multi-vol. transl. series classical works from late Roman, medieval near eastern, patristic and early Christian ch. periods Princeton U., 1998, Cath. U. Am., 1998, U. Calif., Berkely, 1998; rsch. prof. Old and New Testamen bibl. lit. commentary, 1998. *Over twenty years as a top-notch commercial industrial real estate investor, manager, broker and developer. Major achievements include financing venture capital, large scale investments and developments in hotel shopping center markets and through use of applying long-range capital through refinancing of existing mortgages principals net yields. Leading consultant and speaker on business and economic issues that are influenced by Federal Government policies. Also leading expert on corporate governance and speaker issues affecting corporate directors and shareholders.* Author: (10 vol. manuscript) History of Ecumenical Doctrines and Canon Law of Church; editorial bd. Internat. Tax Jour., 1993; author: Publishers National Endowment for Arts and Humanities Classical Translations: Latin, Greek, and Byzantine Literary Texts for Modern Theological-Philosophical Analysis of Social Issues; Essays on Issues of Religious Ethics and Social, Public Policy Issues, 1995, 96, others; editorial bd. Internat. Tax Jour., 1993, Melrose Press: Internat. Firm; contbr. articles to profl. jours. Dir., vice chmn. Downtown Assn. San Francisco; councillor, dir. Atlantic Coun. U.S., 1984—; corp. counsel, chmn. spl. arbitrator's tribunal on U.S.-Brazil trade, fin. and banking rels. Inter-Am. Comml. Arbitration Commn., Washington; chmn. nat. adv. com. U.S.-Mid. East rels. U.S. Mid. East Policy Coun., U.S. State Dept., Washington, 1989—; mem. Pres. Bush's Adv. Commn. on Econ. and Public Policy Priorities, Washington, 1989; mem. conf. bd. Mid. East Policy Coun., U.S. State Dept., Washington, 1994—; elected mem. Coun. of Scholars U.S. Libr. Congress, Washington; bd. dirs. Internat. Diplomacy Coun., San Francisco Opera, Ballet, Symphony Assns. Recipient Cmty. Svc. honors Mayor Dianne Feinstein, San Francisco, 1987, Leadership awards St. Ignatius Coll. Prep., 1984, Calif.'s Gold State award, 1990, AU-ABA Achievement award, 1990, Medal of Honor Order Internat. Ambs. Com. U.S. State Dept. and Foreign Svc. Inst., Washington D.C., World Lifetime Achievement award, Induction 20th Century Millenium Hall Fame and Dist. Leadership Hall Fame Am. Acad. Achievement, 1998, award Superior Talent in Bus. and Arts, Century Dist. Acheivement award, Am. Acad. Achievement, 1998, Internat. Cultural award, 1997, Presdl. Seal Honor, 1997, Decree Internat. Cultural Letters, 1997; named Civic Leader of Yr., Nat. Trust for Hist. Preservation, 1988, 89; named to Presdl. Order of Merit, 1991., Induction U.S. Lib. Congress 500 Leaders of Influence Hall Fame, 1998, Noble Installation Orders of Knighthood Royal British Legions by Queen Elizabeth II, 1998. Fellow World Jurist Assn., World Assn. Judges (Washington); mem. ATLA, Internat. Bar Assn. (various coms., internat. litigation, taxation, labor issue), Am. Arbitration Assn. (panelist, internat. decree), Am. Fgn. Law Assn. (various coms.), Am. Soc. Ch. History, Am. Inst. Archaeology (Boston), Pontifical Inst. Medieval Studies (Toronto, Can.), Am. Hist. Assn., Am. Philol. Assn., Inst. European Law, Medieval Acad. Am., U.S. Supreme Ct. Hist. Soc. (presdl. seal of honor, cultural diploma honor), J Canon Law Soc. U.S., Nat. Planning Assn., Nat. Assn. Scholars (Eminent Scholar of Yr. 1993), Netherlands Arbitration Inst. (mem. Gen. Panels of Arbitrators, mem. Permanent Ct. Arbitration), Calif. Coun. Internat. Trade (GATT com., tax com., legis. com.), Practicing Law Inst., Am. Fgn. Law Assn. (mem. editl. bd. Working Groups on Rsch. Jour. for Legal systems of Africa, Mid. East, Latin Am., EEC and Soviet Union), U.S.-China Bus. Coun. (export com., GATT com., banking and fin. com., import com.), Bay Area Coun. (corp. mem.), Nat. Acad. Conciliators (Spl. award), Internat. Bar (mem. U.S. Group on Model on Insolvency Corp. Acts), Ctr. Internat. Comml. Arbitration, Comml. Club (various positions), Am. Venture Capital Assn., Pacific Venture Capital Assn., Am. Soc. Internat. Law, Washington Fgn. Law Soc., Asia-Pacific Lawyers Assn., Soc. Profls. in Dispute Resolution, British Inst. Internat. and Comparative Law, Internat. Law Assn. (U.S. br.), Commercial Bar Assn. of United Kingdom (London), Inter-Pacific Bar Assn. (Tokyo; mem. arbitration intellectual property, consitutional taxation, labor, legal groups), Inst. European Law Faculty of Laws (United Kingdom), Urban Land Inst. Internat., Mid. East Inst. (Am.-Arab Affairs Coun.), Inter-Am. Bar Assn., 1987—, Calif. Trial Lawyers Assn., Ctr. Reformation Rsch. (co-chmn. Calif. State Com. on U.S.-Mid. East Econ. and Polit. Rels.), Soc. Biblical Lit., Am. Acad. Arts and Letters, Am. Acad. Religion, World Lit. Acad., Coun. Scholars, Am. Com. on U.S.-Japan Rels., Japan Soc. No. Calif., Pan-Am. Assn. San Francisco, Soc. Indsl./Office Realtors, Assn. Entertainment Lawyers London, Royal Chartered Inst. Arbitrators (London), Soc. Indsl. and Office Realtors, Urban Land Inst., San Francisco Realtors Assn., Calif. Realtors Assn., Coun. Fgn. Rels., Chgo. Coun. Fgn. Rels., Conf. Bd., San Francisco Urban and Planning Assn., U.S. Trade Facilitation Coun., Asia Soc., Am. Petroleum Inst., Internat. Platform Assn., San Francisco C. of C. (bus. policy com., pub. policy com., co-chmn. congl. issues study group), Am. Inst. Diplomacy, Overseas Devel. Coun. (Mid. East, Russian Republics, Latin Am. studies group), Internat. Vis. Ctr. (adv. bd.), Fin. Execs. Inst., Nat. Assn. Corp. Dirs., Heritage Found. (bd. dirs.), Archaeological Inst. Am. (fellow coun. near east studies, Egyptology), Am. Literature Judicature Soc., Soc. of Biblical, Nat. Assn. Indsl. and Office Properties, World Literary Acad. (Cambridge, Eng.), Am. Acad. Arts & Letters, Am. Acad. Religion, Pres. Club, Nat. Assn. Bus. Economists, Villa Taverna Club, Palm Beach Yacht Club, Pebble Beach Tennis Club, Calif. Yacht Club, Commonwealth Club, City Club San Francisco, British Bankers Club, London, San Diego Track Club (registered athlete), Crow Canyon Country Club (bd. dirs.), Western Venture Capital Assn., Am. Venture Capital Assn., Authors Guild, Internat. Pen Soc., diplomate-delegate World Econ. Summit Conf., Paris, 1998, IOSECC Conf. Internat. Org. Securities Conf., Paris, 1998. Republican. Roman Catholic; Clubs: Crow Canyon Country Club, The Players. Avocations: theater, social entertainment events, opera, ballet, fine arts. Home: 501 Forest Ave Palo Alto CA 94301-2631 Office: 540 Jones St Ste 201 San Francisco CA 94102-2008

LYNE, DOROTHY-ARDEN, educator; b. Orangeburg, N.Y., Mar. 9, 1928; d. William Henry and Janet More (Freston) Dean; m. Thomas Delmar Lyne, Aug. 16, 1952 (div. June 1982); children: James Delmar, Peter Freston, Jennifer Dean. BA, Ursinus Coll., 1949; MA, Fletcher Sch. Law and Diplomacy, 1950. Assoc. editor World Peace Found., Boston, 1950-51; editorial assoc. Carnegie Endowment Internat. Peace, N.Y.C., 1951-52; dir. Assoc. of Internat. Rels. Clubs, N.Y.C., 1952-53; editor The Town Crier, Westport, Conn., 1966-68; editorial assoc. Machinery Allied Products Inst., Wash., 1959-63; tchr. Helen Keller Mid. Sch., Easton, Conn., 1967-89; vice chmn. Cooperative Ednl. Svcs., Fairfield, 1983-85. Editor: Documents in American Foreign Rels., 1950, Current Rsch. in Internat. Affairs, 1951. Chmn. Westport Zoning Bd. of Appeals, 1976-80, Westport Bd. of Edn., 1985-87; vice chmn. Westport Bd. of Edn., 1980-85; mem. Westport Charter Revision Commn., 1966-67. Republican. Episcopalian.

LYNN, KATHERINE LYN, quality engineer, chemist; b. Nagoya, Japan, June 25, 1954; (parents Am. citizens); d. Jimmie Frank and Barbara Sue (Whiteside) Sutton; m. Richard Shelly Lynn, Feb. 28, 1981. BS in Chemistry cum laude, Calif. State U., Fullerton, 1979. Cert. quality engr. Am. Soc. Quality, cert. quality auditor, cert. quality mgr. Technician U.S. Borax Corp., Anaheim, Calif., 1974-79; chemist Armstrong World Industries, Southgate, Calif., 1979-82; project engr. Hydril Co., Whittier, Calif., 1982-84; sr. quality engr. So. Calif. Gas Co., L.A., 1984—. Patentee fluorspar flotation. Bd. dirs. East Side Christian Ch., 1987-89. Mem. So. Calif. Thermal Analysis Group (chair 1988, sec. 1985-87), Soc. Plastic Engrs., Am. Soc. for Quality Control, Am. Chem. Soc., Sierra Club. Mem. Christian Ch. Avocations: outdoor activities, backpacking, Nordic and Alpine skiing. Home: 5120 Faust Ave Lakewood CA 90713-1924 Office: So Calif Gas Co Box 3249 PO Box 3249 Los Angeles CA 90051-1249

LYNNE, JUDITH, interior designer; b. Beaver Falls, Pa.; d. Clinton Axel August and Irene Lucille (Williams) Stromberg; 1 child, Mark Jonathan Enlow. Student, UCLA, 1979-80. Cert. interior designer, Calif. Owner Judith Lynne Interior Design, Palm Springs, Calif., 1977—. Mem. Am. Soc. Interior Designers (bd. dirs. 1994-95, 97—, pres.-elect 1998—, Disting. Svc. award 1997, Design Excellence award 1998), Ptnrs. Edn., Fashion Group Internat. Office: Judith Lynne Interior Design PO Box 4998 Palm Springs CA 92263

LYON, DANIEL FRANK SOUTHWORTH, lawyer; b. N.Y., July 4, 1936; s. Daniel R. and Leta B. (Boswell) L.; m. Ida M. Hanson-Lyon, Jul. 6, 1954 (dec. 1996); children: Daniel, Sherry, Dennis, Mary, Tom; m. Yvonne C. Hudson-Lyon, Mar. 15, 1997. BS, Milton Coll., 1963; LLB, Blackstone Sch. Law, 1965; JD, Univ. New Mex., 1968. Bar: New Mex. 1968. Deputy sheriff Rock County Sheriff's Dept., Beloit, Wis., 1958; probation/parole officer New Mex. Probation & Parole Bd., Albuquerque, 1964-68; pvt. practice Albuquerque, 1968-71; mgmt. U.S. West Communications, Albuquerque, 1971-91; mem. Bernalillo County Valuation Bd., Albuquerque, 1991-95, New Mex. Adult Parole Bd., Santa Fe, 1995—; arbitrator State Bar of New Mex., 1980—; commn. National Com. on Uniform State Laws, 1972-78. State rep. New Mex., 1970-78; chmn. State Employment Security Commn., 1978-81; del. New Mex. Constitutional Conv., 1989. Mem. State Bar New Mex. (com. mem.), State Real Estate Com., Internat. Right of Way Assn. (dir. 1978). Avocations: traveling, athletic events, watch TV. Home: 9216 Camino Viejo Ln NW Albuquerque NM 87114-5398

LYON, DUSTIN L., artist; b. Idaho Falls, Idaho, Oct. 10, 1951; s. Lawrence Cecil and Marion Allene (Mecham) L.; m. Jessie Nelean marsden, Aug. 19, 1976; children: Travis Nixon, Justin Neal, Mandy Nelean, Heather Danielle. Assoc., Ricks Coll., Rexburg, Idaho, 1977. Fine artist, Idaho and Ariz., 1979—. Exhibited in groups shows at Nebr. Land Show, 1998, Simic Gallery, 1992; featured artist Nebraska-Land Show, 1998. Recipient 3d Place award George Phippen Art Show, Prescott, Ariz., 1984, Purchase award Shoshone Nat. Bank, Cody, Wyo., 1988, Gold Medal, May Gallery, Scottsdale, Ariz., 1998—. Mem. LDS Ch. Avocations: gardening, sports, art collecting, baseball cards. Home: 30408 N 43d St Cave Creek AZ 85311

LYON, RICHARD, mayor, retired naval officer; b. Pasadena, Calif., July 14, 1923; s. Norman Morais and Ruth (Hollis) L.; m. Cynthia Gisslin, Aug. 8, 1975; children: Patricia, Michael, Sean; children by previous marriage: Mary, Edward, Sally, Kathryn, Patrick (dec.), Susan. B.E., Yale U., 1944; M.B.A., Stanford U., 1953. Commd. ensign USN, 1944; advanced through grades to rear adm. SEAL, 1974; served in Pacific and China, World War II; with Underwater Demolition Team Korea; recalled to active duty as dep. chief Naval Res. New Orleans, 1978-81; mem. Chief Naval Ops. Res. Affairs Adv. Bd., 1978-81; exec. v.p. Nat. Assn. Employee Benefits, Newport Beach, Calif., 1981-90; mem. Bd. Control, U.S. Naval Inst., 1978-81; pres. Civil Svc. Commn., San Diego County, 1990—, Oceanside Unified Sch. Bd., 1991; mayor City of Oceanside, 1992—. Pres. bd. trustees Children's Hosp. Orange County, 1965, 72. Decorated Legion of Merit. Mem. Nat. Assn. Securities Dealers (registered prin.), Newport Harbor Yacht Club, Oceanside Yacht Club, Rotary (Anaheim, Calif. pres. 1966). Republican. Episcopalian. Home: 600 S The Strand Oceanside CA 92054-3902

LYONS, GEORGE, religion educator; b. Richmond, Ind., Dec. 9, 1947; s. Galen H. and Georgia M. (Sebby) L.; m. Terre Lynn Hickok, May 24, 1969; children: Kara Joy, Nathanael David. BA, Olivet Nazarene U., 1970; MDiv, Nazarene Theol. Sem., 1973; PhD, Emory U., 1982. Prof. bibl. lit. Olivet Nazarene U., Kankakee, Ill., 1977-91, coord. grad. religion lit. program, 1986-90, chmn. dept. bibl. lit., 1989-91; prof. bibl. lit. N.W. Nazarene Coll., Nampa, Idaho, 1991—; guest lectr. Nazarene Theol. Sem., Kansas City, Mo., 1982, 86, 89, Nazarene Theol. Coll., Brisbane, Australia, 1989-90, 91, 96. Author: Pauline Autobiography, 1985, Holiness in Everyday Life, 1992, More Holiness in Everyday Life, 1996; co-author: A Dictionary of the Bible, 1984; contbr. articles to profl. publs. Mem. doctrine of ch. commn. Ch. of Nazarene, Kansas City, 1985-89, mem. curriculum com., 1990—; coord. Kankakee County Hunger Walk, 1985-90. Mem. Soc. Bibl. Lit., Wesleyan Theol. Soc. (sec. membership com. 1986, 2d v.p. 1992). Home: 4012 Ivy Dr Nampa ID 83686-8852 Office: NW Nazarene Coll Holly And Dewey St Nampa ID 83686

LYONS, TERRENCE ALLAN, merchant banking, investment company executive; b. Grande Prairie, Alta., Can., Aug. 1, 1949; s. Allan Lynnwood and Mildred Helen (Smith) L. B in Applied Sci., U. B.C., 1972; MBA, U. Western Ont., 1974. Registered profl. engr., B.C. Gen. mgr. Southwestern Drug Co., Vancouver, B.C., Can., 1975-76; mgr. planning Versatile Corp., Vancouver, 1976-83, asst. v.p., 1983-86, v.p., dir., 1986-88; pres., mng. ptnr. B.C. Pacific Capital Corp., 1988—; bd. dirs. BRL Enterprises, Inc., Internat. Utility Structures, Ariz. Goldfields Inc., Regional Cable TV, Inc.; pres., chief exec. officer FT Capital Ltd., 1990—; pres., dir. Westfield Minerals Ltd.,

1993—, Northgate Exploration Ltd. Author articles on mfg. tech. Office: BC Pacific Capital Corp Royal Ctr, PO Box 11179 1632-1055 W Georgia St, Vancouver, BC Canada V6E 3R5

LYSINGER, HEATHER J., administrative assistant; b. Portland, Oreg., Aug. 4, 1975; d. Alfred Neil and Pamela Ann (Holcombe) White; m. Myron Eugene Lysinger Jr., May 24, 1998. AA, Bassist Coll., 1995. Office mgr., designer Tom Dearborn Interiors, Inc., Portland, 1994-96; adminstrv. asst. for reports and documentation Benova, Inc., Portland, 1996—. Chair decorating com. Sunnyside Seventh-day Adventist Ch., Portland, 1996—, chair audio/visual com., 1995—, mem. ch. bd., 1995—, mem. facilities com., 1995—, sec. ministry search com., 1995-96, 96-97. Mem. Am. Soc. Interior Designers. Home: 13005 SE 242d Ave Boring OR 97009-7335

MA, FENGCHOW CLARENCE, agricultural engineering consultant; b. Kaifeng, Honan, China, Sept. 4, 1919; came to U.S., 1972; s. Chao-Hsiang and Wen-Chieh (Yang) Ma; m. Fanny Luisa Corvera-Achá, Jan. 20, 1963; 1 child, Fernando. BS in Agr., Nat. Chekiang U., Maytan, Kweichow, China, 1942; postgrad. in agrl. engring., Iowa State U., 1945-46. Cert. profl. agronomist, Republic of China, 1944; registered profl. agrl. engr., Calif. Chief dept. ops. Agrl. Machinery Operation and Mgmt. Office, Shanghai, China, 1946-49; sr. farm machinery specialist Sino-Am. Joint Commn. on Rural Reconstrn., Taipei, Taiwan, Republic of China, 1950-62; agrl. engring. adviser in Bolivia, Peru, Chile, Ecuador, Liberia, Honduras, Grenada, Bangladesh FAO, Rome, 1962-80; consulting agrl. engr. to USAID projects in Guyana & Peru IRI Rsch. Inst., Inc., Stamford, Conn., 1981-82, 83, 85; chief adviser Com. Internat. Tech. Coop., Taipei, 1984-85; pres. FCM Assocs., Inc., 1962—; short consulting missions to Paraguay, Saudi Arabia, Indonesia, Malawi, Swaziland, Barbados, Dominica, Ivory Coast, Vietnam, Philippines, Nicaragua and others. Author papers, studies; contbr. articles to profl. publs. Mem. Am. Soc. Agrl. Engrs. Avocations: reading, stamp and coin collecting. Home: 1004 Azalea Dr Sunnyvale CA 94086-6747 Office: PO Box 70096 Sunnyvale CA 94086-0096

MA, ZACH, artist; b. San Francisco, Dec. 15, 1951; s. Albert and Mari M.; m. Kathryn Fox, Feb. 1, 1992; children: Connie J., Leilah. BFA, San Francisco Art Inst., 1981, MFA, 1983. Artist MTS Inc., San Francisco, 1978—. Tai-Chi Svs. instr., United Way, 1983-97. With USAF, 1971-77. Mem. Tai-Chi Wold Orgn. (spl. mem., cert. instr.). Avocations: Tai-Chi, archery. Home: 1167 S Mayfair Ave Daly City CA 94015-3551

MAATSCH, DEBORAH JOAN, financial company executive, tax advisor; b. Lincoln, Nebr., Mar. 26, 1950; d. Leon F. Forst and Jarolyn J. Hoffman Forst Conrad; m. Gordon F. Maatsch, Mar. 14, 1969; children: Jason, Diana. BS, U. Nebr., 1976; MBA, U. Phoenix, 1997. Acct., supr. U.S. Civil Svc., Heidelberg, Ger., 1971-73; paralegal Mattson Rickets Davies et al, Lincoln, Nebr., 1976-87; tax cons. Lincoln and Denver, 1981—; paralegal Wade Ash Woods & Hill, P.C., Denver, 1986-94; sr. trust adminstr. Investment Trust Co., Denver, 1994-96; compliance officer Nelson, Benson and Zellmer, Inc., 1995-96; pres. DGJD Inc.-Bleachers, 1993—; controller Arena Devel., Inc., 1996—; mem. Denver Trust Officers Assocs., bus. adv. bd. Ponderosa H.S., 1994—; spkr., coord. Nebr. Continuing Legal Edn. Seminars, 1976-86. Contbr. articles to profl. jours. Mem. Doane Coll. Alumni Assn. (dir. 1989-93), Rocky Mt. Legal Assts. (dir., sect. chair 1990-94), Am. Soc. Women Accts. (officer, dir.), Nebr. Assn. Legal Assts. (officer, dir. 1976-87), Colo. Bar Assn. (computer probate sect.), Phi Chi Theta (treas. 1988-89). Avocations: travel, snow skiing, outdoor activities, motorcycles, home decorating. Office: DGJD Inc PO Box 267 Jefferson CO 80456-0267

MABIN, ANN MARIE, artist management executive, consultant; b. Memphis, Apr. 22; d. Jim and Pearline White; m. Robert Mabin (div. 1989); children: Camille, Diane. AA, Wayne State C.C., 1974, BS, 1977; postgrad., UCLA, 1979-81. Artist rels. Motown Records, Detroit, 1968-79; pres. artist mgmt. Mary Jane Prodn., L.A., N.Y.C., 1979-91, Klasact Entertainment, L.A., 1991—; tour cons. Mary Jane Girls, L.A., 1982-87. Author (poem) Smile, 1989 (Golden Poet award 1990); coord. (record album) Street Songs, 1981 (Am. Music award 1982), Mary Jane Girls, 1983 (Am. Music award 1984), Super Freak, 1981 (Grammy award 1991). Vol. Dem. Conv., Detroit, 1975. Mem. Prestigious Women Assn., Starlight Found. (vol.), Braille Inst. for Blind (vol.). Baptist. Avocations: gourmet cooking, nature walks, music, writing.

MACAGBA, RUFINO L., JR., physician, international agency executive; b. San Fernando, Philippines, Feb. 3, 1933; came to U.S., 1974; s. Rufino N. Sr. and Crispina (Lorenzana) M.; m. Victoria D. Reyes, Apr. 10, 1957; children: Carol Lynn, Rufino III, Jonathan, Michelle. MD, U. Philippines, Manila, 1957; MPH, UCLA, 1975. Hosp. adminstr., chief surgeon Lorma Hosp., San Fernando, 1960-74; internat. health advisor World Vision Internat., Calif., 1975-88, exec. mgmt. trainer, 1982-84; pres. Lorma Hosp. and Coll., 1980—, Health Devel. Internat., Calif., 190—; internat. health coord. Food for the Hungry, Scottsdale, Ariz., 1990-95, head internat. tech. and managerial svcs., 1994-95; dir. MBA program Pacific Christian Coll., Fullerton, Calif., 1995—; freelance cons. to World Vision Relief and Devel., Inc., Monrovia, Calif., World Bank, Washington, U. of the Nations, Kona, Hawaii, Mercy Corps Internat., Portland, Oreg., Food for the Hungry Internat. Author books and booklets, including: Health Care Guidelines for Use in Developing Countries, 1977, Hospitals and Primary Health Care, 1984, What World Vision Staff Should Know About AIDS, 1987, (with Mike O. Minodin) Selected Publications for Community Health Care, 1987, also articles. Mem. Nat. Coun. for Internat. Health (bd. dirs. 1978-80), Internat. Hosp. Fedn. (travelling fellow 1982-84), Health Devel. Internat. (pres. 1991-95). Republican. Christian. Avocations: computers, travel, electronics. Home: 10075 Silverado Ct Santee CA 92071-1600 Office: Pacific Christian Coll MBA Program 2500 Nutwood Ave Fullerton CA 92831-3104

MACALISTER, ROBERT STUART, oil company executive; b. L.A., May 22, 1924; s. Robert Stuart and Iris Grace (Doman) MacA.; m. Catherine Vera Willby, Nov. 15, 1947 (dec. 1994); children: Rodney James, Sara Marjorie Pfirrmann; m. Grace V. LeClerc, Dec. 2, 1995. Student, Brighton Coll., Sussex, Eng., 1945; BSME, Calif. Inst. Tech., 1947. Registered profl. engr., Tex. Petroleum engr. Shell Oil Co., 1947-56; mgmt. trainee Royal Dutch Shell, The Hague, Netherlands, 1956-57; with exec. staff, mgr. Shell Oil Co., U.S.A., 1957-68; v.p., ops. mgr. Occidental Petroleum Corp., Tripoli, Libya, 1968-71; mng. dir.various subs. London, 1971-76; mng. dir., pres. Occidental Internat. Oil, Inc., London, 1976-78; pres., chmn. bd. Can. Occidental Petroleum Ltd., Calgary Alberta, 1978-81; mng. dir. Australian Occidental Petroleum Ltd., Sydney, 1982-83, Hamilton Bros. Oil & Gas Ltd., London, 1983-86; petroleum cons. Camarillo, Calif., 1986—; exec. U.K. Offshore Operators, London, 1972-78, 83-86. Cubmaster Boy Scouts Am., Larchmont, N.Y., 1964-65, scoutmaster, Houston, 1965-68. Sgt. U.S. Army, 1944-45, ETO. Mem. Am. Assn. Petroleum Geologists, Soc. Petroleum Engrs., Can. Petroleum Assn. (bd. govs. 1978-81), Las Posas Country Club, Gold Coast Srs., Caltech Torchbearer. Republican. Episcopalian. Avocations: carpentry, crafts, watercolor painting, golfing, gardening. Home and Office: 78 Lopaco Ct Camarillo CA 93010-8846

MACAN, EDWARD L., music educator; b. Rochester, Mich., Dec. 17, 1961; s. Thomas F. and Lena M. (Jones) M.; m. Connie J. Marrufo, June 2, 1984; children: Nicole, Catherine. BM, Oakland U., 1983; MA, U. Calif., Riverside, 1986; PhD, Claremont Grad. Sch., 1991. Prof. Coll. of the Redwoods, Eureka, Calif., 1994—; adj. instr. Chaffey Coll., Rancho Cucamonga, Calif., 1989-90; vis. asst. prof. Whittier Coll., Calif., 1990-93. Author: (book) Rocking the Classics: English Progressive Rock and the Counterculture, 1997; recording artist: (CD) Ed Macan's Hermetic Science, 1997; composer musical compositions, articles. Bd. dirs. Humboldt Arts Coun., Eureka, 1998—.

MACCALLUM, (EDYTHE) LORENE, pharmacist; b. Monte Vista, Colo., Nov. 29, 1928; d. Francis Whittier and Berniece Viola (Martin) Scott; m. David Robertson MacCallum, June 12, 1952; children: Suzanne Rae MacCallum Barslund and Roxanne Kay MacCallum Batenel (twins), Tracy Scott, [illegible] Pharmacy U. Colo., 1950. Registered pharmacist, Colo. Pharmacist Presbyn. Hosp., Denver, 1950, Corner Pharmacy, Lamar, Colo., 1950-53; rsch. pharmacist Nat. Chlorophyll Co., Lamar, 1953; relief pharmacist various stores, Delta, Colo., 1957-59, Farmington, N.Mex., [illegible]

N.Mex., 1971-79; mgr. Med. Arts Pharmacy, Farmington, 1966-67; cons. pharmacist Navajo Hosp., Brethren in Christ Mission, Farmington, 1967-77, sales agt. Norris Realty, Farmington, 1977-78; pharmacist, owner, mgr. Lorene's Pharmacy, Farmington, 1979-88; tax cons. H&R Block, Farmington, 1968; cons. Pub. Svc. Co., N.Mex. Intermediate Clinic, Planned Parenthood, Farmington; first woman registered pharmacist apptd. N.Mex. Bd. Pharm., 1982-92. Author numerous poems for mag. Advisor Order Rainbow for Girls, Farmington, 1975-78. Mem. Nat. Assn. Bds. Pharmacy (com. on internship tng., com. edn., sec., treas. dist. 8, mem. impaired pharmacists adv. com., chmn. impaired pharmacists program N.Mex., 1987—, mem. law enforcement legis. com., chmn. nominating com. 1992), Nat. Assn. Retail Druggists, N.Mex. Pharm. Assn. (mem. exec. coun. 1977-81), Order Eastern Star (Farmington). Methodist. Home and Office: 1301 Camino Sol Farmington NM 87401-8075

MACCAULEY, HUGH BOURNONVILLE, banker; b. Mt. Vernon, N.Y., Mar. 12, 1922; s. Morris Baker and Alma (Gardiner) MacC.; m. Rachael Gleaton, Aug. 30, 1943 (div. May 1980); m. Felice Cooper, Dec. 2, 1980. Student, Rutgers U., 1939-41, Tex. Christian U., 1948-50, U. Omaha, 1957-59. With 102nd Cavalry, Essex Troop N.J. Nat. Guard, 1940-42; commd. 2d lt. U.S. Army, 1943; advanced through grades to col. U.S. Army, USAF, Washington, 1943-73; v.p. Great Am. Securities, San Bernardino, Calif., 1979-94; founder., chmn. bd. Desert Cmty. Bank, Victorville, Calif., 1980-95, chmn. emeritus, 1995; dir. Desert Cmty. bank, Victorville, Calif., 1996—; account exec. Gorian Thornes, Inc., San Bernardino, Calif., 1995-96; bd. dirs. Desert Cmty. Bank. bd. dirs. Air Force Village West, 1986-88; chmn. bd. and CEO Gen. and Mrs. Curtis E. Lemay Found., 1987—. Decorated Air medal, Legion of Merit. Mem. Daedalian Soc., Rotary, Internat. Platform Soc., Balboa Bay Club. Republican. Presbyterian. Avocation: golf. Home: 214 Golden West St Huntington Beach CA 92648

MACCLEAN, WALTER LEE, dentist; b. Sheridan, Wyo., July 10, 1935; s. Edward Satterlee and Eleanor Elizabeth (Weir) Mac.; m. Nancy Lee Strale, Sept. 4, 1965 (div. 1975); children: David Satterlee, Carrie Lynn. BS with honors, U. Wyo., 1957, postgrad., 1958; DMD, U. Oreg., Portland, 1962. Mil. dental adv. Korean Mil. Adv. Group, Wonju, 1962-63; chief dental svc. Dugway Chem. Testing Ctr., Utah, 1965-68; pvt. dental practice Cheyenne, Wyo., 1968-70; assoc. prof. Sheridan Coll., Wyo., 1970-76; staff dentist VA Hosp. Med. Ctr., Ft. Meade, S.D., 1976-93; ret., 1993; cons., lectr. Health Edn. Program Svc., Ft. Meade, 1984-93. With U.S. Army 1962-68. Mem. ADA. Episcopalian. Home: PO Box 450 Hardin MT 59034-0450 also: Highbourne House, 13-15 Marylebone High St, London W1M 3PE, England

MACCORKLE, EMMETT WALLACE, III, insurance agent; b. Portsmouth, Va., Feb. 10, 1942; s. Emmett Wallace and Nelda (Reymann) MacC.; m. Carol Britton, Dec. 27, 1964; children: Jeffrey W., Steven M. BA, Cornell U., 1964. CLU. Agt. Northwestern Mut. Life, San Francisco, 1967-72; dist. agt. Northwestern Mut. Life, San Mateo, 1972-80; pres. MacCorkle Ins. Svcs., San Mateo, 1980—. Mem. Cornell U. Coun., Ithaca, N.Y., 1986-89; mem. Bellarmine Coll. Prep. Bd. Regents, San Jose, Calif., 1988-91; mem. devel. com. Cartoon Art Mus., San Francisco, 1989-90. With USMC, 1964-67, Vietnam. Named Man of Yr., Peninsula Assn. Life Underwriters, San Mateo, 1980. Mem. Bohemian Club (San Francisco), Menlo Circus Club (Menlo Park, Calif.), Cornell Club No. Calif. (pres. 1974). Democrat. Avocations: amateur historian, toastmaster and buckle swasher. Home: 1060 Continental Dr Menlo Park CA 94025-6652 Office: MacCorkle Ins Svcs 1650 Borel Pl Ste 100 San Mateo CA 94402-3507

MACCORMACK, HARRY DILTS PROBJASKI, theater, stage production educator; b. Binghamton, N.Y., Oct. 8, 1942; s. Henry Edward and Naomi Ione (Yager) MacC.; m. Linda Vogelsong, 1967 (div.); children: Lani Cur, Blue Heron; m. Susan Posner, Jan. 1, 1978; m. Sabine Schulte, Apr. 4, 1991. BA, Lewis and Clark Coll., 1964; postgrad., Harvard U., 1964-65; MFA, U. Iowa, 1967. Headmaster Riverrun Live & Learn Cmty., Corvallis, 1970-72; instr. dept. English Oreg. State U., Corvallis, 1967-70, stage prodn. mgr., instr., 1974—; founder, pres., exec. dir. Oreg. Tilth, Salem, 1984-93; writer, poet Sunbow Studios, Corvallis, 1967—; owner, operator Sunbow Farm Organic Produce, Corvallis, 1972—. Author: Call of the Mountains, 1969, The Revolving Door, 1970, Organic Guidelines & Standards, 1986, The Transition Document, 1988. Bd. dirs. Lincoln County Farmers Market, 1986—; founder, past bd. dirs. Corvallis Saturday Market. Rockefeller Found. fellow, 1964; potato video grantee Dept. Environ. Quality, Salem, 1991, Sustain Agr. Iniative N.W. Area Found., St. Paul, 1989-92. Mem. Oreg. Tilth (founder, cons.). Home: 6910 SW Plymouth Dr Corvallis OR 97333 Office: Oreg State Univ Theatre Arts Withycombe Hall Corvallis OR 97331

MACDONALD, ALEXANDER EDWARD, meteorologist; b. Fort Snelling, Minn., Mar. 29, 1945; s. Alexander Colin and Marie Christine (Peterson) MacD.; m. Susan Hayes, June 17, 1969; children: Lee Alexander, Ann Elizabeth, Michael Hayes. BS, Mont. State U., 1967; MS, U. Utah, 1973, PhD, 1975. Meteorologist Nat. Weather Svc., Salt Lake City, 1973-80, NOAA/Forecast Systems Lab., Boulder, Colo., 1980—; dir. NOAA Forecast Systems Lab., 1988—. Capt. USAF, 1967-71. Fellow Am. Meteorol. Soc. (exec. com. 1993-96). Home: 8554 Thunderhead Dr Boulder CO 80302-9381 Office: NOAA/FSL 325 S Broadway St Boulder CO 80303-3464

MACDONALD, ANDREA DENYSE, editor, publisher, genealogist; b. Seattle, Oct. 23, 1953; d. Ples and Thelma Virginia (Crossman) Chaffin; m. Peter Michael MacDonald; children: Michellaine, Christopher, Athena. Layout person graphics Boeing Aerospace Co., Seattle, 1976-81; graphic illustrator Gen. Dynamics, San Diego, 1983-85; advt. coord. Small Bus. Report, Monterey, Calif., 1985-86; publ. mgr. Classmate, Monterey, 1986-87; editor, writer Awa Lau Wahine, Pearl Harbor, Hawaii, 1987-88; editor, writer newsletter Family Backtracking, Port Orchard, Wash., 1996-98; publisher, owner Sandy Moon Publ., Port Orchard, 1998—. Author, publisher: The Becketts of Calais, Maine and Scotland, 1998, The Crossmans of St. Mewan, England, 1998. Founder Wash. State Cemetery Assn., Port Orchard, 1998; svc. unit mgr. Girl Scouts Am., Honolulu, 1987-88. Mem. Assn. Profl. Genealogists, Nat. Geneal. Soc., DAR (chpt. registrar 1998—), Wash. State Geneal. Soc., Pacific N.W. Cornish Soc., Puget Sound Geneal. Soc. Office: Sandy Moon Publ PO Box 103 Port Orchard WA 98366-0103

MACDONALD, ANDREW STEPHEN, management consulting firm executive; b. Fairbanks, Alaska, July 15, 1953; s. Bernard L. and Rosemary (Unger) MacD.; m. Josephine A. Joanne, Aug. 4, 1972; children: Peter, Stephen, Charles. BA in Acctg., Seattle U., 1974. CPA, cert. mgmt. cons. Acct. Boeing Aerospace, Seattle, 1976-79; owner, pres. Triak Corp., Seattle, 1977—; pres. Exec. Cons. Group, Inc., Seattle, 1979—. Mem. AICPA, Inst. Mgmt. Cons., Wash. Soc. CPAs, Columbia Tower Club. Home: 10030 Lake Shore Blvd NE Seattle WA 98125-8158 Office: Exec Cons Group Inc 1111 3d Ave Ste 2700 Seattle WA 98101-3224

MACDONALD, HARRY MARTIN, Presbyterian minister, educator; b. L.A., Mar. 28, 1926; s. Archibald Campbell and Rachel (Martin) MacD.; m. Hope Joan Sevferts, June 15, 1948; children: Thomas, Daniel, Deborah. BA, Westmont Coll., 1948; BDiv, Am. Bapt. Sem. West, L.A., 1951; postgrad., L'Abri, Switzerland, 1961-62; D in Missiology, Trinity Evang. Divinity Sch., Chgo., 1983. Ordained Bapt. Ch., 1951. Staff Young Life Inc., L.A., 1948-55; area dir. Young Life Inc., Seattle, 1955-58, Pitts., 1958-61; gen. dir., founder Alvo Da Mocidade, Brazil, 1962-68; regional dir. Young Life Rocky Mt. Region, 1968-70; internat. dir. Young Life, 1970-80; sr. pastor John Knox Presbyn. Ch., Seattle, 1980-96, pastor emeritus, 1996—; cons. Lithuanian Christian Coll., Klaideda, Lithuania, 1996—; prof. Young Life Tng., Seattle, 1996—. Bd. dirs. INTERDEV, Seattle, 1986—; bd. trustees Whitworth Coll., Spokane, Wash., 1987-96; chmn. Regent Coll. Found., Seattle, 1988-93; bd. govs. Regent Coll., Vancouver, B.C., Can., 1989-98. Avocations: music, golf, travel, writing, speaking. E-mail: missiology@msn.com. Home: 835 SW Channon Dr Seattle WA 98166-3817

MACDONALD, KIRK STEWART, lawyer; b. Glendale, Calif., Oct. 24, 1940; s. Bruce Mace and Phyllis Jeanne MacDonald. BSCE, U. So. Calif., 1970; JD, Western State U., 1982. Bar: Calif. 1982, U.S. Dist. Ct. (cen. dist.) Calif. 1982, U.S. Ct. Appeals (9th cir.) 1982, U.S. Dist. Ct. (no. dist.) Calif. 1984, U.S. Dist. Ct. [illegible]

Pipe Inst., La Mirada, Calif., 1976-82; ptnr. Gill and Baldwin, Glendale, Calif., 1982—. Mem. ABA, L.A. County Bar Assn., Water Environ. Assn., Calif. Water Environ. Assn. Avocations: travel, woodworking. Office: Gill and Baldwin 130 N Brand Blvd Fl 4 Glendale CA 91203-2646

MACDONALD, NORVAL (WOODROW), safety engineer; b. Medford, Oreg., Dec. 8, 1913; s. Orion and Edith (Anderson) MacD.; m. Elizabeth Ann Clifford, Dec. 8, 1937; children: Linda (Mrs. Bob Comings), Peggy (Mrs. Don Lake), Kathleen (Mrs. Michael Nissenberg). Student, U. So. Calif., 1932-34. Registered profl. safety engr., Calif. Safety engr. Todd Shipyards, San Pedro, Calif., 1942-44, Pacific Indemnity Ins. Co., San Francisco, 1944-50; area safety engring. chief safety engr. Indsl. Ind., San Francisco, 1950-76; supervising safety engr. Beaver Ins. Co., 1976-82, v.p. loss control, 1982-88; cons. safety engr. MacDonald and Assocs., 1988-99; tchr. adult evening classes U. San Francisco, 1960-63, Golden Gate U., 1969-76. Contbr. articles to profl. jours.; producer safety training films. Mem. ASME, Am. Soc. Safety Engrs. (pres. San Francisco chpt. 1958, 59), Las Posas Country Club, Masons, Shriners, Am. Soc. Safety Engrs. (pres. 1958-59). Methodist. Home: 1710 Shoreline Dr Camarillo CA 93010-6018

MACDONNELL, KEVIN MICHAEL, pilot; b. Glen Cove, N.Y., Nov. 3, 1959; s. Sean Michael and Mary Noëlle (McEnhill) M. BS in aero. studies, Embry-Riddle Aero. U., 1981. Commd. 2d. lt. USMC, 1981, advanced through grades to capt., 1984-87; pilot Delta Air Lines, L.A., 1988-96; internat. pilot Delta Air Lines, N.Y.C., 1996—. Usher St. John Neumann Ch., Irvine, Calif., 1989—; Big Brother, Orange County, Calif., 1995—; line divsn. officer, USMC, 1984-86, aviation safety officer, USMC, 1986. Mem. So. Calif. Gaelic Athletic Assn. (pres. 1994), Wild Geese Gaelic Athletic Assn. (pres. 1992-96, lt. gov. resolution 1994), Platoon Leaders Class Club (pres. 1979-80). Roman Catholic. Avocations: running, reading, sailing, Irish cultural events, Irish sports. Home: 30 Magellan Aisle Irvine CA 92620-5717

MACDONNELL, PHILIP J., lawyer; b. Boston, Apr. 22, 1948. BA magna cum laude, Harvard U., 1971, JD cum laude, 1974. Bar: Ariz. 1974, U.S. Dist. Ct. Ariz. 1975, U.S. Ct. Appeals (9th cir.) 1976, U.S. Supreme Ct. 1978. Asst. atty. gen. Ariz. Atty. Gen.'s Office, 1975-77, chief counsel special prosecutions divsn., 1977-81; asst. U.S. atty. Dist. Ariz., 1981-85; supt. Ariz. Dept. Liquor Licenses and Control, 1985-87; atty. Jennings, Strouss and Salmon, Phoenix, 1987—. Editor Harvard Law Rev., 1972-73, sr. editor, 1973-74. Office: Jennings Strouss and Salmon 1 Renaissance Sq 2 N Central Ave Fl 1 600 Phoenix AZ 85004-4471*

MACDONOUGH, ROBERT HOWARD, retired consulting engineer, tax consultant; b. Chgo., Jan. 24, 1941; s. John Haaf and Helen Margaret (McWilliams) MacD.; m. Joan Carol Rosecrants, Dec. 28, 1963 (div. Nov. 1975); children: John Haaf, Thomas William, Mark Peter. BS in Engring. Ops., Iowa State U., 1962; MA in Econ., Drake U., 1966. Registered profl. engr., Iowa; enrolled agent. Assoc. Mgmt. Sci. Am., Palo Alto, Calif., 1969; mng. assoc. Theo. Barry & Assoc., Los Angeles, 1970-72; mgr. indsl. engring. Advanced Memory Systems, Sunnyvale, Calif., 1972-73; mgr. planning and engring. Signetics, Sunnyvale, 1973-75; pres. Facilities Cons., Mountain View, Calif., 1976-96; instr. H&R Block; cons. assoc. Shumaker Tax Cons. Mem. Inst. Indsl. Engrs. (sr.), Phi Gamma Delta. Mem. Phi Gamma Delta. Republican.

MACEK, ANNA MICHAELLA, cosmetics executive; b. Lancashire, Eng., Aug. 10, 1950; came to U.S., 1974; d. Wasyl and Maria (Litynska) Flaszczak; m. Frank Macek, Aug. 18, 1977. MA, U. Manchester, Eng., 1973; grad., Ecole des Estheticiennes Inst. de Beaute, Geneva, 1974. Asst. to pres., chief exec. officer Reed-Ingram Corp., N.Y.C., 1974-77; coordinator corp. pub. relations Northrop Corp., Los Angeles, 1978-82; pres. Annastasia Cosmetics, Gardena, Calif., 1983—. Contbr. articles to profl. jours. Mem. Beauty and Barber Supply Inst. Avocations: tennis, gardening.

MACELVAINE, WILLIAM STEPHEN, rancher, consultant; b. Topeka, Sept. 27, 1944; s. Robert Capps and Gretchen (Swatszel) MacE.; m. Susan Lynn Allison, June 14, 1968; children: Dianna, LeeAnn, Steve Jr., Brian. BS in Farm Mgmt., Calif. Poly. State Coll., San Luis Obispo, 1969. Water treatment plant operator I, waste water treatment plant operator II; comml. pilot. Owner, operator Souza Ranch, Morro Bay, Calif., 1965—, Rancho Colina Mobile Home Cmty., Morro Bay, Calif., 1971—; owner MacElvaine Consulting, Morro Bay, 1992—; dir. Mid State Fair Bd., Paso Robles, Calif., 1996—. County supr. dist. 2, Bd. Suprs. San Luis Obispo County, 1979-83; regional commr. So. Ctrl. Region Coastal Commn., San Luis Obispo, Santa Barbara and Ventura Counties, Calif., 1979-81; mem. Calif. Coastal Commn., 1983-92; Rep. nominee from dist. 18, Calif. Sentate, 1994. With Calif. N.G., 1963-69. Mem. San Luis Obispo County Farm Bur., Flying Samaritans (pilot 1990—), Calif. C. of C. Republican. Protestant. Avocations: flying, genealogy, chess, swimming. Home: 1325 Atascadero Rd Morro Bay CA 93442-1803 Office: Rancho Colina Mobile Home Cmty 1045 Atascadero Rd Morro Bay CA 93442-1800

MACER, GEORGE ARMEN, JR., orthopedic hand surgeon; b. Pasadena, Calif., Oct. 17, 1948; s. George A. and Nevart Akullian M.; m. Celeste Angelle Lyons, Mar. 26, 1983; children: Christiana Marilu, Marina Lynn, Emily Sue. BA, U. So. Calif., 1971, MD, 1976. Diplomate Am. Bd. Med. Examiners; diplomate in orthop. surgery and hand surgery Am. Bd. Orthop. Surgery. Intern Meml. Hosp. Med. Ctr., Long Beach, Calif., 1976; resident Orthop. Hosp./U. So. Calif., 1977-81; pvt. practice hand surgery Long Beach, 1983—; asst. clin. prof. orthops. U. So. Calif., L.A., 1983-89, 90—; cons. hand surgery svc. Rancho Los Amigos Hosp. Downey, 1990—; cons. Harbor UCLA Med. Ctr., Torrance, 1983—. Joseph Boyes Hand fellow, 1982; mem. AMA, Calif. Med. Assn., Los Angeles County Med. Assn., Western Orthop. Assn., Am. Soc. for Surgery of Hand, Am. Acad. Orthop. Surgery. Republican. Avocations: boating, skiing, scuba diving, carpentry. Office: 3550 Linden Ave Ste 2 Long Beach CA 90807-4577

MACGINITIE, WALTER HAROLD, psychologist; b. Carmel, Calif., Aug. 14, 1928; s. George Eber and Nettie Lorene (Murray) MacG.; m. Ruth Olive Kilpatrick, Sept. 2, 1950; children: Mary Catherine, Laura Anne. B.A., UCLA, 1949; A.M., Stanford U., 1950; Ph.D., Columbia U., 1960. Tchr. Long Beach (Calif.) Unified Sch. Dist., 1950, 1955-56; mem. faculty Columbia U. Tchrs. Coll., 1959-80, prof. psychology and edn., 1970-80; Lansdowne scholar, prof. edn. U. Victoria, B.C., Can., 1980-84; research assoc. Lexington Sch. Deaf, N.Y.C., 1963-69; mem. sci. adv. bd. Ctr. for Study of Reading, 1977-80, chmn. 1979-80. Co-author: Gates-MacGinitie Reading Tests, 1965, 78, 89, Psychological Foundations of Education, 1968; Editor: Assessment Problems in Reading, 1972; co-editor: Verbal Behavior of the Deaf Child, 1969. Life mem. Calif. PTA. Served with USAF, 1950-54. Fellow APA, AAAS, Am. Psychol. Soc., Nat. Conf. on Rsch. on Language and Literacy, N.Y. Acad. Scis.; mem. Internat. Reading Assn. (pres. 1976-77, Spl. Svc. award 1981), Reading Hall of Fame (pres. 1989-90). Home and Office: PO Box 1789 Friday Harbor WA 98250-1789

MACGREGOR, SHARON EVONNE, university official; b. Pocatello, Idaho, July 16, 1941; d. Willard Robert and Marian (Bartlett) Leisy; m. John Fred Cook, June 19, 1971 (div. Nov. 1980). BEd, No. Mont. Coll., 1970; M in Secondary Edn., U. Alaska, Juneau, 1980; EdD, U. San Francisco, 1987. Cert. secondary sch. tchr., Alaska. Loan officer 1st Nat. Bank, Havre, Mont., 1964-68; adminstrv. asst. Alaska State Legis., Juneau, 1970-71; tchr. Juneau Dist. High Sch., 1971-75; instr. Juneau Dist. Community Coll., 1975-79; assoc. prof. U. Alaska, Juneau, 1979-90, dean Sch. Bus. and Pub. Adminstrn.,, 1986-90; assoc. dean Coll. Tech., Boise (Idaho) State U., 1990—; editor in chief office tech. McGraw Hill Book Gregg Div., N.Y.C., 1983-84; mem. exec. bd. statewide assembly U. Region V Vocat. Assn., 1978-80, del. 1982. Treas. Alaska State Vocat. Assn., 1980-82, pres. elect, 1986, pres., 1987; pres. U. Alaska Juneau Assembly, 1978-80, v.p., 1980-82. No. Mont. Coll. scholar, Havre, 1968-70; named Outstanding Tchr., U. Alaska, 1976. Republican. Avocations: hiking, fishing, skiing, knitting. Home: [illegible] Boise ID [illegible] Office: Boise State U Coll Tech Office Assoc Dean 1910 University Dr Boise ID 83725-0399

[illegible]

Mamolen; m. Bradley K. Shearer, Mar. 18, 1990. B.F.A., San Francisco Art Inst., 1973; B.S., U. State N.Y., 1983; M. Planning, U. So. Calif., 1980; M.A., Calif. State U., L.A., 1984; PhD The Union Insts., 1995, Exec. dir. YWCA of U. So. Calif., L.A., 1980-81; instr. UCLA Extension, 1980, Calif. State U.-Northridge, 1982, Otis Art Inst. of Parsons Sch., L.A., 1979-82; instr. Maricopa Co. Cmty. Coll., 1993-95; facility planner-analyst Steinmann, Grayson, Smylie, L.A., 1981-82; asst. prof., program coord. environ. design program Sch. of Art, E. Carolina U., Greenville, N.C., 1984-86, psychology intern, TASC Inc., Phoenix Ariz., 1994-95, assoc. faculty, Goddard Coll., 1995-97, prof. Walden U. 1996—; mem. faculty Union Inst. Ctr. for Distant Learning, 1993—; project mgr. ednl. tech. & learning Technical U. BC, 1998; psychologist Napa (Calif.) State Hosp., 1997-98; writer, Fannie Mae, Washington, D.C., 1988; field editor Area Development mag., 1989-92; research asst. HUD, San Francisco, 1975; pres., prin. City Arts, L.A., 1978-84, Greenville, N.C., 1984-86, Washington, 1986-90, Machanic & Co., Phoenix, 1992-95, mindymac/Embracing Change, Portland, Oreg., 1998—; computer software trainer Forhan & Wakefield Group, Vienna, Va., 1989-90; instrnl. writer, project mgr. ComputerPrep, Phoenix, 1990-91;quality cons., instrnl. developer AG Comm. Systems, 1992; mental health therapist Salt River Indian Community Mental Health Svc., 1993-94; instructional designer/developer U. Phoenix, 1993-95. Movie reviewer Daily Reflector, Greenville, N.C., 1985, Dissertation: Waiting for Cancer Test Results: Impacts on the Patient & Family, 1996; contbr. articles and book revs. to profl. jours.; one-man shows include Lycoming Coll., Pa., 1974; exhibited in group shows So. Exposure Gallery, San Francisco, 1974, 75, Barnsdall Park Mcpl. Gallery, Los Angeles, 1981, Gray Gallery, E. Carolina U., 1984, 85, 86, Community Council for Arts, Kinston, N.C., 1985, Art League Gallery, Alexandria, Va., 1986, Gallerie Triangle, Washington, 1987, Western Eye, Phoenix Coll., 1991; patentee Stay-Dry Toilet Seat. Peer counselor Bosom Buddies Breast Cancer Hotline, 1993-95; mem. Maricopa County South Area Behavioral Health Adv. Coun., Phoenix, 1993-94; speaker, facilitator Parents Anonymous, Phoenix, 1992. Mem. APA, Am. Psychol. Soc., Am. Soc. Tng. and Devel., Lemon Grove Hist. Soc., Friends of the Libr., The Am. Poet. Democrat. Jewish. Avocations: science, gardening, travel, drawing, photography.

MACHUNG, ANNE, sociologist, writer; b. Long Beach, Calif., Jan. 30, 1947; d. Peter and Alice (Nelson) Machung; m. Ron Rothbart. PhD, Univ. Wis., 1983. Dir. women & work rsch. project Univ. Calif., Berkeley, Calif., 1985-86; dir. vis asst. prof. women's studies Diablo Valley Coll., Pleasanto, Calif., 1987; rsch. analyst Univ. Calif., Berkeley, 1989-92, sr. policy analyst, 1992-96; dir. acad. svcs. San Francisco State Univ., San Francisco, 1996-97; cons. Higher Edn. Policy, Berkeley, 1998. Co-author: The Second Shift, 1989; contbr. articles to profl. jours. Recipient Notable Book of Yr. award N.Y. Times, 1990, Disting. Achievement award Nat. Women's Politica Caucus, 1991. Office: Higher Edn Policy Cons 1003 Keith Ave Berkeley CA 94708-1604

MACIAS, CARLOS, artist; b. Managua, Nicaragua, Nov. 4, 1949; came to U.S., 1983; s. Carlos Perez Mora and Dora M.; m. Veronica Bustamante, May 5, 1985 (div. Sept. 1987); 1 child, Nicole Perez. B, La Salle Inst., Managua, Nicaragua, 1968; JD, U. Centroamericana, Managua, Nicaragua, 1972. Author: Journey to Zakhar, 1973; dir., producer (films) Museum, 1988, Adversaly Yours, 1988. Buddhist. Home: PO Box 67a37 Los Angeles CA 90067-1037

MACINTYRE, PATRICIA COLOMBO, middle school educator; b. San Diego, Jan. 20, 1955; d. Vincent Christopher Colombo and Ellen Louise (Johnson) David; m. John Malcolm MacIntyre, July 25, 1981; children: Ann Marie, Katherine Christine. BA, San Diego State U., 1977; MA in Computer Edn., U.S. Internat. U., 1987. Cert. tchr., Calif. Math. and art tchr. Adams Jr. High Sch., Richmond, Calif., 1979-80; math. and computer tchr. Piedmont (Calif.) Middle Sch., 1980-81, La Jolla (Calif.) Country Day Sch., 1982-85; adminstrv. asst. to headmaster St. Michael's Sch., Newport, R.I., 1981-82; math. tchr. Kubasaki High Sch., Dept. Def. Dependents Sch., Okinawa, Japan, 1989-90; compuer tchr., tech. coord. Palm Middle Sch., Lemon Grove, Calif., 1985—; local telementor Calif. Tech. Project, 1994-95. Selected for KUSI TV's Class Act, 1995, One of 20 Top Tchrs. in San Diego County, 1995; recipient Honoring Our Own award San Diego Sch. Bds. Assn., 1995. Mem. San Diego Computer-Using Educators (grantee 1991), Phi Kappa Phi. Republican. Roman Catholic. Avocations: children, family activities. Office: Palm Middle Sch 8425 Palm St Lemon Grove CA 91945-3314

MACK, BRENDA LEE, sociologist, public relations consulting company executive, media executive; b. Peoria, Ill., Mar. 24; d. William James and Virginia Julia (Pickett) Palmer; m. Rozene Mack, Jan. 13 (div.); 1 child, Kevin Anthony. AA, L.A. City Coll.; BA in Sociology, Calif. State U., L.A., 1980. Ct. clk. City of Blythe, Calif.; ptnr. Mack Trucking Co., Blythe; owner Brenda Mack Enterprises, L.A., 1981—, Mack Media Presents, L.A., 1994—; conflict mediator, artists' rep., cultural sensitivity cons.; lectr., writer, radio and TV personality; prodr., writer, host T.V. talk show Brenda Says; cons. European cmty.; co-originator advt. concept View/Door Project; pub. News from the United States newsletter through U.S. and Europe.Past bd. dirs. Narcotic Symposium, L.A. With WAC, U.S. Army. Mem. Women For, Calif. State U. L.A. Alumni Assn., World Affairs Coun., German-Am. C. of C., European Cmty. Studies Assn. Home: 8749 Cattaraugus Ave Los Angeles CA 90034-2558 Office: PO Box 555942 Los Angeles CA 90055-0942

MACK, CHARLES DANIEL, III, labor union executive; b. Oakland, Calif., Apr. 16, 1942; m. Marlene Helen Fagundes, Oct. 15, 1960; children: Tammy, Kelly, Kerry, Shannon. B.A., San Francisco State Coll., 1964. Truck driver Garrett Freight Lines, Emeryville, Calif., 1962-66; bus. agt. Teamsters Local No. 70, Oakland, 1966-70, sec.-treas., 1972—; legis. rep. Calif. Teamsters Pub. Affairs Council, Sacramento, 1970-71; trustee Western Conf. Teamsters Pension Trust Fund, 1980—, pres. Teamsters' Joint Council 7, San Francisco, 1982—, v.p. western region, 1998—; regional v.p. Internat. Union, 1998; mem. Calif. Inst. for Fed. Policy Rsch., 1993—. Bd. dirs. Econ. Devel. Corp. of Oakland, 1980-90, Calif. Compensation Ins. Fund, San Francisco, 1980-86, Calif. Coun. Econ. and Environ. Balance, The Calif. Found. on Environ. and the Economy.

MACK, J. CURTIS, II, civic organization administrator; b. Los Angeles, Dec. 22, 1944; s. James Curtis and Ahli Christina (Youngren) M.; m. Tamara Jo Kriner, Jan. 23, 1988; children: James Curtis III, Robert Lee. BA cum laude, U. So. Calif., 1967, M in Pub. Adminstrn., 1969, MA, 1976. Asst. to regional dir. VA, Los Angeles, 1973-79; exec. dir. Citizens for the Republic, Santa Monica, Calif., 1979-85; asst. sec. oceans and atmosphere U.S. Dept. Commerce, Washington, 1985-88; pres. Los Angeles World Affairs Coun., 1988—; bd. dirs. Brentwood Bank of Calif. Mem. Pres.'s Commn. on White House Fellowships, 1984-85. Col. USAFR, 1969-99. Mem. Nat. Space Club (bd. dirs. 1987-88). Republican. Episcopalian. Avocation: philatelist. Office: LA World Affairs Coun 911 Wilshire Blvd Ste 1730 Los Angeles CA 90017-3454

MACKAIG, JANET BROWNLEE, artist, printmaker, educator; b. Santa Monica, Calif., July 16, 1931; d. Roy Edward and Lorna (Feckler) Murphy; A.A., Pasadena City Coll., 1964; B.A., Calif. State U., Los Angeles, 1969, M.A., 1971, postgrad., 1975; postgrad. UCLA, 1975; m. Richard Allaire Mackaig, Dec. 15, 1950; children—Janet (Mrs. William Chadwick), Steven Richard. Tchr., Creative Arts Group, Sierra Madre, Calif., 1965-75, Duarte (Calif.) Unified Sch. Dist., 1973-76; tchr. Otis Art Inst., Los Angeles, 1975-76, Saddleback Coll., Mission Viejo, Calif., 1976-78, Laguna Beach Sch. Art, 1980—; one-man shows: Upstairs Gallery, Claremont, Calif., 1969, U. Oreg., 1976, Fine Arts Gallery, Laguna Beach, Calif., 1981, Minot (N.D.) State Coll., 1981; group shows include: Colorprint U.S.A., Tex. Tech. U., 1975, U. Ala., 1975, Pioneer Press Traveling Print Show, Africa, 1975-76, Art-A Multi-Cultural Show, Calif. Mus. Sci. and Industry, 1978, Contemporary Korean Printmakers Assn. Print Show, 1978, Coos Art Mus., Coos Bay, Oreg., 1979, La Grange (Ga.) Coll., 1980, Trenton (N.J.) State Coll., 1980, Internat. Print Biennial, Miami, Fla., 1982, Nat. Printmaking Invitational, San Bernardino, Calif., 1983, Angeles Gate Cultural Ctr., San Pedro, Calif.; represented in permanent collections. Bd. dirs. Womanspace, 1974—. Recipient Calif. Purchase awards Santa Monica Coll., 1973, Calif. State U., Los Angeles, 1976, Calif. Poly. U., Pomona, 1979. Mem. Laguna Beach Art Assn., Calif. Soc. Printmakers, Los Angeles Printmaking Soc. (pres. 1977-78), Los Angeles Inst. Contemporary Art, Print Club Phila., Pasadena Artists Concern. Club: Pioneer Press. Home: 23821 Salvador Bay Monarch Beach CA 92629-4207

MACKAY, PATRICIA MCINTOSH, counselor; b. San Francisco, Sept. 12, 1922; d. William Carroll and Louise Edgerton (Keen) McIntosh; AB in Psychology, U. Calif., Berkeley, 1944, elem. teaching credential, 1951; MA in Psychology, John F. Kennedy U., Orinda, Calif., 1979; PhD in Nutrition, Donsbach U., Huntington Beach, Calif., 1981; m. Alden Thorndike Mackay, Dec. 15, 1945; children—Patricia Louise, James McIntosh, Donald Sage. Cert. marriage, family and child counselor. Elem. tchr. Mt. Diablo Unified Sch. Dist., Concord, Calif., 1950-60; exec. supr. No. Calif. Welcome Wagon Internat., 1960-67; wedding cons. Mackay Creative Svcs., Walnut Creek, Calif., 1969-70; co-owner Courtesy Calls, Greeters and Concord Welcoming Svcs., Walnut Creek, 1971-94; marriage, family and child counselor, nutrition cons., Walnut Creek, 1979—; coord. Alameda and Contra Costa County chpts. Parents United, 1985—, pres. region 2; bd. dirs. New Directions Counseling Ctr., Inc., 1975-81, founder, pres. aux., 1977-79. Bd. dirs. Ministry in the Marketplace, Inc.; founder, dir. Turning Point Counseling; active Walnut Creek Presbyn. Ch.; bd. dirs. counseling dir. Shepherd's Gate-shelter for homeless women and children, 1985-92, Contra Costa County Child Care Coun., 1993, 94, 95. Recipient Individual award New Directions Counseling Ctr., 1978, awards Neo-Life Co. Am. Prestige Club, yearly, 1977-86, Cmty. Svc. award Child Abuse Prevention Coun., 1990, 92, 94. Mem. Assn. Marriage and Family Therapists, Parents United Internat. (pres. region 2, bd. dirs. 1992), U. Calif. Berkeley Alumni (sec. 1979-94), C. of C., Prytanean Alumnae, Delta Gamma. Republican. Club: Soroptimist (dir. 1976, 86) (Walnut Creek). Home: 1101 Scots Ln Walnut Creek CA 94596-5432 Office: 1399 Ygnacio Valley Rd Ste 34 Walnut Creek CA 94598-2815

MACKENZIE, PETER SEAN, instructional designer; b. L.A., Aug. 25, 1954; s. William Duncan and Patricia Ann (Kronschnabel) Mack; m. Carin Willette, Dec. 28, 1983; 1 child, Liam Reynolds. BA, Western Wash. U., 1976. Bus. editor Skagit Valley Herald, Mount Vernon, Wash., 1976-79; mng. editor Stanwood (Wash.)-Camano News, 1979-84; graphic artist Pacific Media Group, Seattle, 1985-90, editor, 1990-94; instnl. designer Mosaix, Inc. (formerly Digital Systems Internat.), Redmond, Wash., 1994—; instr. U. Wash. Exptl. Coll., Seattle, 1990-91, 96-97. Author: Jumper, 1989; rec. artist LP KEZX Album Project, 1987, Victory Music Vol. # 2, 1988; speaker Viacom Cable Pub. Access TV, Seattle, 1990. V.p. Stanwood, Wash. C. of C., 1983. Recipient 1st place newswriting award Wash. Newspaper Pubs. Assn., 1981, 82, 2d place award for comprehensive coverage, 1982, 3d place awards in newswriting, features and spot news, 1983. Mem. Internat. Soc. PErformance Improvement (Pugot Sound chpt.). Avocations: photography, music, political research, philosophy. Home: 316 NW 86th St Seattle WA 98117-3125 Office: Mosaix Inc 6464 185th Ave NE Redmond WA 98052-5032

MACKEY, WAYNE ALLISON, electrical engineer; b. Pitts., Sept. 22, 1955; s. George Allison and Dorothy Jayne (Ross) M.; m. Mary Lou Herbers, Nov. 16, 1984; children: Benjamin Paul, Craig Thomas. BSEE and Econs., Carnegie Mellon U., 1977; MS in Engring., Loyola Marymount U., L.A., 1982. Engr. space and info. systems Raytheon Co., Sudbury, Mass., 1977-78; mem. tech. staff Hughes Aircraft Co., El Segundo, Calif., 1978-84, head tech. sect., 1984-87, sr. scientist, engr., 1987-90, div. sr. scientist, 1990—, team leader event based concurrent engring., 1991—, team leader estimating process improvement, 1992, team leader customer focused quality and orgn. metrics system, 1993, team leader 6 Sigma quality, 1994, team leader RCS supplier devel., 1995; prin. cons., founder CCC Solutions, Manhattan Beach, Calif., 1997—; prin. Product Devel. Consulting Inc., 1997—; team leader 6 Sigma quality, 1994; exec. advisor to Mgmt. Roundtable Inc., 1995, material ops. mgr., 1995; conf. chmn., spkr. Metrics for Product Devel. and Project Mgmt., 1996, 97; team leader best practices supplier cert., 1996; team leader Nat. Metrics Task Force, 1997; mem. Stanford Integrated Mfg. Assn., Stanford Global Supply Chain Forum, MIT Lean Aircraft Initiative, MIT Supplier Sys. and Relationships Focus Group. Inventor automated environ. tester, universal FLIR tester, automatic bid/spread sheet, four steps metric process. Fellow Hughes Corp. Edn. Coun., 1980. Mem. Am. Soc. Quality Control, Assn. Proposal Mgmt. Profls., Tau Beta Pi. Avocations: high end audio equipment, music, skiing, guitar. Office: Product Devel Consulting Inc 1315 10th St Manhattan Beach CA 90266-6035

MACKIE, EDWARD BUCHANAN, lawyer; b. Vancouver, B.C., Can., June 1, 1937; came to U.S., 1939; s. George McKay and Lily Crawford (Home) M.; m. Anne Bachofner, Sept. 30, 1967; children: Erin Leigh, Kevin Reid. BA in Polit. Sci., Yale U., 1959; LLB, U. Wash., 1962. Bar: Wash. 1962, U.S. Dist. Ct. (we. dist.) Wash. 1962, U.S. Ct. Appeals (9th cir.) 1963, U.S. Supreme Ct. 1966. Law clk. to chief justice Wash. Supreme Ct., Olympia, 1962-63; asst. atty. gen. Wash. Atty. Gen.'s Office, Olympia, 1964-69; dep. atty. gen. Wash. Atty. Gen.'s Office, 1969-81, chief dep. atty. gen., 1981-93; instr. Wash. Law Enforcement Tng. Schs., 1965-71; adj. prof. U. Puget Sound Law Sch., Tacoma, 1976-78, Seattle Univ. Law Sch., 1996—; bd. dirs., pres. Wash. State Employees Credit Union, 1970-79; mem. Wash. Jud. Selection Commn., 1976-79; lectr. Ariz. Acad., Phoenix, 1979. Mem. Thurston County Bd. Freeholders, 1979. Mem. ABA, Assn. Govt. Lawyers, Lions. Avocations: skiing. Home: 7925 Zangle Rd NE Olympia WA 98506-9786

MACKINTOSH, FREDERICK ROY, oncologist; b. Miami, Fla., Oct. 4, 1943; s. John Harris and Mary Carlotta (King) MacK.; m. Judith Jane Parnell, Oct. 2, 1961 (div. Aug. 1977); children: Lisa Lynn, Wendy Sue; m. Claudia Lizanne Flournoy, Jan. 7, 1984; 1 child, Gregory Warren. BS, MIT, 1964, PhD, 1968; MD, U. Miami, 1976. Intern then resident in gen. medicine Stanford (Calif.) U., 1976-78, fellow in oncology, 1978-81; asst. prof. med. U. Nev., Reno, 1981-85, assoc. prof., 1985-92, prof. medicine, 1992—. Contbr. articles to profl. jours. Fellow ACP; mem. Am. Soc. Clin. Oncology, Am. Cancer Soc. (pres. Nev. chpt. 1987-89, Washoe chpt. 1988-90), No. Nev. Cancer Coun. (bd. dirs. 1981-92), No. Calif. Cancer Program (bd. dirs. alt. 1983-87, bd. dirs. 1987-91). Avocation: bicycling. Office: Nev Med Group 781 Mill St Reno NV 89502-1320

MACLAUCHLIN, ROBERT KERWIN, communications artist, educator; b. Framingham, Mass., Oct. 8, 1931; s. Charles Lewis and Elinor Frances (Kerwin) MacL.; m. Elizabeth D'Ann Willson, June 13, 1964. BA in Sociology, U. Mass., Amherst, 1954; MEd, Bridgewater State Coll., 1958; MS in Radio and TV, Syracuse U., 1959; PhD in Speech, Radio, TV, Mich. State U., 1969. Personnel trainee Nat. Security Agy., Washington, 1954-55; elem. sch. tchr. Mattapoisett (Mass.) Pub. Schs., 1957-58; asst. prof., dir. programming Maine Ednl. TV Network, Orono, 1959-66; assoc. prof. speech communications, dir. TV-Radio instrn. Colo. State U., Ft. Collins, 1969-76, prof., dir. TV-Radio instrn., 1976-98, prof. emeritus, 1998—; cons. U. Maine, Orono, 1968, Ft. Collins Presbyn. Ch., 1976-78, Sta. KCOL-AM-FM, Ft. Collins, 1978, Pub. Health Assn., Ft. Collins, 1985; archives program guest Maine Pub. Broadcast, Orono, 1983. Festival luncheon spkr. dist. convention Rotary Club, 1998. Served with inf. U.S. Army, 1955-57. Recipient Excellence in Teaching award Mich. State U., 1969, Friend of Broadcasting award Colo. Broadcasters Assn., 1985, Resolution award Colo. Broadcasters Assn., 1997, Oliver P. Pennock Disting. Svc. award Colo. State U., 1997; named Disting. Vis. Prof. U. Vt., Burlington, 1983, A Teacher Who Makes A Difference Denver's Rocky Mountain News, KCNC-TV, 1987. Mem. NATA (panel Colo. chpt. 1989—), Broadcast Edn. Assn. (Industry State chmn. 1981-86, panel 1991—, chmn. faculty internship com. 1991—), Colo. Broadcasters Assn. (edn. com. 1972—, Hall of Fame com. 1980—, human resources com. 1991, Friend of Broadcast award 1985, panelist summer conv. 1994, panelist summer conv. 1995), Broadcast Pioneers (charter mem. Colo. chpt.), Kiwanis (Disting. past pres. 1979-80). Republican. Avocations: outdoor activities. Home: 1407 Country Club Rd Fort Collins CO 80524-1907

MACLEAN, JUDITH E., writer, editor; b. L.A., May 13, 1946; d. Fred M. and Dorothy C. (Schmidt) MacL. BA, Rice U., 1969; postgrad., Duquesne U., 1970-71; postgrad. lang. study, Sorbonne U., 1966. Family therapist Families Together, Pitts., 1974-76; reporter In These Times, Chgo., 1976-77; co-chmn. New Am. Movement, Chgo., 1977-79; editor Am. Soc. on Aging, San Francisco, 1980-85; freelance writer, editor San Francisco, 1986—; instr. U. Calif. Berkeley ext., San Francisco, 1994-95, Support Ctr., San Francisco, 1992-93. Co-author: (book) Women Take Care, 1986; contbr. articles/stories to publs. Newsletter editor: Harvey Milk Lesbian and Gay Dem. Club, San Francisco, 1982-85, polit. action chmn., 1986-87; mem. nat. com. New Am. Movement, Pitts., 1972-76; mem. Nicaragua Solidarity Brigarde, Leon, Nicaragua, 1986. Named Vol. of Yr. Harvey Milk Lesbian and Gay Dem. Club, San Francisco, 1986. Mem. Media Alliance. Avocations: cross-country skiing, backpacking, mini-triathlons, hiking, sea kayaking.

MACLEOD, ALEX, newspaper editor; b. Seattle. Student, Whitman Coll. Night reporter to city editor to asst. mng. editor-news Seattle Times, 1976-84, assoc. mng. editor, 1984-86, mng. editor, 1986—. Office: Seattle Times PO Box 70 Seattle WA 98111*

MACLEOD, DIANNE SACHKO, educator; b. Comox, Canada, Nov. 15, 1941; came to U.S., 1963; d. Samuel Dennis and Pearl Anne (Belyk) S.; m. Norman Macleod, June 27, 1976; 1 child, Alexander. BA (hon.), U. British Columbia, Vancouver, 1963; MA, U. Calif., Berkeley, 1975, PhD, 1981. Asst. dir. Pomeroy Galleries, San Francisco, 1966-69; visual arts coord. Calif. Arts Commn., Sacramento, 1969-71; prof. art history U. Calif., Davis, 1981—; reviewer Getty Post-doctoral Fellowships, Brentwood, Calif., 1995—. Author: Art and the Victorian Middle Class: Money and the Making of Cultural Identity, 1996; co-editor: Orientalism Transposed: The Impact of the Colonies on British Culture, 1998; guest editor Victorian Poetry, 1995; mem. editl. bd. Journal of Pre-Raphaelite and Aesthetic Studies, 1988-95. Mem. edn. com. Britain Meets the Bay, British Consulate, San Francisco, 1997. Fellow Nat. Endowment for the Humanities, 1987; Fulbright-Hays scholar Courtauld Inst., London, 1978-79. Mem. Am. Soc. Aesthetics, Am. Historical Assn., Coll. Art Assn., Interdisciplinary Nineteenth-Century Studies Assn. Democrat. Avocations: reading detective novels, walking, swimming, speaking French. E-mail: dsmacleod@ucdavis.edu. Fax: (510) 428-0695. Home: 340 62d St Oakland CA 94618-1216 Office: Dept Art and Art Hist One Shields Ave Univ Calif Davis CA 95616

MACLEOD, RICHARD PATRICK, foundation administrator; b. Boston, Apr. 2, 1937; s. Thomas Everett and Margaret Gertrude (Fahey) MacL.; children: Kimberly Margaret Hamelin, Richard Alexander MacLeod. BA in Govt., U. Mass., 1960; MA in Internat. Rels., U. So. Calif., 1968. Instr. polit. sci. USAF Acad., 1968-71; Commd. 2d lt. USAF, 1960, advanced through grades to col., 1981; sr. rsch. fellow The Nat. Def. U., Washington, 1978-79; chief Space Policy Br., dep. chief Plans USAF Aerospace Def. Command, 1979-80; exec. officer to the comdr. in chief USAF Aerospace Def. Command, NORAD, 1980-81; chief of staff NORAD, 1981-84, USAF Space Command, 1982-84; ret. U.S. Space Found., 1985; exec. dir. U.S. Space Found., Colorado Springs, Colo., 1985-88; pres. U.S. Space Found., Colorado Springs, 1988-97, dir., 1997—; bd. dirs. Analytical Surveys, Inc., Colorado Springs, 1985—, U.S. Space Found., 1997—; space edn. advisor Coll. Engring. Adv. Coun., U. Colo., Colorado Springs. Author: Peoples War in Thailand, Insurgency in the Modern World, 1980. Mem. White House Space Policy Adv. Bd.; bd. dirs. Pike's Peak Coun. Boy Scouts Am., Colorado Springs; past pres. Colorado Springs Symphony Coun.; past dir. World Affairs Coun., Colorado Springs. Fellow Brit. Interplanetary Soc.; mem. AIA, Air Force Acad. Found. (bd. dirs., trustee), U.S. Space Found. (founding), Aviation Space Writers Assn., Air Force Space Ops. Assn., GPS Internat. Assn., Am. Legion, The Co. of Fifers and Drummers. Office: US Space Found 2860 S Circle Dr Ste 2301 Colorado Springs CO 80906-4184

MACMULLEN, DOUGLAS BURGOYNE, writer, editor, retired army officer, publisher; b. Berkeley, Calif., Dec. 26, 1919; s. T. Douglas and Florence (Burgoyne) MacM.; ed. San Francisco State U., 1937-41, Stanford U., U. Calif., Fgn. Svc. Inst., Strategic Intelligence Sch., Indsl. Coll. of the Armed Forces, Air War Coll., Army Mgmt. Sch.; m. Sherry Bernice Auerbach, Mar. 11, 1942; 1 child, Douglas Burgoyne Jr. Commd. 2d lt. F.A. Res. U.S. Army, 1941; advanced through grades to col. M.I., 1967; Army gen. staff Psychol. Ops. Fgn. Svc., PIO; ret., 1972; exec. editor Am. Rsch. Assoc., Sherman Oaks, Calif.; cons. in communication; accredited corr. Def. Dept. Bd. govs. Monte Vista Grove Homes, Pasadena, Calif., Shriners Hosps. for Crippled Children, L.A.; pres. Clan MacMillan Soc. N.Am., 1973-77, trustee, 1975—; mem. L.A. Olympics Citizens Adv. Commn., 1982-84; mem. L.A. Philanthropic Found.; bd. dirs. Masonic Press Club, L.A., 1975, 84-88; mem. steering com. Mayor L.A. Coun. Internat. Visitors and Sister Cities, 1969; hon. dep. sheriff San Bernardino County, Calif., 1996—; chmn. Los Angeles-Glasgow Sister Cities Ad Hoc Com.; former mem. San Francisco Mayor's Mil. and Naval Affairs Com.; mem. wills and gifts com. Shriners Hosp. Crippled Children, Al Malaikah Temple, L.A., 1974-80; cons. com. on pub. info. Masons Grand Lodge of Calif., 1985-86, 98—. Decorated Legion of Merit, Army Commendation medal (U.S.), Knight Comdr. Order of Polonia Restituta (Free Poland), Red Cross of Constantine; Royal Order Scotland. Mem. Internat. Inst. Strategic Studies, Assn. Former Intelligence Officers (pres. L.A. County chpt.), U.S. Naval Inst., Assn. U.S. Army, Company Mil. Historians, St. Andrew's Soc. Los Angeles (past pres., trustee), Air Force Assn., Coun. Brit. Socs., United Scottish Soc., Chinese Hist. Soc. Am., Chinese Hist. Soc. So. Calif., Ret. Officers Assn., Calif. State Sheriff's Assn., Friends Brit. Lib., Stanford U. Alumni Assn., Calif. Newspaper Pubs. Assn., Nat. Def. Exec. Res., Hereditary Companion Royal Hose of O'Conor (Ireland), Sigma Delta Chi. Republican. Presbyterian. Clubs: Army & Navy Club (Washington). Lodges: Masons (32 deg.), K.T., Shriners (editor, pub. The Al Malaikahan, former imperial news editor Shrine of N.Am.), Quatuor Coronati C.C. Co-author: Psychological Profile of Cambodia, 1971; author-editor: A Sentimental Journey--The History of the First Hundred Years, 1988; numerous other publs. and articles; radio commentator and newspaper columnist on mil., polit. and internat. affairs. Address: PO Box 5201 Sherman Oaks CA 91413-5201

MACNAB, JJ, financial planner, insurance analyst, consultant; b. Encino, Calif., July 17, 1964; m. Eric Kendall, Apr. 28, 1995. BA in Internat. Rels., U. Calif., Berkeley. CFP; chartered life underwriter. Dir. advanced underwriting Equitable Life Ins., San Francisco, 1986-89; fin. planner New Eng. Securities, San Rafael, Calif., 1989-91, Planning & Fin. Advisors, San Francisco, 1991-97; pres. Generic Prodns., San Mateo, Calif., 1996—, MacNab Consulting, San Francisco, 1997—. Editor: (newsletter) Perspectives, 1994-98; author: (newsletter) Planned Giving Today, 1998. Vol. Adult Literacy, Oakland, 1996. Mem. Internat. Assn. Fin. Planners, No. Calif. Planned Giving Coun., Peninsula Estate Planning Coun. Liberterian. Avocations: opera, stained glass, travel. Fax: 415-421-1228. E-mail: jjmacnab@dnai.com. Home: 120 W 3d Ave San Mateo CA 94402 Office: MacNab Consulting 155 Montgomery St Ste 408 San Francisco CA 94104-4109

MACNEAL, RICHARD HENRI, company executive, researcher; b. Warsaw, Ind., Feb. 25, 1923; s. Kenneth F. MacNeal and Marguerite M.J. (Giroud) MacNeal Cummin; m. Carolyn J. Colcord, May 30, 1946; children: Robert K., Bruce E., Paul D. BA, Harvard U., 1943; MS, Calif. Inst. Tech., 1947, PhD, 1949. Asst. prof. Calif. Inst. Tech., Pasadena, 1949-55; engr. Lockheed Calif. Co., Burbank, 1955-56; mgr. Computer Engring. Assocs., Pasadena, 1956-62; CEO MacNeal Schwendler Corp., L.A., 1963-85, 91-96, chmn., 1963-97; mem. adv. bd. NASA, Washington, 1974-75. Author: Electric Circuit Analysis for Elastic Structures, 1962, Finte Elements: Their Designs and Performance, 1993; contbr. articles to profl. jours.; mem. editl. bd. Computers and Structures, 1971-97, Finite Elements in Analysis and Designs, 1985—. Gov. Idyllwild Arts Found., Calif., 1984—, pres., 1987-92. Enlisted U.S. Army, 1943-46. Recipient Elmer A. Sperry award Sperry Found., 1997. Fellow AIAA (Structure Dynamics and Materials award lecture 1982); mem. Nat. Acad. Engring., Calif. Inst. Tech. (disting. alumnus 1998). Avocation: oil painting. Home and Office: 501 Highland Dr La Canada CA 91011-4032

MAC NEIL, JOSEPH NEIL, archbishop; b. Sydney, N.S., Can., Apr. 15, 1924; s. John Martin and Kate (Mac Lean) Mac N. BA, St. Francis Xavier U., Antigonish, N.S., 1944; postgrad., Holy Heart Sem., Halifax, N.S., 1944-48, U. Perugia, 1956, U. Chgo., 1964; JCD, U. St. Thomas, Rome, 1958. Ordained priest Roman Cath. Ch., 1948. Pastor parishes in N.S., 1948-55; officialis Chancery Office, Antigonish, 1958-59; adminstrn. Diocese of Antigonish, 1959-60; rector Cathedral Antigonish, 1961; dir. extension dept. St. Francis Xavier U., Antigonish, 1961-69, v.p., 1962-69; bishop St. John, N.B., Can., 1969-73; chancellor U. St. Thomas, Fredericton, N.B., 1969-73;

archbishop of Edmonton, Alta., 1973—; chmn. Alta Bishops' Conf., 1973—; chmn. bd. Newman Theol. Coll., Edmonton, 1973—, St. Joseph's Coll. U. Alta., Edmonton, 1973—. Vice chmn. N.S. Voluntary Econ. Planning Bd., 1965-69; bd. dirs. Program and Planning Agy., Govt. of N.S., 1969; exec. Atlantic Provinces Econ. Coun., 1968-73, Can. Coun. Rural Devel., 1965-75; bd. dirs. Futures Secretariat, 1981, Ctr. for Human Devel., Toronto, Ont., Can., 1985—; mem. bd. mgmt. Edmonton Gen. Hosp., 1983-92, Edmonton Caritas Health Group, 1992—; mem. Nat. Com. for Can. Participation in Habitat, 1976. Mem. Can. Assn. Adult Edn. (past pres. N.S.), Can. Assn. Dirs. Univ. Extension and Summer Schs. (past pres.), Inst. Rsch. on Pub. Policy (founding mem.), Can. Conf. Cath. Bishops (pres. 1979-81, mem. com. on ecumenism 1985-91, com. on missions 1991-96, mem. permanent coun. 1993-95). Address: Archbishop of Edmonton, 8421 101st Ave, Edmonton, AB Canada T6A 0L1

MACON, CAROL ANN GLOECKLER, micro-computer data base management company executive; b. Milw., Mar. 25, 1942; d. William Theodore and Gwendolyn Martha (Rice) Gloeckler; m. Jerry Lyn Macon, Aug. 28, 1981; children: Christian, Marie. BS in Edn. cum laude, U. Wis., Milw., 1969; postgrad., Midwestern State U., Wichita Falls, Tex., 1977, U. Tex., San Antonio, 1978, U. Colo., Colorado Springs. Tchr. Lubbock, Tex.; patient affairs coord. Cardiac Assocs., Colorado Springs; founder, CFO Macon Systems, Inc., Colorado Springs. Artist, Australia, Tex., Colo. Founding mem., bd. dirs. Pikes Peak Botanic Gardens. Mem. Software Pubs. Assn., Colorado Springs BBB, Colorado Springs Fine Arts Ctr., Pikes Peak Rose Soc. (pres.), Glen Eyrie Garden Soc., Colo. Mountain Club, Kissing Camels Garden Club (pres.), Phi Kappa Phi, Kappa Delta Pi, Sigma Tau Delta, Psi Chi.

MACON, JERRY LYN, software company owner, software publisher; b. Okla., Jan. 10, 1941; s. James Westwood and Mary Isabelle (Hankins) M.; m. Carol Ann Gloeckler, Aug. 28, 1981; children: Heather, Scott, Karla. BS in Physics magna cum laude, Colo. Coll., 1963; MS in Physics, MIT, 1966; MBA in Fin., U. Colo., 1980. Physics instr. U.S. Naval Acad., Annapolis, Md., 1966-69; stockbroker Merrill Lynch, Colorado Springs, 1969-71; dir. systems analysis and programming Colorado Springs Pub. Schs., 1971-80; co-founder, pres. Alpine Software, Inc., Colorado Springs, 1980-82, Macon Systems Inc., Colorado Springs, 1981—. Author: (software) DB Master, 1980, Advanced DB Master, 1981, Advanced DB Master for Windows Version 6.0, 1995. Mem. Colorado Springs Fine Arts Ctr., 1982—, Colorado Springs Better Bus. Bur., 1990—. Cmdr. U&SN, 1966-69. Boettcher Found. scholar, 1959; Woodrow Wilson fellow, 1963; MIT rsch. assistantship, 1964. Mem. Nat. Fedn. Ind. Bus., Software Pubs. Assn., Pikes Peak Rose Soc., Colo. Mountain Club, Phi Beta Kappa. Avocations: mountain climbing, hiking, travel, reading history, growing roses. Office: Macon Sys Inc 724 S Tejon St Colorado Springs CO 80903-4042

MACON, ROBIN JEFFREY, small business owner; b. St. Louis, Sept. 25, 1957; s. robert Teco and Irene E. (Eastlen) M. AA, Forest Park Coll., St. Louis, 1979. Electronic/elec. technician Vocat. Tng. Ctr., St. Louis, 1979-80; owner RJM Prodns., Norwalk, Calif., 1981—; bus. cons. Kele's Ent., St. Louis, 1982-87; bd. advisors Union/Sarah Inc., St. Louis, 1987-89. Bd. dirs. Sickle Cell Found., St. Louis, 1986-89, Helpline Youth Coun., Norwalk, 1995-96. Recipient Plaque, Sickle Cell Found., St. Louis, 1988, award Norwalk Unified Sch. Dist., 1996. Mem. Norwalk C. of C., Club Hollywood (founder, pres. 1998—). Republican. Avocations: walking, jogging, music, meditation. Office: RJM Exec Prodns 11065 Imperial Hwy Apt 16 Norwalk CA 90650-2223

MACPHERSON, SHIRLEY, clinical therapist; b. Bayonne, N.J., June 16, 1934; d. Alexander Phillip and Milldred (Gurstelle) Gottlieb; m. Duncan MacPherson, Jan. 2, 1981; children from previous marriage: Suzanne Lomas, Brett Barber. BS, Columbia U., NYU, 1951; MS, Juilliard Sch. Music, 1955; MEd, Calif. State U., Northridge, 1967; MA in Psychology, Pepperdine U., 1992; PhD in Psychology, Pacific Western U., 1998. Concert pianist Norman Seman Prodns., N.Y.C., 1952-61; indsl. health educator Am. Med. Internat., L.A., 1968-70; cons., lectr. Hosp. Mgmt. Corp., L.A., 1970-80; regional dir. Control Data Corp., L.A., 1980-86; outplacement specialist Ind. Cons., L.A., 1986-90; psychologist, intern Airport Marina Counseling Svcs., L.A., 1990-93; staff psychologist Forensic Psychology Assocs., Sherman Oaks, Calif., 1993-94; staff clin. psychologist Pacific Psychologist Assocs., L.A., 1992-94; clin. therapist MacPherson Relationship Counseling, L.A., 1993—. Author: Rx for Brides, 1990, Understanding Your Man, 1998. Vol. Cmty. Alliance to Support and Empower, L.A., 1994-96, South Bay Free Clinic, L.A., 1995-97; mem. Town and Gown Scholarship program, U. So. Calif., L.A. Mem. AAUW, APA, Calif. Psychol. Assn., L.A. Psychol. Assn., L.A. World Affairs Coun., L.A. Group Psychotherapy Assn. Avocations: French and Italian, Chinese brush painting, piano, studies.

MACPIKE, LORALEE, retired literature educator; b. Beverly Hills, Calif., Mar. 6, 1939; d. Frederick Lea and Loretta Alice (Jazowick) MacP.; m. R. Craig D. Sawyer, June 6, 1960 (div. July 14, 1976); children: Gwynn Anne Sawyer Ostrom. BA, Bryn Mawr Coll., 1960; MA, Calif. State U., 1970; PhD, UCLA, 1976. Asst. prof. U. Hawaii, Honolulu, 1975-78; from assoc. prof. to prof. lit. Calif. State U., San Bernardino, 1978-97; retired, 1998; editor, pub. Lesbian Rev. Books, Hilo, Hawaii, 1994—. Author: Dostoevsky's Dickens, 1981; editor: There's Something I've Been Meaning to Tell You, 1989; contbr. articles to profl. jours. AAUW fellow, 1974.

MACQUEEN, CHER, newscaster, sportscaster; b. Kansas City, Mo., Mar. 20, 1952; . Ira Raymond and Peggy Estelle (Turner) Milks. AA in Liberal Arts, L.A. Valley Coll., 1982; BS in Broadcasting, U. New York, Albany, 1993; grad., Barbizon Sch. of Modeling, 1996. Lic. radio-TV operator. Personnel specialist U.S. Army, Honolulu, Hawaii, 1973-75; adminstrv. specialist U.S. Army, San Francisco, Calif., 1975-77; broadcast journalist U.S. Army, Vicenza, Italy, 1977-80; radio traffic specialist Armed Forces Radio & TV, L.A., 1980-84, radio prodn. specialist, 1984-86; supr. broadcast support specialist Armed Forces Radio & TV, Sun Valley, Calif., 1986-90; broadcast support mgr, Armed Forces Radio & TV, Sun Valley, 1990-91, internal info. mgr., 1991-94, news and sports specialist, 1994—. Mem. DAV (life), Armed Forces Broadcasters Assn. (v.p. L.A., 1991-93). Avocations: handcrafts especially crochet. Home: PO Box 276 Highland CA 92346-0276 Office: Armed Forces Radio & TV Svc 1363 Z St Bldg 2730 Riverside CA 92518-2073

MACUMBER, JOHN PAUL, insurance company executive; b. Macon, Mo., Jan. 21, 1940; s. Rolland Deardorf and Althea Villa (Cason) M.; BA, Cen. Meth. Coll., Fayette, Mo., 1962; Asso. in Risk Mgmt., Ins. Inst. Am., 1978; m. Marilyn Sue Ashe, Nov. 10, 1962; children—Leanne, Cheryl. Casualty underwriter U.S. Fidelity & Guaranty Co., St. Louis, 1962-66; automobile underwriter Am. Indemnity Co., Galveston, Tex., 1966-69; auto casualty underwriter St. Paul Cos., New Orleans, 1969-73; sr. comml. casualty underwriter Chubb/Pacific Indemnity, Portland, Oreg., 1973-75; casualty underwriter Interstate Nat. Corp., L.A., 1975-76, underwriting supr., 1976-78, v.p., br. mgr., Mpls., 1978-82, also v.p. subs. Chgo. Ins. Co.; umbrella/spl. risk supr. Guaranty Nat. Ins. Co., Englewood, Colo., 1982-85; br. mgr. Burns & Wilcox, Ltd.-West, Salt Lake City, 1985-96; v.p. M.J. Kelly Ins. Brokers of Utah, Sandy, 1997—. With USAF, 1962-68. Nat. Methodist scholar, 1958; named Co. Person of Yr. Profl. Ins. Agts Utah, 1991, Ind. Ins. Agts. of Utah, 1996. Mem. Ins. Assn. Utah (sec.-treas. 1992-93, v.p. 1993-94, pres. 1994-95), Profl. Ins. Agts. Utah, Ind. Ins. Agts. Utah, Surplus Line Assn. Utah (bd. dirs. 1994-97), Nat. Assn. Profl. Surplus Lines Offices. Republican. Mem. Unity Ch. of Salt Lake City (v.p., bd. dirs. 1988). Lodges: Optimists (charter pres. 1968) (Friendswood, Tex.); Kiwanis (charter pres. 1979) (Bloomington, Minn.). Clubs: Insurance, Blue Goose (Salt Lake City). Home and Office: 9683 S Buttonwood Dr Sandy UT 84092-3245

MACY, RICHARD J., state supreme court justice; b. Saranac Lake, N.Y., June 2, 1930; m. Emily Ann Macy; children: Anne, Patty, Mark. BS in Bus., U. Wyo., 1955, JD, 1958. Pvt. practice Sundance, Wyo., 1958-85; justice Wyo. Supreme Ct., Cheyenne, 1985—, Crook County atty., 1970-83, mem. Nat. Conf. Commrs. on Uniform State Laws, 1982—. Mem. Sigma Chi (Nat. Outstanding Sig award 1986). Office: Wyo Supreme Ct Supreme Ct Bldg 2301 Capitol Ave Cheyenne WY 82001-3644

MADDEN, DAVID WILLIAM, English language educator; b. San Francisco, Sept. 10, 1950; s. John Joseph and Esther Calvert (Pearce) M.; m. Mary Virginia Davis, Mar. 19, 1977; children: Anne Elizabeth, Margaret Kathleen. Student, St. Mary's Coll., Moraga, Calif., 1968-70; BA, U. Calif., Davis, 1972, MA, 1974, PhD, 1980. Lectr. U. Calif., Davis, 1980-82; asst. prof. Calif. State U., Sacramento, 1982-85, assoc. prof., 1985-90, prof., 1990—. Author: Understanding Paul West, 1993; editor: Critical Essays on Thomas Berger, 1995; guest editor: Review of Contemporary Fiction XI, 1991, Review of Contemporary Fiction XVII, 1997; contbr. articles to profl. jours. Active Am. Cancer Soc., Sacramento, 1986-87, site coun. Jefferson Sch., Sacramento, 1987-94. Recipient Exceptional Merit Svc. award Calif. State U., Sacramento, 1984, Meritorious Performance and Profl. Promise award, Calif. State U., 1987, Capital Svc. Ctr. Coun. award, 1992; Fulbright grantee, 1977-78, Rsch. grantee Calif. State U., Sacramento, 1989-93. Mem. Western Lit. Assn., Am. Com. Irish Studies, Phi Kappa Phi. Democrat. Home: 3201 Lemitar Way Sacramento CA 95833-2756 Office: Calif State U Dept English 6000 J St Sacramento CA 95819-2605

MADDEN, EDWARD P., protective services official. Chief police Flagstaff (Ariz.) Police Dept. Office: Flagstaff Police Dept 120 N Beaver St Flagstaff AZ 86001-5525*

MADDEN, JAMES COOPER, V, management consultant; b. Glen Cove, N.Y., June 18, 1961; s. James Cooper IV and Linda Marie (Lizza) M.; 1 child, Jennifer Louise. Student, Webb Inst. Naval Architecture, Glen Cove, 1979-80; BA cum laude, So. Meth. U., 1983, BBA magna cum laude, 1983. Cert. Soc. Naval Architects and Marine Engrs. Cons. Andersen Cons./Arthur Andersen, Houston, 1983-85, sr. cons., 1985-87; mgr. Andersen Cons./Arthur Andersen, L.A., 1987-90, sr. mgr., 1990-91; prin. Booz-Allen & Hamilton, L.A., 1991-93; v.p. mng. dir. MCI Systemhouse, L.A., 1993-95, pres. U.S. and Mexico ops., 1995-97, CFO, 1997-98; CEO BPO-US, Inc., Newport Beach, Calif., 1998—. Author industry papers. Bd. dirs. Source 2, Cognicase. Scholar Webb Inst. Naval Architecture, 1979-80. Avocations: sailing, snow skiing, travel, reading. Office: BPO-US Inc 5000 Birch St Ste 3000 Newport Beach CA 92660-2140

MADDEN, JAMES GREGORY (GREG), electrical engineer; b. Rochester, Minn.; s. James Fentviose and Clara (Clements) M. BSEE, Purdue U., 1982. Engr. TRW, Redondo Beach, Calif., 1982-83; sect. head TRW, Redondo Beach, 1984-85, sr. engr., 1986-89, CCAFS program chief engr., 1990-94, ADFESS program mgr., 1997—. Office: TRW One Space Pk Redondo Beach CA 96278

MADDEN, PAUL ROBERT, lawyer; b. St. Paul, Nov. 13, 1926; s. Ray Joseph and Margaret (Meyer) M.; m. Rosemary R. Sorel, Aug. 7, 1974; children: Margaret Jane, William, James Patrick, Derek R. Sorel, Lisa T. Sorel. Student, St. Thomas Coll., 1944; AB, U. Minn., 1948; JD, Georgetown U., 1951. Bar: Ariz. 1957, Minn. 1951, D.C. 1951. Assoc. Hamilton & Hamilton, Washington, 1951-55; legal asst. to commr. SEC, Washington, 1955-56; assoc. Lewis and Roca, Phoenix, Ariz., 1957-59, ptnr., 1959-90; ptnr. Beus, Gilbert & Morrill, Phoenix, 1991-94; ptnr. Chapman and Cutler, Phoenix, 1994-97; of counsel Gallagher & Kennedy, 1997—; bd. dirs. Mesa Air Group, Inc., Phoenix, chmn., 1998—. Sec. Minn. Fedn. Coll. Rep. Clubs, 1947-48; chmn. 4th dist. Minn. Young Rep. Club, 1948; nat. co-chmn. Youth for Eisenhower, 1951-52; mem. Ariz. Rep. Com., 1960-62; bd. dirs. Found. Jr. Achievement Ctrl. Ariz., Cath. Community Found., Phoenix, Heritage Hills Homeowners Assn., St. Joseph the Worker; past bd. dirs. Camelback Charitable Trust, The Samaritan Found., Phoenix; past bd. dirs., past. pres. Ariz. Club, Phoenix, 1990-93; past bd. dirs., past chmn. Found. for Sr. Living; past bd. dirs., vice chmn., Cen. Ariz. chpt. ARC; past bd. dirs., vice chmn., Cen. Ariz. chpt. ARC; past bd. dirs., past pres. Jr. Achievement Cen. Ariz., Inc.; mem. nat. bd. vis. U. Ariz. Law Sch. With USNR, 1946-48. Mem. ABA, Ariz. Bar Assn., Maricopa County Bar Assn., Fed. Bar Assn., Fedn. Ins. Counsel, Phi Delta Phi. Clubs: The Barristers (Washington), Arizona. Home: 5847 N 46th St Phoenix AZ 85018-1234 Office: Mesa Air Group Inc 410 N 44th St Ste 700 Phoenix AZ 85008-7608 Office: Gallagher & Kennedy PA 2600 N Central Ave Ste 1800 Phoenix AZ 85004-3099

MADDEN, RICHARD BLAINE, forest products executive; b. Short Hills, N.J., Apr. 27, 1929; s. James L. and Irma (Twining) M.; m. Joan Fairbairn, May 24, 1958; children: John Richard, Lynne Marie, Kathryn Ann, Andrew Twining. B.S., Princeton U., 1951; J.D., U. Mich., 1956; M.B.A., NYU, 1959; PhD (hon.), St. Scholastica Coll., 1994. Bar: Mich. 1956, N.Y. 1958. Gen. asst. treas.'s dept. Socony Mobil Oil Corp., N.Y.C., 1956-57; spl. asst. Socony Mobil Oil Corp., 1958-59, fin. rep., 1960; asst. to pres. Mobil Chem. Co.; also dir. Mobil Chems. Ltd. of Eng., 1960-63; exec. v.p., gen. mgr. Kordite Corp.; also v.p. Mobil Plastics, 1963-66; v.p. Mobil Chem. Co., N.Y.C., 1966-68; group v.p. Mobil Chem. Co., 1968-70; asst. treas. Mobil Oil Corp., 1970-71; chmn. Mobil Oil Estates Ltd., 1970-71; pres., chief exec. Potlatch Corp., San Francisco, 1971-77, chmn. chief exec. officer, 1977-94; ret., 1994; bd. dirs. Potlatch Corp., PG&E Corp., CNF Transp. Inc., URS Corp.; former bd. dirs. Del Monte Corp., AMFAC Inc., Bank Calif. N.A. and BankCal Tri-State Corp.; from lectr. to adj. assoc. prof. fin. NYU, 1960-63; bd. dirs. Hospitaller; v.p. Order of Malta, Western Assn.; bd. govs., mem. adminstrv. compensation, audit & labor rels. com. San Francisco Symphony. Bd. dirs. Smith-Kettlewell Eye Rsch. Inst., trustee emeritus, former chmn. Am. Enterprise Inst.; former mem. bd. Nat. Park Found.; hon. trustee Com. for Econ. Devel. Lt. (j.g.) USNR, 1951-54. Mem. N.Y. Bar Assn., Mich. Bar Assn. Roman Catholic. Clubs: Bohemian (San Francisco); Lagunitas (Ross, Calif.); Metropolitan (Washington).

MADIX, ROBERT JAMES, chemical engineer, educator; b. Beach Grove, Ind., June 22, 1938; s. James L. and Marjorie A. (Strohl) M.; children: Bradley Alan, David Eric, Micella Lynn, Evan Scott. BS, U. Ill., 1961; PhD, U. Calif., 1964. NSF postdoctoral fellow Max Planck Inst., Göttingen, Fed. Republic of Germany, 1964-65; asst. prof, chem. engr. Stanford (Calif.) U., 1965-72, assoc. prof., chem. engr., 1972-77; prof. chem. engring. Stanford U., 1977—, chmn., chem. engr., 1983-87, prof. chemistry, 1981—; cons. Monsanto Chem., St. Louis, 1975-84, Shell Oil Co., Houston, 1985-86; Peter Debye lectureship Cornell U., 1985; Eyring lectr. chemistry Ariz. State U., 1990; Barnett Dodge lectr. Yale U., 1996; disting. prof. lectr. U. Tex., Austin, 1980; Walter Robb Disting. lectr. Penn State U., 1996; chmn. Gordon Rsch. Conf. on Reactions on Surfaces, 1995. Assoc. editor Catalysis Rev., 1986—, Catalysis Letters, 1992—, Rsch. on Chem. Intermediates, 1994—; contbr. numerous articles to profl. jours. Recipient Alpha Chi Sigma award AIChemE, 1990, Paul Emmett award Catalysis Soc. N.Am., 1984, Humboldt U.S. Sr. Scientist prize, 1978; Ford Found. fellow, 1969-72. Mem. Am. Chem. Soc. (Irving Langmuir Disting. Lectr. award 1981, Arthur Adamson award 1997, Henry J. Albert award Precious Metals Inst., 1997), Am. Phys. Soc., Am. Vacuum Soc., AIChE, Calif. Catalysis Soc. Office: Stanford Univ Dept Chemical Engring Stanford CA 94305

MADLANG, RODOLFO MOJICA, retired urologic surgeon; b. Indang, Cavite, The Philippines, Apr. 9, 1918; came to U.S., 1953; s. Simeon Fajardo and Eugenia R. (Mojica) Madlangsacay; m. Lourdes Recto Gregorio, Dec. 8, 1946; children: Cesar, Rodolfo G., Mercy Lynn. AA, U. Philippines, Manila, 1939, MD, 1945. Diplomate Am. Bd. Urology. Resident in gen. surgery Philippine Gen. Hosp., Manila, 1946-49; resident in urology St. Francis Hosp., Peoria, Ill., 1953-55; asst. prof. physiology Far Ea. U. Inst. Medicine, Manila, 1956-58, cons. in urology, 1956-58; attending urologist St. Catherine Hosp., East Chicago, Ind., 1958-81, chief surgery, 1977-79; attending urologist St. Margaret Hosp., Hammond, Ind., 1960-81; chief urology U.S. VA Outpatient Clinic, L.A., 1982-98. Fellow ACS; mem. AMA, Am. Urol. Assn., Pan Pacific Surg. Assn., Assn. Mil. Surgeons of the U.S., Ind. State Med. Assn., N.Y. Acad. Scis. Republican. Roman Catholic.

MADNI, ASAD MOHAMED, engineering executive; b. Bombay, Sept. 8, 1947; came to U.S., 1966; s. Mohamed Taher and Sara Taher (Wadiwalla) M.; Gowhartaj Shahnawaz, Nov. 11, 1976; 1 child, Jamal Asad. Gen. cert. edn., U. Cambridge, Eng., 1964; AAS in Electronics, RCA Insts., Inc., 1968; BS in Engring., UCLA, 1969, MS in Engring., 1972; postgrad. exec. inst., Stanford U., 1984; cert. in engring. mgmt., Calif. Inst. Tech., 1987; PhD in Engring., Calif. Coast U., 1987; [illegible] MIT, 1990 [illegible] Pacific States U., L.A., 1969-71; sr. electronics auditor Pertec Corp., Chatsworth, Calif., 1973-75; project engr., sr. engr., prog. mgr., dir. advanced programs Microwave div. Systron Donner, Van Nuys, Calif., 1975-82, dir. engring., 1982-92; gen. mgr. Microwave and Instrument div. Systron Donner, Van Nuys, Calif., 1985-90; chmn., pres., chief exec. officer Systron Donner Corp., 1990-92; pres., CEO Sensors and Controls Group BEI Electronics, Inc., 1992-93, BEI Motion Sys. Co., 1993-94, BEI Sensors & Sys. Co., 1994—; vice-chmn. IEEE-MTTS, San Fernando Valley chpt., 1991-92, chmn., 1992-94; tech. advisor Test and Measurement World, Boston, 1982-90; adv. Calif. State U. Northridge. Mem. editorial rev. bd., West coast chmn. Microwave Systems News and Communications Tech., 1982-90; contbr. more than 60 articles to numerous tech. publs.; patentee in field. Fellow IEEE; mem. AAAS, NRA (life), Soc. Automotive Engrs., N.Y. Acad. Scis., Assn. Old Crows (life, gold cert. of merit 1992), Calif. Rifle and Pistol Assn. (life), MIT Soc. Sr. Execs. (life), UCLA Alumni Assn. (life), MIT Alumni Assn. (life). Home: 3281 Woodbine St Los Angeles CA 90064-4836 Office: BEI Sensors & Systems Co 13100 Telfair Ave Sylmar CA 91342-3576

MADNICK, MARE T., software company executive; b. Phila., Oct. 8, 1964; s. Irving Leslie Madnick and Eileen Ruth (Spivack) Ansill; m. Dorayn Shanock, Oct. 6, 1994; children: Gabriel Aaron, Daniel Evan. BS in Finance, U. Md. Pres., COO B.L. Software, Inc., L.A., 1991—.

MADRID, PATRICIA ANN, state attorney general, lawyer; b. Las Cruces, N.Mex., Sept. 25, 1946; d. Charles and Virginia (Fitch) M.; m. L. Michael Messina, May 2, 1975; children: Giancarlo Anthony, Elizabeth Jennifer. BA in English and Philosophy, U. N.Mex., 1969; JD, 1973; cert. Nat. Jud. Coll., U. Nev., 1978. Bar: N.Mex. 1973. Teaching asst. U. N.Mex., Albuquerque, 1969-70, Am. Indian Law Ctr., Albuquerque, 1971; law clk. to N.Mex. atty. gen., Santa Fe., 1972; atty. N.Mex. Legislature, Santa Fe, 1974; assoc. Kool, Bloomfield, & Eaves, P.A., Albuquerque, 1974-78; dist. judge 2nd Jud. Dist. State of N.Mex., Albuquerque, 1978-84; presiding judge, 1984; ptnr. Messina, Madrid & Smith, P.A., Albuquerque, 1984-88; atty. gen. State of N. Mex., 1999—. Editor N.Mex. Law Rev., 1972-73. Mem. State rules com. State Democratic Party, N.Mex., 1980, jud. council and credentials com. 1982-83; co-chmn. N.Mex. Carter for Pres. Com., 1980; bd. dirs. Am. Council Young Polit. Leaders, del. to Japan, 1982, Fechin Art Inst., Taos, N.Mex.; Dem. nominee Lt. Gov. N.Mex., 1994; candidate N.Mex. Atty. Gen., 1998. Recipient Respect for Law Commendation, Mayor of Albuquerque, 1979, Hon. Commdr. award U.S. Air Force, 1979, Award of yr., Albuquerque Bus. and Profl. Women; named Outstanding Young Women of Am., 1980-81. Mem. N.Mex. Jud. Council (exec. com. 1982-83), N.Mex. Bar Assn., Hispanic Women's Coun. of N.Mex. (bd. dirs. 1989), N.Mex. Judges Assn., Nat. Assn. Women Judges, U. N.Mex. Alumni Assn. (bd. dirs.), N.Mex. Assn. Women in Govt., N.Mex. Automobile Assn. (bd. dirs.), Mex. Am. Legal Def. and Ednl. Fund (bd. dirs. 1989), Hispanic Women's Council N. Mex. (charter, incorporator 1988). Democrat. Roman Catholic. Home: 2219 Vista Larga Ave NE Albuquerque NM 87106-3731 Office: Office of Atty Gen Battan Meml Bldg 407 Galisteo St Rm 260 Santa Fe NM 87501*

MADRIL, LEE ANN, writer; b. Burbank, Calif., Sept. 16, 1944; d. George Mathew McDougall; 1 child, Francis Michael. Student, Granada Hills (Calif.) Coll., 1962. Freelance writer, 1986-90; shoot out artist, life mem. Bad Co., Auburn, Calif., 1990—; writer Idaho State Newspaper, Just Horses, Indian Valley, 1994—; cons. in authenticity, Calif. State Horsemen, Santa Rosea, 1988-90, Bad Co., 1990. Writer Idaho State Newspaper Just Horses; contbr. articles to profl. jours. Vol. Red Cross, Soques, Calif., 1982, Salinas (Calif.) Valley Meml. Hosp., 1979, Greenpeace, Humane Soc. U.S. Recipient Kodak KINSA award, 1989, winner County and State photo awards, 1993. jem. Calif. State Horseman's Assn. (state champion 1989-90), Silver Spurs, Moose. Republican. Roman Catholic. Avocations: tng. horses, researching Old West data. Home and Office: PO Box 121 Newcastle CA 95658-0121

MADSEN, BARBARA A, state supreme court justice. Justice Washington Supreme Ct., Olympia. *

MADSEN, SUSAN ARRINGTON, writer; b. Logan, Utah, Aug. 25, 1954; d. Leonard J. and Grace F. Arrington; m. Dean Madsen, Aug. 20, 1974; children: Emily, Rebecca, Sarah, Rachel. BS in Journalism, Utah State U., 1975. Mem. adj. faculty Logan Latter-day Saints Inst. Religion, 1991-95. Author: Christmas: A Joyful Heritage, 1984, The Lord Needs a Prophet, 1990, I Walked to Zion: True Stories of Young Pioneers on the Mormon Trail, 1994, Growing Up in Zion: True Stories of Young Pioneers Building the Kingdom, 1996, The Second Rescue: The Story of the Spiritual Rescue of the Willie and Martin Handcart Pioneers, 1998, (with Leonard J. Arrington) Sunbonnet Sisters: True Stories of Mormon Women and Frontier Life, 1984, Mothers of the Prophets, 1987; contbr. numerous articles to Collier's Ency. Yearbooks. Chair Hyde Pk. (Utah) Bd. Adjustments, 1985-94. Honoree Utah State U. Nat. Women's History Week, 1985; recipient Cmty. Svc. award Nat. Daus. Utah Pioneers, 1990. Mem. LDS Ch. Avocations: horseback riding, snow skiing, genealogy, family activities.

MADSON, DAVID JOHN, fundraising executive; b. Mpls., Sept. 29, 1955; s. John Richard and Kleda Rae (Thompson) M.; m. Helen M. DeMichiel, Oct. 5, 1986; 1 child, Antonia Kleda Madson. BS magna cum laude in Visual Comm., U. Minn., Mpls., 1979; postgrad., U. Minn., 1986-87. Advanced cert. fund raiser exec., 1993. Media arts instr. ACTION Cmty. Outreach Program, 1976-77; photography instr. Inver Hills C.C. Program, 1978-84; assoc. dir. devel. Film in the Cities, St. Paul, 1981-84; exec. dir. Boston Film/Video Found., 1984-85; assoc. devel. officer propsect rsch. U. Minn. Found., 1985-86; chief devel. officer Coll. Edn. U. Minn., Mpls., 1987-93, chief devel. officer Cancer Ctr., 1993-95; dir. devel. Sch. Nursing U. Calif., San Francisco, 1995-98, dir. devel. Sch. Dentistry, 1998—; mem. adv. panels Minn. State Arts Bd., St. Paul, 1993-95, Nat. Endowment Arts, Washington, 1991, 93, 94; cons. Jerome Hill Theatre Devel., 1985; prodr. Cable Arts TV Project, 1985; panelist photography fellowships Minn. State Arts Bd., 1985, NEA, 1994; cons. Media Arts Ctr. Project, Artspace, Mpls., 1985-86; cons. nat. satellite distbn. project Deep Dish Pub. Access TV, N.Y.C., 1985-87; panelist McKnight Found./Mpls. Arts Commn., 1986-88; devel. cons. Mgmt. Assistance Project, 1991; media grants rev. panelist Minn. Humanities Commn., 1991; program com. Minn. Coun. on Planned Giving Conf., 1992; co-founder Midwest/Big Ten Edn. Advancement Network, 1991-93. Exhibited in group photography shows at St. Paul Sci. and Art Ctr., 1974, Kennedy Ctr. for Arts, Washington, 1975, Nash Gallery, 1976, 81, Coffman Union Gallery, 1977, 78, Film in the Cities, 1977, Hunt Gallery. Treas. Univ. Film Soc., Mpls., 1981-84, 89-95, KFAI Cmty. Radio, Mpls., 1989-92; pres. Seward Cmty. Coop., Mpls., 1993-95; bd. dirs. United Cerebral Palsy, San Francisco, 1996-99; bd. dirs. Minn. Span Assn., 1988-93; pres. Red Eye Collaboration Theater, Mpls., 1986-91; bd. dirs. Lowertown Cmty. Coun., 1981-83, Palace Theater Co., 1982-84, So. Theater, 1986-89, Friends of Photography Ansel Adams Ctr., 1999—; arts adv. com. City of St. Paul Planning Dept., 1982-84; com. mem. childhood devel. study Citizens League, 1987-88; mem. Chain of Lakes planning com. City of Mpls. Park Bd., 1989; bd. dirs. Powderhorn Cmty. Coun., 1985-90, treas., 1986-88; bd. dirs., co-founder Lowertown Lofts Artist Housing Coop., 1982-90, treas., 1983-88; facilities com. Minn. chpt. Am. Youth Hostels, 1990-93; mem. devel. com. Headwaters Fund, 1990-93; bd. dirs. Prevention Alliance, 1988-93; bd. dirs. Film in the Cities, 1992-95, sec., 1993-95; pres. Berkeley Montessori Sch., 1998—; pres. San Francisco chpt. United Cerebral Palsy Found., 1996-98; mem. local adv. bd. Sta. KPFA-FM, Pacificia Radio, 1998—. Mem. Nat. Assn. Fund Raising Execs. (v.p. edn. Golden Gate chpt. 1996-99, bd. dirs. Minn. chpt. 1993-95, v.p. external affairs 1999—), U. Minn. Alumni Assn. (nat. bd. 1996—, pres. San Francisco charter 1995-98). Avocations: cross country skiing, bicycling. Office: U Calif Box 0248 San Francisco CA 94143

MAEDA, J. A., data processing executive; b. Mansfield, Ohio, Aug. 24, 1940; d. James Shunso and Doris Lucille Maeda; m. Robert Lee Hayes, 1 child, Brian Sentaro Hayes. BS in Math., Purdue U., 1962, postgrad., 1962-63; postgrad., Calif. State U., Northridge, 1968-75; cert. profl. designation in tech. of computer operating systems and tech. of info. processing, UCLA, 1971. Cons. rsch. asst. computer ctr. Purdue U., West Lafayette, Ind., 1962-63; computer operator, sr. tab operator, mem. faculty Calif. State U., Northridge, 1969, programmer cons., tech. asst. II, 1969-70, supr. acad. appli- [illegible] office of the chancellor, 1972-73, tech. support coord. statewide timesharing

tech. support, programmer II, 1973-74, acad. coord., tech. support coord. instrn., computer cons. III, 1974-83; coord. user svcs. info. ctr., mem. tech. staff IV CADAM INC subs. Lockheed Corp., Burbank, Calif., 1983-86, coord. user svcs., tech. specialist computing dept., 1986-87; v.p., bd. dirs. Rainbow Computing, Inc., Northridge, 1976-85; dir. Aki Tech/Design, Northridge, 1976—; mktg. mgr. thaumaturge Taro Quipu Cons., Northridge, 1987—; tech. cons. Digital Computer Cons., Chatsworth, Calif., 1988; computer tech., fin. and bus. mgmt., sys. integration, 1988-90; tech. customer software support Collection Data Sys., Westlake, Calif., 1991; sr. tech. writer Sterling Software Info. Mgmt. Divsn., 1992—. Author, editor more than 375 user publs., tutorials, reference manuals, user guides, CD graphics/packaging; contbr. articles and photos to profl. jours. Mem. IEEE, SHARE, DECUS (ednl. spl. interest group 1977-83, ednl. steering com. RSTS/E 1979-82), Soc. for Tech. Communicators. Avocations: photography, photojournalism, vintage automobiles. Office: Info Mgmt Divsn 5900 Canoga Ave Woodland Hills CA 91367-5009

MAEHL, WILLIAM HARVEY, historian, educator; b. Bklyn., May 28, 1915; s. William Henry and Antoinette Rose (Salamone) M.; m. Josephine Scholl McAllister, Dec. 29, 1941; children: Madeleine, Kathleen. BSc, Northwestern U., 1937, MA, 1939; PhD, U. Chgo., 1946. Asst. prof. history St. Louis U., 1941-42, Tex. A&M U., College Sta., 1943, De Paul U., Chgo., 1944-49; historian Dept. of Def., Karlsruhe, Stuttgart, Fed. Rep. Germany, 1950-52; chief briefing office U.S. hdqrs. U.S. Hdqs. European Command, Frankfurt, Germany, 1952-53; chief historian Arty. Sch., Okla., 1954; with War Plans Office, Hdqs. No. Air Materiel Area for Europe, Burtonwood, Eng., 1954-55; assoc. prof. European history Nebr. Wesleyan U., Lincoln, 1955-57, prof., 1958-62, 65-68; prof. German history Auburn (Ala.) U., 1968-81, prof. emeritus, 1981—; vis. prof. U. Nebr., 1962, U. Auckland, New Zealand, 1963-64, Midwestern U., Wichita Falls, Tex., 1965. Author: German Militarism and Socialism, 1968, History of Germany in Western Civilization, 1979, A World History Syllabus, 3 vols., 1980, August Bebel, Shadow Emperor of the German Workers, 1980, The German Socialist Party: Champion of the First Republic, 1918-33, 1986; author monographs for U.S. Army in Europe, chpts. in books, atomic, biol. and emergency war plans for No. Air Materiel Area for Europe; contbr. poetry to Question of Balance, Tears of Fire, Disting. Poets Am., Best Poems of 1995, Journey of Mind; contbr. articles to profl. jours. Grantee Nebr. Wesleyan U., 1959, Auburn U., 1969-73, 79-80, Am. Philosophical Soc., 1973-74, Deutscher Akademischer Austauschdienst, 1978. Mem. Am. Hist. Assn., Phi Kappa Phi, Phi Alpha Theta.

MAES, KATHRYN GONDER, educator; b. Keyser, W.Va., July 16, 1945; d. Bernard Ignatius and Kathryn Kildow (Wooddell) G.; m. David Brindle, Dec. 18, 1977 (dec. Dec. 1988); m. LeRoy William Maes, Feb. 29, 1992. ADVS, Cen. Sch. Speech & Drama, London, 1986; MA, West Va. Univ., 1971; PhD, Univ. Pitts., 1982. Assoc. prof. W.Va. Univ., Morgantown, 1971-85, Univ. Ill., Champagne, 1985-89; head of voice dept. Nat. Theatre Conservatory, Denver, 1989-92; assoc. prof., chair theatre Univ. Colo., Denver, 1992—; dialect and vocal coach Royal Shakespeare Co., London, 1986, 87, 88, 89, Nat. Theatre of Great Britain, 1986, Royal Exchange Theatre, Manchester, Eng., 1987, Playhouse in the Park, Cin., 1985-89. Director (play) Koch, 1996-98, Burn This, 1997, The Importance of Being Earnest, 1996, As You Like It, 1998. Recipient Univ. Colo. Svc. award Sch.Arts, 1993. Mem. A ssn. Theatre in Higher Edn., Voice & Speech Trainers Assn. (editor 1971-84). Democrat. Roman Catholic. Avocations: golf, hiking, traveling. Home: 1530 S Quebec Way # 23 Denver CO 80231 Office: Univ Colo Campus Box 162 Denver CO 80217-3364

MAES, PETRA JIMENEZ, state supreme court justice; widowed; 4 children. BA, U. N.Mex., 1970, JD, 1973. Bar: N.Mex. 1973. Pvt. pratice law Albuquerque, 1973-75; rep., then office mgr. No. N.Mex. Legal Svcs., 1975-81; dist. judge 1st Jud. Dist. Ct., Santa Fe, Los Alamos, 1981—; chief judge, 1984-87, 92-95. Active S.W. coun. Boy Scouts Am., mem. dist. coms.; presenter pre cana St. John's Cath. Ch.; bd. dirs. Nat. Ctr. on Women and Family Law; chairperson Tri-County Gang Task Force; mem. Gov.'s Task Force on Children and Families, 1991-92; mem. adv. com. Santa Fe County Jail, 1996. Mem. N.Mex. Bar Assn. (elderly law com. 1980-81, alternative dispute resolution com. 1987-92, code of jud. conduct com. 1992—, juvenile cmty. corrections svcs. com. chairperson), Hispanic Nat. Bar Assn., N.Mex. Dist. Judges Assn., N.Mex. Women's Bar Assn., Hispanic Women's Coun. (charter). Office: Supreme Court of New Mexico PO Box 848 Santa Fe NM 87504-0848*

MAESTAS, ALEX WALTER, state agency clerk; b. Espanola, N. Mex., Jan. 18, 1954; s. Mariano E. and Stella Dora M.; m. Carol Paulette Pino, June 26, 1976; children: Andrew Arthur, Pamela Marie, Nicholas Alex. BS, U. N. Mex., 1976; Diploma, Victory Bible Sch. of Ministry, 1993, Ariz. State U., 1997. Ins. cert., 1990-94; cert. elem. tchr., N.Mex. Elem. sch. tchr. Annunciation Sch., Albuquerque, 1979-84, Albuquerque Pub. Schs., 1984-86; statistical analyst Workers' Compensation Adminstrn., Albuquerque, 1986-88, record mgr., 1988-96, clk. of ct. bur. chief, 1996—. Mem. exec. bd. Albuquerque Parochial League, 1980-84; pres. Zia Little League, Albuquerque, 1995-96. Mem. Worker's Compensation Assn. N. Mex., Nat. Assn. Ct. Mgmt. Home: 240 Parsifal St NE Albuquerque NM 87123-2608 Office: N Mex Workers Compensation Adminstrn PO Box 27198 Albuquerque NM 87125-7198

MAGALNICK, ELLIOTT BEN, retail medical supply company executive; b. Cleve., Aug. 19, 1945; s. Joseph Hyman and Ann (Resnick) M.; m. Diane Kerner, May 26, 1968 (div. Feb. 1988); children: Joel A., David A.; m. Judy Banjavic, June 9, 1991; stepchildren: Daniel Banjavic, David Banjavic. BS in Bus. Mgmt., Temple U., 1968. Cert. orthopedic fitter Health Industries Dealer Assn. Retail mgr. Milner Surg. Supply Co., Phila., 1970-72, Colo. Surg. Supply Co., Denver, 1972-73; mgr. non wheelchair retail Wheelchairs, Inc., Englewood, Colo., 1973-77; asst. mgr. ops. Denver Surg. Supply Co., 1977-78; owner, founder The Get Well Shop, Inc., Aurora, Colo., 1978—. Mem. chorus Shir Ami Singers, Denver, 1978-95, Colo. Symphony Orch., Denver, 1986-96; vol. Allied Fedn. Denver, 1984-87; mem. Legion of Merit, Rep. Party, Denver, 1992; donor Belle Bonfils Blood Ctr., 1976—; cantor Temple Micah, Denver, 1991-95, Temple Shalom, Colorado Springs, Colo., 1996-97; parachaplain Jewish Family Svc., Denver, 1998-99. Named Disting. Pres., Optimist Internat., 1987. Mem. Colo. Assn. Med. Equipment Suppliers (dealer mem., mem. state bd.), Health Industries Dealer Assn. (cert. orthopedic fitter, bd. dirs. 1986-87), Luncheon Optimist Club Windsor Gardens (pres. 1986), Masons (master mason Columbine Lodge), Colo. Consistory, El Jebel Temple, Rocky Mtn. Cantors Assn. Jewish. Avocations: bicycling, cross-country skiing, singing, tennis, reading. Office: The Get Well Shop Inc 12028 E Mississippi Ave Aurora CO 80012-3294

MAGDANZ, JAMES SIDNEY, writer; b. Norfolk, Nebr., Oct. 27, 1951; s. Albert Sidney and Mary Jane (Cooley) M.; m. Susan Elizabeth Georgette, Sept. 22, 1987; children: Reid, Grant. B of Journalism, U. Mo., 1973. Editl. page editor Jackson (Tenn.) Sun, 1973-75; picture editor Des Moines Register, 1976-81; social sci. rschr. State of Alaska, Kotzebue, 1981—; writer, photographer Kotzebue, 1981—; cons. Northwest Arctic Sch. Dist., Kotzebue, 1995-97, Nat. Park Svc., Kotzebue, 1998. Author: (children's book) Go Home, River, 1996; photographer: (exhibit) Shungnak, Alaska State Mus., 1982. Fellow Alicia Patterson Found., Washington, 1979; grantee Ella Lyman Cabot Trust, Boston, 1979. Mem. Am. Soc. Media Photographers, Nat. Press Photographers Assn., Soc. of Children's Book Writers and Illustrators. Home: PO Box 278 Kotzebue AK 99752-0278

MAGDOSKU, CHRISTOPHER LEE, civil engineer; b. Beeville, Tex., July 19, 1971; s. Andrew Stephen Magdosku and Robin Lee (Lockwood) Sundberg. BSCE, Calif. State Poly. U., Pomona, 1994; MSCE, Calif. State U., Long Beach, 1996. Engr. in tng., Calif. Lab. asst. Dean White, San Dimas, Calif., 1993-95; tech. trainee engring. dept. City of Whittier, Calif., 1995-96; staff engr. Giles Engring. Assocs., Inc., Anaheim, Calif., 1996, Geofon Inc., Cypress, Calif., 1996-97, Geotech. Profls. Inc., Cypress, Calif., 1997—. Mem. ASCE (assoc.), Pi Sigma Epsilon. Roman Catholic. Achievements include research on slope stability and fire hazards of hillside of San Dimas. Avocations: golf, playing drums, landscaping. Office: Geotech Profls Inc 5736 Corporate Ave Cypress CA 90630-4700

MAGEE, DENNIS, cultural organization administrator; b. Pala, Calif., Oct. 9, 1937; s. Raymond Milton and Prudence Theresa (Golsh) M. BSBA, San Diego State U., San Diego, 1961. Wholesaler Kroshel Industries, San Diego, 1962-69; adminstr. Indian Health Council Inc., Pauma Valley, Calif., 1970—; adv. bd. Masters in Pub. Health Program for Native Americans, U. Calif., Berkeley; bd. trustees Robert F. Kennedy Meml. Found., Washington; bd. dirs. Comprehensive Health Planning Assn. of San Diego, Riverside and Imperial Counties, Nat. Indian Health Bd., Denver; mem. San Diego State U. Athletic Found, San Diego State U. Alumni Assn., San Diego Council of Community Clinics; bd. chair Nature Am. Tng. Assocs., Sacramento, D.Q. U., Davis, Calif., Calif. Rural Indian Health Bd., Sacramento. Bd. dirs. United Way of San Diego County, Nat. Neighborhood Ctrs. Am., N.Y.C., Citizens Equal Opportunity Commn., San Diego, Mental Health Assn., Sacramento, San Diego County Regional Criminal Justice Planning bd.; mem. tribal health coun., Sacramento; mem. San Diego County Human Relations Commn. Recipient Nat. Disting. Cmty. Svc. award Nat. Soc. Workers Techni-Culture Coalition, Cin., 1973, Indian Health Ctr. dedicated to Dennis Magee, 1976, Letter of Commendation Pres. Jimmy Carter, 1980; named One of Ten Outstanding Young Men of San Diego San Diego Jr. C. of C. Mem. Northern San Diego County Associated Cs. of C. (bd. dirs.). Democrat. Roman Catholic. Avocations: sports, bicycling, hunting, bullfighting. Home: Pala Mission Rd PO Box 86 Pala CA 92059-0086 Office: Indian Health Council Inc PO Box 406 Pauma Valley CA 92061-0406

MAGEE, THOMAS ROBERT, musician; b. San Diego, Sept. 2, 1951; s. Robert James and Ruth Elaine (Shultz) M. Grad. high sch., Granada Hills, Calif. Drummer Steve Correll Quartet, Los Angeles, 1968-73, Keith Carradine/Revelation Record Co., Los Angeles, 1972, La Quinta Hotel Orch., Palm Springs, Calif., 1973-74, Dodge Bolton Band, Los Angeles, 1975-76, Harry "The Hipster" Gibson, Los Angeles, 1976, Morton Downey Jr. Show Band, on tour, 1977-78, Coale Johnson Band, San Francisco, 1978, Johnny Black Orch., Los Angeles, 1979-80, Herman Young Quartet, Los Angeles, 1982; freelance musician Los Angeles, 1982—. Harmonica soloist (soundtrack) Easy Movers, 1971, (music video) Never Let You Down by David Bowie, 1987; appeared in documentary film Boogie In Blue, 1990; drummer Buzz Gardner Quartet, 1991-92; mus. dir. play Espiritus de Soma, 1993. Mem. Am. Fedn. Musicians. Avocation: writing.

MAGENTA, MURIEL, artist; b. N.Y.C., Dec. 4, 1932; d. James E. and Sara (Wallman) Gellert; m. Gerald Zimmerman (dec.); children: Jean, Eric Vermilion. BA, Queens Coll., 1953; MA in Art History, Ariz. State U., 1962, MFA in Painting, 1965, PhD, 1970. Prof. art Ariz. State U., 1969—. One woman shows include Ariz. State U., 1976, Phoenix Art Mus., 1977, U. So. Calif., 1978, Marian Locks Gallery, Phila., 1979, Rutgers U., 1981, Yares Gallery, Scottsdale, Ariz., 1981, CitiBank, N.Y.C., 1984, U. Ark., 1984, L.A. Contemporary Exhbns., 1985, Scottsdale Ctr. for the Arts, 1990, 93, Kansas City (Mo.) Art Inst., 1991, Gallery 10, Washington, 1991, Ariz. State U. Art Mus., 1997; group shows include L.A. Inst. Contemporary Art, 1978, Rutgers U., 1981, The Print Club Phila., 1983, Tweed Gallery, Plainfield, N.J., 1984, Tucson Art Mus., Ariz., 1988, Lawndale Art and Performance Ctr., Mus. of Fine Art, Santa Fe, N.Mex., 1990, Ctr. Simone De Beauvoir, Paris, 1992, Medien Operative Berlin, 1992, 8th Cadiz (Spain) Internat. Video Festival, 1992, South Bend (Ind.) Art Ctr., 1992, John Michael Kohler Art Ctr., Sheboygan, Wis., 1992, CAGE, Cin., 1993, Ctr. Simone DeBeauvoir, Paris, 1993, Drexel U., Phila., 1993, Artemisia Gallery, Chgo., 1996, U. Minn., Mpls., 1998, SIGGRAPH, Orlando, 1998, ZKM, Karlsruhe, Germany, 1998; represented in permanent collections Ariz. State U., Valley Nat. Bank, Phoenix, Prudential Life, Scottsdale. Phoenix Art Mus. grantee, 1975-77; Ariz. State U. grantee, 1981-82, 92-93. Mem. NOW, Women's Caucus for Art (nat. pres. 1982-84, Mid-career achievement award 1991), Coll. Art Assn. Am., Mid-Am. Coll. Art Assn., Nat. Women's Polit. Caucus, Women in Animation, Inter-Soc. for the Electronic Arts, SIGGRAPH. Home: 8322 E Virginia Ave Scottsdale AZ 85257-1741 Studio: Ariz State U Inst Studies in Arts Tempe AZ 85287-3302

MAGID, GAIL AVRUM, neurosurgeon, neurosurgery educator; b. Chgo., Oct. 15, 1934; s. Harry M. and Henrietta (Busch) M.; m. Janet Louise Reinhardt, June 15, 1962 (div.); children: Allison Magid London, Jonathan Alward; m. Roseanne Cipra Muirhead, Sept. 4, 1982. BSc, U. Ill., 1954; MD, Chgo. Med. Sch., 1958. Diplomate Am. Bd. Neurol. Surgery. Intern Cook County Hosp., Chgo., 1958-59; resident, then fellow neurol. surgery Mayo Clinic, Rochester, Minn., 1959-61, 63-65; clin. instr. neurosurgery U. Calif., San Francisco, 1965-70, asst. clin. prof., 1970-79, assoc. prof., 1979—; chmn. Dominican Neurol. Inst., Santa Cruz, Calif., 1975—; bd. dirs. Dominican Found.; cons. neurosurgery U.S. Army, San Francisco Gen. Hosp. Assoc. editor: Clinical Neurosurgery, 1974. Bd. dirs. Santa Cruz Symphony Assn., 1983-85, U. Calif. Friends of Arts, Santa Cruz, 1985-86. Served to lt. comdr. USN, 1961-63. Fellow ACS, Internat. Coll. Surgeons; mem. AMA, Calif. Med. Assn., Internat. Soc. Pediatric Neurosurgeons, Am. Assn. Neurol. Surgeons, We. Neurosurg. Soc. (v.p. 1996—), Cong. Neurol. Surgeons, San Francisco Neurol. Soc. (pres.-elect 1991, pres. 1992), St. Francis Yacht Club (San Francisco). Republican. Home: 241 4th Ave Santa Cruz CA 95062-3815 Office: 1661 Soquel Dr Santa Cruz CA 95065-1709

MAGIEREK, DYLAN JAY, marketing professional, consultant, producer; b. Chgo., July 15, 1967; s. Kenneth John Magierek and Helene Ruth Tessler. BA in music bus., San Francisco State U., 1996. Recording industry program certification. Mktg., promotion rep. Sony Media Corp., Oakland, Calif., 1990-91, sales rep., 1991-92; field mktg. rep. Uni Distbn., San Francisco, 1992-94, field account exec., 1994-96; sales, mktg. rep. Universal Music & Video Distbn., San Francisco, 1996—; lectr. music, recording industry program, San Francisco State U., 1997-98. Prodr. compact discs Sisyphus Quits, 1998, Crotchrocket, 1998; recording engr. In Dylan's Bedroom, 1996. Democrat. Avocations: recording music, making short films, volcano rsch., island travel. E-mail: dylmisc@aol.com. Home: 1262 Page St San Francisco CA 94117-3026

MAGNES, HARRY ALAN, physician; b. Orange, N.J., Dec. 3, 1948; s. Sam and Shirley (Daniels) M.; m. Patricia Bruce, Mar. 25, 1989; 1 child, Carlos Fontiveros. AB in Biology magna cum laude, Brown U., 1970; MD, Yale U., 1974; M in Med. Mgmt., Tulane U., 1998; cert. in med. mgmt., Am. Coll. Physician Execs., 1997. Diplomate Am. Bd. Internal Medicine, Am. Bd. Med. Mgmt. Intern, resident internal medicine U. Iowa Hosps. and Clinics, 1974-77; ptnr., med. dir., pres., CEO Gallatin Med. Clinic, Downey, Calif., 1977—; pres., CEO Gallatin Med. Corp., Downey, Calif., 1992-94; med. dir., bd. dirs. Gallatin Med. Found., Downey, Calif., 1993—; staff physician Downey Cmty. Hosp., 1977-96, Presbyn. Intercmty. Hosp., 1992—; clin. instr. Rancho Los Amigos Hosp., Downey, 1981-83; chairperson bd. dirs. Primehealth of So. Calif., 1997-98; bd. dirs. Calif. Health Network, sec.-treas., 1998—; project adv. bd. VA/UCLA/RAND Calif. Med. Group, IPA Governance Project, 1997-98. Author: Rheumatic Fever in Connecticut, 1974. James Manning scholar Brown U., 1968. Mem. Am. Coll. Physician Execs., Healthcare Assn. So. Calif. (chmn. med. dirs. forum 1997-98), Am. Med. Group Assn. (policy com. 1994—, legis. com. 1997—), Med. Group Mgmt. Assn., Phi Beta Kappa, Sigma Xi. Avocation: racquetball. Office: Gallatin Med Found 10720 Paramount Blvd Downey CA 90241

MAGNESS, RHONDA ANN, microbiologist; b. Stockton, Calif., Jan. 30, 1946; d. John Pershing and Dorothy Waneta (Kelley) Wetter; m. Barney LeRoy Bender, Aug. 26, 1965 (div. 1977); m. Gary D. Magness, Mar. 5, 1977; children: Jay D. (dec.), Troy D. BS, Calif. State U., 1977. Lic. clin. lab. scientist Nat. Cert. Agy., Calif., med. technologist; cert. clin. lab. scientist. Med. asst. C. Fred Wilcox, MD, Stockton, 1965-66; clk. typist Dept. of U.S. Army, Ft. Eustis, Va., 1967, Def. Supply Agy., New Orleans, 1967-68; med. asst. James G. Cross, MD, Lodi, Calif., 1969, Arthur A. Kemalyan, MD, Lodi, 1969-71, 72-77; med. sec. Lodi Meml. Hosp., 1972; lab. aide Calif. State U., Sacramento, 1977; phlebotomist St. Joseph's Hosp., Stockton, 1978-79; supr. microbiology Dameron Hosp. Assn., Stockton, 1980—. Active Concerned Women Am., Washington, 1987—. Mem. Calif. Assn. Clin. Lab. Technologists, San Joaquin County Med. Assts. Assn., Nat. Geog. Soc., Nat. Audubon Soc., San Francisco Offshore. Baptist. Lodge: Jobs Daus. (chaplain 1962-63). Avocations: boating, snow and water skiing, birding, sewing, reading. Home: 9627 Knight Ln Stockton CA 95209-1961 Office: Dameron Hosp Lab 525 W Acacia St Stockton CA 95203-2405

MAGOON, NANCY AMELIA, art association administrator, philanthropist; b. N.Y.C., Apr. 19, 1941; d. Jack and Norma Harriet (Hirschl) Parker; m. Robert Cornelius Magoon, Mar. 16, 1978; children: Adam Glick, Peri Curnin. Student, Cornell U., 1958-59. Gallerist Hokin Gallery, Miami, 1986-89; sec. Nat. Found. Advancement in Arts, 1989-94; nat. coun. mem. Aspen Art Mus., 1985—, Aspen Ballet, 1985—; v.p. Ctr. for Fine Arts, Miami, 1984-94, Miami City Ballet, 1990-94. bd. dirs. Cmty. Alliance Against AIDS, 1990-92; coun. mem. Susan Komen Breast Cancer, Aspen, 1994—; hon. trustee Ctr. for Fine Arts, Miami Beach, 1996; trustee Site Santa Fe, 1996. Named one of Outstanding Women in Miami, 1992; NEA grantee, 1995. Avocations: skiing, golf, fly fishing, skeet and clay target shooting.

MAGOWAN, PETER ALDEN, professional baseball team executive, grocery chain executive; b. N.Y.C., Apr. 5, 1942; s. Robert Anderson and Doris (Merrill) M.; m. Jill Tarlau (div. July 1982; children: Kimberley, Margot, Hilary; m. Deborah Johnston, Aug. 14, 1982. BA, Stanford U., 1964; MA, Oxford U., Eng., 1966; postgrad., Johns Hopkins U., 1967-68. Store mgr. Safeway Stores Inc., Washington, 1968-70; dist. mgr. Safeway Stores Inc., Houston, 1970-71; retail ops. mgr. Safeway Stores Inc., Phoenix, 1971-72; divsn. mgr. Safeway Stores Inc., Tulsa, 1973-76; mgr. internat. divsn. Safeway Stores Inc., Toronto, Ont., Can., 1976-78; mgr. western region Safeway Stores Inc., San Francisco, 1978-79; CEO Safeway Stores Inc., Oakland, Calif., 1980-93, chmn. bd. dirs., 1980-98; pres., mng. gen. ptnr. San Francisco Giants, 1993—; bd. dirs. Daimler Chrysler Corp., Caterpillar, Safeway Inc. Office: San Francisco Giants 3 Com Park San Francisco CA 94124-3904

MAGUIRE, GEORGE, theater artistic director, actor, educator; b. Wilmington, Del., Dec. 4, 1946; s. Francis J. and Carolyn (Plummer) M. BS in German, Indiana (Pa.) U., 1968; postgrad., Lewis & Clark Coll., 1969, U. Denver, 1969-70. Actor Gt. Lakes Shakespeare, Cleve., 1977-81, Actors' Theater of Louisville, 1980, Canterbury Tales, N.Y.C., 1980; artistic dir. Solano Coll. Theater, Suisun, Calif., 1989—; actor ACT, San Francisco, 1997. Author: (play) The Enchanted Mesa, 1984; dir.: Equus, The Secret Garden, 1991-93; appeared in (films) The Game, True Crime, Leonard VI, Murder in the First, Fight Club; (TV) Stolen Innocence, others. Mem. adv. bd. Solano Coll. Theater Assn., 1989-98. Recipient 7 San Francisco Drama Logue awards, Samuel French Playwright award, 1984, Bay Area Critics award, 1995. Mem. Theta Xi. Home: 120 Gardenside Dr Apt 301 San Francisco CA 94131-1321 Office: Solano Coll Theater 4000 Suisun Valley Rd Suisun City CA 94585

MAGUIRE, JOHN DAVID, academic administrator, educator, writer; b. Montgomery, Ala., Aug. 7, 1932; s. John Henry and Clyde (Merrill) M.; m. Lillian Louise Parrish, Aug. 29, 1953; children: Catherine Merrill, Mary Elizabeth, Anne King. A.B. magna cum laude, Washington and Lee U., 1953, Litt.D. (hon.), 1979; Fulbright scholar, Edinburgh (Scotland) U., 1953-54; B.D. summa cum laude, Yale, 1956, Ph.D., 1960; postdoctoral research, Yale U. and U. Tübingen, Germany, 1964-65, U. Calif., Berkeley, 1968-69, Silliman U., Philippines, 1976-77; HLD (hon.), Transylvania U., 1990. Dir. Internat. Student Ctr., New Haven, 1956-58; mem. faculty Wesleyan U., Middletown, Conn., 1960-70; asso. provost Wesleyan U., 1967-68; vis. lectr. Pacific Sch. Religion and Grad. Theol. Union, Berkeley, 1968-69; pres. SUNY Coll. at Old Westbury, 1970-81, Claremont (Calif.) Grad. U., 1981-98. Author: The Dance of the Pilgrim: A Christian Style of Life for Today, 1967; also numerous articles. Mem. Conn. adv. com. U.S. Commn. Civil Rights, 1961-70; participant White House Conf. on Civil Rights, 1966; advisor, permanent trustee and 1st chmn. bd. dirs. Martin Luther King Ctr. for Social Change, Atlanta, 1968—; bd. dirs. Nassau County Health and Welfare Coun., 1971-81, pres., 1974-76; trustee United Bd. Christian Higher Edn. in Asia, 1975-81, Inst. Internat. Edn., 1980-86; charter trustee Tomás Rivera Policy Inst., Claremont, Calif., 1984—, vice chmn., 1987-94, treas., 1995—, Assn. Ind. Calif. Colls. and Univs., 1985-98, chmn. 1990-92, mem. exec. com., 1992-98, The Calif. Achievement Coun., 1985-94, chmn. 1990-94, Transylvania U. Bingham Trust, 1987—, Lincoln Found. and Lincoln Inst. of Land Policy, Inc., 1987-94, The JL Found., 1988—, The Bus. Enterprise Trust, 1989—, Ednl. Found. for African Ams., 1991—; bd. dirs. Assn. Am. Colls. and Univs., 1981-86, chmn., 1984-85; bd. dirs. Legal Def. and Edn. Fund, NAACP, 1991—, west coast div., 1981—, Thacher Sch., Ojai, Calif., 1982-94, vice chmn., 1986-90, Salzburg Seminar, 1992-96; charter mem. Pacific Coun. Internat. Policy, 1995—; mem. Am. Com. on U.S.-Soviet Rels., 1981-92, Blue Ribbon Calif. Commn. on Teaching Profession, 1984-86; mem. governing coun. Aspen Inst. Wye Faculty Seminar, 1984-94; mem. Coun. on Fgn. Rels., 1983—; adv. bd. RAND Ctr. Rsch. Immigration Policy, 1994—; mem. Pres.'s Adv. Coun. to Commn. on Calif. Master Plan for Higher Edn., 1986-87, L.A. Ednl. Alliance for Restructuring Now, 1992—, Calif. Bus. Higher Edn. Forum, 1992-98. Recipient Julia A. Archibald High Scholarship award Yale Div. Sch., 1956; Day fellow Yale Grad. Sch., 1956-57; Kent fellow, 1957-60; Howard Found. postdoctoral fellow Brown U. Grad. Sch., 1964-65; Fenn lectr., 7 Asian countries, 1976-77; recipient Conn. Prince Hall Masons' award outstanding contbns. human rights in Conn., 1965; E. Harris Harbison Gt. Tchr. prize Danforth Found., 1968. Fellow Soc. Values Higher Edn. (pres. 1974-81, bd. dirs. 1972-88); mem. Phi Beta Kappa, Omicron Delta Kappa. Democrat. Office: Claremont Grad U 170 E 10th St Claremont CA 91711-5909

MAHADEV, RAJESH, strategic marketing professional; b. Madras, India, Apr. 17, 1966; came to U.S., 1988; s. R.K. and Padma (Alwa) M.; m. Ana Elisa Mendes De Oliveira, Jan. 23, 1992; 1 child, Isabella Beauclair. B. Commerce in Acctg., U. Bangalore (India), 1987; MBA in Mktg. and Fin., U. Denver, 1990. Sr. account exec. Communication Workshop, Bangalore, 1987-88; turnaround specialist Corriere & Assocs., Inc., Englewood, Colo., 1992-94; assoc. dir. U.S. West, Inc., Englewood, Colo., 1994-95; dir. mktg. BPL U.S. West Cellular, Ltd. India, 1996-97; dir. new bus. devel. US West Comm., 1997—. Educator Jr. Achievement of Denver, 1992; amb. Greater Denver Chamber, 1992—. Mem. Am. Mensa Ltd. Avocations: classical piano, elk hunting. Office: US West Comm # 310 1801 California St Ste 3330 Denver CO 80202-2658

MAHADY, ERIC M., artist, animator; b. Raleigh, N.C., Apr. 26, 1963; s. Frederick Joseph Jr. and Mary Andrea Mahady. BS in Indsl. Design, Art Ctr. Coll. Design, Pasadena, Calif., 1989. Designer Warner Bros. Animation, 1990-97; tech. supr., animator H.B.O./Box Office Original Animation, 1996; dir. animation Walt Disney TV, 1997; art dir. Robert Bane Edits./Tamara Bane Gallery, 1998; artist Nickelodeon, Burbank, Calif., 1998—. Avocations: painting, film. Office: Nickelodeon Animation Studio 231 W Olive Ave Burbank CA 91502-1825

MAHAFFEY, KAY P., artist, interior designer, facilities planner; b. Cin., Oct. 16, 1936; d. Frederick and Eva Nell (Cricher) Pfiester; m. Virgil B. Mahaffey (dec.); children: Lynn Elizabeth, Margaret Kay. BS in Edn., U.Cin., 1958, BA in Design, 1958; MA in Art Edn., U. Washington, Seattle, 1972. Art tchr. Various Pub. Schs., Ohio, Wis., Wash., 1958-62; art mobile designer Bucks County C.C., Pa., 1975-76; cons. to legislators N.J. Commn. on the Arts, Trenton, N.J., 1975-78; facilities planning, constrn. Merabank (Bank Am. S.W.), Phoenix, Ariz., 1980-86; asst. prof. Ariz. State U., Coll. Arch. and Design, Tempe, 1987-89; chair interior design N.W. Coll. of Art, Poulsbo, Wash., 1992-97; supr. relocation Puget Sound Energy, Facilities, Bellevue, Wash., 1997—; chair comty. peer outreach com. Ariz. State U. Coll. of Design, Tempe, 1987-89; mem. adv. bd. interior design Northwest Coll. Art, Poulseo, Wash., 1992—. Artist: works exhibited in juried exhbns. Bellevue, Wash., Califl, Pa., Japan and Germany; author: (curricula) Tune in to Where You Live, 1972, Facilities Planning, 1986-87. Organizer Speakers' Bur., N.W. Kidney Ctr., Seattle, 1969-75; co-chair Kappa Kappa Gamma Scottsdale Chpt. Alumni Art Show, 1983, 84; corp. rep. to steering com. Phoenix Ariz. Core Devel., 1984-85; designer, planner Women's Crisis Ctr., Scottsdale, 1986-87. Recipient scholarship Nat. Oceanic Atmospheric Assn., Seattle,1970, grad. fellowship Kappa Kappa Gamma, 1970, award of excellence, N.W. Kidney Ctr., 1972. Mem. Internat. Facility Mgmt. Assn., Am. Soc. Interior Design, Internat. Interior Design Assn. Avocations: skiing, tennis, kayaking, gardening. Home: 18730 94th Ave W Edmonds WA 98020-2320

MAHARIDGE, DALE DIMITRO, journalist, educator; b. Cleve., Oct. 24, 1956; s. Steve and Joan (Kopfstein) M. Student, Cleve. State U., 1974-75.

Free-lance reporter various publs., Cleve., 1976; reporter The Gazette, Medina, Ohio, 1977-78; free-lance reporter Cleve. Plain Dealer, 1978-80; reporter The Sacramento Bee, 1980-91; lectr. Stanford U., Palo Alto, Calif., 1992—. Author: Journey to Nowhere: The Saga of the New Underclass, 1985, repub. with introduction by Bruce Springsteen, 1996, And Their Children After Them, 1989 (Pulitzer Prize for gen. nonfiction 1990), The Last Great American Hobo, 1993, The Coming White Minority: California's Eruptions and the Nation's Future, 1996; editor Unigue Books, 1999; contbr. articles to profl. jours. Nieman fellow Harvard U., 1988; grantee Pope Found., 1994, Freedom Forum, 1995. Democrat. Office: Stanford U Dept Comm Bldg 120 Stanford CA 94305

MAHDAVI, KAMAL B., writer, researcher; b. Esfahan, Iran, Sept. 1, 1933; came to U.S., 1958, naturalized.; s. Ebrahim B. and Ghamar (Jalilian) M. BA, U. Calif., Berkeley, 1964; MA, U Toronto, 1965; postgrad., U. Cambridge, Eng., 1965-69. Cert. coll. tchr., Calif. R&D rschr. U. Stockholm, 1969-71; freelance rschr., writer self-employed, San Francisco, San Diego, 1972—; ind. legal rschr. San Francisco, San Diego, 1980—. Author (as K.M.B. Writer): Technological Innovation: An Efficiency Investigation, 1972; contbr. articles to profl. jours. Civil rights litigant. Avocations: swimming, chess. Office: PO Box 121164 San Diego CA 92112-1164

MAHER, DAVID L., drug store company executive; b. Iowa City, 1939. Grad., U. Iowa, 1964. Pres., vice chmn., COO Am. Stores Co., Salt Lake City. Office: American Stores Co 299 S Main St Salt Lake City UT 84111-2241

MAHER, JOHN FREDERIC (JACK MAHER), TV news executive; b. Denver, May 23, 1954; s. John A. and Pauline Ann (Douglas) M.; m. Rebecca Joyce Loeffel, Aug. 9, 1975; children: Matthew John, Jeffrey Paul, Callie Maureen. BA in Mass Comm., N. Mex. State U., 1977. TV news reporter, anchor KVIA-TV, El Paso, Tex., 1975-78, KBMT-TV, Beaumont, Tex., 1978-80; TV news producer KUSA-TV, Denver, 1980-90, TV news exec. producer, 1990—. Recipient EMMY, NATAS, 1994, 97. Roman Catholic. Avocations: hiking, gardening, piano, history, chess. Office: KUSA-TV 500 Speer Blvd Denver CO 80203

MAHLER, ROBERT LOUIS, soil scientist, educator; b. Huntington Park, Calif., Jan. 7, 1954; s. Robert Alfred and Emily Chonita (Ortega) M.; 1 child, Claudia. BS, Wash. State U., 1976, MS, 1978; PhD, N.C. State U., 1980. Asst. prof., assoc. prof., now prof. soil sci. U. Idaho, Moscow, 1980—, soil fertility researcher, 1980—, extension soil scientist, 1989—, water quality coord., 1990—. Contbr. more than 200 articles to profl. jours. Environ. sciences tchr. Knights of Columbus. Mem. Am. Soc. Agronomy, Soil Sci. Soc. Am., Western Soc. Soil Sci., Rotary, KC, Gamma Sigma Delta (pres. 1989-90). Roman Catholic. Avocations: hiking, camping, collecting baseball cards. Office: U Idaho Soil Sci Divsn Moscow ID 83843

MAHMOOD, AAMER, computer system architect; b. Lahore, Pakistan, Jan. 27, 1956; came to U.S., 1979; s. Muhammad Iftikhar Quereshi and Farakh (Sultana) Iftikhar; m. Samira Aftab, June 28, 1985; children: Muhammad Bilal, Umer Ali. BSEE with honors, U. Engring. & Tech., Lahore, 1979; MSEE, Stanford U., 1980, PhD in Elec. Engring., 1986. Lectr. U. Egnring. & Tech., 1979; teaching asst. Stanford (Calif.) U., 1980-82, rsch. asst., 1983-85; mem. tech. staff Rolm Milspec Computers, San Jose, Calif., 1986-88; mgr., tech. leader CPU and memory systems Amdahl/Advanced Systems, Sunnyvale, Calif., 1988-93; sr. mgr. architect network hardware Cisco Systems, San Jose, 1994—. Contbr. articles to profl. jours. Bd. of Secondary Edn. merit scholar, Lahore, 1971, Bd. of Intermediate Edn. talent scholar, Lahore, 1973. Mem. IEEE (sr.), Assn. Computing Machinery, Stanford Alumni Assn. (life). Home: 1098 Cardinal Way Palo Alto CA 94303-3540

MAHONEY, ANN DICKINSON, fundraiser; b. Topeka, Sept. 12, 1961; d. Jacob Alan II and Ruth (Curd) Dickinson; m. Michael James Mahoney, May 29, 1993; children: James Junius Castle, Catherine Lane. AB in History, Grinnell Coll., 1983; postgrad., McGill U., Montreal, Quebec, Can., 1985. Analyst, corp. fin. dept. E.F. Hutton & Co., Inc., N.Y.C., 1983-85; pres., owner The Dark Side, N.Y.C., 1985-87; asst. dir. individual giving Meml. Sloan-Kettering Cancer Ctr., N.Y.C., 1987-88, dir. spl. gifts, 1988-91; assoc. dir. devel. Sch. Humanities and Scis. Stanford (Calif.) U., 1991-96; ind. fundraising cons., 1996—; devel. asst. regional office Brandeis U., N.Y.C., 1987. Vol. interviewer Grinnell Coll., N.Y.C., San Francisco, 1983—. Mem. Nat. Soc. Fund Raising Execs., Jr. League San Francisco (com. chmn. 1996-98), Pacific Rsch. Inst. for Pub. Policy, Hist. Topeka (Kans.) Assn., Friends of Filoli (Woodside, Calif.), Peninsula Assn. Retarded Children & Adults Aux. (San Mateo, Calif.; bd. dirs. 1998—), Spokane Club (Wash.). Republican. Episcopalian. Avocations: photography, dressage, literature. Office: PO Box 332 Burlingame CA 94011-0332

MAHONEY, BRIAN PURCELL, insurance agency executive; b. Groton, Conn., Aug. 17, 1943; s. Robert John and Irene (Jaskiewicz) M.; m. Linda Carpenter, Aug. 28, 1965; children: Lauren, Peter, Melissa. BA, U. Conn., 1965; cert., Coll. of Ins., 1966. Sales agt. Valley Ins. Agy., Grand Junction, Colo., 1970-78, v.p., 1978-85, exec. v.p., 1985-95; pres. Moody Valley Ins., Grand Junction, 1995—; mem., chmn. Royal Ins. Adv., Denver, 1975-80, Com. Union Ins. Adv., St. Louis, CNA Ins. Pacer Coun., Denver, 1996—. Pres. Grand Junction C. of C., 1982-84; pres., bd. dirs. Grand Junction Lions Club, 1978-82; mem., chmn., founding pres. Grand Junction Riverfront Com. and found., 1997—; bd. dirs. Mesa County Econ. Devel. Coun., Grand Junction, 1985-87, 97—. Named Lion of Yr., Grand Junctions Lions, 1993, Citizen of Yr., Grand Junction Realtors Assn., 1994. Mem. Bookcliff Country Club (bd. dirs. 1996—, v.p. 1997). Republican. Congregational. Avocation: outdoor sports. Home: 2567 G Rd Grand Junction CO 81505-9548 Office: Moody Valley Ins Agy 604 25 Rd Grand Junction CO 81505-1202

MAHONEY, SANDRA LEA, program coordinator; b. Wichita Falls, Tex., June 26, 1957; d. Robert Glen Seabury and Gloria Marie (Wellman) Ellison; m. James Kevin Mahoney Sr., Aug. 1, 1993. BA in Liberal Arts, U. of the Pacific, Stockton, Calif., 1978, MA in English, 1987, EdD, 1997. Instr. lit. Nat. U., Stockton, 1987; instr. English San Joaquin Delta Coll., Stockton, 1987-92; reader GMAT, CBEST tests Ednl. Testing Svc., Oakland, Calif., 1990-95; alt. coord. placement testing U. of the Pacific, Stockton, 1997, 98, instr. writing, 1990-98, instr. mentor seminars, 1994—, coord. retention svcs., 1997—; cons. writing San Joaquin Office of Edn., Stockton, 1998. Mem. Nat. Coun. Tchrs. English, Assn. Supervision and Curriculum Devel., Am. Assn. Higher Edn., Am. Psychol. Assn., Am. Ednl. Rsch. Assn., Phi Delta Kappa. Avocation: writing. Office: U of the Pacific 3601 Pacific Ave Stockton CA 95211

MAHONY, ROGER M. CARDINAL, archbishop; b. Hollywood, Calif., Feb. 27, 1936; s. Victor James and Loretta Marie (Baron) M. A.A., Our Lady Queen of Angels Sem., 1956; B.A., St. John's Sem. Coll., 1958, B.S.T., 1962; M.S.W., Catholic U. Am., 1964. Ordained priest Roman Cath. Ch., 1962, ordained bishop, 1975, created cardinal priest, 1991. Asst. pastor St. John's Cathedral, Fresno, Calif., 1962, 68-73, rector, 1973-80; residence St. Genevieve's Parish, Fresno, Calif., 1964—, adminstr., 1964-67, pastor, 1967-68; titular bishop of Tamascani, aux. bishop of Fresno, 1975-80; chancellor Diocese of Fresno, 1970-77, vicar gen., 1975-80; bishop Diocese of Stockton (Calif.), 1980-85; archbishop Archdiocese of L.A., 1985-91, cardinal priest, 1991—; diocesan dir. Cath. Charities and Social Svc. Fresno, 1964-70, exec. dir. Cath. Welfare Bur., 1964-70; exec. dir. Cath. Welfare Bur. Infant of Prague Adoption Service, 1964-70; chaplain St. Vincent de Paul Soc., Fresno, 1964-70; named chaplain to Pope Paul VI, 1967; mem. faculty extension div. Fresno State U., 1965-67; sec. U.S. Cath. bishops ad hoc com. on farm labor Nat. Conf. Bishops, 1970-75; chmn. com. on pub. welfare and income maintenance Nat. Conf. Cath. Charities, 1969-70; bd. dirs. West Coast Regional Office Bishops Com. for Spanish-speaking, 1967-70; chmn. Calif. Assn. Cath. Charities Dirs., 1965-69; trustee St. Patrick's Sem., Archdiocese of San Francisco, 1974-75; mem. adminstrv. com. Nat. conf. Cath. Bishops, 1976-79, 82-85, 87-90, com. migration and refugees, 1976 [illegible] farm labor, 1981—, com. moral evaluation of deterrence, 1986-88; cons. com., chmn. for ProLife Activities, 1990—; mem. com. social devel. and world peace U.S. Cath. Conf., 1985, chmn. internat. policy sect., 1987-90; com. justice and peace, Pontifical Couns., 1984-89, 90—, pastoral care of migrants and itinerant people, 1986—, social communications, 1989—. Mem. Urban Coalition of Fresno, 1968-72, Fresno County Econ. Opportunities Commn., 1964-65, Fresno County Alcoholic Rehab. Com., 1966-67, Fresno City Charter Rev. Com., 1968-70, Mexican-Am. Council for Better Housing, 1968-72, Fresno Redevel. Agy., 1970-75, L.A. 2000 Com., 1985-88, Fed. Commn. Agrl. Workers, 1987—, Blue Ribbon Com. Affordable Housing City of L.A., 1988; mem. commn. to Draft an Ethics Code for L.A. City Govt., 1989-90; bd. dirs. Fresno Community Workshop, 1965-67; trustee St. Agnes Hosp., Fresno. Named Young Man of Yr. Fresno Jr. C. of C., 1967. Mem. Canon Law Soc. Am., Nat. Assn. Social Workers. Home: 114 E 2nd St Los Angeles CA 90012-3711 Office: Archdiocese of LA 3424 Wilshire Blvd Los Angeles CA 90010-2241*

MAIDEN, EVA WENKART, psychotherapist, school psychologist; b. Vienna, Austria, Apr. 8, 1935; d. Simon I. and Antonia (Taubes) Wenkart; m. Henry George Maiden, Aug. 26, 1956 (div. 1977); children: Peter David, Benjamin Paul; m. Martin Leonard Primack, Jan. 1, 1989. BA, Antioch U., 1957; MA, San Francisco State U., 1967. Cert. sch. psychologist, Calif.; lic. marriage, family and child counselor, Calif. Sch. psychologist Ravenswood Schs., East Palo Alto, Calif., 1967-69; tchr., sch. counselor Richmond (Ind.) Schs., 1969-70; sch. psychologist Yellow Springs (Ohio) Schs., 1970-72, Alum Rock Schs., San Jose, Calif., 1973-85; founder, psychotherapist Midpeninsula Mental Health Svcs., Palo Alto, 1976-91; psychotherapist Palo Alto, 1976—; instr. psychology Cen. State U., Wilberforce, Ohio, 1971; cons. psychologist Children's Hosp., Dayton, Ohio, 1972; counselor re-entry program DeAnza Coll., Cupertino, Calif., 1987. Chair for consciousness raising NOW, Palo Alto, 77-82; group leader women's support group Jewish Comty. Ctr., Palo Alto, 1983-89; v.p. bd. dirs. Tikvah network for Holocaust survivors, San Francisco, 1992—. Fellow Am. Orthopsychiat. Assn.; mem. Calif. Assn. Marriage and Family Therapists, Calif. Assn. Sch. Psychologists. Office: PO Box 6055 Palo Alto CA 94309-6055

MAIER, GERALD JAMES, natural gas transmission and marketing company executive; b. Regina, Sask., Can., Sept. 22, 1928; s. John Joseph and Mary (Passler) M. Student, Notre Dame Coll. (Wilcox), U. Man., U. Alta., U. Western Ont. With petroleum and mining industries Can., U.S., Australia, U.K.; responsible for petroleum ops. Africa, United Arab Emirates, S.E. Asia; chmn. emeritus TransCan. PipeLines, Calgary, 1998—, also bd. dirs.; vice-chmn. NOVA Corp., Calgary, 1998—, also bd. dirs.; bd. dirs. BCE Inc., Bank of N.S., Stream-Flo Industries, Ltd., Petro-Can., XPronet Inc.; past chmn. Can. Nat. Com. for World Petroleum Congresses; chmn. Van Horne Inst. for Internat. Transp. Chmn. bd. dirs. Notre Dame Coll. Named Hon. Col. King's Own Calgary Rgt., Resource Man of Yr. Alta. Chamber of Resources, 1990; recipient Can. Engr.'s Gold medal Can. Coun. Profl. Engrs., 1990, Disting. Alumni award U. Alta., 1992, Mgmt. award McGill U., 1993, Centennial award Alta Assn. Engrs., Geologists and Geophysicists. Fellow Can. Acad. Engring.; mem. Assn. Profl. Engrs., Geologists and Geophysicists Alta. (past pres.), Can. Inst. Mining and Metallurgy (Past Pres.'s Meml. medal 1971). Avocations: golf, downhill skiing, shooting, fishing. Office: TransCan PipeLines Ltd, 801-7 Ave SW/PO Box 2535, Calgary, AB Canada T2P 2N6

MAIERHAUSER, JOSEPH GEORGE, entrepreneur; b. Yankton, S.D., Mar. 23, 1927; s. Joseph and Angela M. (Jung) M.; m. Reta Mae Brockelsby, Nov. 25, 1948 (div. 1965); 1 child, Joe; m. Martha Helen Kuehn, Dec. 10, 1965. Student, U. S.D., Vermillion, 1946, S.D. Sch. Mines and Tech., Rapid City, 1947. Sales mgr. Black Hills Reptile Gardens, Rapid City, S.D., 1949-54; operator Colossal Cave Park, Vail, Ariz., 1956—; ptnr. Sta. KRNR, Roseburg, Oreg., 1961—. Mem. adv. bd. Salvation Army, Tucson, 1979-86; govs. appointee San Pedro Rparian Nat. Cons. Area Adv. Com., 1989—; past pres. So. Ariz. Internat. Livestock Assn., 1987-88; bd. dirs. Friends of Western Art., Tucson; co-founder Pima County Parklands Found.. With U.S. Navy Air Corps., 1944-45. Mem. Mountain Oyster Club (pres. 1989-91, bd. dirs. 1980-83). Republican. Avocation: conservation. Home: Bear Paw Vail AZ 85641 Office: Colossal Cave Mountain Park PO Box D70 Vail AZ 85641-0070

MAIER-LORENTZ, MADELINE MARIE, nurse educator; b. Boulder City, Nev., Oct. 7, 1952; d. William J. and Madeline A. (Menegus) Maier; m. John F. Lorentz, May 22, 1982; 1 child, William Charles Lorentz. BA in Psychology, U. San Francisco, 1974, BSN, 1979; MSN, U. Phoenix, 1998; postgrad., Grad. Sch. Am., 1998—. RN, Calif.; cert. pub. health nurse, Calif. Nurse Davies Med. Ctr., San Francisco, 1979-81; nurse to pvt. practice plastic reconstructive surgeon San Francisco, 1979-81; nurse Richland Meml. Hosp., Columbia, S.C., 1981-82. Vol. election dist. congressman, San Diego, 1993-98. Mem. ANA, ACA, Nat. League Nursing, Am. Acad. Bereavement, Calif. Advocates Nursing Home Reform, Psi Chi, Sigma Theta Tau. Republican. Roman Catholic. Avocations: reading, piano. Home: 11539 Keisha Cv San Diego CA 92126-6604

MAIMON, ELAINE PLASKOW, English educator, university provost; b. Phila., July 28, 1944; d. Louis J. and Gertrude (Canter) Plaskow; m. Morton A. Maimon, Sept. 30, 1967; children: Gillian Blanche, Alan Marcus. AB, U. Pa., 1966, MA, 1967, PhD, 1970. Asst. prof. Haverford (Pa.) Coll., 1971-73; lectr. Beaver Coll., Glenside, Pa., 1973-75, asst. prof., dir. writing, 1975-77, assoc. prof., 1977-83, assoc. dean, 1980-84, assoc. v.p., prof. English, 1984-86; adj. assoc. prof. U. Pa., Phila., 1982-83; assoc. dean of coll. Brown U., Providence, 1986-88; dean, prof. English Queens Coll. CUNY, Flushing, N.Y., 1988-96; provost, v.p., COO Ariz. State U. West, Phoenix, 1996—; nat. bd. cons. NEH, 1977-81; mem. adv. bd. Cox Comms. Co-author: Writing in the Arts and Sciences, 1981; co-editor: Readings in the Arts and Sciences, 1984, Thinking, Reasoning and Writing, 1989. Mem. exec. bd. Sch. to Work, Western Maricopa County, 1996-98; mem. adv. bd. Cox Comm., 1997—. Elaine Maimon award for Excellence in Writing named in her honor Beaver Coll., 1994. Mem. MLA (exec. com., teaching of writing divsn., 1991), Nat. Coun. Tchrs. English (nominating com. 1986-87), ACE Nat. Commn. Women, Conf. on Coll. Composition Comm. (exec. com. 1985-87), Assn. Am. Colls., Phi Beta Kappa. Home: 20726 N 55th Ave Glendale AZ 85308-9342 Office: Ariz State U W PO Box 37100 4701 E Thunderbird Rd Phoenix AZ 85032-5540

MAIN, ROBERT GAIL, communications educator, training consultant, television and film producer, former army officer; b. Bucklin, Mo., Sept. 30, 1932; s. Raymond M. and Inez L. (Olinger) M.; m. Anita Sue Thoroughman, Jan. 31, 1955; children: Robert Bruce, David Keith, Leslie Lorraine. BS magna cum laude, U. Mo., 1954; grad. with honors, Army Command and Gen. Staff Coll., 1967; MA magna cum laude in Communications, Stanford U., 1968; PhD, U. Md., 1978. Commd. 2d lt. U.S. Army, 1954, advanced through grades to lt. col., 1968; mem. faculty Army Command and Gen. Staff Coll., 1968-70; chief speechwriting and info. materials div. U.S. Army Info. Office, 1971, chief broadcast and film div., 1972-73; dir. def. audiovisual activities Office of Info. for Armed Forces, 1973-76, ret., 1976; chmn. dept. comml. design, prof. instructional technology Calif. State U., Chino, 1976—; dir. Inst. Digital Electronic Art; tng. cons. Author: Rogues, Saints and Ordinary People, 1988; contbr. articles on computer based tng. and telecoms. to scientific and profl. jours.; producer: Walking Wounded, TV documentary, 1983; producer Army Info. Films, Army Radio Series, 1972-73. Decorated Legion of Merit, Meritorious Service medal, Commendation medal with oak leaf cluster, combat Inf. Badge; Vietnamese Cross of Gallantry; recipient Freedom Found. awards, 1972, 73, 74; Bronze medal Atlanta Film Festival, 1972; Best of Show award Balt. Film Festival, 1973; Creativity award Chgo. Indsl. Film Festival, 1973; Cine gold award Internat. Film Producers Assn., 1974; named an Outstanding Prof. Calif State U., 1987-88. Mem. Phi Eta Sigma, Alpha Zeta, Phi Delta Gamma, Omicron Delta Kappa, Alpha Gamma Rho.

MAINWARING, WILLIAM LEWIS, publishing company executive, author; b. Portland, Oreg., Jan. 17, 1935; s. Bernard and Jennie (Lewis) M.; m. Mary E. Bell, Aug. 18, 1962; children: Anne Marie, Julia Kathleen, Douglas Bernard. B.S., U. Oreg., 1957; postgrad., Stanford U., 1957-58. With Salem (Oreg.) Capitol Jour., 1958-76, editor, pub., 1962-76; pub. Oreg. [illegible] Partridge Press, Ltd., 1977—; pres. MediAmerica, Inc., Portland, 1981-96, CEO, 1988-96; bd. dirs. MediAmerica, Inc. Author: Exploring the Oregon Coast, 1977, Exploring Oregon's Central and Southern Cascades, 1979, Exploring the Mount Hood Loop, 1992, Government, Oregon-Style, 1996, rev. edit., 1997. Pres. Salem Beautification Coun., 1968, Marion-Polk County United Good Neighbors, 1970, Salem Social Svcs. Commn., 1978-79, Salem Hosp. Found., 1978-81. 2d lt. AUS, 1958; capt. Res. Ret. Mem. Salem Area C. of C. (pres. 1972-73), Oreg. Symphony Soc. Salem (pres. 1973-75), Salem City Club (pres. 1977-78), Sigma Chi. Republican. Presbyterian. Home and Office: 1090 Southridge Pl S Salem OR 97302-5947

MAIOCCHI, ROBERTO, software engineer; b. Milan, Feb. 21, 1960; came to U.S., 1991; s. Guido Maiocchi and Bianca Rolleri. BS, Poly. Milan, 1985, PhD, 1991. Rsch. assoc. Poly. Milan, 1985-91; tech. dir. Rez N8 Prdns., L.A., 1992-94; sr. animator Pacific Data IMages, L.A., 1994; software engr. Walt Disney Feature Animation, Glendale, Calif., 1995-96, Testaro SSA, L.A., 1996—. Fulbright grantee Assn. Cultural Exchanges Italy U.S., 1986. Office: Testarossa 1250 Long Beach Ave Apt 223 Los Angeles CA 90021-2351

MAIROSE, PAUL TIMOTHY, mechanical engineer, consultant; b. Mitchell, S.D., Aug. 4, 1956; s. Joseph E. and Phyllis R. (Glissendorf) M.; m. Connie L. Nickell, Apr. 1, 1989 (dec. June 8, 1992); m. Donna M. Ward, Sept. 10, 1993; children: Carly J., Kevin P. BSME, S.D. Sch. Mines and Tech., 1978; postgrad., Tulane U., 1986. Registered profl. engr., Wash. Mech. engr. UNC Nuclear Industries, Richland, Wash., 1979-80, Wash. Pub. Power Supply System, Richland, 1980-85, 89; cons. La. Power & Light Co., New Orleans, 1985-86, Erin Engring. & Rsch. Inc., Walnut Creek, Calif., 1986-87, Sacramento Mcpl. Utility Dist., 1987-89; mech. engr. GE, Portland, Oreg., 1989-90; sr. cons. Rocky Flats Project Cygna Energy Svcs., 1990-91; v.p. mktg. Data Max, 1991—; pvt. practice cons. engr. Vancouver, Wash., 1991—; project engr. Mactec, Inc., Richland, Wash., 1990-91; pres. Project Tech. Mgmt., 1990—; chief engr. S.W. Air Pollution Control Authority, Vancouver, Wash., 1992—; owner M-n-M Distributing, 1998—; mem. Wash. State Title V Permit Writers Subcom., 1994—, Wash. State New Source Rev. Subcom., 1994—; v.p. M-n-M Distbg., 1998—. Co-author: Topical Report on Extreme Erosion at Yucca Mountain, Nevada, 1993, RACT Evaluation for the Centralia Plant, Centralia, Washington. Mem. polit. action com. Sacramento Mcpl. Utility Dist., 1988. Mem. ASME (assoc.), ASHRAE (assoc.), Aircraft Owners and Pilots Assn., Profl. Assn. Diving Instrs., Air & Waste Mgmt. Assn., Sierra Club, Bards of Bohemia. Republican. Roman Catholic. Avocations: foreign travel, hiking, bicycling, private piloting, scuba diving. Home: 4606 NW 387th St Woodland WA 98674-3423

MAJOR, ALICE JEAN, lawyer; b. Denver; m. Kent H. Major, Feb. 16, 1997; children: David, Thomas, Kassie, Samantha. BS in Bus., U. Colo., 1984, MBA, 1986; JD, U. Kans., 1987. Bar: Mo. 1987, Kans. 1988, U.S. Dist. Ct. Kans. 1988, Colo. 1990, U.S. Dist. Ct. Colo. 1991, U.S. Ct. Appeals (3d cir.) 1993, U.S. Supreme Ct. 1994. Atty. Legal Aid of Western Mo., Kansas City, 1987-88, Spencer, Fane, Britt & Browne, Kansas City, 1988-91; mcpl. and county atty. City and County of Denver, 1991—; spkr. Colorado Springs mtg. Colo. County Attys. Assn., 1992. Vol. Denver Dumb Friends League, Denver, 1996—. Recipient miscellaneous ribbons and awards for paintings. Mem. Alfred A. Arraj Inn of Ct. (barrister mem.). Avocations: art, skiing, fishing. Office: City Attys Office City and County of Denver 1437 Bannock St Rm 353 Denver CO 80202-5375

MAJOR, PATRICK WEBB, III, principal; b. Wai, Maharastra, India, Mar. 12, 1947; s. Patrick W. Jr. and Alice (Seeland) M.; m. Daphnelynn Jantz, June 26, 1971; children: Mindy Joy, Matthew Patrick Webb. BA in BE, Columbia Internat. U., 1969; BA, Biola U., 1972; MA, Point Loma Coll., 1979; postgrad., U. Calif., Irvine. Cert. secondary tchr., adminstr., Calif. Prin. Omega High Sch., Bakersfield, Calif., 1980-84; headmaster Bakersfield (Calif.) Christian Life Schs., 1984-86; prin. North Kern Christian Sch., Wasco, Calif., 1986-88; prin., adminstr. Yucaipa (Calif.) Christian Schs., 1988—. Mem. ASCD, Assn. Christian Schs. Internat. (former dist. rep., exec. bd. mem.), Ctrl. Redwood League (pres. 1985-86), CIF Ctrl Sect., Internat. Fellowship Christian Sch. Adminstrs., Nat. Assn. Elem. Sch. Prins.

MAJOR, ROY COLEMAN, language educator; b. Wyandotte, Mich., June 29, 1945; s. Coleman Joseph and Marjorie Lois (Shenk) M.; m. Elza Arientie de Magalhães, June 12, 1970 (div. Jan. 1993); children: Sylvia Magalhães, Alexander Christopher. BA, U. Akron, 1967; MA, U. Ariz., 1970, Ohio State U., 1976; PhD, Ohio State U., 1979. Instr. English Curso Oxford, Rio de Janeiro, 1971-73, Instituto Brasil-Estados Unidos, Rio de Janeiro, 1971-74; instr. linguistics, English Tchr.'s Tng. Course, Rio de Janeiro, 1971-74; instr. linguistics Pontificia Universidade Católica do Rio de Janeiro, 1972-73; instr. English Universidade Gama Filho, Rio de Janeiro, 1973-74; grad. tchg. asst. Ohio State U., Columbus, 1975-79; lectr. San Diego State U., 1979-81; asst. prof. Wash. State U., Pullman, 1981-87, assoc. prof., 1987-92, dir. TESOL, 1981-92; assoc. prof. Ariz. State U., Tempe, 1992—, dir. programs in linguistics and TESL, 1997—; 1st acad. coord. Intensive Am. Lang. Ctr., Wash. State U., 1983-85, acting dir. undergrad. program linguistics, 1989-90; vis. assoc. prof. U. Hawaii, Honolulu, 1990; vis. assoc. prof. No. Ariz. U., Flagstaff, 1993; lectr. in field. Guest editor: Studies in Second Language Acquisition, 1998; reviewer numerous jours.; reviewer grant proposal NSF, 1994, Social Sci. and Humanities Rsch. Coun. Can., 1986, 87; rschr. second lang. phonology Ontogeny Model, The Similarity Differential Rate Hypothesis; contbr. chpts. to books and articles to profl. jours. Recipient grant Doris Duke Found., 1969, scholarship Fulbright Found., 1982-83, Postdoctoral fellowship NIH, 1985, Travel grant Am. Coun. Learned Socs., 1990. Mem. Linguistics Soc. Am., Am. Assn. Applied Linguistics, TESOL, Ariz. TESOL. Democrat. Avocations: hiking, camping, running, concerts, plays. Office: Ariz State Univ Dept English Tempe AZ 85287-0302

MAK, GILBERT KWOK KWONG, pediatric dentist, researcher; b. Hong Kong, 1963; came to U.S., 1987.; s. Lun and Sze Mak. B in Dental Surgery, U. London, 1986; Licentiate in Dental Surgery, Royal Coll. Surgeons, London, 1987; postgrad. cert. in pediat. dentistry, U. So. Calif., L.A., 1990. Asst. house surgeon Guy's Hops. Dental Sch. U. London, 1986, researcher dept. oral medicine and oral pathology, 1987; resident in pediatric dentistry U. So. Calif., 1987, clin. teaching faculty dept. pediatric dentistry, 1987—; resident in dentistry Children's Hosp. L.A., 1987-90, Long Beach Med. Ctr., 1990; asst. prof. U. So. Calif., L.A., 1990—; pvt. practice L.A., 1990—; attending physician Millier's Children Dental Residency Program Long Beach Meml. Med. Ctr., 1991—; with Dulwich Coll., London, 1980-82; univ. senator U. So. Calif., L.A., 1992-93. Contbr. articles to profl. jours. Recipient Fencing Bronze Proficiency award Amateur Fencing Assn., 1982, Med. Sickness Soc. Elective award Guy's Hosp. Dental Soc., 1986, Malleson Prize for Dental Rsch. Guy's Hosp., London, 1985, NIH Physician Scientist award, 1991—; USPHS grantee, 1987-88, 88-89; Dean's fellow U. Soc. Calif. Sch. Dentistry, 1989-90. Mem. Internat. Assn. for Dental Rsch., Am. Acad. Pediatric Dentistry, ADA, Brit. Soc. for Dental Rsch., Brit. Dental Assn., Am. Soc. Dentistry for Children, Alumni Assn. Student Clinicians of ADA, Calif. Dental Assn., Harbor Dental Soc. Office: PO Box 661059 Arcadia CA 91066-1059

MAKARUK, HANNA EWA, theoretical physicist; b. Warsaw, Poland; d. Leszek Henryk and Halina (Wojnowska) M.; m. Robert Michal Owczarek. MSc, U. Warsaw, 1989; PhD summa cum laude, Polish Acad. Scis., 1994. Rsch. asst. Polish Acad. of Scis. Inst. of Fundamental Technol. Rsch., Warsaw, 1989-94, assoc. prof., 1994—; postdoctoral fellow Los Alamos Nat. Lab., 1996—; lecturing prof. Polish Acad. of Scis., 1995-96. Referee Classical and Quantum Gravity, Jour. of Physics, Jour. of Tech. Physics, Reports on Math. Physics; reviewer Math. Revs.; contbr. articles to profl. jours. Fellowship Kosciuszko Found., N.Y.C., 1996, Japanese Soc. for the Promotion of Sci., 1995; rsch. grant Polish State Com. for Sci., Warsaw, 1995. Mem. Internat. Soc. for Interaction between Math. and Mechanics, Polish Soc. for Applied Electromagnetics, Soc. for Indsl. and Applied Math., Polish Phys. Soc., Am. Math. Soc. Roman Catholic. Achievements include research in the description of conductivity in conducting polymers by multidimensional Dirac equation, spinor structure methods; new algebraic methods in strongly nonlinear problems and field theory; math. methods in theory of neural networks. Office: Los Alamos Nat Lab MS B213 T-13 Los Alamos NM 87545

MAKEPEACE, MARY LOU, mayor; 2 children. BA in Journalism, U. N.D.; MPA, U. Colo., Colorado Springs. Tchr. Am. Sch., Tananarive, Madagascar; asst. to Def. Attaché Am. Embassy, Prague, Czechoslavakia; adult edn. officer Ramstein AFB, Germany; case worker, adminstr. El Paso

County Dept. Social Svcs., 1974-82; exec. dir. Cmty. Coun. Pikes Peak Region, 1982-84; dist. 1 rep. City Colorado Springs, 1985-97, vice mayor, 1997, mayor, 1997—; exofficio mem. Econ. Devel. Coun. Bd. Dirs.; chair Econ. Devel. Com., Task Force City Svcs. to Srs., urban affairs com. Pikes Peak Area Coun. Govts.; apptd. Colo. Space Adv. Coun.; adj. prof. U. Colo.; leader Pikes Peak Program Citizen's Goals. Mem. steering com. Imagination Celebration; sr. advisor Palmer Found., Pikes Peak Partnership; mem. Nat. League Cities Leadership Tng. Coun.; past mem. Colo. Mcpl. League Exec. Bd., 1st United Meth. Ch. Gates Found. fellow, 1992; recipient Svc. Mankind award Centennial Sertoma Club, 1985; named Super Woman Women's Health Ctr., 1988, Best City Councilmem. Springs Mag., 1991. Mem. Am. Soc. Pub. Adminstrn., Pi Alpha Alpha. Office: Office of Mayor and City Coun City Adminstrn Bldg 30 S Nevada Ave Ste 401 Colorado Springs CO 80903-1825*

MAKOWSKI, EDGAR LEONARD, obstetrician and gynecologist; b. Milw., Oct. 27, 1927; s. Adam and Ernestine (Horn) M.; m. Patricia M. Nock, Nov. 1, 1952; children: Peter, James, Ann, Mary, Thomas, Paul. B.S., Marquette U., 1951, M.D., 1954. Intern Deaconess Hosp., Milw., 1954-55; resident in Ob/Gyn U. Minn., Mpls., 1955-59; asst. prof. U. Minn., 1959-66, asso. prof., 1966; asso. prof. Ob/Gyn U. Colo., Denver, 1966-69; prof. U. Colo., 1969-93, chmn. dept., 1976-88, prof. emeritus, 1993—. Contbr. articles to sci. jours., chpts. to books. Served with AUS, 1946-47. NIH spl. fellow in physiology Yale U., 1963. Mem. Am. Gynecol. and Obstet. Soc. (pres.), Am. Coll. Obstetricians and Gynecologists, Soc. Gynecol. Investigators, Central Assn. Obstetricians and Gynecologists, Colo. Soc. Ob/Gyn., Perinatal Research Soc. (pres.). Roman Catholic. Achievements include radioactive microsphere technique for determination of organ blood flow.

MAKUUCHI, MUNIO HOWARD (MUNIO HOWARD TAKAHASHI), artist, poet, educator; b. Seattle, Sept. 7, 1934; s. John and Yutaka and Mary Sumie (Makuuchi) Takahashi; m. Evelyn Faye James, June 21, 1962 (div. 1965); 1 child, James. Student, Valparaiso U., 1953-56, Chgo. Art Inst., 1955, U. Pa., 1965-66; BA in Art, U. Colo., 1961; MA in Intaglio Printmaking, U. Iowa, 1964; MFA in Painting, U. Wis., 1975. Tchr. U. Iowa, Iowa City, East H.S., Rochester, N.Y., 1965; art rehab., adult graphics Kirkwook (Iowa) C.C., 1967-68; asst. chair art dept. U. Wis., Janesville, 1968-72; lectr. Adeyemi Coll. Edn., Ondo, Nigeria, 1977-78, U. Ife, Ife-Ife, Nigeria, 1978-84. Author numerous prose, poems and prints. Numerous gp. and solo exhibitions including Portland Art Mus., 1997, Sergels Gallery, Chgo., 1964, Des Moines Art Mus., 1963, Bellevue (Wash.) Art Museum, U. W. Ill. Library, 1994, Wisc. Acad. Scis., Arts and Letters, Madison, 1990-92. With U.S. Arym, 1956-58. Mem. DAV, Asian Bus. Mgmt., Japanese Am. C. of C., Coll. Club, Am. Legion, Nisei Vets. Com., Japanese Am. Citizen League. Democrat. Lutheran. Avocations: fishing, baskball, cooking, arogamist, dancing, playing pool. Home: 4447 S Frontenac St Seattle WA 98118-3625

MALA, THEODORE ANTHONY, physician, consultant; b. Santa Monica, Calif., Feb. 3, 1946; s. Ray and Galina (Liss) M.; children: Theodore S., Galina T. BA in Philosophy, DePaul U., 1972; MD, Autonomous U., Guadalajara, Mex., 1976; MPH, Harvard U., 1980. Spl. asst. for health affairs Alaska Fedn. Natives, Anchorage, 1977-78; chief health svcs. Alaska State Div. of Corrections, Anchorage, 1978-79; assoc. prof., founder, dir. Inst. for Circumpolar Health Studies, U. Alaska, Anchorage, 1982-90; founder Siberian med. rsch. program U. Alaska, Anchorage, 1982, founder Magadan (USSR) med. rsch. program, 1988; commr. Health and Social Svcs. State of Alaska, Juneau, 1990-93; pres. chief exec. officer Ted Mala, Inc., Anchorage, 1993-97; pres., ptnr. Mexican-Siberian Trading Co., Monterrey, Mex., 1994-96; CEO Confederated Tribes of Grand Ronde, Oreg., 1998—; mem. Alaska rsch. and publs. com. Indian Health Svc., USPHS, 1987-90; advisor Nordic Coun. Meeting, WHO, Greenland, 1985; mem. Internat. Organizing Com., Circumpolar Health Congress, Iceland, 1992-93; chmn. bd. govs. Alaska Psychiat. Inst., Anchorage, 1990-93; cabinet mem. Gov. Walter J. Hickel, Juneau, 1990-93; advisor humanitarian aid to Russian Far East U.S. Dept. State, 1992—; cons. USAID on U.S.-Russian Health Programs, 1994. Former columnist Tundra Times; contbr. articles to profl. jours. Trustee United Way Anchorage, 1978-79; chmn. bd. trustees Alaska Native Coll., 1993-96. Recipient Gov.'s award, 1988, Outstanding Svc. award Alaska Commr. Health, 1979, Ministry of Health citation USSR Govt., 1989, Citation award Alaska State Legislature, 1989, 90, 94, Commendation award State of Alaska, 1990, Alaska State Legislature, 1994, Honor Kempton Svc. to Humanity award, 1989, citation Med. Comty. of Magadan region, USSR, 1989; Nat. Indian fellow U.S. Dept. Edn., 1979. Mem. Assn. Am. Indian Physicians, N.Y. Acad. Scis., Internat. Union for Circumpolar Health (permanent sec.-gen. 1987-90, organizing com. 8th Internat. Congress on Circumpolar Health 1987-90). Avocations: cross-country skiing, hiking, photography, travel. Office: 9615 Grand Ronde Rd Grand Ronde OR 97347

MALCOLM, RICHARD WARD, academic administrator, consultant; b. Columbus, Ohio, July 27, 1933; s. Ralph James and Beatrice (Ward) M.; 1 child, Gwynn Malcolm Socolich. BS, U. Findlay (Ohio), 1956; MA, Ariz. State U., 1960; MEd, U. So. Calif., 1965, EdD, 1966. Acad. dean Martin Coll., Pulaski, Tenn., 1965-67; dean instrn. Arapahoe C.C., Littleton, Colo., 1967-71; chair edn. divsn. Chapman U., Orange, Calif., 1971-80; assoc. prof. U. So. Calif., 1976-77; dean instrn. Mesa (Ariz.) C.C., 1980-91; asst. to provost Chandler (Ariz.)/Gilbert C.C., 1991-92, chair divsn. social and behavioral scis., 1993-96; dir. R & D Williams campus Maricopa C.C., 1998-97; coord. Phoenix Ctr. U. Findlay, 1997—. Author: Mental Measurement Yearbook, 1972. Pres. Ariz. Rail Pasenger Assn., Phoenix, 1984-93. Mem. Am. Assn. Higher Edn., Ariz. Acad. Adminstrv. Assn. (treas. 1991—), Rotary. Methodist. Avocations: reading, travel, hiking, railroading, music. Office: Paradise Valley C C 18401 N 32nd St Phoenix AZ 85032-1210

MALDONADO, EPIFANIO MIKE, school counselor; b. Trinidad, Colo., Mar. 6, 1951; s. Jose Mariano and Rafelita Cecelia (Martinez) M.; m. Theresa Mary Sanchez, July 4, 1971; children: Suzette, Mariano. AA, Trinidad State Jr. Coll., 1971; BA, Adams State Coll., 1973, MA, 1986. Cert. school guidance counselor, Colo. Tchr. Centennial Sch. Dist., San Luis, Colo., 1973-88, counselor, 1988—; parlimentarian Urban Rural, San Luis, 1975-77; dir. Sch. to Career, San Luis, 1996—; chmn. MTM Enterprises, San Luis, 1996—. Bd. dirs. Victim Offender Reconciliation Program, Alamosa, Colo., 1996—. Recipient Outstanding Hunter Edn. Instr., Colo. Divsn. Wildlife, 1986. Mem. NEA, NRA (life), Colo. Edn. Assn., Centennial Edn. Assn. (chmn./treas. 1976-78), N.Am. Hunting Club (life), KC (organizer Easter Egg Hunt 1990-97, vol. Stas. of Cross Shrine and trail 1991-97). Democrat. Roman Catholic. Avocations: hunting, fishing, reading, sports, travel. Home: PO Box 449 San Luis CO 81152-0449 Office: MTM Enterprises 4th and Broadway 256 San Luis CO 81152

MALDONADO, GREGORY MATTHEW, music director, educator; b. Merced, Calif., June 8, 1958; s. Daniel Robert and Elaine Louise (Turrey) M. MusB, UCLA, 1990. Music dir., founder L.A. Baroque Orch., 1986—; mem. faculty U. So. Calif., 1988-97; instr. in Baroque violin UCLA, 1989-91; founder, music dir. La Stravaganza, L.A., Eroica String Quar., L.A., L.A. Fortepiano Trio, L.A. Supporter Greenpeace Internat., San Francisco, 1989, Pesticide Watch, L.A., 1990—. Mem. So. Calif. Early Music Soc. Avocations: travel, hiking, feature films, exotic foods. Home: 2844 Avenel St Los Angeles CA 90039-2071*

MALE, MARY, special education educator; b. Austin, Tex., Feb. 3, 1949; d. Roy Raymond and Carloyn Kate (Conlisk) M.; m. David Brick, Jan. 1, 1998; 1 child, Jonathan Brooks Barclay. BA, U. Tex., 1970, MA, 1973; PhD, U. So. Calif., 1980. Cert. elem., secondary, special edn. tchr. Tchr. Crystal City, Tex., 1971, St. Gerard's Sch., San Antonio, Tex., 1972, Tex. Dept. MHMK, Austin, Tex., 1974-75; program specialist Calif. Regional Resource Ctr., L.A., 1975-79; trainer, coord. Special Edn. Resource Network, L.A., 1979-82; prof. San Jose (Calif.) State U., 1983—; cons., trainer in field. Author: Special Magic, 1988, Technology for Inclusion, 1997. E-mail: mmale@aol.com. Office: San Jose State U 1 Washington Sq San Jose CA 95192-0001

MALHOTRA, NEIL, company executive; b. Sunnyvale, Calif., Jan. 28, 1949; s. Vinod and Neema (Budhiraja) M.; m. Jennifer Harrison, Mar. 17, 1968 (div. May 1972); children: Peter, Robert, Jennifer; m. Helen Carter, July 5, 1973; 1 child, Allen. BA, Harvard U., 1970; MBA, U. Pa., 1974; PhD, Yale U., 1976. Dept. mgr. Univation, Santa Clara, Calif., 1975-80, v.p. mktg., mem. bd. advisors, 1981-87; sr. v.p., mem. bd. advisors Cirrus Logic, Santa Clara, 1987—. Author: The Justice of Capitalism, 1978, Tammany Hall, 1983, The Modern Spoilsmen, 1985, Social Darwinism Today, 1991. Avocations: skiing, reading James Joyce, watching ER, listening to the Beatles, playing golf. Home: 19088 Austin Way Saratoga CA 95070-6405 Office: Cirrus Logic Ext Office 1113 S Park Victoria Dr Milpitas CA 95035-6942

MALIK, SOHAIL, chemistry educator, researcher, consultant; b. Karachi, Pakistan, Nov. 7, 1958; came to U.S., 1986; s. Bakhtiar Malik and Amna Begum; m. Rubina Sial, Jan. 1, 1990; 1 child, Shahbaz. BSc with honors, U. Karachi, 1980, MS, 1982, PhD, 1986; postgrad., Stanford U., 1986-88. Instr. div. chemistry and nephrology, depts. lab. medicine and medicine U. Wash., Seattle, 1988-89, asst. prof. depts. lab. medicine and medicine, 1989-96; head natural products lab. dept. lab. medicine, 1990-96; co-dir. div. chemistry, dept. lab. medicine U. Wash., Seattle, 1991-96; pres., dir. R&D BioFrontiers, Inc., Redmond, Wash., 1996—; postdoctoral rsch. assoc. dept. chemistry Stanford (Calif.) U., 1986-88; peer rev. cons. NIH/Alcohol Drug Abuse and Mental Health Adminstrn. Mem. editorial bd. Current Medicinal Chemistry; contbr. articles to profl. jours.; patentee in field. Fellow Am. Inst. Chemists, Stanford U. scholar, 1986-88. Mem. Am. Assn. Advancement Sci., Am. Chem. Soc., Am. Soc. Pharmacognosy, Internat. Isotope Soc., Acad. Clin. and Lab. Physicians and Scientists. Avocations: reading, travel, music, poetry, photography. Office: BioFrontiers Inc 2661 Bel Red Rd Ste 208 Bellevue WA 98008-2200

MALISH, DAVID MARC, physician; b. Phila., Dec. 29, 1947; s. Irvin and Esther (Divor) M.; (div. 1990); children: Jennifer, Scott; m. Shari Boxer, Sept. 26, 1992; 1 child, Jack. BS, Knox Coll., 1969; MD, Hahnemann U., 1973. Diplomate Am. Bd. Internal Medicine, Am. Bd. Allergy and Immunology. Intern Hahnemann Hosp., Phila., 1973-74; internal medicine resident Monmouth Med. Ctr., Long Branch, N.J., 1974-76; fellow in allergy and immunology Kaiser Found. Hosp.-Sunset facility, UCLA Immunodeficiency Clinic, Children's Hosp., L.A., 1976-78; locum tenems Drs. Cenci and Krall, West Hartford and Hartford, Conn., 1978-79; pvt. practice San Jose, Calif., 1979—; staff internist Monte Villa Hosp., Morgan Hill, Calif., 1979-81; med. dir., staff internist Good Samaritan Recovery Ctr., Good Samaritan Hosp., San Jose, 1991-94, med. cons. Samaritan Pain Ctr., San Jose. Bd. dirs. Am. Lung Soc., Santa Clara, 1980—; med. dir. Camp Superstuff-Asthmatic Camp for Children, 1985—; head pediat. asthma sect. Am. Lung Assn., Santa Clara County, 1994—; mem. fin. bd. for physicians Com. to Reelect Congressman Norm Mineta. Fellow Am. Acad. Allergy and Immunology, Am. Coll. Allergy; mem. Am. Acad. Physicians, Calif. Soc. Addiction Medicine (cert.), Santa Clara Med. Assn. Avocations: photography, art, weight lifting, computers. Fax: (408) 358-6144. Office: 2505 Samaritan Dr Ste 606 San Jose CA 95124-4016

MALKASIAN, SAAKIS WILLIAM STAN, educator; b. Boston, Mar. 16, 1922; s. Tatios and Herisemen Der Sackisian; m. Leanore, June 30, 1951 (dec. Aug. 1995); m. Marilyn I. Riley Sconberg, Oct. 18, 1997; children: Jeffrey, Gary, Melissa. Grad., Northeastern U., Boston, 1942, We. Ill. U., 1950, Boston U., 1953. With Calif. State Athletic Com., Sacramento, 1983-90, Calif. State Bd. Edn., Sacramento, 1990—. Contbr. articles to profl. jours. With USMC, 1943-46. Recipient Journalism award We. Ill. U., 1948. Mem. Ben Ali Shrine, Scotish Rite, Daylight Lodge Mason. Avocations: golf, music, travel. Home: 4001 Pounds Ave Sacramento CA 95821-4030

MALLCHOK, JEANNE, special education educator; b. Detroit, Dec. 3, 1936; d. Edward Lawrence and Marjorie (Kimball) Ruslander; m. Harry Mallchok, July 16, 1960; children: William, Marc, Mindy, Jeff. BA in Edn., Wayne State U., 1960; postgrad. studies, E. Carolina U., 1988-90, We. Oreg. State U., 1991-96. Cert. handicapped learner standard teaching lic.; basic endorsement k-12. Dancer Lemanis-Tillak Ballet Co., 1953-58, dancer-singer summer stock Botsford Inn., Detroit, 1957-58; dancer, vocal soloist Detroit Tambouitzans, 1957-61, 76-80; co-owner Haslett (Mich.) Pharmacy, 1963-83; artistic dir. Childrens Ballet Theatre, Lansing, Mich., 1975-84; choreographer Okems H.S., Lansing Ballet, 1975-84; instr. dance Lansing C.C., 1975-84; owner, instr., mgr. The Ballet Corner, Mich., 1980-86; opera singer Eugene (Oreg.) Opera Co., 1991—; instr. Children and Adult Dance Comty. Ctr., Eugene, 1991—; instr. classical ballet Lansing (Mich.) C.C., 1976-81, Lane C.C., Eugene, Oreg., 1998—. Choreographer for classical ballets (adapted to h.s. or younger age groups)and musicals at Okemos (Mich.). H.S., 1975-84. Bd. dirs. treas. Lansing (Mich.) Ballet Camp; bd. dirs. Children's Ballet Theatre, 1975-84; vol. Morehead City, N.C., 1975-84. Mem. NEA, Oreg. Edn. Assn. Avocations: travel, dancing, biking, hiking. Home: 536 Empress Ave Eugene OR 97405

MALLON, PETER, archbishop; b. Prince Rupert, Can., Dec. 5, 1929; s. Joseph P. and Sheila M. (Keenan) D. Grad., Seminary Christ the King, Burnaby and Mission, B.C. ordained to ministry Roman Cath. Ch., 1956;. Asst. Holy Rosary Cath., Vancouver, B.C., 1956-64, rector, 1966-82; chancellor Archdiocese Vancouver, 1964-65, dir. religious edn., 1971-73; adminstr. Guardian Angels Parish, Vancouver, 1964-65; pastor St. Anthony's, West Vancouver, 1982-89; bishop Nelson, B.C., 1989-95; archbishop of Regina Sask., Can., 1995—. Address: 445 Broad St N, Regina, SK Canada S4R 2X8

MALLORY, GORDEN, music educator; b. Klamath Falls, Oreg., Apr. 15; s. Harrold Mark and Minnie M. B in Music Edn., Willamette U., 1951; M in Music Edn., Northwestern U., 1952. Band dir. various schs., Calif., 1952-64, South Humboldt Schs., Gaberville, Calif., 1964-77, Tehachapi (Calif.) Sch. Dist., 1977-80, The Dalles (Oreg.) Schs., 1980-90, Clayton Valley H.S., Concord, Calif., 1990-91; substitute tchr. Klamath County & City Schs., 1992-96; band dir. Triad Sch., Klamath Falls, 1996-98. Mem. Nat. Music Educators Conf. Avocations: photography, music performance, travel. Home: 5476 Havencrest Dr Klamath Falls OR 97603-3966

MALLORY, LEE WESLEY, English and French language educator, poet; b. San Mateo, Calif., Mar. 16, 1946; s. Lee W. Mallory II and Mary Ann (Gadd) Recor; m. Adell J. Patterson, June 27, 1969 (div. Dec. 1989); children: Misty Ann, Natalee Adell. AA, Orange Coast Coll., 1966; Bachelor's degree, U. Calif., Santa Barbara, 1969; Master's degree, Calif. State U., Long Beach, 1978. Cert. prof. English and French, Calif. Prof. Santa Ana (Calif.) Coll., 1980—; pres. acad. senate Santa Ana Coll., 1986-87, officer faculty bargaining unit, 1987—. Author: (books) 91739, 1970, I Write Your Name, 1990, Full Moon, Empty Hands, 1994, Holiday Sheer, 1997. Pres. Cen. Newport Beach (Calif.) Comty. Assn., 1976-78; co-prodr. Factory Poetry Readings, Costa Mesa, Calif., 1988—; prodr. Poetry at Alta, Newport Beach, 1992—. Capt. U.S. Army, 1973-76. Mem. Assn. Rancho Santiago Coll. Dist. (polit. action officer 1992-98), Phi Beta Kappa. Democrat. Avocations: poetry, long distance running. Office: Santa Ana Coll 17th at Bristol St Santa Ana CA 92706

MALM, ROYCE ELLIOTT, musician; b. Los Angeles, Nov. 22, 1929; s. Albin Nils and Mildred Elizabeth (Aden) M.; Mus.B., U. So. Calif., 1952, M.Mus. in Composition, 1954; m. Enid Elliott Malm; children: Jaime Louise, Lorraine Elise. Tchr. public schs. in Calif., 1957-89; tchr. secondary choral music and music appreciation Burbank (Calif.) Unified Sch. Dist., 1964-89; ret. 1989; mem. Burbank Symphony Assn., 1971-91, pres., 1975-78, exec. dir., 1979—; dir. ch. choirs, 1953—; v.p. Burbank Community Concerts Assn., 1973-75, Symphony League Los Angeles County, 1975-78, Performing Arts Fedn. Burbank, 1977-78; music cons., estate and radio music archivist, recording restoration Cambria Records, 1992—. Composer: Reflections, 1980; others. Served with AUS, 1954-56. Mem. Music Educators Nat. Conf., NEA, Burbank Tchrs. Assn., Calif. Tchrs. Assn., Choral Conductors Guild Calif., So. Calif. Vocal Assn., Pro Musica Sana, Sir Thomas Beecham Soc., Pi Kappa Lambda, Phi Mu Alpha. Democrat. Presbyterian. Home: 5905 Ironwood St Palos Verdes Peninsula CA 90275-1762 Office: Cambria Master Recordings PO Box 374 Lomita CA 90717-0374

MALMGREN, RENÉ LOUISE, educational theater administrator; b. Mpls., Nov. 14, 1938; d. Albert William (dec.) and Hildegarde Ann (Topel) Erickson; m. Donald Elwin Malmgren, Dec. 27, 1958; children: D. Gustaf, Ericka Susan, Beret Kristina. BA in Theatre, Speech and English, Colo. Women's Coll., 1966; MA in Ednl. Adminstrn and Curriculum Devel., U. Colo., 1981. Cert. supt., adminstr., ESL cert., Ariz. Cons. creative drama cultural arts program Denver Pub. Schs., 1970-72; tchr. APS Crawford Elem. Sch., Aurora, Colo., 1972-78; instr. Colo. Women's Coll., Denver, 1974-75; ednl. dir. Colo. Children's Theatre Co., Denver, 1977-86; coord. curriculum Aurora Pub. Schs., 1982-85; asst. dir. instrn. fine arts Tucson Unified Sch. Dist., 1985-90; mng. dir. Ariz. Children's Theatre Co., Tucson, 1990-96; adminstr. svcs. Tucson Ctr. for Performing Arts, 1992-94; editor dramatic arts curriculum Ariz. Dept. Edn., Phoenix, 1989; rev. panelist Ariz. Commn. on Arts, Phoenix, 1986-87. Co-author satellite TV curriculum, 1987; appeared in premier of play The Only Woman Awake, 1984. Del. Colo. Dem. Conv., Denver, 1980; peacekeeper Take Back the Night March-Rape Assistance and Awareness Program, Denver, 1982-84; mem. policy. com. Tucson Cable Arts Channel, 1986-87; mem. edn. com. Tucson Symphony Orch., 1988-92; bd. dirs. Arts and Creativity Early Childhood, 1990-93, Arts Genesis, 1990-92; exec. dir. Fourth Ave. Mchts. Assn., 1996-97; chair English lang. model Fine Arts Tuscon Unified Sch. Dist. Cholla Magnet H.S., 1998—. Mem. ASCD, Nat. Art Edn. Assn., Ariz. Arts Supervisory Coalition, Ariz. Theatre Educators Assn. (bd. dirs. 1985-89, pres. 1988-89), Phi Delta Kappa. Home: 2612 E La Cienega Dr Tucson AZ 85716-1546

MALOHN, DONALD A., manufacturing executive, retired; b. South Bend, Ind., Mar. 26, 1928; s. Harry A. and Opal (Baker) M.; m Myla Claire Lockwood, Feb. 9, 1948; 1 child, Chris. BSEE, Tri-State U., Angola, Ind., 1952. Engr. jet engine div. Studebaker Corp., South Bend, Ind., 1952-54; prodn. rsch. engr. Ford Motor Co., Dearborn, Mich., 1954-61; sr. analytical engr. Solar, San Diego, 1961-62; dept. mgr. Sundstrand Aviation, Denver, 1962-66; asst. dir. engring. Ai Rsch. Mfg. Co., Phoenix, 1966-78; exec. v.p. Tiernay Turbines, Phoenix, 1978-94. Inventor: five patents, 1963; contbr. tech. jours. Mem. ASME, Am.Soc. Metals, Soc. Automotive Engrs., Life Mem. Soc. Republican. Avocations: reading, woodcraft. Home: 7848 E Sage Dr Scottsdale AZ 85250-7648

MALONE, JOHN C., telecommunications executive; b. 1941; m. Leslie. Attended Yale U., Johns Hopkins U. Formerly pres. Jerrold Electronics Corp.; pres., CEO Tele-Comms., Inc., Denver, chmn. and CEO, 1996—. Office: Tele-Comm Inc 5619 Dtc Pkwy Englewood CO 80111-3017*

MALONE, KARL, professional basketball player; b. Summerfield, La., July 24, 1963. Student, La. Tech. U., 1981-85. Basketball player Utah Jazz, 1985—; mem. U.S. Olympic Basketball Team (received Gold medal), 1992. Mem. NBA All-Star team, 1988-94; recipient NBA All-Star Game MVP award, 1989, co-recipient, 1993; mem. All-NBA first team, 1989-94; mem. All-NBA second team, 1988; mem. NBA All-Defensive second team, 1988; mem. NBA All-Rookie Team, 1986; co-leader most seasons (8) with 2000 points, 1987-95; NBA Most Valuable Player, 1997. Office: Utah Jazz Delta Ctr 301 W South Temple Salt Lake City UT 84101-1216*

MALONE, KEVIN CRAIG, physical therapist; b. Burien, Wash., June 29, 1960; s. Frank Leslie and Kathleen Marie M.; m. Veronica Virginia Sophia Hacker, June 15, 1985 (div. Jan. 1991); m. Janine Elizabeth Grandon, Feb. 20, 1993; children: Stephen C., Nathan R. Malone. BS in phys. therapy, U. Wash., 1983. Cert. phys. therapist. Staff therapist Good Samaritan Hosp., Puyallup, Wash., 1983-85; staff therapist Profl. Svcs. for the Injured, Burien, 1985-88, 1st Rehab. & Phys. Therapy, Olympia, Wash., 1988-89, Kent Orthop. & Sports Therapy, Kent, Wash., 1989-92; clinic dir. Covington Phys. Therapy, Kent, 1992-95, Physiotherapy Assocs., Covington, Wash., 1995—. Author, prodr.: (movie) ORG, 1979 (shown at King County Movie Madness, 1979); actor, grip Islands in the Sound, 1981 (included in Bumbershoot Festival, 1982); aut: (physician newsletter) Physiofacts, 1995—. Mem. ch. coun. Renton (Wash.) Christian Ctr. 1998—, missions liaison, 1997—; Rep. precinct committeeman, King County, 1997-98. Mem. Promise Keepers. Mem. 4-Sq. Gospel Ch. Avocations: Bible study, writing (fiction), model rocketry, camping. Home: 12828 SE 186th Pl Renton WA 98058-7919 Office: Physiotherapy Assocs 17615 SE 272d St Ste 110 Covington WA 98042

MALONE, LAURA KAY, multimedia developer; b. Tucson, Mar. 31, 1954; d. Arthur Murray and Margarita (Artschwager) Kay. BA in English and Creative Writing, Oberlin Coll., 1976; MA in Ed. Tech., San Diego State U., 1993. Pvt. practice as therapist L.A., 1979-89; tchr. creative writing Malawi, Africa, 1987-88; multimedia prodn. asst. Interactive Prodn. Assocs., L.A., 1989; game designer Connexus Interactive Media, San Diego, Calif., 1992-93; instrnl. designer Project Vista, San Diego, 1993; creative dir. Bien Logic, Inc., San Diego, 1993-94; game designer Lightspan Partnership, Inc., San Diego, 1994-95; owner, dir. interactive design Digital Asylum, San Diego, 1994-97; sr. exec. prodr. Inspired Arts, Inc., La Jolla, Calif., 1998; web site arch. Online Focus, Cupertino, Calif., 1998—. Designer, artist: (interactive art) Violencia: An Interactive Art Piece on Violence and Beauty in America, 1996, numerous multimedia CD-ROMS and Web sites. Home: 240 Woodland Dr Scotts Valley CA 95066-4820 Office: Online Focus 10051 Pasadena Ave Cupertino CA 95014-5932

MALONE, MICHAEL PETER, academic administrator, historian; b. Pomeroy, Wash., Apr. 18, 1940; s. John Albert and Dolores Frances (Cheyne) M.; m. Kathleen Malone, Apr. 17, 1983; children: John Thomas, Molly Christine. BA in History, Gonzaga U., 1962; PhD in Am. Studies, Wash. State U., Pullman, 1966. Asst. prof. history Tex. A&M U., College Station, 1966-67; asst. prof., prof. history Mont. State U., Bozeman, 1967—, dean grad. studies, 1979-88, v.p. acad. affairs, 1988-90; pres. Mont. State U., 1991—; bd. dirs. Buttrey Food and Drug, Commn. on Colls. of N.W. Assn. of Schs. and Colls. Author: The Battle for Butte, 1981 (Sick award 1981), Historians and The American West, 1983, (with others) Montana: A History of Two Centuries, 1976, 2d edit., 1991, The American West: A 20th Century History, 1989, James J. Hill, Empire Builder of the Northwest, 1995. Mem. Western History Assn., Nat. Assn. State Univs. and Land-Grant Colls. (exec. bd. dirs.). Home: 2310 Springcreek Dr Bozeman MT 59715-6035 Office: Montana State U Bozeman MT 59717

MALONE, MICHAEL WILLIAM, electronics executive, software engineer; b. Belmore L.I., N.Y., Mar. 31, 1956; s. Daniel Joseph Malone and Frances Ann (Reilly) Coppersmith; m. Jane Pauline Raese, Aug. 20, 1988. BS in Elec. Engring. and Computer Sci., U. Colo., 1986. Test engr. Catalina Controls, Longmont, Colo., 1984-86; design engr. Inlab, Inc., Broomfield, Colo., 1986-87, mgr. engring., 1987-89; software engr. UMG, Inc., Golden, Colo., 1989-90, sr. software engr., 1990-91, v.p., 1991-94; sr. software engr. RELA, Boulder, Colo., 1994-98, Aztek-Engring., Inc., Boulder, Colo., 1998—. Developer software. With USN, 1975-79. Avocations: rock climbing, sailing, aikido, skiing. Office: Rela Inc 6175 Longbow Dr Boulder CO 80301-3294

MALONE, ROXANNE ENYEART, artist, educator; b. Topeka, Kans.; d. Clarence J. and Audrey (Wiss) Malone; m. James L. Enyeart, Sept. 7, 1964; children: Mara, Sascha, Megan. BFA, Kans. City Art Inst., 1965; MFA, U. Ariz., 1984. Prof. Pima Coll., Tucson, 1987-89, Rochester (N.Y.) Inst. Tech., 1991-92, Cornell U., Ithaca, N.Y., 1994, Coll. of Santa Fe, N. Mex., 1995-98; mem. advisory com. MIT, Boston, 1993. Artist: Kirlian Photograms, Androgyne Series, 1986 (award 1986), video art, Zen Trilogy, 1987 (award 1987), Plant and Geometric Series, Cibachromes, 1991, Mixed Media, 1997 (award 1997). Mem. art com. Rochester, N.Y. Diocese, 1993-94, arts advocate Women, Montage, Rochester, 1994. Art award Woman's Gallery, Tucson, 1992. Mem. Soc. for Photographic Edn., George Eastman House, Ctr. for Creative Photography. Avocation: horticulture. Office: Coll of Santa Fe 1600 Saint Michaels Dr Santa Fe NM 87505-7615

MALONEY, PATRICK J., petroleum engineer, saloon partner; b. Butte, Mont., Dec. 15, 1954; s. James Patrick and Katherine (Johnson) M.; m. Pavlette R. Duffy, Sept. 29, 1990. BS in Petroleum Engring., Montana Tech. U., 1977; Assoc. degree in Bus. Mgmt., ICS Correspondent Sch., 1987; MS in Petroleum Engring., Montana Tech. U., 1997. Registered profl. engr. Mont. Asst. gas engr. Mont. Power Co., Butte, 1971-78; gas engr. Mont. Power Co., Shelley, Mont., 1978-80; field supt. Mont. Power Co., Cut Bank, Mont.; sr. petroleum engr. Mont. Power Co., Butte, 1985-89, dir. petroleum engring., 1989—; participant in classes and seminars in management skills, hazardous waste disposal, interaction, and personal computer skills at Mont.

Power Co., Butte, 1983—. Home: 500 S Emmett Ave Butte MT 59701-2204 Office: Mont Power Co 40 E Broadway St Butte MT 59701-9394

MALONEY, PATSY LORETTA, university official, nursing educator; b. Murfreesboro, Tenn., Feb. 19, 1952; d. Buford Leon Browning and Ina (Bush) Dubose; m. Richard J. Maloney, July 26, 1975; children: Katherine Nalani, Nathaniel Allen, Elizabeth Maureen. BS in Nursing, U. Md., 1974; MA, Cath. U., 1984, MS in Nursing, 1984; EdD, U. So. Calif., 1994. Commd. 1st lt. U.S. Army, 1974, advanced through grades to lt. col., 1989; asst. chief nurse evenings and nights DeWitt Army Hosp., Ft. Belvoir, Va.; chief nurse, tng. officer 85th EVAC Hosp., Ft. Lee, Va.; clin. head nurse emergency rm./PCU Tripler Army Med. Ctr., Honolulu, chief nursing edn.; chief surg. nursing sect. and acute care nursing sect. Madigan Army Med. Ctr., Tacoma, 1991-94; ret., 1994; dir. Ctr. for Continued Nursing Learning Pacific Luth. U., Tacoma, Wash., 1994—; asst. prof., dir. ctr. for continued nursing learning Pacific Luth. U., Tacoma, 1994—. Mem. Emergency Nurses Assn., Nat. Nursing Staff Devel. Orgn., Assn. Mil. Surgeons, Acad. Med. Surg. Nurses, Sigma Theta Tau, Phi Kappa Phi. Home: 7002 53rd St W University Pl WA 98467-2214 Office: Pacific Luth U Ctr Cont Nursing Learning Tacoma WA 98467

MALOOF, GILES WILSON, academic administrator, educator, author; b. San Bernardino, Calif., Jan. 4, 1932; s. Joseph Peters and Georgia (Wilson) M.; m. Mary Anne Ziniker, Sept. 5, 1958 (dec. Oct. 1976); children: Mary Jane, Margery Jo. BA, U. Calif. at Berkeley, 1953; MA, U. Oreg., 1958; PhD, Oreg. State U., 1962. Petroleum reservoir engr. Creole Petroleum Corp., Venezuela, 1953-54; mathematician electronics div. research dept. U.S. Naval Ordnance Rsch. Lab., Corona, Calif., 1958-59; asst. prof. math. Oreg. State U., Corvallis, 1962-68, rsch. assoc. dept. oceanography, 1963-68, vis. prof. math., 1977-78; prof. math. Boise (Idaho) State U., 1968—, head dept., 1968-75, dean grad. sch., 1970-75; project dir. Dept. Energy Citizens' Workshop Energy Environment Simulator for Eastern Oreg., No. Nev. and Idaho, 1976—. Served with Ordnance Corps, AUS, 1950, 54-56. Author, reviewer of coll. textbooks; contbr. to profl. jours. Recipient Carter award, 1963, Mosser prize, 1966, Oreg. State U. Mem. Math. Assn. Am., Am. Math. Soc., Soc. Indsl. and Applied Math., Northwest Coll. and Univ. Assn. for Sci. (dir. 1973—, pres. 1990-92), Northwest Sci. Assn. (trustee 1977-80), Assoc. Western Univs. (mem. edn. and rsch. com. 1993—), Sigma Xi, Pi Mu Epsilon, Phi Kappa Phi. Home: 1400 Longmont Ave Boise ID 83706-3730

MALOZEMOV, LEONID A., mathematician; b. Russia, Sept. 8, 1961; came to U.S., 1992; s. Aleksander F. and Anna P. Malozemov; m. Tatiana D. Lozinskaia, Dec. 3, 1988; 1 child, Marsha. MS in Stats., Gorky (Russia) U., 1982; PhD in Math., Moscow U., 1989. Asst. prof. Yoshkar-Ola (Russia) Poly. Inst., 1982-85, Moscow Civil Engring. Inst., 1989-92; statistician Kaiser Permanente, Pasadena, Calif., 1996-98; assoc. Aames Fin. Corp., L.A., 1998—; vis. prof. Calif. State U., Northridge, 1994-96. Contbr. articles to profl. jours. H. Bateman fellow Calif. Inst. of Tech. (CALTECH), Pasadena, 1992-94, Humboldt fellow Humboldt Found., Germany, 1994. Achievements include contributions to financial modeling, risk management, the theory of Schrodinger operators; speaking at international congresses and conferences in many countries. Office: Aames Fin Corp 52d Fl 350 S Grand Ave Fl 52D Los Angeles CA 90071-3406

MALPHURS, ROGER EDWARD, biomedical marketing executive; b. Lake Worth, Fla., Dec. 15, 1933; s. Cecil Edward and Muriel Thelma (Ward) M.; m. Carolyn Sue Calapp, Feb. 2, 1963(div. 1993); children: Steven, Brian, Darren, Regina, Victoria. BS, U. Utah, 1961; D of Chiropractic, Palmer Coll. Chiropractic West, 1990. Cert. med. technologist; lic. chiropractor, Calif., Ariz. Supr. spl. chemistry Cen. Pathology Lab., Santa Rosa, Calif., 1968-73; mgr. lab. Cmty. Hosp., Santa Rosa, 1973-76; supr. chem., staff asst. Meml. Hosp., Santa Rosa, 1976-85; pres., CEO R.E. Malphurs Co., Sunnyvale, Calif., 1972—; owner, developer REMCO Mktg. Assocs., Santa Rosa, 1970-71; pvt. commodity trader, 1974—; owner Better Bus. Forms and Typeset, Santa Rosa, 1977-81, commodity pool operator, 1979-80; dept. mgr. immunochemistry Spectra Labs., Fremont, Calif., 1990-95; clin. trials cons. hematology, tech. writer Abbott Diagnostics, Santa Clara, Calif., 1995—. Author: A New, Simple Way to Win at Blackjack, 1972. Served as squadron commdr. CAP USAF Aux., 1982-84. Mem. APHA, Am. Chiropractic Assn., Calif. Chiropractic Assn., Optimists Internat. (youth awards chmn. 1969-74), Toastmasters (sec./treas. 1988-89), Rep. Senatorial Inner Circle. Republican. Avocations: flying, computers, pistol shooting, oil painting, writing.

MALSON, REX RICHARD, drug and health care corporation executive; b. Stanberry, Mo., Nov. 26, 1931; s. Albert J. Curtis and Nellie E. Coburn (Bussey) M.; m. Jimmie S., May 25, 1956 (dec. 1980); children: Richard Gary, Gregory Neil; m. Vicki L., Feb. 10, 1983 (div. Aug. 1984). B.B.A., Ga. State U., 1961; postgrad. grad. exec. program, U. Chgo., 1967; postgrad. exec. program hon., Stanford U., 1983; LHD (hon.), L.I. U., 1989. Gen. transp. mgr. John Sexton & Co., Chgo., 1964-68; dir. distbn. system Keebler Co., Chgo., 1968-73; with drug and health care group McKesson Corp., San Francisco, 1973-92, vice pres., 1984-86, exec. v.p. ops., 1986-89, pres. & chief operating officer, 1989-92, also vice chmn.,bd. dirs.; ret., 1992; bd. dirs. Sunbelt Beverage Co., Balt., Stationers Distbg. Co., Ft. Worth; chmn. bd. dirs. Armor All Products Corp. Served with U.S. Navy, 1951-55, Korea. Mem. Am. Soc. Traffic and Transp. Republican.

MALSON, VERNA LEE, special education educator; b. Buffalo, Wyo., Mar. 29, 1937; d. Guy James and Vera Pearl (Curtis) Mayer; m. Jack Lee Malson, Apr. 20, 1955; children: Daniel Lee, Thomas James, Mark David, Scott Allen. BA in Elem. Edn. and Spl. Edn. magna cum laude, Met. State Coll., Denver, 1975; MA in Learning Disabilities, U. No. Colo., 1977. Cert. tchr., Colo. Tchr.-aide Wyo. State Tng. Sch., Lander, 1967-69; spl. edn. tchr. Bennett Sch. 29J, Colo., 1975-79, chmn. health sci., social studies, 1977-79; spl. edn. tchr. Deer Trail Sch., Colo., 1979—, chmn. careers, gifted and talented, 1979-87, spl. edn./preschool tchr. 1992—; course cons. Regis Coll., Denver, 1990; mem. spl. edn. parent adv. com. East Central Bd. Coop. Ednl. Services, Limon, Colo. Colo. scholar Met. State Coll., 1974; Colo. Dept. Edn. grantee, 1979, 81; recipient Cert. of Achievement, Met. State Coll., 1993. Mem. Council Exceptional Children, Bennett Tchrs. Club (treas. 1977-79), Kappa Delta Pi. Republican. Presbyterian. Avocations: coin collecting; reading; sports. Home: PO Box 208 Edgerton WY 82635-0208 Office: Deer Trail Pub Schs PO Box 26J Deer Trail CO 80105-0026

MALTBY, JOYCE PAULA, actress, educator; b. Chgo., Apr. 2, 1937; d. Joseph J. Millstone and Dorothy (Block) Damond; m. Joseph Maltby Sept. 7, 1958 (div. Dec., 1972); children: Melinda Susan; Rebecca Lynn; m. Norman Charles Boroughs, Dec. 21, 1988. BS, U. Wis., 1959; MFA, U. Hawaii, 1985. Instr. U. Hawaii dept. continuing edn., Honolulu, 1968-71; instr. in theatre Cerro Coso Coll., Ridgecrest, Calif., 1973-76; actress, dir. Various Theatres, Honolulu, Hawaii, 1981-94; asst. prof. theatre Hawaii Pacific U., Kaneohe, Hawaii, 1992—; dir., actress various theatres, Columbia, Mo., Calif., 1973-79; lectr. in theatre, U. Hawaii, Honolulu, 1981-88. Author: (musicals books) Rosie's Place, 1993 (Po' Okela 1994), A Night at Rosie's, 1997. Recipient 3 Po' Okela acting awards Hawaii State Theatre Coun., 1985-94, 6 directing awards, 1986-98, Lifetime Achievement award Hawaii State Theatre Coun., 1998. Mem. SAG, Actors' Equity, Hawaii State Theatre Coun. Home: 205 Aiokoa St Kailua HI 96734-1668

MALTIN, FREDA, retired university administrator; b. Calgary, Alta., Can., June 4, 1923; came to the U.S., 1958; d. Meyers Wolfe and Ida (Kohn) Rosen; m. Manny Maltin, Aug. 25, 1950; 1 child, Richard Allan. Diploma Garbutt's Bus. Coll., Calgary, 1942. Various secretarial and bookkeeping positions, 1951; mem. adminstrv. staff U. So. Calif., 1960-92, asst. to exec. dir. Davidson Conf. Ctr., 1987-92, Grad. Sch. Bus. Adminstrn., 1981-92. Recipient staff achievement award U. So. Calif., 1991. Mem. U. So. Calif. Staff Club (charter), U. So. Calif. Skull and Dagger (hon.), U. So. Calif. Town and Gown.

MALTIN, LEONARD, television commentator, writer; b. N.Y.C., Dec. 18, [illegible] M.; m. Alice Tlusty, Mar. 15, 1975; 1 child, Jessica Bennett. BA, NYU, 1972. Mem. faculty New Sch. for Social Rsch., N.Y.C., 1973-81; curator Am. Acad. Humor, N.Y.C., 1975-76; guest curator dept. film Mus. Modern Art, N.Y.C., 1976; film critic and corr. Entertainment Tonight, Hollywood, Calif., 1982—; columnist Modern Maturity, 1996—; film critic Playboy mag., 1998—; adj. prof. Sch. Cinema & TV, U. So. Calif., 1998—. Author: Movie Comedy Teams, 1970, rev. edit., 1985, Behind the Camera (reprinted as The Art of the Cinematographer), 1971, The Great Movie Shorts (reprinted as Selected Short Subjects), 1971, The Disney Films, 1973, rev. edit., 1995, The Great Movie Comedians, 1978, Of Mice and Magic: A History of American Animated Cartoons, 1980, rev. edit., 1987, The Great American Broadcast, 1997; co-author: Our Gang: The Life and Times of the Little Rascals, 1977, reprinted as The Little Rascals: The Life and Times of Our Gang, 1992; editor: Leonard Maltin's Movie & Video Guide, 1969, rev. annually, Leonard Maltin's Movie Encyclopedia, 1994, Leonard Maltin's Family Film Guide, 1999; producer, writer, host (video) Cartoons for Big Kids, 1989; writer (TV spl.) Fantasia: The Making of a Disney Classic, 1990; writer, host (video) The Making of The Quiet Man, 1992, The Making of High Noon, 1992, Cartoon Madness: The Fantastic Max Fleischer Cartoons, 1993, Cliffhanger!, 1993. Mem. steering com. Hollywood Entertainment Mus., 1989—. Mem. Authors Guild, Soc. for Cinephiles (pres. 1990-91, Man of Yr. 1973), L.A. Film Critics Assn. (pres. 1995-96). Office: care Entertainment Tonight Paramount TV 5555 Melrose Ave Los Angeles CA 90038-3112

MALTZAN, MICHAEL THOMAS, architect; b. Roslyn Heights, N.Y., Oct. 10, 1959; s. William George and Jacqualine (Cain) M.; m. Amy Louise Murphy, Sept. 25, 1988. Student, Wentworth Inst. Tech., 1977-79; BFA, RISD, 1984, BArch, 1985; MArch with letter of distinction, Harvard U., 1988. Lic. architect, Calif. Architect The Architects, Glastonbury, Conn., 1978-80, Williamd D. Warner Assocs., Exeter, R.I., 1980-83, Steven Lerner Assocs., Providence, 1983-84, Schwartz/Silver Assocs., Boston, 1984-86, Machado-Silvetti Assocs., Boston, 1986-88, Frank O. Gehry Assocs., L.A., 1988-95; pvt. practice architecture L.A., 1995—; instr. RISD, Providence, 1987, Harvard U., Cambridge, Mass., 1988; co-instr. UCLA, 1989; invited jury critic Harvard U., RISD, So. Calif. Inst. Architecture, L.A., Ariz. State U., tempe, Calif. Coll. Arts and Crafts, San Francisco, U. SO. Calif., L.A., UCLA, Iowa State U., Ames, Miami (Ohio) U. Prin. works include Unitarian-Universalist Ch., Vernon, Conn., 1979, Providence Riverfront Study, 1982, Harvard Law Sch. Alumni Bldg. Addition, Cambridge, 1984, 330 Congress St. Renovation, Boston, 1985, 280 Summer St. Renovation, Boston, 1986, City of Leonforte, Italy Master Plan, 1987 (Progressive Arch. award), North Park Apt. Complex Renovation, Chevy Chase, Md., 1988, Walt Disney Concert Hall, 1988— (Progressive Arch. award), Culver City (Calif.) Retail Complex Master Plan, 1990, Villa Olympica Retail and Entertainment Complex, Barcelona, Spain, 1992, U. Toledo Art Sch., 1992 (AIA award), Inner-City Arts Sch., L.A., 1994, Harvard West Lake Art Ctr., 1997, Getty Culture Lab., 1997. Recipient Coll. Gold medal AIA. Office: 2801 Hyperion Ave Apt 107 Los Angeles CA 90027-2571

MAMMOLITI, TONY, executive; b. Toronto, Can., Oct. 27, 1965; came to U.S., 1990; s. Domenic and Mariangela (Giovinazzo) M.; children: Nicholas Domenic, Joseph Angelo. Student, U. Toronto, Erindale Campus, 1984-85. From operations mgr. to N.W. regional dir. Canac, Can., U.S., 1986-93; N.W. regional dir. Canac, Redmond, Wash., 1997—; prin., owner Mobili Enterprises, Redmond, Wash., 1993-97. Roman Catholic. Home: 14016 NE 63rd Court Redmond WA 98052 Office: 5817 238th SE Ste 4 Woodinville WA 98072

MAN, LAWRENCE KONG, architect; b. Kowloon, Hong Kong, July 4, 1953; s. Hon-Kwong Man and Sau-Ching Luk. Student, U. Redlands, 1971-72; BArch, U. Oreg., 1977; MArch, Harvard U., 1978. Registered architect, Mass., Calif. Designer, project architect Shepley Bulfinch Richardson & Abbott, Boston, 1978-86; project designer, project architect E. Verner Johnson & Assoc., Boston, 1987-91; owner Lawrence Man Architect, Cambridge, Mass., 1992-95, L.A., 1994—. Prin. works include L.A. schs., Fed. Credit Union, L.A., Pub. Mus. Grand Rapids, Mich. (AIA Grand Valley Disting. Bldg. award 1997), LCP Studio, Somerville, Mass., New Asia Restaurants, Danvers and Arlington, Mass., Tai Pan Restaurant, Cambridge, Mass. (Honor award AIA 1993, New Eng. award Excellence in Architecture 1993, Design Excellence award Nat. Orgn. Minority Architects 1993), Ti-Sales Office, Sudbury, Mass. (Design Excellence award Nat. Orgn. Minority Architects 1993), Dental Clinic, Reading, Mass. (AIA Interior Architecture award 1992, Interior Design Project award Am. Soc. Interior Designers 1991, Boston Exports citation AIA 1990, Boston Soc. of Architects/New Eng. Healthcare Assembly honor award, 1994), Mus. Ctr. Union Terminal, Cin. (Reconstrn. award 1991), Ramesses Pavilion Boston Mus. Sci. (Double Vision award/Double Silver Soc. Environ. Graphics 1990), Smithsonian South Quadrangle Mus., Washington (Boston Exports award/citation AIA 1990, Honor award AIA 1989), U. Vt. Student Ctr., Burlington, Campus Ctr. Study and Libr. addition Franklin & Marshall Coll., Andover (Mass.) Co. Corp. Hdqs., Emerson Hosp., Concord, Mass., pvt. residences, others. Mem. AIA, Am. Assn. Mus., South Pasadena Design Rev. Bds. Avocations: dancing, traveling, music. Home: 1837 Huntington Dr South Pasadena CA 91030-4802

MANARY, RICHARD DEANE, manufacturing executive; b. Des Moines, Nov. 11, 1944; s. Robert Claude and Veronica (Cornwell) M.; m. Eileen Cecile, Aug. 16, 1986; children: Erica (dec.), Matthew, Stephen, Lauren. AA in Indsl. Engring., Southwestern Coll., 1976; BA in History, Calif. State U., San Diego, 1967, BS in Edn., 1973; grad., Stanford U. Bus. Ext., 1991; MBA, Nat. U., 1993. Registered profl. engr., Calif.; cert. elem. tchr., Calif. Mfg. engr. Rohr Industries, San Diego, 1967-78; chief R&D div. Rohr Industries, Riverside, Calif., 1978-80, project mfg. mgr., 1980-84; dep. program mgr. Rohr Industries, Wichita, Kans., 1984-87; mgr. Titan 3d, Titan IV missile programs Rohr Industries, Riverside, 1987-89; program mgr. MD-11 Rohr Industries, 1989-91; gen. program mgr. Boing mil. programs Rohr Industries, Chula Vista, Calif., 1991-95, gen. mgr. Space Products divsn., 1995-97; program mgr. tactical mil. fighters B.F. Goodrich, Chula Vista, 1997-99, dir. ops., 1999—. Contbr. articles to profl. jours. Chmn. employee and community assistance program Rohr Industries, Riverside, 1981-85; adv. Riverside chpt. Jr. Achievement, 1978-79. Mem. Soc. Mfg. Engrs. (sr., assoc., chmn. 1978-79), Soc. Automotive Engrs., Soc. Material and Process Engrs., Am. Soc. Metals, Nat. Mgmt. Assn. (chmn. 1980-81), Aerospace Industries Assn. (space com.), Air Force Assn., KC. Democrat. Roman Catholic. Avocations: backpacking, skiing, stamp collecting, travel, Little League baseball. Home: 4098 Martin Canyon Ct Bonita CA 91902-2562 Office: 850 Lagoon Dr Chula Vista CA 91910-2001

MANASSE, GEORGE H., motion picture and television producer; b. Florence, Italy, Jan. 1, 1938; came to U.S., 1940; s. Ernst Moritz and Marianne (Bernhardt) M.; m. Mary Stewart Minter, May 16, 1967; 1 child, Daniel Ephraim. Student, U. N.C. Mem. Dirs. Guild Am. Home: 4122 Stone Canyon Ave Sherman Oaks CA 91403-4544

MANASSON, VLADIMIR ALEXANDROVICH, physicist; b. Chernovtsy, Ukraine, Mar. 4, 1952; came to U.S., 1991; s. Alexander and Chaya (Finkelsteyn) M.; m. Katrine Kokhanovskaya, Aug. 2, 1975; children: Alexander, Julia. *Father Alexander Manasson, MD, veteran of the World War II, was a highly educated person, who spoke nine languages, and worked as a Chief Medical Officer at a big mental clinic. Mother Chaya Finkelsteyn, MD, PhD, discovered a new form of psychoses caused by a child delivery and found its effective treatment. She also loves to play the paino. Both parents spent a lot of time with their children and had a very strong influence on them.* BSEE, Moscow Inst. Electronic Mfg., 1973, MSEE, 1974; PhD in Physics, Chernovtsy U., 1984. Entr. Acad. of Scis. of the Ukraine Material Sci. Inst., 1975-78, sr. engr., 1978-80, jr. rsch. assoc., 1980-85, sr. rsch. assoc., 1985-90; rsch. scientist Phys. Optics Corp., Torrance, Calif., 1991-94, sr. scientist, 1994-95; leader antenna devel. WaveBand Corp., Torrance, Calif., 1996—. *Vladimir's areas of expertise include semiconductor physics, optoelectronics, and millimeter-wave beam-steering technology. Accomplishments include inventions and developments of various semiconductor devices and electronic systems; including precision photo-dectectors, electro-optic and photo-electric plasma-grating modulators; a tunnel coupling antenna feeder; mechanically, optically and electronically controlled beam-steering millimeter-wave antennas; a laser warning receiver; a skin colorimeter; a [illegible] a cooperative friend/foe discriminator; and a fiber-optic flow-meter. He has managed projects for U.S. Air Force, Army, Navy, BMDO, National Science Foundation, NASA, Department of Transportaiton, Department of Com-[illegible]* Grantee NSF, 1993-94, 97, 98, Dept. Def., 1994, 95, 96, 97, 98, Dept. Transp., 1994, 97, 98, U.S. Dept. Commerce, 1997, Nat. Rsch. Coun./Nat. Acad. of Sci., 1995, 98. Mem. IEEE, Optical Soc. Am., Assn. of Old Crows. Avocations: playing piano, reading, children. Office: 375 Van Ness Ave Torrance CA 90501-1497

MANATT, CHARLES TAYLOR, lawyer; b. Chgo., June 9, 1936. BS, Iowa State U., 1958; JD, George Washington U., 1962. Bar: Calif. 1962, U.S. Supreme Ct. 1967, D.C. 1985. Ptnr. Manatt, Phelps & Phillips, Washington, now chmn. Bd. editors George WAshington Law Rev., 1960-62. Pres. Calif. Bankers Assn.; chmn. Nat. Democratic Inst., Calif. Democratic Com., Nat. Democratic Com., Internat. Found. for Election Sys. Mem. ABA, Calif. State Bar, L.A. County Bar Assn., San Fernando Valley Bar Assn. (pres. 1971-72), Century City Bar Assn., Phi Delta Phi, Delta Sigma Rho. Office: Manatt Phelps & Phillips Trident Ctr E Tower 11355 W Olympic Blvd Los Angeles CA 90064-1614

MANCHESTER, ARTHUR HERSCHELL, English and foreign language educator; b. Aberdeen, Wash., July 25, 1933; s. Forrest E. and Annie (Nuttall) M.; m. Barbara Jane Sanford, Aug. 10, 1962; children: Vance Arthur, Eric Andrew. AB, N.W. Nazarene Coll., Nampa, Idaho, 1955; MA, U. Colo., 1958. Cert. in secondary edn., Oreg. Teaching asst. U. Colo., Boulder, 1957-58; prof. N.W. Nazarene Coll., 1958-60; tchr. R.E. Bennett Jr. H.S., Chehalis, Wash., 1960-62, Gresham (Oreg.) Union H.S., 1962-91; home instr. Multnomah County (Oreg.) Pub. Schs., 1996; home and hosp. tchr. Portland (Oreg.) Pub. Schs., 1991—; tchr. Gresham (Oreg.) Sam Barlow H.S., 1996-97; analytical writing scorer Multnomah County and State of Oreg. Schs., 1987—. Author: Math Puzzles and Games, 1977, 2d edit., 1994. Recipient Dankstipendium, Deutscher Akademischer Austauschdienst, 1956-57, summer stipend NDEA, 1963, Honorarium, NEH, 1978. Mem. NEA, Oreg. Edn. Assn., Confedn. Oreg. Fgn. Lang. Tchrs. (pres. 1981-82, bd. dirs. 1978-80, 82-83). Republican. Nazarene. Avocations: walking, reading, word puzzles. Home: 3039 SE 174th Ave Portland OR 97236-1011

MANCINI, ROBERT KARL, computer analyst, consultant; b. Burbank, Calif., May 13, 1954; s. Alfred Robert and Phyllis Elaine (Pflugel) M.; m. Barbara Diane Bacon, Aug. 4, 1979; children: Benjamin Robert, Bonnie Kathryn, Brandon Peter, Bailey Andrew. BA in Econs., UCLA, 1976; cert. in bibl. studies, Multonmah Sch. of the Bible, 1981; MBA, Santa Clara (Calif.) U., 1987. Process clk. Am. Funds Svc. Co., L.A., 1976-77; exec. asst. Sierra Thrift & Loan Co., San Mateo, Calif., 1977-78; sci. programming specialist Lockheed Missiles & Space Co., Sunnyvale, Calif., 1978-90; mgr. tech. publs. Diversified Software Systems Inc., Morgan Hill, Calif., 1990—; cons. Mancini Computer Svcs., San Jose and Morgan Hill, 1985—; instr. Heald Coll., San Jose, Calif., 1990. Mem. fin. coun. Hillside Ch., 1990-91; mem. blue ribbon budget rev. com. City of Morgan Hill, 1992. Mem. Phi Kappa Sigma (expansion com. 1976-78). Republican. Avocations: tennis, gardening, restoring vintage autos. Home: PO Box 1602 Morgan Hill CA 95038-1602

MANCUSO, VINCE, advertising executive. Chief ifn. officer, sr. v.p. Rubin Postaer & Assocs., Santa Monica, Calif. Office: Rubin Postaer & Assocs 1333 2d St Santa Monica CA 90401*

MANDAVA, BHARGAVI CHANDRA, novelist, poet; b. Hyderabad, India, Apr. 9, 1966; came to U.S., 1971; d. Brahmam and Gouthami (Duggirala) M. BA, NYU, 1988. Author: (novel) Where the Oceans Meet, 1996; contbr. poetry and fiction to numerous anthologies and lit. revs.; contbr. articles and music criticism to various publs. Hotline counselor/advocate L.A. Commn. on Assaults Against Women 1993-94. Recipient Joyce Kilmer prize for mag. journalism NYU, 1987-88; Rudin scholar NYU, 1988; Brody Arts Fund grantee, 1997-98. Mem. Authors Guild, Acad. Am. Poets.

MANDEL, MARTIN LOUIS, lawyer; b. L.A., May 17, 1944; s. Maurice S. and Florence (Byer) M.; m. Duree Dunn, Oct. 16, 1982; 1 child, Max Andrew. BA, U. So. Calif., 1965, JD, 1968; LLM, George Washington U., 1971. Bar: Calif. 1969, U.S. Dist. Ct. (cen. dist.) Calif. 1972, U.S. Ct. Claims, 1971, U.S. Tax Ct. 1971, U.S. Supreme Ct. 1972. With office of gen. csl. IRS, Washington, 1968-72; ptnr. Stephens, Jones, LaFever & Smith, L.A., 1972-77, Stephens, Martin & Mandel, 1977-79, Fields, Fehn, Feinstein & Mandel, 1979-83; sr. v.p., gen. counsel Investment Mortgage Internat., Inc., 1983-84; ptnr. Feinstein, Gourley & Mandel, 1984-85, Mandel & Handin, San Francisco, 1985—; pres. The Mandel Group, 1988—; gen. counsel L.A. Express Football Club, 1983-85; instr. corps. U. West L.A., 1973-83. Mem. ABA, L.A. County Bar Assn., L.A. Athletic Club, Phi Delta Phi. Office: 1510 Fashion Island Blvd San Mateo CA 94404-1596

MANDELIN, MICHAEL FORREST, computer scientist, consultant; b. Greenville, Miss., Oct. 24, 1958; s. Clyde Duane and Ruby Eleanor (Williams) M. AA, Scottsdale (Ariz.) C.C., 1978; BSc, Ariz. State U., Tempe, 1981. Fingerprint examiner FBI, Washington, 1976; pvt. practice Phoenix, 1981-87; office mgmt. sys. City of Scottsdale, Ariz., 1987-89; sr. analyst Mattel Toys, Inc., 1989—. Contbr. articles to profl. jours. Vol. Citizens Constitutional Rights, Phoenix, 1977-79; deputy registrar Maricopa County, Ariz., 1979-81. Recipient Rocky Mountain Collegiate Press award Rocky Mountain Collegiate Press Assn., Denver, 1980. Democrat. Avocations: current events, painting, graphic arts, writing. E-mail: michael.mandelin@gte.net. Home: 4750 N Central Ave Apt 16P Phoenix AZ 85012-1718 Office: Mattel Toys Inc 2424 W Desert Cove Ave Phoenix AZ 85029-4713

MANDELSTEIN, PAUL STANLEY, book publishing executive; b. Bklyn., May 18, 1946; s. Max and Esther (Friedman) M.; m. Cornelia S. Pratt, Feb. 21, 1973 (div. June 1993); children: Zachary, Naomi, Nicolas. Student, Bklyn. Coll., 1965. Pres. Quantum Pub., Mill Valley, Calif., 1984—, The Book Pub. Co., Summertown, Tenn.; mktg. cons. Farm Foods, Summertown, Tenn., 1975—, Solar Electronics, Summertown, 1976—, Shambhala Pubs., 1994—; bus. cons. Audio Scholar, Mendocino, Calif., 1991. Author: The Nightingale and the Wind, 1993, The Lute Player, 1994, The Divorced Father's Survival Guide, 1996. Avocations: tennis, mythology, mythopoetics, basketball, music. Home: 1204 El Cide Ct Mill Valley CA 94941-3401 Office: 65 Main St Saint Johnsbury VT 05819-2204

MANEATIS, GEORGE A., retired utility company executive; b. 1926. BSEE, Stanford U., 1949, MSEE, 1950. With GE, 1950-53; with Pacific Gas & Elec. Co., San Francisco, 1953-91, v.p., 1979-81, sr. v.p., 1981-82, exec. v.p., 1982-86, pres., 1986-91, also bd. dirs. Office: Pacific Gas & Electric Co PO Box 770000 123 Mission St H17F San Francisco CA 94177

MANGAN, TERENCE JOSEPH, police chief; b. Utica, N.Y., Feb. 17, 1938; s. Lawrence and Eloise (Roth) M.; m. Charlotte Mauss, June 19, 1971; children: Sean, Megan. B.A., St. Mary's Coll.,Norwalk, Conn., 1961; M.A., St. Albert's Coll., 1965; postgrad. in Pub. Adminstrn., Adminstrn. Justice, U. So. Calif., 1972-76; Grad. FBI Nat. Acad. Cert. Wash. State Criminal Justice Tng. Commn., Calif. Peace Officers Standards and Tng. Commn.; grad. Northwest Law Enforcement Exec. Command Coll., 1986; cert. Gov.'s Rev. Team Child Abuse Services, 1986. With Seaside (Calif.) Police Dept., 1967-72; with Lakewood (Calif.) Police Dept., 1972-76, chief, dir. community safety, to 1976; chief Bellingham (Wash.) Police Dept., 1976-87; chief Spokane (Wash.) Police Dept., 1987-98; mem. FBI Leadership and Mgmt. Science Unit, FBI Acad., Quantico, Va. 1998-; past chair Wash. State Criminal Justice Tng. Commn.; mem. Mgmt. Adv. Group Organized Crime and Narcotics Enforcement; appointed to Death Investigations Coun., Spl. Task Force on Child Abuse, Gov's Criminal Justice Adv. Bd.; master mentor Waspc's Exec. Leadership Inst., coord. Northwest Law Enforcement Exec. Command Coll. Program; mem. Wash. Law Enforcement Exec. Forum, past chair; mem. Wash. State Inst. Cmty. Oriented Policing; lectr. FBI Acad. Mem. archdiocesan steering com. Ann. Catholic Appeal, 1982; chair fund-raising drives Am. Cancer Soc., Am. Heart Assn., Salvation Army, Easter Seal Soc., Assn. for Retarded Citizens; bd. advs. Holy Names Ctr.; exec. bd. Boy Scouts of Am., Inland Empire Coun.; bd. dirs. Spokane Goodwill [illegible] U.S. Secret Service, 1969, Congressional Com. Internal Security, 1971, Svc. award City of Seaside, 1972, Disting. Svc. award City of Lakewood, also Wash. Assn. Sheriffs and Police Chiefs, 1978-81, Police Officer of Yr. award Nat. Exchange Club, 1979, Lawman of Yr. award Vets. of Foreign Wars, 1980, Law Enforcement Officer of Yr. award Wash. VFW, 1980, Community Ser-

vice award Wash. Toastmasters Internat., 1980, Pres. award Pacific Lutheran U., 1981, Paul Harris fellow Rotary Internat., 1986. Mem. Internat. Assn. Chiefs Police (com. terrorism), Nat. Council Crime and Delinquency, Wash. Assn. Sheriffs and Police Chiefs (past pres.), Internat. Peace Arch Law Enforcement Council. Roman Catholic. Office: Spokane Police Dept Office of the Chief 1100 W Mallon Ave Spokane WA 99260-2043

MANGHAM, CHARLES ADLEY, SR., psychiatrist, psychoanalyst; b. San Antonio, Jan. 17, 1919; s. Arthur Decatur and Emma Evelyna (Flanagan) M.; m. Aileen Muriel Ramberg, Apr. 15, 1944; children: Charles A. Jr., A. Deborah, Joel R. BS, U. Va., 1939, MD, 1942. Diplomate Am. Bd. Psychiatry and Neurology; cert. child and adult psychoanalysis. Intern Virginia Mason Hosp., Seattle, 1942-43; med. officer U.S. Army Med. Corps, 1943-46; resident in medicine Emergency Hosp., Washington, 1946-47; resident in psychiatry Cin. Gen. Hosp., 1947-50; instr. psychiatry U. Wash., Seattle, 1950-51; pvt. practice child psychoanalysis Seattle, 1951—; clin. prof. dept. behavioral scis. U. Wash., 1968—; tng. analyst Seattle Inst. Psychoanalysis. Mem. Assn. Child Psychoanalysis (pres. 1990-92), Am. Psychoanalytic Assn., Wash. State Med. Assn., King County Med. Assn. Avocations: tennis, bicycling, skiing, bridge, stamp collecting. Office: 4033 E Madison St Seattle WA 98112-3104

MANGICARO, RICHARD ALAN, musician; b. Syracuse, N.Y., July 24, 1957; s. Dominic and Hilda (Koch) M. BMus, SUNY, Potsdam, 1985; AA, Onondaga C.C., Syracuse, N.Y., 1977. Artist rels. dir. Paiste Cymbal Co., Brea, Calif., 1988—; customer svc., internal sales rep. various recording and performing groups, 1987-88, drummer, percussionist, vocalist, 1979-86. Recording and performing credits include Glenn Frey, Joe Walsh, Gina Schock, Venice, Jon Butcher, Clear, The Drifters, Rick Monroe Band, Kacee & Condition Groove, Sonja Meyers Band, Sofa, Tin Drum, Groove Congress, Mike Russell, Al Raitano, Murumba, Hal Leonard Pub. Co. Recordings, Jenson Publs. Recordings, Victoria Dolceamore. Avocations: yoga, healthy eating, hiking, bicycling.

MANGUM, GARTH LEROY, economist, educator; b. Delta, Utah, July 23, 1926; s. James L. and Golda (Elder) M.; m. Marion Poll, Nov. 20, 1953; children: Stephen, David, Mary, Elizabeth. BS, Brigham Young U., 1956; MPA, Harvard U., 1958, PhD, 1960; JD, U. Utah, 1989. Instr. econs. Harvard U., 1960; asso. prof. econs. Brigham Young U., 1960-63; sr. staff analyst Presdl. R.R. Commn., 1961; research dir., subcom. employment and manpower U.S. Senate, 1963-64; exec. dir. President's Com. Manpower, 1964-65; exec. sec. Nat. Com. Tech., Automation and Econ. Progress, 1965-66; research prof. econs. George Washington U., 1967-71; co-dir. George Washington U. (Center Manpower Policy Studies), 1967-69; Max McGraw prof. econs. and mgmt. U. Utah, Salt Lake City, 1969-97, prof. emeritus, 1997—, dir. Inst. Human Resource Mgmt., 1969-90; lectr. U. Tel Aviv, Israel, 1969, 84, Am. Seminar at Salzburg, 1975, U. South Africa, 1977, Monash U., Australia, 1984; Spl. mediator Fed. Mediation and Conciliation Service, 1962-63; mem. Adv. Council Vocational Edn., 1966-67; vice chmn. Nat. Manpower Policy Task Force, 1966-69, chmn., 1969-71, mem., 1966-76; mem. Nat. Council on Employment Policy, 1976—, chmn., 1979-81, sec.-treas., 1990—; chmn. Nat. Inst. Career Edn., 1976-81; cons. fed., state and local govts., bus. firms, govts. of, Saudi Arabia, Kuwait, Jordan, Yemen, Bahrain, United Arab Emirates, Indonesia, Yugoslavia, Romania, Uganda, Nigeria, Israel, South Africa, Russia, Korea, China, other countries; cons. AID, ILO, World Bank; also arbitrator. Author: The Operating Engineers: Economic History of a Trade Union, 1964, MDTA, Foundation of Federal Manpower Policy, 1968, The Emergence of Manpower Policy, 1969, Federal Work and Training Program in the 1960's, 1969, Economic Opportunity in the Ghetto, 1970, Human Resources and Labor Markets, 1971, Career Education: What It Is and How To Do It, 1972, A Decade of Manpower Development and Training, 1973, Career Education and the Elementary School Teacher, 1973, Career Education in the Middle/Junior High School, 1973, Manpower Planning for Local Labor Markets, 1974, Career Education for the Academic Classroom, 1975, Employability, Employment and Income, 1976, Career Education in the High School, 1976, Your Child's Career, 1977, The Lingering Crisis of Youth Unemployment, 1978, Coming of Age in the Ghetto, 1978, Job Market Futurity, 1979, The Coal Industry and its Industrial Relations, 1985, Capital and Labor in American Copper, 1992, Labor Struggle in The Post Office, 1992, The Mormons War on Poverty, 1993, Union Resilience in Troubled Times, 1994, Portable Pension Plans for Casual Labor Markets, 1995, Transnational Industrial Marriages, 1996, The Rise, Fall and Replacement of Industry-Wide Bargaining in the Basic Steel Industry, 1996, Programs in Aid of the Poor, 1997, On Being Poor in Utah, 1997; also articles, monographs.; editor: The Manpower Revolution: Its Policy Consequences, 1965, Automation and Economic Progress, 1966, Metropolitan Impact of Manpower Programs, 1973, The T in CETA, 1981, Of Heart and Mind: Social Policy Essays in Honor of Sar A. Levitan, 1996. With USAAF, 1944-45. Mem. Ch. of Jesus Christ of Latter-day Saints (missionary 1950-53, bishop 1971-78). Home: 1539 Preston St Salt Lake City UT 84108-2639

MANINA, MITCHELL RAY, video production company executive, consultant; b. San Francisco; s. Ray and Marie (Topper) M.; divorced; children: Jenifer, Mariah, Jessalyn. Musician Concert Band, 1970-83; video store owner Video Madness, South Lake Tahoe, Calif., 1984-93; video prodn. co. owner VideoQuest (formerly Digital Imagery), South Lake Tahoe, 1986—, bd. dirs., cons. Lake Tahoe Wedding Assn., South Lake Tahoe, 1995; tchr.'s aide in video prodn. Lake Tahoe C.C., South Lake Tahoe, 1994-96. Inventor guitar plug. Recipient award of distinction for TV comml. The Communicator Awards, 1996, Videographer award, 1997, Award of Distinction, 1998, Crystal Award of Excellence, Communicator Awards, 1997, Vision award nat. finalist, 1998. Mem. WEVA Internat., Lake Tahoe Wedding Assns.

MANION, MARY PATRICE, recreation program director; b. Dallas, July 10, 1969; d. James Leo and Camille Jane (MacInnis) M. BS in Fin., Boston Coll., 1991. Assoc. dir. Land, Milw., 1992-94; dir. Adaptive Sports Ctr., Crested Butte, Colo., 1995-98; vol. Land, Milw., 1991-92; mem. steering com. Nat. Disabled Vets. Winter Sports, U. N.C., Crested Butte, 1995—. Fellow Profl. Ski Instrs. of Am., Snow Sports Assn. for Women. Roman Catholic.

MANIT, EDDY C., limousine company executive; b. Bangkok, Thailand, June 9, 1974; arrived in U.S., 1975; s. Songfon and Preeya (Suvaranarat) M. BS, Santa Clara Univ., 1996. Pres. Limo Station, Burungame, Calif., 1994—. Avocations: tennis, weight training, skiing, golf, basketball. Office: Limo Station Inc 1415 Rollins Rd Ste 100 Burlingame CA 94010-2300

MANK, EDWARD WARREN, marketing professional; b. Boothbay Harbor, Maine, Oct. 2, 1962; s. Edward Raymond Jr. and Sandra Gail (Strahan) M. Assoc. in Liberal Arts, C.C. Vt., 1985; cert. ophthalmic technician, Nat. Edn. Ctr., San Francisco, 1992; cert. real estate broker, Am. Sch. Mortgage Banking, Walnut Creek, Calif., 1994. Lic. real estate salesman, Calif.; cert. Am. Bd. Optometry Dispensing. Tng. coord. Burger King Corp., South Burlington, Vt., 1985-87, San Francisco, 1988-89; asst. mgr. Bonanza Family Restaurant, South Burlington, 1987-88; supr. U.S. Census Bur., San Francisco, 1990; sales rep. Viacom Cablevision, San Francisco, 1991; programming researcher NBC, San Francisco, 1992; mktg. cons. Calyx & Corolla, San Francisco, 1993; mktg. rep. Alliance Bancorp, Millbrae, Calif., 1993—. Sustaining mem. Rep. Nat. Com., Washington, 1989—; sponsor Heritage Found., Washington, Cato Inst., Washington. Mem. Acad. Polit. Sci., Coun. Fgn. Rels., World Affairs Coun., Nat. Rifle Assn. (life), Reason Found. Republican. Episcopalian. Home: 3401 E 18th St Apt 3 Oakland CA 94601-3003 Office: Alliance Bancorp 800 El Camino Real Millbrae CA 94030-2010

MANLEY, BARBARA LEE DEAN, occupational health nurse, hospital administrator, safety and health consultant; b. Washington, Nov. 5, 1946; d. Robert L. Dean and Mary L. (Jenkins) Dean Smallwood. BS, St. Mary-of-the-Woods, Terre Haute, Ind., 1973; MA, Central Mich. U., 1981. Cert. occupl. health nurse specialist. Indsl. nurse Ford Motor Co., Indpls., 1973-80; employee health nurse Starplex, Inc., Washington, 1981-84, Doctor's Hosp., Lanham, Md., 1984-85; regional occupational health nurse coordinator Naval Hosp., Long Beach, Calif., 1985-88; project mgr. East Coast Health Care Network, Inc., San Francisco, 1980-84; occupl. health nurse cons. HHS, Washington, 1980-84; occupational health and safety cons., mgr. FPE Group, Torrence, Calif., 1988-91; safety and loss control mgr. Assn. Calif. Hosp. Dists., Sacramento, 1991-93, v.p. loss control svcs., 1993-96; exec. dir. Quantum Inst., Sacramento, 1996—; part-time lectr. Compton (Calif.) Coll., 1986. Vol. ARC, Ft. Lewis, Wash., 1974-76, Ft. Harrison, Ind., 1978-80; counselor Crisis Hot-Line, Laurel, Md., 1981-83, Laurel Boy's and Girls Club, 1981-84. Recipient Navy's Meritorious Civilian Svc. Medal, 1989, Women of Excellence award Long Beach Press-Telegram Newspaper Guild, 1990, LCM Profl. of Yr. Acad. Loss Control Mgmt., 1995. Fellow Acad. Ambulatory Nursing Adminstrs. (Honor plaque 1981); mem. SCVAOHN (chair govt. affairs 1994—), Assn. Exec. Females, Am. Nurses Assn., Nat. Safety Mgmt. Soc. (2d v.p. 1992-96, 1st v.p. 1996—), Am. Assn. Occupational Health Nurses, Assn. Occupl. Healthcare Profls. (sec. 1986-88, conf. chairperson 1988, Outstanding Nurse of Yr. 1987), Fed. Safety and Health Council, Cen. Mich. U. Alumni Assn. (sec. 1985-88), Chi Eta Phi (regional bd. dirs. 1978-81). Presbyterian. Avocations: reading; crocheting; traveling; music. Office: Assn Calif Hosp Dists 2260 Park Towne Cir # Cl Sacramento CA 95825-0416

MANLEY, RICHARD WALTER, insurance executive; b. Malone, N.Y., Dec. 26, 1934; s. Walter E. and Ruth (St. Mary) M.; m. Linda Kimberlin, Dec. 18, 1965; children: Stephanie, Christopher. BS in Bus., U. So. Miss., 1960. Cert. real estate broker. Account exec. Colonial Life and Accident, Hattiesburg, Miss., 1960-63; dist. mgr. Colonial Life and Accident, Oklahoma City, 1963-66; regional dir. Colonial Life and Accident, Denver, 1966-76, zone dir., 1976-82; pres. Commonwealth Gen. Group, Denver, 1982-98, Manley Properties Inc., Denver, 1982-90, Richard W. Manley Commonwealth Gen. Grps., Inc., Denver, 1982—; cons. Capitol Am. Life Ins. Co., Cleve., 1987-96; bd. dirs. (merco) Mercy Hosp., Denver, 1982-87. With USAF, 1956-59. Mem. Cherry Hills C. of C., Rotary, Alpha Tau Omega. Roman Catholic. Avocations: golfing, racquetball, running. Home: 6510 E Lake Pl Englewood CO 80111-4411

MANN, CLAUD PRENTISS, JR., retired television journalist, real estate agent; b. Galveston, Tex., June 30, 1925; s. Claud Prentiss and Henrietta Anno (Cline) M.; m. Loris Lea Padgett, Sept. 18, 1948; children: Beatrice Anno, Claudea Padgett, Claud Prentiss III. BS, U. Houston, 1949. Cert. tchr., Calif.; lic. real estate agt., Wash. Fellow Fund for Adult Edn. Mass Media U. Calif., Berkeley, 1958-59; anchor, reporter, writer, prodr., commentator Sta. KTVU-TV, San Francisco, Oakland, Calif., 1962-87; news dir., anchor, prodr. Sta. KTIE-TV, Oxnard, Santa Barbara, Calif., 1987-88; freelance writer, producer, pub. info. specialist, 1988—; journalism instr. Highline and South Seattle Community Colls., 1990-92. V.p. bd. dirs. Vashon-Maury Sr. Ctr. Recipient No. Calif. Emmy awards for reporting and anchor work, 1975, 76, 77, 79, 81, John Swett award for Edn. Reporting; commendations U.S. State Dept., City of Oakland, City of San Francisco, Calif. State Legis. Mem. AFTRA, NATAS (Silver Circle), Vashon Allied Arts (bd. dirs. 1989-91), Soc. Profl. Journalists. E-mail: cmanX2@AOL.com. Home: 25115 122nd Ave SW Vashon WA 98070-7820

MANN, J. KEITH, arbitrator, law educator, lawyer; b. May 28, 1924; s. William Young and Lillian Myrle (Bailey) M.; m. Virginia McKinnon, July 7, 1950; children: William Christopher, Marilyn Keith, John Kevin, Susan Bailey, Andrew Curry. BS, Ind. U., 1948, LLB, 1949; LLD, Monmouth Coll., 1989. Bar: Ind. 1949, D.C. 1951. Law clk. Justice Wiley Rutledge and Justice Sherman Minton, 1949-50; practice, Washington, 1950; with Wage Stblzn. Bd., 1951; asst. prof. U. Wis., 1952; asst. prof. Stanford U. Law Sch., 1952-54, assoc. prof., 1954-58, prof., 1958-88, prof. emeritus 1988—, assoc. dean, 1961-85, acting dean, 1976, 81-82, cons. to provost, 1986-87; vis. prof. U. Chgo., 1953; mem. sec. of Labor's Adv. Com., 1955-57; mem. Pres.'s Commn. Airlines Controversy, 1961; mem. COLC Aerospace Spl. Panel, 1973-74; chmn., mem. Presdl. Emergency Bds. or Bds. of Inquiry, 1962-63, 67, 71-72; spl. master U.S. vs. Alaska, U.S. Supreme Ct., 1980-97. Ensign USNR, 1944-46. Sunderland fellow U. Mich., 1959-60; scholar in residence Duke U., 1972. Mem. ABA, AAUP, Nat. Acad. Arbitrators, Indsl. Rels. Rsch. Assn., Acad. Law Alumni Fellows Ind. U., Order of Coif, Tau Kappa Epsilon, Phi Delta Phi. Editor book rev. and articles Ind. U. Law Jour., 1948-49. Democrat. Presbyterian. Home: 872 Lathrop Dr Stanford CA 94305-1053 Office: Stanford U Sch Law Stanford CA 94305-8610

MANN, JOAN ELLONA, artist, editor; b. Seattle, Aug. 21, 1931; d. Henry Hughes and Jeanetta Maurine (Baker)) Jacobsen; m. Hugh Mann, Sept. 2, 1955 (div. Aug. 1981); children: Susan, Kristi, Steven, Nancy, Roy. BA in Journalism, U. Wash., 1953, BFA in Sculpture, 1970, MFA in Sculpture, 1985. Reporter East Side Jour., Kirkland, Wash., 1953-55; med. editor Virginia Mason Med. Ctr., Seattle, 1965-69; info. specialist Continuing Edn. News Svc. U. Wash., Seattle, 1969-73; editor Seattle Arts Commn., 1973-77; pub. info. officer King County Arts Commn., Seattle, 1973-90; owner, mgr. Joan Mann, Editor, Seattle. Sculptures include multi-media floor sculpture Trident, Ship of Fools, 1988 (award); shows include U. Wash. Henry Gallery, 1971; group shows include Roscoe Louie Gallery, Seattle, 1975, Univ. Unitarian Gallery, 1978, U. Wash. Henry Gallery, 1987, U. Wash. Meany Hall, 1987, SJW Studios, Seattle, 1988, Seattle Ctr. Opera House, 1988, PNAC, Bellevue, 1988, Ctr. for Contemporary Art, Seattle, 1989. Precinct del. Wash. Dem. Com., Seattle, 1992. Recipient 2d and 3d place ann. awards Wash. Press Women, 1971, 1st prize Ctr. for Contemporary Art, 1989; travel grantee Goethe Inst., Berlin, 1988. Mem. Women in Comm. (Nat. Clarion award 1974), Allied Arts Seattle (adv. bd. 1990—), Seattle Art Mus. Roman Catholic. Avocations: photography, skiing, hiking on beaches, travel.

MANN, MICHAEL MARTIN, electronics company executive; b. N.Y.C., Nov. 28, 1939; s. Herbert and Rosalind (Kaplan) M.; m. Mariel Joy Steinberg, Apr. 25, 1965. BSEE, Calif. Inst. Tech., 1960, MSEE, 1961; PhD in Elec. Engrng. and Physics, U. So. Calif., 1969; MBA, UCLA, 1984. Cert. bus. appraiser, profl. cons., mgmt. cons., lic. real estate broker, Calif. Mgr. high power laser programs office Northrop Corp., Hawthorne, Calif., 1969-76; mgr. high energy laser systems lab. Hughes Aircraft Co., El Segundo, Calif., 1976-78; mgr. E-0 control systems labs. Hughes Aircraft Co., El Segundo, 1978-83, asst. to v.p., space & strategic, 1983-84; exec. v.p. Helionetics Inc., Irvine, Calif., 1984-85, pres., chief exec. officer, 1985-86, also bd. dirs.; ptnr. Mann Kavanaugh Chernove, 1986-87; sr. cons. Arthur D. Little, Inc., 1987-88; chmn. bd., pres., CEO, Blue Marble Devel. Group, Inc., 1988—; exec. assoc. Ctr. Internat. Cooperation and Trade, 1989—; sr. assoc. Corp. Fin. Assocs., 1990—; exec. assoc. Reece and Assocs., 1991—; dir. Reece & Assocs., 1991—; mng. dir. Blue Marble Ptnrs. Ltd, 1991—; chmn. bd. dirs., CEO Blue Marble Ptnrs., 1992—; chmn., CEO, En Compass Techs., Inc., Torrance, Calif., 1994-98; mem. Army Sci. Bd., Dept. Army, Washington, 1986-91; chmn. Ballistic Missile Def. Panel, Directed Energy Weapon Panel, Rsch. and New Initiatives Panel; cons. Office of Sec. of Army, Washington, 1986—, Inst. of Def. Analysis, Washington, 1978—, Dept. Energy, 1988—, Nat. Riverside Rsch. Inst., 1990—; bd. dirs. Datum, Inc.,1988—, Fail-Safe Tech., Corp., 1989-90, Safeguard Health Enterprises, Inc., 1988—, Am. Video Communications, Inc., Meck Industries, Inc., 1987-88, Decade Optical Systems, Inc., 1990—, Forum Mil. Application Directed Energy, 1992—, Am. Bus. Consultants, Inc., 1993—; chmn. bd. Mgmt. Tech., Inc. 1991—, Encompass Tech., Inc., 1994-98; bd. dirs., mem. adv. bd. Micro-Frame, Inc., 1988-91; chmn. bd. HLX Laser, Inc., 1984-86; bd. dirs. Cons's. Roundtable, 1992—, Am. Bus. Cons., Inc., 1993—; rsch. assoc., mem. extension teaching staff U. So. Calif., L.A., 1964-70; chmn. Ballistic Missile Def. Subgroup, 1989-90, Tactical Directed Energy Weapons Subgroup, 1988-90; chmn., chief exec. officer Mgmt. Tech., Inc., 1991—; dir. Am. Bus. Cons., Inc., 1993—; faculty mem. Asia Pacific Inst., 1998—; faculty Nat. Technol. U., 1997—. Contbg. editor, mem. adv. bd. Calif. High-Tech Funding Jour., 1989-90; contbr. over 50 tech. articles to profl. jours.; patentee in field. Mem. adv. com. to Engrng. Sch., Calif. State U., Long Beach, 1985—; chmn. polit. affairs Am. Electronics Assn., Orange County Coun., 1986-87, mem. exec. com., 1986-88; adv. com. several Calif. congressmen, 1985—; mem. dean's coun. UCLA Grad. Sch. Mgmt., 1984-85; bd. dirs. Archimedes Circle U. Soc. Calif., 1983-85, Ctr. for Innovation and Entrepreneurship, 1986-90, Caltech/MIT Venture Forum, 1987-91; chmn. adv. coun. and adj. prof., indsl. and sys. engrng. U. So. Calif., 1996—; mem. bd. examiners Nat. Quality Award, 1998—. Hicks fellow in Indsl. Rels. Calif. Inst. Tech., 1961, Hewlett Packard fellow. Mem. IEEE (sr.), So. Calif. Tech. Execs. Network, Orange County CEO's Network, Orange County CEO's Roundtable, Pres. Roundtable, Nat. Assn. Corp. Dirs., Aerospace-Def. CEO's Roundtable, Am. Def. Preparedness Assn., Security Affairs Support Assn., Acad. Profl. Cons. and Advisors, Internat. Platform Assn., Inst. Mgmt. Cons. (bd. dirs. So. Calif. chpt.), Pres. Assn., Cons. Roundtable, King Harbor Yacht Club. Republican. Avocations: sailing, photography, writing. Home: 4248 Via Alondra Palos Verdes Peninsula CA 90274-1545 Office: Blue Marble Partners 406 Amapola Ave Ste 125 Torrance CA 90501-6217

MANN, NANCY LOUISE (NANCY LOUISE ROBBINS), entrepreneur; b. Chillicothe, Ohio, May 6, 1925; d. Everett Chaney and Pauline Elizabeth R.; m. Kenneth Douglas Mann, June 19, 1949 (div. June 1979); children: Bryan Wilkinson, Laura Elizabeth. BA in Math., UCLA, 1948, MA in Math., 1949, PhD in Biostatistics, 1965. Sr. scientist Rocketdyne Divsn. Rockwell Internat., Canoga Park, Calif., 1962-75; tech. staff Rockwell Sci. Ctr., Thousand Oaks, Calif., 1975-78; rsch. prof. UCLA Biomath., L.A., 1978-87; pres., CEO, owner Quality Enhancement Seminars, Inc., L.A., 1982—; pres., CEO Quality and Productivity, Inc., L.A., 1987—; curriculum adv. UCLA Ext. Dept. of Bus. and Mgmt., L.A., 1991—; mem. com. on Nat. Statistics, Nat. Acad. Scis., Washington, 1978-82; mem adv. bd. to supt. U.S. Naval Posgrad. Sch., Monterey, Calif., 1979-82. Co-author: Methods for Analysis of Reliability and Life Data, 1974; author: Keys to Excellence, 1985, The Story of the Deming Philosophy, 2d edit., 1987, 3d edit., 1989; contbr. articles to profl. jours. Recipient award IEEE Reliability Soc., 1982, ASQC Reliability Divsn., 1986. Fellow Am. Statis. Assn. (v.p. 1982-84); mem. Internat. Statis. Inst. Office: Quality and Productivity Inc 1081 Westwood Blvd # 213 Los Angeles CA 90024-2911

MANN, RICHARD GEORGE, art history educator; b. Derby, Conn., July 26, 1949; s. George Harvey and Alberta Pauline (Jonah) M. BA, Kalamazoo Coll., 1972; MA, U. Minn., 1974; PhD, NYU, 1982. Lectr. art history U. Canterbury, Christchurch, New Zealand, 1983-84; asst. prof. art Rhode Coll., Memphis, 1984-85; asst. prof. art history SUNY, Purchase, N.Y., 1985-87; asst. prof., assoc. prof. art history U. Oreg., Eugene, 1987-91; prof. art San Francisco State U., Sch. Creative Arts, 1991—; vis. lectr. So. MEth. U., Dallas, 1997; cons. in field. Author: Spanish Paintings, 1991, El Greco y su patrous, 1995; contbr. articles to profl. jours. Rsch. granteeOreg. Coun. Humanities, 1991, NEH, 1991, Graham Found., 1993. Mem. Am. Soc. Spanish Art Hist. Studies, No. Calif. Renaissance Soc., Renaissance Soc. Am., Coll. Art Assn. Avocations: collecting posted history of Spanish Cicil War, collecting British stamps, weight lifting. Office: San Francisco State U Art Dept 1600 Holloway Ave San Francisco CA 94132-1722

MANN, WESLEY F., newspaper editor. Editor Investor's Business Daily, L.A., 1984—. Office: Investor's Business Daily 12655 Beatrice St Los Angeles CA 90066-7303*

MANN, ZANE BOYD, editor, publisher; b. St. Paul, Jan. 28, 1924; s. Michael M. and Rose Lee (Reuben) M.; m. Esther Zeesman, Mar. 25, 1945; children: Michael L., Eric F. Personal Fin. Planning, U. Calif., Riverside, 1986. Registered investment advisor Securities and Exch. Commn. Mcpl. fin. cons. Ehlers Mann & Assoc., Mpls., 1956-64; v.p. mcpl. bond underwriter Ebin Robertson, Mpls., 1964-70; v.p. mcpl. dept. Piper Jaffrey & Co., Mpls., 1970-72; ret., 1972; editor, pub. monthly investment newsletter Calif. Mcpl. Bond Advisor, Palm Springs, Calif., 1984—. Author: Fair Winds and Far Places, 1978; contbr. articles to profl. jours. Mem. Twin City Met. Planning Commn., St. Paul, 1958-70; bd. dirs. CORAL, Riverside County, Calif., 1984-91. Staff sgt. U.S. Army, 1942-45. Decorated DFC with cluster, Air medal with cluster, Soldier's medal, Purple Heart U.S. Army Air Corp. Mem. Nat. Fedn. Mcpl. Analysts, Calif. Soc. Mcpl. Analysts, Internat. Combat Camera Assn., Writers Guild Am. (ret.), Com. for the Sci. Investigation of Claims of the Paranormal (assoc.), Royal Corinthian Yacht Club (life, Cowles, Eng.), Mensa., Sports Car Club Am. Avocations: sailing, racing and cruising, scuba, SCCA competition driver, pilot. Home: 1300 E Verbena Dr Palm Springs CA 92262-5873 Office: Calif Mcpl Bond Advisor 1037 S Palm Canyon Dr Palm Springs CA 92264-8378

MANNERS, NANCY, retired mayor; b. Catania, Sicily, Italy; d. Gioacchino Jack and Maria Providenza (Virzi) Marasa; m. George Manners, Dec. 20, 1941; children: Gene David, Nancy Ellen Manners Sieh, Joan Alice. BA in Pub. Adminstrn., U. La Verne, 1979. Asst. city mgr. City of Covina, 1963-74; mcpl. mgmt. cons., 1975-85; mem. city coun. City of West Covina, Calif., 1984-97; pres. Ind. Cities Risk Mgmt. Authority, West Covina, 1988; mayor City of West Covina, 1988-89, 92-93; pres. Ind. Cities Assn., 1989-90. Pres. Covina Coord. Coun., 1970-71, Altrusa Club of Covina-West, 1971-72, Ea. San Gabriel Valley Regional Occupation Program, 1974-76, San Gabriel Valley Planning Com., 1986-87, Mid-Valley Mental Health Coun., 1988-89; regional chmn. San Gabriel Valley Lung Assn., 1971-73; trustee Covina-Valley Unified Sch. Dist., 1973-77; foreman pro tem L.A. County Grand Jury, 1980-81; chmn. L.A. County Solid Waste Mgmt. Com., 1986-89; treas., bd. dirs. San Gabriel Valley Commerce and Cities Consortium, 1991, policy and steering com. Nat. League Cities, 1991-96; chmn. employee rels. policy com. League Calif. Cities; bd. dirs. L.A. County Sanitation Dist., 1992-94, San Gabriel Valley Coun. of Govts., San Gabriel Valley Mosquito Abatement Dist., 1994-97; hon. chair, grand marshall July 4th Parade, City of West Covina, 1997. Named Covina Citizen Yr., 1977, West Covina Citizen Yr., 1983, Woman Yr., Calif. State Legislature, 1990; recipient Woman of Distinction award Today's Woman Forum, 1988, Woman of Achievement award YWCA, 1987, 88, Community Svc. award West Covina C. of C., 1989, Meritorious Pub. Svc. award Rsch. Inst. Claremont McKenna Coll., 1990, Disting. Leader award San Gabriel Valley Boy Scouts of Am., 1997, others. Mem. LWV (pres. San Gabriel Valley 1978-79), Am. Heart Assn. (mem. bd. dirs.), Mcpl. Mgmt. Assocs. of So. Calif. (v.p. 1972-73), Queen of the Valley Hosp. 2100 (pres. 1996-97), Ind. Cities Assn. (v.p. 1988, pres. 1989), West Covina Hist. Soc. (v.p. 1995—), West Covina Rotary (bd. dirs.). Home: 734 N Eileen Ave West Covina CA 91791-1042

MANNING, DANIEL RICARDO, professional basketball player; b. Hattiesburg, Miss., May 17, 1966; s. Ed Manning. Student, U. Kans. Basketball player L.A. Clippers, 1988-94, Atlanta Hawks, 1994, Phoenix Suns, 1994—. Recipient Bronze medal U.S. Olympic Basketball Team, 1988; named Most Outstanding Player NCAA Divsn. I Tournament, 1988, Naismith award, 1988, Wooden award, 1988; named to Sporting News NCAA All-Am. first team, 1987, 88, NBA All-Star Team, 1993-94. First pick overall NCAA draft, 1988; mem. NCAA Divsn. I Championship team, 1988. Office: Phoenix Suns 201 E Jefferson St Phoenix AZ 85004-2412*

MANNINO, J. DAVIS, psychotherapist; b. Patchoque, N.Y., Sept. 27, 1949; s. Joseph I. and Adrienne Adele (Davis) M. BA magna cum laude, SUNY, Stony Brook, 1971; MSW summa cum laude, San Francisco State U., 1974; EdD in Counseling and Ednl. Psychology, U. San Francisco, 1989. Lic. psychotherapist, Calif.; lic. clin. social worker, Calif., marriage, family and child counselor. Instr. U. Malaysia, 1974-76; dir. refugee programs City San Francisco, 1979-82; instr. U. San Francisco, 1979-85; pvt. practice specializing in psychology San Francisco, Sonoma Counties, 1979—; cons. foster care Calif. State Legis., 1980, community rels., San Francisco Police Dept., 1982-87, Hospice Sonoma County, 1990, Sonoma County Mental Health, 1990; forensic task force on AIDS, San Francisco Pub. Health Dept., 1984-85; child abuse investigation supr. City of San Francisco, 1985-88; supr. Reasonable Efforts to Families Unit; project coord. Edna McConnell Clark Found. Family Mediation Demonstration Grant, 1987-88; prof. human sexuality, death and dying, Intro. to Psychology Santa Rosa Jr. Coll., 1990—; commr. Calif. Bd. Behavioral Sci. Examiners, 1990. Author: Grieving Days, Healing Days, 1997, Sexually Speaking, 1998; contbr. articles to profl. jours.; local psychology columnist Art of Caregiving, 1986—. Mem. APA, NASW (diplomate clin. social work), Orthopsychiat. Assn., Am. Assn. Counseling and Devel., Am. Soc. Sex Educators, Counselors and Therapists, Soc. for Sci. Study Sexuality, Calif. Assn. Marriage Family and Child Therapists, Golden Gate Bus. Assn. (ethics com. 1986, Disting. Svc. award, 1985), Am. Assn. Marriage and Family Therapists, Nat. Register Clin. Social Workers, Lions (bd. dirs. San Francisco chpt. 1986). Avocations: running, gym and fitness, writing, gardening. Office: 4597 18th St San Francisco CA 94114-1831 also: PO Box 2880 Guerneville CA 95446-2880

MANNY, BRIAN SCOTT, graphic designer; b. New Bedford, Mass., Dec. 13, 1969; Roland Adrian and Dorothy Ann (Sylvia) M.; m. Karen Lynne Mariani, Mar. 21, 1994. BS in Art summa cum laude, Towson State U., Balt., 1996. Graphic designer Vision Printing, Ventura, Calif., 1997—. Decorated SW Asia serv. medal with two bronze stars, Fleet Marine Force

combat sea service deployment ribbon with three bronze stars. With USN, 1987-92. Democrat. Home: 6250 Telegraph Rd Apt 1002 Ventura CA 93003-4307 Office: Vision Printing 4125 Market St Ste 4 Ventura CA 93003-5642

MANOLAKAS, STANTON PETER, watercolor artist; b. Detroit, July 25, 1946; s. Constantine Stamatios and Angela (Kaloyerpolous) M.; m. Barbara Soldathos, July 25, 1971. Student, Eastman Sch. of Music, 1964-65; BA in Psychology, U. So. Calif., L.A., 1969; postgrad., Calif. State U., Long Beach, 1969-70. Represented by Art Angle's Gallery, Orange, Calif., 1985-94, Gallery 131, Glendale, Calif., 1995—. Exhibited in group show at Zantman Galleries, Carmel, Calif., 1989, Dossin Great Lakes Mus., 1994; demonstration artist City Art exhibit Millard Sheets Gallery, L.A. County Fair, Pomona, Calif., 1994, L.A. Heritage Sq. Mus., 1994, Lake Superior Maritime Mus., Duluth, Minn.; represented in permanent collections Bechtel Industries, San Francisco, Marriott Hotel Corp., Newton, Mass., Gallagher & Heffernan Inc., San Francisco, The Borovay Group, L.A., Datum Inc., Anaheim, Calif., Tarbell Realty Inc., Costa Mesa, Calif., Wolverine Bronze, Roseville, Mich., Dossin Great Lakes Mus., Lake Superior Marine Mus., Little Travis Bay Hist. Soc. Active AFL-CIO County Fedn. of Labor, L.A., 1982-92; mem. Saint Sophia Cathedral Choir, L.A., 1970-82, Burbank Symphony Orch., 1973-76, Glendale (Calif.) Symphony Orch., 1975-77. Republican. Eastern Orthodox. Avocations: distance running, music, photographic collector of historic photos. Home: 2500 Las Flores Dr Los Angeles CA 90041-1021

MANOLIU, MARIA, linguist; b. Galatz, Romania, Mar. 12, 1934; came to U.S., 1978, naturalized, 1987; d. Ion T. and Ana S. (Codescu) Manoliu. BA, French Coll., Galatz, 1951; MA, U. Bucharest, Romania, 1955, PhD, 1966. Asst. prof. Romance linguistics U. Bucharest, 1957-61, assoc. prof., 1961-68, prof., 1968-77; prof. linguistics U. Calif., Davis, 1978—; vis. prof. U. Chgo., 1972-74, H. Heine Universitat, Dusseldorf, 1994; cons. NEH, 1980—; mem. adv. bd. Revue Romane, Copenhagen, 1972—, Romance Philology, Berkeley, Calif., 1984—, Philologica Canariensia, Spain, 1992—. Author: Sistematica Substitutelor, 1968 (Ministry of Edn. award 1968), Gramatica Comparata a limbilor romanice, 1971, El Estructuralismo Lingüístico, 1979, Tipologia e Historia, 1985, Gramatica, Pragmasemantica si Discurs, 1993, Discourse and Pragmatic Constraints on Grammatical Choices. A Grammar of Surprises, 1994; editor-in-chief Bull. de la S.R.L.R., Bucharest, 1975-78; contbr. articles to profl. jours. Recipient Evenimentul award for Outstanding Contbn. to Romanian Culture, 1991; grantee Internat. Com. Linguists, 1972, Fulbright Found., 1972-74, 91, 92, IREX, 1993, U. Calif., 1970—. Mem. MLA, Am. Romanian Acad. (pres. 1982-95, hon. pres. 1995—), Academia Română (hon.), Soc. de Linguistique Romane, Soc. Roumaine de Linguistique Romane (v.p. 1974—), Internat. Assn. Hist. Linguistics, Linguistics Soc. Am., Internat. Assn. Pragmatics, Romanian Studies Assn. Am. (pres. 1986-88). Avocations: tourism, classical music, cinema. Office: U Calif Dept French and Italian 509 Sproul Hall Davis CA 95616

MANSEL, CHARLES MICHAEL LONGLEY, educational consultant, insurance specialist; b. Slough, Eng., Mar. 12, 1939; came to U.S., 1964; s. Charles Bernard and Pearl (Levings) M.; m. Ginger H. Mansel, Aug. 2, 1969; children: Douglas, Kristen. BA, Cambridge U., 1959; LLB, Lausanne (Switzerland) U., 1961. Cert. ins. counselor. Comml. underwriter Farmers Ins. Group, L.A., 1964-69; various mgmt. and mktg. positions San Francisco, 1969-77; owner, risk mgr. Inst. Assocs. No. Calif., Walnut Creek, 1977-95; ind. contractor Nat. Alliance, Austin, Tex., 1995—. Capt. Her Majesty's Svcs., English Army, 1960-62. Recipient Disting. Pilot award Aircraft Owners & Pilots Assn. Air Safety Found., Md., 1989. Avocations: aviation, snow skiing. Home: 706 Tonstad Pl Pleasant Hill CA 94523-1702 Office: c/o Argo Ins Brokers 2300 Contra Costa Blvd Pleasant Hill CA 94523-3918

MANSFIELD, ELAINE SCHULTZ, molecular geneticist, automation specialist; b. Boulder, Colo., Apr. 20, 1954; d. William Varley and Juanita M. (Zingg) M.; m. Gary G. Schultz, Nov. 24, 1983; children: Matthew, Greggory Mark. BA in Molecular Biology, San Jose State U., 1975; MS in Genetics, U. Calif., Berkeley, 1978, PhD in Genetics, 1983. Diplomate Am. Bd. Med. Genetics (fellow), Am. Bd. Clin. Molecular Genetics. Customer cons. IntelliGenetics, Mountain View, Calif., 1983-86; staff scientist Applied Biosys., Foster City, Calif., 1986-93; sr. staff scientist Molecular Dynamics, Sunnyvale, Calif., 1993-98; dir. pharmacogenomics diaDexus, LLC, Santa Clara, Calif., 1998—; lectr. in the field. Author (with others) Mutations in the Human Genome, 1993; contb. to profl. jours.; patentee in field. U. Calif. grantee, Chancellors Patent Fund grantee U. Calif., NIH SBIR grantee, 1995-99. Mem. AAAS, Am. Soc. Human Genetics, Am. Soc. Histocompatibility and Immunogenetics, Women in Sci., Black Masque (pres. 1975). Avocations: skiing, quilting. Office: diaDexus LLC 3303 Octavius Dr Santa Clara CA 95054-3004

MANSFIELD, ROGER LEO, astronomy and space publisher; b. Boston, Feb. 18, 1944; s. Roy D. Sr. and Nellie E. (Venzlovski) M.; m. Alice Lee Waring, Nov. 1, 1969 (div. Mar. 1983); 1 child, Jason Benjamin; m. Karen June Sprout, June 27, 1987. BS in Chemistry with high honors., U. Cin., 1965; MA in Math., U. Nebr., 1972. Chemist Lockheed Missiles & Space Co., Palo Alto, Calif., 1967; orbital analyst USAF, Offutt AFB, Nebr., 1967-73; instr. Dept. of Math. USAF Acad., Colorado Springs, Colo., 1973-74; aerospace engr. Philco-Ford Corp., Palo Alto, 1974-75, Data Dynamics Inc., Mountain View, Calif., 1975-76, Ford Aerospace & Communications Corp., Colorado Springs, 1976-90; prin. engr. Loral Aerospace Corp., Colorado Springs, 1990-95; owner Astron. Data Svc., 1976—; asst. prof. adjoint U. Colo., Colorado Springs, 1996—. Pub. Skywatcher's Almanac, Local Planet Visibility Report, Photographer's Almanac, Comparative Ephemeris, Space Birds, WeatherBirds Utilities; contbr. articles to profl. jours. Mem. Am. Astron. Soc., Math. Assn. Am., Internat. Planetarium Soc., Rocky Mountain Planetarium Assn., Phi Beta Kappa, Phi Eta Sigma. Avocations: satellite tracking and orbital mechanics. Home and Office: 3922 Leisure Ln Colorado Springs CO 80917-3502

MANSOUR, FATEN SPIRONOUS, interior designer, multimedia computer designer, realtor; b. Amman, Jordan, May 8, 1958; came to U.S., 1981; d. Spironous Mansour and Margret Mousa Nijmeh; 1 child, Lara. AS in Bus. Adminstrn., Wasifia Coll., Amman, 1977; AS in Computer Sci., Sec. Bus. Adminstrn., West Valley Coll., 1988; BS in Interior Design, Art, Photography, San Jose State U., 1992, M in Physiology, 1994. Cert. notary pub. Tchr. French Rawdat Al-Sa'adeh, Amman, 1976-78; office mgr. of Min. of Transp. Queen Alia Internat. Airport, Amman, 1977-88; coord. banquets and weddings Marquee Club and Café, San Jose, Calif., 1988-93; interior designer, realtor, multi-media computer designer Esquisite, San Jose, 1992—, desktop pub., 1992—. Prodr. Arab Am. TV, L.A., 1990—. Active Arab Am. Anti-Discrimination Com. Avocations: multi-media painting, photography, poetry, painting, internet cruising. Home: PO Box 10355 San Jose CA 95157-1355 Office: Esquisite PO Box 10355 San Jose CA 95157-1355

MANSOUR, YOUSEF, video specialist; b. Cairo, June 19, 1956; s. Abdou and Sonia (Housef) M.; children: Majo, Monika. Assocs. in Hotel Mgmt., 1976. Dir. Egyptian Security Svc. Agy., Cairo. Home: 2631 W Megan St Chandler AZ 85224-3441

MANSOURI, LOTFOLLAH (LOTFI MANSOURI), opera stage director, administrator; b. Tehran, June 15, 1929; arrived in Can., 1976; s. Hassan and Mehri (Jalili) M.; m. Marjorie Anne Thompson, Sept. 18, 1954; 1 child, Shireen Melinda. AB, UCLA, 1953. Asst. prof. UCLA, 1957-60; resident stage dir. Zurich Opera, 1960-65; chief stage dir. Geneva Opera, 1965-75; gen. dir. Can. Opera Co., Toronto, Ont., 1976-88, San Francisco Opera, 1988—; dramatic coach Music Acad. West, Santa Barbara, Calif., 1959; dir. dramatics Zurich Internat. Opera Studio, 1961-65, Centre Lyrique, Geneva, 1967-72; artistic adviser Tehran Opera, 1973-75; opera adviser Nat. Arts Centre, Ottawa, Ont., 1977; v.p. Opera America, 1979—; operatic cons. dir. [illegible] Francisco Opera (60 prodns.), N.Y.C. Opera, Lyric Opera of Chgo., Canadian Opera Co. (30 new prodns.), Houston Grand Opera, La Scala, Covent Garden, Verona Opera, Kirov Opera, Australian Opera, Vienna Staatsoper, Vienna Volksoper, Salzburg Festival, Amsterdam Opera, Holland Festival, Nice (France) Opera, Festival D'Orange, France, Verona Arena Festival; co-author: An Operatic Life, 1982. Decorated chevalier Order Arts and Letters (France), 1992. Mem. Am. Guild Mus. Artists, Can. Actors Equity Assn. Initiated above-stage projection of subtitles as a simultaneous translation of opera, 1983. Address: Columbia Artists Mngmt Crittenden Division 165 W 57th St New York NY 10019-2201*

MANTE, GEORGE EDWARD, tax administrator; b. Aberdeen, Wash., Sept. 14, 1947; s. George Bernard and Jessie Josephine (Salmi) M. BA, Willamette U., 1969; M of Pub. Adminstrn., Seattle U., 1978; PhD in Philosphy, Univ. Calif., Modesto, 1986; postdoctoral student, Calif. Coast U., 1986—. Cert. secondary tchr., Oreg. Chmn. lang. arts/soc. studies dept. South Umpqua Pub. Schs., Myrtle Creek, Oreg., 1969-72; dep. auditor Grays Harbor County, Montesano, Wash., 1972-73; dir. spl. services Dept. Navy, Pacific Beach, Wash., 1973-74; unemployment ins. tax adminstr. Employment Security, Olympia, Wash., 1975—; trustee The Evergreen State, Olympia; bd. dirs. Grays Harbor County Human Services Bd., Montesano. Bd. dirs. Grays Harbor County Shorelines Hearings Bd., Montesano, Grays Harbor Community Actions Council, Aberdeen; city councilman City of Aberdeen, 1976-79. Mem. Navy League of U.S., Am. Pub. Health Assn., Am. Polit. Sci. Assn., Am. Soc. Pub. Adminstrs., Internat. Assn. Personnel in Employment Security (pres. 1986—) (disting. achievement award, 1986). Republican. Roman Catholic. Lodges: Elks (Loyal Knight 1971-72), KC, Eagles. Avocations: hunting, fishing, golf, duplicate bridge, numismatics. Home: 5506 Windemere Dr SE Olympia WA 98501-5046 Office: Employment Security Dept 212 Maple Park Ave SE Olympia WA 98501-2240

MANTES, GEORGE, state senator; b. Tooele, Utah; m. Mary Ann Ballard, Aug. 25, 1963. BS in Mktg., U. Utah, 1959. Auto dealer Mantes Chevrolet Co., Tooele, 1968—; mem. Utah State Senate, 1990-98, minority whip, 1995-96; mem. Exec. Appropriations com., Nat. Conf. State Legislatures, Tooele County Econ. Devel. Coun. Bd. dirs. Blue Cross/Blue Shield Utah. Mem. Tooele C. of C., Tooele Jaycees (past pres.), Utah Auto Dealers Assn. (past pres.). Democrat. Home: 327 Upland Dr Tooele UT 84074-2849 Office: 1041 N Main St Tooele UT 84074-2141*

MANUEL, CONSORCIO DON CABATINGAN, mechanical engineer, energy conservationist; b. Asturias, Cebu, The Philippines, Feb. 23, 1945; came to U.S., 1967; s. Consorcio Villarin and Maria Yap (Cabatingan) M.; m. Flora Gadi Medina, Mar. 9, 1977; children: Dino Cristopher, Helen Marie, Nicole Puanani. Pre-engrng., La Salle Coll., Bacolod City, The Philippines, 1963; BSME, Mapua Inst. Tech., Manila, 1966; postgrad., N.Mex. State U., 1969-70. Registered profl. engr., The Philippines, Hawaii. Mech. designer Faruk Konuk & Assocs., Honolulu, 1967; asst. plant engr. Del Monte Corp., Honolulu, 1967; prin. Ferris & Hamig, Honolulu, 1970-77; sr. staff engr. Hawaii State Energy Office, Honolulu, 1978-79; chief mech. engr. Group Arch., Honolulu, 1979-80; sr. mech. engr. Belt Collins/Lyons, Honolulu, 1980-82; pres. AECES, Inc., Honolulu, 1982-83, Benjamin S. Notkin, Hawaii, Honolulu, 1983-92, C. Don Manuel/Hawaii, Inc., Kailua, 1992—. Pres. Oahu Filipino Jaycees, Honolulu, 1977; mem. Hawaii Energy Conservation Coun., Honolulu, 1981, Gov.'s Energy Investment Adv. Conf., 1985. Served with U.S. Army, 1968-70. Recipient Energy Engring. Excellence award ASHRAE Hawaii chpt., 1984, spl. recognition award U.S. Dept. of Energy, Washington, 1987, engring. excellence finalist Am. Consulting Engrs. Coun., Washington, 1992, Entrepreneur of Yr. award Filipino C. of Ch. of Hawaii, 1991. Mem. ASHRAE, ASME, Filipino Am. League Engrs. and Architects (Outstanding Engr. of Yr. 1996). Democrat. Roman Catholic. Achievements include the design of a naturally ventilated high rise bldg., designed resort hotel without a cooling tower using waste heat from air conditioning to heat domestic hot water, swimming pool and swimming lagoon; developed domestic solar water heater. Avocations: golf, basketball, scuba diving. Home and Office: C Don Manuel/Hawaii Inc 91-1039 Kanihaalilo St Kapolei HI 96707-3012

MAPES, JEFFREY ROBERT, journalist; b. San Francisco, Nov. 21, 1954; s. James Robert and Phyllis June (Bloemker) M.; m. Karen Jane Minkel, Aug. 20, 1978; children: Katharine, James. BA, San Jose State U., 1976. Reporter Napa (Calif.) Register, 1976-79; Washington corr. Scripps League Newspapers, 1979-83; reporter The Oregonian, Portland, 1984-87, chief polit. reporter, 1987—. Office: The Oregonian 1320 SW Broadway Portland OR 97201-3499*

MAQUET, JACQUES JEROME PIERRE, anthropologist, writer; b. Brussels, Belgium, Aug. 4, 1919; came to U.S., 1967, naturalized, 1974; s. Jerome and Jeanne (Lemoine) M.; m. Emma de Longrée, June 17, 1946; children: Bernard, Denis; m. Gisèle Cambresier, Nov. 13, 1970. JD, U. Louvain, Belgium, 1946, D.Phil., 1948; student, Harvard, 1946-48; PhD, U. London, Eng., 1952; Dr. ès-lettres, Sorbonne, France, 1973. Field anthropologist Inst. Sci. Research in Central Africa, 1949-51; head Inst. Sci. Research in Central Africa (Social Scis. Center), 1951-57; prof. State U. of Congo, Elisabethville, 1957-60; research dir. Ecole pratique des Hautes Etudes, U. Paris, 1961-68; prof. anthropology Case Western Res. U., 1968-71; prof. UCLA, 1971-91, chmn. dept. anthropology, 1978-83, prof. emeritus anthropology, 1991—; vis. prof. Northwestern U., 1956, Harvard, 1964, U. Montreal, 1965, U. Pitts., 1967; extraordinary prof. U. Brussels, 1963-68. Author: The Sociology of Knowledge, 1951, Aide-mémoire d'ethnologie africaine, 1954, Ruanda, 1957, (with others) Elections en Société féodale, 1957, The Premise of Inequality in Ruanda, 1961, Power and Society in Africa, 1971, Civilizations of Black Africa, 1972, Africanity, The Cultural Unity of Black Africa, 1972, Introduction to Aesthetic Anthropology, 1979, The Aesthetic Experience, 1986, L'Anthropologue et l'esthétique, 1993, La Experiencia Estética, 1998; co-editor: (with others) Dictionary of Black African Civilization, 1974. Recipient Waxweiler award Royal Acad. Belgium, 1961; First World Festival of Negro Arts award Dakar, 1966. Mem. Am. Anthrop. Assn., Internat. Assn. Buddhist Studies, Pali Text Soc., AAUP, Fedn. Am. Scientists.

MARABLE, DARWIN WILLIAM, photography educator, writer; b. L.A., Jan. 15, 1937; s. William Williams and Norma Teresa (Phillips) M.; m. Joan Ynez Frazell, May 23, 1964; 1 child, Theresa Simone. BA, U. Calif., Berkeley, 1960; MA in Art History, San Francisco State U., 1972; PhD in History of Photography, U. N.Mex., 1980; studied with, Thomas F. Barrow, Van Deren Coke, Beaumont Newhall, others. Lectr. San Francisco State U., 1976-77, 82, Calif. Coll. Arts and Crafts, Oakland, 1977-78, St. Mary's Coll., Moraga, Calif., 1990-91, 92; instr. U. Calif., Berkeley Ext., 1995—; panelist Calif. Arts Coun., Sacramento, 1986. Contbr. numerous essays, reviews and interviews to prof. publs. including Photo Metro, Artweek, The Washington DC Times, others. Bd. dirs. Diablo Symphony Orch., Walnut Creek, Calif., 1979-81, Lafayette (Calif.) Arts and Scis. Found., 1980-81, Contra Costa Alliance for the Arts, Martinez, Calif., 1980-81; vol. U. Calif. Student-Alumni Mentor Program, Friends of Photography Docent Program. Mem. History of Photography Group, The Friends of Photography, Soc. Photographic Edn. Roman Catholic. Avocations: travel, genealogy. Office: U Calif Berkeley Ext Photography Program 55 Laguna St San Francisco CA 94102-6232

MARANGI, VITO ANTHONY, SR., claim administrator; b. Utica, N.Y., Jan. 1, 1932; s. Gregorio and Carmella (Consoli) Marangi; m. Mary Margaret Lokey, Apr. 10, 1960 (div. July 1973); children: Vito Anthony Jr., Vanetta Gayle, Gregory Alan; m. Diann Louise Bunch, Apr. 11, 1987. BS, SUNY, Potsdam, 1958. Asst. regional claims mgr. Hartford Ins. Group, Fresno, Calif., 1958-67; supervising adjuster Underwriters Adjusting Co., Fresno, 1967-70; home office claim supr. Meritplan Ins. Co., Newport Beach, Calif., 1970-71; appeals referee State of Nev., Reno and Carson City, 1971-73, 76-79; br. mgr. Brown Bros. Adjusters, Reno, 1974-87; ind. ins. adjuster Tony Marangi, Adjuster, Carson City, 1987—; vice chmn., bd. trustees Carson-Tahoe Hosp., 1991-96. Scout master Boy Scouts Am., Utica, N.Y., Fresno, Calif., Carson City, 1953-85. With USN, 1949-53. Mem. Nev. State Claims Assn. (pres., v.p., treas., sec.), No. Nev. Claims Assn. (pres., v.p., [illegible] C. (bus. edn. com. 1987—, transp. com. 1987—). Avocations: photographer, bowling, dancing, classic car owner, musician. Home and Office: PO Box 643 Carson City NV 89702-0643

MARAVICH, MARY LOUISE, realtor; b. Fort Knox, Ky., Jan. 4, 1951; d. John and Bonnie (Balandzic) M. AA in Office Adminstrn., U. Nev., Las Vegas, 1970; BA in Sociology and Psychology, U. So. Calif., 1972; grad. Realtors Inst. Cert. residential specialist. Adminstrv. asst. dept. history U. So. Calif., L.A., 1972-73; asst. pers. supr. Corral Coin Co., Las Vegas, 1973-80; realtor, Americana Group div. Better Homes and Gardens, Las Vegas, 1980-85, Jack Matthews and Co., 1985-93, Realty Execs., Las Vegas, 1993—. Mem. Nev. Assn. Realtors (cert. realtors inst.), Las Vegas Bd. Realtors, Nat. Assn. Realtors, Women's Council of Realtors, Am. Bus. Women's Assn., NAFE, Million Dollar Club, Pres.'s Club. Office: Realty Execs 1903 S Jones Blvd Ste 100 Las Vegas NV 89146-1260

MARBERRY, JAMES FREDRIC, artist, graphic designer; b. Fresno, Calif., Dec. 19, 1938; s. James Parker and Anna Jane (Reiners) M. BFA, Calif. Coll. Arts and Crafts, Oakland, 1964; student, Oakland City Coll., 1960-63. Graphic designer HK Graphics, Oakland, 1965-66, Harry Burum Advt., Fresno, 1966-68, Capal, Deare & Reed, San Francisco, 1969-70, W/T Publ., Bklyn., 1974-78; free-lance graphic designer San Francisco, 1971-74; free-lance illustrator, designer Fresno, 1980-95; tchr. art Fresno Unified Sch. Dist., 1995—. Bd. dirs. Chinatown Art Gallery, Fresno, 1997—, La Grange (Calif.) Art Guide, 1993-94. With U.S. Coast Guard, 1957-59, 63. Avocations: watercolor, oil and acrylic painting, religion.

MARBURGER, GEORGE GERALD, retired naval officer, educator; b. Columbus, Ohio, Jan. 15, 1938; s. George Gerald and Lorena Mae (Runkle) M.; m. Ann Fairfax Adams, Dec. 20, 1960; children: Julie Ann, Elizabeth Ann, George Gerald III, Francis Lee. BS, U.S. Naval Acad., 1960; MS, Ohio State U., 1974. Cert. instr., supr. comty. colls., Calif. Commd. ensign USN, 1960, advanced through grades to capt., 1981, retired, 1990; commanding officer USS Dolphin USN, 1974-76; chief staff officer ComSubron 15, 1976-78; spl. asst. to Sec. Defense USN, Washington, 1984-87; commanding officer USNROTC Ohio State U., Columbus, 1987-90; mgr. Nationwide Fin. Svcs., Columbus, 1991-92; adj. instr. Palomar Coll., San Marcos, Calif., 1995-99. Mem. Naval Submarine League. Home: 3673 Mount Ariane Dr San Diego CA 92111-3904

MARCELYNAS, RICHARD CHADWICK, management consultant; b. New London, Conn., Aug. 21, 1937; s. Anthony F. and Elizabeth A. (Chadwick) M.; m. Betty A. Forray, July 1, 1961; children: Michael R., Thomas R. BA in Bus. Adminstrn., U. Wash., 1961; postgrad. Seattle U., 1971-72. Mgmt. trainee, installation foreman Pacific Bell, Fullerton, Calif., 1964-65; cost acct. Scott Paper Co., Everett, Wash., 1965-68; asst. v.p. pers. and adminstrn. Nat. Pub. Svc. Ins. Co., Seattle, 1968-77; pers. ops. mgr. Olympia Brewing Co., 1977-78; mgr. indsl. rels. Heath Tecna Precision Structures Inc., Kent, Wash., 1978-85; mgmt. con. Pilon Mgmt. Co., Seattle, 1985-90; pers. adminstr. Peninsula Group Olympia, Wash., 1990-94; pres. Chadwick & Assocs., Olympia, 1994—. Served to maj. USMCR, 1961-77. Decorated commendations for bravery and tech. expertise, 1962-64; recipient Seattle chpt. Pacific N.W. Personnel Mgrs. Assn. Bd. Dirs. award, 1975. Mem. Pacific N.W. Personnel Mgrs. Assn. (past pres. Tacoma chpt.), Oreg. Lodging Assn. Office: 623 Sherman St SW Olympia WA 98502-5454

MARCH, ANNETTE MARIE, English and literature educator; b. San Antonio, July 1, 1943; d. Gustave Frederick Mertz and Nadine Zelda Miller; m. Theodore Frank Wrinkle, Aug. 19, 1965 (div. Feb., 1970); 1 child, Miranda. BA, San Jose State U., 1966, MA, 1967; postgrad., U. B.C., Vancouver, Can., 1972. Lectr. U. Brit. Columbia, Vancouver, Can., 1969-70; instr. Calif. Writing Project U. Calif., Santa Cruz, 1977; instr. U. San Francisco, 1986-9#, evaluator, 1989-92; instr. Cabrillo Coll., Aptos, Calif., 1987—; lectr. U. Calif., Santa Cruz, 1989-96, Calif. State U. Monterey Bay, Seaside, Calif., 1997—; writing cons. Defense de Mujeres, Watsonville, Calif., 1996—. Contbg. author: (book) Interdisciplinary Writing Handbook, 1995; editor: (books) Writing as Women Reader, 1971-95, Autobiographical Writing from the Margins, 1995—. Mem. Green Party, 1990—, Peace Action Network, 1990—; facilitator Womens Groups, Santa Cruz, Calif., 1990—; counselor Women's Crisis Support, Santa Cruz., 1996—. Recipient Can. Coun. grant, Ottawa, 1969-70, Harper Collins fellowship, 1993. Mem. MLA, AAUW, Nat. Coun. Tchrs. of English. Avocations: yoga, gardening, hiking, camping. Home: 139 Franklin St Santa Cruz CA 95050 Office: Calif State U Monterey Bay 100 Campus Ctr Seaside CA 93955

MARCHALONIS, JOHN JACOB, immunologist, educator; b. Scranton, Pa., July 22, 1940; s. John Louis and Anna Irene (Stadner) M.; m. Sally Ann Sevy, May 5, 1978; children: Lee, Elizabeth, Emily. A.B. summa cum Laude, Lafayette Coll., 1962; Ph.D., Rockefeller U., 1967. Grad. fellow Rockefeller U., 1962-67; fellow Am. Cancer Soc. Walter and Eliza Hall Inst. Med. Research, 1967-68; asst. prof. biomed. scis. Brown U., 1969-70; head molecular immunology lab. Walter and Eliza Hall Inst. Med. Research, Melbourne, Australia, 1970-76; head cell biology and biochemistry sect. Frederick Cancer Research Ctr., 1977-80; prof. adj. faculty dept. pathology U. Pa., 1977-83; prof., chmn. dept. biochemistry and molecular biology Med. U. S.C., Charleston, 1980-88; prof., chmn. dept. microbiology and immunology U. Ariz., Tucson, 1988—, prof. pathology, 1991—, prof. medicine, 1992—; bd. dirs. Am. Type Tissue Culture Collection. Author: Immunity in Evolution, 1977; editor: Comparative Immunology, 1976, the Lymphocyte: Structure and Function, 1977, (with N. Cohen) Self/Non-Self Discrimination, 1980, (with G.W. Warr) Antibody as a Tool, 1982, The Immunobiology and Molecular Biology of Parasitic Infections, 1983, Antigen-Specific T Cell Receptors and Factors, 1987, The Lymphocyte: Structure and Function, 2d edit., 1987, (with Carol Reinisch) Defense Molecules, 1989, (with Gregory Beck, Edwin L. Cooper and Gail S. Habicht) Primordial Immunity, 1994; edtl. bd. jours. in field. Active Nat. Commn. Damon Runyon-Walter Winchel Cancer Fund. Named among 1,000 most highly cited sci. authors Inst. for Sci. Info.; Frank R. Lillie fellow, 1974; grantee in field. Fellow Am. Inst. Chemists, Am. Acad. Microbiology; mem. AAAS, Am. Assn. Immunology, Am. Soc. Biol. Chemists, Sigma Xi, Phi Beta Kappa. Episcopalian. Achievements include development of microchemical (radioimmunochemical) approaches for proteins and surface receptors of living cells; characterization of immunoglobulin-like antigen receptors of thymus-derived lymphocytes; application of synthetic peptide technology to antibodies, T cell receptors and autoimmunity; pioneered investigation of the molecular evolution of immunity. Home: 5661 N Camino Arturo Tucson AZ 85718-3933 Office: U Ariz Health Sci Ctr Tucson AZ 85724

MARCHI, JON, cattle rancher, exporter, former investment brokerage executive; b. Ann Arbor, Mich., Aug. 6, 1946; s. John Robert and Joan Trimble (Toole) M.; m. Mary Stewart Sale, Aug. 12, 1972; children: Aphia Jessica, Jon Jacob. Student Claremont Men's Coll., 1964-65; BS, U. Mont., 1968, MS, 1972. Sec., treas. Marchi, Marchi & Marchi, Inc., Morris, Ill., 1968-69; account exec. D. A. Davidson & Co., Billings, Mont., 1972-75, asst. v.p., office mgr., 1976-77, v.p. mktg. and adminstrn., Great Falls, Mont., 1977—; sec., dir., v.p. fin. svcs. and exec. devel., D. A. Davidson Realty Corp., Great Falls, 1978-85, chmn. rsch. com., 1980; cattle rancher, Polson, Mont., 1985—; bd. dirs. Big Sky Airlines, Billings, Mont., chmn. bd. dirs., 1995; bd. dirs. Implemax Equipment Co., Inc., Bozeman; bd. dirs. Energy Overthrust Found., Mansfield Found., Mont. Beverages, Mont. Venture Capital Network, Direct Advantage, Inc., Hamilton, Mont., Mont. Naturals Internat., Inc., Eclipse Techs., Inc., Mont. Small Bus. Investment Corp.; chmn., dir. Devel. Corp. Mont., Helena, 1995. Chmn. Mont. Gov.'s Subcom. for Venture Capital Devel., Mont. Cmty. Fin. Corp., Helena; chmn. investment com., State of Mont. Sci. and Tech. Alliance, 1985—; chmn. seed capital com. State of Mont., bd. dirs. job svc. com. Mem. Mont. Peoples Action; sec.-treas. Valley View Assn., 1987—; trustee sch. dist. # 35, Polson, Mont., 1990—, chmn., 1991—; bd. dirs. Mont. Entrepreneurship Ctr., Missoula, Mont., 1990—; pres., dir., sec./treas. Mont. Pvt. Capital Network, Bozeman, Mont., 1990—, pres., 1992—; chmn., dir. Mont. Naturals Internat., Inc., 1991; dir. Mont. State Rural Devel. Coun., 1992, Mont. SBA Adv. Coun., 1992; dir. Ctr. Econ. Renewal and Tech. Transfer Mont. State U., Bozeman, 1994—; del. to White House Conf. on Small Bus., Washington, 1994-95; chmn. Glacier Venture Fund, Helena, Mont., 1996—; mem. investment adv. com. DCC Growth Fund, Washington, 1998—. With U.S. Army, 1969-71. Mem. Nat. Cattlemen's Assn. (fgn. trade com.), Am. [illegible] Assn. (bd. dirs.), Mont. Cattle Feeders Assn., Montana Angus Assn., Western Montana Angus Assn., Am. Angus Assn., Western Mont. Stockgrowers Assn., Securities Industry Assn., Mont. Stock Growers Assn., Mont.

Ambassadors (dir. 1995), Polson C. of C. (dir.), Leadership Great Falls Club, Ski Club, Mont. Club, Helena Wilderness Riders Club, Rotary. Episcopalian. Office: Marchi Angus Ranches 7783 Valley View Rd Polson MT 59860-9302

MARCHIANO, BRUCE JOSEPH, actor; b. L.A., Feb. 5, 1956; s. George Joseph and Eve (Mitchel) M. BA in econs., Calif. State Univ., 1977; JD, Western State Univ., 1980. Bar: Calif. Atty. Aronson & Riddet, Santa Ana, Calif., 1980-82; actor North Hollywood, Calif., 1982—; writer, author Harvest House Publ., Eugene, Oreg., 1997. Actor: Gospel of Matthew, 1993; author: In the Footsteps of Jesus, 1997. Office: Marchiano Films & Ministries 11333 Moorpark St # 171 North Hollywood CA 91602-2618

MARCHINI, CLAUDIA CILLONIZ, artist; b. Lima, Peru, Feb. 3, 1959; came to U.S., 1983; d. Alberto Peschiera and Matilde Spiers (Toledo) Cilloniz; m. Carlos Edwards, Nov. 14, 1983; 1 child, Renzo. BFA in Painting, Memphis Coll. Art, 1987; MFA in Painting, U. Tex., San Antonio, 1989. Part-time mgr. Lung Clinic, Grants Pass, Oreg. Executed mural Oreg. State Capitol bldg., Salem, 1994 (2d place Ea. N.Mex. U. 1997), One woman shows at Foyer Auditorium and Gallery, U. Tex., San Antonio, 1990, GPHS Libr. Gallery, Oreg., 1991, Instituto Cultural Peruano Norteamericano, Lima, 1992, 93, Rogue Gallery, Medford, Oreg., 1992, Portland (Oreg.) State U., 1994, Firehouse Gallery, Grants Pass, Oreg., 1995, D.O.T. N.W., Portland, 1995, Galeria Cecilia Gonzalez, Lima, 1996, Gallery at Stevenson Union, So. Oreg. State Coll., Ashland, 1996, Lisa Harris Gallery, Seattle, 1997, Galeria Cecilia Gonzalez, Lima, Peru, 1998; group exhbns. include Instituto Cultural Peruano Norteamericano, 1988, 110 Broadway, San Antonio, 1988, Mexico-Arte, Austin, Tex., 1988, Bank One, San Antonio, 1989, Rolling Oaks Mall, San Antonio, 1989, Art League Gallery, Beaumont, Tex., 1990, U. Toronto, Can., 1990, Art Gallery at Lower Columbia Coll., 1991, Newport (Oreg.) Visual Arts Ctr., 1991, 92, Grants Pass Mus., 1991, 92, 93, Rogue Gallery, 1991, 92, 95, Stonington Gallery, Seattle, 1992, 93, Wiseman Gallery, Grants Pass, 1993, Paris Gibson Sq. Mus. of Art, Great Falls, Mont., 1993, Ctr. Contemporary Art, Seattle, 1993, Pulliam Deffengaugh Gallery, Portland, 1994, Ctr. for Visual Arts, Oakland, Calif., 1994, Washington State Convention and Trade Ctr., 1995, D.O.T. Northwest, 1995, Graven Images Gallery, Ashland, Oreg., 1995, Portland Mus. of Art, 1995, So. Oreg. Art Exhbn., Grants Pass, 1996, Coleman Gallery, Albuquerque, 1996, Museo de Osma, Lima, 1996, Ea. N.Mex. U., 1997, Ctr. Visual Arts, Oakland, Calif., 1997, Grants Pass Mus., 1998, Ea. N. Mex. Univ., 1998, Museo de Osma, Lima, 1998, Jega Gallery, Ashland, 1998, Lisa Harris Gallery, Seattle, 1998, Grants Pass Mus. Art, Oreg., 1998, Ga. N.Mex. U., 1998, Museo Osma, Lima, 1998 ; represented in various pvt. collections. Recipient 2d place award Ea. N.Mex. U., 1997. Mem. Seattle's Ctr. Contemporary Art, Grants Pass Mus. of Art, Greenpeace, Wofld Wildlife Fund, Arts Coun. So. Oreg., U.S. Squash Racquet Assn. Avocations: squash, hiking, travel, animals. Office: Lung Clinic 874 NE 7th St Grants Pass OR 97526-1635

MARCKWARDT, HAROLD THOMAS, association executive; b. Chgo., May 4, 1920; s. Herman and Carrie (Polachek) M.; AB, U. So. Calif., 1949, AM, 1953; MS, U. Calif., 1970, postgrad., 1970—; m. Patricia Ann Hoffman, Apr. 7, 1945; children: Craig, Diana, Brad, Glenn. Tool and machinery designer Douglas Aircraft, Santa Monica, Cal., 1939-43; playground leader County L.A., 1946-47; cmty. program dir. Hollywood (Calif.) YMCA, 1947-51, dir. cmty. program and bldg., 1952-55; exec. dir. Westchester YMCA, L.A., 1955-63; area dir. Nat. Coun. YMCA, 1963-66, pres. Western Center Assocs., L.A., 1966-89; internat. mgmt. cons., Indonesia, 1985-91, Sri Lanka, 1989; field assoc. Internat. Exec. Service Corps, 1987—. Exec. dir. Calif. Youth and Govt. Statewide Com., 1965, del. seminar UN, 1959. Colliver lectr. U. Pacific, 1965. Trainer, Leadership Devel. Camp, L.A., 1959; mem. Mayor's Steering Com., 1973-75, chmn. Mayor's Facilitators com. Conf. Children, Youth and Sr. Citizens, 1974; mem. employment and tng. subcom. L.A. County Task Force, 1977; mem. Task Force on Equity for Women in Employment, 1976-77; cert. mem. New Zealand Preferred Agent Link Program, 1996—. Served to 1st lt., USAAF, 1943-46, USAF (SAC), 1950-52. Recipient One of Hollywood's Top Ten Young Men award, 1954. Mem. Am. Soc. Tool Engrs. (charter mem.), Pacific S.W. Area YMCA Assn. Profl. Dirs. (pres. 1963-66), Orgn. Devel. Network, Airplane Owner's and Pilots Assn., Am. Soc. Tng. and Devel. (v.p. 1979, pres. 1980), Internat. Fedn. Tng. and Devel. Orgns., Pacific Asia Travel Assn. (exec. bd. 1994-98), Indonesian Bus. Soc., Am. Soc. Travel Agts., Indonesian Trade Mission, World Span-One Club (pres. 1993-94, v.p. 1991-93). Democrat. Author: The Leader Makes The Difference, 1968; Leading Discussion Groups, 1972; How to Make Executive Decisions About Training, 1976; 16 Steps to the Job You Want, 1979; The Quality Circles Kit, 1982. Mem. Australian Tourist Commn. (cert., mem. Australian tourist adv. bd. 1997—). Home: 4216 Colbath Ave Sherman Oaks CA 91423-4210 Office: 4716 Woodman Ave Sherman Oaks CA 91423-2416

MARCUS, H. LOUISE, educator, writer; b. Chgo., Apr. 10, 1928; d. Philip and Dora G. (Abraham) Moshel; m. Bernard Louis Marcus, Mar. 29, 1948; children: Bonnie Gail Marcus Graybill, Donald Lawrence, Leonard Michael, Sally Marcus Rodeman. AA, Wright Jr. Coll., Chgo., 1947; BA, U. Calif., Santa Barbara, 1967. Tchr. Temple B'nai B'rith, Santa Barbara, 1965-72; tutor handicapped Santa Barbara Adult Edn., 1991-94; aide Hollister Sch., Goleta, Calif., 1996—. Writer short stories. Program chmn. Orgn. for Rehab. Tng., 1990-93; pres. Hadassah, 1970-71. Mem. LWV, B'nai B'rith Sisterhood, Elderhostel. Democrat. Jewish. Avocations: writing, gardening, grandchildren.

MARCUS, JANET, city council; married; 3 children. MEd in Counseling and Guidance, U. Ariz.; MA, Radcliffe U.; BA in English, Wellesley Coll. Nat. bd. mem. Common Cause, 1976-79; pres. Planned Parenthood of Southern Ariz., 1985-87; mem. Energy & Environ. Policy Com. Nat. League Cities, 1989—; city coun., 1987-91, Tucson, 1991—. Office: 7575 E Speedway Blvd Tucson AZ 85710-8809*

MARCUS, JEFFREY HOWARD, electronic security system company executive; b. Albany, N.Y., June 4, 1950; s. Paul and Phyllis (Zippert) M.; m. Carol Ellen Marcus, Aug. 28, 1994. BS in Elec. Engring. and Computer Sci., U. Colo., Denver, 1977; MBA, U. Phoenix, Denver, 1985. Specialist counter intelligence U.S. Army, Washington, 1971-73; v.p. engring. Securus, Inc. (formerly Photo-Scan of Colo.), Denver, 1977-81, pres., 1981—; also bd. dirs. Securus (formerly Photo-Scan of Colo.), Denver; bd. dirs. PSA Fin. Svcs., Inc., Westminster; chmn. bd., tech. com. PSA Security NEtwork, Westminster. Democrat. Avocations: traveling, skiing, snorkeling, photography. Office: Securus Inc 12411 E 37th Ave Denver CO 80239-3404

MARCUS, KAREN MELISSA, foreign language educator; b. Vancouver, B.C., Can., Feb. 28, 1956; came to the U.S., 1962; d. Marvin Marcus and Arlen Ingrid (Sahlman) Bishop; m. Jorge Esteban Mezei, Jan. 7, 1984 (div. Mar. 1987). BA in French, BA in Polit. Sci., U. Calif., Santa Barbara, 1978, MA in Polit. Sci., 1981; MA in French, Stanford U., 1984, PhD in French, 1990. Lectr. in French Stanford (Calif.) U., 1989-90; asst. prof. French No. Ariz. U., Flagstaff, 1990-96, assoc. prof. French, 1996—; cons. Houghton Mifflin, 1993, Grand Canyon (Ariz.) Natural History Soc., 1994. Vol., letter writer Amnesty Internat. Urgent Action Network, 1991-95; vol. No. Ariz. Aids Outreach Orgn., Flagstaff, 1994-95. Recipient medal for outstanding achievement in French, Alliance Française, Santa Barbara, 1978; named Scholarship Exch. Student, U. Geneva, Switzerland, 1979-80; doctoral fellow Stanford (Calif.) U., 1981-85. Mem. MLA, Am. Assn. Tchrs. French, Am. Coun. on the Tchg. Fgn. Langs., Am. Literary Translators Assn., Women in French, Coordination Internat. des Chercheurs Sur Les Litteratures Maghrebines, Phi Beta Kappa, Pi Delta Phi, Alpha Lambda Delta. Democrat. Jewish. Avocations: walking, yoga, reading, writing short stories, photography. Office: No Ariz Univ Modern Lang Dept Box 6004 Flagstaff AZ 86011

MARCUS, LAURA L., remote control company executive, hypnotherapist; b. Eugene, Oreg., Sept. 22, 1954; d. Edward Howard Lillie and Marilyn Ann (Malone) Groenig; m. Randy Lee Marcus, June 24, 1972; children: Melisa Lee, Steven Lee, Mandy Lee. Grad., Howard Hamilton Sch. Hypnotism, Albany, Oreg, 1996. Cert. hypnotherapist. Joint owner, adminstr. mktg. Remote Safety Systems, Inc. (Marcus Tech., Inc., Salem, Oreg., 1986—. Contbr., editor orgn. newsletter M.E.D. & C.A., 1985-86. mem. Am. Natural Hygiene Soc., Inc., Nat. Guild Hypnotists.

MARCUS, RUDOLPH ARTHUR, chemist, educator; b. Montreal, July 21, 1923; came to U.S., 1949, naturalized, 1958; s. Myer and Esther (Cohen) M.; m. Laura Hearne, Aug. 27, 1949; children: Alan Rudolph, Kenneth Hearne, Raymond Arthur. BS in Chemistry, McGill U., 1943, PhD in Chemistry, 1946, DSc (hon.), 1988; DSc (hon.), U. Chgo., 1983, Poly. U., 1986, U. Göteborg, Sweden, 1987, U. N.B., Can., 1993, Queens U., Can., 1993, U. Oxford, Eng., 1995, Yokohama Nat. U., 1996, U. N.C., 1996, U. Ill., 1997, Technion-Israel Inst. Tech., 1998. Rsch. staff mem. RDX Project, Montreal, 1944-46; postdoctoral rsch. assoc. NRC of Can., Ottawa, Ont., 1946-49, U. N.C., 1949-51; asst. prof. Poly. Inst. Bklyn., 1951-54, assoc. prof., 1954-58, prof., 1958-64; prof. U. Ill., Urbana, 1964-78; Arthur Amos Noyes prof. chemistry Calif. Inst. Tech., Pasadena, 1978—; vis. prof. theoretical chemistry U. Oxford, 1975-76; Baker lectr. Cornell U., Ithaca, N.Y., 1991; Linnett vis. prof. chemistry Cambridge (Eng.) U., 1996; hon. prof. Fudan U., Shanghai, 1994—; hon prof. Inst. Chemistry Chinese Acad. Scis., Beijing, 1995—; hon. fellow Univ. Coll., Oxford, 1995—; professorial fellow Univ. Coll., Oxford, 1975-76; mem. Courant Inst. Math. Scis., NYU, 1960-61; trustee Gordon Rsch. Confs., 1966-69, chmn. bd. dirs., 1968-69, mem. coun., 1965-68; mem. rev. panel Argonne Nat. Lab., 1966-72, chmn., 1967-68; mem. rev. panel Brookhaven Nat. Lab., 1971-74; mem. rev. com. Radiation Lab., U. Notre Dame, 1975-80; mem. panel on atmospheric chemistry climatic impact com. NAS-NRC, 1975-78, mem. com. kinetics of chem. reactions, 1973-77, chmn., 1975-77, mem. com. chem. scis., 1977-79, mem. com. to survey opportunities in chem. scis., 1982-86; mem. math. panel Internat. Benchmarking of U.S. Rsch. Fields, 1996-97; adv. com. for chemistry NSF, 1977-80, external adv. bd. NSF ctr. Photoinduced Charge Transfer, 1990—, mem. presdl. chairs com., Chile, 1994-96; advisor Ctr. for Molecular Scis., Chinese Acad. Scis. and State Key Lab. for Structural Chemistry of Unstable and Stable Species, Beijing, 1995—; co-hon. pres. 29th Internat. Chemistry Olympiad, 1997. Former mem. editl. bd. Jour. Chem. Physics, Ann. Rev. Phys. Chemistry, Jour. Phys. Chemistry, Accounts Chem. Rsch., Internat. Jour. Chem. Kinetics Molecular Physics, Theoretica Chimica Acta, Chem. Physics Letters, Faraday Trans., Jour. Chem. Soc.; mem. editl. bd. Laser Chemistry, 1982—, Advances in Chem. Physics, 1984—, World Sci. Pub., 1987—, Internat. Revs. in Phys. Chemistry, 1988—, Progress in Physics, Chemistry and Mechanics (China), 1989—, Perkins Transactions 2, Jour. Chem. Soc., 1992—, Chem. Physics Rsch. (India), 1992—, Trends in Chem. Physics Rsch. (India), 1992—; hon. editor Internat. Jour. Quantum Chemistry, 1996—. Alfred P. Sloan fellow, 1960-61, sr. postdoctoral fellow NSF, 1960-61; sr. Fulbright-Hays scholar, 1972; recipient Sr. U.S. Scientist award Alexander von Humboldt-Stiftung, 1976, Electrochem. Soc. Lecture award Electrochem. Soc., 1979, 96, Robinson medal Faraday divsn. Royal Soc. Chemistry, 1982, Centenary medal Faraday divsn., 1988, Chandler medal, Columbia U., 1983, Wolf prize in Chemistry, 1985, Nat. Medal of Sci., 1989, Evans award Ohio State U., 1990, Nobel prize in Chemistry, 1992, Hirshfelder prize in Theoretical Chemistry, U. Wis., 1993, Golden Plate award Am. Acad. Achievement, 1993, Lavoisier medal French Chem. Soc., 1994; named Hon. Citizen, City of Winnipeg, 1994, Treasure of L.A., Ctrl. City Assn., 1995, Desper award U. Cin., 1997. Fellow AAAS, Am. Acad. Arts and Scis. (hon., exec. com. western sect., co-chmn. 1981-84, rsch. and planning com. 1989-91), Internat. Soc. Electrochemistry (hon.), Royal Soc. Chemistry (hon.), Royal Soc. London (hon.), Chinese Acad. Scis. (hon.), Internat. Acad. Quantum Molecular Sci. (hon.), Royal Soc. Can. (hon.); mem. NAS (hon.), Am. Philos. Soc. (hon.), Korean Chem. Soc. (hon.), Am. Phys. Soc., Am. Chem. Soc. (past divsn. chmn., mem. exec. com., mem. adv. bd. petroleum rsch. fund, Irving Langmuir award in chem. physics 1978, Pter Debye award in phys. chemistry 1988, Willard Gibbs medal Chgo. sect. 1988, S.C. Lind Lecture, East Tenn. sect. 1988, Theodore William Richards medal Northwestern sect. 1990, Edgar Fahs Smith award Phila. sect. 1991, Ira Remsen Meml. award Md. sect. 1991, Pauling medal Portland, Oreg., and Puget Sound sect. 1991, Auburn-Kosolapoff award 1996, Theoretical Chemistry award 1997, chem. & Engring. News award 1998). Achievements include responsibility for the Marcus Theory of electron transfer reactions in chemical systems and RRKM theory of unimolecular reactions. Home: 331 S Hill Ave Pasadena CA 91106-3405

MARDIAN, DANIEL, construction company director; b. Pasadena, Calif., Apr. 10, 1917; s. Samuel and Akabe (Lekerian) M.; m. Katherine Evkhanian, Jan. 30, 1942; children: Daniel Jr., Tom, John, Paul, Scott. Student, Pasadena City Coll., 1937; diploma, U.S. Army Engring. Sch., Ft. Belvoir, Va., 1944, U.S. Army Command and Gen. Staff Coll., 1961. Commd. U.S. Army, 1942, advances through grades to lt. col., 1962, ret., 1970; ptnr. Mardian Constrn. Co., Phoenix, 1945-47, exec. v.p., 1947-66, pres., 1966-78, also bd. dirs.; past chmn., mem. Nat. Joint Apprenticeship/Tng. commn. Oper. Engrs., Washington, 1975-78; mem. adv. bd. constrn. programs Ariz. State U., Tempe, 1957—, mem. adv. bd. Coll. Engring., 1957—; mem. adv. bd. constrn. program No. Ariz. U., Flagstaff; bd. dirs. Citibank, Phoenix, 1962-87. Pres. Am. Coun. Constrn. Edn., Monroe, La., 1991-93; past pres., bd. dirs. Fiesta Bowl, Tempe, 1986-92; gen. campaign chmn. United Way, Phoenix, 1967; pres. Met. Phoenix C. of C., 1967-68. Capt. C.E., U.S. Army, 1942-46, PTO, 1970—. Recipient Hall of Fame award Ariz. State U., 1990, medallion of merit, 1984, Excellence in Constrn. award Am. Subcontractors Assn., 1988, Hall of Fame award Nat. Football Found., 1987, Brotherhood award Ariz. chpt. NCCJ, 1981, Fellow award Am. Inst. Constructors, 1996. Mem. Associated Gen. Contractors Am. (life bd. dirs., chmn. yr. award 1970, mem. workforce devel. com., trustee, chmn. laborers tng. com., 1969—), Sun Angel Found. (chmn. 1989-91), Ariz. Acad., Phoenix Country Club (bd. dirs., pres. 1985-86), Phoenix Kiwanis Club (past dir.). Republican. Mem. United Ch. Christ. Avocations: golfing, fishing. Home: 7215 N 3rd St Phoenix AZ 85020-4904 Office: Perini Building Co 360 E Coronado Rd Phoenix AZ 85004-1524

MARDIAN, ROBERT CHARLES, JR., restaurateur; b. Orange, Calif., Feb. 1, 1947; s. Robert Charles Sr. and Dorothy Driscilla (Denniss) M.; m. Jayne Marie Garvin, June 21, 1970 (div. 1977); 1 child, Robert Charles III; m. Kathleen Frances Dixon, Oct. 13, 1984 (div. 1991); children: Alexandra Quinn, Ashley Michele. BA, Stanford U., 1969; MBA, Pepperdine U., 1986. Gen. mgr. Loft Restaurant, San Jose, Calif., 1969-71; chief exec. officer/chmn. bd. Wind & Sea Restaurants, Inc., Dana Point, Calif., 1971—; bd. dirs. Dana Niguel Bank, cons. U.S. Olympic Com., Colorado Springs, 1984-88. Commr. Dana Point Econ. Devel. Mem. Young Pres. Orgn. Republican. Avocations: skiing, surfing, beach volleyball, running, snowboarding. Office: Wind & Sea Restaurants Inc 34699 Golden Lantern St Dana Point CA 92629-2908

MARDON, AUSTIN ALBERT, geographer, writer, researcher; b. Edmonton, Alta., Can., June 25, 1962; came to U.S. 1985; s. Ernest George and May Gertrude (Knowler) m. Stephanie Ngar Ling Liu, 1996. BA in Geography, U. Lethbridge, Alta., 1985; MSc in Geography, S.D. State U., 1988; MEd Edn. Curriculum and Instruction, Tex. A&M U., 1990; grad. work in space sci., U. N.D., 1990. Research scientist NASA/NSF, Antarctica, 1986-87; freelance writer, 1991—; dir. pres. Antarctic Inst. Canada, Edmonton, 1985—; mem. meteorite recovery expedition, Antarctic, 1986-87; mem. Com. Space Rsch. Internat. Com. Sci. Unions. Author/co-author 16 books in areas of space sci., meteorite sci., astronomy, Alberta history, space exploration tech., polar sci., Medieval English history, and geography; contbr. more than 75 articles to profl. jours. With Can. Army, 1981-85, hist. rschr. and cons., Alberta Culture and Multiculturalism, 1989-91. Recipient Antarctic Svc. medal, U.S. Navy, 1987; Duke of Edinburgh medal, Can., 1987; Polar Continental Shelf Proj. Arctic Research grantee, 1988, personal audience with Pope in Rome, 1995, Gov. Generals Caring Canadian Award, 1998. Mem. Am. Meteor Soc., Antarctic Inst. Can. (pres. 1985—), The Explorers Club (internat. fellow), American Polar Soc., Clubhouse Soc. Edn. (chmn. 1993—), Gamma Theta Upsilon (Geography honor soc.), Sigma Pi Sigma (Physics honor soc.). Progressive Conservative. Roman Catholic. E-mail: mardon@freenet.edmonton.ab.ca. Office: Main Post Office, PO Box 1223, Edmonton, AB Canada T5J 2M4

MAREE, WENDY, painter, sculptor; b. Windsor, Eng., Feb. 10, 1938. Student, Windsor & Maidenhead Coll., 1959; studied with Vasco Lazzlo, London, 1959-62. Exhibited in group shows at Windsor Arts Festival, San Bernardino (Calif.) Mus.; one-woman shows include Lake Arrowhead (Calif.) Libr., 1989, Amnesty Internat., Washington, 1990, Phyllis Morris Gallery, Many Horses Gallery, L.A., 1990, Nelson Rockefeller, Palm Springs, Calif., 1992, 94, Stewart Gallery, Rancho Palos Verdes, Calif., Petropavlovsk (Russia) Cultural Mus., Kamchatka, Russia, 1993, Coyle-Coyle Gallery, Blue Jay, Calif., 1995, La Quinta Sculpture Park, Calif., 1995, Avante-Garde Gallery, Palm Springs, 1996, Avante-Garden Gallery, La Jolla, Calif., 1996, Avante Garde Gallery, La Jolla, 1996, Carmichael Gallery, Rancho Mirage, Calif., 1998, Art in the Courtyard, Palm Springs, Calif., 1997, L.G.O. Internat. Galerie des Arts Palm Springs, 1998, others; represented in pvt. collections His Royal Highness Prince Faisal, Saudi Arabia, Gena Rowlands, L.A., John Cassavetes, L.A., Nicky Blairs, L.A., Guilford Glazer, Beverly Hills, Calif., June Allyson, Ojai, Calif., Amnesty Internat., Washington, L.G.O. Internat. Gallery, Palm Springs; commd. Ingleside Inn, Palm Springs. Recipient award San Bernardino County Mus., 1988, Gov. Kamchatka of Russia, 1993. Mem. Artist Guild of Lake Arrowhead. Address: 246 Saturmino Dr Palm Springs CA 92262

MAREI, IBRAHIM, medical technologist; b. Marowe, Sudan, Dec. 6, 1939; s. Hassan and Shafika (Mohamed) M. BS in Chemistry, U. Cairo, 1966; MS in Med. Tech., Calif. State U., 1980. Lic. clinical chemist tech., Calif., clinical lab. tech., Calif. Clinical chemist SmithKline-Beecham, Van Nuys, Calif., 1969-71; supr. ctr. critically ill lab. Hollywood Presbyn. Med. Ctr., L.A., 1971-75; sr. toxicologist, clin. chemist spl. chemistry dept., instr. on the job tng. and edn. new students, tech. staff Reference Labs., Newbury Park, Calif., 1975-88; clin. chemist endochronology dept., med. technologist Smith Kline Biosci. Labs., Van Nuys, Calif., 1988—, gen. supr., 1996; supr. spl. chemistry dept. Specialty Labs., Santa Monica, Calif., 1996—. Mem. Am. Soc. Clinical Pathologists (cert.), Am. Chem. Soc., Am. Assn. Clinical Chemists (cert.), Am. Pub. Health Assn. Calif. Assn. for Med. Lab. Tech. Home: 7441 Hazeltine Ave Apt 107 Van Nuys CA 91405-1486 Office: Specialty Labs 2211 Michigan Ave Santa Monica CA 90404-3900

MARELICK, LIN, graphic arts educator, artist; b. Oakland, Calif., Oct. 26, 1950; d. Andrew Lewis and Katherine Mary (Kukulica) M. BA in art studio, Sonoma State U., 1976; MFA inart studio, U. Ariz., 1981. Graphic arts instr. Econ. Social Opportunities Inc., San Jose, Calif., 1981-85, asst. dir., 1985-87; graphic arts instr. Santa Clara (Calif.) Adult Edn. Ctr., 1987-89, Mission Coll., Santa Clara, 1989—; exec. bd. mem., treas. Acad. Senate Calif. C.C., Sacramento, 1996-98. Editor: The Forum, Sacramento, 1997-98, The Rostrum, 1996-98. Com. mem. Bay Area Mun. Elections, San Jose, Calif., 1987-89; dept. chair Mission Coll., Santa Clara, 1994-98; divsn. chair Mission Coll., 1995-98. Recipient Merit award Sonoma Count Arts Coun., Santa Rosa, Calif., 1976, Chancellor's Recognition award West Valley Mission Coll. Dist., 1997. Mem. Graphic Arts Educators Assn. Avocations: playing tennis, hiking, playing clarinet, singing, going to movies. Office: Mission College 3000 Mission College Blvd Santa Clara CA 95054-1897

MARGARYAN, ALFRED, physical chemistry engineer, material science researcher; b. Tehran, Iran, Apr. 19, 1936; came to U.S., 1988; s. Ashot and Almast (Babakhanian) M.; m. Anahit Kouradjian, Mar. 1, 1968; children: Ashot, Ara. BS, Poly. Inst., Yerevan, Armenia, 1959; MS, Tech. Inst., St. Petersburg, Russia, 1966, DS, 1985. Rsch. engr. Inst. Inorganic Chemistry, Yerevan, 1959-63; asst. prof. Tech. Inst., St. Petersburg, 1963-66; chief scientist Inst. Inorganic Chemistry, 1966-76; sr. rsch. scientist Vavilov State Optical Inst., St. Petersburg, 1976-88; sr. scientist Control Optics Corp., Baldwin Park, Calif., 1988-93; sr. rsch. scientist Material Sci. Co., Glendale, Calif., 1990-93; prof. U. La Verne, Calif., 1991-94; chief scientist U&M Sci. Co., Glendale, 1994—. Author: Germanate Glasses, 1993, Ligands and Modifiers in Vitreous Materials: Spectroscopy of Condensed Systems, 1999; contbr. over 120 articles to profl. jours. Mem. Armenian Soc. Archs. and Scientists, Internat. Soc. Optical Instrumentation Engring. Roman Catholic. Avocations: classical music, sports, arts. Home: 1139 E Maple St Apt 5 Glendale CA 91205-4420 Office: U&M Sci Co 1139 E Maple St Apt 5 Glendale CA 91205-4420

MARGO, KENNETH CRAIG, counselor; b. Oklahoma City, Apr. 22, 1953; s. Marvin Kenneth and Bobbie June (Cravens) M.; m. Laura Leslie Brooks, June 19, 1980. BA in Psychology, Centenary Coll., Shreveport, La., 1975; MEd in Counseling Psychology, Ctrl. State U., Edmond, Okla., 1978. Lic. profl. counselor, Okla., Wyo. Staff psychologist Okla. Children's Meml. Hosp., Oklahoma City, 1978-82; psychologist, clinic dir. Lincoln County Guidance Ctr., Chandler, Okla., 1982-84; pvt. practice Oklahoma City, 1984-86, 89-90; staff psychologist Mental Health Svcs. So. Okla., Ardmore, 1986-88; therapist, staff devel. coord. St. Joseph's Childrens Home, Oklahoma City, 1988-89; supr. outpatient substance abuse program Ctrl. Wyo. Counseling Ctr., Casper, 1990—; exec. dir. Sublette Cmty. Counseling Svcs., Pinedale, Wyo., 1990—. Mem. Okla. Youth and Suicide Task Force, Oklahoma City, Health Planning Commn., Chandler. Mem. ACA, Am. Mental Health Counselors Assn., Wyo. Mental Health Counselors Assn., Wyo. Counseling Assn., Okla. Assn. Counseling & Devel. (pres. 1989). Avocations: computers, canoeing. Office: Sublette Cmty Counseling Svcs PO Box 856 41 1/2 S Franklin Pinedale WY 82941

MARGOLIS, SYLVIA GANZ, retired secondary education educator; b. Norfolk, Va., Aug. 6, 1910; d. Morris Louis and Pauline (Buch) Margolis; m. Irving H. Ganz, Feb. 23, 1941 (dec. Sept. 1969); 1 child, Marshall Louis; m. Morris D. Margolis, Mar. 30, 1974 (dec. May 1977). AB, Coll. William and Mary, 1932; postgrad., UCLA, Calif. State U., Fresno, U. Calif., Long Beach, Sorbonne, Paris. Cert. tchr., Calif., Va. English tchr. YWCA, Richmond, Va., 1937-40; substitute tchr. Am. Dependents' Schs., Germany, 1946-49; tchr. Fresno City Schs., 1951-53, Kern County Schs., Richland, Calif., 1953-66, L.A. Unified Sch. Dist., 1966-76; mem. State Com., Sacramento, 1964-65; del. Nat. Edn. Assn. to World Conf. of Educators, West Berlin, 1975; lectr. numerous orgns. Bd. mem. YWCA, Bay City, Mich., 1943-46; chair United Nations Day, Bakersfield, Calif., 1960; bd. mem. Jewish Fedn. Coun. L.A., 1968-74; vol. tchr. at local C.C., Northridge, Calif., 1980-81; mem. com. Judaic studies at Coll. William and Mary, Williamsburg, Va., 1983-87. Recipient cert. appreciation Girl Scout Coun., Johnstown, Pa., 1942; Fed. Dept. Edn. grantee Univ. Pitts., 1962. Mem. AAUW (edn. rep. 1978-80, San Fernando Valley br. bd. mem. 1979-84, del. to UN Conf. on Women in Copenhagen 1980), Anti-Defamation League, Hadassah (bd. mem. 1978-85), Bridges for Peace (Am.), Coll. William and Mary Alumni Assn. (mem. com. on Judaic studies 1980s), B'nai Brith Women, Phi Kappa Phi, Tau Kappa Alpha. Democrat. Jewish. Avocations: reading, writing poetry, participating in study and discussion groups, traveling. Home: 23801 Calabasas Rd Ste 2033 Calabasas CA 91302-1569

MARGULIES, LEE, newspaper editor. Television editor Los Angeles Times, Calif., 1976—. Office: Los Angeles Times Times Mirror Sq Los Angeles CA 90053*

MARIEN, ROBERT, producer, director, naturalist, photographer; b. San Juan, P.R., Oct. 3, 1952; came to U.S., 1980; s. Jorge Marién and Conchita Herńaiz. BS, U. Sacred Heart, Santurce, P.R., 1976; MS, U. P.R., 1978; MFA, Calif. Inst. Arts, 1982. Producer Dept. Natural Resources, San Juan, 1976-77; film editor Guastella Film Producers, Inc., San Juan, 1977-78; dir. photography Publi Co-Op, San Juan, 1978-79; photographer Expo-Foto 80, San Juan, 1980; prodn. photographer M3 Effects, Inc., North Hollywood, Calif., 1982-83; film research Dennis Film Services, Inc., Hollywood, Calif., 1983-84; cinema coordinator XXIII Olympic Games, Los Angeles, 1984; host spl. shows Universal Studios Tour, Inc., Universal City, Calif., 1984-86; prodn. asst. Columbia Picture Industries, Inc., Burbank, Calif., 1984-86; cameraman Jerry Kramer Prodns., Inc., Hollywood, Calif., 1986; prof. basics of filmmaking Art Ctr. Coll. Design, Pasadena, Calif., 1986-87; producer promotions, copywriter Sta. KVEA-TV, Glendale, Calif., 1986-88; contractor, producer Spanish TV/radio spots The Disney Co., 1989—; owner, photographer Stock Photo Agy., Rom-Ma Stock Images, Pasadena, Calif., 1989—; prof. cinema and scis., documentary prodr. Columbia Coll., Hollywood, 1989-95. Producer, dir., editor: (documentaries) Marine Environments, 1977, The Forests of Puerto Rico, 1978 (Environmental award 1979), (visual essay) Sojourn Earth, 1982 (Gold medal 1982, Filmex 1983, Golden Halo 1984, Gold Lone Star award Houston Internat. Film & Video Festival, 1988); producer, cameraman The VIII PanAmerican Games in Puerto Rico, 1979; producer, cameraman Through the World of Nutrition, 1979; dir. photography, cameraman Chef's Delight, 1983; dir. photography The Puerto Rican Cuatro, 1978, Celebrity On Course, 1985; camera asst. The Computer Question, 1983. Prodr., dir., editor: (documentaries) Marine Environments,

1977, The Forests of Puerto Rico, 1978 (Environmental award 1979), (visual essay) Sojourn Earth, 1982(Gold medal 1982, Filmex 1983, Golden Halo 1984, Gold Lone Star award Houston Internat. Film & Video Festival 1988); prodr., dir. Documentary for Frank Capra Jr., 1997; prodr., cameraman The VIII PanAmerican Games in Puerto Rico, 1979, Through the World of Nutrition, 1979; dir. photography, cameraman Chef's Delight, 1983; dir. photography The Puerto Rican Cuatro, 1978, Celebrity on Course, 1985; camera asst. The Computer Question, 1983. Office: Ro-Ma Stock Images 1003 S Los Robles Ave Pasadena CA 91106-4332

MARIN, PAUL (SOLOMON SCHNEIDER), actor, writer; b. Bklyn., July 20, 1927; s. Hyman and Jennie (Orloff) Schneider; m. Doris Luper, Dec. 16, 1955; 1 child, Tani Schneider Foger. Grad. H.S., Bklyn., 1944. Actor stage, movies, TV, 1956—. Appeared on Broadway in What Every Woman Knows, 1956, Fair Game, 1957, The Tenth Man, 1959-61, Giddeon, 1962, Fiddler on the Roof, 1966-67; motion pictures include Mommie Dearest, The Man Who Wasn't There, Doctors Wives, The Love Machine, The Greatest Story Ever Told, Private Benjamin, Yes, Georgio, Face in the Crowd, Pretty Boy Floyd; appeared in more than 100 TV shows; starred in Superior Court and Incredible Hulk; co-starred in Working, Nowhere Man, Ellen, Moonlighting, Max Headroom, Hunter, The Judge, The White Shadow, Benson; featured in Murder She Wrote, Highway to Heaven, David Letterman Show, Rockford Files; also appeared in Three's Company, Betty White Show, Mannix, Hart to Hart, Mission Impossible, Flamingo Road, Philco Playhouse, Room 222, Streets of San Francisco, Studio One, One Life to Live, General Hospital, As the World Turns; also appeared in regional stage prodns. of Glengarry Glen Ross, Checking Out, Awake and Sing, Plaza Suite, in stock, dinner theater, off-Broadway and L.A. 99-seat theaters and in TV commls.; author: (novel) Spreading the Word or A Mythic Odyssey 1993, (screenplay) Murder Unplanned, 1997. Vol. Wadsworth Va., 1992—; coun. mem. Actor's Equity. With U.S. Navy, 1945-47. Recipient L.A. Weekly award Best Actor in Revival of Yr. Noises Off, 1990. Mem. Acad. Motion Picture Arts and Scis., Acad. TV Arts & Scis.

MARINER, WILLIAM MARTIN, chiropractor; b. Balt., Jan. 2, 1949; s. William Joseph and Ellen (Dexter) M. AA, Phoenix Coll., 1976; BS in Biology, L.A. Coll. of Chiropractic, 1980, D Chiropractic summa cum laude, 1980; DD (hon.), Universal Life Ch., Modesto, Calif., 1986. Health food restaurant mgr. Golden Temple of Conscious Cookery, Tempe, Ariz., 1974-75; health food store mgr. Guru's Grainery, Phoenix, 1975; physical therapist A.R.E. Clinic, Phoenix, 1975-76; research dir., founder G.R.D. Healing Arts Ctr., Phoenix, 1974-77; aminstrv. asst., acad. dean L.A. Coll. Chiropractic, Whittier, Calif., 1977-80; faculty Calif. Acupuncture Coll., L.A., 1978-80; ednl. cons. Avanti Inst., San Francisco, 1985-91; found, dir., head clinician Pacific Healing Arts Ctr., Del Mar, Calif., 1980-93, Mt. Shasta, Calif., 1993—; ednl. cons. John Panama Cons., San Francisco, 1991—. Patentee in field. Co-dir. "We Care We Share" Charitable Orgn., San Diego, 1985-86. Named Outstanding Sr., L.A. Coll. Chiropractic, 1980. Mem. Calif. Chiropractic Assn., Am. Chiropractic Assn., Internat. Coll. Applied Kinesiology, Holistic Dental Assn., Brit. Homopathic Assn. Avocations: Yoga, meditation, personal growth, natural healing methods, cooking. Office: Pacific Healing Arts Ctr PO Box 192 Mount Shasta CA 96067-0192

MARINEZ, FERNANDO, information specialist; b. Morelia, Mexico, Sept. 22, 1962; s. Alejandro and Guadalupe (Fernandez) M. BA, Harvard Coll., 1985; JD, U. Calif., Berkeley, 1993. Info. specialist Putnam, Hayes & Bartlett Inc., Cambridge, Mass., 1985-91; rsch. atty. Farella, Braun & Martel, San Francisco, 1993-95; info. specialist McKinsey & Co., San Francisco, 1995-97; practice knowledge specialist A.T. Kearney Inc., San Francisco, 1997—. Editor La Raza Law Jour., 1992. Nat. Housing Law Project rsch. grantee, Oakland, Calif., 1993. Mem. Special Libr. Assn., Soc. for Competitive Intelligence Profls. Office: A T Kearney Inc 101 California St Ste 1600 San Francisco CA 94111-6100

MARINO, RICHARD J., publishing executive. With Harcourt/Brace/Jovanovich; sr. v.p. advtg. and mktg. ABC Cap Cities Pub. Corp.; assoc. pub. PC World Communications, 1990-92, pub., 1992-94, pres., 1994-96, pres., CEO, 1997—. Office: PC World IDG Comms 501 2nd St Ste 600 San Francisco CA 94107-1469*

MARIO, ERNEST, pharmaceutical company executive; b. Clifton, N.J., June 12, 1938; s. Jerry and Edith (Meijer) M.; m. Mildred Martha Daume, Dec. 10, 1961; children: Christopher Bradley, Gregory Gerald, Jeremy Konrad. B.S. in Pharmacy, Rutgers U., 1961; M.S. in Phys. Scis., U. RI., 1963, Ph.D. in Phys. Scis., 1965. Registered pharmacist, R.I., N.Y. Vice pres. mfg. Smith Kline Corp., Phila., 1975-77; v.p. mfg. ops. U.S. Pharm. Co. (divsn. E. R. Squibb), New Brunswick, N.J., 1977-79; v.p., gen. mgr. chem. div. E. R. Squibb, Princeton, N.J., 1979-81; pres. chem. and engring. div., sr. v.p. Squibb Corp., Princeton, 1981-84; v.p. Squibb Corp., 1984-86; pres., COO Glaxo Inc., 1986-88, chmn., CEO, 1988, chmn., 1989-91; CEO Glaxo Holdings plc, 1989-93, dep. chmn., 1991-93; co-chmn., CEO, Alza Corp., Palo Alto, Calif., 1993-97, chmn., ceo, 1997—; grad. asst., instr. U. R.I., Kingston, 1961-66; research fellow Inst. Neurol. Diseases, Bethesda, Md., 1963-65. Contbr. articles to profl. jours. Trustee Duke U., Rockefeller U., U. R.I. Found.; mem. pres.'s coun. U. R.I.; chmn. Am. Found. for Pharm. Edn.; bd. dirs. Nat. Found. Infectious Diseases, Antigenics, Pharm. Product Devel., Stanford Health Svcs., Tech. Mus. Innovation; mem. Calif. gov.'s coun. on biotech. Office: Alza Corp 950 Page Mill Rd Palo Alto CA 94304-1080

MARION, SUSAN FELICE, educator; b. Norristown, Pa., Mar. 8, 1962; d. Harvey Theodore and Nancy Paula (Brumberg) M. BFA in Film Prodn., NYU, 1984; MEd in Elem. Edn., U. Mass., 1990; EdM in Ednl. Tech., Harvard U., 1992. Film prodn. supr. NYU, N.Y.C., 1985-86; gen. educator Boston Pub. Schs., 1987-90; freelance edn. cons. Boston, 1990-92; ednl. field rschr. Harvard U., Cambridge, Mass., 1990-92; gen. educator Denver Pub. Schs., 1992—; instr. Metropolitan State Coll., Denver, 1998—; cons. Denver Pub. Schs., Denver Post, 1995—, Nat. History Mus. West, Oglalla, Nebr., 1998. Author: Integrated Arts Curriculum Guide, 1993; dir., writer, editor (film) Matinee, 1985. Founder Living History Project, Denver, 1995—. DNP Project grantee Denver Neighborhood Partnership, 1996, 97, 98, Colonial Dames Project grantee Colonial Dames Colo. Chpt., Denver, 1996, 98, Sch. to Career grantee Denver Pub. Schs., 1997-98, Destination Edn. grantee United Airlines/DPS Found., Denver, 1997-98. Mem. NCTE, CCIRA. Home: 1538 S University Blvd Denver CO 80210-2813

MARIUCCI, STEVE, coach professional and college football; b. Iron Mountain, Mich., Nov. 4, 1955; m. Gayle Mariucci; 4 children. Football coach No. Mich. U., 1978-79, Calif. State U., Fullerton, 1980-82; asst. head coach U. Louisville, 1983-84; receivers coach Orlando Renegades U.S. Football League, 1985; quality control coach L.A. Rams, 1985; receivers/spl. teams coach U. So. Calif., L.A., 1986, wide receivers/spl. teams coach, 1987-89, quarterbacks coach, offensive coord., 1990-91; quarterbacks coach Green Bay (Wis.) Packers, 1992-95; head coach Golden Bears U. Calif., 1996—; head coach San Francisco 49ers, 1996—. Office: San Francisco 49ers 4949 Centennial Blvd, Candlestick Point Santa Clara CA 95054-1229*

MARK, ARTHUR, information systems specialist; b. San Francisco, Aug. 1, 1948; s. Bo You and Chew Lin (Oyoung) M.; m. Alice Look, Sept. 1, 1973 (div. Oct. 1987); children: Jennifer, Brandon. BS, Calif. State U., 1971, MS, 1977. Cert. data processing, info. systems auditor, internal auditor. Instr. info. systems Calif. State U., Sacramento, 1978—, Am. River Coll., Sacramento City Coll.; with State of Calif., Sacramento, 1977-85, 88—. Active United Way. Maj. USMC, 1985-88. Mem. MENSA, Inst. Internal Auditors. Republican. Avocations: jogging, tennis, cross-country skiing, personal computers. Home: 8985 Laguna Place Way Elk Grove CA 95758-5366

MARK, KATHLEEN ABBOTT, writer; b. Toronto, Ont., Can., Oct. 4, 1911; came to U.S., 1945; d. Arthur and Clara Barker (Foulkes) Abbott; m. Jordan Carson Mark, Nov. 22, 1935; children: Joan Mary, Thomas, Elizabeth Smith, Graham, Christopher, Mary. Student, U. N.Mex., 1971-73. Free lance writer Los Alamos, N. Mex., 1964—. Author: Meteorite Craters, 1987; contbr. articles to Sea Frontiers. Co-recipient Nininger award U. Ariz., 1974-75. Mem. AAAS, Geol. Soc. Am., Meteoritical Soc., History of Earth Scis. Soc., History of Sci. Soc. Home and Office: 4900 Sandia Dr Los Alamos NM 87544-1850

MARKEL, REX ALLEN, medical facility administrator; b. Oakland, Calif., Jan. 30, 1957; s. James Allen and Dove Rose (Gomes) M.; m. Karen Lynn McHattie, May 17, 1986 (div. Dec. 1992); 1 child, Erik Kenneth; m. Catherine Kenny, May 8, 1993. AA, El Camino Coll., 1988. RN. Nursing asst. Little Co. of Mary Hosp., Torrance, Calif., 1986-87; clin. sys. analyst II Daniel Freeman Hosps., Inc., Inglewood, Calif., 1988—. Mem. Am. Nursing Informatics Assn., Technology Info. Mgmt. Edn. Soc., Beer Can Collectors Am. Democrat. Roman Catholic. Avocations: music, home improvement, off road 4 wheeling, bicycling. Home: 1251 Levinson St Torrance CA 90502-1856

MARKER, MARC LINTHACUM, lawyer, investor; b. Los Angeles, July 19, 1941; s. Clifford Harry and Voris (Linthacum) M.; m. Sandra Vocom. Aug. 29, 1965; children: Victor, Gwendolyn. BA in Econs. and Geography, U. Calif.-Riverside, 1964; JD, U. So. Calif., 1967. Asst. v.p., asst. sec. Security Pacific Nat. Bank, L.A., 1970-73; sr. v.p., chief counsel, sec. Security Pacific Leasing Corp., San Francisco, 1973-92; pres. Security Pacific Leasing Svcs. Corp., San Francisco, 1977-85, dir., 1977-92; bd. dirs., sec. Voris, Inc., 1973-86; bd. dirs. Refiners Petroleum Corp., 1977-81, Security Pacific Leasing Singapore Ltd., 1983-85, Security Pacific Leasing Can. Ltd., 1989-92; lectr. in field. Served to comdr., USCGR. Mem. ABA, Calif. Bar Assn., D.C. Bar Assn. Republican. Lutheran. Club: Army and Navy.

MARKEWICH, GARY STEVEN, dermatologist; b. Houston, Mar. 10, 1944; s. Jake and Florence T. (Herskovitz) M.; m. Rosa Katharina Foster, June 12, 1988; children: Jeffrey, Robert, Aaron, Brandon. BA, U. Tex., 1965, MD, 1969. Diplomate Am. Bd. Dermatology. Dermatologist U.S. Army, Ft. Carson, Colo., 1973-75; pvt. practice Colorado Springs, Colo., 1975-91, Las Vegas, 1991—. Maj. U.S. Army, 1969-75. Office: 2870 S Maryland Pkwy Ste 120 Las Vegas NV 89109-1548

MARKHAM, CHARLES HENRY, neurologist; b. Pasadena, Calif., Dec. 24, 1923; s. Fred Smith and Maziebelle Valeta (Glover) M.; m. Kathleen Tiernan, Sept. 29, 1945 (div. 1971); children: Charles H., Arthur Tiernan, Daphne, James Daniel; m. Lisa Wells Overly, July 10, 1971; children: John Wells, Sara Brennan. Student, Colo. Sch. Mines, 1941-43; AB, Stanford U., 1947, MD, 1951. Intern, med. asst. resident Lane Hosp., San Francisco, 1950-52; fellow in neurology Children's Med. Ctr., Boston, 1952-53; asst. resident Boston City Hosp., 1953-54, chief resident, 1954-55; asst. prof. neurology UCLA Sch. Medicine, 1958-65, assoc. prof., 1965-70, assoc. prof. neurology, 1970-71, prof. neurology, 1971-94, prof. emeritus, 1994—; sci. dir. Dystonia Med. Rsch. Found., Chgo., 1985-94, mem. bd. trustees, 1994—; sci. dir. Hereditary Disease Found., L.A., 1979-81; mem. adv. bd. Am. Parkinson Disease Assn., N.Y.C., 1976-83; attending physician UCLA Sch. Medicine, 1957—, cons. in neurology St. John's Hosp., Santa Monica, Calif., 1960-94. Contbr. articles to profl. jours.; author numerous books and abstracts. Trustee Westlake Sch. for Girls, L.A., 1965-74, St. Matthews Parish Sch., L.A., 1985-87; bd. dirs. Jubilee Christian Acad., 1996—, Wildling Mus., 1997—, Las Positas Park Found., 1998—. With U.S. Army, 1943-45. Grantee NIH, NASA. Mem. Am. Acad. Neurology, AAAS, Am. Bd. Psychiatry and Neurology, Am. Epilepsy Soc., Am. Neurol. Assn., Am. Pain Soc., Am. Soc. for Gravitational and Space Biology, Bárány Soc. (Hallpike-Nylen prize 1990), Internat. Brain Rsch. Orgn., Internat. League Against Epilepsy, L.A. Soc. Neurology and Psychiatry, N.Y. Acad. Scis., Soc. for Neurosci., Western Inst. on Epilepsy, Rsch. Soc. for Parkinson Disease and Movement Disorders (pres. 1984—). Republican. Achievements include research in L-dopa and other therapy for Parkinson's disease, dystonia, brain stem mechanisms for vestibular and quick and slow eye movements, space motion sickness. Office: UCLA Sch Medicine Dept Neurology Los Angeles CA 90095-1769

MARKHAM, REED B., education educator, consultant; b. Alhambra, Calif., Feb. 14, 1957; s. John F. and Reeda (Bjarason) M. BA, Brigham Young U., 1982, MA, 1982; BS, Regents Coll., 1981, MA, 1982; MPA, U. So. Calif., 1983; MA, UCLA, 1989; PhD, Columbia Pacific U., 1991. Mem. faculty Brigham Young U., Provo, Utah, 1984; mem. faculty Calif. State U., Fullerton and Long Beach, 1984, Northridge, 1985; mem. faculty El Camino Coll., Torrance, Calif., 1986, Orange Coast Coll., Costa Mesa, Calif., 1986, Pasadena (Calif.) Coll., 1986, Fullerton (Calif.) Community Coll., 1986; instr., mem. pub. rels. com. Chaffey (Calif.) Coll., 1986-87; prof., CARES dir. Calif. State Poly. U., Pomona, 1987-98; adj. prof. Calif. State U., L.A., 1992-93, dir. Ctr. for Student Retention, 1995—; prof. East L.A. Coll., 1996-98, Salt Lake C.C., 1998—; rsch. asst. to pres. Ctr. for the Study of Cmty. Coll., 1985; mem. faculty Riverside (Calif.) Coll., 1989-90, Rio Hondo (Calif.) Coll., 1989-90, English Lang. Inst., 1994, Calif. Poly Summer Bridge, 1989-95, East L.A. Coll.; adj. prof. Citrus Coll., 1998—; speechwriter U.S. Supreme Ct., Washington, 1980; cons. gifted children program Johns Hopkins U./Scripps Coll., Claremont, Calif., 1987-88; mem. faculty PACE Program East L.A., 1995-96; faculty East L.A. Coll., 1996-97; adj. prof. U. So. Calif., 1998—; prof. Salt Lake C. C., 1998-99. Author: Power Speechwriting, 1983, Power Speaking, 1990, Public Opinion, 1990, Advances in Public Speaking, 1991, Leadership 2000: Success Skills for University Students, 1995, Excellence in Public Speaking, 1997; co-author: Student Retention: Success Models in Higher Education, 1996, Upward Bound Program Grant Proposal, 1996, Making Marriage Magnificent, 1998; editor Trojan in Govt., U. So. Calif., 1983; editl. bd. mem. Edn. Digest, Speaker and Gavel, Innovative Higher End., Pub. Rels. Rev., Nat. Forensic Jour., The Forensic Educator, Clearinghouse for the Contemporary Educator, Hispanic Am. Family Mag.; writer N.Y. times, Christian Sci. Monitor; ednl. columnist San Bernardino (Calif.) Sun., 1992-98. Pres. bd. trustees Regents Coll., 1986. Mem. Doctorate Assn. N.Y. Scholars, Nat. Assn. Pvt. Nontraditional Colls. (accrediting com. 1989—), Pub. Rels. Soc. Am. (dir.-at-large inland empire 1992-93, faculty advisor). LDS. Office: Comm Dept Salt Lake CC PO Box 30808 Salt Lake City UT 84130-0808

MARKHAM, RICHARD GLOVER, research executive; b. Pasadena, Calif., June 18, 1925; s. Fred Smith and Maziebelle (Glover) M.; m. Jonne Louise Pearson, Apr. 29, 1950; children: Janet B., Fred S., Charles R., Richard G., Marilyn A. Student, Stanford U., 1943; BS, Calif. Inst. Tech., Pasadena, 1945; MS, Stanford U., 1947. Pres., owner Aquarium Pump Supply, Prescott, Ariz., 1957-78; 1st v.p., dir. Bank of Prescott, 1981-87; also v.p., bd. dirs. Oxycal Labs., Prescott, 1981-97, ret., 1997. Patentee in field. Mem. Ariz. Dept. Econ. Planning and Devel., 1967-72; treas. Ariz. State Rep. Com., 1970-72; active Ariz. Acad., 1974—; trustee Orme Sch., Mayer, Ariz., 1970-83, Prescott Coll., 1979-83.

MARKIE, SHANE ROBERT, poet; b. Aurora, Colo., Jan. 4, 1965; s. Robert William Markie and Lois May (Hardenbrook) Fisher. Student, Brigham Young U., 1983-85, 89-90. Contbr. poetry to Bell's Letters Mag., 1994-97, Jackhammer Mag., 1995-96, Streetbeat Mag., 1993-96, Writing Dangerous Poetry, 1998. Avocations: reading, downhill skiing, computers, internet.

MARKKULA, A. C., JR., entrepreneur, computer company executive. Co-founder, former pres., chief exec. officer Apple Computer Inc., now chmn. bd. dirs.; founder, vice chmn. Echelon, Los Gatos, Calif. Office: Echelon Corp 4015 Miranda Ave Palo Alto CA 94304*

MARKLEY, RICHARD DELBERT, manufacturing company executive; b. Bennington, Kans., Aug. 26, 1938; s. Claude Delbert and Dorothy Velma (Moody) M.; m. Marilyn Yvonne Welty, Feb. 4, 1962; children: Keith, Matthew. BSEE, Kans. State U., 1960. Trainee Westinghouse Electric Corp., Pitts., 1960-61; sales engr. Westinghouse Electric Corp., various, 1961-76; v.p. Westinghouse Airport Sys. Co., Burlington, Vt., 1976-83; prin., owner CD-3 Equipment Co., Inc., Lakewood, Colo., 1983—, dir. Point Lighting Corp., Simsbury, Conn., 1993—. Active Devel. Disabilities Resource Ctr., Lakewood, Colo., 1975—, chmn. Colo. State Devel. Disabilities Council, Denver, 1975-76. E-mail: dmark@rmi.net. Fax: (303) 980-9887. Home and Office: CD-3 Equipment Co Inc 2770 S Coors Ct Lakewood CO 80228-4958

MARKOVICH, PATRICIA, economist; b. Oakland, Calif.; d. Patrick Joseph and Helen Emily (Prydz) Markovich; BA in Econs., MS in Econs., U. Calif.-Berkeley; postgrad. (Lilly Found. grantee) Stanford U., (NSF grantee) Oreg. Grad. Rsch. Ctr.; children: Michael Sean Treece, Bryan Jeffry Treece, Tiffany Helene Treece. Cert. Emergency Mgmt. Planner. Pub. rels. Pettler Advt., Inc.; pvt. practice polit. and econs. cons.; aide to majority whip Oreg. Ho. of Reps.; lectr., instr., various Calif. instns., Chemeketa (Oreg.) Coll., Portland (Oreg.) State U.; commr. City of Oakland (Calif.), 1970-74; chairperson, bd. dirs. Cable Sta. KCOM; mem. gen. plan commn. City of Piedmont, Calif.; with Oakland Mus. Archives of Calif. Artists. Mem. Internat. Assn. Feminist Economists, Mensa (officer San Francisco region), Bay Area Artists Assn. (coord., founding mem.), Berkeley Art Ctr. Assn., San Francisco Arts Commn. File, Calif. Index for Contemporary Arts, Pro Arts, YLEM: Artists Using Sci. and Tech., NAFE, No. Calif. Pub. Ednl. and Govt. Access Cable TV Com. (founding), Triple Nine Soc., Nat. Coord. Coun. Emergency Mgmt., Am. Econ. Assn., Allied Social Scis. Assn., N.Y. Acad. Scis., Internat. Assn. for Feminist Economists.

MARKS, KEVIN ANDREW, lawyer; b. Neptune, N.J., Feb. 17, 1967; s. Gene R. Sr. and Karen (Hendrickson) M.; m. Leslie Susan Dymond, July 3, 1994. AB, Lafayette Coll., Easton, Pa., 1989; JD, Villanova U., 1993. Bar: Pa., N.J., 1993, Calif., 1996. Mktg. analyst Phoenix Petroleum, King of Prussia, Pa., 1989-90; atty. Hoyle, Morris & Kerr LLP, Phila., 1993-96, Littler Mendelson PC, Oakland, Calif., 1996—. Runner Race for the Cure, Phila., 1996. Mem. Kiwanis. Avocations: golf, wine, cooking. Fax: 510-873-8656. E-mail: kmarks@littler.com. Office: Littler Mendelson PC 1111 Broadway Ste 1510 Oakland CA 94607-4097

MARKS, LEONARD, JR., retired corporate executive; b. N.Y.C., May 22, 1921; s. Leonard M. and Laura (Colegrove) Rose; m. Antonia Saldaña Riley, July 19, 1986; children from previous marriage: Linda, Patricia Anne, Peter K. A.B. in Econs., Drew U., 1942; M.B.A., Harvard U., 1948, D.B.A., 1961. Asst. prof. bus. adminstrn. Harvard U., 1949-55; prof. fin. Stanford U., 1955-64; asst. sec. USAF, Washington, 1964-68; v.p. corp. devel. Times Mirror Co., Los Angeles, 1968-69; sr. v.p. Wells Fargo Bank, San Francisco, 1969-72; exec. v.p. Castle & Cooke Inc., San Francisco, 1972-85; gen. ptnr. Marks-Hoffman Assocs., Venture Capital, 1985-92; ind. corp. dir., 1992-98; bd. dirs. Alexion Pharm. Inc. Co-author: Case Problems in Commercial Bank Management, 1962; contbg.: Credit Management Handbook, 1958. Capt. AUS, 1942-46, ret. brig. gen. USAFR.

MARKS, MARIANNE See SCHAFER, MARIANNE MARKS

MARKS, MICHAEL E., electronics company executive. BA, MA, Oberlin Coll.; MBA, Harvard U. Formerly pres., CEO Metcal Inc.; chmn. bd. dirs. Flextronics, 1993—, CEO, 1994—. Office: Flextronics 2090 Fortune Dr San Jose CA 95131-1823*

MARKS, PETER AMASA, technical consulting company administrator; b. Passaic, N.J., Dec. 5, 1948; s. Amasa and Eunice M.; BS in Design Engring., U. Cin., 1972, MA in Media Communications, 1973, postgrad. in human factors engring. Rsch. asst. dept. mech. engring. U. Cin., 1972; sr. engr. Ford Motor Co., Sharonville, Ohio, 1972-75; prin. Design Insight Cin., 1976—; mng. dir. SDRC TEC Services, Milford, Ohio, 1978-84, dir. product planning and devel., SDRC, Inc., Milford, 1981-84; sr. v.p. ops. Automation Tech., Campbell, Calif., 1985-88; CEO, Design Insight, 1988—. lectr., cons. on product design tech. implementation, U.S., Asia, Europe, also for Am. Mgmt. Assns.; co-founder, head bd of judges Am. Product Excellence (APEX) Awards. Grad. fellow; Gen. Motors grantee in design, 1970; winner nat., internat. competitions for tech. programs. Mem. ASME, IEEE, Soc. Mfg. Engrs., Am. Mgmt. Assn. Office: Design Insight 3760 Old Pilkington Rd Santa Cruz CA 95065-2120

MARKS, ROBERT ARTHUR, lawyer, attorney general; b. Dayton, Ohio, Oct. 9, 1952; s. Arthur Kenneth and Patricia Marks; m. Victoria Scurlock, Oct. 21, 1978; two sons. BA, U. Wis., 1974; JD, U. Cin., 1977. Bar: Ohio 1977, Hawaii 1978, U.S. Ct. Appeals (6th cir.) Ohio 1977, U.S. Ct. Appeals (9th cir.) Hawaii 1978, U.S. Supreme Ct. 1992. Pvt. practice Honolulu, 1978-84; dep. atty. gen. State of Hawaii, Honolulu, 1984-87, supr. dep. atty. gen., 1987-92, 1st dep. atty. gen., 1992, atty. gen., 1992-94; counsel Alston, Hunt, Floyd & Ing, Honolulu, 1995-97, Price, Okamoto Himeno & Lum, Honolulu, 1997—. Office: Price Okamoto Himeno Lum 707 Richards St Ste 728 Honolulu HI 96813-4623

MARKS, SHARON LEA, primary school educator, nurse; b. Arroyo Grande, Calif., June 12, 1942; d. Donald Elmore and Gertrude (Grieb) Shaffer; m. George Conrad Schmidt, June 23, 1963 (div. 1975); children: Kerrilynn, Robert, Marianne; m. Keith Dalton Marks, June 4, 1978; children: Joseph, Erik, Alice. Diploma, Sch. Nursing Samuel Merritt Hosp., 1963; BS in Nursing, Lewis and Clark State Coll., 1984, BS in Mgmt., 1986. RN, Calif.; cert. tchr., Calif. Staff nurse Vesper Meml. Hosp., San Leandro, Calif., 1968-74; night nurse supr. Tuolumne Gen. Hosp., Sonora, Calif., 1975; nurse Orleans (Calif.) Search and Rescue Team, 1975-78; instr. nursing Pasadena (Calif.) City Coll., 1978-79; resource coord. learning ctr. div. health sci. Spokane (Wash.) Community Coll., 1979-84; staff nurse Kootenai Med. Ctr., 1979-85; instr. North Idaho Coll., Coeur d'Alene, 1984-85; staff nurse North Idaho Home Health, Coeur d'Alene, 1985-86; coord. br. office Family Home Care, Spokane, 1986-87; devel., dir. Good Samaritan Home Health Plummer, Idaho and Fairfield, Washington, 1987-88; mgr. patient svcs. VNS Seattle-King County, Tukwila, Wash., 1988-89; co-owner, v.p. The Wooden Boat Shop, Seattle, 1989-97; primary sch. tchr. Marisposa Sch., 1994-95, Corona Sch., 1995-96, West Randall Sch., Fontana, Calif., 1996—; owner Marks and Assocs., 1994—; instr. in emergency med. tech. Orleans campus Coll. Redwoods, Eureka, Calif., 1977-78; book reviewer Brady Co., Besterfield and Assocs., 1994; film reviewer Olympia Media Info. Avocations: travel, gardening, hiking. Office: 35621 Wildwood Canyon Rd Yucaipa CA 92399-5130

MARKS, STANLEY JACOB, lawyer, historian, lecturer, author; b. Chgo., Apr. 26, 1914; s. Samuel and Sarah Marks; m. Ethel Milgrom, Aug. 1, 1936; 1 child, Roberta E. AB, U. Ill., 1934; LLB, JD, John Marshall Law Sch., Chgo., 1937. Bar: Ill. 1939. Pres., chmn. bd. Beauti-Dor, Inc., Chgo., 1939—, Glamour Glass Door, Inc., Chgo., 1939—; pvt. practice Calif., 1964—; internat. and nat. legal and bus. labor cons. L.A., 1964—; lectr. on polit. and social/econ. events worldwide. Author: (with Ethel Marks) The Bear That Walks Like a Man, 1943, Murder Most Foul, 1967, Two Days of Infamy, 1969, Coup d'Etat!, 1970, Through Distorted Mirrors, 1974, Juadism Looks at Christianity, 1986, A Year in the Lives of the Damned, Reagn, Reaganism, 1986, The 1991 U.S. Consumer Market, 1991, Yes, Americans, A Conspiracy Murdered JFK!, 1992, Jews, Judaism and the U.S., 1992, Justice For Whom?, 1996, If this Be Treason, 1996others; playwright: Judgement Day, 1998, Judaism - Civilization's Las Hope, 1998; pub. weekly polit. newsletter Diogenes, 1984, 88, 90. Writer Dem. Nat. Com., 1936, 40, 48, 52, 60, 91, 96. With AUS, 1946-47. Recipient various Army decorations. Mem. Am. Acad. Polit. and Social Scis., Soc. Am. Mil. Engrs., Authors League Am., Libr. of Congress Assn., Anti-Defamation League, Dramatists Guild (life), Masons, Shriners, Anti Discrimination League, World Jewish Congress, Dramatist Guild.

MARKUS, THOMAS BENJAMIN, theatre director, actor; b. Evanston, Ill., Oct. 28, 1934; s. Benjamin and Ruby (Friedman) M.; 1 child, Lindsay. B.A., Pomona Coll., 1956; M.F.A., Tulane U., 1958, Ph.D., 1962. Asst. prof., U. Calif.-Santa Barbara, 1962-69; assoc. prof. CUNY, 1969-71; prof. Temple U., Phila., 1971-78; artistic dir. Theater at Monmouth, Maine, 1977-78, TheatreVirginia, Richmond, 1978-85, Theatre by the Sea, N.H., 1986-87; resident dir. and dramaturg Pioneer Theatre Co., 1988—; prof. Yale U., New Haven, 1986, Fla. State U., 1988, U. Utah, 1988—; guest dir. Lobero Theatre, Santa Barbara, 1967, Roundabout Theatre, N.Y., 1970, Utah Shakespeare Festival, 1964, 66, 67, 80, 90, Festival Theatre, University Park, Pa., 1971, 83, Performing Arts Found., Huntington, N.Y., 1973, Oreg. Shakespeare Festival, Ashland, 1973, Colo. Shakespeare Festival, Boulder, [illegible] Calif. Shakespeare Festival, Berkeley, [illegible] Walnut St. Theatre, [illegible] Merrimack Repertory Theatre, [illegible] of Cyprus, 1997, Hong Kong Repertory Theatre, 1995, Ga. Shakespeare Festival, 1996. Author: The Professional Actor, 1979, An Actor Behaves, 1992, How to Read a Play, 1996, A Novel Approach to Theatre, 1997, Let's Go to

the Theatre, 1997; (play) The Father, 1967, Christmas Carol, 1981, Three Sisters, 1991, A Silly Goose, 1996. Mem. Actors Equity Assn., SAG, AFTRA, Nat. Theatre Conf., Am. Soc. Theatre Research, Shakespeare Theatre Assn. America, Soc. Stage Dirs. and Choreographers. Home: 48 W 300 S # 2005N Salt Lake City UT 84101-2007 Office: U Utah 218 Pioneer Meml Theatre Salt Lake City UT 84112

MARLATT, DOROTHY BARBARA, university dean; b. Tarrytown, N.Y., Dec. 1; d. Joseph S. and Evelyn M. (McGinnis) Porcano; m. Gene R. Marlatt, Aug. 20, 1960; children: David D., Julia Jeanne Marlatt Kelley. BA, Wheaton (Ill.) Coll., 1960; MA, U. Colo., 1966; EdD, Internat. Grad. Sch., St. Louis, 1987. Tchr. Alexandria (Va.) Pub. Schs., 1961-62, Westminster (Colo.) Pub. Schs., 1962-66, Jeffco Pub. Schs., Lakewood, Colo., 1966-69; elem. prin. Denver Pub. Schs., 1970-94; assoc. prof. edn. Rockmont Coll., Lakewood, 1976-93; prof. edn. Colo. Christian U., Lakewood, 1993-98, dean edn., 1994-97; adj. prof. Union Grad. Sch., Cin., 1995—; prin. Twin Peaks Charter Acad., Longmont, Colo., 1997-99. Author: Leadership to a Higher Power, 1998. Recipient Svc. to Youth award YMCA, 1960, Svc. award Big Bros., 1970, Pub. Rels. Recognition award Denver Pub. Schs., 1972. Fellow Acad. Nat. Staff Devel., Inst. for Devel. of Ednl. Activities, Nat. Elem. Sch. Prins. Assn.; mem. Optimists, Kappa Delta Pi. Republican. Presbyterian. Avocation: music.

MARLATT, MICHAEL JAMES, lawyer; b. L.A., Jan. 15, 1957; s. James Raymond and Norma Jean (Greenfield) M.; m. Donna Marie Healey, Apr. 13, 1985. BA, Calif. Poly. U., 1981; JD, Pepperdine U., 1984. Bar: Calif. 1984, U.S. Dist. Ct. (ctrl. dist.) Calif. 1985, U.S. Supreme Ct. 1990. Project liaison U. So. Calif., Sch. Medicine, L.A., 1975-78; documentation rschr. NASA-Jet Propulsion Lab., Pasadena, Calif., 1978-81; ptnr. Thompson & Colegate, Riverside, Calif., 1984—; bd. dirs. Assn. So. Calif. Def. Counsel, L.A., U. Calif., Riverside; lectr. Princeton U., 1993, U. Amsterdam Law Sch., 1994, Loma Linda (Calif.) U. Sch. Medicine, 1991-94, Boston Coll. Law Sch., 1997; chair Am. Legal Sys. Internat. Law Program Civil Litigation U. of Calif., 1997; lectr., spkr. to ins. cos. on health care, 1988—; bd. dirs. Mission Inn Found., v.p.; radio commentator Stas. KCKC, KCAL, and KMEN. Mem. ctr. com. Calif. Rep. Party, Sacramento, 1990-93; bd. dirs. U. Calif., Riverside, pres., 1996-97; bd. dirs. Mission Inn Found., v.p., 1996-97. Mem. So. Calif. Assn. Hosp. Risk Mgrs. (bylaws com. 1996—), Riverside Comty. Hosp., 1999, Victoria Country Club, Phi Alpha Delta. Roman Catholic. Avocations: rare book collecting, collegiate athletics, traveling. Office: Thompson & Colegate PO Box 1299 3610 14th St Riverside CA 92501-3846

MARLBOROUGH, JANET LYNN, healthcare consultant; b. Long Beach, Calif., Mar. 23, 1951; d. Malvin J. and Marion J. (Zolper) M. BSN, Calif. State U., L.A., 1973; MBA, U.S. Internat. U., 1983. Dir. bus. devel. Mercy Hosp. and Med. Ctr., San Diego, 1977-87; adminstrv. dir. Orthopaedic Hosp., L.A., 1987-88; COO Panorama Comty. Hosp., Panorama City, Calif., 1989-90; adminstrv. dir. St. Joseph Hosp., Orange, Calif., 1990-91; reg. mgr. Bedford Internat., Pasadena, Calif., 1991-93; prin. Marlborough Med., Oceanside, Calif., 1993—; spkr. in field. Author: (book) Dynamic Nurse Management, 1987. Bd. dirs. YWCA San Diego County, treas., 1990. Lt. USN, 1973-76. Recipient Tribute to Women and Industry award, 1986. Mem. Med. Group Mgrs. Assn., Women in Health Care Adminstrn. (v.p. 1986). Office: Marlborough Med PO Box 4916 Oceanside CA 92052-4916

MARLER, LARRY JOHN, private investor, leadership consultant; b. Chgo., Sept. 22, 1940; s. Walter William and Lena Inez (Killen) M.; m. Katy Jo Hibbits, Oct. 17, 1962 (div. Apr. 1971); 1 child, Preston Scott; m. Linda Lee Sorg, Sept. 2, 1982. BA, Christian Coll. Am., 1987; MA, Houston Grad. Sch. Theology, 1988; PhD, U.S. Internat. U., San Diego, 1992. Acct. Shell Oil Co., New Orleans, Houston, 1964-73; acctg. supr. We. Geophys. Co. Am., Houston, 1974; payroll supr. Olsen Inc., Houston, 1975-77; corp. credit mgr. Grant Corps., Houston, 1977-82; rschr., student contractor Navy Pers. R&D Ctr., San Diego, 1990-92; entrepreneur Denver, 1992-97; ESL coord., acct. Galilee Bapt. Ch., Denver, 1998—. With USCG, 1959-62. Mem. Am. Psychol. Soc., Am. Soc. Quality Control, Toastmasters Internat. Republican. Protestant. Avocations: reading, jogging, swimming, hiking, downhill skiing.

MARLETT, DE OTIS LORING, retired management consultant; b. Indpls., Apr. 19, 1911; s. Peter Loring and Edna Grace (Lombard) M.; m. Ruth Irene Pillar, Apr. 10, 1932 (dec. Feb., 1969); children: De Otis Neal, Marilynn Ruth; m. Marie Manning Ostrander, May 1, 1970 (dec. Apr. 1982); m. Peggie P. Whittlesey, Jan. 15, 1983 (dec. Oct., 1993); m. Estelle B. Brewer, Sept. 23, 1994. B.A., M.A., U. Wis., 1934; postgrad., Northwestern U., (part time), 1934-39, Harvard U.; postgrad. (Littauer fellow in econs. and govt.), 1946-47. CPA, Wis., 1935. Staff mem. Ill. Commerce Commn., 1934-39; lectr. in econs. and pub. utilities Northwestern U., (part time), 1936-39; staff mem. Bonneville Power Adminstrn., U.S. Dept. Interior, 1939-45, asst. adminstr., 1945-52; acting adminstr. Def. Electric Power Adminstrn., 1950-51; asst. to v.p., gen. mgr. Dicalite and Perlite divs. Great Lakes Carbon Corp., 1952-53; v.p., also gen. mgr. Dicalite, Perlite, Mining and Minerals divs. Gt. Lakes Carbon Corp., 1953-62, v.p. property investment dept., 1962-81; pres., chief exec. officer Great Lakes Properties, Inc., 1981-83, ret., 1983; past pres., dir. Rancho Palos Verdes Corp., G.L.C. Bldg. Corp., Del Amo Energy Co., Torrance Energy Co.; former mem. L.A. arbitration panel N.Y. Stock Exch. Contbr. articles and reports on public utility regulation, operation and mgmt. to profl. jours. Past bd. dirs. United Cerebral Palsy Assn. Los Angeles County; bd. dirs., past co-chmn. So. Calif. region NCCJ, mem. nat. trustee, mem. nat. exec. bd., nat. protestant co-chmn., 1987-90; past mem. Orthopaedic Hosp. Adv. Coun.; past trustee City of Hope; past pres., dir. Los Angeles area coun., past chmn. relationships com., past pres. Sunshine area, pres. Western region Boy Scouts Am., 1978-81, nat. exec. bd., 1978-88, past mem. nat. exec. com., past chmn. properties com., chmn. logistics for world jamboree delegation to Australia, 1987-88; past trustee Nat. Scouting Mus.; mem. internat. com. Baden Powell fellow World Scouting Found., 1984, mem. Benefactors Cir.; past mem. Western Govs. Mining Adv. Coun., Calif. State Mining Bd.; bd. govs. Western div. Am. Mining Congress, chmn., 1962-63; incorporator, past pres., bd. dirs. Torrance Meml. Med. Center Health Care Found.; region III dir., past mem. corp. adminstrn. and fin. com., Los Angeles United Way. Recipient Disting. Service medal U.S. Dept. Interior, 1952; named knight Order of Crown Belgium; commd. Ky. Col.; recipient Silver Beaver, Silver Antelope, Silver Buffalo awards Boy Scouts Am., 1984. Mem. AIME, AICPA, Fin. Execs. Inst., L.A. World Affairs Coun., Wis. Alumni Assn., Perlit Inst. (past pres., dir.), L.A. C. of C. (past dir., chmn. mining com.), Mining Assn. So. Calif. (past pres., dir.), Calif. Mine Operators Assn. (past dir.), Nat. Com. to Preserve Social Security and Medicare, Bldg. Industry Assn. So. Calif., Calif. Club, Portuguese Bend Club (past pres.), Palos Verdes Bay Club (past v.p.), Phi Kappa Phi, Beta Gamma Sigma, Phi Beta Kappa, Beta Alpha Psi, Lambda Alpha Internat. Democrat. Home: 32759 Seagate Dr Unit 204 Rancho Palos Verdes CA 90275-5891

MARLIN, ROBERT MATTHEW, secondary school educator; b. Buffalo, N.Y., June 11, 1940; s. Clarence Lewis and LaVerna (Haentgus) M.; m. Margaret Mary Steve, July, 1962 (div. July 1970); 1 child, Wendy. BEd, U. Alaska, 1967; postgrad., Alaska Pacific U., 1967-71, U. Ga., 1970, U. Salamanca, Spain, 1987, Calif State U., 1984-87. Cert. tchr., Calif. Radio traffic analyst USAF Security Svc., Anchorage, 1958-63; copywriter Anchorage Daily Times, 1963-67; tchr. Anchorage Sch. Dist., 1967-72; mgr. Transamerica Corp., L.A., 1972-84; tchr. L.A. Unified Sch. Dist., 1984—; participant sci. seminar on quality of edn., Pinar de Rio, Cuba, 1995, Matanzas, Cuba, 1996, Manzanillo, Cuba, 1997, Cienfuegos, Cuba, 1998. Bd. dirs. Upward Bound, Alaska Meth. Univ., Anchorage, 1969; vol. counselor Gay and Lesbian Cmty. Svcs. Ctr., L.A., 1975-76; cons. Constl. Rights Found., L.A., 1994—; gay and lesbian edn. commn. site liason L.A. Bd. Edn., 1996—. With USAF, 1958-63. Grantee Dept. Commerce, 1969, NSF, 1970, 71, L.A. Unified Sch. Dist., 1988. Mem. NEA, Gay, Lesbian, Straight Edn. Network, Calif. Tchrs. Assn., United Tchrs. L.A. (gay lesbian issues com.). Democrat. Home: 531 W Avenue 46 Los Angeles CA 90065-5007 Office: Berendo Middle Sch 1157 S Berendo St Los Angeles CA 90006-3301

MARLOW, EDWARD A., career officer; b. Cleve., Nov. 22, 1946; m. Gari Ann Dill, Sept. 20, 1975. *Wife Gari Ann is a breeder, historian and photographer of Arabian Horses. She recieved her B.A. in political science from UCLA in 1969 and is the only granddaughter of aviation pioneer Chester Arthur Elliott.* AA, Long Beach City Coll., 1971; cert., Officer Candidate Sch., Ft. Benning, 1974, Basic Infantry Officer Course, Ft. Benning, 1976; student, Am. Law Inst., N.Y., 1979-80; cert., Advance Armor Officer Course, Ft. Knox, 1982, U.S. Army Command and Gen. Staff Coll., 1986; BS in Bus. Mgmt. and Polit. Sci., SUNY, 1987; MPA, U. So. Calif., 1990; cert., Advance Intelligence Officer Course, Ft. Huachuca, 1991. Registered investment adv. 1978-90 with the Securities and Exchange Commission. Commissioned 2nd lt. infantry U.S. Army, 1974, advanced through grades to maj., 1988; chief real property branch Mil. Dept., Sacramento, 1968—; pres. and dir. TEAM Mgmt. Corp., 1978—. Mng. sr. ptnr. Caribbean Basin Latin Am. Devel. Orgn., Sacramento, 1988-98; trustee Hosp. Relief Fund Caribbean, Inc., Washington, 1989-92; mem. Caribbean Pvt. Sector Disaster Coord. Subcommittee White House Internat. Disaster Adv. Com., 1991-92; sr. ptnr. Caribbean Basin Latin Am. Devel. Orgn. Endowment Group, Sacramento, 1992—; chair bd. trustees CABALADO relief Fund, Inc., 1993-98.Provided disaster assistance and medical equipment to Glendon Hospital, Plymouth, Montserrat, West Indies, 1994-95. Avocations: sailing, fishing.

MARMADUKE, ARTHUR SANDFORD, educational administrator; b. Long Beach, Calif., May 29, 1926; s. William Sandford and Nina Belle (Romberger) M.; m. Carolyn Ann Tilden, Aug. 21, 1949; children: Jennifer, Stephen, Scott. AB, Occidental Coll., 1950; MPA, U. Mich., 1952; DPA (hon.), U. Pacific, 1970. Adminstrv. analyst Office Legis. Analyst Calif. State Legis., Sacramento, 1951-55; dir. admissions Occidental Coll., L.A., 1955-60; dir. Calif. Student Aid Commn., Sacramento, 1960-85; exec. dir. Eureka Project, Sacramento, 1986-90; dir. Independent Solution Project, 1989-91; cons. Weingart Found., 1987, Bush Found., 1985, Marin Ednl. Fund.; vice chmn. nat. task force on student aid programs KEppel Com., 1974-75; chmn. Coll. Scholarship Svc., Coll. Entrance Examination Bd., 1967-69; mem. planning com., dir. Calif. Higher Edn. Policy Ctr., 1991-93. Contbr. author several student aid books. Trustee Sacramento Country Day Sch. Recipient Disting. Service award Calif. Student Fin. Aid Adminstrs., 1982, Raol Wallenberg New Traditional High Sch., San Francisco, 1985, Coll. Bd. Scholarship Service, N.Y.C., 1985. Home: 1516 Del Dayo Dr Carmichael CA 95608-6011

MARMION, SUZANNE MICHELLE, reporter; b. Poughkeepsie, N.Y.; d. Nicholas Gerard Marmion and Gloria Jean Rushton. BA in Women's Studies and English Lit., U. Calif., Berkeley, 1994; MS in Journalism, Columbia U., 1997. Freelance reporter Sta. KQED-FM, San Franciscio, Sta. KPBS-FM, San Diego, Chgo. Tribune; corr. People Weekly, L.A. Contbr. author: U. Calif. Berkeley Poetry Chap Book, 1992. Mem. Soc. Profl. Journalists, Sacramento Press Club, Phi Beta Kappa.

MAROLD, KATHRYN ANN, computer scientist, educator; b. Omaha, May 3, 1944; d. Omer James and Edna Mae (Hansen) Schneider; m. Joseph Louis Marold, June 10, 1967; children: Dean, Patrick. BA, Creighton U., 1966; MSS, U. Denver, 1989, PhD, 1994. Tchr. Omaha Pub. Schs., 1966-68, Kingston (R.I.) Schs., 1969-70, Jefferson County Adult Edn., Arvada, Colo., 1972-74; sys. mgr. Joseph L. Marold, DDS, Arvada, 1970-85; cons. K&K Cons., Arvada, 1985-89; prof. Met. State Coll., Denver, 1989—. Author: Computers & Information Processing, 1993, Beyond the Internet, 1995, Using MS Sorks 4.0: An Introduction to Computing, 1997. Rep. Mayor's Arts Info. Careers Coun., Denver, 1996—. Grantee U. Denver, 1990, Met. State Coll., 1990, 97, U.S. West, 1995. Mem. AAUW, Acad. Computing Machinery, Info. Resource Mgmt. Assn. (editor), Internat. Comm. Assn. Republican. Roman Catholic. Avocations: outdoors, conyon and desert hiking, biking. Home: 3540 Miller Ct Wheat Ridge CO 80033-5665 Office: Metro State Coll Denver PO Box 173362 Denver CO 80217-3362

MARON, ROBERT EDWARD, sales executive; b. Dolliver, Iowa, Sept. 27, 1922; s. Arthur Edward and Della Elizabeth 9Larison) M.; m. Dorotny Jean Lincoln, Nov. 1, 1943 (div. July 1961). Student, Grinnell Coll., 1940-41, Am. U., 1942-43. Art salesperson Leo Block Studio, Chgo., 1947-48; art editor Sears Roebuck, Chgo., 1948-51; salesperson Internat. Mineral and Chemical, Chgo., 1951-62. Author: (book) Charlie, 1976. Pres. Northgate Terrace Sr. Ctr., Oakland, Calif., 1987—. With USN, 1942-47. Mem. DPOE. Republican. Avocations: golf, touring, flying. Office: Northgate Terr Residents Assn 550 24th St Oakland CA 94612-1757

MAROON, MICKEY, clinical social worker; b. Flint, Mich., July 20, 1948; d. Harold Clifford and Dorothy Ruth (Fuller) McDaniel; m. Michael Martin Maroon, Aug. 22, 1970. BA, Bradley U., 1970; MSW, Denver U., 1975. Lic. clin. social worker, Colo.; bd. cert. diplomate. Social worker Ill. Dept. Children and Family Svcs., Peoria, Ill., 1970-73; clin. social worker Adams County Social Svcs., Westminster, Colo., 1975-77, Bethesda Hosp., Denver, 1977-84; pvt. practice Denver, 1979—; clin. cons. Human Svcs., Inc., Denver, 1988-91; vol. faculty Health Sci. Ctr. U. Colo., Denver, 1987—; chair attending social work staff West Pines Hosp., Wheat Ridge, Colo., 1988-89. Recipient Clin. Faculty award U. Colo. Health Scis. Ctr. Dept. Psychiatry, 199, Pacesetter award Nat. Assn. Soc. Workers, 1998. Mem. NASW (pres. Colo. chpt. 1994-96, chair clin. social work com. 1996, Social Worker of Yr. Colo. chpt. 1997, interim exec. dir. 1997—), Colo. Soc. Clin. Social Work (Denver chpt. pres. 1992, state pres. 1993, Cmty. Svc. award 1996).

MARQUAND, BARBARA K., freelance writer; b. Denver, May 13, 1962; d. Kenneth Earl and Betty H. (Farley) M.; m. John Marvin Seelmeyer, May 19, 1990; 1 child, Sara Day Seelmeyer. BA, Colo. State U., Ft. Collins, 1984. Reporter The Sentinel Newspapers, Arvada, Lakewood, Wheat Ridge, Colo., 1984-87, The Greeley (Colo.) Tribune, 1987-89; contbg. editor Chico (Calif.) News and Rev., 1990-92; freelance writer, Grass Valley, Calif., 1992—. Contbr. articles to regional and nat. trade and consumer mags. Vol. tutor Hennessy Sch., Grass Valley, 1992, The Friendship Club, Nevada County Schs., Grass Valley, 1997-98; vol. crisis counselor Catalyst, Chico, 1991. Recipient 2d place award feature writing Calif. Newspaper Pubs. Assn., 1991, 1st place series awrd Colo. Assoc. Editors and Reporters, 1987, numerous others. Mem. LWV (sec. Western Nevada County 1996), Sierra Trailblazers (sec. 1998—), The Women's Group. Episcopalian. Avocations: running, reading, camping, hiking, painting.

MARQUESS, LAWRENCE WADE, lawyer; b. Bloomington, Ind., Mar. 2, 1950; s. Earl Lawrence and Mary Louise (Coberly) M.; m. Barbara Ann Bailey, June 17, 1978; children: Alexander Lawrence, Michael Wade. BSEE, Purdue U., 1973; JD, W.Va. U., 1977. Bar: W.Va. 1977, Tex. 1977, U.S. Dist. Ct. (so. dist.) Tex. 1977, Colo. 1980, U.S. Dist. Ct. Colo. 1980, U.S. Ct. Appeals (10th cir.) 1980, U.S. Supreme Ct. 1984, U.S. Dist. Ct. (no. dist.) Ohio 1988, U.S. Ct. Appeals (DC cir.) 1997. Assoc. Johnson, Bromberg, Leeds & Riggs, Dallas, 1977-79, Bradley, Campbell & Carney, Golden, Colo., 1979-82; ptnr. Bradley, Campbell & Carney, Golden, 1983-84; assoc. Stettner, Miller & Cohn P.C., Denver, 1984-85; ptnr. Stettner, Miller & Cohn P.C., 1985-87, Nelson & Harding, Denver, 1987-88, Heron, Burchette, Ruckert & Rothwell, 1989-90, Harding & Ogborn, 1990-94, Otten, Johnson, Robinson, Neff & Ragonetti, Denver, 1994—; mem. faculty Am. Law Inst. - ABA Advanced Labor and Employment Law Course, 1986, 87. Mem. ABA (labor, antitrust and litigation sects.), ACLU, Colo. Bar Assn. (co-chmn. labor law com. 1989-92), Denver Bar Assn., 1st Jud. Dist. Bar Assn., Sierra Club, Nat. Ry. Hist. Soc. Democrat. Methodist. Home: 11883 W 27th Dr Lakewood CO 80215-7000 Office: Otten Johnson Robinson Neff & Ragonetti 950 17th St Ste 1600 Denver CO 80202-2828

MARQUEZ, MARTINA ZENAIDA, retired elementary education educator; b. Santa Rosa, N.Mex., Nov. 5, 1935; d. Jose Zenon and Adelina (Romero) Sanchez; m. George J. Marquez, June 17, 1972. Student, Mt. St. Scholastica Coll., 1954-56, Regis Coll., 1956-59; BA, Coll. Santa Fe, 1963; MA, U. N.Mex., 1968. Cert. tchr., N.Mex. Elem. tchr. St. Rose Lima Sch., Santa Rosa, 1959-67, Cristo Rey Sch., Santa Fe, 1967-68, Los Lunas (N. Mex.) Consol. Schs., 1975-78, head tchr. adults operation; SER Manpower Devel. Tng. Act, Albuquerque, 1968-71, 73-75; tchr., cons. Regional Resource Ctr., N.Mex. State U., Las Cruces, 1971-72; counselor, coord. Taos (N.Mex.) Career Edn. Program, 1972-73; chpt. I reading tchr. Grants (N.Mex.) & Cibola County Schs., 1978-97; chmn. ethics com. Profl. Standards Commn., N.Mex. Dept. Edn., 1986-88. Dir. choir St. Vivian's Ch., Milan, N.Mex., 1978—; del. Dem. Women's Club, Grants, N.Mex., 1981—; v.p. Literacy Vols. Am. of Cibola County. Named 1991 Cibola County Woman of Achievement 3d Ann. Women's Resource Conf., N.Mex. Tchr. of Yr., 1996; recipient Nat. Educator award Milken Family Found., 1996. Mem. AAUW (bylaws chmn. 1984, Grants Woman of Yr. award 1988), Internat. Reading Assn. (1st v.p. Malpais coun. 1988-89, pres. 1989-90, state pres. 1992-93, dist. 3 facilitator, Local Literacy award 1986, State Literacy award 1987, state pres. N.Mex. 1992-93, N.Mex. State coord. 1997), Delta Kappa Gamma (pres. Psi chpt. 1986-88). Democrat. Roman Catholic. Home: PO Box 11 Bluewater NM 87005-0011

MARRA, JULIE MITCHELL, project administrator, editor; b. Bridgeport, Conn., Sept. 18, 1966; d. Andrew John and Judith Ann Mitchell; m. Stephen Andrew Marra, May 20, 1995. BA, L.I. U., 1988. Asst. editor C.R. Gibson Co., Norwalk, Conn., 1988-90, editor, 1990-94, editl. mgrt., 1994-95; editor, project mgr. Ellison Media Co., Phoenix, 1995—. Home: 13540 E Bayview Dr Scottsdale AZ 85259-5424

MARRIES, DANNY DON, news anchor, reporter; b. Anchorage, Mar. 21, 1972; s. Kurtis Edwin and Julia Frances (Benneti) M.; m. Stephanie Anne Sommerville, July 23, 1976; 1 child, Kurtis Robert. BA in Mass Comm., Mesa State Coll., 1996. News anchor, reporter, weather anchor KREX-TV, Grand Junction, Colo., 1993-96; news anchor, reporter, prodr. KEYC-TV, Mankato, Minn., 1996-97; news anchor, reporter, editl. prodr. KYMA-TV, Yuma, Ariz., 1997—. Sponsorship chmn. United Way Yuma County, 1998; team capt. KYMA-TV, March of Dimes-Walk Am., Yuma, 1998. Recipeint 1st place enterprise news AP, 1997, 1st place best newscast KYMA-TV, AP, 1997. Mem. Order of DeMolay (life, past master councilor 1990—). Avocations: coin collecting, water and snow skiing, PADI certified rescue diver. Office: KYMA-TV 1385 S Pacific Ave Yuma AZ 85365-1725

MARRINGTON, BERNARD HARVEY, retired automotive company executive; b. Vancouver, B.C., Can., Nov. 9, 1928; s. Fredrick George and Constance Marie (hall) M.; m. Patricia Grace Hall, Sept. 3, 1953 (div. 1993); children: Jodie Lynn, Stacey Lee. Student, U. Pitts., 1982, Bethany Coll., W.Va., 1983; BS in Mktg. Mgmt., Pacific Western U., 1985. V.p., sales mgr. W & L of La Mesa, Calif., 1960-66; pres., gen. mgr. W & L of La Mesa, 1966-68; regional mgr. PPG Industries, Inc., L.A., 1977-88, regional mgr. profit ctr., 1988-91; cons. L.A. Unified Sch. Dist., 1972, South Coast Air Quality Mgmt. Dist., El Monte, Calif., 1987-91; adv. com. So. Calif. Regional Occupational Ctr., Torrance, 1978-91; mem. Ford Arbitration bd. U. Wis., 1997-99. Contbr. articles to profl. jours. Sustaining sponsor Ronald Reagan Presdl. Found., Simi, 1987—; sustaining mem. Rep. Nat. Com., L.A., 1985-92, Rep. Presdl. Legion of Merit, 1986-99; del. Rep. Platform Planning com., L.A., 1992; charter mem. Nat. Tax Limitation Com., Washington, 1988, Jarvis Gann Taxpayers Assn., L.A., 1979-99; sponsor Reagan Presdl. Libr., 1986; mem. Ford Arbitration Bd., U. Wis., 1997-99. Recipient Award for Outstanding Community Support, So. Calif. Regional Occupational Ctr., 1986. Episcopalian. Avocations: rose gardening, circus culture, golf, sailing, classical music.

MARROQUIN, ART, reporter; b. West Covina, Calif., Sept. 7, 1974; s. Theresa Ann Marroquin. BA, Calif. State U., Fullerton, 1998. Reporter Inland Valley Daily Bull., Ontario, Calif., 1995-97; corr. San Gabriel Valley Tribune, West Covina, spring 1997; intern San Jose (Calif.) Mercury News, summer 1997; reporter Orange County Register, Anaheim, Calif., 1997-98; intern Oregonian, Portland, summer 1998; reporter L.A. Times, 1998—. Historian Ind. Latino Student Assn., Fullerton, 1996-97, chair pub. rels., 1997-98. Chips Quinn scholar Freedom Forum, Washington, 1997. Mem. Nat. Assn. Hispanic Journalists, Calif. Chicano News Media Assn. (Joel Garcia scholar 1996, 97).

MARROQUIN, PATRICIA, newspaper editor; b. West Covina, Calif., Feb. 1, 1957; d. Humberto Sr. and Josephine (Aragon) M. BS, Calif. State Poly. U., 1980; MA, Stanford U., 1981. Typist San Gabriel Valley Daily Tribune, West Covina, 1974-79; newsletter editor East San Gabriel Valley Consortium, West Covina, 1979-80; copy editing intern The Wall St. Jour., N.Y.C., 1980; copy editor San Jose (Calif.) Mercury News, 1981-86; mng. editor Micro Market World, Menlo Park, Calif., 1987; copy editor L.A. Times, Costa Mesa, Calif., 1987-92; asst. slot editor L.A. Times, Costa Mesa, 1992-93; slot editor L.A. Times, Costa Mesa, Calif., 1993-94, suburban asst. copy chief, 1994-95, slot editor, 1995, business copy editor, news editor, 1996—; co-founder, So. Calif. writer/editor Perspectiva, The Hispanic Newspaper of Record, 1988; fellow Inst. Journalism Edn.'s Mgmt. Tng. Ctr., Northwestern U., Evanston, 1990. Named Journalist of Yr., Soc. Profl. Journalists, 1979-80. Founding mem. Am. Copy Editors; Mem. Nat. Assn. Hispanic Journalists, Calif. Chicano News Media Assn., Orange County Press Club, Society (ACES). Avocations: jogging, photography, computers, web page bldg. Office: LA Times Times Mirror Sq Los Angeles CA 90053

MARROW, DEBORAH, foundation executive, art historian; b. N.Y.C., Oct. 18, 1948; d. Seymour Arthur and Adele (Wolin) M.; m. Michael J. McGuire, June 19, 1971; children: David Marrow McGuire, Anna Marrow McGuire. BA cum laude, U. Pa., 1970, PhD, 1978; MA, Johns Hopkins U., 1972. Resch. asst. Phila. Mus. of Art, 1974-75; mng. editor Chrysalis Mag., L.A., 1978-80; asst. prof. Occidental Coll., L.A., 1979, 81-82; publs. coord. The J. Paul Getty Trust, L.A., 1983-84; program officer The Getty Grant Program, L.A., 1984-86, asst. dir., 1987-89, dir., 1989-99; interim dir. The Getty Res. Inst., 1999—; mem. internat. com. Coun. on Founds., Washington, 1992-96; mem. internat. adv. Group Nat. Endowment for the Arts, 1992; mem. adv. com. Calif. Cmty. Found., L.A., 1991—; mem. Excellence and Equity task force Am. Assn. of Mus., Washington, 1989-91. Author: The Art Patronage of Maria de Medici, 1982; contbr. articles to profl. jours. Chair cultural diversity com. The J. Paul Getty Trust, L.A., 1995—; mem. Save Am.'s com., Nat. Trust for Historic Preservation in partnership with White Ho. Millenium Coun. Samuel H. Kress Found. fellow, N.Y.C., 1975-77. Mem. Coll. Art Assn. of Am., So. Calif. Assn. for Philanthropy (program com., 1988-89, 97), Grantmakers in the Arts, Art Table, Internat. Coun. of Mus., Penn Women (trustee coun.). Office: The Getty Rsch Inst 1200 Getty Center Dr Ste 800 Los Angeles CA 90049-1685

MARROW, MARVA JAN, photographer, writer, video and multimedia producer, web designer, publisher; b. Denver, Apr. 22, 1948; d. Sydney and Helen Berniece (Garber) M. Student, Carnegie-Mellon U., 1965-67. Singer, songwriter RCA Records, Italy, 1972-77; pvt. practice photography Italy and U.S., 1976—; dir. acquisitions RAI TV, L.A., 1990-91; mng. agt. Thomas Angel Prodns., L.A., 1991-94; represented by Shooting Star Photo Agy., Agenzia Marka, Agenzia Masi, Italy, Unipboto Press Internat., Japan; corr., photographer Italian TV Guide, Milan, 1979-97; collaborator, photographer for other U.S. and European publs., radio and TV; TV news and documentary prodr. RAI TV, 1990—. Composer numerous songs for Italian pop artists, including Lucio Battisti, Battiato, Premiata Forneria Marconi (PFM), Patty Pravo, 1972—; author: (photobook) Inside the L.A. Artist, 1988; project dir. (CD-ROM) Digital Art Mus., 1994—; prodr. (CD-ROM) The Kat's Meow, 1996, The Top Dog, 1996, The World of Makeup, 1996; prodr., designer, publ.: (on-line mag.) allpets.com, 1996—; designer Bev's Beautyrama for Am. online; contbr. photographs for covers and articles to nat. and internat. mags. Mem. Motion Picture Assn. of Am., Fgn. Press Assn. Democrat. Avocations: cooking, travel, art, breeding and showing pedigreed cats. Home and Studio: 2080 N Garfield Ave Altadena CA 91001-2959 Office: Ayzenberg Group 39 E Walnut St Pasadena CA 91103-3832

MARRS, LINDA DIANE, manufacturing executive; b. Portland, Oreg., May 4, 1964; d. David Gilbert and Diane (Sause) A. BA in Econs., U. Wash., 1991. Office mgr. Hawaii Wood Preserving Co., Kahului, 1984-85, v.p., 1987-94, pres., 1994—; with inventory control dept. Monarch Bldg. Supply, Kahului, 1986-87. Adminstrv. asst. I Have A Dream Program, Kahului, 1990-91; mem. area com. Spl. Olympics Maui County, 1993—; unified softball coach Spl. Olympics, 1994. Mem. Am. Wood Preservers Assn., Maui Contrs. Women's Aux. (pres. 1996—), Chi Omega (pres. Phi chpt. 1985). Republican. Mem. Christian Ch. Avocations: reading, skiing, golfing, spectator sports. Home: 125 Akea Pl Kula HI 96790-9526 Office: Hawaii Wood Preserving Co 356 Hanakai St Kahului HI 96732-2407

MARSDEN, GUY TALBOT, light sculptor, electronics engineer, products design consultant; b. Boston, May 19, 1955; s. Peter Bernard and Jo Mary

(Horry) M. BFA, Md. Inst. Coll. Art, 1976. Display engr. Md. Sci. Ctr., Balt., 1977-79; pvt. practice spl. effects tech., various films L.A., 1979-85; proprietor Art Tec, engring. for the artists, L.A., 1985—; light sculptor, 1986—. Prin. works include electronic-kinetic shows Mus. Neon Art, L.A., 1985, 87, 88, 89, 90, 91, Am. Light Art, Tokyo, 1989; one man show, 1989. Avocation: windsurfing.

MARSH, DONALD PETE, hospital chaplain; b. Redfield, S.D., Dec. 9, 1951; s. Vernon Glen Marsh and Esther Virgina (Bramble) Parrish; m. Vickie Lynn Schwersinske, Dec. 17, 1978; children: Rebecca, Amy. BA magna cum laude, Columbia Union Coll., 1974; MDiv, Andrews U., 1979; postgrad., Fuller Theol. Sem., 1992—. Pastor Mich. Conf. Seventh-Day Adventists, Lansing, 1978-84, Chesapeake Conf. Seventh-Day Adventists, Gambrills, Md., 1985-89; chaplain resident Holy Cross Hosp., Silver Spring, Md., 1989-90; dir. pastoral care Avista Adventist Hosp., Louisville, Colo., 1990—; chmn. ethics com. Avista Hosp., Louisville, 1992—; mem. task force Centura Health Spiritual Documentation, 1996—, Colo. Coalition for Healthcare Decisions, Denver, 1994-96, steering com. Centura Health Living Beyond Illness, 1997—. Mem. Assn. Profl. Chaplains, Colo. Soc. Patient Reps., Seventh-Day Adventists Healthcare Chaplains Assn. (treas. 1995—), Kiwanis. Avocations: music, bicycling, photography. Office: Avista Adventist Hosp 100 Health Park Dr Louisville CO 80027

MARSH, JOHN HARRISON, environmental planner, lawyer; b. Auburn, Wash., June 25, 1954; s. F. A. Buzz and Margery Ann (Greene) M.; m. Debra Rose Raniere, June 18, 1977; children: Jenna Rose, Christian John. BS in Fisheries Scis., Oreg. State U., 1977; JD, Lewis & Clark Coll., 1985, cert. natural resources and environ. law, 1985. Bar: Oreg. 1986. Rsch. asst. EPA, Corvallis, Oreg., 1975-77; fisheries biologist Nat. Marine Fisheries Svc., Portland, Oreg., 1977-78, Oreg. Dept. Fish and Wildlife, Astoria, 1978; pub. info. officer, enhancement coord. Columbia River Inter-Tribal Fish Commn., Portland, 1978-79, fisheries ecologist, 1979-85; system planning coord. N.W. Power Planning Coun., Portland, 1985-96, mgr. habitat and prodn., 1996—, coor. Enhancement Act; instr. sci. and tech. of watershed mgmt. Portland State U., 1997; speaker, expert witness in field; guest lectr. Lewis and Clark Coll., 1984, 95, Portland State U., 1995, 96, 98; field leader streamkeeper program Oreg. Trout, 1997, 98. Contbr. articles to profl. publs. Organizer food drive Friends of Seasonal Workers, 1987; chair ann. NPPC food drive Sunshine Divsn., 1987—; bd. dirs. Panavista Park Homeowners Assn., 1991-93, mem. archtl. rev. com., 1990—, chair, 1991—; Riverwest Ch. lead Sunday sch. instr. grades 5-6, 1992-96, adult Bible study instr., 1995—, Kinship leader, 1994-98, Mex. Youth Mission team, 1994, 95, libr. coord., 1995—; asst. scoutmaster Boy Scouts Am., 1972-73; mem. steering com. Sharing Columbia: Partnerships for Action, 1989. Mem. Am. Fisheries Soc. (cert. profl. fisheries scientist, exec. com. Portland chpt. 1981-84, v.p. 1981-82, pres. 1982-83, chair legis. com. Oreg. chpt. 1988-89, program com. 1980-81, riparian com. Western div. 1982-83, convenor various sessions, mem. native peoples fisheries com. 1982-88, chair 1984-86, resolutions com. 1985-86, strategic plan devel com., 1993-95, other coms.), Oreg. State Bar Assn., Native Am. Fish and Wildlife Assn., Oreg. Wine Brotherhood (chair Benefit Auction and Barrel Tasting 1995), Great Lovers of Wine Soc. Oreg. (pres. 1988). Avocations: fishing, hunting, wine, cooking. Office: NW Power Planning Coun 851 SW 6th Ave Ste 1100 Portland OR 97204-1387

MARSH, KATHERINE CYNTHIA, writer, journalist, poet; b. Salem, Oreg., Apr. 23, 1956; d. Emanuel Louis and Mary Elizabeth (Dooper) M. Student, Chemeketa C.C., Salem, 1976, 86, U. Oreg., 1977-78; AA, Linn-Benton C.C., Albany, Oreg., 1986. Freelance writer Salem, 1976-77, 85-86; freelance corr. The Oreg. Herald, Albany, 1979; reporter The Willamette Valley Examiner, Salem, 1984-85, The Commuter, Albany, 1985-86; corr. Sr. News, Salem, 1988-90, Keizer(Oreg.)/South Salem Times, 1989-90; freelancer, corr. The West Side, Salem, 1989-90; reviewer bus. publs.; collaborator various books, 1994—. Contbr. essays, poetry to jours., revs., series In Touch Mag., 1998. Recipient Poetry award Nashville Newsletter, 1979, 81, Soc. Am. Poets, 1994; listed in Poets and Writers, 1997. Mem. Poets Guild, Internat. Women's Writing Guild. Office: PO Box 613 Salem OR 97308-0613

MARSH, MALCOLM F., federal judge; b. Portland, Oreg., Sept. 24, 1928; m. Shari Marsh. BS, U. Oreg., 1952, LLB, 1954, JD, 1971. Bar: Oreg. 1954, U.S. Dist. Ct. Oreg. 1955, U.S. Ct. Appeals (9th cir.) 1968. Ptnr. Clark & Marsh, Lindauer & McClinton (and predecessors), Salem, Oreg., 1954-87; judge U.S. Dist. Ct. Oreg., Portland, 1987—. With U.S. Army, 1946-47. Fellow Am. Coll. Trial Lawyers; mem. ABA, Oreg. Bar Assn. Office: US Dist Ct 1507 US Courthouse 1000 SW 3d Ave Portland OR 97204*

MARSH, MARY ELIZABETH TAYLOR, recreation administrator, dietitian, nutritionist; b. Medina, N.Y., Dec. 10, 1933; d. Glenn Aaron and Viola Hazel (Lansill) Grimes; m. Wilbur Alvin Fredlund, Apr. 12, 1952 (div. Jan. 1980); 1 child, Wilbur Jr.; m. Frederick Herbert Taylor, Mar. 15, 1981 (dec. Dec. 1996); children: Martha Dayton, Jean Grout, Beth Stern, Cindy Hey, Carol McLellan, Cheryl Dearborn, Robert Marsh, Marilyn Dobbs, Janice Russell, Gordon Marsh, Margaret Hana; m. Earl R. Marsh, Apr. 4, 1998. BS in Food and Nutrition, SUCB, Buffalo, 1973; MEd in Health Sci. Edn. and Evaluation, SUNY, 1978. Registered dietitian, 1977. Diet cook Niagara Sanitorium, Lockport, N.Y., 1953-56; cook Mount View Hosp., Lockport, N.Y., 1956-60, asst. dietitian, 1960-73, dietitian, food svc. dir., 1973-79, cons. dietitian, 1979-81; instr. Erie Community Coll., Williamsville, N.Y., 1979-81; sch. lunch coord. Nye County Sch. Dist., Tonopah, Nev., 1982-93; retired Nye County Sch. Dist., 1993; food svc. mgmt. cons., fin. mgmt. advisor pvt. practice, 1994—; activity dir. Preferred Equitity Corp. Recreation Vehicle Resort, Pahrump, Nev., 1993-95; tchr. maturing body and nutrition Nev. Cmty. Coll., Pahrump, Fall 1997; nutritionist Equal Opportunity Bd. Clark County, Las Vegas, 1997—; cons. dietitian Nye Gen. Hosp., Tonopah, 1983-88; adj. instr. Erie C.C., Williamsville, 1978-79, So. Nev. C.C., 1997; nutrition instr. for coop. extension Clark County C.C., 1990—; cons. Group Purchasing Network N.Y. Hosp. Administr., Buffalo, 1975-79, vice-chmn. adv. com., 1976-78; cons. BOCES, Lockport, 1979-81. Nutrition counselor Migrant Workers Clinic, Lockports, 1974-80; mem. Western N.Y. Soc. for Hosp. Food Svc. Adminstrn., 1974-81; nutritionist Niagara County Nutrition Adv. Com., 1977-81; mem. Helping Hands, Pahrump, 1997—; nutritionist Equal Opportunity Bd. Clark County, 1997. Recipient Outstanding Woman of the Yr., YWCA-UAW Lockport, 1981, Disting. Health Care Food Adminstrn. Recognition award Am. Soc. for Hosp. Food Svc. Adminstrs., 1979, USDA award Outstanding Lunch Program in Nev. and Western Region, 1986, 91. Mem. Am. Assn. Ret. Persons, Am. Sch. Food Svc. Assn. (bd. dirs. 1987, 92-93, cert. dir. II 1987, 5-yr. planning com. 1990, mem. ann. confs. 1988), Am. Dietetic Assn. (nat. referral system for registered dietitians 1992-93), So. Nev. Dietetic Assn. (pres. 1985-86), Nev. Food Svc. Assn. (participant ann. meetings 1990-93), Nutrition Today Soc., Nev. Sch. Food Svcs. Assn. (dietary guidelines com. 1991-93), Pahrump Kawians. Republican. Lutheran. Avocations: travel, knitting, crocheting, sewing. Home: 481 N Murphy St Pahrump NV 89048-3851

MARSH, MARY VIRGINIA, artist; b. Portland, Oreg., Sept. 5, 1956; d. William Elliot and Virginia Brown (Simpson) M.; m. Tony Victor Bellaver, Sept. 2, 1994. BFA, Acad. Art Coll., San Francisco, 1985; MA, San Francisco Art Inst., 1992. Exhbns. include San Francisco Art Inst., 1991, San Francisco Arts Commn., 1992, Smith Gallery, Santa Cruz, Calif., 1998, San Jose Mus. Art, 1998. Studio: Pier 70 The Noonan Bldg San Francisco CA 94107

MARSH, PAUL NORTON, non-profit executive; b. Shreveport, La., Mar. 18, 1969; s. Thad Norton and Patricia Anne (Cunningham) M.; m. Rebecca Anne Wells, Aug. 1, 1992. 1 child, Connor Levi. BA in Polit. Sci., Tex. Luth. U., 1992. Cmty. svc. coord. Seguin (Tex.) Housing Authority, 1992-93; exec. dir. Seguin Activity Ctr. 1993-94; dir. of devel. Tex. Luth. U. Seguin, 1994-97; dir. devel. Rainbow Trail Luth. Camp, Colorado Springs, 1997— . Firefighter, v.p. Seguin Vol. Fire Dept., 1993-97. Mem. Assn. of Luth. Devel. Execs. Lutheran. Avocation: backpacking. Office: Rainbow Trail Luth Camp 1901 N Union Blvd Ste 215 Colorado Springs CO 80909-1101

MARSH, STEPHEN SEABROOKE, writer, journalist; b. Cin.; s. Charles Seabrooke and Margery I.; m. Christine Louise Reed, June 29, 1990. BA, U. Denver, 1974. Freelance writer Atlanta Constn., 1979-81, Atlanta Mag., 1979-81; staff writer Up the Creek Weekly, Denver, 1982-84, Rocky Mountain Bus. Jour., Denver, 1984-86, Denver Bus. Jour., 1986-88; corr. Money Mag., N.Y.C., 1986-98; spl. corr. Life Mag., N.Y.C., 1988-93; media cons. Russell Karsh & Hagen, 1989-91, others; guest lectr. Jefferson County Pub. Schs., 1991-92, Colo. State U., 1992. Author: Retaliation, 1981, Palace of the Puzzle Kings, 1997, DRAK-18, 1998; co-author (screenplay) Boulder Beings, 1990. Recipient Best Story of Yr. award Colo. Press Assn., 1985, Investigative Reporting award Soc. Profl. Journalists, 1985, Spot News Reporting award, 1985, Fountainhead Media award Soc. Mktg. Profl. Svcs., 1987. Mem. Denver Bd. Realtors. Avocations: music, photography, hiking, fly fishing, skiing.

MARSHAK, HARRY, physician, plastic surgeon; b. L.A., Oct. 1, 1961; s. Herbert and Pearl (Engelson) M. BS, U. Calif., Riverside, 1981; MD, UCLA, 1984. Diplomate Am. Bd. Surgery, Am. Bd. Plastic Surgery. Pvt. practice Beverly Hills, Calif., 1991—. Fellow ACS (hon.), Internat. Coll. Surgeons; mem. Am. Soc. Plastic and Reconstructive Surgeons, Calif. Soc. Plastic Surgery. Republican. Avocations: sports. Office: 120 S Spalding Dr Ste 300 Beverly Hills CA 90212-1800

MARSHALL, ARTHUR K., lawyer, judge, arbitrator, educator, writer; b. N.Y.C., Oct. 7, 1911. BS, CUNY, 1933; LLB, St. John's U., N.Y.C., 1936; LL.M., So. Calif. U., 1952. Bar: N.Y. State 1937, Calif. 1947. Practice law N.Y.C., 1937-43, Los Angeles, 1947-50; atty. VA, Los Angeles, 1947-50; tax counsel Calif. Bd. Equalization, Sacramento, 1950-51; inheritance tax atty. State Controller, Los Angeles, 1951-53; commr. Superior Ct. Los Angeles County, 1953-62; judge Municipal Ct., Los Angeles jud. dist., 1962-63, Superior Ct., Los Angeles, 1963-81; supervising judge probate dept. Superior Ct., 1968-69, appellate dept., 1973-77; presiding judge Appellate Dept., 1976-77; pvt. practice arbitrator, mediator, judge pro tem, 1981—; acting asst. prof. law UCLA, 1954-59; grad. faculty U. So. Calif., 1955-75; lectr. Continuing Edn. of the Bar; mem. Calif. Law Revision Commn., 1984—, chmn., 1986-87, 92-93, 98-99, vice chmn. 1983, 85, 98; chmn. com. on efficiency and econs. Conf. Calif. Judges, past chmn. spl. action com. on ct. improvement; past chmn. probate law cons. group Calif. Bd. Legal Specialization. Author: Joint Tenancy Taxwise and Otherwise, 1953, Branch Courts, 1959, California State and Local Taxation Text, 2 vols., 1962, rev. edit., 1969, supplement, 1979, 2d edito., 1981, Triple Choice Method, 1964, California State and Local Taxation Forms, 2 vols., 1961-75, rev. edit., 1996, California Probate Procedure, 1961, 5th rev. edit., 1994, Guide to Procedure Before Trial, 1975; contbr. articles to profl. jours. Mem. Town Hall. With AUS, 1943-46; lt. col. JAGC, USAR ret. Named Judge of Yr. Lawyers Club L.A. County, 1975; first recipient Arthur K. Marshall award established by estate planning, trust and probate sect. L.A. Bar Assn., 1981, Disting. Jud. Career award L.A. Lawyers Club, award L.A. County Bd. Suprs., 1981. Fellow Am. Bar Found.; mem. ABA (probate litigation com. real property, probate and trust sect.), Am. Arbitration Assn. (mem. nat. panel of arbitrators), Internat. Acad. Estate and Trust Law (academician, founder, 1st pres., now chancellor), Calif. State Bar (advisor to exec. com. real property, probate and trust sect. 1970-83), Santa Monica Bar Assn. (pres. 1960), Westwood Bar Assn. (pres. 1959), L.A. Bar Assn., Am. Legion (comdr. 1971-72), U. So. Calif. Law Alumni Assn. (pres. 1969-70), Phi Alpha Delta (1st justice alumni chpt.). Office: 300 S Grand Ave 28th flr Los Angeles CA 90071-3110

MARSHALL, CAROL SYDNEY, labor market analyst, employment counselor; b. N.Y.C., Nov. 21, 1930; d. Charles Herbert and Tillie (Muriel) Helman; m. Bogdan Branislav Denitch, 1952 (div. 1954); m. Charles Marshall, Oct. 9, 1954 (div. Aug. 1973); children: Katrina, Peter Morgan Helman, Bonnie Sophia Brip, Athena. Student, Antioch Coll., 1948-50, Hunter Coll., 1953-61, U. Mo., 1967-68; AB in Geography & Urban Planning with honors & distinction, San Diego State U., 1971, postgrad., 1972-73. Copy person, cub reporter Chgo. Sun-Times, 1949-50; adminstrv. asst. Hudson Guild Child Care Ctr., N.Y.C., 1951-54; rsch. asst. City of Antioch Planning Dept., Calif., 1971-72; planning aide San Diego County Planning Dept., 1972-73; labor market analyst Labor Market Info. Divsn. Calif. Employment Devel. Dept., San Francisco, 1973-94; employment rep. Job Svc. Calif. Employment Devel. Dept., San Francisco, 1994—; speaker, panelist on labor mkt. issues, 1985-94; labor mkt. rsch. cons. San Francisco Pvt. Industry Coun., 1986-94, San Mateo Pvt. Industry Coun., 1986-91, Alameda County Econ. Devel. Bd., 1991-94; mem. profl. working group Health Occupations Study Nat. Ctr. for Rsch. in Vocat. Edn., Berkeley, Calif., 1989-91; mem. adv. bd. Dept. Health Info. Tech. City Coll. San Francisco, 1992-94. Contbr. articles to profl. jours. Mem. Young Peoples Socialist League, N.Y.C., 1947-54, nat. sec., 1952-53; mem. Young Socialist League, N.Y.C. 1954-62; organizer, co-founder San Diego State U.Child Care Ctr., 1971. Mem. Dem. Socialists of Am. (East Bay exec. com.), Ctr. for Sci. in the Pub. Interest, Pub. Citizens Health Rsch. Group, East Bay Bicycle Coalition, San Francisco Bicycle Coalition, League of Am. Bicyclists. Jewish. Avocations: bicycling, classic rock & roll, photography, theatre. Office: Calif Employment Devel Dept Job Svc 363 Civic Dr Pleasant Hill CA 94523-1920

MARSHALL, CONRAD JOSEPH, entrepreneur; b. Detroit, Dec. 23, 1934; s. Edward Louis Fedak and Maria Magdalena Berzsenyi; m. Dorothy Genieve Karnafil, Dec. 1, 1956 (div. 1963); children: Conrad Joseph Jr., Kevin Conrad, Lisa Marie; m. Beryle Elizabeth Callahan, June 15, 1965 (div. 1972); children: Brent Jasmer, Farah Elizabeth. Diploma, Naval Air Tech. Tng. Ctr., Norman, Okla., 1952; student, Wayne State U., 1956-59; Diploma, L.A. Police Acad., 1961. Dir. mktg. Gulf Devel., Torrance, Calif., 1980-83; sales mgr. Baldwin Piano Co., Santa Monica, Calif., 1977-80; dir. mktg., v.p. Western Hose, Inc., L.A., 1971-76; city letter carrier U.S. Post Office, L.A., 1969-71; writer freelance L.A., 1966—; police officer L.A. Police Dept., 1961-66; asst. sales mgr. Wesson Oil Co., Detroit, 1958-60; agt. Life Ins. Co. of Va., Wayne, Mich., 1956-58; pres. Am. Vision Mktg., L.A., 1990—, Con-Mar Prodns., L.A., 1983—; sr. v.p. Pacific Acquisition Group, 1992—. Invest. Admin. HealthCom, Int., 1993—; pres. Midway TV Co., 1994—; tech. advisor Lion's Gate Films, Westwood, Calif., 1970-74, Medicine Wheel Prodns., Hollywood, Calif., 1965-75; mng. gen. ptnr. Encino Wireless #1, 1994—; CEO Midway TV Inc., 1995; v.p. nat. bus. affairs MMA Internat., 1997; v.p. mktg. Kidkritter, Inc., 1998. Author: (series) "Dial Hot Line", 1967, (screenplay) "Heads Across the Border", 1968, "The Fool Card", 1970, "Probable Cause", 1972; co-author: The Fedak File, 1995; albums include Song Shark, 1992, Conrad Marshall Quintet, 1991. Campaign vol. Dem. Ctrl. Com., L.A., 1976, Rep. Ctrl. Com., 1994. Mem. Screen Actors Guild, Internat. Platform Assn. Avocations: poetry, song writing, club singing, philosophy, theology. Home: 11853 Kling St Valley Vlg CA 91607-4073 Office: Con-Mar Prodns 2026 Holly Hill Ter Hollywood CA 90068-3812

MARSHALL, CONSUELO BLAND, federal judge; b. Knoxville, Tenn., Sept. 28, 1936; d. Clyde Theodore and Annie (Brown) Arnold; m. George Edward Marshall, Aug. 30, 1959; children: Michael Edward, Laurie Ann. AA, L.A. City Coll., 1956; BA, Howard U., 1958, LLB, 1961. Bar: Calif. 1962. Dep. atty. City of L.A., 1962-67; assoc. Cochran & Atkins, L.A., 1968-70; commr. L.A. Superior Ct., 1971-76; judge Inglewood Mcpl. Ct., 1976-77, L.A. Superior Ct., 1977-80, U.S. Dist. Ct. Central Dist. Calif., L.A., 1980—; lectr. U.S. Information Agy. in Yugoslavia, Greece and Italy, 1984, in Nigera and Ghana, 1991, in Ghana, 1992. Contbr. articles to profl. jours.; notes editor Law Jour. Howard U. Mem. adv. bd. Richstone Child Abuse Center. Recipient Judicial Excellence award Criminal Cts. Bar Assn., 1992, Ernestine Stalhut award; named Criminal Ct. Judge of Yr., U.S. Dist. Ct., 1997; rsch. fellow Howard U. Law Sch., 1959-60. Mem. State Bar Calif., Century City Bar Assn., Calif. Women Lawyers Assn., Calif. Assn. Black Lawyers, Calif. Judges Assn., Black Women Lawyers Assn., Los Angeles County Bar Assn., Nat. Assn. Women Judges, NAACP, Urban League, Beta Phi Sigma. Office: US Dist Ct 312 N Spring St Ste 243-p Los Angeles CA 90012-4701

MARSHALL, DONALD THOMAS, medical technologist; b. Omaha, June 0, 1951; s. William A. and Alma J. (Jorgensen) M.; m. Beverly Ann Everett, Sept. 22, 1990. Med. tech., Pikes Peak Inst. Med. Tech., 1977; EMT, Pikes Peak C.C., Colorado Springs, 1979; PhD of Religion, Universal Life Ch., 1995, D of Metaphysics (hon.), 1995. Registered med. technologist; cert. chmn. labor technologist 11 raj and med lab recristian bit donoph i happ in Plains, Cheyenne Wells, Colo., 1977-79; med. lab. technician Conejos County Hosp., La Jara, Colo., 1979-84; med. technologist Nat. Health Lab., Englewood, Colo., 1984-91; lab. tech. cons., quality assurance officer Cmty. Health Svcs. Denver Health, Denver, 1996—, med. technologist, 1996—. EMT, fireman La Jara Vol. Fire Dept., 1979-84, Meritorious Svc. Citation, 1983. Mem. Am. Med. Technologists, Masons (worshipful master 1994). Republican.

MARSHALL, JAMES KENNETH, academic administrator; b. Providence, Dec. 25, 1952; s. James William and Eileen Frances (O'Connell) M.; m. Mary H. Jackson, Mar. 17, 1987. BA in Chemistry, SUNY, Plattsburgh, 1974; MBA in Fin., U. R.I., 1977; postgrad., U. Wash., 1978-79. Fin. instr. U. R.I., Kingston, 1978; teaching assoc. U. Wash., Seattle, 1978-79; asst. dir. facilities mgmt. U. Colo., Boulder, 1979-86, dir. buying and contracting, 1986-90; transp. mgr. Town of Vail, Colo., 1991-92; v.p. Women at the Wheel Automotive Cons. and Consumer Edn. Svc., Bozeman, Mont., 1990-96; assoc. dir. computing and network svcs. U. Colo., Boulder, 1996-98, dir. IT user support, 1998—; honorarium instr. U. Colo., Denver, 1981-85; bd. dirs. Minority Enterprises, Inc., 1988-90. Contbr. chpt. to book on plant administration. Recipient Job Well Done award U. Colo. Boulder Dept. Facilities Mgmt., 1983. Mem. Beta Gamma Sigma, Phi Kappa Phi. Avocations: skiing, climbing, fishing, golf, cycling. Office: U Colo PO Box 379 Boulder CO 80309-0379

MARSHALL, JOHN PAUL, broadcast technologist; came to U.S., 1967; Degree, U. Grenoble, France, 1963; student, U. Munich, 1964-65, San Francisco State, 1969-71, John O'Connell Tech. Inst., 1973-74. Cert. novell administr., cert. broadcast technologist. Mem. faculty law and econ. scis. U. Grenoble, 1963-64; mem. Expo '67 staff City of Montreal, Que., Can., 1967; filmmaker Cinemalab, San Francisco, 1970; engr. film and TV Able Studios, San Francisco, 1971-73; radio and TV engr. Sta. KALW-FM (Nat. Pub. Radio), San Francisco, 1973-74; broadcast engr. Sta. KRON-TV (NBC), San Francisco, 1974-91; intern Centre d'Informatique et de Maintenance Automatisme, 1993; founder Marshall U.S.A., San Francisco, 1994; freelance broadcast engr. KPIX-TV (CBS), KGO-Radio (ABC), KSFO-Radio (ABC), KPST-TV, San Francisco, 1995—, also Sta. KPST-TV (Home Shopping Network), San Francisco; freelance audio visual tech. advisor, San Francisco area, 1975—, lectr. radio, TV, motion pictures, 1975—, cons. customized electronic effects; tech. advisor, assoc. Broadkast Skills Bank. Translator tech. pubs. and manuals, 1975—. Mus. dir., participant in theater prodns., 1950-59; active Boy Scouts Am. Govt. of France scholar, 1960-63. Mem. Rolls Royce Owners Club Found. (life), Internet Soc., Soc. Broadcast Engrs. (cert. broadcast technologist), Elec. Tech. Assn. Avocations: classical pianist, polyglot, world traveler. Office: 298 4th Ave Ste 419 San Francisco CA 94118-2468

MARSHALL, JUDY K., lay worker; b. L.A., Apr. 19, 1958; d. Gregory and Mary Cal-Ida (Linn) M. Student, Concordia Luth. Coll., 1976, 77, Moorpark Coll., 1977-79, St. Louis U., 1979, 80. Tchr. Sunday sch. Luth. Ch., Thousand Oaks, Calif., 1986-90; co-leader Conejo Valley Luth. Singles, Thousand Oaks, 1987-89; leader Conejo Valley Luth. Singles, Thousand Oaks, Calif., 1989-90; sec. Luth. Ch.-Mo. Synod Singles Ministry, 1989-90; cons. Pacific S.W. Dist. Luth. Ch.-Mo. Synod, Irvine, Calif., 1990—; owner Wine & Roses Catering, Newbury Park, Calif., 1985—; co-dir. Single Retreat, Luth. Ch.-Mo. Synod, Thousand Oaks, 1985-90; sec. ch. coun. Redeemer Luth., Thousand Oaks, 1986-89. Vol. Hospice of Conejo, Thousand Oaks, 1982-83, Big Bros./Big Sisters, Thousand Oaks, 1985, Luth. Social Svcs., Thousand Oaks, 1988-90, Zoe Christian Ctr. for Homeless, 1990. Democrat. Office: Wine & Roses Catering 4265 Greenwood St Newbury Park CA 91320-5230

MARSHALL, L. B., clinical lab scientist; b. Chgo., Feb. 10; s. Gillman and Ethel (Robinson) M.; m. Esther Wood, Sept. 28, 1961; children: Lester B. III, Kiti B., Lelani. AA City Coll. San Francisco, 1957; BS in Podiatric Medicine, U. Puget Sound, 1961; ScD, London Inst., Eng., 1972. Pres., Med. Offices Health Svcs. Group Inc., San Francisco, 1964—. Mem. NAACP. With U.S. Army, 1947-53. Decorated Bronze Star, Med. Combat Badge; recipient Cert. Appreciation Pres. Nixon, 1973, Urban League, 1973, Calif. Dept. Human Resources, 1973. Mem. Am. Calif. Assns. Med. Technologists, Oyster Point Yacht Club, Press Club, Commonwealth Club (San Francisco).

MARSHALL, MARY JONES, civic worker; b. Billings, Mont.; d. Leroy Nathaniel and Janet (Currie) Dailey; m. Harvey Bradley Jones, Nov. 15, 1952 (dec. 1989); children: Dailey, Janet Currie, Ellis Bradley; m. Boyd T. Marshall, June 27, 1990. Student, Carleton Coll., 1943-44, U. Mont., 1944-46, UCLA, 1959. Owner Mary Jones Interiors. Founder, treas. Jr. Art Council, L.A. County Mus., 1953-55, v.p., 1955-56; mem. costume council Pasadena (Calif.) Philharm.; co-founder Art Rental Gallery, 1953, chmn. art and architecture tour, 1955; founding mem., sec. Art Alliance, Pasadena Art Mus., 1955-56; benefit chmn. Pasadena Girls Club, 1959, bd. dirs., 1958-60; chmn. L.A. Tennis Patron's Assn. Benefit, 1965; sustaining Jr. League Pasadena; mem. docent council L.A. County Mus.; mem. costume council L.A. County Mus. Art., program chmn. 20th Century Greatest Designers; mem. blue ribbon com. L.A. Music Ctr.; benefit chmn. Venice com. Internat. Fund for Monuments, 1971; bd. dirs. Art Ctr. 100, Pasadena, 1988—; pres. The Pres.'s L.A. Children's Bur., 1989; co-chmn. benefit Harvard Coll. Scholarship Fund, 1974, steering com. benefit, 1987, Otis Art Inst., 1975, 90th Anniversary of Children's Bureau of L.A., 1994; mem. Harvard-Radcliffe scholarship dinner com., 1985; mem. adv. bd. Estelle Doheny Eye Found., 1976, chmn. benefit, 1980; adv. bd. Loyola U. Sch. Fine Arts, L.A. Art Ctr. Sch. Design, Pasadena, Calif., 1987—; patron chmn. Benefit Achievement Rewards for Coll. Scientists, 1988; chmn. com. Sch. Am. Ballet Benefit, 1988, N.Y.C.; bd. dirs. Founders Music Ctr., L.A., 1977-81; mem. nat. adv. council Sch. Am. Ballet, N.Y.C., nat. co-chmn. gala, 1980; adv. council on fine arts Loyola-Marymount U.; mem. L.A. Olympic Com., 1984, The Colleagues; founding mem. Mus. Contemporary Art, 1986; chmn. The Pres.'s Benefit L.A. Children's Bur., 1990; exec. com. L.A. Alive for L.A. Music Ctr., 1992; mem. exec. com. Children's Bur. of L.A. Found., 1992; chmn. award dinner Phoenix House, 1994, 96; bd. dirs. Andrews Sch. Gerontology, U. So. Calif., 1996—, Leakey Found., 1996—; bd. regents Children's Hosp. L.A., 1996—. Mem. Am. Parkinson Disease Assn. (steering com. 1991), Valley Hunt Club (Pasadena), Calif. Club (L.A.), Kappa Alpha Theta. Home: 10375 Wilshire Blvd Ste 8B Los Angeles CA 90024-4712

MARSHALL, MERYL C(ORINBLIT), television producer, lawyer; b. Los Angeles, Oct. 16, 1949; d. Jack and Nita (Green) Corinblit; BA, UCLA, 1971; JD, Loyola Marymount U., L.A., 1974. Bar: Calif. 1974. Dep. pub. defender County of L.A., 1975-77; sole practice, L.A., 1977-78; ptnr. Markman and Marshall, L.A., 1978-79; sr. atty. NBC, Burbank, Calif., 1979-80, dir. programs, talent contracts bus. affairs, 1980, asst. gen. atty., N.Y.C., 1980-82, v.p., compliance and practices, Burbank, 1982, v.p. program affairs, Group W Prodns., 1987-89, sr. v.p. future images, 1989-91, TV producer, Meryl Marshall Prodns., 1991-93; pres. Two Oceans Entertainment Group, 1991—. Chmn., Nat. Women's Polit. Caucus, Westside, Calif., 1978-80; mem. Calif. Dem. Ctrl. Com., 1978-79; mem. Hollywood Women's Polit. Com., 1988. Mem. Acad. TV Arts and Scis. (treas. 1985, 93-97, bd. govs. 1989—, pres. 1997—), Women in Film. Democrat. Jewish. Home: 4528 Camellia Ave North Hollywood CA 91602-1908 Office: Two Oceans Entertainment Group 15060 Ventura Blvd Ste 400 Sherman Oaks CA 91403-2423

MARSHALL, RICHARD CEDRIC, architect; b. Portland, Oreg., Dec. 21; s. Cedric Edward Marshall and Dena Elizabeth (Forsberg) Betts; m. Kathryn Roeckel, Apr. 12, 1958 (div. Apr. 1988); children: Paul Vik, Rolf Coursen. BS in Forestry, U. Calif. Berkeley, 1941; cert. in physics/meteorology, UCLA, 1943; BA in Architecture, U. Calif. Berkeley, 1950; student, Ecole des Beaux Arts, Paris, 1947-48. Lic. architecture and meteorology, Calif. Acting head dept. architecture U. Calcutta, Howrah, India, 1955-56; faculty mem. U. Calif., Berkeley, 1961-62; ptnr. Marshall, Leefe and Ehrenkrantz, Architects, San Francisco, 1960-63; exec. v.p. Architecture & Associated Professions, San Francisco, 1963-71; architect advisor for Africa UNESCO, Paris, 1970-72; ptnr. Marshall & Bowles, Architects, San Francisco, 1964-74; pvt. practice architecture San Francisco, 1973—; chmn. bd. Marshall/Lee Inc. Architects, San Francisco, 1982—; guest lectr. various universities throughout 1998 a design architect span chm. 1978

80; author: Prototypes for Africa, 1971-72; contbr. articles to profl. jours. Patron mem. CORE, San Francisco, 1978-86; dir. Cmty. Music Ctr., San Francisco, 1975-76; mem. adv. bd. Can. Coll., Redwood City, Calif., 1974-76; dir., chmn., planner Telegraph Hill Dwellers, San Francisco, 1994-97. Capt. USAAF, 1942-46, ETO. Fellow AIA (chmn. sch. facilities local, state, nat. 1965-79, chmn. fellowship com. 1980, 81, 83); mem. Am. Arbitration Assn. (arbitrator 1987—), Telegraph Hill Dwellers Assn. (planning and zoning chmn. 1992—). Democrat. Episcopalian. Avocations: gardening, travel, photography, civic activities. Office: 888 Post St San Francisco CA 94109-6013

MARSHALL, ROBERT HERMAN, economics educator; b. Harrisburg, Pa., Dec. 6, 1929; s. Mathias and Mary (Bubich) M.; m. Billie Marie Sullivan, May 31, 1958; children: Mellisa Frances, Howard Hylton, Robert Charles. A.B. magna cum laude, Franklin and Marshall Coll., 1951; M.A., Ohio State U., 1952, Ph.D., 1957. Teaching asst. Ohio State U., 1952-57; mem. faculty, then prof. econs. U. Ariz., Tucson, 1957-95, prof. emeritus, 1995; dir. Internat. Bus. Studies Project, 1969-71; research observer Sci.-Industry Program, Hughes Aircraft Co., Tucson, summer 1959. Author: Commercial Banking in Arizona: Structure and Performance Since World War II, 1966, (with others) The Monetary Process, 2d edit. 1980. Bd. dirs. Com. for Econ. Opportunity, Tucson, 1968-69. Faculty fellow Pacific Coast Banking Sch., summer 1974. Mem. Am. Econ. Assn., Phi Beta Kappa, Beta Gamma Sigma, Pi Gamma Mu, Phi Kappa Phi, Delta Sigma Pi. Democrat. Roman Catholic. Home: 6700 N Abington Rd Tucson AZ 85743-9795

MARSHALL, ROBERTA NAVARRE, middle school educator; b. Martinez, Calif., Sept. 26, 1949; d. Robert Frank and Navarre (Baggett) M. BS, Calif. Polytech. State U., 1971; MS in voc. edn., Calif. State U., 1981. Cert. secondary educator, Calif. Consumer-homemaking tchr. Hanford (Calif.) H.S., 1972-73, Eagle Mountain (Calif.) H.S., 1974-79, Solano Jr. H.S., Vallejo, Calif., 1980—; co-chairperson applied acads. dept. Solano Jr. H.S., Vallejo; competitive recognition events coord. FHA-HERO Region 3, 1991-95; workshop presenter. Middle grades curriculum task force Calif. Dept. Edn., Sacramento, 1987-88. Recipient home econs. curriculum grants, 1985-86, 89-90; named Tchr. of Yr. Elks Lodge, 1988-89. Mem. Calif. Tchrs. Assn., Home Econs. Tchrs. Assn. Calif. (v.p. 1991-93), Am. Assn. Univ. Women, Am. Voc. Assn., Am. Assn. Family & Consumer Scis., Future Homemakers of Am. (adv. 1972), Home Econs. Related Occupations, Delat Kappa Gamma (Theta Iota chpt.). Avocations: reading, needlework, walking, traveling. Home: 5038 Brittany Dr Suisun City CA 94585-6855 Office: Solano Jr H S 1025 Corcoran Ave Vallejo CA 94589-1844

MARSHALL, SCOTT, advertising agency executive. V.p. Ogilvy & Mather, N.Y.C., sr. v.p., 1986-88; pres. Cole & Weber, Inc., Seattle; now pres. Hal Riney & Ptnrs., Inc., San Francisco. Office: Hal Riney & Ptnrs 2001 Embarcadero San Francisco CA 94133-1534*

MARSHALL, SHARON BOWERS, nursing educator, director clinical trials; b. Alameda, Calif.; d. Stanley Jay and Rosalie Kathryn (Soldati) Bowers; m. Lawrence F. Marshall; children: Derek, Kathryn, Samantha. BS in Nursing, San Francisco State U., 1970. Charge nurse med./surg. unit Mt. Zion Hosp., San Francisco, 1970-73, charge nurse med./surg. ICU, 1973-75; clin. nurse U. Calif. San Diego Med. Ctr., 1975-78, coordinator neurotrauma study, 1978-79, project coordinator Nat. Traumatic Coma Data Bank, 1979-88, project mgr. Comprehensive Cen. Nervous System Injury Ctr., 1979-86, mgr. neurotrauma research, 1984-91; asst. clin. prof. neurol. surg. U. Calif. San Diego Sch. Medicine, 1992—; study dir. Internat. Tirilazad Study, 1991-95; prin. investigator Internat. Selfotel Trial, 1994-96. Author: Head Injury, 1981, Neuroscience Critical Care: Pathophysiology and Patient Management, 1990; contbr. articles to profl. jours. Mem. Internat. Soc. Study of Traumatic Brain Injury, Am. Assn. Neurosci. Nursing. Avocations: skiing, traveling. Office: 4130 La Jolla Village Dr La Jolla CA 92037-9121

MARSHALL, WILLIAM GERALD, English language educator; b. Statesville, N.C., Oct. 19, 1948; s. William E. and Mary (Rowell) M.; m. Debra Ventura (div.). BA, Lenoir-Rhyne Coll., 1970; MA, Appalachian State U., 1972; PhD, SUNY, Binghamton, 1977. Prof. English U. Hawaii, Honolulu, 1977—. Author: The Resotration Mind, 1997, A Great Stage of Fools: Theatricality and Madness in the Plays of William Wycherley, 1993, author articles on Restoration and Eighteenth Century lit. Mem. MLA, Masons. Avocations: walking, symphony. Office: U Hawaii Dept English Honolulu HI 96822

MARSHALL, WILLIAM PATRICK, lawyer, croupier; b. Colorado Springs, Colo., Oct. 2, 1956; s. Jerome Francisand Paula Susan (Brown) M.; m. Susan Lee Bibeau, Dec. 2, 1987; children: Charity Marie, Shannon Rose, Lauren Lee. BA, Calif. State U., Sacramento, 1978; JD, Southland U., 1983. Bar: Calif. 1989. Bacarrat croupier Harrah's Casino Resort, Stateline, Nev., 1983—; pvt. practice South Lake Tahoe, Calif., 1996—; rep. bd. rev. Harrah's Casino Resort, 1994—. Organizer, spokesman Save the Trees Com., Elk Grove, Calif., 1976; legal svcs. rep. Voluntary Action Ctr., South Lake Tahoe, 1989-93; bi-weekly clinic atty. Legal Svcs. of North Calif., South Lake Tahoe, 1993-96. Recipient Nate Blank award Voluntary Action Ctr., 1991. Mem. Legion of Mary (pres. 1994-95, local founder), Confraternity of Mary. Republican. Roman Catholic. Office: Office of Will Marshall 1014 Blue Lake Ave PO Box 13737 South Lake Tahoe CA 96151-3737

MARSTON, MICHAEL, urban economist, asset management executive; b. Oakland, Calif., Dec. 4, 1936; s. Lester Woodbury and Josephine (Janovic) M.; m. Alexandra Lynn Geyer, Apr. 30, 1966; children: John, Elizabeth. BA, U. Calif., Berkeley, 1959; postgrad. London Sch. Econs., 1961-63. V.p. Larry Smith & Co., San Francisco, 1969-72, exec. v.p. urban econ. divsn., 1969-72; chmn. bd. Keyser Marston Assocs., Inc., San Francisco, 1973-87; gen. ptnr. The Sequoia Partnership, 1979-91; pres. Marston Vineyard and Winery, 1982—, Marston Assocs., Inc., 1982—, The Ctr. for Individual and Instnl. Renewal, 1996—. Cert. rev. appraiser Nat. Assn. Rev. Appraisers and Mortgage Underwriters, 1984—. Chmn., San Francisco Waterfront Com., 1969-86; chmn. fin. com., bd. dirs., mem. exec. com., treas. San Francisco Planning and Urban Rsch. Assn., 1976-87, Napa Valley Vintners, 1986—, mem. gov. affairs com.; trustee Cathedral Sch. for Boys, 1981-82, Marin Country Day Sch., 1984-90; v.p. St. Luke's Sch., 1986-91; pres. Presidio Heights Assn. of Neighbors, 1983-84; chmn. Presidio Com. 1991—; v.p., bd. dirs., mem. exec. com. People for Open Space, 1972-87; mem. Gov.'s Issue Analysis Com. and Speakers Bur., 1966; mem. speakers bur. Am. Embassy, London, 1961-63; v.p., bd. dirs. Dem. Forum, 1968-72; v.p., trustee Youth for Service. Served to lt. USNR. Mem. Napa Valley Vintners, Urban Land Inst., World Congress Land Policy (paper in field), Order of Golden Bear, Chevalier du Tastevin, Bohemian Club, Pacific Union Club, Lambda Alpha. Contbr. articles to profl. jours. Home: 3375 Jackson St San Francisco CA 94118-2018

MARTIEN, NORMAN GERALD (JERRY MARTIEN), creative writing and English educator, carpenter; b. Calif., Nov. 29, 1939; s. Norman and Lucille (Montijo) M.; m. Glenda Reeley, July 1960 (div.); children: Philip, Robert; m Jenny Finch, Mar. 1998. Carpenter, 1978—; poet Calif. Poet-In-The-Schs., 1980—; instr. Humboldt State U., Arcata, Calif., 1995—. Author: Shell Game, 1996, (poems) Pieces in Place, 1999; editor Upriver Downriver, 1985-90; contbr. poems and articles to profl. jours. Sec. Resist, St. Louis, 1968-70; founding mem. The Same Old People, Arcata, 1972—; mem. Dunes Adv. Com., Humboldt County, 1991-94; bd. dirs. Planet Drum Found., San Francisco, 1998—. Home and Office: PO Box 1051 Arcata CA 95518

MARTIN, AGNES, artist; b. Maklin, Sask., Can., 1912; came to U.S., 1932, naturalized, 1950; Student, Western Wash. State Coll., 1935-38; BS, Columbia U., 1942, MFA, 1952. One-woman shows include Betty Parsons Gallery, N.Y.C., 1958, 59, 61, Robert Elkon Gallery, N.Y.C., 1961, 63, 72, 76, Nicolas Wilder Gallery, Los Angeles, 1963-66, 67, Visual Arts Ctr., N.Y.C., 1971, Kunstraum, Munich, 1973, Inst. Contemporary Art U. Pa., Phila., 1973, Pace Gallery, N.Y.C., 1975, 76, 77, 78, 79, 80-81, 81, 83, 84, 85, 86, 89, 91, 92, 94, 95, Mayor Gallery, London, 1978, 84, Galerie Rudolf Zwirner, Cologne, Fed. Republic Germany, 1978, Harcus/Krakow Gallery, Boston, 1978, Margo Leavin Gallery, Los Angeles, 1979, 85, Mus. N.Mex., Santa Fe, 1979, Richard Gray Gallery, Chgo., 1981, Garry Anderson Gallery, Sydney, Australia, 1986, Waddington Galleries Ltd., London, 1986, Stedelijk Mus., Amsterdam, 1991, Whitney Mus. Am. Art, N.Y.C., 1992; exhibited in group shows at Carnegie Inst., Pitts., 1961, Whitney Mus. Am. Art, N.Y.C., 1962, 66, 67, 74, 77, 92, Tooth Gallery, London, 1962, Gallery Modern Art, Washington, 1963, Wadsworth Atheneum, Hartford, Conn., 1963, Solomon R. Guggenheim Mus., N.Y.C., 1965, 66, 76, Mead Corp., 1965-67, Mus. Modern Art, N.Y.C., 1967, 76, 85, Inst. Contemporary Art, Phila., 1967, Detroit Inst. Art, 1967, Corcoran Gallery Art, Washington, 1967, 81, Finch Mus., N.Y., 1968, Phila. Mus., 1968, Zurich Art Mus., Switzerland, 1969, Ill. Bell Telephone Co., Chgo., 1970, Mus. Contemporary Art, Chgo., 1971, Inst. Contemporary Art U. Pa., Phila., 1972, Randolph-Macon Coll., N.C., 1972, Kassel, Fed. Republic Germany, 1972, Stedelijk Mus., Amsterdam, 1975, U. Mass., Amherst, 1976, Venice Biennale, Italy, 1976, 80, Cleve. Mus. Art, 1978, Albright-Knox Gallery, Buffalo, 1978, Inst. Contemporary Art, Boston, 1979, Art Inst. Chgo., 1979, San Francisco Mus. Modern Art, 1980, ROSC Internat. Art Exhbn., Dublin, Ireland, 1980, Marilyn Pearl Gallery, N.Y.C., 1983, Kemper Gallery, Kansas City Art Inst., 1985, Am. Acad. and Inst. Arts and Letters, N.Y.C., 1985, Charles Cowles Gallery, N.Y.C., 1986, Moody Gallery Art U. Ala., Birmingham, 1986, Butler Inst. Am. Art, 1986, Art Gallery Western Australia, Perth, 1986, Mus. Contemporary Art, Los Angeles, 1986, Boston Fine Arts Mus., 1989; represented in permanent collections Mus. of Modern Art, N.Y.C., Albright-Knox Gallery, Aldrich Mus., Ridgefield, Conn., Art Gallery Ont., Can., Australian Nat. Gallery, Canberra, Grey Art Gallery and Study Ctr., N.Y.C., Solomon R. Guggenheim Mus., High Mus. Art, Atlanta, Hirshhorn Mus. and Sculpture Garden, Washington, Israel Mus., Jerusalem, La Jolla (Calif.) Mus. Contemporary Art, Los Angeles County Mus. Art, Mus. Art R.I. Sch. Design, Providence, Mus. Modern Art, Neuegalerie der Stadt, Aachen, Fed. Republic Germany, Norton Simon Mus. Art at Pasadena, Calif., Stedelijk Mus., Amsterdam, The Netherlands, 1992, Mus. Modern Art, paris, 1992, Tate Gallery, London, Wadsworth Atheneum, Walker Art Ctr., Mpls., Whitney Mus. Am. Art, 1993, Sofia, Madrid, 1993, Huosten, 1993, Worcester (Mass.) Art Mus., Yale U. Art Gallery, New Haven; subject of various articles. Office: 414 Placitas Rd # 37 Taos NM 97571-2513

MARTIN, CLYDE VERNE, psychiatrist; b. Coffeyville, Kans., Apr. 7, 1933; s. Howard Verne and Elfrieda Louise (Moehn) M.; m. Barbara Jean McNeilly, June 24, 1956; children: Kent Clyde, Kristin Claire, Kerry Constance, Kyle Curtis. Student Coffeyville Coll., 1951-52; AB, U. Kans., 1955; MD, 1958; MA, Webster Coll., St. Louis, 1977; JD, Thomas Jefferson Coll. Law, Los Angeles, 1985. Diplomate Am. Bd. Psychiatry and Neurology. Intern, Lewis Gale Hosp., Roanoke, Va., 1958-59; resident in psychiatry U. Kans. Med. Ctr., Kansas City, 1959-62, Fresno br. U. Calif.-San Francisco, 1978; staff psychiatrist Neurol. Hosp., Kansas City, 1962; practice medicine specializing in psychiatry, Kansas City, Mo., 1964-84; founder, med. dir., pres. bd. dirs. Mid-Continent Psychiat. Hosp., Olathe, Kans., 1972-84; adj. prof. psychology Baker U., Baldwin City, Kans., 1969-84; staff psychiatrist Atascadero State Hosp., Calif., 1984-85; clin. prof. psychiatry U. Calif., San Francisco, 1985—; chief psychiatrist Calif. Med. Facility, Vacaville, 1985-87; pres., editor Corrective and Social Psychiatry, Olathe, 1970-84, Atascadero, 1984-85, Fairfield, 1985-97. Contbr. articles to profl. jours. Bd. dirs. Meth. Youthville, Newton, Kans. 1965-75, Spofford Home, Kansas City, 1974-78. Served to capt. USAF, 1962-64, ret. col. USAFR. Oxford Law & Soc. scholar, 1993. Fellow Am. Psychiat. Assn. (life), Royal Soc. Health (London), Am. Assn. Mental Health Profls. in Corrections, World Assn. Social Psychiatry, Am. Orthopsychiat. Assn.; mem. AMA, Assn. for Advancement Psychotherapy, Am. Assn. Sex Educators, Counselors and Therapists (cert.), Assn. Mental Health Adminstrs. (cert.), Marines Meml. Club, San Francisco, Capitol Hill Club, Washington D.C., St. James Club, London, Phi Beta Pi, Pi Kappa Alpha. Methodist (del. Kans. East Conf. 1972-80, bd. global ministries 1974-80). Office: PO Box 3365 Fairfield CA 94533-0587

MARTIN, CONNIE RUTH, lawyer; b. Clovis, N.Mex., Sept. 9, 1955; d. Lynn Latimer and Marian Ruth (Pierce) M.; m. Daniel A. Patterson, Nov. 21, 1987; step-children: David Patterson, Dana Patterson. B in Univ. Studies, Ea. N.Mex. U., 1976, MEd, 1977; JD, U. Mo., Kansas City, 1981. Bar: N.Mex. 1981, U.S. Dist. Ct. N.Mex. 1981. Asst. dist. atty. State of N.Mex., Farmington, 1981-84; ptnr. Tansey, Rosebrough, Gerding & Strother, PC, Farmington, 1984-93; pvt. practice Connie R. Martin, P.C., Farmington, 1993-94; domestic violence commr. 11th Judicial Dist. Ct., State of N.Mex., 1993-94; with Jeffrey B. Diamond Law Firm, Carlsbad, N. Mex., 1994-96; assoc. Sager, Curran, Sturges and Tepper PC, Las Cruces, N. Mex., 1996-97, Holt & Babington PC, Las Cruces, 1997—; dep. med. investigator State of N.Mex., Farmington, 1981-84; instr. San Juan Coll., 1987, N.Mex. State U., 1995; spkr. N.Mex. Jud. Edn. Ctr., 1993-94; chair paralegal program adv. com., 1988, Adv Com., St Francis Clin., Presbyterian Med. Svs., 1994-96; bd. Bar Examiners State of N.Mex., 1989—, vice-chair, 1995-97, chair, 1997—; asst. bar counsel Disciplinary Bd.; mem. profl. adv. com. Meml. Med. Ctr. Found., 1997—; mem. So. N.Mex. Estate Planning Coun., 1997—. Bd. dirs., exec. com. San Juan County Econ. Opportunity Coun., Farmington, 1982-83; bd. dirs. Four Corners Substance Abuse Coun., Farmington, 1984, N.Mex. Newspapers, Inc.; chmn. Cmty. Corrections-Intensive Supervision Panel, Farmington, 1987-88; jud. selection com. mem. San Juan County, 1991, Chavez County, 1995; nominating com. Supreme Ct./Ct of Appeals, 1991-96. Recipient Distinguished Svcs. award for Outstanding Young Woman San Juan County Jaycees, 1984. Mem. N.Mex. Bar. Assn. (bd. dirs. elder law sect. 1993-96, peer rev. task force 1994-95, asst. to new lawyers com. 1986-87, local bar com. 1988, bd. dirs. young lawyers divsn. 1989-91, bd. dirs. real property probate and trust sect. 1994-97), San Juan County Bar Assn. (treas. 1985-87, v.p. 1987, pres. 1988), Farmington C. of C. (bd. dirs. 1991-93). Republican. Baptist. Avocations: health, fitness, reading. Office: PO Box 2699 Las Cruces NM 88004-2699

MARTIN, DERRICK, basketball player; b. Mar. 6, 1971. Guard L.A. Clippers. Office: c/o LA Clippers 3939 S Figueroa St Los Angeles CA 90037-1200

MARTIN, DONALD WALTER, author, publisher; b. Grants Pass, Oreg., Apr. 22, 1934; s. George E. and Irma Ann (Dallas) M.; m. Kathleen Elizabeth Murphy, July, 1970 (div. May 1979); children: Daniel Clayton, Kimberly Ann; m. Betty Woo, Mar. 18, 1985. Enlisted USMC, 1952; advanced through grades to staff sgt. USMC, Japan, Republic of Korea, Republic of China, 1956-61; reporter Blade-Tribune, Oceanside, Calif., 1961-65; entertainment editor Press-Courier, Oxnard, Calif., 1965-69; mng. editor Argus-Courier, Petaluma, Calif., 1969-70; assoc. editor Motorland mag., San Francisco, 1970-88; founder, prin., CEO Pine Cone Press, Inc., Columbia, Calif., 1988—. Author: Best of San Francisco, 1986, 90, 94, Best of the Gold Country, 1987, 92, San Francisco's Ultimate Dining Guide, 1988, Inside Francisco, 1991, Best of the Wine Country, 1991, 95, Oregon Discovery Guide, 1993, 95, 96, Northern California Discovery Guide, 1993, The Ultimate Wine Book, 1993, Washington Discovery Guide, 1994, Utah Discovery Guide, 1995, Adventure Cruising, 1996, Arizona Discovery Guide, 1996, Arizona in Your Future, 1991, 93, 97, The Toll-Free Traveler, 1997, Las Vegas: The Best of Glitter City, 1997, 98, New Mexico Discovery Guide, 1998, California-Nevada Roads Less Traveled, 1999, San Diego: The Best of Sunshine City, 1999. Recipient Diane Seely award Ventura County Theatre Council, 1968. Mem. Soc. Am. Travel Writers. Republican. Avocations: traveling, hiking, white water rafting, biking. Home: 631 Stephanie St # 138 Henderson NV 89014-2633

MARTIN, ERNEST LEE, academic administrator, historian, theologian, writer; b. Meeker, Okla., Apr. 20, 1932; s. Joel Chester and Lula Mae (Quinn) M.; m. Helen Rose Smith, Aug. 26, 1957 (div. 1980); children: Kathryn, Phyllis, Samuel; m. Ramona Jean Kinsey, June 27, 1987. BA, Ambassador U., 1958, MA, 1960, PhD, 1966. Dean faculty Ambassador U., St. Albans, Eng., 1965-72; chmn. dept. theology Ambassador U., Pasadena, Calif., 1972-74; dir. Found. for Bibl. Rsch., Pasadena, 1974-84, Acad. for Scriptural Knowledge, Portland, 1985—; dir. 450 coll. students with Prof. Benjamin Mazar Herodian Western Wall archaeol. excavations, Jerusalem, 1969-74. Author: Birth of Christ Recalculated, 1978, 2d edit., 1980, The Original Bible Restored, 1984, Secrets of Golgotha, 1987, 2d edit., 1996, The Star That Astonished the World, 1996, 101 Bible Secrets That Christians Do Not Know, 1993, The People That History Forgot, 1993, The Place of the New Third Temple, 1994, Restoring the Original Bible, 1994, The Biblical Manual, 1995, ABC's of the Gospel, 1997, The Essentials of New Testament Doctrine, 1999, The Temples that Jerusalem Forgot, 1999, Angels-The Fictions and the Facts, 1999. Tech. sgt. USAF, 1950-54. Mem. SBL (advisor to Original Bible Project), Planetarium Soc. E-mail: doctor@askelm.com. Home: PO Box 25000 Portland OR 97298-0990 Office: Assocs for Scriptural Knowledge 4804 SW Scholls Ferry Rd Portland OR 97225-1668

MARTIN, GEORGE, psychologist, educator; b. L.A., May 8, 1940; s. George Leonard and Margaret (Padigamus) M.; m. Penny Harrell, June 22, 1963 (div. 1986); children: Jeni, Kimberle. BA, UCLA, 1965; MA, Calif. State U., L.A., 1967; MS, Calif. State U., Fullerton, 1994. Systems analyst L.A. Dept. Water & Power, 1965-67; project coord. L.A. Police Dept., 1967-70, edn. cons., 1980-83; alcohol researcher Pomona (Calif.) Coll., 1970-73; tng. systems researcher Lanterman State Hosp., Pomona, 1973-77; prof. psychology Mt. San Antonio Coll., Walnut, Calif., 1970—, dir. rsch., 1986-94. Contbr. articles to profl. jours. Rsch. dir. Orange County Dem. Party, 1985-86. With U.S. Army, 1959-61. Grantee Nat. Inst. Law Enforcement, 1967-70, Nat. Inst. Alcohol, 1970-74. Mem. APA, NSA. Avocations: photography, computers. Home: 1313 N Grand Ave Ste 326 Walnut CA 91789-1317 Office: Mt San Antonio Coll 1100 N Grand Ave Walnut CA 91789-1341

MARTIN, GEORGE, consulting engineer. BS, U. Birmingham, England, 1951; PhD, U. Birmingham, 1955. Chief cons. engr. John Gardom & Co., Derby, England, 1952-56; tech. mgr. Chromizing Co., L.A., 1956-57; chief metallurgist Honolulu Oil Co., L.A., 1957-61; program mgr. Rockwell Internat., L.A., 1961-70; br. chief advanced mfg. tech. McDonnell-Douglas Astronautics, Santa Monica, Calif., 1970-72; pres. Creative Crafts, Inc., Santa Monica, Calif., 1974—; adj. prof. engring. U. Calif., L.A., 1974-90, 57-90. Contbr. articles to profl. jours. Capt. Brit. Mil., 1941-47. Mem. I Mech. Engrs. (U.K.). Office: George Martin Assocs 1223 Wilshire Blvd # 353 Santa Monica CA 90403-5400

MARTIN, GEORGE FRANCIS, lawyer; b. Yuba City, Calif., July 7, 1944; s. John Severd and Albina Marie M.; m. Linda Louise D'Aoust, Mar. 17, 1968; children: Brandon, Bry. BA in Govt., Calif. State U., Sacramento, 1968; JD, U. Calif., Davis, 1971. Bar: Calif. Adminstr. asst. Assemblyman E. Richard Barnes, Sacramento, 1967-68; with Borton, Petrini & Conron, Bakersfield, Calif., 1971—; mng. gen. ptnr. Borton, Petrini & Conron, Bakersfield, 1977—; dean Calif. Pacific Sch. Law, Bakersfield, 1993-95; holdings numerous ventures, partnerships; lectr. in field; founder, owner theatrical bus. Mgmt. by Martin, Inc., Shower of Stars, Frantic Records, 1962-67. Editor-in-chief Verdict Jour. of Law, 1984-85, Calif. Def. Mag.; newspaper reporter Appeal Democrat, Marysville, Calif., 1959-62. Former vice chmn. Kern County Rep. Ctrl. Com.; past pres. So. Calif. Def. Counsel; past chmn. Ctrl. Calif. Heart Inst.; bd. dirs. Calif. State U. at Bakersfield Found., chair, 1998; bd. dirs. Calif. Coun. Partnerships, Kern Econ. Devel. Corp; mem. adv. bd. Automobile Club So. Calif.; chmn. adv. bd. Witkin Legal Inst. Mem. Greater Bakersfield C. of C. (bd. dirs., past pres.). Office: Borton Petrini & Conron 1600 Truxtun Ave Bakersfield CA 93301-5111

MARTIN, GILBERT EDWARD, historian, writer; b. New Orleans, Apr. 13, 1923; s. Cornelius and Mary (Anderson) M.; m. Geraldine Theresa Aubert, Sept. 14, 1946 (div.); children: Gwendolyn, Gilbert, Gerald, Gail, Gary, Guy, Ginger. Grad., Chgo. Tech. Coll. Ext., 1952. Pvt. practice arch., builder New Orleans, 1952-57, Detroit, 1957-81. Author, pub.: Creoles—A Shattered Nation, 1981, Passe Pour Blanc, 1993, Creole Chronology, 1994, Creole Treaty Rights, 1995. Initiator La. Reclamation Movement, 1998. Cpl. USMC, 1942-45. Avocations: shooting pool, doing video documentaries at the Veterans Home. Home: PO Box 1200 Yountville CA 94599-1297

MARTIN, JANE EVERETTE, financial company executive; b. Hopewell, Va., Jan. 14, 1943; d. Robert Thornton and Myrtle Iola (Dale) Tuggle; m. Thomas Joy Martin, June 27, 1964 (div. Mar. 1970); children: Michael Joy, David Thomas. Student, William and Mary Coll., 1961-63. Sales asst. Merrill Lynch, Palo Alto, Calif., 1976-77; mem. staff broker's trading desk E.F. Hutton, Palo Alto, 1977-81, asst. v.p., 1981-87; pres. Jane Martin Assocs., Palo Alto, 1987-94, Shooting Star Pictures, Palo Alto, 1993—; exec. dir. Managed Futures Assn., Palo Alto, 1991—; bd. dirs. Frederick Gilbert & Assocs., Redwood City, Calif. Address: Managed Futures Assn 1200 19th St NW Ste 300 Washington DC 20036-2428

MARTIN, JOHN STEWART, software engineer; b. Tacoma, June 20, 1965; s. Richard and Catherine Jesse (Stewart) M.; m. Tami Renee Ewing, Feb. 25, 1992; 1 child, Devon Irene. Grad. high sch., Portland, Oreg. Rsch. asst. Inst. Neurosci. U. Oreg., Eugene, 1990-93; asst. dir. software devel. Covox, Inc., Eugene, 1993-95; pres. EIJA, Inc., Eugene, 1995—. Creator: (Internet virtual world) Singlenesia, 1991. Mem. Eugene Area C. of C. Avocations: radio controlled model aircraft, collecting music, robotics. Office: Singlenesia Software 2852 Willamette St Ste 502 Eugene OR 97405-8200

MARTIN, JOSEPH, JR., retired lawyer, former ambassador; b. San Francisco, May 21, 1915; m. Ellen Chamberlain Martin, July 5, 1946; children: Luther Greene, Ellen Myers. AB, Yale U., 1936, LLB, 1939. Assoc. Cadwalader, Wickersham & Taft, N.Y.C., 1939-41; ptnr. Wallace, Garrison, Norton & Ray, San Francisco, 1946-55, Pettit & Martin, San Francisco, 1955-70, 73-95; gen. counsel FTC, Washington, 1970-71; ambassador, U.S. rep. Disarmament Conf., Geneva, 1971-76; ret.; mem. Pres.'s Adv. Com. for Arms Control and Disarmament, 1974-78. Pres. Pub. Utilities Commn., San Francisco, 1956-60; Rep. nat. committeeman for Calif., 1960-64; treas. Rep. Party Calif., 1956-58; bd. dirs. Patrons of Art and Music, Calif. Palace of Legion of Honor, 1958-70, pres., 1963-68; bd. dirs. Arms Control Assn., 1977-84; pres. Friends of Legal Assistance to Elderly, 1983-87. Lt. comdr. USNR, 1941-46. Recipient Ofcl. commendation for Outstanding Service as Gen. Counsel FTC, 1973, Distinguished Honor award U.S. ACDA, 1973, Lifetime Achievement award Legal Assistance to the Elderly, 1981. Fellow Am. Bar Found. Clubs: Burlingame Country, Pacific Union. Home: 331 Greer Rd Woodside CA 94062-4207

MARTIN, JOY ANNE, clinical psychologist, consultant; b. Andover, Mass.; d. Edward and Ethel Mae (McGonigle) Fengya. BS, Boston U., 1966, EdM, 1976; PhD, Calif. Sch. Profl. Psychology, 1988; cert. in Adv. Tng. Program in Psychoanalytic Psychotherapy, San Diego Psychoanalytic Soc. and Inst., 1997. Lic. psychologist, Calif. Tchr. Dept. Def. Dependent Schs., Japan, Fed. Republic Germany, 1972-83; grad. asst. Old Dominion U., Norfolk, Va., 1983-84; clin. practitioner inpatient substance abuse program U.S. Naval Air Sta., Mirimar, Calif., 1985-86; pvt. practice La Jolla, Calif., 1986—; fellow Mercy Hosp. and Med. Ctr., San Diego, 1988-89; clin. psychologist HIV/Infectious Disease divsn. Naval Med. Ctr., San Diego, 1990—, Psychiat. Ctrs. San Diego, 1988—. Mem. APA (western regional trainer HIV office for psychology edn., mem. mil. task force HIV office for psychology edn.), Am. Acad. Exprts Traumatic Stress, Assn. for the Advancement of Psychology, Nat. Register Health Svc. Providers in Psychology, Calif. Psychol. Assn., San Diego Acad. Psychologists, Calif. Sch. Profl. Psychology Alumni Assn. (bd. dirs.), Sierra Club. Avocations: skiing, cycling, travel, camping.

MARTIN, JUNE JOHNSON CALDWELL, journalist; b. Toledo, Oct. 6; d. John Franklin and Eunice Imogene (Fish) Johnson; m. Erskine Caldwell, Dec. 21, 1942 (div. Dec. 1955); 1 child, Jay Erskine; m. Keith Martin, May 5, 1966. AA, Phoenix Jr. Coll., 1939-41; BA, U. Ariz., 1941-43, 53-59; student Ariz. State U., 1939, 40. Free-lance writer, 1944—; columnist Ariz. Daily Star, 1956-59; editor Ariz. Alumnus mag., Tucson, 1959-70; book reviewer, columnist Ariz. Daily Star, Tucson, 1970-94; ind. book reviewer and audio tape columnist, Tucson, 1994—; panelist, co-producer TV news show Tucson Press Club, 1954-55, pres., 1958; co-founder Ariz. Daily Star Ann. Book & Author Event. Contbg. author: Rocky Mountain Cities, 1949; contbr. articles to World Book Ency., and various mags. Mem. Tucson CD Com., 1961; vol. campaigns of Samuel Goddard, U.S. Rep. Morris Udall, U.S. ambassador and Ariz. gov. Raul Castro. Recipient award Nat. Headliners Club, 1959, Ariz. Press Club award, 1957-59, 96, Am. Alumni Council, 1966, 70. Mem. Nat. Book Critics Circle, Jr. League of Tucson, Tucson Urban League, PEN U.S.A. West, Planned Parenthood of So. Ariz., Pi Beta Phi. Democrat. Methodist. Club: Tucson Press. Home: Desert Foothills Sta PO Box 65388 Tucson AZ 85728-5388

MARTIN, LEONARD AUSTIN, II, music educator; b. McCook, Nebr., July 18, 1949; s. Austin Berwell and Marie Elizabeth (Kimbro) M. BA summa cum laude, Metro State Coll. Denver, 1971; MA, Denver U., 1972, PhD, 1984. Cert. tchr., adminstr., Colo. Music instr. Cross Exec. Sch. Music, Aurora, Colo., 1965—, Peetz (Colo.) elem. and secondary schs., 1972, 5 area sch. dists., Denver, 1973, Adams County Sch. Dist. 12, Denver, 1974-94; prof. U. Colo., Denver, 1990—, U. No. Colo., 1996—, Adams State Coll., 1996—, U. Phoenix, 1997—; mem. faculty tchr. edn. program U. Denver, 1994—, prof. Educator's Inst., 1994—. Author: High School Music Theory, 1978, Basic Music Theory, 1989, A Curriculum for Educational Licensure, 1994; contbr. articles to profl. jours. Youth choir dir. Faith Presbyn. Ch., Aurora, 1973-75, substitute dir. adult choir, 1987-90; mem. worship team, mem. choir Cornerstone Cmty. Ch., Glendale, Colo., 1991-93; substitute dir., Presbyn. Ch. Aurora, 1995-97 (choir dir. 1998—); cornetist Aurora Summer Cmty. Band, 1965-71; mem. Colo. All-State Band, 1967; choir dir. Aurora First Presbyn. Ch., 1998—. Mem. NEA, ASCD, Colo. Edn. Assn., Music Educators Nat. Conf., Colo. Music Educators Assn., Denver Musicians Soc. (pres.), Nat. Geog. Soc. Republican. Presbyterian. Avocations: collecting chime/strike clocks, elephants, silent 8 mm movies, swimming, bowling.

MARTIN, LEONARDO SAN JUAN, urologist, surgeon; b. Macati, Rizal, The Philippines, Nov. 26, 1926; came to U.S., 1953; s. Nemesio Martin and Felicidad San Juan; m. Helen Mary Dougherty, May 24, 1958; children: Leonard, John and David (twins), Mark, Regina Mary, Daniel. AA, U. The Philippines, 1947; MD, U. Santo Tomas, Manila, The Philippines, 1952. Diplomate Am. Bd. Urology; cert. physician and surgeon, Calif. Resident in urology Phila. Gen. Hosp., 1954-57; fellow in urology Mass. Gen. Hosp., Boston, 1957-59; urologist Manila Specialists Med. Ctr., 1959-63; instr. urology U. Santo Tomas, 1959-63; assoc. cancer urologist Roswell Pk. Meml. Hosp., Buffalo, 1963-65; urologist Sunnyvale (Calif.) Med. Ctr., 1965-94; mem. clin. tchg. staff Stanford (Calif.) Med. Ctr., 1965-94; cons. urology Los Altos, 1994—; commr., med. expert Calif. Med. Bd. Licensure, Sacramento, 1987—. Contbr. 37 articles to profl. jours. Bd. dirs. Flint Cultural Ctr., Cupertino, Calif., 1970-80. Named one of 10 Outstanding Young Men, Jaycees, The Philippines, 1960, Disting. Men of Medicine, U. The Philippines Coll. Medicine, 1960. Fellow ACS (cert. merit 1964); mem. AMA (cert. Inc. merit 1964), Am. Urol. Assn. (western sect., cert. merit 1964), Am. Assn. Clin. Urologists, Philippine-Am. Urol. Soc. (founding pres. 1972), U. Santo Tomas Med. Alumni Assn. in Am. (pres. 1996-97), Boys and Girls Club of Am. (bd. dirs. Santa Clara county unit Calif.). Republican. Roman Catholic. Avocations: oil painting, piano and organ, stained glass, tennis, golf. Home and Office: 1931 Deodora Dr Los Altos CA 94024-7055

MARTIN, LINDE BENISON, artist, interior designer; b. Erlangen, Germany, Jan. 2, 1930; came to U.S., 1953; d. Michael and Thea (Jetzelsberger) Kuchenreuther; m. James Bruce Martin, Nov. 16, 1966 (div.); 1 child, Cornelia Johnson. Student, Sorbonne, Paris, 1947-50, Cabrillo Coll., Aptos, Calif., 1961-65, San Jose (Calif.) State U., 1965. Tchr. Creativity Workshop, Zurich, 1988-90. *I have experimented in many art forms and excelled in all. I am a gardener and have artistically developed the harmony in my garden. I am featured in the University of California's Art & Garden Tour. My paintings are lyrical abstractions in oil on linen that invite the viewer to partake in the creation of the art. My work has been described as a palatte for the viewer to create and see with. Ms. Linde's says her paintings posses a timeless essance of creativity that will endure as a monument of the freedom and creativity of the human vision.* Exhibited works in solo shows at Redding Gallery, Carmel, Calif., 1963, Jungain Ctr., San Francisco, 1973, Stanford U., 1975, Carmel Gallery Fine Arts, 1985, Kunsthalle, Nuremberg, Germany, 1991, U. Calif. Santa Cruz Women's Ctr., 1993, Christ Luth. Ch., Tiberon, Calif., U. Phoenix, Santa Cruz, 1994, others; group shows include Vorpal Gallery, San Francisco, Open Studios Art Tour, Santa Cruz, O Gallery, Westport, Conn., Syntex Corp., San Jose, Met. Art Care, Los Altos, Calif., Mus. Modern Art, Miami, Fla., Montreal Internat. Competition, San Jose, Wax Lander Galleries, Santa Fe, 1997; represented in collections at U. Phoenix., U. Calif. at Santa Cruz, First Congl. Ch., Santa Cruz, also pvt. collections including that of Itzac Perlman, N.Y.C.; commns. include watercolor illustration for children's books, art glass windows and paintings. Named Best Artist of 1996 Spectra Art Mag., Grand Prize Crabby Award Art Calendar Mag., 1998. Avocations: gardening, reading, theater, classical music. E-mail: rocky2@got.net. Home: 244 Seaborg Pl Santa Cruz CA 95060-3133

MARTIN, LOREN WINSTON, physician; b. Albertsville, Ala., Apr. 20, 1938; s. Loren d. and Byrda G. (Crotwell) M.; m. Vivian Elizabeth Sanger Martin, Dec. 29, 1960; children: Lori Ann, Karen Lynn, James Winston. BA in Chemistry, Duke U., 1959; MD, U. Tenn., 1962. Lic. physician, Ariz. Rotating internship Fitzsimons Army Hosp., Denver, 1963; med. residency Honolulu, 1964-67; med. officer U.S. Army, 1962-70; fellowship allergy U. Colo., Denver, 1970-71; pvt. practice Tucson, 1971—. Decorated Bronze Star. Fellow Am. Acad. Allergy & Immunology, Am. Coll. Allergy & Immunology; mem. Pima County Med. Soc. Republican. Office: 5300 E Erickson Dr Ste 120 Tucson AZ 85712-2809

MARTIN, MICHAEL, publisher; b. Fort Lauderdale, Fla., Aug. 30, 1960; s. Earl Perkinson and Patricia Veronica Martin. BA in Journalism, San Francisco State U., 1993. Reporter Ind. Newspaper Group, Burlingame, Calif., 1993-94; pub. San Francisco Observer, 1995—. Big Bros. Glide Meml. Ch., San Francisco, 1990—. Mem. Soc. Profl. Journalists (Mark of Excellence award 1992). Avocations: sailing, windsurfing, scuba diving, hiking, yoga. Office: San Francisco Observer 459 Fulton St Ste 303 San Francisco CA 94102-4318

MARTIN, MICHAEL ALBERT, surveillance agent; b. Akron, Ohio, Feb. 29, 1940; s. Albert Leo and Beatrice Marie (Flasck) M.; m. Jeanine E. Johnson, June 10, 1972 (div. Dec. 1976). Hotel Sch. diploma, Universal Schs., Miami, Fla., 1969. Security officer Boyd Group, California Hotel, Las Vegas, Nev., 1991-98; surveillance agt. Boyd Group, California Hotel, Las Vegas, 1999—. Author: Atlantis Secrets Revealed, 1994, Hilltop Country Songbook, 1997, (poetry) Noet You Poet, 1995; author (songs) To Eva My Love, Western Song, Your Song of Love, Reaching Out; contbr. to The Best Poems of 1995, The Best Poems of 1997, The Best Poems of the 90s. Staff sgt. USAF, 1964-68. Recipient Ednl. awards USAF, 1964-65, others; named to the Internat. Poetry Hall of Fame, 1996. Mem. Internat. Soc. Poets (hon., 13 Editors Choice award for poetry), Am. Legion, Masons (Scottish Rite pres. 1973—), Shriners. Democrat. Roman Catholic. Avocations: travel, photography, book writing, poetry writing, song writing. Home: Duck Creek Village 5330 Duralite St # 103 Las Vegas NV 89122-7364 Office: Calif Hotel and Casino PO Box 630 Las Vegas NV 89125

MARTIN, MYRON GREGORY, foundation administrator; b. Houston, Jan. 14, 1958; s. Monty Gene and Vera Mae (Saurage) M. MusB, U. North Tex., 1980; MBA, Golden Gate U., 1989. Various sales and mktg. positions Baldwin Piano Co., N.Y.C., 1980-1990, dir. concert and artists, 1990-95; exec. dir. Liberace Found., Las Vegas, Nev., 1995-98; dir. U. Las Vegas, 1998—. Mem. adv. bd. Thelonious Monk Inst., Washington, D.C., 1994-95; bd. dirs. Cystic Fibrosis Found., Chgo., 1990, Liberace Found., 1993-95, Museums and Attractions, Las Vegas, 1996—. Recipient Special award Cystic Fibrosis Found., 1990. Mem. Nev. Mus. Assn. (bd. dirs. 1997—). Avocations: tennis, judging scholarship pageants for Miss America organization. Home: 5121 Breakers Ln Las Vegas NV 89113-1311 Office: U Las Vegas Performing Art Ctr 4505 Maryland Pky Las Vegas NV 89154-9901*

MARTIN, NORMAN FRANCIS, public relations executive; b. Half Moon Bay, Calif., July 8, 1914; s. Frank A. and Mary (Phillips) M. AB in Philosophy, Gonzaga U. Spokane, 1941; MA in Philosophy, 1942; STL in Theology, Colegio Maximo de San Miguel, Buenos Aires, 1948; MA in History magna cum laude, U. of Americas, Mexico City, 1950; D in History magna cum laude, Natl. U., Mexico City, 1957. Prof. English and History Colegio Centro America, Granada, Nicaragua, 1942-43; prof. English [illegible] History Santa Clara (Calif.) U., 1958-80, dir. Grad. Fellowships, 1973-78, dir. Spl. Projects, 1978-89, prof. Emeritus History, 1980, asst. to pres. U. Rels., 1989—. Author: Vagabundos en la Nueva Espana, 1957; editor: Instruccion del Virrey Croix a Bucareli, 1960, Instruccion del Virrey Ortega, 1965; contbr. articles to profl. jours. Bd. trustees Santa Clara (Calif.) U., 1978-83, O'Connor Hosp. found., San Jose, 1989-95; bd. fellows Santa Clara (Calif.) U., 1983-93; juvenile adv. bd. Santa Clara (Calif.) City Police Dept., 1984-94. Recipient Guggenheim fellowship John Simon Guggenheim found., N.Y.C., 1961-62, Nat. Endowment for Humanities, NEH, Washington, 1968-69. Mem. Jesuit Order in Cath. Ch., Am. Hist. Soc., Am. Cath. Hist. Soc., Latin Am. Studies Assn., Phi Alpha Theta. Republican. Roman Catholic. Avocations: classical music, swimming. Home: Nobili Hall Santa Clara University Santa Clara CA 95053-1600 Office: Varsi Hall Santa Clara University Santa Clara CA 95053-1400

MARTIN, PATRICIA ANN, music educator; b. Salinas, Calif., Mar. 11, 1939; d. Kenneth Duane and Hazel Gertrude (Setser) Lowe; m. Raymond Dalton Martin, Aug. 22, 1959; children: William Dalton, Brian David. BA, Calif. State U., 1965. Choir accompanist Salinas Christian Ch., 1954-57; choir accompanist North Fresno Christian Ch., Fresno, Calif., 1957-93, organist, 1965-96, choir dir., 1968-70; tchr. music pvt. lessons Fresno, 1962—; tchr. music Mountain View Christian Sch., Fresno, 1992-93; organist for weddings, various chs., Fresno, 1962-96; dir. bell choir North Fresno Christian Ch., 1985-86, dir. ministry, 1989-90. Composer songs, piano teaching pieces, 1974—; contbr. poetry to anthologies, 1981—. Mem. AAUW, Am. Guild Organists (sec. 1978-79), Calif. Fedn. Music Clubs (pres. 1988-91), Music Tchrs. Assn. Calif. (state chmn. Cal-Plan 1981-83, pres. 1983-85, condr. workshops 1978—, dir. pianorama 1976-88), Jr. Music Festival (pres. 1987-91, performer in New Wrinkles Sr. Theatre 1993—). Republican.

MARTIN, PERRY CLYDE, electronic specialist, soil scientist; b. Orem, Utah, Aug. 10, 1950; s. Albert Clyde and Wanda Burneta (Atchison) M.; children from previous marriage: T.S., Terradi Burneta; m. Winefreda Hopkins, Nov. 4, 1995. B in Biophysics Rsch., Westminster Coll., 1983; student, Utah State U., 1986. Expeditor Western Div. EDO Corp., Salt Lake City, 1980-83; electronics specialist Hill Air Force Base, Clearfield, Utah, 1983—; creator, owner Thai-Berry Park, Clearfield, 1988—. Chmn. bd. dirs. Western Youth Clearfield, 1989—. Avocation: computers. Home: 458 E 450 S Clearfield UT 84015-1736

MARTIN, PRESTON, financial services executive; b. L.A., Dec. 5, 1923; s. Oscar and Gaynell (Horne) M.; 1 child, Pier Preston. BS in Fin., U. So. Calif., 1947, MBA, 1948; PhD in Monetary Econs., U. Ind., 1952. Prof. fin. Grad. Sch. Bus. Adminstrn. U. So. Calif., 1950-60; prin. in housebldg. firm, 1952-56; with mortgage fin. and consumer fin. instns., 1954-57; commr. savs. and loan State of Calif., 1967-69; chmn. Fed. Home Loan Bank Bd., Washington, 1969-72; founder, CEO PMI Mortgage Ins. Co., 1972-80; chmn., CEO Seraco Group subs. Sears, Roebuck & Co., 1980-81, also bd. dirs. parent co.; chmn., CEO WestFed Holdings Inc., L.A., 1986-92, SoCal Holdings, Inc., L.A., 1987-93, H.F. Holdings, Inc., San Francisco, 1986; vice-chmn. Fed. Res. Bd., Washington, 1982-86; founder Fed. Home Loan Mortgage Corp.; prof. bus. econ. and fin. Inst. per lo Studio Organizitzatione Aziendale, Italy. Author: Principles and Practices of Real Estate, 1959. Mem. President's Commn. on Housing, 1980-81; prin. Coun. Excellence in Govt., Washington. Recipient House and Home award, 1969, award Engring. News Record, 1971, Turntable award Nat. Assn. Home Builders, 1973. Mem. Lambda Chi Alpha. Presbyterian. *

MARTIN, RICHARD H., national park service executive. Supt. Death Valley (Calif.) Nat. Park. Office: Death Valley Nat Park PO Box 579 Death Valley CA 92328-0579*

MARTIN, ROBERT BURTON, management and marketing consultant; b. Takoma Park, Md., Mar. 17, 1935; s. Herbert Lester and Lenora Marie (Sponseller) M.; m. Mary Lou Rushworth, Sept. 7, 1959 (div. Dec. 1982); children: Laurajean, Kenneth, Donna Beth. BEE, Cornell U., 1958; MS, Northwestern U., 1966, PhD, 1967. Dir. mgmt. systems Denver and Rio Grande Western R.R., 1967-71; v.p. Mgmt. Design Assoc., Denver, 1971-79; owner Martin & Assoc., Denver, 1979—; founder Martin Aquatics, LLC, Denver, 1993—; treas. Rocky Mountain chpt. Inst. of Mgmt. Sci., Denver, 1968-70; opening speaker AICPAs, Las Vegas, Nev., 1988. Author, pub.: (newsletter) Martin Reports, 1981-90, Bob Martin-Chris Frederiksen Marketing and Management Report for CPAs, 1990-94. Served to lt. USN, 1958-63. Mem. Inst. Mgmt. Cons., Alpha Pi Mu, Sigma Xi. Avocations: hiking, camping, ultralight aviation, watersports. Home and Office: PO Box 6886 Denver CO 80206-0886

MARTIN, ROBERT MICHAEL, lawyer; b. N.Y.C., Nov. 28, 1922; s. Charles Augustus and Mary Corcoran (Shannon) M.; m. Monica Maria Schmid, Jan. 22, 1951; children: Tara J., C. Brian, Stacy D. BA, Amherst Coll., 1949; grad. cert., Trinity Coll., Dublin, Ireland, 1950; JD, U. So. Calif., 1965; diploma in law, Nat. D.A. Coll., 1973. Bar: Calif. 1966. Mem. faculty Chadwick Sch., Rolling Hills, Calif., 1952-56; mgmt. Servo-Mechanisms, Torrance, Calif., 1956-58, Systems Devel.Corp., Santa Monica, Calif., 1958-62, Douglas Missile & Space, Santa Monica, Calif., 1962-63; v.p. Automation Svc. Co., Beverly Hills, 1963-65; dep. pub. defender L.A. County, 1965-67, spl. asst. dist. atty., dept dist atty., 1971-93; chief counsel, exec. officer Calif. Alcohol Beverage Control Bd., 1967-69; state dir. Calif. Dept. of Social Welfare, Sacramento, 1969-71; ptnr. Donahue, Donahue and Martin, Redondo Beach, Calif., 1995—; instr. travel law West L.A. Coll. Author: Automation in Medicine. Sgt. U.S. Army Air Corp., 1942-45. Mem. Calif. Bar Assn., Calif. Dist. Atty. Assn., Irish-Am. Bar Assn., Asia-Pacific Lawyers Assn., Internat. Forum of Travel and Tourism Advocates, Air Force Assn., 454th Bombardment Group Assn., Amherst Coll. Alumni Assn., U. So. Calif. Alumni Assn. Republican. Avocations: travel, golf, body surfing, tennis, flying. Office: Donahue Donahue and Martin 116 Avenue I Fl 2 Redondo Beach CA 90277-5401

MARTIN, STEVE, national park service officer. Supt. Denali Nat. Park, Alaska. Office: Denali Nat Park PO Box 9 Denali National Park AK 99755-0009*

MARTIN, WILFRED WESLEY FINNY, psychologist, property owner and manager; b. Rock Lake, N.D., Dec. 3, 1917; s. William Isaac and Anna Liisa (Hendrickson-Juntunen) M.; m. Stella Helland, Sept. 25, 1943; children: Sydney Wayne, William Allan. BA, Jamestown Coll., 1940; army specialized tng. program, Hamilton Coll., 1944; MS, EdD, U. So. Calif., 1956. Highsch. prin., coach pub. sch., Nekoma, N.D., 1940-42; contact rep., psychologist VA, L.A., 1946-49, psychologist, chief rehab., 1972-77; guidance dir. Moorhead (Minn.) Pub. Schs., 1951-53; instr. Concordia Coll., Moorhead, 1951-53; from intern to resident Fargo (N.D.) VA Hosp., 1953-58; psychologist VA, Fargo, 1953-58; assoc. Sci. Rsch. Assoc./IBM, Boulder, Colo., 1958-65; regional dir. Sci. Rsch. Assoc./IBM, L.A., 1966-72; owner, mgr. Martin Investments, Huntington Beach, Calif., 1977—; adjutant U. Miss., Oxford, 1942; trustee Wilfred W. and Stella Martin Trust, Huntington Beach, 1991. Author: Veterans Administration Work Simplification, 1948, 57. Charter mem. Rep. Presdl. Task Force, 1980; adv. sr. ptnrs. bd. dirs. U. Calif. Med. Sch., Irvine, 1990; donor Dr. and Mrs. W.W. Martin Endowment, Jamestown Coll., N.D., 1985; mem. Assocs. of James Ford Bell Libr., U. Minn. With U.S. Army, 1942-45. Mem. Am. Psychol. Assn., Cardinal & Gold U. So. Calif., Jamestown Coll. Heritage Circle (charter), Suomi Coll. Second Century Soc., Elks. Republican. Lutheran. Avocations: reading, Finnish heritage, swimming, sports, card playing. Home: PO Box 5445 Huntington Beach CA 92615-5445

MARTINETTI, RONALD ANTHONY, lawyer; b. N.Y.C., Aug. 13, 1945; s. Alfred Joseph and Frances Ann (Battipaglia) M. Student, U. Chgo., 1981-82; JD, U. So. Calif., 1982. Bar: Calif. 1982; U.S. Dist. Ct. (cen. and no. dists.) Calif. 1982, U.S. Dist. Ct. Ariz., 1992; U.S. Ct. Appeals (9th cir.) 1982. Ptnr. Kazanjian & Martinetti, Glendale, Calif., 1986—; co-founder Am. Legends Website, 1996, Am. Legends Pub., 1996. Author: James Dean Story, 1995; co-author: Rights of Owners of Lost, Stolen or Destroyed Instruments Under UCC Section3-804: Can They Be Holders in Due Course, [illegible] New Leader, 1968-76. Vol. trial lawyer Bet Tzedek Legal Svcs., 1987—; judge pro tem L.A. Superior Ct., 1994—. Mem. Calif. Bar Assn. Roman Catholic. Office: Kazanjian & Martinetti 520 E Wilson Ave Glendale CA 91206-4374

MARTINEZ, ALEX, state supreme court justice; b. Denver, CO, Apr. 1, 1951; m. Kathy Carter; children: Julia, Maggie. Diploma, Phillips Exeter Acad., N.H., 1969; student, Reed Coll., 1969-72; BA, U. Colo., 1973, JD, 1976. Bar: Colo. 1976. Dep. state pub. defender Pueblo and Denver, 1976-83; county ct. judge Pueblo, 1983-88, dist. ct. judge, 1988-97; justice Colo. Supreme Ct., Denver, 1997—; Supreme Ct. liaison Colo. Criminal Rules Com., Colo. Criminal Jury Instrns.; chmn. Child Welfare Appeals Workgroup, 1997; mem. standing com. Integrated Info. Svcs. Chmn. Pueblo adv. bd. Packard Found., 1993-96; chmn. site-based governing coun. Pueblo Sch. Arts and Scis., 1994-95; mem. site-based governing coun. Roncalli Mid. Sch., 1993-94; bd. dirs. Colo. U. Law Alumni. Mem. Colo. Bar Assn. (regional v.p. 1995-96), Colo. Hispanic Bar Assn., Pueblo Bar Assn. (mem. exec. coun. 1994-96), Pueblo Hispanic Bar Assn. E-mail: AJMarti@aol.com. Office: Colo Supreme Ct 2 E 14th Ave Rm 430 Denver CO 80203-2115

MARTINEZ, ALMA R., actor, director; b. Monclova, Coahuila, Mex.. Student, U. Guadalajara-Artes Plasticas, Mex., 1972-73, Ibero-Am. U., Mex., 1976, Centro U. Teatro, Mexico City, 1976-77; BA in Theatre, Whittier Coll., 1984; MFA in Acting, U. So. Calif., 1995; postgrad., Stanford U., 1994—; student, Jerzy Grotowski Para Theatre, Berkeley, Calif., 1977, Lee Strasberg Theatre Inst., Hollywood, Calif., 1982, Royal Acad. Dramatic Arts, London, Eng., 1987, Mnouchkine/Theatre du Soleil, Paris, 1993. Appeared in plays including In the Summer House, Lincoln Ctr., N.Y.C., Greencard, Joyce Theatre, N.Y.C., Zoot Suit, Mark Taper Forum, L.A., Bocon, Mark Taper Forum, L.A., Macbeth, Oreg. Shakespeare Festival, The Skin of Our Teeth, Oreg. Shakespeare Festival, Hello Dolly, Long Beach Civic Light Opera, A Christmas Carol, South Coast Repertory, House of Blue Leaves, Pasadena Playhouse, Sundance Inst., Sundance, Utah, Fuente Ovejuna, Berkeley Repertory Theatre, Burning Patience, San Diego Repertory Theatre, Marriage of Figaro, Ariz. Theatre Co., Sons of Don Juan, Asolo Theatre, Fla., Wait Until Dark, Pa. Stage Co., La Carpa de los Rasquachis, Teatro Campesino; TV appearances include Gen. Hosp., St. Elsewhere, Twilight Zone, Sequin, Corridos (Peabody award), Tough Love, Dress Gray, The Boys, In a Child's Name, The Gambler Returns, Quiet Killer, The New Adam 12 (series regular), 500 Nations, Nash Bridges (guest star); film appearances include Jacaranda, The Novice, Trial by Terror, Dollie Dearest, Maria's Story, For A Loves One, Soldado Razo, Shattered Image, Zoot Suit, Barbarosa, Born in East L.A., Under Fire, among others; dir. (plays) Bed of Stone, 1996, La Gran Carpa de los Rasquachis, 1997. Active Assistance with Alcohol and Sobriety Uniting Latinas, United L.Am. Youth, Med. Aid for El Salvador, Save the Children, the Christian Children's Fund; vol. and charity work in refugee camps in Ethiopia, India, Thailand, Sri Lanka, and The Philippines; bd. dirs. Ctrl. Am. Refugee Ctr. El Teatro Compresing. Recipient Cert. of Appreciation El Teatro Campesino, 1978, Recognition award Barrio Sta., 1980, Alumni Hall of Fame, El Rancho H.S., 1982, Outstanding Hispanic Alumni award Whittier Coll., 1984; co-recipient with Anthony Quinn and Edward James Olmos Hispanic Entertainer of Yr., The Equitable Co., 1987; Escobedo fellow Stanford U., 1996, Dorothy Danforth Compton Rsch. fellow, 1996. Mem. Nat. Acad. of Television Arts & Scis., AFTRA, SAG (John Dales scholar 1995-96, 98), TCG, Assn. for Theatre in Higher Edn., Nat. Theatre Conf. E-mail: bneducda@leland.stanford.edu. Office: PO Box 8986 Stanford CA 94309-8986 Agent: c/o Paul Kohner Inc 9300 Wilshire Blvd Ste 555 Beverly Hills CA 90212-3211

MARTINEZ, ANTHONY JOSEPH, real estate appraiser; b. San Pedro, Calif., Nov. 2, 1947; s. Antonio Jose and Frances (Gonzales) M.; m. Judith Lyn Miller, July 24, 1971; children: Ronda Adrienne, Amanda Elizabeth, Melanie Melissa. AA, Cerritos Coll., 1968; BA, U. Americas, Mexico City, 1970. Cert. secondary tchr., Calif.; cert. gen. real estate appraiser, Ariz. Corp. officer Canyon Savs. & Loan, Prescott, Ariz., 1976-80; Ariz. dir. Nat. Assn. Ind. Fee Appraisers, Phoenix, 1989-91; with bd. dirs. Ariz. State Bd. Appraisal, Phoenix, 1990-96, chmn., 1990-94; owner RAM Enterprises, Prescott, 1980-86, A.J. Martinez & Assocs., Prescott, 1986—; instr. Yavapai Coll., Prescott, 1973—; chmn. Bus. Adv. Coun. Yavapai Coll., 1988-89; with accredited residential sq. footage stds. com. Am. Nat. Stds. Instn., 1995-96. Tech. editor: Principios De La De Bienes Raicdes Residenciales, 1983. Charter mem. Prescott Town Hall. Mem. Nat. Assn. Ind. Fee Appraisers (sr., cert. instr. 1984—), Assn. Regulatory Ofcls. (nat. pres. 1994-95), Outward Bound-Prescott (bd. dirs. 1976-80), West Yavapai Guidance Clinic (bd. dirs. 1978-84), Prescott Sister Cities Assn. (pres. 1975-78), Lions (pres. Prescott Sunrise club 1979-80). Republican. Lutheran. Avocations: reading, camping, hunting. Office: Anthony J Martinez & Assocs PO Box 4195 Prescott AZ 86302-4195

MARTINEZ, BONNIE YVONNE, retired social services worker; b. Billings, Mont., Apr. 16, 1925; d. John Aaron and Dorothy Vernon (Best) Lewis; m. Antonio Avalos Martinez, Jan. 6, 1950 (div. Nov. 1974); children: Karla Dababneh, Yvette A., Anthony K., Robin M., Dana M., Lance M., Maria B. Van Haren. Grad. in Cosmetology, Edison Tech., 1950; student, Rocky Mountain Coll., 1970. Clk. Prudential Ins., L.A., 1967-68; crime/traffic auditor L.A. Police Dept., 1968-70; clk. Dept. Motor Vehicles, L.A., 1970-71; comty. action social worker Billings, 1971-74; eligibility technician San Diego County Welfare, 1974-76, Yellowstone County Welfare, Billings, 1976-91. House rep. State of Mont., Helena, 1994—, bd. Liftt, Rape Task Force, Granparents Raising Grandchildren. Mem. Hispanics and Friends Phyllis Wheatley (pres. 1971). Republican. Pentecostal. Avocations: people, betterment of society. Home: 769 Fallow Ln Billings MT 59102-7000

MARTINEZ, CARLA ANN, word processor; b. Espanola, N.Mex., Oct. 28, 1961; d. Frank Roy and Cecilia Ann Martinez. AAS in Word Processing, No. N.Mex. C.C., Espanola, 1983; BS in Bus. Adminstrn., U. Phoenix, Albuquerque, 1997. Sec. Rio Arriba County, Espanola, 1979; police dispatcher Rio Arriba County Sheriffs, Espanola, 1979; sec. II Zia Co., Los Alamos, N.Mex., 1983-85; word processor Los Alamos Nat. Lab., 1985—. Mem. Onate Fiesta Coun., Espanola, 1985; chmn. Democrats for Progress, 1997-98, campaign mgr. Co. Treas. Robin Roybal, Espanola, 1994, 96; campaign treas. State Rep. Debbie Rodella, Espanola, 1992, mem. 4th of July Fireworks Com., Espanola, 1990, Mayor Richard Lucero Re-Election Campaign, Espanola, 1990, Christmas Farolito Display Com., Espanola, 1988; chmn. Fight Back Across N.Mex., Espanola, 1985-87, St. Judes Roadblock, Espanola, 1988, Muscular Dystrophy Telethon, Espanola, 1986. Recipient certs. of appreciation Gov. N.Mex., Santa Fe, 1986, Sec. of State, Santa Fe, 1986. Mem. Office Edn. Assn. (sec. 1981-83), N.Mex. Office Edn. Assn. (state parliamentarian 1981-82), No. N.Mex. Search Bd. (v.p. 1981-83), Espanola Valley Jaycees (sec. 1986-87, Jaycee of Yr. 1987), U.S. Jr. C. of C. (Charles E. Kulp Meml. award 1989, 50 Mem. Recruiter award 1989), N.Mex. Jaycees (chpt. pres. 1988-89, program mgr. 1986-88, region B dir., 1987-88, v.p. cmty. devel. 1989-90, v.p. enrollment and growth 1990-91, v.p. mgmt. devel. 1991-92, Chpt. Pres. of yr. 1989, Program Mgr. of Yr. 1988, Region Dir. Yr. 1988, V.P. of Yr. 1991). Democrat. Roman Catholic. Avocations: softball, softball umpiring, dancing, tennis, running. Home: PO Box 1120 Espanola NM 87532-1120

MARTINEZ, EDGAR, professional baseball player; b. N.Y.C., Jan. 2, 1963. Student, American Coll., Puerto Rico. Baseball player Seattle Mariners, 1982—. Named. to Am. League All-Star Team, 1992, 95, 96, Am. League Silver Slugger Team, 1992, 95. Am. League Batting Champion, 1992, 95. Office: Seattle Mariners Kingdome 83 King St Seattle WA 98104-2875*

MARTINEZ, GAYLE FRANCES, protective services official; b. Joplin, Mo., June 25, 1954; d. Jackie Ray Jackson and Shirley Joann (Williams) Jackson Hulett; m. Randy Louis Brown (div. Sept. 1974); 1 child, Randy Louis Brown II; m. Alan John Dwinells, July 15, 1975 (div. Sept. 1977); children: Christopher Ray Dwinells. AA, Longview Coll., 1979; indsl. drafting cert., Marin County Adult Sch., 1984; BA, Sacramento State Coll., 1989. Cert. peace officer. Computer operator JC Penney, Kans., 1977-81; air cargo specialist USAF, 1980-92; ins. agent Prudential, Richmond, Calif., 1983-85; peace officer Calif. State Prison, Vacaville, 1985—; trainer Calif. [illegible] convalescent home therapy dogs. Author: Whispers in the Wind. Mem. Calif. Correctional Peace Officers Assn. (union rep.). Democrat. Assembly of God. Avocations: sewing, interior decorating, bowling, piano. Home: 599 Greenwood Dr Vacaville CA 95687-6215

MARTINEZ, JOHN STANLEY, entrepreneur; b. Phila., Apr. 14, 1930; s. Joseph Vincent and Helen Leeds (Simpson) M.; m. Britta K. Ponder, Dec. 29, 1987; children: John Jr., Joseph G., Mary Lynn. BChemE, Rensselaer Poly. Inst., 1951; diploma, Oak Ridge Sch. Reactor Tech., 1957; PhD, U. Calif., Berkeley, 1962. Rsch. engr. N.Am. Aviation Co., Santa Susanna, Calif., 1954-55, Jet Propulsion Lab., Calif. Inst. Tech., Pasadena, Calif., 1955-61; rsch. assoc. Livermore (Calif.) Nat. Lab., 1959-61; with TRW Systems Group, Redondo Beach, Calif., 1961-76, mgr. high energy laser bus. area, 1970-76; pres. Physics Internat. Co., San Leandro, Calif., 1976-84, Jamar Enterprises, Moraga, Calif., 1970—, HLX Laser Inc., San Diego, 1986-87, Air-Sea Comm. Corp., San Diego, 1988-89; pres., CEO Jamar Tech. Co., San Diego, 1987-89, Calif. Jamar, Inc., 1989-92; chmn. Surgilase, Inc., Warwick, R.I., 1991-94; CEO, chmn. Jmar Industries, San Diego, 1993-98; chmn. Jmar Precision Sys., Inc., Chatsworth, Calif., 1993-98, Jmar Semiconductor Inc., Irvine, Calif., 1997—; CEO, chmn. Jmar Technols., Inc., San Diego, 1998—; supervisory dir. Pisces Internat., Netherlands, 1982-84; pres., chmn. Hermosa Entertainment Corp., Hermosa Beach, Calif., 1969-72;. Contbr. articles to profl. publs.; patentee in field. Chmn. Hermosa Beach City Improvement Commn., 1968-70. Capt. USMC, 1951-54, Korea. AEC fellow, 1958, Ford Found. fellow, 1960. Mem. IEEE, Sigma Xi, Tau Beta Pi. Avocations: skiing, bicycling. Home: PO Box 1030 Del Mar CA 92014-1030 Office: 3956 Sorrento Valley Blvd San Diego CA 92121-1403

MARTÍNEZ, LEE ANNE, aquatic ecologist, biology educator; b. Lake Arrowhead, Calif., 1957; d. Daniel and Barbara Martínez. BA in Aquatic Biology, U. Calif., Santa Barbara, 1979; MA in Biol. Oceanography, U. Calif., Santa Cruz, 1982; PhD in Aquatic Ecology, Cornell U., 1987. Thord-Gray fellow Scandinavian Am. Soc., Lund, Sweden, 1987; Pres.'s fellow U. Calif., Santa Barbara, 1988-89, lectr., 1989-90; Ford Found. postdoctoral fellow dept. entomology U. Calif., Riverside, 1990-93; assoc. prof. biology U. So. Colo., 1993—; bd. dirs. Marine Edn. Consortium, Santa Barbara, 1988-90; fellowship reviewer Grad. Women in Sci., 1990-93, grad. fellowship NSF, 1996—. Regents scholar U. Calif., Santa Barbara, 1977-79, Fulbright sr. rschr, 1998; Pres.' fellow, 1978, Grad. fellow NSF, 1980-85; grantee NSF, 1984, Ford Found., 1986-87, 90-91, Fulbright Sr. Rsch. grantee 1998; recipient R.H. Whittaker award Field of Ecology and Evolution, Cornell U., 1983. Mem. Am. Soc. Limnology and Oceanography (travel grantee 1985), Grad. Women in Sci. (Award for Excellence 1983), N.Am. Benthological Soc. (Wildco award, hon. mention 1984), Soc. Adv. Chicanos and Nat. Ams. in Sci. (bd. dirs. 1996-98), Sigma Xi (grant-in-aid 1983). Achievements include demonstration of novel symbiosis between open-ocean planktonic diatom mats (algae) and endosymbiotic nitrogen-fixing bacteria. Office: U So Colo 2200 Bonforte Blvd Pueblo CO 81001-4901

MARTINEZ, MARCOS LOUIS, humanities educator; b. Fairview, N.Mex., Oct. 8, 1955. BA, U. N.Mex., 1979, MA, 1987; diploma, Julliard Sch., 1983. Cert. master tchr. Suzuki method actor tng., 1991. Artistic dir. La Compania Teatro Albuquerque, 1988-91; assoc. prof. theater Calif. State U., San Marcos, 1992—; founder, dir. Teatro Consejo, Albuquerque, 1986-87, Latino Ensemble San Diego, artistic dir., 1996—; grants panel NEA, Washington, 1993, 96, Calif. Arts Coun., Sacramento, 1997. Co-adaptor, prodr. You Say Chaquehue, 1989; dir., playwright Poaching, 1994; actor Last Angry Brown Hat, 1996; co-author, actor Holy Dirt, 1997. Mem. adv. com. San Diego Repertory Theater, 1993-98, Ctr. Cultural Raza, San Diego, 1994. Grantee Rockefeller Found., 1989, McCune Found., 1993, Healy Found., 1994, Fox Found., 1996, U.S.-Mex. Culture Found., 1997. Mem. Screen Actors Guild. Democrat. Roman Catholic. Avocations: fishing, hunting, running, skiing. Office: Calif State U San Marcos CA 92096

MARTINEZ, MARIA DOLORES, pediatrician; b. Cifuentes, Cuba, Mar. 16, 1959; d. Demetrio and Alba Silvia (Perez) M.; m. James David Marple, Apr. 25, 1992. MD, U. Navarra, Pamplona, Spain, 1984. Med. diplomate. Resident in pediatrics Moses Cone Hosp., Greensboro, N.C., 1986-89; pvt. practice Charlotte, N.C., 1989-93, Mooresville, N.C., 1993-96; pediat. pulmonary fellow Univ. Med. Hosp., Tucson. Mem. AMA, Am. Acad. Pediatrics, N.C. Med. Soc., Mecklenburg County Med. Soc. Republican. Roman Catholic. Avocations: horseback riding, travel. Office: Univ Med Hosp 1501 Campbell Ave Tucson AZ 85741

MARTINEZ, MARIE E., poet; b. Mankato, Minn., Apr. 27, 1942, d. William R. and Hazel A. Sargent; m. Robert Loch, Aug. 26, 1961 (div. Aug. 1975); children: Julie Adams, Robert Loch, Jackie Loch, Jayne Rincon; m. Ernest C. Martinez, June 10, 1984 (wid.). Author: (poetry) Famous poets of 20th Century, 1996, Poetic Voices of America, 1998, others. Recipient 14 Editor Choice awards Internat. Soc. of Poets, 1995-98. Mem. Internat. Soc. of Poets. Avocations: gardening, quilting, reading, antiques, fishing and camping. Home: 7215 Inca St Denver CO 80221-2712

MARTINEZ, MATTHEW GILBERT, congressman; b. Walsenburg, Colo., Feb. 14, 1929; children: Matthew, Diane, Susan, Michael, Carol Ann. Cert of competence, Los Angeles Trade Tech. Sch., 1959. Small businessman and bldg. contractor; mem. 97th-106th Congresses from 30th (now 31st) Calif. dist., 1982—; mem. edn. and labor com., fgn. affairs com. Mem. Monterey Park Planning Commn., 1971-74; mayor City of Monterey Park, 1974-75; mem. Monterey Park City Council, 1974-80, Calif. State Assembly, 1980-82; bd. dirs. San Gabriel Valley YMCA. Served with USMC, 1947-50. Mem. Congl. Hispanic Caucus, Hispanic Am. Democrats, Nat. Assn. Latino Elected and Apptd. Ofcls., Communications Workers Am., VFW, Am. Legion, Latin Bus. Assn., Monterey Park C. of C., Navy League (dir.). Democrat. Lodge: Rotary. Office: US Ho of Reps 2234 Rayburn Bldg Ofc Washington DC 20515-0531*

MARTINEZ, PATRICIA ANN, middle school educator, administrator; b. Phoenix, Oct. 12, 1963; d. Jack Leon and Eleanor Jean (Gripman) McMullen; m. Gerald Marc Martinez, Aug. 11, 1984. BA, Calif. State U., 1986, MA magna cum laude, 1994. Cert. tchr. Calif. Tchr. St. Athanasius Elem. Sch., Long Beach, Calif., 1987-93; vice prin. St. Athanasius Elem. Sch., Long Beach, 1990-93; lang. arts specialist Washington Mid. Schs., Long Beach, 1993-96, spl. edn. tchr., 1996-97, U.S. history tchr., 1997—; mentor tchr. St. Athanasius Elem. Sch., Long Beach, 1988-90, mem. restructuring team, family leader Site-Based Decision Making Com., new-tchr. coach. Mem. ACLU, Greenpeace, 1988—; mem. Focus on Youth. Mem. ASCD, NEA, AAUW, Nat. Cath. Edn. Assn., Internat. Reading Assn., Internat. Platform Assn., Tchrs. Assn. Long Beach, Calif. Tchrs. Assn., Kappa Delta Pi, Phi Kappa Phi. Democrat. Lutheran. Avocations: volleyball, weight-lifting, Stephen King books, church choir, skiing. Home: 3601 Gardenia Ave Long Beach CA 90807-4303 Office: Washington Mid Sch 1450 Cedar Ave Long Beach CA 90813-1705

MARTINEZ, RAY, museum director. Dir. Ghost Ranch Living Mus., Albuquerque. Office: Ghost Ranch Living Mus Carson National Forest US Hwy 84: HCR 77 Box 15 Abiquiu NM 87510-9802*

MARTÍNEZ, VALERIE LYNNE, poet, educator; b. Santa Fe, June 26, 1961; d. José Ramon and Exilda Marie (Trujillo) M. BA in English, Vassar Coll., 1983; MFA in Poetry, U. Ariz., 1989. Adj. faculty U. Ariz., Tucson, 1990-92; prin. Bah'i Primary Sch., Mbabane, Swaziland, 1993; tchr. English U-Tech H.S., Big Bend, Swaziland, 1994-95; adj. faculty U. N.Mex., Albuquerque, 1996; prof. English N.Mex. Highlands U., Las Vegas, 1996—; dir. N.Mex. Highlands Writing Ctr., Las Vegas, 1996—. Editor: Reinventing the Enemy's Language, 1997; contbr. (anthology of poetry) The Best American Poetry, 1996, 1997, Touching the Fire, 1998; contbr. poetry to mags. and periodicals. Children's tennis instr., 1984—. Mem. Acad. Am. Poets. Office: NMex Highlands Univ Dept English and Philosophy Mortimer Hall Las Vegas NM 87701

MARTINEZ, WILLIAM, JR., Spanish langauge educator, multicultural issues consultant; b. National City, Calif., Feb. 6, 1961; s. William and Beatrice (Lara) M.; m. Eriko Ishikawa, Dec. 23, 1993. BA, San Diego State U., 1986, MA, 1988; PhD, U. Calif., Irvine, 1993. Tchg. asst. San Diego State U., 1986-88; tchg. assoc. U. Calif., Irvine, 1989-92, Pres.'s dissertation fellow, 1992-93; asst. prof. Spanish Calif. Poly. State U., San Luis Obispo, 1993-97, assoc. prof. Spanish, 1997—; chair student affairs com. Calif. State Internat. Programs, Long Beach, 1996—; vice chair acad. senate Calif. Poly. State U., 1997-98; cons. Calif. State U. Task Force on Globalization, Long Beach, 1997. Editor (mag.) Cultures, 1996—; contbr. articles to profl. jours. Participant/cons. Mex. Coun. Gen. Task Force, Santa Maria, Calif., 1996-97; scholar-in-residence San Luis Arts Coun., 1997—. Mem. MLA, L.Am. Studies Assn., Assn. Calif. Lang. Profls., Ctrl. Coast Assn. Lang. Profls., Philol. Assn. Pacific, Phi Beta Kappa, Sigma Delta Phi, Golden Key. Avocations: photography, poetry writing. Office: Calif Poly State Univ San Luis Obispo CA 93407

MARTINI, ROBERT EDWARD, wholesale pharmaceutical and medical supplies company executive; b. Hackensack, N.J., 1932. BS, Ohio State U., 1954. With Bergen Brunswig Corp., Orange, Calif., 1956-92, v.p., 1962-69, exec. v.p., 1969-81, pres., 1981-92, CEO, 1990-97; chmn. Bergen Brunswig Corp., Orange, 1992—; chmn. exec. com. Bergen Brunswig Corp. Capt. USAF, 1954.

MARTINS-GREEN, MANUELA, cell biologist; b. Luso, Moxico, Angola, Dec. 30, 1947; came to U.S., 1973; d. Joaquim P. and Maria Alice (Marques) Martins; m. Harry W. Green, II, May 15, 1975; children: Alice, Harry, Maria Green. BS, U. Lisbon, 1970; MS, U. Calif., Riverside, 1975; PhD, U. Calif., Davis, 1987. Chief scientist EM lab Agronomical Sta., Oeiras, Portugal, 1970-73; electron microscopist, dept. ophthalmology U. Calif., Davis, 1975-82; postdoctoral researcher Lawrence Berkeley Lab., U. Calif., 1987-88, rsch. scientist, 1992-93; adj. asst. prof. Rockefeller U., 1991-92; asst. prof. biology U. Calif., Riverside, 1993—; vis. lectr. U. Wuhan, China, 1988. Contbr. articles to profl. jours., books. Recipient Nat. Rsch. Svc. award, 1988-91, NIH traineeship, 1986-87; Fulbright Travel grantee Internat. Exch. Scholars, Riverside, 1973, NIH grantee, 1992—. Mem. Am. Cancer Soc., Am. Soc. for Cell Biology, Am. Soc. Devel. Biology, Cytokine Soc., Women for Cell Biology, Wound Healing Soc., Phi Kappa Phi. Avocations: travel, hiking. Office: U Calif Dept Cell Biology and Neuroscis Riverside CA 92521

MARTINSON, CONSTANCE FRYE, television program hostess, producer; b. Boston, Apr. 11, 1932; d. Edward and Rosalind Helen (Sperber) Frye; m. Leslie Herbert Martinson, Sept. 24, 1955; 1 child, Julianna Martinson Carner. BA in English Lit., Wellesley Coll., 1953. Dir. pub. relations Coro Found., Los Angeles, 1974-79; producer/host KHJ Dimensions, Los Angeles, 1979-81, Connie Martinson Talks Books, Los Angeles, 1981—; instr. dept. humanities UCLA, 1981—; moderator, instr. Univ. Judaism; celebrity advisor Book Fair-Music Ctr., L.A., 1986; advisor, moderator L.A. Times Festival of Books, 1996; bd. dirs. Friends of English UCLA; TV rep. L.A. Pub. Libr. L.A. Cityview, Sta. WNYE, Channel Am. Author Dramatization of Wellesley After Images, 1974; book editor, columnist Calif. Press Bur. Syndicate, 1986—; columnist Beverly Hills Courier, 1997—. Pres. Mayor's adv. council on volunteerism, Los Angeles, 1981-82; chmn. community affairs dept. Town Hall of Calif., Los Angeles, 1981-85; bd. dirs. legal def. fund NAACP, Los Angeles, 1981-84. Mem. Women in Cable, Am. Film Inst., Jewish TV Network (bd. dirs. 1985-87), PEN, Nat. Book Critics Assn., Wellesley Coll. Club (pres. 1979-81), Mulholland Tennis Club. Democrat. Jewish. Avocations: tennis, theater, reading. Home and Office: 2288 Coldwater Canyon Dr Beverly Hills CA 90210-1756

MARTINSON, STEVEN DELMAR, German studies educator; b. Puyallup, Wash., Aug. 10, 1949; s. Robert Delmar and Ruth Marie (Brackman) M.; m. Elizabeth Timmermans, Aug. 23, 1975; children: Elisa, Eric, Lori. BA, Seattle Pacific U., 1971; MA, U. Wash., 1973, PhD, 1977. Asst. prof. Northwestern U., Evanston, 1977-80, UCLA, 1980-88; assoc. prof. U. Ariz., Tucson, 1988-91, prof. dept. of German Studies, 1991—, spl. asst. dean's office Coll. of Humanities, 1996-98. Author: Harmonious Tensions: The Writings of Friedrich Schiller, 1996 (Choice award 1997), Between Luther and Münzer: The Peasant Revolt in German Drama and Thought, 1988, On Imitation, Imagination and Beauty. A Critical Reassessment of the Concept of the Literary Artist During the Early German Aufklärung, 1977, also articles. Chmn. Faith Luth. Ch. and Sch., Tucson, 1997-98. Rsch. fellow Alexander von Humboldt Found., Bonn, Germany, 1990-91; study grantee German Acad. Exch. Svc., Bonn, 1982. Mem. MLA, Am. Soc. 18th Century Studies, Am. Assn. Tchrs. German, Alexander von Humboldt Assn. Am., The Lessing Soc. Avocations: guitar, fishing, hiking. Home: 10525 E Calle Vaqueros Tucson AZ 85749 Office: U Ariz Dept German Studies Tucson AZ 85721

MARTONE, FREDERICK J., state supreme court justice; b. Fall River, Mass., Nov. 8, 1943. BS, Coll. Holy Cross, 1965; JD, U. Notre Dame, 1972; LLM, Harvard U., 1975. Bar: Mass. 1972, Ariz. 1974, U.S. Dist. Ct. Mass. 1973, U.S. Dist. Ct. Ariz. 1974, U.S. Ct. Appeals (1st cir.) 1973, U.S. Ct. Appeals (9th cir.) 1974, U.S. Supreme Ct. 1977. Law clk. to Hon. Edward F. Hennessey Mass. Supreme Judicial Ct., 1972-73; pvt. practice Phoenix, 1973-85; assoc. presiding judge Superior Ct. Ariz., Maricopa County; judge Superior Ct. Ariz., Maricopa County, Phoenix, 1985-92; justice Supreme Ct. Ariz., Phoenix, 1992—. Editor notes and comments Notre Dame Lawyer, 1970-72; contbr. articles to profl. jours. Capt. USAF, 1965-69. Mem. ABA, Ariz. Judges Assn., Maricopa County Bar Assn. Office: Supreme Ct Arizona 1501 W Washington St Phoenix AZ 85007-3231

MARTS, ALBERT LEE, choirmaster, rehabilitation counselor; b. Wichita, Kans., Oct. 23, 1950; s. Albert L. and Thalia Nian (Filby) M.; m. Pamella Ann McFarland, Nov. 20, 1971 (div. Jan. 1990); children: Damien, Dominique; m. Barbara Lea Jackson, July 7, 1990; stepchildren: Benjamin, Matthew. BS in Bible and Psychology, Manahttan Christian Coll., 1973; MA in Psychology, Eastern N.Mex. U., 1976; D Christian Counseling, Bethany Theol. Sem., 1974. Ordained to ministry Christian Ch., 1987. Minister Latham (Kans.) Christian Ch., 1970-71, Farmington (Kans.) Christian Ch., 1972-73; youth minister Southside Christian Ch., Kansas City, Mo., 1971-72; choirmaster Cannon AFB (N.Mex.) Chapel, 1983-89, St. James Episcopal Ch., Clovis, N.Mex., 1990—; vocat. rehab. counselor div. Vocat. Rehab., Clovis, 1989—. Mem. Assn. Applied Psychophysiology and Biofeedback, Rotary (pres. Clovis chpt. 1987-88).

MARTY, LAWRENCE A., magistrate; b. Leigh, Nebr., June 17, 1926. Student Wayne State U., 1944-46, Creighton Sch. Law, 1946-48; J.D., U.Wyo., 1954. Bar: Wyo. 1954. Sole practice, Green River, Wyo., 1954-67; ptnr. Mart & Clark, Green River, 1967-74; ptnr. Marty & Ragsdale, Green River, 1975—; judge Green River Mcpl. Ct., 1956-58; U.S. Magistrate Dist. Wyo., 1958—. Alt. del. Rep. Nat. Conv., 1964. Mem. ABA, Wyo. Bar Assn., Sweetwater County Bar Assn. Office: 20 E Flaming Gorge Way Green River WY 82935-4210

MARTZ, JUDY HELEN, state official; b. Big Timber, Mont., July 28, 1943; m. Harry Martz, June 23, 1965; children: Justin, Stacey. Owner, operator Martz Disposal Svc., 1971—; skater U.S. World Speed Skating Team, Japan, 1963, U.S. Olympic Team, Innsbruck, Austria, 1964; exec. dir. U.S. High Altitude Speed Skating Ctr., Butte, Mont., 1985-89; field rep. Senator Conrad Burns, 1989-96; lt. gov. State of Mont., 1996—; coach Mont. Amateur Speed Skating Assn.; bd. dirs. Youth Hockey Assn.; pres. adv. bd. U.S. Internat. Speed Skating Assn. Bd dirs. St. James Cmty. Hosp., Legion Oasis HUD Housing Project. Named Miss Rodeo Mont., 1963; inducted Butte Sports Hall of Fame, 1987.

MARTZEN, PHILIP D., physicist, software developer; b. Dinuba, Calif., Oct. 23, 1948; s. Dave and Vivian M.; m. Eloise Thompson, Jan. 29, 1972 (div. May 1988); Children: Natashya, Kinarii; m. Cynthia Stapp Landriz, July 1, 1995 (div. May 1997). BS, U. Calif., Santa Barbara, 1973, PhD, 1979. Staff mem. Geodynamics Corp., Santa Barbara, Calif., 1979-95; cons. Frontier Tech. Inc., Santa Barbara, Calif., 1996; cons. speech tech. lab. Panasonic, Santa Barbara, 1997; sr. mem. tech. staff Aerospace Corp., El Segundo, Calif., 1997—. Contbr. to profl. jours. V.p. REACTS, Santa Barbara, 1995-96; mem. Sci. and Engering. Coun. Santa Barbara, 1995—. Republican. Episcopalian. Avocations: golf, rock climbing, sailing, hiking. Home: 4166 San Martin Way Santa Barbara CA 93110-1429

MARUYAMA, TOMOKO, curator educator; b. Fujisawa, Kanagawa, Japan, Mar. 27, 1966; came to U.S., 1970; d. Hideo and Junko (Kato) M. BS, Cornell U., 1988; cert. completion Japanese lang., Soka U., Hachioji, Tokyo, 1993; MA, U. Chgo., 1994. Assoc. curator edn. Mus. Photog. Arts, San Diego, 1996—; asst. curator photography Tokyo Fuji Art Mus., Hachioji, 1995—. Author: Points of Entry, 1995, Moneywork$, 1997, various curriculum resources, 1995-97. Office: Mus Photographic Arts 1649 El Prado San Diego CA 92101-1662

MARVIN, BARBARA JOYCE, writer; b. Garden City, N.Y., July 31, 1954; d. Roland Reed Jr. and Ruth Doris (Henze) Hummel; m. Lewis Beach Marvin III, July 5, 1977; children: Lewis Beach Marvin IV, Henze Louise, Maximilian Gardner. BA in English Lit., Finch Coll., 1975; postgrad., Marymouht Manhattan, 1975, Adelphi U., 1975. ballerina Malibu Ballet by the Sea, 1980-98; owner animal sanctuary Moonfire Ranch, Malibu, 1957—. Author: Tales from Moonfire, 4 vols., 1995-98; author short stories, hist. love tales. Mem. Pacific Asian Mus., Malibu Libr. Mem. Met. Club (N.Y.), Malibu Ballet Soc. Republican. Avocations: ballet, exotic animals, vegetarianism, poetry and prose, fashion modeling. Home and Office: 23852 Pacific Coast Hwy # 349 Malibu CA 90265-4879

MARX, MARY M., museum director; b. Englewood, N.J., May 29, 1962; d. James F. and Joanne Marax. BA, Reed Coll., Portland, Oreg., 1984. Rsch. biologist Reed Coll., Portland, 1984-85, U. Calif., San Francisco, 1985-88; program dir. East Bay Conservation Corps, Oakland, Calif., 1989-91; program dir. Museum of Children's Art, Oakland, 1989-96, exec. dir., 1996—; cons. MM Cons., Oakland, 1995—. Contbr. articles to profl. jours. Commnr. City of Oakland Cultural Affairs, chmn. arts and edn. com., 1996—; co-chair Oakland Unified Sch. Dist. Arts and Edn. task force, 1997—; mem. steering com. Prescott Neighborhood Collaborative, 1995—; moderator City of Cerkeley C. of C. Panet, 1997; bd. dirs. Sports$Kids, 1996-98, Textile Werks, 1996-98; mentor Oakland H.S. Visual Arts Acad. program, 1994-96. Mem. Art Table. Avocations: running, cycling, gardening, skiing. Office: Museum of Children's Art 560 2nd St Oakland CA 94607-3502

MARZULLO, RICK JAMES, artist, educator; b. Inglewood, Calif., May 23, 1959; m. Linda Petersen, Feb. 12, 1983; 1 child: James Thomas. Graphic artist Solvang, Calif., 1975—; owner, papercutter Solvang Papirklip, Solvang, 1995—; tchr., lectr. Elderhostel Internat., Solvang, 1994—; lectr. Farstrup-Mortensen Lecture Series, Solvang, 1997. Prin. works include wrought iron gate design Bethania Lutheran Ch., Solvang, stained glass windows; represented in permanent collections Rebild Nat. Park Soc., Denmark, Hans Christian Andersen Mus., Elverhøj Danish Heritage Mus., Solvang; exhibited in numerous local one-man shows. Active Elverhøj Danish Heritage Mus., 1992—, Danish Immigrant Mus., Elk Horn, Iowa, 1996. Named 1st place for annual Christmas card design Danish Immigrant Mus., Elk Horn, 1996. Mem. Solvang Danish Days Found. (lectr., demonstrator 1992—), Papirets Kunstnere (guild), Guild Am. Papercutters. Avocations: heraldry, architecture, Scandinavian folk art, art history, design and decorative arts. Office: Solvang Papirklip PO Box 612 Solvang CA 93464-0612

MASCAREÑAS, ROBERT JAMES, communications executive, electrical engineer; b. Santa Fe, Aug. 27, 1970; s. William Robert and Connie S. (Salazar) M. BSEE, U. N.Mex., 1995; postgrad. in elec. engring., Cornell U., 1996—. Tech. staff Sandia Nat. Labs., Albuquerque, 1995-97; owner Shockwave 97-Internet Consulting Svcs., Albuquerque, 1997—. Recipient Outstanding Sr. award NASA Tng. Project U. N.Mex., 1995, Outstanding Mentor award, 1995; recipient Internat. Rotary Youth Leadership award, 1987. Mem. IEEE, N.Y. Acad. Scis. Avocations: home recording studio, weightlifting. Office: Shockwave 97 Internet Consulting Svcs PO Box 30161 Albuquerque NM 87190-0161

MASHALIDIS, EFSTATHIOS STEVE, aeronautics educator, educational consultant; b. Drama, Macedonia, Greece, Feb. 13, 1955; came to U.S., 1995; s. Konstantinos and Helen (Chrisidis) M.; m. Paraskevi Voula Bakas, Oct. 16, 1978; 1 child, Helen. BA, York U., 1983; MA, U. Toronto, Ont., Can., 1985, EdD, 1994. Rschr. OISE, Toronto, 1993-94; ednl. cons. Toronto, 1994-95; adj. faculty Phoenix Coll., 1995-96; faculty assoc. Ariz. State U. West, Phoenix, 1996—; asst. prof. Embry-Riddle Aero. U., Phoenix, 1996—; tchr. Peel Bd. Edn Mississauga, Ont., 1990-91. Author: The Nature of Human Mind and Thought: An Essay on Consciousness and Its Modes, 1994; consulting editor: Dialogs: An Interactive Jour. of the Scis., Philosophy and Theology. Founding mem. Nat. Coun. for Excellence in Critical Thinking Instrn., 1992—, Nat. Assn. Multicultural Assn., Phoenix, 1997-98. Mem. AAUP, Assn. Process Philosophy Edn. (assoc. exec. sec.), Assn. Integrative Studies, Internat. Network Philosophers Edn., Philosophy Edn. Soc., Am. Philos. Assn. Greek Orthodox. Avocations: movies, travel, cultures, books, science fiction. Office: Embry-Riddle Aeronautical U 2625 E Air Ln Phoenix AZ 85034-2626

MASKELL, DONALD ANDREW, contracts administrator; b. San Bernadino, Calif., June 22, 1963; s. Howard Andrew Maskell and Gloria Evelyn (Iglesias) White. BA, U. Puget Sound, 1985. Adminstrv. asst. State of Wash., Kent, 1986-87; data analyst Boeing Co., Seattle, 1987-93, engring. contract requirements coord., 1993—, requirements support specialist. Mem Elks. Republican. Presbyterian. Avocations: travel, computers, golf, theater, history.

MASLAND, LYNNE S., university official; b. Boston, Nov. 18, 1940; d. Keith Arnold and Camilla (Puleston) Shangraw; m. Edwin Grant Masland, Sept. 19, 1960 (div. 1975); children: Mary Conklin, Molly Allison; m. Steven Alan Mayo, July 1, 1995. Student, Mt. Holyoke Coll., South Hadley, Mass., 1958-60; BA, U. Calif., Riverside, 1970; MA, U. Calif., 1971; PhD, U. B.C., Vancouver, Can., 1994. Asst. pub. rels. dir. Inter-Am. U., San German, P.R., 1963-64; asst. to dir. elem. edn. Govt. of Am. Samoa, Pago Pago, 1966-68; project dir., cons. Wash. Commn. for Humanities, Seattle, 1976-80; exec. editor N.W. Happenings Mag., Greenbank, Wash., 1980-84; media specialist Western Wash. U., Bellingham, 1984-88; dir. pub. info. Western Wash. U., 1988—; cons. William O. Douglas Inst., Seattle, 1984, Whatcom Mus. History and Art, Bellingham, 1977; instr. U. Nebr., Omaha, 1972-86, Western Wash. U., 1972-86; asst. adj. prof. Fairhaven Coll/. 1995—. Editor: The Human Touch: Folklore of the Northwest Corner, 1979, Proceedings: The Art in Living, 1980, Reports to the Mayor on the State of the Arts in Bellingham, 1980-81; contbr. numerous articles to profl. jours. Pres. LWV, Whatcom County, Bellingham, 1977-79; bd. dirs. N.W. Concert Assn., 1981-83, Wash. State Folklife Coun., 1985-90; docent Nat. Gallery, Washington, 1969; bd. dirs. Sta. KZAZ, nat. pub. radio, Bellingham, 1992-93; bd. dirs. Mt. Baker Family Medicine. Univ. grad. fellow U. B.C., 1990-94. Mem. Wash. Press Assn. (pres. 4th Corner chpt. 1987-88, Superior Performance award 1986), Can. Comparative Lit. Assn., Coun. for Advancement and Support Edn. (Case Dist. VIII Gold award for Media Rels.), Whatcom Comm. Assn., Mount Baker Family Med. (bd. dirs.), Bellingham City Club, Rotary (bd. dirs. 1992-94). Episcopalian. Avocations: boating, gardening, travel, piano. Office: Western Wash U High St Bellingham WA 98225

MASLANSKY, CAROL JEANNE, toxicologist; b. N.Y.C., Mar. 3, 1949; d. Paul Jeremiah and Jeanne Marie (Filiatrault) Lane; m. Steven Paul Maslansky, May 28, 1973. BA, SUNY, 1971; PhD, N.Y. Med. Coll., 1983. Diplomate Am. Bd. Toxicology; cert. gen. toxicology. Asst. entomologist N.Y. State Dept. Health, White Plains, 1973-74; sr. biologist Am. Health Found., Valhalla, N.Y., 1974-76; rsch. fellow N.Y. Med. Coll., Valhalla, 1977-83, Albert Einstein Coll. Medicine, Bronx, N.Y., 1983; copr. toxicologist Texaco, Inc., Beacon, N.Y., 1984-85; prin. GeoEnviron. Cons., Inc., White Plains, N.Y., 1982-97, Maslansky GeoEnviron. Inc., Prescott, Ariz., 1997—; lectr. in entomology Westchester County Parks and Preserves, 1973-96, lectr. toxicology and hazardous materials, 1985—. Author: Air Monitoring Instrumentation, 1993, Health and Safety at Hazardous Waste Sites, 1997, (with others) Training for Hazardous Materials Team Members, 1991 (manual, video) The Poison Control Response to Chemical Emergencies, 1993. Mem. Harrison (N.Y.) Vol. Ambulance Corps., 1986-91, Westchester County (N.Y.) Hazardous Materials Response Team, 1987-96. Monsanto Fund Fellowship in Toxicology, 1988-90; grad. fellowship N.Y. Med. Coll., 1977-83. Mem. AAAS, Nat. Environ. Health Assn., N.Y. Acad. Sci., Am. Coll. Toxicology, Am. Indsl. Hygiene Assn., Environ. Mutagen Soc. Achievements include participation in development of genetic toxicity assays to identify potential carcinogens; rsch. on air monitoring instrumentation at hazardous materials sites, health and safety for hazardous waste site workers, environmental and chemical toxicology, genetic toxicology.

MASLIN, HARRY, recording industry executive, producer; b. Phila., Apr. 4, 1948; s. Philip and Sarah (Jacobs) M. Rec. engr. Regent Sound, N.Y.C.,

1969-71; chief engr. Hit Factory Studios, N.Y.C., 1971-73, 74-75; rec. engr. Record Plant Studios, N.Y.C., 1973-74; record producer HRM Prodns., Hollywood, Calif., 1975—; co-owner, pres. Image Rec. Studios, Hollywood, 1983—. Recipient 20 gold and platinum records Rec. Industry Assn. of Am. Mem. Nat. Acad. Rec. Arts and Scis., ASCAP, Audio Engring. Soc. Office: Image Rec Studios 1020 N Sycamore Ave Los Angeles CA 90038-2308

MASON, DANA ELAINE, marketing manager; b. Cleveland, Ohio, Nov. 19, 1970; d. Shephard and Elaine Inez (King) M. BSJ, Ohio Univ. Asst. mktg. dir. Eller Media, Cleve., 1993-95; A&R coord. Priority Records, L.A., 1995-96, advt. mgr., 1996-97, mktg. mgr., 1997—; cons. Longevity Records, L.A., 1995-96. Mem. L.A. Music Network. Avocations: graphic design, media planning, buying consultant. Home: 11825 Magnolia Blvd Apt 116 Valley Village CA 91607-2875

MASON, DEAN TOWLE, cardiologist; b. Berkeley, Calif., Sept. 20, 1932; s. Ira Jenckes and Florence Mabel (Towle) M.; m. Maureen O'Brien, June 22, 1957; children: Kathleen, Alison. BA in Chemistry, Duke U., 1954, MD, 1958. Diplomate Am. Bd. Internal Medicine, Am. Bd. Cardiovasc. Diseases, Nat. Bd. Med. Examiners. Intern, then resident in medicine Johns Hopkins Hosp., 1958-61; clin. assoc. cardiology br., sr. asst. surgeon USPHS, Nat. Heart Inst., NIH, 1961-63, asst. sect. dir. cardiovascular diagnosis, attending physician, sr. investigator cardiology br., 1963-68; prof. medicine, prof. physiology, chief cardiovascular medicine U. Calif. Med. Sch., Davis-Sacramento Med. Center, 1968-82; dir. cardiac ctr. Cedars Med. Ctr., Miami, Fla., 1982-83; physician-in chief Western Heart Inst., San Francisco, 1983—; chmn. dept. cardiovascular medicine St. Mary's Med. Ctr., San Francisco, 1986-98; co-chmn. cardiovascular-renal drugs U.S. Pharmacopeia Com. Revision, 1970-75; mem. life scis. com. NASA; med. rsch. rev. bd. VA, NIH; vis. prof. numerous univs., cons. in field; mem. Am. Cardiovascular Splty. Cert. Bd., 1970-78. Editor-in-chief Am. Heart Jour., 1980-96; contbr. numerous articles to med. jours. Recipient rsch. award Am. Therapeutic Soc., 1965; Theodore and Susan B. Cummings Humanitarian award Dept. State-Am. Coll. Cardiology, 1972, 73, 75, 78; Skylab Achievement award NASA, 1974; U. Calif. Faculty Rsch. award, 1978, Award of Honor Wisdom Soc., 1997, Medal of Honor Winston Churchill Soc., 1998, Armand Hammer Creative Genius award, 1998, Dwight D. Eisenhower Admirable Am. of Achievement award, 1998; named Outstanding Prof. U. Calif. Med. Sch., Davis, 1972. Master Am. Coll. Cardiology (pres. 1977-78); fellow A.C.P., Am. Heart Assn., Am. Coll. Chest Physicians, Royal Soc. Medicine; mem. Am. Soc. Clin. Investigation, Am. Physiol. Soc., Am. Soc. Pharmacology and Exptl. Therapeutics (Exptl. Therapeutics award 1973), Am. Fedn. Clin. Research, N.Y. Acad. Scis., Am. Assn. U. Cardiologists, Am. Soc. Clin. Pharmacology and Therapeutics, We. Assn. Physicians, AAUP, We. Soc. Clin. Research (past pres.), Phi Beta Kappa, Alpha Omega Alpha. Republican. Methodist. Club: El Marcero Country. Home: 44725 Country Club Dr El Macero CA 95618-1047 Office: Western Heart Inst St Mary's Med Ctr 450 Stanyan St San Francisco CA 94117-1079

MASON, FRANK HENRY, III, automobile company executive, leasing company executive; b. Paris, Tenn., Nov. 16, 1936; s. Frank H. and Dorothy (Carter) M.; children—Robert C., William C. B.E.E., Vanderbilt U., 1958; M.S. in Indsl. Mgmt., MIT, 1965. With Ford Motor Co., 1965-71, asst. controller Ford Brazil, Sao Paulo, Brazil, 1971-74, mgr. overseas financing dept., Dearborn, Mich., 1974-76, asst. controller engine div., 1976-78, mgr. facilities and mgmt. services, 1978-81; controller Ford Motor Credit Co., Dearborn, 1981-87; dir. finance Ford Fin. Services Group, Dearborn, 1987-89; exec. v.p., chief fin. officer U.S. Leasing, Internat., San Francisco, 1989-92; ret. 1992. Served to lt. USN, 1958-63.

MASON, GREG, publishing executive. Pub. PC Computing, San Francisco. Office: PC Computing 50 Beale St Ste 13 San Francisco CA 94105-1819*

MASON, JAMES ALBERT, museum director, former university dean; b. Eureka, Utah, 1929; married, 1956; 3 children. BA, Brigham Young U., 1955, MA, 1957; EdD, Ariz. State U., 1970. Cons., clinician in fine arts, 1955—; former chmn. dept. music Brigham Young U., Provo, dean Coll. Fine Arts and Communications, 1982-93; dir. Mus. of Art Brigham Young U., 1993-96; retired, 1996; vis. prof., lectr. Ind. U., Northwestern U., Cin. Coll.-Conservatory, U. Tex., Central Conservatory, Beijing, Internat. Soc. Music Edn., Warsaw; chmn. nat. symposium Applications of Psychology to the Teaching and Learning of Music; chmn., bd. dirs. The Barlow Endowment for Music Composition; co-founder, 1st pres. Utah Valley Symphony Orch.; past condr. Utah Valley Youth Orch.; bd. trustees Utah Opera Co.; commr. Utah Centennial of Statehood. Editor: The Instrumentalist, Orch. News, Utah Music Educator, Research News column, Jour. Research in Music Edn. Bd. dirs. Presser Found. Mem. Music Educators Nat. Conf. (past nat. pres., council), Nat. Music Council (past bd. dirs.), Am. Music Conf. (past bd. dirs.).

MASON, JOHANNA HENDRIKA ANNEKE, retired secondary education educator; b. Indramajoe, Indonesia, Feb. 17, 1932; came to U.S., 1957; d. Johannes Simon and Hendrika Jacoba (De Vroedt) Vermeulen; m. Alfred Bob Markholt, Feb., 1958 (div. Dec. 1966); children: Bob, Anneke, Joe Ralph, Lee Markholt; m. Rollin Mason, 1968 (div. 1978). French lang. diploma with top honors, Paris Alliance Française, 1952; BA in Philosophy summa cum laude, U. Puget Sound, 1976, MA in Comparative Lit., 1979, BA in Edn., 1988. Cert. pub. sch. tchr. 4-12. Adminstrv. asst. to pres. N.V. Nutricia, Zoetermeer, The Netherlands, 1953-57; pvt. sec. Grad. Sch. Bus. Harvard U., Cambridge, Mass., 1957; adminstrv. asst., lectr. humanities divsn. U. Puget Sound, Tacoma, 1966-88; tchr. English and French h.s. and mid. sch. Tacoma, 1988-94; mem. pres. staff orgn. U. Puget Sound, Tacoma, 1978-80, budget task force, 1981-86. Author: (poetry compilation) Journey, 1981, A Handfull of Bubbles, 1981, Echoes, Mirrors, Reflections, 1983; contbr. poetry to lit. mags. Mem. city's task force on hate crimes, Tacoma, 1992, translator, 1974-90; spkr., mem. Unitarian Universalist Assn., Tacoma, 1994—; mem. Tacoma Art Mus. Mem. So. Poverty Law Ctr., Amnesty Internat., Coun. Indian Nations, Phi Kappa Phi (nat. com. on comms. 1991-94, pres. chpt. 1973-77). Avocations: reading, hiking, theater, needlework, poetry.

MASON, MARSHALL W., theater director, educator; b. Amarillo, Tex., Feb. 24, 1940; s. Marvin Marshall and Lorine (Chrisman) M. B.S. in Speech, Northwestern U., 1961. Prof. Ariz. State U., 1994—; chief drama critic New Times, Phoenix, 1994-96. Founder, artistic dir. Circle Repertory Co., 1969-87, guest artistic dir., Ctr. Theater Group, 1988; dir. Broadway prodns. Redwood Curtain, 1993, The Seagull, 1992, Solitary Confinement, 1992, Burn This, 1987, As Is, 1985 (Drama Desk award, Tony nomination), Passion, 1983, Angels Fall, 1983 (Tony nomination), Fifth of July, 1981 (Tony nomination), Talley's Folly, 1980, (Pulitzer Prize, N.Y. Drama Critics Circle award, Tony nomination), Murder at the Howard Johnsons, 1979, Gemini, 1977, Knock Knock, 1976 (Tony nomination); Off-Broadway prodns. Sympathetic Magic, 1997, Robbers, 1997, Cakewalk, 1996, A Poster of the Cosmos/The Moonshot Tape, 1994, The Destiny of Me, 1992, Sunshine, 1989, Talley and Son, 1985, Childe Byron, 1980, Hamlet, 1979, Serenading Louie, 1976 (Obie award), Knock Knock, 1976 (Obie award), The Mound Builders, 1975 (Obie award), Battle of Angeles, 1974 (Obie award), The Sea Horse, 1974, The Hot L Baltimore, 1973 (Obie award); dir. numerous prodns. including Who's Afraid of Virginia Woolf?, Tokyo, 1985, Talley's Folly, 1982, London, Home Free! and The Madness of Lady Bright, 1968, London, Nat. Tour Sleuth, 1988, Summer and Smoke, 1988, Whisper in the Mind, 1990, King Lear, 1998, The Elephant Man, London, 1998, Long Day's Journey into Night, 1998; dir. numerous TV prodns. including Picnic, 1986, Kennedy's Children, 1982, The Fifth of July, 1983. Recipient Vernon Rice award, 1975, Drama Desk award, 1977, Margo Jones award, 1977, Outer Critics Circle award, 1978, Theatre World award, 1979, Shubert's Vaughan award, 1980, Obie award for Sustained Achievement, 1983, Inge Festival award for lifetime achievement, 1990, Last Frontier award, 1994, award Ariz. Press Club, 1995, Erwin Piscator award, 1996. Mem. Soc. Stage Dirs. and Choreographers (pres. 1983-85), Dirs. Guild Am., Actors Equity Assn., Coll. Fellow of Am. Theater. Address: 1948 E Ellis [illegible]

MASON, PAUL ALEXANDER, astronomer; b. Lafayette, La., July 13, 1962; s. David E. and Betty (Oxford) M.; m. Denise R. Baker, May 15, 1983 (div. 1987). BS in Physics and Math., U. Ariz., 1987, BS in Astronomy, 1987; MS in Physics, La. State U., 1992; PhD in Astronomy, Case Western Res. U., 1996. Rsch. asst. U. Ariz., Tucson, 1986-88; teaching asst. La. State U., Baton Rouge, 1988-91, rsch. asst., 1991-92; postdoctoral fellow in astrophysics N.Mex. State U., Las Cruces, 1996—; dir. Picture Rocks Obs., Tilden, Tex. Contbr. articles to profl. jours. Grantee La. Space Consortium, 1992, NASA, 1996; Towson Meml. scholar, 1994-95. Mem. Am. Astron. Soc., Astron. Soc. Pacific. Achievements include discovery of many properties of the complex magnetic cataclysmic variable star BY Cam; research in magnetic cataclysmic variables, low-mass X-ray binaries, and gamma ray bursts. Home: 910 S Tornillo St # 4 Las Cruces NM 88001-3362 Office: NMSU Astronomy PO Box 30001 Las Cruces NM 88003-8001

MASRI, MERLE SID, biochemist, consultant; b. Jerusalem, Palestine, Sept. 12, 1927; came to U.S., 1947; s. Said Rajab and Fatima (Muneimné) M.; m. Maryjean Loretta Anderson, June 28, 1952 (div. 1974); children: Kristin Corinne, Allan Eric, Wendy Joan, Heather Anderson. BA in Physiology, U. Calif., Berkeley, 1950; PhD in Mammalian Physiology and Biochemistry, U. Calif. Berkeley, 1953. Rsch. asst. Dept. Physiology, Univ. Calif., Berkeley, 1950-53; predoctoral fellow Baxter Labs., Berkeley, 1952-53; rsch. assoc. hematology Med. Rsch. Inst., Michael Reese Hosp., Chgo., 1954-56; sr. rsch. biochemist Agrl. Rsch. Svc., USDA, Berkeley, 1956-87; supervisory rsch. scientist Agrl. Rsch. Svc., USDA, N.D. State U. Sta., Fargo, N.D., 1987-89; pvt. practice as cons. Emeryville, Calif., 1989—; lectr. numerous confs. Contbr. articles to profl. jours. and books. Recipient Spl. Svc. and Merit awards USDA, 1966, 76, 77, Superior Svc. award USDA, 1977. Mem. AAAS, Am. Chem. Soc., Am. Oil Chemists Soc., Am. Assn. Cereal Chemists, N.Y. Acad. Scis., Inst. Food Technologists, Commonwealth Club Calif., Internat. Platform Assn., World Affairs Coun. of No. Calif., Sigma Xi. Achievements include patents for detoxification of aflatoxin in agricultural crops, improved dyeability of cotton fabrics and reduced dye and electrolyte discharge in plant effluent, new closed-circuit raw wool scouring technology to conserve water and energy and control pollution, synthesis and use of polymers for wastewater treatment, and for enzyme immobilization, toxic heavy metals removal and textile finishing treatment, non-polluting new technology for scouring raw wool in a closed circuit with water recycling and re-use and waste effluent control; studied chlorination of water in food processing operations and water re-use and recycle and the generation of mutagens and means of improving disinfection efficiency and reducing mutagen formation, cereal technology and wheat and durum quality, carbohydrate chemistry, fermentation and enology; discovered new methods and reagents for protein and amino acid residue modification and analysis, new mammalian metabolic pathways; developed other non-polluting textile finishing treatments. Home: 9 Commodore Dr Emeryville CA 94608-1652

MASSARO, MIKE, advertising executive. COO, exec. v.p. Goldberg, Moser & O'Neill, San Francisco, Calif., 1988—. Office: 77 Maiden Ln San Francisco CA 94108-5414*

MASSEE, ROBERT LEWIS, visual arts educator, freelance photographer; b. White Sulphur Springs, Mont., Feb. 5, 1965; s. Jerry and Ruth M. BA, U. Mont., 1989, MA, 1993. Video prodn. asst. U. Mont., Missoula, 1988-93; promotions producer, dir. KECI-TV, Missoula, 1990-93; newscast dir. KTVQ-TV, Billings, Mont., 1993-94; telecomms. specialist, adj. prof. Mont. State U., Billings, 1994—; audio tech. TNN, Nashville; camera operator Fox Sports Northwest, Seattle. Producer, dir. docudrama Date Rape: Where Seduction Ends and Abuse Begins, 1993, documentry Gateway Park Project, 1995. Vol. Cmty. TV Channel 7, Billings, Mont., 1994—. Recipient Very Special People award Bright and Beautiful, Billings, 1996. Avocations: skiing, golf, auto racing. E-mail: tcúrm@vixen.emcmt.edu. Fax: 406-657-2090. Office: Montana State U Billings 1500 N 30th St Billings MT 59101-0245

MASSEY, HENRY P., JR., lawyer; b. Montclair, N.J., Sept. 2, 1939. AB, Cornell U., 1961, JD with distinction, 1968. Bar: Calif. 1969. Assoc. Jackson, Tufts, Cole & Black, San Francisco, 1968-72, ptnr., 1973-82; ptnr. Wilson Sonsini Goodrich & Rosati, Palo Alto, Calif., 1982—. Bd. editors Cornell Law Rev., 1967-68. Mem. ABA (sects. on corp., banking and bus. law, taxation law), State Bar Calif. (mem. corps. com. bus. law sect. 1979-82), Order of Coif, Phi Kappa Phi. Office: Wilson Sonsini Goodrich & Rosati 650 Page Mill Rd Palo Alto CA 94304-1050

MASSEY, PAUL J., newspaper publisher; m. Jane Massey; children: Paul Jr., Mark, Jennifer, Moira. BS in Printing Mgmt., Carnegie Mellon U., 1956; MS in Acctg., Bentley Coll. Acctg. and Fin., 1978. Publisher various newspapers, Boston, Cleve., elsewhere, 1972-92, Fairbanks (Alaska) Daily News-Miner, 1992—; adv. bd. Alaska Airlines, Fairbanks Internat. Airport. Bd. dirs. Fairbanks Cmty. Food Bank, Festival Fairbanks, Fairbanks Mus. Expansion Com., Fairbanks Shakespeare Theater; mem. bd. visitors, U. Alaska Fairbanks; mem. leadership adv. coun. UAF; co-chair United Way Drive, Fairbanks, 1997. Mem. Fairbanks Rotary Club, Fairbanks C. of C. (bd. dirs.). Office: Fairbanks Daily News-Miner 200 N Cushman St Fairbanks AK 99701-2832

MASSIER, PAUL FERDINAND, mechanical engineer; b. Pocatello, Idaho, July 22, 1923; s. John and Kathryn (Arki) M.; m. Miriam Parks, May 1, 1948 (dec. Aug. 1975); children: Marilyn Massier Schwegler, Paulette Massier Holden; m. Dorothy Hedlund Wright, Sept. 12, 1978. *Grandfather Reverend Ferdinand Massier pioneered the Baptist missionary movement in the Austrian provinces of Bukovina and Galicia during the late 1800's and early 1900's. Father John Massier immigrated to the U.S. from Bukovina in 1903; mother Katie from Croatia-Slavonia in 1906. In 1951, father was elected "Deacon for Life" by First Baptist Church in Pocatello, Idaho. Mother was an excellent cook and loved gardening. Daughter Marilyn, a flutist, was awarded "Musician of the Year" at Arcadia, California High School; where daughter Paulette, a violinist, was Concert Mistress of the orchestra. Both toured Europe with the American Youth Symphony Orchestra.* Cert. engring., U. Idaho (so. br.), 1943; BSME, U. Colo., 1948; MSME, MIT, 1949. Engr. Pan-Am. Refining Corp., Texas City, Tex., 1948; design engr. Maytag Co., Newton, Iowa, 1949-50; research engr. Boeing Co., Seattle, 1951-55; sr. research engr., supr. and dep. sect. mgr. Jet Propulsion Lab. Calif. Inst. Tech., Pasadena, 1955-84, task mgr., 1984-88, mem. tech. staff, 1989-94. *Over 40 years of engineering research and supervision led to concepts and analysis of "far out" rocket propulsion systems such as anti-matter, laser, nuclear, and metastable states; evaluation of cooling capabilities of numerous conceivable liquid propellants for rocket engines; understanding of the formation of cenospheres during the combustion of heavy oils by analysis of electron microscope photo images; analysis and experimentation of pulsating blood flow through partially blocked human coronary arteries; development of a protocol for the use of artificial heart valves in humans; development of gas turbines for use as engines in trucks and boats, and as air compressors.* Contbr. articles to profl. jours. Moderator Arcadia Congl. Ch., 1996-98; mem. Arcadia High Sch. Music Club, 1966-71. With U.S. Army, 1943-46. Recipient Apollo Achievement award NASA, 1969, Basic Noise Rsch. award NASA, 1980, Life Mem. Svc. award Calif. PTA, 1970, Layman of Yr. award Arcadia Congl. Ch., 1971, Mil. Unit Citation award, 1946. Fellow AIAA (assoc., Sustained Svc. award 1980-81); mem. N.Y. Acad. Scis., Planetary Soc., Order of the Engr., Sigma Xi, Tau Beta Pi, Pi Tau Sigma, Sigma Tau. Congregationalist. Achievements include 50% reduction of cooling requirements for rocket engines, experimental evaluation of heat transfer from thermally ionized gases at temperatures up to 13,000 degrees; development of criteria for the design of supersonic diffusers for rocket engine testing at ground level; reduction of noise from aircraft jet engines, utilization of alternative fuels: combustion of heavy oils and formation of cenospheres. Avocations: travelog and documentary film production and presentations, genealogy and family history research, antiques, collecting sheet music. Home: 1000 N 1st Ave Arcadia CA 91006-2533

MASTERS, ELAINE, educator, writer; b. Kansas City, Kans., Oct. 6, 1932; d. David Shepherd and Stella Frances (Ragan) M.; m. Donald Ramon Masters, Apr. 27, 1951; children: David, Vicki, Jennifer, Kevin. BS in Edn. with honors, U. Mo., Kansas City, 1968. [illegible] Am. Sch., Manila, 1956-57; tchr. grade 5 Escuela Gloria Felix, Caracas, Venezuela, 1960-62; tchr. grade 6 Okinawa Christian Sch., Urasoe, 1968-70; tchr. grade 5 Flint Hill Elem. Sch., Vienna, Va., 1970-73, tchr. Bible Inst. Hawaii, Honolulu, 1991-92; dir. Christian edn. St. Thomas United Meth. Ch., 1983-84; tchr. children's ministries Salvation Army, Kaneohe, Hawaii, 1991-94; evangelist, Hong Kong, Malaysia, Nigeria, Thailand, Russia; seminar leader on Bible and Christian living, Hong Kong, Malaysia, Nigeria, Thailand; advisor Pentecostal Assemblies of Tribes, Chiang Mai, Thailand, 1991—; lectr. Christian Writers Workshop, 1993—. Author: Ali and the Ghost Tiger, 1967, Teach Us To Pray, 1970, Day Camp and Day Care Handbook, 1989, The Thief in Chinatown, 1998, Footloose the Mongoose and the Jumping Flea, 1999; contbr. articles to mags. and newspapers; inventor cricket transposer tool for musicians. Mem. spkrs. bur. Alzheimer's Assn., Honolulu, 1991-97. Mem. Women's Aglow Fellowship Internat., Soc. Children's Book Writers and Illustrators (regional advisor State of Hawaii 1996-98). Avocations: travel, Hawaiian culture, Thai and hill tribes culture, foreign languages. Home: 2355 Ala Wai Blvd Apt 502 Honolulu HI 96815-3404

MASTERS, LARRY JAMES, SR., lapidary educator; b. Port Angeles, Wash., Nov. 5, 1946; s. Caroline Eva Castle; m. Linda Louise, July 16, 1990; children: Larry Jr., Jason, James, Tammy, Catheline, Angela. AAS, Mohave C.C., Bullhead City, Ariz., 1995. Cert. tchr., Ariz. Instr. lapidary sci./art Mohave C.C., Bullhead City, Ariz., 1995—. Sgt. USMC, 1964-77. Mem. Silver Colo. River Rock Club (display chmn. 1996-98), Environ. Club Bullhead City (pres. 1996—). Baptist. Avocations: rock collecting, miniature car collecting, environmental club. Home: 4608 Calle Amigo Fort Mohave AZ 86427

MASTERSON, LINDA HISTEN, medical company executive; b. N.Y.C., May 21, 1951; d. George and Dorothy (Postler) Riddell; m. Robert P. Masterson, March 6, 1982; m. William J. Histen, May 24, 1971 (div. 1979). BS in med. tech., U. R.I., 1973; MS in microbiology, U. Md., 1977; student, Wharton U. Pa., Phila., 1988. Med. technologist various hosps., 1972-78; microbiology specialist Gen. Diagnostics, Warner-Lambert, Morris Plains, N.J., 1978-80; from tech. sales rep. to dir. internat. mktg. Micro-Scan, Baxter Internat., Sacramento, 1980-87; dir. mktg. Ortho Diagnostics, Johnson & Johnson, Raritan, N.J., 1987-89; sr. v.p. mktg/sales GenProbe, San Diego, 1989-92; v.p. mktg./sales Bio Star, Boulder, Colo., 1992-93; exec. v.p. Cholestech Inc., Hayward, Calif., 1994—; bd. dirs. U.S. Alcohol Testing of Am., Inc., Rancho Cucamonga, Calif. Tribute to women in industry Young Women's Christian Assn., N.J., 1989. Mem. Biomedical Mktg. Assn., Med. Mktg. Assn., Phi Kappa Phi. Avocations: skiing, kayaking, racketball. Office: Cholestech Inc 5347 Investment Blvd Hayward CA 94541-9999

MASTRINI, JANE REED, social worker, consultant; b. Lincoln, Nebr., July 23, 1948; d. William Scott and Ellen (Daly) Cromwell; m. Charles James Mastrini, July 19, 1969. BA, Western State Coll., Gunnison, Colo., 1970; MSW, U. Denver, 1980. Lic. social worker Colo.; cert. alcohol counselor Colo. and nat. Tchr. Flandreau (S.D.) Indian Sch., 1970; social worker S.D. Dept. Welfare, Pierre, 1970-75; child care worker Sacred Heart Home, Pueblo, Colo., 1975-76; counselor Fisher Peak Alcohol Treatment Ctr., Trinidad, Colo., 1976-77; family therapist West Nebr. Gen. Hosp., Scottsbluff, 1980-81; adolescent coord. St. Luke's Hosp., Denver, 1981-86; exec. dir. New Beginnings At Denver, Lakewood, Colo., 1986-90; pres. Counseling Dimensions of Colo., Denver, 1990-92; trainer Mile High Inst., 1987-93; outpatient mgr. Arapahoe House, 1992-94; therapist Kaiser Permanente, Denver, 1994—; cons. Colo. Counseling Consortium, Denver, 1984-90; field work supr. U. Denver, 1983—. Lectr., group leader Colo. Teen Inst., Denver, 1984-85, Westminster (Colo.) DARE Bd., 1998—. Mem. NASW (cert.), P.E.O. (pres. 1984-87, 94-95), Colo. Counseling Consortium, Colo. Assn. Addiction Treatment Programs (v.p. 1991-92), Westminster Dare Bd., 1998—. Democrat. Episcopalian. Avocations: hiking, reading. Home: 5738 W 116th Pl Westminster CO 80020-5948 Office: Kaiser Permanente CDTP 10230 E Dakota Ave Denver CO 80231-1312

MASTROLIA, LILYAN SPITZER, educator; b. Bklyn., Mar. 28, 1934; d. Samuel R. and Lena (Rosenbaum) Spitzer; m. Edmund J. Mastrolia, Aug. 28, 1956; children: John Alan, Philip Louis. BS in Chemistry cum laude, Bklyn. Coll., 1955; postgrad., U. So. Calif., 1955-56; MEd, Calif. State U., Los Angeles, 1957; postgrad., Calif. State U., Sacramento, 1959-60, 80-81. Tchr. Los Angeles Unified Sch. Dist., 1957-58, Folsom Unified Sch. Dist., 1958-59, San Juan Unified Sch. Dist., Carmichael, Calif., 1960-89; sci. chmn. Barrett Intermediate Sch., Carmichael, 1970-84, Mills Jr. High Sch., Rancho Cordova, Calif., 1959-63. Author poetry and book revs.; co-author Physical Science, 1979; contbr. articles to profl. jours. Facilitator reaching out Drug Abuse Prevention, 1984. Grantee NSF, 1960, 83, 84, Am. Cancer Soc. 1984. Mem. Nat. Sci. Tchrs. Assn., Nat. Writers Club, Computer Writers Assn., Nat. League Am. Penwomen (pres. 1985), Calif. Writers Club (pres. 1981-82), Internat. Food, Wine and Travel Writer's Assn., Computer Press Assn., Am. Med. Writer's Assn., Nat. Writer's Club. Avocation: tennis.

MASTRONARDE, DONALD JOHN, classicist, educator; b. Hartford, Conn., Nov. 13, 1948; s. Richard Francis and Salvatrice Dolores (Carpino) M.; m. Joan Karen Langdon, June 20, 1971; children: Andrew, Nicholas. BA, Amherst Coll., 1969; BA with honors, Oxford (Eng.) U., 1971; PhD, U. Toronto, Can., 1974. Asst. prof. classics U. Calif., Berkeley, 1973-79, assoc. prof. classics, 1979-84, prof. classics, 1984—, dept. chair classics, 1993—. Author: (textbook, software) Introduction to Attic Greek, 1993, 95, (monographs) Contact and Discontinuity: Some Conventions of Speech and Action on the Greek Tragic Stage, 1979, Euripides.Phoenissae, 1994 (Charles J. Goodwin award of merit Am. Philol. Assn. 1997); co-author: (monograph) The Textual Tradition of Euripides Phoinissai, 1982; mem., chair editl. bd. U. Calif. Publs.: Classical Studies, 1988-93; chair editl. bd. Classical Antiquity, 1992-96. Fellow Am. Coun. Learned Socs., 1978, 96, John Simon Guggenheim Found., 1984. Mem. Am. Philol. Assn., Soc. for the Promotion of Hellenic Studies. E-mail: pinax@socrates.berkeley.edu. Fax: 510-643-2959. Office: Dept Classics 2520 Univ Calif Berkeley CA 94720-2520

MASUDA, YOSHINORI, systems analyst; b. Kasai, Hyogo, Japan, Apr. 6, 1953; came to U.S., 1977, naturalized, 1993; s. Saburo and Mitsuyo (Masuda) M. BL, Kobe U., Japan, 1977; MBA, U. San Francisco, 1980. Gen. mgr. Kotobuki Trading Co., San Francisco, 1980-85; distbn. analyst Kikkoman Internat. Inc., San Francisco, 1986-87, mgr. mgmt. info. system, 1987-88, mgr. electronic data interchange, 1988-93, mgr. distbn./customer svc./electronic data interchange, 1993—. Mem. Japanese C. of C. No. Calif. Govt. Rels., Beta Gamma Sigma. Avocations: skiing, scuba diving, travel. Home: 480 Wellesley Ave Mill Valley CA 94941-3540 Office: Kikkoman Internat Inc 50 California St Ste 3600 San Francisco CA 94111-4760

MATAN, LILLIAN KATHLEEN, educator, designer; b. Boston, Aug. 18, 1937; d. George Francis and Lillian May (Herbert) Archambault; m. Joseph A. Matan, Aug. 6, 1960; children: Maria, Meg, Tony, Elizabeth, Joan, Molly. BS, Seton Hall Coll., 1960; MA, San Francisco State U., 1984; postgrad. studies, U. San Francisco. Tchr. St. Jone de Chantal, Bethesda, Md., 1956-60; tchr. home econs. Surrottsville (Md.) H.S., 1960-61; tchr., head home econs. dept. Bruswick (Md.) H.S., 1972-73; designer Dudley Kelley and Assocs., San Francisco, Calif., 1976-84; designer (prin.) K. Matan Antiques and Interiors, Ross, Calif., 1985-87; designer Charles Lester Assocs., San Francisco, 1987-88; dean of students St. Rose Acad., San Francisco, 1988-90; dir., asst. devel. The Branson Sch., Ross, Calif., 1990-92; prin. St. Anselm Sch., San Anselmo, Calif., 1993-94; adminstrv. head Ring Mt. Day Sch., Tiburon, Calif., 1995-96; sabbatical, 1997-98; ednl. cons. Head Start, Frederick County, Md., 1972-73. Pres. Cath. Charities, Marin County, Calif.; mem. Ecumenical Assn. for Housing, Marin County. Mem. KM (dame), ASID, Am. Assn. Interior Design (cert. interior designer Calif.), Am. Assn. Family and Consumer Scis., Serra Club, Phi Delta Kappa. Democrat. Roman Catholic. Home: PO Box 1140 Ross CA 94957-1140

MATANGA, GEORGE BWALYA, hydrologist; b. Kitwe, Zambia; came to U.S., 1967; s. Christopher and Magdalena (Bwalya) M.; m. Akraporn Prakobphol, July 12, 1989. BS, Calif. State U., 1971; MS, U. Calif., [illegible] Postdoctoral fellow Waterloo Ctr. Groundwater Rsch., Ont., Can., 1980-82; rsch. fellow U. Zimbabwe, Harare, 1982-83; rschr. U. Calif., Davis, 1983-84; vis. prof. Oreg. State U., Corvallis, 1984-86; groundwater modeler McLaren/Hart, Rancho Cordova, Calif., 1986-91; sr. staff engr. Radian Internat., Sacramento, Calif., 1991—. Avocations: jogging, bicycling, reading,

backpacking. Office: Radian Internat 10389 Old Placerville Rd Sacramento CA 95827-2506

MATARAZZO, HARRIS STARR, lawyer; b. Portland, Oreg., July 24, 1957; s. Joseph Dominic and Ruth Wood (Gadbois) M.; m. Judith Grace Hudson, Jan. 2, 1988. AB in Polit. Sci., Brown U., 1979; JD, Northwestern Sch. Law, Portland, 1983. Bar: Oreg. 1986, U.S. Dist. Ct. Oreg. 1986, U.S. Ct. Appeals (9th cir.) 1986, U.S. Supreme Ct. 1992. With Aitchison, Imperati, Paull, Barnett and Sherwood, Portland, 1986; assoc. Parks & Bauer, Salem, Oreg., 1987-88; pvt. practice Portland, 1988—; sprk. Mental Health and the Law conf. Med. Ednl. Svcs., Inc., 1995, 96. Contbr. to Criminal Law Handbook, 1994, 98. Mem. Hist. Preservation League Oreg., Portland, 1984—, Oreg. State Pub. Interest Rsch. Group, Portland, 1985—, The Old Ch. Soc., Portland, 1986; bd. dirs. Bosco Milligan Found., 1992—, Rape Survivors Inc., 1994, Lincoln H.S. Alumni Assn., 1995—, Morrison Ctr., 1996—, Network Housing, Inc., 1998—, Oreg. Advocacy Ctr., 1998, Italian Businessmen's Club, 1998—, InAct, Inc., 1998—; mem. vestry Trinity Epsicopal Ch., 1992-95; mem. Oreg. Advocacy Ctr. Mental Health Adv. Coun., 1996—; mem. planned giving com. Multnomah County Libr., 1997—. Mem. ABA, Fed. Bar Assn., Oreg. State Bar Assn., Oreg. Criminal Def. Lawyers Assn. (spkr. State of Mind. conf. 1990), Multnomah County Bar Assn. Office: Bank Am Fin Ctr 121 SW Morrison St Ste 1020 Portland OR 97204-3140

MATARÉ, HERBERT F., physicist, consultant; b. Aachen, Germany, Sept. 22, 1912; came to U.S., 1953; s. Josef P. and Paula (Broicher) M.; m. Ursula Krenzien, Dec. 1939; children: Felicitas, Vitus; m. Elise Walbert, Dec. 1983; 1 child, Victor B. BS in Physics, Chemistry and Math., Aachen U. Geneva, 1933; MS in Tech. Physics, U. Aachen, 1939; PhD in Electronics, Tech. U. Berlin, 1942; PhD in Solid State Physics summa cum laude, Ecole Normale Supérieure, Paris, 1950. Asst. prof. physics & electronics Tech. U. Aachen, 1936, 45; head of microwave receiver lab. Telefunken, A.G., Berlin, 1939-46; mgr. semicondr. lab. Westinghouse, Paris, 1946-52; founder, pres. Intermetall Corp., Düsseldorf, Fed. Republic Germany, 1952-56; head semincondr. R & D, corp. rsch. labs. Gen. Telephone & Electronics Co., N.Y.C., 1956-59; dir. rsch. semicondr. dept. Tekade, Nürnberg, Fed. Republic Germany, 1959-61; head quantum physics dept. rsch. labs. Bendix Corp., Southfield, Mich., 1961-64; tech. dir., acting mgr. hybrid microelectronics rsch. labs. Lear Siegler, Santa Monica, Calif., 1963-64; asst. chief engr. advance electronics dept. Douglas Aircraft Co., Santa Monica, 1964-66; tech. dir. McDonnell Douglas Missile Div., 1964-69; sci. advisor to solid state electronics group Autonetics (Rockwell Internat.), Anaheim, Calif., 1966-69; pres. Internat. Solid State Electronics Cons., L.A., 1973—; prof. electronics U. Buenos Aires, 1953-54; vis. prof. UCLA, 1968-69, Calif. State U., Fullerton, 1969-70; dir. Compound Crystals Ltd., London, 1989—; cons. UN Indsl. Devel. Orgn. to 15 Indian insts. and semiconductor cos. with conf. talks at India Inst. Tech., New Delhi and Bombay, 1978. Author: Receiver Sensitivity in the UHF, 1951, Defect Electronics in Semiconductors, 1971, Conscientious Evolution, 1978, Energy, Facts and Future, 1989, (with P. Faber) Renewable Energies, 1993; patentee first European transistor, first vacuum growth of silicon crystals with levitation, growth of bicrystals, first low temperature transistor with bicrystals, optical heterodyning with bicrystals, first crystal TV transmission link, first color TV transmission over fiber with LEDs and bicrystals, liquid phase epitaxy for LEDs and batch process for III-V-solar cells; contbr. over 100 articles to profl. jours. Fellow IEEE (life); mem. AAAS, IEEE Nuclear Plasma Scis. Soc., IEEE Power Engring. Soc., Inst. for Advancement of Man (hon.), Am. Phys. Soc. (solid state div.), Electrochem. Soc., Am. Vacuum Soc. (thin film div.), Materials Rsch. Soc., N.Y. Acad. Scis. (emeritus). Avocations: astrophysics, biology, classical music, piano. Office: ISSEC PO Box 2661 Malibu CA 90265-7661

MATAS, MYRA DOROTHEA, interior architect and designer; b. San Francisco, Mar. 21, 1938; d. Arthur Joseph and Marjorie Dorothy (Johnson) Anderson; m. Michael Richard Matas Jr., Mar. 15, 1958; children: Michael Richard III, Kenneth Scott. Cert. interior design, Canada Coll.; cert. interior design, Calif. Owner, operator Miquel's Antiques Co., Millbrae, Calif., 1969-70, Miguel's Antiques & Interiors Co., Burlingame, Calif., 1970-79, Country Elegance Antiques & Interiors Co., Menlo Park, Calif., 1979-84, La France Boutique Co., 1979-84; owner, operator, interior designer, architect, kitchen and bath designer Myra D. Matas Interior Design, San Francisco, 1984—, Lafayette, La., 1994—; mgr. La France Imports, Inc., 1982-92; pres., gen. contractor Artisans 3 Inc., Burlingame, 1988-92; gen. contractor Matas Constr., Millbrae, 1993—; instr. interior design dept. Canada Coll. Mem. Calif. Coun. Interior Design. Contbr. articles in field to profl. jours. Office: Ste 340 101 Henry Adams St San Francisco CA 94103-5213 also: 324 rue Jefferson Lafayette LA 70501

MATASEJE, VERONICA JULIA, sales executive; b. St. Ann's, Ontario, Can., Apr. 5, 1949; came to U.S., 1985; d. John and Anna Veronica M. Grad. H.S., Smithville, Can. Clk. typist, typesetter Crown Life Ins. Co., Toronto, Can., 1966-70; typesetter Toronto Life/Calendar Mag., 1970-71; typesetter, exec. sec. Cerebrus Prodns. Ltd., Toronto, 1971-74; pres. Veron Prodns. Ltd., Toronto, 1975-81, Acclaim Records Inc., Toronto, 1981-88; pvt. health care provider Las Vegas, Nev., 1989-94; retail sales mgr. Top Cats, Las Vegas, Nev., 1994—. Campaign vol. Dist. Atty., Las Vegas, 1994; vol. pilot Angel Planes, Las Vegas, 1989. Avocations: gardening, interior design, showing cats, travel. Home: 4326 Caliente St Las Vegas NV 89119-5801 Office: Top Cats PO Box 61173 Las Vegas NV 89160-1173

MATELIC, CANDACE TANGORRA, museum studies educator, consultant, museum director; b. Detroit, Aug. 21, 1952; d. Paul Eugene and Madeline Marie (Tangora) M.; m. Steven Joseph Mrozek, Sept. 17, 1983 (div. Sept. 1987); 1 child, Madeline Rose. BA, U. Mich., 1974; MA, SUNY, Oneonta, 1977; postgrad., SUNY, Albany. Interpretive specialist Living History Farms, Des Moines, 1978-80; mgr. adult edn. Henry Ford Mus./Greenfield Village, Dearborn, Mich., 1981-82, mgr. interpretive tng., 1982-84; dir., prof. mus. studies Cooperstown grad. program SUNY, Oneonta, 1985-94; exec. dir. Mission Houses Mus., Honolulu, 1994-96, Historic St. Mary's City, Md., 1997-98; cons. history mus., 1979—; lectr., tchr. nat. and regional confs., workshops, seminars, 1979—; grant reviewer Nat. Endowment for the Humanities and Inst. for Mus. Svc., Washington, 1982—. Author: (with others) Exhibition Reader, 1992; co-author: A Pictorical History of Food in Iowa, 1980, Survey of 1200-Plus Museum Studies Graduates, 1988; contbr. articles and videos on mus. interpretation and tng., 1979—; author conf. proceedings. Trustee Motown Hist. Mus., 1989—; bd. dirs. Hawaii Youth Opera Chorus, 1996. Mem. Am. Assn. State and Local History (sec., bd. dirs. 1988-93, program chmn. ann meeting 1988, mem. edn. com. 1996—, co-chair task force on edn. and tng. 1994-96), Assn. Living Hist. Farms and Agrl. Mus. (bd. dirs. 1980-88, pres. 1985, John T. Schlebecker award Lifetime Disting. Svc. 1996), Midwest Open Air Mus. Coordinating Coun. (founder, bd. dirs., pres. 1978-80), Am. Assn. Museums (mus. studies com. 1986-94), Internat. Coun. Museums, Nat. Trust for Hist. Preservation, Hawaii Museums Assn. (bd. dirs. 1994-96), So. Md. Mus. Assn. (bd. dirs. 1997-98), Cath. Hist. Soc., St. Mary's County Hist. Soc., Rotary. Democrat. Roman Catholic.

MATERA, FRANCES LORINE, elementary educator; b. Eustis, Nebr., June 28, 1926; d. Frank Daniel and Marie Mathilda (Hess) Daiss; m. Daniel Matera, Dec. 27, 1973; children: Richard William Post, Mary Jane Post Craig. BS in Edn., Concordia Tchrs. Coll., Seward, Nebr., 1956; MEd, U. Oreg., 1963; Luth. tchrs. diploma, Concordia Tchrs. Coll., Seward, 1947. Elementary tchr. Our Savior's Luth. Ch., Colorado Springs, Colo., 1954-57; tchr. 5th grade Monterey (Calif.) Pub. Schs., 1957-59; tchr. 1st grade Roseburg (Oreg.) Schs., 1959-60; tchr. several schs. Palm Springs (Calif.) Unified Sch. Dist., 1960-73; tchr. 3rd grade Vista del Monte Sch., Palm Springs, Calif., 1973-93; ret., 1993. Named Tchr. of the Yr., Palm Springs Unified Schs. Mem. Kappa Kappa Iota (chpt. and state pres.).

MATHEIS, LAWRENCE PAUL, association executive, public health consultant; b. St. Louis, Apr. 11, 1948; s. Lawrence Paul and Theresa (Lady) M.; m. Mary Francis Manning, Apr. 2, 1947; 1 child, Michelle Marie Whitaker. AB, Washington U., St. Louis, 1976, MSW, 1978. Sr. cmty. assoc. Greater St. Louis Health Sys. Agy., 1976-79; dir. planning and implementation Cardinal Health Agy., Lumberton, N.C., 1979-81; exec. dir. Clark County Health Sys. Agy., Las Vegas, 1981-86; instr. health policy U. Nev., Las Vegas, 1982—; exec. dir. Nev. State Med. Assn., Reno, 1982—; instr. health policy Coll. St. Francis, Las Vegas, 1986; instr. stats. C.C. of So. Nev., Las Vegas, 1983-86; state health adminstr. State of Nev., Carson City, 1986-88; chair Nev. Health Issues Coalition, 1988—. Newspaper columnist Las Vegas Rev., 1984-86; contbr. chpt. to book. Bd. dirs. Nev. Tobacco Prevention Coalition, Las Vegas. Sgt. U.S. Army, 1970-73. Mem. Am. Soc. Assn. Execs., Am., Assn. Med. Soc. Execs. Unitarian-Universalist. Avocations: creative writing, chess. Home: 5276 Rambling Rd Las Vegas NV 89120-1346 Office: Nev State Med Assn 2590 E Russell Rd Las Vegas NV 89120-2417

MATHER, E. COTTON, geography educator; b. West Branch, IA, Jan. 3, 1918; s. Anders Vetti and Alleda (Zwickey) M.; m. Julia Marie Eiler, Dec. 23, 1944; children: Cotton Vetti, J'Lee Alleda. AB, U. Ill., Champaign, 1940, MS, 1941; PhD, U. Wis., Madison, 1950. Geographer Army Map Svc., Washington, 1941; rsch. analyst Office of Strategic Svcs., Washington, 1942-44; instr. U. Wis., Madison, Wis., 1945-46; assoc. to full prof., dept. chmn. U. Minn., Mpls., 1957-85; pres. N.Mex. Geog. Soc., Mesilla, N.Mex., 1985-94; vis. prof. numerous univs. U.S., Can., overseas, 1959-88. Co-editor: Atlas of Kentucky, 1977, (14) International Geographical Guidebooks of North America, 1992; co-author: India, Cultural Patterns and Processes, 1982, Prairie Border Country, 1980, Upper Coulee Country, 1975, St. Croix Border Country, 1968, Beyond the Great Divide, 1992, Registered Places of New Mexico, 1994, Japanese Landscapes. Recipient research award, Assn. of Am. Geographers, 1954, Ford Found., 1964, 65. Fellow Royal Geog. Soc.; mem. Assn. Am. Geographers, Pierce County Geog. Soc., Internat. Geog. Union, N.Mex. Geog. Soc., Ctr. Am. Places (dir.), Explorers Club. Home: PO Box 1184 Mesilla NM 88046-1184 Office: NMex Geograph Soc PO Box 1201 Mesilla NM 88046-1201

MATHES, DONALD ELY, international consultant; b. St. Louis, June 1, 1933; s. Arthur and Julia Edith (Geigher) M.; m. Libbie Pauline Seltzer, July 10, 1960; children: Joshua D., Michael A. BA, Colgate U., Hamilton, N.Y., 1955; MA, Washington U., St. Louis, 1962; postgrad., Sch. Adv. Internat. Studies, Washington, 1973-74. Press attache U.S. Embassy, Lima, Peru, 1969-71; dir. pub. affairs U.S. Consulate Gen., Sao Paulo, Brazil, 1974-79; dir. press office Latin Am. bur. State Dept., Washington, 1979-81; sr. policy officer Policy Staff/USIA, Washington, 1982-83; dep. dir. Policy Staff/USIA, 1983-86; asst. press. sec. The White House, Washington, 1986-87; dir. Fast Media Guidance/USIA, Washington, 1987; internat. cons. Bethesda, Md., 1988-89; sr. assoc. Macro Systems, Inc., Silver Spring, Md., 1990—. Lt. (j.g.) USN, 1956-58. Recipient Superior Honor award, USIA, 1986, Career Achievement award, 1987. Mem. Am. Fgn. Svc. Assn. Republican. Jewish. Avocations: skiing, golf, hiking, reading. Home: PO Box 882079 Steamboat Springs CO 80488-2079

MATHESON, JAMES HUGH, musician, educator; b. L.A., Feb. 21, 1932; s. Hugh Angus and Fannie Stella (Robinson) M.; m. Joyce Helen Hornsby, June 26, 1954; children: Michael Hugh, Mark Allan. BA, San Francisco State U., 1957. English hornist Boston Pops Tour Orch., 1956; oboist/English Horn personel mgr. Portland (Oreg.) Symphony, 1957-62; oboist San Francisco Symphony, 1962-80; prin. oboist San Francisco Opera, 1962—; lectr. San Francisco State U., 1978—, Stanford (Calif.) U., 1984—; musician/oboist Anchor Chamber Players, San Francisco, 1982-96, Stanford Woodwind Quintet, 1987—; mem., bd. dirs. Musicians' Union # 6, San Francisco, 1972-82. Sgt. U.S. Army, 1951-54. Democrat. Avocations: repair and maintenance of music instruments.

MATHEWS, ANNE JONES, consultant, library educator and administrator; b. Phila.; d. Edmond Fulton and Anne Ruth (Reichner) Jones; m. Frank Samuel Mathews, June 16, 1951; children: Lisa Anne Mathews-Bingham, David Morgan, Lynne Elizabeth Bietenhader-Mathews, Alison Fulton Sawyer. AB, Wheaton Coll., 1949; MA, U. Denver, 1965, PhD, 1977. Field staff Intervarsity Christian Fellowship, Chgo., 1949-51; interviewer supr. Colo. Market Rsch. Svcs., Denver, 1952-64; reference libr. Oreg. State U., Corvallis, 1965-67; program dir. Ctrl. Colo. Libr. Sys., Denver, 1969-70; inst. dir. U.S. Office of Edn., Inst. Grant, 1979; dir. pub. rels. Grad. Sch. Librarianship and Info. Mgmt. U. Denver, 1970-76, dir. continuing edn., 1977-80, from assoc. prof. to prof., 1977-85; dir. office libr. programs, office ednl. rsch., improvement U.S. Dept. Edn., Washington, 1986-91; dir. Nat. Libr. Edn., Washington, 1992-94; cons. Acad. Ednl. Devel., Washington, 1994—; vis. lectr. Simmons Coll. Sch. Libr. Sci., Boston, 1977; cons. USIA, 1984-85, mem. book and libr. adv. com., 1981-91; faculty assoc. Danforth Found., 1974-84; speaker in field; mem. secondary sch. curriculum com. Jefferson County Pub. Schs., Colo., 1976-78; mem. adv. com. Golden H.S., 1973-77; mem. adv. coun. White House Conf. on Librs. and Info. Svcs., 1991; del. Internat. Fedn. Libr. Assn., 1984-93. Author, editor 6 books; contbr. articles to profl. jours., numerous chpts. to books. Mem. rural librs. and humanities program Colo. planning and resource bd. NEH, 1982-83; bd. mgrs. Friends Found. of Denver Pub. Libr., 1976-82; pres. Faculty Women's Club, Colo. Sch. Mines, 1963-64; bd. dirs. Jefferson County Libr. Found., 1997—; mem. Engl. Speaking Union (Denver chpt. 1995—). Mem. ALA (visionary leaders com. 1987-89, coun. mem. 1979-83, com on accreditation 1984-85, orientation com. 1974-77, 83-84, pub. rels. com.), Am. Soc. Info. Sci. (pub. rels. chmn. 1971), Mountain Plains Libr. Assn. (profl. devel. com. 1979-80, pub. rels. and publs. com. 1973-75, continuing edn. com. 1973-76), Colo. Libr. Assn. (pres. 1974, bd. dirs. 1973-75, continuing edn. com. 1976-80), Assn. Libr. & Info. Sci. Edn. (communication com. 1978-80, program com. 1977-78), Cosmos Club (Washington). Avocations: travel, reading, antique collecting, mus. & gallery activities. Home: 492 Mount Evans Rd Golden CO 80401-9626

MATHEWS, BARBARA EDITH, gynecologist; b. Santa Barbara, Calif., Oct. 5, 1946; d. Joseph Chesley and Pearl (Cieri) Mathews; AB, U. Calif., 1969; MD, Tufts U., 1972. Diplomate Am. Bd. Ob-Gyn. Intern, Cottage Hosp., Santa Barbara, 1972-73, Santa Barbara Gen. Hosp., 1972-73; resident in ob-gyn Beth Israel Hosp., Boston, 1973-77; clin. fellow in ob-gyn Harvard U., 1973-76, instr., 1976-77; gynecologist Sansum Med. Clinic, Santa Barbara, 1977-98; faculty mem. ann. postgrad. course Harvard Med. Sch.; bd. dirs. Sansum Med. Clinic, 1989-96, vice chmn. bd. dirs., 1994-96; dir. ann. postgrad course UCLA Med. Sch. Bd. dirs. Meml. Rehab. Found., Santa Barbara, Channel City Club, Santa Barbara, Music Acad. of the West, Santa Barbara, St. Francis Med. Ctr., Santa Barbara; mem. citizen's continuing edn. adv. council Santa Barbara C.C.; moderator Santa Barbara Cottage Hosp. Cmty. Health Forum. Fellow ACS, Am. Coll. Ob-gyn.; mem. AMA, Am. Soc. Colposcopy and Cervical Pathology (dir. 1982-84), Harvard U. Alumni Assn., Tri-counties Obstet. and Gynecol. Soc. (pres. 1981-82), Phi Beta Kappa. Clubs: Birnam Wood Golf (Santa Barbara). Author: (with L. Burke) Colposcopy in Clinical Practice, 1977; contbg. author Manual of Ambulatory Surgery, 1982. Home: 2105 Anacapa St Santa Barbara CA 93105-3503 Office: 2235 De La Vina St Santa Barbara CA 93105-3815

MATHEWS, BONNIE L., psychologist; b. Oakdale, Calif., May 18, 1945; d. John Frederick and Dorothy (Bailey) Webber; m. William M. Mathews (div.). BS, Calif. State U., 1980; MS, Loma Linda U., 1982; D of Psychology, Calif. Grad. Inst., 1993. Clin. psychologist, Calif. Intern Goodwill Industries Vocat. Rehab. Ctr., Sacramento, 1979, Diogenes Youth Svcs., Sacramento, 1980, Calif. Rehab. Ctr., Norco, Calif., 1980-81, Christian Counseling Ctr., La Sierra, Calif., 1980-82, Loma Linda (Calif.) U. Med. Ctr., 1981, Loma Linda U. Clinic, 1981-82; psychologist pvt. practice, San Bernardino, Calif., 1982—; asst. prof. dept. social rels., marriage & family therapy Loma Linda U. Grad. Sch., 1985—; asst. dir. The Counseling Team, San Bernardino, 1985—; clin. supr. staf trainees Christian Counseling Ctr., La Sierra, 1992—. Mem. APA, Am. Assn. Marriage & Family Therapy, Am. Critical Incident Stress Found., Calif. Assn. Marriage & Family Therapy, Calif. Peace Officers Assn., Calif. State Sheriff's Assn., Internat. Assn. Chiefs of Police. Avocations: ballroom dancing, home improvements. Office: 1881 Bus Ctr Dr San Bernardino CA 92408

MATHEWS, CAROLINE MARIE, secondary education educator; b. L.A., Nov. 21, 1940; d. Ralph Harold and Louise Alberta (Sickler) Mittendorf; div.; children: Jodi Kynette Hawley, Lisa Marie Hawley. BA in Bus., Calif. State U., L.A., 1968; MA in Bus., Humboldt State U., 1976. Cert. tchr., Calif. Tchr. U.S. history Fortuna (Calif.) H.S., 1968—, chmn. adv. com., 1973-83; presenter Calvary Chapel Women's Confs., 1995—. Treas. Stage 3 Dance Co., Arcata, Calif., 1980-85; vol. Humboldt County Assn. for the Retarded Camp and Activity program, 1969-79. Fellow Stanford U., 1985, Sonoma State U., 1991. Mem. Hwa Rang Do World Assn., Delta Pi Epsilon. Avocations: photography, backpacking, oil painting, quilting, poetry. Office: Fortuna HS 379 12th St Fortuna CA 95540-2357

MATHEWS, STANTON TERRY, lawyer; b. May 28, 1952; m. Lisa Diane Earls, Jan. 15, 1977; children: Amy Marie, Adriane Rene, Britton Lafe, Garret Tyler. BA, Brigham Young U., 1976; JD, Western State U. Coll. Law, 1981; cert. in aviation litig., Nat. Jud. Coll., Reno, Nev. Pvt. practice law Laguna Hills, Calif., 1981—; judge pro tem Orange County Superior Ct. Mem. ATLA, Orange County Bar Assn. (lectr. 1990—), Calif. Trial Lawyers Assn., Consumer Attys. of Calif., Diplomate Million Dollar Advocates Forum, Western Trial Lawyers Assn., Orange County Trial Lawyers, Orange County Coll. Trial Advocacy. Office: 24012 Calle De La Plata Ste 320 Laguna Hills CA 92653-7624

MATHEWS, WILLIAM EDWARD, neurological surgeon, educator; b. Indpls., July 12, 1934; s. Ples Leo and Roxie Elizabeth (Allen) M.; m. Eleanor Jayne Comer, Aug. 24, 1956 (div. 1976); children: Valerie, Clarissa, Marie, Blair; m. Carol Ann Koza, Sept. 12, 1987; 1 child, William Kyle. BS, Ball State U., 1958; DO, Kirksville Coll. Osteo. Med., 1961; MD, U. Calif., Irvine, 1962; fellow, Armed Forces Trauma Sch., Ft. Sam Houston, Tex., 1967-68. Diplomate Am. Bd. Neurol. and Orthopedic Surgery, Am. Bd. Pain Mgmt., Am. Bd. Indsl. Medicine, Am. Bd. Spinal Surgeons (v.p. 1990-92), Am. Bd. Forensic Medicine, Am. Bd. Traumatic Stress. Intern Kirksville (Mo.) Osteopathic Hosp., 1961-62; resident neurosurgery Los Angeles County Gen. Hosp., 1962-67; with Brookes Army Hosp., Ft. Sam Houston, 1967-68; with 8th field hosp. U.S. Army Neurosurgeon C.O. & 933 Med. Corp, Vietnam, 1968-69; chief neurosurgery Kaiser Med. Group, Walnut Creek, Calif., 1969-77; staff neurosurgeon Mt. Diablo Med. Ctr., Concord, Calif., 1977—; NIH student rsch. fellow, 1959-61; chief resident neurosurgery Los Angeles County Gen. Hosp., 1962-67; asst. prof. Krksville Coll. Osteopathic Medicine, 1958-62; asst. lecturing prof. Neuroanatomy U. Calif. Coll. of Medicine, 1962-65; sec. Am. Fedn. Med. Edn., 1997—; chmn. Am. Bd. Spinal Surgery, 1998. Author: (jour./book) Intracerebral Missile Injuries, 1972, Early Return to Work Following Cervical Disc Surgery, 1991, Iatrogenic Tethering of the Spinal Cord, 1998; contbr. articles to profl. jours. Mem. adv. com. Rep. Presdl. Selection Com.Maj. U.S. Army, 1967-69, Vietnam. Recipient Disting. Svc. award Internat. Biography, 1987; scholar Psi Sigma Alpha, 1989. Fellow Congress Neurol. Surgeons (joint sect. on neurotrauma), Royal Coll. Medicine, Am. Acad. Neurologic and Orthopedic Surgeons (pres. 1981-82, bd. dirs. 1990-97), Internat. Coll. Surgeons; mem. AMA, Calif. Med. Assn., San Francisco Neurologic, Contra Costa County Med. Soc. Roman Catholic. Avocations: pin and ink art, golf, gardening.

MATHEWSON, JUDITH JEANNE, special education educator; b. Normandy, Mo., May 4, 1954; d. Robert Edward and Jeanne Eileen (Parcels) M. AA, Kansas City C.C., 1974; BS in Psychology (Secondary Edn.) and Journalism, Kans. State U., 1976; MS in Psychology and Spl. Edn., Emporia State U., 1979. Cert. secondary tchr., Alaska, Kans. Spl. edn. tchr. Wichita Pub. Schs., 1978-79; tchr. severely emotionally disturbed students Whaley Ctr., Anchorage, 1979-83; tchr. Clark Jr. H.S., Anchorage, 1983-86, King Career Ctr., Anchorage, 1986-91; spl. edn. vocat. tchr. Chugiak H.S., Eagle River, 1994—; adj. faculty Def. Equal Opportunity Mgmt. Inst., Patrick AFB, Fla., 1989-91; lead instr., cons. Youth Corps Challenge Program Alaska Nat. Guard, Ft. Richardson, 1993-95; evening H.S. tchr. Anchorage Sch. Dist., 1991. Contbr. articles to newspapers and newsletters. Active Eagle River (Alaska) Boys and Girls Club, 1991-94; v.p. Alaska Coun. on Prevention Drug and Alcohol Abuse, Inc., Anchorage, 1986-93; usher Alaska Ctr. for Performing Arts, Anchorage, 1989—; diversity trainer Anchorage Sch. Dist., 1989—, tchr. rep., 1990. Capt. Alaska ANG, 1986—. Decorated Air Force Commendation medal, Achievement medal, Alaska Cmty. Svc. award, 1994. Mem. Holy Fools Clowning Group (treas. 1986—), Anchorage Woman's Club, Coun. for Exceptional Children (v.p. 1976—), Alaska NG Officers Assn. Roman Catholic. Avocations: computers, travel, teaching, skiing, bicycling. Home: 19412 3rd St Eagle River AK 99577-8421

MATHIAS, BETTY JANE, communications and community affairs consultant, writer, editor, lecturer; b. East Ely, Nev., Oct. 22, 1923; d. Royal F. and Dollie B. (Bowman) M.; student Merritt Bus. Sch., 1941, 42, San Francisco State U., 1941-42; 1 child, Dena. Asst. publicity dir. Oakland (Calif.) Area War Chest and Community Chest, 1943-46; pub. rels. Am. Legion, Oakland, 1946-47; asst. to pub. rels. dir. Cen. Bank of Oakland, 1947-49; pub. rels. dir. East Bay chpt. of Nat. Safety Council, 1949-51; propr., mgr. Mathias Pub. Rels. Agy., Oakland, 1951-60; gen. assignment reporter and teen news editor Daily Rev., Hayward, Calif., 1960-62; freelance pub. rels. and writing, Oakland, 1962-66, 67-69; dir. corp. communications Systech Fin. Corp., Walnut Creek, Calif., 1969-71; v.p. corp. communications Consol. Capital companies, Oakland, 1972-79, v.p. community affairs, Emeryville, Calif., 1981-84, v.p. spl. projects, 1984-85; v.p., dir. Consol. Capital Realty Svcs., Inc., Oakland, 1973-77; v.p., dir. Centennial Adv. Corp., Oakland, 1976-77; communications cons., 1979—; cons. Mountainair Realty, Cameron Park, Calif., 1986-87; pub. rels. coord. Tuolumne County Visitors Bur., 1989-90; lectr. in field; bd. dirs. Oakland YWCA, 1944-45, ARC, Oakland, So. Alameda County chpt., 1967-69, Family Ctr., Children's Hosp. Med. Ctr. No. Calif., 1982-85, March of Dimes, 1983-85, Equestrian Ctr. of Walnut Creek, Calif., 1983-84, also sec.; adult and publs. adv. Internat. Order of the Rainbow for Girls, 1953-78; communications arts adv. com. Ohlone (Calif.) Coll., 1979-85, chmn., 1982-84; mem. adv. bd. dept. mass communications Calif. State U.-Hayward, 1985; pres. San Francisco Bay Area chpt. Nat. Reyes Syndrome Found., 1981-86; vol. staff Columbia Actors' Repertory, Columbia, Calif., 1986-87, 89; mem. exec. bd., editor newsletter Tuolumne County Dem. Club, 1987; publicity chmn. 4th of July celebration Tuolumne County C. of C., 1988; vol. children's dept. Tuolumne County Pub. Libr., 1993—; vol. Annual Cmty. Christmas Eve Dinner, Sonora, Calif., 1988-96; mem. adv. com. Ride Away Ctr. for Therapeutic Riding for the Handicapped, 1995-96, vol., Hold Your Horses Therapeutic Riding Acad., 1997; vol. Tuolumne County Visitors Bur. and Film Commn., 1996—. Recipient Grand Cross of Color award Internat. Order of Rainbow for Girls, 1955. Order Eastern Star (life, worthy matron 1952, publicity chmn. Calif. state 1955), Editor East Bay Mag., 1966-67, TIA Traveler, 1969, Concepts, 1979-83. Home: 20575 Gopher Dr Sonora CA 95370-9034

MATHIAS, LESLIE MICHAEL, electronic manufacturing company executive; b. Bombay, Dec. 17, 1935; came to U.S., 1957; s. Paschal Lawrence and Dulcine (D'Souza) M.; m. Vivian Mae Doolittle, Dec. 16, 1962. BSc, U. Bombay, 1957; BS, San Jose (Calif.) State U., 1961. Elec. engr. Indian Standard Metal, Bombay, 1957; sales engr. Bleisch Engring. and Tool, Mt. View, Calif., 1958-60; gen. mgr. Meadows Terminal Bds., Cupertino, Calif., 1961-63; prodn. mgr. Sharidon Corp., Menlo Park, Calif., 1963-67, Videx Corp., Sunnyvale, Calif., 1967-68, Data Tech. Corp., Mt. View, 1968-69; pres. L.G.M. Mfg., Inc., Mt. View, 1969-83; pvt. practice plating cons. Los Altos, Calif., 1983-87; materials mgr. Excel Cirs., Santa Clara, Calif., 1987-91, 93-98, acct. mgr., 1991-93, materials mgr., 1993-98; buyer Planned Parenthood, San Jose, Calif., 1998—. Social chmn. Internat. Students, San Jose, 1958-59. Mem. Nat. Fedn. Ind. Bus., Calif. Cirs. Assn., Better Bus. Bur., Purchasing Assn., U.S. C. of C. Roman Catholic. Avocations: computer hacker, electronics, reading, med. jours. Home: 20664 Mapletree Pl Cupertino CA 95014-0449

MATHRE, LAWRENCE GERHARD, minister, federal agency administrator; b. Vancouver, B.C., Can., Mar. 24, 1925; s. Lawrence Alfred and Nellie Josephine (Thompson) M.; m. Blanche Kathleen Brudevold, Sept. 2, 1951; children: James Lawrence, Jerome Keigh, John Mark, Joel David. BA, St. Olaf Coll., 1948; MDiv., Luther Sem., 1952; MA, Phillips U., 1962. Ordained to ministry Evang. Luth. Ch. in Am., 1952. Pastor First Luth. Ch., Fargo, N.D., 1952-54, Bethlehem Luth. Ch., Buffalo Center, Iowa, 1952-57; founder, pastor Prince of Peace Luth. Ch., Oklahoma City, 1957-63; chaplain fed. prison system U.S. Dept. Justice, Okla., Wash., Ill. and Calif., 1963-73; chaplain dir. Western and N.C. regions U.S. Dept. Justice, 1973-83; pastor Hope Luth Ch., San Mateo, Calif., 1984-87, Zion Luth. Ch., Stockton, Calif., 1987-91; ret., 1991; assoc. prof. Pacific Luth. U., Parkland, Wash., 1970-72; chaplain St. Joseph's Regional Med. Ctr. With AUS, 1943-45, ETO. Decorated Bronze Star. Mem. Am. Protestant Correctional Chaplains Assn. (nat. pres. 1974), Am. Correctional Chaplains Assn. (nat. pres. 1977), Assn. Clin. Pastoral Edn. (regional chmn. 1979-83, v.p. 1977-79, treas. 1984-89), Winnebago Itasc Travelers (chaplain), Lions

(chaplain San Mateo club 1985-87). Republican. Home: 2228 Meadow Lake Dr Stockton CA 95207-4578 Winter Address: 78469 Indigo La Quinta CA 92253

MATHUR, ASHOK, telecommunications engineer, educator, researcher; b. Gorakhpur, Uttar Pradesh, India; came to U.S., 1979; s. Raj Swarup and Savitri Mathur; m. Jayanti Srivastava, May 31, 1978; children: Menka, Puja. BS, U. Agra, India, 1963, MS, 1965; PhD, U. Southampton, Hampshire, Eng., 1974. Cert. telecommunications engr., Calif.· teaching credential, Calif. Lectr. upper atmospheric physics Kanpur, India, 1965-68; doctoral researcher U. Southampton, 1968-73; postdoctoral research fellow U. Poitiers, Vienne, France, 1973-74; assoc. prof., research supr U. Kanpur, 1974-79; mem. tech. staff telecomms. sci. and engring. divsn. Jet Propulsion Lab. Calif. Inst. Tech., Pasadena, 1979-92; prin. systems engr. applied tech. divsn. Computer Scis. Corp., Pasadena, 1992-94. Contbr. numerous publs. to profl. jours.; mem. editorial bd. Acta Ciencia Indica Jour., 1975-78. Recipient 10-Yr. Svc. award Jet Propulsion Lab. Calif. Inst. Tech., 1990, Overseas Students award Brit. Coun., London, 1968, Délégation Générale a la Recherche Scientifique et Technique award, Paris, 1973, cert. of merit for disting. svcs. Internat. Biographical Ctr., Cambridge, Eng., 1988, Group Achievement award NASA, 1991. Mem. IEEE (sr.), AIAA (vice chmn. pub. policy San Gabriel Valley, sec. L.A. 1987-92), The European Phys. Soc., Calif. Inst. Tech. Mgmt. Club, Armed Forces Comms. and Electronics Assn. Avocations: photography, traveling, reading. Home: 1923 Huntington Dr Unit B Duarte CA 91010-2659 Office: Hughes Electronics/DIRECTV Inc MS RE/R8/N353 2230 E Imperial Hwy El Segundo CA 90245-3531

MATIN, A., microbiology educator, consultant; b. Delhi, India, May 8, 1941; came to U.S., 1964, naturalized, 1983; s. Mohammed and Zohra (Begum) Said; m. Mimi Keyhan, June 21, 1968. BS, U. Karachi, Pakistan, 1960, MS, 1962; PhD, UCLA, 1969. Lectr. St. Joseph's Coll., Karachi, 1962-64; research assoc. UCLA, 1964-71; sci. officer U. Groningen, Kerklaan, The Netherlands, 1971-75; from asst. prof. to full prof. microbiology and immunology Stanford U., Calif., 1975—; prof. Western Hazardous Substances Rsch. Ctr. Stanford U., 1981—; cons. Engenics, 1982-84, Monsanto, 1984-86, Chlorox, 1992-93; chmn. Stanford Recombinant DNA panel; mem. Accreditation Bd. for Engring. and Tech.; mem. internat. adv. com., Internat. Workshop on Molecular Biology of Stress Response: Meml. Found., Banaras U. and German Min. of Rsch., mem. panel Yucca Mountain Microbial Activity, Dept. of Energy, mem. study sect.; participant DOE, NABIR program draft panel; convenor of microbiol. workshop and confs.; rev. panel DOE environ. mgmt. program; mem. rev. panels DOE NABIR program, mem. Stanford Biosafety Panel; keynote spkr., adv. bd. several internat. confs.; lectr. in field. Mem. editl. bd. Jour. Bacteriology, Ann. Rev. Microbiol., Jour. Microbiology; reviewer NSF and other grants; contbr. numerous publs. to sci. jours. Fulbright fellow, 1964-71; recipient rsch. awards NSF, 1981-92, Ctr. for Biotech. Rsch., 1981-85, EPA, 1981—, NIH, 1989-92, U.N. Tokten, 1987, DOE, 1993—, Dept. Agri., 1995-97. Fellow Am. Acad. Microbiology; mem. AAAS, AAUP, Am Soc. for Microbiology (Found. lectr. 1991-93), Soc. Indsl. Microbiology, No. Soc. Indsl. Microbiology (bd. dirs.), Biophys. Soc., Am. Chem. Soc. Avocations: reading, music, hiking. Home: 690 Coronado Ave Stanford CA 94305-1039 Office: Stanford U Fairchild Sci Bldg Dept Microbiology & Immunology Stanford CA 94305-5124

MATISOFF, MARTIN ALLEN, medical editor, writer; b. Hollywood, Calif., Mar. 28, 1957; s. Bernard S. and Louise A. (Breskin) M.; m. Sharon B. Plotkin, Dec. 5, 1982. BA, Western Ill. Univ., 1998. Materials, processes engr. Litton Data Systems, Van Nuys, Calif., 1981-83; design engr. Fastener Tech., North Hollywood, Calif., 1983; applications programer Singer Librascope, Glendale, Calif., 1983-88; components engr. Ocean Tech. Inc., Burbank, Calif., 1988; tech. writer Gen. Micro Systems, Montclair, Calif., 1988-90; publ. mgr. EQE Internat., Irvine, Calif., 1990-93; medical editor Lippincott-Raven Press, N.Y., 1993-98; editor-in-chief Nutralife, Anaheim, Calif., 1998—; freelance writer, Orange, Calif., 1993—. Author poems; contbr. articles to profl. jours. Recipient Eng. Honors award Sigma Tau Delta, 1997. Mem. Am. Assn. Advancement of Sci., Assn. Advancement of Medical Instrumentation, Soc. Profl. Journalists. Jewish. Avocations: poetry, reading, cello, gardening, writing. Office: Nutralife 1383 E Gene Autry Way Anaheim CA 92805

MATLEY, BENVENUTO GILBERT (BEN MATLEY), computer engineer, educator, consultant; b. Monroe, La., Sept. 8, 1930; s. Welcome Gilbert and Lucette Marie (Renaud) M.; m. Patricia Jean McWilliams, June 21, 1959; children: Elizabeth, Katherine, John, Stephen, Richard, David. AB, San Diego State U., 1960; MBA, U. So. Calif., 1964; EdD, Nova U., 1980. Cert. data processor. Mathematician, engr. various data processing and computing firms, San Diego and L.A., 1956-64; sr. computer systems engr. Nortronics div. Northrop Corp., Hawthorne, Calif., 1964-69; prof. data processing and math. Ventura (Calif.) Coll., 1969—; lectr. in mgmt. and computer sci. West Coast U., L.A., 1982—; software cons, ednl. cons., Ventura, 1972—. Author: Principles of Elementary Algebra: A Language and Equations Approach, 1991; sr. author: National Computer Policies, 1988; contbr. chpts. to books, articles to profl. jours. Active Ventura County coun. Boy Scouts Am., 1979-82; cons. Calif. Luth. U., Thousand Oaks, Calif., 1989. Lt. (j.g.) USNR, 1952-55, Europe. Profiled in In the Beginning: Recollections of Software Pioneers, 1998. Mem. IEEE Computer Soc. (Disting Visitor 1988-91), Assn. for Computing Machinery, Math. Assn. Am. Avocation: writing. Office: Ventura Coll 4667 Telegraph Rd Ventura CA 93003-3872

MATOSSIAN, JESSE NERSES, physicist; b. L.A., Feb. 2, 1952; s. Hagop Sarkis and Alice Elizabeth (Barsoomian) M. BS in Physics, U. So. Calif., L.A., 1975; MS in Physics, Stevens Inst. Tech., Hoboken, N.J., 1976; PhD in Physics, Stevens Inst. Tech., 1983. Mem. tech. staff Hughes Rsch. Labs., Plasma Physics Lab., Malibu, Calif., 1983-91, sr. mem. tech. staff, sr. rsch. staff physicist, 1992—. Reviewer Jour. Propulsion and Power, 1987-91; contbr. over 45 articles to profl. jours. and tech. publs.; 10 patents, 10 patents pending in field. Patrom mem. L.A. County Mus. of Art; bd. dirs. Graphic Arts Coun. Mem. AIAA, IEEE, Am. Phys. Soc. (life), N.Y. Acad. Scis., Sigma Xi. Avocations: art history, collecting 19th and 20th century European paintings and 16th century engravings, classical music, travel.

MATOVICH, MITCHEL JOSEPH, JR., motion picture producer, executive; b. Watsonville, Calif., Dec. 16, 1927; s. Mitchel Joseph and Mildred Florence (Ingrom) M.; widowed, 1968; divorced, 1983; children: Wayne, Mark, Laura; m. Patte Dee Matovich, 1989. Student, San Jose State U., 1946-49. Mechanical designer Stanford Rsch. Inst., Menlo Park, Calif., 1955-59; rsch. specialist Lockheed Missiles & Space Co., Sunnyvale, Calif., 1959-70; mgr. NASA and Dept. of Def. bus. sect. Engineered Systems Div. FMC Corp., San Jose, Calif., 1970-77; pres. and chief exec. officer Morton Co. Div. of Haycor Corp., Hayward, Calif., 1977-82; pres. Concept Devel. Co., Newark, Calif., 1982-89, Matovich Prodns., Hollywood, Calif., 1987—, Stereotronics Inc., Beverly Hills, Calif., 1988—; pres. Matovich Prodns., 1989—, Movietown Pictures, 1997—; co-owner Vagabond Theatre, L.A., 1990-91. Author: The Image Machine, and other novels, feature length screenplays, stories for screenplays, short stories; author and artist childrens book series; producer, dir. (feature film) Deadly Delusions; producer (feature films) Lightning in a Bottle, 1993 (Gold award Houston Film Festival, Award of Excellence Film Adv. Bd.), I Don't Buy Kisses Anymore, 1992 (named Best Ind. Feature Houston Internat. Film Festival, Award of Excellence Film Adv. Bd., Angel award Excellence in Media, Top Applause award Santa Clarita Valley Internat. Film Festival 1994); co-producer: Social Suicide; co-inventor: Stereotronics 3-D Video System; patentee in field. Chmn. bd. Santa Clarita Internat. Film Festival, 1995; bd. dirs. Interguild Credit Union. With USN, 1945-46, 51-52, Korea. Mem. Acad. TV Arts and Scis., Soc. Motion Picture and TV Engrs., Dirs. Guild, Producers' Guild (bd. dirs.), Mensa, Intertel. Avocations: flying, scuba diving, writing, travel, art. Home: 10802 W Sandpiper Pl #11 Newhall CA 91321 Office: Matovich Prodns Inc PO Box 5744 Beverly Hills CA 90209-5744

MATSCH, RICHARD P., judge; b. Burlington, Iowa, June 8, 1930. A.B., U. Mich., 1951, J.D., 1953. Bar: Colo. Asst. U.S. atty. Colo., 1959-61; dep. city atty. City and County of Denver, 1961-63; judge U.S. Bankruptcy Ct., Colo., 1965-74; judge U.S. Dist. Ct. for Colo., 1974-94, chief judge, 1994—; [illegible] Judicial Conf. of the U.S. 1991-94; mem. com. on criminal law, 1988-94; mem. bd. dirs. Fed. Judicial Ctr., 1995—. Served with U.S. Army, 1953-55. Mem. ABA, Am. Judicature Soc. Office: US Court House 1929 Stout St Denver CO 80294*

MATSON, FLOYD WILLIAM, humanities educator, writer; b. Honolulu, Aug. 31, 1921; s. Floyd Emerson and Esther Gwendolyn (Gould) M.; m. Carla Black, June 20, 1955 (div. July 1972); children: Catherine Ann, Stephen Dale. BA in Comm., U. Calif., Berkeley, 1950, MA in Polit. Sci., 1953, PhD in Polit. Sci., 1960. News reporter Honolulu Star Bull., 1940-41; tech. writer Adel Precision Products Corp., Burbank, Calif., 1942; press analyst U.S. Occupation Hdqs., Tokyo, 1946-47; instr. speech U. Calif., Berkeley, 1951-55; resident adminstr. Far East Program U. Calif., Tokyo, 1955-56; assoc. prof. Am. studies U. Hawaii, Honolulu, 1966-68, prof. Am. studies, 1968—; lectr. speech U. Calif., Berkeley, 1956-65; vis. assoc. prof. polit. sci. U. Hawaii, Honolulu, 1965-66; cons. Stanford Rsch. Inst., Palo Alto, Calif., 1968-74. Author: The Broken Image, 1964 (Book Find Club award 1965), The Idea of Man, 1976; co-author: Prejudice, War, and the Constitution, 1954 (Woodrow Wilson award 1955), The Dehumanization of Man, 1983; editorial advisor Jour. Humanistic Psychology, 1972—, mem. editorial bd. Biography Jour., 1980—. Tech. sergeant U.S. Army Air Corps, 1943-46, Okinawa. Recipient Humanist Service award Am. Humanist Assn., 1972; grantee Japanese Sci. Found., 1976. Mem. Nat. Fedn. Blind (cons. and historian), Nat. Fedn. Blind Hawaii (treas., Eva Smyth award 1969), Am. Studies Assn., Am. Humanist Assn. Democrat. Avocations: reading, swimming, film collecting. Office: U Hawaii 1819 East-West Rd Honolulu HI 96822

MATSUDA, CRAIG SHIN, journalist; b. Denver, Feb. 14, 1956; s. Kenji and Daisy (Haruye) M. BS in Journalism, Northwestern U., 1977, MS in Journalism, 1978. Copyeditor Houston Chronicle, 1978; reporter, asst. suburban editor Miami Herald, 1978-83; Sunday metro editor Denver Post, 1983-88; asst. fgn. editor L.A. Times, 1988—. Mem. Asian Am. Journalists Assn. (nat. bd. dirs. 1998—), Newspaper Assn. Am. (diversity com. 1998—), Maynard Inst. Journalism Edn., The Asia Soc. Office: LA Times Times Mirror Sq Los Angeles CA 90053

MATSUI, DOROTHY NOBUKO, elementary education educator; b. Honolulu, Jan. 9, 1954; d. Katsura and Tamiko (Sakai) M. Student, U. Hawaii, Honolulu, 1972-76, postgrad., 1982; BEd, U. Alaska, Anchorage, 1979, MEd in Spl. Edn., 1986. Clerical asst. U. Hawaii Manoa Disbursing Office, Anchorage, 1974-76; passenger service agt. Japan Air Lines, Anchorage, 1980; bilingual tutor Anchorage Sch. Dist., 1980, elem. sch. tchr., 1980—; facilitator for juvenile justice courses Anchorage Sch. Dist., Anchorage Police Dept., Alaska Pacific U., 1992-93; mem. adv. bd. Anchorage Law-Related Edn. Advancement Project. Vol. Providence Hosp., Anchorage, 1986, Humana Hosp., Anchorage, 1984, Spl. Olympics, Anchorage, 1981, Municipality Anchorage, 1978, Easter Seal Soc. Hawaii, 1975. Mem. NAFE, NEA, Alaska Edn. Assn., Smithsonian Nat. Assoc. Program, Nat. Space Soc., Smithsonian Air and Space Assn., World Aerospace Edn. Orgn., Internat. Platform Assn., Nat. Trust for Hist. Preservation, Nat. Audubon Soc., Planetary Soc., Cousteau Soc., Alaska Coun. for the Social Studies, Alaska Coun. Tchrs. Math., World Inst. Achievment, U.S. Olympic Soc., Women's Inner Circle Achievement, U. Alaska Alumni Assn., World Wildlife Fund, Japanese-Am. Nat. Mus., Alpha Delta Kappa (treas. Alpha chpt. 1988-92, corr. sec. 1993-96, sgt. at arms 1996-98). Avocations: reading, sports, learning. Office: Anchorage Sch Dist 7001 Cranberry St Anchorage AK 99502-7145

MATSUI, JIRO, importer, wholesaler, small business owner; b. Honolulu, Hawaii, Apr. 5, 1919; s. Juro and Tsuta (Murai) M.; m. Barbara Toshiko Tanji; children: Kenneth Jiro, Alan Kiyoshi, Carol Ritsu. BA, U. Hawaii, 1949. Owner Honolulu Aquarium and Pet Supply, Honolulu, 1946-77, Bird House, Honolulu, 1957-61; owner, pres., chmn. Petland, Inc., Honolulu, 1961—, Pets Pacifica, Inc., Honolulu, 1977—, Global Pet Industries, Honolulu, 1975—; organizer, coord. first Pet Consumer Show in U.S., 1979, pres. 1979-82; first Internat. Pet Show; cons. Japan Pet Product Mfr. Assn. Fair, Japan, 1981—. Pres. Waikiki Vets. Club, Kapahulu, Oahu, Hawaii, 1948-66, Waiana (Oahu) Farmers, 1948-88; sr. adv. com. plants and animals State of Hawaii, 1974—. Sgt. U.S. Army, 1941-46. Decorated Bronze Star; named retailer of yr. Retail Merchants of Hawaii, 1993. Mem. Am. Pet Soc. (pres. 1979-82, chmn. 1989-92), World Wide Pet Supply Assn. (bd. dirs. 1974-93, pres. 1989-90, Edward B. Price award 1982), Honolulu C. of C. (bd. dirs. 1974—), Merchants of Hawaii. Avocations: fishing, gardening,. Office: Pets Pacifica Inc 94-486 Ukee St Waipahu HI 96797-4211

MATSUI, ROBERT TAKEO, congressman; b. Sacramento, Sept. 17, 1941; s. Yasuji and Alice (Nagata) M.; m. Doris Kazue Okada, Sept. 17, 1966; 1 child, Brian Robert. AB in Polit. Sci, U. Calif., Berkeley, 1963; JD, U. Calif., San Francisco, 1966. Bar: Calif. 1967. Practiced law Sacramento, 1967-78; mem. Sacramento City Council, 1971-78, vice mayor, 1977; mem. 96th-106th Congresses from 5th Calif. dist., 1979—; ranking minority mem., mem. ways and means subcom. on oversight; dep. chair Dem. Nat. Com., 1995—; chmn. profl. bus. forum Dem. Congl. Campaign Com.; congl. liaison nat. fin. council Dem. Nat. Com.; mem. adv. council on fiscal policy Am. Enterprise Inst. chmn. Profl. Bus. Forum of the Dem. Congl. Co. and Com.; congl. liaison Nat. Fin. Council, Dem. Nat. Com.; mem. Am. Enterprise Inst. Adv. Council on Fiscal Policy. Named Young Man of Yr. Jr. C. of C., 1973; recipient Disting. Service award, 1973. Mem. Sacramento Japanese Am. Citizens League (pres. 1969), Sacramento Met. C. of C. (dir. 1976). Democrat. Clubs: 20-30 (Sacramento) (pres. 1972), Rotary (Sacramento). Office: US Ho of Reps 2308 Rayburn HOB Washington DC 20515-0505*

MATSUMORI, DOUGLAS, lawyer; b. Salt Lake City, Oct. 22, 1947. BS, U. Utah, 1973; JD, Harvard U., 1976. With Ray, Quinney & Nebeker P.C., Salt Lake City. Mem. Utah State Bar, Phi Beta Kappa. Office: Ray Quinney & Nebeker 79 S Main St Ste 400 Salt Lake City UT 84111-1996

MATSUNAGA, GEOFFREY DEAN, lawyer; b. L.A., Sept. 30, 1949; s. Hideo Arthur and Yuri (Yamazaki) M.; m. Masako Inoue, Aug. 20, 1981; children: Ayako, Hideko, Lisa Fumi. BS, USAF Acad., 1971; MBA, UCLA, 1972; postgrad., Inter U. Ctr. Japanese Lang. Studies, 1979-80; JD, U. Calif., Berkeley, 1982. Bar: Calif. 1982, U.S. Dist. Ct. (cen. dist.) Calif. 1982, N.Y. 1983, U.S. Dist. Ct. (so. dist.) N.Y. 1983. Jud. extern U.S. Dist. Ct. (cen. dist.), L.A., 1981; assoc. Milbank, Tweed, Hadley & McCloy, N.Y.C., 1982-84, Tokyo, 1984-87; assoc. Sidley & Austin, Tokyo, 1987-88, L.A., 1988-91; counsel Sheppard, Mullin, Richter & Hampton, L.A., 1991-94; ptnr. Kagei & Matsunaga, L.A., 1995—. Founding bd. dirs. Futures Industry Assn., Japan, 1987; counsel East West Players, 1992-95. Lt. USN, 1972-78. Japan Found. fellow, Tokyo, 1979-80. Mem. Japan Bus. Assn. Southern Calif., Japan Am. Soc. So. Calif. (adv. bd. South Bay 1992-95). Episcopalian. Avocation: hiking, classical music. Office: Kagei & Matsunaga 19191 S Vermont Ave Ste 420 Torrance CA 90502-1051

MATSUOKA, ERIC TAKAO, mathematics educator; b. Honolulu, May 9, 1967; s. Kenneth Tamotsu and Hilda Sumie (Hino) M. BA in Math. with distinction, U. Hawaii, 1987, MA in Math., 1994. Acctg. clk. Wayne Choo, CPA, Honolulu, 1987-88; lab. instr. in math. Leeward Community Coll., Pearl City, Hawaii, 1988-91, lectr. in math., 1989-94; contr. Computronics, Honolulu, 1989-93; instr. math., 1994—. Mem. Math. Assn. Am. (Instnl. award 1987). Avocations: bowling, gemstones, jewelry, computers, mathematics. Office: Leeward CC 96-045 Ala Ike St Pearl City HI 96782-3366

MATSUURA, KENNETH RAY, counselor, articulation officer; b. Urbana, Ill., July 17, 1954; s. George Shigeo and Sally Sueko (Kawasaki) M.; m. Peggy Ai Iwata, May 27, 1995. BA, U. Calif., Santa Barbara, 1976; MA, UCLA, 1978, PhD, 1996. Career counselor Calif. State U. Dominguez Hills, Carson, 1984-85; grad. recruitment coord. U. Calif., Irvine, 1985-90; counselor/articulation officer Cerritos Coll., [illegible] Calif., 1988—; [illegible] accreditation teams Western Assn. Schs. and Colls., L.A., 1994; program reviewer Am. Coll. Pers. Assn. Ann. conf., Washington, 1988; presenter to confs. UCLA Grad. Advancement Program fellow, 1977-78. Avocations: singing, music. Home: 1066 Boston Dr Pasadena CA 91107-5917 Office: Cerritos College 11110 Alondra Blvd Norwalk CA 90650-6298

MATTATHIL, GEORGE PAUL, communications specialist, consultant; b. Kottayam, India, May 12, 1957; came to U.S., 1985; s. Paul and Annamma M. Bs, U. Kerala (India), 1973-78; MS, Indian Inst. Tech., 1978-82. Project engr. Tekelec, Calabasas, Calif., 1986-89; sr. systems analyst Security Pacific Automation, L.A., 1989-90; sr. design. engr. Telenova, Camarillo, Calif., 1990-91; cons. Raynet, Menlo Park, Calif., 1991, Larse, Santa Clara, Calif., 1991—, NEC, 1992—, Level One Comm., Sacramento, 1994—, DigitalLink, 1994—, Verilink, San Jose, 1994—, Telebit, Sunnyvale, 1995—, Hitachi, San Jose, 1995—, C-Cor Electronics, Fremont, 1996, Xylan, Calabasas, Calif., 1996—, GoDigital Telecomm., Fremont, 1996—. Nat. Sci. Talent scholar, India, 1975-80. Mem. IEEE, Profl. and Tech. Cons. Assn., Assn. Computing Machinery, Software Forum, Soc. Telecom. Cons. Avocations: photography, biking. Office: Silicom Inc PO Box 2264 Cupertino CA 95015-2264

MATTES, MARTIN ANTHONY, lawyer; b. San Francisco, June 18, 1946; s. Hans Adam and Marion Jane (Burge) M.; m. Catherine Elvira Garzio, May 26, 1984; children: Nicholas Anthony, Daniel Joseph, Thomas George. BA, Stanford U., 1968; postgrad., U. Chgo., 1968-69, U. Bonn, Fed. Republic Germany, 1971; JD, U. Calif., Berkeley, 1974. Bar: Calif. 1974, U.S. Ct. Appeals (D.C., 5th and 9th cirs.) 1978, U.S. Dist. Ct. (no. dist.) Calif. 1979, U.S. Dist. Ct. (ea. dist.) Calif. 1991. Asst. legal officer Internat. Union Conservation of Nature and Natural Resources, Bonn, 1974-76; staff counsel Calif. Pub. Utilities Commn., San Francisco, 1976-79, legal advisor to pres., 1979-82, adminstrv. law judge, 1983, asst. chief adminstrv. law judge, 1983-86; ptnr. Graham & James, San Francisco, 1986-98, Nossaman Guthner Knox Elliott, LLP, San Francisco, 1998—; mem. adv. group. to Calif. Senate Subcom. on Pub. Utilities Commn. Procedural Reform, 1994. Mng. editor Ecology Law Quar., 1973-74; contbr. articles to profl. publs. Mem. Conf. Calif. Pub. Utility Counsel (treas. 1988-90, v.p. 1990-91, pres. 1991-92), Internat. Coun. Environ. Law, San Francisco Bar Assn. Office: Nossaman Guthner Knox Elliott LLP 50 California St 34th Fl San Francisco CA 94111*

MATTESON, BARBARA ANN VANCE, secondary education educator; b. Ft. Collins, Colo., Mar. 1, 1940; d. Wilford Walton and Louise (Hinchliffe) Vance; m. David Russell Matteson, Apr. 9, 1961 (dec. Oct. 12, 1988); 1 child, Deborah Jean. BA, U. No. Colo., 1965; postgrad., U. Colo., 1967-78, Colo. State U., 1967-78, U. Wyo., 1978—. Tchr. reading and lang. arts Westminster (Colo.) H.S., 1968-78; tchr. reading and lang. arts Natrona County H.S., Casper, Wyo., 1978—, chmn. dept. lang. arts, 1981-87; tchr. Natrona Acad., 1994—; coord. secondary lang. arts Natrona County Sch. Dist. 1, 1992-95, writing assessment facilitator, 1992-93. Named Outstanding Educator, Natrona County Sch. Dist. 1, 1990. Mem. ASCD, Nat. Coun. Tchrs. English, Wyo. ASCD, Delta Kappa Gamma. Avocations: reading, travel, dollhouses. Home: 2700 Belmont Rd Casper WY 82604-4644 Office: Natrona County HS 930 S Elm St Casper WY 82601-3603

MATTESON, ROBERT JAMES, music company executive, talent agent; b. Glendale, Calif., Nov. 24, 1951; s. William Robert Matteson and Claire Ann (Mitchell) Holt. Grad. h.s., Hollywood, Calif. Computer tape libr. Arco Corp., L.A., 1980; talent agt. Four Star Agy., L.A., 1976-79, The Casting Agy., Palm Springs, Calif., 1987-94; pres. Four Star Concerts, Inc., L.A., 1971—. Author, dir. (film) Satan's Playground, 1978; author: The Aristocracy Collection of Autographs, 1996. Mem. Desert Blind Assn., Palm Springs, 1987—. Mem. Pres.'s Club. Avocations: tennis, music, film collector and star photo collecting. Office: Four Star Concerts Inc 431 S Palm Canyon Dr # 101 Palm Springs CA 92262-7303

MATTEUCCI, DOMINICK VINCENT, real estate developer; b. Trenton, N.J., Oct. 19, 1924; s. Vincent Joseph and Anna Marie (Zoda) M.; BS, Coll. of William and Mary, 1948; BS, Mass. Inst. Tech., 1950. Registered profl. engr., Calif.; lic. gen. bldg. contractor, real estate broker; m. Emma Irene DeGuia, Mar. 2, 1968; children: Felisa Anna, Vincent Eriberto. Owner, Matteucci Devel. Co., Newport Beach, Calif.; pres. Nat. Investment Brokerage Co., Newport Beach. Home: 2104 Felipe Newport Beach CA 92660-4040 Office: PO Box 10474 Newport Beach CA 92658-0474

MATTEUCCI, SHERRY SCHEEL, lawyer; b. Columbus, Mont., Aug. 17, 1947; d. Gerald F. and Shirley Scheel; m. William L. Matteucci, Dec. 26, 1969 (div. June 1976); children: Cory, Cody. Student, Kinman Bus. U., 1965-66, Mont. State U., 1967-69, Gonzaga U., 1971-72; BS, Eastern Wash. State U., 1973; JD, U. Mont., 1979. Bar: Mont., U.S. Dist. Ct. Mont., U.S. Ct. Appeals (9th cir.), U.S. Supreme Ct. Mont. Spl. asst. Commr. Higher Edn., 1974-76; assoc. Crowley, Haughey, Hanson, Toole & Dietrich, Billings, Mont., 1979-83, ptnr., 1984-93; U.S. atty. Dist. of Mont., Billings, 1993—; bd. visitors U. Mont. Law Sch., 1988—. Mem. editorial bd. U. Mont. Law Rev., 1977-78, contbg. editor, 1978-79. Bd. dirs. Big Bros. & Sisters, Billings, 1982-85, City/County Library Bd., Billings, 1983-93, Billings Community Cable Corp., 1986, chmn., 1987; vice chmn., bd. dirs. Parmley Billings Library Found. Named one of Outstanding Young Women in Am., 1983. Mem. ABA, State Bar Mont. (chmn. jud. polling com. 1985-87, chmn. women's law sect. 1985-86, trustee, sec., treas. 1988—), Yellowstone County Bar Assn. (dir. 1984-87, pres.-elect 1986-87, pres. 1987-88), Billings C. of C. (leadership com. 1986, legis. affairs com. 1984). Democrat. Mem. Unitarian Ch. Home: 1804 Virginia Ln Billings MT 59102-3626 Office: U.S. Attorney Western Federal Savings & Loan Bldg 2929 3rd Ave N Billings MT 59101-1944*

MATTHAU, CHARLES MARCUS, film director; b. N.Y.C., Dec. 10, 1965; s. Walter and Carol M. BA, U. So. Calif., 1986. Pres. The Matthau Co., L.A., 1987—; bd. govs. Cedar Sinai Med. Ctr., L.A. Dir. motion picture Doin' Time on Planet Earth, 1990 (Saturn award Coun. Film Orgns., Silver Scroll award Acad. Sci. Fiction); dir., prodr. TV show Mrs. Lambert Remembers Love, 1993 (Golden Angel award Best TV Spl. 1993, Golden Medal award Best Drama Prodn. 1993, Grand award The Houston Internat. Film Festival); dir., prodr. motion picture The Grass Harp, 1996 (recipient Best Dir. Family Film awards 1996); dir. The Marriage Fool, 1998; dir. over 50 feature shorts. Nat. spokesperson Am. Lung Assn., L.A., 1989—; active Action on Smoking and Health, Washington, 1986—. Recipient Cine award, Coun. Non-Theatrical Events, Washington, 1985, Golden Seal award, London Amateur Film Festival, 1986, Platinum Circle award Am. Film Inst. Mem. Dirs. Guild Am.

MATTHEW, LYN, sales and marketing executive consultant, educator; b. Long Beach, Calif., Dec. 15, 1936; d. Harold G. and Beatrice (Hunt) M.; m. Wayne Thomas Castleberry, Aug. 12, 1961 (div. Jan. 1976); children: Melanie, Cheryl, Nicole, Matthew. BS, U. Calif.-Davis, 1958; MA, Ariz. State U., 1979. Cert. hotel sales exec., 1988, meeting profl. Pres., Davlyn Cons. Found., Scottsdale, Ariz., 1979-82; cons., vis. prof. The Art Bus., Scottsdale, 1982—; pres., dir. sales and mktg. Embassy Stes., Scottsdale, 1987-98, bd. trustees Hotel Sales and Mktg. Assn. Internat. Found., 1988—, chmn., 1991-93, mem. exec. com., 1993—; vis. prof. Maricopa C.C., Phoenix, 1979—, Ariz. State U., Tempe, 1980-83; cons. Women's Caucus for Art, Phoenix, 1983-88. Bd. dirs. Rossom House and Heritage Square Found., Phoenix, 1987-88. Author: The Business Aspects of Art, Book I, 1979, Book II, 1979; Marketing Strategies for the Creative Artist, 1985. Mem. Women Image Now (Achievement and Contbn. in Visual Arts award 1983), Women in Higher Edn., Nat. Women's Caucus for Art (v.p. 1981-83), Ariz. Women's Caucus for Art (pres. 1980-82, hon. advisor 1986-87), Ariz. Vocat. Edn. Assn. (sec. 1978-80), Ariz. Visionary Artists (treas. 1987-89), Hotel Sales and Mktg. Assn. Internat. (pres. Great Phoenix chpt. 1988-89, regional dir. 1989-90, bd. dirs. 1985-90), CHME (profl. designation tng. chair, certification commr.), Meeting Planners Internat. (v.p. Ariz. Sunbelt chpt. 1989-91, pres. 1991-92, Supplier of Yr. award 1988, CMP certification trainer), Soc. Govt. Meeting Planners (charter bd. dirs. 1987, Sam Gilmer award 1992, nat. conf. co-chmn. 1993-94), Ariz. Visionary Artists (treas. 1987-88), Ariz. Acad. Performing Arts (v.p. bd. dirs. 1987-88, pres. 1988-89).

MATTHEW, NEIL EDWARD, artist, educator; b. Anderson, Ind., Jan. 19, [illegible] Dec. 22, 1963. BA in Edn., Ariz. State U., 1949; MFA, Ind. U., 1955; postgrad., U. Iowa, 1957-58, State Acad. of Fine Arts, Stuttgart, Germany, 1959-60. Tchr., art Covington (Ind.) Jr. H.S., 1949-50, Clay H.S., South Bend, Ind., 1955-57; instr. art Ind. U., [illegible] prof. art. Ind. U., Indpls., 1964-71; asst. to assoc. prof. art Herron Sch. Art/

Ind. U. Purdue U., Indpls., 1971-87, assoc. prof. emeritus, 1987—; art exhbit judge Kokomo Art Assn., Ind., 1970; rschr. for salary studies AAUP, Ind. U. Purdue U., 1970s, others. Painter oils, acrylics, and watercolors, 1945—; printmaker etching and woodcuts, 1953—; photographer; one-man shows include: Lyman-Snodgrass Gallery, Indpls., 1984, Lieber's Gallery, Indpls., 1962, 68, Purdue U. Gallery, 1962, Ind. U. Med. Ctr., Indpls., 1966, Ind. U. at Kokomo, 1967, Ind. U. Purdue U. Archives and Libr., 1996, 98, others; group shows include: Ind. Arts Competition, 1988, Purdue U., 1966, 69, Libr. of Congress, 1956, 58, 59, numerous others; work represented at Lieber's Gallery, Indpls., 1959-73, Assoc. Am. Artists, N.Y.C., 1965-72, Lyman-Snodgrass Gallery, Indpls., 1984-85, Ruschman Gallery, Indpls., 1989—; permanent collections include: U. Ariz. Mus. of Art, Tucson, Ctr. for Creative Photograhy, Tucson, Archives, Ind. U. -Purdue U. at Indpls., Depauw U., Greencastle, Ind., others. Pvt. first class U.S. Army, 1950-52. Named Outstanding Art Grad., Ariz. State U., Tempe, 1949; recipient tuition scholarship U. Iowa, Iowa City, 1957-58; Fulbright grantee, Stuttgart, 1959-60. Mem. Soc. Ind. Pioneers, Coll. Art Assn., Ctr. for Creative Photography, Assocs. of Art History (bd. dirs. 1991-97), Fulbright Assn. Republican. Presbyterian. Avocations: travel, reading, art history, fiction. Home: 5233 North Via Sempreverde Tucson AZ 85750-5967

MATTHEWS, DARYL BRUCE, psychiatrist; b. Cleve., Sept. 26, 1947; s. David Earle and Esther Ann (Seifter) M.; m. Esther Solomon, Dec. 24, 1979; children: Max, Jacob. BA in Human Biology, Johns Hopkins U., 1969, MD, 1973, PhD in Sociology, 1977. Diplomate Am. Bd. Psychiatry and Neurology, Am. Bd. Forensic Psychiatry. Asst. prof. psychiatry Boston U., 1976-81; assoc. prof. U. Va., Charlottesville, 1981-82; assoc. clin. prof. U. Hawaii, Honolulu, 1982-90; prof., dir. edn. U. Ark., 1990-95; clin. prof. U. Hawaii, Honolulu, 1995—. Author: Disposable Patients, 1981; contbr. articles to profl. jours. Jewish. Office: 4224 Waialae Ave Ste 5 Honolulu HI 96816-5307

MATTHEWS, ESTHER ELIZABETH, education educator, consultant; b. Princeton, Mass., June 20, 1918; d. Ralph Edgar and Julia Ellen (Cronin) M. BS in Edn., Worcester State Coll., 1940; EdM, Harvard U., 1943, EdD, 1960. Tchr. various Mass. schs., 1942-47; guidance dir. Holden (Mass.) Pub. Schs., 1947-53, Wareham (Mass.) Pub. Schs., 1954-57; counselor Newton (Mass.) High Sch., 1957-60, head counselor, 1960-66; assoc. prof. edn. U. Oreg., 1966-70, prof. edn., 1970-80, prof. emerita, 1980—; vis. prof. U. Toronto, Ont., Can., summer 1971; lectr. on edn. Harvard U., 1963-66; cons. in field; lectr. various colls. and univs. Author book chpts.; contbr. numerous articles to profl. jours. and papers to conf. proc.; featured in spl. issue of Oreg. Counseling Assn. Jour., 1998. Mem. ACD (Recognition for Contbn. to Promote Human Rights 1987), World Future Soc., Nat. Vocat. Guidance Assn. (pres. 1974-75, chair nat. com. 1966-67, sec. 1967-68, bd. trustees 1968-71, editl. bd. Vocat. Guidance Quar. 1966-68), Oreg. Pers. and Guidance Assn. (Leona Tyler award 1973, Disting. Svc. award 1979), Oreg. Career Devel. Assn. (Disting. Svc. award 1987, Esther E. Matthews Ann. award for outstanding contbn. to career devel. in Oreg. established in her honor 1993). Home: 832 Lariat Dr Eugene OR 97401-6438

MATTHEWS, EUGENE EDWARD, artist; b. Davenport, Iowa, Mar. 22, 1931; s. Nickolas Arthur and Velma (Schroeder) M.; m. Wanda Lee Miller, Sept. 14, 1952; children: Anthony Lee, Daniel Nickolas. Student, Bradley U., 1948-51; BFA, U. Iowa, 1953, MFA, 1957. Prof. fine arts grad. faculty U. Colo., Boulder, 1961-96, prof. fine arts emeritus, 1996—, dir. vis. artists program, 1985-96; vis. artist Am. Acad. Rome, 1989. One-man shows include U. Wis., Milw., 1960, Brena Gallery, Denver, 1963, 65, 67, 70, 74, 76, 78, 80, 83, 88, Colorado Springs Fine Arts Ctr., 1967, Sheldon Art Gallery, U. Nebr., 1968, Denver Art Mus., 1972, James Yu Gallery, N.Y.C., 1973, 77, Dubins Gallery, L.A., 1981, Galeria Rysunku, Poznan, 1983, CU Art Galleries, U. Colo., Boulder, 1996, Rule Art Gallery, Denver, 1998; exhibited in numerous group shows U.S., Europe, Africa, Asia; internat. watercolor exhbn. New Orleans, 1983, Louvre, Paris, Met. Mus. of Art, N.Y.C., Internat. Art Ctr., Kyoto, Japan, Mus. of Modern Art, Rijeka, Yugoslavia, Taipei Fine Arts Mus., Taiwan, Republic of China, Internat. Watercolor Biennial-East/West, Champaign, Ill., 1997; represented in permanent collections Nat. Mus. Am. Art, Washington, Denver Art Mus., Butler Inst. Am. Art, Chrysler Art Mus., others. Recipient Penello d'Argento award Acitrezza Internazionale, 1958, S.P.Q.R. Cup of Rome, Roma Olimpionica Internazionale, 1959, Gold medal of honor Nat. Arts Club, N.Y.C., 1969, Bicentennial award Rocky Mountain Nat. Watercolor Exhbn., 1976, Am. Drawings IV Purchase award, 1982, others; fellow in painting Am. Acad. Rome, 1957-60, U. Colo. Creative Rsch. fellow, 1966-67. Mem. Watercolor U.S.A. Honor Soc. (charter). Home: 720 Hawthorn Ave Boulder CO 80304-2140

MATTHEWS, GLENNA CHRISTINE, historian; b. L.A., Nov. 7, 1938; d. Glen Leslie and Alberta Marie (Nicolais) Ingles; m. James Duncan Matthews (div. Jan. 1978); children: Karen, David. BA, San Jose State U., 1969; MA, Stanford U., 1971, PhD, 1977. Assoc. prof. history Okla. State U., 1978-85. Author: Just a Housewife, 1987, The Rise of Public Woman, 1992; co-author: Running as a Woman, 1993. Recipient The Sierra prize Western Assn. Women Historians; NEH fellow, 1998—. Mem. Am. Hist. Assn., Orgn. Am. Historians.

MATTHEWS, JENNIFER LEE, music industry executive; b. San Bernardino, Calif., Apr. 26, 1968; d. Clint Lee and Marie Irene (Logsdon) M. BA in Comm., San Francisco State U., 1990; BA, Calif. Inst. Integral Studies, 1997. West Coast promotions mgr. Polygram Records, San Francisco, 1988-89; regional mktg. mgr. Virgin Records Am., Beverly Hills, Calif., 1989-91, nat. dir. alternative mktg., 1991-94, dir. mktg., 1994-96; dir. mktg. Hearts of Space, Sausalito, Calif., 1996—. Music supr. (film) Angel's Share, 1998; film mem. The Way Home, 1997. Mem. NOW. Avocations: dancing, snowboarding, music. Office: Hearts of Space 1 Harbor Dr Ste 201 Sausalito CA 94965-1434

MATTHEWS, JUSTUS, composer, music educator; b. Peoria, Ill., Jan. 13, 1945; s. Charles Matthews and Dorothea (Maurer) M.; m. Barbara Matthews, Aug. 15, 1971; children: David, Laura. BA, Calif. State U., Northridge, 1967, MA, 1968; PhD, SUNY, Buffalo, 1971. Prof. Calif. State U., Long Beach, 1971—. Office: Calif State U Music Dept Long Beach CA 90840

MATTHEWS, LYDIA ANN, art history educator; b. N.Y.C., June 22, 1959; d. Alexander and Anna (Koutsatsias) M. BA magna cum laude, Colo. Coll., 1981; postgrad., U. London, 1983; MA, U. Calif., Berkeley, 1987. Instr. studio art Bemis Art Sch., Colorado Springs, 1980-82; tchg. assoc. U. Calif., Berkeley, 1983-86; lectr. Humboldt State U., Arcata, Calif., 1987-89, 92, San Francisco Art Inst., 1990-92, San Francisco State U., 1990-91; asst. prof. Calif. Coll. Arts & Crafts, Oakland and San Francisco, 1992-97, assoc. prof., 1997—; co-adminstr. Expanding Am. Art History to Reflect Multiethnic Diversity, San Francisco Art Inst., 1990-92; mem. curatorial adv. bd. So. Exposure, San Francisco, 1998—; panelist Women's Caucus for Art, Oakland, Calif., 1992; advisor, panelist, juror San Francisco Arts Commn., San Francisco, 1994, 96, 97; mem. steering com. San Francisco Bay Area for Freedom of Expression, 1990-92. Author, editor: (book) Site to Sight: Mapping Bay Area Visual Culture, 1995; co-author: (interactive CD-ROM) Bay Area Art Finder, 1995; contbr. articles to profl. jours. Recipient No. Calif. Grantmaker's award San Francisco Art Commn., 1995; Humanities and Sci. Rsch. Travel grantee Calif. Coll. Arts & Crafts, 1993, 95, 97, Tchg. Devel. grantee, 1998. Mem. Coll. Art Assn., San Francisco Mus. Modern Art (advisor edn. dept., workshop leader 1995-97, Soc. for Encouragement of Contemporary Art grantee 1995), Yerba Buena Ctr. for Arts (curatorial adv. bd. 1992-98), Headlands Ctr. for Arts (dir. pub. programs, curatorial adv. bd. 1993-97), Found. for Advanced Critical Studies, 2AES: Ctr. for Critical Arch./Art, Phi Beta Kappa. Democrat. Avocations: dancing, gardening, creative writing, drawing. Office: Calif Coll of Arts & Crafts 5212 Broadway Oakland CA 94618

MATTHEWS, NORMAN SHERWOOD, JR., insurance company executive; b. San Antonio, Tex., Apr. 23, 1944; s. Norman Sherwood and Alice Ann (Hathaway) M.; student Middle Tenn. State U., 1962-64, Ventura Coll., 1965, Calif. State U., Northridge, 1965-66, U. Md., 1968-70; BBA, U. Tex., 1972; postgrad. U. Hawaii, 1977-79; m. Masayo Nakamura, Sept. 1, 1970; children: Debbie Ann, Scott Tsuyoshi. CPA, Hawaii; cert. internal auditor. Research asst. State Farm Ins. Co., Murfreesboro, Tenn., 1963-64; inventory control analyst Minn. Mining & Mfg. Co., Camarillo, Calif., 1964-65; sr. acct. Peat, Marwick, Mitchell & Co., Honolulu, 1973-75; dir. mgmt. analysis Hawaii Med. Service Assn., Honolulu, 1975—, asst. v.p. mgmt. analysis and security, 1989-98, v.p., compliance officer, 1998—. With USAF, 1966-70. Decorated Air medal with 8 oak leaf clusters. Mem. AICPA, Inst. Mgmt. Accts., Inst. Internal Auditors, Info. Sys. Audit and Control Assn. Home: 2724 Kahoaloha Ln Apt 1903 Honolulu HI 96826-3338 Office: Hawaii Med Svc Assn 818 Keeaumoku St Honolulu HI 96814-2365

MATTHEWS, SCOTT, record producer; b. Sacramento, July 25, 1955; s. Thomas and Maggie Mathews; m. Kolleen Ezzelle, June 23, 1991; children: Wilson, Ava Grace. Grad., Encina H.S., 1973. Record prodr. Hit or Myth Prodns., San Rafael, Calif., 1975—. Recipient Platinum and Gold Records, RIAA, 1977-99, Grammy nominations, 1993. Mem. NARAS, BMI. Avocation: visiting home in Palm Springs and ranch in Napa, Calif. Office: Hit or Myth Prodns 36 Lisbon St San Rafael CA 94901

MATTHEWS, WARREN WAYNE, state supreme court justice; b. Santa Cruz, Calif., Apr. 5, 1939; s. Warren Wayne and Ruth Ann (Maginnis) M.; m. Donna Stearns, Aug. 17, 1963; children: Holly Maginnis, Meredith Sample. A.B., Stanford U., 1961; LL.B., Harvard U., 1964. Bar: Alaska 1965. Assoc. firm Burr, Boney & Pease, Anchorage, 1964-69, Matthews & Dunn, Matthews, Dunn and Baily, Anchorage, 1969-77; assoc. justice Alaska Supreme Ct., Anchorage, 1977—, justice, chief justice. Bd. dirs. Alaska Legal Services Corp., 1969-70. Mem. Alaska Bar Assn. (bd. govs. 1974-77), ABA, Anchorage Bar Assn. *

MATTIS, DANIEL CHARLES, physicist, educator; b. Brussels, Sept. 8, 1932; came to U.S., 1941; s. Joseph and Lucie (Applebaum) M. BS, MIT, 1953; MS, U. Ill., 1954, PhD, 1957. Mem. rsch. staff IBM, N.Y.C., 1958-65; prof. Belfer Grad. Sch. of Yeshiva U., N.Y.C., 1965-78; Thomas Potts prof. Polytech. U., N.Y.C., 1978-80; prof. U. Utah, Salt Lake City, Utah, 1980—; Wei-Loon vis. prof. Chinese U. Hong Kong, 1997. Author: (books) Theory of Magnetism, Vol. 1, 1981, Vol. 2, 1985, Many Body Theory, 1994; mem. editl. bd. Internat. Jour. Modern Physics; contbr. articles to profl. jours. Fellow Am. Phys. Soc. Achievements include 2 patents over 200 tech. papers. Office: U Utah Dept Physics Salt Lake City UT 84112

MATTONI, RUDOLF HEINRICH THEODOR, conservation biologist; b. Venice, Calif., Oct. 6, 1927; s. Andre Mattoni and Elvira Mildred Kressler; m. Diana H. Donald, June 6 (div. May 1967); children: Nicholas, Adriano; m. Leona S. Stoltz, June 20, 1968; 1 child, Carlo. BS, U. Calif., Berkeley, 1950; MA, UCLA, 1953, PhD, 1957. Rsch. assoc. dept. botany UCLA, 1955-61; rsch. assoc. N.Am. Aviation, L.A., 1961-65; rsch. dir. NUS Corp., Hawthorne, Calif., 1965-69; dir. Agri Sci. Labs, Inc., L.A., 1969-83; pres. Agresearch, Inc., L.A., 1977—; lectr. dept. geography UCLA, 1993—. Author: (booklet) Butterflies of Los Angeles, 1992; editor: (sci. jour.) Jr. Research on Lepidoptera, 1977—. Pres. Royce 270, L.A., 1984-86; bd. dirs. Long Beach (Calif.) Opera, 1984-96. Recipient spl. award for conservation Def. Logistics Agy., 1996, Nat. Wildlife Fedn., 1997, Dept. Def., 1998, spl. recognition for conservation U.S. Fish and Wildlife, 1996. Avocations: classical music, economics. Office: UCLA Dept Geography Los Angeles CA 90095-1524

MATTSON, VERNON WILLIAMS, theology educator; b. Salt Lake City, Jan. 15, 1934; s. Vernon W. and Ellen (Williams) M.; m. Georgia M. Jensen, Dec. 19, 1958; children—Anna, Denise, Shane, David, Paul, Steven. B.S., Brigham Young U., 1960, M.R.E., 1969. Tchr., Ch. Jesus Christ of Latter-day Saints, Salt Lake City, 1960—, lectr., 1977—; pres. Buried Records Prodns., Salt Lake City, 1978—. Author: The Dead Sea Scrolls and Other Important Discoveries, 1979. Served with USN, 1952-54. Mem. Am. Schs. Oriental Research, Soc. Early Hist. Archeology, Found. Ancient Research and Mormon Studies. Republican. Home: 3439 W 7260 S West Jordan UT 84084-2719

MATUS, NANCY LOUISE, artist; b. Wichita, Kans., Jan. 22, 1955; d. Joseph John and Josephine Emily (Kulina) M.; m. Kenneth Lee Walker, Feb. 14, 1990. AA, Phoenix Coll., 1980; student, U. Ariz., 1978, 79, Ariz. State U., 1984, 85. Exhibited in group shows Ariz. Sate Capitol, Phoenix, 1985, Movimento Artistico del Rio Salado Gallery, Phoenix, 1986, 87, 89, 91, 92, Tempe (Ariz.) Arts Ctr., 1987, U. Ariz., Phoenix, 1987, Nat. Acrylic Painters Assn., Long Beach, Calif., 1996; represented in numerous pvt. collections, including corp. loan to City of Phoenix, City Hall, 1998; work represented in Best of Acyrlic Painting, 1996, Creative Inspirations, 1997. Mem. Nat. Acrylic Painters Assn. (signature), Cottonwood Country Club. Address: 25802 S Cloverland Dr Chandler AZ 85248-6875

MATUSZAK, DAVID F., secondary education educator, writer; b. Upland, Calif., Sept. 2, 1953; s. Frank S. and Vera (Thurston) M.; 1 child, Christopher. BA, Calif. State U., Long Beach, 1975, MA, 1980; EdD, Pacific Western U., 1993. Instr. Yucaipa (Calif.) High Sch., 1977—. Author: Nelson Point: Portrait of a Northern Gold Rush Town, 1993, The Cowboy's Trail Guide to Westerns, 1998. Pres., CEO The Friends of Live Oak Canyon, 1990—. Avocations: surfing, snowboarding, outdoorsman.

MATZDORFF, JAMES ARTHUR, investment banker, financier; b. Kansas City, Mo., Jan. 3, 1956. BS, U. So. Calif., 1978; MBA, Loyola U., Los Angeles, 1980. Comml. loan officer Bank of Am., Los Angeles, 1976-78; mng. dir. James A. Matzdorff & Co., Beverly Hills, Calif., 1978—. Mem. Rep. Nat. Com., 1980—. Mem. Am. Fin. Assn., Mercedes Benz Car Club, BMW Motorcycle Internat., Phi Delta Theta. Avocations: tennis, sailing, karate, skiing, sport target shooting. Office: 9903 Santa Monica Blvd Ste 374 Beverly Hills CA 90212-1671

MAUL, TERRY LEE, psychologist, educator; b. San Francisco, May 6, 1946; s. Chester Lloyd and Clella Lucille (Hobbs) M.; AB, U. Calif., Berkeley, 1967, MA, 1968, PhD, 1970; student Coll. San Mateo, 1964-65; m. Gail Ann Retallick, June 27, 1970 (div. Dec. 1986); 1 son, Andrew Eliot. Prof. psychology San Bernardino Valley Coll., San Bernardino, Calif., 1970—, chmn. dept., 1979-82, 96-97; researcher self-actualization. Mem. AAUP (chpt. pres. 1971-73), Am. Psychol. Assn., Audubon Soc., Mensa, Nature Conservancy, Wilderness Soc., Sierra Club. Democrat. Author: (with Eva Conrad) Introduction to Experimental Psychology, 1981; (with Gail Maul) Beyond Limit: Ways to Growth and Freedom, 1983; contbg. author other psychol. texts. Office: San Bernardino Valley Coll 701 S Mount Vernon Ave San Bernardino CA 92410-2705

MAULDIN, JEAN HUMPHRIES, aviation company executive; b. Gordonville, Tex., Aug. 16, 1923; d. James Wiley and Lena Leota (Noel-Crain) Humphries; B.S., Hardin Simmons U., 1943; M.S., U. So. Calif., 1961; postgrad. Westfield Coll., U. London, 1977-78, Warnborough Coll., Oxford, Eng., 1977-78; m. William Henry Mauldin, Feb. 28, 1942; children—Bruce Patrick, William Timothy III. Psychol. counselor social services 1st Baptist Ch., 1953-57; pres. Mauldin and Staff, public relations, Los Angeles, 1957-78; pres. Stardust Aviation, Inc., Santa Ana, Calif., 1962—. Mem. Calif. Democratic Council, 1953-83; rep. 69th Assembly Dist. Caucus to Calif. Dem. State Central com. exec. bd., 1957—, Orange County Dem. Central Com., 1960—; mem. U.S. Congl. Peace Adv. Bd., 1981—; del. Dem. Nat. Conv., 1974, 78, Dem. Mid-Term Conv., 1976, 78, 82, 86, Dem. Nat. Issues Conf.; mem. nat. advisor U.S. Congl. Adv. Bd. Am. Security Council; pres. Santa Ana Friends of Public Library, 1973-76, McFadden Friends of Library, Santa Ana, 1976-80; chmn. cancer crusade Am. Cancer Soc., Orange County, 1974; mem. exec. bd. Lisa Hist. Preservation Soc., 1970—; lay leader Protestant Episcopal Ch. Am., Trinity Ch., Tustin, Calif. Named Woman of Yr., Key Woman in Politics, Calif. Dem. Party, 1960-80. Am. Mgmt. Assn. (pres.'s club), Bus. and Profl. Women Am., Exptl. Aircraft and Pilots Assn., Nat. Women's Polit. Caucus, Dem. Coalition Central Coms., Calif. Friends of Library (life), Women's Missionary Soc. (chmn.), LWV, Nat. Fedn. Dem. Women, Calif. Fedn. County Central Com. Mems., Internat. Platform Assn., Peace Through Strength, Oceanic Soc., Nat. Audubon Soc., Sierra Club, Nat. Wildlife Fedn., Internat. Amnesty Assn., Am. Security Council, Nat. Women's Pilot. Club: U. So. Calif. Ski, Town Hall of Calif. Author: Cliff Winters, The Pilot, The Man, 1961; The consummate Barnstormer, 1962; The Daredevil Clown, 1965. Home: 1013 S Elliott Pl Santa Ana CA 92704-2224 also: 102 E 45th St Savannah GA 31405-2115 Office: 16542 Mount Kibby St Fountain Valley CA 92708-2437

MAUPIN, BILL, state supreme court justice; children: Allison, Michael. BA, U. Nev., 1968; JD, U. Ariz., 1971. Atty., ptnr. Thorndal, Backus, Maupin and Armstrong, Las Vegas, 1976-93; judge 8th Jud. Dist. Clark County, 1993-97; assoc. justice Supreme Ct. Nev., 1997—; bd. govs. Nev. State Bar, 1991-95. Recipient highest rating for Retention as Dist. Ct. Judge, 1994, 96, Highest Qualitative Ratings, 1996, Las Vegas Review Jour., Clark County Bar Assn.; highest rating as Supreme Ct. Justice Clark County Bar Assn. and Las Vegas Rev. Jour. judicial poll, 1998. Mem. Nev. Supreme Ct. (study com. to review jud. elections, chmn. 1995, alternate dispute resolution implementation com. chmn. 1992-96). Office: Supreme Ct Bldg Carson City NV 89710

MAURER, ROBERT MICHAEL, medical company executive; b. Boston, July 6, 1952; s. Robert Distler and Barbara Anne (Mansfield) M.; m. Jae Young Sim, Oct. 31, 1982; children: Andrew, Joanne, Stephen. BA, Carleton Coll., 1974; MBA, Harvard U., 1980. Sales rep. diagnostic div. Abbott Labs., North Chicago, Ill., 1974-78, area mgr. diagnostic div. Far East, 1980-85, cancer mktg. mgr. diagnostic div., 1985-86, venture mgr. psychiat. and neurology diagnostic div., 1986-90, mgr. bus. planning diagnostic divsn., 1990-91; COO, CFO Molecular Geriatrics, Lake Bluff, Ill., 1992; COO, 1993-95; v.p. bus. devel. Avigen Alameda (Calif.) Co., 1996—. Office: Avigen Co Ste 1000 1201 Harbor Bay Pky Alameda CA 94502

MAURICE, DON, personal care industry executive; b. Peoria, Ill., Aug. 29, 1932; s. Imajean (Webster) Crayton; m. Cindalu Jackson, Aug. 31, 1990. Student, Loma Linda U., 1984-86; cert. paralegal studies, Calif. State U., San Bernardino, 1994. Lic. hair stylist, skin therapist; cert. paralegal, notary pub. Owner 2 schs. in advanced hair designs, San Diego, 1962-64, D & M Enterprises, Advt. Agy., 1964-78; now cons. D&M Enterprises Advt. Agy.; dist. mgr. AqRo Matic Co. Water Purification Systems, San Diego, 1972-75; profl. sales educator Staypower Industries, San Diego, 1972-76, 3d v.p., 1975-76; regional bus. cons. Estheticians Pharmacology Rsch., Garden Grove, Calif., 1975-81; owner, operator Don Maurice Hair Designs, Hemet, Calif., 1980-83; dir., operator Hair Sytles by Maurice, Loma Linda, Calif., 1984-88; owner, pres. Grooming Dynamics, Redlands, Calif., 1988—; bus. cons. Yogurt Place, Paradise Valley, Ariz., 1978-79, others; regular guest Channel 6/Channel 8, San Diego, 1968-78; cons. infomercial Pre-Paid Legal Svcs., Inc., 1994—. Author: The New Look For Men, 1967, The Art of Men's Hair Styling, 1968 (accepted by Library of Congress), Baldness, To Be or Not To Be, 1989. Promoter Spl. Olympics, Hemet, 1981. Sgt. U.S. Army, 1950-53, Korea. Decorated Purple Heart, 1952; named Leading Businessman in His Profession, Union and Evening Tribune, 1969. Mem. Internat. Platform Assn., Christian Businessmen's Assn. Avocations: writing, sculpting, art, sports, music. Office: Grooming Dynamics PO Box 1279 Loma Linda CA 92354-1279

MAURIELLO, BRIAN DOMINICK, educational media and television producer, writer and director; b. Johnson City, N.Y., Dec. 3, 1973; s. Vincent James Mauriello and Judith Ann (Herceg) Matos. BS, Ithaca Coll., 1996. Freelance prodr. Clear View video, Sandy Hook, Conn., 1988-92; TV tchg. asst. Ithaca (N.Y.) Coll., 1993-96; contract prodn. staff Kinney Shoes Multi-Media Svcs., N.Y.C., 1994, Housing Authority Ins., Cheshire, Conn., 1995; tech. tng. developer Telxon Corp., Akron, Ohio, 1996; writer, prodr., dir. Interlink New Media, N. Canton and Akron, Ohio, 1996-97; series post-prodn. mgr. ABC/Kane Prodns. Internat. Inc., L.A., 1997-98; writer, prodr., dir. Observision Films, L.A., 1998; technical tng. program specialist Am. Isuzu Motors, Inc., Cerritos, Calif., 1998—; instr. automotive tech. Rio Hondo Coll., Whittier, Calif., 1999—; cons. Gossa Vision Prodns., Ithaca, 1992-94. Writer, producer, dir. TV documentary Which Way EJ?, 1996, others, also TV commls. Recipient several found. awards for bus. and citizenship, 1988-92. Mem. Internat. Documentary Assn., Internat. TV Assn. (judge 1995). Roman Catholic. Avocations: photography, travel, automobile restoration. Home: 5340 Falls Way # P Buena Park CA 90621

MAURO, RICHARD FRANK, lawyer, investment manager; b. Hawthorne, Nev., July 21, 1945; s. Frank Joseph and Dolores D. (Kreimeyer) M.; m. LaVonne M. Madden, Aug. 28, 1965; 1 child, Lindsay Anne. AB, Brown U., 1967; JD summa cum laude, U. Denver, 1970. Bar: Colo. 1970. Assoc. Dawson, Nagel, Sherman & Howard, Denver, 1970-72; assoc. Van Cise, Freeman, Tooley & McClearn, Denver, 1972-73, ptnr., 1973-74; ptnr. Hall & Evans, Denver, 1974-81, Morrison & Forester, Denver, 1981-84; of counsel Parcel & Mauro, P.C., Denver, 1984—; pres. Parcel, Mauro & Hultin, P.C., Denver, 1988-90; of counsel Parcel, Mauro P.C., Denver, 1992—; pres. Sundance Oil Exploration Co., 1985-88; exec. v.p. Castle Group, Inc., 1992-97; adj. prof. U. Denver Coll. Law, 1981-84. Symposium editor: Denver Law Jour., 1969-70; editor: Colorado Corporation Manual; contbr. articles to legal jours. Pres. Colo. Open Space Coun., 1974; mem. law alumni coun. U. Denver Coll. Law, 1988-91. Francis Wayland scholar, 1967; recipient various Am. jurisprudence awards. Mem. ABA, Colo. Bar Assn., Denver Bar Assn., Colo. Assn. Corp. Counsel. (pres. 1974-75), Am. Arbitration Assn. (comml. arbitrator), Order St. Ives, Denver Athletic Club (bd. dirs. 1986-89). Home: 2552 E Alameda Ave Unit 128 Denver CO 80209-3330 Office: 1801 California St Ste 3600 Denver CO 80202-2636

MAUS, JOHN ANDREW, computer systems engineer; b. Whittier, Calif., July 13, 1945; s. Kenneth Waring and Bertha Estella (Eckman) M.; M. Diana Barba, April 16, 1977 (div. May 1, 1983); m. Colette An Moschelle, Nov. 23, 1985; stepchildren: BreAnn, Adam; children: Steven Andrew, Terra An. BA in Physics, U. Calif., Riverside, 1963-67; MS in Physics, San Diego State U., 1967-70. Cert. data processor, 1983. Programmer, analyst San Diego State Found., 1970-72; instr. bus. San Diego State U., 1971-73; systems programmer San Diego State U., San Diego, 1971-74; data processing mgr. M.H. Golden Co., San Diego, 1974-79; computer systems engr. Hewlett-Packard Co., Spokane, Wash., 1979-84, sr. systems engr., 1984-86, network systems engr., 1986-89, sr. tech. cons., 1989-93; UNIX high availability cons. Hewlett-Packard Co., Spokane, 1994—, sr. tech. cons. high availability, 1999—; physics lab. asst. USDA Salinity Lab., Riverside, 1965-67; underwater acoustics programmer Naval Undersea Ctr., San Diego, 1967-70; programmer San Diego Inst. Pathology, 1972-76; adv. com. Computer Sci. Bus. Applications North Idaho Coll., 1989-96; mem. career network U. Calif., Riverside, 1990—; dist. tech. com. Nine Mile Falls (Wash.) Sch., 1994-97. Author: INTEREX Conference Proceedings, 1989; co-author: Chemical Physics Letters, 1971, Electronic and Atomic Collisions, 1971. Merit badge counselor Spokane chpt. Boy Scouts Am., 1983—. Mem. Assn. Computing Machinery (founder Spokane chpt., chpt. chmn. 1980-82, service award 1981). Avocations: internat. travel, skiing, computers. Home: 12417 W Sunridge Dr Nine Mile Falls WA 99026-9311 Office: Hewlett-Packard Co 1121 N Argonne Rd Ste 121 Spokane WA 99212-2686

MAUTER, WARREN EUGENE, chemist, business development manager; b. Denver, Aug. 27, 1953; s. Jacob Martin and Harriette June (Kaiser) M.; m. Deborah Lee Long, Jan. 22, 1983 (div. 1987). BS in Chemistry, Met. State Coll., 1976; MS in Material Sci. and Engring., U. Colo., 1980, MBA, 1986. Cert. rsch. technician, rsch. chemist. Rsch. chemist Manville Corp., Denver, 1973-80, group leader, 1980-83; applications mgr. Cardinal Chem., Columbia, S.C., 1983-84; prin. Alpine Cons., Denver, 1984-88; corp. mgr. COBE Labs., Inc., Lakewood, Colo., 1988—; instr. econs. and fin. U. Colo. Coll. Engring, 1987-89; mem. industry adv. coun. U. Colo. Coll. Engring., Denver, 1989-92; mem. bd. advisors. Shuck Found., 1986-88; mem. Colo. State U. Engring. Adv. Coun., 1997—; print dir. Colo. Venture Ctrs. Guild, 1996. Bd. reviewers Jour. Vinyl Tech., 1981-83; contbr. articles to profl. jours. Sci. and Tech. Colo. scholar Met. State Coll., 1971-74. Mem. ASTM, Soc. Plastics Engrs. (bd. dirs. vinyl div. 1982-86), Nat. Sanitation Found. (industry adv. bd. 1980-84), Am. Chem. Soc., Colo. Mountain Club, U. Colo. Execs. Club (Denver, v.p. 1987, pres. 1988). Republican. Avocations: Alpine mountaineering, sailing, competitive running. Home: 1649 S Marion St Denver CO 80210-2752 Office: COBE Labs Inc 1185 Oak St Lakewood CO 80215-4407

MAUZY, MICHAEL PHILIP, environmental consultant, chemical engineer; b. Keyser, W.Va., Nov. 14, 1928; s. Frank and Margery Ola (Nelson) M.; m. Nancy Shepherd Watson, Mar. 27, 1949; children: Michael P. Jr., Jeffrey A., Rebecca A. BSChemE, Va. Poly. Inst., 1950; MSChemE,

U. Tenn., 1951. Registered profl. engr., Va., Ill. With Monsanto Co., St. Louis, 1951-71, dir. engring. and mfg., 1968-71, mgr. comml. devel. Kummer Corp., Creve Coeur, Mo., 1971-72; mgr. labs. Ill. EPA, Springfield, 1972-73, mgr. water pollution control, 1973-74, mgr. environ. programs, 1974-77, dir., 1977-81; v.p. Roy F. Weston, Inc., West Chester, Pa., 1981-88, Vernon Hills, Ill., 1988-93, Albuquerque, 1993-96; also bd. dirs. Roy F. Weston, Inc., West Chester, Pa.; mgr. The Pangaea Group, LLC, Albuquerque, 1996—; bd. dirs. DeTox Internat. Corp., St. Charles, Ill.; provider Congl. testimony, 1974-81; presenter various workshops, symposia and seminars, 1974—. Contbr. articles on environ. mgmt. to profl. publs., 1974—. Mem. Ohio River Valley Water Sanitary Commn., Cin., 1976-81. 1st lt. U.S. Army, 1951-53. Recipient Environ. Quality award Region V, U.S. EPA, Chgo., 1976, Disting. Svc. award Cons. Engrs. Coun. of Ill., 1978, Ill. award Ill. Assn. Sanitary Dists., 1979, Clarence W. Klassen award Ill. Assn. Water Pollution Control Ops., 1984. Mem. Am. Pub. Works Assn., Am. Inst. Chem. Engring., Water Pollution Control Assn., Am. Mgmt. Assn. Avocations: reading, travel, home improvements.

MAXEY, DIANE MEADOWS, artist; b. Lufkin, Tex., Feb. 26, 1943; d. Warren Gaston and Jackie Meadows; m. William Brant Maxey, Sept. 5, 1964; children: Dananne, Robert Warren. BA in Art and Edn., U. North Tex., 1965; postgrad., U. Tex., Arlington, Tex. Tech U., Lubbock; studied with Al Brouilette, Bud Biggs, Edgar Whitney, Dick Phillips, Robert E. Wood, Rex. Brandt, Milford Zornes. Art tchr. Dallas Pub. Schs., 1965-66; substitute tchr. Arlington Pub. Schs., 1969-72; pvt. classes San Angelo, Tex., 1973-77; owner Maxi Watercolor Studio, Paradise Valley, 1978—, Bandanna Tours, Scottsdale, 1988-91; mem. staff Scottsdale Artist Sch., The Sherman Art Ctr.; tchr. numerous watercolor workshops for different local schs. and internat. tours cos. Exhibited at Gold Nuggett Art Gallery, Wickenburg, Ariz., Long Gallery, Scottsdale, Ariz., Elizabeth Hains Gallery, Scottsdale; featured artist in Freshening Your Paintings with New Techniques, Fresh Flowers The Best of Flower Painting, The Best of Watercolor 2, The Best of Watercolor Composition, Splash 5; featured in Internat. Artist Mag., 1998. Dir. visual ministry First So. Bapt. Ch., Scottsdale, 1988-95. Recipient numerous awards. Mem. Western Fedn. Watercolor Soc. (gen. chmn. 1981-82), Southwestern Watercolor Assn. (signature), Ariz. Artist Guild (hon. life; pres. 1982-83), Ariz. Watercolor Assn., Tex. Watercolor Assn. (signature), 22 x 30 Profl. Critique Group. Avocations: gardening, travel. Home and Office: Maxi Watercolor Studio 7540 N Lakeside Ln Paradise Valley AZ 85253-2857

MAXSON, ROBERT C., university president. Former sr. v.p. acad. affairs U. Houston Systems, Houston; pres. U. Nev., Las Vegas, 1984-94, Calif. State U., Long Beach, 1994—. Office: Calif St Univ Long Beach SSA 300 1250 N Bellflower Blvd Long Beach CA 90840-0006*

MAXWELL, DONALD STANLEY, retired publishing executive; b. L.A., May 30, 1930; s. Harold Stanley and Margaret (Trenam) M.; m. Martha Helen Winn, Dec. 5, 1952; children: Sylvia Louise, Cynthia Lynn, Bruce Stanley, Bradley Erl, Walter James, Wesley Richard, Amy Bernice. Student, Long Beach City Coll., 1948-50; BBA, Woodbury Coll., 1956; D of Bus. Adminstrn. (hon.), Woodbury U., 1991. CPA. Ptnr. Robert McDavid & Co. (CPAs), L.A., 1955-61; controller Petersen Pub. Co., L.A., 1961-68; v.p. fin. Petersen Pub. Co., 1969; controller L.A. Times, 1969-79; v.p. Los Angeles Times, 1977-79, v.p. fin., 1979-81; asst. treas. Times Mirror Co., 1971-82, v.p., controller, 1982-87, v.p., chief acctg. officer, 1987-93, v.p., 1993, exec. dir. fin. program, 1993-95; ret., 1995. Trustee Woodbury U., 1981-97, chmn. bd. trustees, 1984-87. Served with AUS, 1950-52. Mem. Fin. Execs. Inst. (dir. 1979-82, pres. L.A. chpt. 1973-74), Internat. Newspaper Fin. Execs. (dir. 1978-82, pres. 1980-81), Am. Inst. CPAs, Calif. Soc. CPAs, Am. Horse Council, Internat. Arabian Horse Assn., Arabian Horse Assn. So. Calif., Friendly Hills Country Club. Republican. Baptist. Home: 2160 Le Flore Dr La Habra Heights CA 90631-8020

MAXWELL, FLOYD DAWSON, research engineer, consultant; b. Athens, Ga., Mar. 12, 1935; s. Archie Lee Maxwell and Samantha Lee Willingham; m. Roberta Marie Runnestrand, Aug. 4, 1975; children: Michael R., Pamela J. BSEE, U. Ariz., 1961; PhD, U. Calif., Riverside, 1974; postgrad., UCLA. Electronic engr. Naval Ordinance Lab., Corona, Calif., 1961-69, br. head, 1967-69; rsch. engr. Forest Fire Lab., Riverside, 1969-74; rsch. assoc. U. Calif., Riverside, 1971-74; tech. staff The Aerospace Corp., El Segundo, Calif., 1974-75, mgr., sr. engr. specialist, 1975—; cons. USN, Corona, Justice Dept., Riverside, 1969-74, Atty. Gen., Sacramento, 1979-81, INMARSAT, London, 1994; lectr. grad. studies U. So. Calif., L.A., 1980-83. Planning commr. City of Riverside, 1974-75; pres. South Shores Homeowners Assn., 1977-88; bd. dirs. Palos Verdes (Calif.) Land Conserv, 1988—. Recipient Outstanding Young Men of Am. award Jr. C. of C., 1966. Mem. AAAS, Combustion Inst. (bd. dirs. 1970-80), Sigma Xi. Achievements include patent for near infrared system for imaging forest fires through smoke. Office: The Aerospace Corp 2350 E El Segundo Blvd El Segundo CA 90245-4691

MAXWELL, PAMELA JOY, clinical psychologist; b. Riverside, Calif., Dec. 28, 1962; d. F.D. Maxwell and Mary J. Schoonmaker. BA, Calif. State U., Northridge, 1985, MA, 1987; PhD, Calif. Sch. Profl. Psychology, 1990. Lic. psychologist, Calif. Program coord. The HELP Group, Sherman Oaks, Calif., 1991-94, program supr., 1993-94, cmty. therapist, 1996—; clin. field coord. Supportive Counseling Care, Manhattan Beach, Calif., 1994-96; psychologist Mullikin Med. Ctrs., Glendale, Calif., 1996—; pvt. practice psychologist La Cañada, Calif., 1997—. Cmty. vol. LA Works. Mem. APA.

MAXWELL, RAYMOND ROGER, accountant; b. Parmer County, Tex., Jan. 7, 1918; s. Frederick W. and Hazel Belle (Rogers) M.; m. Jeanne Hollarn, June 16, 1945 (dec. Dec. 1987); children: Donald R., Bruce Edward, Sabrina G. Ed.B., Western Ill. State Tchrs Coll., 1941; MBA in Acctg., U. Fla., 1949; postgrad., UCLA, 1965-68. CPA, Fla., Calif. Asst. to bus. mgr. Western Ill. State Tchrs. Coll., Macomb, 1939-41; apprentice acct. Charles H. Lindfors, CPA, Ft. Lauderdale, Fla., 1946-48; acct./auditor Frederic Dunn-Rankin & Co. CPA, Miami, Fla., 1948-49; CPA staff Charles Costar, CPA, Miami, 1951; resident auditor/CPA prin. Raymond R. Maxwell CPA, Ft. Lauderdale, 1951-56; supt. pub. instrn. Broward County, Ft. Lauderdale, 1956-61; staff asst. in fin. North Am. Aviation, Inc., El Segundo, Calif., 1961-65; acctg. prin. Raymond R. Maxwell, CPA, Whittier, Calif., 1968—; part-time rsch. asst. UCLA, 1965, teaching asst., 1966, 67; instr. Calif. Poly., 1967. Active precinct election bds., Whittier, L.A. County, 1989; 1st reader First Ch. of Christ, Scientist, Whittier, 1990-92, 96-98, exec. bd., 1989, exec. bd. chmn., 1993, participant Bible Explorations, 1991-92. 1st lt. USAAF, 1942-46. Republican. Avocations: dancing, swimming, computers. Office: 8235 Painter Ave Whittier CA 90602-3108

MAXWELL-BROGDON, FLORENCE MORENCY, school administrator, educational adviser; b. Spring Park, Minn., Nov. 11, 1929; d. William Frederick and Florence Ruth (LaBrie) Maxwell; m. John Carl Brogdon, Mar. 13, 1957; children: Carole Alexandra, Cecily Ann, Daphne Diana. B.A., Calif. State U., L.A., 1955; MS, U. So. Calif., 1957; postgrad. Columbia Pacific U., San Rafael, Calif., 1982-86. Cert. tchr., Calif. Dir. Rodeo Sch., L.A., 1961-64; lectr. Media Features, Culver City, Calif., 1964—; dir. La Playa Sch., Culver City, 1968-75; founding dir. Venture Sch., Culver City, 1974—, also chmn. bd.; bd. dirs., v.p. Parent Coop. Preschools, Baie d'Urfe Que., Can., 1964—; del. to Ednl. Symposium, Moscow-St. Petersburg, 1992, U.S./China Joint Conf. on Edn., Beijing, 1992, Internat. Confedn. of Prins., Geneva, 1993, Internat. Conf., Berlin, 1994. Author: Let Me Tell You, 1973; Wet'n Squishy, 1973; Balancing Act, 1977; (as Morency Maxwell) Framed in Silver, 1985; (column) What Parents Want to Know, 1961—; editor: Calif. Preschooler, 1961-74; contbr. articles to profl. jours. Treas. Democrat Congl. Primary, Culver City, 1972. Mem. Calif. Council Parent Schs. (bd. dirs. 1961-74), Parent Coop. Preschools Internat. (advisor 1975—), Pen Ctr. USA West, Mystery Writers of Am. (affiliate), Internat. Platform Assn., Nat. Assn. Secondary Sch. Prins., Libertarian. Home: 10814 Molony Rd Culver City CA 90230-5451 Office: Venture Sch 5333 Sepulveda Blvd Culver City CA 90230-5015

MAY, CLIFFORD DANIEL, newspaper editor, journalist; m. Lou Ann Brunwasser; children: Miranda Rose, Evan Phillip Barr. Cert. in Russian lang. and lit., U. Leningrad, 1973; BA, [illegible], 1973; M Journalism, Columbia U., 1975, M Internat. Affairs, 1975. Assoc. editor Newsweek, 1975-78; roving fgn. corr. Hearst Newpapers, 1978-79; sr. editor Am. edit. Geo mag., 1979-80; gen. editor Sunday Mag., Washington corr. N.Y. Times, 1980-89; chief West Africa bur. N.Y. Times, Abidjan, Ivory Coast, 1984; assoc. editor Rocky Mountain News, Denver, 1989-97; comms. dir. Rep. Nat. Com., Washington, 1997—; spl. corr. CBS Radio News, Bill Moyers' Jour./Internat. Report-PBS-TV, 1970's; host, prodr. Roundtable, Sta. KRMA, Colo.; freelance writer, 1979-89. Contbg. editor World Press Rev. Mag.; host, prodr. roundtable Sta. KRMA, Denver, 1994—; host Race for the Presidency TCI News, 1995-96. Avocations: downhill skiing, outdoor activities. Office: Rep Nat Com 310 1st St SE Washington DC 20082-0002

MAY, KATHERINE (KAKI HEINEMANN), author; b. St. Louis; d. Herbert N. and Elsa S. (Straus) Arnstein; BS, Washington U., St. Louis, 1950, MA (Arts and Scis. Faculty award 1950), 1956; m. Morton D. May, 1937; children: David A., Philip F.; m. Sol Heinemann, July 8, 1950; 1 child, Kate Heinemann Taucher. Freelance writer, poet, 1960—; prof. English, U. Tex., El Paso, 1968-74; condr. poetry readings, workshops, 1968—; mem. El Paso Art Resources Dept. Bd., 1980-81; author: Brandings, 1968; Some Inhuman Familiars, 1983; taping for Poetry Collection of Library of Congress, 1982. Mem. PEN, Nat. Soc. Arts and Letters. Home: 111 Emerson St Apt 1423 Denver CO 80218-3791

MAY, MICHAEL WAYNE, technical school executive; b. Springhill, La., Mar. 31, 1949; s. Willie Wilmer and Ethel Florene (Sigler) M. Student So. Ark. U., 1968-70, La. Tech. U., 1970-71. Prodn. dir. Sta. KKAM, Pueblo, Colo., 1973-75; quality control dir. Sta. KBOZ, Bozeman, Mont., 1975-78; music dir., dir. rsch., disk jockey Sta. KOOK, Billings, Mont., 1978-80; founder, operator May Tech. Coll., Billings, Great Falls, 1980—; owner Sta. KMAY, Billings, Mont. Mem. Career Coll. Assn. (state capt. for Mont.). Author: Building with the Basics: Radio Personality Development, 1979, Radio Personality Basics, 1992. Home: 80 Skyline Dr Billings MT 59105-3038 Office: PO Box 127 Billings MT 59103-0127

MAY, PHILIP ALAN, sociology educator; b. Bethesda, Md., Nov. 6, 1947; s. Everette Lee and Marie (Lee) M.; m. Doreen Ann Garcia, Sept. 5, 1972; children: Katrina Ruth, Marie Ann. BA in Sociology, Catawba Coll., 1969; MA in Sociology, Wake Forest U., 1971; PhD in Sociology, U. Mont., 1976. NIMH predoctoral fellow U. Mont., Missoula, 1973-76; dir. health stats. and rsch. Navajo Health Authority, Window Rock, Ariz., 1976-78; asst. prof. U. N.Mex., Albuquerque, 1978-82, assoc. prof., 1982-89, prof., 1989—, dir. Ctr. on Alcoholism, Substance Abuse and Addictions, 1990—; mem. fetal alcohol syndrome study com., Inst. of Medicine/Nat. Acad. Scis., 1994-96; cons. various govt. agys., 1976—; dir. Nat. Indian Fetal Alcohol Syndrome Prevention Program, Albuquerque, 1979-85; mem. adv. bd. Nat. Orgn. on Fetal Alcohol Syndrome, Washington, 1990—; rsch. assoc. Nat. Ctr. for Am. Indian and Alaska Native Mental Health Rsch., 1986—. Contbr. chpts. to books and articles to profl. jours. Mem. Ctrl. United Meth. Ch., Albuquerque, 1980-90, 98—, First United Meth. Ch., Albuquerque, 1990-97, Bd. Edn. Laguna Pueblo, N.Mex. Lt. USPHS, 1970-73. Recipient Spl. Recognition award U.S. Indian Health Svc., 1992, award Navajo Tribe and U.S. Indian Health Svc., 1992, Human Rights Promotion award UN Assn., 1994, Program award for Contbns. to Mental Health of Am. Indians, U.S. Indian Health Svc., 1996. Mem. APHA, Am. Sociol. Assn., Population Ref. Bur., Coll. on Problems of Drug Dependence, Rsch. Soc. Alcoholism. Home: 4610 Idlewilde Ln SE Albuquerque NM 87108-3422 Office: U NMex CASAA 2350 Alamo Ave SE Albuquerque NM 87106-3202

MAY, ROBERT, sales executive; b. Harlem, Holland, Oct. 22, 1932; s. Robert Sr. and Pat (Riley) M. MA, Oxford (Eng.) U., 1956, PhD, 1964. V.p. sales Pjb, Cotati, Calif. Lt. col. USMC, 1951-76. Avocations: music, theatre, bridge, fencing.

MAY, STEPHEN JAMES, communications educator, writer; b. Toronto, Ont., Can., Sept. 10, 1946; s. Thomas and Claire (Thompson) M.; m. Caroline Casteel, Sept. 27, 1947; 1 child, Trevor. BA, Calif. State U., Carson, 1975; MA, Calif. State U., L.A., 1977; DLitt, Internat. U., London, 1990. Prof. and chair dept. of Englist and Lit. Pikes Peak C.C., Colorado Springs, Colo., 1980-91; prof. Colo. N.W. C.C., Craig, 1992-98; chair dept. of English and Lit. Pikes Peak C.C., Colorado Springs, Colo., 1998—; advisor Internat. Biog. Ctr., Cambridge, Eng., 1989-95. Author: Pilgrimage, 1987, Fire From the Skies, 1990, Footloose, 1993, Zane Grey, 1997, Lone Rider, 1999; contbr. to profl. jours. including SouthWest Art, Ohio Review. Mem. Western Writers Am., Colo. Authors League, Zane Grey Soc., Soc. S.W. Authors, C.C. Humanities. Avocations: travelig, writing, drawing. Home: 5546 Escondido Dr Colorado Springs CO 80918

MAYBAY, DUANE CHARLES, recycling systems executive; b. Ft. Dodge, Iowa, Oct. 5, 1922; s. John H. and Florabel (Hibbard) Lungren; m. Mary Tribble Parrish, Dec. 18, 1947 (div. Oct. 1972); children: Tina Biggs, Karen Woodward. BA in Mktg., U. Wis., 1948. Product engr. Gates Rubber Co., Denver, 1948-50; asst. dir. sales & mktg. Hi-C divsn. Hi-C and Snow Crop Divsn. Minute Maid Corp., N.Y.C., 1951-63; mktg. dir. Knudsen Foods, L.A., 1963-70; owner Mountain Foods, Altadena, Calif., 1970-76, Maybay Recycling Sys., Irvine, Calif., 1976-84; ptnr. Resource Recovery Sys., Irvine, 1984—. Served to lt. col. U.S. Army Air Corps, 1943-45, Italy. Avocation: antiques. Home: 104 Pergola Irvine CA 92612-1704 Office: Resource Recovery Sys PO Box 17426 Irvine CA 92623-7426

MAYBERRY, PATRICIA ANN TINTHOFF, artist, educator, interior designer; b. Urbana, Ill., Oct. 19, 1940; d. Fred S. and Alyce L. (Tyler) Tinthoff; m. William Thomas Mayberry, July 16, 1962; children: Michael, Karrin. BA, DePauw U., 1962. Cert. K-12 art tchr., Ariz. Tchr. Maplewood Elem. Sch., Rantoul, Ill., 1962-65; artist, propr. Custom Welded Jewelry and Sculpture, Scottsdale, 1970-78; tchr. art Pueblo Elem. Community Sch., Scottsdale, 1973-74; propr. Panache Interior Design, Scottsdale, 1979-87, Artforms, Paradise Valley, Ariz., 1987—; tchr., propr. Children's Art Sch., Paradise Valley, 1975—; juror South Mountain Magnet Sch. for Arts, Phoenix, 1990, 91, 92, 93, 94, Horizons Show, Shemer Art Ctr., Phoenix, 1991, 92, sr. show Phoenix Union High Sch. Dist., 1995; lectr. art Sun City West Art Club, 1998, No. Ariz. Watercolor Assn., 1998. Exhibited at Western Fedn. Watercolor Show, Corpus Christi, Tex., 1991, El Paso (Tex.) Mus. Art, 1992; one woman show Joe Wilcox Fine Arts, 1998; two woman show Ch. of Beatitudes, Phoenix, Ariz., 1991-92, West Valley Art Mus., 1996, Meijers Art Gallery, Scottsdale, Ariz., 1999; three person show Citibank Tower, Phoenix, 1993; exhibited in group shows for Nat. Watercolor Soc. at Muckenthaler Cultural Ctr., Fullerton, Calif., 1994, Joslyn Fine Arts Ctr., Torrance, Calif., 1995; permanent collections include Maricopa County C.C., Baker, Livermore & Quinn Pvt. Collections. Recipient purchase award Maricopa County C.C.'s, 1987, Nat. Okla. Watercolor Investment award, 1996. Mem. Nat. Watercolor Soc. (signature mem.), Ariz. Artists Guild (3d v.p. 1988-90, pres. 1990-92), Ariz. Watercolor Assn. (2d v.p. 1989-90, bd. dirs. 1994-98, Best of Show award 1989, 94, 96, Disting. Merit award 1991, 92, 95, Juror's Choice award 1994, royal mem.), Contemporary Watercolor Assn. (sec. 1991-92, Merit award 1991), 22x30 Watercolor Group, Alpha Omicron Pi (pres. collegiate chpt. 1961-62, pres. alumni chpt. 1974-75). Republican. Avocations: skiing, aerobics. Home and Studio: 8818 N 66th Pl Paradise Valley AZ 85253-2302

MAYER, EDWARD MAXIMILIAN, architect; b. Bandung, West Java, Indonesia, Feb. 22, 1932; came to U.S., 1956; s. Wilhelm and Christina Rosina (Kepel) M.; m. Camille J. Mayer; children: Jaqueline, Duane, Christine, Joel, Wendy. BA, Eastlands Coll., London, 1962; MA, U. Eng. (Oxford), 1965; PhD, Met. Coll., London, 1972. Cert. interior designer, Wash. Commd. 2d. lt. USAF, 1950, advanced through grades to lt. col., 1952-72; jet pilot USAF, Royal Netherlands Air Force, 1952-72; arch., designer Smiths Inc., Oakland, Calif., 1957-72, USAF HQ PACAF, Hickam AFB, Hawaii, 1972-91, U.S. Army Corps Engrs., Pentagon, Va., 1991-95, U.S. Govt., Las Vegas, Nev., 1995—. Mem. Internat. Interior Design Assn. Avocations: music, photography, reading, fishing. Home: 613 Rancho Del Mar Way North Las Vegas NV 89031

MAYER, ELIZABETH BILLMIRE, educational administrator; B.Ed., Nat. Coll. Edn., Evanston, Ill., 1953; M.A. in Liberal Studies, Wesleyan U., 1970. Teaching asst. Hull House, Chgo., 1950-51; teaching scholar Nat. Coll. Edn. Demonstration Sch., 1952-53; pre-sch. tchr. St. Matthew's Sch., Pacific Palisades, Calif., 1959-63, tchr. 2d grade, 1963-67; librarian Chandler Sch., Pasadena, Calif., 1971-72, tchr. 4th grade, 1972-80, curriculum coordinator 1st-8th grades, 1979-80; tchr. 4th-6th grades Inst. for Experimentation in Tchr. Edn., SUNY-Cortland, 1980; asst. prof. edn. SUNY-Cortland, 1980-82; founder, headmistress The Mayer Sch., Ithaca, N.Y., 1982-92, Ariz. State U., Tempe, 1992—, Coll. Edn., 1992-94, faculty liaison Acad. Affairs, 1994—. Mem. Nat. Council Tchrs. Math., Nat. Council Tchrs. English, Nat. Sci. Tchrs. Assn., Rotary Internat. (mem. bd. dirs. 1994-96), Phi Delta Kappa (officer 1980-81, 92-96), Mem. Leadership America, class of 1995. Office: Ariz State U PO Box 870101 Tempe AZ 85287-0101

MAYER, GEORGE ROY, educator; b. National City, Calif., Aug. 28, 1940; s. George Eberly and Helen Janet (Knight) M.; m. Barbara Ann Fife, Sept. 9, 1964 (div. June 1986); children: Kevin Roy, Debbie Rae Ann; m. Jocelyn Volk Finn, Aug. 3, 1986. BA, San Diego State U., 1962; MA, Ind. U., 1965, EdD, 1966. Cert. sch. psychologist; cert. behavior analyst. Sch. counselor, psychologist Ind. U., Bloomington, 1964-66; asst. prof. guidance and ednl. psychology So. Ill. U., Carbondale, 1966-69; profl. edn. Calif. State U., L.A., 1966—; cons. in field; mem. adv. bd. Dept. Spl. Edn., L.A., 1986—, Alamansor Edn. Ctr., Alhambra, Calif., 1986-90, Jay Nolan Ctr. for Autism, Newhall, Calif., 1975-86; lectr. in field; mem. study group on youth violence prevention Nat. Ctr. for Injury Prevention and Control, Divsn. Violence Prevention of the Ctrs. for Disease Control and Prevention, 1998. Author: Classroom Management: A California Resource Guide; co-author: Behavior Analysis for Lasting Change, 1991; contbr. articles to profl. jours. Recipient Outstanding Prof. award Calif. State U.-L.A., 1988; U.S. Dept. Edn. grantee, 1996—. Mem. Assn. for Behavior Analysis, Nat. Assn. Sch. Psychologists, Calif. Assn. Behavior Analysis (pres., Outstanding Contbr. to Behavior Analysis award 1997), Cambridge Ctr. for Behavioral Studies (adv. bd.), Calif. Assn. Sch. Psychologists (chmn. practitioners conf. 1994—). Avocations: horseback riding, fishing, swimming. Home: 10600 Pinyon Ave Tujunga CA 91042-1517

MAYER, HERBERT CARLETON, JR., computer consultant; b. Newton, Mass., Aug. 2, 1922; s. Herbert Carleton and Elsie Marie (Hauser) M.; m. Maryetta Brodkord, Aug. 21, 1948; children: Judith Marie, Christine Louise. BS, Parsons Coll., 1943; MS, U. Iowa, 1947; PhD, U. So. Calif., 1975. Instr. math. U. Idaho, Moscow, 1947-48, U. Utah, Salt Lake City, 1949-51; edn. adminstr. Gen. Electric co., Richland, Wash., 1951-59; systems engr., univ. industry specialist IBM, Chgo., 1959-81; assoc. prof. mgmt. info. systems Wash. State U., Pullman, 1980-82; assoc. prof. U. Wis.-Parkside, Kenosha, 1982-85, Eastern Wash. U., Cheney, 1985-90; adj. prof. mgmt. U. Tex., El Paso, 1976-78. Pres. Tri-City Heights Assn., Kennewick, Wash., 1956-58, PTA, Kennewick, 1957-58; v.p. Kennewick Sch. Bd., 1958-59, pres., 1959. Mem. Math. Assn. Am., Internat. Assn. Computing in Edn., Am. Soc. Engring. Edn., Data Processing Mgmt. Assn. (bd. dirs., sec. Spokane chpt. 1988, v.p. edn. Spokane chpt. 1989, v.p. student chpt. 1990), Manito Lions Spokane (membership chmn. 1991-92, program chmn. 1992-93, v.p. 1993-98), Phi Delta Kappa (found. chmn. Spokane chpt. 1992-94). Home: 3334 S Bernard St Spokane WA 99203-1636

MAYER, PATRICIA JAYNE, financial officer, management accountant; b. Chgo., Apr. 27, 1950; d. Arthur and Ruth (Greenberger) Hersh; m. William A. Mayer Jr., Apr. 30, 1971. AA, Diablo Valley Coll., 1970; BSBA, Calif. State U., Hayward, 1975. Cert. mgmt. acct. Staff acct., auditor Elmer Fox Westheimer and Co., Oakland, Calif., 1976; supervising auditor Auditor's Office County of Alameda, Oakland, 1976-78; asst. acctg. mgr. CBS Retail Stores doing bus. as Pacific Stereo, Emeryville, Calif., 1978-79; contr. Oakland Unified Sch. Dist., 1979-84; v.p. fin., CFO YMCA, San Francisco, 1984-96; v.p. fin. customer segments Charles Schwab & Co., San Francisco, 1996—; instr. acctg. to staff YMCA, San Francisco, 1984-96, CBS Retail Stores, 1978-79. Draft counselor Mt. Diablo Peace Ctr., Walnut Creek, Calif., 1970-72; dep. registrar of voters Contra Costa County Registrar's Office, Martinez, Calif., 1972-77. Mem. Fin. Execs. Inst. (bd. dirs. San Francisco chpt.), Inst. Mgmt. Accts. (pres.-elect Diablo Valley chpt. 1995—, pres. 1995-96), Dalmatian Club No. Calif., Dalmation Club Am. Democrat. Jewish. Avocations: showing and breeding Dalmatians, playing Tex. Hold 'Em poker tournaments. Office: Charles Schwab & Co 101 Montgomery St Ste 200 San Francisco CA 94104-4175

MAYER, ROBERT ANTHONY, retired college president; b. N.Y.C., Oct. 30, 1933; s. Ernest John and Theresa Margaret (Mazura) M.; m. Laura Wiley Christ, Apr. 30, 1960. BA magna cum laude, Fairleigh Dickinson U., 1955; MA, NYU, 1967. With N.J. Bank and Trust Co., Paterson, 1955-61; mgr. advt. dept. N.J. Bank and Trust Co., 1959-61; program supr. advt. dept. Mobil Oil Co., N.Y.C., 1961-62; asst. to dir. Latin Am. program Ford Found., N.Y.C., 1963-65; asst. rep. Ford Found., Brazil, 1965-67; asst. to v.p. adminstrn., 1967-73; officer in charge logistical services Ford Found., 1968-73; asst. dir. programs N.Y. Community Trust, N.Y.C., 1973-76; exec. dir. N.Y. State Council on the Arts, N.Y.C., 1976-79; mgmt. cons. N.Y.C., 1979-80; dir. Internat. Mus. Photography, George Eastman House, Rochester, N.Y., 1980-89, mgmt. cons., 1989-90; pres. Cleve. Inst. of Art, 1990-97—. Mem. editorial adv. bd.: Grants mag., 1978-80; author: (plays) La Borgia, 1971; Alijandru, 1971, They'll Grow No Roses, 1975. Mem. state program adv. panel NEA, 1977-80; mem. Mayor's Com. on Cultural Policy, N.Y.C., 1974-75; mem. pres.'s adv. com. Bklyn. campus, L.I. U., 1978-79; bd. dirs. Fedn. Protestant Welfare Agys., N.Y.C., 1977-79, Arts for Greater Rochester, 1981-83, Garth Fagan's Dance Theatre, 1982-86; trustee Internat. Mus. Photography, 1981-89, Lacoste Sch. Arts, France, 1991-96, sec., 1994-96; mem. dean's adv. com. Grad. Sch. Social Welfare, Fordham U., 1976; mem. N.Y. State Motion Picure and TV Devel. Adv. Bd., 1984-87, N.Y. State Martin Luther King Jr. Commn., 1985-90, Cleve. Coun. Cultural Affairs, 1992-94; chmn. Greater Cleve. Regional Transit Authority Arts in Transit Com., 1992-95; bd. dirs. Friends of Ariz. State U. Ctr. for Latin Am. Studies, 1997—. Recipient Nat. award on advocacy for girls Girls Clubs Am., 1976. Mem. Nat. Assembly Art Agys. (bd. dirs. 1977-79, 1st vice chmn. 1978-79), Alliance Ind. Colls. Art (bd. dirs. 1983-91, vice chmn. 1986-87, sec. 1987-89), N.Y. State Assn. Museums (bd. councilors 1983-86, pres. 1986-89), Assn. Ind. Colls. Art and Design (bd. dirs. 1991-97, exec. com. 1991-93, 96-97). Home: 2704 N 60th St Scottsdale AZ 85257-1012

MAYEUR, ROBERT GORDON, music educator, guitarist; b. Houston, Mar. 23, 1932; s. Rutherford Louis and Zelta Viva (Benschoter) M.; m. Dora Guilda, Aug. 1, 1986; children: Gabrielle, Suzanne. BA, U. North Tex., 1954; MA, UCLA, 1965. Instr. music Santa Monica (Calif.) Coll., 1972-79; prof. music L.A. Valley Coll., Van Nuys, 1979—. Composer Rock City, 1966, The Guitar Thru The Ages, 1974, The Guitar and Jazz, 1975, The Guitar Ensemble, 1986, vol. II, 1998. With U.S. Army, 1964-67. Mem. Am. Fedn. Musicians (life), Guitar Found. Am. (v.p. 1974-98). Home: 5777 Tanner Ridge Ave Westlake Village CA 91362 Office: LA Valley Coll 5800 Fulton Ave Van Nuys CA 91401

MAYFIELD, SANDRA JEANNE, recreational therapist, consultant; b. Mpls., Aug. 28, 1942; d. Glen Douglas and Ellynore (Kukko) M. BS in Recreation, San Jose State U., 1967, MS in Therapeutic Recreation, 1979. Cert. recreation therapist, Calif., therapeutic recreation specialist. Recreation asst. supr. Sunnyvale (Calif.) Park and Recreation Dept., 1960-67; dir. recreation Santa Clara Valley Med. Ctr., San Jose, Calif., 1967—; lectr. San Francisco State U., 1976-78; instr. San Jose State U., 1986-88, Tex. Women's U., Denton, 1989; cons. Western Med., Hayward, Calif., 1978-79; bd. dirs. Horizons West; chmn., presenter numerous local, state and nat. workshops and conf. sessions; mem. steering com. Coma to Community Bain Trauma Conf., 1988-95; Calif. Bd. Rec. personnel certification, 1993—. Author: Protocols in Therapeutic Recreation, 1989, Quality Assurance and Continuous Quality Improvement, 1992; co-author: Facilitating a Desired Leisure Lifestyle, 1987. Recipient Disting. Recreation Alumnus award San Jose State U., 1983, Alumnus of Yr. award dept. recreation and leisure studies, 1988. Mem. Nat. Therapeutic Recreation Soc. (bd. dirs. 1983-89, pres. 1988-89, Disting. Svc. award 1993), Calif. Park and Recreation Soc. (pres. therapeutic recreation sect. 1981-83, state bd. dirs. 1981-83, chmn. recreation therapy licensure task force 1983-95, Outstanding Therapeutic Recreator award 1985, Citation 1988, Fellowship award 1993). Democrat. Avocations: [illegible]. Office: Santa Clara Valley Med Ctr 751 S Bascom Ave San Jose CA 95128-2604

MAYNARD, KENNETH DOUGLAS, architect; b. Hackensack, N.J., Aug. 16, 1931; s. Douglas Harry and Eva (Whiting) M.; m. Myrna Myrtle James, Feb. 4, 1956; children: Colin, Vivien Noll. Cert. in Architecture, U. Natal, Durban, Republic of South Africa, 1958. Registered architect Alaska. Draftsman Morross & Graff, Johannesburg, Republic of South Africa, 1950-51, Anglo-Am. Corp., Johannesburg, Republic of South Africa, 1951-54, Moir & Llewellyn, Empangeni, Zululand, Republic of South Africa, 1955-57; architect Pearse Aneck-Hahn & Bristol, Johannesburg, 1957-60, Manley & Mayer, Anchorage, 1960-61, FAA, Anchorage, 1961-62, Crittenden Cassetta Wirum & Jacobs, Anchorage, 1962-65; prin. Schultz & Maynard, Anchorage, 1965-68, Kenneth Maynard Assocs., Anchorage, 1968-78; pres. Maynard & Partch, Anchorage, 1978-96; prin. USKH, Inc., Anchorage, 1996—. Active Western Alaska Coun. Boy Scouts. Am., Anchorage, 1965-84; bd. dirs. Salvation Army Adv. Bd., Anchorage, 1981-87, Anchorage Mus. Assn., 1969-86, Anchorage Opera Co., 1983-90; chmn. Mayor's Comprehensive Homeless Program Strategy Group, 1992-94. Fellow AIA (pres. Alaska chpt. 1969, N.W. regional rep. for nat. com. on design 1976-89); mem. Constrn. Specification Inst. (pres. Cook Inlet chpt. 1993-94), Soc. Am. Mil. Engrs. Republican. Avocation: tennis. Home: 2237 Forest Park Dr Anchorage AK 99517-1324 Office: USKH 2515 A St Anchorage AK 99503-2776

MAYNARD, MICHAEL, librarian; b. Yuma, Ariz., July 8, 1955; s. Ernest Ray and Refugio (Guerrero) M. AAS in Electronic Tech., Phoenix Coll., 1986; BA in German, Ariz. State U., 1989; postgrad., U. Leipzig, 1990, Eberhard-Karls U., Tubingen, Germany, 1990-91; MLS, U. Ariz., 1992. Electronics technician USN, 1977-83; asst. libr. Chapel Libr., Venice, Fla., 1983-84; security officer Anderson Agy., Phoenix, 1984-89; grad. asst. U. Ariz., Tuscon, 1989-90, libr. asst. main libr. acquisitions dept., 1992; asst. libr. Internat. Bapt. Coll., Tempe, Ariz., 1992-94; head libr. Fitch Libr., Mesa, Ariz., 1994-97; libr. II Ariz. Dept. Corrections, Douglas, 1997—. *Mr. Maynard studied Classical Philology in graduate school. He passed the rigorous Prufung zum Nachweise fur deutsche Sprachkenntnis in Germany. He studied in Tucson, Arizona, but was unable to commute or pay rent there. He slept in his car while he was a full time student of Library Science. He earned his Master of Library Science degree and then completed two semesters of Koine Greek at International Baptist College and 16 semester hours of French at Mesa Community College with a 4.0 GPA. He has seven years experience working in libraries. He became director of Comma Publications in 1995. His book (ISBN 1-886971-05-6) is being sold worldwide.* Author: History of the Debate Over I John 5:7-8, 1995. With USN, 1977-83. Scholar U. Ariz., 1989-90, Herman Weinel scholar, 1990. Mem. ALA, Assn. Christian Librs., Ariz. Libr. Assn. Baptist. Avocations: foreign languages, long distance running, nutrition, collecting biographical sketches, New Testament textual criticism. E-mail: receptus@sprynet.com. Home: PO Box 1544 Douglas AZ 85608-1544 Office: Comma Publs PO Box 1625 Tempe AZ 85280-1625

MAYNARD, WAYNE, landscape architect; b. Interlochen, Mich., Sept. 10, 1938; s. Harold Harry and Donna Deane M.; m. Nancy Rose Bech, June 15, 1962 (div. 1976). AA, Monterey Peninsula Jr. Coll., 1958; BS in Landscape Architecture, Calif. State Polytech, 1963; M of Landscape Architecture, U. Mich., 1966. Lic. landscape architect, Calif.,. Designer San Diego City Sch. Dist., 1963-64; assoc. prof. dept. landscape architecture N.C. State U., Raleigh, 1966-72; forest planning officer USDA, Forest Svc., San Bernardino, Calif., 1972-79; owner Valley Planning Cons., Merced, Calif., 1979-92; landscape architect pvt. practice, Merced, Calif., 1992—. Com. mem. U. Calif., Merced, 1990—; project mgr. Merced Youth Sports Complex, 1990-95; chmn. Merced Beautification Com., 1993-95; bd. dirs. Merced Farmland Trust, 1995—. Mem. Am. Soc. Landscape ARchitects, Rotary, Merced City Chamber. Avocations: painting, reading, travel, golf. Office: 36644 Road 197 Woodlake CA 93286-9685

MAYOL, RICHARD THOMAS, advertising executive, political consultant; b. Springfield, Ill., Oct. 30, 1949; s. Richard McFaren and Marjorie (Maddex) M. AA, Springfield Coll., 1969; BS, U. Tulsa, 1972. Co-owner First Tuesday Inc., Phoenix, 1976-85; pres. Mayol and Assocs., Phoenix, 1985—; CEO New West Policy Group, Prescott, Ariz., 1993—; cons. Dem. candidates, Dem. candidates ballot issues, corp. pub. policy Western U.S., Nev. Dem Party, Ariz. Dem Party, Del Webb Corp., Open Primary Elections, Now Initiative, Johnson for Gov. Mem. Phoenix Film Commn., 1985—. Mem. Am. Assn. Polit. Cons., Phoenix Grand Prix Commn. Avocations: photography, writing, horseback riding. Home and Office: 348 Moreland Cir Prescott AZ 86303-4035 also: 223 Union St Prescott AZ 86303-3806

MAYOR, BABETTE ROBIN, artist, art educator; b. Warwick, R.I., May 27, 1952; d. Adrian Lester and Elfriede Maria (Barwitz) M; m. John Edward Morgan; children: Heidi, Cooper. AA, Chaffey Coll., Alta Loma, Calif., 1972; BA, U. Calif. Riverside, 1974; MFA, Claremont Grad. Sch., 1978. Adj. prof. Chaffey Coll., Alta Loma, Calif., 1977, '79; adj. prof. of art Mt. San Antonio Coll., Walnut, Calif., 1978-82; sr. graphic designer U. La Verne, Calif., 1981-90; adj. prof. art U. La Verne, 1988-90; assoc. prof. art Calif. State Polytech. U., Pomona, 1990-98; free lance artist/graphic designer Rancho Cucamonga Calif., 1979—; organizer, curator student art exhibitions with Coll. Environ. Design Glass Gallery, Calif. Poly Tech, Pomona, 1994, 95, 96, co-organizer with Patric D. Prince and Patrick Merril digital art exhbns. in Kellogg U. Art Gallery, 1996, 97. Artist: work exhibited at Arco Ctr. for Visual Art, L.A., 1979, Mt. San Antonio Coll. Art Gallery, Walnut, Calif., 1979, Pasadena Festival of Arts 5th ann. Juried Show, Ambassador Coll., 1980 (hon. mention), Villa Senor Art Gallery, San Bernardino, Calif., 1983 (2-person show), Norman F. Feldheym Ctrl. Libr. Art Galleries, San Bernardino, 1987, U. La Verne Faculty Exhbn., Da Gallery, Pomona, Calif., 1989, W. Keith and Janet Kellogg U. Art. Gallery, 1991, 92, 93, 94, 95, 96, 97, CGS Gallery, Claremont, Calif., 1994, Kohn Turner Art Gallery, L.A., 1995, Brewery Annex Gallery, L.A., 1996, Riverside C.C. Art Gallery, 1996.; designer: Fgn. Lang. Brochure, 1983 (Creativity award 1983). Cons., educator OCCUR, Ontario, Calif., 1995; mem. Calif. Youth Authority Trade Adv., 1990—. Home: 13992 Glendora Dr Rancho Cucamonga CA 91739-2181 Office: Calif State Polytech U 3801 W Temple Ave Pomona CA 91768-2557

MAYS, JAMES, JR., physician; b. Pine Bluff, Ark., May 1, 1938; s. Talmadge and Edna (Motley) M.; children: James Jr., James Earl, James T.O., James Eddie. BS/BA, U. Ark., Pine Bluff, 1961; MD, U. Ark., Little Rock, 1965. Tng. in cardiology UCLA and U. Calif., Irvine, to 1972; chief of cardiology, chief CCU Martin Luther King Hosp., L.A., 1972-75, chief cmty. edn., 1975-77; practice medicine specializing in cardiology, L.A., 1977—; pres. High Blood Pressure Found., L.A., 1977—, Adopt-A-Family Found., L.A., 1981—, Mays Med. Clinics, L.A., 1978—; chancellor, pres. Tech. Health Careers Sch., L.A., 1980-85. Author: Mercy Is King, 1977, Chameleon, 1980, Radian, 1981, Trapped, 1987, Justice on TV (The O.J. Simpson Trial), 1997. Capt. U.S. Army, 1966-68. Recipient awards. Mem. NAACP, PUSH, Masons, Kappa Alpha Psi. Avocations: sports, writing.

MAYTUM, HARRY RODELL, retired physician; b. Alexandria, S.D., Jan. 25, 1913; s. Wellington James and Lillian May (Syferd) M.; m. Louetta Susanna Stoltz, Apr. 27, 1937; children: James, Nancy, Joan. BS magna cum laude, U. Wis., 1936, MD, 1938. Intern Alameda County Hosp., Oakland, Calif., 1938-39, resident in surgery, 1946-47; resident in surgery Merced County Hosp., Merced, Calif., 1939-41; pvt. practice, Merced, 1947-95; ret., 1995; chief staff Mercy Hosp., Merced, Merced County Hosp. Bd. dirs. Merced County Mosquito Abatement Dist., 1954-64. Lt col. M.C., USAAF, 1941-47, ETO. Fellow Am. Geriatric Soc., Am. Acad. Family Practice (charter); mem. AMA, Calif. Med. Assn. (Plessner Meml. award 1992), Merced-Mariposa County Med. Soc. (pres.. 1955), Merced C. of C. (bd. dirs. 1973-77, former chmn. health affairs com., Merced Citizen of Yr. award 1989), Kiwanis (pres. Merced 1953), Elks, Phi Beta Kappa, Alpha Omega Alpha. Republican. Avocations: wood carving, furniture restoration, lapidarist. Home: 3460 R St Merced CA 95348-2359

MAZUREK, JOSEPH P., state attorney general, former state legislator; b. San Diego, July 27, 1948; B.A., U. Mont., 1970, J.D., 1975; m. Patty Mazurek; 3 children. Bar: Mont. 1975; atty. Gough, Shanahan, Johnson, and Waterman, Helena, Mont.; mem. Mont. Senate from 23d Dist., 1981-92; Senate pres., 1991-92; atty. gen., State of Mont., 1993—; mem. Revenue Oversight Com., 1983-92; chmn. Senate Judiciary Com.; assoc. editor Mont. Law Rev., 1974-75. Served with U.S. Army, 1970-72. Mem. ABA, Beta Gamma Sigma, Phi Delta Phi, Phi Delta Theta. Office: Justice Bldg PO Box 201401 215 N Sanders St Helena MT 45620-1401*

MAZZA, DAVID ANTHONY, communications and media professional; b. Burbank, Calif., Nov. 4, 1952; s. Joseph Anthony and Bonita Maxine (Nickle) M. Chief investigator Davis, Wright, Tremaine, Portland, Oreg., 1980-90; freelance writer, rschr. Portland, 1990-96; media dir. Jobs with Justice, Portland, 1993-96; comm. dir. Oreg. Pub. Employees Union, Salem, 1996—. Author: God, Land and Politics, 1992. Mem. living wage com. City of Portland, 1993-94, mem. Mayor Katz' transition team, 1992-94; mem. adv. bd. Oreg. Future, Portland, 1996-98; mem. citizens adv. com. Westside Bypass Study, Portland, 1992-96. With USN, 1971-77. Mem. Comm. Workers Am., Sierra Club (bd. dirs. Oreg. chpt. 1988-92, chair/environ. activist 1990-92, chair nat. com. on resource use 1990-92). Avocation: oil painting. Office: Oreg Pub Employees Union PO Box 12159 Salem OR 97309-0159

MAZZETTI, ROBERT F., real estate manager, retired orthopedic surgeon; b. San Francisco, Sept. 29, 1930; children: Mark, Robert Alan, Michelle. BA, U. Calif., San Francisco, 1952, MD, 1955. Diplomate Am. Bd. Orth. Surgery. Pvt. practice orth. surgeon Santa Barbara, Calif., 1962-98.

MCADAMS, FRANK JOSEPH, III, communications educator; b. Chgo., Nov. 18, 1940; s. Frank Joseph Jr. and Mary Irene (Geary) McA.; m. Patty Ann Rafferty, Dec. 27, 1966. BS, Loyola U., Chgo., 1967; MFA, UCLA, 1979. Instr. UCLA, 1981—, U. Calif., Irvine, 1989—; adj. prof. Sch. of Cinema, U. So. Calif., L.A., 1991—; mem. judging panel Diane Thomas Awards, UCLA, 1986—; mem. screenwriting adv. bd. U. Calif.-Irvine Extension, 1995—. Screenwriter: California Rain, 1978, Stagecoach Bravo, 1979. Precinct capt. Clinton-Gore, Orange County, Calif., 1992. Capt. USMC, 1966-69. Recipient award for best newspaper col. Orange County Press Club, 1974, HM for Best Series, 1974, Sam Goldwyn Screenwriting award Sam Goldwyn Found., 1978, 79. Mem. Writers Guild of Am. W., UCLA Theater Arts Alumni Assn., PEN Ctr. USA West. Democrat. Roman Catholic. Office: MAGLA PO Box 1511 Hollywood CA 90078-1511

MCAFEE, IVAN PAUL, III, editor; b. Denver, Oct. 23, 1955; s. I. Paul Jr. and Shirley Naomi (Anderson) McA.; m. Aimee Suzanne Kepner, Apr. 24, 1976; children: Harmony, Megan, Tessie. BA in English, Biola U., 1978. City editor S.E. News-Signal, South Gate, Calif., 1983-85; asst. city editor City News Svc., Hollywood, Calif., 1986-88; city editor Inland Valley Daily Bull., Ontario, Calif., 1988-90; bus. editor Inland Valley Daily Bull., Ontario, 1990-95; editor The Bus. Press, Ontario, 1995—. Mem. So. Profl. Journalists (dir. Inland So. Calif. Pro chpt. 1997—, Best Bus. Story award 1994, Best Feature Story award 1996, Best Tech. Story award 1998), Soc. Am. Bus. Writers and Editors. Avocations: Internet research, competitive roller skating, fiction writing. Office: The Bus Press 3700 Inland Empire Blvd Ste 450 Ontario CA 91764-4914

MCALISTER, MICHAEL H., architect; b. Calif., May 22; s. Doyle R. and Mary E. McAlister. AA, Bakersfield Coll.; BArch, Calif. Polytech. U. Planning techinition Bakersfield City Hall, 1963; carpenter Del Webb Corp., Kern City, Calif., 1964; architectural draftsman Goss & Choy Architects, Bakersfield, 1965-67; architect, v.p. D.G.C. & Assocs., Bakersfield, 1971-80; dir. architecture, v.p. N.B.A. & Assocs., Architects, Bakersfield, 1980-83; architect, pres. Michael H. McAlister, A.I.A., Bakersfield, 1983—; nephrology design cons. for various treatment groups and hosps., 1987—. Commr., architectural advisor Historic Preservation Commn., Bakersfield, 1986-87; bd. dirs. Camp Fire Coun., Kern County, Calif., 1980-84. Recipient Architectural Pub. Bldg. Hist. award Beautiful Bakersfield Com., City of Bakersfield's City Coun. and Hist. Preservation Commn., 1985, 87, Exterior Environ. Design Excellence Bakersfield C. of C., 1988, Comml. Design Excellence award, 1984, Design Excellence and Beautification award City of Taft, Calif., 1989, Design Excellence award State of Nev., 1992. Mem. AIA (Calif. Coun., Golden Empire chpt.). Avocations: horseback riding, art and sculpture. Office: 5030 Office Park Dr Ste B Bakersfield CA 93309-0612

MCANINCH, JACK WELDON, urological surgeon, educator; b. Merkel, Tex., Mar. 17, 1936; s. Weldon Thomas and Margaret (Canon) McA.; m. Barbara B. Buchanan, Dec. 29, 1960 (div. Aug. 1972); m. Burnet B. Sumner, Dec. 29, 1987; children: David A., Todd G., Brendan J. BS, Tex. Tech U., 1958; MS, U. Idaho, 1960; MD, U. Tex., 1964. Diplomate Am. Bd. Urology (trustee 1991-97, pres. 1996-97). Commd. capt. U.S. Army, 1964-66, advanced through grades to col., 1977, ret., 1977; col. USAR; intern then resident Letterman Army Med. Ctr., San Francisco, 1964-69; chief urol. surgery San Francisco Gen. Hosp., 1977—; prof. urol. surgery U. Calif., San Francisco, 1977—. Editor: Urogenital Trauma, 1985, Urologic Clinics of North America, 1989, Smith's General Urology, 1995; section editor: Early Care of the Injured Patient, 1990, Traumatic and Reconstructive Urology, 1996. Col. US Army, 1964-72. Recipient Disting. Alumnus award Tex. Tech U., 1994; named Disting. Alumnus U. Idaho, 1997. Fellow ACS (gov. 1992-97); mem. Am. Urol. Assn. (pres. we. sect. 1992-93, bd. dirs. 1990—, pres. 1996-97), Genitourinary Reconstructive Surgeons (pres.), Am. Assn. Surgery Trauma (v.p.), Soc. Univ. Urologists, Am. Bd. Urology (pres. 1996-97). Office: San Francisco Gen Hosp Dept Urology 1001 Potrero Ave Dept Urology San Francisco CA 94110-3594

MCBAIN, DIANE JEAN, actress, writer, newspaper columnist; b. Cleve., May 18, 1941; d. Walter George and Cleo Lida (Ferguson) McB.; m. Rodney L. Burke (div.); 1 child, Evan Andrew. Student, Antioch U., Los Angeles, 1985-87. Film, TV actress, 1957—; actress Warner Bros. Studios, 1959-64; freelance actress, 1976-81; owner Superior Interiors, 1964-68; screen writer, 1979—; treas., producer, prodn. coordinator Pied Piper Prodns., Inc., 1980-83, also bd. dirs.; freelance writer, photographer, 1982—; bd. dirs. The Response Ctr., L.A., counselor, 1985-89; treas. Theater for Youth Project, 1981; with Project Angel Food, 1989-92; nat. bd. dirs. Screen Actors Guild, 1999—. Appeared in films including Ice Palace, Parrish, Claudelle Inglish, A Distant Trumpet, The Caretakers, Donner Pass, Mary, Mary, I Sailed to Tahiti, Spinout, The Delta Factor, Thunder Alley, Wicked, Wicked, The Puppet Master, Cab to Canada, Invisible Mom, II, The Path, April V; TV shows include Dallas, Eight Is Enough, Hawaii Five-O, Grizzly Adams Christman Spl., Knight Rider, Air Wolf, Days of Our Lives, Marcus Welby, M.D., Police Story, Charlie's Angels, Matt Houston, Jake and the Fat Man, General Hospital, Sabrina, The Teenage Witch, Dr. Quinn, Medicine Woman; TV movie Donner Pass; theater prodns. include Who's Happy Now, The Tender Trap, The Glass Menagerie, Star Spangled Girl, Cahuenga Hill. Mem. exec. com. Iris Cantor Ctr. for Breast Imaging, 1990—; Stephen minister All Sts. Episcopal Ch., Beverly Hills, Calif., 1987; bd. dirs. exec. com. Justiceville, Homeless, U.S.A.; adminstr., project mgr. for C.Y.T./Blue Star Prodns., Paramount Studios, L.A. Democrat. Avocations: photography, traveling, aerobics, art.

MCBEATH, GERALD ALAN, political science educator, researcher; b. Mpls., Sept. 13, 1942; s. Gordon Stanley and Astrid Elvira (Hjelmeir) McB.; m. Jenifer Huang, June 7, 1970; children: Bowen, Rowena. BA, U. Chgo., 1963, MA, 1964; PhD, U. Calif., Berkeley, 1970. Vis. asst. prof. polit. sci. Rutgers Coll., New Brunswick, N.J., 1970-72; asst. prof. John Jay Coll., CUNY, N.Y.C., 1972-74, 75-76; assoc. prof. Nat. Chengchi U., Mucha, Taipei, Taiwan, 1974-75; prof. U. Alaska, Fairbanks, 1976—, dept. chair, 1980-85, 97-99, acting dean coll. liberal arts, 1991-93, dir. faculty devel., 1990-92; cons. Inst. Social and Econ. Rsch., Anchorage, 1976-77; contract rschr. Alaska Dept. Natural Resources, Alaska Dept. Edn., Nat. Inst. Edn., others; staff dir. task force on internat. trade policy Rep. Conf., U.S. Senate. Sr. author: Dynamics of Alaska Native Self-Government, 1980; author monograph: North Slope Borough Government and Policymaking, 1981; jr. author: Alaska's Urban and Rural Governments, 1984; sr. editor Alaska State Government and Politics, 1987; co-author: Alaska Politics and Government, 1994 (Am. Assn. State & Local History Commendation cert. 1995); author: The Alaska State Constitution, 1997, Wealth and Freedom: Taiwan's New Political Economy, 1998; editor: Alaska's Rural Development, 1982. Mem. bd. edn. Fairbanks North Star Borough, 1986-95, pres. 1989-90, 93-94, treas., 1991-93. Recipient Emil Usibelli Disting. Svc. award 1993; Chiang Ching-Kuo Found. fellow, 1995-97; named Outstanding Faculty Mem., Assn. Students U. Alaska, Fairbanks, 1979, Alumni Assn. U. Alaska, Fairbanks, 1981; grantee Nat. Inst. Edn., 1980-83, Alaska Coun. on Sci. and Tech., 1982-84, Spencer Found., 1987-88, Chiang Ching-Kuo Found., 1995-97. Mem. Asian Studies on Pacific Coast (program chmn. 1983, bd. dirs. 1982-83), Assn. Asian Studies, Western Polit. Sci. Assn. (mem. editl. bd. Western Govtl. Rschr.), Am. Polit. Sci. Assn., Fairbanks N. Star Borough Bd. Edn. Democrat. Home: 1777 Red Fox Dr Fairbanks AK 99709-6625 Office: U Ala Dept Polit Sci Fairbanks AK 99775

MCBRATNEY, TIMOTHY MICHAEL, mortgage banker; b. Pasadena, Calif., Dec. 30, 1958; s. John Bryson and Charleen (Gerhardt) McB.; m. Diane Martha D'Agostino, Mar. 14, 1998. BS, U. Oreg., 1981. Mgmt. trainee 1st Nat. Bank Anchorage, 1982-83; constrn. lender Nat. Bank Alaska, Anchorage, 1983-86; mortgage banker Lomas & Nettleton, Anchorage, 1986-87, Norwest Mortgage, Inc., Portland, Oreg., 1987—. Republican. Presbyterian. Avocations: golf, windsurfing, martial arts.

MCBRIDE, BONNIE TARBELL, investor relations executive; b. San Jose, Calif., Nov. 13, 1968; d. John Arthur and Barbara Farnum (Tarbell) McB. BA, U. Calif., Berkeley, 1990; MBA in Fin., U. Calif., Davis, 1995. Corp. paralegal Wilson, Sonsini, Goodrich & Rosati, Palo Alto, Calif., 1990-93; fin. analyst Level One Comms., Sacramento, Calif., 1994-95; sr. fin. analyst Intel Corp., Santa Clara, Calif., 1995-96; sr. acct. exec., cons. Fin. Rels. Bd., San Francisco, 1996-97; dir. investor rels. Cirrus Logic, Inc., Fremont, Calif., 1997—. Avocations: golf, marathon running, fly fishing. Fax: (510) 249-4230. E-mail: bonnie@corp.cirrus.com. Office: Cirrus Logic Inc 3100 W Warren Ave Fremont CA 94538-6419

MCCABE, MONICA JANE, oncological nurse; b. Anaheim, Calif.; d. Thurman Huston and Marcia Diane (Gandy) Walker; m. Roger Alan McCabe, July 27, 1985; children: Justin Robert, Sarah Jane. Assoc. Nursing, N.Mex. State U., Alamogordo, 1993. RN, N.Mex., Ariz. Med.-surg. nurse Meml. Med. Ctr., Las Cruces, N.Mex., 1993-94; oncology nurse Dr. Bishnu Rauth, Las Cruces, 1994-95; oncology and bone marrow transplant nurse Univ. Med. Ctr., Tucson, 1995—, mem. reengring. core team, 1996; nurse clinician Nat. Med. Care Homecare, Tucson, 1995-96; oncology nurse specialist Ariz. Oncology Assocs., Tucson, 1998—; unit asst. liaison Univ. Med. Ctr., 1996-98, clin. practice com. cost containment com, 1997, Keystone computer trainer, 1997, lectr. in oncology, 1997-98; computer cons. Meml. Med. Ctr., Las Cruces, 1994; mem. Caring Environ. Patient Edn. Team. Mem. ANA, Ariz. Nursing Assn., N.Mex. Nurses Assn., Oncology Nursing Soc. (cert. Oncology Nursing Cert. Corp. subs.), So. Ariz. Oncology Nursing Soc. (pres.- elect 1999—). Avocations: outdoor activities, ceramics, computers. Home: PO Box 91198 Tucson AZ 85752-1198

MCCAIG, JEFFREY JAMES, transportation company executive; b. Moose Jaw, Sask., July 5, 1951; s. John Robert and Anne Shorrocks (Glass) McC.; m. Marilyn Graves, July 7, 1983; children: Robbert Angus, Scott Thomas, Christa Mae. Student, Can. Jr. Coll. Lausanne, Switzerland, 1970; AB, Harvard Coll., 1973; LLB, Osgoode Hall Law Sch., Can., 1976; MSc in Mgmt., Leland Stanford Jr. U., 1984. Assoc. MacKimmie Matthews, 1976-81; owner, sr. officer Jeffrey J. McCaig Profl. Corp., 1981-83; v.p. planning and corp. devel. Trimac, Calgary, Alta., Can., 1983-87, exec. v.p., 1987-90, pres., 1990-94, pres., CEO, 1994—; chmn. Bovar, Inc., Calgary, 1994—; bd. dirs. Bovar, Inc., chmn. bd. dirs. Trimac Corp., Richland Petroleum Corp., Tetonka Drilling Inc., Conf. Bd. Can., ATA Found. Mem. Law Soc. Alta., Young Pres.'s Orgn., Calgary Golf and Country Club, Calgary Petroleum Club, Glencoe Club, 400 Club. Home: 708 Riverdale Ave SW, Calgary, AB Canada T2S OY3 Office: Trimac Corp, 800 5 Ave SW Ste 2100, Calgary, AB Canada T2P 5A3

MCCAIN, JOHN SIDNEY, III, senator; b. Panama Canal Zone, Aug. 29, 1936; s. John Sidney and Roberta (Wright) McC.; m. Cindy Hensley, May 17, 1980; children: Doug, Andy, Sidney, Meghan, Jack, Jimmy, Bridget. Grad. U.S. Naval Acad., 1958; grad., Nat. War Coll., 1973-74. Commd. ensign U.S. Navy, 1958, capt., navy pilot, 1977; prisoner of war Hanoi, Vietnam, 1967-73; dir. Navy Senate Liaison Office, Washington, 1977-81; mem. 98th-99th Congress from 1st Ariz. Dist.; U.S. senator from Ariz., 1987—, mem. armed svcs. com., chmn. commerce, sci. and transp. com., Indian affairs com., nat. rep. senatorial com. Bd. dirs. Community Assistance League, Phoenix, 1981-82. Decorated Legion of Merit, decorated Silver Star, Bronze Star, Purple Heart, D.F.C., Vietnamese Legion of Honor. Mem. Am. Legion, VFW. Republican. Episcopalian. Office: US Senate Office 241 Russell Washington DC 20510

MCCAIN, WARREN EARL, retired supermarket company executive; b. Logan, Kans., Dec. 17, 1925. A.A., Oreg. State U., 1948; postgrad., U. Ill. Supr. sales Mountain States Wholesale Co., 1951-59; with Albertson's Inc., Boise, Idaho, owner, operator supermarkets, 1959—, became mgr. non-foods, 1959, mgr. store, 1962-65, supr. merchandise, 1965-67, dir. intermountain region, 1967-68, v.p. ops., 1968-72, exec. v.p., 1972-74, pres., 1974-84, chmn. bd., chief exec. officer, 1976-94, also dir.; dir. Idaho 1st Nat. Bank. Office: Albertson's Inc PO Box 20 250 E Parkcenter Blvd Boise ID 83706-3999*

MCCALL, WILLIAM CALDER, oil and chemical company executive; b. Hoquiam, Wash., Feb. 1, 1906; s. Dougall Hugh and Hughena (Calder) McC.; m. Marian Hall, Mar. 22, 1946; children—Ernest, Robert. Student U. Oreg., 1924-28; LHD Lewis & Clark Coll., 1992. Asst. sales mgr. Anaconda Sales Co., Chgo., 1932-39; chmn. McCall Oil & Chem. Corp., Portland, Oreg., 1939—, Gt. Western Chem. Co., Portland, 1975—; dir. Oreg. Bank, Portland, King Broadcasting Co., Seattle. Pres. Oreg. Art Mus., Portland; trustee Lewis and Clark Coll., Portland; exec. v.p. Oreg. Symphony Soc.; dir. Oreg. Health Scis. Found., Good Samaritan Hosp. Found., Portland. Republican. Episcopalian. Clubs: Eldorado Country (Indian Wells, Calif.) (pres. 1978-79); Arlington (Portland); Pacific-Union (San Francisco); Los Angeles Country, Vintage (Palm Desert, Calif.), Waverley Country, Rainier (Seattle). Office: McCall Oil and Chem Corp 808 SW 15th Ave Portland OR 97205-1993

MCCAMBRIDGE, DENNIS, marshal. Chief dep. U.S. marshal U.S. Dist. Ct., Boise. Office: Fed Bldg and US Courthouse 550 W Fort St MSC 10 Boise ID 83724-0101

MCCANN, JACK ARLAND, former construction and mining equipment company executive, consultant; b. Chestnut, Ill., Apr. 16, 1926; s. Keith Ogden and Miriam Imogene McC.; m. Marian Adele Gordon, Mar. 31, 1956; 1 child, Christopher John. A.B., Bradley U., 1950. Mgr. Washington Office, R.G. LeTourneau Inc., 1950-58; mgr. def. and spl. products Westinghouse Air Brake Co., 1958-64, mgr. nat. accounts, 1964-67, mng. dir. Belgian plant and European mktg., 1967-70; gen. sales mgr. WABCO div. Am. Standard Inc., Peoria, Ill., 1970-73, v.p. mktg., 1973-80, v.p. staff, 1980-82; ret., 1982; now cons. Vestryman St. Francis-in-Valley Episcopal Ch., Green Valley Ariz.

MCCANN, KIM LOU M., theater educator, director; b. Joplin, Mo., Dec. 8, 1954; d. James Cleland McCann and Mary Earline (Campbell) Kelley; m. Robert V. Sutton, June 11, 1976 (div. June 1983). AA in Drama, Diablo Valley Coll., 1974; BA in Theater, Calif. State U., Sacramento, 1976; MFA in Drama, U. Calif., Davis, 1981. Instr. Short Ctr. South, Sacramento, Calif., 1982—; lectr., resident dir. Sacramento City Coll., 1984—. Dir. Twelfth Night, 1994, Love's Labour's Lost, 1995, Hamlet, 1996, Cyrano DeBergerac, 1997, Measure for Measure, 1998, and 50 others; actor in over 100 prodns. including Dancing at Lughnasa, Our Town, Hay Fever, Midsummer Night's Dream, others. Chmn. bd. dirs. Sacramento City Actors Theater, 1985—. Mem. Sacramento Area Regional Theatre Alliance (Elly award 1985, 87, 91, 96). Avocations: pets, music, reading. Office: Sacramento City College 3835 Freeport Blvd Sacramento CA 95822-1386

MCCARGAR, ELEANOR BARKER, portrait painter; b. Presque Isle, Maine, Aug. 30, 1913; d. Roy and Lucy Ellen (Hayward) Barker; m. John Albert McCargar, Feb. 18, 1947; children: Margaret, Lucy, Mary. Cert. elem. sch. tchg., Aroostook State Normal Sch., Presque Isle, 1933; student, Acadia U., 1935-36; B of Sociology, Colby Coll., 1937; summer student, Harvard U., 1939; and, Cambridge Sch. Art, 1939; studied portrait painting with Kenneth Washburn, Thomas Leighton, Maria von Ridelstein, Jean Henry, 1957-67. Ltd. svc. credential in fine and applied arts and related

techs. Calif. C.C. Tchr. sci. and geography Limestone (Maine) Jr. H.S., 1937-41; ins. claim adjuster Liberty Mut. Ins. Co., Boston, 1941-42, Portland, Maine, 1943; ARC hosp. worker 20th Gen. Hosp., Ledo, Assam, India, 1944-45; portrait painter Burlingame and Apple Valley, Calif., 1958—. Commns. include more than 650 portraits in 10 states and 4 fgn. countries. Recipient M. Grumbacher Inc. Merit award for outstanding contbn. to arts, 1977; named Univ. of Maine Disting. Alumnus in Arts, 1981. Avocations: canoeing, camping, travel, studying.

MCCARTHY, LAURENCE JAMES, physician, pathologist; b. Boston, Aug. 11, 1934; s. Theodore Clifford and Mary Barrett (Moran) McC.; m. Cynthia Marion DeRoch, Aug. 28, 1978; children: Laurence J. Jr., Jeffrey A., Karen E., Patrick K., Ryan N. BA, Yale U., 1956; student, Georgetown U. Sch. Med., 1956-58; MD, Harvard U., 1960; MS, U. Minn., 1965. Cert. Am. Bd. Pathology, 1965. Intern Boston City Hosp., 1960-61; resident in pathology Mayo Clinic, Rochester, Minn., 1961-65; pathologist Honolulu Heart Program, 1965-67; chief pathology Kelsey-Seybold Clinic, Houston, 1967-68; clin. asst. pathologist M.D. Anderson Hosp., Houston, 1967-68; chief pathology Straub Clinic, Honolulu, 1968-72; assoc. pathologist Wilcox Hosp., Lihue, Hawaii, 1972-74; chief pathology A.R. Gould Hosp., Presque Isle, Maine, 1975-78; assoc. pathologist Kuakini Med. Ctr., Honolulu, 1978—. Med. dir. USPHS, 1965-67. Fellow Coll. Am. Pathologists, Am. Soc. Clin. Pathologists; mem. AMA, Hawaii Soc. Pathologists (pres. 1970), Am. Acad. Forensic Sci., Hawaii Med. Assn., Honolulu County Med. Soc. (del. 1982-83). Roman Catholic. Home: 249 Kaelepulu Dr Kailua HI 96734-3311 Office: Kuakini Med Ctr 347 N Kuakini St Honolulu HI 96817-2306

MCCARTHY, MARIE GERALDINE, program director, coordinator, educator; b. San Francisco, Nov. 7, 1940; d. Emmett Francis and Marie Delores (Costello) McC.; children: Peter, Robert, Todd Brockman. BA, Lone Mountain Coll., 1962; MA, Dominican Coll., San Rafael, Calif., 1972. Gen. secondary credential; cert. cmty. coll. chief adminstrv. officer, supr., history, basic edn., spl. edn., profl. edn. educator, counselor. Coord., counselor Work Incentive Program, Employment Devel. Dept., Marin County, Calif., 1970-72; coord., instr. Neighborhood Youth Corps Program, Marin County, Calif., 1972-74; coord. Marin City Project Area Com., Marin County, Calif., 1978-79; coord. basic skills program Coll. of Marin, Kentfield, Calif., 1973-79, edn. cons., 1980-83, pres. acad. senate, 1993—, coord. Disabled Students Program, 1984—; faculty advisor Challenged Students Club, Coll. of Marin, Kentfield, 1983—, exec. coun. United Profs. of Marin, Local 1610, 1984-92, mem. staff devel. com., 1986-88, event coord. ann. student fundraiser for students with disabilities, 1985—, dist. psychol. disabilities task force, 1994—, dist. councilmem. Faculty Assn. Calif. C.C.s, 1994—, dist. budget com., 1994—, dist. master planning com., 1994—, mem. crisis intervention team, 1990—, editor DSPS Forum, 1995—; exec. com. Statewide Acad. Senate, 1995-96. Author: How To Learn To Study: Bridging the Study Skills Gap, 1982, The Faculty Handbook on Disabilities, 1993. Bd. dirs., v.p. CENTERFORCE, 1992—; bd. dirs. Marin Coalition, Marin Athletic Found., 1992—, Marin Ctr. for Ind. Living, 1994—, EXODUS, 1992—, sec.; past v.p. Bay Faculty Assn.; founder Youth Helping Homeless, 1990—; mem. Alliance for the Mentally Ill., 1994—, JERICHO, 1994—; founding bd. dirs. INSPIRIT, 1984—. Recipient Spl. Achievement award Calif. Youth Soccer Assn., 1980, Marin County Mother of Yr. award, 1984, Spl. Recognition awards The Indoor Sports Club for Physically Handicapped, 1984, 88-90, 92-93, Mom Makes the Difference honoree Carter Hawley Hale Stores, Inc., 1994, Cert. of Recognition, Marin Human Rights Commn., 1994, Hayward award, 1995, Buckelew Partnership award, 1995, Disting. Faculty award Com. Alumni Assn., 1995. Mem. AAUW, Calif. Assn. Postsecondary Educators for the Disabled, Faculty Assn. Calif. C.C.'s, Amnesty Internat. Platform Assoc., AHEAD, Commonwealth Club Calif., U.S. Soccer Fedn. Avocations: piano, singing, hiking, aerobics, meditation. Home: 6004 Shelter Bay Ave Mill Valley CA 94941-3040 Office: Coll of Marin College Ave Kentfield CA 94904

MCCARTHY, WILLIAM ROBERT, minister; b. Tacoma, Wash., Nov. 17, 1941; s. Denward Sylvester and Florence Elizabeth (Lohan) McC.; m. Bernice Bigler, Apr. 22, 1962; children: Brian Edward Earl, Sean David. BS, Oreg. State U., 1966; MDiv, Nashotah House, 1975. Ordained deacon Episcopal Ch., 1975, priest, 1975. Curate St. Michael's Ch., Barrington, Ill., 1975-77; vicar St. Anselm's Ch., Park Ridge, Ill., 1977-81; rector Christ Ch. Parish, Waukegan, Ill., 1981-89, Ch. of Good Samaritan, Corvallis, Oreg., 1989—; diocesan cursillo officer Diocese Chgo., 1977-85; spiritual dir. Ecumenical Cursillo Community, Chgo., 1977-83; mem. steering com. Happenings in Christianity, Chgo., 1978-80; chmn. Bishop's Adv. Commn. on Renewal and Evangelism, Chgo., 1983-85; mem. diocesan coun. Diocese of Oreg., 1991-93; bd. dirs. Oreg. Episcopal clergy Assn., 1990-93; standing com. Diocese of Oreg., 1994-97. Contbr. articles to profl. jours. Bd. mem. Waukegan Area Crime Stoppers, 1982-85; founder, chmn. FOCUS 90 Com. for Downtown Devel., 1988-89; charter bd. dirs. Waukegan Downtown Assn., 1983-89, v.p., 1986-87, pres., 1987-88; founder, exec. dir. Share/Food Waukegan Area, 1985-89; bd. dirs. YMCA of Lake County, 1985-89; trustee Good Samaritan Hosp., Corvallis, 1989—; vice chair bd. Samaritan Health Svcs., 1998—. With USNR, 1962-65. Mem. Assn. for Psychol. Type, Rotary, Masons, Phi Sigma Kappa. Office: Ch of the Good Samaritan 333 NW 35th St Corvallis OR 97330-4908

MCCARTNEY, PATRICK KEVIN, newspaper editor, writer; b. L.A., Sept. 9, 1948; s. Warren Phil and Mildred Pauline (Weiler) McC. BA, U. San Diego, 1970; MA, U. So. Calif., 1983. Statis. analyst L.A. County Probation Dept., Downey, Calif., 1973-79; writer Free Venice (Calif.) Beachhead, 1984-88; editor Westchester (Calif.) Jour., 1987-88; reporter Blade-Citizen newspaper, Solana Beach, Calif., 1988-89; staff writer Press-Courier, Oxnard, Calif., 1990-91; corr. L.A. Times, Ventura, Calif., 1991-94; mng. editor North Lake Tahoe Bonanza, Incline Village, Nev., 1994-96; sr. writer Tahoe Daily Tribune, South Lake Tahoe, Calif., 1996—. Pres. Venice Town Coun., 1984-86; candidate for L.A. City Coun., 1987. Mem. Venice Hist. Soc. (co-founder, bd. dirs. 1986-88), Encinitas Hist. Soc. (bd. dirs. 1989). Avocations: hiking, outdoor sports, natural science, Calif. history. Home: 12116 Persimmon Ter Auburn CA 95603-3826

MCCARTY, ROBERT CLARKE, mathematician; b. Mountain View, Calif., Apr. 29, 1922; s. John Emmet and Eldora Lydia (Freeman) McC.; m. Netta Cassen, July 29, 1945 (div. Oct. 1968) 1 child, Stephanie Ann; m. Rita Ransier, July 29, 1969; children: Michael Wayne, Teresa Kay, Kathleen Gail. BA in Math., San Jose Sate U., 1950; MS in Math. and Statistics, U. Wash., 1957; PhD in Math., Pacific Western U., 1990. Staff mathematician Boeing Rsch. Labs., Seattle, 1952-59; rsch. mathematician Stanford Rsch. Inst., Menlo Park, Calif., 1959-70; pres., cons. McCarty and Assocs., Gilroy, Calif., 1976—; sr. staff scientist ESL-TRW Corp., Sunnyvale, Calif., 1984-87; prin. staff scientist ARGO Systems, Sunnyvale, 1987-93; cons. in math., orchard mgmt.; sci. advisor to Congresswoman Zoe Lofgren, sci. com. US Congress, 1994—; rsch. proxy for Prof. A.S. Paulraj, Dept. Elec. Engring., Info. Scis., Stanford U., 1993-95; sr. rsch. mathematician Aires Corp., Arlington, Va., 1994-96. Contbr. articles to profl. jours. Lt. USCGR, 1941-52. Mem. Sigma Xi. Avocations: HAM radio, rifle and pistol marksmanship, swimming. Home and Office: 9425 Marcella Ave Gilroy CA 95020-9085

MCCAULEY, KEVIN BRUCE, minister; b. San Jose, Calif., May 19, 1954; s. Bruce and Marie (Gallaway) McC.; m. Georga Ann Fonner, June 25, 1977; children: Jennifer, Ryan, Kyle, Sean. AA, West Valley Community Coll., 1974; BA, San Diego State U., 1976; MA, U. San Francisco, 1980. Ordained to ministry Ind. Bible Ch., 1986. Tchr., vice prin. Los Gatos (Calif.) Christian Sch., 1977-84; pastor Christian edn. Crossroads Bible Ch., San Jose, 1982—; chmn. Christian Leaders and Sunday Sch., San Jose, 1989—. Author: (curriculum) Christian Influences on American History, 1980; chair editorial com. West mag., 1990. Active Coalition of Christians in Govt., San Jose; mem. Citizens for Excellence in Edn., Costa Mesa, Calif., 1991. Mem. Nat. Assn. Evangs., Greater San Jose Assn. Evangs. (exec. com. 1990—), Child Evangelism Fellowship (adv. com. 1989—), Profl. Assn. Christian Educators, Nat. Assn. Christian Educators, Awana (dir. San Jose chpt.). Democrat. Home: 48 Park Fletcher Pl San Jose CA 95136-2403 Office: Crossroads Bible Ch 600 Meridian Ave Ste 202 San Jose CA 95126-3427

MCCAW, BRUCE R., insurance executive, airline and communications executive; b. Washington, June 26, 1946; s. J. Elroy and Marion O. (Oliver) McC. Student Colo. Coll., 1964-66, U. Wash., 1967-68. Lic. ins. broker, comml. pilot. Pres. Jet Air Corp., Everett, Wash., 1968-72, Delta Aviation Ins. Brokers Inc., Bellevue, Wash., 1972-80; v.p. and dir. McCaw Communications Cos. Inc., Bellevue, 1969—, Horizon Air Industries Inc., Seattle, 1981-87; chmn. Westar Ins. Group Inc., Bellevue, 1979—; vice chmn. Forbes Westar Inc., 1986—, pres. PacWest Racing Group, 1993—; barnstormer Mus. of Flight, Seattle, 1983—; exec. dir. Assn. Am. Air Travel Clubs, Bellevue, 1974-79. Bd. trustees Poncho, Seattle, 1983-84; dir. Lynnwood Rotary Air Show, Everett, 1968-77; aviation chmn. Everett C. of C. Recipient Disting. Alumnus Achievement award Lakeside Sch., Seattle, 1984. Mem. Nat. Bus. Aircraft Assn., Aviation Ins. Assn., Regional Airline Assn. Republican. Episcopalian. Lodge: Rotary.*

MCCAW, CRAIG O., communications executive; b. Centralia, Wash., 1949. Grad., Stanford U., 1971. Pilot; chmn., CEO McCaw Cellular Comm., Inc., 1968-88; chmn. bd. dirs., CEO McCaw Cellular Comm., Inc., Kirkland, Wash., 1982-94; chmn., CEO Lin Broadcasting Co., 1990—; founder, chief, co-exec. officer Teledesic Corp., Kirkland, 1990—; chmn., CEO NEXTLINK Comm. Inc., Eagle River Inc. *

MCCAWLEY, WILLIAM DALE, II, accountant, writer, ethnohistorian; b. Long Beach, Calif., Nov. 26, 1952; s. William Dale and Antoinette Gertrude (Wolke) M.; children: Michael Breier, Jonathan William. BA, Calif. State U., Long Beach, 1974. Cert. elem. tchr., Calif. CFO, dir. finance and adminstrn. McDonnell Douglas Physician Sys. Co., Gardena, Calif., 1981-88; dir. adminstrn. U. Phoenix, Fountain Valley, Calif., 1988-89; sr. accountant Robert-John Industries, Huntington Beach, Calif., 1989-91; asst. controller Tallon Termite & Pest Control, Long Beach, Calif., 1991-95; cons. LSA Assoc. Inc., Irvine, Calif., 1995-96; acctg. mgr. Microage Computer Ctr., Fountain Valley, Calif., 1997—; cons. Channell Islands Nat. Park, Ventura, Calif., 1991—, Rancho Los Alamitos Historical Ranch and Gardens, Long Beach, 1993—. Author: The First Angelinos: The Gabrielino Indians of Los Angeles, 1996 (cert. commendation Am. Assn. State and Local History 1997). Avocations: photography, hiking, reading, astronomy. Home: 14672 Monroe St Midway City CA 92655

MCCLAIN, RICHARD STAN, cinematographer; b. Los Angeles, Oct. 7, 1951; m. Kim Girard, Nov. 7, 1987. Founder Pasadena Camera Sys., Inc. Aerial cameraman: (feature films) The Client, Contact, Letters From a Killer, I Love Trouble, Lightning Jack, Tombstone, Falling Down, Heart and Soul, So, I Married an Axe Murderer, The Good Son, Made in America, This Boy's Life, Fearless, Passenger 57, Wind, At Play in the Fields of the Lord, The Right Stuff, The Iceman, Rambo, Firebirds, Wind, Basic Instinct, Innerspace, Buster, U2 Rattle and Hum, Crazy People, The Hunt for Red October, The Doors, Flatliners, Nell, Murder in the First, Drop Zone, Get Shorty, The Money Train; (TV shows) Magnum P.I., Airwolf. Recipient Best Cinematography award London Internat. Advt. Awards, 1993, Telly award (2), 1993, (1), 1994. N.Y. Festival Silver award, 1993, Telly award (2) 1994, (4) 1995, (2), 1996. Mem. Internat. Cinematographers Guild, Screen Actors Guild, Dirs. Guild Am., Soc. Operating Cameramen (pres.).

MCCLARY, JAMES DALY, retired contractor; b. Boise, Idaho, July 19, 1917; s. Neil Hamaker and Myrtle (Daly) McC.; m. Mary Jane Munger, Feb. 2, 1939; children: Pamela, John. Student, Boise Jr. Coll., 1934-36, AA, 1957; AB, Stanford U., 1938; LLD, Gonzaga U., 1976. Laborer to supt. Morrison-Knudsen Co., Inc., Boise, 1932-42, project mgr., asst. dist. mgr., 1942- 47; gen. mgr. Mexican subs. Morrison-Knudsen Co., Inc., 1947-51, asst. to gen. mgr., 1951-53, asst. gen. mgr., 1953-60, dir., 1955-78, v.p., 1956-60, exec. v.p., 1960-72, chmn. bd., 1972-78; mem., vice chmn. Idaho Permanent Bldg. Fund Adv. Council, 1961-64, chmn., 1964-71. Treas. Idaho Rep. Cen. Com., 1964-70; presdl. elector, 1968; trustee Boise Jr. Coll., 1960-83, vice chmn., 1967-73, chmn., 1973-83; bd. dirs. Boise State U. Found., Inc., 1964-91, pres., 1970-81; bd. dirs. AGC Edn. and Rsch. Found., 1974-91, pres., 1974-90; elector Hall of Fame for Great Ams., 1976—; trustee St. Alphonsus Regional Med. Ctr., 1976-82, vice chmn., 1981-82. Recipient George Washington medal of honor Freedoms Found., Valley Forge, Pa., 1977, Disting. Alumnus award Boise State U., 1988, Silver medallion, 1996; decorated Chevalier and Legion of Honor, Order of DeMolay; named Disting. Alumnus of Yr. Boise State U. Alumni Assn., 1971, Ky. Col. Fellow ASCE, Am. Inst. Constructors; mem. Internat. Rd. Fedn. (bd. dirs. 1972-78, vice chmn. 1977-78), Soc. Am. Mil. Engrs., Assoc. Gen. Contractors Am. (bd. dirs. 1958—, mem. exec. com. 1961-78, pres. 1972), Cons. Constructors Coun. Am., Newcomen Soc., Conf. Bd. (sr. mem.), Idaho Assn. Commerce and Industry (bd. dirs., chmn. 1974-77, Harwood award 1994), Moles (hon., mem. award for Outstanding Achievement in Constrn. 1978), Hillcrest Country Club (bd. dirs. 1965-67, 69, pres. 1967), Arid Club (mem. exec. com. 1966), Ariz. Club (Scottsdale), Ariz. Country Club (Phoenix), Univ. Club (Mexico City), Stanford Club (Washington). Episcopalian. Home: 4903 Roberts Rd Boise ID 83705-2805

MCCLATCHY, JAMES B., editor, newspaper publisher; b. Sacramento; s. Carlos K. and Phebe (Briggs) McC.; m. Susan Brewster; children: Carlos F., William B. B.A., Stanford U.; M.S., Columbia U. Pub. McClatchy Newspapers, Sacramento.; past pres., dir. InterAm. Press Assn.; dir. Capital Region Inst., Sacramento; pres. Ctrl. Valley Found. Trustee Nat. Ctr. Internat. Schs. Office: McClatchy Newspapers 21st & Q Sts Sacramento CA 95813

MCCLELLAN, CATHERINE ANN, costume designer, educator; b. Phoenix, Ariz., Apr. 4, 1952; d. Ralph Holland and Marilyn LaRae (Breese) M. BA, Brigham Young U., 1975; MFA, U. Ariz., Tucson, 1989. Costume shop supr., make up artist Osmond Studios, Orem, UT, 1977-79; designer, costume shop mgr., adj. faculty No. Ariz. U., Flagstaff, 1982-84; costume shop asst. Ariz. Theatre Co., Tucson, 1986-1989; adj. faculty, costume shop supr. Syracuse Stage/Syracuse U., N.Y., 1989-91; guest faculty No. Ill. U., DeKalb, 1991-92; costume shop mgr. Walnut St. Theatre, Phila., 1992-94; costume studio mgr. Brigham Young U., Provo, UT, 1995—; poster presentation Mob Cap Constrn., U.S. Inst. for Theatre Tech., Long Beach, Calif., 1998. Mem. U.S. Inst. For Theatre Tech., Theta Alpha Phi, Alpha Psi Omega. Mem. LDS Ch. Avocations: drawing, painting, patchwork, quilt design, reading, singing, weaving. Office: DAP Costume Studio F-315 HFAC BYU Provo UT 84602

MCCLELLAN, CRAIG RENE, lawyer; b. Portland, Oreg., June 28, 1947; s. Charles Russell and Annette Irene (Benedict) McC.; m. Susan Armistead Nash, June 7, 1975; children: Ryan Alexander, Shannon Lea. BS in Econs., U. Oreg., 1969; JD magna cum laude, Calif. We. U., 1976. Bar: Calif. 1976, U.S. Dist. Ct. (so. dist.) Calif. 1976, U.S. Dist. Ct. (ea., ctrl., no. dists.) Calif. 1991, U.S. Supreme Ct. 1991. Compliance specialist Cost of Living Coun. and Price Commn., Washington, 1972-73, dir. Oil Policy subcom., 1973; ptnr. Luce, Forward, Hamilton & Scripps, San Diego, 1976-87; owner McClellan & Brown, San Diego, 1987—. Chmn. annual fundraising auction KPBS, 1984. Capt. USMC, 1969-72. Mem. Assn. Trial Lawyers Am., Am. Bd. Trial Advocates, Am. Inns of Ct. (master), Calif. State Bar Assn., San Diego County Bar Assn., Calif. Trial Lawyers Assn. (bd. govs. 1985-87), San Diego Trial Lawyers Assn. (bd. dirs. 1983-90), Nat. Forensics League, Phi Gamma Delta, Phi Alpha Delta. Presbyterian. Avocations: reading, running, tennis, chess, civic activities. Office: McClellan & Brown 1144 State St San Diego CA 92101-3529

MCCLELLAND, CRAIG ALEXANDER, architect, educator, business owner; b. Renton, Wash., Nov. 3, 1962; s. James Richard and Carol Anne (Hawkins) McC.; m. Kamilla Kuroda, June 25, 1989. BArch, U. Wash.; MArch, U. Ill. Lic. architect. Technician III, Wash. State Dept. Transportation, Seattle, 1985; project mgr. Van Horne and Van Horne, Seattle, 1986-87, Alexander Sasonoff, Seattle, 1989-91; arch. James and Scherer, Olympia, Wash., 1991-96; owner, arch. Alexander Archs., Olympia, 1996—; prof. South Sound C.C., Olympia, 1998—; project arch. BJSS, Olympia, 1997—. Amb. Olympia C. of C., 1997, Shelton C. of C., 1997. Mem. AIA. Avocations: mountaineering, construction, reading, writing. Home and Office: 110 SE Eagles Nest Dr Shelton WA 98584-9261

MCCLELLAND, KAMILLA KURODA, news reporter, proofreader, book agent; b. Bozeman, Mont., June 16, 1964; d. Yasumasa and Alice (Kassis) Kuroda; m. Craig Alexander McClelland, June 25, 1989. BA in Asian Studies, U. Calif., Berkeley, 1987; MS in Print News, U. Ill., Champaign-Urbana, 1989. Legis. aide Hawaii State Ho. of Reps., Honolulu, 1987; grad. asst. U. Ill. Dept. Journalism, Champaign, 1987-89; asst. op-ed editor The Daily Illini, Champaign, 1988-89; reporter AP, Seattle, 1989, Tacoma News Tribune, 1989-90; bus. news reporter The Olympian, Olympia, Wash., 1990-97; editor-in-chief Friday edit. N.Am. Post (formerly N.W. Nikkei), Seattle, 1997-98; asst. editor South Sound Bus. Examiner, Tacoma, Wash., 1998—; proofreader Minerva Rsch., Inc., Honolulu, 1982—. Vol. Am.-Arab Anti Disc Com., Berkeley, Calif., 1984-87, Capital City Marathon, Olympia, 1993-95, Olympia Symphony, 1996, Black Hills Triathalon, 1993—, Olympia Chamber Orch., 1996; active Japanese Am. Citizens League, Honolulu, also Berkeley, 1983-89. Recipient Recognition awards for newswriting Gannett, 1991, 92, 95, 1st Pl., Best of Gannett award for bus. and consumer reporting, 1994, Well Done Bus. Reporting Gannett award, 1995, 2nd place bus. and consumer reporting Best of Gannett award, 1995. Mem. Asian Am. Journalists Assn., Soc. Profl. Journalists (2d pl. award Bus. Features Pacific Northwest Excellence Journalism comp. 1996). Avocations: hiking, camping, martial arts, raising rabbits, backpacking. Offices: N Am Post Friday Edit PO Box 3173 Seattle WA 98114-3173

MCCLENDON, IRVIN LEE, SR., company executive, computer consultant, writer and editor; b. Waco, Tex., June 12, 1945; s. Irvin Nicholas and Evelyn Lucile (Maycumber) McC.; divorced; children: Michael Boyd, Irvin Lee Jr., Laura Ann, Paul Nicholas, Richard Lester. Student El Camino Coll., 1961-63, U. So. Calif., 1962-66; BA in Math., Calif. State U.-Fullerton, 1970, postgrad. in bus. adminstrn., 1971-76; cert. nat. security mgmt. Indsl. Coll. Armed Forces, 1974; postgrad. in religion Summit Sch. Theology, 1982-84. Engring. lab. asst. Rockwell Internat. Corp., Anaheim, Calif., 1967-68, test data analyst, 1968, assoc. computer programmer, 1968-70, mem. tech. staff, 1970-82; systems programmer A-Auto-trol Tech. Corp., Denver, 1982-84, sr. tech. writer, 1984-86; sr. tech. writer, editor Colo. Data Systems, Inc., Englewood, Colo., 1986-87; engring. writer III CalComp subs. Lockheed Co., Hudson, N.H., 1987; sr. tech. writer CDI Corp., Arvada, Colo., 1987-88; staff cons. CAP GEMINI AM., Englewood, 1989; sr. tech./instrnl. writer & editor TTS Inc., Aurora, Colo., 1990-96, sr. multimedia developer, 1996-97; gen. mgr., chief editor The Berkeley Group, LLC, Denver, 1997—; writer Am. Resume Ctr., Northglenn, Colo., 1997-98. Sec. of governing bd. Yorba Linda Libr. Dist., 1972-77; mem. St. Paul's United Meth. Ch., Denver, 1997—, mem. The Colorado Chorale, 1988, 97-98; trustee Ch. of God (Seventh Day), Bloomington, Calif., 1979-81, treas., 1980-81, mem. Calif. State U. and Coll. Statewide Alumni Coun., 1976-77; 2d v.p. Orange County chpt. Calif. Spl. Dists. Assn., 1976, pres., 1977; mem. Adams County Rep. Ctrl. Com., 1984-90, Denver County Rep. Ctrl. Com., 1992-95; tech. support adviser to chmn. Colo. Rep. Com., 1997-98. With USAFR, 1967-71. USAF Nat. Merit scholar, 1963-67. Mem. Calif. Assn. Libr. Trustees and Commrs. (exec. bd., So. Calif. rep. 1976-77), Nat. Eagle Scout Assn. (life), Bible Sabbath Assn. (life), Calif. State U.-Fullerton Alumni Assn. (dir. 1975-77). Republican.

MCCLENNEN, MIRIAM J., former state official; b. Seattle, Sept. 16, 1923; d. Phillip and Frieda (Golub) Jacobs; m. Louis McClennen, Apr. 25, 1969; stepchildren: Peter Adams, James C.A., Helen, Persis, Crane, Emery. BA, U. Wash., 1945; MBA, Northwestern U., 1947. Exec. trainee Marshall Field & Co., Chgo., 1945-47; buyer Frederick & Nelson (subs. of Marshall Field), 1949-57; fashion coordinator, buyer Levy Bros., Burlingame/San Mateo, Calif., 1957-63; buyer Goldwaters, Phoenix, 1963-67; adminstrv. asst. to pres. Ariz. State Senate, Phoenix, 1973-76; dir. publs. Office of Sec. of State, Phoenix, 1976-87; chairwoman legis. subcom. adminstrv. procedure Ariz. State Legislature, Phoenix, 1984-85. Original compiler, codifier, editor publ. Ariz. Adminstrv. Code, 1973-87, Ariz. Adminstrv. Register, 1976-87. Bd. dirs., mem. Phoenix Art Mus. League, 1972-90; bd. dirs., mem. exec. bd. Phoenix Symphony Guild, 1969-88; bd. dirs., sec. Combined Met. Phoenix Arts and Scis., 1974-90, mem. adv. bd., 1990-95; bd. dirs. Phoenix Art Coun., 1973-78, Master Apprentice Programs, 1980-83; bd. dirs., mem. exec. com. Heard Mus., 1982-88, 90—, chmn. publs. com., 1982-88, chmn. exhibit and edn. com., 1990-93; mem. adv. bd. Ariz. State Hist. Records, 1987-90, Ariz. Commn. on Arts, 1989-96, Phoenix Art Mus., 1966—, dir.'s circle, 1988—; bd. dirs. Arizonans for Cultural Devel., 1996—; mem. Cape Mus. of Fine Arts, 1996—. Recipient Disting. Svc. award Atty. Gen. Ariz., 1987, Outstanding Svc. to People, Ariz. State Senate, 1987, Nat. Assn. Secs. of State award, 1987. Mem. English Speaking Union, Nat. Soc. Arts and Letters, Charter 100 (bd. dirs. 1981-85), Phoenix Country Club, Ariz. Club, Eastward Ho! Country Club (Chatham, Mass.). Home: 5311 N La Plaza Cir Phoenix AZ 85012-1415 also (summer): 2267 Rte 28 Harwich MA 02645

MCCLOSKEY, ROBIN ANN, artist, educator; b. Camden, N.J., Mar. 26, 1955; d. John William and Anita Isabel (Morales) McC.; m. Keith W. Hartman, Dec. 27, 1954. BA, U. N.C., Charlotte, 1977; MFA, Pa. State U., 1984. Instr. art Cabrillo Coll., Aptos, Calif., 1994-95; Dayton-Hudson vis. artist Carleton Coll., Northfield, Minn., 1995; instr. art City Coll. San Francisco, 1996—. Mem. Calif. Soc. Printmakers, Women's Caucus for Art.

MCCLOUD, MEVELYN ANN, personal caregiver; b. Portland, Oreg., June 18, 1949; d. Melvin Everett and Florence Ella (Neasley) McC.; m. Marcus Lamont O'Ray, Nov. 24, 1971 (wid. Mar. 1973); 1 child, Lena Marie. Office clk. Everybody's Records, Portland, 1976-78; cashier, mixologist Dorothy's medallion, New Orleans, 1978-80; acctg. officer Delgado C.C., New Orleans, 1980-85; appointment sec. Olin Mills, Houston, 1986; sales agt., interviewer Market Decision Corp., Portland, 1987-88; bookkeeper Assn. for Retarded Citizens of Multi County, Portland, 1988-92; personal asst. Portland, 1992—; copy editor Advocate Newspaper, Gresham, Oreg., 1994-95. Editor-in-chief: Venture Mag., 1994-95. Recipient Excellence in Publ. award Assoc. Students of MHCC, Gresham, 1995, Golden Poet award World of Poetry Soc., Sacramento, 1991. Mem. Phi Theta Kappa. Avocations: photography, writing, cinema, reading. Home: PO Box 285 Portland OR 97207-0285

MCCLUNE, MICHAEL MARLYN, real estate executive; b. Denver, July 12, 1950; s. Raymond Earl and Lorraine Elva (Bohm) McC.; m. Elizabeth Ann Butler, Sept. 18, 1982; children: Kristin Elizabeth, Michael Ryan. BSCE magna cum laude, U. So. Calif., 1972, MBA, 1974. Lic. real estate broker, Calif. Real estate investment broker Vistar Fin., Marina del Rey, Calif., 1979-81; program bus. mgr. Hughes Aircraft Co., El Segundo, Calif., 1981-85; v.p. LaSalle Ptnrs. Ltd., L.A., 1985-93; pres., CEO, New Am. Asset Mgmt. Svcs., Long Beach, Calif., 1993-97; pres. New Am. Cons. Svcs., Long Beach, 1993-97; regional v.p. LaSalle Ptnrs. Mgmt. Svcs., Inc., 1998; nat. dir. real estate svcs. EPS Solutions, Newport Beach, Calif., 1999—. Capt. USAF, 1974-79. Mem. Bldg. Owners and Mgrs. Assn. Greater L.A. (bd. dirs. 1994—, chmn. bd. dirs. 1995-96, President's award 1993), Long Beach Mgrs. Assn. (v.p. 1988-90), Rotary, Tau Beta Pi. Avocations: family, tennis, golf. Office: EPS Solutions 3723 Birch St Ste 5 Newport Beach CA 92660

MCCLURE, EVELYN SUSAN, historian, photographer; b. Milw., Mar. 11, 1940; d. Henry F. and Blanche E. Schuster; m. John C. McClure, Oct. 26, 1967; 1 child, Heather. BS, U. Wis., 1964. Cert. fine art photography, U. Calif. Adminstrv. asst. Northwestern U., Chgo., 1964-66, KGO-TV, San Francisco, 1966-70, Crocker Bank, San Francisco, 1980-86, Wells Fargo Bank, San Francisco, 1986-93; pub. Belle View Press, Sebastopol, Calif., 1993—. Author, photographer: Sebastopol, California - History, Homes & People 1855-1920, 1995 (Historic Scholarship award Sonoma County Hist. Soc. 1997). Exhbn. com. Sebastopol Ctr. Arts, 1995-97; bd. mem., publicity chair, newsletter editor, vol. Western Sonoma County Hist. Soc., Sebastopol, 1996. Roman Catholic. Avocation: gardening.

MCCLURE, JAMES A., lawyer, retired senator; b. Payette, Idaho, Dec. 27, 1924; s. W. R. and Marie McC.; m. Louise Miller; children: Marilyn, Kenneth, David. JD, U. Idaho, 1950; DL (hon.), Coll. Idaho, 1986. Mem. Idaho State Senate, 1961-66; asst. majority leader, 1965-66; city atty. City of Payette, Idaho; pros. atty. Payette County, Idaho; mem. 90th-92nd Congresses 1st Idaho Dist., 1967-73; senator Idaho, 1973-90; chmn. Energy and Natural Resources Com., 1981-86; mem. Com. on Rules and Adminstrn., Com. on Appropriations; pres. McClure, Gerard & Neuenschwander, Inc., Washington, 1990—; ptnr. Givens, Pursley, & Huntley, Boise, Idaho, 1990—. Trustee Kennedy Ctr., Meth. Ch. Mem. Elks, Masons, Kiwanis, Phi Alpha Delta. Methodist. Office: McClure Gerard & Neuenschwander

Inc 201 Maryland Ave NE Washington DC 20002-5703 also: Givens Pursley & Huntley Ste 200 Park Pl 277 N 6th St Ste 200 Boise ID 83702-7720*

MCCLURE, ROBERT COKE, financial consultant, minister; b. Berkeley, Calif., Nov. 22, 1954; s. Frank Edward and Augusta Anne (Tolles) McC.; m. Trudy M. Winterfield, Mar. 22, 1980 (div. Mar. 1990); children: Frank, Catherine, David. BA, Dartmouth Coll., 1976; MDiv, Princeton (N.J.) Theol. Sem., 1980. Series 7 security license, N.Y Stock Exch. Parish min. Rexburg and St. Anthony Cmty. Chs., Idaho, 1980-86, 1st Presbyn. Ch., Pocatello, Idaho, 1986-93; fin. cons. A.G. Edwards and Sons Inc., Pocatello, 1994—; part-time min. Montpelier (Idaho) Cmty. Ch., 1995—; moderator Kendall Presbyn. Ch., 1983-84. Bd. dirs. CASA program, Pocatello, 1989-95, Snake River Alliance, Idaho, 1996—; co-chmn. Downtown Cmty. Ctr. Com., Pocatello, 1998—. Mem. Rotary (bd. dirs. Pocatello chpt. 1998—, Paul Harris fellow 1988). Democrat. Avocations: fly fishing, back packing, computers, historical reading. Office: AG Edwards and Sons Inc 201 N Main Pocatello ID 83204

MCCLURE, WILLIAM OWEN, biologist; b. Yakima, Wash., Sept. 29, 1937; s. Rexford Delmont and Ruth Josephine (Owen) McC.; m. Pamela Preston Harris, Mar. 9, 1968 (div. 1979); children: Heather Harris, Rexford Owen; m. Sara Joan Rorke, July 27, 1980. BSc, Calif. Inst. Tech., 1959; PhD, U. Wash., 1964. Postdoctoral fellow Rockefeller U., N.Y.C., 1964-65; rsch. assoc. Rockefeller U., 1965-68; asst. prof. U. Ill., Urbana, 1968-75; assoc. prof. U. So. Calif., L.A., 1975-79; prof. biology, prof. neurology U. So. Calif., 1979—; v.p. sci. affairs Nelson Rsch. & Devel. Co., Irvine, Calif., 1981-82; acting v.p. rsch. & devel. Nelson Rsch. & Devel. Co., 1985-86; dir. program. neurol. info. sci. U. So. Calif., 1982-92, dir. program in psychobiology, 1991—; dir. cellular biology U. So. Calif., 1979-81, dir. neurobiology, 1982-88, dir. prog. psychobiology, 1991—; cons. in field; dir. Marine & Freshwater Biomed. Ctr., U. So. Calif., 1982-83; co-dir. Baja Calif. Expedition of the R/V Alpha Helix, 1974, others; chmn. Winter Conf. on Brain Rsch., 1979, 80, others; lectr. in field; sci. adv. bd. Nelson R & D, 1972-91; mem. bd. commentators Brain and Behavioral Scis., 1978—. Editor or author 3 books; co-editor: Wednesday Night at the Lab; patentee in field; mem. editorial bd. Neurochem. Rsch., 1975-81, Jour. Neurochemistry, 1977-84, Jour. Neurosci. Rsch., 1980-86; contbr. over 100 articles to profl. jours. Bd. dirs. San Pedro and Peninsula Hosp. Found., 1989-95, Faculty Ctr., U. So. Calif., 1991-95, San Pedro Health Svcs., 1992-97. Recipient John R. Hubbard award Univ. Assoc., 1993, Assocs. award for Outstanding Tchg., Univ. Assocs., 1994; Scripps Inst. fellow, 1958, NIH fellow, 1959-64, 64 -65, Alfred P. Sloan fellow, 1972-76, others; recipient rsch. grants, various sources, 1968—; Intersci. Rsch. Inst. fellow, 1989. Mem. AAAS, Am. Soc. Neurochemistry, Soc. for Neurosci., Am. Soc. Biol. Chemistry and Molecular Biology, Internat. Soc. Neurochemistry, Assn. Neurosci. Depts. and Programs, Univ. Park Investment Group, Bay Surgical Soc., N.Y. Acad. Scis. Republican. Presbyterian. Avocations: computing, travel. Home: 30533 Rhone Dr Palos Verdes Peninsula CA 90275-5742 Office: U So Calif Dept Biol Scis Los Angeles CA 90089

MCCOLLEY, STEVEN RICHARD, nurse anesthetist; b. Ogden, Utah; s. Eldon Dale and Beverly Jean (Deamer) McC.; m. Deborah Lynn Hiatt, Apr. 1, 1994; children: Forest, Aaron, Chandler. BS in respiratory therapy, Weber State Coll., Ogden, 1982; MA in biology, U. Mo., Kans. City, 1987; DSc in health counseling, Clayton Sch. Natural Nursing, Birmingham, Ala., 1994. Cert. registered nurse anesthetist. Supr. respiratory therapy McKay-Dee Hosp., Ogden, 1981-85; staff RN, SICU McKay-Dee Hosp., 1984-85; student nurse anesthetist Truman Med. Ctr., Kans. City, 1985-87; staff nurse anesthetist Kaiser-Permanente-Fontana, Fontana, Calif., 1987-88; freelance nurse anesthetist Ogden, 1988-94; staff nurse anesthetist VA Med. Ctr., Salt Lake City, 1994—. Capt. U.S. Army, 1990-91. Mem. Utah Assn. Nurse Anesthetists (pres. 1992-94, editor newsletter 1992—, author by-laws 1992), Am. Assn. Nurse Anesthetists (resolutions com. 1995—), Internat. Anesthesia Rsch. Soc., Soc. for Cardiovascular Anesthetists. Mem. LDS Ch. Avocations: karate, flying, musical instruments, family. Home: 1296 S 200 E Kaysville UT 84037-3706

MCCOLLUM, ALVIN AUGUST, real estate company executive; b. L.A., Jan. 20, 1920; s. Nile Clarkson and Ida Martha (Kuhlman) McC.; m. Maxine Eleanor Seeberg, July 29, 1944; children: Robert Michael, James Alan, Patricia Kathleen. BA, UCLA, 1941; postgrad., U.S. Naval Acad., 1946, Southwestern U., 1949-50. Exec. v.p., dir. Strout Realty, N.Y.C., 1948-61, Del E. Webb Corp., Phoenix, 1961-67; pres., dir. Sahara Nev. Corp., Las Vegas, 1964-67, Devel. Svcs., Inc., Scottsdale, Ariz., 1967-69; pres., chmn. Recreation Leisure Land, Inc., Scottsdale, 1969-71; asst. pres., dir. A.J. Industries, Inc., L.A., 1971-74; pres., dir. Carefree (Ariz.) Ranch, Inc., 1974-76; pres., bd. dir. Cons. Internat., Scottsdale, 1976—; chmn. CEO Greenway Environ. Svs., Inc., Gilbert, Ariz., 1992—; pres., bd. dirs. Combined Assets, Inc., Westlake Village, Calif., First Realty Fin., Inc., L.A., Corp. Capital Resources, Inc., Westlake Village. Bd. dirs. Admiral Nimitz Found., Fredericksburg, Tex., 1970—, Boys Club Las Vegas, 1964-68, United Fund, Las Vegas, 1966; co-chmn. NCCJ, Las Vegas, 1966; elder Presbyn. Ch. USA, 1954—. Lt. USN, 1943-48, PTO. Mem. Masons, Shriners, Am. Legion, Mt. Shadows Country Club (bd. dirs. 1962-64). Republican. Avocations: golf, swimming, camping, sailing. Home: 215 N Power Rd Unit 180 Mesa AZ 85205-8442 Office: Greenway Environ Svcs Inc 644 E Southern Ave Ste 204 Mesa AZ 85204-4934

MCCOLM, GEORGE LESTER, international agricultural consultant, journalist; b. Colby, Kans., Aug. 2, 1911; s. Theodore Harrison and Jane (Speirs) McC.; m. Emma Victoria Davis, Aug. 9, 1936 (dec. Sept. 1959); children: Carol Ann, Patricia Alice; m. Elizabeth Jane Gunder Funderburg, May 1, 1975. BS in Agr., Kans. State U., 1935; postgrad., U. Ariz., 1961-64. Cert. profl. agronomist. Various soil conservation and agrl. positions, 1935-41; dir. crop. prodn. War Relocation Authority, Topaz, Utah, 1942-43; soil conservationist Bur. Indian Affairs, Shiprock and Window Rock, Ariz., 1947-52; soil conservationist Bur. Indian Affairs, Shiprock, 1949-52, dir. nursery, 1953-57; dir. B Square Ranch Expt. Sta., Farmington, N.Mex., 1958-61; educator U. Ariz., 1961-66; with U.S. Dept. State, India, 1964-66; tech. rep. internat. Mekong River devel. com. U.S. Dept. State, Vietnam, 1966-72; rancher Lewiston, Calif., 1973-87; owner Lewiston Nursery, 1987—; part-time agrl. advisor Mex. Govt., 1976-81; with Office Strategic Svcs. in WWII conf., Washington, D.C., 1991. Contbr. articles to sci. jours. Bd. dirs. Trinity County Fair Assn. Lt. USNR, 1944-46, PTO; chief agrl. officer, Joint Chiefs of Staff, planning invasion and occupation of Japan, 1944-45; USN officer directing civilian govt. Ponape Island, 1946. Mem. NRA, CAST, Am. Soc. Agronomy and Soil Sci., Calif. Soc. Agronomy and Soil Sci., Am. Asst. Ret. Persons, Lewiston C. of C., Am. Legion, Alpha Gamma Rho, 4-H Club (Edison medal). Republican. Methodist. Avocations: fishing, fly tying, history research. Home: PO Box 330 Lewiston CA 96052-0330 Office: Lewiston Nursery Deadwood Rd Lewiston CA 96052

MCCONNEL, RICHARD APPLETON, aerospace company official; b. Rochester, Pa., May 29, 1933; s. Richard Appleton Sr. and Dorothy (Merriman) McC.; m. Mary Francis McInnis, 1964 (div. 1984); children: Amy Ellen, Sarah Catherine; m. Penny Kendzie, 1993. BS in Naval Engring., U.S. Naval Acad., 1957; MS in Aerospace Engring., USN Postgrad. Sch., 1966. Commd. ensign USN, 1957; naval aviator Operation ASW, 1959-63, 68-71, 75-79; asst. prof. math. U.S. Naval Acad., 1966-68; program mgr. P3C update Naval Air Devel. Ctr., 1971-75; range program mgr. Pacific Missile Test Ctr., 1979-82; ret. USN, 1982; program mgr. Electromagnetic Systems div. Raytheon Co., Goleta, Calif., 1982-87; sr. engr. SRS Techs., Inc., Camarillo, Calif., 1987-92, High Tech. Solutions, Inc., Camarillo, Calif., 1992—. Mem. Internat. Test and Evaluation Assn., Assn. Old Crows. Republican. Office: High Tech Solutions 1000 Paseo Camarillo # S120 Camarillo CA 93010-6021

MCCONNELL, DANA LOU, middle school educator; b. L.A., Sept. 17, 1952; d. Frank and Elnora (Winger) Rodgers; m. Michael John McConnell, July 7, 1973. BA, Brigham Young U., 1975; BS, BA, So. Utah U., 1991. Recreational therapist Care Ctr., Orem, Utah, 1975-77; tchr. Nebo Sch. Dist., Spanish Fork, Utah, 1991-96; tchr. Washington Sch. Dist., St. George, Utah, 1996—, mem. adv. bd., 1998—; mem. sch. adv. bd., Spanish Fork, 1991-96, libr. adv. bd., 1995-96. Young women pres. ch. ward Ch. of Jesus Christ of Latter Day Sts., 1992-96. Mem. Elks. Home: 120 Mesa Vista Ct Ivins UT 84738-6026

MCCONNELL, DENNIS EARL, director of information technology, nuclear engine; b. Benton Harbor, Mich., Aug. 6, 1965; s. Kenneth Earl McConnell and Diana Marie (Hall) Bodnar; m. Lisette Marie Richter, Oct. 25, 1989. BS in Nuclear Engring., MIT, 1986. Nuclear refuel engr. Westinghouse-Nuclear Svcs. Divsn., Monroeville, Pa., 1986-88; pres. Video Design Software, San Diego, 1988-90; dir. info. tech. Nolte and Assocs., Inc., Sacramento, 1990—; cons. Rippey Corp., El Dorado Hills, Calif., Am. Lung Assn., Sacramento. Mem. IEEE. Fax: (916) 641-0800. E-mail: dennis.mcconnell@nolte.com. Home: 1822 Bridgecreek Dr Sacramento CA 95833 Office: Nolte and Assocs Inc Ste 200 1750 Creekside Oaks Dr Sacramento CA 95833

MCCORD, RICHARD COLSON, writer, journalist; b. Charlotte, N.C., Apr. 15, 1941; s. James Richard and Paula (Colson) McC.; m. Laurel Ann Knowles, Jan. 1, 1970; (div. Dec. 4, 1981). BA, Vanderbilt U., 1964. Reporter, editor Newsday, Long Island, N.Y., 1967-71, The New Mexican, Santa Fe, N. Mex., 1972-73; editor, publisher The Santa Fe Reporter, 1974-88; free lance writer Santa Fe, N. Mex., 1988—; newspaper cons., Santa Fe, N. Mex., 1988—; acting editor Door County Advocate, Sturgeon Bay, Wis., 1995-96; writing instr. U. N. Mex., 1998. Author: (book) The Chain Gang, 1996 (2d pl. Mott award 1997). Recipient 2d place editorial writing Pulitzer Prize Com., N.Y.C., 1982, Eugene Cervi award Internat. Soc. Weekly Newspaper Editors, 1984, 1st place editorial writing Nat. Newspaper Assn., Washington, 1987, Gerald Loeb award Loeb Found., L.A., 1990. Mem. PEN, N. Mex., Phi Beta Kappa, Omicron Delta Kappa. Avocations: hiking, camping, travel. Home: 327 W Houghton St Santa Fe NM 87501-4348

MCCORD, VINCENT ABBOTT, JR., electronics industry executive; b. Nashville, July 24, 1946; s. Vincent Abbott and Mary Helen (Kropf) McC.; m. Nancy Elizabeth Stark, Nov. 17, 1973; children: Hunter Stark, Haven Elizabeth. BS in Math., Ga. Inst. Tech., 1969; MBA, Harvard U., 1974. Mktg. rep. IBM, L.A., 1974-78; fin. exec. IBM, White Plains, N.Y., 1978-82, San Jose, Calif., 1982-88; fin. exec. Conner Peripherals, Inc., San Jose, 1988-91, LSI Logic, Inc., Milpitas, Calif., 1991-96; CFO QuickLogic, Inc., Santa Clara, Calif., 1996—. Bd. dirs. City Lights Theatre Co., San Jose, 1987-89. Capt. USAF, 1969-72. Republican. Episcopalian. Avocations: theatre acting, singing, reading, jogging, writing. Home: 965 Foxswallow Ct San Jose CA 95120-2115 Office: 2933 Bunker Hill Ln Santa Clara CA 95054-1124

MCCORKLE, ROBERT ELLSWORTH, agribusiness educator; b. Salinas, Calif., Apr. 3, 1938; s. Stanley Harold and Muriel Eugenia (Vosti) McC.; m. Mary E. McCorkle, June 26, 1965; children: Bonnie Kathleen, Robyn Krystyna. BSc in Farm Mgmt., Calif. Poly. State U., San Luis Obispo, 1960; MSc in Agrl. Econs., U. Calif., Davis, 1962; postgrad., U. Wis., 1969, Oreg. State U., 1966. Rsch. statistician U. Calif., Davis, 1960-62; asst. prof. agrl. bus. Calif. Poly. State U., San Luis Obispo, 1962-66, dir. internat. edn., 1970-74, asst. prof. agrl. mgmt., 1969-76, prof. agribus., 1976—; chief farm mgmt. officer Ministry Agr., Lusaka, Zambia, 1967-69; dir., owner McCorkle Farms, Inc., Willows, Calif., 1970—; vis. prof. Mich. State U., U.S. AID, Washington, 1984-85; dir., owner McCorkle Trucking, Glenn, Calif., 1988—; agrl. economist U.S. AID-Redso ESA, Nairobi, Kenya, 1984-85. Author: Guide for Farming in Zambia, 1968. Pres. Cabrillo Property Owners Assn., Los Osos, Calif., 1976-78; vol. Atty. Gen.'s Adv. Com., Calif., 1972-74. U.S. Peace Corps strategy grantee, Washington, 1976—. Mem. Am. Agrl. Econs. Assn., Am. Soc. Farm Mgrs. and Rural Appraisers, Western Agrl. Econs. Assn., Calif. Poly. Farm Mgmt. Club, Calif. Poly. Alumni Assn., Blue Key, Alpha Zeta (founding mem., sr. advisor Delta chpt., nat. high coun. chronicler, sec.-treas., bd. dirs.), Nat. Alpha Zeta Found. (bd. dirs.). Republican. Episcopalian. Avocations: hunting, fishing. Office: Calif Poly State U San Luis Obispo CA 93407

MC CORMAC, WESTON ARTHUR, retired educator, retired career officer; b. Tacoma, Mar. 5, 1911; s. Jesse Carney and Jessie (Myron) McC.; BA, Golden Gate U., MBA, 1968; diploma Nat. War Coll., 1956; MPA, U. So. Calif., 1972; MA, Calif. Poly. State U., 1975. m. Mary Jeanne Rapinac, Sept. 5, 1941. Account exec. Merrill, Lynch, Pierce, Fenner & Beane, Tacoma, Seattle, 1929-40; commd. lt. U.S. Army, 1940, advanced through grades to col., 1946; asst. chief of staff 7th Army G 1, 1952-54; comdg. officer 35th F.A. Group, Germany, 1956-58; dep. chief of staff V Corps, 1958-60, asst. chief of staff G 1, Pacific, 1962-65; ret., 1966; prof. bus., dept. chmn. Calif. Poly. State U., San Luis Obispo, 1968-80, ret., 1980. Decorated Legion of Merit with 2 oak leaf clusters, Silver Star, Bronze Star medal, Commendation medal with oak leaf cluster. Fellow Fin. Analysts Fedn.; mem. Los Angeles Soc. Fin. Analysts. Home: 16732 Lew Allen Cir Riverside CA 92518-2909

MCCORMICK, ALMA HEFLIN, writer, retired educator, psychologist; b. Winona, Mo., Sept. 2, 1910; d. Irvin Elgin and Nora Edith (Kelley) Heflin; m. Archie Thomas Edward McCormick, July 14, 1942 (dec.); children: Thomas James, Kelly Jean. BA, Ea. Wash. Coll., 1936, EdM, 1949; PhD, Clayton U., 1977. Originator dept. severely mentally retarded Tri-City Public Schs., Richland, Wash., 1953, Parkland, Wash., 1955; co-founder, dir. Adastra Sch. for Gifted Children, Seattle, 1957-64; author profl. publs., novels; contbr. articles to various publs., 1937—. Mem. Am. Psychol. Assn., OX 5 Aviation Pioneers, Kappa Delta Pi. Republican. Roman Catholic. Editor: Cub Flyer, Western Story Mag., Wild West Weekly; assoc. editor: Mexico City Daily News (English sect. of Novedades). One of the first Am. woman test pilot's, 1942. Home and Office: 341 W Vananda Ave Ajo AZ 85321-2746

MCCORMICK, BETTY LEONORA, accountant; b. Missoula, Mont., July 18, 1961; d. George Oliver and Betty June (Dolton) Welch; m. 1993. BBA, U. Mont., 1983. CPA, Mont. Staff acct. Ellis & Assocs., Boise, Idaho, 1984; acct. Glacier Electric Coop., Cut Bank, Mont., 1984-86, office mgr., 1986—; income tax cons. Mem. AICPA, Beta Gamma Sigma. Democrat. Roman Catholic. Avocations: skiing, sewing, reading, hunting. Office: Glacier Electric Coop Inc 410 E Main St Cut Bank MT 59427-3012

MCCORMICK, FLOYD GUY, JR., agricultural educator, college administrator; b. Center, Colo., July 3, 1927; s. Floyd Guy and Gladys (Weir) McC.; m. Constance P. Slane; children: Angela Lynn, Craig Alan, Kim Ann, Robert Guy. BS, Colo. State U., 1950, MEd, 1959; PhD, Ohio State U., 1964. Tchr. vocat. agr. State of Colo., 1956-62; asst. prof. agrl. edn. Ohio State U., 1964-67; mem. com. agr. edn. com. edn. in agr. and natural resources Nat. Acad. Scis., 1967-69; prof. agrl. edn., head dept. U. Ariz., 1967-89, prof. emeritus, dept. head emeritus, 1990—; cons. in-svc. edn., div. vocat. edn. Ohio Dept. Edn., 1963-64; vis. prof. Colo. State U., 1973, U. Sierra Leone, Njala Univ. Coll., 1989; external examiner U. Sierra Leone, 1984, 85, 87; adv. trustee Am. Inst. Cooperatives, Washington, 1985-88; mem. Nat. Coun. Vocat. and Tech. Edn. in Agr., Washington, 1985-88. Co-author: Teacher Education in Agriculture, 1982, Supervised Occupational Experience Handbook, 1982; author: The Power of Positive Teaching, 1994, also instrl. units, tech. bulls., articles in profl. jours.; spl. editor: Agrl. Edn. mag., 1970-74. Trustee Nat. FFA Found. Served with USNR, 1945-46. Named hon. state farmer Colo., 1958, Ariz., 1968, Am. farmer, 1972; recipient Centennial award Ohio State U., 1970, E.B. Knight award NACTA Jour., 1980, Regional Outstanding Tchr. award Nat. Assn. Coll. Tchrs. Agr., 1989, also fellow, 1988, VIP citation Nat. FFA Assn., 1990, Diamond Anniversary award Ohio State U., 1992. Mem. Am. Vocat Assn. (mem. policy com. agrl. edn. divsn. 1976-79, v.p. divsn. 1985-88, chmn. membership com. 1980-83, sec. agrl. edn. divsn. 1983-86, pres. 1985-88, outstanding svc. awrd 1989), Nat. Vocat. Agr. Tchrs. Assn. (life, Outstanding Svc. award Region I 1974, 83, 96), Am. Assn. Tchr. Educators in Agr. (disting. lectr. 1984, editor newsletter 1975-76, pres. 1976-77, Disting. Svc. award 1978, 88, Rsch. award western region rsch. 1988), Alpha Zeta, Alpha Tau Alpha (hon.), Gamma Sigma Delta, Phi Delta Kappa, Epsilon Pi Tau. Home: 6933 E Paseo San Andres Tucson AZ 85710-2203

MCCORMICK, HOMER L., JR., lawyer; b. Frederick, Md., Nov. 11, 1928; s. Homer Lee McCormick and Rosebelle Irene Biser; m. Jacquelyn R.; children: Deidre Ann and Thomas Lee. Student, George Washington U., 1946-48; AB, San Jose State U., 1951; JD, U. Calif., San Francisco, 1961. Bar: Calif. 1961, U.S. Dist. Ct. Ctrl. Dist. Calif. 1972, U.S. Dist. Ct. No. Calif. 1961, U.S. Dist. Ct., So. Dist. Calif. 1976, U.S. Dist. Ct. of Appeals (9th cir. 1961), U.S. Tax Ct. 1977, U.S. Ct. Claims 1977, U.S. Supreme Ct. 1977. Atty. Holiway Jones State of Calif., 1961-63; atty. assoc. Rutan & Tucker, Santa Ana, Calif., 1963-66, atty. ptnr., 1966-70; atty., sr. ptnr. Rutan & Tucker, Costa Mesa, Calif., 1970-88, dept. head pub. law, 1974-88, mng. ptnr., 1984-88; founding ptnr., sr. ptnr. McCormick, Kidman & Behrens, Costa Mesa, 1988—; Arbitrator Am. Arbitration Assn., 1966-88; judge pro tem Orange County Superior Ct., 1975, 81, 84; spkr., lectr. Cal. Continuing Edn. of the Bar, 1976-88; profl. designation Internat. Right of Way Assn.; elected mem. Cal. Condemnation Lawyers, 1994—. Contbg. author: Real Property Remedies, 1982; contbr. articles to profl. jours. Mem. bd. govs. Bus. Com. Arts, Orange County Philharm. Soc. Lt. USMCR, 1951-56; pilot, Korea. Named Alumnus of Year Hastings Law Sch., 1992. Mem. ABA (com. chair 1991), Am. Bd. Trial Adv. (pres. O.C. chpt. 1973), Orange City Atty. Assn. (pres. 1972), Fed. Bar Assoc., Consumer Attys. Calif., Am. Judicature Soc., Orange County Bar Assn. (com. chair 1991-92), Orange County Bus. Trial Lawyers, Order Coif, Thurston Soc., Hastings Alumni Assn. (pres. 1973), Springs Country Club, Delta Theta Pi. Republican. Episcopalian. Avocations: boating, fishing, flying, golf, foreign travel.

MCCORMICK, LAWRENCE RAY, adult education educator; b. Peoria, Ill., Mar. 17, 1947; s. George and Wavie (Styles) McC.; m. Laurie Donna, May 31, 1975; children: Timothy R., Joseph E. BA, Calif. State U., Long Beach, 1974, MA, 1976; MDiv, Ref. Theol. Sem., 1979; PhD, U. So. Calif., 1992. Prof. Azusa (Calif.) Pacific U., 1985-97. With U.S. Army, 1967-69. Mem. Speech Comm. Assn., Religious Speech Comm. Assn. Avocations: skiing, camping, antiques. Office: Azusa Pacific U 901 E Alosta Ave Azusa CA 91702-2769

MCCORMICK, RICHARD, telecommunications company executive; b. Fort Dodge, Iowa, July 4, 1940; s. Elmo Eugene and Virgilla (Lawler) McC.; m. Mary Patricia Smola, June 29, 1963; children: John Richard, Matthew David, Megan Ann, Katherine Maura. B.S. in Elec. Engring., Iowa State U., 1961. With Bell Telephone Co., 1961-85; N.D. v.p., CEO Northwestern Bell Telephone Co., Fargo, 1974-77; asst. v.p. human resources AT&T, Basking Ridge, N.J., 1977-78; sr. v.p. Northwestern Bell, Omaha, 1978-82, pres., CEO, 1982-85; exec. v.p. U S West Inc., Englewood, Colo., 1985-86, pres., COO, 1986-90, pres., CEO, 1990-91, chmn., pres., CEO, 1992—; bd. dirs. Norwest Corp., United Airlines Corp. Mem. Phi Gamma Delta. Office: U S West Inc Ste 230 3200 Cherry Creek Ln Dr S Denver CO 80209*

MCCORMICK, RICHARD LEVIS, academic administrator; b. New Brunswick, N.J., Dec. 26, 1947; s. Richard Patrick and Katheryne Crook (Levis) McC.; m. Suzanne Dee Lebsock, Aug. 30, 1984; children: Elizabeth, Michael. BA in Am. Studies, Amherst Coll., 1969; PhD in History, Yale U., 1976. From asst. prof. to prof. Rutgers U., New Brunswick, N.J., 1976-92; dean Faculty Arts and Scis. Rutgers U., New Brunswick, 1989-92; exec. vice chancellor, provost, vice chancellor acad. affair U. N.C., Chapel Hill, 1992-95; pres. U. Wash., Seattle, 1995—. Author: From Realignment to Reform: Political Change in New York State, 1893-1910, 1981, The Party Period and Public Policy: American Politics from the Age of Jackson to the Progressive Era, 1986. Rsch. fellow Am. Coun. Learned Socs., 1978-79, fellow John Simon Guggenheim Meml. Found., 1985. Mem. Phi Beta Kappa. Home: 806 36th Ave E Seattle WA 98112-4320 Office: Univ Wash Seattle WA 98195

MCCOSKER, DUNCAN EARLE, art educator; b. L.A., July 6, 1944; s. Joseph Samuel and Betty Eleanor (Hoyt) McC.; m. Hun-mi Cho, May 10, 1993. BA in Math., Occidental Coll., 1965; MA in Math., U. So. Calif.; MFA in Design, Calif. Inst. of Arts. Prof. of art U. San Diego, Calif., 1994—; Artist-in-residence, vis. scholar Am. Acad. in Rome, 1997; artist-in-residence, Cite Internat. des arts, Paris, 1990, 97. One-person exhbn. Carpenter Ctr./Harvard U., 1996, Worcester Mus., 1989, Chrysler Mus., 1985, Mus. of Photographic Arts, 1984. Home: 1018 Santa Barbara St San Diego CA 92107-4109

MCCOWN, LINDA JEAN, medical technology educator; b. Pitts., Mar. 18, 1953; d. William Earnest and Mary Elizabeth McC. BS, Pa. State U., 1975; MS, U. Pitts., 1979. Cert. med. technologist, clin. lab. scientist. Microbiology aide Pa. State U., University Park, 1973-74; med. technologist, asst. supr., rsch. technologist Children's Hosp. of Pitts., 1975-80; asst. prof. med. tech., assoc. program dir. Ctrl. Wash. U., Ellensburg, 1980—; critiquer, insp. Nat. Accreditation Agy. for Clin. Lab. Scis., Chgo., 1984—; test item writer Nat. Cert. Agy., Lenexa, Kans., 1989—; recruiter Am. Soc. Clin. Pathologists, Chgo., 1988—; guest lectr. physician asst. program U. Wash., Seattle, 1996—. Contbr. articles to profl. jours. Stephen ministry, deacon First Presbyn. Ch., Yakima, Wash., 1992-98; bd. dirs. The Campbell Farm, Wapato, Wash., 1990-95; rally chmn. Heifer Project Internat., Wapato, 1991-94. Mem. Am. Soc. for Med. Tech. (mem. commn. on accreditation 1988-91), Wash. State Soc. for Clin. Lab. Sci. (conv. chair 1992, edn. chair 1986-94, 95-96, Pres.'s award 1992, convention hospitality chair and cons. 1998), Columbia Basin Soc. Clin. Lab. Sci. (pres-elect 1993, pres. 1994-95), Omicron Sigma. Avocations: photography, tennis, travel, music. Home: 1305 Jefferson Ave Yakima WA 98902-2528 Office: Ctrl Wash U Ctr Med Tech 1120 W Spruce St Yakima WA 98902-3218

MCCOY, EUGENE LYNN, civil engineer; b. Ridgefield, Wash., Apr. 9, 1926; s. Eugene Victor McCoy and Thelma Lucinda (Ayres) Martin; m. Marcia Helen Schear, Sept. 14, 1955 (div. 1974); children: Thomas Edwin, Susan Lynn, Molly Kay (dec.). AS, Lower Columbia Coll., 1948; BS, Wash. State U., 1950; MS, U. Wash., 1955. Registered profl. engr., Wash. Successively civil engr. soils, chief soils engr. sect., chief geotech. br. Portland (Oreg.) dist., chief geotech. br. North Pacific div. U.S. Army Corps. Engrs., 1955-85; staff cons. Shannon and Wilson, Portland, 1985-88, Cornforth Cons. Inc., Tigard, Oreg., 1988—; tech. specialist delegation for design of Longtan Dam, U.S. Army Corps. Engrs., Beijing, 1981, People to People's delegation Dams and Tunnels, 1987. Contbr. articles to profl jours. Active camp com. Campfire Girls, 4-H Clubs, Oregon City; vol. Loaves and Fishes, Oreg. State U. Ext., AARP Tax Aid. Radio officer U.S. Merchant Marine, 1944-46; with U.S. Army, 1950-52. Mem. ASCE, U.S. Com. Large Dams, Oreg. Master Gardener. Democrat. Unitarian. Avocations: gardening, hiking, skiing, forestry. Home: 20551 S Fischers Mill Rd Oregon City OR 97045-9646 Office: Cornforth Cons Inc 10250 SW Greenburg Rd Ste 111 Portland OR 97223-5460

MCCOY, HARRY E., II, lawyer; b. Parkersburg, W.Va., June 27, 1938. BA, U. Utah, 1967, JD, 1970. Bar: Utah 1970, Tex. 1974. Ptnr. Ballard Spahr Andrews & Ingersoll, LLP, Salt Lake City; founding dir. ARDA Internat. Found., 1983—; bd. dirs., chair legis. coun., Am. Resort Devel. Assn. Mem. Utah State Bar. E-mail: mccoy2@ballardspahr.com. Office: Ballard Spahr Andrews & Ingersoll LLP 201 S Main St Ste 1200 Salt Lake City UT 84111-2210

MCCOY, JAMES JOSEPH, journalist; b. Canton, Ohio, Mar. 27, 1954; s. James Mark and Kathleen Loretta (O'Connor) McC.; m. Louise Kim Coates, Feb. 18, 1989; children: Kelsey Anne, James Ryland. BA in journalism/speech, U. Hawaii, 1977. Reporter Honolulu Star-Bull., 1977-82; reporter Sta. KHON-TV, Honolulu, 1982-91; mng. editor Sta. KHON-TV, 1992-96, news dir., 1996—. Office: Sta KHON-TV 1170 Auahi St Honolulu HI 96814-4917

MC COY, LOIS CLARK, emergency services professional, retired county official, magazine editor; b. New Haven, Oct. 1, 1920; m. Herbert Irving McCoy, Oct. 17, 1943; children: Whitney, Kevin, Marianne, Tori, Debra, Sally, Daniel. BS, Skidmore Coll., 1942; student Nat. Search and Rescue Sch., 1974. Asst. buyer R.H. Macy & Co., N.Y.C., 1942-44, assoc. buyer, 1944-48; instr. Mountain Medicine & Survival, U. Calif. at San Diego, 1973-74; cons. editor Search & Rescue Mag., 1975; cons. editor, Rescue Mag., 1988-97; editor Press On Newsletter, 1992—, coord. San Diego Mountain Rescue Team, La Jolla, Calif., 1973-75; exec. sec. Nat. Assn. for Search and Rescue, Inc., Nashville and La Jolla, 1975-80, comptr., 1980-82; disaster officer San Diego County, 1980-86, Santa Barbara County, 1986-91, ret. Contbr. editor Rescue Mag., 1989-97, editor-in-chief Response! mag., 1982-86; pres. Nat. Inst. Urban Search & Rescue, 1983—; editor Press On! Electronic mag., 1994—; mem. adv. bd. Hazard Montly, 1991—; cons. law enforcement div.; Calif. Office Emergency Svcs., 1976-77; pres. San Diego Com. for Los Angeles Philharmonic Orch., 1957-58. Bd. dirs. Search and Rescue of the Californias, 1976-77, Nat. Assn. for Search and Rescue, Inc.,

1980-87, pres., 1985-87, trustee, 1987-90, mem. Calif. OES strategic com., 1992-96; CEO Nat. Inst. For Urban Search, 1989—; mem. Gov.'s Task Force on Earthquwakes, 1981-82, Earthquake Preparedness Task Force, Seismic Safety Commn., 1982-85. Recipient Hal Foss award for outstanding service to search and rescue, 1982, Diamond Safety award for outstanding work in emergency services, 1996. Mem. IEEE, Armed Forces Comm. and Electronics Assoc., Nat. Assn. for Search & Rescue (life, Svc. award 1985), San Diego Mountain Rescue Team (hon. life), Santa Barbara Amateur Radio Club. Episcopalian. Author: Search and Rescue Glossary, 1974; contbr. to profl jours. E-mail: niusr@ix.netcom.com. Office: PO Box 91648 Santa Barbara CA 93190-1648

MCCOY, SHAWN ALOYSIOUS, musician; b. L.A., Mar. 18, 1973; s. John Michael and Claire Fredrica (Wall) McC. Writer, singer (CD) Out of Order, 1992; band leader (CD) Intentional Infliction of Emotional Distress, 1993, Eye CARamba, 1995, Killem Gillem 1000 Lbs., 1998. Mem. Bands for Bread, Manhattan Beach, 1992. Roman Catholic. Office: Out of Order 2422 Ripley Ave Redondo Beach CA 90278-5149

MCCOY-SHAY, DONNA CAROL, telecommunication manager; b. Carthage, Mo., Feb. 13, 1952; d. Vernon and LaVerne McCoy; m. Douglas W. Shay. BS in Biology, Mo. So. State Coll., 1976. Park ranger Dept. of Interior-Nat. Park Svc., Diamond, Mo., 1971-77; installer We. Electric, Joplin, Mo., 1977-83; field installations supr. No. Telcom, Inc., Denver, 1984-90; tech. field mgr. U.S. West Comm., Phoenix, 1990—. Mem. NAFE, Women's Club, Mo. So. State Coll. Alumni Assn., Beta Sigma Phi. Avocations: arts and crafts, photography. Home: 30035 N 47th St Cave Creek AZ 85331-7828 Office: US West Comm 3033 N 3rd St Rm 406 Phoenix AZ 85012-3088

MCCRAVEN, EVA STEWART MAPES, health service administrator; b. L.A., Sept. 26, 1936; d. Paul Melvin and Wilma Zech (Ziegler) Stewart; m. Carl Clarke McCraven, Mar. 18, 1978; children: David Anthony, Lawrence James, Maria Lynn Mapes. ABS magna cum laude, Calif. State U., Northridge, 1974, MS, Cambridge Grad. Sch. Psychology, 1987; PhD, 1991. Dir. spl. projects Pacoima Meml. Hosp., 1969-71, dir. health edn., 1971-74; asst. exec. dir., v.p., Hillview Community Mental Health Center, Lakeview Terrace, Calif., 1974—, dir. clin. svcs.; past dir. dept. consultation and edn. Hillview Ctr., developer, mgr. long-term residential program, 1986-90; former program mgr. Crisis Residential Program, Transitional Residential Program and Day Treatment Program for mentally ill offenders, past. dir. mentally ill offenders svcs.; former program dir. Valley Homeless Shelter Mental Health Counseling Program; dir. Integrated Services Agy., Hillview Mental Health Ctr., Inc., 1993—, dir. clin. programs, 1996—; Former pres. San Fernando Valley Coordinating Coun. Area Assn., Sunland-Jujunga Coordinating Coun.; bd. advisors Pacoinia Sr. Citizens Multi-Purpose Ctr.; bd. dirs. N.E. Valley Health Corp., 1970-73, Golden State Community Mental Health Ctr., 1970-73. Recipient Resolution of Commendation award State of Calif., 1988, Commendation award, 1988, Spl. Mayor's plaque, 1988, Commendation awards for community svcs. City of L.A., 1989, County of L.A., 1989, Calif. State Assembly, 1989, Calif. State Senate, 1989, award Sunland-Tujunga Police Support Coun., 1989, Woman of Achievement award Sunland-Tujunga BPW, 1990. Mem. Am. Pub. Health Assn., Valley Univ. Women, Health Services Adminstrn. Alumni Assn. (former v.p.), Sunland-Jujunga Bus. and Profl. Women, LWV. Office: Hillview Community Mental Health Ctr 11500 Eldridge Ave San Fernando CA 91342-6523

MCCRAY, DOROTHY WESTABY, artist and educator; b. Madison, S.D., Oct. 13, 1915; d. Robert Spencer and Annie Mary (Otter) Westaby; m. Francis F. McCray, Aug. 6, 1938 (dec. Jan. 1960); 1 child, Peter Michael. BA, State U. of Iowa, 1937, MA in Painting, 1939; MFA in Printmaking, Calif. Coll. Arts and Crafts, Oakland, 1955. Prof. art Western N.Mex. U., Silver City, 1948-81, prof. emeritus, 1981—; profl. painter/printmaker McCray Studios, Silver City. Solo exhbns. include Mezzanine Gallery, Oakland, Calif., Art Directions Gallery, N.Y.C., Lebanon Valley Coll., Pa., Coralles Art Assn., N.Mex., Richard Levy Gallery, Albuquerque, numerous others; group exhbns. include Art Inst. Chgo., 1940-41, Phila. Acad., 1941, Kansas City Art Inst., 1941, 42, Smithsonian Inst., Washington, 1941, 58, Am. Fine Arts Gallery, N.Y.C., 1943, Joslyn Meml. Art Mus., Omaha, 1947, Mus. Fine Arts, Santa Fe, 1950, 51, 52, 53, 54, 56, 57, 58, 59, 63, 66, Oakland (Calif.) Art Mus., 1955, Cin. Art Mus., 1956, 58, NAD, Newton, Kans., 1956, Dallas Mus. Fine Arts, 1956, 58, Roswell (N.Mex.) Art Mus., 1958, Bradley U., Peoria, Ill., 1960, Highlands U., Las Vegas, 1960, Bklyn. Mus., 1961, Pa. Acad. Art, Phila., 1965, Museo de Arte Historia, Juarez, Mexico, 1978, The Shellfish Collection, Silver City, N.Mex., 1990, 91, Deming (N.Mex.) Ctr. for Arts, 1991, Grant County Art Guild, Pinos Altos, N.Mex., 1991, 92, Carlsbad (N.Mex.) Mus. and Art Ctr., 1992, Richard Levy Gallery, Albuquerque, 1992, Jonathon Green Gallery, Naples, Fla., numerous others; represented in pvt. and mus. collections throughout the United States. Named Hon. Citizen of S.D., 1983; Western N.Mex. U. Art Building named Dorothy McCray Art Building, 1982; recipient N.Mex. Gov.'s Award for Excellence and Contbns. to the Arts, 1992, numerous art awards in exhbns. Office: PO Box 322 Silver City NM 88062-0322

MCCREADY, KENNETH FRANK, past electric utility executive; b. Edmonton, Alta., Can., Oct. 9, 1939; s. Ralph and Lilian McCready; children: John, Janet, Brian. BSc, U. Alta., 1963. Supr. data processing and systems Calgary (Alta.) Power Ltd., 1965-67, supr. rates and contracts, 1967-68, adminstrv. asst. to exec. v.p., 1968-72, asst. mgr. mgmt. cons. div., 1972-75; mgr. mgmt. systems dept., gen. mgr. Montreal Engring. Co., Calgary, 1975-76; v.p. adminstrn. Calgary (Alta.) Power Ltd., 1976-80; sr. v.p. ops. TransAlta Utilities, Calgary, 1980-85, pres., COO, 1985-89, also bd. dirs., 1988-96; pres., CEO TransAlta Corp., 1989-96; CEO TransAlta Energy Corp., 1989-96; pres. K. F. McCready & Assocs. Ltd., Calgary, 1996—; bd. dirs. PanCan. Petroleum Ltd., Hewlett Packard (Can.) Ltd., ABB Asea Brown Boveri Environment adv. bd., Zurich, Marigold Found. Ltd., Calgary, Tech. Devel. Corp., Ottawa, Dynamotive Technologies, Corp., Computer Modelling Group, Calgary, Can. Environ. Tech. Advancement Corp., Calgary, Internat. Inst. Sustainable Devel., Winnipeg; past chmn. Conf. Bd. Can.; past chmn. bd. Advanced Computing Techs., Inc.; mem. Dow Chem. Corp. Adv. Coun., Midland, Tata Energy Rsch. Inst. adv. bd., Washington. Past dep. chmn. bd. govs. So. Alta. Inst. Tech.; past chair Alta. Round Table on Environment and Econ.; past mem. com. on trade and environment Govt. Can. Internat. Trade Adv.; past pres. Western Electric Power and Light Assn.; past chair environ. task force Bus. Coun. Nat. Issues. Mem. Assn. Profl. Engrs., Geologists and Geophysicists of Alta., Ranchmen's Club. Avocations: computers, cycling, photography.

MCCREARY, DEBORAH DENNIS, oncology nurse; b. Washington, Ohio, Oct. 6, 1952; d. Eldon Hugh Dennis and Janice Sylvia (North) Saunders; m. James Leo McCreary, May 21, 1988. BSN, Ohio State Sch. Nursing, 1976. Nurse Ohio State U. Hosp., Columbus, 1976-77; asst. head nurse Riverside Meth. Hosp., Columbus, 1977-80; nurse Good Samaritan Hosp., San Jose, Calif., 1980-82; asst. head nurse Valley West Hosp., San Jose, 1982; outpatient oncology nurse Southbay Med. Oncology, San Jose, 1982-88; oncology nurse specialist, office mgr. Menlo Med. Clinic, Menlo Park, Calif., 1988—; cons. Schering Corp., Dallas, 1991, Berlix, Menlo Park, 1992, spkr., 1994, Ortho Biotech, San Francisco, 1995. Mem. Oncology Nursing Soc. (Santa Clara chpt. sec. 1982-84, membership chair 1984-85, cert. oncology nurse). Republican. Avocations: classical music, piano, gourmet cooking, hiking, travel. Home: 23750 Ravensbury Ave Los Altos CA 94024-6341 Office: Menlo Med Clinic 1300 Crane St Menlo Park CA 94025-4260

MCCRONE, ALISTAIR WILLIAM, university president; b. Regina, Can., Oct. 7, 1931. BA, U. Sask., 1953; MSc, U. Nebr., 1955; PhD, U. Kans., 1961. Instr. geology NYU, 1959-61, asst. prof., 1961-64, assoc. prof., 1964-69, prof., 1969-70, supr. Rsch. Ship Sea Owl on L.I. Sound, 1959-64; asst. dir. univ. program NYU, Sterling Forest, 1965-66; resident master Rubin Internat. Residence Hall NYU, 1966-69, chmn. dept. geology, 1966-69, assoc. dean Grad. Sch. Arts and Scis., 1969-70; prof. geology, acad. v.p. U. Pacific, 1970-74, acting pres., 1971; prof. geology, pres. Calif. State U. Sys. Humboldt State U., Arcata, 1974—, mem. sys. exec. coun. Calif. State U. Sys., 1974—, acad. senate Humboldt State U., 1974—, mem. chancellor's com. on innovative programs, 1974-76, trustees' task force on off-campus instrn., 1973-76, exec. com. Chancellor's Coun. of Pres., 1976-79, Calif. state dir. Am. Assn. State Colls. and Univs., 1977-80, mem. Commn. on Edn. Telecomm., 1983-86; chair Calif. State U. Statewide Task Force on Earthquake and Emergency preparedness, 1985-88, 95; chmn., mem. accreditation teams Western Assn. Schs. and Colls.; chair com. on energy and environ. Am. Assn. State Colls. and Univs., 1980-84; chair program com. Western Coll.Assn., 1983-84, panelist, 1983; mem. bd. dirs. Assn. Am. Colls., 1989-93, chair, 1992-93. Contbr. articles to profl. jours.; lectr. on geology Sunrise Semester program CBS Nat. Network, 1969-70; various appearances on local TV stas. Bd. trustees Presbyn. Hosp.-Pacific Med. Ctr., San Francisco, 1971-74; mem. Calif. Coun. for Humanities, 1977-82; mem. local campaign bd. United Way, 1977-83; mem. Am. Friends Wilton Park, 1980—; bd. dirs. Humboldt Convention and Visitors Bur., 1980-87, Redwood Empire Assn., 1983-87; bd. dirs. Calif. State Automobile Assn., 1988—, Am. Automobile Assn., 1990-93; bd. trustees Calif. State Parks Found., 1994—. Shell fellow in geology U. Nebr., 1954-55; Danforth assoc. NYU, 1964. Fellow Calif. Acad. Scis.; mem. AAAS, Geol. Soc. Am., Am. Assn. U. Adminstrs. (nat. bd. 1986-89, 96—), Rotary, St. Andrews Soc. N.Y. (life), Sigma Xi (pres. NYU chpt. 1967-69), Phi Kappa Phi. Avocation: golf. Office: Humboldt State U Univ Campus Arcata CA 95521

MCCUAIG, IAN CARRUTHERS, fundraising consultant; b. Orillia, Ont., Can., Mar. 5, 1962; came to U.S., 1992; s. Alan Hayes and Elizabeth Louise (Bonnell) McC.; m. Sarah Elizabeth Robertson, July 2, 1994. Student, Royal Conservatory of Music, Toronto, Ont., 1983; BA in Internat. Rels., U. Toronto, 1990; CSPG, Calif. State U., 1997. Cert. specialist planned giving. Devel. cons. UN Assn., Toronto, 1988-89; account exec. Gordon L. Goldie Co., Ltd., Toronto, 1989-92; cons. Marts & Lundy, Inc., San Francisco, 1992-96; sr. dir. Devel. Goodwill, San Francisco, 1996—. Contbr. articles to profl. publs. Nat. sec. Amnesty Internat. Can., Ottawa, Ont., 1986-88; chair human rights com. UN Assn., Toronto, 1988-89; elder Timothy Eaton Meml. Ch., Toronto, 1984-92; deacon Calvary Presbyn. Ch., San Francisco, 1992-96; mem. Dem. Nat. Com. Mem. World Affairs Coun., Nat. Soc. Fundraising Execs. (cert., v.p. Golden Gate chpt., mem. nat. acad.), Internat. Diplomacy Coun., Nat. Com. on Planned Giving Can.-Am. C. of C., St. Francis Yacht Club, Commonwealth Club of Calif. Avocation: sailing. Office: Goodwill 1500 Mission St San Francisco CA 94103-2513

MCCUBBIN, SHARON ANGLIN, elementary school educator; b. Fullerton, Calif., Nov. 20, 1948; d. Floyd Calvin and Grace Ann Anglin; m. David Paul White (div. 1990); children: Julie, Adrian, Matthew; m. Robert Patrick McCubbin, July 13, 1991. BA, U. Calif., 1973; MEd, Cleveland State U., 1993. Cert. clear multiple subject profl. pre-K, Calif., elem. Montessori tchr., early childhood edn. Tchr. Primanti Montessori, Orange, Calif., 1977-81; tchr., adminstr. Montessori of Orange, 1981-83, Tustin Hills Montessori, Santa Ana, Calif., 1983-89; tchr., cons. for Montessori programs Irvine (Calif.) Unified Sch. Dist., 1990—; Montessori elem. mentor tchr., 1990—; cons. title VII programs Irvine Unified Sch. Dist., 1990—, GATE adv. bd. mem.; cons. for early childhood programs to local corps. Asst. Jr. Disabled Programs, Orange, 1988—. Mem. ASCD, AAUW, Assn. Montessori Internat., Assn. Montessori Internat./U.S.A., Assn. Montessori Internat. Elem. Alumni Assn. (regional rep. 1984), Am. Montessori Soc., N.Am. Montessori Tchrs. Assn., Pvt. Sch. Adminstrs., U. Calif.-Irvine Alumni Assn., Calif. Tchrs. Assn., Irvine Tchrs. Assn. Home: 19082 Ervin Ln Santa Ana CA 92705-2828 Office: Irvine Unified Sch Dist 5050 Barranca Pkwy Irvine CA 92604-4698 also: Santiago Hills Elem 29 Christamon W Irvine CA 92620-1836

MCCUBBIN, SUSAN BRUBECK, real estate executive, lawyer; b. Decatur, Ill., Mar. 16, 1948; d. Rodney Earl Brubeck and Marilyn Jean (McMahon) Hopkins; 1 child, Martin Charles Jr.; m. William James McCubbin, May 30, 1987. LLB, Western State U., Fullerton, Calif., 1977. Bar: CAlif. 1977; lic. real estate broker, Calif. Ptnr. Blue Chip Constrn. Co., Santa Ana, Calif., 1969-73; pres. Brubeck Co., San Francisco and Newport Beach, Calif., 1973-78; sole practice San Francisco, 1978-79; sr. mktg. cons., broker Grubb & Ellis Co., San Francisco, 1979-87; pres. Greenwich Corp., San Rafael, Calif., 1987—; broker assoc. Fox & Carskadon, Mill Valley, Calif. Columnist Automotive Age Mag., 1974-75. Chmn. U.S. Senate Primary Campaign, Orange County, Calif., 1976. Republican. Avocations: computers/videography, tennis, historical study, travel, music.

MCCULLOUGH, EDWARD EUGENE, patent agent, inventor; b. Baldwin, N.D., June 4, 1923; s. Elmer Ellsworth and Emma Izelda (Nixon) McC. BA, U. Minn., 1957; postgrad., Utah State U., 1965. Machine designer Sperry Rand Corp., Mpls., 1952-58; patent adminstr. Thiokol Corp., Brigham City, Utah, 1958-86; patent cons. Thiokol Corp., Brigham City, 1986; pvt. practice, 1986—. Patentee instruments for making perspective drawings, apparatus for forming ignition surfaces in solid propellant motors, passive communications satellite or similar article, flexible bearings and process for their manufacture, rocket nozzel support and pivoting system, cavity-shaping machine, others. Pianist Aldersgate Meth. Ch., Brigham City, 1959—. Staff Sgt. U.S. Army, 1949-52. Decorated two battle stars. Avocations: philosophy, music composition, hiking in the mountains. Home: PO Box 46 Brigham City UT 84302

MCCULLOUGH, GAYLE JEAN, graphic artist, publisher; b. Mare Island, Calif., Feb. 7, 1943; d. Earl Martin and Dorothy Clare (Vincent) Hoos; m. Norris Henry Hill; m. James Arthur McCullough, Feb. 19, 1979; children: Kareena Jean, Michael Earl, Michelle Lin. AA in Graphic Arts, Sacramento City Coll., 1970. Composing operator Cal-West Life Ins., Sacramento, 1972-75; sr. graphic artist Dept. Social Svcs. State of Calif., Sacramento, 1975—; mem. AOA implementation team State COSS, Sacramento, 1993—, mem. equal employment opportunity disabled adv. bd., 1986-87. Author, illustrator: Feud for Thought, 1993; author: Everything Hearing People Know About Deafness, 1994, What's Next?, 1994; author, illustrator, pub. (mag.) Life After Deafness, 1993-94. V.p. cmty. coun. NorCal Ctr. on Deafness, Sacramento, 1993-94. Recipient Swimming and Diving Champion award Sacramento City and County, 1957-59, Gold Keys for Art award Brueners & Hallmark Cards, 1959, 60; grantee Bank of Am., 1970. Mem. Calif. Assn. Late Deafened Adults (bd. dirs. 1993-94), Assn. Late Deafened Adults Sacramento (pres., founder 1990—). Avocations: oil painting, art, swimming, tennis. Home: 6773 Starboard Way Sacramento CA 95831-2413 Office: COSS MS 7-182 744 P St Sacramento CA 95814-6413

MCCUNE, ELLIS E., retired university system chief administrator, higher education consultant; b. Houston, July 17, 1921; s. Ellis E. and Ruth (Mason) McC.; m. Hilda May Whiteman, Feb. 8, 1946; 1 son, James Donald. Student, Sam Houston State U., 1940-42; B.A., UCLA, 1948, Ph.D., 1957; LHD, Golden Gate U., 1994. Teaching asst. UCLA, 1949-51; from instr. to assoc. prof. polit. sci. Occidental Coll., Los Angeles, 1951-59; chmn. applied politics and econs. curriculum Occidental Coll., 1951-56; asst. prof. Calif. State U., Northridge, 1959-61, assoc. prof., chmn. dept. polit. sci., 1961-63, prof., 1963, dean letters and sci., 1963; dean acad. planning Calif. State Univs. and Colls., 1963-67; pres. Calif. State U., Hayward, 1967-90, pres. emeritus, 1991—; acting chancellor The Calif. State U. System, 1990-91, ret., 1991; cons. govtl. units and agys.; lectr., panelist; mem. Calif. State Scholarship and Loan Commn., 1964-68, chmn., 1967-68; pres. Govtl. Adminstrn. Group Los Angeles, 1959; chair planning com., mem. exec. com., bd. dirs. Eden Med. Ctr. Found., 1994—, pres.-elect, 1995-97, pres., 1997—; bd. dirs. Hayward Area Hist. Soc., 1998—. Chmn. univs. and colls. div. United Bay Area Crusade, 1969-70, 73-74; bd. dirs. Oakland (Calif.) Museum Assn., 1974-77, 86-88, Hayward Area Hist. Soc., 1998—; vice chmn. higher edn. div., East Bay United Way, 1989-90; mem. arts adv. council, 1986-87, devel. com., 1988-89, Bay Area Urban League, bd. trust Calif. Coun. Econ. Edn. No. sect., Emergency Shelter Program Adv. Coun., Hayward Area Hist. Assn., NAACP Hayward chpt.; trustee Calif. Council Econ. Edn.; sec. bd. dirs. Eden Community Found., 1978-79; rsch. fellow Haynes Found, 1957. With USAAF, 1942-46. Mem. Am. Coun. Edn. (adv. com. 1970-72, inst. coll. & univ. adminstrs. 1973-74, bd. dirs. 1985-86), Western Assn. Schs. and Colls. (accrediting commn. sr. colls. and univs. 1974-78, chmn., 1978-82, pres. 1979-81), N.W. Assn. Schs. and Colls. (commn. colls. 1974-80), Assn. Am. Colls. (bd. dirs. 1972-75, vice chmn. 1975-76), Assn. Western Univs. (bd. dirs.), Coun. Postsecondary Accreditation (bd. dirs. 1977-80, exec. com. 1979-80, chmn. 1985-87, immediate past chmn., 1988-89, chmn. com. recognition 1982-84), Am. Assn. State Colls. and Univs. (chmn. accreditation com. 1983-86, com. acad. pers. and acad. freedom 1987-88, com. on acad. affairs 1988-91), Calif. Coun. Edn. (trustee), Western Polit. Sci. Assn. (exec. coun. 1958-61), Hayward C. of C. (dir. 1968-71, 73-76, 77-80, 82-85, 86-90), Regional Assn. East Bay Colls. and Univs. (exec. com. 1974-90, sec. 1975-76, 87-88, vice chmn. 1976-77, 84-85, chmn. 1977-79, 85-86), Rotary, Phi Beta Kappa, Pi Gamma Mu, Pi Sigma Alpha. Club: Bohemian (San Francisco). Fax: 510-537-3581. E-mail: EMcCune@worldnet.att.net. Home: 22012 Sevilla Rd # 85 Hayward CA 94541-2735 Office: Calif State U Pres Emeritus LI 3167 Hayward CA 94542-3053

MCCURDY, JOHN, developmental caregiver; b. Carthage, Mo., Jan. 24, 1946; s. John and Louise (Fowler) McC.; m. Nancy M. Lacey, Jan. 5, 1971 (div. June 1972); 1 child, John; m. Terry A. Weir, Mar. 29, 1980. Student, U. Colo., 1967-68, U. Mont., 1977-80. Machinist Goldco Mfg. Co. Inc., Denver, 1972-75; shipping and warehouse worker Christie Transfer and Storage Co., Butte, Mont., 1975-78; maintenance worker 4 B's Restaurant, Butte, Mont., 1980-84; account exec. Drillco Oil and Gas Investments, Gulfport, Miss., 1984-88; stand examiner U.S. Forest Svc., Butte, 1988-89; salesman Aire Inc., Anaconda, Mont., 1989-91; resident care aide Mont. Devel. Ctr., Boulder, Mont., 1991—; salesman Town and Country Advt. Co., Denver, 1965-68. Mem. Lions, Gulf Coast, Miss., 1985-88. With U.S. Army, 1968-72. Mem. U.S. Naval Inst., Acad. Polit. Sci., Coun. Fgn. Rels. Republican. Baptist. Avocations: reading, martial arts, skiing, boating, hunting. Home: 26 Basin Creek Rd Butte MT 59701-9704 Office: Mont Devel Ctr PO Box 87 Boulder MT 59632-0087

MCDADE, DONNA MARIE, writer; b. Cleve., Apr. 29, 1949; d. Daniel and Frieda (Dresp) Forkapa; 1 child, Jason C. Gorman. Student, Bowling Green U., 1967-68. LPN, Ariz. Oper. rm. technician Parma (Ohio) Hosp., 1969-71; with ER staff Providence Gen. Hosp., 1971; with ICU-CCU staff St. Josephs Hosp., Reading, Pa., 1972; operating room technician Reading Hosp., 1973-75; with CCU staff Parma Cmty. Hosp., 1975-76; with ICU, CCU, MICU and ER staffs U. Med. Ctr., 1977-79, with ER staff, 1983; with ICU, CCU, MICU and ER staffs Tucson Med. Ctr., 1977-79, with radiation oncology staff Ariz. Health Scis. Ctr., 1989-94; with ER staff Meml. Hosp., Colorado Springs, Colo., 1981-83; mgr. patient rels., triage nurse Cigna Healthplan, Tucson, 1984-89; lectr. in field. Writer poetry; contbr. articles to profl. jours. Recipient Nurse of Yr. award U.M.C. Tucson Achievements, 1991, Achievement awards 1992, 93, 94, 95.

MCDADE, JAMES RUSSELL, management consultant; b. Dallas, Jan. 15, 1925; s. Marion W. and Jeannette (Reneau) McD.; m. Sandra Lee Bushey, Sep. 10, 1955. BSEE, So. Meth. U., Dallas, 1947; MBA, Northwestern U., Evanston, Ill., 1950. Asst. to pres. Davidson Corp., Chgo., 1951-52; asst. to pres. Mergenthaler Linotype Co., Bklyn., 1952-53, comml. works mgr., 1953-56; chief indsl. engr. Tex. Instruments, Inc., Dallas, 1956-57, product gen. mgr., 1958-60, v.p., 1961-64; chmn. bd. McDade Properties Co., Aspen (Colo.), Denver, Dallas, 1964—; bd. dirs. Pitkin County Bank, Aspen; chmn. bd. dirs. Harley-Davidson Tex., Westec Security of Aspen, Aspen Security, Inc. Founding mem. Aspen Art Mus., 1980; mem. Ballet Aspen, 1980—; pres. club Aspen Valley Hosp., 1984—. Served to 1st lt. USAF, 1943-46. Mem. Rep. Senatorial Inner Circle, Am. Mgmt. Assn., Presidents Assn. Avocations: skiing, horseback riding, camping, swimming. Home and Office: 1000 Red Mountain Rd PO Box 9090 Aspen CO 81612-9090

MCDANIEL, JOSEPH CHANDLER, lawyer; b. Covington, Va., Mar. 24, 1950; s. Everts Hardin and Betty (Chandler) McD.; m. Sandra Lee Bonds, Dec. 27, 1976; children: Sean Kenneth, Caitlin Bonds. BA in Philosophy, Ariz. State U., 1974, JD, 1980. Bar: Ariz. 1980, U.S. Dist. Ct. Ariz. 1981; cert. specialist bankruptcy law Ariz. Bd. Legal Specialization, cert. specialist consumer bankruptcy law Am. Bankruptcy Bd. Specialization, cert. specialist bus. bankruptcy law. Law clk. U.S. Bankruptcy Ct., Phoenix, 1980-82; pvt. practice Phoenix, 1982-84; ptnr. McDaniel and Jaburg, P.C., Phoenix, 1984-89, McDaniel and Lee, Phoenix, 1989-91, McDaniel & Gan, P.C., 1991-93, McDaniel & Kaup, P.C., 1993-94, Lerch, McDaniel & Kaup, P.L.C., 1994-96, Lerch, McDaniel, DelPrimn & Kaup, P.L.C., 1996—; lectr. in field; mem. Scriveners Com. Local Rules of Ct. for Dist. of Ariz. Bankruptcy Cts., Phoenix, 1980. Author: A Guide to Researching Bankruptcy Law, 1980; editor: (with others) Arizona Civil Remedies, 1982; lectr. in field. Bd. dirs. St. Patrick's Day Parade, 1988-89, Irish Cultural Assn. Phoenix, 1988-89. Mem. ABA (gen. practice sect. bankruptcy com., chmn., sr. vice chmn. membership com. pubs. bd.), Ariz. Bar Assn. (lectr., co-chmn. continuing legal edn. com., bankruptcy sect. 1987-88, chmn. 1988-89, co-chmn. jud. rels. com. 1990-92), Maricopa County Bankruptcy Practitioners (chmn.), Ariz. Bankruptcy Coalition (bd. dirs. 1986—, chair speakers com. 1994-96), Maricopa County Bar Assn., Am. Bankruptcy Inst. Democrat. Roman Catholic. Avocations: computer tech., chess, hiking. Office: Lerch McDaniel DelPrimn Kaup PLC 2700 N Central Ave Ste 1500 Phoenix AZ 85004-1185

MCDANIEL, RICKEY DAVID, senior living executive; b. Rochester, Minn., Apr. 10, 1946; s. Malcolm David and Elaine (Lee) McD.; m. Shelley Ann Sorensen, May 10, 1980; children: Michael, Mathew, Joseph. AA, Rochester Jr. Coll., 1966; BA, Winona State U., 1969. Clin. mgr. St. Mary's Hosp., Rochester, Minn., 1971-74; long term care adminstr. Roderick Enterprises, Inc., Portland, Oreg., 1974-78; regional dir. Roderick Enterprises, Inc., Portland, 1978-80, v.p. ops., 1980-84; pres. Health Sys. Mgmt. and Devel., L.A., 1984-86; ops. dir. Brim Enterprises, Inc., Portland, 1987-88, v.p., 1988-92, sr. v.p., 1992-93; pres. Brim Sr. Living, Inc., Portland, 1993-97; sr. v.p. Encore Sr. Living, LLC, 1997—, also bd. dirs., exec. com.; bd. dirs. Brim Homestead, Inc., Portland, Dominican Life Care Svcs., Portland, Belmar, Inc., Portland, also v.p. 1989—; pres. Care Mgmt., Inc., A Fla. Employee Leasing Corp., 1991—; developer Alzheimer patients care and housing program, 1993—. Cpl. USMC, 1969-71. Republican. Lutheran. Avocations: ice hockey, coaching basketball, baseballand hockey. Home: 12620 SE Callahan Rd Portland OR 97236-6165 Office: Brim Inc 305 NE 102nd Ave Portland OR 97220-4199

MCDANIEL, ROGER D., electrical company executive. Pres., CEO Integrated Process Equipment, San Jose, Calif. Office: Integrated Process Equipment 911 Bern Ct Ste 110 San Jose CA 95112-1236*

MCDAVID, DOUGLAS WARREN, systems consultant; b. San Francisco, Feb. 25, 1947; s. James Etheridge and Elizabeth Rae (Warren) McD.; m. Nancy Kathleen Somers, June 1968 (div. 1982); 1 child, Amy Kemp; m. Carleen Ann Richmond, Feb. 14, 1987; 1 child, Amanda Claire. BA in Sociology, U. Calif., Santa Cruz, 1969; MA in Libr. Sci., San Jose State U., 1972. Libr. Palo Alto (Calif.) City Libr., 1969-81; systems analyst Tymnet (Tymshare), Cupertino, Calif., 1981-84; mgr. systems architecture Tymnet McDonnell Douglas, San Jose, Calif., 1984-86; data modeling cons. Fireman's Fund Ins., Terra Linda, Calif., 1986-87, Bank of Calif., San Francisco, 1988; systems cons. Pacific Bell, San Ramon, Calif., 1989-93; prin. Integrated Info., 1994—; dir. Computer Resources Group, San Francisco; spkr. Entity/Relationship Conf. Internat., Burlingame, Calif., 1991, DAMA Internat. Conf., 1994—; sr. cons. in bus. semantic modeling for object oriented applications IBM Corp., 1994—; 1996 spkr. Bus. Rules Conf. OOPSLA, IBM Object Technology Conf., Ind. Labor & Mgmt. Coun. Assoc. editor: Handbook of Object Technology. Mem. IEEE, Assn. for Computing Machinery, Data Adminstrn. Mgmt. Assn. (San Francisco bd. dirs. 1987-91, Sacramento bd. dirs. 1992, speaker 1991, 92), Data Processing Mgmt. Assn. (speaker 1992), Am. Assn. Artificial Intelligence (speaker 1993). Avocations: golf, gardening, creative writing, investing, swimming. Home and Office: 8611 Kingslynn Ct Elk Grove CA 95624-3135

MCDERMOTT, DAVID (JOHN), artist, writer, photographer; b. Wrangell, Alaska, Apr. 8, 1958; s. A.W. and Margaret (Price) McD.; m. Rebeca Reyna, Dec. 29, 1978; children: Amy, Rachel, Kelly. Student, Seattle Pacific Coll., 1976-77. Nat. registered and cert. emergency med. technician; cert. instr. NRA; lic. 3rd class boiler operator. Pres., owner Mut. Devel. Co., Ketchikan, 1980—; facitlities supr. U. Alaska, 1995—; fireman, emergency med. technician Ketchikan Vol. Fire Dept., 1989-91; contbg. cons. bodybldg. books and mags., 1986—; feature article Musclemag Internat. mag., 1990. Artist ltd. edit. art print series, 1977—. Recipient Expert Rifleman award U.S. Govt., 1973, 1st, 2d & 3d Profl. Painting prizes Arts Guild Show, 1995. Mem. NEA (del. state/nat. governing assemblies), Ketchikan Edn. Assn. (exec. bd. 1992-94, pres. 1994—), Nat. Assn. EMTs, Nat. Soc. EMT-Paramedics, Nat. Soc. EMS Adminstrs., Soc. EMT Tech. Instr./Coords. Avocations: weightlifting, motorcycling, target shooting. Home: 620

Anderson Dr Ketchikan AK 99901-5404 Office: Mut Devel Co 627 Carlanna Ketchikan AK 99901-5620

MCDERMOTT, JAMES A., congressman, psychiatrist; b. Chicago, Ill., Dec. 28, 1936; children: Katherine, James. BS, Wheaton Coll., 1958; MD, U. Ill., 1963. Intern Buffalo Gen. Hosp., 1963-64; resident in adult psychiatry U. Ill. Hosps., Chgo., 1964-66; resident in child psychiatry U. Wash. Hosps., Seattle, 1966-68; asst. clin. prof. dept. psychiatry U. Wash., Seattle, 1970-83; mem. Wash. Ho. of Reps., 1971-72, Wash. Senate, 1975-87; regional med. officer U.S. Fgn. Svc., 1987-88; mem. 101st-106th Congresses from 7th Wash. dist., 1989—; former chmn. standards of ofcl. conduct com. 101st-105th Congresses from 7th Wash. dist., mem. ways and means com., budget com.; mem. exec. and edn. com. Nat. Conf. State Legislatures, chair ethics com. Mem. Wash. State Arts Commn., Wash. Coun. for Prevention Child Abuse and Neglect; Dem. nominee for gov., 1980. Lt. comdr. M.C., USN, 1968-70. Mem. Am. Psychiat. Assn., Wash. State Med. Assn., King County Med. Soc. Democrat. Episcopalian. Office: US Ho of Reps 2349 Rayburn HOB Washington DC 20515-4707*

MCDEVITT, CHARLES FRANCIS, state supreme court justice; b. Pocatello, Idaho, Jan. 5, 1932; s. Bernard A. and Margaret (Hermann) McD.; m. Virginia L. Heller, Aug. 14, 1954; children: Eileen A., Kathryn A., Brian A., Sheila A., Terrence A., Neil A., Kendal A. LLB, U. Idaho, 1956. Bar: Idaho 1956. Ptnr. Richards, Haga & Eberle, Boise, 1956-62; gen. counsel, asst. sec. Boise Cascade Corp., 1962-65; mem. Idaho State Legislature, 1963-66; sec., gen. counsel Boise Cascade Corp., 1965-67, v.p. sec., 1967-68; pres. Beck Industries, 1968-70; group v.p. Singer Co., N.Y.C., 1970-72, exec. v.p., 1973-76; pub. defender Ada County, Boise, 1976-78; co-founder Givens, McDevitt, Pursley & Webb, Boise, 1978-89; justice Idaho Supreme Ct., Boise, 1989-97, chief justice, 1993-97; ptnr., founder McDevitt & Miller, LLP, Boise, 1997—; served on Gov.'s Select Com. on Taxation, Boise, 1988-89; mem. State Select Com. on Campaign Ethics and Campaign Finances, State Select Com. on Legis. Compensation. Home: 4940 Boise River Ln Boise ID 83706-5706 Office: McDevitt & Miller LLP 537 W Bannock St Ste 215 Boise ID 83702-5968

MCDONALD, ALAN ANGUS, federal judge; b. Harrah, Wash., Dec. 13, 1927; s. Angus and Nell (Britt) McD.; m. Ruby K., Aug. 22, 1949; children: Janelle Jo, Saralee Sue, Stacy. BS, U. Wash., 1950, LLB, 1952. Dep. pros. atty. Yakima County, Wash., 1952-54; assoc. Halverson & Applegate, Yakima, 1954-56; ptnr. Halverson, Applegate & McDonald, Yakima, 1956-85; judge U.S. Dist. Ct. (ea. dist.) Wash., Yakima, 1985-95, sr. judge, 1995—. Fellow Am. Coll. Trial Lawyers; Yakima C. of C. (bd. dirs.). Clubs: Yakima Country, Royal Duck (Yakima). Office: US Dist Ct PO Box 2706 Yakima WA 98907-2706

MCDONALD, CRAYDON DEAN, psychologist; b. Denver, Dec. 22, 1946; s. Donald D. and Irene (Dunlavy) McD.; m. Laurie Weston, Dec. 4, 1982; children: Ian, Brendan, Tavis, Morgaine. *Eighth generation descendant of Andrew McDonald who emigrated from Scotland to what is now called West Virginia following the Battle of Culloden. Father Donald D. (02.07.21-06.11.80) fought as a US Marine in 21 battles culminating in Black Hill, Iwo Jima Volcanic Islands. Spouse, Laurie Weston, MD (10.04.51-), is Board-certified in Adult (ABPN), Adolescent (ABAP), and Geriatric (ABPN subspecialty) Psychiatry. The children attend a Waldorf School. As a family, plans are being made for a circumnavigation with a 60' sloop in 2004. Craydon's extra time is currently invested in writing a self-help trilogy.* BFA, Parsons Sch. Design, N.Y.C., 1970; MDiv cum laude, St. Paul Sch. Theology, Kansas City, Mo., 1979; D of Ministry, Wesley Theol. Sem., Washington, 1982; PhD, Boston U., 1987. Diplomate Am. Bd. Profl. Psychology; lic. psychologist, Mass., Wis., Ill., Ariz.; approved supr. Am. Assn. Marriage & Family Therapy; ordained to ministry United Meth. Ch., 1982. Psychologist Worcester (Mass.) Pastoral Counseling Ctr., 1982-87; assoc. prof., asst. program dir. Loyola U., Chgo., 1987-88; clin. psychologist Lake Geneva, Wis., 1987-93; psychology faculty No. Ariz. U., 1993—; chief psychologist Drs. McDonald, Weston & Assocs., 1982—; examiner Am. Bd. Profl. Psychology. Author: Personality and Cognitive Theology, 1982, Type A Coronary Prone Behavior and Narcissism, 1987. Fellow The Acad. Family Psychology (bd. dirs.); mem. APA (program com. divsn. 43), Human Factors Soc., Am. Assn. Pastoral Counselors. Democrat. Home: 3115 W Tina Ln Flagstaff AZ 86001-0926 Office: Ste C 1100 N San Francisco St Flagstaff AZ 86001-3260

MCDONALD, DOUGLAS ROBERT, non profit agency executive; b. San Francisco, May 27, 1949; s. Robert Angus and Shirley Anne (Beine) McD.; m. Karen Bachanas, June 24, 1978; children: Jennifer, Cameron. AB, Stanford Univ., 1971; MBA, Santa Clara Univ., 1974. Dist. exec. Boy Scouts Am., San Mateo, Calif., 1971-74; exec. Boy Scouts Am., Palo Alto, Calif., 1974-76; regional sales mgr. Baron Data Systems, San Leandro, Calif., 1976-81; field dir./COO Boy Scouts Am., San Mateo, Calif., 1981-86; assoc. reg. dir. Boy Scouts Am., Sunnyvale, Calif., 1986-88; Scout exec./CEO Boy Scouts Am., Stockton, Calif., 1988-92; scout exec./CEO Boy Scouts Am., San Jose, Calif., 1992—. Recipient Paul Harris fellow Rotary Internat., 1990, James E. West fellow Boy Scouts Am., 1993. Mem. Nat. Soc. Fund Raising Execs., Sigma Alpha Epsilon, Alpha Phi Omega, Silicon Valley Planned Giving Coun., Rotary Internat. Republican. Roman Catholic. Avocations: travel, computers, investments. Office: Boy Scouts Am PO Box 28547 San Jose CA 95159-8547

MCDONALD, HENRY (HARRY MCDONALD), research center administrator; b. Glasgow, Scotland, Jan. 24, 1937; came to U.S., 1965, naturalized U.S. citizen.; m. June McDonald; 3 children. BS in Aero. Engring., U. Glasgow, 1960, DEng, 1985, hon. degree, 1997. Supr. wind tunnel testing Brit. Aircraft Corp., Wharton, Eng., 1960-65; rsch. engr. United Techs. Rsch. Ctr., East Hartford, Conn., 1965-76; founder pres., CEO, Sci. Rsch. Assocs. Inc., Glastonbury, Conn., 1976-92; prof. mech. engring. Pa. State U., State College, 1991-96, asst. dir. computational scis. Applied Rsch. Lab., 1991-96; dir. NASA Ames Rsch. Ctr., Moffett Field, Calif., 1996—; former mem. adv. panels in aero. field. Contbr. numerous articles on aero. R & D to sci. jours. Former mem. RAF Res. Co-recipient Small Businessman of Yr. award for high tech. State of Conn. Mem. aero. assns. Achievements include co-patentee of novel ultra-high frequency ventilator providing life support to critically ill patients suffering from adult respiratory distress syndrome; research on heat transfer and gas dynamics relative to aircraft engine performance and design. Avocation: sailing. Office: NASA Ames Rsch Ctr Office Dir Mail Stop 200 Moffett Field CA 94035-1000*

MCDONALD, JAMES JOHN, JR., lawyer; b. Cin., Feb. 15, 1960; s. James J. and Mary P. (Sweeney) McD. BA, New Coll. USF, 1981; JD, Georgetown U., 1984. Bar: Ga. 1984, Calif. 1990, U.S. Ct. Appeals (5th, 9th and 11th cirs.) 1985, U.S. Dist. Ct. (2nd, 7th dist.). Assoc. Fisher & Phillips, Atlanta, 1984-90, ptnr., 1990—; editor: Mental and Emotional Injuries in Employment Litigation (Bur. of Nat. Affairs), 1994; editl. bd.: Employee Relations Law Jour., N.Y., 1994—. Contbr. articles to ednl. publs. Mem. ABA, Am. Psychol. Assn., Am. Coll. Forensic Psychiatry. Republican. Avocations: photography, sailing. Office: Fisher & Phillips 4675 Macarthur Ct Ste 550 Newport Beach CA 92660-8836

MCDONALD, JOHN N., JR., retired reporter, copy editor, consultant; b. Long Beach, Calif., Oct. 8, 1923; s. John N. and Elizabeth A. (Henzler) McD.; m. Maxine E. McDonald, Aug. 14, 1931; children: Stephen, Linda, Douglas, Terri. BA, San Diego State U., 1950. Sportswriter, copy editor San Diego Union, 1950-89; mktg. dir. San Diego Auto Mus., 1991-94; radio, TV coord. Los Angeles County Fair, Pomona, Calif., 1982-91; asst. pub. rels. dir. Del Mar (Calif.) Fair, 1955-59, 77-81; pub. rels. dir. Nat. Date Festival, Indio, Calif., 1983-85, Calif. Midwinter Fair, Imperial, 1982-85; cons. Hall Champions Mus., San Diego, 1996-98; cons. pub. rels. Del Mar Motorcycle Races, 1994-95; cons. mktg. Antique Auto Races, San Diego, 1989-92; promoter Demolition Derbies, San Bernadino, Calif., 1985-90. Author: Under the Green, 1978; co-author, editor: Green Dragons, 1998. Yeoman 1st class USN, 1942-47. Mem. Am. Auto Racing Writers/Broadcasters (pres. 1970-73, bd. mem.), San Diego Press Club, Sigma Delta Chi. Avocations: writing, gardening. Home: 7266 Horner St San Diego CA 92120-1915

MCDONALD, JOSEPH LEE, insurance broker; b. Bremerton, Wash., Aug. 15, 1931; s. Joseph Okane and Ida Elizabeth (Finholm) McD.; m. Glorietta Maness, Jan. 22, 1954 (dec. 1984); children: Holly Ann Chaffin, Andrew Lee McDonald; m. Beverly Mae Falkner, June 22, 1986. BS, U. Wash., 1954. Various mgmt. positions AT&T, 1956-62; broker, ptnr. McDonald & McGarry Co., Seattle, 1962-84; ptnr., exec. McDonald Ins. Group, Kirkland, Wash., 1984—; v.p., bd. dirs. Chimayo Inc., Seattle, 1990-94, Santa Fe Food Corp., Seattle, 1991-96. City councilman City of Bellevue, 1971-75; commr. Water Dist. #97, Bellevue, 1967-71, Lake Hills Sewer Dist., Bellevue, 1965-71; pres. Wash. State Assn. of Sewer Dists., Seattle, 1969. With U.S. Army, 1954-56. Mem. Coll. Club of Seattle, Overlake Golf and Country Club, Western Assn. of Ins. Brokers, Ind. Ins. Agts. Assn., Seattle Master Builders Assn., Nat. Wildlife Fedn., Nature Conservancy, Apt. Assn. of Seattle and King County, Roche Harbor Yacht Club, Chi Phi. Avocations: skiing, sailing, tennis. Home: 7235 91st Pl SE Mercer Island WA 98040-5803 Office: McDonald Ins Group 416 6th St S Kirkland WA 98033-6718

MCDONALD, MARIANNE, classicist; b. Chgo., Jan. 2, 1937; d. Eugene Francis and Inez (Riddle) McD.; children: Eugene, Conrad, Bryan, Bridget, Kirstie (dec.), Hiroshi. BA magna cum laude, Bryn Mawr Coll., 1958; MA, U. Chgo., 1960; PhD, U. Calif., Irvine, 1975, doctorate (hon.) Am. Coll. Greece, 1988, hon. diploma Am. Archaeological Assn. Teaching asst. classics U. Calif., Irvine, 1974, D Litt (hon.) U. Athens, Greece, 1994, U. Dublin, 1994, Aristotle U., U. Thessalonika, 1997. instr. Greek, Latin and English, mythology, modern cinema, 1975-79, founder, rsch. fellow Thesaurus Linguae Graecae Project, 1975-97; bd. dir. Centrum. Bd. dirs. Am. Coll. of Greece, 1981-90, Scripps Hosp., 1981; Am. Sch. Classical Studies, 1986—; mem. bd. overseers U. Calif. San Diego, 1985—; nat. bd. advisors Am. Biog. Inst., 1982—; pres. Soc. for the Preservation of the Greek Heritage, 1990—; founder Hajime Mori Chair for Japanese Studies, U. Calif., San Diego, 1985, McDonald Ctr. for Alcohol and Substance Abuse, 1984, Thesaurus Linguarum Hiberniae, 1991—; vis. prof. U. Dublin, 1990—, U. Ulster, Ireland, 1997; adj. prof. theatre U. Calif., San Diego, 1990, prof. theatre and classics, 1994 . Recipient Ellen Browning Scripps Humanitarian award, 1975; Disting. Svc. award U. Calif.-Irvine, 1982, Irvine medal, 1987, 3rd Prize Midwest Poetry Ctr. Contest, 1987; named one of the Community Leaders Am., 1979-80, Philanthropist of Yr., 1985, Headliner San Diego Press Club, 1985, Philanthropist of Yr. Honorary Nat. Conf. Christians and Jews, 1986, Woman of Distinction Salvation Army, 1986, Eleventh Woman Living Legacy, 1986, Woman of Yr. AHEPA, 1988, San Diego Woman of Distinction, 1990, Woman of Yr. AXIOS, 1991; recipient Bravissimo gold medal San Diego Opera, 1990, Gold Medal Soc. Internationalization of Greek Lang., 1990, Athens medal, 1991, Piraeus medal, 1991, award Desmoi, 1992, award Hellenic Assn of Univ. Women, 1992, Academy of Achievement award AHEPA, 1992, Woman of Delphi award European Cultural Ctr. Delphi, 1992, Civis Universitatis award U. Calif. San Diego, 1993, Hypatia award Hellenic U. Women, 1993, Am.-Ireland Fund Heritage award, 1994, Contribution to Greek Letters award Aristotle U. Thessaloniki, 1994, Mirabella Mag. Readers Choice One of 1000 Women for the Nineties, 1994, Order of the Phoenix, Greece, 1994, citations from U.S. Congress and Calif. Senate, Alexander the Gt. award Hellenic Cultural Soc., 1995, made hon. citizen of Delphi and gold medal of the Amphiktuonon, Delphi, Greece, 1995, award European Cultural Ctr. of Delphi, 1995, Women Who Mean Bus. award for Fine Arts San Diego Bus. Jour., 1995. Vol. of Decade Women's International Ctr., 1994, 96, Gold Star award San Diego Arts League, 1997. Mem. MLA, AAUP, Am. Philol. Assn., Soc. for the Preservation of the Greek Heritage (pres.), Libr. of Am., Am. Classical League, Philol. Assn. Pacific Coast, Am. Comparative Lit. Assn., Modern and Classical Lang. Assn. So. Calif., Hellenic Soc., Calif. Fgn. Lang. Tchrs. Assn., Internat. Platform Assn., Greek Language Found., Royal Irish Acad., Greece's Order of the Phoenix (commdr. 1994), KPBS Producers Club, Hellenic Univ. Club (bd. dir.). Author: Terms for Happiness in Euripides, 1978, Semilemmatized Concordances to Euripides' Alcestis, 1977, Cyclops, Andromache, Medea, 1978, Heraclidae, Hippolytus, 1979, Hecuba, 1984, Hercules Furens, 1984, Electra, 1984, Ion, 1985, Trojan Women, 1988, Iphigenia in Taurus, 1988, Euripides in Cinema: The Heart Made Visible, 1983; translator: The Cost of Kindness and Other Fabulous Tales (Shinichi Hoshi), 1986, (chpt.) Views of Clytemnestra, Ancient and Modern, 1990, Classics and Cinema, 1990, Modern Critical Theory and Classical Literature, 1994, A Challenge to Democracy, 1994, Ancient Sun/Modern Light: Greek Drama on the Modern Stage, 1990, Star Myths: Tales of the Constellations, 1996; contbr. numerous articles to profl. jours. Avocations: karate, harp (medieval), skiing, diving. Home: PO Box 929 Rancho Santa Fe CA 92067-0929 Office: U Calif at San Diego Dept Theatre La Jolla CA 92093

MCDONALD, MARY KATHLEEN, secondary anatomy and physiology educator; b. Hays, Kans., May 5, 1947; d. Isidore and Adolphine (Gabel) Pfannenstiel; m. Thomas Robert McDonald, Mar. 6, 1970; children: Michael, Patrick. BS in Gen. Sci., Ft. Hays U., 1969; cert. secondary edn., Grand Canyon U., Phoenix, 1986; MEd in Adminstrn., Ariz. State U., 1991. Cert. med. technologist; cert. secondary sci. tchr., adminstr., cmty. coll. tchr. Med. technologist Luth. Med. Ctr., Wheatridge, Colo., 1974-84, Good Samaritan Hosp., Phoenix, 1984-85; sci. tchr. Fremont Jr. H.S., Mesa, Ariz., 1986-96, chairperson sci. dept., 1986-96; tchr. Rio Salado C.C., 1996; tchr. advanced placement anatomy and physiology Westwood H.S., Mesa Pub. Schs., 1996—; mem. sch. adv. com., chairperson student behavior com. Westwood H.S., Mesa Pub. Schs.; mem. educator selection com, mentor program, portfolio writing com. Career Ladder Program, Mesa Pub. Schs., 1987-93; mem. dist. AIDS Com., Mesa Pub. Schs., 1994-95, parent adv. coun., 1996-97. Commr., den leader, com. chairperson Boy Scouts, Arvada, Colo., 1979-83. Mem. NEA, Mesa Edn. Assn.

MCDONALD, ROSCOE, JR., minister, artist, writer; b. Ft. Worth, Sept. 11, 1947; s. Roscoe Sr. and Jennie May (Garlend) McD.; m. JoAann K. Fields, Feb. 28, 1969 (div. Feb. 1985); children: Lavord D., Muhammad A., Davion D. Student, Riverside Jr. Coll., L.A., 1970-72, L.A. C.C., 1973-75, Calif. State U., L.A., 1978-80. 1st v.p. NAACP, Lancaster, Calif., 1985-86; asst. pastor Whosoever Will Christian Ch., Palmdale, Calif., 1986-94, First Bapt., Lillerock, Calif., 1986-94; founder Ministry for Youth of Am. Broadcasting Network, Dallas, 1994—; amb. Promise Keepers Men's Ministry, Littlerock, Calif., 1996-97; sales rep. Sprint Phone Co., 1986-94. With U.S. Army, 1968-70. Mem. So. Calif. Gospel Announcers Assn. Avocations: writing, reading, singing, track and field. Home: 37562 115th E Littlerock CA 93543

MCDONALD, THOMAS EDWIN, JR., electrical engineer; b. Wapanucka, Okla., June 19, 1939; s. Thomas Edwin and Rosamond Bell (Enoch) McD.; m. Myrna Kay Booth, Sept. 10, 1961; children: Stephen Thomas, Jennifer Kay, Sarah Lynn. BSEE, U. Okla., 1962, MSEE, 1963; PhDEE, U. Colo., 1969. Registered profl. engr., N.Mex. Asst. prof. elec. engring. U. Okla., Norman, 1969-70; planning engr. Okla. Gas and Electric Co., Oklahoma City, 1970-72; staff mem. Los Alamos (N.Mex.) Nat. Lab., 1972—, group leader, 1974-80, program mgr., 1980-92; program mgr. Centurion program Los Alamos (N.Mex.) Nat. Lab., Los Alamos, 1986-90; dep. program dir. inertial confinement fusion program Los Alamos (N.Mex.) Nat. Lab., 1990-92, program coord. mine detection and laser tech., 1992-93; project mgr. Nat. Ctr. for Advanced Mfg. Tech., 1993-96, project leader high-speed electronic imaging tech. devel., 1996—; adj. prof. elec. engring. U. Okla., 1970-72; cons. Los Alamos Tech. Assocs., 1980—, mgr. design sect., 1980-81. Rschr. in inertial confinement fusion, high-speed electronic imaging and neutron radiography; contbr. articles to profl. jours. Bd. dirs., mem. United Ch. Los Alamos, 1987— (chmn. fin. bd.), chmn. bd. elders, 1992. Served to capt. U.S. Army, 1963-67. Mem. IEEE (chmn. Los Alamos sect.), AAAS, Soc. for Info. Display, Soc. Photo-Optical Instrumentation Engrs., Los Alamos Gymnastics Club (treas., bd. dirs. 1980-88), Rotary (sec. Los Alamos, pres. 1999), Sigma Xi, Eta Kappa Nu. Republican. Avocation: computer science. Home: 4200 Ridgeway Dr Los Alamos NM 87544-1956 Office: Los Alamos Nat Lab PO Box 1663 Los Alamos NM 87544-0600

MCDONALD, TIM, professional football player; b. Fresno, Calif., Jan. 6, 1965. Student, U. So. Calif. With St. Louis Cardinals, 1987; safety Phoenix Cardinals (formerly St. Louis Cardinals), 1988-92; with S.F. 49ers, 1993—. Named defense back The Sporting News All-America team, 1985. Played in Pro Bowl, 1989, 1991, 92, 93. Office: San Francisco 49ers 3Com Park at Candlestick Pt 4949 Centennial Blvd Santa Clara CA 95054-1229*

MCDONNELL, JOSEPH ANTHONY, sculptor, critic; b. Detroit, Oct. 20, 1936; s. William Francis and Virginia (Kirchner) McD.; children—Elizabeth Drew, Julia, Elena, Sophia. B.F.A., U. Notre Dame, 1958, M.F.A., 1959; postgrad. Accademeia Belli Arte-Florence-Italy, 1961. Faculty, Coll. New Rochelle, N.Y., 1982-83; assoc. editor, critic Art World, N.Y.C., 1984—; sculptor fountain: Homage to Great Lakes, Milw. Pub. Mus., 1965, Solar Disc II, 1984, Tallyrand Bldgs., Tarrytown, N.Y., Stele I, Irving, Tex., 1983; exhibitions: Andre Emmeich Gallery, N.Y., 1993-95, Maxwell Davidson Gallery, N.Y., 1994-98, Nardin Gallery, N.Y., 1997; collections: Snite Museum U. Notre Dame, Museum of Permian Basin, Midland, Tex., U. Mich. Museum, Dearborn, Bruce Museum, Stamford, Conn. Recipient award as artist improving environment, HUD, 1972. Mem. Sculptors Guild, Club: Century Assocs. Home: 946 Federal Ave E Seattle WA 98102-4531

MCDONOUGH, RUSSELL CHARLES, retired state supreme court justice; b. Glendive, Mont., Dec. 7, 1924; s. Roy James and Elsie Marie (Johnson) McD.; m. Dora Jean Bidwell, Mar. 17, 1946; children: Ann Remmich, Michael, Kay Jensen, Kevin, Daniel, Mary Garfield. JD, George Washington U., 1949. Bar: Mont. 1950. Pvt. practice Glendive, Mont., 1950-83; judge Gen. Jurisdiction State of Montana, Glendive, 1983-87; justice Mont. Supreme Ct., Helena, 1987-93, ret., 1993. City atty. City of Glendive, 1953-57; county atty. Dawson County, Mon., 1957-63; del. Mont. Constl. Conv., Helena, 1972. 1st lt. AC, U.S. Army, 1943-45, ETO. Decorated DFC. Mem. Mont. Bar Assn. Roman Catholic. Home: 1805 Joslyn St Trlr 131 Helena MT 59601-0158

MCDOUGALL, JACQUELYN MARIE HORAN, therapist; b. Wenatchee, Wash., Sept. 24, 1924; d. John Rankin and Helen Frampton (Vandivort) Horan; m. Robert Duncan McDougall, Jan. 24, 1947 (div. July 1976); children: Douglas, Stuart, Scott. BA, Wash. State U., 1946. Lic. therapist, Wash.; cert. nat. addiction counselor II. Pres. oper. bd. Ctr. for Alcohol/Drug Treatment, Wenatchee, 1983-85; sec. Wash. State Coun. on Alcoholism, 1988-89, supr. out-patient svcs., 1989-90. Treas. Allied Arts, Wenatchee, 1984; pres. Rep. Women, Wash., 1969-70.

MCDOWELL, JENNIFER, sociologist, composer, playwright, publisher; b. Albuquerque; d. Willard A. and Margaret Frances (Garrison) McD.; m. Milton Loventhal, July 2, 1973. BA, U. Calif., 1957; MA, San Diego State U., 1958; postgrad., Sorbonne, Paris, 1959; MLS, U. Calif., 1963; PhD, U. Oreg., 1973. Tchr. English Abraham Lincoln H.S., San Jose, Calif., 1960-61; free-lance editor Soviet field, Berkeley, Calif., 1961-63; rsch. asst. sociology U. Oreg., Eugene, 1964-66; editor, pub. Merlin Papers, San Jose, 1969—, Merlin Press, San Jose, 1973—; rsch. cons. sociology San Jose, 1973—; music pub. Lipstick and Toy Balloons Pub. Co., San Jose, 1978—; composer Paramount Pictures, 1982-88, Lipstick and Toy Balloons Music, 1998—; tchr. writing workshops; poetry readings, 1969-73; co-producer radio show lit. and culture Sta. KALX, Berkeley, 1971-72. Author: (with Milton Loventhal) Black Politics: A Study and Annotated Bibliography of the Mississippi Freedom Democratic Party, 1971 (featured at Smithsonian Inst. Spl. Event 1992), Contemporary Women Poets, 1977, Ronnie Goose Rhymes for Grown-Ups, 1984; co-author: (plays off-off Broadway) Betsy and Phyllis, 1986, Mack the Knife Your Friendly Dentist, 1986, The Estrogen Party To End War, 1986, The Oatmeal Party Comes To Order, 1986, (plays) Betsy Meets the Wacky Iraqui, 1991, Bella and Phyllis, 1994; contbr. poems, plays, essays, articles, short stories, and book revs. to lit. mags., news mags. and anthologies; rschr. women's autobiog. writings, contemporary writing in poetry, Soviet studies, civil rights movement, and George Orwell, 1962—; writer: (songs) Money Makes a Woman Free, 1976, 3 songs featured in Parade of Am. Music; co-creator mus. comedy Russia's Secret Plot To Take Back Alaska, 1988, Intern Girl, 1998. Recipient 8 awards Am. Song Festival, 1976-79, Bill Casey Award in Letters, 1980; doctoral fellow AAUW, 1971-73; grantee Calif. Arts Coun., 1976-77. Mem. Am. Assn. for Advancement of Slavic Studies, Soc. Sci. Study of Religion, No. Calif. Songwriters Assn., Am. Sociol. Assn., Dramatists Guild, Phi Beta Kappa, Sigma Alpha Iota, Beta Phi Mu, Kappa Kappa Gamma. Democrat. Office: care Merlin Press PO Box 5602 San Jose CA 95150-5602

MCDOWELL, MARCIA ANN, security professional; b. Toronto, Ont., Can., May 14, 1956; came to U.S., 1956; d. William James and Thelma Rose (Smith) McD. BS, Thomas A. Edison State Coll., 1993, postgrad., U. Phoenix, 1996—. Provincial constable Ont. (Can.) Provincial Police; spl. svcs. officer Ann Arbor (Mich.) City Police; profl. dealer Bicycle Club Casino, Bell Gardens, Calif.; owner, instr. Gold Coast Sch. Dealing, Downey, Calif.; instr. C.C. South Nev., Las Vegas; surveillance specialist Sahara Hotel & Casino, Las Vegas; lectr. in field. Author: Techniques of Casino Surveillance, 1995, Signature Bets-A Guide to Recognizing Roulette Advantage Play, 1996. Recipient Arnold Fletcher award Thomas A. Edison State Coll., Trenton, N.J., 1993. Mem. Am. Mgmt. Assn. Avocations: paleoanthropology, paleobiology, music, gardening.

MCDOWELL, RICHARD LOUIS, university administrator, management educator; b. Battle Creek, Mich., Oct. 22, 1938; s. Louis Dwight and Jane (Shoults) M.; m. Sally Bray, June 12, 1971 (dec. July 1997); children: Katherine Elizabeth, James Scott, Megan Sue. SB, MIT, 1960, SM, 1966; PhD, Tufts U., 1974. Asst. dir., dir. Boston Area Seminar for Internat. Students, 1963-71 summers; asst. to Dean Student Affairs and Admissions MIT, Cambridge, 1960-66; teaching and rsch. asst. polit. sci. Tufts U., Medford, Mass., 1966-68; instr. Bentley Coll., Waltham, Mass., 1968-70; asst. prof. govt. Bentley Coll., Waltham, 1970-73; assoc. prof. pub. adminstrn. Suffolk U., Boston, 1973-74, dean and prof. bus. and pub. adminstrn. Sch. of Mgmt., 1974-91; dean, prof. Sch. Bus. and Econs. Chapman U., Orange, Calif., 1991—; bd. dirs. South Boston Savs. Bank, Boston Bancorp, Orange County Forum Family Solutions. Sect. chmn. United Way, Boston, 1982-84, 86; mem. adv. com. to Sec. of Elder Affairs, Commonwealth of Mass., Boston, 1962-86; bd. dirs. Mass Halfway Housese, Inc., Boston, 1984-91, Orange County Forum, 1992—, Family Solutions, 1993—. Mem. Am. Soc. Pub. Adminstrn. (nat. coun. 1977-80), Am. Assembly Coll. Schs. of Bus. (bd. dirs. 1987-89), Nat. Assn. Schs. Pub. Affairs and Adminstrn. (exec. com. 1979-81). E-mail: rlm2727@aol.com. Home: 27 E Yale Loop Irvine CA 92604-3365 Office: Chapman Univ Orange CA 92666-1032

MCDOWELL, ROBERT MICHAEL, management consultant; b. Dubuque, Iowa, Mar. 19, 1961; s. James Patrick and Barbara Jean (Bradley) McD. BS in Indsl. Engring., Iowa State U., 1983. Indsl. engr. 3M Corp., Knoxville, Iowa, 1984-86; chief exec. officer, pres. McDowell Enterprises, Cudahy, Wis., 1986—; pres., chief exec. officer McAid, Ltd., Cudahy, 1986—; cons. McGraw-Edison, Milw., 1987—. Advisor Knoxville Jr. Achievement, 1984, v.p. 1985; active Ams. for Legal Reform. Recipient Citizenship award ABA, 1979. Mem. Inst. Indsl. Engrs. Avocation: reading. Home and Office: PO Box 54307 Phoenix AZ 85078-4307

MCDOWELL, RONALD WILES, artist; b. Geneva, N.Y., Feb. 26, 1956; s. Wiles Trime and Shirley Dell (Williams) McD.; m. Sheila Mae Murphy, June 15, 1974; children: Nichorai Winston, Amethyst Tierra. Grad., Central H.S., Cheyenne, Wyo., 1974. Invited isntr. Art Students League, Denver, 1995. Exhibited in one-man show at Am. Nat. Bank, Cheyenne, 1972; group shows include N.Mex. Tapestry, Albuquerque, 1983, Art USA, Colo., 1986, New West Show, Indpls., 1990, Gov.;s Invitational, Loveland, Colo., 1990, Miniatures-N.Mex. Art Mus., Albuquerque, 1990-97, Haley Meml. Libr. Show, Midland, Tex., 1996-98, others; pub. artist U. Tex., Tex. Tech U.; contbg. artist: Best of Portrait Painting, 1998; subject of articles in Art of the West, Focus Santa Fe. Recipient numerous awards for art. Avocations: tennis, cake decorating. Office: PO Box 7612 Loveland CO 80537-0612

MCDOWELL, SHERRIE LORRAINE, secondary education educator; b. Manchester, Ky., Apr. 20, 1948; d. Alonzo and Madge Loudean (Christensen) Garrison; m. Gary Lynn McDowell, July 11, 1970; 1 child, Marc Ryan. BA, U. No. Colo., 1970; MA, Lesley Coll., 1989; postgrad., U. Wyo. Cert. tchr., Wyo. Tchr. English St. Mary's Cath. Sch., Cheyenne, Wyo., 1971-72; instr. homebound program Laramie County Sch. Dist., Cheyenne, 1978-84; English instr. Cen. High Sch., Cheyenne, 1984—; Wyo. coach Nat. Tournament of Acad. Excellence, 1988-90. Mem. NEA (Assembly rep. 1993-98, cadre trainer state level women's leadership tng. program 1995—), AAUW (sec. 1975-77), Wyo. Edn. Assn. (chair profl. standards and practices commn. 1995—, chair summer Inst. 1996—, co-chmn. local activities Read

Across Am.), Nat. Coun. Tchrs. English (recorder Boston Conv. 1996), Cheyenne Tchrs. Edn. Assn. (edn. assn. del. 1992—, chair instrnl. issues 1995, co-chair pub. rels. 1988-90, editor ACCENTS 1988-90, sec. 1995-96), Wyo. Assn. Tchrs. English (presenter), Wyo. Chautauqua Soc. (pres. 1985-86, bd. dirs. 1984-85), Delta Kappa Gamma (state scholarship chair 1989-90, pres. chpt. 1988-90). Home: 100 Grandview Ct Cheyenne WY 82009-4912 Office: Ctrl H S 5500 Education Dr Cheyenne WY 82009-4098

MCDOWELL, T.J. RIDER, pharmaceutical executive; b. Princeton, N.J., Sept. 15, 1960; s. S.H. and R.M. (Thoms) McD.; m. Victoria Cross Knight, July 27, 1991. Student, The Lawrenceville (N.J.) Sch., 1972-76, Art Student's League, N.Y.C., 1983-85. Investigative reporter Premiere Mag., N.Y.C., 1990's, Calif. Mag., L.A., 1990's, San Francisco Chronicle, 1990's; CEO, founder Knight-McDowell Labs., Carmel, Calif., 1995—. Author: Wimbledon, 1987 (Internat. Best Seller), The Mercy Man, 1988, Forest Hills, 1989; author, prodr. feature film: The Angel of Pennsylvania Avenue, 1996. Nat. screenwriting grantee Nat. Endowment for Arts, 1989. Mem. Chelsea Arts Club. Mem. Green Party. Avocations: tennis, sculpting, fox hunting. Office: Lake-McDowell Labs PO Box 2884 Carmel CA 93921-2884

MCEACHERN, SUSAN MARY, computer company executive; b. Royal Oak, Mich., May 3, 1960; d. Donald Keith and Lois Jean (Robison) McE.; m. James Paul Corbett, Jan. 8, 1983 (div. 1995). BS, Mich. State U., 1982; MBA, New Mex. State U., 1985. From acct. adminstr. trainee to acct. adminstr. IBM, El Paso, Tex., 1985-89; customer support rep. IBM, Southfield, Mich., 1989-90; sr. adminstrv. specialist IBM, Southfield, 1991-92, adv. customer support rep., 1992-93; fin. analyst IBM, Boulder, Colo., 1993-95, database adminstr., analyst, 1995, team leader, 1995—; cons. Integrated Sys. Solutions Co., Dallas, 1990-93. Author: Treasury of Poetry, 1992; editor-in-chief Online Newsletter for Polycystic Ovarian Syndrome Assn., 1998—; asst. editor Bull. for Nat. Polycystic Ovarian Syndrome Assn., 1998—; prin. flutist PSC Players, 1997—; profl. flutist Longmont-Boulder Players, 1996—. Vol. supr. Easter Seals, Southfield Mich., El Paso, Tex., 1978-88, Crisis Pregnancy, Las Cruces, New Mex., 1982-86, Multiple Sclerosis, Mich., 1983, Longmont (Colo.) Vol. Assn., 1994. Recipient Photography award Mich. State Fair, 1991, 92. Mem. IBM PC Club, Creative Designs (pres. 1994—, Nat. Sci. and Engring. vol. rep. 1994), Polycystic Ovarian Syndrome Assn. (pres. Colo. chpt. 1997—), Women of the Moose (chair health awareness 1998—). Avocations: computers, swimming, white-water rafting, photography, flute. Home: PO Box 6043 Longmont CO 80501-2077

MCELROY, LEO FRANCIS, communications consultant, journalist; b. Los Angeles, Oct. 12, 1932; s. Leo Francis and Helen Evelyn (Silliman) McE.; m. Dorothy Frances Montgomery, Nov. 3, 1956 (div. 1981); children: James, Maureen, Michael, Kathleen; m. Judith Marie Lewis, May 30, 1992. BS in English, Loyola U., L.A. 1953. News dir. KFI, KRLA, KABC Radio, L.A., 1964-72; pub. affairs host Sta. KCET, Pub. TV, L.A., 1967-74; v.p. Sta. KROQ AM/FM, L.A., 1972-74; polit. editor Sta. KABC-TV, L.A., 1974-81; pres. McElroy Communications, L.A. and Sacramento, 1981—; pres. sec. Lt. Gov.'s Office, Sacramento, 1982-84; chmn. Calif. AP Broadcasters, 1972-74; cons. State Office Migrant Edn., Sacramento, 1974, Californians for Water, L.A. , 1982, Calif. Water Protection Coun., Sacramento, 1982, Planning and Conservation League, Sacramento, 1984—, Common Cause, Sacramento, 1988—. Author: Uneasy Partners, 1984; author plays: Mermaid Tavern, 1956, To Bury Caesar (Christopher award 1952), 1952, Rocket to Olympus, 1960, The Code of Whiskey King, 1995. State del. Western Am. Assembly on Prison Reform, Berkeley, Calif., 1973; chmn. State Disaster Info. Task Force; Calif., 1973-74; campaign media cons. statewide issues, various candidates, Sacramento, L.A., 1981—; bd. dirs. Vols. in Victim Assistance, Sacramento, 1984, Rescue Alliance, Sacramento, 1987-92, Mental Health Assn., Sacramento, 1985-89, Leukemia Soc., 1992-97. Recipient Gabriel award Cath. Archdiocese, L.A., 1972, Golden Mike award Radio-TV News Assn., L.A., 1973; Hon. Resolution, Calif. State Assembly, Sacramento, 1981. Mem. ASCAP, AFTRA, Screen Actors Guild, Am. Assn. Polit. Cons. Mem. Reform Party. Roman Catholic. Home: 2262 Swarthmore Dr Sacramento CA 95825 Office: McElroy Comm 2410 K St Ste C Sacramento CA 95816-5002

MCELYEA, ULYSSES, JR., veterinarian; b. Ft. Collins, Colo., Oct. 29, 1941; s. Ulysses and Hazel (Hall) McE.; m. Rexanna Bell, Dec. 29, 1975 (div. 1980). BS in Pharmacy, U. N.Mex., 1963; DVM, Colorado State U., 1967, MS, 1968. Diplomate Am. Bd. Vet. Practicioners; cert. in companion animals. Owner Alta Vista Animal Clinic, Las Cruces, N.Mex., 1970—; bd. dirs. N.Mex. Acad. Vet. Practice, Albuquerque, bd. dirs. state of N.Mex. Bd. Vet. Examiners, v.p., 1988-98, vice chair, 1992, chair, 1992-96, Bank of the Rio Grande. Pres. Las Cruces Community Theater, 1974; founder, bd. dirs. Dona Ann Arts Coun., Las Cruces, 1976-80. Capt. U.S. Army, 1968-70. Mem. AVMA, Am. Pharm. Assn., Am. Assn. Feline Practitioners, Am. Soc. Vet. Ophthalmologists, N.Mex. Vet. Med. Assn. (bd. dirs. 1976-82), So. N.Mex. Vet. Assn. (pres. 1974, 84), N.Mex. State U. Athletic Assn. 9bd. dirs. 1976—, pres.-elect 1992-93, pres. 1993-94), N.Mex. State U. Pres.'s Assn. 9bd. dirs. 1988-91), U. N.Mex. Alumni Assn. (bd. dirs. 1976-80). Democrat. Home: 2635 Fairway Dr Las Cruces NM 88011-5044 Office: Alta Vista Animal Clinic 725 S Solano Dr Las Cruces NM 88001-3244

MCEUEN, JOHN, musician, guitarist. Formerly with Nitty Gritty Dirt Band; now solo artist. Author music scores for: The Good Ole Boys, An Actor's Life for Me, 1995, A Night in the Ozarks, The Music of the Wild West (Western Heritage award 1994, Internat. Film Festival Gold award 1994), The Man Outside, Wild and Crazy Guy, Comedy Is Not Pretty, Chuck's Country Lightning, Paint Your Wagon, For Singles Only, Badrock, Take It To The Limit, National Geographic's Braving Alaska (nominated Emmy 1993); recordings include Best of...String Wizard's Picks, String Wizards II (nominated Grammy 1992), String Wizards, Music of the Wild West, Will The Circle Be Unbroken, and 22 albums with Nitty Gritty Dirt Band (4 gold records, 20 hits); producer, writer, performer (music videos) Return to Dismal Swam;, Miner's Night Out; producer: John McEuen & Friends, Austin City Limits, Rocky Muntain Opry, Music of the Wild West, Against the Wind, Bluegrass Festival, Soundstage. Recipient Houston Film Festival Silver Star award, 1993, Internat. Film Festival Gold Best Special award 1994, Western Heritage Best Album award Cowboy Hall Fame, 1994; nominated: Grammy award String Wizards II, 1992, Emmy (score) Braving Alaska for National Geographic/PBS, 1993.

MCEVOY-JAMIL, PATRICIA ANN, English language educator; b. Butler, Pa., June 26, 1955; d. Joseph Lawrence McEvoy and Janet Ann (McConnell) Beier; m. M. Jamal Jamil, Nov. 23, 1977; 1 child, Amirah M. MA in TESOL, Monterey Inst. Internat. Studies, 1984; MA in English, Coll. Notre Dame, 1995; EdD, U. San Francisco, 1996. Calif. C.C. credential for life. Instr. ESL City Coll. San Francisco, 1989—, Canada Coll., Redwood City, Calif., 1989—; lectr. ESL Stanford (Calif.) U., 1989—, Coll. Notre Dame, Belmont, Calif., 1991—; presenter in field. Recipient ELITE Patron of Honor award ELITE Stanford (Calif.) Hosp., 1989, 90. Mem. Nat. Coun. Tchrs. English, Calif. Tchrs. English to Speakers of Other Langs., Phi Delta Kappa. Avocations: tennis, swimming, bicycling.

MCEWAN, ANGELA, court interpreter; b. L.A., Apr. 23, 1937; d. Louis and Edna VanZanten; m. Guillermo Patricio McEwan-Alvarado, Dec. 21, 1956; children: William, Carlos. BA in English, U. Mary Hardin-Baylor, Belton, Tex., 1972; MA in Spanish, U. Calif.-Irvine, 1976. Cert. ct. interpreter, Calif. Bilingual editor Doubleday Multimedia, Santa Ana, Calif., 1975-76, Nat. Multilingual, Multicultural Materials Devel. Ctr., Pomona, Calif., 1976-77; tchg. asst. in Spanish U. Calif., Irvine, 1973-76; ct. interpreter U.S. Dist. Ct., L.A., 1980—, L.A. Superior Ct., Long Beach, 1984—; tchr., translator Calif. State U., Long Beach, 1996; Spanish translator Transcultural Comm., Bloomfield, N.J., 1993—; guest lectr. UCLA, U. Calif.-San Diego, Calif. State U., Long Beach, 1994-96, mentor legal interpreting UCLA Ext., 1996; advisor translation program U. Calif.-Irvine Ext., 1997-98; cons./interpreter testing Coop. Pers. Svcs., Sacramento, 1989— Transl.: (books) Erotic Study/Estudio Erotico, 1996, Book of the XXXIX Steps, 1997 (Luz Bilingual prize 1997); author stories and essays in Spanish. Interpreter Olympic Organizing Com., L.A., 1984. Mem. Am. Lit. Translators Assn., PEN Ctr. West, Am. Translators Assn. (editl. com. Beacons 1997), Calif. Ct. Interpreters Assn. (L.A. chpt. vice chair 1989), Nat. Assn. of Judiciary Interpreters and Translators, Hispanics for L.A. Opera (adv. bd. 1995—). Avocations: travel, reading, gardening.

MCFADDEN, ROBERT CLYDE, real estate broker; b. Fullerton, Calif., Oct. 22, 1949; s. John W. and Beverly (Cross) McF.; m. Tina McFadden, Oct. 20, 1991 (div. Oct. 1995); children: Julie, Robert C., Carson, Shawnee. AA, Western Nev. C.C. Real estate broker Champions, Inc., Carson City, Nev., 1978—; mobile home dealer Champions, Inc., Carson City, 1985—. Restored 1862 St. Charles hotel across from Nev. capitol, 1995, Mills Mansion, 1998, home used in The Shootist, last John Wayne movie, 1991. Candidate for mayor of Carson City, 1992, 96. With U.S. Army, 1970-72. Mem. Nev. Art Mus., Nev. Mus., Nev. Hist. Soc. Republican. Achievements include donation of $30,000 to Va.-Truckee R.R. reconstruction; designing of 30-mile running trail around Carson City, 1996. Home: 500 Mountain St Carson City NV 89703-4158

MCFARLAND, DONALD JOE, hardware engineer; b. Oak Creek, Colo., Dec. 8, 1932; s. Donald Coleman McFarland and Barbara (Yirsa) Schwabe; m. Betty Irene Johnson, Nov. 17, 1951; children: Donald J. Jr., Diana D., Cheryl R. BSEE, Okla. State U., 1958. Elec. engr. Rockedyne divsn. N.Am. Aviation, Canoga Park, Calif., 1958-60; elec. engr. space and info. divsn. N.Am. Aviation, Lakewood, Calif., 1964-66; elec. engr. Lockheed Missile & Space, Van Nuys, Calif., 1960-64; sys. engr. Northrip Space Lab., Hawthorn, Calif., 1964-66; sr. elec. engr. MTS Jet Propulsion Lab., Pasadena, 1966—. Cpl. USMC, 1952-54. Achievements include design and testing of rocket engine test bed controls; prodn. of various items of surveillance satellite and polaris missile operational support equipment, mariner and voyager attitude control subsy. operational support equipment, drop dynamics module for Spacelab Three, drop physics module for U.S. Microgravity Lab. One, tempus incandescence measuring instrument for Internat. Microgravity Lab. One; design of a Martian surface seismometer prototype design, production and testing of Apollo and Lunar Exploration Module factory and launch Automatic Checkout Equipment. Home: 3705 Elderberry Cir Grand Junction CO 81506-8485 Office: Jet Propulsion Lab 4800 Oak Grove Dr Pasadena CA 91109-8001

MCFARLAND, JON WELDON, retired county commissioner; b. Wenatchee, Wash., Aug. 23, 1938; s. Charles Edward and Maud Elizabeth (Brennan) McF.; m. Kay Annette Erbes, Apr. 5, 1956; children: Colleen, Michael, Heather. BS in Edn., Eastern Wash. State U., 1961; MS in Personnel Adminstrn., George Washington U., 1966; Grad., Command and Gen. Staff Coll., Fort Leavenworth, Kans., 1970, U.S. Army War Coll., Carlisle Barracks, Pa., 1980. Commd. U.S. Army, 1961, advanced through grades to col., 1981, retired, 1988; ops. officer European Hdqtrs. U.S. Army, Heidelberg, Fed. Republic Germany, 1980-83; commdr. 16th mil. police brigade U.S. Army, Fort Bragg, N.C., 1983-85, provost marshal 18th Airborne Corps, 1983-85; asst. commandant, commdr. of troops U.S. Army Mil. Police Sch., Fort McClellan, Ala., 1985-88; county commr. Columbia County, Wash., 1989-96; dir., owner Mr. Mc's Direct Mktg. Svcs., 1992—; owner, dir. Spectro-Optics of Ea. Wash., Dayton, 1994—; Wash. staff for courthouse security, 1995-96; vice chmn. Southeastern Emergency Med. and Trauma Coun., Wash., 1990-94, chmn., 1995-97, 99—; chmn. Columbia County Bd. Commrs., 1990, 96; bd. dirs. Emergency Mgmt. Svcs., Columbia County. Author: History of Civil Disturbance 1960-68, 1969. Bd. dirs. Columbia County Pub. Health Dist., Dayton, 1989-96, chmn., 1995-96; bd. dirs. Project Timothy Pub. Svcs., bd. dirs., Columbia County Health Found., 1989—; vice chmn. Palouse Econ. Devel. Corp., 1990-92, chmn., 1993-95; bd. trustees Walla Walla C.C., 1998—. Decorated Legion of Merit, Bronze Star, numerous others. Mem. Assn. U.S. Army, Wash. State Assn. Counties, U.S. Army War Coll. Found., Kiwanis (bd. dirs. Dayton 1990—). Democrat. Roman Catholic. Avocations: woodworking, pottery, fishing, hunting, travel. Home: 150 S Touchet Rd Dayton WA 99328-8741 Office: Columbia County 205 S 4th St Dayton WA 99328-1411

MCFARLAND, KEVIN JOHN, foundation administrator; b. Mt. Clement, Mich., Mar. 18, 1958; s. Chuck Paul and Myrna (Bell) McF.; m. Betty Ann Bolton, Nov. 26, 1976; children: Michelle, Michael, Melinda. BS in Bibl. Studies magna cum laude, Abilene Christian U., Tex., 1980; postgrad., Tex. Tech. U., 1980-81, Stanford U., 1982-83. Resident asst. Abilene (Tex.) State Sch., 1976-78; pvt. landscaping bus. Abilene, 1978-80; research assoc., home and family life dept. Tex. Tech. U., Lubbock, 1980-81; youth and family minister Redwood City (Calif.) Ch. of Christ, 1981-84; pres. Manna Internat. Relief and Devel. Corp., Redwood City, 1984—. Bd. dirs. Am. Coun. Voluntary Internat. Action; dir. Inst. Cooperation Internat. Devel.; mem. Amnesty Internat., Bread for the World. Mem. Nat. Honor Soc., Cultural Survival, Soc. Internat. Devel. Global Affairs Coun., Inst. Cooperation Internat. Devel. (bd. dirs., founder, exec. dir.), Inst. Cultural Affairs, Acad. Polit. Sci., Evang. for Social Action, ALpha Chi. Home: 1193 Hudson St Redwood City CA 94061-2208 Office: Manna Internat PO Box 3507 Redwood City CA 94064-3507

MC FARLAND, NORMAN FRANCIS, bishop; b. Martinez, Calif., Feb. 21, 1922; student St. Patrick's Sem., Menlo Park, Calif.; J.C.D., Cath. U. Am. Ordained priest Roman Catholic Ch., 1946, consecrated bishop, 1970; titular bishop of Bida and aux. bishop of San Francisco, 1970-74; apostolic adminstr. Diocese of Reno, 1974-76; bishop Diocese of Reno-Las Vegas, 1976-87, Diocese of Orange, Calif., 1987-98. Office: 200 W La Veta Ave Orange CA 92866-1936

MCFARLAND, RONALD EARL, educator, writer, literary critic; b. Bellaire, Ohio, Sept. 22, 1942; s. Earl Alexander and Mary Maxine (Stullenburger) McF.; m. Elsie Roseland Watson; children: Kimberley Ellen, Jennifer Lynn, Jonathan Ronald. AA, Brevard Jr. Coll., Cocoa, Fla., 1962; BA, Fla. State U., Tallahassee, 1963, MA, 1965; PhD, U. Ill., 1970. Instr. English Sam Houston State Coll., Huntsville, Tex., 1965-67; from asst. prof. to prof. English, U. Idaho, Moscow, 1970—; exch. prof. English, Ohio U., Athens, 1985-86; manuscript reviewer Am. Indian Quar., Norman, Okla., 1994—. Author: (poetry) The Haunting Familiarity of Things, 1993, (critical study) The World of David Wagoner, 1997; editor Idaho's Poetry, 1988, Norman Maclean, 1988. Chmn. Moscow (Idaho) Arts Commn., 1980-81; chmn. soccer competition Idaho Spl. Olympics, Moscow, 1985, 87, 89; tournament coord. U. Idaho Internat. Soccer Tournament, Moscow, 1990—; moderator Celebrating Writers Among Us, Moscow, 1997, 98. Recipient Libr. Faculty award U. Idaho Libr., 1984, Burlington-No. Faculty Achievement award U. Idaho, 1990, Disting. Alumnus award Brevard C.C., Melbourne, Fla., 1996; Idaho State writer-in-residence Idaho Commn. on the Arts, Boise, 1985-86. Mem. Acad. Am. Poets, U.S. Soccer Fedn. (referee). Democrat. Methodist. Avocations: fly fishing, bird hunting, stamp collecting, militaria, collecting vintage military weapons. Home: 857 E 8th St Moscow ID 83843-3535 Office: U Idaho Dept English Dept English Moscow ID 83844

MCFARLAND, WILLELLYN SHAW, artist, educator; b. Compton, Calif., Nov. 14, 1934; d. William Bruce Shaw and Brenda Marguerite McKee; m. Jim McFarland, Apr. 9, 1960; children: Craig, Robin, Shawn. BFA, U. So. Calif., L.A., 1956; tchg. credentials, Calif. State U., Long Beach, 1978. Lifetime credentials in spl. secondary art, gen. jr. h.s., Calif. Tchr. elem. edn. Montebello Sch. Dist., 1972-92; adult sch. tchr. El Rancho Unified Sch. Dist., 1982-98; tchr. Downey (Calif.) Sch. Dist., 1983—; advisor Artists Mag., 1996. Featured in book Artists of California, 1993. Mem. Nat. Watercolor Soc. (pres., exhbn. dir. 1991-92, 96-97, chmn. selection jury 1998 Ann. Exhbn. 1998, exhibited in juried art exhbns. 1995, coord. sec., advisor 1997-98), Women Painters West (exhibited in juried exhbns. 1986). Avocations: golf, painting on location. Home: 7937 E 4th Pl Downey CA 90241

MCFARLANE, WILLIAM JOHN, management consultant; b. Edinburgh, Scotland, Nov. 27, 1949; came to U.S., 1985; s. David Duncan and Doreen (Penney) McF.; children: Robert William, Aran James; m. Isae Wada, Apr. 8, 1998. Grad., Dundee Coll. Tech., 1980; MBA, U. Edinburgh, 1984. V.p. Associated Travel Network, Chgo., 1985-86; gen. mgr. Corp-Net Internat., Libertyville, Ill., 1986-88; v.p. Galileo N.Am., Rosemont, Ill., 1988-90; prin. Bill McFarlane & Assocs., Norcross, Ga., 1990-93; pres., CEO AQUA Software Products, Inc., Santa Ana, Calif., 1993-96; prin. Bill McFarlane & Assocs., Inc., Mill Valley, Calif., 1997—. Contbr. articles to trade mags. Republican. Avocations: travel, computers, world events. E-mail: Bill@BillMcFarlane.com. Home: 17 Ethel Ave Mill Valley CA 94941

MCFARLANE, WILLIS MCKEE, buffalo company executive; b. Cleve., May 27, 1933. BA in Econs. cum laude, Amherst Coll., 1955. Exec. Nowthwestern Mut. Life Ins., 1955-60; ptnr. life ins. co. Files, Cristal, and McFarlane, 1956—; founder AIRCOA, Cleve., 1968-79, Denver, 1979-90; co-owner Denver Buffalo Mktg. Co., 1990—, Buffalo Bar, Idaho Springs, 1995—. Chmn. bd. dirs. Colo. Symphony Orch.; bd. dirs. Colo. Wildlife Heritage Found. Mem. Cherry Hills Country Club. Office: Denver Buffalo Co 1120 Lincoln St Ste 905 Denver CO 80203-2138*

MCGANN, JOHN MILTON, real estate executive; b. Omaha, Mar. 18, 1948; s. John Byron and Donna M. (Rehnquist) McG.; m. Barbara June Scott, June 2, 1978. BSBA, cert. real estate, U. Nebr., Omaha, 1971. Property mgr. Boetel & Co., Omaha, 1971-73; asst. office bldg. mgr. The Irvine Co., Newport Beach, Calif., 1973-74; property mgr. Harbor Investment Co., Corona Del Mar, Calif., 1974-76, Robert A. McNeil Corp., Santa Ana, Calif., 1976-78; gen. mgr. Daon Mgmt., Newport Beach, 1978-80; v.p. August Mgmt. Inc., Long Beach, Calif., 1980-82, Calif. Fed. Asst. Mgmt., L.A., 1982-83; pres. Wespac Mgmt. Realty Corp., Newport Beach, 1983-87; v.p., dir. asset mgmt., pres. CalFed Asset Mgmt. Co., L.A., 1987-90; v.p. com. ops. Pinnacle Realty (formerly Sovereign/Ring), Santa Monica, 1990-95; pres., ptnr. Churchill McGann, LLC, 1995-97; pres. McGann Enterprises Inc., Churchill McGann & Roundtable Pizza, Long Beach, Calif., 1997—. Mem. Inst. Real Estate Mgmt. (L.A. chpt., cert. property mgr.), Internat. Coun. Shopping Ctrs. (cert. shopping ctr. mgr.), Lambda Chi Alpha, Delta Sigma Pi, Rho Epsilon (pres.). Republican. Mem. Christian Sci. Ch. Home: 3834 Pine Ave Long Beach CA 90807 Office: McGann Enterprises Inc. Churchill McGann 4201 Long Beach Blvd #306 Long Beach CA 90807-2021 also: Roundtable Pizza 5250 Faculty Ave Lakewood CA 90712

MCGARRIGLE, ROGER WILLIAM, civil and structural engineer; b. Portland, Oreg., Apr. 20, 1940; s. John Frances and Florence Alberta (Hancock) McG.; m. Janet Boone, Dec. 16, 1943; 1 child, Kellee McGarrigle Patey. BS in Applied Sci./Structures, Portland State U., 1966. Consulting engr. Portland, 1971-86; ptnr. Van Domelen/Looijenga/McGarrigle/Knauf, Portland, 1986-95; pvt. practice Portland, 1995—. Projects include structural repairs to the Portland Bldg. and seismic strengthening of some Portland, Oregon City, McMinnville, Forest Grove Sch. Dist. facilities and Willamette U., Oreg. State U., U. Portland, Western Oreg. State Coll., and Pacific U. bldgs. and designs for new constrn. of comml. and indsl. bldgs. and site improvements. Mem. City of Gresham Bldg. Code Bd. of Appeals. Named to Acad. of Disting. Alumni Portland State U., 1997. Mem. ASCE, Structural Engrs. Assn. of Oreg. (life, past pres.), Western States Coun. of Structural Engrs. Assns. (past pres., past rep. to Bldg. Seismic Safety Coun.), Oreg. Seismic Safety Policy Adv. Commn. (past chair), Structural Adv. Bd., Portland Bur. Bldgs. (past chair), Earthquake Engring. Rsch. Inst., Am. Concrete Inst., Am. Pub. Works Assn., Consulting Engrs. Coun. of Oreg., Soc. Am. Mil. Engrs., Internat. Conf. Bldg. Officials, Nat. Trust for Historic Preservation. Fax: (503) 248-4340. E-mail: mcgar engr@aol.com. Office: Roger McGarrigle PE 1630 SW Harbor Way Ste 305 Portland OR 97201

MCGARY, RITA ROSE, social worker; b. Frenchville, Me., Sept. 18, 1927; d. Joseph N. and Lula (Labbe) Babin; m. Lawrence E. McGary; children: Philip, Robert, Kathleen. BA in Sociology, Rivier Coll., 1949; MEd, U. Va., 1978; MSW, U. Nev., 1994. Lic. social worker, Nev., nat. cert. counselor, clin. mental health counselor. Tchr. Fort Kent (Me.) H.S., 1949-51; dir., tchr. Nursery Sch., Palembang, Indonesia, 1954-56; tchr. Am. Sch., Asunción, 1963-66; tchr. for homebound Fairfax County Pub. Schs., Fairfax, Va., 1971-74, presenter workshop, cons., case mgr., vis. tchr., 1980-92, sch. social worker, conflict mediator, 1990-92; case mgr. Washoe County Sch. Dist., Reno, 1994—; mediator Fairfax County Family Ct., Fairfax, Va.,1 991-92; case mgr., program coord. Family Resource Ctr., Reno, 1996; social work intern Nev. State Prison, Nev. Women's State Prison, 1993, VA Med. Ctr. and Vet. Ctr., Reno, Nev., 1994, 1994; mem. Child Abuse and Neglect Task Force, Reno, 1998; dir. Miguel Ribera Family Resource Ctr., Reno, 1998; adj. prof. U. Nev., Reno; presenter in field. Contbr. article to profl. jour. Election worker Dem. Party, Va., 1984; sch. rep. Hisp. Multidisciplinary Team Child Protective Svcs., Fairfax, Va., 1990-92; coord. V.A. Day of Svc. for Homeless, 1994; field exec. Girl Scout Coun. Nation's Capital, Washington, 1975-79. Recipient Excellence in Edn. Dept. of Cmty. Action, Fairfax, Va., 1991. Mem. AAUW, NASW, NOW, Sch. Social Work Assn. Am., Nev. Sch. Social Work Assn. (chairperson 1998), So. Poverty Law Ctr., People for Am. Way, Phi Kappa Phi. Home: 1539 Foster Dr Reno NV 89509-1211

MCGAVIN, JOCK CAMPBELL, airframe design engineer; b. L.A., Sept. 14, 1917; s. Campbell and Irene (LeMarr) McG.; m. Catherine Marcelle Glew, Jan. 12, 1952; 1 child, James Campbell. AA, L.A. City Coll., 1950; AB, U. So. Calif., 1970, MS, 1975; PhD, Calif. Coast U., 1989. Airframe design engr. Rockwell Internat. Corp., L.A., 1946-82; ret., 1982; sr. design engr. X-15 airplane, Apollo Command Module, space shuttle, others. Vol. mem. pub. involvement subcom. Puget Sound Water Quality Authority, Seattle, 1987-89; commd. Ky. Col., ETO svc., 1994. Capt. C.E. U.S. Army, 1940-46, ETO. Recipient Apollo Achievement award NASA, 1969; named to Honorable Order of Ky. Colonels. Mem. Soc. for History Astronomy, Izaak Walton League Am. (pres. Greater Seattle chpt. 1991-93, vol. worker environ. projects 1985—), U. So. Calif. N.W. Alumni Club (pres. 1987-89). Avocations: world travel, history of astronomy, radio-controlled model airplanes. Home: 12939 NE 146th Pl Woodinville WA 98072-4632

MCGEE, ANASTASIA GUINIVIERE, visual effects coordinator; b. Riverside, Calif., May 19, 1964; d. Gordon Edward Pflug and Delores Anne (Bell) Stromberg; 1 child. BA in Comm., U. Calif., San Diego, 1985; BFA in Film, Art Ctr. Coll., 1988. Personal asst. Peloria Corp., L.A., 1988-89; temp. asst. Right Connections, L.A., 1989-90; park films coord. Buena Vista Visual Efx, Burbank, Calif., 1990-92, coord. park films and libr. restoration, 1992-94, visual effects coord., 1994-96; dept. coord. Buena Vista Imaging, Burbank, 1996—; mem. adv. bd. Disney U., Burbank, 1994—; mem. steering com. Disney Vols., Burbank, 1995-98. Recipient 5-Yrs. Continuous Svc. award Walt Disney Co., 1995. Office: Buena Vista Imaging 500 S Buena Vista St Burbank CA 91521-0001

MCGEE, CRAIG HESLIN, insurance company executive; b. Port Angeles, Wash., June 4, 1926; s. Herbert Milton and Caryl (Heslin) McG.; m. Dorothy Jean Smith, Feb. 24, 1951; children: Caryl, Leslie, Galen. AB, Whitman Coll., 1950; JD, U. Wash., 1954. Adjuster/examiner Allstate Ins. Co., Seattle, 1955-60; dist. claims mgr. Allstate Ins. Co., Phoenix, 1960-65; claims supr. Pemco Mutual Ins. Co., Seattle, 1965-69, mgr. claim dept., 1969-91, govt. affairs rep., 1992—. Bd. dirs. Parent Anonymous Washington State, Seattle, 1982-88. With U.S. Army, 1944-46, 50-51. Mem. Pacific Claim Execs. Assn. (pres. 1977-78, bd. dirs. 1974-79), Queen City Yacht Club (chair 1988-91, Man of Yr. 1991), Wash. Athletic Club. Avocation: sailing.

MCGEE, JAMES F., lawyer; b. N.Y.C., Sept. 19, 1950; s. James F. and Elizabeth J. (Mooney) M.; m. Annamarie Saunders, Feb. 13, 1988; children: James, Brooke Nicole. BS, U. Penn., 1972; JD, Western State U., Fullerton, Calif., 1980. Bar: Calif. 1980. Founder McGee & Assocs., Newport Beach, Calif., 1980—. Chmn. Laguna Beach Bd. Adjustment, 1985-87, Laguna Beach Architecture Review Bd., 1985-87; pres. Junior All Am. Football, 1997; pres. Pelican Hill Cmty. Assn., 1995-97; pres. Newport Coast Cmty. Assn., 1997; chief Indian Guides Chumash Tribe, 1996-97; chief Newport Beach-Costa Mesa YMCA Indian Guides Dolphin Nation, 1997. Recipient 20-30 Internat. So. Calif. Man of Yr., 1985. Mem. ABA, ATLA, Calif. Bar Assn., Orange County Bar Assn., Calif. Trial Lawyers Assn., Orange County Trial Lawyers Assn. Avocations: sports, flying, public speaking. Office: 23 Corp Plaza Ste 230 Newport Beach CA 92660

MCGEE, MICHAEL JAY, fire marshal, educator; b. Ft. Worth, June 9, 1952; s. Cecil Carl McGee and Helen Ruth (Peeples) McGee-Furrh; m. Carol Lee Garbarino, Sept. 18, 1982; children: Megan Rose, John Michael, Molly Caitlin. Student, U. Tex., 1970-73, Western Oreg. State U., 1983; AAS in Fire Protection Tech., Colo. Mountain Coll., 1990. Lic. fire suppression systems insp., Colo., vocat. educator, Colo.; cert. hazardous materials technician, Colo., 1992, EMT, Colo.; cert. fire safety hazardous materials instr., evaluator. Driver Massengale Co., Austin, Tex., 1970-73; gen. mgr. Sundae Palace, Austin, 1973-74; staff mem. Young Life, Colorado Springs,

Colo., 1970-75; mgr. Broadmoor Mgmt. Co., Vail, Colo., 1974-76; technician Vail Cable Communications, 1976-77; fire marshal Vail Fire Dept., 1977—, fire sci. coord., 1995—, emergency med. program coord., 1996—; v.p. HAZPRO (Hazardous Materials and Fire Safety Consulting Firm), 1996—; dist. rep. Joint Coun. Fire Dist. Colo., 1983-85; co-chmn. Eagle County Hazardous Materials, 1984-85, mem. planning com., 1987-90; mem. accountability com. Eagle County Sch. Dist., 1991-96, mem. budget rev. com., 1991-93, vice chair accountability com. 1992-93, chmn. accountability com., 1993-96; mem. policy rev. com., 1993-96, bldg. coord., team coach Odyssey of the Mind at Eaglevalle Elem. Sch., 1995; invited dir. workshops Colo. Dept. Edn. Dist. Accountability Convention, Colo. Springs, 1995. Chmn. Eagle County chpt. ARC, 1980-83, disaster chmn., 1977-80; tng. officer Eagle Vol. Fire Dept., 1988-90; mem. parish coun. St. Mary's Parish, Eagle County, 1989-90; mem. citizen's adv. com. Colo. Mountain Coll., 1990-91, bd. dirs. 1990; bldg. coord., team coach Odessey of the Mind, Eagle Valley Elem. Sch., 1994-95, 97-98, 98-99, coach, 1997-98; mem. facilities master planning com. Engle County Sch. Dist., 1996-97; mem. planning com. 1999 World Alpine Ski Championships. Mem. Internat. Assn. Arson Investigators (Colo. chpt.), Internat. Platform Assn., Nat. Fire Protection Assn., Colo. State Fire Marshals Assn., Colo. State Fire Chiefs Assn. Office: Vail Fire Dept 42 W Meadow Dr Vail CO 81657-5000

MCGEE, WINSTON EUGENE, artist; b. Salem, Ill., Sept. 4, 1924; s. Elmer Clifford and Ida Evelyn (Chezchin) McG.; m. Susan Cutler Kelley; children: Chaunda Wild, Lindsay McGee. B Journalism, U. Mo., Columbia, 1948, MA, 1949; postgrad., École Superieure Beaux Arts, Paris, 1951. Art dir. Nat. Cathedral, Washington, 1951; chair art dept. Lake Erie Coll., Painesville, Ohio, 1952-69; exch. advisor Ecole des Beaux Arts, Nice, France, 1962; dir. study ctr. U. Caen, France, 1968; chair art dept. Cleve. State U., 1970-76; chair art dept. Calif. State U. Stanislaus, Turlock, 1976-95, prof. emeritus, 1997—; pres., owner Winsu Prodns., Turlock, 1982-92. Represented in permanent collections including Holmes Collection, Dallas, Portland Art Mus., Calif. Palace Legion of Honor, San Francisco Achenbach Found., Calif. Wall, Calif. State U. San Francisco Campus. Pres. New Orgn. for Visual Arts, Cleve., 1974, Turlock Arts Commn., 1978-80. With U.S. Army, 1942-47, ETO. Fulbright scholar, 1951; recipient Gold medal Acad. Italia delle Arte, 1963. Fellow Internat. Inst. Arts and Letters (life); mem. Turlock City Arts Commn., Turlock Golf and Country Club. Republican. Methodist. Avocations: golf, swimming, walking. Home: 1710 Smith Dr Turlock CA 95382-2825 Office: Next Door Studio 244 Broadway Turlock CA 95380

MCGEHAN, FREDERICK PARSONS, JR., public affairs executive; b. Hartford, Conn., Oct. 20, 1941; s. Frederick Parsons and Doris Gertrude (Clough) McG.; m. Barbara Joan Beckley, Nov. 11, 1967; children: John Patrick, Matthew Robert, Anne Elizabeth. BS in English, Holy Cross Coll., 1963; MS in Journalism, Columbia U., 1964. Reporter Providence Jour., 1964-66; sci. reporter Newhouse News Svc., Washington, 1966-68, Balt. Sun, 1968-74; pub. affairs specialist Nat. Bur. Standards, Gaithersburg, Md., 1974-77, Boulder, Colo., 1977-85; pub. affairs dir. Nat. Inst. Standards & Tech., Boulder, 1985—. Sgt. U.S. Army, 1964-70. Mem. Boulder Press Club. Democrat. Roman Catholic. Avocations: skiing, hiking. Office: Nat Inst Standards & Tech 325 Broadway St Boulder CO 80303-3337

MCGIHON, MICHAEL EDWIN, sheet metal manufacturing executive; b. Long Beach, Calif., July 31, 1949; s. Alvin Frances and Edna Lona (Windes) McG.; m. Phyllis Rachel Tiner, Aug. 15, 1970; 1 child, Scott Del. Student, Long Beach C.C., 1971. Apprentice McGihon Sheet Metal, Long Beach, 1967-71, journeyman, foreman, 1971-91, pres., 1991—, cons. R&D, 1985—. Mem. Aircraft Owners and Pilots Assn., Long Beach Ski Club (asst. v.p. 1992-93). Democrat. Lutheran. Avocations: scuba diving, skiing, boating, travel, flying. Home: 2901 N Heather Rd Long Beach CA 90815-1052

MCGILLICUDDY, JOAN MARIE, psychotherapist, consultant; b. Chgo., June 23, 1952; d. James Neal and Muriel (Joy) McG. BA, U. Ariz., 1974, MS, 1976; PhD, Walden U., 1996. Cert. nat. counselor. Counselor ACTION, Tucson, 1976; counselor, clin. supr. Behavioral Health Agy. Cen. Ariz., Casa Grande, 1976-81; instr. psychology Cen. Ariz. Coll., Casa Grande, 1978-83; therapist, co-dir. Helping Assocs., Inc., Casa Grande, 1982—, v.p., sec., 1982—; cert. instr. Silva Method Mind Devel., Tucson, 1986—. Mem. Mayor's Com. for Handicapped, Casa Grande, 1989-90, Human Svcs. Planning, Casa Grande, 1985-95. Named Outstanding Am. Lectr. Silva Mind Internat., 1988-97. Mem. ACA. Avocations: jogging, singing. Office: Helping Assocs Inc 1901 N Trekell Rd Casa Grande AZ 85222-1706

MCGILVRAY, GERI SIGLER, artist; b. San Jose, Calif., Feb. 22, 1942; d. Charles Agustas and Vivian May (Croy) Sigler; m. Greg John Tilden, Jan. 8, 1963 (div. 1971); children: Maureen Bernadette, Charles Eugene. AA, San Francisco City Coll., 1962; student, San Francisco State U., 1963. Cert. tchr., Calif. Tchr. Palo Alto, Calif., 1971-79. Artist: paintings exhibited at Flower and Art Show, Redwood City, Calif., 1966, (2d and 3d pl. awards), Palo Alto Art Club Town and Country Show, 1969 (hon. mention), 1971 (hon. mention), 1972 (1st pl.),s one-woman show Art Factory, Palo Alto, 1973, group show at St. Michael's Alley, Palo Alto, 1989, one woman show at Palo Alto Med. Clin., 1996 (also filmed and televised in Palo Alto, Menlo Park and Atherton), exhibited at Virtual Gallery, Palo Alto, 1996, 97, 98, Open Studio, Palo Alto, 1996, Oakland Art and Wine Festival, 1997, Borders Books, Palo Alto, 1997, Encore Gallery (now Virtual Gallery), Los Gatos, Calif., 1997, Palo Atlo Cafe, 1997, Mus. West San Francisco, 1997, commd. drawing Palo Alto City Coun., 1998; her work has also been published in Calif. newspapers and art mags. and TV program Front & Center. Recipient awards Menlo Park Hist. Comm., 1976. Mem. Pacific Art League (numerous awards for paintings 1972), Women's Caucus Arts. Avocations: painting, volleyball, camping, biking, singing. Home: 2533 Middlefield Rd Palo Alto CA 94301-4031 Office: Geri McGilvray Art Studio 2533 Middlefield Rd Palo Alto CA 94301-4031

MCGINNIS, MICHAEL PATRICK, psychotherapist; b. Madison, Wis., Oct. 4, 1950; s. James and Patricia Jane (Cole) McG.; m. Carol Ann Bailey, Aug. 8, 1982; children: Arielle Dominque, Chandra Eden. Student, U. Wis., 1968-69, U. Maine, 1971-73; BA, Sonoma State U., 1980, MA, 1984. Cert. marriage, family and child counselor, Calif. Offset printer Portland (Maine) Printing Co., 1970-71, Pronto Prints, Madison, 1972-74; mental health specialist Sheltered Workshop, Madison, 1975-77; mental health worker social svc. dept. Treatment Alternatives to Street Crimes, Santa Rosa, Calif., 1977-79; counselor Nat. Coun. on Alcoholism, Santa Rosa, 1978-79, exec. dir. Sonoma County, 1979-81; counselor, trainer Sonoma County Family Svc. Agy., Santa Rosa, 1981-86; pvt. practice, Healdsburg, Calif., 1985—; trainer, cons. domestic violence treatment Calif. Dept. Mental Health, 1979-84, YWCA Women's Emergency Shelter, Santa Rosa, 1980-86. Mem. Calif. Assn. Marriage and Family Therapists (clin.), Am. Profl. Soc. on Abuse on Children (clin.), Calif. Profl. Soc. on Abuse of Children (clin.). Democrat. Avocations: fishing, investing, reading. Home and Office: 610 Alta Vista Dr Healdsburg CA 95448-4651

MCGIRR, JACKELEN RICHARDSON, clothing designer; b. San Francisco, July 13, 1941; d. Jack Covell and Helen (York) Richardson; m. Douglas Jones, Dec. 22, 1969 (div. 1982); 1 child, Jackelen Anne; m. Wesley Neil McGirr, Feb. 7, 1987. BA, Calif. State U., Sacramento, 1963, gen. secondary credential, 1964; lic. in real estate, Fresno State Coll., 1965; MA in Clothing Design, Pacific Union Coll., 1968. Tchr. home econs. Kingsburg (Calif.) High Sch., 1963-65, Napa (Calif.) Valley Unified Sch. Dist., 1965-82; ptnr. Bottle Shop, St. Helena, Calif., 1965-71; clothing designer Alturas, Calif., 1982-88; owner, mgr. Jackelen Custom Designed Garments, St. Helena, 1988—, Jackelen Jewelry, St. Helena, 1990—; cons. on cottage industry Coll. Siskeyou, Weed, Calif., 1983-85, Lassen Coll., Susanville, Calif., 1984. Exhibited designs Calif. State Fair, 1986—. Mem. Alturas Tourism Com., 1983-88. Mem. AAUW, Order of Ea. Star. Republican. Presbyterian. Home and Office: 2080 Spring Mountain Rd Saint Helena CA 94574-1763

MCGLAUGHLIN, THOMAS HOWARD, publisher, retired naval officer; b. Cin., Jan. 12, 1928; s. George Godden and Cordelia (Herrlinger) McG.; m. Moana Maharam-Stone, Jan. 4, 1984. BS in Elec. Engring., U.S. Naval Acad., 1950. Lic. master mariner. Commd. ensign U.S. Navy, 1950, advanced through grades to capt., 1970; White House aide to Pres. John F. Kennedy, Washington, 1960-63; exec. officer USS Prichett, Long Beach, Calif., 1963-65; comdg. officer USS Maddox, Long Beach, 1965-67; exec. officer USS Boston, Boston, 1967-70; chief naval ops. Comdr.-in-Chief, Pacific, Honolulu, 1970-74; chief of staff Mil. Sealift Command, N.Y.C., 1974-79; ret. U.S. Navy, 1979; pres. Falmouth Press, Honolulu, 1983—; marine surveyor R.W. Dickieson Internat., Inc., Honolulu, 1982—; master M.V. Rella Mae, Honolulu, 1981-90, Royal Taipan, Cebu, Philippines, 1990. Hon. police chief Boston Police Dept., 1969. Decorated Bronze Star; recipient medal for Outstanding Svc., Am. Legion, Pitts., 1942. Mem. Nat. Def. Transp. Assn., VFW (life), U.S. Naval Acad. Alumni Assn. (life), The Retired Officers Assn. Republican. Presbyterian. Avocations: flying, scuba diving. Home: The Royal Iolani #1702 581 Kamoku St Honolulu HI 96826-5250 Office: RW Dickieson Internat Inc 46-208 Kahuhipa St Kaneohe HI 96744-3905

MCGLYNN, BETTY HOAG, art historian; b. Deer Lodge, Mont., Apr. 28, 1914; d. Arthur James and Elizabeth Tangye (Davey) Lochrie; m. Paul Sterling Hoag, Dec. 28, 1936 (div. 1967); children: Peter Lochrie Hoag, Jane Hoag Brown, Robert Doane Hoag; m. Thomas Arnold McGlynn, July 28, 1973. BA, Stanford U., 1936; MA, U. So. Calif., 1967. Cert. secondary tchr., Calif. Rsch. dir. So. Calif. Archives of Am. Art, L.A., 1964-67, Carmel (Calif.) Mus. Art, 1967-69; dir. Triton Mus. Art, Santa Clara, Calif., 1970; archivist, libr. San Mateo County (Calif.) Hist. Soc. Mus., 1972-74; cons. Monterey Peninsula Mus. Art, Calif., 1964—; tchr. art extension Monterey Peninsula Coll., Calif., 1970, San Jose City Coll., 1971; lectr. in field. Author: The World of Mary DeNeale Morgan, 1970, Carmel Art Association: A History, 1987; contbg. author: Plein Air Painters of California, The North, 1986, Orchid Art and The Orchid Isle, 1982, Hawaiian Island Artists and Friends of the Arts, 1989, Jo Mora: Spokesman for the Old West, 1998; editor, author of jours. La Peninsula (San Mateo County Hist. Soc.), 1971-75, Noticias (Monterey History and Art Assn.), 1983-88, 95; author of booklets; contbr. articles to profl. jours. Appraiser art work City of Carmel, 1967, adv. bd. Art in Pub. Places, 1997-98; appraiser art work City of Monterey, 1981; mem. Friends of Harrison Meml. Libr., Carmel, Friends of Sunset Found., Carmel, Pacific Grove Art Ctr., Monterey Bay Aquarium. Mem. AAUW, Butte (Mont.) Arts Chateau, Carmel Art Assn. (hon.), Carmel Heritage Soc., Carmel Found., Carmel Residents Assn., Chinese Hist. Soc., Monterey History and Art Assn. (art cons.), Monterey Mus. Art (mem. acquisitions bd.), Gallatin County Hist. Soc. (Mont.), Stanford Alumni Assn., Robinson Jeffers Tor House Found. (art cons.), Hawaiian Hist. Soc., Mont. Hist. Soc., Nat. Mus. of Women in Arts, The Westerners, P.E.O., Book Club of Calif. Republican. Avocations: research archives and library. Home and Office: PO Box 7189 Carmel CA 93921-7189

MCGOVERN, DAVID CARR, lawyer; b. Taunton, Mass., Sept. 3, 1946; s. James Edward and Dorothea Elizabeth (Carr) McG.; m. Pamela Lee Compton, Mar. 22, 1975; 1 child, William David. AB, Coll. of Holy Cross, 1968; JD, U. Va., 1979. Bar: Calif. 1980, U.S. Dist. Ct. (ctrl. dist.) Calif. 1980, U.S. Dist. Ct. (so. dist.) Calif. 1981. Assoc. Rosenfeld, Meyer and Susman, Beverly Hills, Calif., 1979-81; ptnr. Engstrom, Lipscomb and Lack, L.A., 1981-90, Haight, Brown and Bonesteel LLP, Santa Monica, Calif., 1990—. Bd. dirs. United Cerebral Palsy/Spastic Children's Found., L.A., 1985-94; men's com. John Tracy Clinic Women's Aux., L.A., 1988-94; founding mem. Friends of John Tracy Clinic, L.A., 1996—; benefit com. Boys and Girls Club Venice, Calif., 1994—. Mem. ABA, State Bar Calif., Aviation Ins. Assn. Avocations: running, reading, coaching youth basketball, travel. Fax: (310) 829-5117. E-mail: mcgoverd@hbblaw.com. Home: 7812 W 80th St Playa del Rey CA 90293-7905 Office: Haight Brown and Bonesteel LLP 1620 26th St Ste 4000N Santa Monica CA 90404-4013

MC GOVERN, WALTER T., federal judge; b. Seattle, May 24, 1922; s. C. Arthur and Anne Marie (Thies) McG.; m. Rita Marie Olsen, June 29, 1946; children: Katrina M., Shawn E., A. Renee. B.A., U. Wash., 1949, LL.B., 1950. Bar: Wash. 1950. Practiced law in Seattle, 1950-59; mem. firm Kerr, McCord, Greenleaf & Moen; judge Municipal Ct., Seattle, 1959-65, Superior Ct., Wash., 1965-68, Wash. Supreme Ct., 1968-71; judge U.S. Dist. Ct. (we. dist.) Wash., 1971-87, chief judge, 1975-87, sr. judge, 1987—; mem. subcom. on supporting personnel Jud. Conf. U.S., 1981-87, chmn. subcom., 1983, mem. adminstrn. com., 1983-87, chmn. jud. resources com., 1987-91. Mem. Am. Judicature Soc., Wash. State Superior Ct. Judges Assn., Seattle King County Bar Assn. (treas.), Phi Delta Phi. Club: Seattle Tennis (pres. 1968). Office: US Dist Ct US Courthouse 5th Fl 1010 5th Ave Ste 215 Seattle WA 98104-1189

MCGOWAN, THOMAS RANDOLPH, retired religious organization executive; b. Balt., Apr. 19, 1926; s. Robert and Mary (Miller) McG.; m. Bernice A. Bernard, May 20, 1967 (dec. Nov. 1981); children: Howard, James, Terry; m. Roedean Olivia Oden, Feb. 9, 1985; children: Karen White, Kevin, Kurt. AA, Oakland Jr. Coll., 1964; postgrad., San Francisco State Coll., 1964-68; BS, U. Md., 1978. Lt. security police Oakland (Calif.) Army Base, 1955-60; chief motor pool San Francisco Procurement Agy., Oakland, 1960-64, contract specialist, 1964-68; contract specialist Harry Diamond Labs., Washington, 1968-79, br. chief procurement divsn., 1972-79; chief procurement directorate Yuma (Ariz.) Proving Ground, 1979-82; dir. ecumenism Roman Cath. Diocese of Oakland, 1983—; dir. African Am. Cath. Pastoral Ctr., Diocese of Oakland, 1991—. Convenor Interreligious Coun. of Oakland, 1988—; trustee Greater Oakland Interfaith Network, 1989-92; mem. East Oakland Renewal Task Force, 1990—; bd. dir. Columbia (Md.) Found., 1972-74, chmn., 1975-79; div. Bd. Cons., Graymoor, N.Y., 1990—; bd. dirs. Thea Bowman Manor, Oakland, 1989—, St. Mary's Ctr. With U.S. Army, 1944-46. Mem. Knights of Peter Claver, Rotary. Democrat. Avocations: tennis, woodworking. Home: 139 Pinto Dr Vallejo CA 94591-8451

MCGOWN, JOHN, JR., lawyer; b. Bowling Green, Ky., June 15, 1949; s. John Stanley and Margaret (Deatherage) McG.; m. Mary Grunewald, Apr. 20, 1978; children: Erin Margaret, Brenna Kathryn. BS, U. Ky., 1971; JD, U. Colo., 1974; LLM in Taxation, U. Denver, 1981. Bar: Colo. 1975, U.S. Tax Ct. 1981, Idaho 1982;. Dep. dist. atty. Weld County, Colo., 1974-78; assoc. Montgomery, Little, Young, Campbell, & McGrew, Denver, 1979-80; rschr. appellate divsn. IRS, Denver, 1980-81; mem. staff tax dept. Price Waterhouse, Denver, 1981-82; ptnr. Hawley, Troxell, Ennis & Hawley, LLP, Boise, Idaho, 1982—; adj. prof. Boise State U., 1983; guest lecturer U. Idaho Coll. Law, Moscow, 1990; guest speaker various tax seminars, 1983—. Contbr. over 50 articles to profl. jours. Bd. dirs. Assn. for Retarded Citizens Ada County, Inc., 1987-93, pres. 1991-92, Assoc. Taxpayers Idaho, Inc., 1993—, exec. com., 1995—; audit review panel United Way Ada County, 1986-91; IRS vol. tax asst. program 1982, 87. Fellow Am. Coll. of Trust and Estate Counsel; mem. ABA (taxation sect.), Idaho State Bar Assn. (founding mem., taxation probate and trust law sect.), Idaho Soc. CPAs (fed. and state taxation com. 1984-89, bus. legis. com. 1989-91), Boise Bar Assn., Toastmasters (pres. 1991), Beta Gamma Sigma, Sigma Chi. Home: 1824 N 19th St Boise ID 83702-0707 Office: Hawley Troxell Ennis & Hawley LLP 877 Main St Boise ID 83702-5883

MCGRATH, PATRICK JOSEPH, bishop; b. Dublin, Ireland, July 11, 1945; came to U.S., 1970; Grad., St. John's Coll. Sem., Waterford, Ireland; student, Lateran U., Rome. Ordained priest Roman Cath. Ch., 1970, titular bishop of Allegheny. Aux. bishop Archdiocese San Francisco, 1989—. Office: Archdiocese San Francisco Chancery Office 445 Church St San Francisco CA 94114*

MCGRATH, SHERYL LYNNETTE, executive director non-profit organization; b. Kenosha, Wis., Sept. 11, 1962; d. George John and Lola LaVaughn (Moen) McGrath. AA, Spokane (Wash.) Coll. C.C., 1982; BA, Ea. Wash. U., 1984, MA, 1986; cert., Grantsmanship Tng. Ctr. Inst., L.A., Calif., 1997, People's Law Sch., Spokane, Wash., 1997. Gen. mgr. 1881 restaurant Sheraton Hotel, Spokane, Wash., 1986-88; acct. coord. Estee Lauder/Nordstrom, San Diego, 1988-90; dir. retail ops. The Salvation Army, Spokane, Wash., 1990-94; exec. dir. Cancer Patient Care, Spokane, 1994—; goodwill ambassador Caterina Wineries, Spokane, 1990—; pub. speaker to orgns., industries, groups for Cancer Patient Care; TV show hostess, Cancer Patient Care TCI Comm., Spokane, 1998—. Campaign com. United Way, Spokane, 1996-97; v.p. Rep. Action Club, Spokane, 1997—, coord. candidate forum 1997, senator appreciation reception, 1997, campaign com. Rep. Duane Sommers 6th dist., 1998; VIP participant Yakima Tng. Facility Wash. State Nat. Guard, 1998; bd. dirs., co-chair expansion com. Spokane Luth. Sch., 1998; chair Spokane County Rep. Party, 1999—. Recipient Key Nat. Art award, Spokane, Wash., 1978. 2d runner up Mrs. Washington Internat., Spokane, 1993, also Comty. Svc. award 1993, 2d runner up Mrs. Washington Am., 1995, Ms Wash. Am. Woman, Ms Am. Woman, 1995. Mem. NRA, Spokane Ecolog. Soc., Spokane C. of C. (Agora bus. excellence award 1998), Rotary South Spokane (social com. chair 1997, exec. sec. 1998, pres.-elect 2000). Avocations: painting, piano, wine tasting, event planning, creative projects. Home: 4006 S Perry St Spokane WA 99203-4271 Office: Cancer Patient Care 124 E Treat Spokane WA 99202

MCGREGOR, RUTH VAN ROEKEL, state supreme court justice; b. Le Mars, Iowa, Apr. 4, 1943; d. Bernard and Marie Frances (Janssen) Van Roekel; m. Robert James McGregor, Aug. 15, 1965. BA, U. Iowa, 1964, MA, 1965; JD, Ariz. State U., 1974. Bar: Ariz. 1974, U.S. Dist. Ct. Ariz. 1974, U.S. Ct. Appeals (9th cir.), U.S. Supreme Ct. 1982. Assoc. Fennemore, Craig, von Ammon, Udall & Powers, Phoenix, 1974-79, ptnr., 1980-81, 82-89; law clk. to justice Sandra Day O'Connor U.S. Supreme Ct., Washington, 1981-82; mem. disciplinary commn. Ariz. Supreme Ct., 1984—. Mem., newsletter editor Charter 100, Phoenix, 1981—; bd. dirs., mem. Ctr. for Law in Pub. Interest, Phoenix, 1977-80. Mem. ABA (chmn. state memberships 1985—), Ariz. Bar Assn. (disciplinary com. 1984—). Democrat. Lutheran. Club: Soroptomists. Office: Arizona Supreme Court 1501 W Washington St Phoenix AZ 85007-3231*

MCGROGAN, MICHAEL PATRICK, molecular and cell biologist; b. San Francisco, Apr. 4, 1947; s. John Thomas and Veneta Almeta (Wideman) McG.; m. Sharol Kay Hudson, Sept. 13, 1969; 1 child, Melissa Catherine. Student, U. Mo., St. Louis, 1965-67; BA in Microbiology, U. Mo., Columbia, 1969; student, St. Louis U., 1971-73; PhD in Molecular and Cell Biology, Washington U., St. Louis, 1977. Postdoctoral rschr. Wash. U. Med. Sch., St. Louis, 1977-78; NCI postdoctoral fellow dept. bio. scis. Stanford (Calif.) U., 1978-81; scientist, rsch. group leader molecular biology dept. Cetus Corp., Emeryville, Calif., 1981-85; sr. scientist, rsch. group leader molecular biology dept. InVitron Corp., Redwood City, Calif., 1985-90; dir., sr. staff scientist Dept. of Gene Expression, Berlex Biosci., Alameda, Calif., 1990-93; chief scientific officer Sierra BioSource, Gilroy, Calif., 1993-96; dir. R&D Layton BioSci., Gilroy, Calif., 1996-98, v.p. R&D, 1998—; project leader Interleukin 2 (IL-2) Cetus Corp., 1982-84; primary investigator Protease Nexin, InVitron Corp., Redwood City, 1986-88; rsch. leader for granulocyte proteins project, 1988-90; developer human hNT-Neuron products. Contbr. articles to profl. jours.; patentee in field. Fellow NDEA, St. Louis U., 1971; rsch. grantee NIH, Wash. U., 1973, SBIR grantee. Mem. AAAS, Am. Soc. of Microbiology. Office: Layton BioSci 1180-C Day Rd Gilroy CA 95020-9308

MCGUIRE, JAMES CHARLES, aircraft company executive; b. St. Louis, Aug. 8, 1917; s. John Patrick and Anna Beulah (Erbar) McG.; AB, Washington U., St. Louis, 1949, MA (Univ. fellow), 1953, PhD, 1954; m. Eunice Leota Sloop, Mar. 21, 1942 (div. June 1948); 1 child: Judith Lynn; m. Ingrid Elisabeth Getreu, Sept. 16, 1954. Research assoc. Ohio State U., 1953-56; rsch. psychologist Aeromed. Lab., Wright-Patterson AFB, Ohio, 1956-59; group supr. Boeing Airplane Co., Seattle, 1959-61; dept. mgr. Internat. Electric Corp., Paramus, N.J., 1961-62; sr. human factors scientist System Devel. Corp., Santa Monica, Calif., 1962-67; v.p. Booz-Allen Applied Rsch., Saigon, Vietnam, 1967-72; v.p. Assoc. Cons. Internat., Saigon, 1972-75, Bethesda, Md., 1975-78; br. chief Human Factors, System Tech. Devel., 1978-82; prin. staff engr. tech. modernization methodology Douglas Aircraft Co., Long Beach, Calif., 1982-85; program mgr. cockpit automation tech. program, Northrop Aircraft div., Hawthorne, Calif., 1985-87; sect. mgr. aircraft programs human factors engring. dept. Douglas Aircraft Co., Long Beach, 1987-90, sr. staff engr. Crew Systems Tech., 1990-93; prin. engr. tech. McDonnell Douglas Aerospace Transport Aircraft, 1993-94; prin. engr.-scientist, crew sys. tech., Phantom Works, Boeing Co., 1995—, DeltaIV Rocket Internat. Space Sta.; lectr. Nat. Def. Coll., Vietnamese Armed Forces, Saigon, 1971. Served with AUS, 1940-46. Decorated Bronze Star medal with oak leaf cluster; recipient Tech. Svc. First Class medal Republic South Vietnam Armed Forces, 1968. Mem. Am. Psychol. Assn., IEEE, Computer Soc. of IEEE, Human Factors and Ergonomics Soc., Am. Assn. Artificial Intelligence, Phi Beta Kappa, Sigma Xi. Republican. Home: 23201 Mindanao Cir Dana Point CA 92629-3625 Office: Boeing Info Space and Def Sys Mail code C078-0422 2401 E Wardlow Rd Long Beach CA 90807-5309

MCGUIRE, MICHAEL ALLEN, artist, educator; b. Columbus, Ohio, Dec. 22, 1946; s. Hetsel Stewart and Agnes Marie (Whitesel) McG. Student, Columbus Coll. Art and Design, 1958-60; BA, Ohio U., 1970; postgrad., Santa Monica City Coll., 1972, Santa Fe C.C., 1997—. Art therapist Columbus State Mental Hosp., 1970-72; artist, illustrator freelance, L.A. and Santa Fe, 1972—; fine artist in painting Santa Fe, 1974—; illustrator John Muir Publs., Santa Fe, 1978-81; animation artist Animated Images, Bandelier Films, UMA Mirage Prodns., 1984-88; freelance muralist, Santa Fe, 1975-80; art tchr. Brentwood Art Ctr., L.A., 1971-74, Valdes Art Instrn..N.Mex. Artists Assn., Santa Fe, 1982—. Artist: Cosmic Erotica, 1972, Creation Compositions, 1973; featured artist Best of Wildlife Art, 1997, 99, 99; exhibited in shows at Ind. State Mus., Indpls., N.Mex. Art League, Albuquerque, Governor's Gallery, Santa Fe, Variant Gallery, Taos, N.Mex., N.Mex. State Fair, Fine Arts Complex, Albuquerque, Leigh Yawkey Woodson Art Mus., Wausau, Wis., Rotary Club of Colorado Springs, Colo., numerous others. Recipient numerous awards for art. Mem. N.Mex. Watercolor Soc. (signature mem.). Avocations: computer graphics and animation, tennis, golf, bonsai, parrots. E-mail: vistaman@earthlink.net. Home and Studio: 3356 Cerrillos Rd Santa Fe NM 87505-7201

MCGUIRE, MICHAEL FRANCIS, plastic and reconstructive surgeon; b. St. Louis, Oct. 4, 1946; s. Arthur Patrick and Virginia Claribel (Gannon) McG. BA, Columbia U., 1968, MD, 1972. Diplomate Am. Bd. Surgery, Am. Bd. Plastic Surgery. Intern UCLA, 1972-73, resident in gen. surgery, 1973-77, resident in plastic surgery, 1978-80; fellow in plastic surgery rsch. Stanford (Calif.) U., 1977-78; traveling fellow in plastic surgery Gt. Britain, 1980; chief plastic surgery L.A. County-Olive View Med. Ctr., Sylmar, Calif., 1980-85; pvt. practice Santa Monica, Calif., 1980—; chief plastic surgery St. John's Health Ctr., 1990—; asst. clin. prof. surgery UCLA, 1980-97, assoc. clin. prof., 1998—; bd. dirs. Calif. Med. Rev., Inc., sec.-treas., 1997, v.p., 1997—; chmn. surg. rev. St. Johns Health Ctr., 1996-98; pres. Pacific Coast Plastic Surgery Ctr., 1988—. Charter patron L.A. Music Ctr. Opera, 1983—; sponsoring patron Los Angeles County Art Mus., 1986—; patron Colleague Helpers in Philanthropic Svc., Bel Air, Calif., 1987, 93, 95; pres. Found. for Surg. Reconstrn., 1996—. Fellow ACS, Royal Soc. Medicine; mem. Am. Soc. Plastic and Reconstructive Surgeons (membership chmn. 1997—), Am. Soc. Aesthetic Plastic Surgery (ethics chmn. 1998—), L.A. County Med. Assn. (v.p. 1995-97, sec.-treas. 1997—), Calif. Med. Assn. (del., exec. com., splty. delegation 1994—), Calif. Soc. Plastic Surgery (exec. com., auditor 1988-89, program chmn. 1990, exec. coun. 1991-94, treas. 1994-97, v.p. 1997-98, acting pres. 1997, pres.-elect 1998-99, pres. 1999—), Am. Assn. Accreditation of Ambulatory Surgery (facilities ops. com. 1995-96, bd. dirs. 1996, treas. 1996-98, sec. 1998—), Alpha Omega Alpha. Avocations: golf, travel, collecting antique Irish glass, opera, modern art. Office: 1301 20th St Ste 460 Santa Monica CA 90404-2054

MCGUIRE, MICHAEL JOHN, environmental engineer; b. San Antonio, June 29, 1947; s. James Brendan and Opal Mary (Brady) McG.; BS in Civil Engring., U. Pa., 1969; MS in Environ Engring., Drexel U., 1972, PhD in Environ. Engring., 1977; diplomate Am. Acad. Environ. Engring.; m. Deborah Marrow, June 19, 1971; children: David, Anna. San. engr. Phila. Water Dept., 1969-73; rsch. assoc. Drexel U., Phila., 1976-77; prin. engr. Brown & Caldwell Cons. Engrs., Pasadena, Calif., 1977-79; water quality engr. Met. Water Dist. of So. Calif., L.A., 1979-84, water quality mgr., 1984-86, dir. water quality, 1986-90, asst. gen. mgr., 1990-92; pres. McGuire Environ. Cons., Inc., Santa Monica, Calif., 1992—; cons. to subcom. on adsorbents, safe drinking water com. Nat. Acad. Scis., 1978-79, Natl. Rsch. Council, Drinking Water Contaminants (comm. mem.) 1998; cons. mem. Techs. Workgroup USEPA, DBP Reg Neg, 1992-93. Registered profl. engr., Pa., N.J., Calif., Ariz. Mem. Am. Water Works Assn. (Acad. Achievement award 1978, edn. div. chmn. 1982-83, chair taste and odor com. 1993-98,

Calif.-Nev. sect., chmn. water quality and resources div. 1982-83, governing bd. 1984-87, 89-96, exec. com. 1989-96, chmn. 1991-92, nat. dir. 1993-96, trustee Research Found. 1983-86, nat. v.p. 1994-96, nat. exec. com. 1994-96, Fuller award 1994), Am. Chem. Soc., ASCE, Internat. Water Supply Assn., Internat. Assn. on Water Quality (specialist group on taste and odor control 1982—, chmn. organizing com. 1991, off-flavor symposium 1987-91), Internat. Ozone Assn. (internat. bd. dirs. 1992-95), Sigma Xi, Sigma Nu, Sigma Tau. Editor: (with I.H. Suffet) Activated Carbon Adsorption of Organics From the Aqueous Phase, 2 vols., 1980; Treatment of Water by Granular Activated Carbon, 1983; contbr. articles to profl. jours. Office: McGuire Environ Cons Inc 1919 Santa Monica Blvd Santa Monica CA 90404-1950

MCGUIRE, MICHAEL WILLIAM, communications executive; b. Pomona, Calif., Aug. 1, 1960; s. Frederick L. and Anna Belle (Crum) McG.; m. Victoria Jean Von Tobel; children: Gordon, Michael Jr. BA in Polit. Sci., U. San Diego, 1984. Spokesman, dir. Congl. affairs Voice of Am., Washington, 1986-88; owner, chief exec. officer McGuire Rsch. Svcs., Las Vegas, Denver and, San Francisco, 1988—; cons. various U.S. and multinat. corps. Cons. various candidates for pub. office, 1988. Mem. Hiwan Golf Club. Home: 34123 Upper Bear Creek Rd Evergreen CO 80439-7816

MCGULPIN, ELIZABETH JANE, nurse; b. Toledo, Oct. 18, 1932; d. James Orville and Leah Fayne (Helton) Welden; m. David Nelson Buster, Apr. 9, 1956 (div. Nov. 1960); children: David Hugh, James Ray, Mark Stephen; m. Fredrick Gordon McGulpin, Oct. 7, 1973. AA in Nursing, Pasadena City Coll., 1968. RN, Wash. Lic. nurse Las Encinas Hosp., Pasadena, Calif.; nurse Hopi Indian Reservation HEW, Keams Canyon, Ariz., 1969-70; nurse, enterostomal therapist Pasadena Vis. Nurse Assn., 1972-74; nurse Seattle King County Pub. Health, 1977-81; home care nurse Victorville, Calif., 1983-85; nurse Adult Family Home, Woodinville, Wash., 1986—; vol. nurse, counselor Child Protective Svcs., Victorville, 1984; realtor Century 21, Lynden, Wash., 1993—. Vol. nurse Am. Cancer Soc., Pasadena, 1973-75, United Ostomy Assn., Los Angeles, Victorville, 1973-84; RN, ARC, 1996—. Am. Cancer Soc. grantee. Mem. Nat. Assn. Realtors, Wash. Assn. Realtors, Whatcom County Assn. Realtors, Vis. Nurse Assn. (Enterostomal Therpay grantee 1973). Avocations: reading, gardening, travel. Home: 106 Kale St Everson WA 98247-9660

MCHENRY, ANITA PETEI, historian, archaeologist; b. Coffeyville, Kans., Mar. 2, 1949; d. Woodrow Wilson Gordon and Erva Odile (Crevier) Hardy; m. Gray Richard McHenry, Dec. 12, 1981; children: Carrie Ann, Thomas Owen. BS in Anthropology, U. Calif., Riverside, 1992; MA in History, U. San Diego, 1997. Archaeologist, historian Gallegos & Assocs., Carlsbad, Calif., 1990-96; pub., owner GP Mktg., Escondido, Calif., 1996—; vol. archivist Valley Ctr. (Calif.) Libr., 1996—; v.p. hist. com. Friends of Valley Ctr. Libr., 1996—. Author: History of Valley Center, 1997. Mem. Nat. Trust Historic Preservation. Recipient fellowship grant U. San Diego, 1995-96. Mem. Soc. Calif. Archaeology, San Diego Hist. Soc., Smithsonian Assn., San Diego County Archaeol. Soc., Phi Alpha Theta. Avocations: historical research, genealogy, archaeology, reading. Home and Office: GP Mktg 28338 Mountain Meadow Rd Escondido CA 92026-6907

MCHENRY, HENRY MALCOLM, anthropologist, educator; b. Los Angeles, May 19, 1944; s. Dean Eugene and Emma Jane (Snyder) McH.; m. Linda Jean Conway, June 25, 1966; children: Lindsay Jean, Annalisa Jane. BA, U. Calif., Davis, 1966, MA, 1967; PhD, Harvard U., 1972. Asst. prof. anthropology U. Calif., Davis, 1971-76, assoc. prof. anthropology, 1976-81, prof. anthropology, 1981—, chmn. dept. anthropology, 1984-88. Fellow Am. Anthrop. Assn., Calif. Acad. Sci.; mem. Am. Assn. Phys. Anthropologists (exec. com. 1981-85), Soc. Study Evolution, Soc. Vertebrate Paleontology, Phi Beta Kappa, Phi Kappa Phi. Democrat. Buddhist. Avocation: winemaker. Home: 330 11th St Davis CA 95616-2010 Office: U of Calif Davis Dept Of Anthropology Davis CA 95616

MCHENRY, JULIE, communications executive. BJ, U. Mo.; MBA in Mktg., U. Portland. Adv. prog. supr. Tektronix, Inc., Beaverton, Oreg.; acct. exec. Regis McKenna Inc., Portland, Oreg.; co-founder, v.p. The Waggener Group; co-founder Global Tech. Comm., Wilson McHenry Co.; spkr. in field. Office: Wilson McHenry Co 393 Vintage Park Dr Ste 140 Foster City CA 94404*

MCHENRY, PATRICIA ROSE, state agency administrator; b. Burbank, Calif., Mar. 24, 1950; d. Clarence U. and Neota Etta (Common) Benton. BA with distinction, U. N.Mex., 1977. Office mgr. S.W. Cable TV, Espanola, N.Mex., 1978-79; exec. asst. Baha'i' Internat. Ctr., Haifa, Israel, 1980-83; exec. mgmt. analyst N.Mex. Dept. Fin. and Adminstrn., Santa Fe, 1979, exec. budget analyst, 1983-85; sr. fiscal analyst N.Mex. Legis. Fin. Com., Santa Fe, 1985-88; dep. dir. adminstrv. svcs. divsn. N.Mex. Dept. Corrections, Santa Fe, 1988-89; adminstr. data processing N.Mex. Human Svc. Dept., Santa Fe, 1990-92; dep. dir. property control divsn. N.Mex. Gen. Svc. Dept., Santa Fe, 1992—. V.p. Mil. Hist. Found. N.Mex. Mem. Baha'i' Faith. Office: NMex Gen Svc Dept Property Control Divsn 1100 S Saint Francis Dr Santa Fe NM 87505-4147

MCHUGH, BETSY BALDWIN, sociologist, educator, journalist, business owner; b. Concord, N.H., 1928; d. Walter Killenbeck and Eliza Alice (Hunt) Slater; m. Michael Joseph McHugh, Dec. 19, 1954; children: Betsy, Michael. MusB in Vocal Music, Syracuse (N.Y.) U., 1954; grad. student, Cornell U. Tchr. pub. schs. Juneau, Alaska, 1966-85; owner, founder Cashè Pub. Co., Tampa, Fla., and Juneau, 1986—, Nikish Ki Lodges and Youth Camps subsidiaries Baldwin Enterprises. Named one of Alaska's Outstanding Educators, Gov. Alaska Woman's Commn., 1985, Uno of Yr., 1993, 94, Internat. Una of Yr., 1993, 94, one of 2000 Most Notable Women, 1994, Better Profl. WOmen, 1993, 94. Mem. Can. Nat. Libr., Nat. Press Club, Bus. Assn. N.Y. State, Libr. of Congress, Can. Bus., D.C. C. of C., Mex. C. of C., Sigma Delta Chi. Avocations: snorkeling, writing, sociology, dancing, music.

MC HUGH, MARGARET ANN GLOE, psychologist; b. Salt Lake City, Nov. 8, 1920; d. Harold Henry and Olive (Warenski) Gloe; m. William T. McHugh, Oct. 1, 1943; children: Mary Margaret McHugh-Shuford, William Michael, Michelle McHugh Sprague. BA, U. Utah, 1942; MA in Counseling and Guidance, Idaho State U., 1964; PhD in Counseling Psychology, U. Oreg., 1970. Lic. psychologist; nat. cert. counselor . Tchr. kindergarten, Idaho Falls, Idaho, 1951-62, tchr. high sch. English, 1962-63; counselor Counseling Center, Idaho State U., Pocatello, 1964-67; instr. U. Oreg., Eugene, 1967-70; asst. prof. U. Victoria, B.C., Can., 1970-76; therapist Peninsula Counseling Center, Port Angeles and Sequim, Wash., 1976-81, McHugh & Assocs. Counseling Center, 1981—, ret. 1995. Served with WAVES, 1943-44. Mem. APA, ACA, Am. Assn. Marriage and Family Therapy, Wash. Psychol. Assn. (rsch. women issues, rels's., depression and women, sexual abuse, adults with childhood and abuse trauma). Home: 1175 Cameron Rd Sequim WA 98382-7501

MCHUGH, PETER, mayor; b. Boston; m. Gail Marie Parnagian; children: Sean Michael, Tatia Marie. Student, Boston U. Sch. Bus. Adminstrn., 1963; BS in Bus. Adminstrn., UCLA, 1969. With IBM, 1964; mem. city coun. Milpitas, Calif., 1976-78, 82-90; mayor Milpitas, 1978-82, 90-96; bd. suprs. dist. 3 County of Santa Clara, 1996—. Recipient numerous honors and acknowledgments for cmty. svc. including Calif. State Assembly, Calif. State Senate, U.S. Congress. Office: 70 W Hedding St Fl 10 San Jose CA 95110-1705*

MCINNIS, SCOTT STEVE, congressman, lawyer; b. Glenwood Springs, Colo., May 9, 1953; s. Kohler McInnis and Carol Kreir; m. Lori McInnis; children: Daxon, Tessa, Andrea. BA, Ft. Lewis Coll., 1975; JD, St. Mary's Law Sch., 1980. Atty. Delaney & Balcomb P.C., Glenwood Springs, Colo., 1981—; mem. Colo. Ho. of Reps., 1984-93; majority leader, 1990-93; mem. 103d-106th Congresses from 3d Colo. Dist., 1993—; chmn. agri. livestock and natural resources com., 1988-90; mem. rules com. Recipient Florence Sabin award, 1984, Guardian of Small Bus. award Nat. Fed. Ind. Bus., 1990, Lee Atwater Leadership award, 1991, and various awards from United Vets. Country; named Legislator of Decade and Legislator of Yr. by Colo. Ski Country and Colo. Wildlife Found. Mem. Elks, Rotary, Phi Delta Phi. Republican. Roman Catholic. Office: US Ho of Reps 215 Cannon HOB Washington DC 20515-0603*

MCINNIS, SUSAN MUSÉ, corporate communications manager; b. Seattle, July 22, 1955; d. Emmett Emory Jr. and Florence Howardine (McAteer) McI. BSBA, U. Denver, 1977; cert. in environ. design, UCLA, 1985; MA in Journalism, Calif. State U., Fullerton, 1992. Researcher Denver Gen. Hosp., summer 1973; mktg. coord. 3M Bus. Products, Emeryville, Calif., 1978-79; spl. libr. Reel Grobman & Assocs., L.A., 1981-83; tchr. Mayfield Sr. Sch., Pasadena, Calif., 1985-87; advt. coord. Reynolds Advt., 1987; cmty. and employee rels. mgr. Calif.-Am. Water Co. (oper. co. Am. Water Works), San Marino, Calif., 1988—. Mem. Am. Water Works Assn. (cert. water distbn.), Pub. Rels. Soc. Am., Kiwanis (pres. Duarte, Calif. chpt. 1994-95).

MCINTIRE, WILLIAM ALLAN, communications executive, special effects supervisor; b. Long Beach, Calif., Dec. 29, 1946; s. Calvin William McIntire and Ivy Rosalind (Boyd) Wagner; m. Kathryn Dugger, May 7, 1977; children: William Raymond, Jessica Louise. Student, Valley Jr. Coll., Long Beach City Coll. Format advisor Reb Foster Assocs., Beverly Hills, Calif., 1960-65, gen. mgr. music publ., sound engr., 1970-73; gen. mgr. music publ., sound engr. A&R Three Dog Night, 1971-73; mgr. equipment mfg. div., sound reinforcement engr. Pirate Sound, Inc., Hollywood, Calif., 1973-76; chief engr., TV prodn. tech. supr. Mobile Video Prodns., Portland, Oreg., 1976-80; owner, tech. support Creative Tech. Services, Portland, 1980-84; prodn. tech. supr., prodn. mgr. MPI Prodns., Portland, 1984-87; TV engr., prodn. ops., camera operator Sta. KPTV-TV, Portland, 1987; owner William A. McIntire Entreprises, Portland; song screening staff Am. Song Festival, 1975; camera shader Portland Trailblazers TV, 1980-81. Produced spl. effects, lighting, equipments and electronics for numerous films, TV and stage; spl. effects supr. numerous music videos and commls.; inventor various electronic devices and Magic Gadgets and Magic Boxes trademark. Mem. Audio Engring. Soc., Soc. Motion Picture and TV Engrs., soc. Broadcast Engrs., Oreg. Media Prodn. Assn. Office: William A McIntire Enterprises PO Box 4244 Portland OR 97208-4244

MCINTYRE, JERILYN SUE, academic administrator; m. W. David Smith. Student, Stanford U., Italy, 1962; AB in History with distinction, Stanford U., 1964, MA in Journalism, 1965, cert. Summer Radio-TV Inst., 1965, tchrs. cert., 1968; PhD in Comms., U. Washington, 1973; postgrad. Inst. Ednl. Mgmt., Harvard U., 1993. Corr. World News Bureau McGraw-Hill Pub. Co., L.A.; asst. prof. dept. mass comm. Chico (Calif.) State Coll., 1968-70; asst. prof. Sch. Journalism U. Iowa, Iowa City, 1973-77; acting dir. divsn. journalism and mass comm. U. Utah, Salt Lake City, 1978-79, assoc. prof., prof. dept. comm., 1977—, assoc. dean Coll. Humanities, 1984-88, assoc. v.p. acad. affairs, 1988-90, interium pres., 1991-98, v.p. acad. affairs, 1990—; dir. Wall St. Jour. Publs. workshop Chico State Coll., 1968; mem. ednl. adv. bd. NFL, 1996—; mem. exec. com. coun. acad. affairs Nat. Assn. State Univs. and Land Grant Colls., 1995—, chair-elect, 1996-97; mem. steering com. Utah Edn. Network, 1995—. Editl. asst. Chemical Week Mag., 1965-66, World News Bureau, 1966-67; mem. editl. bd. Journalism History; past mem. editl. bd. Comms. Peports, Critical Studies in Mass Comm., Journalism Monographs, Jour. Comm. Inquiry, Journalism Quarterly, Western Jour. Speech Comm.; contbr. articles to profl. jours., chpts. to books. Mem. Utah Women's Forum, pub. awareness and comm. com. Utah Partnership Edn. and Econ. Devel., others. Pub. Rels. Soc. Am. fellow, 1968, U. Washington grantee, 1972, 73, U. Iowa grantee, 1976, U. Utah grantee, 1981, 82, David P. Gardner fellow, 1984; recipient Yesterday's Girl Scout Today's Successful Woman award Utah Girl Scout Coun., 1996. Mem. AAUW (Dist. Woman Utah Salt Lake City chpt. 1994), Assn. Fedn in Journalism and Mass Comm. (mem. com. on status women 1979-80, sec. and editor CLIO 1979-80, vice head hist. divsn. office 1980-91, head 1981-82, mem. publs. com. 1981-84, mem. adv. com. 1981-82, mem. standing com. on rsch. 1989-95), Rotary (Salt Lake City chpt., chmn. sch. and edn. com.), Kappa Tau Alpha (pres. U. Utah chpt.). Office: U Utah Salt Lake City UT 84112

MCINTYRE, LISA JEAN, sociologist, educator; b. Sedro Woolley, Wash., Apr. 14, 1953; d. David Gillespie and Jean Francis McI. BA, Smith Coll., 1975; MA, U. Chgo., 1978, PhD, 1986. Asst. prof. sociology Wash. State U., Pullman, 1987-93, assoc. prof. sociology, 1993—. Author: The Public Defender, 1987, Law in the Sociological Enterprise, 1994, The Practical Skeptic: Core Concepts in Sociology, 1999; author, editor: Families & Law, 1993. Mem. Am. Sociol. Assn., Sociologists for Women in Soc., Law & Soc. Assn. Office: Wash State U Dept Sociology Pullman WA 99164-4020

MCINTYRE, LOUISE S., income tax consultant; b. Cin., Jan. 29, 1924; d. George Washington and Bertha (McDaniels) Sullivan; m. Harry McIntyre Jr., Jan. 18, 1947; children: Carol L., Patricia A., Harriet L., Harry J., Brenda R. AA, Mira Costa Coll., Oceanside, Calif., 1972; grad. in auditing, Nat. Tax Practice Inst., 1989. Enrolled agt. Hydraulic testor Paterson Field, Fairfield, Ohio, 1942-45; control clk. Hickam Field, Honolulu, 1945-47; clk.-typist Patterson Field, Fairfield, 1947-49, Camp LeJeune, Jacksonville, N.C., 1951-56; sec., bookkeeper Mission Bowl, Oceanside, 1973-79; income tax cons. Oceanside, 1974—. Mem. Oceanside Human Rels. Commn., 1970; bd. dirs. Armed Forces YMCA, Oceanside, 1969-71, Oceanside Christian Women's Club, 1988-91, North County Concert Assn. Aux., 1993-96; active PTA, Girl Scout U.S. Mem. Inland Soc. Tax Cons. (bd. dirs. 1988—), Am. Soc. Women Accts. (v.p. 1989-90), Enrolled Agts. Palomar, Nat. Assn. Enrolled Agts., Nat. Soc. Pub. Accts., Calif. Assn. Ind. Accts., Palmquist PTA (hon. life). Avocations: bowling, dancing, crafts, interior decorating, cake decorating. Home: 328 Camelot Dr Oceanside CA 92054-4515

MCINTYRE, NORMAN F., petroleum industry executive; b. Pangman, Sask., Can., Oct. 21, 1945; s. Donald and Jean (Cruickshank) McI.; m. Lana Jean, June 10, 1967; children: Jason Lee, Spencer James. BSc in Petroleum Engring., U. Wyo., 1971; MS in Mgmt., MIT, 1991. Various positions with Mobil Oil, U.S., Can., to 1982; group mgr. engring. offshore divsn. Petro-Can., 1982-83, gen. mgr. frontier devel. offshore divsn., 1983, v.p. frontier devel., 1983-86, v.p. prodn. devel., 1986-89; sr. v.p. western region Petro-Can. Products, 1989-90; pres. Petro-Can. Resources, Calgary, Alta., Can., 1990-95, exec. v.p., 1995—; chmn., dir. Panarctic Oils Ltd.; dir. Petroleum Transmission Co., 1997. Campaign chair United Way of Calgary and Area. Mem. Can. Assn. of Petroleum Producers (chmn. 1998), Assn. of Profl. Engineers, Geologists and Geophysists of Alberta, Assn. Profl. Engrs. Office: Petro-Canada, 150-6th Ave SW PO Box 2844, Calgary, AB Canada T2P 3E3

MCINTYRE, ROBERT WHEELER, conservation organization executive; b. Chgo., Aug. 26, 1936; s. Henry Langenberg and Winifred (Wheeler) McI.; m. Emily Beardsley Taylor, Oct. 12, 1961 (div. 1985); children: W. Burley, Nancy T., Oliver W., Shanna L., Amanda K.; m. Miriam de Jesus Zarate, June 23, 1990 (div. 1998). AB in Sociology, Stanford U., 1959; MBA, Harvard U., 1964. Loan analyst Wells Fargo Bank, San Francisco, 1964-65; supr. budget analysis Ford Aerospace, Palo Alto, Calif., 1965-69; controller Allied Life Scis., San Leandro, Calif., 1969-70; ptnr. Diplomat Mfg. Co., Palo Alto, 1970-71; staff cons. Opportunity Through Ownership, San Francisco, 1971-72; gen. mgr. Quality Metal Finishers, San Francisco, 1972-73; sr. v.p., chief fin. officer The Trust for Pub. Land, San Francisco, 1973—. Adv. bd. Peninsula Open Space Trust, Menlo Park, 1978—, Resource Renewal Inst., Sausalito, 1988—, Wter Heritage Trust, Sausalito, 1988—, Dorothy Erskine Open Space Fund, San Francisco, 1978—; bd. dirs. Environ. Vols., Palo Alto, 1980—; bd. dirs., treas. Robert C. Wheeler Found., Palo Alto, 1965—. Lt. (j.g.) USNR, 1959-62. Recipient Presdl. Citation award, The Trust for Pub. Land, 1988, Spl. Svc. award, Environ. Vols., 1989. Mem. Harvard Club N.Y., Harvard Club Boston, San Francisco Tennis Club, USS Coral Sea Assn. Avocations: hiking, backpacking, tennis, travel. Office: The Trust for Public Land 116 New Montgomery St Fl 4 San Francisco CA 94105-3607

MC KAUGHAN, HOWARD PAUL, linguistics educator; b. Canoga Park, Calif., July 5, 1922; s. Paul and Edith (Barton) McK.; m. Barbara Jean Budroe, Dec. 25, 1943; children: Edith (Mrs. Daniel Skene Santoro), Charlotte (Ms. Charlotte Barnhart), Patricia (Mrs. Stephen B. Pike), Barbara (Mrs. Ronald Chester Bell), Judith (Ms. Judith D. Achilles). AB, UCLA, 1945, MTh, Dallas Theol. Sem., 1946; MA, Cornell U., 1952, PhD, 1957. Mem. linguistic rsch. team Summer Inst. Linguistics, Mexico, 1946-52; asso. dir. Summer Inst. Linguistics, Philippines, also assoc. dir. summer sessions U. N.D., 1952-57, dir. Philippine br., 1957-61; rsch. asst. prof. anthropology U. Wash., 1961-62; rsch. assoc. prof., 1962-63; assoc. prof. linguistics U. Hawaii, 1963-64, prof. linguistics, 1964-88, prof. emeritus, 1988—, chmn. dept., 1963-66, dir. Pacific and Asian Linguistics Inst., 1964, 1966-69, assoc. dean grad. div., 1965-72, dean grad. div., dir. rsch., 1972-79, acting chancellor, 1979, interim vice chancellor acad. affairs, 1981-82, acting dir rsch., 1982-84, acting dean grad. div., 1982-83, dean, 1984-87, dir. rsch. rels., 1987-88; lectr. linguistics U. Philippines, summers, 1954, 60; Fulbright vis. prof. Philippine Normal Coll.-Ateneo-De La Salle Consortium, Philippines, 1977, De La Salle U., Philippines, 1992; vis. prof. linguistics Bukidnon State Coll., Malaybalay, Philippines, 1993, 94; linguistic cons. Summer Inst. Linguistics, Malaysia branch, 1995—; prin. Wycliffe Sch. Linguistics, summers 1953, 61; vis. prof. Australian Nat. U., Canberra, 1970; adj. prof. linguistics U. Okla., summers 1984, 85, 86; vis. prof., head dept. linguistics Payap U., Chiang Mai, Thailand, 1989-90. Sr. scholar East-West Ctr., Honolulu, 1964; NDEA Maranao-Philippines research grantee, 1963-65; Office of Edn. Hawaii English grantee, 1965-66; NSF Jeh Language of South Vietnam grantee, 1969-70, Maranao Linguistic Studies, 1971-72, numerous other research grants. Mem. linguistic socs. Am., Philippines, Western Assn. Grad. Schs. (pres. 1978), Hawaii, Linguistic Circle N.Y., Philippine Assn. Lang. Tchrs., Hawaii Govt. Employees Assn., Phi Beta Kappa, Phi Kappa Phi. Author (with B. McKaughan): Chatino Dictionary, 1951; (with J. Forster) Ilocano: An Intensive Language Course, 1952; The Inflection and Syntax of Maranao Verbs, 1959; (with B. Macaraya): A Maranao Dictionary, 1967, rev. edit., 1996. Editor: Pali Language Texts: Philippines, 21 vols., 1971; The Languages of the Eastern Family of the East New Guinea Highlands Stock, 1973; Maranao Stories, 1995; Stories from the Darangen, 1995; contbr. articles, chpts. to books, sci. jours. Home: 420 S Hill Rd Mcminnville OR 97128-9105

MCKAY, ALICE VITALICH, academic administrator; b. Seattle, Sept. 6, 1947; d. Jack S. and Phyllis (Bourne) Vitalich; m. Larry W. McKay, Aug. 14, 1973 (div. Jan. 1983). BA, Wash. State U., 1969; MEd, U. Nev., Las Vegas, 1975; EdD, U. Nev., Reno, 1986. High sch. tchr. Clark County Sch. Dist., Las Vegas, 1972-77, specialist women's sports, 1977-80, high sch. counselor, 1980-84, high sch. asst. prin., 1984-95; dir. Project Lead U. Nev., Reno, 1995—; pres. Lotus Profit, Inc., Las Vegas, 1985-86; dir. Nev. Project Lead. Sec. exec. bd. Gang Alternatives Partnership, 1993—. Mem. Am. Assn. Counseling and Devel. (committee on women 1985—), Nev. State Counseling and Devel. (pres. 1985-86), Nat. Assn. Female Execs., AAUW, Phi Delta Kappa (exec. bd. 1980-82). Avocations: skiing, golf. Office: U Nev Coll Edn Reno NV 89557-0217

MCKAY, GLEN (GLEN GUMMESS), audio-visual specialist; b. L.A., Mar. 4, 1954; s. Glen H. and Evelyn (Hennesey) Gummess; m. Margo Polinski, Sept. 25, 1982; children: Matthew, Alicia. BA in Broadcast Journalism, U. So. Calif., 1976; Master in Ednl. Tech. Leadership, George Washington U., 1998. Radio news dir. Sta. KYKK/KZOR-FM, Hobbs, N.Mex., 1980-87; news corr. Sta. KBIM-TV, Roswell, N.Mex., 1987-90; audio visual coord. N.Mex. Jr. Coll., Hobbs, 1990—; web page cons. Estacado Libr. Info. Network, Hobbs, 1998. Author, dir. (video prodn.) Lemons to Lemonade, 1994 (1st place award AECT 1995); author, editor (radio documentary) Waste Isolation Pilot Plant, 1983 (Best Documentary award N.Mex. AP 1984). Mem. com. Troop 340 Boy Scouts Am., Hobbs, 1997-98; v.p. St. Helena Sch. Parent Sch. Assn., Hobbs, 1998—. Mem. Assn. Edn. and Comm. Tech. Roman Catholic. Avocations: swimming, hiking, books, movies. E-mail: gummess@wtaccess.com. Fax: 505-392-3668. Office: NMex Jr Coll 5317 N Lovington Hwy Hobbs NM 88240-9121

MCKAY, JOHN, lawyer; b. Seattle, June 19, 1956; s. John Larkin and Kathleen (Tierney) M. BA, U. Wash., 1978; JD, Creighton U., 1982. Bar: Wash. 1982, U.S. Dist. Ct. (we. dist.) Wash. 1982, U.S. Supreme Ct. 1990, U.S. Ct. Appeals (9th cir.) 1990. Ptnr. Lane Powell Spears Lubersky, Seattle, 1982-92, Cairncross & Hempelmann, Seattle, 1992-97; pres. Legal Svcs. Corp., Washington, 1997—. White House fellow, Washington, 1989-90. Mem. ABA (bd. govs. 1991-94), Wash. State Bar Assn. (pres. young lawyers divsn. 1988-89). Republican. Roman Catholic. Avocations: soccer, golf.

MCKAY, MONROE GUNN, federal judge; b. Huntsville, Utah, May 30, 1928; s. James Gunn and Elizabeth (Peterson) McK.; m. Lucile A. Kinnison, Aug. 6, 1954; children: Michele, Valanne, Margaret, James, Melanie, Nathan, Bruce, Lisa, Monroe. B.S., Brigham Young U., 1957; J.D., U. Chgo., 1960. Bar: Ariz. 1961. Law clk. Ariz. Supreme Ct., 1960-61; assoc. firm Lewis & Roca, Phoenix, 1961-66; ptnr. Lewis & Roca, 1968-74; assoc. prof. Brigham Young U., 1974-76, prof., 1976-77; judge U.S. Ct. Appeals for 10th Cir., Denver, 1977-91, chief judge, 1991-94, sr. judge, 1994—. Mem. Phoenix Community Council Juvenile Problems, 1968-74; pres. Ariz. Assn. for Health and Welfare, 1970-72; dir. Peace Corps, Malawi, Africa, 1966-68; bd. dirs., pres. Maricopa county Legal Aid Soc., 1972-74. Served with USMCR, 1946-48. Mem. ABA, Ariz. Bar Assn., Maricopa County Bar Assn., Am. Law Inst., Am. Judicature Soc., Order of Coif, Blue Key, Phi Kappa Phi. Mem. LDS Ch. Office: US Ct Appeals for 10th Cir Fed Bldg 125 S State St Ste 6012 Salt Lake City UT 84138-1114*

MCKAY, TOM, political organization administrator. Chmn. Rep. Party Alaska, Anchorage. Office: Rep Party Alaska 1001 West Firewood Ln Anchorage AK 99503*

MCKAY, W. COLIN, playwright, screenwriter, educator; b. San Francisco, June 22, 1948; s. Wallace Crawford and Olive Margaret McKay; m. Cary Larson, Dec. 7, 1971; children: W. Kirk and W. Conan (twins). Tchr. Bakersfield (Calif.) Coll.; dir. theater East Los Angeles Coll., Monterey Park, Calif.; playwright in residence Blue Sphere Aliance, Hollywood, Calif., 1997. Author: Nagasaki Dust, 1992 (Best New Play award Theatre Ctr. Group), Shadow War, 1997 (Charlotte Rep Festival award), Gentleman's War, 1998, Children of Shame, 1998; co-author: (with George Cybulski) Snitch, 1995.

MCKEE, CATHERINE LYNCH, law educator, lawyer; b. Boston, June 7, 1962; d. Robert Emmett and Anne Gayle (Tanner) Lynch; m. Bert K. McKee Jr., Dec. 25, 1990; children: Timothy Kingston, Shannon Lancaster. BA in Biol. Sci., U. Calif. Berkeley, 1984; JD, U. San Diego, 1988. Bar: Calif. 1988, U.S. Dist. Ct. (cen., so. and ea. dists.) Calif. 1989, U.S. Ct. Appeals (9th cir.) 1989. Assoc. Parkinson, Wolf, Lazar & Leo, L.A., 1988-89, McCormick & Mitchell, San Diego, 1989-91; prof. Mt. San Antonio Coll., Walnut, Calif., 1994—; certification review hearing officer, Orange County, 1994—. Contbr. weekly newspaper column, 1993—; prodr., star videos An Attorney's Guide to Legal Research on the Internet, 1999; co-author: Jeff and Catherine's World's Best List of Legal (and Law-related) Internet Sites. Chair scholarship com. U. Calif. Alumni Assn., Diamond Bar, 1995—. Named Cmty. Person of Yr. Diamond Bar C. of C., 1995. Mem. ABA, State Bar Calif. (probation monitor 1993—), Ea. Bar Assn. L.A., Am. Inns of Ct., Calif. Assn. Lanterman-Petris-Short Hearing Officers. Avocations: weight lifting, photography, reading. Office: Mount San Antonio Coll 1100 N Grand Ave Walnut CA 91789-1341

MC KEE, JOHN ANGUS, oil company executive; b. Toronto, Ont., Can., Aug. 31, 1935; s. John William and Margaret Enid (Phippen) McK.; m. Susan Elizabeth Harley, May 30, 1970; children: John Andrew, Mary Susan. Student, U. Toronto, 1954-58, Upper Can. Coll., Port Hope, Ont., Trinity Coll. Sch., Port Hope, Ont. With Dominion Securities Corp. Ltd., Toronto, 1958-60; mng. dir. Patino Mining Group, Toronto and London, Eng., 1960-71; with Consolidated Tin Smelters, Brit. Tin Investment Corp., Amalagamated Metal Corp., 1964-71; pres. J. Angus McKee & Assoc., 1971-93; pres., chief exec. officer Can. Occidental Petroleum Ltd., 1983-93; bd. dirs., chmn. Gulfstream Resources Can., Ltd., Calgary, Alta., 1993—; dir. Conor Pacific Environ. Techs. Inc., Big Rock Brewery Ltd., Hankin Atlas Industries Ltd., Stone & Webster Can. Ltd., Stone & Webster, Inc.; bd. govs. Trinity Coll. Sch.. Mem. Toronto Club, York Club, Badminton and Racquet Club, Ranchmen's Club, Calgary Petroleum Club, Knickerbocker Club (N.Y.C.), Craigleith Ski Club, Internat. Order of St. Hubert, Goodwood Club, Alpha Delta Phi [illegible]. Office: Gulf[illegible] Resources Ltd, 855 2d St SW 34th Fl, Calgary, AB Canada T2P 4J8

MCKEE, JOHN MORRISON, broadcast executive; b. Winnipeg, Man., Can., Sept. 2, 1951; s. Gordon John Frederick and Lee Rae (Morrison) M.; m. Susan Leslie Lewis, Apr. 13, 1974; children: Sean Adam, Jessica Lee, Trevor James. BA, U. Winnipeg, 1975. Store mgr. Eaton's of Can., 1975-79; gen. mktg. mgr. Hudson Bay Co., Can., 1979-90; v.p. sales and mktg. CUC Broadcasting Ltd., Can., 1990-92; v.p. gen. mgr. DIRECTV Can., 1992-95; sr. v.p. spl. markets DIRECTV, Inc., El Segundo, Calif., 1995—; sr. cons. Toronto (Can.) Retail Cons.; bd. dirs. St. Elizabeth's Vis. Nurses, Can., Power DIRECTV, Inc., Bandits Fashion Stores. Home: 28025 Lobrook Dr Rncho Pls Vrd CA 90275-3131 Office: DIRECTV Inc 2300 E Imperial Hwy El Segundo CA 90245-2813

MCKEE, ROBIN MELINDA, theatre director; b. Paris, Oct. 12, 1960; came to U.S., 1963; d. Robert Wesley and Susan Viola (Edwards) McK.; m. David Vincent Huscher, Feb. 1981 (div.); m. Robert Evans Walker, Aug. 15, 1987. BA in Drama with honors, U. Calif., Irvine, 1981; MA in Theatre Arts, Calif. State U., Sacramento, 1984; postgrad., Brit. Theatre Assn., London, 1990. Artistic dir. Sacramento Exptl. Theatre, 1982-84; asst. dir. Mark Taper Forum, L.A., 1989-90, assoc. spl. projects, 1989-90; producing dir. Telluride (Colo.) Repertory Theatre Co., 1994-95. coordinating prodr. Taper Lab '89: New Work Festival, L.A.; guest dir. Santa Paula Theater Ctr., Santa Paula, Calif., 1989, 91, Loyola Marymount U., L.A., 1991, The Sheridan Opera House, 1994, Sierra Repertory Co., Sonora, Calif., 1994, Sunset Ctr., Carmel, 1995, 96, The Western Stage, Salinas, Calif., 1995, 96, Colo. Shakespeare Festival, Boulder, 1997; co-prodr.: Mark Taper Forum, 1990; dir. Odyssey Theatre, L.A., 1991, (club tour) "Weill Thoughts" Stephaniem Vlahos Sings, L.A., 1991, L.A. Music Ctr. Opera, 1991, 92, Audrey Skirball-Kenis Theatre Assn. Matrix Theater, L.A., 1992, Telluride Theatre Festival, L.A., 1989-93 (Best Prodn., Best Direction awards), The Western Stage, Salinas, Calif., 1993, GroveMont Playhouse, Monterey, Calif., 1993, Sunset Ctr., Carmel, 1993; line prodr. Multicultural Spoken Word Festival, L.A., 1992, The Sheridan Opera House, Telluride, 1995; dir./dramaturge Polygram, Inc., L.A., 1991-93, Colo. Shakespeare Festival, Boulder, Colo., 1996; prodr. Telluride REP, 1994; dir./prodr. Telluride REP, 1995, Velvet Stages Prodns., Telluride, 1996; (film and video) 1st asst. dir. Lover's Lane and Daybreak; (film and video) dir. observer Married People, George, Going Places; Down Home, Home Improvement; (film and video) acting coach Goldilocks and the Three Bears; dir./exec. prodr. Telluride REP, 1995; prodr. Telluride REP, 1995; dir. O Solo Mio Festival, San Francisco, 1996, The Rocky Mountain Christmas, 1996; producing artistic dir. Carmel-by-the-Sea, 1997. Office: Carmel Performing Arts Festival PO Box 221473 Carmel CA 93922-1473

MCKEE, ROGER CURTIS, retired federal magistrate judge; b. Waterloo, Iowa, Feb. 11, 1931; s. James A. and Leonace (Burrell) McK.; m. Roberta Jeanne Orvis, Sept. 3, 1954; children: Andrea Jane, Brian Curtis, Paul Robert. BA, State Coll. of Iowa, 1955; MA, U. Ill., 1960; JD, U. San Diego, 1968. Bar: Calif. 1970, U.S. Dist. Ct. (so. dist.) Calif. 1969, U.S. Ct. Appeals (9th cir.) 1971. Telegrapher, agt. Ill. Cen. R.R., 1950-55; tng. asst. No. Ill. Gas Co., Aurora, 1959-60; with indsl. rels. dept. Convair div. Gen. Dynamics Corp., San Diego, 1960-68; contract adminstr. and supr. Datagraphix div. Gen. Dynamics Corp., San Diego, 1968-69, asst. counsel, 1969-70; ptnr. Powell & McKee, San Diego, 1970-75, Millsberg, Dickstein & McKee, San Diego, 1975-83; magistrate judge U.S. Dist. Ct. for So. Dist. Calif., San Diego, 1983-97; presiding magistrate judge, 1993-97. Bd. trustees So. Calif. Presbyn. Homes, L.A., 1979-81; moderator Presbytery of San Diego, 1980. Capt. USNR, 1949-85. Mem. Calif. Bar Assn., Fed. Magistrate Judges Assn., Navy League U.S., Naval Res. Officers Assn., Res. Officers Assn., Dixieland Jazz Soc. (bd. dirs. San Diego chpt. 1984—). Republican.

MCKEEVER, MIKE PIERCE, economics and business educator; b. Glendale, Calif., Mar. 3, 1941; s. Samuel Pierce and Martha Frances (Darby) McK.; m. Jeanetta Ross, Oct. 20, 1964 (div. June 1970); 1 child, Nancy; m. Marjorie Alice McKean, Dec. 17, 1970; children: Michael P. Jr., Johnathan Brooks. BA with honors, Whittier (Calif.) Coll., 1963; MS in Econs., London Sch. Econs., 1966. Life credential bus., econs., social sci. Calif. C.C. Owner Counseling Brokerage Group, Santa Rosa, Calif., 1980-84, Bus. Plan Workshop, Santa Rosa, 1980-95; asst. prof. econs. and bus. Armstrong U., Berkeley, Calif., 1995-97; founder McKeever Inst. Econ. Policy Analysis, Berkeley, 1995—. Author: How to Write a Business Plan, 1981, Conceptual Economics, 1993. Dir. Inst. Small Bus. Dept. Sonoma State U., 1981; pres. We Care, Santa Rosa, 1984; chmn. adv. com. Suppression of Drug Abuse in Schs. Sonoma County, Santa Rosa, 1985. Recipient award Role Recognition-Downtown Devel., Santa Rosa City Coun., 1983; named Vol. of Yr. Santa Rosa City Schs., 1984. Avocations: men's senior baseball league player and coach. Home and Office: 1511 Woolsey St Berkeley CA 94703-2321

MCKEIGHEN, RONALD EUGENE, physicist; b. Marion, Ill., Oct. 17, 1942; s. George A. and Aileen (Keach) McK.; m. Loretta M. Ward, Sept. 3, 1966; children: Kevin, Christy. BS in Engring. Physics, U. Ill., 1964, MS in Nuclear Engring., 1965, PhD in Physics, 1971. Postdoctoral in cancer rsch. and nuclear medicine Oak Ridge Nat. Lab., 1972-73; sr. prin. rsch. scientist Searle/Siemens Ultrasound, Des Plaines, 1973-79; sr. R&D engr. KB-Aerotech, Lewistown, Pa., 1979-83; staff scientist Advanced Diagnostic Rsch., Tempe, Ariz., 1983-85; prin. staff engr. Motorola Space Elect, Scottsdale, Ariz., 1985-86; mgr. advanced devel. Advanced Tech. Labs., Bothel, Wash., 1986-93; dir. advanced devel. Acoustic Imaging inc., Phoenix, 1993—. Contbr. articles to profl. jours. and chpts. to books. Spl. fellow in nuclear engrng. AEC. Mem. IEEE. Mem. Pentecostal Ch. Achievements include patent for concept of digital beamformer for ultrasonic phased array, developed ultrasonic transducer arrays and sensors. Home: 1432 E Desert Flower Ln Phoenix AZ 85048-5932 Office: Acoustic Imaging 10027 S 51st St Ste 101 Phoenix AZ 85044-5207

MCKELLOP, HARRY A., biomechanical engineering educator; b. L.A., Nov. 7, 1945; s. Thomas and Opal Nina (Brown) McK.; m. Tovya Wager, Nov. 5, 1989; 1 child, Rachelle Tashi. BS in Mech. Engring., UCLA, 1970, MS in Mech. Engring., 1972; PhD in Mech. Engring., U. So. Calif., 1988. Adj. asst. prof. surgery U. Calif., 1979-80; instr. rsch. orthopaedics U. So. Calif., L.A., 1980-89; dir. JVL Orthopaedic Rsch. Ctr., L.A., 1993—, asst. prof. orthopaedics, 1989-95, asst. prof. rsch. biomed. engring., 1989-95, assoc. prof. rsch. orthopaedics and biomed., 1995—, dir. rsch., 1994—; v.p. rsch. Orthopaedic Hosp., L.A., 1996—. Contbr. articles to profl. jours. Recipient John Charnley award, 1994; NIH grantee, 1994-97; awardee Kappa Delta, 1998. Fellow Am. Inst. Med. and Biol. Engring.; mem. Orthopaedic Rsch. Soc., Am. Acad. Orthopaedic Surgeons, Hip Soc. Achievements include development of wear resistant Polythylene for Joint Replacements; developed total system for fixing complex femur fractures. Office: Orthopaedic Hospital 2400 S Flower St Los Angeles CA 90007-2629

MCKELVY, MICHAEL JOHN, materials chemist, research scientist; b. Berkeley, Calif., Apr. 19, 1954; s. Andy Milton and Dagmar Marie (Johnson) McK.; m. Margaret Knight Riddall, Aug. 2, 1975; children: Robin, Adam, Evan. BS in Chemistry, U. Calif., Berkeley, 1975; MS in Chemistry, Ariz. State U., 1981, PhD in Chemistry, 1985. Engr. crystal growing lab., ctr. solid state sci. Ariz. State U., Tempe, 1976-82, materials sci. engr. II, 1982-84, rsch. specialist, 1984-90, mgr. materials facility, 1986-94, rsch. scientist, 1990—, affiliate assoc. prof. sci. & engring. of materials program, 1993—, dir. materials facility, 1994—, dir. Goldwater materials sci. labs., 1995—, acting dir. ctr. solid state sci., 1997; invited asst. prof. Institut des Matériaux de Nantes, U. Nantes, France, 1993; proposal reviewer Petroleum Rsch. Fund, Washington, 1992-94. Contbr. articles to profl. jours.; manuscript reviewer Chemistry of Materials, 1994—, Jour. Physics and Chemistry of Solids, 1995, Jour. Solid State Chemistry, 1996—, Molecular Crystals and Liquid Crystals, 1997—, Jour. Am. Chem. Soc., 1998—. Coach Chandler (Ariz.) Youth Baseball, 1988-95, Chandler Am. Little League, 1996-97; chair Cub Scout pack com., Boy Scouts Am., Mesa, Ariz., 1992, mem. Boy Scout com., Chandler, 1993-95. Rsch. grantee NSF, 1986—, Petroleum Rsch. Fund, 1992-95, Dept. Energy, 1995—. Mem. Am. Chem. Soc., Materials Rsch. Soc. Democrat. Presbyterian. Achievements include patent for Chemical Switch and Method for Detection of Chemical Components; co-development of atomic-level imaging of Lamellar Intercalation Reaction processes using dynamic high-resolution transmission electron microscopy and scanning tunneling microscopy/spectroscopy; research in new materials synthesis, materials reaction mechanisms, carbon dioxide mineral sequestration, intercalation chemistry, thermal chemistry and analysis, materials sci. edn. Office: Ariz State U Ctr for Solid State Science Tempe AZ 85287-1704

MCKENNA, FREDERICK GREGORY, lawyer, consultant; b. Chgo., Oct. 4, 1952; s. Frederick Hilary and Jean Elizabeth (Henneberry) McK.; m. Cornelia Ann Burns, Nov. 17, 1984; children: Kieran Padraig, Conor Burns. BA with honors, Coll. Holy Cross, 1974; JD, Georgetown U., 1978; postgrad., U. Nev., Las Vegas, U. Denver. Bar: D.C. 1978, Md. 1981, Nev. 1986, U.S. Supreme Ct. 1987, Colo. 1993. Assoc. Joseph, McDermott et al, Washington, 1979-82, Hudson & Creyke, Washington, 1982-85; sr. counsel Reynolds Elec. & Engring. Co., Inc., Las Vegas, 1985-90; dep. gen. counsel EG&G Rocky Flats, Golden, Colo., 1990-92, v.p., gen. counsel, 1992-96; spl. counsel Hall & Evans, Denver, 1996—. Mem. Community Svc. Commn., Md., 1984-85. Mem. ABA, D.C. Bar Assn. (D.C. procurement com.), Mensa. Republican. Roman Catholic. Avocations: weightlifting, science history. Home: 5954 Wood Sorrel Way Littleton CO 80123-6758 Office: Hall & Evans 1200 17th St Ste 1700 Denver CO 80202-5817

MCKENNA, JEANETTE ANN, archaeologist; b. N.Y.C., Aug. 6, 1953; d. Edward Patrick and Ann Jeanette (O'Brien) McKenna; children: Stephanie Jane, Daniel Glen Edward. AA in Phys. Edn., Mount San Antonio Jr. Coll., 1974; BA in Anthropology, Calif. State U., Fullerton, 1977, MA in Anthropology, 1982; postgrad., Ariz. State U., 1981-84, U. Calif., Riverside, 1991-92. Field archaeologist Archaeol. Rsch., Inc., Costa Mesa, Calif., 1976-79; rsch. asst. Calif. State U., 1979; lab. dir. Environ. Rsch. Archaeologists, L.A., 1978-79; staff archaeologist Ariz. State U., Tempe, 1979-82; rsch. archaeologist Soil Systems, Inc., Phoenix, 1982-84, Sci. Resource Surveys, Huntington Beach, Calif., 1984-87; co-owner, prin. Hatheway & McKenna, Mission Viejo, Calif., 1987-89; owner, prin. McKenna et al., Whittier, Calif., 1989—; dir. Divsn. Cultural Resource Mgmt. Svcs. EIP Assocs., Chino, Calif., 1996-97. Contbr. numerous articles to profl. jours. and reports. Bd. dirs. Whittier Conservancy, 1987-98, interim treas., 1994, pres., 1994-95, bd. dirs. Residents' Voice, 1998—. Recipient Gov.'s award for Hist. Preservation/Calif., The Whittier Conservancy, 1995. Mem. Soc. Profl. Archaeologists (bd. dirs. 1993-97), Archaeol. Inst. Am., Am. Soc. Conservation Archaeology, Am. Mus. Natural History, Soc. Am. Anthropology, Ariz. Archaeol. Coun., Ariz. Hist. Found., Calif. Hist. Soc., Nat. Arbor Day Found., Nat. Parks and Conservation Assn., Nat. Trust for Historic Preservation, Soc. Calif. Archaeology, Soc. Hist. Archaeology, S.W. Mus. Assn., Wilderness Soc., Whittier Conservancy, Southwestern Anthrop. Assn., Gene Autry Western Heritage Mus. Assn., Nature Conservancy, Smithsonian Assocs., Sierra Club, otehrs. Democrat. Roman Catholic. Avocations: traveling, reading, hiking, camping, gardening. Office: McKenna et al 6008 Friends Ave Whittier CA 90601-3724

MCKENNA, SUZANNE, performing arts educator; b. St. Johns, Ariz., May 31, 1942; 1 child, Nöe. BS, Brigham Young U., 1964; MA, Ea. N.Mex. U., 1977; PhD, U. Utah, 1986. Prodn. dir. Kailua H.S.; assembly dir. Bonneville Jr. H.S.; debate coach Olympus H.S.; grad. tchg. asst. Ea. N.Mex. U. Theatre; speech-drama chair Brighton H.S.; grad. tchg. asst. U. Utah; drama instr. Mission San Jose H.S.; prof. Salt Lake C.C., Salt Lake City; spkr. in field.

MCKEON, ELAINE, museum administrator. Chmn. San Francisco Mus. of Modern Art, Calif. Office: San Francisco Mus Modern Art 151 3rd St San Francisco CA 94103-3159*

MCKEON, HOWARD P. (BUCK MCKEON), congressman, former mayor; b. L.A.; m. Patricia; 6 children. BS, Brigham Young U. Mem. Coun. City of Santa Clarita, Calif., 1987-92, mayor, 1987-88; mem. 103rd-105th Congresses from 25th Calif. dist., 1993—; founding dir., chmn. Valencia Nat. Bank; co-owner Howard & Phil's Western Wear, Inc. Hon. chmn. Leukemia Soc. Celebrity program, 1990, Red Cross Community Support Campaign, 1992; active Dist. Com. Boy Scouts Am.; chmn., trustee William S. Hart Sch. dist., 1979-87; chmn., dir. Henry Mayo Newhall Meml. Hosp., 1983-88; mem. Calif. Rep. State Ctrl. Com., 1988-92; bd. dirs. Santa Clarita Valley Sml. Bus. Devel. Ctr., 1990-92, Canyon Country C. of C., 1988-92. Office: US Ho of Reps 2242 Rayburn Ho Ofc Bldg Washington DC 20515

MCKERAHAN, KARIN E., investment company executive; b. Montclair, N.J., June 21, 1965; d. Robert M. and Pamela R. (Beyer) Danek; m. Kelly I. McKerahan, Aug. 1, 1987. BA, Marietta Coll., 1987; MBA, Capital U., 1995. CFP, Ohio. With McKerahan Fin. Svcs., Temecula, Calif. Active S.W. Adv. Com. for Alternatives to Domestic Violence, Temecula, 1997—. Mem. Nat. Assn. Pers. Fin. Advisors, Inst. Cert. Fin. Planners, Soroptomist Club (v.p. 1998—), Murrieta C. of C. (amb. 1996—). E-mail: mckerahan@ez2.net. Office: McKerahan Fin Svcs 43537 Ridge Park Dr Ste 102 Temecula CA 92590-3613

MCKIBBEN, HOWARD D., federal judge; b. Apr. 1, 1940; s. James D. and Bernice McKibben; m. Mary Ann McKibben, July 2, 1966; children: Mark, Susan. BS, Bradley U., 1962; MPA, U. Pitts., 1964; JD, U. Mich., 1967. Assoc. George W. Abbott Law Office, 1967-71; dep. dist. atty. Douglas County, Nev., 1969-71, dist. atty., 1971-77; dist. ct. judge State of Nev., 1977-84; judge U.S. Dist. Ct. Nev., Reno, 1984—. Mem. Nev. Bar Assn., Am. Inns of Ct. (pres. Nev. chpt. 1986-88). Methodist. Avocations: tennis, golf, racquetball. Home: PO Box 588 Verdi NV 89439-0588 Office: US Dist Ct 400 S Virginia St Ste 804 Reno NV 89501-2197

MCKIBBEN, RYAN TIMOTHY, newspaper executive; b. Watertown, S.D., June 25, 1958; s. Bernard Dean and Patricia Martha (Loehr) McK.; m. Mary Elizabeth O'Donnell, Oct. 3, 1981; children: Sean Robert, Michael Patrick. Grad. high sch., Janesville, Wis. Classified advt. exec. Green Bay (Wis.) Press Gazette, 1977-79; display advt. exec. Racine (Wis.) Jour. Times, 1979-80; advt. dir. Oshkosh (Wis.) Northwestern, 1980-82, dir. sales/mktg., 1982-84; advt. dir. Reno Gazette-Jour., 1984-85, Madison (Wis.) Newspapers Inc., 1985-88; v.p., advt. dir., sr. v.p. advt. and mktg. Denver Post, 1988-90, exec. v.p., gen. mgr., 1990-93, pub., 1993-98; pres. Western Color Print, Denver, 1998—; bd. dirs. Newspapers First, N.Y.C. Mem. mktg. com. Metro Area Boys Clubs, Denver, 1988—; bd. dirs. Nat. Jewish Ctr. for Immunology and Respiratory Medicine, Denver, Denver Metro Conv. Bur., Denver Ctr. for Performing Arts, Colo. Symphony, Colo. Forum, Colo. Concer, Castle Pines Golf Club. Mem. Am. Press Inst., Newspaper Advt. Coop. Network (bd. dirs. 1989—), Internat. Newspaper Advt./Mktg. Execs., (com. mem. 1989—), Denver Advt. Fedn., Boys and Girls Club, Columbine Country Club. Republican. Roman Catholic. Home: 5350 S Race Ct Littleton CO 80121-1430 Office: Western Color Print 1600 Stout St Ste 1520 Denver CO 80202*

MCKIM, HARRIET MEGCHELSEN, education educator; b. Keokuk, Iowa, Oct. 17, 1919; d. Herbert John and Florence Josephine (Ottowa) Megchelsen; m. Lanier McClure, Nov. 1, 1944 (div. 1948); 1 child, Janet Gray; m. L.A. McKim, July 28, 1950 (div. 1968). BA, Calif. State U., Sacramento, 1952; MA, U. So. Calif., 1963, EdD, 1979. Tchr., prin. Cumberland County Schs., Crossville, Tenn., 1939-42; sec. Tenn. Valley Authority, Oak Ridge Def. Plant, Mare Island Naval Shipyard and Cal-West Ins., 1942-52; tchr., vice-prin., reading specialist, dir. ESEA I various pub. schs., Oxnard, Orcutt, Sacramento, Edwards AFB, Calif. and Spokane, Wash., 1950-64; coord. Yuba City and Yuba County Schs., 1964-70; cons. Calif. Dept. Edn., 1970-83; part-time instr. Alan Hancock Community Coll., Santa Maria, Calif., Sacramento City Coll., Polytech. U., San Luis Obispo, Calif., U. Calif., Davis, Santa Barbara, 1964-84; supr. student tchrs. Calif. State U., Sacramento, 1984; adj. prof. edn. Nat. U., Sacramento, 1986-88; rep. Child Devel. Assocs., 1992—. Vol. tchr. ARC parenting classes, Sacramento, 1984-85; docent, spkr. Crocker Art Mus.; vol. Loaves and Fishes; bd. dirs. Elderhostel Calif. State U.; docent Sacramento History Ctr.; deacon Fremont Presbyn. Ch.; bd. mem. Sacramento World Affairs Coun. Mem. AAUW, Nat. Assn. Edn. Young Children, Calif. Ret. Tchrs., Am. Assn. Ret. Persons, Profs. of Early Childhood Edn., Sacramento Affiliates, Amnesty Internat., Sierra Club, Delta Kappa Gamma, Phi Delta Kappa. Avocations: watercolor painting, writing, gardening, traveling. Address: 5332 State Ave Sacramento CA 95819-1738

MCKINLEY, DONALD ROBERT, former school system administrator, education advisor; b. Cottonwood, Idaho, Nov. 17, 1924; s. Howard R. and Elsie May (Wortman) McK.; m. Margaret Faye Burson, March 27, 1948; children: Constance, Kathryn, Philip. BS, U. Idaho, 1948, MS, 1953; EdD, Wash. State U., 1958. Tchr. music and govt. Grangeville (Idaho) Sch. Dist., Idaho, 1948-50; tchr. music and math. Cajon Valley Sch. Dist., El Cajon, Calif., 1952-56; supt.-prin. Ferndale (Calif.) H.S. Dist., 1957-59; prin. Davis (Calif.) Sr. H.S., 1959-67; asst. supt. Davis Unified Sch. Dist., 1967-70; supt. Placer Union H.S. Dist., Auburn, Calif., 1970-72, San Ramon Valley Sch. Dist., Danville, Calif., 1972-73; chief dep. state supt. Calif. State Dept. Edn., Sacramento, 1973-83; sales and regional mgr. WICAT Edn. Sys., Provo, Utah, 1983-86; mktg. advisor Edn. Sys. Corp., San Diego, 1986-89; edn. advisor Photo & Sound Co., San Francisco, 1989-92, Edunetics Corp., Arlington, Va., 1992-94; search cons. Wilson Riles & Assocs., Sacramento, Calif., 1990—; chmn. Coun. of Chief State Sch. Officers-Study Commn., Washington, 1975-76; mem. Sec. of Edn. Adv. Com., Washington, 1981-86; cons. Optical Data Corp., 1995—, Ameri Data Corp., 1995-96. Lt. USN, 1943-46, World War II, 1950-52, Korea. Mem. Am. Assn. Sch. Adminstrs., Calif. Assn. Secondary Sch. Adminstrs. (pres. 1969-70), Assn. Calif. Sch. Adminstrs. (pres. 1971-72). Avocations: golf, fishing, travel. Home: 5332 Adelaide Way Sacramento CA 95841-4304

MCKINLEY, EILEEN BALDWIN, elementary education educator; b. San Ysidro, Calif., Sept. 15, 1913; d. Charles Raymond I and Mattie (Seaman) Baldwin; m. James Clarence McKinley, July 31, 1943 (dec. Aug. 1990); children: Ann LeBaron, Mary Margaret. AB, U. Calif., Berkeley, 1936; cert. in tchg., San Francisco State Coll., 1938. Tchr. Calif. Dept. Edn., Richmond, Mendocino Dept. Edn., Ukiah, Calif., San Pablo (Calif.) Dept. Edn.; caseworker Wash. Dept. Welfare, Chehalis; tchr. Lewis County Edn., Chehalis. Active Wenatchee Brethren Bapt. Ch. Mem. DAR. Republican. Avocations: quilt making, reading, church activities. Home: 1040 Gellatly Ave Wenatchee WA 98801-3249

MCKINLEY, JOSEPH WARNER, health science facility executive; b. Champaign, Ill., Jan. 9, 1943; s. Lyle Warner and Eloise M. (Coleman) McK. BS, Georgetown U., 1968; MBA, George Washington U., 1973. Asst. adminstr. Weiss Meml. Hosp., Chgo., 1973-75; assoc. v.p. Rockford (Ill.) Meml. Hosp., 1975-78; v.p. ops. Phoenix Meml. Hosp., 1978-84, exec. v.p., CEO, 1984-88; exec. v.p. St. Francis Med. Ctr., Lynwood, Calif., 1988-90; CEO Meridian Point Rehab. Hosp., Scottsdale, Ariz., 1990-95, St. Agnes Med. Ctr./Nazareth Hosp., Phila., 1995-96; prin./owner Lawrenz Cons., Phoenix, 1996—. Capt. U.S. Army, 1968-71, Vietnam. Mem. Am. Coll. of Healthcare Execs., Ariz. Club. Republican. Episcopalian. Home: 6 Colonia Miramonte Paradise Valley AZ 85253

MCKINLEY, PATRICK, prosecutor. Chief of police Fullerton, Calif.; now asst. dist. atty. County of Santa Barbara. Office: Office of District Atty Courthouse 1105 Santa Barbara St Santa Barbara CA 93101*

MCKINNEY, GEORGE D., JR., pastor, bishop; b. Jonesboro, Ark., Aug. 9, 1932; m. Jean Carleen Brown, June 15, 1957; children: George A., Grant A., Gregory A., Gordon A., Glenn A. BA in Sociology, Ark. State U., Pine Bluff, 1954; MA in Philosophy of Christianity, Oberlin Coll., 1956; student Grad. Sch. Social Work, U. Mich., 1957-58; PhD, Calif. Grad. Sch. Theology, 1974. Founder, pastor St. Stephen's Ch. of God in Christ, San Diego, 1962—; bishop 2d. Ecclesiastical So. Jurisdiction, 1985—; pvt. practice mariage, family and child counselor, 1971-85; cons. Cmty. Welfare Coun., 1968-71; sr. probation officer San Diego County, 1959-65; dir. Chagrin Falls Park Cmty. Ctr., Toledo, 1955-56. Author books and articles. Founder Am. Urban U., San Diego, St. Stephen's Christian Sch., 1978, St. Stephen's Retirement Ctr., 1979, St. Stephen's Daycare Ctr., 1963, others. Recipient Legacy award NAACP, 1995. Mem. Nat. Assn. Evangelicals, Nat. Black Evangelical Assn., Environment for Social Action, Morris Cerullo World Evangelism, Pacific Inst. Cmty. Orgn., Religious Alliance Against Pornography, Rotary (Mr. San Diego 1995), Urban League, others. Office: 5825 Imperial Ave San Diego CA 92114-4118

MCKINNEY, MONICA LORRAINE, media/communications company executive; b. San Diego, June 22; d. Ricardo John and Jeannette Elizabeth (Mark) McK. BBA in Mgmt., U. Miami, 1984. Computer instr., operator ADIA, Inc., San Diego and Atlanta, 1985-90; internat. tng. and devel. coord. Coca-Cola Co., Atlanta, 1990-92; pres. film, video, print prodn., telecom. software devel. MLM Comm., Inc., Atlanta and Las Vegas, 1990—. Graphic designer promotional campaign material, 1984 (plaque 1985); writer, prodr., dir. Drug's In The Work Place, 1992 (various awards 1992); prodr., dir. nat. radio spl. Crack Down, 1994 (trophy 1995, The Communicator award 1997, The Videographer award 1998, Silver Telly award 1998, Outstanding People of the 20th Century medal 1999); creator, host, prodr. TV series CELEBS, 1995; actress various TV and film feature prodns. Vol. drug prevention program Nat. Ctr. Tng. and Devel., Miami, 1985; prodr. AIDS fund concerts, Atlanta, 1993; internat. media liaison 25th Anniversary Martin Luther King Jr. Ctr., Atlanta, 1992. Recipient Outstanding People of the 20th Century medal, 1999. Mem. NAFE, Internat. TV Assn. (chair exec. com. 1990—, VidFest Bumper award 1991), Am. Women in Radio and TV (chair 1992-93), Small Bus. Adminstrn./NSET (dir. comms. 1996—, grant 1995), T.R.E.T.ment, Inc. (pub. rels. chair 1995—, bd. dirs., cert. 1997), Woman Inc. Democrat. Avocations: horseback riding, photography, print and runway modeling. Office: MLM Comm Inc 5445 W Reno Ave Ste 1811 Las Vegas NV 89118-1571

MC KINNEY, ROBERT MOODY, newspaper editor and publisher; b. Shattuck, Okla., Aug. 28, 1910; s. Edwin S. and Eva (Moody) McK.; married, 1943; 1 child, Mrs. Meade Martin; m. Marie-Louise de Montmollin, May 7, 1970 (dec. Jan. 1998). AB, U. Okla., 1932; LLD, U. N.Mex., 1964. Investment analyst Standard Stats. Co., Inc. (now Standard and Poor's Co.), 1932-34; ptnr. Young-Kolbe & Co., 1934-38, Robert R. Young & Co., 1938-42; exec. v.p., treas. Pathe Film Co., 1934-39, Allegheny Corp., 1936-42, Pittston Corp. and subs., 1936-42; v.p. Fremkir Corp., 1937-50, Allan Corp., 1937-50; exec. v.p., treas. Mo. Pacific R.R., 1938-42; ptnr. Scheffmeyer, McKinney & Co., 1945-50; editor, pub. Santa Fe New Mexican, 1949—; chmn. bd. The New Mexican, Inc., 1949—; profl. corp. dir. 10 N.Y.S.E. cos., 1934-86; chmn. Robert Moody Found.; chmn. N.Mex. Econ. Devel. Commn. and Water Resources Devel. Bd., 1949-51; asst. sec. U.S. Dept. Interior, 1951-52; chmn. panel to report to Congress on impact of Peaceful Uses of Atomic Energy, 1955-56; permanent U.S. rep. to Internat. Atomic Energy Agy., Vienna, 1957-58; U.S. rep. Internat. Conf. Peaceful Uses Atomic Energy, Geneva, 1958; U.S. ambassador to, Switzerland, 1961-63; exec. officer Presdl. Task Force on Internat. Investments, 1963-64; chmn. Presdl. Commn. on Travel, 1968; chmn. bd. visitors U. Okla., 1968-72; U.S. rep. Internat. Centre Settlement Investment Disputes, Washington, 1967-74. Author: Hymn to Wreckage: A Picaresque Interpretation of History, 1947, The Scientific Foundation for European Integration, 1959, On Increasing Effectiveness of Western Science and Technology, 1959, The Red Challenge to Technological Renewal, 1960, Review of the International Atomic Policies and Programs of the United States, 1960, The Toad and the Water Witch, 1985, Variations on a Marxist Interpretation of Culture, 1986. Lt. USNR, 1942-45. Recipient Disting. Service medal U.S. Dept. Treasury, 1968, Disting. Service medal U. Okla., 1972. Mem. Am. Soc. Newspaper Editors, Coun. Fgn. Rels., Coun. of Am. Ambs., Newspaper Assn. of Am., Phi Beta Kappa, Phi Gamma Delta. Democrat. Episcopalian. Clubs: Chevy Chase (Md.); Metropolitan (Washington); University, Brook, Century, Links, Knickerbocker, River (N.Y.C.). Home: Wind Fields 39850 Snickersville Tpke Middleburg VA 20117-3002 Office: PO Box 1705 Santa Fe NM 87504-1705

MCKINNON, JAMES BUCKNER, real estate sales executive, writer, researcher; b. Tacoma, Dec. 5, 1916; s. James Mitchell and Rochelle Lenore (Buckner) McK.; m. Mary C. Corbitt, Dec. 1961 (div. June 1963); 1 child, James H.C.; m. Marylyn Adelle Coote, Mar. 12, 1967 (div. May 1977); 1 child, Michelyn; m. Martha Sackmann, June 12, 1977. BA in Internat. Studies, U. Wash., 1983, H.M. Jackson Sch. Police detective Los Angeles Police Dept., 1946-50; bn. security officer 1st med. bn. 1st Marine div. Fleet Marine Force, 1950-53; owner, operator, mgr., dir. promotional sales The Saucy Dog Drive-In, Venice, Calif., 1953-63; salesman new car sales and leasing Burien Mercury, Seattle, 1963-66; real estate salesman and appraiser various firms Seattle, 1966—; instr., lectr. U.S. Naval Support Activity,

Sandpoint, Wash., 1964-74; mem., lectr. NRC 11-8, Naval Postgrad. Sch., Monterey, Calif., 1975-76; Burien Mercury announcer KOMO TV. Author: (poetry) On the Threshold of a Dream, Vol. III, 1992, Best Poems of the 90's, 1992; contbr. to anthologies: Where Words Haven't Spoken, 1993, Fire From Within, 1994; contbr. articles to various newspapers and mil. jours. Mem. br. adv. com. Wash. State YMCA, Seattle, 1994—, treas., 1986-94, 95, mem. so. dist. fin. bd., 1989-93, 94, 95-96. With USN, 1939-53, PTO, Korea. Recipient Wilmer Culver Meml. award Culver Alumni Fictioneers, Seattle, 1979, Silver Poet award World of Poetry Press, 1986, Golden Poet award, 1987-92, Best Poet of the 90's Nat. Libr. of Poetry, 1992, First Place with Editor's Preference award Creative Arts and Scis. Enterprises, 1996; Occidental Coll. scholar, 1935; named to Honorable Order Ky. Cols., 1976; named One of Best New Poets, Am. Poetry Assn. Anthology, 1988; inducted into the Internat. Poetry Hall of Fame, 1996. Mem. Internat. Soc. Authors and Artists (1st place award for 1997 poem), Internat. Platform Assn., U.S. Naval Inst. (life), Internat. Soc. Poets (life), N.W. Writers Conf., Ret. Officers Assn. (life), Mensa, Acad. Am. Poets, KP, Masons. Republican. Home: 2312 41st Ave SW Seattle WA 98116-2060

MCKINSTRY, RONALD EUGENE, lawyer; b. Bakersfield, Calif., Aug. 11, 1926; s. Melville Jack and Lillian Agatha (Saner) McK.; m. Shirley Danner, June 19, 1948; children: Michael R., Jill I. McKinstry Epperson, Jeffrey A., Carol A. McKinstry Sundquist. BS, U. Wash., 1950, JD, 1951. Bar: Wash. 1951, U.S. Ct. Claims 1970, U.S. Ct. Appeals (D.C. cir.) 1981, U.S. Supreme Ct. 1982. Assoc. Evans, McLaren, Lane, Powell & Beeks, Seattle, 1951-55, Bogle, Bogle & Gates, Seattle, 1955-61; ptnr. Bogle & Gates, Seattle, 1962-91, chmn. litigation dept., 1970-91; sr. trial ptnr. Ellis Li & McKinstry, Seattle, 1992—; apptd. spl. master by U.S. Dist. Ct. (we. dist.) Wash., 1976-81, apptd. settlement mediator, 1980—. Editor-in-chief Washington Civil Procedure Before Trial Deskbook, 1981, Supplement to Deskbook, 1986; contbr. articles to profl. jours. Attends Christ Meml. Ch., Poulsbo, Wash. With USN, 1944-46, PTO. Recipient Svc. award Western Ctr. for Law and Religious Freedom, 1990. Fellow Am. Coll. Trial Lawyers (regent 1978-82); mem. ABA, Internat. Assn. Def. Counsel (mem. exec. com. 1974-78, voted Best Lawyers in Am. NAIFEH, 1983-98), AAA Club Wash. (mem. exec. com. 1983-98), Seattle Tennis Club. Republican. Christ Meml. Ch. Avocations: golf, traveling. Office: Ellis Li & McKinstry 3700 First Interstate Ctr 999 3rd Ave Seattle WA 98104-4001

MCKNIGHT, LENORE RAVIN, child psychiatrist; b. Denver, May 15, 1943; d. Abe and Rose (Steed) Ravin; m. Robert Lee McKnight, July 22, 1967; children: Richard Rex, Janet Rose. Student, Occidental Coll., 1961-63; BA, U. Colo., 1965, postgrad. in medicine, 1965-67; MD, U. Calif., San Francisco, 1969. Diplomate Am. Bd. Psychiatry and Neurology. Cert. adult and child psychiatrist Am. Bd. Psychiatry. Intern pediatrics Children's Hosp., San Francisco, 1969-70; resident in gen. psychiatry Langley Porter Neuropsychiat. Inst., 1970-73, fellow child psychiatry, 1972-74; child psychiatrist Youth Guidance Center, San Francisco, 1974-74; pvt. practice medicine specializing in child psychiatry, Walnut Creek, Calif., 1974-93; asst. clin. prof. Langley Porter Neuropsychiat. Inst., 1974—; asst. clin. prof. psychiatry U. Calif. San Francisco Med. Ctr. Internat.; med. dir. CPC Walnut Creek (Calif.) Hosp., 1990-93. Insts. Edn. fellow U. Edinburgh, 1964; NIH grantee to study childhood nutrition, 1966. Fellow Am. Acad. Child and Adolescent Psychiatry; mem. Am. Coll. Physician Execs., Internat. Arabian Horse Assn., Diablo Arabian Horse Assn. Avocation: breeding Arabian Horses. Office: Kaiser Martinez Inpat Psych 200 Muir Rd Martinez CA 94553-4672

MC KNIGHT, WILLIAM WARREN, JR., publisher; b. Normal, Ill., June 9, 1913; s. William Warren and Isabel Alida (Travis) McK.; m. Alice McGuire, Oct. 30, 1937; children: William Warren, III, Michael Joe, John James. B.S. in Bus. Adminstrn., Northwestern U., 1938. With McKnight Pub. Co., Bloomington, Ill., 1938-83; sec.-treas. McKnight Pub. Co., 1949-56, pres., 1956-67, chmn. bd., 1968-79; bd. dirs. Gen. Telephone Co. Ill., Champion Fed. Savs. & Loan Assn., chmn. bd. Pres. Bloomington Rotary Club, 1952, Bloomington C. of C., 1954; mem. Ill. Commn. Higher Edn., 1956-60; chmn. Bloomington-Normal Airport Authority, 1965-70, CETA Pvt. Industry Council Ill. Balance of State, 1979-81. Served with USNR, 1942-46. Recipient Disting. Service award Bloomington Kiwanis Club, 1963, Disting. Service award Normal C. of C., 1973; Good Govt. award Bloomington Jaycees, 1970; Edn. Constrn. award Edn. Council Graphic Arts Industry, 1974; Disting. Alumni award Ill. State U., 1978; Disting. Service award Spirit of McLean County, 1982; Disting. Service citation Epsilon Pi Tau, 1983; award of Merit Am. Vocat. Assn., 1990; disting. assoc. award Coun. on Tech. Tchr. Edn., 1995. Mem. Graphic Arts Edn. Assn., Internat. Tech. Edn. Assn., Nat. Assn. Indsl. and Tech. Tchrs. Educators, Ill. C. of C. (dir. 1964-69), Ill. Mfrs. Assn. (dir. 1954-62). Republican. Presbyterian. Clubs: Coll. Alumni, Bloomington Country. Home (winter): 7788 E Stallion Rd Scottsdale AZ 85258-3485

MCKUSICK, MARSHALL KIRK, computer scientist; b. Wilmington, Del., Jan. 19, 1954; s. Blaine Chase and Marjorie Jane (Kirk) McK.; domestic ptnr. Eric P. Allman. BSEE with distinction, Cornell U., 1976; MS in Bus. Adminstrn., U. Calif., Berkeley, 1979, MS in Computer Sci., 1980, PhD in Computer Sci., 1984. System designer Hughes Aircraft Co., 1977-79; software cons., 1982—; rsch. computer scientist U. Calif., Berkeley, 1984-93. Author: The Design and Implementation of the 4.4BSD Operating System, 1996 (trans. into German, 1997, Japanese, 1997, French, 1997); contbr. articles to profl. publs. Mem. IEEE, Usenix Assn. (Lifetime Achievement award 1992, pres. 1990-92, bd. dirs. 1986-92), Assn. Computing Machinery. Democrat. Avocations: swimming, scuba diving, wine collecting. Office: 1614 Oxford St Berkeley CA 94709-1608

MCLANE, FREDERICK BERG, lawyer; b. Long Beach, Calif., July 24, 1941; s. Adrian B. and Arlie K. (Burrell) McL.; m. Lois C. Roberts, Jan. 28, 1967; children: Willard, Anita. BA, Stanford U., 1963; LLB, Yale U., 1966. Bar: Calif. 1967, U.S. Dist. Ct. (cen. dist.) Calif. 1967. Assoc. prof. law U. Miss., Oxford, 1966-68; assoc. O'Melveny & Myers, L.A., 1968-74, ptnr., 1975—; com. of counsel HUD, Los Angeles, 1979-84; lectr. in field. Pres., bd. dirs. Legal Aid Found., L.A., 1974-83; deacon Congl. Ch., Sherman Oaks, Calif., 1979-83; vice-chair L.A. Music Ctr., Unified Fund, 1992-94; bd. dirs. Calif. Sci. Ctr. Found., 1991—. Mem. ABA (banking com., fed. regulation of securities com.), Calif. Bar Assn. (fin. insts. com., uniform comml. codes), L.A. Bar Assn., Order of Coif, Calif. Club (L.A.), L.A. Country Club, Lakeside Golf Club (L.A.). Democrat. Avocations: golf, walking, reading. Office: O'Melveny & Myers 400 S Hope St Los Angeles CA 90071-2899

MCLAREN, ARCHIE CAMPBELL, JR., marketing executive; b. Atlanta, Sept. 25, 1942; s. Archie Campbell and Virginia Lynn (Sides) McL.; m. Georgia Mae Blunt, 1969 (div. 1971); 1 child, Leslie Michelle; m. Yvette Rubio, June 17, 1995. BA, Vanderbilt U., 1964; JD, Memphis State U., 1968. Clk. FBI, Memphis, 1965-66; tchr., tennis coach Memphis U. Sch., 1966-68; tchr. Hunt High Sch., Columbus, Miss., 1968-69; tennis coach Miss. State U., Starkville, Miss., 1968-69; concierge The Roosevelt Hotel, New Orleans, 1969-70; sales rep. West Pub. Co., St. Paul, 1970-84, adminstr. internat. mktg. The Orient, 1985-90; freelance wine cons., 1985—; cons. Calif. Ctrl. Coast Wine Growers Assn., Santa MAria, 1987-91; lectr. advanced wine appreciation Calif. Poly. U. Extended Edn., San Luis Obispo, 1986-90; dir. KCBX Ctrl. Coast Wine Classic, San Luis Obispo, 1985—, KHPR Wine Classic, Honolulu, 1987-91, Winesong, Ft. Bragg, Calif., 1987-96, WETA Washington Wine Classic, 1989-90, KCRW Summerday, 1991, Santa Barbara Wine Auction, 1997-98, auction dir., 1992-94, 97, 98—; auction cons. Am. Inst. of Wine And Food, 1994—; chmn. Edna Valley Arroyo Grande Valley Vinters' Assn., 1999. Host talk show Pub. Radio Sta. KCBX, San Luis Obispo, 1984—; columnist (newspaper) San Luis Obispo Telegram-Tribune, 1992-95, New Times San Luis Obispo, 1995-96; contbg. writer: Adventures in Dining, 1994-95, Santa Barbara Mag., 1998—. Bd. dirs. Avila Beach County Water Dist., 1992-95, pres., 1992-94; bd. dirs. San Luis Obispo (Calif.) Mozart Festival, 1988-92, pres., 1991-92; dir. Internat. Festival Champagne and Sparkling Wine, 1992—; mem. Avila Valley Adv. Coun., 1993-95; bd. dirs. Guild South County Ctr. for Performing Arts, 1993-94. Mem. Calif. Cen. Coast Wine Soc. (pres. 1985), Am. Soc. Wine Educators, German Wine Soc. Honolulu, Vintners Club San Francisco, Avila Bay Wine Soc., Cen. Coast Chaine des Rotisseurs (chpt. pres. 1987, 88, 89), Marin County Food and Wine Soc., Internat. Food, Wine & Travel Writers' Assn., Austrian Wine Brotherhood, Avila Bay Club. Avocations: racquetball, tennis, squash racquets, collecting wine, basketball. Office: PO Box 790 Avila Beach CA 93424-0790

MCLARNAN, DONALD EDWARD, banker, corporation executive; b. Nashua, Iowa, Dec. 19, 1906; s. Samuel and Grace (Prudhon) McL.; m. Virginia Rickard, May 5, 1939; children: Marilyn, Marcia, Roxane. A.B., U. So. Calif., 1930; grad., Southwestern U. Law Sch., 1933; postgrad., Cambridge U. Trust appraiser, property mgr. Security-Pacific Nat. Bank, Los Angeles, 1935-54; regional dir. SBA for, So. Calif., Ariz., Nev., 1954-61; area adminstr. SBA for, Alaska, Western U.S., Hawaii, Guam, Samoa, U.S. Trust Terr., 1969-73; pres. Am. MARC, Inc. (offshore oil drillers and mfr. diesel engines), 1961-63, Terminal Drilling & Prodn. Co., Haney & Williams Drilling Co., Western Offshore, 1961-63; v.p., dir. Edgemar Dairy, Santa Monica Dairy Co., 1954-70; founder, pres., chmn. bd. Mission Nat. Bank, 1963-67; pres. Demco Trading Co., Mut. Trading Co.; dir. Coast Fed. Savs. & Loan; cons. numerous corps.; guest lectr. various univs. Contbr. articles on mgmt. and fin. to profl. jours. Chmn. fed. agys. div. Community Chest, 1956; nat. pres. Teachers Day, 1956; bd. councillors U. So. Calif.; founder, chmn., pres. Soc. Care and Protection Injured Innocent; adv. bd. Los Angeles City Coll.; bd. dirs. Calif. Easter Seal Soc.; nat. chmn. U. So. Calif. Drug Abuse Program. Recipient Los Angeles City and County Civic Leadership award, 1959. Mem. Nat. Assn. People with Disabilities (pres.); Mem. Skull and Dagger, Delta Chi. Clubs: Mason (Los Angeles) (K.T., Shriner), Los Angeles (Los Angeles), Jonathan (Los Angeles). Home: 135 S Norton Ave Los Angeles CA 90004-3916 Office: 1111 Crenshaw Blvd Los Angeles CA 90019-3112

MCLAUGHLIN, GLEN, financial services company executive; b. Shawnee, Okla., Dec. 21, 1934; s. Champe and Mattie Bet (Jenkins) McL.; m. Ellen Marr Schnake, Aug. 29, 1964; children: Helen Elizabeth, Glen Wallace. B.B.A., U. Okla., 1956; M.B.A., Harvard U., 1964. Asst. treas. Foremost-McKesson, Inc., San Francisco, 1964-69; exec. v.p., dir. MacFarlane's Candies, Oakland, Calif., 1969-70; dir. fin. and adminstrn. Memorex Corp., London, 1970-71; sr. v.p. fin. Four-Phase Systems, Inc., Cupertino, Calif., 1971-82; pres., chmn. Four-Phase Fin., Inc., Cupertino, 1977-82; chmn. bd. Four-Phase Systems, Ltd., Toronto, Ont., Can., 1977-82, Four-Phase Systems Internat., Inc., 1977-82, DeAnza Ins. Co. Ltd., Cayman Islands, 1979-82; gen. ptnr. Matrix Ptnrs., L.P., San Jose and Boston, 1982-86; chmn. bd. Venture Leasing Assocs., 1986—; chmn. bd. dirs. Cupertino Nat. Bank, Calif., 1990-96; dir. Greater Bay Bancorp, Palo Alto, Calif., 1996—. Author: The Mapping of California as an Island, 1995. Served USAF 1956-62, USAFR 1964-65 (capt. and pilot), pres. Jr. Achievement Santa Clara County, 1978-79, chmn. bd., 1980-81; chmn. bd. Jr. Achievement Found. Santa Clara County, 1980-87; mem. bus. sch. adv. bd. U. Santa Clara, 1981-84; pres. Boy Scouts Am., Santa Clara County, 1986-87, mem. exec. coun., 1982—, pres. No. Calif. Area, 1988-91; pres. BSA Meml. Found., 1991-95; mem. pvt. sector investment adv. panel City of San Jose, 1984-92; bd. visitors Sch. Acctg., Coll. Bus. Adminstrn., U. Okla., 1991-94, endowed chair in bus. ethics, 1997, bd. advs., 1998—; trustee Gould Acad., Bethel, Maine, 1993—, O'Connor Hosp. Found., San Jose, 1994-97; bd. dirs. Am. Cancer Soc., Santa Clara County, 1994-98, Libr. Congress Map Divn., Phillips Soc., 1995—, co-chair, 1998—; founding angel Band of Angels, Silicon Valley, Calif., 1995—. Recipient Silver Leadership award Jr. Achievement, 1981, Silver Beaver award Boy Scouts Am., 1985, Silver Antelope award Boy Scouts Am., 1990, Disting. Eagle Scout award Boy Scouts Am., 1994, pub. svc. citations Calif. State Senate, Calif. State Assembly, Santa Clara County Suprs.; Baden-Powell World fellow, 1986; decorated Order of St. John, 1989. Fellow Royal Geog. Soc.; mem. Fin. Execs. Inst., English Speaking Union, Commonwealth Club, Harvard U. Bus. Sch. Club, Roxburghe Club, Book Club Calif., Beta Gamma Sigma, Sigma Alpha Epsilon. Home: 14016 Camino Barco Saratoga CA 95070-5661

MCLAUGHLIN, JAMES DANIEL, architect; b. Spokane, Wash., Oct. 2, 1947; s. Robert Francis and Patricia (O'Connel) McL.; B.Arch., U. Idaho, 1971; m. Willa Kay Pace, Aug. 19, 1972; children: Jamie Marie, Robert James. Project architect Neil M. Wright, Architect, AIA, Sun Valley, Idaho, 1971-74, McMillan & Hayes, Architects, Sun Valley, 1974-75; now pres., prin. McLaughlin Architects Chartered, Sun Valley. Prin. works include Oakridge Apts., Moscow, Idaho (Excellence in Design award AIA), Walnut Ave. Mall, Ketchum, Idaho (Excellence in Design award AIA, 1987), McMahan Residence, Sun Valley (Excellence in Design award AIA, 1987). Chmn., Ketchum Planning and Zoning Commn., Ketchum Planning Commn., Ketchum Zoning Commn.; chmn. Sun Valley Planning and Zoning Commn.; vice-chmn. Idaho Archtl. Licensing Bd. Served to 1st lt. U.S. Army. Registered architect, 10 states including Idaho. Mem. AIA , Nat. Coun. Archtl. Registration Bds., Nat. Home Builders Assn., Ketchum-Sun Valley C. of C. (dir.). Roman Catholic. Club: Rotary. Prin. archtl. works include James West Residence, First Fed. Savs., Fox Bldg. Rehab., Walnut Ave. Mall, First St. Office Bldg. Home: PO Box 6 Lot # 5 Red Cliffs Subdivsn Ketchum ID 83340-0006 Office: McLaughlin Architects Chartered PO Box 479 Sun Valley ID 83353-0479

MCLAUGHLIN, JERRY DEWAYNE, obstetrician, gynecologist; b. Lubbock, Tex., Nov. 22, 1964; s. Jerry DeWayne and Jennie Ruth (Jones) McC.; m. Sundi Karalyne Jones, Mar. 5, 1988; children: Mykel Jerry, Melody Hope. BS in Chemistry cum laude, Tex. Tech. U., 1986; MD, U. Tex., 1991. Diplomate Am. Bd. OB-Gyn. Resident ob-gyn Tex. Tech. U. Affil. Hosps., Lubbock, 1991-95; ob-gyn St. Mary Med. Ctr., Hobbs, 1995—. Bd. dirs. Lea County Perinatal Project, Hobbs, 1997—; leadership team Nat. Coalition Against Domestic Violence, Albuquerque, 1997—. Mem. AMA (Physician Recognition award 1995, Young Physician Rep. 1997—), ACOG (jr. fellow), N.Mex. med. Soc. (councilor 1997—), Lea County Med. Soc. (sec. 1995—), Southwest Ob-Gyn Soc. (councilor 1995—), Rotary. Democrat. Baptist. Avocations: reading, model car building, computers. Home: 413 E Abo Dr Hobbs NM 88240-3401 Office: St Mary Med Ctr 2410 N Fowler St Hobbs NM 88240-2347

MCLAUGHLIN, JOSEPH MAILEY, lawyer; b. L.A., July 10, 1928; s. James Aloysius and Cecilia Ann (Mailey) McL.; m. Beverly Jane Walker, July 24, 1949; children: Stephen Joseph, Lawrence James, Suzanne Carol, Eileen Louise. JD, Loyola U., L.A., 1955. Bar: Calif. 1955, U.S. Supreme Ct. 1959. Mem. firm McLaughlin and Irvin, L.A., 1955—; lectr. labor relations Loyola U., L.A., 1958-60, mem. bd. visitors law sch., 1987—; pres. Food Employers Coun., Inc., 1984-89; pres. L.A. Stock Exch., 1972. Contbg. author: Labor Law for General Practitioners, 1960. Served to 1st lt. USAF, 1951-53. Mem. San Francisco, Long Beach, Los Angeles County, Fed., Am., Internat., Inter-Am. bar assns., State Bar Calif., Am. Judicature Soc., Assn. Bus. Trial Lawyers, Am. Soc. Internat. Law, Calif. Club. Office: 11957 Wood Ranch Rd Granada Hills CA 91344-2144

MCLAUGHLIN, LINDA LEE HODGE, federal judge; b. 1942. BA, Stanford U., 1963; LLB, U. Calif., Berkeley, 1966. With Keatinge & Sterling, L.A., 1966-70, Richards, Martin & McLaughlin, Beverly Hills and Newport Beach, Calif., 1970-73, Bergland, Martin & McLaughlin, Newport Beach, 1973-76, Bergland & McLaughlin, Costa Mesa, Calif., 1976-80; judge North Orange County Mcpl. Ct., Fullerton, Calif., 1980-82, Orange County Superior Ct., Santa Ana, Calif., 1982-92, U.S. Dist. Ct. (ctrl. dist.) Calif., Santa Ana, 1992—; mem. adv. com. jud. forms Jud. Coun., 1978—, mem. adv. com. gender bias in cts., 1987-90. Mem. governing bd. Victim-Witness Assistance Program Orange County. Mem. Nat. Assn. Women Judges, Calif. State Bar Assn. (mem. com. profl. ethics 1976-80, disciplinary referee dist. 8 1978-80), Calif. Women Lawyers (gov. dist. 8 1978-80), Calif. Judges Assn. (chair civil law and procedure com. 1985-86), Orange County Bar Assn. (mem. com. adminstrn. justice 1975-78, client rels. com. 1978-80, com. jud. appointments 1979-80), Orange County Women Lawyers, Boalt Hall Alumni Assn., Stanford U. Alumni Assn., Cap and Gown Hon. Soc. Office: US District Court 751 W Santa Ana Blvd Rm 713 Santa Ana CA 92701-4509

MCLAUGHLIN, MARGUERITE P., state senator, logging company executive; b. Matchwood, Mich., Oct. 15, 1928; d. Harvey Martin and Luella Margaret (Livingston) Miller; m. George Bruce McLaughlin, 1947; children: Pamela, Bruce Jr., Cynthia. Owner, operator contract logging firm, Orofino, Idaho; mem. Idaho Ho. of Reps., 1978-80; mem. Idaho Senate, 8th term., asst. Dem. leader, 1990, 91, 92, 93, dem. leader, 1997—; chair Democrat Caucus, 1995—. mem. Senate Fin. Com., 1987—, Gov.'s Adv. Coun. Workers Compensation, 1990-96, State of Idaho Endowment Fund Investment Bd., 1991-95, legis. coun., 1989-94, 95—. State of Idaho Job Tng. Coun., 1989-98, state ins. fund commn., 1 998—. Trustee Joint Sch. Dist. 171, 1976-80; pres. Orofino Celebration, Inc. Office: Idaho State Senate State Capital Boise ID 83720

MCLEAN, HUGH ANGUS, management consultant; b. Salt Lake City, Feb. 19, 1925; s. George Mark and Rose (Powell) McL.; m. Martha Lane Green, Nov. 23, 1949; children: Michael Hugh, Merrie Smithson. Student, U. Kans., 1943-44; BSME, Iowa State U., 1946; postgrad., U. Utah, 1946, 61-66. Registered profl. engr., Utah. With Utah Oil Refining Co., Boise, Idaho, Twin Falls, Idaho and Salt Lake City, 1953-61, Am. Oil Co., Salt Lake City and 11 western states, 1961-66; cons. Standard Oil (Ind.), Chgo., 1966-69; v.p. Mahler Assocs., Midland Park, N.J., 1969-76; pres. McLean Mgmt. Systems, Wyckoff, N.J., 1976-84, Heber City, Utah, 1984—. Author: There Is a Better Way to Manage, 1982, Developmental Dialogues, 1972, Career Planning Program, 1975; creator, host (TV) live shows and commls., 1956-57; creator stewardship mgmt. system, 1987. Rep. election judge, Salt Lake City, 1964, Operation Eagle Eye, Chgo., 1968; pub. communications dir. Ch. Jesus Christ Latter-Day Saints, N.Y. metro area, 1981-84; introduced SAFE HOMES in county and state, 1987; chmn. bd. dirs. Town Hall Playhouse, 1990-96; elected Daniel Twp. Planning Commn., 1996—. Served to lt. (j.g.) USNR, 1943-46. Recipient Silver award Am. Petroleum Inst., 1957. Mem. Am. Soc. Tng. Devel. (chmn. N.Y. metro chpt. field trips 1972-74). Home: PO Box 251 Heber City UT 84032-0251 Office: McLean Mgmt Systems PO Box 251 Heber City UT 84032-0251

MCLEAN, HULDA HOOVER, volunteer, conservationist, naturalist, artist; b. Palo Alto, Calif., Aug. 19, 1906; d. Theodore Jesse and Mildred (Brooke) Hoover; m. Charles Alexander McLean (dec. 1981); children: Charles Alexander, Allan Hoover, Robertson Brooke. BA, Stanford U., 1927. Rancher Santa Cruz County, Calif., 1943-85; v.p. Waddell Creek Assn., Davenport, Calif., 1985—; vol. mgr. Waddell Creek Ranger Sta., Davenport, 1993—. Author: Uncle Bert, 1975, Hulda's World, 1848-1884, 1989, Tidedrift Shells of Monterey Bay, 1995, The Herbert Hoover Family, 1996. Pres. Calif. Coun. Youth, Sacramento, 1961-65; mem. Santa Cruz County Bd. Suprs., 1956-63, foreman county grand jury, 1980-81; vol. Calif. Dept. Parks and Recreation, 1975—; conservation chmn. Native Daus. of Golden West, 1990-96. Recipient Superior Achievement award Calif. Dept. Parks and Recreation, 1996. Mem. DAR (conservation chmn. 1985—, Conservation award 1990), LWV (pres. Calif . 1941-43), AAUW, Am. Pen Women, Soroptimists Internat. (Woman of Achievement, 1965, Woman of Distinction, 1998), Santa Cruz Bus. and Profl. Women (Woman of Yr. Santa Cruz County 1982), Santa Cruz Art League, Santa Cruz C. of C (Woman of Yr. 1998). Home: 512 Walnut Ave Santa Cruz CA 95060-3636

MCLEAN, ROBIN JENNIFER, marketing, advertising professional; b. Denver, Dec. 15, 1960; d. Robert Earl and Marjorie Lee (Worland) McL. BA, U. Denver, 1983, postgrad., 1986—. Prodn. asst. Sta. KOA, Denver; advt. intern Colle & McVoy, Englewood, Colo.; advt. sales rep. Dow Jones & Co., Inc., Englewood, 1983-85; acct. exec. Univ. Graphics, Inc., Englewood, 1985-86; v.p. Columbine Mktg., Denver, 1986-90; acct. exec. Century Media, 1990-91; dir. advertising, mktg. Cherry Creek Locale, Denver, 1992-95; owner, investigator Alpine Investigations, 1995—; advisor U. Denver, 1985—; mktg. and pub. rels. cons. U.S. West, Inc. Mem. Denver Mus. of Natural History, Denver Botanical Gardens. Republican. Roman Catholic. Avocations: skiing, swimming, hiking, dancing, reading. Home: 270 Glencoe St Denver CO 80220-5716

MCLEOD, JAMES RICHARD, English language educator; b. Spokane, Wash., Jan. 8, 1942; s. Richard Leland and Bernice Lola (Smith) McL.; m. Judith Ann Osterberg Sylte, June 11, 1982; children: Anne, Brock, Rory, John. BA in English, U. Wash., 1966; MA in English, Ea. Wash. U., 1969. Cert. tchr., Wash. Psychiat. group worker Ryther Child Ctr., Seattle, 1961-63; tchr. Cen. Valley Sch. Dist., Spokane, 1966-69; prof. English North Idaho Coll., Coeur d'Alene, 1970—, dir. Scottish studies program, 1982-90; coord. two-yr. coll. programs, mem. exec. com. Associated Writing Programs, 1974-75. Author: Theodore Roethke: A Manuscript Checklist, 1971, Theodore Roethke: A Bibliography, 1973, Mysterious Lake Pend Oreille and Its Monster, 1987; contbr. to scholarly publs., author numerous poems. Bd. dirs., Kootenai County Coun. Alcoholism, Coeur d'Alene, 1977-80; mem.-at-large, United Ministries in Higher Edn., Seattle, 1979-85; cubmaster, Kootenai County coun. Boy Scouts Am., 1983-84; coord., Kootenai County Centennial Com., Ft. Sherman Day, Coeur d'Alene, 1988-90; evaluator Oral History of Coeur d'Alene Indian Project, Idaho Humanities Coun., 1992-93. Named honored author, Wash. State Arts Commn., 1972, Idaho State Library, Boise, 1976. Mem. Community Coll. Humanities Assn., Nat. Trust Scotland, Clan MacLeod Soc. USA (nat. v.p. 1982-86), Wash. Poets Assn. (bd. dirs. 1973-76), Spokane Piobaireachd Soc. (treas. 1983-91), North Idaho Coll. Rowing Club (advisor 1988—), North Idaho Coll. Cryptozoology Club. Democrat. Episcopalian. Avocations: racquetball, travel, genealogy, writing poetry, Scots music. E-mail: jrmcleod@nidc.edu. Home: 701 S 12th St Coeur D Alene ID 83814-3815 Office: North Idaho Coll 1000 W Garden Ave Coeur D Alene ID 83814-2161

MCLEOD, JOHN HUGH, JR., mechanical and electrical engineer; b. Hattiesburg, Miss., Feb. 27, 1911; s. John Hugh and Martha (Caldwell) McL.; m. Suzette Boutell, 1951; children: John Hugh III, Robert Boutell. BS, Tulane U., 1933. Registered profl. engr., Calif. Engr. various firms, 1933-39; field engr. Taylor Instrument Co., Rochester, N.Y., 1940-42; rsch. and devel. engr. Leeds & Northrup Co., Phila., 1943-47; sect. head guidance systems and guided missiles U.S. Naval Air Missile Test Ctr., Point Mugu, Calif., 1947-56; design specialist Gen. Dynamics/Astronautics, San Diego, 1956-63, cons., 1963-64; pvt. practice mech. and elec. engring. cons., La Jolla, Calif., 1964—; disting. vis. prof. Calif. State U. Chico, 1975; mem. exec. com. Fall Joint Computer Conf. Am. Fedn. Info. Processing Socs., 1965. Co-founder San Diego Symposium for Biomed. Engring., 1961. Author: Simulation: The Dynamic Modeling of Ideas and Systems with Computers, 1968, Computer Modeling and Simulation: Principles of Good Practice, 1982; editor, pub.: Simulation Council Newsletter, 1952-55; editor: Simulation, 1963-74; assoc. editor Instruments & Control Systems, 1955-63, Behavioral Sci., 1973—; tech. editor Simulation in the Service of Soc., 1971—; co-author: Large-Scale Models for Policy Evaluation, 1977. With USN, 1942-43. Recipient Sr. Sci. Simulation award Electronic Assocs., Inc., 1965, TIMS award Inst. Mgmt. Scis., 1986; NEH, NSF grantee, 1983; McLeod Inst. Simulation Sci. named in his honor at 18 acad. instns. including Calif. State U., Chico, U. Calgary, Can., U. Ottawa, Can., U. Ghent, Belgium, Istituto per la Recerca, Naples, Italy, Polish Acad. Scis., Warsaw, U. Edinburgh, Scotland, Beijing U. Aeronautics and Astronautics, Riga Tech. U., Latvia, Hungarian Acad. Scis., Budapest. Mem. IEEE, AAAS, Soc. Computer Simulation (founder, chmn. com. on profl. ethics, publs. advisor, John McLeod award 1987). E-mail: mcleod@sdsc.edu. Home: 8484 La Jolla Shores Dr La Jolla CA 92037-3019 Office: Soc Computer Simulation PO Box 17900 San Diego CA 92177-7900

MCLOONE, JAMES BRIAN, psychiatrist, educator; b. Phoenix, Ariz., Mar. 21, 1950; s. John Joseph and Lorraine Suzette (Hughes) McL.; children: Katherine Ann, Brian Bathe. BA, U. Ariz., 1972; MD, George Washington U., 1976. Diplomate Am. Bd. Psychiatry and Neurology. Inpatient med. dir. Maricopa Med. Ctr., Phoenix, 1980-81; dir. psychiatry residency Good Samaritan Regional Med. Ctr., Phoenix, 1981—, chmn. dept. psychiatry, 1992—; assoc. prof. clin. psychiatry U. Ariz. Coll. Medicine, Tucson, 1982—, assoc. head dept. psychiatry for acad. and clin. affairs, Phoenix campus, 1997—; chair med. edn. com. Good Samaritan Regional Med. Ctr., Phoenix, 1990—, exec. com., 1992—. Mem. Men's Art Coun. Phoenix Art Mus., 1981-87; student advisor U. Ariz. Coll. Medicine, Tucson, 1982—, Brophy Coll. Prep., Phoenix, 1982—; cons. Maricopa Mental Health Assn., Phoenix, 1990—. Fellow Am. Psychiatric Assn.; mem. Am. Assn. Dirs. Psychiat. Residency Tng., Assn. Geropsychiatrists, Paradise Valley C. C., Alpha Omega Alpha. Roman Catholic. Avocations: golf, gardening. Office: Good Samaritan Reg Med Ctr 925 E Mcdowell Rd Phoenix AZ 85006-2579

MCLURKIN, THOMAS CORNELIUS, JR., lawyer; b. L.A., July 28, 1954; s. Thomas Cornelius and Willie Mae (O'Connor) McL.; m. Charmaine Dubo. BA, U. So. Calif., 1976, MPA, 1980, PhD in Pub. Adminstrn., 1998; JD, U. LaVerne, 1982. Bar: Calif. 1984; U.S. Dist. Ct. (ctrl. dist.) Calif.

1984, U.S. Dist. Ct. Hawaii 1984, U.S. Ct. Appeals (9th cir.) 1984, U.S. Dist. Ct. (ea., no. and so. dists.) Calif. 1985, U.S. Tax Ct. 1988, U.S. Ct. Mil. Appeals 1989, U.S. Army Ct. Mil. Rev. 1993, U.S. Supreme Ct., 1995. Law clk. dept. water and power City of L.A., 1979-82; jud. clk. cen. dist. U.S. Dist. Ct., L.A., 1982-83; law clk. Office City Atty., L.A., 1983-84, dep. city atty., 1984—. Author (with others): Facts in American History, 1968, 2nd edit. 1989, Eagle Scout, 1970. Mem. L.A. World Affairs Coun., 1980—, Smithsonian Assocs.; bd. dirs. L.A. Area coun. Boy Scouts Am., Hillsides Homes for Children; provisional patron Tournament of Roses Assn., Pasadena, 1994—; mem. Verdugo Hills Area coun. Boy Scouts Am. Mem. ABA, ALA, ASPA, Los Angeles County Bar Assn., Assn. Trial Lawyers Am., Langston Law Assn. L.A., U. So. Calif. Gen. Alumni Assn. (bd. govs. exec. bd. 1986-90), U. So. Calif. Black Alumni Assn.-Ebonics (pres. 1988-89), U. So. Calif. Pres.'s Cir., Elks, Am. Legion, Phi Alpha Delta, Kappa Alpha Psi. Republican. United Methodist. Avocations: sailing, tennis, volunteer work, American and world history. Office: LA City Atty Office 200 N Main St Ste 1700 Los Angeles CA 90012

MCMAHON, BRIAN, publishing executive. Pub. Car and Driver Hachette Filipacchi Mags., Inc., Ann Arbor, Mich. Office: Hachette Filipacchi Mags Inc 1499 Monrovia Ave Newport Beach CA 92663-2752 also: 2002 Hog Back Rd Ann Arbor MI 48105*

MCMAHON, CRAIG ROGER, magistrate; b. Meriden, Conn., July 5, 1950. BA, George Washington U., 1972; JD, New Eng. Sch. Law, Boston, 1976. Magistrate Alaska Ct. Sys., Bethel, 1977—. Office: Alaska Ct Sys PO Box 130 Bethel AK 99559-0130

MCMAHON, JOHN WILLIAM, sculptor; b. Honolulu, May 12, 1938; s. John William McM. and Catherine (Stores) Fifita; m. Hui Ping, June 17, 1995; children: Erin K., Alison J. Student, UCLA; BA, Calif. State U., Northridge, 1976. Commd. 2d lt. USCG, 1976. Mem. Res. Officers Assn., Pacific Rim Sculptors. Avocations: biking, hiking, surfing. Home: 30 Quail Ridge Dr Atascadero CA 93422-4555

MCMANIS, JAMES, lawyer; b. Haverhill, Mass., May 28, 1943; s. Charles and Yvonne (Zinn) McM.; m. Sara Wigh, Mar. 30, 1968. BA, Stanford U., Palo Alto, Calif., 1964; JD, U. Calif., Berkeley, 1967. Bar: Calif. 1967, U.S. Dist. Ct. (no. dist.) Calif. 1967, U.S. Ct. Appeals (9th cir.) 1967, U.S. Supreme Ct. 1971. Dep. dist. atty. Santa Clara County Dist. Atty., 1968-71; mem. McManis, Faulkner & Morgan, San Jose, Calif., 1971—; spl. master tech. equities litigation, 1987—; spl. examiner State Bar Calif., 1995-98; prof. law Lincoln U. Law Sch., San Jose, 1972-82; lectr. Calif. Continuing Edn. of Bar, 1989-90; instr. U. Calif. Law Sch., 1992-96, Stanford U. Sch. Law, 1994-99. Pres. Santa Clara County Bar Assn. Law Found., 1996, dir., 1987—. Fellow Am. Coll. Trial Lawyers; mem. ABA, State Bar Calif., Calif. Trial Lawyers Assn., Santa Clara County Bar Assn., Boalt Hall Alumni Assn. Avocations: history, books, travel, running. Fax: 408-279-3244. E-mail: jmcmanis@mfmlaw.com. Office: McManis Faulkner & Morgan Inc 160 W Santa Clara St Fl 10 San Jose CA 95113-1701

MC MANUS, PHILIP JAMES, advocate, human rights, peace-building activist; b. San Francisco, Oct. 23, 1951; s. William Marian and Marion Arnold (Smith) McM.; m. Betsy Fairbanks; children: Timothy, Kevin, Maria Rosa. Latin Am. program coord. Resource Ctr. for Nonviolence, Santa Cruz, Calif., 1978-96; chmn. U.S. Fellowship of Reconciliation Task Force on Latin Am. and the Caribbean, Santa Cruz, 1986—, Internat. Svc. for Peace (SIPAZ), Santa Cruz, 1995—; cons. IF, Watsonville, Calif., 1996—; staff Witness for Peace, Nicaragua, 1983-84; vol. Servicio Paz y Justicia en Am. Latina, Ecuador, 1991-92. Editor: Relentless Persistence, 1991; contbr. articles on process of change in Latin Am.; Prodn. Coord. (documentary film) The Faithful Revolution: Vatican II, 1995. Judge Pfeffer Peace Prize, 1995—. Office: SIPAZ PO Box 2415 Santa Cruz CA 95063-2415

MCMILLAN, LARRY DONALD, engineering executive; b. Trout Lake, Mich., June 10, 1936; s. Ira Duncan and Lilly Bell (Reed) McM.; m. Theresa Ann Mayer, June 25, 1955 (div. July 1975); children: Aaron, Keith, Curt, Adam, Kent, Craig, Andrea; m. Victoria Jeanne Cronin, Nov. 5, 1977. BSEE, Aquinas Coll., Grand Rapids, Mich., 1965; MSEE, Ariz. State U., 1972; postgrad., U. Colo., Colorado Springs, 1990-97. Elec. engring. mgr. Motorola, Inc., Phoenix, 1966-76; mgr. process engring. Am. Microsys., Inc., Santa Clara, Calif., 1976-77; dir. engring. Nat. Cash Register Corp., Colorado Springs, 1977-79; v.p., gen. mgr. microtech. ops. Storage Tech. Corp., Louisville, Colo., 1979-80; v.p. Stephenson Western, Inc., Aurora, Colo., 1980-82; engring. mgr. Honeywell, Inc., Colorado Springs, 1982-84; v.p. rsch. and devel., corp. founder Ramtron Corp., Colorado Springs, 1984-88; CEO, pres., corp. founder Symetrix Corp., Colorado Springs, 1988—; adj. prof. Mich. Technol. U., Houghton, 1986-88. Co-author: (chpt.) Ferroelectric Ceramics, 1993; contbr. articles to Integrated Ferroelectrics, Nature, Jour. Integrated Ferroelectrics, Condensed Matter News, Nikkei Electronics, Ferroelectrics, Jour. Applied Physics, Applied Physics Letters. Achievements include patents for Method of Making Barium Strontium Titanate, Integrated Circuit Capacitors and Process for Making the Same, Process for Making Metal Oxides, Metal Polyoxyalkylated Precursor Solutions in an Octane Solvent and Method of Making the Same, Ferroelectric Integrated Circuit, Precursors and Processes for Making Metal Oxides, Memory with Ferroellectric Capacitor Connectable to Transistor Gate, Ferroelectric Memory and Non-Volatile Memory Cell for Same, Misted Deposition Apparatus for Fabrication an Integrated Circuit, Non-Volatile Memory, Ferroelectric Dielectric Memory Cell can Switch at Least GIG Cycles and has Low Fatigue, ABO3 Structured Solid Solutions Mixed and Average Perovskites for High Dielectric Constant DRAMs and Capacitors, Precursors and Processes for Making Metal Oxides, Low Temperature Process for Fabricationg Layered Superlattice Materials and Making Electronic Devices Including Same, others. Home: 3005 Blodgett Dr Colorado Springs CO 80919-4510 Office: Symetrix Corp 5055 Mark Dabling Blvd Colorado Springs CO 80918-3862

MCMILLAN, MONTY HAYES, filmmaker, security analyst; b. Beaumont, Tex., Nov. 25, 1949; s. Carl Alvin and Bonnie Jean (Hayes) McM. Student, U. Tex., 1968-73. Pres., prodr. Thor Projects, Inc., Austin, Tex., 1974-78; pres., prodr., dir. Synergy Pictures, Hollywood, Calif., 1987—; freelance filmaker, 1971—; cons., tchr. TV3 Malaysia, Kuala Lumpur, 1986; rsch. analyst Hughes Aircraft, El Segundo, Calif., 1991-96, Navy League, El Segundo, 1993, Army War Coll. Nat. Security Forum, 1993, Army War Coll. Nat. Security Seminars, 1997. Dir. Life on the Slope, S2 Prodns., Prudhoe Bay, Alaska, 1985-86, America's Army, Washington, 1996; co-prodr., photographer Dhammazedi Bell, Rangoon, Burma, 1995-96; screewriter (screenplays) The Cuban Circuit, 1979, The Aztec Highway, 1986; prodr., dir. Command Briefing-U.S. Army Signal Command, 1998; contbr. articles to Voices mag., 1997. Mem. Cmty. Emergency Response Team, L.A., 1995—; media photographer Houston Intertribal Coun., 1986. Mem. Internat. Alliance Stage and Theatrical Employees, L.A. World Affairs Coun. Democrat. Episcopalian. Avocations: cooking, collecting baseball cards, photography, travel. Home and Office: Synergy Pictures 1304 Mariposa Austin TX 78704

MCMILLAN, TERRY L., writer, educator; b. Port Huron, Mich., Oct. 18, 1951; d. Edward McMillan and Madeline Washington Tillman; 1 child, Solomon Welch. BA in Journalism, U. Calif., Berkeley, 1979; MFA, Columbia Univ., N.Y.C., 1979. Instr. U. Wyoming, Laramie, 1987-90; prof. U. Ariz., Tucson, 1990-92. Author: Mama, 1987, Disappearing Acts, 1989, Waiting to Exhale, 1992, How Stella Got Her Groove Back, 1996; editor: Breaking Ice: An Anthology of Contemporary African-American Fiction, 1990; screenwriter (with Ron Bass) (movie) Waiting to Exhale, 1995. Recipient National Endowment for the Arts fellowship, 1988.

MCMILLIN, WILLIAM RAY, real estate broker; b. Warren, Ohio, July 7, 1942; s. Delbert C. and Hope E. McM.; children: Michael, Maya. BS in math., Stanford, 1964, MA in edn., 1965; postgrad., Syracuse, 1970-73. Tchr. San Francisco Unified Sch. Dist., 1964-70; adminstrv. asst. Syracuse Univ., 1971-73; prin. Fonda-Fultonville Ctr. Sch. Dist., N.Y., 1973-74; planning specialist, optional ednl. programs. rep. Western N.Y. Regional Office for Ednl. Planning, 1974-75; coord. N.Y. State External H.S. Diploma program Syracuse Univ. Rsch. Corp., civ, 1976; broker assoc. Grubb & Ellis Co. Commercial Real Estate Svcs., San Jose, Calif., 1977-92; commercial real estate broker Marcus & Millichap, Palo Alto, Calif., 1992—; cons. Onondage-Madison Bd. Cooperative Edn. Svcs., N.y., 1976, math. lab. specialist Syracuse City Schs., 1971, athletic dir. San Francisco Dept. Parks & Recreation, 1967-68; h.s. math. tchr. Mountain View Los Altos Unified Sch. Dist., 1965, 68. Bd. pres. Newark Unified Sch. Dist., 1997; pres. Lake Area Residents Assn., 1997, 98; treas. Fremont Dem. Forum, Fremont, Calif., 1998; bd. dirs. Alameda County Sch. Bd. Assn., 1994-98, v.p., 1998. Democrat. Avocations: tennis, skiing, flying. Home: 35321 Cheviot Ct Newark CA 94560-1424 Office: Marcus & Millichap 2626 Hanover St Palo Alto CA 94304-1132

MCMILLON, BILLY JOE, writer, educator; b. Baldwyn, Miss., Jan. 25, 1942; s. Miles Booker and Beulah Mae (Mabry) McM.; m. Sandra Gayle Clem, 1961 (div. 1966); 1 child, Kimberly Ellen; m. Mary Heather Roeseler, Feb. 21, 1970; children: Matthew Arthur, Kevin Myles. AB in Social Studies, Sacramento State Coll., 1966; MA in Spl. Edn. and Counseling, Sonoma State Coll., 1977. Tchr. grades 4-8 Copperopolis Elem. Sch., San Andreas, Calif., 1964-65; tchr. English and social studies Stanislaus Jr. H.S., Modesto, Calif., 1965-68; guidance counselor, dorm adminstr. boarding sch. Bur. Indian Affairs, Greasewood, Ariz., 1968-69; tchr. Sonoma (Calif.) County Office Edn., 1969-79; tchr. depts. psychology and edn. Sonoma State U., 1973-78; tchr. learning disabilities group Wright Sch. Dist., Santa Rosa, Calif., 1979-83; tchr. various workshops including ext. faculty Sonoma State U., 1993—; substitute tchr. West County Union H.S. Dist., 1995—. Author: California's Underwater State Parks, 1982, The Old Lodges and Hotels of Our National Parks, 1983, Fairs and Festivals of California, Hawaii, and Nevada, 1985, Volunteer Vactaions, 1st edit., 1987, 6th edit., 1997, Wilderness U., 1992, Nature Nearby, 1990, The Archaeology Handbook, 1991, Best Hikes With Children, 1992, Best Hikes With Children North Bay, 1992, Best Hikes With Children South Bay, 1992, Best Hikes With Children Around Sacramento, 1993, Country Roads of Florida, 1994, Seasonal Guide to Natural Year, 1995, Great Outdoor Getaways, 1995, Birding Arizona, 1996, Camping With Kids, 1996, Florida With Kids, 1998; contbr. over 400 articles to newspapers and mags.; columnist Travels on a Slightly Tilted Planet, 1994, 95; TV appearances include CBS This Morning, NBC Nightly News, CNN's International Hour and Morning Report. Coach basketball, baseball, and soccer, various h.s. and youth leagues, 1960—. Mem. NEA, Outdoor Writers Calif., Calif. Tchrs. Assn. Avocations: photography, hiking, traveling, blacksmithing.

MCMULLIN, LINDA SUE, English language educator; b. Casper, Wyo., Jan. 16, 1951; d. Kendrick A. and Eunice Katherine (Wilson) McM.; m. David Vernon Hunt, Dec. 18, 1989. BA, Lewis and Clark Coll., 1973; MA, U. Ariz., 1976. Cert. lifetime cmty. coll. educator, Calif. Tchr. English Centro Colombo-Am., Bucaramanga, Colombia, 1976-77, acad. dir., 1977-78; instr. ESL Am. Lang. Acad., Pocatello, Idaho, 1978-80, Bridge Internat. Sch., Denver, 1980-84; prof. ESL Imperial Valley Coll., Imperial, Calif., 1985—; v.p. acad. senate Imperial Valley Coll., 1989-91, mem. Title III writing team, 1997-98. Co-author: Classroom Research Techniques, 1990. Deacon 1st Presbyn. Ch., El Centro, sec., 1995—. Mem. TESOL, Calif. Tchrs. Assn. (sec. Imperial Valley Coll. chpt. 1989-91). Avocation: camping. Home: 600 Wensley Ave El Centro CA 92243-3957 Office: Imperial Valley Coll Hwy III and Aten Rd Imperial CA 92251

MCMURDO, C(HARLES) GREGORY, state official, lawyer; b. Klamath Falls, Oreg., Apr. 30, 1946; s. Charles Andrew and Juanita Berniece (Bell) McM.; B.A., Oreg. State U., 1968, J.D., Lewis and Clark Coll., 1972. Bar: Oreg. 1972, U.S. Dist. Ct. Oreg. 1975, U.S. Ct. Appeals (9th cir.) 1980, U.S. Supreme Ct. 1984. Legal counsel Oreg. Ho. of Reps., Salem, 1972-76; asst. sect. state State of Oreg., Salem, 1976-81, dep. sec. state, 1981-85; mem. Workers Compensation Bd., 1985-88; dir of govt. rels, Metro, Portland, 1988-90; dep. supt. of pub. instrn., State of Oreg., 1990—. Mem. Oreg. State Bar. Republican. Episcopalian. Office: Oreg Dept of Edn Pub Svc Bldg 255 Capitol St NE Salem OR 97310-1341

MCMURRAY, RON, political association executive. Chmn. Idaho State Rep. Party, 1995—. *

MCNABB, ROBERT HENRY, minister; b. Charles City, Iowa, Jan. 28, 1917; s. John Henry and Gail (Gants) McNabb; m. Doris Jean Patrick, Oct. 25, 1947; children: Daniel, Allen, Roy, Gail, Marjori. BA, Cornell Coll., 1943; STB, Boston U., 1946, postgrad., 1946-47. Ordained to ministry Meth. Ch., 1945. Min. United Meth. Ch., Greeley, Iowa, 1947-49; missionary United Meth. Ch., Honolulu, 1949-55; min. Oreg.-Idaho conf. United Meth. Ch., 1955-74; missionary United Meth. Ch., Juneau, Alaska, 1974-80; min. United Meth. Ch., Ontario, Oreg., 1980-83, Palmerston-North, New Zealand, 1983-84; min. Cen. Christian Ch., United Ch. of Christ, 1984-86; min. Olaa 1st Hawaiian Ch. Cen. Christian Ch., 1986-88; min. Hilo Ch. Hilo Coast United Christian Ch., 1986-95; senate chaplain Alaska State Senate, Juneau, 1976-78; chaplain Jr. CAP, Juneau, 1978-80. Mem. Rotary (pres.-elect Ontario 1983), Kiwanis, Lions. Democrat.

MCNALLY, CONNIE BENSON, editor, publisher, antiques dealer; b. Chgo.; d. Peter D. and Joanna Agriostathes; m. Dick Benson, Nov. 19, 1955 (div. mar. 1961); 1 child, Douglas; m. William C. McNally, July 27th, 1995. Student, Univ. Wis., 1954-55; BA, Baylor, 1962. Midwest supr. Slenderella Internat., Chgo., 1955-59; dir. John Roberts Powers Sch., Dallas, 1960-62; backgammon tchr., profl. Racquet Club, Palm Springs, Calif., 1969-75, La Costa (Calif.) Resort, 1973-75; antique dealer Palm Springs, 1975—; ptnr. Carriage Trade Antiques, 1975-78; owner, mgr. McNally Co. Antiques, 1978—; editor, pub. Silver Mag., Inc., Rancho Santa Fe, Calif., 1993—. Mem. Am. Assn. Antique Dealers, Antique Dealers Assn. Calif., Country Firends (vol. chair 1985-87, area dir. 1988-89, publicity chair 1990-91, program chair 1992-93, corr. sec. 1994-95, bd. dirs.), Social Svc. League La Jolla, Soc. Am. Silversmiths, Rancho Santa Fe Rep. Women's Club. Avocations: equestrian, gourmet cook. Office: Silver Mag Inc PO Box 9690 Rancho Santa Fe CA 92067-4690

MCNALLY, THOMAS P., theater educator; b. Denver, Aug. 14, 1946; s. Bernard Edward and Dorothy Ann (Reardon) McN.; m. Sheila Lee Stone, Aug. 24, 1972; 1 child, Gillian Bridget. BA in Philosophy, English and Drama, Regis Coll., 1969; MFA in Acting and Directing, U. Denver, 1972. Artistic dir. McNally Prodns., Denver, 1971-73; prof., chair Loretto Heights Coll., Denver, 1973-81; prod., tchr. MFA program, dir. Pa. State U., State College, Pa., 1981-88; prof., chair, artistic dir. U. No. Colo. and Little Theatre of the Rockies, Greeley, 1988—; guest dir. Camden (Maine) Shakespeare Co., 1982, Grosse Pointe (Mich.) Players, 1990—, Arvada (Colo.) Ctr. for the Arts, 1991, Denver Civic Theater, 1994; spkr., presenter confs. in field. Author: Acting: The Active Process, 1997. Bd. dirs. higher edn. coun. Denver Ctr. Theatre Co., 1993—. Recipient Program of Excellence award Colo. State Legislature, 1998. Mem. Actors Equity Assn., Ednl. Theatre Assn. (Founders award 1992), Alliance for Theatre in Higher Edn., Alliance of Colo. Theatre (bd. dirs. 1988-92, Higher Edn. Educator of Yr. 1994). Democrat. Roman Catholic. Avocations: films, golf. Home: 4406 W 17th St Greeley CO 80634-3328

MCNAMARA, BRENDA NORMA, secondary education educator; b. Blackpool, Lancashire, Eng., Aug. 8, 1945; came to U.S., 1946; d. Milford Hampson and Nola (Welsby) Jones; m. Michael James McNamara, July 19, 1969. BA in History, Calif. State U., Long Beach, 1967; postgrad., Calif. State U., various campuses, 1967—. Cert. secondary tchr. and lang. devel. specialist, Calif. Tchr. history West High Sch., Torrance, Calif., 1968—, dept. chair, 1989—; cons. Calif. State Dept. Edn. Golden State Examination in History, 1998; cons. in field. Co-author: World History, 1988. Western Internat. Studies Consortium grantee, 1988. Mem. Calif. Tchrs. Assn., Calif. Coun. for Social Studies, Torrance Tchrs. Assn. (bd. dirs. 1992—), South Bay Coun. for Social Studies, Nat. Tchrs. Assn., Nat. Coun. for Social Studies, Am. Historical Assn. Avocations: travel, theater, mystery reading, gourmet cooking. Office: West H S 20401 Victor St Torrance CA 90503-2297

MCNAMARA, JAMES ANTHONY, architect; b. Camden, N.J., May 11, 1954; s. John Francis and Margaret (Noon) McN.; m. Loretta Lewis, June 2, 1980; children: Colleen, Kerry. BA in Architecture, U. N.Mex., 1978. Registered architect, Tex., N.Mex. Architect CRSS, Houston, 1978-87, FMSM Architects, Albuquerque, 1988-95; prin., architect Pohde May Keller McNamara, Albuquerque, 1995—. Mem. N.Mex. Health Care Task Force, Santa Fe, 1995-96. Mem. AIA (treas. 1995-97), Nat. Coun. Archtl. Registration Bds. Avocation: furniture designing/crafting. Home: 1201 Calle Del Ranchero NE Albuquerque NM 87106-1907 Office: Rohde May Keller McNamara 900 Gold Ave SW # 1100 Albuquerque NM 87102-3043

MCNAMARA, STEPHEN, newspaper executive; b. Chgo., July 9, 1934; s. Robert Charles McNamara Jr. and Susan (Deuel) Shattuck; m. Hanne Morgensen Petterson, Feb. 21, 1960 (div. Aug. 1968); children: Lise, Natalie, Kevin; m. Kay Copeland, June 10, 1978; children: Christopher, Morgan. AB in Am. History, Princeton U., 1955. Reporter Winston-Salem (N.C.) Jour., 1955-57; sports writer Miami Herald, 1957-59; contbg. European editor Car & Driver, N.Y.C., 1960; asst. news editor, exec. sports editor, Sunday editor San Francisco Examiner, 1961-67; CEO, editor, pub. Pacific Sun, Mill Valley, Calif., 1967—; co-pub. The Ark, Tiburon, Calif., 1987—; pres. Marin Sun Printing Co., Mill Valley, 1967-93; mng. gen. ptnr. Sunrise Investment Co., Mill Valley, 1980—; vis. lectr. San Francisco State U., 1967; mem. innovation and planning commn. Calif. Dept. Edn., Sacramento, 1980; co-founder, pres. Marin Solar Village Corp., Mill Valley, 1976—, Marin Cmty. Video, Mill Valley, 1973-78. Mem. Soc. Profl. Journalists, Nat. Assn. Alternative Newsweeklies (pres. 1978-81), Calif. Assn. Alternative Newsweeklies (pres. 1990-92), Calif. Soc. Newspaper Editors (pres. 1985-86, bd. dirs. 1983-93), Calif. Newspaper Pubs. Assn. (bd. dirs. 1989-93), San Francisco Press Club (1st place newspaper writing award 1967, 3-2d place awards), Cap and Gown Club (Princeton U.). Democrat. Home: 2 Bradford Way Mill Valley CA 94941-1111 Office: Pacific Sun Pub 21 Corte Madera Ave Mill Valley CA 94941-1800

MCNAMARA, TOM, scientific consulting corporation executive; b. Battle Creek, Mich., May 23, 1944; s. George P. (stepfather) and Mildred E. Lunt. Grad. in Chemistry, Boston U., 1966; M.B.A., Northeastern U., 1970; m. Ellen K. LaRue, Sept. 24, 1977; 1 child, George Lunt. With corp. planning dept. Reynolds Aluminum, Richmond, Va., 1970-72; sr. cons. Technomic Cons., Chgo., 1972-74; founder, pres. NUVENTURES Cons., Inc., Chgo. and San Diego, 1975—; speaker trade convs. and confs. worldwide; frequent guest TV and radio talk shows; on water advisor Am.'s Cup, 1988, 91, 94. Author: Henry Lunt and The Ranger, 1991, Henry Lunt and The Spymaster, 1994, Skull and Crossbones, 1997; co-author: America's Changing Workforce, 1990; editor: George and The Pitching Machine, 1994; contbr. articles to profl. publs. Rep. nominee Ill. Gen. Assembly, 1974, 76; mem. various coms. United Fund and Chgo. Assn. Commerce and Industry, 1975-79; Spokesman 200th Anniversary U.S. Bill of Rights tour, 1991. 1st lt. Ordnance Corps, U.S. Army, 1966-69. Recipient Presdl. Commendation for heroism, 1974, Commendation award Chgo. Police Dept., 1974, Pulitzer Prize nominee, 1991. Mem. Acacia, Bahia Corinthian Yacht Club, San Diego Tennis and Racquet Club. Contbr. articles to profl. publs. Office: PO Box 2489 La Jolla CA 92038-2489

MCNAMEE, STEPHEN M., federal judge; b. 1942. B.A., U. Cinn., 1964; M.A., J.D., U. Ariz., 1969. U.S. atty. Dist. of Ariz., Phoenix, 1985-90; judge U.S. Dist. Ct. Ariz., Phoenix, 1990—. Office: City of Phoenix US Court Hse & Fed Bldg 230 N 1st Ave Phoenix AZ 85025-0230*

MCNARY, SUE TUSHINGHAM, artist; b. Collingswood, N.J., Dec. 9, 1942; d. Herbert Wallis and Marty Louise (Brown) Tushingham; m. William Francis McNary III, Apr. 5, 1962 (dec. 1982); children: William Wallis, Glenn Michael. AA, Columbia Coll., 1961; student, Mich. State U., 1968-69. Gallery owner Hotel del Coronado, Calif., 1984—; commd. cover artist Childrens Home Soc. of Calif., San Diego, 1991, Kennedy Pub., Coronado, 1988, 95; commd. mural artist Village Elem. Sch., Coronado, 1992, San Diego Visitor and Conv. Bur., 1993; commd. artist USN, Coronado, 1993-94, Hotel del Coronado, 1995, Portal Pub. Co., 1991, Sunset Mktg. Pub., 1992, Bentley Ho. Pub., 1995; v.p., bd. dirs. Delta, Coronado, 1993-95. juried exhibitor N.Y. Art Expo, N.Y.C., 1989-92; commd. mural Coronado golf course, Meml. Clubhouse, 1997. Mem. San Diego Visitor and Conv. Bur., San Diego, 1985—; artist Childrens Sch. Found., 1988—; bd. dirs. San Diego County Art Coun., San Diego, 1984-88, San Diego Art Inst., 1975-79. Mem. Coronado Rotary Club, The Charter 100, Coronado Investment Club (v.p.), Connections, Del Mar Turf Club. Methodist. Avocations: stock market, aerobics, skiing, dancing. Home: 1500 Orange Ave Coronado CA 92118-2918 Office: Sue Tushingham McNary Art Gallery Hotel del Coronado Coronado CA 92118

MC NEALY, SCOTT, computer company executive; b. 1954. BA, Harvard U., 1976; MBA, Stanford U., 1980. With Rockwell Internat. Corp., Troy, Mich., 1976-78, sales engr.; staff engr. FMC Corp., Chgo., 1980-81; dir. ops. Onyx Systems, San Jose, Calif., 1981-82; chmn. bd., pres., CEO, Sun Microsystems Inc., Mountain View, Calif., 1982—, also bd. dirs., 1985. Office: Sun Microsystems Inc 2550 Garcia Ave Mountain View CA 94043-1100

MCNULTY, JAMES F., export company executive. BS in Engring., U.S. Mil. Acad., 1964; MS in Nuc. Physics, Ohio State U., 1970; MS in Mgmt., MIT, 1985. Rsch. assoc. Lawrence Livermore Nat. Lab., 1972-74; asst. dir. Office Mil. Applications U.S. Dept. Energy, 1978-80; officer nuc. weapon requirements Ops. and Plans Office Dept. U.S. Army, 1980-82, sys. mgr. Pershing II Missle Sys., 1982-84, program mgr. ground based laser sys., 1985-88; dir. bus. devel. Parsons Corp., 1988-89; v.p. Parsons Corp., Washington, 1991-92; sr. v.p., mgr. sys. divsn. Parsons Corp., 1992-95, pres. infrastructure and tech. group, 1996; pres., CEO Parsons Corp., Pasadena, Calif., 1996—. Office: Parsons Corp 100 W Walnut St Pasadena CA 91124-0001*

MCNUTT, STEPHEN RUSSELL, volcanologist, geophysical scientist; b. Hartford, Conn., Dec. 21, 1954; s. Elmer Ellsworth and Leona (LaPointe) McN. BA, Wesleyan U., Middletown, Conn., 1977; MA, Columbia U., 1982, MPhil, 1984, PhD, 1985. Sr. seismologist Calif. Div. Mines and Geology, Sacramento, 1984-91; rsch. prof. U. Alaska, Fairbanks, 1991—; cons. U. Costa Rica, San José, 1982—, U. Nat. Automata de Mexico, 1994—. Contbr. articles to profl. jours. Mem. Seismol. Soc. Am., Am. Geophys. Union, Internat. Assn. Volcanology and Chemistry of Earth's Interior (U.S. nat. com. chmn. 1996—), Buffalo Chips Running Club (Sacramento, bd. dirs. 1986-90). Democrat. Roman Catholic. Avocations: running, skiing, music, philately, drawing cartoons. Office: U Alaska Geophys Inst Alaska Volcano Obs PO Box 757320 Fairbanks AK 99775-7320

MC PHERSON, ROLF KENNEDY, clergyman, church official; b. Providence, Mar. 23, 1913; s. Harold S. and Aimee (Semple) McP.; m. Lorna De Smith, July 21, 1931 (dec.); children—Marlene (dec.), Kay; m. Evangeline Carmichael, Jan. 31, 1997. Grad., So. Cal. Radio Inst., 1933; D.D. (hon.), L.I.F.E. Bible Coll., 1944; LLD (hon.), L.I.F.E. Bible Coll., Los Angeles, 1988. Ordained to ministry Internat. Ch. Foursquare Gospel, 1940. Pres. Internat. Ch. Foursquare Gospel, L.A., 1944-88, dir., 1944-92; pres. emeritus, 1988—; pres., dir. L.I.F.E. Bible Coll., Inc., L.A., 1944-88. Mem. Echo Park Evangelistic Assn. (pres. 1944—). Office: Internat Ch Foursquare Gospel 1910 W Sunset Blvd Ste 200 Los Angeles CA 90026-3295

MCQUERN, MARCIA ALICE, newspaper publishing executive; b. Riverside, Calif., Sept. 3, 1942; d. Arthur Carlyle and Dorothy Louise (Krupke) Knopf; m. Lynn Morris McQuern, June 7, 1969. BA in Polit. Sci., U. Calif., Santa Barbara, 1964; MS in Journalism, Northwestern U., 1966. Reporter The Press-Enterprise, Riverside, 1966-72, city editor, 1972-74, capitol corr., 1975-78, dep. mng. editor news, 1984-85, mng. editor news, 1985-87, exec. editor, 1988-94, pres., 1992—; editor, publisher, 1994—; asst. metro editor The Sacramento Bee, 1974-75; editor state and polit. news The San Diego Union, 1978-79, city editor, 1979-84; juror Pulitzer Prize in Journalism, 1982, 83, 92, 93. Mem. editorial bd. Calif. Lawyer mag., San Francisco, 1983-88. Bd. advisors U. Calif.-Berkeley Grad. Sch. Journalism, 1991-96, U. Calif.-Riverside Grad. Sch. Mgmt., 1994—; pres. Riverside Cmty. Coll. Found., 1996-98; trustee U. Calif. Riverside Found., 1996—. Recipient Journalism award Calif. State Bar Assn., 1967, Sweepstakes award Twin Counties Press Club, Riverside and San Bernardino, 1972, Athena award YWCA, 1994. Mem. Am. Soc. Newspaper Editors (bd. dirs. 1992-98), Calif. Soc. Newspaper Editors (bd. 1988-95), Calif. Newspaper Pubs. Assn. (bd. dirs. 1992—), Calif. Press Assn. (bd. dirs. 1996—), Soc. Profl. Journalists, U. Calif.-Santa Barbara Alumni Assn. (bd. dirs. 1983-89). Home: 5717 Bedford

Dr Riverside CA 92506-3404 Office: Press-Enterprise Co 3512 14th St Riverside CA 92501-3878

MCQUILLIN, RICHARD ROSS, management consultant; b. Elyria, Ohio, Oct. 15, 1956; s. Wayne Rupp and Frana Rose (Romp) McQ.; m. Riko Koga; children: Richard K., Sean K. BS, Ohio State U., 1979; MS, U. So. Calif., L.A., 1983; MBA, UCLA, 1990. Sr. staff mem. TRW Inc., Redondo Beach, Calif., 1979-88; sr. cons. Deloitte & Touche, L.A., 1990-91; cons. mgr. NetBase Computing, El Segundo, Calif., 1993—. Treas., controller Patio Creek Homeowners Assn., Torrance, Calif., 1986-91, pres. 1991—; pres. TRW Investment Club, Redondo Beach, 1984-87. UCLA fellow, 1989. Mem. IEEE, Beta Gamma Sigma. Home: 19028 Entradero Ave Torrance CA 90503-1360 Office: NetBase Computing Inc 2101 Rosecrans Ave Ste 5250 El Segundo CA 90245-4742

MCRAE, HAMILTON EUGENE, III, lawyer; b. Midland, Tex., Oct. 29, 1937; s. Hamilton Eugene and Adrian (Hagaman) McR.; m. Betty Hawkins, Aug. 27, 1960; children: Elizabeth Ann, Stephanie Adrian, Scott Hawkins. BSEE, U. Ariz., 1961; student, USAF Electronics Sch., 1961-62; postgrad., U. Redlands, Calif., 1962-63; JD with honors and distinction, U. Ariz., 1967; LHD (hon.), Sterling Coll., 1992; vis. fellow, Darwin Coll. and Martin Ctr., Cambridge (Eng.) U., 1996-97. Bar: Ariz. 1967, U.S. Supreme Ct. 1979; cert. real estate specialist, Ariz. Elec. engr. Salt River Project, Phoenix, 1961; assoc. Jennings, Strouss & Salmon, Phoenix, 1967-71, ptnr., 1971-85, chmn. real estate dept., 1980-85, mem. policy com., 1982-85, mem. fin. com., 1981-85, chmn. bus. devel. com., 1982-85; ptnr. and co-founder Stuckey & McRae, Phoenix, 1985—; co-founder, chmn. bd. Republic Cos., Phoenix, 1985—; magistrate Paradise Valley, Ariz., 1983-85; juvenile referee Superior Ct., 1983-85; pres., dir. Phoenix Realty & Trust Co., 1970—; officer Indsl. Devel. Corp. Maricopa County, 1972-86; instr. and lectr. in real estate; officer, bd. dirs. other corps.; adj. prof. Frank Lloyd Wright Sch. Architecture, Scottsdale, Ariz., 1989—; instr. Ariz. State U. Coll. Architecture and Environ. Design; lead instr. ten-state-bar seminar on Advanced Real Estate Transactions, 1992; evaluation com. for cert. real estate specialist Ariz. Bar, 1994-96; mem. real estate adv. commn. Ariz. Bar, 1996-97. Exec. prodr. film documentary on relief and devel. in Africa, 1990; contbr. articles to profl. jours. Elder Valley Presbyn. Ch., Scottsdale, Ariz., 1973-75, 82—, 96-98, chair evangelism com. 1973-74, corp. pres., 1974-75, 84-85, trustee, 1973-75, 82-85, chmn. exec. com., 1984, mem. mission com. 1993—, chmn. 1998; trustee Upward Found., Phoenix, 1977-80, Valley Presbyn. Found., 1982-83, Ariz. Acad., 1971—; trustee, mem. exec. com. Phi Gamma Delta Ednl. Found., Washington, 1974-84; trustee Phi Gamma Delta Internat., 1984-86; bd. dirs. Archon, 1986-87; founder, trustee, pres. McRae Found., 1980—; bd. dirs. Food for Hungry Inc. (Internat. Relief), 1985-95, exec. com., 1986-95, chmn. bd. dirs., 1987-92; chmn. bd. dirs. Food for Hungry Internat., 1993-95, pres. adv. coun., 1995—; trustee, mem. exec. com. Ariz. Mus. Sci. and Tech., 1984—, 1st v.p., 1985-86, pres., 1986-88, chmn. bd. dirs., 1988-90, exec. com. 1984-90, exhibits com. 1990—; Lambda Alpha Internat. Hon. Land Econs. Soc, 1988—; sec.-treas. Ariz. State U. Coun. for Design Excellence, 1989-90, bd. dirs. 1988—, pres. 1990-91; mem. Crisis Nursery Office of the Chair, 1988-89, Maricopa Community Colls. Found., 1988—, sec. 1990-91, 2d v.p. 1993-94, 1st v.p. and pres. elect 1994-95, pres. 1995—, capital campaign cabinet, 1995-96, mem. nominating com., 1997, Phoenix Cmty. Alliance, 1988-90, Interchurch Ctr. Corp., 1987-90, Western Art Assocs., bd. dirs., 1989-91, Phoenix Com. on Fgn. Rels., 1988—, U. Ariz. Pres.'s Club, 1984—, chmn., 1991-92; bd. dirs. Econ. Club of Phoenix, 1987— , sec.-treas., 1991-92, v.p., 1992-93, pres. 1993-94; bd. dirs. Ctrl. Ariz. Shelter Svcs., 1995—, Ariz. Community Found., 1996—, invest. com., 1996, exec. com. 1997—, treas. 1997—, chair nominating com. 1997-98, vice chair bd. dirs., 1999—, chair devel. com., 1999—, mem. Elsner scholarship com., 1999—; founding mem. Alliance linking poverty and homelessness, 1996-98, bd. dirs., 1996—, mem. exec. com., 1996—, co-chair long range planning com., 1997-98; mem. adv. bd. Help Wanted USA, 1990-92; vol. fund raiser YMCA, Salvation Army, others; bd. dirs. Frank Lloyd Wright Found., 1992—, chair fin. com. 1997—, chmn. bd. dirs., 1998—; mem. Taliesin Coun., 1985—; bd. dirs. Taliesin Arch., 1992-98, Taliesin Conservation Com. (Wis.), 1992; founding mem. Frank Lloyd Wright Soc., 1993—; mem. fin. com. Kyl for Congress, 1985-92, bd. dir. campaign bd. Kyl for U.S. Senate, 1993-94, 99—; Senator Kyl Council, 1995—; campaign com. Symington for Gov. '90, 1989-90, mem. gubernatorial adv. bd., 1990Gov.'s Selection Com. for State Revenue Dir., 1993; mem. bond com. City of Phoenix, 1987-88; mem. Ariz. State U. Coun. of 100, 1985-89, investment com., 1985-89; bd. govs. Twelve Who Care Hon Kachina, 1991; mem. adv. coun. Maricopa County Sports Authority, 1989-93; mem. Ariz. Coalition for Tomorrow, 1990-92; founding mem., bd. dirs. Waste Not Inc., 1990-94, pres., 1990-92, chmn., 1992-94, adv. bd. 1996—; bd. dirs. Garden Homes at Teton Pines Home Owners Assn., 1996—; selected as bearer for the Olympic Torch Relay Team, 1996. 1st lt. USAF, 1961-64,. Recipient various mil. award; 1st place award Ariz. Bar exam, 1967. Mem. ABA, AIEE, AIME, Ariz. Bar Assn., Maricopa County Bar Assn., U. Ariz. Alumni Assn., Nat. Soc. Fund Raising Execs. (Philanthropy award Ariz. chpt. 1991, 97), Clan McRae Soc. N.Am. Phoenix Exec. Club, Internat. Platform Assn., Am. Friends of the U. Cambridge (Eng.), Jackson Hole Racquet Club, Teton Pines Country Club, Tau Beta Pi. Republican. Home: 8101 N 47th St Paradise Vly AZ 85253-2907 Office: Republic Cos 2425 E Camelback Rd Ste 900 Phoenix AZ 85016-4285

MCREE, DUNCAN EVERETT, molecular biologist, researcher; b. San Francisco, Feb. 5, 1957; s. John Everett and Joan Marie (Kilburn) McR.; m. Janice Anne Yuwiler, May 15, 1983; children: Alexander Marc, Kevin Lawrence, Alisa Laura. BS, U. Calif., Davis, 1978; PhD in Biochemistry, Duke U., 1984. Helen Hay Whitney fellow The Scripps Rsch. Inst., La Jolla, Calif., 1985-89, asst. mem., 1989—. Author: Practical Protein Crystallography, 1993, (software) Xtal View, 1992. Calif. State scholar, 1975-77; NIH grantee, 1990-98. Avocations: computer programing, model railroading, R/C model airplanes. Office: The Scripps Rsch Inst MB4 10666 N Torrey Pines Rd La Jolla CA 92037-1027

MCREYNOLDS, GREGG CLYDE, lawyer; b. Omaha, July 19, 1954; s. Zach A. and Mary M. (McCulloh) McR.; m. Dianne Worth McReynolds; children: Elizabeth, Heather, Kevin. BA, St. Johns Coll., Santa Fe, N.Mex., 1976; JD, U. N.Mex., 1979. Bar: N/Mex. 1979, Colo. 1982. Atty. Menig & Sager, Albuquerque, Anderson & Campbell, Denver, pvt. practice; instr. advocacy U. Colo. Law Sch., Boulder, 1992—. Author: Primer on Employment Law, 1990; contbr. articles to profl. jours. Commr. Parks, Trails Commn., Greenwood Village, 1994-97; mem. Sundance Hills Metro Dist. Bd., 1997—. Recipient Nat. Hon. Soc. award, 1972. Mem. ABA, Colo. Bar Assn., Denver Bar Assn. Office: 7720 E Belleview Ave Ste 200 Englewood CO 80111-2614

MCVEIGH-PETTIGREW, SHARON CHRISTINE, communications consultant; b. San Francisco, Feb. 6, 1949; d. Martin Allen and Frances (Roddy) McVeigh; m. John Wallace Pettigrew, Mar. 27, 1971; children: Benjamin Thomas, Margaret Mary. B.A. with honors, U. Calif.-Berkeley, 1971; diploma of edn. Monash U., Australia, 1975; M.B.A., Golden Gate U., 1985. Tchr., adminstr. Victorian Edn. Dept., Victoria, Australia, 1972-79; supr. Network Control Ctr., GTE Sprint Communications, Burlingame, Calif., 1979-81, mgr. customer assistance, 1981-84, mgr. state legis. ops., 1984-85, dir. revenue programs, 1986-87; communications cons. Flores, Pettigrew & Co., San Mateo, Calif., 1987-89; mgr. telemarketing Apple Computer, Inc., Cupertino, Calif., 1989-94; prin. The Call Ctr. Group, San Mateo, Calif., 1995—; telecomm. cons. PPG Svcs., 1994—; telecomm. spkr. Dept. Consumer Affairs, Sacramento, 1984. Panelist Wash. Gov.'s Citizens Council, 1984; founding mem. Maroondah Women's Shelter, Victoria, 1978; organizer nat. conf. Bus. Women and the Polit. Process, New Orleans, 1986; mem. sch. bd. Boronia Tech. Sch., Victoria, 1979. Recipient Tchr. Spl. Responsibilities award Victoria Edn. Dept., 1979. Mem. Women in Telecommunications (panel moderator San Francisco 1984), Am. Mgmt. Assn., Peninsula Profl. Women's Network, Am. Telemktg. Assn. (bd. dirs. 1992), Women's Econ. Action League. Democrat. Roman Catholic.

MCVEY, GARY JAMES, film curator; b. N.Y.C., Mar. 5, 1952; s. James Andrew and Alice Catherine (Kelly) M.; m. Meryl Senatt, Feb. 18, 1989; children: Evan H., Kara F. BFA, NYU, 1973. Tech. dir. Bleeker St. Cinema, N.Y.C., 1974-77; chief rschr. Alexander Jacobs Prodns., L.A., 1978-81; gen. mgr. Filmex, L.A., 1982-86; dir. film festivals Am. Film Inst., L.A., 1986-96; exec. dir. Am. Cinema Found., L.A., 1997—; adv. bd. Israel Film Festival, N.Y., L.A., 1991—, Motion Picture Centennial, L.A., 1994-96; film critic Soho News, N.Y.C., 1975-77. Author: (screenplay) Inside Story, 1986; creator Cinematheque Series, USA Ind. Showcase, 1991. Recipient Key Art award The Hollywood Reporter, 1995, 98; Merit scholar Nat. Merit Scholarship Corp., 1969-73. Office: American Cinema Foundation 9911 West Pico Blvd Los Angeles CA 90035

MCWAID-HARRAH, DIANA MEGAN, health service administrator; b. Torrance, Calif., Nov. 11, 1964; d. Frederick Hatton and Delphine Alieen (Aycock) McWaid; m. Jeffrey Lloyd Harrah, Mar. 13, 1993. BA, Calif. State U., Fullerton, 1988; MS, Calif. State U., Long Beach, 1990. Cert. Am. Health Info. Assn. Office mgr. Cedars-Sinai Med. Ctr., L.A., 1988-90; practice mgr. Med. Group of Beverly Hills, L.A., 1991-92; dir. health info. svcs. Little Co. of Mary Hosp., Torrance, Calif., 1992-97; field and client support mgr. ImageStat Corp., Santa Monica, 1997—; cons. Ind. MSO, Torrance, 1995. Mem. cmty. emergency safety team Calif. Hts. Neighborhood Assn., Long Beach, 1996. Mem. Nat. Mgmt. Assn. (chpt. sec. 1995-96, chpt. pres. 1996-97), So. Calif. Health Info. Assn. (edn. com. chair 1995-96, 96-97), Calif. Health Info. Assn. (membership com. 1996-97. Avocations: cooking, gardening, sports. Office: ImageStat Corp 2950 31st St Ste 220 Santa Monica CA 90405-3095

MCWILLIAMS, BEATRIZ DURAN, communications educator; b. Chula Vista, Calif., Nov. 15, 1969; d. Donald Albert and Maria (Duran) McW. BA in Comms., San Diego State U., 1992; MS in Comms., So. Ill. U., 1993. Instr. Southwestern Coll., Chula Vista, 1993-95, Palomar coll., San Marcos, Calif., 1993-95; prof. Miracosta Coll., Oceanside, Calif., 1995—; acad. advisor Latina Leadership Network, Mira Costa Coll., Oceanside, 1996—. Mem. Speech Comms. Assn., Western States Comms. Assn., Internat. Comms. Assn., Am. Comm. Assn.

MCWRIGHT, MICHAEL J., historic site administrator; b. Mandan, N.D., July 5, 1950. Mem. pk. svc. staff Colo. region, 1974-75; facility mgr. Grant-Kohrs Ranch Nat. Hist. Site, Deerlodge, Mont., 1975—. Office: Grant-Kohrs Ranch National Historic Site PO Box 790 Deer Lodge MT 59722-1075*

MEAD, JERRY DALE, wine expert, writer; b. Rogers, Ark., May 14, 1939; s. Lloyd Willard and Mary Frances (Boyd) M.; m. Linda Elizabeth Gallentine, Aug. 31, 1957; children—Loretta Jean, Jerry Dion, Sean Darren. Wine expert, cons. and writer, San Francisco, 1969-91, Carson City, Nev., 1991—; founder Wine Investigation for Novices and Oenophiles (WINO). Founder Orange County Fair com. wine competition; founder, chmn. New World Internat. Wine Competition. Recipient Perpetual Trophy for Excellence in Wine Writing, Calif. Assn. Winegrape Growers, 1985. Author syndicated column Mead on Wine; pub. WINO newsletter, The Wine Trader; contbr. numerous articles to nat. and regional publs.

MEAD, TERRY EILEEN, practice management hospital consultant, CEO; b. Portland, Oreg., Mar. 14, 1950; d. Everett L. and Jean (Nonken) Richardson; divorced; 1 child, Sean Knute Wade Adcock. AA summa cum laude, Seattle U., 1972; postgrad., U. Wash., 1971. Project mgr. Assoc. Univ. Physician, Seattle, 1971-74; pathology supr. Swedish Hosp., Seattle, 1974-77; svcs. supr. Transamerica, Seattle, 1977-78; various mgmt. positions Providence Hosp., Seattle, 1978-83; CEO Mead's Med. Mgmt. Inc. Cons. Firm, Chiloquin, Oreg., 1980—; adminstr. Evergreen Surg. Ctr., Kirkland, Wash., 1983-86; bus. mgr. Ketchikan (Alaska) Gen. Hosp., 1986—; instr. U. Alaska, Ketchikan, 1990; adminstr. Bethel (Alaska) Family Clinic, 1994-96; CEO Southeast Oreg. Rural Health Network, 1996-98; pres. Mead's Med. Mgmt. Inc., 1980—; sec. S.E. adv. bd. U. Alaska, Ketchikan, 1987-94; cons. to hosps. and physicians, Wash., Alaska, Oreg., 1980—; mgr. Practice Mgmt. Cons., Seattle, 1982-83; mem. Klamath County Health Care Task Force, 1997. Mem. City Charter Rev. Com., Ketchikan, 1990-94; High Sch. Facilities Com. Ketchikan, 1990; S.E. dir. search com. U. Alaska, Ketchikan, 1990; treas. Calvary Bible Ch., Ketchikan, 1989-91; bd. dirs. S.E. Alaska Symphony, 1992-94, Jr. Achievement, 1992-93; chmn. fin. com. City of Bethel, 1994-96; mem. Klamath County Blue Ribbon Health Task Force, 1997. Mem. Rotary Internat. Avocations: computers, politics, fishing, music, writing. Home and Office: 516 3d St Mukilteo WA 98275

MEAD, TRAY C., museum director; b. Mesa, Ariz., Apr. 1, 1950; s. Norman Wesley and Peggy Lee (Barrows) M.; Barbara Celaya, Feb. 9, 1981; children: Michael Adam, Kristiana Nicole. BA in Edn., Ariz. State U., 1973. Cert. tchr., Ariz. Publisher Ariz. Northland Mag., Flagstaff, 1973-77; mus. dir. Mesa Southwest Mus., 1977—; founding dir. Ariz. Fed. Credit Union, Phoenix, 1980-85. Author: Mesa, Beneath the Superstitions, 1988, Sirrine House Story, 1992; editor: Mesa Grande, 1979, Capturing the Canyon, 1987; field editor Ariz. White Mountain Mag., 1965—; contbg. editor Tonto Trails Mag., 1970—. Founding dir. Mesa Conv. and Tourism Bureau, 1989—; founding chmn. S.W. Svc. Corp., Phoenix, 1981-85; bd. dirs., founding pres. Arts in Mesa, 1980—. Recipient Excellence award Centennial Com., 1978, Golden Quill award Caligraphic Soc. Ariz., 1987, Native Am. Heritage award U.S.M.C. Netherlands, 1991; named Hon. Medicine Man, Ft. Apache Tribe, 1973, Hon. Chmn. Mesa Parade, Mayor City of Mesa, 1980. Mem. Nat. Trust Hist. Preservation, Am. Assn. State and Local Histories, Am. Assn. Mus., Mus. Assn. Ariz. (founding mem., v.p. 1982—), Ctrl. Ariz. Mus. Assn. (founding pres. 1978—), Mesa C. of C. (com. chmn. 1979-89). Avocations: sculpting, painting, hiking, reading. Home: 370 E Pinon Way Gilbert AZ 85234-4573 Office: Mesa Southwest Museum 53 North McDonald Dr Mesa AZ 85201-7325*

MEADE, KENNETH JOHN, realty company owner, broker; b. N.Y.C., Nov. 25, 1925; s. John Joseph and Blanche (Woodworth) M.; m. Alice Elizabeth (Steinmann), Nov. 8, 1952; children: Steven, Janet, Patricia. Student, N.Y. Inst. Fin., 1960-62. Cert. real estate residential broker. Sales broker Del Webb Devel., Sun City, Ariz., 1974-82; mgr. Mull Realty Inc., Sun City, Ariz., 1982-83; broker, owner 6 offices Ken Meade Realty Inc., Sun City, Ariz., 1983—; dir., treas. Sun City Bd. Realtors, 1988—. Bd. dirs., v.p. Sun City Ambs., 1988—. With USN, 1942-45. Mem. Nat. Assn. Realtors, Ariz. Assn. Realtors, Dale Carnegie Club (past instr. sales course, Outstanding Achievment 1964). Republican. Lutheran. Avocations: stock market technics, charts, sales psychology. Home: 13306 W Meeker Blvd Sun City West AZ 85375-3815 Office: Ken Meade Realty Inc 17001 N Del Webb Blvd Sun City AZ 85373-1804

MEAGHER, MICHAEL, radiologist; b. New Rochelle, N.Y., Oct. 24, 1942; s. Joseph Aloysius and Elizabeth (Ahern) M.; m. Martha Batten Mitchell, 1968; children: Kelly, Courtney. Student, Rensselaer Poly. Inst., 1960-62; AB with distinction, U. Rochester, 1964; MD, Stanford U., 1969. Diplomate Am. Bd. Radiology, Nat. Bd. Med. Examiners. Intern in medicine Cornell U., N.Y. Hosp., 1969-70; jr. asst. resident in diagnostic radiology U. Wash., Seattle, 1970-71, sr. asst. resident diagnostic radiology, 1973-74, resident diagnostic radiology, 1974-75; active staff mem. dept. radiology Queen's Med. Ctr., Honolulu, 1975—, Leahi Hosp., Honolulu, 1981—, Kahuku (Hawaii) Hosp., 1988—; pres. Radiology Assocs., Inc., 1978, 81-84, 90; chmn. dept. radiology Queen's Med. Ctr., 1979-80, 82-86, 88-90, dir. dept. radiology, 1985-91, dir. magnetic resonance imaging, 1991—, chmn. cancer com., 1980-82; mem. med. staff Hawaii Health Tech. Magnetic Resonance Imaging Facility, Honolulu, 1986—, chief of staff, 1978; clin. instr. dept. radiology U. Hawaii Sch. Medicine, 1983-89, clin. assoc. prof., 1989-93, clin. prof., 1993-97, chmn., prof., 1997—, asst. rsch. prof. Cancer Rsch. Ctr. Hawaii, 1989—; clin. asst. prof. dept. radiology U. Wash. Sch. Medicine, 1980-88; presenter in fld. Contbr. articles to profl. publs. Chmn. high tech. adv. com. State Health Planning and Devel. Agy., 1983—; bd. dirs. Friends of Hawaii Pub. TV, 1979-81; pres., CEO Queen's Health Care Plan, Honolulu, 1985-89, chmn. bd. dirs., 1989-91; bd. dirs. Managed Care Mgmt., Inc., Honolulu, 1990; v.p. bd. dirs. Hawaii Opera Theatre, 1990-91, treas., 1991—. Lt. comdr. USN, 1971-73. NIH fellow, 1966; Kaiser Found. grantee, 1967. Fellow Am. Coll. Radiology; mem. AMA, Hawaii State Radiol. Soc. (sec.-treas. 1978-79, v.p. 1979-80, pres. 1980-81), Radiol. Soc. N.Am., Soc. Computer Applications in Radiology (charter), Am. Roentgen Ray Soc. Home: 1234 Maunawili Rd Kailua HI 96734-4042 Office: Queen's Med Ctr Dept Radiology Honolulu HI 96813

MEALS, PAMELA F., publishing executive; 1 child, Laura. Student, We. Oreg. State Coll. With advtsg. The Oreg. Statesman and Capital Jour., Salem; advtsg. mgr. The Idaho Statesman, Boise, 1979, pres., publ., 1994-99; publ. Coffeyville (Kans.) Jour., 1979-82, The Palladium-Item, Richmond, Ind., 1982-85, The Olympian, Olympia, Wash., 1985-94, Bellingham Herald, Bellingham, Wash., 1999—. Bd. dirs. Boise Pub. Schs. Edn. Found., Idaho Shakespeare Festival, Albertson Coll. Annual Fund, FUNDSY, William Allen White Found. Mem. Boise Area C. of C. (bd. dirs.), Rotary Club, Idaho Bus. Coun., Pacific N.W. Newspaper Assn. (bd. dirs.), Newspaper Assn. Am. Office: The Bellingham Herald 1155 N State St Bellingham WA 98225*

MEANS, LANE LEWIS, entertainer; b. Livermore, Calif., Jan. 8, 1951; d. Richard Leroy and Norma Lillian (Ghiozzi) Lewis; m. David Albert Means, Apr. 30, 1984. BA in Phys. Edn., Calif. State U., Chico, 1973; BA in Dance, U. Calif., Irvine, 1975, MFA, 1977. Dancer Penrod-Plastino Movement Theater, Irvine, 1977-80, America by Nite, Bangkok, Manila and Japan, 1980, Penthouse Pet Revue, Reno, 1981, Bal du Moulin Rouge, Reno, 1981-82, Hello Hollywood, Ito, Japan, 1982-83; ice skater Razzle Dazzle, Reno, 1984-85, Las Vegas on Ice, Acapulco, Mex., 1986—; choreographer, dance instr. Directions in Dance, Torrance, Calif., 1977-78, Irvine Acad. Performing Arts, 1978; choreographer Kenai Alaska Jr. Miss Fashion Show, 1991-97; guest artist Kenai Peninsula Coll. Dancers, 1990; adj. faculty, dance instr., choreographer Kenai Peninsula Coll., 1991; advisor Kenaitze-Dena'ing Jabila'ina Dancers, asst. dance leader; dir., choreographer Skyview H.S. Skylight Dancers, 1998; dir. Kenai Swing Golden Girls, 1998-99; mem. Fireweed Dancers, 1998. Treatment specialist Kenai Peninsula Community Care Ctr., 1988-90. Home and Office: PO Box 1363 Kenai AK 99611-1363

MEANS, NATRONE JERMAINE, professional football player; b. Apr. 26, 1972. Student, U. N.C. Running back San Diego Chargers, 1991-96, 98—, Jacksonville Jaguars, 1996-97, San Diego Chargers, 1998-. Selected to Pro Bowl, 1994. Mem. San Diego Chargers AFC Champions, 1994. Office: San Diego Chargers PO Box 609609 San Diego CA 92160-9609*

MEARS, LINDA SHAW, artist; b. L.A., Apr. 23, 1949; d. Richard Frank and Lorae Veda (Lenhart) Shaw; m. Barney Edward Jensen, Aug. 18, 1983 (div. Aug. 1988); 1 child, Amy Rae Jensen Mears; m. Charles Everts Mears, July 22, 1989; 1 child, Elizabeth Ann Mears. AA, Sacramento (Calif.) City Coll., 1986. RN; lic. vocat. nurse. Nurse various, Sacramento, L.A., 1970-89; artist, 1987—. Works exhibited at Celebrity Centre Internat., Hollywood, 1993, Galerie Je Revins, Westport, Conn., 1996—, Yvon Daigle Galerie Art Naif, Quebec, 1996—, Galerie Pro Arte Kasper, Switzerland, 1992, 98, Uruguary Exhbn. of Am. Art, 1998-2001, toad Hall Galleries, Cooperstown, N.Y., N.Y.C., 1987—, Jay Johnson Am.'s Folk Heritage Gallery, N.Y.C., 1987-92, Frank J. Miele Gallery, N.Y.C., 1992—; oil paintings in permanent collection of Le Musee d'Art Internat. Yvon-M. Daigle, Quebec; oil paintings in the permanent collection of Musee d'Art Internat. Pyrenees, Rousillon, France; calendars for The Time Factory, Indpls., 1998—; group of oil paintings featured in "The Education of a Speculator" by Victor Niederhoffer, 1997; art on Christmas cards by Hallmark Cards, Inc., 1993—, calendars by Golden Turtle Press, 1991—, calendars at Japanese banks, Pacific Press Svcs., 1988—; art included in books "Naive Art Celebrates Mother Nature," 1999, "Naive Art Gallery," 1991. Mem. L.A. County Art Mus. Mem. Folk Art Mus. N.Y.C., Folk Art Soc. E-mail: mearsarts@earthlink.net. Home: Linda Mears Studio 23460 Hamlin St West Hills CA 91307-3331 Office: Linda Mears Studio 23460 Hamlin St West Hills CA 91307-3331

MEAUX, ALAN DOUGLAS, facilities technician, sculptor; b. Joliet, Ill., Sept. 10, 1951; s. Berry Lee and Luella Ann (Ferguson) M.; m. Letta Sue Nygaard, Sept. 15, 1984; children: Ashley Nicole, Lacey Marie. Student, Joliet Jr. Coll., 1969-71, Bradley U., 1971-72, U.S. Dept. Agr. Grad. Sch., 1972, Skagit Valley Coll., 1983-85. Photographer J.J.C. Blazer, Joliet Herald News, Joliet, 1969-71; auto mechanic Pohanka Olds and Fiat, Hillcrest Heights, Md., 1972-74, Hoffman Olds and Rolls Royce, Hartford, Conn., 1974-75; carpenter Klappenbach Constrn. Co., Moscow, Idaho, 1975-79; property mgr. Olympic Builders, Oak Harbor, Wash., 1979-86; maintenance technician Troubleshooters Inc., Oak Harbor, 1986-87; facilities technician Island County Govt., Coupeville, Wash., 1987—; chmn. safety com. Island County Govt., 1997, 98; bronze sculptor Ronin Art Prodns., Oak Harbor, 1979—; appraiser class A Mid-Am. Appraisers Assn., Springfield, Mo., 1986—; bd. dirs. North West Token Kai, U. Wash., Seattle, 1989—, lectr., 1985; contbr. Nanka Token Kai, L.A., 1985—. Author: Japanese Samurai Weapons, 1989; prin. works exhibited at Mini Guild Children's Orthopedic Show, Ballard, Wash., 1986, Worldfest/Ethnic Heritage Coun., Seattle, 1988, 89, 90, Stanwood (Wash.) Invitational Art Show, 1988. Mem. NRA (life), Law Enforcement Alliance Am. (life), Japanese Sword Soc. U.S. (life), N.W. Token Kai (charter, bd. dirs. 1989-91), Western Mus. Conf., Wash. Mus. Assn., Ethnic Heritage Coun., Nanka Token Kai, Japan Soc., Wash. Arms Collectors Assn., North Whidbey Sportmen's Assn. (chmn. range com., trustee), Leisure Acres Water Assn. (pres. 1998—), Internat. Defensive Pistol Assn., Ctrl. Whidbey Sportmen's Club. Avocations: hunting, fishing, woodworking, reading, collecting Japanese antiques. Office: Ronin Art Prodns PO Box 1271 Oak Harbor WA 98277-1271

MECHAM, GLENN JEFFERSON, lawyer, mayor; b. Logan, Utah, Dec. 11, 1935; s. Everett H. and Lillie (Dunford) M.; m. Mae Parson, June 5, 1957; children: Jeff B., Scott R., Marcia, Suzanne. BS, Utah State U., 1957; JD, U. Utah, 1961; grad. Air Command and Staff Coll., Air War Coll., 1984. Bar: Utah 1961, Supreme Ct. U.S., U.S. Ct. Appeals (10th Cir.), U.S. Dist. Ct. Utah, U.S. Ct. Claims. Gen. practice law, 1961-65; atty. Duchesne County, Utah, 1962, City of Duchesne, 1962; city judge Roy City, Utah, 1963-66; judge City of Ogden, Utah, 1966-69, mayor, 1992—; lectr. law and govt. Stevens-Henager Coll., Ogden, 1963-75; asst. U.S. atty., 1969-72; ptnr. Mecham & Richards, Ogden, Utah, 1972-82; pres. Penn Mountain Mining Co., South Pacific Internat. Bank, Ltd.; mem. Bur. Justice Stats. Adv. Bd., U.S. Dept. Justice, U.S. Conf. Mayors. Chmn. Ogden City Housing Authority; chmn. bd. trustees Utah State U., Space Dynamics Lab. Utah State U.; mem. adv. coun. Fed. Home Loan Bank; pres. Utah League Cities and Towns, 1981-82; vice chmn. Wasatch Front Reg. Coun. Col. USAF, 1957. Mem. ABA, Weber County Bar Assn. (pres. 1966-68), Utah Bar Assn., Am. Judicature Soc., Weber County Bar Legal Svcs. (chmn. bd. trustees 1966-69), Utah Assn. Mcpl. Judges (sec.), Sigma Chi, Phi Alpha Delta. Home: 1715 Darling St Ogden UT 84403-0556 Office: City of Ogden 2484 Washington Blvd Ste 300 Ogden UT 84401-2319

MEDAK, WALTER HANS, lawyer; b. Vienna, Austria, May 10, 1915; came to U.S., 1938; s. Hugo and Grete (Figdor) M.; m. Edith Rhodes, 1944 (div. 1957); 1 child, Ronald Harvard; m. Renée Rasens, 1996. Grad., Acad. of Commerce, Vienna, 1934, U. Vienna, 1938; postgrad., U. Ga., 1939-40; MA in Econs., U. Calif., Berkeley, 1949; JD, Harvard U., 1948. Prodn. mgr. Mabs, Inc., L.A., 1942-43; prodn. engr. Kaiser Co., Richmond, Calif., 1943-45; atty. Belli & Medak, Walnut Creek, Calif., 1957-59; pvt. practice law Walnut Creek and Moraga, Calif., 1950—; bd. dirs. Snyder/Newell, Inc., San Francisco; bd. dirs. Carnelian Woods, Carnelian Bay, Calif., pres., 1974-90. Mem. ABA, Calif. County Bar Assn., Assn. Trial Lawyers Am., Calif. Trial Lawyers Assn., Harvard Club (chmn. admissions and scholarship com. San Francisco chpt. 1973-74). Avocations: skiing, swimming, music, travel. Home and Office: 2830 Regent St Berkeley CA 94705-2134

MEDEARIS, ROGER NORMAN, artist; b. Fayette, Mo., Mar. 6, 1920; s. Thomas Whittier and Mara (Miller) M.; m. Elizabeth Burrall Sterling, Jan. 16, 1976; 1 son, Thomas Whittier, III. Pupil of, Thomas Hart Benton, 1938-41. One-man exhbns. include Kende Galleries, N.Y.C., 1949, 50, Capricorn Galleries, Bethesda, Md., 1971, 78, 81, 84, 94; group exhbns. include AAA Galleries, Met. Mus. Art, NAD, N.Y.C., Carnegie Mellon U., Pitts., Butler Inst. Am. Art, Youngstown, Ohio, Albrecht-Kemper Mus. Art, St. Joseph, Mo., Spencer Mus. Art, Lawrence, Kans., many others; represented in numerous pvt. and public collections, including, D.C. Mcpl. Ct., Nat. Mus. Am. Art, Washington, Nelson-Atkins Mus. Art, Kansas City, Butler Inst. Am. Art., Hunt Inst., Pitts., Albrecht-Kemper Art Mus., St. Joseph, Mo., Beach Mus., Kans. State U., Manhattan, El Paso Mus. of Art; commd. by Nat. Recreation & Park Assn., 1982, Print Club Albany, 1994; work reviewed in various articles, monographs. With USN Dept., 1942-45, AUS, 1945-46. Address: 2270 Melville Dr San Marino CA 91108-2612 also: care William A. Karges Fine Art Los Angeles CA 90000

MEDLAND, MAURICE BLUE, writer, educator; b. Centerville, Iowa, Sept. 29, 1936; s. William C. and Avis N. (Blue) M.; m. Karen A. McFarland, Aug. 7, 1965; children: Melissa A., Steven W. BS, Truman State U., 1961; MBA, Pepperdine U., 1977. Mgmt. sys. analyst Rockwell Internat. Corp., Downey, Calif., 1961-70; dir. Fluor Corp., Irvine, Calif., 1970-85; v.p. PacifiCare Health Sys., Cypress, Calif., 1985-87; novelist Calif., 1987—; instr. U. Calif., Irvine, 1998—; adv. Calif. State U. Fullerton Writer's Program, 1998—. Author: Point of Honor, 1997. With USN, 1954-57. Recipient Apollo Achievement award NASA, 1969. Mem. The Authors Guild. E-mail: mmedland@msn.com. Fax: (714) 779-9831. Home: 19842 Villager Cir Yorba Linda CA 92886-4454

MEDOFF, MARK HOWARD, playwright, screenwriter, novelist; b. Mt. Carmel, Ill., Mar. 18, 1940; s. Lawrence Ray and Thelma Irene (Butt) M.; m. Stephanie Thorne, June 24, 1972; children: Debra, Rachel, Jessica. B.A., U. Miami, Fla., 1962; M.A., Stanford U., 1966; D.H.L., Gallaudet Coll., 1981. Instr. English and drama N.Mex. State U., 1966-79, dramatist in residence, 1974—, head dept. drama, 1978-87, prof. drama, 1979-93, artistic dir., 1982-87; artistic dir. Am. S.W. Theatre Co., 1984-87. Author: (plays) When You Comin' Back, Red Ryder?, 1974, The Wager, 1975, The Kramer, 1975, The Halloween Bandit, 1978, The Conversion of Aaron Weiss, 1978, Firekeeper, 1978, The Last Chance Saloon, 1979, Children of a Lesser God, 1980 (Soc. West Theatres best play award 1982), The Majestic Kid, 1981, The Hands of Its Enemy, 1984, Kringle's Window, 1985, The Heart Outright, 1986 (novel) Dreams of Long Lasting: (films) When You Comin' Back, Red Ryder?, 1979, Off Beat, 1986, Apology, 1986, Children of a Lesser God, 1986, Good Guys Wear Black, 1978, Clara's Heart, 1988, The Majestic Kid, 1988, City of Joy, 1992, Homage, 1995, Santa Fe, 1997; works appear in Best Plays, 1973-74, 75-75, 79-80, Best Short Plays, 1975, The Homage that Follows, 1987; plays Stumps, 1989, Stefanie Hero, 1990, Showdown On Rio Road, 1995, Gila, 1995, A Christmas Carousel, 1996, Crunch Time, 1996, Gunfighters, A Gulf War Chronicle, 1997. Guggenheim fellow, 1974-75; recipient Obie award, Drama Desk award, Outer Critics Circle award, Media award Pres.'s Com. Employment Handicapped, Tony award; Oscar award nominee for Best Screenplay for Children of A Lesser God, 1987. Mem. SAG, Dramatists Guild, Writers Guild Am., Actors Equity Assn., Pen. Office: PO Box 3072 Las Cruces NM 88003-3072

MEDUSKI, JERZY WINCENTY, nutritionist, biochemist; b. Kalusz, Poland, Oct. 29, 1918; s. Dobieslaw Antoni and Katarzyna (Barbowska) M.; came to U.S., 1962, naturalized, 1969; M.D., Warsaw (Poland) Med. Sch., 1946; Ph.D. in Biochemistry, U. Lodz (Poland), 1951; 1 child, Jerzy Dobieslaw. Organizer, chief pharmacology labs. Polish Nat. Inst. Hygiene, Warsaw, 1945-52, organizer, head lab. of intermediary metabolism, 1952-59; asso. prof. biochemistry Warsaw Med. Sch., 1955-59; asst. prof. neurology U. So. Calif. Sch. Medicine, Los Angeles, 1973—; pres. Nutritional Cons. Group, Inc. Mem. Los Angeles County Bd. Suprs. Task Force on Nutrition. WHO fellow, Holland, Scotland, 1948-49; research grantee, USSR, 1956. Mem. Polish Acad. Sci. (sci. sec. biochem. com. 1952-59), Polish Med. Assn. (sci. sec. nat. bd. 1958-59), Polish Biochem. Soc. (founding mem.), Biochem. Soc. London, Royal Soc. Chem. London, Internat. Soc. on Toxinology, AMA, Am. Soc. Microbiology, Internat. Soc. on Oxygen Transport to Tissues, Sigma Xi. Author 3 books on biochemistry; contbr. more than 80 articles to internat. jours.; author textbook on nutritional biochemistry, 1977. Home: 1922 12th St Santa Monica CA 90404-4604 Office: U So Calif Sch Medicine 2025 Zonal Ave Los Angeles CA 90033-1034

MEECH, KAREN JEAN, astronomer; b. Denver, July 9, 1959; d. Lloyd Augustus and Patricia Ann (Marshall) M. BA cum laude in Physics, Rice U., 1981; PhD in Planetary Astronomy, MIT, 1987. Rsch. asst. Maria Mitchell Obs., Nantucket, Mass., 1978, Am. Assn. Variable Star Observation, Cambridge, Mass., 1979, 81-82; rsch. asst. archaeoastronomy EARTHWATCH, Cusco, Peru, 1980; univ. lab. asst. molecular physics Rice U., Houston, 1980-81, quantum physics grader, 1980-81; rsch. asst. Am. Assn. Variable Star Observers, 1981-82; rsch. specialist MIT, Cambridge, 1981-82, grad. teaching asst., 1982-86, grad. rsch. asst., 1986-87; asst. astronomer Inst. for Astronomy, Honolulu, 1987-91, assoc. astronomer, 1992—; mem. IFA Computer Adv. Com., 1991-93, IFA Endowment Com., 1991, U. Rsch. Coun., 1990-93, NASA Planetary Astronomy Com. II, 1993-94, NASA Planetary Sci. Data Steering Group, 1993-96, IFA Admissions Com., 1992-97, NASA Planetary Astronomy Rev. Panel, 1990-91, Cerro Tololo Interamerican Obs. user's Com., 1991-94, USIA Internat. Teleconf., 1991, NASA Keck Planetary Mgmt. Ops. Working Group, 1996—, Com. on Planetary Lunar Exploration, 1998—, Annie Jump Cannon Award Com., 1995-97, U. Hawaii Faculty Senate, 1995-97; chair IFA S cholarship Com., 1991; interviewer Rice U. Alumni, 1989—; telescope allocation com. referee Kitt Peak Nat. Obs., 1995—; reviewer. Contbr. articles to Astron. Jour., Astrophys. Jour., Sci., Icarus, Nature, Bull. Am. Astronomy Soc., Info. Bull. Variable Stars, Minor Planet Circular, IAU Circular. Safety diver U. Hawaii Scuba class, 1988-90; vol. Honolulu Zool. Soc. Zoo Fun Run, 1991-92; active dept. edn. H.S. Student Career Program, Honolulu, 1988; organizer H.S. Tchr.-Student Asst. Workshops, 1993-95, 99—; local organizing chair divsn. Planetary Astronomy meeting, Kona, Hawaii, 1995, Bioastronomy meeting, Kona, Hawaii, 1999; judge Hawaii State Sci. Fair, 1992—; bd. dirs. Kilolokahi, 1995—. Scholar Bd. of Govs., 1980, Grad. Student Rschrs. fellow NASA, 1986-87; recipient Annie Jump Cannon award in Astronomy, 1988, Harold C. Urey prize in Astronomy Am. Astron. Soc., 1994, Heaps prize in Physics, 1981; asteroid 4367 named in her honor, 1996. Mem. Am. Astron. Soc. (divsn. planetary scis., 1995, Asteroid 4367 named Meech in her honor), Internat. Astron. Union-Commn. 15 (nat. com. 1997—), Am. Assn. Variable Star Observers. Achievements include co-discovery of the outburst of Halley's comet at the longest distance from the sun for a recorded outburst; discovery of cometary activity on object 2060 Chiron; investigator Hubble space telescope. Office: Inst for Astronomy 2680 Woodlawn Dr Honolulu HI 96822-1897

MEECHAM, WILLIAM JAMES, ophthalmologist; b. Ann Arbor, Mich., Nov. 30, 1958; s. William Coryell and Barbara (Brown) M.; m. Amanda Roberts. AB in Zoology, U. Calif., Berkeley, 1980, MA in Biophysics, 1983; MD, U. Calif., San Francisco, 1987. Diplomate Nat. Bd. Med. Examiners, Am. Bd. Ophthalmology. Med. intern Cabrini Med. Ctr., N.Y.C., 1987-88; resident in ophthalmology U. Calif., San Francisco, 1988-91, ocular oncology fellow, 1991-92, clin. asst. prof., 1991—, ocular plastics fellow, 1992-93; sr. physician depts. ophthalmology and mohs surgery Kaiser Permanente, San Rafael, 1993—. Contbr. articles to profl. publs.; editor-in-chief U. Calif.-San Francisco Synapse, 1984-85. Fellow ACS, Am. Acad. Ophthalmology, Am. Soc. Ophthalmic Plastic and Reconstructive Surgeons. Avocation: ceramic sculpture. Office: 99 Montecillo Rd San Rafael CA 94903-3308

MEEHAN, MICHAEL JOSEPH, lawyer; b. St. Louis, Aug. 28, 1942; s. Joseph Michael and Frances (Taylor) M.; m. Sharon Kay McHenry (div. 1988); m. Patricia Ann Shive, July 8, 1989. BS in Engring., U.S. Coast Guard Acad., 1964; JD with high distinction, U. Ariz., 1971. Bar: Ariz. 1971, U.S. Ct. Appeals (6th, 8th, 9th and 10th cirs.), U.S. Supreme Ct. 1975. Law clk. Assoc. Justice William H. Rehnquist, U.S. Supreme Ct., 1972; assoc. Molloy, Jones & Donahue, P.C., Tucson, 1971-75, shareholder, 1975-93; chmn. exec. com., head trial dept., 1986-93; founder Meehan & Assocs., Tucson, 1993—; mem. fed. appellate rules adv. com. Jud. Conf. U.S., 1994—. Author chpt. on appellate advocacy: State Bar of Arizona Appellate Practice Handbook. Fellow Am. Acad. Appellate Lawyers; mem. ABA (sect. on litig., sect. on intellectual property), Ariz. Bar Assn. (exec. coun., chair appellate practice sect. 1995—). Republican. Lutheran. Avocation: golf. Office: Meehan & Assocs PO Box 1671 Tucson AZ 85702-1671

MEEKS, MARK ANTHONY, minister; b. Dallas, Sept. 24, 1946; s. Frederick Earl and Lillie Mae (Chaddick) M.; m. Debra Ann Yeager, Oct. 30, 1985; children: Jessica, Lillian, Sonya. AA, Dallas Bapt. Coll., 1967; BA, U. Tex. at Arlington, 1969; postgrad., Southwestern Bapt. Sem., 1969-72; MDiv, So. Bapt. Sem., 1973. Ordained to ministry Bapt. Ch., 1973. Pastor Grace Bapt. Ch., Heidelberg, Germany, 1973-76; co-dir. Karis Community, Denver, 1978-80; spiritual leader Capitol Heights Presbyn. Ch., Denver, 1979—; mem. ecumenical ministry team Capitol Heights Presbyn and Ten-Thirty Cath. Community, Denver, 1982-92. Regional coord. Amnesty Internat., Denver. Mem. Capitol Hill United Ministries (pres. 1986-91, chaplain 1991-94, pres. 1998—), Colo. Alliance for the Mentally Ill, Sierra Club, Colo. Environ. Coalition, Assets Based Cmty. Devel. Religious Netowrk, Dietrich Bonhoeffer Soc. Home: 399 Blackbird Dr Bailey CO 80421-2077 Office: Capitol Heights Presbyn Ch 1100 Fillmore St Denver CO 80206-3334

MEHDIZADEH, PARVIZ, insurance company executive; b. Tehran, Iran, Sept. 15, 1934; came to U.S., 1981; s. Alexander and Sedigheh (Siavooshy) M.; m. Manijeh Sadri, Sept. 12, 1961; children: Sheida, Peyman, Pejman. BS, Forestry Sch., Tehran, 1958; MS, N.C. State U., 1963, PhD, 1966. Pres. Rsch. Inst. Natural Resources, Tehran, 1968-73; assoc. prof. U. Tehran, 1973-74; prof. environ. sci. U. Tabriz, Iran, 1974-76; chmn. resolution com. FAO, Rome, 1976-77; chmn. natural resources Ctrl. Treaty Orgn., Ankars, Turkey, 1977-78; spl. adviser to sec. Ministry of Agr., Tehran, 1978-79; dist. mgr. Am. Family Life Assurance Co., Beverly Hills, Calif., 1981—; v.p. Point Internat. Corp. Inc., Los Angeles, 1986—; pres. ZMS Fin. Network Corp. Inc., Beverly Hills, Calif., 1995-98, Active Universal Corp., 1998—; cons. Ministry of Sci., Tehran, 1972-75, UN U., Tokyo, 1975-76; gen. agt. AFLAC, 1995. Author: Flowering Plants of Semi-Arid Regions, 1976, Economizing of Water Use in Agriculture, 1977; editor Khandamhayeh Hafteh, 1979. Mem. U.S. Senatorial Club, Washington, 1984; charter mem. Rep. Presdl. Task Force, Washington, 1984. Mem. Life Underwriters Assn. (L.A. chpt., Health Ins. Quality award 1985, 88, 89), Rotary (chmn. dist. 5280 1992, Paul Harris Fellow award 1989). Avocations: tennis, golf.

MEHLMAN, LON DOUGLAS, information systems specialist; b. Los Angeles, Apr. 29, 1959; s. Anton and Diane Mehlman. BA, UCLA, 1981; MBA, Pepperdine U., 1983. Systems programmer Ticom Systems Inc., Century City, Calif., 1978-81; systems analyst NCR Corp., Century City, 1981-83; sr. systems analyst Tandem Computers Inc., L.A., 1983-91; sr. computer scientist Computer Scis. Corp., El Segundo, Calif., 1991-97; dir. info. tech., CIO Globe Cast Comms. N.Am., Culver City, Calif., 1997—. Author: Establishing an Enterprise Information Systems Infrastructure, 1995, Implimenting TQM, 1995, Lessons Learned from the Navstar GPS Engineering Management System Project, 1997. Mem. Am. Mgmt. Assn., Assn. for Info. and Image Mgmt., Armed Forces Communications and Electronics Assn., Sierra Club, Phi Delta Theta. Avocations: golf, tennis, sailing, skiing, world travel. Office: Globe Cast Comms NAm 3872 Keystone Ave Culver City CA 90232-3305

MEHRING, CLINTON WARREN, engineering executive; b. New Haven, Ind., Feb. 14, 1924; s. Fred Emmett and Florence Edith (Hutson) M.; m. Carol Jane Adams, Mar. 9, 1946; children—James Warren, Charles David, John Steven (dec.), Martha Jane. B.S., Case Inst. Tech., 1950; M.S., U. Colo., 1956. Registered profl. engr., Wyo., Colo., Nev. Design engr. U. S. Bur Reclamation, Denver, 1950-56; design engr. Tipton & Kalmbach, Denver, 1956-58; asst. resident engr. Tipton & Kalmbach, Quito, Equador, 1959-61; asst. chief design engr. Tipton & Kalmbach, Lahore, Pakistan, 1962-65; v.p. Tipton & Kalmbach, Denver, 1966-73, exec. v.p., 1973-79, pres., 1979—, also bd. dirs. Served with AUS, 1943-45. Recipient Theta Tau award as outstanding grad. Case Inst. Tech., 1950. Fellow ASCE (life); mem. Am. Cons. Engrs. Coun., U.S. Com. on Large Dams, Am. Concrete Inst., U.S. Com. Irrigation and Drainage (life), Sigma Xi, Tau Beta Pi, Theta Tau, Sigma Chi, Blue Key. Methodist. Club: Denver Athletic. Home: 1821 Mt Zion Dr Golden CO 80401-1733 Office: 1331 17th St Denver CO 80202-1566

MEHRING, MARGARET, filmmaker, retired educator; b. Milbank, S.D., Sept. 3, 1925; d. Robert Dunbrack and Bernice (Case) Jones; m. William Samuel Mehring, June 21, 1947 (dec. June 1958); 1 child, William Dunbrack. BA, Lawrence Coll., 1947; MS in Edn., U. So. Calif., 1972, PhD in Cinema, 1978. Writer, dir., prodr. Mehring Prodns., L.A., 1953—; mem. faculty U. So. Calif. Sch. Cinema and TV, L.A., 1959-91, dir. filmic writing program, 1978-91, dir. emerita, 1991—; media edn. cons. Oglala Lakota Coll., Pine Ridge Indian Reservation, Kyle, S.D., 1996—. Author: The Screenplay, 1989; writer, dir., prodr. numerous ednl., documentary and indsl. tng. films for Employers Ins. Wausau, 1955, 57, 59-62, Golden State Ins. Co., 1964, Techno Electric Mfg. Co., 1965, Calif. Dept. Social Welfare, 1967, Andersen Windowall Corp., 1969, Golden State Mut. Life Ins. Co., 1983; writer, dir. ednl. films for MLA, U. So. Calif., 1959-60, John Tracy Clinic, 1961-62, Calif. Dept. Social Welfare, 1963-64, Am. Assn. Ret. Persons and Nat. Ret. Tchrs. Assn., 1965-67, Profl. Rsch., Inc., 1968, Acad. Comm. Facility, UCLA, 1969, ednl. sound film strips dept. daytime programs ans spl. projects UCLA Ext., 1971, San Diego County Dept. Edn., 1972, Iran film series Instrnl. Media Ctr., Mich. State U., 1975-77; writer films Who's Behind the Wheel, Part 1, 1966, Part II, 1967, Mayday, Mayday, 1970, The Man, Part I, 1972, Part II, 1973, How To Manage Your resources-Safety, Part I, 1973, Part II, 1974 (all for USAF), Immunity-The Power To Resist a Disease, 1970. Pres. El Moro Dem. Club, Los Osos, Calif., 1994-95; bd. dirs. Ctrl. Coast Women's Polit. Com., San Luis Obispo, Calif., 1995-96; vol. Global Vols.-Poland, 1995; vol. instr. Oglala Lakota Coll., Pine Ridge Indian Reservation, Kyle, S.D., 1995, vol. cons., designer degree media program, 1998—; project dir. First Amendment/Blacklist Project. Mem. Univ. Film and Video Assn., Script Coalition for Industry, Profls. and Tchrs., Delta Kappa Alpha (assoc.). Home and Office: PO Box 6171 Los Osos CA 93412-6171

MEHTA, BRINDA J., foreign languages educator; b. Maharashtra, India, Aug. 6, 1959; came to U.S., 1982; d. Jagadish Manubhai and Kunda (Tipnis) M. BA in French Lit. with honors, Elphinstone Coll., Bombay, India, 1979; MA in French Lit. with honors, U. Bombay, 1982; PhD in French Lit., Brown U., 1988. French instr. Queen Mary H.S., Bombay, 1981-82; sr. tchg. asst. French studies Brown U., Providence, 1983-88, tchg. fellow in French Summer Acad., 1987, French instr. Brown Learning Cmty., 1986-88; asst. prof. French Eckerd Coll., St. Petersburg, Fla., 1988-92; assoc. prof. French Mills Coll., Oakland, Calif., 1992—; presenter lang. and lit. Rollins Coll., Winter Park, Fla., 1989, 90, 92, Duquesne U., 1989, Fla. State U., 1991, MLA Ann. Conv., San Francisco, 1991, MIFLC, Blacksburg, Va., 1992, 19th Ann. African Lit. Assn., Guadeloupe, 1993, 20th Ann. meeting, Accra, Ghana, 1994, 25th Ann. conf., Columbus, Ohio, 22nd Ann. Conf., SUNY, Stony Brook, 1996, 24th Ann. conf. U. Tex., Austin, 1998, C.I.E.F. Conf., Quebec City, 1994, Soyinka Festival, Lagos, Nigeria, 1994, Mt. Carmel Women's Coll., Bangalore, India, 1994, Assn. for Commonwealth Lit. and Lang. Studies Conf., Kelaniya, Sri Lanka, 1995, Fourth World Conf. on Women in Beijing, China, 1995, U. Calif., Berkeley, 1996, Fla. Internat. U., Miami, 1996, Mich. State U., East Lansing, 1997, Hammamet, Tunisia, 1997, 5th Internat. Conf. of Arab Women's Solidarity Assn., Cairo, Egypt, 1997, I.C.A.S.E.L., Mysore, India, 1998, 6th Internat. conf. Caribbean Women Writers and Scholars, Grand Anse, Grenada, 1998, 1st Internat. Conf. Caribbean Lit., Nassau, The Bahamas, 1998; scholar-in-residence Inist. for Gender Studies U. W.I., St. Augustine, Trinidad, 1999. Author: Corps Infirme, Corps Infame: La Femme dans le Roman Balzacien, 1992; author chpts. to books; contbr. articles to profl. jours. Am. Coun. Learned Socs. Rsch. fellow, 1998; affiliated scholar Beatrice Bain Rsch. Group on Gender, U. Calif., Berkeley, 1998. Mem. MLA, Am. Assn. Tchrs. French, African Lit. Assn., Assn. Caribbean Women Writers and Scholars, Women in French Assn., Assn. Caribbean Studies, Assn. Commonwealth Studies. Hindu. Avocations: music, film, travel, theatre, reading. Office: Mills Coll 5000 MacArthur Blvd Oakland CA 94613

MEI, TOM Y. K., lawyer; b. Kuantan, Malaysia, July 24, 1940; came to U.S., 1958.; s. Hung Po and Hannah (Chung) M.; m. Margene Suzuki Mei, Sept. 1964; children: Rodney, Todd. BA in econ., Calif. State U. at L.A., 1963; JD, Western State U. Coll. Law, 1975. Bar: Calif. 1976. Claim rep. CNA Ins., L.A., 1964-66; claim supr. CNA Ins., San Diego, 1966-76; assoc. attorney Murchison & Cumming, Santa Ana, 1976-88, ptnr., 1988—; pres. San Diego Claims Mgr. Council, 1973. Mem. Am. Bd. Trial Advocates (bd. dirs.), Defense Rsch. Inst., Orange County Bar Assoc. Avocation: snow sking and traveling. Office: Murchison & Cumming 200 W Santa Ana Blvd Ste 801 Santa Ana CA 92701-4134

MEIER, THOMAS JOSEPH, museum director, author; b. Denver, June 23, 1939; s. Henry Joseph and Helen Miriam (Croke) M.; m. Beverly Joyce Loeffler, June 8, 1963; children: Thomas, John. BS in Edn., U. Colo., 1964. Cert. tchr., Colo. Space mgmt. dir. U. Colo., Boulder, 1966-69; owner Sturtz & Copeland, Boulder, 1969-77; historian and writer Mesa Press, Boulder, 1977-90; dir. Boulder Mus. History, 1990—. Author: The Pictureman, 1994, (booklet) The Early History of Boulder 1993, contbr. articles to profl. jours. Mem. mass transit com. City of Boulder, 1973; mem. City Planning Bd., Boulder, 1974-75, City Landmark Bd., Boulder, 1974-75. Served with USMC, 1957-60. Mem. Boulder Hist. Soc. (pres. 1985), Colo. Hist. Soc. Home: 2850 Vassar Dr Boulder CO 80303-5737 Office: Boulder Mus of History 1206 Euclid Ave Boulder CO 80302-7224

MEIGEL, DAVID WALTER, career officer, retired musician; b. Chgo., Feb. 27, 1957; s. Thomas Arent and Annie Elizabeth (Thomas) M. Diploma, USAF NCO Leadership Sch., Chanute AFB, Ill., 1981, USAF/CAP SQD Officer Sch., 1987, USAF NCO Acad., Norton AFB, Calif., 1991. Enlisted USAF, 1976; commd. staff sgt. to 2d lt. CAP, Travis AFB, Calif., 1986; advanced through grades to tech. sgt. USAF, 1989; percussionist 724th USAF Band, McChord AFB, Wash., 1976-78, 752d USAF Band, Elmendorf AFB, Alaska, 1978-80, 505th USAF Band, Chanute AFB, Ill., 1980-84, 504th USAF Band, Travis AFB, 1984-90; prin. percussionist, chief of adminstrn. Am.'s Band in Blue, USAF, Travis AFB, 1990-92. Prin. percussionist San Diego (Calif.) Civic Orch., 1973-76, Poway (Calif.) High Sch. Band, 1974-75; percussionist Anchorage (Alaska) Civic Opera, 1979-80, Anchorage (Alaska) Scottish Soc., 1979-80, Fairfield Civic Theatre, Fairfield, Calif., 1984—; communications officer USAF Civil Air Patrol, Travis AFB, 1986—. Recipient Gov.'s medal Youkon Internat. Invitational Scottish Games, Whitehorse City Coun., B.C., 1980; decorated USAF Achievement medal 1989, 93, USAF Commendation medal 1986, Comdrs. Commendation medal; named one of Outstanding Young Men Am., 1988, 92. Mem. CAP, USAF Aux. Avocations: amateur radio, golf, bowling, computer ops. Home: 3600 Data Dr Apt 544 Rancho Cordova CA 95670-7938

MEIGHAN, STUART SPENCE, hospital consultant, internist, writer; b. Glasgow, Scotland, Jan. 30, 1923; came to U.S., 1962; s. Stuart Spence and Annie Louise (Brown) M; m. Anne Stewart Henderson, Nov. 4, 1952 (div. 1968); children: Jane Spence, Stuart Spence; m. Louise Rhys McGregor, July 7, 1985. MB, U. Glasgow, 1945. Registrar, sr. registrar Nat. Health Svc., U.K., 1948-57; sr. staff mem. Allan Blair Meml. Clinic, Regina, Sask., Can., 1957-62; internist Cleland Clinic, Oregon City, Oreg., 1962-64; dir. med. affairs Good Samaritan Hosp., Portland, Oreg., 1964-78; pres. Spence Meighan and Assocs., Portland, 1978—; cons. several hosps. and orgns. Contbr. over 100 articles to profl. jours. Lt. Royal Navy, 1946-48. Recipient Disting. Svc. award Am. Soc. Internal Medicine. Fellow Am. Coll. Physicians, Royal Coll. Physicians. Avocations: sailing, tennis, theater, rugby football, music. Home and Office: 408 NW Rainier Ter Portland OR 97210-3347

MEIGS, JOHN LIGGET, artist; b. Chgo., May 10, 1916; s. James L. and Mary Margaret (Cookly) M.; 1 adopted son, Clinton Taylor (dec.). Student, U. Redlands, 1933-34, Gand Chaumier Acad., Paris. 50 one-man shows in U.S., France; author: Peter Hurd The Lithographs, Peter Hurd Sketch Book, Cowboy in American Graphics; contbr. numerous articles to profl. jours. With USN, 1951, PTO. Avocations: book collector, original art collector. Home and Office: PO Box 107 San Patricio NM 88348-0107

MEIKLEJOHN, ALVIN J., JR., state senator, lawyer, accountant.; b. Omaha, June 18, 1923; B.S., J.D., U. Denver, 1951; m. Lorraine J. Meiklejohn; children: Pamela Ann, Shelley Lou, Bruce Ian, Scott Alvin. Mem. Colo. Senate from 19th dist., 1976-96, chmn. com. edn.; mem. Edn. Commn. of States, 1981-96, chmn. Colo. Commn. on Ach. in Edn., 1995, mem., 1993-96. Mem. Jefferson Sch. Dist. No. R-1 Bd. Edn., 1971-77, pres., 1973-77; commr. Commn. on Uniform State Laws, 1988-96. Served to capt. U.S. Army, 1940-46; to maj. USAF, 1947-51. Mem. Colo. Soc. CPA's, Arvada C. of C. Republican. Clubs: Masons, Shriners. Home: 7540 Kline Dr Arvada CO 80005-3732 Office: Jones & Keller PC 1625 Broadway Ste 1600 Denver CO 80202-4727

MEINDL, ROBERT JAMES, English language educator; b. Wausau, Wis., Sept. 17, 1936; s. George Martin and Adeline Emilie (Goetsch) M.; m. Victoria Lynn Chavez; children: Karin Rose, George Andrew, Damian Kurt, Erika Wittmer, Christopher Smith, Gabrielle Remelia. BS, U. Wis., 1958; MA, U. Conn., 1960; PhD, Tulane U., 1965; postdoctoral studies, U. Calif., Berkeley, 1967-68, Goethe Inst., Liblar, Germany, 1879, U. Cologne, Germany, 1970. Teaching asst. U. Conn., Storrs, 1958-60; teaching fellow Tulane U., 1960-62; lectr. U. Wis., Green Bay, 1963-65; from asst. to full prof. English Calif. State U., Sacramento, 1965—. Translator: Studies in John Gower, 1981; book rev. editor Studia Mystica Jour., 1984-89; contbr. numerous articles to profl. jours. With USNR, 1953-61, 79-96. Nat. Endowment for the Humanities fellow Stanford U., 1982. Mem. MLA, Medieval Acad. Am., Medieval Assn. of Pacific, Early English Text Soc., John Gower Soc., New Chaucer Soc. Home: 2301 Pennland Dr Sacramento CA 95825-0329 Office: Calif State U 6000 J St Sacramento CA 95819-2605

MEISSINGER, ELLEN MURRAY, artist, educator; b. Raleigh, N.C., June 19, 1947; d. William Don and Sarah (Elliott) Murray; m. Lonnie Dean Meissinger, Jan. 10, 1975; children: Logan Don, Jordan Daniel. BFA, U. N.C., Greensboro, 1969, MFA, 1971. Prof. Okla. State U., Stillwater, 1971-86, Ariz. State U. Sch. of Art, Tempe, 1986—; juror Rocky Mountain Nat. Water Media Exhibit, Foothills Art Ctr., Golden, Colo., 1997; mem. painting and print commn. Ariz. State U., Tempe, 1997. Invitational exhbns. include Am. Still Life Painting, 1998, Watercolor Now V/Springfield Art Mus., 1997; featured in books: Best of Watercolor Painting Composition, 1997, Best of Watercolor Painting Texture, 1997. Mem. Nat. Watercolor Soc., Watercolor USA Honor Soc. (pres. 1993-95, bd. dirs. 1995-97), Coll. Art Assn. Avocation: gardening. Office: Ariz State U Sch of Art PO Box 871505 Tempe AZ 85287-1505

MEISTER, JOHN EDWARD, JR., consultant, technical educator, systems analyst; b. Elgin, Ill., Nov. 17, 1956; s. John Edward and Marilyn Barbara (Futter) M.; m. Rebecca Marie Buehner, Nov. 15, 1975; children: Christine Marie, Mark Christopher. AA, Cen. Tex. Coll., 1979, U. Md., 1980; BS cum laude, U. Md., 1981; postgrad., Western Conservative Baptist Sem., 1982-83. Enlisted U.S. Army, 1974, advance through grades to staff sgt., 1980; electronics technician Frankfurt, Fed. Republic of Germany, 1974-77; maintenance supr. Darmstadt, Fed. Republic of Germany, 1978-81; transferred from 232d Signal Co. Telecommunications, 1981; instr. U.S. Army Signal Sch., Ft. Gordon, Ga., 1981-82; resigned U.S. Army, 1982; sr. electronics instr. ITT Tech. Inst., Portland, Oreg., 1982-83; equipment engring. and engring. svcs. technician Intel Corp., Aloha, Oreg., 1983-85; ind. lifetime AMSOIL Dealer, Snohomish, Wash., 1983—; electronic designer Boeing Electronics Co., Everett, Wash., 1985-89; systems analyst Boeing Comml. Airplanes, Everett, 1989-95; telecomm. designer UNIX Network Boeing Info. and Support Svcs., 1995; UNIX instr. Boeing Info. & Support Svcs., Delivery Sys. Cert. and Tng., Bellevue, Wash., 1995-96; cons. Clearview Cons., Snohomish, Wash., 1996—; sr. engring. CAD Syss. adminstr. Intermec Corp., Everett, Wash., 1997—; instr. computing Boeing Off-Hour Tng., 1994-96; electronics engr. Innovative Designs and Electronic Sys. Techs., Portland, 1982-85; UNIX specialist. Bd. dirs. Machias Ridge East Homeowner's Assn., 1988-91; fin. advisor Jr. Achievement, Everett High Sch., 1988-89. Mem. NRA, Pacific N.W. 4-Wheel Dr. Assn. Republican. Baptist. Avocations: photography, automotive mechanics, full-size Jeeps. E-mail: john@virtual-cafe.com; web server: wagoneers.com. Home and Office: 14809 State Route 9 SE Snohomish WA 98296-8784

MEITZLER, LELAND KEITH, executive editor; b. Enumclaw, Wash., Apr. 13, 1950; s. Theodore Canfield and Virginia Francis (Cornett-Feller) M.; m. Patty Sue Daffern, Sept. 1, 1968; children: Leland Neal, Dale Ralph. AA with honors, Green River C.C., Auburn, Wash., 1983. Mgr. Meitzler's Greenhouse & Nursery, Puyallup, Wash., 1970-72; sales mgr. Meitzler's Wholesale Greenhouses, Orting, Wash., 1972-75; terminal mgr. Green Thumb Products Corp., Apopka, Fla., 1975-76; owner, mgr. Northwest Tropicals, South Prairie, Wash., 1976-82; pres. Meico Assocs., South Prairie, Wash., 1982-84; co-founder, pres. Heritage Quest Mag., Orting, 1985-92; mng. editor Heritage Quest Mag., Bountiful, Utah, 1992-95, exec. editor, 1996—; touring editor Am. Geneal. Lending Libr., Bountiful, 1993—. Mem. Assn. Profl. Genealogists, Tacoma-Pierce County Geneal. Soc. (corr. sec. 1982-83, pres. 1983-85), South Prairie Hist. Soc. (pres. 1982-85). Republican. Avocations: country music, touring by motor home,

genealogy. Office: Am Genealogy Lending Libr PO Box 329 Bountiful UT 84011-0329 Address: PO Box 40 Orting WA 98360-0040

MEKELBURG, BRIAN PHILLIP, dermatologist; b. L.A., May 3, 1952; s. A. Alfred Mekelburg and Frances Selma Stearns; m. Nancy Yates (div. Aug. 1993); 1 child, Griffin. BA, Pomona Coll., 1973; MD, Tufts U., 1977. Diplomate Am. Bd. Dermatology. Resident in internal medicine UCLA-Harbor Med. Ctr., Torrance, Calif., 1977-80; resident in dermatology UCLA-Wadsworth VA Med. Ctr., L.A., 1980-83; pvt. practice L.A., 1983—; clin. chief divsn. dermatology dept. medicine Cedars-Sinai Med. Ctr., L.A., 1992-96; asst. clin. prof. medicine UCLA Sch. Medicine, L.A., 1983—. Fellow Am. Acad. Dermatology, Am. Soc. Dermatologic Surgery, N.Am. Soc. Phlebology. Avocations: guitar playing, tennis, sailing. Office: # 1035 E 8631 W 3d St Los Angeles CA 90048

MELBOURNE, ROBERT ERNEST, civil engineer; b. Oceanside, Calif., July 17, 1989; s. Thomas Powell and Helen Millicent (Plausse) M.; m. Jeanne Edith Kuhn, Apr. 8, 1961; children: Ann Teresa Farley, Maria Helen, Steven Thomas, Louise Clare Vance. BSCE, U. So. Calif., 1951, PhD in History, 1996; MSCE, Stanford U., 1955; MA in History, U. San Diego, 1990. Registered civil engr., Calif. Engr. Morrison-Knudsen Co., Boise, Noxon, Mont., 1955-57, J.E. Haddock Ltd., Pasadena, Calif., 1957-58; pres. R.E. Melbourne Co. Inc., San Luis Rey, Calif., 1958-66; designer, chief engr. San Diego County Water Authority, San Diego, 1966-90; mil. historian in pvt. practice, 1990—; mem. adv. bd. Colorado River Bd., L.A., 1967-83. Commr. Oceanside Historic Preservation, 1997—. Lt. USN, 1951-54, PTO. Fellow ASCE; mem. U.S. Naval Inst., Soc. Am. Mil. Engrs. Soc. Mil. History, Navy League of U.S., Marine Corps Heritage Found. Republican. Roman Catholic. Home: PO Box 9 San Luis Rey CA 92068

MELDMAN, MARGERY LYNN, writer, photographer; b. Milw., May 8, 1936; d. Herman and Miriam (Cony) Scholl; m. Burt A. Meldman, June 11, 1955; children: Sharon, Michael, Debbie. Columnist Phoenix Ctrl. News, 1974-77; freelance travel and environ. writer, 1994—; travel writer Phoenix Home and Garden Mag., 1995—; columnist Westbrook Villager, 1996—. Author: Confessions of a Life Underwriter's Wife, 1976; co-author: Crossing the Border Fast and Easy, 1992. Named communicator of achievement Ariz. Press Women, 1997. Mem. Ariz. Press Women (v.p. 1993-95, pres. 1995-97), Nat. Fedn. Press Women, Soc. Profl. Journalists, Internat. Food Wine & Travel Writers Assn. Avocations: travel, reading, birding. Home: 8652 W Sequoia Dr Peoria AZ 85382-8638

MELENDY, RICHARD FRANCIS, entertainer, artist; b. Pasadena, Calif., Aug. 13, 1968; s. Richard Albert and Marjorie Frances (Weston) M.; m. Robert Charles Howard, May 10, 1997. AA, Pasadena City Coll., 1990; BA magna cum laude, U. So. Calif., L.A., 1992. Owner, entertainer, fine artist Melendy Entertainment Svcs., La Canada, 1992—; mem. Pasadena Arts Coun., 1995—, adv. bd. mem., 1996—. Vol. entertainer Childrens Hosp., L.A., 1997—; vol. Camp Ronald McDonald. Recipient Ebell of L.A. award, 1991. Mem. World Clown Assn., L.A. Guild Puppetry (performer), Carrousel of Clowns, Golden Key. Avocations: unicycling, visual art drawing and painting, pantomine, clowning, juggling. Home: 309 Inverness Dr La Canada CA 91011-4142

MELICH, DORIS S., public service worker; b. Salt Lake City, Apr. 8, 1913; d. Edward Harrison and Marie Cushing Snyder; m. Mitchell Melich, June 3, 1935; children: Tanya Marie Melich Silverman, Michael E., Nancy Lynne, Robert Allen. BA in Western History, U. Utah, 1934. Mem. Nat. Commn. Arthritis and Related Musculoskeltal Diseases, 1974-76, Nat. Arthritis Adv. Bd., 1977-84, 86-90; Utah del. Nat. Ho. of Dels. Arthritis Found., 1982-87; pres. Utah Arthritis Found. Bd., 1975-78, v.p., 1968-69, 73-74; Utah rep. Arthritis Found. Govt. Affairs, 1983—. Leader, founder 1st Girl Scouts Lone Troop U.S., Moab, Utah, 1947, regional selections com., 1958-67; active Utah Ballet Guild, Salt Lake Art Ctr., Utah Arts Coun., 1988—, Utah State Rep. Women, YWCA; trustee emeritus Arthritus Found. Recipient Pyramid award Nat. Arthritis Found., 1986, Utah Girl Scouts Regional award, 1987, Thanks Badge, 1963, Merit Honor award U. Utah Emeritus Club, 1978, Minute Man award Utah N.G., 1985; named to Nat. Women's Wall of Fame, Seneca Falls, N.Y., 1993. Mem. AAUW, Nat. Assistance League of Salt Lake City (charter mem.), Utah Women's Forum, Order Ea. Star, Alpha Delta Pi, Beta Sigma Phi (sponsor). Home: 900 Donner Way Apt 708 Salt Lake City UT 84108-2112

MELLOR, RONALD JOHN, history educator; b. Bklyn., Sept. 30, 1940; s. Ronald Green and Eleanor Teresa (Walsh) M.; m. Anne Tidaback Kostelanetz, June 7, 1969; 1 child, Ronald Blake. AB, Fordham Coll., 1962; cert., U. Louvain, Belgium, 1961; AM, Princeton U., 1964, PhD in Classics, 1968. Asst. prof. Classics Stanford (Calif.) U., 1965-75; assoc. prof. history UCLA, 1976-82, prof. history, 1982—; vice-chmn. history UCLA, 1991-92, chmn. history, 1992-97; visitor Princeton Inst. Advanced Studies, 1997-98. Author: Thea Rhome, 1975, Tacitus, 1993, Tacitus and the Classical Tradition, 1995, The Roman Historians, 1999; editor: From Augustus to Nero: The First Dynasty of Imperial Rome, 1990, The Historians of Ancient Rome, 1997, The Roman Historians, 1999. Fellow NEH, 1969, Am. Coun. Learned Socs., 1972, Humanities Rsch. Ctr. Australian Nat. U., Canberra, Australia, 1990; hon. fellow U. Coll. London, Eng., 1969, 72, 83-85. Mem. Am. Hist. Assn., Am. Philol. Assn., Am. Inst. Archaeology, Assn. Ancient Historians, Soc. for the Promotion of Roman Studies. Democrat. Avocations: opera, travel, theater, tennis. Home: 2620 Mandeville Canyon Rd Los Angeles CA 90049-1473 Office: UCLA Dept History 405 Hilgard Ave Los Angeles CA 90095-9000

MELNICK, ALICE JEAN (AJ MELNICK), counselor; b. St. Louis, Dec. 25, 1931; d. Nathan and Henrietta (Hausfater) Fisher; BJ, U. Tex., Austin, 1952; MEd, U. North Tex., 1974; m. Harold Melnick, May 24, 1953; children: Susan, Vikki, Patrice. Lic. profl. counselor. Reporter, San Antonio Light, 1952-53; instr. journalism project Upward Bound, So. Meth. U., Dallas, 1967-71; instr. writing El Centro Dallas County Community Coll., Dallas, part time 1972-74; instr. human devel. Richland Community Coll., Dallas, part-time 1974-79; tchr. English, journalism and psychology Dallas Ind. Sch. Dist., 1969-81; counselor Ursuline Acad., 1981-94; part-time instr. human devel. Santa Fe C.C. Freelance photographer. Mem. Dallas Sports Car Club, N. Mex. Jewish Hist. Soc., Temple Beth Shalom. Jewish. Home: 101 Monte Alto Rd Santa Fe NM 87505-8865

MELOAN, TAYLOR WELLS, marketing educator; b. St. Louis, July 31, 1919; s. Taylor Wells and Edith (Graham) M.; m. Anna Geraldine Leukering, Dec. 17, 1944 (div. 1974); children: Michael David, Steven Lee; m. Jane Innes Bierlich, Jan. 30, 1975. B.S. cum laude, St. Louis U., 1949; M.B.A., Washington U., St. Louis, 1950; D of Bus. Admin., Ind. U., 1953. Advt. mgr. Herz Corp., St. Louis, 1941-42; sales promotion supr. Liggett & Myers Tobacco Co., St. Louis, 1942-43; asst. prof. mktg. U. Okla., Norman, 1953; asst., then assoc. prof. mktg. Ind. U., Bloomington, 1953-59; prof., chmn. dept. mktg. U. So. Calif., Los Angeles, 1959-69, prof. mktg., 1969-92, Robert E. Brooker prof. mktg., 1970-79, Robert E. Brooker disting. prof. mktg. emeritus, 1991—; disting. emeritus prof. U. So. Calif., L.A., 1997—, dean Sch. Bus. Adminstrn., 1969-71, assoc. v.p. acad. adminstrn. and research, 1971-81; prof. bus. adminstrn. U. Karachi, Pakistan, 1962; vis. prof. mktg. Istituto Post U. Per Lo Studio Dell Organizzazione Aziendale, Turin, Italy, 1964, U. Hawaii, 1993, Madrid Bus. Sch., 1993; disting. vis. prof. U. Witwatersrand, Johannesburg, 1978, U. Hawaii, 1993; editl. advisor bus. adminstrn. Houghton Mifflin Co., Boston, 1959-73; cons. to industry and govt., 1953; bd. dirs Inst. Shipboard Edn. Author: New Career Opportunities, 1978, Innovation Strategy and Management, 1979, Direct Marketing: Vehicle for Department Store Expansion, 1984, Preparing the Exporting Entrepreneur, 1986, The New Competition: Dilemma of Department Stores in the 1980's, 1987, Franchise Marketing: A Retrospective and Prospective View of a Contractual Vertical Marketing System, 1988; co-author: Managerial Marketing, 1970, Internationalizing the Business Curriculum, 1968, Handbook of Modern Marketing, contbg. author, 1986; co-author, co-editor: International and Global Marketing: Concepts and Cases, 1994, International and Global Marketing Concepts and Cases, Vol. 2, 1997; bd. editors Jour. Mktg., 1965-72. Trustee World Affairs Coun. Orange County, [illegible] (pres. L.A. chpt. 1963-64), Order of Artus, Beta Gamma Sigma, Delta Pi Epsilon, Calif. Yacht Club, Univ. Club, Rotary. Home: 59 Lakefront Irvine CA 92604-4683 Office: U So Calif Dept Mktg Los Angeles CA 90089-1421

MELSHEIMER, HAROLD, obstetrician, gynecologist; b. Legenfeld, Germany, June 11, 1927; came to U.S., 1955; naturalized, 1960; s. Louis and Hella Leonie (Schwehr) Peterman; m. Norma Sykes Sabrina, Nov. 27, 1967; children: Laura, Linda. BS, Marburg U., West Germany, 1951, MD, 1954. Diplomate Am. Bd. Ob-Gyn. Intern Baden County Hosp., West Germany, 1954-55, St. Mary's Hosp. Med. Ctr., Long Beach, Calif., 1955-56; resident Queens Hosp. Med. Ctr., Honolulu, 1956-57, Calif. Hosp. Med. Ctr., L.A., 1957-59; pvt. practice ob-gyn. Encino, Calif., 1959-87; ret.; former dept. chief, now hon. staff mem. Am. Med. Internat. Med. Ctr., Tarzana, Calif., Encino Hosp.; founder Technion Inst. of Tech. Contbr. articles to profl. jours. Operational mem. USCG Aux., 1971. Recipient cert. of honor Wisdom Soc.; named Hon. Citizen, Rep. of Korea, 1966. Fellow ACS (life), Am. Coll. Ob-Gyn., Internat. Coll. Surgeons; mem. AMA, Calif. Med. Assn., L.A. County Med. Assn., Am. Physicians Fellowship for Israel Med. Assn., N.Y. Acad. Scis., Braemar Country Club. Avocations: travel, art, history, sailing. Home: 25660 Deertrail Dr Tehachapi CA 93561-9140

MELTEBEKE, RENETTE, career counselor; b. Portland, Oreg., Apr. 20, 1948; d. Rene and Gretchen (Hartwig) M. BS in Sociology, Portland State U., 1970; MA in Counseling Psychology, Lewis and Clark Coll., 1985. Lic. profl. counselor, Oreg.; nat. cert. counselor. Secondary tchr. Portland Pub. Schs., 1970-80; project coord. Multi-Wash CETA, Hillsboro, Oreg., 1980-81; coop. edn. specialist Portland C.C., 1981-91; pvt. practice career counseling, owner Career Guidance Specialists, Lake Oswego, Oreg., 1988—; mem. adj. faculty Marylhurst (Oreg.) Coll., 1989-93, Portland State U., 1994—; assoc. Drake Beam Morin Inc., Portland, 1993-96; career cons. Managed Health Network, 1994—, Career Devel. Svcs., 1990—, Life Dimensions, Inc., 1994; presenter Internat. Conf., St. Petersburg, Russia, 1995. Rotating columnist Lake Oswego Rev., 1995—; creator video presentation on work in Am. in 5 langs., 1981. Pres. Citizens for Quality Living, Sherwood, Oreg., 1989; mem. Leadership Roundtable on Sustainability for Sherwood, 1994-95; bd. dirs. Bus. for Social Responsibility for Oreg. and Southwestern Wash., 1999%. Recipient Esther Matthews award for outstanding contbn. to field of career devel., 1998. Mem. Assn. for Psychol. Type, Nat. Career Devel. Assn., Oreg. Career Devel. Assn. (pres. 1990), Assn. for Humanistic Psychology (presenter nat. conf. Tacoma 1996), Willamette Writers. Avocations: walking, swimming, bicycling, cross-country skiing, photography. Home: 890 SE Merryman St Sherwood OR 97140-9746 Office: Career Guidance Specialists 15800 Boones Ferry Rd Ste C104 Lake Oswego OR 97035-3492

MELTON, BRAD RAY, editor, researcher, writer, historian; b. Charleston, Ill., Dec. 13, 1971; m. Jennifer Lynn Peters, Dec. 14, 1996. BA in Mass Comm., Prescott Coll., 1997; postgrad. in History, Ariz. State U., 1997—. Ops. coord. Ariz. Hwys., Phoenix, 1994—; editor-in-chief Ariz. Style Mag., Phoenix, 1995-96; editl. asst. Ariz. Hwys., Book Divsn., Phoenix, 1998—; asst. editor Documentary Editing, dept. history Ariz. State U., Tempe, 1998—. Rschr. (TV spls.) Copperstate Chronicles, 1995-97; contbr. articles to profl. jours. Recipient scholarship Prescott Coll., 1996, scholarship Ariz. Bd. Regents, 1998—. Mem. Soc. Profl. Journalists (scholarship 1996), Ariz. Hist. Found., Western History Assn., Nat. Coun. Pub. History, Phi Alpha Theta. Lutheran. Avocations: photography, desktop publishing, hiking, hockey, travel. Office: Ariz Hwys 2039 W Lewis Ave Phoenix AZ 85009

MELTON, CHERYL ANN, educator, small business owner; b. Bklyn., Jan. 5, 1949; d. Raymond Franklin and Irene Louise (Cotton) Blair; m. Gilbert Edmund Melton, Aug. 26, 1972; children: Byron Adrian, Brandie Alicia. BS in Edn., Ohio State U., 1971; MS in Edn., Nazareth Coll., Rochester, N.Y., 1976; postgrad., Calif. State U., 1998. Prof. clear multiple subject teaching credential, Calif.; clear cross-cultural acad. and lang. devel. cert., Calif. Elem. tchr. N.Y.C. Bd. Edn., Bklyn., 1971-72, Rochester City Sch. Dist., 1973-84; elem. tchr. Long Beach (Calif.) Unified Sch. Dist., 1984-90, lang. arts specialist, 1990—, reading recovery tchr., 1992—, mentor tchr., 1996—; regional reading specialist Los Angeles County Office of Edn., 1996—; mem. Sch. Program Improvement Leadership Team, Long Beach, 1990—; adv. bd. Scholastic, Inc.-Literacy Place, 1994-95; summer facilitator trainer Early Literacy Inservice Course, 1995; participant Calif. State U.-Long Beach South Basin Writing Project's Think Tank, summer 1996; instr. masters reading specialist program Sch. Edn. U. LaVerne. Chmn. membership devel. Jr. League Long Beach, 1991-92, mem. by-laws task force, 1992-93, adv. future planning, 1989—, selected mentor, 1991—, sustaining advisor placement com., 1994-95, sustainer coun. mem., 1995—; chosen del. Jr. League Dallas. Scholar Calif. literature project Calif. State U., Dominguez Hills, 1992. Mem. Tchrs. Assn. Long Beach, Nat. Coun. Tchrs. English, Nat. Coun. Negro Women, Links (Orange County chpt. Inc., co-chair model initiative youth project 1994, 95, 96, 97, 98, co-chair Journey into Possibilities, Rochester chpt., charter), Jack and Jill of Am. (charter Long Beach chpt.), Internat. Reading Assn., Reading Recovery Coun. N.Am., Beach Cities Reading Assn., Calif. Reading Assn., Nat. Coun. Tchrs. English, English Coun. of Long Beach, Delta Sigma Theta (charter, Long Beach alumnae). Democrat. Baptist. Avocations: travel, reading magazines, networking, literacy. Home: 4508 Hazelnut Ave Seal Beach CA 90740-2918

MELTON, ROBERT W., JR., communications educator; b. Berkeley, Calif., Feb. 2, 1954; s. Robert W. and Innes (McElrath) M.; m. Katherine Ruth Brame, Mar. 26, 1977; children: Sarah Katherine, Timothy Alden, James Alexander. AA, Santa Rosa (Calif.) Jr. Coll., 1974; BS in Journalism, U. Oreg., 1976; MS in Edn., Portland State U., 1996. Reporter, photographer East Oregonian, Pendleton, Oreg., 1976-78; student tchr. South Eugene (Oreg.) H.S., 1979; tchr Roseburg (Oreg.) Sr. H.S., 1979-84; tchr. Wilson H.S., Portland, 1984-94; assoc. prof. U. Iowa, Iowa City, 1992—; tchr. Benson Poly. H.S., Portland, 1994—; adj. asst. prof. U. Oreg., Eugene, 1983-84; bd. dirs. ReDesign Inst., Inc., Dallas. Author: Publications Stylebook, 1985; editor: Teacher Resource Notebook, 1989; co-author: Advertising A-Z, 1991, The Second Page, 1992. Vol. bd. Portland Ctr. Stage, 1994-96, vol., 1992—. Recipient Pioneer award Nat. Scholastic Press Assn., 1994, 5 Yr. Vol. award Portland Ctr. Stage, 1996; named Disting. adviser Dow Jones Newspaper Fund, 1988. Mem. NEA, Journalism Edn. Assn. (v.p. 1997—, bd. dirs. 1987—, Merit medal 1991), Oreg. Edn. Assn., Oreg. Journalism Edn. Assn. (pres. 1984-88), Portland Assn. Tchrs. (bldg. rep. 1997—). United Methodist. Avocations: travel, photography, theater, writing, speaking. Home: 2607 SW Bertha Blvd Portland OR 97201-1986 Office: Benson Poly HS 546 NE 12th Ave Portland OR 97232-2719

MELTON, WILLIAM RAY, JR., insurance company executive; b. Detroit, Mich., Nov. 24, 1920; s. William Ray and Marguerite (Hale) M.; m. Cleola May Smith, Jul. 19, 1942; children: Judith Ann, Carole Jean, Nancy Sue, Patricia Louise. BA in speech, Univ. Southern Calif., 1950, MS in ednl. psychology, 1952. Production mgr. CTB/McGraw Hill, Monterey, Calif., 1948-63; 2nd v.p. sales promotion Transamerica Occidental Life Ins. Co., L.A., 1967-83; lectr. in creative writing Whittier Coll., Whittier, Calif., 1990-91. Author: Nine Lives to Pompeii, 1974, I Get My Best Ideas in Bed, 1971; contbr. articles to profl. jours. With Army Air Corps, 1942-46, ETO. Recipient Best Novel By Orange County Author award Univ. Calif., Irvine, 1975. Mem. Archaeological Inst. Am., Agatha Christie Soc., PEN Internat., Orange County Press Club, Mystery Writers of Am., Phi Delta Kappa. Republican. Protestant. Avocations: travel, reading, big band music, movies, genealogy, archaeology. Home: 1310 Ironwood St La Habra CA 90631-7458

MELVIN, JAY WAYNE, computer programmer; b. Oak Park, Ill., Feb. 3, 1946; s. Kendred Wayne and Margarita Alice (Pérez) M.; m. Linda Hansen, Dec. 10, 1980. MA in Urban Studies, Claremont (Calif.) Grad. Sch., 1975, postgrad., 1977. Hot line/prodn. mgr. Forth, Inc., Hermosa Beach, Calif., 1981-85; sr. software engr. Maxtor Corp., San Jose, Calif., 1986-88; computer programmer Tracor-Ultron Labs., San Jose, 1988-90, Comtech Labs., Palo Alto, Calif., 1990-92; programmer, team leader, mgr. software devel. lab. Omnipoint Corp., Colorado Springs, Colo., 1992-96; mgr. applications integration lab. Pacific Bell Mobile Svcs., Pleasanton, Calif., 1996-98; network controller, network ops. ctr. Pacific Bell Mobile Svcs., Pleasanton, 1998; cons. phenomenoLOGIC, La Honda, Calif., 1985-92, infoPATH, La Honda, 1990— . Contbr. articles to profl. jours. Peace Corps vol. U.S. State [illegible] Calif. Dept. Forestry, Kings Mountain, 1986-88; fire dept. lt. Vol. Fire Brigade, La Honda, San Mateo, 1988-94; radio operator Mil. Affiliate Radio Svc., Jackson, Miss., 1962-64. Recipient Beyond War award, 1987; grad. fellowship Law Enforcement Adminstrn. Assn., 1975-77. Mem. IEEE, Amateur Radio Relay League (life), Amateur Satellite Corp. (life), Forth Interest Group, Assn. of Computing Machinery, Pi Sigma Alpha. Avocation: amateur radio astronomy. Home and Office: PO Box 333 La Honda CA 94020-0333

MENDE, HOWARD SHIGEHARU, mechanical engineer; b. Hilo, Hawaii, Nov. 19, 1947; s. Tsutomu and Harue (Kubomitsu) M. BSME, U. Hawaii, 1969; MSME, U. So. Calif., 1975. Registered profl. engr., Calif. Mem. tech. staff I Rockwell Internat., Anaheim, Calif., 1970-71; mem. tech. staff I Rockwell Internat., L.A., 1971-73, mem. tech. staff II, 1973-77, mem. tech. staff IV, 1984-86; devel. engr. AiRsch. Mfg. Co., Torrance, Calif., 1977-83; mech. engr. Def. Contracts Mgmt. Dist. West, Santa Ana, Calif., 1987-94, electronics engr., 1994—; lectr. Pacific States U., L.A., 1974-75. Mem. ASME. Democrat. Buddhist. Home: 1946 W 180th Pl Torrance CA 90504-4417 Office: Def Contracts Mgmt 2525 W 190th St Torrance CA 90504-6002

MENDELSON, ALAN CHARLES, lawyer; b. San Francisco, Mar. 27, 1948; s. Samuel Mendelson and Rita Rosalie (Spindel) Brown; children: Jonathan Daniel, David Gary; m. Agnés Marie Barbariol. BA with great distinction, U. Calif., Berkeley, 1969; JD cum laude, Harvard U., 1973. Bar: Calif. 1973. Assoc. Cooley Godward LLP, San Francisco, 1973-80; ptnr. Cooley Godward LLP, Palo Alto, 1980—, mng. ptnr., 1990-95, 96-97; sec. gen. counsel Amgen Inc., Thousand Oaks, Calif., 1990-91; acting gen. counsel Cadence Design Sys., Inc., San Jose, Calif., 1995-96; bd. dirs. Isis Pharms. Inc., CoCensys, Inc.; sec. Walker Interactive Sys., 1982—, PetsMart, 1986—, Axys Pharm. Corp., 1993—, Aviron, 1992—; mem. mgmt. com. Cooley Godward, LLP; chmn. Cos. Practice Group, 1990—, Life Sci. Group, 1998—. Chmn. Piedmont (Calif.) Civil Svc. Commn., 1978-80; den leader Boy Scouts Am., Menlo Park, Calif.; fundraiser Crystal Springs Upland Sch., Hillsborough, Calif., Harvard Law Sch. Fund, Berkeley, Lucille Packard Children's Hosp.; coach Menlo Park Little League, 1982-86; pres., mem. exec. com., bd. dirs. No. Calif. chpt. Nat. Kidney Found., 1986-98. With USAR, 1969-75. Recipient Disting. Svc. award Nat. Kidney Found., 1992; named U. Calif. Berkeley Alumni scholar, 1966, Scaife Found. scholar, 1966, One of 100 Most Influential Attys. in U.S. Nat. Law Jour., 1994, 97, (Best Lawyers in Am., 1993-98). Mem. Bohemian Club, Phi Beta Kappa. Jewish. Home: 76 De Bell Dr Atherton CA 94027-2253 Office: Cooley Godward LLP 5 Palo Alto Sq 3000 El Camino Real Palo Alto CA 94306-2120

MENDELSON, BRADDON LEIGH, film producer; b. Northridge, Calif., Aug. 23, 1961; s. Donald and Judith Carol (Rose) M.; m. Heather Lynn Westcott, Apr. 5, 1998. BA in TV-Film, Calif. State U., 1983. Freelance film prodr. various, L.A., 1991—, screenplay writer, 1991—, TV writer, 1987—, stage dir., 1992—, music video prodr., 1998—, music video writer, 1998; comedy writer Warner Bros. TV, 1999—; pres., CEO Noisivision, Inc. Prodr.: (feature films) Boogie Boy, 1997, Inside Edge, 1993; writer: (TV series) Who's The Boss, 1987; dir.: Golden Mike Awards, 1983; writer/dir.: (stage show) The Riot Act, 1995; contbr. articles to profl. jours. Recipient Am.'s Best/6th An. Writing Competition award The Writers Found., 1995, Achievement award in Fine Arts, Bank of Am., 1979. Mem. Writers Guild of Am., Am. Fedn. of Radio and TV Artists.

MENDELWAGER, GREG, video production company executive; b. N.Y.C., Jan. 14, 1950; s. Jack and Lucille (Levine) Mendelwager; m. Yolanda Trujillo, Aug. 26, 1990. BS, U. N.Mex., 1972; student, Parsons Sch. Design, N.Y.C., 1982-83. Mktg. dir. Select Films, N.Y.C., 1972-78; asst. mgr. domestic ops. Viacom Internat., N.Y.C., 1979-83; v.p. sales and mktg. IVM Prodns., N.Y.C., 1983; dir. internat. sales FilmLife, Moonaachie, N.J., 1984; mktg. mgr., asst. to COO Elmo Mfg. Corp., New Hyde Park, N.Y., 1984-85; corp. v.p. Select Audio Visual Inc., N.Y.C., 1985-96; pres. Riverbend Prodns., Albuquerque, 1997—. Mem. Internat. TV. Assn., Soc. Motion Picture & TV Engrs. Jewish. Avocation: archaeology. Office: Riverbend Prodns 4116 Bluestem Ct NW Albuquerque NM 87114-5517

MENDENHALL, CARROL CLAY, physician; b. Missouri Valley, Iowa, July 26, 1916; s. Clay and Maude (Watts) M.; student U. So. Calif., 1942-44, Chapman Coll., 1946-47, Los Angeles City Coll., 1947-48; D.O., Coll. Osteo. Physicians and Surgeons, 1952; M.D., Calif. Coll. Medicine, 1962; m. Lucille Yvonne Bonvouloir, June 14, 1946 (div. July 1957); 1 son, Gregory Bruce; m. 2d, Barbara Marilyn Huggett-Davis, Sept. 28, 1974. Intern, Los Angeles County Osteo. Hosp., 1952-53; gen. practice medicine, 1953-82, specializing in weight control, Gardena, Calif., 1961-74, specializing in stress disorders and psychosomatic medicine, Ft. Worth, 1974-78, specializing in integral medicine and surgery, Santa Clara, Calif., 1978—; med. dir. Green's Pharms., Long Beach, Calif., 1956-64; v.p. Internat. Pharm. Mfg. Co., Inc., San Pedro, Calif., 1965-66; pres. Chemico of Gardena, Inc., 1964-69; staff Gardena Hosp.; active staff O'Connor Hosp., San Jose, Calif., 1979—; tchr., lectr. biofeedback, prevention and treatment of stress, creative thought; founder, dir. Eclectic Weight Control Workshop, 1971-74, Longevity Learning, Longevity Learning Seminars, 1980; past mem. adv. bd. dirs. L.A. Nat. Bank. Cadre med. dir. Gardena Civil Def., 1953-54, asst. to chief med. dir., 1954-60, chief med. and first aid services, 1960-64. Served as pharmacist's mate USNR, 1944-46. Fellow Royal Soc. Health, Am. Acad. Med. Preventics, Am. Acad. Homeopathic Medicine; mem. Calif. Med. Assn., Santa Clara County Med. Soc., Acupuncture Research Inst. (also alumni assn.), Los Aficionados de Los Angeles (pres. 1964-66), Am. Soc. Clin. Hypnosis. Flamenco Soc. No. Calif. (bd. dirs. 1986—). Address: 1653 Milroy Pl San Jose CA 95124-4723

MENDEZ, CELESTINO GALO, mathematics educator; b. Havana, Cuba, Oct. 16, 1944; s. Celestino Andres and Georgina (Fernandez) M.; came to U.S., 1962, naturalized, 1970; BA, Benedictine Coll., 1965; MA, U. Colo., 1968, PhD, 1974, MBA, 1979; m. Mary Ann Koplau, Aug. 21, 1971; children: Mark Michael, Matthew Maximilian. Asst. prof. maths. scis. Met. State Coll., Denver, 1971-77, assoc. prof., 1977-82, prof., 1982—, chmn. dept. math. scis., 1980-82; adminstrv. intern office v.p. for acad. affairs Met. State Coll., 1989-90. Mem. advt. rev. bd. Met. Denver, 1973-79; parish outreach rep. S.E. deanery, Denver Cath. Cmty. Svcs., 1976-78; mem. social ministries com. St. Thomas More Cath. Ch., Denver, 1976-78, vice-chmn., 1977-78, mem. parish council, 1977-78; del. Adams County Rep. Conv., 1972, 74, 1994, Colo. 4th Congl. Dist. Conv., 1974, Colo. Rep. Conv., 1982, 88, 90, 92, 96, Douglas County Rep. Conv., 1980, 82, 84, 88, 90, 92, 94, 96; alt. del. Colo. Rep. Conv., 1974, 76, 84, 5th Congl. dist. conv., 1976, mem. rules com., 1978, 80, precinct committeeman Douglas County Rep. Com., 1976-78, 89-92, mem. cen. com., 1976-78, 89-92; dist. 29 Rep. party candidate Colo. State Senate, 1990; mem. Colo. Rep. Leadership program, 1989-90, bd. dirs., 1990—; Douglas county chmn. Rep. Nat. Hispanic Assembly, 1989—; bd. dirs. Rocky Mountain Better Bus. Bur., 1975-79, Rowley Downs Homeowners Assn., 1976-78; trustee Hispanic U. Am., 1975-78; councilman Town of Parker (Colo.), 1981-84, chmn. budget and fin. com. 1981-84; chmn. joint budget com. Town of Parker-Parker Water and Sanitation Dist. Bds., 1982-84; commr. Douglas County Planning Commn., 1993—; dir. Mile High Young Scholars Program, 1995-98. Recipient U. Colo. Grad. Sch. excellence in teaching award, 1965-67; grantee Benedictine Coll., 1964-65, Math. Assn. Am. SUMMA grantee Carnegie Found. N.Y., 1994, NSF, 1995—. Mem. Math. Assn. Am. (referee rsch. notes sect. Am. Math. Monthly 1981-82, gov. Rocky Mountain section 1993-96, investment com. 1995—, devel. com. 1995—, task force on reps. 1994-96), Am. Math. Soc., Nat. Coun. Tchrs. of Math., Colo. Coun. Tchrs. of Maths. (bd. dirs. 1994—), Colo. Internat. Edn. Assn., Assoc. Faculties of State Insts. Higher Edn. in Colo. (v.p. 1971-73). Republican. Roman Catholic. Assoc. editor Denver Metro. Jour. Math. and Computer Sci., 1993—; contbr. articles to profl. jours. including Am. Math. Monthly, Procs. Am. Math. Soc., Am. Math. Monthly, Jour. Personalized Instruction, Denver Met. Jour. Math. and Computer Sci., and newspapers. Home: 39 Hummingbird Dr Castle Rock CO 80104-9047 Office: PO Box 173362 Denver CO 80217-3362

MENDIUS, PATRICIA DODD WINTER, editor, educator, writer; b. Davenport, Iowa, July 9, 1924; d. Otho Edward and Helen Rose (Dodd) Winter; m. John Richard Mendius, June 19, 1947; children: Richard, Catherine M. Grubel, Louise, Karen M. Choojian. BA cum laude, UCLA, 1946; MA cum laude, U. N.Mex., 1966. Cert. secondary edn. tchr., Calif.,

N.Mex. English teaching asst. UCLA, 1946-47; English tchr. Marlborough Sch. for Girls, L.A., 1947-50, Aztec (N.Mex.) High Sch., 1953-55, Farmington (N.Mex.) High Sch., 1955-63; chair English dept. Los Alamos (N.Mex.) High Sch., 1963-86; sr. technical writer, editor Los Alamos Nat. Lab., 1987—; adj. prof. English, U. N.Mex., Los Alamos, 1970-72, Albuquerque, 1982-85; English cons. S.W. Regional Coll. Bd., Austin, Tex., 1975—; writer, editor, cons. advanced placement English test devel. com. Nat. Coll. Bd., 1982-86, reader, 1982-86, project equality cons., 1985-88; book selection cons. Scholastic mag., 1980-82. Author: Preparing for the Advanced Placement English Exams, 1975; editor Los Alamos Arts Coun. bull., 1986-91. Chair Los Alamos Art in Pub. Places Bd., 1987-92; chair adv. bd. trustees U. N.Mex., Los Alamos, 1987-93; pres. Los Alamos Concert Assn., 1972-73, 95—; chair Los Alamos Mesa Pub. Libr. Bd., 1990-94, chair endowment com., 1995—. Mem. Soc. Tech. Communicators, AAUW (pres. 1961-63, state bd. dirs. 1959-63, Los Alamos coordinating coun. 1992-93, pres. 1993-94), DAR, Order Ea. Star, Mortar Bd., Phi Beta Kappa (pres. Los Alamos chpt. 1969-72, v.p. 1996-97), Phi Kappa Phi, Delta Kappa Gamma, Gamma Phi Beta. Avocations: swimming, reading, hiking, astronomy, singing. Home: 124 Rover Blvd Los Alamos NM 87544-3634 Office: Los Alamos Nat Lab Diamond Dr Los Alamos NM 87544

MENDOZA, PEGGY ANN GILBERT, elementary education educator, writer; b. L.A.; d. James and Dorothy Elizabeth (Backus) Gilbert; m. Tommy Bravo Mendoza, July 10, 1982; 1 child, Caitlin Elizabeth. Assocs., Long Beach City Coll., 1982; BA, Calif. State U., Long Beach, 1985. Cert. tchr., Calif. Elem. tchr. Mark Keppel Sch., Paramount, Calif., 1987-89, Hamilton Sch., Anza, Calif., 1989-92, Hemet (Calif.) Elem. Sch., 1992-93; mid. sch. tchr. Cottonwood Sch., Aguanga, Calif., 1993-96, independent study program tchr., coord., 1996-98; creative mag. advisor Cottonwood Sch., 1993-94, yearbook advisor, 1993-94, 94-95, 95-96, acad. decatholon coach, 1995, 96; program quality review Hemet Unified Sch. Dist., 1996. Author: White Dove Remembers, 1996. Mem. Calif. Tchr.'s Assn., Hemet Tchr.'s Assn. Democrat. Roman Catholic. Avocations: writing, doll collecting, home improvements. Home: 49780 Kiowa Dr Aguanga CA 92536-9741

MENKIN, CHRISTOPHER (KIT MENKIN), leasing company executive; b. Manhattan, N.Y., Jan. 1, 1942; s. Lawrence and Columbia (Riland) M.; children: Dashiel, Tascha, Ashley. Student, Julliard Sch. of Music, 1960, Santa Monica Coll., 1959-61, UCLA, 1961-64. News editor, dir. Sta. KRFC Radio, San Francisco, 1964-67; adminstrv. asst. to assemblyman Leo J. Ryan South San Francisco, 1967-68; mng. editor Sta. KGO TV News, San Francisco, 1968-69; news producer west coast Sta. ABC TV, Los Angeles, 1969; city mgr. City of San Bruno (Calif.), 1970; owner Menkin & Assocs., Santa Clara, Calif., 1971—; sr. ptnr. Am. Leasing, Santa Clara, 1971—; ptnr. Medallon Leasing, Santa Clara, 1974-80; pres. Monte Sereno Wine Co., Santa Clara, 1978—; dir. Meridian Nat. Bank, 1982-84. Chmn. nominating com. San Jose (Calif.) Symphony, 1988—; sec. Salvation Army, Santa Clara, 1968—, bd. dirs., 1990—, bd. dirs. San Jose chpt., 1990, vice chmn. county adv. bd., 1992; bd. dirs. Cmty. Against Substance Abuse, Los Gatos, Calif., 1988—, Valley Inst. of Theater Arts, Saratoga, Calif., 1987-88, San Jose Trolley, 1988—; vice chmn. Salvation Army Rehab. Bd., 1997. Mem. United Assn. Equipment Leasing (regional chmn. 1992-95, membership chmn. 1994-95, dir. 1996—), Credit Women Internat. (1st male pres.), Santa Clara Valley Wine Soc. (pres. 1988), Credit Profls. Santa Clara Valley (pres. 1990-91), Assn. Credit Grantors (past pres.), Santa Clara C. of C. (pres. 1973-76), Bay Area Exec. Club (sec.), Confrerie de la Chaine de Rotisseurs (charge de presse 1992-95), Royal Rose Soc. Gt. Britain (rep. No. Calif. 1990—). Democrat. Avocations: Rosarian, gardening, wine collecting, music, books. Office: Am Leasing 348 Mathew St Santa Clara CA 95050-3114

MENNELLA, VINCENT ALFRED, automotive manufacturing and airplane company executive; b. Teaneck, N.J., Oct. 7, 1922; s. Francis Anthony and Henrietta Vernard (Dickson) M.; B.A. in Acctg., U. Wash., 1948; m. Madeleine Olson, Aug. 18, 1945; children—Bruce, Cynthia, Mark, Scott, Chris. Sales and bus. mgmt. positions Ford div. Ford Motor Co., 1949-55; founder, pres. Southgate Ford, Seattle, 1955-80; pres. Flightcraft, Inc., Seattle, 1973-86; chmn. bd. Stanley Garage Door Co., 1981-86, Zman Magnetics, 1990—. Former chmn. March of Dimes. Served to capt. USNR, 1942-45. Republican. Roman Catholic. Clubs: Rainier Golf, Seattle Tennis, Rotary (past pres.). Home: 1400 SW 171st Pl Seattle WA 98166-3453

MENZIES, LEILA KAY, college official; b. Gary, Ind., Mar. 3, 1947; d. Walter Wayne and Hazel (Annadown) Leonard. BA in History, UCLA, 1969; MBA in Mgmt. and Stats., Calif. State U., Dominguez Hills, 1980. Asst. bus. mgr. housing, conf. dir. U. Calif., Davis, 1976-78; gen. mgr. housing UCLA, 1978-80; dir. budget and ops. for housing U. Cin., 1980-84; sales rep., owner Yurika Foods, Mich., 1983-84; dean fin. and adminstrv. svcs. Coll. Ea. Utah, Price, 1984-88; v.p. L.A. Harbor Coll., Wilmington, Calif., 1988—. Lay del. Calif.-Pacific Ann. Conf., United Meth. Ch., 1990, 91, 92. Mem. Nat. Assn. Coll. and Univ. Bus. Officers (community coll. com. 1990-92), Western Assn. Coll. and Univ. Bus. Officers (chmn. community coll. com. 1991-92, participant Exec. Leadership Inst. 1992), L.A. C.C. Dist. (mgmt. retreat planning com. 1992), Geneal. Soc. Pa., Wilmington Hist. Soc. Office: LA Harbor Coll 1111 Figueroa Pl Wilmington CA 90744-2311

MENZIES, THOMAS NEAL, art consultant, art critic; b. Long Beach, Calif., Mar. 1, 1945; s. Thomas Warren and Frances (Starks) M. BA, U. Calif., Irvine, 1972; MA, U. So. Calif., 1978. Libr. dir. Parsons Sch. Design, L.A., 1980-82; art coord. Hirsch/Bedner & Assocs., Santa Monica, Calif., 1982-84; pres. Neal Menzies Contemporary Art Inc., L.A., 1984—. Contbg. editor ARTWEEK mag., Oakland, Calif., 1979-83. Charter Founder, Mus. Contemporary Art, L.A.; docent Venice (Calif.) Art Walk. Mem. So. Calif. Art Writers Assn., L.A. Contemporary Exhbns. (friend), Pres.' Circle, L.A. County Mus. of Art. Office: 170 S La Brea Ave Los Angeles CA 90036-2910

MERA, CSABA LESLIE, medical director, consultant; b. Szeged, Hungary, Sept. 28, 1949; came to U.S., 1968; s. Zoltan and Klára Irén (Jobba) M.; m. Jo Ann Mcelmurry, Aug. 18, 1968 (div. Dec. 1980); children: Todd, Trent; m. Patricia Anne Hastings, June 27, 1981; children: Steven, Patrick. BA, Andrews U., 1968; MD, Loma Linda U., 1972. Diplomate Am. Bd. Pediatrics. Asst. dir. emergency dept. Loma Linda (Calif.) U. Med. Ctr., 1973-75, asst. prof. emergency medicine, 1977-80; physician emergency dept. San Antonio Cmty. Hosp., Upland, Calif., 1975-77; resident, fellow in pediatrics Hosp. for Sick Children, Toronto, Ont., Can., 1980-83; pediatrician San Luis Med. Clinic, San Luis Obispo, Calif., 1983-85; pvt. practice Lompoc, Calif., 1985-89; pediatrician CIGNA Healthcare, Orange, Calif., 1989-94, chmn. pediatric dept., 1992-94, med. dir., 1994-96; asst. clin. prof. U. Calif., Irvine, 1990—; med. dir. Pacificare Calif., Cypress, 1996-98, Ultra Link, Costa Mesa, 1998—, Life Trac, Mpls., 1998—. Patentee in field. Fellow Royal Coll. Physicians, Am. Acad. Pediatrics; mem. Am. Coll. Physician Execs., MENSA Internatl., MHP (Managed Healthcare Profl.), CPUR (Cert. Profl. in Utilization Review), ABQAURP (Amer. Bd. of Quality Assurance and Utilization Review Phys.), Alpha Omega Alpha. Avocations: running, playing and coaching soccer, vegetarian gourmet cooking, collecting music CD's. E-mail: cmera@home.com. Office: Ultralink 535 Anton Blvd Ste 900 Costa Mesa CA 92626-7109

MERCER, JOHN A., state legislator; b. Missoula, Mont., Jan. 21, 1957; m. Tine Mercer; children: Thomas, Michael. BA in Bus., U. Mont., 1979; JD, Northwestern U., 1982. Pvt. practice Polson, Mont., 1982; mem. Mont. Ho. of Reps., 1984—, minority whip, 1989-90, minority leader, 1991-92, house spkr., 1993—, mem. rules com., mem. legis. administrv. com. E-mail: house@state.mt.us. Office: PO Box 460 Polson MT 59860 Office: PO Box 200400 Helena MT 59620-0400

MERCER, MARGARET TEELE, medical and film industry marketing executive; b. Bronxville, N.Y., Sept. 10, 1962; d. William Earl Jr. and Judith (Forster) M.; m. Robert Mitchell Fromcheck, May 23, 1993. BS, U. Colo., 1985. Assoc. product mgr. Prescription Products divsn. Fisons Pharms., Denver, 1988-92; mktg. mgr. HealthScan Products, Cedar Grove, N.J., 1992-93; account exec. Sandler Comm., N.Y.C., 1993-94; mktg. dir. Proctor Cos., Littleton, Colo., 1995—. Youth leader Calvary Ch., Denver, 1988-91. Mem. NAFE, Healthcare Bus. Assn. Avocations: athletics, travel, reading. Home: 2 Rose Clover Littleton CO 80127-2220

MERCER, TOBY, artist; b. Mont., Feb. 11, 1947. Bachelor's degree, U. Mont., 1969. Artist Kalispell, Mont., 1975—. E-mail: tobymerc@p-tinet.net.

MERCER, WILLIAM EARL, museum curator; b. Annaheim, Calif., May 14, 1960; s. Robert Oakley and Rowena June (Ill) M. BA in Anthropology, Calif. State U., Northridge, 1983, BA in History, 1983; MA in Mus. Studies, Tex. Tech U., 1986; postgrad., U. N.Mex., 1989-93. Asst. curator Buffalo Bill Hist. Ctr., Cody, Wyo., 1986-87; mus. tech. Nat. Park Svc., Albuquerque, 1989-93; curator art of Africa and the Americas Cin. Art Mus., 1993-96; curator Native Am. art Portland (Oreg.) Mus., 1997—. Author mus. exhbn. catalogs: Singing the Clay, 1994, These Good Things, 1997. Mem. Am. Assn. Mus., Native Am. Art Studies Assn. (sec./treas. 1995—). Office: Portland Art Mus 1219 SW Park Ave Portland OR 97205-2486

MERCHANT, ROLAND SAMUEL, SR., hospital administrator, educator; b. N.Y.C., Apr. 18, 1929; s. Samuel and Eleta (McLymont) M.; m. Audrey Bartley, June 6, 1970; children: Orelia Eleta, Roland Samuel, Huey Bartley. BA, NYU, 1957, MA, 1960; MS, Columbia U., 1963, MSHA, 1974. Asst. statistician N.Y.C. Dept. Health, 1957-60, statistician, 1960-63; statistician N.Y. Tb and Health Assn., N.Y.C., 1963-65; biostatistician, adminstrv. coord. Inst. Surg. Studies, Montefiore Hosp., Bronx, N.Y., 1965-72; resident in adminstrn. Roosevelt Hosp., N.Y.C., 1973-74; dir. health and hosp. mgmt. Dept. Health, City of N.Y., 1974-76; from asst. adminstr. to adminstr. West Adams Cmty. Hosp., L.A., 1976; spl. asst. to assoc. v.p. for med. affairs Stanford U. Hosp., Calif., 1977-82, dir. office mgmt. and strategic planning, 1982-85, dir. mgmt. planning, 1986-90; v.p. strategic planning Cedars-Sinai Med. Ctr., L.A., 1990-94; cons. Roland Merchant & Assocs., L.A., 1994—; clin. assoc. prof. dept. family, community and preventive medicine Stanford U., 1986-88, dept. health rsch. and policy Stanford U. Med. Sch., 1988-90. With U.S. Army. 1951-53. USPHS fellow. Fellow Am. Coll. Healthcare Execs., APHA; mem. Am. Hosp. Assn., Nat. Assn. Health Svcs. Execs., N.Y. Acad. Scis. Home: 27335 Park Vista Rd Agoura Hills CA 91301-3639 Office: Roland Merchant & Assocs 27335 Park Vista Rd Agoura Hills CA 91301-3639

MERCURIO, EDWARD PETER, natural science educator; b. Orange, Calif., Dec. 28, 1944; s. Peter Amadeo and Jeanne (Monteleone) M.; m. Jeanne Roussel Gable, Oct. 18, 1980 (div. Dec. 1984); 1 child, Katherine Roussel; m. Patricia Ann Kahler, Apr. 12, 1987; children: Peter Edward, Rose Sierra. BA, UCLA, 1967, MA, 1970, CPhil, 1978. Research asst. UCLA, 1971, teaching asst., 1968-71; instructional assoc. Golden West Coll., Huntington Beach, Calif., 1972-73; cons. Monterey County Planning Dept., Salinas, Calif., 1980; prof. Hartnell Coll., Salinas, Calif., 1973—; photographer in field, Calif., 1961—; lectr. in field, Calif., 1970—; cons. in field, 1980—. Fellow Woodrow Wilson Nat. Fellowship Found., 1967. Mem. AAAS, Sierra Club. Democrat. Avocations: writing and performing original songs, hiking, backpacking, plant and animal breeding, mountain bicycle riding. Home: 647 Wilson St Salinas CA 93901-1346 Office: Hartnell Coll 156 Homestead Ave Salinas CA 93901-1628

MEREDITH, THOMAS KIRKPATRICK, publisher, inventor; b. L.A., Feb. 24, 1947; s. Corwyn Kirkpatrick and Carolyn Teresa (LaCava) M.; m. Angelita Villa Alvarez, Jan. 6, 1965 (div. June 1969); children: Thomas Kirkpatrick, Angela Hope. Student, Tushita/Tibetan Retreat Ctr., McCloud Gange, India, 1981, Bodhgaya (India) Stupa, 1981, Manjushri Inst., Ulverston, Eng., 1978-82. Ordained Buddhist monk, 1978-82. Publisher World Patriot Enterprises, Santa Cruz, Calif.; supporting actor Grad. Film Project/Wash. State U., Olympia, 1994; background specialist CBS TV movie Thrill, 1996. Author: Argosy, 1967; author/compiler series: Lust for Innocence, 1996; inventor power source, pub. safety device. Counsellor, Psychiat. Halfway House, Berkeley, Calif., 1972-73; mem. Santa Cruz County Intergroup, Capitola, Calif., 1996-98; co-founder/facilitator J.A.D.E. Ctr./Ataskadero (Calif.) State Hosp., 1974-76. Found. for the Preservation of the Mahayana Tradition scholar, Kathmandu, Nepal, 1978-82. Avocations: community television studio production, acting in community theater, collecting sculpture and statuary. Office: World Patriot Enterprises 322 Rigg St Ste 8 Santa Cruz CA 95060-3541

MERENDINO, K. ALVIN, surgical educator; b. Clarksburg, W.Va., Dec. 3, 1914; s. Biagio and Cira (Bivona) M.; m. Shirley Emojane Hill, July 6, 1943; children: Cira Anne Watts, Nancy Jane Napuunoa, Susan Hill Mitchell, Nina Merendino-Sarich, Maria King Merendino-Stillwell. BA, Ohio U., 1936, LLD (hon.), 1967; MD, Yale U., 1940; PhD, U. Minn., 1946. Diplomate Am. Bd. Surgery, Am. Bd. Thoracic Surgery. Intern Cin. Gen. Hosp., 1940-41; resident U. Minn. Hosp., Mpls., 1941-45; rsch. asst. Dr. Owen H. Wangensteen, 1942-43; trainee Nat. Cancer Inst., 1943-45; dir. program in postgrad. med. edn. in surgery Ancker Hosp., St. Paul, 1946-48; instr. dept. surgery U. Minn., Mpls., 1944-45, asst. prof. dept. surgery, 1945-48; assoc. prof. dept. surgery U. Wash., Seattle, 1949-55, dir. exptl. surgery labs., dept. surgery, 1950-72, prof. dept. surgery, 1955-81, prof. emeritus, 1981—, prof. and adminstrv. officer dept. surgery, 1957-64, prof., chmn., 1965-72; chmn. dept. surgery King Faisal Specialist and Rsch. Ctgr., Riyadh, Saudi Arabia, 1976, dir. med. affairs, 1976-79, dir. Cancer Therapy Inst., spl. cons. to Coun., supr. for exec. mgmt., assoc. dir. med. affairs, 1981-82; dir. ops. King Faisal Med. City, Riyadh, 1981-85; mem. adv. com. for med. rsch., Boeing Airplane Co., 1959-67, chmn., 1962l cons. Children's Orthopedic Hosp., Seattle, 1972-82; mem. adv. com. on heart disease and surgery for crippled children's svc., Wash. State Dept. Health and Div. Vocational Rehab., 1961; mem. surgery study sect. NIH, 1958-62, subcom. on prosthetic valves for cardiac surgery, chm. 1st Nat. Conf., 1960, mem. adv. com. 2d Nat. Conf. on Prosthetic Heart Valves, 1969, Surgery A study sect. chmn., 1970-72, Nat. Heart and Lung Inst. Tng. Com., 1965-69; cons. VA, Seattle, 1949-59, 65-81; mem. adv. com. on hosps. and clinics, USPHS, 1963-66; mem. surgery test com. Nat. Bd. Med. Examiners, 1963-67; mem. surgery resident rev. com., Conf. Com. on Grad. Edn. in Surgery, 1963-73, vice-chmn., 1972-73; chmn. 2d Saudi Arabian Med. Conf., Riyadh, 1978; mem. com. on postgrad. med. edn., Kingdom of Saudi Arabia Ministry of Health, 1978-79. Editor in chief: Prosthetic Valves for Cardiac Surgery, 1961; assoc. editor: Prosthetic Heart Valves, 1969; mem. editorial bd. Am. Jour. Surgery,. 1958-83, Jour. Surg. Rsch., 1961-69, Pacific Medicine and Surgery, 1964-68, King Faisal Hosp. Medicine Jour. (renamed Annals of Saudi Medicine), 1981-85; contbr. articles to profl. jours., chpts. to books; producer movies on surgery. Recipient cert. of merit Ohio U. Alumni Assn., 1957, Outstanding W.Va. Italian-Am. award W.Va. Italian Heritage Festival Inc., Clarksburg, W.Va., 1984, Spirit of Freedom award A. James Mancin, Sec. State W.Va., 1984, Disting. W. Virginian award State of W.Va., 1984, John Baird Thomas Meml. award Ohio U.; named Surgery Alumnus of Yr., U. Minn., 1981, Disting. Citizen Wash. State, Lt. Gov. John Cherberg, 1981; NIH grantee, 1951-76. Fellow ACS (numerous coms., bds.), Soc. of Univ. Surgeons (councilman at large 3 yrs.), Internat. Soc. Surgery; mem. Am. Surg. Assn. (adv. mem. com. 1959-64, v.p. 1972-73), Am. Assn. for Thoracic Surgery, Halsted Soc., Henry N. Harkins Surg. Soc., N. Pacific Coast Surg. Assn., Seattle Surg. Soc. (honored special tribute annual meeting 1997), So. Surg. Soc. (Arthur H. Shipley award 1972), Am. Bd. Surgery 1958-64 (vice chmn. 1962-63, chmn. 1963-64, emeritus 1964—); University Club, Seattle Golf Club, Phi Beta Kappa, Sigma Xi, Beta Theta Pi (sec., pres.), Phi Beta Pi (hon.). Republican. Episcopalian. Avocations: golf, fly fishing, bird hunting, gardening. Home: The Highlands Seattle WA 98177 Office: U Wash Sch Med Dept Surgery Seattle WA 98195

MERIAM, JAMES LATHROP, mechanical engineering educator; b. Columbia, Mo., Mar. 25, 1917; s. Junius Lathrop and Mary (Bone) M.; m. Julia Ellen Powers, Dec. 25, 1940; children: Mary Ellen Seitz Kaschub, Melissa Lee Bullard. B in Engring., Yale U., 1939, M in Engring., 1941, PhD, 1942. Registered mech. engr., Calif. Asst. instr. Yale U., 1940-42; with Pratt and Whitney Aircraft Co., summer 1940, Gen. Electric Co., summer 1942; mem. faculty U. Calif.-Berkeley, Berkeley, 1942-63, asst. dean grad. studies, 1952-56, prof. engring. mechanics, 1954-63, chmn. div. mechanics and design, 1959-61, chmn. faculty Coll. Engring, 1961-62; prof. engring. mech. Duke U., 1963-72, dir. research and devel., dean Sch. Engring., 1963-69; prof. mech. engring. Calif. Poly State U., San Luis Obispo, 1972-80; ret. Calif. Poly State U., 1980; vis. prof. U. Calif.-Santa Barbara, Santa Barbara, 1980-90; cons. in field, 1946—. Author: Mechanics, Part I, Statics, 2d edit., 1959, Mechanics, Part II, Dynamics, 2d edit., 1959, Dynamics, 1966, 2d edit., 1971, Statics, 1966, 2d edit., 1971, Statics SI-Version, Dynamics SI-Version, 1975, Engineering Mechanics, Vol. 1, Vol. 2, SI/English version, 1978, SI version, 1980, 2d edit., SI/English version, 1986 (with L.G. Kraige) SI version, 1987, 93, 97, SI/English version, 4th edit., 1997, also numerous papers. Lt. (j.g.) USCGR, 1944-45. Recipient award advancement basic and applied sci. Yale Engring. Assn., 1952, Outstanding Faculty award Tau Beta Pi, 1963. Fellow ASME (charter, life mem.), Am. Soc. Engring. Edn. (life mem., chmn. grad. studies divsn. 1959-60, mem. coun. 1960-63, chmn. mechanics divsn. 1974-75, Outstanding Svc. award Southeastern sect. 1975, Disting. Educator award 1978, Hon. Membership award 1982, Svc. award 1989, Lamme award 1992, Centennial medallion 1993); mem. Sigma Xi, Tau Beta Pi, Pi Tau Sigma. Home: 4312 Marina Dr Santa Barbara CA 93110-2434

MERIDITH, DENISE PATRICIA, government official; b. N.Y.C., Apr. 14, 1952; d. Glenarva C. and Dorothy (Sawyer) M. BS, Cornell U., 1973; MPA, USC, 1993. Various positions Bur. Land Mgmt., various locations, 1973-79, chief div. resources, Alexandria, Va., 1980-83, dep. state dir., 1983-86, dep. state dir. Santa Fe, 1986-89; assoc. state dir., Calif., 1989-91; state dir. Ea. States, 1991-93; dep. dir BLM, Washington, 1993-95, state dir. Ariz., 1995—. Pres. Greater Phoenix Black C. of C., Phoenix Black bd. dirs., Girl Scouts bd. dirs. Recipient Ray Gildea Conservation award Soil Conservation Service, 1972; Spl. Achievement award, Bur. Land Mgmt., 1980, Meritorious Service award Dept. Interior, 1987. Mem. Wildlife Soc. (cert.), Soc. Am. Foresters, Soc. Range Mgmt., Audobon Soc., Federally Employed Women, Nat. Assn. Female Execs., LWV, Cornell Coun. Avocations: photography, writing, art, movies, public speaking. Home: PO Box 7305 Phoenix AZ 85011-7305 Office: Bur Land Mgmt 222 N Central Ave Phoenix AZ 85004

MERING, JOHN VOLLMER, retired history educator; b. Kansas City, Mo., Feb. 21, 1931; s. Ray Delaplane and Clara F. (Vollmer) M.; m. Ellen Westfall, Oct. 24, 1954; children: Clay, Ellen Curtis, Margaret Vollmer, Sarah Rollins. BS in Edn., U. Mo., 1953, PhD in History, 1960. Assoc. prof. history U. Fla., Gainesville, 1960-66; assoc. prof. U. N.D., Grand Forks, 1966-69; prof. U. Ariz., Tucson, 1969-84, prof. emeritus, 1984—. Author: Whig Party in Missouri, 1967; contbr. articles to profl. publs. 1st lt. U.S. Army, 1954-56. Episcopalian. Home and Office: 1940 E Elm St Tucson AZ 85719-4326

MERK, ELIZABETH THOLE, investment company executive; b. Salt Lake City, July 29, 1950; d. John Bernard and Emily Josephine (Knotek) Thole; 1 child, William Lance Ulich; m. J. Eliot Merk, July 26, 1996. BA, U. Hawaii, Hilo, 1984, paralegal cert. cum laude, 1989; postgrad.in bus. administrn., U. Hawaii, Manoa, 1985-86. Lic. ins. agt. Hawaii; registered investment advisor, stock brokerage prin. Regional rep. Lightolier, Inc., Salt Lake City, 1978-80; group sales rep. FHP/Utah, Salt Lake City, 1980-81; health net rep. Blue Cross Corp., L.A., 1981-82; v.p. fin. Bus. Support Systems, Hilo, 1983-89; rep. Prudential Ins. and Fin. Svcs., Honolulu, 1989-97; registered rep. Pruco Securities Corp. subs. Prudential Ins. & Fin. Svcs., 1989-97; acct. exec. Dean Witter Reynolds, 1997-98; pres., CEO, registered prin. Elizabeth Merk Investments, 1998—; investment advisor, stockbroker. Docent Lyman House, 1984-85, L.A. County Mus. of Art, 1980-81, S.L.C. Art Mus., 1970-80; bd. dirs. YWCA, Hawaii Island, 1980-91, 1st v.p., 1988. Named YWCA Vol. of Yr., 1991; recipient Nat. Quality award 1991, 92, 93, 94, Nat. Sales Achievement award 1992, 93; Paul Harris fellow Rotary Internat., 1997. Fellow Life Underwriters Tng. Coun.; mem. AAUW (fundraiser chmn. Kona chpt. 1992, bd. dirs. Hilo chpt. 1987-89, cmty. area rep. 1989), Am. Bus. Women's Assn. (past pres. Nani O Hilo chpt. 1995-96, treas. 1997—, cmty. svc. chmn. 1993-95, membership chmn. 1996-97, audit com. chmn. 1997, audit com. chmn. Kanoelani chpt. 1992, program chmn. Hilo chpt. 1985, expansion com. Hilo Lehua chpt. 1985, Steven Bufton grantee 1985, ways and means com. 1984, memberships chmn. Lehua chpt. 1983, mem. Inner Circle 1997), Nat. Assn. Life Underwriters (legis. rep. West Hawaii 1995-97), Million Dollar Round Table (provisional mem. 1991, qualifying mem. 1992-95), Soroptimist (mem.-at-large). Roman Catholic.

MERRIGAN, MARY ELLEN, sales executive, radio station executive; b. Maryville, Mo., July 7, 1951; d. James Robert and Coletta Marie (Seipel) M. BA in Speech, Northwest Mo. State U., 1973. Account exec. Sta. WMKC Radio, Oshkosh, Wis., 1973-74, Sta. KHAK Radio, Cedar Rapids, Iowa, 1974-77; account exec. Sta. KARN Radio, Little Rock, 1977-79, sales mgr., 1979-80; account exec. Sta. KCKN Radio, Kansas City, Kans., 1980-81; account exec. Sta. KMJQ Radio, Houston, 1981-85, sales mgr., 1985-86, gen. sales mgr., 1986-88; broadcast sales cons. Merrigan Enterprises, Houston, 1988-89; v.p., gen. mgr. Sta. KKSS Radio, Albuquerque, 1989—; gen. mgr. Sta. KRQS Radio, 1998—, Sta. KDZZ Radio, 1998—; bd. dirs., West Corp., 1993-97; part-owner SignPro of N.Mex., 1995—, Great Locations, 1996—. Bd. dirs. YMCA, 1990-94; hostess Leukemia Soc. Celebrity Waiters Luncheon, 1991, 92; vice chair YMCA, 1994. Named Vol. of Yr., Met. YMCA Bd., 1992. Mem. NAT, N.Mex. Mus. Natural History, Albuquerque Radio Broadcasters Assn. (chair), N.Mex. Broadcasters Assn. (pres.). Avocations: bicycling, reading, needlepoint. Office: Sta KKSS Radio 5301 Central Ave NE Ste 1200 Albuquerque NM 87108-1517

MERRILL, DEAN ROGER, publishing executive; b. L.A., Dec. 17, 1943; s. Raymond and Mary (Frantz) M.; m. Grace L. Danielson, June 25, 1966; children: Nathan, Rhonda, Tricia. B in Theology, Chgo. Bible Coll., 1964; MA, Syracuse U., 1970. Ordained to ministry Fellowship of Christian Assemblies, 1965. Various editorial positions Campus Life Mag., Wheaton, Ill., 1965-69, 71-73; dir. univ. info. Oral Roberts U., Tulsa, Okla., 1970-71; exec. editor Creation House Pubs., Carol Stream, Ill., 1973-74; various editorial positions David C. Cook. Pub. Co., Elgin, Ill., 1974-81; sr. editor Leadership Jour., Carol Stream, 1981-85; editor, v.p. Christian Herald Mag., Chappaqua, N.Y., 1985-89; v.p. periodicals Focus on the Family, Colorado Springs, Colo., 1989-96; v.p., pub. Internat. Bible Soc., Colorado Springs, 1997—. Author: The God Who Won't Let Go, 1998, Sinners in the Hands of an Angry Church, 1997. Mem. Evangelical Press Assn. (pres. 1985-87). Avocation: music. Office: Internat Bible Soc 1820 Jet Stream Dr Colorado Springs CO 80921-3618

MERRILL, THOMAS M., produce executive; b. 1929. With Merrill Farms, 1945—, now pres., CEO. Office: Merrill Farms PO Box 659 1067 Merrill St Salinas CA 93902*

MERRILL, THOMAS ST. JOHN, medical photographer; b. Jersey City, N.J., Feb. 21, 1946; s. Willard St. John and Frances Minnie (Havlieck) M.; m. Marie Knoetig, Mar. 19, 1967; children: Monica Marie-Rose, Michelle St. John. Student, Fairleigh Dickenson U., 1963-64, Germain Sch. Photography, 1967-68; AA, Saddleback Coll., 1990; student, Mt. San Antonio Coll., 1990-92; BS in Bus. Adminstrn., U. Phoenix, 1995. Cert. retinal angiographer. Photography asst. VA Hosp., N.Y.C., 1968; dept. head, photography Manhatten Eye, Ear and Throat Hosp., N.Y.C., 1968-69; med. photographer Don Allen Studio, N.Y.C., 1969-71; sr. ophthalmic photographer Mt. Sinai Sch. Medicine, N.Y.C., 1971-76; ophthalmic photographer U. Calif., Irvine, 1976-86; photographer Allergan Inc., Irvine, 1986-89; owner, pres. The Med. Image, Chino, Calif., 1983—; sr. med. photographer Providence St. Joseph Med. Ctr., Burbank, Calif., 1991—. Mem. Luth. Hour Rose Float Com., Pasadena, Calif. With U.S. Army, 1964-67, Vietnam. Mem. Biol. Photographic Assn. (fellow 1991, chmn. so. Calif. chpt. 1990-92), Ophthalmic Photographers' Soc., VFW (life), AMVETS. Avocations: Rose parade float operator. Home: 4395 Goldenrod Ct Chino CA 91710-1618 Office: Saint Joseph Med Ctr 501 S Buena Vista St Burbank CA 91505-4809

MERRIM, LOUISE MEYEROWITZ, artist, actress; b. N.Y.C.; d. Leo and Jeanette (Harris) Meyerowitz; m. Lewis Jay Merrim, June 27, 1948; children: Stephanie, Andrea Merrim Goff (dec.). BFA, Pratt Inst., 1947; MFA, Columbia U., 1951; postgrad., Post Coll., 1971-72, New Sch., 1977-78. Art tchr. pub. schs., N.Y.C., 1947-51, Port Washington, N.Y., 1970-83. One-woman shows include Plandome Gallery, L.I., Isis Gallery, N.Y., San Diego art Inst., Pan Pacific Hotel, San Diego; exhibited in group shows at Nassau County Fine Arts Mus. (Bronze award), Heckscher Mus. (Nora Mirmont award), Nat. Acad., Nat. Assn. Women Artists (Medal of Honor, Charlotte Whinston award), Audubon Artists (Stephen Hirsch Meml. award), Cork

Gallery, Warner Comm. Gallery, L.I. Art Tchrs. (two awards of excellence), L.I. Art Tchrs. Award Winners Show, Pt. Washington Libr. Invitational, Glen Cove (2nd prize), Manhasset Art Assn. (best in show, five 1st prizes), San Diego Art Inst., San Diego Mus. Art (Gold award), Oceanside Mus. Art, Hank Baum Gallery, San Francisco, Tarbox Gallery, Clark Gallery, Knowles Gallery, San Diego, Golden Pacific Arts Gallery, San Diego, Henry Chastain Gallery, Scottsdale; appeared in numerous theatrical prodns. including Fiddler on the Roof, Barefoot in the Park, N.Y., Anything Goes, The Musical Comedy Murders of 1940, Anastasia (Drama award), Fiddler on the Roof, The Music Man, What's Wrong With this Picture?, Marvin's Room, San Diego, The Foreigner; dir. Under Milkwood; dir., appeared in Spoon River Anthology. Mem. Nat. Assn. Women Artists, N.Y. Soc. of Women Artists, Contemporary Artists Guild of N.Y., Audubon Artist (N.Y.), San Diego Art Inst., Artists Guild of San Diego Art Mus. (pres. 1993), Artists Equity, Actors Alliance. Avocations: tennis, poetry, travel. Home: 3330 Caminito Vasto La Jolla CA 92037-2929

MERRING, ROBERT ALAN, lawyer; b. Middletown, N.Y., Oct. 5, 1951; s. Merton Joseph and Mabel Ruth M.; m. Lynn S. Connor, Mar. 16, 1996. Student, Ohio Wesleyan U., 1969-70; A.B. with distinction and dept. honors, Stanford U., 1973; JD in Internat. and Fgn. Law with honors, Columbia U., 1977; cert. Pepperdine Sch. Law, Inst. for Dispute Resolution, 1996. Bar: Calif. 1977, U.S. Dist. Ct. (cen. dist.) Calif. 1978, U.S. Dist. Ct. (so. and ea. dists.) Calif. 1980, U.S. Ct. Appeals (9th cir.) 1980, U.S. Dist. Ct. (no. dist.) Calif. 1983, U.S. Supreme Ct. 1987, Colo. 1989. Assoc. Pacht, Ross, Warne, Bernhard & Sears, Inc., L.A., 1977-79, Donovan Leisure Newton & Irvine, L.A., 1979-81, Cutler and Cutler, L.A., 1983-88, Friedemann & Hart, Irvine, 1988-89; pvt. practice Newport Beach and Irvine, Calif., 1989—; mem. San Diego-Orange County Am. Arbitration Assn. panel comml. arbitrators, 1993—; civil arbitrator, judge pro tem Orange County Superior Ct., 1993—; mediator U.S. Bankruptcy Ct. (ctrl. dist.) Calif., 1996—; mediator Orange County Superior Ct., 1998—; clin. prof. Loyola U. Law Sch., Los Angeles, 1981-82. Editor Columbia Jour. Transnat. Law, 1976-77. Columbia U. Internat. fellow, 1975-76. Mem. ABA, Orange County Bar Assn., Assn. Bus. Trial Lawyers, Internat. Trademark Assn., Am. Arbitration Assn., State Bar of Calif. (del. 1998—). Home: 1300 Park Newport Apt 217 Newport Beach CA 92660-5031

MERSEL, MARJORIE KATHRYN PEDERSEN, lawyer; b. Manila, Utah, June 17, 1923; d. Leo Henry and Kathryn Anna (Reed) Pedersen; AB, U. Calif., 1948; LLB, U. San Francisco, 1948; m. Jules Mersel, Apr. 12, 1950; 1 son, Jonathan. Admitted to D.C. bar, 1952, Calif. bar, 1955; Marjorie Kathryn Pedersen Mersel, atty., Beverly Hills, Calif., 1961-71; staff counsel Dept. Real Estate State of Calif., Los Angeles, 1971—. Active L.A.-Guangzhou Sister City. Mem. Beverly Hills Bar Assn., L.A. County Bar Assn., Trial Lawyers Assn., So. Calif. Women Lawyers Assn. (treas. 1962-63), L.A.-Guangzhou Sister City Assn., Beverly Hills C. of C., World Affairs Coun., Current Affairs Forum, L.A. Athletic Club, Sierra Club. Home: 13007 Hartsook St Sherman Oaks CA 91423-1616 Office: Dept Real Estate 107 S Broadway Ste 8107 Los Angeles CA 90012-4671

MERTA, PAUL JAMES, cartoonist, photographer, engineer, restauranteur, real estate developer; b. Bakersfield, Calif., July 16, 1939; s. Stanley Franklin and Mary Ann (Herman) M.; AA, Bakersfield Jr. Coll., 1962; BS in Engring., San Jose State Coll., 1962. Cartoonist nat. mags., 1959—; civilian electronics engr. Air Force/Missiles, San Bernardino, Calif., 1962-65; electronics countermeasures engr., acquisition program mgr. Air Logistics Command, Sacramento, 1965-90; ret.; TV film, video animator, producer, owner Merge Films, 1965—; photographer, owner The Photo Poster Factory, Sacramento, 1971—; owner restaurant La Rosa Blanca, Sacramento, 1979-91; ptnr. Kolinski and Merta Hawaiian Estates, 1981—; polit. cartoonist Calif. Jour., 1958-59, Sacramento Union Newspaper, 1974-94, Sacramento Legal Jour., 1979. Home: 1965 3rd Ave Sacramento CA 95818-3003 Office: 1005 12th St Sacramento CA 95814-3920

MESCHKOW, JORDAN MARK, patent lawyer; b. Bklyn., Mar. 25, 1957; s. Gerald Meschkow and Florence Y. (Katz) Silverman; m. Susan G. Scher, Aug. 10, 1980; children: Sasha Hayley, Alisha Sadie. BS in Biology, SUNY, Stony Brook, 1979; JD, Chgo. Kent Coll. Law, 1982. Bar: Ariz. 1982, Fla. 1983; registered U.S. Patent and Trademark Office 1983. Assoc. James F. Duffy, Patent Atty., Phoenix, Ariz., 1982; ptnr. Duffy & Meschkow, Phoenix, 1983-84; sole practice Phoenix, 1984-92; sr. ptnr. Meschkow & Gresham, Plc., Phoenix, 1992—; frequent talk radio guest and spkr. at seminars on patent, trademark and copyright law. Contbr. article series to profl. jours.; patentee in field. Exec. bd. City of Phoenix Fire Pub. Awareness League, 1996—. Mem. Am. Intellectual Property Law Assn., State Bar Ariz. (intellectual property sect. 1982—), State Bar Fla. Avocations: gardening, motorcycling, bicycling, skating, swimming. E-mail: M&Gpatent@mcimail.com. Office: 5727 N 7th St Ste 409 Phoenix AZ 85014-5818

MESLOH, WARREN HENRY, civil and environmental engineer; b. Deshler, Nebr., Mar. 17, 1949; s. Herbert Frederick and Elna Florence (Petersen) M.; m. Barbara Jane Anderson, Sept. 7, 1969; children: Christopher Troy, Courtney James. BS, U. Kans., 1975; postgrad., Kans. State U., 1976-77. Registered profl. engr. Colo., Kans., Nebr.; cert. expert witness Am. Consulting Engrs. Coun. Project mgr. Wilson & Co. Engrs., Salina, Kans., 1975-80, process design dir., 1980-82; engring. dir. Taranto, Stanton & Tagge, Fort Collins, Colo., 1982-85; pres. The Engring. Co., Fort Collins, Colo., 1985—; mem. civil engring. adv. bd. Kans. U., Lawrence, 1982—. Contbg. author (book) Pumping Station Design, 1989, (water pollution control manual) Manual of Practice No. OM-2, 1991, ACEC Certified Exper Witness, 1996; contbr. articles to profl. jours. Cub master Boy Scouts Am., Salina, 1980-81; active Luth. Ch., 1982—; vol. Paralyzed Vets. Orgn., Fort Collins, 1985—; pres. Foothills Green Pool Assn., Fort Collins, 1987-88. Sgt. U.S. Army, 1971-73, Germany. Named Outstanding Engr.-In-Tng. NSPE, 1978. Mem. Am. Pub. Works Assn., Am. Water Works Assn., Water Pollution Control Fedn., Fort Collins Country Club. Republican. Avocations: golf, boating, snow skiing. Office: The Engring Co 2310 E Prospect Rd Fort Collins CO 80525-9770

MESSER, ANGELA, systems development executive; b. Hartlepool, Eng., Dec. 29, 1960; came to U.S., 1991; d. Andrew and Marguerite Thornton (Bruce) M.; Richard John Burdett, Aug. 16, 1986 (div. 1988); m. Gregory Gene Weinman, Feb. 24, 1994. BS with honors in Computation, U. Manchester, Eng., 1983. Computer programmer Brit. Steel Corp., Redcar, Eng., 1979-80; analyst programmer Internat. Computers Ltd., Bracknell, Eng., 1983-85; systems analyst Visa Internat., London, 1985-88, supr. systems devel., 1988-91; project mgr. Visa Internat., San Mateo, Calif., 1991-92; bus. mgr. Visa Internat., San Mateo, 1992-94, dir., 1994-95, v.p. clearing and settlement, 1995-96, sr. v.p. clearing and settlement applications devel., 1996—. Mem. NAFE, Mensa. Avocations: gardening, golf, skiing, classical music. Home: 2100 Coronet Blvd Belmont CA 94002-1619 Office: Visa Internat PO Box 8999 San Francisco CA 94128-8999

MESSINGER, CORA R., funeral director; b. Chickasha, Okla., Sept. 28, 1930; d. George Franklin and Addie (Jewett) Ross; m. Paul R. Messinger, Nov. 23, 1950;children: H. Kendrick, David William. Student, U. Ariz., 1957. Asst. control records dept. Valley Nat. Bank, Phoenix, 1948-50; engring. coord. Air Rsch. Mfg., Phoenix, 1954-56; owner Messinger Mortuary and Chapel, Scottsdale, Ariz., 1959—; owner, corp. sec., treas. Messinger Ins. Agy., Inc., Scottsdale, 1985—. Rep. dist. chmn., Scottsdale and East Phoenix, 1964-69; mem. Scottsdale Meml. Hosp. Aux., 1961—, YMCA bd., 1972-80, Scottsdale Indian Art bd., 1962-68. Mem. Boyce Thomson Arboretum, Desert Bot. Gardens, Arizona Club, Phoenix Art Mus., USTA. Republican. Roman Catholic. Avocations: tennis, gardening, Western art. Office: Messinger Mortuary Inc 7601 E Indian School Rd Scottsdale AZ 85251-3607

MESSINGER, J. HENRY, lawyer; b. N.Y.C., Sept. 7, 1944; s. Benjamin and Edna (Balser) M.; m. Karen Gilbert D'Abo, Feb. 5, 1977 (div.); 1 child, Alan Toby. BA, Union Coll., 1965, JD, NYU, 1968, MA in Edn., 1969, MA in Polit. Sci., U. N.Mex. 1996. Bar: N.Y. 1968, N.Mex. 1973, U.S. Tax Ct. 1973. Pvt. practice, Woodstock, N.Y., 1970-72; assoc. Stephen Natelson, Esq., Taos, 1972-73; ptnr. Natelson & Messinger, Taos, 1974-75; pvt. practice, Taos, 1976-94, Albuquerque, 1994—. Bd. dirs. Taos Sch. Music, 1982-97, R.C. Gorman Found., 1986—; bd. dirs. Taos Valley Sch., 1979-82, pres. 1980-81. Mem. ABA, Am. Polit. Sci. Assn., Law and Soc. Assn. Office: 809 Branding Iron St SE Albuquerque NM 87123-4207

MESSMER, HAROLD MAXIMILIAN, JR., financial services executive; b. Jackson, Miss., Feb. 20, 1946; s. Harold Maximilian and Margaret (Dee) M.; m. Marcia Elizabeth Nesmith, Apr. 5, 1973; children: Michael Christopher, Matthew Gordon. A.B. summa cum laude, Loyola U., 1967; J.D. cum laude, NYU, 1970. Ptnr. corp. law and securities O'Melveny & Myers, Los Angeles, 1970-81; sr. v.p., gen. counsel Pacific Holding Corp., Los Angeles, 1981-82; pres., chief operating officer Pacific Holding Corp., 1982-85; pres., dir., chief operating officer Cannon Mills Co. (subs.), Kannapolis, N.C., 1982-85; chmn., dir. Castle & Cook Inc., San Francisco, 1985; chmn., pres., chief exec. officer Robert Half Internat. Inc., San Francisco, 1985—; dir. Nat. Bank N.C., Charlotte; adj. prof. Claremont Grad. Sch. Bus.(exec. mgmt. program), 1979-82; bd. dirs. Health Care Property Investors, Los Angeles, BF Enterprises Inc., N.C. Nat. Bank, Charlotte. Trustee Davidson (N.C.) Coll., 1984—; appointee Pres. Reagan's Adv. Com. on Trade Negotiations, 1985-87. Served with USAR, 1971-75. Mem. ABA, Los Angeles County Bar Assn., Calif. Bar Assn. Served with USAR, 1971-75. Office: Robert Half Internat Inc 2884 Sand Hill Rd Ste 200 Menlo Park CA 94025-7059

METCALF, JACK, congressman, retired state senator; b. Marysville, Wash., Nov. 30, 1927; s. John Read and Eunice (Grannis) M.; m. Norma Jean Grant, Oct. 3, 1948; children: Marta Jean, Gayle Marie, Lea Lynn, Beverlee Ann. Student U. Wash., 1944-45, 47; BA, BEd, Pacific Luth. U., 1951. Tchr., Elma (Wash.) pub. schs., 1951-52, Everett (Wash.) pub schs., 1952-81; mem. Wash. Ho. of Reps., 1960-64; mem. Wash. Senate, 1966-74, 80-92, U.S. congressman, 106th Congress 2nd Dist., Washington, 1995—; chmn. environment and natural resources com., 1988-92; mem. domestic & internat. monetary policy, fin. instns. & consumer credit, aviation, surface transp. coms. Chmn. Honest Money for Am. Mem. Council State Govts., Wash. Edn. Assn. (dir. 1959-61), Wash. Assn. Profl. Educators (state v.p. 1979-81, state pres. 1977-79). Mem. Nat. Conf. State Legislatures, Western States Recycling Coalition, South Whidbey Kiwanis, Deer Lagoon Grange. Republican. Home: 3273 E Saratoga Rd Langley WA 98260-9694 Office: US House Reps 1510 Longworth Bldg Washington DC 20515-4702*

METCALF, RICHARD LEE, computer consultant; b. Phillippi, W.Va., Sept. 21, 1946; s. Henry DeForest and Ruth Amy (Gardner) M.; m. Sandra Kay Williamson (div. Aug. 1985); 1 child, Arthur Lynn; m. Kin Wolson Kim, Nov. 22, 1985; 1 child, Andrew Jackson. AA, Columbia Coll., 1980. Asst. project mgr. Comarco, Inc., Petersburg, Va., 1988-95; system adminstr. Mashell Telecom, Eatonville, Wash., 1996-97; tech. cons. Wash. State Libr., Olympia, 1997—. Prodr. music products, 1970—, Exptl. Music Fest, 1996—. With U.S. Army, 1964-88. Avocations: poetry, music. Home: 5308 65th Ave SE Lacey WA 98513-5007 Office: Washington State Libr 4224 6th Ave SE Lacey WA 98503-1024

METCALF, VIRGIL ALONZO, economics educator; b. Branch, Ark., Jan. 4, 1936; s. Wallace Lance and Luella J. (Yancey) M.; m. Janice Ann Maples, July 2, 1958; children: Deborah Ann, Robert Alan. BS in Gen. Agr., U. Ark., 1958, MS in Agrl. Econs., 1960; Diploma in Econs., U. Copenhagen, 1960; PhD in Agrl. Econs., U. Mo., 1964. Asst. prof. U. Mo., Columbia, 1964-65, asst. to chancellor, 1964-69, assoc. prof., 1965-69, prof., exec. asst. to the chancellor, 1969-71; prof. econs., v.p. adminstrn. Ariz. State U., Tempe, 1971-81, prof. Sch. Agribus. and Natural Resources, 1981-88, prof. internat. bus. Coll. of Bus., 1988—; asst. to the chancellor U. Mo., 1964-69, coord. internat. programs and studies, 1965-69, mem. budget com., 1965-71, chmn., co-chmn. several task forces; cons. Ford Found., Bogota, Colombia, 1966-67; mem. negotiating team U.S. Agy. for Internat. Devel., Mauritania, 1982, cons., Cameroon, 1983, agrl. rsch. specialist, India, 1984, agribus. cons., Guatemala, 1987, 88, asst. dir. Reform Coops. Credit Project, El Salvador, 1987-90; co-dir. USIA univ. linkage grant Cath. U., Bolivia, 1984-89; cons. World Vision Internat., Mozambique, 1989. Contbr. numerous articles to profl. jours. Mem. City of Tempe U. Hayden Butte Project Area Com., 1979; bd. commrs. Columbia Redevel. Authority; mem. workable project com. City of Columbia Housing Authority. Econs. officer USAR, 1963, econ. analyst, 1964-66. Fulbright grantee U. Copenhagen, 1959-60, U. Kiril Metodij, Yugoslavia, 1973. Mem. Am. Assn. Agrl. Economists, Soc. for Internat. Devel., Samaritans (chmn. 1976, bd. dirs. 1976, mem. task force of health svc. bd. trustees 1974, health svc. 1974-78, chmn. program subcom. 1975), Kiwanis, Blue Key, Gamma Sigma Delta, Alpha Zeta, Alpha Tau Alpha. Democrat. Home: 1357 W Crystal Springs Dr Gilbert AZ 85233-6606 Office: Ariz State U Coll Bus Tempe AZ 85287

METCALF, WAYNE C., insurance commissioner; m. Shirley Umada Metcalf. BA in Polit. Sci., U. Hawaii, 1975; JD, 1978; student, Tufts U., 1992-93. Atty. pvt. practice, 1979—; spl. cons. UN, 1994; ins. commr. Dept. Commerce and Consumer Affairs State Hawaii, 1994-97, 99—; staff Senate Jud. Com., 1973-75; staff dir. Senate Pres.'s Office, 1975-78; vice-chmn. House Com. on Jud., 1984-86; chmn. House Com. on Jud., 1986-92;; mem. house coms. Comsuner Protection and Commerce, 1984-92, Land Use and Hawaiian Affairs Plannong, 1984-86, Labor and Pub. Employment Transp., 1985-88, Housing, Health Humand Svcs, 1988-90, Housing, Health, 1990-92. Recipient Disting. Alumni award U. hawaii, 1988, Disting. Legislator award, Nat. Dem. State LEgis. Leaders Assn., 1988; named one of Hawaii's five best legislators by polit. columnist Dan Boylan, 1990, 92. Office: Insurance Divsn Dept Commerce and Consumer Affairs PO Box 3614 250 S King St Fl 5 Honolulu HI 96811-4505*

METHVIN, W(ARREN) NEAL, JR., court administrator; b. Laramie, Wyo., Apr. 22, 1947; s. Warren Neal and Lela Mae (Hardy) M.; m. Dorothy Marie McConnell, June 29, 1973 (div.); m. Linda Carol Attaway, Feb. 23, 1980; 1 child, Melissa Lieann. AS, Chaffee Coll., Alta Loma, Calif., 1971; MS, San Diego State U., 1975; ThD (hon.), Universal Life Ch., Modesto, Calif., 1976. Supervising clk. Office of County Clk., San Diego, 1978-80; adminstrv. asst. San Diego Superior Ct., 1980-82, chief dep. jury commr., 1982-96, coord. jury svcs., 1996—. Mem. exec. bd. County Employees Charitable Orgn., San Diego, 1982—; pres. Homeowners Assn., San Diego, 1989-95. Sgt. U.S. Army, 1967-69. Mem. Nat. Assn. Trial Ct. Adminstrs., Pub. Employees Bowling Assn. (pres. 1985-89). Republican. Baptist. Avocations: reading, tennis, bowling. Office: San Diego Superior Ct 330 W Broadway San Diego CA 92101-3825

METLTZOFF, NANCY JEAN, education educator; b. N.Y.C., Mar. 26, 1952; d. Julian and Judith (Novikoff) M.; children: Kimberly, Adam, Jesse Buckingham. PhD, U. Oreg. Coord. Super Summer Program, Eugene, Oreg., 1989; dir. Starts Program, Eugene, 1990-91; asst. prof. of edn. Willamette U., Salem, Oreg., 1991-93; coord. grad. program, asst. prof. edn. Pacific U., Eugene, 1994—. Author: (novel) A Sense of Balance, 1978. Mem. Am. Edn. Rsch. Assn., Educators for Social Responsibility. Avocation: dance. Office: Pacific U 40 E Broadway Eugene OR 97401-3135

METOYER, JOSEP PHANOR, JR., minister, marketing executive; b. Natchitoches, La., Sept. 24, 1948; s. Joseph Phanor Sr. and Velma Veronica (Conant) M.; m. Beverly Jean McKillian, Nov. 26, 1977; children: David, Monica, Fred, Nicol, Sharyl. BS, Biola U., 1994. Ordained to ministry Virginia Islands Bapt. Mission., Inc. Account exec. KABC TV, Hollywood, Calif., KABC Radio, L.A., KMPC Radio, Hollywood; coop. sales dir. KFWB Radio, Hollywood; sports sales dir. KFI Radio, L.A., Nederlander Sports Mktg., L.A.; pres., CEO KLM Sports, Santa Monica, Calif.; mem. adv. bd. Santa Monica C.C., 1996—, Ctr. for Healthy Aging, Santa Monica, 1997—. Mem. West Side Mins. Alliance, Santa Monica, 1995—; historian Western State Bapt. Conv., L.A., 1996—; dir. adv. bd. YMCA Santa Monica, 1997—. Recipient Leadership award County L.A., 1995, Spritual Leader award League United Latin Assn., 1998. Mem. Congress Christian Edn. (Ctrl. Dist. Assn. pres. 1997—), Rotary (Santa Monica dir. 1997—, Outstanding Leader 1998). Democrat. Avocation: fishing. Home: 2430 Cloverfield Blvd Santa Monica CA 90405-1825 Office: Calvary Bapt Ch 1502 20th St Santa Monica CA 90404-3176

METSKER, THOMAS CHARLES, map company executive; b. Tacoma, May 24, 1927; s. Charles Thomas and Emily Rose (Fleming) M.; m. Patricia Jeanne Rossiter; children: Mark F., Thad C., Kimberly J., Ty Thomas. BA in Bus., U. Puget Sound, 1951. Pres. Metsker Map Co., Tacoma, 1942—. Del. Wash. state convs. Rep. Party, 1960-70. With USN, 1945-47. Roman Catholic. Avocations: hunting, fishing, golf, skiing. Home: 3012 N Narrows Dr Unit 6 Tacoma WA 98407-1556 Office: Metsker Map Co 9616 40th Ave SW Tacoma WA 98499-4302

METTE, JOE, museum director. Dir. California State Capitol Mus., Sacramento, Calif.; dist. supt. pks. and recreation dist. office San Luis Obispo (Calif.) Coast Dist., 1998—. Office: Pks and Recreation Dist Office 3220 S Higuera St Ste 311 San Luis Obispo CA 93401*

METZ, MARY SEAWELL, university dean, retired college president; b. Rockhill, S.C., May 7, 1937; d. Columbus Jackson and Mary (Dunlap) Seawell; m. F. Eugene Metz, Dec. 21, 1957; 1 dau., Mary Eugena. BA summa cum laude in French and English, Furman U., 1958; postgrad., Institut Phonetique, Paris, 1962-63, Sorbonne, Paris, 1962-63; PhD magna cum laude in French, La. State U., 1966; HHD (hon.), Furman U., 1984; LLD (hon.), Chapman Coll., 1985; DLT (hon.), Converse Coll., 1988. Instr. French La. State U., 1965-66, asst. prof., 1966-67, 1968-72, assoc. prof., 1972-76, dir. elem. and intermediate French programs, 1966-74, spl. asst. to chancellor, 1974-75, asst. to chancellor, 1975-76; prof. French Hood Coll., Frederick, Md., 1976-81, provost, dean acad. affairs, 1976-81; pres. Mills Coll., Oakland, Calif., 1981-90; dean of extension U. Calif., Berkeley, 1991-98; ret., 1998; pres. S.H. Cowell Found., San Fransisco, 1999—; vis. asst. prof. U. Calif.-Berkeley, 1967-68; mem. commn. on leadership devel. Am. Coun. on Edn., 1981-90, adv. coun. Stanford Rsch. Inst., 1985-90, adv. coun. Grad. Sch. Bus., Stanford U.; assoc. Gannett Ctr. for Media Studies, 1985—; bd. dirs. PG&E, Pacific Telesis, PacTel & PacBell, Union Bank, Longs Drug Stores, S.H. Cowell Found. Author: Reflets du monde francais, 1971, 78, Cahier d'exercices: Reflets du monde francais, 1972, 78, (with Helstrom) Le Francais a decouvrir, 1972, 78, Le Francais a vivre, 1972, 78, Cahier d'exercices: Le Francais a vivre, 1972, 78; standardized tests; mem. editorial bd.: Liberal Edn., 1982—. Trustee Am. Conservatory Theater. NDEA fellow, 1960-62, 1963-64; Fulbright fellow, 1962-63; Am. Council Edn. fellow, 1974-75. Mem. Western Coll. Assn. (v.p. 1982-84, pres. 1984-86), Assn. Ind. Calif. Colls. and Univs. (exec. com. 1982-90), Nat. Assn. Ind. Colls. and Univs. (govt. rels. adv. coun. 1982-85), So. Conf. Lang. Teaching (chmn. 1976-77), World Affairs Coun. No. Calif. (bd. dirs. 1984-93), Bus.-Higher Edn. Forum, Women's Forum West, Women's Coll. Coalition (exec. com. 1984-88), Phi Kappa Phi, Phi Beta Kappa. Address: PO Box 686 Stinson Beach CA 94970-0686 also: 9 Regulus Ct Alameda CA 94501 Office: SH Cowell Found 120 Montgomery St San Francisco CA 94102

METZ, STEVEN WILLIAM, small business owner; b. Inglewood, Calif., Nov. 30, 1946; s. Glenn Ludwig and Kathleen Martha (Peterson) M.; m. Michelle Marie McArthur, Aug. 11, 1989; 1 child, Glenn Christian. Student, Fullerton Coll., Calif. Supt. Oahu Interiors, Honolulu, 1969-71, Hackel Bros., Miami, Fla., 1971-73; exec. v.p. Tru-Cut Inc., Brea, Calif., 1974-82; gen. mgr. The Louvre', Grass Valley, Calif., 1983-85; mfg. engring. mgr. Rexnord Aerospace, Torrance, Calif., 1986-87; pres., founder Metz/Calcoa Inc., Torrance, Calif., 1987—; mfg. rep. consul Orange County Spring, Anaheim, 1987—, TALSCO, 1994—, Precision Resources, 1994—, GEMTECH, 1994—; mfg. rep. consul Alard Machine Products, Gardena, Calif., 1988—, v.p. spl. projects, 1997—. Charter mem. Rep. Presdl. Task Force, 1991—; mem. L.A. Coun. on World Affairs, 1991-92. With U.S. Army, 1966-68. Recipient Appreciation awards DAV, 1968, Soc. Mfg. Engrs., 1991. Fellow Soc. Carbide Engrs.; mem. Soc. Carbide and Tool Engrs. (chpt. pres. 1980-82, Appreciation award 1981), Rep. Presdl. Legion of Merit. Avocations: golf, swimming, riding, boating.

METZKER, GARY HOWARD, executive news editor; b. Phila., Nov. 23, 1953; s. Raymond and Nanette (Baider) M. BA in Journalism, U. Mo., 1976. Sports writer Wilmington (Del.) News Jour., 1973-76; sports writer, copy editor Columbia (Mo.) Daily Tribune, 1976-77; sports news editor Clearwater (Fla.) Sun, 1977-79, Fla. Times Union, Jacksonville, 1979-81; asst. sports editor L.A. Herald Examiner, 1981-83; sports news editor Long Beach (Calif.) Press Telegram, 1983-84; exec. news editor, sports editor, metro news editor L.A. Times, 1984—. Recipient Best Layouts Daily, Sunday, Special Section award AP Sports Editors, 1976, 77, 78, 85, 86, 87, Best Layouts Headlines award L.A. Press Club, 1981, 86, 91, 97, Mem. Staff Spot News Pulitzer prize Columbia U., N.Y., 1992, 94, 97. Mem. Aerobics Fitness Assn. Am. Jewish. Avocations: teaching aerobics. Office: Los Angeles Times Times Mirror Square Los Angeles CA 90053

METZNER, RICHARD JOEL, psychiatrist, psychopharmacologist, educator; b. L.A., Feb. 15, 1942; s. Robert Gerson and Esther Rebecca (Groper) M.; children: Jeffrey Anthony, David Jonathan; m. Leila Kirkley, June 26, 1993. BA, Stanford U., 1963; MD, Johns Hopkins U., 1967. Intern, Roosevelt Hosp., N.Y.C., 1967-68; resident in psychiatry Stanford U. Med. Center, 1968-71; staff psychiatrist div. manpower and tng. NIMH-St. Elizabeths Hosp., Washington, 1971-73; chief audiovisual edn. system VA Med. Center Brentwood, L.A., 1973-79, chmn. VA Dist. 26 Edn. Task Force, 1976-78; asst. prof. psychiatry UCLA Neuropsychiat. Inst., 1973-80, assoc. clin. prof., 1980-96, clin. prof., 1996—, lectr. Sch. Social Welfare, 1975-84; pvt. practice medicine specializing in psychiatry, Bethesda, Md., 1972-73, L.A., 1973—, Sedona, Ariz., 1997—; dir. Western Inst. Psychiatry, L.A., 1977—; pres. Psychiat. Resource Network, Inc., 1984-90; Served with USPHS, 1968-71. Recipient 6 awards for film and videotape prodns., 1976-80; diplomate Am. Bd. Psychiatry and Neurology (cons. 1974-78, producer audiovisual exam. programs 1975-77). Fellow Am. Psychiat. Assn.; mem. So. Calif. Psychiat. Soc., Mental Health Careerists Assn. (chmn. 1972-73), Phi Beta Kappa. Democrat. Jewish. Contbr. numerous articles to profl. publs., 1963—; producer, writer numerous films and videotapes, 1970—.

MEUNIER, ROBERT RAYMOND, research electrical engineer, optical engineer; b. Hollywood, Calif., Mar. 27, 1957; s. Raymond Robert and Anna Marie (Rapp) M. ASD in Laser Electro-Optics, Pasadena (Calif.) City Coll., 1984; BS in Mgmt., Pepperdine U., 1993. Lab. asst. Jet Propulsion Lab., Pasadena, Calif., 1984-85; rsch. engr. satellite sys. Rockwell Internat., Seal Beach, Calif., 1985-89; electro-optical engr. Cymbolic Scis. Internat., Irvine, Calif., 1989-90; project engr. OCA Applied Optics, Garden Grove, Calif., 1990-92; owner, program mgr. Integrated Scientific, Mission Viejo, Calif., 1992—; sr. sys. test engr. Rocketdyne Corp., Granada Hills, Calif., 1994—. Mem. Laser Inst. Am., Soc. Photo-optical Instrumentation Engrs., L.A. Collegiate Coun. (alumnus), Inter Orgnl. Coun. (founder, chmn. 1981-82), Nat. Mgmt. Assn., Internat. Platform Assn., Lions Club, Inventors Forum, Sigma Pi. Republican. Roman Catholic.

MEWES, JENNIFER ROBYN, counselor; b. Bellflower, Calif., Feb. 26, 1969; d. Robert John Charles and Bess Elizabeth (May) M. BA in psychology, UCLA, 1991; MEd in counseling, Springfield (Mass.) Coll., 1993; postgrad., U. Ariz., 1993—. Adminstrv. asst. U. Ariz., Tucson, 1995-96; sr. acad. advisor U. Ariz., 1996-97, outreach counselor, 1997—; adj. faculty Pima C.C., Tucson, 1997—. Mem. APA, Nat. Assn. Acad. Advisors for Athletes, Assn. for the Advancement of Applied Psychology. Office: U Ariz PO Box 210096 Tucson AZ 85721-0096

MEYER, BARBARA ANN, tax specialist; b. Indpls., Mar. 20, 1924; d. Horace Wright and Sibyl Conklin (Lindley) Townsend; m. Robert James Scott, Dec. 15, 1941 (dec. 1949); children: Sue Meyer Suppiger, Randolph David, Steven James; m. Fred J. Meyer, Jan. 3, 1950; 1 child, Johanna Laura Meyer-Mitchell. Student, U. Md., 1958-60, Big Bend C.C., 1965-69. Cert. enrolled agent, U.S. Treasury, 1980. Owner, mgr. Meyer Tax. Svc., Coulee Dam, Wash., 1969-94, cons., 1994—; enrolled agent emeritus; income tax tchr. Big Bend C.C., Coulee Dam, 1975-80. Contbr. articles to newspapers. Chair svc. to mil. families ARC, Ephrata, Wash., 1941—, Roosevelt History Month, Grand Coulee, 1995-96; bd. chmn. Pub. Hosp. Dist. #6, Grand Coulee, 1990-94. Mem. Nat. Assn. Enrolled Agents, Wash. State Soc. Enrolled Agents (v.p. 1984—, bd. dirs. 1985-88), Am. Cancer Soc. (bd. dirs. 1995—), Calif. Soc. Enrolled Agents (affiliate), Grand Coulee C. of C. (life, hon., pres. 1979-80), Grand Coulee Yacht Club (life, hon.), Grand Coulee Dam Rotary (pres. 1992-93). Democrat. Avocations: cooking, gardening, bird watching. Home: 201 Columbia Ave Coulee Dam WA 99116-1436 Office: Meyer Tax Svc 102 Stevens Ave Coulee Dam WA 99116-1503

MEYER, C. RICHARD, architect. BArch, U. Calif., Berkeley, 1968. Registered architect, Wash. With The Callison Partnership, Seattle, 1977—, dir. quality assurance; mem. adv. bd. cert. program project mgmt. U. Wash.; contracts rev. panelist Soc. Archtl. Adminstrs.; mem. faculty Pacific real estate symposium N.W. Real Estate Inst.; guest lectr. Archtl. Registration Exam. Seminar; guest lectr. coll. architecture and urban planning U. Wash.; guest panelist Internat. Conf. of Bldg. Ofcls. Nat. Conf., 1991. Mem. AIA (treas. Seattle chpt., mem. steering com. Pacific NW regional conf., vice-chair nat. risk mgmt. com., mem. steering com. nat. practice com., liaison to Am. Arbitration Assn.), Nat. Inst. Bldg. Scis. Office: The Callison Partnership Ltd 1420 5th Ave Ste 2400 Seattle WA 98101-2343*

MEYER, CAROLYN MAE, writer children's books; b. Lewistown, Pa., June 8, 1935; d. Harry Victor and Sara Elizabeth (Knepp) M.; m. Joseph Smrcka, June 4, 1960 (div. 1973); children: Alan, John, Christopher; m. E.A. Mares, May 30, 1987. BA, Bucknell U., 1957. Author: Voices of South Africa, 1986, White Lilacs, 1993, Where the Broken Heart Still Beats, 1992, more than 40 others. Home: 202 Edith Blvd NE Albuquerque NM 87102

MEYER, CHARLES G., museum director. Exec. dir. Bakersfield (Calif.) Mus. Art, 1995—. Office: Bakersfield Mus Art PO Box 1911 Bakersfield CA 93303-1911*

MEYER, CHRISTOPHER HAWKINS, lawyer; b. Springfield, Mo., Sept. 29, 1952; s. Richard DeWitt and Nancy (Hawkins) M.; m. Karen Anne Adams, Aug. 8, 1987; 1 child, C. Andrew Meyer. BA in Econs. magna cum laude, U. Mich., 1977, JD cum laude, 1981. Bar: D.C. 1981, U.S. Ct. Appeals (D.C. cir.) 1982, U.S. Ct. Appeals (9th cir.) 1983, Colo. 1985, U.S. Ct. Appeals (10th cir.) 1985, Idaho, U.S. Ct. Appeals (8th cir.). Counsel water resources program Nat. Wildlife Fedn., Washington, 1981-84; assoc. prof. adjoint, counsel Rocky Mountain Natural Resources Clinic Nat. Wildlife Fedn., Boulder, Colo., 1984-91; ptnr. Givens Pursley, Boise, 1991—. *Mr. Meyer is a partner in the law firm Givens Pursley LLP in Boise, Idaho. His practice emphasizes natural resources, environmental, water, constitutional and administrative law. He has written extensively on these subjects and is a frequent speaker throughout the country. Before joining Givens Pursley in 1991, he was an adjunct professor at the University of Colorado Law School, where he taught advanced water law and negotiation. He has earned Martindale-Hubbell's highest rating ("AV") for practicing attorneys.* Contbr. articles to profl. publs. Mem. steering com. Idaho Environ. Forum; bd. dirs. Idaho Food Bank, Treasure Valley Land Trust. Recipient Lawyer of Yr. award Environ. Policy Inst., 1984, Water Conservationist of Yr. Nebr. Wildlife Fedn., 1989. Mem. Phi Beta Kappa. Democrat. Roman Catholic. Home: 2460 E Bergeson St Boise ID 83706-6012 Office: Givens Pursley LLP 277 N 6th St Ste 200 Boise ID 83702-7720

MEYER, DANIEL KRAMER, real estate executive; b. Denver, July 15, 1957; s. Milton Edward and Mary (Kramer) M. Student, Met. State Coll., Denver, 1977-78, U. Colo., 1978-80. Ptnr., developer RM & M II (Ltd. Partnership), Englewood, Colo., 1981-87; pres. Centennial Mortgage and Investment, Ltd., Englewood, Colo., 1984-87; prin. Capriole Properties, Greenwood Village, Colo., 1983—. Alumni mem. bd. trustees Kent Denver Country Day Sch., 1981-83; sec. dist. 37 ctrl. and vacancy com. Colo. Ho. of Reps., 1991-92. Recipient Pamela Davis Beardsley devel. award Kent Denver Sch., 1995. Mem. Greenwood Athletic Club. Republican. Avocations: climbing, rollerblading, political economy, 20th century English lit., metaphysics.

MEYER, DEANNIE, artist; b. Roseburg, Oreg., Sept. 20, 1938; d. Robert and Roberta June (Horning) Laughlin; m. Richard C. Meyer, June 12, 1958; children: Daniel Vernon, Kirk Lynn, Robert Otto. AA, Shasta Coll., Redding, Calif., 1994; BFA, Calif. Coll. of Arts & Crafts, Oakland, 1996. Legal sec. Redding, 1965-84. Recent exhbns. include Calif. State Fair, 1997 (merit award), 1996 (merit award), 1995 (merit award), 1994 (merit award), 1992 (merit award), Pa. Watercolor Soc., 1996 (2d pl. award), Calif. Coll. Arts & Crafts, 1996, 1995, 1994, Old City Hall Gallery (2-person show), 1995, Redding Mus. of Art & History, 1994, 1993, 1992, Shasta Coll. Gallery, 1994, 1993, 1992. Vol. Little League, Weaverville, Calif., 1962-65, and Redding, 1965-70, Cub Scouts and Boys Scouts Am., Redding, 1966-70. Republican. Avocations: photography, piano. Home: 1377 Dominion Dr Redding CA 96002-3616

MEYER, DENNIS ROBERT, physician; b. Cin., Jan. 27, 1943; s. Earl D. and Orvinne (Price) M.; m. Judith Margaret Laird, Oct. 27, 1942; children: John-anderson L., Amanda Leilani. BA, Northwestern U., 1964, MD, 1968. Resident in medicine Cook County Hosp., Chgo., 1968-70, Tripler Med. Ctr., Honolulu, 1970-71; fellow in tropical medicine SEATO Rsch. Lab., Bangkok, Thailand, 1971-72; asst. prof., clin. prof. medicine U. Hawaii, Honolulu, 1977—; pvt. practice Med. Assocs., Honolulu, 1977—. Bd. dirs. Am. Heart Assn., Honolulu, 1980-85, Am. Diabetes Assn., Honolulu, 1982-86; chmn. Hawaii Symphony Orch., Honolulu, 1993-96; pres. Waialae G.C. Assn., Honolulu, 1992-94. With U.S. Army, 1972-77. Knighted Niadh Nask, 1994. Fellow ACP; mem. Rotary (bd. dirs. 1990-93, v.p. 1995-96), Waikiki Yacht Club, Pacific Club. Republican. Episcopalian. Avocations: history, sailing, skiing, travel. Home: 914 Waiholo St Honolulu HI 96821-1226 Office: Med Assocs Ltd 1380 Lusitana St Honolulu HI 96813-2449

MEYER, DIANA LYNN, clinical nurse specialist; b. Fairborn, Ohio, June 10, 1955; d. Jerome and Vivian Shirley (Storm) Cohen; m. William Douglas Meyer, Mar. 13, 1979; children: Aaron Douglas, Jordan Cameron. ASN, SUNY, N.Y.C., 1984; BSN, Calif. State U., Fullerton, 1992; MSN, UCLA, 1996. Cert. emergency nurse, BCEN, critical care RN, AACN. RN Children's Hosp. L.A., 1985-90, U. Calif., Irvine, 1990-94; pre-hosp. care coord. U. Calif. Med. Ctr., Orange, 1994-96; clinical nurse specialist Friendly Hills Regional Med. Ctr., La Habra, Calif., 1996-97, dir. patient care svcs., 1997—; educator CME Assocs., Orange, 1990—; cons. Creative Programs Unltd., Orange, 1992—. Editor (newsletter) Orange Coast Rhythms, 1996—. Mem. Emergency Nurses Assn. (sci. review panel 1996, 97), Calif. Emergency Nurses Assn. (dir.-at-large 1996-97, pres.-elect 1997-98, pres. 1998—, Donald Kelleher scholarship 1995), Orange Coast Emergency Nurses Assn. (pres. 1995, Emergency Nurse of Yr. 1995), Long Beach Emergency Nurses Assn. (Gary Sparger Meml. scholarship). Address: Frendly Hill Health Care Net 1034 W Feather River Way Orange CA 92865-2021

MEYER, FREDERICK G., lawyer; b. Temple, Tex., 1945. BA, Dartmouth Coll., 1967; JD, Columbia U., 1970; LLM, NYU, 1979. Bar: Conn. 1970, N.Y. 1971, Colo. 1979. Atty. Holland & Hart, Denver, Reinhart, Boerner, Van Deuren, Norris & Rieselbach, P.C., Denver, 1998—; vis. lectr. grad. tax program law sch. U. Denver, 1982-83. Co-author: Colorado Probate: Beyond the Basics, 1984, Colorado Probate & Estate Planning, 1986, An Attorney's Look at Tax Planing for the Small Business Owner, Rancher and Farmer: Asset Protection Planning, 1996; co-editor: Colorado Estate Planning Handbook, rev. edit., 1989; editor trust and estate forum Colo. Lawyer, 1981-82; contbr. articles to profl. jours. Fellow Am. Coll. Trust and Estate Counsel, Colo. Bar Found.; mem. ABA (vice chair agrl. tax com. 1996-97), Greater Denver Tax Counsels Assn., Rocky Mountain Estate Planning Counsel (pres. 1987). Office: Reinhart Boerner Van Deuren Norris and Rieselbach PC 1700 Lincoln St Ste 3725 Denver CO 80203-4537

MEYER, GEORGE WILBUR, internist, health facility administrator; b. Cleve., Apr. 30, 1941; s. George Wilbur and Emily Fuller (Campbell) M.; m. Carolyn Edwards Garrett, Apr. 8, 1967; children: Robert James, Elizabeth Jackson, Dobro Goodale. BS, MIT, 1962; MD, Tulane Med. Sch., 1966. Intern So. Pacific Hosps. Inc., San Francisco, 1966-67; resident Pacific Presbyn. Med. Ctr., San Francisco, 1969-72; commd. 1st lt. USAF, advanced through grades to col., 1980; fellow in gastroenterology David Grant USAF Med. Ctr., Travis AFB, Calif., 1974-76; asst. chair dept. medicine USAF Med. Ctr., Keesler AFB, Miss., 1976-78; asst. prof. dept. medicine Uniformed Svcs. Univ., Bethesda, Md., 1978-80; chair dept. medicine Wright Patterson AFB, Dayton, Ohio, 1980-82; chief of medicine Wilford Hall USAF Med. Ctr., Lackland AFB, Tex., 1982-86; chief clin. svcs. USAF Acad., Colo., 1986-88; comdr. 1st Med. Group, Langley AFB, Va., 1988-89, 86th Med. Group, Ramstein AFB, Germany, 1989-92; program dir. internal medicine Ga. Bapt. Med. Ctr., Atlanta, 1993-97; assoc. clin. prof. medicine U. Calif., Davis, 1998—; cons. Walter Reed Army Med. Ctr., Washington, 1978-80, Nat. Naval Med. Ctr., Bethesda, 1978-80; assoc. prof. Wright State U. Sch. Medicine, Dayton, 1980-82; cons. Dayton VA Med. Ctr., 1980-82; clin. assoc. prof. medicine U. Tex. Health Sci. Ctr., San Antonio, 1982-86, Med. Coll. Ga., Augusta, 1993-97; cons. dept. corp. med. divsn. state of Calif., 1997-99. Mem. editl. bd. Gastrointestinal Endoscopy, 1993-97, On-Line Jour. of Digestive Health, 1998—; book review editor Practical Gastroenterology, 1999; contbr. articles and revs. to profl. jours. and chpts. to books. Mem. leadership com. Am. Cancer Soc., Ramstein AFB, 1989-93, bd. dirs. Atlanta City Unit, 1995-97, Ga. divsn. 1996-97, El Paso Teller Unit, Colorado Springs, 1986-88, Bexar Metro Unit, San Antonio, 1984-86; adv. com. United Health Svcs., Dayton, 1980-82. Fellow ACP, Am. Coll. Gastroenterology; mem. Am. Soc. for Gastro Endoscopy, Am. Gastrointestinal Assn. Avocations: squash, tennis, scuba, stamps.

MEYER, GREG CHARLES, psychiatrist; b. Bismarck, N.D., Aug. 17, 1935; s. Oscar Clarence and Agnes Josephine (Pearson) M. Degree in profl. engrng., Colo. Sch. Mines, 1958, Alexander Hamilton Bus. Inst., 1960; MME, U. So. Calif., 1965; MD, Marquette U., 1970. Diplomate Am. Bd. Psychiatry and Neurology, Am. Bd. Forensic Medicine. Engr. Minuteman-Thiokol, Brigham City, Utah, 1958-61; sr. engr. Saturn S-II N.Am. Aviation, Downey, Calif., 1962-65; design specialist Titan-Martin, Denver, 1965-66; rotating intern Weld Country Gen. Hosp., Greenly, Colo., 1970-71; psychiatric resident Ariz. State Hosp., Phoenix, 1971-74, psychiatrist, 1974-76; pvt. practice Mesa-Tempe, Ariz., 1975—; psychiatrist Ariz. Ctrl. Med. Ctr., 1995—; med. dir. Ctrl. Ariz. Med. Ctr., 1997-99; chmn. psychiatry Desert Samaritan Hosp., Mesa, 1982-86, 90-94, chmn. joint mental health, 1981-83, mem. edn. com., 1979-82, quality assurance com., 1979; exec. com. Desert Vista Hosp., Mesa, 1988-94, chief of staff, 1989; chmn. psychiatry Mesa Luth. Hosp., 1984-85, exec. com., 1984-85; mng. ptnr. Desert Samaritan Med. Bldg. II, Mesa, 1985-86; rsch., edn. com. East Valley Camel Back Hosp., 1989-90, quality assurance com., 1985; med. dir. Ctrl. Ariz. Med. Ctr., 1997-99. Co-discoverer Larson-Meyer Transform. Coach Pop Warner Football, 1974. With USMCR, 1953-59. Mem. AMA, Am. Psychiat. Assn., Ariz. Med. Assn., Ariz. Psychiat. Assn., Phoenix Psychiat. Coun., Maricopa County Med. Assn., Christian Med./Dental Assn., Triple Nine Soc., SCV, Wingfield Family Soc. Republican. Lutheran. Avocations: multi engine instrument pilot, sailing, computers, canoeing, photography.

MEYER, JAROLD ALAN, oil company research executive; b. Phoenix, July 28, 1938; s. Lester M. and Anita (Walker) M.; m. Diane Louise Wheeler; children: Ronald Alan, Sharon Lynne. BSChemE, Calif. Inst. Tech., 1960, MS, 1961. Mgr. process devel. Chevron Rsch., Richmond, Calif., 1978-82; tech. mgr. Chevron U.S.A., El Segundo, Calif., 1982-84; v.p. process rsch. Chevron Rsch., Richmond, 1984-86, pres., 1986—; sr. v.p. Chevron Rsch. and Tech., Richmond, 1990-93; ret., 1993; prin. J.A. Meyer Assocs., Martinez, Calif., 1993—; bd. dirs. Solvent Refined Coal Internat., Inc., San Francisco; mem. adv. bd. Surface Sci. and Catalysis Program Ctr. for Advanced Materials, Lawrence Berkeley Lab., 1988-91; mem. adv. coun. Lawrence Hall Sci., 1989-94; indsl. advisor Accreditation bd. for Engring. and Tech. Inventor petroleum catalysts; contbr. articles to profl. jours. Bd. visitors U. Calif., Davis, 1986-93, trustee found., 1989—. Mem. Nat. Acad. Engring., Am. Chem. Soc., Nat. Petroleum Refining Assn., Indsl. Rsch. Inst., Conf. Bd. Internat. Rsch. Mgmt. Coun., Accreditation Bd. for Engring. and Tech. Indsl. Advisor, Sigma Xi, Tau Beta Pi. Avocations: electronics design and constrn., photography. Home and Office: 849 Corte Briones Martinez CA 94553-5950

MEYER, JEFFREY THORE, music educator; b. Buffalo, Minn., Apr. 26, 1963; s. Thore Peter and Joyce Ida (Vergin) M. m. Kelly JoLayne Deach, Mar. 19, 1988; children: Layne, Kurt, Weston. BMus, Wheaton Coll., 1985; MA, U. Minn., 1990, postgrad., 1998. Asst. prof. music Simpson Coll., Redding, Calif., 1994—; piano performer, 1981—; choir dir., 1986—. Contbr. article to Garland Ency. of World Music; composer mus. works. Pres.' scholar Wheaton Coll., 1981-85; fellow U. Minn., 1988, NEH, 1995. Mem. Am. Musicol. Soc., Coll. Music Soc., Soc. for Ethnomusicology, Nat. Assn. Schs. Music. Avocations: tennis, camping, hiking, golf, astronomy. Home: 1585 Arroyo Manor Dr Redding CA 96003-9217 Office: Simpson Coll 2211 College View Dr Redding CA 96003-8601

MEYER, JEROME J., diversified technology company executive; b. Caledonia, Minn., Feb. 18, 1938; s. Herbert J. and Edna (Staggemeyer) M.; m. Sandra Ann Beaudoin, June 18, 1960; children—Randall Lee, Lisa Ann, Michelle Lynn. Student, Hamline U., 1956-58; B.A., U. Minn., 1960. Devel. engr. Firestone Tire & Rubber Co., Akron, Ohio, 1960-61; v.p., gen. mgr. Sperry Univac, St. Paul, 1961-79; group v.p. Honeywell, Inc., Mpls., 1979-84; pres., chief operating officer Varian Assocs., Palo Alto, Calif., 1984-86, also bd. dirs.; pres., chief exec. officer Honeywell Inc., 1986-90; from pres. to chmn., CEO Tektronix Inc., Beaverton, Oreg., 1990—; bd. dirs. Oreg. Pub. Broadcasting, Esterline Tech., Oregon Bus. Coun., AMP, Std. Ins. Co. Trustee Oreg. Grad. Inst., Willamette U., Oreg. Children's Found. Mem. Oregon Golf Club. Avocation: golf. Office: Tektronix Inc PO Box 1000 26600 SW Parkway Ave Wilsonville OR 97070-9297

MEYER, JOSEPH B., state official, former academic administrator; b. Casper, Wyo., 1941; m. Mary Orr; children: Vincent, Warren. Student, Colo. Sch. Mines; BA, U. Wyo., 1964, JD, 1967; postgrad., Northwestern U., 1968. Dep. county atty. Fremont County, Wyo., 1967-69; assoc. Smith and Meyer, 1968-71; asst. dir. legis. svc. office State of Wyo., Cheyenne, 1971-87, atty. gen., 1987-95; spl. asst. to pres. Univ. Wyo., Laramie, 1995—; sec. of state State of Wyoming, 1999—; conductor numerous govt. studies on state codes including Wyo. probate, criminal, state adminstrn., banking, domestic rels., game and fish, state instn., employment security, worker's compensation, motor vehicle, others; conductor legis. rev. of adminstrv. rules; negotiator with Office of Surface Mining for Wyo. state preemption; instr. Wyo. Coll. Law, fall 1986; lectr. Rocky Mountain Mineral Law Found., 1977; chmn. Conf. Western Atty. Gen., 1992-93; mem. exec. com. Nat. Assn. Attys. Gen. Bd. dirs. Cheyenne Jr. League, 1982-85, Jessup PTO, 1980-81; instr. Boy Scouts Am. Mem. Rotary. Congregationalist. Avocations: golf, tennis, gardening, wood carving, rock hunting. Office: Univ Wyoming External Rels PO Box 3315 Laramie WY 82071-3315 also: State Capital Bldg Cheyenne WY 82002-0020*

MEYER, JUDITH ANNE, health facility administrator; b. Flushing, N.Y., Dec. 12, 1940; d. Frederick J. and Kathryn M. (Geiger) W.; m. John H. Meyer, Jan. 19, 1962; children: John, Jessica. BA in Comparative Linguistics, Queens Coll., 1961; MS in Communication Disorders, So. Conn. State Coll., 1981. Sch. clin. cons. Litchfield (Conn.) Pub. Schs., Waterury (Conn.) Pub. Schs., 1978-89; pvt. practice Northwestern Conn., 1982-89; image cons. Image In Focus, Litchfield, 1987-90; dir. care provider Novacare, Inc., Valley Forge, Pa., 1989-92; regional speech-lang. pathology coord. Rehability (name now Am. Rehab. Svcs.), Meridian, Conn., 1993-94; corp. dir. long-term care devel. Am. Rehab. Svcs., Inc., Brentwood, Tenn., 1995-96; v.p. ops., dir. clin. svcs. Orthop. and Neurol. Rehab., Inc., Los Gatos, Calif., 1996—. Freelance corr. Sta. WSNG-AM-FM, Litchfield, 1989-91. Dir. christian edn. 1st Congl. Ch., 1980-84, me. bd. deacons, 1986-89; mem. Planning & Zoning Bd., Litchfield, 1985—; vol. Weanto Nogue Trust, Cornwall, Conn., 1989-92. Mem. Nat. Assn. Support Long-Term Care (mem. bd. govs., mem. rehab. coalition, chair mulit-level membership com.), Am. Speech/Lang. Hearing Assn. (ACE award 1993), Mensa. Avocations: naturalist, Special Olympics coach, ski instructor, hiking, gardening. Office: ONR Inc 200 S Santa Cruz Ave Los Gatos CA 95030-6700

MEYER, M. E. JOSEPH, III, small business owner; b. Ft. Campbell, Ky.; s. Milton Edward Jr. and Mary Charlotte (Kramer) M. BA in Humanities, U. Colo., 1974; cert. massage therapy, Boulder Sch. Massage Therapy, 1980; student, Hakomi Inst., Boulder and Munich, 1982-84. Ski instr. Geneva Basin, Squaw Pass, Arapaho Basin, Keystone, Colo., 1967-71; instr. guitar Musikschule Schöneberg, West Berlin, Federal Republic of Germany, 1977-81; instr. guitar (docent) Conservatory in West Berlin, 1978-81; pvt. practice massage therapy, instr. Oslo, Copenhagen, Stockholm, Berlin, Munich, Aspen, Colo., Reykjavik, Iceland, 1981-85; fgn. editor Aspen Daily News, 1986; instr. German Colo. Mountain Coll., Aspen, 1986-87; dir., loan officer Centennial Mortgage Investments, Englewood, Colo., 1986-87; dir., owner Aspen Therapeutic Massage Assocs., Englewood, 1986-92; owner Aspen Fitness Assocs., Englewood, 1992—; dir. massage therapy tng. Delta Med. Inst., Arvada, Colo., 1997—; dir. massage therapy Greenwood Athletic Club, Englewood, 1986-92; massage therapist Aspen Valley Hosp., 1983-86, World Disabled Ski Championship, Winter Park, Colo., 1990; translator World Cup Ski Races, Aspen, 1986-87. Contbr. articles to profl. jours.; scriptor, actor instructional video The Swedish Massage, 1987; exec. producer video Seated Aerobic Workout, 1992. Mem. Clean Air Adv. Bd., Aspen, 1985-87; ski guide Blind outdoor Leadership Devel., Aspen, 1985-87; vol. Monoski & Sitski Tether, Nat. Sports Ctr. for Disabled, Winter Park, Colo., 1990-92. Mem. Am. Massage Therapy Assn. (conf. coord., bd. dirs. Colo. chpt.), Hakomi Inst., II Bass, Opera Colo. (chorus 1992—), Colo. Symphony Orch. (chorus 1991—), Japan Am. Soc. Colo., Alliance Francaise, Mensa. Republican. Avocations: skiing, triathlon, singing, foreign languages. Office: Aspen Fitness Assocs 1550 Larimer St # 110 Denver CO 80202-1602

MEYER, MICHAEL C., diversified company executive; b. Phoenix, Apr. 4, 1956; s. John H. and Lee (Booher) M. BS in Mgmt., Ariz. State U., 1982; postgrad., U. N.Mex., 1983-84. Adminstr. bldg. and grounds Internat. Tel. & Tel., Phoenix, 1976-80; bldg. supr. Intel, Albuquerque, 1982-83, mgr. info. systems, 1983-84; ops. mgr. MCM & Assocs., Phoenix, 1984-86; pres., bd. dirs. Facility Ops. Group (FOG), Tempe, Ariz., 1986—, chief exec. officer, 1988—; sr. ptnr. MCM & Assocs. Internat. Cons. Co.; bd. dirs. Digicom. Mem. Internat. Facility Mgmt. Assn. (bd. dirs.), Telecommunications Assn., Tempe C. of C., Phoenix C. of C., Rotary. Avocations: sailing, golf, camping. Office: Facility Ops Group 2730 S Hardy Dr Tempe AZ 85282-3338

MEYER, MICHAEL EDWIN, lawyer; b. Chgo., Oct. 23, 1942; s. Leon S. and Janet (Gorden) M.; m. Catherine Dieffenbach, Nov. 21, 1982; children: Linda, Mollie, Patrick, Kellie. BS, U. Wis., 1964; JD, U. Chgo., 1967. Bar: Calif. 1968, U.S. Supreme Ct. 1973. Assoc. Lillick & McHose, L.A., 1967-73, ptnr., 1974-90, mng. ptnr., 1986-87; ptnr. Pillsbury Madison Sutro, 1990—, mem. mgmt. com., 1990-92; chmn. Pillsbury Madison Sutro, L.A., 1999—; judge pro tem Beverly Hills Mcpl. Ct., Calif., 1976-79, Los Angeles Mcpl. Ct., 1980-86; lectr. in field. Bd. dirs. Bldg. Owners and Mgrs. Assn. Greater L.A., L.A. coun. Boy Scouts Am., L.A. Sports and Entertainment Commn.; pub. counsel United Way Greater L.A., Los Angeles County Bar Found., trustee, 1997—. Recipient Good Scout award L.A. coun. Boy Scouts Am., 1992, Man of Yr. award United Way, 1996. Mem. ABA, Am. Arbitration Assn. (arbitrator), Calif. Bar Assn., Los Angeles County Bar Assn. (trustee 1997—), L.A. Bar Assn., U. Chgo. Alumni Assn. So. Calif. (pres. 1980-82), Calif. Club, U. L.A. Club (dir. 1979-85, pres. 1984-85), L.A. Country Club. Jewish. Home: 759 31st St Manhattan Beach CA 90266-3456 Office: Pillsbury Madison Sutro 725 S Figueroa St Los Angeles CA 90017-5524

MEYER, RACHEL ABIJAH, foundation director, artist, theorist, poet; b. Job's Corners, Pa., Aug. 18, 1963; d. Jacob Owen and Velma Ruth (Foreman) M.; children: Andrew Carson, Peter Franklin. Student, Lebanon Valley Coll. Restaurant owner Purcy's Place, Ono, Pa.; restaurant mgr. King's Table Buffet, Citrus Heights, Calif.; product finalizer TransWorld Enterprises, Blaine, Wash.; dir., support svcs. adminstr. Tacticar Found., Sacramento, 1991—; tchr. Tacticar Inst., 1995; chair Coniresms, Sacramento, 1996—. Author: Year of the Unicorn, 1994. Avocations: researching, writing, painting. Studio: 2013 Kathryn Way Sacramento CA 95821-5517

MEYER, ROBERT LEE, secondary education educator; b. St. Joseph, Mo., July 9, 1952; s. Robert James and Jerry Lee (Patterson) M.; m. Barbara Anita Stickles, Aug. 2, 1986. BS in Edn., Mo. Western State Coll., 1974; MA in Edn., U.S. Internat. U., 1988. Cert. tchr., Calif., Mo.; cert. specialist learning handicapped, resource specialist cert., adminstr., Calif. Spl. edn. tchr., learning handicapped Mann Jr. High Sch., San Diego, 1978-80, Serra High Sch., San Diego, 1980-84, Morse High Sch., San Diego, 1984-85; magnet seminar tchr. Bell Jr. High Sch., San Diego, 1985-91; project resource tchr., dir. student activities Serra High Sch., San Diego, 1991-94, resource specialist, 1994-95; magnet coord. Ctr. for Sci., Math. and Computer Tech. Samuel Gompers Secondary Sch., San Diego, 1995-97; dean of students, attendance coord. Scripps Ranch H.S., non-athletic event coord., 1997-98; asst. prin. Mountain Empire Jr./Sr. H.S., 1998—; chmn. resource com. Western Assn. Schs. & Colls. accreditation Serra High Sch., San Diego, 1995, chmn. process com. Western Assn. Schs. and Colls. accreditation Gompers Secondary Sch., San Diego, 1996-97, sch. site coun., 1992-97, gov. team mem., 1992-95, chair spl. edn. dept., 1983, mem. sch. leadership team, 1992-95, sr. class advisor, 1994-95, liaison Partnerships in Edn., 1996-97; monitor City Schs. Race Human Rels. Monitoring Team, 1991-92, African Am. students pupil advocate program adv. coun., 1995-97; restructuring coord. Senate Bill 1274 Grant, 1993-95, resource specialist, 1994-95; chmn. process com. Western Assn. Schs. and Colls. accreditation Gompers Sec. Sch., adv. com. mem. African Am. students program; co-chmn. race/human rels. com. Scripps Ranch H.S., 1997-98. Contbr.: (book) History of Andrew Meyer Family, 1989. Alternate del. Dem. Party 6th Dist. and State Conventions, Holt County, Mo., 1976; mem. Nat. Conf. Minitown Race/Human Rels. Camp Coord., Scripps Ranch H.S. Mem. Assn. Calif. Sch. Adminstrs., Delta Chi. Democrat. Roman Catholic. Avocations: collecting political buttons, antiques, travel.

MEYER, ROBERTA, mediator, communication consultant; b. San Francisco, July 27, 1936; d. Theodore Robert and Virginia (Organ) M.; m. G. William Sheldon; children: Megan McDougall Radeski, Deborah Ann Guerra. Student, U. Utah, 1974. Cert. mediator. Founder, pres., exec. dir. Roberta Meyer Communication Cons., Inc., San Francisco, 1977—; presenter numerous workshops in field of alcoholism and communication; nat. speaker Nat. Found. for Alcolhism Communicaton; keynote speaker Calif. Women's Commn. on Alcoholism, 1981; mem. adv. bd. Soviet Am. Alliance on Alcoholism and Other Addictions. Author: Facts About Booze and Other Drugs, 1980, The Parent Connection: How To Communicate With Your Child About Alcohol and Other Drugs, 1984, Listen to the Heart, 1989, (film) Understanding Addiction, 1988, Better Relationships Through Effective Communication, 1991; numerous radio and TV appearances; creator, dir. Meyer Method dance program for ballroom dancers, One Meyer Method dance trng. video, 1998. Mem. adv. bd. Marin Svcs. for Women, 1980; vol. Pacific Med. Ctr., San Francisco Ballet Aux.; mem. N.Y.C. & San Francisco Ballet Cos., 1950-56; mem. faculty San Francisco Ballet Sch., 1956-65; founder, dir. Ballet Arts of San Francisco, 1965-78, San Francisco Ballroom Dance Theatre, 1994—. Recipient award Optimists Club, 1978; named 56th Point of Light, Pres. Bush, 1990. Mem. Nat. Ctr. for Collaborative Planning and Community Svc. (cert.), Nat. Coun. on Alcoholism (co-chmn. pub. info. com. 1985—, v.p. Bay area 1988—, bd. dirs. Teen Kick Off 1987—, Alcoholism and Drug Rsch. Communications Ctr. 1990—; pres. 1988—, creator, cons. youth aware program 1974—), San Francisco Womens Rehab. Assn. (pres. 1975-76), Nat. Coun. on Alcoholism and Drug Dependence Calif. (pres. 1988-91), Childrens Theatre Assn., San Francisco C. of C.

MEYER, ROGER PAUL, physician; b. Atlanta, Mar. 30, 1950; s. Leonard Arthur and Janet Elanor (Miller) M.; children: Seth E., Hilary R. BA in Psychology with honors, U. N.C., 1972; MD, Med. Coll. Ga., 1976; postgrad., U. N.Mex., 1980. Physician in pvt. practice Carson Med. Group, Carson City, Nev., 1980—; chief of staff Carson Tahoe Hosp., 1986-87, chmn. dpt. ob-gyn., 1990-91; v.p. Nev. Physicians Rev. Orgn., 1987; dir. Physicians Managed Care IPA; sec. Nev. First Care Ins. Co. Fellow Am. Coll. Ob.-Gyn. (Nev. legislature liaison 1991); mem. Am. Acad. Reproductive Medicine, Am. Coll. Physician Execs. Democrat. Jewish. Avocations: skiing, fishing, golf. Office: Carson Med Group 1200 N Mountain St Carson City NV 89703-3824

MEYER-BORDERS, JANET LOUISE, artist; b. Shreveport, La., June 20, 1955; d. Russell Barton Meyer and Shirley Ann (Emerson) Rydberg; m. Steven Fredric Cogliano, Apr. 21, 1975 (div. Apr. 1981); 1 child, Jeremy Steven Borders; m. Douglas Harold Borders, June 26, 1982; 1 child, Heather Nicole Borders. AA, Coll. of the Desert, 1983; student, Saddleback Coll., 1990; BA in Art and Art History, U. Calif., Santa Cruz, 1993. docent, artist Long Marine Lab., Santa Cruz, 1992—. Tchr. Lawndale (Calif.) Unified Schs., 1976-77; with Employment Devel. Dept., Mammoth Lakes, Calif., 1978-79, Standard Mortgage Co., Palm Desert, Calif., 1980-82, IBM, Gilroy, Calif., 1983-84, Holidy Host RV Ctr., Scotts Valley, Calif., 1985-86; sec. Classic Framing Constrn. Co., Irvine, Calif., 1988-89; co-owner Santa Cruz Constrn., 1993—. One woman shows include Bridge Gallery, 1992, St.

George Expresso, S.C., 1994; Group shows include Saddleback Coll., Calif., 1990, Rt. 66 Gallup, N.Mex., 1990, UCSC Student Ctr., Calif., 1991, 92, 93, Squid Festival, Santa Cruz, Calif., 1991. Mem. Western Arts Assn. Conservators. Democrat. Roman Catholic. Avocations: oil painting, etching, drawing, matting and framing art, collecting art. Home: 213 Continental St Santa Cruz CA 95060-6065

MEYERS, ANN ELIZABETH, sports broadcaster; b. San Diego, Mar. 26, 1955; d. Robert Eugene and Patricia Ann (Burke); m. Donald Scott Drysdale, Nov. 1, 1986; children: Donald Scott Jr., Darren John, Drew Ann. Grad., UCLA, 1978. Profl. basketball player N.J. Gems, 1979-80; profl. basketball player Ind. Pacers NBA, 1979; sports broadcaster Ind. Pacers, 1979-80; sportscaster men's basketball U. Hawaii, Honolulu, 1981-82; sportscaster men's and women's basketball UCLA, 1982-84, 89—; sportscaster volleyball, basketball, softball, tennis ESPN, 1981—; sportscaster Olympic Games ABC, L.A., 1984; sportscaster volleyball, softball, tennis, basketball, soccer Sportsvision, 1985-87; sportscaster volleyball, basketball, softball Prime Ticket, 1985-97; sportscaster CBS-TV, 1991—, ESPN Women's Basketball, Fox Women's Basketball, WNBA-NBC World Championships; sportscaster Goodwill Games, WTBS, 1986, 90; sportscaster basketball NBC and ESPN, 1996-97, WNBA, NBA, ESSPN, 1996-98. Winner Silver medal Montreal Olympics, 1976, Gold medal Pan Am. Games, 1975, Silver medal, 1979, All-Am. UCLA, 1975, 76, 77, 78; 1st woman named to Hall of Fame UCLA, 1987; named to Women's Sports Hall of Fame, 1987, Orange County Sports Hall of Fame, 1985, Calif. H.S. Hall of Fame, 1990, Basketball Hall of Fame, 1993, Nat. H.S. Hall of Fame, 1995, NBC Hoop It Up, 1995, 96, 97, Cath. Youth Orgn. Hall of Fame, 1996, Women's Basketball Hall of Fame, 1999. Office: care Lampros and Roberts 16615 Lark Ave Ste 101 Los Gatos CA 95032-7645

MEYERS, DIANA LEE, public relations and fundraising consultant; b. Bremerton, Wash., July 27, 1937; d. Albert Earl and Evelyn Francis (Baldauf) Clark. BA in English and History, U. Calif., Santa Barbara, 1960. Office mgr. Alfred Millard Hist. Research, Santa Barbara, 1959-64; adminstrv. asst. Puritan Cos., Santa Barbara, 1964-75; ops. officer MacElhenny/Levy Real Estate, Santa Barbara, 1975-76; pub. rels. and devel. officer Cancer Found. Santa Barbara, 1976-84; owner Diana L. Meyers Consulting Svcs., Santa Barbara, 1984—. Contbr. articles to profl. jours. Assoc. Compton Internat. Fundraising, Ltd., 1996. Mem. AAUW (named gift award 1981), Nat. Soc. Fund Raising Execs. (Profl. Fundraiser of Yr. 1993), Santa Barbara Assocs., Santa Barbara C. of C. (Recognition award 1989), Santa Barbara Advt. Club (Silver medal award 1987), Univ. Club, U. Calif. Santa Barbara Alumni Assn., U. Calif. Santa Barbara Affiliates, Bus. and Industry Assocs., Channel City Club. Republican. Unitarian. Avocations: civic involvement, gourmet cuisine, theatre, music, art. Office: 928 Carpinteria St Ste 10 Santa Barbara CA 93103-3477 *Died Jan. 14, 1998.*

MEYERS, HOWARD CRAIG, lawyer; b. Chgo., Nov. 15, 1951; s. Spencer M. and Joyce L. (Dresdner) M. BA in English, Ariz. State U., 1973, JD, 1977. Bar: Ariz. 1977; cert. bus. bankruptcy specialist Am. Bankruptcy Bd. Cert., cert. bankruptcy specialist State Bar Ariz.; cert. creditors rights specialist, Am. Bankruptcy Bd. Cert. Of counsel Burch & Cracchiolo, P.A., Phoenix, Ariz. Mem. ABA, Comml. Law League of Am., Am. Bankruptcy Inst., State Bar Ariz. (debtor-creditor com.), Maricopa County Bar Assn., Internat. Council of Shopping Ctrs. Republican. E-mail: howard.meyers@azbar.org. Home: 6711 E Camelback Rd Unit 65 Scottsdale AZ 85251-2067 Office: PO Box 16882 702 E Osborn Rd Ste 200 Phoenix AZ 85014-5281

MEYERS, MARLENE O., hospital administrator; m. Eugene Meyers; children: Lori, Lisa, Dean. BSN, U. Sask., 1962; postgrad., U. Oslo, Norway, 1973; MSc, U. Calgary, Alta., Can., 1976; postgrad., Harvard U., 1980, U. Wis., 1985, U. Western Ont., Can., 1993. Various nursing positions Alta. and B.C., Can., 1962-69; instr., chair Mount Royal Coll. Allied Health, Calgary, 1969-82; asst. exec. dir. Rockyview Hosp., Calgary, 1982-85; v.p. patient svcs. Calgary Gen. Hosp., 1985-91, pres., CEO, 1991-95; pres., CEO Meyers and Assocs. Health Care Mgmt. Cons., Calgary, 1995—; surveyor Can. Coun. on Health Facilities Accreditation, 1986-97. Rotary Intl. Named Calgary Woman of Yr. in field of Health, 1982; recipient Heritage of Svc. award, 1992. Mem. Alta. Assn. RNs (hon. mem., 1996), Can. Coll. Health Svcs. Orgn., Can. Exec. Svcs. Orgn., Can. Soc. for Internat. Health (bd. dirs. 1997—). Home: 244 Osprey Cir Hope ID 83836 Office: 10464 E Cannon Dr Scottsdale AZ 85258-4929

MEYERS, THEDA MARIA, textile company executive; b. Bremen, Germany, Feb. 16; came to U.S. 1957; d. Johann-Friedrich and Christophina E.L.J. (Fentrohs) Ficke; m. Laurence Jay Meyers, Oct. 2, 1960 (div. 1970); 1 child, Jayson Bennett. Dipl., U. Bremen, 1956; student, Fashion Inst. Tech., N.Y.C., 1960. Artist-stylist Rosewood Fabrics, N.Y.C., 1960-62; textile stylist Belding Corticelli, N.Y.C., 1962-65; chief designer Jerry Mann of Calif., L.A., 1969-74; fashion designer Sunbow Ltd., Prisma Corp., L.A., 1974-81, Frig & Frag Inc., L.A., 1981-83, Jonathan Martin, L.A., 1983-85; textile stylist, v.p. design E.M.D.A.Y., Inc., L.A., 1985-92; cons. Theda Meyers Consultancy, L.A., 1993—; part-time tchr. Fashion Inst. of Design & Merchandising, L.A., to 1974; part-time judge Trade Tech. Coll., L.A. to 1981; textile designer extensive nat. and internat. experience in womenswear apparel design and textile design. designer Calif. apparel. Mem. NAFE. Avocations: fine arts, theater. Office: 38 Saint Tropez Laguna Niguel CA 92677-2768

MEYERSON, BARBARA TOBIAS, elementary school educator; b. Rockville Centre, N.Y., May 17, 1928; d. Sol and Hermine (Sternberg) Tobias; m. Daniel Meyerson, Sept. 4, 1962 (dec. Apr. 1989); children: George D., Barbara Meyerson Ayers. BEd, SUNY, New Paltz, 1948; postgrad., NYU, Hofstra U. Tchr. kindergarten Dix Hills (N.Y.) pub. schs., Hicksville (N.Y.) pub. schs., Valley Stream (N.Y.) pub. schs.; tchr. 6th grade Flushing (N.Y.) Bd. Edn. Dist. commr. Boy Scouts Am., mem. tng. staff, organizer new units; founder, sec. Repertory Theatre, Rio Rancho, N.Mex.; bd. dirs. Italian Am. Assn., Rio Rancho; vol. Rio Rancho City Hall Pub. Offices; vol. reading and spl. edn. classes RRPS. Mem. ACE, VFW Aux. (pres.), United Fedn. Tchrs. Home: 6127 Cottontail Rd NE Rio Rancho NM 87124-1545

MEYERSON, BRUCE ELLIOT, lawyer; b. N.Y.C., Apr. 10, 1947. BS, Ariz. State U., 1968; JD, Georgetown U., 1972. Bar: Ariz. 1972. Exec. dir. Ariz. Ctr. for Law in Pub. Interest, 1974-82; judge Ariz. Ct. Appeals, 1982-86; gen. counsel Ariz. State U., 1986-90; ptnr. Steptoe & Johnson, Phoenix; adj. prof. law Ariz. State U., 1985-88. Mem. nat. governing bd. Common Cause, 1978-81; bd. dirs. Community Legal Svcs., 1979-81; chair ad hoc com. on human rels. City of Phoenix, 1984. Office: Steptoe & Johnson 40 N Central Ave 24th Fl Phoenix AZ 85004-4424

MEYERSON, GREGORY Z., judge, lawyer; b. Bklyn., Sept. 14, 1948; s. Fred and Shirley (Kahn) M.; m. Sandy Meyerson, June 15, 1975; 1 child, David E. BA, U. Ariz., 1970, JD, 1973. Bar: Ariz. 1973, U.S. Dist. Ct. Ariz. 1973. Trial specialist NLRB, Phoenix, 1973-87; U.S. immigration judge U.S. Dept. Justice, Harlingen, Tex., 1988-93; U.S. adminstrv. law judge Social Security Adminstrn., Phoenix, 1993—, hearing office chief adminstrv. law judge, 1995—. Mem. State Bar Ariz. Home: 1550 E Redfield Rd Phoenix AZ 85022-4595 Office: Social Security Adminstrn 3737 N 7th St Ste 200 Phoenix AZ 85014-5078

MIAN, GUO, electrical engineer; b. Shanghai, Feb. 6, 1957; came to U.S., 1987; s. Wenseng Mian and Guorong Sun; m. Ann Wang, Nov. 1, 1989. BS in Physics, Shanghai U. Sci. & Tech., 1982; MS in Physics, Western Ill. U., 1989; DSc in Elec. Engring., Washington U., 1992. Mgr. Rec. Media Lab. Magnetic Rec. Ctr., Shanghai (China) Ctrl. Chem. Ltd., 1982-85; vis. scientist materials sci. lab. Keio U., Yokohama, Japan, 1985-87; sr. rsch. elec. engring. Quantum Corp., Milpitas, Calif., 1992-93, Conner Peripherals, San Jose, Calif., 1993-95; sr. mgr. HDD R&D Ctr. Samsung Info. Sys. Am., San Jose, Calif., 1995—. Contbr. articles to Jour. Materials Sci., IEEE Trans. Magnetics, Jour. Magnetism & Magnetic Materials, Jour. Applied Physics, Japanese Jour. Applied Physics, Jour. Japanese Magnetic Soc. Recipient C & C Promotion award Found. for C & C Promotion, Tokyo, 1986. Mem. IEEE, IEEE Magnetics Soc., IEEE Computer Soc., Am. Phys. Soc. Achievements include discovery of transverse correlation length in magnetic thin film media, a linear relationship between correlation function of media noise and an off track displacement of a recording head, an algorithm to determine an autocorrelation signal to noise ratio for an arbitratry data sequence in time domain, an algorithm to determine a nonlinear bit shift in high density magnetic storage by a time domain correlation analysis which has been implemented in Lecory 7200 and 9350 digital scopes, an in-situ measurement of exchange coupling of magnetic thin film, mechanism of residual stress forming and releasing in electronic ceramics processing; inventor in field. Home: 105 Serra Way # 362 Milpitas CA 95035-5206

MIAN, LAL SHAH, entomologist, educator; b. Pakistan, Mar. 4, 1945; s. Mohammad Shah M.; m. Judith Anne Conatser, Dec. 26, 1983; children: David Shah and Adam Shah. BSc in Agrl. with honors, U. Peshawar, 1967, MSc in Agrl. with honors, 1972; MS in Agrl., Am. U., Beirut, Lebanon, 1974; PhD in Entomology, U. Calif., Riverside, 1982. Registered Environ. Health Specialist. Tech. asst. forest entomology Forest Rsch. Inst., Peshawar, 1967-68; instr. entomology U. Peshawar, 1969-72, lectr. entomology, 1974-77; vector ecologist San Bernardino (Calif.) County Vector Control Program Pub. Health Dept., 1986—; adj. lectr. Calif. State U., San Bernardino, 1993, 95, 98. Author: (with others) Distribution, Transport and Fate of the Insecticides Malathion and Parathion in the Environment, 1981, Interagency Guidelines for the Surveillance and Control of Selected Vector-borne Pathogens in California, 1995; reviewer Environ. Entomology, Jour. of Econ. Entomology, Annals of Entomological Soc.Am., 1980-85; assoc. editor Bull. Soc. Vector Ecology, 1991-92; editl. bd. Wing Beats, 1992-94, Bull. Soc. Vector Ecology, 1992—. contbr. more than 55 articles to profl. jours.; numerous interviews to newsmedia. Elected mem. U. Senate Lectrs. Constituency, 1976-77, U. Syndicate 23-mem Governing Body, 1976-77; mem. Curriculum Com. Faculty Agrl., 1975-76, Resident Dir. Tchr. Student Ctr., 1975-77, Chancellor's Search Com. for Dean Coll. Natural and Agrl. Scis. U. Calif., 1981, Grad. Student Coun. U. Calif., 1981, Student Mini-Grant Adv. Com. U. Calif. Coop. Ext., 1981-82. Recipient postdoctoral fellow in mosquito rsch. U. Calif., 1982-83, 84-85, 85-86; assistantship in mosquito rsch. U. Calif., 1981-82; Dawood Found. scholar U. Peshawar, 1962-63, Directorate of Edn. scholar, U. Peshawar, 1962-67, Dept. Agrl. scholar U. Peshawar, 1964-67, U.S. Aid scholar Am. U., 1972-74, Ctrl. Overseas scholarship U. Calif., 1977-82. Mem. AAAS, Internat. N.W. Conf. Diseases in Nature Communicable to Man, Am. Registry Profl. Entomologists, Am. Mosquito Control Assn. (recertification and tng. com., 1992-94, recertification com., 1994-95, pub. rels., edn. com. 1998), Entomol. Soc. Am., N.Y. Acad. Scis., Mosquito and Vector Control Assn. Calif. (disease control subcom. Vector control com., 1990-93, pubs. com., 1990-94, tng. and cert., 1991-97, chem. control com., 1993-97, Africanized Honey Bee Ad Hoc Com., 1995-97, procs., 1997), Calif. Environ. Health Assn., Entomological Assn. So. Calif., San Bernardino County Africanized Honey Bee Task Force, Statewide Africanized Honey Bee Stearing Com., Soc. Vector Ecology (pubs. com., 1988, local arrangements com., 1993, program com. ednl. programs in Vector control com., 1993), Big Bear Valley (coordinated resource mgmt. plan group, 1993-94), Rathbun Tech. Adv. Com., Sigma Xi. Democrat. Office: San Bernardino County Vector Control Program 2355 E 5th St San Bernardino CA 92410-5201

MICCO, TERI RENÉ, artist; b. Hutchinson, Kans., Mar. 10, 1959; d. Alexander James and Sybil Ruth (Mathes) M. BFA, Washington U., 1981; MFA, Sch. of Visual Arts, 1989. Graphic artist Denver Ctr. Theatre Co. & NTC, Denver, 1984-85; theatre reviewer Westword Newspaper, Denver, 1985-86; graphic designer, illustrator Teri Micco Design and Illustration, Denver, 1986-87; designer, prodn. artist WBMG, Working Woman mag., SVA Press, N.Y.C., 1988-89; asst. prof. No. Ariz. U., Flagstaff, 1989-92, Boise State U., 1992-97; artist Boise, 1997-98, Las Vegas, N.Mex., 1998—; juror student area competition Nat. PTA Reflections Program, Boise, 1994; panelist Boise State U., 1993, 95; project creator, coord. Artists for Transcendence, Boise, 1997-98, Las Vegas, N.Mex., 1998—. Co-author, designer: Force(s)/Modalities: International Book and Art Exhibit, 1996 (Internat. Juried competition); artist, author, designer A Booker's Dozen: Idaho Center For the Book, 1994. Vol. East End Neighborhood Assn., Boise, 1992-95. Grantee Idaho Commn. on the Arts, 1995, Idaho Commn. on the Arts, 1998; recipient Award of Excellence U. Coll. Designers Assn., 1994, Excellence in Publ. Format Design and Column Illustration Art Dirs. Club of Denver, 1984. Mem. Boise Art Mus., Arts for Idaho, Coll. Art Assn., East End Neighborhood Assn. Avocations: playing flute and clarinet, walking in nature.

MICHAEL, CECIL FRANCIS, JR., pediatrician; b. Albuquerque, June 3, 1950; s. Cecil F. and Gene (Clairmont) M.; m. Karen Sara Dworkin, June 28, 1975; children: Kristen, Jonathan. BA in Chemistry, U. N.M., 1972, MD, 1976. Resident in pediats. Phoenix Affiliated Pediat. Program, 1976-79; pvt. practice Cactus Children's Clinic, Glendale, Ariz., 1979—; chmn. pediat. dept. Thunderbird Samaritan Hosp., Glendale, 1981-83; mem. grievance com. Maricopa County Med. Soc., Phoenix, 1987. Contbr. article to profl. jour. Recipient Top Doctor Nurse's List award, Phoenix Mag. Poll, 1997, Top Doctor Doctor's Poll, 1998. Fellow Am. Acad. Pediats.; mem. AMA, Ariz. Med. Assn., Maricopa County Med. Soc. Democrat. Roman Catholic. Avocations: golf, exercise, gardening, mountain biking. Office: Cactus Childrens Clinic 5310 W Thunderbird Glendale AZ 85306

MICHAEL, ERNEST ARTHUR, mathematics educator; b. Zurich, Switzerland, Aug. 26, 1925; came to U.S., 1939; s. Jakob and Erna (Sondheimer) M.; m. Colette Verger Davis, 1956 (div. 1966); children: Alan, David, Gerard; m. Erika Goodman Joseph, Dec. 4, 1966; children: Hillary, Joshua. B.A., Cornell U., 1947; M.A., Harvard U., 1948; Ph.D., U. Chgo., 1951. Mem. faculty dept. math. U. Wash., Seattle, 1953—; asst. prof. U. Wash., 1953-56, assoc. prof., 1956-60, prof., 1960-93, prof. emeritus, 1993—; mem. Inst. for Advanced Study, Princeton, 1951-52, 56-57, 60-61, 68, Math. Research Inst., E.T.H., Zürich, 1973-74; vis. prof. U. Stuttgart, Ger., 1978-79, U. Munich, Fed. Republic Germany, 1987, 88, 92-93. Editor: Procs. Am. Math. Soc., 1968-71, Topology and Its Applications, 1972-94, Set-Valued Analysis, 1993—; contbr. articles to profl. jours. Served with USNR, 1944-46. Grantee AEC; Grantee Office Nav. Research; Grantee NSF; Grantee Guggenheim Found.; Grantee Humboldt Found. Mem. Am. Math. Soc., Math. Assn. Am., ACLU, Amnesty Internat. Jewish. Home: 16751 15th Ave NW Seattle WA 98177-3842 Office: U Washington Dept Math Box 354350 Seattle WA 98195-4350

MICHAEL, GARY G., retail supermarket and drug chain executive; b. 1940; married. BS in Bus., U. Idaho, 1962. Staff acct. Ernst & Ernst, CPA's, 1964-66; with Albertson's, Inc., Boise, Idaho, 1966—, acct., 1966-68, asst. controller, 1968-71, controller, 1971-72, v.p., controller, 1972-74, sr. v.p. fin., treas., 1974-76, exec. v.p., 1976-84, vice chmn., CFO, corp. devel. officer, 1984-91, chmn., CEO, 1991—; also dir. Albertson's, Inc. Served to 1st lt. U.S. Army, 1962-64. Office: Albertsons Inc PO Box 20 250 E Parkcenter Blvd Boise ID 83706-3999*

MICHAEL, JAMES DANIEL, computer scientist; b. Peoria, Ill., May 27, 1957; s. Thomas Proctor and Mary Lou (Wagner) M.; m. Judith Ann O'Donnell, June 23, 1979. BS in Psychology, U. Calif., Davis, 1978. Teller Bank of Am., Davis, 1978-79, Fresno, Calif., 1979; computer operator Fresno County Computer Svcs., 1979-81; computer programmer Gesco Corp., Fresno, 1981-83, systems programmer, 1983-89; mgr. IBM operating systems Calif. State U., Fresno, 1989—. Co-author: The Porter Tract - An Historical and Architectural Survey, 1990; contbr. articles to profl. publs. Mem. Fresno City and County Hist. Soc., 1989—; founding mem. Landmarks Preservation Coun., Fresno, 1991—, Tree Fresno, 1987—; mem. Fresno Zool. Soc. Mem. Assn. for Computing Machinery, Nat. Systems Programmer Assn. Democrat. Avocations: historic home restoration, music, Irish language studies, gardening. Office: Calif State U CCMS 2225 E San Ramon Ave Fresno CA 93740-8029

MICHAELS, PATRICK FRANCIS, broadcasting company executive; b. Superior, Wis., Nov. 5, 1925; s. Julian and Kathryn Elizabeth (Keating) M.; AA, U. Melbourne, 1943; BA, Golden State U., 1954; PhD, London U., 1964; m. Paula Naomi Bowen, May 1, 1960; children—Stephanie Michelle, Patricia Erin. War corr. CBS; news editor King Broadcasting, 1945-50; war corr. Mid-East Internat. News Service, 1947-49; war corr. MBS, Korea, 1950-53; news dir. Sta. WDSU-AM-FM-TV, 1953-54; fgn. corr. NBC, S. Am., 1954-56; news dir. Sta. KWIZ, 1956-59; commentator ABC, Los Angeles, 1959-62; fgn. corr. Am. News Services, London, 1962-64; news commentator McFadden Dartell Sta. KCDQ, 1964-68; news commentator ABC, San Francisco, 1968-70; news dir. Sta. KWIZ, Santa Ana, Calif., 1970-74, station mgr., 1974-81; pres. Sta. KWRM, Corona, Calif., Sta. KQLH, San Bernardino, Calif., 1981-88; chmn. Michaels Media, Huntington Beach, Calif., 1988—. Bd. dirs. Econ. Devel. Corp. Mem. Nat. Assn. Broadcasters (bd. dirs.), Calif. Broadcasters Assn. (v.p.), Am. Fedn. TV and Radio Artists, Orange County Broadcasters Assn. (pres.), Sigma Delta Chi (ethics com.). Republican. Clubs: Rotary, Balboa Bay (bd. govs.), South Shore Yacht, Internat. Yachting Fellowship of Rotarians (staff commodore). Home: PO Box 832 Corona Del Mar CA 92625-0832

MICHAL, RONALD JAMES, physicist; b. Compton, Calif., Oct. 26, 1953; s. James Victor and Joy Aileen (Rogers) M.; m. Monica Jewel Anderson, Feb. 9, 1974 (div. Jan. 1983); children: Kenneth James, Debra Jewel, Michal; m. Valerie Jean Lowe, Oct. 19, 1984; children: Katherine Marie, Christopher Paul Miller. AA Physics, Fullerton (Calif.) C.C., 1976; BA Physics, Calif. State U., Fullerton, 1978; MA Physics, Calif. State U., Long Beach, 1981. Cert. community coll. tchr., Calif. Engr./scientist McDonnell Douglas, Huntington Beach, Calif., 1978-88; sr. engr. Smith Industries, Grand Rapids, Mich., 1988-90; engr. specialist Litton Guidance and Control, Woodland Hills, Calif., 1991—; instr. Fullerton Coll., 1981-88. Contbr. articles to profl. jours. Mem. Astron. Soc. Pacific, Planetary Soc., Internat. Planetarium Soc., High-Desert Astron. Soc. Republican. Achievements include patents for apparatus for reducing magnetic field effects in fiber optic gyros; fiber-optic senor, optical fiber sensing systems having acoustical modulation, reciprocally switched four modulator systems. Home: PO Box 152 1016 Apple St Wrightwood CA 92397 Office: Litton Guidance and Control 5500 Canoga Ave Woodland Hills CA 91367-6621

MICHALKO, JAMES PAUL, library association administrator; b. Cleve., May 13, 1950; s. Paul James and Lillian (Fanta) M.; 1 child, Alexandra. BA, Georgetown U., 1971; MLS, MBA, U. Chgo., 1974. Asst. to v.p., adminstrn. Technicare Inc. (formerly BCC Industries), Cleve., 1971-72; asst dir., adminstrn. U. Pa. Librs., Phila., 1974-80; dir. bus. and fin. Rsch. Librs. Group, Stanford, Calif., 1980-85, v.p. fin. and adminstrn., 1985-87, acting pres., 1988-89; pres. Rsch. Librs. Group, Mountain View, Calif., 1989—. Contbr. to Libr. Quar., Coll. & Rsch. Librs.; reviewer for Libr. Quar., Coll. & Rsch. Librs., Acad. of Mgmt. Rev., Jour. Acad. Librarianship, Jour. Libr. Adminstrn. Office: Rsch Librs Group Inc 1200 Villa St Mountain View CA 94041-1106

MICHAUD, GERALD FREDRICK, media advocacy nonprofit executive; b. Rochester, N.Y., June 16, 1949; s. Eric Joseph and Dorothy (Daigle) M. BA magna cum laude, U. Detroit, 1971, MA, 1975; postgrad., Loyola U., New Orleans, 1975. Asst. dir., writer Alba House Communications, Canfield, Ohio, 1972-73; dir. Alba House Media, Detroit, 1973-75; pub. rels. Youth for Understanding, Ann Arbor, Mich., 1975-79; editor EDM Digest, Farmington, Mich., 1978-80; creative dir., v.p. Dimon and Assocs. Advt., Burbank, Calif., 1980-87; exec. dir. End Hunger Network, Beverly Hills, Calif., 1987-95; v.p. creative svcs. Optima Direct, Vienna, Va., 1995—; bd. dirs., pres. End Hunger Network, Santa Monica. Graphic designer (TV spl.) End Hunger Televent, 1983, Live Aid, 1985; editor jour. Nutrition, 1985-87. Co-chmn. Prime Time to End Hunger, 1989. Recipient John Vismara award U. Detroit, 1971, Pioneer Gold award Creative Direct Mktg. Guild West, 1993, Gold Maxi award Direct Mktg. Assn. Washington. Democrat. Roman Catholic. Home: 440 Estado Way Novato CA 94945-1306 Office: End Hunger Network 365 Sycamore Rd Santa Monica CA 90402-1121

MICHAUDON, ANDRÉ FRANCISQUE, physicist; b. Cavaillon, Vaucluse, France, May 14, 1929; s. Maurice Louis and Jeanne Francoise (Chatal) M.; children: Claire Hello, Helene Caron. Engring. degree, Ecole Supérieure Ingenieurs Arts et Métiers, Paris, 1951, Ecole Supérieure Electricite, Paris, 1953; DSc, U. Paris, 1964. Rsch. engr. Le Materiel Teléphonique, Boulogne, France, 1954-56; group leader Commissariat à Energie Atomique, Cen Saclay, France, 1956-64, 65-72; theorist MIT, Cambridge, 1964-65; div. head Commissariat à Energie Atomique, Bruyeres le Chalel, France, 1972-79; dept. dept. head Commissariat à l'Energie Atomique, Limeil, France, 1979-83; French co-dir. Inst. Laue Langevin, Grenoble, France, 1983-89; prof. Inst. Nat. des Scis. et Techniques Nucléaires, Saclay, Orsay, France, 1969-84; physicist Los Alamos Nat. Lab., 1989—; mem. exec. coun. European Sci. Found., Strasbourg, France, 1987-90; mem. adv. coun. Cen. Bur. for Nuclear Measurements EU, Geel, Belgium, 1990-95; cons. Orgn. for Econ. Cooperation and Devel., Paris, 1989-92. Author, editor: Nuclear Fission, 1981; co-gen. editor: Neutron Sources, 1983, Neutron Radiative Capture, 1984, Probability & Statistics, 1991; contbr. articles to profl. jours. Lt. French Navy, 1953-54. Recipient written congratulations Minister of the Navy, France, 1954, award Acad. des Sciences, Paris, 1980; named knight Order of Merit, Paris, 1984. Fellow Am. Phys. Soc., Am. Nuclear Soc.; mem. Soc. Francaise de Physique, N.Y. Acad. Scis. Avocations: music, tennis, skiing, golf, hiking. Home: 211 W Water St Santa Fe NM 87501-6201 Office: Los Alamos Nat Lab Lansce 3 MS H 855 Los Alamos NM 87545

MICHEL, DIANE LOUISE, social sciences educator; b. San Jose, Calif.; d. Stephen Price and Desdemona (Van Meter) Webb; children: Suzanne Karen Downing, Stephen Webb Radke. Student, San Jose State Coll., 1952-54, 57-59; BS in Psychology, Portland (Oreg.) State U., 1975; PhD in Ednl. Psychology, U. Oreg., 1987. Instr. Mt. Hood C.C., Gresham, Oreg., 1976-78, Portland State U., 1976-79, U. Oreg., 1980-81; grad. tchrs. aide Oreg. State U., 1982-85; tchg. asst. De Anza Coll., Cupertino, Calif., 1987-88; instr. Palo Verde Coll., Blythe, Calif., 1988—; mem. Calif. statewide acad. senate, 1996-98. Mem. NEA (pres. 1998-99), Faculty Assn. Calif. Cmty. Colls., Mus. of Tolerance, Amnesty Internat. Mem. Soc. of Friends. Office: Palo Verde Coll 811 W Chanslorway Blythe CA 92226

MICHEL, JAMES WESLEY, family practice physician, nutritional consultant; b. Boulder, Colo., June 19, 1946; s. Lester Allen and Martha Lilly (Brown) M.; m. Linda Carroll Goody, June 27, 1970 (div. Nov. 1986); m. June Irene Briggs Rand Villalvazo, June 18, 1988; children: Cynthia Renee, Marcus Allen, Matthew Alexander, Martin Andrew, Macajan Adam. BS, Harvey Mudd Coll., 1968; MD, Wayne State U., 1976. Intern U. Colo., resident; physician USPHS, Westcliffe, Colo., 1979-82, Shaw Health Ctr., Hollywood, Calif., 1982-89; med. dir. Primus Med. Clinic, Monterey, Calif., 1989-92; pvt. practice Carmel, Calif., 1992—; staff phys. Cmty. Hosp. Monterey Peninsula, 1992—. Bd. dirs. Monterey Hostel Soc., 1998; clerical asst. St. James Episcopal Ch., chalice bearer, 1996-98, reader, 1996-98. Fellow Am. Acad. Family Physicians. Avocations: scuba, railroading, hostelling. Home: PO Box 3697 Carmel CA 93921-3697 Office: PO Box 4947 Carmel CA 93921-4947

MICHEL, MARY ANN KEDZUF, nursing educator; b. Evergreen Park, Ill., June 1, 1939; d. John Roman and Mary (Bassar) Kedzuf; m. Jean Paul Michel, 1974. Diploma in nursing, Little Company of Mary Hosp., Evergreen Park, 1960; BS in nursing, Loyola U., Chgo., 1964; MS, No. Ill. U., 1968, EdD, 1971. Staff nurse Little Co. of Mary Hosp., 1960-64; instr. Little Co. of Mary Hosp. (Sch. Nursing), 1964-67, No. Ill. U., DeKalb, 1968-69; asst. prof. No. Ill. U., 1969-71; chmn. dept. nursing U. Nev., Las Vegas, 1971-73; prof. nursing U. Nev., 1975—, dean Coll. Health Scis., 1973-90; pres. PERC, Inc.; mgmt. cons., 1993—; mgmt. cons. Nev. Donor Network, 1993; mem. So. Nev. Health Manpower Task Force, 1975; mem. manpower com. Plan Devel. Commn., Clark County Health Sys. Agy., 1977-79, mem. governing body, 1981-86; mem. Nev. Health Coordinating Coun., Western Inst. Nursing, 1971-85; mem. coordinating com. assembly instnl. adminstrs. dept. allied health edn. and accreditation AMA, 1985-88; mem. bd. advisors So. Nev. Vocat. Tech. Ctr., 1976-80; sec.-treas. Nev. Donor Network, 1988-89, bd. dirs., 1986-90, chmn. bd., 1988-90. Contbr. articles to profl. jours. Trustee Desert Spring Hosp., Las Vegas, 1976-85; bd. dirs. Nathan Adelson Hospice, 1982-88, Bridge Counseling Assocs., 1982, Everywoman's Ctr., 1984-86; chmn. Nev. Commn. on Nursing Edn., 1972-73, Nursing Articulation Com., 1972-73, Yr. of Nurse Com., 1978; moderator Invitational Conf. Continuing Edn., Am. Soc. Allied Health Professions, 1978; mgmt. cons. Nev. Donor Network, 1994—, Donor Organ Recovery Svc., Transplant Recipient Internat. Orgn., S.W. Eye Bank, S.W. Tissue Bank. Named Outstanding Alumnus, Loyola U., 1983; NIMH fellow, 1967-68. Fellow Am. Soc. Allied Health Professions, 1991, (chmn. nat. resolutions com. 1981-84, treas. 1988-90, sec's. award com. 1982-83, 92-93, nat. by-laws com. 1985,

conv. chmn. 1987); mem. AAUP, Am. Nurses Assn., Nev. Nurses Assn. (dir. 1975-77, treas. 1977-79, conv. chmn. 1978), So. Nev. Area Health Edn. Coun., Western Health Deans (co-organizer 1985, chair, 1988-90), Nat. League Nursing, Nev. Heart Assn., So. Nev. Mem. Hosps. (mem. nursing recruitment com. 1981-83, mem. nursing practice com. 1983-85), Las Vegas C. of C. (named Woman of Yr. Edn.) 1988, Slovak Catholic Sokols, Phi Kappa Phi (chpt. sec. 1981-83, pres.-elect 1983, pres. 1984, v.p. Western region 1989-95, editl. bd. jour. Nat. Forum 1989-93), Alpha Beta Gamma (hon.), Sigma Theta Tau, Zeta Kappa. Office: U Nev Las Vegas 4505 S Maryland Pky Las Vegas NV 89154-9900

MICHELS, DOUG, executive. Pres., CEO SCO, Santa Cruz, Calif. Office: 425 Encinal St PO Box 1900 Santa Cruz CA 95061-1900*

MICKELSON, SIG, broadcasting executive, educator; b. Clinton, Minn., May 24, 1913; s. Olaf and Harriet (Reinholdson) M.; m. Maybelle Brown, June 8, 1940 (dec. Apr., 1985); children: Karen Ann (Mrs. Christiaan De Brauw), Alan; m. Elena Mier y Teran, June 14, 1986. B.A., Augustana Coll., 1934, LLD, 1987; M.A., U. Minn., 1940. With CBS, N.Y.C., 1943-61; pres. CBS News, 1954-61; v.p., dir. Time-Life Broadcast, Inc., N.Y.C., 1961-70. Ency. Brit. Ednl. Corp., Chgo., 1970-72; prof., chmn. editorial dept. Medill Sch. Journalism, Northwestern U., Evanston, Ill., 1972-75; pres. RFE/RL, Inc., Washington, 1975-78; Disting. vis. prof. San Diego State U., 1978-79, exec. dir. Ctr. for Communications, 1979-82, adj. prof, 1984-90, Van Deerlin prof. communications, 1989-90; pres. San Diego Communications Coun., 1989-90; Manship prof. journalism La. State U., 1991-93, disting. prof. comm., 1994—; rsch. fellow Hoover Instn., 1981—; advisor Nat. News Coun., 1973-80; ex-officio Bd. Internat. Broadcasting, 1975-78; dir. Stauffer Comms. Inc., 1979-95. Author: The Electric Mirror, 1972, America's Other Voice, 1983, The First Amendment: The Challenge of New Technology, 1989, From Whistle Stop to Sound Bite, 1989, The Northern Pacific Railroad and the Selling of the West, 1993, The Decade That Shaped TV News: CBS in the 1950s, 1998. Bd. regents Augustana Coll., 1983-95. Mem. Radio TV News Dirs. Assn. (founder, v.p. 1946-48, pres. 1948-49), Internat. Inst. for Comm. (founder, chmn. 1970-71, chmn. exec. com. 1967-70, 71-73), Coun. on Fgn. Rels. Clubs: Century Assn. (N.Y.C.); Cosmos (Washington). Home: 6443 Pasatiempo Ave San Diego CA 92120-3823

MIDDLEBROOKS, EDDIE JOE, environmental engineer; b. Crawford County, Ga., Oct. 16, 1932; s. Robert Harold and Jewell LaVerne (Dixon) M.; m. Charlotte Linda Hardy, Dec. 6, 1958; 1 child, Linda Tracey. BCE, U. Fla., 1956, MS, 1960; PhD, Miss. State U., 1966. Registered profl. engr., Ariz., Miss., Utah; registered land surveyor, Fla. Asst. san. engr. USPHS, Cin., 1956-58; field engr. T.T. Jones Constrn. Co., Atlanta, 1958-59; grad. teaching asst. U. Fla., 1959-60; research asst. U. Ariz., 1960-61; asst. prof., then assoc. prof. Miss. State U., 1962-67; research engr., asst. dir. San. Engring. Research Lab., U. Calif.-Berkeley, 1968-70; prof. Utah State U., Logan, 1970-82, dean Coll. Engring., 1974-82; Newman chair natural resources engring. Clemson U., 1982-83; provost, v.p. acad. affairs Tenn. Tech. U., 1983-88; provost, v.p. acad. affairs U. Tulsa, 1988-90, prof. chem. engring., 1988-92, Trustees prof. chem. engring., 1990-92, acting pres., 1990; prof. civil engring. U. Nevada, Reno, 1992-97; mem. nat. drinking water adv. council EPA, 1981-83; cons. EPA, UN Indsl. Devel. Orgn., Calif. Water Resources Control Bd., also numerous indsl. and engring. firms. Author: Modeling the Eutrophication Process, 1974, Statistical Calculations-How To Solve Statistical Problems, 1976, Biostimulation and Nutrient Assessment, 1976, Water Supply Engineering Design, 1977, Lagoon Information Source Book, 1978, Industrial Pollution Control, Vol. 1: Agro-Industries, 1979, Wastewater Collection and Treatment: Principles and Practices, 1979, Water Reuse, 1982, Wastewater Stabilization Lagoon Design, Performance and Upgrading, 1982, Reverse Osmosis Treatment of Drinking Water, 1986, Pollution Control in the Petrochemicals Industry, 1987, Natural Systems for Waste Management and Treatment, 1988, 2d edit., 1995; mem. editl. adv. bd. Lewis Pubs. Inc., Environment Internat., Environ. Abstracts; contbr. tech. articles to profl. jours. Fellow ASCE; mem. AAAS, Water Environment Fedn. (dir. 1979-81, 91-92), Eddy medal 1969), Assn. Environ. Engring. Profs. (pres. 1974), Utah Water Pollution Control Assn. (pres. 1976), Internat. Assn. on Water Quality, Am. Soc. Engring. Edn., Am. Acad. Environ. Engrs. (diplomate, trustee 1992-95, v.p. 1995, pres. 1997-98), Sigma Xi, Omicron Delta Kappa, Phi Kappa Phi (Disting. mem.), Tau Beta Pi, Sigma Tau. Home and Office: 360 Blackhawk Ln Lafayette CO 80026-9392

MIDDLETON, ANTHONY WAYNE, JR., urologist, educator; b. Salt Lake City, May 6, 1939; s. Anthony Wayne and Dolores Caravena (Lowry) M.; m. Carol Samuelson, Oct. 23, 1970; children: Anthony Wayne, Suzanne, Kathryn, Jane, Michelle. BS, U. Utah, 1963; MD, Cornell U., 1966. Intern, U. Utah Hosps., Salt Lake City, 1966-67; resident in urology Mass. Gen. Hosp., Boston, 1970-74; practice urology Middleton Urol. Assos., Salt Lake City, 1974—; mem. staff Primary Children's Hosp., staff pres., 1981-82; mem. staff Latter-Day Saints Hosp., chmn. divsn. urology, 1995—; chmn. divsn. of urology Salt Lake Regional Med. Ctr. 1977-79, 84-86, assoc. clin. prof. surgery U. Utah Med. Coll., 1977—; vice chmn. bd. govs. Utah Med. Self-Ins. Assn., 1980-81, 96—, chmn. 1985-87; chmn. med. adv. bd. Uroquest Co., 1996—. Bd. dirs. Utah chpt. Am. Cancer Soc., 1978-86; bishop, later stake presidency Ch. Jesus Christ Latter-day Saints; vice chmn. Utah Med. Polit. Action Com., 1978-81, chmn., 1981-83; chmn. Utah Physicians for Reagan, 1983-84; mem. U. Utah Coll. Medicine Dean's Search Com., 1983-84; bd. dirs. Utah Symphony, 1985—, Primary Children's Found., 1989-96. Capt. USAF, 1968-70. Editor (monthly pub.) AACU-FAX, 1992—; assoc. editor Millenial Star Brit. LDS mag. 1960-61. Mem. ACS, Utah Med. Assn. (pres. 87-88, disting. svc. award 1993), Am. Urologic Assn. (socioecons. com. 1987-90, chmn. western sect. socioecons. com. 1989-90, western sect. health policy com. chmn., 1990—), AMA (alt. del. to House of Dels. 1987-88, 89-92, 94, 96-98; del. 1998—), Salt Lake County Med. Assn. (sec. 1965-67, pres. liaison com. 1980-81, pres.-elect 1981-83, pres. 1984), Utah Urol. Assn. (pres. 1976-77), Salt Lake Surg. Soc. (treas. 1977-78), Am. Assn. Clin. Urologists (bd. dirs. 1989-90, nat. pres. elect 1990-91, pres. 1991-92, nat. bd. chmn. urologic polit. action com. UROPAC, 1992-98), Phi Beta Kappa, Alpha Omega Alpha, Beta Theta Pi (chpt. pres. Gamma Beta 1962). Republican. Contbr. articles to profl. jours. Home: 2798 Chancellor Pl Salt Lake City UT 84108-2835 Office: 1060 East 1st South Salt Lake City UT 84102-1501

MIDDLETON, MICHAEL JOHN, civil engineer; b. N.Y.C., May 14, 1953; s. Vincent Aloysius and Mary Hilda (Lehane) M. BS in Civil Engring., U. Calif., Davis, 1975. Registered profl. engr., Calif., Wash., Hawaii. Project mgr. G.A. Fitch & Assoc., Concord, Calif., 1975-78, v.p., 1978-80; project mgr. Santina & Thompson, Inc., Concord, 1980-83, dir. engring., 1983-88, sr. v.p., 1988—. scholar, Calif. Scholarship Fedn., 1971. Mem. ASCE, Nat. Soc. Profl. Engrs., Soc. Am. Mil. Engrs. Roman Catholic. Home: 1409 Bel Air Dr Apt A Concord CA 94521-5348 Office: Santina & Thompson Inc 1355 Willow Way Ste 280 Concord CA 94520-8113

MIDDLETON-DOWNING, LAURA, psychiatric social worker, artist, small business owner; b. Edinburg, Ind., Apr. 20, 1935; d. John Thomas Jr. and Rowene Elizabeth (Baker) Middleton; m. George Charles Downing, 1974 (div. 1986). BA in English Lit., U. Colo., 1966, MFA, 1969, BA in Psychology, 1988; MSW, U. Denver, 1992; Doctor of Clin. Hypnotherapy, Am. Inst. Hypnotherapy, 1995. Cert. clin. hypnotherapist, Calif.; cert. past-life therapist, Colo. Profl. artist Silver Plume and Boulder, Colo., 1965—; profl. photographer Silver Plume, Boulder, 1975—; art tchr. U. Colo., Boulder and Longmont, 1971-73; mem. survey crew Bur. of Land Mgmt., Empire, Colo., 1984-85; cons. social work and psychotherapy Boulder, 1992—; med. social worker Good Samaritan Health Agy., Boulder, 1993-97; pvt. practice clin. hypnotherapy Boulder, 1995—, pvt. practice past-life therapist, 1995—; ind. distbr. Super Blue Green Algae, 1996—; pres. Phoenix LG, Inc. Author, photographer Frontiers, Vol. IV, No. 1, 1979; works exhibited in 15 one-woman shows, 1969—; numerous group exhbns. including group exhbn., Colo. History Mus., Denver, 1997-98. Trustee Town of Silver Plume, Colo., 1975-84; co-founder, pres. Alma Holm Rogers Nat. Orgn. Women, Clear Creek County, 1975-82; mem. Ctrl. Mountain Coun., Clear Creek County, 1980; chairperson Mary Ellen Barnes Cmty. Ctr. Project, Silver Plume, Colo., 1983; vol. Rape Crisis Team, Boulder, 1989-90, Child & Family Advocacy Program, Boulder, 1992-97; adv. bd. mem. Good Samaritan Agy., Boulder, 1993-97; caring minister vol. First Congl. Ch., Boulder, 1995-98; founding mem. Front Range Women in the Visual Arts, Boulder, Colo. Recipient Juried Exhbn. Merit award Colo. Women in the Arts, 1979; Women's Incentive scholar U. Colo., Boulder, 1989; Grad. Sch. Social Work scholar U. Denver, 1991; Colo. Grad. grantee U. Denver, 1992. Mem. NASW, DAR, Colo. Advs. for Responsible Mental Health Svcs., Eye Movement Desensitization Reprocessing Network, Assn. for Past-Life Rsch. and Therapies, Inc. (Colo. group leader), Natural Resources Def. Coun., The Nature Conservancy, Bus. Women's Leadership Group, Psi Chi. Avocations: inline skating, scuba diving, photography, travel, volunteerism. Office: PO Box 2312 Boulder CO 80306-2312

MIDDLEWOOD, MARTIN EUGENE, technical communications specialist, writer, consultant; b. Galesburg, Ill., Mar. 21, 1947; s. Martin and Bernetta Maxine (Henderson) M.; m. Mona Marie Jarmer, Sept. 10, 1971; children: Erin, Martha, Emily, Margaret. BA, Ea. Wash. U., 1973, MA, 1980. Writer tech. manuals Tektronix, Inc., Beaverton, Oreg., 1976-77, tech. writer, 1977-79, sr. tech. writer, 1979-82, supr. pub. rels., 1982-84, mgr. pub. rels., 1984-85; mgr. mktg. communications Tektronix, Inc., Vancouver, Wash., 1985-86; dir. info. strategy and svcs. Waggener Edstrom, Portland, Oreg., 1986-98; pub. Cognizer Report, Portland, Oreg., 1990-94; chmn. adv. bd. sci. and tech. writing, Clark Coll., Vancouver, 1984—; owner communications cons. firm, Vancouver, 1978—. Author: (ednl. brochure series) Oscilloscope Measurements, 1979 (award of excellence Willamette Valley chpt., Network Svcing., won Awd. of Distinction, 1980, Soc. Tech. Communication, 1980); contbr. articles to profl. jours. Served with USMC, 1967-70. Recipient cert. recognition Clark Coll., Vancouver, 1984, 86, 89, 92-98, award of excellence Pacific N.W. chpt. Internat. Assn. Bus. Communicators, 1985. Mem. Soc. Tech. Communication (sr., pres. Willamette Valley chpt. 1983-85, award of recognition 1986, chpt. pub. achievement award 1985, awards of distinction, 1980, 81). Avocation: photography. Home and Office: 1107 SE 98th Ave Vancouver WA 98664-4119

MIDKIFF, DONALD WAYNE, program manager; b. Post, Tex., Sept. 26, 1940; s. Colvert Crockett Midkiff and Judy M. (Poss) Hinckley; m. Olga Maria Androvitch, June 21, 1961 (div. 1968); m. Manbeth Jean Crowell, Apr. 29, 1979. BS in Tech. Mgmt., Denver Tech. Coll., 1988; MS in Mgmt., Colo. Tech. U., 1994, MBA, 1998. With USAF, 1960, advanced through grades to sgt., 1968; electronics supr. Lockheed Aircraft, Jidda, Saudi Arabia, 1969-71; site mgr. Kentron Hawaii, Ltd., Pleiku, South Vietnam, 1971-73; supr. Kentron, Kwajalein, Marshall Islands, 1973-80, range ops. engr., 1980-84; ops. supr. Kentron PRC, Maui, Hawaii, 1984-85; ops. mgr. Kentron PRC, Colorado Springs, Colo., 1985-87; divsn. security mgr. PRC, Colorado Springs, Colo., 1987-89; program mgr. PRC Inc., Colorado Springs, Colo., 1989—; advisor Denver Tech. Coll., Colorado Springs, 1991—. CPR instr. Am. Red Cross, 1980-86; pres. Kwajalein Dive Club, 1981-83, Kwajalein Tennis Club, 1978-80. Recipient Group Achievement award NASA, 1992. Mem. AFCEA, Mensa, Nat. Contract Mgmt. Assn., Profl. Assn. Diving Instrs. (dive master). Republican. Avocations: golf, tennis, trap shooting, scuba diving, reading. Office: PRC Inc 985 Space Center Dr Ste 260 Colorado Springs CO 80915-3642

MIDYETT, MICHAEL BURTON, contractor; b. Wolfratshausen, Bavaria, Germany, Mar. 8, 1960; came to U.S., 1962; s. Burton Robert and Emma kthryn (Streck) M.; m. Julie Kay Rienstra, May 28, 1986; children: Blakelee Jane, Michael Burton William. Laborer, leadman El Paso Precast, Colorado Springs, Colo., 1980-85; sales rep. El Paso Precast/Carder Concrete, Colorado Springs & Denver, 1985-90; sales mgr. Barbour Concrete/Pavers, Independence, Mo., 1990-94; gen. mgr. Pavestone Co., Denver, 1995—. Mem. Am. Pub. Works Assn., Am. Soc. Landscape Archiects, Home Builders Assn., Colo. Contractors Assn., Associated Landscape Contractors Colo., Mo. Concrete Assn. (pres. divsn. 1992-93). Avocations: fly fishing, golf, back packing, baseball, tennis. Office: Pavestone Co 9401 E 96th Ave Henderson CO 80640-8420

MIEL, VICKY ANN, city official; b. South Bend, Ind., June 20, 1951; d. Lawrence Paul Miel and Virginia Ann (Yeagley) Hernandez. BS, Ariz. State U., 1985. Word processing coordinator City of Phoenix, 1977-78, word processing adminstr., 1978-83, chief dep. city clk., 1983-88, city clk. dir., 1988—; assoc. prof. Phoenix Community Coll., 1982-83, Mesa (Ariz.) Community Coll., 1983; speaker in field, Boston, Santa Fe, Los Angeles, N.Y.C. and St. Paul, 1980—. Author: Phoenix Document Request Form, 1985, Developing Successful Systems Users, 1986. Judge Future Bus. Leaders Am. at Ariz. State U., Tempe, 1984; bd. dirs. Fire and Life Safety League, Phoenix, 1984. Recipient Gold Plaque, Word Processing Systems Mag., Mpls., 1980, Green Light Productivity award City of Phoenix, 1981, Honor Soc. Achievement award Internat. Word Processing Assn., 1981, 1st Ann. Grand Prize Records Mgmt. Internat. Inst. Mcpl. Clks., 1990, Olsten Award for Excellence in Records Mgmt., 1991, Tech. Award of Excellence, 1995. Mem. ASPA, Assn. Info. Systems Profls. (internat. dir. 1982-84), Internat. Inst. Mcpl. Clks. (cert., 2d v.p. 1996-97, 1st v.p. 1997-98, pres. 1998-99, tech. award of excellence 1995), Am. Records Mgrs. Assn., Assn. Image Mgmt., Am. Mgmt. Assn. Office: City of Phoenix 200 W Washington St Ste 1500 Phoenix AZ 85003-1611

MIEUX, DONNA MARIE, special education educator; b. L.A., Feb. 10, 1949; d. Donald Lee and Alma Olivia (Johnson) Troy; m. Isom (Ike) Mieux, June 9, 1972; children: Kendra Desiree, Andre Donald. BA in Sociology, U. Calif., Santa Barbara, 1971, MA in Spl. Edn., U. Akron, 1976; EdD, Nova Southeastern U., 1993. Cert. spl. edn.; cert. tchr. Lang. enrichment tchr. L.A. Unified Sch. Dist., 1972-74; resource specialist Whittier (Calif.) City Sch. Dist., 1976-79; resource specialist Hacienda La Puente (Calif.) Unified Sch. Dist., 1979—, mentor. tchr., 1993—, tchr. severely handicapped, 1989-92, artist-of-the-month developer, stamp club sponsor, 1988-90; developer, coord. before sch. tutorial program for at-risk students, 1990—; adj. faculty psychology The Union Inst., L.A., 1994—; instr. writing Mt. San Antonio Coll., Walnut, Calif., 1994—. Sunday sch. tchr. United Ch. of Christ, Claremont, Calif., 1989-93; mem. PTA, La Puente, 1972—; vol. Rancho Los Amigos Hosp., Brownies, Girl Scouts USA, various sports activities, 1969—. Recipient scholarship Compton Tchrs. Assn., 1967, Martin Luther King scholarship Calif. Tchrs. Assn., 1990; fellow Occidental Coll., 1971. Mem. Nat. Tchrs. Assn., Calif. Tchrs. Assn. Democrat. Avocations: sculpturing, writing, viewing high quality foreign movies, tennis. Office: Palm Elem Sch 14740 Palm Ave Hacienda Heights CA 91745

MIGDEN, CHESTER L., professional society administrator; b. N.Y.C., May 21, 1921; s. Albert and Louise (Jawer) M.; m. Dina Vohl, July 22, 1944; children: Barbara, Ann, Amy. B.A., CCNY, 1941; LL.B., Columbia U., 1947. Bar: N.Y. State 1947. Atty. NLRB, N.Y.C., 1947-51; various positions Screen Actors Guild Inc., Hollywood, 1952-81; nat. exec. sec. Screen Actors Guild Inc., 1973-81; v.p. Internat. Fedn. Actors, 1973-81, Calif. Labor Fedn., 1974-81, Associated Actors and Artistes Am., 1973-81; exec. dir. Assn. Talent Agts., 1982-94; ret., 1994; officer, trustee Producers-Screen Actors Guild pension, welfare plans, 1960-81; v.p. Motion Picture and TV Fund, 1975—; instr. extension program UCLA. Contbr. articles to profl. jours. Mem. Acad. Motion Picture Arts and Scis., Am. Arbitration Assn. (arbitrator), Labor Rels. Cons. Democrat. *

MIGUEL DESOUSA, LINDA J., critical care nurse, nursing educator; b. Honolulu, Dec. 6, 1946; d. Gregory and Irene N. (Calasa) Furtado; children: Joseph H. Miguel Jr., Brett A. Miguel. ADN, Maui Community Coll., Kahului, Hawaii, 1980; BSN, U. Hawaii, 1987, MS, 1990. RN, Hawaii. Charge nurse ICU-CCU Maui Meml. Hosp., Wailuku, 1980-88; nursing instr. Maui Community Coll., Kahului, 1988; unit supr.-coronary care Straub Clinic and Hosp., Honolulu, 1988-90; nursing instr. Kapiolani Community Coll., Honolulu, 1990-92; edn. dir. Waianae Health Acad., 1992-97; nursing svcs. mgr. Kula Hosp., Maui, 1997—; researcher in field. Contbr. articles to profl. jours. Outer Island Students Spl. Nursing scholar, 1988-90, Rsch. scholarship, 1989. Mem. AACN, Hawaii Nurses Assn., Hawaii Soc. for Cardiovascular and Pulmonary Rehab., Assn. Am. Women in C. C.s, Sigma Theta Tau. Office: 204 Kula Hwy Kula HI 96790-9471

MIHALOEW, DONALD MICHAEL, marriage and family therapist, educator; b. Ambridge, Pa., July 5, 1938; s. Michael and Rose Marie (DiNovo) M.; married Aug. 1970 (div. Oct. 1988); children: Christine R., Andreya L.; m. Betty J. Kellow, Sept. 1991; stepchildren: Shannon L., Misty M. BA, Westminster Coll., 1961; MDiv, Princeton (N.J.) Theol. Sem., 1964; MA, U. Oreg., 1971, EdD, 1991. Lic. marriage and family therapist, Oreg.; cert. family life educator, Nat. Coun. on Family Rels. Adj. asst. prof. Lane C.C., Eugene, Oreg., 1976-97, U. Oreg., Eugene, 1977-91, Lewis and Clark Coll., Portland, Oreg., 1991-99, Portland State U., 1991-99, N.W. Christian Coll., Eugene, 1997-98; pvt. practice Eugene, 1980—; counselor, program coord. Lane County Juvenile Ct., Eugene, 1968-80; adj. asst. prof. Independence (Kans.) C.C., 1964. Contbr. articles on family process to various publs. Bd. dirs. Chruchill Child Care Coalition, Eugene, 1980-90; asst. pastor Independence Presbyn. Ch., 1964. Recipient Bullard Social Interest award Oreg. Soc. Individual Psychology, 1998. Mem. Oreg. Assn. Marriage and Family Therapy (bd. dirs. 1998), Am. Assn. Marriage and Family Therapy. Avocations: home remodeling, backpacking, boating, camping, softball. Office: Western Oreg Inst Marriage and Family Studies 1849 Willamette St Ste 11 Eugene OR 97401

MIKALOW, ALFRED ALEXANDER, II, deep sea diver, marine surveyor, marine diving consultant; b. N.Y.C., Jan. 19, 1921; m. Janice Brenner, Aug. 1, 1960; children: Alfred Alexander, Jon Alfred. Student Rutgers U., 1940; MS, U. Calif., Berkeley, 1948; MA, Rochdale U. (Can.), 1950. Owner Coastal Diving Co., Oakland, Calif., 1950—, Divers Supply, Oakland, 1952—; dir. Coastal Sch. Deep Sea Diving, Oakland, 1950—; capt. and master rsch. vessel Coastal Researcher I; mem. Marine Inspection Bur., Oakland. marine diving contractor, cons. Mem. adv. bd. Medic Alert Found., Turlock, Calif., 1960—. Lt. comdr. USN, 1941-47, PTO, 49-50, Korea. Decorated Purple Heart, Silver Star. Mem. Divers Assn. Am. (pres. 1970-74), Treasury Recovery, Inc. (pres. 1972-75), Internat. Assn. Profl. Divers, Assn. Diving Contractors, Calif. Assn. Pvt. Edn. (no. v.p. 1971-72), Authors Guild, Internat. Game Fish Assn., U.S. Navy League, U.S. Res. Officers Assn., Tailhook Assn., U.S. Submarine Vets. WWII, Explorer Club (San Francisco), Calif. Assn. Marine Surveyors (pres. 1988—), Soc. Naval Archs. and Marine Engrs. (assoc.), Masons, Lions. Author: Fell's Guide to Sunken Treasure Ships of the World, 1972; (with H. Rieseberg) The Knight from Maine, 1974. Office: 320 29th Ave Oakland CA 94601-2104

MIKEL, THOMAS KELLY, JR., laboratory administrator; b. East Chicago, Ind., Aug. 27, 1946; s. Thomas Kelly and Anne Katherine (Vrazo) M.; BA, San Jose State U., 1973; MA, U. Calif.-Santa Barbara, 1975. Asst. dir. Santa Barbara Underseas Found., 1975-76; marine biologist PJB Labs., Ventura, Calif., 1976-81; lab. dir. CRL Environ., Ventura, 1981-88; lab. dir. ABC Labs, Ventura, 1988—; instr. oceanography Ventura Coll., 1980-81. Chair joint task group, section author 20th edit. Std. Methods Examination Water & Wastewater APHA, 1996. With U.S. Army, 1968-70. Mem. Assn. Environ. Profls., Soc. Population Ecologists, ASTME (rsch. contbr. 10th ann. symposium 1986), Soc. Environ. Toxicology and Chemistry. Biol. coord. Anacapa Underwater Natural trail U.S. Nat. Park Svc., 1976; designer ecol. restoration program of upper Newport Bay, Orange County, Calif., 1978; rsch. contbr. 3d Internat. Artificial Reef Conf., Newport Beach, Calif., 1983, Ann. Conf. Am. Petroleum Inst., Houston. Democrat.

MIKLOWITZ, PAUL STEPHEN, philosophy educator; b. Calif., June 18, 1956; s. Julius and Gloria Elaine (Dubov) M.; m. Marija Bozic, March 14, 1988; 1 child, Sabina. BA, U. Calif., Santa Cruz, 1977; MA, U. Chgo., 1979; MPhil, Yale U., 1985, PhD, 1988. Instr. Mt. St. Mary Coll., Newburgh, N.Y., 1979-80, Yale U., New Haven, Conn., 1985-88; prof. Calif. Polytech. State U., San Luis Obispo, Calif., 1988—; bioethics com. French Hosp. Med. Ctr., San Luis Obispo, Calif., 1990—. Author: Metaphysics To Metafictions, 1998; contbr. articles to profl. jours. Campaign capt. United Way, San Luis Obispo. Prize Tchg. fellow Yale U., New Haven, Conn., 1985, Andrew W. Mellon fellow Rice U., Houston, 1988. Mem. Am. Assn. U. Professors, The Nietzsche Soc. Avocations: photography. Office: Calif Polytech State U San Luis Obispo CA 93407

MILAN, MARJORIE LUCILLE, early childhood education educator; b. Ludlow, Colo., June 24, 1926; d. John B. and Barbara (Zenonian) Pinamont; m. John Francis Milan, June 18, 1949; children: Barbara, J. Mark, Kevin. BA, U. Colo., 1947, MA, 1978; PhD, U. Denver, 1983. Cert. tchr., adminstr., supt., Colo. Tchr. Boulder (Colo.) Pub. Schs., 1947-49, Denver Pub. Schs., 1949-51, 67—; adminstr. T. Tot Kindergarten, Denver, 1951-55; tchr. Colo. Women's Coll., Denver, 1956-57; adminstr. Associated Schs., Denver, 1956-67; adv. bd. George Washington Carver Nursery, Denver, 1960-85. Mem. Assn. Childhood Edn. (state bd. 1960—, Hall of Excellence 1991), Rotary (pres. chpt. 1994-95), Philanthropic Ednl. Orgn., Phi Delta Kappa, Delta Kappa Gamma. Avocations: swimming, music. Home: 1775 Lee St Lakewood CO 80215-2855

MILANOVICH, NORMA JOANNE, educational company executive; b. Littlefork, Minn., June 4, 1945; d. Lyle Albert and Loretta (Leona) Drake; m. Rudolph William Milanovich, Mar. 18, 1943 (dec.); 1 child, Rudolph William Jr. BS in Home Econs., U. Wis., Stout, 1968; MA in Curriculum and Instrn., U. Houston, 1973, EdD in Curriculum and Program Devel., 1982. Instr. human svcs. dept. U. Houston, 1971-75; dir. videos project U. N.Mex., Albuquerque, 1976-78, dir. vocat. edn. equity ctr., 1978-88, asst. prof. occupational edn., 1982-88, coord. occupational vocat. edn. programs, 1983-88, dir. consortium rsch. and devel. in occupational edn., 1984-88; pres. Alpha Connection Tng. Corp., Albuquerque, 1988—; adj. instr. Cen. Tng. Acad., Dept. Energy, Wackenhut; mem. faculty U. Phoenix; adj. faculty So. Ill. U., Lesley Coll., Boston. Author: Model Equitable Behavior in the Classroom, 1983, Handbook for Vocational-Technical Certification in New Mexico, 1985, A Vision for Kansas: Systems of Measures and Standards of Performance, 1992, Workplace Skills: The Employability Factor, 1993; editor: Choosing What's Best for You, 1982, A Handbook for Handling Conflict in the Classroom, 1983, Starting Out...A Job Finding Handbook for Teen Parents, Going to Work...Job Rights for Teens; author: JTPA Strategic Marketing Plan, 1990, We, The Arcturians, 1990, Sacred Journey to Atlantis, 1991, The Light Shall Set You Free, 1996; editor: Majestic Raise newsletter, 1996, Celestial Voices newsletter, 1991-96. Bd. dirs. Albuquerque Single Parent Occupational Scholarship Program, 1984-86; del. Youth for Understanding Internat. Program, 1985-90; mem. adv. bd. Southwestern Indian Poly. Inst., 1984-88; com. mem. Region VI Consumer Exch. Com., 1982-84; ednl. lectures, tng., tour dir. internat. study tours to Japan, Austria, Korea, India, Nepal, Mex., Eng., Greece, Egypt, Australia, New Zealand, Fed. Republic Germany, Israel, Guatemala, Peru, Bolivia, Chile, Easter Island, Tibet, China, Hong Kong, Turkey, Italy, Russia, Ukraine, Sweden, Norway, France, Kenya, Tanzania, Zimbabwe, North Pole Arctic Region, Antarctica, Argentina, Ireland, Scotland, New Zealand, Fiji, Australia, Bali, Palau, The Amazon, Galapagos Islands. Grantee N.Mex. Dept. Edn., 1976-78, 78-86, 83-86, HEW, 1979, 80, 81, 83, 84, 85, 86, 87. Mem. ASTD, Am. Vocat. Assn., Vocat. Edn. Equity Coun., Nat. Coalition for Sex Equity Edn., Am. Home Econs. Assn., Inst. Noetic Scis., N.Mex. Home Econs. Assn., N.Mex. Vocat. Edn. Assn., N.Mex. Adv. Coun. on Vocat. Edn., Greater Albuquerque C. of C., NAFE, Phi Delta Kappa, Phi Upsilon Omicron, Phi Theta Kappa. Democrat. Roman Catholic.

MILAVSKY, HAROLD PHILLIP, real estate executive; b. Limerick, Sask., Can., Jan. 25, 1931; s. Jack and Clara M. B in Commerce, U. Sask., Saskatoon, Can., 1953; LLD (hon.), U. Sask., 1995, U. Calgary, 1995. Chief acct., treas., controller Loram Internat. Ltd. div. Mannix Co. Ltd., Calgary, Alta., Can., 1956-65; v.p., chief fin. officer Power Corp. Devels. Ltd., Calgary, Alta., Can., 1965-69; exec. v.p., bd. dirs. Great West Internat. Equities Ltd. (name now Trizec Corp. Ltd.), Calgary, Alta., Can., 1976-94; pres. Trizec Corp. Ltd., Calgary, Alta., Can., 1976-86, bd. dirs., 1976-94, chmn., 1986-93; chmn. Quantico Capital Corp., Calgary, 1994—; bd. dirs. Citadel Diversified Mgmt., Ltd., Calgary, ENMAX Corp., Telus Corp., Edmonton, Encal Energy, Inc., Calgary, Prime West Energy Inc., Calgary, Aspen Properties, Ltd., Calgary, Torode Realty, Ltd., Calgary, TransCanada Pipe-Lines, Ltd., Calgary. Past dir. Terry Fox Humanitarian Award Program; past dir. Conf. Bd. Can.; past. gov. Acctg. Edn. Found. Alta.; hon. col. 14th Svc. Battalion, Calgary; bd. dirs. Tennis Can. Recipient Commemorative medal B'nai Brith, 1992. Fellow Inst. Chartered Accts. Alta.; mem. Inst. Chartered Accts. Sask., Can. Inst. Pub. Real Estate Cos. (past pres., bd. dirs.), Can. C. of C. (past chmn.), Internat. Profl. Hockey Alumni (founding dir.), Petroleum Club, Ranchmen's Club. Avocations: skiing, tennis, horseback riding. Office: Quantico Capital Corp, 1920-855 Second St SW, Calgary, AB Canada T2P 4J7

MILES, DON CLIFFORD, architect; b. Ft. Knox, Ky., Sept. 17, 1942; s. Don and Kathrine Eva (Gray) M.; m. Pamela Wait, Aug. 6, 1972; children:

Katherine Wait, Lesley Gray, Nicole Conel. BArch with honors, U. Wash., 1966; MArch, M of City Planning in Urban Design, Harvard U., 1971. Registered architect, Wash. Assoc. ptnr. Zimmer, Gunsul, Frasca Partnership, Seattle; cons., lectr. numerous orgns., cities, corps. Prin. projects include Pedestrian Corridor, Major Pub. Open Spaces, CBD Transit Ctr., Bellevue, Wash., Banfield Light Rail Project, Portland, Boise (Idaho) Downtown Major Pub. Open Space, Street Improvements and Transit Malls, Honolulu Rapid Transit Project, Revitalization of State St., Chgo., Midway Corridor Project, Mpls., High Capacity Transit Project, Seattle, Ctrl. Orange County Aerial Fixed Guideway, Mission Valley West Extension Light Rail Project, San Diego, Master Plan for Capitol of State of Wash., Seattle Union Sta. Redevel. Plan, Weyerhauser Corp. Campus, Quadrant Corp. site, Lake Union, Seattle, Whitman Coll. Bd. dirs., founder Project for Pub. Spaces, 1975—; bd. dirs Seattle Children's Mus., 1978-82; trustee Queen Ann Community Coun., 1978-80. Fellow AIA, Inst. Urban Design. Avocations: skiing, jogging. Home: 611 W Comstock St Seattle WA 98119-3422 Office: Zimmer Gunsul Frasca 1191 2nd Ave Ste 800 Seattle WA 98101-2949*

MILES, DONALD F., lawyer; b. Marysville, Calif., Apr. 11, 1949. AB with honors, Stanford U., 1971; JD, U. Calif., San Francisco, 1974. Bar: Calif. 1974, U.S. Dist. Ct. (no. dist.) Calif. 1974, U.S. Dist. Ct. (ea. dist.) Calif. 1977, U.S. Dist. Ct. (so. dist.) Calif. 1986, U.S. Supreme Ct. 1987, U.S. Dist. Ct. (ctrl. dist.) Calif. 1991. Law clk. to Hon. William P. Clark Jr. Supreme Ct. Calif. 1974-75; mem. Howard, Rice, Nemerovski, Canady, Falk & Rabkin, P.C., San Francisco; spl. master U.S. Dist. Ct. (no. dist.) Calif.; instr., adj. faculty mem. Hastings Coll. Law U. Calif.; faculty mem., bd. dirs. Hastings Nat. Coll. Advocacy; mem. adv. com. Calif. Legis. Joint Com. Tort Liability. Author: (with others) Civil Procedure During Trial, vol. II, 1984, 95, California Liability Insurance Practice, 1991, Continuing Education of the Bar Action Guide, 1991; author, narrator: (videotape) Laying a Foundation to Introduce Evidence, 1989; contbr. articles to profl. jours. Bd. chmn. The Glenwood Sch. Found. Mem. ABA (sect. torts and ins. practice), State Bar Calif., Assn. Def. Counsel No. Calif., Bar Assn. of San Francisco, Internat. Assn. Def. Counsel, Def. Rsch. Inst., Thurston Soc., Order of Coif. Office: Howard Rice Nemerovski Canady Falk & Rabkin PC 3 Embarcadero Ctr Ste 7 San Francisco CA 94111-4003

MILES, MARGARET MELANIE, historian, educator; b. Detroit, Sept. 16, 1952; d. Richard D. and Dione M. AB, U. Mich., 1973; MA, Princeton U., 1976, PhD, 1980. Excavator Am. Sch. Classical Studies, Athens, Greece, 1980-82; vis. asst. prof. U. Calif., Berkeley, 1982-87, Intercollegiate Ctr. Classical Studies, Rome, 1988-90, Smith Coll., Northampton, Mass., 1991-92; asst. then assoc. prof. U. Calif., Irvine, 1992—. John Williams White fellow Am. Sch. Classical Studies, 1976-77, Rome Prize fellow Am. Acad. Rome, 1987-88, Mellon fellow Inst. Advanced Study, 1990-91, NEH fellow, 1996-97; grantee Am. Philos. Soc., 1983, Am. Coun. Learned Socs., 1985. Mem. Archeol. Inst. Am. (Olivia James fellow 1979-80), Coll. Art Assn. Office: Dept History Sch Humanities U Calif Irvine CA 92697-2785

MILES, RICHARD ROBERT, art historian, writer; b. Tokyo, Apr. 1, 1939; s. Robert Henri and Eleanor Alfrida (Child) Perreau-Saussine. BA, UCLA, 1972. Novelist, screenwriter various, 1965-72; ptr. Meilinki Enterprises Ltd., 1980—; pres. Burbank (Calif.) Tchrs. Assn., 1984-85; bd. dirs. Balcom Trading Co., Tokyo, 1979-82. Author: That Cold Day in the Park, 1965 (Dell Book award 1965), Angel Loves Nobody, 1967 (Samuel Goldwyn award UCLA, 1969); (art history) Prints of Paul Jacoulet, 1982, Elizabeth Keith-The Prints, 1989, The Watercolors of Paul Jacoulet, 1992, others. Mem. Internat. Soc. of Fine Art Appraisers, New Eng. Appraisers Assn., Writers Guild of Am. West, Acad. of Am. Poets. Office: Meilinki Enterprises Ltd 214 N Bowling Green Way Los Angeles CA 90049-2816

MILES, SAMUEL I(SRAEL), psychiatrist, educator; b. Munich, Mar. 4, 1949; came to U.S. 1949; s. Henry and Renee (Ringel) M.; m. Denise Marie Robey, June 26, 1977; children: Jonathan David, Justin Alexander. BS, CCNY, 1970; MD, N.Y. Med. Coll., 1974; PhD, So. Calif. Psychoanalytic Inst., 1986. Diplomate Am. Bd. Psychiatry and Neurology with added qualifications in forensic psychiatry and addiction psychiatry. Intern D.C. Gen. Hosp., Washington, 1974-75; resident in psychiatry Cedars-Sinai Med. Ctr., Los Angeles, 1975-78; practice medicine specializing in psychiatry Los Angeles, 1978—; ind. med. examiner Calif. Dept. Indsl. Relations, 1984-91, qualified med. examiner, 1991—; asst. clin. prof. psychiatry UCLA Sch. Medicine, 1978-97, assoc. clin. prof., 1998—; assoc. clin. chief psychiatry Cedars-Sinai Med. Ctr., 1998—; mem. faculty So. Calif. Psychoanalytic Inst., 1986—; mem. psychiat. panel Superior Ct. Los Angeles County, 1990—, Fed. Ct., 1990—. Fellow Am. Acad. Psychoanalysis, Am. Orthopsychiat. Assn.; mem. Acad. Psychiatry and the Law, Am. Coll. Legal Medicine, Calif. Psychiat. Assn. (mem. managed care com. 1991-96), So. Calif. Psychiat. Soc. (coun. rep. 1985-88, 92-95, chairperson pvt. practice com. 1988-92, sec. 1991-92, mem. worker's compensation com. 1992—, treas. 1997-98), So. Calif. Psychoanalytic Inst. (pres. clin. assocs. orgn. 1981-82, mem. admissions com. 1988—, mem. ethics stds. com. 1991-92, chair ethics stds. com. 1993-98, mem. exec. com. 1993-98). Jewish. Avocations: aviation, swimming. Office: 8631 W 3rd St Ste 425E Los Angeles CA 90048-5908

MILEY, DOUGLAS HENRY, artist; b. Continental, Ohio, Apr. 4, 1941; s. Henry Cecil and Mary Alice (Vannoy) M.; m. Lilly B. Sandige, Oct. 23, 1993. Grad., Continental H.S., 1959. Illustrator U.S. Army, 1963-65; Campbell's Soup, Napoleon, Ohio, 1966-77; conservator art restoration Prescott, Ariz., 1979-84; artist, 1984—. Named Artist of Yr., Southwest Artist's Assn., 1995. Protestant. Avocations: walking, traveling, reading, pencil drawing. Home: 1900 Forest Meadows Dr Prescott AZ 86303

MILEY, EDWARD RANDALL, lawyer; b. Misawa Air Base, Amori, Japan, May 9, 1967; s. Edward Hamsell and Donna Lee (Larson) M.; m. Stefany Ann Tewell, Aug. 30, 1997. BA, Austin Coll., Sherman, Tex., 1989; MBA, U. Tex., Dallas, 1992, MA, 1992; JD, Calif. Western Sch. of Law, 1995. Nar: Calif. 1995, U.S. Dist. Ct. (so. dist.) Calif. 1995, Nev. 1996, U.S. Dist. Ct. Nev. 1996, U.S. Ct. Appeals (9th cir.) 1996. Assoc. Vannah Costello Canepa Wiese & Riedy, Las Vegas, Nev., 1995-96, Gugino & Schwartz, Las Vegas, 1996-97; sr. assoc. Gillock Koning Markley & Killebrew, Las Vegas, 1997—; mem. So. Nev. disciplinary bd. State Bar of Nev., Las Vegas, 1996—, mem. fee dispute com., 1998—, mem. consumer affairs and protection com., 1998—, exec. counsel for young lawyers sect.; State Bar of Nev., 1997—. Mem. ABA, ATLA, Fed. Bar Assn., Clark County Bar Assn., Las Vegas C. of C., Rotary. Republican. Avocations: golf, tennis, squash. Office: Gillock Konong Markley & Killebrew 1640 Alta Dr Ste 2 Las Vegas NV 89106-4165

MILGRIM, DARROW A., insurance broker, recreation consultant; b. Chgo., Apr. 30, 1945; s. David and Miriam (Glickman) M.; m. Laurie Stevens, Apr. 15, 1984; children: Derick, Jared, Kayla. BA, Calif. State U., San Bernardino, 1968; postgrad., U. So. Calif., 1972. Accredited in adv.; cert. ins. counselor; cert. sch. administr. Tchr. Rialto (Calif.) Unified Sch. Dist., 1969-70, Las Virgenes Unified Sch. Dist., Westlake Village, Calif., 1970-78; instr. Calif. State U., Northridge, Calif., 1980-84; ins. broker, exec. v.p. Speare Ins. Brokers, Blade Ins. Svcs., Brentwood, Calif., 1984—; dir. Calamigos Star C Ranch Summer Camp, Malibu, Calif., Calamigos Environ. Edn. Ctr., Malibu. Editor: Legislation and Regulations for Organized Camps, 1987. Pres. Camping Adv. Coun., Long Beach, 1985-87; bd. dirs. Calif. Collaboration for Youth, Sacramento, 1985—, Camp Ronald McDonald for Good Times, 1989-95; commr. dept. parks and recreation City of Agoura Hills, Calif., 1987-93; cons. So. Calif. Children's Cancer Svcs. So. Calif. sect., chmn. nat. legis. com. Martinsville, Ind., 1980-98, nat. bd. dirs. 1990-95, legis. liaison, regional honor 1986), Ins. Brokers and Agts. of L.A. Coun. Office: Speare and Co Ins Brokers PO Box 250024 Los Angeles CA 90025-0660

MILIOZZI, PAOLO, electrical engineer; b. Macerata, Italy, Nov. 22, 1967; s. Antonio and Teresa Miliozzi; m. Ana Maria Isabel Hernandez, July 19, 1997. Laurea summa cum laude, U. Bologna, Italy, 1992; PhD, U. Padova, Italy, 1996. Grad. student rschr. U. Padova, 1992-94; grad. student rschr. U. Calif., Berkeley, 1994-95, rsch. engring. fellow, 1995-96; design automation engr. Rockwell Internat., Newport Beach, Calif., 1996—. Contbr. articles to profl. jours. Am William Penn Fisher 1995-96. Recipient scholarship

Edn. Abroad Program, U. Calif., 1994. Mem. IEEE. Roman Catholic. Avocations: photography, volleyball, scuba diving, swimming. Office: Rockwell Internat 4311 Jamboree Rd MC 510-301 Newport Beach CA 92660-3007

MILLAR, RICHARD WILLIAM, JR., lawyer; b. L.A., May 11, 1938. LLB, U. San Francisco, 1966. Bar: Calif. 1967, U.S. Dist. Ct. (cen. dist.) Calif. 1967, U.S. Dist. Ct. (no. dist.) Calif. 1969, U.S. Dist. Ct. (so. dist.) Calif. 1973, U.S. Supreme Ct. Assoc. Iverson & Hogoboom, Los Angeles, 1967-72; ptnr. Eilers, Stewart, Pangman & Millar, Newport Beach, Calif., 1973-75, Millar & Heckman, Newport Beach, 1975-77, Millar, Hodges & Bemis, Newport Beach, 1979—. Fellow Am. Bar Found.; mem. ABA (litigation sect., trial practice com., ho. of dels. 1990—), Calif. Bar Assn. (lectr. CLE), Orange County Bar Assn. (sec. 1999, chmn. bus. litig. sect. 1981, chmn. judiciary com. 1988-90, sec. 1999), Balboa Bay Club, Bohemian Club (San Francisco), Pacific Club. Home: 2546 Crestview Dr Newport Beach CA 92663-5625 Office: Millar Hodges & Bemis One Newport Pl Ste # 900 Newport Beach CA 92660

MILLAR, ROBERT, artist; b. L.A., Mar. 6, 1958; s. Thomas A. and Josephine E. (Alford) M. BA, Calif. State U., Northridge, 1980. Exhibited work at L.A. Metro Rail Sta., 1990 (progressive Arch. citation 1992), Newport Harbor Art Mus., 1991, Rose Theatre Site, London, 1992, S.D. Alvarado Filtration Plant, 1993. Arts commr. City of Manhattan Beach, Calif., 1985-94; mem. pub. art adv. com. Calif. Arts Coun., 1992. Grantee Pollock-Krasner Found., 1989. Studio: PO Box 515 Manhattan Beach CA 90267-0515

MILLARD, MALCOLM STUART, retired lawyer; b. Highland Park, Ill., Mar. 22, 1914; s. Everett L. and Elizabeth (Boynton) M.; m. Joanne T. Blakeman; 1 child, Anne W. Benjamin. BA, Harvard U., 1936; JD, Northwestern U., 1939. Bar: Ill. 1939, Calif. 1951. Ptnr. Farr & Millard, Carmel, Calif., 1951-55, Millard, Tourangeau, Morris & Staples, P.C., Carmel, 1955-91; ptnr. Millard, Morris & Staples, Carmel, 1991-94, ret., 1994; dir. Leslie Salt Co., 1975-81. Trustee Community Hosp. of Monterey Peninsula, 1982-88, Monterey Inst. Fgn. Studies, 1955-76, Community Found. Monterey County, 1988—; pres. Community Chest of Monterey Peninsula, 1958. Served to lt. USN, 1943-46. Mem. Monterey Inst. Internat. Relations (hon. lifetime trustee 1982—; hon. DHL 1991), Ill. State Bar, Calif. State Bar, Monterey County Bar Assn. (pres.), Old Capital Club, Harvard Club. Avocations: environmental interests, travel, ranching.

MILLARD, NEAL STEVEN, lawyer; b. Dallas, June 6, 1947; s. Bernard and Adele (Marks) M.; m. Janet Keast, Mar. 12, 1994; 1 child, Kendall Layne. BA cum laude, UCLA, 1969; JD, U. Chgo., 1972. Bar: Calif. 1972, U.S. Dist. Ct. (cen. dist.) Calif. 1973, U.S. Tax Ct. 1973, U.S. Ct. Appeals (9th cir.) 1987, N.Y. 1990. Assoc. Willis, Butler & Schiefly, Los Angeles, 1972-75; ptnr. Morrison & Foerster, Los Angeles, 1975-84, Jones, Day, Reavis & Pogue, Los Angeles, 1984-93, White & Case, L.A., 1993—; instr. Calif. State Coll., San Bernardino, 1975-76; lectr. Practising Law Inst., N.Y.C., 1983-90, Calif. Edn. of Bar, 1987-90; adj. prof. USC Law Ctr., 1994—. Citizens adv. com. L.A. Olympics, 1982-84; trustee Altadena (Calif.) Libr. Dist., 1985-86; bd. dirs. Woodcraft Rangers, L.A., 1982-90, pres., 1986-88; bd. dirs. L.A. County Bar Found., 1990—, pres., 1997-98; mem. Energy Commn. of County and Cities of L.A., 1995—; bd. dirs. Inner City Law Ctr., 1996—. Mem. ABA, Calif. Bar Assn., N.Y. State Bar Assn., L.A. County Bar Assn. (trustee 1985-87), Pub. Counsel (bd. dirs. 1984-87, 90-93), U. Chgo. Law Alumni Assn. (pres. 1998—). Calif. Club, Phi Beta Kappa, Pi Gamma Mu, Phi Delta Phi. Office: White and Case 633 W 5th St Ste 1900 Los Angeles CA 90071-2087

MILLARD, OLIVIA, fundraiser; b. Highland Park, Ill., Jan. 13, 1959; d. Everett Lee and Mary Hyde M.; m. William Richard Waldman, Dec. 23, 1997. AA, Simons Rock Coll., 1978; BA, U. Colo., 1981; JD, Cornell U., 1984. Bar: N.Y., Mass. Assoc. LeBoeuf, Lamb, Leiby & McRae, N.Y.C., 1984-87; exec. dir. Lower Hudson chpt. The Nature Conservancy, Mt. Kisco, N.Y., 1987-97; Western regional dir. devel. The Nature Conservancy, Santa Fe, N.Mex., 1997—; co-chair Hudson River Adv. Bd., Pres.'s Coun. on Sustainable Devel., Westchester County, N.Y., 1994-97; chair region 3 N.Y. Open Space Adv. Com., New Paltz, N.Y., 1994-97; founder (with others) Friends of the Great Swamp, Patterson, N.Y., 1989-97; founding trustee Sterling Forest Resources, Goshen, N.Y., 1994-97. Avocations: gardening, sailing. Office: The Nature Conservancy 212 E Marcy St Ste 200 Santa Fe NM 87501-2049

MILLBROOKE, ANNE, historian; b. St. Helens, Oreg., Feb. 10, 1952; d. Arne Myllyluoma and Marjut (Wrangen) Howard. BA, Boise State Coll., 1973; MA, U. Wis., 1975; PhD, U. Pa., 1981. Cert. archivist Acad. Cert. Archivists. Info. specialist Nat. Bur. Standards, Gaithersburg, Md., 1978-79; historian Conn. Coordinating Com. for the Promotion of History, 1980-81; program assoc. Conn. Humanities Coun., Middletown, Conn., 1981; asst. corp. historian and archivist United Techs. Corp., Hartford, Conn., 1981-83; mgr. archive and hist. resource ctr., 1983-91; vis. assoc. prof. Wesleyan U., Middletown, Conn., 1992-94; cons. historian, 1992—; NSF vis. prof. Mont. State U., 1994-96; history prof. Northwest Campus UAF, 1999—. Mem. Nat. Coun. on Pub. History, History of Earth Scis. Soc., History Sci. Soc., Soc. for History of Tech., Soc. Am. Archivists, Am. Hist. Assn.

MILLENDER-MCDONALD, JUANITA, congresswoman, former school system administrator; b. Birmingham, Ala., Sept. 7, 1938; d. Shelly and Everlina (Dortch) M.; m. James McDonald III, July 26, 1955; children: Valeria, Angela, Sherryll, Michael, Roderick. BS, U. Redlands, Calif., 1980; MS in Edn., Calif. State U., L.A., 1986; postgrad., U. So. Calif. Manuscript editor Calif. State Dept. Edn., Sacramento; dir. gender equity programs L.A. Unified Sch. Dist.; mem. 106th Congress from 37th Calif dist., Washington, 1996—, mem. small bus. com., transp. and infrastructure com. City councilwoman, Carson; bd. dirs. S.C.L.C. Pvt. Industry Coun. Policy Bd., West Basin Mcpl. Water Dist., Cities Legis. League (vice chmn.; mem. Nat. Women's Polit. Caucus; mem. adv. bd. Comparative Ethnic Study, Calif.; founder, exec. dir. Young Advocates So. Calif. Mem. NEA, Nat. Assn. Minority Polit. Women, NAFE, Nat. Fedn. Bus. and Profl. Women, Assn. Calif. Sch. Adminstrs., Am. Mgmt. Assn., Nat. Coun. Jewish Women, Carson C. of C., Phi Delta Kappa. Office: US House of Reps 419 Cannon Bldg Washington DC 20515-0531*

MILLER, ANNE KATHLEEN, training company executive, technical marketing consultant; b. Denver, Sept. 15, 1942; d. John Henry and Kathryn Elizabeth (Doherty) Meyer; m. Edgar Earle Miller, Aug. 20, 1966 (div. Aug. 1976); children: Sheila Anne, Rebecca Elizabeth; m. Warren Ross Landry, Dec. 11, 1982 (dec. Oct. 1990). BS in Chemistry, St. Mary Coll. Leavenworth, Kans., 1964. Cert. jr. coll., secondary tchr., Calif. Lectr. San Jose (Calif.) State U., 1978-82; product mgr. Jasco Chem., Mountain View, Calif., 1979-82; v.p., gen. mgr. Micropel, Hayward, Calif., 1982-84; product mgr. Cambridge Instruments, Santa Clara, Calif., 1984-86; product mktg. mgr. KLA Instruments, Santa Clara, Calif., 1986-87; pres., owner Meyland Enterprises, Redwood City, Calif., 1987—; Semiconductor Svc. Tng. Orgn., Redwood City, Calif., 1988—. Inventor formation of optical film. Mem. Soc. Photo Optical Instrumentation Engrs., Am. Chem. Soc., Semiconductor Industry Equipment Materials Internat., Am. Electronics Assn. Office: Semiconductor Svcs 735 Hillcrest Way Redwood City CA 94062-3453

MILLER, BARBARA SHAW, investment consultant, real estate appraiser; b. Passaic, N.J., Oct. 31, 1933; d. Clifford Ledger and Irene Marie (Langerin) Shaw; m. Crandon E. Caufield, Feb. 10, 1955 (div. May 1960); m. Thomas Joseph Miller, July 3, 1963; children: William, Charles, Katharine. Diploma, NYU, 1955. Cert. real estate appraiser. Exec. sec. adminstrv. asst. Associated Msde. Corp., N.Y.C., 1955-58, 61-70; chief appraiser Western Savings & Loan, Phoenix, 1971-80, Southwest Savings & Loan, Phoenix, 1980-86; cons. Sun Lakes (Ariz.) Mktg., 1986-88, Miller Assocs., Phoenix, 1988—. Ethics com. mem. Appraisal Inst. Rev. Com., Chgo., 1972—; hon. prof. Beijing Bus Art Coll China 1998; cons devel & constrn administry ctr Dalian Xinghai Bay, China, 1998. Author: Real Estate Appraisal Kit, 1981, State Arizona Women's Services Handbook, 1989. Dir. internat. affairs, Golden Eagle Found., Vancouver, Can., 1997—; amb., advisor H. Martin Found., Jakarta, Indonesia, 1997—; dir. Saharia Med. Rsch., Phoenix, 1997—. Mem. World League Freedom & Democracy (chmn. int. com. 1996). Repub

can. Roman Catholic. Avocations: writing, painting. Office: Miller Assocs Inc PO Box 32424 Phoenix AZ 85064-2424

MILLER, BARBARA STALLCUP, development consultant; b. Montague, Calif., Sept. 4, 1919; d. Joseph Nathaniel and Maybelle (Needham) Stallcup; m. Leland F. Miller, May 16, 1946; children: Paula Kay, Susan Lee, Daniel Joseph, Alison Jean. B.A., U. Oreg., 1942. Women's editor Eugene (Oreg.) Daily News, 1941-43; law clk. to J. Everett Barr, Yreka, Calif., 1943-45; mgr. Yreka C. of C., 1945-46; Northwest supr. Louis Harris and Assocs., Portland, Oreg., 1959-62; dir. pub. relations and fund raising Columbia River council Girl Scouts U.S.A., 1962-67; pvt. practice pub. relations cons., Portland, 1967-72; adviser of student publs., asst. prof. communications U. Portland, 1967-72, dir. pub. relations and info., asst. prof. communications, 1972-78, dir. devel., 1978-79; exec.dir. devel., 1979-83; assoc. dir. St. Vincent Med. Found., 1983-88; dir. planned giving Good Samaritan Found., 1988-95; planned giving cons., 1995—. Pres. bd. dirs. Vols. of Am. of Oreg., Inc., 1980-84, pres. regional adv. bd., 1982-84; chmn. bd. dirs S.E. Mental Health Network, 1984-88; nat. bd. dirs. Vols. of Am., 1984-96; pres., bd. dirs. Vol. Bur. Greater Portland, 1991-93; mem. U. Oreg. Journalism Advancement Coun., 1991—; named Oasis Sr. Role Model, 1992. Recipient Presdl. Citation, Oreg. Communicators assn., 1973, Matrix award, 1976, 80, Miltner award U. Portland, 1977, Communicator of Achievement award Oreg. Press Women, 1992, Willamette Valley Devel. Officers award, 1992 (Barbara Stallcup Miller Profl. Achievement award, 1992), Mem. Nat. Coast Trail Assn. (pres. bd. dirs. 1997—), Nat. Soc. Fundraising Execs., Nat. Planned Giving Coun, Women in Comm. (NW regional v.p. 1973-75, Offbeat award 1988), Nat. Fedn. Press Women, Oreg. Press Women (dist. dir.), Pub. Rels. Soc. Am. (dir. local chpt., Marsh award 1989), Oreg. Fedn. Womens Clubs (communications chmn. 1978-80), Alpha Xi Delta (found. trustee, editor 1988-95). Unitarian. Clubs: Portland Zenith (pres. 1975-76, 81-82). Contbr. articles to profl. jours. Home and Office: 1706 Boca Ratan Dr Lake Oswego OR 97034-1624

MILLER, BRUCE, advertising executive. Pres, new bus. contact Suissa Miller Advt, L.A. Office: Suissa Miller Advt 11601 Wilshire Blvd Fl 16 Los Angeles CA 90025-1770*

MILLER, CAROLE ANN LYONS, editor, publisher, marketing specialist; b. Newton, Mass., Aug. 1; d. Markham Harold and Ursula Patricia (Foley) Lyons; m. David Thomas Miller, July 4, 1978. BA, Boston U., 1964; bus. cert., Hickox Sch., Boston, 1964; cert. advt. and mktg. profl. UCLA, 1973; cert. retail mgmt. profl. Ind. U., 1976. Editor Triangle Topics, Pacific Telephone, L.A.; programmer L.A. Cen. Area Speakers' Bur., 1964-66; mng. editor/mktg. dir. Teen mag., L.A. and N.Y.C., 1966-76; advt. dir. L.S. Ayres & Co., Indpls., 1976-78; v.p. mktg. The Denver, 1978-79; founder, editor, pub. Clockwise mag., Ventura, Calif., 1979-85; mktg. mgr. pub. rels. and spl. events Robinson's Dept. Stores, L.A., 1985-87, exec. v.p. dir. mktg. Harrison Svcs., 1987-93; pres. divsn. Miller & Miller Carole Ann Lyons Mktg., Camino, Calif., 1993—; instr. retail advt. Ind. U., 1977-78. Recipient Pres.'s award Advt. Women of N.Y., 1974; Seklemian award 1977; Pub. Svc. Addy award, 1978. Mem., Advt. Women N.Y., Calif. Videographers Assn., Retail Advt. & Mktg. Assn., Fashion Group Internat., Bay Area Integrated Mktg., San Francisco Fashion Group, San Francisco Direct Mktg. Assn. UCLA Alumni Assn., Internat. TV Videographer's Assn. (Sacramento chpt.). Editor: Sek Says, 1979.

MILLER, CHARLES DALY, self-adhesive materials company executive; b. Hartford, Conn., 1928; married. Grad., Johns Hopkins U. Sales and mktg. mgr. Yale & Towne Mfg. Co., 1949-59; assoc. Booz, Allen & Hamilton, 1959-64; with Avery Internat. Corp., Pasadena, Calif., 1964—; v.p., mng. dir. Materials Europe, 1965-68; v.p. Fasson Internat. Ops., 1968; group v.p. materials group Avery Internat. Corp., Pasadena, 1969-75, pres., bd. dirs., COO, 1975-77, pres., CEO, 1977-83; chmn., CEO Avery Dennison Corp. (formerly Avery Internat. Corp.), Pasadena, 1983-98, chmn., 1998—. Office: Avery Dennison Corp PO Box 7090 Pasadena CA 91109-7090

MILLER, CHARLES WALLACE, historian, environmental geologist; b. Phoenix, July 7, 1946; s. Charles W. and Emabel O. Miller; m. Connie Raschke, June 3, 1972; 1 child, Geoffrey Wallace. BA, U. Md., 1969; MA, U. Tex., 1970; BS, SUNY, Albany, 1978; PhD, Union Inst., 1990. Tchr. pub. schs. San Antonio, 1971-76; instr. San Antonio Coll., 1972-78, St. Mary's Univ., San Antonio, 1976-78, Cochise Coll., Sierra Vista, Az., 1989-90; environ. geologist U.S. Geol. Survey, Metairie, La., 1978-80; field geologist U.S. Bur. Land Mgmt., Moab, Utah, 1980-84; historian U.S. Bur. Reclamation, Salt Lake City, 1990-94; environ. scientist USAF, Tucson, 1994—; mineral cons., Tucson, 1984-89; instr. Pima C.C., 1998—. Author: Stake Your Claim! The Tale of America's Enduring Mining Law, 1991, The Spirit of the Pioneers Still Rules, 1997, The Automobile Gold Rushes, 1998; contbr. articles to profl. jours. Vol. Christ Comty. Ch., Tucson, also various youth orgns. including Boy Scouts; group coord. Combined Fed. Campaign. Mem. Nat. Eagle Scout Assn., Mining History Assn., Mensa, Hist. Soc. Golden Key, Phi Alpha Theta, Pi Sigma Alpha. Avocations: backpacking, scuba diving, photgraphy. Home: 9501 E Walnut Tree Dr Tucson AZ 85749-8437 Office: USAF 355 CES/CEVA Davis Monthan A F B AZ 85707

MILLER, CLARA BURR, education educator; b. Higganum, Conn., July 19, 1912; d. Eugene Orlando and Mabel (Clark) Burr; m. James Golden Miller, Sept. 19, 1942; children: Clara Elizabeth, Eugenia Manelle. BA, Mt. Holyoke Coll., 1933; MA, Columbia U., 1942. Cert. tchr., Conn., N.Y., Pa., Ariz. Tchr. Suffield (Conn.) Jr. High Sch., 1934-36, Rockville (Conn.) High Sch., 1936-41, Buckeley High Sch., Hartford, Conn., 1941-42, Pitts. Schs., 1952-55, Winchester-Thurston Sch., Pitts., 1955-58, Vail-Deane Sch., Elizabeth, N.J., 1955-69, Kingman (Ariz.) High Sch., 1971-76; mem. res. faculty Mohave C.C., Kingman, 1978-84; pres. bd. edn., clk. Mohave Union H.S. Dist. 30, 1983-91, bd. dirs., 1983-94; bd. dirs. Mohave Mental Health Clinic, v.p. bd. dirs., 1988, pres. bd. dirs., 1989-90. Author: Trails, Rails and Tales, 1981, (with others) Short Stories, 1984. Bd. dirs. No. Ariz. Comprehensive Guidance Ctr., Flagstaff, 1985-90, Kingman Aid to Abused People; sec. Good Samaritan Assn., Inc., Kingman, 1979-95; pres. Ch. Women United, 1972-74, Presbyn. Women, 1987; elected elder session Kingman Presbyn. Ch., 1983-95; mem. Mohave County Cmty. Action Bd., Western Ariz. Coun. Govts.; coord. League Friendship Indians and Other Americans, 1981-95; co-chmn. Women Making History Com., 1981-95; elected head, Montview Manor social activities, 1996-98, bd. mgrs., 1998—; elected deacon, Montview Blvd. Presbyn. Ch., 1997—. Recipient Nat. Community Svc. award Mohave County Ret. Tchrs Assn., 1987, Leta Glancy/Cecil Lockhart-Smith award No. Ariz. Comprehensive Guidance Ctr., 1990; named one of Women Making History Kingman Multi-Club Com., 1985. Mem. NEA, AAUW (pres. 1979-81), Ariz. Edn. Assn., Ariz. Sch. Bds. Assn., Soc. Profl. Journalists, Mohave County Ret. Tchrs Assn. (v.p. 1991-93, pres. 1993-95), Footprinters. Democrat. Avocations: traveling, oil painting, writing, reading, church activities. Home: 1663 Steele St Denver CO 80206-1727

MILLER, CLIFFORD JOEL, lawyer; b. L.A., Oct. 31, 1947; s. Eugene and Marian (Millman) M. BA, U. Calif., Irvine, 1969; JD, Pepperdine U., 1973. Bar: Calif. 1974, Hawaii 1974, U.S. Dist. Ct. Hawaii 1974. Ptnr. Rice, Lee & Wong, Honolulu, 1974-80, Goodsill Anderson Quinn & Stifel, Honolulu, 1980-89, McCorriston, Miller & Mukai, Honolulu, 1989—. Mem. ABA, Calif. Bar Assn., Hawaii Bar Assn., Am. Coll. Real Estate Lawyers. Avocations: sailing, volleyball, swimming, skiing. Office: McCorriston Miho Miller Mukai 5 Waterfront Plz 500 Ala Moana Blvd Ste 400 Honolulu HI 96813-4989

MILLER, CORBIN RUSSELL, investment company executive; b. Huntington, W.Va., Apr. 6, 1948; s. Corbin Russell and Ernestine (Thorne) M.; m. Kathryn Ann Anderson, Sept. 16, 1978. AB cum laude, Princeton (N.J.) U., 1971. Trainee Morgan Guaranty Trust Co., N.Y.C., 1972-74, asst. treas., 1974-77, asst. v.p.; Morgan Guaranty Trust Co., N.Y.C., 1974-77, asst. treas.; J. Henry Schroder Corp., N.Y.C., 1979-83, J. Henry Schroder Bank & Trust, N.Y.C., 1983-87; sr. v.p. IBI Schroder Bank & Trust Co., N.Y.C., 1987-90; pres. Kosla Techs. Corp., Pleasanton, Calif., 1990-91; mng. dir. Regent Ptnrs. Inc., N.Y.C. and Denver, 1991-92; exec. v.p. S.N. Phelps & Co., Greenwich, Conn., 1992-95; exec. v.p., CFO, dir. Carey Internat., Inc., Washington, 1995-96. pres Lombard North Am., Inc., San Francisco, 1997—; bd. dirs. Lombard Invest ments, Inc. I and Farm Indonesia American Most Comp Fund rural bank

Bd. dirs. Met. Opera Guild, N.Y.C., 1994—. Mem. Am. Soc. Order St. John of Jerusalem (chancellor 1999—), Met. Opera Club (pres. 1992-94), Knickerbocker Club, Rockaway Hunting Club, Racquet and Tennis Club, The Brook. Republican. Episcopalian. Avocation: golf. Home: 920 Powell St San Francisco CA 94108 Office: Lombard North Am Inc 600 Montgomery St Fl 36 San Francisco CA 94111-2702

MILLER, CORINNE, lawyer; b. Newcastle, Wyo., Jan. 8, 1958; d. Edwin Jay Prell and Kay Darlene (Bayne) Burgener; m. James Robert Miller; 1 child, Alan Vincent Burke II. AAS, Casper Coll., 1979; BS, U. Wyo., 1983, JD, 1988. Bar: Wyo. 1989, U.S. Dist. Ct. Wyo. 1989, U.S. Ct. Appeals (10th cir.) 1993. Jud. law clk. 7th Dist. Ct., Casper, Wyo., 1988-89; asst. pub. defender State of Wyo., Gillette, 1989-91; pvt. practice, Casper, 1991—. Office: 111 W 2d St Ste 603 Casper WY 82601-2469

MILLER, DARLENE LOUISE, wardrobe consultant, educator; b. Stayton, Oreg., May 13, 1936; d. Robert LaFollet Wirth and Rova Marie Jackson; m. Russell Eugene Miller, Aug. 10, 1958; 1 child, Brenda Carlene Ruble. BS in Home Econs. Edn., Oreg. State U., 1958. Cert. tchr. h.s. Tchr. homemaking St. Paul (Oreg.) H.S., 1958-59, Dayton (Oreg.) H.S., 1959-61; tchr. adult edn. Missoula (Mont.) County Sch. Dist., 1977-97; instr. U. Mont., Missoula, 1982, Mesa (Ariz.) C.C., 1993-98; tchr. adult edn. Missoula Vo-Tech., 1994-96; color-wardrobe cons., Missoula, 1980-98; profl. seamstress, Oreg. and Mont., 1960-98; presenter seminars in field. Author, pub.: Your Shape, Your Clothes and You, 1993, 2d edit., 1995; designer Just for You clothing, 1997, 98. Grad. Leadership Missoula, 1989. Mem. Am. Sewing Guild, INN Nat. Spkrs. Assn., Profl. Assn. Custom Clothiers, Missoula Businesswomens Network, C. of C. Avocations: hiking, skiing, reading, knitting, needlework. Home and Office: Clothes for You 6 Rosebud Ln Missoula MT 59801-8414

MILLER, DAVID ALLEN, physicist; b. Galion, Ohio, Sept. 3, 1963; s. Richard Allen and Dorothy S. (Stoyanovich) M.; m. Regina Denise Fulkerson, Mar. 16, 1987; 1 child, Christopher David. BS, Bowling Green (Ohio) U., 1985, Tex. A&M U., 1987; MS, U. Md., 1994. Commd. 2d lt. USAF, 1986, advanced through grades to maj., 1990, ret., 1996; comdr., chief of staff Palehua Solar Obs., Honolulu, Hawaii, 1996—; team chief Air Force Space Forecast Ctr., Falcon, Colo., 1994-96, v.p. booster club, 1995. Contbg. author, editor: Maryland Pilot Earth Science and Technology Education Network, 1994. Vol. St. Andrew's Epis. Cathedral, Honolulu, 1996—; earth sci. instr. Md. High Sch. Tchrs., 1993-94; clean air forecaster U. Md., College Park, 1993-94, trooper, stable mgr. cavalry, 1993; sailor Pacific Yacht Club, Hickam AFB, 1997—. Decorated Commendation medal, first oak leaf. Mem. AAAS, Air Force Space Command Officers Club, Am. Phys. Soc. Achievements include development of technique to forecast spacecraft internal changing conditions. Home: 92-1240 Kaleo Pl Kapolei HI 96707-1535 Office: Palehua Solar Obs 10 Hickam Ct Hickam AFB HI 96853-5252

MILLER, DAVID WAYNE, construction inspector, coordinator; b. Yuba City, Calif., June 23, 1949; s. Lloyd Wayne and Beverly Lorene (Ryan) M.; children: Quinlan Kenneth, Erin Patricia, Justin Michael Francis. AA in Constrn. Tech., Delta, 1985; BA in Art, Calif. State U., Hayward, 1989. Cert. tech. transfer and commercialization Internat. Conf. Bldg. Ofcls./Internat. Assn. Plumbing and Mech. Ofcls. Uniform Plumbing Code; cert. mgmt., cert. inspector. Plumber/fitter local 492 United Assn. Pipe Trades, Stockton, Calif., 1972—; plumber/fitter Lawrence Livermore Nat. Lab., Livermore, Calif., 1983-87, estimator, 1987-90; owner Moon Studios, 1976-80, Moonraker, 1991—. Author: (short story) Morgan's Tide, 1982, (Fremont C. of C. lit.) History of Fremont, 1982—; contbr. articles to CitySports, 1982. Sgt. U.S. Army, 1969-71, Vietnam. Mem. Lawrence Livermore Armed Force Vets. Assn., (founder, pres. 1986), Toastmasters.

MILLER, DENIS ROBERT, radio personality, broadcast executive; b. Camden, N.J., May 27, 1959; s. Robert and Elise Miller; m. Gail Kearney, Sept. 1, 1995; children: Travis, Sarah, Kate. BA in Radio-TV, Calif. State U., Fresno, 1984. On-air personality Sunny Country 102, Santa Maria, Calif., 1986-88, KHAY Radio, Ventura, Calif., 1988-89; comms. operator Ventura County Fire, Ventura, 1989-94; on-air personality, program dir., prodn. dir. Sunny Country 102, 1994-98; pres. Reelsounds Inc., 1994—. Avocations: softball, golf, computer design. Home: 1141 George Dr Santa Maria CA 93455-5120 Office: Bayliss Broadcasting 2215 Skyway Dr Santa Maria CA 93455-1118

MILLER, DIANE WILMARTH, human resources director; b. Clarinda, Iowa, Mar. 12, 1940; d. Donald and Floy Pauline (Madden) W.; m. Robert Nolen Miller, Aug. 21, 1965; children: Robert Wilmarth, Anne Elizabeth. AA, Colo. Women's Coll., 1960; BBA, U. Iowa, 1962; MA, U. No. Colo., 1994. Cert. tchr., Colo.; vocat. credential, Colo.; cert. sr. profl. in human resources. Sec.-counselor U. S.C., Myrtle Beach AFB, 1968-69; instr. U. S.C., Conway, 1967-69; tchr. bus. Poudre Sch. Dist. R-1, Ft. Collins, Colo., 1970-71; travel cons. United Bank Travel Svc., Greeley, Colo., 1972-74; dir. human resources Aims Community Coll., Greeley, 1984—; instr. part-time Aims Community Coll., Greeley, 1972—. Active 1st Congl. Ch., Greeley. Mem. Coll. Univ. Pers. Assn., Coll. Univ. Pers. Assn. Colo., No. Colo. Human Resources Assn., Soc. Human Resource Mgmt., Philanthropic Ednl. Orgn. (pres. 1988-89), Women's Panhellenic Assn. (pres. 1983-84), Scroll and Fan Club (pres. 1985-86), WTK Club, Questers. Home: 3530 Wagon Trail Pl Greeley CO 80634-3405 Office: Aims Cmty Coll PO Box 69 Greeley CO 80632-0069

MILLER, DONNA JEAN, nursing educator; b. L.A., Feb. 9, 1958; d. Lawrence John and Margaret Irene (Mariano) Miller. BA, Creighton U., 1980; diploma in nursing, U. So. Calif., 1983; BSN, Calif. State U., 1990, MSN, 1996. RN, Calif.; cert. critical care nurse. Staff nurse ICU/ER Daniel Freeman Meml. Hosp., Inglewood, Calif., 1984-93; edn. specialist Daniel Freeman Meml. Hosp., 1993—; clin. instr. Mt. St. Mary's Coll., L.A., 1992-93. BLS, ACLS instr. Am. Heart Assn. Mem. Assn. Critical Care Nurses, Sigma Theta Tau, Phi Kappa Phi. Office: Daniel Freeman Meml Hosp 333 N Prairie Ave Inglewood CA 90301-4501

MILLER, DONNA PAT, library administrator, consultant; b. Lindale, Tex., Dec. 13, 1948; ž; d. Donald Edward and Patsy Ruth (Dykes) Pool; m. James D. Miller, Aug. 17, 1991; children: James Jr., John, Julie, Jaynie. BS in Music, Tex. Woman's U., 1971, MA in Music, 1976; MLS, U. North Tex., 1987. Cert. music and learning resources tchr. Band dir. Grapevine (Tex.) Mid. Sch., 1971-77; pvt. music tchr. Mesquite, Tex., 1978-79; band dir. T.W. Browne Mid. Sch., Dallas, 1979-84, Vanston Mid. Sch., Mesquite, 1984-86; elem. libr. McKenzie Elem. Sch., Mesquite, 1986-90, Reinhardt Elem. Sch., Dallas, 1990-91, Range Elem. Sch., Mesquite, 1991-92; dir. libr. svcs. Mesquite Ind. Sch. Dist., 1992-95; libr. dir. Craig-Moffat County Pub. Libr., Craig, Colo., 1995—; adj. prof. Tex. Woman's U., Denton, 1993—; mem. sci. adv. bd. Gale Rsch., Inc., Detroit, 1993—; cons. Region V Edn. Svc. Ctr., Beaumont, Tex., 1994—. Author: Developing an Integrated Libr. Program Reviewer Booklist Mag., 1986—, The Book Report Mag., 1992—; contbr. articles to mags. Mem. ALA, ASCD, Tex. Libr. Assn., Phi Delta Kappa, Beta Phi Mu. Avocations: running, reading, writing, music. Office: Craig-Moffat County Libr 570 Green St Craig CO 81625-3028

MILLER, DWIGHT RICHARD, cosmetologist, corporate executive, hair designer; b. Johnstown, Pa., Jan. 24, 1943. Grad., Comer & Doran Sch., San Diego; DSci. (hon.), London Inst. for Applied Rsch., 1973. Cert. aromatherapist; lic. cosmetologist., instr.; Brit. Mastercraftsman. Styles dir. Marinello-Comer, Hollywood, Calif., 1965-67; expert Pivot Point Internat., Chgo., 1967-68; styles dir. Lapins, L.A., 1969; dir. Redken, L.A., 1970, Vidal Sassoon, London, 1971-74; world amb. Pivot Point, New Zealand and Australia, 1974-75; internat. artistic dir. Pivot Point, Chgo., 1975-78; internat. dir., co-founder Hair Artists Inst. & Registry, 1978-81; internat. artistic dir. Zotos Internat., Darien, Conn., 1981-87, Matrix Essentials, Inc., Solon, Ohio, 1987-92; bd. dirs., founder, v.p. creative Anasazi Exclusive Salon Products, Inc., Dubuque, Iowa, 1992-96; pres. Anasazi Salon Sys., Santa Fe, N.Mex., 1996-98; cons., 1998—; judge hairdressing competitions including Norwegian Masters, Australian Nat. Championships; pres. Intercrimpers, London, 1974-75. Author: Sculptic Cutting Pivot Point 75, Prismatics, 1983, Milady's Standard System of Salon Skills, 1998; prod., dir. 15 documentaries, numerous tech. and industry videos; contbr. articles, photographs to popular mags.; developer several profl. product lines including Vidal Sassoon-London, Design Freedom, Bain de Terre, Ultra Bond, Vavoom!, Systeme Biolage. Cons. American Crew, Anasazi; with USMC, 1960-64. Named Artistic Dir. Yr. Am. Salon mag.; presented with Order of White Elephant, 1976; recipient London Gold Cup for Best Presentation London Beauty Festival, 1982, Dr. Everett G. McDonough award for Excellence in Permanent Waving, World Master award Art and Fashion Group, 1992. Mem. Cercle des Arts et Techniques de la Coiffure, Intercoiffure, Haute Coiffure Franchaise, Soc. Cosmetic Chemists, Hair Artists Great Britain, Internat. Assn. Trichogists, Nat. Cosmetologists Assn. (HairAmerica, cert. instr.), Am. Soc. Phytotherapy and Aromatherapy, HairChicago (hon.), Art and Fashion Group (pres. 1993), 'Dressers MC (pres. 1990—), London's Alternative Hair Club (patron), The Salon Assn., Am. Beauty Assn., Beauty and Barber Suppy Inst. Home and Office: 707 Don Gaspar Ave Santa Fe NM 87501-4429

MILLER, ELEANOR, English language and literature educator; b. Mill Valley, Calif.. BA with honors, U. Nev., 1966, PhD in English with honors, 1970. Instr. English Valley Coll., San Bernardino, Calif., 1983-84, Crafton Hills Coll., Redlands, Calif., 1984-86, Coll. of the Desert, Palm Springs, Calif., 1986-90; prof. English Composition & Literature So. Nev. C.C., Las Vegas, 1990—; chair teaching-learning excellence com. So. Nev. C.C., Las Vegas, 1991-94, new faculty mentor, 1995—. Author: English Placement Grading, 1991, CCSN Writing Across the Curriculum, 1994, New Faculty Mentoring, 1997, Teaching Excellence, 1998. Advisor/participant Women's Re-entry Ctr., Palm Springs/Las Vegas, 1989-94; vol. Womyn's Festival Com., U. Nev., Las Vegas, 1994—; mem. adv. bd. Collegiate Press, 1998—. Mem. AAUW, Nat. Coun. Tchrs. English, Nev. State Tchrs. English, Nev. Adult Edn. Assn., Nev. Humanities Com., Mountain Plains Adult Edn. Assn., U. Nev. Alumni Assn., Women in Comm., Phi Kappa Phi.. Avocations: reading, travel. Office: So Nev CC 3200 E Cheyenne Ave North Las Vegas NV 89030-4228

MILLER, EUGENE H., lawyer; b. Chgo., Dec. 21, 1947; s. Clifford and Birdie M.; m. Judith Miriam Bolef, June 15, 1969; children: Adam, Rachel. BS, U. Ill., 1969, JD, 1973. Bar: Ill. 1973, Calif. 1973, U.S. Dist. Ct. (no. dist.) Calif. 1973, U.S. Supreme Ct. 1977, U.S. Tax Ct. 1983. Acct. Lester Witte, Chgo., 1969-70, Price Waterhouse, Oakland, Calif., 1973-74; atty. Heizel, Leighton, Brunn & Deal, Oakland, 1974-77, Brunn, Leighton & Miller, Oakland, 1977-79; atty. Miller, Starr & Regalia, Oakland, 1980—, mng. ptnr. Author: (with others) Closely Held Corporations, 1988. Office: Miller Starr & Regalia 5th Fl 1331 N California Blvd Fl 5 Walnut Creek CA 94596-4537

MILLER, FRANKLIN EMRICK, software engineer, project engineer; b. Greenville, Ohio, Aug. 12, 1946; s. Rollin Linde and E. Evelyn (Emrick) M.; m. Sandra Lewis, Dec. 20, 1969; children: William Rollin, Rose Mary. BS in Math. and Physics, Otterbein Coll., 1969; MEd in Ednl. Psychology and Counseling, Wayne State U., 1975; PhD in Ednl. Psychology, Computer Stats., U. Denver, 1984. Lic. pvt. pilot FAA. Commd. U.S. Air Force, 1969, advanced through grades to capt.; space surveillance officer SLBM, Maine, 1970-71, BMEWS Thule, Greenland, 1971-72; chief instr./systems analyst, Correlation Ctr. 440L, McGuire AFB, N.J., 1972-73; site space surveillance officer, Aviano, Italy, 1973-75; chief Defense Support Program support programming unit, Colo., 1975-79; chief applications support programming DSP, South Australia, 1979-81, ret., 1988; software engr. Aerojet Electro Systems Corp., Aurora, Colo., 1981-88. Bd. dirs., Aurora Community Mental Health Ctr., 1976-79; vol. counselor Comitis Crisis Ctr., YMCA, Aurora, 1976-78. Mem. Am. Psychol. Assn. (div. Applied Experimental and Engring. Psychologists), Denver Astron. Soc. (sec. 1994-96), Soc. Personality Assessment, Phi Delta Kappa. Republican. Author: The Preliminary Online Rorschach Test Manual, 1980; contbr. article to profl. jour. Recipient Corp. award for improving Desert Storm performance, 1991. Office: The Aerospace Corp Buckley Ang Base 18300 E Crested Butte Ave Aurora CO 80011-9518

MILLER, GARDNER HARTMANN, paralegal; b. Strasbourg, France, Mar. 26, 1934; came to U.S., 1934; s. L. Gardner and Elisabeth Lydia (Fischer) M.; m. Frances Carroll Rothe, June 20, 1955 (div. July 1960); 1 child, Catherine Louise Miller Hudson; m. Marlyn Jeanette Wiggins, Dec. 31, 1967, 1 child, Andrea Marlise. BA in Polit. Sci., UCLA, 1955; B of Fgn. Trade, Thunderbird Grad. Sch., 1960; AS in Legal Asst. Studies, Albuquerque Tech. Vocat. Inst., 1989. Fgn. trade analyst U.S. Dept. of Commerce, L.A., 1960-62; market analyst Douglas Aircraft Co., Santa Monica, Calif., 1962-66; field office mgr. McDonnell Douglas Corp., San Bernardino, Calif., 1966-70; regional mktg. mgr. Tracor, Inc., San Bernardino, 1970-72; dir. mktg. Dikewood Corp., Albuquerque, 1972-84, Deuel and Assocs., Albuquerque, 1984-88; paralegal specialist Criminal divsn. U.S. Atty., Albuquerque, 1989—. Inventor, patentee TruStroke Putting Aid. Naval aviator USNR, 1955-81, capt. USNR ret. Recipient Spl. Achievement award U.S. Dept. of Justice, 1992, Meritorious award, 1996, Outstanding Performance awards, 1997, 98. Mem. State Bar of N.Mex. (legal assts. divsn.), N.Mex. Alliance of Profession Paralegals (bd. dirs. 1993-95), Legal Assts. of N.Mex. (bd. dirs. 1991-93). Avocations: golf, skiing. Office: US Attys Office 201 3d St NW Ste 900 Albuquerque NM 87102-3155

MILLER, GARY IVAN, architect; b. Denver, June 1, 1964; s. Terry Miller; m. Bonnie louise Green, Aug. 24, 1985; children: Benjamin, Nicole, Nathan. Student, Metro State Coll., Denver, 1982-83, U. Colo., Denver, 1983-85. Prin. Denver Accu-Tech Planning & Design, Westminster, Colo., 1982—. Trustee Fairview Bapt. Ch., Denver, 1987—. Mem. Home Builders Assn. Office: Denver Accu-Tech Planning & Design 12018 Melody Dr Denver CO 80234-4212

MILLER, GEORGE, mayor; b. Detroit, 1922; m. Roslyn Girard; 4 children. BA, U. Ariz., 1947, MEd, 1952. Tchr. high schs., owner, prin. painting contracting co., until 1989; mayor City of Tucson, 1991—. Active mem. Dem. Party So. Ariz., 1960—, treas. Pima County div., state chmn. Presdl. Del. Selection Reform Commn.; bd. dirs. Tucson Jewish Community Ctr., Anti-Defamation League of B'nai B'rith; councilman Tucson City Coun., 1977-91, also vice mayor. With USMC, WWII. Decorated Purple Heart; recipient Recognition award United Way, Cmty. Svcs. Support award Chicano Por La Causa (2), Met. Edn. Commn. Crystal Apple award, cert. appreciation San Ignacio Yaqui Coun., Old Pasqua, Dr. Martin Luther King Jr. Keep the Dream Alive award, 1995; named Father of Yr. 1995, Man of Yr. So. Ariz. Home Builders Assn., Outstanding Pub. Ofcl. Ariz. Parks and Recreation Assn., 1995. Office: Office of Mayor PO Box 21270 Tucson AZ 85726-7210*

MILLER, GEORGE, congressman; b. Richmond, Calif., May 17, 1945; s. George and Dorothy (Rumsey) M.; m. Cynthia Caccavo, 1964; children: George, Stephen. B.A., San Francisco State Coll., 1968; J.D., U. Calif., Davis, 1972. Legis. counsel Calif. senate majority leader, 1969-73; mem. 94th-106th Congresses from 7th Calif. dist., 1975—, mem. edn. and workforce resources com.; chmn. subcom. on oversight and investigations, 1985—, chmn. subcom. on labor stds., 1981-84, chmn. select com. on children, youth and families, 1983-91, chmn. com. on natural resources, 1991-94; mem. com. on edn. and lab., dep. majority whip, 1989-94; vice chair Dem. Policy Com., 1995—. Mem. Calif. Bar Assn. Office: House of Representatives 2205 Rayburn Bldg Washington DC 20515-0507*

MILLER, GEORGIA ELLEN, business owner; b. Seattle; d. George Rynd Sr. and Mary Edith (Martin) M. BE, UCLA, 1934, MEd, 1956. Tchr. Punahou Sch., Honolulu, 1948-74; owner Miller's Bus. Svcs., Honolulu, 1975—. Bd. dirs. Waikiki Improvement Assn., Honolulu, 1980-98, Waikiki Cmty. Ctr., Honolulu, 1992-95; pres. Waikiki Residents Assn., Honolulu, 1978—; mem. State Constitutional Conv., Hawaii, 1997; sec. Waikiki Neighborhood Bd., 1980-86, v.p., 1990—, acting chair, 1992-93; county chmn. Oahu (Hawaii) Rep. Party, 1976; founding mem. Waikiki Neighbook Bd., officer; lobbyist Waikiki Residents Assn. Recipinet Kilohana award for Outstanding Vol. Svc. Gov. Coyetano, 1996. Mem. Bus. and Profl. Women (pres. 1973, legis. chair 1980, 88, state lobbyist 1988-97), AAUW, Alpha Chi Omega, Pi Lambda Theta. Mem. United Ch. of Christ. Avocations: gardening, historic preservation. Home: 2415 Ala Wai Blvd Apt 1603 Honolulu HI 96815-3409 Office: Millers Bus Svcs 1720 Ala Moana Blvd Apt B4C Honolulu HI 96815-1347

MILLER, GREGORY ALAN, artist, writer; b. Denver, Nov. 4, 1946; s. Alan Duane and Betty Darlene (Tengwald) M.; m. Karen Ilene Petras, May 1, 1983; children: Petra, Jana. Student, U. Colo., Boulder and Denver, U. Hawaii. Freelance artist, Boulder, Colo., late 1960s, San Francisco, 1970s; corp. officer KPM Mgmt., Arvada, colo., 1998. Painter murals and other works in various locations, 1970-90; author: Antilia Princess, 1996, Earthfood the Planet, 1997. Vol. Libertarian Party, Jefferson County. Recipient various awards for art. Avocations: travel, gardening, study, building. Home: 5215 Dover St Arvada CO 80002-3429

MILLER, GREGORY KENT, structural engineer; b. Anaconda, Mont., July 6, 1951; s. Robert Bruce and Lois Patricia (Arvish) M. BS in Civil Engring./Engring. Mechanics, Mont. State U., 1973, MS in Engring. Mechanics, 1974. Project engr. U.S. Energy R&D Adminstrn., Idaho Falls, Idaho, 1974-77; structural engr. EG&G Idaho, Inc., Idaho Falls, 1977-93, supr., 1993-94; supr. Lockheed Martin Idaho Technologies Co., Idaho Falls, 1994—. Contbr. articles to profl. jours. including Internat. Jour. of Impact Engring., Jour. of Nuclear Materials, Internat. Jour. of Solids and Structures, Jour. of Nuclear Sci. and Tech. Mem. ASME (com. mem. boiler and pressure vessel code sect. III 1995—), Tau Beta Pi, Phi Kappa Phi (Sr. of Yr. 1973). Achievements include research on advanced modeling and analysis methods for evaluating failure of fuel particles in high-temperature gas-cooled reactors; contributed to technology for analyzing complex material behavior in pressure vessels; advanced methods for evaluating containers bearing nuclear materials for impact loads associated with accidental drop events. Office: Lockheed Martin Idaho Technologies Co PO Box 1625 Idaho Falls ID 83415-0001

MILLER, HAROLD WILLIAM, nuclear geochemist; b. Walton, N.Y., Apr. 21, 1920; s. Harold Frank and Vera Leona (Simons) M. BS in Chemistry, U. Mich., 1943; MS in Chemistry, U. Colo., 1948, postgrad. Control chemist Linde Air Products Co., Buffalo, 1943-46; analytical research chemist Gen. Electric Co., Richland, Wash., 1948-51; research chemist Phillips Petroleum Co., Idaho Falls, Idaho, 1953-56; with Anaconda (Mont.) Copper Co., 1956; tech. dir., v.p. U.S. Yttrium Co., Laramie, Wyo., 1956-57; tech. dir. Colo. div. The Wah Chang Co., Boulder, Colo., 1957-58; analytical chemist The Climax (Colo.) Molybdenum Co., 1959; with research and devel. The Colo. Sch. of Mines Research Found., Golden, 1960-62; cons. Boulder, 1960—; sr. research physicist Dow Chem. Co., Golden, 1963-73; bd. dirs. Sweeney Mining and Milling Corp., Boulder; cons. Hendricks Mining and Milling Co., Boulder; instr. nuclear physics and nuclear chemistry Rocky Flats Plant, U. Colo. Contbr. numerous articles to profl. jours. Recipient Lifetime Achievement award Boulder County Metal Mining Assn., 1990. Mem. Sigma Xi. Avocations: mineralogy, western U.S. mining history. Home and Office: PO Box 1092 Boulder CO 80306-1092

MILLER, HARRIET SANDERS, art center director, retired; b. N.Y.C., Apr. 18, 1926; d. Herman and Dorothy (Silbert) S.; m. Milton H. Miller, June 27, 1948; children—Bruce, Jeffrey, Marcie. B.A., Ind. U., 1947; M.A., Columbia U., 1949; M.S., U. Wis., 1962, M.F.A., 1967. Dir. art sch. Madison Art Ctr., Wis., 1963-72; acting dir. Center for Continuing Edn., Vancouver, B.C., 1975-76; mem. fine arts faculty Douglas Coll., Vancouver, 1972-78; exec. dir. Palos Verdes Arts Center, Calif., 1978-84; dir. Junior Arts Center, Los Angeles, 1984-98; one woman exhibits at Gallery 7, Vancouver, 1978, Gallery 1, Toronto, Ont., 1977, Linda Farris Gallery, Seattle, 1975, Galerie Allen, Vancouver, 1973.

MILLER, JAY ANTHONY, minister; b. Baldwin Park, Calif., Dec. 15, 1959; s. Allen Roger and Barbara Anne (Offinga) M.; m. Gayle Jean Taylor, July 16, 1983; children: Abram Anthony, Kaleb Nathanael. Tjitse Taylor. BA, So. Calif. Coll., 1981; MA, Azusa Pacific U., 1982; postgrad., Westminster Sem., Escondido, Calif., 1983; ThD, Bethany Theol. Sem., Dothan, Ala., 1986; MDiv, Azusa Pacific U., 1992. Lic. to ministry Friends Ch., 1982, ordained, 1986; ordained by Am. Bapt. Chs. in U.S.A., 1988. Youth pastor Glendora (Calif.) Friends Ch., 1980-81; sr. pastor Santee (Calif.) Friends Ch., 1982-84, Alhambra (Calif.) Friends Ch., 1987-88; asst. pastor Garden Grove (Calif.) Friends Ch., 1985-87; sr. pastor 1st Bapt. Ch. of Orange, Monrovia, Calif., 1989-92, 92-97, 1st Bapt. Ch., Orange, Calif., 1992-97, Lincoln Ave. Bapt. Ch., Orange, Calif., 1998—; Christian edn. cons. Friends Chs., Whittier, Calif., 1985-88; regional chmn. evangelism Am. Bapt. Chs., Covina, Calif., 1990-92; adj. faculty Golden Gate Bapt. Theol. Sem., 1998—. Talk show host KGER, 1994-96, KBRT, 1996-97. Chaplain Tustin (Calif.) Community Hosp., 1981, Alhambra Police Dept., 1987-91, Monrovia Police Dept., 1991; pres. Monrovia Police Chaplains. Recipient commmendation City of MOnrovia, 1990. Mem. Am. Bapt. Chs. MMins. Coun., Monrovia Mins. Assn. Office: Lincoln Ave Bapt Ch 1310 E Lincoln Ave Orange CA 92565

MILLER, JEAN RUTH, librarian; b. St. Helena, Calif., Aug. 4, 1927; d. William Leonard and Jean (Stanton) M. BA, Occidental Coll., 1950; MLS, U. So. Calif., Los Angeles, 1952. Base librarian USAF, Wethersfield, Eng., 1952-55; post librarian USMC Air Sta., El Toro, Calif., 1955-63; data systems librarian Autonetics (Rockwell), Anaheim, Calif., 1963-65; mgr. library services Beckman Instruments, Inc., Fullerton, Calif., 1966-93; mem. adv. com. Library Technician Program, Fullerton Coll., 1969—. Author: (bibliography) Field Air Traffic Control, 1965, Electrical Shock Hazards, 1974. Chair Fullerton Are U. So. Calif. Scholarship Alumni Interview Program, Fullerton, 1974—. Mem. IEEE, So. Calif. Assn. Law Libraries, Med. Library Group of So. Calif., Spl. Libraries Assn. (pres. So. Calif. chpt. 1975-76, chair Sci./Tech. Div. 1985-86). Republican. Avocations: travel, reading, swimming. Home: 4701 E Fairfield St Anaheim CA 92807-3651

MILLER, JEFFREY LATOURETTE, architect; b. Portland, June 9, 1951; s. George Manual and Lucile Clay Latourette Miller; m. Molly Polk Finch, Mar. 21, 1975 (div. Aug. 1984); m. Elizabeth Ann Stark, June 11, 1988; children: Henry Latourette, Lucile Katherine. BS, Boston U., 1972; MArch, U. Wash., 1977. Draftsman Martin Soderstrom & Matteson, Portland, 1977-79; draftsman, designer John Thodos, Portland, 1980-81; architect pvt. practice, Portland, 1982—. Dir. Portland Civic Theatre, 1977-80, Artquake, 1978-80, Portland Ctr. Visual Arts, 1980-82, Activities Coun. Portland Art Mus., 1985-86, Berry Botanic Gardens, Portland, 1996—; vol. Highlands Archtl. Rev. Com., Greenhart, Oreg., 1990-92; pres. Greenhart Homeowners Assn., 1985-92. Mem. AIA, Univ. Club, Multnomah Athletic Club, Racquet Club Portland. Democrat. Episcopalian. Avocations: landscape design, squash, running, swimming. Office: 10 NW Macleay Blvd Portland OR 97210-3322

MILLER, JILL MARIE, psychoanalyst; b. Denver, Mar. 1, 1953; d. Wilbur C. and Viretta Ann (Shaw) M. BA, U. Denver, 1974, MSW, 1979; grad. child and adolescent psychoanalyst, Anna Freud Ctr., London, 1989; PhD, U. London, 1993; grad. adult psychoanalyst, Denver Psychoanalytic Inst., 1996. Bd. cert. diplomate clin. social work; cert. child, adolescent, adult psychoanalyst Am. Psychoanalytic Assn. Clin. social worker Cath. Cmty. Svcs., Denver, 1979-83, Mt. Airy Psychiat. Hosp., Denver, 1983-85; pvt. practice clin. social worker Denver, 1982-85, pvt. practice psychoanalyst, 1991—; faculty mem. Denver Psychoanalytic Inst., Colo. Ctr. for Psychoanalytic Studies, 1991—; clin. instr. dept. psychiatry U. Colo. Med. Sch., Denver, 1994-98, asst. clin. prof. 1998—. Contbr. to books. Recipient prize for outstanding clin. paper The Anna Freud Ctr., London, 1987, Brandt Steele award The Denver Inst. for Psychoanalysis, 1998; Dorothy Burlingham scholar The Anna Freud Ctr., London, 1989, 90. Mem. Assn. Child Psychoanalysis (bd. mem., councillor 1996-99), Denver Inst. for Psychoanalysis (assoc. dir. child and adolescent tng. 1995-98, dir. child and adolescent tng. 1998, dir. 1999—), Colo. Ctr. for Psychoanalytic Studies (bd. mem. 1991-94). Avocations: outdoor activities, tennis, hiking. Office: 240 Saint Paul St Ste 315 Denver CO 80206-5115

MILLER, JOAN WENDY, financial advisor; b. Cleve., Oct. 11, 1948; d. Sidney and Claire Roth; m. William S. Comanor, Dec. 15, 1991; children: Lauren, Gregory. BA in Sociology, U. Calif., Berkeley, 1970. Cert. tchr., Calif.; lic. ins. specialist N.Y. Stock Exch., Calif. Account rep. Dean Witter Reynolds, Santa Monica, Calif., 1980-85; v.p. investments Great Western (now Washington Mut.), L.A., 1985-90; v.p. sr. investment specialist Bank of Am., L.A., 1990-96; fin. cons. Fin. Network Investment Corp., L.A., 1996—; unit trust coord. Dean Witter Reynolds, Santa Monica, 1982-84; spkr. in field. Pres. Temple Israel Sisterhood, Hollywood, Calif., 1992; v.p. Friends

of Wonderland Ave. Sch., L.A., 1995-96. Avocations: marathon running, French, cooking. Home: 519 S Arden Blvd Los Angeles CA 90020-4737 Office: Fin Network Investment Corp 3807 Wilshire Blvd Ste 1040 Los Angeles CA 90010-3111

MILLER, JOSEPH ARTHUR, retired manufacturing engineer, educator, consultant; b. Brattleboro, Vt., Aug. 28, 1933; s. Joseph Maynard and Marjorie Antoinette (Hammerberg) M.; m. Ardene Hedwig Barker, Aug. 19, 1956; children: Stephanie L., Jocelyn A., Shana L., Gregory J. BS in Agrl., Andrews U., Berrien Springs, Mich., 1955; MS in Agrl. Mechs., Mich. State U., 1959; EdD in Vocat. Edn., UCLA, 1973. Constrn. engr. Thornton Bldg. & Supply, Inc., Williamston, Mich., 1959-63, C & B Silo Co., Charlotte, Mich., 1963-64; instr. and dir. retraining Lansing (Mich.) C.C., 1964-68; asst. prof./prog. coord./coop coord. San Jose State U., 1968-79; mfg. specialist Lockheed Martin Missiles and Space (and predecessor cos.), Sunnyvale, Calif., 1979-81, rsch. specialist, 1981-88, NASA project mgr., 1982-83, staff engr., 1988-96, rsch. staff engr., 1996-98, coord. flexible mfg. system simulation project, 1994-96, team mem. federally funded AIMS Agile Mfg. project, 1995-97, team mem. corp funded machining outsource initative project, 1995-97, coord. productivity improvement program, 1996-98; agrl. engring. cons. USDA Poultry Expt. Sta., 1960-62; computer numerical control cons. Dynamechtronics, Inc., Sunnyvale, 1987-90; machining cons. Lockheed, Space Sys. Div., 1986-96; instr. computer numerical control DeAnza Coll., Cupertino, Calif., 1985-88, Labor Employment Tng. Corp., San Jose, Calif., 1988-93; instr. computer-aided mfg. and non traditional machining San Jose (Calif.) State U., 1994—; team leader Pursuit of Excellence machine tool project Lockheed Martin Missiles and Space, Sunnyvale, Calif., 1990-95, coord. safety award program, 1997-98, mem. quality awareness program screening com., 1998. Author: Student Manual for CNC Lathe, 1990; contbr. articles to profl. jours. Career counselor Pacific Union Coll., Angwin, Calif., 1985-92. UCLA fellow, 1969-73. Mem. Soc. Mfg. Engrs. (sr. mem. 1980-92, chmn. edn. com. local chpt. 1984-85, career guidance counselor 1986-88), Nat. Assn. Indsl. Tech. (pres. industry divsn. 1987-88, bd. cert. 1991-92, mem., chmn. accreditation visitation teams 1984—), Calif. Assn. Indsl. Tech. (pres. 1974-75, 84-85), Am. Soc. Indsl. Tech. (pres. 1980-81, mfg. engring. & constrn. cons. 1998—). Seventh-day Adventist. Avocations: violin, camping, designing and building homes. Home: PO Box 190 Berry Creek CA 95916-0190

MILLER, LARRY H., professional sports team executive, automobile dealer; b. Salt Lake City; m. Gail Miller; 5 children. Formerly with auto parts bus., Denver and Salt Lake City; now owner auto dealerships, Salt Lake City, Albuquerque, Denver and Phoenix; part-owner Utah Jazz, NBA, Salt Lake City, 1985-86, owner, 1986—. Office: care Utah Jazz 301 W South Temple Salt Lake City UT 84101-1216 Office: Larry H Miller Group 5650 S State St Murray UT 84107-6131*

MILLER, LEE ROBERT, video director; b. N.Y.C., Apr. 12, 1951; s. Eugene and Ruth N. Miller. Degree in Psychology, U. Washington, 1973. Ind. rec. engr. Los Angeles, 1974-86; chief rec. engr. One Pass Film/Video, San Francisco, 1986-87; owner Miller Video & Film, Novato, Calif. rec. engr. for seven gold records by artists including Willie Nelson, Julio Iglesias, Jazzercise, Muddy Track (Neil Young), (TV spls.) Fats Domino Live in Concert, Ricky Nelson Live at the Universal Ampitheatre, Los Angeles; Peter, Paul, and Mary's 25th Anniversary Spl., (TV shows) Cagney and Lacey, Dynasty, Fall Guy, Seven Brides for Seven Brothers, (films) The Black Hole, The Last Starfighter, King of the Gypsies, Zoot Suit. Mem. Cinema Audio Soc., Nat. Assn. Rec. Arts Scis. Home: 475 Wilson Ave Novato CA 94947-4239

MILLER, LETA ELLEN, musicologist, flutist, educator; b. Burbank, Calif., Sept. 30, 1947; d. Morris and Hortense (Goldstone) Zuckerman; m. Alan K. Miller, June 29, 1969; children: Joel Ira, Rebecca Sharon. BA in Music with great distinction, Stanford U., 1969; MusM in Music History, Hartt Coll. Music, 1971; PhD in Musicology, Stanford U., 1978. Prof. music U. Calif., Santa Cruz, 1980—. Author: (with A. Cohen) Music in the Paris Academy of Sciences, 1666-1793, 1979, Music in the Royal Society of London, 1660-1806, 1987, (with F. Lieberman) Lou Harrison: Composing a World, 1998; author, editor Chansons from the French Provinces (1530-1550), vol. 1, Lyon, 1980, vol. 2, The Northern Region, 1983, Thirty-six Chansons by French Provincial Composers (1529-1550), 1981, Gioseppe Caimo: Madrigali and Canzoni for Four and Five Voices, 1990, Lou Harrison: Selected Keyboard and Chamber Music, 1937-94, 1998; contbr. articles to profl. jours.; numerous recs. on renaissance, baroque and modern flute. Recipient grant Nat. Endowment for Arts, 1989, 92, 94, grant Nat. Endowment for Humanities, 1995, music rec. grant Copland Fund, 1996. Jewish. Home: 107 Iowa Dr Santa Cruz CA 95060-2446

MILLER, LORRAINE, business owner. BA in History, U. Utah. Lab. technician U. Utah Med. Ctr., 1972-75; pres. Cactus & Tropicals, Inc., Salt Lake City, 1975—; mem. adv. bd. Utah Securities Commn., 1994; panelist Am. Arbitration Assn., 1991; pres., bd. dirs. Phoenix Inst., 1986-87. Vol. VISTA, 1966-69; mem. Gov.'s Task Force Entrepreneurism, 1988, Gov.'s Task Force Work Force Devel., 1994; mentor Women's Network Entrepreneurial Tng., Small Bus. Adminstrn., 1990; mem. adv. bd. Utah Dem. Health Care Task Force, 1991, Women's Bus. Devel. Office State of Utah, 1990-92; employer Supportive Employment for the Handicapped, 1990-92. Recipient Pathfinder award Salt Lake C. of C., 1986, Women of Achievement award YWCA, 1992; named Nat. Small Bus. Person of Yr. by U.S. Small Bus. Adminstrn., 1994. Mem. Nat. Assn. Women's Bus. Owners (pres. Salt Lake chpt. 1992), Utah Assn. Women's Bus. Owners (pres. 1992, 1st v.p. 1991, bd. dirs. 1985, 89-90, named Woman Bus. Owner of Yr. 1987), Wasatch Cactus & Succulent Soc. (co-founder). Office: Cactus & Tropicals of Utah 2735 S 2000 E Salt Lake City UT 84109-1749

MILLER, MAYNARD MALCOLM, geologist, educator, research institute director, explorer, state legislator; b. Seattle, Jan. 23, 1921; s. Joseph Anthony and Juanita Queena (Davison) M.; m. Joan Walsh, Sept. 15, 1951; children: Ross McCord, Lance Davison. BS magna cum laude, Harvard U., 1943; MA, Columbia U., 1948; PhD (Fulbright scholar), St. John's Coll., Cambridge U., Eng., 1957; student, Naval War Coll., Air War Coll., Oak Ridge Inst. Nuclear Sci.; D of Sci. (hon.), U. Alaska, 1990. Registered profl. geologist, Idaho. Asst. prof. naval sci. Princeton (N.J.) U., 1946; geologist Gulf Oil Co., Cuba, 1947; rsch. assoc., coordinator, dir. Office Naval Rsch. project Am. Geog. Soc., N.Y.C., 1948-53; staff scientist Swiss Fed. Inst. for Snow and Avalanche Rsch., Davos, 1952-53; instr. dept. geography Cambridge U., 1953-54, 56; assoc. producer, field unit dir. film Seven Wonders of the World for Cinerama Corp., Europe, Asia, Africa, Middle East, 1954-55; rsch. assoc. Lamont Geol. Obs., N.Y.C., 1955-57; sr. scientist dept. geology Columbia U., N.Y.C., 1957-59; asst. prof. geology Mich. State U., East Lansing, 1959-61, assoc. prof., 1961-63; prof. Mich. State U., 1963-75; dean Coll. Mines and Earth Resources U. Idaho, Moscow, 1975-88, prof. geology, dir. Glaciological and Arctic Scis. Inst., 1975—; dir., state geologist Idaho Geol. Survey, 1975-88; elected rep. Legislature of State of Idaho, Boise, 1992—; prin. investigator, geol. cons. sci. contracts and projects for govt. agys., univs., pvt. corps., geographic socs., 1946—; geophys. cons. Nat. Park Svc., NASA, USAF, Nat. Acad. Sci.; organizer leader USAF-Harvard Mt. St. Elias Expdn., 1946; chief geologist Am. Mt. Everest Expdn., Nepal, 1963; dir. Nat. Geographic Soc. Alaskan Glacier Commemorative Project, 1964—; organizer field leader Nat. Geographic Soc. Joint U.S.-Can. Mt. Kennedy Yukon Meml. Mapping Expdn., 1965, Muséo Argentino de Ciencias Naturales, Patagonian expdn. and glacier study for Inst.. Geologico del Peru & Am. Geog. Soc., 1949-50, participant adv. missions People's Republic of China, 1981, 86, 88, geol. expdns. Himalaya, Nepal, 1963, 84, 87, USAF mission to Ellesmere Land and Polar Sea, 1951; organizer, ops. officer USN-LTA blimp geophysics flight to North Pole area for Office Naval Rsch., 58; prin. investigator U.S. Naval Oceanographic Office Rsch. Ice Island T-3 Polar Sea, 1967-68, 70-73; dir. lunar field sta. simulation program USAF-Boeing Co., 1959-60; co-prin. investigator Nat. Geographic Soc. 30 Yr. Remap of Lemon & Taku Glaciers, Juneau Icefield, 1989-92; exec. dir. Found. for Glacier and Environ. Rsch., Pacific Sci. Ctr., Seattle, 1955-95, chmn., 1992—, pres., 1955-85, trustee, 1960—, organizer, dir. Juneau (Alaska) Icefield Rsch. Program (JIRP), 1946—; cons. Dept. Hwys. State of Alaska, 1965; chmn., exec. dir. World Ctr. for Exploration Found., N.Y.C., 1969-71; dir. [illegible] 1976-89; [illegible] JSHS program U.S. Army Rsch. Office and Acad. Applied Sci., 1982-89; sci. dir. U.S. Army Rsch. Office-Nat. Sci. and Humanities Symposia program, 1991—; disting. guest prof. China U. Geoscis., Wuhan, 1981-88, Changchun U. Earth Scis., People's Republic of China, 1988—; adj. prof. U. Alaska, 1986—. Author: Field Manual of Glaciological and Arctic Sciences; co-author books on Alaskan glaciers and Nepal geology; contbr. over 200 reports, sci. papers to profl. jours., ency. articles, chpts. to books, monographs; prodr., nat. lectr. films and videos. Past mem. nat. exploring com., nat. sea exploring com. Boy Scouts Am.; past mem. nat. adv. bd. Embry Riddle Aero. U.; bd. dirs. Idaho Rsch. Found.; pres. state divsn. Mich. UN Assn., 1970-73; mem. Centennial and Health Environ. Commns., Moscow, Idaho, 1987—. With USN, 1943-46, PTO. Decorated 11 campaign and battle stars; named Leader of Tomorrow Seattle C. of C. and Time mag., 1953, one of Ten Outstanding Young Men U.S. Jaycees, 1954; recipient commendation for lunar environ. study USAF, 1960, Hubbard medal (co-recipient with Mt. Everest expdn. team) Nat. Geog. Soc., 1963, Elisha Kent Kane Gold medal Geog. Soc. Phila., 1964, Karo award Soc. Mil. Engrs., 1966, Franklin L. Burr award Nat. Geog. Soc., 1967, Commendation Boy Scouts Am., 1970, Disting. Svc. commendation plaque UN Assn. U.S., Disting. Svc. commendation State of Mich. Legis., 1975, Outstanding Civilian Svc. medal U.S. Army Rsch. Office, 1977, Outstanding Leadership in Minerals Edn. commendations Idaho Mining Assn., 1985, 87, Nat. Disting. Tchg. award Assn. Am. Geographers, 1996; recipient numerous grants NSF, Nat. Geog. Soc., NASA, Murdock Found., others, 1948—. Fellow Geol. Soc. Am., Arctic Inst. N.Am., Explorers Club; mem. councilor AAAS (Pacific divsn. 1978-88), AIME, Am. Geophys. Union, Internat. Glaciological Soc. (past councilor), ASME (hon. nat. lectr.), Assn. of Am. State Geologists (hon.), Am. Legis. Exchange Coun., Am. Assn. Amateur Oarsmen (life), Am. Alpine Club (past councilor, life mem.), Alpine Club (London), Appalachian Club (hon. corr.), Brit. Mountaineering Assn. (hon., past v.p.), The Mountaineers (hon.), Cambridge U. Mountaineering Club (hon.), Himalyan Club (Calcutta), English Speaking Union (nat. lectr.), Naval Res. Assn. (life), Dutch Treat Club, Circumnavigators Club (life), Adventurers Club N.Y. (medalist), Am. Legion, Harvard Club (N.Y.C. and Seattle), Sigma Xi, Phi Beta Kappa (pres. Epsilon chpt. Mich. State U. 1969-70), Phi Kappa Phi. Republican. Methodist. Avocations: skiing, mountaineering, photography. Home: 514 E 1st St Moscow ID 83843-2814 Office: U Idaho Coll Mines & Earth Resources Mines Bldg Rm 204 Moscow ID 83844 also: House of Reps Idaho State House Boise ID 83720 also: Found for Glacier and Environ Rsch 514 E 1st St Moscow ID 83843-2814

MILLER, MICKEY LESTER, retired school administrator; b. Albuquerque, July 26, 1920; s. Chester Lester and Myra Easter (Cassidy) M.; m. Louise Dean Miller, Aug. 30, 1946; children: Linda Miller Kelly, Lee Miller Parks, Lynne Miller Carson. BS, U. N.Mex., 1944; MS, Columbia U., 1949. Coach, tchr. math. Jefferson Jr. H.S., Albuquerque, 1946-49; coach, dept. chair, athletic dir. Highland H.S., Albuquerque, 1949-64, asst. prin., 1964-70; dist. program coord. Albuquerque Pub. Schs., 1970-90; ret., 1990. Author: Guide to Administration of Secondary Athletics, 1990; author brochures, handbooks, articles. Pub. mem. N.Mex. Bd. Dentistry, 1992—; recommending scout Pitts. Pirates Baseball, 1985—. With USN, 1942-46. Recipient Honor award S.W. Dist. Am. Alliance Health, Phys. Edn., Recreation and Dance, 1971, N.Mex. Coaches Assn., 1981, Hall of Fame award N.Mex. Activities Assn., 1985; named Retiree of Yr., S.W. Dist. Am. Alliance Health, Phys. Edn., Recreation and Dance, 1994; named to U. N.Mex. Alumni Lettermen Hall of Honor, 1994; named to Albuquerque Sports Hall of Fame, 1995. Mem. AAHPERD (life, budget/nominating rep. 1985, honor award 1999), U. N.Mex. Alumni Assn., U. N.Mex. LOBO Lettermen Club (pres., treas. 1972). Democrat. Methodist. Avocations: golf, travel, baseball scouting. Home: 1201 Richmond Dr NE Albuquerque NM 87106-2023

MILLER, NORMAN CHARLES, JR., journalism educator; b. Pitts., Oct. 2, 1934; s. Norman Charles and Elizabeth (Burns) M.; m. Mollie Rudy, June 15, 1957; children—Norman III, Mary Ellen, Teri, Scott. B.A., Pa. State U., 1956. Reporter Wall Street Jour., San Francisco, 1960-63; reporter Wall Street Jour., N.Y.C., 1963-64; bur. chief Wall Street Jour., Detroit, 1964-66; Washington corr. Wall Street Jour., 1966-72, Washington Bur. chief, 1973-83; nat. editor Los Angeles Times, 1983-97; freelance writer, 1997—; lectr. journalism U. So. Calif., 1997—. Author: The Great Salad Oil Swindle, 1965. Served to lt. (j.g.) USN, 1956-60. Recipient Disting. Alumnus award Pa. State U., 1978; George Polk Meml. award L.I. U., 1963; Pulitzer Prize, 1964. Roman Catholic. Club: Gridiron (Washington). Avocation: tennis.

MILLER, PAIGE, port executive. Pres. Port of Seattle, commr., 1998—. Office: Office of the Commn 211 Alaskan Way S Pier 69 Seattle WA 98104

MILLER, PAMELA LYNN, sales director; b. Elmhurst, Ill., Sept. 14, 1958; d. Gilbert Jack and Joan Leona (Friedberg) Mintz; m. Arthur Neal Miller, Mar. 5, 1994. BS, Ariz. State U., 1980. Virologist Automated Pathology, Inc., Phoenix, Ariz., 1980-81; territory mgr. MetPath Lab., Inc. (Corning, Inc.), Phoenix, Ariz., 1981-91; regional sales dir. Lab. Corp. of Am., Phoenix, 1991—; advisor med. home project Acad. Pediat., Phoenix, 1995. Vol. Phoenix Children's Cancer Ctr., 1990—. Avocations: golf, travel.

MILLER, RANNE B., lawyer; b. Claremore, Okla., Aug. 22, 1940. BBA, U. Wash., 1963; JD, U. N.Mex., 1967. Bar: N.Mex. 1967. Sr. ptnr. Miller, Stratvert, Torgerson & Schlenker, Albuquerque, 20 yrs. Bd. editors Nat. Resources Jour., 1966-67. Fellow N.Mex. State Bar Found.; mem. Am. Bd. Trial Advocates (pres. N.Mex. chpt. 1976-77), Am. Coll. Trial Lawyers, Fed. Bar Com., State Bar N.Mex., Albuquerque Bar Assn., Phi Kappa Phi. Office: Miller Stratvert Torgerson & Schlenker PO Box 25687 Albuquerque NM 87125*

MILLER, RICHARD ALAN, agricultural consultant, hypnotherapist; b. Everett, Wash., Mar. 16, 1944; s. John Harrison and Katheryn Ada (Nelson) M.; m. Patricia Merz, June 30, 1964 (div. 1972); 1 child, Paula Anne. BS in Physics, Washington State U., 1966; Degree in Fluidics (hon.), MIT, 1967; MS in Physics, U. Del., 1968; engr. in tng./profl. engr., U. Wash., 1969. Cert. giophysicist, 1972, hypnotherapist, 1987. Physicist instruments products div. Dupont, Wilmington, Del., 1966-68; physicist The Boeing Co./MASD, Seattle, 1968-71; biophysicist dept. anesthesiology U. Wash., Seattle, 1971-73; owner, mgr. The Beltane Corp., Inc., Seattle, 1973-80; ltd. ptnr. Western Herb Farms/Country Spice, Seattle, 1980-82; owner, mgr., writer Orgn. Advancement of Knowledge, Grants Pass, Oreg., 1983—; owner, mgr., broker Northwest Bots., Inc., Grants Pass, 1987—; ptnr., mgr., telemktg. program Florals, N.W., Grants Pass & Vancouver, B.C., Can., 1994; ptnr., mgr. broker Nat. Collection Co., Grants Pass & Denman, Can., 1992; ptnr., mgr. telemktg. program N.W. Naturals, Inc., Grants Pass, 1991; ptnr., sales mgr. Coltsfoot, Inc., Grants Pass, 1986—; advisor Ariz. Herb Growers Assn., Phoenix, 1988—; mem. New Crops Devel. Oreg. Dept. Agriculture; cons. in field; lectr. in field. Author: The Magical Mushroom Handbook, 1977, The Magical and Ritual Use of Herbs, 1978, The Magical and Ritual Use of Herbs, 1983, German edit., Spanish edit., 1995, The Potential of Herbs as a Cash Crop, 1985, The Magical and Ritual Use of Aphrodisiacs, 1985, German hardback and softback edit., 1992, The Magical and Ritual Use of Perfumes, 1990, German hardback edit., 1991, Spanish softback edit., 1990, Native Plants of Commercial Importance, 1991, The Modern Alchemist, 1991, Pantheon: Archetypal Gods in Daily Living, 1992, The Diamond Body: A Modern Alchemical View of the Philosopher's Stone, 1992, The Modern Alchemist, 1994, spl. hardback edit., 1995; contbr. articles to profl. jours., chpts. to books. Amb. All Am. City, Grants Pass, 1987—. Small Bus. Innovative Rsch. grantee USDA, 1986, Neighborhood Devel. grantee SBA, 1977, USDA grantee, 1985, 95. Mem. Am. Coun. Hypnotist Examiners, Masons. Home and Office: Northwest Botanicals Inc 493 Coutant Ln Grants Pass OR 97527-6104

MILLER, RICHARD FRANKLIN, educational consultant, researcher; b. San Francisco, Sept. 9, 1927; s. Henry G. and Hulda M. M. AB, San Francisco State U., 1950; MA, U. Calif.-Berkeley, 1964, EdD, 1970. Cert. secondary tchr., gen. supr. Calif. With San Francisco Unified Sch. Dist., 1956-89, tchr. bus. edn., econs. and social studies Mission H.S., 1967-89, adminstr. career edn. program, 1970-80; ednl. cons., 1989—. Mem. San Francisco Symphony, Fine Arts Mus. Soc. Served to sgt., U.S. Army, 1952-54. Fellow in edn. U. Calif.-Berkeley, 1974-76. Mem. ASCD, United Educators San Francisco, Phi Delta Kappa. Democrat. Unitarian.

MILLER, ROBERT CARMI, JR., microbiology educator, university administrator; b. Elgin, Ill., Aug. 10, 1942; s. Robert C. and Melba I. (Steinke) M.; m. Patricia A. Black, Aug. 29, 1964; children: Geoffrey T., Christopher J. BS in Physics, Trinity Coll., Hartford, Conn., 1964; MS in Biophysics, Pa. State U., 1965; PhD in Molecular Biology, U. Pa., 1969. USPHS trainee U. Pa., Phila., 1966-69; postdoctoral fellow U. Wis., Madison, 1969-70; rsch. assoc., Am. Cancer Soc. postdoctoral fellow MIT, Cambridge, 1970-71; asst. assoc. prof. U. B.C., Vancouver, 1971-79, prof. microbiology, 1980—, head dept. microbiology, 1982-85, dean sci., 1985-88, v.p. rsch., 1988-95, univ. senate, 1985-88; assoc. vice provost for rsch., dir. technology transfer U. Wash., Seattle, 1995—; vis. prof. Inst. Molecular Biology, U. Geneva, Switzerland, 1976; mem. grants com. on genetics Med. Rsch. Coun., 1980-82; mem. Grants Panel A Nat. Cancer Inst., 1981-85; biotech. com. B.C. Sci. Coun., 1981-87, univ./industry program grant com., 1987-92; biotech. com. Med. Rsch. Coun., 1983; assoc. com. for biotech. NRC, 1983-86; strategic grant com. biotech. NSERC, 1985-87; bd. dirs. Paprican, Discovery Found., Sci. Coun. B.C., TRIUMF. Assoc. editor Virology, 1974-85, Jour. Virology, 1975-84; contbr. 100 articles to profl. jours.; author research papers. Recipient gold medal Nat. Sci. Coun. B.C., 1993; grantee Natural Sci. and Engring. Rsch. Coun., 1971-96, Med. Rsch. Coun., 1981, 86-89, Nat. Cancer Inst., 1982-86. Office: Univ Wash Office Tech Transfer 1107 NE 45th St Ste 200 Seattle WA 98105-4631*

MILLER, ROBERT G., retail company executive; b. 1944. With Albertson's Inc., 1961-89, exec. v.p. retail ops., 1989-91; chmn. bd., pres., CEO Fred Meyer Inc., Portland, Oreg., 1991—. Office: Fred Meyer Inc 3800 SE 22nd Ave Portland OR 97202-2999*

MILLER, ROBERT JOSEPH, governor, lawyer; b. Evanston, Ill., Mar. 30, 1945; s. Ross Wendell and Coletta Jane (Doyle) M.; m. Sandra Ann Searles, Oct. 17, 1949; children: Ross, Corrine, Megan. BA in Polit. Sci., U. Santa Clara, 1967; JD, Loyola U., Los Angeles, 1971. First legal advisor Las Vegas (Nev.) Met. Police Dept., 1973-75; justice of the peace Las Vegas Twp., 1975-78; dep. dist. atty. Clark County, Las Vegas, 1971-73, dist. atty., 1979-86; lt. gov. State of Nev., 1987-89, gov., 1989-98, 1991-98; sr. ptnr. Jones Vargas, Las Vegas, 1999—. Chmn. Nev. Commn. on Econ. Devel., Carson City, 1987-91, Nev. Commn. on Tourism, Carson City, 1987-91; mem. Pres. Reagan's Task Force on Victims of Crime, 1982; chmn. Nev. divsn. Am. Cancer Soc., 1988-90. Mem. Nat. Dist. Attys. Assn. (pres. 1984-85), Western Govs. Assn. (chmn. 1993-94), Nat. Govs. Assn. (vice chmn. exec. com. 1995-96, chmn. 1996-97, past chmn. com. on justice and pub. safety, chmn. legal affairs com. 1992-94, lead gov. on transp. 1992—), Nev. Dist. Attys. Assn. (pres. 1979, 83). Democrat. Roman Catholic. Office: Jones Vargas 3rd Fl S 3773 Howard Hughes Pky Las Vegas NV 89109*

MILLER, ROBERT SCOTT, mental health administrator, social worker; b. Seattle, Dec. 12, 1947; s. Bert Lester and Carol Theresa (Gustafson) M.; m. Karen Ann Staake, Nov. 12, 1977; children: Sarah, Megan, Emily. BA in Sociology cum laude, Seattle Pacific U., 1970; AM in Social Work, U. Chgo., 1972; MA in Human Resources Mgmt., Pepperdine U., 1977. Cert. social worker, Wash. Br. supr. Wash. State Dept. Social and Health Svcs., Oak Harbor and Anacortes, 1975-78; supr. casework Wash. State Dept. Social and Health Svcs., Everett, 1973-75; lectr., coord. rural community mental health project U. Wash., Seattle, 1978-83; exec. dir. Armed Svcs. YMCA, Oak Harbor, 1984-86; area dir. United Way of Island County, Oak Harbor, 1986-88, exec. dir., 1988-92; exec. dir. Saratoga Community Mental Health, Coupeville, Wash., 1992-93; outpatient therapist, attention-deficit/hyperactivity disorder mental health specialist Cath. Cmty. Svcs. Northwest, Oak Harbor, Wash., 1993-96; dir. Cath. Cmty. Svcs. Northwest, Oak Harbor and Mount Vernon, Wash., 1996—; clin. dir. Cath. Cmty. Svcs. N.W., Everett, Wash., 1998—; part-time instr. sociology Chapman U. Naval Air Sta. Whidbey Island, Orange, Calif., 1988-95; mem. adv. bd. Island Family Health Ctr., Oak Harbor, 1990-91. *Robert Miller researched with J. Ray: Rural Community Mental Health: The Scope of Practice, Worker Satisfaction, and Implications for Training, University of Washington (1982). He presented paper The Role Transition of Professionals Moving to Rural Locales, NATO Symposium on Role Transitions, University Wisconsin, 1982. He designed first crisis nursery in Washington (1983). One of first two male presidents of a Business & Professional Women's club (1986). He received McDonald's Program Achievment Awards for YMCA latchkey program, and community indoctrination tour for Whidbey Island Naval Air Station personnel (1986).* Contbr. articles to profl. jours. Bd. dirs. Puget Sound chpt. Huntington's Disease Soc. Am., 1989-93, pres., 1991, fundraising chmn., 1989-91, v.p., 1990; mem. adv. bd. United Ways Wash., 1991-92; chmn. Island County bd. emergency food and shelter program Fed. Emergency Mgmt. Agy.; vice chmn. Cmty. Resource Network, Oak Harbor, 1991; mem. steering com. Greater Oak Harbor Econ. Summit, 1991; mem. strategic planning com. Whidbey Gen. Hosp., Coupeville, 1992-93; mem. exec. com. Mt. Baker coun. Boy Scouts Am., 1993; bd. dirs. Opportunity Coun., Bellingham, 1993-94; bd. dirs. Concerts on the Cove, Coupeville, 1993-96, v.p., 1994-95; mem. Oak Harbor Citizen's Comprehensive Plan Task Force, 1994; mem. Readiness to Learn Coupeville Cmty. Team, 1996; risk mgmt. subcom. chair Assoc. Provider Network, 1997-98; mem. child study team Island County, 1996—, child protective team, 1997—; mem. profl. adv. coun. Pregnancy Care Clinic, Oak Harbor, 1998-99. Recipient outstanding svc. award Armed Svcs. YMCA of U.S., Dallas, 1985, two program merit awards McDonald's Corp., Oak Harbor, 1986; named Alumni of a Growing Vision, Seattle Pacific U., 1991, Diplomat of Yr. Greater Oak Harbor C. of C., 1991. Mem. NASW (bd. dirs. Wash. chpt. 1982-85), Wash. Assn. Social Welfare (pres. 1975-76), Acad. Cert. Social Workers, Sunrise Rotary Club (sec. Oak Harbor chpt. 1998—). Lutheran. Avocations: reading, genealogy, camping, fishing, computers. E-mail: bobm@ccsww.org. Home: 2450 S Rocky Way Coupeville WA 98239-9610 Office: Cath Community Svcs NW 1918 Everett Ave Everett WA 98201

MILLER, ROBERT STEVEN, secondary school educator; b. Van Nuys, Calif., Aug. 9, 1963; s. Frederick Earl and Mary (Brash) M. AA, L.A. Valley Coll., 1984; BSBA, Calif. State U., 1987, MA in History, 1990. Cert. substitute tchr., 1993-96. Study group leader, study skills researcher Ednl. Opportunity Program Calif. State U., L.A., 1989-93, faculty mem. History Dept., lectr., 1990-92; sec., treas. Agate/Amethyst World, Inc., Van Nuys, Calif., 1986-91, v.p., 1992-96; with Summer Bridge Program Calif. State U., L.A., 1994-96; tchr. history Chatsworth (Calif.) H.S., 1996—. Mng. editor (jour.) Perspectives, 1990, editor-in-chief, 1991. Jake Gimbel scholar, 1989. Mem. Am. Historians Assn., The Soc. for Historians of Am. Fgn. Rels., Phi Alpha Theta (v.p. 1990, pres. 1991, Eta Xi chpt., Ledeboer Family scholar 1989), Pi Sigma Epsilon (v.p. 1986-87, pres. 1988 Phi chpt.), Mu Kappa Tau (pres. and founder 1989, Calif State U. LA chpt.). Democrat. Roman Catholic. Home: 13750 Runnymede St Van Nuys CA 91405-1515 Office: Chatsworth HS 10027 Lurline Ave Chatsworth CA 91311-3153

MILLER, RONALD EDKER, land use planner, artist; b. Cambridge, Mass., July 5, 1919; s. Norman Edker and Lillian Isabella (Wright) M.; m. Dorothy Mildred Lowe, Jan. 3, 1942 (div. Nov. 1948); children: Ronald, Cheryl; m. Betty Lou Tiger, oct. 1, 1949; children: John, Rebecca, Jeffrey, Janet, Sally. Student, Art Inst. of Boston, 1945, Feener Tech. Sch., Boston, 1946; BS in Art, Lewis & Clark Coll., 1952. Surveyor Stevens & Coon Engrs., Portland, 1941; surveyor and engr. drafting Bonneville Power Adminstr., Portland, 1947-49; urban design planner Multnomah County Planning, Portland, 1952-65; land use planner Bur. of Indian Affairs, Portland, 1965-74; land use planning cons., Portland, 1975-98; art instr., Portland, 1975-98. Master sgt. USMC, Army Air Force, ETO, 1941-45. Mem. Am. Inst. Planners, Masons (50 Yr. medal Blue Lodge 1997). Avocations: visual arts, model making, fencing, tennis. Home: 2950 SW Sunset Blvd Portland OR 97201-1279

MILLER, RONALD GRANT, journalist; b. Santa Cruz, Calif., Feb. 28, 1939; s. Fred Robert and Evelyn Lenora Miller; m. Darla-Jean Irene Rode, Nov. 2, 1963. AA, Monterey Peninsula Coll., 1958; BA, San Jose State U., 1961. Reporter Santa Cruz (Calif.) Sentinel, 1959-62; reporter, chief news bur. San Jose (Calif.) Mercury News, 1962-77, editor T.V., 1977-99, syndicated TV columnist Knight Ridder Syndicate, 1978-99; journalist, author, 1998—; commentator, critic Sta. KLOK, San Jose, 1981-83; panelist, guest speaker various orgns., 1978—; nat. judge Cableace awards, 1987. Author: (foreword) Les Brown's Encyclopedia of Television, 1992; co-author: Masterpiece Theatre, 1995, Author: Mystery! A Celebration, 1996 (Agatha,

Anthony, and Macavity award nominee 1996-97); contbr. articles and short fiction to various mags. Recipient Nat. Spot News Photo award Sigma Delta Chi, 1961, Outstanding Alumnus award San Jose State U. Dept. Journalism and Mass Comm., 1985, Nat. Headline award Press Club Atlantic City, 1994. Mem. TV Critics Assn. (nat. pres. 1981). Democrat. Home and Office: 1554 Arbor Ave Los Altos CA 94024-5913

MILLER, ROSEMARY MARGARET, accountant; b. Jersey City, Jan. 3, 1935; d. Joseph John and Marguerite (Delatush) Corbin; m. James Noyes Orton, 1956 (div. 1977); m. Julian Allen Miller, Oct. 14, 1978 (dec. 1993); children: Alexandria Lynn Hayes, Jennifer Ann Orton Cole. Student Barnard Coll., 1953-54, Rutgers U., Newark, 1954-56, Howard U., 1962-63, No. Va. Community Coll., 1976-83; AA, Thomas A. Edison State Coll., 1981; BS in Acctg., U. Md., 1987; cert. H & R Block, 1981; cert. tax profl. Am. Inst. Tax Studies. Bookkeeper Gen. Electronics, Inc., Washington, 1970-73; cost acct. Radiation Systems, Inc., Sterling, Va., 1973-80; acct. Bilsom Internat., Inc., Reston, Va., 1980-83; sales mgr. Bay Country Homes, Inc., Fruitland, Md., 1984; sr. staff acct. Snow, Powell & Meade, Salisbury, Md., 1985-86; acct. Meadows Hydraulics, Inc., Fruitland, Md., 1987-88; acct. Porter & Powell CPAs, Salisbury, 1988-93; owner, prin. RCOM Cons., acctg., bookeeping, taxes, Princess Anne, Md. Mem. Accreditation Council for Accountancy (accredited 1981), Nat. Soc. Public Accts., Inst. Mgmt. Accts., Nat. Soc. Tax Profls. (cert. tax profl. 1994). Democrat. Lutheran. Office: 240 E Ruth Ave Apt 103 Phoenix AZ 85020-3173

MILLER, SEAN JEFFREY, information systems specialist; b. Derby, Conn., Aug. 20, 1969; s. Jeffrey James and Betty (DePanfilis) M. BA cum laude, Columbia U., 1992. Network adminstr. Voith Sulzer, Portland, Oreg., 1994-97; IS mgr. Wacom Tech., Vancouver, 1997-98. Author: (novel) The Naysayer's Yearbook, 1998. Avocations: sanskrit, yoga, Spanish, poetry.

MILLER, SUZANNE MARIE, law librarian, educator; b. Sioux Falls, S.D., Feb. 25, 1954; d. John Gordon and Dorothy Margaret (Sabatka) M.; 1 child, Altinay Marie. B.A. in English, U. S.D., 1975; M.A. in Library Sci., U. Denver, 1976; postgrad. in polit. sci. U. LaVerne, 1980, postgrad. in law, 1984. Librarian II, U. S.D. Sch. of Law, Vermillion, 1977-78; law libr. U. LaVerne, Calif., 1978-85, instr. in law, 1980-85; asst. libr. tech. svcs. McGeorge Sch. Law, 1985—, prof. advanced legal rsch., 1994—. Co-author (with Elizabeth J. Pokorny) U.S. Government Documents: A Practical Guide for Library Assistants in Academic and Public Libraries, 1988; contbr. chpt. to book, articles to profl. jours. Recipient Am. Jurisprudence award Bancroft Whitney Pub. Co., 1983. Mem. Am. Assn. Law Librs., So. Calif. Assn. Law Libs. (arrangements com. 1981-82), Innovacq Users Group (chairperson, 1986-88), No. Calif. Assn. Law Librs. (mem. program com., inst. 1988), Western Pacific Assn. Law Librs. (sec. 1990-94, pres. elect 1994-95, pres. 1995-96, local arrangements chair 1997). Roman Catholic. Home: 4030 Jeffrey Ave Sacramento CA 95820-2551 Office: U of the Pacific McGeorge Sch Law Library 3200 5th Ave Sacramento CA 95817-2705

MILLER, TIMOTHY ALDEN, plastic and reconstructive surgeon; b. Inglewood, Calif., Dec. 11, 1938; s. Henry Bernard and Florence Algena (Maddock) M.; 1 child, Matthew Christopher. Student, U. Calif., Berkeley; MD, UCLA, 1963. Diplomate Am. Bd. Surgery, Am. Bd. Plastic Surgery (dir. 1991-97). Intern Vanderbilt U. Hosp., Nashville, 1963-64; resident in surgery, dept. surg. pathology UCLA, 1966-67, resident, then chief resident gen. and thoracics sugery, 1967-69, acting asst. prof., 1969-70, prof. surgery, 1981—; asst. surg. resident John Hopkins Hosp., 1967; fellow plastic and reconstructive surgery U. Pitts., 1970-72; chief plastic surgery West L.A. VA Med. Ctr., 1973—. Author: (novel) Practice to Deceive, 1991; assoc. editor Jour. Plastic & Reconstructive Surgery, 1987-93, co-editor, 1994—. Trustee Children's Inst. Internat., 1995—. Capt. U.S. Army, 1964-66, Vietnam. Decorated Bronze Star; recipient Thomas Symington award Pitts. Acad. Medicine, 1971. Mem. Am. Soc. for Plastic Surgery (co-editor Jour. Plastic and Reconstructive Surgery), Am. Soc. for Aesthetic Plastic Surgery (bd. dirs. 1990-95), Plastic Surgery Ednl. Found. (bd. dirs. 1991-95). Office: UCLA Med Ctr 200 Medical Plz Ste 669 Los Angeles CA 90095-6960

MILLER, VEL, artist; b. Nekoosa, Wis., Jan. 22, 1936; d. Clarence Alvin Krause and Celia Mae (Houston) Clark; m. Warren Eugene Miller, Apr. 30, 1955; children: Jennifer, Andrea, Matthew, Stuart. Student, Valley Coll., Art League L.A. Exhbns. include Stamford (Tex.) Art Found., Haley Libr., Midland, Tex., Peppertree Ranch, Santa Ynez, Calif., Mountain Oyster Club, Tucson, Cowboy Outdoor Gathering, Paso Robles, Cattlemans Show, San Luis Obispo, Calif., Buffalo Trails Gallery, Jackson, Wyo., Shared Visions Gallery, Delray Beach, Fla., Judith Hale Gallery, Los Olivos, Calif., Western Interpretations Gallery, Atascadero, Calif., Hahn Gallery, Scottsdale, Ariz.; represented in permanent collections at Home Savings and Loan L.A., Glendale (Ariz.) Coll., Cavalry Mus., Samore, France; also pvt. collections. Recipient Best of Show award San Fernando Valley Art Club, San Gabriel Art Assn., Death Valley Invitational Show, numerous others. Mem. Am. Woman Artist (founder), Oil Painters Am.

MILLER, WALKER DAVID, judge; m. Susanne Hauk; 3 children. LLB, U. Colo., 1963; M Comp L, U. Chgo., 1965. Bar: Colo., 1963. Asst. prof. Sch. Law, U. Kans., Lawrence, 1966-69; ptnr. Miller & Ruyle, Greeley, Colo., 1969, Miller, Ruyle, Steinmark & Shade, Greeley, 1970-74; pvt. practice $DS. Dist. Ct. Colo., Greeley, 1974-92; ptnr. Karowsky, Witwer, Miller and Oldenburg, Greeley, 1992-96; judge U.S. Dist. Ct. Colo., Denver, 1996—. Office: US Dist Ct Colo 1929 Stout St Rm C-530 Denver CO 80294-0001

MILLER, WARREN EDWARD, political scientist; b. Hawarden, Iowa, Mar. 26, 1924; s. John Carroll and Mildred Ovedia (Lien) M.; m. Ruth S. Jones, May 1981; children by previous marriage: Jeffrey Ralph, Jennifer Louise. B.S., U. Oreg., 1948, M.S., 1950; Ph.D., Maxwell Sch. Citizenship and Public Affairs, Syracuse U., 1954; Ph.D. (hon.), U. Goteborg, Sweden, 1972. Asst. study dir. Survey Research Ctr., Inst. Social Research, U. Mich., 1951-53, study dir., 1953-56, research assoc., 1956-59, program dir., 1959-68, research coordinator polit. behavior program, 1968-70, prin. investigator nat. election studies, 1977—; dir. Ctr. Polit. Studies, Inst. Social Research, 1970-81; program dir. Ctr. Polit. Studies, 1982-93; asst. prof. polit. sci. Ctr. Polit. Studies, Inst. Social Research, 1956-58, asso. prof., 1958-63, prof., 1963-93, Arthur W. Bromage prof. polit. sci., 1981-82; prof. polit. sci. Ariz. State U., 1981—; fellow Ctr. Advanced Study in Behavioral Scis., 1961-62; exec. dir. Inter-univ. Consortium for Polit. and Social Rsch., 1962-70, assoc. dir., 1978—; vis. prof. U. Tilburg, Netherlands, 1973, U. Geneva, 1973, European U. Inst., Florence, Italy, 1979; vis. Disting. prof. Ariz. State U., 1981; trustee Inst. Am. Univs., 1970—; Regents' prof., Ariz. State U., 1988—. Author: (with others) books including The Voter Decides, 1954, American Voter, 1960, Elections and the Political Order, 1966, (with T.E. Levitin) Leadership and Change: Presidential Elections from 1952-1976, 77, (with M.K. Jennings) Parties in Transition, 1986, Without Consent, 1988, (with others) The American National Election Studies Data Sourcebook, 1952-1978, 80, The American National Election Studies Data Sourcebook, 1952-86, 89; (with J. Merrill Shanks) The New American Voter, 1996; contbr. (with others) articles to profl. publs.; editl. bd.: (with others) Am. Polit. Sci. Rev, 1966-71, Computers and the Humanities, 1969-71, Social Science History, 1976-91, Social Science Rev., 1973; editorial adv. bd.: (with others) Sage Electoral Studies Yearbook, 1974. Served with USAAF, 1943-46. Recipient Disting. Alumnus award Maxwell Sch. Citizenship and Public Affairs, Syracuse U., 1974, Disting. Faculty Achievement award U. Mich., 1977; honored in the creation of the Warren E. Miller award for Intellectual Accomplishment and Svc. Am. Polit. Sci. Assn. sect. on Elecions, Pub. Opionion and Voting Behavior, 1995, creation of the Warren E. Miller award for Meritorious Svc. to Social Scis. Inter-Univ. Consortium for Polit. and Social Rsch., 1993. Fellow Am. Acad. Arts and Scis.; mem. AAAS, Am. Polit. Sci. Assn. (pres. 1979-80, Frank J. Goodnow Disting. Svc. award 1998), Internat. Polit. Sci. Assn. (coun. 1969-73), M.W. Polit. Sci. Assn., Internat. Soc. Polit. Psychology, So. Polit. Sci. Assn., Social Sci. History Assn. (pres. 1979-80), Norwegian Acad. Sci. and Letters. Office: Ariz State U Dept Polit Sci Tempe AZ 85287

MILLER, WILLIAM ELWOOD, mining company executive; b. Bend, Oreg., May 9, 1919; s. Harry Adelbert and Sarah (Heyburn) M.; B.A., Stanford, 1941, M.B.A., 1947; m. Constance Alban Crosby, July 2, 1955; children: William, Constance, Harold, Mary, Sarah Crosby, Charles Crosby, Helen, Harry. Owner and operator Central Oregon Pumice Co., Bend, 1948—; pres. The Miller Lumber Co., Bend, The Miller Ranch Co., Bend, Miller Tree Farm. Commr., City of Bend, 1959-62, mayor, 1960. Bd. dirs. Central Oreg. Coll.; pres. Central Oreg. Coll. Found., 1956-57; dir. Central Oregon Coll. Area Ednl. Dist., 1961-65, chmn., 1964-65; bd. govs. Ore. Dept. Geology and Mineral Industries, 1971-75. Served with A.C., USNR, 1942-45. Decorated D.F.C., Air medal. Mem. Central Oreg. (v.p. 1954), Bend (pres. 1954) C. of C., Bend Golf Club, Rotary (dir. Bend 1955-56), Kappa Sigma. Republican. Episcopalian. Home: 527 NW Congress St Bend OR 97701-2509 Office: 110 NE Greenwood Ave Bend OR 97701-4602

MILLER, WILLIAM FREDERICK, research company executive, educator, business consultant; b. Vincennes, Ind., Nov. 19, 1925; s. William and Elsie M. (Everts) M.; m. Patty J. Smith, June 19, 1949; 1 son, Rodney Wayne. Student, Vincennes U., 1946-47; BS, Purdue U., 1949, MS, 1951, PhD, 1956; DSc (hon.), 1972. Mem. staff Argonne Nat. Lab., 1955-64, assoc. physicist, 1956-59, dir. applied math. div., 1959-64; prof. computer sci. Stanford U., Palo Alto, Calif., 1965-97; Herbert Hoover prof. pub. and pvt. mgmt. emeritus Stanford U., 1997—, assoc. provost for computing, 1968-70, v.p. for rsch., 1970-71, v.p., provost, 1971-78; mem. Stanford Assocs., 1972—; pres., CEO SRI Internat., Menlo Park, Calif., 1979-90; chmn. bd., CEO SRI Devel. Co., Menlo Park, David Sarnoff Rsch. Ctr., Inc., Princeton, N.J.; bd. dirs. Inprise Corp.; chmn. bd. dirs. Whowhere, Inc., 1997-98, Sentris Corp.; professiorial lectr. applied math. U. Chgo., 1962-64; vis. prof. math. Purdue U., 1962-63; vis. scholar Ctr. for Advanced Study in Behavioral Scis., 1976; fellow McKenna Group; mem. adv. coun. BHP Internat., 1990-97; mem. computer sci. and engring bd. NAS, 1968-71; mem. Nat. Sci. Bd., 1982-88; mem. corp. com. computers in edn. Brown UU., 1971-79; mem. policy bd. EDUCOM Planning Coun. on Computing in Edn., 1974-79, chmn., 1974-76; mem. ednl. adv. bd. Guggenheim Meml. Found., 1976-80; mem. com. postdoctoral and doctoral rsch. staff NRC, 1977-80, mem. computer sci. and telecom.; dir. Fund Am., 1977-91, Fireman's Fund Ins., 1977-91, Wells Fargo Bank and Co., 1996-97, Varian Assocs. Inc., 1973-96, Veo Systems Inc., 1996-99. Assoc. editor: Pattern Recognition Jour, 1968-72, Jour. Computational Physics, 1970-74. Served to 2d lt. F.A. AUS, 1943-46. Recipient Frederic B. Whitman award United Way Bay Area, 1982, Sarnoff Founders medal, 1997, David Packard Civic Entrepreneurship Team award, 1998. Fellow IEEE, Am. Acad. Arts and Scis., AAAS; mem. Am. Math. Soc., Am. Phys. Soc., Soc. Indsl. and Applied Math., Assn. Computing Machinery, Nat. Acad. Engring., Sigma Xi, Tau Beta Pi (Eminent Engr. 1989). Office: Stanford U Grad Sch Bus Stanford CA 94305

MILLER, ZOYA DICKINS (MRS. HILLIARD EVE MILLER, JR.), civic worker; b. Washington, July 15, 1923; d. Randolph and Zoya Pavlovna (Klementinovska) Dickins; m. Hilliard Eve Miller, Jr., Dec. 6, 1943; children: Jeffrey Arnot, Hilliard Eve III. Grad. Stuart Sch. Costume Design, Washington, 1942; student Sophie Newcomb Coll., 1944, New Eng. Conservatory Music, 1946, Colo. Coll., 1965; grad. Internat. Sch. Reading, 1969. Instr. Stuart Summer Sch. Costume Design, Washington, 1942; fashion coord. Julius Garfinckel, Washington, 1942-43; fashion coord., cons. Mademoiselle mag., 1942-44; star TV show Cowbelle Kitchen, 1957-58, Flair for Living, 1958-59; model mags. and comml. films, also nat. comml. recs., 1956—; dir. devel. Webb-Waring Inst. for Biomedical Rsch., Denver, 1973—. Contbr. articles, lectures on health care systems and fund raising. Mem. exec. com., bd. dirs. El Paso County chpt. Am. Lung Assn., Colo., 1954-63; mem. exec. com. Am. Lung Assn. Colo., 1965-84, bd. dirs. 1965-87, chmn. radio and TV coun., 1963-70, mem. med. affairs com., 1965-70, pres., 1965-66, procurer found. funds, 1965-70; developer nat. radio ednl. prodns. for internat. use Am. Lung Assn., 1963-70, coord. statewide pulmonary screening programs Colo., other states, 1965-72; chmn. benefit fund raising El Paso County Cancer Soc., 1963; co-founder, coord. Colorado Springs Debutante Ball, 1967—; coord. Nat. Gov.'s Conf. Ball, 1969; mem. exec. com. Colo. Gov.'s Comprehensive Health Planning Coun., 1967-74, chmn., 1971-72; chmn. Colo. Chronic Care Com., 1969-73, chmn. fund raising, 1970-72, chmn. spl. com. congl. studies on nat. health bills, 1971-73; mem. Colo.-Wyo. Regional Med. Program Adv. Coun., 1969-73; mem. Colo. Med. Found. Consumers Adv. Coun., 1972-78; mem. decorative arts com. Colorado Springs Fine Arts Ctr., 1972-75; founder, state coord. Nov. Noel Pediatrics Benefit Am. Lung Assn., 1973-87; founder, chmn. bd. dirs. Newborn Hope, Inc., 1987—; mem. adv. bd. Wagon Wheel Girl Scouts, 1991—, Cmty. in Schs., 1995—; mem. cmty. adv. coun. Beth-El Nursing Sch., 1998. Zoya Dickins Miller Vol. of Yr. award established Am. Lung Assn. of Colo., 1979; recipient James J. Waring award Colo. Conf. on Respiratory Disease Workers, 1963, Nat. Pub. Rels. award Am. Lung Assn., 1979, Gold Double Bar Cross award, 1980, 83, Jefferson award Am. Inst. Pub. Svc., 1991, Thousand Points of Light award The White House, 1992, Recognition award So. Colo. Women's C. of C., 1994, Silver Spur Community award Pikes Peak Range Riders, 1994, Silver Bell award Assistance League Colorado Springs, 1996, Svc. to Mankind award Centennial Sertoma Club, 1997, Help Can't Wait award Pikes Peak chpt. ARC, 1997, Cmty. Weaver award The Independent News, 1997, Apgar award Colo. March of Dimes, 1998; named Humanitarian of Yr., Am. Lung Assn. of Colo., 1987, One of 50 Most Influential Women in Colorado Springs by Gazette Telegraph Newspaper, 1990, One of 6 Leading Ladies Colo. Homes & Lifestyles Mag., 1991. Lic. pvt. pilot. Mem. Colo. Assn. Fund Raisers, Denver Round Table for Planned Giving, Nat. Soc. Fund Raising Execs., Nat. Cowbell Assn. (El Paso county pres. 1954, TV chmn., chmn. nat. Father of Yr. contest Colo. 1956-57), Broadmoor Garden Club. Home: 74 W Cheyenne Mountain Blvd Colorado Springs CO 80906-4336

MILLICKER, GEORGE HENRY, interior designer; b. Peekskill, N.Y., May 20, 1932; s. Daniel Joseph adn Anastasia (Phelan) M. BA, Pratt Inst., 1954, MA, 1955. Assoc. designer Samson Berman Assocs., N.Y.C., 1955-56, 59-62; interior designer Conn-Pozen Design Assocs., Phoenix, 1962-64, Jim Coles & Assoc., Phoenix, 1964-66; sr. project designer Cannell & Chaffin, L.A., 1966-87; design cons. Millicker & Salisbury, Newport Beach, Dana Point, Calif., 1987—. Prin. works include interiors of Bank of Am., L.A., 1972-74, Ore-Ida Foods, Boise, Idaho, 1978-79, Kings County (Calif.) Ctr., 1976-77, exec. fls. Crocker Bank, L.A., 1984-85, Allied Signal Aerospace Co., Torrance, Calif., 1987-97, Moog Inc. Aircraft Group-Torrance Ops., 1995—, Hughes Telecomm. & Space--Battery Ops., 1998—, Moog Inc. Schaeffer Magnetics-Chatsworth Ops. With U.S. Army, 1956-58. Mem. ASID. Avocations: painting, hiking. Office: Millicker & Salisbury 34001 Ruby Lantern St # B Dana Point CA 92629-2513

MILLIGAN, RONALD E., journalist; b. Oakland, Calif., Feb. 12, 1927; s. Edgar Dewitt and Arline Claudia (Mahar) M.; m. Damita Hope Prado, July 12, 1952 (wid. Dec. 1953); children: Marina, Erin. BS, U. Calif., Berkeley, 1951; MA, Columbia U., 1970. Reporter Group W News, N.Y.C., 1966-69; reporter radio and tv network ABC, N.Y.C., 1970-71; reporter radio and tv stas. WTIC TV AM FM news, Hartford, Conn., 1972-77; gen. mgr. Conn. Radio Info. Svc., Wethersfield, Conn., 1978-86; reporter Calif. State U., Carson and Long Beach, 1986-90, Wave Newspapers, L.A., 1991-98, Daily Breeze, Torrance, Calif., 1998; with Calif. State U., Long Beach, 1998—. With USN, 1945-46, PTO. Mem. Radio TV News Assn., Soc. Profl. Journalists. Home: 8401 23rd St Westminster CA 92683 Office: Calif State U 1250 Bellflower Blvd Long Beach CA 90840

MILLIKEN, JOHN GORDON, research economist; b. Denver, May 12, 1927; s. William Boyd and Margaret Irene (Marsh) M.; m. Marie Violet Machell, June 13, 1953; children: Karen Marie, Douglas Gordon, David Tait, Anne Alain. BS, Yale U., 1949, BEng, 1950; MS, U. Colo., 1966, PhD, 1969. Registered profl. engr., Colo. Engr. U.S. Bur. Reclamation, Denver, 1950-55; asst. to plant mgr. Stanley Aviation Corp., Denver, 1955-56; prin. mgmt. engr., dept. mgr. Martin-Marietta Aerospace Divsn., Denver, 1956-64; mgmt. engr. Safeway Stores, Inc., Denver, 1964-66; sr. rsch. economist, prof., assoc. div. head U. Denver Rsch. Inst., 1966-86; pres. Univ. Senate, 1980-81; prin. Milliken Chapman Rsch. Group, Inc., Littleton, Colo., 1986-88, Milliken Rsch. Group, Inc., Littleton, 1988—; vis. fellow sci. policy rsch. unit U. Sussex, Eng., 1975-76; bd. dirs. Sci. Mgmt. Corp.; cons. mgmt. engr. Author: Aerospace Management Techniques, 1971, Federal Incentives for Innovation, 1974, Recycling Municipal Wastewater, 1977, Water and Energy in Colorado's Future, 1981, Metropolitan Water Management, 1981, Technological Innovation and Economic Vitality, 1983, Water Management in the Denver, Colorado Urban Area, 1988, Benefits and Costs of Oxygenated Fuels in Colorado, 1990, Water Transfer Alternatives Study, 1994, Colorado Springs Water Resources Plan Alternative Assessment Study, 1995, Colorado Springs Utilities Wastewater Infrastructure Alternatives Study, 1998; contbr. articles to profl. jours. Bd. dirs. S.E. Englewood Water Dist., 1963—, South Englewood San. Dist., 1965—; bd. dirs. South Suburban Pk. and Recreation Dist., 1971-96, chmn., 1990-92; chmn. Dem. Com. of Arapahoe County, 1969-71, 5th Congl. Dist. Colo., 1972-73, 74-75; mem. exec. com. Colo. Faculty Adv. Coun., 1981-85; mem. Garrison Diversion Unit Commn., 1984; trustee Colo. Local Govt. Liquid Asset Trust, 1986—, chmn., 1991-93; bd. dirs. Colo. Spl. Dist. Assn. Property and Liability Pool, 1989—, pres. 1997-98. With M.C., U.S. Army, 1945-46. Recipient Adlai E. Stevenson Meml. award, 1981, cert. of Appreciation for svc. to Nation, U.S. Sec. Interior, 1984, hon. title "Amicus Universitatis," U. Denver, 1994, Disting. Svc. award Spl. Dist. Assn. Colo., 1995; Milliken Park named in his honor for svcs. to Littleton cmty., 1996. Mem. Acad. Mgmt., Nat. Assn. Bus. Economists, Yale Sci. and Engring. Assn., Am. Water Works Assn., Sigma Xi, Tau Beta Pi, Beta Gamma Sigma, Sigma Iota Epsilon. Congregationalist. Home and Office: 6502 S Ogden St Littleton CO 80121-2561

MILLIN, LAURA JEANNE, museum director; b. Elgin, Ill., June 11, 1954; d. Douglas Joseph and PAtricia Ruth (Feragen) M. BA in Interdisciplinary Studies, The Evergreen State Coll., 1978. Dir. On The Boards, Seattle, 1979; art dir. City Fair Merocenter YMCA, Seattle, 1980; dir. Ctr. on Contemporary Art, Seattle, 1981; co-owner Art in Form Bookstore, Seattle, 1981-89; co-dir. 3d internat festical of films by women dirs. Seattle Art Mus.. & 911 Contemporary Arts, 1988; auction coord. Allied Arts of Seattle, 1989; dir. Missoula (Mont.) Mus. of the Arts, 1990—; dir. Visual AIDS Missoula Missoula Mus. of the Arts, 1989; curator Radio COCA, Ctr. on Contemproary Art, Seattle, 1986, co-curator, 1981, 83; lectr. in field. Co-editor: AnOther (ind. feminist newspaper), Seattle, 1989, editor: (exhibition catalog) James Turrell: Four Light Installations, 1981. Bd. dirs. Internat. Festival of Films by Women Dirs., Seattle, 1987, 89, Nine One One Comtemporary Arts Ctr., Seattle, 1981-87, bd. chmn. 1981-85; bd. advisors REFLEX (art mag.), Seattle, 1988-89, Ctr. on Contemporary Art, Seattle, 1983-86; state vis. Mont. Arts Coun., Missoula, 1991, NEA, Mpls., 1988, Chgo., 1987; ; panelist Mont. Arts Coun., Helena, 1990; cons. Seattle Arts Commn., 1989, juror, 1985. Home: 1721 S 9th St W Missoula MT 59801-3432 Office: Missoula Mus of the Arts 335 N Pattee St Missoula MT 59802-4520*

MILLIS, ROBERT LOWELL, astronomer; b. Martinsville, Ill., Sept. 12, 1941; married, 1965; 2 children. BA, Ea. Ill. U., 1963; PhD in Astronomy, U. Wis., 1968. Astronomer Lowell Obs., Flagstaff, Ariz., 1967-86, assoc. dir., 1986-90, dir., 1990—. Mem. Am. Astron. Soc., Internat. Astronomy Union, Divsn. Planetary Sci. (sec.-treas. 1985-88, chmn. 1994-95). Achievements include research in planetary satellites and ring systems; occultation studies of solar system objects; research on comets. Office: Lowell Observatory 1400 W Mars Hill Rd Flagstaff AZ 86001-4499*

MILLON, JEAN-PIERRE, health care executive; b. Paris, June 30, 1950; s. Andre and Marie-France (Parachaud) M.; m. Monique Triffoz, Dec. 15, 1979; children: Sebastien, Véronique. B in Econ, U. Lyons, France, 1974; degree in ME, Ecole Centrale, Lyons, 1974; M in Mgmt., Northwestern U., 1976. Head fin. planning dept. Eli Lilly France, Strasbourg, 1976-78; fin. planning mgr. Eli Lilly France, Paris, 1978-80; fin. advisor Eli Lilly Europe, London, 1980-81; fin. dir. Eli Lilly Benelux, Brussels, 1981-82, Eli Lilly Germany, Badhomburg, 1982-85; gen. mgr. Carribbean and Ctrl. Am. Eli Lilly Co., San Juan, P.R., 1985-88; dir. mkt. rsch. and planning Eli Lilly Co., Indpls., 1988-91, dir. strategic planning, 1991-92; pres. Eli Lilly Japan, Kobe, 1992-95; pres., CEO PCS Health Systems, Scottsdale, Ariz., 1995—. V.P. Am. C. of C., Tokyo, 1993-95; mem. Scottsdale Leadership Coun., 1996—; bd. dirs. Phoenix Symphony, exec. com., 1996—; advisor Thunderbird Internat. Sch. Bd., 1995—, Ariz. State U., 1995—; mem. Kellogg Grad. Sch. Advisor Bd., 1996—; bd. trustee Barrows Neurol. Found., 1997—. Avocations: skiing, traveling. Office: PCS Health Systems 9501 E Shea Blvd Scottsdale AZ 85260-6704

MILLS, BECKY, park administrator. BA, Swarthmore Coll.; MSW, U. Calif., Berkeley. Cmty. and individual social work, 1963-69; adminstrv. analyst Statewide Pres.'s Office U. Calif., 1969-72; exec. dir. Advocates for Women Econ. Devel. Ctr., 1972-76; cons. in fundraising and tng. Stanford U., Girl Scouts USA, others, 1976-78; equal opportunity mgr., chief youth programs Western Regional Nat. Park Svc., 1978-95; supr. Gt. Basin Nat. Park, 1995—. Office: Great Basin Nat Pk Hwy 488 Baker NV 89311*

MILLS, CAROL MARGARET, business consultant, public relations consultant; b. Salt Lake City, Aug. 31, 1943; d. Samuel Lawrence and Beth (Neilson) M.; BS magna cum laude, U. Utah, 1965. With W.S. Hatch Co., Woods Cross, Utah, 1965-87, corp. sec., 1970-87, traffic mgr., 1969-87, dir. publicity, 1974-87; cons. various orgns., 1988—; dir. Hatch Svc. Corp., 1972-87, Nat. Tank Truck Carriers, Inc., Washington, 1977-88; bd. dirs. Intermountain Tariff Bur. Inc., 1978-88, chmn., 1981-82, 1986-87, bd. dirs. Mountainwest Venture Group. Fund raiser March of Dimes, Am. Cancer Soc., Am. Heart Assn.; active senatorial campaign, 1976, gubernatorial campaign, 1984, 88, congl. campaign, 1990, 92, 94, vice chair voting dist., 1988-90, congl. campaign, 1994; chmn. 1990-92, chmn. party caucus legis. dist.; witness transp. com. Utah State Legislature, 1984, 85; apptd. by gov. to bd. trustees Utah Tech. Fin. Corp., 1986—, corp. sec., mem. exec. com., 1988—; mem. expdn. to Antarctica, 1996, Titanic '96 expdn. Recipient svc. awards W.S. Hatch Co., 1971, 80; mem. Pioneer Theatre Guild, 1985—; V.I.P. capt. Easter Seal Telethon, 1989, 90, recipient Outstanding Vol. Svc. award Easter Seal Soc. Utah, 1989, 90. Mem. Nat. Tank Truck Carriers Transp. Club Salt Lake City, Am. Trucking Assn. (mem. pub. rels. coun.), Utah Motor Transport Assn. (bd. dirs. 1982-88), Internat. Platform Assn., Traveler's Century Club, Titanic Internat., Beta Gamma Sigma, Phi Kappa Phi, Phi Chi Theta. Home and Office: 77 Edgecombe Dr Salt Lake City UT 84103-2219

MILLS, DALE DOUGLAS, journalist; b. Seattle, Oct. 4, 1930; d. Donald Emery and Antoinette (Kinleyside) Douglas; m. William Russell Mills, Aug. 13, 1955; children—Lida Susan, William Tad Jr., Peter Donald, Jane Douglas. B.A., U. Wash., 1952. Reporter, Seattle Times, 1954-55, 1974-83; asst. librarian Harvard U., 1955-56; editor Puget Soundings mag., 1968-71. Author: (satire) Deliver Us From Squid Roe, 1995. Mem. com. sign control Seattle City Council, 1970-72; research dir. Bruce Chapman City Council campaign, 1971; bd. mgrs. King County Juvenile Ct.; trustee Allied Arts Seattle; bd. dirs. King County Council for Prevention of Child Abuse and Neglect. Recipient awards for excellence in reporting Wash. Press Assn., Nat. Fedn. Press Women, Allied Daily Newspapers, C.B. Blethen Meml. award for disting. investigative reporting, Excellence award Soc. Profl. Journalists/Sigma Delta Chi. Mem. Jr. League Seattle, Seattle Yacht Club, Helen T. Bush Children's Hosp. Guild, Kappa Kappa Gamma.

MILLS, JENNIFER LYNN, technical support analyst; b. Albuquerque, Sept. 12, 1962; d. Kenneth Dean and Jean Ellen (Easley) M. A of Tech. Arts and Computer Info. Svcs., Edmonds C.C., Lynnwood, Wash., 1989. Tech. support analyst Revelation Technologies, Inc., Bellevue, Wash., 1992-94; contract cons. CJ Enterprises, Los Alamos, N.Mex., 1994; tech. support analyst Lovelace Biomedical Rsch. Inst., Albuquerque, 1995, Inhalation Toxicology Rsch. Inst., Albuquerque, 1995, BASIS Internat., Ltd., Albuquerque, 1995—. Mem. Sigma Chi, Alpha Alpha Tau. Avocations: reading, animal care, hiking, motorcycling, arts and crafts. Office: BASIS Internat Ltd 5901 Jefferson NE Albuquerque NM 87109

MILLS, KATHLEEN CLAIRE, anthropology and mathematics educator; b. Pitts., Dec. 27, 1948; d. Clair I. and Ruth (McDowell) Wilson; m. William G. Mills, May 27, 1978; 1 child, David Lee. AS, Kilgore Coll., 1968; BS, Met. State Coll., Denver, 1982; MA in Secondary Edn., U. Colo., 1987, MA in Anthropology, 1989. Staff U.S. Geol. Survey, Denver, 1980-82; computer application specialist Petroleum Info., Englewood, Colo., 1982-83; entry level geologist La. Land and Exploration, Denver, 1983-86; prof. anthropology and math. C.C. of Aurora, 1987-96, GED coord., 1996; prof. anthropology Red Rocks C.C., 1994-98; svc. rep. Merrill Lynch, Englewood, 1996—; excavation supr. Caesarea Maritima, Israel, 1989-96. Drafter U.S. Oil and Gas Map, 1981. Mem. Am. Schs. Oriental Rsch., Denver Natural History Mus., Archaeol. Inst. Am. Colo. Archaeol. Soc., Nat. Geog. Soc. Avocations: bicycling, reading, hiking, travel. Home: 7946 E Mexico Ave Denver

CO 80231-5687 Office: Janus 3773 Cherry Creek North Dr Denver CO 80209-3804

MILLS, LAWRENCE, lawyer, business and transportation consultant; b. Salt Lake City, Aug. 15, 1932; s. Samuel L. and Beth (Neilson) M. BS, U. Utah, 1955, JD, 1956. Bar: Utah 1956, ICC 1961, U.S. Supreme Ct. 1963. With W.S. Hatch Co. Inc., Woods Cross, Utah, 1947-89, gen. mgr., 1963-89, v.p., 1970-89, also dir.; bd. dirs. Nat. Tank Truck Carriers, Inc., Washington, 1963—, pres., 1974-75, chmn. bd., 1975-76; mem. motor carrier adv. com. Utah State Dept. Transp., 1979—; keynote speaker Rocky Mountain Safety Suprs. Conf., 1976; mem. expedition to Antartica, 1996, Titanic Expedition, 1996. Contbr. articles to legal and profl. jours. and transp. publs. Del. to County and State Convs., Utah, 1970-72; v.p. Utah Safety Coun., 1979-82, bd. dirs., 1979—, pres., 1983-84; mem. Utah Gov's Adv. Com. on Small Bus.; capt. Easter Seal Telethon, 1989, 90; state vice chmn. High Frontier, 1987—; mem. adv. com. Utah State Indsl. Commn., 1988—, chmn. com. studying health care cost containment and reporting requirements 1990—; mem. expdn. to Antarctica, 1996, Titanic '96 expedition. Recipient Safety Dir. award Nat. Tank Carriers Co., 1967, Outstanding Svc. and Contbn. award, 1995, Trophy award W.S. Hatch Co., 1975, Disting. Svc. award Utah State Indsl. Commn., 1992, Outstanding Svc. award Utah Safety Coun., 1994. Mem. Salt Lake County Bar Assn., Utah Motor Transport Assn. (dir. 1967—, pres. 1974-76, Outstanding Achievement Award 1989), Utah Hwy. Users Assn. (dir. 1981—), Indsl. Rels. Coun. (dir. 1974—), Salt Lake City C. of C., U.S. Jaycees (life Senator 1969—, ambassador 1977—, pres. Utah Senate 1979-80, Henry Giessenbier fellow 1989), Nat. Petroleum Coun., Utah Associated Gen. Contractors (assoc. 1975-77, 88—), Silver Tank Club, Hillsdale Coll. President's Club, Traveler's Century Club. Home and Office: 77 Edgecombe Dr Salt Lake City UT 84103-2219

MILNE, THOMAS JOHN, writer, retired career officer; b. Toronto, Ont., Can., Nov. 26, 1947; s. John Grant and Lucille Cecilia (Egg) M.; m. Marilou Tandiama Abano, Apr. 16, 1986; 1 child, Christine. A in Arts, Fulleton Coll., 1977. Advanced through grades to sgt. USAF, 1969; stationed at Malmstrom AFB Mont., 1966-68; served in 35th Combat Support Group Vietnam, 1969; commd. ensign USN, 1979, advanced through grades to sgt., 1996; served in USS Harold E. Holt USN, Pearl Harbor, 1979-83; served in USS Horne USN, San Diego, 1983-84; instr. USN, Fleet Combat Tng. Ctr., San Diego, 1985-87; served in USS Wabash USN, Long Beach, Calif., 1987-89, served in USS Lockwood, 1989-93; leading chief, cons. Navy Personnel Rsch. and Devel. Ctr., San Deigo, 1993-96; retired USN, 1996. Author: Micro-Management is for Mushrooms, 1996. Recipient 1st place Rice Speech Award Lincoln Meml. U., 1970. Mem. Silent Valley Club, Adventure Club No. Am. Avocations: hiking, camping, singing, reading history books. Home: 16618 Newbrook Cir Cerritos CA 90703-1410 Office: Marine Clerks Union ILWU Local 63 6615 E Pacific Coast Hwy Long Beach CA 90803-4211

MILNER, CLYDE A., II, historian; b. Durham, N.C., Oct. 19, 1948; s. Charles Fremont and Eloyse (Sargent) M.; m. Carol Ann O'Connor, Aug. 14, 1977; children: Catherine Carol, Charles Clyde. AB, U. N.C., 1971; MA, Yale U., 1973, MPhil, 1974, PhD, 1979. Admissions counselor Guilford Coll., Greensboro, N.C., 1968-70; acting instr. Yale U., New Haven, Conn., 1974-75; research fellow McNickle Ctr., Chgo., 1975-76; instr. Utah State U., Logan, 1976-79, asst. prof., 1979-82, assoc. prof., 1982-88, prof., 1988—; dir. Mountain West Ctr. for Regional Studies, 1997—; reader of manuscripts History Book Club, Inc., 1986—; exec. dir. Am. Studies program, Utah State U., 1997—. Author: With Good Intentions, 1982; editor: Major Problems in the History of the American West, 1989, co-editor 2d edit., 1997; editor: A New Significance: Re-envisioning the History of the American West, 1996; assoc. editor The Western Hist. Quar., 1984-87, co-editor, 1987-89, editor, 1990-97, exec. editor, 1998—; co-editor: Churchmen and the Western Indians, 1985, Trails: Toward a New Western History, 1991, Oxford History of the American West, 1994 (Western Heritage award for non-fiction Nat. Cowboy Hall of Fame 1994, Caughey Western History Assn. award for best book on history of Am. West 1995). Recipient Paladen Writing award The Montana Mag. Western History, 1987, Faculty Svc. award Associated Students Utah State U., 1987, Outstanding Social Science Researcher award Utah State U., 1983, (with Carol A. O'Connor) Charles Redd prize Utah Acad. Scis., Arts and Letters, 1996. Mem. Western History Assn., Orgn. Am. Historians, Phi Alpha Theta, Phi Beta Kappa. Society of Friends. Home: 1675 E 1400 N Logan UT 84341-2975 Office: Utah State U Dept of History Logan UT 84322

MILNER, DANIEL PAUL, publishing executive, composer, producer; b. San Diego, June 17, 1952; s. Gerald Herbert and Dolores Rose (Englund) M. Student, U. Minn., 1970-72. Freelance rec. engr. various studios, Los Angeles, Mpls., 1966-68, 72-78; rec. artist 20th Century Records, Los Angeles, 1970-74, record producer, 1972-74; staff songwriter Warner Bros. Records, Los Angeles, 1973-76; chief rec. engr. Studio West Rec., San Diego, Los Angeles, 1978-83; owner, exec. prodr. Milner and Sullivan Music, San Diego, Los Angeles, 1982-89; owner, pres. Wintermoon Music, San Diego, Los Angeles, 1983—; owner, exec. prodr. Broadcast Design Group, 1996—; music dir. The Arthur Co., L.A., 1978-92; audio cons. Studio C, San Diego, 1984-92, Wanna Be Doll Corp., 1986—; judge Clio Awards com., 1987-88. Composer, producer, arranger, engr.: (TV scores) Ace Diamond Private Eye, 1985, Safe at Home, 1984-87, Rocky Road, 1984-87, Down to Earth, 1983-86, The O'Briens, 1987, Here to Stay, 1987, Airwolf, 1986-88, The Munsters, 1987-90, The American Gladiators, 1993-97, (pilots) On the Line, 1985, Safe at Home, 1984, Operation Watchdog, 1987, (jingles) Budweiser, NBC Theme Song, Michelob, Firestone, thousands more; engr., producer: (feature film scores) A Minor Miracle, Happy Hour, Iced. Bd. dirs. Wildlife Rehabilitation, San Diego, 1978-84; mem. San Diego Zool. Soc., 1985-90; music producer United Way, San Diego, 1986-87, San Diego Pops Orch., 1986; conductorial mem. San Diego Pops Summer Orch. (Golden Baton 1985). Recipient 20 Clio nominations, 1 Emmy nomination, 21 Internat. Broadcast awards, 12 Addys, 1 Chgo. Film Festval, 6 Tellys, 2 N.Y. Film Festival, 3 Best in West, 1 Golden Peel, 28 Las Vegas Addys, 2 N.Y. Andys, 71 Utah Fedn., 3 Beldings, hundreds more. Mem. BMI, Am. Fedn. Musicians, San Diego Advt. Club (11 Homburg awards 1980—), San Diego Communicating Arts Group (8 awards 1984—). Roman Catholic. Avocations: falconry, jet-skiing, painting, pigeon racing. Office: Wintermoon Music 12432 Kestrel St San Diego CA 92129-3535

MILONE, ANTHONY M., bishop; b. Omaha, Sept. 24, 1932. Grad., North American Coll. (Rome). Ordained priest Roman Catholic Ch., 1957. Ordained titular bishop of Plestia and aux. bishop Diocese of Omaha, 1982; bishop Diocese of Great Falls-Billings, Great Falls, Mont., 1987—. Office: Diocese of Gt Falls-Billings PO Box 1399 121 23rd St S Great Falls MT 59403*

MILOSZ, CZESLAW, poet, author, educator; b. Lithuania, June 30, 1911; came to U.S., 1960, naturalized, 1970; s. Aleksander and Weronika (Kunat) M. M Juris, U. Wilno, Lithuania, 1934; LittD (hon.), U. Mich., 1977; honoris causa, Brandeis U., 1985, Harvard U., 1989, Jaqellonian U., Poland, 1989, U. Rome, Italy, 1992. Programmer Polish Nat. Radio, 1935-39; diplomatic service Polish Fgn. Affairs Ministry, Warsaw, 1945-50; vis. lectr. U. Calif., Berkeley, 1960-61; prof. Slavic langs. and lits. U. Calif., 1961-78, prof. emeritus, 1978—. Author: The Captive Mind, 1953, Native Realm, 1968, Post-War Polish Poetry, 1965, The History of Polish Literature, 1969, Selected Poems, 1972, Bells in Winter, 1978, The Issa Valley, 1981, Separate Notebooks, 1984, The Land of Ulro, 1984, The Unattainable Earth, 1985, Collected Poems, 1988, Provinces, 1991, Beginning With My Streets, 1992, A Year of the Hunter, 1994, Facing the River, 1995, A Book of Luminous Things, 1996, Striving Towards Being, 1996. Recipient Prix Littéraire Européen Les Guildes du Livre, Geneva, 1953, Neustadt Internat. prize for lit. U. Okla., 1978, citation U. Calif., Berkeley, 1978, Nobel prize for lit., 1980, Nat. Medal of Arts, 1990; Nat. Culture Fund fellow, 1934-35; Guggenheim fellow, 1976. Mem. AAAS, Am. Acad. Arts and Scis., Am. Acad and Inst. Arts and Letters, Polish Inst. Letters and Scis. in Am., PEN Club in Exile. Office: U Calif Dept Slavic Langs Lits Berkeley CA 94720

MILTON, CORINNE HOLM, art history educator; b. Nogales, Ariz., Oct. 16, 1928; d. Walter and Louise (Oates) Holm; m. Lee B. Milton, July 17, 1950 (dec. Oct. 1986); children: Bruce, Marina, Alan, Stuart. BA in Polit. Sci., U. Ariz., 1951, MLS, 1982; tchg. cert., U. N.Mex., 1973. Cert. secondary sch. tchr., Ariz., C.C. tchr., Ariz., Calif. Real estate sales agt. Walter Holm & Co., 1951-67; French and history tchr. Dept. State Overseas Schs., Washington, 1968-76; Sci. Tran Sci. Translating Co., Santa Barbara, Calif., 1976-78; libr. City of Nogales, 1982-83, City of Tucson, 1990-93; lectr. U. Ariz. Extension, Tucson, 1984—; Spanish instr. Pima Coll., Tucson, 1990-93; mem. Ariz.-Sonora Gov.'s Commn., Phoenix, 1993—; evaluator Ariz. Coun. for Humanities. Author, abstracter ABC Clio Press, 1976-78. Mem. Ariz. Opera Guild, 1989-96; bd. dirs. Hilltop Gallery, Nogales, 1989—; hostess, translator Tuscon Internat. Vis. Coun., 1994-96; lectr. on art history to cmty. schs. and retirement homes, Tucson, 1989—. Mem. UN Coun., Tucson Mus. Art (docent 1989—), Sunbelt World Trade Assn., Pimeria Alta Hist. Soc., Sierra Club. Democrat. Episcopalian. Avocations: hiking, raising greyhounds. Home: 6981 E Jagged Canyon Pl Tucson AZ 85750-6196

MINAMI, ROBERT YOSHIO, artist, graphic designer; b. Seattle, May 1, 1919; s. Kichitaro and Suma (Fujita) M.; m. Shizu Tashiro, May 30, 1953; 1 child, Ken. Artist; student, Art Inst., Chgo., 1957, Am. Acad. Art, Chgo., 1980-81. Graphic artist Filmack Studios, Chgo., 1945-48, S. Taylor & Leavitt Assocs., Chgo., 1949-50; head graphic designer NBC-TV, Chgo., 1950-82; fine artist Robert Minami's Studio, Oceanside, Calif., 1983—; artist Goodman Theatre Design, Chgo., 1955-56; mem. Oceanside Mus. Art Exhbn. Com.; art instr. Mus. Sch. Art, Oceanside, 1997-98. Exhibits include Oceanside Mus. Art, 1996. Active Supporters for City Couns., Oceanside, 1984—. Recipient Merit award Artist Guild Chgo., 1956, People's Choice award Carlsbad Oceanside Art League, 1986, Dick Blick award, 1992, 1st place award Mixed Media Collage, 1993, Nat. Watercolor award Watercolor West, 1994, Best of Watercolor Painting, Texture award, 1997. Mem. San Diego Watercolor Soc., United Scenic Artists (life), Am. Fine Art Connection, San Diego Art Inst., Nat. Watercolor Soc. (assoc.), Watercolor West Juried Assn. Avocations: painting, travel, movies, concerts, opera.

MINANEL, SHELLEY, writer, artist; b. New Rochelle, N.Y., Jan. 4, 1923; parents Benjamin and Mary (Regelson) Lipman. Student, Cooper Union Art, 1939-42. Pres. S. Minanel & Assocs., Marina Del Rey, Calif., 1980—; author Papier-Mache Press, Watsonville, Calif., 1987—; mem. adv. bd. Internat. Biog. Ctr., Cambridge, Eng., 1997—. Artist: (book) Artist's Market, 1985; contbr. poetry to anthologies including When I Am an Old Woman I Will Wear Purple, 1987, I Am Becoming the Woman I Want, 1994, There Is No Place Like Home for the Holidays, 1997; contbr. poetry and artwork to publs. including Sailing, Read Me, Light, Redbook, Pacific Yachting, Personal Computer Age, Editor's Desk, Aerobics Mag., Writer's Bloc. Mem. Pub. Citizen, Washington, 1996—. Recipient 2d pl. award for poetry N.Mex. Poetry Soc., 1989, Hon. Mention for poetry Writer's Market Digest, 1997. Mem. Sierra Club. Avocations: reading, bicycling, songwriting. Home: # 370C 14021 Marquesas Way Marina Del Rey CA 90292-6047 Office: S Minanel Assocs 1402 Marquesas Way Marina Del Rey CA 90292

MINAR, PAUL G., design consultant; b. Phoenix, July 12, 1932; s. Aaron Crowther and Ione Anna (Schmid) Mortensen. Student, Ariz. State U., 1950-54, John F. Kennedy U., 1978-80, Antioch West U., 1980. Sound effects technician, TV stage mgr. Sta. KHJ-AM-TV, L.A., 1955-63; displayer W.&J. Sloane Furniture Co., Beverly Hills, Calif., 1963-66, Bullock's Dept. Store, L.A., 1966-68, Macy's Dept. Store, San Francisco, 1968-70; interior designer Lloyd's Furniture Co., San Diego, 1970-71, Bonynge's Furniture Co., Oakland, Calif., 1971-72, Breuner's Furniture Co., Oakland, 1972-74; design cons. The Other Artist, San Francisco, 1974—; archival rschr. and conservation Petaluma Hist. Mus., 1994—; profl. numerologist; lectr. in onomatology. Author: Numerology For People Who Dont Understand It, 1997. Writer, producer (documentary) The Modern Nursing Home, 1959. Vol. talent agt. San Francisco Symphony Black and White Ball, 1983; bd. dirs. Akasha Personal Projects; mem. Fine Arts Mus. of San Francisco. Mem. Inst. Noetic Scis., Petaluma Mus. Assn. Democrat. Roman Catholic. Avocations: wilderness exploration, tennis, classical music, parapsychology, world history. Office: The Other Artist 3200 Buchanan St San Francisco CA 94123-3517

MINDELL, EARL LAWRENCE, nutritionist, author; b. St. Boniface, Man., Can., Jan. 20, 1940; s. William and Minerva Sybil (Galsky) M.; came to U.S., 1965, naturalized, 1972; BS in Pharmacy, N.D. State U., 1963; PhD in Nutrition, Pacific We. U., 1985; masner herbalist Dominion Herbal Coll., 1995; m. Gail Andrea Jaffe, May 16, 1971; children: Evan Louis-Ashley, Alanna Dayan. Pres. Adanac Mgmt. Inc., 1979—; instr. Dale Carnegie course; lectr. on nutrition, radio and TV. Mem. Beverly Hills, Rancho Park, Western Los Angeles (dir.) regional chambers commerce, Calif., Am. pharm. assns., Am. Acad. Gen. Pharm. Practice, Am. Inst. for History of Pharmacy, Am. Nutrition Soc., Internat. Coll. Applied Nutrition, Nutrition Found., Nat. Health Fedn., Orthomolecular Med. Assn., Internat. Acad. Preventive Medicine. Clubs: City of Hope, Beverly Hills Rotary, Masons, Shriners. Author: Earl Mindell's Vitamin Bible, Parents Nutrition Bible, Earl Mindell's Quick and Easy Guide to Better Health, Earl Mindell's Pill Bible, Earl Mindell's Shaping Up with Vitamins, Earl Mindell's Safe Eating, Earl Mindell's Herb Bible, Mindell's Food as Medicine, Earl Mindell's Soy Miracle, 1995, Anti-Aging Bible, 1996, Secret Remedies, 1997, Supplement Bible, 1998, Nutrition and Health for Your Dog, 1998, Prescription Alternatives, 1998; columnist Let's Live mag., The Vitamin Supplement (Can.), The Vitamin Connection (U.K.), Healthy N' Fit; contbr. articles on nutrition to profl. jours. Fellow Brit. Homeopathic Inst., Scottish Inst. Homeopathy. Home: 244 S El Camino Dr Beverly Hills CA 90212-3809 Office: 170 S Beverly Dr Beverly Hills CA 90212-3003

MINE, HILARY ANNE, telecommunications company executive, consultant; b. Portland, Oreg., Aug. 21, 1961; d. Lewis Stuart Keizer and Ann Christina (Kelly) Mine; m. Jon Charles Evans, Jan. 10, 1997; 1 child, Kelly Anne. BA in Econs., Reed Coll., 1983; MBA in Bus. Analysis, San Francisco State U., 1990. Analyst Berkeley Roundtable on Internat. Economy, U. Calif., Berkeley, 1984-85, program mgr. Engring. Sys. Rsch. Ctr., 1985-88; project mgr., computer cons. San Francisco State U., 1988-89; bus. planning analyst Chips and Techs., Inc., 1989-90; rsch. dir. info. techs. Frost & Sullivan, 1990-92; prin. Info. Techs. Cons., 1992-94; dir. global cons. No. Bus. Info./Datapro, 1994-96; sr. v.p. Probe Rsch., Inc., Folsom, Calif., 1996—. Tutor St. John's Tutoring Ctr., 1988; asst. edn. coord. Planned Parenthood, 1990-91. Mem. IEEE, NAFE. Avocations: cooking, kayaking, travel, Simcity. Office: Probe Rsch Inc 9580 Oak Avenue Pkwy Ste 7-170 Folsom CA 95630-1888

MINERBI, LUCIANO MARIO LAURO, urban and regional planning educator, consultant, community volunteer; b. Milan, Italy, Aug. 13, 1941; came to U.S., 1967, permanent resident, 1971; s. Giulio and Beatrice (Tosi) M.; m. Daniela Rocco, June 18, 1975; children: Lahela, Makia, Mareva. D in Architecture, Poly. U., Milan, 1966; cert. Harvard U., 1967, 1970; M in Urban Planning, U. Wash., 1969. Rschr. Istituto Lombardo Studi Economici e Sociali, Milan, 1967; asst. prof. U. Hawaii, Honolulu, 1969-73, assoc. prof., 1973-80, prof., 1980—; vis. prof. U. Venice, Italy, 1972-74; planning cons., Milan, 1967-69, Honolulu, 1969—; adj. rsch. assoc. East West Ctr., 1984; expert UN Tech. Coop. Roster, 1973—; cons. UN Statis. Office, Govt. of Fiji, 1980-83, UN Ctr. Regional Devel., Nagoya, Japan, 1984-89, Environ. Planning Tng., Solomon Islands and U.S. Aid, 1987, Tonga, 1989, Nat. Coastal Devel. Inst., 1990-91, Impact on Tourism in the Pacific Islands Greenpeace, 1991-92, Hawaii State Dept. Health, Dept. Lands and Natural Resources, 1992-93, Gov.'s Molokai Subsistence and Fishponds Restoration Task Forces, State Dept. Lands and Natural Resources Hawaii, 1993-94, Local Cultural Assessment for Environ. Risk Rankings State Dept. Health, 1992-93, Impact of Geothermal Devel. on Native Hawaiians Oak Ridge Nat. Lab.- U.S. Dept. of Energy, 1993-94, Training on cmty bldg., Queen LiLi'Uokalani Children Ctr., 1994, 1997-98, Externality impact of energy devel. on native Hawaiians, 1996, Costal zone mgmt. and village planning in Am. Samoa Govt. and U.S. Dept. Interior, Native Hawaiians access rights State Hawaii Dept. Bus. Econ. Dev. and Tourism, 1998. contbr. articles and chpts. to nat. and internat. profl. jours. and books; author, editor reports on urban and land devel. and land readjustment, community and indigenous based planning and sustainable urban environment, cultural risk assessment, native Hawaiian sacred places, historic preservation, alternative and responsible tourism in Hawaii, S. Pacific and Asia. Chmn. planning com. Moiliili Community Ctr., Honolulu, 1982-83; vice chmn. bd. dirs. Neighborhood Bd. 8 Honolulu, 1977-79; bd. dirs. Moiliili Community Ctr., 1980-83; mem. City and County Adv. Com. on Mixed Uses, Honolulu, 1982, Aloha United Way unit coord., 1986—, Neighborhood Reinvestment Corp., 1986; commr. Housing and Community Devel., City and County Honolulu, 1987-91; mem. Hawaii Ecumenical Coalition on Tourism, 1989—, S.M. Matsunaga Inst. for Peace, U. Hawaii, 1988—, exec. com. mem., 1989, 91-92; advisor to several native Hawaiian community groups. Mellon fellow U. Wash., 1967-69; grantee East-West Ctr. and U. Hawaii, 1981, 84-85; research fellow East-West Ctr., 1984; instrnl. research mentioned in various State of Hawaii legis. resolutions, 1979-86. Mem. Am. Inst. Cert. Planners (charter), Soc. Internat. Devel., AIA (assoc.). Roman Catholic. Office: U Hawaii Dept Urban and Regional Planning Social Sciences Bldg Honolulu HI 96822

MINGER, TERRELL JOHN, public administration and natural resource institute executive; b. Canton, Ohio, Oct. 7, 1942; s. John Wilson and Margaret Rose M.; m. Judith R. Arnold, Aug. 7, 1965; 1 child, Gabriella Sophia. BA, Baker U., 1966; MPA, Kans. U., 1969; Urban Exec. Program, MIT, 1975; Loeb fellow Harvard U., 1976-77; Exec. Devel. Program, Stanford U., 1979; MBA, U. Colo., 1983. Asst. dir. admissions Baker U., 1966-67; asst. city mgr. City of Boulder, Colo., 1968-69; city mgr. City of Vail, Colo., 1969-79; pres., chief exec. officer Whistler Village Land Co., Vancouver, B.C., Can., 1979-81; v.p., gen. mgr. Cumberland S.W. Inc., Denver, 1981-83; exec. asst., dep. chief of staff to Gov. Colo., 1983-87; pres., chief exec. officer Sundance (Utah) Inst. for Resource Mgmt., 1986—; pres., chief exec. officer Sundance Enterprises Ltd., 1988-91; adj. prof. grad. sch. pub. affairs U. Colo., 1983—, Sch. Bus. U. Denver, 1992—; bd. dirs. Colo. Open Lands, Inc., 1986—; participant UN Conf. on Environment and Devel., Rio de Janeiro, 1992; chmn. environ. adv. bd. Wal-Mart, Inc., 1990—; co-chmn. task force sustainable consumption World Bus. Coun. Sustainable Devel.; co-chmn. N.Am. Telecom./Environ. Taskforce; chmn. Environ. Excellence Task Force Telecomm. Industry; environ. advisor Salt Lake City Olympic Com.; bd. dirs. Piton Found., 1996. Editor: Greenhouse/ Glasnost—The Global Warming Crisis, 1990. Spl. del. UN Habitat Conf. Human Settlements, spl. rep. to UN Environment Program, 1992, coord. UN Global Youth Forum, 1993, 94, co-chmn. conf. on environment and marketing, N.Y.C., 1993; founder Vail Symposium; co-founder, bd. dirs. Colo. Park Found., 1985—; founding mem. Greenhouse/Glasnost U.S./ USSR Teleconf. with Soviet Acad. Scis., 1989—; mem. pres. task force Commn. on Sustainable Devel., 1994—; co-chmn. Golf and Environ. Conf., Pebble Beach, Calif., 1995; founder, pres. Western Rendezvous, 1995—. Nat. finalist White House Fellowship, 1978; named one of B.C.'s Top Bus. Leaders for the '80's, 1980. Mem. Urban Land Inst., Colo. Acad. Pub. Adminstrn. (charter, founding mem. 1988), Colo. City Mgmt. Assn., Internat. City Mgrs. Assn. (Mgmt. Innovation award 1974-76), Western Gov.'s Assn. (staff coun., chmn. adv. com. 1985-86), Flatirons Athletic Club. Editor: Vail Symposium Papers, 1970-79; author, editor: Growth Alternatives for Rocky Mountain West, 1976; Future of Human Settlements in the West, 1977. Home: 785 6th St Boulder CO 80302-7416 Office: Ctr for Resource Mgmt 1410 Grant St Ste 307C Denver CO 80203-1846

MINICK, KARAN FRIEDA, writer; b. L.A., July 13, 1935; d. Louis and Frieda (Karan) M.; divorced. BA, U. Calif., Berkeley, 1957, postgrad., 1964-65; JD, U. So. Calif., L.A., 1960. Bar: Calif., U.S. Supreme Ct. Lawyer State Bar of Calif., San Francisco, 1961-63, U.S. Dept. of Labor, Washington, 1966-70, San Joaquin County Counsel, Stockton, Calif., 1970-77; pvt. practice Stockton, 1977-90; real estate agt. Coldwell Banker, Stockton, 1990; law prof. Humphreys Coll. of Law, Stockton, 1963-65; tchr. bus. law Delta C.C., Stockton, 1982-85; mem. adv. com. to State Hist. Preservation Commn., 1974-76; mem. State Assn. of Pub. Guardians, Coroners, Calif., 1972-76. Columnist: Fed. Bar News, 1967-69; author: The Quiet Revolution, 1989, Tomorrow is a Promise, 1993, The Angels Club, 1996, Making Good Time, 1996, Wooden Men, 1998. Chair Pvt. Industry Coun., Stockton, 1982; mem. State Bar Com. on Ct. Rules and Procedure, Calif., 1978-81; bd. dirs. Stockton Cmty. Coun., 1972-76, Cmty. Action Coun., 1973-74. Recipient Internat. Legal Exch. Program ABA, Australia, 1977. Home: 5216 Basilica Dr Apt 290 Stockton CA 95207-6041

MINK, PATSY TAKEMOTO, congresswoman; b. Paia, Maui, Hawaii, Dec. 6, 1927; d. Suematsu and Mitama (Tateyama) Takemoto; m. John Francis Mink, Jan. 27, 1951; 1 child, Gwendolyn. Student, Wilson Coll., 1946, U. Nebr., 1947; BA, U. Hawaii, 1948; LLD, U. Chgo., 1951; DHL (hon.), Chaminade Coll., 1975, Syracuse U., 1976, Whitman Coll., 1981. Bar: Hawaii. Pvt. practice Honolulu, 1953-65; lectr. U. Hawaii, 1952-56, 59-62, 79-80; atty. Territorial Ho. of Reps., 1955; mem. Hawaii Ho. of Reps., 1956-58, Ter. Hawaii Senate, 1958-59, Hawaii State Senate, 1962-64, 89th-94th Congresses from 2nd Hawaii dist., 101st-106th Congresses from 2d dist. Hawaii, 1990—; mem. edn. and workforce com., mem. budget com.; mem. govt. reform com., mem. U.S. del. to UN Law of Sea, 1975-76, Internat. Woman's Yr., 1975, UN Environ. Program, 1977, Internat. Whaling Commn., 1977; asst. sec. of state U.S. Dept. State, 1977-78. Charter pres. Young Dem. Club Oahu, 1954-56, Ter. Hawaii Young Dems., 1956-58; del. Dem. Nat. Conv., 1960, 72, 80; nat. v.p. Young Dem. Clubs Am., 1957-59; v.p. Ams. for Dem. Action, 1974-76, nat. pres., 1978-81; mem. nat. adv. com. White House Conf. on Families, 1979-80; mem. nat. adv. coun. Federally Employed Women. Recipient Leadership for Freedom award Roosevelt Coll., Chgo., 1968, Alii award 4-H Clubs Hawaii, 1969, Nisei of Biennium award, Freedom award Honolulu chpt. NAACP, 1971, Disting. Humanitarian award YWCA, St. Louis, 1972, Creative Leadership in Women's Rights award NEA, 1977, Human Rights award Am. Fedn. Tchrs., 1975, Feminist of Yr. award Feminist Majority Found., 1991, Margaret Brent award ABA, 1992, Outstanding Woman of Yr. award Nat. Assn. Profl. Am. Women, 1992, Environ. Leadership award Nat. League Conservation Voters, 1993, Jessie Bernard Wise Women award Ctr. for Women Policy Studies, 1993, Hawaii's Health Mother award, 1994, Hispanic Health Leadership award, 1995, Women Work! Nat. Network for Women's Employment, 1995, Women at Work Pub. Policy award, 1995, Justice in Action award Asian Am. Legal Def. and Edn. Fund, 1996, Daniel K. Inouye award Hawaii Psychol. Assn., 1996, Indsl. Union Dept. Lewis-Murray-Reuther Social Justice award AFL-CIO, 1996, Top Rating for Global Internat. Trade Watch, Pub. Citizens/Nat. Farmers Union/Friends of the Earth, 1996, award Inferfaith IMPACT for Justice and Peace, 1996, Hawaii Coun. on Lang. Planning and Policy cert. for opposition to English-only legislation, 1996, Hawai'i Women Lawyers Lifetime Achievement award 1997, Legis. Leadership award Nat. Assn. of WIC Dirs., 1997. Office: US Ho of Reps 2135 Rayburn HOB Washington DC 20515-1102*

MINKIN, BARRY HOWARD, management consultant, writer, speaker; b. N.Y.C., Dec. 7, 1940; s. Isadore and Reba (Weiss) M.; m. Wendy Kagan, Dec. 22, 1963 (div. 1982); children: Brett, Melissa. BA, Hofstra U., 1962; MBA, CCNY, 1968. Cert. bus. opportunity appraiser. Asst. v.p. mktg. Cocoa-Cola Bottling, N.Y.C., 1962-64; asst. to pres. Slant Fin. Corp., Greenvale, N.Y., 1964-68, gen. mgr., 1968-73; sr. mgmt. cons. Stanford Rsch. Inst., Menlo Park, Calif., 1973-83; prin. Minkin Affiliates, Redwood City, Calif., 1983—; chmn. bd. dirs. Immuna Rx, Evanston, Ill., 1998—. Author: Status of Biotechnology, 1987, Econoquake, 1993, Future In Sight, 1995. Recipient Presdl. Citation HEW, 1968, Achievement award ASTD, 1971, Leadership award, 1972. Office: Minkin Affiliates 4000 Farm Hill Blvd Ste 110 Redwood City CA 94061

MINNERLY, ROBERT WARD, retired headmaster; b. Yonkers, N.Y., Mar. 21, 1935; s. Richard Warren and Margaret Marion (DeBrocky) M.; m. Sandra Overmire, June 12, 1957; children: Scott Ward, John Robert, Sydney Sue. AB, Brown U., 1957; MAT, U. Tex., Arlington, 1980. Tchr., coach Rumsey Hall Sch., Washington, Conn., 1962-64; tchr., coach Berkshire Sch., Sheffield, Mass., 1964-70, asst. head, 1969-70, headmaster, 1970-76; dir. Salisbury (Conn.) Summer Sch. Reading and English, 1970; prin. upper sch. Ft. Worth Country Day Sch., 1976-86; headmaster Charles Wright Acad., Tacoma, Wash., 1986-96; ednl. cons. The Edn. Group, 1996—; cons. Tarrant County Coalition on Substance Abuse, 1982-84; mem. mayor's task force Tacoma Edn. Summit, 1991-92. Contbr. articles to profl. jours. Bd. dirs. Tacoma/Pierce County Good Will Games Art Coun., 1989; mem. exec. com. Am. Leadership Forum, 1991-93; bd. dirs. Broadway Ctr. for Performing Arts, Tacoma, 1988-94, 96-98; mem. exec. com., 1990-93; elected Wash. State Bd. Edn., 1996—. Named Adminstr. of Yr. Wash. Journalism Edn. Assn., 1991. Mem. Pacific N.W. Assn. Ind. Schs. (chmn. long-range planning com. 1989-92, exec. com. 1990-92, 91, v.p. 1994). Republican. Presbyterian. Home and Office: 4214 39th Avenue Ct NW Gig Harbor WA 98335-8029

MINNERY, DAVID JEFFREY, sculptor; b. Mountain View, Calif., Sept. 24, 1969; s. David Frances and Rosemarie (Kroupa) M. BFA, Sch. Art Inst. Chgo., 1991. Prin. works exhibited at varius locations. Mem. Internat. Sculpture Soc., Pacific Am. League Palo Alto. Avocations: cooking, mountain biking, gardening, computers. Home: 780 N 1st Ave Apt C Upland CA 91786-4759

MINNICH, DIANE KAY, state bar executive; b. Iowa City, Feb. 17, 1956; d. Ralph Maynard Minnich and Kathryn Jane (Obye) Tompkins. BA in Behavioral Sci., San Jose State U., 1978. Tutorial program coord./instr. Operation SHARE/La Valley Coll., Van Nuys, Calif., 1979-81; field exec. Silver Sage Girl Scout Coun., Boise, Idaho, 1981-85; continuing legal edn. dir. Idaho State Bar/Idaho Law Found. Inc., Boise, 1985-88, dep. dir., 1988-90, exec. dir., 1990—; mem. adv. bd. legal asst. program Boise State U. Mem. Assn. CLE Adminstrs., Chgo., 1985-90; bd. dirs. Silver Sage coun. Girl Scouts, Boise, 1990-93, mem. nominating com., 1990-94, 97—, chair nominating com., 1991-92; mem. legal asst. program adv. bd. Boise State U. Named one of Outstanding Young Women in Am., 1991. Mem. Nat. Orgn. Bar Execs. (membership com. 1992-97, chair 1996-97), Zonta Club Boise (pres. 1991-92, bd. dirs. 1989-93, chair comms. com.), Rotary Club Boise (chair mem. com. 1994-97, bd. dirs. 1996-97). Avocations: softball, jogging, golf. Office: Idaho State Bar/Idaho Law Found PO Box 895 525 W Jefferson St Boise ID 83702-5931

MINNICH, JOSEPH EDWARD, tourist railway consultant; b. Swanton, Ohio, Sept. 13, 1932; s. Charles and Leila (Gaiman) M.; m. Frances Katherine Searcy, Feb. 6, 1977; children: Christopher, Susan, Teresa. Student, U. Toledo, 1956-58, Am. U., 1969. Ins. broker Wright Russell & Bay Co., Toledo, 1961-67; ch. adminstr. St. Paul's Luth. Ch., Toledo, 1968-80; pres. Toledo Lake Erie & Western R.R., 1978-81, Heritage R.R. Co., 1981-83; exec. v.p. Centennial Rail, Ltd., Denver, 1981-94, chmn. bd. dirs., 1994—; v.p. Airpower West Ltd., 1992-95. Author: Steam Locomotives in the United States, 1985, Historic Diesels in the United States, 1988; editor Trainline mag., 1979-95. V.p. Airpower West, Ltd., 1992-95. Sgt. USAF, 1951-55. Nat. Assn. Ch. Bus. Adminstrs. fellow, 1971. Mem. Tourist Ry. Assn. (bd. dirs. 1984-95, Disting. Svc. award 1991), Colo. Ry. Mus. Republican. Lutheran. Home: 3641 S Yampa St Aurora CO 80013-3527 Office: Centennial Rail Ltd PO Box 460393 Aurora CO 80046-0393

MINNIE, MARY VIRGINIA, social worker, educator, retired; b. Eau Claire, Wis., Feb. 16, 1922; d. Herman Joseph and Virginia Martha (Strong) M. BA, U. Wis., 1944; MA, U. Chgo., 1949, Case Western Reserve U., 1956. Lic. clin. social worker, Calif. Supr. day care Wis. Children Youth, Madison, 1949-57; coordinator child study project Child Guidance Clinic, Grand Rapids, Mich., 1957-60; faculty, community services Pacific Oaks Coll., Pasadena, Calif., 1960-70; pvt. practice specializing in social work various cities, Calif., 1970-78; ednl. cons. So. Calif. Health Care, North Hollywood, Calif., 1978-94; ret., 1994; med. social worker Kaiser Permanente Home Health, Downey, Calif., 1985-87; assoc. Baby Sitters Guild, Inc., 1987-94; cons. Home Health, 1987-90; ind. cons., 1998-94, ret., 1994; pres. Midwest Assn. Nursery Edn., Grand Rapids, 1958-60; bd. dirs., sec. So. Calif. Health Care, North Hollywood; bd. dirs., v.p. Baby Sitters Guild Inc., South Pasadena, 1986-94; cons. project Head Start Office Econ. Opportunity, Washington, 1965-70. Mem. Soc. Clin. Social Workers, Nat. Assn. Social Workers, Nat. Assn. Edn. Young Children (1960-62). Democrat. Club: Altrusa (Laguna Beach, Calif.) (pres. 1984-87). Avocations: music, travel, tennis, swimming, walking. Home and Office: 2225 Silver Oak Way Hemet CA 92545-8126

MINOR, HALSEY M., computer company executive. Degree, U. Va. Founder Global Pub. Corp.; chmn., CEO CNET: The Computer Network, 1992—. Office: C-Net The Computer Network 150 Chestnut St San Francisco CA 94111-1004*

MINOR, JOHN T., III, computer science educator; b. Fulton, Mo., Nov. 17, 1950; s. John T. and Ruth Edna (Neuenschwander) M. BA in math., Rice U., 1973; PhD in computer sci., U. Tex., 1979. Asst. prof. U. Okla., Norman, 1979-85; assoc. prof. U. Nev. Las Vegas, 1985-90, chmn. computer sci. dept., 1990-93, assoc. prof., 1993—; manuscript reviewer J. Wiley & Sons, 1986-87; cons./expert witness Gaming Control Bd., Las Vegas, 1990, Parnell & Assocs., Las Vegas, 1991-92, Gentile & Assocs., 1993. Task Force co-chmn. Advanced Techs. Magnet H.S., Las Vegas, 1991-94. Recipient postdoctoral fellowship USAF, Rome, N.Y., 1984, Army Rsch. Office grant, 1986-91. Mem. Assn. for Computing Machinery (treas. 1989-90), Am. Assn. for Artificial Intelligence, Assn. for Automated Reasoning, Spring Mountains Assn., Phi Kappa Phi, Upsilon Pi Epsilon. Office: U Nev Las Vegas PO Box 4019 Las Vegas NV 89127-0019

MINOR, VERNON HYDE, art history educator; b. Steubenville, Ohio, Feb. 24, 1945; s. Merrill Radcliffe and Elna Maria (Wagner) M.; m. Heather Hyde, July 8, 1994; children: Samuel, William. BA, Kent State U.; PhD, U. Kans. Prof. art history U. Colo., Boulder, 1976—. Author: Art History's History, 1994, Passive Tranquility The Sculpture of Filippo Della Valle, 1997. Mem. Coll. Art Assn. Home: 1145 Berea Dr Boulder CO 80303-6637 Office: U Colo CB 318 Boulder CO 80309-0318

MINTO, FLORAN KAY, sculptor; b. Oklahoma City, July 16, 1941; d. James H. and Mary Ruth (Houston) Waggoner; m. Arlo Waldon Minto, Aug. 4, 1962 (div. Oct. 1992); children: Trenton Traver, Tyler Waldon. BFA, U. Okla., 1963; postgrad. in arts studies, various colls. Exhbns. include: Art.Rage.Us Main Libr., San Francisco, 1998, Glenbow Mus., Calgary, Can., 1996, Webster U., St. Louis, 1995, The Butler Inst. of Am. Art, Youngstown, Ohio, 1995, Vern Riffe Ctr. for Govt. and the Performing Arts, Columbus, Ohio, 1994, Sunbird Gallery, Bend, Oreg., 1994, U.S. Ho. of Reps., Washington, 1993, 5th Street Gallery, Reno, Nev., 1992, Sierra Art Ctr., Reno, 1991, Art Gallery, Lassen C.C., Susanville, Calif., 1990, 92, Gallery 1002, Susanville, 1991, Fine Arts Show, Eagleville, Calif., 1990, others. Vice-pres. bd. dirs. Breast Cancer Action Group, Burlington, Vt., 1994-95. Recipient Outstanding Performance award Lassen C.C., 1992, Rock Welding award, 1990, sculpture awards Redding Arts Festival, Calif., 1965, Philbrook Art Ctr., Tulsa, 1963, Mus. of Art, U. Okla., 1963, others; work featured in various jours. and art catalogues. Mem. Internat. Sculpture Ctr., Lassen C.C. Welding Guild, Modoc County Art Ctr., Nev. Mus. of Art, Delta Phi Delta. Avocations: horseback riding, cross-country skiing, hunting, reading. Home: PO Box 223 Eagleville CA 96110-0223

MINTS, GRIGORI EFROIM, specialist in mathematical logic; b. Leningrad, USSR, June 7, 1939; s. Efroim B. and Lea M. (Novick) M.; m. Maryanna Rozenfeld, July 21, 1987; 1 child, Anna. Diploma, Leinigrad U., 1961, PhD, 1965, ScD, 1989. Rsch. assoc. Steklov Inst. Math., Leningrad, 1961-79; with Nauka Pubs., Leningrad, 1979-85; sr. rsch. assoc. Inst. Cybernetics, Tallinn, Estonia, 1985-91; prof. dept. philosophy Stanford (Calif.) U., 1991—; mem. adv. bd. Jour. Symbolic Logic, 1987-90; mem. editorial bd. Jour. Symbolic Computation, 1983-96, Jour. of Functional Programming, 1990-95; mem. program orgn. com. Logic in Computer Sci., 1991-94, ASL mtg. March 1997, Conf. on Automated Deduction, Logic Programming and Automated Reasoning. Editor: Mathematical Investigation of Logical Deduction, 1967, COLOG-88, 1989, Logic Colloquium, 1996; Jour. Logic and Computation, 1991—; contbr. articles to profl. jours. Mem. Assn. Symbolic Logic (mem. coun. 1990-93), Internat. Union History and Philosophy and Sci. (assessor 1991-95), Annals of Pure and Applied Logic (mem. editorial bd. 1980-89).

MINTZ, MARSHALL GARY, lawyer; b. Detroit, May 28, 1947. BA, UCLA, 1968, JD, 1971. Bar: Calif. 1972. Law clk. appellate dept L.A. County Superior Ct., 1971-72; ptnr. Kelly Lytton Mintz & Vann, L.A., Calif., 1995—; moderator, panelist Calif. Continuing Edn. of Bar, 1980—; mem. arbitration adminstrv. com. L.A. County Superior Ct., 1979, mem. 1984 Olympics spl. settlement panel. Mem. ABA, State Bar Calif., L.A. County Bar Assn. (arbitrator arbitration and client rels. com. 1978-99), Assn. Bus. Trial Lawyers (bd. govs. 1976-77, program chmn. 1976). Office: Kelly Lytton Mintz & Vann LLP Ste 1450 1900 Avenue Of The Stars Los Angeles CA 90067-4488

MINUDRI, REGINA URSULA, librarian, consultant; b. San Francisco, May 9, 1937; d. John C. and Molly (Halter) M. BA, San Francisco Coll. for Women, 1958; MLS, U. Calif.-Berkeley, 1959. Reference libr. Menlo Park (Calif.) Pub. Libr., 1959-62; regional libr. Santa Clara County (Calif.) Libr., 1962-68; project coord. Fed. Young Adult Libr. Svcs. Project, Mountain View, Calif., 1968-71; dir. profl. services Alameda County (Calif.) Libr., 1971, asst. county libr., 1972-77; libr. dir. Berkeley Pub. Libr., 1977-94; city librarian, San Francisco Pub. Libr., 1997—; lectr. U. San Francisco, 1970-72, U. Calif., Berkeley, 1977-81, 91-93; lectr. San Jose State U., 1994—; cons., 1975—; adv. bd. Miles Cutter Ednl., 1992—. Bd. dirs. No. Calif. ACLU, 1994-96, Cmty. Memory, 1989-91, Berkeley Cmty. Fund, 1994—, chair youth com., 1994—, Berkeley Pub. Libr. Found. Bd., 1996—; mem. bd. mgrs. cen. br. Berkeley YMCA, 1988-93. Recipient proclamation Mayor of Berkeley, 1985, 86, 94, Citation of Merit Calif. State Assembly, 1994; named Woman of Yr. Alameda County North chpt. Nat. Women's Polit. Caucus, 1986, Outstanding Alumna U. Calif. Sch. Libr. and Info. Scis., Berkeley, 1987. Mem. ALA (pres. 1986-87, exec. bd. 1980-89, coun. 1979-88, 90-94, Grolier award 1974), Calif. Libr. Assn. (pres. 1981, coun. 1965-69, 79-82), LWV (dir. Berkeley chpt. 1980-81, v.p. comm. svcs. 1995-97). Author: Getting It Together, A Young Adult Bibliography, 1970; contbr. articles to publs. including School Libr. Jour., Wilson Libr. Bull. Office: Reality Mgmt 836 The Alameda Berkeley CA 94707-1916 also: San Francisco Pub Libr 100 Larkin St San Francisco CA 94102-4705

MINZNER, DEAN FREDERICK, aviation company executive; b. Winchester, Mass., July 20, 1945; s. Frederick Louis and Winifred (Hughes) M.; B.A., Franklin and Marshall Coll., 1967; M.B.A., Columbia U., 1972. Dist. exec. Greater N.Y. councils Boy Scouts Am., N.Y.C., 1972-76; sales exec. Coast Avia, Long Beach, Calif., 1976-78, Performance Aircraft, Inc., Hayward, Calif., 1978; owner, pres. Western Aviation Consultants, Inc., Hayward, 1978-82, Cal-Pacific Assocs., Inc., Hayward, 1979—, Cal-Pacific Enterprises, Hayward, 1982—. Mem. Assn. M.B.A. Execs., Columbia U. Grad. Sch. Bus. Alumni Assn., Aircraft Owners and Pilots Assn. Office: PO Box 6206 Hayward CA 94540-6206

MINZNER, PAMELA B., state supreme court justice; b. Meridian, Miss., Nov. 19, 1943. BA cum laude, Miami U., 1965; LLB, Harvard U., 1968. Bar: Mass. 1968, N.Mex. 1972. Pvt. practice Mass., 1968-71, Albuquerque, 1971-73; adj. prof. law U. N.Mex., Albuquerque, 1972-73, asst. prof., 1973-77, assoc. prof., 1977-80, prof. law, 1980-84; judge N.Mex. Ct. Appeals, Albuquerque, 1984-94; justice N.Mex. Supreme Ct., Santa Fe, 1994—, chief justice, 1998—; mem. faculty Inst. Preparativo Legal U., N.Mex. Sch. Law, 1975, 79; participant NEH Summer Seminar for Law Tchrs. Stanford Law Sch., 1982, U. Chgo. Law Sch., 1978. Author: (with Robert T. Laurence) A Student's Guide to Estates in Land and Future Interests: Text, Examples, Problems & Answers, 1981, 2d edit. 1993. Mem. ABA, State Bar N.Mex. (co-editor newsletter 1979-83, bd. dirs. 1978-79, 83-84, sect. on women's legal rights and obligations), Gamma Phi Beta. Democrat. Avocations: reading, bridge, movies. Office: NMex Supreme Ct PO Box 848 Santa Fe NM 87504-0848*

MIRANDA, MONTY MITCHELL, film director; b. Hahn, Germany, Nov. 3, 1966; s. Eugene Fredrick Miranda and Janice (Cassina) Heyden. BS, U. Colo., 1990. Dir., ptnr. Incite Films, Denver, 1992—. Dir. more than 120 TV commls., short films, documentaries, others, 1992—; screenwriter: Landlocked, Curve, others. Recipient Pub. Svc. award Am. Advt. Fedn., 1992, Alfie award Denver Ad Fedn., 1992, Best of Show Golds Ad Show, 1993, six Judge's Choice Gold award, 1998. Office: Incite Films 1425 W 13th Ave Denver CO 80204-2448

MIRCHANDANI, VINOD, engineering executive; b. Japla, India, Mar. 18, 1956; came to U.S., 1980; s. Lal and Saju (Aduani)M.; m. Gail Ruth Marshall M.; children: Nicole, Neal, Cade. BSME, BITS, Pilani, 1978; MSME, Stanford U., 1982; MSMOT NTU, Ga. Tech./Lehigh, Atlanta, 1997. Design engr. M.A.N., Nurnberg, W. Germany, 1978-79; project engr. Terminal Data Corp., Woodland Hills, Calif., 1982-85; product engr. IBIS, Westlake, Calif., 1985-87; mgr. Xerox, El Segundo, Calif., 1987-94; product devel. mgr., 1994—. Contbr. articles to profl. jours.; patentee in field. Mem. Soc. Photographic Imaging Engrs. Avocations: tennis, hiking. Office: Xerox 701 S Aviation Blvd El Segundo CA 90245-4898

MIRICH, DAVID GAGE, secondary education language educator; b. Rock Springs, Wyo., June 17, 1956; s. John Jack and Kay Marie (Garvin) M. Student, U. de Filologia, Sevilla, Spain, 1981-82; BA in Psychology, Dakota Western U., 1981; teaching cert., U. Colo., 1989; postgrad., U. de Complutense, Madrid, 1991, Universidad de Salamanca, Spain, 1993; MA in Bilingual/Spl. Edn., U. Colo., 1995; postgrad., 1994—. Pvt. practice tchr., interpreter Sevilla, 1981-83; tchr. bilingual Horace Mann Middle Sch., Denver (Colo.) Pub. Schs., 1989-92; tchr. bilingual/ESOL coord. North High Sch., Denver (Colo.) Pub. Schs., 1992—; tchr. on spl. assignment, secondary bilingual and ESOL edn. Denver Pub. Schs., 1994-95. Founder, chmn. Boulderiety Conv., Boulder, Colo., 1989-92; candidate Boulder Valley Sch. Bd., 1989; founder, pres. Front Range Children's Orthodontic Fund, Denver, 1991-92. With USN, 1974-75. Named Vol. of Week., Vol. Boulder (Colo.) County, 1987, Hero of the Week, Rocky Mountain News, 1994. Mem. Nat. Assn. Bilingual Edn. (Nat. Bilingual Tchr. of Yr. 1994), Colo. Assn. Bilingual Edn. (v.p. 1993-95, Colo. Bilingual Tchr. of Yr., 1994). Avocations: horses, breeding dogs, languages, travel, real estate restoration. Home: 2224 Hooker St Denver CO 80211-5043 Office: West HS 9th and Elati Sts Denver CO 80203

MIRIKITANI, JOHN MASA, foundation administrator; b. Honolulu, Nov. 24, 1962; s. Clifford Kunio and Helene M. AB, U. Calif., Berkeley, 1985; JD, U. Mich., 1990; AB, U. Calif., Berkeley, 1985; postgrad., U. Hawaii; AA in Am. Econs. summa cum laude, Econ. Inst., 1997; MA in Econs. with honors, Yale U., 1998, postgrad., 1998—. Policy analyst intern Sloan Found. for Pub. Policy and Mgmt./U. Calif., Berkeley, 1984; policy analyst legis. bus. devel. com. State of Hawaii, Honolulu, 1988-89; founder, pres. John and Clifford Mirikitani Found., Honolulu, 1988—; sponsor Mirikitani Lectrs. in law and econs. edn., U. Hawaii, Manoa, Honolulu, 1989-91; med. researcher, 1992—; tchg. fellow Yale U. Candidate for State Bd. Edn., State Hawaii, 1992, 94; sponsor local broadcast Sesame St. PBS, Concerts for Youth Honolulu Symphony. Recipient fellowship Harvard Kennedy Sch. of Govt., 1985. Mem. Am. Law and Econs. Assn., Phi Beta Kappa. Avocations: internat. investing, chess, weightlifitng, nutrition, ichthyology. Home: 2336 Oahu Ave Honolulu HI 96822-1965

MIRISOLA, LISA HEINEMANN, air quality engineer; b. Glendale, Calif., Mar. 25, 1963; d. J. Herbert and Betty Jane (Howson) Heinemann; m. Daniel Carl Mirisola, June 27, 1987; 1 child, Ian Cataldo. BSME, UCLA, 1986. Cert. engr.-in-tng., Calif. Air quality engr. South Coast Air Quality Mgmt. Dist., Diamond Bar, Calif., 1988—. Chancellor's scholar UCLA, 1981. Mem. ASME, NSPE, Soc. Women Engrs. Office: South Coast Air Quality Mgmt Dist 21865 Copley Dr Diamond Bar CA 91765-4178

MIRK, JUDY ANN, retired elementary educator; b. Victorville, Calif., June 10, 1944; d. Richard Nesbit and Corrine (Berghoefer). BA in Social Sci., San Jose (Calif.) State U., 1966, cert. in teaching, 1967; MA in Edn., Calif. State U., Chico, 1980; student, marriage and family counseling, John F. Kennedy U., CA. Cert. elem. edn. tchr., Calif. Tchr. Cupertino (Calif.) Union Sch. Dist., 1967-95; lead tchr. lang. arts Dilworth Sch., San Jose, 1988-90, mem. supt.'s adv. team, 1986-90, mem. student study team, 1987-95; ret.; mem. student study team, 1987-95; mem. Dilworth Sch. Site Coun., 1981-95. Mem. The Camp Fellowship. Mem. Daytime Drama Guild (charter), Phi Mu. Republican. Avocations: photography, birdwatching. Home: 2075 Redwood Dr Santa Cruz CA 95060-1238

MIRONE-BARTZ, DAWN, secondary school and community college educator; b. Mt. Vernon, N.Y., Sept. 21, 1963; d. Robert and Joann Mirone (Perrotta) M.; m. Greg Bartz; 1 child, Katherine. BA in Journalism and Speech Comm., U. R.I., 1985; MA in Social Sci. Edn., Columbia U., 1987; cert. in social scis. and English, Calif. State U., Long Beach, 1991; postgrad., U. Mass., 1995, Calif. State U., Fullerton, 1996—. Cert. tchr., Calif, N.Y. Reporter Std. Times, North Kingstown, R.I., 1984-85; tchg. asst. Greenwich (Conn.) H.S., 1985-86; journalism and English tchr. Evander Childs H.S., Bronx, 1986-88; dir. edn. Bellwood Med. Health Ctr., Bellflower, Calif., 1988-89; social sci. and English tchr. Regency H.S., Long Beach, 1989-90; social sci., English, speech, and journalism tchr. Laguna Beach (Calif.) H.S., 1990—, activities dir., 1992-95, mem. scholarship com., 1991, 94; journalism instr. Saddleback Coll., Mission Viejo, Calif., 1994-97; cultural diversity coord. Laguna Beach (Calif.) H.S., 1993-96. Mem. citywide youth violence commn. City of Laguna Beach/Sch. Dist., 1992-94; sch. coord. Close Up Washington, Laguna Beach, 1991—. Recipient Nat. Svc. award PTA, 1993; grantee Laguna Beach City Coun., 1992, Recognition award for Journalism, 1994. Mem. Am. Polit. Sci. Assn., Am. Scholastic Press Assn. (1st pl. award 1994, 95, 96, 97), Journalism Education Assn., Quill & Scroll Soc. (Internat. 1st pl. award 1994, 2d place 1996), Columbia U. Press Assn. (2d pl. award 1997). Avocations: motor cross racing, skiing, rollerblading. Office: Laguna Beach HS 625 Park Ave Laguna Beach CA 92651-2340

MIRSKY, PHYLLIS SIMON, librarian; b. Petach Tikva, Israel, Dec. 18, 1940; d. Allan and Lea (Prizant) Simon; m. Edward Mirsky, Oct. 21, 1967; 1 child, Seth (dec.). BS in Social Welfare, Ohio State U., 1962; postgrad., Columbia U., 1962-63; AMLS, U. Mich., 1965. Caseworker field placement Children's Aid Soc., N.Y.C., 1962-63; hosp. libr. hosp. and instns. divsn. Cleve. Pub. Libr., 1963-64; reference libr. UCLA Biomed. Libr., 1965-68, reference/acquisitions libr., 1968-69, head cons./continuing edn. Pacific S.W. Regl. Med. Libr. Sv., 1969-71, asst. dir. Pacific S.W. Regl. Med. Libr. Sv., 1971-73, faculty coord. Biomed. Libr. program Cen. San Joaquin Valley Area Health Edn. Ctr., 1973-77, assoc. dir. Pacific S.W. Regl. Med. Libr. Sv., 1973-79; head reference sect., coord. libr. assoc. program Nat. Libr. of Medicine, Bethesda, Md., 1979-81; asst. univ. libr., scis. U. Calif.-San Diego, La Jolla, 1981-86, acting univ. libr., 1985, 92-93, asst. univ. libr. adminstrv. and pub. svcs., 1986-87, assoc. univ. libr. adminstrv. and pub. svcs., 1987-92, assoc. univ. libr., 1993-95; dep. univ. libr., 1995—; guest lectr. Libr. Schs. UCLA and U. So. Calif., 1967-78, Grad. Sch. Libr. Sci. Cath. U., Washington, 1980, Grad. Sch. Libr. and Info. Sci. UCLA, 1984; mem. task force on role of spl. libr. nationwide network and coop. programs Nat. Commn. on Libr. and Info. Svcs./Spl. Libr. Assn., 1981-83; facilitator AASLD/MLA Guidelines Scenario Writing Session, L.A., 1984; mem. users coun. OCLC Online Computer Libr. Ctr., Inc., 1991-94; U. Calif.-San Diego rep. Coalition for Networked Info., 1992—; instr. Assn. Rsch. Librs., Office Mgmt. Studies, Mgmt. Inst., 1987; peer reviewer Coll. Libr. Tech. and Cooperation Grant Program U.S. Dept. Edn., 1988-94; cons. Nat. Libr. Medicine, Bethesda, Md., 1988, San Diego Mus. Contemporary Art Libr., La Jolla, Calif., 1993, Salk Inst., 1995; mem. Libr. of Congress Network Adv. Com., 1994-96, chair steering com., 1995-96. Contbr. articles to profl. jours. and bulls. Mem. fin. com. City of Del Mar, 1995-98, chair, 1997-98. NIH fellow Columbia U., 1962-63; sr. fellow UCLA/Coun. on Libr. Resources, 1987. Fellow Med. Libr. Assn. (bd. dirs. 1977-80); mem. ALA (site visitors panel com. on accreditation 1990-92, libr. adminstrn. and mgmt. assn. 1990-92), Med. Libr. Group Soc. Calif. and Ariz. (sec. 1970-71, v.p. 1971-72, pres. 1972-73), Documentation Abstracts, Inc. (bd. dirs. 1985-90, vice chair bd. dirs. 1988-90), Med. Libr. Assn. (pres. 1984-85), U. Mich. Sch. Libr. Sci. Alumni Assn. Office: U Calif-San Diego Univ Libr 0175G 9500 Gilman Dr La Jolla CA 92093-5003

MIRZA, ZAKIR HUSSAIN, aerospace company consultant; b. Jullundar, India, Dec. 15, 1947; arrived in Can., 1971, came to U.S., 1977; s. Mohammad Hussain and Kaniz Fatima Mirza; m. Naveeda J. Mirza, Aug. 26, 1977; children: Noreen, Hassan, Nadeem. BSc in Physics/Maths., U. Panjab, Lahore, Pakistan, 1968, MSc in Physics, 1970. Test engr. Bendix Corp., Windsor, Ont., Can., 1971-79; mgr. instrumentation engring. Nat. Tech. Sys., Saugus, Calif., 1979-82; sr. instrumentation engr. Wyle Labs., Norco, Calif., 1982-84; sr. test engr. Rohr Corp., Chula Vista, Calif., 1984-87; cons. various clients including Hughes Space and Comm. Co., El Segundo, Calif., Ledtronics, Torrance, Calif., Teledyne Continental Motors, Muskegon, Mich., FMC Corp., San Jose, Calif., Stewart and Stevenson, Houston, Morton Thiokol, Brigham City, Utah, 1987—. Fellow Inst. Advancement Engring., AIAA (assoc., chair-elect L.A. chpt., 1998-99). Republican. Islam. Avocations: flying fixed wing aircraft, swimming. Home: 4952 Blackhorse Rd Rancho Palos Verdes CA 90275-3760 Office: Hughes Space & Comm 1950 E Imperial Hwy El Segundo CA 90245-2701

MISA, KENNETH FRANKLIN, management consultant; b. Jamaica, N.Y., Sept. 24, 1939; s. Frank J. and Mary M. (Soszka) M.; BS cum laude in Psychology, Fairfield U., 1961; MS in Psychology, Purdue U., 1963; PhD in Psychology (Fellow 1963-66), St. John's U., 1966. Staff psychologist Rohrer, Hibler & Replogle, Los Angeles, 1966-67; assoc. A.T. Kearney, Inc., Los Angeles, 1968-71, sr. assoc., 1972-74, prin., 1975-78, v.p., partner, 1979-86; pres. HR Cons. Group, 1987—. Cert. mgmt. cons.; lic. psychologist, Calif. Mem. Am. Psychol. Assn., Am. Psychol. Soc., Calif. State Psychol. Assn., Soc. for Human Resources Mgmt., Human Resources Planning Soc., Indsl. Rels. Rsch. Assn., Soc. for Indsl. and Organizational Psychology, World Affairs Coun. of L.A., Town Hall of So. Calif., Glendale C. of C., Jonathan Club. Republican. Roman Catholic. Home: 804 S Orange Grove Blvd Pasadena CA 91105-1715 Office: HR Cons Group 100 N Brand Blvd Ste 200 Glendale CA 91203-2642

MISCHER, DONALD LEO, television director and producer; b. San Antonio, Mar. 5, 1940; s. Elmer Frederick and Lillian Alma. B.A., U. Tex., 1961, M.A., 1963. Mem. faculty U. Tex., 1962-63; producer/dir. USIA, Washington, 1965-68; with Charles Guggenheim Prodns., 1969-71; pres. Don Mischer Prodns., pres. Mischer Enterprises, Inc., Beverly Hills, Calif., prodr., dir., and program packager for network television programs, 1971—. Television programs include: The Opening and Closing Ceremonies of the 1996 Centennial Olympic Games, Atlanta, The Kennedy Center Honors: A Celebration of the Performing Arts (Emmy Awards 1981, 87); The Tony Awards (Emmy Awards 1987-88); Michael Jackson's Super Bowl XXVII Halftime Show; Baryshnikov by Tharp (Emmy Award 1985); Gregory Hines, Tap Dance America; Carnegie Hall: Live at 100; It's Garry Shandling's Show; Mowtown 25: Yesterday, Today, Tomorrow (Emmy Award 1983); The Muppets Celebrate Jim Henson; Motown Returns to the Apollo (Emmy Award 1985); Baryshnikov in Hollywood, Goldie and Liza Together, Shirley MacLaine—Illusions, Making Television Dance with Twyla Tharp, An Evening with Robin Williams, Am. Film Inst. Salute to Gene Kelly; producer additional programs with Bob Hope (Bob Hope: The First 90 Years - Emmy award Outstanding Variety, Music or Comedy Special, 1993), Barbara Walters, Goldie Hawn, others. Recipient: Primetime Emmy awards (10), Director's Guild awards for Outstanding Directorial Achiement (8), NAACP Image awards (3), Peabody award, Golden Rose of Montreux award, Gabriel award, Ohio State award. Mem. Dirs. Guild Am., Nat. Acad. TV Arts and Scis. Gov., Am. Film Inst. Office: Brillstein-Grey Entertainment 9150 Wilshire Blvd Ste 350 Beverly Hills CA 90212-3453*

MISH, MICHAEL, composer, writer, motivational speaker; b. L.A., Nov. 14, 1949; s. Abe and Cynthia (Anastasio) M.; m. Maya Korenn Mish, Aug. 6, 1994 (dec. Nov. 1994). AA, L.A. Valley Jr. Coll., Van Nuys; student, San Jose (Calif.) State U. Owner Mish Mash Music, Ashland, Oreg., 1988—; freelance spkr. Author (musicals) The Magic Stone, 1993, Growin/, 1997; host environ. spl., NBC, 1990.

MISHKIN, MARJORIE WONG, aviation and marketing consultant; b. L.A., Oct. 28, 1940; d. Thomas A. and Mayme M. (Moe) Wong; children: Barbara Joanne Brewer, Cynthia Anne; m. David Gordon Mishkin, Jan. 6, 1991. BA, Goucher Coll., 1962; MA, U. Calif. at Berkeley, 1965. Research economist Fed. Reserve Bank San Francisco, 1964-65; bus. cons., travel industry, 1968-74; marketing analyst The Flying Tiger Line Inc., Los Angeles, 1974-76, systems analyst, 1976-77, mgr. mgmt. reporting and performance analysis, 1977-78; dir. passenger pricing and fare devel. Continental Airlines, 1978-80, dir. internat. pricing, 1980-83; aviation and mktg. cons. Chen & Assocs., 1983—, dir. practice devel. Greenberg, Glusker, Fields, Claman & Machtinger, 1989-90; fin. cons. Solomon Smith Barney; bd. dirs. Continental Fed. Credit Union. Trustee, chmn. devel. Marlborough Sch.; trustee, deacon 1st Congl. Ch. of Los Angeles; mem. evaluation com. Am. Heart Assn. Danforth Found. assoc., 1968-79. Mem. Nat. Mgmt. Assn. (membership chmn.), World Affairs Council L.A., L.A. Libr. Assn. (v.p., treas.), Town Hall Calif., U. Calif. Alumni Assn., Marlborough Alumni Assn. Republican. Home: Ste 406 10430 Wilshire Blvd Ste 406 Los Angeles CA 90024-4652

MISKUS, MICHAEL ANTHONY, electrical engineer, consultant; b. East Chicago, Ind., Dec. 10, 1950; s. Paul and Josephine Miskus; m. Daphne Christine Headley, Nov. 19, 1998. BS, Purdue U., 1972; AAS in Elec. Engring. Tech., Purdue U., Indpls., 1972, MA in Orgnl. Mgmt., U Phoenix, 1996, postgrad., 1997; cert. mgmt. Ind. U., 1972, Ind. Central Coll., 1974; MA in Orgnl. Mgmt. U. Phoenix, 1996; PhD in Orgnl. Behavior, Columbia U., 1998. Cert. plant engr.; registered environ. assessor REA, Calif. Service engr. Reliance Electric & Engring. Co., Hammond, Ind., 1972-73; maintenance supr., maintenance mgr. Diamond Chain Co./AMSTED Industries, Indpls., 1973-76; primary and facilities elec. engr. Johnson & Johnson Baby Products Co., Park Forest South, Ill., 1976-81; prin. Miskus Cons., indsl./comml. elec. cons., 1979—; plant and facilities engring. mgr. Sherwin Williams Co., Chgo. Emulsion Plant, Chgo., 1981-85; with Miscon Assocs., Riverside, Calif., 1985—; acting dir. plant and facilities engring. Bourns Inc., 1982-90; facility mgr. Cardiovascular Devices Inc., 3M Health-care, 1990—; mgr. Metrology and Corp. Metrology Lab & ISO 9000, 3M, St. Paul; facilities ops. mgr. Press Enterprise, Riverside, 1997—; instr., lectr. EET program Moraine Valley C.C., Palos Hills, Ill., 1979; instr. cert. program plant engring. U. Calif.; lectr. energy engring., bldg. automation systems Prairie State Coll., Chicago Heights, Ill., 1980—; mem. adj. faculty, faculty adv. bd. Orange Coast Coll., Costa Mesa, Calif.; commr., chmn. Riverside Energy Commn., 1988—; mem. Elec. Industry Evaluation Panel. Mem. faculty adv. bd. Moraine Valley C.C., 1980—. Mem. IEEE, Am. Inst. Plant Engrs. (pres. Pomona chpt. 1989—, chmn. western region VI membership, chmn. nat. coun. stds. labs. region II Twin Cities sect. 1995—), Assn. Facility Engrs. (pres. Inland Empire chpt. III 1997—), Assn. Energy Engrs., Assn. Energy Engrs. (sr., So. Calif. chpt.), Assn. Profl. Energy Mgrs. (bd. dirs. Orange County chpt. 1992), Illuminating Engring. Soc. N.Am., Internat. Platform Assn., 3M Global plant engring. steering com., ops. sub-com.; Riverside C. of C. Club: Purdue Alumni Org. of L.A. (v.p. Inland chpt.), Purdue Club L.A. (v.p. Inland Empire sect.). Office: PO Box 55525 Riverside CA 92517-0525

MISNER, CHARLOTTE BLANCHE RUCKMAN, community organization administrator; b. Gifford, Idaho, Aug. 30, 1937; d. Richard Steele and Arizona (Hill) Ruckman; m. G. Arthur Misner, Jr., Aug. 29, 1959; children: Michelle, Mary, Jennifer. BS in Psychology, U. Idaho, 1959. Vol. numerous orgns. India, Mexico, The Philippines, 1962-70; sec., v.p., pres., trustee St. Luke's Hosp., Manila, 1970-84; founding mem., 3d v.p., pres. Am. Women's Club of Philippines, 1980-84; exec. dir. Friends of Oakland (Calif.) Parks and Recreation, 1986-92, 1992—. Active Lincoln Child Ctr., Oakland, 1984—. Recipient Vol. Svc. award Women's Bd. St. Luke's Hosp., 1977, Mid. Sch. Vol. award Internat. Sch.-Manila, 1980. Me. Alpha Gamma Delta (alumnae treas., pres. East Bay 1985-89, province dir. alumnae 1989-98, bd. dirs. alumni devel. 1998—), Cum Laude Soc. (hon.). Home: 481 Ellita Ave Oakland CA 94610-4808 Office: Friends of Oakland Parks & Recreation 1520 Lakeside Dr Oakland CA 94612-4521

MISSAL, STEPHEN JOSEPH, art educator, portraitist; b. Albuquerque, Apr. 23, 1948; s. Joshua Morton and Pegge Lenore (McComb) M.; m. Elizabeth Sperry; children: David J., Kele M. B.F.A., Wichita State U., 1970, M.F.A., 1972. Head art dept. White Mountain Sch., Littleton, N.H., 1972-74; mem. art faculty Northeast Mo. State U., Kirksville, Mo., 1974-77; free-lance artist Denver, 1977-79; mem. art faculty Scottsdale Community Coll., Ariz., 1979-84, Mesa Community Coll., Phoenix Coll., 1984—; mem. faculty, head of drawing Art Inst. Phoenix, 1996—; interim graphic design chmn., 1998—; art adjudicator, 1974—; staff artist Scottsdale Daily Progress, 1979-85; stage set designer Phoenix Little Theatre, 1978, Scottsdale Stagebrush Theatre, 1981. Illustrator: The Field Guide to Rock Climbing and Mountaineering, 1974—. Exhibited in group shows Tulsa Midwest Competition, 1972 (purchase award), 1972, Tulsa Invitational Show (purchase award), 1973, 14th Midwest Exhbn., Joslyn Art Mus., Omaha (purchase award), 1976, Festival VIII (Scottsdale Ctr. for Arts award), 1977. Violinist Dartmouth Coll. Civic Symphony, 1972-74, Scottsdale Civic Orch., 1979—. Mem. Nat. Coll. Art Assn., Midwest Coll. Art Assn. Office: Art Inst Phoenix 7233 W Dunlap Phoenix AZ 85021

MITCHELL, BETTIE PHAENON, religious organization administrator; b. Colorado Springs, Colo., June 6, 1934; d. Roy William and Laura Lee (Costin) Roberts; m. Gerald Mitchell, May 3, 1952; children: Michelle Smith, Laura Sweitz, Jennie Grenzer, Mohammad Bader. BS in Edn., Lewis & Clark Coll., 1954; postgrad., Portland State U., 1962-72; MA in Religion summa cum laude, Warner Pacific Coll., 1979. Cert. counselor, Oreg. Elem. tchr. Quincy Sch. Dist., Clatskanie, Oreg., 1955-56; substitute tchr. Beaverton (Oreg.) and Washington County Schs., 1956-77; tchr. of the Bible Portland (Oreg.) C.C., 1974-92; counseling and healing ministry, 1977-79; founder, exec. dir. Good Samaritan Ministries, Beaverton, 1979-88, founder, internat. exec. dir., 1988—; tchr. Christian Renewal Ctr. Workshops, 1977-85; spkr., presenter in field; leader tours in the Mid. East; developing counselor edn. programs Pakistan, Ukraine, Jordan, Egypt, Kenya, Uganda, Tanzania, Zambia, Malawi, South Africa, Nigeria, Burundi, Sierra Leone, India, Bangladesh, Rwanda, Singapore, Jordan. Author: Who Is My Neighbor? A Parable, 1988, The Power of Conflict and Sacrifice, A Therapy Manual for Christian Marriage, 1988, Good Samaritan Training Handbook, 1989, Be Still and Listen to His Voice, The Story of Prayer and Faith, 1990, A Need for Understanding - International Counselor Training Manual, 1993. Mem. Israel Task Force, Portland, 1974-80; Leader Camp Fire Internat., 1962-73, elem. sch. coord., 1962-68; asst. dir. Washington County Civil Def., 1961-63; precinct committeewoman Rep. Party, 1960; bd. dirs. Beaverton Fish, 1966-74; v.p. NCCJ, Portland, 1983-85; chmn., speaker's bur. Near East Task Force for Israel; chmn. fire bond issue campaign City of Beaverton, mgr. mayoral campaign, 1960; sunday sch. tchr., speaker, organizer Sharing and Caring program Bethel Ch., 1974-79. Mem. Am. Christian Counseling Assn., Christian Assn. for Psychol. Studies, Oreg. Counseling Assn. Republican. Fax: 503-646-8898. E-mail: goodsam@cuhu.net. Avocations: historical research, writing, photography, Biblical archaeology, correspondence. Home: 6550 SW Imperial Dr Beaverton OR 97008-5311 Office: Good Samaritan Ministries 7929 SW Cirrus Dr Ste 23 Beaverton OR 97008-5971

MITCHELL, DAVID CAMPBELL, inventor, corporate executive; b. Sacramento, Dec. 11, 1957; s. Alan Campbell and Lorraine May (Grant) M.; m. Lanette Pearson; children: David Kirk, Travis, Holly Ann. Student, U. Utah, 1973-74, Brigham Young U. Rsch. dir. Flex Inc., Williston, N.D., 1976-78; with Deseret Industries, Salt Lake City, 1978-81; head R&D Pro Biotiks Labs., Ogden, Utah, 1981—, Melaleuca, Idaho Falls, Idaho, 1987-89; pres., chmn. David C. Mitchell Med. Rsch. Inst., Salt Lake City, 1980—; rsch. cons. U. Utah Rsch. Park, Salt Lake City, 1981—; environ. cons. Hi-Valley Chem., Salt Lake City, 1988—; v.p. Mitchell Products, Orem, Utah, 1989—. Inventor, 125 patents in vitamins, cosmetics, pharmaceuticals, arthritis, cancer, psoriasis, scars and wounds, artificial sweeteners, pain killers, anti-depressants and related biochemistries. Vol. Freeman Inst., Salt Lake City, 1980-87; vol. supr. Granite Bakery (Feed the Poor), Salt Lake City, 1982-87; active rehab. handicapped Deseret Industries, Salt Lake City, 1978-81; pres., young adults rep. Latter-day Saints Ch., Salt Lake City, 1977-78. Scholar NSF, 1973; named one of Outstanding Young Men of Am., 1989. Fellow AAAS, ACS, N.Y. Acad. Scis. Home and Office: PO Box 901690 Sandy UT 84090-1690

MITCHELL, GENEVA BROOKE, hypnotherapist; b. Ringgold, Tex., Feb. 15, 1929; d. Roy Banks and Willie Jewel (Lemons) Shaw; m. Roy David Mitchell, Nov. 30, 1947; children: Ronald, Donald, Joel, Pamela, Annette. Cert. master hypnotist Hypnosis Tng. Inst., L.A., 1980, cert. hypnotherapist, 1983; cert. in advanced investigative and forensic hypnosis Tex. A&M U., 1982; D. Clin. Hypnosis, Am. Inst. Hypnotherapy, Calif., 1989. Chiropractic asst. Alamogordo, N.Mex., 1962-79; hypnotherapist Alamogordo Hypnosis and Counseling Ctr., 1980-92; mgr. Shaw Mobile Home Park, 1986—; mng. ptnr. Shaw, Mitchell & Mallory, Albuquerque, 1986, mgr., 1987-88; hypnotherapist M&M Horses Corp., Tularosa, N.Mex., 1985-92; owner A New Image Hypnosis Ctr., Albuquerque, retired, 1992; pres. N.Mex. Chiropractic Aux., 1984-85; mem. Am. Council Hypnotist Examiners, 1980-83, hypnotist for tape series, instr. New Forever Trim Life Loss Program. Author: Take The Power, 1991. Charter pres. La Sertoma, Alamogordo, 1957; pres. Oregon sch. PTA, Alamogordo, 1958, La Luz Sch. Parents Club, N.Mex., 1962; sec. N.Mex. Jr. Rodeo Assn., 1964; co-founder Du Sch. La Luz, 1960; mem. N.Mex. Gov.'s Council on Youth, 1960; bd. dirs. Otero County Jr. Rodeo Assn., N.Mex., 1968; dir. self-hypnosis sch.; speaker Am. Bd. Hypnotherapy Conv., 1991. Recipient Speakers award Life Found., 1984. Mem. Am Assn. Profl. Hypnotherapists, Ladies for Life (Appreciation award 1984, 90), N.Mex. Ladies Life Fellowship (pres. 1983, bd. dirs. 1985), S.W. Hypnotherapy Examining Bd., Internat. Chiropractic Assn. Aux. (pres. 1994—, conv. chmn. 1993), Ladies for Life Chiropractic Orgn. (pres. elect 1993). Avocations: golf, painting, swimming, martial arts, writing.

MITCHELL, GLORIA JEAN, elementary school principal, educator; b. Plant City, Fla., Oct. 14, 1945; d. Jessie Mae (Anderson) Smith; m. Thero Mitchell, Sept. 19, 1969; children: Tarra Shariss Patrick, Thero Jr. BS, Bethune-Cookman Coll., 1967; MA, U. Detroit, 1974; postgrad., U. Wash., 1990. Cert. tchr., adminstr. Wash. Tchr. Dade County Schs., Miami, Fla., 1967-71, Agana (Guam) Presch., 1971-72, Detroit Pub. Schs., 1973-76, Prince Williams Schs., Dale City, Va., 1976-81; counselor/tchr. State of Alaska, Ketchikan, 1981-85; tchr. Bellevue (Wash.) Schs., 1985-90, tchr., prin., 1992—; bd. dirs. YMCA Bothell, Wash., chair sustaining drive, 1994-95; bd. dirs. Cascadia C.C., Bothell. Recipient Golden Acorn award PTA-Lake Hills Schs., 1986, Golden Apple award KCTS TV, Seattle, 1994-95; named West Field Vol. of Yr., YMCA, Bothell, Wash., 1987, Woman of Yr., Woodinville (Wash.) Region II Prin. of Yr., Bellevue, 1994. Mem. ASCD, Nat. Alliance Black Sch. Educators, Wash. Alliance Black Sch. Educators,. Avocations; needle point, golf, comty. volunteerism. Office: Bellevue Pub Schs 14220 SE 12th St Bellevue WA 98007-4103

MITCHELL, JERRY MICHAEL, biologist; b. Borger, Tex., Nov. 24, 1955; s. James C. and JoAnn (Huffine) M.; m. Cassy Ann Mulford, Apr. 2, 1949; 1 child, Hanna Carry. BS in Wildlife Biology, West Tex. A&M U., 1977, MS in Biology, 1979. Resource mgmt. technician Nat. Park Svc., Zion Nat. Park, Utah, 1979, resource mgmt. specialist, to 1988; chief planning and backcountry programs Nat. Park Svc., Grand Canyon Nat. Park, Ariz., 1988-93, acting chief resources mgmt. divsn., 1990-91; chief cultural resource mgmt. Nat. Park Svc., Yosemite Nat. Park, Calif., 1993-96, chief gen. mgmt. plan implementation office of supt., 1997—; Nat. Park Svc. coord. Interagy. Glen Canyon Environ. Studies, 1989-93; park coord. Yosemite Valley Implementation Plan, 1995—; tech. writer Colo. River Mgmt. Plan, 1989, Grand Canyon R.R. Els, 1989-93, Glen Canyon Dam Els, 1989-93. Contbr. articles to profl. jours. Mem. George Wright Soc., Park Steward Assn. Avocations: drawing, woodworking, gardening. Office: Nat Pk Svc PO Box 25287 12795 W Alameda Pkwy Denver CO 80225

MITCHELL, JOHN HENDERSON, management consultant, retired career officer; b. Atlanta, Sept. 9, 1933; s. William Lloyd and Jessie (Henderson) M.; m. Joan Ann Cameron, Apr. 8, 1961; children: John Cameron, Christopher Lloyd, Colin MacKenzie. BABA, St. Bonaventure U., 1956, PhD in Sci., 1991; MA in Pub. Adminstrn., Shippensburg State U., 1973. Commd. 2d lt. U.S. Army, 1956, advanced through grades to maj. gen., 1982; comdr. 8th Bn., 6th Arty., 1st Inf. divsn. U.S. Army, Vietnam, 1968; chief officer assignments Field Arty. br. Officer Pers. Directorate, U.S. Army, Washington; chief of staff 8th divsn. U.S. Army, 1973-75; asst. dept. chief of staff for personnel, Hdqrs. U.S. Army Europe and 7th Army U.S. Army, Heidelberg, Germany, 1975-77; comdr. Arty. divsn., chief of staff 1st Inf. divsn. U.S. Army, Ft. Riley, Kans., 1977-79; comdr., Field Command, Def. Nuclear Agy. U.S. Army, Kirtland AFB, N.Mex., 1979-81; dir. Human Resources Devel. Office, dept. chief staff for pers. U.S. Army, Washington; U.S. comdr. Berlin, 1984-88; ret., 1989; pres. Intersys., Inc., Englewood, Colo., 1989-94, Pease, Orr, Mitchell Enterprises, Colorado Springs, Colo., 1994-97; chmn. Berlin Sculpture Fund, Denver, 1997—. Bd. dirs. Nat. Safety Coun., 1982-84. Decorated D.S.M. with oak leaf cluster, Legion of Merit with oak leaf cluster, D.F.C. with oak leaf cluster, Bronze Star with oak leaf cluster and V., Air medals. Mem. Assn. U.S. Army, VFW, Army Navy Club, Army War Coll. Alumni, Soc. of First Inf. Div. Republican. Roman Catholic. Avocations: tennis, history, reading. Home: 375 Hidden Creek Dr Colorado Springs CO 80906-4386

MITCHELL, JOSEPH PATRICK, architect; b. Bellingham, Wash., Sept. 29, 1939; s. Joseph Henry and Jessie Delila (Smith) M.; student Western Wash. State Coll., 1957-59; BA, U. Wash., 1963, BArch, 1965; m. Marilyn Ruth Jorgenson, June 23, 1962; children: Amy Evangeline, Kirk Patrick, Scott Henry. Assoc. designer, draftsman, project architect Beckwith Spangler Davis, Bellevue, Wash., 1965-70; prin. J. Patrick Mitchell, AIA & Assoc./Architects/Planners/Cons., Kirkland, Wash., 1970—. Chmn. long range planning com. Lake Retreat Camp, 1965-93; chartered mem., bldg. chmn. Northshore Baptist Ch., 1969, 80-96, elder, 1984-90; mem. bd. extension and central com. Columbia Baptist Conf., 1977-83; Northshore Bapt. Ch. del. Bapt. World Alliance 16th Congress, Seoul, Korea, 1990, 17th Cong., Buenos Aires, Argentina, 1995; trustee Bakke Libr./Cultural Ctr., 1994-96; vice moderator Columbia Baptist Conf., 1995-96, moderator, 1996-97, ch. ministries overseer bd., pres., 1997—; chartered mem., Cascade Cmty. Ch., 1997—, mem. Deming Hist. Cemetery Assn., 1997—, IFRRA Arch. Edn. Tour, Finland and St. Petersburg, 1998. Recipient Internat. Architectural Design award St. John Vianney Parish, 1989. Cert. Nat. Council Archtl. Registration Bds. Mem. AIA, Constrn. Specification Inst., Interfaith Forum Religion, Art, and Architecture (archtl. edn. tour Finland and St. Petersburg 1998), Nat. Fedn. Ind. Bus., Christian Camping Internat., Wash. Farm Forestry Assn., Deming Hist. Cemetary Assn., Woodinville C. of C., Kirkland C. of C. Republican. Office: 12620 120th Ave NE Ste 208 Kirkland WA 98034-7511

MITCHELL, KATHLEEN ANN, illustrator, graphic designer; b. Cin., July 27, 1948; d. Gerald Paige and Velma Alice (Bleier) Clary; m. Terence Nigel Mitchell, Feb. 2, 1977; children: Jessica Rose, Alexander Christien. BSc in Design, U. Cin., 1971. Graphic designer Lippincott & Margulies, N.Y.C., 1971, Allied Internat., London, 1972, Moura-George Briggs, London, 1973-75; art dir., photographer Phonograph Record Mag., L.A., 1976-77; ptnr. Walter Morgan Assocs., Santa Monica, Calif., 1977-80; illustrator Artists Internat., L.A. and N.Y.C., 1983—. Illustrator: (books) Once Upon a Cat, 1983, Jane Eyre, 1983, Alice in Wonderland, 1986, The Wizard of Oz, 1987, The Secret Garden, 1987, Kittens, Kittens, Kittens, 1987, My Bible Alphabet, 1987, The Christmas Story, 1989, Silent Night, 1989, The First Christmas, 1992, Aladdin and the Magic Lamp, 1993, Cinderella, 1993, Cats, 1994, Friendships, 1994, Thoughts, 1994, Beauty and the Beast, 1995, Joseph and the Dream Coat, 1995, Dogs, 1995, My Little Flower, 1995, The Joy of Christmas, 1995, There's a Ghost in the House, 1996, Puss in Boots, 1997, My Secret Valentine, 1997, Valentine Thoughts, 1997, Sleeping Beauty, 1997, The Wild Swans, 1998, The Story of Moses, 1999, Honesty, 1999. Democrat. Avocations: art, antiques. Home: 1040 22nd St Santa Monica CA 90403-4518

MITCHELL, LUCILLE ANNE, retired elementary school educator; b. Dayton Corners, Ill., Oct. 19, 1928; d. Roy Rollin and Edna May (Whitehouse) Sheppard; m. Donald L. Mitchell; children: David, Diane, Barbara Rock, Patricia Reaves. BSin Edn., Augustana Coll., 1966; MS in Edn., Western Ill. U., 1972, Edn. Specialist, 1974. Tchr. Carbon Cliff (Ill.) Elem. Sch., 1962-65, Moline (Ill.) Bd. Edn., 1967-92; mem. textbook selection com. Moline Bd. Edn., 1967-84; tchr. of gifted Moline Bd. Edn., 1985-87. Named Ill. Master Tchr., State of Ill., 1984. Mem. Ill. Edn. Assn. (various coms.), Moline Edn. Assn. (various coms.), Delta Kappa Gamma (program chmn. 1978-79, recording sec. 1980-81). Avocations: organ, piano, oil and water color painting. Home: 9614 W Timberline Dr Sun City AZ 85351-2923

MITCHELL, MICHAEL KIEHL, elementary and secondary education educator, minister; b. Phila., Pa., Oct. 27, 1932; s. Robert Bartow and Louise Room (Keyser) M.; m. Gloria (Nell) Wilburn, Nov. 12, 1960; children: Donald Kiehl, Robert Alan. B in Edn., U. Miami, 1955; MEd, Tex. A&M U., 1975, PhD, 1978; grad., Internat. Sch. Christian Comm. Cert. elem. and secondary edn., Fla., Tex., Alaska; lic. comml. pilot. Tchr. math Dade County Pub. Schs., Miami Springs, Fla., 1955-60; tchr. elem. Greenwood Sch. Dist., Midland, Tex., 1961-63; from tchr. social studies, English to tng. coord. Midland (Tex.) Sch. Dist., 1963-73; prin. rsch. investigator Tex. A&M U., College Station, 1977-78; project dir. Edn. Profl. Devel. Consortium, Richardson, Tex., 1978-79; sr. rsch. scientist Am. Airlines, Dallas, 1979-83; pres. North Rsch. Inc., Anchorage, Alaska, 1983-84; vocat. edn. curriculum specialist Anchorage Sch. Dist., 1984-87; sci. tchr., dept. head McLaughlin Youth Ctr. Anchorage (Alaska) Sch. Dist., 1987—; adj. prof. U. Alaska, Anchorage, 1987-89; evaluation team N.W. Accreditation Assn., Anchorage, 1985; asst. min. United Meth. ch., 1990-94; min. Christian Cmty. Fellowship, 1994—; deacon First Congl. Ch., Anchorage; instr. Flight and Ground Sch. Dir., v.p. Anchorage Comty. Theater, 1984-89; marriage commr. 3d Jud. Dist. Alaska, Anchorage, 1989-93; vol. United Way, Anchorage, 1984-90, Tony Knowles for Gov. Campaign, Anchorage, 1990, 94, Mark Begich for Mcpl. Assembly Campaign, 1991, Cheryl Clementson for Mcpl. Assembly Campaign, 1993. With U.S. Army, 1946-47. Tex. Edn. Agy. fellow, Austin, 1975, Ednl. Profl. Devel. fellow, 1975-78. Mem. NEA, NRA (life), Anchorage Edn. Assn., Am. Correctional Edn. Assn., Alaska Airmans Assn. (life, bd. dirs. 1983-89), Screen Actors Guild, Mensa (life), Am. Legion (life), Clowns of Am., Nat. Sci. Tchrs. Assn., Alaska Sci. Tchrs. Assn., Alaskan Aviation Safety Found., Tex. Assn. Aerospace Tchrs. (life), Former Students Assn. Tex. A&M U., Vets. Underaged Mil. Svc. (life), Am. Legion (life), Phi Delta Kappa, Phi Kappa Phi. Libertarian. Avocations: commercial pilot, professional acting, FAA accident prevention counselor. Home: 6626 Foothill Dr Anchorage AK 99504-2620 Office: McLaughlin Youth Cen High 2600 Providence Dr Anchorage AK 99508-4613

MITCHELL, RIE ROGERS, psychologist, counseling educator; b. Tucson, Feb. 1, 1940; d. Martin Smith and Lavaun (Peterson) Rogers; student Mills Coll., 1958-59; BS, U. Utah, 1962, MS, 1963; postgrad. San Diego State U., 1965-66; MA, UCLA, 1969, PhD, 1969. Registered play therapist, supr.; cert. sandplay therapist; diplomate Am. Bd. Psychology, 1992; m. Rex C. Mitchell, Mar. 16, 1961; 1 child, Scott Rogers. Tchr., Coronado (Calif.) Unified Sch. Dist., 1964-65; sch. psychologist Glendale (Calif.) Unified Sch. Dist., 1968-70; psychologist Glendale Guidance Clinic, 1970-77; asst. prof. ednl. psychology Calif. State U., Northridge, 1970-74, asso. prof., 1974-78, prof., 1978—, chmn. dept. ednl. psychology, 1976-80, acting exec. asst. to pres., 1981-82; acting exec. asst. to pres. Calif. State U., Dominguez Hills, 1978-79; cons. to various Calif. sch. dists.; pvt. practice psychology, Calabasas, Calif. Recipient Outstanding Educator award Maharishi Soc., 1978; Woman of Yr. award U. Utah, 1962, Profl. Leadership award Western Assn. Counselor Edn., 1990, Disting. Tching. award Calif. Univ., Northridge, 1994. Mem. Calif. Assn. Counselor Edn., Supervision and Adminstrn. (dir. 1976-77), Western Assn. Counselor Edn. and Supervision (officer 1978-82, pres. 1980-81, profl. leadership award, 1990), Assn. Counselor Edn. and Supervision (dir. 1980-81, program chmn. 1981-82, treas. 1983-86, Presdl. award 1986, Leadership award 1987), UCLA Doctoral Alumni Assn. (pres. 1974-76), Am. Psychol. Assn., Am. Ednl. Research Assn., Calif. Women in Higher Edn. (pres. chpt. 1977-78), Calif. Concerns (treas. 1984-86), Sandplay Therapists Am. (bylaws chmn. 1995—, exceptions chmn. 1995-96, fin. officer 1996—), Pi Lambda Theta (pres. chpt. 1970-71, chairwoman nat. resolutions 1971-73), Sandplay Therapist of Am. (fin. officer 1996—, bd. mem. 1993—, media chair, 1995, bylaws chair, 1994-96, exceptions com. chair, 1995-96). Author: Sandplay: Past Present & Future, 1994; contbr. numerous articles on group process, sandplay, counselor edn. to profl. jours. Home: 4503 Alta Tupelo Dr Calabasas CA 91302-2516 Office: Calif State U Counselor Edn Dept Northridge CA 91330

MITCHELL, ROBERT CAMPBELL, nuclear consultant; b. West Point, N.Y., Mar. 28, 1940; s. Herbert V. and Beatrice Cheeseman (Campbell) M.; m. Mardeene Burr, Aug. 19, 1963 (div. Dec. 1983); children: Wendolyn, Dawnelle; m. Patricia Johnson, Aug. 17, 1987. B of Engring., Stevens Inst. Tech., 1962; MEE, Rensselaer Poly. Inst., 1965. Registered profl. engr., Calif. Design/ops. engr. Knolls Atomic Power Lab., Schenectady, N.Y., 1962-67; prin. tng. engr. Nuclear Energy Div. Gen. Electric Co., San Jose, Calif., 1967-72, project engr., 1972-75, mgr. advanced projects, 1975-77, project mgr., 1977-87, licensing mgr., 1987-95; pvt. cons. Tucson, 1995—. Contbr. articles to profl. jours. Nominee White House fellow Gen. Electric Co., San Jose, 1973. Mem. Elfun Soc. Republican. Avocations: photography, bridge, golf, computers. Home and Office: 2140 E Bighorn Mt Dr Tucson AZ 85737

MITCHELL, THOMAS, journal editor; m. Janice Mitchell; children: Jeffery, Jay. Grad., Colo. State U. City editor Mid-Cities Daily News, Hurst, Tex.; editor Lewisville (Tex.) Daily Leader; city editor Shreveport (La.) Jour.; night city editor The Miami News; mng. editor Las Vegas Rev.-Jour., 1989-92, editor, 1992—. Recipient First place prize for editl. writing Best of the West journalism competition, 1990, First place prize Nev. Press Assn., 1995. Mem. Am. Soc. Newspaper Editors, Investigative Reporters and Editors. Office: 1111 W Bonanza Rd Las Vegas NV 89106*

MITCHELL, THOMAS EDWARD, JR., communications cabling executive; b. Sacramento, Apr. 12, 1946; s. Thomas Edward and Violet Mae (Southall) M.; m. Terri Kathleen Vance, Apr. 20, 1969; children: Anthony E., Brian C. BA, Nat. U., 1987, MBA, 1988. Enlisted USMC, 1966, advanced through grades to maj., 1980, retired, 1989; sr. exec. Nat. Decision Sys., Encinitas, Calif., 1989-90, Equifax Mktg. Decision Sys., San Dieto, 1990-93; pres., COO Holocomm Sys. Inc., San Diego, 1993—; bd. dirs. Cal-Pacific Steel Structure Inc., Hawaii, Calif. Contbr. articles to profl. jours.; patentee in field. Dir. Toys for Tots, L.A./ORange Counties, Calif., 1974-77. Recipient Silver Star medal U.S. Pres., 1968, Meritorious Svc. medal, Joint Chiefs of Staff Commendation medal, others. Mem. World Trade Assn. (assoc. 1989—), Am. Legion, Internat. Platform Assn. Avocations: restoring old cars, racquetball, golf, history. Home: 3264 Chase Ct Oceanside CA 92056-3809 Office: Holcomm Sys Inc 2131 Palomar Airport Rd Ste 150 Carlsbad CA 92009-1434

MITCHELL, WAYNE LEE, health care administrator; b. Rapid City, S.D., Mar. 25, 1937; s. Albert C. and Elizabeth Isabelle (Nagel) M.; m. Marie Galletti; BA, U. Redlands (Calif.), 1959; MSW, Ariz. State U., 1970, EdD, 1979. Profl. social worker various county, state, and fed. agys., 1962-70, Bur. Indian Affairs, Phoenix, 1970-77, USPHS, 1977-79; asst. prof. Ariz. State U., 1979-84; with USPHS, Phoenix, 1984—; lectr. in field. Bd. dirs. Phoenix Indian Cmty. Sch., 1973-75, ATLATL, 1995-98; bd. dirs. Phoenix Indian Ctr., 1974-79, Cmty. Svc. award, 1977; mem. Phoenix Area Health Adv. Bd., 1975; mem. Community Behavioral Mental Health Bd., 1976-80; mem. bd. trustees Heard Mus. of Anthropology, Phoenix, Ariz., 1996; mem. bd. dirs. Partnership for Cmty. Devel. Ariz. State U.-West, 1996—. Bd. dirs. Ctrl. Ariz. Health Sys. Agy., 1982-85; mem. Fgn. Rels. Com. Phoenix. With USCG, 1960-62. Recipient Cmty. Svc. award Ariz. Temple of Islam, 1980, Ariz. State U., 1996, Dir. Excellence award Phoenix Area IHS Dir., 1992, 93. Mem. NASW, NAACP, Fgn. Rels. Coun., Am. Hosp. Assn., U.S.-China Assn., Kappa Delta Pi, Phi Delta Kappa, Chi Sigma Chi, Nucleus Club. Congregationalist. Democrat. Contbr. articles to publs. Home: PO Box 9592 Phoenix AZ 85068-9592 Office: DHHS-IHS Two Renaissance Sq 40 N Central Ave Phoenix AZ 85004-4424

MITCHELL-CHAVEZ, BETTIANNE (BA MITCHELL-CHAVEZ), franchise executive; b. Washington, Nov. 27, 1952; d. Noriar and Marylou (Lenk) Pahigian; m. John J. Stabers (div.); 1 child, John Chad; m. Robert Franklin Chavez, Mar. 11, 1991; stepchildren: Andrea, Julia. BS in English cum laude, Suffolk U. Cert. Wilson sales trainer; cert. in Brian Tracy sales and sales mgmt. instrn.; cert. instr. internat. bus., sales mgmt. Sr. account rep. Letter Men Inc., pub., mktg., advt., Burlington, Mass., 1978-82; mgr. Boston sales br. The Boston Herald, 1982-83; telemktg. ter. mgr. Compugraphic Corp. div. AGFA Corp., Wilmington, Mass., 1983-85; pres., mktg. cons. Advance Inc., mktg., recruitment and search co., Marlboro, Mass., 1985-88; dir. sales devel. AlphaGraphics Printshops of Future Inc. affiliate R.R. Donnelly and Sons, Tucson, v.p. tng. and support, 1991-93, v.p. franchise devel., 1993-94; COO, software developer and licensor INVZN, 1994—; adj. bus. prof. Pima C.C.; presenter in field. Mem. ASTD, NAFE, AAUW, Ariz. Franchisor and Licensor Assn. (bd. dirs., program chairperson 1994—, licensor, liaison to Internat. Franchisor Assn. 1993—, pres.-elect, bd. dirs.), The Consortium, Inc. (CEO, founder). Avocations: networking, public speaking, travel, scuba diving, golf. Address: 1338 N Palmsprings Dr Gilbert AZ 85234-8511

MITHUN, MARIANNE, linguist, researcher, educator; b. Bremerton, Wash., Apr. 8, 1940; d. Omer Lloyd George and Ruth Eleonor (Trueblood) M.; m. Wallace L. Chafe, Jan. 25, 1985. BA, Pomona Coll., 1969; MA, Yale U., 1972, M Philosophy, 1972, PhD, 1974. Prof. linguistics SUNY, Albany, 1973-85, U. Calif., Santa Barbara, 1986—; vis. prof. Université du Quebec, Can., 1973-82, Yale U., New Haven, 1980, Wake Forest U., Winston-Salem, N.C., 1975, U. Calif., Berkeley, 1981-86. Author: The Languages of Native

America, 1979, Montague, Grammar, Philosophy and Linguistics, 1979; contbr. numerous articles on linguistics to profl. jours. Fellow Am. Anthrop. Assn. (bd. dirs., exec. com., adminstrn. adv. com. 1982—); mem. Linguistic Soc. Am., Soc. Study Indigenous Langs. of Ams. (exec. bd. 1982-83, pres. elect 1991-92), Soc. Linguistic Anthropology (pres. 1982-84), Linguistic Soc. Am. (exec. bd. 1991—). Office: U Calif Dept Linguistics Santa Barbara CA 93106

MITIO, JOHN, III, state agency administrator; b. Michigan City, Ind., Jan. 15, 1950; s. John Mitio Jr. and Bonnie Gloria (Pearce) Morse; stepson of Eugene A. Morse; m. Judy Sena, Nov. 25, 1971 (div. 1985); m. Gail Stefl, Sept. 5, 1987 (div. 1995); 1 child, Kevin Michael. AA in Liberal Arts, N.Mex. State U., Alamogordo, 1976; BA in Anthropology, N.Mex. State U., Las Cruces, 1979. Engr. aide U.S. Civil Service, Alamogordo, 1974-75, Dynalectron Corp., Alamogordo, 1976; law enforcement campus police N.Mex. State U., Las Cruces, 1977-79; eligibility worker human svcs. dept. State of N. Mex., Albuquerque, 1984-86; medicaid planner human svcs. dept. State of N. Mex., Santa Fe, 1986-97; mgr. pub. rels. Cone Mil. Surplus, 1997—. Sgt. USAF, 1969-73, 1st lt., 79-83. Decorated Nat. Def. Svc. medal, Armed Forces Expeditionary medal, Air Force Overseas Svc. medal, Air Force Good Conduct medal. Mem. Planetary Soc., World Future Soc., Nat. Space Soc. Republican. Roman Catholic. Avocations: opera, skiing, winemaking. Home: PO Box 16094 Santa Fe NM 87506-6094 Office: Human Svcs Dept PO Box 2348 2500 Cerrillos Rd Santa Fe NM 87505-3260

MITKOV, IGOR, physicist; b. Moscow, July 19, 1966; came to U.S., 1996; s. Vladimir and Zoya (Markus) Beilin; m. Rosa Lisin, Oct. 4, 1995; 1 child, Michael. MS, Moscow State U., 1989; PhD, Hebrew U. Jerusalem, 1996. Rschr. Moscow State U., 1989-91; tchg. asst. Hebrew U. Jerusalem, 1992-96; rsch. assoc. Los Alamos (N.Mex.) Nat. Lab., 1996—. Contbr. articles to profl. jours. Recipient scholarship Moscow State U., 1987, prize USSR Acad. Sci., 1988, scholarship Jerusalem Post Found., 1992. Mem. Am. Geophys. Union.

MITRA, SANJIT KUMAR, electrical and computer engineering educator; b. Calcutta, West Bengal, India, Nov. 26, 1935; came to U.S., 1958; MS in Tech., U. Calcutta, 1956; MS, U. Calif., Berkeley, 1960, PhD, 1962; D of Tech. (hon.), Tampere (Finland) U., 1987. Asst. engr. Indian Statis. Inst., Calcutta, 1956-58; from teaching asst. to assoc. Univ. Calif., Berkeley, 1958-62; asst. prof. Cornell U., Ithaca, N.Y., 1962-65; mem. tech. staff Bell Telephone Labs., Holmdel, N.J., 1965-67; prof. U. Calif., Davis, 1967-77; prof. elec. and computer engring. U. Calif., Santa Barbara, 1977—, chmn. dept. elec. and computer engring., 1979-82; dir. Ctr. for Info. Processing Rsch., 1993-96; cons. Lawrence Livermore (Calif.) Nat. Lab., 1974-95; cons. editor Van Nostrand Reinhold Co., N.Y.C., 1977-88; mem. adv. bd. Coll. Engring. Rice U., Houston, 1986-89; mem. adv. coun. Rsch. Inst. for Math. and Computing Sci., U. Groningen, The Netherlands, 1995—; mem. adv. bd. Internat. Signal Processing Ctr., Tampere U. of Tech., Finland, 1997—; external assessor Faculty of Engring., U. Putra Malaysia, Serdang, 1997—. Author: Analysis and Synthesis of Linear Active Networks, 1969, Digital and Analog Integrated Circuits, 1980; co-editor: Modern Filter Theory and Design, 1973, Two-Dimensional Digital Signal Processing, 1978, Miniaturized and Integrated Filters, 1989, Multidimensional Processing of Video Signals, 1992, Handbook for Digital Signal Processing, 1993, Digital Signal Processing: A Computer-Based Approach, 1997, Nonuniform Discrete Fourier Transform and Its Signal Processing Applications, 1998, Digital Signal Processing Laboratory Using MATLAB, 1999. Named Disting. Fulbright Prof., Coun. for Internat. Exch. of Scholars, 1984, 86, 88, Disting. Sr. Scientist, Humboldt Found., 1989. Fellow AAAS, IEEE (Edn. award Crcts. and Systems Soc. 1988, disting. lectr. Crcts. and Systems Soc. 1991-96, Tech. achievement award Signal Processing Soc. 1996), Internat. Soc. Optical Engring.; mem. Am. Soc. for Engring. Edn. (F.E. Terman award 1973, AT&T Found. award 1985), European Assn. for Signal Processing. Achievements include patents for two-port newtorks for realizing transfer functions; non-reciprocal wave translating device; discrete cosine transform-based image coding and decoding method; method and apparatus for multipath channel shaping; method and apparatus for multipath channel shaping. Office: Univ Calif Dept Elec Computer Eng Santa Barbara CA 93106

MITTAL, MANMOHAN, design and technology engineer; b. Muzaffarnagar, India, Sept. 5, 1950; came to U.S., 1981; s. Keder Nath and Prakash (Wati) M.; m. Shashi Rani, Jan. 28, 1976; children: Vivek, Vibhav. BSEE, Inst. Tech. Banaras Hindu U., Varanasi, India, 1971; MASEE, U. Ottawa, Ont., Can., 1981; PhD in Elec. and Computer Engring., Wash. State U., 1984. Electronics engr. IIMS Banaras Hindu U., 1971-73; design engr. Bharat Heavy Elecs. Ltd., Haridwar, India, 1973-79; grad. rsch./teaching asst. Wash. State U., Pullman and U. Ottawa, 1979-84; DA mgr. CAE design automation Silicon Systems, Inc., Tustin, Calif., 1984-88; mgr. std. cell design automation Vitesse Semiconductor Corp., Camarillo, Calif., 1988-94; sole proprietor, cons. 2M Soft Tech. Group, Thousand Oaks, Calif., 1994-96; sr. dir. VLSI core design group C-Cube Micro Systems, Milpitas, Calif., 1996-99; v.p. engring. Duet Techs., San Jose, Calif., 1999—. Contbr. tech. papers to profl. jours. U. medal Inst. Tech., Banaras Hindu U., 1972; fellow U. Ottawa, 1979-81; grantee Wash. State U., 1981-84. Mem. IEEE (sr., sec. exec. com. Orange County chpt. 1985-88, mem. tech. program. com., custom integrated cirs. conf. 1988-94, bipolar circuits and tech. conf. 1985-90), N.Y. Acad. Scis., Assn. Computing Machines, Sigma Xi, Tau Beta Pi. Hindu. Achievements include patent for Incremental Hierarchical Netlist Extraction Tool. Avocations: traveling, badminton, tennis. Office: Duet Techs Inc 2698 Orchard Pky San Jose CA 95134

MIYASAKI, SHUICHI, lawyer; b. Paauilo, Hawaii, Aug. 6, 1928; s. Torakichi and Teyo (Kimura) M.; m. Pearl Takeko Saiki, Sept. 11, 1954; children: Joy Michiko, Miles Tadashi, Jan Keiko, Ann Yoshie. BSCE, U. Hawaii-Honolulu, 1951; JD, U. Minn., 1957; LLM in Taxation, Georgetown U., 1959; grad. Army War Coll., 1973. Bar: Minn. 1957, Hawaii 1959, U.S. Supreme Ct. 1980. Examiner, U.S. Patent Office, 1957-59; dep. atty. gen. State of Hawaii, 1960-61; mem., dir., sec./treas. Okumura Takushi Funaki & Wee, Honolulu, 1961-90; pvt. practice, Honolulu, 1991—; atty. Hawaii Senate, 1961, chief counsel ways and means com., 1962, chief counsel judiciary com., 1967-70; civil engr. Japan Constrn. Agy., Tokyo, 1953-54; staff judge adv., col. USAR, Ft. DeRussy, Hawaii, 1968-79; local legal counsel Jaycees, 1962; lectr. Nat. Assn. Pub. Accts. Hawaii Chpt. Ann. Conv., 1990, 94, Mid Pacific Inst. Found., Honolulu, 1990, Econ. Study Club of Hawaii, 1990, Meiji Life Ins. Co. Japan, 1992, Cent. YMCA, 1992, City Bank Honolulu, 1997. Legis. chmn. armed services com. C. of C. of Hawaii, 1973; instl. rep. Aloha council Boy Scouts Am., 1963-78; exec. com., sec., dir. Legal Aid Soc. Hawaii, 1970-72; state v.p. Hawaii Jaycees, 1964-65; dir., legal counsel St. Louis Heights Community Assn., 1963, 65, 73, 91—; dir., legal counsel Citizens Study Club for Naturalization of Citizens, 1963-68; advisory bd. Project Dana Honolulu, 1991—, vice chair 91, 92; life mem. Res. Officers Assn. U.S. Served to 1st lt., AUS, 1951-54. Decorated Meritorious Service medal with oak leaf cluster. Mem. ABA, Hawaii Bar Assn., U.S. Patent Office Soc., Hawaii Estate Planning Council, Rotary, Central YMCA Club, Waikiki Athletic Club, Army Golf Assn., Elks, Phi Delta Phi. Office: 1001 Bishop St Ste 1030 Honolulu HI 96813-3408

MIYATA, KEIJIRO, culinary arts educator; b. Tokyo, Mar. 8, 1951; came to U.S., 1967; s. Yataro Miyata and Hekkiken (Liu) Choy; m. Connie Joyce Nelson, Mar. 8, 1976; children: Michelle, Kelly, Adam. Assoc. in Occupational Study, Culinary Inst. Am., Hyde Park, N.Y., 1972, cert. of nutrition, 1991; cert., Seattle Wine Sch., 1991. Cert. exec. chef; cert. culinary educator. Garde mgr. Mid-Pacific Country Club, Kailua, Hawaii, 1972; working chef Waikiki Yacht Club, Honolulu, 1972-74, Sagano Japanese Restaurant, New Rochelle, N.Y., 1974-76; asst. pastry chef Rye Town (N.Y.) Hilton Hotel, 1976-77; working chef The Explorer, Everett, Wash., 1977-79; exec. chef Holiday Inn, Everett, 1979-81, Mill Creek (Wash.) Country Club, 1981; culinary art instr. Everett Community Coll., 1981-85, North Seattle (Wash.) Community Coll., 1985-90, Seattle Cen. Community Coll., 1990—; cons. Chalon Corp., Redmond, Wash., Chiang-Mai Restaurant, Mukilteo, Wash., 1988, Holiday Inn Crown Plaza, Seattle, Satsuma Japanese Restaurant, 1996. Participant Nagano Winter Olympic Ice Sculpture Festival, Karuizawa, Japan, 1998. Recipient Gold awards Am. Culinary Fedn., Oreg. State Chef's Assn., Portland, 1983, Gold and Bronze medals World Culinary Olympic, Frankfurt, Germany, 1984, 88, Grand Champion award U.S. Nat. Ice Carving Contest, N.Y.C., 1986, 2d place award All Japan Ice Carving Assn., Asahikawa, 1988, Ednl. Excellence award Oreg. and Wash. Community Coll. Couns. Wash. Fedn. of Tchrs. & Am. Fedn. of Tchrs., AFL-CIO, 1988, 89; ACF Seafood Challenge State finalist, Charlotte, N.C., 1989, New Orleans, 1990; 1st place Pacific Rim Invitational World Ice Sculpting Classic, 1989; 1st place Seymour Ice Sculpting Competition, 1991; 1st place 3d Ann. Internat. Ice Sculpting Competition, Lake Louise, Alta., Can., 1993, Award of Excellence Wash. Fedn. Tchrs./Am. Fedn. Tchrs./AFL-CIO, 1993, 1st place Wash. State Seafood Festival Recipe Contest, Shelton, Wash., 1993, Grand Cahmpion, 1994, 1st place ICE ART'94 Ice Sculpting Competition, Fairbanks, Alaska, 1994, Most Artistic award AsahiKawa Internat. Ice Sculpting Competition, 1996, 1st place IceCarver's Choice, People's Choice Awards--8th Internat. Ice Carving Championship, Anchorage, Alask, 1997; selected as Snow Sculpting Team Mem. of Sister City of Portland, Internat. Snow Sculpting Competition, Sapporo, Japan, 1997; participant Nagano Winter Olympic Ice Sculpture Festival, Karuizawa, Japan, 1998, 1st place People's Choice awards 6th annual Internat. Ice Sculpting competition, Lake Louise, Alberta, Canada, 1999. Mem. Wash. State Chefs Assn. (bd. dirs. 1982, 83, 86, 87, 88, cert. chmn. 1986-92, Chef of Yr. 1986), Am. Acad. Chefs, Nat. Ice Carving Assn. Office: Seattle Cen Community Coll 1701 Broadway Seattle WA 98122-2413

MIZER, RICHARD ANTHONY, technology company executive; b. San Francisco, Jan. 7, 1952; s. Conrad Xavier and Sally Jo (Hagan) M. BA in Bioengring. and Econs., U. Calif., San Diego, 1977. Founding ptnr. Microdoctors, Palo Alto, Calif., 1974-94; mgr., ptnr. K-Family Corp. dba Harlow's Night Club, Fremont, Calif., 1977-79, Restaurants Unique Inc. dba Bourbon St., Mountain View, Calif., 1980-83; engring. mgr. Pacific Bell, San Ramon, Calif., 1983-89; tech. staff advanced tech. Pacific Bell, 1989-92, developer advanced video svcs., 1992-96; asst. v.p. Nuko Info. Sys., Inc., San Jose, Calif., 1996-98; pres., CEO Digital Ventures Diversified Inc., San Jose, Calif., 1998—. Exec. prodr.: Cinema of the Future sm, 1992; assoc. prodr. Soccer Fest: World Cup Soccer Final in HDTV to Europe and U.S. theaters from Pasadena Rose Bowl, 1994; exec. in chg. prodn. 50th Anniversary of Signing of UN Charter, 1995. Mem. security staff Republican Task Force, San Francisco, 1984, tech. staff U.S. Olympic Com., Los Angeles, 1984. Mem. IEEE, Nat. Assn. Broadcasters, Soc. Motion Picture and TV Engrs. (western region gov. 1999—). Roman Catholic. Avocations: martial arts, auto racing, skiing, triathelon. Office: Digital Ventures Diversified Inc Palo Alto Bus Park 1121 San Antonio Rd D202 Palo Alto CA 94303-4311

MIZIKER, RONALD DENNIS, television producer; b. Cleve., Oct. 14, 1941; s. John and Irene (Marusa) M.; m. Bonnie Lou Walston, Aug. 22, 1964 (div. May 1997); children: Robert, Ryan. BA in TV and Comm., U. N.Mex., 1965; postgrad., U. So. Calif., 1965-66. Prodr., dir. Sta. KNME-TV, Albuquerque, 1963-65; with advt. dept. Armstrong Floors, Lancaster, Pa., 1966-68; TV prodr. Avco Broadcasting, Cin., 1968-69; dir. show devel. Disneyland and Walt Disney World, Burbank, Calif., 1969-79; prodr. Walt Disney Prodns., Burbank, 1979-82; v.p. original programming Disney Channel, Burbank, 1982-84; pres., creative dir. Miziker & Co. Inc., Burbank, 1984—. Prodr. Perry Como Christmas Spl., 1981 (Emmy award); (TV series) Five Mile Creek, 1983 (ACE award), By George, 1996 (Emmy award); creative dir. Rockin' Robin, 1996 (Thea award). Prodr. coverage of funeral of Pres. Richard M. Nixon, Calif. and internat., 1993; media cons. Reagan/Bush campaign, 1980, 84, Reagan White Ho., 1980-86. Mem. Nat. Acad. TV, Themed Entertainment Assn. (com. chair 1995), Hollywood Radio and TV Soc. Republican. Office: Miziker & Co Inc 4110 W Riverside Dr Burbank CA 91505-4143

MIZUGUCHI, NORMAN, state official; b. Hilo, Hawaii, May 26, 1939; m. Harriet Mizuguchi; 1 child, Reid. BS, Springfield Coll.; MS, Mich. State U.; PhD, U. Utah. Mem. state house State of Hawaii, 1974-78, state senator, 1978—; pres. Hawaiian Emporium Inc., Sundance Circle Inc.; tchr., edn. officer Dept. of Edn. Sec. Pearl city Makule Softball League; mem. Barbers Point coun., Navy League, Hawaiian Edn. Coun., Hui Kokua Kinipopo Booster Club, Japanese Am. Citizens League Honolulu, Aiea Hongwanji. Democrat. Office: Hawaiian Senate Hawaii State Capitol Rm 003 415 S Beretania St Honolulu HI 96813*

MIZUKI, BRIAN TODD, video engineer; b. Pasadena, Calif., Dec. 27, 1955; s. Hiroshi George and Tazuko (Itow) M.; children: Leslie, Todd, Mark. AA, Pasadena City Coll., 1978. Student aide Pasadena (Calif.) Unified Sch. District, 1974-75; student asst., student counselor Asian-Affairs Office Pasadena (Calif.) City Coll., 1976-78; student asst. KPCS-FM Pasadena City Coll., 1975-76; student broadcast engr. KNBC, Burbank, Calif., 1978-80; vidio engr. Pan Pacific Video Prodns., Altadena, Calif., 1978—. Mem. Pasadena City Coll. Soc. Motion Pictures, TV (alumni coord.). Presbyn. Avocations: electronics, ham radio communications, model rail trains, videography, photography. Home and Office: Pan Pacific Video Productions 348 Laun St Altadena CA 91001-5540

MIZUNO, ALEX T., artist, graphic designer, film maker, illustrator, bilinguist; b. Tokyo, Sept. 27, 1955; came to the U.S., 1979; s. Akio and Shizue (Nakane) M. BA, Nihon U., Tokyo, 1978, City Coll. San Francisco, 1983. Prodn. artist Tenjo-Sajiki Theatre Group, Tokyo, 1978-79; prodn. mgr. Terayama Prodn., Tokyo, 1978-79; voice-over artist 20th Century Fox, Tri Star Pictures, others, San Francisco, 1980—; illustrator Paramount, MacroMedia, others, San Francisco, 1984 ; decoration artist No. Calif. Cherry Blossom Festival, San Francisco, 1988—; prodn. coord. Video for Apple, Readers Digest, others, San Francisco, 1993—. Film maker Previously Lost Lovers of America, 1984 (award Palo Alto Film Festival 1985), video for Apple Computer; contbr. articles to mags. Mem. Pacific Film Archive. Avocations: films, art, music, theater. Office: Alexs Arts and Comm 140 Harold Ave San Francisco CA 94112-2334

MJELDE, MICHAEL JAY, title company executive, writer; b. Bremerton, Wash., Dec. 1, 1938; s. Joseph Nordahl and Bertha Louise (Croes) M.; m. Wylla Rae Mjelde, Sept. 22, 1962; children: Michael John (dec.), Arina L. Caton, Heather L. Allison, Debi Randall, Sharla R. Grad. high sch., Bremerton. Engring. technician Safeco Title Ins., Seattle, 1963-71, Jones Bassi Engrs., Mercer Island, Wash., 1971-72; engring. technician Land Title Co. of Kitsap, Bremerton, 1972-77, asst. mgr., 1977-91, mgr. Kitsap County, 1992-93; exec. v.p. Land Title Co. of Kitsap, Silverdale, Wash., 1994—. Author: Glory of the Seas, 1970, Clipper Ship Captain, 1997; co-author: Seabeck: Tides Out Table's Set, 1993; editor Sea Chest, 1991—. Home: PO Box 968 Seabeck WA 98380-0968

MJOLSNESS, RAYMOND CHARLES, retired physicist, researcher; b. Chgo., Apr. 22, 1933; s. Raymond and Emma Pearl (McCormick) Veseth; m. Patricia M. McGeary, Oct. 7, 1957; children: Eric, Ingrid, Kirsten. BA, Reed Coll., 1953, Oxford (Eng.) U., 1955; PhD, Princeton U., 1963. Rsch. assoc. Los Alamos (N.Mex.) Nat. Lab., 1958-61; asst. prof. math. Reed Coll., Portland, Oreg., 1961-62; staff scientist GE Space Sci. Ctr., King of Prussia, Pa., 1962-63; staff mem. Los Alamos Nat. Lab., 1963-67; assoc. prof. astronomy Pa. State U., State College, 1967-69; staff mem. Los Alamos Nat. Lab., 1969-92; adj. prof. physics Los Alamos Nat. Lab., 1983-84. Contbr. articles to profl. jours. including Phys. Rev., Physics of Fluids, Turbulent Shear Flow II. Mem. Am. Phys. Soc. Achievements include research in plasma stability theory, and collision theory, electron-atom and electron-molecule collisions, cosmology, hydrodynamics (turbulence, stability theory, code development, low gravity flows), and foundations of quantum mechanics. Avocations: jogging, weightlifting, music, chess, investing. Home: 207 Dos Brazos St Los Alamos NM 87544-2426

MKRYAN, SONYA, geophysicist, researcher, educator; b. Beyrouth, Lebanon, Mar. 1, 1935; arrived in U.S., 1979; m. Vahram and Marie (Topalian) Faradjian; m. Karapet Mkryan, Apr. 11, 1970; children: Marine, Anahit, Lusine. MS in Physics, Pedagogical Inst., 1956; PhD in Physics and Math., Tbilicy State U., 1970. Physics, math. tchr. H.S., Ghaltakchi, 1952-53; librerian Ores Dept., Leninakan, Armenia, 1954-59; geophysicst, rschr. Inst. of Geophysics Engring. Seismology, Leninakan, 1960-70; assoc. prof. of physics Polytech. Inst., Kirovakan, Armenia, 1970-79; mech. inspector Robertshaw Co., Anaheim, Calif., 1980-82; tchr. Pasadena (Calif.) Sch. Dist., 1983-86; eligibility worker, acting supr. Dept. of Pub. Svcs., Glendale, Calif., 1986-97; social worker in home supportive svcs. Glendale, 1997—. Author: (poetry) Ups and Downs of Life, 1987, Incessant Melodies, 1992, Light and Darkness, 1997, (novels) Eternities Travelers, 1998; one-person shows include: Tekeyan Gallere, Pasadena, Calif., 1989, Pasadena Union of Marash Armenians Hall, 1982-95; group shows: Altadena, Pasadena, Downy, Glendale, Ambassador Hotel, La. (second prize 1987), Wilshir Ebeu, La., 1988. Mem. Armenian Writers Union in Calif., Internat. Soc. of Poets, Nat. Libr. of Poets, Armenian Allied Arts Assn. (First prize 1982, 84, 85, 87, 91), Armenian Radio and TV Com. Avocations: writing, walking, reading, cooking, dancing. Home: 2723 N Lake Ave Altadena CA 91001

MOBERLY, LINDEN EMERY, educational administrator; b. Laramie, Wyo., Jan. 4, 1923; s. Linden E. and Ruth (Gathercole) M. BS, Coll. Emporia, 1952; MS, Kans. State Tchrs. Coll., 1954; m. Viola F. Mosher, Apr. 29, 1949. Tchr. sci., Florence, Kans., 1952-54, Concordia, Kans., 1954-56, Grand Junction, Colo., 1957-60; asst. prin. Orchard Mesa Jr. High Sch., Grand Junction, 1960-66, prin., 1967-84; field cons. Nat. Assn. Secondary Sch. Prins., 1985—. Sgt. USMC, 1941-46. Recipient Outstanding Secondary Prin. award Colo. Assn. Sch. Execs., 1978. Mem. NEA, VFW, Nat. Assn. Secondary Prins. (bd. dir. 1979-83), Colo. Edn. Assn. (bd.dir. 1968-71), Colo. North Central Assn. Colls. and Secondary Schs., Colo. Assn. Secondary Sch. Prins. (bd. dir. 1974-77), Lions, Sons of the Revolution, Marine Corps League (life), VFW (life), Masons (award of Excellence 1990). Home: 2256 Kingston Rd Grand Junction CO 81503-1221

MOBLEY, PATRICIA ANN (TRISH MOBLEY), lay church worker, church secretary; b. Barstow, Calif., Apr. 22, 1943; d. Jesse Ralph and Elizabeth (Gard) Mobley; m. Jerry D. Smith, 1962 (div. 1978); children: Paul David Smith, Susanne Rachelle Reid; m. Robert Joseph Misenheimer, Mar. 22, 1985 (div. Nov. 1985). Student, Life Bible Coll., L.A., 1960-62. Pianist, leader high sch. youth group Foursquare Ch., Barstow, 1959-61; pianist, coord. jr. ch., Foursquare Ch., Arlington, Calif., 1964-66; pianist, tchr. Grace Bapt. Ch., Newhall, Calif., 1971-75; pianist, jr. high dir. choir 1st Bapt. Ch., Lake Arrowhead, Calif., 1975-78; pianist, mem. cabinet, visitation team, tchr. 1st Bapt. Ch. Singles Ministry, Pomona, Calif., 1978-85, pianist, mem. Regional Single Adult Task Force, leader, 1988-90; pianist, tchr., mem. bd. curriculum devel. 1st Evang. Free Ch., Single Parent Fellowship, Fullerton, Calif., 1985-88; sec. Todd Meml. Chapel, Pomona, 1984—. Mem. Com. to Re-call Clay Bryant, Pomona, 1989; treas. Com. to Elect Bob Jackson, Pomona, 1991. Barstow Bus. and Profl. Women's scholar, 1961. Mem. Nat. Notary Assn. (cert.). Republican.

MOCKARY, PETER ERNEST, clinical laboratory scientist, researcher, medical writer; b. Zghorta, Lebanon, Jan. 6, 1931; came to U.S., 1953; s. Ernest Peter and Evelyn (Kaddo) M.; m. Yvette Fadlallah, Aug. 27, 1955; children: Ernest, Evelyn, Paula, Vincent, Marguerite. BA in Philosophy, Coll. des Freres, Tripoli, Lebanon, 1948; BA in Medicine, Am. U. Beirut, 1950, postgrad., 1950-52. Cert. clin. lab. scientist, Calif.; cert. clin. lab. scientist Nat. Certification Agy. Chief hematology unit VA Wadsworth Med. Ctr., West Los Angeles, Calif., 1956-81; CEO Phoenicia Trading Co., 1981-88; dir. Coagulation Lab., Orthopaedic Hosp., L.A., 1988-97; lab. supr. Westside Hosp., L.A., 1964-79; lectr. hematology UCLA, West Los Angeles, 1970-78. Pres. World Lebanese Cultural Union, L.A., 1978-79. With U.S. Army, 1954-56. Recipient outstanding performance award lab. svc. VA Wadsworth Med. Ctr., 1972-76. Republican. Roman Catholic. Avocations: billiards, reading, classical music. Home: 3103 Gilmerton Ave Los Angeles CA 90064-4319

MOCTEZUMA-BENDER, LISA BETH, book distributor executive, art agent; b. Huntington, N.Y., May 14, 1966; d. Michael Henry and Rhoda Sharon (Lipschitz) Bender; m. Edgardo Moctezuma, Oct. 28, 1990; children: Cloe Beth, Jacob Ross; 1 stepchild, Deseret Moctezuma. BA in Italian and Spanish Lang. and Lit., Brandeis U., 1988. Exec. Latin Am. Book Source, Inc., Chula Vista, Calif. Office: Latin Am Book Source Inc 48 Las Flores Dr Chula Vista CA 91910-1964

MODER, LISA MARIE, software engineer, manufacturing process engineer; b. Muchengladbach, Germany, Apr. 18, 1965; came to U.S., 1967; d. John Andrew and Sue Elaine (Anderson) Bondch; m. David Lincoln Moder, May 2, 1987; children: Daniel Lee, Sean Michael, Christopher James. BSEE Tech., Met. State Coll., 1990. Software engr. Erbtec Engring., Boulder, Colo., 1989—. Mem. IEEE. Democrat. Avocations: collecting, creating elec. gadgets, computer games. Home: 3355 Newland St Wheat Ridge CO 80033-6440 Office: Erbtec Engring 2760 29th St Ste 100 Boulder CO 80301-1202

MOE, ANDREW IRVING, veterinarian; b. Tacoma, Jan. 2, 1927; s. Ole Andrew and Ingeborg (Gordham) M.; BS in Biology, U. Puget Sound, 1949; BA, Wash. State U., 1953, DVM 1954; m. Dorothy Clara Becker, June 25, 1950; children: Sylvia Moe McGowan, Pamela Moe Barker, Joyce. Meat cutter Art Hansen, Tacoma, 1943-48; gen. practice as veterinarian Baronti Vet. Hosp., Eugene, Oreg., 1956-57; veterinarian, regulatory Calif. Animal Health br. Calif. Dept. Food and Agr. Resident veterinarian II, Modesto, Calif., 1957-64, acting veterinarian-in-charge Modesto Dist. Office (veterinarian III), 1976-77, ret., 1990—. Watersafety instr. ARC, 1958-61. Capt., Vet. Corps., 1954-56, 62; comdr. 417th Med. Svc. Flight Res. (AFRES), 1965-66, 71-73; lt. col. Biomed. Scis. Corps USAF, ret., 1982. Recipient Chief Veterinarian badge, 1975. Mem. VFW (life; comdr. post 4144 1998-99), No. San Joaquin Vet. Med. Assn. (pres. 1979), Calif. Acad. Vet. Medicine (charter), Res. Officers Assn. (life), Ret. Officers Assn. (life), Assn. Mil. Surgeons U.S. (life), U.S. Animal Health Assn., Sons of Norway, Shriners (bd. dirs., dir. Modesto Shrine 1995), Masons (Illustrious Master Modesto chpt. 1983, Allied Masonic degrees, pres. Modesto Masonic Luncheon Club 1991, 98, Meritorious Svc. medal 1992), Scottish Rite (pres. Ctrl. Valley 1997), Internat. Order of the Rainbow for Girls, Presido Yacht Club of Sausalito (Calif.), Theta Chi, Alpha Psi. Lutheran (del. 102d Synod 1961). Home: 161 Norwegian Ave Modesto CA 95350-3542

MOE, ORVILLE LEROY, racetrack executive; b. Spokane, Wash., Nov. 26, 1936; s. Clarence Orville and Georgia Maria (Lombard) M.; m. Deonne Wesley Schultz, Jan. 11, 1953; children: Kathleen June, Susan Marie, Terry Ann. Co-owner Moe's Sudden Svc. Fuel Co., Spokane, Wash., 1956-74; sec. Gold Res. Mining Corp., Spokane, 1973-89, Bonanza Gold Corp., Spokane, 1973-85; pres., founder Spokane Raceway Park, Inc., 1971—; regional v.p. Am. Hot Rod Assn., Kansas, Mo., 1968-84, mktg. dir., 1978-84; co-producer Internat. Car Show Assn., Spokane, 1969-90. Co-producer Spokane Auto Boat Speed Show, 1964—. Mem. Nat. Rep. Senatorial Com., 1984—; mem., trustee Rep. Presdl. Task Force, mem. 1992 Presdl. Trust Rep. Nat. Com. Mem. ISCA, Eagles, Am. Hot Rod Assn. (exec. v.p. Spokane, Wash. 1986—), Internat. Footprint Assn., Am. Auto Racing Assn. (regional v.p.). Republican. Avocations: auto racing, mining, collecting and rebuilding autos, fishing, ice hockey. Office: Spokane Raceway Park Inc 101 N Hayford Rd Spokane WA 99224-9510

MOE, STANLEY ALLEN, architect, consultant; b. Fargo, N.D., May 28, 1914; s. Ole Arnold and Freda Emily (Pape) M.; m. Doris Lucille Anderson, May 25, 1937; children: Willa Moe Crouse, Myra Moe Galther. BArch, U. Minn., 1936; D of Engring. (hon.), U. N.D., 1993. lic. architect several states; cert. Nat. Coun. Archtl. Registration Bds. Project architect several firms in Midwest, 1936-42; project architect U.S. Army Corps Engrs., Africa, 1942-43; ptnr. H.S. Starin, Architects & Engrs., Duluth, Minn., 1943-47; sr. ptnr. Moe & Larsen, Architects & Engrs., L.A., 1947-54; ptnr., gen. mgr., exec. v.p. Daniel, Mann, Johnson & Mendenall, L.A., 1954-71, corp. v.p., 1972-79; prin. Stanley A. Moe, AIA, L.A., 1979—; dir. design of major mil. projects in Eritrea, Sudan, Egypt, Yemen for Allied Forces, 1942-43; chmn. control com. DMJM & Assocs., 1958-63; project dir. Space Shuttle facilities Kennedy Space Ctr., 1973; project dir. for design of aircraft maintenance complex Iranian Aircraft Industries, 1978; project mgr. for design of major med. facility program Min. of Def. and Aviation, Saudi Arabia, 1975-76; project mgr. design of Boufarik Internat. Airport, Algeria, 1983; dir. design prototype, tng. & operational facilities Titan I Intercontinental Ballistic Missiles Program USAF, 1958-63. Pres. San. Fernando Valley Young Reps., 1952, Van Nuys (Calif.) Jaycees, 1950. Recipient Dsting. Svc. award for cmty. svc. Van Nuys Jaycees, 1949, Sioux award U. N.D. Alumni Assn., 1985, Trustees Soc. award U. Minn., 1992. Mem. AIA (Calif. coun.), Delta Tau Delta. Republican. Presbyterian. Avocations: world travel, hunting, fishing, historic restoration, woodworking. Home and Office: 447 S Plymouth Blvd Los Angeles CA 90020-4706

MOELLER, RICHARD ROBERT, political science educator; b. Euclid, Ohio, Nov. 8, 1966; m. Loralie Davis, April 9, 1994. BA, Baldwin-Wallace Coll., 1989; MA, George Washington U., 1991; PhD, U. Edinburgh, Scotland, 1995. Political analyst Schoman and Spates Internat., Silver Spring, Md., 1995—; lectr. U. Nev., Las Vegas, 1996-98; asst. prof. The Metropolitan State Coll. Denver, Colo., 1998—. Author: (with others) Political Parties and the European Union, 1996; contbr. articles to profl. jours.; creator web site U. Nev., Las Vegas, 1996-98. Mem. selection team Military Acad. State of Nev., Las Vegas, 1998; lectr. Social Studies Council Nev., Las Vegas, 1997. Mem. Am. Political Sci. Assn., German Studies Assn., Ohio Assn. Economists Political Scientists, Lambda Chi Alpha. E-mail: rmoeller@yahoo.com. Fax: 303-556-2716. Office: The Metropolitan Coll Denver Political Sci PO Box 173362 Denver CO 80217-3362

MOERBEEK, STANLEY LEONARD, lawyer; b. Toronto, Ont., Can., Nov. 12, 1951; came to U.S., 1953; s. John Jacob and Mary Emily Moerbeek; m. Carol Annette Mordaunt, Apr. 17, 1982; children: Sarah, Noah. BA magna cum laude, Calif. State U., Fullerton, 1974; student, U. San Diego-Sorbonne, Paris, 1977; JD, Loyola U., 1979. Bar: Calif. 1980; cert. in internat. bus. transactions, bankruptcy and bus. rehab., and civil trial practice. From law clk. to assoc. McAlpin Doonan & Seese, Covina, Calif., 1977-81; assoc. Robert L. Baker, Pasadena, Calif., 1981-82, Miller Bush & Minnott, Fullerton, 1982-83; prin. Law Office of Stanley L. Moerbeek, Fullerton, 1984—; judge pro tem Orange County Superior Ct., Calif., 1984—; notary pub., lt. gov. 9th cir. law student divsn. ABA, 1979. Mem. Heritage Found., Washington, 1989—. Calif. Gov.'s Office scholar, 1970; recipient Plaque of Appreciation, Fullerton Kiwanis, 1983. Mem. Calif. Assn. Realtors (referral panel atty. 1985—), Orange County Bar Assn. (Coll. of Trial Advocacy 1985), Orange L.A. County Bar Assns., Calif. C. of C., Phi Kappa Phi. Roman Catholic. Avocations: history, politics, sports. Office: 1370 N Brea Blvd Ste 210 Fullerton CA 92835-4128

MOFFATT, HUGH MCCULLOCH, JR., hospital administrator, physical therapist; b. Steubenville, Ohio, Oct. 11, 1933; s. Hugh McCulloch and Agnes Elizabeth (Bickerstaff) M.; m. Ruth Anne Colvin, Aug. 16, 1958; children: David, Susan. AB, Asbury Coll., 1958; cert. in phys. therapy, Duke U., 1963. Lic. in phys. therapy and health care adminstrn. Commd. officer USPHS, 1964, advanced through grades to capt.; therapist USPHS, N.Y.C., 1964-66, Sitka, Alaska, 1970-72; therapist cons. USPHS, Atlanta, 1968-70; clinic adminstr. USPHS, Kayenta, Ariz., 1972-73; hosp. dir. USPHS, Sitka, 1973-78; therapist cons. Idaho Dept. Health, Boise, 1966-68; contract health officer USPHS, Anchorage, 1978-89, ret., 1989; phys. therapy cons. Ocean Beach Hosp., Ilwaco, Wash., 1989—, Harbors Home Health Svcs., Aberdeen, Wash., 1990—; therapist cons. Our Lady of Compassion Care Ctr., Anchorage, 1979—, Alaska Native Med. Ctr., Anchorage, 1988—. With U.S. Army, 1955-57. Mem. Am. Phys. Therapy Assn., Commd. Officers Assn. USPHS, Res. Officers Assn., Ret. Officers Assn., Am. Assn. Individual Investors, Am. Assn. Ret. Persons, Eagles. Avocations: automobile repairs, woodworking, camping, fishing, church choir.

MOFFATT, ROBERT HENRY, accountant, publisher, writer, consultant; b. Montreal, Que., Can., June 30, 1930; came to U.S., 1968, naturalized, 1973; s. James Bigelow and Edwige Edith M.; m. Hannelore Mann, Jan. 7, 1989. Student Loyola Coll., Montreal, Que., 1948-52, Acadia U., 1962, UCLA, 1970, 72. Lic. in air navigation, Can.; enrolled agt., Dept. Treasury. Mng. editor, pub. Kings-Annapolis Wings, 1961-66; pres., Valley Pubs. Ltd., Kingston, N.S., Can., 1961-67 exec. dir. Maritime Motor Transport Assn. and editor Maritime Truck Transport Rev., Moncton, N.B., Can., 1967-68; dir. custom products div. Wolf-Brown Inc., Los Angeles, 1968-77; newsletter pub, writer, 1980—; pvt. practice tax acctg., Los Angeles, 1970—; secular humanist. Columnist, author editorials in mags. Clk., author constn. Village of Greenwood, N.S., 1961-63; chmn. bd. commrs., 1963-66; publicity chmn. Voluntary Econ. Planning Program, province N.S., 1965-66. Served to lt. Can. Air Force, 1954-60. Mem. Nat. Assn. Enrolled Agts. (newsletter editor, bd. dirs.), Nat. Soc. Pub. Accts (accredited in taxation), Calif. Soc. Enrolled Agts. Home and Office: 7509 W 88th St Los Angeles CA 90045-3408

MOFFETT, FRANK CARDWELL, architect, civil engineer, real estate developer; b. Houston, Dec. 9, 1931; s. Ferrell Orlando and Jewell Bernice (Williams) M.; BArch, U. Tex., 1958; m. Annie Doris Thorn, Aug. 1, 1952 (div.); children: David Cardwell (dec.), Douglas Howard; m. Darlene Adele Alm Sayan, June 7, 1985 (div.); m. Jennie Bob Hays Bergstrom, July 4, 1995 (div.). Architect with archtl. firms, Seattle, Harmon, Pray & Detrich, Arnold G. Gangnes, Ralf E. Decker, Roland Terry & Assocs., 1958-64; ptnr. Heideman & Moffett, AIA, Seattle, 1964-71; chief architect Wash. State Dept. Hwys., Olympia, 1971-77, Wash. State Dept. Transp., 1977-87; owner The Moffett Co., Olympia, 1974—; founder, treas. TAA, Inc., Olympia, 1987-90, pres., 1991—; advisor Wash. State Bldg. Code Council, 1975-95; instr. civil engring. tech. Olympia Tech. Community Coll., 1975-77; adv. mem. archtl. barriers subcom. Internat. Conf. Building Ofcls.; presenter in field; archtl. works include hdqrs. Gen. Telephone Directory Co., Everett, Wash., 1964; Edmonds Unitarian Ch., 1966; tenant devel. Seattle Hdqrs. Office, Seattle-First Nat. Bank, 1968-70; Wash. State Dept. Transp. Area Hdqrs. Offices, Mt. Vernon, Selah, Raymond, Colfax and Port Orchard 1973-87; Materials Lab., Spokane, Wash., 1974; Olympic Meml. Gardens, Tumwater, Wash., 1988, City Anacortes emergency power stas., 1989, L. Albert Residence, 1990, F. Gasperetti Residence, 1991; archtl. barriers cons. State of Alaska, 1978, State of Wash., 1972-94. Chmn. Planning Commn. of Mountlake Terr., Wash., 1963, 64, mem., 1961-67; mem. State of Wash. Gov.'s Task Force on Wilderness, 1972-75, Heritage Park Task Force, Olympia, Wash., 1986—; trustee Cascade Symphony Orch., 1971; incorporating pres. United Singles, Olympia, 1978-79; capt. CAP, pub. affairs officer Olympia Squadron; mem. nat. panel profl. advisors to Nat. Multiple Sclerosis Soc., 1993—; bd. dirs. Wash. Coalition Citizens with Disabilities, 1997—. With USN, 1951-54. Registered architect, Alaska, Calif., Wash., profl. engr., Wash.; cert. Nat. Council Archtl. Registration Bds., U.S. Dept. Def., Fallout Shelter Analysis, environ. engring. Fellow ASCE; mem. AIA (dir. S.W. Wash. chpt. 1980-82, pres.-elect 1985, pres. 1986, dir. Wash. council 1986, architects in govt. nat. com. 1978-87, chmn. N.W. and Pacific region conf. 1991), Am. Public Works Assn., Inst. Bldgs. and Grounds, Constrn. Specifications Inst., Am. Arbitration Assn. (invited panelist), Gen. Soc. Mayflower Descs. (gov. Wash. Soc. 1982-83), Nat. Huguenot Soc. (pres. Wash. Soc. 1981-83, 85-87, 95—), Olympia Geneal. Soc. (pres. 1978-80), SAR (state treas. 1984-85), SCV, Sons and Daus. of Pilgrims, (gov. Wash. Soc. 1984), Order of Magna Charta, Aircraft Owners' and Pilots' Assn., Rotary (pres. Edmonds, 1969-70), Olympia, Coll. Club of Seattle. Co-author: An Illustrated Handbook for Barrier-Free Design, 4th Edit., 1989, Accessibility Design for All, 1992, 2nd edit., 1995, 3d edit., 1998; Housing and Building Accessibility: The Law in Washington, 1992. Republican. Baptist. Home and Office: PO Box 2422 Olympia WA 98507-2422

MOFFITT, DONALD EUGENE, transportation company executive; b. Terre Haute, Ind., May 22, 1932; s. James Robert and Margaret Mary (Long) M.; m. Billie Duffy, Feb. 21, 1989; 1 child, Jaime. BA, Ind. State U., 1954; postgrad., Ind. U., 1956; grad., Advanced Mgmt. Program, Harvard U., 1972. Acct. Foster Freight Lines, Indpls., 1955-56; with Consol. Freightways Inc., San Francisco, 1956-88, v.p. planning, 1961-69; v.p. fin., motor carrier subs. Consol. Freightways Corp. Del., 1969-75; v.p. fin., treas. parent co. Consol. Freightways Inc., San Francisco, 1975-81; exec. v.p. Consol. Freightways Inc., Palo Alto, Calif., 1981-86; vice chmn. parent co. bd. Consol. Freightways, Inc., Palo Alto, Calif., 1986-88; chmn., CEO Circle Express, Indpls., 1988-90; pres., CEO Consol. Freightways, Inc., Palo Alto, Calif., 1990-96; chmn., CEO Consol. Freightways, Inc. (name now CNF Transp. Inc.), Palo Alto, Calif., 1995—, also bd. dirs.; chmn. bd. dirs. all subsidiaries CNF Transport, 1990—; chmn., pres., CEO CNF Transp. Inc., 1996—. Bd. dirs. Bay Area Coun., Calif. Bus. Roundtable, Conf. Bd., Boy Scouts Am., ARC, Hoover Instn.; bd. dirs., exec. com. Hwy. Users Fedn.; bd. trustees Automotive Safety Found.; bus. adv. coun. Northwestern U. Transp. Ctr. Mem. Nat. C. of C. (vice-chmn., bd. dirs.). Office: CNF Transp Inc 3240 Hillview Ave Palo Alto CA 94304-1201

MOFFITT, JOHN FRANCIS, art history educator, writer; b. San Francisco, Feb. 25, 1940. BFA, Calif. Coll. Arts and Crafts, 1962; MA in Art History, Calif State U., San Francisco, 1963; PhD, U. Madrid, 1966. Asst. prof. art and art history East Carolina U., Greenville, N.C., 1966-68, [illegible] prof. to prof. history of art N.Mex. State U., Las Cruces, 1969-96, prof. art history emeritus, 1996—. Author: Spanish Painting, 1973, Occultism in Avant-Garde Art: The Case of Joseph Beuys, 1988, Velázquez, práctica e idea: Estudios dispersos, 1991, Art Forgery: The Case of the Lady of Elche, 1995, Spanish edit., 1996, The Arts in Spain, 1999, Spanish edit., 1999; co-author: O Brave New People: The European Invention of the American Indian, 1996. E-mail: moffitj@nmsu.edu.

MOGG, DONALD WHITEHEAD, chemist; b. La Grange, Ill., Feb. 11, 1924; s. Harold William and Margaret (Whitehead) M.; B.S., Allegheny Coll., 1944; postgrad. Harvard U., 1946-47. Asst. chemist Gt. Lakes Carbon Corp., Morton Grove, Ill., 1947-48, chemist, 1948-53, research chemist, 1953-56, project supr., 1956-59, sect. head, 1959-63; sect. head Gt. Lakes Research Corp., Elizabethton, Tenn., 1963-66; research and devel. mgr. bldg. products div. Grefco, Inc., Torrance, Calif., 1966-68, corp. research and devel. mgr., 1968-72, group mgr., 1972-81, sr. research assoc., 1981-82. Served with U.S. Army, 1944-46. Mem. Am. Chem. Soc., AAAS, Phi Beta Kappa, Phi Kappa Psi. Presbyterian. U.S. and fgn. patentee in field of bldg. products. Home: 3823 Ingraham St Apt B202 San Diego CA 92109-6460

MOGHADAM, AMIR, consultant, educational administrator. BSME, U. London, 1983; PhD in Aeronautical Engring., U. Cambridge, 1987. Postdoctoral rschr. U. Calif., Santa Barbara, 1987-88; asst. prof. Northrop U., L.A., 1988-91, v.p. faculty senate, 1990-91; acad. and ednl. adminstrv. positions Northrop-Rice Inst. of Tech., Inglewood, Calif., 1991-96, dean/campus dir., 1996-98; pres., CEO Aeronautics Innovation Inc., Irvine, Calif., 1993—; dir. student affairs, info. and computer sci. U. Calif., Irvine, 1998—. Contbr. articles to profl. jours. Mem. AIAA, Am. Soc. Engring. Edn., Tau Alpha Pi, Tau Beta Pi, Sigma Gamma Tau. Office: Info and Computer Sci U Calif Irvine Irvine CA 92697-3425

MOGULOF, MELVIN BERNARD, consultant; b. N.Y.C., June 17, 1926; s. Nathan and Ida (Platkin) M.; m. Mildred Edith Goldfarb, June 3, 1956; children: Daniel, Dena. BS, Denver U., 1949; MA, Syracuse U., 1950; MS, U. Conn., 1956; PhD, Brandeis U., 1963. Program officer Pres.'s Commn. on Juvenile Delinquency, Washington, 1963-64; regional mgr. community action program OEO, San Francisco, 1964-66; regional dir. model cities program HUD, San Francisco, 1966-68; assoc. prof. San Francisco State Coll., 1968-69; sr. rsch. assoc. The Urban Inst., Washington, 1969-74; exec. dir. community svcs. Fedn. Jewish Philanthropies, N.Y.C., 1974-76; exec. v.p. Jewish Fedn. East Bay, Oakland, Calif., 1980-86; chief exec. officer Koret Found., San Francisco, 1986-88; dir. task force Pres.'s Adv. Com. on Exec. Orgn., Washington, 1970; cons. Kaiser Found., Packard Found., Osher Found., Bay Vision 20/20 Commn. Author: Governing Metropolitan Areas, 1973, Saving the Coast, 1974; contbr. 35 articles to profl. jours., 10 book chpts. Sgt. U.S. Army, 1944-46. Sr. Fulbright lectr. U.S. Fulbright Commn., London, 1971-72, Jerusalem, Israel, 1976-77. Mem. Mayor's Drug Task Force, Berkeley, 1989; bd. dirs. Berkeley Dispute Resolution Svc., 1989. Jewish.

MOHLER, JAMES WILLIAM, minister; b. Lynwood, Calif., Nov. 8, 1955; s. Lionel Louis and Shelia (Howard) M.; m. Miriam Ruth Moses, Aug. 23, 1980. MusB cum laude, Biola U., 1979, postgrad., 1995; MA in Christian Edn., Talbot Sem., 1984. Ordained to ministry Am. Bapt. Ch., 1986. Min. to jrs., middlers 1st Bapt. Ch., Downey, Calif., 1977-86; min. children and youth 1st Bapt. Ch., Scottsdale, Ariz., 1986—; adj. prof. Biola U., La Mirada, Calif., 1985-86; leader Tonto Rim Am. Bapt. Camp, Payson, Ariz., 1986—. Mem. project area com. City of Downey, 1985-86. Recipient Scholastic Recognition award, nat. Assn. Profs. of Christian Edn. Avocations: camping, racquetball, music, puppetry. Office: 1st Bapt Ch 7025 E Osborn Rd Scottsdale AZ 85251-6324

MOHR, JOHN LUTHER, biologist, environmental consultant; b. Reading, Pa., Dec. 1, 1911; s. Luther Seth and Anna Elizabeth (Davis) M.; m. Frances Edith Christensen, Nov. 23, 1939; children: Jeremy John, Christopher Charles. AB in Biology, Bucknell U., 1933; student, Oberlin Coll., 1933-34; PhD in Zoology, U. Calif., Berkeley, 1939. Research asso. Pacific Islands Research, Stanford, 1942-44; rsch. assoc. Allan Hancock Found., U. So. Calif., 1944-46, asst. prof., 1946-47, asst. prof. dept. biology, 1947-54, asso. prof., 1954-57, prof., 1957-77; chmn. dept., 1960-62, prof. emeritus, 1977—; vis. prof. summers U. Wash. Friday Harbor Labs., 1956, '57; rsch. assoc. vertebrate zoology Natural History Mus., Los Angeles County, 1996—; marine borer and pollution surveys harbors So. Calif., 1948-51, arctic marine biol. research, 1952-71; chief marine zool. group U.S. Antarctic research ship Eltanin in Drake Passage, 1962, in South Pacific sector, 1965; research deontology in sci. and academia; researcher on parasitic protozoans of anurans, crustaceans, elephants; analysis of agy. and industry documents, ethics and derelictions of steward agy., sci. and tech. orgns. as they relate to offshore and coastal onshore oil activities, environ. effects of oil spill dispersants and offshore oil industry discharges and naturally occurring radioactive material NORMs. Active People for the Am. Way; mem. Biol. Stain Commn., 1948-80, trustee, 1971-80, emeritus trustee, 1981—, v.p., 1976-80. Recipient Guggenheim fellowship, 1957-58. Fellow AAAS (coun. 1964-73), So. Calif. Acad. Scis., Sigma Xi (exec. com. 1964-67, 68, 69, chpt.-at-large bd. 1968-69); mem. Am. Micros. Soc., Marine Biol. Assn. U.K. (life), Am. Soc. Parasitologists, Western Soc. Naturalists (pres. 1960-61), Soc. Protozoologists, Soc. Integrative and Comparative Biology, Ecol. Soc. Am., Calif. Native Plant Soc., Assn. Forest Svc. Employees Environ. Ethics, Common Cause, Huxleyan, Sierra Club, Phi Sigma, Theta Upsilon Omega. Home: 3819 Chanson Dr Los Angeles CA 90043-1601

MOHRDICK, EUNICE MARIE, nurse, consultant, health educator; b. Alameda, Calif.; d. Walter William and Eunice Marie (Connors) M. BS in Nursing Edn., U. San Francisco, 1955; MA in Edn. spl interest, San Francisco State Coll., 1967; Pub. Health Cert., U. Calif., San Francisco, 1968; EdD, Western Colo. U., 1977. RN, Calif. Supr. oper. rm. St. John's Hosp., Oxnard, Calif., 1947-50, supr. maternity, delivery and nursery rms., 1950-53; nurse, supr. St. Mary's Hosp., San Francisco, 1943-45, supr., instr., 1955-60, 62-65; asst. dir. nursing, tchr. nursing history St Mary's Coll. of Nursing, San Francisco, 1953-55; tchr. home nursing Mercy High Sch., San Francisco, 1960-61; tchr. Health, Family Life San Francisco Unified Schs., 1968-83; tchr. holistic health Contra Costa Coll., 1981-86; cons. pvt. practice Albany, Calif., 1986—; tchr. El Cerrito (Calif.) Senior Ctr., 1986-88. Author: Elementary Teacher Handbook, How to Teach Sex Education, Grades, 4,5,6, 1977. Mem. Madonna Guild, San Francisco, 1986—, v.p., 1989—; mem. Half Notes' Singing Club to Sick and Spl. Needy, 1970—. Recipient Title I Grant U. Calif. San Francisco, 1968, Workshop Grant for Culture Inter-relationship Study, Singapore, UNESCO, Washington U., St. Louis, 1973. Mem. AAUW, San Francisco State U. Alumna, U. San Francisco Nursing Alumni (charter mem., bd. dirs. 1974-88), Mensa. Republican. Roman Catholic. Avocations: painting, piano, travel, swimming, investing. Home & Office: 205 Lewers St Honolulu HI 96815-1939

MOINI, HOSSEIN, mechanical engineer, educator, consultant; b. Tehran, Iran, Sept. 9, 1955; came to U.S., 1978; m. Bahareh Aurang, June 4, 1989. BS, Arya-Mehr U. of Tech., Tehran, 1978; PhD, U. Calif., Santa Barbara, 1986. Rsch., tchg. asst. U. Calif., Santa Barbara, 1980-85, lectr., 1986, numerical analyst, 1987; prof. Calif. State U., Fullerton, 1987—; cons. in field. Contbr. articles to profl. jours. Rsch. grantee Hughes Aircraft, Fullerton, Calif., 1989, Instrumentation grantee NSF, Washington, 1996, Rsch. grantee Boeing Co., Long Beach, Calif., 1997, Lockheed Martin Corp., Sunnyvale, Calif., 1997-98. Mem. ASME, AIAA, Internat. Soc. Pharmaceutical Engrs., Am. Soc. Engring. Edn., Honor Soc. Internat. Scholars. Avocations: sailing, volleyball, biking. Office: California State U Mech Engineering Dept 800 N State College Blvd Fullerton CA 92831-3547

MOJAS, KATHLEEN MARIE, psychologist; b. Santa Monica, Calif., July 1, 1961; d. Peter William and Mary Elizabeth Mojas. BA in Comms., UCLA, 1987; PhD in Clin. Psychology, Calif. Grad. Inst., 1992. Lic. psychologist, Calif., 1994. Intern, tutor, counselor Dr. Gardner Child Psychologist, Brentwood, Calif., 1988-90; psychol. asst. Calif. Grad. Inst. [illegible] Beverly Hills, Calif., 1989-94, seminar leader, spkr., writer, 1989—; rsch. asst. UCLA, 1987, Artists and Educators for Self-Esteem, L.A., 1987-89, Dick Clark Prodns., L.A., 1987; behavior edn. counselor Nutrisys., Northridge, Calif., 1986-87, media psychologist nat. talk, news shows. Contbr. articles to profl. jours., mags. Assoc. mem. APA, Golden Key. Democrat. Avocations: astronomy, painting, hiking, reading, writing. Office: 449 S Beverly Dr Ste 212 Beverly Hills CA 90212-4428

MOLINA, WILLIAM H., cinematographer, director; b. Mexico City, May 20, 1962; came to U.S., 1976; s. Edward A. and Mary (Poole) M. BA in Film, TV, Trinity U., 1984. Cameraman Hayes Prodns., Inc., San Antonio, 1982-85; freelance cinematographer, L.A., 1987—. Dir., dir. photography: (films) Revelation, 1981 (Acad. Motion Picture Arts and Scis. Regional Student Films award 1982), The Diverse Reflection, 1983 (Artist Alliance award 1984); cinematographer: (feature films) Helicopter Cowboy, 1987, The Channeler, 1990, Teenage Exorcist, 1990, Dance With Death, 1990, Tinsel, 1990, In the Heat of Passion, 1991, Munchie, 1991, Stepmonster, 1992, Place, 1993, Destination Vegas, 1994, Oceans of Air, 1992; dir., cinematographer: (feature films) Where Truth Lies, 1996, Dusting Cliff Seven, 1996, Dillinger in Paradise, 1997, Tap Water, 1998, Last Assassins, 1998, Yellow Badge of Courage, 1998; cinematographer (films) Le Baton, 1994, El Artista, 1997, Reducing Stanley, 1997. Recipient Bronze medal Internat. N.Y. Film and Video Festival, 1985, Gold award Houston Film Festival, 1991, Artist Achievement award in cinematography Internat. Photographers Guild Film Showcase, 1996; Univ. Film and Video Assn. grantee, 1983; recipient Gold award Flagstaff Internat. Film Festival, 1998. Mem. Soc. Operating Cameramen (treas.), Internat. Photographers Guild. Avocations: soccer, aviation.

MOLINA VILLACORTA, RAFAEL ANTONIO, investment company executive; b. Sept. 5, 1963; s. Rafael Antonio and Rosa Isabel (Villacorta) M.; m. Maria Asuncion Cornejo, Sept. 28, 1985; children: Elisa Maria, Rafael Augusto, Cristia Adolfo, Leonardo Paolo. AA, Sacramento City Coll., 1983; BS, Golden Gate U., 1994. CFO MVM Investments, Sacramento, 1983-85; adminstr. State of Calif., Sacramento, 1985-93; CEO, mng. dir. C & T Investments, Dixon, Calif., 1988—; managing dir. Data Systems, Los Altos, Calif., 1996—; dir. MAM Co., Sacramento, 1985—; CEO, dir. Del Sol Investments, Dixon, 1989-98. Mem. Calif. State Employees Assn., Sacramento, 1985, Am. Mgmt. Assn., Sacramento, 1991; pres. St. Peter's Ch., Dixon, 1992. Recipient Outstanding Achievement award Calif. Dept. Health Svcs., 1988, Primary Clinics, 1990. Mem. Am. Mgmt. Assn., Network Profl. Assn., Tele-Comms. Assn., Calif. Microcomputers Users. Roman Catholic. Avocations: travel, computers, reading. Office: C & T Investments Co 358 E A St Dixon CA 95620-3535

MOLINSKY, BERT, tax consultant; b. Bronx, N.Y., Feb. 25, 1938; s. Joseph and Ida G. (Rosenberg) M.; m. Donna L. Thurman, June 26, 1964; children: Avery, Lucy, Lois, Sarah. Student, U. Ariz., 1956-61, Diablo Valley Coll., 1986-88, Calif. State U., Hayward, 1988-92. CFP; CLU; ChFC; Enrolled Agt. Field supt. INA Life, Phoenix, 1966-72; regional life mgr. Sentry Life Ins. Co., Oklahoma City, 1972-73, Mpls., 1973-75, San Francisco, 1975-78; mgr. Acacia Mutual Life, Oakland, Calif., 1978-80; gen. agt. Am. United Life, Concord, Calif., 1980-82; owner East Bay Triple Check Tax Svcs., Walnut Creek, Calif., 1982—, Triple Check Tax and Fin. Svc., Peoria, Ariz., 1993—; instr. Golden Gate U. CPD, San Francisco, 1983-93, Mt. Diablo Sch. Dist., Concord, 1986-93; faculty Coll. for Fin. Planning, Denver, 1983—; bd. dirs. Triple Check Licensee Coun. Contbr. articles to profl. jours. Nat. dir. U.S. Jaycees, Phoenix, 1967; pres. Bnai Brith Coun. of Lodges, San Francisco, 1986. With USNR, 1955-72. Named Jaycee of Yr. Ariz. Jaycees, 1967. Fellow Nat. Tax Practice Inst.; mem. Enrolled Agts., East Bay Assn Life Underwriters (pres. 1985-86), Nat. Assn. Enrolled Agts., Peoria Sunset Lions (past pres.), Ariz. State Enrolled Agts. Assn. (pres. 1997—), Nat. Assn. Enrolled Agents (nat. by-laws chmn., mem. affiliates task force, 1997-99). Avocation: sports. Office: Plaza Del Rio Ctr 9401 W Thunderbird Rd Ste 140 Peoria AZ 85381-4817 also: PO Box 100 Peoria AZ 85380-0100

MOLLMAN, JOHN PETER, book publisher, consultant electronic publishing; b. Belleville, Ill., Feb. 8, 1931; s. Kenneth John and Maurine (Farrow) M.; children—Sarah Chase, Eric Cleburne. BA, Washington U., St. Louis, 1952. Advt. specialist Gen. Electric Co., Schenectady and Boston, 1952-54; mgr. Enterprise Printing Co., Millstadt, Ill., 1956-66; gen. mgr. Monarch Pub. Co., N.Y.C., 1966-67; dir. prodn. Harper & Row Pubs., N.Y.C., 1967-74; pub. Harper's Mag. Press, N.Y.C., 1971-74; v.p. prodn. Random House Inc., N.Y.C., 1974-81; sr. v.p. World Book-Childcraft Inc., Chgo., 1981-88; pres. World Book Pub., 1988-91; pub. cons., 1991-92; dir. intellectual property devel. Multimedia Publishing Microsoft, 1992-96; cons. in electronic pub. Carmel, Calif., 1996—; bd. dirs. Helicon Pub. Co., Oxford, Eng. Mem. vis. com. Washington U.; mem. pub. com. Art Inst. Chgo. With U.S. Army, 1954-56. Mem. Golf Club at Quali Lodge, Sigma Delta Chi, Omicron Delta Kappa. Unitarian. Home: 25340 Vista Del Pinos Carmel CA 93923-8804

MOLONEY, STEPHEN MICHAEL, lawyer; b. L.A., July 1, 1949; s. Donald Joseph and Madeline Marie (Sartoris) M.; m. Nancy Paula Barile, Jan. 15, 1972; children: Michael, John, Kathleen. Student, St. John's Sem., Camarillo, Calif., 1967-69; BS, U. Santa Clara, 1971, JD, 1975. Bar: Calif. 1975, U.S. Dist. Ct. (cen. dist.) Calif. 1976, U.S. Supreme Ct. 1990. Assoc. Gilbert, Kelly, Crowley & Jennett, L.A., 1975-80, from ptnr. to sr. ptnr., 1980—; arbitrator, settlement officer L.A. Superior Ct., 1985—. Contbr. articles to profl. jours. Dir. Calif. Def. Polit. Action Com., Sacramento, 1991—. With USAR. Recipient Svc. award to Pres. of So. Calif. Def. Counsel, Def. Rsch. Inst., Chgo., 1992. Mem. Assn. So. Calif. Def. Counsel (pres. 1992-93), Calif. Def. Counsel (dir. 1991—), L.A. County Bar Assn. (vols. in parole, 1976-77, exec. com. alternative dispute resolution com. 1992-96), Oakmont Country Club, La Quinta Resort and Club. Democrat. Roman Catholic. Avocations: politics, golf, reading, travel. Office: Gilbert Kelly Crowley & Jennett 1200 Wilshire Blvd Ste 6 Los Angeles CA 90017-1908

MONACO, PAUL, academic administrator, educator, artist, writer; b. Niskayuna, N.Y., Sept. 11, 1942; s. Angelo M. and Birdena (O'Melia) M.; m. Victoria O'Donnell, 1993. BS, Columbia U., 1965; MA, U. N.C., 1966; PhD, Brandeis U., 1974. Asst. prof. hist. Brandeis U., Waltham, Mass., 1973-75; prof. arts and humanities U. Tex., Dallas, 1975-85, dir. grad. studies arts and humanities, 1976-80; dept. head, prof. media and theatre arts Mont. State U., Bozeman, 1985—; bd. dirs. U. Film and Video Assn., 1988-91, 95-96, Bozeman Film Festival, 1985— (pres. 1987-90); mem. Hist. Preservation Com., Bozeman, 1988-90, Mont. Com. for Humanities, Missoula, 1989-93; regional coord. Nicholls Screenwriting Awards, 1989-91. Author: Cinema and Soc., Modern Europe Culture..., 1993, Ribbons in Time, 1988 (ALC Outstanding Acad. Book award 1988), Understanding Society, Culture and Television, 1998; prodr., dir.: Montana: 2d Century, 1990-96 (Mont. broadcasters award 1991), Bison in the Killing Fields, 1996; prodr., dir., co-writer: Home to Montana, 1988; dir. I Often Thought of Berlin, 1989, Way of the Trout Women, 1994, Gary Strobel: A Portrait, 1996, War and Work, 1997. Bd. dirs. Mont. Ballet Co., Bozeman, 1986-90; mem. selection com. Fulbright Found., Germany, 1996, 97. Recipient Fulbright Prof. award U.S., Germany, 1982-83, 92. Mem. PKP (pres. Mt. State U. chpt. 1998—). Home: 290 Low Bench Rd Gallatin Gateway MT 59730-9741 Office: Mt State Univ Visual Communications Bldg Bozeman MT 59717

MONAHAN, LEONARD FRANCIS, musician, singer, composer, publisher; b. Toledo, Aug. 19, 1948; s. Leonard Francis and Theresa Margaret (Geraldo) M.; m. Elaine Ann Welling, Oct. 14, 1978. BS in Psychology and Philosophy, U. Toledo, 1980. Musician, writer Len Monahan Prodns., Toledo, 1971-75; musician, composer, publisher World Airwave Music, Toledo, 1975—; founder Red Dog Records Label. Recipient Internat. Recognition of Christmas Music. Mem. Broadcast Music Inc., Internat. Platform Assn., Nat. Assn. Independent Recording Distbrs. Author: If You Were Big and I Were Small, 1971, The Land of Echoing Fountains, 1972, Sending You My Thoughts, 1987, Another Road, 1987, Tapping at Your Window, 1988; composer numerous songs. Home: Catania Regency 2151 Carlmont Dr Apt 102 Belmont CA 94002-3408 Office: F-Hall 8535 8-1 Delta OH 43515

MONARCHI, DAVID EDWARD, management scientist, information scientist, educator; b. Miami Beach, Fla., July 31, 1944; s. Joseph Louis and Elizabeth Rose (Muller) M.; BS in Engring. Physics, Colo. Sch. of Mines,

1966; PhD (NDEA fellow), U. Ariz., 1972; 1 child by previous marriage, David Edward. Asst. dir. of Bus. Rsch. Divsn., U. Colo., Boulder, 1972-75, asst. prof. mgmt. sci./info. systems, 1972-75, assoc. prof. mgmt. sci. and info. systems, 1975-97, prof. info. systems, 1997—; assoc. dir. Bus. Rsch. Divsn., 1975-80, dir. Divsn. Info. Sci. Rsch., 1982-84; prin. investigator of socio-econ. environ. systems for govtl. agys., and local govt. orgns., State of Colo., also info. systems for pvt. firms, 1972-77, use of virtual reality in distance learning Colo. Commn. Higher Edn., 1996—. Mem. Gov.'s Energy Task Force Com., 1974. Mem. IEEE, Inst. for Mgmt. Sci., Assn. Computing Machinery, Am. Assn. Artificial Intelligence. Contbr. numerous articles on socio-econ. modeling, object-oriented systems and artificial intelligence to profl. jours. Home: 32 Benthaven Pl Boulder CO 80303-6210 Office: U Colo Grad Sch Bus Boulder CO 80309-0419

MONARY, MICHAEL ANTHONY, horticulturist; b. East Greenwich, R.I., Nov. 7, 1951; s. Dan Campbell and Marguerite Lula (Welsh) M. Groundsman City of Santa Clara, Calif., 1972-77; cons. Santa Clara County, Calif., 1977-98; ideaman Livermore Lab., Santa Clara, 1984, NASA Ames Rsch. Ctr., Mountain View, Calif., 1984. designer of nuclear weapon, automatic weapon clip, aparatus for travel to and in space.

MONDRUS, MARTIN, artist, retired educator; b. L.A., May 9, 1925; s. Isador and Anna (Ratner) M.; m. Eloisa Ferrer, Feb. 26, 1948; children: Madalyn, Margarita Engle. BA, Calif. State U., L.A., 1953; MFA, Claremont Grad. Sch., Calif., 1955. Part-time art instr. Pasadena (Calif.) City Coll., 1948-53; art instr. Humboldt State Coll., Arcata, Calif., 1955; art instr., prof. art, prof. emeritus Glendale (Calif.) C.C., 1956-90, divsn. chair art and music, 1988-90; adj. faculty Glendale C.C., 1990—. One man shows include Claremont (Calif.) Grad. Sch., 1956, Glendale Coll. Art Gallery, 1971, Brand Libr. Art Ctr., Glendale, 1974, Riverside (Calif.) Art Ctr. & Mus., 1978, Westwood (Calif.) Ctr. of the Arts, 1982, San Bernardino County Mus., Redlands, Calif., 1985, Burbank (Calif.) Creative Arts Ctr., 1986, Carnegie Art Mus., Oxnard, Calif., 1988, Glendale Coll., 1989, Senior Eye Gallery, Long Beach, Calif., 1990, 95; retrospective exhbn. Downey Mus. Art, Downey, Calif., 1991; exhibited in group shows in U.S., Japan, Korea, Germany, Israel; executed mural Glendale Coll., 1989. With U.S. Merchant Marine, 1943-46, PTO. Mem. Anti Defamation League, World Jewish Congress, Pasadena Soc. Artists (pres. 1962, 92, 93, hon. mem.), L.A. Printmaking Soc., Long Beach Arts, Fine Arts Fedn., Am. Legion, Am. Jewish War Vets. Democrat. Avocations: tennis, attending concerts and ballet performances. Home: 929 Olancha Dr Los Angeles CA 90065-4231

MONEIM, MOHEB S., orthopaedic surgeon, educator; b. Cairo, May 14, 1941; came to U.S., 1970; m. Brigitte Moneim; children: Omar, Sonya. MD, Cairo U., 1963. Diplomate Am. Bd. Orthop. Surgery; lic. physician, N.Mex., Tex. Orthop. resident Duke U. Med. Ctr., Durham, N.C., 1972-75, Greenville (S.C.) Shriners Hosp., 1974-75; hand fellow, instr. surgery Hosp. for Spl. Surgery, Cornell Med. Coll., N.Y.C., 1975-76; pvt. practice Albuquerque, 1976—; attending orthop. surgeon U. N.Mex. Med. Ctr., Albuquerque, 1976—, chief of staff, 1991-93; chief divsn. hand surgery dept. orthop. and rehab. U. N.Mex., Albuquerque, 1990—, prof. and chmn., 1991—. Contbr. articles to profl. jours., chpts. to books. Col., aide-de-camp Gov. gary Carruthers, Santa Fe, N.Mex., 1990; bd. trustees Univ. Hosp., Albuquerque, 1993-95. Fellow Royal Coll. Surgeons of Can.; mem. Am. Orthop. Assn., Am. Soc. for Surgery of the Hand (chmn. hand surgery fellowship com. 1992-94), Am. Acad. Orthop. Surgeons, Royal Coll. Physicians and Surgeons of Can., Alpha Omega Alpha. Office: Univ New Mex Health Sci Ctr Dept Orthop and Rehab 915 Camino de Salude NE Albuquerque NM 87131

MONGE, ROGER EDUARDO, writer; b. Esteli, Nicaragua, Aug. 20, 1932; s. Elias and Irene (Zelaya) M.; m. Rosa Adela Aguilar, Jul. 30, 1962 (div. 1984)a; children: Adela Irene, Maria Dolores, Roger. Law student, Univ. Nacional, Leon, Nicaragua, 1951-54; agronomist, Escuela de Agronomial, Managua, Nicaragua, 1954-57. Agricultural extension agt. Agriculture Min., Managua, 1957-60; agricultural banking National Bank, Managua, 1960-70; framing Boaco, Nicaragua, 1970-80; dairy producer Guatemala, 1980-83; logistics Nicaraguan Democratic Force, Danli, Honduras, 1983; adminstrv. control Demorcatic Revolutionary Alliance, San Jose, Costa Rica, 1984-88; security agt. Delta Enterprises, La Puenta, Calif., 1990-94; writer L.A., 1994—. Author: Quien Paga los Elotes, 1995, El Viaje, 1996, Acuantos Gringos Matestes Senor Don Pedron, 1998. Mem. Masonic Lodge. Republican. Roman Catholic. Avocations: reading, classical music, gastronomy, parapsychology, history research. Home: 666 N Vendome St Apt 7 Los Angeles CA 90026-3756

MONK, DIANA CHARLA, artist, stable owner; b. Visalia, Calif., Feb. 25, 1927; d. Charles Edward and Viola Genevieve (Shea) Williams; m. James Alfred Monk, Aug. 11, 1951; children: Kiloran, Sydney, Geoffrey, Anne, Eric. *Grandparents David and Ann Shea (nee Maher) emigrated from Ireland to Canada in the late 1800s. Settled in Idaho and ran a horse ranch in Sheaville. They were the primary suppliers of horses for Buffalo Bill's Traveling Horse Show. David and his brother Cornelius were the first to herd longhorn cattle from Texas to Idaho. Viola graduated Reed College in Oregon. She married Charles Williams a graduate of U.C. Davis. They had two children, Diana and Barbara (deceased). James Alfred Monk attended Sydney Sussex College at Cambridge University. Kiloran Margaret, born 1952, B.A. San Francisco State University; Sydney Charles, born 1954, B.A. Sonoma State University; James Geoffrey, born 1954, M.S. from U.C. Berkeley; Anne Patricia, born 1955, B.S. from U.C. Berkeley; Eric David, born 1960, owner of Asilomar Products and Eric Monk and Associates.* Student, U. Pacific, 1946-47, Sacramento Coll., 1947-48, Calif. Coll. Fine Arts, San Francisco, 1948-51, Calif. Coll. Arts & Crafts, Oakland, 1972. Art tchr. Mt. Diablo Sch. Dist., Concord, Calif., 1958-63; pvt. art tchr. Lafayette, Calif., 1963-70; gallery dir. Jason Aver Gallery, San Francisco, 1970-72; owner, mgr. Monk & Lee Assocs., Lafayette, 1973-80; stable owner, mgr. Longacre Tng. Stables, Santa Rosa, Calif., 1989—. One-person shows include John F. Kennedy U., Orinda, Calif., Civic Arts Gallery, Walnut Creek, Calif., Vallery Art Gallery, Walnut Creek, Sea Ranch Gallery, Gualala, Calif., Jason Aver Gallery, San Francisco; exhibited in group shows at Oakland (Calif.) Art Mus., Crocker Nat. Art Gallery, Sacramento, Le Salon des Nations, Paris. Chair bd. dirs. Walnut Creek (Calif.) Civic Arts, 1972-74, advisor to dir., 1968-72; exhibit chmn. Valley Art Gallery, Walnut Creek, 1977-78; juror Women's Art Show, Walnut Creek, 1970, Oakland Calif. Art. Home and Office: Longacre Tng Stables 1702 Willowside Rd Santa Rosa CA 95401-3922

MONSON, THOMAS SPENCER, church official, former publishing company executive; b. Salt Lake City, Aug. 21, 1927; s. George Spencer and Gladys (Condie) M.; m. Frances Beverly Johnson, Oct. 7, 1948; children—Thomas L., Ann Frances, Clark Spencer. BS with honors in mktg, U. Utah, 1948; MBA, Brigham Young U., 1974, LLD (hon.), 1981. With Deseret News Press, Salt Lake City, 1948-64; mgr. Deseret News Press, 1962-64; mem. Council Twelve Apostles, Ch. of Jesus Christ of Latter Day Saints, 1963-85, bishop, 1950-55; pres. Canadian Mission, 1959-62; chmn. bd. Deseret News Pub. Co., 1977-96; vice chmn. Deseret Mgmt. Corp.; pres. Printing Industry Utah, 1958; bd. dirs. Printing Industry Am., 1958-64; mem. Utah exec. bd. U.S. West Communications. Mem. Utah Bd. Regents; mem. nat. exec. bd. Boy Scouts Am.; trustee Brigham Young U. With USNR, 1945-46. Recipient Recognition award, 1964, Disting. Alumnus award U. Utah, 1966; Silver Beaver award Boy Scouts Am., 1971; Silver Buffalo award, 1978; Bronze Wolf award World Orgn. of the Scout Movement, 1993. Mem. Utah Assn. Sales Execs., U. Utah Alumni Assn. (dir.), Salt Lake Advt. Club, Alpha Kappa Psi. Club: Exchange (Salt Lake City). Office: LDS Ch 47 E South Temple Salt Lake City UT 84150-1005

MONTAG, DAVID MOSES, telecommunications company executive; b. Los Angeles, Apr. 30, 1939; s. Gustave and Esther (Kessler) M.; children: Daniel Gershon, Esther Yael, Michael Menachem. student UCLA, 1957-61. Tech. writer L.H. Butcher Co., Los Angeles, 1961; phys. sci. lab. technician East Los Angeles Coll., Monterey Park, 1961—, planetarium lectr., 1963-78; pres., dir. Or Chadash, Inc., Monterey Park, 1968—; owner EDUCOMP, Monterey Park, Calif., 1980—; cons. David M. Montag & Assocs., Monterey Park, 1993—; pres. Aquinas Computer Corp.; v.p. Wireless Optical Networks, San Diego, 1996—. ednl. cons. for computer-assisted instrn.; v.p., bd. dirs. Coll. Religious Conf., 1968-92. Mem. AIAA, Assn. of Orthodox Jewish Scientists, Laser Inst. Am., Internat. Soc. Tech. in Edn., Physics Instructional Resource Assn. Home and Office: PO Box 384 Monterey Park CA 91754-0384

MONTAGUE, SIDNEY JAMES, real estate developer; b. Denver, Oct. 3, 1950; s. Jerome Edward and Donna Sherrill (Nixon) M.; m. Mary Francis Terry, Dec. 26,1987; stepchildren: Jonathan Ramsey Shockley, Britt Elizabeth Shockley; children: Noah Reimer. BA in Econs., Midland Luth. Coll., Fremont, Nebr., 1972. Loan counselor Am. Nat. Bank, Denver, 1972-74; loan officer First Nat. Bank Denver, 1974-79; exec. v.p. Buell Devel. Corp., Denver, 1979-84; v.p. The Writer Corp., Denver, 1985-86; pres. Mondevco Inc., Littleton, Colo., 1986-87; devel. mgr. Perini Land & Devel. Co., Phoenix, 1987-91; v.p. Perini Land & Devel. Co., San Francisco, 1991-94; prin. Farrmont Realty Group, Inc., 1994-96; sr. v.p. Orsett Properties Ariz., 1996—. Republican. Avocations: sailing, scuba diving, flying, golf. Office: 1440 E Missouri #265 Phoenix AZ 85014

MONTE, WILLIAM DAVID, education educator; b. San Diego, Aug. 17, 1958; s. Thomas Gilbert Monte and Lisa Ruth Veale; m. Amy Lisa Schuenemann, Jan. 9, 1982; children: Sarah Nicole, William David. BS in Ministry, Bethany Coll., Santa Cruz, Calif., 1981; MA in Theology, Fuller Theol. Sem., Pasadena, Calif., 1987; MA in Edn., Claremont (Calif.) Grad. Sch., 1991, postgrad., 1992—. Cert. multiple subjects, Calif. Tchr. Mira Mesa Christian Sch., San Diego, 1982-83; tchr. ESL Armenean Social Svc. Ctr., L.A., 1988-89; substitute tchr. Baldwin Park (Calif.) Unified Sch. Dist., 1988-89; tchr. Upland (Calif.) Unified Sch. Dist., 1989-94; faculty assoc. office tchr. edn. Claremont Grad. Sch., 1994—; adj. faculty dept. edn. Whittier Coll., 1995—; founder, pres. ednl. cons. firm DIDASKEIN, San Dimas, Calif., 1986—. Contbr. articles to profl. jours. AB 1470 Tch. grantee State of Calif., 1990-91; Minority Student fellow Claremont Grad. Sch., 1992-93. Mem. Religious Edn. Assn., Computer Using Eductors, Assn. for Moral Edn., Assn. for Religion and Intellectual Life, Pi Lambda Theta,. Avocations: computers/multimedia, tennis, photography, creative writing, model building. Home: 538 Andover Ave San Dimas CA 91773-3201 Office: Claremont Grad Sch 121 E 10th St Claremont CA 91711-3911

MONTEAU, NORMAN KEITH, gemologist; b. Balt., Dec. 20, 1957; s. Milton Keith and Vieva Regina (Williams) M.; m. Sandra Lynn Staub, Dec. 7, 1987. Cert. diamond grading, Gemol. Inst., 1981, cert. colored stone grading, 1982, cert. gem identification, 1982. Numerous certs. fro Gemol. Inst. Am. Owner, founder Monteau Gemol. Svcs., Woodland Hills, Calif., 1987-91, pres., 1992—; owner, pres. Am. Internat. Gemologists, Beverly Hills, Calif., 1993—; mng. ptnr. The William Staub Co., L.A., 1994—; appraiser to Archdiocese of L.A., Cath. Ch., 1993—; arbitrator State Farm Ins. Co., 1993—, lectr. nat. retail jewelry stores, insurance cos. others on gemology and values, 1992—; advisor to ins. cos. in Calif. for earthquake property damage assessment, 1994, expert witness L.A. Mcpl. Ct., 1995; jewelry appraiser County of Los Angeles, 1996—; mem. Ptnrs. for Internat. Edn. and Tng./U.S. AID, 1996. Contbr. articles to profl. jours. Recipient Excellence award Aetna Ins. Co., 1992; honored guest of bd. govs. Gemol. Inst. Am., Carlsbad, Calif., 1996. Mem. Nat. Assn. Jewelry Appraisers, Am. Soc. Appraisers, Gemol. Inst. Am. (mem. Pres.'s Cir. 1992—), Calif. Jewelers Assn., Alumni Assn. Gemol. Inst. Am. (charter), Jewelers Bd. of Trade, Woodland Hills C. of C. Avocations: racquetball, mountain climbing, water skiing, jet car racing, white water rafting. Office: Monteau Gemol Svcs 21250 Califa St Ste 203 Woodland Hills CA 91367-5042

MONTERO, DARREL MARTIN, sociologist, social worker, educator; b. Sacramento, Mar. 4, 1946; s. Frank and Ann Naake; m. Tara Kathleen McLaughlin, July 6, 1975; children: David Paul, Lynn Elizabeth, Laura Ann, Emily Kathryn. AB, Calif. State U., 1970; MA, UCLA, 1972, PhD, 1974. Postgrad. researcher Japanese-Am. Research Project UCLA, 1971-73, dir. research, 1973-75; assoc. head Program on Comparative Ethnic Studies, Survey Research Ctr. UCLA, 1973-75; asst. prof. sociology Case Western Res. U., Cleve., 1975-76; asst. prof. urban studies, research sociologist Pub. Opinion Survey, dir. urban ethnic research program U. Md., College Park, 1976-79; assoc. prof. Ariz. State U., Tempe, 1979—; cons. rsch. sect. Viewer Sponsored TV Found., Los Angeles, Berrien E. Moore Law Office, Inc., Gardena, Calif., 1973, Bur. for Social Sci. Research, Inc., Washington, Friends of the Family, Ltd., Nat. Sci. Found. Author: Japanese Americans: Changing Patterns of Ethnic Affiliation Over Three Generations, 1980, Urban Studies, 1978, Vietnamese Americans: Patterns of Resettlement and Socioeconomic Adaptation in the United States, 1979, Social Problems, 1988; mem. editorial bd. Humanity and Society, 1978-80; contbr. articles to profl. jours. Served with U.S. Army, 1966-72. Mem. Am. Sociol. Assn., Am. Assn. Pub. Opinion Research (exec. council, standards com.), Am. Ednl. Research Assn., Council on Social Work Edn., Soc. Study of Social Problems, D.C. Sociol. Soc., Am. Soc. Pub. Adminstrn., Nat. Assn. Social Workers, Pacific Sociol. Assn. Office: Ariz State Univ Sch Social Work Tempe AZ 85281

MONTFORT, MATTHEW CHARLES, musician, music educator, writer; b. Denver, Feb. 12, 1958; s. Charles Dubois and Constance (Whitnell) M. MA in World Music, Antioch U., 1995. Leader, dir. Ancient Future, Kentfield, Ohio, 1978—; tchr. Blue Bear Sch. of Music, San Francisco, 1988—. Author: Ancient Traditions - Future Possibilities, 1985; wedmaster: http: www.ancient-future.com, 1995—. Named Colo. Outstanding Youth Guitarist, 1976; recipient Louis Armstrong Jazz award, H.S. Band Assn., 1976, Indie award Nat. Assn. Ind. Record Distrbrs., 1984, Number 4 Contemporary Inst. Release award Tower Pulse Mag., 1994. Office: Ancient Future PO Box 264 Kentfield CA 94914-0264

MONTGOMERY, ELIZABETH ANNE, English language educator; b. Santa Monica, Calif., Nov. 5, 1965; d. William Fairbairn and Janice Lynn (Winkler) M. BA in Lit., Claremont McKenna Coll., 1987, MA in Edn., 1995. Cert. tchr., Calif. Tchr. English Berlitz Internat., Beverly Hills, Calif., 1990; tchr. ESL Canoga Park (Calif.) H.S., 1990-91; tchr. English Inlingua Lang. Sch., Fribourg, Switzerland, 1991, Berlitz Internat., Berne, Switzerland, 1991; tchr. English-ESL Internat. Sch. Berne, 1991-92; writer Flintridge Cons., Pasadena, Calif., 1992-93; tchr. English Pomona (Calif.) H.S., 1993—; mem. Task Force on Proficiency Testing, Pomona, 1994-95. Watson fellow Thomas J. Watson Found., 1987-88. Mem. ASCD, NEA, Calif. Tchrs. Assn., Calif. Assn. for Bilingual Edn., Nat. Coun. Tchrs. English, Associated Pomona Tchrs. Home: # 184 1781 Appleton Way Pomona CA 91767-3519 Office: Pomona H S 475 Bangor St Pomona CA 91767-2443

MONTGOMERY, JAMES FISCHER, savings and loan association executive; b. Topeka, Nov. 30, 1934; s. James Maurice and Frieda Ellen (Fischer) M.; m. Diane Dealey; children: Michael James, Jeffrey Allen, Andrew Steven, John Gregory. BA in Acctg., UCLA, 1957. With Price, Waterhouse & Co., C.P.A.'s, Los Angeles, 1957-60; controller Conejo Valley Devel. Co., Thousand Oaks, Calif., 1960; asst. to pres. Gt. Western Fin. Corp., Beverly Hills, Calif., 1960-64; pres. United Financial Corp of Calif., Los Angeles, 1964-75; chmn., CEO Great Western Financial Corp., Chatsworth, Calif., 1975-96; now chmn. bd. dirs. Great Western Financial Corp., Chatsworth, Calif., 1996-97; chmn., CEO Frontier Bank, Park City, Utah, 1997—; fin. v.p., treas. United Fin. Corp., Los Angeles, 1964-69, exec. v.p., 1969-74, pres., 1975; pres. Citizens Savs. & Loan Assn., Los Angeles, 1970-75. Served with AUS, 1958-60. Office: Frontier Bank PO Box 981180 Park City UT 84098-1180*

MONTGOMERY, JANET K., newspaper editor; b. Carrington, N.D., Nov. 18, 1968; d. Guy E. and Kathleen K. (Klink) M.; m. Carl Jasper Eugene Warensoury, Aug. 16, 1997. BS, U. Wyo., 1994. Reporter Jackson Hole Guide, Jackson, Wyo.; reporter Pinedale (Wyo.) Roundup, editor. Playwright Close to Home, 1992. Writer Rendez Vous Com., Pinedale, 1998; instr. Fremont Yacht Club, Pinedale, 1998. Office: Pinedale Roundup PO Box 100 Pinedale WY 82941-0100

MONTGOMERY, NANCY VINCENT, English as a second Language educator; b. Beardstown, Ill., Apr. 24, 1946; d. James Earl and Thelma Margaret (Wardell) Vincent; m. James Thomas Montgomery, Dec. 16, 1967; children: Allison, Jeff. BS, So. Ill. U., 1968; MEd, U. N. Tex., 1986, E. Tex. State U., 1992. Cert. tchr. elem. edn., ESL, mid-mgmt. adminstrn. Tchr. Granite City (Ill.) Pub. Schs., 1968-74, Met. Christian Sch., Dallas, 1975-79, Jakarta (Indonesia) Internat. Sch., 1980-82, Dallas Ind. Sch. Dist., 1982—; project leader Dallas Ind. Sch. Dist., 1988, leadership devel. acad., 1990, alternative cert. mentor, 1991—, staff devel. assoc., 1993; adj. instr. Dallas C.C. Dist., 1991—; del. to Citizen to Citizen Amb. Program to Russia for Reading Edn. Author: (literacy program) Language Acquisition, 1990, Intergenerational Literacy, 1993. Pres. coun. So. Ill. U., Carbondale. Named Finalist, Perot Found. Excellence in Teaching, 1988, 91, Outstanding Tchr., Kiwanis Club, 1993; grantee Am. Airlines, 1990, Jr. Svc. League, 1993; named Tchr. of Yr., 1994-95. Mem. Internat. Reading Assn. (Dallas coun. bldg. rep.), ASCD, Nat. Staff Devel. Coun., Tex. Jr. Coll. Tchrs. Assn., Tex. Assn. Improvement of Reading, Tex. State Reading Assn. Avocations: world traveling, studying tribal cultures, reading, physical fitness. Home: 1999 Broadway Ste 4300 Denver CO 80202-5726

MONTGOMERY, ROBERT LOUIS, chemical engineer; b. San Francisco, Nov. 20, 1935; s. Louis Clyde and Fay Elythe (Myers) M.; m. Patricia Helen Cook, Mar. 17, 1962; children: Cynthia Elaine, Jeanette Louise, Cecelia Irene, Howard Edwin. BS in Chemistry, U. Calif., Berkeley, 1956; PhD in Phys. Chemistry, Okla. State U., 1975. Registered profl. engr., Kans., Tex., Colo. Phys. chemist U.S. Bur. Mines, Reno, 1956-62; NSF predoctoral fellow Okla. State U., Stillwater, 1963-66; sr. engr. Boeing Co., Wichita, Kans., 1966-75; postdoctoral fellow Rice U., Houston, 1975-77, sr. research assoc., 1982-84; tech. data engr. M.W. Kellogg Co., Houston, 1977-82; staff engr. Martin Marietta, Denver, 1984-94. Contbr. articles to profl. jours. Mem. Am. Chem. Soc., Am. Soc. for Metals, Profl. Engrs. Colo., Sigma Xi. Avocations: amateur radio, skiing. Home: 9933 Fairwood St Littleton CO 80125-8811

MONTGOMERY, ROBIN VERA, realtor; b. Boise, Idaho, July 21, 1928; d. Bruce Cameron and Grace Evangeline (Matthews) M.; m. Lewis Robert Goldberg, June 10, 1956 (div. June 1978); children: Timothy, Holly, Randall. BA in Journalism, U. Mich., 1957; BArch, U. Oreg., 1972. Architect Robin's Roost, Eugene & Florence, Oreg., 1972-82; realtor Exclusive Realtors, L.A., 1989—. Program chair Hadassah, Eugene, 1968; pres. Elec. Wires Underground, Eugene, 1967. With USN, 1949-53. Mem. Calif. Assn. Realtors, Theta Sigma Phi. Democrat. Avocations: hiking, films, writing, concerts. Home: 1334 S Carmelina Ave Apt 7 Los Angeles CA 90025-1919

MONTGOMERY, SETH DAVID, retired state supreme court chief justice; b. Santa Fe, Feb. 16, 1937; s. Andrew Kaye and Ruth (Champion) M.; m. Margaret Cook, Oct. 29, 1960; children: Andrew Seth, Charles Hope, David Lewis. AB, Princeton U., 1959; LLB, Stanford U., 1965. Bar: N.M. 1965. Ptnr. Montgomery & Andrews, P.A., Santa Fe, 1965-89, of counsel, 1994—; justice N.Mex. Supreme Ct., 1989-94, chief justice, 1994; adj. prof. law U. N.Mex. Sch. Law, Albuquerque, 1970-71; chmn. N.Mex. adv. coun. Legal Svcs. Corp., Santa Fe, 1976-89. Bd. visitors Stanford U. Sch. Law, 1967-70, 82-85, U. N.Mex. Sch. Law, 1982-89; pres., chmn. Santa Fe Opera, 1981-86; pres. Santa Fe Opera Found., 1986-89; chmn., vice chmn. Sch. Am. Rsch., Santa Fe, 1985-89; bd. dirs. New Vistas, Santa Fe, 1986-89, First Interstate Bank of Santa Fe, 1977-89, Old Cienega Village Mus., 1980-89. Lt. (j.g.) USN, 1959-62. Named Citizen of Yr., Santa Fe C. of C., 1986, Sunwest Bank of Santa Fe, 1994; recipient Disting. Cmty. Svc. award Anti-Defamation League, 1991, Western Area Outstanding Achievement award Nat. Multiple Sclerosis Soc., 1992, award for advancement of law N.Mex. Trial Lawyers, 1994, Award for Outstanding Judge Albuquerque Bar Assn., 1994. Fellow Am. Coll. Trial Lawyers, Am. Coll. Trust and Estate Counsel, Am. Bar Endowment, N.Mex. Bar Assn. (bd. bar commrs. 1986-89, sec., treas. 1988-89, Professionalism award 1993); mem. ABA, Am. Judicature Soc. Democrat.

MONTONE, KENNETH ALAN, art director, creative director, consultant; b. Chgo., Aug. 30, 1938; s. George Joseph and Beatrice Mabel (Calcott) M.; m. Patricia Joan Klapperich, Feb. 1, 1964; children: James Paul, Ian Andrew, Paul Matthew, Anne Elizabeth. BFA with honors, U. Ill., 1963. Graphic designer U. Ill. Press, Champaign, 1962-63; staff graphic designer ABC-TV, Chgo., 1963-65; art dir. McCann-Erickson, Inc., Sydney, Australia, 1965-67; staff graphic designer CBS-TV, Chgo., 1967-69; syndicated cartoonist, "Kiwi" Chgo. Tribune-N.Y. News Syndicate; art dir. McCann-Erickson, Inc., Portland, Oreg., 1969-80; creative dir. Morton Advt., Portland, 1980-84, Ken Montone & Assocs., Portland, 1984—. Art dir.: "Celebrate" series, 1980. With USN, 1956-59. Recipient Reata Howard Trombley award Portland Ad Fedn., 1983, Art Dirs. Club award N.Y. Ad, 1983, Best in West award Am. Advt. Fedn., 1983. Mem. Advt. Industry Emergency Fund (bd. dirs.), Portland Ad Fedn., Advt. Museum. Avocations: walking, drawing, traveling. Home and Office: Ken Montone & Assocs 165 NW 95th Ave Portland OR 97229-6303

MONTOYA, MICHAEL A., state treasurer, accountant; b. Albuquerque, May 4, 1952; s. Orlando (Reno) and Nancy (Maestas) M. BS, U. Colo., 1982. CPA, N.Mex. Tax mgr. Ernst and Young, Albuquerque, 1985-90; dep. state auditor State of N.Mex., Santa Fe, 1993-94, treas., 1995—. V.p., bd. dirs. Albuquerque Hispano C. of C., 1986-90; bd. dirs. Belen (N.Mex.) C. of C., 1986-90; bd. dirs. Healthnet of N.Mex., Albuquerque, 1987-90, Recreational Health Occupl. Ctr., Inc., Albuquerque, 1986-90. Mem. AICPAs, Assn. Hispanic CPAs. Democrat. Avocations: racquetball, hunting, fishing. Home: PO Box 414 Los Lunas NM 87031-0414 Office: NMex State Treasurer PO Box 608 Santa Fe NM 87504-0608*

MOODY, JOHN HENRY, minister; b. Seattle, Aug. 10, 1945; s. Henry Thornton Jr. and Ruby Fern (Johnson) M.; m. Melody Ann Hentiksen, Aug. 5, 1967; children: Eric John, Anna Marlene. BA in Psychology, Pacific Luth. U., 1967; MDiv, Luther Theol. Sem., 1971; D of Ministry, San Francisco Theol. Sem., 1977. Ordained to ministry Luth. Ch., 1972. Exec. dir. Tri-Cities Chaplaincy, Kennewick, Wash., 1971-86, Interfaith Ministries Hawaii, Honolulu, 1987—; exec. bd. Widowed Persons Wash., Seattle, 1973-78, Hospice Hawaii, Honolulu, 1988—; chmn. Pacific Region ACPE, L.A., 1991—; cons. Epsisc. Ministries & Alaska PAcific U., Salt Lake City, 1987-91, Alaska Pacific U., Anchorage, 1986-90. Contbr. articles to profl. jours. Chaplain Civil Air Patrol, Honolulu, 1989—. Fellow Coll. Chaplains (cert. chmn. Hawaii 1989—); mem. Assn. Mental Health Clergy, Assn. Clin. Pastoral Edn. (cert. supr. health clergy 1981). Avocations: hiking, golf, travel, jogging. Home: 1382 Kamahele St Apt A Kailua HI 96734-3345 Office: Interfaith Ministries 2229 N School St Ste 210 Honolulu HI 96819-2588

MOON, HAROLD WARREN, JR., professional football player; b. L.A., Nov. 18, 1956; m. Felicia Hendricks; children: Joshua, Jeffrey, Chelsea, Blair. Degree in comm., U. Wash., 1978. With Edmonton Eskimos, 1978-84, Houston Oilers, 1984-94, Minn. Vikings, 1994-97, Seattle Seahawks, 1997—. Named to Pro Bowl, 1988-93, Sporting News NFL All-Pro team, 1990. AFC Passing Leader, 1992; holds NFL single-season records for most passes attempted-665, 1991; most passes completed-404, 1991, sheares NFL single game record for most times sacked-12, 1985; shares NFL single season records for most games with 300 or more yards passing-9, 1990, most fumbles-18, 1990; Played in Grey Cup CFL Championship Game 1978-82. Address: Seattle Seahawks 11220 NE 53rd St Kirkland WA 98033-7505*

MOON, MATTHEW ELLIOTT, record company executive; b. Missoula, Mont., Oct. 15, 1967; s. Michael Elliott Moon and Chara Robin (Boehm) Tully; m. Virginia Anne Benson, May 2, 1998. GED, Seattle. Computer programmer Wash. State Human Rights Commn., Olympia, 1988-93; owner Kill Rock Stars, Olympia, 1991—. Poet, singer: (compact disc) Won't You Dance with this Man?, 1996; singer: (compact disc) Witchypoo, 1994. Avocations: music, poetry. Office: Kill Rock Stars # 418 120 State Ave NE # 418 Olympia WA 98501-1131

MOON, RONALD T. Y., state supreme court justice; b. Sept. 4, 1940; m. Stella H. Moon. B in Psychology and Sociology, Coe Coll., 1962; LLB, U. Iowa, 1965. Bailiff, law clk. to Chief Judge Martin Pence U.S. Dist. Ct., 1965-66; dep. prosecutor City and County of Honolulu, 1966-68; assoc. Libkuman, Ventura, Ayabe, Chong & Nishimoto (predecessor firm Libkuman, Ventura, Moon & Ayabe), Honolulu, 1968-72, ptnr., 1972-82; judge 9th div. 1st cir., Cir. Ct., State of Hawaii, Honolulu, 1982-90; assoc. justice Supreme Ct., State of Hawaii, Honolulu, 1990-93; chief justice Supreme Ct., State of Hawaii, 1993—; apptd. arbitration judge 1st cir. cir. ct.; adj. prof. law U. Hawaii, 1986, 87, 88; lectr., guest spkr. numerous events. Mem. ABA, Hawaii Bar Assn., Assn. Trial Lawyers Am., Am. Bd. Trial Advocates (pres. 1986-93, nat. sec. 1989-91), Am. Inns of Cts. IV

(bencher 1983—), Am. Judicature Soc., Hawaii Trial Judges' Assn. Office: Supreme Ct Hawaii 417 S King St Honolulu HI 96813-2902

MOON, SPENCER, author, program consultant, educator; b. Talladega, Ala., May 11, 1948; s. Glascoe McCann and Florence Edna (Moon) Jackson. Baccalaureate in Filmmaking, Antioch Coll., 1977; MA in Film and Video Production, Columbia Pacific U., 1989. Film editor Sta. KPIX-TV, San Francisco, 1977-79, stage mgr., technician, 1979-91; prof. African-Am. studies dept. City Coll., San Francisco, 1995—; cons. Black Filmmkaers Hall of Fame, Oakland, Calif., 1985-91, San Francisco Internat. Film Festival, 1986-90; artist in residence Calif. Arts Coun., San Bruno, 1986-89; program cons. KMTP-TV, 1991. Author: Reel Black Talk: A Sourcebook of 50 American Filmmakers, 1997; co-author: Blacks in Hollywood: Five Favorable Years, 1987-1991, 1992; producer, dir.: (film) Strivin' and Survivin', 1977, (videos) Interracialism: The National Denial, 1981, 5 Days In July, 1986, Art From Jail, 1989; contbr. articles to profl. jours. Mem. Film Arts Found., Assn. Ind. Video and Film, Bay Area Black Media Coalition (life, svc. award 1984, media award 1997), Internat. Alliance Theatrical Stage Employees (journeyman local 16). Home and Office: Realize Your Energy 766 1/2 Hayes St San Francisco CA 94102-4132

MOONEY, JEROME HENRI, lawyer; b. Salt Lake City, Aug. 7, 1944; s. Jerome Henri and Bonnie (Shepherd) M.; m. Carolyn Lasrich, Aug. 10, 1965 (div. Dec. 1978); 1 child, Dierdre Nicole; m. Kaitlyn Cardon, Sept. 23, 1995. BS, U. Utah, 1966, JD, 1972. Bar: Utah 1972, Calif. 1998, U.S. Ct. Appeals (10th cir.) 1974, U.S. Supreme 1984. Sole practice Salt Lake City, 1972-75, 79-83; sr. ptnr. Mooney, Jorgenson & Nakamura, Salt Lake City, 1975-78, Mooney & Smith, Salt Lake City, 1983-87, Mooney & Assoc., Salt Lake City, 1987-94, Mooney Law Firm, Salt Lake City, 1995—; bd. dirs. Mooney Real Estate, Salt Lake City. Mem. Gov.'s Coun. on Vet. Affiars, Salt Lake City, 1982-89; trustee Project Realty, Salt Lake City, 1976—, P.E.A.C.E.; FDA sponsor Project Reality, 1994—; vice chair State Mil. Acad. Assoc., 1992-93. Mem. ABA (criminal justice sect. U.S. Sentencing Commn. com.), Utah Bar Assn. (chmn. criminal bar sect. 1987-88), Utah NG Assn. (trustee 1976), 1st Amendment Lawyers Assn. (v.p. 1986-88, pres. 1988-89), Nat. Assn. Criminal Def. Lawyers, Families Against Mandatory Minimums (adv. coun.), VFW. Democrat. Jewish. Avocations: sailng, computers. Home: 128 I St Salt Lake City UT 84103-3418 Office: Larsen & Mooney Law 50 W Broadway Ste 100 Salt Lake City UT 84101-2020*

MOONEY, ROSLYN PAULA, computer company executive; b. Chgo., June 5, 1963; d. Morton Irving and Lorraine Ruth (Borman) Wax; m. James Finbarr Mooney, Sept. 7, 1996. BBA in Mktg., U. Iowa, 1985. Distbn. mgr. Merisel, Moonachie, N.J., 1989-90; dist. mgr. Merisel, Wood Dale, Ill., 1990-91; maj. account exec. Merisel, El Segundo, Calif., 1991-92, dir. consumer products, 1992-93, dir. maj. accounts, 1993-94, dir. sales ops., 1994-96, v.p. strategic ops., 1996-98; v.p. comml. channel Merisel, 1999—. Avocations: golf, running, skiing, traveling. Home: 1902A Pullman Ln Redondo Beach CA 90278-4813 Office: Merisel 200 Continental Blvd El Segundo CA 90245-4510

MOORE, BRUCE, executive. Pres., CEO Quspex Mgmt., Santa Clara. Office: 2300 Central Expy Santa Clara CA 95050-2516*

MOORE, C. BRADLEY, chemistry educator; b. Boston, Dec. 7, 1939; s. Charles Walden and Dorothy (Lutz) M.; m. Penelope Williamson Percival, Aug. 27, 1960; children: Megan Bradley, Scott Woodward. BA magna cum laude, Harvard U., 1960; PhD, U. Calif., Berkeley, 1963. Predoctoral fellow NSF, 1960-63; asst. prof. chemistry U. Calif., Berkeley, 1963-68, assoc. prof., 1968-72, prof., 1972—, vice chmn. dept., 1971-75, chmn. dept. chemistry, 1982-86, dean Coll. Chemistry, 1988-94; professeur associé Faculté des Scis., Paris, 1970, 75; Miller Rsch. Prof. U. Calif., Berkeley, 1972-73, 87-88; vis. prof. Inst. for Molecular Sci., Okazaki, Japan, 1979, Fudan U., Shanghai, 1979, adv. prof., 1988—; vis. fellow Joint Inst. for Lab. Astrophysics, U. Colo., Boulder, 1981-82; faculty sr. scientist, dir. (Chemical Sci. Div.) Lawrence Berkeley Nat. Lab., 1974—, divsn. dir., 1998—: mem. editl. bd. Jour. Chem. Physics, 1973-75, Chem. Physics Letters, 1980-85, Jour. Phys. Chemistry, 1981-87, Laser Chemistry, 1982—. Editor: Chemical and Biochemical Applications of Lasers; assoc. editor Annual Review of Physical Chemistry, 1985-90; contbr. articles to profl. jours. Trustee Sci. Svc., 1995—. Recipient Coblentz award, 1973, E.O. Lawrence Meml. award U.S. Dept. Energy, 1986, Lippincott award, 1987, 1st award Inter-Am. Photochem. Soc., 1988; nat. scholar Harvard U., 1958-60; fellow Alfred P. Sloan Found., 1968, Guggenheim Found., 1969, Humboldt Rsch. award for Sr. U.S. Scientists, 1994. Fellow AAAS, Am. Acad. Arts and Scis., Am. Phys. Soc. (Plyler award 1994); mem. NSF adv. com. for education and human resources directorate, chair subcom. policy and planning 1997—, NAS (chmn. com. undergrad. sci. edn. 1993-97), Am. Chem. Soc. (past chmn. divsn. phys. chemistry, Calif. sect. award 1977). Avocation: cycling. Home: 936 Oxford St Berkeley CA 94707-2435 Office: U Calif Dept Chemistry 211 Lewis Hall Berkeley CA 94720-1460

MOORE, CARLETON BRYANT, geochemistry educator; b. N.Y.C., Sept. 1, 1932; s. Eldridge Carleton and Mabel Florence (Drake) M.; m. Jane Elizabeth Strouse, July 25, 1959; children—Barbara Jeanne, Robert Carleton. BS, Alfred U., 1954, DSc (hon.), 1977; PhD, Cal. Inst. Tech., 1960. Asst. prof. geology Wesleyan U., Middletown, Conn., 1959-61; mem. faculty Ariz. State U., Tempe, 1961—; nat. rsch. coun. rsch. assoc. NASA Ames Rsch. Ctr., 1974; prof., dir. Ctr. for Meteorite Studies Ariz. State U., Regents' prof., 1988—; vis. prof. Stanford U., 1974; Prin. investigator Apollo 11-17; preliminary exam. team Lunar Receiving Lab., Apollo, 12-17. Author: Cosmic Debris, 1969, Meteorites, 1971, Principles of Geochemistry, 1982, Grundzügeder Geochemie, 1985; editor: Researches on Meteorites, 1961, Jour. Meteoritical Soc.; contbr. articles to profl. jours. Fellow Am. Geophys. Union, Ariz.-Nev. Acad. Sci. (pres. 1979-80), Meteoritical Soc. (life hon., pres. 1966-68), Geol. Soc. Am., Mineral. Soc. Am., AAAS (council 1967-70); mem. Geochem. Soc., Am. Chem. Soc., Am. Ceramic Soc., Sigma Xi. Home: 507 E Del Rio Dr Tempe AZ 85282-3764 Office: Ariz State U Ctr for Meteorite Studies Tempe AZ 85287-2504

MOORE, CHARLES AUGUST, JR., psychologist; b. Medford, Oreg., Feb. 22, 1944; s. Charles August and Bernadine (Newlun) M. BS, Lewis and Clark Coll., 1965; MA, U. Colo., 1967, PhD, 1972. Lic. psychologist, Calif., Oreg. Teaching asst. U. Colo., Boulder, 1965-66, 70-71, rsch. asst., counselor, practicum supr., 1966-67, 71-72; asst. psychologist State Home and Tng. Sch., Grand Junction, Colo., 1967; intern in psychology Camarillo (Calif.) State Hosp., 1968-69; psychology assoc., program psychologist Camarillo Drug Abuse Program (The Family), 1969-70; intern in psychology Oxnard (Calif.) Mental Health Ctr., 1969; clin. psychologist, dir. intern tng. Rural Clinics, Reno, 1972; clin. psychologist Kern County Mental Health Svcs., Bakersfield, Calif., 1972-74; clin., cons. psychologist San Diego County Mental Health Svcs., 1974-88; pvt. practice La Jolla (Calif.) Clinic, 1976-78; August Ctr., Chula Vista, Calif., 1978-85; staff psychologist Dept. Vet.'s Affairs Domiciliary, White City, Oreg., 1988—; guest lectr. Calif. State Coll., Bakersfield, 1973-74; mem. Health Systems Agy. Mental Health Task Force, 1979; mem. doctoral dissertation com. U.S. Internat. U., 1975-76; mem. mental health task force San Diego County Bd. Suprs., 1979. Contbr. articles to profl. jours. Mem. Univ. City Community Coun., San Diego, 1976-78; bd. dirs. Pub. Employees Assn., 1976-77. Recipient Experiment in Internat. Living European Study award Lewis and Clark Coll., 1962; USPHS fellow, 1967-68; U. Colo. Grad. Sch. Rsch. grantee, 1971; recipient Hands and Heart award Dept. Vets. Affairs, 1989-90, Domiciliary Spl. Contbn. and Outstanding Performance awards, 1990, 91. Mem. APA, Am. Psychology and Law Soc., Calif. Psychol. Assn., Western Psychol. Assn., San Diego County Psychol. Assn., Assn. County Clin. Psychologists San Diego, San Diego Psychology and Law Soc., San Diego Soc. Clin. Psychologists. Office: Dept VA Domiciliary Psychology Svc 8495 Crater Lake Hwy White City OR 97503-3011

MOORE, CHRISTOPHER MINOR, lawyer; b. L.A., Oct. 12, 1938; s. Prentiss Elder and Josephine (French) M.; m. Gillian Reed, Sept. 29, 1965; children: Stephanie Kja Conn, Carrie Christine McKay. AB, Stanford U., 1961; JD, Harvard U., 1964. Dep. county counsel Los Angeles County Counsel, 1965-66; ptnr. Moore & Lindelof, L.A., 1966-69, Burkley & Moore, Torrance, Calif., 1969-74; pvt. practice Law Offices of Christopher Moore, Torrance, 1974-81; ptnr. Burkley, Moore, Greenberg & Lyman, Torrance, 1981-90; prin. Christopher M. Moore & Assoc., Torrance, 1990—. Mem. bd. edn. Palos Verdes (Calif.) Peninsula Unified Sch. Dist., 1972-77. Fellow Am. Coll. Trust and Estate Counsel, Am. Acad. Matrimonial Lawyers; mem. L.A. Yacht Club. Avocations: sailing, golf. Office: Christopher Moore & Assoc 21515 Hawthorne Blvd Ste 490 Torrance CA 90503-6525

MOORE, DAN STERLING, insurance executive, sales trainer; b. Lincoln, Nebr., June 27, 1956; s. Jack Leroy and Carolyn Marie (Bachman) M.; m. Marla Janine Collister, June 2, 1979; children: Tyler David, Anna Rose. Student, Red Rocks Coll., 1977. Lic. ins. exec. Asst. mgr. European Health Spa, Englewood, Colo., 1975-78; sales mgr. Colo. Nat. Homes, Westminster, 1979-80; sales assoc. Dale Carnegie, Denver, 1981; sales mgr. Paramount Fabrics, Denver, 1981-84; sales assoc. Mighty Distbg., Arvada, Colo., 1984-87; divsn. mgr. Nat. Assn. for Self Employed/United Group Assn., Englewood, Colo., 1987—; divsn. mgr. Communicating for Agr. Assn., 1993-98, Am. Bus. Coalition, 1997—, Am. for Financial Security, 1999—. Leader, trainer Alpine Rescue Team, Evergreen, Colo., 1971-74; minister Jehovah's Witnesses, 1972—. Avocations: golf, skiing, backpacking, scuba diving, tennis. Home: 892 Nob Hill Trl Franktown CO 80116-7917 Office: Nat Assn Self Employed/United Group 10579 W Bradford Rd Ste 100 Littleton CO 80127-4247

MOORE, DANIEL ALTON, JR., retired state supreme court justice; b. 1933. BBA, U. Notre Dame, 1955; JD, U. Denver, 1961. Dist. ct. magistrate judge Alaska, 1961-62; pvt. practice law, 1962-80; judge 3d Jud. Dist. Superior Ct., 1980-83; justice Alaska Supreme Ct., Anchorage, 1983-92, chief justice, 1992-95; ret., 1995; mediator for J.A.M.S./Endispute, 1996—.

MOORE, DONALD WALTER, academic administrator, school librarian; b. Culver City, Calif., June 9, 1942; s. Raymond Owen and Jewel Elizabeth (Young) M.; m. Dagmar Ulbrich, Mar. 28, 1968; 1 child, Michael. AA, L.A. Valley Coll., 1967; BA in History, Calif. State U., Northridge, 1970; MA in Learning Disability, Calif. State U., 1973; MLS, U. So. Calif., 1974. Part time librarian L.A. Pierce Coll., Woodland Hills, Calif., 1974—; instr. vocat. edn. act program L.A. Trade Tech. Coll., 1978-80, pres.'s staff asst., 1983-87; instr. learning skills L.A. City Coll., 1987-88, dir. amnesty edn., 1988-92, dir. Citizenship Ctr., 1992—; adj. instr. computer sci. L.A. Trade-Tech. Coll., 1983—, Coll. of the Canyons, Valencia, Calif., 1996—. Author: Cavalrymen, 1983; contbr. fiction, articles, revs. to various publs. Mem. Ednl. Writers Am., Co. Mil. Historians, Edpress, Little Big Horn Assn. Republican. Roman Catholic. Avocations: writing, collecting U.S. frontier military memorabilia, computing. Office: LA City Coll Citizenship Program 855 N Vermont Ave Los Angeles CA 90029-3516

MOORE, ELIZABETH JANE, banker; b. Long Branch, N.J., Dec. 14, 1940; d. Robert William and Ruth Elizabeth (Dunphy) Marton; m. Gerard George Moore, Mar. 3, 1962; children: Christine Marie, Stephanie Ann, Gerard Marton, Paul Henry George, Barbara Jean. BBA, U. Phoenix, 1987. Charge card specialist Valley Nat. Bank, Phoenix, 1971-74, corp. trust specialist, 1974-80; trust specialist Valley Nat. Bank, Prescott, Ariz., 1980-86, trust adminstr., sr. client svcs. officer, 1986-89; asst. v.p. Advantage Trust, Prescott, Ariz., 1989-93; v.p. Bank One Ariz., Phoenix, 1993-96, relationship mgr., 1998—. Pres., bd. dirs. Prescott Fine Arts Assn., 1998-99; bd. dirs. Ctrl. Yavapai County (Ariz.) Fire Dist., 1988-89, clk., 1989—, chair bd. dirs., 1990-91; bd. dirs. Yavapai Humane Soc., 1989-91, 97—, 1st v.p., treas., 1990-91; chair bd. dirs. Vol. Firefighters Relief and Pension Fund, 1989-91; chair bd. dirs. Ctrl. Yavapai Pub. Safety Pers., 1991; ops. mgr., dir. Trinity Luth. Ch. Christian Preschool and Childcare Ctr., 1997-98; mem. Phoenix Pub. Libr. Recipient 1st Place Photo Contest award Parade mag., 1992. Mem. Yavapai County Legal Secs. Assn. (treas. 1983-85, gov. 1985-86, Legal Sec. of Yr. 1984), U. Phoenix Network for Profl. Devel. (chartered), Friday Club. Avocations: bear collecting, crafts, exercise. Home: 3002 Pleasant Valley Ct Prescott AZ 86305-4150 Office: 302 W Gurley St Prescott AZ 86301

MOORE, EVERETT LEROY, library administrator; b. Eugene, Oreg., May 24, 1918; s. Clinton L. Moore and Elsie LaVerne (Crowder) Morgan; m. Fern Irene Owen, July 13, 1942; children: David LeRoy, Richard Eugene, Patricia Elaine. BA, Wheaton Coll., 1949; MA, Pasadena Coll., 1954; MA in Libr. Sci., Vanderbilt U., 1960; PhD, U. So. Calif., 1973. Cert. C.C. chief adminstrv. officer, Calif. Libr. Evangel Coll., Springfield, Mo., 1955-57; head tech. svcs. North Coastal Regional Libr., Tillamook, Oreg., 1957-60; head social sci. and bus. libr. Calif. State U., Chico, 1960-62; dir. libr. svcs. Coll. of the Desert, Palm Desert, Calif., 1962-75; dir. univ. libr. Am. U. Cairo, 1970-72; dir. libr. svcs. Woodbury U., L.A., 1976-87, dir. libr. svcs., prof. emeritus, 1987—; pres. so. region Jr. Coll. Round Table, Calif. Libr. Assn., Sacramento, 1965-66; chair tech. svcs. com. Calif. C.C. Libr. Coop., 1968-70, chmn. Desert area, 1974-75. Contbr. to profl. jours. Avocations: reading, computers, politics. Home: 1322 E Avenue Q12 Palmdale CA 93550-5168

MOORE, GORDON E., electronics company executive; b. San Francisco, Calif., Jan. 3, 1929; s. Walter Harold and Florence Almira (Williamson) M.; m. Betty I. Whittaker, Sept. 9, 1950; children: Kenneth, Steven. BS in Chemistry, U. Calif., 1950; PhD in Chemistry and Physics, Calif. Inst. Tech., 1954. Mem. tech. staff Shockley Semicondr. Lab., 1956-57; mgr. engring. Fairchild Camera & Instrument Corp., 1957-59, dir. research and devel., 1959-68; exec. v.p. Intel Corp., Santa Clara, Calif., 1968-75; pres., chief exec. officer Intel Corp., 1975-79, chmn., chief exec. officer, 1979-87, chmn., 1987-95, chmn. emeritus, 1995—; bd. dirs. Varian Assocs. Inc., Transamerica Corp. Fellow IEEE (Founders medal 1997); mem. Nat. Acad. Engring., Am. Phys. Soc. Office: Intel Corp 2200 Mission College Blvd Santa Clara CA 95052*

MOORE, JAMES C., museum director. Dir. Albuquerque Mus. Office: Albuquerque Mus 2000 Mountain Rd NW Albuquerque NM 87104*

MOORE, JAMES R., lawyer; b. Longview, Wash., Sept. 14, 1944; s. James Carlton and Virginia (Rice) M.; m. Patricia Riley, Aug. 25, 1967 (div. 1978); 1 child, Katherine M.; m. Christine M. Monkman, July 14, 1979 (div. 1996); stepchildren: Amy McKenna, John McKenna; 1 foster child, Zia Sunseri; m. Kathryn Lindquist, Aug. 26, 1996; stepchildren: Matthew Elggren, Adam Elggren, Erin Elggren, David Heilner. BA, Whitman Coll., 1966; JD, Duke U., 1969. Bar: Wash. 1970, U.S. Ct. Appeals (4th cir.) 1972, U.S. Supreme Ct. 1973, U.S. Ct. Appeals (9th cir.) 1974, D.C., 1995. Law clk. to Hon. J. Barnes U.S. Ct. Appeals (9th cir.), L.A., 1969-70; trial atty. pollution control, land/natural resources div. U.S. Dept. Justice, Washington, 1970-74; asst. U.S. atty. U.S. Atty.'s Office, Seattle, 1974-82; regional counsel U.S. EPA Region 10, Seattle, 1982-87; counsel Perkins Coie, Seattle, 1987-88, ptnr., 1989-98; of counsel Perkins Coie, 1999—; trainer, speaker on environ. litigation, negotiation and law; sr. environ. counsel Huntmen Chem. Co., 1999—. Contbr. articles to profl. jours. Bd. dirs. Environ. Law Inst., 1995—; chair audit com. Whitman Coll., 1994—. Mem. ABA (sect. natural resources 1987—), Wash. State Bar Assn. (environ. and land use sect. 1974—, spl. dist. coun. 1988-95). Democrat. Office: Huntsmen Chem Co 500 Huntsmen Way Salt Lake City UT 84108 also: 607 14th St NW Washington DC 20005-2000

MOORE, JOE GILBERT, manufacturing company executive; b. Kansas City, Mo., Sept. 7, 1939; s. Gilbert and Margaret (Seibel) M.; m. Audrey Marie Jasmen, 1970; children: Steven, Allen. AA, Mt. San Antonio Jr. Coll., Walnut, Calif., 1961. Owner Hardbacker, Lake Havasu City, Ariz., 1996—; owner Book Exch., Montclair, Calif, 1970-96. Served with U.S. Army, 1962-65.

MOORE, JOHN D., management consultant; b. Mt. Pleasant, Iowa, Apr. 7, 1937; s. Burris P. and Esther I. (Copenhaver) M.; m. Karen K. Kriegel, June 19, 1957; children: Charles A., Michael J., Susan K., David J. AB, Muscatine Community Coll., 1961; BBA, Augustana Coll., 1966; postgrad. U. Iowa, 1966-68. Office mgr. Stanley Engring., Muscatine, Iowa, 1966-64; pers. mgr. Oscar Mayer & Co., Davenport and Perry, Iowa, 1964-68; Midwest regional mgr. A. S. Hansen, Lake Bluff, Ill., 1968-73; legal adminstr. Gardner, Carton & Douglas, Chgo., 1973-78, Heller Ehrman White & McAuliffe, San Francisco, 1978-84; v.p. and dir. Hildebrandt, Inc., Walnut Creek, Calif., 1984-90; pres. Moore Cons. Inc., 1990—. Pres., Libertyville (Ill.) High Sch. Bd., 1974, Libertyville Ecumenical Council, 1975; bd. dirs. Libertyville YMCA, 1969-71. Recipient Muscatine Disting. Service award, 1963; named Outstanding State V.P., Iowa Jaycees, 1964; Outstanding Nat. Dir., U.S. Jaycees, 1965. Mem. Assn. of Legal Adminstrs. (regional v.p. 1977-78, nat. v.p. 1979-81, nat. pres. 1982-83), Found. Assn. of Legal Adminstrs. (pres. 1986-88), Golden Gate Assn. Legal Adminstrs. Republican. Methodist. Home and Office: 2632 Quiet Place Dr Walnut Creek CA 94598-4440

MOORE, JUSTIN EDWARD, data processing executive; b. West Hartford, Conn., June 17, 1952; s. Walter Joseph and Victoria Mary (Calcagni) M. BS in Mgmt. Sci., Fla. Inst. Tech., 1974. Systems assoc. Travelers Ins., Hartford, Conn., 1974-77; data processing programmer R.J. Reynolds Inc., Winston-Salem, N.C., 1977-78; programmer/analyst Sea-Land Svc., Elizabeth, N.J., 1978-79; mgr. market analysis Sea-Land Svc., Oakland, Calif., 1979-82; asst. v.p., dir. application systems Fox Capital Mgmt. Corp., Foster City, Calif., 1982-86; mgr. bus. svcs. dept mktg. and pricing Am. Pres. Cos., Ltd., Oakland, 1987-88, dir. mktg. and pricing systems, 1988-89; dir. systems devel. The Office Club, Concord, Calif., 1989-91; dir. MIS Revo, Inc., Mountain View, Calif., 1992-93; account mgr. Imrex Computer Systems, Inc., South San Francisco, 1993-94; project mgr. Exigent Computer Group, Inc., San Ramon, Calif., 1994—. Democrat. Roman Catholic. Avocations: golf, personal computing, investment mgmt. Home: 5214 Jomar Dr Concord CA 94521-2343 Office: Exigent Computer Group Inc 4000 Executive Pky San Ramon CA 94583-4257

MOORE, LAURIE ALISON, expressive arts therapist, hypnotherapist; b. Berkeley, Calif., July 27, 1962; d. Ralph Joseph Jr. and Coralie Zella (Berman) M. AA, Bard Coll., 1982; BA, U. Calif., Santa Cruz, 1991; MA, Lesley Coll., 1996; PhD, Summit U., 1999. Cert. hypnotherapist Twin Lakes Coll. Healing Arts; lic. marriage, family and child counselor. Marriage, family and child counselor intern Calif.; performace art dir. Gardens of Muscular Earth, Santa Cruz, Calif., 1988-94; hypnotherapist Transformations, Santa Cruz, Calif., 1990—; therapist intern Lipton Day Treatment, Leominsler, Mass., 1994-95, U. Vt., Burlington, 1995-96; teen theatre dir. Middlebury (Vt.) Counseling Ctr., 1995-96; instr. Calif. State U., Chico, 1996—, San Francisco State U., 1996—, U. Vt., 1996—, Johnson (Vt.) State U., 1996—, Santa Clara (Calif.) State U., 1996—; expressive arts therapist Elysium Wellness Ctr., Aptos, Calif., 1996-98; workshop facilitator, 1978—; cons., 1982—. Performer variety of cafes, benefits, plays and radio shows, 1989-96; musician (tape) Tough Skins and Sweet Fruit, 1991; author Dear Dr. Laurie column, 1998—; contbr. articles, stories, and poetry to newspapers and profl. jours. Vol. Theatre for Teen Learning, Fredrick Tutle Mid. Sch., Burlington, 1995-96; sch. performing arts resource tchr., 1997-98. Jewish. Avocations: yoga, dance, music, art, meditation. Office: Linden Plz Ste 309 20 S Santa Cruz Ave Los Gatos CA 95030

MOORE, MARY FRENCH (MUFFY MOORE), potter, community activist; b. N.Y.C., Feb. 25, 1938; d. John and Rhoda (Teagle) Walker French; m. Alan Baird Minier, Oct. 9, 1982; children: Jonathan Corbet, Jennifer Corbet, Michael Corbet. BA cum laude, Colo. U., 1964. Ceramics mfr., Wilson, Wyo., 1969-82, Cheyenne, Wyo., 1982—; commr. County of Teton (Wyo.), 1976-83, chmn. bd. commrs., 1981, 83, mem. dept. pub. assistance and social svc., 1976-82, mem. recreation bd., 1978-81, water quality adv. bd., 1976-82. Bd. dirs. Teton Sci. Sch., 1968-83, vice chmn., 1979-81, chmn., 1982; bd. dirs. Grand Teton Music Festival, 1963-68, Teton Energy Coun., 1978-83, Whitney Gallery of Western Art, Cody, Wyo., 1995—, Opera Colo., 1998—; mem. water quality adv. bd. Wyo. Dept. Environ. Quality, 1979-83; Dem. precinct committeewoman, 1978-81; mem. Wyo. Dem. Cen. Com., 1981-83; vice chmn. Laramie County Dem. Cen. Com., 1983-84, Wyo. Dem. nat. committeewoman, 1984-87; chmn. Wyo. Dem. Party, 1987-89; del. Dem. Nat. Conv., 1984, 88, mem. fairness commn. Dem. Nat. Com., 1985, vice-chairwoman western caucus, 1986-89; chmn. platform com. Wyo. Dem. Conv., 1982; mem. Wyo. Dept. Environ. Quality Land Quality Adv. Bd., 1983-86; mem. Gov.'s Steering Com. on Troubled Youth, 1982, dem. nat. com. Compliance Assistance Commn., 1986-87; exec. com. Assn. of State Dem. Chairs, 1989; mem. Wyo. Coun. on the Arts, 1989-95, chmn., 1994-95, Dem. Nat. Com. Jud. Coun., 1989—; legis. aide for Gov. Wyo., 1985, 86; project coord. Gov.'s Com. on Childrens' Svcs., 1985-86; bd. dirs. Wyo. Outdoor Coun., 1984-85; polit. dir., dep. mgr. Schuster for Congress, 1994-95. Recipient Woman of Yr. award Jackson Hole Bus. and Profl. Women, 1981, Dem. of Yr. Nellie Tayloe Ross award, Wyo. Dems., 1990. Mem. Alden Kindred of Am., Jackson Hole Art Assn. (bd. dirs., vice chmn. 1981, chmn. 1982), Assn. State Dem. Chairs, Soc. Mayflower Descendents, Pi Sigma Alpha. Home: 8907 Cowpoke Rd Cheyenne WY 82009-1234

MOORE, MATTHEW EMERSON, environmental program planning management specialist; b. Tuscaloosa, Ala., Aug. 5, 1964; s. Charles Thomas Moore Sr. and Annabel (Owens) Moore Allen; m. Anne Goldthwaite Dorr, March 20, 1993. BS, No. Ariz. U., 1987; MA, Claremont Grad. Sch., 1989. Mem. policy clinic team Ctr. for Politics and Policy, Claremont (Calif.) Grad. Sch., 1987-89; rsch. asst. Rose Inst. State and Local Govt., Claremont, 1989; analyst, asst. planner LSA Assocs., Inc., Irvine, Calif., 1989-90; project mgr. Urban Vision, Irvine, 1991-93; regional water quality mgmt. planning coord. Ariz. Dept. Environ. Quality, Phoenix, 1994; sr. air quality analyst Idaho Divsn. Environ. Quality, Boise, 1994-98; sr. transp. planner Idaho Transp. Dept., 1998—; mem. Sch. Renewable Natural Resources master's thesis com. U. Ariz., Tucson, 1994. Author: Lead Agency CEQA Procedures Survey Results, 1991; co-author: Taxes, Trees and Transit; California's Response to CO2-Induced Climate Change, 1990, Curbing Air Pollution in the South Coast Air Basin, 1989; editor-at-large: Multiple Resource Mgmt. Plan for El Cipres, Ensenada, Mex., 1994. Founding pres. Explorer Post 477, Boy Scouts Am., Tempe, Ariz., 1980-82; interpretive specialist Walnut Canyon Nat. Monument, Flagstaff, Ariz., 1987; mem. drought planning adv. bd. City of Claremont, 1988-89; mem. leadership coun. First United Meth. Ch., Boise. Mem. Am. Planning Assn., Am. Polit. Sci. Assn., Nat. Assn. Environ. Profls., Internat. Assn. Impact Assessment. Methodist. Avocations: sailing, surfing, reading, hiking, biking.

MOORE, OMAR KHAYYAM, experimental sociologist; b. Helper, Utah, Feb. 11, 1920; s. John Gustav and Mary Jo (Crowley) M.; m. Ruth Garnand, Nov. 19, 1942; 1 child, Venn. BA, Doane Coll., 1942; MA, Washington U., St. Louis, 1946, PhD, 1949. Instr. Washington U., St. Louis, 1949-52; teaching assoc. Northwestern U., Evanston, Ill., 1950-51; rsch. asst., prof. sociology Tufts Coll., Medford, Mass., 1952-53; researcher Naval Rsch. Lab., Washington, 1953-54; asst. prof. sociology Yale U., New Haven, 1954-57, assoc. prof. sociology, 1957-63; prof. psychology Rutgers U., New Brunswick, N.J., 1963-65; prof. social psychology, sociology U. Pitts., 1965-71, prof. sociology, 1971-89, prof. emeritus, 1989—; scholar-in-residence Nat. Learning Ctr.'s Capital Children's Mus., Washington, 1989-90; pres. Responsive Environ. Found., Inc., Estes Park, Colo., 1962—; assessor of rsch. projects The Social Scis. and Humanities Rsch. Coun. Can., 1982—; adj. prof. U. Colo., Boulder, 1992—. Contbg. editor Educational Technology; contbr. numerous articles to profl. jours.; patentee in field; motion picture producer and director. Recipient Award The Nat. Soc. for Programmed Instruction, 1965, Award Doane Coll Builder Award, 1967, Ednl. Award Urban Youth Action, Inc., 1969, Award House of Culture, 1975, Cert. of Appreciation, 1986, Cert. of Appreciation D.C. Pub. Schs., 1987, da Vinci Award Inst. for the Achievement of Human Potential, 1988, Cert. of Appreciation Capital Children's Museum, 1988, award Jack & Jill of America Found., 1988, Cert. of Appreciation U.S. Dept. of Edn., 1988, Cert. of Appreciation D.C. Pub. Schs., 1990, Person of Yr. in Ednl. Tech. award Ednl. Tech. mag., 1990. Mem. AAAS, Am. Math. Soc., Am. Psychol. Assn., Internat. Sociol. Assn., Am. Sociol. Assn., Assn. for Symbolic Logic, Assn. for Anthrop. Study of Play, Philosophy Sci. Assn., Psychonomics Soc., Soc. for Applied Sociology, Soc. for Exact Philosophy, Math. Assn. Am. Republican. Avocation: mountaineering. Home and Office: 2341 Upper High Dr PO Box 1673 Estes Park CO 80517-1673

MOORE, RICHARD, academic administrator; m. Susan Moore; children: Betsy, Parker. BS in Busn. Claremont Men's Coll., 1955; PhD, 1965; MBA, U. Calif., 1956. Asst. prof. mktg. San Jose (Calif.) State U., 1959-61; instr., divsn. dir. San Bernardino Valley (Calif.) Coll., 1961-66; dean instrn. Moorpark Coll., Calif., 1966-74; pres., supt. Santa Monica (Calif.) Coll., 1974-94; pres. C.C. So. Nev., Las Vegas, 1994—. Active C.C. H.S. program Clark County Sch. Dist., Boys & Girls Clubs, Learning and Earning

Program, Weekend Coll., Silver Sage Coll., Peace Officers Acad., Video Distance Edn., other acad. programs. Lt. U.S. Army, 1957-59. Office: C C So Nev 3200 E Cheyenne Ave North Las Vegas NV 89030*

MOORE, RICHARD KENNETH, high school librarian, columnist; b. Hanford, Calif., July 29, 1948; s. Alan Stewart and Beatrice Mary (Nixon) M.; m. Karen Monroe, May 25, 1973 (dec. Oct. 1994); children: Kenneth Eliot, Larkin Michelle. BA in English, Calif. State U., Long Beach, 1971. Cert. libr., Calif. Libr. Torrance (Calif.) H.S., 1973-91, Bolsa Grande H.S., Garden Grove, Calif., 1991—. Poetry columnist Libr. Talk Mag., 1987-91, sch. libr. column in Calif. Librs. newsletter of Calif. Libr. Assn., 1992—; contbr. articles and revs. to profl. jours. Calif. Assn. Sch. Librs. scholar, 1972. Mem. ALA, Calif. Libr. Assn., Calif. Sch. Libr. Assn. Republican. Episcopalian. Avocations: poetry, politics, family, chocolate. E-mail: RichardGuy@AOL.Com. Office: Bolsa Grande HS 9401 Westminster Ave Garden Grove CA 92844-2901

MOORE, ROB, professional football player; b. N.Y.C., Oct. 27, 1968. BS in Psychology, Syracuse U., 1990. With N.Y. Jets, 1990-94; wide receiver Ariz. Cardinals, Phoenix, 1994—. Named to Sporting News Coll. All-Am. Team, 1989, NFL Pro Bowl Team, 1994. Office: Ariz Cardinals PO Box 888 Tempe AZ 85280-0888*

MOORE, ROGER ALBERT, JR., archaeologist; b. Tampa, Fla., Dec. 18, 1946; s. Roger Albert Moore and Frieda E. (Heil) Hutchison; m. Susan Kay Waters, Sept. 8, 1978; children: Tabitha Rose, Roxie Ann. BA in Anthropology, Ohio State U., 1972; student, U. Tenn., 1974-75; MA in Anthropology, Ea. N.Mex. U., 1981. Lic. archael. surveyor, N.Mex., Colo., Utah, Wyo., Ariz. Crew chief, field foreman U. Tenn., Knoxville, 1973-74, excavator, lab. asst., 1974-75; excavator, lab. asst. Cahokia Mounds State Park, Collinsville, Ill., 1974; lithic analyst Ea. N.Mex. U., Portales, 1975-78; lab. dir. U. Colo., Cortez, 1978-79; field dir. ESCA-Tech, Inc., Ridgeway, Colo., 1980; lab. dir. Navajo Nat. Archaeology Dept., Farmington, N.Mex., 1980-82; supervisory archaeologist San Juan County Mus. Assn., Bloomfield, N.Mex., 1982-88; owner, prin. investigator Moore Anthropol. Rsch., Aztec, N.Mex., 1988—; owner Southwest Archaeol. Svcs., Aztec, N.Mex., 1996—; instr. San Juan Coll., Farmington, 1983; mem. strategic action team Aztec Mcpl. Sch. Dist., 1995. Co-author: Old Dallas Historical Archaeology Project, 1987; contbr. articles to profl. jours. Vol. Portales (N.Mex.) Food Coopr., 1976-78, Salmon Ruin Mus., Bloomfield, 1982-88, Bonds for Books Plus Com., Aztec, 1994; mem. lithic dictionary com. N.Mex. Archaeol. Coun., 1989—; chmn. com. B.L.M. Cultural Adv. Group, Farmington, 1991—; mem. Aztec H.S. parent adv. com., 1996-97. Mem. Soc. Am. Archaeology (life), N.Mex. Archaeol. Coun., Archaeol. Soc. N.Mex. (cert., Archaeol. Achievement award 1994, bd. dirs. 1998—), Ariz. Archaeol. and Hist. Soc., Tenn. Anthropol. Assn. (life), San Juan County Mus. Assn. (bd. dirs. 1993-95), Nat.Trust for Hist. Preservation, Aztec C. of C. (bd. dirs. 1995-97), San Juan Archaeol. Soc., Phi Kappa Phi. Republican. Presbyterian. Avocations: running, hiking, tennis, reading. Office: Moore Anthropol Rsch PO Box 1156 Aztec NM 87410-1156

MOORE, ROSEMARY KUULEI, headmaster; b. San Diego, Apr. 16, 1955; d. Edward James and Rina Larn (Young) M.; m. Lance Wesley Holter, June 16, 1994; children: Ian Everest Yannell, Jade River Holter, Sean Maru Yannell, Michael McKinley Yannell. Student, U. So. Calif., L.A., 1975, U. Hawaii, Kahului, 1980. Project coord. Hawaiian Sea Village, Amfac Property Corp., Kaanapali, 1979-80; shopping ctr. mgr. Whalers Village, Amfac Property Corp., Kaanapali, 1980-83; comm. mgr., adminstrv. dir. Amfac Property Corp., Kaanapali, 1983, property mgr., 1983-85; v.p. Kahikinui (Hawaii) Homes Project, 1990-93; chair, com. rels. dir. Haleakala Waldorf Sch., Kula, Hawaii, 1991-92; headmaster Haleakala Waldorf Sch., Kula, 1992—. Author: Lightworker, 1990, Mikey & Cocoa are Friends, 1992; contbr. articles to profl. jours. Coord. hwy. beautification Dept. Transp., Maui, 1992—; mem. steering com. Valley Isle Voters Assn., Maui, 1994. Mem. Nat. Wildlife Soc., Cousteau Soc. Avocations: writing, surfing, skin diving, hiking, camping. Office: Haleakala Waldorf Sch RR 2 Kula HI 96790-9802

MOORE, STANLEY WAYNE, political science professor; b. Camden, N.J., Feb. 11, 1937; s. Frank Stafford and Alma Beatrice (Law) M.; m. Nancy Joan Crawford, Sept. 1, 1961; children: David Crawford, Andrea Katrina, Stanley Edward Stafford Moore, Sonia Elizabeth. AB magna cum laude, Wheaton (Ill.) Coll., 1959; MA and PhD in Govt., Claremont (Calif.) Grad. Sch., 1971. Asst. prof. polit. sci. Calif. State U.-Stainslaus, Turlock, 1967-69, Monterey (Calif.) Inst. for Internat. Studies, 1969-72; vis. assoc. U. Redlands, Calif., 1972-73; assoc. prof. Pepperdine U., Malibu, Calif., 1973-79, prof. polit. sci., 1979—; pres. Calif. Ctr. for Edn. in Pub. Affairs, Inc., 1991—. Author: A Child's Political World: A Longitudinal Perspective, 1985; contbr. articles to profl. jours. Scoutmaster troop 761 Boy Scouts Am., 1981-92; vice chmn. Ventura County Air Pollution Control Bd., 1981-92; mem. Ventura County Beyond the Yr. 2,000 Commn., 1988-90; bd. mem. Calif. Bicentennial Found. for U.S. Constn., 1987-91; mem. Nat. Dem. Com., Calif. Dem. Com.; mem. Christians in Polit. Sci.; bd. dirs. L.A. chpt. Christians for Biblical Equality. 1995—. Recipient Medal of Honor, Boy Scouts Am., 1989; grantee Spencer Found. Chgo., 1979, 81. Fellow Am. Sci. Affiliation; mem. Am. Polit. Sci. Assn., Western Polit. Sci. Assn., So. Calif. Polit. Sci. Assn. (pres. 1988—), So. Calif. Soc. for Internat. Devel. (pres. 1988—), Coun. Soc. for Internat. Devel., Sierra, Audubon Soc., Nature Conservancy, Nat. Wildlife Fedn. Presbyterian (elder). Avocations: backpacking, fishing, photography, reading, ch. activities. E-mail: revdrmoore@earthlink.net. Office: Pepperdine U Dept Polit Sci Malibu CA 90263

MOORE, TERESA MARGARET, artist; b. St. Paul, Aug. 26, 1963; d. Leo J. and Dorothy Moore. AA in Theater, Fine Arts, Scottsdale Coll., 1985. set designer Exit Theatre, San Francisco, 1998. One-woman shows include Visual Arts Ctr., Phoenix, 1989, Trojanowska Gallery, San Francisco, 1992, 93, 94, Greenwood Gallery, Seattle, 1995, Bastoky Gallery, Seattle, 1996, Sixteen, N.Y.C., 1997, Old Fed. Res. Bank, San Francisco Enrico's, 1998; group exhibits include Galleria Paolucci, Rome, 1988, Galleria Bianco Oro, Rome, 1988, Fina Cocina, Phoenix, 1989, 90, Galaxy Gallery, Miami Beach, Fla., 1989, 93, 94, Ariz. Mus. for Youth, Mesa, 1989, 90, Phoenix Union Gallery, 1990, Gallery Genesis, Chgo., 1990, Bay Area Discovery Mus., Sausalito, Calif., 1994, Nat. Mus. on Women in the Arts Libr. and Archives, Washington, 1996—, Objects and Images Gallery, Bronxville, N.Y., 1998, Phoenix Hotel, San Francisco, 1998, Liss Gallery, Toronto, Can., 1998. Avocations: theatre, bat watching and conservation, collecting pulp paperback books.

MOORE, TERRY WAYNE, high technology venture management consultant; b. North Kingston, R.I., Feb. 26, 1957; s. Robert Wendell and Marilyn (Rose) M. BS in Engring., U. Fla., 1981; MBA, U. San Diego, 1993; postgrad., U. Calif., San Diego, 1994. Sr. materials engr. U.S. Dept. Def., Alameda, Calif., 1981-85, program mgr., 1985-87; staff engr., scientist Gen. Atomics, La Jolla, Calif., 1987-89, project mgr., 1989-92, mktg. program mgr., 1992-93; owner Moore Consulting Co., San Diego, 1994—; entrepreneur Venture Mgmt., Moore Cons. Co., San Diego, 1990—; new high tech. ventures cons. for emerging growth and start up cos., 1991—; mem. dirs. database com. Internat. Forum Corp. Dirs., 1995—, program com., 1995—, membership com., 196—, improving dir. effectiveness cert.; mem. San Diego Regional Tech. Alliance, Calif. State Office Strategic Tech. Devel. Trade and Commerce; mem. Team Dennis Conner's Am.'s Cup Syndicate, 1995, crew mem. Stars and Stripes, winner Pacific Class Nat. Championships, 1995. Judge San Diego Sci. Fair, 1989—; rep. Neighborhood Watch, La Costa, Calif., 1989—; vol. fund raiser Am. Cancer Soc., Epilepsy Soc., United Way, U. Calif. San Diego Cancer Ctr. Found. Mem. Am. Soc. for Materials Internat. (sec.-treas. 1990-92, vice chmn. 1993-94, chmn. 1994-95, past chmn. 1995-96, bd. dirs. 1989—, nat. chpt ops. com., chmn. computer subcom. 1991—, chmn. 1994-95), Project Mgmt. Inst. (sec. 1993-94, treas. 1994-95, bd. dirs. 1993—), Nat. Bd. Cert. Project Mgmt. Profl. (cert.), San Diego Engring. Soc. (program chmn. bd. dirs. 1995-96), Soc. Advancement of Material and Process Engring., San Diego Venture Mgmt. Group, MIT Enterprise Forum (mem. panel selection com.), Found. for Enterprise Devel., San Diego Yacht Club. Republican. Presbyterian. Avocations: financial investments, ocean yacht racing, reading, triathlons, private pilot. Home and Office: 905 Orchid Way Carlsbad CA 92009-4830

MOORE, THOMAS SCOTT, lawyer; b. Portland, Oreg., Nov. 17, 1937; s. Harry Alburn and Geraldine Elizabeth (Scott) M.; m. Saundra L. Wagner, Sept. 7, 1957 (div. 1974); children: Cindy, Kristin, Thomas, Victoria, Wendy; m. Alice H. Zeisz, Nov. 5, 1976; 1 child, Alice G. BA, Willamette U., 1959, JD cum laude, 1962. Bar: Oregon 1962. Pvt. practice Portland, 1962—. Contbr. articles to law jours. Republican. Avocation: tennis. Office: 4425 SW Corbett Ave Portland OR 97201-4206

MOORE, WALTER DENGEL, rapid transit system professional; b. Chgo., Sept. 16, 1936; s. Walter D. and Velma Louise (Rhode) M.; m. Sandra M. Stetzel, Jan. 23, 1965 (div. 1980); children: Thomas, Timothy; m. Janice Masilun, Nov. 30, 1996. BA in Liberal Arts and Scis., U. Ill., 1958; BSEE, Ill. Inst. Tech., 1972. Supt. maintenance of way Chgo. Transit Authority, 1963-89; supr. track and rail tech. support Met. Transp. Assn. Los Angeles County, L.A., 1989—. With U.S. Army, 1958-60. Mem. Am. Pub. Transp. Assn. (vice chmn. power com. 1974-75), Am. Ry. Engring. Assn. (vice chmn. subcom. on power signals and comm. 1990—), Underwater Soc. Am. (N.Am. record in spear-fishing 1988), Calif. Pub. Utilities Commn. (gen. order 1995), Nat. Rsch. Coun., NAS (transp. rsch. bd.), Nat. Acad. Engrs. (project C3 and D6 light rail track manual). Avocations: free diving, theater. Home: 12741 Andy St Cerritos CA 90703-6044 Office: Met Transp Assn L A County 320 S Santa Fe Ave Los Angeles CA 90013-1812

MOORE, WILLIS HENRY ALLPHIN, history and geography educator; b. N.Y.C., Dec. 14, 1940; s. Carl Allphin and Mary Catherine (Moody) M.; m. Alison Mae Dingley; children: Patrick Kakela, Michael Kirby, Catherine Malia. BA Letters, U. Okla., 1962; MEd in Adminstrn., U. Hawaii, 1971. Teaching asst. dept. history U. Hawaii, 1962-64; dir. edn. Bernice P. Bishop Mus., Honolulu, 1967-76; pres. Hawaii Geog. Soc., Honolulu, 1976-78, exec. sec., editor, 1978—; mem. Hawaii Com. for Humanities, 1976-78; producer, narrator film-lecture programs Nat. Audubon Soc. and travelogue forums; instr. in history, geography and polit. sci. Chaminade U. of Honolulu, 1986—; lectr. elderhostel U. Hawaii, Hawaii Pacific U.; instr. Hawaii Prison Sys. Co-author/co-editor: Hawaii Parklands, Sociological History of Honolulu, Total Solar Eclipse over Hawaii, 1991, Christmas Comes to Hawaii; contbr. articles to Honolulu Advertiser, Pacific Daily News, Guam, Pacific Mag., Honolulu Star-Bull. Lay reader St. Andrew's Cathedral. Mem. Am. Corrections Assn., Internat. Map Trade Assn., Am. Assn. State and Local History, Am. Mus. Assn., Pacific Sci. Assn., Hawaii Mus. Assn. (pres. 1972-74), Hawaii Pub. Radio, Am. Guild Organists, Soc. Profls. in Dispute Resolution, Sierra Club (chmn. Hawaii chpt. 1973-75), Hawaiian Hist. Soc., Nat. Soc. Arts and Letters. Office: PO Box 1698 Honolulu HI 96806-1698

MOORHEAD, CARLOS J., former congressman; b. Long Beach, Calif., May 6, 1922; s. Carlos Arthur and Florence (Gravers) M.; m. Valery Joan Tyler, July 19, 1969; children: Theresa, Catharine, Steven, Teri, Paul. BA, UCLA, 1943; JD, U. So. Calif., 1949. Bar: Calif. 1949, U.S. Supreme Ct. 1973. Pvt. practice law Glendale, Calif., 1949-72; dir. Lawyers Reference Service, Glendale, 1950-66; mem. 93d-104th Congresses from 22d (now 27th) Dist. Calif., 1973-96; mem. judiciary com., chmn. subcom. on cts. and intellectual property, vice chmn. commerce com., mem. subcom. on energy & power, subcom. on telecomm. & fin.; dean Calif. Congl. Rep. Delegation; apptd. to Fed. Cts. Study Com. Pres. Glendale Hi-Twelve Club; mem. Verdugo Hills council Boy Scouts Am.; mem. Calif. Assembly, 1967-72; mem. Calif. Law Revision Commn., 1971-72; pres. 43d Dist. Republican Assembly, Glendale Young Republicans; mem. Los Angeles County Rep. Central Com., Calif. Rep. Central Com.; pres. Glendale La Crescenta Camp Fire Girls, Inc. Served to lt. col. AUS, 1942-46. Recipient Man of Yr. award USO, 1979. Mem. Calif. Bar Assn., L.A. County Bar Assn., Glendale Bar Assn. (past pres.), Glendale C. of C., Masons, Shriners, Lions, Moose, VFW. Presbyterian. Office: 511 E Harvard St Ste 5 Glendale CA 91205-1184

MOORMAN, BRIDGET ANNE, clinical systems engineer; b. Chandler, Ariz., Mar. 11, 1964; d. Michael Oakley Moorman and Susan G. (Royce) Fowler. BS in Mech. Engring., Ariz. State U., 1985; MS in Biomed. Engring, Renssaeler Polytech., Hartford (Conn.) Grad. Ctr., 1991. Cert. clin. engring. Internat. Cert. Commn. Power engr. Western Area Power Adminstrn., Phoenix, 1985-86; ground system mgr., satellites USAF Defense Meteorol. Satellite Program, L.A., 1986-89; clin. engr. intern Hartford (Conn.) Hosp., 1989-91; rsch. aide, biomech. U. Calif., San Diego, 1991-92; clin. engr. U. Ariz Med. Ctr., Tucson, 1992-95; clin. systems engr. Kaiser Found. Hosps., Berkeley, Calif., 1995—; mech. engr. USAF Reserve, 1989—. Engring. mentor Women in Sci. and Engring., Tucson, 1994-95, Telementor Women in Medicine; Biology, 1996-92. Capt. USAF, 1986-97. Recipient clin. engring. internship, grad. scholarship Hartford Hosp., 1989. Mem. Soc. Women Engrs. (pres. Tucson sect. 1994-95, chair program com. nat. conv. 1999), Tau Beta Pi. Avocations: flying (instrument rating), skiing, cooking, reading, hiking.

MOOSBURNER, NANCY, nutritionist; b. Houston, Tex., Apr. 6, 1943; d. Henry Fenno and Shirley Louise (McCandless) Laughton; m. Stephen Weinert, Nov. 1964 (div. Nov. 1974); children: Catherine, Jeffery; m. Otto Moosburner, Feb. 7, 1976; 1 child, Brian. BS, U. Nev., Reno, 1979, MS, 1982. Cert. sch. bus. ofcl. Wash. Assn. Sch. Bus. Ofcls. Edn. specialist Nev. Dept. of Edn., Carson City, 1980-83, state dir., 1983-84; sch. nutrition program supr. Douglas Co. Sch. Dist., Minden, Nev., 1987-93, dir. sch. nutrition St. Helens (Oreg.) Sch. Dist., 1993-94; instr. Truckee Meadows C.C., Reno, Nev., 1982-83, Portland C.C., St. Helens, 1993-94; child nutrition program supr. Auburn (Wash.) Sch. Dist., 1994—; state pres Nev. Sch. Food Svc. Assn., Minden, 1992-93. Contbr. articles to profl. jours. Recipient Excellence in Food Svc. award U.S. Dept. Agri., 1989; named Outstanding Women of Am., 1977. Mem. Am. Dietetic Assn., Am. Sch. Food Svc. Assn. (dir. West region 1991-93, exec. bd. dirs.), Soc. for Nutrition Edn., Am. Family and Consumer Svcs. Assn., Oreg. Sch. Food Svc. Assn. (pub. comm. 1993-94), Wash. Sch. Food Svc. Assn. (exec. bd. dirs. 1997—, spl. projects chair, state chair industry seminar 1997). Democrat. Avocations: bee keeping, gardening, antiques, cooking, walking. Home: PO Box 2628 Longview WA 98632-8665

MOOSE, CHARLES A., state official; b. Aug. 11, 1953. BA in U.S. History, U. N.C., 1975; MA in Pub. Adminstrn., Portland State U., 1984, PhD in Urban Studies and Criminology, 1993; grad., FBI Nat. Acad. Patrol officer Portland Police Dept., 1975-81, sergeant, 1981-84, lieutenant, 1984-91, capt. of No. Precinct, 1991-92, dep. chief of Ops. Branch, 1992-93, chief of police, 1993—. Bd. dirs. Boys and Girls Club of Portland, Comprehensive Options for Drug Abusers; mem. funding allocation com. Black United Fund Oreg.; mem. Multnomah County Cmty. Action Commn., Police Exec. Rsch. Forum, Bd. Pub. Safety Standards and Tng., Gov.'s Drug and Violent Crime Policy Bd., Gov.'s Juvenile Justice Task Force; bd. dirs. Portland State U. Mem. Am. Soc. Criminology, Nat. Orgn. of Black Law Enforcement Execs., Soc. of Police Futurists Internat., Internat. Assn. Chiefs of Police. Address: Police Bureau 1111 SW 2nd Ave Portland OR 97204-3232*

MOOSSA, A. R., surgery educator; b. Port Louis, Mauritius, Oct. 10, 1939; s. Yacoob and Maude (Rochecoute) M.; m. Denise Willoughby, Dec. 28, 1973; children: Pierre, Noel, Claude, Valentine. BS, U. Liverpool, Eng., 1962, MD (hon.), 1965; postgrad., Johns Hopkins U., 1972-73, U. Chgo., 1973-74. Intern Liverpool Royal Infirmary, 1965-66; resident United Liverpool Hosps. and Alder Hey Children's Hosp., 1966-72; from asst. prof. surgery to assoc. prof. U. Chgo., 1975-77, prof., dir. surg. rsch., chief gen. surgery svc., vice chmn. dept., 1977-83; chmn. dept. surgery U. Calif.-San Diego Med. Ctr., 1983—; Litchfield lectr. U., Oxford, Eng., 1978; praelector in surgery U. Dundee, Scotland, 1979; Hampson Trust vis. prof. U. Liverpool, Eng., 1992, G.B. Ong. vis. prof. U. Hong Kong, 1993, Philip Sandblon vis. prof. U. Lund, Sweden. Editor: Tumors of the Pancreas, 1982, Essential Surgical Practice, 1983, 3d edit., 1995, Comprehensive Textbook of Oncology, 1985, 2d edit., 1991, Gastrointestinal Emergencies, 1985, Problems in General Surgery, 1989, Operative Colorectal Surgery, 1993. Fellow Royal Coll. Surgeons (Hunterian prof. 1977); mem. ACS, Am. Surg. Assn., Soc. Univ. Surgeons, Am. Soc. Clin. Oncology. Office: U Calif San Diego Med Ctr 200 W Arbor Dr San Diego CA 92103-1911

MORAIN, CLAUDIA MITCHELL, journalist; b. Boulder, Colo., July 26, 1956; d. William Frazee and Charlotte Lou (Kaysen) Mitchell; m. Daniel Doyle John Morain, Jan. 31, 1981; children: Anthony, Clara, Elizabeth. BA magna cum laude, U. Wash., 1977. Reporter The Jour.-American, Bellevue, Wash., 1978-81, L.A. Daily News, Van Nuys, Calif., 1981; med. writer The Register, Santa Ana, Calif., 1981-82; assoc. prodr. KCET-TV (PBS), L.A., 1982; writer, editor L.A., San Francisco and, Palo Alto, 1982-87; health writer San Jose (Calif.) Mercury News, 1987-89; med. writer, editor Davis, Calif., 1989—; journalism lectr. San Francisco State U., 1986, U. So. Calif., L.A., 1984. Author: (booklet) Understanding Asthma; editor: (chpts.) Core Concepts in Health; contbr. more than 1000 articles to newspapers and mags. Recipient C. Everett Koop Media award for Outstanding Single News or Feature Story, AHA, 1994, 95, Media Achievement award Calif. Media Assn., 1989, J.C. Penney-Mo. Spl. award, 1981. Mem. Am. Med. Writers Assn., Am. Soc. Profl. Journalists, Phi Beta Kappa. Avocations: cooking, hiking, travel, reading.

MORALES, SANDRA LEE, educator; b. Sunnyside, N.Y., Oct. 15, 1934; d. John Joseph and Mabel Marnes (O'Brien) Lee; m. Hernan Morales, July 19, 1958; children: Martita Morales Sageser, Anita Morales Frost, Michael, Kathryn, Christina. BA in Chemistry, St. John's U., 1955; MS in Sci. Edn., U. Colo., 1972. Tchr. sci. St. Joseph's High Sch., Bklyn., 1955-56; tchr. algebra, biology All Saints High Sch., Bklyn., 1956; tchr. physics, gen. sci., math. Adelphi Acad., Bklyn., 1956-58; tchr. A.P. chemistry, gen. sci., sr. sci. Antilles H.S., San Juan, P.R., 1958-64, head dept. chemistry, 1962-64; sci. dept. head, tchr. life scis., earth scis. Pauline Meml. Sch., Colorado Springs, Colo., 1981-95; tutor pvt. practice, Colorado Springs, Colo., 1995—. Mem. Pauline Meml. PTO, 1973-95, pres., 1977-79; bd. dirs. Pointe Sublime Water Bd., Colorado Springs, 1980-92; pres. Colorado Springs Intercity Tennis, 1977-79; vol. Humane Soc., Colorado Springs, 1996—, Outdoor Colo., 1996—. Mem. AAUW, Colo. Tennis Assn., Am. Audubon Soc. Republican. Roman Catholic. Avocations: hiking, photography, tennis, astronomy, bird watching.

MORAMARCO, FRED STEPHEN, English writing educator, editor; b. Bklyn., July 13, 1938; s. Stephen and Nina (Toriello) M.; m. Sheila Sobell, Aug. 15, 1964 (div. Aug. 1988); children: Stephen, Nicholas. BA, L.I. U., 1964; MA, U. Utah, 1966, PhD, 1969, cert. Am. studies, 1969. Asst. prof. English San Diego State U., 1969-71, assoc. prof. English, 1971-75, prof. English, 1975—, dir. Sch. Lit., 1974-78, dir. MA in Liberal Arts Program, 1985-88, dir. grad. studies English, 1989-92; Fulbright lectr. U. Cattolian, Milan, 1973; editor Poetry Internat., San Diego State U., 1996—. Co-author: Modern American Poetry, 1989, Containing Multitudes, 1998; co-editor: Men of Our Time: Male Poetry in Contemporary America, 1992; editor Poetry Internat., 1997-98. Mem. Am. Acad. Poets, Am. Lit. Assn., Calif. Faculty Assn., Italian-Am. Cmty. Assn. Democrat. Avocations: gourmet cooking, multimedia technology, piano playing. Office: Dept English San Diego State Univ San Diego CA 92182-0001

MORAN, ROBERT EARL, JR., sports journalist; b. Columbia, S.C., Dec. 24, 1952; s. Robert Earl and Viola Esther (Quarles) M. BS in Journalism, Ohio U., 1974. Reporter, columnist Ariz. Daily Star, Tucson, 1974-87, The Tribune, Mesa, Ariz., 1987—. Mem. NAACP, So. Poverty Law Ctr. Mem. Football Writers Assn. Am. (bd. dirs. 1995-96, 3d Place award 1992), U.S. Basketball Writers Assn., Nat. Sportscasters Sportswriters Assn. (1st Place award 1983, 94, 97). Democrat. A.M.E. Avocations: travel, model cars, tennis. Home: 2970 N Oregon St Unit 16 Chandler AZ 85224-7754 Office: The Tribune 120 W 1st Ave Mesa AZ 85210-1312

MORAN, THOMAS HARRY, university administrator; b. Milw., Oct. 21, 1937; s. Harry Edward and Edna Agnes Moran; BS, U. Wis., 1964, MA, 1972, PhD, 1974; m. Barbara Ellen Saklad, June 10, 1969; children: David Thomas, Karen Ellen. Dir. capital budgeting Wis. Dept. Adminstrn., 1962-64; exec. dir. Wis. Higher Ednl. Aids Bd., 1964-69; spl. cons. tax policy Wis. Dept. Revenue, 1973-74; dep. dir. Wis. Manpower Coun., Office of Gov., 1974-76; v.p. bus. and fin., treas. U. Detroit, 1976-78; exec. assoc. v.p. health affairs U. So. Calif., L.A., 1979-87; v.p. bus. affairs, 1988—. USN fellow, 1957-59; U.S. Office Edn. rsch. fellow, 1973. Mem. Am. Assn. Higher Edn., Phi Kappa Phi. Office: U So Calif 200 Town & Gown University Park Los Angeles CA 90007

MORAND, BLAISE E., bishop; b. Tecumseh, Ont., Can., Sept. 12, 1932. Ordained priest Roman Cath. Ch., 1958. Ordained coadjutor bishop Diocese of Prince Albert, Sask., Can., 1981, bishop, 1983—. Office: Diocese of Prince Albert, 1415 4th Ave W, Prince Albert, SK Canada S6V 5H1*

MORANG, DIANE JUDY, writer, television producer, business entrepreneur; b. Chgo., Apr. 28, 1942; d. Anthony Thomas Morang and Laura Ann Andrzejczak. Student, Stevens Finishing Sch., Chgo., 1956, Fox Bus. Coll., 1959-60, UCLA, 1967-69. Mem. staff Chgo. Sun Times, Daily News, 1957, Drury Ln. Theatre, Chgo., 1961-62, AM Show ABC-TV, Hollywood, Calif., 1970-71; chair, mem. judging panel Regional Emmy awards, 1989, judge 2 categories, 1985. Author: How to Get into the Movies, 1978; author, creator: The Rainbow Keyboard, 1991; creator: The Best Kids' Show in the World; contbr. numerous articles to newspapers, mags. Bd. dirs., mem. scholarship com. Ariz. Bruins UCLA Alumni Assn.; mem. Nat. Mus. Women in the Arts, Washington. Mem. NATAS (mem. Hollywood Emmy-award winning team Hollywood, Calif. 1971), Nat. Women's Hall of Fame, Seneca Falls, N.Y., Ariz. Authors Assn. (bd. dirs.). Roman Catholic.

MORE, PHILIP HARVEY BIRNBAUM, business administration educator; b. San Diego, Jan. 21, 1944; s. Louis and Ruth Laureen (Bay) B.; m. Marlin Sue Van Every, Dec. 26, 1964; 1 child, Brian Philip. BA, U. Calif., Berkeley, 1965; PhD, U. Wash., 1975. Analyst Los Angeles County Civil Service Commn., 1965-67; teaching assoc. U. Wash., Seattle, 1972-74; asst. prof. bus. adminstrn. Ind. U., Bloomington, 1975-80, assoc. prof., 1980-85; prof. Ind. U., Bloomington, 1986, U. So. Calif., 1986—; resident dir. J.F.K. Inst., Tiburg U., The Netherlands; vis. scholar Polish Acad. Scis., Tokyo U., SDA Bocconi, Milan, Italy, Seoul Nat. U., Korea, Dartmouth Coll. Co-author: Organization Theory: A Structural and Behavioral Analysis, Modern Management Techniques for Engineers and Scientists, International Research Management: Studies in Interdisciplinary Methods From Business, Government and Academics, 1990; assoc. editor IEEE Transaction on Engring. Mgmt. jour.; contbr. articles to profl. jours., book revs., sects. to books, invited papers Germany, Poland, Eng., Can., Thailand, Hong Kong, Korea. Served with USAF, 1967-71. Recipient DBA Assn. Teaching award Ind. U., 1978; NSF fellow, 1974-75, N.Y. Acad. Scis. fellow, 1981; U. Hong Kong Sr. Fulbright scholar, 1981-82. Mem. Acad. of Mgmt. (pres. tech. and innovation mgmt. div. 1989-90), Engring. Mgmt. Soc., Inst. Ops. Rsch. and Mgmt. Scis., Internat. Assn. for Study of Interdisciplinary Research, Beta Gamma Sigma, Beta Alpha Psi, Sigma Iota Epsilon, Sigma Chi. Methodist. Office: U So Calif Grad Sch Bus Admistrn Los Angeles CA 90089-1421

MOREAU, JOSEPH ANTHONY, educational administrator; b. Mt. Holly, N.J., July 20, 1962; s. Albert and Lois Elizabeth (Luthi) M. BA, U. Calif., San Diego, 1983; Cert., UCLA, 1986; MA, Calif. State U., L.A., 1995. Prodn. mgr. Hughes Aircraft Co., El Segundo, Calif., 1983-86; freelance producer La Jolla, Calif., 1986-87; sr. ptnr., mgr. Venice (Calif.) Prodn. and Design, 1987-91; media specialist Sussman-Prejza & Co., Culver City, Calif., 1988-89; supr. Pasadena (Calif.) City Coll. Instructional Resources Ctr., 1990-97; assoc. dean learning resources West Hills Coll., Coalinga, Calif., 1997—. Avocations: woodworking, restoring antique cars. Office: West Hill Coll 300 W Cherry Ln Coalinga CA 93210-1301

MOREL, JOHN A., oil and gas consulting company owner, geologist; b. Chgo., Mar. 20, 1947; s. Walter and Lucille Morel; m. Felice Morel; children: Michael, Katherine, Daniel, Stephen. BS in Physics, Ill. Inst. Tech., 1969; MS in Physics, U. Wyo., 1972, PhD in Geology, 1978. Lic. profl. geologist, Wyo. Project geophysicist Amoco Product Co., Denver, 1974-80; geologist Davis Oil Co., Denver, 1980-81; exploration mgr. Gary-Williams Co., Denver, 1981-87; geologist Basin Expl., Denver, 1994, 95; cons., owner Foxpark Oil & Gas, Denver, 1987—; spkr. in field. Contbr. numerous papers to profl. jours. Tenor with Colo. Symphony Orch. Chorus, 1991-96. Mem. Am. Assn. Petroleum Geology (cert. petroleum geologist), Soc. Exploration Geophysics, Geol. Soc. Am., Wyo. Geol. Assn., Rocky Mountain Assn. Geology, Denver Geophys. Soc. Office: Foxpark Oil & Gas Inc 2792 S Fillmore St Denver CO 80210-6419

MORENO, GUILLERMO FERNANDEZ, minister; b. San Antonio, Aug. 28, 1948; s. Willie Luna and Frances (Fernandez) M.; m. Delia Guerra, June 6, 1971; 1 child, Guillermo. BA, U. Calif. L.A., 1976, MA, 1978; MA, Bob Jones U., 1981, PhD, 1988. Ordained to ministry Christian Ch. Min. Latin Am. Coun. of Christian Chs., Brownsville, Tex., 1967—; pastor Latin Am. Coun. of Christian Chs., Brownsville, 1969—. Latin Am. Coun. of Christian Chs. Galena, L.A., 1988—; instr. Cladic Sem., L.A., 1969—; choir dir. Cladic Sem., L.A., 1967-79; evangelist Latin Am. Coun. Christian Chs., U.S.A., summers 1968—; vis. instr. Clases Biblicas, Monterrey, Mex., summers, 1975—; mgr. Cladic Bible Book store, L.A., 1984-86; exec. editor Expositor Dominical Cladic, 1993—. Author Bible Doctrine seminar; contbr. articles to profl. jours. Mem. Sigma Delta Pi Spanish Honor Soc. (lifetime), Bob Jones U. Alumni Assn. Republican. Home: 1255 Watson Ave Wilmington CA 90744-2853

MORENO, MANUEL D., bishop; Educator U. of Calif., L.A., St. John's Sem., Camarillo, Calif. Ordained priest Roman Cath. church, 1961. Ordained aux. bishop of Los Angeles, titular bishop of Tanagra, 1977; installed as bishop of Tucson, 1982—. Office: Diocese of Tucson PO Box 31 Tucson AZ 85702*

MOREY, MELINDA GRACE, artist; b. Torrance, Calif., Apr. 11, 1963; d. Thomas Hugh Morey and Carolyn Jolly (Givens) Bodine; m. Chester Alan Fergursky, Sept. 5, 1998. BFA in Studio Art summa cum laude, U. Ariz., 1998. Freelance artist Calif., 1983-86; scenic artist Santa Fe (N.Mex.) Opera, 1987; mural artist Evans and Brown Co., Inc., San Francisco, 1988-91. Mural artist, 1991-98. Pres. Cen. Arts Collective, Tucson, 1997-98. Undergrad. rsch. grantee U. Ariz., 1997, recipient award of acad. excellence, 1998. Avocations: yoga, surfing, bodysurfing, photography, travel.

MOREY, ROBERT HARDY, communications executive; b. Milw., Sept. 5, 1956; s. Lloyd W. and Ruby C. (McElhaney) M. AA, Ricks Coll., 1978; BA, Brigham Young U., 1983. Program dir. Sta. KABE-FM, Orem, Utah, 1982-83, sales mgr., 1983; nat. mgr. ops Tiffany Prodns. Internat., Salt Lake City, 1983-84; account exec. Osmond Media Corp., Orem, 1984; corp. sec., bd. dirs. Positive Communications, Inc., Orem, 1984—; chief exec. officer, 1987—; gen. mgr. Sta. KSRR, Orem, 1985—; pres. K-Star Satellite Network, Orem, 1986—; Broadcast Media Svcs., Orem, 1989-93; gen. mgr. Sta. KMGR, Salt Lake City, 1993; ops. mgr. KQMB-FM, Salt Lake City, 1994-95, gen. mgr., 1995-98; guest lectr. various colls. and univs., 1981—. Chmn. Rep. voting dist., Orem, 1984. Recipient Community Service award Utah Valley Community Coll., 1983; named one of Outstanding Young Men in Am. U.S. Jaycees, 1983. Avocations: reading, collecting stamps. Home: PO Box 828 Orem UT 84059-0828 Office: Sta KSRR Ventura Media Ctr 1240 E 800 N Orem UT 84097-4318

MORGAN, AUDREY, architect; b. Neenah, Wis., Oct. 19, 1931; d. Andrew John Charles Hopfensperger and Melda Lily (Radtke) Anderson; m. Earl Adrian Morgan (div); children: Michael A. Morgan, Nancy Lee Morgan, Diana Lou Hansen, Susan Lynn Heiner. BA, U. Wash., 1955. Registered architect, Wash., Oreg.; cert. NCARB. Project mgr. The Austin Co., Renton, Wash., 1972-75; med. facilities architect The NBBJ Group, Seattle, 1975-79; architect constrn. rev. unit Wash. State Divsn. Health, Olympia, 1979-81; project dir., med. planner John Graham & Co., Seattle, 1981-83; pvt. practice architecture, Ocean Shores, Wash., 1983—; also health care facility cons., code analyst. Contbg. author: Guidelines for Construction and Equipment for Hospitals and Medical Facilities; Co-editor: Design Consideration for Mental Health Facilities; contbr. articles to profl. jours. and govt. papers; prin. works include quality assurance coord. for design phase Madigan Army Med. Ctr., Ft. Lewis, Wash.; med. planner and code analyst Rockwood Clinic, Spokane, Wash., Comprehensive Health Care Clinic for Yakima Indian Nation, Toppenish, Wash.; code analyst S.W. Wash. Hosps., Vancouver; med. planner Pacific Cataract & Lazer Inst. Chehalis & Kennewick, Wash; med. planner facilities for child, adult, juvenile and forensic psychiatric patients., States of Wash. and Oreg. expert witness litigation cases involving mental health facilities. Cons. on property mgmt. Totem council Girl Scouts U.S.A., Seattle, 1969-84, troop leader cons., trainer, 1961-74; mem. Wash. State Bldg. Code Coun., tech. adv. group for non-residential bldgs., Barier Free Com. Tech. adv. group for Ams. with Disabilites Act; assoc. mem. Wash State Fire Marshals Tech. Adv. Group. Mem. AIA (nat. acad. architecture for health 1980—, subcoms. codes and standards, chair mental health com., 1989-92, and numerous other coms., founding mem. Wash. council AIA architecture for health panel 1981—, recorder 1981-84, vice chmn., 1987, chmn. 1988, bd. dirs. S.W. Wash. chpt. 1983-84), Nat. Fire Protection Assn., Am. Soc. Value Engrs., Am. Hosp. Assn., Assn. Western Hosps., Wash. State Hosp. Assn., Wash. State Soc. Hosp. Engrs. (hon.), Seattle Womens Sailing Assn., Audubon Soc., Alpha Omicron Pi. Lutheran. Clubs: Coronado 25 Fleet 13 (Seattle) (past sec., bull. editor); GSA 25 Plus. Home and Office: PO Box 1990 Ocean Shores WA 98569-1990 also: 904 Falls Of Clyde Loop SE Ocean Shores WA 98569-9542

MORGAN, BYRON ALBERT, filmmaker, writer; b. L.A., Feb. 3, 1921; s. Albert Byron and Gladys Ruth (McIntosh) M.; m. Patricia Ann McLaughlin, Feb. 24, 1954 (div. 1981); children: Melissa, Marya, Patricia, Heather, Laura, Byron Jr., John, Peter, Jonathan, Mark; m. Dell Verlon, Sept. 30, 1991. BS, Loyola Marymount U., 1959; MA, UCLA, 1959. Enlisted USN, 1942, advanced through grades to lt., photographer, 1950-54, ret., 1954; writer, instr. Syracuse (N.Y.) U. Overseas project, Iran, 1954-55; chief scriptwriting divsn. Naval Photographic Ctr., 1955-57; press officer, film writer, dir., prodr. Nat. Adv. Com. for Aeronautics, 1957-58; chief audiovisual motion picture writer, dir., prodr. NASA, 1958-65; pres. Byron Morgan Assocs., Inc., Santa Monica, Calif., 1965—; founder Cinema 8 Corp., 1969-70; filmwriter, dir. numerous films U.S. Army Med. Inst. Rsch., 1970-72; TV dir. programs for various govt. agys. U.S. Army Audio Visual Agy., 1972-74; writer, dir., prodr. NASA, 1974—; writer, tech. advisor Space, Paramount Pictures, 1984-85. Filmmaker Beating the Heat, 1958, Ariel, 1962 (Chris award), Steps to Saturn, 1963 (Chris award), America in Space: The First Five Years, 1964 (Cert. of Merit award XII Internat. Festival of Mountain Climbing and Exploration Films, Trent, Italy), Project Apollo: Manned Flight to the Moon, 1964 (Chris award, 2d pl. Nat. Visual Presentation Assn.), X-15, 1965 (1st prize with USSR Une Aile d'Or Festival Mondial du Film Aeronautique et Spatial, Vichy, France), The World Was There, 1965 (1st prize Fedn. Aeronautique, King Constantine and Queen Frederika of Greece Spl. Presentation), Research Project X-15, 1965 (1st prize Aeronautics Fedn. Aeronautique), Rise of the Soviet Navy, 1967 (Golden Eagle award Coun. on Internat. Nontheatrical Events CINE), Aeronautics: Space in the 70s, 1971 (Golden Eagle award Coun. on Internat. Nontheatrical Events CINE, Gold Camera award 1st pl. U.S. Indsl. Film Festival, Trazzo d'Oro and Diploma al Merito Cinematografico XVII Rassegna Internat. Elettronica Nucleare E Teleradiocinematografica), Flight of Apollo XI, 1971 (Golden Eagle award Coun. on Internat. Nontheatrical Events CINE), Living Space, 1972 (Golden Eagle award Coun. on Internat. Nontheatrical Events CINE, 1st prize Mil. Festival Rome), Apollo-Soyuz, 1975 (Chris Bronze Plaque award 23rd Columbus (Ohio) Film Festival, certs.), If One Today: Two Tomorrow, 1976 (Golden Eagle award Coun. on Internat. Nontheatrical Events CINE), Images of Life, 1977 (gold award Internat. Film and TV Festival, Bronze medal V.I. Internat. Film Festival, Chris Plaque Columbus (Ohio) Film Festival), among others. 1st pres. Young Dems. 15th Dist., Hollywood, 1948. Mem. Alliance L.A. Playwrights, SAG, Dramatists Guild, St. John of Jerusalem (treas. 1984), L.A. Tennis Club. Roman Catholic. Avocations: tennis, playwriting. Home: 28681 Teton Ln Lake Arrowhead CA 92352 Office: 535 W 4th #201 Long Beach CA 90801

MORGAN, CHARLES EDWARD PHILLIP, bank executive; b. Wichita, Kans., Nov. 3, 1916; s. Wells C. Morgan and Mary E. (Brown) Allredge; m. Elizabeth Ann Brown, Oct. 14, 1945 (div. Dec. 1972); children—Valerie Donahue, Renee Tompkins. Student U. Wichita, 1935; student bus. administrn. U. Calif., Berkley, 1962. Teller First Nat. Bank, Santa Fe, 1936; v.p./br. mgr. Wells Fargo Bank, Sacramento, 1948-76; sr. v.p. Capitol Bank of Commerce, Sacramento, 1976-86. Served to 1st lt. USAF, 1942-45. Mem. Masons, Shriners. Democrat. Mem. Christian Ch. Home: 1111 Alvarado Ave Apt 302 Davis CA 95616-0918

MORGAN, DAVID FORBES, minister; b. Toronto, Ont., Can., Aug. 3, 1930; came to U.S., 1954; s. Forbes Alexander and Ruth (Bamford) M.; m. Delores Mae Storhaug, Sept. 7, 1956; children: Roxanne Ruth, David Forbes II. BA, Rocky Mt. Coll.; ThB, Coll. of the Rockies, MDiv; postgrad. Bishop's Sch. Theology; LittD (hon.). Temple Coll., 1956, D.C. Nat. Coll. Ordained priest. Pres., Coll. of the Rockies, Denver, 1960-73; founder and rector Prior Order of Christ Centered Ministries, Denver, 1973—; canon pastor St. John's Cathedral, Denver, 1982-96, canon at large, 1996—; bd. dirs. Internat. Contemplative Outreach, Ltd., mem. internat. faculty. Author: Christ Centered Ministries, A Response to God's Call, 1973; Songs with A Message, 1956. Clubs: Oratory of the Good Shepherd, Denver Botanic Garden. Home: 740 Clarkson St Denver CO 80218-3204 Office: St Johns Cathedral 1313 Clarkson St Denver CO 80218-1806

MORGAN, DIRCK, broadcast journalist; b. L.A., Feb. 3, 1954; s. Phillip Barton and Katherine (Ramirez) Segall; m. Ellen Tomoye Matsumoto, Dec. 1, 1993; 1 child, Makena Sunao. AA, Pierce Coll., 1973. Assignment editor KFWB/Group W. Westinghouse, L.A., 1972-74; corp. comm. specialist Northrop Corp., L.A., 1975-78; news dir. Stas. KARM, KFIG, Fresno, Calif., 1978-84; editor, anchor Sta. KGIL, L.A., 1984-85; fin. anchor Sta. KWHY-TV, L.A., 1985-87; cmty. resources specialist Optimist Boys Home, L.A., 1985-87; reporter Sta. KFWB, CBS, L.A., 1988—; media crisis mgmt. specialist L.A. County Fire Dept., 1990—, L.A. Police Dept., 1991—, LAUSD, 1996, Calif. State Mil. Res., L.A., 1990-95. Helicopter airborne reporter, 1988-91, broadcast series on L.A. riots, 1992 (L.A. Press Club award), L.A. Police Dept. Ballistics, 1994 (L.A. Press Club award), Radio TV News Assn.: 15 golden mikes. Instr., announcer Kenkojuku World Karate, L.A., 1984-92; host Nissei Week, L.A., 1990-98. Recipient 15 Golden Mike awards Radio and TV News Assn. Mem. L.A. Police Protective League (hon. life). Avocations: karate, Japanese koi fish, firearms, classic cars. Office: KFWB/CBS 6230 Yucca St Los Angeles CA 90028-5295

MORGAN, JACK ADRIEN, plant physiologist; b. San Francisco, Mar. 2, 1950; s. William Harold and Mildred Margaret (Clink) M.; m. Teresa Ann Hymer, Aug. 22, 1972; children: Ross Hymer, Reed William. BS in Biology, N.Mex. State U., 1975; MS in Agronomy, U. Ga., 1978, PhD in Agronomy, 1981. Rsch. assoc. U. Ga., Athens, 1975-81; plant physiologist USDA-Agrl. Rsch. Svc., Ft. Collins, Colo., 1981—. Contbr. articles to profl. jours. Sci. Excha. grantee USDA-Orgn. for Internat. Coop. Devel., Italy, 1991, 93; rsch. grantee USDA-Coop. State Rsch. Svc., 1992-94, NSF, 1996-98. Mem. Agronomy Soc. Am., Crop Sci. Soc. Am. (assoc. editor), Ecology Soc. Am., Italian Jour. Agronomy (assoc. editor), Sigma Xi. Democrat. Mennonite. Avocations: hiking, singing, guitar, reading. Home: 4401 Whippeny Dr Fort Collins CO 80526-5258 Office: USDA-ARS Crops Rsch Lab 1701 Centre Ave Fort Collins CO 80526-2083

MORGAN, JACK M., lawyer; b. Portales, N.Mex., Jan. 15, 1924; s. George Albert and Mary Rosana (Baker) M.; BBA, U. Tex. 1948; LLB, 1950; m. Peggy Flynn Cummings, 1947; children: Marilyn, Rebecca, Claudia, Jack. Admitted to N.Mex. bar, 1950; sole practice law, Farmington, N.Mex., 1956—; bd. dirs. First Place Fin. Corp., First Nat. Bank, Farmington, N.Mex.; mem. N.Mex. State Senate, 1973-88 Served with USN, 1942-46. Mem. N.Mex. Bar Assn., S.W. Regional Energy Council (past chmn.), Kiwanis, Elks. Republican. Office: PO Box 2151 Farmington NM 87499-2151

MORGAN, JAMES L., artist; b. Gouldburg, Pa., June 26, 1920; s. Lee James and Edith (Eldard) M.; m. M. Jean, July 5, 1943 (dec. Apr. 1966); children: James L. III (dec.), Mary Jane, Robert A.; m. Helen M., Sept. 30, 1969. BA, SUNY, 1974; MFA, U. N.C., 1987. Represented in permanent collections at IBM, Raleigh, N.C. Home: 2673 Congress Way Medford OR 97504-8509

MORGAN, LANNY, musician; b. Des Moines, Mar. 30, 1934; s. Harold Ira and Ruth (Maddick) M.; m. Marty Shelton Morgan; children: Breck, Wynter. Student, L.A. (Calif.) City Coll., 1952. instr. Stanford U. Summer Jazz Workshops, L.A. Jazz Workshop, Grove Sch. Music, Many others; guest artist, instr. at coll., high schs. throughout U.S.; played on recordings, films, TV; guest solo U.K. clubs, festivals. Played lead alto saxophone with Maynard Ferguson, Rey de Michele Orch., Oliver Nelson, Bill Holman Band, Bob Florence Band, Supersax; appeared, recorded Steely Dan, Natalie Cole, Diane Schurr, Shirley Horn, Andy Williams, Mel Torme, Frank Sinatra, Julie Andrews, and many others; lead quartet/quintet in L.A.; recordings include Lanny Morgan Quartet, 1993, Pacific Standard, 1997. With U.S. Army, 1957-59. Home: 6470 Gaviota Ave Van Nuys CA 91406-6401

MORGAN, MARK QUENTEN, astronomer, astrophysics educator; b. Topeka, Dec. 27, 1950; s. Walter Quenten and Barbara Gene (Haynes) M. BA in Astronomy, San Diego State U., 1972; PhD in Astronomy, U. Addison, Ont., Can., 1976. Jet engine and power plant engr. N.Am. Aviation, Palmdale, Calif., 1966-68; astron. observer San Diego State U., 1970-74; engr., solar observer U. Md.-Clark Lake Radio Obs., Borrego Springs, Calif., 1978-82; engr., lectr. Sci. Atlanta, San Diego, 1979—. Inventor continuous wave laser, 1965, high intensity sound acoustic screening system, 1979. Mem. Inst. Environ. Scis., Acoustic Soc. Am., Astrophys. Soc. Am., Union Concerned Scientists, Planetary Soc. Office: Sci Atlanta PO Box 4254 San Diego CA 92164-4254

MORGAN, MICHAEL BREWSTER, publishing company executive; b. L.A., Dec. 30, 1953; s. Brewster Bowen and Eleanor (Boysen) M.; m. Debra Hunter, July 20, 1986. BA, Conn. Coll., 1975. Coll. sales rep. Addison Wesley Pub. Co., Chapel Hill, N.C., 1977-81; sponsoring editor Addison Wesley Pub. Co., Reading, Mass., 1981-84; chief exec. officer Morgan Kaufmann Pubs., San Francisco, Calif., 1984—. Mem. Am. Assn. for Artificial Intelligence, Assn. for Computing Machinery. Office: Morgan Kaufmann Pubs 340 Pine St San Francisco CA 94104-3205*

MORGAN, NEIL, author, newspaper editor, lecturer, columnist; b. Smithfield, N.C., Feb. 27, 1924; s. Samuel Lewis and Isabelle (Robeson) M.; m. Caryl Lawrence, 1945 (div. 1954); m. Katharine Starkey, 1955 (div. 1962); m. Judith Blakely, 1964; 1 child, Jill. AB, Wake Forest Coll., 1943. Columnist San Diego Daily Jour., 1946-50; columnist San Diego Evening Tribune, 1950-92, assoc. editor, 1977-81, editor, 1981-92; assoc. editor, sr. columnist San Diego Union-Tribune, 1992—; syndicated columnist Morgan Jour., Copley News Service, 1958—; lectr.; cons. on Calif. affairs Bank of Am., Sunset mag. Author: My San Diego, 1951, It Began With a Roar, 1953, Know Your Doctor, 1954, Crosstown, 1955, My San Diego 1960, 1959, Westward Tilt, 1963, Neil Morgan's San Diego, 1964, The Pacific States, 1967, The California Syndrome, 1969, (with Robert Witty) Marines of Margarita, 1970, The Unconventional City, 1972, (with Tom Blair) Yesterday's San Diego, 1976, This Great Land, 1983, Above San Diego, 1990, (with Judith Morgan) Dr. Seuss & Mr. Geisel, 1995, (with Judith Morgan) Roger: The Biography of Roger Revelle, 1997; contbr. non-fiction articles to Nat. Geog., Esquire, Redbook, Reader's Digest, Holiday, Harper's, Travel and Leisure, Ency. Brit. Lt. USNR, 1943-46. Recipient Ernie Pyle Meml. award, 1957, Bill Corum Meml. award, 1961, Disting. Svc. citation Wake Forest U., 1966, grand award for travel writing Pacific Area Travel Assn., 1972, 78, Fourth Estate award San Diego State U., 1988, The Morgan award Leadership Edn. Awareness Devel. San Diego, 1993; co-recipient Ellen and Roger Revelle award, 1986; named Outstanding Young Man of Yr. San Diego, 1959, 1st place news commentary, Calif. News Pub. Assn., 1993, Harold Keen award, 1996. Mem. Authors Guild, Am. Soc. Newspaper Editors, Soc. Profl. Journalists, Soc. of Am. Travel Writers, Bohemian Club, Phi Beta Kappa. Home: 7930 Prospect Pl La Jolla CA 92037-3721 Office: PO Box 191 San Diego CA 92112-4106

MORGAN, NICHOLAS ISAAC, civil and environmental engineer, consultant; b. N.Y.C., Mar. 10, 1960; s. David Eisek Morgan and Alice Leslie (Blackstone) Gerard; m. Sloane, M. Smith, Sept. 10, 1994; 1 child, J. Gerard. BA in Civil Engring., U. Calif., Berkeley, 1982; MS in Civil Engring., U. Wash., Seattle, 1984. Civil engr. Kennedy/Jenks Cons., San Francisco, 1985-88; sr. engr. CH2M Hill, Bellevue, Wash., 1988—; project engr. U.S. EPA, Seattle, Washington, 1982-84; coord. regional superfund fed. facilities U.S. EPA Region 9, San Francisco, 1984-88; strategic planning coord. U.S. EPA, Washington, 1988-94; U.S. coord. internat. toxic trade campaign Greenpeace Internat., Washington, 1994-95; pres. Nicholas Morgan and Assocs., The Greenmill

MORGAN, PAUL EVAN, architect; b. L.A., Nov. 30, 1961; s. Normand Evan and Priscilla Josephine (Ibach) M.; m. Cynthia Lynne Burrell, Mar. 12, 1994. BA in Anthropology, UCLA, 1986; MArch, U. Colo., Denver, 1989. Lic. architect, Calif. Intern architect Anderson Mason Dale, Denver, 1988-89; intern architect John Ferguson and Assocs., L.A., 1989-92, job capt., CAD mgr., 1992-94, project architect, 94—. Mem. UCLA Alumni Assn., UCLA Alumni Band. Democrat. Presbyterian. Avocations: golf, skiing, reading, travel, music. Home: 6100 W 76th St Los Angeles CA 90045-1638 Office: John Ferguson and Assocs 2440 S Sepulveda Blvd Los Angeles CA 90064-1744

MORGAN, RONALD WILLIAM, sales executive; b. Redlands, Calif.; s. Liberty W. and Eleanor L. Morgan; m. Debra Ann Lein, Nov. 30, 1991. AA in Machine Shop, Valley Coll., 1973; BA in Bus., Calif. State U., San Bernardino, 1977. Sales mgr. Combined Ins., Redlands, 1976-77; ter. sales mgr. Bullard Safety, L.A., 1977-79; sales engr. H.E.S. Machine Tool, Whittier, Calif., 1979-81, Machinery Sales, L.A., 1981-89; regional mgr. Ingersoll Rand Water Jet, Yorba Linda, Calif., 1989-91; ter. sales mgr. Machinery Sales, L.A., 1991-93; dist. mgr. Ellison Machinery, L.A., 1993-94; regional mgr. Daewoo Machinery, L.A., 1995—. With USCGR. Mem. Soc. Mfg. Engrs., Sons Am. Revolution. Avocations: travel, boats, motorcycles. Office: Daewoo Machinery 10395 Slusher Dr Santa Fe Springs CA 90670-7352

MORGAN, STANLEY CHARLES, plastic and reconstructive surgeon; b. Phoenix, July 23, 1935; s. Fred Charles and Hazel (King) M.; m. Doris Anne Duke, Sept. 8, 1956; children: Pamela Anne, Cheryl Lynn, Mark Thomas. BS, U. Ariz.; MD, St. Louis Sch. Medicine. Diplomate Am. Bd. Plastic Surgery. Intern UCLA Ctr. Health Svcs., 1961-62, resident plastic surgery, 1966-68; resident gen. surgery Wadsworth Vets. Hosp., L.A., 1962-66; practice medicine specializing in plastic surgery Pasadena, Calif., 1970—; asst. clin. prof. U. So. Calif. Sch. Medicine, Los Angeles, 1981—, UCLA Ctr. Health Scis., 1970-81. Lt. col. U.S. Army, 1968-70. Fellow ACS, Am. Soc. Plastic and Reconstructive Surgeons, Am. Soc. Aesthetic Plastic Surgery, Calif. Soc. Plastic Surgeons. Office: 10 Congress St Ste 407 Pasadena CA 91105-3023

MORGENROTH, EARL EUGENE, entrepreneur; b. Sidney, Mont., May 7, 1936; s. Frank and Leona (Ellison) M.; m. Noella Nichols, Aug. 2, 1958; children: Dolores Roxanna, David Jonathan, Denise Christine. BS, U. Mont., 1961. From salesman to gen. mgr. Sta. KGVO-AM Radio, Missoula, Mont., 1958-65; sales mgr. Stas. KGVO-TV, KTVM-TV and KCFW-TV, Missoula, Butte, Kalispell, Mont., 1965-66, gen. mgr., 1966-68; gen. mgr. Sta. KCOY-TV, Santa Maria, Calif., 1968-69; v.p., gen. mgr. Western Broadcasting Co., Missoula, 1966-69, gen. mgr., pres., 1969-81; gen. mgr. pres. numerous cos., Mont., Calif. Idaho, P.R., Ga., 1966-84; pres., chmn. Western Broadcasting Co., Missoula, 1981-84, Western Communications, Inc., Reno, 1984-90; prin. Western Investments, Reno, 1984—; chmn. Western Fin., Inc., Morgenroth Music Ctrs., Inc., Mont., Mont. Band Instruments, Inc.; chmn. E & B Music Co., Times Square, Inc., Rio de Plumas Ranches, LLC. Mem. Mont. Bank Bd., Helena; commencement spkr. U. Mont., 1988; bd. dirs. U. Mont. Found., 1985-95. With U.S. Army, 1954-57. Named Boss of Yr. Santa Maria Valley J.C.s, 1968, Alumni of Yr., U. Mont. Bus. Sch., 1998. Mem. U. Mont. Century Club (pres.), Missoula C. of C. (pres.), Rocky Mountain Broadcasters Assn. (pres.), Craighead Wildlife-Wildlands Inst. (bd. dirs. 1991-97), Boone and Crockett Club (first v.p. devel.), Grizzly Riders Internat. (bd. dirs., v.p.), Bldg. A Scholastic Heritage (bd. dirs. 1987-97). Republican. Methodist.

MORGENROTH, ROBERT WILLIAM, producer; b. Pitts., Jan. 29, 1957; s. William Mason Morgenroth and June Marie Carr; m. Linda Ann Culliton; children: Christiana Lee, Thomas James. BS in Bus. Mgmt., W.Va. Weslyan Coll., 1977; postgrad., Ariz. State U., 1980; cert. in directing, producing, UCLA Extension, 1987. Producer Media Prodns., USA, Denver, 1981-83, v.p. prodn., gen. mgr., 1983-85; pres. prodn. Media Prodns., USA, L.A., 1985-86; asst. prodn. exec. New World Prodns., L.A., 1986-87; ind. producer, prodn. mgr. L.A., 1987—; owner E=MC2, Inc. (Visual Effects Co.), L.A., 1990—. Author mktg. column in 'N Sync mag., 1984-85. Recipient Award of Excellence U.S. Indsl. Film Festival, 1985. Mem. Am. Film Inst., Writers, Dirs., Producers Assn., Colo. Film and Video Assn. (pres. 1985-86). Democrat. Avocations: travel, scuba diving, skiing. Office: 710 Ivy St Glendale CA 91204-1004

MORGENSEN, JERRY LYNN, construction company executive; b. Lubbock, Tex., July 9, 1942; s. J.J. and Zelline (Butler) M.; m. Linda Dee Austin, Apr. 17, 1965; children: Angela, Nicole. BCE, Tex. Tech U., 1965. Area engr. E.I. Dupont Co., Orange, Tex., 1965-67; div. engr. E.I. Dupont Co., La Place, La., 1967-73; project mgr. Hensel Phelps Constrn. Co., Greeley, Colo., 1973-78, area mgr., 1978-80, v.p., 1980-85, pres., CEO, 1985—. Office: Hensel Phelps Constrn Co 420 Sixth Ave PO Box O Greeley CO 80632

MORGENSTERN, NORBERT RUBIN, civil engineering educator; b. Toronto, Ont., Can., May 25, 1935; s. Joel and Bella (Skornik) M.; m. Patricia Elizabeth Gooderham, Dec. 28, 1960; children: Sarah Alexandra, Katherine Victoria, David Michael Gooderham. BASc, U. Toronto, 1956, DEng h.c., 1983; DIC, Imperial Coll. Sci., 1964; PhD, U. London, 1964; DSc h.c., Queen's U., 1989. Rsch. asst., lectr. civil engring. Imperial Coll. Sci. and Tech., London, 1958-68; prof. civil engring. U. Alta., Edmonton, Can., 1968-83, Univ. prof., 1983—, chmn. dept. civil engring., 1994-97; cons. engr., 1961—. Contbr. articles to profl. jours. Bd. dirs. Young Naturalists Found., 1977-82, Edmonton Symphony Soc., 1978-85. Athlone fellow, 1956; recipient prize Brit. Geotech. Soc., 1961, 66, Huber prize ASCE, 1971, Legget award Can. Geotech. Soc., 1979, Alta. order of Excellence, 1991. Fellow Royal Soc. Can., Can. Acad. Engring.; mem. U.S. Nat. Acad. Engring. (fgn. assoc.), Royal Acad. Engring. (fgn. mem.), Cancian Geosci. Coun. (pres. 1983), Can. Geotechnical Soc. (pres. 1989-91), Internat. Soc. for Soil Mechanics and Found. Engring. (pres. 1989-94), Royal Glenora Club, Athenaeum (London), various other profl. assns. Home: 106 Laurier Dr, Edmonton, AB Canada T5R 5P6 Office: U Alta, Dept Civil Engring, Edmonton, AB Canada T6G 2G7

MORGENTHALER, PATRICIA B., visual artist; b. Wilburton, Okla., Sept. 25, 1924; d. Fred Yother and Ethel Inez (May) Neal; m. Fred Warren Morgenthaler, Sept. 5, 1943 (div. 1987); children: Ronald Warren, Wayne William, John Robert. Ba, Calif. State U., Fullerton, 1976; MFA, Claremont (Calif.) Grad. Sch., 1978. One women shows include Hunt-Wesson Adminstrv. Complex, 1974, Riverside Art Ctr., 1974, Laguna Art Mus., 1974, 75, Brand Libr. Art Gallery, 1974, Downey Mus. of Art, 1974, L.A. Mcpl. Gallery, 1974, Long Beach Art Assn., 1975, Hillcrest Invitational, Whittier, Claif., 1975, Floating Gallery, Santa Ana, Calif., 1975, Brea Civic Cultural Ctr. Gallery, 1975, Muckenthaler Cultrual Ctr., Fullerton, Calif., 1975, Ctr. Gallery-Calif. State U. Fullerton, 1975, Arnold Gallery, Newport, Calif., Newport Beach City Hall, Whitter Art Gallery, Whittier, Calif., Ctr. Gallery, U. of Calif., Irvine, Libra Gallery, Claremont, Calif., 1977, Calif. Mus. Sci. and Industry, 1978, Mus. Libra Gallery, 1978, Los Angeles County Mus. Art Rental Gallery, 1979, Pacific Design Ctr., 1981, Brea Civic Cultural Ctr. Gallery, 1983, Downey Mus. of Art, 1984, Orlando Gallery, 1985, Chrysalis Gallery, Claremont, 1985, Studio Art Sale Benefit, Fullerton, 1986, Soc. Western Artists, Fresno, 1988, Rancho Santiago Coll. 1988, Orange County Women's Invitational, Anahcim, Calif., 1988, Orange County Ctr. for Contemporary Art Auction, 1989, Calif. State U. Alumni/Art Alliance Auction, 1989, Hunt Beach Br. Libr., Fullerton, 1990. Teaching fellow Claremont Grad. Sch., 1977-78. Office: Morgenthaler Studio 501 W Hermosa Dr Fullerton CA 92835-1403

MORIMOTO, CARL NOBORU, computer system engineer, crystallographer; b. Hiroshima, Japan, Mar. 31, 1942; came to U.S., 1957; naturalized

ized, 1965; s. Toshiyuki and Teruko (Hirano) M.; m. Helen Kiyomi Yoshizaki, June 28, 1969; children: Matthew Ken, Justin Ray. BA, U. Hawaii, 1965; PhD, U. Wash., 1970. Research assoc. dept. chemistry Mich. State U., East Lansing, 1970-72; postdoctoral fellow dept. biochemistry and biophysics Tex. A&M U., College Station, 1972-75; sr. sci. programmer Syntex Analytical Instruments Inc., Cupertino, Calif., 1975-78; prin. programmer analyst, software engring. mgr. Control Data Corp., Sunnyvale, Calif., 1978-83; mem. profl. staff GE Aerospace, San Jose, Calif., 1983-93; prin. engr. GE Nuclear Energy, San Jose, 1993-97; mem. tech. staff Silicon Graphics, Inc., Mountain View, Calif., 1997-98; contractor GE Nuclear Energy, San Jose, Calif., 1998—. Mem. Am. Crytallographic Assn., Assn. Computing Machinery, Am. Chem. Soc., Sigma Xi. Am. Baptist. Home: 4003 Hamilton Park Dr San Jose CA 95130-1223

MORIN, PAULA MARIE YVETTE (MARYAN MORIN), photographer, artist, photo researcher; b. Hollywood, Calif., Feb. 4, 1945; d. Charles Eugene Robert Anthony Joseph and Mary Elsa (Hoffmann) M.; m. Robert C. McCamey, 1970 (div. 1974); children: Marc Richard McCamey, Ian Eugene McCamey. BA in Fine Art magna cum laude, So. Oreg. Univ., Ashland, 1978; cert. secondary tchr., So. Oreg. Univ./U. Wash., Ashland and Seattle, 1990. Photographer, oral historian Circle Sky Prodns., Talent, Oreg., 1979-81; photographer U. Mont., Missoula, 1981-82; owner, photographer Heritage Photo Works LLC, Prescott, Ariz., 1991-96, Hamilton, Mont., 1991-96; artist, photographer Paula Morin Photo Art and Looking Glass Images, Missoula, 1997—; field rschr. Oreg. Folk Arts, Oreg. Art Commn., Salem, 1979; mem. adj. faculty Prescott (Ariz.) Coll., 1993; founding dir. N.W. Exposure Photography Inc., Ashland, Oreg., 1979; arts pro cons. Mont. Arts Coun., 1999. Represented in permanent collections of Casa Grande (Ariz.) Mus., 1993 and Mt. Angel Abbey (Oreg.). Profl. devel. grantee Ariz. Commn. on Arts, Phoenix, 1993. Mem. Mont. Hist. Soc. Roman Catholic. Avocations: horsemanship, outdoor life, travel. Office: Paula Morin Photo Art LLC PO Box 8222 Missoula MT 59807-8222

MORITA, TOSHIYASU, technology professional; b. Tokyo, Feb. 8, 1967; s. Hiroshi and Fusako (Ishikawa) M. Grad. high sch., 1985. Programmer Origin Systems, Inc., Austin, Tex., 1987; engr. Cyclops Electronics, Boerne, 1988-90; programmer Taito R&D, Bothell, Wash., 1990; mgr. new tech. LucasArts Entertainment, San Rafael, Calif., 1990-93; tech. dir. Sega Tech. Inst., Redwood City, Calif., 1993-94, Sega of Am., Redwood City, 1994-96, SegaSoft, Redwood City, 1996-97; dir. tech. Sega Am., Redwood City, 1997—. Mem. IEEE Computer Soc. (affiliate), Mensa.

MORITZ, TIMOTHY BOVIE, psychiatrist; b. Portsmouth, Ohio, July 26, 1936; s. Charles Raymond and Elisabeth Bovie (Morgan) M., m. Joyce Elizabeth Rasmussen, Oct. 13, 1962 (div. Sept. 1969); children: Elizabeth Wynne, Laura Morgan; m. Antoinette Tanasichuk, Oct. 31, 1981; children: David Michael, Stephanie Lysbeth. *Brother Roger is a gynecologist in Dayton and pioneered in treatment of fertility. Brother Michael is an attorney in Columbus listed in "Who's Who in America". Brother Jeffrey is an engineer with Hewlett-Packard in Santa Rosa. Daughter Lisa is a health research administrator at New York University. Daughter Laura Tresca is a teacher in the Boston area. Wife Antoinette, a teacher in Columbus, with a master's degree from Ohio State and additional graduate work at University of Georgia, has subsequently devoted herself to raising her children. Son David and daughter Stephanie are students in Las Vegas.* BA, Ohio State U., 1959; MD, Cornell U., 1963. Diplomate Am. Bd. Psychiatry and Neurology. Intern in medicine N.Y. Hosp., N.Y.C., 1963-64, resident in psychiatry, 1964-67; spl. asst. to dir. NIMH, Bethesda, Md., 1967-69; dir. Community Mental Health Ctr., Rockland County, N.Y., 1970-74, Ohio Dept. Mental Health, Columbus, Ohio, 1975-81; med. dir. psychiatry Miami Valley Hosp., Dayton, Ohio, 1981-82; med. dir. N.E. Ga. Community Mental Health Ctr., Athens, Ga., 1982-83, Charter Vista Hosp., Fayetteville, Ark., 1983-87; clin. dir. adult psychiatry Charter Hosp., Las Vegas, Nev., 1987-94; pvt. practice psychiatry Las Vegas, Nev., 1987—; prof. Wright State U., Dayton, Ohio, 1981-82; asst. prof. Cornell U., N.Y.C., 1970-73; cons. NIMH, Rockville, Md., 1973-83. *After he provided 6 years of leadership improving its state and community mental health, mental retardation, and drug abuse services, the State of Ohio recognized his contributions by renaming its Central Ohio Forensic Psychiatric Hospital as "The Timothy B. Moritz Forensic Psychiatric Hospital". During his 16 years of fulltime public service as a psychiatrist at the federal, state, and community levels, he received recognition for leadership in developing comprehensive community services and improved state services. Since 1983 he has been fulltime in the private practice of psychiatry devoted to providing the best possible quality treatment to individual patients.* Author: (chpt.) Rehabilitation Medicine and Psychiatry, 1976; mem. editorial bd. Directions in Psychiatry, 1981—. Dir. dept. mental health and mental retardation Gov.'s Cabinet, State of Ohio, Columbus, 1975-81. Recipient Svc. award Ohio Senate, 1981, Svc. Achievement award Ohio Gov., 1981. Fellow Am. Psychiat. Assn. (Disting. Svc. award 1981); mem. AMA, Nev. Assn. Psychiat. Physicians, Nev. State Med. Assn., Clark County Med. Soc., Cornell U. Med. Coll. Alumni Assn. Office: Timothy B Moritz MD 3150 N Tenaya Way Ste 415 Las Vegas NV 89128-0463

MORLER, EDWARD EDWIN, small business owner; b. Oak Park, Ill., May 7, 1940; s. Edwin Edward and Malva Ida (Pospicil) M.; m. Denise Dawson, Oct. 28, 1993. BS, Ill. Inst. of Tech., 1962; MBA, U. Chgo., 1968; PhD, U. Md., 1973. Cons. Fry Consultants, Inc., Chgo., 1968-69; dir. adminstrv. svcs. Airline Pilots Assn., Washington, 1969-71; spl. cons. Dept. Labor, Washington, 1972; cons. Washington, 1973-76, Effective Comm. Skills, Inc., N.Y.C., 1976-78; founder, chmn. Morler Internat., Inc., Sonoma, Calif., 1978—. Lt. U.S. Navy, 1962-66,. Avocations: artist in oils, golf, writing. Office: Morler Internat Inc 1140 Brockman Dr Sonoma CA 95476

MORRIS, BRIAN, advertising executive. Pres. Dailey & Assoc., L.A., Calif. Office: Dailey & Assoc 8687 Melrose Ave West Hollywood CA 90069*

MORRIS, BRUCE DORIAN, technical writer, literary historian, educator; b. San Francisco, July 10, 1947; s. William and Helen S. (Jorgensen) M. AA, Coll. San Mateo, Calif., 1968; BA in English and Linguistics, San Francisco State Coll., 1969; MA in English Lit., San Francisco State U., 1972; PhD, U. Denver, 1977. Grad. teaching fellow dept. English U. Denver, 1973-77; asst. instr. Pacific Crest Outward Bound Sch., Portland, Oreg., 1978; jr. tech. writer Harris-Farinon, San Carlos, Calif., 1979-82; sr. tech. writer Verilink Corp., San Jose, Calif., 1985-88, Tektronix Corp., Mountain View, Calif., 1988-90, MorComm Tech. Writing Svcs., Belmont, Calif., 1991—, MorComm Press, Belmont, Calif., 1992—; sr. tech writer Alpha Lab Telco Syss., Fremont, Calif., 1994-96; sr. tech. writer Carrier Access Corp., Boulder, Colo., 1996-97; ind. contractor Fujitsu Network Tech. Profl. Svcs. Divsn., Campbell, Calif., 1998—. Author: Sport Climber's Guide to Skyline Boulevard, 1995; editor: Arthur Symons: Letters to Yeats, 1989. Calif. State grad. fellow. Mem. MLA, Internat. Platform Soc., Soc. for Tech. Comm., Irish-Am. Cultural Inst., Am. Alpine Club, Access Fund, Commonwealth Club of Calif., Alpha Gamma Sigma. Avocations: rock climbing, bicycle racing. Home and Office: MorComm Press and Tech Writing Svcs 2221 Thurm Ave Belmont CA 94002-1547

MORRIS, DAVID JOHN, mining engineer, consultant, mining executive; b. Seattle, May 6, 1945; s. Jack Abraham and Alice Jean (Hanson) M.; m. Melania F. Kearney, July 28, 1978; children: Whitney Elizabeth, Benton James, Sienna Elise. BA in Math. and Physics, Whitman Coll., 1968; BS in Mining Engring., Columbia U., 1968. Registered profl. engr., Colo., Utah, Wash. Mining engr. Union Oil of Calif., Los Angeles, 1968-69; mining engr. John T. Boyd Co., Denver, 1974-76, sr. mining engr., 1976-78, v.p., mgr., 1978-87; sr. cons., 1998—; mng. ptnr. Palmer Coaking Coal Co., Black Diamond, Wash., 1976-82, 90—; pres. Pacific Coast Coal Co., Black Diamond, Wash., 1982—, Pacific Hydropower Devel., Inc., Seattle, Wash., 1995—. Mem. Bd. Overseers Whitman Coll., Walla Walla, Wash., 1986—, vice chair, 1993-95, chmn. Rep. campaign for Whitman, Denver, 1985; coach youth athletics. Served as lt. USN, 1969-74, Vietnam. Henry Krumb scholar Columbia U., N.Y.C., 1967-68. Mem. NSPE, Soc. Mining Engrs. (admissions com. 1985-88, Howard Eavenson award com. 1984-87, Woomer award com. 1990-93, chair 1993—, Ramsay award com. 1992-95, chair 1995—), Nat. Coal Assn. (bd. dirs. 1990—, exec. com. 1993-94, 96—), Nat. Coal Coun. (appointed by Sec. of Energy 1992, 94, 96), Nat. Mining Assn. (bd. dirs. 1995—), Seattle C. of C. (chmn. energy com. 1991-94), Western Rugby Football Union (sec. 1980), Broadmoor Golf Club, Rotary. Republican. Avocations: golf, hunting, fishing, gardening, handball. Home: 3711 E Madison St Seattle WA 98112-3838 Office: Pacific Coast Coal Co Inc PO Box 450 Black Diamond WA 98010-0450

MORRIS, DONALD CHARLES, commercial real estate mergers and acquisitions; b. Iowa City, Nov. 15, 1951; s. Lucien Ellis and Jean (Pinder) M.; m. Barbara Louise Small, Apr. 28, 1973 (div. Apr. 1980); m. Jana Susan Moyer, Aug. 28, 1982; children: Alexander Charles, Elisa Jean. Student, Cantab Coll., Toronto, Can., 1970-71; BSC, U. Guelph, Can., 1974; MSC, U. Guelph, 1975; PhD, U. B.C., Vancouver, 1978. Instr. U. B.C., Vancouver, 1975-77; pres. Morley Internat., Inc., Seattle, 1976-81; self-employed Comml. Investment Real Estate, Seattle, 1981-83; v.p., regional mgr. DKB Corp., Seattle, 1983-86; pres. Morris Devel. Svcs., Inc., Seattle, 1986—, Washington Group, Inc., Seattle, 1986—. Bd. dirs. Perservation Action, Washington, 1985-90; mem. Nat. Trust for Historic Preservation. Mem. Nat. Assn. Realtors, Wash. Assn. Realtors. Avocations: skiing, sailing, boating. Office: Wash Group Morris Devel PO Box 4584 Rollingbay WA 98061-0584

MORRIS, ELIZABETH TREAT, physical therapist; b. Hartford, Conn., Feb. 20, 1936; d. Charles Wells and Marion Louise (Case) Treat; BS in Phys. Therapy, U. Conn., 1960; m. David Breck Morris, July 10, 1961; children: Russell Charles, Jeffrey David. Phys. therapist Crippled Children's Clinic No. Va., Arlington, 1960-62, Shriners Hosp. Crippled Children, Salt Lake City, 1967-69, Holy Cross Hosp., Salt Lake City, 1970-74; pvt. practice phys. therapy, Salt Lake City, 1975—. Mem. nominating com. YWCA, Salt Lake City. Mem. Am. Phys. Therapy Assn., Am. Congress Rehab. Medicine, Am. Alliance for Health, Phys. Edn., Recreation & Dance, Nat. Speakers Assn., Utah Speakers Assn., Salt Lake Area C. of C., Friendship Force Utah, U.S. Figure Skating Assn., Toastmasters Internat., Internat. Assn. for the Study Pain, Internat. Platform Assn., World Confederation Phys. Therapy, Medart Internat. Home: 4177 Mathews Way Salt Lake City UT 84124-4021 Office: PO Box 526186 Salt Lake City UT 84152-6186

MORRIS, HENRY ARTHUR, JR., export company executive, consultant; b. Phila., May 26, 1923; s. Henry A. Sr. and Eleanor (Samuel) M.; widowed; 1 child, Henry A. III; m. Farideh R. Ranjandish, Feb. 9, 1991. BA, Lycoming Coll., 1952; LLB, Cath. U., 1954. Pres., chief exec. officer Am. Funding Int., Inc., Beverly Hills, Calif., 1956—; bd. dirs. McLean Agro-Indsl., Arlington, Va., Am. Housing Internat., Inc., Fairfax, Va.; chief exec. officer Export Cons., Inc., West L.A., 1983—. With U.S. Army, 1943-45, Europe. Democrat. Roman Catholic. Avocations: fox hunting, golf. Office: Am Funding Internat Inc PO Box 2085 Beverly Hills CA 90213-2085

MORRIS, JAMES, national monument official. Supt. Craters of the Moon Nat. Monument, Arco, Idaho. Office: Craters of the Moon Nat Monument PO Box 29 Arco ID 83213-0029*

MORRIS, JOHN DAVID, research institute administrator, geology educator; b. Mpls., Dec. 7, 1946; s. Henry Madison and Mary Louise (Beach) M.; m. Dalta Jan Eads, Sept. 3, 1977; children: Chara Mischelle, Timothy Adam, Beth Anna. BSCE, Va. Tech., 1969; MS in Geol. Engring., U. Okla., 1977, PhD in Geol. Engring., 1980. Civil engr. City of L.A. Pub. Works, 1969-75; adj. rsch. scientist Inst. for Creation Rsch., Santee, Calif., 1972-84; prof. geology Inst. for Creation Rsch., Santee, 1984-95, pres., 1995—; asst. prof. geol. engr. U. Okla., 1980-84. Author: The Young Earth, 1994, Noah's Ark and Ararat Adventures, 1994 (Gold Medal 1994); co-author: Modern Creation Trilogy, 1996; contbr. articles to profl. jours. Republican. Mem. Bible Ch. Office: Inst for Creation Rsch 10946 Woodside Ave N Santee CA 92071-2833

MORRIS, JOHN THEODORE, planning official; b. Denver, Jan. 18, 1929; s. Theodore Ora and Daisy Allison (McDonald) M.; BFA, Denver U., 1955; m. Dolores Irene Seaman, June 21, 1951; children: Holly Lee, Heather Ann, Heidi Jo, Douglas Fraser. Apprentice landscape architect S.R. DeBoer & Co., Denver, summer 1949, planning technician (part-time), 1954-55; sr. planner and assoc. Trafton Bean & Assocs., Boulder, Colo., 1955-62; prin. Land Planning Assocs., planning cons., Boulder, 1962-65; planning dir. and park coord. Boulder County, 1965-67; sch. planner Boulder Valley Sch. Dist., 1967-84, also dir. planning and engring., 1967-84, supr. facility improvement program, 1969-84; pvt. sch. planning cons., 1984—; cons. U. Colo. Bur. Ednl. Field Svcs., 1974. Bd. dirs. Historic Boulder, 1974-76; mem. parks and recreation adv. com. Denver Regional Coun. Govts., 1975-84. Served with USCG, 1950-53. Mem. Am. Inst. Cert. Planners, Am. Planning Assn., Longmont Artist Guild. Home and Office: 7647 32nd St Boulder CO 80302-9327

MORRIS, KARLENE EKSTRUM, interior design educator; b. Kimball, S.D., Mar. 4, 1938; d. Carl Leonard and Caren (Johnson) Ekstrum; m. Robert Swift Morris, July 30, 1965; 1 child, Ingrid Caren. BS, S.D.State U., 1960; MA, Calif. State U.-Long Beach, 1964; postgrad., UCLA, Calif. State U. developer interior design program San Antonio Coll., Walnut, Calif. Tchr. Woodrow Wilson High Sch., L.A., 1960-61, Pioneer High Sch., Whittier, Calif., 1961-64; prof. interior design Mt. San Antonio Coll., Walnut, Calif., 1966—, developer interior design program San Antonio Coll., Walnut, Calif., 1966—. Recipient Outstanding Home Econs. Dept. award Chancellors Office L.A. Cmty. Colls., 1984, Excellence in Edn.-Regional Interior Design Program, Calif. Cmty. Colls., 1997; grantee Illuminating Engrs. N.Am., 1987. Mem. Am. Soc. Interior Designers, Interior Design Educators Coun. Republican. Lutheran. Avocations: needlework, gardening, travel, reading. Home: 3643 Yorkshire Rd Pasadena CA 91107-5434

MORRIS, ROBERT, writer; b. Levelland, Tex., Feb. 6, 1933; s. Arthur Garfield and Vera (Gardener) M.; m. Mary Pauline Erschoen, Sept. 15, 1965 (div. 1991); 1 child, Peter Jason. BS, U. Houston, 1960. Instr. fiction Glendale C.C.; reporter Southwest Wave, L.A., 1961-63; deputy probation officer L.A. County, 1963-85. Author: Hit and Run, 1986. Bd. dirs. Penny Lane Found. With U.S. Army, 1953-55. Recipient L.A. Weekly Critics award, 1988. Home and office: 2200 N Beachwood Dr Hollywood CA 90068

MORRIS, STEPHEN ALLEN, elementary school educator; b. Garden Grove, Calif., Mar. 2, 1957; s. Eddie Melvin and Lesta Joy (Birdsall) M.; m. MariLynn Edith; stepchildren: Tyler, Trevor. BS in Phys. Edn., Calif. State U., Fullerton, 1987. Cert. tchr., Calif. Elem. tchr. Riverside (Calif.) Unified Sch. Dist., 1990—; lectr. Calif. Elem. Edn. Assn., Torrance, 1994—, The Edn. Ctr., Torrance, 1994—; cons. Inland Area Math. Project, Riverside, 1992—. Author: Everything You Wanted to Know About Division...In a Day!, 1993. Mem. Benjamin Franklin Elem. Sch. Site Coun., Riverside, 1992. Mem. ASCD, Nat. Coun. Tchrs. Math., Calif. Math. Coun. Baptist. Avocations: running, cycling, silkscreening. Home: 6823 Laurelbrook Dr Riverside CA 92506-6268 Office: Ben Franklin Elem Sch 19661 Orange Terrace Pky Riverside CA 92508-3256

MORRISON, ELLEN M., writer, researcher; b. Marysville, Calif., Apr. 17, 1954; d. Louis Arch and Mildred Claire (Hansen) Morrison; m. Kenneth William Lann, Jun. 26, 1976; 1 child, Mallory. BA, UCLA, 1977; MA, U. Chgo., 1982, PhD, 1979-87. Rsch. asst. U. Chgo., 1980-82, rsch. analyst, 1982-84; project dir. Northwestern U., Evanston, Ill., 1984-87; postdoctoral fellow U. Calif., San Francisco, 1988-90; program dir. Inst. for the Future, Menlo Park, Calif., 1990-95; author San Carlos, Calif., 1995—. Co-author: Strategic Choices For America's Hospitals (book of the year 1990), 1990; Contbr. articles to profl. jours. Mem. NOW, Amnesty Internat., Greenpeace. Democrat. Avocations: public education support, community theatre, jogging, skiing, tennis. Home and Office: 142 Plymouth Ave San Carlos CA 94070-1621

MORRISON, GLENN LESLIE, minister; b. Cortez, Colo., Feb. 26, 1929; s. Ward Carl Morrison and Alma Irene (Butler) Anderson; m. Beverely Joanne Buck, Aug. 26, 1949; children: David Mark, Betty Jo Morrison Mullen, Gary Alan, Judith Lynn Morrison Oltmann, Stephen Scott. Student, San Diego State U., 1948-49, Chabot Coll., 1968-69. Ordained to ministry Evang. Ch. Alliance, 1961. Dir. counseling and follow-up Oakland (Calif.) Youth for Christ, 1954-56; pres. Follow Up Ministries, Inc., Castro Valley, Calif., 1956—; assoc. pastor 1st Covenant Ch., Oakland, 1956-58; exec. dir. East Bay Youth for Christ, Oakland, 1960-66; supervising chaplain Alameda County (Calif.) Probation Dept., 1971-90; vol. chaplain Alameda County Sheriff's Dept., 1971—; seminar leader Calif. Dept. Corrections, Sacramento, 1978—, mem. chaplains coordinating com., 1988—; founder, dir. God Squad Vol. Program for Prison Workers, 1972—. *Glenn Morrison began his ministry to prisoners in 1949 as volunteer chaplain at Camp Minniewawa, a state prison camp near San Diego, California. In 1956 he helped found Follow Up Ministries, a non-profit California corporation with volunteer outreach in several states and foreign countries. A 28 lesson corresponence Bible course is available to prisoners around the world. Morrison's years of service in the correctional field, his expertise in working with prisoners and volunteers, and his cordial relations with institutional officials have earned him the respect and trust of leaders in this fast-growing mission field.* Author: Scripture Investigation Course, 1956. Mem. Am. Correctional Assn., Am. Protestant Correctional Chaplains Assn. (regional pres., sec. 1980-86, nat. sec. 1986-88, nat. 2nd v.p. 1996-98). Office: Follow Up Ministries Inc PO Box 2514 Castro Valley CA 94546-0514

MORRISON, GUS (ANGUS HUGH MORRISON), mayor, engineer; b. Buffalo, Sept. 13, 1935; s. John Weir and Mary (Norton) M.; m. Joy Rita Hallenbarter, Feb. 7, 1959; children: Frank, Gloria, Heather. Technician Bell Aircraft Corp., Niagara Falls, N.Y., 1956-58; technician Lockheed Missiles and Space Corp., Sunnyvale, Calif., 1958-63, test engr., 1963-78, group engr., 1978-86, dept. mgr., 1986—; mayor Fremont, Calif., 1994—. Mayor Fremont, Calif., 1985—, council mem., 1978-85, planning commr., 1977-78; bd. dirs. Tri City Ecology Ctr., 1976—. Served with USN, 1953-56. Democrat. Roman Catholic. Avocations: computers, photography, seriography. Office: Office of Mayor PO Box 5006 Fremont CA 94537-5006*

MORRISON, JAMES R., art educator, sculptor; b. Lancaster, Pa., Jan. 8, 1953; s. Clifford R. and E. Jane (Gephart) M.; m. Lisa Ann Foltz, May 30, 1981; children: Erica Marie, James Jr. BS in Art Ed. magna cum laude, U. Pa., Millersville, 1985, MEd in Art, 1990. Cert. tchr., Calif. and Pa. Art tchr. Thaddeus Stevens Sch. of Tech., Lancaster, Pa., 1989-91, Arroyo Seco Jr. H.S., Valencia, Calif., 1991—; Prod. Asst. to sculptor Ike Hay, 1981-90; juror Lititz Art Show, 1988. One-man show Millersville Univ., 1989; group shows at Millersville Univ., 1988,89, Cmty. gallery, Lancaster, Pa., 1988, 89, 90, Hollywood Arts Coun., 1994, L.A. Art Assoc., 1994-95, Eighth Muse Gallery, West Hollywood, Calif., 1995, Desmond Gallery, West Hollywiid, 1995, Claremont Grad. U., 1997; numerous others; represented in numerous private collections. Office: Arroyo Seco Jr HS N Vista Del Gado Dr Valencia CA 91354

MORRISON, JEAN, geochemist, geology educator; b. New Milford, Conn., May 19, 1958; d. Milnor Bowden and Etta Marie (Hayball) M.; m. James Lawford Anderson, June 6, 1992; children: Sarah Marie, James Milnor. BA, Colgate U., 1980; MS, U. Ga., 1983; PhD, U. Wis., 1988. Asst. prof. U. So. Calif., L.A., 1988-95, assoc. prof., 1995—; vis. assoc. prof. Calif. Tech., Pasadena, 1996-97. Editor, author/co-author: Jour. Meta Geology, 1997; contbr. articles to sci. jours. Mem. Geol. Soc. of Am., Am. Geophys. Union, Mineralogic Soc. of Am. Office: Univ So Calif Los Angeles CA 90089-0740

MORRISON, KEITH ANTHONY, artist; b. Linstead, St. Catherine, Jamaica, May 20, 1942; came to U.S., 1945; s. Noel Albert and Beatrice Louise (McPherson) M. BFA, Art Inst. Chgo., 1963, MFA, 1965. Asst. prof. Fisk U., Nashville, 1967-68; chmn. art dept. DePaul U., Chgo., 1969-71; assoc. prof. U. Ill., Chgo., 1971-73, assoc. dean Coll. of Architecture & Art, 1973-78; prof. art U. Md., College Park, 1979-88, chmn. art dept., 1988—; dean San Francisco Sri Inst., 1992-94, dean Coll. Creative Arts San Francisco State U., 1994-96; dean Coll. Arts Humanities U. Md., 1997; dean Coll. Creative Arts San Fransisco State U., 1997—; visual arts cons. Ill. State Arts Coun., Chgo., 1971-75, D.C. Arts Coun. Washington, 1986; visual panelist Md. State Arts Coun., 1986; bd. dirs. Washington Project for the Arts. Contbr. articles to profl. jours.; one-man shows include Washington, Chgo., L.A., Boston, N.Y.C.; exhibited in many group shows including Art Inst. Chgo., Bronx Museum, N.Y.C., De Young Muesum, San Francisco, Museum Art, Chgo., Penn. Museum Art, Caribbean Biannul, 1996, Museum Modern Art, Monterey, Mex., 1991, 93; represented in numerous pub. and pvt. collections. Recipient Internat. Painting award Orgn. of African Unity, Liberia, 1978, Bicentennial Painting award City of Chgo., 1976, Teaching award Danforth Found., St. Louis, 1969-70, Ford Found. Grad. Student award Art Inst., Chgo. 1963-65. Mem. Coll. Art Assn. of Am. Avocation: tennis. Home: 750 Gonzalez Dr Apt 10H San Francisco CA 94132-2214 Office: San Francisco State U 1600 Holloway Ave San Francisco CA 94132-1722

MORRISON, MARTHA KAYE, photolithography engineer, executive; b. San Jose, Calif., Oct. 5, 1955; d. Myrle K. and Arthena R. Morrison; 1 child, Katherine A. AA, West Valley Coll., Saratoga, Calif., 1978. Prodn. worker Signetics Co., Sunnyvale, Calif., 1973-75, equipment engr., 1976-78, 79-80, prodn. supr., 1978-79; expediter Monolithic Memories, Sunnyvale, 1975-76; photolithography engr. KTI Chems., 1980-81; founder, chief engr., CEO Optalign, Inc., Livermore, Forest Ranch, Calif., 1981—; participant West Valley Coll. Tennis Team # 1 Singles and Doubles, 1976-78; regional profl. ranking NCTA Opens Singles/Doubles, 1982-85, 93, 94, 95, 96, 97, 98, rankings 15-20 singles/#2-#8 doubles, instr. tennis Chico Racquet Club, 1994, Butte Creek Country Club, 1995—; participant exhbn. tennis match with Rosie Cosals and Billie Jean King, 1994, 95. Dir. benefit Boys & Girls Club of Chico. Named Champion Chico Open Finalist Woodridge Open, 1994, 1993 #2 NCTA Women's Open Doubles, Doubles #3, 1994, Tracy Open, 1996, Vacaville Open, 1998. Mem. USPTA (cert.), Tennis Profl. Chico Racquet Club, Butte Creek Country Club. Office: PO Box 718 Forest Ranch CA 95942-0718

MORRISON, MURDO DONALD, architect; b. Detroit, Feb. 21, 1919; s. Alexander and Johanna (Macaulay) M.; BArch, Lawrence Tech. U., 1943; m. Judy D. Morrison; children from previous marriage—Paula L., Reed A., Anne H. Individual practice architecture, Detroit, 1949, Klamath Falls, Oreg., 1949-65, Oakland, Calif., 1965-78; ptnr. Morrison Assocs., San Francisco, 1978-85, Burlingame, Calif., 1985-89, Redwood City, Calif., 1989—; v.p. Lakeridge Corp., 1968—, Oreg. Bd. Archtl. Examiners, 1961-65, chmn., 1964. Mem. Town Council Klamath Falls, 1955-57; co-chmn. Oakland Pride Com., 1968-77; mem. Redwood City Gen. Plan Com., 1986, Redwood City Design Rev. Com., 1991—, Emerald Hills Design Rev. Bd., 1990-97. Served with USN, 1943-46. Recipient Progressive Architecture award, 1955, Alumni of Yr. award Lawrence Inst., 1965. Mem. AIA (treas. East Bay, chmn. Oakland chpt., dir. San Mateo county chpt. 1996—). Presbyterian. Architect: Gilliam County Courthouse (Progressive Architecture design award), 1955, Chiloquin (Oreg.) Elem. Sch., 1963, Lakeridge Office Bldg., Reno, 1984, Provident Cen. Credit Union Bldg., Monterey, Calif., 1986, Embarcadero Fed. Credit Union, San Francisco, 1991, Warrick Residence, The Sea Ranch, Calif., 1996, Spectre Industries Office Bldg., Milpitas, Calif., 1997, Rosenbaum Residency, Los Altos Hills, Calif., 1998, others; master planner Lakeridge, a 945-acre cmty. in Reno, v.p. devel., 1963—. Home and Office: 3645 Jefferson Ave Redwood City CA 94062-3149

MORRISON, ROBERT CLIFTON, artist; b. Billings, Mont., Aug. 13, 1924; s. Lloyd Clifton and Elsie Genevive (Talgo) M.; m. Berta Frances McPike, June 16, 1948; children: James, Barbara, Judith, Bruce. BA, Carleton Coll., Northfield, Minn., 1949; MA, U. N.Mex., 1951. Arts supr. Billing Pub. Schs., 1957-67; prof. art Rocky Mt. Coll., Billings, 1967-87, acad. dean, 1985-86; artist, 1965—. One-person shows and invitational exhibits include U. Oreg. Art Gallery, Eugene, 1960, Mont. Hist. Soc., Helena, 1962, Mus. of the Plains Indian, Browning, Mont., 1969, Western Art Gallery, Albuquerque, 1972, JPL Gallery, London, 1975, Yellowstone Art Mus., Billings, Mont., 1978, Waterworks Gallery, Miles City, Mont., 1986, The Billings Clinic Gallery, 1988, Paris Gibson Art Mus., Great Falls, Mont., 1995, Carbon County Arts Guild, Red Lodge, Mont., 1996, 98, Smithsonian Instn., Washington, 1996, 97; represented in pvt. and pub. collections in U.S., Eng., Denmark and Norway. Bd. dirs. Western Heritage Ctr., Billings, 1982-91; mem. Mont. Arts Coun., Helena, 1977-82, 97—. With inf. AUS, 1943-46, ETO.

MORRISON, ROBERT LEE, physical scientist; b. Omaha, Nov. 22, 1932; s. Robert Alton and Lulu Irene (Ross) M.; m. Sharon Faith Galliher, Feb.

19, 1966; children: Dennis, Karyn, Cheryl, Tamara, Traci. BA, U. Pacific, Stockton, Calif., 1957, MS, 1960. Chief chemist Gallo Winery, Modesto, Calif., 1957-66; rsch. scientist Lawrence Livermore Nat. Lab., Livermore, Calif., 1966-69, sr. rsch. scientist, 1973-93; pres. Poolinator, Inc., Gardena, Calif., 1970-72; owner R.L. Morrison Techs., Modesto, 1993—; cons., speaker, presenter in field. Contbr. numerous articles to profl. jours.; patentee in field. Recipinet Excellence in Nuclear Weapons award U.S. Dept. Energy, 1990, others. Mem. Am. Chem. Soc. Avocations: flying, skiing, scuba diving, photography. Home: 1117 Springcreek Dr Modesto CA 95355-4820

MORRISON, ROGER BARRON, geologist; b. Madison, Wis., Mar. 26, 1914; s. Frank Barron and Elsie Rhea (Bullard) M.; BA, Cornell U., 1933, MS, 1934; postgrad. U. Calif., Berkeley, 1934-35, Stanford U., 1935-38; PhD, U. Nev., 1964; m. Harriet Louise Williams, Apr. 7, 1941 (deceased Feb. 1991); children: John Christopher, Peter Hallock and Craig Brewster (twins). Registered profl. geologist, Wyo. Geologist U.S. Geol. Survey, 1939-76; vis. adj. prof. dept. geoscis. U. Ariz., 1976-81, Mackay Sch. Mines, U. Nev., Reno, 1984-86; cons. geologist; pres. Morrison and Assocs., Ltd., 1978—; prin. investigator 2 Landsat-1 and 2 Skylab earth resources investigation projects NASA, 1972-75. Fellow Geol. Soc. Am.; mem. AAAS, Internat. Union Quaternary Rsch. (mem. Holocene and paleopedology commns., chmn. work group on pedostratigraphy), Am. Soc. Photogrammetry and Remote Sensing, Am. Soc. Agronomy, Soil Sci. Soc. Am., Internat. Soil Sci. Soc., Am. Quaternary Assn., Colo. Sci. Soc., Geol. Soc. of Nev. Author 3 books, co-author one book, co-editor 2 books; editor: Quaternary Nonglacial Geology, Conterminous U.S., Geol. Soc. Am. Centennial Series, vol. K-2, 1991; mem. editorial bd. Catena, 1973-88; contbr. over 150 articles to profl. jours. Research includes Quaternary geology and geomorphology, hydrogeology, environ. geology, neotectonics, remote sensing of Earth resources, paleoclimatology, pedostratigraphy. Office: 13150 W 9th Ave Golden CO 80401-4201

MORRISON, WILLIAM FOSDICK, business educator, retired electrical company executive; b. Bridgeport, Conn., Mar. 14, 1935; s. Robert Louis and Helen Fosdick (Mulroney) M.; m. E. Drake Miller, Dec. 14, 1957 (div. Sept. 1972); children: Donna Drake, Deanne Fosdick, William Fosdick; m. Carol Ann Stover, Nov. 20, 1972. BA in Econs., Trinity Coll., 1957. Mgr. purchasing dept. Westinghouse Electric Co., Lima, Ohio, 1960-68; mgr. mfg. Westinghouse Electric Co., Upper Sandusky, Ohio, 1969; gen. mgr. Westinghouse Electric Co., Gurabo, P.R., 1970-71; mgr. tng. Westinghouse Electric Co., Pitts., 1972-84; program mgr. Westinghouse Electric Co., Sunnyvale, Calif., 1984-89, procurement project dir., 1990-94; prof. San Jose State U., Calif., 1993—, Golden Gate U., San Francisco, 1995—; lead negotiator Advanced Micro Devices, Santa Clara, Calif., 1995-97; prof. U. Calif., Berkeley, 1996—, Menlo Coll., 1998—; negotiation cons. and trainer, 1969—; lead negotiator ReSound Corp., 1998—. Author: The Pre-Negotiation Planning Book, 1985, The Human Side of Negotiations, 1994; contbr. articles to profl. jours. Bd. dirs. Valley Inst. of the Theatre Arts, Saratoga, Calif., 1986-90, Manhattan Playhouse, 1989-94; chmn. Sensory Access Found. Golf Tournament, 1995-96. Served to capt. USAFR, 1958-64; mem. protocol office World Cup USA, 1994. Named Man of the Yr. Midwest Lacrosse Coaches Assn., 1983, recipient Service award U.S. Lacrosse Assn., 1982. Mem. Nat. Assn. Purchasing Mgmt. (pres. Lima chpt. 1966-67, dir. nat. affairs 1967-68, dist. treas. 1968-70). Club: Sunnyvale Golf Assn. (vice-chmn. 1985, chmn. 1986, 93, handicap scorer 1992-93). Lodge: Elks. Avocation: golf. E-mail: wfmorrison@earthlink.net. Home: 3902 Duncan Pl Palo Alto CA 94306-4550 Office: San Jose State U Coll of Bus 1 Washington Sq San Jose CA 95112-3613

MORRISSEY, JOHN CARROLL, SR., lawyer; b. N.Y.C., Sept. 2, 1914; s. Edward Joseph and Estelle (Caine) M.; m. Eileen Colligan, Oct. 14, 1950; children: Jonathan Edward, Ellen (Mrs. James A. Jenkins), Katherine, John, Patricia, Richard, Brian, Peter. BA magna cum laude, Yale U., 1937, LLB, 1940; JSD, N.Y. U., 1951; grad., Command and Gen. Staff Sch., 1944. Bar: N.Y. State 1940, D.C. 1953, Calif. 1954, U.S. Supreme Ct. 1944. Asso. firm Dorsey and Adams, 1940-41, Dorsey, Adams and Walker, 1946-50; counsel Office of Sec. of Def., Dept. Def., Washington, 1950-52; acting gen. counsel def. Electric Power Adminstrn., 1952-53; atty. Pacific Gas and Electric Co., San Francisco, 1953-70; assoc. gen. counsel Pacific Gas and Electric Co., 1970-74, v.p., gen. counsel, 1975-80; individual practice law San Francisco, 1980—; dir. Gas Lines, Inc. Bd. dirs. Legal Aid Soc., San Francisco; chmn. Golden Gate dist. Boy Scouts Am., 1973-75; commr. Human Rights Commn. of San Francisco, 1976-89, chmn., 1980-82; chmn. Cath. Social Svc. of San Francisco, 1966-68; adv. com. Archdiocesean Legal Affairs, 1981—; regent Archdiocesan Sch. of Theology, St. Patrick's Sem., 1994—; dir. Presidio Preservation Assn., 1995—. Served to col. F.A. U.S. Army, 1941-46. Decorated Bronze star, Army Commendation medal. Mem. NAS, AAAS, ABA, Calif. State Bar Assn., Fed. Power Bar Assn., N.Y. Acad. Scis., Calif. Conf. Pub. Utility Counsel, Pacific Coast Electric Assn., Pacific Coast Gas Assn., Econ. Round Table of San Francisco, World Affairs Council, San Francisco C. of C., Calif. State C. of C., Harold Brunn Soc. Med. Rsch., Electric Club, Serra Club, Commonwealth Club, Yale Club of San Francisco (pres. 1989-90), Pacific-Union Club, Sometimes Tuesday Club, Sovereign Mil. Order Malta, Phi Beta Kappa. Roman Catholic. Home: 2030 Jackson St San Francisco CA 94109-2840 Office: PO Box 77000 123 Mission St Rm 1709 San Francisco CA 94105-1551

MORROW, CHERYLLE ANN, accountant, bankruptcy, consultant; b. Sydney, Australia, July 3, 1950; came to U.S., 1973; d. Norman H. and Esther A. E. (Jarrett) Wilson. Student, U. Hawaii, 1975; diploma Granville Tech. Coll., Sydney, 1967. Acct., asst. treas. Bus. Investment, Ltd., Honolulu, 1975-77; owner Lanikai Musical Instruments, Honolulu, 1980-86, Cherylle A. Morrow Profl. Svcs., Honolulu, 1981—; fin. managerial cons. E.A. Buck Co., Inc., Honolulu, 1981-84; contr., asst. trustee THC Fin. Corp., Honolulu, 1977-84, bankruptcy trustee, 1984-92; v.p., sec., treas. Innervation, Inc., 1989—; panel mem. Chpt. 7 Trustees dist. Hawaii U.S. Depart. Justice, 1988-91; co-chair Small Bus. Hawaii Legis. Action Com., 1990-92; dir./treas. Women's Fin. Resource Ctr., 1997—. Mem. Small Bus. Hawaii PAC, Lanikai Community Assn., Arts Coun. Hawaii; vol., mem. Therapeutic Horsemanship for Handicapped, program chair, 1990-92, vice chair, 1990-95, chair, 1995—; vol., mem. Small Bus. Adminstrn. Women in Bus. Com. 1987—; vol. tax preparer IRS VITA, 1990—, site coord., 1993—; mem. Bus. Task Force Regulatory Reform, Hawaii, 1996—; mem. working group Task Force Econ. Revitalization, Hawaii, 1997 acct. exec. U.S. Small Bus. Adminstrn., 1997. Recipient City and County of Honolulu award, State of Hawaii award, 1996, 97, Women in Bus. Advocate award U.S. Small Bus. Adminstrn., 1996, Small Bus. Booster award Small Bus. Hawaii, 1996, City and County of Honolulu award U.S. Small Bus. Adminstrn., 1997, Acct. Adv. award. Mem. AARP (vol. tax preparer TCE 1991—), NAFE, Australian-Am. C. of C. (bd. dir. 1985-92, corp. sec. 1986-92, v.p. 1988-92), Pacific Islands Assn. Women (corp. sec./treas. 1988-90), Pacific Islands Assn. (asst. treas. 1988—), Associated Builders and Contractors (Hawaii chptr., mem. vol. com. 1997—), Soc. Fire Protection Engrs. (Hawaii chptr.), Instrumentation Soc. Am., Nat. Fedn. Ind. Bus. Avocations: reading, music, dancing, sailing, gardening. Office: Innervation, Inc 145 Hekili St Ste 300 Kailua HI 96734-2846

MORROW, RONALD EDWARD, editor, publisher; b. Sidney, Ohio, July 16, 1949; s. Sam and Anna Lee (Haynes) M.; m. Roberta Ellen Morrow, Aug. 29, 1981; children: Michael David, Shawna Kelly. BA in English and Philosophy, U. Colo., 1998. Editor Climbing Art, LaPorte, Colo., 1977-78; editor, pub. Climbing Art, Denver, 1978—. Democrat. Avocations: mountain climbing, running. Office: Climbing Art 6390 E Floyd Dr Denver CO 80222-7638

MORROW, WINSTON VAUGHAN, financial executive; b. Grand Rapids, Mich., Mar. 22, 1924; s. Winston V. and Selma (von Egloffstein) M.; m. Margaret Ellen Staples, June 25, 1948 (div.); children: Thomas Christopher, Mark Staples; m. Edith Burrows Ulrich, Mar. 2, 1990. AB cum laude, Williams Coll., 1947; JD, Harvard U., 1950. Bar: R.I. 1950. Assoc. atty. Edwards & Angell, Providence, 1950-57; exec. v.p., asst. treas., gen. counsel, bd. dirs. Avis, Inc. and subs., 1957-61; v.p., gen. mgr. Rent A Car div. Avis, Inc., 1962-64, pres., bd. dirs., 1964-75; chmn., chief exec. officer, bd. dirs. Avis, Inc. and Avis Rent A Car System, Inc., 1965-77; chmn., pres., bd. dirs. Telecredit Inc. and subs., 1976-80, pres. Westwood Equities Corp., L.A., 1981-95, CEO, 1984-95, also bd. dirs.; chmn., pres., chief exec. officer Ticor Title Ins. Co., 1982-91, also bd. dirs.; chmn. TRTS Data Svcs. Inc., 1985-91, bd. dirs. AECOM Tech. Corp., L.A., 1990—; dir. William & Scott, Inc., 1994-96; mem. Pres.'s Industry and Govt. Spl. Travel Task Force, 1968, travel adv. bd. U.S. Travel Svcs., 1968-76, L.A. City-wide Airport Adv. Com., 1983-85; co-chmn. L.A. Transp. Coalition, 1985-91. Mem. juvenile delinquency task force Nat. Coun. Crime and Delinquency, 1985-86, L.A. Mayor's Bus. Coun., 1983-86, Housing Roundtable, Washington, 1983-85; chmn., pres. Spring St. Found., 1991—; bd. dirs. Police Found., Washington, 1983-91; trustee Com. for Econ. Devel., Washington, 1987-91; trustee Adelphi U., 1970-75. Decorated Stella Della Solidarieta Italy, Gold Tourism medal Austria). Mem. Fed. Bar Assn., R.I. Bar Assn., Car and Truck Rental Leasing Assn. (nat. pres. 1961-63), Am. Land Title Assn. (bd. govs. 1989-90), L.A. Area C. of C. (bd. dirs. 1983-90), Williams Club, L.A. Tennis Club, Phi Beta Kappa, Kappa Alpha. Home: 4056 Farmouth Dr Los Angeles CA 90027-1314 also: Meadowview Farm Cushing Corners Rd Freedom NH 03836-0221

MORRY, G. RICHARD, retired lawyer; b. Seattle, Mar. 2, 1943. BA cum laude, U. Wash., 1965, JD with honors, 1970. Bar: Wash. 1971, Hawaii 1973, U.S. Ct. Appeals (9th cir.) 1973, U.S. Supreme Ct. 1974. Ptnr. Rush Moore Craven Sutton Morry & Beh, Honolulu, of counsel, 1998—; pres. Hawaii Inst. for CLE, 1996. Exec. editor Wash. Law Rev., 1969-70; bd. editors Hawaii Bar Jour., 1975-97. Mem. ABA, Wash. State Bar Assn., Hawaii State Bar Assn., Am. Judicature Soc., Maritime Law Assn. of U.S. Address: Rush Moore Craven Sutton Morry & Beh 20th Fl Hawaii Tower 745 Fort Street Mall Honolulu HI 96813-3800*

MORSE, JOHN MOORE, architect, planner; b. Brookline, Mass., Aug. 23, 1911; s. Arthur Moore and Helen (Stearns) M.; m. Emily Hall (dec. 1988); children: David Hall, Catherine Morse Wikkerink; m. Helen Taverniti, Aug. 5, 1989. AB, Harvard U., 1934, MArch, 1940. Registered architect, Wash. Tchr. Loomis Sch., Windsor, Conn., 1934-36; ptnr. Bassetti & Morse, Seattle, 1947-62; prin. John Morse & Assocs., Seattle, 1962-78; ptnr. Morse Stafford Ptnrship., Seattle, 1978-85; prin. John Morse Architect & Planner, Seattle, 1985—. Mem. King County (Wash.) Planning Commn., 1965-70, Design Rev. Bd., Mill Creek, Wash., 1987-89; chmn. Seattle Urban Design Bd., 1966; bd. dirs. Cornish Coll. Arts, Seattle, 1974-80. Fellow AIA (pres. Seattle chpt. 1969, Seattle chpt. medal 1996, various local and nat. awards). Democrat. Office: 7027 32nd Ave NE Seattle WA 98115-5906

MORSE, JUDY, science foundation administrator. Exec. dir. Arboretum Foundation, Los Angeles County Arboreta and Botanic Gardens, Arcadia, Calif. Office: Los Angeles County Arboretum Found 301 N Baldwin Ave Arcadia CA 91007-2697*

MORSE, KAREN WILLIAMS, academic administrator; b. Monroe, Mich., May 8, 1940; m. Joseph G. Morse; children: Robert G., Geoffrey E. BS, Denison U., 1962; MS, U. Mich., 1964, PhD, 1967; DSc (hon.), Denison U., 1990. Rsch. chemist Ballistic Rsch. Lab., Aberdeen Proving Ground, Md., 1966-68; lectr. chemistry dept. Utah State U., Logan, 1968-69, from asst. to assoc. prof. chemistry, 1969-83, prof. chemistry dept., 1983-93, dept. head Coll. Sci., 1981-88, dean Coll. Sci., 1988-89, univ. provost, 1989-93; pres. Western Wash. U., Bellingham, 1993—; mem., chair Grad. Record Exam in chemistry com., Princeton, N.J., 1980-89, Gov.'s Sci. Coun., Salt Lake City, 1986-93, Gov.'s Coun. on Fusion, 1989-91, ACS Com. on Profl. Tng., 1984-92; cons. 1993; nat. ChemLinks adv. com. NSF, 1995; bd. advisor's orgn. com. 2008 summer Olympic Games, Seattle, 1995; faculty Am. Assn. State Colls. and Univs. Pres.'s Acad., 1995, 96; chair Wash. Coun. of Pres., 1995-96; bd. dirs. Whatcom State Bank. Contbr. articles to profl. jours. Mem. Cache County Sch. Dist. Found., Cache Valley, Logan, 1988-93; swim coach, soccer coach; trustee First United Presbyn. Ch., Logan, 1979-81, 82-85; adv. bd. Sci. Discovery Ctr., Logan, 1993, KCTS-TV, Bellingham, 1996—; mem. bd. dirs. United Way, Whatcom County, 1993—; exec. com. Bellingham-Whatcom Econ. Devel. Com., 1993—. Recipient Disting. Alumni in Residence award U. Mich., 1989, Francis P. Garvan and John M. Olin medal, 1997. Fellow AAAS; mem. Am. Chem. Soc. (Utah award Salt Lake City and Cen. dists. 1988, Garvan-Olin medal 1997), Am. Assn. State Colls. and Univs. (mem. policy and purposes com. 1995, chair 1996), Bus. and Profl. Women Club (pres. 1984-85), Philanthropic Edn. Orgn., Phi Beta Kappa, Sigma Xi, Phi Beta Kappa Assocs., Phi Kappa Phi, Beta Gamma Sigma. Avocations: skiing, biking, photography. Office: Western Washington Univ Office of Pres 516 High St Bellingham WA 98225-9000*

MORSE, LOWELL WESLEY, banking and real estate executive; b. West Palm Beach, Fla., May 1, 1937; s. Alton and Blanche (Yelverton) M.; m. Vera Giacalone, June 22, 1958; children: Lowell Wesley, Stephen D., Michael S. BS, U. Santa Clara, 1968; grad., Def. Lang. Inst., Monterey, Calif., 1959. Russian linguist U.S. Army Security Agy., 1957-60; asst. city mgr. City of Pacific Grove, Calif., 1961-66; city mgr. Town of Los Altos Hills, Calif., 1967-69; chmn. Morse & Assocs., Inc., Portland, Oreg., 1972—; founder, dir. Comerica Bank Calif., San Jose, 1979—; dir. Internat. Family Entertainment; dir. Body By Jake, Inc., 1998; chmn. Cypress Ventures Inc., Portland, The Bagel Basket, Inc.; chmn. bd. trustees Regent U. Served with U.S. Army, 1957-60. Home: 6205 SW Meridian Way Tualatin OR 97062-6750 Office: 5335 Meadows Rd Ste 365 Lake Oswego OR 97035-3114

MORSE, RICHARD, social scientist; b. Boston, Oct. 12, 1922; s. Stearns and Helen Ward (Field) M.; m. Romola Thomas Chowdhry, June 23, 1949; children: Ashok Daniel, Martha Sunita Kelly. *Romola Chowdhry Morse, wife, mother, educator, writer, civic organizer. Born in Fatehgarh, India, of Christian, Hindu, and Muslim heritage. Basic belief: The equality of all human beings, and the cooperation of all nations and groups toward establishment of world peace and nurturing. Schooled in India and Ceylon. BA King's College, London. MEd Cambridge University. Deputy director, WAC (India). Professor of English Literature, Isabella Thoburn College, and of Eastern Philosophy at Bradford College. Chairperson church and school committees. President/Vice President YWCA Rangoon, Bombay, New Delhi, Mid-Peninsula, Lawrence. President UNA/USA Hawaii Division. Author, Kristo: The Turbulence and Romance of Changing India. National Library of Poetry awards, 1996-97.* A.B., Dartmouth Coll., 1946; postgrad., Banaras Hindu U., Aligarh Muslim U., Gokhale Inst. Politics and Econs., India, 1947, Columbia, 1950; A.M., ABD, Harvard, 1958. Edn. officer ECA, Burma, 1950-53; asst. rep. Ford Found., Burma, 1954-56; sr. internat. economist Stanford Research Inst., Menlo Park, Calif., 1958-64, 66-69; cons. Ford Found., India, 1964-66; indsl. devel. cons. Andover, Mass., 1969-74; rsch. assoc., sr. fellow, co-coord. Participatory Devel. Group East West Ctr., Honolulu, 1974-94; sr. fellow emeritus East West Ctr., Honolulu, 1994—; study dir. NAS and Nat. Acad. Engring. Internat. Panel on Internat. Industrialization Inst., 1972-73; chmn. bd. govs. Inst. Current World Affairs, 1972-74, trustee, 1988-91; bd. dirs. Inst. World Affairs, 1988-91, mem. adv. coun., 1992—; co-founder, dir. Hawaii Entrepreneurship Tng. and Devel. Inst., 1977—; mem. adv. com. Immigrant Ctr. Enterprise Project, Honolulu, 1992-96; ptnr.-founder Kalimat Moosilauke Pubs., 1996—. Author (with Eugene Staley): Modern Small Industry for Developing Countries, 1965; author: Village Voices in Rural Development and Energy Planning, 1987; co-editor: Grassroot Horizons: Connecting Participatory Development Initiatives East and West, 1995. Served with AUS, 1942-45. Fellow Inst. Current World Affairs, 1946-49; recipient certificate of honor Hawaii Ho. of Reps., 1994. Mem. Am. Econ. Assn., Am. Agrl. Econs. Assn., Am. Assn. Asian Studies, Economists Allied for Arms Reduction, UN Assn. (exec. bd. Hawaii divsn.). Home: 1621 Halekoa Dr Honolulu HI 96821-1126 Office: 1777 E West Rd Honolulu HI 96822-2323

MORSE, RICHARD JAY, human resources and organizational development consultant, manufacturers' representative company executive; b. Detroit, Aug. 2, 1933; s. Maurice and Belle Rosalyn (Jacobson) M. BA, U. Va., 1955; MA in Clin. Psychology, Calif. State U., L.A., 1967. Area pers. adminstr. Gen. Tel. Co. of Calif., Santa Monica, 1957-67; sr. v.p. human resources The Dekins Co., Glendale, Calif., 1967-83, pvt. cons. human resources and orgn. devel. Cambria, 1983—. Contbr. articles to profl. jours. Fund raiser various orgns., So. Calif., 1970—. Mem. Internat. Soc. Performance Improvement (founding mem. 1958—). Republican. Jewish. Avocations: travel, tennis, walking, swimming. Home and Office: 6410 Cambria Pines Rd Cambria CA 93428-2009

MORTEN, RALPH EDWARD, police officer, bomb technician; b. Yankton, S.D., Aug. 23, 1950; s. Claude Leslie and Evelyn Madeline (Steele) M.; m. Alison Joan Squire, Apr. 3, 1982; children: Joshua, Lauren, Sarah, Erin. BS in Criminal Justice Adminstrn., Calif. State U., 1983. Cert. tchr. C.C. level, Calif. Police officer Phoenix Police Dept., 1974-79, L.A. Police, 1979—; pres. The Morten Group, Upland, Calif., 1995—; firearms cons. Nat. Tactical Officers Assn., LaMirada, Calif., 1986-90, Internat. Assn. Chiefs Police, Washington, 1986-91; firearms, security cons. R.M. Consulting, Upland, Calif., 1989—; del., union rep., LA Police Protective League, 1994—. Inventor: Robotic Forklift (remote control), 1995. Baseball coach Little League, Upland, Calif., 1994—. With USMC, 1971-73. Recipient medal of valor L.A. Police Dept., 1990; named Officer of Yr. Internat. Footprint Assn., L.A., 1990. Mem. Internat. Assn. Bomb Technicians and Investigations, Peace Officers Assn. L.A. County. Republican. Methodist. Avocations: running, weight tng., coaching baseball, softball, shooting. Office: LA Police Dept 150 N Los Angeles St Los Angeles CA 90012-3302

MORTENSEN, GORDON LOUIS, artist, printmaker; b. Arnegard, N.D., Apr. 27, 1938; s. Gunner and Otillia Ernestine (Reiner) M.; m. Phoebe Hollis Hansen, Apr. 10, 1965 (div. 1968); m. Linda Johanna Sisson, Dec. 7, 1969. BFA, Mpls. Coll. Art and Design, 1964; postgrad., U. Minn., 1969-72. One-man shows include Minn. Mus., St. Paul, 1967, Concept Art Gallery Pitts., 1981, 83, 85, 87, 89, 91, 93, C.G. Rein Galleries, Mpls., 1978, 80, 85, 89, 91, 93, others; exhibited in group shows Miami U., Oxford, Ohio (1st place award 1977), Phila. Print Club (George Bunker award 1977), 12th Nat. Silvermine Guild Print Exhbn., New Canaan, Comm., 1976, 78, 80, 83, 86, 94, 96 (Hearsch Mag. award 1978, Purchase award 1983, 86), 4th Miami Internat. Print Biennial (4th place award 1980), Rockford Internat., 1981, 85 (Juror's award 1981), Boston Printmakers Nat. Exhbn., 1977, 79, 80, 81, 83, 97 (Purchase award 1977, 79, 83, Juror's Accomodation), others; represented permanent collections, Achenbach Found. Graphic Arts at Palace Legion of Honor, San Francisco, Bklyn. Mus., Phila. Mus. Art, Libr. of Congress, Minn. Mus. Art, Met. Mus. and Art Ctr., Miami, Fla., Mus. Am. Art, Washington, Art Inst. Chgo., Mus. Art at Carnegie-Mellon Inst., Pitts., Walker Art Ctr., Mpls., Dulin Gallery Art, Knoxville, Tenn., numerous corp. collections; profiled in numerous art jours. Served with USMC, 1957-60. Mem. Boston Printmakers, Phila. Print Club, L.A. Printmaking Soc., Albany Print Club, Am. Print Alliance. Home and Office: 4153 Crest Rd Pebble Beach CA 93953-3052

MORTENSEN, WILLIAM S., banking executive; b. 1932. Chmn. bd., pres., CEO 1st Fed. Bank Calif., Santa Monica, 1955—, CEO, until 1997, chmn., bd., 1999—; CEO, pres. Babette Heinbuch, 1997—. Office: 1st Fed Bank Calif 401 Wilshire Blvd Santa Monica CA 90401-1416*

MORTILLA, MICHAEL DANIEL, composer; m. Beth Burleson, May 21, 1983. Co. pianist Martha Graham Dance Co., N.Y.C., 1979-86; faculty, prin. musician U. Calif., Santa Barbara, 1986-99; owner MIDI Life Crisis, Santa Barbara, 1989—. Composer (silent film scores) The Chaplin Mutuals, 1989, (1996 Olympic Games) Easy Street, 1996, (1st Internet film broadcast) The Rink, 1997, (numerous TV and radio) NPR, PBS, BBC, VOM, 1988—. Mentor artist Arts Fund, Santa Barbara, 1995-98; grant panel reviewer Arts Commn., Santa Barbara, 1993. Recipient Collaborative Artist grant Nat. Endowment of Arts, 1988, Collaborative Artist grant Mass. Coun. on Arts, 1988, 89, Meet the Composer, 1988-99, Ind. Artist award Arts Fund, 1992. Mem. Broadcast Music Inc. (assoc.), Am. Music Ctr., Soc. Composers and Lyricists, Internat. Guild Musicians in Dance, Film Music Network. E-mail: Mortilla@west.net. Office: MIDI Life Crisis PO Box 1266 Santa Barbara CA 93102

MORTIMER, DAVID WILLIAM, communications engineer; b. Redding, Calif., June 8, 1962; s. Walter L. and Phyllis B. (Winters) M.; m. Jenene McGhie, Sept. 20, 1997. BSEE, Brigham Young U., 1988; MBA, Syracuse U., 1997. Devel. engr. Scala Electronics, Medford, Oreg., 1988-89; asst. sta. mgr. Holzkirchen Radio Free Europe/Radio Liberty, Munich, 1989-90; asst. sta. mgr. Spain Radio Free Europe/Radio Liberty, Playa de Pals, 1990-93; ops. dir. Portugal Radio Free Europe/Radio Liberty, Lisbon, 1993-95; tech. asst. Radio Free Europe/Radio Liberty, Prague, Czech Republic, 1995; acting mng. dir. Portugal Radio Free Europe/Radio Liberty, Lisbon, 1995. Mem. IEEE, Aircraft Owners and Pilots Assn., Nat. Eagle Scout Assn. (life.).

MORTIMER, KENNETH P., academic administrator. Pres. Western Wash. U., Bellingham, 1988-93, U. Hawaii Sys., Honolulu, 1993—. Office: U Hawaii Sys Bachmann Hall 202 2444 Dole St Honolulu HI 96822-2302*

MORTIMER, WENDELL REED, JR., judge; b. Alhambra, Calif., Apr. 7, 1937; s. Wendell Reed and Blanche (Wilson) M.; m. Cecilia Vick, Aug. 11, 1962; children: Michelle Dawn, Kimberly Grace. AB, Occidental Coll., 1958; JD, U. So. Calif., L.A., 1965. Bar: Calif. 1966. Trial atty. legal divsn. Legal div. State of Calif., L.A., 1965-73; assoc. Thelen, Marrin, Johnson & Bridges, L.A., 1973-76, ptnr., 1976-93; pvt. practice San Marino, Calif., 1994-95; judge L.A. Superior Ct., 1995—; mem. exec. com. L.A. Superior Ct. With U.S. Army, 1960-62. Mem. ABA, Los Angeles County Bar Assn., Pasadena Bar Assn., Calif. Judges Assn., Am. Judicature Soc., Am. Judges Assn., Legion Lex., ABOTA. Home: 1420 San Marino Ave San Marino CA 91108-2042

MORTON, CLAUDETTE, education administrator; b. Billings, Mont., Jan. 21, 1940; d. Hugh Wesley and Timey Delacy (Hopper) M.; m. Larry Roy Johnson, July 5, 1959 (div. 1987); 1 child, Eric Roy Johnson; m. George Miller, Sept. 3, 1987. BA in Drama, U. Mont., 1963, MA in Drama, 1964, EdD in Edn., 1990. Cert. tchr., adminstrv., Mont. Tchr. English, supr. Moorhead (Minn.) State U., 1964-65; sub. tchr. Missoula and Glassgow (Mont.) Sch. Dists., 1965-70; English tchr., dir. speech, drama Glasgow H.S., 1970-78; English specialist, liaison to county supr. Office of Public Instrn., Helena, Mont., 1978-86; exec. sec. and state agy. dir. Bd. of Pub. Edn., Helena, 1986-90; dir. Mont. rural edn. ctr. and western Mont. coll. assoc. prof. edn. U. Mont., Dillon, 1990-96; exec. dir. Mont. Small Schs. Alliance, Helena, 1996—; mem. rural edn. adv. com. Northwest Reginal Edn. Lab., Portland, 1991-96, adv. bd. Ctr. for Study of Small and Rural Schs. U. Okla., 1993—; mem. Blue Ribbon Schs. Panel, U.S. Dept. Edn., 1994, 96—. Editor: Visions: Healthy Living for the 21 Century, 1992; contbr. articles to profl. jours. Mem. Ch. Pub. Policy Mont. Arts Coun., 1978-86, chair Mont. Cult. Advocacy, 1982-86; state. pres. AAUW, Mont., 1988-90, theatre content ch. arts assessment planning com. Coun. of Chief State Sch. Officers. Mem. Nat. Assessment Ednl. Progress (arts assessment, oversight com.), Nat. Rural Edn. Assn. (Howard A. Dawson award for svc. 1995), Nat. Coun. of Tchrs. of English, Am. Assn. Colls. of Tchr. Educators, Am. Edn. Rsch. Assn., Mont. Alliance for Arts Edn., Delta Kappa Gamma, Phi Delta Kappa. Democrat. Congregationalist. Avocations: travel, hiking, cross country skiing, politics. the arts. Office: Mont Small Schs Alliance 1 S Montana Ave Helena MT 59601-5178

MORTON, LAUREL ANNE, elementary education educator; b. Cin., July 27, 1954; d. James William and Rosemary (Danner) M. BA in Social Sci., Calif. State U.-Stanislaus, Turlock, 1978; teaching credential, Calif. State Polytech U., Pomona, 1986; MA in Edn., Calif. State Poly. U., Pomona, 1992. Cert. tchr., Calif., Colo. Sr. loan clk. Shearson Am. Express Mortgage Corp., Newport Beach, Calif., 1978-82; adminstrv. asst. Investco Corp., Santa Barbara, Calif., 1982-83; supr. loan servicing dept. County Savs. Bank, Santa Barbara, 1983-84; comm. asst. Fuller Theol. Sem., Pasadena, Calif., 1984-85; elem. tchr. Howard Sch., Ontario, Calif., 1986-91; tchr. Bon View Elem. Sch., Ontario, 1992—, 4th grade team leader, 1993-94, track leader, 1995-96. Tchr. sponsor Performing Arts Club, Bon View Elem. Sch., 1996-97, 97-98. Mem. Nat. Honor Soc., Phi Kappa Phi, Zeta Tau Alpha. Avocations: tennis, theater, dancing, travel, museums or venues of educational interest. Home: 1919 Stonehouse Rd Sierra Madre CA 91024-1409 Office: Bon View Elem Sch 2121 S Bon View Ave Ontario CA 91761-5530

MORTON, LINDA, mayor; b. Dec. 7, 1944; married; 2 children. BA with honors, U. Nebr., 1966. Tchr. Sunnyvale (Calif.) Elem. Sch., 1967-69, Jefferson County (Colo.) Sch. Dist., 1966-67, 69-70; realtor various cos., 1979-91. Mem. city coun. City of Lakewood, 1981-91, mayor, 1991—; chair Denver Metro Mayors Caucus, 1996-97; [illegible] Blue Ribbon Panel on State Transp. Needs, 1995; represented Lakewood on Bd. Denver

Regional Coun. of Govts., from 1981, chair, 1986-87; chair Jefferson County C. of C., 1989-90; apptd. by Gov. Colo. to Met. Air Quality Coun., 1985; bd. dirs. Nat. Assn. Regional Coun. Govts., 1986-90, CML, 1993—; bd. mem. Nat. League Cities, Colo. Mcpl. Bd., 1995—. Recipient John V. Christensen Meml. award, 1995; named Outstanding Elected Ofcl. West C.of C., 1987, 97. Fax: 987-7063. Office: City of Lakewood 445 S Allison Pkwy Lakewood CO 80226-3105

MOSBY, DOROTHEA SUSAN, municipal official; b. Sacramento, Calif., May 13, 1948; d. William Laurence and Esther Ida (Lux) M. AA in Sociology, Bakersfield (Calif.) Coll., 1966-69; BS in Recreation, San Jose State U., 1969-72; MPA, Calif. State U. Dominguez Hills, Carson, 1980-82. Asst. dept. pers. officer San Jose Pks. and Recreation Dept., 1972-73, neighborhood ctr. dir., 1973-74; sr. recreation leader Santa Monica Recreation and Pks. Dept., 1974-76, recreation supr., 1976-83; head bus. divsn. Santa Monica Recreation and Parks Dept., 1983-88; bus. adminstr. Santa Monica Cultural & Recreation Svcs., 1988-91; dir. pks. and recreation City of South Gate, Calif., 1991—; bd. dirs., officer Santa Monica City Employees Fed. Credit Union, 1980-89, pres. 1986-87; mem. citizens adv. com. L.A. Olympic Organizing Com., 1982-84. Mem. choir, flute soloist Pilgrim Luth. Ch., Santa Monica, 1974—, treas. Luth. ch. coun., 1984-86; vol. driver XXIII Olympiad, Los Angeles, 1984; contbr. local housing assistance U.S. Olympic Com., Los Angeles, 1984; mem. adv. com. Windsor Sq. Hancock Park Hist. Soc., Los Angeles, 1983, dir. Christmas carolling, 1980—, chmn. Olympic com., 1984, bd. trustees, 1984-90, chmn. pub. programs, 1985, co-chmn. pub. programs, 1986, co-vice chair, 1987, chmn., 1988, 89; Downey Symphony Guild; bd. dirs. Downey Symphony; mem. Samuel C. May Grad. Student Rsch. Paper Judging Com., Western Govt. Rsch. Assn., 1994. Recipient Outstanding Profl. of Yr. award Los Angeles Basin Pk. and Recreation Commrs. and Bd. Mems., 1993. Mem. Calif. Pk. and Recreation Soc. (bd. dirs. 1979-82, 86, mem. Calif bd. pk. and recreation pers. 1990-92, Scholarship Found. Bd. 1992—, chair 1996, 97, 98—, dist. 10 v.p. 1994, 95, 96, Dist. 10 Spl. Recognition award 1998), Nat. Recreation and Pk. Assn., Mgmt. Team Assocs. (sec., treas. 1979-83), Western Govtl. Rsch. Assn., Nat. Assn. Univ. Women, South Gate C. of C., Kiwanis Club (pres.), Chi Kappa Rho (pres. 1986), Pi Alpha Alpha. Avocations: flute, piano, reading, bicycling, tennis. Home: 9329 Elm Vista Dr Apt 103 Downey CA 90242-2992 Office: City of South Gate Dept Pks and Recreation 4900 Southern Ave South Gate CA 90280-3462

MOSBY, RALPH JOSEPH, minister; b. Kansas City, Mo., Feb. 11, 1931; s. Ralph Mosby Sr. and Ruth (Robinson) Collier; m. Kathleen Theresa Johnson, May 29, 1971; children: Audwin Joaquin, Gregory Johnson. BA, Redlands U., 1962; MDiv, Am. Bapt. Sem., 1968; PhD, Calif. Grad. Sch. Theology, 1973. Ordained to ministry Bapt. Ch.; cert. adult edn. tchr. (life). Assoc. min. Trinity Bapt. Ch., L.A., 1965-71; sr. pastor Immanuel Bapt. Ch., L.A., 1971-73, St. John Bapt. Ch., Long Beach, Calif., 1974—; instr. Am. Bapt. Sem. of West, Covina, Calif., 1968-69, Angeles Bible Coll., Hawthorne, Calif., 1974-75, L.A. Trade Tech. Coll., 1974-80, Long Beach City Coll., 1974-90. Bd. dirs. Long Beach Area Citizenship Involved, 1975—, Cable Com. Adv. Commn., Long Beach, 1983—, African Am. Coordinating Coun., Long Beach, 1989—; pres. Long Beach Housing Action Assn., 1976-78. Recipient Commendation of Svc. award County of L.A., City of Long Beach, 1983-86. Mem. South Coast Ecumenical Coun. (pres. 1988-89 Pastor of Yr. 1984), Christian Fellowship Union of Chs. (pres. 1985-88), Black Am. Bapt. of Pacific S.W. (pres. 1985-88, Svc. award 1988), Theta Alpha Phi. Home: 4350 Cerritos Ave Long Beach CA 90807-2462

MOSELEY, JOHN TRAVIS, university administrator, research physicist; b. New Orleans, Feb. 26, 1942; s. Fred Baker and Lily Gay (Lord) M.; m. Belva McCall Hudson, Aug. 11 1964 (div. June 1979); m. Susan Diane Callow, Aug. 6, 1979; children: Melanie Lord, John Mark, Stephanie Marie, Shannon Eleanor. BS in Physics, Ga. Inst. Tech., 1964, MS in Physics, 1966, PhD in Physics, 1969. Asst. prof. physics U. West Fla., Pensacola, 1968-69; sr. physicist SRI Internat., Menlo Park, Calif., 1969-75, program mgr., 1976-79; vis. prof. U. Paris, 1975-76; assoc. prof. U. Oreg., Eugene, 1979-81, dir. chem. physics inst., 1980-84, prof. physics, 1984—, head physics dept., 1984-85, v.p. rsch., 1985-94, v.p. acad. affairs, provost, 1994—; mem. exec. com., coun. on acad. affairs NASULGC, 1994—, chair, 1996-97; bd. dirs. Oreg. Resource and Tech., Portland; mem. com. on Atomic and Molecular Sci., 1983-85. Contbr. numerous articles to profl. jours. Mem. So. Willamette Rsch. Corridor, Eugene, 1985—, Lane Econ. Devel. Com., Eugene, 1988-94; bd. dirs. Eugene/Springfield Metro Partnership, 1985—, Oreg. Bach Festival, Eugene, 1987-94, Eugene Arts Found., 1995-97. Recipient Doctoral Thesis award Sigma Xi, 1969; Fulbright fellow, 1975; numerous rsch. grants, 1969—. Fellow AAAS, Am. Physical Soc.; mem. AAUW, Am. Chem. Soc. Avocations: skiing, backpacking. Home: 2140 Essex Ln Eugene OR 97403-1851 Office: U Oreg Office of VP Acad Affairs and Provost Eugene OR 97403-1258

MOSES, ELBERT RAYMOND, JR., speech and dramatic arts educator; b. New Concord, Ohio, Mar. 31, 1908; s. Elbert Raymond Sr. and Helen Martha (Miller) M.; m. Mary Miller Sterrett, Sept. 21, 1933 (dec. Sept. 1984); 1 child, James Elbert (dec.); m. Caroline Mae Entenman, June 19, 1985. AB, U. Pitts., 1932; MS, U. Mich., 1934, PhD, 1936. Instr. U. N.C., Greensboro, 1936-38; asst. prof. Ohio State U., Columbus, 1938-46; assoc. prof. Ea. Ill. State U., Charleston, 1946 56; asst. prof. Mich. State U., E. Lansing, Mich., 1956-59; prof. Clarion (Pa.) State Coll., 1959-71, chmn. dept. speech and dramatic arts, 1959—, emeritus prof., 1971—; Fulbright lectr. State Dept. U.S. Cebu Normal Sch., Cebu City, Philippine Islands, 1955-56; vis. prof. phonetics U. Mo., summer 1968; hon. sec.'s advocate dept. of aging State of Pa., Harrisburg, 1980-81. Author: Guide to Effective Speaking, 1957, Phonetics: A History and Interpretation, 1964, Three Attributes of God, 1983, Adventure in Reasoning, 1988, Beating the Odds, 1992, In Pursuit of Life, 1996; poems included in Best Poems of the 90s, 1992, in two web pages; contbr. articles to profl. jours.. Del. 3d World Congress Phoneticians, Tokyo, 1976; mem. nat. adv. com. fng. students and tchrs. HEW; del. to Internat. Congress Soc. Logopedics and Phoniatre, Vienna, 1965; liaison rep. to Peace Corps; pres. County Libr. Bd.; past exec. dir. Clarion County United Way; commr. Boy Scouts Am., 1976-77; pres. Venango County Adv. Coun. for Aging, 1978-79. Maj. AUS, 1942-46, lt. col. AUS, ret. Recipient Ret. Sr. Vol. Program Vol. of Yr. award No. Ariz. Coun. Govts., 1989, Spl. award Speech Comm. Assn., 1989, Endowment Benefactor award, 1991; 6 Diamong Pin of Melvin Jones Found., Internat. Lions, Life Mem. for outstanding svc. Yavapai Hills Lions, Best Male Songwriter, Poet of Yr. awards Entertainer Network Nashville, 1994, Listing Achievement in Entertainer-Indi-Assn. as Most Consistent Golden Poet of Nashville, 1995, EIA Platinum Poet, 1995, 96, Best Legendary Poet, 1996, EIA Diamond Poet, 1998; named to Internat. Poetry Hall of Fame. Fellow United Writers Assn.; mem. Ariz. Comm. Support System, Quarter Century Wireless Assn., Soc. Wireless Pioneers, Mil. Affiliate Radio System, Hospitalier Order of St. John of Jerusalem, Knights Hospitalier, Knightly and Mil. Order of St. Eugene of Trebizond (chevalier), Soverign and Mil. Order of St. Stephen the Matyr (comdr.), Knightly Assn. of St. George the Matyr, Ordre Chevaliers du Sinai, Hist. File, VFW (comdr.), Am. Legion (comdr.), Rotary (pres. 1966-67, dist. gov. 1973-74), Order of White Shrine of Jerusalem, Niadh Nask (Marshall of Kilbonane), Internat. Chivalric Inst., Confedn. of Chivalry (life, mem. grand coun.), Ordre Souverain et Militaire de la Milice du Saint Sepulcre (chevalier grand cross), Sovereign World Order of White Cross (lord of knights, dist. commdr. Ariz.), Prescott High Twelve Club (pres. 1990), Morse Telegraph Club, Inc., 21st Century Club (charter), The Old Old Timers Club, Phi Delta Kappa (Svc. Key 1978). Republican. Methodist. Avocation: ham radio. Home: 2001 Rocky Dells Dr Prescott AZ 86303-5685

MOSES, GLORIA JEAN, artist; b. St. Louis, Apr. 10, 1940; d. Harry and Pearl (Greenberg) Wittelstein; children: Joel Michael, Glenna Marie, Sharon Madeline. Student, Santa Monica City Coll., L.A., 1961-63, Washington U., St. Louis, 1957-61. Artist Saddle and Bridle Mag., St. Louis, 1957-61; self employed, 1961—. Exhibited works at County Mus. L.A. Art Rental Gallery, Long Beach Mus., 1961—, Orlando Gallery, L.A., 1987, 94, 96, 97, 98 Ariana Gallery, Detroit, 1994—, Vallery Miller Gallery, Palm Springs, 1994—, Parham Teapot Gallery, 1998. Mem. Nat. Watercolor Soc. (signature, bd. dirs. 1982), Watercolor USA (Patron award 1980), Nat. Print Soc., Ceramic Soc. Democrat. Jewish. Avocations: reading, gardening, piano, cooking. Office: Moses and Assocs 493 S Robertson Blvd Beverly Hills CA 90211-3624

MOSES, KIM M, film producer, director; b. North Hollywood, Calif., July 28, 1956; d. John Moses and Beverly (Hartwig) Ford; m. Joe Montana, Jan. 4, 1975 (div.); m. Ian Sander; children: Aaron Sander, Declan Moses Sander. Diploma in Paralegal, Georgetown U., 1977, BA in Liberal Arts, 1979. Congl. aide, paralegal U.S. Congress, Washington, 1977-83; news desk for summer Olympics, ABC Sports, L.A., 1984; news desk for winter Olympics, ABC Sports, Sarajevo, 1984; with Ohlmeyer Prodns., N.Y.C., L.A., 1985-93. Prodr. (film) How'd They Do That?, 1993, Power Boat Racing with Don Johnson, 1991, Comic Strip Live, 1994, My World on Video, 1990; prodr. (TV) The Extreme Edge, 1992, Disney's Christmas on Ice 1991; exec. prodr. (TV) Stolen Babies, 1994, Chasing the Dragon, 1996, (series) N.Y. News, 1995, (pilot) Legacy, 1997; exec. prodr. (series) Profiler, 1996-98, co-writer (with Ian Sander), 1998, dir., 1998, exec. cons., 1998-99; exec. prodr.: (TV series) Brimstone, 1998.

MOSES, STEPHEN DAVID, real estate investment professional; b. Phila., Nov. 24, 1934; s. Lester Jacob and Rosalie (Berg) M.; divorced; children: Kathy, Bobby. BS in Econs., Franklin & Marshall Coll., 1955; JD cum laude, Harvard Law Sch., 1958. Former v.p., sec. City Constrn. Corp. (subs. Kidder, Peabody and Prudential); exec. Boise Cascade Corp., 1967-71; temporary judge Mcpl. Ct. of Calif./L.A. Dist.; chmn. bd. dirs. Stephen Moses Interests, L.A., 1981—; bd. dirs. ICN Pharms., Inc.; mem. Pres. Nixon's Task Force on Low Income Housing; adv. Pres. Johnson's Commn. on Urban Housing; cons. U.S. Ho. Reps. Sub-Com. on Housing; adv. on housing Prime Minister of Yugoslavia, others. Trustee, chmn. investment com. Franklin & marshall Coll.; trustee, former chmn. coms. UCLA; bd. vis. Hebrew Union Coll.; bd. dirs. Calif. State U. Inst., v.p. Fraternity of Friends of L.A. County Music Ctr.; bd. dirs. Dem. Nat. Com., nat. fin. co-chmn., nat. fin. vice-chmn., western fin. chmn.; bd. dirs. Dem. Bus. Coun.; western chmn. Al Gore for Pres. Campaign; nat. fin. co-chmn. Tsonges for Pres. Campaign; co-fin. chmn. Gary Hart for Pres. Campaign. Recipient Housing Man of Yr., Nat. Housing Conf., Civic Achievement award Am. Jewish Com., Couple of Yr. (with wife, Kitty) Big Sisters of L.A.

MOSHER, SALLY EKENBERG, lawyer, musician; b. N.Y.C., July 26, 1934; d. Leslie Joseph and Frances Josephine (McArdle) Ekenberg; m. James Kimberly Mosher, Aug. 13, 1960 (dec. Aug. 1982). MusB, Manhattanville Coll., 1956; postgrad., Hofstra U., 1958-60, U. So. Calif., 1971-73; JD, U. So. Calif., 1981. Bar: Calif., 1982. Musician, pianist, tchr., 1957-74; music critic Pasadena Star-News, 1967-72; mgr. Contrasts Concerts, Pasadena Art Mus., 1971-72; rep. Occidental Life Ins. Co., Pasadena, 1975-78; v.p. James K. Mosher Co., Pasadena, 1961-82, pres., 1982—; pres. Oakhill Enterprises, Pasadena, 1984—; assoc. White-Howell, Inc., Pasadena, 1984-94; real estate broker, 1984-96; harpsichordist, lectr., composer, 1994—; pub. Silver Wheels Pub., ASCAP. Musician (CD recs.) William Byrd: Songs, Dances, Battles, Games, 1995, From Now On: New Directions For Harpsichord, 1998; contbr. articles to various publs. Bd. dirs. Jr. League Pasadena, 1966-67, Encounters Concerts, Pasadena, 1966-72, U. So. Calif. Friends of Music, L.A., 1973-76, Calif. Music Theatre, 1988-90, Pasadena Hist. Soc., 1989-91, I Cantori, 1989-91; bd. dirs. Pasadena Arts Coun., 1986-92, pres., 1989-92, chair adv. bd., 1992-93; v.p., bd. dirs. Pasadena Chamber Orch., 1986-88, pres., 1987-88; mem. Calif. 200 Coun. for Bicentennial of U.S. Constn., 1987-90; mem. Endowment Adv. Commn., Pasadena, 1988-90; bd. dirs. Foothill Area Cmty. Svcs., 1990-95, treas., 1991, vice chair, 1992-94, chair, 1994-95. Manhattanville Coll. hon. scholar, 1952-56. Mem. ABA, Calif. Bar Assn., Assocs. of Calif. Inst. Tech., Athenaeum, Kappa Gamma Pi, Mu Phi Epsilon, Phi Alpha Delta. Fax: (626) 795-3146. E-mail: sally@cyberverse.com. Home: 1260 Rancheros Rd Pasadena CA 91103-2759

MOSK, STANLEY, state supreme court justice; b. San Antonio, TX, Sept. 4, 1912; s. Paul and Minna (Perl) M.; m. Edna Mitchell, Sept. 27, 1937 (dec.); 1 child, Richard Mitchell; m. Susan Hines, Aug. 27, 1982 (div.); m. Kaygey Kash, Jan. 15, 1995. Student, U. Tex., 1931; PhB, U. Chgo., 1933; postgrad., U. Chgo. Law Sch., 1934; JD, Southwestern U., 1935; postgrad., The Hague Acad. Internat. Law, 1970, U. Pacific, 1970; LLD, U. San Diego, 1971, U. Santa Clara, 1976, Calif. Western U., 1984, Whittier Coll. Law, 1993, Pepperdine U., 1995, Western State U., San Diego, 1995. Bar: Calif. 1935, U.S. Supreme Ct. 1956. Practiced in Los Angeles, until 1939; exec. sec. to gov. Calif., 1939-42; judge Superior Ct. Los Angeles County, 1943-58; pro tem justice Dist. Ct. Appeal, Calif., 1954; atty. gen. Calif., also head state dept. justice, 1959-64; justice Supreme Ct. Calif., 1964—; mem. Jud. Coun. Calif., 1973-75, Internat. Commn. Jurists. Author: Democracy in America-Day by Day, 1995. Chmn. San Francisco Internat. Film Festival, 1967; mem. Dem. Nat. Com., Calif., 1960-64; mem. bd. regents U. Calif., 1940; pres. Vista Del Mar Child Care Svc., 1954-58; bd. dirs. San Francisco Law Sch., 1971-73, San Francisco Regional Cancer Found., 1980-83. With AUS, WWII. Recipient Disting. Alumnus award U. Chgo., 1958, 93. Mem. ABA, Nat. Assn. Attys. Gen. (exec. bd. 1964), Western Assn. Attys. Gen. (pres. 1963), L.A. Bar Assn., San Francisco Bar Assn., Am. Legion, Manuscript Soc., Calif. Hist. Soc., Am. Judicature Soc., Inst. Jud. Adminstrn., U. Chgo. Alumni Assn. No. Calif. (pres. 1957-58, 67), Order of Coif (hon.), B'nai B'rith, Hillcrest Country Club (L.A.), Commonwealth Club, Beverly Hills Tennis Club. Office: Supreme Ct Calif 350 Mcallister St San Francisco CA 94102-4712

MOSKOWITZ, SEYMOUR, investment company executive, consultant, engineering executive, scientist; b. Paterson, N.J., May 26, 1935; s. David and Ruth (Abrams) M.; m. Gloria Jean Vocale, Jan. 22, 1978; 1 child, Audrey Lyn. BSEE, N.J. Inst. Tech., 1956; MSEE, U. So. Calif., 1962, PhD in Elec. Engring., 1969. Lt. USAF, 1956-59; chief scientist, lab. mgr. Hughes GM, El Segundo, Calif., 1959-87, Denver, 1959-87; exec. scientist Atlantic Rsch. Corp., Rockville, Md., 1987-93; account exec. Dean Witter Reynolds, Denver, 1993-95; v.p. Bidwell & Riddle Investment Adv., Englewood, Colo., 1996—; cons. M2 Assocs., Aurora, Colo., 1987-93; pres. Imagineering Assocs., Englewood, Colol., 1988-93. Contbr. articles to profl. jours. Bd. dirs. Rocky Mountain Children's Law Ctr., Denver, 1990—, Maccabi USA/Sports for Israel, Phila., 1994—. Ranked sr. tennis player USTA, 1980—. Mem. Greenwood Athletic Club, Tau Beta Pi, Eta Kappa Nu, Phi Eta Sigma. Home: 5633 E Southmoor Cir Englewood CO 80111-1042 Office: Bidwell & Riddle Investment Adv 8400 E Prentice Ave Ste 1401 Englewood CO 80111-2926

MOSKUS, JERRY RAY, academic administrator, educator; b. Springfield, Ill., Dec. 10, 1942; s. Raymond Charles and Jean (Riley) M.; m. Virginia Dieckmann Moskus, July 2, 1986; children: Elizabeth, Jane, Jennifer, Julianne, Jonathan. BS in English, Ill. State U., 1965, MS in English, 1968, PhD in Edn. Adminstrn., 1983. Tchr. English Saybrook (Ill.) Arrowsmith High Sch., 1966-69; instr. Lincoln Land Community Coll., Springfield, 1969-71, asst. to pres., 1971-73, dir. rsch., 1973-75, dean, 1975-84, v.p. acad. svcs., 1984-85; exec. v.p. Des Moines Area Community Coll., Ankeny, Iowa, 1985-90; pres. Lane Community Coll., Eugene, Oreg., 1990—; temp. asst. prof. Iowa State U., Ames, 1989. Bd. dirs. Vachel Lindsay Assn., Springfield, 1983-85, Iowa Children's & Family Svcs., Des Moines, 1986-90; bd. dirs. United Way of Lane County, 1990—. Mem. So. Willamette Pvt. Industry Coun. (bd. dirs. 1990—), League for Innovation in The Community Coll., Springfield Rotary, Phi Delta Kappa, Sigma Tau Delta. Office: Lane Community Coll 4000 E 30th Ave Eugene OR 97405-0640

MOSQUEIRA, CHARLOTTE MARIANNE, dietitian; b. L.A., July 26, 1937; d. Leo and Magdalene Tollefson; children: Mark, Michael. BS, St. Olaf Coll., 1959; postgrad. U. Oreg. Med. Sch., 1959-60; MA, Central Mich. U., 1980. Registered dietitian. Dir. dietetics Riverside Meth. Hosp., Columbus, Ohio, 1977-79; dir. nutrition and food svc. Fresno (Calif.) Community Hosp. and Med. Ctr., 1980-91; mem. faculty Dept. Enology and Food Sci., Calif. State U., Fresno, 1984-93; dir. nutritional svc. Emanuel Med. Ctr., Turlock, Calif., 1991-97, Bapt. Med. Ctr., Little Rock, 1997. Mem. Am. Dietetic Assn., Calif. Dietetic Assn. Lutheran.

MOSS, DEBRA LEE, special education educator; b. L.A., June 15, 1952; d. Boris and Mildred Rose (Volk) Elkin; divorced; children: Ryan Adam, Lauren Nicole, Rebecca Anne. BA in Psychology, UCLA, 1973; MA in Spl. Edn., Calif. State U., L.A., 1977. Cert. elem. tchr. severely handicapped, learning handicapped and jr. coll. tchr., Calif. Tchr. spl. edn. UCLA Neuropsychiat. Inst., 1972-75, demonstration tchr., curriculum coord., 1975-78; edn. specialist Harbor Regional Ctr. for Developmentally Disabled, Torrance, Calif., 1978-82; ednl. cons. North L.A. Regional Ctr. for Developmentally Disabled, Panorama City, Calif., 1982-87; behavior specialist L.A. Unified Sch. Dist., 1987-91, program specialist, 1991-92, support staff spl. edn. mid. schs., 1992-93, inclusion facilitator, 1993-98, program specialist, 1998—; hon. lectr. West Valley Occupational Ctr., 1986—; tutor spl. edn., L.A., 1973—; behavior specialist to families, 1985—. Contbr. articles to profl. jours. Mem. Am. Assn. on Retardation, Nat. Assn. for Autistic Children and Adults, Coun. for Exceptional Children. Democrat. Office: LA USD West Valley Spl Edn Svc Unit 6505 Zelzah Ave Reseda CA 91335-6221

MOSS, ERIC OWEN, architect; b. L.A., July 25, 1943. BA, UCLA, 1965; MArch with honors, U. Calif., Berkeley, 1968, Harvard U., 1972. Prof. design So. Calif. Inst. Architecture, 1974—; prin. Eric Owen Moss Archs., Culver City, Calif., 1975—; Eliot Noyes chair Harvard U., Cambridge, Mass., 1990; Eero Saarinen chair Yale U., New Haven, 1991; lectr. Hirshhorn Mus. Symposium, Washington, 1990, Nat. AIA Conv., 1990, Mus. Contemporary Art, L.A., 1991, N.Y. Archtl. League, 1991, Archtl. Assn. Ireland, Dublin, Archtl. Assn., London, 1991, Royal Coll. Art, London, 1991, Smithsonian Inst., Washington, 1992, U. Calif., Berkeley, 1992, Osterreichiaches Mus. fur Angewandte Kunst, Vienna, Austria, 1992, UCLA, 1992, Royal Danish Acad. Fine Arts, Copenhagen, 1993, U. Lund, Sweden, 1993, Mus. Finnish Architecture, Helsinki, 1993, Royal Acad. Arts, London, 1993, U. Pa., Phila., 1994, others; tchr. U. Tex., Austin, 1983, Wash. U., St. Louis, 1984, U. Ill., Chgo., 1985, Tulane U., New Orleans, 1985, U. Minn., Mpls., 1985, Columbia U., N.Y.C., 1986, Rice U., Houston, 1988; participant various confs. Exhbns. of work include World Biennial of Architecture, Sofia, Bulgaria, 1989, Salle des Tirages du Credit Foncier de France, Paris, 1990, Bartlett Sch. Architecture and Urban Design, London, 1991, Gallery of Functional Art, Santa Monica, Calif., 1992, GA Gallery, Tokyo, 1992, Mus. fur Gestaltung Zurich, Switzerland, 1993, Santa Monica (Calif.) Mus. Art, 1993, Fonds Regional D'Art Contemporain du Centre, 1993, Aspen (Colo.) Art Mus., 1993, Centro de Arte y Comunicacion, Buenos Aires, 1993, Contemporary Arts Ctr., Cin., 1993, Philippe Uzzan Galerie, Paris, 1993, Contemporary Arts Ctr., Tours, France, 1993, Internat. Exhbn. Contemporary Architecture, Havana, Cuba, 1994, others. Recipient Progressive Architecture Design award, 1978, 92, Winning Interior Archtl. Record award, 1984, Interiors Design award, 1991. Fellow AIA (L.A. awards 1977, 79, 83, 88, 90, Calif. Coun. awards 1981, 86, 88, L.A. Honor awards 1991, Nat. Honor awards 88, 89, Calif. Coun. Urban Design/Adaptive Re-Use awards 1991, Nat. Interior Design awards 1992, 94, L.A. Design awards 1992, 93). Subject of monographs and numerous articles in mags. and jours. Office: 8557 Higuera St Culver City CA 90232-2535*

MOSS, GARNER MCKENZIE, art director, media executive, designer; b. Torrance, Calif., Dec. 15, 1964; s. McKenzie and Peppy (Frisone) M. BS, Calif. Poly., 1989. Freelance designer San Luis Obispo, Calif., 1982-87; designer EasyAd, San Luis Obispo, Calif., 1987-88; jr. art dir. Lewis Galoob Toys, San Luis Obispo, Calif., 1989-90; designer, illustrator Lucas Films Games, San Rafael, Calif., 1988-92; creative dir. Terris & Jaye, San Francisco, Calif., 1990-95; designer IMSI, San Rafael, Calif., 1993-95; creative dir., ptnr. Impact Media Group, San Francisco, 1993—; mem. adv. bd. Calif. Poly., Calif. State U., San Luis Obispo, 1995—. Recipient 18 Nat. Polly awards Nat. Polit. Awards for Design, 1990-95, Logotype award Print Mag. Nat. Design Bd., 1990, Prints Best Logos and Symbols #3 Print Mag. Nat. Design Bd., 1991. Roman Catholic. Avocations: skiing, illustration, robot building and competing. Office: Impact Media Group South Train Car 300 De Haro St San Francisco CA 94103-5144

MOSS, LYNDA BOURQUE, museum director. Dir. Western Heritage Ctr., Billings, Mont. Office: Western Heritage Ctr 2822 Montana Ave Billings MT 59101-2305*

MOSS, RICHARD B., pediatrician; b. N.Y.C., Oct. 30, 1949. MD, SUNY, Downstate, 1975. Intern Children's Meml. Hosp., Chgo., 1975-76, resident, 1976-77; fellow Stanford (Calif.) U. Med. Sch., 1977-79, 80-81; now pediatrician Lucile Salter Packard Children's Hosp., Palo Alto, Calif.; prof. pediats. Stanford U. Med. Sch. Office: Stanford U Sch Med Ctr Dept Pediats Stanford CA 94305-5119

MOSS, STEVE HOYLE, television and film producer and director; b. Abilene, Tex., Oct. 7, 1950; s. Hoyle Gene and Boots (Jobe) M.; m. Deborah Sue Brooks, May 10, 1991. Student, Tex. Tech U., Lubbock, 1969-72. Owner Ski Shop, Lubbock, 1971-82; profl. skier Chevrolet Freestyle, 1971-78; prodr., dir. Steve Moss Prodns., Dallas and L.A., 1983—; prodr. World Pro Ski Tour & World Pro Snowboard Tour, TNN, Nashville, 1997—. Prodr. feature film Convict Cowboy, 1985; dir. music videos. Recipient MTV Music Video award, 1985, 86, 88, Golde Eagle award N.Y. Film Festival, 1985. Office: 14754 Bassett St Van Nuys CA 91405-3840

MOSS, SUSAN HECHT, artist, writer; b. Chgo., May 6, 1944; d. Benjamin Franklin and Amy (Hecht) M.; m. Glen Galloway, Jan. 15, 1964 (div. Sept. 1974). BA in Art/Psychology with honors, U. Nev., 1966; MFA, Otis Art Inst., 1970. spkr. on breast cancer. Author: Keep Your Breasts! Preventing Breast Cancer the Natural Way, 1994, 5th edit., 1998; contbr. poetry to profl. publs.; exhibited in permanent collections at L.A. County Mus. of Art, Skirball Mus., L.A., Laguna Mus. of Art.; exhibited David Findlay Gallery, N.Y., Albright-Knox Mus., Forum Gallery, N.Y. Mem. Cancer Ctrl. Soc. (spkr. 1996), Nat. Breast Cancer Coalition. Democrat. Jewish. Avocations: swimming, weight-lifting, hiking, booksigning, creating videos on breast cancer prevention. Studio: 4767 York Blvd Los Angeles CA 90042-1648 Home: 1879 Montiflora Ave Los Angeles CA 90041-2016

MOSSMAN, THOMAS MELLISH, JR., television manager; b. Honolulu, Nov. 20, 1938; s. Thomas Mellish and Marian (Ledwith) M.; children: Thomas Mellish III, James Michael; m. Jan Carla MacAlister, Dec. 31, 1989. Student, U. Hawaii, 1954-57; BA, U. Denver, 1958, MA, 1965. Producer-dir. KRMA-TV, Denver, 1960-64, KCET-TV, L.A., 1964-72; pres. Mosaic Films, L.A., 1972-73; prodn. and operations dir. KLCS-TV, L.A., 1973-78, station mgr., 1978-87, 96—; dept. dir. Archdiocese of L.A., 1987-96; sta. mgr. KLCS-TV, L.A., 1996—; instr. Calif. State U., Northridge, 1981—; chairperson, founder L.A. Community TV, 1987-95. Chmn. exec. bd. Regional Ednl. TV Adv. Coun., 1989-93; chmn., founding mem., chmn. Alliance for Distance Edn. in Calif., 1991-95; pres. Cath. TV Network, 1993-96; bd. dirs. L.A. Cable TV Access Corp. Mem. NATAS, Dirs. Guild Am., Alliance for Community Media. Episcopalian. Office: KLCS-TV 1061 W Temple St Los Angeles CA 90012-1513

MOSTELLER, JAMES WILBUR, III, data processing executive; b. Ft. Riley, Kans., June 21, 1940; s. James Wilbur, Jr., and Ruth Renfro (Thompson) M.; B.S. in Econs., Rensselaer Poly. Inst., 1962; M.B.A., Temple U., 1971; m. Sandra Josephine Stevenson, Oct. 13, 1962; children—Margaret, Steven, Michael. Data processing systems analyst, Philco-Ford, Ft. Washington, Pa., 1966-69; data processing analyst and supr., Merck Sharp & Dohme, West Point, Pa., 1969-75, dir. mgmt. info. systems KELCO div. Merck and Co., San Diego, 1975-87; dir. info. mgmt. Advanced Systems div. United Technologies, San Diego, 1987-88; computer scientist Navy Personnel Research and Devel. Ctr., San Diego, 1988-97; head prodn. sys. Navy SPAWAR Sys. Ctr., San Diego, 1997—. Bd. dirs. New Horizons Montessori Sch., Ft. Washington, Pa., 1974-75; leader youth programs North County YMCA, 1977-81; mem. San Diego Research Park Com., 1978-86; 1st. v.p., mem. exec. com. San Diego Space and Sci. Found., 1985-92. With USN, 1962-66, capt. Res., 1966-93. Cert. in data processing. Mem. Data Processing Mgmt. Assn., Assn. Systems Mgmt., Naval Res. Assn. (life), U.S. Naval Inst. (life), Beta Gamma Sigma, Sigma Alpha Epsilon (chpt. pres. 1961-62), La Playa Yacht Club 1999—. Office: Navy SPAWAR Sys Ctr D0298 San Diego CA 92152-5001

MOTE, GORDON EDWARD, health facility administrator; b. Chlumonie, Bolivia, Dec. 5, 1943; came to U.S., 1944; s. Robert Grant and Caroline Elizabeth (Heubach) M.; m. Patricia Louise Hoss, June 18, 1968 (div. July 1984); 1 child, Gregory Edward; m. Raylene Louise Parrett, Oct. 13, 1985. BA in Biology, Loma Linda U., 1968; MBA, Century U., 1988, PhD, 1995. Field dir., staff biologist World Life Rsch. Inst., Colton, Calif., 1967-68; dept. mgr., instr. biology Loma Linda U., Riverside, Calif., 1970-73; dir. ops. Versitron Industries, Riverside, 1973-78; asst. to v.p. Zee Med. Products, Irvine, Calif., 1978-80; adminstr. Bio-Labs., Colton, 1980, Stout &

Perkins Acctg. Corp., Redlands, Calif., 1981-84; contr. Riverside-San Bernardino County Indian Health, Banning, Calif., 1987-88; mgmt. and health care cons. Profl. Mgmt. Solutions, Grand Terrace, Calif., 1984—; pres., exec. dir. Integrated Life Style Mgmt., Grand Terrace, 1993—; bd. dirs. Cyric Software, San Diego, 1991—, Pac-Tech Sys. Inc., Calimesa, Calif., 1994—; instr. Nat. Assn. Underwater Instructors, 1971—. Mem. Am. Mgmt. Assn. Avocations: sailing, skin and scuba diving, bicycling, kayaking. Home and Office: 35667 Oleander Ave Yucaipa CA 92399-9412

MOTHERSHEAD, J. LELAND, III, dean; b. Boston, Jan. 10, 1939; s. John L. Jr. and Elizabeth Rankin (Crossett) M.; m. Therese Petkelis, June 23, 1963; 1 child, John Leland VI. BA, Carleton Coll., 1960; MA in Tchg., Brown U., 1963. Tchr. Tabor Acad., Marion, Mass., 1962-63, Chadwick Sch., Rolling Hills, Calif., 1963-66; tchr., adminstr. Flintridge (Calif.) Prep. Sch., 1966-75, head lower sch., 1972-74, dir. student affairs, 1974-75; tchr. Southwestern Acad., San Marino, Calif., 1979-83, dean, 1983—. Mem. Rotary (pres. San Marino Club 1994-95, gov. dist. 5300 1998—). Avocation: building historic wooden ship models. Home: 1145 Oak Grove Ave San Marino CA 91108-1028 Office: Southwestern Acad 2800 Monterey Rd San Marino CA 91108-1798

MOTSENBOCKER, REX ALAN, construction company executive; b. Norman, Okla., Dec. 14, 1962; s. Rex Albert and Nondace Nadine (Bonner) M.; m. Karla Doreen Miller, Nov. 14, 1992. BS in Bus., Calif. State U., Sacramento, 1984; BS in Constrn. Engring., Ariz. State U., 1986; MBA in Fin. magna cum laude, Western Internat. U., Phoenix, 1994; postgrad., So. Calif. U., Newport, 1994—. Cert. fin. cons. Project coord. Tibshraeny Bros., Mesa, Ariz., 1986; project mgr. Joe E. Woods, Tempe, Ariz., 1986-87; project engr. Sundt Corp., Phoenix, 1987—; pres. Master Investments, Phoenix, 1994—; CFO Master Builders Devel., LLC, Las Vegas, Nev., 1994—; mgr., CFO Remington Estates Devel., L.L.C., Phoenix, 1995—; bd. dirs. bullion Recovery Sys., Inc., Phoenix. Author: Financial Aspects of Investing in Mexico, 1994. Team leader Senator McCain Re-election Campaign, Phoenix, 1992-94; project dir. Christmas in April, Phoenix, 1989-93. Mem. Project Mgrs. Inst. (v.p. membership 1990—), Am. Mgrs. Assn., Constrn. Mgmt. Assn., Phoenix C. of C., Nat. Asbestoc Council, Ariz. State U. Alumni Assn. (v.p. bd. 1994—), Delta Mu Delta (v.p. 1993—). Republican. Avocations: triathlons, singing. Home: 15833 N 7th Dr Phoenix AZ 85023-4435

MOTT, JUNE MARJORIE, school system administrator; b. Faribault, Minn., Mar. 8, 1920; d. David C. and Tillie W. (Nelson) Shifflett; m. Elwood Knight Mott, Oct. 18, 1958. BS, U. Minn., 1943, MA, 1948. Tchr. high schs. in Minn., 1943-46, 48-53, 54-57; script writer, Hollywood, Calif., 1953-54; tchr. English, creative writing and journalism Mt. Miguel High Sch., Spring Valley, Calif., 1957-86, chmn. English dept., 1964-71, chmn. Dist. English council, 1967-68; mem. Press Bur., Grossmont (Calif.) High Sch. Dist., 1958-86; elected to Grossmont Union High Sch. Governing Bd., 1986—, clk. sch. bd., 1989, v.p. governing bd., 1989-90, 93, pres. sch. bd., 1991-92, v.p., 1992-93, pres. governing bd., 1993-94, v.p., 1998; scriptwriter TV prodn. Lamp Unto My Feet, Jam Dandy Corp.; free-lance writer, cons. travel writer, photographer; editor, publ Listening Heart, 1989. Author, editor in field. Vice chmn. polit. action San Diego County Regional Resource Ctr., 1980-81; mem. S.D. Bd. of Alcohol and Drug Abuse Prevention, 1990—, Curriculum Com. Grossmont Dist., 1990—, Site Facilities Com., Master Planning Com., 1992—, East County Issues and Mgmt. Com., 1990—, East County Women in Edn.; apptd. del. Calif. Sch. Bds. Assn., 1992—, del. assembly, 1992—, elected to region 17 del. assembly, 1993—; v.p., pub. rels. chmn. Lemon Grove Luth. Ch., 1962-78, 89—, v.p., 1993, pres. 1994, chair concert series, 1997—. Writing project fellow U. Calif., San Diego, 1978; named Outstanding Journalism Tchr., State of Calif., Outstanding Humanities Tchr., San Diego County, Tchr. of Yr. for San Diego County, 1978; U. Cambridge scholar, 1982; Woman of Yr. Lemon Grove Soroptimists, 1990. Mem. ASCD, NEA, AAUW, Nat. Council Tchrs. English, Nat. Journalism Assn., Calif. Assn. Tchrs. English, Calif. Tchrs. Assn., So. Calif. Journalism Assn., Calif. Sch. Bds. Assn. (elected del. region 17, del. assembly 1993—), Calif. Elected Women's Assn. for Edn. Rsch. (ednl. cons. 1990), San Diego County Journalism Educators Assn. (pres. 1975-76), Grossmont Edn. Assn. (pres. 1978-80), Greater San Diego Council Tchrs. English, Nat. Writers Club, Am. Guild Theatre Organists, Am. Guild Organists, Palomar Chpt. Organ Soc., San Diego Mus. of Art, Lemon Grove Hist. Soc., Spreckels Organ Soc., Calif. Retired Tchrs. Assn. (membership chairwoman 1986-89, pres. chpt. # 69 1989-94, parlimentarian 1992-93, chair bylaws 1996—), Lemon Grove C. of C. (mem. econ. devel. com. 1994—), Nat. Sch. Bds. Assn., Order Ea. Star, Kiwanis (pres. elect Lemon grove chpt. 1992, program chmn., pres. 1993-94), Sigma Delta Chi, Delta Kappa Gamma (pres. Theta Gamma chpt. 1993—). Democrat. Home and Office: 2885 New Jersey Ave Lemon Grove CA 91945-2826

MOTTER, THOMAS FRANKLIN, medical products executive; b. Modesto, Calif., June 27, 1948; s. Thomas Dean and Beverley June (Mosier) M.; m. Wanda Lenice Parker, Feb. 9, 1968 (div. Jan. 1972); children: Eric Franklin, Katrina Lenice; m. Jerry Ann Averill, Oct. 24, 1976; children: Heidi Marika, Courtney Averill. *Original surname spelled Matter. Johannes immigrated to America in 1751 on English ship Edinborough. He was an orphan and came with Uncle Adtam. Originally from Basil Switzerland via Altdorf and Alteckendorf, Haut Rhin then Bas Rhine, Alsace then Palatinate. Came to Lancaster, Pennsylvania, fought under Washington in French-Indian War. Moved up Susquahanna after War and settled in Lykens Valley near Berrysburg. Johannes and Johannes Jr. fought in 10th Regiment, Pennsylvania Line under Anthony Wayne. Buried in heroes monument, St.John's Hill Church, Berrysburg. Johannes Jr.'s brother Michael was Grandfather of Margaret "Rebecca" Motter, Grandmother of Dwight David Eisenhower, Allied Commander WWII and 34th President of United States.* AA, Cabrillo Jr. Coll., Santa Cruz, Calif., 1968; BA, Stephens Coll., 1970; MBA, Pepperdine U., 1975. Social worker County of Santa Cruz and Amador, 1970-77; nat. dir. mktg. Humphrey Instruments/SmithKline, San Leandro, Calif., 1978-88; internat. gen. mgr. HGM Med. Lasers, Salt Lake City, 1988-89; pres., CEO Paradigm Med. Industries Inc., Salt Lake City, 1989—. *Mr. Motter has dedicated his life in service to the sick and poor. First as a Social Worker in Child Protective Services and Crisis Intervention for seven years in California. Most recently as Chairman, Founder, CEO and President of Paradigm Medical which he took public on the Nasdaq in 1996. He was Captain, Armor during the Vietnam War and was recognized recently for Knighthood by the Catholic Church and the Knights of the Hospital of St. John of Jerusalem. He is active in the Anglican Catholic Church and is primarily responsible for recent technological advances in Catardt Surgery and Glaucoma Diagnosis and management, by God's grace.* Mem. Nat. Ski Patrol, Stockton, 1973-79; v.p. Sandy (Utah) Pony Baseball, 1994-95; coach Kearns (Utah) Am. Legion Baseball, 1995-96. Capt. U.S. Army, 1970-76. Named. Mem. Nat. Adult Baseball Assn. (mem. Nat. Championship team), Am. Legion, Sons of the Am. Revolution Utah State Chpt., Knight Orthodox Order of the Knights of the Hosp. of St. John of Jerusalem. Episcopalian. Avocations: skiing, hardball baseball, coaching, fly fishing, hunting. Office: Paradigm Med Industries Inc 1127 W 2320 S Ste A Salt Lake City UT 84119-1551

MOTULSKY, ARNO GUNTHER, geneticist, physician, educator; b. Fischhausen, Germany, July 5, 1923; came to U.S., 1941; s. Herman and Rena (Sass) Molton; m. Gretel C. Stern, Mar. 22, 1945; children: Judy, Harvey, Arlene. Student, Cen. YMCA Coll., Chgo., 1941-43, Yale U., 1943-44; BS, U. Ill., 1945, MD, 1947, DSc (hon.), 1982, MD (hon.), 1991. Diplomate Am. Bd. Internal Medicine, Am. Bd. Med. Genetics. Intern, fellow, resident Michael Reese Hosp., Chgo., 1947-51; staff mem. charge clin. investigation dept. hematology Army Med. Service Grad. Sch., Walter Reed Army Med. Ctr., Washington, 1952-53; research assoc. internal medicine George Washington U. Sch. Medicine, 1952-53; from instr. to assoc. prof. dept. medicine U. Wash. Sch. Medicine, Seattle, 1953-61, prof. medicine, prof. genetics, 1961—; head div. med. genetics, dir. genetics clinic Univ. Hosp., Seattle, 1959-89; dir. Ctr. for Inherited Diseases, Seattle, 1972-90; attending physician Univ. Hosp., Seattle; cons. Pres.'s Commn. for Study of Ethical Problems in Medicine and Biomed. and Behavioral Research, 1979-83; cons. various coms. NRC, NIH, WHO, others. Editor Am. Jour. Human Genetics, 1969-75, Human Genetics, 1969-97. Commonwealth Fund fellow in human genetics Univ. Coll., London, 1957-58; John and Mary Markle scholar in med. sci., 1957-62; fellow Ctr. Advanced Study in Behavioral Scis., Stanford U., 1976-77, Inst. Advanced Study, Berlin, 1984. Fellow ACP, AAAS; mem. NAS, Internat. Soc. Hematology, Am. Fedn. Clin. Research, Genetics Soc. Am., Western Soc. Clin. Research, Am. Soc. Human Genetics, Am. Soc. Clin. Investigation, Am. Assn. Physicians, Inst. of Medicine, Am. Acad. Arts and Scis. Home: 4347 53rd Ave NE Seattle WA 98105-4938 Office: U Wash Divsn Med Genetics PO Box 356423 Seattle WA 98195-6423

MOU, THOMAS WILLIAM, physician, medical educator and consultant; b. Phila., May 17, 1920; s. Thomas Simonsen and Ellen Marie (Mathiesen) M.; m. Marie Elizabeth Hartmann, Dec. 29, 1945 (div. Oct., 1976); children: Susan, Roberta; m. M. Delma Jane Schreiber, Nov. 11, 1976. BSc in Bacteriology, Phila. Coll. Pharm & Sci., 1941; MD, U. Rochester, 1950. Diplomate Nat. Bd. Med. Examiners. Instr. medicine and bacteriology U. Rochester (N.Y.) Sch. of Medicine, 1954-56; asst. prof. preventive medicine to prof. cmty. medicine SUNY at Syracuse, 1956-70; exec. dean to assoc chancellor health sci. SUNY Ctrl. Adminstrn., Albany, 1970-77; dean clin. campus W. Va. U., Charleston, 1977-85; pres. Ednl. Commn. for Fgn. Med. Grads., Phila., 1986-88; dean emeritus W. Va. U. Med. Ctr., Morgantown, 1986—; geriatric practice Adult Medicine Specialists, Pueblo, Colo., 1990—; cons. Carnegie Commn. for Advancement of Tchg., Princeton, N.J., 1987-88, Charles A. Dana Found., N.Y.C., 1988, Geriatric Pharmacy Inst. of Phila. Coll. of Pharmacy and Sci., 1988. Contbr. 36 article or presentations to profl. jours or sci. confs. Trustee Phila. Coll. Pharmacy and Sci., 1972-81. Capt. Sanitary Corps, 1941-45. Recipient Disting. Alumnus award Phila. Coll. Pharmacy and Sci., 1975, award of distinction and honor Ben Franklin Soc. SUNY, N.Y.C., 1975, Koch medal Am. Optometric Soc., N.Y.C., 1976; T.W. Mou Endowed Lectureship W. Va. U., Charleston, 1985. Fellow Am. Coll. Physicians, Am. Coll. Preventive Medicine, Phila. Coll. Physicians. Avocations: violin, travel. Home: 3050 Valleybrook Ln Colorado Springs CO 80904-1154 Office: Adult Medicine Specialists 314 W 16th St Pueblo CO 81003-2728

MOULD, DIANE RENEE, pharmacologist; b. Englewood, N.J., Oct. 6, 1960; d. Spencer Herbert and Beverly Ann (Fortunato) M. BS in Chem. Biology, Stevens Inst. Tech., 1983; PhD of Pharmaceutics, Ohio State U., 1989. Rsch. asst. Stevens Inst. Tech., Hoboken, N.J., 1979-83; sci. rsch. assoc. Lederle Labs., Pearle River, N.Y., 1983-84; tchg. asst. Coll. Pharmacy Ohio State U., Columbus, 1984-90; clin. rsch. investigator Hoffmann-La Roche, Nutley, N.J., 1990—; cons. Projection Rsch., Clifton, N.J., 1992—, Knorr Co., Smoke Rise Kinnelon, N.J., 1983-90. Contbr. articles to profl. jours. Fellow Am. Found. Pharm. Edn., 1986-89. Fellow Phi Kappa Phi (award 1985); mem. Am. Assn. Pharm. Sci., Am. Soc. Clin. Pharmacology and Therapeutics, Drug Info. Assn. Avocations: painting, music, weight lifting, photography, parachuting.

MOULE, WILLIAM NELSON, electrical engineer; b. Highland Park, Mich., Sept. 13, 1924; s. Hollis Creager and Kate DeEtte (Hill) M.; m. Barbara Ann Bagley, June 27, 1953; children: Janice Louise, Robert Hollis (dec.), Linda Anne, Nancy Lynn Moule Moles. BSEE, Mich. State U., 1949; MSEE, U. Pa., 1957. Reg. profl. engr., N.J. Design engr. Radio Corp. of Am., Camden, N.J., 1949-59; sr. design engr. Radio Corp. of Am., Moorestown, N.J., 1959-67; sr. engr. Emerson Elec. Co., St. Louis, 1967-70, Emerson Elec. Rantec Divsn., Calabasas, Calif., 1970; sr. staff engr. Raytheon Co., Santa Barbara, Calif., 1970-73, ITT Gilfillan, Van Nuys, Calif., 1973, Jet Propulsion Lab., Pasadena, Calif., 1973-79; sr. rsch devel. engr. Lockheed Advanced Devel. Co., Burbank, Calif., 1979—. Patentee numerous inventions, 1956—. Dir. nat. alumni bd. Mich. State U., East Lansing, 1984-87; pres. Big Ten Club of So. Calif., L.A., 1992. Staff sgt. USAAF, 1943-46. Mem. IEEE (sr., L.A. chpt. sec., treas. Antennas and Propagation soc. 1987-89, vice chmn. 1989-90, chmn. 1990-91), 305th Bombardment Group Meml. Assn. (life). Democrat. Presbyn. Avocations: travel, photography, genealogy. Home: 5831 Fitzpatrick Rd Calabasas CA 91302-1104 Office: Lockheed Martin Skunk Works 1011 Lockheed Way Palmdale CA 93599-0001

MOULIN, JANE ANN FREEMAN, ethnomusicology educator, researcher; b. Oak Park, Ill., Mar. 4, 1946; d. James Frederic and Georgia Charlotte (Rahn) Freeman; m. Jacques Edouard Moulin, Apr. 26, 1975; children: Jean-Philippe Keala, Marie-Chantal Mahala. BA in Music cum laude, U. Hawaii, 1969; MA in Music, UCLA, 1971; PhD in Music, U. Calif., Santa Barbara, 1991. Libr. Music Libr UCLA, 1970-71; tchr. English English Companions, Osaka, Japan, 1972; dancer Te Maeva and Tahiti Nui, Papeete, Tahiti, 1973-76; rsch. fellow U. Auckland, New Zealand, 1989; fellow East-West Ctr., Honolulu, 1984-85, 91; assoc. prof. Hawaii Loa Coll., Kaneohe, 1980-92; prof. U. Hawaii, Honolulu, 1992—; dir. Europa Early Music Consort, Honolulu, 1981—; primary rschr. field work in French Polynesia, 1973-77, 85, 89, 95, 98; cons. Video series Dancing, WNET Channel 13, N.Y.C., 1989-92. Author: The Dance of Tahiti, 1979, Music of the Southern Marquesas Islands, 1994, (audio catalog) Music of the Southern Marquesas Islands, 1991, ency. and jour. articles on Tahitian and Marquesan performing arts; editl. bd. Jour. Perfect Beat, 1993—, Pacific Islands Monograph Series, 1997—; bd. dirs. Hawaii Assn. Music Socs., Honolulu, 1983-88. Bd. dirs. Tahiti-USA Assn., Honolulu, 1997—; mem. adv. bd. folk arts State Found. Culture and Arts, Honolulu, 1985-87. Recipient Regents' fellowship U. Calif., 1970-71, 88-89, rsch. grant UNESCO/Archives of Maori and Pacific Music, Auckland, 1989, regents' award for excellence in tchg. U. Hawaii, Honolulu, 1997, First Prize Thèse-Pac Assn. Competition, New Caledonia, 1994. Mem. Soc. Ethomusicology (mem. coun. 1995-97), Internat. Coun. Traditional Music, Polynesia Soc., Pacific Arts Assn., Viola da Gamba Soc. Am. Avocations: Tahitian dance, hula, consort playing. Office: U Hawaii Music Dept 2411 Dole St Honolulu HI 96822-2329

MOULTHROP, REBECCA LEE STILPHEN, elementary education educator; b. Lubbock, Tex., Mar. 5, 1944; d. Lee Edward and Geraldine (Lansford) Stilphen; m. John Stephen Martin Moulthrop, June 1967 (div. 1968); 1 child, Paul Martin. BS in edn., U. New Mex., 1966; MS in reading edn., Calif. State U., Fullerton, 1971; postgrad., U. LaVerne. Elem. tchr. Arnold Heights Elem. Sch., Moreno Valley, Calif., 1966-67, Hawthorn Elem. Sch., El Monte, Calif., 1968-69; chap. 1 reading specialist Posey Elem. Sch., Lubbock, 1971-72; elem. tchr. Arnold Heights Elem. Sch., Moreno Valley, 1972-74, Sunnymead Elem. Sch., Moreno Valley, 1974-80, Moreno Elem. Sch., Moreno Valley, 1980-88; chap. 1 program coord. Edgemont Elem. Sch., Moreno Valley, 1988-91; elem. tchr. Sunnymeadows Elem. Sch., Moreno Valley, 1991—; assertive discipline cons. Moreno Valley (Calif.) Unified Sch. Dist., 1979-85, mentor/tchr., 1985-89, adminstrn. designee/trainee, 1988-95; effective tchg./supervision coach Riverside (Calif.) County Sch. Office, 1984-87. Mem. NEA, Calif. Reading Assn., Internat. Reading Assn., Reading Edn. Guild, Delta Kappa Gamma, Phi Delta Kappa. Avocations: traveling, dancing, painting. Home: 23820 Ironwood Ave Unit 56 Moreno Valley CA 92557-8109 Office: Moreno Valley Unif Sch Dist 13911 Perris Blvd Moreno Valley CA 92553-4306

MOULTON, CANDY LEE, writer; b. Laramie, Wyo., Oct. 22, 1955; d. Arthur Warren and Betty Marie (Herring) Vyvey; m. Stephen Edward Moulton, Aug. 13, 1977; children: Shawn Reed, Erin Marie. AA, N.W. C.C., 1976; BS, U. Wyo., 1978. Reporter Saratoga (Wyo.) Sun, 1973-78, editor, 1978-82; editor WWA Roundup mag., Encampment, Wyo., 1996—. Author: Steamboat, 1992, Wason Wheels, 1995 (1st Pl.), Legacy of the Tetons, 1994 (1st Pl.), Roadside History of Wyoming, 1995, Salt Lake City Uncovered, 1997, The Grand Encampment, 1997, Roadside History of Nebraska, 1997. Sec., treas. Encampment Centennial Com., 1987-98. Mem. Wyo. Press Women (pres., 1st v.p., 2d v.p., 3d v.p., sec. 1978-98, Communicator of Achievement 1995), Wyo. Writers (v.p., pres.), Nat. Fedn. of Press Women, Western Writers of Am., Women Writing the West, Oreg-Calif. Trail Assn., NW Coll. Alumni Assn. Avocations: hiking, camping, reading. Home and Office: PO Box 29 Encampment WY 82325-0029

MOUNTAIN, CLIFTON FLETCHER, surgeon, educator; b. Toledo, Apr. 15, 1924; s. Ira Fletcher and Mary (Stone) M.; children: Karen Lockerby, Clifton Fletcher, Jeffrey Richardson. AB, Harvard U., 1947; MD, Boston U., 1951. Diplomate Am. Bd. Surgery. Dir. dept. statis. rsch. Boston U., 1947-50, cons. rsch. analyst Mass. Dept. Pub. Health, 1951-53; intern U. Chgo. Clinics, 1954, resident, 1955-58, instr. surgery, 1958-59; sr. fellow thoracic surgery Houston, 1959; mem. staff U. Tex. Anderson Cancer Ctr.; asst. prof. thoracic surgery U. Tex., 1960-73, assoc. prof surgery, 1973-76, prof., 1976-94, prof. emeritus, 1995Ô, prof. surgery Sch. Medicine, 1987Ô, chief sect. thoracic surgery, 1970-79, chmn. thoracic oncology, 1979-84, chmn. dept. thoracic surgery, 1980-85, cons. dept. thoracic and cardiovascular surgery, 1996Ô, chmn. program in biomath. and computer sci., 1962-64, Mike Hogg vis. lectr. in S.Am., 1967; prof. surgery U. Calif., San Diego, 1996Ô; mem. sci. mission on cancer USSR, 1970-78, and Japan, 1976-84; mem. com. health, rsch. and edn. facilities Houston Cmty. Coun., 1964-78; cons. Am. Joint Com. on Cancer Staging and End Result Reporting, 1964-74, Tex. Heart Inst., 1994-96; mem. Am. Joint Com. on Cancer, 1974-86, chmn. lung and esophagus task force; mem. working party on lung cancer and chmn. com. on surgery Nat. Clin. Trials Lung Cancer Study Group, NIH, 1971-76; mem. plans and scope com. cancer therapy Nat. Cancer Inst., 1972-75, mem. lung cancer study group, 1977-89, chmn. steering com., 1973-75, mem. bd. sci. counselors divsn. cancer treatment, 1972-75; hon. cons. Shanghai Chest Hosp. and Lung Cancer Ctr., Nat. Cancer Inst. of Brazil; sr. cons. Houston Thorax Inst., 1994-96. Editor The New Physician, 1955-59; mem. editorial bd. Yearbook of Cancer, 1960-88, Internat. Trends in Gen. Thoracic Surgery, 1984-91; contbr. articles to profl. jours., chpts. to textbooks. Chmn. profl. adv. com. Harris County Mental Health Assn.; bd. dirs. Harris County chpt. Am. Cancer Soc. Lt. USNR, 1942-46. Recipient award Soviet Acad. Sci., 1977, Garcia Meml. medal Philippine Coll. Surgeons, 1982, Disting. Alumni award Boston U., 1988, Disting. Achievement U. Tex. M.D. Anderson Cancer Ctr., 1990, Disting. Svc. award Internat. Assn. for the Study of Lung Cancer, 1991, Disting. Alumnus award Boston U. Sch. of Medicine, 1992, ALCASE Internat. award for excellence, 1997, Rudolf Nissen medal German Soc. Cardiovascular and Thoracic Surgery, 1998; named hon. pres. First Internat. Congress on Thoracic Surgery, 1997. Fellow ACS, Am. Coll. Chest Physicians (chmn. com. cancer 1967-75), Am. Assn. Thoracic Surgery, Inst. Environ. Scis., N.Y. Acad. Sci., Assn. Thoracic and Cardiovascular Surgeons of Asia (hon.), Hellenic Cancer Soc. (hon.), Chilean Soc. Respiratory Diseases (hon., hon. pres. 1982); mem. AAAS, Am. Assn. Carcer Rsch., AMA, So. Med. Assn., Am. Thoracic Soc., Soc. Thoracic Surgeons, Soc. Biomed. Computing, Am. Fedn. Clin. Rsch., Internat. Assn. Study Lung Cancer (pres. 1976-78), Am. Radium Soc., European Soc. Thoracic Surgeons, Pan-Am. Med. Assn., Houston Surg. Soc., Soc. Surg. Oncology, James Ewing Soc., Sigma Xi. Achievements include conception and development of program for application of mathematics and computers to the life sciences, of resource for experimental designs, applied statistics and computational support; first clinical use of physiologic adhesives in thoracic surgery; demonstration of clinical behavior of undifferentiated small cell lung cancer; first laser resection of lung tissue at thoracotomy; development of international system for staging of lung cancer.

MOUSER, ANDREW LEE, film company executive; b. Mt. Shasta, Calif., Nov. 18, 1959; s. Andrew Mouser and Eula Mae (Lorriette) Sweatt; 1 child, Emily. BS, Nat. U., 1989. Systems cons. Mouser Comms., L.A., 1991-94; CEO Info-Techs., L.A., 1994—; chief tech. officer Centropolis Entertainment, Sony Studios, Culver City, Calif., 1994—. With USN, 1976-86. Mem. Profl. Cons. Orgn., Mensa. Republican. Home: 4095 Glencoe Ave # 101 Marina Dl Rey CA 90292-5607 Office: Centropolis Entertainment Sony Studios 10201 W Pico Blvd Los Angeles CA 90064-2606

MOUSSEUX, RENATE, language educator; b. Stuttgart, Germany, Oct. 27, 1942; came to U.S., 1964; d. Emile and Gertrud Muller; m. Patrick Mousseux, Dec. 12, 1974; 1 child, Marc. BA, Padagogische Hochschule, Germany; MA, Grand Canyon U.; BL French, German, ESL, Phoenix U. Cert. French, German, psychology, bilingual French, ESL, secondary grades 7-12, Ariz., Calif. Prof. German Berlitz Sch. Lang., Sherman Oaks, Calif., 1966-67, Thunderbird Grad. Sch. Internat. Mgmt., Glendale, Ariz., 1968-72; prof. German and French Scottsdale Dist. H.S., 1980—; prof. French and German Rio Salado C.C., 1976-86; prof. French Scottsdale C.C., 1990-96, U. Phoenix, 1991—, 1991—; lit. and talent agt., co-prodr. for film and lit., 1991—, editor, pub. poetry books, 1991—; distbr. Native Am. Music; bus. lang. trainer, course developer various corps.; trainer student tchrs. Ariz. State U., Ottawa U. Author: Accellerated French (Vive le Francais), 1989, Accellerated German (Willkommen Deutsch), 1990, Accellerated Spanish (Viva el Espanol), 1991, Accellerated Japanese (Moshi Moshi), 1991, Accellerated English (Hello English), 1992. With Essential Skills Com. Ariz. State Bd. Edn. Recipient Ariz. Fgn. Lang. Tchr. of Yr. award Ariz. Assn. Fgn. Lang. Tchrs., 1986, Exceptional Mentorship Skills award Ariz. State U., 1994, Excellence in Mentorship cert. Ariz. State U., 1995; named Tchr. of Yr., U.S. West Outstanding Tchr. Program, 1989, Nat. Day of Excellence award 1996, award in leadership and quality in edn. ASCD, 1990. Mem. NEA, Nat. Geographic Soc., Am. Assn. Tchrs. German, Alliance Francaise, French Tchrs. Assn., Cultural Heritage Alliance, Ariz. Fgn. Lang. Assn., Scottsdale Edn. Assn. Avocation: reading, writing, psychology, anthropology. Home: 15611 N Boulder Dr Fountain Hls AZ 85268-1814 Office: Chaparral High School 6935 E Gold Dust Ave Scottsdale AZ 85253-1484

MOWERY, GERALD EUGENE, publisher, writer; b. Buena, Wash., Mar. 7, 1927; s. Jennings Bryan and Opal Mae Mowery; children: Colleen, Theresa, Rhonda, Laura, Victoria, Charles, Peggy. Degree in bus., Kinmen's U. Lic. pub. acct., Wash. Supr. Boeing Airplane Co., Seattle, 1968-78; owner Jerry's Coin, Book and Frame Shops, Puyallup, Wash., 1978-85, Rudolph Maurer Pub., Puyallup, Wash., 1985—. Author and pub. more than 120 books including All Matter Originates from Electrons and Positrons, 1981, The Fascinating .000249008 Atomic Mass Particle, The 27 Unacknowledged Elements, 1983, E=GM Squared, 1994, The Revised Periodic Table of Elements, The .000249088 Atomic Mass Particle, 1998; co-author with Gene Buck: The Entrepreneurs Favorite Short Stories, Favorite Poems, Favorite Facts and Stuff;author, publ. Adjusted Periodic Table of Elements, 1982, 93, 97, 98. Achievements include defining the atomic mass make up of sub atomic particles and their relationship to carbon 12, defining light as a .0001245445 atomic mass particle and heat as a .000249089 atomic mass particle; prepared (atomic mass) sub atomic particle table. Avocations: philosophical thinking, stamp collecting, writing stories and poems. Office: Rudolph Maurer Pub 8212 110th St E Puyallup WA 98373

MOYA, ROSEMARY MERCEDES, mental health administrator; b. Santa Fe, Aug. 11, 1957; d. Willie and Mercedes Sadie Ramona (Rivera) Padilla; m. Raymond Anthony Moya, Aug. 9, 1980; children: Joslyn Monique, Alyssa Nichole. BS in Edn., U. N.Mex., 1979, MPA, 1990. Adminstrv. asst. Hubbard Broadcasting, Albuquerque, 1980; staff asst. N.Mex. Mcpl. League, Santa Fe, 1980-81; staff asst. Div. Mental Health/Dept. of Health, Santa Fe, 1981-82, pers. adminstr., 1982-84, planner, 1981-88, health program mgr., 1988-91, chief community programs bur., 1991—. Parent vol. St. Francis Cath. Sch., 1990—; vol. Am. Cancer Soc., 1993, Easter Seals, Santa Fe, 1991; sec. liturgy com. Santa Maria de la Paz Cath. Com., 1991-94, chair liturgy com., 1994—, mem. bldg. com., 1991-94, mem. art selection com., 1992-94. N.Mex. Mcpl. League scholar, 1987-90; named Woman of Yr., Girls Club, Santa Fe, 1987. Mem. NAFE, Nat. Orgn. for Victim Assistance, Pi Alpha Alpha, Phi Kappa Phi. Democrat. Roman Catholic. Avocations: volleyball, skiing, tennis, camping, reading. Office: Dept Health/Div Mental Hlth 1190 S Saint Francis Dr Santa Fe NM 87505-4182

MOYER, CRAIG ALAN, lawyer; b. Bethlehem, Pa., Oct. 17, 1955; s. Charles Alvin and Doris Mae (Schantz) M.; m. Candace Darrow Brigham, May 3, 1986; 1 stepchild, Jason; 1 child, Chelsea A. BA, U. So. Calif., 1977; JD, U. Calif., L.A., 1980. Bar: Calif. 1980, U.S. Dist. Ct. (cen. dist.) Calif. 1980. Assoc. Nossaman, Krueger et al, L.A., 1980-83, Finley, Kumble et al, Beverly Hills, Calif., 1983-85; ptnr. Demetriou, Del Guercio, Springer & Moyer, L.A., 1985—; instr. Air Resources Bd. Symposium, Sacramento, 1985—, U. Calif., Santa Barbara, 1989—; lectr. Hazmat Conf., Long Beach, Calif., 1986—, Pacific Automotive Show, Reno, Nev., 1989—; lectr. hazardous materials, environ. law UCLA; lectr. environ. law U. Calif., Santa Barbara; lectr. hazardous materials regulatory framework U. Calif., Santa Barbara. Co-author: Hazard Communication Handbook: A Right to Know Compliance Guide, 1990, Clean Air Act Handbook, 1991, Brownfields: A Practical Guide to the Cleanup, Transfer and Redevelopment of Contaminated Property, 1997; contbr. articles to profl. jours. Pres. Calif. Pub. Interest Rsch. Group, L.A., 1979-80. Mem. ABA (natural resources sect.), Calif. Bar Assn., L.A. County Bar Assn. (environ. law sect., chmn. legis. rev. com., mem. exec. com.), Tau Kappa Epsilon (pres. L.A. chpt. 1975-76, Outstanding Alumnus 1983). Republican. Avocation: bicycling. Office: Demetriou Del Guercio Springer & Moyer Chase Plz 801 S Grand Ave Fl 10 Los Angeles CA 90017-4613

MOYER, J. KEITH, newspaper editor. Exec. editor The Fresno (Calif.) Bee, pub., 1997—. Office: The Fresno Bee 1626 E St Fresno CA 93786-0002*

MOYERS, WILLIAM TAYLOR, artist; b. Atlanta, Dec. 11, 1916; s. William Taylor and Sarah Frances (McKinnon) M.; m. Neva Irene Anderson, Mar. 20, 1943; children: Joanne, William Taylor, Charles, John. BA, Adams State Coll., Alamosa, Colo., 1939; postgrad., Otis Art Inst., L.A., 1939; Dr. (hon.), Adams State Coll., 1992. Artist Walt Disney Prodns., Burbank, Calif., 1939-40; free lance illustrator, 1946-62. One man show Nat. Cowboy Hall of Fame, 1973; group show Phoenix Art Mus., CAA Shows, 1973-90. Bd. dirs. Albuquerque Arts Bd., 1985, Adams State Coll. Found., 1974—, Cowboy Artists of Am. Mus., Kerrville, Tex., 1984-89. Capt. U.S. Army, 1942-46. Recipient illustration award Ltd. Edits. Club, N.Y.C., 1945, sculpture awards Cowboy Artists Am., 1968-84, silver medal for watercolor, 1989, 91, gold medal for watercolor, 1993; named Artist of Yr., Tucson Festival Soc., 1991. Mem. Cowboy Artists of Am. (pres. 1971-72, 83-84, 88-89). Presbyterian. Avocation: book collecting. Home: 1407 Morningside Dr NE Albuquerque NM 87110-5639

MOYLAN, JAY RICHARD, medical products executive; b. Greenfield, Mass., Dec. 20, 1950; s. Richard J. and Margaret M. (McCarthy) M.; m. Sharon J. Slater, June 18, 1976; children: Jaimee, Shauna. AA in Liberal Arts, Greenfield Community Coll., 1972; AS in Respiratory Therapy, Springfield Tech. Community C., 1975; BS in Health Care Mgmt., U. Mass., 1983. Staff respiratory therapist Mercy Hosp., Springfield, Mass., 1973-74; respiratory therapy supr. Brattleboro (Vt.) Meml. Hosp., 1974-75; dir. cardiopulmonary svc. Farren Meml. Hosp., Turners Falls, Mass., 1975-83; cardiopulmonary sales rep. Erich Jeager, Inc., Rockford, Ill., 1983-85; cardiovascular sales rep. Electro Catheter Corp., Rahway, N.J., 1985-86; cardiopulmonary sales specialist Sensor Medics Corp., Yorba Linda, Calif., 1986-95; sys. sales dir. OmniCell Technologies, Inc., Palo Alto, Calif., 1995—; chmn. Coun. Pulmonary Svc. Mgrs., Springfield, 1980-81. Chmn. Cath. Stewardship Appeal Holy Trinity Parish, Greenfield, 1989; bd. dirs. cen. Mass. chpt. Am. Lung Assn., 1981-83; treas. FMH Credit Union, 1980-83; councilor Mass. Thoracic Soc., 1995—. Recipient Achievement award Mass. Soc. Respiratory Care, 1989. Mem. Coun. Pulmonary Svc. Mgrs. (Lifetime Mem. award), Am. Coll. Sports Medicine, Am. Assn. Respiratory Care (registered, rev. com. 1991), Am. Registry Diagnostic Med. Sonographers (registered), Nat. Bd. Respiratory Care (cert.), Nat. Soc. Cardiopulmonary Tech. (cert.), Mass. Thoracic Soc., Mass. Lung Assn., New Eng. Soc. for Healthcare Materials Mgmt., Mass. chpt. Health Care Fin. Mgmt. Assn. Avocations: skiing, golf.

MOYLAN, STEVE, publishing executive. Pub., CEO Infoworld, San Mateo, Calif. Office: Infoworld Pub 155 Bovet Rd Ste 800 San Mateo CA 94402-3115*

MOZENA, JOHN DANIEL, podiatrist; b. Salem, Oreg., June 9, 1956; s. Joseph Iner and Mary Teresa (Delaney) M.; m. Elizabeth Ann Hintz, June 2, 1979; children: Christine Hintz, Michelle Delaney. Student, U. Oreg., 1974-79; B in Basic Med. Scis., Calif. Coll. Podiatric Medicine, D in Podiatric Medicine, 1983. Diplomate Am. Bd. Podiatric Surgery. Resident in surg. podiatry Hillside Hosp., San Diego, 1983-84; pvt. practice podiatry Portland, Oreg., 1984—; dir. residency Med. Ctr. Hosp., Portland, 1985-91; lectr. Nat. Podiatric Assn. Seminar, 1990, Am. Coll. Gen. Practitioners, 1991, Am. Coll. Family Physician, 1995. Cons. editor Podiatry Mgmt. mag., 1994-98; contbr. articles to profl. jours.; patentee sports shoe cleat design, 1985. Podiatric adv. coun. Oreg. Bd. Med. Examiners, 1994-97. Fellow Am Coll. Ambulatory Foot Surgeons, Am. Coll. Foot Surgeons. Republican. Roman Catholic. Avocations: softball, basketball, piano, jogging, electric bass guitar, coaching children's sports programs. Office: Town Ctr Foot Clinic 8305 SE Monterey Ave Ste 101 Portland OR 97266-7728

MRACKY, RONALD SYDNEY, marketing and promotion executive, travel consultant; b. Sydney, Australia, Oct. 22, 1932; came to U.S., 1947, naturalized, 1957; s. Joseph and Anna (Janousek) M.; m. Sylvia Frommer, Jan. 1, 1960; children: Enid Hillevi, Jason Adam. Student, English Inst., Prague, Czechoslovakia, 1943-47; grad., Parsons Sch. Design, N.Y.C., 1950-53; postgrad., NYU, 1952-53. Designer D. Deskey Assocs., N.Y.C., 1953-54; art dir., designer ABC-TV, Hollywood, Calif., 1956-57; creative dir. Neal Advt. Assocs., L.A., 1957-59; pres. Richter & Mracky Design Assocs., L.A., 1959-68; pres., CEO Richter & Mracky-Bates div. Ted Bates & Co., L.A., 1968-73, pres., CEO Regency Fin., Internat. Fin. Svcs., Beverly Hills, Calif., 1974-76; sr. ptnr. Sylron Internat., L.A., 1973—; mgmt. dir. for N.Am. Standard Advt.-Tokyo, L.A., 1978-91; CEO Standard/Worldwide Cons. Group, Los Angeles and Tokyo, 1981-87; officer, bd. dirs. Theme Resorts, Inc., Denver, 1979—; prin., officer Prodn. Travel & Tours, Universal City, 1981—, Eques Ltd., L.A., 1988—; mng. ptnr. GO! Pubs., 1993—; cons. in field; exec. dir. Inst. for Internat. Studies and Devel., L.A., 1976-77;. Contbr. articles to profl. jours.; mem. editl. bd., mktg. dir. The African Times and Africa Quar., 1990—. With U.S. Army, 1954-56. Recipient nat. and internat. awards design and mktg. Mem. Am. Mktg. Assn., African Travel Assn. (amb.-at-large, pres. So. Calif. chpt.), L.A. Publicity Club, Pacific Asia Travel Assn., S.Am. Travel Assn., Am. Soc. Travel Agents. Office: 10554 Riverside Dr Toluca Lake CA 91602-2441

MRAZEK, DAVID ANTON, documentary producer; b. Chgo., May 6, 1963; s. George Joseph and Patricia (Aldred) M.; m. Teresa Mae Fitzgerald, Aug. 22, 1997. BA in English with high distinction, U. Ill., 1985; MFA in Film and T.V. Prodn., U. So. Calif., 1990. Prodr., dir., writer (documentary film) My Prague Spring, 1993 (Gold award Houston Internat. Film Festival 1993); prodr., writer The Great War, PBS, 1996 (Peabody award 1997, Emmy award 1997); prodr., writer Intimate Strangers-Unseen Life on Earth, PBS, 1998. Mem. Writer's Guild of Am., League of Conservation Voters, Internat. Documentary Assn. Avocations: cross country skiing, hiking. Home: 387 Wenham Rd Pasadena CA 91107

MU, XIAO-CHUN, computer company executive; b. Tianjin, China, Mar. 23, 1957; parents Guoguang and Yuanxiang Chi; m. Pei-yang Yan, June 2, 1984; children: Wendy, Kevin. BS, Nankai U., Tianjin, China, 1981; PhD, Pa. State U., 1986. Engr. Dept. mgr. Intel Corp., Santa Clara, Calif., 1986—; univ. mentor Semiconductor Rsch. Corp., N.C. Contbr. over 50 articles to profl. jours.; patentee in field. Mem. Electrochem. Soc. Avocations: tennis, bicycling. Fax: (408) 765-2949. E-mail: xiao-chunmu@ccm.sc.intel.com. Home: 19685 Via Escuela Dr Saratoga CA 95070-4441 Office: M/S: SC1-03 3065 Bowers Ave Santa Clara CA 95054-3202

MUBARAK, SCOTT J., pediatric orthopedic surgeon; b. Ft. Smith, Ark.; m. Sandy Mubarak. BS, Ripon Coll., 1968; MD, U. Wis., 1971. Pres. orthop. CAMG, San Diego; dir. orthop. Children's Hosp., San Diego; clin. prof. orthop. U. Calif., San Diego; physician pediat. orthop. Hosp. for Sick Children, Toronto, Can., 1977. Author: Compartment Syndromes, 1980; contbr. over 95 articles to profl. jours. Mem. Pediat. Orthop. Soc. N.Am., Scoliosis Rsch. Soc., AOA, Kappa Delta. Office: Childrens Associated Med Group 33030 Children Way # 410 San Diego CA 92123

MUCICA, MARY ANN, editor, educator; b. Little Falls, N.Y.; d. Anthony August and Stella Mary (Novogurski) Pellerito; m. Robert Mucica; children: Gwendolyn, Debbie, Amy. BS in Journalism, Calif. State U., Northridge, 1982. Assoc. editor Valley Mag., Van Nuys, Calif., 1980-83, Calif. Travel, Van Nuys, Calif., 1983, Landscape & Irrigation, Van Nuys, Calif., 1984; exec. editor Weider Publications Muscle & Fitness Mag., Woodland Hills, Calif., 1984—; prof. Calif. State U., Northridge, 1982-90; lectr. in field. vol. internship program Calif. State U., Northridge, 1984—. Office: Weider Publications Muscle & Fitness Mag 21100 Erwin St Woodland Hills CA 91367-3712

MUDDU, SUDHAKAR, computer engineer, researcher; b. Kakinada, India, June 15, 1968; Came to U.S., 1990; s. Venkata Rao and Vijaya (Akundi) M.; m. Suneela, Padma, Tatpudi, Mar. 13, 1998. BTech in Electronic Engring., Indian Inst. Tech., Madras, 1990; MS in Computer Sci., UCLA, 1993, PhD in Computer Sci., 1996. Tech. application engr. Intel Corp., Santa Clara, Calif., 1992, cons. engr., 1993; rsch. scientist IBM TJ Watson Rsch. Ctr., Yorktown Hts., N.Y., 1994; mem. tech. staff AT&T Bell Labs., Holmdel, N.J., 1995, Silicon Graphics Inc., Mountain View, Calif., 1996—. Patentee in field. Fredrick M. Adler fellow Yale U., 1990-91; Nat. Merit scholar Indian Govt., 1983-85. Mem. IEEE. Hindu. Office: Silicon Graphics Inc PO Box 7311 MS 40L 175 2011 N Shoreline Blvd Mountain View CA 94043-1389

MUEDEKING, HARRIET LAURA, secondary education educator, retired; b. Superior, Nebr., Jan. 9, 1915; d. Herman August and Madge Mae (Lamm) Rollwagen; m. George Herbert Muedeking, June 26, 1941; children: Miriam Heyer, George. AA, St. Paul Luth. Coll., 1935; BA, Hamline U., 1937; MA, St. Thomas U., 1978. Tchr. Medford (Minn.) H.S., 1937-41; jr. h.s. tchr. Richmond (Calif.) H.S., 1959-66; h.s. tchr. Mpls. Pub. Schs., 1967-80; tcr. Calif. Literacy, Napa, 1992-96. Contbr. articles to profl. jours. Republican. Lutheran. Avocations: sewing, computer, Internet. Home: 4414 Springwood Dr Napa CA 94558-1724

MUEGGE, LYN, advertising executive. CFO, exec. v.p. Publicis & Hal Riney (formerly Hal Riney & Ptnrs. Inc.), San Francisco. Office: Publicis & Hal Riney 2001 The Embarcadero San Francisco CA 94133-1534

MUELLER, FRANK JOHN, retired editor; b. St. Louis, June 28, 1917; s. Frank Henry and Friedericka (Wunsch) M.; m. Edith Marie Church, Jan. 30, 1946; children: Anita Rushlau, Daniel, Becky Lariviere. Asst. city editor Star-Times, St. Louis, 1946-50, asst. sports editor, 1950-51; copy editor Houston Post, 1951-54, asst. news editor, 1954-55; copy editor Detroit News, 1955-56, cable editor, 1956-65, editor nat. & internat. news, 1965-81. Author: (play) Mercy, Mercy, Mercy, 1980. 1st lt. U.S. Army Air Force, 1941-45. Republican. Roman Catholic. Home: 8064 E Madero Ave Mesa AZ 85208-5185

MUELLER, GERRY DAMON ADENT, publisher, editor; b. Tacoma Park, Md., Apr. 30, 1953; s. Richard Mueller and Geraldine Deloris Damon; children: Damon Eric, Michael David. AA, Paradise Valley C.C., Tempe, AZ, 1996; BA of Journalism, Ariz. State U., Tempe, 1996, MA of Mass Comm., 1998. CEO Good Times Publ. Corp., Phoenix, AZ, 1994—; editor Desert Times, Phoenix, AZ, 1995—. Mem. Soc. Profl. Journalists (pres. 1996—), Phi Theta Kappa. Home and Office: Apt 1090 4901 E Kelton Ln Scottsdale AZ 85254

MUELLER, KEITH RICHARD, advertising executive; b. Chgo., Mar. 17, 1957; s. Richard Edward M. and Bette (Bachman) Hall. BS in TV/Radio, Ithaca Coll., 1979. Supr. on-air ops. Showtime Entertainment Co., N.Y.C., 1981-82, prodn. supr., 1982-83; supr. broadcast ops. United Satellite Communications, Inc., N.Y.C., 1983-85; exec. producer Weekly Shopping Network, Inc., N.Y.C., 1986; pres. Video Billboards N.Y./N.J., Edgewater, N.J., 1986-88; producer NBC TV Network, N.Y.C., 1988-90; pres. Keith Mueller Prodns., Newport Beach, Calif., 1990—; exec. dir. The 900 Advertising Club, Newport Beach, Calif., 1990—; judge Clio awards, N.Y.C., 1983-88. Mem. Nat. Acad. TV Arts and Scis., Nat. Assn. Info. Svcs. Home: 4240 Park Newport Apt 414 Newport Beach CA 92660-6046 Office: Keith Mueller Prodns PO Box 5048 Newport Beach CA 92662-5048

MUELLER, PAMELA SUE, secondary school educator; b. Mpls., Sept. 29, 1947; d. Milton Samuel and Elizabeth Jane (Lamb) Boyd; m. William Attebery, Aug. 4, 1968 (div. Feb. 1984); children: Matthew Attebery, Margot Attebery, Wilson Attebery; m. David Michael Mueller; 1 child, Heidi. BA in Edn., U. Wash., 1969; MA in Tech. Edn., City U., Seattle, 1995. Tchr. 7th grade lang. arts James Madison Jr. H.S., Seattle, 1968-69; tchr. English, reading, drama Cleveland H.S., Seattle, 1969-72; tchr. 6th. grade Vista and Fairhaven Mid. Sch., Bellingham, Wash., 1979-80; tchr. honors English, reading, drama Bellingham H.S., 1984—, Squalicum High, Bellingham; dir. various plays Bellingham H.S. Choir dir. Immanuel Luth. Ch., Everson, Wash., 1997—; mem. Whatcom Chorale, Bellingham, 1982—. Avocations: motorcycling, reading, theatre, music. Home: 5501 Sand Rd Bellingham WA 98226-9514 Office: Squalicum High 3773 E Mcleod Rd Bellingham WA 98226-7728

MUENCH, LOTHAR WILHELM, electrical engineer, consultant; b. Karlstadt, Germany, Aug. 9, 1953; came to U.S., 1994; s. Bernhard Anton and Auguste (Weidner) M.; m. Prayad Pomsuwan, Aug. 8, 1985; children: Direk, Sebastian, Johannes. Student, Fachober Sch., Wurzburg, Germany, 1970-72; diploma in engring., Fachober Sch., Aalen, Germany, 1977. Cert. Dept. Tech. Econ. Cooperation, Bangkok. Svc. engr. Siemens Med., Erlangen, Germany, 1977-79, sr. engr. CAT Scan,, 1979-82; cons. Rsch. Inst. Health Scis., Chiang Mai (Thailand) U., 1982-85; project mgr. Kontron Bildanalyse, Munich, 1986-90; mgr. R&D, Tomtec GmbH, Munich, 1990-94; mgr. advanced products divsn. Tomtec Inc., Boulder, Colo., 1994—; founder Next Dimension Imaging, Longmont, Calif., 1997—; cons. dept. pediat. Oxford (Eng.) U., 1984. Third world vol. for tech. expertise German. Vol. Svc., Berlin, 1982-85. With German Air Force, 1973-74. Mem. NEMA (mem. Dicom com. 1996). Achievements include contributions to the design, development and deployment of the first ultrasound computer tomography system for cardiologic and non-cardiologic diagnostics. Home: 1752 Drake St Longmont CO 80503-1604 Office: 1752 Drake St Longmont CO 80503-1604

MUGLER, LARRY GEORGE, regional planner; b. Chgo., June 22, 1946; s. Warren Franklin and Elaine Mae (Mittag) M.; m. Judy Ann Allison, Aug. 3, 1968; children: Jonathan, Allison. BSCE, Northwestern U., 1968; postgrad., Evang. Theol. Sem., 1968-70; MS in Urban and Regional Planning, U. Wis., 1972. Planning analyst State of Wis., Madison, 1970-72; dir. community devel. Cen. Okla. Econ. Devel. Dist., Shawnee, 1972-74; planner Denver Regional Council of Govts., 1974-80, dir. environ. services, 1980-83, dir. devel. services, 1983—. Contbr. chpt. on pub. works mgmt. to book. Pres. bd. dirs. Leawood Met. Recreation and Park Dist., Littleton, Colo., 1978-98; chair planning and rsch. com., bd. stewards Rocky Mountain Conf. The United Meth. Ch. Named one of Outstanding Young Men in Am., Jaycees, 1974; Lasker Found. fellow, 1971; recipient Disting. Svc. award Spl. Dist. Assn. of Colo., 1989. Mem. Am. Planning Assn. (sec. Colo. chpt. 1970-96), ASCE (subcom. chmn. 1985-86, 88-91, div. exec. com. 1991—, vice chair 1994-96, chair 1996), Am. Inst. Cert. Planners, Urban Land Inst. Republican. Methodist. Avocations: soccer referee, choir. Office: Denver Regional Coun Govts 2480 W 26th Ave Ste 200B Denver CO 80211-5326

MUHAMMAD, KHALEEDAH, entrepreneur, sales and marketing consultant, community activist; b. Berkeley, Calif., Nov. 2, 1943; d. Samuel Taylor Odom and Robbie Lee (Taylor) Gordon; children: Raymie, Jamal; m. Ansar El Muhammad, June 12, 1974; children: Tamishi, Ansar El II. BA, Los Angeles State Coll., 1965; postgrad., Calif. State, Hayward, 1971-72. Caseworker Pacoima (Calif.) Child Guidance Clinic, 1965-68; probation officer Los Angeles Probation Dept., 1968-72; ednl. opportunity program counselor U. Calif., Berkeley, 1974-79; community cons. YWCA, Richmond, Calif., 1979-81; owner, sales mgr. Touch of Class Boutique, Richmond, 1981-84; owner, mktg. cons. Nature's Co., Richmond, 1982-84; owner Unique Home Services, Richmond, 1984—; part-owner, mktg. cons. Cora's Kitchen, Oakland, Calif., 1987—, Halal Mktg. Services, Oakland, 1987—; sales, mktg. cons. The Fox Factory, Richmond, 1985-87. Author: (pamphlet) It's Not Easy Being a Parent, 1979. Vice chairperson Unity Orgn., Richmond, 1979-83; founder People United For Coops., Richmond, 1983; bd. dirs. Richmond chpt. Reading Is Fundamental, 1979-83, Minority Arts Network, Contra Costa, Calif., 1987; ct. apptd. spl. rep. Adv. for Wards of the Ct., 1990-91; co-founder Loving Care Inc.; exec. dir. Ansari House Residential Treatment Facility for Teenage Girls. Mem. Nat. Assn. Female Execs. Democrat. Islam. Avocations: gourmet cooking, gardening. Home: 147 Downie Dr Vallejo CA 94589-1933 Office: 123 12th St Richmond CA 94801-3527

MUHM, JOHN ROBERT, radiologist; b. Bradenton, Fla., Jan. 25, 1944; s. Robert C. and Betty Lou (Stucker) M.; m. Alexia A. Larson, June 15, 1968 (div. Sept. 1993); children: John Robert Jr., Amy Elizabeth, Leah Larson, Matthew Alexander; m. Marjorie L. Cox, Aug. 17, 1996; 1 child, Alexander Dean. Student, Colo. State U., 1961-64; MD, U. Colo., 1968. Diplomate Am. Coll. Radiology. Diagnostic radiologist Mayo Clinic, Rochester, Minn., 1974-87; chmn. radiology dept. Mayo Clinic, Scottsdale, Ariz., 1985-95; diagnostic radiologist Mayo Clinic, Scottsdale, 1987—; dir. radiology residencey program, Mayo Clinic, 1977-84. Contbr. more than 40 scientific papers, 2 book chpts., 1975—. Capt. U.S. Army, 1970-72. Fellow Am. Coll. Radiology; mem. AMA, Radiological Soc. N.Am. (dir. chest refresher course com. Oak Brook, Ill., 1988-92), Am. Roentgen Ray Soc., fellow Am. Coll. Chest Physicians, Soc. Thoracic Surgery, Am. Soc. Nuclear Cardiology. Republican. Roman Catholic. Avocations: reading, skiing, tennis, hiking, gardening. Home: 16427 N 108th Way Scottsdale AZ 85259-9107 Office: Mayo Clinic Scottsdale 13400 E Shea Blvd Scottsdale AZ 85259-5499

MUICO-MERCURIO, LUISA, critical care nurse; b. Caloocan, Manila, Philippines, Nov. 17, 1955; d. Amado B. and Eustaquia (Buenavista) Muico; m. Wilfred Tongson Mercurio, Dec. 28, 1974; children: Elyjah Matthew, Kristoffer Ross, Mercurio. ADN, Harbor City Coll., 1978; BSN, Calif. State U., 1990, postgrad., 1992—. Cert. ACLS instr., BLS instr; CCRN; cert. pub. health nurse. Staff nurse ICU Long Beach (Calif.) Meml. Med. Ctr., 1978-80; staff nurse CVT/ICU Cedar Sinai Med. Ctr., L.A., 1980-84; staff nurse ICU, CCU, emergency rm., cath. lab. Long Beach Cmty. Hosp., 1982-86; ICU, CCU coord. Pioneer Hosp., Artesia, Calif., 1986-87; staff nurse CSU Kaiser-Permanente, L.A., 1988-90, pub. health nurse, 1990, asst. dept. adminstr., 1990-92; asst. dept. adminstr. Kaiser-Permanente, Sunset and Bellflower, Calif.; cardiovascular/thoracic surgery nurse coord. Kay Med. Group/Hosp. Good Samaritan, L.A., 1992—; adminstrv. supr. Barlow Respiratory Hosp., L.A., 1993; staff nurse critical care unit UCLA, 1994—, staff nurse liver transplant unit, 1996—; nursing faculty Pacific Coast Coll., 1994—, ICU-Kaweah Delta Dist. Hosp., Visalia, Calif., 1996—; adminstr., cons. Welco Guest Homes, Porterville, Calif., 1996—. Named to Dean's list Harbor City Coll., 1976-78, Dean's list Calif. State U., 1988-90. Mem. AACN (cert.), Nat. Golden Key Honor Soc., Nursing Honor Soc., Sigma Theta Tau (Nu Mu chpt.). Republican. Avocations: small arms competition, Hapkido, racquetball competition, singing.

MUKERJI, TAPAN, geophysicist, researcher; b. Varanasi, India, May 3, 1965; came to U.S., 1989; s. Girija Prasad and Manju (Banerjee) M. BSc in Physics, Banaras Hindu U., Varanasi, India, 1986, MSc in Geophysics, 1989; PhD in Geophysics, Stanford U., 1995. Rsch. and tchg. asst. Stanford U., 1990-95, rschr., 1995—. Co-author: The Rock Physics Handbook; contbr. articles to profl. jours. Fellow Coun. Sci. and Indsl. Rsch., India, 1989, Green fellow Stanford U., 1989-90, Haider fellow Stanford U., 1997. Mem. IEEE, Am. Geophys. Union, Am. Phys. Soc., Soc. Exploration Geophysicists. Achievements include work with new theoretical model for estimating velocity dispersion in anisotropic rock; scale dependent wave propagation in heterogeneous media; new strategies for quantifying uncertainty in rock physics; multi-disciplinary time lapse seismic monitoring. Avocations: science, music. Office: Rock Physics Lab Geophysics Dept Stanford U Stanford CA 94305

MULAC, PAMELA ANN, priest, pastoral counselor; b. Salem, Ohio, Dec. 6, 1944; d. Elmer John and Dorothy Adelaide (McGee) M.; m. George Robert Larsen, Aug. 8, 1987. Student, Bryn Mawr Coll., 1962-64; AB, U. Chgo., 1966; MDiv, Seabury-Western Theol. Sem., 1974; PhD, Garrett Evang. Theol. Sem., Northwestern U., 1988. Ordained to ministry Episcopal Ch. as priest, 1978. Asst. deacon, priest St. Luke's Ch., Evanston, Ill., 1974-84; asst. priest St. Mark's Ch., Upland, Calif., 1984-88, St. Ambrose Ch., Claremont, Calif., 1988-90; assoc. priest for pastoral care All Saints Ch., Pasadena, Calif., 1991-93; asst. interim pastor St. George's, La Canada, Calif., 1994-95; chaplain Foothill Presbyn. Hosp., Glendon, Calif., 1994-95; interim pastor St. Timothy's Ch., Apple Valley, Calif., 1995-96; interim rector St. Michael's Ch., Riverside, Calif., 1996—; pastoral counselor Swedish Covenant Hosp., Chgo., 1975-84; adj. lectr. Seabury-Western Theol. Sem., Evanston, 1981-82, trustee, 1981-84; pastoral counselor Walnut (Calif.) Valley Counseling Ctr., 1984-89; adj. lectr. marriage and family therapy program Azusa Pacific U., 1988-89, adj. lectr. operation impact, 1991-92; adj. prof. Sch. of Theology at Claremont, 1994-95; adj. prof. Episc. Theology Sch., Claremont, 1994-96. Bd. dirs. Cathedral Shelter Chgo., 1980-84; co-chairperson Leader's Sch. Cursillo, Chgo., 1981-83; mem. Commn. on Alcoholism, Diocese of L.A., 1985-87. Episcopal Ch. Found. fellow, 1978-81. Mem. Am. Assn. Pastoral Counselors (sec. Pacific region 1984-85, treas. 1984-91, fin. chair 1988-91), Assn. Clin. Pastoral Edn. Home and Office: 1439 Bonnie Jean Ln La Habra Heights CA 90631-8665

MULASE, MOTOHICO, mathematics educator; b. Kanazawa, Japan, Oct. 11, 1954; came to U.S., 1982; s. Ken-Ichi and Mieko (Yamamoto) M.; m. Sayuri Kamiya, Sept. 10, 1982; children: Kimihico Chris, Paul Norihico, Yurika. BS, U. Tokyo, 1978; MS, Kyoto U., 1980, DSc, 1985. Rsch. assoc. Nagoya (Japan) U., 1980-85; JMS fellow Harvard U., Cambridge, Mass., 1982-83; vis. asst. prof. SUNY, Stony Brook, 1984-85; Hedrick asst. prof. UCLA, 1985-88; asst. prof. Temple U., Phila., 1988-89; assoc. prof. U. Calif., Davis, 1989-91, prof., 1991—, vice chair dept. math., 1995-96, chair dept. math., 1998—; mem. Math. Scis. Rsch. Inst., Berkeley, Calif., 1982-84, Inst. for Advanced Study, Princeton, N.J., 1988-89; vis. prof. Max-Planck Inst. for Math., Bonn, Germany, 1991-92, Kyoto U., 1993, 94, Humboldt U., Berlin, Germany, 1995, 96. Contbr. articles to profl. jours. Treas. Port of Sacramento Japanese Sch., 1990-91. Mem. Math. Soc. Japan, Am. Math. Soc. (com. on internat. affairs 1993-96). Avocation: music. Office: U Calif Dept Math Davis CA 95616

MULKEY, KAREN LANDRY, actress, artist, educator, writer; b. Mpls., Dec. 4, 1950; d. William Barrett and Eileen Marie (Jorgenson) Nienaber; m. Christian Homer Mulkey Jr., July 25, 1981; children: Amelia, Elizabeth. BA, U. Minn., 1972, postgrad., 1972-74. Actress Guthrie Theater, Mpls., 1975-78, 80, Denver Ctr. Theater, 1980, St Elsewhere, MTM Prodns., L.A., 1983-85, South Coast Repertory, Costa Mesa, Calif., 1990, 95, 96; tchr., coach for child actors Center State L.A., 1997—; tchr. Beyond Borders, L.A., 1997—. Write ind. screenplays; creating a body of artwork in the Calif. Impressionistic style; writer, actress film Patti Rocks, 1987; appeared in films including Full Moon Rising, Amanda, Mindgames; appeared in TV vilms On the Wings of Ealges, Lois Gibbs and the Love Canal, Right to Die; appeared in TV episodes Chgo. Hope, Beverly HIlls 90210, Picket Fences, Melrose Place, Cagney and Lacey, others. Bush fellow, 1973. Mem. SAG, AFTRA, Actors Equity Assn. Democrat. Lutheran. Office: Paradigm 10100 Santa Monica Blvd Los Angeles CA 90067-4003

MULKEY, SHARON RENEE, gerontology nurse; b. Miles City, Mont., Apr. 14, 1954; d. Otto and Elvera Marie (Haglof) Neuhardt; m. Monty W. Mulkey, Oct. 9, 1976; children: Levi, Candice, Shane. BS in Nursing, Mont. State U., 1976. RN, Calif. Staff nurse, charge nurse VA Hosp., Miles City, Mont., 1976-77; staff nurse obstetrics labor and delivery Munster (Ind.) Cmty. Hosp., 1982-83; nurse mgr. Thousand Oaks Health Care, 1986-88; unit mgr. rehab. Semi Valley (Calif.) Adventist Hosp., 1988-89, DON TCU, 1989-91; DON Pleasant Valley Hosp. Extended Care Vacility and Neuro Ctr., 1991-93; dir. nurses Victoria Care Ctr., Ventura, Calif., 1993—; clin. supr. Procare Home Health, Oxnard, Calif., 1996-97; staff nurse acute rehab. Los Robles East Campus Rehab. Unit, Westlake, Calif., 1998, TCU charge nurse, 1998—. Mem. ANA, Nat. Gerontol. Nursing Assn., Internat. Platform Assn., Alpha Tau Delta (pres. 1973-75), Phi Kappa Phi. Home: 3461 Pembridge St Thousand Oaks CA 91360-4565

MULLAHEY, RAMONA KAM YUEN, land use planner, educator; b. Hilo, Hawaii, Nov. 1, 1945. BA, U. Hawaii, 1967, M Urban and Regional Planning, 1976. Sole proprietor Honolulu, 1976-87; prin. Mullahey & Mullahey, Honolulu, 1987—; nat. speaker on K-12 design edn. to variety internat., nat., regional orgns.; lectr. urban and regional planning U. Hawaii. Author: (book and video) Maintaining A Sense of Place Community Workbook, 1987, Community as a Learning Resource, 1994; editor newsletter Am. Planning Assn. Resources, 1990—. Mem. Rental Housing Trust Fund Commn., Hawaii, 1993—. Recipient Pub. Edn. award Am. Planning Assn., Hawaii chpt., 1993; Nat. Endowment for Arts grantee, Washington, 1986, 92, 94, local grantee; named 1 of 12 Nat. Women Leaders in K-12 Design Edn., The Urban Network. Mem. ASCD, Nat. Trust Historic Preservation (Nat. Preservation Honor award 1988), Am. Planning Assn. (pres. Hawaii chpt. 1992-93, immediate past pres. 1993—, Disting. Leadership award Hawaii Chpt. 1994), Orgn. Am. Leaders (pres. 1990-91), C. of C. of Hawaii (edn. coun.). Avocation: photography. Home and Office: PO Box 1348 Honolulu HI 96807-1348

MULLARKEY, MARY J., state supreme court justice; b. New London, Wis., Sept. 28, 1943; d. John Clifford and Isabelle A. (Steffes) M.; m. Thomas E. Korson, July 24, 1971; 1 child, Andrew Steffes Korson. BA, St. Norbert Coll., 1965; LLB, Harvard U., 1968; LLD (hon.), St. Norbert Coll., 1989. Bar: Wis. 1968, Colo. 1974. Atty.-advisor U.S. Dept. Interior, Washington, 1968-73; asst. regional atty. EEOC, Denver, 1973-75; 1st atty. gen. Colo. Dept. Law, Denver, 1975-79, solicitor gen., 1979-82; legal advisor to Gov. Lamm State of Colo., Denver, 1982-85; ptnr. Mullarkey & Seymour, Denver, 1985-87; justice Colo. Supreme Ct., Denver, 1987—, chief justice, 1998—. Recipient Alumni award St. Norbert Coll., De Pere, Wis., 1980, Alma Mater award, 1993. Fellow ABA Found., Colo. Bar Found.; mem. ABA, Colo. Bar Assn., Colo. Women's Bar Assn. (recognition award 1986), Denver Bar Assn., Thompson G. Marsh Inn of Ct. (pres. 1993-94). Office: Supreme Ct Colo Colorado State Judicial Bldg 2 E 14th Ave Denver CO 80203-2115

MULLEN, LAWRENCE JAMES, journalism educator; b. Schenectady, N.Y., Feb. 2, 1960; s. Thomas Stephen and Dorothy Jean (Riley) M.; m. Barbara Ann Spanjers, Dec. 14, 1990. BA, Buffalo State Coll., 1982; MA, U. Md., 1987; PhD, U. Iowa, 1992. Asst. prof. Augustana Coll., Sioux Falls, S.D., 1992-94; asst. prof. U. Nev. Las Vegas, 1994—; cons. Rowland, Jasa & Dahl, Overland Park, Kans., 1996. Contbr. articles to profl. jours. Mem. Nat. Comm. Assn., Internat. Comm. Assn., Broadcast Edn. Assn., Assn. for Edn. in Journalism and Mass Comm., Am. Assn. Pub. Opinion Rsch. Democrat. Roman Catholic. Avocations: ballroom dancing, chess, tai chi chuan. Home: 8450 W Charleston Blvd Las Vegas NV 89117-9010 Office: U Nev Las Vegas 4505 S Maryland Pkwy Las Vegas NV 89154-9900

MULLEN, ROD, nonprofit organization executive; b. Puyallup, Wash., Aug. 2, 1943; s. Charles Rodney and Grace Violet (Fritsch) M.; m. Lois Fern Tobiska, May 3, 1963 (div. Jan. 1977); children: Cristina, Charles, Moneka; m. Naya Arbiter, Oct. 17, 1977. Student, U. Idaho, 1961-63; AB in Polit. Sci., U. Calif., Berkeley, 1966; postgrad., San Francisco Art Inst., 1968. Dir. Oakland (Calif.) facility Synanon Found., Inc., 1971-72, dir. San Francisco facility, 1972-73, dir. Tomales Bay (Calif.) facility, 1976-78, dir. Synanon edn. programs, 1973-76; treatment dir. nat. programs Vision Quest, Inc., Tucson, 1981-82; dir. resources and devel. Amity, Inc., Tucson, 1982-84, exec. dir., 1984-95; founder, pres., CEO, Amity Found. of Calif., Porterville, Calif., 1995—; mem. Nat. Adv. Com. on Substance Abuse Prevention, 1990-92, 93-96; mem. sci. adv. bd. Ctr. for Therapeutic Cmty. Rsch., Nat. Devel. and Rsch. Insts., N.Y.C., 1991—; cons. Calif. Office Criminal Justice Planning, Sacramento, 1993; prin. investigator program Nat. Inst. on Drug Abuse, 1990-93. *Mr. Mullen has a 30-year career providing national leadership using the therapeutic community model for addicted women and their children; adolescents with lengthy histories of substance abuse and violent behaviors, and adult and adolescent addicts in incarcerated settings. Mullen directs Amity's recidivism reduction program at the RJ Donovan Correctional Facility in San Diego, cited by the Office of National Drug Control policy, Department of Justice, Center for Addiction and Substance Abuse at Columbia University, and numerous others for the ability to significantly reduce recidivism and violent behviors in inmates, saving millions of dollars per year and providing a national model.* Contbr. numerous articles to profl. publs., chpts. to books. Mem. Am. Correctional Assn., Therapeutic Coms. of Am., Calif. Assn. of Therapeutic Comtys. (sec.). Fax: (209) 783-2846. E-mail: rodm@amityfound.com. Office: Amity Found Calif PO Box 713 Porterville CA 93258-0713

MULLER, CAROLYN BUE, physical therapist, volunteer; b. Crosby, N.D., Feb. 24; d. Sigurd Christian and Eleanor (Rushfeldt) Bue; m. Willard Chester Muller, Jan. 27, 1945; children: Marolyn Jean, Barbara Anne, Nancy Eleanor. BA, St. Olaf Coll., 1940; cert. in phys. therapy, Harvard U., 1944. Assoc. dir. younger girls and phys. edn. sect. YWCA, Syracuse, N.Y., 1940-43; phys. therapist Valley Forge Hosp., Phoenixville, Pa., 1944-45; med. records libr. Trust Territory of Pacific Islands, Truk, Caroline Islands, 1951-52; founder, prin. organizer Am. Cmty. Sch., Truk, 1952, Lincoln Sch., Katmandu, Nepal, 1956, Am. Cmty. Sch., Mogadiscio, Somali Republic, 1958, Kampala, Uganda, 1966; panelist workshop Wash. Commn. for Humanities, Yakima, 1996. Author: Living in Uganda, 1967; cartographer: Maudie - An Oregon Trail Childhood, 1993. Charter registrar Clallam County Mus. and Hist. Soc., Port Angeles, Wash., 1977-87; vol. reading tutor Port Angeles Sch. Dist., 1980—; cmty. coord. UNICEF, Port Angeles, 1982-85; rep. Target Wash. Seminar, Seattle, 1984; rep. Asia-Can. Women in Mgmt. Conf., Victoria, B.C., Can., 1985; regional judge Wash. State Nat. History Day Contest, Port Angeles, 1985—; selection judge Wash. State Inquiring Mind Lecture Series, Seattle, 1989, 90, 96, organizer/coord., Inquiring Mind Lecture Series 1983—; state judge Nat. History Day Contest, Ellensburg, Wash., 1993—; bd. dirs. Wash. State Friends of the Humanities, 1991-94; trustee Wash. Commn. for the Humanities, 1995-97; pres. Am. Women's Club, Katmandu, 1957-58, Mogadiscio, 1959-60; v.p. Internat. Women's Club, Saigon, South Vietnam, 1971; mem. selection com. Evergreen State Soc. Awards, 1998, 99. Recipient Women Making a Difference award Soroptimist Internat., 1984, Outstanding Vol. award Citizens' Ednl. Ctr. N.W., 1988, Evergreen award Evergreen State Soc., 1992. Mem. AAUW (br. pres. 1980-84, Edn. Found. scholarship in her name 1996). PEO (rec. sec. 1984-85, v.p. 1985-86, pres. 1987-89, chaplain 1994, Internat. Peace scholarship in her name 1990, state chmn. Internat. Peace scholarship 1989-90). Avocations: growing flowers, cross-country walking, oil painting, reading, travel. Home: 3624 S Mount Angeles Rd Port Angeles WA 98362-8910

MULLER, DAVID WEBSTER, architectural designer; b. Norwich, Conn., Aug. 25, 1956; s. Richard Johnson and Barbara Alice (Reading) M.; m. Susan Akers, Dec. 31, 1989; 1 stepchild, Shannon. BA in Polit. Sci., George Washington U., 1978. Rsch. assoc. Rep. Nat. Com., Washington, 1978-80, dep. dir. spl. projects, 1981-83; western field dir. Nat. Rep. Congl. Com., Washington, 1983-85; v.p. Russo Watts & Rollins, Sacramento, Calif., 1985-86; campaign mgr. Chavez for U.S. Senate, Silver Spring, Md., 1986; v.p. Russo Watts & Rollins, Sacramento, 1987-89; cons. Sacramento, 1989, pvt. investor, 1990—; archtl. design and restoration Muller/West, 1990—. Mem. Nat. Coun. for Arts and Scis. George Washington U. Mem. San Francisco Yacht Club. Avocations: sailing, photography, writing fiction, international travel, kayaking. Home and Office: Muller/West 1309 Dolphin Terrace Corona Del Mar CA 92625-5945

MULLER, JEROME KENNETH, photographer, art director, editor; b. Amityville, N.Y., July 18, 1934; s. Alphons and Helen (Haberl) M.; m. Nora Marie Nestor, Dec. 21, 1974. BS, Marquette U., 1961; postgrad., Calif. State U., Fullerton, 1985-86; MA, Nat. U., San Diego, 1988; postgrad., Newport Psychoanalytic Inst., 1988-90. Comml. and editorial photographer N.Y.C., 1952-55; mng. editor Country Beautiful mag., Milw., 1961-62, Reprodns. Rev. mag., N.Y.C., 1967-68; editor, art dir. Orange County (Calif.) Illustrated, Newport Beach, 1962-67, art editor, 1970-79, exec. editor, art dir., 1968-69; owner, CEO Creative Svcs. Advt. Agy., Newport Beach, 1969-79; founder, CEO Mus. Graphics, Costa Mesa, Calif., 1978—; tchr. photography Lindenhurst (N.Y.) High Sch., 1952-54, comic art U. Calif., Irvine, 1979, publ. design Orange Coast Coll., Costa Mesa, Calif., 1997—; guest curator 50th Anniversary Exhbn. Mickey Mouse, 1928-78, The Bowers Mus., Santa Ana, Calif., 1978; organized Moving Image Exhbn. Mus. Sci. and Industry, Chgo., Cooper-Hewitt Mus., N.Y.C., William Rockhill Nelson Gallery, Kansas City, 1981; collector original works outstanding Am. cartoonists at major mus. One-man shows include Souk Gallery, Newport Beach, 1970, Gallery 2, Santa Ana, Calif., 1972, Cannery Gallery, Newport Beach, 1974, Mus. Graphics Gallery, 1993, White Gallery Portland State U., 1996, U. Calif., Irvine, 1997, Nat. Telephone and Comm., Irvine, Calif., 1998; author: Rex Brandt, 1972; contbr. photographs and articles to mags. Served with USAF, 1956-57. Recipient two silver medals 20th Ann. Exhbn. Advt. and Editorial Art in West, 1965. Mem. APA, Mus. Modern Art (N.Y.C.), Met. Mus. Art, Art Mus. Assn. Am., L.A. Press Club, Newport Beach Tennis Club, Orange County Mus. Art, Alpha Sigma Nu. Home: 2438 Bowdoin Pl Costa Mesa CA 92626-6304 Office: PO Box 10743 Costa Mesa CA 92627-0234

MULLER, LAWRENCE GEORGE, communications consultant; b. San Francisco; s. Lawrence George Mullen Sr. and Agnes L. Meenan. AA, Skyline Coll., 1972, BA, Calif. State U., Hayward, 1974; MA with highest distinction Calif. State U., L.A., 1976. Cert. assoc. in claims, assoc. in ins., suprvisory. mgmt. Claims adjuster Crawford & Co., San Francisco, 1980-85; litigation adjuster Maryland Casualty, Sacramento, 1985-90; corp. claims trainer Claims Unltd. Weil & Co., Oakland, Calif., 1990-93; risk mgr. MV Transp., San Francisco, 1993-95; with Infinity Ins. Co., 1997-98; comm. cons. San Francisco, 1974—; arbitrator, mediator BBB, Oakland and San Francisco; profl. spkr Toastmasters, Calif.; comm. cons. to law enforcement and banks, Calif. Co-author: (comm. strategies) Just for the Sake of Argument, 1985; author: (comm. analysis) The Use of Ritual to Promote Officer Safety, 1990; contbr. poetry to anthologies. Grief counselor CFM, Vaccaville, 1989-98; baseball umpire Am. Softball Assn./No. Calif. Athletic Assn., Fresno and Daly City, 1988-90; dist. bd. dirs. Kiros Prison Ministry, 1990-97. Named Outstanding Toastmaster, Dist. 33, 1979-82. Mem. Pi Kappa Delta (nat. debate Gold Medal 1973, hon. Forensic Fraternity Orders of Debate, Speaking and Instruction). Avocations: photography, computers, logic problems. Home: 15 Lake Vista Ave Daly City CA 94015-1013 Office: L G Muller Jr Speech Comms Inc 1953 Manor Pl Ste 1 Fairfield CA 94533-4152

MULLIGAN, ERLINDA RITA, medical, surgical nurse; b. Gallup, N.Mex., June 11, 1954; d. Reginaldo Fred and M. Maggie (Apodaca) Gallegos; m. Michael Joseph Mulligan,; children: Raymond Fredrick, Margaret Rose, Erin Pablo, Kimberly Edel. ADN, U. N.Mex., Gallup, 1988. RN, N.Mex., Ariz.; cert. med.-surg. nurse Am. Nurses Credentialing Ctr. Nurse Rehoboth McKinley Christian Hosp., Gallup, 1988-89, nurse I, 1989-90, nurse II, rep. med.-surg. and pediat. units, 1990-91, nurse III, 1991-92, nurse IV, 1992-95, surg./med. specialist, 1993—, home health nurse, 1994-97, psychiatric nurse, 1993-94; clin. nurse dept. ob-gyn. Gallup (N.Mex.) Indian Med. Ctr. Indian Health Svc., 1997—. Active St. Francis Ch., Gallup, 1954—, mem. choir, 1991-94; active St. Francis Sch. PTO, Gallup, 1982-92; mem. Right to Life Com. of N.Mex., 1992-94, sec. Gallup chpt., 1993-94. Roman Catholic. Avocations: reading, exercising, sewing, gardening, parenting. Home: 205 E Logan Ave Gallup NM 87301-6133

MULLIGAN, KATHLEEN ANN, dancer, choreographer, educator; b. Fresno, Calif.; d. John C. and Barbara Jean (Tanner) M. BA in Cosmetology, Fresno City Coll., 1978; student, Calif. State U., Fresno, 1976-78. Cosmetologist Picadilly Coiffures, Fresno, 1978-80; owner, instr. Fresno Sch. Ballet, 1980-83; computer bookkeeper Advance Paper Box Co., L.A., 1984-88; dancer Terri Lewis Dance Co., L.A., 1985-89; bookkeeper Richard Robert, CPA, Inc., Fresno, Calif., 1988-89; sr. acct., collection mgr. Manco Abbott Inc., Fresno, 1990—; dancer, choreographer Fresno Civic Ballet, Fresno Cmty. Theatre, 1975-85; tchr. ballet and jazz, choreographer CM Sch. Performing Arts. Avocations: travel, water sports, golf. Home: 7166 N Fruit Ave Apt 108 Fresno CA 93711-0742

MULLINS, RUTH GLADYS, nurse; b. Westville, N.S., Can., Aug. 25, 1943; d. William G. and Gladys H.; came to U.S., 1949, naturalized, 1955; student Tex. Womans U., 1961-64; BS in Nursing, Calif. State U.-Long Beach, 1966; MSN, UCLA, 1973; PhD, Columbia Pacific U.; m. Leonard E. Mullins, Aug. 27, 1963; children: Deborah R., Catherine M., Leonard III. Pub. health nurse, L.A. County Health Dept., 1967-68; nurse Meml. Hosp. Med. Center, Long Beach, 1968-72; dir. pediatric nurse practitioner program Calif. State U., Long Beach, 1973-97, asst. prof., 1975-80, assoc. prof., 1980-85, prof., 1985—; health svc. credential coord. Sch. Nursing Calif. State U., Long Beach, Calif., chmn., 1979-81, coord. grad. programs, 1985-92; mem. Calif. Maternal, Child and Adolescent Health Bd., 1977-84; vice chair Long Beach/Orange County Health Consortium, 1984-85, chair 1985-86. Tng. grantee HHS, Divsn. Nursing Calif. Dept. Health; cert. pediatric nurse practitioner. Fellow Nat. Assn. Pediatric Nurse Assocs. and Practitioners (exec. bd., pres. 1990-91), Nat. Fedn. Nursing Specialty Orgns. (sec. 1991-93); mem. APHA, Nat. Alliance Nurse Practitioners (governing body 1990-92), Assn. Faculties Pediatric Nurse Practitioner Programs, L.A. and Orange County Assn. Pediatric Nurse Practitioners and Assocs. (treas. 1998), Am. Assn. U. Faculty, Ambulatory Pediatric Assn. Democrat. Methodist. Author: (with B. Nelms) Growth and Development: A Primary Health Care Approach; contbg. author: Quick Reference to Pediatric Nursing, 1984; asst. editor Jour. Pediatric Health Care. Home: 6382 Heil Ave Huntington Beach CA 92647-4232 Office: Calif State U Dept Nursing 1250 N Bellflower Blvd Long Beach CA 90840-0001

MULLIS, KARY BANKS, biochemist; b. Lenoir, N.C., Dec. 28, 1944; s. Cecil Banks Mullis and Bernice Alberta (Barker) Fredericks; children: Christopher, Jeremy, Louise. BS in Chemistry, Ga. Inst. Tech, 1966; PhD in Biochemistry, U. Calif., Berkeley, 1973; DSc (hon.), U. S.C., 1994. Lectr. biochemistry U. Calif., Berkeley, 1972; postdoctoral fellow U. Calif., San Francisco, 1977-79, U. Kans. Med. Sch., Kansas City, 1973-76; scientist Cetus Corp., Emeryville, Calif., 1979-86; dir. molecular biology Xytronyx, Inc., San Diego, 1986-88; cons. Specialty Labs, Inc., Amersham, Inc., Chiron Inc. and various others, Calif., 1988-96; chmn. StarGene, Inc., San Rafael, Calif.; v.p. Histotec, Inc., Cedar Rapids, Iowa; v.p. molecular biology chemistry Vyrex Inc., La Jolla, Calif.; Disting. vis. prof. U. S.C. Coll. of Sci. and Math. Contbr. articles to profl. jours.; patentee in field. Recipient Preis Biochemische Analytik award German Soc. Clin. Chem., 1990, Allan award Am. Soc. of Human Genetics, 1990, award Gairdner Found. Internat., 1991, Nat. Biotech. award, 1991, Robert Koch award, 1992, Chiron Corp. Biotechnology Rsch. award Am. Soc. Microbiology, 1992, Japan prize Sci. and Tech. Found. Japan, 1993, Nobel Prize in Chemistry, Nobel Foundation, 1993; named Calif. Scientist of Yr., 1992, Scientist of Yr., R&D Mag., 1991. Mem. Am. Chem. Soc., Am. Acad. Achievement, Inst. Further Study (dir. 1983—). Achievements include invention of Polymerase Chain Reaction (PCR). Office: Vyrex Inc 2159 Avenida de la Palaya La Jolla CA 92037-5924*

MULTHAUP, MERREL KEYES, artist; b. Cedar Rapids, Iowa, Sept. 27, 1922; d. Stephen Dows and Edna Gertrude (Gard) Keyes; m. Robert Hansen Multhaup, Apr. 7, 1944; children: Eric Stephen, Robert Bruce. Student fine art, State U. of Iowa, 1942-43; student color theory, Rice U., 1971. Mem. teaching faculty Summit (N.J.) Art Assn., 1956-60; art instr. studio classes Springfield, N.J., 1954-55, Bloomfield (N.J.) Art Group, 1955-56, Westport, Conn., 1962-63; mem. teaching faculty Hunterdon Art Ctr., Clinton, N.J., 1985-92. One woman exhbns. include Coriell Gallery, 1995; exhibited in group shows at Nat. Assn. Women Artists, N.Y.C., 1957-97 (awards in figure painting), Hartford (Conn.) Athanaeum Mus., 1961 (1st prize), Highgate Gallery, N.Y.C., Waverly Gallery, N.Y.C., Leicester Gallery, London, Silvermine Gallery, Conn., Pendut Gallery, Tex., Benedict Gallery, Sidney Rothman Gallery, N.J., Stamford (Conn.) Mus., Bridgeport (Conn.) Mus., Montclair (N.J.) Mus., Newark Mus., Coriell Gallery, Albuquerque; included in traveling exhibit Nat. Assn. Women Artists, 1996—, Travel USA, 1999, New World Art Ctr., N.Y.C., 1998, 99, Gallery Art 54, N.Y.C., 1997; also numerous commd. portraits, U.S., Eng., Australia. Bd. dirs., exhbn. chmn. Summit Art Assn., 1950-60, Silvermine Guild of Art, New Canaan, Conn., 1960-64; bd. dirs. Artist's Equity of N.J., 1977-84, chmn. state-wide event, 1983, 86; artist's adv. coun. Hunterdon Art Ctr., Clinton, 1988-92; pres. Four Hills Neighbors, 1998—. Recipient awards in juried exhbns. in Iowa, Pa., N.J., Conn., N.Y.C. Mem. Nat. Mus. for Women in Arts (charter mem.), Nat. Assn. Women Artists Inc. (awards for figure painting 1957, 80, 89), Albuquerque United Artists. Avocations: entertaining, sewing, singing, playing the piano and reading, dancing. Home and Studio: 1321 Stagecoach Rd SE Albuquerque NM 87123-4320

MULVANEY, JAMES FRANCIS, lawyer; b. Chgo., Nov. 2, 1922; m. Mary Ruth Rinderer, 1945; 7 children. BS, Loyola U., Chgo., 1942, JD, 1948. Atty. Chgo., 1948-55, San Diego, Calif., 1956-62; exec. v.p. U.S. Nat. Bank, 1963-72, pres., CEO, 1972-73; pres. San Diego Baseball Co., 1955-68; v.p., gen. counsel San Diego Padres Nat. League, 1968-73; sr. ptnr. Mulvaney, Kahan & Barry, San Diego, 1974—; chmn., CEO Chela Fin., San Francisco, 1983—. Bd. vis. U. San Diego Sch. Law, 1971-88; chmn. United Way Internat., 1991-94, mem. exec. com., United Way Am., 1987-93, various officers; co-chmn. San Diego Organizing Project, 1983—; bd. dirs. World SHARE, Inc., 1986-92, Old Globe Theatre London, Del Mar Charities, [illegible] San Diego award, 1991, First Annual Spirit of Charity award Cath. Community Svcs., 1984, Brotherhood award Nat. Conf. Christians and Jews, Inc., 1983, Citizen of Yr. award Jr. C. of C. and The City Club, 1983, numerous others. Mem. San Diego County Bar Found. (treas., Outstanding Svc. award 1988), ABA, Calif. State Bar Assn., Ill. State Bar Assn., San Diego C. of C., San Diego Coun. on World Affairs, The City Club of San Diego, Navy League. Office: Mulvaney Kahan & Barry 401 W A St Fl 17 San Diego CA 92101-7901

MULVEY, GERALD JOHN, telecommunication engineering administrator, meteorologist educator; b. Cambria Heights, N.Y., Dec. 20, 1949; s. George Patrick and Estelle Florence M.; m. Katherine Louise Strick, July 7, 1973. BS in Physics, York Coll., Jamaica, N.Y., 1971; MS in Atmospheric Sci., SUNY, Albany, 1973; PhD in Atmospheric Sci., Colo. State U., 1977. Cert. cons. meteorologist, CCM. Rsch. assoc. dept. atmospheric sci. Colo. State U., 1977-78; mgr. dept. atmospheric physics Meteorology Rsch., Inc., Altadena, Calif., 1978-80; sr. rsch. engr. Lockheed Martin Missiles and Space, Sunnyvale, Calif., 1980-97; advanced programs mgr. Lockheed Martin Western Devel. Labs., 1997-98; lectr. dept. geoscis. San Francisco State U., 1995-98; advanced programs mgr. Lockheed Martin Global Telecom., Sunnyvale, Calif., 1998—. Co-author: Environmental Impacts of Artificial Ice Nucleating Agents, 1978; contbr. articles to profl. jours. including Analytical Chemistry and Jour. Applied Meteorology. Commr. Cupertino (Calif.) Libr. Commn., 1989-93. Mem. AAAS, Am. Meteorological Soc., Internat. Soc. Measurement and Control (v.p. Santa Clara valley 1996-97), Sigma Xi. Roman Catholic. Achievements include development of long range transport of active cloud nucleating agents. Office: Lockheed Martin Global Telecomunications 1260 Crossman Ave # Ms82 Sunnyvale CA 94089-1116

MULVIHILL, PETER JAMES, fire protection engineer; b. Honolulu, Jan. 24, 1956; s. James H. and Jane A. (Norton) M. BSCE, Worcester (Mass.) Poly. Inst., 1978. Registered profl. engr. Fire Protection, Nev. Sr. engr. Indsl. Risk Insurers, San Francisco, 1978-84; fire protection engr. Aerojet Gen. Corp., Sacramento, 1984-87, Reno Fire Dept., 1987-93; bn. chief Boise (Idaho) Fire Dept., 1993-95; cons. Rolf Jensen & Assocs., Inc., Lehi, Utah, 1995-96; fire protection engr. Rolf Jensen & Assocs., Inc., Las Vegas, Nev., 1996—; part-time instr. univ. extension U. Calif., Davis, 1993-95, Truckee Meadows Community Coll., Reno, 1988-93. Commr. Gov.'s Blue Ribbon Commn. to Study Adequacy of State Regulations Concerning Highly Combustible Materials, Carson City, Nev., 1988. Mem. Soc. Fire Protection Engrs., No. Nev. Fire Marshals Assn. (pres. 1992-93), Nat. Fire Protection Assn. (alt. mem. com. air conditioning), Internat. Assn. Fire Chiefs, Utah Fire Marshals Assn.. Office: 101 Convention Center Dr Las Vegas NV 89109-2001

MUMFORD, CHRISTOPHER GREENE, corporate financial executive; b. Washington, Oct. 21, 1945; s. Milton C. and Dorothea L. (Greene) M.; B.A., Stanford U., 1968, M.B.A., 1975. Cons., Internat. Tech. Resources Inc., 1974; asst. v.p. Wells Fargo Bank, San Francisco, 1975-78; treas. Arcata Corp., San Francisco, 1978-82, v.p. fin., 1982-87, exec. v.p. fin., 1987-94. gen. ptnr. Scarff, Sears & Assocs., San Francisco, 1986-95, mng. dir. Questor Ptnrs. Fund, L.P., San Francisco, 1995-98; v.p. bd. dirs. Triangle Pacific Corp., Dallas, 1986-88, Norton Enterprises Inc., Salt Lake City, 1988-90; bd. dirs. Community Home Med. Enterprises, Inc., Grass Valley, Calif., Crown Pacific Ltd., Portland, Oreg., IMPCO Technologies Inc., Cerritos, Calif. Office: 601 California St Ste 1450 San Francisco CA 94108-2805

MUND, GERALDINE, judge; b. L.A., July 7, 1943; d. Charles J. and Pearl (London) M. BA, Brandeis U., 1965; MS, Smith Coll., 1967; JD, Loyola U., 1977. Bar: Calif. 1977. Bankruptcy judge U.S. Ctrl. Dist. Calif., 1984—, bankruptcy chief judge, 1997—. Past pres. Temple Israel, Hollywood, Calif.; mem. Bd. Jewish Fedn. Coun. of Greater L.A. Mem. ABA, L.A. County Bar Assn. Office: 21041 Burbank Blvd Woodland Hills CA 91367-6606

MUNGIA, SALVADOR ALEJO, JR., lawyer; b. Tacoma, Feb. 19, 1959; s. Salvador Alejo Sr. and Susie (Tamaki) M. BA, Pacific Luth. U., 1981; JD, Georgetown U., 1984. Bar: Wash. 1984, U.S. Dist. Ct. (we. dist.) Wash. 1985, U.S. Ct. Appeals (9th cir.) 1986, U.S. Supreme Ct. 1992. Law clk. to Justice Fred Dore Wash. State Supreme Ct., Olympia, 1984-85; law clerk to Hon. Carolyn R. Dimmick U.S. Dist. Ct. (we. dist.) Wash., Seattle, 1985-86; assoc. Gordon, Thomas, Honeywell, Malanca, Peterson & Daheim, Tacoma, 1986-91, ptnr., 1991—; adj. prof. Pacific Luth. U., 1993-94. Vol. atty. ACLU, Tacoma, 1986—, bd. dirs., 1987-92; commr. Tacoma Human Rights Commn., 1990-96; bd. dirs. Legal Aid for Washington, 1992-96, life bd. dirs., 1997—. Mem. ABA, Wash. State Bar Assn., Fed. Bar Assn. Western Wash., Tacoma-Pierce County Bar Assn. (pres. 1999), Pierce County Young Lawyers Assn. (trustee 1988-90), Wash. Alpine Club, Tacoma Lawn Tennis Club, Tacoma Club. Avocations: mountain climbing, skiing, tennis, running. Home: 615 N C St Tacoma WA 98403-2810 Office: Gordon Thomas Honeywell Malance Peterson & Daheim PO Box 1157 Tacoma WA 98401-1157

MUNITZ, BARRY, foundation administrator; b. Bklyn., July 26, 1941; s. Raymond J. and Vivian L. (LeVoff) M.; m. Anne Tomfohrde, Dec. 15, 1987. BA, Bklyn. Coll., 1963; MA, Princeton U., 1965, PhD, 1968; cert., U. Leiden, Netherlands, 1962. Asst. prof. lit. and drama U. Calif., Berkeley, 1966-68; staff assoc. Carnegie Commn. Higher Edn., 1968-70; mem. presdl. staff, then assoc. provost U. Ill. System, 1970-72, acad. v.p., 1972-76; v.p., dean faculties Central campus U. Houston, 1976-77, chancellor, 1977-82, chmn. coordinating bd. faculty workload, 1976-80; chmn. Tex. Long Range Planning, 1980-82; pres., COO Federated Devel. Co., 1982-91; vice chmn. Maxxam Inc., L.A., 1982-91; chancellor Calif. State U. System, Long Beach, Calif., 1991-98; prof. English lit. Calif. State U., L.A., 1991—; pres., CEO J.Paul Getty Trust, L.A., 1998—; bd. dirs. Sta. KCET-TV, Am. Coun. on Edn., Nat. Bus. Higher Edn. Forum, SunAmerica Inc., SLM Holdings; cons. in presdl. evaluation and univ. governance. Author: The Assessment of Institutional Leadership, 1977, also articles, monographs. Mem. task force NSF. Recipient Disting. Alumnus award Bklyn. Coll., 1979, U. Houston Alumni Pres.'s medal, 1981; Woodrow Wilson fellow, 1963. Mem. Young Pres. Orgn., Heritage Club, Phi Beta Kappa. Office: J Paul Getty Trust Ste 400 1200 Getty Center Dr Los Angeles CA 90049-1681

MUNLU, KAMIL CEMAL, military logistician, educator; b. Istanbul, Turkey, July 14, 1954; came to U.S., 1981; s. Adnan and Jale Sidika (Konari) M. BA in Econs., Calif. State U., Long Beach, 1983; MBA in Bus. Adminstrn., Nat. U., San Diego, 1986, MS in Logistics, 1988; M in Internat. Bus. Adminstrn., U.S. Internat. U., San Diego, 1990; DPA, U. La Verne, Calif., 1995. Buyer Onder Ltd., Ankara, Turkey, 1972-78; mgr. JAKL, Inc., Birmingham, England, 1979-81; rep. Aydinlar Cons., Ankara, 1984-93; logistics specialist, project efficiency coord. Hill Industries, Inc., Chatsworth, Calif., 1993-95; v.p. materials mgmt. Kale Logistics Internat., Ankara, 1995-98; adj. prof. Woodbury U., Burbank, Calif., 1998—; cons. spl. projects logistical support Onder, Ltd., Ankara, 1996-98. Mem. Turkish Army, 1984-85. Mem. Turkish Businessman Club, Turkish Tng. Orgn. for Higher Edn. Avocations: art, boating, golfing, reading, travel. Home: 10 Lindero Ave Long Beach CA 90803-2459

MUNN, WILLIAM CHARLES, II, psychiatrist; b. Flint, Mich., Aug. 9, 1938; s. Elton Albert and Rita May (Coykendall) M.; student Flint Jr. Coll., 1958-59, U. Detroit, 1959-61; M.D., Wayne State U., 1965; children by previous marriage—Jude Michael, Rachel Marie, Alexander Winston. Intern David Grant USAF Med. Center, Travis AFB, Calif., 1965-66; resident in psychiatry Letterman Army Hosp., San Francisco, 1967-70; practice medicine, specializing in psychiatry, Fairfield, Calif., 1972—; chief in-patient psychiatry David Grant Med. Center, 1970-71, chmn. dept. mental health, 1971-72; psychiat. cons. Fairfield-Suisun Unified Sch. Dist., 1971—, Fairfield Hosp. and Clinic, 1971, N. Bay Med. Ctr.(formerly Intercommunity Hosp.), Fairfield, 1971—, Casey Family Program, 1980—, Solano County Coroner's Office, 1981; asst. clin. prof. psychiatry U. Calif., San Francisco, 1976—; cons. Vaca Valley Hosp., Vacaville, Calif., 1988—, VA Hosp., San Francisco, 1976, David Grant USAF Hosp., 1976. Served to maj., M.C., USAF, 1964-72, flight surgeon, chief public health, chief phys. exam. center McGuire AFB, N.J., 1966-67. Diplomate Am. Bd. Psychiatry and Neurology (examiner). Mem. Am. Psychiat. Assn., No. Calif. Psychiat. Soc., E. Bay Psychiat. Assn. Fax: 707-422-8920. Office: 1245 Travis Blvd Ste E Fairfield CA 94533-4842

MUNOZ, JOHN JOSEPH, retired transportation company executive; b. Salinas, Calif., Jan. 18, 1932; s. John Fernando and Naomal (Smith) M.; m. Phyllis Taylor, Feb. 6, 1961 (div. 1978); children: Sam, Kathy, Toni; m. Rachel Canales, Nov. 24, 1979; children: Michelle, Monique. AA, Allan

Hancock Coll., 1956; student, San Jose State U., 1981, Western Sierra Law Sch. Ops. mgr. So. Pacific Milling Co., Santa Maria, Calif., 1971-77; cons. Govt., Venezuela, 1977-78; fleet supt. Granite Rock Co., San Jose, Calif., 1978-80; plant mgr. Granite Constrn. Co., Greenfield, Calif., 1980-85; mgr. transpn. Ball, Ball. & Brosmer Inc., Danville, Calif., 1985-86; ops. mgr., bd. dirs. Sorrento Ready Mix Co., Del Mar, Calif., 1986-89; trans. cons. Greenfield, Calif., 1991-96; ret., 1996; cons. Dept. Agrl. Devel., Maricaibo, Venezuela, 1976—. Commr. Planning Commn., Greenfield, Calif., 1982-85; mem. fund raising com. Broccoli Festival, Greenfield, 1983-85; dir. Soledad Prison Vocat. Tng., 1982-85. Lt. 11th Ranger Airborne, U.S. Army, 1950-52, Korea. Mem. Am. Concrete Inst., Calif. Trucking Assn., Los Californianos, Rotary, Lions, Elks. Republican. Avocations: hunting, fishing, auto racing. Home and Office: PO Box 3654 Greenfield CA 93927-3654

MUÑOZ, MONICA, journalist; b. Mex. City, Feb. 7, 1965; came to U.S., 1966; d. Mario Mendoza Muñoz and Marilyn (Smith) Tom. AA, Riverside (Calif.) City Coll., 1992; BA in Journalism, Tex. Tech. U., 1995. Police dispatcher San Diego (Calif.) Police, 1984-92; producer KGTV, San Diego, 1996-97; writer, producer KNXV-TV, Phoenix, 1997-98; assignment editor NBC, San Diego, 1998—. Avocations: reading, jogging, handcrafts. Office: 8330 Engineer Rd San Diego CA 92171

MUNRO, MALCOLM GORDON, obstetrician, gynecologist, educator; b. Woodstock, Ont., Can., Mar. 22, 1952; came to U.S., 1991; s. Charles Gordon and Maribelle (Logie) M.; m. Sandra June Brander-Smith, Nov. 17, 1990; children: Tyler Gordon, Megan Danielle. MD, U. Western Ont., London, 1975. Diplomate Am. Bd. Ob-Gyn. Intern Royal Columbian Hosp., New Westminster, B.C., 1975-76; resident ob.-gyn, U. Western Ont., London, 1976-77; resident U. B.C., Vancouver, 1978-80, clin. fellow gyneolgic. oncology, 1980-81, clin. instr. ob-gyn., 1981-83; asst. clin. prof. UCLA, Vancouver, 1983-89; assoc. clin. prof. U. B.C., Vancouver, 1988-92; assoc. prof. UCLA, 1991-95, prof., 1995—, assoc. chmn. dept. ob/gyn., 1994-95; chmn. ob-gyn. sect. B.C. Med. Assn., Vancouver, 1984-88, Rsch. Coordinating Com. Grace Hosp., Vancouver; founding co-chmn. Gynecologic Studies Group, Washington, 1993—; cons. Cancer Control Agy., B.C., 1981-91, Ethicon Endosuture Core Cons. Group, 1992-96; chmn. STOP-DUB Clin. Trial, 1996-2001. Author: (book) Gynecology, A Practical Approach, 1990; contbr. articles to profl. jours., chpts. to books; inventor, patentee laparoscopic loop electrodes, 1993; mem. editl. bd. Treating the Female Patient, 1988-94, Jour. of Gynecologic Technique, 1993—; reviewer Obstetrics and Gynecology, 1990—, Fertil Steril, 1993—, Am. Jour. Managed Care, 1996—; mem. ad hoc rev. com. Jour. Am. Assn. Gynecologic Laparoscopists, 1994—. Med. dir. Planned Parenthood, Vancouver, 1980-85; founding dir. U. B.C. Coop. Osteoporosis Program, 1987-91, Multidisciplinary Osteoporosis Clinic, U. Hosp., Vancouver, 1987-91. Recipient Appreciation cert. Planned Parenthood of B.C., 1991; grantee Vancouver Found., 1988, P.W. Woodward Found., 1988, Ethicon Endosurgery, 1992, NIH/NIAID AIDS and Cervical Neoplasia co-investigator, 1992-94, 96, study chair AHCPR/GSG. Fellow Royal Coll. Surgeons Can., Soc. Obstetricians and Gynecologists Can.; mem. Can. Fertility and Andrology Soc., Am. Fertility Soc., Am. Assn. Gynecologic Laparoscopists, Am. Coll. Obstetricians and Gynecologists (vice-chair B.C. section VIII 1987-90). Office: UCLA Med Ctr 14445 Olive View Dr Sylmar CA 91342-1437

MUNRO, RALPH DAVIES, state government official; b. Bainbridge Island, Wash., June 25, 1943; s. George Alexander and Elizabeth (Troll) M.; m. Karen Hansen, Feb. 17, 1973; 1 son, George Alexander. BA in History and Edn. (scholar), Western Wash. U. Indsl. engr. Boeing Co., 1966-68; sales mgr. Continental Host, Inc.; asst. dep. dir. ACTION Agy., 1971; spl. asst. to gov. State of Wash., 1970-76; gen. mgr. Tillicum Enterprises & Food Services Co.; dir. Found. for Handicapped, 1976-80; pres. Northwest Highlands Tree Farm; sec. of state State of Wash., 1980—. Chmn. community service com. Seattle Rotary Club 4; founder 1st pres. Rotary Youth Job Employment Center, Seattle. Named Man of Yr. Assn. Retarded Citizens, Seattle, 1970. Mem. Nat. Assn. Secs. State (pres.), Nat. Assn. Retarded Children, Wash. Historic Mus. (dir.), Wash. Trust Historic Preservation (founder), Nature Conservancy. Republican. Lutheran. Office: Sec of State Legislative Bldg PO Box 40220 Olympia WA 98504-0220

MUNSON, LUCILLE MARGUERITE (MRS. ARTHUR E. MUNSON), real estate broker; b. Norwood, Ohio, Mar. 26, 1914; d. Frank and Fairy (Wicks) Wirick; R.N., Lafayette (Ind.) Home Hosp., 1937; A.B., San Diego State U., 1963, student Purdue U., Kans. Wesleyan U.; m. Arthur E. Munson, Dec. 24, 1937; children—Barbara Munson Papke, Judith Munson Andrews, Edmund Arthur. Staff and pvt. nurse Lafayette Home Hosp., 1937-41; indsl. nurse Lakey Foundry & Machine Co., Muskegon, Mich., 1950-51, Continental Motors Corp., Muskegon, 1951-52; nurse Girl Scout Camp, Grand Haven, Mich., 1948-49; owner Munson Realty, San Diego, 1964—. Mem. San Diego County Grand Jury, 1975-76, 80-81, Calif. Grand Jurors Assn. (charter). Office: 2999 Mission Blvd Ste 102 San Diego CA 92109-8076

MUNSON, WILLIAM CRAWFORD, III, civil engineer; b. Hartford, Conn., Nov. 17, 1966; s. William Crawford Munson and Milicent Yevette (Wolfson) Kari; m. Laurine Marie Denney; children: Amber Renalea Jones, Lisa June Smith. AS, Yuba C.C., Marysville, Calif., 1991; BS, Calif. Poly. State U., 1994. Tech. asst. Academic Computing Svcs., San Luis Obispo, Calif., 1992-93; gen. mgr. Straight "A" Painters, Inc., San Luis Obispo, Calif., 1993-94; project engr. John Paoluccio Consulting Engrs., Inc., Modesto, Calif., 1995—. Mem. Assn. Facilities Engring. (pres.). Avocations: automobile racing, sailing, flying, wine tasting, darts. Office: John Paoluccio Consulting Engrs Inc 5038 Salida Blvd Salida CA 95368-9403

MUNSTERTEIGER, KAY DIANE, speech and language pathologist; b. Newcastle, Wyo., June 2, 1956; d. Donald Francis and Janice Mathilda (Emerson) M. BS, U. Wyo., 1978; MS, U. Nev., Reno, 1980. Speech lang. pathologist No. Nev. Speech lang. Clinic, Reno, 1980-82, Washakie County Sch. Dist. 1, Worland, Wyo., 1982—; pvt. practice speech pathologist Worland, 1982—; speech lang. pathologist, cons. Washakie County Sch. Dist. 2, Tensleep, Wyo., 1984-85; speech lang. pathologist Spl. Touch Presch., Worland, 1985-86, 89-93, Rehab Visions, 1995—, Symphony Rehab. Svcs., 1997—; pres. bd. examiners Speech Pathology and Audiology, 1988-93. Mem. Pub. Sch. Caucus. Mem. NEA, State Edn. Assn., Am. Speech Lang. Hearing Assn., Wyo. Speech Lang. Hearing Assn., Nat. Stuttering Project, Pub. Sch. Caucus, Assn. Childhood Edn. Internat., Phi Kappa Phi. Democrat. Roman Catholic. Avocations: traveling, reading, crafts. Office: Washakie County Sch Dist # 1 1900 Howell Worland WY 82401-3520

MURANAKA, HIDEO, artist, educator; b. Mitaka, Tokyo, Japan, Feb. 4, 1946; s. Nobukichi and Hisae M. BFA, Tokyo Nat. U. of Fine Arts, 1970, MFA, 1972. Calif. Community Coll.- Instr. Cred. Drawing accepted for The Pacific Coast States Collection from the v.p. house, Washington, 1980, Nat. Mus. Art, Bklyn. Mus., Achenbach Found., Calif. Palace of Legion of Hon., Yergeau-Musee Internat. d'Art (Can.). Mem. Democratic Nat. Comm., Wash., 1985—. Recipient second prize Iternat. Art Exhbn. Museo Hosio, Italy, 1984, V.J.'s Artist award Palm Springs Desert Mus., 1995; named to Hist. Preservation Am. Hall of Fame. Mem. Oakland Mus. Assn., The Fine Arts Mus. San Francisco, Lepidopterist's Soc. Avocations: collecting butterflies, music. Home: 179 Oak St Apt W San Francisco CA 94102-5948

MURANE, WILLIAM EDWARD, lawyer; b. Denver, Mar. 4, 1933; s. Edward E. and Theodora (Wilson) M.; m. Rosemarie Palmerone, Mar. 26, 1960; children: Edward Wheelock, Peter Davenport, Alexander Phelps. AB, Dartmouth Coll., 1954; LLB, Stanford U., 1957. Bar: Wyo. 1957, Colo. 1958, D.C. 1978, U.S. Supreme Ct. 1977. Assoc. then ptnr. Holland & Hart, Denver, 1961-69; dep. gen. counsel U.S. Dept. Commerce, Washington, 1969-71; gen. counsel FDIC, Washington, 1971-72; ptnr. Holland & Hart, Denver, 1972—; pub. mem. Adminstrv. Conf. of the U.S., Washington, 1978-81. Bd. dirs. Ctr. for Law and Rsch., Denver, 1973-76, Acad. in the Wilderness, Denver, 1986—; trustee Colo. Symphony Orch., 1994—; mem. bd. visitors Stanford U. Law Sch. Capt. USAF, 1958-61. Fellow Am. Coll. Trial Lawyers; mem. ABA (ho of dels. 1991-96), U. Club, Cactus Club. Republican. Avocations: fishing, classical music. Office: Holland & Hart 555 17th St Ste 3200 Denver CO 80202-3950

MURATORE, MARILYN ANN, contractor; b. San Francisco, June 26, 1941; d. Thomas James and Camille Catherine (Bacigalupi) Dennison; m. Richard Peter Muratore, Oct. 25, 1959 (div. 1995); 1 child, Tamara Ann. Treas. Peter D. Scatena, Inc., San Francisco, 1974-84; v.p., sec. Muratore Corp., San Francisco, 1985-91, chmn. bd., sec., 1991-96; owner Muratore Assocs., San Francisco, 1997—. Active Com. to Reelect Dick Claire for Mayor, Redwood City, Calif., 1991. Mem. Am. Bldg. Contractors Assn. (bd. dirs. 1992—, pres. San Francisco chpt. 1997), Pacific Contractors Assn. (bd. dirs. 1997—), San Francisco C. of C. Avocations: boating, swimming, skiing. Office: Muratore Assocs 250 Alameda De Las Pulgas Redwood City CA 94062-2833

MURDOCK, DAVID H., diversified company executive; b. Kansas City, Mo., Apr. 10, 1923; m. Maria Ferrer, Apr., 1992. LLD (hon.), Pepperdine U., 1978; LHD (hon.), U. Nebr., 1984, Hawaii Loa Coll., 1989. Sole proprietor, chmn., chief exec. officer Pacific Holding Co., L.A.; chmn. Dole Food Co. (formerly Castle & Cooke, Inc.), L.A., 1985—, also bd. dirs. Trustee Asia Soc., N.Y.C., L.A.; founder, bd. dirs. Found. for Advanced Brain Studies, L.A.; bd. visitors UCLA Grad. Sch. Mgmt.;bd. govs. Performing Arts Coun. of Music Ctr., L.A.; bd. govs. East-West Ctr., L.A.; patron Met. Opera, N.Y.C. With USAAC, 1943-45. Mem. Regency Club (founder, pres.) Bel-Air Bay Country Club, Sherwood Country Club (founder, pres.), Met. Club (N.Y.C.). Office: Dole Food Co Inc 31355 Oak Crest Dr Westlake Village CA 91361-4679 also: Pacific Holding Co 10900 Wilshire Blvd Ste 1600 Los Angeles CA 90024-6535*

MURDOCK, PAMELA ERVILLA, travel and advertising company executive, b. Los Angeles, Dec. 3, 1940; d. John James and Chloe Conger (Keefe) M.; children: Cheryl, Kim. BA, U. Colo., 1962. Pres., Dolphin Travel, Denver, 1972-87; owner, pres. Mile Hi Tours, Denver, 1973—, MH Internat., 1987—, Mile-Hi Advt. Agy., 1986—. Bd. dirs. Rocky Mountain chpt. Juvenile Diabetes Found. Internat.; exec. bd. Rocky Mtn. Father's Day Coun., 1998. Named Wholesaler of Yr., Las Vegas Conv. and Visitors Authority, 1984. Recipient Leadership award Nat. Multiple Sclerosis Soc., 1996. Mem. NAFE, Am. Soc. Travel Agts., Nat. Fedn. Independent Businessmen. Republican. Home: 5565 E Vassar Ave Denver CO 80222-6239 Office: Mile Hi Tours Inc 2160 S Clermont St Denver CO 80222-5007

MURIAN, RICHARD MILLER, book company executive; b. East St. Louis, Ill., Sept. 17, 1937; s. Richard Miller Jr. and Margaret Keyes (Gregory) M.; m. Judith Lee, Aug. 11, 1961 (dec. Apr. 1992); 1 child, Jennifer Ann. BA, U. Calif., Davis, 1969; MLS, U. Calif., Berkeley, 1972; MA, Calif. State U., Sacramento, 1975; MDiv, Trinity Evang., 1977. Cert. history instr., libr. sci. instr., Calif. History reader Calif. State U., Sacramento, 1965-66; history reader U. Calif., Davis, 1966-68, philosophy rschr., 1968-69; bibliographer Argus Books, Sacramento, 1970-71; rsch. dir. Nat. Judical Coll., Reno, 1971-72; libr. Calif. State U., Sacramento, 1972-76; tv talk show host Richard Murian Show, L.A., 1979-80; pres. Alcuin Books, Ltd., Phoenix, 1981—; bd. dirs. Guild of Ariz. Antiquarian Books; pres. East Valley Assn. Evangs., Mesa, Ariz., 1984-86; cons. Ariz. Hist. Soc., 1993—. Contbr. articles to profl. jours. Active U. Calif. Riverside Libr., 1981-83, KAET (PBS), 1988—, Ariz. State U., 1989—. Recipient Sidney B. Mitchell fellowship U. Calif., Berkeley, 1971. Mem. Am. Assn. Mus., Am. Soc. Appraisers, Ariz. Preservation Found., Grand Canyon Nature Assn., Internat. Platform Assn., Ariz. Publ. Book Assn. (awards com.), Phi Kappa Phi. Democrat. Presbyterian. Avocations: fgn. films, jazz. Office: Alcuin Books Ltd 115 W Camelback Rd Phoenix AZ 85013-2519

MURILLO, VELDA JEAN, social worker, counselor; b. Miller, S.D., Dec. 8, 1943; d. Royal Gerald and Marion Elizabeth (Porter) Matson; m. Daniel John Murillo, June 25, 1967 (div. Dec. 1987); 1 child, Damon Michael. BS, S.D. State U., 1965; MA, Calif. State U., Bakersfield, 1980. Cert. marriage, family and child counselor. Social worker adult svcs. Kern County Dept. Welfare, Bakersfield, 1965-78, social worker child protective svcs., 1978-84; asst. coord. sexual abuse program Kern County Dist. Atty., Bakersfield, 1985-91, coord. sexual abuse program, 1991—; Mem. Calif. Sexual Assault Investigators, 1982-84, Kern Child Abuse Prevention Coun., Bakersfield, 1982-84; co-developer, presenter Children's Self Help Project, Bakersfield, 1982-87; cons. mem. Sexual Assault Adv. Com., Bakersfield, 1991-96. Democrat. Avocations: spiritual healing, travel, metaphysical pursuits, Reiki (master). Office: Kern County Dist Atty 1215 Truxtun Ave Bakersfield CA 93301-4619

MURKOWSKI, FRANK HUGHES, senator; b. Seattle, Mar. 28, 1933; s. Frank Michael and Helen (Hughes) M.; m. Nancy R. Gore, Aug. 28, 1954; children: Carol Victoria Murkowski Sturgulewski, Lisa Ann Murkowski Martell, Frank Michael, Eileen Marie Murkowski Van Wyhe, Mary Catherine Murkowski Judson, Brian Patrick. Student, Santa Clara U., 1952-53; BA in Econs, Seattle U., 1955. With Pacific Nat. Bank of Seattle, 1957-58, Nat. Bank of Alaska, Anchorage, 1959-67; asst. v.p., mgr. Nat. Bank of Alaska (Wrangell br.), 1963-66; v.p. charge bus. devel. Nat. Bank of Alaska, Anchorage, 1966-67; commr. dept. econ. devel. State of Alaska, Juneau, 1967-70; pres. Alaska Nat. Bank, Fairbanks, 1971-80; mem. U.S. Senate from Alaska, Washington, D.C., 1981—; chmn. Com. on Energy and Natural Resources; mem. Com. on Fin., Vets Affairs Com., Indian Affairs Com., Japan-US Friendship Com.; Rep. nominee for U.S. Congress from Alaska, 1970. Former v.p. B.C. and Alaska Bd. Trade; mem. U.S. Holocaust Mus. Coun. Served with U.S. Coast Guard, 1955-57. Mem. AAA, AMVETS, NRA, Am. Legion, Polish Legion Am. Vets., Ducks Unltd., Res. Officer's Assn., Alaska Geog. Soc., Alaska World Affairs Coun., Fairbanks Hist. Preservation Found., Coalition Am. Vets., Alaska Native Brotherhood, Naval Athletic Assn., Am. Bankers Assn., Alaska Bankers Assn. (pres. 1973), Young Pres.'s Orgn., Alaska C. of C. (pres. 1977), Anchorage C. of C. (bd. dirs. 1966), B.C. C. of C., Fairbanks C. of C. (bd. dirs. 1973-78), Pioneers of Alaska, Internat. Alaska Nippon Kai, Capital Hill Club, Shilla Club, Army Athletic Club, Congl. Staff Club, Diamond Athletic Club, Washington Athletic Club, Elks, Lions. Office: US Senate 322 Hart Senate Bldg Washington DC 20510

MURLIN, WILLIAM EWELL, audiovisual specialist; b. Mpls., Apr. 28, 1941; s. William Raymond and Jean Helen (Ewell) M.; m. Beatrice C. MacMillan, June 13, 1964 (div. Dec. 1990); children: I. Jeffry William, G. Andrew John. BA, Wash. State U., 1963. Announcer KGY Radio, Olympia, Wash., 1963-65; reporter KMED Radio, Medford, Oreg., 1965-67, KMED TV, Medford, Oreg., 1967-69, KEX Radio, Portland, Oreg., 1969-73; news dir. KOIN Radio, Portland, Oreg., 1973-75; reporter KATU TV, Portland, Oreg., 1975-77; assignment editor, reporter KOIN TV, Portland, Oreg., 1977-79; audio-visual specialist Bonneville Power Adminstrn., Portland, Oreg., 1979—; bd. dirs. Assn. Multi-Image, Portland, 1987. Editor: Woody Guthrie-Roll On Columbia, The Columbia River Collection, 1987; editor (rec.) Woody Guthrie-The Columbia River Collection, 1987. Recipient Superior Accomplishment award U.S. Dept. Energy, 1991. Mem. Internat. TV Assn. Avocations: folk music, backpacking, camping. Office: Bonneville Power Adminstrn PO Box (CGMV-B1) Portland OR 97208-3621

MURPHEY, MICHAEL MARTIN, country western singer, songwriter; b. Tex., Mar. 14, 1945; married; children: Ryan, Brennan, Laura Lynn. Attended, UCLA. Profl. musician, 1962—; with Lewis & Clark Expedition, 1966-70; adj. prof. music and Am. studies Utah State U. Songwriter for Monkees, Kenny Rogers, Nitty Gritty Dirt Band; pop hit Wildfire, 1975, What's Forever For, Carolina in the Pines, Love Affairs, Still Taking Chances; founder Westfest Annual celebration; albums: Geronimo's Cadillac, 1971, Blue Sky Night Thunder, 1981, The Best of Michael Martin Murphey, 1981, The Heart Never Lies, 1986, Tonight We Ride, 1986, Americana, 1987, River of Time, 1988, Land of Enchantment, 1989, Best of County Michael Martin Murphey, 1990, Cowboy Songs, 1990, Cowboy Christmas: Cowboy Songs II, 1991, Cowboy Songs III, 1993, Americas Horses, 1994 (re-released as The Horse Legends, 1997), Sagebrush Symphony, 1995, Cowboy Songs Four, 1998. Named Best New Artist, County Music Assn., Acad. County Music; recipient Grammy nomination for a Face in the Crowd, Nat. Am. Video award for She Wants, award Cowboy Hall of Fame (3), 1990-92, 95, 96, 99, Western Heritage awards (5), Golden Smoky award Nat. Forest Svc., 1998. Office: PO Box FFF Taos NM 87571-2550

MURPHY, CLAIRE RUDOLF, author, consultant; b. Spokane, Wash., Mar. 9, 1951; d. Kermit Max and Frances Claire (Collins) R.; m. Robert Patrick Murphy, June 9, 1979; children: Conor, Megan. BA in History, Santa Clara U., 1973; MFA in Creative Writing, U. Alaska, 1988. Cert. tchr., Calif., Alaska, Wash. Tchr. secondary lang. arts St. Mary's (Alaska) Sch., 1974-77; tchr. lang. arts North Pole H.S., Fairbanks, Alaska, 1977-82, Ryan Mid. Sch., Fairbanks, 1982-83; instr. adult learning programs Fairbanks Correctional Ctr., 1983-89; adj. prof. U. Alaska, Fairbanks, 1989-90; dir. Young Writers Inst., Fairbanks, 1993-98; writing cons. Alaska State Writing Consortium, 1983-98; freelance writer Spokane, 1998—; instr. writing Eastern Wash. U., Spokane, 1999—; mem. curriculum adv. bd. Fairbanks Sch. Dist., 1997-98. Author: Friendship Across Arctic Waters: Alaskan Cub Scouts Meet Their Soviet Neighbors, 1991, To the Summit, 1992, The Prince and the Salmon People, 1993, Gold Star Sister, 1994, A Child's Alaska, 1994 (Parents Coun. selection, Sequoyah Children's Book award 1996-97, Caribou Girl, 1998; co-author: (with Jane Haigh) Gold Rush Women, 1997. Recipient Contbrn. to Literacy in Alaska award Alaska Ctr. for the Book, Anchorage, 1998. Mem. Soc. Children's Book Writers and Illustrators, Author's Guild. Democrat. Roman Catholic. Avocations: sports, music. Home: 1514 E 19th Ave Spokane WA 99203

MURPHY, FRANCIS SEWARD, journalist; b. Portland, Oreg., Sept. 9, 1914; s. Francis H. and Blanche (Livesay) M.; BA, Reed Coll., 1936; m. Clare Eastham Cooke, Sept. 20, 1974. With The Oregonian, Portland, 1936-79, TV editor, Behind the Mike columnist, 1952-79. Archeol. explorer Mayan ruins, Yucatan, Mex., 1950—, mem. Am. Quintana Roo Expdn., 1965, 66, 68. With U.S. Army, 1942-46. Author: Dragon Mask Temples in Central Yucatan, 1988. Mem. Am. Philatelic Soc. (life), Royal Asiatic Soc., City Club (bd. govs. 1950, 64-66), Explorers Club, Am. Club of Hong Kong, Oreg. Hist. Soc., Soc. Am. Archeaology, Am. Philatelic Soc., Hong Kong Philatelic Soc., World Wide Fund Nature, Royal Hong Kong Jockey Club. Democrat. Congregationalist. Home: 4213 NE 32nd Ave Portland OR 97211-7149

MURPHY, KELLY, test and operations staff; b. Orlando, Fla., Aug. 27, 1954; m. Wendy J. Brewster; children: Kellen B., McKenna B. BS in Human Resource Mgmt., Kennedy-Western U., 1997. Cert. radiol. monitor; lic. ionizing radiation equipment operator NRC. Metrologist USMC Marine Air Wing, various locations, 1973-77, ITT Arctic Svcs., Thule AB, Greenland, 1977-79; flight test avionics Boeing Aircraft Co., Seattle, 1979-83; environ. test staff Boeing Missile Sys., Seattle, 1983-84; test and ops. staff Free Electron Laser Boeing Aerospace Co., Seattle, 1984-95; test and ops. staff S.Q.U.I.D. tech. demonstration Boeing Def., Seattle, 1995-96; test and ops. staff Digital Flight Controls Boeing Comml. Airplane Group, Seattle, 1996—; cons. vacuum tech. Great Circle Tech. Svcs., 1990—. Mem. Am. Vacuum Soc. Office: Boeing Comml Airplane Group PO Box 3707 Seattle WA 98124-2207

MURPHY, MARY ANN, human services administrator; b. Salt Lake City, Feb. 13, 1943; d. Wallace L. and Irene (Hummer) Matlock; m. Robert A. Glatzer, Dec. 31, 1977; children: Gabriela, Jessica, Nicholas. BA, U. Wash., 1964; MS, Ea. Wash. U., 1975. House counselor Ryther Child Ctr., Seattle, 1966-67; tchr. presch. Head Start, L.A. and Seattle, 1967-70, Children's Orthopedic Hosp., Seattle, 1970-72; faculty Ea. Wash. U., Cheney, 1973-82; exec. dir. Youth Help Assn., Spokane, Wash., 1983-88; mgr. regional ctr. for child abuse and neglect Deaconess Med. Ctr., Spokane, 1988-97; dir. Casey Family Ptnrs., Spokane, 1997—; pres. Wash. State Alliance for Children, Youth and Families, Seattle, 1985-87; chairperson Gov.'s Juvenile Justice Adv. Commn., Olympia, Wash., 1987—. Mem. Nat. Coun. on Juvenile Justice, 1994. Recipient Alumni Achievement award Ea. Wash. U., 1994; named Outstanding Women Leader in Health Care YWCA, 1992, Outstanding Children's Advocate, Wash. State Children's Alliance, 1996. Avocations: reading, swimming, backpacking. Home: 1950 W Clarke Ave Spokane WA 99201-1306 Office: Casey Family Ptnrs 613 S Washington St Spokane WA 99204-2517

MURPHY, MICHAEL J., architect; b. L.A., May 8, 1927; s. Michael J. and Alta M.; widowed, June 1993; children: Marc, Michele. Arch. San Bernardino, Calif., 1968-87, Hiller & Murphy, San Bernardino, Calif., 1968-78, Parsons & Murphy, 1978-82; owner, prin. arch. Michael J. Murphy, San Bernardino, Calif., 1986—; design cons. Chin & Murphy, San Bernardino, 1970-97; lectr. U. Calif., Riverside, 1972-78, pres. Butterfield Constrn., 1975-77, Dramus Constrn., 1976-77; pres., part owner Tee & Murphy Enterprise, Inc., 1980-83; v.p., part owner Archtl. Computer Svcs., 1980-86; mem. archtl. com. Indian Knolls Estates, Foothill Vista Estates #1 and #2; bd. dirs., arch. Ricksha Express, Inc. Princ. works include 210 Baskin-Robbins 31 Flavors. nat. and internat., 1974-80; also numerous apts., comml. bldgs., chs., condominiums, med. complexes, motels, pools and cabanas, restaurants, schs.; master plan for planned city of 21 square miles Toltec, Ariz., master planned 2 miles ocean front San Felipe, Mex., and others in Calif. Civitan Little League, 1968, Mayors Coun. Internat. Friendship, 1975-88, Mayors Coun., San Bernardino City, 1975-93, Emergency Med. Svcs. Activity, Inc., 1978-85; bd. dirs. Lighthouse for Blind, 1973-77, San Bernardino City Tournament of Roses Parade Com., 1980-83; com. mem. San Bernardino Expo 81, 1977. Sgt. 1st USN, 1944-46. Recipient citizens of Yr. Award, LWV, San Bernardino, 1982. Calif. Coun. AIA Calif., Assn. Bldg. Professions (pres. 1981-84), Am. Inst. Bldg. Designers (pres., 1964-66). E-mail: murfeearch@aol.com. Office: Michael J Murphy AIA 2601 Del Rosa Ave Ste 220 San Bernardino CA 92404-4415

MURPHY, MICHAEL JOSEPH, state official; b. Seattle, May 24, 1947; s. John Anthony and Helen Elizabeth (Domick) M.; m. Theresa Ann Smith. BA in History, Seattle U., 1969; MBA, Pacific Luth. U., 1978. Chief adjudicator vet.'s program Office of the State Treas., Olympia, Wash., 1972-75, adminstr. pub. deposit protection commn., 1975-81, internal auditor to state treas., 1981-87; treas. Thurston County, Olympia, 1987-96, State of Wash., Olympia, 1997—; mem. adv. bd. asset/liability com. Twin County Credit Union, Olympia, 1987-96; instr. profl. orgns., govt. Treas. Thurston County Dems., 1973-77. Mem. Wash. Assn. County Treasurers (bd. dirs., officer 1987-96, legis. coord. 1989-96, Pres. award 1994), Wash. Assn. County Ofcls. (bd. dirs. 1989-90), Wash. Mcpl. Treasurers Assn. (bd. dirs. 1990—, Cert. Excellence for investment policy 1992), Wash. Fin. Officers Assn. (profl. fin. officer 1988—, bd. dirs. 1997—), Nat. Assn. State Treasurers, Olympia Yacht Club, Olympia Country and Golf Club, Valley Athletic Club. Roman Catholic. Avocations: sailing, golf, travel. Home: PO Box 1342 Olympia WA 98507-1342 Office: Legis Bldg 2d Fl Wash State Treas Olympia WA 98504-0200

MURPHY, MICHAEL R., federal judge; b. Denver, Aug. 6, 1947; s. Roland and Mary Cecilia (Maloney) M.; m. Maureen Elizabeth Donnelly, Aug. 22, 1970; children: Amy Christina, Michael Donnelly. BA in History, Creighton U., 1969; JD, U. Wyo., 1972. Bar: Wyo. 1972, U.S. Ct. Appeals (10th cir.) 1972, Utah 1973, U.S. Dist. Ct. Utah 1974, U.S. Dist. Ct. Wyo. 1976, U.S. Ct. Appeals (5th cir.) 1976, U.S. Tax Ct. 1980, U.S. Ct. Appeals (9th cir.) 1981, U.S. Ct. Appeals (fed. cir.) 1984. Law clk. to chief judge U.S. Ct. Appeals (10th cir.), Salt Lake City, 1972-73; with Jones, Waldo, Holbrook & McDonough, Salt Lake City, 1973-86; judge 3d Dist. Ct., Salt Lake City, 1986-95, pres. judge, 1990-95; judge U.S. Ct. Appeals (10th cir.), Salt Lake City, 1995—; mem. adv. com. on rules of civil procedure Utah Supreme Ct., 1985-95, mem. bd. dist. ct. judges, 1989-90; mem. Utah State Sentencing commn., 1993-95, Utah Adv. Com. on child Support Guidelines, 1989-95, chair 1993-95; mem. Utah Child Sexual Abuse Task Force, 1989-93. Recipient Freedom of Info. award, Soc. Profl. Journalists, 1989, Utah Minority Bar Assn. award, 1995, alumni Achievement citation, Creighton U., 1997; named Judge of Yr., Utah State Bar, 1992. Fellow Am. Bar Found.; mem. ABA (editl. bd. Judges' Jour. 1997—), Utah Bar Assn. (chmn. alternative dispute resolution com. 1985-88), Sutherland Inn of Ct. II (past pres.). Roman Catholic. Office: 5438 Federal Bldg 125 S State St Salt Lake City UT 84138-1102*

MURPHY, MILLENE FREEMAN, psychiatric rehabilitation nurse, business executive; b. Idaho Falls, Idaho, Feb. 3, 1941; d. Eson Milton and Maurine (Dustin) Freeman; m. Stanley Dee Murphy, Aug. 24, 1962; children: Madison Dee, D'Lene, Eric Daniel, Aaron Milton, William Stanley, Sarah Anne, Nona Reen. BSN, Brigham Young U., 1963; MS in Psychiatric Nursing, U. Utah, 1970; PhD in Neuropsychology, Brigham Young U., 1982. Advanced practice RN. Nurses aid LDS Hosp., Idaho Falls, Idaho, 1959-63; pub. health nurse Salt Lake City Health Dept., 1963-64; staff nurse

LDS Hosp., Salt Lake City, 1964-68; instr. nursing Brigham Young U., Provo, 1965-67, asst. prof., 1970-83; assoc. prof., dir. nursing SEMO U., Cape Girardeau, Mo., 1983-85; assoc. prof. Brigham Young U., 1985-96; founder, pres. Wellness Consultation and Edn. Inc., Richfield, Utah, 1992—; pres. Psychiat. Rehab. Nurses Inc., Nine Mile Falls, Wash.; co-founder Three R's Wellness Program for psychiatric rehab.; founder, adminstr. Adelaide's House, Richfield. Author: (with others) How to Enter the World of Psychosis, 1994, Recovering from Psychosis; A Wellness Approach, 1996, My Symptom Management Workbook: A Wellness Expedition, 1996. Coach Payson Youth Soccer Program, 1990-93; mem. Sevier County Planning Com., Utah Coalition for Aging and Mental Health. Mem. ANA, Am. Psychiatric Nurses Assn., Soc. Edn. and Rsch. Psychiatric Nursing, Utah Psycho-Social Nursing Orgn. (pres., chair 1988-92), Utah Coun. Psychiatric Nurses (pres. 1997—), Phi Kappa Phi, Sigma Theta Tau, Sigma Xi. Mem. LDS Ch. Avocations: family history, genealogy, travel. Home: PO Box 13 Richfield UT 84701-0013

MURPHY, PHILIP EDWARD, broadcast executive; b. Chgo., May 11, 1945; s. Edward Curtis and Mary Francis (D'Incecco) M.; m. Carol Jean Sefton, Mar. 11, 1967 (div. 1985); children: Mandy Jean, Patrick Jeffrey; life ptnr. Robert G. McCracken, 1985—. BS, Ind. U., 1967. Prodn. mgr. Sta. WFIU-FM, Bloomington, Ind., 1968; news reporter, photographer, editor Sta. WTHR-TV, Indpls., 1969, sr. account exec., 1970-80; acct. exec. Blair TV, L.A., 1980-81; pres. Am. Spot Cable Corp., Hollywood, Calif., 1981-82; sr. v.p. TV group ops., overseer asset protection program Paramount Pictures, Hollywood, 1982—; responsible for tech. preparation and distbn. material provided to worldwide electronic ancillary markets United Paramount Network Ops.; spkr. film preservation, in field; advisor Libr. of Congress, Washington, Nat. Archives, Washington. Lighting designer Civic Theatre, Indpls., 1979; tech. dir. Footlite Mus., Indpls., 1970-78; bd. dirs. Cathedral Arts, Indpls., 1978-80. Mem. Assn. Moving Image Archivists, Human Rights Campaign (Washington), Gay and Lesbian Alliance Against Defamation L.A., Hollywood Supports Assn., Soc. Motion Picture and TV Engrs. Avocations: photography, videography, audio, theatre. Office: Paramount Pictures TV Stage 3/212 5555 Melrose Ave Los Angeles CA 90038-3197

MURPHY, RONDO A., retired sales professional; b. Nampa, Idaho, Dec. 21, 1933; s. Thomas Hugh and Iona (Williams) M.; m. Peggy Murphy, June 5, 1958 (div.); 1 child, Clynn R.; m. Nancy Lee Peake, Oct. 17, 1964; children: David, Tracey, Ronda, Yvette, Collette, Tarea. AA, Ricks Coll., 1958; student, U. Utah, 1963-64. Lic. real estate agt., Utah; lic. life ins. agt., Idaho. Sales and mgmt. positions Hall-Perry Machinery Co., Great Falls, Mont., 1958-63; salesman Western Rd. Machinery Co., Salt Lake City, 1964-69; v.p., gen. mgr. Wyo. Equipment Co., Casper, 1969-70; salesman Scott Machinery Co., Salt Lake City, 1970-75, SKI Equipment Co., Salt Lake City, 1976-78, Professional Investment Co., Salt Lake City, 1978-81; rancher Grantsville (Utah) Land & Livestock, 1982-86; asst. supt. McDivitt & Street Co., Charlotte, N.C., 1986-89; ticket sales agt. Disneyland, Anaheim, Calif., 1990-94. Author: Relativity of Knowledge, 1976, Bible Relativity, 1998. Sgt. USAF, 1952-56, Korea. Mem. Lions. Avocations: spectator sports, basketball, football, volleyball, golf. Home: 3050 W Ball Rd Spc 18 Anaheim CA 92804-3847

MURRAY, ALICE PEARL, data processing company executive; b. Clearfield, Pa., Aug. 4, 1932; d. James Clifford and Leah Mae (Williams) M.; BS, Pa. State U., 1954. With IBM, 1954—, systems svc. rep., Pitts., 1954-56, computer test ctr. rep., Endicott, N.Y., 1956-58, edn. devel. coord., Endicott, 1958-59, adv. instr., L.A., 1959-63, staff instr., L.A., 1963-68, exec. edn. coord., 1968-74, sr. instr. Info. Systems Mgmt. Inst., L.A., 1974-84, sr. edn. rep. IBM Americas Far East Corp., 1984-87; sr. staff mem. customer exec. edn., 1989; cons., 1990-95; ind. cons., 1995—; coord. exhibit Calif. State Mus. Sci. and Industry; guest speaker before civic and profl. groups; guest instr. various univs. and colls.; profl. lectr. Recipient Distinguished Educator award IBM, 1974, also Outstanding Professionalism award, 1975; hon. citizen Tex., Alaska. Mem. Los Angeles County Art Mus., Pa. State Alumni Assn., Wilshire Country Club, Assistance League of So. Calif., L.A. Libr. Found., Delta Delta Delta. Republican. Home and Office: 514 S Gramercy Pl Los Angeles CA 90020-4969

MURRAY, DONALD EUGENE, plastic surgeon; b. Dillon, Mont., May 30, 1937; s. Ned Charles and Ruth Adelaide (McFarland) M.; m. Charla Leavens Murray, June 18, 1961; children: Thomas Allan, Carol Ann. BS in Quantitative Biology, MIT, 1959; MD, Stanford Sch. of Medicine, 1964. Diplomate Am. Bd. Plastic Surgery, Nat. Bd. Med. Examiners; lic. Mont. Straight surgery internship Palo Alto-Stanford Med. Ctr., Calif., 1964-65; asst. resident gen. surgery Stanford U. Sch. of Medicine, Palo Alto, Calif., 1965-66, fellow in rehabilitaion surgery, 1966-67, resident gen. surgery, 1967-68, chief resident plastic and reconstructive surgery, 1969-70; chief resident gen. surgery San Mateo Gen. Hosp./Stanford U. Sch. of Medicine, Calif., 1968; chief resident head and neck surgery Roswell Park Meml. Inst., Buffalo, N.Y., 1969; fellow plastic and reconstructive surgery Royal Melbourne Hosp., Australia, 1970-71; honorary plastic and reconstructive surgeon Middlemore Hosp., Auckland, New Zealand, 1971; pvt. practice Missoula, Mont., 1971—; chief of surgery Missoula Cmty. Hosp., 1974, St. Patrick's Hosp., 1977; trainee in VRA summer Clin. Tng. Program Rehab. Medicine Stanford Med. Ctr., 1962; clin. clk. St. Thomas' Hosp. Cardiovasc. Surgery, London, England, 1963; mem. Mont. State Comprehensive Health Planning Coun., Mont. Fedn. for Med. Care (instl. rev. steering com. 1976-86, bd. dirs. 1982-88), Mont. Physicians' Svc. Adjudication Com., 1979, Mont. Medicare Adv. Com., 1992-95; surgery com. Missoula Cmty. Hosp., 1973, 86, surgery com. St. Patrick's Hosp., 1975-78, 88-89, pres. elect med. staff, 1981, pres. med. staff, 1982, quality assurance com., 1981 (chmn. 1983), by-laws revision com., 1985; chmn. Health Facilities Com. State of Mont. Dept. of Health & Environ. Scis., 1973-75, credentials com. St. Patrick's Hosp., 1986-88; faculty affiliate Dept. Comm. Sci. & Disorders U. Mont., 1975-90; adv. com. Missoula Tech. Ctr., 1977; orgnl. com. Mont. Health Sys. Agy., 1977; burn chmn. Western Mont. Emergency Med. Svcs. Coun., 1978; assoc. mem. Am. Soc. of Clin. Hypnosis, 1982. Mem. Missoula Symphony Assn. (bd. dirs. 1980-87, pres. 1986). Fellow ACS (com. on applicants 1980—); mem. AMA, Am. Soc. of Plastic and Reconstructive Surgeons (annotated bibliography com. 1979-82), Am. Cleft Palate Assn., Northwest Soc. of Plastic Surgeons, Rocky Mountain Assn. of Plastic and Reconstructive Surgeons (nominating com. 1979, pres. elect 1989, pres. 1990), Mont. Cleft Palate Assn. (pres. 1974), Mont. Med. Assn. (joint med. legal panel 1976-78, malpractice panel 1978, profl. liability com. 1980-86), Western Mont. Med. Soc. (v.p. 1974, pres. elect 1975, pres. 1976). Avocations: skiing, mountain bike riding, classical music. Office: 614 W Spruce St Missoula MT 59802-4002

MURRAY, JAMES ALAN, urban and environmental consultant, investor; b. Evansville, Ind., Oct. 2, 1942; s. William Dewey and Dorothy Marie (Gleason) M.; BS, U. N.Mex., 1964; MBA, Harvard U., 1969; MA (NDEA fellow), U. Oreg., 1971, PhD, 1972; children: Heidi Lynn, Paul Alan, Kendra Leigh. Dir. fin. City of Boulder (Colo.), 1972-73, dir. adminstrv. svcs., 1973-74; v.p. Briscoe, Maphis, Murray & Lamont, Inc., Boulder, 1974-78, pres., 1978-84, also dir.; dir. fin. City and County of Denver, 1984-86, chief exec. officer, 1986-87, asst. to mayor, 1987-89; pres., dir. Murray Lamont & Assocs., Inc., 1990-98; pres., dir. Colo. Scientific Investments, Inc., 1993-96; chmn. Lanzhou Murray Clothing Co., China, 1994-95, Lanzhou Murray Electronics Co., Ltd., China, 1995—; adj. assoc. prof. Grad. Sch. Public Affairs, U. Colo., Boulder, 1972-80, Denver, 1985-91. Mem. open space adv. com. City of Boulder, 1972-74; bd. dirs. Met. Denver Sewage Authority, 1984-85; Colo. Baseball Commn., 1989-93. Mem. ASPA, Am. Econ. Assn., Western Econ. Assn., Water Pollution Control Fedn., Denver Athletic Club, Kappa Mu Epsilon, Pi Alpha Alpha. Home: 99 S Downing St Apt 602 Denver CO 80209-2407

MURRAY, JEAN RUPP, communications executive, author; b. Portland, Oreg., Aug. 29, 1943; d. Edward Howard and Dorothy Eugenia (Ross) Brown. BA in English, Portland State U., 1965. Cert. tchr., Oreg. Tchr., dept. head Beaverton (Oreg.) Sch. Dist., 1967-88; pres., founder Write Communications, Portland, 1988—; adj. faculty Portland C.C., Concordia U., Portland State U.; nat. trainer, cons.State of Oreg., City of Portland, Nike, Inc., Oreg. Health Scis. U., Oreg. Mil. Acad., Oreg. Fin. Instns. Assn., Freightliner, Automated Data Processing, others, 1988—; spkr. Tektronix, Fred Meyer, Pacific Power, Am. Inst. of Banking, Utah Power, Pacific Telecom, Inc., other; writing dir. U.S. Army C.E., USDA Forest Svcs., PacifiCare, others, 1989-90. Author: Flawless Grammar at Your Fingertips: An Instant Guide to Perfect Grammar for Everybody in Business, 1994; TV appearances include Stas. KATU-TV and KGW-TV. Vol. Dove Lewis Emergency Vet. Clinic, Portland, 1989—, Doerbecher Children's Hosp., Oreg. Humane Soc. Mem. ASTD, Oreg. Speakers Assn. (pres. bd. dirs. 1997—), Nat. Speakers Assn., Ctr. for Marine Conservation. Republican. Avocations: target-shooting, travel, animal. E-mail: http://www.paws4thoughts.com. Office: Write Comm 14657 SW Teal Blvd # 200 Beaverton OR 97007-6194

MURRAY, KATHLEEN ELLEN, writer; b. Chgo., Feb. 23, 1946; d. John Joseph and Marie Agnes (Stoltzman) M.; B.A., Calif. State U., Sacramento, 1973; A.A., Am. River Coll., 1968. File clk. Allstate Ins. Co., Sacramento, 1964-66; clk. typist Calif. Hwy. Patrol, Sacramento, 1968-69; copy editor Sacramento Bee, 1971-95; instr. Calif. State U., Sacramento, 1975-76. Newspaper Fund intern, scholar, 1971. Home: PO Box 606 Nevada City CA 95959-0606

MURRAY, MICHAEL KENT, lawyer; b. Missoula, Mont., Feb. 14, 1948; s. Paul R. and Virginia F. Murray; m. Jennifer C. Pinkerton, Apr. 16, 1983; children: Britton M., Spencer J. BA, U. Calif., Santa Barbara, 1970; JD, U. Santa Clara, 1974. Bar: Wash. 1974, U.S. Ct. Claims 1975, U.S. Tax Ct. 1976, U.S. Dist. Ct. Wash. 1977, U.S. Ct. Appeals (fed. cir.) 1982. Trial atty. honor law grad. program U.S. Dept. Justice, Washington, 1974-76; atty. Foster Pepper & Riviera, Seattle, 1976-79; ptnr. Foster Pepper & Riviera, Seattle and Bellevue, 1980-86; ptnr.-in-charge Foster Pepper & Riviera, Bellevue, 1983-86; atty., pres. Michael K. Murray, P.S., Seattle, 1986—; pres. N.W. Properties Devel. Corp., Seattle, 1986-92; of counsel Lasher Holzapfel Sperry & Ebberson, Seattle, 1992—. Articles editor Santa Clara Lawyer, U. Santa Clara Sch. Law, 1973-74. Trustee Pacific Northwest Ballet, Seattle, 1979-81; dir. Bellevue Downtown Assn., 1984-87. Mem. Wash. State Bar Assn., King County Bar Assn., Seattle Yacht Club, Seattle Tennis Club. Avocations: sailing, fly fishing, biking, computing. Home: 1570 9th Ave N Edmonds WA 98020-2627 Office: Lasher Holzapfel Sperry & Ebberson 601 Union St Ste 2600 Seattle WA 98101-2302

MURRAY, PATTY, senator; b. Bothell, Wash., Oct. 10, 1950; d. David L. and Beverly A. (McLaughlin) Johns; m. Robert R. Murray, June 2, 1972; children: Randy P., Sara A. BA, Wash. State U., 1972. Sec. various cos., Seattle, 1972-76; citizen lobbyist various ednl. groups, Seattle, 1983-88; legis. lobbyist Orgn. for Parent Edn., Seattle, 1977-84; instr. Shoreline Community Coll., Seattle, 1984—; mem. Wash. State Senate, Seattle, 1989-92, U.S. Senate, Washington, 1993—; mem. Appropriations Com. ranking minority mem. subcom. mil. constrn.; vice chmn. Senate Dem. Policy Com.; mem. Com. on Labor and Human Resources, Budget Com., Senate Dem. Tech. and Comms. Com., Com. on Vets. Affairs. Mem. bd. Shoreline Sch., Seattle, 1985-89; mem. steering com. Demonstration for Edn., Seattle, 1987; founder, chmn. Orgn. for Parent Edn., Wash., 1981-85; 1st Congl. rep. Wash. Women United, 1983-85. Recipient Recognition of Svc. to Children award Shoreline PTA Coun., 1986, Golden Acorn Svc. award, 1989; Outstanding Svc. award Wash. Women United, 1986, Outstanding Svc. to Pub. Edn. award Citizens Ednl. Ctr. NW, Seattle, 1987. Democrat. Office: US Senate 111 Russell Senate Office Bldg Washington DC 20510-4704*

MURRAY TUXILL, SUZANNE, accountant; b. Frankfurt, Germany, Aug. 12, 1970; (parents Am. citizens); d. Peter A. and Suzanne Marie (Falzo) M.; married, May 31, 1997. BBA in Acctg., Siena Coll., 1992. CPA, N.Y., Tex. Assoc. acct. Bollam Sheedy Torani & Co., LLP, Albany, N.Y., 1992-95, Margolis & Co., PC, Bala Cynwyd, Pa., 1995-96; sr. fin. analyst Morven Ptnrs. LP, Dallas, 1996-97; sr. acct. E Entertainment TV, L.A., 1997—. Asst. vol. Arsenal City Run, Watervliet, N.Y., 1992-93. Mem. Inst. Mgmt. Accts. (dir. student activities Albany chpt. 1994-95, mem. pub. rels. com. Phila. chpt. 1995—). Home: 12412 Texas Ave # 303 Los Angeles CA 90025-1963 Office: El Entertainment TV 5670 Wilshire Blvd Los Angeles CA 90036-5679

MUSGRAVE, CHARLES EDWARD, retired music director, correctional official; b. Alton, Ill., Nov. 17, 1932; s. Clay Everett and Fannie Adeline (Peek) M.; m. Barbara Jean Robertson, Aug. 11, 1952 (div. Feb. 1971); children: Michael David, Debra Ann; m. Toby Elaine Riley, Aug. 18, 1973. B in Mus. Edn., Shurtleff Coll., 1954; MS, U. Ill., 1957; postgrad., U. No. Colo., 1970. Cert. tchr., Ill., Ind. Tchr. music Alton (Ill.) Pub. Schs., 1953-67; v.p. Monticello Coll., Godfrey, Ill., 1967-69; asst. to v.p. U. No. Colo., Greeley, 1970; chmn. dept. music Duneland Sch. Corp., Chesterton, Ind., 1970-72; dir. devel. Interlochen (Mich.) Arts Acad., 1972-73; v.p. Musart Corp., Chgo., 1973-74; dir. music and coll. coord. Ind. State Prison, Michigan City, 1974-95; ret., 1995; assoc. dir. music Willowbrook Meth. Ch., Sun City, Ariz., 1996—; condr. Sun City (Ariz.) Concert Band, 1997—; mem., asst. condr. Salt River Brass Band, Phoenix, 1997—; condr. Renaissance Brass Band, Sun City, Az., 1997—; vice chmn. La Porter Fed. Credit Union, Michigan City, 1975-96; facility coordinator adult continuing edn. Ind. U. Author: Fussell's Individual Technique Guide, 1973, (music) Why Only on Christmas, 1981. Rep. committeeman, Chesterton, 1976-95, del. to state conv., Ind., 1978-89; mem. Porter County (Ind.) Planning Commn., 1984-85; chmn. govt. workers sect. United Way, Michigan City, 1981-90; mem. Ind. Gov.'s Adv. Com., 1983; minister of music 1st United Meth. Ch., Chesterton, 1978-91; bd. dirs. Five Lakes Conservation Club, Wolcottville, Ind., 1983-95; bd. dirs., v.p. Valparaiso Cmty. Concerts Assn., 1986-95. Grantee Systems Mgmt. U. W. Va., U. Chgo., 1979. Mem. Correctional Edn. Assn. (Internat. Tchr. of Yr. 1981), Ind. Soc. Chgo., LaGrange Country Club, Masons, Shriners, Scottish Rite, Phi Delta Kappa. Avocations: golf, photography, computers. Home: 9815 Evergreen Dr Sun City AZ 85373-2169 also: 7230 S 175 E Wolcottville IN 46795-9590

MUSICH, ROBERT LORIN, motivational speaker; b. Glendale, Calif., Feb. 15, 1969; s. Richard and Zola (Nickel) M. BA, La Salle U., M. Sr. asst. mgr. Am. Gen. Fin., Upland, Calif., 1988-89; mgmt./corp. trainer Mortgage Link, Pasadena, 1989-94; mgr. AT&T, L.A., 1994-96; owner Musich & Assocs., West Covina, Calif., 1989—. Singer (tenor) So. Calif. Mormon Choir, 1994—; cand. Calif. State Assembly, 59th Dist., 1995; vol. Am. Cancer Soc., 1994-96; coach Youth League Football, 1987-92; elder's quorum pres. LDS Ch., sec., 1992-93, 2d and 1st counselor, 1995-96, mem. stake single adult com., 1993-95, mem. regional single adult com. bi-regional chmn., 1993-95. Republican. Avocations: singing, dancing, theatre, volleyball, football. Office: Musich and Associates 3447 E Hillhaven Dr West Covina CA 91791-1718

MUSIHIN, KONSTANTIN K., electrical engineer; b. Harbin, China, June 17, 1927; s. Konstantin N. and Alexandra A. (Lapitsky) M.; m. Natalia Krilova, Oct. 18, 1964; 1 child, Nicholas; came to U.S., 1967, naturalized, 1973; student YMCA Inst., 1942, North Manchurian U., 1945, Harbin Poly. Inst., 1948. Registered profl. engr., Calif., N.Y., Pa., Wash. Asst. prof. Harbin Poly. Inst., 1950-53; elec. engr. Moinho Santista, Sao Paulo, Brazil, 1955-60; constrn. project mgr. Caterpillar-Brazil, Santo Amaro, 1960-61; mech. engr. Matarazzo Industries, Sao Paulo, 1961-62; chief of works Vidrobras, St. Gobain, Brazil, 1962-64; project engr. Brown Boveri, Sao Paulo, 1965-67; sr. engr. Kaiser Engrs., Oakland, Calif., 1967-73; sr. engr. Bechtel Power Corp., San Francisco, 1973-75; supr. power and control San Francisco Bay Area Rapid Transit, Oakland, 1976-78; chief elec. engr. L.K. Comstock Engring. Co., San Francisco, 1978-79; prin. engr. Morrison Knudsen Co., San Francisco, 1979-84; prin. engr. Brown and Caldwell, Cons. Engrs., Pleasant Hill, Calif., 1984-85; cons. engr. Pacific Gas and Electric Co., San Francisco, 1986-89; sr. engr. Bechtel Corp., San Francisco, 1989—. Mem. IEEE (sr.), Nat., Calif. socs. profl. engrs., Instituto de Engenharia de Sao Paulo. Mem. Christian Orthodox Ch. Home: 5666 Ocean View Dr Oakland CA 94618-1533

MUSMANN, KLAUS, librarian; b. Magdeburg, Germany, June 27, 1935; came to U.S., 1957; s. Ernst Hans and Eva (Grunow) M.; m. Gladys H. Arakawa, June 15, 1963 (div. 1973); children: Carlton, Michelle; m. Lois Geneva Steele, Dec. 27, 1986. BA, Wayne State U., 1962; MALS, U. Mich., 1963; MA, Mich. State U., 1967; PhD, U. So. Calif., 1981. Libr. Detroit Pub. Libr., 1962-65; asst. serials libr. Mich. State U., East Lansing, 1965-67; head of acquisitions Los Angeles County Law Libr., L.A., 1968-84; coll. devel. libr. U. Redlands, Calif., 1984—, acting dir., 1994-96, dir., 1996—. Author: Helen and Vernon Farquhar Collection: A Bibliography, 1987, Diffusion of Innovations, 1989, Technological Innovations in Libraries, 1850-1950, 1993; contbr. articles to profl. jours. Grantee Coun. on Libr. Resources, 1990. Mem. ALA, Assn. Coll. and Rsch. Librs., Soc. for History of Tech., Fortnightly Club. Avocations: photography, travel. Home: 220 W Highland Ave Redlands CA 92373-6768 Office: Univ of Redlands Redlands CA 92374

MUSSEHL, ROBERT CLARENCE, lawyer; b. Washington, May 1, 1936; s. Chester Carl and Clara Cecelia (Greenwalt) Mussehl; children: Debra Lee, David Lee, Omar Chung; spouse: Misook Chung, Mar. 22, 1987. BA, Am. U., 1964, JD, 1966. Bar: Wash. 1967, U.S. Dist. Ct. (we. dist.) Wash. 1967, U.S. Ct. Appeals (9th cir.) 1968, U.S Supreme Ct. 1971. Sr. ptnr. Thom, Mussehl, Navoni, Hoff, Pierson & Ryder, Seattle, 1967-78, Neubauer & Mussehl, Seattle, 1978-80, Mussehl & Rosenberg, Seattle, 1980—; speaker law convs. and other profl. orgns.; moot ct. judge Nat. Appelate Advocacy Competition, San Francisco, 1987; panel mem. ABA Symposium on Compulsory Jurisdiction of World Ct., San Francisco, 1987; chmn. bd., chief exec. officer The Seattle Smashers profl. volleyball club, 1976-80. Contbr. numerous articles to legal pubs. Mem. Wash. Vol. Lawyers for Arts, 1976-80; statewide chair Lawyers for Durning for Gov., 1976; mem. task force on the single adult and Ch. Ch. Coun. Greater Seattle, 1976-78; bd. dirs. Wash. State Pub. Interest Law Ctr., 1976-81; founder, immediate past chair Lawyers Helping Hungry Children campaign, Wash. State Lawyers Campaign for Hunger Relief, 1991—. Recipient Jefferson award for pub. svc. State of Wash., 1997. Fellow Am. Bar Found., Am. Acad. Matrimonial Lawyers; mem. ABA (ho. of dels. 1979-91, spl. adv. com. on internat. activities 1989-91, chair marriage and family counseling and conciliation com. family law sect. 1981-83, mem. world order under law standing com. 1983-89, chair, 1986-89, chair ad hoc com. on the assembly 1986-89, mem. assembly resolutions com. 1979-91, mem. blue ribbon com. for world ct. 1987-88, mem. standing com. on dispute resolution, 1992-93; exec. coun. sect. dispute resolution 1993-95, asst. budget officer, 1995-97, budget officer 1997—, Achievement award), Wash. State Bar Assn. (exec. com. family law sect. 1973-75, chmn. internat. law com. 1974-76, sec.-treas., exec. com. world peace through law sect. 1980—, chair 1981-82, mem. edit. bd. Family Law Deskbook 1987-89), Wash. State Trial Lawyers Assn., Seattle-King County Bar Assn. (family law sect. 1971-90, other coms. 1970—, chmn. young lawyers sect. 1971-72, sec. 1972-73, trustee), Am. Arbitration Assn. (panel arbitrators), World Assn. Lawyers of World Peace Through Law Ctr. (founding mem.), Heritage Club YMCA Greater Seattle (charter 1977—), UN Assn. U.S.A. (bd. dirs. Seattle chpt. 1989-91). Avocations: biking, tennis, weight training, painting, religious studies. Home: One Pacific Tower 2000 1st Ave Apt 902 Seattle WA 98121-2167 Office: 1111 3rd Ave Ste 2626 Seattle WA 98101-3219

MUSTACCHI, PIERO, physician, educator; b. Cairo, May 29, 1920; came to U.S., 1947; naturalized, 1962; s. Gino and Gilda (Rieti) M.; m. Dora Lisa Ancona, Sept. 26, 1948; children: Roberto, Michael. BS in Humanities, U. Florence, Italy, 1938; postgrad. in anatomy, Eleve Interne, U. Lausanne, Switzerland, 1938-39; MB, ChB, Fouad I U., Cairo, Egypt, 1944, grad. in Arabic lang. and lit., 1946; D Medicine and Surgery, U. Pisa, 1986; D Honoris Causa, U. Aix-Marseilles, France, 1988; hon. degree, U. Alexandria, Egypt, 1985. Qualified med. examiner, Calif. Indsl. Accident Commn., 1994. House officer English Hosp., Ch. Missionary Soc., Cairo, Egypt, 1945-47; clin. affiliate U. Calif., San Francisco, 1947-48; intern Franklin Hosp., San Francisco, 1948-49; resident in pathology U. Calif., San Francisco, 1949-51; resident in medicine Meml. Ctr. Cancer and Allied Diseases, N.Y.C., 1951-53; rsch. epidemiologist Dept. HEW, Nat. Cancer Inst., Bethesda, Md., 1955-57; cons. allergy clinic U. Calif., San Francisco, 1957-70, clin. prof. medicine and preventive medicine, 1970-90, clin. prof. medicine and epidemiology, 1990-96, head occupl. epidemiology, 1975-90, head divsn. internat. health edn. dept. epidemiology and internat. health, 1985-90; médecin agréé, official physician Consulate Gen. of France, San Fransisco, 1995—; med. cons., vis. prof. numerous edn. and profl. instns., including U. Marseilles, 1981, 82, U. Pisa, Italy, 1983, U. Gabon, 1984, U. Siena, Italy, 1985, work clinic U. Calif., 1975-84, Ctr for Rehab. and Occupl. Health U. Calif., San Francisco, 1984-93; cons. numerous worldwide govtl. agys.; ofcl. physician French Consulate Gen., San Francisco, 1995. Contbr. chpts. to books, articles to profl. jours. Editorial bd. Medecine d'Afrique Noire, Ospedali d'Italia. Served with USN, USPHS, 1953-55. Decorated Order of Merit (Commander) (Italy), Ordre de la Legion d'Honneur (France), Medal of St. John of Jerusalem, Sovereign Order of Malta, Order of the Republic (Egypt); Scroll, Leonardo da Vinci Soc., San Francisco, 1965; award Internat. Inst. Oakland, 1964; Hon. Vice Consul. Italy, 1971-90. Fellow ACP, Am. Soc. Environ. and Occupational Health; mem. AAAS, Am. Assn. Cancer Rsch., Calif. Soc. Allergy and Immunology, Calif. Med. Assn., San Francisco Med. Soc., West Coast Allergy Soc. (founding), Mex. Congress on Hypertension (corr.), Internat. Assn. Med. Rsch. and Continuing Edn. (U.S. rep.), Acad. Italiana della Cucina. Democrat. Avocations: mathematics, music, languages. Home: 3344 Laguna St San Francisco CA 94123-2208 Office: U Calif Parnassus Ave San Francisco CA 94143 also: 3838 California St San Francisco CA 94118-1522

MUTSCHLER, HERBERT FREDERICK, retired librarian; b. Eureka, S.D., Nov. 28, 1919; s. Frederick and Helena (Oster) M.; m. Lucille I. Gross, Aug. 18, 1945; 1 dau., Linda M. B.A., Jamestown Coll., 1947; M.A., Western Res. U., 1949, M.S., 1952. Tchr. history high sch. Lemmon, S.D., 1947-48; asst. librarian Royal Oak (Mich.) Libr., 1952-55; head librarian Hamtramck (Mich.) Libr., 1955-56; head public svcs. Wayne County Libr. System, Wayne, Mich., 1956-59; asst. county librarian Wayne County Libr. System, 1960-62; dir. King County Libr. System, Seattle, 1963-89; library bldg. cons. Wayne County Libr., 1956-62, Wash. State Libr., 1966—; cons. Salt Lake County Libr., Pierce County Libr., North Olympic Libr.; lectr. U. Wash. Sch. Librarianship, 1970-71; bldg. cons. Hoquiam (Wash.) Libr., Olympic (Wash.) Regional Libr., Camas (Wash.) Pub. Libr., N. Cen. (Wash.) Regional Libr., Spokane (Wash.) County Libr., Enumclaw (Wash.) Libr., Puyallup (Wash.) Pub. Libr., Kennewick (Wash.) Pub. Libr., Lopez Island (Wash.) Libr. Contbr. articles profl. jours. Mem. Foss Home and Village Bd. Trustees, 1989—; bd. dirs. King County Libr. Sys. Found. With AUS, 1941-45; to capt. 1950-52. Decorated Silver Star, Bronze Star with cluster, Purple Heart, Presdl. Unit Citation. Mem. ALA (councilor at large 1965-69, chpt. councilor 1971-75, pres. library adminstrv. div. 1974-75), Pacific N.W. Library Assn., Wash. Library Assn. (exec. bd. 1964-65, 69-71, pres. 1967-69). Republican. Lutheran. Club: City, Municipal League. Lodge: Kiwanis. Home: 5300 128th Ave SE Bellevue WA 98006-2952

MYBECK, RICHARD RAYMOND, lawyer; b. Chgo., Dec. 5, 1928; s. Walter Raymond and Genevieve Lucille (Carlsten) M.; m. Betty Jane Engle, Aug. 23, 1952; children: Walter R. II, Wendy Sue, Lucinda Jeanne, Amanda Jane (dec.), Candace Christine, Sara Melinda. BChE, Purdue U., 1950, BS in Engring. Law, 1953; JD, Ind. U., 1953. Bar: Ind. 1953, Wis. 1954, Ill. 1962, Ariz. 1973; registered U.S. patent atty., patent agt., Can. Patent trainee, atty. Allis Chalmers Mfg. Co., West Allis, Wis., 1953-57, patent atty., 1957-62; atty. Koehring Corp., Milw., 1957; patent atty. Armour and Co., Chgo., 1962-71; sr. patent atty. Greyhound Corp., Chgo., Phoenix, 1971-77; sr. counsel Armour Pharmaceutical Co., Phoenix, Scottsdale, Ariz., 1977-81; pvt. practice Scottsdale, 1981—; pres., bd. dirs. Farmakeia, Inc., Scottsdale, Hoosier Investment Co., Scottsdale; dir. Ariz. State Rsch. Inst., 1988-97. Councilman Town of Paradise Valley, Ariz., 1988-92, commr., chmn. planning and zoning commn., 1981-88, mem. chmn. bd. adjustment, 1974-81; lay speaker United Meth. Ch., 1954—. Named to Hall of Fame Oak Park (Ill.) Youth Baseball, 1987; recipient Degentesh award Forest Park (Ill.) VFW, 1969. Mem. ABA, Ariz. Bar Assn. (chmn. various sects.), Ill. Bar Assn., Wis. Bar Assn., Intellectual Property Assn. Chgo., Ariz. Patent Law Assn., Purdue Alumni Assn. (dir. region 15 1993-95), Culver Legion, Ind. U. Alumni Assn., Elks, Masons, Tau Kappa Epsilon, Sigma Delta Kappa. Methodist. E-mail: Richard.Mybeck@azbar.org. Fax: (602) 483-7452. Home: 4901 E Tomahawk Trl Paradise Vly AZ 85253-2030 Office: 8010 E Morgan Trl Ste 10 Scottsdale AZ 85258-1234

MYCUE, EDWARD, writer, publisher, editor, book seller; b. Niagara Falls, N.Y., Mar. 21, 1937; s. John Powers and Ruth Agnes (Taylor) M. AS in Pre-Law, Arlington State Jr. Coll., 1957; BA, North Tex. State U., 1959, postgrad., 1959-60; postgrad., Boston U., 1960-61. Rsch. asst. dept. polit. sci. North Tex. State U., 1958, teaching fellow in govt., 1959-60; endl. TV

programming intern Sta. WGBH-TV, Boston, 1960-61; cons. intergovernmental personnel rels. U.S. Dept. Health, Edn., and Welfare, Washington, 1962-68; freelance writer, traveling lectr. Europe, 1968-70; assoc. mgr., pub. Panjandrum Books and Press, 1972-76; asst. mgr. bookshops and publs. dept. Fine Arts Mus. San Francisco, 1976-81; book buyer Grace Cathedral Book Shop, San Francisco, 1981-94; pub. Norton-Coker Press, Took mag., Took Modern Poetry, 1988—; tchr. high sch., asst. headmaster Acherensua Secondary Sch., U.S. Peace Corps., Ghana, 1961.; instr. Am. lit. Internat. People's Coll., Denmark, 1969; instr. writing program Folsom Prison, 1972-73; MacDowell Colony fellow writer-in-residence Peterborough (N.H.) High Sch., 1974. Author: (poetry) Her Children Come Home Too, 1972, Damage Within The Community, 1973, Chronicle, 1974, Root, Route & Range, 1977, Root, Route & Range: The Song Returns, 1979, The Singing Man My Father Gave Me, 1980, Edward, 1987, Unity, 1987, Grate Country, 1988, No One For Free, 1988, The Torn Star (A Vision), 1988, Next Year's Words, 1989, Pink Garden, Brown Trees, 1990, No One 6, 1991, Idolino, 1991, Life Is Built From The Inside Out, 1993, Because We Speak the Same Language, 1995, Nights Boats, 1999, works pub. in (anthologies) The Male Muse, 1973, 14 Voices, 1975, For David Gascoyne, 1981, Poly, 1989, Round Glow of Family Nest,1989, How The Net Is Gripped, 1992, Rhysling Anthology, 1992, Terminal Velocities, 1993; contbr poetry to Akros, Arenaria, Backspace, Bellingham Rev., Berleley Poetry Review, Contact II, Detail, European Judaism, Five Leaves Left, Grasslands, Green's Mag., Hammers, Heaven Bone, Hippycore, Industrial Sabatoge/Curvd H&2, Il Segnale, James White Review, Krax, La Broca, Fuel, LINQ, Matilda, Meanjin, Mensuel, New York Quarterly, La Carta de Qliver, Nicolau, Poetry South, Poetry Ireland Review, Barddoni, Caliban, Carbuncle, Cups, Oxygen, Exquisite Corpse, Midwest Quarterly, EOTU, Echo Room, Antigonish Review, Fuel, Le Miracle Tatoue, Frank, Euthanesia Roses, Plain Brown Wrapper, Riverside Quarterly, Outrigger, Pearl, My Favorite Sentence, Panjandrum, Beyond Baroque, Tight, Talisman, Xavier Review, Xizquil, Villiage Idiot, Wyoming, Hub of the Wheel, Capilano Review, Wallace Stevens Jour., Washington Review, Stand. MacDowell Colony fellow Peterborough, N.H., 1974, Lowell Inst. fellow Boston, 1960-61. Mem. PEN. Home and Office: PO Box 640543 San Francisco CA 94164-0543

MYERS, CHARLOTTE WILL, biology educator; b. Harbor Beach, Mich., Jan. 5, 1930; d. Louis John and Ruth (Sageman) Wills; m. John Jay Myers, Dec. 27, 1958; children: Sandra, Andrew, Susan Ruth. BA in Biology, U. Mich., 1951, MS in Edn., 1952. Tchr. biology Birmingham (Mich.) Pub. Schs., 1952-59; tchr. art pvt. practice, Birmingham, 1962-78, Santa Fe, 1979—; instr. Oakland U. , Pontiac, Mich., 1975-77; demonstrator, coord. Internat. Porcelain Art Teaching, Birmingham and Santa Fe, 1972—. V.p. PTA, Birmingham, 1957; founder Future Tchrs., Birmingham, 1956; area chmn. Muscular Dystrophy, Birmingham, 1963-64; leader Girl Scouts Am., Birmingham, 1969-71. Mem. N.Mex. State Fedn. Porcelain Artists (sec. 1986—), Mich. China Painting Tchrs. Orgn. (pres. 1973-77), Rocky Mountain Outdoor Writers & Photographers (bd. dirs. 1995—), Internat. Porcelain Arts Tchrs., Artists Equity (treas. 1981-83), Porcelain Arts Club (pres. 1979-81, treas. 1987-89). Democrat. Presbyterian. Avocations: gardening, needlework, travel. Home and Office: 9 Cibola Cir Santa Fe NM 87505-9006

MYERS, CINDY L., museum director. Exec. dir. Phoenix Mus. History, 1996—. Office: Phoenix Mus History 105 N 5th St Phoenix AZ 85004-4404*

MYERS, CLAUDIA BOLES, educational foundation executive; b. Nashville, Aug. 15, 1952; d. Claude C. and Marilyn (Davis) Boles; m. Richard J. Myers, May 25, 1974; children: Megan Coleen, Lauren Mary. B in Social Work, U. Kans., 1974, M in Social Work, 1975. Sch. social worker Shawnee Mission (Kans.) Schs., 1974-76, Jefferson County Schs., Lakewood, Colo., 1976-77; fundraiser Am. Lung Assn., Denver, 1986-90; dir. devel. Am. Heart Assn., Denver, 1990-94; exec. dir. Cherry Creek Schs. Found., Englewood, Colo., 1994—. Delegate Rep. State Assembly, Denver, 1998. Mem. Colo. Assn. Non-Profit Orgs., Colo. Consortium Edn. Founds., Greenwood Village C. of C. (bd. dirs. 1996-98). Avocations: golf, skiing, softball, reading. Office: Cherry Creek Schools Foundation 4700 S Yosemite St Englewood CO 80111-1307

MYERS, DOUGLAS GEORGE, zoological society administrator; b. L.A., Aug. 30, 1949; s. George Walter and Daydeen (Schroeder) M.; m. Barbara Firestone Myers, Nov. 30, 1980; children: Amy, Andrew. BA, Christopher Newport Coll., 1981. Tour and show supr. Annheuser-Busch (Bird Sanctuary), Van Nuys, Calif., 1970-74, mgr. zool. ops., 1974-75, asst. mgr. ops., 1975-77, mgr. ops., 1977-78; gen. services mgr. Annheuser-Busch (Old Country), Williamsburg, Va., 1978-80, park ops. dir., 1980-81; gen. mgr. wild animal park Zool. Soc. San Diego, 1981-83, dep. dir. ops., 1983-85, exec. dir., 1985—; cons. in field. Mem. adv. com. of pres.' assn. Am. Mgmt. Assn. Fellow Am. Assn. Zool. Parks and Aquariums (profl., bd. dirs.), Internat. Union Dirs. Zool. Gardens; mem. Internat. Assn. Amusement Parks and Attractions, Am. Mgmt. Assn. (adv. com. pres. assn.), Calif. Assn. Zoos and Aquariums, Mus. Trustee Assn., Rotary. Lodge: Rotary. Office: San Diego Zoo PO Box 551 San Diego CA 92112-0551

MYERS, ELIZABETH ROUSE, management consultant; b. Grand Island, Nebr., July 14, 1923; d. William Wayne Rouse and Lulu Zella Trout; m. Richard Roland Myers, June 25, 1943; children: Diane Marie Berndt, Richard Wayne. Student, Kearny State Tchrs. Coll., Nebr., 1942-43. Draftsman Borg-Warner Corp., Kalamazoo, 1944; acct. CFI Steel Corp., Pueblo, Colo., 1950-52; sec., treas. Standard Paint, Yakima, Wash., 1954-86; pres. Pied Piper Childrens Books, Yakima, Wash., 1985-96; federal oil leases, 1980—; docent Yakima Valley Mus. & Gilbert House, Wash. 1984—. Editor: H.S. Paper. Tchr., supt. First Presbyn. Ch., Yakima, Wash., 1958-70; mem. bd. Parent Tchrs.; bd. dirs., teen chmn. YWCA; pres. Gilbert House. Mem. Yakima Valley Mus. (awarded Doll 1985, Show 1986, vol. of yr. 1994). Republican. Presbyterian. Avocations: gardening, doll and toy collecting, world traveling, walking, flying. Home: 106 N 25th Ave Yakima WA 98902-2807

MYERS, ELMER, psychiatric social worker; b. Blackwell, Ark., Nov. 12, 1926; s. Chester Elmer Myers and Irene (Davenport) Lewis; widowed; children: Elmer Jr., Keith, Kevin. BA, U. Kans., 1951, MA, 1962; student, U. Calif., Santa Barbara, 1977-78. Psychiat. social worker Hastings (Nebr.) State Hosp., 1960-62; psychiat. social worker State of Calif., Sacramento, 1962-75, supr. psychiat. social worker, 1975-80; supr. psychiat. social worker Alta Calif. Regional Ctr., Sacramento, 1980-85; exec. dir. Tri-County Family Services, Yuba City, Calif., 1966-69; cons. to 3 convalescent Hosps., Marysville, Calif., 1969-71; lectr. Yuba Coll., Marysville, 1971-76; assoc. prof. Calif. State U., Chico, 1972-73; cons. in field, Marysville, 1985—; group therapist Depot Homeless Shelter, 1996—, counselor 1995—. Juror Yuba County Grand Jury, Marysville, 1965, 87-88; sec. Y's Men's Club, Yuba City, 1964-65; chmn. Tri-County Home Health Agy., Yuba City, 1974-76; vice-chmn. Gateway Projects, Inc., Yuba City, 1974-75; bd. dirs. Christian Assistance Network, 1993, Habitat for Humanity, 1993, Yuba County Truancy Bd., Marysville, 1964-67, Golden Empire Health Sys. Agy., Sacramento, 1972-76, Youth Svcs. Bur., Yuba City, 1967, Bi-County Mental Retardation Planning Bd., Yuba City, 1972, Yuba County Juvenile Justice Commn., Marysville, 1982-90, Am. Cancer Soc., Marysville, 1985-92, Yuba County Rep. Ctrl. Com., 1983-90, Salvation Army, 1990—, facilittor care project, 1992; asst. dir. Marysville Adult Activity Ctr., 1990—; active Yuba-Sutter United Way, 1971-73, 91-92, Tri-County Ethnic Forum, sec., 1991-1993;steering com. Yuba County Sr. Ctr. Assn., 1992, 95—; chmn. Yuba County Cmty. Svcs. Commn., 1997-99; pres. Yuba-Sutter Gleaners, 1997—, Yuba-Sutter Commn. on Aging, 1996. Recipient Cert. Spl. Recognition Calif. Rehab. Planning Project, 1969, Cert. Spl. Recognition State of Calif., 1967; Cert. Spl. Recognition Alta Calif. Regional Ctrs., 1985. Mem. Nat. Assn. Social Workers (cert.), Kern County Mental Health Assn. (chmn. 1978-79). Lodge: Rotary (bd. dirs. Marysville club 1975-76). Avocations: fgn. lang. study, gardening, reading, computers. Home and Office: 3920 State Highway 20 Marysville CA 95901-9003

MYERS, GREGORY EDWIN, aerospace engineer; b. Harrisburg, Pa., Jan. 1, 1960; s. Bernard Eugene and Joyce (Calhoun) M.; m. Susan Ann Hayslett, Dec. 30, 1983; children: Kimberly, Benjamin. BS in Aerospace Engring., U. Mich., 1981; MS in Aerospace Engring., Air Force Inst. Tech., 1982. Aerospace engr. Sperry Comml. Flight Systems group Honeywell, Inc., Phoenix, 1987-90; sr. project engr. satellite systems ops. Honeywell, Inc., Glendale, Ariz., 1990-92; sr. project engr. air transport systems Honeywell, Inc., Phoenix, 1992-93, prin. engr., 1993-97; prin. software engr. Orbital Scis. Corp., Chandler, Ariz., 1997—, sr. prin. software engr., 1999—; presenter in field. Contbr. articles to profl. jours. Mem. Aviation Week Rsch. Adv. Panel, 1990-91. Recipient Certs. of Recognition and Appreciation Lompoc Valley Festival Assn., Inc., 1983, Arnold Air Soc. (comdr. 1979), Cert. of Appreciation Instrument Soc. Am., 1991. Mem. AIAA (sr.). Lutheran. Avocations: softball, tennis, reading, computer programming. Office: Orbital Scis Corp 3380 S Price Rd Chandler AZ 85248-3534

MYERS, HARDY, state attorney general, lawyer; b. Electric Mills, Miss., Oct. 25, 1939; m. Mary Ann Thalhofer, 1962; children: Hardy III, Christopher, Jonathan. AB with distinction, U. Miss., 1961; LLB, U. Oreg., 1964. Bar: Oreg., U.S. Ct. of Appeals (9th cir.), U.S. Dist. Ct. Law clerk U.S. Dist. Judge William G. East, 1964-65; pvt. practice Stoel Rives LLP, 1965-96; atty. gen. State of Oregon, 1997—; mem. Oreg. Ho. of Reps., 1975-85, speaker of the ho., 1979-83. Pres. Portland City Planning Commn., 1973-74; chair Oreg. Jail Project, 1984-86, Citizens' Task Force on Mass Transit Policy, 1985-86, Oreg. Criminal Justice Coun., 1987-91, Portland Future Focus, 1990-91, Metro Charter com., 1991-92, task force on state employee benefits, 1994; co-chair gov. task force on state employee compensation, 1995. Office: Oreg Atty Gen Justice Dept 1162 Court St NE Salem OR 97310-1320*

MYERS, KATHERINE DONNA, writer, publisher; b. L.A., Nov. 10, 1925; d. John Allen Myers and Eulah Caldwell (Myers) Harris; m. Thomas Miller, Feb. 2, 1944 (div. 1963); children: Kathleen JoAnn Content, David Thomas. Teaching credential in bus. edn., U. So. Calif., L.A., 1975; postgrad., Loyola U., Paris, 1980. Cert. pub. adminstr. Dep. field assessor L.A. County Tax Assessor, L.A., 1944-60; sec. L.A. Unified Sch. Dist., 1960-70; br. sec. bank Crocker Nat. Bank, L.A., 1970-78; instr. legal sec. Southland Coll., L.A., 1975-78; exec. sec. ABC, L.A., 1978-89; v.p. spl. projects Glendale (Calif.) TV Studios, 1990-92; writer, publisher Eagles Wings Publishing Co., L.A., 1992—; owner, pres. Success Secretarial Seminar, L.A., 1980-84; pub., author Eagle's Wings Pub. Co., L.A., 1992—; wedding cons., counselor Crenshaw United Meth. Ch., L.A., 1993—. Author, pub.: Wedding Bells, A New Peal, 1994; (instrnl. book) Productivity Guide, Bilingual Special Education, 1980; (biography) The Eagle Flies on Friday, 1988, (hist. newsletter) Eagle Reader's Newsletter, 1993; author: (tech. booklet) Ronnie Knows about Sickle Cell, 1973 (Founder's award 1973). Troop leader, adminstr. Girl Scouts Am., L.A., 1956; chmn. sickle cell com. MLK Hosp. Guild, L.A., 1974; den mother Boy Scouts Am., 1960; lifetime mem. PTA, L.A., 1960. Recipient THANKS badge Girl Scouts Am., 1959, Founder's award MLK Jr. Hosp. Guild, 1974. Mem. Photo Friends Ctrl. Libr., Wilshire C. of C. (bd. dirs. 1980). Democrat. United Methodist. Avocations: health walking, supporting illiteracy programs, short story writing. Home and Office: Eagle Wings Publ Co 3939 Marlton Ave Apt 401 Los Angeles CA 90008-1771

MYERS, KATHLEEN ANNE, pediatrics nurse; b. Tacoma, Wash., July 23, 1970; d. David Arthur and Carol Susan (Frederick) M. Student, N.W. Nazarene Coll., Nampa, Idaho, 1988-89; BSN, Seattle Pacific U., 1993, grad. student in MSN program, 1997—. Cert. pediatric nurse; cert. BLS, PALS. Mem. nursing staff pediat. Yakima (Wash.) Valley Meml. Hosp., 1993—. Mem. Assembly of God Ch. Avocations: aerobics, fishing, sewing.

MYERS, PATRICIA SEITTERS, journalist, author, editor; b. Akron, Ohio; d. Lamoine Bitterman and Elizabeth Helen (Myers) Seitters; m. Gerald R. McElfresh (div.); children: Stephen D., Philip S., Suzanne C. BA, U. Akron; fellow, Northwestern U. Reporter Cleve. Plain Dealer, 1960-62; reporter, editor Mesa (Ariz.) Tribune, 1965-72, editor, staff writer, 1979-86; reporter, editor Scottsdale (Ariz.) Progress, 1972-79; editor at large Phoenix Mag., 1986-88, sr. staff writer, restaurant critic, 1988-89; pres., speaker Steps to Success Seminars, Scottsdale, 1985-88; faculty assoc. Ariz. State U., Tempe, 1974-77, 88, Mesa Community Coll., 1985; freelance writer various publs., 1972—; reporter, Ariz. corr. Time mag., 1978-79; food editor Arizona Republic, Phoenix, 1989-94, entertainment writer, 1994-95, arts and entertainment writer, 1995-97; food editor Phoenix Gazette, 1989-94, arts and entertainment writer, 1995-97; free-lance writer, cons. Myers Productions, 1997—; entertainment editor, restaurant columnist Phoenix Rising Mag., 1998—. Author (book) Scottsdale: Jewel in the Desert, 1984 (1st pl. nat. award 1986), (slide-illustrated audio-tape) Women Journalists in America, 1976; contbg. editor Japanese Gardens, 1979; writer, host video interviews Inside Interviews, 1982-87; contbr. writer All Music Guide to Jazz, 1994, Music Hound Guide to Jazz, 1998. Cons. hist. exhibits City of Scottsdale, 1986-88; mem. adv. bd. Sedona Jazz on the Rocks. recipient Ariz. Newspapers Assn. Best Entry (writing) awards, 1974, 79, 84, Nat. Better Newspapers Assn. Best Serious Column award, 1983, Nat. Press Women writing awards (13), 1966—; Ariz. Edn. Assn. awards, 1967 71. Mem. Ariz. Press Women (pres. 1970-71, Woman of Achievement award 1986), Impact for Enterprising Women (Celebration of Success winner 1987), Jazz Journalists Assn., Jazz in Ariz. Inc. (founder, pres. 1980-81), Ariz. Women in Food and Wine, Scottsdale Hist. Soc. (mem. adv. bd.), Mortar Bd. Alumni (program chair Valley of the Sun chpt. 1982), Alliance Francaise. Home: PO Box 4201 Scottsdale AZ 85261-4201

MYERS, ROBERT GEAROLD, developmental test executive, flight test engineer; b. Santa Fe, Mar. 12, 1935; s. Franklin Gearold and Nadine Cathrine (Torrey) M.; children: Paul Wayne, Laura Ellen; m. Sherry Kay Myers, Jan. 31, 1998. BSME, N.Mex. State U., 1958; MBA, Golden Gate U., 1974. Engring. officer Air Force Res., 1959-86; engring. mgr. Boeing Devel. Projects, Seattle, 1958-84; B-1B sys. engring. mgr., base mgr. Boeing Mojave Test Ctr., Edwards AFB, Calif., 1984-88, base mgr., 1989-91; v.p. B2 Flight Test Mil. Aircraft Sys. divsn. Test Labs. Northrop Grumman, Edwards AFB, Calif., 1991-98; ret. Northrop Grumman, Century City, Calif., 1999. Recipient Tech. Laureatte Aviation Week and Space Tech., 1997. Fellow ASME; mem. AIAA. Avocations: softball, skiing, backpacking, hunting. Home: PO Box 1659 Tehachapi CA 93581-1659

MYERS, WALTER E., protective services official. Chief of police Salem, Oreg. Office: 555 Liberty St SE Rm 130 Salem OR 97301-3513*

MYERSON, ALAN, director, film and television writer; b. Cleve., Aug. 8, 1936; s. Seymour A. and Vivien I. (Caplin) M.; m. Irene Ryan, June 2, 1962; 1 son, Lincoln; m. Leigh French, Apr. 15, 1977; children: Sierra Jasmine French-Myerson, Darcy Anna French-Myerson. Student, Pepperdine Coll., 1956-57, UCLA, 1957. mem. drama faculty U. Calif., Berkeley, 1966, San Francisco State U., 1967. Dir. Broadway and Off Broadway Prodns., 1958-64, including This Music Crept By Me Upon the Waters, The Committee; dir.: Second City, N.Y.C. and Chgo., 1961, 62; founder, producer, dir. The Committee, San Francisco, L.A. and N.Y., 1963-74; dir.: (films) Steelyard Blues, 1972, Private Lessons, 1981, Police Academy 5, 1988, It's Showtime, 1976; numerous TV shows, 1975—, including Laverne and Shirley, Rhoda, Bob Newhart Show, Welcome Back, Kotter, Fame, Crime Story, Dynasty, Miami Vice, Hunter, Sisters, Picket Fences, The Larry Sanders Show, Frazier, Friends; TV films The Love Boat, 1976, Hi, Honey, I'm Dead, 1991, Bad Attitudes, 1991, Holiday Affair, 1996. Active in civil rights, anti-war, anti-nuclear power movements, 1957—. Recipient Emmy nomination 1997. Mem. Acad. Motion Picture Arts and Scis., Acad. TV Arts and Scis., Dirs. Guild Am.

MYHREN, TRYGVE EDWARD, communications company executive; b. Palmerton, Pa., Jan. 3, 1937; s. Arne Johannes and Anita (Blatz) M.; m. Carol Jane Enman, Aug. 8, 1964; children: Erik, Kirsten, Tor; m. 2d Victoria Hamilton, Nov. 14, 1981; 1 stepchild, Paige. BA in Philosophy and Polit. Sci., Dartmouth Coll., 1958, MBA, 1959. Sales mgr., unit mgr. Procter and Gamble, Cin., 1963-65; sr. cons. Glendinning Cos., Westport, Conn., 1965-69; pres. Auberge Vintners, 1970-73; exec. v.p. Mktg. Continental, Westport, 1969-73; v.p., gen. mgr. CRM, Inc., Del Mar, Calif., 1973-75; from v.p. mktg. to pres. Am. TV and Comm. Corp., Englewood, Colo., 1975-80, chmn. bd., CEO, 1981-88; v.p., then exec. v.p. Time Inc., N.Y.C., 1981-88; mem. exec. com., treas., vice chmn., then chmn. bd. dirs. Nat. Cable TV Assn., Washington, 1982-91; mem. adv. com. on HDTV, FCC, 1987-89, pres. Providence Jour. Co., pres., 1990-96; bd. dirs. Advanced Mktg. Svcs., Inc., La Jolla, Calif., ; Founders Funds, Inc., J. D. Edwards, Inc., Verio, Inc., Formus Inc., Nat. Cable TV Ctr., Denver, Cable Labs, Inc., Boulder, Colo., Peapod, Inc., Skokie, Ill.; pres. Myhren Media, 1989—, Greenwood Cable Mgmt., 1989-91; pres., CEO King Broadcast Co., 1991-96. Mem. Colo. Forum, 1984-91, chmn. higher edn. com., 1986; bd. dirs., co-founder Colo. Bus. Com. for the Arts, 1985-91; mem. exec. coun. Found. for Commemoration U.S. Constn., 1987-90; mem. Nat. GED Task Force, 1987-90, Colo. Baseball Commn., 1989-91, Colo. Film Commn., 1989-91; trustee Nat. Jewish Hosp., 1989— (Humanitarian award 1996), R.I. Hosp., 1991-95, Lifespan Health Sys., 1994-97, U. Denver, 1996—, U.S. Ski and Snowboard Team Found., 1998—; chmn. Local Organizing Commn. 1995 NCAA Hockey Championship. Lt. (j.g.) USNR, 1959-63. Recipient Disting. Leader award Nat. Cable TV Assn., 1988, ann. humanitarian award Nat. Jewish Hosp., 1996. Mem. Cable TV Adminstrn. and Mktg. Soc. (pres. 1978-79, Grand Tam award 1985, One of A Kind award 1994), Cable Adv. Bur. (co-founder 1978), Cable TV Pioneers. Episcopalian. Address: Myhren Media Inc 280 Detroit St # 200 Denver CO 80206-4807

MYLNECHUK, LARRY HERBERT, financial executive; b. Littlefork, Minn., Mar. 9, 1948; s. William and Marjorie (Raco) M.; m. Sandy L. Henderson, Mar. 14, 1970; children: Kendra Elizabeth, Scott William. BA, Lewis & Clark Coll., Portland, 1970; JD, Lewis & Clark Coll., 1974. Legal specialist Oreg. Dept. Edn., Salem, 1976-82; sr. v.p., dir. Morley Capital Mgmt. Inc., Portland, 1982-89; founder, pres. Integra Assocs., Inc., Lake Oswego, Oreg., 1989—; exec. dir. The Stable Value Assn., Inc., Lake Oswego, 1990-96; cons. Hueler Analytics, Inc., Mpls., 1989—; conf. chmn. GIC Nat. Forum Conf., Washington, 1993-95; guest lectr. Portland State U., 1978, U. Oreg., 1980. Contbr. articles to profl. jours. Founder Woodstock Neighborhood Assn., 1975; mem. Multnomah County (Oreg.) Charter Rev. Commn., 1978, Tualatin (Oreg.) City Coun., 1980-84, Portland Com. on Fgn. Rels., 1976—, bd. dirs., 1993-96; mem. Gov.'s Commn. on Adminstrv. Hearings, State of Oreg., 1988-89; trustee St. Francis of Assisi Endowment Fund, 1993; vestry mem., lay eucharistic min., del. State Episcopal Conv., 1996; mem. Diocesan Coun., 1996-98; chmn. corp. fundraising Lake Oswego Children's Choir. Fellow NEH, 1979, edn. policy fellow George Washington U., 1980. Mem. SAR (pres. Lewis and Clark chpt.), Western Pension Conf., Assn. Soc. Execs., World Affairs Coun. Oreg., Citizen Amb. Program to Western Europe, Gen. Soc. The War of 1812, Soc. Colonial Wars, Sons and Daus. of Pilgrims, Oreg. Soc. Sons of the Revolution (co-founder, treas. 1996), Internat. Bus. Forum (mem. adv. bd. 1996), Sons of the Bench and Bar (charter), SAR (pres. Oreg. State Soc. 1997, nat. trustee 1997-98, v.p. Gen.-Pacific dist. 1999—), N.Am. Soc. of Securities Adminstrs. (profl. stds. com. 1998), Soc. Magna Charta Barons. Democrat. Episcopalian. Avocations: hiking, diving. Office: Integra Assocs Inc PO Box 1594 Lake Oswego OR 97035-0013

MYRICK, HELEN ESTELLE, civic worker; b. Vancouver, B.C., Can., Feb. 4, 1952; came to U.S., 1964; d. Guy Vernon and Vera Loretto (Tacey) M. BA in Cmty. Svcs., Seattle U., 1973; MPA, Pacific Luth. U., 1984. Counselor Renton (Wash.) Area Youth Svcs., 1973-79; probation officer Kitsap County, Bremerton, Wash., 1979-82; social worker III, Wash. State Dept. Social and Health Svcs., Tacoma, 1982-85; mgr. human resources Tacoma-Pierce County Health Dept., 1985-93; legis. aide Wash. State Ho. of Reps., Olympia, 1993-94; polit. cons. Save Our Sealife Initiative Campaign, Tacoma, 1994-95; cons., project mgr. Greater Pierce County Cmty. Network, Tacoma, 1995—; owner The People's Bus.; employment counselor King County Work Tng. Program, Seattle, summer 1995; owner The People's Bus. Mem. adv. bd. Pierce County Cmty. Action Agy., 1987-95, Tacoma Hate Crimes Task Force, 1991-93; adult advisor Students Against Violence Everywhere, Federal Way, Wash., 1994-95; candidate Wash. State Ho. of Reps., 1990, 94; bd. dirs. Wash. State Women's Polit. Caucus, Seattle, 1993-95, endorsement chmn., 1995-97; rep. legis. action com. 30th Dist. Dems., Federal Way, 1992-94; bd. dirs. Port of Tacoma Citizen's Work Group, 1995—; bd. dirs. Federal Way Youth and Family Svcs., 1990—, also past pres.; mem. tech. adv. bd. Family Policy Coun., 1995—; commr. City of Tacoma Human Rights Commn., 1996. Recipient Disting. Svc. award N.W. Dispatch newspaper, 1991; leadership fellow Tacoma-Pierce County C. of C., 1988-89. Mem. NOW, Coalition To Stop Gun Violence, Toastmasters (Most Enthusiastic Speaker award Tacoma 1990), City Club Tacoma (bd. dirs. 1991—). Home and Office: 15411 9th Ave E Tacoma WA 98445-1291

NACHMAN, RICHARD JOSEPH, management training executive; b. Washington, Sept. 18, 1944; s. Joseph Frank and Rosemary (Anderson) N.; m. Nancy Ruth Hodgson, Feb. 4, 1966 (div. Oct. 1975); children: Russell J., Kirk L.; m. Christina Maria Schulz, Jan. 2, 1979; 1 child, William C. Hoff. BA, U. Colo., 1968. Program dir. mgmt. edn. Grad. Sch. Bus. U. Mich., Ann Arbor, 1968-70; dir. Ctr. Mgmt. and Tech. Programs Sch. Bus. U. Colo., Boulder, 1970-74; pres. Mgmt. Rsch. Corp., Loveland, 1974—, RJN and Assocs., Loveland, 1977—. Contbr. articles to profl. publs.; prodr. seminars, video tng. materials The One Minute Manager, The Art of Negotiating, Japanese Manufacturing Techniques, World Class Manufacturing. Bd. dirs. World Missionary Press, Hand of Help, Inc., Good News Svc. Inc. Republican. Avocations: travel, fishing, skiing, camping.

NACHT, SERGIO, biochemist; b. Buenos Aires, Apr. 13, 1934; came to U.S., 1965; s. Oscar and Carmen (Scheiner) N.; m. Beatriz Kahan, Dec. 21, 1958; children: Marcelo H., Gabriel A., Mariana S., Sandra M. BA in Chemistry, U. Buenos Aires, 1958, MS in Biochemistry, 1960, PhD in Biochemistry, 1964. Asst. prof. biochemistry U. Buenos Aires, 1960-64; asst. prof. medicine U. Utah, Salt Lake City, 1965-70; rsch. scientist Alza Corp., Palo Alto, Calif., 1970-73; sr. investigator Richardson-Vicks Inc., Mt. Vernon, N.Y., 1973-76; asst. dir., dir. rsch. Richardson-Vicks Inc., Mt. Vernon, 1976-83; dir. biomed. rsch. Richardson-Vicks Inc., Shelton, Conn., 1983-87; sr. v.p. rsch. and devel. Advanced Polymer Systems, Redwood City, Calif., 1987-93, sr. v.p. sci. and tech., 1993-98, sr. v.p. dermatology and skin care, 1998—; lectr. dermatology dept. SUNY Downstate Med. Ctr., Bklyn., 1977-87. Contbr. articles to profl. jours.; patentee in field. Mem. Soc. Investigative Dermatology, Soc. Cosmetic Chemists (award 1981), Dermatology Found., Am. Physiological Soc., Am. Acad. Dermatology. Democrat. Jewish. Home: 409 Wembley Ct Redwood City CA 94061-4308

NACHT, STEVE JERRY, geologist; b. Cleve., July 8, 1948; s. Max and Elfrida (Kamm) N.; m. Patricia Katherine Osicka, Aug. 3, 1976; 1 child, David Martin. BS in Geology, Kent State U., 1971, MS in Geology, 1973; MS in Urban Studies, Cleve. State U., 1979. Registered geologist, S.C., Va., Wyo.; environ. assessor, Calif.; cert. geologist, Ind.; lic. drinking water treatment class III, Ohio; cert. environ. mgr., Nev. Geologist Cleve. Utilities Dept., 1974-78; geologist, hydrologist Dalton, Dalton & Newport, Cleve., 1979-82; prin. scientist Lockheed-Emsco, Las Vegas, Nev., 1983-86; sr. geologist, project mgr. Earth Tech. Inc., Long Beach, Calif., 1986-87, The MARK Group, Las Vegas, 1987-90; dir. waste tech., sr. geologist Reynolds Elec. & Engring. Co., Las Vegas, 1990-92, chief environ. remediation sect., 1992-95; asst. project mgr. Bechtel Nev. Corp., Las Vegas, 1996-97, project mgr., 1997—. Contbr. articles to profl. jours. Mem. AAAS, ASTM (groundwater com., past chmn. sect., well maintenance, rehab. and decommissioning sect.), Am. Inst. Profl. Geologists (cert.), Assn. Ground Water Scientists and Engrs., Assn. Engring. Geologists, Project Mgmt. Profl. (cert.), Project Mgmt. Inst. Home: 4184 Del Rosa Ct Las Vegas NV 89121-5011 Office: Bechtel Nev PO Box 98521 Las Vegas NV 89193-8521

NADY, JOHN, electronics company executive; b. Agfalva, Hungary, Feb. 13, 1945; came to U.S., 1951; s. John and Hermine Nady. BSEE, Calif. Inst. Tech., 1965; MSEE, U. Calif., Berkeley, 1968. Elec. engr. Lawrence Radiation Lab., Livermore, 1966-71, Westinghouse Corp., Oakland, Calif., 1971-72; owner, chief exec. officer Nady Systems, Inc., Oakland, Calif., 1976—, Calif. Concerts, Inc., Oakland, Calif., 1985-93. Patentee in field. Recipient Emmy award Pioneering Devel. Wireless Microphones, 1996. Mem. Nat. Assn. Broadcasters, Audio Engring. Soc., Nat. Assn. Music Merchants. Avocations: electric guitar, skiing, tennis, golfing, softball. Office: Nady Systems Inc 6701 Shellmound St Emeryville CA 94608-1023

NAGANO, KENT GEORGE, conductor; b. Morro Bay, Calif.. B.A. Sociology & Music (high honors), U of Calif., Santa Cruz; MA in Composition, San Francisco State U.; studied with, Laszlo Varga. Former asst. Opera Co. Boston; former prin. guest condr. Ensemble InterContemporain & the Dutch Radio Orch.; mus. dir. & condr. Berkeley Symphony, 1978—; mus. dir.

Opéra de Lyon, 1989—; assoc. prin. & guest condr. LSO, London, England, 1990; mus. dir., prin. condr. designate Hallé Orch., England, 1991-94; mus. dir., prin. condr. Hallé Orch., 1994—. has performed with numerous orchestras around the world; recordings include: Songs of the Auvergne, Peter and the Wolf, Turandot and Arlecchino (Grammy nom.), La Boheme, Dialogues of the Carelites, The Death of Klinghoffer (Grammy nom.), Love for Three Oranges (Grammy nom.), Susannah (Grammy award), La damnation de Faust, The Rite of Spring, Rodrgue et chimene. Recipient Seaver/NEA Conducting award, 1985; Record of Yr. award Gramophone; named "officer" of France's Order of Arts and Letters, 1993. Office: Vincent Farrell & Assocs 157 W 57th St New York NY 10019*

NAGEL, DARYL DAVID, retail executive; b. Arlington, Minn., Apr. 13, 1939; s. Paul Charles and Frieda L. (Oldenburg) N.; m. Joan Clare Dacey, Dec. 23, 1961; children: Kelly, Andrew, Maureen. BME, U. Minn., 1962; diploma in Advanced Mgmt. Program, Harvard U., 1978. Asst. mdse. mgr. Res. Supply Co., Mpls., 1962-65; mdse. mgr. Reserve Supply Co., Mpls., 1965-66, v.p., gen. mgr., 1966-69; v.p. area gen. mgr. United Bldg. Ctrs., Winona, Minn., 1969-78, exec. v.p., chief ops. officer, 1978-84, pres., chief exec. officer, 1984-87; pres., CEO Lanoga Corp., Seattle, 1987—; bd. dirs. Lanoga Corp., Seattle, 1987—, Badger Foundry, Winona, 1984-87. Bd. dirs. United Way, Winona, 1978-84; chmn. Home Ctr. Inst., 1997—. Mem. Home Ctr. Leadership Coun., C. of C. (bd. dirs. 1964-69, 73, 78), Sahalee Country Club. Republican. Lutheran. Avocations: golf, gardening, skiing. Office: Lanoga Corp PO Box 97040 Redmond WA 98073-9740

NAGEL, JEROME KAUB, architect; b. Denver, Dec. 26, 1923; s. Fritz Andrew and Josephine (Gaylord) N.; m. Cynthia Fels, Sept. 1, 1951; children—Peter Barry, James Gaylord. B.Arch., Yale U., 1949. Registered architect, Colo. Prin. J.K. Nagel Architect, Denver, 1953-61, Rogers & Nagel, Denver, 1961-66, Rogers, Nagel, Langhart, Architects, 1966-77, Interplan Inc., 1969-77; pres. Nagel Investment Co.; dir. Bank Western, Denver, Field Devel. Corp., Denver. Mem. Colo. Hwy. Commn., chmn., 1982-83; bd. dirs. Planned Parenthood Fed. Am. Inc., N.Y.C., 1974-78, Rocky Mountain Planned Parenthood, Denver, 1972-76, Colo. chpt. ARC, 1957-60, 80-81, Denver Santa Claus Shop, 1987-91; mem. panel arbitrators Am. Arbitration Assn., 1962—; chmn. Colo. Bicycling Adv., Denver Bicycling Adv. Bd. Bd. Served to 1st lt. AC U.S. Army Air Corps, 1943-45. Decorated D.F.C., Air medal with 11 oak leaf clusters. Mem. AIA (nat. life; sec. chpt. 1960-61, pres. 1962-63), Denver Country Club (bd. dirs. 1983-86), Univ. Club (bd. dirs. 1962-66) Mile High Club, Denver Rotary Club Found. (pres. 1992-93), Denver Athletic Club. Episcopalian. Home: 67 Eudora St Denver CO 80220-6311

NAGEL, STANLEY BLAIR, retired construction and investment executive; b. Bklyn., Mar. 19, 1928; s. Robert Arthur and Renee Ann Nagel; children: Scott Alan, Robert Arthur. BBA, U. Oreg., 1950. With constrn. dept. Nagel Investment, Portland, Oreg., 1955-58, pres., 1956—; pres. R.A. Constrn., Portland, 1956—; buyer May Co., Portland, 1958-72; gen. mgr. Portland Outdoor Store, 1972-75; owner Nagels Nursery & Greenhouses, Portland, 1975—; pres. E & S Distbrs., Portland, 1982—; ret., 1996. Co-inventor pizza machine (patent pending). 2d lt. U.S. Army, 1952-55. Republican. Jewish. Avocations: photography, Malt scotch collector. Home and Office: 5353 SW Martha St Portland OR 97221-1840

NAGLER, MICHAEL NICHOLAS, classics and comparative literature educator; b. N.Y.C., Jan. 20, 1937; s. Harold and Dorothy Judith (Nocks) N.; m. Roberta Ann Robbins (div. May 1983); children: Jessica, Joshua. BA, NYU, 1960; MA, U. Calif., Berkeley, 1962, PhD, 1966. Instr. San Francisco State U., 1963-65; prof. classics, peace studies and comparative lit. U. Calif., Berkeley, 1966-91, prof. emeritus, 1991—. Author: Spontaneity and Tradition, 1974, America Without Violence, 1982; co-author: The Upanishads, 1987; contbr. articles to profl. publs. Pres. bd. dirs. METTA Ctrs. for Nonviolence Edn. Fellow Am. Coun. Learned Socs., NIH; MacArthur Found. grantee, 1988. Mem. Am. Philolog. Soc. (editor Oral Tradition). Office: U Calif Classics Dept Berkeley CA 94720

NAGLESTAD, FREDERIC ALLEN, legislative advocate; b. Sioux City, Iowa, Jan. 13, 1929; s. Ole T. and Evelyn Elizabeth (Erschen) N.; student (scholar) U. Chgo., 1947-49; m. Beverly Minnette Shellberg, Feb. 14, 1958; children—Patricia Minnette, Catherine Janette. Pub. affairs, pub. relations, newscaster, announcer KSCJ-radio, Sioux City, Iowa, 1949-51; producer, dir., newscaster, announcer WOW-TV, Omaha, 1953-57; program mgr. WCPO-TV, Cin., 1957-58; mgr. KNTV-TV, San Jose, Calif., 1958-61; owner Results Employment Agy., San Jose, 1961-75; legis. advocate Naglestad Assocs., Calif Assn. Employers, Calif. Automotive Wholesalers Assn., Air Quality Products, Calif. Assn. Wholesalers-Distbrs., State Alliance Bd. Equalization Reform, Quakemaster, many others, 1969—. Pres. Calif. Employment Assn., 1970-72. Asst. concertmaster Sioux City Symphony Orch., 1945-47. Sgt. AUS, 1951-53. Recognized for outstanding contbn. to better employment law, Resolution State Calif. Legislature, 1971. Office: 3991 Fair Oaks Blvd Sacramento CA 95864-7254

NAGTALON-MILLER, HELEN ROSETE, humanities educator; b. Honolulu, June 27, 1928; d. Dionicio Reyes and Fausta Dumbrigue (Rosete) N.; m. Robert Lee Ruley Miller, June 15, 1952. BEd, U. Hawaii, 1951; Diplôme, The Sorbonne, Paris, 1962; MA, U. Hawaii, 1967; PhD, Ohio State U., 1972. Cert. secondary education educator. Tchr. humanities Hawaii State Dept. Edn., Honolulu, 1951-63; supr. student tchrs. French lab. sch. Coll. of Edn. U. Hawaii, Honolulu, 1963-66, instr. French, coord. French courses Coll. Arts and Scis., 1966-69; teaching asst. Coll. Edn. Ohio State U., Columbus, 1970-72; instr. French lab. sch. Coll. Edn. U. Hawaii, Honolulu, 1974-76; adminstr. bilingual-bicultural edn. project Hawaii State Dept. Edn., Honolulu, 1976-77; coord. disadvantaged minority recruitment program Sch. Social Work, U. Hawaii, Honolulu, 1977-84; coord. tutor tng. program U. Hawaii, Honolulu, 1984-86; program dir. Multicultural Multifunctional Resource Ctr., Honolulu, 1986-87; vis. prof. Sch. Pub. Health, ret. U. Hawaii, Honolulu, 1987-92; bd. dirs. Hawaii Assn. Lang. Tchrs., Honolulu, 1963-66, Hawaii Com. for the Humanities, 1977-83; mem. statewide adv. coun. State Mental Health Adv. Com., Honolulu, 1977-82; task force mem. Underrepresentation of Filipinos in Higher Edn., Honolulu, 1984-86. Author: (with others) Notable Women in Hawaii, 1984; contbr. articles to profl. jours. Chairperson edn. and counseling subcom. First Gov.'s Commn. on Status of Women, Honolulu, 1964; vice chairperson Honolulu County Com. on the Status of Women, 1975-76, Hawaii State Dr. Martin Luther King Jr. Commn., Honolulu, 1982-85; pres. Filipino-Am. Hist. Soc. of Hawaii, 1980—; mem. Hawaii State Adv. Com. to U.S. Commn. on Civil Rights, 1981—, chairperson, 1982-85; bd. dirs. Japanese Am. Citizens League Honolulu chpt., 1990—, mem. Hawaiian Sovereignty com., 1994—, Protect Our Constitution, Hawaii; mem. Pro-Choice Polit. Action Com., 1989-92. Women of Distinction, Honolulu County Com. on Status of Women, 1982; recipient Nat. Edn. Assn. award for Leadership in Asian and Pacific Island Affairs, NEA, 1985, Alan F. Saunders award ACLU in Hawaii, 1986, Disting. Alumni award U. Hawaii Alumni Affairs Office, 1994. Mem. Filipino Am. Nat. Hist. Soc., Filipino Coalition for Solidarity, Gabriela Network (Hawaii chpt.), Filipino Cmty. Ctr., Philippine Centennial Coordinating Com./Hawaii, NOW, Alliance Française of Hawaii, Rainbow Peace Fund. Democrat. Avocations: social-political advocacy, reading, classical music, theater, literary presentations. Home and Office: 3201 Beaumont Woods Pl Honolulu HI 96822-1423

NAGY, STEPHEN MEARS, JR., physician, allergist; b. Yonkers, N.Y., Apr. 1, 1939; s. Stephen Mears and Olga (Zahoruiko) N.; m. Branda Yu Nagy, 1966; children: Catherine, Stephen III. BA, Princeton U., 1960; MD, Tufts U., 1964. Diplomate Am. Bd. Internal Medicine, Am. Bd. Allergy and Immunology. Pvt. practice Sacramento, Calif., 1971-99; prof. Sch. Medicine U. Calif., Davis, 1974—. Author, editor Evaluation & Management of Allergic and Asthmatic Diseases, 1981; mem. editl. bd. Clinical Reviews in Allergy; creator Famous Teachings in Modern Medicine Allergy Series slide collection. Capt. U.S. Army, 1966-68, Vietnam. Fellow Am. Acad. Allergy, Am. Coll. Allergy; mem. CMA, Sacramento-El Dorado Med. Soc. (bd. dirs. 1971-95). Avocations: cycling, book collecting, opera, racquet ball, fencing. Office: 4801 J St Ste A Sacramento CA 95819-3746

NAJJAR, TAMARA LITCHFIELD, mail order business owner; b. Elgin, Ill., June 2, 1958; d. Kelmar Thomas and Betty Joan (Light) Litchfield; m. Idris M. Najjar, Jan. 5, 1986; children: Zakariya, Suraya, Ali. AS in Fire Protection, AS in Safety, We. Ky. U., Bowling Green, 1983. Lic. cosmetologist. Asst. supr. Opryland USA Inc., Nashville, 1983-86; asst. mgr. Hitachi Am., Nashville, 1986-91; owner, mgr. TJ Designs, Riverside, Calif., 1993—. Author, pub.: Beauty Shop in A Book, 1993. Fundraising chair Islamic Acad., Riverside, 1993-94, yearbook organizer, 1993. Mem. Mosque of Riverside. Democrat. Muslim. Avocations: couponing and rebating, gardening, decorating. Home and Office: 273 Newell Dr Riverside CA 92507-3106

NAKABAYASHI, NICHOLAS TAKATERU, retired retail executive; b. Honolulu, Feb. 25, 1920; s. Denji and Ume (Teraoka) N. BS, Utah State U., 1949; MS, U. Ill., 1953, PhD, 1959. Rsch. asst. U. Ill., Urbana, 1953-59; jr. rsch. physiologist UCLA, 1959-61, asst. rsch. physiologist, 1961-64; rsch. fellow Calif. Inst. Tech., Pasadena, 1961-64; sec.-treas. Underwater Rsch. Corp., L.A., 1962-64; rsch. asst. dept. ob/gyn U. Mich. Med. Ctr., Ann Arbor, 1964-70; biologist VA Hosp., Wadsworth, 1971-72; instr. San Gabriel Adult Sch., Calif., 1971-78; supr. serology VA Hosp., Long Beach, Calif., 1972-74; owner Regent Liquor Store, L.A., 1974-79; pres., treas. Regent Liquor, Inc., L.A., 1979-85; ret.; tutor Waikiki Lifelong Learning Ctr. Kapiolani C.C., Honolulu, 1993—. NIH grantee, 1967, 69. Mem. N.Y. Acad. Sci., 100th Inf. Battalion Vets. Club. Avocations: calligraphy, Hawaiiana. Home: 516 Kamoku St Apt 302 Honolulu HI 96826-5101 Office: Waikiki Lifelong Learning Ctr Kaliolani C C 2301 Kuhio Ave Ste 212 Honolulu HI 96815-2970

NAKAGAWA, ALLEN DONALD, radiologic technologist; b. N.Y.C., Mar. 14, 1955; s. Walter Tsunehiko and Alyce Tsuneko (Kinoshita) N. BS in Environ. Studies, St. John's U., Jamaica, N.Y., 1977; MS in Marine Biology, C.W. Post Coll., 1980. Cert. radiologic technologist, in fluoroscopy, Calif.; cert. Am. Registry Radiol. Technologists. Research asst. environ. studies St. John's U., 1976-78; lab. asst. Bur. Water Surveillance, Nassau Co. of Health Dept., Wantaugh, N.Y., 1978; clin. endocrinology asst. U. Calif. VA Hosp., San Francisco, 1981-83; student technologist St. Mary's Hosp., San Francisco, 1985-86; radiologic technologist Mt. Zion Hosp., San Francisco, 1986-88; sr. radiologic technologist U. Calif., San Francisco, 1989—, urosurg. radiologic technologists, 1988-89; attendee U. Calif. San Francisco Trauma and Emergency Radiology Conf., 1995, U. Calif. San Francisco Musculoskeletal MRI Conf., 1996. Mem. AAAS, ACLU, Calif. Soc. Radiologic Technologists, Marine Mammal Ctr., Calif. Acad. Scis., Japanese-Am. Nat. Mus., Sigma Xi. Democrat. Methodist. Avocations: assisting handicapped, photography, music, computer illustration, studying advanced technology.

NAKAHATA, TADAKA, retired consulting engineer, land surveyor; b. Kauai, Hawaii, Nov. 24, 1924; s. Tadao and Yae (Ohta) N.; BS in Civil Engring., U. Hawaii, 1951; m. Clara S. Sakanashi, June 23, 1956; children—Leanne A. Nikaido, Holly E. Chung, Merry Y. Ifuku. Engr./surveyor B.H. McKeague & Assos., Honolulu, 1951-55, Harland Bartholomew & Assos., Honolulu, 1955-56, Paul Low Engring. Co., Honolulu, 1956-59, Nakahata, Kaneshige, Imata & Assos., 1959-63; owner T. Nakahata, Honolulu, 1964-83, ret., 1983; mem. Hawaii Bd. Registration of Architects, Engrs. and Land Surveyors, 1980-83. With AUS, 1946-47. Mem. ASCE, Am. Congress Surveying and Mapping, Nat. Soc. Profl. Engrs. Mem. Makiki Christian Ch.

NAKAKI, THOMAS, information systems specialist; b. L.A., Nov. 1, 1960; s. Hidetaka and Mary Kimeko N. BS in Geophysics, UCLA, 1982, MS in Geophysics and Space Physics, 1985. LAN adminstr. Veritest, Santa Monica, Calif., 1993-95; MIS dir. Veritest, Santa Monica, 1995—; network engr. A.R.C., El Segundo, Calif., 1997—. Stage mgr. Bel Canto Opera Co., West L.A., 1993—. Roman Catholic. Office: Veritest 3420 Ocean Park Blvd Ste 2030 Santa Monica CA 90405-3322

NAKAMOTO, CAROLYN MATSUE, principal; b. Hilo, Hawaii, Oct. 28, 1947; d. Matsuichi and Kiyoko Sugimoto; m. Glenn Sunao Nakamoto, June 15, 1985. BEd in Secondary Edn., U. Hawaii, 1969, MEd in Ednl. Adminstrn., 1994. Cert. prof. sch. adminstr., Hawaii; cert. profl. tchr. secondary tchr. phys. sci. and gen. sci., Hawaii. Tchr. sci. Kalani H.S., Honolulu, 1971-77, Kaiser H.S., Honolulu, 1977-87; vice-prin. McKinley H.S., Honolulu, 1987-90; acting prin. Royal Elem., Honolulu, 1989; prin. Hahaione Elem., Honolulu, 1990—. Mem. ASCD, Nat. Assn. Secondary Sch. Prins., Phi Delta Kappa, Delta Kappa Gamma.

NAKANISHI, DON TOSHIAKI, Asian American studies educator, writer; b. L.A., Aug. 14, 1949; m. Marsha Hirano; 1 child, Thomas. BA in Polit Sci. cum laude, Yale U., 1971; PhD in Polit. Sci., Harvard U., 1978. Prof., dir. Asian Am. Studies Ctr. UCLA; researcher Social Sci. Rsch. Coun. of N.Y. and the Japan Soc. for the Promotion of Sci. of Tokyo Joint-Project on Am.-Japanese Mut. Images, 1971-73; mem. Asian Am. task force for social studies guideline evaluation, Calif. State Dept. Edn., 1973; guest spkr. Ctr. for the Study of Ednl. Policy, Grad. Sch. Edn., Harvard U., 1974, Metropathways, Ethni-City Sch. Desegregation Program, Boston, 1974; researcher, co-project chair Hispanic Urban Ctr., Project Sch. Desegregation, L.A., 1974. Author: (with others) Mutual Images: Essays in American-Japan Relations, 1975, Eliminating Racism, 1988, Racial and Ethnic Politics in California, 1991; author: In Search of a New Paradigm: Minorities in the Context of International Politics, 1975, The Education of Asian and Pacific Americans: Historical Perspectives and Prescriptions for the Future, 1983, The UCLA Asian Pacific American Voter Registration Study, 1986; contbr. articles to profl. jours. Chair Yale U. Alumni Schs. Com. of So. Calif., 1978—; bd. dirs. Altamed and La Clinica Familiar Del Barrio of East L.A., 1982—; commr. Bd. Transp. Commrs., City of L.A., 1984-90; v.p. Friends of the Little Tokyo Pub. Libr., 1986-88; co-chair nat. scholars adv. com. Japanese Am. Nat. Mus., 1987—; mem., bd. govs. Assn. of Yale Alumni, 1988-91; mem. exec. coun. Mayor's LA's Best Afterscl. Program, City of Los Angeles, 1988-90. Rsch. fellow Japan Soc. for the Promotion of Sci., 1978; recipient Nat. Scholars awrd for Outstanding Rsch. Article on Asian Pacific Am. Edn., Nat. Assn. for Asian and Pacific Am. Edn., 1985, Civil Rights Impace award Asian Am. Legal Ctr. of So. Calif., 1989; grantee Chancellors' Challenge in the Arts and Humanities, 1991, Calif. Policy Seminar, 1992, U. Calif. Pacific Rim Studies, 1992. Mem. Nat. Assn. for Interdisciplinary Ethnic Studies (bd. dirs. 1976-79), Assn. Asian Am. Studies (nat. pres. 1983-85), Nat. Assn. for Asian and Pacific Am. Edn. (exec. bd. dirs., v.p. 1983—). Office: UCLA Asian Am Studies Ctr 3230 Campbell Ave Los Angeles CA 90095

NAKANO, ROY Y., writer; b. Hilo, Hawaii, July 31, 1921; s. Toraki and Yoshi (Yano) N.; m. Tokiko Hideko Takahashi, Aug. 18, 1947. Grad., Hilo H.S., 1940. Logistics procurement agt. FAA, Honolulu, 1951-83. With U.S. Army, 1944-47. Avocations: music, writing, swimming, hiking. Home: 1557 Alewa Dr Honolulu HI 96817-1206

NAKAYAMA, PAULA AIKO, state supreme court justice; b. Honolulu, Oct. 19, 1953; m. Charles W. Totto; children: Elizabeth Murakami, Alexander Totto. BS, U. Calif., Davis, 1975; JD, U. Calif., 1979. Bar: Hawaii 1979. Dep. pros. atty. City and County of Honolulu, 1979-82; ptnr. Shim, Tam & Kirimitsu, Honolulu, 1982-92; judge 1st Cir. Ct. State of Hawaii, Oahu, 1992-93; justice State of Hawaii Supreme Ct., Honolulu, 1993—. Mem. Am. Judicature Soc., Hawaii Bar Assn., Sons and Daughters of 442. Office: Ali'iolani Hale Hawaii Supreme Ct 417 S King St Honolulu HI 96813-4720*

NALDER, ERIC CHRISTOPHER, investigative reporter; b. Coulee Dam, Wash., Mar. 2, 1946; s. Philip Richard and Mibs Dorothy (Aurdal) N.; m. Jan Christiansen, Dec. 20, 1968; 1 child, Britt Hillary. BA in Communications, U. Wash., 1968. News editor Whidbey News-Times, Oak Harbor, Wash., 1971; reporter Lynnwood (Wash.) Enterprise, 1972, Everett Herald, Lynnwood, 1972-75, gen. assignment reporter Seattle Post-Intelligencer, 1975-78, edn. writer, 1977-78, investigative reporter, 1978-83; chief investigative reporter Seattle Times, 1983—. Author: Tankers Full of Trouble, 1994. Recipient Edn. Writers Assn. award Charles Stewart Mott Found., 1978, Hearst Comty. Svc. award, 1978, C.B. Blethen awards (13), Outstanding Govt. Reporting award Seattle Mcpl. League, Pub. Svc. in Journalism award Sigma Delta Chi, 1987, Edward J. Meeman award Scripps Howard Found., 1987, Thomas Stokes award, Washington Journalism Ctr., 1990, Pulitzer prize for nat. reporting, 1990, Nat. Headline award, 1991, AP Sports Editors' Investigative Reporting award, 1992, Pub. Svc. award AP Mags. Editors Assn., 1992, Goldsmith prize for investigative reporting, 1992, Worth Bingham prize for investigative reporting, 1992, Headliner award, 1992, Investigative Reporters and Editors award, 1992, 95, Silver Gavel award ABA, 1995, Pulitzer prize for investigative reporting, 1997, John B. Oakes award for disting. environ. journalism, 1998. Mem. Investigative Reporters and Editors, Pacific N.W. Newspaper Guild. Avocation: downhill skiing. Office: Seattle Times 1120 John St Seattle WA 98109-5321 Address: PO Box 70 Seattle WA 98111-0070

NAMKUNG, XHANA MARIE, advertising executive; b. San Diego, Jan. 15, 1964; d. Paul S. Namkung and Leota Carolyn (Hamilton) Kotler. AA magna cum laude, L.A. Valley Coll., Van Nuys, Calif., 1984; BA with distinction, U. Hawaii, 1988. Office mgr. Kingsound Studios, North Hollywood, Calif., 1984-85; adminstrv. office mgr. Western Equipment Dist. Co., Van Nuys, Calif., 1984-90; legal sec. Northridge, Calif., 1989-92; lead student svc. rep. Learning Tree U., Chatsworth, Calif., 1991-93; exec. asst. fin. EMI Music Distbn., Woodland Hills, Calif., 1992-94, rsch. corr. nat. advt., 1994-95, sr. coord. nat. advt., 1995—. Vol. Musicares, L.A., 1995—. Mem. Women in Comm., Inc. Avocations: music, pop culture, travelling, hiking. Office: EMI Music Distbn 21700 Oxnard St Ste 700 Woodland Hills CA 91367-3617

NANAO, KENJILO, artist, educator; b. Aomori, Japan, July 26, 1929; came to U.S., 1960; s. Yosaburo Hirano and Tama Nanao; m. Gail Carol Chadell, Aug. 24, 1965; 1 child, Max Harunobu. Student, Nihon U., Tokyo, 1950-53, Calif. Sch. Fine Arts, San Francisco, 1960-63; MFA, San Francisco Art Inst., 1970. Lectr. art San Jose (Calif.) State U., 1970; prof. art Calif. State U., Hayward, 1970-91, prof. emeritus, 1991—; vis. prof. U. N.H., 1973, Stanford U., 1992. One-man shows include Tsubaki Kindai Gallery, Tokyo, 1965, Smith Andersen Gallery, Palo Alto, Calif., 1971, 74, 78, 90, 98, Santa Barbara Mus., 1972, Achenbach Found. Legion Honor, 1973, Dubins Gallery, L.A., 1985, 86, 89, 92, others; exhibited in group shows at Gump's Gallery, San Francisco, 1971-76, Anchorage Fine Arts and Hist. Mus., 1976, Bklyn. Mus., 1976, 78, Crocker Art Mus., Sacramento, Calif., 1980, Palo Alto Cultural Ctr., 1992, Galerie Sho, Tokyo, 1994, J.J. Brookings Gallery, San Francisco, 1997, others; represented in permanent collections Biblioteque National, Paris, Mus. Modern Art, N.Y.C., Libr. of Congress, Washington, Nat. Gallery of Art, Washington, others. Recipient 4 Purchase prizes Honolulu Acad. Arts, 1973-78, Purchase prize City of Phila., 1973, Bklyn. Mus. Art, 1972; Ford Found. grantee, 1968; Nat. Endowment for the Arts fellow, 1980. Home: 640 Santa Rosa Ave Berkeley CA 94707-1547

NANCE, JOHN JOSEPH, lawyer, writer, air safety analyst, broadcaster, consultant; b. Dallas, July 5, 1946; s. Joseph Turner and Margrette (Grubbs) N.; m. Benita Ann Priest, July 26, 1968; children: Dawn Michelle, Bridgitte Cathleen, Christopher Sean. BA, So. Meth. U., 1968, JD, 1969; grad., USAF Undergrad. Pilot Tng., Williams AFB, Ariz., 1971. Bar: Tex. 1970, U.S. Ct. Appeals (fed. cir.), 1994. News reporter, broadcaster, newsman various papers and stas. Honolulu and Dallas, 1957-66; radio news anchorman Sta. WFAA-AM, Dallas, 1966-70; newsman including on camera Sta. WFAA-TV, Dallas; pvt. practice law Dallas, 1970—; news dir. Newscom Network, Dallas, 1970; airline pilot Braniff Internat. Airways, Dallas, 1975-82, Alaska Airlines, Inc., Seattle, 1985—; chmn., pres. Exec. Transport, Inc., Tacoma, 1979-85; chmn., chief exec. officer EMEX Corp., Kent, Wash., 1987—; mng. ptnr. Phoenix Ptnrs., Ltd., Tacoma, Wash., 1995—; project devel. assoc. Columbia Tristar TV, 1997—; sr. ptnr. Nance & Carmichael, PLLC, Austin, Tex., 1997—; project devel. assoc. Columbia TriStar TV, 1997—; profl. speaker Human Mgmt., 1984—, Teamwork and Comms. in the Med. Profession; airline safety, advocate Ind. Cons., earthquake preparedness spokesman Ind. Cons.; dir. steering com. Found. for Issues Resolution in Sci. Tech., Seattle, 1987-89; speaker Northwestern Transp. Ctr. Deregulation and Safety Conf., 1987; cons. NOVA Why Planes Crash, PBS, 1987, ABC World News Tonight Crash of US AIR 427, 1994; aviation analyst ABC-TV and radio, 1995—; aviation editor: ABC Good Morning Am., 1995—; broadcast analyst, 1986—; spkr. in field. Author: Splash of Colors, 1984, Blind Trust, 1986 (Wash. Gov.'s award 1987), On Shaky Ground, 1988, Final Approach, 1990, What Goes Up, 1991, Scorpion Strike, 1982, Operating Handbook USAF Air Carrier Safety and Inspection Office, 1991, Phoenix Rising, 1994, Pandora's Clock, 1995, Medusa's Child, 1997, The Last Hostage, 1998; contbr. to Transportation Deregulation in the U.S., 1988; aviation editor: ABC Good Morning Am., 1995—; appeared in Sheep on the Runway Tacoma Little Theater, 1975; tech. advisor, actor Pandora's Clock NBC mini-series, 1996; appeared in Medusa's Child, ABC Mini-series, 1997; prodr., writer, dir. USAF Video Prodns.: ANG Introduction to CRM, 1992, USAF SOC CRM Program, 1992, Test and Evaluation CRM, 1993, The Teamwork Connection, 1996. Prs. Fox Glen Homeowners Assn., Tacoma, 1974-77; cons. Congl. Office Tech. Assessment, Tacoma, 1987; witness numerous air safety hearings U.S. Congress, Washington, 1986-88; bd. dirs. St. Charles Borromeo Sch., Tacoma, 1975-78, Nat. Patient Safety Found. of AMA, 1997—; mem. Mayor's Vets. Task Force, Tacoma, 1991; bd. advisors Jour. Air Law and Commerce So. Meth. Sch. Law, 1995—, exec. bd. Sch. of Law, 1998—; bd. advisors Pacific Northwest Writer's Conf., 1994—; mem. adv. bd. supply and logistics mgmt. program Portland State U., 1997—; exec. bd. mem. SMU Sch. Law, 1998—. Capt. USAFR, 1975-94; lt. col. Persian Gulf. Decorated Merit Svc. medal; named Airline Safety Man of Year Wash. State Div. of Aeronautics, 1987. Fellow Chartered Inst. Transport (Canberra, Australia); mem. ABA, SAG, Tex. Bar Assn., Author's Guild Am., Res. Officers Assn. (life), Aircraft Owners' and Pilots' Assn., Phi Alpha Delta, Delta Chi. Home and Office: John Nance Prodns 4512 87th Ave W Tacoma WA 98466-1920 Office: Phoenix Ptnrs Ltd PO Box 24465 Federal Way WA 98093-1465

NANCE, ROBERT LEWIS, oil company executive; b. Dallas, July 10, 1936; s. Melvin Renfro Nance and Ruth Natlie (Seibert) Nowlin; m. Penni Jane Warfel; children: Robert Scott, Amy Louise, Catherine Leslie. BS, So. Meth. U., 1959; LLD (hon.), Rocky Mountain Coll., 1989. V.p. geology Oliver & West Cons., Dallas, 1960-66; ptnr. Nance & Larue Cons., Dallas, 1966-69; pres., CEO Nance Petroleum Corp., Billings, Mont., 1969—; bd. dirs. First Interstate BancSystems, MDU Resources, Rocky Mountain Coll., Billings, chmn., 1986-91; mem. Nat. Petroleum Coun., 1992-94; chmn. Petroleum Technology Transfer Coun. Coun. pres. Am. Luth. Ch., Billings, 1980; trustee, chmn. Deaconess Med. Ctr., Billings; chmn. Deaconess Billings Clinic Healty Sys. Recipient Hall of Fame award Rocky Mountain Coll. Alumni, 1987, Disting. Svc. Trusteeship, Assn. Governing Bds. Univs. Colls., 1988. Mem. Am. Assn. Petroleum Geologists, Ind. Petroleum Assn. Am. (exec. com., nat. bd. govs.), Ind. Petroleum Assn. Mountain States (v.p. Mont. 1977-79), Mont. Petroleum Assn., Hilands Golf Club, Billings Petroleum Club. Avocations: fly fishing, scuba diving, skiing. Office: Nance Petroleum Corp PO Box 7168 550 N 31st St Billings MT 59103

NANDAGOPAL, MALLUR R., engineer; b. Kolar, Karnataka, India, May 14, 1938; came to U.S., 1976; s. M. Ramanuja Iyengar and Garudammal; m. Sreedharani K. Ramamurthy; children: Radha, Meena, Sudha. BS, Cen. Coll., Bangalore, India, 1958; B of Tech., Indian Inst. Tech., Bombay, 1962; ME, Indian Inst. Sci., Bangalore, 1963, PhD, 1974. Registered profl. engr., Wash. Mem. faculty Indian Inst. Sci., 1963-77; engr. City of Spokane, Wash., 1977—; coord. summer sch. Indian Inst. Sci., 1974-75. Contbr. articles to profl. jours. Mem. restoration adv. bd. Fairchild AFB. Mem. IEEE (sr., Engr. of Yr. award 1995), Inst. Sci. (sec. Staff Club 1972-74), Fed. Emergency Mgmt. Agy. (mitigation com.). Hindu. Avocations: tennis, astrology, reading, movies. Home: 410 E Shiloh Hills Dr Spokane WA 99208-5819

NANTO, ROXANNA LYNN, marketing professional, management consultant; b. Hanford, Calif., Dec. 17, 1952; d. Lawson Gene Brooks and Bernice (Page) Jackson; m. Harvey Ken Nanto, Mar. 23, 1970; 1 child, Shea Kiyoshi. AA, Chemeketa Community Coll., 1976; BSBA, Idaho State U., 1978. PBX operator Telephone Answer Bus. Svc., Moses Lake, Wash., 1965-75; edn. coord. MimiCassia Community Edn., Rupert, Idaho, 1976-77; office mgr. Lockwood Corp., Rupert, Idaho, 1977-78; cost acct. Keyes Fibre Co., Wenatchee, Wash., 1978-80; acctg. office mgr. Armstrong & Armstrong, Wenatchee, Wash., 1980-81; office mgr. Cascade Cable Constrn. Inc., East Wenatchee, Wash., 1981-83; interviewer, counselor Wash. Employment Security, Wenatchee, 1983-84; pres. chief exec. officer Regional Health Care

Plus, East Wenatchee, 1986-88; dist. career coord. Eastmont Sch. Dist., East Wenatchee, 1984-90; prin. Career Cons., 1988-90; exec. dir. Wenatchee Valley Coll. Found., 1990-91; ednl. cons. Sunbelt Consortium, East Wenatchee, 1991-93; cons. CC Cons. Assocs., 1993—; ptnr. Cmty. Devel. Mktg. and Mgmt. Resource Group, Wenatchee, Wash., 1994—; also bd. dirs. Cmty. Devel. Mktg. and Mgmt. Resource Group, Wenatchee; ptnr. Bus. Consulting and Rsch., Malaga, Wash., 1997—; speaker North Cen. Washington Profl. Women, Wenatche, 1987, Wen Career Women's Network, Wenatchee, 1990, Wenatchee Valley Rotary, 1990, Meeting the Challenge of Workforce 2000, Seattle, 1993; cons., speaker Wash. State Sch. Dirs., Seattle, 1987; speaker Wenatchee C. of C., 1989; sec. Constrn. Coun. of North Cen. Washington, Wenatchee, 1981-83; bd. dirs. Gen. Vocat. Adv. Bd., Wenatchee, 1986-88, Washington Family Ind. Program, Olympia, 1989—; mem. econ. devel. coun. Grant County, 1992—; ptnr. low income housing devel. Bus. Cons. & Rsch., Wenatchee, 1996—. Mem. at large career Women's Network, 1984—, mem. Econ. Devel. Coun. of No. Cen. Washington; mem. Steering Com. to Retain Judge Small. Recipient Nat. Paragon award, 1991; grantee Nat. Career Devel. Guidelines Wash. State, 1989; named Wenatchee Valley Coll. Vocat. Contbr. of Yr., 1991. Fellow Dem. Women's Club; mem. Nat. Assn. Career Counselors, Nat. Assn. Pvt. Career Counselors, Nat. Coun. Resource Devel., NCW Estate Planning Coun. Avocations: self improvement books, staff and organizational development, motivational audio tapes, housing development for elderly and special needs individuals. Home and Office: 2961 Riviera Blvd Malaga WA 98828-9733

NAPLES, CAESAR JOSEPH, law/public policy educator, lawyer, consultant; b. Buffalo, Sept. 4, 1938; s. Caesar M. and Fannie A. (Occhipinti) N.; children: Jennifer, Caesar; m. Sandra L. Harrison, July 16, 1983. AB, Yale U., 1960; JD, SUNY, 1963. Bar: N.Y. 1963, Fla. 1977, Calif. 1988, U.S. Supreme Ct. 1965. Assoc. Moot & Sprague, Buffalo, 1965-69; asst. dir., employee rels. N.Y. Gov. Office, Albany, 1969-71; asst. v. chancellor SUNY, Albany, 1971-75; vice chancellor and gen. counsel Fla. State U. System, 1975-82; v. chancellor Calif. State U. System, 1983-92; vice chancellor emeritus Calif. State U., 1992—; prof. law and fin. Calif. State U. System, Long Beach, 1983—; bd. dirs., gen. counsel Walden U., Mpls. and Naples, Fla., 1993—; cons. Govt. of Australia, U. Nev. Sys., Assn. Can. Colls. and Univs., Que., also other univs. and colls. Contbr. articles to profl. jours.; co-author: Romanov Succession, 1989 with J.Victor Baldridge. Bd. dirs., gen. counsel Walden U., 1997—; mem. Metlife Resources Adv. Bd., 1986—, chmn., 1992—; mem. Meml. Heart Inst. Long Beach Meml. Hosp., 1993—, bd. dirs., chmn. 1998—, found. bd., 1996—; bd. dirs. Calif. Acad. Math. and Scis., 1995—. Capt. U.S. Army, 1963-65. Mem. Acad Pers. Adminstrn. (founder), Nat. Ctr. for Study Collective Bargaining Higher Edn. (bd. dirs.). Avocations: opera, tennis. E-mail: cjnaples@csulb.edu. Fax: 310-798-0065. Office: 816 N Juanita Ave Ste B Redondo Beach CA 90277-2200

NAPLES, SUSAN LORRAINE, property management company executive; b. Claremont, N.H., May 15, 1949; d. Robert William Gerrie and Margaret Lorraine (Leavitt) Baney; 1 child, Clinton Eric. Student pub. schs. Santa Ana, Calif. Cert. cmty. assn. mgr., profl. cmty. assn. mgr. Project dir., personnel dir. Cmty. Devel. Council Santa Ana, 1974-76; founding exec. dir. Women's Transitional Living Ctr., Orange, Calif., 1976-78; sr. account exec. Profl. Cmty. Mgmt., El Toro, Calif., 1978-81; CEO Cardinal Property Mgmt., Inc., Anaheim, 1981—. Co-author: How to Start a Shelter for Battered Women, 1977. Participant White House Conf. on Domestic Violence, 1977; founder, dir. Calif. Assn. Cmty. Mgrs., 1992-96, AIDS Walk Orange County, 1991-92; del. Dem. Nat. Conv., 1992, 96; mem. Dem. Found. Orange County, 1992—, vice-chair, 1994-96, treas., 1996—; mem. Orange County Dem. Ctrl. Com., 1991-96, Calif. Dem. Ctrl. Com., 1992-96, mem. exec. bd., 1993-94. Mem. NOW (co-chair Orange County chpt. 1976, co-coordinator domestic violence task force Calif. chpt. 1977), NAFE, Nat. Women's Polit. Caucus, Assn. Traditional Hooking Artists. Office: Cardinal Property Mgmt Inc 1290 N Hancock St Ste 103 Anaheim CA 92807-1982

NAPOLITANO, JANET ANN, prosecutor; b. N.Y.C., Nov. 29, 1957; d. Leonard Michael and Jane Marie (Winer) N. BS, U. Santa Clara, Calif., 1979; JD, U. Va., 1983. Bar: Ariz. 1984, U.S. Dist. Ct. Ariz. 1984, Ct. Appeals (9th cir.) 1984, U.S. Ct. Appeals (10th cir.) 1988. Law clk. to hon. Mary Schroeder U.S Ct. Appeals (9th Cir.), 1983-84; assoc. Lewis & Roca, Phoenix, 1984-89, ptnr., 1989-93; U.S. atty. Dist. Ariz., Phoenix, 1993-97; atty. Lewis and Roca, Phoenix, 1997—; mem. Atty. Gen.'s Adv. Com., 1993—, chair, 1995-96. Vice-chair Ariz. Dem. Party, 1991-92; mem. Dem. Nat. Com., 1991-92; State Bd. Tech. Registration, 1989-92; Phoenix Design Standards Rev. Com., 1989-91; bd. dirs. Ariz. Cmty. Legal Svcs. Corp., 1987-92; bd. regents Santa Clara U., 1992—. Truman Scholarship Found. scholar, 1977. Mem. ABA, Am. Law Inst., Ariz. Bar Assn., Maricopa County Bar Assn., Am. Judicature Soc., Ariz. State Bar (chmn. civil practice and procedure com. 1991-92), Phi Beta Kappa, Alpha Sigma Nu. Avocations: hiking, trekking, travel, reading, film. Office: PO Box 2525 Phoenix AZ 85002-2525

NARAMORE, JAMES JOSEPH, family practice physician, educator; b. Gillette, Wyo., Nov. 29, 1949; s. Kenneth Chester and Joan (Biggerstaff) N.; m. Karen Rae Buttermore, July 9, 1972; children: Lindsay, Marissa, Jessica, Marcus. BA with highest achievement in Biology, John Brown U., Siloam Springs, Ark., 1972; MD with family practice honors, U. Utah, 1977. Diplomate Am. Bd. Family Practice. Resident in family practice U. Nebr., Omaha, 1977-80, chief resident; pvt. practice, Gillette, 1981—; mem. staff Campbell County Meml. Hosp., Gillette, 1980—, chief staff, 1986, chief dept. family practice, 1990-91; instr. dept. human medicine U. Wyo., 1983-86, clin. assoc. prof. family practice, 1986—; ptnr., co-founder Med. Arts Lab., Gillette, 1981—; med. dir. Campbell County Detention Ctr., 1988—; med. dir. Pioneer Manor Nursing Home, Gillette, 1989—; aviation med. examiner FAA, Oklahoma City, 1986—; cons. on occupational medicine to numerous industries, Campbell County, 1986—; adv. coun. Wyo. Bd. Medicine, 1993—. Charter mem. Gillette Area Leadership Inst., 1986-87; chmn. missions com. Grace Bible Ch., Gillette, 1983—, chmn. bd. elders, 1989—. Mem. Am. Acad. Family Physicians, Wyo. Med. Soc., Campbell County Med. Soc. (pres. 1983-84), Gillette C. of C. (bd. dirs. 1987-90), Toastmasters (pres. Gillette 1992, Competent Toastmaster award 1986—, Able Toastmaster Bronze award 1996). Republican. Avocations: snow skiing, bicycling, photography, reading, travel. Home: 1214 Hilltop Ct Gillette WY 82718-5625 Office: Family Health 407 S Medical Arts Ct Ste D Gillette WY 82716-3372

NARAYANAMURTI, VENKATESH, research administrator; b. Bangalore, Karnataka, India, Sept. 9, 1939; came to U.S., 1961; s. Duraiswami and Janaki (Subramaniam) N.; m. Jayalakshmi Krishnayya, Aug. 23, 1961; children: Arjun, Ranjini, Krishna. BSc, MSc, St. Stephen's Coll., Delhi, India, 1958; PhD, Cornell U., 1965. Instr., rsch. assoc. Cornell U., Ithaca, N.Y., 1965-68; mem. tech. staff AT&T Bell Labs., Murray Hill, N.J., 1968-76, dept.head, 1976-81, dir., 1981-87; v.p. rsch. Sandia Nat. Labs., Albuquerque, 1987-92; dean engring. U. Calif., Santa Barbara, 1992—; chmn. microelectric bd. Jet Propulsion Lab., Pasadena, Calif., 1988—; chmn. condensed matter and materials phys. panel NRC, 1996; mem. U. Calif. Pres.' Coun. for Nat. Labs., 1995—; bd. dirs. Serpal Interface, Inc., Santa Clara, Calif., 1997—; mem. NAE Pub. Info. Adv. Bd., 1993—, NSF Dir.'s Strategic Planning Bd., 1994—, Los Alamos Nat. Lab. Adv. Bd. for Materials and Indsl. Partnerships, 1994—. Author more than 130 publs.; patentee in field. Fellow IEEE, AAAS, Am. Phys. Soc., Indian Acad. Scis.; mem. NAE, Royal Swedish Acad. Engring. Scis. (fgn.). Avocations: long distance running, squash. Office: U Calif Dept Engring Santa Barbara CA 93106

NARULA, MOHAN LAL, realtor; b. Ferozepur, India, Feb. 2, 1939; came to U.S., 1962; s. Ram Dyal and Pemeshwari Narula; m. Sylvia Conway, Aug. 31, 1968; children: Rabinder, Rajinder. BS, Panjab U., India, 1960; BSME, Calif. Poly. State U., San Luis Obispo, 1965; MS in Engring., Calif. State U., Northridge, 1970. Engr. Abex Corp., Oxnard, Calif., 1965-69; salesman, realtor Walker & Lee, Oxnard, Calif., 1970-73; owner, realtor Narula Co. Realtors, Oxnard, Calif., 1973—. Mem. Cert. Comml. Investment Mem. (designate 1979), Oxnard Harbor Bd. Realtors (mem. profl. standard com. 1980-89), Los Angeles Cert. Comml. Investment Mem. (bd. dirs., treas. 1985). Home: 2830 W Hill St Oxnard CA 93035-2522 Office: Narula Co Realtor 3201 Samuel Ave Ste 7 Oxnard CA 93033-5334

NASH, PAUL LESLIE, ceramic art educator; b. Van Nuys, Calif., Aug. 8, 1949; s. Irving and Emily Nash; m. Kendra Ozaki, Mar. 15, 1975 (div. Mar. 1996); children: Dylan, Ian. BFA with honors, Chouinard Art Inst., 1971; MA in Tchg., RISD, 1973. Instr. art-ceramics Windward C.C. U. Hawaii, Kanehoe, 1985-90, asst. prof., 1990-95, assoc. prof., 1995—; studio artist, 1971—. Guest artist Queen Emma Gallery, 1997; exhibited in numerous shows, including Marietta Coll., 1976-78, So. Calif. Exposition, Del Mar, 1976, Internat. Art Festival, L.A., 1978, Canyon Gallery Two, L.A., 1979, 81, Garendo Gallery, Studio City, 1980, 81, Hawaii Craftsmen Show, 1982, Raku Ho'olaule'a, 1984, 86, 89, 90, 92, Hon. Artist's Guild, 1989, Kagawa Jr. Coll., Japan, 1990, 91, Contemporary Mus., U. Hawaii, 1990-91, Windward C.C., 1991, 94, 96, U. Hawaii, Manoa, 1995, Queen Emma Gallery, 1999, others. Art advisor Windward C.C. Ceramics Club, 1983—. Mem. Hawaii Craftsman Assn. (bd. dirs. 1998—, v.p. 1999—). Avocations: guitar, writing music, folk rock. Office: Windward CC 45-720 Keaahala Rd Kaneohe HI 96744-3528

NASH, STEVEN ALAN, museum curator, art historian; b. Wadsworth, Ohio, Apr. 8, 1944; s. Frank W. N. and LaDema (Siffert) N.; m. Carol Ostrowski, June 14, 1969; children: Colin H., Jessica K. BA, Dartmouth Coll., 1966; PhD, Stanford U., 1973. Curator Albright-Knox Art Gallery, Buffalo, 1973-80; dep. dir., chief curator Dallas Mus. Art, 1980-88; assoc. dir., chief curator, European Arts Fine Arts Mus. of San Francisco, 1988—; panelist Nat. Endowment for the Arts, Washington, 1986—, Inst. Mus. Svcs., Washington, 1979—; bd. dirs. Oberlin (Ohio) Intermus. Conservation Labs., 1976-80. Author: Catalogue: Albright-Knox Art Gallery, 1976, Ben Nicholson, 1977, Naum Gabo: Constructivism, 1986, Century of Modern Sculpture, 1987. Bd. dirs. Lakehill Prep. Sch., Dallas, 1987-88, Buffalo Archtl. Guidebook, 1979-80. Mus. Profl. fellow Nat. Endowment for Arts, 1980; fellow Mabelle McLeod Lewis Found., 1970-71. Mem. Coll. Art Assn., Am. Assn. Mus., Dartmouth Alumni Club. Office: Fine Arts Mus San Francisco Legion of Honor Lincoln Pk San Francisco CA 94121-1693*

NASO, VALERIE JOAN, automobile dealership executive, travel company operator, artist, photographer, writer; b. Stockton, Calif., Aug. 19, 1941; d. Alan Robert and Natalie Grace (Gardner) McKittrick Naso; m. Peter Joralemon, May 31, 1971 (div.). Student pub. schs., Piedmont, Calif. Cert. graphoanalyst. Pres., Naso Motor Co. (formerly Broadway Cadillacs, Oakland, Calif.) Bishop, Calif., 1964—; freelance artist, 1965—; owner, operator Wooden Horse Antiques, Bishop, 1970-82; editor, writer, photographer Sierra Life Mag., Bishop, 1980-83; freelance writer, photographer, 1972—; owner, operator Boredom Tours, Bishop, 1981—; owner, sole photographer, Renaissance Photography, N.Y.C. and Bishop, Calif., 1982—, Keyboard Colors, 1986; cons. graphoanalyst, 1976—. Fiction, non-fiction work pub. in Horse and Horseman, Am. Horseman, Horse & Rider Mag., Cameo Mag., Desert Mag., Sierra Life Mag. Mem. Nat. Assn. Female Execs., Authors Guild, Inc., Authors League Am., Am. Film Inst., Archives of Am. Art, Lalique Soc. Am., Musical Box Soc. Internat., Alliance Francaise (N.Y. chpt.), Bishop C. of C., Victorian Soc. Am., Nat. Trust for Hist. Preservation, Am. Craft Coun., Nat. Rifle Assn. Clubs: Cadillac LaSalle (nat. and so. calif. chpts.); Wagner Soc. (N.Y.C.). Office: 783 N Main St Bishop CA 93514-2427 also: PO Box 1625 Bishop CA 93515-1625

NASON, DOLORES IRENE, computer company executive, counselor, eucharistic minister; b. Seattle; d. William Joseph Lockinger and Ruby Irene (Church) Gilstrap; m. George Malcolm Nason Jr.; children: George Malcolm III, Scott James, Lance William, Natalie Joan. Student, Long Beach (Calif.) City Coll.; cert. in Religious Edn. for elem tchrs., Immaculate Heart Coll., cert. teaching, cert. secondary teaching; attended, Salesian Sem. Buyer J. C. Penney Co., Barstow, Calif.; prin. St. Cyprian Confraternity of Christian Doctrine Elem. Sch., Long Beach; prin. summer sch. St. Cyprian Confraternity of Christian Doctrine Elem. Sch., Long Beach; pres. St. Cyprian Confraternity Orgn., Long Beach; dist. co-chmn. L.A. Diocese; v.p. Nason & Assocs., Inc., Long Beach, 1978—; pres. L.A. County Commn. on Obscenity & Pornography, 1984—; eucharistic minister St. Cyprian Ch., Long Beach, 1985—; bd. dirs. L.A. County Children's Svcs., 1988—; social svcs. counselor Disabled Resources Ctr., Inc., Long Beach, 1992—; vol. Meml. Children's Hosp., Long Beach, 1977—; mem. scholarship com. Long Beach City Coll., 1984-90, Calif. State U., Long Beach, 1984-90. Mem. devel. bd. St. Joseph High Sch., 1987—; pres. St. Cyprian's Parish Coun., 1962—; mem. Long Beach Civic Light Opera, 1973-96, Assistance League of Long Beach, 1976—. Mem. U. of Pacific Club, KC (Family of Month award 1988). Roman Catholic. Avocations: physical fitness, theater, choir, travel.

NASVIK-DENNISON, ANNA, artist; b. St. Paul; d. Peter Olson and Hattie Mathilda (Swenson) Nasvik; m. Roger Bennett, Nov. 7, 1936 (dec. June 1996); children: Lynne, Kristin. Student, Coll. of St. Catherine, St. Paul, 1925, St. Paul Sch. of Art, 1927, Art Student's League, 1932. Tchr. art St. Joseph's Acad., St. Paul, 1926-30; freelance fashion illustrator N.Y.C., 1930-64; artist syndicated page The Fashion Syndicate, N.Y.C., 1934-38; mem. nat. art bd. Nat. League Am. Pen Women, 1990-92. One woman shows include Colbert Galleries, Sherbrooke St., Mont., Can., 1979, Gallery Milhalis, Sherbrooke St., Mont., 1984, T. Eaton Foyer des Arts, Mont., 1982-87, Venable-Neslage Gallerie, Washington, 1979-84, Lido Galleries, Scottsdale, Ariz., 1988, Hilltop Galleries, Nogales, Ariz., 1991 (top painting award, People's Choice award), 1995, Maiden Ln. Gallery, San Francisco, 1991, Hilltop Gallery, Nogales, 1995 (hon. mention Tubac Ctr. of Arts 1995, hon. mention 1998), 96. Named Woman of Art, Foyer des Arts, 1982; winner 3 top awards Ariz. juried show, Nat. League Am. Pen Women, 1989; recipient 3 People's Choice award Hilltop Galleries, 1991. Mem. Nat. Mus. Women in Arts, Santa Cruz Valley Art Assn., Lakeshore Assn. of Art, Nat. League of Pen Women (3 Top awards 1989, nat. bd. dirs. 1990—), Pen Women Sonora Desert. Avocations: ballroom dancing, aerobics, church, people, painting. Home and Office: 231 W Paseo Adobe Green Valley AZ 85614-3462

NATHAN, LAURA E., sociology educator; b. L.A., Oct. 28, 1951; d. Monroe and Sheila (Solomon) Engelberg; m. Mark D. Nathan, April 9, 1978; children: Justin. BA in Sociology, U. Calif., Santa Barbara, 1973; MA in Sociology, U. Calif., L.A., 1975, PhD in Sociology, 1981. Teaching assoc. in sociology Univ. Calif., L.A., 1975-76; acting asst. prof. sociology Calif. State Univ., Fullerton, Calif., 1977-81; coord., instr. Univ. Calif., L.A., 1979-80; assoc. prof. sociology and psychology Antelope Valley Coll., Lancaster, Calif., 1981-82; asst. prof. sociology Mills Coll., Oakland, Calif., 1982-87; assoc. prof. sociology Mills Coll., Oakland, 1987-93; prof. of sociology Mills Coll., Oakland, Calif., 1993—, Robert J. and Ann B. Wert prof. of sociology, 1993—; lectr. in sociology and womens studies Calif. State Univ., Long Beach, 1978; program evaluator U.S. Dept. Health, Edn. and Welfare, L.A., 1974-75, program dir. 1975-76; mem. conf. planning com. Womens Leadership Conf., Mills Coll., also com. chair, 1992-93; bd. dirs. Am. Cancer Soc., Alameda County, Calif., 1985—. Author: (with others) Secondary Analysis of Survey Data, 1985; contbr. chpts. to books. Regents Rsch. grantee, 1979, Mellon Found. grantee, 1983, Faculty Devel. Rsch. grantee Mills. Coll., 1985, 86, 87, 90, 91, 94, 95, W.K. Kellogg Nat. fellow, 1988, Thornton Bradshaw Humanities fellow Claremont Grad. Sch., 1990; recipient Disting. Leadership award Am. Cancer Soc., 1995, ten Broek Soc. award for Excellence in Teaching, 1996. Mem. Pacific Sociol. Assn. (mem. nominating com. 1985-88, mem. program com. 1995—), Am. Sociol. Assn. (membership com. 1988-92), Soc. for the Study of Social Problems (chmn. poverty, class inequality div. 1987-88). Jewish. Avocations: traveling, mysteries, vol. work. Office: Mills Coll 5000 Macarthur Blvd Oakland CA 94613-1301

NATHANSON, THEODORE HERZL, aeronautical engineer, architect; b. Montreal, Que., Can., Apr. 20, 1923; came to U.S., 1949; naturalized, 1983; s. Henry and Minnie (Goldberg) N.; student McGill U., 1940-42; SB in Aero. Engring., MIT, 1944; MArch, Harvard U., 1955. Research engr. Noorduyn Aviation Ltd., Montreal, 1944-45; stress engr. Canadair Ltd., Montreal, 1945-46; structural engr. A.V. Roe (Can.) Ltd., Malton, Ont., 1946-47; with Mies van der Rohe, Chgo., summer 1949, R. Buckminster Fuller, Forest Hills, N.Y., summer 1951; cons. engr. and architect, Montreal, Boston, Los Angeles, 1955—; mem. tech. staff Rockwell Internat., 1979-92, structural analysis and advanced design Space Transp. Systems div., Downey, Calif., 1979-86, mission ops. and advanced concepts Space Sta. Systems div., 1986-87, space sta. elec. power system Rocketdyne div., Canoga Park, Calif., 1987-92; cons. Aerospace Engr., L.A., 1992—; lectr. architecture, McGill U., 1967-68. Fellow Brit. Interplanetary Soc.; mem. Order Engrs. Que., Order Architects Que., Soc. Am. Registered Architects, Nat. Soc. Profl. Engrs., AIAA, AIA (assoc.), Royal Archtl. Inst. Can., Nat. Mgmt. Assn., Copley Soc. of Boston, MIT Club of So. Calif. (bd. govs.), Can. Soc. (Los Angeles). Projects and models included in group shows: Mus. Fine Arts, Springfield, Mass., 1961, N.Y. World's Fair, 1965, Winterfest, Boston, 1966, Boston Artists' Project '70. Jewish. Home: 225 S Olive St Apt 1502 Los Angeles CA 90012-4906

NATHWANI, BHARAT NAROTTAM, pathologist, consultant; b. Bombay, Jan. 20, 1945; came to U.S., 1972; s. Narottam Pragji and Bharati N. (Lakhani) N. MBBS, Grant Med. Coll., Bombay, 1969, MD in Pathology, 1972. Intern Grant Med. Coll., Bombay U., 1968-69; asst. prof. pathology Grant Med. Coll., 1972; fellow in hematology Cook County Hosp., Chgo., 1972-73; resident in pathology Rush U., Chgo., 1973-74; fellow in hematopathology City of Hope Med. Ctr., Duarte, Calif., 1975-76, pathologist, 1977-84; prof. pathology, chief hematopathology U. So. Calif., L.A., 1984—. Contbr. numerous articles to profl. jours. Recipient Grant awards Nat. Libr. Medicine, Bethesda, Md., Nat. Cancer Inst., 1991. Mem. AAAS, Internat. Acad. Pathology, Am. Soc. Clin. Pathology, Am. Soc. Hematology, Am. Soc. Oncology. Office: U So Calif Sch Medicine HMR 209 2011 Zonal Ave Los Angeles CA 90033-1034

NATT, THEODORE MCCLELLAND, newspaper editor, publisher; b. Portland, Oreg., Mar. 28, 1941; s. Theodore Manfred and Martha Sue (McClelland) N.; B.S., U. Oreg., 1963; postgrad. Stanford, 1966-67; M. Diane Gail Shields, Dec. 27, 1962; children—Theodore McClelland, Lorena Sue, David Morris, Morgan Sadler. Reporter, Walla Walla (Wash.) Union-Bull., 1963-64, Oregonian, Portland, 1964-65; news editor St. Helens (Oreg.) Sentinel-Mist, 1965-66; asso. editor Daily News, Longview, Wash., 1968-71, mng. editor, 1971-74, editor, publisher, 1974—; dir., sec., exec. v.p. Longview Pub. Co., 1971-86; pres., chief exec. officer Westmedia Corp., Longview, 1986—. Mem. adv. com. Wash. Dept. Social and Health Services, 1972-74; mem. bd. visitors John S. Knight Fellowships, Stanford U.; pres. Allied Daily Newspapers, 1985-88. Stanford U. profl. journalism fellow, 1966-67; Pulitzer prize juror, 1977, 83, 84, 93, 94. Recipient Pulitzer prize, 1981. Mem. Wash. Asso. Press Assn. (pres. 1974-75), Soc. Profl. Journalists, Am. Soc. Newspaper Editors (dir. 1988-91), AP Mng. Editors Assn. (pres. 1984), Coun. Fgn. Rels., Washington Athletic Club (Seattle), Rainier Club (Seattle), Longview Country Club, Nat. Press Club (Washington), Kappa Sigma, Sigma Delta Chi (Disting. Service award 1981). Democrat. Episcopalian. Office: The Daily News PO Box 189 Longview WA 98632-7118

NAU, CHARLES JOHN, lawyer; b. Chgo., Mar. 12, 1947; s. Charles J. and Roma (Murphy) N. BA maxima cum laude, U. Notre Dame, 1969, LLD cum laude, 1974. Bar: N.Y. 1975, Calif. 1983, France, 1979. Gen. counsel Syntex Labs., Inc., Palo Alto, Calif., 1983-94; dir. govt. affairs ALZA Corp., Palo Alto, Calif., 1995—; cons. Nat. Inst. Drug Abuse CDC, Washington, 1990, legal advisor Nat. Leadership Coalition on AIDS, Washington, 1990—; del. EEC-UNESCO Internat. Conf. AIDS in the Workplace, Paris, 1992. Chair SYNPAC, Palo Alto, 1986-94; del. Dem. Nat. Convention, N.Y., 1980; exec. dir. Dems. Abroad, 1984. Mem. Nat. Health Care Attorneys. Office: ALZA Corp PO Box 10950 Palo Alto CA 94303-0802

NAUGHTEN, ROBERT NORMAN, pediatrician; b. Stockton, Calif., Oct. 13, 1928; s. Norman Stafford and Junetta (Doherty) N.; m. Ann Louise Charkins, June 26, 1954; children: Robert James, Annette Marie Naughten-Dessel, Patricia Louise Schoof. AA, San Jose City Coll., San Jose, Calif., 1948; BA, U. Calif., Berkeley, 1950; MA, Stanford U., 1955; MD, Hahnemann U., 1959. Lic. physician and surgeon, Calif. Intern Highland-Alameda County Hosp., Oakland, Calif., 1959-60; rsch. fellow Nat. Cancer Inst., Stanford, Calif., 1960-61; resident pediat. Stanford Med. Ctr., 1961-63; pvt. practice specializing in pediat. Los Gatos, Calif., 1963—; instr. Santa Clara Valley Med. Ctr., San Jose, 1963—, Dept. of Pediat., Stanford, 1963-73; cons. drug abuse San Jose Police Dept., 1963-68; cons. child abuse Dist. Atty., San Jose, 1984 ; cons. dept. social svcs. State of Calif., 1989—. Contbr. articles to profl. jours. Bd. dirs., v.p. Outreach and Escort, Inc., San Jose, 1985-88. Named Alumnus of Yr. San Jose City Coll., 1967, Chef of the West Sunset Mag., 1989; fellow Coll. of Physicians, Phila., 1986. Mem. AMA, Calif. Assn., Santa Clara Med. Assn. (v.p. 1986-88), Am. Acad. Pediatrics, Am. Acad. Allergy and Clin. Immunology, Calif. Alumni Assn. (Berkeley), Stanford Alumni Assn., Commonwealth Club (San Francisco), Soc. of the Sigma Xi. Democrat. Roman Catholic. Avocations: gourmet cooking, stamp collecting, sailing, art. Home: 13601 Riverdale Dr Saratoga CA 95070-5229 Office: 777 Knowles Dr Ste 3 Los Gatos CA 95032-1417

NAUGOLNYKH, KONSTANTIN ALEKSANDROVICH, physicist; b. Baku, Russia, Oct. 7, 1932; s. Leonid A. Prilipko and Valentina Naugolnykh; m. Alla E. Vovk, May 19, 1959; 1 child, Tatiana K. PhD, N. Andreev Acoustics Inst., Moscow, 1959, D, 1971, prof., 1980. Scientific researcher Acoustics Inst., Moscow, 1959-63; vis. prof. Brown Univ., Providence, R.I., 1963-64; sr. researcher Acoustics Inst., Moscow, 1965-80; head of lab. N. Andreev Acoustics Inst., Moscow, 1980-94; rsch. assoc. NOAA/ERL/ETL/CU, Boulder, Colo., 1994—. Co-author: Electric Disharges in Water, 1971, Nonlinear Wave Processes in Acoustics, 1990; patentee in field. Fellow Acoustical Soc. Am., Russian Acoustical Soc. (v.p. 1992-94); mem. Nat. Oceanic & Atmospheric Adminstrn., Environ. Rsch. Lab., Environ. Tech. Lab. Avocations: skiing, windsurfing. Home: 4990 Meredith Way Apt 203 Boulder CO 80303-1191 Office: 325 Broadway St Boulder CO 80303-3337

NAVA, YOLANDA MARGOT, broadcast journalist, author; b. L.A., Nov. 23, 1944; d. Roberto Nava and Consuelo (Chavira) Stepsis; m. Art Torres, May, 1975 (div. July 1993); children: Joaquin Nava Torres, Danielle Nava Torres. BA, UCLA, 1967, postgrad., 1968-70. Credentialed C.C. educator. Tchr. h.s. L.A. Unified Sch. Dist., 1968-70; instr. sociology Santa Monica (Calif.) Coll., 1970-71; project dir. Neighborhood Youth Corps United Way, L.A., 1971-73; career opportunity devel. specialist Calif. State Univs.-Colls., L.A., 1973-74; host "Impacto" KNBC-TV, Burbank, Calif., 1973-74; prodr., host "Saturday" KNBC-TV, Burbank, 1974-75, co-host "Sunday", 1983-85; news anchor, reporter KTXL-TV, Sacramento, Calif., 1977-79, KXTV-TV, Sacramento, 1979-81; west coast reporter, nat. host "Latin Tempo" La Raza Prodn. Ctr., Washington, 1983-86; news reporter, host "2-the-Point" KCBS-TV, L.A., 1987-89; v.p., owner Ponce Nicasio Broadcasting, Inc./KCMY Channel 29, Sacramento, 1990-95; host Life and Times Tonight, KCET-TV, L.A., 1998—; cons. pub. info. L.A. Unified Sch. Dist., 1990-97. Author: Chicanas in the Media, 1981, Hispanics in the Media, 1986, It's All in the Frijoles: Famous latinos Share Real Life Stories, Time-Tested Dichos, Favorite Folktales and Inspiring Words of Wisdom, 1999; weekly columnist Eastern Group Publs., L.A., 1995—. Bd. dirs. YWCA Greater L.A., 1993-98, L.A. Area Boy Scout Coun., 1992—, Bella Lewitsky Dance Co., L.A., 1991-98; mem. adv. com. L.A. Chamber Orch., 1992—, bd. mem. Eastside Family & Child Ctr., 1995—. Recipient Emmy award Acad. TV Arts & Scis., 1988; named one of 5 Women of Achievement, L.A. Times, 1986, one of 25 Top Hispanic Leaders, L.A. Herald Examiner, 1983, one of 100 Top Women in Calif., 1983. Mem. Trusteeship for Women, Women in Film, Nat. Assn. Hispanic Journalists, Calif. Coun. Adult Educators, Comision Femenil Mexicana Nacional (founder, pres. 1973-75). Democrat. Mem. Ch. Religious Sci. Avocations: gardening, hiking, travel, theater, arts. Office: 4401 Sunset Blvd Los Angeles CA 90027

NAVARRO, MANUEL, protective services official; b. Oakland, Calif.. AA in Fire Sci., BA in Pub. Adminstrn. Cert. master fire instr., Colo. Fire fighter, 1966-67, Lawrence Radiation Lab. Fire Dept., 1967-72; various positions to asst. chief Oakland (Calif.) Fire Dept., 1972-93; fire chief Colorado Springs (Colo.) Fire Dept., 1993-94; mem. FEMA Urban Search and Rescue Mgmt. and Control Com. Mem. Mex.-Am. Polit. Assn. (chairperson). Office: Colorado Springs Fire Dept 31 S Weber St Colorado Springs CO 80903-1913

NAVICKAS, JOHN, fluid dynamics engineer, researcher, consultant; b. Raseiniai, Lithuania, Nov. 26, 1933; came to U.S., 1949; s. John and Ona (Remeikis) N.; m. Marija D. Masionis Navickas, Sept. 1, 1985; children: Rima, Rymante, Tadas, Dalia. BS, UCLA, 1957; MS, 1961. Assoc. tech. fellow The Boeing Co., Huntington Beach, Calif., 1957—; cons. Lloyd's Registry of Shipping, Eng., 1982, Am. Bur. Shipping, 1992, Nippon Kokan, Japan, 1979-82, Lithuania Acad. Sci., 1978, 82. Editor: Conference Proceedings Computational Experiments, 1989; author more than 35 articles on

multi-phase fluid dynamics, computational methods and space systems. Com. mem. Lithuanian Childrens Hope, L.A., 1992—. Capt. U.S. Army, 1957-65. Mem. ASME, AIAA.

NAYLOR, BRUCE GORDON, museum director; b. Midale, Sask., Can., Aug. 19, 1950; s. John Raymond Naylor and Mary Lynn (Frisby) Redeberg; m. Marlene Johnstone, Dec. 19, 1981 (dec. July 1992); m. Judith Jeune, June 11, 1994; children: John Raymond, Connor Harold. BS with high honors, U. Sask., 1972; PhD, U. Alta., 1978. Postdoctoral fellow U. Toronto, Ont., 1978-80; lectr. U. Calif., Berkeley, 1979; asst. prof. U. Alta., Edmonton, 1980-82; curator Tyrrell Mus., Drumheller, Alta., 1982-86; asst. dir. Royal Tyrrell Mus., Drumheller, 1986-92; dir., 1992—; adj. prof. U. Alta., 1983—; sen. U. Calgary, Alta., 1989-90; bd. dirs. Yoho-Burgess Shale Rsch. Found. Contbr. articles to sci. publs. Operating grantee Nat. Sci. & Engring. Rsch. Coun., Ottawa, 1981-82. Fellow Geol. Assn.; mem. Soc. Vertebrate Paleontology. Avocations: horseback riding, gardening. Office: Royal Tyrrell Mus, Box 7500, Drumheller, AB Canada T0J 0Y0

NAYLOR, THOMAS EVERETT, account administrator; b. Grand Junction, Colo., Jan. 1, 1939; s. Everett E. and Berneice I. (Anderson) N. AA, Mesa Coll., 1959; BS, U. Colo., 1961. CPA, Colo. Loan officer trainee Nat. State Bank, Boulder, Colo., 1961-62; acct. Ideal Basic, Denver, 1962-63; auditor Alexander Lindsay, CPA, Denver, 1963-64; acct. U. Colo., Boulder, 1964-65, head acct., 1965-67, fin. officer, 1967-68, adminstrv. svc. officer, 1968-70, asst. dir. housing-budget/finances, 1970—; pvt. practice acctg., Boulder, 1984—. With USAR, 1961-67. Fellow Colo. Soc. CPAs, Assn. Intermountain Housing Officers, Assn. Coll. and Univ. Housing Officers. Avocations: sports, history, stamps, fine arts.

NAYLOR-JACKSON, JERRY, public relations consultant, retired, entertainer, broadcaster; b. Chalk Mountain, Tex., Mar. 6, 1939; s. William Guy and Mary Bernice (Lummus) Jackson; m. Pamela Ann Robinson, Jan. 30, 1966; children: Geoffrey K. Naylor, Kelli A. Naylor-Dobrzynski, Gregory K. Naylor. Grad., Elkins Electronics Inst., Dallas, 1957; student, U. Md., Fed. Republic of Germany, 1957-58. Life first class radio/TV engring. lic. FCC. Broadcaster various local TV and AM radio stas. San Angelo, Texas, 1955-57; lead singer Buddy Holly and the Crickets, 1960-65; solo entertainer, performer, recording artist and producer, 1965-87; sr. v.p. corp. devel. Newslink Internat. Satellite Broadcast Comms. Co., Inc., Washington, 1986-88; pres. Internat. Syndications, Inc. subs. Newslink Inc., Washington, 1986-88; pres., CEO, owner The Jerry Naylor Co., McMinnville, Oreg., 1984—; v.p. capital programs, sr. cons. Calif. Luth. Univ., Thousand Oaks, 1990-92; sr. cons., dir. ann. fund Calif. Luth. U., 1989-90; polit./media cons. various Rep. candidates and orgns., 1968-92; cons. to Violeta Barrios de Chamarro, Pres. of Republic of Nicaragua, 1990-92; disc jockey Sta. KHEY-AM, Sta. KINT-AM, El Paso, Tex., 1959; on-air personality Sta. KRLA-AM, Sta. KDAY-AM, L.A., 1960; on-air disc jockey, air personality, celebrity host KLAC-AM, L.A., 1974-83; on-camera and voice-over spokesman for Safeway Stores, Inc., Avis Rent-a-Car, Mut. of Omaha, Wrigley Co., 1968-83; U.S. presdl. appointee, chmn. Job Tng. Partnership Act work group/youth at risk subcom. Nat. Commn. for Employment Policy, 1985-91; nat. dir. spl. events Reagan for Pres., 1979-81; apptd. mem. commn. for employment policy Pres. Ronald Reagan, 1985-91. Recording artist maj. labels including CBS Records, Motown Records, Warner Bros. Records, EMI Records, 1965-84; host weekly nat. and internat. radio program Continental Country (Number 1 syndicated country music radio show in Am., Billboard Mag., Country Music Assn., 1974), (weekly variety show) Music City, USA, 1966-67. Nat. dir. spl. events Reagan for Pres., 1975-76, 79-80; sr. cons. to White House, 1988, 89-92. With U.S. Army, 1957-58, Germany. Named to Top 40 Male Vocalists of Yr., Billboard Mag., 1970, named #1 Rock Group (Crickets), Billboard Mag./New Musical Express Mag., 1958, 62. Mem. NARAS, Country Music Assn., Acad. Country Music (Telly award for TV documentary 1991, 92), Phi Kappa Phi (alumni). Avocation: writing prose and poetry. Home and Office: Jerry Naylor Co 1279 SW Russ Ln Mcminnville OR 97128-5699

NAZAIRE, MICHEL HARRY, physician; b. Jérémie, Haiti, Sept. 29, 1939; s. Joseph and Hermance N.; m. Nicole Lamarque, Dec. 28, 1968; children: Hannick and Carline (twins). *Daughters Carline and Hannick, born in 1970, are living in New York: Carline is currently employed as administrative assistant by Rheinbraun Thyssen Inc. Hannick is a student at City College, studying education-early childhood.* Grad., Coll. St. Louis de Gonzague, 1959; MD Faculty of Medicine and Pharmacology, State U. Haiti, 1966. Intern State U. Hosp., Port-Au-Prince, Haiti, 1965-66; resident physician Sanitarium, Port-Au-Prince, Haiti, 1966-68; practice medicine specializing in pneumology, 1966-68; practice medicine specializing in pneumo-physiology Port-Au-Prince, 1966—; physician fellow Klinik Havelhohe, West Berlin, 1969-70, 89-91; attending physician Sanitarium, Port-Au-Prince, 1976-91; Dep. mem. Internat. Parliament for Safety and Peace, envoy-at-large Internat. State Parliament, mem. global environ. technol. newtwork Who. Contbr. articles to Jour. Indsl. Hygiene, Pneumology and Respiratory Protection. Fellow Internat. Soc. for Respiratory Protection, Am. Coll. Chest Physicians (assoc), mem. Am. Pub. Health Assn., Am. Conf. Govtl. Indsl. Hygienists, Internat. Union Against Tuberculosis, Internat. Platform Assn., Physicians for Social Responsibility. Address: 6407 S 12th St Apt 1711 Tacoma WA 98465-1983 also: 1115-21 Dorchester Rd #3C Brooklyn NY 11218

NAZZARO, DAVID ALFRED, sales executive; b. Malden, Mass., Sept. 15, 1940; s. Alfred Anthony and Louise (Cunningham) N.; m. Jane Valentine, June 26, 1971; one child, David Thomas. BME, U.S. Mcht. Marine Acad., 1962; MS, Columbia U., 1965; MBA, Pepperdine U., 1975. Regional mgr. Turbo Power and Marine Systems Union Techs., Hardford, Conn., 1965-74; mgr. bus. devel S & Q Corp., San Francisco, 1974-78; v.p. and gen. mgr. Con-Val, Oakland, Calif., 1978-85; pres. and chief exec. officer Dasa Controls, Belmont, Calif., 1985-87; mgr. bus. devel Johnson Yokogawa Corp., San Francisco, 1987-94; prin. Nazzaro and Assocs. Fin. Cons., 1994—; bd. dirs. Community Action Agy., 1998—, Peninsula Exch. Contbr. papers to profl. publs. Bd. dirs. Clearview Homeowners Assn., San Mateo, 1976; pres. St. Bartholomew's Parish Council, San Mateo, 1986. Lt. USNR, 1963-69. Sr. Mem. Instrument Soc. Am. (pres. No. Calif. Sect. 1987-88); mem. ASME, Am. Water Works Assn., Elks, Jaycees, St. Bartholomew's Mens Club (pres. 1977). Avocations: skiing, tennis, racquetball, handball, bridge. E-mail: danazzaro@aol.com. Home: 30 Tollridge Ct San Mateo CA 94402-3730

NEAL, ALBERT HARVEY, retired minister; b. Morganton, Ark., Apr. 4, 1925; s. Albert Wilburn ad Alma Fay (Bittle) N.; m. Barbara Jean Sly, Oct. 28, 1946 (div. June 1984); children: Brenda L. Wood, Linda Caroll, Ronda Jean Easter; m. Betty Lu Dunn Beasley, Sept. 25, 1987. DD (hon.), Sch. Bible Theology, San Jacinto, Calif., 1989. Ordained to ministry Pentecostal Ch. of God, 1950. Pastor Yreka, Calif., Farmersville, Calif., 1949-55; dir. Indian missions, 1955-65; dist. supt. Pacific NW Dist., 1965-77; world missions field rep., 1977-79; pastor Longview, Wash., 1979-82, Grover City, Calif., Kelseyville, Calif., 1982-90; area sales dir. Bennie Harris Assocs., 1973-91; asst. gen. supt. Pentecostal Ch. of God, Joplin, Mo., 1973-77. With USN, 1942-46, PTO. Decorated Presdl. Unit Citation, Philippines Liberation with 2 stars, South Pacific ribbon with 9 stars. Republican. Home: 2500 Kay St Ceres CA 95307-3408

NEAL, JAMES MADISON, JR., retired editor and educator; b. Oklahoma City, Aug. 6, 1925; s. James Madison and Tillie Belle (Milliken) N.; m. Caroline Dorothy Becker (dec. Dec. 1991); children: Charles, James W., Jody, Carolyn. BA, U. Okla., 1949; MA, S.D. State U., 1970. Editor various newspapers, Colo., Nebr. and Okla., 1949-59; wire editor Rapid City Journal, Rapid City, S.D., 1959-67; instr. S.D. State U., Brookings, S.D., 1967-71; asst. prof. U. Nebr., Lincoln, 1971-73, assoc. prof., 1973-90, S.D. chmn. AP Mng. Editors Assn., 1962-64. Mem. ACLU (bd. dirs. Nebr. affiliate 1979-82, Ariz. affiliate 1994), VFW, Soc. Profl. Journalists, Investigative Reporters and Editors. Unitarian. Avocations: painting, travel. Home: 360 Rimrock Cir Prescott AZ 86303-5544

NEAL, PHILIP MARK, diversified manufacturing executive; b. San Diego, Aug. 28, 1940; s. Philip Mark and Florence Elizabeth (Anderson) N.; children. Brian, Kevin. B.A., Pomona Coll., 1962, M.B.A., Stanford U., 1964. high financial planning and analyst CBD, Hollywood, 1964-66, cons.

McKinsey & Co., L.A., 1966-73; v.p., contr. Avery Internat. Corp., L.A., 1974-78; sr. v.p. fin. Avery Internat. Corp., Pasadena, Calif., 1979-88, group v.p. materials group, 1988-90, exec. pres., 1990, pres., COO, 1990-98, pres., CEO, 1998—; bd. dirs. Ind. Colls. of So. Calif. Trustee Pomona Coll.; gov. Town Hall of Calif. Bd. Govs. mem. Fin. Execs. Inst. Republican. Episcopalian. Office: Avery Dennison Corp PO Box 7090 150 N Orange Grove Blvd Pasadena CA 91103-3534

NEAL, SHEILA DIANNE, university adminstrator; b. Phoenix, Nov. 9, 1959; came to U.S., 1959; d. William Wally and Pearlene (Coit) Wright; divorced; children: Melvin Louis II, Cecelia Pearlene. BS in Elem. Edn., Grand Canyon U., Phoenix, 1994, MA TESL, 1998; MEd in Ednl. Leadership, No. Ariz. U., Flagstaff, 1997. With Salt River Project, Tempe, Ariz., 1981-91; ESL tchr. Scottsdale (Ariz.) Pub. Sch. Dist., 1995-96; spl. programs coord. Grand Canyon U., Phoenix, 1996—, adj. prof., 1997—. Mem. NAACP. Democrat. Baptist. Avocations: singing, cooking, reading, exercising. Office: Grand Canyon U 3300 W Camelback Rd Phoenix AZ 85017-1097

NEAL-PARKER, SHIRLEY ANITA, obstetrician and gynecologist; b. Washington, Aug. 28, 1949; d. Leon Walker and Pearl Anita (Shelton) Neal; m. Andre Cowan Dasent, June 21, 1971 (div. Feb. 1978); 1 child, Erika Michelle Dasent; m. James Carl Parker, Feb. 11, 1979; 1 child, Amirah Nabeehah. BS in Biology, Am. U., 1971; MD, Hahnemann U., 1979. Med. lic. Md., W.Va., Calif., Wash. Intern Howard U. Hosp., 1979-80, resident, 1980-84; physician Nat. Health Svc. Corp., Charleston, W. Va., 1984-86; clin. instr. W. Va. U., Charleston, 1985-86; pvt. practice ob./gyn. Sacramento, 1986-95; pvt. practice Chehalis, Wash., 1995—; chair dept. perinatology Providence Centralia Hosp., 1999—; chair dept. perinatology Providence Centralia Hosp., 1999—. Mem. bd. Ruth Rosenberg Dance Ensemble, Sacramento, 1992-95, S.W. Washington Ballet Ctr., 1995—, Human Response Network, Chehalis, 1995-97. Mem. Am. Assn. Gynecologic Laparoscopists, Am. Productive Health Profls., Nat. Med. Assn., Am. Med. Women's Assn. (comty. svc. award Mother Hale br. 1994), Nat. Assn. Gynecol. Laparoscopists, Nat. Assn. Reproductive Profls., Wash. State Med. Assn., Lewis County Med. Soc., Soroptomist Internat. Avocations: traveling, reading, crocheting, collecting ethnic dolls, magnets. Home: 221 Vista Rd Chehalis WA 98532-8766 Office: PO Box 997 171 S Market Blvd Chehalis WA 98532-3037

NEAR, TIMOTHY, theater director. Grad., San Francisco State U., Acad. Music and Dramatic Art, London. Artistic dir. San Jose Repertory Theatre, 1986—; past actress, dir. with numerous prestigious theaters including The Guthrie Theatre, Berkeley (Calif.) Repertory Theater, La Jolla (Calif.) Playhouse, The Alliance Theatre, Atlanta, The Mark Taper Forum, L.A., Ford's Theatre, Washington, Repertory Theatr of St. Louis, N.Y. Shakespeare Festival, Stage West, Mass. Dir. Ghosts on Fire, La Jolla Playhouse (DramaLogue award), Singer in the Storm, Mark Taper Forum (DramaLogue award), Thunder Knocking on the Door (DramaLogue award). Recipient 1997 Woman of Achievement in the Arts, San Jose Mercury News and The Woman's Fund. Office: San Jose Repertory Theatre 101 Paseo de San Antonio San Jose CA 95113-2603

NEARY, PATRICIA ELINOR, ballet director; b. Miami, Fla.; d. James Elliott and Elinor (Mitsitz) N. Corps de ballet Nat. Ballet of Can., Toronto, Ont., 1957-60; prin. dancer N.Y.C. Ballet, 1960-68; ballerina Geneva Ballet (Switzerland), 1968-70, ballet dir., 1973-78; guest artist Stuttgart Ballet, Germany, 1968-70; asst. ballet dir., ballerina West Berlin Ballet, 1970-73; ballet dir. Zurich Ballet (Switzerland), 1978-86, La Scala di Milano ballet co., Italy, 1986-88; tchr., Balanchine ballets, Balanchine Trust, 1987—.

NEBELKOPF, ETHAN, psychologist; b. N.Y.C., June 13, 1946; s. Jacob and Fannie (Carver) N.; m. Karen Horrocks, July 27, 1976; children: Demian David, Sarah Dawn. BA, CCNY, 1966; MA, U. Mich., 1969; PhD, Summit U., 1989. Social worker Project Headstart, N.Y.C., 1965; coord. Project Outreach, Ann Arbor, 1968-69; program dir. White Bird Clinic, Eugene, Oreg., 1971-75; counseling supr. Teledyne Econ. Devel. Corp., San Diego, 1976-79; dir. planning and edn. Walden House, San Francisco, 1979-89, dir. tng., 1990-93; program evaluator United Indian Nations, Oakland, Calif., 1994-96; clin. dir. Indian Health Ctr. Santa Clara Valley, San Jose, Calif., 1997—; adj. prof. dept. social work San Francisco State U., 1982-87; cons. Berkeley (Calif.) Holistic Health Ctr., 1979-84, Medicine Wheel Healing Co-op, San Diego, 1976-79; alternate del. Nat. Free Clinic Coun., Eugene, 1972-74; clin. dir. Urban Indian Health Bd., Oakland, Calif., 1997. Author: White Bird Flies to Phoenix, 1973, The New Herbalism, 1980, The Herbal Connection, 1981, Hope Not Dope, 1990. Mem. Mayor's Task Force on Drugs, San Francisco, 1988; mem. treatment com. Gov.'s Policy Coun. on Drugs, Sacramento, 1989; task force Human Svcs. Tng., Salem, Oreg., 1972; organizer West Eugene Bozo Assn., 1973; founder Green Psychology, 1993. Named Outstanding Young Man of Am., U.S. Jaycees, 1980; recipient Silver Key, House Plan Assn., 1966. Fellow Am. Orthopsychiat. Assn.; mem. Calif. Assn. Family Therapists, World Fedn. of Therapeutic Communities, Nat. Writer's Club, N.Y. Acad. Scis., Internat. Assn. for Human Rels. Lab. Tng., Calif. Assn. of Drug Programs and Profls. (pres. 1988-90), Phi Beta Kappa. Avocations: herbs, rocks, cactus, yoga, baseball cards. Office: 6641 Simson St Oakland CA 94605-2220

NEDNEY, JOE, football player; b. San Jose, Mar. 22, 1973. Kicker Ariz. Cardinals, Phoenix. Office: c/o Ariz Cardinals PO Box 888 Phoenix AZ 85001-0888

NEECE, ROBERT BARRY, lawyer; b. Cleve., Jan. 17, 1948; s. Gus Warlick and Mary Elizabeth (Davis) N. BA, U. Colo., 1970; JD with honors, U. Ark., 1978; postgrad., Columbia U., 1978-79. Bar: Ark. 1978, Colo. 1978, U.S. Dist. Ct. Colo. 1978. Assoc. Sch. of Law Columbia U., N.Y.C., 1978-79; jud. clk. Colo. Ct. Appeals, Denver, 1980-81; assoc. Sherman & Howard, Denver, 1981-86, Senn & Hoth, Denver, 1986-87; ptnr. Pred and Miller, Denver, 1987-91; spl. counsel Burns, Wall, Smith and Mueller, P.C., Denver, 1992—; vis. adjunct prof. law Willamette U. Sch. of Law, Salem, Oreg., 1979-80; lectr. in law U. Denver Coll. of Law, 1985-88; mem. faculty Nat. Ctr. for Preventive Law, Denver, 1988-89, Nat. Bus. Inst., Inc., Eau Claire, Wis., 1991—; mem. Colo. Bus. Corp. Act Com., pre-law exec. com. U. No. Colo.; bd. dirs. Intellectual Tech., Inc., San Diego. Co-author: Negotiating Business Transactions, 1988, Considerations in Buying or Selling a Business in Colorado, 1991, 92. Merrill fellow Columbia U., 1978. Mem. ABA, Colo. Bar Assn., Denver Bar Assn., The University Club, Phi Alpha Delta.

NEEDLEMAN, JACOB, philosophy educator, writer; b. Phila., Oct. 6, 1934; s. Benjamin and Ida (Seltzer) N.; m. Carla Satzman, Aug. 30, 1959 (div. 1989); children: Raphael, Eve; m. Gail Anderson, Dec. 1990. BA, Harvard U., 1956; grad., U. Freiburg, 1957-58; PhD, Yale U., 1961. Clin. psychology trainee New Haven (Conn.) Veterans Hosp. Adminstrn., 1960-61; rsch. assoc. Rockefeller Inst., N.Y., 1961-62; from asst. prof. to assoc. prof. philosophy San Francisco State U., 1962-66, prof philosophy, 1967—, chair dept. philosophy, 1968-69; vis. scholar Union Theol. Seminary, 1967-68; dir. Ctr. Study New Religions, 1977-83; lectr. psychiatry, cons. med. ethics U. Calif., 1981-84. Author: Being-in-the-World, 1963, The New Religions, 1970, Religion for a New Generation, 1973, A Sense of the Cosmos, 1975, On the Way to Self-Knowledge: Sacred Tradition and Psychotherapy, 1976, Lost Christianity, 1980, Consciousness and Tradition, 1982, The Heart of Philosophy, 1982, Sorcerers, 1986, Sin and Scientism, 1986, Lost Christianity: A Journey of Rediscovery to the Centre of Christian Experience, 1990, Money and the Meaning of Life, 1991, Modern Esoteric Spirituality, 1992, The Way of the Physician, 1993, The Indestructible Question, 1994, A Little Book on Love, 1996, Time and the Soul, 1998; (trans.) The Primary World of Senses, 1963, Essays on Ego Psychology, 1964; editor Care of Patients with Fatal Illness, 1969, The Sword of Gnosis, 1973, Sacred Tradition and Present Need, 1974, Understanding the New Religions, 1978, Speaking of My Life: The Art of Living in the Cultural Revolution, 1979, Real Philosophy: An Anthology of the Universal Search for Meaning, 1991; contbr. Death and Bereavement, 1969, To Live Within, 1971, My Life with a Benjamin Family, 1972, The New Man, 1972, The Essential Meaning of the Kabbalah, 1973, The Phenomenon of Death. Grantee Religion in Higher Edn., 1967-68, Marsden Found., Ella Lyman Cabot Trust, 1969, Marsda Found, Far West Inst., 1975, Fulbright scholar Germany, 1957-58, Fels Found. fellow Summit 1991 fellow Rockefeller Found. Humanities 1971.

78. Office: San Francisco State U Dept Philosophy 1600 Holloway Ave San Francisco CA 94132-1722

NEELD, MICHAEL EARL, legislative staff administrator; b. Portland, Oreg., May 13, 1955; s. Carl Eugene and Frances Karlene (Riggers) N.; m. Ann Pelissier. BA in Journalism and Polit. Scis., U. Oreg., 1977. Advt. rep. Post Publs., Camas, Wash., 1977; chpt. cons. Kappa Sigma Internat. Fraternity, Charlottesville, Va., 1977-79; fundraising dir. Am. Cancer Soc., Richmond, Va., 1979-80; news editor, polit. rep. Sta. KYXI, Portland, 1980-84; comms. dir. Moshofsky for Congress, Portland, 1984; pub. info. officer Wash. State Ho. of Reps., Olympia, 1984-85; comms. dir. Paulus for Gov., Portland, 1985-86; sr. info. officer Wash. State Ho. of Reps., Olympia, 1986-91, rep. staff coord., 1991-96, pub. rels. coord., 1996—; founder, ptnr. Pacific N.W. Advocates Pub. Affairs Cons., Olympia, 1989—; instr. polit. strategy, tactics, fundraising and media Wash. State Rep. Party, Tukwila, 1991-92; campaign dir. House Rep. Orgnl. Com., Olympia, 1991-92. Recipient Best Coverage of Breaking News award Oreg. AP/Broadcast, 1982. Mem. U. Oreg. Alumni Assn., Trumpeters, City Club of Portland, Fremont Grove Soc. (founder), Indian Summer Golf and Country Club (v.p. 1998—), Kappa Sigma (alumni, housing corp. bd. dirs. 1980-84). Presbyterian. Avocations: politics, reading, golf. Home: 7224 Deerfield Park Dr NE Olympia WA 98516-2135 Office: Wash Ho of Reps B-5 John L O'Brien Bldg PO Box 40600 Olympia WA 98504-0600

NEFF, JOHN, recording engineer, producer; b. Birmingham, Mich., Mar. 13, 1951; s. Robert Leslie Joseph and Mary Therese (McElvarr) N.; m. Nancy Louise Boocks, Aug. 29, 1987; children: Jennifer Lyn Neff, Bryan C. Groves, Kenneth John Neff. Student, Oakland Community Coll., Auburn Hills, Mich., 1970-72. Freelance recording artist, session musician Detroit, 1965-73; freelance record producer Toronto, Phoenix, L.A., 1974-79; radio announcer, engr. Stas. KVIB, KHEI, KMVI, KLHI, KAOI, 1981-88; record producer Maui Recorders, Kula, Hawaii, 1986-92; cons. studio design Roadrunner Audio Svcs., Glendale, Ariz., 1993-96; studio engring. cons. TEC:ton, L.A., 1996-97; chief engr., studio mgr. David Lynch's Asymmetrical Prodns., Hollywood, 1997—; rec. engr. for David Lynch, Walter Becker, Donald Fagen (Steely Dan), Buffy Ste Marie, Willie Nelson, Sagan Lewis; touring musician Detroit, Toronto, Phoenix, L.A., 1969-79; studio monitor design for Kenny "Baby Face" Edmonds, Brian Austin Green; tech. cons. to David Lynch, Fox Scoring Stage; film mixer The Straight Story (David Lynch). Recipient Grammy award nomination for Kamakiriad, 1994. Mem. ASCAP, Audio Engring Soc. (cert.), Am. Fedn. Musicians. Avocations: photography, hiking, travel. Home: 30428 Star Canyon Pl Castaic CA 91384 Office: Asymmetrical Prodns PO Box 931540 Hollywood CA 90093

NEFF, LESTER LEROY, administrator, minister; b. Medford, Oreg., Nov. 20, 1923; s. James Asher and Ruth (Turnbow) N.; m. Avon Maxine Bostwick, Aug. 15, 1942; children: Lawrence Dale, Carol Lee, Donald Leroy. BA, Ambassador Coll., 1959, MA in Theology, 1962. Inspector Retail Credit Co., Atlanta, 1946-55; dept. mgr. Worldwide Ch. of God, Pasadena, Calif., 1955-64, 1971-73; bus. mgr. Ambassador Coll., Big Sandy, Tex., 1964-71, 73-76; pastor Worldwide Ch. of God, Pasadena, Calif., 1976-79, ministerial administr., 1979-81; sec. Ambassador U., Big Sandy, Tex., 1990-95; ret., 1995. Treas. Worldwide Ch. God, 1981-90, sec. 1981-95. Sgt. USAAF, 1943-46.

NEGLEY, FLOYD ROLLIN, genealogist, retired army officer and civilian military employee; b. Ashland, Nebr., Apr. 26, 1924; s. Floyd Carroll and Margaret (Miners) N.; m. Teresa Mitsuko Ohashi, Mar. 12, 1954; children: Teresa Kei, Caroline Yumi. Japanese lang. student, U. Army Lang. Sch., Monterey, Calif., 1956-57; student in computer scis., U. Ariz., 1959-61; BS in Econs., Sophia U. Tokyo, 1965. Intelligence analyst U.S. Army, Tokyo, Okinawa, Japan, 1949-59; automated comm. maintenance officer U.S. Army, various cities, 1969-70; automated comm. analyst U.S. Army, Ft. Huachua, Ariz., 1970-92; genealogist Tucson, 1970—; advisor Armed Forces Comm.-Electronics Assn., Tokyo/Ft. Huachuca, 1961-92; computer advisor Japanese Army/Air Force, Tokyo, 1963-67; owner Japan Food Mart, Tucson, 1971-80; owner, property mgr. Negley Svcs., Tucson, 1970—; indexer mortality/natality for Pima County, Ariz., 1987-97. Author 5 books on Negley U.S. history and genealogy, 1986-88; author, indexer 2 books, 1994-96; translator (Japanese fiction) A Bamboo Doll, 1967. Pres. Pima-Cochise Commuters, Inc., Tucson, 1988, advisor, 1971-91; various offices Aztec Toastmasters, Tucson, 1992—, Thunder Mountain Toastmasters, Ft. Huachuca, 1982-91. Named Disting. Toastmaster, Toastmasters Internat., 1995, state 4-H champion, Nebr. 4-H Clubs, Lincoln, 1943. Mem. SAR, Ariz. Geneal. Soc. (pres. 1985-87, editor Copper State Bull. 1987—). Avocations: indexing, swimming, travel, gardening. Home: 2726 E Waverly St Tucson AZ 85716-3083

NEIMANN, ALBERT ALEXANDER, mathematician, business owner; b. Torrington, Wyo., Nov. 29, 1939; s. Alexander and Lydia (Temple) N.; m. Barbara Jean Maw, May 6, 1967; children: Debbie, Todd, Amy, Kelly,. BA, Willamette U., 1967. Mathematician Keyport (Wash.) Naval Torpedo Sta., 1968-70; math. statistician Concord (Calif.) Naval Weapons Sta., 1970-85, engring. statistician, 1985-94; bus. owner Antioch Sports Cards and Collectibles, A&T Sports Cards, Calif., 1994—. Mgr. Little League Baseball, Antioch, Calif., 1977-84, Little League Softball, Antioch, 1984-87; Sunday sch. tchr. Grace Bapt. Ch., 1979-90; statistician Antioch H.S., 1985-89. Recipient Performance award Concord Naval Weapons Sta., 1978, 88-94. Mem. Am. Statis. Assn., Math. Assn. Am., Am. Soc. for Quality Control, Nat. Coun. Tchrs. Math. Avocations: jogging, electronics, reading, gardening, basketball. Office: Antioch Sports Cards & Collectibles 2550 Somersville Rd Antioch CA 94509-8700

NEINAS, CHARLES MERRILL, athletic association executive; b. Marshfield, Wis., Jan. 18, 1932; s. Arthur Oscar and Blanche Amelia (Reeder) N.; children: Andrew, Toby. B.S., U. Wis., 1957. Asst. exec. dir. Nat. Collegiate Athletic Assn., Kansas City, Mo., 1961-71; commr. Big Eight Conf., Kansas City, 1971-81; exec. dir. Coll. Football Assn., 1981—; Dr. Patricia L. Pacey prof. econs. U. Colo., Boulder, 1981—, econ. cons., 1981—; adviser Am. Football Coaches Assn., 1997—. Served with USNR, 1952-54. Home: 4977 Idylwild Trl Boulder CO 80301-3651 Office: Neinas Sports Svcs 6688 Gunpark Dr Boulder CO 80301-3372

NELIPOVICH, SANDRA GRASSI, artist; b. Oak Park, Ill., Nov. 22, 1939; d. Alessandro and Lena Mary (Ascareggi) Grassi; m. John Nelipovich Jr., Aug. 19, 1973. BFA in Art Edn., U. Ill., 1961; postgrad., Northwestern U., 1963, Gonzaga U., Florence, Italy, 1966, Art Inst. Chgo., 1968; diploma, Accademia Universale Alessandro Magno, Prato, Italy, 1983. Tchr. art Edgewood Jr. High Sch., Highland Park, Ill., 1961-62, Emerson Sch. Jr. High Sch., Oak Park, 1962-77; batik artist Calif., 1977—; illustrator Jolly Robin Publ. Co., Anaheim, Calif., 1988—; supr. student tchrs., Oak Park, 1970-75; adult edn. tchr. ESL, ceramics, Anaheim, Ill., 1974; mem. curriculum action group on human dignity, EEO workshop demonstration, Oak Park, 1975-76; guest lectr. Muckenthaler Ctr., Fullerton, Calif., 1980, 92, Niguel Art Group, Dana Point, Calif., 1989, Carlsbad A.A., 1990, ARt League, Oceanside Art Group, 1992; 2d v.p. Anaheim Hills Women's Club, 1990-91, rec. sec. 1991-92; fabric designer for fashion designer Barbara Jax, 1987. One-Woman shows include Lawry's Calif. Ctr., L.A., 1981-83, Whittier (Calif.) Mus. 1985-86, Anaheim Cultural Ctr., 1986-88, Ill. Inst. Tech. Chgo., 1989, Muckenthaler Cultural Ctr., Fullerton, 1990; also gallery exhibits in Oak Brook, 1982, La Habra, Calif., 1983, Millard Sheets Gallery, Pomona, Calif., 1996; represented in permanent collections McDonald's Corp., Oak Brook, Glenkirk Sch., Deerfield, Ill., Emerson Sch., Oak Park, galleries in Laguna Beach, Calif., Maui, Hawaii, Mich., N.J.; poster designer Saratoga Fine Arts. Active Assistance League, Anaheim, Calif., 1992—; 2d v.p. ways and means cons., 1995-96, 97-98. Recipient numerous awards, purchase prizes, 1979—; featured in Calif. Art Rev., Artists of So. Calif. Vol. II, Nat. Artists' Network, 1992. Mem. AAUW (hospitality chmn. 1984-85), Soc. Children's Book Writers and Illustrators, Assistance League Anaheim, Orange Art Assn. (jury chmn. 1980). Roman Catholic. Avocations: photography, travel. Home and Office: 5742 E Calle Cedro Anaheim CA 92807-3207

NELLERMOE, LESLIE CAROL, lawyer; b. Oakland, Calif., Jan. 26, 1954; d. Carrol Warden and Flora Finn (Behring) Fin m Darrell Ray Nellermoe,

Aug. 9, 1986; 1 child, Devin Anne. BS cum laude, Wash. State U., 1975; JD cum laude, Willamette U., 1978. Bar: Wash. 1978, U.S. Dist. Ct. (ea. dist.) Wash. 1979, U.S. Dist. Ct. (we. dist.) Wash. 1983. Staff atty. Wash. Ct. Appeals, Spokane, 1978-79; asst. atty. gen. Wash. Atty. Gen. Office, Spokane, 1979-83, Olympia, 1983-85; assoc. Syrdal, Danelo, Klein, Myre & Woods, Seattle, 1985-88; ptnr. Heller Ehrman White & McAuliffe, Seattle, 1990—. Bd. dirs. N.W. Environ. Bus. Coun., 1996—, Campfire Boys & Girls, Seattle, 1991-97. Mem. ABA, Wash. State Bar Assn., King County Bar Assn., Wash. Environ. Industry Assn. (bd. dirs.). Office: Heller Ehrman White & McAuliffe 701 5th Ave 6100 Columbia Ctr Seattle WA 98104-7043*

NELSON, ALAN JAN, minister, evangelist; b. Los Angeles, Sept. 18, 1944; s. Arthur Leonard and Laura Nelson; A.A., Los Angeles Valley City Coll., 1965; B.S., San Franando Valley State Coll., 1967; M.S., Calif. State Coll., Los Angeles, 1969. Actor, 1962—, screen writer, 1978—, comic, 1965—, stuntman, 1975—, film producer, 1979—; asst. adminstr. Oak Hill Learning Services, Lakeview Terrace, Calif., 1970; dir. community services City of South El Monte (Calif.), 1971; v.p. Ev Gray Lighting Co., Van Nuys, Calif., 1972-75; hosp. adminstr. Los Angeles Met. Hosp., 1976; exec. dir. Search Consortium, West Los Angeles, 1977-79; pres. AGVA, N.Y.C., 1979-83; pres. L & N Prodns. Inc., Van Nuys, 1975—; pres. A.J.N. Hallelujah, Inc., 1981—; 4th v.p. Theatre Authority Inc., 1980-83; corp. cons. entertainment field, 1975-78; evangelist, 1975—. V.p. West Los Angeles Coordinating Coun., 1977; mem. El Monte Coordinating Coun., 1971. Recipient Mid-Wilshire Optimists Outstanding Service award, 1980, Outstanding Service plaque AGVA, 1981, citation for advancement of variety artist State of N.J., 1981, Golden Mask award Hollywood Appreciation Soc., 1982. Mem. Screen Actors Guild, Actors and Artists Am. Assoc. (5th v.p. 1980-83). Democrat. Club: Friars.

NELSON, ALLEN F., investor relations company executive; b. Portland, Oreg., Oct. 17, 1943; s. Roy August and MIldred Mary (Jensen) N.; m. Johanna Molenaar, Dec. 8, 1973. BS, U. Iowa, 1965, MA, 1968. V.p. Shareholder Comm. Corp., N.Y.C., 1970-72; v.p. Trafalgar Capital Corp., N.Y.C., 1973; pres. Nelson, Lasky & Co., Inc., N.Y.C., 1974-76; account exec. Corp. Comm., Inc., Seattle, 1976-77; pres. Allen Nelson & Co., Inc., Seattle, 1977—. Mem. Fin. Analysts Fedn., Nat. Investor Rels. Inst., Nat. Security Traders Assn., Practicing Law Inst., Pub. Rels. Soc. Am., Am. Soc. Corp. Secs., Can Corp. Shareholder Svcs. Assn., Ranier Club, Montana Club, Vancouver Club. Home: 4400 Beach Dr SW Seattle WA 98116-3937 Office: Allen Nelson & Co Inc PO Box 16157 Seattle WA 98116-0157

NELSON, ANITA JOSETTE, educator; b. San Francisco, June 10, 1938; d. George Emanuel and Yvonne Louise (Borel) N. BA, San Francisco State Coll., 1960; MA, U. Denver, 1969. Dir. Community Ctr., Nurenberg, W.Ger., 1961-63; dir. program spl. services Cmty. Ctr., Tokyo, 1964-66; resident counselor U. Denver, 1967-69; dir. student activities Maricopa (Ariz.) Tech. Coll., 1969-72, coach women's varsity tennis, coordinator campus activities, 1972-75; counselor, prof., fgn. student advisor Scottsdale (Ariz.) C.C., 1975-94, divsn. chair counseling, 1989-91, emeritus faculty, 1994. Named Phoenix Mgmt. Council Rehabilitator of Year, 1977. Republican. Home: 351 Molino Ave Mill Valley CA 94941-2767

NELSON, ANNA MASTERTON, writer, digital effects artist; b. West Covina, Calif., July 16; d. Richard Frederick and Mary Winifred (Denk) N. BA in Psychology, U. So. Calif., L.A., 1994. Dialogue writer Gelula, 1998-99; writer, libr. Fox Broadcasting Corp., 1996-97; writer's asst., sr. v.p. devel. Dick Clark Prodns., Inc., 1992-95; asst. to dir. Gettysburg, 1991; adminstrv. asst. Acuity Entertainment, 1990; rsch. session supr. Columbia Broadcasting Sys., 1989; lectr. dept. anthropology U. So. Calif., L.A., 1994—. Active Malibu (Calif.) Rep. Womens Club, 1993—, Project AIDS, L.A., 1993-95, Project Angel Food, 1997—. Office: PO Box 1982 Studio City CA 91614-0982

NELSON, BARBARA JONES, food service and theatre professional; b. Augusta, Ga., Feb. 3, 1954; d. Robert F. and Margaret H. (Hill) Jones; divorced; children: Candice, Russell. Diploma, Dallas Fashion Mdse. Coll. Pres. Bo-Mar, Inc., Gallup, N.Mex., Cinebar, Inc. Mem. McKinley County Rep. Party, Gallup, 1991—; sec. Gallup Downtown Devel. Group.; sec. McKinley County Crimestoppers Bd. Named Employer of Yr. by Connections/Nat. Assn. Retarded Citizens, Durango, Colo., 1991, N.Mex. Mainstreet Vol. of Yr., 1995, Woman of Yr., AAUW, 1995. Mem. NAFE, Soroptimist, Am. Mgmt. Assn., Nat. Restaurant Assn., Nat. Fedn. Ind. Bus., Gallup-McKinley C. of C. (sec.). Episcopalian. Avocations: travel, photography. Office: Bo-Mar Inc 914 E 66th Gallup NM 87301-5557

NELSON, BRYAN H(ERBERT), non-profit agency administrator; b. Yakima, Wash., July 3, 1956; s. Herbert B. and Marilyn A. (Cupper) N.; m. Sandra Exley, June 11, 1993; children from previous marriage: Christofer A., Bryanne E. BEd, Ea. Wash. U., 1977, MS in Speech Pathology, 1978. Speech pathologist Ednl. Svc. Dist. 101, Spokane, Wash., 1978-83, coord. speech pathology, 1983-84, coord. inservice tng., 1985; processor fruit broker Herb Nelson Inc., Yakima, 1985-88; coord. early childhood and spl. edn. programs Selah (Wash.) Sch. Dist., 1989-92, coord. spl. edn., 1989-92; dir. New Directions, EPIC, 1992-97; gen. ptnr. Nelson Perkins Assocs., Yakima, 1990-93; dir. New Directions-Epic, Yakima, Wash., 1992-97; cons. ABC Sch. Supply Inc., Yakima, 1997—; guest lectr. Ea. Wash. U., Cheney, 1984-85; chmn. very spl. arts festival Ednl. Svc. Dist 101, 1985, on-site coord. IDEAS conv., 1983. Bd. dirs., chmn. citizens adv. bd. Yakima Vocat. Skill Ctr., 1988-89; mem. gen. adv. com. Yakima Vocat. Coop.; mem. allocation panel United Way, Yakima, 1974, loaned exec., 1990; mem. exec. com. Yakima County Birth to Six, 1989-90; mem. Health Svcs. Adv. com. Oreg. Child Devel. Coalition, 1997—. Avocations: reading, golf, skiing, refinishing furniture. Office: ABC School Supply 7303 Perry St Yakima WA 98908-2013

NELSON, BRYCE EAMES, journalist, educator; b. Reno, Nev., Dec. 16, 1937; s. H.V. and Jennie Nelson; m. Martha Streiff, Sept. 23, 1961; children: Kristin, Matthew. BA, Harvard Coll., 1959; MPhil (Rhodes Scholar), U. Oxford, Eng., 1962. Instr. U. Pitts., 1962-63; fgn. affairs asst. Senator Frank Church, Washington, 1963-65; reporter Washington Post, 1965-66, Sci. Mag., Washington, 1966-69; midwest bur. chief, corr. L.A. Times, Chgo., Washington, 1969-82; writer human behavior N.Y. Times, 1982-84; prof. journalism U. So. Calif., L.A., 1984—; dir. U. So. Calif. Sch. Journalism, 1984-88. Mem. editl. bd. Am. Oxonian, Claremont, Calif., 1996—. Recipient award Calif. Assoc. Press Contest for Investigative Reporting, 1980, Disting. Contbr. award APA, 1983, Deutsch award for Disting. Journalism Am. Orthopsychiat. Assn., 1970. Mem. Assn. Am. Rhodes Scholars, Soc. Profl. Journalists, Assn. Edn. in Journalism and Mass Comm., Am. Hist. Assn., We. History Assn. Episcopalian. Avocations: hiking, biking, music, movies, swimming. Office: Univ So Calif Sch Journalism Annenberg Sch Los Angeles CA 90089-0281

NELSON, CARL ALFRED, author, international business educator; b. Pitts., Oct. 11, 1930; s. Alfred Helge Nelson and Isabel Alice (Younger) Newbauer; m. Barbara Long, June 2, 1956; children: Jennifer, Allison, Monica. BS, U.S. Naval Acad., 1956; MS, U.S. Naval Post Grad., 1967; student, US Naval War Coll., 1970; D of Bus. Adminstrn., U.S. Internat. U., 1984. Enlisted USN, 1949, advanced through grades to capt., 1956-82; comdr. USS Worden CG-18, 4 others; v.p., dir. AMMEX Cons., Chula Vista, Calif., 1985-86; pres. Global Bus. & Trade, San Diego, 1982—; prof. Internat. Sch. Mgmt.; worldwide lectr. Author: Your Own Import-Export Business: Winning the Trade Game, 1988, Import-Export: How to Get Started in International Trade, 1989, 2d edit., 1995, Global Success, 1990, Managing Globally; A Complete Guide to Competing Worldwide, 1993, Protocol for Profit, 1998, International Business, 1998, Exporting, 1999, The Advisor, 1999; numerous short stories and articles. Pres. Chula Vista Boys Club, 1988; exec. bd. dirs. Calif. Dem. Party, 1992-97, pres. S.D. Writers/Editors Guild, 1998. Decorated Legion of Merit, Bronze Star, Air medals; named Alumni of Yr., U.S. Internat. U., 1989. Mem. Assn. Global Bus., Acad. Internat. Bus., San Diego World Trade Assn., Authors's Guild of Am., Chula Vista C. of C. (dir. 1984-90, Internat. Focus award 1988), Optimist Club. Home: 1385 Don Carlos Ct Chula Vista CA 91910-7130

NELSON, CAROLYN MARIE, artist; b. Oak Park, Ill., Jan. 4, 1945; d. Carl Lewis and Mary Wilma (Clark) Eilers; m. Michael Woodrick, June 5, 1970 (div. Sept. 1977); children: Katrina, Matthew; m. Stephen Paul Nelson, Aug. 31, 1985. Student, Palm Beach Art Inst., West Palm Beach, Fla., 1962-65, Palm Beach Jr. Coll., Lake Worth, Fla., 1964-65, Maude King Sch. Art, West Palm Beach, Fla., 1959-69, Cerritos (Calif.) Coll., 1987. Owner, instr. art sch. and gallery, Lake Park, Fla., 1972-80; artist, instr. Scottsdale (Ariz.) Ctr. of Arts, 1982; artist Contracting Agys., Los Angeles, 1983-85; asst. dir. fine art Adamson-Duvannes Galleries, Los Angeles, 1985-86; artist, dir. Gateways to History, Los Angeles, 1986—; art dir. Studio 3, Lake Park, Fla., 1974-80; artistic dir. Steve's Stitchery, Los Angeles, 1988—. Artist cartoons AMA, 1976, typography Christmas in Dixie parade float (trophy 1978), painting NASA, 1977, graphics Kenyatia U. Narobi, 1979, Getty Oil Co., 1984, Medical Illustrating, 1989. Medical Illustration, 1990; engring. asst. airplane flight manual for MD-11 comml. aircraft; major exhibit in watercolor, Laguna Beach, Calif., 1990. Commr. City of Norwalk, Calif., Am. Heritage/Bicentennial Commn. Fellow Los Angeles County Mus., Gallery One Guild (v.p. 1977-78). Lutheran. Home: 1840 S Gaffey St San Pedro CA 90731-5361

NELSON, CONNIE RAE, pharmacy education director, educator; b. Lewistown, Mont., Aug. 19, 1950; d. Ward Wallace and Violet May (Charette) Dickson; m. Alan C. Nelson, July 23, 1977; children: Russell Robert, Nicole Elaine. Pharmacy asst. level A degree, Clover Park Vocat. Tech. Inst., Tacoma, 1979; student in pharmacology Bates Vocat. Tech. Inst., Tacoma, 1982. Lic. pharmacy asst. level A. Druggist clk. Thrifty Drugs, Tacoma, 1972-79; intern in hematology, oncology, pediatrics Madigan Army Med. Ctr., Tacoma, 1979-80; pharmacy asst. A, St. Joseph Hosp., Tacoma, 1979-84; pharmacy instr. Clover Park Vocat. Tech. Inst., Tacoma, 1984-93; pharmacy dept. dir. Eton Tech. Inst., Federal Way, Wash., 1993-94; ednl. task force pharmacy bd. Wash. State, 1993-95, co-chmn. Wash. State Ednl. Task Force, 1995; pharmacy curriculum cons., 1993—. Archtl. and land development West Tapps Maintenance Co., Sumner, Wash., 1979-86, legal and pub. affairs mem., 1984-86, pres., 1985-90. Mem. Wash. State Soc. Pharmacy Assts., Pharmpac (legis. rep. for assts. 1986), Wash. State Soc. Hosp. Pharmacists (pres. Pharmacy Asst. chpt. 1984-95), Wash. State Soc. Pharmacy Assts. (founder, pres. 1985—, legal and pub. affairs chmn. 1987—, legis. chmn. 1987-95, exec. dir. 1991—). Avocations: lecturing, camping, horticulture. Home: 18710 58th St E Sumner WA 98390-6808

NELSON, DOROTHY WRIGHT (MRS. JAMES F. NELSON), federal judge; b. San Pedro, Calif., Sept. 30, 1928; d. Harry Earl and Lorna Amy Wright; m. James Frank Nelson, Dec. 27, 1950; children: Franklin Wright, Lorna Jean. B.A., UCLA, 1950, J.D., 1953; LL.M., U. So. Calif., 1956; LLD honoris causa, U. San Diego, 1997, U. So. Calif., 1983, Georgetown U., 1988, Whittier U., 1989, U. Santa Clara, 1990; LLD (honoris causa), Whittier U., 1989. Bar: Calif. 1954. Research assoc. fellow U. So. Calif., 1953-56; instr., 1957, asst. prof., 1958-61, assoc. prof., 1961-67, prof., 1967, assoc. dean., 1965-67, dean., 1967-80; judge U.S. Ct. Appeals (9th cir.), 1979-95, sr. judge, 1995—; cons. Project STAR, Law Enforcement Assistance Adminstrn.; mem. select com. on internal procedures of Calif. Supreme Ct., 1987—; co-chair Sino-Am. Seminar on Mediation and Arbitration, Beijing, 1992; dir. Dialogue on Transition to a Global Soc., Weinacht, Switzerland, 1992. Author: Judicial Adminstration and The Administration of Justice, 1973, (with Christopher Goelz and Meredith Watts) Federal Ninth Circuit Civil Appellate Practice, 1995; Contbr. articles to profl. jours. Co-chmn. Confronting Myths in Edn. for Pres. Nixon's White House Conf. on Children, Pres. Carter's Commn. for Pension Policy, 1974-80, Pres. Reagan's Madison Trust; bd. visitors U.S. Air Force Acad., 1978; bd. dirs. Council on Legal Edn. for Profl. Responsibility, 1971-80, Constnl. Right Found., Am. Nat. Inst. for Social Advancement, Pacific Oaks Coll., Childrens Sch. & Rsch. Ctr., 1996-98; adv. bd. Nat. Center for State Cts., 1971-73, World Law Inst., 1997—; chmn. bd. Western Justice Ctr., 1986—; mem. adv. com. Nat. Jud. Edn. Program to promote equality for women and men in cts.; bd. advisors Tahirih Justice Inst., Washington, 1998—; chair 9th Cir. Standing Com. on ADR, 1998—. Named Law Alumnus of Yr. UCLA, 1967, Disting. Jurist, Ind. U. Law, 1994; recipient Profl. Achievement award, 1969; named Times Woman of Yr., 1968; recipient U. Judaism Humanitarian award, 1973; AWARE Internat. award, 1970; Ernestine Stalhut Outstanding Woman Lawyer award, 1972; Pub. Svc. award Coro Found., 1978, Pax Orbis ex Jure medallion World Peace thru Law Ctr., 1975, Hollzer Human Rights award Jewish Fedn. Coun., L.A., 1988, Medal of Honor UCLA, 1993, Emil Gumpert Jud. ADR Recognition award L.A. County Bar Assn., 1996, Julia Morgan award YWCA Pasadena, 1997; Lustman fellow Yale U. 1977. Fellow Am. Bar Found., Davenport Coll., Yale U.; mem. Bar Calif. (bd. dirs. continuing edn. bar commn. 1967-74), Am. Judicature Soc. (dir., Justice award 1985), Assn. Am. Law Schs. (chmn. com. edn. in jud. adminstrn.), Am. Bar Assn. (sect. on jud. adminstrn., chmn. com. on edn. in jud. adminstrn. 1973-89), Phi Beta Kappa, Order of Coif (nat. v.p. 1974-76), Jud. Conf. U.S. (com. to consider standards for admission to practice in fed. cts. 1976-79). Office: US Ct Appeals Cir 125 S Grand Ave Ste 303 Pasadena CA 91105-1621*

NELSON, DREW VERNON, mechanical engineering educator; b. Elizabeth, N.J., Oct. 11, 1947; s. Andrew K. and Myra G. (Kempson) N. BSME, Stanford U., 1968, MSME, 1970, PhDME, 1978. Research asst. Stanford U., Calif., 1971-74, asst. prof., 1978-83, assoc. prof., 1983-96; prof. Stanford U., 1996—; engr. Gen. Electric Co., Sunnyvale, Calif., 1975-76, sr. engr., 1977-78; cons. in field. Co-editor: Fatigue Design Handbook, 1989; contbr. articles to profl. jours. Recipient Spergel Meml. award for Most Outstanding Paper, 32d Internat. Wire and Cable Symposium, 1984, Hetenyi award for Best Rsch. Paper Pub in 1994 in the jour. Exptl. Mechanics. Mem. ASTM, Soc. Automotive Engrs., Soc. for Exptl. Mechanics, Sigma Xi, Tau Beta Pi. Home: 840 Cabot Ct San Carlos CA 94070-3464 Office: Stanford U Dept Mech Engring Stanford CA 94305-4021

NELSON, FRANCES PATRICIA, food service executive; b. Denver, Jan. 15, 1948; d. Wilbur Jordan and Margaret Emma Anna (Kruger) Cannon; m. Kenneth Roy Nelson, Sept. 2, 1972; children: Krista, Erin, Michael. BS, Colo. State U., 1970; MA, U. No. Colo., 1981. Asst. dir. child nutrition Colo. Dept. Edn., Denver, 1971-77; dir. nutrition svc. Denver Head Start, 1981-83; dir. food svc. Englewood (Colo.) Pub. Schs., 1988-91, Jefferson County Schs., Golden, Colo., 1991—; cons. Wildwood Child Care, Englewood, 1984-88, Mile High Child Care Assn., Denver, 1981-83, Colo. Dept. Edn., Denver, 1976, Denver Pub. Schs., 1979. Contbr. articles to profl. jours. Leader Girl Scouts Am., Denver, 1982-88, Boy Scouts Am., 1991; team adminstr. Aurora (Colo.) Soccer Club, 1981-88. Mem. Am. Dietetic Assn., Am. Sch. Food Svc. Assn., Colo. Sch. Food Svc. Assn. (pres.-elect 1991-92, pres. 1992-93). Home: 6227 S Netherland Cir Aurora CO 80016-1323 Office: Jefferson County Pub Schs 1829 Denver West Dr # 27 Golden CO 80401-3120

NELSON, GEORGE DARRELL, theatre and film educator; b. Calgary, Alta., Can., Dec. 27, 1954; came to U.S., 1966; s. George Edgar and Audrey (Broadhead) N.; m. Leslie Jo Bell, Mar. 18, 1977; children: Justin Marcus, MacLain Darrell, Jordan Derek, Courtney Marie, George Tyler, Aaron Joseph, Marshall Christian, Audrey Dianna. BA, Brigham Young U., 1977; MFA, U. Wash., 1979; PhD (hon.), U. Okabogi, Iowa, 1998. Assoc. prof. dept. theatre and film Brigham Young U., Provo, Utah; pres., CEO Clime Internat., Provo, 1992—; chmn. bd. NCTI, Phoenix, 1983-92; bd. dirs. Insight Learning Found., Phoenix, 1996—. Author: (plays) Outside In, 1979 (Best New Play award CTAA Region 9), Showtime, 1998; (personality test) Who Are Hue, 1992; dir. film Understanding Styles, 1995. Mormon. Office: Brigham Young U D-581 HFAC Provo UT 84602

NELSON, HAROLD BERNHARD, museum director; b. Providence, R.I., May 14, 1947; s. Harold B. and Eleanor (Lavina) N. BA, Bowdoin Coll., 1969; MA, U. Del., 1972. Rsch. fellow NMAA Smithsonian Inst., Washington, 1976-77; curator Am. art Mus. Art & Archeol., U. Mo., Columbia, 1977-79; registrar Solomon R. Guggenheim Mus., N.Y.C., 1979-83; exhibition program dir. Am. Fedn. Arts, N.Y.C., 1983-89; dir. Long Beach (Calif.) Mus. of Art, 1989—; juror Annual Art Exhibition Mus. Art, Sci. & Industry, Bridgeport, Conn., 1988, Annual Art Exhibition, Clark County Dist. Libr., Las Vegas, Nev., 1984; speaker Am. Assn. Mus. Annual Conf., Detroit, 1985, annual meeting Western Mus. Conf., Portland, Oreg., 1987, Grantmakers in Art Symposium, N.Y.C., 1986, annual meeting Western Mus. Conf., Salt Lake City, 1985; mem. adv. com. APA, Assn. Sci. and Tech. Ctrs.; panelist Aid to Spl. Exhibitions, NEA, Washington, 1986; participant Am. Legal Assn., ABA Conf., San Francisco, 1986; observer, respondent Mus. Symposium, NEA, Dallas, 1985. Author: Sounding the Depths: 150 Years of American Seascape, 1989, New Visions: Selina Trieff, 1997, Bountiful Harvest: American Decorative Arts from the Gail-Oxford Collection, 1997, For a New Nation: American Decorative Arts from the Gail-Oxford Collection, 1998. Office: Long Beach Mus Art 2300 E Ocean Blvd Long Beach CA 90803-2442

NELSON, HARRY, journalist, medical writer; b. Interlachen, Fla., Apr. 18, 1923; s. Knut Alfred and Edith Farr (Wilkes) N.; m. Diane Gabriella Meerschaert, Aug. 29, 1948 (div. 1977); children—Tanya Ann, Lawrence Stephen, Ronald Gerard, James Anthony, John Christopher; m. Gita Doris Wheelis, Jan. 29, 1984. B.A., U. So. Calif., 1949. Reporter, photographer Bakersfield Press, Calif., 1949; reporter, photographer Bakersfield Community Chest, Calif., 1949; promotion writer Los Angeles Times, 1949-57, reporter, 1957-58, med. writer, 1958-88, sr. writer, 1977-80; freelance med. writer, 1988—; staff writer Milbank Meml. Fund, 1993—. Charter mem. bd. dirs. Los Angeles County Comprehensive Health Planning Assn., Los Angeles, 1968-69. Served with USAAF, 1941-45. Recipient spl. commendation AMA, 1974, John Hancock award John Hancock Ins. Co., 1978, Journalism award Am. Acad. Pediatrics, 1979, Disting. Svc. by non-physician award Calif. Med. Assn., 1988, Lifetime Achievement in med. writing award AMA, 1988, Peter Lisagor award for exemplary journalism Chgo. Headliners Club, 1988. Mem. Nat. Assn. Sci. Writers (pres. 1966). Avocations: sailing; hiking; ceramics. Address: Med Writers Internat PO Box N 14016 Yellowstone Dr Frazier Park CA 93222

NELSON, HELEN MARTHA, retired library director; b. Anaconda, Mont., Dec. 20, 1929; d. Ole Bertin and Caroline Helen (Massey) N. BA with honors, U. Mont., 1951; MLS, U. Wash., 1960. Asst. documents and serials libr. U. Mont., Missoula, 1951-52; tchr. English and history, libr. Laurel H.S., 1952-54; tchr. English, libr. Beaverhead County H.S., 1954-56; tchr. English, journalism Anaconda Sr. H.S., 1956-59; libr., adminstr. U.S. Army, 1960-68; libr. dir. Oceanside (Calif.) Libr., 1968-94; chmn. Serra Coop. Libr., 1973-74, 84-85, 90-91; mem. coun. Serra Coop. Sys., 1969-94. Chmn. Christian Sponsors, Oceanside, 1975; congl. pres. King of Kings Luth. Ch., Oceanside, 1974, 77, 84, mem. coun. 1971-77, 82-84, 92-94; bd. dirs. Oceanside/Carlsbad ARC, 1970-71; del. Calif. Gov.'s Conf. Librs. and Info. Sci. Mem. ALA, AAUW, LWV, Mont. Libr. Assn., Calif. Libr. Assn. (coun. 1978-80, v.p. Palomar chpt. 1978), Pub. Libr. Execs. of So. Calif., Oceanside C. of C., Calif. Inst. Libr. (bd. dirs. 1978-80). Avocations: photography, travel, crewel embroidery.

NELSON, IVORY VANCE, academic administrator; b. Curtis, La., June 11, 1934; s. Elijah H. and Mattie (White) N.; m. Patricia Robbins, Dec. 27, 1985; children: Cherlyn, Karyn, Eric Beatty, Kim Beatty. BS with distinction, Grambling (La.) State U., 1959; PhD with distinction, U. Kans., 1963. Assoc. prof. chemistry So. U., Baton Rouge, 1963-67, head div. sci., 1966-68; prof. chemistry Prairie View (Tex.) A&M U., 1968-83, asst. acad. dean, 1968-72, v.p. rsch., 1972-82, acting pres., 1982-83; exec. asst. Tex. A&M U. System, College Station, 1983-86; chancellor Alamo C.C. Dist., San Antonio, 1986-92; pres. Cen. Wash. U., Ellensburg, 1992—; DuPont teaching fellow U. Kans., 1959; rsch. chemist Am. Oil Co., 1962; sr. rsch. chemist Union Carbide Co., 1969; vis. prof. U. Autonomous Guadalajara, Mex., 1966, Loyola U., 1967; Fulbright lectr., 1966; cons. evaluation coms. Oak Ridge (Tenn.) Assoc. Univs., NSF, Nat. Coun. for Accreditation Tchr. Edn., So. Assn. Colls. and Schs.; mem. regional policy coms. on minorities Western Interstate Com. on Higher Edn., 1986-88; mem. exec. com. Nat. Assn. State Univs. and Land Grant Colls., 1980-82. Contbr. articles to profl. jours. Bd. dirs. Target 90, Goals San Antonio, 1987-89, coun. of pres.NAIDA,(1993-96) Commn. on Student Learning, Wash., 1992—, United Way San Antonio, 1987-89, Alamo Area coun. Boy Scouts Am., 1987-89, San Antonio Symphony Soc., 1987-91, Key Bank of Wash.; mem. bd. dirs. assn. Western U., (1995—) mem. com. fir jud. reform State of Tex., 1991; mem. edn. adv. bd. Tex. Rsch. Park, 1987-89; bd. givs. Am. Inst. for character Edn., Inc., 1988-91; mem. adv. com. Tex. Ho. of Reps., 1978; chmn. United Way Campaign Tex. A&M U. System, 1984, others. Staff sgt. USAF, 1951-55, Korea. T.H. Harris scholar Grambling State U., 1959; fellow Nat. Urban League, 1969. Mem. AAAS, Am. Chem. Soc., Tex. Acad. Sci., NAACP, Phi Beta Kappa, Sigma Xi, Phi Lambda Upsilon, Beta Kappa Chi, Alpha Mu Gamma, Kappa Delta Pi, Sigma Pi Sigma, Omega Psi Phi, Sigma Pi Phi, Phi Kappa Phi. Avocations: fishing, photography, sports. Home: 211 E 10th Ave Ellensburg WA 98926-2911 Office: Office of Pres Cen Wash U Ellensburg WA 98926

NELSON, JAMES C, state supreme court justice; m. Chari Werner; 2 children. BBA, U. Idaho, 1966; JD cum laude, George Washington U., 1974. Fin. analyst SEC, Washington; pvt. practice Cut Bank; county atty. Glacier County; justice Mont. Supreme Ct., 1993—; former mem. State Bd. Oil and Gas Conservation, also chmn.; former mem. State Gaming Adv. Counsel, Gov. Adv. Coun. on Corrections and Criminal Justice Policy; liaison to Commn. of Cts. of Ltd. Jurisdiction, mem. adv. com. Ct. Assessment Program. Served U.S. Army. Office: Justice Bldg Supreme Ct of Mont 215 N Sanders St Rm 315 Helena MT 59620*

NELSON, KENNETH ARTHUR, electrical engineer; b. Coeur d'Alene, Idaho, Apr. 18, 1942; s. Elton Arthur and Maxine Edna (Barnes) N.; m. Sharon Fay Paynter, Sept. 2, 1962; children: Neva Kenine, Krena Krista, Kelina Kara, Kimberly Kay. BSEE, U. Idaho, 1965; cert., Alexander Hamilton Inst., 1970. Registered profl. engr., Calif., Idaho. With GE, various locations, 1965-75; sr. mfg. engr. Jenn-Air Corp., Indpls., 1975-79; plant engr. A.O. Smith Corp., Newark, Calif., 1979-82; dir. facilities Memorex Corp., Santa Clara, Calif., 1982-88; with Scenic Mgmt. Corp., Tracy, Calif., 1988—; instr. Profl. Engring. Inst., San Carlos, Calif., 1985-88, ITT Ednl. Svcs., Inc., Hayward, Calif.; founder Scenic Mgmt., Livermore, Calif., 1985—. Inventor in field. Mem. IEEE, Am. Soc. Metals Internat. Republican. Lutheran. Avocations: fishing, camping, hunting. Home: 1585 Hoot Owl Ct Tracy CA 95376-4396

NELSON, L. BRUCE, lawyer; b. Mpls., Aug. 6, 1946; s. Leo W. and Sylvia E. Nelson; m. Nancy E. Cook, Aug. 23, 1969; 1 child, Andrew C. AB, Hamilton Coll., 1968; JD, U. Colo., 1971. Bar: Colo., D.C., U.S. Ct. Appeals (10th cir.). Assoc./ptnr. Sherman & Howard, Denver, 1972-83; dir., shareholder Isaacson, et al, Denver, 1983-91; counsel Inverness Properties, Denver, 1991-94; dir., shareholder Ducker, Montgomery, et al, Denver, 1994—; clk. Judge Jean Breitenstein, 10th Cir. Ct. Appeals, Denver, 1971. Mem. ABA, Colo. Bar Assn., Colo. Corp. Counsel. Office: Ducker Montgomery Ste 1500 1560 Broadway Denver CO 80202

NELSON, MARY CARROLL, artist, author; b. Bryan, Tex., Apr. 24, 1929; d. James Vincent and Mary Elizabeth (Langton) Carroll; m. Edwin Blakely Nelson, June 27, 1950; children: Patricia Ann, Edwin Blakely. BA in Fine Arts, Barnard Coll., 1950; MA, U. N.Mex., 1963. Juror Am. Artist Golden Anniversary Nat. Art Competition, 1987, Don Ruffin Meml. Art Exhbn., Ariz., 1989, N.Mex. Arts and Crafts Fair, 1989, 96; guest instr. continuing edn. U. N.Mex., 1991; conf., organizer Affirming Wholeness, The Art and Healing Experience, San Antonio, 1992, Artists of the Spirit Symposium, 1994. Group shows include N.Mex. Mus. Fine Arts Biennial, 1987, N.Mex. Lightworks, 1990, Level to Level, Layering, Ohio, 1987, Artist as Shaman, Ohio, 1990, The Healing Experience, Mass., 1991, A Gathering of Voices, Calif., 1991, Art is for Healing, The Universal Link, San Antonio, Tex., 1992, Biennial, Fuller Lodge Art Ctr. Los Alamos, N.Mex., 1993, Layering, Albuquerque, 1993, Crossings, Bradford, Mass., 1994, The Layered Perspective, Fayetteville, Ark., 1994, Tree of Life, San Miguel de Allende, Mex., 1996, Honoree, Magnifico, Albuquerque, 1997, Guardian Spirits, Marlborough, Eng., 1997, Memories in Multi-Media, Columbus, Ohio, 1998, Objects, Agora Gallery, N.Y.C., 1998, Celtic Connections, Mass., 1998; represented in pvt. collections in: U.S., Fed. Republic of Germany, Eng. and Australia; author: American Indian Biography Series, 1971-76, (with Robert E. Wood) Watercolor Workshop, 1974, (with Ramon Kelley) Ramon Kelley Paints Portraits and Figures, 1977, The Legendary Artists of Taos, 1980, (catalog) American Art in Peking, 1981, Masters of Western Art, 1982, Connecting, The Art of Beth Ames Swartz, 1984, Artists of the Spirit, 1994, Doris Steider, A Vision of Silence, 1997, Beyond Fear, A Toltec's Guide to Freedom and Joy, 1997, (catalog) Layering, An Art of Time and Space,

1985, (catalog) Layering/Connecting, 1987; contbg. editor Am. Artist, 1976-91, Southwest Art, 1987-91; editor (video) Layering, 1990; arts correspondent Albuquerque Jour., 1991-93; contbr. One Source Sacred Journeys, 1997, Bridging Time and Space, Essays on Layered Art, 1998. Mem. Albuquerque Arts Bd., 1984-88. Mem. Soc. Layerists in Multi-Media (founder 1982). Home: 1408 Georgia St NE Albuquerque NM 87110-6861

NELSON, MICHAEL RICHARD, artist, designer, photographer; b. Galesburg, Ill., Aug. 17, 1947; s. Melvin Richard and Dorothy (Jordan) N.; m. Ardis Rosiak, Apr. 4, 1971 (div. June 1981); 1 child, Joshua Jordan; m. Susan Chieco, Feb. 23, 1990. BA, Western Ill. U., 1970, MA, 1973. Prin. Michael Nelson Graphics, L.A., 1974-78; ptnr. Nelson and Sixta, L.A., 1978—. Served with U.S. Army, 1971-73, Vietnam. Democrat. Avocations: painting, photography, golf. Home: 4036 Glenalbyn Dr Los Angeles CA 90065-3115 Office: Nelson and Sixta 1150 Brea Canyon Rd Walnut CA 91789-3906

NELSON, NANCY ELEANOR, pediatrician, educator; b. El Paso, Apr. 4, 1933; d. Harry Hamilton and Helen Maude (Murphy) N. BA magna cum laude, U. Colo., 1955, MD, 1959. Intern, Case Western Res. U. Hosp., 1959-60, resident, 1960-63; pvt. practice medicine specializing in pediats., Denver, 1963-70; clin. prof. U. Colo. Sch. Medicine, Denver, 1988—, assoc. dean student affairs U. Colo. Sch. Medicine, 1988—. Mem. Am. Acad. Pediats., AMA (sect. med. schs. governing coun. 1994-96), Denver Med. Soc. (pres. 1983-84), Colo. Med. Soc. (bd. dirs. 1985-88, mem. jud. coun. 1992—, mem. liason com. med. edn. 1995—). Office: 4200 E 9th Ave Denver CO 80220-3706

NELSON, NEVIN MARY, interior designer; b. Cleve., Nov. 5, 1941; d. Arthur George Reinker and Barbara Phyllis (Gunn) Parks; m. Wayne Nelson (div. 1969); children: Doug, Brian. BA in Interior Design, U. Colo., 1964. Prin. Nevin Nelson Design, Boulder, Colo., 1966-70, Vail, Colo., 1970—; program chmn. Questers Antique Study Group, Boulder, 1969. Coord. Bob Kirscht for Gov. campaign, Eagle County, Colo., 1986; state del. Rep. Nat. Conv., 1986-88; county coord. George Bush for U.S. Pres. campaign, 1988, 92; chmn. Eagle County Reps., 1989-93; v.p. bd. dirs. Park Lane Condo Assn., Denver, 1995-96; pres. Save Our Imperiled Land, Vail, 1998. Mem. Am. Soc. Interior Designers. Episcopalian. Avocations: party planning, cooking, reading, travel, skiing. Home: PO Box 1212 Vail CO 81658-1212 Office: 2498 Arosa Dr Vail CO 81657-4276

NELSON, PAULA MORRISON BRONSON, educator; b. Memphis, Mar. 26, 1944; d. Fred Ford and Julia (Morrison) Bronson: m. Jack Marvin Nelson, July 13, 1968; children: Eric Allen, Kelly Susan. BS, U. N.Mex., 1967; MA, U. Colo., Denver, 1985. Physical edn. tchr. Grant Union Sch. Dist., Sacramento, 1967-68; physical edn. tchr. Denver Pub. Schs., 1968-74, with program for pupil assistance, 1974-80; tchr. ESL Douglas County Pub. Schs., Parker, Colo., 1982-83; chpt. 1 reading specialist Denver Pub. Schs., 1983-96, computer/reading specialist, 1996-98, reading specialist, gifted and talented tchr., 1998—; demonstration tchr. Colo. Edn. Assn., 1970-72; mem. curriculum com. Denver Pub. Schs., 1970-72; mem. Douglas County Accountability Com., Castle Rock, Colo., 1986-92; mem. educators rev. panel Edn. for Freedom; computer trainer Denver Pub. Schs. Tech. Team, 1992—. Co-author: Gymnastics Teacher's Guide Elementary Physical Education, 1973, Applauding Our Constitution, 1989; editorial reviewer G is for Geography, Children's Literature and the Five Themes. 1993; producer slide shows Brotherhood, 1986, We the People...Our Dream Lives On, 1987, Celebration of Cultures, 1988. Named Pub. Edn. Coalition grantee, Denver, 1987, 88, 89, 90, grantee Rocky Mountain Global Edn. Project, 1987, Wake Forest Law Sch., Winston-Salem, N.C., 1988, 89, 90, 92; recipient chpt. II grant, 1991, Tech. grant, 1993, Three R's of Freedom award State Dept. Edn., 1987, Nat. Recognition award Commn. on Bicentennial of Constitution., 1987, Distinguished Tchr. award City of Denver, 1994. Mem. Windstar Found., Colo. Coun. Internat. Reading, Internat. Reading Assn., Colo. Coun. for the Social Studies, Tech. in Edn., Am. Fedn. Tchrs., Denver Fedn. Tchrs. Republican. Methodist. Avocations: snow and water skiing, tennis. Home: 10488 E Meadow Run Parker CO 80134-6220

NELSON, RANDALL ERLAND, surgeon; b. Hastings, Nebr., Dec. 28, 1948; s. Marvin Erland and Faith Constance (Morrison) N.; m. Carolyn Joy Kaufman, Feb. 28, 1976. BS in Chemistry cum laude, So. Nazarene U., 1971; MD, U. Nebr., 1975; MS in Surgery, U. Ill., Chgo., 1979. Diplomate Nat. Bd. Med. Examiners, Am. Bd. Surgery. Intern in gen. surgery Strong Meml. Hosp., Rochester, N.Y., 1975-76; resident in gen. surgery U. Rochester Affiliated Hosps., 1976-78, Rush-Presbyn.-St. Luke's Med. Ctr., Chgo., 1978-81; gen. surgeon Surg. Group San Jose, Calif., 1981—; instr. gen. surgery U. Rochester Sch. Medicine and Dentistry, 1975-78, Rush Med. Coll., Chgo., 1978-80; adj. attending surgeon Rush-Presbyn.-St. Luke's Med. Ctr., 1980-81. Mem. Rep. Nat. Com., Washington, 1984—. Fellow ACS, Southwestern Surg. Congress; mem. Calif. Med. Assn., Santa Clara County Med. Soc., San Jose Surg. Soc., U.S. C. of C., Circle-K Club, Phi Delta Lambda. Republican. Avocations: photography, traveling, bicycling, collecting coins and stamps. Office: Surg Group of San Jose 2101 Forest Ave Ste 124 San Jose CA 95128-1424

NELSON, ROBERT WILLIAM, theater arts educator; b. Spanish Fork, Utah, May 14, 1935; s. Robert Arthur Nelson and Edme Hunter Dotson; m. Kathleen Caldwell, May 29, 1964; children: Kevin, Pamela, Jeffrey, Julietta, Jeannette. BA, Brigham Young U., 1960, MA, 1965; postgrad., U. Colo., Boulder, 1969-70. Tchr. theater and speech Tooele (Utah) H.S., 1960-62; prof. theater arts Ricks Coll., Rexburg, Idaho, 1964—, chair theater dept., 1971-80, acting chair theater dept., 1983-84. Dir., scenic designer, lighting designer numerous plays and musicals. With U.S. Army, 1953-61. Mem. Rocky Mountain Theater Assn. (bd. dirs. 1984-94). Mem. Ch. of LDS. Avocation: photography. Home: 52 Ash Ave Rexburg ID 83440-2006 Office: Ricks Coll #220 Snow Bldg Rexburg ID 83460

NELSON, RODNEY ELLSWORTH, judge; b. Mpls., July 4, 1934; s. Gustaf Arthur and Thea Amanda (Aslakson) N.; m. Shari Lee Dennis, Aug. 15, 1964; children: Amanda Lee, Braden Ellsworth. BA, U. Minn., 1956; LLB, Columbia U., 1960. Bar: Calif., 1961. Ptnr. Nelson, Ritchie & Gill, Los Angeles, 1979-82, Loo, Meredith & McMillan, Los Angeles, 1983-85, Bryan, Cave, McPheeters & McRoberts, Los Angeles, 1986—. Republican. Presbyterian. Home: 11525 Bellagio Rd Los Angeles CA 90049-2110 Office: Los Angeles Superior Ct 111 N Hill St Dept 46 Los Angeles CA 90012

NELSON, THOMAS G., federal judge; b. 1936. Student, Univ. Idaho, 1955-59, LLB, 1962. Ptnr. Parry, Robertson, and Daly, Twin Falls, Idaho, 1965-79, Nelson, Rosholt, Robertson, Tolman and Tucker, Twin Falls, from 1979; judge U.S. Cir. of Appeals (9th cir.), Boise, Idaho, 1990—. With Idaho Air N.G., 1962-65, USAR, 1965-68. Mem. ABA (ho. of dels. 1974, 87-89), Am. Bar Found., Am. Coll. Trial Lawyers, Idaho State Bar (pres., bd. commrs.), Idaho Assn. Def. Counsel, Am. Bd. Trial Advocates (pres. Idaho chpt.), Phi Alpha Delta, Idaho Law Found. Office: US Ct Appeals 9th Circuit 304 N Eighth St PO Box 1339 Boise ID 83701-1339*

NELSON, WALTER WILLIAM, computer programmer, consultant; b. Seattle, May 7, 1954; s. Arne A. and Helen R. (Truitt) N.; m. Paula E. Truax, Dec. 21, 1985. BA in Zoology, U. Wash., 1976, BS in Psychology, 1977; PhC in Psychology, U. Minn., 1982. Systems analyst Dept. of Social and Health Svcs., State of Wash., Seattle, 1986-89; computer info. cons. Dept. of Health, State of Wash., Seattle, 1989-90; pres. Data Dimensions, Inc. (name now Nelson Consulting, Inc.), Seattle, 1990—; pres. Tech. Alliance, Renton, Wash., 1990-91, Nelson Family Homes, Inc., 1996—, Women's Fin. Resources, Inc., 1998—. Contbr. articles to profl. jours. Mem. Tech Alliance, Berkeley Macintosh Users Group, Seattle Downtown Macintosh Bus. Users Group, 4th Dimension Spl. Interest Group (founder, pres. 1990—). Avocations: tennis, golf, thoroughbred horse racing. Office: Nelson Consulting Inc 6729 20th Ave NW Seattle WA 98117-5707

NELSON, WILLIAM RANKIN, surgeon, educator; b. Charlottesville, Va., Dec. 12, 1921; s. Hugh Thomas and Edith (Rankin) N.; m. Nancy Laidley, Mar. 17, 1956 (div. 1979); children: Robin Page Nelson Russel, Susan Kimberly Nelson Wright, Anne Rankin Nelson Cron; m. Pamela Morgan Phelps, July 5, 1984. BA, U. Va., 1943, MD, 1945. Diplomate Am. Bd. Surgery. Intern Vanderbilt U. Hosp., Nashille, 1945-46; resident in surgery U. Va. Hosp., Charlottesville, 1949-51; fellow surg. oncology Meml. Sloan Kettering Cancer Ctr., N.Y.C., 1951-55; instr. U. Colo. Sch. Medicine, Denver, 1955-57; asst. clin. prof. U. Colo. Sch. Medicine, 1962-87, clin. prof. surgery, 1987—; asst. prof. Med. Coll. Va., Richmond, 1957-62; mem. exec. com. U. Colo. Cancer Ctr.; mem. nat. bd., nat. exec. com. Am. Cancer Soc. Contbr. articles to profl. jours. and chpts. to textbooks. Capt. USAAF, 1946-48. Recipient Nat. Div. award Am. Cancer Soc., 1979. Fellow Am. Coll. Surgeons (bd. govs. 1984-89); mem. AMA, Internat. Soc. Surgery, Brit. Assn. Surg. Oncology, Royal Soc. Medicine (U.K.), Soc. Surg. Oncology (pres. 1975-76), Soc. Head and Neck Surgeons (pres. 1986-87), Am. Cancer Soc. (pres. Colo. div. 1975-77, exec. com., nat. bd. dirs., del. dir. from Colo. div. 1985-94), Am. Soc. Clin. Oncology, Western Surg. Assn. Colo. Med. Soc., Denver Med. Soc., Denver Acad. Surgery, Rocky Mt. Oncology Soc., Univ. Club, Rotary. Republican. Episcopalian. Avocations: skiing, backpacking, travel, bicycling, fly fishing.

NEMETZ, PETER NEWMAN, policy analysis educator, economics researcher; b. Vancouver, B.C., Can., Feb. 19, 1944; s. Nathan Theodore and Bel Nemetz; m. Roma E.S. Kellock, July 16, 1994; 1 stepchild, Fiona Susan. BA in Econs. and Polit. Sci., U. B.C., 1966; AM in Econs., Harvard U., 1969, PhD in Econs., 1973. Teaching fellow, tutor Harvard U., Cambridge, Mass., 1971-73; lectr. Sch. Planning, U. B.C., Vancouver, 1973-75, asst. prof. to assoc. prof. policy analysis, 1975-96, prof., 1996—, chmn., 1984-90; nonresident faculty Green Coll., 1993-94, 95-97, St. John's Coll., 1997—; postdoctoral fellow Westwater Rsch. Centre, Vancouver, 1973-75; vis. scientist, dept. med. stats. and epidemiol. Mayo Clinic, 1986-88, sr. visiting scientist Dept. of Health Scis. Rsch. Mayo Clinic, 1988—; cons. consumer and corp. affairs, Can., 1977-80; program chmn. The Vancouver Inst., 1990—; mem. rsch. mgmt. com. Ctr. Health Svcs and Policy Rsch., U. B.C., 1990—, mgmt. com. Ctr. Southeast Asia Rsch., 1992—; bd. dirs. U. B.C. Press, 1993—; faculty assoc. U. B.C. dept. resource mgmt. and envirin. studies, 1979—, Ctr. Japanese Studies, 1992—, dept. healthcare and epidemiology; selection com. U. B.C. Rhodes Scholarship, 1991-98; mem. U. B.C. Senate, 1998—; assoc. Ctr. Pacific Basin Monetary and Econ. Studies, Econ. Rsch. Dept., Fed. Reserve Bank of San Francisco, 1991—. Mem. bd. mgmt. BC-Yukon divsn. Can. Nat. Inst. for Blind., 1992-94. Editor Jour. Bus. Adminstrn., 1978—. Contbr. articles to sci. jours. Grantee Natural Scis. and Engrng. Rsch. Coun. of Can., 1976-92, Consumer and Corp. Affairs Can., 1978-80, Econ. Coun. of Can., 1979-80, Max Bell Found., 1982-84. Mem. Inst. Resources and the Environ. (assoc.), Am. Econ. Assn. Jewish. Clubs: Harvard of B.C. (pres. 1986-94), Vancouver Club. Avocations: swimming; photography. Office: Univ British Columbia, Faculty of Commerce, Vancouver, BC Canada V6T 1Z2

NEMIR, DONALD PHILIP, lawyer; b. Oakland, Calif., Oct. 31, 1931; s. Philip F. and Mary (Shavor) N. AB, U. Calif., Berkeley, 1957, JD, 1960. Bar: Calif. 1961, U.S. Dist. Ct. (no. dist.) Calif. 1961, U.S. Ct. Appeals (9th cir.) 1961, U.S. Dist. Ct. (ctrl. dist.) Calif. 1975, U.S. Supreme Ct. 1980. Pvt. practice, San Francisco, 1961—; pres. Law Offices of Donald Nemir, A Profl. Corp. Mem. Calif. State Bar Assn. Home: PO Box 1089 Mill Valley CA 94942-1089

NEMIRO, BEVERLY MIRIUM ANDERSON, author, educator; b. St. Paul, May 29, 1925; d. Martin and Anna Mae (Oshanyk) Anderson; m. Jerome Morton Nemiro, Feb. 10, 1951 (div. May 1975); children: Guy Samuel, Lee Anna, Dee Martin. Student Reed Coll., 1943-44; BA, U. Colo., 1947; postgrad., U. Denver. Tchr., Seattle Pub. Schs., 1945-46; fashion coord., dir. Denver Dry Goods Co., 1948-51; fashion dir. Denver Market Week Assn., 1952-53; free-lance writer, Denver, 1958—; moderator TV program Your Preschool Child, Denver, 1955-56; instr. writing and communications U. Colo. Denver Ctr., 1970—, U. Calif., San Diego, 1976-78, Met. State Coll., 1985; dir. pub. relations Fairmont Hotel, Denver, 1979-80; free lance fashion and TV model; author, co-author: The Complete Book of High Altitude Baking, 1961, Colorado a la Carte, 1963, Colorado a la Carte, Series II, 1966, (with Donna Hamilton) The High Altitude Cookbook, 1969, The Busy People's Cookbook, 1971 (Better Homes and Gardens Book Club selection 1971), Where to Eat in Colorado, 1967, Lunch Box Cookbook, 1965, Complete Book of High Altitude Baking, 1961, (under name Beverly Anderson) Single After 50, 1978, The New High Altitude Cookbook, 1980. Co-founder, pres. Jr. Symphony Guild, Denver, 1959-60; active Friends of Denver Libr., Opera Colo. Recipient Top Hand award Colo. Authors' League, 1969, 72, 79-82, 100 Best Best Books of Yr. award N.Y. Times, 1969, 71; named one of Colo.'s Women of Yr., Denver Post, 1964. Mem. Am. Soc. Journalists and Authors, Colo. Authors League (dir. 1969-79), Authors Guild, Authors League Am., Friends Denver Library, Opera Colo. Guild, Rotary, Kappa Alpha Theta. Address: Park Towers 1299 Gilpin St # 15 W Denver CO 80218

NEMIROFF, MAXINE CELIA, art educator, gallery owner, consultant; b. Chgo., Feb. 11, 1935; d. Oscar Bernard and Martha (Mann) Kessler; m. Paul Rubenstein, June 26, 1955 (div. 1974); children: Daniel, Peter, Anthony; m. Allan Nemiroff, Dec. 24, 1979. BA, U. So. Calif., 1955; MA, UCLA, 1974. Sr. instr. UCLA, 1974-92; dir., curator art gallery Doolittle Theater, Los Angeles, 1985-86; owner Nemiroff Deutsch Fine Art, Santa Monica, Calif.; leader of worldwide art tours; cons. L'Ermitage Hotel Group, Beverly Hills, Calif., 1982—, Broadway Dept. Stores, So. Calif., 1979—, Security Pacific Bank, Calif., 1978—, Am. Airlines, Calif. Pizza Kitchen Restaurants; art chmn. UCLA Thieves Market, Century City, 1960—, L.A. Music Ctr. Mercado, 1982—; lectr. in field. Apptd. bd. dirs. Dublin (Calif.) Fine Arts Found., 1989; mem. Calif. Govs. Adv. Coun. for Women, 1992; mem. art selection com. Calif. State Office Bldgs., 1997—. Named Woman of Yr. UCLA Panhellenic Council, 1982, Instr. of Yr. UCLA Dept. Arts, 1984; elected to Fashion Circle of the Costume Coun., L.A. County Mus. Art, 1997—. Mem. L.A. County Mus. Art Coun., UCLA Art Coun., UCLA Art Coun. Docents, Alpha Epsilon Phi (alumnus of yr. 1983). Avocations: tennis, horseback riding, skiing, piano and guitar.

NEMIROFF, PAUL RAPHAEL, producer, director; b. N.Y.C., Sept. 2, 1932; s. Sam and Anne (Weinstein) N.; m. Maxine Rich Nemiroff, Aug. 15, 1954; children: Audrey Robin, Steven Brian. BA, Cornell U., 1954. Prodn. asst. CBS TV Network, N.Y.C., 1956-58; TV comml. producer Young & Rubicam, Inc., N.Y.C., 1958-62; asst. producer Columbia Pictures, Inc., Hollywood, Calif., 1962; prodn. mgr. Wilding Pictures, Inc., N.Y.C., 1962-63, Allen Funt, N.Y.C., 1963; dir., producer N.Y.C., 1963-65, Filmex, Inc., N.Y.C., 1965-68; producer Pelican Films, Inc., N.Y.C., 1968-69, Quality Presentations, Inc., N.Y.C., 1969-72; dir., producer Townhouse Prodns., Inc., N.Y.C., 1973-79; dir., producer, owner Paul Nemiroff Prodns., Inc., 1979—; dir., producer N.Y. Internat. Film and TV Festival, 1975, 76, 78, 80, 83, 84, U.S. Indsl. Film Festival, 1976, 77, Two Cine Golden Eagles, 1980, 86, Cindy, 1978, Interim, 1981, 83, 85. 1st lt. U.S. Army, 1954-56. Numerous awards for films. Mem. Internat. Assn. of Bus. Communicators (award of excellence 1980, 81). Jewish. Avocations: bass fishing, gardening. Office: 18697 N 95th Way Scottsdale AZ 85255-5551

NEMO, FRED, artist; b. Seattle, Wash., Dec. 4, 1949; s. Stimson Bullitt and Carolyn (Kizer) Woodbridge; children: Crystal Bullitt, Melita Bullitt, Prairie Rose Zelano. Choreographer, prin. dancer Hazel, 1992-98. Rep., plaintiff, Critical Mass, Portland, Oreg., 1994-99. E-mail: diputs@teleport.com.

NEPOTE, MENDES ALFRED, secondary education educator, retired; b. Camino, Calif., May 8, 1915; s. Andrew G.B. and Veneranda C. (Davi) N.; m. Mary Antoinette Fernandez, Nov. 10, 1938; children: Doris Ann, Michel Elaine. BA in Edn., San Jose State U., 1938; MA in Edn., Stanford U., 1960. Cert. tchr. secondary edn., Calif. Tchr. Lodi (Calif.) Unified Sch. Dist., 1938-76. Author: An Introduction to Language Learning, 1974. Bd. dirs. Lodi Sister City Commn., 1969-98, Pacific Italian Alliance, Stockton, Calif., 1979-98. With US Coast Guard, 1942-68. Mem. Calif. Tchrs. Assn. (life), Ret. Officers Assn. (life). Republican. Roman Catholic. Avocations: golfing, stained glass, woodworking, lapidary. Home: 200 S Orange Ave Lodi CA 95240-3330

NEPPE, VERNON MICHAEL, neuropsychiatrist, psychopharmacologist, author, educator; b. Johannesburg, Transvaal, Rep. South Africa, Apr. 16, 1951; came to U.S., 1986; s. Solly Louis and Molly (Hesselsohn) N., m. Elisabeth Selma Schachter, May 29, 1977; children: Jonathan, Shari. BA, U. South Africa, 1976; MB, BCh, U. Witwatersrand, Johannesburg, 1973, diploma in psychol. medicine, 1976, M in Medicine, 1979, PhD in Medicine, 1981; MD, U.S., 1982. Diplomate Am. Bd. Psychiatry and Neurology, Am. Bd. Geriatric Psychiatry, Am. Bd. Forensic Psychiatry, Am. Bd. Forensic Examiners, Am. Bd. Forensic Medicine; registered psychiatry specialist U.S., Republic of South Africa, Can. Specialist in tng. dept. psychiatry U. Witwatersrand, Johannesburg, 1974-80; sr. cons. U. Witwatersrand Med. Sch., Johannesburg, 1980-82, 83-85; neuropsychiatry fellow Cornell U., N.Y.C., 1982-83; div. dir. U. Wash. Med. Sch., Seattle, 1986-92; dir. Pacific Neuropsychiat. Inst., Seattle, 1992—; mem. clin. faculty dept. psychiatry and behavioral scis. U. Wash. Med. Sch., 1992—; adj. prof. psychiatry St. Louis U. Sch. of Medicine, dept. psychiatry and human behavior, 1994—; attending physician N.W. Hosp., 1992—; neuropsychiatry cons. South African Brain Rsch. Inst., Johannesburg, 1985—; chief rsch. cons. Epilepsy Inst., N.Y.C., 1989; mem. faculty lectr. Epilepsy: Refining Med. treatment, 1993-94. Author: The Psychology of Dèjà Vu, 1983, Innovative Psychopharmacotherapy, 1990, Cry the Beloved Mind: A Voyage of Hope, 1999, (text) BROCAS SCAN, 1992; (with others) 33 book chpts.; editor 14 jours. issues; contbr. articles to profl. jours. Recipient Rupert Sheldrake prize for rsch. design (2d prize) award New Scientist, 1983, Marius Valkhoff medal South African Soc. for Psychical Rsch., 1982, George Elkin Bequest for Med. Rsch., U. Witwatersrand, 1980; named Overseas Travelling fellow, 1982-83. Fellow Psychiatry Coll. South Africa (faculty), Royal Coll. Physicians of Can., North Pacific Soc. for Neurology, Neurosurgery and Psychiatry, Coll. Internat. Neuropharmacologicum, Am. Coll. Forensic Examiners; mem. AMA, Parapsychologic Assn., Am. Psychiat. Assn. (U.S. transcultural collaborator diagnostic and statis. manual 1985-86, cons. organic brain disorders 1988—), Am. Epilepsy Soc., Soc. Biol. Psychiatry, Can. Psychiat. Assn., Soc. Sci. Exploration, Am. soc. Clin. Psychopharmacology, Am. Neuropsychiat. Assn. Jewish. Avocations: chess, table tennis, tennis, computers, scrabble. Office: Pacific Neuropsychiat Inst c/o Brainquest Press # 236 4756 University Village Pl NE Seattle WA 98105

NERCISSIANTZ, ARA Z., chemistry researcher; b. Oct. 17, 1952; s. Zaven N.; 1 child. BA, U. So. Calif., 1976; MS, U. Calif., Santa Barbara, 1977; PhD, Columbia U., Pacifica, Calif., 1989; MBA, U. La Verne, Calif., 1997. Chemist Morton Thioker Corp., Tustin, Calif., 1982-85; process engr. Allegheny Internat., Anaheim, Calif., 1985-86; group leader Cargill Corp., Lynwood, Calif., 1986-89; prin. scientist Courtaulds Aerospace, Burbank, Calif., 1989-94; dir. rsch. McGean-Rohco Co., Downey, Calif., 1994—. Inventor in field. Fellow Am. Inst. Chemists (cert.); mem. Am. Chem. Soc., Nat. Certification Commn. Home: PO Box 898 Glendale CA 91209-0898

NESBITT, PAUL EDWARD, historian, author, educator; b. Balt., Dec. 25, 1943; s. William Ervin and Margaret Caroline (Shaw) N.; m. Donna Jean Coppock, Aug. 15, 1966 (dec. 1972); children: Erik-Paul A., Janelle M., m. Pamela Jean Lichty, May 25, 1974 (div. 1983); m. Anita Louise Wood, Dec. 8, 1984 (div. 1989); m. Paula Jane Sawyer, May 7, 1994. AB, U. Wash., 1965; MA, Wash. State U., 1968, PhD (hon.), 1970; PhD, U. Calgary, Alta., Can., 1972. Reader in Anthropology, U. Wash., 1965, grad. rschr.-tchr. Wash. State U., 1966-68, instr., Tacoma C.C., Wash., 1968-69; grad. rschr.-tchr. U. Calgary, 1969-71; exec. Hudson's Bay Co., Calgary, 1971; prof. Western Oreg. U., Monmouth, 1971-74; state historian State of Calif., Sacramento, 1974-97, ret. 1997; dir. Am. Sch. of Interior Design, San Francisco, 1974, HBC Bow Fort Rsch., Morley, Atla., 1970-71; instr. Am. River Coll., Sacramento, 1980-86; exec. mgr. Calif. State Govt. United Way Campaign, 1986, 87, also bd. dirs., mem. fiscal and communication coms., El Dorado County and Sacramento chpts., 1988—; designer, cultural rsch. cons. pvt. contracts western states, 1960—; exec. dir. Heritage Areas Assn., 1993—, pres. bd. dir., 1994—. Contbr. articles to prof. jours. Fellow Am. Anthropl. Assn.; mem. Calif. Hist. Soc., Am. Inst. of Interior Designers (profl. 1974-77, bd. dirs. energy planning and devel. cos. 1986-88), AIA (Cen. Valley chpt. 1975-77), Rotary. Home: 3177 Clark St Placerville CA 95667-6405

NESMITH, AUDREY MARIE, retired military housing manager, writer; b. Washington, Apr. 6, 1937; d. John Wallace and Elsie Mae (Welsh) Cullins; m. Adolfo Mier Delhierro, May 11, 1960; (dec. Mar., 1978), children: Alicia Marie Delhierro Carver, Julia Mae Delhierro Crawford; m. Benjamin Rea Nesmith, Jan. 9, 1985. Student, U. Md., 1982-86. Chief bachelor officers qtrs. U.S. Army White Sands Missile Range, WSMR, N. Mex., 1978-80; chief housing referral office U.S. Army, Ft. Sam Houston, Tex., 1980-82; chief housing divsn. U.S. Army-U.S. Army Mil. Command, Garmsich, Fed. Republic Germany, 1982-85; dep. dir. housing divsn. U.S. Navy Washington Naval Dist., 1985-89; Equal Employment Opportunity officer, Garmisch, Fed. Republic Germany, 1984-85; v.p. Profl. Housing Mgmt. Assn., Garmisch, 1983-84. Author: (book) Loved into Life, 1985. Treas. First Ch. Christian and Missionary Alliance, 1994-96. Republican. Avocations: writing, reading, theatre, films, opera. Home: 1533 Merion Way Apt 26E Seal Beach CA 90740-4967

NESS, JAMES JOSEPH, law enforcement educator; b. Stevens Point, Wis., July 6, 1941; s. Lawrence Joseph and Eleanor Thresa (Hojnacki) Niespodziani; m. Sandra Jean Peters Feverston, Apr. 11, 1964 (div. Sept. 1985); 1 child, Peter James; m. Ellyn Katherine Buikema, Nov. 29, 1986; 1 child, Jamie (dec.). BA in Liberal Arts, Northeastern Ill. U., 1975; MS in Law Enforcement, So. Ill. U., 1979, PhD in Ednl. Admin., 1989. Patrol officer Wis. Dells Police, 1964-66, Drake U. Police, Des Moines, 1966-69; police lt. Triton Police Dept., River Grove, Ill., 1969-77; rschr. So. Ill. U., Carbondale, 1977-79, dir. police mgmt. study, 1979-81, prof. law enforcement, 1983-89; chief of police Villa Grove (Ill.) Police, 1981-83; dir. AJ programs Barton County C.C., Great Bend, Kans., 1989-95; dean of academics Haitian Nat. Police Tng. Ctr., Port-au-Prince, Haiti, 1995; internat. police task force UN, Bosnia, Yugoslavia, 1996-97; dean acad. Commonwealth Internat. U., Mesa, Ariz., 1997—. Author: Introduction to Law Enforcement, 1994; contr. articles to profl. jours. Staff sgt., USAF, 1959-64. Mem. Internat. Assn. Chiefs of Police, Central Kans. Ct. Appointed Spl. Advocates (pres. 1990-94), Ctrl. Kans. Cmty. Corrections (pres. 1993-95). Avocations: civil war reenactor, trail riding. Home: 6335 E Brown Rd Unit 1122 Mesa AZ 85205-5622 Office: Commonwealth Internat U 1457 W Southern Ave Ste 8 Mesa AZ 85202-4852

NESTLER, JANICE RAE, health facility administrator, educator; b. San Diego, Feb. 5, 1947; d. James Goddard MacBride and Philonise Anne (Whistler) Williams; m. Gary Wayne Messer, Sept. 15, 1967 (div. Jan. 1975); children: Troy Edward, Travis Robert; m. Richard Charles Nestler, Mar. 21, 1979; children: Christie Ann, Laura Suzanne. BS in Pub. Health Edn., Oreg. State U., 1978. Prevention program devel. staff Marion County Mental Health Dept., Salem, Oreg., 1976-78; exec. dir. Eastside Adult Day Svcs., Bellevue, Wash., 1984—; bd. dirs. work force devel. com. Nat. Coun. on the Aging/Nat. Title V Contractor Nat. Adult Day Svcs. Assn.; bd. dirs. home and comty.-based svcs. com. Am. Assn. of Homes and Svcs. for the Aging, Wash. Adult Day Svcs. Assn. Mem. Nat. Adult Day Svcs. Assn. (chmn.), Bellevue Breakfast Rotary (Rotarian of Yr. 1997). Avocations: reading, travel, gardening, antiquing. Office: Eastside Adult Day Svcs 12831 NE 21st Pl Bellevue WA 98005-1909

NETHERCUTT, GEORGE RECTOR, JR., congressman, lawyer; b. Spokane, Wash., Oct. 4, 1944; s. George Rector and Nancy N.; m. Mary Beth Socha Nethercutt, Apr. 2., 1977; children: Meredith, Elliott. BA in English, Wash. State U., 1967; JD, Gonzaga U., 1971. Bar: D.C. 1972. Law clk. to Hon. Raymond Plummer U.S. Dist. Ct. Alaska, Anchorage, 1971; staff counsel to U.S. Senator Ted Stevens Washington, 1972, chief of staff to U.S. Senator Ted Stevens, 1972-76; pvt. practice Spokane, Wash., 1977-94; mem. 104th Congress from 5th Wash. dist., Washington, 1994—; mem. house appropriations and sci. coms. Chmn. Spokane County Rep. Party, 1990-94, co-founder Vanessa Behan Crisis Nursery, pres. Spokane Juvenile Diabetes Found., 1993-94. Mem. Masons (lodge #34), Lions Club (Spokane Ctrl.), Sigma Nu. Republican. Presbyterian. Avocations: running, handball, squash. Office: US House Reps 1527 Longworth Bldg Ofc Bldg Washington DC 20515-4705

NETT, LOUISE MARY, nursing educator, consultant; b. Sept. 25, 1938. Diploma, St. Cloud Sch. Nursing, 1959; cert. in therapy program, Gen. Rose Hosp., Denver, 1967. Staff nurse med. unit Mt. Sinai Hosp., Mpls., 1959-60; [illegible]

emergency rm. staff nurse Colo. Gen. Hosp., Denver, 1961-62; head nurse Outpatient Clinic Charity Hosp., New Orleans, 1962-64; dir. respiratory care U. Colo. Health Scis. Ctr., Denver, 1965-85, pulmonary program specialist Webb-Waring Lung Inst., 1985-89; rsch. assoc. Presbyn./St. Luke's Ctr. for Health Scis. Edn., Denver, 1989—; clins. assoc. prof. nursing U. Colo. Sch. Nursing, Denver; adj. asst. prof. U. Kans. Sch. Allied Health; instr. medicine pulmonary divsn. U. Colo. Sch. Medicine, Denver, 1980-89; mem. Nat. Heart, Lung, and Blood Inst. adv. coun., NIH, 1979-82, mem. safety and data monitoring bd. for early intervention for chronic obstructive pulmonary disease, lung divsn., 1985-91; mem. clin. practice guidelines for smoking cessation and presentation panel Agy. for Health Care Policy and Rsch., 1994; dir. numerous courses, confs. in field; worldwide lectr. assns., symposia, confs., TV, convs., meetings, workshops; internat. cons. hosps., health depts., 1975—; local, regional lectr. through med. programs Am. Lung Assn., Am. Cancer Soc. Colo., cmty. hosps., businesses. Author: (with T.L. Petty) For Those Who Live and Breathe with Emphysema and Chronic Bronchitis, 1967, 2d edit., 1971, Enjoying Life with Emphysema, 1984, 2d edit., 1987 (Am. Jour. Nursing Book of Yr. award 1987), Rational Respiratory Therapy, 1988; mem. editl. bd. Heart and Lung Jour., 1972-87, Respiratory Times Newsletter, 1986-88, Jour. Home Health Care Practice, 1988; contbr. articles to profl. jours., chpts. to books. Mem. subcom. on nursing Am. Lung Assn., 1975-76; mem. exec. bd. dirs. Colo. divsn. Am. Cancer Soc., 1984—, chairperson pub. edn. com., 1985-86; mem. exec. com. Am. Stop Smoking Intervention Study, 1991-94, mem. alliance bd. Recipient Rocky Mountain Tobacco Free Challenge Regional award for treatment of nicotine addiction program, 1989, award for ednl. seminars, 1989, award in profl. end., 1992, award for outstanding work in developing and promoting smoking cessation, 1992, profl. educator award, 1993, award for nicotine treatment network, 1993. Mem. ANA, Am. Assn. for Respiratory Care (health promotion com. 1987—, internat. liaison com. 1987-90, Charles H. Hudson Pub. Respiratory Health award 1991), Am. Assn. of Cardio Vascular and Pulmonary Rehab., Am. Thoracic Soc. (ad hoc com. role of non-physician in respiratory care 1972, respiratory therapy com. 1972-74, program planning com. 1989), Behavioral Medicine Soc., Colo. Trudeau Soc. (v.p. 1981, pres.-elect 1982, pres. 1983), Colo. Pub. Health Assn., Internat. Oxygen Club, Internat. Soc. for Humor Studies, Soc. of European Pnemonology. Office: 1850 High St Denver CO 80218

NETTELHORST, ROBIN PAUL, academic administrator, writer; b. Ohio, Mar. 14, 1957; s. Paul Merrit and Naomi Jean (Saylor) N.; m. Ruth Williamson, June 25, 1983; children: Vanessa Rachel, Nichole Antoinette, Sarah Brittany. BA, L.A. Bapt. Coll., 1979; MA, UCLA, 1983. Lectr. Christian Heritage Coll., El Cagon, Calif., 1984; lectr. old testament and bibl. langs. L.A. Bapt. Coll., 1984-87; novelist, 1987—; v.p. Quartz Hill (Calif.) Sch. Theology, 1992—; webmaster Quartz Hill Sch. Theology, 1996—. Editor Quartz Hill Jour. Theology, 1994—; author short stories; contbr. articles to mags. Ordained deacon Quartz Hill Cmty. Ch., 1987—. Mem. Am. Acad. Religion, Soc. Bibl. Lit. Baptist. Avocations: camping, reading, philately, numismatics. E-mail: robin@theology.edu. Office: Quartz Hill Sch Theology 43543 51st St W Quartz Hill CA 93536-5608

NETTLESHIP, LOIS ELLEN, history educator; b. Bklyn., June 14, 1942; d. Charles and Ethel (Bernstein) Shankman; m. William. A. Nettleship, Aug. 14, 1966; children: Elizabeth, Anna. BA, Sarah Lawrence Coll., 1964; MA, Columbia U., 1966; DPhil., U. Sussex, Eng., 1976. Mem. faculty Johnson County Community Coll., Overland Park, Kans., 1975-91, Fullerton (Calif.) Coll., 1991—; dir. Johnson County Ctr. for Local History, Overland Park, Kans., 1983-91; tchr. Great Plains and Western U.S. history Columbia U., summer 1990. Author numerous books on local Kans. history, 1986-91; contbr. articles to profl. jours. Mem. Johnson County Bicentennial Commn., 1987-88. Woodrow Wilson Found. fellow 1964, NEH fellow 1980, 82; named Innovator of Yr. League for Innovation, 1984. Mem. Kans. Com. for the Humanities (bd. dirs. 1987-90), Kans. Hist. Tchrs. Assn. (pres. 1987-88), Kans. State Hist. Soc. (editorial com. 1988-90). Avocation: music. Home: 526 Pinehurst Ave Placentia CA 92870-4450

NETZEL, PAUL ARTHUR, fund raising management executive, consultant; b. Tacoma, Sept. 11, 1941; s. Marden Arthur and Audrey Rose (Jones) N.; BS in Group Work Edn., George Williams Coll., 1963; m. Diane Viscount, Mar. 21, 1963; children: Paul M., Shari Ann. Program dir. S. Pasadena-San Marino (Calif.) YMCA, 1963-66; exec. dir. camp and youth programs Wenatchee (Wash.) YMCA, 1966-67; exec. dir. Culver-Palms Family YMCA, Culver City, Calif., 1967-73; v.p. met. fin. devel. YMCA Met. Los Angeles, 1973-78, exec. v.p. devel., 1979-85; pres. bd. dirs. YMCA Employees Credit Union, 1977-80; chmn. N.Am. Fellowship of YMCA Devel. Officers, 1980-83; adj. faculty U. So. Calif. Coll. Continuing Edn., 1983-86, Loyola Marymount U., L.A., 1986-90, Calif. State U., L.A., 1991-92, UCLA Extension, 1991—; chmn., CEO Netzel Assocs., Inc., 1985—; pvt. practice cons., fund raiser. Chmn. Culver-Palms YMCA, Culver City, 1991-93, chmn. 1989-91, bd. mgrs. 1985—; pres. bd. Culver City Guidance Clinic, 1971-74; mem. Culver City Bd. Edn., 1975-79, pres., 1977-78; mem. Culver City Edn. Found., 1982-91; bd. dirs. Los Angeles Psychiat. Svc., 1971-74, Goodwill Industries of So. Calif., 1993-97; mem. Culver City Council, 1980-88, vice-mayor, 1980-82, 84-85, mayor, 1982-83, 86-87; mem. Culver City Redevel. Agy., 1980-88, chmn., 1983-84, 87-88, vice chmn, 1985-86; bd. dirs. Los Angeles County Sanitation Dists., 1982-83, 85-87, Western Region United Way, 1986-93, vice chmn, 1991-92; chmn. bd. dirs. Calif. Youth Model Legislature, 1987-92; mem. World Affairs Coun., 1989—; mem. adv. bd. Automobile Club of So. Calif., 1996—. Recipient Man of Yr. award Culver City C. of C., 1972. Mem. Nat. Soc. Fund Raising Execs. (nat. bd. dirs. 1989-91, vice chmn. 1994, v.p. bd. dirs. Greater L.A. chpt. 1986-88, pres. bd. dirs. 1989-90, Profl. of Yr. 1983), Calif. Club, Rotary (L.A. # 5, pres. 1992-93, treas. L.A. found. 1995-96), Rotary Internat. (gov. dist. 5280 1997-98), Mountain Gate Country. Address: Netzel Assocs Inc 9696 Culver Blvd Ste 204 Culver City CA 90232-2753

NEU, CARL HERBERT, JR., management consultant; b. Miami Beach, Fla., Sept. 4, 1937; s. Carl Herbert and Catherine Mary (Miller) N.; BS, MIT, 1959; MBA, Harvard U., 1961; m. Carmen Mercedes Smith, Feb. 8, 1964; children—Carl Bartley, David Conrad. Cert. profl. mgmt. cons. Indsl. liaison officer MIT, Cambridge, 1967-69; coord. forward planning Gates Rubber Co., Denver, 1969-71; pres., co-founder Dyna-Com Resources, Lakewood, Colo., 1971-77; pres., founder Neu & Co., Lakewood, 1977—; mng. dir. Pro-Med Mgmt. Systems, Lakewood, 1981—; lectr. Grad. Sch. Pub. Affairs, U. Colo. Denver, 1982-84. Mem. exec. coun. Episcopal Diocese Colo., 1974; mem. Lakewood City Coun., 1975-80, pres., 1976; chmn. Lakewood City Charter Commn., 1982, Lakewood Civic Found., Inc., 1986-91; pres. Lakewood on Parade, 1978, bd. dirs., 1978-80; pres. Classic Chorale, Denver, 1979, bd. dirs., 1978-83; pres. Lakewood Pub. Bldg. Authority, 1983—; bd. dirs. Metro State Coll. of Denver Found., 1990—, treas., 1994-97; bd. dirs. Kaiser Permanente Health Adv. Com., 1990—, chair, 1997. With U.S. Army, 1961-67. Decorated Bronze Star medal, Army Commendation medal; recipient Arthur Page award AT&T, 1979; Kettering Found. grantee, 1979-80. Mem. Internat. City Mgrs. Assn., Lakewood-So. Jefferson County C. of C. (bd. dirs. 1983-89, chmn. 1988, chmn. 1987-88), Jefferson County C. of C. (chmn. 1988). Republican. Episcopalian. Contbr. articles to profl. jours. Home: 8169 W Baker Ave Denver CO 80227-3129

NEUDECKER, STEPHEN K., marine ecologist, museum professional. BS in Zoology, U. Ky., 1974; MS in Biology, U. Guam, 1978; PhD in Marine Ecology, U. Calif., Davis, 1982; grad. Mus. Mgmt. Inst., U. Calif., Berkeley, 1993. Project scientist U. Guam Marine Lab., Mangilao, 1975-77; marine environ. cons. Santa Fe Engrs. and Yamada Engrs., Guam and Tokyo, 1977-78, Dames and Moore, Inc., San Francisco, 1983; cons., sr. scientist Ecol. Analysts, Inc., Concord and Lafayette, Calif., 1979-80, 82-84; sr. scientist, lab. coord. Lockheed Engring. and Mgmt. Svcs. Co., Las Vegas, 1984; cons., sr. project mgr. Henwood Energy Svcs., Sacramento, 1985-86; prin. Environ. Cons. Svcs., Davis and Bonita, Calif., 1984—; exec. dir. Bayfront Conservancy Trust, Chula Vista, Calif., 1984—. Contbr. numerous articles to profl. jours. Mem. AAAS, Am. Assn. Mus., Am. Zoo and Aquarium Assn., Ecol. Soc. Am. (cert. sr. ecologist), Am. Soc. Icthyologists and Herpetologists, Bonita Sunrise Rotary (past pres.), Internat. Wine and Food Soc. (past pres. Chula Vista chpt.), Sigma Xi. Office: Chula Vista Nature Ctr 1000 Gunpowder Point Dr Chula Vista CA 91910-1201

NEUHARTH, DANIEL J., II, psychotherapist; b. Sioux Falls, S.D., Nov. 10, 1953; s. Allen Harold and Loretta Faye (Helgeland) N. BA, Duke U., 1975; MS in Journalism, Northwestern U., 1978; MA, John F. Kennedy U., 1988; PhD in Clin. Psychology, Calif. Sch. Profl. Psychology, 1992. Lic. marriage, family and child counselor. Reporter USA Today, Washington, 1982-83; lectr. San Diego State U., 1983-84; talk show host KSDO-AM, San Diego, 1983-84; pres. Dialogues, San Francisco, 1987—; psychotherapist pvt. practice, San Francisco, 1992—; vis. prof. U. Fla., Gainesville, 1980-81, U. Hawaii, Honolulu, 1981-82; adj. faculty U. San Francisco, 1989—. Host, prodr. radio talk show Saturday Night People, 1984; Author: If You Had Controlling Parents, 1998, (with others) Confessions of an S.O.B., 1989. Office: Dialogues PO Box 1022 Fairfax CA 94978-1022

NEUHAUSER, PHILIPP DANTON, corporate communications specialist; b. Bklyn., Dec. 27, 1929; s. Louis R. and Katherine (Miller) N.; m. Mary Virginia Rose Neuhauser, Nov. 8, 1953; children: Michael, Stephen, Charlene, Philipp II. BS, Woodbury U., 1955. Promoter Curtis Circulation Co., San Diego, 1955-57; writer, producer, dir. Gen. Dynamics Convair, San Diego, 1957-62; multi-media prodn. mgr. jet propulsion lab. Calif. Inst. Tech., Pasadena, Calif., 1962—; instr. Pasadena Jr. Coll., 1965-80; pres. Associated Retirees Caltech/Jet Propulsion Lab. Contbr. articles to profl. jours. Lifetime charter mem. Def. Info. Sch., Ft. Benjamin Harrison, Ind., 1989—. With USN, 1948-52. Recipient Gold medal Internat. Film and TV Festival, 1983, Gold Camera award U.S. Indsl. Film Festival, 1983, 2 Disting. Tech. Communications Soc. Technical Communications, 1983; named to Def. Info. Sch. Hall of Fame Ft. Benjamin Harrison, 1991. Mem. Audio Visual Mgmt. Assn. (regional dir. 1984-86, disting. achievement award, 1982), Assn. Multi-Image, Am. Aviation Historical Soc., U.S. Space and Rocket Pioneers, Aerospace Edn. Assn., Comm. Media Mgmt. Assn. Republican. Roman Catholic. Club: E Clampus Vitus (Pasadena). Avocations: raquetball, gold mining. Home: 10931 Quill Ave Sunland CA 91040-2322 Office: Calif Inst Tech Jet Propulsion Lab 4800 Oak Grove Dr Pasadena CA 91109-8001

NEUMANN, HERMAN ERNEST, elementary and special education educator; b. Winona, Minn., Nov. 11, 1931; s. Herman Ferdinand and Dena Matilda (Peterson) N.; m. Juanita Evelyn, Sept. 11, 1954; children: Mary Evelyn, Herman Ernest Jr., Martin Andrew, Amy Louise. BS, Winona State U., 1961; MA, Calif. State U., Bakersfield, 1976; postgrad., San Jose U., 1977, Calif. State U., San Barbara, 1978. Cert. early childhood, spl. edn., elem. edn., ESL instr. Classroom tchr. grades K-6, resource specialist Bakersfield (Calif.) City Schs., 1980-82; classroom tchr. Kern County, Bakersfield, 1982-84; resource specialist Bakersfield (Calif.) City Schs., 1984-92; lectr. in edn. Calif. State U., Bakersfield, 1994—. Contbr. articles to profl. jours. 1st class airman USAF, 1952-56. NSF fellow, 1966, Internat. Biog. Assn. fellow, Cambridge, Eng., 1993; named to Hall of Fame Teaching Excellence Kern County, 1990, Tchr. of Yr., 1990. Mem. NEA (grantee 1969), Bakersfield Elem. Tchrs. Assn., ASCD, Calif. Tchrs. Assn. Home: 5219 Cedarbrook Ln Bakersfield CA 93313-2719 Office: Bakersfield City Schs 1300 Baker St Bakersfield CA 93305-4326

NEUMANN, LINDA KAY, marketing executive; b. Wyandotte, Mich., Feb. 5, 1959; d. Michael and Raelene Fern (Bongart) Goldman; m. David Dewain Neumann, Mar. 31, 1980; children: Rachel Anne, Kyle Wayne. Student, Mesa C.C., San Diego, 1976-86; grad. with honors, Bank Mktg. Sch., 1991. Mail clk., securities clk. Hawaiian Trust Co. Ltd., Honolulu, 1977-78, supr., 1979-81; securities vault clk., bank card clk. Union Bank Calif., San Diego, 1981-82, sales adminstrv. asst., 1983-86, mktg. adminstrv. asst., mktg. officer, 1986-88, from mktg. asst. v.p. to mktg. v.p., 1992-94, mktg. v.p., mgr., 1994-99, bus. and sales planning mgr., v.p., 1996—; chmn. San Diego Ednl. Coun. Am. Banking Assn. Am. Inst. Banking, 1996-97. Pres. Rolling Hills Elem. PTA, 1995-96; parliamentarian Deer Canyon Elem. PTA. Mem. Direct Mktg. Assn., Advt. Club San Diego, San Diego Direct Mktg. Assn., Bank Mktg. Assn. Office: Union Bank Calif 530 B St Ste 950 San Diego CA 92101-4404

NEUMANN, NANCY RUTH, studio educator; b. L.A., Feb. 1, 1948; d. Robert Thomas and Frances Andersen; m. Bernd Fritz Dietmar Neumann, June 26, 1971; children: Peter, Christina, Linda, Christoph, Karin. BA, U. Calif., Riverside, 1969; MA, Sorbonne U., Paris, 1971; credentials, Calif. State U., San Bernardino, 1985. Cert. community coll. tchr., various subjects, Calif., studio tchr., Calif. Missionary, reading instr. Maroua, Cameroon, Africa, 1971-73; instr. Pasadena (Calif.) City Coll., 1974-75; secondary tchr. Riverside (Calif.) Christian Sch., 1985-86; studio tchr. Vista Films, Culver City, 1986, Hollywood (Calif.) Studios, 1986-88, Paramount Studios, Hollywood, Calif., 1986-93, MGM - Lorimar Prodns., Culver City, Calif., 1986-91, Universal Studios, Universal City, Calif., 1986-90, R.J. Louis Prodns., Burbank, Calif., 1987, Michael Landon Prodns., Culver City, 1987-88, Carsey-Werner Prodns., L.A., 1988; instr. Riverside Community Coll., 1988; studio tchr. Bob Booker Prodns., Hollywood, 1988-90, Walt Disney Prodns., Burbank, 1992—; exec. producer Am. Pictures, Riverside, 1989—; studio tchr. NBC Prodns., Burbank, 1990, 20th Century Fox, 1993—; pvt. tutor, Riverside, L.A., 1987—; drama coach Grace Ch., Riverside, 1981-82, Magnolia Ave. Bapt. Ch. Riverside, 1986-89. Author: several plays, 1981-89; writer 70 songs, 1968—. Coach mock trial Riverside Christian H.S., 1985-86; choir dir. Riverside Christian Sch., 1985-86; Sunday Sch. tchr. Grace Bapt. Ch., Harvest Christian Fellowship, Riverside, Magnolia Ave. Bapt. Ch., 1968-92, Wheat, Oil and Wine Christian Fellowship, Riverside, Sunday sch. supt., 1992-93; children's choir dir. Grace Bapt. Ch., 1981-82. Recipient Golden Star Halo award, Star Sapphire Halo award, Jeanie Golden Halo award for acting and teaching So. Calif. Motion Picture Coun., 1994. Mem. Nat. Assn. Christian Educators, Internat. Alliance of Theatre and Stage Employees, Internat. Platform Assn., Greater L.A. World Trade Ctr. Assn., Sons of Norway (study scholar 1967), Delta Phi Alpha. Republican. Avocations: photography, music, travel, production of films and videos. Home: 1787 Prince Albert Dr Riverside CA 92507-5852 Office: Walt Disney Studios 500 S Buena Vista St Burbank CA 91521-0004

NEUMANN, PETER GABRIEL, computer scientist; b. N.Y.C., Sept. 21, 1932; s. J.B. and Elsa (Schmid) N.; m. Elizabeth Susan Neumann; 1 child, Helen K. AB, Harvard U., 1954, SM, 1955; Dr rerum naturarum, Technisch Hochschule, Darmstadt, Fed. Republic Germany, 1960; PhD, Harvard U., 1961. Mem. tech. staff Bell Labs, Murray Hill, N.J., 1960-70; Mackay lectr. Stanford U., 1964, U. Calif., Berkeley, 1970-71; computer scientist SRI Internat., Menlo Park, Calif., 1971—. Author: Computer-Related Risks, 1995. Fulbright grantee, 1958-60. Fellow AAAS, IEEE, Assn. for Computing (editor jour. 1976-93, chmn. com. on computers and pub. policy 1985—). Avocations: music, tai chi, holistic health. Office: SRI Internat EL-243 333 Ravenswood Ave Menlo Park CA 94025-3493

NEUMAYR, SHARON, land developer, writer; b. Parkston, S.D., July 27, 1942; d. Herbert and Edna K. (Schumacher) N. BS in Edn., No. State U., Aberdeen, S.D., 1964; MA, Western State Coll., Gunnison, Colo., 1970. Cert. profl. tchr. Colo. Tchr. English Marshall (Minn.) High Sch., 1964-67, Risley Jr. High, Pueblo, Colo., 1967-73, Ctrl. High Sch., Pueblo, 1973-95; tchr. composition/lit. Pueblo C.C., 1991-95; tchr. composition U. So. Colo., Pueblo, 1994; land developer Pueblo County, 1996—. Author: (workbooks) American Literature Activities, 1992, World Literature Activities, 1994. Bd. dirs. Pueblo Ballet, 1987-89, Pueblo Symphony, 1989-93, Animal Welfare, Pueblo, 1993-95. Mem. NEA, Nat. Coun. Tchrs. of English. Democrat. Avocations: gardening, reading, hiking, biking. Home: PO Box 1653 Pueblo CO 81002-1653

NEUMUELLER, ANDERS J.F., newspaper editor, writer; b. Stockholm, Sweden, Apr. 8, 1946; arrived in Can., 1982; s. Hans F. and Agneta K. (Horn af Aminne) N.; m. Hamida J. Jamal, July 15, 1977; children: Mina, Sofia. BA, Uppsala (Sweden) U., 1971; diploma in internat. mktg., Coll. Distributive Trades, London, 1973. Art dir. Scandecor, Uppsala, 1975-78; writer Diverse, Stockholm, 1978-82; prin. The Creative Dept., Vancouver, B.C., 1982-86; editor Swedish Press, Vancouver, 1986—; founder, editor Scandinavian Press, Vancouver, 1994—. Author: Posters, 1978, 2d edit., 1979, God Jul, 1980, Herr Svensson, 1982, others. Founder Sweden House Soc., Vancouver, 1988. Mem. Uasa Order of Am. Avocations: skiing, travel. Office: Swedish Press Inc, 1294 W 7th Ave, Vancouver, BC Canada V6H 1B6

NEVILLE-HARRIS, ALICE ALMEDA (ALICE ALMEDA AHNA), retired critical care nurse; b. N.Y.C., Nov. 19, 1933; d. Anthony and Bessie Beatrice (Brown) Harris; m. James Edward Neville, May 21, 1951 (dec. June 30, 1963); children: Mary Ann, Wallace Lee, Denise Leona, James Edward, Clyde Leo. AA, West L.A. C.C., 1981; BA, John Jay Coll., N.Y.C., 1983. CCCN. Psychiat. nurse Bronx Mcpl. Hosp., N.Y.C., 1956-67; thoracic surgery nurse Sloane Kettering, N.Y.C., 1968-69; prison health nurse N.Y.C., 1968-77; home care nurse Norrell Registry, Van Nuys, Calif., 1979-78; CCRN Crenshaw Hosp., L.A., 1982-93. Author-dir.: (play) God's Watchin' You, 1995; contbr. poetry to anthologies. with NAACP, SCLC, Vols. Am., Mayor Lindsey Prison Health Task Force, 1969. Inducted World of Poets Hall of Fame World of Poetry Press, 1986. Mem. Internat. Poet Soc. (life), Internat. Black Writers and Artists (bd. dirs. 1995—). Democrat. Avocations: motivating youth, chess, folk tales, story telling. Home: 1124 W 82nd St Los Angeles CA 90044-3520

NEVIN, DAVID WRIGHT, real estate broker, mortgage broker; b. Culver City, Calif., July 27, 1947; s. Wilbur D. and Anita J. (Hulderman) N.; m. Shirley Grimes, Nov. 12, 1977; children: Jenny, David Wright Jr. BA, Calif. State Poly. U., 1974. Rural manpower asst. employment devel. State Calif., Riverside, 1970-74; pers. mgr. Lindsay Olive Growers, Calif., 1974-79; employee rels. mgr. Morton Salt Co., Newark, Calif., 1979-80; real estate salesman Valley Realty, Fremont, Calif., 1980, The Property Profls., Fremont, Calif., 1980-85; owner Nevin & Nevin, Inc., 1984-88, CitiDesign, 1989—; co-owner Brokers Exch., Inc., 1985-86; dir., officer CitiBrokers Real Estate, Inc., 1986-94; owner Nevin Fin/Mortgage Exchange 1992—; br. mgr. Brandt Property Mgmt. Group, 1994-95; mgr. Internat. Trade Corp., Saigon, Vietnam, 1997—. Sustaining mem. Rep. Nat. Com., Washington, 1984; mem. Presdl. Task Force, Washington, 1984, Fremont Cmty. Ch. Served with U.S. Army, 1967-69. Mem. Realtors Nat. Mktg. Inst. (real estate brokerage coun.), Internat. Real Estate Fedn., So. Alameda County Bd. Realtors (local govt. rels. com. 1983-86). Address: 1292 Marguerite St Livermore CA 94550-4242

NEVLING, HARRY REED, health care human resources executive; b. Rochester, Minn., Sept. 15, 1946; s. Edwin Reid and Ruth Margaret (Mulvihill) N.; m. Joanne Carol Meyer, Nov. 26, 1976; 1 son, Terry John. AA, Rochester Community Coll., 1973; BA cum laude, U. Winona, 1974; MBA, U. Colo., 1990. Pers. rep. Rochester Meth. Hosp., 1974-75; dist. mgr. Internat. Dairy Queen Corp., 1975-76; with David Realty Corp., Littleton, Colo., 1976-83, v.p., 1979-83, gen. mgr., 1981-83, Longmont (Colo.), United Hosp., 1977—; pers. dir., 1977-87, dir. human resources, 1988-95, v.p. human resources, 1995—; cons. Front Range Community Coll. of Denver, 1983-85; prin. Harry R. Nevling-Broker, 1983-85, 95—; v.p. Realty Mart Internat., Inc., 1985-93, Dist. chmn. Am. Party, 1973-74, St. Vrain Valley Sch. Dist., Health Occupations Adv. Com. 1977—, chmn. 1979-85, Vocat. Edn. Adv. Coun. 1986-91, pres. 1986-91; with Citizen Amb. People to People Program, Hungary, Czech Republic, Germany, 1991; mem. exec. com. Nat. Health Care Skills Stds. Project, 1993-95; spkr., presenter in fiCo-author: Healthcare Reform: The Human Resources Cornerstone to Successful Reform, 1992. Served to capt. U.S. Army, 1965-72; Vietnam. Decorated D.F.C., Bronze Star with oakleaf cluster, Air medal (22, valor device); recipient Rescue citation for lifesaving Boeing Co., 1969, Helping Hand award United Way, 1974, Outstanding Service award, 1979, cert. of appreciation, 1982, Disting. Young Alumni award Winona State U., 1989. Mem. VFW (past post comdr.), Longmont Area Human Resources Assn., 1980-89, Boulder Area Human Resource Assn., 1978—, Mountain States VHA (pers. com. 1989—, chmn. 1989-93), Colo. Healthcare Assn. for Human Resource Mgmt. (sec. 1980, pres. elect 1981, pres. 1981-82, exec. com. 1986—), Am. Soc. for Healthcare Human Resources Adminstrn. (ann. meeting chmn. 1985-86, regional dir. 1986-90, legis. and labor liaison 1988-90, chpt. rels. com. 1990-91, pres. elect 1991-92, pres. 92-93, immediate past pres. 1993-95, exec. com. 1991-95, chmn. nominating com. 1994-95, chmn. conflict of interest com., 1994-95, orgnl. transition task force 1994-95, nat. nominating com. 1996, Bylaws com. 1992-93, 96-97, Disting. Svc. award 1996), Soc. Human Resource Mgmt., Human Resource Cert. Inst. (sr. profl. in human resources), Mt. State VHA (pers. com. 1989—, chmn. 1989-93), Vietnam Helicopter Pilots Assn.; bd. mem. Boulder Bus. Dependent Care Assn., 1995—, pres. 1996. Home: 2346 Eagleview Cir Longmont CO 80501-7797 Office: Longmont United Hosp 1950 Mountain View Ave Longmont CO 80501-3129

NEW, DEBRA MARIE, choreographer; b. Glendale, Calif., Nov. 10, 1951; d. C. Gordon and Mildred Marie (Cavin) Smith; m. Robert Larry New, Nov. 11, 1977. BA in Dance/Choreography, U. Calif., Irvine, 1973; pvt. studies, with Eugene Loring, Antony Tudor. Specialty dancer Folies Bergere, Las Vegas, 1975-78, 80; lead/Adagio Barry Ashton, St. Louis, 1979, Alan Lee, Valley Forge, Pa., 1982; dancer Playboy/Peter Jackson Prodn., Atlantic City, 1982; choreographer Tips Movie, L.A., 1984; co-creator New Sounds Prodn., Palm Springs, 1987; prodr. New Sounds Prodn., L.A., 1990; adj. prof., choreographer Coll. of the Desert, Palm Desert, 1992-98. Choreographer numerous shows for festivals, etc., also co-writer. Founder, dir. Palm Desert Dance Under the Stars Festival, 1998. Recipient Govs. scholar award State of Calif., 1969; named Artist of the Yr. Keyboard mag., 1987. Mem. Calif. Tchrs. Assn., Am. Fedn. Aerobics Assn. Home and Office: 71-586 Sahara Rd Rancho Mirage CA 92270

NEWACHECK, DAVID JOHN, lawyer; b. San Francisco, Dec. 8, 1953; s. John Elmer and Estere Ruth Sybil (Nelson) N.; m. Dorothea Quandt, June 2, 1990. AB in English, U. Calif., Berkeley, 1976; JD, Pepperdine U., 1979; MBA, Calif. State U., Hayward, 1982; LLM in Tax, Golden Gate U., 1987. Bar: Calif. 1979, D.C. 1985, N.Y. 1987, U.S. Dist. Ct. (no. dist.) Calif. 1979, U.S. Ct. Appeals (9th cir.) 1979, U.S. Supreme Ct. 1984. Tax cons. Pannell, Kerr and Forster, San Francisco, 1982-83; lawyer, writer, editor Matthew Bender and Co., San Francisco, 1983—; instr. taxation Oakland (Calif.) Coll. of Law, 1993—; lawyer, tax cons., fin. planner San Leandro, Calif., 1983—; bd. dirs. Aztec Custom Co., Orinda, Calif., 1983—; cons. software Collier Bankruptcy Filing Sys., 1984. Author/editor: (treatises) Ill. Tax Service, 1985, Ohio State Taxation, 1985, N.J. Tax Service, 1986, Pa. Tax Service, 1986, Calif. Closely Held Corps., 1987, Texas Tax Service, 1988; author: (software) Tax Source 1040 Tax Preparation, 1987, Texas Tax Service 1988, California Taxation, 1989, 2d edit., 1990, Bender's Federal Tax Service, 1989, Texas Litigation Guide, 1993, Family Law: Texas Practice & Procedure, 1993, Texas Transaction Guide, 1994, Ohio Corporation Law, 1994, Michigan Corporation Law, 1994, Massachusetts Corporation Law, 1994. Mem. youth com. Shepherd of the Valley Luth. Ch., Orinda, 1980-85, ch. coun., 1980-82; bd. dirs. Oakland Coll. Law, treas., CFO, 1997—. Mem. ABA, Internat. Platform Assn., State Bar Assn. Calif., Alameda County Bar Assn., U. Calif. Alumni Assn., U. Calif. Band Alumni Assn., Kiwanis Club San Leandro (bd. dirs. 1998—), Commonwealth Club (San Francisco chpt.), Mensa. Republican. Avocations: music, competitive running, sports. Home: 5141 Vannoy Ave Castro Valley CA 94546-2558 Office: 438 Estudillo Ave San Leandro CA 94577-4908

NEWBERG, DOROTHY BECK (MRS. WILLIAM C. NEWBERG), portrait artist; b. Detroit, May 30, 1919; d. Charles William and Mary (Labedz) Beck; student Detroit Conservatory Music, 1938; m. William C. Newberg, Nov. 3, 1939; children: Judith Bookwalter Bracken, Robert Charles, James William, William Charles. Trustee Detroit Adventure, 1967-71, originator A Drop in Bucket Program for artistically talented inner-city children. Cmty. outreach coord. Reno Police Dept.; bd. dirs. Bloomfield Art Assn., 1960-62, trustee 1965-67; bd. dirs. Your Heritage House, 1972-75, Franklin Wright Settlement, 1972-75, Meadowbrook Art Gallery, Oakland U., 1973-75, Sierra Nevada Mus. Art, 1978-80, NCCJ; mem. adv. bd. Gang Alternatives Partnership Adv. Bd. Recipient Heart of Gold award, 1969; Mich. vol. leadership award, 1969, Outstanding Vol. award City of Reno, 1989-90. Mem. Nevada Mus. Art, No. Nev. Black Cultural Awareness Soc. (bd. dirs.), Hispanic 500 C. of C. No. Nev. Roman Catholic. Home: 2000 Dant Blvd Reno NV 89509-5193

NEWBERG, WILLIAM CHARLES, stock broker, real estate broker, automotive engineer; b. Seattle, Dec. 17, 1910; s. Charles John and Anna Elizabeth (Anderson) N.; BSME, U. Wash., 1933; MME, Chrysler Inst. Engring., 1935; LLB (hon.), Parsons Coll., 1958; m. Dorothy Beck, Nov. 3, 1939; children: Judith N. Newberg Bookwalter, Robert Charles, James William, William Charles. Salesman, Am. Auto Co., Seattle, 1932-33; student

engr. Chrysler Corp., Detroit, 1933-35, exptl. engr., 1935-42, chief engr. Chgo. plant, 1942-45, mem. subs. ops. staff, Detroit, 1945-47, pres. airtemp divsn., Dayton, Ohio, 1947-50, v.p., dir. Dodge divsn., Detroit, 1950-51, pres. Dodge divsn., 1951-56, group v.p., Detroit, 1956-58, exec. v.p., 1958-60, pres., 1960; corp. dir. Detroit Bank & Trust, Detroit, 1955-60; corp. cons., Detroit, 1960-76; realtor Myers Realty, Inc., Reno, 1976-79; owner Bill Newberg Realty, 1979—; account exec. Allied Capital Corp., Reno, 1980—; chmn. Newberg Corp., 1982; treas. Perfect "10" Industries. Elder, St. John's Presbyn. Ch., Reno, 1976—; mem. exec. bd. Detroit Area coun. Boy Scouts Am., 1955-74, Nev. Area coun. Boy Scouts Am., 1976—; Mich. state chmn. March of Dimes, 1967-68. Mem. Soc. Automotive Engrs., Am. Def. Preparedness Assn. (life), Automotive Orgn. Team (life), U. Wash. Alumni Assn. (life), Newcomen Soc., Franklin Inst., Alpha Tau Omega. Clubs: Prospectors, Harley Owners Group. Home: 2000 Dant Blvd Reno NV 89509-5193

NEWBERRY, CONRAD FLOYDE, aerospace engineering educator; b. Neodesha, Kans., Nov. 10, 1931; s. Ragan McGregor and Audra Anitia (Newmaster) N.; m. Sarah Louise Thonn, Jan. 26, 1958; children: Conrad Floyde Jr., Thomas Edwin, Susan Louise. AA, Independence Jr. Coll., 1951; BEME in Aero. Sequence, U. So. Calif., 1957; MSME, Calif. State U., Los Angeles, 1971, MA in Edn., 1974; D.Environ. Sci. and Engring., UCLA, 1985. Registered profl. engr., Calif., Kans., N.C., Tex.; chartered engr., U.K. Mathematician L.A. divsn. N.Am. Aviation Inc., 1951-53, jr. engr., 1953-54, engr., 1954-57, sr. engr., 1957-64; asst. prof. aerospace engring. Calif. State Poly. U., Pomona, 1964-70, assoc. prof. aerospace engring., 1970-75, prof. aerospace engring., 1975-90, prof. emeritus, 1990—; staff engr. EPA, 1980-82; engring. specialist space transp. systems div. Rockwell Internat. Corp., 1984-90; prof. aeronautics and astronautics Naval Postgrad. Sch., Monterey, Calif., 1990—, acad. assoc. space systems engring., 1992-94. Recipient John Leland Atwood award as outstanding aerospace engring. educator AIAA/Am. Soc. Engring. Edn., 1986, Fred Merryfield Design award ASEE, 1997. Fellow AIAA (dep. dir. edn. region VI 1976-79, dep. dir. career enhancement 1982-91, chmn. L.A. sect. 1989-90, chmn. Point Lobos sect. 1990-91, chmn. acad. affairs com. 1990-93, dir. tech.-aircraft sys. 1990-93), Inst. Advancement Engring., Brit. Interplanetary Soc.; mem. IEEE, AAAS, ASME, NSPE, Royal Aero. Soc., Calif. Soc. Profl. Engrs., Am. Acad. Environ. Engrs. (cert. air pollution control engr.), Am. Soc. Engring. Edn. (chmn. aerospace divsn. 1979-80, divsn. exec. com. 1976-80, 89-94, exec. com. ocean and marine engring. divsn. 1982-85, 90-97, program chmn. 1991-93, chmn. 1993-95, chmn. and mem. bd. dirs. PIC II 1995-97), Am. Soc. Pub. Adminstrn., Am. Meteorol. Soc., U.S. Naval Inst., Am. Helicopter Soc., Soc. Naval Architects and Marine Engrs., Air and Waste Mgmt. Assn., Inst. Environ. Scis., Exptl. Aircraft Assn., Water Environ. Fedn., Soc. Automotive Engr., Soc. Allied Weight Engrs., Assn. Unmanned Vehicle Sys., Calif. Water Pollution Control Assn., Nat. Assn. Environ. Profls., Am. Soc. Naval Engrs., SAFE, SID, Planetary Soc., Tau Beta Pi, Sigma Gamma Tau, Kappa Delta Pi. Democrat. Mem. Christian Ch. (Disciples of Christ). Achievements include research on aircraft, space craft, missiles, and engine design, waveriders, aircrew centered system design and related impacts on exergy, quality, concurrent engineering, cost and environmental controls. Home: 9463 Willow Oak Rd Salinas CA 93907-1037 Office: Naval Postgrad Sch Dept Aeronautics and Astronautics AA/Ne 699 Dyer Rd Monterey CA 93943-5106

NEWCOMB, BRUCE, state legislator, farmer, rancher; b. Burley, Idaho, Mar. 2, 1940; m. Celia Gould; 5 children. Student, N.W. Christian Coll., Stanford; BS, U. Oreg. Mem. Idaho Ho. of Reps., Boise, 1987, past majority leader, caucus chmn., house spkr. Methodist. Avocations: fly fishing, hunting, family. Fax: 208-334-2491. E-mail: infocenter@lso.state.id.us. Office: State Capitol Boise ID 83720-0038

NEWCOMBE, ALAN GEORGE, plant pathologist; b. Toronto, Aug. 11, 1953; came to the U.S., 1991; s. Alan G. and Hanna (Hammerschlag) N.; m. Frances Schips, July 30, 1977; children: Felice G., Claire L. BS, McGill U., 1983; PhD, U. Guelph, 1988. Postdoctoral rsch. assoc. Agriculture Canada, Winnipeg, 1988-91; rsch. assoc. in plant pathology Washington State U., Puyallup, 1991—. Contbr. articles to profl. jours. Grantee USDA, 1992—, DOE, 1995—. Mem. Am. Phytopathological Soc. Achievements include research in hybrid poplar pathogens and the genetics of resistance to them. Office: Wash State U 7612 Pioneer Way E Puyallup WA 98371-4989

NEWE, RALPH AXEL, career officer, consultant; b. Aschaffenburg, Bavaria, Germany, Mar. 15, 1966; came to U.S., 1979; s. Bernd and Bernie N.; m. Alyson Claire Haeger, Nov. 29, 1995. BA in Polit. Sci. and German, U. N. Mex., 1991; postgrad. studies, Holy Names Coll., Oakland, Calif., 1998—. Sgt. US Army, 1985-88; 2d engr. USN, Norfolk, Va., 1992-94; navigator USN, San Diego, 1995-97; cons. Andersen Consulting, San Francisco, 1997—; climbing instr. D.O.D., Berchtesgarden, Germany, 1984; mem. Andersen Cons. Customer Relationship Mgmt. Practice. Lt. USN, 1991-97. Decorated Army Commendation medal with oak leaf cluster, Army Achievement medal, Navy Achievement medals. Mem. VFW, DAV, Project Mgmt. Inst. Democrat. Avocation: flying.

NEWELL, MICHAEL STEPHEN, finance company executive, international finance, protective services consultant; b. Denver, Dec. 22, 1949; s. Henry Michael and Marlene (McRae) N.; m. Linda Margaret Wolfe, Sept. 19, 1987; children: Katherine Margaret, Brittany Nicole; children from previous marriage: Troy, Angela, Michael, Jennifer. Grad., Denver Police Acad., 1972; CO Real Estate Lic., Real Estate Prep., 1977; HHD (hon.), Am. Acad. Inst. Pub. Theology, 1997. Cert. peace officer, Colo. Police officer Denver Police Dept., 1972-79; prin. Michael Newell & Assocs., Denver, 1979-82; sr. account exec. Am. Protection Industries, Los Angeles, 1982-84; chief exec. officer Newco Fin., Huntington Beach, Calif., 1984—; chmn. The Newco Internat. Group/Newco Fin., Huntington Beach; with VALUES Self Improvement Program, Fountain Valley; bd. dirs. Lifesong Self-Esteem workshops, Huntington Beach.; expert witness stalking crimes and preadtor control techniques; condr. seminars on stalker suppression, stalking survival, threat mgmt. in the workplace. Author: The Securtiy Manual, 1995, Stalker Suppression, 1996, Stalking Rescue, The Book of F.A.T.E. (From Abuse to Empowerment), (video prodns.) The Personal Protection Technique, 1995, Stalking Survival, 1995; author, facilitator: Your Paradigm Shift. Founder, bd. dirs. Law Enforcement Support Assn., Denver, 1981; bd. dirs. Crisis Action Network/Stalking Rescue. Served with U.S. Army, 1968-71, Viet Nam. Decorated Bronze Star, Viet Svc. medal with clusters; recipient Pres.'s Nat. Patriotism medal Am. Police Hall of Fame, Nat. Assn. Chiefs Police, 1996, Knight Chevalier The Venerable Order of Michael the Archangel, others; named "The Real Life Equalizer", CBS News/48 Hours. Republican. Mem. Religious Sci. Ch. Avocations: music, photography, travel. Office: Internat Risk Cons PO Box 558 Littleton CO 80160-0558

NEWHALL, BARBARA FALCONER, writer, journalist; d. David Bishop and Catherine Ann Falconer; m. Jonathan Newhall, Mar. 5, 1977; children: Peter Falconer, Christina Falconer. BA, U. Mich.; Cert. in German Lang. and Culture, U. Heidelberg, Germany. Copy editor, reporter San Francisco Chronicle, 1972-80; feature writer, columnist Oakland (Calif.) Tribune, 1980-92; religion reporter Contra Costa Times, Walnut Creek, Calif., 1992-96; writer, journalist freelance, Oakland, 1997—. Recipient 1st Place award for humor San Francisco Press Club, 1990. Mem. Religion Newswriters Assn., East Bay Press Club, Delta Delta Delta. Episcopalian. Avocations: photography, travel, swimming, hiking.

NEWHOUSE, THEODORE, newspaper executive. V.p. The Oregonian, Portland. Office: The Oregonian 1320 SW Broadway Portland OR 97201*

NEWKIRK, RAYMOND LESLIE, management consultant; b. Shreveport, La., July 13, 1944; s. Raymond Clay and Dorothy Emily (Parker) N.; m. Pellcisima Guese Calma, Jan. 19, 1985. AA, Dayton Community Coll., 1973; BS in Behavioral Sci., N.Y. Inst. Tech., 1976; MS in Philosophy, Columbia Pacific U., 1980, PhD in Behavioral Sci., 1982; PhD in Human [illegible] MA in Clin. Psychology, Calif. Coast U., 1997. Clin. intern Fielding Inst., 1995; chief exec. officer, cons. Newkirk & Assocs., Ft. Lauderdale, Fla., 1980-84; head dept. ADP Royal Saudi Naval Forces, Jeddah, 1984-86; pres., cons. Internat. Assn. Info. Mgmt., Santa Clara, [illegible] quality analyst Quality Assurance Inst., Orlando, Fla.,

1986—; prin. cons. Info. Impact Internat., Nashville, 1988—; pres., CEO Sys. Mgmt. Inst., Pleasant Hill, Calif., 1987; pres., COO P.Q. Info. Group, Egmont ann Hoeff, The Netherlands, 1992-94; pres., CEO Systems Mgmt. Inst., 1994—; prin. Forum 2000, 1996—; dep. gov. Am. Biog. Inst., 1995. Author: Chronicles of the Making of A Philosopher, 1983; contbr. articles to profl. jours. Speaker, mem. Union for Concerned Scientists, San Francisco, 1988. Fellow Brit. Inst. Mgmt., Internat. Biog. Assn.; mem. Assn. Systems Mgmt., Assn. Profl. Cons., Planetary Soc., Columbia Pacific Alumni Assn. (pres. Mid-east chpt. 1985), Assn. Computing Machinery, IEEE Computer Soc., Am. Biograph. Inst. (dep. gov. 1995), Phi Theta Kappa (outstanding scholar award 1973), Confedn. of Chivalry (knight). Roman Catholic. Avocations: writing, classical guitar, tennis, weight lifting. Home: 95 Greenock Ln Pleasant Hill CA 94523-2083

NEWLAND, RUTH LAURA, small business owner; b. Ellensburg, Wash., June 4, 1949; d. George J. and Ruth Marjorie (Porter) N. BA, Cen. Wash. State Coll., 1970, MEd, 1972; EdS, Vanderbilt U., 1973; PhD, Columbia Pacific U., 1981. Tchr. Union Gap (Wash.) Sch., 1970-71; owner Newland Ranch Gravel Co., Yakima, Wash., 1998; ptnr. Arnold Artificial Limb, Yakima, 1981-86; owner, pres. Arnold Artificial Limb, Yakima and Richland, Wash., 1986—; owner Newland Ranch, Yakima, 1969—. Contbg. mem. Nat. Dem. Com., Irish Nat. Caucus Found.; mem. Pub. Citizen, We The People, Nat. Humane Edn. Soc.; charter mem. Nat. Mus. Am. Indian. George Washington scholar Masons, Yakima, 1967. Mem. NAFE, NOW, Am. Orthotic and Prosthetic Assn., Internat. Platform Assn., Nat. Antivisection Soc. (life), Vanderbilt U. Alumni Assn., Peabody Coll. Alumni Assn., Columbia Pacific U. Alumni Assn., World Wildlife Fund, Nat. Audubon Soc., Greenpeace, Mus. Fine Arts, Humane Soc. U.S., Wilderness Soc., Nature Conservancy, People for Ethical Treatment of Animals, Amnesty Internat., The Windstar Found., Rodale Inst., Sierra Club (life), Emily's List. Democrat. Avocations: reading, gardening, sewing, handcrafts, people. Home: 2004 Riverside Rd Yakima WA 98901-9526 Office: Arnold Artificial Limb 9 S 12th Ave Yakima WA 98902-3106

NEWLIN, DOUGLAS RANDAL, learning products engineer; b. Denver, Mar. 26, 1940; s. Loren Randall and Nola Berniece (Paris) N.; m. Sandra Temple, June 22, 1968; children: Jason Britt, Jeremy Owen. BS in Journalism, U. Colo., 1968. Advt. prodn. mgr. Am. Sheep Producers Council, Denver, 1968-70; promotion dir. Sta. KLZ-AM-FM, Denver, 1970-71; account mgr. Curran-Morton Advt., Denver, 1971-72; advt. and sales promotion specialist Gates Rubber Co., Denver, 1972-78; mktg. communications mgr. Hewlett Packard Co., Ft. Collins, Colo., 1978-90; learning products engr., 1990—; vis. lectr. U. Colo., Boulder, 1972-73, statis. quality control course George Washington U., Washington, 1984; web page designer. Author hardware and software catalogs, 1984-90, UNIX Tech. Documentation, 1990—; U.S. newsletter editor Ted Heath Music Appreciation Soc. of U.K. (Eng.); contbr. articles to profl. jours. Pres. Lake Sherwood Homeowners Assn., Ft. Collins, 1982; treas. Lake Sherwood Lake Com., Ft. Collins, 1983-85. Served with U.S. Army, 1959-61. Recipient Gold Key award Bus. and Profl. Advt. Assn., 1976. Mem. Big Bands Internat. Republican. Avocation: bicycling. Home: 4112 Mt Vernon Ct Fort Collins CO 80525-3335 Office: Hewlett Packard Co 3404 E Harmony Rd Fort Collins CO 80528-9599

NEWLIN, L. MAX, parks and recreation director; b. June 4, 1942. BS, Wilmington Coll., 1968. Mgr. Massacre Rocks State Pk., American Falls, Idaho, 1996—. Exec. dir. Friends Massacre Rocks Inc.; v.p. S.E. Idaho Travel Coun. Idaho Parks and Recreation Assn. fellow, 1990. Mem. Power County/Am. Falls Hist. Soc. (chmn.). Office: Massacre Rocks State Pk 3592 North Park Ln American Falls ID 83211-5556*

NEWMAN, ANITA NADINE, surgeon; b. Honolulu, June 13, 1949; d. William Reece Elton and Margie Ruth (Pollard) Newman; m. Frank E.X. Ward, Sept. 9, 1995; children: Justin Ellis, Chelsea Newman, Andrew Frank, Tyler William. AB, Stanford U., 1971; MD, Dartmouth Coll., 1975. Diplomate Am. Bd. Otolaryngology. Intern, then resident in gen. surgery Northwestern Meml. Hosp., Chgo., 1975-77, resident in otolaryngology, 1977-78; resident UCLA Hosp. and Clinics, 1979-82, assoc. prof., 1982-96; surgeon USC Head and Neck Group, 1997—, staff surgeon Wadsworth VA Hosp., L.A., 1982-84; rsch. fellow in neurotology UCLA, 1984-88. Contbr. articles to profl. jours. Mem. alumni admissions support com. Darmouth Med. Sch. Alumni Coun., 1983-87. Fellow ACS; mem. Am. Acad. Otolaryngology, Am. Med. Women's Assn., Los Angeles County Med. Women's Assn., Assn. Rsch. in Otolaryngology, Stanford Women's Honor Soc. Democrat. Office: U So Calif Healthcare Consultation 1510 San Pablo St Ste 201 Los Angeles CA 90033

NEWMAN, CRAIG ALAN, media executive, lawyer; b. Detroit, June 29, 1957; s. Norman and Ruth (Chodoroff) N.; m. Susan Marcie Lipton, Mar. 22, 1987; children: Rachel Ariel, Jonathan Ross. BS, Ariz. State U., 1979; MA, U. Mo., 1981; JD, U. Detroit, 1984. Law clk. to Chief U.S. Dist. Judge Philip Pratt U.S. Dist. Ct. (ea. dist.) Mich., 1984-86; assoc. Cahill Gordon & Reindel, N.Y.C., 1986-89; ptnr. Arnold & Porter, N.Y.C., 1989-95; sr. v.p., gen. counsel Americast, L.A. and N.Y.C., 1996—. Editor-in-chief U. Detroit Law Rev., 1983-84; contbr. articles to profl. publs. Recipient Nathan Burkam award ASCAP, 1984, Clarence Burton scholarship U. Detroit, 1983-84, Outstanding Grad. in Journalism Soc. Profl. Journalists, 1979. Mem. N.Y. State Bar Assn., D.C. Bar Assn., Mich. Bar Assn. Office: Americast 10880 Wilshire Blvd Ste 1750 Los Angeles CA 90024-4118

NEWMAN, DEAN GORDON, business consultant; b. North Branch, Iowa, Mar. 17, 1929; s. Floyd William and Hazel Jane (Covault) N.; m. Maggie; B.A., Simpson Coll., 1950; M.B.A. (Hicks fellow), Stanford U., 1952; children—Gary Dean, Craig William. Trainee, Gen. Electric, Schenectady, 1952, Syracuse, N.Y., 1955-56, Chgo., 1956-58; mem. employee and community relations staff, Chgo., 1958-62, mgr. employee and community relations, Milw., 1962-67, DeKalb, Ill., 1967-69; v.p. employee and pub. relations United Nuclear Corp., Elmsford, N.Y., 1969-71; v.p. employee and indsl. relations Apache Corp., Mpls., 1971-83, v.p. human resources and communications, 1983-87 ; v.p. mktg. Nelson Cons. Group, Mpls., 1989-92; chmn. Linear Fitness Systems, Inc., Allenspark, Colo., 1998—. Pres. Apache Found., 1973-87 ; v.p., bd. dirs. Boys Clubs of Mpls., 1978-85; chmn. Boys and Girls Club of Mpls., 1985-88, exec. com., 1988-89; v.p. fin., bd. dirs. Boys and Girls Club Larimer County, 1993-96; vice chmn. Bus. Econs. Edn. Found., 1986-88, chmn. fin. com., 1988-89; Served with USNR, 1952-55; Korea. Mem. Nat. Assn. Mfrs. (dir. 1981-87), Alpha Tau Omega, Epsilon Sigma, Sigma Tau Delta, Pi Gamma Mu. Republican. Methodist. Home and Office: 125 County Road 84 W Allenspark CO 80510-9713

NEWMAN, EDGAR LEON, historian, educator; b. New Orleans, Jan. 21, 1939; s. Isidore and Anna N. children: Jonathan, Suzanne; m. Linda Loeb Clark, Apr. 21, 1989. BA, Yale U., 1962; PhD, U. Chgo., 1969. Asst. prof. N.Mex. State U., Las Cruces, 1969-75, assoc. prof. history, 1975—; lectr. U. Peking, 1985. Editor H-France. Fulbright fellow, 1965-66; Am. Philos. Soc. fellow, 1971; Nat. Endowment for Humanities fellow, 1975-76. Mem. Western Soc. for French History (pres. 1977-78, governing coun. 1990-92, 96—, gov. chair 1996-98), Societe d'histoire de la Revolution de 1848 (comite directeur), Soc. Scis. History Assn., French Hist. Studies Assn., Am. Hist. Assn. (annotator for France bibliographical survey 1815-52). Editor: Historical Dictionary of France from the 1815 Restoration to the Second Empire; contbr. Dictionnaire de Biographie Française, Dictionnaire du Movement Ouvrier Français, Jour. of History of Ideas, Jour. Modern History, Dictionary of Am. Biography, others. E-mail: enewman@nmsu.edu Office: NMex State U PO Box 3H Las Cruces NM 88004-0003

NEWMAN, HARRY CHARLES, family practice physician; b. Portland, Oreg., June 26, 1944; s. Leonard Anton and Opal (Massey) N. Student, Whitworth Coll., 1962-64; BA, U. Oreg., 1967, MD, 1972; postgrad., Uppsala (Sweden), 1978-79. Diplomate Nat. Bd. Med. Examiners, Am. Bd. Family Practice, Am. Bd. Internal Medicine, Am. Bd. Pathology; cert. ACLS, ATLS, NALS, PALS, BALS. [illegible] pathology U. Calif. San Francisco Med. Ctr., San Francisco, 1972-76; chief resident in pathology Beth Israel Med. Ctr., N.Y.C., 1979-80; fellow in pathology Meml. Sloan-Kettering Cancer Ctr., N.Y.C., 1980-82; fellow in immunohematology U. Medicine and Dentistry, Newark, 1982-83; attending pathologist White Plains (N.Y.) Hosp., 1983-86; resident in family practice

Niagara Falls (N.Y.) Hosp., 1986-89; family practice physician Indian Health Svc., Pine Ridge, S.D., 1989-92, Redwood Family Practice, Eureka, Calif., 1994—; geriatric fellow La Grange (Ill.) Hosp., 1992-94; observing pathologist Södersjukhuset, Stockholm, 1979. Contbr. articles t med. publs. Fellow Am. Acad. Family Practice, Calif. Med. Assn.; mem. Phi Beta Kappa. Avocation: poetry readings. Home: 4515 Valley West Blvd Apt H Arcata CA 95521-7424 Office: Redwood Family Practice 2350 Buhne St Eureka CA 95501-3205

NEWMAN, JULLIANA, marketing executive; b. Huntington, N.Y., June 5, 1957; d. Coleman and Lillian (Saboe) Newell; m. John Sherfy Newman, Nov. 7, 1988; children: Ana, Anders, Hayley. AA, Suffolk County Community, Selden, N.Y., 1978; BA, Queens (N.Y.) Coll., 1980; postgrad., CUNY, 1980-82. Prodn. editor Plenum Press, N.Y.C., 1982-83; mng. editor LeJacq Pub., N.Y.C., 1984-86; mng. editor/project dir. Audio Visual Med. Mktg., N.Y.C., 1986-88; editorial dir. Haymarket Doyma, N.Y.C., 1988-90; dir. healthcare communication Macmillan Healthcare Info., Florham Park, N.J., 1990-91; communications specialist PCS, Inc., Scottsdale, Ariz., 1991-93; v.p. mktg. ValueRx, Albuquerque, 1993—; founder Jour. of Outcomes Mgmt., 1994; developer software Pro Tracker; editorial dir. Diagnostek Report, 1993—, PRN: Information As Needed, 1993—; cons. Nat. Asthma Edn. Program, Bethesda, Med., 1991, Asthma and Allergy Found., Washignton, 1991, Pres.'s Coun. on Phys. Fitness and Sports, Washington, 1991. Cert. editor of Life Scis. Vol. Pres.'s Coun. on Phys. Fitness and Sports, Washington, 1991—. Ednl. grantee Connaught Labs., 1991, Allen & Hanburys, Research Triangle Park, N.C., 1991, 92. Mem. Coun. of Biology Editors, Am. Med. Writers Assn., NAFE, Am. Heart Assn., Arthritis Found., Nat. Council on Prescription Drug Programs. Democrat. Lutheran. Avocations: traveling, creative writing, gourmet cooking. Office: Diagnostek Inc 4500 Alexander Blvd NE Albuquerque NM 87107-6805

NEWMAN, KATHARINE DEALY, author, consultant; b. Phila., Aug. 17, 1911; d. Creswell Victor and Harriet Elizabeth (Hetherington) Dealy; m. Morton Newman, May 11, 1946 (div. 1968); children: Deborah Silverstein, Blaze. BS in Edn. summa cum laude, Temple U., 1933; MA in English, U. Pa., 1937, PhD in English, 1961. Cert. secondary and coll. English educator, Commonwealth of Pa. Tchr. Phila. High Schs., 1933-46, 49-50; asst. prof. U. Minn., Mpls., 1946-47, Temple U. C.C., Phila., 1959; assoc. prof. Moore Coll. Art, Phila., 1961-63; tchr. Abington (Pa.) High Sch., 1963-67; prof. West Chester (Pa.) State U., 1967-77; cons. Inst. for Ethnic Studies, West Chester U., 1975-77; exch. prof. Cheyney State (Pa.) U., 1971, San Dieguito Adult Sch., 1993-94; cons. in field. Author: The Gentleman's Novelist: Robert Plumer Ward, 1765-1846, 1961, The American Equation: Literature in a Multi-Ethnic Culture, 1971, Ethnic American Short Stories, 1975, The Girl of the Golden West, 1978, Never Without a Song, 1995; contbr. articles to profl. jours. Named Outstanding Bd. Mem. Jr. League, 1987; Coordinating Coun. Literary Mags. Editor fellow, 1980. Mem. MLA (emeritus), Soc. for Study of Multi-Ethnic Lit. of U.S. (founder, officer 1973, editor newsletter 1973-77, editor MELUS jour. 1977-81, editor emeritus 1983—, Contbn. award 1982), Inst. for Ethnic Studies (founder, chmn. 1975-77), Episc. Svc. Alliance (co-founder 1978, bd. dirs. 1978-87, v.p. 1982, 86, pres. 1983-84, cert. appreciation 1987). Democrat. Episcopalian. Home: 910 Bonita Dr Encinitas CA 92024-3805

NEWMAN, MARC ALAN, electrical engineer; b. Jasper, Ind., Nov. 21, 1955; s. Leonard Jay and P. Louise (Shainberg) N.; m. Shelley Jane Martin, Aug. 13, 1977; 1 child, Kelsey Renée. BSEE, Purdue U., 1977, MSEE, 1979. Sr. elec. engr. Sperry Corp. Flight Systems, Phoenix, 1979-85; staff engr. Motorola Inc., Tempe, Ariz., 1985-88, Quincy St. Corp., Phoenix, 1988-89; prin. staff scientist Motorola Inc., Chandler, Ariz., 1989-91, Scottsdale, Ariz., 1991—; Prolog and artificial intelligence expert Motorola Inc., Tempe, Chandler and Scottsdale, 1985—. Patentee in field. Mem. IEEE, The Assn. for Logic Programming (London), Am. Assn. Artificial Intelligence, Ariz. Artificial Intelligence Assn. (founder), Internat. Platform Assn., Phi Sigma Kappa, Eta Kappa Nu. Achievements include patent combining expert system with artificial neural network, a patent for cell phone security device, a patent for evaluating patents for legal errors; patent for interfacing cellular telephones to personal computers. Avocations: fine music, photography, astronomy, mountain bicycling, travel. Home: 7411 S Rita Ln Estate 110 Tempe AZ 85283-4790 Office: Motorola Inc 8201 E Mcdowell Rd Scottsdale AZ 85257-3893

NEWMAN, MICHAEL RODNEY, lawyer; b. N.Y.C., Oct. 2, 1945; s. Morris and Helen Gloria (Hendler) N.; m. Cheryl Jeanne Anker, June 11, 1967; children: Hillary Abra, Nicole Brooke. Student NASA Inst. Space Physics, Columbia U., 1964; BA, U. Denver, 1967; JD, U. Chgo., 1970. Bar: Calif. 1971, U.S. Dist. Ct. (cen. dist.) Calif. 1972, U.S. Ct. Appeals (9th cir.) 1974, U.S. Dist. Ct. (no. dist.) Calif. 1975, U.S. Supreme Ct. 1978, U.S. Dist. Ct. (so. dist.) Calif. 1979, U.S. Tax Ct. 1979, U.S. Dist. Ct. (ea. dist.) Calif. 1983. Assoc. David Daar, 1971-76; ptnr. Daar & Newman, 1976-78, Miller & Daar, 1978-88, Miller, Daar & Newman, 1988-89, Daar & Newman, 1989—; judge pro tem L.A. Mcpl. Ct., 1982—, L.A. Superior Ct., 1988—; mem. Consulegis, EEIG. Facilitator First and Second Ann. German-Am. Strategic Partnership Conf.; mem. Internat. Commerce Com. L.A. Area C. of C.; lectr. Ea. Claims Conf., Ea. Life Claims Conf., Nat. Health Care Anti-Fraud Assn., AIA Conf. on Ins. Fraud, Consulegis A.G.M.'s Paris, 1997, Madrid, 1998; mem. L.A. Citizens Organizing Com. for Olympic Summer Games, 1984, mem. govtl. liaison adv. commn. 1984; mem. So. Calif. Com. for Olympic Summer Games, 1984; cert. ofcl. Athletics Congress of U.S., co-chmn. legal com. S.P.A-T.A.C, chief finish judge; trustee Massada lodge B'nai Brith. Recipient NYU Bronze medal in Physics, 1962, Maths. award USN Sci., 1963. Mem. ABA (multi-dist. litigation subcom., com. on class actions), Los Angeles County Bar Assn. (chmn. attys. errors and omissions prevention com., mem. cts. com. litigation sect.), Conf. Ins. Counsel, So. Pacific Assn., TAC (bd. dirs., Disting. Svc. award 1988), Porter Valley Country Club. Office: 865 S Figueroa St Ste 2500 Los Angeles CA 90017-2567

NEWMAN, MURRAY ARTHUR, aquarium administrator; b. Chgo., Mar. 6, 1924; emigrated to Can., 1953, naturalized, 1970; s. Paul Jones and Virginia (Murray) N.; m. Katherine Greene Rose, Aug. 8, 1952; 1 child, Susan. B.Sc., U. Chgo., 1949; postgrad., U. Hawaii, 1950; M.A., U. Calif., Berkeley, 1951; Ph.D., U. B.C. (Can.), Vancouver, 1960. Curator fisheries UCLA, 1951-53, Ichthyology Museum, U. B.C., 1953-56; curator Vancouver Public Aquarium, 1956-66, dir., 1966-93; pres. Mana Aquarium Cons.; fgn. adv. Nat. Mus./Aquarium Project, Taiwan; past chmn. adv. com. Western Can. Univs. Marine Biol. Soc.; co-chmn. Enoshima (Japan) Internat. Aquarium Symposium, 1997; spl. advisor Enoshima Aquariaum, 1998. Author: Life in a Fishbowl: Confessions of an Aquarium Director, 1994. Served with USN, 1943-46. Decorated Order of Can.; recipient Man of Yr. award City of Vancouver, 1964; Centennial award Govt. Can., 1967, cert. of merit, 1988; Harold J. Merilees award Vancouver Visitors Bur., 1976, 75 Achievers award, 1987, Silver Bravery medal Royal Soc. Canada, 1992, Canada 125 medal, 1992. Mem. Am. Assn. Zool. Parks and Aquariums, Internat. Union Dirs. Zool. Gardens, Can. Assn. Zool. Parks and Aquariums (pres. 1978-79), Vancouver Club, Round Table Club. Office: Vancouver Pub Aquarium, PO Box 3232, Vancouver, BC Canada V6B 3X8

NEWMAN, RICHARD, engineering executive. With Cahn Gengr Inc., L.A., 1960-77; pres. of subsidiary Daniel Mann Johnnson & Mendenhall, L.A., 1977-88; pres. Aecom Tech Corp., L.A., 1989—, now chmn. bd. dirs., pres., CEO. Office: Aecom Tech Corp 3250 Wilshire Blvd # 5 Los Angeles CA 90010-1577*

NEWMAN, RUTH TANTLINGER, artist; b. Hooker, Okla., May 28, 1910; d. Walter Warren and Jean Louise (Hayward) Tantlinger; m. John Vincent Newman; children: Peter Vincent, Michael John. Student, Pomona Coll; BFA, UCLA, 1932; postgrad., Instituto Allende, U. Guanajuato, Mex. Art tchr. Santa Ana (Calif.) Schs., 1933-34, Santa Ana Adult Edn., 1934-40; watercolor tchr. Ventura (Calif.) Recreation Ctr., 1941-50; pvt. tchr. [illegible] History and Art, 1993, Santa Barbara Art Assn., Ojai Art Ctr., Ventura Art Club, Oxnard (Calif.) Art Club, Art Club of Westlake Village, Thousand Oaks (Calif.) Art Club, others; commd. to paint 12 Calif. Missions, 1958, watercolors at San Juan Bautista Retreat House, Calif., [illegible] Bernardino, Mallorca, Spain; book featuring reproductions of selected works,

Ruth Newman: A Lifetime of Art, introduced at her solo show in Ventura Mus., 1993. Mem. Westlake Village Art Guild, Thousand Oaks Art Club, Buena Ventura Art Club (charter). Home: 32120 Oakshore Dr Westlake Village CA 91361-3808

NEWMAN, STANLEY RAY, oil refining company executive; b. Milo, Idaho, Mar. 5, 1923; s. Franklin Hughes and Ethel Amelda (Crowley) N.; student Tex. A&M U, 1944-45; B.S., U. Utah, 1947, Ph.D., 1952. m. Rosa Klein, May 27, 1961 (div. Mar. 1980); children: Trudy Lynn, Susan Louise, Karen Elizabeth, Paul Daniel, Phillip John; m. Madelyn Wycherly, Jan. 10, 1991; children: Heidi, Heather, Amy. With Texaco Res. Ctr., Beacon, N.Y., 1951-82, technologist, 1973-77, sr. technologist research mfg.-fuels, 1977-82, profl. cons. on fuels and chems., 1983-91. Chmn., Planning Bd., Village of Fishkill, N.Y., 1973- 77; village trustee, 1990-92; mem. Dutchess County Solid Waste Mgmt. Bd., 1974-76. With inf. Signal Corps U.S. Army, 1944-46. Mem. AAAS, N.Y. Acad. Sci., Dutchess County Geneal. Soc. (pres. 1981-87, exec. v.p. 1987-88), N.Y. Fruit Testing Assn., Sigma Xi (pres. Texaco Res. Ctr. br. 1980-81). Republican. Mormon. Patentee in field. Home: 285 Plantation Cir Idaho Falls ID 83404-7990

NEWQUIST, DONALD STEWART, designer, technical director, consultant; b. Frankfort, Ky., May 25, 1953; s. Edward Wallace N. and Jeanne Gayle (Utterback) Caddy; m. Linda Susan Carter, Oct. 10, 1987. BA, Centre Coll. of Ky., Danville, 1975; MA, U. Nev., Las Vegas, 1979; postgrad., U. Nev. Cert. Nat. Coun. Qualifications for Lighting Professions. Grad. fellow Ctr. Coll. of Ky., 1975-76; grad. teaching asst. U. Nev., Las Vegas, 1976-78; instr. tech. theater Clark County Community Coll., N. Las Vegas, Nev., 1978-80; tech. supr. City of Las Vegas, 1979-91; adminstr. Las Vegas Civic Ballet, 1988-90; engring. analyst City of Las Vegas Project Unit, 1991; lighting designer T.J. Krob Cons. Engrs., Las Vegas, 1991—; tech. dir. USAF Base Talent Show, Davis-Monthan AFB, Ariz., 1986, 87; tech. cons. USAF Recreation Ctr., Nellis AFB, Nev., 1982-85; resident designer Ecdysis Dance Theater, Las Vegas, 1980-84; mem. Lorenzi Park Amphitheater Task Force, Las Vegas, 1988. Designer: stage renovation, Reed Whipple Cultural Ctr., 1981; stage addition, Charleston Heights Arts Ctr., 1980. Lic. lay reader, Christ Episcopal Ch., Las Vegas, 1981—. Mem. Illuminating Engring. Soc. N.Am. (sect. treas. 1989-90, sect. pres. 1990-92, bi-regional conf. chmn., regional v.p. 1994-96, dir. 1995-96). Republican. Avocation: travel. Office: TJ Krob Cons Engrs 1919 S Jones Blvd Ste B Las Vegas NV 89146-1299

NEWSHAM, DAVID P., protective services official; b. Long Beach, Calif., Oct. 11, 1942. BA in Mgmt., U. Redlands. From police res. officer to capt. Burbank (Calif.) Police Dept., 1970-90, chief of police, 1990—; chmn. dept. master plan task force Burbank Police Dept., 1990-95. Bd. dirs. YMCA, Burbank, ARC, Boy Scouts Am., Am. Heart Assn. With USAF, 1960-64. Mem. Internat. Assn. Chiefs Police, Calif. Peace Officers Assn., L.A. County Police Chiefs Assn., San Gabriel Valley Police Chiefs Assn., Burbank Police Officers Assn., Profl. Helicopter Pilots Assn. Avocations: boating, skiing, automobile restoration, piloting. Office: Office Chief of Police 272 E Olive Ave Burbank CA 91502-1231 also: PO Box 6459 Burbank CA 91510*

NEWSTEAD, ROBERT RICHARD, urologist; b. Detroit, Sept. 16, 1935; s. Oran Henry and Agnes Audery (Lewandowski) N.; m. Marie Carmela LiPuma, Aug. 5, 1961; children: Elizabeth Marie, Peter Joseph, Angela Agnes, Paul Michael. Student, Coll. Idaho, 1955-57, Quincy Coll., 1957-58; MD, Loyola U., Chgo., 1963. Intern Walter Reed Gen. Hosp., Washington, 1963-64; resident U. Iowa, Iowa City, 1967-71; urologist Urology Clinic Yakima, Wash., 1971-84, pres., 1984—; chief of staff Yakima Valley Meml. Hosp., 1995—; chief of surgery St. Elizabeth Med. Ctr., Yakima, 1980-81, Yakima Valley Hosp., 1978-79. Bd. dirs. St. Elizabeth Found., Yakima, 1983-93, The Capital Theater, 1987-93, Boy Scouts Am., Yakima, 1982-86. Capt. U.S. Army, 1962-67. Fellow Am. Cancer Soc., Iowa City, 1969-70, Am. Cancer Soc., 1961; named one of Outstanding Young Men Am., 1968. Fellow Am. Bd. Urology, ACS, Am. Urol. Assn., Wash. State Urol. Bd. (mem. at large exec. com.); mem. AMA, Rubin Flocks Soc. (pres. 1985-86), Yakima Surgical Soc. (pres. 1982-83), Yakima County Med. Soc. (pres. 1989-90), Rotary. Roman Catholic. Avocations: art, skiing, golf. Home: 814 Conestoga Blvd Yakima WA 98908-2419 Office: Urology Clinic Yakima 111 S 11th Ave Yakima WA 98902-3203

NEWTON, ERIC C., dance educator; b. Washington, Aug. 14, 1948; s. Carl Richardson and Edna patricia (Pettis) N. MA, U. Leiden, The Netherlands, 1987. Dancer Repertory Dance Theater, Salt Lake City, 1968-72; prin. dancer Martha Graham Dance Co., N.Y.C., 1973-77; dancer Netherlands Dance Theater, The Hague, 1977-82; instr. Rotterdam (The Netherlands) Dance Acad., 1982-86, 89-95, U. N.Mex., Albuquerque, 1996—; freelance translator, The Netherlands, 1988-94. Bd. dirs. Albuquerque Arts Alliance, 1996—.

NEWTON, PAUL E., electrical company executive. Pres., CEO Boole & Babbage, San Jose, Calif. Office: Boole & Babbage 3131 Zanker Rd San Jose CA 95134-1933*

NEY, CHARLES STEPHEN, theatre educator; b. Indpls., July 27, 1951; s. Linus Harold and Ruth (Capps) N.; m. Michelle Stakelum, Feb. 2, 1978; children: Rachel, Cameron. BFA, Ill. Wesleyan U., 1973; MFA, So. Metholdist U., Dallas, 1976; PhD, U. Ill., 1989. Artistic dir. Manhattan Clearinghouse, Dallas, 1976-79; adminstrv. asst. to theatre head U. Ill., Champaign-Urbana, 1980-82; owner Wordmaster, Austin, Tex., 1982-85; asst. prof. St. Edward's U., Austin, Tex., 1985-90, assoc. prof., 1990-93; assoc. prof. U. Idaho, Moscow, 1993-95, chair theatre, 1995—; producing artistic dir. Idaho Repertory Theatre, Moscow, 1995—; Invitation to perform at Kennedy Ctr., 1996. Dir.: (plays) Chicago, 1990 (Austin Cir. of Theatres Best Musical 1990), Fences, 1991 (Best Drama Austin Cir. of Theatres 1991), Top Girls, 1995 (artistic achievement KC/ACTF 1996), Females Seeking..., 1997 (artistic achievement KC/ACTF 1998). Recipient Bravo award Austin C. of C., 1991, Best Prodn. award Austin Cir. of Theatres, 1987. Mem. Assn. Theatre in Higher Edn., Northwest Drama Conf. Avocation: gardening. Office: U Idaho Dept Theatre Arts Moscow ID 83844-3074

NEY, MICHAEL JAMES, lawyer; b. Oakland, Calif., Nov. 20, 1943; s. George William and Monica Patricia (Ford) N.; m. Jamie Sue Deren, July 13, 1968; children: Molly, Deren. B of Sci. and Commerce, Santa Clara U., 1965; JD, John F. Kennedy U., 1971. Bar: Calif. 1972, U.S. Dist. Ct. (no. dist.) Calif. 1972. Dep. dist. atty. County of Alameda, Oakland, 1972-73; assoc. Helzel, Leighton, Brunn & Deal, Oakland, 1973-75; ptnr. McNamara, Houston, Dodge, McClure & Ney, Walnut Creek, Calif., 1975—; judge pro tem Contra Costa County Superior Ct. Mem. ABA, Am. Arbitration Assn. (panel mem.), Am. Bd. Trial Advs., Calif. Bar Assn., No. Calif. Assn. Def. Counsel (bd. dirs.), Contra Costa Bar Assn. Roman Catholic. Home: 1031 Via Nueva Lafayette CA 94549-2726 Office: McNamara Houston Dodge McClure & Ney 1211 Newell Ave Walnut Creek CA 94596-5331

NG, LAWRENCE MING-LOY, pediatrician; b. Hong Kong, Mar. 21, 1940; came to U.S., 1967, naturalized, 1977; s. John Iu-cheung and Mary Wing (Wong) N.; m. Bella May Ha Kan, June 25, 1971; children: Jennifer Wing-mui, Jessica Wing-yee. B in Medicine, U. Hong Kong, 1965, B in Surgery, 1965. House physician Queen Elizabeth Hosp., Hong Kong, 1965-66, med. officer, 1966-67; resident physician Children's Hosp. of Los Angeles, 1967-68; resident physician Children's Hosp. Med. Center, Oakland, Calif., 1968-70, fellow in pediatric cardiology, 1970-72, now mem. teaching staff; practice medicine, specializing in pediatrics and pediatric cardiology, San Leandro, Calif., 1972—, Oakland, Calif., 1982—; mng. ptnr. Pediatric Med. Assocs. of East Bay, 1990—; chief of pediatrics Oakland Hosp., 1974-77; chief of pediatrics Vesper Meml. Hosp., 1977-79, sec. staff, 1984, v.p. staff, 1985; chief pediatrics Meml. Hosp., San Leandro, 1986-88; founder Pediatric Assocs. of East Bay, 1990; bd. dirs. Children's First Healthcar Network, 1997—. Active Republican Party. Diplomate Am. Bd. Pediatrics. Fellow Am. Acad. Pediatrics; mem. AMA, Calif. Med. Assn., Am. Heart Assn., Alameda County Assn. Primary Care Practitioners (membership chmn. 1993-97, sec. treas. 1994-97), Los Angeles Pediatric Soc., East Bay Pediatric Soc., Smithsonian Assocs., Nat. Geog. Soc., Orgn. Chinese Ams. (chpt. pres. 1984), Chinese-Am. Physicians Soc. (co-founder, sec. 1980, pres. 1983, exec. dir. 1997—), Fedn. Chinese Med. Socs. (dir. 1998—), Chinese-Am. Polit. Assn. (life), Ethnic Health Inst. (bd. dirs. 1998—), Oakland Mus. Assns., Oakland Chinatown C. of C. (bd. dirs. 1986-91, adv. bd. 1992—); Oakland Asian Cultural Ctr. (dir. 1996—, treas. 1996—), Hong Kong U. Alumni Assn. (sec. No. Calif. chpt. 1992-96, pres. 1997—), Ethnic Health Inst. (bd. dirs. 1998—), Children's First Healthcare Network (bd. dirs. 1997—), Stanford U. Alumni Assn. (life), Chancellor's Assocs. U. Calif. at Berkeley, Chancellor's Assocs. U. Calif. at San Francisco, Commonwealth Club, Consumers' Union (life); Chinese Am. Golf Club. Buddhist. Office: 345 9th St Ste 204 Oakland CA 94607-4206 also: 101 Callan Ave Ste 401 San Leandro CA 94577-4523

NG, WING CHIU, accountant, computer software consultant, educator, activist; b. Hong Kong, Hong Kong, Oct. 14, 1947; came to U.S., 1966; s. Bing Nuen and Oi Ying (Lee) Ng. BS, Yale U., 1969, MS, 1969; PhD, NYU, 1972. CPA, Hawaii. Rsch. assoc. SUNY, Stony Brook, 1972-74; asst. prof. U. Md., College Park, 1974-76; rsch. physicist U. Bonn, Fed. Republic of Germany, 1976-78; chartered acct. Richter, Usher & Vineberg, Montreal, Can., 1978-80; pvt. practice Honolulu, Hawaii, 1980—; pres. Bowen, Ng & Co., Honolulu, 1983-84, Asia-Am. Investment, Inc., Honolulu, 1983—, Mathematica Pacific, Inc., Honolulu, 1984—; part-time prof. U. Hawaii, Honolulu, 1982—; ptnr. Advance Realty Investment, Honolulu, 1980—; dir. S & L Internat., Inc., Honolulu, 1987—. Creator: (computer software) Time Billing, 1984, Dbase General Ledger, 1987, Dbase Payroll, 1987, Dbase Accounts Receivable, 1989; co-author: Draft Constitution of the Federal Republic of China, 1994. Dir. Orgn. of Chinese Ams., Honolulu, 1984-86, Fedn. for a Dem. China, Honolulu, 1990—, Hong Kong, 1991—; dir. Alliance Hong Kong Chinese in U.S., 1995—. Included in Prominent People of Hawaii, Delta Pub. Co., 1988. Mem. AICPA, Hong Kong Soc. Accts., Hawaiian Trail & Mountain Club (auditor 1987—). Democrat. Buddhist. Avocations: hining, the internet. Office: 1149 Bethel St Ste 306 Honolulu HI 96813-2210

NGO, DAVID QUAT, electrical engineer; b. Bac-Giang, Vietnam, Jan. 9, 1947; came to U.S., 1975; m. Hang Mong, July 8, 1978; children: Nancy, Lynda. BSEE, Phu-Tho Inst. Tech., Saigon, South Vietnam, 1971, Lehigh U., 1979; MSEE, Pa. State U., 1981. Chief engr. Dept. Pub. Works & Comm., Saigon, 1971-75; rsch. asst. Pa. State U., State College, 1979-81; sr. engr. Allied-Bendix Aerospace, Columbia, Md., 1981-87; sr. system engr. E-Systems, Inc., Greenville, Tex., 1987-94; staff engr. Motorola, Inc., Scottsdale, Ariz., 1994—. Recipient Silver Snoopy award NASA, 1984. Mem. IEEE. Avocations: jogging, fishing, tennis, reading. Office: Motorola Inc 8201 E Mcdowell Rd Scottsdale AZ 85257-3893

NGUYEN, ANN CAC KHUE, pharmaceutical and medicinal chemist; b. Kieu Moc, Sontay, Vietnam; d. Nguyen Van Soan and Luu Thi Hieu. BS, U. Saigon, 1973; MS, San Francisco State U., 1978; PhD, U. Calif., San Francisco, 1983. Teaching and research asst. U. Calif., San Francisco, 1978-83, postdoctoral fellow, 1983-86; research scientist U. Calif., 1987—. Contbr. articles to profl. jours. Recipient Nat. Research Service award, NIH, 1981-83; Regents fellow U. Calif., San Francisco, 1978-81. Mem. AAAS, Am. Chem. Soc., N.Y. Acad. Scis., Bay Area Enzyme Mechanism Group, Am. Assn. Pharm. Scientists. Roman Catholic. Home: 1488 Portola Dr San Francisco CA 94127-1409 Office: U Calif Box 0446 San Francisco CA 94143

NGUYEN, GIANG DAI, artist, sculptor, graphic artist, muralist; b. Hanoi, Vietnam, May 21, 1944; came to U.S., 1992; s. Bui Dinh and Luan Thi (Le) N.; m. Thuy Bich Cao, Dec. 1976 (div. May 1985); children: Anh Nhat, Lan Thuy; m. Nguyen Tuoi Thi, Oct. 24, 1998. Grad. Sch. Art, Hanoi, 1965; AA, Coll. Art, Hanoi, 1968; BA, Coll. Art, Moscow, 1974. Supervisory artist advtg. and exhibiting co., Hanoi, 1975-78; lectr. Coll. Art, Hanoi, 1978-80; polit. prisoner Hanoi, 1980-87; polit. refugee Hong Kong, 1988-91; artist Seattle, 1992—. Pvt. collections in U.S., Japan, Can., Hong Kong, France; collection in Mus. of Art, Voronezh, Russia; murals include USA Today, Seattle, 1995, American Jazz, Seattle, 1994, Traditions of Vietnamese Culture, Seattle, 1992, Old Medicine of the Philippines, Battayon, 1991; exhbns. include Chinese Galley: Asian artists group show, Seattle, 1996, University Friends Ctr., Seattle, 1994, solo show at Pillar Point, Hong Kong, 1991, internat. group show at mus., Sophia, Bulgaria, 1977, group show Moscow, 1972; inventor of Upside Down art. Named Most Talented Artist of the World in internat. competition Stockholm, 1997; winner 3rd prize 1st Internat. Drawing Contest World of Art, 1997, 3rd prize Internat. Competition, Stockholm, 1997, 3rd prize Wash. State Conv. Ctr. group show, 1993, Best Contemporary Art CD-ROM--juried collection, 1996. Mem. Vietnamese Artist Assn. of N.W. U.S.A., S.E. Effective Devel., Inc. Home: 6854 Holly Park Dr S #501 Seattle WA 98118-3219

NGUYEN, KING XUAN, language educator; b. Hue, Vietnam, Dec. 20, 1930; came to U.S., 1975; s. Duong Xuan Nguyen and Thi Thi Ton-Nu. BA, U. Saigon, 1960, LLB, 1963; MEd, Boise State U., 1980. Tchr. Boise Sch. Dist., 1975-95; lectr. S.E. Asian Studies Summer Inst./U. Wash., 1992, 93, U. Wis., 1994, Ariz. State U., 1996, 97; spl. lectr. Boise State U., 1975-77. Col. Vietnamese Air Force to 1975. Recipient Red Apple Award for Outstanding Svc. to Edn., Boise, 1990. Mem. NEA, Idaho Edn. Assn., Boise Edn. Assn., Consortium Tchrs. Southeast Asian Langs., Assn. of TESOL. Home: 9674 W Pattie Ct Boise ID 83704-2824

NGUYEN, LAM DUC, business executive, consultant; b. Ninh Binh, Vietnam, July 20, 1945; came to the U.S., 1975; s. Phuong-Duc and Thien-Thi Nguyen; m. Trang Thu Nghiem, June 17, 1978; children: Katherine, Andrew, Alexander. BA, U. Saigon, 1968; diploma in TEFL, U. Sydney, Australia, 1973; postgrad., Furman U., 1977, San Jose State U., 1980; AS in Computer Sci., Condie Coll., 1981; MS in Telecomm. Sys. Mgmt., Nat. U., Calif., 1996, postgrad., 1997—. Cert. Emergency Specialist Tchg. credential ESL grades K-12; Calif. C.C. tchg. credential for ltd. svcs. in basic edn.; Calif. C.C. instr. credential in computer scis. Materials/mfg. sys. analyst, project leader Shugart Corp., Sunnyvale, Calif., 1979-84; mgr. programming and sys. devel. Televideo Sys., Inc., San Jose, Calif., 1984-86; sales and mktg. sys. analyst, project leader Spectra-Physics, San Jose, 1986; project mgr. U.S. Wind Power, Livermore, Calif., 1986-87; asst. mgr. ops. Burger King Corp., San Jose, 1987-88; dir. programs, dep. exec. dir. IRCC Inc., San Jose, 1988-93; pres., founder WIN-Visions, San Jose, 1993—; asst. chief tng. team Combined Document Exploitation Ctr., 1965-68; lang. instr. Military Asst. Command Civil Ops. for Rural Devel. Strategies/USAID, Bien Hoa, Vietnam, 1968-69; tchr. ESL/EFL Vietnamese-Am. Assn., Saigon, 1970-75; lectr. med. English U. Saigon-Med. Coll., 1974-75; spl. asst. to dir. refugee liaison officer, chief interpreter staff Refugee Camp, Eglin AFB, Fla., 1975; refugee camp mgmt. counselor Indochinese Inter-Agy. Task Force, U.S. State Dept., Indiantown Gap Refugee Camp, Pa., 1975; statis. quality control Michelin Tire Corp., S.C., 1976-78, others; part-time ESL instr. Foothill-De Anza Coll., San Jose, Calif., 1979-80; bilingual elem. and ESL tchr. San Jose Unified Sch. Dist., 1979-80; spkr., panelist in field. Co-author: Affirmative Action and Viet Community, 1996; author: Annotated Bibliography of Selected Materials for Family/Community Involvement, 1997; editor VIET mag., Thi Truong Tu Do mag.; co-editor, reporter Tin Bien News; contbr. articles to profl. jours.; host, prodr. ednl. radio shows. Active Nat. Asian Pacific Islanders Am. Adv. Coun., Democratic Nat. Com., 1991—, San Jose City Mayor's Gang Prevention Policy Team, 1992—, Coalition of Asian Pacific-Ams., No. Calif., 1992—, Nat. Immigration Forum, 1994; nat. co-chair Nat. Vietnamese-Am. Voter's League, 1992—, Nat. League Indochinese Am. Voters, 1992—; pres. Vietnamese-Ams. Civic Action Com., 1992—; mem., contbr. World Affairs Coun., 1993—; mem. adv. com. on voter registration and Get Out To Vote, Santa Clara County, co-chair, 1993, 94; mem. Dem. Congl. Campaign Com., 1992—; charter mem. Senate Task Force, 1992—; mem. Dem. Nat. Com.; mem. nat. steering com. Clinton/Gore, 1996; mem. Calif. State Adv. Coun. Refugee Assistance, 1992—, mem. various coms.; chair Vietnamese-Ams. Com. for Clinton/Gore, No. Calif., 1992, 96; chair fund raising com. Tet Festival, 1988-91, spl. event com., 1992-97; leader Vietnamese Ams. Dukakis' Presdl. Campaign, 1988; mem. Nat. Asian Pacific Am. Governing Coun., Clinton/Gore, 1996. Recipient Appreciation cert. Nat. ARC, 1975, Appreciation cert. and letter of commendation Refugee Liaison Office, USAF, 1975, Achievement cert. Dept. Army, 1975, Outstand Svc. to Refugee citation World YMCA, 1975, Peter Casey Asian Am. Leadership award, 1987, Letter of Commendation, Senator Art Torres, 1989, Letter Commendation, Santa Clara County Greater Ave. for Independence/Refugee Employment and Social Svcs. Adminstrn., 1990, Appreciation cert. State Calif. Dept. Social Svcs., 1990, Appreciation Cert. Calif. Dept. Health Svcs., Tobacco Control, 1991, Appreciation cert. U. Berkeley, Extended Foods and Nutrition Edn. Program, 1991, Merit award Coalition of Nationalist Vietnamese Orgns. of No. Calif., 1991, Leadership award No. Calif. Asian Pacific Americans, 1992, Cmty. Svc. award City of San Jose, 1993, Spirit of Democracy award State of Calif., 1994. Democrat. Buddhist. Avocations: bilingual ballot, civil and human rights, writing, reading, traveling. Home and Office: WIN-Visions 4864 Miramar Ave San Jose CA 95129-1004

NGUYEN, LAN KIM, software engineer; b. Saigon, July 5, 1960; parents Hai Kim Dang and My Thi Nguyen. BSEE, Cornell U., 1983; MA in Physics, SUNY, Buffalo, 1985, MSEE, 1986. Software engineer McDonnell Douglas Astronautics, Huntington Beach, Calif., 1986—. scholar Cornell U., 1982-83. Mem. Eta Kappa Nu. Avocations: sports, music. Office: 9188 Bolsa Ave Westminster CA 92683-5556

NGUYEN, MAI, aerospace engineer; b. Saigon, Vietnam, June 13, 1947; came to U.S., 1975; s. Ngat Van and Le Thi Nguyen; m. Thanh-Mai Thi Pham, July 30, 1975; children: Mary, Minh Q., Emily. BSChemE, Calif. State Poly. U., Pomona, 1979, MS in Engring., 1986. Registered profl. engr., Calif. Mem. tech. staff Space divsn. Rockwell, Downey, Calif., 1979-93, engring. specialist, 1993-97; sr. engring. specialist Boeing Reusable Space Sys., Downey, 1997—. Recipient Outstanding Engring. Merit award Orange County Engring. Coun., 1998, Group Achievement award NASA, 1989, 92, 96, 97, 98. Fellow Inst. for Advancement of Engring.; mem. Tau Beta Pi. Republican. Buddhist. Avocations: movies, travel, music. Home: 1801 Chantilly Ln Fullerton CA 92833-1291 Office: Boeing Reusable Space Sys Mail Code AE70 12214 Lakewood Blvd Downey CA 90242-2693

NGUYEN, TAI ANH, minister. Supt. Vietnamese Ministry Dist. of the Christian and Missionary Alliance, 1989. Office: 2275 W Lincoln Ave Anaheim CA 92801-6551*

NGUYEN, THINH VAN, physician; b. Vietnam, Apr. 16, 1948; came to U.S., 1971; s. Thao Van and Phuong Thi (Tran) N.; m. Phi Thi Ho, Jan. 2, 1973; children: Anh-Quan, Andrew. BS, U. Saigon, 1970; MS, U. Mo., 1973; MD, U. Tex., 1982. Diplomate Am. Bd. Internal Medicine, Am. Acad. Pain Mgmt., Fed. Lic. Examination. Rsch. asst. U. Tex. Med. Sch., Dallas, 1974-78; intern U. Tex. Med. Br., Galveston, 1982-83, resident, 1983-85; internist Family Health Plan, Inc., Long Beach, Calif., 1985-88, internist, area chief, 1988-89; pvt. practice San Jose, Calif., 1990—; chmn. quality assurance/UM com. Premier Care of No. Calif. Med. Group, Inc., 1996—; chmn. interdisciplinary com. Charter Cmty. Hosp., Hawaiian Gardens, Calif., 1988-89, San Jose Med. Ctr., 1993—. Fellow Am. Acad. Otolaryngic Allergy (affiliate), Am. Soc. Laser Med. Surgery, 1998—; mem. ACP, AMA, Am. Acad. Pain Mgmt., Calif. Assn. Med. Dirs. (bd. dirs. 1988-92), Calif. Med. Assn., Santa Clara County Med. Assn. Office: 2470 Alvin Ave Ste 5 San Jose CA 95121-1664

NGUYEN, TIEN MANH, communications systems engineer; b. Saigon, Vietnam, Apr. 5, 1957; came to the U.S., 1975; s. Hung The and Bi Thi (Luu) N.; m. Thu Hang Thi, Dec. 28 1986. BS in Engring., Calif. State U., Fullerton, 1979, MS in Engring., 1980; MSEE, U. Calif., San Diego, 1982; PhD in Elec. Engring., Columbia Pacific U., 1986; MA in Math., Claremont Grad. Sch., 1993, PhD in Engring. Math., 1995. Cert. electro magnetic compatibility engr., mfg. technologist. Tchg. asst. U. Calif., San Diego, 1982-83; chief automated mfg. dept. ITT Ednl. Svcs., West Covina, Calif., 1983-85; tech. staff Jet Propulsion Lab., Pasadena, Calif., 1985-96; engring. specialist The Aerospace Corp., El Segundo, Calif., 1996-97, sect. mgr., 1997—; prin. tech. advisor Internat. Consultative Com. for Space Data Systems (CCSDS), Pasadena, 1985-90, 93-96. Editor: Proceedings of Consultative Com. for Space Data Systems, Radio Frequency & Modulation, 1989, 94, VACET Tech. Jour., 1996—; contbr. over 70 articles to profl. jours. Grad. rep. EECS dept. U. Calif., San Diego, 1982-83; NASA del. to internat. Consultative Com. for Space Data Systems, 1986—. San Diego fellow, 1980-82, Long Beach Found. scholar Calif. State U., recipient Bendix Mgmt. Club award, 1987, NASA Hon. award, 1988, over 23 NASA monetary awards, 1989-96, 2 NASA Hon. awards, 1993, West Bond prize award for best PhD dissertation, 1995. Mem. IEEE (sr., vice chmn. 1987-94, session chmn. internat. symposium on electro magnetic compatibility 1986, internat. conf. on telecomm. 1995, session organizer and chmn., award 1986, 95, student activities chair Orange County Sect., 1996-97, 3 Aerospace Invention Disclosure awards 1998, 2 Aerospace Performance awards 1998), AIAA (sr.), AAAS, Soc. Mfg. Engrs., Am. Math. Soc., Armed Forces Commn. and Electronics Assn., Vietnamese-Am. Sci. and Profl. Engring. Soc. (chmn. bd. dirs. 1995-96, planning chair and tech. program chair conf. 1996, presenter in field, editor VASPES '96 Conf. Proc.), Vietnamese Assn. for Computing, Engring., Tech., and Sci. (gen. co-chmn. Viet-Tech. Internat. Conf. 1996 (editor-in-chief VACETS Tech. Jour. 1996-97, mem. steering com. 1997, elected mem. exec. com. 1997-98), N.Y. Acad. Scis., U.S. Naval Inst., Phi Kappa Phi, Sigma Xi. Republican. Buddhist. Achievements include patent for technique to resolve phase ambiguity for QPSK systems; development of new algorithms to design communications systems for space applications; development of future standards for space data systems. Home: 1501 Maxzim Ave Fullerton CA 92833-4511 Office: The Aerospace Corp 2350 E El Segundo Blvd El Segundo CA 90245-4691

NI, MAO-LIN, electrical engineer; b. Shijiazhuang, China, Nov. 1, 1963; s. Jin Ni and Xiangrui Lu; m. Ying Chen, Feb. 17, 1991; 1 child, Chenyu. BS, Hebei Inst. Mech./Elec. Engr., Shijiazhuang, 1983; MS in Control Engring., Harbin (China) Inst. Tech., 1988; PhD in Control Engring., Chinese Acad. Space Tech., Beijing, 1992; postgrad., U. Calif., Davis, 1997—. Elec. engr. Tianjin Inst. Cement Industry, China, 1983-86; sr. control engr. Beijing Inst. Control Engring., China, 1992-97. Grantee NSF China, 1994, N.Y. Acad. Scis., 1995. Avocations: table tennis, music. Office: U Calif Dept Maths Davis CA 95616

NIBLEY, ROBERT RICKS, retired lawyer; b. Salt Lake City, Sept. 24, 1913; s. Joel and Teresa (Taylor) N.; m. Lee Allen, Jan. 31, 1945 (dec.); children—Jane, Annette. A.B., U. Utah, 1934; J.D., Loyola U., Los Angeles, 1942. Bar: Calif. bar 1943. Accountant Nat. Parks Airways, Salt Lake City, 1934-37, Western Air Lines, Los Angeles, 1937-40; asst. mgr. market research dept. Lockheed Aircraft Corp., Burbank, Calif., 1940-43; asso. firm Hill, Farrer and Burrill, Los Angeles, 1946-53; partner Hill, Farrer and Burrill, 1953-70, of counsel, 1971-78. Served from ensign to lt. comdr. USNR, 1943-46. Mem. ABA, L.A. Bar Assn., Calif. Club, Phi Delta Phi, Phi Kappa Phi, Phi Delta Theta. Home: 4860 Ambrose Ave Los Angeles CA 90027-1866

NICCUM, ERYNN RUTH, artist; b. San Francisco, Sept. 8, 1970; d. Richard Lyn and Grace Hattie (Pecher) N. Site dir. arts City of Palo Alto, Calif., 1987-90; cons. Reprint Mint, Palo Alto, 1990-96; freelance portrait artist Mountain View, Calif., 1993—; office mgr. Lady Bug Messenger, Palo Alto, 1996—; owner, operator Cats Claw Herbal, Mountain View, 1995—. Avocations: animal rights, collecting antique cat paraphernalia, tattoos. Home: 395 Sierra Vista Ave Apt 26 Mountain View CA 94043-2924

NICHOLAS, FREDERICK M., lawyer; b. N.Y.C., May 30, 1920; s. Benjamin L. and Rose F. (Nechols) N.; m. Eleanore Berman, Sept. 2, 1951 (div. 1963); children: Deborah, Jan, Tony; m. Joan Fields, Jan. 2, 1983. AB, U. So. Calif., 1947; postgrad., U. Chgo., 1949-50; JD, U. So. Calif., 1952. Bar: Calif. 1952, U.S. Dist. Ct. Calif. 1952, U.S. Ct. Appeals (9th cir.) 1952. Assoc. Loeb & Loeb, L.A., 1952-56; ptnr. Swerdlow, Glikbarg & Nicholas, Beverly Hills, Calif., 1956-62; pvt. practice Beverly Hills, 1962-80; pres., atty. Hapsmith Co., Beverly Hills, 1980—; bd. dirs. Malibu Grand Prix, L.A., 1982-90; gen. counsel Beverly Hills Realty Bd., 1971-79; founder, pres. Pub. Counsel, L.A., 1970-73. Author: Commercial Real Property Lease Practice, 1976. Chmn. Mus. Contemporary Art, L.A., 1987-93, chmn. com. Walt Disney Concert Hall, L.A., 1987-95; trustee Music Ctr. L.A. County, 1987-95, L.A. Philharm. Assn., 1987-95; chmn. Calif. Pub. Broadcasting Commn., Sacramento, 1972-78; pres. Maple Ctr., 1977-79. Recipient Citizen of Yr. award Beverly Hills Bd. Realtors, 1978, Man of Yr. award Maple Ctr., 1980, Pub. Svc. award Coro Found., 1988, The Medici award L.A. C. of C., 1990, Founders award Pub. Counsel, 1990, Trustees award Calif. Inst. Arts, 1993, City of Angels award L.A. Ctrl. Bus. Assn.; named Outstanding Founder in Philanthropy, Nat. Philanthropy Day Com., 1990. Mem. Beverly Hills Bar Assn. (bd. govs. 1970-76, Disting. Svc. award 1974, 81, Exceptional Svc.

award 1986), Beverly Hills C. of C. (Man of Yr. 1983). Home: 1001 Maybrook Dr Beverly Hills CA 90210-2715 Office: Hapsmith Co 9300 Wilshire Blvd Beverly Hills CA 90212-3213

NICHOLS, ALBERT MYRON, minister; b. Creston, Iowa, Oct. 17, 1914; s. Albert Maurice and Lou (Myers) N.; m. Phyllis Cochran, June 28, 1939; children: Byron Albert, Phillip Garrett. AB, UCLA, 1936; BS, San Francisco Theol. Sem., 1940; DD, Occidental Coll., 1952. Ordained to ministry United Presbyn. Ch. in U.S.A., 1940. Pastor chs. North Hollywood, Calif., 1940-43; assoc. pastor Pasadena (Calif.) Presbyn. Ch., 1943-57; pastor 1st Presbyn. Ch., Pendleton, Oreg., 1957-82; ret. 1st Presbyn. Ch., Pendleton, 1982; chmn. gen. assembly com. on responsible marriage and parenthood United Presbyn. Ch. in U.S.A., 1959-62, mem. Bd. Christian Edn., 1969-72; mem. 1st coun. Synod of Pacific; moderator Oreg. Synod, 1968, 69; stated clk. Ea. Oreg. Presbytery, 1975—. Pres. Pasadena Child Guidance Clinic, 1955-57; trustee San Francisco Theol. Sem., 1963-84; life trustee Lewis and Clark Coll., Portland, Oreg.; mem. Pendleton City Recreation Commn., 1965—; founding bd. dirs. Presbyn. Intercommunity Hosp., Whittier, Calif.; mem. State of Oreg. Health Coun., 1985-88, State Trauma Adv. Bd., 1987-91; chmn. City of Pendleton Capital Improvements Commn., 1983—. Named 1st Citizen of Pendleton, 1984. Home: 1013 NW 12th St Pendleton OR 97801-1235

NICHOLS, ANDREW WILKINSON, public health physician, educator; b. Bardstown, Ky., Jan. 29, 1937; s. Andrew Wilkinson and Catherine May (Garrison) N.; m. Ann Marie Weaver, June 1965; children: Catherine Ann, Michael Garrison, Miles Andrew. AB, Swarthmore Coll., 1959; MD, Stanford U., 1964; MPH, Harvard U., 1970. Diplomate Am. Bd. Preventive Medicine, Am. Bd. Family Practice. Asst. resident in medicine, then resident in medicine St. Luke's Hosp., N.Y.C., 1964-66, 68-69; med. officer U.S. Peace Corps, Lima, Peru, 1966-68; prof. family & community medicine U. Ariz., Tucson, 1970—, dir. Rural Health Office, 1980—; mem. Ariz. State Ho. Reps., 1992—; pres. Ariz.-Mex. Border Health Found., Tucson, 1985—, U.S.-Mex. Border Health Assn., El Paso, Tex., 1989-90, Nat. Orgn. AHEC Program Dirs., Washington, 1991-93, Ariz. Pub. Health Assn., 1982-83; chmn. bd. dirs. Jour. Rural Health, Kansas City, Mo., 1988, 89, 90; dir. Ariz. Area Health Edn. Ctr., 1984—, S.W. Border Rural Health Rsch. Ctr., 1988—, WHO Collaborating Ctr. Rural and Border Health, 1992—. Co-author: Public Health and Community Medicine, 1980; contbr. articles to health pubis. Bd. dirs. Habitat for Humanity, Tucson, 1979-93, div. higher edn. Christian Ch., St. Louis, 1988-92. Robert Wood Johnson Found. Health Policy fellow, 1977-78; sr. fellow Fogaty Internat. Ctr.-NIH, 1985-87; named Outstanding Health Worker of Yr. U.S.-Mex. Border Health Assn., 1986. Fellow Am. Coll. Preventive Medicine, Am. Acad. Family Physicians. Mem. Disciples of Christ Ch. Avocation: photography. Home: 4556 N Flecha Dr Tucson AZ 85718-6726 Office: Univ Ariz Health Sci Ctr 2501 E Elm St Tucson AZ 85716-3416

NICHOLS, DAVID LAWRENCE, television writer, producer; b. Columbia, S.C., Sept. 14, 1954; s. John Edward Jr. and Patricia Ann (Downey) N.; m. Sarah Jane Landstrom, Mar. 28, 1982; 1 child, Sydney Marie. BFA magna cum laude, Syracuse U., 1975. Story editor Eisenhower and Lutz, CBS-TV, Studio City, Calif., 1987-88; prodr. Live In, CBS-TV, Hollywood, Calif., 1989-90; supr. prodr. Evening Shade, CBS-TV, Studio City, 1990-93; co-exec. prodr. Hearts Afire, CBS-TV, Studio City, 1993-94, Grace Under Fire, ABC-TV, Studio City, 1996-97; exec. prodr. Caroline in the City, NBC-TV, Studio City, 1997-98. Co-author (play) Town Full of Heroes; contbr. articles to L.A. Times, 1978-80; performer The Colony Studio Theatre, L.A., 1976-80, The Groundlings improv theatre, L.A., 1984-86. Mem. AFTRA, SAG, Acad. T.V. Arts and Scis., Actors Equity Assn., Writers Guild of Am. (West).

NICHOLS, EDWARD IVAN, corporate training company executive; b. Boise, Idaho, Mar. 10, 1943; s. Edward Loren Wellman and Betty Jane (Nelson) Nichols. B in Music Edn., Idaho State U., 1968. Music tchr. Granite Sch. Dist., Salt Lake City, 1969-70; leader, musician, singer, comic Sunrise, various, 1971-78; inventory mgr. Sight and Sound, Denver, 1978-81; prin., owner Comedy Works, Denver, 1981-93, Colo. Jazz Workshop, Denver, 1987—, Court Jesters, Denver, 1996—. Co-author: Manual for Becoming A Jester, 1999. Bd. dirs. First Entertainment, Denver, 1988-93, Gift of Jazz, Denver, 1995-97. Mem. Internat. Assn. Jazz Educators. Office: Court Jesters PO Box 9311 Denver CO 80209-0311

NICHOLS, ELIZABETH L(UELLA), genealogist, writer, publisher, researcher, consultant; b. Chase City, Va., May 26, 1937; d. Clyde Redmond Nichols Sr. and Besse Luella Bolton. Student, Brigham Young U., 1955-56; Secretarial degree, Howard Bus. Coll., Shelby, N.C., 1959. Accredited genealogist. With dept. family history LDS Ch., Salt Lake City, 1970—, sys. user specialist,, sr. corr. specialist, libr. ref. cons., writer, editor, lectr., 1981-95; sr. ref. cons. LDS Ch., 1996—; owner Family History Educators, Salt Lake City, 1990—; lectr. in field. Author: The Genesis of Your Genealogy: Step-by-Step Instruction for the Beginner in Family History, 1969, 4th edit., 1998, Genealogy in the Computer Age: Understanding Family Search: vol. 1: Ancestral File, the International Genealogical Index (IGI), and the Social Security Death Index, rev. edit., 1994, Genealogy in the Computer Age: Understanding FamilySearch, vol. 2: Personal Ancestral File, Family History Library Catalog, More Resource Files, and Using Them All in Harmony, 1997; co-author: Exciting Things are Happening: A Survey Report of North American Family History Activity, 1980; author Family Exaltation and You, 1972, rev., 1973, Stake Training Outline for Teachers, 1972, Records Submission Manual, 1973, How to Trace CFI (IGI) Batch Numbers, Research Paper Series F, no. 5, 1977, Submitting Names, 1987, Teaching Family Heritage in Four Weeks: A Course Outline, 1990, Finding Your Relationship to a Known Relative, rev. edit., 1993, Christian Holiday Verses, 1993; author (with others) Boy Scouts: Genealogy, 1988; contbr. articles to profl. jours., chpts. to books. Mem. DAR (Utah state registrar 1992-95, state chmn. geneal. records 1989-92), Nat. Writers Assn., Nat. Geneal. Soc., New England Hist. Geneal. Soc., Utah Geneal. Assn. (asoc. editor Geneal. Jour. 1970s, sec. to bd. dirs. 1970s), Pubs. Mktg. Assn. Mormon. Avocations: enjoying extended family and friends, reading, personal family history, writing poetry. Home: 8 Hillside Ave # 105 Salt Lake City UT 84103 Office: Family History Educators PO Box 510606 Salt Lake City UT 84151-0606 also: LDS Ch Dept Family History 250T Church Office Bldg Salt Lake City UT 84150-3400

NICHOLS, MARK EDWARD, engineer; b. Schenectady, N.Y., Sept. 3, 1950; s. John Burton and Betty Jane (Paulsen) N.; m. Cornelia Rocas. BS in Engring. Physics, U. Calif., Berkeley, 1972; MS in Sci. and Engring. Mgmt., West Coast U., 1984; postgrad., Ind. Coll. Armed Forces, 1977. Cert. in Nat. Security Mgmt. Inst. and mech. technician Wetzel-Moreau Engring. Co., Inglewood, Calif., 1970-71; sales engr., supr. United Tech. Industries/Turbocooler Divsn., Manhattan Beach, Calif., 1972-73; wind tunnel test engr. Space Divsn. Rockwell Internat., Downey, Calif., 1973-76; flight and sys. engr. Space Sys. Divsn. Rockwell Internat., Palmdale, Calif., 1976-78; aero. test engr. Space Sys. Divsn. Rockwell Internat., Downey, 1980-85, project engr. payloads-cargo integration Aerospace Divsn., 1985-96; flight test integration engr. Gen. Dynamics/Convair, San Diego, 1978-80; project engr. mission/manifest integration requirements Boeing N.Am., 1996—; instr. Aerodynamics and Aeronautics, Adv. Career Tng., Downey, 1986—; instrnl. aide, lectr. Discover-E, Downey, 1992—. Columnist, Long Beach Press-Telegram, 1987-90. With USN, 1968-69. Judge L.A. County and Calif. State Sci. and Engring. Fairs, 1987—. Recipient Achievement award Bank of Am., 1968, Silver Snoopy Achievement award NASA, 1978; Gov.'s scholar, 1968. Mem. ASME, AIAA, Nat. Mgmt. Assn., Am. Legion #270, Planetary Soc., Moose #1739, Los Amigos Men's Club. Republican. Avocations: golf, skiing, sailing, travel, motorcycling. Home: 11682 Lakewood Blvd Downey CA 90241-5272 Office: Boeing NAm 12214 Lakewood Blvd Downey CA 90242-2693

NICHOLS, RICHARD ALAN, ecologist; b. L.A., Apr. 18, 1951; s. Harry Alfred and Sheila Helen (Davidson) N.; m. Claudia Denise Evans, May 12, [illegible] Range Mgmt., U. Calif., Davis, 1983. Cert. rangeland mgr., Calif.; cert. profl. in erosion and sediment control. Botanist U.S. Forest Svc., Yreka, Canby, Calif., 1981-82; postgrad. rsch. asst. U. Calif., Davis, 1983-84; range conservationist U.S. Dept. Interior Bur. Land Mgmt., Caliente, Nev., 1984-86; range conservationist 1st Strategic Aerospace Divsn., Vandenberg AFB, Calif., 1986-87, natural resources planner, 1987-88; sr. botanist Western Ecol. Svcs. Co., Novato, Calif., 1988-91; sr. program mgr. Fugro Inc., Roseville, Calif., 1991-95; dir. natural resources EIP Assocs., San Francisco, 1995—; cons. Delta in-channel island group San Francsico Estuary Project, Sacramento, 1996—. Contbr. articles to profl. jours. Recipient Sustained Superior Performance award USAF, 1990-91. Mem. Internat. Erosion Control Assn., Calif. Native Grass Assn. (bd. dirs. 1997—), Soc. Ecol. Restoration, Calif. Native Plant Soc., Soc. Range Mgmt., Constrn. Materials Assn. Calif. (environ. and safety com. 1998). Democrat. Episcopalian. Achievements include successful application of biotech. bank stabilization on a major California river; founder mitigation com. and chief coastal dune restoration planner for Peace Keeper/Rail Garrison Project. Avocations: hiking, fishing, reading. Home: 550 Battery St Apt 1114 San Francisco CA 94111-2325 Office: EIP Assocs 601 Montgomery St Ste 500 San Francisco CA 94111-2642

NICHOLS, VANCE EVERETT, minister, principal; b. San Diego, Feb. 3, 1959; s. Kermit Don Nichols and Veora Rachel (Huffman) Nichols-Wilson; m. Janet Louise Perkins, June 9, 1984; children: Joel Vance, Joshua Paul. BS in Radio and TV, San Diego State U., 1986. Producer, creative cons. Horizon Gate Prodns., Spring Valley, Calif., 1985-86; prin. sch. ministries Calvary So. Bapt. Ch./Calvary Christian Schs., San Diego, 1986-89; elem. prin., dir. devel. Riverside (Calif.) Christian High Sch., 1989—; pastor Tamarind Ave. Bapt. Ch., Fontana, Calif., 1989-91; arbitrator Christian Conciliation Ct., San Diego, 1989; seminar leader Assn. Christian Schs. Internat., Anaheim, Calif., 1990—. Wrote, produced, and directed various motion pictures; author numerous short stories and poems. Active Nat. Right to Life, San Diego, Riverside, 1987—. Recipient numerous domestic, internat. film and scholastic journalism awards. Mem. Internat. Fellowship Christian Sch. Adminstrs., Calvary Arrowhead So. Bapt. Assn. (exec. bd. 1989-91). Republican. Home: 10556 Rouselle Dr Mira Loma CA 91752-1392 Office: Riverside Christian High Sch 3532 Monroe St Riverside CA 92504-3320

NICHOLSON, LOREN LEE, journalism educator, author; b. Denver, Mar. 26, 1922; s. James Garfield and Eva Elsie (Burt) N.; m. Patricia Henley, Mar. 19, 1945 (div. Apr. 1979); m. Bernice Bingham Loughran, Feb. 26, 1983. AB in Journalism, San Jose (Calif.) State U., 1945; MBA, Stanford U., 1947, postgrad., 1956, 57, 58. Accounts exec. John P. Scripps Newspapers, Watsonville, Calif., 1945-47; advt. corr. Sunset Mag., San Francisco, 1947-49; advt. dir. Scripps Newspapers, Redding, Calif., 1949-56; prof. journalism Calif. Poly. State U., San Luis Obispo, Calif., 1956-91; pres. Calif. Heritage Pub. Assocs., San Luis Obispo, 1992-97. Editor La Vista, 1968-74 (Hist. award 1974); author: Rails Across The Ranchos, 1980, 2nd edit., 1994, Old Picture Postcards, 1989, Romualdo Pacheco's California, 1990, Glimpses of Childhood, 1995. Recipient creative grant Calif. State Poly. U., San Luis Obispo, 1972, fellowships Huntington Libr., San Marino, Calif., 1977, Aluminum Co. Am., Pitts., 1980, Outstanding Community Svc. award, Daughters of the Am. Revolution, 1999. Mem. Retired Active Men (pres. 1995), South County Hist. Soc. (pres. 1997-98), San Luis Obispo County Hist. Soc. (pres. 1964, 80), Calif. Conf. Hist. Socs. (regional v.p. 1966). Democrat. Congregationalist. Avocations: photography, tour organizing, travel.

NICHOLSON, MARILYN LEE, arts administrator; b. San Jose, Calif., Feb. 7, 1949; d. John Hart Nicholson and Betty Ann (Price) Shepardson; m. Neal Luit Evenhuis. BA in English and History, U. Ariz., 1972; BFA in Studio, U. Hawaii-Manoa, Honolulu, 1977, MA in English, 1977, AS, 1984. Edn. coord., dir. Bishop Mus. Arts and Crafts Sch., Honolulu, 1977-79; owner Fiber Arts Store, Kailua, Hawaii, 1978-82; field coord. Hawaii State Found. on Culture and Arts, Honolulu, 1981-85; exec. dir. Sedona (Ariz.) Arts Ctr., 1986-92, Volcano (Hawaii) Art Ctr., 1992—; mem. bd. artist selection com. Ariz. Indian Living Treasures, 1988-92; bd. dirs., treas. Sedona Cultural Arts Ctr., 1987-92; conf. speaker Nat. Assembly Arts Agys., 1988. Founding Chmn. Sedona Gallery Assn., 1990-92; mem. com. Sedona Acad., 1986-92; mem. steering com. community plan City of Sedona, 1989-91; commr. Arts & Cultural Ctr., Sedona, 1989-91; mem. exec. com. planning Volcano Community Assn., 1993-96. Recipient Mayor's award for Disting. Svc., Sedona City Coun., 1992. Mem. Hawaii Mus. Assn. (bd. dirs. 1995—), Cooper Ctr. Coun. (bd. dirs. 1992—), Aloha Festivals-Hawaii Island (bd. dirs. 1992—). Office: Volcano Art Ctr PO Box 104 Hawaii National Park HI 96718-0104

NICKENS, CATHERINE ARLENE, retired nurse, freelance writer; b. Litchfield, Ill., Oct. 30, 1932; d. Harley Lloyd Moore and Ida Mae Reynolds; m. Carl Roland Nickens, Sept. 4, 1954 (div. Apr. 1975); children: Linda Dianne, Carl Roland Jr., Karen Patricia, Eric Moore. Nursing diploma, St. Joseph's Hosp., 1954. RN, Calif. Staff nurse St. Joseph's Hosp., Alton, Ill., 1954-55; staff nurse St. Mary's Hosp., Streator, Ill., 1962-68, supr., acting dir., 1968-70; nursing supr. Illini Hosp., Silvis, Ill., 1970-74; office nurse pediatrician's office Silvis, 1974-75; staff nurse telemetry/drug abuse North Miami Gen. Hosp., Miami, Fla., 1975-80; staff nurse, relief supr. Petaluma (Calif.) Valley Hosp., 1981-97; participant women's health study Brigham and Women's Hosp., Boston, 1994—. Author: (hist. fiction) The Thoroughly Compromised Bride, 1991 (award 1992), The Highwayman, 1993 (award 1994). Mem. ACLU, N.Y.C., 1995, Parents, Families and Friends of Lesbians and Gays, Washington, 1994—, Nat. Mus. of Am. Indian/Smithsonian Instn., Washington, 1996-97; friend of the quilt NAMES Project Meml. Quilt, San Francisco, 1992—; mem. friendship cir. Am. Found. for AIDS Rsch., Washington, 1994—; vol. Santa Rosa Police Dept., 1997—. Mem. Romance Writers of Am. (mentor to unpublished writers 1995—). Avocations: reading, traveling, needlework, doll-making. Home and office: 105 Olive St Santa Rosa CA 95401-6241

NICKERSON, DOUGLAS BLAIN, mechanical engineer, consultant; b. Sacramento, Jan. 6, 1917; s. Edward Douglas and Lottie (Bocarde) N.; m. Elizabeth Greenwood Green, June 18, 1943; children: Nancy Elizabeth, Bruce Greenwood, Katherine Grace. BSME, Calif. Inst. Tech., 1940. Registered engr., Calif. Design engr. Lockheed Aircraft Corp., Burbank, Calif., 1940-46; sr. engr. Aerojet Engring. Corp., Azusa, Calif., 1946-52; chief engr. Hydro-Aire divsn. Crane, Burbank, 1952-61; prin. engr. Aerojet Gen. Corp., Azusa, 1961-65; engring. cons. Pasadena, Calif., 1965-81; pres. Stress Analysis Assn., Inc., Pasadena, 1981-85; cons. Pasadena, 1985—; chmn. A16-A aircraft fuel pump com. Soc. Automotive Engrs., 1954-57. Author computer programs; contbr. articles to procs. and confs. Chmn. Young Rep. Club, La Canada, 1954. Named Engr. of Month, Engr. of So. Calif., 1973. Fellow ASME mem. code com.-pumps 1980-90, chmn. code com.-pumps 1990—, mem. code com.-subgroup design 1990—, mem. code com.-nuclear power 1994—)' mem. AAAS, Soc. Naval and Marine Engrs. Achievements include: design, development, test and evaluation of automatic emergency fuel system for jet powered airplane; pioneer work in development of American rocket turbopumps; developed Hydro-Aire Hi V/L aircraft fuel booster; patentee valve, pump bearing assembly, fuel pump bearing. Office: # 1115 # 452 E Foothill Blvd Pasadena CA 91107

NICKUM, MARY JOSEPHINE, journal editor; b. Richmond, Ind., Nov. 6, 1945; d. Joseph and Mary (McGaffney) Stumreiter; m. Richard Erle Lewis, Jan. 11, 1969 (div. Apr. 1985); children: Darrel Jay Lewis, Ryan Alois Lewis; m. John Gerald Nickum, Aug. 16, 1985. BA, Northland Coll., 1967; MLib., U. Wash., 1968; MA in Interdisciplinary Studies, Oreg. State U., 1983. Libr. U.S. EPA, Duluth, Minn., 1968-74; fish/ocean libr. Oreg. State U., Corvallis, 1974-82; editor Am. Fish Soc., Bethesda, Md., 1982-85; project mgr. Fish & Wildlife Reference Svc., Rockville, Md., 1985-92; divsn. mgr. Maxima Corp., Lanham, Md., 1992-93; assoc. editor World Aquaculture, Bozeman, Mont., 1995—; editor Intermountain Jour. Scis., Bozeman, 1996—; Book reviewer Libr. Jour., 1988—; columnist, contbr. articles to No. Aquaculture, 1995—; contbr. articles to Aquaculture Mag., 1998. Mem. Am. Fisheries Soc., Spl. Librs. Assn., Mont. Acad. Sci., Coun. Biology Editors, Bus. and Profl. Women (group sec. 1996-97). Republican. Roman Catholic. Avocations: reading, knitting, travel. Home: 33 Hoffer Ln [illegible]

NICLAS, KARL BERNHARD, electronics engineer; b. Ludenscheid, Germany, Nov. 11, 1930; came to the U.S., 1962; s. Karl Bernhard and Helene (Winterhoff) N.; m. Elka Bach, May 30, 1956; children: Joshua, Daniel. MS in Engring., Tech. U., Aachen, Germany, 1956, D in Engring., 1960. Project engr. Telefunken GmbH, Ulm, Germany, 1956-58, asst. mgr. lab., 1958-62; sr. project engr. GE Co., Palo Alto, Calif., 1962-63; mem. tech. staff Watkins-Johnson Co., Palo Alto, 1963-65, head low-noise tube sect., 1965-67, mgr. tube divsn., 1967-76, cons., 1976-90, prin. scientist, cons., 1990-97; ind. cons. Portola Vally, Calif., 1997—. Contbg. author: Low-Noise Transistors and Amplifiers, 1981, Monolithic Microwave Integrated Circuits, 1985; mem. editl. bd.: Transactions, Microwave Theory and Techniques, 1987—. Recipient Outstanding Publs. award German Soc. Radio Engrs., 1962, Microwave prize IEEE, 1985. Mem. Microwave Theory and Techniques Soc. (sr.), Electron Devices Soc. (sr.), Solid-State Circuits Soc. (sr.). Achievements include eight patents in areas of microwave tubes, electromagnetic wave propagation and semiconductor devices; invented microwave matrix amplifier.

NICOL, ROBERT DUNCAN, architect; b. La Jolla, Calif., Sept. 16, 1936; s. Duncan and Catherine (Muffly) N.; m. Susann Kay Larson; 1 child, Jennifer E. AA, Principia Coll., 1956; BArch, U. Calif., Berkeley, 1961. Registered arch., Ariz., Calif., Mont., Wash. Designer Kawneer Mfg. Co., Richmond, Calif., 1961-62, Claude Oakland, San Francisco, 1962-64; project arch. David T. Johnson, Oakland, Calif., 1964-68; pvt. practice Oakland, Calif., 1968—. Mem. bd. appeals City of Alameda, 1971-73, vice chair planning commn., 1973-77, founder, chair, vice chair design rev. bd., 1974-80, founder, chair, vice chair hist. adv. bd., 1976—, co-founder, chair, vice chair mayor's com. for handicapped, 1980-86; mem. Calif. State Access Bd., 1995—. Recipient Design award Am. Registered Archs., 1969, Harper Plz. Design award Calif. Bldg. Ofcls. Assn., 1985. Fellow AIA; mem. Soc. Am. Registered Archs., Nat. Coun. Archtl. Registration Bds. (sr.), Alexander Graham Bell Assn. for Deaf (lectr.), Oral Hearing Impaired Sec., San Leandro Hist. Railway Soc. (founder, charter mem., chair, vice-chair), Alameda Jr. C. of C. (project dir. 1969), Alameda Victorian Preservation Soc. Republican. Office: 455 17th St Oakland CA 94612-2101*

NICOLAI, EUGENE RALPH, public relations consultant, editor, writer; b. Renton, Wash., June 26, 1911; s. Eugene George and Josephine (Heidinger) N.; student U. Wash., 1929, Whitman Coll., 1929-30; B.A., U. Wash., 1934; postgrad. Am. U., 1942; M.A., George Washington U., 1965; m. Helen Margaret Manogue, June 5, 1935; 1 son, Paul Eugene. Editor, U. Wash. Daily, Seattle, 1934; asst. city editor, writer, nat. def. editor Seattle Times, 1934-41; writer Sta. KJR, Seattle, 1937-39; writer, editor, safety edn. officer Bur. Mines, Washington, 1941-45; news dir. Grand Coulee Dam and Columbia Basin Project, Washington, 1945-50; regional info. dir. Bur. Mines, Denver and Pitts., 1950-55, asst. chief mineral reports, Washington, 1955-61, news dir. office of oil and gas, 1956-57; sr. info. officer, later sr. public info. officer Office Sec. Interior, Washington, 1961-71, staff White House Nat. Conf. on Natural Beauty, spl. detail to White House, 1971, ret.; now public relations cons., tech. editor, writer. Formerly safety policy adviser Interior Dept.; com. mem. Internat. Cooperation Year, State Dept., 1971. With George Washington U. Alumni Found.; founder, mng. dir. Josephine Nature Preserve; pres. Media Assocs. Bd. dirs. Wash. State Council on Alcoholism; adviser Pierce Transit Authority, Pierce County Growth Mgmt., Pierce County Ethics Commn. Named Disting. Alumnus, recipient Penrose award, both Whitman Coll., 1979. Mem. Nature Conservancy, Wash. Environ. Council, Nat. Audubon Soc. (Am. Belgian Tervuren dist. rep.), Crook County (Oreg.) Hist. Soc., Washington State Hist. Soc., Emerald Shores Assn, Sigma Delta Chi, Pi Kappa Alpha. Presbyn. Clubs: George Washington U., Purdy (pres.). Lodge: Masons. Author: The Middle East Emergency Committee; editor: Fed. Conservation Yearbooks. Home: 9809 N Seminole Dr Spokane WA 99208-8608

NICOLAI, THOMAS R., lawyer; b. Frazer, Mich., Dec. 1, 1943. BA cum laude, Kalamazoo Coll., 1965; JD, U. Mich., 1970. Bar: Ill. 1972, Oreg. 1973. Fellow in Econs. U. Bonn., Germany, 1965-67; fellow Alexander von Humbolt Found. at Max Planck Inst. for Fgn. and Internat. Patent, Copyright and Unfair Competition Law, Munich, West Germany, 1970-72; ptr. Stoel Rives LLP, Portland, Oreg., 1973—. Mem. ABA (mem. real property, probate and trust law, bus. law and internat. law and practice sects.), Phi Beta Kappa, Phi Alpha Delta. Office: Stoel Rives LLP 900 SW 5th Ave Ste 2300 Portland OR 97204-1232

NIEBEL, JAMES DENHART, sculptor, retired urology educator; b. San Francisco, Dec. 20, 1922; s. Hebert Lee and Helen Lucille (Denhart) N.; m. Janice Folsom (div.); m. Peggy Dewar (div.); m. Mary Metteer (div.); m. Elena Cruz Clayton, Sept. 27, 1993; children: Christie, Gregory, Alan, Stuart, Cameron. BS in Chem. Engring., Stanford U., 1943; MD, Harvard U., 1949. Diplomate Am. Bd. Urology. Refinery engr. Union Oil Co., Wilmington, Calif., 1943-45; intern, resident Stanford Hosps., San Francisco, 1949-51, 53-57; pvt. practice in urology Monterey, Calif., 1957-71, 74-83; assoc. prof. urology Kampala, Uganda, 1972-73; asst. prof. urology Stanford (Calif.) Med. Sch., 1984-90; urologist Flying Drs., Mex., 1978-85, St. Jude Hosp., Saint Lucia, W. I., 1986, Yichang Med. Sch. Shanghai Med. Sch., China, 1988. Sculptor one-man shows Mendocino Art Ctr., Soleil Gallery, Carmel Valley, Calif., Gio Gallery, Santa Fe. Bd. dirs. Mendocino (Calif.) Music Festival, Mendocino Hist. Rsch. 1st Lt. M.C., U.S. Army, 1951-53. Mem. ACLU Pacific Biol. Lab. (Monterey), Sierra Club. Home: Box 950 44960 Ukiah St Mendocino CA 95460-0950

NIEDERAUER, GEORGE H., bishop; b. Los Angeles, CA, June 14, 1936; s. George and Elaine N. B.A. Philosophy, St. John's Seminary, Camarillo, CA, 1959; B.A. Sacred Theology, Catholic U., Washington, DC, 1962; M.A. English Lit., Loyola U., Los Angeles, CA, 1962; Ph.D. English Lit., USC, 1966. ordained priest April 30, 1962; named prelate of honor (monsignor) 1984; named bishop of Diocese of Salt Lake City, Nov. 3, 1994. Asst. pastor Our Lady of the Assumption Parish, Claremont, CA, 1962-63; priest in residence Holy Name of Jesus Parish, Los Angeles, CA, 1963-65; instr. English Lit. St. John's Seminary Coll., Camarillo, CA, 1965-79; instr. of English Lit. Mt. St. Mary's Coll., Los Angeles, CA, 1967-74; English Dept. chmn. St. John's Seminary Coll., Camarillo, CA, 1968-77; spiritual dir. St. John's Seminary Coll., 1972-79; part-time instr. of Spiritual Theology St. John's Seminary Theologate, 1976-79, full-time instr. of Spiritual Theology, 1979-87; part-time instr. of English Lit. St. John's Seminary Coll., 1979-92; rector St. John's Seminary, 1987-92, spiritual dir., 1979-95; co-dir. Cardinal Manning House of Prayer for Priests, Los Angeles, CA, 1992-95; bishop Salt Lake City, 1995—; mem. Nat. Fedn. of Spiritual Dirs. (pres. 1975-77); mem. Alpha Sigma Nu (Jesuit Honor Soc. - LMU Chapter); pres. Western Assn. of Spiritual Dirs., 1973-75; mem. bd. of the Comm. of Priests' Retreat, Archdiocese of Los Angeles; mem. select comm. for the revision of the U.S. Catholic Conf. "Program for Priestly Formation" 3rd edition; mem. Vatican Visitation Team for Theologates; speaker World Vision Internat, Fuller Theological Seminary, Calif. Lutheran Coll.; mem. Camarillo Ministerial Assn. Avocations include: classical music, stamp collecting, reading, film appreciation. Office: Chancery Office 27 C St Salt Lake City UT 84103-2302*

NIEDERMAN, KIM, marketing professional; b. Chgo., Oct. 12, 1951; s. Howard I. and Rochelle (Levin) N. BA in Mktg., U. Denver, 1973. V.p. Howard Parlor Furniture Co., Chgo., 1974-79; dist. mgr. Wang Labs., Lowell, Mass., 1979-84; pres. Hallmark Industries, Algonquin, Ill., 1984-90; regional mgr. Cisco Systems, 1991—; bd. dirs. Pool-Am., Algonquin, ASA Mfg., Algonquin. Mem. The Exec. Com. Avocations: golf, downhill skiing, racquetball, horse show jumping, jogging.

NIEHAUS, ED, executive. Pres., CEO Neuhaus Ryan Wong, Inc., South San Francisco. Office: 601 Gateway Blvd Ste 900 South San Francisco CA 94080-7009

NIELSEN, BOJE TURIN, landscape architect; b. Copenhagen, Denmark, Oct. 9, 1944; came to U.S., 1946; s. Poul and Grete N.; m. L. Carol; 1 child, Kelsey Dana. AAS, Hudson Valley Coll., 1964; BS, U. Mass., 1975, M of Landscape Architecture, 1978. Landscape architect Forest Svc., USDA, [illegible] 1978-80, Forest Svc., USDA, Deerlodge NAt. Forest, Mont., 1980-94, Forest Svc., USDA, Carson Nat. Forest, N.Mex., 1994-96, Forest Svc., USDA, Clearwater/Nez Perce Nat. Forest, Idaho, 1996—. Chmn. bd. dirs. Friends of Urban Forest, Butte, Mont., 1986-94. Mem. Am. Soc. Landscape

Architects (trustee 1992-94, chpt. dir. 1977—), Masons. Home: 2245 Sunlite Ln Missoula MT 59804-6300 Office: Clearwater/Nez Perce Nat Forest USDA RR 2 Box 475 Grangeville ID 83530-9699

NIELSEN, CHERIE SUE, elementary educator; b. Bingham Canyon, Utah, Nov. 9, 1947; d. Merrill Abindadi and Eva Elizabeth (Christensen) Nelson; m. Mark Andrew Nielsen, June 27, 1969; children: Travis, Jennifer, Trent, Denise, Marlene. AS, Snow Coll., 1968; BS, Brigham Young U., 1988. Cert. elem. tchr., gifted and talented endorsement, Utah. 4th grade tchr. Granite Sch. Dist., Salt Lake City, 1988-92, 5th grade tchr., 1992—; tchr. asst. Pioneer Elem. Sch., West Valley, Utah, 1992-94, art tchr., 1990—. V.p. coun. level PTA, Salt Lake City, 1993-94. Named Disting. Tchr. Utah State Senate, 1994. Republican. Mem. LDS Ch. Avocations: reading, quilting, watercolor, art, crafts. Office: Pioneer Elem Sch 3860 S 3380 W Salt Lake City UT 84119-4442

NIELSEN, JENNIFER LEE, molecular ecologist, researcher; b. Balt., Mar. 21, 1946; d. Leo Jay and Mary Marriott (Mules) N.; divorced; children: Nadja Ochs, Allisha Ochs. MFA, Ecole des Beaux Arts, Paris, 1968; BS, Evergreen State Coll., 1987; MS, U. Calif., Berkeley, 1990, PhD, 1994. Artist Seattle, 1969-78; fish biologist Weyerhaeuser Co., Tacoma, Wash., 1978-89; resource cons. Berkeley, 1989-90; rsch. biologist USDA-Forest Svc., Albany, Calif., 1990-99; vis. scientist Stanford U., Pacific Grove, Calif., 1994-99; rsch. assoc. Calif. State U.Mosslanding Marie Sta., 1995—; adj. prof. U. Calif., Berkeley, 1998; supervisory rsch. fishery biologist U.S. Geol. Svc., BRD, Alaska Biol. Sci. Ctr., Anchorage, 1999—. Editor: Evolution and the Aquatic Ecosystem, 1995; contbr. over 50 articles to profl. jours.; paintings exhibited at Metro. Mus. Modern Art, 1966; represented in numerous pvt. collections, U.S. and Europe. Mem. Am. Fisheries Soc. (pres. chpt. 1993-94, genetics sect. pres. 1998—), Molecular Marine Biology and Biotech. (regional editor 1995), Animal Behaviour Soc. (policy com. 1993-94). Avocations: painting, cooking, gardening, rock climbing, sailing. Office: Biol Sci Ctr 1011 E Tudor Rd Anchorage AK 99503-6103

NIELSEN, NIELS LAWRENCE, visual effects design and production, art director; b. El Paso, Tex., May 10, 1954; s. Svend Erik Nielsen and Elizabeth Ann (Hunicke) Bogart; m. Teresa Jo Hunt, Feb. 21, 1994; 1 child, Sylkie Wilson-Nielsen. BFA, U. Wis., Milw., 1978; ed. advanced film studies, Am. Film Inst., Hollywood, Calif., 1983. Project art dir. Harmonyland, Landmark Entertainment, Oita, Japan, 1989-91; asst. art dir. Lost City Palace, Sun Internat., Sun City, South Africa, 1991-92; art dir. Silver Legacy Casino, Circus-Circus, Reno, 1994; miniature effects supr. The Fifth Element Digital Domain, Venice, Calif., 1996; crew chief From the Earth to the Moon, Hunter Gratzner, Inc., L.A., 1997-98; art dir., project mgr. Star Trek World Tour, Paramount Pictures, Hollywood, 1997-98. Dir., prodr.: (documentary) The Gods of Beauty, 1995 (Cindy Silver award 1996); writer (screenplay) Celeste, 1995 (World Fest Gold award 1996); writer, dir.: (motion picture) Venus on the Halfshell, 1998. Wis. Arts Bd., Nat. Endowment for Arts funding grantee, Madison, 1982-83. Mem. Ind. Feature Project, Internat. Documentary Assn. Democrat. Home: 1215 Carlton Way Venice CA 90291-4001

NIELSEN, VERA BAGLEY, retired teacher, librarian; b. Greenwich, Utah, Oct. 13, 1916; d. James Alvin and Diantha Matilda (Anderson) Bagley; m. Byron Woodland, May 17, 1941 (dec. Feb. 1944); 1 child, Kathleen Myrle, m. Leland Nielsen, Sept. 12, 1952 (dec. Jan. 1993); 1 child, James Cary. AB magna cum laude, Brigham Young U., 1937, MA, 1949. Cert. tchr. 1st class elem., librarian, media specialist, supervisory/adminstrn. Tchr., librarian Franklin Sch., Provo, Utah, 1937, Maeser Sch., Provo, 1944-45, Wasatch Sch., Provo, 1952-58, Provost Sch., Provo, 1959-62; demonstraton tchr. Lab. Sch. Brigham Young U., Provo, 1945-49, tchr. film classics, 1957-58; media specialist Grandview Sch., Provo, 1949-52, Rock Canyon Sch., Provo, 1962-83; instr. libr. Coll. Edn., Provo, summers; instr. Coll. Edn. U. Utah, Salt Lake City, 1958-59; subtitute tchr. Cyprus High Sch., Magna, Utah, 1944; cons. workshops Salt Lake City Sch. Dist., 1957, Utah Edn. Assn., Salt Lake City, 1982-93. Contbr. articles to profl. publs.; editor Family Bull., Bagley Family Orgn., 1976-93; cons. Fascinating Tales Series, ARO Pub. Co., 1981-82. Sec. Orem (Utah) Boosters City Coun., 1970-80; with publicity Miss Orem Scholarship Pageant, 1984-94; sec. Utah County Dem. Party, 1984-92, treas., 1992-95. Recipient Disting. Svc. award Kiwanis Club, Provo, 1978, Vol. Svc. award Utah Gov.'s Commn., Salt Lake City, 1993. Mem. AAUW (br. pres., 1944, 76, state pres. 1968-70, regional dir. 1987-89, editor state bull. 1975-79, 90-94, Disting. Woman award Utah State chpt. 1986,), Assn. Childhood Edn. (pres., historian 1970), Ret. Sch. Employees (unit pres., 1983, , NRTA state coord. 1983-87, state pres. 1993-95), Gen. Federated Women's Clubs (state treas., 1992-94, v.p. 94—), Women's Divsn. C. of C. (sec. 1994, treas. 95), Women's Coun. Provo (pres. 1985-87, Delta Literary honor, 1991, parliamentarian, 1992), League of Women Voters, Phi Delta Kappa (treas., officer 1980, Kappan of Yr. Brigham Young U. chpt. 1987). Mormon.

NIELSEN, WILLIAM FREMMING, federal judge; b. 1934. BA, U. Wash., 1956, LLB, 1963. Law clk. to Hon. Charles L. Powell U.S. Dist. Ct. (ea. dist.) Wash., 1963-64; mem. firm Paine, Hamblen, Coffin, Brooke & Miller, 1964-91; judge to chief judge U.S. Dist. Ct. (ea. dist.) Wash., Spokane, 1991—. Lt. col. USAFR. Fellow Am. Coll. Trial Lawyers; mem. ABA, Wash. State Bar Assn., Spokane County Bar Assn. (pres. 1981-82), Fed. Bar Assn. (pres. 1988), Spokane County Legal Svcs. Corp. (past pres.), Lawyer Pilot Bar Assn., Assn. Trial Lawyers Am., Wash. State Trial Lawyers Assn., Assn. Def. Trial Attys., Am. Inns of Ct., Charles L. Powell Inn (pres. 1987), The Spokane Club, Rotary, Alpha Delta Phi, Phi Delta Phi. Office: US Dist Ct PO Box 2208 920 W Riverside Ave 9th Fl Spokane WA 99210-2208*

NIELSON, BARBARA BROADHEAD, special education administrator; b. Nephi, Utah, Apr. 9, 1931; d. Elmer Robert and Anna Else (Rassmussen) Broadhead; m. Gordon Leon Nielson, Jan. 5, 1953; children: Victoria, Ellen, Margo, Peggy, Thomas, Lyle, Clark. BS cum laude, Brigham Young U., 1965-67, MS, 1972-74, DEd, 1988-92. Cert. prof. elem., early childhood and spl. edn. tchr., adminstr. Elem. and kindergarten tchr. Tintic Sch. Dist., Eureka, Utah, 1966-68; spl. edn. tchr. Millard Sch. Dist., Delta, Utah, 1968-77, elem. prin., 1977-91, chpt. I dir., 1991-92, spl. edn. dir., coord. at-risk programs, 1992—; co-owner Booster Edn. Svc., Delta, 1973-75; mem. Utah Sch. Accreditation Com., Salt Lake City, 1980-85, Career Ladder Coun., Delta, 1984-92; dir. Millard Sch. Dist. Edn. Found., Delta, 1991-92. Author: A Systematic Instructional Reading Approach for Parent of School Ate Children, 1973, (games) Tic-Tac-Toe Phonics, 1973; co-author: Booster Math Materials, 1973; contbr. articles to profl. jours. Active Sierra club, Utah, 1990-94, Ashgrove Cement County Community Coun., Nephi-Delta, 1990-94, West Millard Recreation Coun., Delta, 1980-90; lobbyist, co-writer hazardous waste siting criteria Millard County Concerned Citizens for State of Utah, 1988-94. Named Outstanding Spl. Edn. Tchr., Utah State Office Edn., Salt Lake City, 1973, 74-75; recipient Disting. Svc. in Edn. award Utah State Legis., Salt Lake City, 1991. Mem. Utah Edn. Assn. (profl. rights and responsibility com. 1977-79), So. Utah Educators Assn. (coun. mem. 1974-78), U. Adminstrv. Womens Assn., Delta Rotary, Prins. Acad. of Utah, Delta Kappa Gamma (regional dir. 1973-74). Republican. Mem. Latter Day Saints. Avocations: environmentalist, reading, gardening, travel, history/genealogy. Home: PO Box 38085 295 Juniper St Leamington UT 84638 Office: Millard Sch Dist PO Box 666 Delta UT 84624-0666

NIELSON, THEO GILBERT, law enforcement official, university official; b. Roosevelt, Utah, June 29, 1938; s. John Gilbert and Mazie (Alexander) N.; m. Martha Perez, May 22, 1961; children: Lucille Marie, Sherry Lou, Mark Andrew, Rex Alexander, Theo Gilbert Jr., Cristal Ina, Gregory Angus, Mazie Leah, Rosanna Alma. Grad., FBI Nat. Acad., 1970; BA, Ariz. State U., 1975, MS, 1977. Officer Univ. Police, Ariz. State U., Tempe, 1963-67, sgt., 1967-70, lt., 1970-79; chief police Douglas (Ariz.) Police Dept., 1979-82; div. adminstr. Ariz. Criminal Intelligence Systems Agy., Tucson, 1982-84; dir. campus safety and security No. Ariz. U., Flagstaff, 1984-92; chief of capitol police Ariz. Dept. Adminstrn., Phoenix, 1992—. Mem. Am. Soc. for Indsl. Security (chmn. No. Ariz. chpt. 1987), Internat. Assn. Chiefs Police, Internat. Assn. Campus Law Enforcement Adminstrs., Ariz. Assn. Campus Law Enforcement (pres. 1989-90). Republican. Mormon. Avocations: genealogy, hiking, grandchildren. Home: 3335 E Hampton Ave Mesa AZ 85204-6410 Office: Ariz State Capitol Police 1700 W Washington St Ste B15 Phoenix AZ 85007-2812

NIEMI, JANICE, lawyer, former state legislator; b. Flint, Mich., Sept. 18, 1928; d. Richard Jesse and Norma (Bell) Bailey; m. Preston Niemi, Feb. 4, 1953 (divorced 1987); children—Ries, Patricia. BA, U. Wash., 1950, LLB, 1967; postgrad. U. Mich., 1950-52; cert. Hague Acad. Internat. Law, Netherlands, 1954. Bar: Wash. 1968. Assoc. firm Powell, Livengood, Dunlap & Silverdale, Kirkland, Wash., 1968; staff atty. Legal Service Ctr., Seattle, 1968-70; judge Seattle Dist. Ct., 1971-72, King County Superior Ct., Seattle, 1973-78; acting gen. counsel, dep. gen. counsel SBA, Washington, 1979-81; mem. Wash. State Ho. of Reps., Olympia, 1983-87, chmn. com. on state govt., 1984; mem. Wash. State Senate, 1987-95; sole practice, Seattle, 1981-94; superior ct. judge King County, 1995—, chief criminal judge, 1997—; mem. White House Fellows Regional Selection Panel, Seattle, 1974-77, chmn., 1976, 77; incorporator Sound Savs. & Loan, Seattle, 1975. Bd. dirs. Allied Arts, Seattle, 1971-78, Ctr. Contemporary Art, Seattle, 1981-83, Women's Network, Seattle, 1981-84, Pub. Defender Assn., Seattle, 1982-84; bd. visitors dept. psychology U. Wash., Seattle, 1983-87, bd. visitors dept sociology, 1988-98; mem. adv. bd. Tacoma Art Mus., 1987—. Named Woman of Yr. in Law, Past Pres.'s Assn., Seattle, 1971; Woman of Yr., Matrix Table, Seattle, 1973, Capitol Hill Bus. and Profl. Women, 1975. Mem. Wash. State Bar Assn., Wash. Women Lawyers. Democrat. Home: PO Box 20516 Seattle WA 98102-1516

NIERENBERG, NORMAN, urban land economist, retired state official; b. Chgo., May 8, 1919; s. Isadore Isaac and Sadie Sarah (Dorfman) N.; m. Nanette Joyce Fortgang, Feb. 9, 1950; children: Andrew Paul, Claudia Robin. AA, U. Chgo., 1939; AB, Calif. State Coll., L.A., 1952; MA, U. So. Calif., 1956. Lic. real estate broker, Calif.; cert. supr. and coll. instr., Calif. Right-of-way agt. Calif. Dept. Transp., L.A., 1951-61, 85-90; sr. agt. Calif. Dept. Transp., San Francisco, 1988-89; instr. UCLA, 1960-61, 67-75, 81-85; coord. continuing edn. in real estate U. Calif., Berkeley, 1961-64; coord. econ. benefits study Salton Sea, Calif. Dept. Water Resources, L.A., 1968-69; regional economist L.A. dist. CE, 1970-75, chief economist, 1981-85; regional economist Bd. Engrs. for Rivers and Harbors, Ft. Belvoir, Va., 1975-81; faculty resource person Oakland Project, Ford Found., U. Calif., Berkeley, 1962-64; project reviewer EPA, Washington, 1972-73. Editor: History of 82d Fighter Control Squadron, 1945; assoc. editor Right of Way Nat. Mag., 1952-55. Capt. USAAF, 1942-46, ETO, Lt. Col. USAFR ret. Mem. NEA, Am. Econ. Assn., Calif. Tchrs. Assn., Calif. Assn. Real Estate Tchrs. (bd. dirs. 1962), L.A. Coll. Tchrs. Assn., Ret. Officers Assn., Omicron Delta Epsilon. Democrat. Jewish. Home: Unit 4 21931 Burbank Blvd Apt 4 Woodland Hills CA 91367-6456

NIERENBERG, WILLIAM AARON, oceanography educator; b. N.Y.C., Feb. 13, 1919; s. Joseph and Minnie (Drucker) N.; m. Edith Meyerson, Nov. 21, 1941; children—Victoria Jean (Mrs. Tschinkel), Nicolas Clarke Eugene. Aaron Naumberg scholar, U. Paris, 1937-38; B.S., CCNY, 1939; M.A., Columbia U., 1942, Ph.D. (NRC predoctoral fellow), 1947. Tutor CCNY, 1939-42; sect. leader Manhattan Project, 1942-45; instr. physics Columbia U., 1946-48; asst. prof. physics U. Mich., 1948-50; assoc. prof. physics U. Calif. at Berkeley, 1950-53, prof., 1954-65; dir. Scripps Instn. Oceanography, 1965-86, dir. emeritus, 1986—; vice chancellor for marine scis. U. Calif. at San Diego, 1969-86; dir. Hudson Labs., Columbia, 1953-54; assoc. prof. U. Paris, 1960-62, asst. sec. gen. NATO for sci. affairs, 1960-62; spl. cons. Exec. Office Pres., 1958-60; sr. cons. White House Office Sci. and Tech. Policy, 1976-78. Contbr. papers to profl. jours. E.O. Lawrence lectr. Nat. Acad. Sci., 1958, Miller Found. fellow, 1957-59, Sloan Found. fellow, 1958, Fulbright fellow, 1960-61; mem. U.S. Nat. Commn. UNESCO, 1964-68, Calif. Adv. Com. on Marine and Coastal Resources, 1967-71; adviser-at-large U.S. Dept. State, 1968—; mem. Nat. Sci. Bd., 1972-78, 82-88, cons., 1988-89; chmn. USNC/PSA, NRC, 1988—; mem. Nat. Adv. Com. on Oceans and Atmosphere, 1971-77, chmn., 1971-75; mem. sci. and tech. adv. Council Calif. Assembly; mem. adv. council NASA, 1978-83, chmn. adv. council, 1978-82. NATO Sr. Sci. fellow, 1969; Decorated officer Nat. Order of Merit France; recipient Golden Dolphin award Assn. Artistico Letteraria Internazionale, Disting. Pub. Service medal NASA, 1982, Delmer S. Fahrney medal The Franklin Inst., 1987, Compass award Marine Tech. Soc., 1975. Fellow Am. Phys. Soc. (coun., sec. Pacific Coast sect. 1955-64); mem. Am. Acad. Arts and Scis., NAE, NAS (coun. 1973—), Am. Philos. Soc., Sigma Xi (pres. 1981-82, Procter prize 1977). Home: PO Box 927269 San Diego CA 92192-7269 Office: U Calif Scripps Instn Oceanography 0221 La Jolla CA 92093

NIES, KEVIN ALLISON, physics educator; b. N.Y.C., Apr. 23, 1949; d. Russell Albert and Signe Marie (Rasmussen) N. BS in Physics, U. Calif., Santa Barbara, 1972; postgrad., UCLA, 1979, Pasadena City Coll., 1980-81, Calif. State U., Northridge, 1985-90. Tchg. credential, Calif.; lic. FCC radio telephone 2d class. Rsch. assoc. level 2 UCLA Brain Inst., L.A., summer 1973; TV technician, engr. NBC, N.Y.C., 1978; founder, dir. Calif. Video Inst., L.A., 1980—; tchr. secondary edn. L.A. Unified Sch. Dist., 1985—; judge sci. fair San Fernando H.S., Slymar, Calif., 1994; instr. video prodn. Calif. Video Inst., L.A., 1982-85; mem. Assn. Women in Sci., L.A., 1978-83, 94, NSTA, 1985-88, Nat. Orgn. Broadcasting Engrs. and Technicians, 1978-80. Author: From Priestess to Physician, 1996; author, dir.: (video series) Women Physicists and Their Research, 1981, (video programs) Voyager: The Inside Story, 1982, Scientists in Space, 1983, Working Under Volcanos, 1984, Rendezvous with a Comet, 1985; author, illustrator: (book) From Sorceress to Scientist, 1990; webmaster The Hypatia Inst. Mem. Mus. of Tolerance, L.A., 1995-96. Mem. NOW, United Tchrs. L.A., Nat. Alliance of Breast Cancer Orgns., UCLA Alumni Assn. Democrat. Office: The Calif Video Inst PO Box 572019 Tarzana CA 91357-2019

NIESLUCHOWSKI, WITOLD S., cardiovascular and thoracic surgeon; b. Warsaw, Poland, Mar. 2, 1944; came to U.S., 1975; s. Stanislaw Leon and Izabela Anna (Swierczynska) N.; m. Bonnie Jean Thomas, Apr. 15, 1978; children: Jason Brian, Christopher Thomas, Megan Jean, Jennifer Anne. MD, Warsaw Med. Sch., 1967. With Akademicki Zwiazek Sportowy, Warsaw, 1961-75; cardiovascular surgeon Oxnard (Calif.) Hosp., 1975—. Mem. Oxnard Humanitarians, 1987—; bd. dirs. Am. Heart Assn., Camarillo, Calif., 1988—. Fellow ACS, Am. Coll. Cardiologists; mem. Soc. for Thoracic Surgeons. Club: Cabrillo Tennis (Camarillo). Office: 1700 N Rose Ave Ste 420 Oxnard CA 93030-7656

NIEVES, CARMEN, emergency services coordinator; b. Biddeford, Maine, Aug. 26, 1950; d. Roland E. and Yvette T. (Lessard) Therrien; m. Jose E. Nieves, June 27, 1987. Cert. mgmt., Riverside City Coll., 1996. Cert. emergency mgr. Police svcs. rep. Riverside (Calif.) Police, 1986-91, emer. svc. coord., 1991—. Adv. com. local gov., 1990-97; chair mgmt. adv. group City of Riverside, 1997—. Mem. Western Riverside Emer. Council (chair. 1993—), Emergency Mgrs. Assn. (chair 1997—), Calif. Emergency Svcs. Assn., Earthquake Survival Program. Office: Riverside Police 4102 Orange St Riverside CA 92501-3671

NIKLASON, LUCILLE VIOLA, retired psychologist, marriage & family therapist; b. Glenham, S.D., Aug. 7, 1929; d. Jonas Eugene and Dorothy Hanna (Schlomer) Beckman; m. Lowell T. Niklason, Mar. 23, 1950; children: Loren T., Michael L., Peggy J. Miller. BS, S.D. State U., 1951; MS, U. Utah, 1967, PhD, 1984. Cert. tchr., counselor and sch. psychologist, Utah; lic. marriage and family therapist, Utah. Substitute tchr. various pub. schs., Auburn, Wash., 1958-66; sch. psychologist Davis County Schs., 1968-83, 86-94, dir. placement in spl. edn., 1983-85; tchr. marriage classes Weber State U., Ogden, Utah, 1985; spkr. childrearing Young Women's Orgn., IRS, Ogden, 1994-97; presenter in field. Contbr. articles to profl. jours. Mem. Nat. Assn. Sch. Psychologists, Utah Assn. Sch. Psychologists (sec. 1981-84, del. to nat. orgn. 1983). Avocations: swimming, rafting, water color painting. Home: 1639 Oakcrest Dr Ogden UT 84403-3131

NIKU, SAEED BENJAMIN, engineering educator; b. Tehran, Iran, Jan. 4, 1953; came to U.S., 1975; s. Saleh and Sara (Broukhim) N.; m. Shohreh Soleiman Zadeh, July 5, 1987; children: Adam, Alan. BSME, Tehran Poly., 1975; MSME, Stanford U., 1976; PhD, U. Calif., Davis, 1982. Registered profl. engr., Calif. Design engr. Atomic Energy Orgn. of Iran, Tehran, 1976-77; sr. engr. Aliaf Co., Tehran, 1977-79; prof. engring. Calif. Poly. State U., San Luis Obispo, 1983—; rsch. engr. Mentor Corp., Santa Barbara, Calif., 1984 (summer), Naval Civil Engring. Lab. Port Hueneme, Calif., 1989-90 (summers). Mem. ASME, Am. Soc. Engring. Edn. Office: Calif Poly State Univ Dept Mech Engring San Luis Obispo CA 93407

NILLES, DARRELL LERAD, artist, inventor, architect; b. Madison, Wis., Nov. 30, 1957; s. Fred and Agnes Nilles. BArch., U. Minn., 1981. Architect LKA Ptnrs., Colorado Springs, Colo., 1983-86; architect, designer Wolff Lang Christopher, Rancho Cucamonga, Calif., 1986-89, Hill Pinkert, Irvine, Calif., 1989, Wimberly Allison Tony Goo, Newport Beach, Calif., 1989-91; owner, artist, inventor Nilles Studios, Orange, Calif., 1991-95; architect, curator art exhibits RTKL Internat., L.A., 1994-98; owner, artist LeRad Studios, L.A., 1995—; student project juror U. Calif., Fullerton, 1993-94; guest art exhibit curator L.A. Art Assn., 1998. Exhibited in shows at L.A. Art Assn., 1991, Fine Arts Inst., San Bernardino County Mus., Redlands, Calif., 1993, Irvine (Calif.) Fine Art Ctr., 1994, numerous others. Mem. Internat. Sculpture Ctr., L.A. Contemporary Exhbns. Avocations: tennis, hiking, biking, swimming.

NILLES, JOHN MATHIAS (JACK NILLES), futurist; b. Evanston, Ill., Aug. 25, 1932; s. Elmer Edward and Hazel Evelyn Nilles; m. Laila Padorr, July 8, 1957. BA magna cum laude, Lawrence Coll., 1954; MS in Engring., UCLA, Los Angeles, 1964. Sr. engr. Raytheon Mfg. Co., Santa Barbara, Calif., 1956-58; section head. Ramo-Woodridge Corp., L.A., 1958-59; project engr. Space Technology Lab., L.A., 1960; dir. The Aerospace Corp., L.A., 1961-67; sr. systems engr. TRW Systems, L.A., 1967-69; assoc. group dir. The Aerospace Corp., L.A., 1969-72; dir. interdisciplinary programs U. So. Calif., L.A., 1972-81, dir. info. technology program, 1981-89; pres. JALA Internat. Inc., L.A., 1980—; coord. EC Telework Forum, Madrid, 1992—; dir. Telecommuting Adv. Coun., L.A., 1991-97, pres., 1993-94; chmn. Telecommuting Rsch. Inst., Inc., L.A., 1990—. Author: The Telecommunications Transportation Tradeoff, 1976, Japanese edit., 1977, Exploring the World of the Personal Computer, 1982, French edit., 1985, Micros and Modems, 1983, French edit., 1986, Making Telecommuting Happen, 1994, Portuguese edit., 1997, Managing Telework, 1998. Capt. USAF, 1954-56. Recipient Rod Rose award Soc. Rsch. Adminstrs., 1976, Environ. Pride award L.A. Mag., 1993, Environ. Achievement award Renew Am., 1994-96, Commendation, L.A. County Bd. Suprs., 1997; inducted into Telework Hall of Fame, 1998. Mem. IEEE, IEEE Computer Soc., AAAS, Assn. Computing Machinery, Inst. Ops. Rsch. and Mgmt. Scis., World Future Soc., Calif. Yacht Club. Avocations: sailing, photography. E-mail: jnilles@jala.com. Office: JALA Internat Inc 971 Stonehill Ln Los Angeles CA 90049-1412

NING, XUE-HAN (HSUEH-HAN NING), physiologist, researcher; b. Peng-Lai, Shandong, People's Republic of China, Apr. 15, 1936; came to U.S., 1984; s. Yi-Xing and Liu Ning; m. Jian-Xin Fan, May 28, 1967; 1 child, Di Fan. *Grandfather Xi-Quan was a doctor of traditional Chinese medicine and master of Si-Nai-Tang (the meaning is "seek truth from facts") Chinese Pharmacy. Father Yi-Xing was the general manager of Li-Hua Textile Mill, Tsingdao, China. Wife Jian-Xin Fan, MD Shanghai First Medical College, 1960. She is an emeritus doctor and associate research professor in Shanghai Research Institute of Sports Science. She was a research scientist in the Research and Training Group of high jumper Zhu Jian-Hua, who broke the world record 3 times. Daughter Di Fan is the manager,administration of GE FanucAutomation Shanghai JV.* MD, Shanghai 1st Med. Coll., People's Republic of China, 1960. Rsch. fellow Shanghai Inst. Physiology, 1960-72, leader cardiovasc. rsch. group, 1973-83, head, assoc. prof. cardiovasc. rsch. unit, 1984-87, prof. and chair hypoxia dept., 1988-90, vice chairperson academic com., 1988-90; NIH internat. rsch. fellow U. Mich., Ann Arbor, 1984-87, vis. prof., hon. prof., rsch. investigator, 1990-95; prof. and dir. Hypoxia Physiology Lab. Academia Sinica, Shanghai, 1989—; acting leader, High Altitude Physiology Group, Chinese mountaineering and sci. expdn. team to Mt. Everest, 1975; leader High Altitude Physiology Group, Dept. Metall. Industry of China and Ry. Engring. Corps, 1979; vis. prof. dept. physiology Mich. State U., East Lansing, 1989-90; vis. prof. dcpt. pediat. U. Wash., Seattle, 1994-97; affiliate prof., rsch. scientist Children's Hosp. and Regional Med. Ctr., Seattle, 1997—. *As acting leader of the physiological group in the Chinese Mountaineering Team in 1975, he and his colleagues became the first in the world to succeed in taking electrocardiograms of mountaineers who had reached heights of 7600 meters, 8200 meters, 8680 meters, and the summit from sea level. They also demonstrated the relationship between cardiac function and high altitude performance. Over 39 years cardiovascular research, specially refer to hypoxia and ischemia, recently he has demonstrated that a temperature threshold exists in the myocardial protection, and that the threshold-temperature preserves function and signaling for mitochondrial biogenesis during subsequent ischemia.* Author: High Altitude Physiology and Medicine, 1981, Reports on Scientific Expedition to Mt. Qomolungma, High Altitude Physiology, 1980, Environment and Ecology of Qinghai-Xizang (Tibet) Plateau, 1982; mem. editl. bd. Chinese Jour. Applied Physiology, 1984—, Acta Physiologica, 1988—; contbr. articles to profl. jours. Recipient Merit award Shanghai Sci. Congress, 1977, All-China Sci. Congress, Beijing, 1978, Super Class award Academia Sinica, Beijing, 1986, 1st Class award Nat. Natural Scis., Beijing, 1987, # 1 Best Article award Tzu-Chi Med. Jour., Taiwan, 1995. Mem. Am. Physiol. Soc., Internat. Soc. Heart Rsch., Royal Soc. Medicine, Shanghai Assn. Physiol. (bd. dirs. 1988—), Chinese Assn. Physiol. (com. applied physiology 1984—, com. blood, cardiovascular, respiratory and renal physiology 1988—), Chinese Soc. Medicine, Chinese Soc. Biomed. Engring. Achievements include research in predictive evaluation of mountaineering performance, paradox phenomenon of cardiac pump function injury after climbing or giving oxygen, blood flow-metabolism-function relationship of heart during hypoxia and ischemia, effect of medicinal herbs on cardiac performance, cardiovascular adaptation and resistance to hypoxia and ischemia, Hypothermic adaptation protects heart from subsequent ischemia; the critical temperature 30 degrees celsius for modulating myocardial metabolism to resist ischemia, first electrocardiograph recording at summit of Mt. Everest. Home: 7033 43rd Ave NE Seattle WA 98115-6015 Office: U Wash Dept Pediatrics Box 356320 1959 NE Pacific St Seattle WA 98195-0001

NINNEMANN, JOHN LOUIS, biology educator, college dean; b. Chgo., June 10, 1944; s. Milton Carl and Bernice Helen (Sharp) N.; m. Laura Lorayne Danielson, June 30, 1979; children: Scot John, Kristi Marie. BA, St. Olaf Coll., 1966; MS, N.D. State U., 1968; PhD, Colo. State U., 1971. Asst. prof. microbiology Weber State Coll., Ogden, Utah, 1971-73; postdoctoral rsch. fellow Sloan-Kettering Inst. for Cancer Rsch., N.Y.C., 1973-75; asst. prof. surgery U. Calif., San Diego, 1975-80, assoc. adj. prof., 1984-88; assoc. prof. surgery U. Utah, Salt Lake City, 1980-84; assoc. prof. biology Adams State Coll., Alamosa, Colo., 1988-92, prof., chmn. dept. biology, 1992-94, dean, prof., 1994-98; dean Coll. Scis., prof. biol. scis. Ctrl. Wash. U., Ellensburg, 1998—. Editor: The Immune Consequences of Thermal Injury, 1981, Traumatic Injury: Infection and Other Immunologic Sequelae, 1983, Prostaglandins, Leukotrienes, and the Immune Response, 1988, (with E. Faist and D.R. Green) Immune Consequences of Trauma, Shock, and Sepsis: Mechanisms and Therapeutic Approaches, 1989; contbr. chpt. to: Current Topics in Burn Care, 1983, The Nature, Cellular and Biochemical Basis and Management of Immunodeficiencies, 1987, Basic Research and Clinical Aspects of Pseudomonas Aeruginosa, 1987, Lipid Mediators in the Immunology of Shock, 1987; (with others) Organ Preservation for Transplantation, 1981, Principles of Organ Transplantation, 1989; contbr. numerous articles to sci. jours. Bd. dirs. Univ. Press Colo., 1990; mem. Coun. Colls. of Arts and Scis., 1994—. Faculty Devel. award NSF, 1971-72, Rsch. Career Devel. award NIH, 1975-80, Pres.'s Continuing Edn. award Am. Burn Assn., 1986-87. Mem. Am. Soc. Microbiology, Am. Assn. Immunologists, Transplantation Soc., N.Y. Acad. Scis., So. Utah Wilderness Alliance, Sierra Club, Sigma Xi, Beta Beta Beta. Democrat. Presbyterian. Avocations: black and white photography, playing violin. Office: Dean Coll of the Scis Ctrl Wash Univ 400 E 8th Ave Ellensburg WA 98926

NINNEMANN, THOMAS GEORGE, broadcast educator; b. Chgo., Apr. 13, 1950; s. Milton Charles and Bernice Helen (Sharp) N.; m. Nancy Gail Rogers, Aug. 12, 1972; children: Stephanie Christine, Peter Christopher. BA, U. No. Colo., 1972. Dir. news. Sta. KGLN, Glenwood Springs, Colo., 1972-73; program mgr. Sta. KKEP, Estes Park, Colo., 1973-74; ops. mgr. Sta. WMST-AM-FM, Mt. Sterling, Ky., 1974-75; dir. news Sta. KPIK-AM-FM, Colorado Springs, Colo., 1975-77; news stringer AP, UPI, various stas., Colorado Springs, Colo., 1977-78; mgr. driver edn., safety dept. Am. Automobile Assn., Denver, 1978-81; pres. mkt. rschr. Rampart

Range Broadcasting Inc., Castle Rock, Colo., 1981-83; news editor Sta. KDEN, Denver, 1983-84; dir. news Stas. KSGT and KMTN-FM, Jackson, Wyo., 1984-94; instr. TV/prodr. dist. TV programming Teton County Sch. Dist., Jackson, 1989—; panelist Yellowstone Fire Rev., Yellowstone Nat. Pk., 1989; contract spokesperson on fire safety Bridger-Teton Nat. Forest, Jackson, 1990-97; seasonal pub. affairs specialist Grand Teton Nat. Park, summers 1995—. Asst. scoutmaster, then scoutmaster Boy Scouts Am., Castle Rock, Colo., 1979-84, mem. dist. com., 1984-93; vice chair Teton County Centennial Com., Jackson, 1989; co-founder, mgr. Jackson Hole Cmty. Band, 1989—; charter mem., mem. coun. Shepherd of the Mountains Luth. Ch.; active Jackson Hole Brass Quintet, 1985—; mem. local com. Christian Ministry in Nat. Parks, 1988-96; mem. pub. adv. com. Wyo. Pub. Radio, 1990—; com. mem. Jackson divsn. Am. Heart Assn., 1994-95. Recipient Tony Bevinette Friend of Wyo. Tourism award Wyo. Travel Commn., 1993, Bronze Smokey award U.S. Forest Svc., 1998; co-recipient Wyo. News Station of Yr. award AP, 1990; named Colo. Broadcast Newsman of Yr. AP, 1976. Avocations: instrumental music, camping, furniture refinishing, local history. Home: PO Box 1050 Jackson WY 83001-1050 Office: Jackson Hole HS PO Box 568 Jackson WY 83001-0568

NINOS, NICHOLAS PETER, retired career officer, physician; b. Chgo., May 11, 1936; s. Peter Spiros and Ann (Lesczynsky) N. BA in Art, Bradley U., 1958, BS in Chemistry, 1959; MD, U. Ill., Chgo., 1963. Diplomate Am. Bd. Internal Med., Am. Bd. Cardiology, Am. Bd. Critical Care Medicne. Intern Cook County Hosp., Chgo., 1963-64, resident in internal medicine, 1964-67, fellow in cardiology, 1967-68; commd. capt. U.S. Army, 1968, advanced through grades to col., 1979; chief dept. medicine U.S. Army Community Hosp. U.S. Army, Bremerhaven, Fed. Republic Germany, 1968-69, Wurzberg, Fed. Republic Germany, 1969-72; chief critical care Letterman Army Med. Ctr., San Francisco, 1976-91; dep. comdr. San Francisco med. command Letterman Army Med. Ctr./Naval Hosp. of Oakland, San Francisco and Oakland, Calif., 1988-90; ret., 1991; assoc. prof. medicine and surgery Uniformed Svcs. U. Health Scis., Bethesda, Md., 1981-91; critical care medicine cons. to U.S. Army Surgeon Gen., 1981-91; lectr. in field. Author: (jour.) Ethics, 1988; co-editor: Nutrition, 1988, Problems in Critical Care, Nutrition Support; mem. editl. bd. Jour. Critical Care Medicine, 1988-91; illustrator: Medical Decision Making, 1988. 2d v.p. Twin Springs Condominium Homeowners Assn., Palm Springs, Calif., 1993-94, sec., 1994-96; ch. bd. councilman St. George Orthodox Ch. of the Desert, Palm Desert, Calif., 1993-95; active Palm Springs Comm., 1993—; bd. dirs. Mizell Sr. Ctr., Palm Springs, 1996—, 1st v.p., 1997—. Decorated Legion of Merit, Meritorious Svc. medal with oak leaf cluster. Fellow Am. Coll. Critical Care Medicine (mem. bd. regents 1989-94, chmn. 1989-91); mem. AMA, Soc. Critical Care Medicine (pres. uniformed svcs. sect. 1987-90, Shubin/Weil award 1988), Soc. Med. Cons. to Armed Forces (assoc.), Inst. Critical Care Medicine (exec. v.p. 1991-92), Toastmasters Internat. (sec.-treas. Palm Springs chpt. 1993-94, pres. 1994, gov. area D-3 1994-95, divsn. D dist. 12 gov. 1995-96, spkrs. bur. dist. 12 1994-96). Avocations: art, skiing, jogging, traveling, music.

NISH, ALBERT RAYMOND, JR., retired newspaper editor; b. San Bernardino, Calif., Mar. 16, 1922; s. Albert Raymond and Mabel Claire (Shay) N.; m. Lois Maxine Ringgenberg, June 21, 1942; children: Steven Raymond, Richard Henry, Kathleen Lorie Jenner. Student San Bernardino Valley Jr. Coll., 1939-41, U. Calif., Berkeley, 1941-42, Wash. State Coll., 1943; Am. Press Inst., 1977. Pony wire editor AP, San Francisco, 1941-42; reporter Chico Record, Calif., 1945-46, Berkeley Daily Gazette, Calif., 1946-48; valley editor Modesto Bee, Calif., 1948-60, asst. mng. editor, 1960-62, mng. editor, 1962-85. Served as fighter pilot USAAC, 1942-45, PTO. Decorated DFC.

NISHIMOTO, MARC MAKOTO, research chemist; b. Wailuku, Hawaii, Apr. 2, 1959; s. Sadao and Asaye (Flores) N.; m. Dina Sachie Shinozuka, Feb. 19, 1988; children: Eric Keith, Gregory Jordan. BS in Chemistry, Seattle U., 1981; MS in Chemistry, U. Wash., 1983, PhD in Chemistry, 1986. Teaching asst. U. Wash., Seattle, 1981-83; postdoctoral fellow Oreg. State U., Corvallis, 1987-88; chemist Nat. Marine Fisheries Svc., Seattle, 1983-87, rsch. chemist, 1988-94; chemist Maui Pineapple Co., Kahului, Hawaii, 1994-95, product safety officer, 1995-96, R&D coord., 1996-97, dept. head, 1997—; reviewer fellowship com. Soc. Environ. Toxicology and Chemistry, 1991—. Contbr. articles to sci. publs.; reviewer Ctr. Indoor Air Rsch. Recipient Outstanding Performance award Nat. Marine Fisheries Svc., 1984, Superior Performance award, 1985, Cert. of Merit, 1990, New Investigator award Air Force Office Sci. Rsch. and Soc. Environ. Toxicology and Chemistry, 1990. Mem. Am. Chem. Soc., Inst. Food Tech., Alpha Sigma Nu. Achievements include research in metabolism of xenobiotics in marine organisms, structure of major DNA adduct formed by fish liver enzymes using chromatography and low temperature fluorescence spectroscopy, level of oxidative DNA damage in marine organisms undergoing oxidative stress, changes in glutathione homeostasis in liver of fish exposed to pro-oxidant chemicals, exposure of fish to xenobiotics. Office: Maui Pineapple Co 120 Kane St Kahului HI 96732

NISHIOKA, GARY JIM, facial plastic surgeon; b. Hood River, Oreg., Oct. 23, 1955; s. Jim Zenshi and Michi (Miwa) N.; m. Linda Thornton, May 22, 1982; 1 child, Ryder. BS in Biology, U. Oreg., 1978; DMD, Oreg. Health Sci. U., 1982; MD, U. Tex. Health Sci. Ctr., 1990. Diplomate Am. Bd. Oral and Maxillofacial Surgery. Resident in hosp. dentistry Oreg. Health Svc. U., Portland, 1982-83; intern in anesthesiology U. Tex. Health Sci. Ctr., San Antonio, 1982-86, resident, 1984-87; intern in gen. surgery U. Mo., Columbia, 1990-91, resident in otolaryngology, 1991-95; fellow in facial plastic and reconstructive surgery Seattle, 1995—. Contbr. articles to profl. jours. Fellow Am. Bd. Otolaryngology; mem. Am. Acad. Facial Plastic and Reconstructive Surgery, Am. Acad. Otolaryngology-Head and Neck Surgery. Roman Catholic. Avocations: collecting Japanese swords, skiing, martial arts, travel. Office: 600 Broadway Ste 280 Seattle WA 98122-5371

NISHIOKA, TERUO (TED NISHIOKA), electrical engineer; b. Crystal City, Tex., Sept. 6, 1945; s. Kazuto Benjamin and Kofumi (Shinkawa) N.; m. Suzanne Nayeko Hayashi, June 24, 1978; 1 child, Stephanie. BSEE, Calif. State Poly. U., 1970. Engr. Salt River Project, Phoenix, 1970-72, Pacific Gas and Electric, San Francisco, 1972-74; power plant engr. Wismer and Becker, Sacramento, 1975-78; sr. elec. engr. Ariz. Pub. Svc., Phoenix, 1978—. Author: Underground Cable Thermal Backfill, 1981. Active Japanese-Am. Citizens League, Phoenix, 1978—, bd. dirs. 1991—; v.p. Ariz. Buddhist Ch., Phoenix, 1987-88, pres., 1989-91; mem. Matsuri steering com., 1992—. With U.S. Army, 1966-68. Mem. IEEE, Power Engring. Soc., Elec. Insulation Soc. Avocations: hunting, jogging, swimming, dancing, tennis. Office: Ariz Pub Svc PO Box 53999 Phoenix AZ 85072-3999

NISHITANI, MARTHA, dancer; b. Seattle, Feb. 27, 1920; d. Denjiro and Jin (Aoto) N. B.A. in Comparative Arts, U. Wash., 1958; studied with, Eleanor King, Mary Ann Wells, Perry Mansfield, Cornish Sch., Conn. Coll. Sch. Dance, Long Beach State U. Founder, dir. Martha Nishitani Modern Dance Sch. and Co., Seattle, 1950—; dance dir. Helen Bush Sch. and Central YWCA, 1951-54; choreographer U. Wash. Opera Theater, 1955-65, Intiman Theater, 1972—; dance instr. Elementary and Secondary Edn. Act Program, 1966; dance specialist spl. edn. program Shoreline Pub. Schs., 1970-72; condr. workshops and concerts King County Youth Correctional Instns., 1972-73; Dance adv. counsel Wash. Cultural Enrichment Program; dance adv. bd. Seattle Parks and Recreation. Dancer Eleanor King Co., Seattle, 1946-50, dance films, 1946-51, Channel 9, Ednl. TV, 1967-68; lectr. demonstrator numerous colls., festivals, convs., childrens theater.; author articles on dance; one of the subjects: A Celebration of 100 Years of Dance in Washington, 1989. Trustee Allied Arts Seattle, 1967. Recipient Theta Sigma Phi Matrix Table award, 1968, Asian Am. Living Treasure award Northwest Asian Am. Theater, 1984; listed Dance Archives, N.Y.C. Libr., 1991, N.Y.C. Lincoln Ctr. Dance Archives, 1991, U. Wash. Libr. Archives, 1993, exhibit of Japanese Am. Women of Achievement, Burke Mus., 1997, 46th Anniversary of Martha Nishitani Modern Dance Sch.; selected for DENSHO-the [illegible] 1961-63), Com. Research in Dance, Seattle Art Mus., Internat. Dance Alliance (adv. council 1984), Smithsonian Assos., Progressive Animal Welfare Soc. Address: 4205 University Way NE PO Box 45264 Seattle WA 98145-0264

NISKANEN, PAUL MCCORD, travel company executive; b. Bend, Oreg., July 6, 1943; s. William Arthur and Nina Elizabeth (McCord) N.; m. Christine Campbell; 1 son, Tapio. Student U. Freiburg, Germany, 1963-64; BA, Stanford U., 1965; MBA, U. Chgo., 1966. Fin. analyst Kimberly-Clark Corp., Neenah, Wis., 1966-68; bus. mgr. Avent Inc. subs. Kimberly-Clark Corp., Tucson, 1968-70; v.p., gen. mgr. Pacific Trailways Bus. Line, Portland, Oreg., 1970-81; chmn. bd., owner Niskanen & Jones, Inc., Moab, Utah, 1982—, Perspectives, Inc., Portland; co-owner Cruise Masters, Beaverton, Oreg., 1989—. Apptd. consul for Finland, 1980—; active Gov.'s Travel Adv. Com., Salem, Oreg., 1976-81; 1st pres. Oreg. Hospitality and Visitors Assn., Portland, 1977-78; bd. dirs. Suomi Coll., Hancock, Mich., 1981—; nat. co-chmn. Dole for Pres. Com., 1987; co-chmn. Vistory 88; mem. adv. bd. Cunard Line, 1996-98. Decorated knight 1st Class Order White Rose Republic of Finland. Mem. Scandinavian Heritage Found. (bd. dirs. 1984). Republican. Home: 4366 SW Hewett Blvd Portland OR 97221-3107 Office: Cruise Masters 2730 SW Cedar Hills Blvd Beaverton OR 97005-1355

NISSEL, MARTIN, radiologist, consultant; b. N.Y.C., July 29, 1921; s. Samuel David and Etta Rebecca (Ostrie) N.; m. Beatrice Goldberg, Dec. 26, 1943; children: Philippa Lyn, Jeremy Michael. BA, NYU, 1941; MD, N.Y. Med. Coll., 1944. Diplomate Am. Bd. Radiology. Intern Met. Hosp., N.Y.C., 1944-45, Lincoln Hosp., N.Y.C., 1947-48; resident in radiology Bronx Hosp., 1948-50, attending radiologist, 1952-54; resident in radiotherapy Montefiore Hosp., Bronx, 1950-51, attending radiotherapist, 1954-65; attending radiologist Buffalo (N.Y.) VA Hosp., 1951-52; attending radiotherapist Univ. Hosp. Boston City Hosp., 1965-69; asst. prof. radiology Boston U. Sch. of Medicine, 1965-69; chief radiotherapist,dir. radiation ctr. Brookside Hosp., San Pablo, Calif., 1969-77; group leader, radiopharm. drugs FDA, Rockville, Md., 1977-86; pvt. cons. radiopharm. drug devel., 1986—. Contbr. articles to profl. jours. Lectr. Am. Cancer Soc., Contra Costa County, Calif., 1973-76. Capt. MC AUS, 1945-47, Korea. Recipient Contra Costa County Speakers Bur. award Am. Cancer Soc., 1973, 76, Responsible Person for Radiol. Health Program for Radiopharm. Drugs award FDA, 1980-86. Mem. Am. Coll. Radiology, Radiol. Soc. N.Am. Avocations; photography, model train building, travel. Office: PO Box 5537 Eugene OR 97405-0537

NISSENSON, ALLEN RICHARD, physician, educator; b. Chgo., Dec. 10, 1946; s. Harry and Sylvia Lillian (Chapnitsky) N.; m. Charna H. Karp, May 28, 1978; 1 child, Ariel Rose. BS in Medicine, Northwestern U., 1967, MD, 1971. Diplomate Am. Bd. Internal Medicine, bd. cert. internal medicine and nephrology. Intern in medicine Michael Reese Hosp. and Med. Ctr., Chgo., 1971-72, resident in internal medicine, 1972-74; fellowship in nephrology Northwestern U., Chgo., 1974-76; assoc. medicine Northwestern U. Med. Sch., Chgo., 1976-77; asst. prof. medicine UCLA Sch. Medicine, 1977-82, assoc. prof. medicine, 1982-88, prof. medicine, 1988—; dir. dialysis program UCLA Ctr. for the Health Scis., 1977—, med. dir. renal mgmt. strategies; adj. attending physician Northwestern Meml. Hosp., Chgo., 1976-77; asst. attending physician UCLA Ctr. for Health Scis., 1977-82, assoc. attending physician, 1988—; attending physician nephrology Wadsworth VA Hosp., 1978—; cons. on peritoneal dialysis Baxter-Travenol Labs., 1981—; mem. nephrology adv. com. Nephrology Nursing Edn. Grant, Calif. State U., 1983-90; vice chmn. Forum of End Stage Renal Disease Networks, 1988-91; mem. sci. adv. bd. Nat. Kidney Found., 1989-91, chmn. coun. on clin. nephrology, dialysis and transplantation, 1989-91; cons. on End Stage Renal Disease reimbursement Rand Corp., 1990—, others. Editor-in-chief Advances in Renal Replacement Therapy, 1993—; mem. editl. bd. Dialysis and Transplantation, 1978—, UCLA Health Insights, 1981-89, Perspectives in Peritoneal Dialysis, 1983—, Internat. Jour. Artificial Organs, 1984—, Seminars in Dialysis, 1987—, Am. Jour. Nephrology, 1989—, Am. Jour. Kidney Diseases, 1989—, Geriat. Nephrology and Urology Jour., 1989—; mem. editl. adv. bd. Contemporary Dialysis, 1983—, Nephrology Practice Today, 1989—, Hematopoietic Therapy Index and Revs., 1993—, Primary Care Reports, 1994—; editl. cons. Am. Jour. Nephrology, 1981-88; contbr. chpts. to books, abstracts and articles to profl. publs. Recipient Nat. Kidney Found. So. Calif. Cmty. Svc. award, 1981; Robert Wood Johnson policy fellow Office of Sen. Paul Wellstone, 1994-95. Fellow ACP; mem. Am. Soc. for Artifical Internal Organs, Am. Fedn. for Clin. Rsch., Am. Soc. Nephrology, Internat. Soc. Nephrology, Internat. Soc. Artificial Organs, Western Soc. for Clin. Investigation, European Dialysis and Transplant Assn., N.Am. Soc. for Dialysis and Transplantation, Renal Physicians' Assn. (bd. dirs. 1993—, sec. bd. dirs. 1994—), Calif. Renal Physicians (bd. dirs. 1987—). Office: UCLA Med Ctr Dialysis Ctr Ste 565-59 200 Medical Plaza Los Angeles CA 90024-6945

NISSINEN, MIKKO PEKKA, dancer; b. Helsinki, Finland, Mar. 4, 1962; came to U.S., 1987; s. Pekka and Pirkko (Pulkkinen) N. Grad., Finnish Nat. Ballet Sch., 1977; postgrad., Leningrad Acad. Ballet Sch., 1979-80. Mem. corps de ballet Finnish Nat. Ballet, Helsinki, 1977-79, soloist, 1980-82; grand sujete Dutch Nat. Ballet, Amsterdam, The Netherlands, 1982-84; soloist Basel (Switzerland) Ballet, 1984-87; soloist San Francisco Ballet, 1987-88, prin. dancer, 1988-96; artistic dir. Marin Ballet, 1996-97, Alberta Ballet, Calgary, Can., 1998—; guest artist La Bayadere, Nat. Ballet Can., 1989, Oberlin Dance Collective, 1993; advisor to sch. dir. Nat. Ballet Sch., Toronto, Ont., Can., 1992; bd. dirs. Le Don Des Etoiles, 1989—; guest tchr. Royal Acad. of Dancing, 1993, Kennedy Ctr. Ednl. Program, 1994, Nat. Ballet Sch., Toronto, 1994; lectr. on dance history and state of dance today Stanord U., St. Mary's Coll., Christensen Soc. Repertoire as dancer includes (with San Francisco Ballet) The Sleeping Beauty, Swan Lake, Bizet Pas de Deux, Handel-a Celebration, Haffner Symphony, Con Brio, Ballet d'Isoline, Giuliani: Variations on a Theme, Tchaikovsky Pas de Deux, Symphony in C, Theme and Variations, Ballo della Regina, The Nutcracker, Airs de Ballet, Variations de Ballet, Rodin, Rodeo, Maelstrom, Dark Elegies, Harvest Moon, Napoli, Job, The Wanderer Fantasy, In the middle, somewhat elevated, Calcium Light Night, Le Corsaire Pas de Deux, Dreams of Harmony, Pulcinella, The Dream; (with other cos.) Don Quixote, Giselle, A Midsummer Night's Dream, Les Biches, Sleeping Beauty, Pyrrich Dances, Masse, Le Tombeau de Couperin, Symphony in C, The Four Temperaments, The Prodigal Son, Rodin, Pierrot Lunaire, La Fille mal gardée, Swan Lake, Henze, Five Tangos, In and Out, Bits and Pieces, Jeu de Cartes; appeared in the Canadian Internat. Ballet Gala, 1989, 90, 91, 92, 93, 94, 95, Reykjavik Arts Festival, 1990, Internat. Ballet Gala, Kuodio, Finland, 1992, Internat. Ballet Gala, Vail, Colo., 1993, Night of Stars Ballet Gala, Helsinki, 1993; profiled in nat. and internat. radio and TV programs, including CNN Worldwide Report, 1992; featured on cover of Dance Mag., 1992; choreographer Full Evening Nutcracker, 1996. Recipient 1st prize 1st Nat. Dance Competition Kuopio, Finland, 1978. Office: Nat Cristie Ctr, 141-18th Ave SW, Alberta, AB Canada T25 0B8

NITZ, FREDERIC WILLIAM, electronics company executive; b. St. Louis, June 22, 1943; s. Arthur Carl Paul and Dorothy Louise (Kahm) N.; m. Kathleen Sue Rapp, June 8, 1968; children: Frederic Theodore, Anna Louise. AS, Coll. Marin, 1970; BS in Electronics, Calif. Poly. State U., San Luis Obispo, 1972. Electronic engr. Sierra Electronics, Menlo Park, Calif., 1973-77, RCA, Somerville, N.J., 1977-79; engring. mgr. EGG-Geometrics, Sunnyvale, Calif., 1979-83; v.p. engring. Basic Measuring Insts., Foster City, Calif., 1983-91; exec. v.p. Reliable Power Meters, Los Gatos, Calif., 1991—; cons. in field, Boulder Creek, Calif., 1978—. Patentee in field. Bd. dirs. San Lorenzo Valley Water Dist., Boulder Creek, 1983—, Water Policy Task Force, Santa Cruz County, Calif., 1983-84. With U.S. Army, 1965-67. Democrat. Lutheran. Home: 24 Taryn Ct Scotts Valley CA 95066-3837 Office: Reliable Power Meters 400 Blossom Hill Rd Los Gatos CA 95032-4511

NIX, NANCY JEAN, librarian, designer; b. Denver; d. James Frederik and Josephine (Britt) N. AB in History, U. So. Calif., L.A., 1959, MLS, 1960. Exhibited in group shows including Iemoto Historical Flower Arrangement Exhibit, 1992, 97. Mem. guiding com. Art Assn. Egg and the Eye Gallery and Restaurant, 1973-76; participant Arts & Humanities Symposium, Palm Desert, Calif., 1974; patron cultural symposium L.A. Garden Club, 1975. Recipient Kakan Monpyo award Ikenobo Ikebana Soc. Floral Art, 1988. [illegible] Japanese Am. Citizens League (historian, exec. bd. L.A. Downtown chpt. 1990—, chpt. historian), Japanese Am. Nat. Mus. (charter), Japanese Am. Cultural and Cmty. Ctr, L.A. Nisei (Woman of Yr. Selection Com. 1990—). Republican. Jewish.

NIXON, ROBERT OBEY, SR., business educator; b. Pitts., Feb. 14, 1922; s. Frank Obey and Margurite (Van Buren) N.; m. Marilyn Cavanagh, Oct. 25, 1944 (dec. 1990); children: Nan Nixon Friend, Robert Obey, Jr., Dwight Cavanagh. BS in bus. adminstrn., U. Pitts., 1948; MS, Ohio State U., 1964; MBA, U. Phoenix, 1984. Commd. 2d lt. USAF, 1943, advanced through grades to col., 1970, master navigator WWII, Korea, Vietnam; sales, adminstrn. U.S. Rubber Corp., Pitts., 1940-41; asst. engr. Am. Bridge Corp., Pitts., 1941-42; underwriter, sales Penn Mutual Life Ins. Corp., Pitts., 1945-50; capt., nav. instr. USAF Reserves, 1945-50; ret. USAF Col., divsn. chief Joint Chiefs of Staff, 1973; educator, cons. U. Ariz., 1973-79; bus. dept. chmn., coord., founder weekend coll. Pima C.C., Tucson, 1979-90, prof. mgmt., 1991-98, coord. weekend coll. program, 1991—; adj. faculty Pima C.C., 1998—; founder, pres. Multiple Adv. Group ednl. cons., Tucson, 1978—. Author: Source Document: On Accelerated Courses and Programs at Accredited Two- and Four-Year Colleges and Universities, 1996; contbr. articles to profl. jours. Mem. Soc. Logistics Engrs. (sr., charter mem.), Phi Delta Theta. Presbyterian. Avocations: tennis, hiking, swimming. E-mail: eb58271@goodnet.com; bnixon@pimacc.pima.edu. Home: 1824 S Regina Cleri Dr Tucson AZ 85710-8664

NIZAMI, TARIQ AHMED, investment company executive; b. Karachi, Pakistan, Aug. 23, 1958; s. Zilley Ahmad and Birgis (Talat) N.; m. Yasmin Nizami, 1995. BS in Bus. Adminstrn., Calif. State U., L.A., 1981, MBA in Mktg., 1983. Product mgr. Cal Switch, Gardena, Calif., 1980-82; ops. mgr. Computer Valley, Walnut, Calif., 1982-84; prin., dir. Computerland, Diamond Bar, Calif., 1984—; pres. Ampak Investments, Brea, Calif.; CEO Pakistan Northern Ins. Co. Ltd. Recipient Gold medal U.S. Pres., 1989. Republican. Muslim. Avocations: computer games, exotic cars. Office: 3 Pine Dr Brea CA 92621-5541

NIZZE, JUDITH ANNE, retired physician assistant; b. L.A., Nov. 1, 1942; d. Robert George and Charlotte Ann (Wise) Swan; m. Norbert Adolph Otto Paul Nizze, Dec. 31, 1966. BA, UCLA, 1966, postgrad., 1966-76; grad. physician asst. tng. program, Charles R. Drew Sch. Postgrad., L.A., 1979; BS, Calif. State U., Dominguez, 1980. Cert. physician asst., Calif. Staff rsch. assoc. I-II Wadsworth Vet. Hosp., L.A., 1965-71; staff rsch. assoc. III-IV John Wayne Clinic Jonsson Comprehensive Cancer Ctr., UCLA, 1971-78; clin. asst. Robert S. Ozeran, Gardena, Calif., 1978; physician asst. family practice Fred Chasan, Torrance, Calif., 1980-82; sr. physician asst. Donald L. Morton prof., chief surg. oncology Jonsson Comprehensive Cancer Ctr., UCLA, 1983-91; administrv. dir. immunotherapy John Wayne Cancer Inst., Santa Monica, Calif., 1991-98; ret.; cons. cilin. rsch. orgn. devel. John Wayne Cancer Inst., 1998—. Contbr. articles to profl. jours. Fellow Am. Acad. Physician Assts., Am. Assn. Surgeons Assts., Calif. Acad. Physician Assts.; mem. AAUW, Assn. Physician Assts. in Oncology. Republican. Presbyterian. Avocations: sailing, tennis, skiing, photography, computers. Home: Ste J 13243 Fiji Way Marina Del Rey CA 90292-7079

NOBLE, LAWRENCE ALAN, artist; b. Tampa, Fla., Nov. 11, 1948; s. Clymer Marlay and Mary Alice (Cortes) N.; m. Elizabeth Wearden, May 22, 1982; children: Casey Josephine, John Marlay. Student, Tex. Acad. Art, 1969, Houston Mus. Fine Art Sch., 1974-75. Illustrator U.S. Army, Ft. Sheridan, Ill., 1970, San Francisco, 1971; staff artist, promotion dept. The Houston Chronicle, Houston, 1972; art dir., designer, illustrator Middaugh Assocs., Houston, 1973; freelance illustrator Noble Studio, Houston, 1973-88; designer, sculptor Noble Studio, Crestline, Calif., 1988—; sculptor, com. mem. San Bernardino County Peace Officers Meml. Com., San Bernardino, 1995—, designer sculptor Victor Salmones galleries, 1995—, sculptor, com. mem. Jack Benny Meml. Com., 1992-93, Ft. Sheridan Centennial Com., 1989-90. *L. Alan Noble, owner of Noble Studio, a 25-year-old company, specializes in design and sculpture. He was featured on the cover and in an article of "American Artist" magazine, March 1983. Noble Studio has sculpted a monument to Civil War General Philip H. Sheridan, and has designed the Star Wars Chess Set for the Danbury Mint. He produced a life-size bronze of actress Lillian Russell and the Car of the Year award for "Playboy" magazine. He also sculpted the Daytona 500 trophy. He is the designer and one of two sculptors selected to build a monument for California Firefighters. His wife, Elizabeth works with him at Noble Studio.* Sculptor, designer various art galleries. Hon. firefighter City of Redlands Fire Dept., 1997; marshall 4th July Parade Crestline Resorts C. of C., 1996, vol. McGovern for Pres., Dem. party, 1972. With U.S. Army, 1969-71. Recipient 4th U.S. Army Leadership and Integrity medal, 1986. Mem. Nat. Sculptors Soc., Internat. Sculpture Ctr., Calif. Profl. Firefighters, Star Wars Fan Club, Star Trek Fan Club. Republican. Roman Catholic. Avocations: surfing, reading, history. Office: Noble Studio PO Box 2229 Crestline CA 92325-2229

NOBLE, MARION ELLEN, retired home economist; b. Blanchardville, Wis., Feb. 18, 1914; d. Dwight Eldridge and Doris Edna (Parkinson) Baker; m. B. Frank Smyth (dec. 1979); children: William, Ann Smyth Marris, Robert, Larry, Margaret Smyth Decker; m. George C. Noble, 1981. BS, U. Wis., Madison, 1936. V.p. Smyth Bus Systems, Canton, Ohio, 1950; womens editor Radio Station WFAH, Alliance, Ohio, 1952-58; home economist extension svc. Stark County, Ohio State U., Canton, 1961-70. Contbr. articles to profl. jours. Named Woman of the Year Urban League, Canton, 1964. Mem. AAUW, Nat. Assn. Extension Home Economists, Pacific Pioneer Broadcasters, Home Econs. Club, Thimble Collectors Internat., Thimble Collectors San Diego, Ladies Oriental Shrine N.Am., Phi Upsilon Omicron, Epsilon Sigma Phi. Republican. Methodist. Avocations: needlework, collecting thimbles and antique sewing items. Home: 3240 San Amadeo Apt A Laguna Hills CA 92653-3037

NOBLE, PHILLIP D., lawyer; b. Oakland, Calif., Aug. 1, 1946. BA, AD in Bus., U. Wash., 1968, JD, 1971. Bar: Wash. 1971. Law clk. to Hon. Morell Sharp Wash. State Supreme Ct., 1971, U.S. Dist. Ct. (we. dist.) Wash., 1972; ptnr. Helsell, Fetterman LLP, Seattle, 1978—. Editor: Justice on Trial, 1971. Mem. ABA, Wash. State Bar Assn., Seattle-King County Bar Assn. Office: Helsell Fetterman LLP 1500 Puget Sound Plz PO Box 21846 Seattle WA 98111

NOBLE, RICHARD LLOYD, lawyer; b. Oklahoma City, Oct. 11, 1939; s. Samuel Lloyd and Eloise Joyce (Millard) N. AB with distinction, Stanford, 1961, LLB, 1964. Bar: Calif. 1964. Assoc. firm Cooper, White & Cooper, San Francisco, 1965-67; assoc., ptnr. firm Voegelin, Barton, Harris & Callister, Los Angeles, 1967-70; ptnr. Noble & Campbell, Los Angeles, San Francisco, 1970—; dir. Langdale Corp., L.A., Gt. Pacific Fin. Co., Sacramento; lectr. Tax Inst. U. So. Calif., 1970; mem. bd. law and bus. program Stanford Law Sch. Contbr. articles to legal jours. Bd. govs. St. Thomas Aquinas Coll. Recipient Hilmer Dehlman Jr. award Stanford Law Sch., 1962; Benjamin Harrison fellow Stanford U., 1967. Mem. ABA, State Bar Calif., L.A. Bar Assn., San Francisco Bar Assn., Commercial Club (San Francisco), Petroleum Club (L.A.), Capitol Hill Club (Washington), Pi Sigma Alpha. Republican. Home: 2222 Ave Of Stars Los Angeles CA 90067-5655 Office: Noble & Campbell 333 N Grand Ave Los Angeles CA 90012-2622

NOBLE, SUSAN ELVIRA, nurse; b. San Francisco, July 27, 1962; d. Brice Esker Noble and Teresita (Cui) Calixto. BSN, Humboldt State U., 1993. RN, Calif. Night supr., relief cmty. psychiat. ctrs. CPC Belmont (Calif.) Hills Hosp., 1993-95; clin. coord. psychiatry/Asian Focus Unit San Francisco Gen. Hosp., 1995-97; prin. adminstrv. analyst, coord. psychiat. utilization rev. U. Calif., San Francisco Gen. Hosp., 1997—. Republican. Roman Catholic. Office: San Francisco Gen Hosp Utilization Rev Psychiatry 1001 Potrero Ave Rm 7m3 San Francisco CA 94110-3594

NOBLIT, BETTY JEAN, publishing technician; b. St. Elmo, Ill., June 12, 1948; d. Clyde W. and Lucille M. (Haggard) N. Grad. in restaurant and club food mgmt., LaSalle U., 1973; grad., Am. Sch. Travel, 1975. Teletype puncher Sarasota (Fla.) Herald-Tribune, 1968-70, Pueblo Chieftain, 1970—; [illegible] personal corr. Prime Min. Indira Gandhi. Active Mahatma Gandhi Ctr. for Peace and Nonviolence, Pueblo, Colo. Mem. Nat. Geog. Soc., Colo. Hist. Soc., Gandhi Ctr. Peace and Nonviolence Pueblo. Home: 1 Cambridge Ave Apt 4B Pueblo CO 81005-2024

NOEBEL, DAVID ARTHUR, minister, educator; b. Oshkosh, Wis., Aug. 27, 1936; s. Arthur William and Dorothy Helen (Schaeffer) N.; m. Alice Maren Koch, Aug. 24, 1957; children: Brent David, Joy. BA, Hope Coll., 1959; postgrad., U. Wis., 1959-63; MA, U. Tulsa, 1971; LLD (hon.), Am. Christian Coll., Tulsa, 1974. Ordained to ministry Christian Ch., 1963. Pastor Grace Bible Ch., Madison, Wis., 1959-63, Christian Crusade Ch., Tulsa, 1963-71; v.p. Am. Christian Coll., Tulsa, 1971-74, pres., 1974-78; pres. Summit Ministries, Manitou Springs, Colo., 1978—. Author: The Marxist Minstrels, 1974, The Homosexual Revolution, 1977, Understanding the Times, 1991. Rep. candidate for Congress, Madison, 1962. Mem. Am. Philos. Assn., Assn. Christian Philosphers, Coun. Nat. Policy. Home: 111 Mohawk St Manitou Springs CO 80829-2007 Office: Summit Ministries PO Box 207 Manitou Springs CO 80829-0207

NOETH, LOUISE ANN, journalist; b. Evergreen Park, Ill., Nov. 17, 1954; d. Cy John and Alice Rose (Bobrovich) N.; m. Michael T. Lanigan, Aug. 29, 1992. Editor Petersen Pub. Co., Inc., Calif., 1980; assoc. pub., editor Autoscene Mag., Westlake Village, Calif., 1981; investigative editor Four Wheeler Mag., Canoga Park, Calif., 1982—; owner, founder Landspeed Prodns., 1984; automotive writer, columnist Press-Courier Newspaper, Oxnard, Calif., 1992-94, Ventura County Newspapers, 1994-95, L.A. Times, 1995; Car Craft Mag., 1994—; with EG&G, Inc., 1992; auto writer, columnist Ventura County Newspapers, 1994-95; adminstr. Spirit of Am. World Land Speed Record Team, 1996—; cons. Spirit Am. World Speed Record Team, Pontiac Motor divsn. Land Rover N.Am., others; mem. Green Mamba Racing Team, Reseda, Calif., 1978—, Sports Illustrated, Chgo. Tribune; graphic art commns. for Wallenius Lines, Harbortown Resort, Radisson Hotels, GTE, Ferro Corp., Nikon Profl. Svcs., Kodak Profl. Network, Forbes mag., SEA, Sailing. Author: Ventura County Destination Guide: Channel Islands Harbor Retrospect; editor: Hot Rod Performance and Custom, 1979; prodr.: Renewing Pride, Schoolroom in Paradise, Heritage Square; contbr. articles to numerous automotive mags.; photography exhibited at Ventura Village Art Gallery, 1994, Ventura County Mus. History and Art, 1991, Ventura County Nat. Bank, 1990, 92, Ventura County Fair, 1990 (spl. non-competition award profl. category), Internet Cafe, 1996—; represented in permanent collection Harbor Town Marina Resort Gallery. Mem. project R.A.F.T. Russians and Ams. for Teamwork, Buffalo Bill's West Show; mem. bd. dirs., pub. chair Carnegie Art Mus., 1995—. Recipient Moto award in investigative news category, Automotive Journalism Conference, 1983-84, 96, Silver Medallion feature writing mag., 1997, 98, pub. rels., 1996, photography, 1998. Mem. Tallship Californian Quarter deck Comm., Oxnard C. of C., Edn. Comm. Youth Edn. Motivation Program, Internat. Motor Press Assn. (sec. 1986—), Specialty Equipment Market Assn. (pub. relations com. 1983, suspension and tire com. 1984-85), Am. Auto Racing Writers and Broadcasters Assn.

NOGUCHI, HIDEO, insurance agency executive; b. Kyoto, Japan, Jan. 17, 1945; s. Tasao and Ishiko (Tsujii) N.; m. Eleanor Kazuko Horii, May 7, 1970; children: Mark H.Y., Mitchell H.Y. BBA, U. Hawaii, 1969. Buyer RCA Purchasing Co., Tokyo, 1969-73; ins. specialist Continental Ins. Agy., Honolulu, 1973-82; pres. Noguchi & Assocs., Inc., Honolulu, 1983—; cons. Recipient Nat. New Agt. Leadership award CNA Corp., 1974, Agt. of Yr. award Continental Ins. Agy., annually 1973-81, Key Club award CNA Co., 1975, 79-81. Mem. Nat. Assn. Life Underwriters, Honolulu Assn. Life Underwriters, Million Dollar Round Table, Internat. Platform Assn., Elks. Home: 3678 Woodlawn Terrace Pl Honolulu HI 96822-1475 Office: 1314 S King St Ste 560 Honolulu HI 96814-1978

NOKES, JOHN RICHARD, retired newspaper editor, author; b. Portland, Oreg., Feb. 23, 1915; s. James Abraham and Bernice Alfaretta (Bailey) N.; m. Evelyn Junkin, Sept. 13, 1936; children: Richard Gregory, William G., Gail (Mrs. William M. Hulden), Douglas J., Kathy E. B.S., Linfield Coll., 1936, LHD (hon.), 1988. With The Oregonian, Portland, 1936-82, city editor, 1950-65, asst. mng. editor, 1965-71, mng. editor, 1971-75, editor, 1975-82; disting. vis. prof. journalism Linfield Coll., 1982-85; cons. editor The Hong Kong Standard, 1994. Author: American Form of Government, 1939, Columbia's River: The Voyages of Robert Gray 1787-1793, 1991, Almost a Hero: The Voyages of John Meares to China, Hawaii and the Pacific Northwest, 1998; editor Oreg. Edn. Jour., 1944. Bd. dirs. Portland U.S.O., 1968-72, U.S. Coast Guard Acad. Found., 1972-74, Portland Opera Assn., 1976-78; trustee Linfield Coll., 1977-93; v.p. Oreg. UN Assn., 1983-85, chmn. Oreg. UN Day, 1983. Lt. (j.g.) USNR, 1944-46; comdr. Res. (ret.). Mem. Navy League U.S. (pres. Portland coun. 1969-71), Linfield Coll. Alumni Assn. (pres. 1940), World Affairs Coun. Oreg. (pres. 1973-74), AP Mng. Editors Assn. (dir. 1973-80), Am. Soc. Newspaper Editors, N.W. China Coun., Sigma Delta Chi (pres. Willamette Valley chpt. 1975-76). Republican. Methodist. Club: Multnomah Athletic (Portland). Home: 14650 SW 103rd Ave Tigard OR 97224-4740

NOLAN, BENJAMIN BURKE, retired civil engineer; b. Detroit, Oct. 6, 1931; s. Benjamin Augustus and Helen Louise (Boughey) N.; m. Katherine Mary Zeman, may 14, 1961. BSCE, U. Calif., Berkeley, 1958. Registered civil engr., Calif. City engr. City of Newport Beach, Calif., 1965-78, pub. works dir., 1978-94; mem. Orange County Transp. Authority, Calif., 1978-94, Transp. Corridor Agys., Orange County, 1984-94; active City Engrs. Assn., Orange County, 1965-94. With USAF, 1951-53, France. Mem. ASCE (life), Am. Pub. Works Assn. Achievements include participation in creation of Orange County Transp. Corridor Agys.; beach erosion solutions; hwy. and bridge constrn. and widening; coastal estuary restoration; harbor facilities and ocean pier improvements; water supply, sanitary sewerage, and storm drainage improvements; and publ. parks and bldgs. constrn. Home: 614 Hassett St Brookings OR 97415-8206

NOLAN, DAVID CHARLES, lawyer, mediator; b. San Mateo, Calif., Oct. 12, 1940; s. Clarence Charles and Leona Henrietta (Lindeman) N.; m. Cynthia Ann James, Feb. 20, 1971; children: Matthew, John, Scott. AB, Stanford U., 1962; JD, U. Calif., Berkeley, 1965. Bar: Calif. 1966, U.S. Ct. Appeals (9th cir.) 1971, U.S. Ct. Appeals (D.C. cir.) 1975, U.S. Dist. Ct. (no. dist.) Calif. 1969, U.S. Dist. Ct. (D.C. cir.) 1970, U.S. Tax Ct., U.S. Supreme Ct. 1972. Ptnr. Graham & James, San Francisco, 1968-93; sole practitioner Walnut Creek, Calif., 1993—. Bd. dirs., officer Family Homes for Retarded, Belmont, Calif., 1978-81; founding dir. Orinda (Calif.) Baseball Assn., 1982-86; commr. Diablo Valley Baseball League, Martinez, Calif., 1983-90. Lt. comdr. USCG, 1965-68. Mem. ABA, Calif. Bar Assn., Contra Costa County Bar Assn., No. Calif. Mediation Assn., Assn. Transp. Practitioners, Commonwealth Club, Maritime Law Assn., Order of Coif. Fax: 925-937-5442. Home: 12 E Altarinda Dr Orinda CA 94563-2406 Office: Ste 830 1990 N California Blvd Walnut Creek CA 94596-3840

NOLAN, JAMES MICHAEL, fire chief; b. Orlando, Fla., Sept. 30, 1943; s. James Douglas and Marjorie Kathleen (Rouse) N.; m. Patricia Ann Fenwick Nolan, Jan. 31, 1969; children: Michael Douglas, Teresa Kathleen. AA in Fire Sci., U. Alaska, 1977; exec. fire officer, Nat. Fire Acad., 1993. Hazardous Materials Incident Mgr. Fed. Emergency Mgmt. Agency. Computer technician KLM Office Machines, Anchorage, Alaska, 1969-73; firefighter Anchorage Fire Dept., 1973-76, fire apparatus engr., 1976-80, fire capt., 1980-84, sr. fire capt., 1984-86, battalion chief, tng., 1986-88, battalion chief, 1988, deputy chief, chief of ops., 1988-94, fire chief, 1994—; chmn. Anchorage Police & Fire Ret. Bd., 1982; mem. Anchorage Regional Fire Tng. Ctr. Bd., 1984-89; mem. State of Alaska Fire Svc. Tng. award Com., 1986-90; adj. instr. in Fire Sci. U. Alaska, Anchorage, 1982-85. Contbr. articles and photographs to book. Chmn. 457 Deferred Compensation Bd., Anchorage, 1995—; mem . Local Chpt. Am. Red Cross, 1995—; mem. Emergency Planning Commn., 1995, Environ. Quality Control Com., 1994—. Mem. Nat. Fire Protection Assn., Alaska State Fire Chiefs Assn., Internat. Assn. of Fire Chiefs, Anchorage Area Interagnecoy Emergency Mgmt. Assn. (pres. 1994—). Avocations: photography, scuba diving, fishing, shooting. Office: Anchorage Fire Dept 1301 E 80th Ave Anchorage AK 99518-3399*

NOLAN, MARK GREGORY, advertising executive; b. San Francisco, July 3, 1958; m. Robyn Lynn Nolan, June 7, 1980. Founder, chief exec. officer Mark Nolan & Assocs., Inc., Citrus Heights, Calif., 1981-87; v.p., ptnr. Nolan Mktg. Group Inc., Citrus Heights, 1987—; mktg. dir., ptnr. Fin. Mktg. Corp., Citrus Heights, 1989—; keynote speaker Marin Self-Pubs. Assn., Ross, Calif., 1986; featured speaker Community Entrepreneurs Assn., Sacramento, 1986, home-based bus. conf., 1991; treas. COSMEP, San Francisco, 1986-88; lectr. UCLA, 1987. Author: The Instant Marketing Plan, 1995; co-author: Health Secrets of the Rich and Famous, 1998, editor: Info. Mktg., 1985-87. Mem. Better Bus. Bur., Eagle Scouts. Mem. S.C. Publicists Assn., Community Entrepreneurs Assn., Internat. Assn. Self-Pubs. (treas. 1986-88), Com. of Small Mag. Editors and Pubs., C. of C., Turtles, Oregon Advt. Club, Entrepreneurs Am., Active 20-30 Club. Avocations: wine appreciation, classic automobiles. Office: Nolan Mktg Group Inc PO Box 2570 Fair Oaks CA 95628-9570

NOLAN, OWEN, professional hockey player; b. Belfast, Northern Ireland, Feb. 12, 1972. Selected 1st round NHL entry draft Que. Nordiques, 190, right wing, 1990-96; right wing San Jose Sharks, 1996—; named to OHL All-Star 1st team, 1989-90; played in NHL All-Star Game 1992, 96. Recipient Emms Family award, 1988-89, Jim Mahon Meml. Trophy, 1989-90. Office: care San Jose Sharks 525 W Santa Clara St San Jose CA 95113-1520*

NOLAN, WILLIAM FRANCIS, writer; b. Kansas City, Mo., Mar. 6, 1928; s. Michael Cahill and Bernadette Mariana (Kelly) N.; m. Cameron Nolan, Mar. 6, 1970. Student, Kansas City Art Inst., 1946-47, San Diego State Coll., 1947-48, Los Angeles City Coll., 1953; diploma in Sci. Fiction (hon.), Am. River Coll., 1975. Greeting card designer and cartoonist Hall Bros., Kansas City, Mo., 1945; outdoor mural painter San Diego, 1949-50; aircraft inspector Convair, San Diego, 1950-52; credit asst. Blake, Moffitt and Towne Paper Co., Los Angeles, 1953-54; employment Interviewer Calif. State Dept. Employment, Inglewood, 1954-56; freelance writer Calif., 1956—; managing editor Gamma mag., Los Angeles, 1963-64; lectr. colls., libraries, writing classes, 1963—; book reviewer Los Angeles Times, 1964-70. Author: Barney Oldfield, 1961, Phil Hill: Yankee Champion, 1962, Impact 20, 1963, Men of Thunder, 1964, John Huston: King Rebel, 1965, Sinners and Supermen, 1965, Death is for Losers, 1968, The White Cad Cross-Up, 1969, Dashiell Hammett: A Casebook, 1969, Space for Hire, 1971, Steve McQueen: Star on Wheels, 1972, Carnival of Speed, 1973, Hemingway: Last Days of the Lion, 1974, Alien Horizons, 1974, The Ray Bradbury Companion, 1975, Wonderworlds, 1977, Logan's World, 1977, Logan's Search, 1980, Hammett: A Life at the Edge, 1983, McQueen, 1984, Things Beyond Midnight, 1984, Look Out for Space, 1985, The Black Mask Boys, 1985, Max Brand Western Giant, 1986, Logan: A Trilogy, 1986, The Work of Charles Beaumont, 1986, Dark Encounters, 1986, Rio Renegades, 1989, How to Write Horror Fiction, 1990, Blood Sky, 1991, Helltracks, 1991, 3 for Space, 1992, Helle on Wheels, 1992, The Black Mask Murders, 1994, Night Shapes, 1995, The Marble Orchard, 1996, The Brothers Challis, 1996, Sharks Never Sleep, 1998, The Winchester Horror, 1999; co-author: (with John Fitch) Adventure on Wheels, 1959, (with George C. Johnson) Logan's Run, 1967, (with R. Reginald) The Work of William F. Nolan, 1988; editor the Ray Bradbury Review, 1952, Omnibus of Speed, 1958, When Engines Roar, 1964, The Pseudo-People, 1965, Man Against Tomorrow, 1965, 3 to the Highest Power, 1968, A Wilderness of Stars, 1969, The Future is Now, 1970, A Sea of Space, 1970, The Edge of Forever, 1971, The Human Equation, 1971, Science Fiction Origins, 1980, Max Brand's Best Western Stories, 1981, Max Brand's Best Western Stories II, 1985, Max Brand's Best Western Stories III, 1987, Urban Horrors, 1990, The Bradbury Chronicles, 1991, Tales of the Wild West, 1997, California Sorcery, 1999, More Tales of the Wild West, 1999; screenwriter: (with George C. Johnson) Logan's Run, 1976 (Best Sci. Fiction Film of Yr. Acad. Science Fiction, Fantasy and Horror), (with Dan Curtis) Burnt Offerings, 1976 (Best Horror Film of Yr. Acad. Sci. Fiction, Fantasy and Horror); teleplays (TV) Brain Wave, 1959, Vanishing Act, 1959, Black Belt, 1960, The Joy of Living, 1971, The Norliss Tapes, 1973, Melvin Purvis, G-Man, 1974, The Turn of the Screw, 1974, Trilogy of Terror (Golden Medallion award, 1975), The Kansas City Massacre, 1975, Sky Heist, 1975, Logan's Run, 1977, First Loss, 1981, Bridge Across Time, 1985, Trilogy of Terror II, 1996; actor, co-writer (film) The Legend of Machine Gun Kelly, 1975; actor (film) The Intruder, 1962. Adv. bd. First Printings of Am. Authors, 1977. Recipient Edgar Allan Poe Spl. Award Scroll, 1970, 72. Mem. Writers Guild Am., Mystery Writers Am. (motion picure awards com.), Sci. Fiction Writers Am., Private Eye Writers Am., Horror Writers Am., Private Eye Writers Am., Dashiell Hammett Soc. San Francisco (co-founder), The Hemingway Soc. (charter), First Printings of Am. Authors (adv. bd.), The Popular Culture Archives Bowling Green (Ohio) State U. (adv. bd. dirs.). Avocations: collecting books by 20th century Am. authors, drawing, painting. Office: Warner Hollywood Studios c/o Vince Gerardis Formosa Bldg Rm 10 1041 N Formosa Ave West Hollywood CA 90046

NOLTE, SYLVIA ANN POE, education educator, program director; b. Kansas City, Kans., Oct. 17, 1936; d. James Fidel and Lemmah Lee (Harrison) Poe; m. Maurice Griffith Nolte, June 15, 1957; children: Baya Clare, Kurt D. BA, U. Mo., 1959; MA, U. Colo., 1976, EdD, 1986. Lic. prin., adminstr., Colo. Dept. Edn. Elem. tchr. Center Sch. Dist., Kansas City, Mo., 1957-58, Columbia (Mo.) Pub. Schs., 1958-61, 66-69; elem. tchr. Colorado Springs (Colo.) Dist. 11, 1972-80, instrnl. supr., 1980-82; asst. supt. Cheyenne Mountain Sch. Dist., Colorado Springs, 1982-88, elem. prin., 1988-94; asst. prof., dir. tchr. edn. U. Colo., Colorado Springs, 1994—; mem. strategic planning com. on minority recruitment Harrison Sch. Dist., 1996—; dir. Regional Licensing Assistance Ctr., Colo. Dept. Edn., Colorado Springs, 1997—. Mem. ASCD, Assn. Tchr. Educators, Internat. Reading Assn., Colo. Assn. Tchr. Educators (sec., pres. 1998), Rotary (pres. Rampart Range club 1996), Phi Delta Kappa (sec., pres. 1994). Democrat. Presbyterian. Avocations: gardening, reading, opera, jazz. Home: 153 Mayhurst Ave Colorado Springs CO 80906-3055 Office: Univ Colo 1420 Austin Bluffs Pkwy Colorado Springs CO 80918-3733

NOONAN, JOHN T., JR., federal judge, legal educator; b. Boston, Oct. 24, 1926; s. John T. and Marie (Shea) N.; m. Mary Lee Bennett, Dec. 27, 1967; children: John Kenneth, Rebecca Lee, Susanna Bain. B.A., Harvard U., 1946, LL.B., 1954; student, Cambridge U., 1946-47; M.A., Cath. U. Am., 1949, Ph.D., 1951, LHD, 1980; LL.D., U. Santa Clara, 1974, U. Notre Dame, 1976, Loyola U. South, 1978; LHD, Holy Cross Coll., 1980; LL.D., St. Louis U., 1981, U. San Francisco, 1985; student, Holy Cross Coll., 1980, Cath. U. Am., 1980, Gonzaga U., 1986, U. San Francisco, 1986. Bar: Mass. 1954, U.S. Supreme Ct. 1971. Mem. spl. staff Nat. Security Council, 1954-55; pvt. practice Herrick & Smith, Boston, 1955-60; prof. law U. Notre Dame, 1961-66; prof. law U. Calif., Berkeley, 1967-86, chmn. religious studies, 1970-73, chmn. medieval studies, 1978-79; judge U.S. Ct. Appeals (9th cir.), San Francisco, 1985-96, sr. judge, 1996—; Oliver Wendell Holmes, Jr. lectr. Harvard U. Law Sch., 1972, Pope John XXIII lectr. Cath. U. Law Sch., 1973, Cardinal Bellarmine lectr. St. Louis U. Div. Sch., 1973, Baum lectr. U. Ill., 1988, Strassberger lectr. U. Tex., 1989; chmn. bd. Games Rsch., Inc., 1961-76; overseer Harvard U., 1991—. Author: The Scholastic Analyst of Usury, 1957; Contraception: A History of Its Treatment by the Catholic Theologians and Canonists, 1965; Power to Dissolve, 1972; Persons and Masks of the Law, 1976; The Antelope, 1977; A Private Choice, 1979; Bribes, 1984; editor: Natural Law Forum, 1961-70, Am. Jour. Jurisprudence, 1970, The Morality of Abortion, 1970. Chmn. Brookline Redevel. Authority, Mass., 1958-62; cons. Papal Commn. on Family, 1965-66, Ford Found., Indonesian Legal Program, 1968; NIH, 1973, NIH, 1974; expert Presdl. Commn. on Population and Am. Future, 1971; cons. U.S. Cath. Conf., 1979-86; sec., treas. Inst. for Research in Medieval Canon Law, 1970-88; pres. Thomas More-Jacques Maritain Inst., 1977—; trustee Population Council, 1969-76, Phi Kappa Found., 1970-76, Grad. Theol. Union, 1970-73, U. San Francisco, 1971-75; mem. com. theol. edn. Yale U., 1972-77; exec. com. Cath. Commn. Intellectual and Cultural Affairs, 1972-75; bd. dirs. Ctr. for Human Values in the Health Scis., 1969-71, S.W. Intergroup Relations Council, 1970-72, Inst. for Study Ethical Issues, 1971-73. Recipient St. Thomas More award U. San Francisco, 1974, Christian Culture medal, 1975, Laetare medal U. Notre Dame, 1984, Campion medal Cath. Book Club, 1987; Guggenheim fellow, 1965-66, 79-80, Laetare medal U. Notre Dame, 1984, Campion medal, 1987, Alemany medal Western Dominican Province, 1988; Ctr. for advanced Studies in Behavioral Scis. fellow, 1973-74; Wilson Ctr. fellow, 1979-80. Fellow Am. Acad. Arts and Scis., Am. Soc. Legal Historians (hon.); mem. Am. Soc. Polit. and Legal Philosophy (v.p. 1964), Canon Law Soc. Am. (gov. 1970-72), Am. Law Inst., Phi Beta Kappa (senator United chpts. 1970-72, pres. Alpha of Calif. chpt. 1972-73). Office: US Ct Appeals 9th Cir PO Box 193939 San Francisco CA 94119-3939*

NOONAN, WILLIAM DONALD, physician, lawyer; b. Kansas City, Mo., Oct. 18, 1955; s. Robert Owen and Patricia Ruth Noonan. AB, Princeton (N.J.) U., 1977; JD, U. Mo., Kansas City, 1980; postgrad., Tulane U., 1981-83; MD magna cum laude, Oreg. Health Scis. U., 1991. Bar: Mo. 1980, U.S. Ct. Appeals (5th cir.) 1982, U.S. Patent & Trademark Office 1982, U.S. Ct. Appeals (D.C. cir.) 1984, Oreg. 1985, U.S. Ct. Appeals (9th Cir.) 1985. Assoc. Shurgue, Mion, Zinn, Washington, 1983-84, Keaty & Keaty, New Orleans, 1984-85; ptnr. Klarquist, Sparkman, Portland, Oreg., 1985—; intern in internal medicine Portland Providence Med. Ctr., 1993-94; resident in ophthalomology Casey Eye Inst., Portland, 1994-95; adj. prof. patent law Tulane U., New Orleans, 1984-85, U. Oreg., 1992-93. Casenotes editor U. Mo. Law Rev., 1979. Nat. Merit scholar. Mem. ABA, AMA (Leadership award 1994), Alpha Omega Alpha (pres. Oreg. chpt. 1990-91). Republican. Avocation: raising horses, mountain climbing, hiking. Office: Klarquist Sparkman 121 SW Salmon 1600 World Trade Ctr Portland OR 97201

NOORDA, RAYMOND J., computer software company executive; b. Ogden, Utah.. BSEE, Utah, 1949. CEO Novell Inc., 1982-94; chmn. MTI Inc, Anaheim, Calif., 1994—. Office: MTI Technology Corp 4905 E La Palma Ave Anaheim CA 92807-1915*

NOPAR, ALAN SCOTT, lawyer; b. Chgo., Nov. 14, 1951; s. Myron E. and Evelyn R. Nopar. BS, U. Ill., 1976; JD, Stanford U., 1979. Bar: Ariz. 1979, U.S. Dist. Ct. Ariz. 1980, U.S. Ct. Appeals (9th cir.) 1980, U.S. Supreme Ct. 1982, Calif. 1989; CPA, Ill. Assoc. O'Connor, Cavanagh, Anderson, Westover, Killingsworth & Beshears P.A., Phoenix, 1979-85, ptnr., 1985-87; of counsel Tower, Byrne & Beaugureau, Phoenix, 1987-88; ptnr. Minutillo & Gorman, San Jose, Calif., 1989-91, Bosco, Blau, Ward & Nopar, San Jose, 1991-96; exec. v.p., gen. counsel, dir. AmeriNet Fin. Systems, Inc., Ontario, Calif., 1996-97; sole practice law San Jose, 1997—. Mem. Ariz. Rep. Caucus, Phoenix, 1984-88. Mem. AICPA, ABA (bus. law and law practice mgmt. sects., mem. forum com. on franchising), Ariz. Bar Assn. (bus. law sect.), Calif. State Bar Assn. (bus. law sect.). Avocations: golf, skiing. Office: 100 Park Center Plz Ste 530 San Jose CA 95113-2232

NORA, JAMES JACKSON, physician, author, educator; b. Chgo., June 26, 1928; s. Joseph James and Mae Henrietta (Jackson) N.; m. Barbara June Fluhrer, Sept. 7, 1949 (div. 1963); children: Wendy Alison, Penelope Welbon, Marianne Leslie; m. Audrey Faye Hart, Apr. 9, 1966; children: James Jackson Jr., Elizabeth Hart Nora. AB, Harvard U., 1950; MD, Yale U., 1954; MPH, U. Calif., Berkeley, 1978. Diplomate Am. Bd. Pediatrics, Am. Bd. Cardiology, Am. Bd. Med. Genetics. Intern Detroit Receiving Hosp., 1954-55; resident in pediatrics U. Wis. Hosps., Madison, 1959-61, fellow in cardiology, 1962-64; fellow in genetics McGill U. Children's Hosp., Montreal, Can., 1964-65; assoc. prof. pediatrics Baylor Coll. Medicine, Houston, 1965-71; prof. genetics, preventive medicine and pediatrics U. Colo. Med. Sch., Denver, 1971—; dir. genetics Rose Med. Ctr., Denver, 1980—; dir. pediatric cardiology and cardiovascular tng. U. Colo. Sch. Medicine, 1971-78; mem. task force Nat. Heart and Lung Program, Bethesda, Md., 1973; cons. WHO, Geneva, 1983—; mem. U.S.-U.S.S.R. Exchange Program on Heart Disease, Moscow and Leningrad, 1975. Author: The Whole Heart Book, 1980, 2d rev. edit., 1989; (with F.C. Fraser) Medical Genetics, 4th rev. edit., 1994, Genetics of Man, 2d rev. edit., 1986, Cardiovascular Diseases: Genetics, Epidemiology and Prevention, 1991; (novels) The Upstart Spring, 1989, The Psi Delegation, 1989, The Hemingway Sabbatical, 1996. Com. mem. March of Dimes, Am. Heart Assn., Boy Scouts Am. Served to lt. USAAC, 1945-47. Grantee Nat. Heart, Lung and Blood Inst., Nat. Inst. Child Health and Human Devel., Am. Heart Assn., NIH; recipient Virginia Apgar Meml. award. Fellow Am. Coll. Cardiology, Am. Acad. Pediatrics, Am. Coll. Med. Genetics; mem. Am. Pediatric Soc., Soc. Pediatric Rsch., Am. Heart Assn., Teratology Soc., Transplantation Soc., Am. Soc. Human Genetics, Authors Guild, Authors League, Acad. Am. Poets, Mystery Writers Am., Rocky Mountain Harvard Club. Democrat. Presbyterian. Avocations: writing fiction, poetry.

NORBECK, JANE S., nursing educator; b. Redfield, S.D., Feb. 20, 1942; d. Sterling M. and Helen L. (Williamson) N.; m. Paul J. Gorman, June 28, 1970; 1 child Sara J. Gorman. BA in Psychology, U. Minn., 1965, BSN, 1965; MS, U. Calif., San Francisco, 1971, DNSc, 1975. Psychiat. nurse Colo. Psychiat. Hosp., Denver, 1965-66, Langley Porter Hosp., San Francisco, 1966-67; pub. health nurse San Francisco Health Dept., 1968-69; prof. U. Calif. Sch. of Nursing, San Francisco, 1975—, dept. chair, 1984-89, dean, 1989-99; chair study sect. Nat. Inst. of Nursing Rsch., 1990-93, mem. editl. bd. Archives of Psychiat. Nursing, 1985-95, Rsch. in Nursing and Health, 1987—. Co-editor: Annual Review of Nursing Research, 1996-97; contbr. articles to profl. jours. Mem. ANA, Am. Acad. Nursing, Am. Orgn. Nursing Exec., Am. Assn. Coll. Nursing, Inst. of Medicine, Sigma Theta Tau. Office: U Calif Sch Nursing 521 Parnassus Ave San Francisco CA 94143-0604

NORD, MYRTLE SELMA, writer, researcher; b. Lane, S.D., Mar. 13, 1918; d. Carl Frederick Schaefer and Minna Anna (Meyer) Scandrett; m. Warren E. Nord, Aug. 10, 1938. BA, Fort Lewis Coll., 1972. Sec. Anaconda Mining, Robeau, S.D., 1935; waitress Rapid City, S.D., 1935-38; office mgr. Farmers Ins. Group, Durango, Colo., 1947-62; ret. Farmers Ins. Group, Durango, 1962. Author: Tell Me a Story, 1956, Inspiring Stories, 1975, Prospectives on Mass Communciations, 1982, Main Currents in Communications, 1986, Leadville's Chicken Bill, 1977, The Searcher, 1993-94 (plays) Five Under Cover 4, 1983, Celebrations 3, 1986, Virtue of Necessity, 1982 (stage plays) Tomorrow = X2, Sound Another Trumpet, 1976 (serials) Children's Friend, Missing Red Envelope, 1950-51, The Blue Triangle, 1952-53, (musicals) Getting It 2-Gether, 1982, No Patsy Like a Dame, 1985, High Blonde Pressure, 1986, Katie's Capers in the Mining Camp, 1989. Mem. Nat. League of Am. Pen Women (state pres. 1966-68), Mystery Writers of Am. Avocations: herbs, music, outdoors. Home: 37658 S Meander Ct Tucson AZ 85739-1048 Office: 37658 S Meander Ct Tucson AZ 85739-1048

NORDBY, JON JORGEN, forensic scientist, educator; b. Madison, Wis., Nov. 14, 1948; s. Eugene Jorgen and Olive Marie (Jensen) N.; m. Kimberly Kay Washburn, Mar. 21, 1992. BA cum laude, St. Olaf Coll., 1970; MA, U. Mass., 1975, PhD, 1977. Assoc. prof. Pacific Luth. U., Tacoma, Wash., 1977—; cons. Final Analysis, Tacoma, 1985—, Coroner's Svc. Forensic Unit, B.C., Can., 1988—, Pierce County Med. Examiner, Tacoma, 1992-97 (med. investigator 1988-92), King County Med. Examiner, Seattle, 1993—, Puyallup (Wash.) Police Dept., 1996—. Editor Synthese, 1989; contbr. articles to profl. jours.; spkr. in field. Team mem. Nat. Disaster Med. Sys. Office Emergency Preparedness, Pacific Rim Region, 1998; deacon, choir mem. Immanuel Presbyn. Ch., Tacoma, 1984-88. Fellow Woodrow Wilson Fellowship Found., Phila., 1970, Rockefeller Found., N.Y., 1970; rsch. fellow Dept. Forensic Med. Guy's Hosp., London, 1994. Fellow Am. Acad. Forensic Scis. (meritorious svc. award 1994, multidisciplinary symposium svc. award 1995, plenary session co-chair svc. award 1997, edn. council 1988, chair memberships discipline com. 1992-94, sec. 1997, ethics com. 1998); mem. Internat. Assn. Bloodstain Pattern Analysts (assoc. editor newsletter 1997), Internat. Criminal Justice Law Enforcement Expert Sys. Assn. (pres. 1991), Assn. Crime Scene Reconstruction, Can. Soc. Forensic Sci., Philosophy of Sci. Assn., Pacific N.W. Forensic Sci. Study Group, Vintage Chevrolet Club Am., Buick Club Am., Vesterheim Mus. Avocations: auto restoration, outboard motor restoration, carpentry, fishing, canoeing. Office: Final Analysis PO Box 6888 Tacoma WA 98407

NORDGREN, WILLIAM BENNETT, engineering executive; b. Salt Lake City, Mar. 5, 1960; s. Kent Widstoe and Eliza (Schmuhl) N.; m. Carolyn B. Erickson, June 26, 1981; children: William Tyson, Cameron Lynn, Cassy Erin. BS, Brigham Young U., 1986, MS, 1989. Engr. Boeing Airplanes Co., Seattle, 1986-88; pres. CIM Engring. Assocs., Orem, Utah, 1988-89; v.p. engring. Prodn. Modeling Corp., Orem, 1989-93; pres. F & H Simulations, Inc., Orem, 1993—. Developer, polar coordinant mill. Mem. Soc. Mfg. Engrs., Inst. Indsl. Engrs. Republican. Mem. LDS Ch. Avocations: fishing, camping, sports. Office: PO Box 658 Orem UT 84059-0658

NORDMEYER, MARY BETSY, retired vocational educator; b. New Haven, May 19, 1939; d. George and Barbara Stedman (Thompson) N. ABPhil, Wheaton Coll., Norton, Mass., 1960; MA, San Jose State U., 1968; AS in Computer Sci., West Valley Coll., 1985. Cert. tchr. spl. edn., Calif.; cert. secondary tchr., Calif. Instr. English Santa Clara (Calif.) Unified Sch. Dist., 1965-77, vocat. specialist, 1977-99, dir. project work ability, 1984-99, also mem. cmty. adv. com.; facilitator Project Work-Ability, Region 5, 1985-86, sec., 1988-90. Author poetry, 1960, Career and Vocat. Edn. for

Students With Spl. Needs, 1986; author/designer Career English, 1974, Career Information, 1975. Recipient Outstanding Secondary Educator award, 1975, Award of Excellence, Nat. Assn. Vocat. Edn., 1984; named Tchr. of Yr. in Spl. Edn., Santa Clara Unified Sch. Dist., 1984-85. Mem. Calif. Assn. Work Experience Educators, Sierra Club, Epsilon Eta Sigma. Democrat. Avocations: backpacking, skiing, mountain climbing, computers, gardening. Home: 14920 Sobey Rd Saratoga CA 95070-6236 Office: Santa Clara Unified Sch Dist 1889 Lawrence Rd Santa Clara CA 95051-2166

NORDQUIST, JOAN MARIE, bibliographer, indexer, researcher; b. San Jose, Calif., Nov. 23, 1937; d. Kenneth James and Evelyn C. (Wood) Beam; m. Gilbert Nelson Nordquist, Oct. 12, 1963; 1 child, Diana Artemis. BA, San Jose State U., 1959, MLS, 1976. Library researcher Encyclopaedia Britannica, Chgo., 1962-74; librarian Santa Cruz (Calif.) Pub. Library, 1975-78; indexer, bibliographer, cons. Reference and Research Services, Santa Cruz, 1982—; research specialist U. Calif., Santa Cruz, 1980-85. Editor, indexer: Audiovisuals for Women, 1980 (Choice Best Acad. Books of Yr. 1980-81), The Left Index, 1982—, Social Theory: A Bibliographic Series, 1986—, Contemporary Social Issues: A Bibliographic Series, 1986—, City on a Hill Index, 1970—. Avocation: reading. Office: Reference and Research Services 511 Lincoln St Santa Cruz CA 95060-3621

NORDSTROM, BRUCE A., department store executive; b. 1933; married. BA, U. Wash., 1956. With Nordstrom, Inc., Seattle, 1956—, v.p., 1964-70, pres., 1970-75, chmn., 1975-77, co-chmn., 1977—, dir. Office: Nordstrom Inc 1501 5th Ave Seattle WA 98101-1603

NORDSTROM, JOHN N., department store executive; b. 1937; married. BA, U. Wash., 1958. With Nordstrom, Inc., Seattle, 1958—, v.p., 1965-70, exec. v.p., 1970-75, pres., 1975-77, co-chmn., 1977—, dir.; bd. dirs. Fed. Res. Bank San Francisco. Office: Nordstrom Inc 1501 5th Ave Seattle WA 98101-1603

NORDT, SEAN PATRICK, clinical toxicologist; b. Port Jefferson, N.Y., Nov. 6, 1967; s. Kenneth Albert and Mary Anne (Ryan) N.; m. Lisa Elaine Vivero, Feb. 2, 1997. BS, St. John's U., Jamaica, N.Y., 1993, DPharm, 1995. Lic. pharmacist Calif., N.Y., Fla.; diplomate Am. Bd. Applied Toxicology. Asst. dir. San Diego divsn. Calif. Poison Control Sys., 1995—; asst. clin. prof. U. Calif., San Diego; cons. San Diego Zoo, 1995—, Sea World San Diego, 1995—, 3E Co., San Diego, 1995—. Contbr. chpts. to books. Texaco Postdoctoral fellow Am. Acad. Clin. Toxicology, 1996. Mem. Am. Acad. Clin. Toxicology, Am. Assn. Poison Control Ctrs., Am. Coll. Clin. Pharmacy, Nat. Assn. Against Health Fraud. Achievements include pharmacokinetic analysis of medications, laboratory interactions and assays, toxicity case reports and research. Office: Calif Poison Control System 200 W Arbor Dr San Diego CA 92103-1911

NOREHAD, ERNEST A., physician; b. Chgo., Oct. 31, 1935; m. Judith L. Norehad; children: Paul, Christopher, Matthew. BA, Kenyon Coll., 1957; MD, U. Chgo., 1962. Physician Evergreen urology, Kirkland, Wash. Councilman Hunts Point City Coun., Wash., 1982-86; commr. Water Dist. 17, Hunts Point, 1980-98. Capt. USAF, 1966-72. Avocation: flying. Office: 12815 120 NE 1 Kirkland WA

NORKIN, MARK MITCHELL, sales executive; b. Whittier, Calif., Nov. 19, 1955; s. Cleo Donald and Carol Mathis. Grad., Gemmological Inst. Am., 1976. Gemmologist Slavicks Jewelers, Newport Beach, Calif., 1976-77; apprentice Troy Sheet Metal Works, Montebello, Calif., 1977-79, journeyman, 1979-80, foreman, 1980-82, project engr., 1982-85, v.p. sales and engring., 1985—; bd. dirs. Troy Sheet Metal. Republican. Avocations: gardening, computers. Office: 1026 S Vail Ave Montebello CA 90640-6020

NORMAN, E. GLADYS, business computer educator, consultant; b. Oklahoma City, June 13, 1933; d. Joseph Eldon and Mildred Lou (Truitt) Biggs; m. Joseph R.R. Radeck, Mar. 1, 1953 (div. Aug. 1962); children: Jody Matti, Ray Norman, Warren Norman (dec. May 1993), Dana Norman; m. Leslie P. Norman, Aug. 26, 1963 (dec. Feb. 1994); 1 child, Elayne Pearce. Student, Fresno (Calif.) State Coll., 1951-52, UCLA, 1956-59, Linfield Coll., 1986-95. Math. aid U.S. Naval Weapons Ctr., China Lake, Calif., 1952-56, computing systems specialist, 1957-68; systems programmer Oreg. Motor Vehicles Dept., Salem, 1968-69; instr. in data processing, dir. Computer Programming Ctr., Salem, 1969-72; instr. in data processing Merritt-Davis Bus. Coll., Salem, 1972-73; sr. programmer, analyst Teledyne Wah Chang, Albany, Oreg., 1973-79; sr. systems analyst Oreg. Dept. Vets. Affairs, Albany, 1979-80; instr. in bus. computers Linn-Benton Community Coll., Albany, 1980-95; ret., 1995; computer cons. for LBCC Ret. Sr. Vol. Program, 1995—; presenter computer software seminars State of Oreg., 1991-93, Oreg. Credit Assoc. Conf., 1991, Oreg. Regional Users Group Conf., 1992; computer tchr. Linn-Benton C.C., 1999; computer cons. Oremet-Wah Chang, 1996-99, Oreg. State Yr. 2000 Project, 1997-98; computer cons. in field. Mem. Data Processing Mgmt. Assn. (bd. dirs. 1977-84, 89-95, region sect. 1995-96, assoc. v.p. 1988, Diamond Individual Performance award 1985). Assn. Info. Tech. Profls. (treas. 1999). Democrat. Avocations: drawing, painting, sewing.

NORMAN, JOHN BARSTOW, JR., designer, educator; b. Paloa, Kans., Feb. 5, 1940; s. John B. and Ruby Maxine (Johnson) N.; m. Roberta Jeanne Martin, June 6, 1967; children: John Barstow III, Elizabeth Jeanne. BFA, U. Kans., 1962, MFA, 1966. Designer and illustrator Advt. Design, Kansas City, Mo., 1962-64; asst. instr. U. Kans., Lawrence, 1964-66; art dir. Hallmark Cards, Inc., Kansas City, Mo., 1966-69; instr. dept. art U. Denver, 1969-73, asst. prof., 1973-78, assoc. prof., 1978-93, Disting. prof., 1980 , prof. emeritus, 1993—; sr. designer Mo. Coun. Arts and Humanities, 1966-67; cons. designer Rocky Mountain Bank Note Corp., Denver, 1971—, Signage Identity System, U. Denver; bd. dirs. communications U. Denver; tech. cons. Denver Art Mus., 1974—, designed exhbns., 1974-75; adv., cons. Jefferson County (Colo.) Sch., System, 1976—; chmn. Design and Sculpture Exhbn., Colo. Celebration of the Arts, 1975-76. One man shows include: Gallery Cortina, Aspen, Colo., 1983; commd. works include: Jedda, Saudi Arabia, Synegistics Corp., Denver; represented in permanent collections Pasadena Ctr. for the Arts, N.Y. Art Dirs. Club, Calif. State U./Fiber Collection, Pasadena (Calif.) Ctr. for the Arts, 1984, N.Y. Art Dirs. Club, 1985 Midland Art Coun./Fiber Collection, 1985, Geologic Soc. Am.; represented in traveling exhbns. L.A. Art Dirs. Show and N.Y. Art Dirs. Show, U.S., Europe, Japan, 1985; fearured in Denver Post, 1984, Post Electric City Mag., 1984, Rocky Mt. News, 1984, Douglas County Press, 1984, Mile High Cable Vision, 1985, Sta. KWGN-TV, 1985, Les Krantz's Am. Artists, 1988, Illustrated Survey of Leading Contemporaries, 1988, U.S. Surface Design Jour., 1988; co-work represented in film collection Mus. Modern Art, N.Y.C.; selected fashion show designs displayed to Sister City dels., Denver, 1987. Co-recipient Silver Medal award N.Y. Internat. Film and Video Competition, 1976, Design awards Coun. Advancement and Support of Edn., 1969, 71, 73, 76, Honor Mention award L.A. Art Dirs. Club, 1984, Honor Mention award N.Y. Art Dirs. Club, 1984, Native Am. Wearable Art Competition, 1985, 5th pl. Nat. Wind Sail Am. Banners Competition, Midland, Mich., 1985, also awards for surface designs in Colo. Ctr. for the Arts Wearable Art Competition, 1984-85, Foothills Art Gallery Nat. Wearable Art Competition, 1984-85, Fashion Group of Denver Competition, 1984-85. Mem. Art Dirs. Club Denver (Gold medals 1974-82, Best of Show Gold medal 1983, Honor Mention award, 1984, 3 Gold medals 1989), Univ. Art Dirs. Assn. Home: PO Box 302 PO Box 507 Lake George CO 80827-0507 Office: U Denver Sch Art 2121 E Asbury Ave Denver CO 80210-4303

NORMAN, JOHN EDWARD, petroleum landman; b. Denver, May 22, 1922; s. John Edward and Ella (Warren) N.; m. Hope Sabin, Sept. 5, 1946; children—J. Thomas, Gerould W., Nancy E., Susan G., Douglas E. BSBA, U. Denver, 1949, MBA, 1972. Clk., bookkeeper Capitol Life Ins. Co., Denver, 1940-42, 45-46; salesman Security Life and Accident Co., Denver, 1947; bookkeeper Central Bank and Trust Co., Denver, 1947-50; automobile [illegible] Oil [illegible] landman, 1985; ind. investor 1985—. Lectr. pub. lands Colo. Sch. Mines, 1968-85; lectr. mineral titles and landmen's role in oil industry Casper Coll., 1969-71. Mem. Casper Mcpl. Band Commn., 1965-71, mem. band, 1961-71, mgr., 1968-71; former musician, bd. dirs. Casper Civic Symphony; former bd. dirs. Jefferson Symphony, performing mem., 1972-75. Served with AUS, World War II. Mem. Am. Assn. Petroleum Landmen (dir. at large, chmn. publs. for regional dir.), Wyo. Assn. Petroleum Landmen (pres.), Denver Assn. Petroleum Landmen, Rocky Mountain Oil and Gas Assn. (pub. lands com. 1981-85), Rocky Mountain Petroleum Pioneers. Episcopalian (mem. choir, vestryman, past dir. acolytes). Club: Elks. Home and Office: 2710 S Jay St Denver CO 80227-3856

NORMAN, NITA VEGAMORA, librarian, educator, storyteller; b. Sariaya, Philippines, Aug. 29; came to U.S., 1968; d. Romualdo and Leoncia (Cereza) Vegamora; m. Michael B. Norman, June 15, 1972. BS in Edn., U. Santo Tomas, 1965; Rosary Coll.MLS, 1975, 1975; M in Edn., Storytelling, Reading, Eastern Tenn. State U., 1995. Sch. tchr. Quiapo Parochial Sch., Manila, 1965-68; asst. libr. Cen. States Inst. of Addiction, Chgo., 1970-75; out-reach libr. Chgo. Pub. Libr., 1975-77, branch head, 1977-83; branch mgr. Phoenix Pub. Libr., 1983—. Speaker in field. Named Libr. of the Year., Friende of the Chgo. Pub. Libr., 1980; recipient Outstnading Pub. Svc. award City of Phoenix , 1985, Disting. Svc. award Murphy Elem. Sch., Phoenix, 1990; Contbn. to Literacy award Hamilton Sch., Phoenix, 1993-94. Mem. ALA (local program com. Chgo. 1978), Pub. Libr. Assn. (alternative edn. program com. 1985—, multilingual libr. svcs. com. 1985—), Reforma (libr. svcs. to Spanish speaking), Ariz. State Libr. Assn. (libr. svcs. to Spanish speaking round table 1983—), Asian Pacific Am. Library Assn. Democrat. Home: 1513 W Culver St Phoenix AZ 85007-1823 Office: Mesquite Br Libr 4525 Paradise Valley Pkwy N Phoenix AZ 85000

NORMAN, SHERI HANNA, artist, educator, cartographer; b. Chgo., Dec. 15, 1940; d. L.J. and Margaret Maxine (Kuyper Fleischer) Hanna; m. Donald Lloyd Norman, Febr. 28, 1963 (div. 1996); 1 child, Ronald Wayne Norman. BA, U. Wyo., Laramie, 1963; attended, Dayton (Ohio) Art Inst., 1975; MFA, San Francisco Art Inst., 1993. Substitute tchr. Arlington, Va. and Yellow Springs, Ohio Pub. Sch. Dists., 1965-71; tech. illustrator, draftsperson U. Tex. Austin, Geotek, Inc., Denver, 1976-85; cartographer British Petroleum, San Francisco, 1985-87; draftsperson Earth Scis. Assocs., Palo Alto, Calif., 1988-92; intern, printmaking asst. Crown Point Press, San Francisco, 1991-92; freelance cartographer San Francisco, 1993—; educator pub. printmaking & papermaking workshops, San Francisco, 1995-96, Napa, Calif., 1997—; pub. printmaking demonstrations San Francisco Women Artists Gallery, 1995, 96; leader pub. nature/women's ceremony-ritual, San Francisco, 1991-93; artist in residence Villa Montalvo Ctr. for the Arts, Saratoga, Calif., 1996, Dorland Mountain Arts Colony, Temecula, Calif., 1996. Author, illustrator: (book) Envisioning An Unbroken Arc, 1992, Vol. 11, 1992; participating artist San Francisco Bay Area Presses, Visual Arts Ctr., Bluffton (Ohio) Coll., 1996; contbg. artist Visual Aid's BIG DEAL, San Francisco, 1996, 97, Florence Crittenton Svcs., San Francisco, 1995, San Francisco Women Artists Gallery, 1995-97. Mem. Calif. Soc. Printmakers (mem. exhbn. com. 1995), No. Calif. Women's Caucus For Art, Graphic Arts Workshop, Arts Coun. Napa Valley. Avocations: ongoing nature studies, early mythologies and desert travel, advocacy. Home and Studio: 2834 Monticello Rd Napa CA 94558-9614

NORRIS, JUNE RUDOLPH, minister; b. Trinidad, Colo., June 30, 1922; d. Ernest Ellsworth and Bessie Mildred (Dawson) Rudolph; m. Willard M. Norris, Feb. 12, 1938 (div. Sept. 1966); children: Gene Curtis, Paul Martin, Dixie June. Student, East L.A. Coll., 1968-74, Samaritan Bible Sch., L.A., 1972-74. Lic. Universal Fellowship Met. Community Chs., 1973, ordained 1974. Staff clergy Met. Community Ch., L.A., 1972-80; pastor Met. Community Ch., Fayetteville, N.C., 1980-81, St. John's Met. Community Ch., Raleigh, N.C., 1981-88, Ch. Holy Spirit of Met. Community Ch., Des Moines, 1989-93; office mgr. W.M. Norris Constrn., Orlando, Fla., 1961-66; clk. outpatient div. Fla. Hosp., Orlando, 1966-67; supr. White Meml. Med. Ctr., L.A., 1968-76; mem. staff Met. Community Ch., San Diego, 1993-96, Boulder, Colo., 1996—. Contbr. articles to Front Page jour. Mem. team to testify state legis. com. for gay/lesbian rights St. John's Met. Community Ch., 1985. Recipient Disting. Svc. award Universal Fellowship Met. Community Ch., 1991, appreciation White People Healing Racism, 1991. Mem. Hosp. Credit Mgrs. Assn. (pres. 1970-71), Mensa. Avocations: bowling, scrabble, sports.

NORRIS, RAYMOND MICHAEL, lawyer; b. Chgo., Dec. 14, 1948; s. William Patrick and Nellie (Scanlon) N.; m. Maxine Anne Flom, Aug. 16, 1951; children: Michael, Erin, David. BA, U. Toronto, 1977; LLB, York U., Toronto, 1981; MCL, George Washington U., 1982. Bar: Ariz. 1982, U.D. Dist. Ct. Ariz. 1983, U.S. Ct. Appeals (9th cir.) 1985. Assoc. Treon Strick Lucia & Aguirre, Phoenix, 1982-86, shareholder atty., 1986-93; founder, v.p. Norris & O'Daniel, Phoenix, 1993—; judge pro tempore Maricopa County Superior Ct., Phoenix, 1995—. Former pres., bd. dirs. Hope Ctr. for Head Injury, Phoenix, 1985-91; bd. dirs. P.R.I.D.E., Phoenix; mem. vol. lawyers program Pro Bono Legal Svcs., Phoenix, 1994—; mem. legis. com. Gov.'s Coun. on Spine and Head Injuries, 1993—. Mem. ATLA, Ariz. State Bar Assn., Phoenix Trial Lawyers Assn. (bd. dirs.), Ariz. Trial Lawyers Assn. Democrat. Avocations: golf, humor, fitness, little league coaching. Home: 106 E Colt Rd Tempe AZ 85284-2386 Office: Norris and O'Daniel PA 2302 N 3rd St Phoenix AZ 85004-1301

NORRIS, WILLIAM ALBERT, former federal judge; b. Turtle Creek, Pa., Aug. 30, 1927; s. George and Florence (Clive) N.; m. Merry Wright, Nov. 23, 1974; children: Barbara, Donald, Kim, Alison; m. Jane Jelenko. Student, U. Wis., 1945; B.A., Princeton U., 1951; J.D., Stanford U., 1954. Bar: Calif. and D.C. 1955. Assoc. firm Northcutt Ely, Washington, 1954-55; law clk. to Justice William O. Douglas U.S. Supreme Ct., Washington, 1955-56; sr. mem. firm Tuttle & Taylor, Inc., L.A., 1956-80; judge U.S. Ct. Appeals (9th cir.), L.A., 1980-94, sr. judge, 1994-97; spl. counsel Pres.' Kennedy's Com. on Airlines Controversy, 1961; mem., v.p. Calif. State Bd. Edn., 1961-67. Trustee Calif. State Colls., 1967-72; pres. L.A. Bd. Police Commrs., 1973-74; Democratic nominee for atty. gen. State of Calif., 1974; founding pres. bd. trustees Mus. Contemporary Art, L.A., 1979—; trustee Craft and Folk Art Mus., 1979—. With USN, 1945-47. Home: 1473 Oriole Dr West Hollywood CA 90069-1155

NORTON, DUNBAR SUTTON, economic developer; b. Hoquiam, Wash., Jan. 30, 1926; s. Percy Dunbar and Anna Fedelia (Sutton) N.; m. Kathleen Margaret Mullarky, Dec. 21, 1948 (dec. Apr. 1994); children: Priscilla K., Rebecca C., Jennifer A., Douglas S.; m. Mary Ethel Wolff, May 25, 1996. Student, U. Oreg., 1946-48; diploma, U.S. Army Command & Gen. Staff, 1964. Enlisted U.S. Army, 1944, commd. 2d lt., 1948, advanced through grades to lt. col., ret., 1974; dir. econ. devel. dept. Yuma (Ariz.) County C. of C., 1974-83; exec. v.p. Lakin Enterprises, Yuma, 1983-87; owner Norton Cons., Yuma, 1987—; dir. Lower Colo. River Rsch. Ctr., Ariz. West Coll./No. Ariz. U., Yuma, 1998—; corp. mem. Greater Yuma Econ. Devel. Corp., 1984-96, vice chmn., 1993-95. Mem. Yuma County Indsl. Devel. Authority, 1984-90, 92—, pres., 1992—; chmn. fundraising com. Yuma Cross Park Coun., 1984-88, sec., 1988-90, v.p., 1990-92, bd. dirs., 1982-96; bd. dirs. Yuma Leadership, 1984-93, Yuma Youth Leadership, 1993-96; chmn. devel. com. Yuma County Airport Authority, 1985-92, v.p., 1992—; vice chmn. Yuma Main St. Bd., 1988-90, Yuma County Geog. Info. Sys. Task Force, 1991-95, Yuma Kids Voting, 1990-91, bd. dirs. Ariz. Partnership Air Transp., 1990-96, v.p. 1993-95; bd. dirs. Yuma County Civic Trusteeship, 1993-95; chmn. The Southwest Inst., 1995-96, What's Best for Our Kids, 1995-96, Yuma Sch. Dist. No. 1 New Elem. Sch. Planning Com., 1996-97; mem. bd. trustees Yuma county Libr., 1996—. Decorated Legion of merit with oak leaf cluster, Bronze Star, Meritorious Svc. and Army Commendation Medal with Oak Leaf Cluster. Mem. Ariz. Assn. for Econ. Devel. (bd. dirs. 1975-82, pres. 1982-83, legis. affairs com. 1987—, Developer of Yr. 1977), Yuma Execs. Assn. (sec.-treas., exec. dir. 1987—). Republican. Episcopalian. Avocations: golf, swimming, singing. Home and Office: 12267 E Del Norte Yuma AZ 85367-7356 also: AWC/NAU-Yuma Fine Arts Bldg PO Box 929 Yuma AZ 85366-0929

NORTON, GOLDY See GOLDSTEIN, NORTON MAURICE

[illegible] d. Dale Francis and Ruby Grace (Gehlhar) N. BA, U. Minn., 1972; postgrad. U. Md., 1978; cert. acctg. U.S. Dept. Agr. Grad. Sch., 1978; MBA, Calif. State Poly. U.-Pomona, 1989. CPA, Md. Securities transactions analyst Bur. of Pub. Debt., Washington, 1972-79, internal auditor, 1979-81; internal auditor IRS, Washington, 1981; sr. acct. World Vision Internat., Monrovia, Calif., 1981-83, acctg. supr., 1983-87; sr. systems liaison coord., Home Savs. Am., 1987-97, sys. auditor, 1997—; cons. (vol.) info. systems John M. Perkins Found., Pasadena, Calif., 1985-86. Author (poetry): Ode to Joyce, 1985 (Golden Poet award 1985). Second v.p. chpt. Nat. Treasury Employees Union, Washington, 1978, editor chpt. newsletter; mem. M-2 Prisoners Sponsorship Program, Chino, Calif., 1984-86. Recipient Spl. Achievement award Dept. Treasury, 1976, Superior Performance award, 1977-78; Charles and Ellora Alliss scholar, 1968. Mem. Angel Flight, Flying Samaritans. Avocations: flying, chess, racquetball, whitewater rafting.

NORVELL, THOMAS VERNON, minister; b. Lake Charles, La., Oct. 19, 1955; s. Thomas Vern and Barbara Joyce (Grant) N.; m. Alica Nell Reynolds, Sept. 9, 1978; children: Thomas Vernon, Carey Lane. BS in Psychology/Religion, Ea. N.Mex. U., 1978; MDiv, Golden Gate Bapt. Theol. Sem., 1981. Ordained to ministry So. Bapt. Conv., 1982. Min. edn. Capital City Bapt. Ch., Sacramento, 1981-89; assoc. pastor edn. and adminstrn. First Bapt. Ch., Fair Oaks, Calif., 1989—. Bd. dirs., treas. Support Abused Victims Early, Sacramento, 1986-90. Recipient Award of Excellence Cosumnes River Coll., 1989; cert. appreciation Superior Ct., Calif., 1988. Mem. Western Bapt. Religious Educators Assn. (chmn. program 1986-88). Office: First Bapt Ch 4401 San Juan Ave Fair Oaks CA 95628-5611

NOSLER, ROBERT AMOS, sports company executive; b. Ashland, Oreg., Apr. 21, 1946; s. John Amos and Louise (Booz) N.; m. Joan Kathleen Hilliard, July 15, 1967; children: Christie Lynn, Jill Ann, John Robert. Student, U. Oreg., 1965. V.p., gen. mgr. Nosler Bullets, Inc., Bend, Oreg., 1974-88; pres., chief exec. officer Nosler Bullets, Inc., 1988-90; pres., CEO Nosler, Inc., Bend, 1990—. Editor: Nosler Reloading Manual #1, 1976. Bd. dirs. Bend C. of C., 1984-88, treas., 1988; chmn. Central Oreg. Welcome Ctr. Steering Com., 1988. With USN, 1966-70; trustee Ctrl. Oreg. Community Coll. Found., 1992—; trustee Nat. Rifle Assn. Found., 1997—. Recipient Pres.' award Bend C. of C., 1984, 87, 88. Mem. Nat. Reloading Mfrs. Assn. (bd. dirs. 1982-86, 90-93, pres. 1984-86), Oreg. Grad. Inst. Sci. & Tech. Chief Exec. Roundtable, Greater Bend Rotary (dir. 1989-91). Republican. Lutheran. Avocations: hunting, outdoors, sports. Office: Nosler Inc 107 SW Columbia St Bend OR 97702-1014

NOTT, CAROLYN MARY, water entertainment technology executive; b. London, Jan. 1, 1939; came to U.S., 1981; d. William Francis Bell and Joan Evelyn (Tomson) N.; m. E. Gerard Schurmann, May 26, 1973. Lic., Royal Acad. Music, London, 1960. Editor Consensus and Review, London, 1961-63; asst. editor Records and Rec., London, 1965-67; freelance music journalist U.K. and USA mags., 1967—; broadcaster Radio Telefis Eireann, Dublin, Ireland, 1967-71; freelance promotion Novello and Co. Ltd., London, 1971-73; dir. mktg. WET Design, L.A., 1989-90, v.p. bus. devel., 1990—; mem. com. Redcliffe Concerts, London, 1977-80; real estate cons. Jon Douglas, L.A., 1987-89; dir. bd. WET Design, 1995-96. Contbr. articles to profl. jours. Mem. Ch. of Eng. Avocations: writing, music, travel, reading, cooking.

NOTTINGHAM, EDWARD WILLIS, JR., federal judge; b. Denver, Jan. 9, 1948; s. Edward Willis and Willie Newton (Gullett) N.; m. Cheryl Ann Card, June 6, 1970 (div. Feb. 1981); children: Amelia Charlene, Edward Willis III; m. Janis Ellen Chapman, Aug. 18, 1984 (div. Dec. 1998); 1 child, Spencer Chapman. AB, Cornell U., 1969; JD, U. Colo., 1972. Bar: Colo. 1972, U.S. Dist. Ct. Colo. 1972, U.S. Ct. Appeals (10th cir.) 1973. Law clk. to presiding judge U.S. Dist. Ct. Colo., Denver, 1972-73; assoc. Sherman & Howard, Denver, 1973-76, 78-80, ptnr., 1980-87; ptnr. Beckner & Nottingham, Grand Junction, Colo., 1987-89; asst. U.S. atty. U.S. Dept. Justice, Denver, 1976-78; U.S. dist. judge Dist. of Colo., Denver, 1989—. Bd. dirs. Beaver Creek Met. Dist., Avon, Colo., 1980-88, Justice Info. Ctr., Denver, 1985-87, 21st Jud. Dist. Victim Compensation Fund, Grand Junction, Colo., 1987-89. Mem. ABA, Colo. Bar Assn. (chmn. criminal law sect. 1983-85, chmn. ethics com. 1988-89), Order of Coif, Denver Athletic Club, Delta Sigma Rho, Tau Kappa Alpha. Episcopalian. Office: US Dist Ct 1929 Stout St Denver CO 80294-0001

NOVALES-LI, PHILIPP, neuropharmacologist; b. Manila, Philippines, May 27, 1962; s. Angelita Tobillo de Novales-Li. DMSc, PhD, Gifu U. Sch. Medicine, Japan, 1989; DPhil, U. Oxford, U.K., 1993. Rsch. fellow U. Oxford, U.K., 1990-94; fellow U. So. Calif. Sch. Medicine, L.A., 1994, project mgr., 1995; pres. St. Hugh's Coll. MCR, U. Oxford, 1991, exec. officer, 1992, pharmacology tutor, 1993; cons. Novales-Li Rsch., Ltd., 1994. Columnist Manila Bull., 1994-95; contbr. articles to sci. jours. Monbusho Rsch. scholar Ministry Edn. & Culture, Tokyo, 1986-89; recipient Outstanding Youth award City of Manila, 1979, ORS award CVCP, London, 1989-92. Mem. Internat. Brain Rsch. Orgn., World Fedn. Mental Health, European Neuroscis. Assn., Oxford Union Soc., Gridiron Club, Oxford Soc. (hon. sec. So. Calif. 1995), Phi Kappa Phi, Phi Epsilon, Phi Sigma (Acad. Excellence in Biol. award 1984). Home: 1201 Maria Orosa St, Ermita Manila 1000, The Philippines Office: 3225 Promontory Cir San Ramon CA 94583-1262 also: U So Calif Sch Medicine 1540 Alcazar St # 205 Los Angeles CA 90033-4500

NOVARRO, LEONARD ANTHONY, writer; b. Bklyn., Dec. 22, 1941; s. Anthony Joseph and Frances Yvonne (Kupidlowski) N.; m. Ellen Virginia Burns, Mar. 11, 1973. BS, St. Peter's Coll., 1963. Reporter, copy editor S.I. (N.Y.) Advance, 1966-73; bur. chief, reporter, asst. nat. fgn. editor Orlando (Fla.) Sentinel, 1973-78; asst. news editor Galette-Telegraph, Colorado Springs, Colo., 1978-79; investigative reporter, features editor Memphis press Scimitar, 1979-84; writer, features editor San Diego Tribune, 1984-92; pvt. practice writing and editing San Diego, 1992—; adviser San Diego State U. Daily Aztec Newspaper, 1993—; designer ACLU Newsletter, San Diego, 1993—, San Diego Hist. Soc. Newsletter, 1996-98. Pvt. U.S. Army, 1964-65. Recipient Newspaper Reporting award Herbert Bayard Swope Meml. Awards, 1977, John Finney award UPI, 1981, Media award for human rels. Nat. Conf. Christians and Jews, 1990, Cmty. Svc. award Soc. Profl. Journalists, 1991. Mem. San Diego Press Club (various writing awards), Am. Legion, Disabled Am. Vets. (life). Democrat. Avocations: playing guitar, writing music.

NOVICK, MICHAEL, adult education educator, author; b. Bklyn., Feb. 9, 1947; s. Ben and Charlotte Novick. BA cum laude, CUNY, Bklyn., 1969; postgrad., UCLA, 1985. Cert. tchr., Calif. Tchr. Puerto Rican H.S., Inc., Chgo., 1978-81, Chgo. City Colls., Inst. for Latin Progress, 1980-81; tchr., adult edn., ELS San Francisco, 1981-82; tchr. Hollywood Cmty. Adult Sch., L.A., 1982-93, Bassett Adult Sch., La Puente, Calif., 1985—, Ctrl. Adult H.S., 1993—; mem. adult edn. task force L.A. Unified Sch. Dist./United Tchrs. L.A., 1990—; chmn. subcom. United. Tchrs. L.A., 1989—. Author: White Lies White Power, 1996; contbr. articles to profl. jours. Mem. Calif. Assn. Tchrs. of English to Speakers of Other Langs., Valley Interfaith Coun. Office: PART PO Box 1055 Culver City CA 90232-1055

NOVICK, STUART ALLAN, owner business consulting firm; b. Savannah, Ga., Aug. 21, 1944; s. Jehiel and Dorothy Ruth (Selicovitz) N.; m. Francesca Julita Lim, June 22, 1986 (div. Mar. 1993); 1 child, Casey Adam. Grad., Stanford U., 1967. Mgr. Chico-San, Inc., Seattle, 1969-72; bus. mgr. Seventh Inn, Boston, 1972-74; owner, mgr. Simulsense, Seattle, 1974-77, More Time! Good Time!, Honolulu, 1977-80; pres. Foodpower, Honolulu, 1980-83, Profitability Cons., Honolulu, 1983-88, Novick and Einstein Advt., Honolulu, 1988-96; owner Profitability World, Honolulu, 1996—. Pub. Hawaii Environ. Gazette, 1994-95. Coord. Gov.'s Energy Awards Program, 1991; chmn. Hunger Project Found., Honolulu, 1977-80; coord. Pau Hunger Found., Honolulu, 1980-81; co-founder, coord. Partnership for the Environment, 1992-95. Mem. Exch. Club (coord. Hilo 1990-91). Avocations: photography, running, writing, cooking, speaking.

NOWITZKY, MARK ALBIN, computer programmer; b. Encino, Calif., [illegible] Systems, Canoga Park, Calif., 1981-86, Great Western Bank, Northridge, Calif., 1986-92; software developer Legent Corp., Woodlands Hills, Calif., 1992-93; adv. programmer Boole & Babbage, San Jose, Calif., 1993-94; pres. NowitzKonsult Co., West Hills, Calif., 1989—; cons. Keane, Inc., Long

Beach, Calif., 1995—. Inventor in field. Avocations: classical & jazz trombone, classical piano. Home: 451 Ivy St Glendale CA 91204-1242

NOWLAN, DANIEL RALPH, engineering executive; b. Hammond, Ind., Feb. 23, 1947; s. Kenneth Edwin and Patricia Jane (Prendergast) N.; m. Sharon Louise Greichunos, Sept. 7, 1968; children: Daniel Ralph Jr., Kevin Anthony, Cynthia Ann. BSEE, Purdue U., 1969, MSEE, 1969. Engr./scientist McDonnell Douglas Astronautics Co, Santa Monica, Calif., 1969-75; engring. mgr. McDonnell Douglas Aerospace-West, Huntington Beach, Calif., 1975-96; tax preparer Tax Corp. of Am., Montrose, Calif., 1975-76; cons. in field; MDC fellow McDonnell Douglas Aerospace-West, 1996-97; sr. mgr., Boeing tech. fellow Boeing Co., 1997—. Eucharistic minister to convalescent homes St. Vincent De Paul Soc., Huntington Beach, 1993—; youth soccer coach Am. Youth Soccer Orgn., Westminster and Huntington Beach, 1975-82; bldg. fund dr. capt. St. Vincent De Paul Cath. Ch., Huntington Beach, 1979, 82, 97. Recipient Popular Sci. Achievement award, 1993, Space Frontier award, 1994, Engring. Project Achievement award, L.A. & Orange County Engring. Coun., 1994. Mem. AIAA (sr.), IEEE, Phi Kappa Theta, Tau Beta Pi, Eta Kappa Nu, Phi Eta Sigma. Roman Catholic. Avocations: arranging music for piano and keyboard, study of modern physics, study of philosophy. Home: 15931 Diamond St Westminster CA 92683-7203 Office: The Boeing Co M/C:HO13-C306 5301 Bolsa Ave Huntington Beach CA 92647-2048

NOWOSATKO, JEROME RAYMOND, software engineer; b. Detroit, Apr. 30, 1965; s. Raymond Peter and Sophie Helen (Pendzik) N. AA in Computer Sci., U. Md., Naples, Italy, 1989, BS in Info. Systems, 1989; MS in Software Engring., Colo. Tech., 1996. Cert. data processor, sys. profl., computing profl. Commd. E-4 U.S. Army, 1984; software engr. Compuware Corp., Detroit, 1990-91, Columbus, Ohio, 1991-92, Colorado Springs, 1992-97; pres., owner NOVUS Profl. Svcs. Inc., Colorado Springs, 1997—. Mem. Data Processing Mgmt. Assn., Inst. for Certification of Computing Profls., Project Mgmt. Inst., Buckley Sch. Forensic Soc. Republican. Roman Catholic. Avocations: hiking, scuba diving, reading, mountain biking, skiing. Home: 7215 Big Valley Ct Colorado Springs CO 80919-1035 Office: NOVUS Profl Svcs 7215 Big Valley Ct Colorado Springs CO 80919-1035

NOYES, PHILIP PATTERSON, ophthalmologist, retired; b. L.A., May 6, 1927; s. Bernard Clifford and Harriet Hazeltine (Patterson) N.; m. Eveline Green Bowers, Oct. 2, 1965; children: Katherine Marie, Elizabeth Lynn. AB, UCLA, 1949, MSc, 1957; MD, Duke U., 1961. Diplomate Am. Bd. Ophthalmology. Lab technician Atomic Energy Project, UCLA, 1950-57; lab asst. dept. physiology UCLA Sch. Medicine, 1957-58, scientist, dept. nuclear medicine, 1961; rotating intern VA Hosp., West Los Angeles, 1961-62; resident in ophthalmology Presbyn. Med. Ctr., San Francisco, 1962-65; pvt. practice ophthalmology San Francisco, 1965-96, San Leandro, 1965-96; chief ophthalmology Drs. Hosp., San Leandro, Vesper Meml. Hosp., San Leandro; chief staff and bd. dirs. San Leandro Hosp., 1992-94. Capt. USPHS. Fellow Am. Acad. Ophthalmology; mem. East Bay Ophthalmology Soc. (past pres.), Sigma Xi. Republican. Episcopalian. Avocations: ham radio, lapidary. Home: 1689 Regent Dr San Leandro CA 94577-5323

NUCE, MADONNA MARIE, career officer; b. Denver, Jan. 15, 1952; d. Donald William and Marie Dorothy (Ruscio) N.; m. Edward Ray Geron, Oct. 9, 1982; 1 child, Maria Louise. BA, U. No. Colo., 1974; grad., Command and Gen. Staff Coll., Ft. Leavenworth, 1993. Enlisted U.S. Army N.G., 1973; commd. 2d lt. U.S. Army, 1981, advanced through grades to col., 1998; adminstrv. supply tech. Colo. Army N.G., Denver, 1974-79; supply technician Colo. Army N.G., Golden, Colo., 1979-81; tng. officer Colo. Army N.G., Aurora, Colo., 1981-84, adminstrv. officer, 1984-85; maintenance officer Colo. Army N.G., Golden, Colo., 1985-86, asst. supply officer, 1986-91, data processing chief, 1991-92, supply mgmt. officer, 1992-93, comptr., 1993-94, dep. dir. maintenance, 1994-96; logistics officer Colo. Army N.G., 1996-97; exec. officer 89th troop command Colo. Army N.G., Golden, 1997-98; dir. maintenance Colo. Army N.G., 1998—. Group leader 5th grade Archdiocese of Denver Jr. Great Books Program, St. Anne Sch., 1987-89, group leader 7th grade Holy Family, 1991-92; bd. dirs. 9 Health Fair, Denver, 1985-90. Mem. Colo. N.G. Assn. (sec. 1981-83, bd. dirs. 1983-85), Assn. U.S. Army (treas. 1986-88), Colo. Artists Assn. Roman Catholic. Avocations: reading, skiing, watercolor painting. Office: HQ STARC Colo Army NG 6848 S Revere Pkwy Englewood CO 80112-3904

NUGENT, ROBERT J., JR., fast food company executive; b. 1942. BBA, U. Cin., 1964. loan officer Citizens Savs., 1964-67; asst. v.p. Gem City Savs., 1967-69; v.p. Ponderosa System Inc., 1969-78, Ky. Fried Chicken, 1978-79; v.p. Foodmaker Inc., San Diego, from 1979, exec. v.p. ops., mktg., 1985-95; CEO, pres. Foodmaker Inc., 1995—. Office: Foodmaker Inc 9330 Balboa Ave San Diego CA 92123-1598

NULL, THOMAS BLANTON, recording producer; b. Waco, Tex., July 9, 1941; s. Thomas Blanton Sr. and Dorothy (Caldwell) N. BA in English, Journalism, U. Mo., 1963. Co-founder Varese Sarabande Records, 1978—; pres. Citadel Records Corp., 1993—; CD-producer Bay Cities Records, Santa Monica, Calif., 1989-90, Phoenix Records, N.Y.C., 1989, Urania Records, N.Y.C., 1987-89; CD prodn. cons. MCA Records, Universal City, Calif., 1990—. Producer soundtrack album film Ghost (recipient Platinum Record award Recording Industry Assn. Am. 1990); exec. prodr. film Ballad of a Gunfighter, 1998. Avocations: classical LP and CD collecting, large antique auto collecting, model cars. Office: Citadel Records 7230 Hinds Ave North Hollywood CA 91605-3701

NUMANO, ALLEN STANISLAUS MOTOYUKI, musician, writer; came to U.S., 1974; Grad., St. Joseph's Coll., Colombo, Ceylon, 1929; postgrad., Worcester Coll., Oxford, Eng., 1940, Royal Coll. Music, London, 1940. Sr. examiner, translator Gen. Hdqs. Supreme Comdr. for Allied Powers, Tokyo, 1945-47; cons., chief tech. translator U.S.-Japanese joint venture Pfizer Taito Co. Ltd., Tokyo, 1954-68; lectr. English composition Sophia U., Tokyo, 1967-68; founder Safilta Tech. Translation Svc., 1969—. Author: (as A.L.A. Corenanda) Music and Reminiscences, 1982-83; translator: All About Christmas (Maymie R. Krythe), 1962; pioneering originator in new field of study Mentalogy; contbr. concert revs., recital critiques and mus. news briefs Nippon Times (now Japan Times), also articles to Times of Ceylon, Organic Forum, Indian Labour Rev.; pencil sketches exhibited at 55th Ann. Exhbn. of Ceylon Soc. of Arts, Colombo, 1952; performed as violinist at Royal Coll. Hall, Colombo, 1940; inventor tech. innovations. Del. Sr. Citizens of Honolulu to Gov.'s State Conf. on Aging. Recipient Gov.'s Cert. of Appreciation, 1980, certs. of appreciation Pres. Ronald Reagan and Pres. George Bush; named Citizen of Yr. 1994 Principality of Hutt River Province Australia. Fellow Inst. Linguists; mem. Soc. Authors, London (assoc.), Translator's Assn., London, Smithsonian Instn. (nat. mem.), George Bush Presdl. Libr. Mus.

NUNES, TANNY LUANN, preschool educator; b. Waukegan, Ill., Mar. 7, 1958; d. Frances Joseph and Bette Caryl (Rogers) McDonnell; m. Patrick Paul Nunes, Feb. 9, 1985; children: Beau, Nick, Casey. AA in Early Childhood Edn., Yuba Coll., 1998. Nanny Martin Family, Folsom, Calif., 1980-83; presch. art tchr. Little Folk U., Folsom, Calif., 1983-85. Author numerous poems. Actress, dancer, writer Lakeport (Calif.) Cmty. Players, 1993—; grief support facilitator Hospice Svcs., Lakeport, 1993-95. Named Poet of Month, Lake County Art Coun., Calif., 1997. Avocations: reading, writing, camping, conversing, cooking ethnic food. Home: 4588 Hawaina Way Kelseyville CA 95451-9756

NUNIS, DOYCE BLACKMAN, JR., historian, educator; b. Cedartown, Ga., May 30, 1924; s. Doyce Blackman and Winnie Ethel (Morris) N. B.A., U. Calif., Los Angeles, 1947; M.S., U. So. Calif., 1950, M.Ed., 1952, Ph.D., 1958. Lectr. U. So. Calif., 1951-56; instr. El Camino Coll., 1956-59; asst. prof. edn. and history UCLA, 1959-65; assoc. prof. history U. So. Calif., 1965-68, prof., 1968-89, emeritus, 1989—; disting. prof. emeritus, 1993; asst. research historian U. Calif., Los Angeles, 1959-63; asso. U. Calif., 1963-65, lectr., 1960-61, asst. prof. edn. and history, 1961-64, asso. prof., 1964-65. Author: Andrew Sublette, Rocky Mountain Prince, 1960, Josiah Belden, 1841 California Overland Pioneer, 1962, The Golden Frontier: The Recollections of Herman Francis Rinehart, 1851-69, 1962, The California Diary of Faxon Dean Atherton, 1836-39, 1964, Letters of a Young Miner, 1964, The Journal of James H. Bull, 1965, The Trials of Isaac Graham, 1967, The Medical Journey of Pierre Garnier in California, 1851, 1967, Past is Prologue, 1968, Hudson's Bay Company's First Fur Brigade to the Sacramento Valley, 1968, Sketches of a Journey on Two Oceans by H.J.A. Alric, 1850-1867, 1971, San Francisco 1856 Vigilance Committee: Three Views, 1971, The Drawings of Ignatio Tirsh, Los Angeles and Its Environs in the 20th Century, A Bibliography, 1973, A History of American Political Thought, 2 vols, 1975, The Mexican War in Baja California, 1977, Henry Hoyt's A Frontier Doctor, 1979, Los Angeles from the Days of the Old Pueblo, 1981, The 1769 Transit of Venus, 1982, The Missionary Letters of Jacob Baegert, 1982, Men, Medicine and Water, 1982, Southern California Historical Anthology, 1984, George Coe's Frontier Fighter, 1984, Life of Tom Horn, 1987, A Guide to the History of California, 1989, Great Doctors of Medicine, 1990, The Bidwell-Bartleson Party, 1991, The Life of Tom Horn Revisited, 1992, Southern California's Spanish Heritage, 1992, Southern California Local History, A Gathering of W.W. Robinson's Writings, 1993, From Mexican Days to the Gold Rush, 1993, Tales of Mexican California, 1994, Women in the Life of Southern California, 1996, Hispanic California Revisited, 1996, The Presidio of San Francisco under Spain and Mexico, 1775-1848, 1996, Mission San Fernando, Rey de España: A Bicentennial Tribute, 1997; editor So. Calif. Quar., 1962—; contbr. articles to profl. jours. Trustee Mission Santa Barbara Archives-Libr., 1970—, pres., 1972—. Decorated Benemerenti, Papal medal, 1984; recipient Distinction award Calif. Com. for Promotion of History, 1985, Merit award Calif. Conf. Hist. Socs., 1986, Franciscan Hist. award, 1990, Disting. Emeritus award U. So. Calif., 1993, Knight Comdr. of St. Gregory, 1993, Order of Isabel the Cath. (Spanish Govt.), 1995, Oscar Lewis award Book Club of Calif., 1996, benefactor award, Franciscans, 1949benefactor's award Province of St. Barbara 1999; Henry E. Huntington Libr. grantee-in-aid, 1960, Am. Philos. Soc. grantee, 1969; Guggenheim fellow, 1963-64. Fellow Calif. Hist. Soc. (trustee 1987-93, v.p. 1989-93, Henry R. Wagner award 1988), fellow Hist. Soc. So. Calif.; mem. Am. Antiquarian Soc., Am. Hist. Assn., Orgn. Am. Historians, Western Hist. Assn., Zamorano Club, L.A. Corral Westerners, Phi Alpha Theta, Pi Sigma Alpha.

NUSBAUM, ELLEN JANE, technology professional; b. Chgo., Apr. 4, 1961; d. Joseph Alan Ettinger and Diane Frank; m. Roger Lewis Nusbaum, Nov. 27, 1988; 1 child, Jillian Eva. BA in journalism, U. Ariz., 1983. Tech. editor Garret Turbine Engine Co., Phoenix, 1986-87; tech. writer Wang Informatics, Phoenix, 1987-89; computer cons. Phoenix, 1989-93; project mgr. Computerprep, Phoenix, 1993-94; sr. project mgr. Computerprep, 1994-96, ILT program mgr., 1996-97, devel. mgr., 1997, engring. mgr., 1997-98, engring. dir., 1998—; grad. Supr.'s Acad., Ariz. Govt. Tng. Svc., Phoenix, 1995; regional judge Odyssey of the Mind, 1996. Contbg. writer food and travel features, Cox Newspapers, Inc. Recipient scholarship for editl. writing William Randolph Hearst Nat. Awards, 1983. Mem. NAFE. Avocations: writing children's books, screenwriting, food and travel writing. Office: Computerprep 410 N 44th St Ste 600 Phoenix AZ 85008

NUSBAUM, GEOFFREY DEAN, psychotherapist; b. Berkeley, Calif., Apr. 1, 1946; s. Wayne Dale and Jeanne (Hankins) N.; m. Barbara Ann Pierfy, June 1, 1986; 1 child, Michael Wayne. BA, Washington U., St. Louis, 1967; MA, Hartford Sem. Fdn. Consortium, 1971, PhD, 1978. Diplomate Am. Bd. Med. Psychotherapy; cert. therapist Am. Assn. for Marriage and Family Therapy; lic. therapist, N.J. Pvt. practice Marlton, N.J. and Phila., 1972—; cons. N.Y. Fertility Rsch. Found., N.Y.C., 1978-83, Bancroft Sch., Haddonfield, N.J., 1983-87; fellow Internat. Coun. Sex. Edn. and Parenthood Am. U. Author: Community, Self Identity, 1978; peer manuscript reviewer to sci. jours. Bd. dirs. Calcutta House AIDS Hospice. Mem. Am. Soc. for Reproductive Medicine, Am. Soc. for Psychosomatic Ob-Gyn., N.Y. Acad. Scis.

NUSS, WILLIAM MARTIN (BILL NUSS), television producer, writer; b. Lawrence, N.Y., Mar. 29, 1954; s. David Bernard and Nadia Sybil (Messing) N. BS, Northwestern U., 1976. Freelance TV writer James at 15, Eight is Enough, Good Times, Welcome Back Kotter, Fernwood Tonite, Hollywood, Calif., 1976-78, v.p. NBC Entertainment, Burbank, Calif., 1978-82; writer Metromedia Producers Corp., 1982-84; producer, story editor, writer Riptide, The A-Team Stephen J. Cannell Prodns., Hollywood, 1985-90, exec. producer 21 Jump Street, Booker, 1985-90; exec. producer Hat Squad, 1992, Renegade, 1993-95; creator, exec. producer, Pacific Blue, 1997. Recipient NAACP award, Asian-Am. award, Newman Found. award, NCCJ Imagen award, Media Access award. Mem. Nat. Acad. TV Arts and Scis., Hollywood Radio and TV Soc.

NUSSBAUM, JON KIMBAL, defense contractor executive; b. Muncie, Ind., Sept. 21, 1957; s. Alvin A. and Maxine E. (Meyer) N.; 1 child, J. Ethan; m. Kelly Ann Nussbaum, Sept. 1, 1998; stepchildren: Julianne E., Kiley N. Buffington, Shelby A. Buffington. BS, U.S. Mil. Acad., 1980. Commd. 2d lt. U.S. Army, 1980, advanced through grades to capt., 1984, resigned, 1988; mgr. advanced programs Alcoa Def. Systems, Inc., San Diego, 1988-89; sr. mgr. bus. devel. McDonnell Douglas Techs., Inc., San Diego, 1989-92; dir., bus. devel. land systems, signature tech. divsn. Sci. Applications Internat. Corp., San Diego, 1992-94, mgr. signature tech. divsn., 1994—, site mgr., program mgr.; self-employed def. cons., Temecula, Calif., 1990—. With USAR. Mem. Am. Def. Preparedness Assn., U.S. Armor Assn., West. Point Assn. Grads., Res. Officers Assn., West Point Soc. of the Inland Empire (treas. 1991—). Republican. Avocations: bicycling, running. Office: Sci Applications Internat Corp 10260 Campus Point Dr San Diego CA 92121-1522

NUSSBERGER, CLINT JOSEPH, career officer; b. Medford, Wis., Aug. 24, 1968; s. James Joseph and Kathleen Rose (Murray) N.; m. Leann Christine Kuns, May 25, 1991; children: Brittany Kaye, Mark Joseph. BA in Polit. Sci., U. Wis., 1993. Enlisted USMC, 1986, commd. 2d lt., 1993; advanced through grades to capt., 1997. Campaign worker Young Reps., Prentice, Wis., 1984; pres. Semper Fidelis Soc., Madison, Wis., 1992-93. Avocations: reading, history, running, geneology, studying Arabic. Home: 205 Cassino Rd Seaside CA 93955-6429

NUTT, JOHN GORDON, neurologist, educator; b. Orlando, Fla., Aug. 26, 1943; s. John Gordon and Margaret (Davenport) N.; m. McKay Brown, June 13, 1970. BA in Biochemistry, Rice U., 1965; MS in Pharmacology, Baylor Coll. Med., 1970, MD, 1970. Diplomate Am. Bd. Psychiatry and Neurology. Intern in internal med. U. Oreg., Portland, 1970-71; mem. staff NIMH Addiction Rsch. Ctr., Lexington, Ky., 1971-73; resident in neurology U. Wash., Seattle, 1973-76; clin. assoc. Nat. Inst. Neurol. Communicative Disorders and Stroke, Bethesda, Md., 1976-78; from asst. prof. to prof. Oreg. Health Sci. U., Portland, 1978-88, prof. neurology, 1988—; dir. Parkinson Ctr. of Oreg., Portland, 1992—; rsch. adv. bd. Essential Blepharospasm Found., 1983-97; assessment com. Am. Acad. Neurology, 1997—; lectr. in field. Author: 100 Maxims-Parkinson's Disease, 1992; author of over 52 chpts. in books; mem. editl. bd. Movement Disorder, Reviews in Neurosci., Ann Neurology, Parkinsonism & Related, 1997—; contbr. 99 articles to profl. jours. Recipient Excellence award Nat. Parkinson's Found. Ctr., Portland; Levodopa Pharmacokientics grantee NIH, 1984-00, Peripheral & Ctrl. Postural Disorders grantee NIH, NIA, P.I. Horak-Dow Neurol. Inst., 1995-00, Nat. Parkinson's Found. Ctr. Excellence grantee NIH, 96-00. Fellow Am. Acad. Neurology (sci. issues com. 1978—); mem. Am. Acad. Neurology (v.p. movement disorder sect. 1998-00), Am. Neurol. Assn. (membership com. 1986-88), Movement Disorder Soc. (exec. com. 1991-95, 99—). Avocations: white water and sea Kayaking. Office: Oregon Health Sciences U Dept Neurology 3181 SW Sam Jackson Park Rd Portland OR 97201-3011

NUTTALL, MICHAEL LEE, engineer, educator; b. Salem, Mass.; s. Leonard John IV and Ethel (Pecukonis) N.; m. Susan Patricia Wade, July 12, 1988; children: Leonard John VI, Andrew Norman, Michelle Leigh, Patricia Katherine. BSChemE, Brigham Young U., 1987; MEE, U. Utah, 1994. Japanese linguist Utah Army N.G., Provo, 1984-87; math tutor Utah Valley C.C., Provo, 1987; engr. Micron Tech., Boise, Idaho, 1988-89, lead engr., 1989-91, process devel. engr., 1994—; instr. Salt Lake C.C., Salt Lake City, 1991-92. Patentee in field. Home: 1469 N Deep Creek Way Meridian ID 83642-4215 Office: Micro Tech 8000 Federal Way Boise ID 83716-9632

NUTTER, WILLIAM SCOTT, business consultant, real estate agent; b. Bryn Mawr, Pa.. Bachelor, Okla. State U., 1966, Master, 1968; postgrad., UCLA, 1970. Lic. real estate agt., Calif.; lic. employment agy. specialist, Calif.; cert. rehab./worker's compensation specialist Am. Personnel and Guidance Assn. Cons. Orange County, Calif.; bd. dirs. Group Nine Corp., Hollywood, Trails West Corp., Orange County, Sage Coach Campers, Inc., Orange County; chair linkages com. Orange County Manpower Adv. Bd. Co-author: Coordinating Education and Rehabilitation, 1971; co-author 1st non-welfare grant for Asian refugees. Commr., Calif. Worksite Edn. and Tng. Act, Orange County, 1979-82; working conf. coord. for minority-handicapped svcs. Calif. State U., Northridge, 1974; state rep. Counselor Adv. Com., Sacramento, 1974-76. With USAF, 1968-71. Recipient Achievement award Orange County Donor Program, 1970, Chancellor's award Golden West Coll. Mem. Orange County Personnel and Guidance Assn. (exec. bd.). Avocations: multi-hull sailing (univ. sailing team capt.), riding (Morgans), fencing (univ. team co-capt.), music (violin), Flying Aggies (nat. 1st place). Home: PO Box 2082 Anaheim CA 92814-0082

NUTZLE, FUTZIE (BRUCE JOHN KLEINSMITH), artist, author, cartoonist; b. Lakewood, Ohio, Feb. 21, 1942; s. Adrian Ralph and Naomi Irene (Rupert) Kleinsmith; children: Adrian David, Arielle Justine and Tess Alexandra (twins). Represented by The Pope Gallery, Santa Cruz, Calif. Author: Modern Loafer, Thames and Hudson, 1981, (authobiography) Futzie Nutzle, 1983, Earthquake, 1989, Run the World: 50 Cents Chronicle Books, 1991; illustrator: The Armies Encamped Beyond Unfinished Avenues (Morton Marcus), 1977, Box of Nothing, 1982, The Duke of Chemical Birds (Howard McCord), 1989, Book of Solutions, 1990, Fact and Friction, 1990, Managing for the 90s, 1992, Soundbites for Success, 1994; feature cartoonist Rolling Stone, N.Y.C., 1975-80, The Japan Times, Tokyo and L.A., 1986—, The Prague Post, Czechoslovakia, 1991—; contbr. exhbns. include Inaugural, 1966, Cupola, 1967, Rolling Renaissance, San Francisco, 1968, 100 Acres, O.K. Harris 1971, N.Y.C., San Francisco Mus. Art, 1972, Indpls. and Cin. Mus. Art, 1975, Leica, L.A., 1978, Santa Barbara Mus. Annex, Calif., 1978, Swope, Santa Monica, West Beach Cafe, Venice, Calif., 1985, Les Oranges, Santa Monica, Correspondence Sch., 1970-78, 1st Ann. Art-A-Thon, N.Y.C., 1985, Am. Epiphany with Phillip Hefferton, 1986, Polit. Cartoon Show, Braunstein, San Francisco, Komsomolskaya Pravda, 1988, retrospective Eloise Packard Smith, 1990, exemplary contemporary, Cowell, U. Calif. Santa Cruz, 1991, Silicon Graphics Inc., Computer Graphics for NAB, Las Vegas, 1993, Prague Eco-Fair, 1991; represented in pvt. and pub. collections (complete archives) Spl. Collections, McHenry Libr., U. Calif., Santa Cruz, Mus. Modern Art, N.Y.C., San Francisco Mus. Modern Art, Oakland Mus., San Francisco Mus. Cartoon Art, Whitney Mus. Am. Art, N.Y.C. regular contbr. The Japan Times. Ltd., Tokyo. Address: PO Box 325 Aromas CA 95004-0325

NUVEEN, JOHN SEPTIMUS, cultural affairs organization executive; b. Evanston, Ill., Feb. 21, 1934; s. John and Grace Bennet N.; children: John, Octavius, Nuveen. Pastor Amagansett (N.Y.) Presbyn. Ch., 1962-63; mem. Iona Community, Ch. of Scotland, Glasgow, 1959-60; pres. Ctr. for Arts, Religion, Edn., Berkeley, Calif., 1988—; bd. dirs. Soc. for Arts, Religion and Contemporary Culture, N.Y.C.; vis. scholar Grad. Theol. Union, Berkeley, 1981-82. Author: Poems for Dreamers, 1986. Active Saco Valley Environ. Svc. Project. Mem. Am. Acad. Religion. Home and Office: 1563 Solano Ave # 133 Berkeley CA 94707-2116

NYCUM, SUSAN HUBBELL, lawyer. BA, Ohio Wesleyan U., 1956; JD, Duquesne U., 1960; postgrad., Stanford U. Bar: Pa. 1962, U.S. Supreme Ct. 1967, Calif. 1974. Sole practice law Pitts., 1962-65; designer, adminstr. legal rsch. sys. U. Pitts., Aspen Sys. Corp., Pitts., 1965-68; mgr. ops. Computer Ctr., Carnegie Mellon U., Pitts., 1968-69; dir. computer facility Computer Ctr., Stanford U., Calif., 1969-72, Stanford Law and Computer fellow, 1972-73; cons. in computers and law, 1973-74; sr. assoc. MacLeod, Fuller, Muir & Godwin, Los Altos, Los Angeles and London, 1974-75; ptnr. Chickering & Gregory, San Francisco, 1975-80; ptnr.-in-charge high tech. group Gaston Snow & Ely Bartlett, Boston, NYC, Phoenix, San Francisco, Calif., 1980-86; mng. ptnr. Palo Alto office Kadison, Pfaelzer, Woodard, Quinn & Rossi, Los Angeles, Washington, Newport Beach, Palo Alto, Calif., 1986-87; sr. ptnr., chmn. U.S. intellectual property/info. tech. practice group Baker & McKenzie, Palo Alto, 1987—, mem. U.S. leadership team, 1987-97, mem. Asia Pacific regional coun., 1995—; trustee EDUCOM, 1978-81; mem. adv. com. for high tech. Ariz. State U. Law Sch., Santa Clara U. Law Sch., Stanford Law Sch., U. So. Calif. Law Ctr., law sch. Harvard U., U. Calif.; U.S. State Dept. del. OECD Conf. on Nat. Vulnerabilities, Spain, 1981; invited speaker Telecom, Geneva, 1983; lectr. N.Y. Law Jour., 1975—, Law & Bus., 1975—, Practicing Law Inst., 1975—; chmn. Office of Tech. Assessment Task Force on Nat. Info. Sys., 1979-80. Author:(with Bigelow) Your Computer and the Law, 1975, (with Bosworth) Legal Protection for Software, 1985, (with Collins and Gilbert) Women Leading, 1987; contbr. monographs, articles to profl. publs. Mem. Town of Portola Valley Open Space Acquisition Com., Calif., 1977; mem. Jr. League of Palo Alto, chmn. evening div., 1975-76. NSF and Dept. Justice grantee for studies on computer abuse, 1972—. Fellow Assn. Computer Machinery (mem. at large of coun. 1976-80, nat. lectr. 1977—, chmn. standing com. on legal issues 1975—, mem. blue ribbon com. on rationalization of internat. propr. rights protection on info. processing devel. in the '90s 1990—), Coll. Law Practice Mgmt.; mem. ABA (chmn. sect. on sci. and tech. 1979-80), Internat. Bar Assn. (U.S. mem. computer com. of corps. sect.), Computer Law Assn. (v.p. 1983-85, pres. 1986—, bd. dirs. 1975—), Calif. State Bar Assn. (founder first chmn. econs. of law sect., vice chmn. law and computers com.), Nat. Conf. Lawyers and Scientists (rep. ABA), Strategic Forum on Intellectual Property Issues in Software of NAS, Internat. Coun. for Computer Comm. (gov. 1998). Home: 35 Granada Ct Portola Valley CA 94028 Office: Baker & McKenzie PO Box 60309 Palo Alto CA 94306-0309

NYE, ERIC WILLIAM, English language and literature educator; b. Omaha, July 31, 1952; s. William Frank and Mary Roberta (Lueder) N.; m. Carol Denison Frost, Dec. 21, 1980; children: Charles William, Ellen Mary. BA, St. Olaf Coll., 1974; MA, U. Chgo., 1976, PhD, 1983; postgrad., Queens' Coll., Cambridge, England, 1979-82. Tutor in coll. writing com. U. Chgo., 1976-79, tchg. intern, 1978; tutor Am. lit. Cambridge (Eng.) U., 1979-82; asst. prof. English U. Wyo., Laramie, 1983-89, assoc. prof., 1989—; v.p., bd. dirs. Plainview Tel. Co., Nebr.; hon. vis. fellow U. Edinburgh (Scotland) Inst. for Advanced Studies in the Humanities, 1987; guest lectr. NEH summer Inst., Laramie, Wyo., 1985, Carlyle Soc. of Edinburgh, 1987, Wordsworth summer Conf., Grasmere, Eng., 1988, cons. NEH. Contbr. articles and reviews to profl. jours. Mem. Am. Friends of Cambridge U., Friends of Cambridge U. Libr. (life), Gen. Soc. Mayflower Descendants; elected mem. Wyo. Coun. for Humanities, 1992-96, mem. exec. com., 1993-94; mem. adv. bd. Wyo. Ctr. for the Book, 1995—; leader Boy Scouts Am. Named Nat. Merit Scholar St. Olaf Coll., 1970-74; recipient Amb. Fellowship, Rotary Found., 1979-80, grant Am. Coun. of Learned Socs., 1988, Disting. Alumnus award, Lincoln (Neb.) E. High Sch., 1986. Mem. MLA (del. assembly 1991-93), Bibliog. Soc. London, Assn. for Computers and the Humanities, Assn. for Lit. and Linguistic Computing, Assn. Literary Scholars and Critics, Coleridge Soc. (life), Friends of Dove Cottage (life), Jane Austen Soc. N.Am. (life), Charles Lamb Soc., Carlyle Soc. (life), Rsch. Soc. for Victorian Periodicals, Soc. for History of Authorship, Reading, and Pub., Wyo. State Hist. Soc. (life), The Victorians Inst., The Tennyson Soc., Royal Oak Found., Penn Club (London), Queens' Coll. Club (Cambridge) Phi Beta Kappa (pres., v.p., sec. Wyo. chpt. 1988-98). Home: 1495 Apache Dr Laramie WY 82072-6966 Office: U Wyo Dept English PO Box 3353 Laramie WY 82071-3353

NYE, GENE WARREN, retired art educator; b. Sacramento, July 3, 1939; s. Charles Frederick and Dorthy Dell Nye; m. Alena Mae Nye, Sept. 20, 1974; children: Dirk, Ronni, Anthony, Timothy. AA, American River Coll., Sacramento, 1962; AB, Sacramento State U., 1964; cert. Secondary Art Tchr., U. Calif., Berkeley, 1966. Printer Roseville (Calif.) Press Tribune, 1957-60; typographer Oakland (Calif.) Tribune, 1960-65; tchr. art Long Beach (Calif.) Unified Sch. Dist., 1965-67; tchr., chair art dept. Woodland (Calif.) Unified Sch. Dist., 1967-98; retired, 1998; freelance artist Wildcat Art, Sacramento, 1985—; cons. in field; workshop presenter. Author: (workbook set and video) Posters Made EZ, 1990. Mem. task force Constn. Revision of CADA, L.A., 1988-89. Named to Calif. Assn. Dirs. of Activities Hall of Fame, 1992. Mem. NEA (life), Calif. Tchrs. Assn., Calif. Retired Tchrs. Assn., Woodland Edn. Assn. (v.p. 1971-72), Calif. Art Edn. Assn., Nat. Art Edn. Assn., Calif. League Mid. Schs., U. Calif.-Berkeley Alumni Assn. (life). Home: 2200 Eastern Ave Sacramento CA 95864-0805

NYE, W. MARCUS W., lawyer; b. N.Y.C., Aug. 3, 1945; s. Walter R. and Nora (McLaren) N.; m. Eva Johnson; children: Robbie, Stephanie, Philip, Jennifer. BA, Harvard U., 1967; JD, U. Idaho, 1974. Bar: Idaho 1974, U.S. Dist. Ct. Idaho 1974, U.S. Ct. Appeals (9th cir.) 1980; lic. pilot. Ptnr. Racine, Olson, Nye, Budge & Bailey, Pocatello, Idaho, 1974—; vis. prof. law U. Idaho, Moscow, 1984; adj. prof. Coll. Engring. Idaho State U., 1993—; bd. dirs. Idaho State U. Found. Recipient Alumni Svc. award U. Idaho, 1988. Fellow ABA (mem. ho. dels. 1988—, state chmn. ho. of dels. 1991—, bd. of govs. 1997—), Am. Bar Found. (stat. chmn. 1992-95); mem. Am. Bd. Trial Advs., Am. Coll. Trial Lawyers, Idaho Bar Assn. (commr. 1985—, pres. bd. commrs. 1987-88), Idaho Def. Counsel Assn. (pres. 1982), Idaho State Centennial Found. (commr. 1985-90), 6th Dist. Bar Assn. (pres. 1982). Avocation: flying. Home: 173 S 15th Ave Pocatello ID 83201-4056 Office: Racine Olson et al Budge & Bailey PO Box 1391 Pocatello ID 83204-1391

NYIRI, JOSEPH ANTON, sculptor, art educator; b. Racine, Wis., May 24, 1937; s. Joseph Anton Nyiri and Dorothy Marion (Larson) Zink; m. Laura Lee Primeau, Aug. 29, 1959 (dec. Mar. 1982); children: Krista, Nicole, Page; m. Melissa Trent, July 28, 1985. BA, U. Wis., 1959, MS, 1961. Tchr. art Madison (Wis.) Sch. Dist., 1959-62; art cons. San Diego Unified Schs., 1962-65, dist. resource tchr., 1965-73, regional tchr. occupational art, 1973-76, mentor tchr., 1985-95; sculptor San Diego, 1962—, fine arts cons., 1966—; head dept. art edn. Serra H.S., San Diego, 1976-95; tchr. art Zool. Soc. San Diego, 1991-95; ret., 1995; cons. gifted and talented edn. program San Diego City Schs., 1995—, gifted programs Escondido, Calif. and Poway, Calif. Schs., 1995—, Boston Schs., 1996-98, Romana, Calif. Pub. Schs., 1997—; instr. art U. Calif. at San Diego, La Jolla, 1967-80, San Diego State U. Extension, 1969—; fine art restorer, 1963—, lectr. art and art edn., 1963—; pvt. art tchr. San Diego City Zoo. Exhibited sculpture in numerous one-man, two-person, juried and invitational shows, 1960—, U. Mex.-Baja Calif., 1983; rev. Calif. Art Rev., 1989. Active Art Guild San Diego Mus. Art; bd. dirs. San Diego Art Inst. Sgt. Wis. N.G., 1955-61. Named One of 3 Tchrs. of Yr., San Diego County, 1983, One of Outstanding Art Tchrs. in U.S., RISD, 1984, Secondary Tchr. of Yr., San Diego City Schs., 1982; recipient creativity award Pacific Inst., 1969. Mem. Arts/Worth: Nat. Coun. Art (charter), Allied Craftsmen San Diego, Internat. Platform Assn., San Diego Art Inst. (bd. dirs.), San Diego Mus. Art (mem. Art Guild), Zool. Soc. San Diego. Democrat. Mem. Christian Ch. Avocations: running, hiking, travel, reading, writing poetry. Office: 3525 Albatross St San Diego CA 92103-4807 Also: Zool Soc San Diego Edn Dept PO Box 551 San Diego CA 92112-0551

NYMAN, DAVID HAROLD, retired nuclear engineer; b. Aberdeen, Wash., May 21, 1938; s. Carl Victor and Elsie Ingagord (Laaksonen) N. Assoc., Grays Harbor Coll., 1958; BSMetE, U. Wash., 1961, MSMetE, 1963. Engr. GE Co., Richland, Wash., 1963-68; engring. specialist United Nuclear Corp., New Haven, 1968-73; mgr. Westinghouse Hanford subs. Westinghouse Corp., Richland, 1973-96; ret., 1996. Contbr. articles to profl jours. Mem. Robotics Internat. of Soc. Mfg. Engrs. (div. chmn. 1985-86, tech. v.p. 1986-88), Robots West Conf. (adv. com. 1984, vice-chmn. 1986, Pres.'s award 1989), Am. Nuclear Soc. (chmn. meetings, proceedings, and transactions com. 1992-96), Am. Soc. Metals., Inst. Nuclear Materials Mgmt., Columbia Basin Dog Tng. Club (pres. 1982-84), Richland Kennel Club, West Highland White Terrier Club of Puget Sound, West Highland White Terrier Club Am. (obedience com. 1982-88), Am. Kennel Club (judge tracking dog excellent tests). Republican. Lutheran.

NYQUIST, MAURICE OTTO, government agency administrator and scientist; b. Fairmont, Minn., May 30, 1944; s. Carl Arther and Wilda Yvette (Freitag) N.; m. Mary Maud Magee, Aug. 8, 1977; children: Gretchen, Beth. BS in Biology, Hamline U., 1966; MA in Biology, Mankato State U., 1968; PhD in Zoology, Wash. State U., 1973. Asst. prof. zoology Wash. State U., Pullman, 1973-74; scientist Nat. Park Svc., Lakewood, Colo., 1974-76, mgr., 1979-93; mgr., scientist Nat. Biol. Svc., Denver, 1993-96, USGS, Denver, 1996—; mem. peer rev. coms. for academia, govt. and pvt. industry; agy. rep. Fed. Geographic Data Com., chair biol. data working group. Dir. prodn. interactive computer exhibit on remote sensing for Denver Mus. Nat. History; contbr. sci. articles to profl. jours. Bd. dirs. Nat. Park Service Equal Employment Opportunity Com., Denver, 1981, chmn., 1982. Recipient Mgrs. award Nat. Park Service, Lakewood, 1981, Performance Commendation award, 1988; research grantee Nat. Rifle Assn., 1972. Fellow Am. Soc. Potogrammetry and Remote Sensing (exec. com., bd. dirs. 1988-90, v.p. 1992, pres.-elect 1993, pres. 1994, asst. dir. remote sensing applications divsn. 1985-87); mem. Am. Congress on Surveying and Mapping (joint satellite mapping and remote sensing com.), The Wildlife Soc., GRASS Users Group (steering com. 1986—, treas. 1987—), ELAS Users Group (co-chmn. 1985-86, chmn. 1986-87), Sigma Xi. Avocations: tennis, skiing, soccer.

OAK, CLAIRE MORISSET, artist, educator; b. St. Georges, Quebec, Can., May 31, 1921; came to U.S., 1945; d. Louis and Bernadette (Coulombe) Morisset; m. Alan Ben Oak, July 2, 1947. Student, Ecole des Beaux Arts, 1938-42, Parsons Sch. Design, N.Y.C., 1945, Art Students League, N.Y.C., 1945-46. Staff artist Henry Morgan & R. Simpson, Montreal, 1942-45; artist illustrator W.B. Golovin Advt. Agy., N.Y.C., 1947-49; freelance illustrator Arnold Constable & Advt. Agy., N.Y.C., 1948-50, Le Jardin des Modes, Paris, 1950-51, May & Co., L.A., 1956, Katten & Marengo Advt., Stockton, Calif., 1962-84; pvt. practice illustrator, designer San Joaquin Valley, Calif., 1984-92; art instr. San Joaquin Delta Coll., Stockton, 1973—; owner Fashion Illustrator's Workshop, N.Y.C., 1953-54; instr. Bauder Coll., Sacramento, 1975-76; painting workshop leader Lodi Art Ctr., 1991—; watercolor workshop leader D'Pharr Painting Adventures, Virginia City, Nev., 1992; ongoing watercolor workshop Galerie Iona, Stockton, Calif., 1993—. Named S.B. Anthony Woman of Achievement in the Arts, U. Pacific, 1982. Mem. Stockton Art League, Lodi Art Ctr., Ctrl. Calif. Art League, The League of Carmichael Artists, Delta Watercolor Soc. (bd. mem. 1988—). Avocations: outdoor painting, drawing from a model. Home: 2140 Waudman Ave Stockton CA 95209-1755

OAKES, TERRY LOUIS, retail clothing store executive; b. Denver, June 12, 1953; s. Robert Walter and Stella Marie (Ray) O.; m. Cynthia Alison Bailey, Jan. 10, 1981; children: Madeleine Bailey, Robert Alan. BBA, So. Meth. U., 1975. Dept. mgr. Woolf Bros., Dallas, 1975-76; buyer I.K.O. Dry Goods, Denver, 1976-79, gen. sales mgr., 1979-81, exec. v.p., mdse. mgr., 1981-86; nat. sales mgr. Fresh Squeeze div. Bayly Corp., Denver, 1986-88; owner, pres. Bolderdash, Denver, 1988—; tchr., mem. adv. bd. fashion mdse. divsn. Colo. Inst. Art., Denver, 1991—. Bd. dirs. Vail Racquet Club, Vail, Colo. Mem. Vail Racquet Club (bd. dirs.). Democrat. Presbyterian. Home: 5390 S Geneva St Englewood CO 80111-6205 Office: Bolderdash 2817 E 3rd Ave Denver CO 80206-4905

OAKLEY, CAROLYN LE, state legislator, small business owner; b. Portland, Oreg., June 28, 1942; d. George Thomas and Ruth Alveta Victoria (Engberg) Penketh; children: Christine, Michelle. BS in Edn., Oreg. State U., 1965. Educator Linn County (Oreg.) Schs., 1965-76; owner Linn County Tractor, 1965-90; mem. Oreg. Legis. Assembly, Salem, 1989—, asst. majority leader, 1993—, majority whip, 1994; mem. exec. bd. Oreg. Retail Coun., 1987-90. Chmn. Linn County Rep. Ctrl. Com., 1982-84; chmn. bd. dirs. North Albany Svc. Dist., 1988-90; chair Salvation Army, Linn and Benton Counties, 1987—; vice chmn. bd. trustees Linn-Benton C.C. Found., 1987—; pres. Women for Agr., Linn and Benton Counties, 1984-86; mem. STRIDE Leadership Round Table, 1991—; state chair Am. Legis. Exch. Coun., 1991-96; nat. bd. dirs., 199-99, exec. com., 1995, 1st vice chair, 1998; mem. Edn. Commn. of the States, 1991—, com. policies and priorities, 1993—, steering com., 1998—, exec. com., 1998; mem. Leadership Coun. on Higher Edn., 1995—; mem. nat. policy bd. Danforth Found., 1995—; state dir., Women in Govt., 1996—; state dir., Nat. Order Women Legislators, 1993—; hon. mem. Linn-Benton Compact Bd., 1993—; active Linn County Criminal Justice Coun., 1994—. Named Woman of Yr. Albany chpt. Beta Sigma Phi, 1970. Mem. Nat Conf State Legislators (chmn. edn. com. 1992—), Albany C. of C. (bd. dirs. 1986-93, 96—), Linn County Rep. women (legis. chmn. 1982-91). Republican. Methodist. Avocations: gardening, camping. Home: 3197 [illegible] Capital Salem OR 97310

OAKLEY, DAVID STERLING, physics educator, consultant; b. Denver, Apr. 2, 1938; s. Gary Addison and JoAnn (Williams) O.; m. Barbara JoAnn Quinn, Apr. 5, 1986; children: David Addison, Andrew Timothy, Madeleine. BA, Colo. U., 1981; MA, Tex. U., 1985, PhD, 1987. Rsch. assoc. Colo. U., Boulder, 1987-89; asst. prof. Lewis and Clark Coll., Portland, Oreg., 1989-93; assoc. prof. Colo. Christian U., Lakewood, 1993—; dir. rsch. Safe Air Monitoring Systems, Inc., Denver, 1989—. Contbr. articles to profl. jours. Youth counselor Young Life, Austin, Tex., 1981-87; mem. So. Utah Wilderness Alliance, Salt Lake City, 1986—, Oreg. Rivers Coun., Portland, 1992—. Mem. Am. Phys. Soc. Presbyterian. Achievements include patent in method for detecting hydrogen containing compounds, detection of natural gas and household radon; research in correlation between solar neutrino flux and solar magnetic fields, in nuclear structure, role of space-time in Christian theology. Office: Colo Christian Univ 180 S Garrison St Lakewood CO 80226-1053

OAKS, LUCY MOBERLEY, retired social worker; b. Lexington, Ky., May 10, 1935; d. Shelton Neville Moberley and Jane Emison (Roberts) Meadors; m. William Bryant Oaks, Nov. 10, 1956; children: Bryant, Michael, Kevin, Richard, Deborah. BA in Social Work, U. Ky., 1957; MA in Counseling Psychology, Bowie (Md.) State Coll., 1979. Cert. mental health counselor, Wash. Youth dir. Calvary Bapt. Ch., Renton, Wash., 1960-64, ch. tng. dir., 1980-87; youth dir. Temple Bapt. Ch., Redlands, Calif., 1965-68, Calvary Bapt. Ch., Morgantown, W.Va., 1971-73; cmty. coll. parent educator Bellevue (Wash.) Cmty. Coll., 1980-89; pvt. counselor Renton, 1980-90; Christians social svcs. dir. Puget Sound Bapt. Assn., Federal Way, Wash., 1984-87; program dir. ACAP Child and Family Svcs., Auburn, Wash., 1989-93; assoc. dir. ACAP Child and Family Svcs., Auburn, 1994-96; retired, 1996; parent instr. APPLE Parenting, Auburn, 1990-92; seminar presenter, Puget Sound, Wash., 1980-95; therapeutic program cons. ACAP Child and Family Svcs., 1996-97; cons. Mary Kay Cosmetics, 1996—. Bd. trustee Valley Cmty. Players, Renton, 1995; bd. dirs. Calvary Bapt. Ch., Renton, 1981-87; featured spkr. parent edn. Puget Sound Area, 1988-96; cons. therapeutic program ACAP Child and Family Svcs., 1996-97. Mem. Puget Sound Adlerian Soc. (bd. dirs. 1981-83), Kiwanis (chmn. interclub com., membership chmn. 1994-95). Democrat. Avocations: drama, reading, walking, traveling, bowling. Home: 2218 177th Pl NE Redmond WA 98052-6071

OATES, JOYCE MARIE, psychiatrist; b. Salt Lake City, Mar. 31, 1948; d. Douglas Francis and Lois Joy (Allgaier) O. *Great-Grandfather Robert Askew, 1865-1937, was a union organizer in Michigan 1895-1901, and friend to Samuel Gompers, AFL President. He moved to Utah after black-listed, eventually working for the U.S. Post Office, where he organized a local union. He immigrated from England during the Panic of 1893. He is listed in American Labors Who's Who 1924 and featured in American Federationist, February 1900. Grandmother Hannah Askew-Oates raised three children by herself when widowed. Parents Doulgas Francis Oates and wife Lois Allgair-Oates, and siblings Donna, William, and Diane went on proselytizing missions for the LDS Church.* BS magna cum laude, U. Utah, 1970, MD, 1974. Diplomate Am. Bd. Psychiatry and Neurology. Intern Pa. Hosp., Phila., 1974-75; resident in psychiatry Inst. of Pa. Hosp., Phila., 1975-78; physician Intensive Treatment unit Copper Mountain Community Mental Health Ctr., Salt Lake City, 1978-79; pvt. practice psychiatry Salt Lake City, 1980-88; med. dir. psychiatry Yuma (Ariz.) Reg. Med. Ctr., 1988-90; psychiatrist locum tenens CompHealth, Salt Lake City, 1990; pvt. practice psychiatrist Las Vegas, 1990—; med. dir. Cinnamon Hills residential treatment, 1993—; med. dir., part owner Vista Treatment Ctr., St. George, Utah, 1995-96. *Joyce Marie Oates is the oldest of six children and worked her way through undergraduate and medical school. She has done considerable genealogy on her ancestors and has written and published life histories of her grandparents and parents. Besides working as Medical Director for a community mental health and intensive treatment center, a hospital psychiatric unit, a private treatment residential center and having a successful private office and hospital practice, she has worked with troubled, drug-addicted and delinquent adolescents.* Mem. Latter Day Saints. Avocations: writing, weaving, spinning.

O'BERG, ROBERT MYRON, minister; b. Long Beach, Calif., Apr. 21, 1961; s. Robert Ronald and Carolyn Ruth (Smith) O'B.; m. Kristen Johnson, Mar. 22, 1986; children: Erin Kristine, Robert William. BA, U. Calif., Riverside, 1983; MA, Claremont Grad. Sch., 1990; MDiv, Pacific Luth. Theol. Sem., 1991. Ordained to ministry Luth. Ch., 1991. Assoc. pastor Our Saviour Luth. Ch., Evang. Luth. Ch. in Am., Simi Valley, Calif., 1991—; book reviewer Augsburg Fortress Pub. House; initial interviewer multi-synodical candidacy com. Evang. Luth. Ch. in Am.; relief chaplain Simi Valley Hosp. and Health Care Svcs.; convener Simi Valley Ecumenical Coun. (Luth., Episcopal and Roman Cath.), 1993-95. Mem. steering com. Luth. Social Svcs. Cen. Coast, 1993; bd. dirs. Vols. for You, 1997—. Recipient Disting. Svc. award Luth. Social Svcs., 1993; named Pastor of Day, Sta. KKLA-FM, 1995. Mem. Aid Assn. for Lutherans, Luth. Brotherhood, U. Calif.-Riverside Alumni Assn., Claremont Grad. Sch. Alumni Assn., Pacific Luth. Theol. Sem. Alumni Assn. Democrat. Avocations: writing, reading history and historical fiction, ancient languages, hunting, music. Home: 6439 Sibley St Simi Valley CA 93063-3857 Office: Our Saviour Luth Ch 4191 Cochran St Simi Valley CA 93063-2347

OBERLANDER, CORNELIA HAHN, landscape architect; b. Muelheim-Ruhr, Germany, June 20, 1924; arrived in U.S., 1939; d. Franz and Lotte Beate (Jastrow) H.; m. H. Peter Oberlander, Jan. 2, 1953; children: Judith A., Timothy A., Wendy E. BA, Smith Coll., 1944; B of Landscape Architecture, Harvard U., 1947; LLD (hon.), U. British Columbia, 1991. guest prof. U. B.C. Dept. Landscape Architecture, 1992; lectr. for guided tour Renaissance Gardens of No. Italy, Smith Coll. Alumni Assn., 1988; mem. adv. com. on design Nat. Capital Commn., 1975-82; mem. adv. panel, co-founder Children's Play Resource Centre, Vancouver, 1978—; lectr. in field. Prin. works include C.K. Choi Bldg., Inst. Asian Rsch., U. B.C., 1992-96, New Pub. Library, 1992—, Thunderbird Housing, U. B.C., 1992—, Kwantlen Coll., 1991—, Cariboo Coll., 1991—, N.W. Territories Legis. Bldg., 1991—, UN Peacekeeping Meml., 1990—, Ritsumeikan U. B.C. Ho., 1990—, Ottawa City Hall, 1989—, Environ. Sci. Bd., Ward Environ. Garden, Trent U., 1989—, Nat. Gallery Can., 1983-88, Canadian Chancery, Washington D.C., 1983-89. Recipient medal Smith Coll., 1982, Regional Honor award and Nat. Merit award Christopher Phillips Landcape Architects, Inc., 1992, Allied Arts medal Royal Archtl. Inst. Can., 1995, Nat. Gallery of Can., Ottawa, Ontario, Can. Chancery Am. Assn. of Nurseymen, 1990, Grand award for L'Ambassade du Can., Landscape Contractors Assn., 1989, Can. Architect award of Excellence, Matsuzaki Wright Architects, Inc., 1989, Amenity award City of Vancouver for Robson Square, 1986, Citation award Can. Soc. of Architects for Chancery & Nat. Gallery, 1990. Fellow Am. Soc. Landscape Architects, Can. Soc. Landscape Architects; mem. Order of Can., Royal Can. Acad. Arts, Archtl. Inst. B.C. (hon.). Home: 1372 Acadia Rd, Vancouver, BC Canada V6T 1P6

OBERSTEIN, MARYDALE, geriatric specialist; b. Red Wing, Minn., Dec. 30; d. Dale Robert and Jean Ebba-Marie (Holmquist) Johnson; children: Kirk Robert, Mark Paul, MaryJean. Student, U. Oreg., 1961-62, Portland State U., 1962-64, Long Beach State U., 1974-76. Cert. geriatric specialist, Calif. Florist, owner Sunshine Flowers, Santa Ana, Calif., 1982—; pvt. duty nurse Aides in Action, Costa Mesa, Calif., 1985-87; owner, activity dir., adminstr. Lovelight Christian Home for the Elderly, Santa Ana, 1987—; activity dir. Bristol Care Nursing Home, Santa Ana, 1985-88; evangelist, speaker radio show Sta. KPRZ-FM, Anaheim, Calif., 1985-88; adminstr. Leisure Lodge Resort Care for Elderly in Lake Forest, Lake Forest, Calif., 1996—; nursing home activist in reforming laws to eliminate bad homes, 1984-90; founder, tchr. hugging classes/laughter therapy terminally ill patients, 1987—; founder healing and touch therapy laughter Therapy, 1991-93; bd. dirs. Performing Arts Ctr.; speaker for enlightenment and healing. Author (rewrite) Title 22 Nursing Home Reform Law, Little Hoover Commn.; model, actress and voiceovers. Bd. dirs. Orange County Coun. on Aging, 1984—; chairperson Helping Hands, 1985—, Pat Robertson Com., 1988, George Bush Presdl. Campaign, Orange County, 1988; bd. dirs., v.p. Women Aglow Orange County, 1985—; evanglist, pub. spkr., v.p. Women Aglow Huntington Beach; active with laughter therapy and hugging classes [illegible] 1984-85, Gold medal Pres. Clinton, 1994; named Woman of Yr., Kiwanis, 1985, ABI, 1990, Woman of Decade, Am. Biog. Soc., 1995, Little Hoover Commn., 1995; honored AM L.A. TV Show, Lt. Gov. McCarthy, 1984. Mem. Calif. Assn. Residential Care Homes, Orange County Epilepsy Soc. (bd. dirs. 1986—), Calif. Assn. Long Term Facilities. Home: 2050 Oak St Santa Ana CA 92707-2921

OBERTI, SYLVIA MARÍE ANTOINETTE, rehabilitation counselor and administrator, career advisor, textile consultant; b. Fresno, Calif., Dec. 29, 1952. BA in Communicative Disorders, Calif. State U.-Fresno, 1976, MA in Rehab. Counseling, 1977. Cert. rehab. counselor Commn. Rehab. Counselors; cert. life tchr. community coll., nat. cert. counselor; Diplomate Am. Bd. Disability Analysts. Sr. rehab. cons. Crawford Rehab. Services, Inc., Emeryville, Calif., 1978-80; vocat. rehab. counselor Rehab. Assocs., Inc., San Leandro, Calif., 1980-81; owner, textile cons. Rugs and Carpets of the Orient, Oakland, Calif., 1979—; exec. dir. TheOberti Co., Oakland and San Jose, Calif., 1981—; cons. to industry, ins. cos., disabled, ADA; tchr. job seeking skills to the disabled; expert witness in the field. Bd. dirs., treas. Pacific Basin Sch. Textile Arts, 1982-86; active Calif. Assn. Physically Handicapped, Inc., 1976—; fundraising chairperson CARP, 1990; fund raiser Special Olympics, 1992-95; fund raiser Nat. Breast Cancer Coalition, 1996; bd. mem. Alameda County Health Care Found., 1998-99. HEW grantee, 1976-77; first woman to solo and finish Mille Miglia, 1992; recipient Pacific Region Community Svc. Trophy Ferrari Club Am., 1992, Silver award Musical Watch Veteran Car Club Mille Miglia Organizers, 1992, 93, 3d of U.S.A., 1993; named to Women's Hall of Fame-Outstanding Woman of Yr. in Sports and Athletics, Alameda County, 1996. Mem. Am. Counseling Assn., Am. Rehab. Counseling Assn. , Internat. Round Table Advancement of Counseling, Nat. Rehab. Counseling Assn., LWV. Office: 3629 Grand Ave Ste 101 Oakland CA 94610-2009

OBNINSKY, VICTOR PETER, lawyer; b. San Rafael, Calif., Oct. 12, 1944; s. Peter Victor and Anne Bartholdi (Donston) O.; m. Clara Alice Bechtel, June 8, 1969; children: Mari, Warren. BA, Columbia U., 1966; JD, U. Calif., Hastings, 1969. Bar: Calif. 1970. Sole practice, Novato, Calif., 1970—; arbitrator Marin County Superior Ct., San Rafael, 1979—; superior ct. judge pro tem, 1979—; lectr. real estate and partnership law. Author: The Russians in Early California, 1966. Bd. dirs. Calif. Young Reps., 1968-69, Richardson Bay San. Dist., 1974-75, Marin County Legal Aid Soc., 1976-78; baseball coach Little League, Babe Ruth League, 1970-84; mem. nat. panel consumer arbitrators Better Bus. Bur., 1974-88; leader Boy Scouts Am., 1970-84; permanent sec. Phillips Acad. Class of 1962, 1987—; mem. Phillips Acad. Alumni Council, 1991-95; bd. community advisors Buck Ctr. for Rsch. on Aging. Mem. ABA, State Bar Calif., Marin County Bar Assn. (bd. dirs. 1985-91, treas. 1987-88, pres.-elect 1989, pres. 1990), Phi Delta Phi, Phi Gamma Delta. Republican. Russian Orthodox. Office: 2 Commercial Blvd Ste 103 Novato CA 94949-6121

O'BRIAN, BONNIE JEAN, library services supervisor; b. Great Bend, Kans., Oct. 19, 1940; d. Claude Marion and Mildred Geraldine (Schmaider) Baker; m. Patrick Gilbert Gibson (div.); 1 child, Debra Kathleen; m. John Robinson O'Brian, Nov. 2, 1968. BS, UCLA, 1961; MS, Calif. State U., Northridge, 1977; Credential in Libr. Media Svcs., Calif. State U., Long Beach, 1978. Libr. L.A. Unified Sch. Dist., Northridge, 1978-84; supr. chpt. 2 L.A. Unified Sch. Dist., L.A., 1984, coord. field libr., 1984-87, supr. libr. svcs., 1987—; asst. prof. libr. sci. Calif. State U., L.A.; condr. workshops in field. Recipient N.W. Valley Parent Tchr. Student award 1978, San Fernando Valley Reading Assn. Myrtle Shirley Reading Motivation award 1986. Mem. ALA, Am. Assn. Sch. Librs., Calif. Sch. Libr. Assn. (pres.), So. Calif. Coun. on Lit. for Children and Young People, White House Conf. on Libr. and Info. Svcs. Republican. Office: Los Angeles Unifed Sch Dist 1320 W 3rd St Los Angeles CA 90017-1410

O'BRIEN, BETTY ALICE, theological librarian, researcher; b. Kingsburg, Calif., June 12, 1932; d. Robert Herbert and Alice Dorothy (Larson) Peterson; m. Elmer John O'Brien, July 2, 1966. AA, North Pk. Coll., 1952; diploma, North Pk. Theol. Sem., 1954; BA, Northwestern U., 1956; MLS, U. Calif., Berkeley, 1957. Asst. libr. North Pk. Theol. Sem., Chgo., 1957-69; libr. St. Leonard Coll., Dayton, Ohio, 1971-84; rschr. United Theol. Sem., Dayton, 1986-96, reference coord., 1991-96; libr. Frasier Meadows Manor, 1997—. Editor: Religion Index 2: Festschriften 1960-69, 1980. Mem. Am. Theol. Libr. Assn. (bd. dirs. 1981-91, editor Summary Proc. 1982-91), Ohio Theol. Libr. Assn. (sec. 1972-76, chairperson 1978-79), Meth. Librs. Fellowship (v.p. 1989-91, pres. 1991-93). Mem. United Meth. Ch.

O'BRIEN, ELMER JOHN, librarian, educator; b. Kemmerer, Wyo., Apr. 8, 1932; s. Ernest and Emily Catherine (Reinhart) O'B.; m. Betty Alice Peterson, July 2, 1966. A.B., Birmingham So. Coll., 1954; Th.M., Iliff Sch. Theology, 1957; M.A., U. Denver, 1961. Ordained to ministry Methodist Ch., 1957; pastor Meth. Ch., Pagosa Springs, Colo., 1957-60; circulation-reference librarian Boston U. Sch. Theology, Boston, 1961-65; asst. librarian Garrett-Evang. Theol. Sem., Evanston, Ill., 1965-69; librarian, prof. United Theol. Sem., Dayton, Ohio, 1969-96, prof. emeritus, 1996—; abstractor Am. Bibliog. Center, 1969-73; dir. Ctr. for Evang. United Brethren Heritage, 1979-96; chmn. div. exec. com. Dayton-Miami Valley Libr. Consortium, 1983-84; rsch. assoc. Am. Antiquarian Soc., 1990. Author: Bibliography of Festschriften in Religion Published Since 1960, 1972, Religion Index Two: Festschriften, 1960-69; contbg. author: Communication and Change in American Religious History, 1993, Essays in Celebration of the First Fifty Years, 1996; pub. Meth. Revs. Index, 1818-1985, 1989-91; contbr. essay to profl. jour. Recipient theol. and scholarship award Assn. Theol. Schs. in U.S. and Can., 1990-91; Assn. Theol. Schs. in U.S. and Can. library staff devel. grantee, 1976-77, United Meth. Ch. Bd. Higher Edn. and Ministry research grantee, 1984-85. Mem. ALA, Acad. Libr. Assn. Ohio, Am. Theol. Libr. Assn. (head bur. personnel and placement 1969-73, dir. 1973-76, v.p. 1977-78, pres. 1978-79), Am. Antiquarian Soc. (rsch. assoc. 1990), Delta Sigma Phi, Omicron Delta Kappa, Eta Sigma Phi, Kappa Phi Kappa. Club: Torch Internat. (v.p. Dayton club 1981-82, pres. 1982-83). Home: 4840 Thunderbird Dr Apt 281 Boulder CO 80303-3829

O'BRIEN, HAROLD ALOYSIUS, JR., nuclear chemist, physics researcher, consultant; b. Dallas, May 17, 1936; s. Harold Aloysius and Adelaide (Esser) O'B.; m. Ann Akard, Aug. 22, 1958; children: Walter, Sheri, Matthew. BA, U. Tex., 1959; MS, N.Mex. State U., 1961; PhD, U. Tenn., 1968. Hon. diplomate Am. Bd. Sci. in Nuclear Medicine. Rsch. scientist Oak Ridge (Tenn.) Nat. Lab., 1962-68; mem. rsch. staff Los Alamos Nat. Lab., 1968-74, 86-93, asssoc. group leader, 1974-80, group leader, 1980-85; sr. tech. mgr. Sci. Applications Internat. Corp., Los Alamos, 1994—; pres. O'Brien & Assocs., Los Alamos, 1994—; vis. scientist Lawrence Berkeley (Calif.) Lab., 1985-86, Lawrence Livermore (Calif.) Lab., 1985-86, U. Calif., Davis, 1985-86; bd. dirs. Am. Bd. Sci. in Nuclear Medicine, 1976-85, pres., 1983-85; bd. dirs. Rho Med, Inc., Albuquerque, 1987-95; mem. subcom. on nuclear and radio chemistry NAS-NRC, 1974-78; mem. spl. study sect. NIH, 1976. Contbr. numerous articles to profl. jours., chpts. to books; patentee in field. Chmn. N.Mex. Radiation Tech. Adv. Coun., Santa Fe, 1974-85, 90—. Mem. Am. Chem. Soc. (exec. com. 1981-84), AAAS, Soc. Nuclear Medicine (trustee 1975-76, bd. dirs. Edn. and Rsch. Found. 1985-98). Avocations: skiing, golf. Fax: 505-672-1685. E-mail: hobrien@mesatop.com. Home: 107 La Senda Rd Los Alamos NM 87544-3819 Office: O'Brien & Assocs 107 La Senda Rd Los Alamos NM 87544-3819

O'BRIEN, JACK GEORGE, artistic director; b. Saginaw, Mich., June 18, 1939; s. J. George and Evelyn (MacArthur Martens) O'B. A.B., U. Mich., 1961, M.A., 1962. Asst. dir. APA Repertory Theatre, N.Y.C., 1963-67; asso. dir. APA Repertory Theatre, 1967-69; worked with San Diego Nat. Shakespeare Festival, 1969-82, A.C.T., 1970-80, Loretto Hilton, 1975, Ahmanson, Los Angeles, 1978-80, San Francisco Opera, Houston Grand Opera, Washington Opera Soc.; artistic dir. N.Y.C. Opera, 1982. Lyricist: Broadway prodn. The Selling of the President, 1972; dir.: on Broadway Porgy and Bess (Tony award nominee 1977), Most Happy Fella, Street Scene, Two Shakespearean Actors, 1993, Damn Yankees, 1994, Hapgood, 1994, others; artistic dir.: Old Globe Theatre, San Diego, 1981. Mem. Actors' Equity, Am. Soc. Composers and Performers, Soc. Stage Dirs. and Choreographers, Dirs. Guild Am.

O'BRIEN, JUDY, art museum official. Pres. Denver Art Mus. Office: Denver Art Mus 100 W 14th Avenue Pkwy Denver [illegible]

O'BRIEN, KEVIN E., lawyer; b. Teaneck, N.J., Nov. 22, 1952. BA, U. Notre Dame, 1975; JD, U. Denver, 1977. Bar: Colo. 1980. Mem. Hall &

Evans, L.L.C., Denver, 1984—; instr. Nat. Inst. Trial Advocacy, 1987. With USAR, 1972-78. Office: Hall & Evans LLC 1200 17th St Ste 1700 Denver CO 80202-5817

O'BRIEN, MARGE ETT, museum administrator; b. Hazleton, Pa., July 14, 1938; d. Gideon E. and Margurite (Pryor) Davis; m. Robert W. O'Brien, June 6, 1958; children: Robert D., Kevin J., William G. Student, Pa. State U., 1956-57; AA, Calif. State U., Dominquez Hills, 1978, BA, 1981, MA, 1983. Tchr. Pre-Sch. Co-op., San Pedro, Calif., 1977-79; dir. Drum Barracks Civil War Mus., Wilmington, Calif., 1986—; cons. Wilmington (Calif.) Hist. Soc., 1989—. Editor Highlands Homeowners newspaper, 1973. Mem. Am. Mus. Assn., Southwestern Mus. Assn., USAF Space Div. Wife's Club (pres. 1976-77). Republican. Lutheran. Office: Drum Barracks Civil War Mus 1052 N Banning Blvd Wilmington CA 90744-4604*

O'BRIEN, RAYMOND FRANCIS, transportation executive; b. Atchison, Kans., May 31, 1922; s. James C. and Anna M. (Wagner) O'B.; m. Mary Ann Baugher, Sept. 3, 1947; children: James B., William T., Kathleen A., Christopher R. B.S. in Bus. Adminstrn., U. Mo., 1948; grad., Advanced Mgmt. Program, Harvard, 1966. Accountant-auditor Peat, Marwick, Mitchell & Co., Kansas City, Mo., 1948-52; contr., treas. Riss & Co., Kansas City, Mo., 1952-58; regional contr. Consol. Freightways Corp. of Del., Indpls., also, Akron, Ohio, 1958-61; contr. Consol. Freightways, Inc., San Francisco, 1961—; v.p., treas. Consol. Freightways, Inc., 1962-63, bd. dirs., 1966, v.p. fin., 1967-69, exec. v.p., 1969-75, pres., 1975—, chief exec. officer, 1977-88, 90-91, chmn., 1988—; now chmn. emeritus CNF Transportation; pres. CF Motor Freight subs. Consol. Freightways, Inc., 1973; dir. Transam. Corp., Watkins-Johnson, Inc.; past chmn. WesternHwy. Inst., Champion Road Machinery, Ltd. Former mem. bus. adv. bd. Northwestern U., U. Calif., Berkeley; bd. dirs., regent, former chmn. bd. trustees St. Mary's Coll.; bd. dirs., regent Charles Armstrong Sch., 1991—; mem. Pres.'s Adv. Herbert Hoover Boys and Girls Club; dir. Boy Scouts Am. Bay Area Coun.; adv. coun. Nat. Commn. Against Drunk Driving. Served to 1st lt. USAAF, 1942-45. Recipient Disting. Svc. Citation Automotive Hall Fame, 1991; named Outstanding Chief Exec. five times Financial World Mag. Mem. Am. Trucking Assn. (bd. dirs. Found., exec. com.), Pacific Union Club, World Trade Club, Commonwealth Club (San Francisco), Burning Tree Country Club, Menlo Country Club. Home: 26347 Esperanza Dr Los Altos CA 94022-2601 Office: CNF Transportation 3000 Sand Hill Rd Menlo Park CA 94025-7113*

O'BRIEN, ROBERT JOHN, information technology consultant; b. Junee, NSW, Australia, Jan. 15, 1940; s. Arthur Edward and Esma Jean (Crane) O'B.; m. Carol Marea Vincent, Aug. 26, 1961 (div. Feb. 1988); children: Sean Robert, Meagan Marea; m. Patricia Ann Hafford Rood, Dec. 1, 1997; children: Mark Dutton Hafford, Lauren Melyn Hafford. Student, U. New Eng., Armidale, Australia, 1954. Field svcs. engr. Internat. Computers Ltd., Sydney, 1960-67; sys. devel. mgr. Malleys Ltd., Auburn, Australia, 1967-79; acct. exec. Hewlett-Packard Australia Ltd., North Ryde, 1979-88, Co-Cam Computer Sys., St. Leonards, Australia, 1988-94; sales support specialist Southmark Computer Sys., Chatsworth, Australia, 1994-97; info. tech. cons. Ft. Collins, Colo., 1997-98, Managed Bus. Solutions, Ft. Collins, 1998—. Umpire U.S. Field Hockey Assn.; project restoration coord. NSW Rail Transport Mus., Thirlmere, Australia, 1975-97. Avocations: field hockey, skiing, skin diving, hot air ballooning. Fax: (970) 207-9834. E-mail: bobob@compuserve.com. Home: 3230 Silverwood Dr Fort Collins CO 80525-2863 Office: Manages Bus Solutions 214 S College Ave Ste 2 Fort Collins CO 80524-2870

O'BRIEN, THOMAS JOSEPH, bishop; b. Indpls., Nov. 29, 1935. Grad., St. Meinrad Coll. Sem. Ordained priest Roman Catholic Ch., 1961. Bishop of Phoenix, 1982—. Office: Catholic Diocese of Phoenix 400 E Monroe St Phoenix AZ 85004-2376*

O'BYRNE, MICHAEL, management consultant; b. Butte, Mont., Dec. 26, 1938; s. Michael E. and Margaret F. (Turner) O'B.; m. Penny L. Graham, Nov. 14, 1964; children: Jennifer L. McLellan, Gregory M. O'Byrne, Andrew G. O'Byrne. BSME, U. Wash., 1961. Cert. engr., Wash. V.p. PACCAR, Inc., Bellevue, Wash., 1969-84; pres. Mobi-Dock, Inc., Mercer Island, Wash., 1985-86; ptnr. The Catalyst Group, Mercer Island, 1986-89; pres. Raima Corp., Bellevue, 1988-89, Pacific North Equipment Co., Kent, Wash., 1990-95; cons. Master Performance, Inc., Bellevue, 1995—. Council mem. Hunts Point, Wash., 1980-97; mem. bd. dirs. Mcpl. League of King County, Seattle, 1994-95; dist. chmn. Boy Scouts Am., Seattle, 1994-98; pres. USO Puget Sound Area, 1997—. Lt. comdr. USN, 1961-69. Mem. Soc. Automotive Engrs., Assoc. Equipment Distributors (chpt. pres. 1994-95), Rotary Internat., Seattle Yacht Club. Republican. Avocations: sailing, skiing, fishing. Home and Office: 4224 Hunts Point Rd Bellevue WA 98004-1106

OCANSEY, AARON AKROFI, game designer; b. Ada, Ghana, Africa, Sept. 16, 1949; came to U.S., 1969, s. Alfred Natea Ocansey and Grace Tay; m. Shirley Donaldson, Nov. 23, 1974 (div. Aug. 1990); children: Denis, Aba, Daniela; m. Gloria Jean Penrice, Aug. 25, 1992; 1 child, Layo Penrice. Stage III Level Acctg., Royal Inst. Tech., Accra, New Town, 1969. Cert. of Appreciation, Pres. Ronald Reagan, 1988. Acct. London Agy., Westwood, Calif., 1974-76, Kindle Inc., Inglewood, Calif., 1984-92, Rotex Exch., Gardena, Calif., 1990-92, Trak Auto Corp., Ontario, Calif., 1992; officer Advance Tech., Hollywood, Calif., 1992—; game designer Ocansey Ocean Inc., Accra, 1989—. Designer: (bd. games) Elmina Game, 1996, Ghana Empire Game, 1998. Avocation: game designing. Home: 16240 Vaquero Ct Riverside CA 92504-5856 Office: Ocansey Ocean, PO Box 6559, Accra Ghana

OCCHIATO, MICHAEL ANTHONY, city official; b. Pueblo, Colo.; s. Joseph Michael and Joan Occhiato; m. Peggy Ann Stefonowicz, June 27, 1964 (div. Sept. 1983); children: Michael, James, Jennifer; m. Patsy Gay Payne, June 2, 1984 (div. Sept. 1995); children: Kim Carr, Jerry Don Webb. BBA, U. Denver, 1961; MBA, U. Colo., 1984; postgrad., U. So. Colo. Sales mgr. Tivoli Brewing co., Denver, 1965-67, acting brewmaster, prodn. control mgr., 1967-68, plant mgr., 1968-69; adminstrv. mgr. King Resources Co., Denver, 1969-70; ops. mgr. Canners Inc., Pepsi-Cola Bottling Co., Pueblo, 1970-76; pres. Pepsi-Cola Bottling Co., Pueblo, 1978-82; gen. mgr. Pepsi-Cola Bottling Group div. PepsiCo., Pueblo, 1982, area v.p., 1982-83; ind. cons. Pueblo, 1983—; broker assoc. Sound Venture Realty, Pueblo, 1996-98, Jones Healy Better Homes & Gardens, 1998—; v.p. Colo. Soft Drink Assn., 1978, pres., 1979; regional dir. Pepsi Cola Mgmt. Inst. divsn. Pepsi Co., 1979-82; pres. Ethnic Foods Internat. dba Taco Rancho, Pueblo; chmn. Weifang (China) Sister City Del., 1991—; bd. dirs. HMO So. Colo. Health Plan, 1988-93, Pueblo Diversified Industries; rancher, 1976—; land devel. real estate broker assoc., 1996—. V.p. Colo. Soft Drink Assn., 1979-80, pres., 1980-81; mem. coun. City of Pueblo, 1978-93, pres., 1986, 87, 90, 91; mem. bd. health, 1978-80, regional planning commn., 1980-81, Pueblo Action Inc., 1978-80, Pueblo Planning and Zoning Commn., 1985; chmn. Pueblo Area Coun. Govts., 1980-82; mem. Pueblo Econ. Devel. Corp., 1983-91; chmn. fundraising Pueblo chpt. Am. Heart Assn., 1983—; bd. dirs. El Pueblo Boys Ranch, 1971-73; del. 1st World Conf. Local Elected Orcls. to 1st UN Internat. Coun. for Local Environ. Initiative; active Earth Wise Pueblo, 1991. Lt. USN, 1961-65. Mem. So. Colo. Emergency Med. Technicians Assn. (pres. 1975), Am. Saler Assn., Am. Quarter Horse Assn., Colo. Cattle Assn., Pueblo C. of C., Rotary, Pi Kappa Alpha (v.p. 1960). Home and Office: 11 Harrogate Ter Pueblo CO 81001-1723

OCHOA, ARMANDO, bishop; b. Oxnard, Calif., Apr. 3, 1943. Grad., Ventura (Calif.) Coll., St. John's Coll., Camarillo, Calif. Ordained priest Roman Cath. Ch., 1970. Titular bishop of Sitifi Calif.; aux. bishop, vicar gen. L.A., 1987-96; bishop Diocese of Tex., El Paso, 1996—. Office: 3424 Wilshire Blvd Los Angeles CA 90010-2241*

OCHSNER, JEFFREY KARL, architect, educator; b. Milw., Sept. 25, 1950; s. Richard Stanley and Mary Anne (Zaccardi) O.; m. Sandra Lynn Perkins, Aug. 5, 1979. Student, Calif. Inst. Tech., 1968-69; BA in Architecture, Rice U., 1973, M in Architecture, 1976. Registered architect, Texas, Wis., Wash. Designer Gunnar Birkerts & Assoc., Birmingham, Mich., 1973-74; architect various, Houston, Milw., Madison, Wis., 1976-81; architect, mgr. Houston Transit Cons., Houston, 1981-83; prin., owner Ochsner Assoc., Architects, Houston, 1984-87; lectr. U. Wash., Seattle, 1988-92, asst. prof., 1992-95, assoc. prof., 1995-99, prof., 1999—, chair, 1996—; vis. lectr. Rice U., Houston, 1980-86. Author: H. H. Richardson: Complete Architectural Works, 1982; editor, co-author: Shaping Seattle Architecture: A Historical Guide to the Architects, 1994; mem. editl. bd. ARCADE: Northwest Jour. for Architecture & Design, 1988-92, Jour. of Archtl. Edn., 1990-95. Fellow Am. Inst. Architects (Houston chpt., Honor award 1984); mem. Nat. Trust Historic Preservation, Soc. Archtl. Historians, College Art Assn., Congress of New Urbanism, Vernacular Architecture Forum. Office: Dept Architecture Univ Washington PO Box 355720 Seattle WA 98195-5720

OCKEY, RONALD J., lawyer; b. Green River, Wyo., June 12, 1934; s. Theron G. and Ruby O. (Sackett) O.; m. Arline M. Hawkins, Nov. 27, 1957; children: Carolyn S. Ockey Baggett, Deborah K. Ockey Christiansen, David, Kathleen M. Ockey Hellewell, Valerie Ockey Sachs, Robert. B.A., U. Utah, 1959, postgrad. 1959-60; J.D. with honors, George Washington U., 1966. Bar: Colo. 1967, Utah 1968, U.S. Dist. Ct. Colo. 1967, U.S. Dist. Ct. Utah 1968, U.S. Ct. Appeals (10th cir.) 1969, U.S. Ct. Claims 1987. Missionary to France for Mormon Ch., 1954-57; law clk. to judge U.S. Dist. Ct. Colo., 1966-67; assoc. ptnr., shareholder, v.p., treas., dir. Jones, Waldo, Holbrook & McDonough, Salt Lake City, 1967-91, pres., IntelliTrans Internat. Corp., 1992-94; mem. Utah Ho. Reps., 1988-90, Utah State Senate, 1991-94; of counsel Mackey Price & Williams, Salt Lake City, 1995-98, asst. atty. gen., Utah, 1998—; trustee SmartUTAH, Inc., 1995—, Utah Tech. Fin. Corp., 1995-98; lectr. in securities, pub. fin. and bankruptcy law. State govtl. affairs chmn. Utah Jaycees, 1969; del. state Rep. Convs., 1972-74, 1976-78, 1980-82, 84-86, 94-96, del. Salt Lake County Rep. Conv., 1978-80, 88-92; sec. Wright for Gov. campaign, 1980; legis. dist. chmn. Utah Rep. Party, 1983-87; trustee Food for Poland, 1981-85, pres., trustee, Unity to Assist Humanity Alliance, 1992-95; bd. dirs. Utah Opera Co., 1991-94; trustee Utah Info. Tech. Assn., 1991—; bd. dir., mem. exec. com. Smart Utah, Inc., 1995—. Lt. U.S. Army, 1960-66; to capt. Judge Adv. Gen. USAR, 1966-81. Mem. Utah State Bar Assn. (various coms.), , Nat. Assn. Bond Lawyers (chmn. com. on state legislation 1982-85), George Washington U. Law Alumni Assn. (bd. dirs. 1981-85), Order of Coif, Salt Lake Rotary, Phi Delta Phi. Contbr. articles on law to profl. jours.; mem. editorial bd. Utah Bar Jour., 1973-75; mem. staff and bd. editors George Washington Law Rev., 1964-66. Home: 4502 Crest Oak Cir Salt Lake City UT 84124-3825

O'CONNELL, HUGH MELLEN, JR., retired architect; b. Oak Park, Ill., Nov. 29, 1929; s. Hugh M. and Helen Mae (Evans) O'C.; m. Frances Ann Small, Apr. 13, 1957; children—Patricia Lynn, Susan Marie, Jeanette Maureen. Designer, John Mackel. Student mech. engring., Purdue U., 1948-50; B.S. in Archtl. Engring, U. Ill., 1953. Registered architect, Ariz., Calif., La., Nev., Nat. Council Archtl. Registration Bds. Structural engr. Los Angeles, 1955-57; architect Harnish & Morgan & Causey, Ontario, Calif., 1957-63; self-employed architect Ventura, Calif., 1963-69; architect Andrews/O'Connell, Ventura, 1970-78; dir. engring. div. Naval Constrn. Bn. Center, Port Hueneme, Calif., 1978-91; supervisory architect Naval Constrn. Bn. Center, Port Hueneme, 1991-93; ret., 1993; mem. tech. adv. com. Ventura Coll., 1965-78; sec. Oxnard Citizens' Adv. Com., 1969-79, v.p., 1970-72, pres., 1972—; chmn. Oxnard Beautification Com., 1969, 74, Oxnard Cmty. Block Grant adv. com., 1975-76; mem. Oxnard Planning Commn., 1976-86, vice chmn., 1978-79, chmn., 1980-81. Mem. Oxnard Art-in-Pub. Places Commn., 1988—. Served with AUS, 1953-55. Mem. AIA (emeritus, pres. Ventura chpt. 1973), Am. Concrete Inst., Soc. Am. Registered Architects (Design award 1968, dir. 1970), Am. Legion, Soc. for Preservation and Encouragement of Barbershop Quartet Singing in Am. (chpt. pres. 1979, chpt. sec. 1980-83), Acad. Model Aeros. (#9190 1948—), Channel Islands Condors Club (treas. 1986—), Sports Flyers Assn., Alpha Rho Chi (Anthemios chpt.). Presbyterian (elder 1963, deacon 1967). Lodges: Kiwanis (pres. 1969, div. sec. 1974-75), Elks. Home and Office: 520 Ivywood Dr Oxnard CA 93030-3527

O'CONNELL, MARY ANN, state senator, business owner; b. Albuquerque, Aug. 3, 1934; d. James Aubrey and Dorothy Nell (Batsel) Gray; m. Robert Emmett O'Connell, Feb. 21, 1977; children: Jeffery Crampton, Gray Crampton. Student, U. N.Mex., Internat. Coun. Shopping Ctrs. Exec. dir. Blvd. Shopping Ctr., Las Vegas, Nev., 1968-76, Citizen Pvt. Enterprise, Las Vegas, 1976; media supr. Southwest Advt., Las Vegas, 1977—; owner, operator Meadows Inn, Las Vegas, 1985 , 3 Christian bookstores, Las Vegas, 1985—; state senator Nev. Senate, 1985—; chmn. govtl. affairs; vice chmn. commerce and labor; mem. taxation com.; vice chmn. Legis. Commn., 1985-86, 95-96; mem., 1987-88, 91-93, mem. edn. com. to rewritten standards; commr. Edn. Commn. States; rep. Nat. Conf. State Legislators; past vice chair State Mental Hygiene & Mental Retardation Adv. Bd.. Pres. explorer div. Boulder Dam Area coun. Boy Scouts Am., Las Vegas, 1979-80, former mem. exec. bd. mem. adv. bd. Boulder Dam chpt.; pres., bd. dirs. Citizens Pvt. Enterprise, Las Vegas, 1982-84, Secret Witness, Las Vegas, 1081-82; vice chmn. Gov.'s Mental Health-Mental Retardation, Nev., 1983—; past mem. community adv. bd. Care Unit Hosp., Las Vegas; past mem. adv. bd. Kidney Found., Milligan Coll., Charter Hosp.; tchr. Young Adult Sunday Sch. Recipient Commendation award Mayor O. Grayson, Las Vegas, 1975, Outstanding Citizenship award Bd. Realtors, 1975, Silver Beaver award Boy Scouts Am., 1980, Free Enterprise award Greater Las Vegas C. of C., Federated Employers Assn., Downtown Breakfast Exch., 1988, Award of Excellence for Women in Politics, 1989, Legislator of Yr. award Bldg. and Trades, 1991, Legislator of Yr. award Nat. ASA Trade Assn., 1991, 94, Guardian of Liberty award Nev. Coalition of Conservative Citizens, 1991, Internat. Maxi Awards Promotional Excellence, Guardian of Small Bus. award Nat. Fedn. Ind. Bus., 1995-96; named Legislator of Yr., Nev. Retail Assn., 1992; inducted into Nev. Vets. Citizens Hall of Fame, 1999. Mem. Retail Mchts. Assn. (former pres., bd. dirs.), Taxpayers Assn. (bd. dirs.), Greater Las Vegas C. of C. (past pres., bd. dirs., Woman of Achievement Politics women's coun. 1988). Republican. Mem. Christian Ch. Avocations: china painting, reading. Home: 7225 Montecito Cir Las Vegas NV 89120-3118 Office: Nev Legislature Senate 401 S Carson St Carson City NV 89701-4747

O'CONNELL, MEGAN GERARD, visual designer, educator; b. St. Paul, Minn., Jan. 22, 1964; d. John James and Jeanne Mary (Carlstrom) O.; m. Leon Bernard Johnson, Sept. 6, 1996; children: Marlowe, Leander. BA in Book Arts (magna cum laude), U. Minn., 1988; MA in Intermedia, U. Iowa, 1993, MFA, 1994. Intern Metropolitan Mus. Art, N.Y.C., 1986; instr. Walker Art Ctr., Mpls., 1986-90, Minn. Ctr. Book Arts, Mpls., 1988-90; asst. antiquarian Rulon-Miller Books, St. Paul, Minn., 1989-90; instr. U. Iowa, Iowa City, 1990-94; asst. prof. U. Oreg., Eugene, 1994—. Author, publisher: Blanket Terms, 1991, Oceans of Everything, 1994, My Independent Industry, 1995, The Grass Is..., 1996. Mem. Internat. Union Mail Artists, Coll. Art Assn., Creative Material Group, Ctr. Book Arts, Motelhaus, Inc. (coord. 1997—), Phi Beta Kappa. Home: 950 W 11th Ave Eugene OR 97402-5238

O'CONNELL, TAAFFE CANNON, actress, publishing executive; b. Providence; d. Joseph Ceril and Edith Ethelyn (Dent) O'C. BA, U. Miss., MFA. Regional supr. Gloria Marshall Figure Salons, S.C.; v.p., co-founder Doc Sox Inc., Pacific Palisades, Calif., 1988-90; pres., founder Canoco Pub., L.A., 1991—, 1-800-266-DYNE, L.A., 1992-93. Film appearances include Men Without Dates, Dangerous, Hot Chili, Cheech & Chong Nice Dreams, Rocky II, Galaxy of Terror, New Years Evil, Rich Man Poor Man Book I, Caged Fury; TV appearances include Malubu Branch, General Hospital, Dangerous Women, Dallas, Knight and Daye, The New Gidget, Knight Rider, Three's Company, Dr. Joyce Brothers Show, Blansky's Beauties, Peter Lupus Show, Fix-It City, Happy Days, Laverne & Shirley, Wonder Woman, The Incredible Hulk; theater appearances include Too True to be Good, Damn Yankees, Anastasia, Star Spangled Girl, The Beaux Stratagem, The Canterbury Tales; founder, pub. Astrocaster, 1991, Power Agent, 1993; Jan. founder Rising Star Distbn. and Canoco Prodns., 1999—. Mem. Screen Actors' Guild, Am. Fedn. TV Radio Artists, Actor's Equity, Actor's Forum (bd. dirs. 1985-94). Avocations: singing, spinning, sailing, traveling. E-mail: industryedge@earthlink.net. Office: Canoco Pub 11611 Chenault St Ste 118 Los Angeles CA 90049-4574

O'CONNER, LORETTA RAE, lawyer; b. Denver, Dec. 23, 1958; d. Ronald Lee and Norma Jareene (Warner) Barkdoll; m. George Ellis Bentley, Dec. 31, 1976 (div. 1979); m. Donald Hugh O'Conner, Feb. 3, 1987; children: Justin Lee, Brandon Craig. AS, Denver Acad. Ct. Reporting, 1983; BA summa cum laude, Regis U., 1992; JD, U. Colo., 1996. Bar: Colo., 1996. Ct. reporter Denver, 1983-87; dist. ct. reporter Jud. Dept., State of Colo., Pueblo, 1987-91; ct. reporter Pueblo, 1991-93; student atty. Pueblo County Legal Svcs.; pvt. practice Pueblo, 1997—; contact atty. State of Colo.; contract rep. Jud. Dept., State of Colo. Chief justice Student Govt. Ct., U. So. Colo., Pueblo, 1992; trained facilitator Kettering Found., Pub. Policy Inst., Dayton, Ohio, 1992; sec. So. Colo. Registered Interpretors for Deaf, Pueblo, 1991. President's scholar U. So. Colo., 1991-92, Alumni Assn. scholar, 1991-92; grantee Kettering Found., 1992; Colo. Legislature grantee and scholar Regis U., 1992; Colo. Legislature grantee U. Colo. Sch. Law, 1993-95, Dean's scholar, Dazzo Scholar, King scholar U. Colo. Sch. Law, 1993-96. Mem. ATLA, ABA, Nat. Ct. Reporters Assn., Colo. Trial Lawyers Assn., Colo. Bar Assn., Colo. Womens Bar Assn., Colo. Ct. Reporters Assn., Pueblo County Bas Assn., Boulder Bar Assn., Golden Key Soc., Phi Delta Phi (clk. 1994-95). Avocations: reading, writing novels. Fax: (719) 584-2233. Home: 15 Mayweed Ct Pueblo CO 81001-1134 Office: O'Conner Law Bldg 426 W 10th St Pueblo CO 81003

O'CONNOR, BETTY LOU, service executive; b. Phoenix, Oct. 29, 1927; d. George Eliot and Tillie Edith (Miller) Miller; m. William Spoeri O'Connor, Oct. 10, 1948 (dec. Feb. 1994); children: Thomas W., William K., Kelli Anne. Student, U. So. Calif., 1946-48, Calif. State U., Los Angeles, 1949-50. V.p. O'Connor Food Svcs., Inc., Jack in the Box Restaurants, Granada Hills, Calif., 1983-93; pres. O'Connor Food Svcs., Inc., Granada Hills, Calif., 1994—, Western Restaurant Mgmt. Co., Granada Hills, 1986—; sec. C.E.O. Foods, Inc., Victorville, Calif.; pres. City Snippers, Inc., Santa Clarita, Calif.; mem. adv. bd. Bank of Granada Hills; bd. dirs. Nat. Franchise Purchasing Coop., nc. Recipient Frannie award Foodmaker, Inc., Northridge, Calif., 1984, First Rate award, 1992. Mem. Jack in the Box Franchisee Assn., Spurs Hon. (sec. U. So. Calif. 1947-48), Associated Women Students (sec. U. So. Calif. 1946-47), Gamma Alpha Chi (v.p. 1947-48), Chi Omega. Republican. Roman Catholic. Avocation: sewing. Office: Western Restaurant Mgmt Co 17545 Chatsworth St Granada Hills CA 91344-5720

O'CONNOR, BIRGIT CHRISTEL HELEN, artist; b. Hamburg, Germany, Oct. 14, 1958; arrived in U.S., 1959; d. Helmut Erwin and Christel Ilona (Kloth) Wiegandt; m. Danial James O'Connor, July 1, 1978; children: James Danial, Nicholas John Francis. Grad. high sch., Mill Valley. Transport aid Marin Gen. Hosp., Greenbrae, Calif., 1977-78; art tchr. Bolinas, Calif., 1998—. Represented in collections at Gallery Mack, Palm Desert, Calif., Seattle, Gallerie de Monde, Hong Kong. Recipient First Pl. Best of Show Calif. State Expo, 1997, First Pl. Napa Town Country Fair, 1997, Best of Show Petaluma Sonoma Marin Fair, 1997, Internat. award of excellence Magnum Opus, 1998, Best of Show Wasco-Aqua Media, 1998, Silver award EWWS, Nat. award, 1998, Corp. award Catherine Wolfe Art Club, 1998. Mem. La. Watercolor Soc. (1st Pl. internat. 1998, Holbein award 1998), Bolinas Living Artist, Marin Art Coun. Avocations: gardening, fishing. Home and Office: PO Box 828 Bolinas CA 94924-0828

O'CONNOR, BONNIE LYNN, executive director; b. Riverside, Calif., Nov. 11, 1965; d. Eugene and Anna Kathryn (Alexander) Aldrighetti; m. Timothy Allen O'Connor, Apr. 22, 1989. AA, Valley Coll., 1989; BS, Univ. Redlands, 1992; postgrad., Calif. State Univ., 1998—. Adminstrv. mgr. Highland Sr. Ctr.; exec. dir. Children's Fund. Mem. chamber leadership program San Bernardino, 1996-97; bd. dirs. Humane Soc., bd. dirs., pres. Volunteer Ctr., San Bernardino. Recipient Scholarship award Am. Soc. Pub. Adminstrn.; named Future Bus. Leader Sun Newspaper, 1998. Mem. Nat. Soc. Fundraising Exec. Avocations: hiking, travel, reading, environmental issues. Office: Children's Fund 385 North Arrowhead Ave San Bernardino CA 92415

O'CONNOR, KARL WILLIAM (GOODYEAR JOHNSON), lawyer; b. Washington, Aug. 1, 1931; s. Hector and Lucile (Johnson) O'C.; m. Sylvia Gasbarri, Mar. 23, 1951 (dec.); m. Judith Ann Byers, July 22, 1972 (div. 1983); m. Eleanor Celler, Aug. 3, 1984 (div. 1986); m. Alma Hepner, Jan. 1, 1987 (div. 1996); children: Blair, Frances, Brian, Brendan. BA, U. Va., 1952, JD, 1958. Bar: Va. 1958, D.C. 1959, Am. Samoa 1976, Calif. 1977, Oreg. 1993. Law clk. U.S. Dist. Ct. Va., Abingdon, 1958-59; practice law Washington, 1959-61; trial atty. U.S. Dept. Justice, Washington, 1961-65; dep. dir. Men's Job Corps OEO, Washington, 1965-67; mem. civil rights div. Dept. of Justice, chief criminal sect., prin. dep. asst. atty. gen., 1967-75, spl. counsel for intelligence coordination, 1975; v.p., counsel Assn. of Motion Picture and Television Producers, Hollywood, Calif., 1975-76; assoc. justice Am. Samoa, 1976, chief justice, 1977-78; sr. trial atty. GSA Task Force, Dept. Justice, 1978-81; insp. gen. CSA, 1981-82; spl. counsel Merit Systems Protection Bd., Washington, 1983-86; U.S. atty. for Guam and the No. Marianas, 1986-89, ret.; pvt. practice Medford, Oreg., 1989—; Am. counsel O'Reilly Vernier Ltd., Hong Kong, 1992-93; ptnr. O'Connor & Vernier, Medford, Oreg., 1993-94; pvt. practice Medford, 1994—. Served with USMC, 1952-55. Mem. Oreg. Bar Assn., D.C. Bar Assn., Va. Bar Assn., Calif. Bar Assn., Am. Samoa Bar Assn., Soc. Colonial Wars, Phi Alpha Delta, Sigma Nu. Home: Box 126 305 N 6th St Jacksonville OR 97530 Office: 916 W 10th St Medford OR 97501-3018

O'CONNOR, KEVIN THOMAS, archdiocese development official; b. Dubuque, Iowa, Oct. 9, 1950; s. Francis John and Marion Helen (Rhomberg) O'C.; m. Abbie J. O'Connor, July 17, 1993; 1 child, Sean Francis. BS, Regis Coll., Denver, 1973. Spl. agt. Northwestern Mut. Life, Denver, 1973-78; account exec. Blue Cross/Blue Shield of Colo., Denver, 1978-82; pres., owner O'Connor Ins. Cons., Denver, 1982-92; dir. devel. Archdiocese of Denver, 1992-95, mgr. Cath. appeal, 1995-96; dir. devel. Archdiocese L.A., 1996—. Chmn. Regis Coll. Telefund, Denver, 1987-88, 90-91; treas., 1st vice chmn. Serra Trust Fund for Vocations, 1988-93, chmn., 1993-96; mem. fin. coun. St. James Parish, 1988-95, chmn. autumn bazaar, 1985, 87, mem. choir, 1993-95; sec. Mother Teresa Com., 1989. Recipient Share Serra Comm. award Serra Internat., 1989, Spl. Project award Dist. 6, 1986, 88, Spl. Recognition award, 1989, Outstanding Serran award, 1995, Jan Berbers award, 1996, Alumni Svc. award Regis Coll., 1990, Disting. Alumnus award Walhert H.S., 1994. Mem. Serra Club Greeley (chmn. founders com. 1996), Serra Club Pueblo (co-chmn. founders com. 1992), Serra Club Colorado Springs (co-chmn. founders com. 1994), Serra Club L.A., Serra Internat. (bd. trustees 1997—, sec. bd. 1998-2000). Roman Catholic. Avocations: golf, tennis, mountain climbing, handball, running. Home: 3510 Fallenleaf Pl Glendale CA 91206-4803 Office: Archdiocese LA 3424 Wilshire Blvd Los Angeles CA 90010-2241

O'CONNOR, MICHAEL ARTHUR, music publishing executive; b. Santa Monica, Calif., June 29, 1953; s. Vern Lee and Carmen (Cardenas) O'C. BA in Polit. Sci., UCLA, 1976. Profl. mgr. Rick Nelson Music, Los Angeles, 1976-78, Glen Campbell Music, Los Angeles, 1978-80; owner Michael O'Connor Music, Los Angeles, 1980—; staff writer MCA Music Publ., 1996; co-pub. BMG Music, 1998. Pub.: (songs) My Body Keeps Changing My Mind by Johnny Mathis and Karen Carpenter, 1980, You Never Gave Up on Me as recorded by Crystal Gayle, 1982, Manhunt from Flashdance soundtrack, 1983, I Do Believe in You as recorded by Kenny Rogers, 1984, The Ronnie Reagan Rag for the Presdl. Inaugural Gala, 1984; composer Stop and Think for Miami Vice TV show, 1986. Recipient spl. citation Ala. Gov. George Wallace, 1986; offered own div. at Motown Records by founder Berry Gordy, 1986. Mem. ASCAP, Broadcast Music, Inc. Home and Office: PO Box 1869 Studio City CA 91614-0869

O'CONNOR, SHEILA ANNE, freelance writer; b. Paisley, Scotland, Jan. 20, 1960; came to the U.S., 1988; d. Brian Aubrey Witham and Margaret Kirk (Reid) Davies; m. Frank Donal O'Connor, Aug. 9, 1986; children: David Michael, Andrew James, Christine Charlotte. BA in French and German, Strathclyde U., 1980, postgrad. diploma in office studies, 1981, MBA, 1992. Office asst. BBC, London, 1982-83; asst. to mng. dir. Unimatic Engrs. Ltd., London, 1983-84; freelance word processing operator London, 1984-88; staff asst. Internat. Monetary Fund, Washington, 1988-94; prin. Internat. Media Assn., Washington, 1988—. Contbr. numerous articles to various publs. Mem. Am. Mktg. Assn., Bay Area Travel Writers Assn., Calif. Writers Club. Avocations: animals, travel. Home and Office: 2531 39th Ave San Francisco CA 94116-2752

ODA, YOSHIO, physician, internist; b. Papaaloa, Hawaii, Jan. 14, 1933; s. Hakuai and Usako (Yamamoto) O.; AB, Cornell U., 1955; MD, U. Chgo.,

1959. Diplomate Am. Bd. Internal Medicine. Intern U. Chgo. Clinics, 1959-60; resident in pathology U. Chgo., 1960-62, Queen's Hosp., Hawaii, 1962-63, Long Beach (Calif.) VA Hosp., 1963-65; resident in allergy, immunology U. Colo. Med. Center, 1966-67; pvt. practice, L.A., 1965-66; pvt. practice internal medicine, allergy and immunology, Honolulu, 1970—; asst. clin. prof. medicine U. Hawaii, Honolulu, 1970—. Maj., AUS, 1968-70. Mem. ACP, Am. Acad. Allergy. Office: Piikoi Med Bldg 1024 Piikoi St Honolulu HI 96814-1925

ODELL, JOHN H., construction company executive; b. Toledo, Oct. 31, 1955; s. John H. and Doris Irene Odell; m. Kathryn Lau, Oct. 1, 1988; children: Ceara, Heather, Victoria. B of Environ. Design, U. Miami, Oxford, Ohio, 1977. Staff architect Richard Halford and Assocs., Santa Fe, 1978-79; ptnr. B.O.A. Constrn., Santa Fe, 1980-84; owner John H. Odell Constrn., Santa Fe, 1985—; v.p. Los Pintores Inc., Santa Fe, 1990-92; pres. Uncle Joey's Food Svcs. Inc., 1991—, John H. Odell Assocs. Inc., Santa Fe, 1995—. Musician Santa Fe Community Orch., 1982, Huntington Community Orch., Huntington, W.Va., 1972-73. Recipient Historic Preservation award City of Santa Fe, 1997. Mem. AIA (assoc., treas., bd. dirs. Santa Fe chpt. yearly 1988-95, mem. liaison com. on design 1987—, Cmty. Svc. award 1993), Vine and Wine Soc. (N.Mex. No. Rio Grande chpt. pres., bd. dirs., v.p.), Nat. Assn. of Home Builders. Avocations: skiing, scuba, handball, racquetball. Home: PO Box 2967 Santa Fe NM 87504-2967 Office: John H Odell Assn 729 Dunlap St Santa Fe NM 87501-2541

ODEN, ROBERT RUDOLPH, surgeon; b. Chgo., Dec. 2, 1922; s. Rudolph J.E. and Olga H. (Wahlquist) O.; m. Nancy Clow; children: Louise, Boyd, Beach, Lisbeth. BS, U. Ill., 1943; MD, Northwestern U., 1947, MS in Anatomy, 1947. Intern Augustana Hosp., Chgo., 1947-48, resident in surgery, 1948-49; resident in orthopaedics Hines Vets. Hosp., Chgo., 1949-51; resident in children's orthopaedics Shriner's Hosp., 1953-54; pvt. practice Chgo., 1954-57, Aspen, Colo., 1957—; clin. assoc. prof. in orthopaedics U. Colo.; orthopaedic surgeon U.S. Olympic Com., 1960, 72, 76, 80. Assoc. editor: Clin. Orthopaedics and Related Rsch. Trustee U.S. Ski Ednl. Found., 1967-82, Aspen Valley Hosp., 1978-86; founder Aspen Orthopaedic and Sports Medicine Pub. Found., 1985, Aspen Inst. for Theol. Futures, 1978, Great Tchrs. and Preachers Series Christ Episc. Ch., 1989; mem. organizing com. Aspen World Cup, 1976-92; founder, trustee Pitkin County Bank, 1983—; founder Aspen Pitkin Employee Housing, 1975. Recipient Blegan award for most outstanding svc. to U.S. skiing, 1985, Halsted award U.S. Ski Assn., 1987, inducted into Aspen Hall of Fame, 1996. Mem. Am. Acad. Orthopaedic Surgeons, ACS, Internat. Coll. Surgeons, Western Orthopaedic Assn., SICOT, Am. Assn. Bone & Joint Surgeons, Rocky Mountain Traumatologic Soc., Canadian Orthopaedic Assn., Am. Orthopaedic Soc. for Sports Medicine, Internat. Ski Safety Soc., ACL Study Group, Internat. Soc. Knee, Internat. Knee Inst., Phi Beta Kappa. Home: PO Box 660 Aspen CO 81612-0660 also: PO Box 172 Captiva FL 33924-0172 Office: 100 E Main St Aspen CO 81611-1778

ODER, BROECK NEWTON, school emergency management consultant; b. Ill., Apr. 20, 1953; s. Bruce Newton and Mary Louise (Roe) O.; m. Jolene Marie Peragine, June 28, 1975 (dec. June 1979). BA in History, U. San Diego, 1974, MA in History, 1975; postgrad., U. N.Mex., 1976-79. Life C.C. teaching credential, Calif. Rsch. asst. to pres. U. San Diego, 1975; grad. asst. U. N.Mex., Albuquerque, 1976-79; tchr. history, chmn. dept. Santa Catalina Sch., Monterey, Calif., 1979—, asst. dean students, 1981-83, dir. ind. study, 1981-95, dean students, 1983-91, dir. emergency planning, 1986—, dean campus affairs, 1991-94, dir. security, 1994—; mem. disaster preparedness coun. Monterey County Office Edn., 1988—; chair Diocesan Sch. Emergency Preparedness Coun., 1991—. Mem. bd. of tchrs. The Concord Rev.; contbr. articles to profl. publs. Participant Jail and Bail, Am. Cancer Soc., Monterey, 1988, 89; reviewer sch. emergency plans, Monterey, 1989—. Recipient award of merit San Diego Hist. Soc., 1975, Outstanding Tchr. award U. Chgo., 1985, Outstanding Young Educator award Monterey Peninsula Jaycees, 1988, resolution of commendation Calif. Senate Rules Com., 1988, cert. of commendation Calif. Gov.'s Office Emergency Svcs., 1991, nat. cert. of achievement Fed. Emergency Mgmt. Agy., 1991, Outstanding High Sch. Tchr. award Tufts U., 1998, High Sch. Tchr. of Excellence, U. Calif. at San Diego, 1998. Mem. ACLU, NAACP, NRA (life), Congress Racial Equality, Am. Hist. Assn., Orgn. Am. Historians, Nat. Coun. on History Edn., Soc. for History Edn., Second Amendment Found., Law Enforcement Alliance Am., Phi Alpha Theta. Avocations: reading, sports, target shooting. Office: Santa Catalina Sch 1500 Mark Thomas Dr Monterey CA 93940-5291

ODERMAN, JEFFREY M., lawyer; b. Orange, N.J., Oct. 30, 1949. BA summa cum laude, UCLA, 1971; JD, Stanford U., 1974. Bar: Calif. 1975, U.S. Supreme Ct., U.S. Ct. Appeals (9th cir.), U.S. Dist. Ct. (ctrl. and no. dists.) Calif. Mem. Rutan & Tucker, Costa Mesa, Calif. Mem. State Bar Calif., Phi Beta Kappa, Order of Coif. Office: Rutan & Tucker PO Box 1950 611 Anton Blvd Ste 1400 Costa Mesa CA 92626-1998

ODERMATT, DIANA B., development officer; b. Hollywood, Calif., Nov. 25, 1938; d. Harold and Mary H. (Wilson) Birtwistle; m. Robert Allen Odermatt, June 9, 1960; children: Kristin Odermatt Lee, Kyle David Odermatt. BA, Mills Coll., 1960. Assoc. dir. admissions Mills Coll., Oakland, Calif., 1978-82; dean admissions and fin. aid Mills Coll., Oakland, 1982-85; dir. devel. Head-Royce Sch., Oakland, 1985-91; major gift officer univ. rels. U. Calif., Berkeley, 1992-95, cons. Coll. Environ. Design, 1995-96; dir. devel. Bentley Sch., Oakland, 1996—; tchr., trainer Coun. for the Advancement and Support of Edn., Washington, 1980-93; bd. mem. European Coun. Ind. Schs., Washington, 1982-85; cons. The Coll. Bd., N.Y.C., 1985-92. Contbr. articles to profl. jours. Home: 39 Drury Ln Berkeley CA 94705-1615 Office: Bentley Sch 1 Hiller Dr Oakland CA 94618-2301

ODOM, GEORGE COSBY, JR., retired religion educator; b. Sebree, Ky., Aug. 30, 1922; s. George Cosby and Connie Bell (Walker) O.; m. Harriet Aileen Zimmer, Mar. 18, 1944; children: Melodie Joy, Denis Lee, Georgette June and Gloria Jane (twins.). BTh, No. Bapt. Theol. Sem., Chgo., 1951; MA, Baylor U., 1952; LHD (hon.), Sioux Empire Coll., Hawarden, Iowa, 1966. Ordained to ministry Conservative Bapt. Assn. Am., 1950; cert. fgn. missionary. Missionary, tchr. Conservative Bapt. Fgn. Missionary Soc., Wheaton, Ill., 1952-87; prof. Theol. Sem. Batista do Nordeste, Floriano, Piaui, Brazil, 1957-68; tchr., ch. planter State of Piaui, 1969-87; ret., 1987; Bible tchr. Sunset Villa Nursing Home, Roswell, N.Mex., 1987—; acting chaplain Sub-Ets World War II, Roswell, 1988—. With USNR, 1942-45, PTO. Recipient plaque Brazilian Bapt. Conv., 1987. Mem. VFW, Pecos Valley U.S. Submarine Vets. World War II (life). Republican. Home: 802 S Plains Park Dr Roswell NM 88201-3619

ODOM, SCOTT J., college administrator, educator; b. Oak Park, Ill., Sept. 10, 1958; s. Bruce Stuart and Patricia (Keleher) O.; m. Christine M. Callinan, Apr. 7, 1990; children: Zachary, Rachel, Georgia. BA, SUNY, Purchase, 1988; MA, Loyola Marymount U., L.A., 1995. Fin. aid adminstr. Loyola Marymount U., L.A., 1989-92, admissions and fin. aid adminstr., 1992-98, instr. English, 1995—. Author theatre criticism L.A. Theatres Mag., 1994-96; author cultural criticism Daily Web Mag., 1995-97; contbr. fiction and poetry to mags.; on-air personality, theater critic KXLU Radio, 1990-97. Democrat. Roman Catholic. Avocation: guitar. Home: 5643 W 79th St Los Angeles CA 90045-3305 Office: Loyola Marymount U 7900 Loyola Blvd Los Angeles CA 90045-2699

O'DONNELL, BARBARA SPENCE, nurse; b. Lincoln, Nebr., Sept. 13, 1940; d. Alton Kenneth and Alma Mae (Benjamin) Jorgensen; m. J. Daniel O'Donnell, Jan. 14, 1984; children: Robert Lloyd, Jacki Ann. BSN cum laude, Ariz. State U., 1976. RN, Ariz. Charge nurse Carl T. Hayden VA Med. Ctr., Phoenix, 1978-84, emergency rm. charge nurse, 1984—; oncology nurse educator VA Hosp., Phoenix, 1978—; mem. nursing edn. bd., 1992—, trauma bd., 1996—; mem. forensic nursing bd. S.W. Region, Phoenix, 1996—. Co-author: Life Support-Spreading It's Wings, 1996 (Trauma award 1996). Mem. Internat. Forensic Nurses Assn., Emergency Nurses Assn., Assn. Critical Care Nurses Assn., Am. Cancer Soc., Sigma Theta Tau. Avocations: artist, reading. Home: 409 W Kings Ave Phoenix AZ 85023-3541

O'DONNELL, EDWARD EARL, physicist; b. Hobbs, N.Mex., Sept. 16, 1937; s. Thomas E. and Bessie L. (Rhodes) O'D.; m. H. Kathryn Jones; children: Damon L., Dari L., Doran L., Devon L. BS, N.Mex. State U., 1961, MS, 1963, PhD, 1965. Rsch. scientist Kaman Scis. Corp., Colorado Springs, Colo., 1965-74, Sci. Applications Internat. Corp., Colorado Springs, 1974-81; v.p. Sci. Applications Internat. Corp., Albuquerque, N.Mex., 1981—; mentor, program mgr. Sci. Applications Internat. Corp., Albuquerque, 1994—. Contbr. articles to profl. jours. Recipient Citation, U.S. Navy, 1996. Mem. AIAA. Avocations: fishing, reading. Home: 757 Highway 98 E # 14-141 Destin FL 32541-2561 Office: Sci Applications Internat Corp 2109 Airpark Rd SE Albuquerque NM 87106-3258

O'DONNELL, VICTORIA JEAN, communication educator; b. Greensburg, Pa., Feb. 12, 1938; d. Victor C. and Helen A. (Detar) O'D.; children from previous marriage: Christopher O'Donnell Stupp, Browning William Stupp; m. Paul M. Monaco, Apr. 9, 1993. BA, Pa. State U., 1959, MA, 1961, PhD, 1968. Asst. prof. comm. Midwestern State U., Wichita Falls, Tex., 1965-67; prof. dept. chair comm. U. No. Tex., Denton, 1967-89; prof., dept. chair comms. Ore. State U., Corvallis, 1989-91; prof. comm., basic course dir. Mont. State U., Bozeman, 1991-93, prof. comm., dir. honors program, 1993—; prof. Am. Inst. Fgn. Studies, London, 1988; cons. Arco Oil & Gas, Dallas, 1983-86, Federal Emergency Mgrs. Agy., Salt Lake City, 1986; speechwriter Sen. Mae Yih, Salem, Ore., 1989-91; steering com. Ore. Alliance Film & TV Educators, 1990-91; expert witness tobacco litig., Tex., 1997; participant Western Regional Honors Conf. Author: Introduction to Public Communication, 1992, 2d edit., 1993; co-author: Persuasion, 1982, Propaganda and Persuasion, 1986, 3d edit., 1999; prodr.: (video) Women, War and Work, 1994; mem. editl. bd. Am. Comm. Jour.; scriptwriter: The Howl of the Wolf, 1997; narrator (PBS TV) Gary Strobel, Bison in the Killing Field. Bd. dirs. Friends of the Family, Denton, 1987-89; bd. dirs. Bozeman Film Festival, 1991—, v.p., 1997-98, pres., 1998—; del. Tex. Dem. Convention, Denton, 1976. Grantee Mont. Com. for the Humanities, 1993, Oreg. Coun. for the Humanities, 1991, NEH, 1977. Mem. Nat. Collegiate Honors Coun. (co-chair Portz Fund com.), Nat. Comm. Assn., Internat. Comm. Assn., Western States Comm. Assn., Co-chair, portz fund commi. NCHC. Home: 290 Low Bench Rd Gallatin Gateway MT 59730-9741 Office: Mont State U U Honors Program Bozeman MT 59717-2140

O'DONNELL, WILLIAM THOMAS, management consultant; b. Latrobe, Pa., Feb. 22, 1939; s. William Regis and Kathryn Ann (Coneff) O'D.; m. Judith Koetke, Oct. 1, 1965; children: William Thomas, William Patrick, Allison Rose, Kevin Raymond. Student Ea. N.Mex. U., 1958-61; student in mktg. John Carroll U., 1961-65, Ill. Inst. Tech., 1965-66; BSBA, U. Phoenix, 1982, MBA with distinction, 1984; postgrad. Union Inst., 1996. Various sales positions Hickok Elec. Instrument Co., Cleve., 1961-65, Fairchild Semicondr., Mpls., 1965-67; Transitron Semicondr., Mpls., 1967-69; regional sales mgr. Burroughs Corp., Plainfield, N.J., 1967-71; mktg. mgr. Owens-Ill. Co., 1972-73, v.p. mktg. Pantek Co., subs. Owens-Ill. Co., Lewistown, Pa., 1973-75, v.p. mktg., nat. sales mgr., Toledo, 1975-76; mktg. mgr. Govt. Electronics div. group Motorola Co., Scottsdale, Ariz., 1976-80, U.S. mktg. mgr. radar positioning systems Motorola Govt. Electronics Group, 1981—; gen. mgr. J.K. Internat., Scottsdale, 1980-81; mgmt. cons. Pres. Cambridge Group, 1987—; v.p. mktg. Pinnacle Surg. Products, 1989; v.p. mktg., Kroy, Inc., 1992-94; mgmt. cons., 1994—; v.p. mktg. and bus. devel. Kroy Inc., 1992, v.p. mktg. Process Control Tech., Inc., 1996—; adj. prof. Union Grad. Sch.; guest lectr. U. Mich. Grad. Sch. Bus. Adminstrn.; instr., chair strategic mgmt. U. Phoenix, 1988, pres. faculty, 1989—, area chair mktg., 1995—; Scottsdale Community Coll., Paradise Valley Community Coll.; talk show host Sta. KFNN, 1992-95. Area chair-gen. mgmt. Union Grad. Sch. Maricopa Community Coll., U. Phoenix. Chmn., Rep. Precinct, Burnsville, Minn., 1968-70; city fin. chmn., Burnsville; dir. community devel. U.S. Jaycees, Mpls., 1968-69; mem. Scottsdale 2000 Com. With USAF, 1957-61. Recipient Outstanding Performance award Maricopa Community Coll. System, 1987, Faciliation award, Maricopa Community Coll., Citation for Faciliation Ability U. Phoenix, 1986, 90, 93; named Hon. Citizen, Donaldsville, La., 1978; others. Mem. Am. Mktg. Assn., Afro-Am. Small Bus. Assn. (bd. dirs.), Phoenix Indian Ctr., Inc. (bd. dirs. 1994), Amateur Athletic Union (swimming ofcl. 1980-82), Phoenix Execs. Club, U. Phoenix Faculty Club (bd. dirs., pres. 1988-91, recipient Presdl. Designation award, officer), North Cape Yacht Club, Scottsdale Racquet Club, Toftnees Country Club. Roman Catholic. Home: 8650 E Via Del Arbor Scottsdale AZ 85258-3526

O'DOWD, DONALD DAVY, retired university president; b. Manchester, N.H., Jan. 23, 1927; s. Hugh Davy and Laura (Morin) O'D.; m. Janet Louise Fithian, Aug. 23, 1953; children: Daniel D., Diane K., James E., John M. BA summa cum laude, Dartmouth Coll., 1951; postgrad. (Fulbright fellow), U. Edinburgh, Scotland, 1951-52; MA, Harvard U., 1955, PhD, 1957. Instr., asst. prof. psychology, dean freshmen Wesleyan U., Middletown, Conn., 1955-60; assoc. prof., prof. of psychology, dean Univ. Oakland Univ., Rochester, Mich., 1960-65, provost, 1965-70; pres. Oakland U., Rochester, Mich., 1970-80; exec. vice chancellor SUNY, Albany, 1980-84; pres. U. of Alaska Statewide System, 1984-90. Sr. cons. Assn. Governing Bds. Univs. and Colls. Carnegie Corp. fellow, 1965-66. Mem. APA, AAAS, Phi Beta Kappa, Sigma Xi. Home and Office: 1550 La Vista Del Oceano Santa Barbara CA 93109-1739

OEMLER, AUGUSTUS, JR., astronomer; b. Savannah, Ga., Aug. 15, 1945; s. Augustus and Isabelle Redding (Clarke) O.; children: W. Clarke, Bryan S. AB, Princeton U., 1969; MS, Calif. Inst. Tech., 1970, PhD, 1974. Postdoctoral assoc. Kitt Peak Nat. Obs., Tucson, 1974-75; instr. astronomy Yale U., New Haven, 1975-77, asst. prof., 1977-79, assoc. prof., 1979-83, prof., 1983-96, chmn. dept., 1988-96; dir. Obs. Carnegie Instn. Washington, Pasadena, Calif., 1996—. Contbr. articles to profl. jours. Alfred P. Sloan fellow, 1978-80. Mem. Am. Astronom. Soc., Internat. Astronom. Union. Republican. Roman Catholic. Home: 741 Burleigh Dr Pasadena CA 91105-2241 Office: Carnegie Obs 813 Santa Barbara St Pasadena CA 91101-1232

OESTING, DAVID W., lawyer; b. Chgo., Aug. 6, 1944. AB, Earlham Coll., 1967; JD, Wash. U., 1970. Bar: Wash. 1970, Alaska 1981. Ptnr. in charge of Anchorage Office Davis Wright Tremaine, Anchorage, 1980—. Editor-in-chief Wash. U. Law Quarterly, 1969-70. Mem. ABA, Wash. State Bar Assn., Alaska Bar Assn., Anchorage Bar Assn., Order of Coif. Office: Davis Wright Tremaine 701 W 8th Ave Ste 800 Anchorage AK 99501-3408

OETTINGER, ROBERT ALLAN, foundation executive, writer; b. L.A., Dec. 17, 1950; s. Larry Justin and Audrey Eileen Oettinger; m. Eve Simon, Apr. 16, 1983; children: Daniel, Emily. BA, U. So. Calif., 1973. Dir. pub. rels. Am. Diabetes Assn., L.A., 1977-84; assoc. campaign dir. Motion Picture & TV Fund, L.A., 1984-88; pres., founder Celebrity Outreach Found., Agoura Hills, Calif., 1988—. Editor: Happy Birthday Hollywood, 1984; writer, producer (documentary) Flying Tigers, Combat Camera. Pres., entertainment com. L.A. Partnership Ethical Charity, 1992; baseball mgr. Woodland Hills (Calif.) Recreational Ctr., 1992—; coms. com. Am. Lung Assn., L.A., 1982-83; bd. dirs. Publicity Club L.A., 1980-82, Roar Foundation, Acton, Calif., 1994—, Goodwill Industries, L.A., 1990-91. Avocations: photography, travel, sports. Office: Celebrity Outreach Found 28708 Roadside Dr Ste F Agoura Hills CA 91301-3300

OFTE, DONALD, retired environmental executive, consultant; b. N.Y.C., Aug. 23, 1929; s. Sverre and Ingeborg Ofte; m. Margaret Mae McHenney, July 23, 1955; children: Marc Christian, Nancy Carolyn Appleby, Kirk Donald Jr. BA in Chemistry, Dana Coll., 1952; postgrad. study metall. engring., Ohio State U., 1958-60. Jr. chemist Inst. Atomic Research, Ames, Iowa, 1952-53; sr. research chemist Monsanto Research Corp., Miamisburg, Ohio, 1958-66; ops. engr. AEC, Miamisburg, 1966-69; br. chief, div. dir. ops. office AEC, Albuquerque, 1969-73; mgr. Pinellas area office AEC, Largo, Fla., 1973-79; mgr. Rocky Flats area office Dept. Energy, Golden, Colo., 1979-82; asst. mgr. devel. and prodn. Dept. Energy, Albuquerque, 1982-83, dep. mgr. ops. office, 1983-84; prin. dep. asst. sec. Dept. Energy Defense Programs, Washington, 1984-87; mgr. ops. office Dept. Energy, Idaho Falls, Idaho, 1987-89; mgmt. cons. Idaho Falls, 1989-92; v.p. govt. ops. United Engrs. & Constructors (Raytheon Engrs. & Constrn.), Denver, 1992-93; v.p. Adv. Scis., Inc., Albuquerque, 1993-94; pres. FERMCO (also known as Fluor Daniel, Fernald), Cin., 1994-96; ret., 1996; v.p. Fluor-Daniel, Inc., 1994-96, affiliate prof. Idaho State U., 1990-92, bd. dirs. Denver Fed. Exec. Bd., 1979-82. Author: (with others) Plutonium 1960, 1965, Physicochemical Methods in Metallurgical Research; contbr. articles to profl. jours. on metallurgy and ceramics. Campaign chmn. United Way Pinellas, St. Petersburg, Fla., 1978; bd. dirs. Bonneville County United Way, Idaho Rsch. Found.; mem. adv. bd. Teton Peaks Council Boy Scouts of Am., 1987-92, Eastern Idaho Tech. Coll.; chmn. Excellence in Edn. Fund Com., 1990-92; vice chmn., bd. dirs. Rio Grande Ch. ARC, Albuquerque, 1982-84. Served to lt. (j.g.) USN, 1953-57. Recipient citation AEC for Apollo 12 SNAP 27 Radioisotope Generator, 1969, High Quality Performance award AEC, 1968, Group Achievement award NASA, 1972; Meritorious Svc. award Dept. Energy, 1985, Disting. Career Svc. award, 1989. Mem. Am. Chem. Soc., Am. Nuclear Soc., Am. Soc. Metals, Nat. Contract Mgmt. Assn., Am. Soc. Pub. Adminstrs., Suncoast Archeol. Soc., Idaho Falls C. of C. (bd. dirs., cmty. svc. award 1990), Rotary Internat. (Paul Harris fellow). Avocations: reading, bridge, gardening, golf. Home: 1129 Salamanca St NW Albuquerque NM 87107-5643

OGBURN, HUGH BELL, chemical engineer, consultant; b. Lexington, Va., July 13, 1923; s. Sihon Cicero Jr. and Bettie Mae (Bell) O.; m. Anne Wotherspoon, Mar. 2, 1946 (div.); children: Margaret Mathews Berenson, Scott A.; m. Nancy Wrenn Petersen, Sept. 5, 1974. B.S., Princeton U., 1944, M.S., 1947, Ph.D., 1954. Sect. dir. research and devel. dept. Atlantic Refining Co., Phila., 1950-61; mgr. process engring. M.W. Kellogg Co., N.Y.C., London, 1961-67; dir. research and engring. Union Carbide Corp., N.Y.C., 1967-69; dir. new bus. devel. Weyerhaeuser Co., Tacoma, 1969-72; pres. H.B. Ogburn Assoc., Greenwich, Conn. and Honolulu, 1971—; v.p., dir. Incontrade Inc., Stamford, Conn., 1973-78; v.p. Pacific Resources Inc., Honolulu, 1978-83; chmn. Pacific Oasis, Los Angeles, 1983-85; dir. Danmore Corp., Planning Research Corp.; cons. AEC; prof. chem. engring. Drexel U., Phila., 1951-61. Contbr. articles to profl. jours.; patentee in field. Pres. bd. trustees Woman's Hosp., Phila., 1954-62, Kapiolani Women's and Children's Med. Ctr., 1980-90; mem. adv. bd. Princeton U., 1960-70. Served to lt. j.g. USNR, 1942-46, PTO. Mem. AIChE, Am. Chem. Soc., Research Engrs. Soc., Pacific (Honolulu) Club, Greenwich Field (Conn.) Club, Princeton (N.Y.C.) Club, Phi Beta Kappa, Sigma Xi, Tau Beta Pi. Republican. Presbyterian. Home and Office: 4340 Pahoa Ave Apt 16 A Honolulu HI 96816-5032

OGDEN, JEAN LUCILLE, sales executive; b. Chgo., Jan. 20, 1950; d. George William and Mary Elizabeth (MacKenzie) Anderson; m. Michael Jude Ogden, Aug. 27, 1977 (div. Dec. 1983). BA with honors, U. Calif., Santa Barbara, 1971. Sales rep. Am. Hosp. Supply Co., Irvine, Calif., 1975-77, Abbott Labs., HPD, L.A., 1977-78, Gillette Co., Albququerque, 1978-79, Unitek Corp., Monrovia, Calif., 1979-86, Nat. Patent Dental Products, San Diego, 1986-87; area mgr. Branson Ultrasonics Corp., L.A., 1987—. Mem., co-chair Nat. Multiple Sclerosis Soc., San Diego, 1983—; mem. Am. Cancer Soc., San Diego, 1985—, Zool. Soc., San Diego, 1984-85. Named one of Outstanding Young Women in Am., 1984. Mem. AAUW, NAFE, Med. Mktg. Assn., Salesmasters Albuquerque, Soroptimist Internat. (officer Carlsbad and Oceanside, Calif. chpt. 1983-85), Alpha Phi (house corp. bd. Long Beach chpt. 1974-75, chpt. advisor 1975-76). Republican. Avocations: sailing, skiing, bridge. Office: Branson Ultrasonics Corp 12955 E Perez Pl La Puente CA 91746-1414

OGDEN, VALERIA MUNSON, management consultant, state representative; b. Okanogan, Wash., Feb. 11, 1924; d. Ivan Bodwell and Pearle (Wilson) Munson; m. Daniel Miller Ogden Jr., Dec. 28, 1946; children: Janeth Lee Ogden Martin, Patricia Jo Ogden Hunter, Daniel Munson Ogden. BA magna cum laude, Wash. State U., 1946. Exec. dir. Potomac Coun. Camp Fire, Washington, 1964-68, Ft. Collins (Colo.) United Way, 1969-73, Designing Tomorrow Today, Ft. Collins, 1973-74, Poudre Valley Community Edn. Assn., Ft. Collins, 1977-78; pres. Valeria M. Ogden, Inc., Kensington, Md., 1978-81; nat. field cons. Camp Fire, Inc., Kansas City, Mo., 1980-81; exec. dir. Nat. Capital Area YWCA, Washington, 1981-84, Clark County YWCA, Vancouver, Wash., 1985-89; pvt. practice mgmt. cons. Vancouver, 1989—; mem. Wash. Ho. of Reps., 1991—; mem. adj. faculty pub. adminstrn. program Lewis and Clark Coll., Portland (Oreg.) State U., 1979-94; mem. Pvt. Industry Coun., Vancouver, 1986-95; mem. regional Svcs. Network Bd. Mental Health, 1993—. Author: Camp Fire Membership, 1980. County vice chmn. Larimer County Dems., Ft. Collins, 1974-75; mem. precinct com. Clark County Dems., Vancouver, 1986-88; mem. Wash. State Coun. Vol. Action, Olympia, 1986-90; treas. Mortar Bd. Nat. Found., Vancouver, 1987-96; bd. dirs. Clark County Coun. for Homeless, Vancouver, 1989—, chmn., 1994; bd. dirs. Wash. Wil life and Recreation Coalition, 1995—, Human Svcs. Coun., 1996—; chair arts and tourism com. Nat. Coun. State Legis., 1996-97; bd. Wash. State Hist. Soc., 1996—. Named Citizen of Yr. Ft. Collins Bd. of Realtors, 1975; recipient Gulick award Camp Fire Inc., 1956, Alumna Achievement award Wash. State U. Alumni Assn., 1988; named YWCA Woman of Achievement, 1991. Mem. Internat. Assn. Vol. Adminstrs. (pres. Boulder 1989-90), Nat. Assn. YWCA Exec. Dirs. (nat. bd. nominating com. 1988-90), Sci. and Society Assn. (bd. dirs. 1993-97), Women in Action, Philanthropic and Ednl. Orgn., Phi Beta Kappa. Democrat. Avocation: hiking, travel. Home: 3118 NE Royal Oak Dr Vancouver WA 98662-7435 Office: Legislative Bldg State Ave NE Rm 410 Olympia WA 98504-1134

OGG, R. DANFORTH, lawyer, commercial fishing administrator, fisherman; b. Berkeley, Calif., Mar. 25, 1949; s. Robert D. Ogg and Phyllis Idon (Aasgaard) Washington (dec.); m. Susan Mary Jeffrey, May 14, 1952; children: Sara May Klemzak, Alex Jeffrey Klemzak. BA in History, U. Calif., Berkeley, 1972; JD, U. Idaho, 1985. Builder Silver Elbow, Kodiak, Alaska, 1976—; pvt. practice law Kodiak, 1985—; comml. fisherman Beargarden Fisheries, Kodiak, 1987—; exec. dir. Alaskan Oceans, Seas, Fisheries Rsch. Found., Kodiak, 1998—. Mem. planning and zoning com. Kodiak Island Borough, 1976-78, assembly mem., 1978-80, mayor, 1980-81; v.p. bd. regents U. Alaska, 1993—. Mem. N.W. Setnetters Assn. (bd. dirs., pres. 1989-92), Monashka Bay Rd. Dist. (bd. dirs., sec. 1986-92), Selective Svc. U.S. (bd. mem. 1980—, chair 1984-86). Avocations: sculpting, painting, walking, building. Home: PO Box 2754 Kodiak AK 99615-2754 Office: PO Box 1968 Kodiak AK 99615-1968

OGG, WILSON REID, lawyer, mediator, arbitrator, real estate and financial consultant, poet, retired judge, lyricist, curator, publisher, educator, philosopher, social scientist, parapsychologist; b. Alhambra, Calif., Feb. 26, 1928; s. James Brooks and Mary (Wilson) O. Student Pasadena Jr. Coll., 1946; A.B., U. Calif. at Berkeley, 1949, J.D., 1952; Cultural D in Philosophy of Law, World Univ. Roundtable, 1983. Bar: Calif. Assoc. trust Dept. Wells Fargo Bank, San Francisco, 1954-55; pvt. practice law, Berkeley, 1955—; adminstrv. law judge, 1974-93; real estate broker, cons., 1974—; curator-in-residence Pinebrook, 1964—; owner Pinebrook Press, Berkeley, Calif., 1988—; rsch. atty., legal editor dept. of continuing edn. of bar U. Calif. Extension, 1958-63; psychology instr. 25th Sta. Hosp., Taegu, Korea, 1954; English instr. Taegu English Lang. Inst., Taegu, 1954. Trustee World U., 1976-80; dir. admissions Internat. Soc. for Phil. Enquiry, 1981-84; dep. dir. gen. Internat. Biographical Centre, Eng., 1986—; dep. gov. Am. Biographical Inst. Research Assn., 1986—; ind. rep. Excel Comm., Inc. Served with AUS, 1952-54. Cert. community coll. instr. Mem. VFW, AAAS, ABA, ASCAP, State Bar Calif., San Francisco Bar Assn., Am. Arbitration Assn. (nat. panel arbitrators), Calif. Soc. Psychical Study (pres., chmn. bd. 1963-65), Internat. Soc. Unified Sci., Internat. Soc. Poets. (life), Internat. Platform Assn., Amnesty Internat., Am. Civil Liberties Union, Intertel, Internat. Soc. Individual Liberty, Triple Nine Soc., Wisdom Soc., Inst. Noetic Scis., Men's Inner Circle of Achievement, Truman Libr. Inst. (hon.), Am. Legion, City Commons Club (Berkeley), Commonwealth Club of Calif., Town Hall Club of Calif., Marines Meml. Club, Masons, Shriners, Elks. Unitarian. Contbr. numerous articles profl. jours; contbr. poetry to various mags. including American Poetry Anthology Vol. VI Number 5, Hearts on Fire: A Treasury of Poems on Love, Vol. IV, 1987, New Voices in American Poetry, 1987, The Best Poems of the 90's, Distinguished Poets of America, The Poetry of Life A Treasury of Moments Am. Poetry Anthology, Vol. VII, 1988, Nat. Libr. Poets, 1992, Disting. Poets Of Am., 1993, The Best Modern Writer of 1994, Parnassus of World Poets, 1994, 95, 96, Best Poems of 1995, 96, 97, 98; elected Internat. Poetry Hall Fame Nat. Libr. Poetry, 1997. Home: Pinebrook 8 Bret Harte Way Berkeley CA 94708-1611 Office: 1104 Keith Ave Berkeley CA 94708-1607 also: 39831 Liberty St Fremont CA 94538-1501 Judge Ogg's career combines outstanding achievement in the legal

profession with a major analysis of the problems of distinguishing co-existence from causality medicine and science. He has also formulated the two-way flow theory of matter and consciousness under which principles of quantum mechanics, black notes, light, expansion and contraction of manifestation, and physical and biological evolutions are derivative from the basic postulates of the theory.

OGILVIE, LLOYD JOHN, clergyman; b. Kenosha, Wis., Sept. 2, 1930; s. Vard Spencer and Katherine (Jacobson) O.; m. Mary Jane Jenkins, Mar. 25, 1951. B.A., Lake Forest Coll., 1952, Garrett Theol. Sem., 1956; postgrad., New Coll., U. Edinburgh, Scotland, 1955-56; D.D., Whitworth Coll., 1973; L.H.D., U. Redlands, 1974; D.Humanities, Moravian Coll., 1975; LLD, Ea. U., 1988. Ordained to ministry Presbyn. Ch., 1956; student pastor Gurnee, Ill., 1952-56; first pastor Winnetka (Ill.) Presbyn. Ch., 1956-62; pastor 1st Presbyn. Ch., Bethlehem, Pa., 1962-72, 1st Presbyn. Ch., Hollywood, Calif., 1972—; preacher Chgo. Sunday Evening Club, 1962—, also frequent radio and TV personality weekly syndicated TV program Let God Love You. Author: A Life Full of Surprises, 1969, Let God Love You, 1974, If I Should Wake Before I Die, 1973, Lord of the Ups and Downs, 1974, You've Got Charisma, 1975, Cup of Wonder, 1976, Life Without Limits, 1976, Drumbeat of Love, 1977, When God First Thought of You, 1978, The Autobiography of God, 1979, The Bush Is Still Burning, 1980, The Radiance of the Inner Splendor, 1980, Congratulations, God Believes in You, 1981, Life as it Was Meant to Be, 1981, The Beauty of Love, The Beauty of Friendship, 1981, The Beauty of Caring, The Beauty of Sharing, 1981, God's Best for My Life, 1981, God's Will in Your Life, 1982, Ask Him Anything, 1982, Commentary on Book of Acts, 1983, Praying with Power, 1983, Falling into Greatness, 1983, Freedom in the Spirit, 1984, Making Stress Work For You, 1984, The Lord of the Impossible, 1984, Why Not Accept Christ's Healing and Wholeness, 1984, If God Cares, Why Do I Still Have Problems?, 1985, Understanding the Hard Sayings of Jesus, 1986, 12 Steps to Living Without Fear, 1987, A Future and a Hope, 1988, Enjoying God, 1990, Silent Strength, 1990, The Lord of the Loose Ends, 1991; gen. editor: Communicator's Commentary of the Bible, 1982; host: (TV and radio program) Let God Love You. Office: 1760 N Gower St Los Angeles CA 90028-5422

OGLE, DAVID WILLIAM, art educator, sculptor, ceramist; b. Richmond, Calif., May 17, 1944; s. Robert Ray Sr. and Dorothy Aileen (Reynolds) O.; m. Carol Jo Gudenkauf, July 7, 1968; 1 child: Ashley Christina. AA in Art, Contra Costa Coll., San Pablo, Calif., 1964; BA in Ceramics, San Jose State U., 1969, MA in Sculpture, 1970; postgrad., San Francisco State U., 1988. Cert. instr. art C.C., Calif. Owner David Ogle Ceramics and Sculpture, Los Gatos, Calif., 1968—; instr., art lab. technician West Valley Coll., Campbell, Calif., 1971-72; instr. art West Valley Coll., Saratoga, Calif., 1973—; chmn. dept. sculpture West Valley Coll., Saratoga, 1973—, chmn. dept. art, 1976-78, chmn. ceramics, 1978—; foundry apprentice San Francisco Art Foundry, 1974-75; lectr. Corcoran Sch. Art, Washington, 1976—, San Jose State U., Calif. 1986—; chmn. Olympiad of Arts Coll. Divsn., Saratoga, 1993-97. Contbg. author Ceramics Monthly Mag., 1985-97; author: Workbook for Ceramics, 1997; one-man shows include San Jose Mus., 1979; exhibited in group shows at San Francisco Mus. Modern Art, Oakland Mus., De Young Mus., Triton Mus., Los Gatos Mus., Crocker Mus., Arts Coun. Gt. Britain-White Chapel Gallery, Musee d'Art Moderne, Paris, France, La Jolla Mus., Palo Alto Cultural Ctr., Esther Robles Gallery, L.A., William Sawyer Gallery, San Francisco, Smith-Anderson Gallery, Palo Alto, Calif., Fendrick Gallery, Washington, Gargoyle Gallery, Aspen, Colo., Jalbert Gallery, Saratoga; represented in permanent collections Addison Gallery Am. Art, Brit. Coun. for Arts; prin. works include Figurescapes, Chi the Vital Spirit, Fates and the Unknown Artist; represented in numerous pvt. collections. Mentor 2" Off to Coll. program West Valley Coll., 1993—; vol. Young Authors program VanMeter Elem. Sch., Los Gatos, 1990-92; vol. Montalvo Art Assn., Saratoga, 1992; active San Francisco Mus. Modern Art, 1975-97. Recipient numerous sculpture awards, Calif., 1970-80; grantee sabbatical West Valley Coll., 1981-82, profl. growth and devel. grantee West Valley Coll., 1996. Mem. Nat. Coun. Edn. for Ceramic Arts, Faculty Assn. C.C., Los Gatos Athletic Club. Avocations: skiing, racquetball, landscaping, writing, home design and construction. Home: 16555 Topping Way Los Gatos CA 95032-5645 Office: West Valley Coll 14000 Fruitvale Ave Saratoga CA 95070-5640

OGLE, JAMES, performing company executive; m. Mary Davis; children: Matthew, Ryan. Student, Nat. ConservatoryMusic; studied with Seiji Ozawa, Leonard Bernstein, Andre Previn, Sir Collin Davis, Boston. Music dir. Boise Philharmnonic Assn., Idaho; assoc. condr. N.C. Symphony; condr.-in-residence Appalachian State U. Cannon Music Camp; guest condr. Music from Bear Valley, Winston-Salem Symphony, South Bend Symphony, Nebr. Chamber Orchestra; guest clinician and condr. La. State U. Symphony Orchestra and Wind Ensemble; guest artist-in-residence U. N.C.; founder, condr., artistic dir. summer residence N.C. Symphony, 1982-94.. Recipient James Bland Meml. Scholarship, Malko Internat. Condr. award, 1974. Mem. Downtown Rotary Club. Office: Boise Philharmonic Assn 516 S 9th St Ste C Boise ID 83702-7005*

OGLE, MADELINE ANN BRIGHT, realtor, investment counselor; b. Fresno, Calif., Jan. 5, 1926; m. Dale A. Mart (dec.); m. George H. Sciaroni (dec.); m. Richard P. Bright (div.); m. Jerome C. Ogle (div. Jan. 1989). Student, Fresno State U., 1956-58; BA, San Francisco State U., 1959; postgrad., Coll. of San Mateo, 1969-71. Cert. investment counselor, 1979. Asst. mgr. customer relations Sears and Roebuck Co., 1954-55; bookkeeper, clk. Innes Reliable Leather Goods, 1955-56; bookkeeper Langendorf Bakeries, 1956; ins. clk. Assigned Risk, San Francisco, 1959-60; mgr., owner Madeline's Dog Salon and Boutique, Santa Clara, Calif., 1961-86; assoc. realtor Santa Rosa, Calif., 1979; founder Madson PetCare Ctrs. Inc., 1990—. Author: From Problems to Profits, 1995, The Madson Management System for Pet Grooming Salons, 1989. Mem. Friend's of Trition Mus., 1975-77; Citizen's Adv. Bd., Santa Clara, 1971; mem. Hist. Preservation Comn., 1971—, chmn. Goals Comn.; lobbyist Target State Lic. for dog grooming, Calif., 1966-71. Recipient Contributions to City of Santa Clara award 1969. Mem. State of Calif. Dept. Real Estate, United Dog Groomers, Inc. (v.p. 1966-71), Soroptimists of Santa Clara (mayor's rep. 1971, chmn. community services com., fundraiser 1982), Santa Clara Women's Club, Calif. Fedn. of Women's Club,. Home and office: 13082 Mono Way # 230 Sonora CA 95370-5338

OH, TAI KEUN, business educator; b. Seoul, Korea, Mar. 25, 1934; s. Chin Young and Eui Kyung (Yun) O.; came to U.S., 1958, naturalized, 1969; B.A., Seijo U., 1957; M.A., No. Ill. U., 1961; M.L.S., U. Wis., 1965, Ph.D., 1970; m. Gretchen Brenneke, Dec. 26, 1964; children: Erica, Elizabeth, Emily. Asst. prof. mgmt. Roosevelt U., Chgo., 1969-73; assoc. prof. Calif. State U., Fullerton, 1973-76, prof. mgmt., 1976—; vis. prof. U. Hawaii, 1983-84, 86; advisor Pacific Asian Mgmt. Inst., U. Hawaii; internat. referee Asia-Pacific Jour. of Mgmt., 1990—; cons. Calty Design Research, Inc. subs. Toyota Motor Corp. The Employers Group; seminar leader and speaker. Named Outstanding Prof., Sch. Bus. Adminstrn. and Econs., Calif. State U., Fullerton, 1976, 78. NSF grantee, 1968-69, recipient Exceptional Merit Service award Calif. State U., 1984, Meritorious Performance and Profl. Promise award Calif. State U., 1987. Mem. Acad. Mgmt., Indsl. Relations Research Assn., Acad. Internat. Bus. Editorial bd. Acad. Mgmt. Rev., 1978-81; contbg. author: Ency. Profl. Mgmt., 1978, Handbook of Management 1985; contbr. articles to profl. jours. Home: 2044 E Eucalyptus Ln Brea CA 92821-5911 Office: Calif State U Dept Mgmt Fullerton CA 92634

O'HAGAN, WILLIAM GORDON, state agency administrator; b. Allentown, N.J., Oct. 12, 1943; s. Forrest Allen and Voncile Arline (Linton) O'H.; m. Marcia Helen Beck, Aug. 12, 1947 (div. Oct. 1985). Grad. high sch., Azusa, Calif., 1962. Owner Richfield Oil Co., Baldwin Park, Calif., 1970-72; mgr. Am. Teaching Aids, Covina, Calif., 1972-88; owner Bill's Auto Repair Co., Covina, 1988-93; mechanic, 1993-95; supr./foreman Public Auction Agy. of Calif., 1996—. Block commander Neighborhood Watch, Covina. Republican. Baptist. Home: 163 N Marcile Ave Glendora CA 91741-2453

O'HARA, MARY MARGARET, artist; b. Detroit, Feb. 21, 1909; d. John J. and Mildred Mary (Scherff) Schultz; m. H. Richard O'Hara, Oct. 6, 1932; children: John Galen, H. Richard Jr. BA in Drawing, Painting and Illustration, Sch. Art Inst. Chgo., 1930; postgrad., Corcoran Gallery, Washington, 1942-45. Painter Vogue Studios, Chgo., 1931-32; v.p. Pacific Coach Ambulance Co., Burlingame, Calif., 1960-80. Commd. portrait artist. Mem. Burlingame Art Soc. (pres., v.p.), 50 Art Club. Republican. Christian Scientist. Avocations: photography, house design. Home and Office: 3594 Lake Park Dr Santa Rosa CA 95403-0116

O'HARE, MARILYNN RYAN, artist; b. Berkeley, Calif., Aug. 6, 1926; d. Lawrence and Linnie Marie (Ryan) Atkins; m. Lawrence Bernard O'Hare, Sept. 20, 1947; children: Timothy Lawrence, Kevin Roy, Shannon John, Kacey Sophia, Kelly Katherine. Student, Jean Turner Art Sch., San Francisco, 1944, 45, 46. Artist Cherubs children's dept. store, San Francisco, 1946, 47, Emporium Art Dept., San Francisco, 1947-54; freelance artist Capwells-Emporium, Liberty House, San Francisco, Oakland, 1955-64; artist-in-residence, coord. art program Childrens Fairyland USA, Oakland, 1962—; commissioned painting for Moffit Hosp., San Francisco, 1970, Havens Sch. Libr., Piedmont, Calif., 1975. Painter children's portraits; designer greeting cards; executed murals Children's Fairyland, Oakland, 1965, 66, 73, Kaiser Hosp., Martinez, Calif., 1974. Vol. art tchr. Oakland Pub. Schs., 1958-62; vol. Oak Mus., 1965—, Convelescant Hosp., Berkeley, Calif., 1975-97. Named Mother of Yr., City of Oakland, 1993. Mem. Oakland Art Assn. Democrat. Avocations: reading, craft design, garage sales. Home: 3361 Burdeck Dr Oakland CA 94602-2624

O'HEARN, MICHAEL JOHN, lawyer; b. Akron, Ohio, Jan. 29, 1952; s. Leo Ambrose and Margaret Elizabeth (Clark) O'H. *Great-great-grandfather John O'Hearn arrived in Manitowoc County, Wisconsin circa 1850 from County Kilkenny, Ireland, the son of Daniel O'Hearn of Kilkenny believed to be descended from a 10th Century eponymous ancestor Eachthighearna who was a brother of the 11th Century Ard Ri Brian Boru of Counties Limerick and Clare. John's descendants were dairy farmers in Maple Grove near Brillion, Wisconsin. Father was in the U.S. Navy V-12 program and later became a chemical engineer and lawyer. Mother is descended from Clarks and Murphys of County Cork, Ireland who settled in Grand Chute, now Appleton, Wisconsin. She became a registered nurse.* BA in Econs., UCLA, 1975; postgrad., U. San Diego, 1977; JD, San Fernando Valley Coll. Law, 1979; postgrad., Holy Apostles Sem., 1993-94. Bar: Calif. 1979, U.S. Dist. Ct. (cen. dist.) Calif. 1979. Document analyst Mellonics Info. Ctr., Litton Industries, Canoga Park, Calif., 1977-79; pvt. practice Encino, Calif., 1979-80; atty. VISTA/Grey Law Inc., L.A., 1980-81; assoc. Donald E. Chadwick & Assocs., Woodland Hills, Calif., 1981-84, Law Offices of Laurence Ring, Beverly Hills, Calif., 1984-85; atty., in-house counsel Coastal Ins. Co., Van Nuys, Calif., 1985-89; atty. Citrus Glen Apts., Ventura, Calif., 1989-92; pvt. practice Ventura County, Calif., 1992—; arbitrator, 1995—; propr., property mgr. Channel Islands Village Mgmt. Co., 1998—. Recipient Cert. of Appreciation, Agy. for Vol. Svc., 1981, San Fernando Valley Walk for Life, 1988, Cert. of Appreciation, Arbitrator for the Superior and Mcpl. Cts., Ventura County Jud. Dist., 1996. Mem. KC, Ventura County Bar Assn., Ventura County Trial Lawyers Assn., Secular Franciscan Order. Republican. Roman Catholic. Avocation: golf. Home: 1741 Fisher Dr Apt 201 Oxnard CA 93035-3008 Office: 3650 Ketch Ave Oxnard CA 93035-3029

OHM, DAVID LEE, school principal; b. Fremont, Nebr., Feb. 18, 1948; s. Harold Jason and Jayne Ann (Fustenau) O.; m. Anita Jane Shepp, Aug. 21, 1975; children: Jason Edward, Janine Lael. BS in Edn., Oreg. State U., 1970; MS in Counseling, Portland (Oreg.) State U., 1974, MS in Adminstrn., 1978. Cert. counselor. Various counseling, tchg. postitions Oreg., 1970-85, asst. prin. Roseburg (Oreg.) H.S., 1985-92, co-prin., 1992-93; dir. secondary edn. Roseburg Sch. Dist., 1993-95; prin. East Sutherlin Sch., Sutherlin, Oreg., 1995—; chair Gov.'s Coun. on Alcohol and Drug Abuse, Oreg., 1987-92; mem. Pub. Safety Coord. Coun., Douglas County, Oreg., 1995-98, mem. Juvenile Adv. Coun., 1987—, mem. County Commr.'s Adv. Bd., 1988. Recipient Youth Svcs. award Columbia Douglas Med. Ctr., Roseburg, 1988, Svc. award State of Oreg., 1991, Hon. Chpt. Farmer award FFA, Roseburg, 1987, 95. Mem. Nat. Elem. Prins. Assn., Oreg. Reading Assn., Conf. Oreg. Sch. Adminstrs. Avocations: reading, fishing, rodeo. Office: East Sch PO Box E 323 E 3d Sutherlin OR 97479

OHMAN, DIANA J., state official, former school system administrator; b. Sheridan, Wyo., Oct. 3, 1950; d. Arden and Doris Marie (Carstens) Mahin. AA, Casper Coll., 1970; BA, U. Wyo., 1972, MEd, 1977, postgrad., 1979—. Tchr. kindergarten Natrona County Sch. Dist., Casper, Wyo., 1971-72; tchr. rural sch. K-8 Campbell County Sch. Dist., Gillette, Wyo., 1972-80, rural prin. K-8, 1980-82, prin. K-6, 1982-84, assoc. dir. instrn., 1984-87; dir. K-12 Goshen County Migrant Program, Torrington, Wyo., 1988-89; prin. K-2 Goshen County Sch. Dist., Torrington, Wyo., 1987-90; state supt. pub. instrn. State of Wyo., Cheyenne, 1991-94, secretary of state, 1995-98; chmn. Campbell County Mental Health Task Force, 1986-87; mem. Legis. Task Force on Edn. of Handicapped 3-5 Yr. Olds, 1988-89. State Committeewoman Wyo. Rep. Party, 1985-88. Recipient Wyo. Elem. Prin. of Yr. award, 1990; named Campbell County Tchr. of Yr. 1980, Campbell County Profl. Bus. Woman of Yr. 1984, Outstanding Young Woman in Am., 1983. Mem. Coun. of Chief of State Sch. Officers (Washington chpt.), Internat. Reading Assn., Wyo. Assn. of Sch. Adminstrs., N.Am. Securities Adminstrs. Assn., Kappa Delta Pi, Phi Kappa Phi, Phi Delta Kappa. Republican. Lutheran. Office: Sec State Office State Capitol Cheyenne WY 82002-0020*

OISHI, CALVIN SHIZUO, orthopedic surgeon; b. Honolulu, Mar. 2, 1961; s. Masaichi and Kazumae (Ichiuji) O.; m. Selma Hiroko Yonamine, Feb. 1, 1992; children: Sarah, Nathaniel. BA in Biology, Pomona Coll., 1983; MD, U. Calif., San Diego, 1987. Diplomate Am. Bd. Orthopedic Surgery. Intern in surgery U. Calif., San Francisco, 1987-88, resident in orthop., 1988-92; fellow in total joint replacement Scripps Clinic and Rsch. Found., 1992-93; orthop. surgeon Orthop. Assocs. of Hawaii Inc., Honolulu, 1993—; asst. clin. prof. orthop. surgery, U. Hawaii, Manoa, 1993—; mem. knee design team Exactech, Gainesville, Fla., 1994—. Contbr. articles to profl. jours. NCAA scholar Pomona Coll., 1983; U. Calif. med. sch. grantee, 1984. Fellow Am. Acad. Orthop. Surgeons; mem. Hawaii Orthop. Assn., Hawaii Med. Assn., Leroy C. Abbott Orthop. Soc. Methodist. Avocations: golf, weightlifting, swimming. Office: Orthop Assocs of Hawaii Inc 1380 Lusitana St Ste 604 Honolulu HI 96813-2449

O'JACK, HELEN MARGARET, clinical social worker; b. Denver, Jan. 31, 1951; d. Herbert Henry and Lillian Anna (Meyer) Thimm; m. William Schmeling, July 24, 1982 (div. Dec. 1992); children: Dustin William Schmeling, Alexander Thimm Schmeling; m. Stanislav G. O'Jack, June 16, 1995. BA in Psychology, U. Colo., 1973; MSW, U. Denver, 1982. Lic. clin. social worker, Wyo. Peer counselor Met. C.C., Omaha, 1975-76; outreach worker South Omaha Crisis Ctr., 1976-77; child care worker Mt. St. Vincent's Youth Home, Denver, 1978-81; social work intern health scs. ctr. U. Colo., Denver, 1981-82; coord. crisis line Vol. Info. Referral Service, Rock Springs, Wyo., 1983-85; clin. social worker, coord. elderly svcs. S.W. Counseling Svc., Rock Springs, 1985-92; med. social worker Wyo. Home Health Care, Rock Springs, 1986-95; pvt. practice, 1992—; facilitator Alzheimer's Family Support Group, Rock Springs, 1983-92; social work cons. Castle Rock Convalescent Ctr., Green River, Wyo., 1990, Sage View Care Ctr., 1992-95; sch. social worker Desert View Sch., 1992—. Mem. NASW (regional rep. on bd. dirs. Wyo. chpt. 1991-92), ACSW. Democrat. Avocations: racquetball, cross-country skiing, camping, hiking. Office: Desert View Elem Sweetwater Sch Dist # 1 PO Box 1089 Rock Springs WY 82902-1089

OKAMURA, HIDEO, manufacturing executive; b. Kochi-City, Japan, May 30, 1943; came to U.S., 1968; s. Junki and Hiroka Okamura; divorced; 1 child, Jennifer H. Prodn. mgr. Power Axle Corp., Compton, Calif., 1984-87; dir. tech. prodn. Dynamic Axle Co., Inc., Long Beach, Calif., 1988-90; mng. dir. Aragon Engring., Inc., Rancho Dominguez, Calif., 1991-96. *Early 1984, set up front wheel drive axle rebuilding factory for Power Axle Corporation. PAC's annual sales reached 3.3 million, 1986. November 1987, organized Dynamic Axle, Inc. July 1989, sold company to trading company, Boston, stayed with company until end of 1990. At same time, 1988-91, ran DSK Trading Co. importing used engine, brake caliper etc. March 1991, Japanese Trading Co. invested 4.5 million in his expertise, organized Aragon Engineering, Inc. Annual sales of this company reached 15 million, 1994. 1996, started Transpower Technologies, Inc. to serve all axle rebuilder nationwide with modification technologies which their excess inventory turned into hard to get items.* Mem. Am. Soc. of Metal, Acad. of Magical Arts, Inc. Avocations: scuba diving, landscaping, photography, golf, travel. Home: 16889 Helena Cir Fountain Vly CA 92708-2815 Office: Transpower Technologies Inc 6301 Orangethorpe Ave Buena Park CA 90620-1340

O'KEEFE, MARK DAVID, state official; b. Pittston, Pa., July 10, 1952; s. Gervase Frances and Anne Regina (Faltyn) O'K.; m. Lucy Bliss Dayton, Sept. 24, 1983; children: Margaret, Angus, Greer. BA in Environ. Studies, Calif. State U., Sacramento, 1977; MS in Environ. Studies, U. Mont., 1984. Mgr. adjudication program Mont. Dept. Nat. Resources, Helena, 1979-81, dir. water devel., 1981-83; owner, operator Glacier Wilderness Guides, West Glacier, Mont., 1983-89; mem. Mont. Ho. Reps., Helena, 1989-92; state auditor State of Mont., Helena, 1993—. Bd. dirs. Boyd Andrew Chem. Dependency Treatment Ctr., Helena, 1991—. With U.S. Army, 1971-73. Democrat. Avocations: backpacking, jogging, rafting, fly fishing. Home: 531 Power St Helena MT 59601-6115 Office: State Auditors Office PO Box 4009 Helena MT 59604-4009*

O'KEEFE, TERENCE MICHAEL, writer, producer, director feature films; b. Worcester, Mass., Dec. 30, 1959; s. James R. and Carol A. (Petty) O'K. Student, St. Thomas Aquinas Coll., Sparkill, N.Y., 1977-79; BS in Pub. Communications, Northeastern U., Boston, 1982; MA in Film Prodn., Loyola Marymount U., 1987. Pres. Video Services, Boston, 1979-82, Vanguard Prodns., Culver City, Calif., 1982—. Author: (poetry) Arspoetica, 1982, (screenplays) Ramous IV, 1986, Defiance, Wanted, Trailer Park, The Guard Never Sleeps, The Case Of The Missing Corpse; producer short film The Dog Ate It (Acad. award for Best short film, 1st pl. Houston Film Festival); producer, writer, dir. film Defiance, 1987; writer, producer, dir., editor music video: Girl on a Swing for EMI recording artists Lions & Ghosts; producer music video: Tell Her I Said? for recording group Jasper; co-playright, producer, dir. (stage play) Actors and Other Animals; producer feature films We the People, The Bad Pack; producer, dir. feature film Cross Dreams; writer, dir.: (feature film) Wanted, 1998. Calif. State U. fellow, 1985-85; recipient Film award Keltonborn Found., 1987, 1st Place award Charlestown Film Festival, Cine Gold award, 1st place award at Houston Film Festival, Telly award Best Comml. Mem. SAG, Am. Assn. Producers, Poetry Soc. Am., Ind. Film Project West. Avocations: golfing, scuba diving. Office: Vanguard Prodns 12111 Beatrice St Culver City CA 90230-6214

O'KELLY, CRYSTAL KATHLEEN, secondary education educator, television producer; b. Pomona, Calif., Dec. 10, 1957; d. Guy Lewis and Doris Lowell (Schmidt) O. BS in Comm., Calif. Poly. U., 1984. Trainer, server CNC Orgn., Rancho Cucamonga, Calif., 1977-84; cons. Grubb & Ellis, Ontario, Calif., 1985; salesperson Nordstrom, Montclair, Calif., 1986; sr. analyst Gen. Dynamics, Pomona, 1986-90; asst. dir. Crystal Cathedral, Garden Grove, Calif., 1996; prodr., on-air talent Claremont (Calif.) Pub. Access TV, 1991—; substitute tchr. Claremont Unified Sch. Dist., 1993—; staff writer Poly Post, Pomona, 1981-82; chmn. bd., 1995-97, bd. mem. Claremont Pub. Access TV, 1994—. Ind. prodr., dir., host, writer, editor, TV show People to Know, a show dedicated to excellence in TV and the arts, 1994—. Vol., co-host fundraiser Claremont Pub. Access TV, 1991—, co-host, fundraiser Sta. CPAT and The Prodrs. Club, Claremont, 1991-93; various other cmty. and mun. projects. Recipient Calif. State scholar, 1976, Basic Edn. Opportunity grantee, 1978. Mem. Toastmasters (v.p. 1997—), Toastmasters Club 12, Pomona Valley Art Assn., Claremont Tennis Club. Protestant. Avocations: painting, dancing, acting, art collecting, photography. Office: People to Know PO Box 992 Claremont CA 91711-0992

OKEN, ALAN IRWIN, record company executive; b. Bklyn., Dec. 1, 1945; 1 child, Richard. BA in Sociology, Calif. State U., Northridge, 1968; JD, Loyola U., Los Angeles, 1971. Bar: Calif. Ptnr. Oken and Klugman, Hollywood, Calif., 1972-79; exec. dir. artistic devel. A & M Records, Hollywood, 1979-88; artist mgr. Rave-Ups, Liz Story, Big Dish, George Howard, 1988-94; co-owner Available Entertainment, Hollywood, 1993—; Bar: Calif., 1972. Mem. Nat. Acad. Rec. Arts and Scis. (bd dirs. 1985—). Office: Available Entertainment 6683 W Sunset Blvd Ste 1 Hollywood CA 90028-7122

OKIMOTO, DAVID, social welfare administrator; s. Frank S. and Hatsue (Toyoshima) O.; m. Dina Lui; children: Cynthia, Michael, Sharon. BS, U. Wash., 1972, MSW, 1975. Therapist Harborview Mental Health, Seattle, 1972-73; planner King County, Seattle, 1974-75; exec. dir. Asian Counseling & Referral Svc., Seattle, 1976-85; dir. dept. human resources City of Seattle, 1985-90; exec. dir. Atlantic St. Ctr., Seattle, 1990—. Chmn. Asia Task Force on Youth, Seattle, 1992—; vice-chmn. Edn. Svc. Dist., Seattle, 1992—, Minority Exec. Dirs. Coalition, 1997-98. Named Disting. Alumnus, U. Wash. Sch. Social Work, 1998, Hometown Hero, KOMO TV and Radio, Seattle, 1995. Democrat. United Methodist. Avocations: skiing, fishing, golf, basketball. Office: Atlantic St Ctr 2103 S Atlantic St Seattle WA 98144

OKLOBDZIJA, VOJIN G., electrical engineer, educator; b. Lika, Yugoslavia, Apr. 28, 1948; came to U.S., 1976; s. Gojko and Danica (Pop-Tosic) O.; m. Huong Nguyen, Nov. 3, 1978; 1 child, Stanisha N. MSEE, U. Belgrade, Yugoslavia, 1971; MSc, UCLA, 1978, PhD, 1982. Rschr. Inst. Physics, Belgrade, 1971-73, Inst. Automation Electronics, Yugoslavia, 1973-74; asst. prof. dept. elec. engring. U. Belgrade, 1974-76; rsch. staff T.J. Watson Rsch. Ctr., IBM, N.Y.C., 1982-91; prof. U. Calif., Davis, 1991—; pres., CEO Integration Corp.; adj. prof. San Francisco State U., 1989—, U. Belgrade, 1990—. Author: (chpt.) Engineering Handbook, 1993, 3d edit., 1997, Computer Engineering, 1995, High Performance System Design, 1999. Fulbright scholar, 1976, prof., 1991. Fellow IEEE, mem. AAUP, ACLU, N.Y. Acad. Scis. Achievements include patent on register-renaming mechanism applied on super-scalar computers today. Home: 1442A Walnut St # 412 Berkeley CA 94709-1405 Office: U Calif Dept Elec and Computer Engring Davis CA 95616

OKSENBERG, MICHEL CHARLES, political scientist, educator; b. Antwerp, Belgium, Oct. 12, 1938; came to U.S., 1939, naturalized, 1945; s. Israel Aron and Klara (Safier) O.; m. Lois Elinor Clarenbach, June 16, 1962; children—David Aron, Deborah Ann. B.A., Swarthmore Coll., 1960; M.A., Columbia, 1963, Ph.D., 1969. Asst. prof. polit. sci. Stanford (Calif.) U., 1966-68; asst. prof. polit. sci. Columbia U., N.Y.C., 1968-71; asso. prof. Columbia U., 1972-74; asso. prof. polit. sci. U. Mich., Ann Arbor, 1973-76, prof., 1977-91, adj. prof., 1991-95, dir. Ctr. for Chinese Studies, 1989-92; mem. staff Nat. Security Council, Washington, 1977-80; chmn. joint com. on contemporary China Social Sci Research Council/Am. Council Learned Socs., 1980-84; pres. East-West Ctr., Honolulu, 1992-95; sr. fellow Asia Pacific Rsch. Ctr., 1995—; prof. polit. science Stanford U., 1995—; bd. dirs. Nat. Com. on U.S.-China Rels., 1976-77, 81-92, 94—; bd. dirs. Com. on Scholarly Comms. with People's Rep. of China, 1980-91; chmn. Social Sci. Rsch. Coun. Com. on Internat. Peace and Security, 1989-92; mem. Trilateral Commn., 1989—. Author: China: The Convulsive Society, 1971, (with Robert Oxnam) China and America, 1977; editor: China's Developmental Experience, 1973, (with Robert Oxnam) The Dragon and the Eagle, 1978, (with Kenneth Lieberthal) Policy Making in China: Leaders, Structures and Processes, 1988, (with Harold Jacobson) China's Entry in the IMF, World Bank, and GATT, 1990, Beijing Spring, 1990, (with Yoichi Funabashi and Heinrich Weiss) An Emerging China in a World of Interdependence, 1994, (with Elizabeth Economy) China Joins the World, 1999; mem. editorial bd. China Quar., 1970—, Chinese Law and Govt., 1972—. Mem. bd. mgrs. Swarthmore Coll., 1970-74. Mem. Am. Polit. Sci. Assn., Assn. Asian Studies (dir. 1970-74), Council on Fgn. Relations, Asia Soc. (dir. China Council 1975-77). Office: Asia Pacific Rsch Ctr 200 Encina Hall Stanford CA 94305

OKUMA, ALBERT AKIRA, JR., architect; b. Cleve., Feb. 10, 1946; s. Albert Akira Sr. and Reiko (Suwa) O.; m. Janice Shirley Bono, July 17, 1971; children: Reiko Dawn, Benjamin Scott. BS in Archtl. Engring, Calif. Poly. State U., San Luis Obispo, 1970, BArch, 1975; edn1. facility planning cert., U. Calif., Riverside, 1990. Lic. architect, Calif., Mont., Ariz., Ill., Nev., N.Mex., Oreg., Maine; cert. Nat. Coun. Archtl. Bds. Architect USN, Point Mugu, Calif., 1975-76; designer Wilson Stroh Wilson Architects, Santa Paula, Calif., 1976-79; architect, project mgr. W.J. Kulwiec AIA & Assocs., Camarillo, Calif., 1979-83, Wilson & Conrad Architects, Ojai, Calif., 1983-

84, Dziak, Immel & Lauterbach Services Inc., Oxnard, Calif., 1984-85; ptnr. Conrad & Okuma Architects, Oxnard, 1985-96; architect So. Calif. Edison/ Edison Internat., Ventura, 1996—; commr. Calif. Bd. Archtl. Examiners, 1985—, City of San Buenaventura Hist. Preservation Commn., 1990-94, chmn., 1991-93, City of San Buenaventura Planning Commn., 1994—, City of San Buenaventura Design Rev. Com., 1994—, vice chair 1994—; peer reviewer Am. Cons. Engrs. Coun., 1987—; lectr. U. Calif. Ext., Riverside, 1991—. Prin. works include Hobson Bros. Bldg. (reconstrn. and preservation), Ventura, Calif., (Design for Excellence award 1991, Historic Bldg. of Yr. award 1992, Archtl. Rev. Design award 1993), Oxnard (Calif.) Main Post Office Renovation (Design for Excellence award 1994). Mem. Spiritual Assembly Baha'is of Ventura, Calif., 1978—, treas., 1978-79, 84, 86-88, chmn., 1992-93; treas.'s rep. Nat. Spiritual Assembly Baha'is U.S., Wilmette, Ill., 1981-91, dist. tchg. com., 1992-93; treas. Parents and Advs. for Gifted Edn., 1988-89; chmn. Ventura Unified Sch. Dist. Citizens Budget Adv. Com., 1990-92, adult edn. adv. com., 1992; mem. City of San Buenaventura specific plan citizens com., 1990-93, multicultural/cmty. heritage task force of the cultural arts plan com., 1991-92, strategic planning citizens adv. com., 1992-93; emergency svcs. vol. State of Calif., 1994—. 1st lt. U.S. Army, 1971-73. Mem. AIA (chpt. bd. dirs. 1976-79, 81—, chpt. sec. 1981, v.p. 1982, pres. 1983, Intern Devel. Program Outstanding Firm award 1993), Am. Planning Assn., Internat. Conf. Bldg. Ofcls., Nat. Trust for Hist. Preservation, Calif. Preservation Found., Constrn. Specifications Inst., Design Methods Group, Coalition for Adequate Sch. Housing, Coun. Ednl. Facility Planners Internat., Structural Engrs. Assn. So. Calif. (affiliate), Ventura County Econ. Devel. Assn. (impact II adv. com. 1993-94, edn. com. 1992-94), Calif. Polytech. State U. Alumni Assn. (life), Toastmasters Internat. Office: So Calif Edison/Edison Internat New Constrn Svcs/EE 10180 Telegraph Rd Ventura CA 93004-1703

OLAH, GEORGE ANDREW, chemist, educator; b. Budapest, Hungary, May 22, 1927; came to U.S., 1964, naturalized, 1970; . Julius and Magda (Krasznai) O.; m. Judith Agnes Lengyel, July 9, 1949; children: George John, Ronald Peter. PhD, Tech. U. Budapest, 1949, D (hon.), 1989; DSc (hon.), U. Durham, 1988, U. Munich, 1990, U. Crete, Greece, 1994, U. Szeged, Hungary, 1995, U. Veszprem, Hungary, 1995, Case Western Res. U., 1995, U. So. Calif., 1995, U. Montpellier, 1996, State U. N.Y., 1998. Mem. faculty Tech. U. Budapest, 1949-54; assoc. dir. Ctrl. Chem. Rsch. Inst., Hungarian Acad. Scis., 1954-56; rsch. scientist Dow Chem. Can. Ltd., 1957-64, Dow Chem. Co., Framingham, Mass., 1964-65; prof. chemistry Case Western Res. U., Cleve., 1965-69, C.F. Mabery prof. rsch., 1969-77; Donald P. and Katherine B. Loker disting. prof. chemistry, dir. Hydrocarbon Rsch. Inst., U. So. Calif., L.A., 1977—; vis. prof. chemistry Ohio State U., 1963, U. Heidelberg, Germany, 1965, U. Colo., 1969, Swiss Fed. Inst. Tech., 1972, U. Munich, 1973, U. London, 1973-79, L. Pasteur U., Strasbourg, 1974, U. Paris, 1981; hon. vis. lectr. U. London, 1981; cons. to industry. Author: Friedel-Crafts Reactions, Vols. I-IV, 1963-64; (with P. Schleyer) Carbonium Ions, Vols. I-V, 1969-76, Friedel-Crafts Chemistry, 1973, Carbocations and Electrophilic Reactions, 1973, Halonium Ions, 1975; (with G.K.S. Prakash and J. Somer) Superacids, 1984; (with Prakash, R.E. Williams, L.D. Field and K. Wade) Hypercarbon Chemistry, 1987; (with R. Malthotra and S.C. Narang) Nitration, 1989, Cage Hydrocarbons, 1990; (with Wade and Williams) Electron Deficient Boron and Carbon Clusters, 1991; (with Chambers and Prakash) Synthetic Fluorine Chemistry, 1992; (with Molnar) Hydrocarbon Chemistry, 1995 (with Laali, Wang, Prakash) Orium Ions, 1998; also chpts. in books, numerous papers in field; patentee in field. Recipient Alexander von Humboldt Sr. U.S. Scientist award, 1979, Calif. Scientist of Yr. award, 1989, Pioneer of Chemistry award Am. Inst. Chemists, 1993; Mendeleev medal Russian Acad. Scis., 1992, Kapitsa medal Russian Acad. Natural Scis., 1995; Nobel prize in Chemistry, 1994; Guggenheim fellow 1972, 88. Fellow AAAS, Chem. Inst. Can., Brit. Chem. Soc. (hon., Centenary lectr. 1978); ; mem. NAS, Italian NAS Lincei, Royal Soc. London (fgn.), Royal Soc. Can., European Acad. Arts, Scis. and Humanities, Royal Chem. Soc. (hon.), Italy Chem. Soc. (hon.), Hungarian Acad. Sci. (hon.), Am. Chem. Soc. (award petroleum chemistry 1964, Leo Hendrik Baekeland award N.J. sect. 1966, Morley medal Cleve. sect. 1970, award Synthetic organic chemistry 1979, Roger Adams award in organic chemistry 1989), German Chem. Soc. Home: 2252 Gloaming Way Beverly Hills CA 90210-1717 Office: U So Calif Labor Hydrocarbon Rsch Inst Los Angeles CA 90007

OLANDER, HELEN RINKER, retired educator; b. Wakeeney, Kans., Aug. 11, 1919; d. Harry Monroe and Marjorie Josephine (Gibson) Rinker; children: Harry III, Kurt. BA in History, U. Mo., Kansas City, 1966. participant Peace Corps, Sri Lanka, 1997-98. Mem. Peace Corps, Sri Lanka, 1997-98. With WAVES, 1942-44. Mem. Gamma Phi Beta. Democrat.

OLDFIELD, FRANK EUGENE, retired aerospace engineering executive; b. Ft. Morgan, Colo., Apr. 20, 1931; s. Henry Johnstone and Florence Ona (King) O.; m. Mary Rose Barrett, Sept. 20, 1975; children: Vanessa L. Lawson, Perry D. BS in Electronics, San Diego State U., 1958. Aerospace engr. Teledyne Ryan Aero., San Diego, 1958-63, computer sys. mgr., 1963-68, advanced projects dir., 1968-88, v.p., chief engr., 1988-93, ret., 1993—; aerospace cons. AAI Corp., Hunt Valley, Md., 1988-94. Author: (book) Mankind Metamorphosis, 1997. Mem., v.p., treas., pres. Smoketree Condo. Assn., 1988-98. Sgt. U.S. Army, 1955-58. Recipient Pioneer award Assn. for Unmanned Vehicle Sys., 1987; tribute to Frank Oldfield recorded in Congl. Records, Ho. of Reps., 1987. Mem. NRA, Early Am. Coppers. Republican. Home: 6050 Henderson Dr Unit 14 La Mesa CA 91942-4012

OLDHAM, ELAINE DOROTHEA, retired elementary and middle school educator; b. Coalinga, Calif., June 29, 1931; d. Claude Smith Oldham and Dorothy Elaine (Hill) Wilkins. AB in History, U. Calif., Berkeley, 1953; MS in Sch. Adminstrn., Calif. State U., Hayward, 1976; postgrad. U. Calif., Berkeley, Harvard U., Mills Coll. Tchr. Piedmont Unified Sch. Dist., Calif., 1956-94, ret., 1994. Pres., bd. dirs. Camron-Stanford House Preservation Assn., 1979-86, adminstrv. v.p., bd. dirs., 1976-79, 86—; mem. various civic and community support groups; bd. dirs. Anne Martin Children's Ctr., Lincoln Child Ctr., pres. Acacia br. Children's Hosp., Oakland, No. Light Sch. Aux., East Bay League II of San Francisco Symphony, sec. Piedmont Hist. Soc. Mem. Am. Assn. Museums, Am. Assn. Mus. Trustees, Internat. Council Museums, Inst. Internat. Edn., Am. Assn. State and Local History, Am. Decorative Arts Forum, Oakland Mus. Assn. (women's bd.), DAR (regent, Outstanding Tchr. Am. History award), Colonial Dames Am., Magna Charta Dames, Daus. of Confederacy (bd. dirs., scholarship chair), Calif. Hist. Soc., Hugeunot Soc. (bd. dirs., scholarship chair), Plantagenet Soc., Order of Washington, Colonial Order of Crown, Americans of Royal Descent, Order St. George and Descs. of Knights of Garter, San Francisco Garden Club, San Francisco Antiques Show (com. mem.), U. Calif. Alumni Assn. (co-chmn. and chmn. of 10th and 25th yr. class reunion coms.), Internat. Diplomacy Coun. (San Francisco chpt.), Internat. Churchill Soc., English Speaking Union, Pacific Mus. Soc., Prytanean Alumnae Assn. (bd. dirs.), Phi Delta Kappa, Delta Kappa Gamma. Republican. Episcopalian. Clubs: Harvard (San Francisco), Bellevue (Oakland), San Francisco Garden Club.

OLDHAM, MAXINE JERNIGAN, real estate broker; b. Whittier, Calif., Oct. 13, 1923; d. John K. and Lela Hessie (Mears) Jernigan; m. Laurance Montgomery Oldham, Oct. 28, 1941; 1 child, John Laurence. AA, San Diego City Coll., 1973; student Western State U. Law, San Diego, 1976-77, LaSalle U., 1977-78; grad. Realtors Inst., Sacramento, 1978. Mgr. Edin Harig Realty, LaMesa, Calif., 1966-70; tchr. Bd. Edn., San Diego, 1959-66; mgr. Julia Cave Real Estate, San Diego, 1970-73; salesman Computer Realty, San Diego, 1973-74; owner Shelter Island Realty, San Diego, 1974—. Author: Jernigan History, 1982, Mears Geneology, 1985, Fustons of Colonial America, 1988, Sissoms. Mem. Civil Svc. Commn., San Diego, 1957-58. Recipient Outstanding Speaker award Dale Carnegie. Mem. Nat. Assn. Realtors, Calif. Assn. Realtors, San Diego Bd. Realtors, San Diego Apt. Assn., Internationale des Professions Immobilieres (internat. platform speaker), DAR (vice regent Linares chpt.), Colonial Dames 17th Century, Internat. Fedn. Univ. Women. Republican. Roman Catholic. Avocations: music, theater, painting, geneology, continuing edn. Home: 3348 Lowell St San Diego CA 92106-1715 Office: Shelter Island Realty 2810 Lytton St San Diego CA 92110-4810

OLDSHUE, PAUL FREDERICK, financial executive; b. Chgo., Nov. 4, 1949; s. James Young and Betty Ann (Wiersema) O.; m. Mary Elizabeth Holl, July 12, 1975; children: Emily Jane, Andrew Armstrong, Abigail Anne. BA, Williams Coll., Williamstown, Mass., 1971; MBA, NYU, 1978. With Chem. Bank, N.Y.C., 1973-78, asst. sec., 1976-78; with Orbanco Fin. Svc. Corp., 1978-83, v.p., treas., 1980-83; exec. v.p. Oreg. Bank, Portland, 1984-88; v.p. syndications PacifiCorp Fin. Svcs., Inc., 1988-90; exec. v.p. U.S. Bancorp, Portland, 1991—. Mem. Fin. Execs. Inst., Multnomah Athletic Club (Portland). Republican.

O'LEARY, BRIAN TODD, writer; b. Boston, Jan. 27, 1940; s. Fred and Mary Mablel (Todd) O'L.; m. Joyce Whitehead, June 20, 1964 (div. 1976); children: Brian Jr., Erin. BA in Physics, Williams Coll., 1961; MA in Astronomy, Georgetown U., 1964; PhD in Astronomy, U. Calif., 1967. Scientist, astronaut NASA, Houston, 1967-68; asst. prof. astronomy Cornell U., Ithaca, N.Y., 1968-71, Hampshire Coll., U. Mass., Amherst, 1972-75; spl. cons. on energy U.S. Ho. of Reps., Washington, 1975; assoc. rsch. faculty Princeton (N.J.) U., 1975-80. Author: The Making on an Ex-Astronaut, 1970 (Best Young Adult Book of 1970, ALA), Mars 1999, 1987, Exploring Inner & Outer Space, 1989, The Second Coming of Science, 1992, Miracle in the Void, 1996. Speech writer and advisor to various U.S. presdl. candidates. Fellow AAAS; mem. Internat. Assn. for New Sci. (co-founder, bd. dirs. 1989—). Avocations: piano, cartooning, hiking, yoga, speaking. Office: Ste 21-200 1993 S Kihei Rd Kihei HI 96753

O'LEARY, PEGGY RENÉ, accountant; b. Billings, Mont., Dec. 6, 1951; d. Paul Eugene and Norma Dean (Metcalf) O'L.; m. Kim Patric Johnson, Mar. 19, 1983. BS, Mont. State U., 1976. CPA, Mont. Staff acct. Peat Marwick Main, Billings, 1976-80; dir. fin. Billings Clinic, 1980-95; chief ops. officer Billings Sch. Dist. 2, 1996—. Div. leader youth support campaign YMCA, Billings, 1987-88, 92-93, bd. dirs., 1988-94, sec. bd., 1989-94; vol. Big Brother and Sister, 1995—. Mem. Billings C. of C. (sch. tax com. 1982-88), Pink Chips Investment Club (treas. 1987-88). Republican. Roman Catholic. Avocations: running, golf, swimming, bicycling. Home: 4565 Pine Cove Rd Billings MT 59106-1332 Office: Billings Sch Dist 2 415 N 30th St Billings MT 59101-1298

O'LEARY, PRENTICE L., lawyer; b. L.A., May 6, 1942. BA, UCLA, 1965, JD, 1968. Bar: Calif. 1969. Ptnr. Sheppard, Mullin, Richter & Hampton, L.A., 1974—. Bd. dirs. Legal Aid Found. L.A., 1987-93. Mem. ABA (bus. bankruptcy com.), State Bar Calif., Los Angles County Bar Assn. (chmn. bankruptcy com., chmn. comml. law and bankrupt sect. 1985-86), Am. Coll. Bankruptcy Profls., Order of Coif. Office: Sheppard Mullin Richter & Hampton 333 S Hope St Fl 48 Los Angeles CA 90071-1406*

OLES, STUART GREGORY, lawyer; b. Seattle, Dec. 15, 1924; s. Floyd and Helen Louise (La Violette) O.; B.S. magna cum laude, U. Wash., 1947, J.D., 1948; m. Ilse Hanewald, Feb. 12, 1954; children: Douglas, Karl, Stephen. Admitted to Wash. bar, 1949, U.S. Supreme Ct. bar, 1960; dep. pros. atty. King County (Wash.), 1949, chief civil dept., 1949-50; gen. practice law, Seattle, 1950-95; sr. partner firm Oles, Morrison & Rinker and predecessor, 1955-90, of counsel, 1991-95. Author: A View From the Rock, 1994, On Behalf of My Clients--a Lawyer's Life, 1998. Chmn. Seattle Community Concert Assn., 1955; pres. Friends Seattle Pub. Library, 1956; mem. Wash. Pub. Disclosure Commn., 1973-75; trustee Ch. Div. Sch. of Pacific, Berkeley, Calif., 1974-75; mem. bd. curators Wash. State Hist. Soc., 1983; former mem. Seattle Symphony Bd.; pres. King County Ct. House Rep. Club, 1950, U. Wash. Young Rep. Club, 1947; Wash. conv. floor leader Taft, 1952, Goldwater, 1964; Wash. chmn. Citizens for Goldwater, 1964; chmn. King County Rep. convs., 1966, 68, 76, 84, 86, 88, 90, 92, 96, Wash. State Rep. Conv., 1980. Served with USMCR, 1943-45. Mem. ABA (past regional vice chmn. pub. contract law sect.), Wash. Bar Assn., Order of Coif, Scabbard and Blade, Am. Legion, Kapoho Beach Club (pres.), Am. Highland Cattle Assn. (v.p. and dir.), Phi Beta Kappa, Phi Alpha Delta. Episcopalian (vestryman, lay-reader), Home: 22715 SE 43rd Ct Issaquah WA 98029-5200 Office: Oles Morrison & Rinker 701 5th Ave Ste 3300 Seattle WA 98104-7082 also: RR 2 Pahoa HI 96778-9802

OLIPHANT, CHARLES ROMIG, physician; b. Waukegan, Ill., Sept. 10, 1917; s. Charles L. and Mary (Goss) R.; student St. Louis U., 1936-40; m. Claire E. Canavan, Nov. 7, 1942; children: James R., Cathy Rose, Mary G., William D. Student, St. Louis U., 1936-40, MD, 1943; postgrad. Naval Med. Sch., 1946. Intern, Nat. Naval Med. Ctr., Bethesda, Md., 1943; pvt. practice medicine and surgery, San Diego, 1947—; pres., CEO Midway Med. Enterprises; former chief staff Balboa Hosp., Doctors Hosp., Cabrillo Med. Ctr.; chief staff emeritus Sharp Cabrillo Hosp.; mem. staff Mercy Hosp., Children's Hosp., Paradise Valley Hosp., Sharp Meml. Hosp.; sec. Sharp Sr. Health Care, S.D.; mem. exec. bd., program chmn. San Diego Power Squadron, 1985-93, 95. Charter mem. Am. Bd. Family Practice. Served with M.C., USN, 1943-47. Recipient Golden Staff award Sharp Cabrillo Hosp. Med. Staff, 1990. Fellow Am. Geriatrics Soc. (emeritus), Am. Acad. Family Practice, Am. Assn. Abdominal Surgeons; mem. AMA, Calif. Med. Assn., Am. Acad. Family Physicians (past pres. San Diego chpt., del. Calif. chpt.), San Diego Med. Soc., Public Health League, Navy League, San Diego Power Squadron (past comdr.), SAR. Clubs: San Diego Yacht, Cameron Highlanders. Home: 4310 Trias St San Diego CA 92103-1127

OLIVA, STEPHEN EDWARD, resource conservationist, lawyer; b. San Rafael, Calif., Jan. 31, 1946; s. George Verdelli Jr. and Dorothy Margaret (Austin) O.; m. Susan Rebecca Ellis, May 5, 1984; children: Stephanie, Mary. BA, U. Calif., Santa Barbara, 1972; JD, U. of the Pacific, 1992. Bar: Calif. 1993, U.S. Dist. Ct. (ea. dist.) Calif. 1993. Naturalist Calif. Dept. Transp., San Francisco, 1973-76; planner Calif. Energy Commn., Sacramento, 1976, Calif. Air Resources Bd., Sacramento, 1976-79; spl. asst. to sec. The Resources Agy., Sacramento, 1979-80; spl. asst. Calif. Dept. Conservation, Sacramento, 1980, mgr. land conservation unit, 1981-87; spl. asst. Calif. Dept. Forestry, Sacramento, 1980-81; chief Office Land Conservation Calif. Dept. Conservation, Sacramento, 1987-89, dep. chief Calif. div. of recycling, 1989-91, environ. coord., 1991-92, staff counsel, legal office, 1992—; mem. governing bd. Calif. Tahoe Regional Planning Agy., South Lake Tahoe, 1979-81; mem. policy adv. com. Sacramento County Local Agy. Formation Commn., 1988-89. Served with U.S. Army, 1966-68, Vietnam. Mem. ABA, Calif. State Bar, Sacramento County Bar Assn. Democrat. Avocations: snorkeling, photography. E-mail: soliva@consrv.ca.gov. Office: Calif Dept Conservation 801 K St MS 24-03 Sacramento CA 95814-3500

OLIVER, BARBARA JEANNE, social services administrator; b. Altadena, Calif., Aug. 21, 1947; m. Ivan J. Spielfogel, Sept. 25, 1968 (div. Feb. 1974); children: Jason, Andrea; m. John L. Oliver , Aug. 25, 1974. Exec. dir. Prevent Child Abuse Orange County, Tustin, Calif., 1989—; mem. steering com. Families and Children Together (FACT) Orange County, Santa Ana, Calif., 1995—; mem. adv. bd. S. Orange County Family Resource Ctr., Mission Viejo, Calif., 1996—. Co-author: (book) The Healing Relationship, 1989; (pamphlet) Stepping Out of Chaos, 1989. Founder Youth Offender Recovery Program, Whittier, Calif., 1989-94; bd. dirs. Calif. Consortium Prevent Child Abuse, Sacramento, 1992-97. Mem. Nat. Assn. Women Bus. Owners (Youth Adv. award 1996), Child Sexual Abuse Network (Outstanding Svc. to Sexually Abused 1992), Calif. Youth Authority (Outstanding Victim Awareness Svcs. 1992). Fax: 714-258-2048. E-mail: bjoexecdir@aol.com. Office: Prevent Child Abuse Orange County 1431 Warner Ave Ste D Tustin CA 92780

OLIVER, DAN DAVID, banker; b. Walla Walla, Wash., Mar. 11, 1952; s. Harold Allen and Nydia Jane (Munns) O.; children: Ana Mary, Whitney Leigh. Student, Univ. Coll., Cardiff, Wales, 1972-73; BA in Pre-Law (hons.), Wash. State U., 1974; MBA in Taxation, Golden Gate U., 1979; JD, Western State U., 1978; grad. with trust specialization, Pacific Coast Banking Sch., U. Wash., Seattle, 1987; grad. Banking Law Sch., George Mason U., Washington, 1993; grad. Nat. Compliance Sch., U. Okla., 1994, nat. grad. Sch. Compliance Mgmt., 1997. Tax acct. John F. Forbes & Co., San Francisco, 1979-81; cat skinner James Francis Munns Farms, Inc., Prescott, Wash., 1981-82; law clk. Sherwood, Tugman, Gose & Roser, Walla Walla, 1975-79; trust adminstrv. asst. Baker-Boyer Nat. Bank, Walla Walla, 1982-83, asst. trust officer, 1984, trust officer, 1985, asst. v.p., legal counsel, 1986, asst. v.p., legal/compliance officer, 1987, v.p. and legal/compliance officer, 1988—, v.p., legal counsel, compliance mgr., 1990, also chmn. bd. dirs. Milton Turf Farm, Inc., West Richland, Wash., sr. v.p., sec., legal counsel, 1988-92; mem. Baker Boyer Bancorp Year 2000 Taskforce, 1998—; trip organizer/ group leader diving expedition to Cozumel, Mexico, 1998, vet. of ten Caribean SCUBA diving trips to remote locations in Belize, Honduras, Saba, St. Kitts, Mexico, Bahamas and Cayman Islands, 1993-99. Commr. Walla Walla City Housing Authority, 1992—, vice chmn., 1997-98; mem. Homeless Coalition, 1994—; bd. dirs. Prescott Sch. Dist., 1983-87, vice chmn., 1985, chmn., 1986; vol. spirits religious program St. Patrick's Cath. Ch., 1990-94; mem. Walla Walla Park and Recreation Adv. Bd., 1991-92, vice chmn., 1992; chmn. Park Improvement Com. for Irrigation, 1992; chmn. Walla Walla Area Com. for Housing, 1991-94; linesman Youth Soccer League; sch. vol. Prospect Point Elem. Sch.; organizer, co-chmn. DeSales H.S. Class of 1970 Reunion, 1995, chmn., treas. 2000 Reunion; mem. panel govt. and politics seminar Leadership Walla Walla, 1994; vice-chmn. Walla Walla City-County Regional Housing Com., 1997-98, chmn. 1998—. Mem. Am. Bankers Assn., Nat. Assn. Housing and Redevel. Ofcls., Wash. Bankers Assn. (symposium panelist 1996, compliance com. 1990—, vice chmn. 1994-95, cmty. reinvestment act panel 1994, compliance symposium panelist of local experts), Walla Walla Valley Estate Planning Coun. (bd. dirs. 1986-87, treas. 1987-88, sec. 1988-89, v.p. 1989-90, pres. 1990-91), Nat. Arbor Day Found., Columbia Rural Elec. Assn., Nat. Assn. Underwater Instrs. (life, master diver, rescue diver, open water I and II, advanced certs., cert. CPR, first aid, and oxygen provider, advanced cert. 1993—, ref. environ. edn. found. 1994—, instr. certification 1997), Bergevin Family Reunion and Edn. Assn. (treas. 1993-96), Frenchtown Found. (charter), Walla Walla Men's Group (treas.), Walla Walla Exch. Club, Beta Sigma Phi. Avocations: scuba diving, swimming, underwater photography, SCUBA kayaking, travel. Office: Baker-Boyer Nat Bank Main and 2d Sts Walla Walla WA 99362

OLIVER, JOHN EDWARD, bank strategic management and training consultant; b. Bedford, Eng., Apr. 14, 1951; came to U.S., 1978; s. Fred K. and Marjorie F. (Brown) O.; m. Jacqueline L. Alcock, Oct. 7, 1972; 1 child, Sophie Rose. Student, Mander Coll., Bedford, 1968-71. Mgr.'s asst. Nat. Westminster Bank, Bedford, 1971-73; credit analyst Kleinwort Benson Ltd., London, 1973-76; mktg. coord. Amex Bank Ltd., London, 1976-78; v.p. Continental Ill. Energy Devel. Corp., Houston, 1978-85; pres. Laurel Mgmt. Systems Inc., San Francisco, 1986—; cons. various U.S. and internat. banks including Merita Bank, London, 1985—; bank edn. cons. Bank Am., San Francisco, 1986—; advisor Am. Inst. Banking, San Francisco, 1994—. Author: What Really is Expected of Me?-The Role of the Community Bank Director, 1995, Strategic Bank Management in a Risk Environment, 1995. Mem. ASTD, Assn. Bank Trainers and Cons. Office: Laurel Mgmt Systems Inc 3933 20th St San Francisco CA 94114-2906

OLIVER, JOYCE ANNE, journalist, editorial consultant, columnist; b. Coral Gables, Fla., Sept. 19, 1958; d. John Joseph and Rosalie Cecile (Mack) O. BA in Communications, Calif. State U., Fullerton, 1980, MBA, 1990. Corp. editor Norris Industries Inc., Huntington Beach, Calif., 1979-82; pres. J.A. Oliver Assocs., La Habra Heights, Calif., 1982—; corp. editorial cons. Norris Industries, 1982, Better Methods Cons., Huntington Harbour, Calif., 1982-83, Summit Group, Orange, Calif., 1982-83, UDS, Encinitas, Calif., 1983-84, MacroMarketing, Costa Mesa, Calif., 1985-86, PM Software, Huntington Beach, Calif., 1985-86, CompuQuote, Canoga Park, Calif., 1985-86, Nat. Semicondr. Can. Ltd., Mississauga, Ont., Can., 1986, Maclean Hunter Ltd., Toronto, Ont., 1986-90; Frame Inc., Fullerton, Calif., 1987-88, The Johnson-Layton Co., L.A., 1988-89, Corp. Rsch. Inc., Chgo., 1988, Axon Group, Horsham, Pa., 1990-91, Am. Mktg. Assn., Chgo., 1990-92, Kenzaikai Co., Ltd., Tokyo, 1991, Penton Pub., Cleve., 1991, Bus. Computer Pub., Inc., Peterborough, N.H., 1991-92, Helmers Pub., Inc., Peterborough, 1992, Schnell Pub., Co., Inc., N.Y.C., 1992-93, Diversified Pub. Group, Carol Stream, Ill., 1993; mem. Rsch. Coun. of Scripps Clinic and Rsch. Found., 1987-92. Contbg. editor Computer Merchandising/ Resell, 1982-85, Computer Reselling, 1985, Reseller Mgmt., 1987-89; contbg. editor Can. Electronics Engring., 1986-90, west coast editor, 1990, Chem. Bus. mag., 1992-93; spl. feature editor Cleve. Inst. Electronics publ. The Electron, 1986-89; bus. columnist Mktg. News, 1990-92; contbr. articles to profl. jours. and mags. Bd. dirs. Action Comms., 1993—. Mem. IEEE, Internat. Platform Assn., Soc. Photo-optical Instrumentation Engrs., Inst. Mgmt. Scis., Nat. Writers Club (profl.), Internat. Mktg. Assn., Soc. Profl. Journalists, L.A. World Affairs Coun. Republican. Roman Catholic. Avocations: sailing, water skiing. Office: 2045 Fullerton Rd La Habra CA 90631-8213

OLIVER, MARY ANNE MCPHERSON, religion educator; b. Montgomery, Ala., Nov. 21, 1935; d. James Curtis and Margaret Sinclair (Miller) McPherson; m. Raymond Davies Oliver, Aug. 28, 1959; children: Kathryn Sinclair, Nathan McPherson. BA, U. Ala., Tuscaloosa, 1956; cert., Sorbonne, Paris, 1958; MA, U. Wis., 1959; PhD, Grad. Theol. Union, Berkeley, Calif., 1972. Tchr., 1972—; instr. U. Calif., Berkeley, St. Mary's Coll., Moraga, Calif., 1973; adj. faculty San Francisco Theol. Sem., San Anselmo, 1977-81; lectr. San Jose (Calif.) State U., 1980-81, San Francisco State U., 1985-86; adj. prof. dept. liberal arts John F. Kennedy U., Orinda, Calif., 1987-95; vis. prof. Gen. Theol. Sem., N.Y.C., 1995. Author: History of Good Shepherd Episcopal Mission, 1978, Conjugal Spirituality: The Primacy of Mutual Love in Christian Tradition, 1994; contbr. articles to profl. jours. Rep. Ala. Coun. on Human Rels., Mobile, 1958; active deanery, conv. Good Shepherd Episc. Ch., Berkeley, Calif., 1970-75; rep. U. Calif. Fgn. Student Hospitality, Berkeley, 1965-70; vol. tchr. Berkeley pub. schs., 1965-73; mentor Edn. for Ministry, Univ. of the South, 1993-97. Mem. Am. Acad. Religion, Conf. on Christianity and Lit. Democrat. Home: 1632 Grant St Berkeley CA 94703-1356

OLIVER, NANCY LEBKICHER, artist, retired elementary education educator; b. Stockton, Calif., 1939; d. John B. and Marjorie Lebkicher; m. Douglas C. Oliver, 1963; children: Charles, Elaine. BA with honors, San Jose State U., 1961. Summer playground dir. Recreation Dept., Redwood City, Calif., 1956-61; 1st grade tchr. Redwood City (Calif.) Elem. Sch. Dist., 1961-63; kindergarten tchr. Ukiah (Calif.) Unified Sch. Dist., 1963-67; assoc. tchr. kindergarten San Carlos (Calif.) Elem. Sch. Dist., 1976-81; shopper for dept. store Macy's, San Francisco, 1975-82. Sunday sch. dir. St. Peter's Episcopal Ch., Redwood City, 1973-78; active White Oaks PTA, San Carlos, 1973-81, newsletter editor, 1978-81; leader Girl Scouts U.S.A., San Carlos, 1978-81. Mem. AAUW (San Carlos br. newsletter editor 1972-74, editor historic tour booklet 1981, editor historic resources booklet 1989, chmn. historic preservation sect. 1979—, pres. Willits br. 1966-67), San Carlos Heritage Assn. (founder, dir. 1995—), Sequoia H.S. Alumni Assn. (founding sec., membership chmn., centennial coord., pres. 1996-98, Unsung Hero award 1998), Internat. Order Rainbow Girls (grand officer Calif. 1957-58, mother advisor Redwood City 1987-89), SeriPrinters. Democrat. Episcopalian. Avocations: needlework, historic preservation activities, walking, calligraphy, classical music. Home: 147 Belvedere Ave San Carlos CA 94070-4818

OLIVER, ROBERT WARNER, economics educator; b. L.A., Oct. 26, 1922; s. Ernest Warner and Elnore May (McConnell) O.; m. Darlene Hubbard, July 1, 1946 (dec. Mar. 1987); children: Lesley Joanne Oliver McClelland, Stewart Warner; m. Jean Tupman Smock, July 15, 1989. AB, U. So. Calif., 1943, AM, 1948; AM, Princeton U., 1950, PhD, 1958. Tchg. asst. U. So. Calif., 1946-47; instr. Princeton U., 1947-50, Pomona Coll., L.A., Calif., 1950-52; asst. prof. U. So. Calif., L.A., 1952-56; economist Stanford Rsch. Inst., South Pasadena, Calif., 1956-59; mem. faculty dept. econs. Calif. Inst. Tech., 1959-88, prof. econs., 1973-88, prof. emeritus, 1988—; urban economist World Bank, Washington, 1970-71; cons. Brookings Instn., 1961, OECD, Paris, 1979; vis. prof. U. So. Calif., 1985; vis. scholar Pembrook Coll., Cambridge (Eng.) U., 1989-90. Author: An Economic Survey of Pasadena, 1959, International Economic Cooperation and the World Bank, 1975, reissued with new intro., 1996, Bretton Woods: A Retrospective Essay, 1985, Oral History Project: The World Bank, 1986; contbg. author: Ency. of Econs., 1981, 93, George Woods and the World Bank, 1995. Mem. Human Rels. Com. City of Pasadena, 1964-65, Planning Commn., 1972-75, 91-95; bd. dirs. Pasadena City Coun., 1965-69; mem. Utilities Adv. Commn., 1981-88, 96—, Strategic Planning Com., 1985; pres. Pasadena Beautiful Found., 1972-74; bd. dirs. Pasadena Minority History Found., 1984—, Jackie Robinson Meml. Found., 1992—, UN Assn. Pasadena chpt., 1996—; trustee Pasadena Hist. Soc., 1992-94. Lt. (j.g.) USN, 1942-46. Social Sci. rsch. fellow London Sch. Econs., 1954-55; Rockefeller Found. fellow, 1974, 91; Danforth assoc., 1981; recipient Outstanding Tchg. award, 1982, Master of the Student Houses, 1997; [illegible]

Royal Econs. Assn., Athenaeum Club, Phi Beta Kappa, Phi Kappa Phi, Delta Tau Delta. Democrat. Methodist. Home: 3197 San Pasqual St Pasadena CA 91107-5330 Office: 1201 E California Blvd Pasadena CA 91125-0001

OLIVER, TRAVIS, advertising agency executive. COO Alcone Mktg. Group, Irvine, Calif. Office: Alcone Mktg Group 15 Whatney Irvine CA 92618-2808*

OLLMAN, ARTHUR LEE, museum director, photographer; b. Milw., Mar. 6, 1947; s. Benn and Shirley O. B.A., U. Wis., 1969; student, San Francisco Art Inst., 1974; M.F.A., Lone Mountain Coll., 1977. Instr. San Francisco Mus. Modern Art, 1976-78, Chabot Coll., 1977-83; mus. dir. Mus. Photog. Arts, San Diego. Founder, dir., producer Photo History Video Project; author: Samuel Bourne, Images of India, 1983, Arnold Newman, Five Decades, 1986, William Klein: An American in Paris, 1987, Revelaciones, The Art of Manuel Alvarez Bravo, 1990, Fata Morgana: The American Way of Life, 1992, Seduced by Life: The Art of Lou Stoumen, 1992, Points of Entry: A Nation of Strangers, 1995; exhibited in one-man shows including Grapestake Gallery, San Francisco, 1979, Centre Georges Pompidou, Musee Nat. D'Art et De Culture, Paris, 1979, Inst. Contemporary Art, Boston, 1985, Night: Photograph Gallery, N.Y.C., 1981, Kodak Gallery, Tokyo, 1988; exhibited in group shows at Milw. Art Ctr., 1979, U. Hawaii, 1979-81, San Francisco Mus. Modern Art, 1980, Monas Heiroglyphicas, Milan, Italy, 1978, Mus. Modern Art, N.Y.C., 1978, Whitney Mus. Am. Art, N.Y.C., 1981, Detroit Inst. Arts, 1994, Mus. Contemporary Art, L.A., 1994, Tower of David Museum, Jerusalem, 1996; represented in permanent collections, including, Mus. Modern Art, N.Y.C, Centre Georges Pompidou, Bibliotheque Nationale, Paris, Tokyo Inst. Polytechnics, Met. Mus. Art, N.Y.C., Nat. Mus. Am. Art, Washington, Chase-Manhattan collection, N.Y.C., J. Paul Getty Mus., L.A. NEA fellow, 1979; Calif. Arts Council grantee, 1977-78, NEA grantee, 1978, exhbn. aid grantee, 1979-80. Mem. San Francisco CAMERAWORK (pres. bd. dirs. 1978-83), Am. Assn. Mus. Jewish. Address: 4310 Goldfinch St San Diego CA 92103-1315 also: Mus Photographic Arts (MOPA) Balboa Park 1649 El Prado San Diego CA 92101*

OLLSON, MICKEY LOUIS, zoo owner; b. Phoenix, May 12, 1941; s. William Archie and Edith Iris (Curnow) O.; m. Donna Marie Ollson, Dec. 5, 1965 (div. Feb. 1975); children: Micalin, Louis Michael. AA, Phoenix Coll., 1961; BS, Ariz. State U., 1963. Owner, dir. Ollson's Exotic Animal Farm, Glendale, Ariz., 1965-83, Wildlife World Zoo, Glendale, 1983—. Contbr. articles to profl. publs. Mem. Am. Assn. Zool. Parks and Aquariums (profl.), Am. Fedn. Aviculture (v.p. 1976-77), Am. Game Bird Fedn. (bd. dirs. 1988—, pres. 1984-89, Outstanding Mem. of Yr. award 1968), Internat. Soc. Zooculturists (charter; treas. 1987-88), Am. Pheasant and Waterfowl Soc. (bd. dirs. 1972-78), Avondale-Goodyear-Litchfield Park C. of C. (bd. dirs. 1985-88), Kappa Sigma (pres. Rho chpt. 1964). Republican. Office: Wildlife World Zoo 16501 W Northern Ave Litchfield Park AZ 85340-9466*

OLMSTED, RONALD DAVID, non-profit organization consultant; b. Portland, Oreg., June 27, 1937; s. Clifford Wolford and Ruth Emily (Driesner) O.; m. Susan Mary Spare, Dec. 27, 1961 (div. June 1972); 1 child, Craig William. Student, Lewis and Clark Coll., 1955-57, U. So. Calif., L.A., 1959-62. V.p., exec. dir. L.A. Ctr. for Internat. Visitors, 1961-67; assoc. dir. devel. U. Chgo., 1967-71; v.p. devel. and pub. affairs Northwestern Meml. Hosp., Chgo., 1971-79; dir. devel. Marimed Found., Honolulu, 1989-93; exec. dir. Alzheimer's Assn., Honolulu, 1995-96; cons. on health, edn. and human svc. orgns., Ill., Mich., Oreg., Hawaii, 1979—; mem. Honolulu Mayor's Com. on People with Disabilities, 1995-96. Contbr. articles on African travels and African affairs to profl. publs. Co-founder, treas. Civic Found. of Chelsea, Mich., 1982-83; treas. Chelsea Area C. of C., 1981-83; trustee Harris Sch., Chgo., 1972-73, Ogden Dunes (Ind.) Town Bd., 1971-72; bd. dirs. United Way Porter County, Ind., 1969-71; mem. L.A. Com. on Fgn. Rels., 1965-69; bd. dirs. Am. Friends of Africa, 1965-68, Nat. Coun. for Cmty. Svcs. to Internat. Visitors, 1965-67; mem. exec. com. L.A. Mayor's Coun. for Internat. Visitors and Sister Cities, 1964-68; vice chmn. Greater L.A. Com. Internat. Student Svcs., 1966. Recipient Koa Anvil award Pub. Rels. Soc. Am.-Honolulu, 1992, multiple awards Assn. Am. Colls., 1975-79, multiple MacEachern awards Am. Acad. Hosp. Pub. Rels., 1974-79, multiple awards Nat. Assn. for Hosp. Devel., 1975-79. Mem. Nat. Soc. Fund Raising Execs. Presbyterian. Avocations: cooking, gardening, sailing, wines. Home and Office: 469 Ena Rd Apt 1506 Honolulu HI 96815-1710

OLNEY, WARREN, IV, journalist; b. Berkeley, Calif., Sept. 2, 1937; s. Warren III and Elizabeth (Bazata) O.; m. Marsha Temple; children: Jennifer, Lise, David, Stephanie, Christopher. BA magna cum laude, Amherst Coll., 1959. State capitol corres. McClatchy Broadcasting, Sacramento, 1966; state capitol corres. Sta. KRON-TV, San Francisco, 1967; Washington corres. CBS owned stas., 1967; reporter/anchor Sta. WTOP-TV, Washington, 1967-69; state capitol corres. Sta. KNXT-TV, L.A., 1969-72; polit. editor/anchor Sta. KNXT-TV, 1972-75, Sta. KNBC-TV, 1975-81; polit. editor/investigative reporter Sta. KABC-TV, 1981-85; polit. editor/anchor Sta. KCBS-TV, 1985-88; anchor Sta. KCOP-TV, 1988-91; host "Which Way, L.A.?" Sta. KCRW-FM (nat. pub. radio), 1992—. Sr. fellow UCLA Sch. Pub. Policy, 1997-99. Named Treasure of L.A. Downtown Ctrl. City Assn., 1996. Mem. Soc. Profl. Journalists (Nat. 1st Amendment award Washington 1994), L.A. Press Club (Joseph Quinn award Broadcast Journalist of Yr. 1985, 97). Office: Sta KCRW FM 1900 Pico Blvd Santa Monica CA 90405

OLPIN, ROBERT SPENCER, art history educator; b. Palo Alto, Calif., Aug. 30, 1940; s. Ralph Smith and Ethel Lucille (Harman) O.; m. Mary Florence Catharine Reynolds, Aug. 24, 1963; children: Mary Courtney, Cristin Lee, Catharine Elizabeth, Carrie Jean. BS, U. Utah, 1963; AM, Boston U., 1965, PhD, 1971. Lectr. art history Boston U., 1965-67; asst. prof. U. Utah, Salt Lake City, 1967-72, assoc. prof., 1972-76, prof., 1976—, chmn. dept., 1975-82, dir. art history program, 1968-76, 83-84, dean Coll. Fine Arts, 1987-97; cons. curator Am. and English art Utah Mus. Fine Arts, 1973—. Grantee U. Utah, 1972, 85, Utah Mus. Fine Arts, 1975, Utah Bicentennial Commn., 1975, Ford Found., 1975, Utah Endowment for Humanities, 1984, 85, Quinney Found., 1986, U. Utah, 1987, State Utah, 1989, Christensen Found., 1993, Eccles Found, 1994, 95; dist. ed., Utah U., 1997; trustee Pioneer State Theatre Found., 1988-97; vice chair Utah Arts Coun., 1993-95, chair, 1995-98, mem., 1998—, Utah Sci. Ctr. Authority, 1995-97; vice chair adv. bd. U. Utah Fine Arts, 1996-97, chair, 1997-98, mem., 1998—; vice chair Salt Lake County Zoo, Arts and Parks Funding Com., 1998—; co-dir. Utah Fine Arts Inst., 1998—. Mem. NASULGC (commn. on the arts, 1989-93), Utah Arts Coun., Utah Sci. Authority, Archives Am. Art Smithsonian Instn., Coll. Art Assn. Am., Utah Acad. Scis. Arts Letters, Assn. Historians Am. Art, Internat. Coun. Fine Arts Deans, 1987-97, Phi Kappa Phi, Sigma Nu. Republican. Mormon. Author: Alexander Helwig Wyant, 1836-92, 1968, Mainstreams/Reflections-American/Utah Architecture, 1973, American Painting Around 1850, 1976, Art-Life of Utah, 1977, Dictionary of Utah Art, 1980, A Retrospective of Utah Art, 1981, Waldo Midgley: Birds, Animals, People, Things, 1984, A Basket of Chips, 1985, The Works of Alexander Helwig Wyant, 1986, Salt Lake County Fine Arts Collection, 1987, Signs and Symbols...Utah Art, 1988, J.A.F. Everett, 1989, George Dibble, 1989, Utah Art, 1991, Utah Painting and Sculpture, 1997, Artists Utah, 1998; contbd. articles to profl. jours. including Utah, State of the Arts, 1993, Utah History Ency., 1994, Macmillan's Dictionary of Art, 1996, Garland's Dutch Art Ency., 1997; writer, host (TV documentary, textbook) Art Life of Utah, 1999. Home: 887 Woodshire Ave Salt Lake City UT 84107-7639 Office: U Utah Dept Art/Art History 1 University Of Utah Salt Lake City UT 84112-1107

OLSCHWANG, ALAN PAUL, lawyer; b. Chgo., Jan. 30, 1942; s. Morton James and Ida (Ginsberg) O.; m. Barbara Claire Miller, Aug. 22, 1965; children: Elliot, Deborah, Jeffrey. B.S., U. Ill., 1963, J.D., 1966. Bar: Ill. 1966, N.Y. 1984, Calif. 1992. Law clk. Ill. Supreme Ct., Bloomington, 1966-67; assoc. Sidley & Austin, and predecessor, Chgo., 1967-73; with Montgomery Ward & Co., Inc., Chgo., 1973-81, assoc. gen. counsel, asst. sec., 1979-81; ptnr. Seki, Jarvis & Lynch, Chgo., 1981-84, dir., mem. exec. com.; exec. v.p., gen. counsel, sec. Mitsubishi Electronics Am., Inc., N.Y.C., 1983-91, Cypress, Calif., 1991—. Mem. ABA, Am. Corp. Counsel Assn., Calif. Bar Assn., Ill. Bar Assn., Chgo. Bar Assn., N.Y. State Bar Assn., Bar Assn. of City of N.Y., Am. Arbitration Assn. (panel arbitrators). Office: Mitsubishi Electronics Am Inc 5665 Plaza Dr Cypress CA 90630-5023

OLSEN, CLIFFORD WAYNE, retired physical chemist, consultant; b. Placerville, Calif., Jan. 15, 1936; s. Christian William and Elsie May (Bishop) O.; m. Margaret Clara Gobel, June 16, 1962 (div. 1986); children: Anne Katherine Olsen Cordes, Charlotte Marie; m. Nancy Mayhew Kruger, July 21, 1990 (div. 1994). AA, Grant Tech. Coll., Sacramento, 1955; BA, U. Calif.-Davis, 1957, PhD, 1962. Physicist, project leader, program leader, task leader Lawrence Livermore Nat. Lab., Calif., 1962-93; ret., 1993, lab. assoc., 1993-95, 96—; cons. Holmes & Narver, 1995, Keystone Internat., 1996-97, Am. Techs. Inc., 1997, Profl. Analysis, Inc., 1997—; mem. Containment Evaluation Panel, U.S. Dept. Energy, 1984—, mem. Cadre for Joint Nuclear Verification Tests, 1988; organizer, editor procs. for 2nd through 7th Symposiums on Containment of Underground Nuclear Detonations, 1983-93. Contbr. articles to profl. jours. Mem. bd. convocators Calif. Luth. U., 1976-78. Recipient Chevalier Degree, Order of DeMolay, 1953, Eagle Scout, 1952. Mem. AAAS, Am. Radio Relay League, Seismol. Soc. Am., Livermore Amateur Radio Klub (pres. 1994-96), Sigma Xi, Alpha Gamma Sigma (life), Gamma Alpha (U. Calif.-Davis chpt. pres. 1960-61). Democrat. Lutheran. Avocations: photography, amateur radio, music, cooking.

OLSEN, DAVID MAGNOR, chemistry and astronomy educator; b. Deadwood, S.D., July 23, 1941; s. Russell Alvin and Dorothy M. Olson; m. Muriel Jean Bigler, Aug. 24, 1963; children: Merritt, Chad. BS, Luther Coll., 1963; MS in Nat. Sci., U. S.D., 1967. Instr. sci., math. Augustana Acad., Canton, S.D., 1963-66; instr. chemistry Iowa Lakes Community Coll., Estherville, Iowa, 1967-69; instr. chemistry Merced (Calif.) Coll., 1969—, instr. astronomy, 1975—, div. chmn., 1978-88, coord. environ. hazardous materials tech., 1989—. Trustee Merced Union High Sch. Dist., 1983—, pres., 1986-87, 97. Mem. NEA, Am. Chem. Soc., Astron. Soc. of the Pacific, Calif. Tchrs. Assn., Planetary Soc., Calif. State Mining and Mineral Mus. Assn. (bd. dirs., sec. 1990-93), Nat. Space Soc., Merced Coll. Faculty Assn. (pres. 1975, 93, 94, treas. 1980-90, 96, 97, bd. dirs., sec. 1990-91), Castle Challenger Learning Ctr. Found. (bd. dirs.), Merced Track Club (exec. bd. 1981), M Star Lodge, Sons of Norway (v.p. 1983), Rotary Internat. Democrat. Lutheran. Home: 973 Idaho Dr Merced CA 95340-2513 Office: Merced Coll 3600 M St Merced CA 95348-2806

OLSEN, DEBORAH ANDREÉ, agriculturist, researcher, consultant; b. St. Paul, Minn., Feb. 15, 1954; d. Merritt Donald and Andreé Phyllis (Dutiel) Butler; m. Phillip David Leroy Olson, 1982. Degree in mktg., ITT Tech., 1973; good lab. practices, Internat. Ctr. Health Environ., 1989. V.p. Profl. Agrl. Cons., Palm Desert, Calif., 1986—; cons. El Ato Chem., Phila., 1989—, DuPont, Wilmington, Del., 1991—, Zeneca, Wilmington, 1994—; adv. bd. Roadside Weed Spokane (Wash.) County, 1991-93. Avocations: watercolors, golf, tennis, cross-stitch, RVing. Home and Office: 42908 Scirocco Rd Palm Desert CA 92211-7697

OLSEN, GREG SCOTT, chiropractor; b. Anaheim, Calif., June 28, 1968; s. John Carlos and Gloria (Brownmiller) Frazier. D Chiropractic, L.A. Coll. Chiropractic, Whittier, Calif., 1994. Pvt. practice, Huntington Beach, Calif., 1994; postgrad. tchg. asst. Internat. Coll. Applied Kinesiology, L.A., 1995—. Mem. Am. Chiropractic Assn., Internat. Chiropractic Assn., Internat. Coll. Applied Kinesiology, Calif. Chiropractic Assn. Avocations: running, bicycling, snow skiing, dancing. Office: GO Chiropractic 16052 Beach Blvd Ste 140 Huntington Beach CA 92647-3844

OLSEN, HARRIS LELAND, real estate and international business executive, educator, diplomat; b. Rochester, N.H., Dec. 8, 1947; s. Harries Edwin and Eva Alma (Turmelle) O.; m. Mimi Kwi Sun Yi, Mar. 15, 1953; children: Garin Lee, Gavin Yi, Sook Ja. AS, SUNY, Albany, 1983, BS, 1988; MA in Polit. Sci., U. Hawaii, 1990; PhD in Internat. Bus. Adminstrn., Kennedy Western U., Idaho, 1993. Enlisted USN, 1967, advanced through grades to; served in various nuclear power capacities USN, Conn., 1971-76, Hawaii, 1976-87; ret. USN, 1987; v.p. Waiono Land Corp., Honolulu, 1981-92, dir., 1993-95; v.p. Asian Pacific Electricity, Honolulu, 1988-89, Kapano Land Assocs., Honolulu, 1988-92, 94-95, MLY Networks, Inc., Honolulu, 1989—, THO Consultants Cor., 1991—, Clarix Internat. Corp., 1994; staff cons. Mariner-Icemakers, Honolulu, 1982-84, Transpacific Energy Corp., Honolulu, 1982-84; dir. Asian Pacific Devel. Bank, 1983; sr. cons. Western Rsch. Assocs., Honolulu, 1984-87, 94-95; quality assurance cons. Asian Pacific, Inc., Honolulu, 1987-88; instr., lectr. Asian history and culture U. Chaminade in Honolulu, 1991; nuclear reactor plant specialist Pearl Harbor Emergency Recall Team, 1991-95; instr. nuclear reactor theory Pearl Harbor, Hawaii, 1992-95; v.p. Schwartz, Inc., 1992-98, dir. Schwartz Jewelry Sch., 1996-98; cons. Waiono/Kapano Devel. Co., 1993; bd. dirs., sec. Pacific Internat. Engring. Corp., 1994-95; Keiretsu sec. Global Ocean Cons., Inc. and Assocs., 1994-95; joint venture Premier Fisheries Pty. Ltd., Papua New Guinea, 1995-98; cons. BFD Devel. Group, 1995-96; co-drafter Nat. Tuna Industry Devel. Plan for Papua New Guinea, 1995; quality analyst, Pearl Harbor, 1995; rep. for Min. for Fisheries, Papua New Guinea, Bi-lateral Fisheries Access Rights Japan and Papua New Guinea, 1996-97, drafter Bi-Lateral Fishing Treaty Japan and Papua New Guinea, 1996; U.S. del. to 4th World Tuna Conf., Manila, 1995, U.S. del. to 5th Aquatic Coninent Conf., Maui, Hawaii, 1995, 6th, 1996; apptd. rep. Abau Electorate, Papua New Guinea Timber Sales, 1995-98; apptd. hon. consul gen. and trade rep., dep. trade min. for Govt. of Papua New Guinea in Honolulu, 1996—; bd. dirs. Island Art; cons. Pew Global Devel. Corp., 1998—. Inventor, alternate power supply system; contbr. articles to profl. publs. Head coach USN Men's Softball, Honolulu, 1978-79; pres. Pearl Harbor (Hawaii) Welfare and Recreation Com., 1983-84; mem. Bishop Mus, Rep. Senatorial Inner Cir.; commd. hon. consul gen. Ind. State Papua New Guinea, 1996; mem. Consular Corps of Hawaii. Named Alumnus of Yr., Kennedy Western U., 1993; recipient Citation of Leadership, Rep. Nat. Com., 1996, Letter of Commendation for Svc. During Aitape Tidal Wave Disaster in Papua New Guinea, 1998. Mem. AAAS, Internat. Fedn. Profl. and Tech. Engrs., Am. Polit. Sci. Assn., N.Y. Acad. Scis., USCG Aux., Am. Legion, Fleet Res. Assn., Navy League, U.S. Naval Inst., Alliance Francaise Hawaii, UN Assn., Honolulu Acad. Arts, Plaza Club, Delta Epsilon Sigma. Republican. Roman Catholic and Buddhist. Avocations: chess, philosophy, Japanese haiku poetry, native American cultures. E-mail: HarryTho@aol.com. Home: 94-1025 Anania Cir Apt 56 Mililani HI 96789-2045 Office: The Blaisdell Bldg 1154 Fort Street Mall Ste 300 Honolulu HI 96813-2712

OLSEN, JOHN DAVID, computer consultant; b. Berkeley, Calif., June 13, 1962; s. John David Chilcote and Sharyn Olsen. Student, U. Wash. Product mgr. Microsoft Corp., Redmond, Wash., 1990-97, Paris, 1995-97. Mem. World Affairs Coun., English Speaking Union, U.S. Rowing Assn., Pi Kappa Alpha. Avocations: rowing, tennis. Home: 1346 N Gardner St Los Angeles CA 90046-4108

OLSEN, MARK NORMAN, small business owner; b. Seattle, Mar. 3, 1947; s. Norman Henry and Agnes Carolyn (Hansen) O.; m. Antoinette Marie Korman, June 20, 1991. Student, U. Wash., Western Wash. U., 1965-67, BHM Tech. Coll., 1968. Cert. autobody journeyman, estimator, inter-industry conf. auto collision repair. Mgr. body shop Fraser Chevrolet, Bellingham, Wash., 1967-83; owner Olsen Auto Body, Bellingham, 1983—. Bd. dirs. Bellingham Tech. Coll. Mem. Auto Body Craftsman (treas.). Home: 1117 N Shore Dr Bellingham WA 98226-9420 Office: Olsen Auto Body 1919 Humboldt St Bellingham WA 98225-4204

OLSEN, STEPHEN RAYMOND, lawyer; b. Livermore, Calif., July 20, 1943; s. Alrae and Wilma F. (Brown) O.; m. Lynn Price, Aug. 25, 1962. AA, Santa Rosa (Calif.) Jr. Coll., 1971; JD, Empire Coll., 1985. Bar: Calif. 1986. Chief assessment stds. County of Sonoma, Santa Rosa, 1978-84, assessor, 1984-86; pvt. practice Santa Rosa, 1986—. Bd. dirs. Bennett Ridge Mut. Water Co., Santa Rosa, 1984-89. Radioman 1/C USN, 1966-70. Mem. Calif. Bar Assn., Sonoma County Bar Assn. (bd. dirs. 1993-98, com. mem. intellectual property sect. 1997—), Santa Rosa C. of C. (edn. com.), Calif. Orgn. of Retired Assessors, Rotary (bd. dirs. 1996—). Avocations: carriage driving (pres. Carriage Assn. Am.). Office: 1301 Farmers Ln Ste 201 Santa Rosa CA 95405-6744

OLSEN-ESTIE, JEANNE LINDELL, golf course owner; b. Everett, Wash., July 17, 1946; d. Carmen David Lindell and Violet Louise (Harris) Johnson; m. Wayne William Olsen, Dec. 22, 1984 (dec. Apr. 1993); children: Kenda, Justin; m. John Gary Estie, Nov. 5, 1994. Grad., Lee Sch. Cosmetology, 1966, Everett Beauty Sch., 1968, Everett Plz. Sch. Cosmetology, 1987. With Marysville (Wash.) Police Dept., 1967-72, Durham Transp., 1979-87; owner, mgr. Olsen's Riverside Golf Course and Olsen's Golf Equipment, 1979—. Active Maryfest, Marysville, 1976-78. Mem. Nat. Granite Ware Collectors, Everett Antique Club, Hummel Club Collectors, Elks (treas. local lodge #479). Avocations: golfing, collecting and restoring antiques, singing. Home and Office: 7612 Beverly Blvd Everett WA 98203-6701

OLSHEN, ABRAHAM CHARLES, actuarial consultant; b. Portland, Oreg., Apr. 20, 1913; m. Dorothy Olds, June 21, 1934; children: Richard Allen, Beverly Ann Jacobs. AB, Reed Coll., 1933; MS, U. Iowa, 1935, PhD, 1937. Chief statistician City Planning Commn., Portland, Oreg., 1933-34; rsch. asst. math. dept. U. Iowa, 1934-37; biometrics asst. Med. Ctr., 1936-37; actuary, chief examiner Oreg. Ins. Dept., 1937-42, 45-46; actuary West Coast Life Ins. Co., San Francisco, 1946—, chief actuary, 1953-63, v.p., 1947—, 1st v.p., 1963-67, senior v.p., 1967-68, bd. dirs., 1955-68; cons. actuarial and ins. mgmt., pres. Olshen & Assocs., San Francisco, 1979—; bd. dirs. Home Federal Savs. & Loan Assn., San Francisco, 1972-85, vice-chmn. bd. 1979-85, bd. chmn. 1985-86; guest lectr. various univs. Contbg. writer Ency. Britannica, Underwriters' Report, The Nat. Underwriter, Life Underwriters Mag., Annals of Math. Stats., other publs. Mem. Calif. com. Health Ins. Coun., U. Calif. Med. Care Adminstrn. com., San Mateo County Retirement Bd. (1975-77). Rsch. assoc. Div. of War Rsch., 1942-44, Ops. Rsch. Gp., H/Q Comdr.-in-Chief, U.S. Fleet, 1944-45. Recipient U.S. Navy Ordnance Devel. award, 1945, Disting. Service award U.S. Office of Sci. Rsch. & Devel., 1945, Presdl. Cert. Merit, 1947. Fellow AAAS, Sigma Xi; mem. Health Ins. Assn. Am. (mem., past chmn. Blanks Com., actuarial & stat. com.), Actuarial Club of Pacific States (past pres.), Actuarial Club of San Francisco (past pres.), Am. Acad. of Actuaries (charter), Am. Math. Soc., Am. Risk and Ins. Assn., Calif. Math. Coun., Commonwealth Club (life), Fellow Conf. of Actuaries in Public Practice, Inst. Mgmt. Scis., Inst. Math. Stats., Internat. Actuarial Assn., Internat. Assn. Consulting Actuaries, Internat. Cong. Actuaries, Ops. Rsch. Soc. (charter), San Francisco Press Club (life). Office: Olshen & Assocs 760 Market St Ste 739 San Francisco CA 94102-2302

OLSON, BETTY-JEAN, retired elementary education educator; b. Camas, Wash., Apr. 26, 1934; d. Earl Raymond and Mabel Anna (Burden) Clemons; m. Arthur H. Geda, Dec. 31, 1957; children: Ann C. Geda, Scott A. Geda; m. Conrad A. Olson, June 14, 1980. AA, Clark Coll., 1954; BA in Edn., Cen. Wash. Coll. Edn., 1956; MEd, No. Monn. Coll., 1975. Cert. elem. tchr. class I, Mont., supr. K-9 class III. Supervising tchr., demo. teaching No. Mont. Coll.; kindergarten, 1st grade instr. Glasgow, Mont.; supervisor, head tchr. Reading Lab, Glasgow AFB, Mont.; 1st grade instr., kindergarten tchr., elem. adminstr. K-7 Medicine Lake (Mont.) Dist. 7; now ret.; certification stds. and practices Adv. Coun. to the State Bd. Pub. Edn.; mem. bd. examiners Nat. Coun. for Accred. of Tchr. Edn., adv. com. Western Mont. Coll., U. Mont.; grad. spkr. Medicine Lake, 1998; v.i.p. Day Spkr., Plentywood; workshop leader and presenter in field. Mem. Sheridan County Community Protective Svcs. Com., Med-Lake Scholarship Com.; mem. Treasure State coun. Girl Scouts U.S.A., 1998. Recipient Golden Kay Profl. award Glasgow Edn. Assn., Outstanding Svc. award NE Mont. Reading Coun., State Merit Award Tchr. Nat. Coun. of Geographic Tchrs., Outstanding Svc. award Fort Peck Fine Arts Coun.; named Tchr. of Mo. KUMV-TV Channel 8, 1998. Mem. NEA, ASCD, Internat. Reading Assn., Nat. Coun. Social Studies, Nat. Elem. Prin. Assn., Medicine Lake Edn. Assn. (past pres.), Mont. Edn. Assn. (rev. bd., officerships), Mont. Elem. Prin., N.E. Mont. Reading Coun. (v.p.), Delta Kappa Gamma (state pres., chpt. pres., exec. bd., committeeships, mem. internat. exec. bd., inspirational spkr.). Home: 108 E Antelope Antelope MT 59211-9607

OLSON, DWIGHT CLARANCE, computer infosystems executive; b. Los Angeles, Apr. 18, 1943; s. Melvin F. and Mildred I. (Lund) O.; m. Lois E. Monson, May 29, 1965; children: Spencer, Jonathan. BS, Augsburg U., 1965, teaching cert., 1966. Programmer Sperry-Univac, St. Paul, Minn., 1966-68; product line mgr. Control Data Corp., Mpls. and San Diego, 1968-78; mgr. System Sci. Software, San Diego, 1968-79; dir. MAE Cons., San Diego, 1979-80; mgr. template Megatek, San Diego, 1980-83; v.p. Data Securities Internat., San Diego, 1983—; also bd. dirs. Patentee in field. Mem. Assn. Data Processing Service Orgns., Gamma Phi Omega. Lutheran. Avocations: stamps, woodworking, reading. Office: Data Securities Internat Inc 9555 Chesapeake Dr San Diego CA 92123-1304

OLSON, EARLE OLIVER, marketing and sales executive, consultant; b. Fargo, N.D., Feb. 12, 1959; s. Daniel Elias and Ellen Marie (Endersbee) O.; m. Patricia Ann McManus, Mar. 14, 1987; children: Melissa Anne, Danielle Marie. BS, St. Cloud (Minn.) State U., 1982; MBA, U. Redlands, 1996. Product mgr. divsn. electronic components Deutsch, Banning, Calif., 1981-83; product mgr. Souriau Inc., Paris and Valencia, Calif., 1987-89, sales exec. Electronic Supply, Riverside, Calif.; corp. market mgr. Cypress Electronics, Buena Park, Calif., 1983-87; v.p. N.Am. market AB Electronics Ltd., South Wales, 1989-92; sales exec. AMP Inc., Diamond Bar, Calif., 1992-95; regional product mgr. AMP Inc., Cupertino, Calif., 1995—; cons. on mil. and aerospace electronics and optics. Mem. Optical Soc. Am., World Airline Entertainment Assn., Airlines Electronic Engring. Com., Aero. Radio. Avocations: snow skiing, photography, travel, reading, computer applications. Home: 68 Azalea Dr Hershey PA 17033-2602 Office: AMP Inc 3333 Corporate Terrace Dr Diamond Bar CA 91765-4702

OLSON, FLOYD P., service company executive; b. Glencoe, Minn., May 12, 1932; s. Oscar Peter and Hazel Anna (Wolff) O.; m. Sandra Rae Larson, Feb. 5, 1955; children: Douglas, David, Clayton, Sarah. BS, U. Minn., 1954. Mgmt. trainee Wilson Meat Packing Co., Albert Lea, Minn., 1957-60; dept. mgr. Wilson Meat Packing Co., Memphis, 1960-62; area mgr. Wilson Meat Packing Co., Sao Paulo, Brazil, 1962-69; plant mgr. Wilson Meat Packing Co., Oklahoma City, 1969-76; pres. Gol-Pak Corp., Oneida, N.Y., 1976-78; asst. West Coast mgr. Hygrade Food Products, Tacoma, Wash., 1978-79; owner, dir. Servpro, Gig Harbor, Wash., 1979—; bd. mem. Peninsula Light Co., Gig Harbor, 1992-95; state dir. Servpro Industries, Wash., 1982—. Organizer Jr. Achievement, Albert Lea, Minn., 1959; pres. couns. ch., 1975-74. With U.S. Army, 1955-57. Mem. Rotary Internat. (pres. Gig Harbor 1990-91, presdl. citation 1996, dist. gov. 1994-95, zone chmn. 1996-97, Paul Harris fellow 1993). Republican. Avocations: motorhoming, golf, travel.

OLSON, KENNETH PAUL, rehabilitation counselor; b. Providence, June 26, 1935; s. Gustave Frederick and Beatrice Evelyn (Backstrom) O.; m. Judith Luellan Hazard, Nov. 12, 1965; children: Glenn Edward Johnson. BA in Sociology, U. Denver, 1960; MA in Sociology, U. Colo., 1973. Cert. rehab. counselor, vocat. specialist; lic. profl. counselor, Colo. Exec. dir. Goodwill Industries, Colorado Springs, Co., 1960-65, San Francisco, 1965, Ft. Worth, 1966-70; counselor II Colo. Div. Rehab., Colorado Springs, 1972-83; pres. Olson Vocat. Svcs., Colorado Springs, 1983-97; pvt. practice vocat. cons. Colorado Springs, 1997—; vocational expert Social Security Adminstn., Denver, 1984—; rehab counselor U.S. Dept. Labor, Denver, 1984-89. V.p. Bus. Arts Ctr., Manitou Springs, 1988-89; councilman Manitou Springs, 1975-78; bd. dirs. Econ. Devel. Com., Manitou Springs, 1998—; chmn. Health Adv. Coun., Pikes Peak Region, 1979-80; mem. Commn. for Rehab. Counselor Cert., 1979-85, Bd. for Rehab. Cert., 1984-86; pres. Manitou Art Project, 1994-95; mem. acountability com. Cmty. Prep. Sch., Manitou Springs Devel. Co., 1998—. Fellow Nat. Rehab. Counseling Assn.; mem. Colo. Rehab. Counseling Assn. (pres. 1979, named Counselor of Yr. 1976), Great Plains Rehab. Assn. (pres. 1982-83), Colo. Rehab. Assn., El Paso County Assn. Lic. Profl. Counselors (treas. 1994-96), Colorado Springs C. of C. (Small Bus. Person of Yr. award 1991), Manitou Springs C. of C. (pres. 1986). Home: PO Box 226 Manitou Springs CO 80829-0226 Office: Kenneth P Olson MA CRC LPC 121 E Pikes Peak Ave Ste 448 Colorado Springs CO 80903-1814

OLSON, MARIAN KATHERINE, emergency management executive, consultant, publisher, information broker; b. Tulsa, Oct. 15, 1933; d. Sherwood Joseph and Katherine M. (Miller) Lahman; m. Ronald Keith Olson, Oct 27, 1956, (dec. May 1991). BA in Polit. Sci., U. Colo., 1954, MA in Elem. Edn., 1962; EdD in Ednl. Adminstrn., U. Tulsa, 1969. Tchr. public schs., Wyo., Colo., Mont., 1958-67; teaching fellow, adj. instr. edn. U. Tulsa, 1968-69;

asst. prof. edn. Eastern Mont. State Coll., 1970; program assoc. research adminstrn. Mont. State U., 1970-75; on leave with Energy Policy Office of White House, then with Fed. Energy Adminstrn., 1973-74; with Dept. Energy, and predecessor, 1975—, program analyst, 1975-79, chief planning and environ. compliance br., 1979-83; regional dir. Region VIII Fed. Emergency Mgmt. Agy., 1987-93; exec. dir. Search and Rescue Dogs of the U.S., 1993—; pres. Western Healthclaims, Inc., Golden, Co.; pres. Marian Olson Assocs., Bannack Pub. Co.; mem. Colo. Nat. Hazards Mitigation Coun. Contbr. articles in field. Grantee Okla. Consortium Higher Edn., 1969, NIMH, 1974. Mem. Internat. Assn. Emergency Mgrs., Am. Soc. for Info. Sci., Am. Assn. Budget and Program Analysis, Assn. of Contingency Planners, Nat. Inst. Urban Search and Rescue (bd. dirs.), Nat. Assn. for Search and Rescue, Colo. Search and Rescue, Search and Rescue Dogs of U.S., Colo. Emergency Mgmt. Assn., Front Range Rescue Dogs, Colo. State Fire Chiefs Assn., Kappa Delta Pi, Phi Alpha Theta, Kappa Alpha Theta. Republican. Home: 203 Iowa Dr Golden CO 80403-1337 Office: 203 Iowa Dr Ste B Golden CO 80403-1337

OLSON, MAXINE LOUISE, artist, lecturer; b. Kingsburg, Calif., June 29, 1931; d. Alfred and Lena A. Marshall; divorced; children: Todd Olson, Terry Olson. BA, Calif. State U., Fresno, 1973, MA, 1975. Asst. prof. U. Ga., Athens, 1986-89; lectr. Coll. of Sequoias, Visalia, Calif., 1973-96; lectr. Fresno City Coll., 1990, Calif. State U., Fresno, intermittently 1973-96; tchr. U. Ga., Contona, Italy, 1987, 93; 6th Annual MicroPubl. Graphics, San Francisco, 1998, The World's Women On-Line United Nations Conf., Beijing, China, 1995. Exhibited works at Oakland Mus., Palazzo Casali, Venice, Italy, Forum Gallery, N.Y.C., Soho 20, N.Y., The World's Women on-line/UN 4th World Conf. on Women, Beijing, China, William Sawyer Gallery, Palm Springs Mus., Calif., Silicon Gallery, Pa. Recipient Gold award Art of Calif. Mag., 1992, IDN Design award, 1997-98. Mem. Coll. Art Assn. Roman Catholic. Avocations: painting, drawing, digital art. Home: 1555 Lincoln St Kingsburg CA 93631-1804

OLSON, ROBERT HOWARD, lawyer; b. Indpls., July 6, 1944; s. Robert Howard and Jacquline (Wells) O.; m. Diane Carol Thorsen, Aug. 13, 1966; children: Jeffrey, Christopher. BA in Govt. summa cum laude, Ind. U., 1966; JD cum laude, Harvard U., 1969. Bar: U.S. Dist. Ct. (no. dist.) Ohio 1970, U.S. Dist. Ct. (no. Dist.) Ind. 1970, U.S. Dist. Ct. (so. Dist.) Ohio 1971, U.S. Supreme Ct. 1973, Ariz. 1985. Assoc. Squire, Sanders & Dempsey, L.L.P., Cleve., 1969, 70-71, 76-81, ptnr., 1981—, ptnr., Phoenix, 1985—; sr. law clk. U.S. Dist. Ct., No. Dist. Ind. 1969-70; chief civil rights div. Ohio Atty. Gen.'s Office, Columbus, 1971-73, chief consumer protection, 1973-75, chief counsel, 1975, 1st asst. (chief of staff), 1975-76; instr. Law Sch., Ohio State U., Columbus, 1974; mem. Cen. Phoenix com. to advise city council and mayor, 1987-89; bd. dirs. Orpheum Theater Found., 1989—, sec., 1989-90, pres., 1990-97, mem. exec. com., 1997—; bd. dirs. The Ariz. Ctr. for Law in the Pub. Interest, 1988—, mem. exec. com., 1990-94, 97—, treas. 1992-93, 97—, v.p., 1993-94; mem. Ariz. Ctr. for Disability Law, 1994-96, treas. 1994-95; mem. Valley Leadership Class XIV, Ariz. Town Hall, 1977. Author monograph on financing infrastructure, 1983; also law rev. articles on civil rights, consumer protection. Bd. dirs. 1st Unitarian Ch. Phoenix, 1998—, v.p., 1987-89, pres. 1998—; bd. dirs. 1st Unitarian Ch. Found., 1987-93, pres., 1990-93. Named Arts Advocate of Yr. Bus. Vols. Arts/Phoenix, 1997. Mem. Ariz. State Bar Assn., Phi Beta Kappa. Democrat. Home: 5201 E Paradise Dr Scottsdale AZ 85254-4746 Office: Squire Sanders & Dempsey LLP 40 N Central Ave Ste 2700 Phoenix AZ 85004-4498

OLSON, RONALD CHARLES, aerospace executive; b. Sioux Falls, S.D., Jan. 23, 1937; s. Arthur Helmer and Myrtle Esther (Gustafson) O.; m. Barbara Jean Newcomb, Apr. 7, 1957; children: Bradley Charles, Jodi Lynn. AA, North Idaho Coll., 1956; BS in EE, U. Idaho, 1958; grad. sr. exec. mgmt. program, MIT, 1988. Design engr. Boeing Aerospace, Seattle, 1958-72, engring. mgr., 1973-83; postgrad. in mgmt. MIT, Seattle, 1988; program mgr. Boeing Defense and Space Group, Seattle, 1985-95; pres., gen. mgr. Sea Launch Co., LDC, Seattle, Cayman Islands, 1995-97; v.p. Boeing Comml. Space Co., Seattle, Cayman Islands, 1995-97; exec. v.p. Boeing Comml. Space Co., Seattle, 1997—; mem. engring. adv. bd. U. Idaho Coll. Engring., Moscow, 1988-95, chmn. bd., 1991-95. Recipient Gen. Ira C. Eaker, Air Force Assn., Vandenburg AFB, 1985; inductee U. Idaho Alumni Hall of Fame, 1998. Mem. Boeing Mgmt. Assn. (sec. 1981-85), Big Band Dance Club (instr. 1980-85), Twin Lakes Golf & Country Club. Republican. Lutheran. Avocations: golf, travel. Home: 1206 184th Avenue Ct E Sumner WA 98390-6443 Office: Boeing Info Space & Def Systems PO Box 3999 Seattle WA 98124-2499

OLSON, STEVEN STANLEY, social service executive; b. Longview, Wash., Aug. 5, 1950; s. Robert Martin and Martha Virginia (Duffin) O.; 1 child, Derek Thomas Dailey. BA, Wash. State U., 1972; MEd, Auburn U., 1977; postgrad., Seattle U., 1981-83. Cert. rehabilitation mgmt. Agrl. extensionist Action/Peace Corps, Popayan, Colombia, 1972-73; supr. Stonebelt Ctr. for the Mentally Retarded, Bloomington, Ind., 1974; adjustment counselor Exceptional Industries, Bowling Green, Ky., 1974-75; vocat. evaluator Exceptional Industries, 1975-76; alcohol counselor E. Ala. Mental Health, Opelika, 1976; intern Auburn Univ./Ptnrs. of the Americas, Guatemala City, Guatemala, 1976; planner, researcher Marion County Mental Health, Salem, Oreg., 1977-78; assoc. dir. Reliable Enterprises, Centralia, Wash., 1979-80; exec. dir. Reliable Enterprises, 1980-98; cons. in field, 1998—; v.p. govt. affairs Rehab. Enterprises Wash., Olympia, 1984-86, chmn. regional rep., 1986-89, pres., 1990-91; treas. Arc of Wash., Olympia, 1983-85, govt. affairs chmn., 1983-89, v.p., 1989-90, sec., 1996-97; adv. coun. Lewis/Mason/Thurston Area Agy. on Aging, 1993—. Contbr. articles to Vocat. Evaluation and Work Adjustment Bull., 1976, Rehab. World, 1977. Treas. Communities United for Reponsible Energy, Lewis County, Wash., 1979—; vice chairperson Wash. Solar Coun., Olympia, Wash., 1980-83; co-chair Early Childhood Help Orgn., Olympia, 1988. Home: 4333 Maytown Rd SW Olympia WA 98512-9239

OLSON, WILLIAM THOMAS, business executive, educator, consultant; b. Coeur d'Alene, Idaho, May 1, 1940; s. William Anthony and Julia Glenn (Hunter) O.; BA, U. N.Mex., 1968; postgrad. U. Va., 1968-72; m. Diana Jean Dodds, Aug. 22, 1962; children: Kristin Ann (dec.), Kira Lynn. Cert. mgmt. cons. Intelligence agt. U.S. Army, 1962-65; asso. editor Newspaper Printing Corp., Albuquerque, 1965-66; news and pub. affairs dir. Sta. KUNM-FM, U. N.M., 1966-68; news person KOAT-TV, Albuquerque, 1968; news dir. WCHV Radio, Charlottesville, Va., 1968-69; moderator, producer Radio-TV Center, U. Va., 1969-73; columnist The Jefferson Jour., Charlottesville, Va., 1972; instr. history U. Va., 1971-73; information specialist Wash. State U. Cooperative Ext. Service, Pullman, 1973-77, instr. Sch. Communications, 1976-77, asst. dir., Wash. Energy Ext. Service, 1977-79; founder, pres. Inland N.W. Soc. Consulting Profls., 1995-96; dir. Spokane County Head Start, 1979-84; adminstr. Community Colls. of Spokane, 1984-89, dir. critical Thinking Project, 1988-89; pres. Effective Mgmt. Systems Corp., 1987-92, CEO, chmn., bd. dirs., 1992—. Dir. Connoisseur Concerts Assn., 1983-86, pres. 1985-86; dir. West Cen. Community Devel. Assn., pres., 1985-86; dir. Spokane Community Ctrs. Found., 1986—; mem. Mayor's budget com. City of Spokane, 1988-89. Served with AUS, 1962-65. Mem. Am. Soc. Quality Goal/QPC, Wash. Family Independence Program 1990-92, Inst. Mgmt. Conss. (mem. 1995—); founding pres., mem. Inland Northwest Soc. of Consulting Profls., 1995—; Author TV documentary (with Ken Fielding): The Golden Years?, 1973; film (with B. Dale Harrison and Lorraine Kingdon) New Directions Out of the Culture of Poverty, 1974. Office: 2018 E 14th Ave Spokane WA 99202-3562

OLSSON, RONALD ARTHUR, computer science educator; b. Huntington, N.Y., Nov. 16, 1955; s. Ronald Alfred and Dorothy Gertrude (Hofmann) O. BA and MA, SUNY, 1977; MS, Cornell U., 1979; PhD, U. Ariz., 1986. Teaching asst. Cornell U., Ithaca, N.Y., 1977-79, rsch. asst., 1979; lectr. SUNY, Brockport, 1979-81; rsch. assoc. U. Ariz., Tucson, 1981-86; prof., vice chair Computer Sci. Dept. U. Calif., Davis, 1986—. Author (book) The SR Programming Language: Concurrency in Practice, 1993; contbr. articles to profl. jours. Grantee MICRO U. Calif., 1987-92, NSF, 1988-96, Dept. Energy, 1988-92, Advanced Rsch. Projects Agy., 1993—. Mem. Assn. for Computing Machinery. Avocations: bicycling, hiking, cross-country skiing, movies. Home: 2741 Brandywine Pl Davis CA 95616-2904 Office: U Calif Dept Computer Sci Davis CA 95616-8562

OLVERA, CARLOS NELSON, mechanical engineer, executive; b. Antioch, Calif., Aug. 16, 1942; s. Manuel Olvera and Faye Ames; m. Pamela Lords, Oct. 20, 1966 (div. 1979); children: Jason, Jared, Jamie, Janel; m. Georgelean Suitter, Mar. 19, 1983. BSME, Brigham Young U., 1972. Registered profl. engr., Calif., Idaho. Mgr. Westinghouse, Idaho Falls, Idaho, 1972-83; sr. engr. So. Calif. Edison, San Clemente, Calif., 1983-97; v.p., bd. dirs. SAI Engrs., inc., Santa Clara, Calif., 1997—; v.p. constrn. SAI Geothermal, Inc., Santa Clara, 1997—; cons. SAI, Inc., 1990-97. Author: Los Olvera, Journey to America. Chmn. Dana Point (Calif.) Planning Commn., 1990; pres. Dana Point Hist. Soc., 1992. Served with USN, 1963-69, USNR, 1974-90, comdr. ret. Mem. ASME. Home: 24901 Danafir Dana Point CA 92629-3153 Office: SAI Geothermal Inc 2118 Walsh Ave Ste 150 Santa Clara CA 95050-2569

O'MALLEY, PETER, professional baseball club executive; b. N.Y.C., Dec. 12, 1937; s. Walter F. and Kay (Hanson) O'M.; m. Annette Zacho, July 10, 1971; children: Katherine, Kevin, Brian. B.S. in Econs, U. Pa., 1960. Dir. Dodgertown, Vero Beach, Fla., 1962-64; pres., gen. mgr. Spokane Baseball Club, 1965-66; v.p. Los Angeles Dodgers Baseball Club, 1967-68, exec. v.p., from 1968; pres. Los Angeles Dodgers, Inc., 1970—, also bd. dirs.; bd. dirs. Tidings newspaper. Bd. dirs. L.A. Police Meml. Found., L.A. World Affairs Coun., Jackie Robinson Found., L.A.-Gungzhou (Republic of China) Sister City Assn., Amateur Athletic Found.; pres. Little League Found.; active L.A. County Bd. Govs., Music Ctr., So. Calif. Com. for the Olympic Games. Mem. Korean-Am. C. of C. of L.A. Office: LA Dodgers 1000 Elysian Park Ave Los Angeles CA 90012-1112*

O'MALLEY, THOMAS PATRICK, academic administrator; b. Milton, Mass., Mar. 1, 1930; s. Austin and Ann Marie (Feeney) O'M. BA, Boston Coll., 1951; MA, Fordham U., 1953; STL, Coll. St.-Albert de Louvain, 1962; LittD, U. Nijmegen, 1967; LLD (hon.), John Carroll U., 1988, Sogang U., Seoul, Rep. of Korea, 1996. Entered Soc. of Jesus, 1952. Instr. classics Coll. of Holy Cross, Worcester, Mass., 1956-58; asst. prof., chmn. dept. classics Boston Coll., 1967-69, assoc. prof., chmn. dept. theology, 1969-73; dean Boston Coll. (Coll. Arts and Scis.), 1973-80; pres. John Carroll U., Cleve., 1980-88; vis. prof. Cath. Inst. W. Africa, 1988-89; assoc. editor AMERICA, N.Y.C., 1989-90; rector Jesuit Com. Fairfield U., 1990-91; pres. Loyola Marymount U., L.A., 1991-99. Author: Tertullian and the Bible, 1967. Trustee Boston Theol. Inst., 1969-73, Fairfield U., 1971-82, 89-91, John Carroll U., 1976-88, Xavier U., 1980-86, U. Detroit, 1982-88, Boston Coll. H.S., 1986-88, Boys Hope, 1986-88, Loyola Marymount U., 1991—, St. Joseph's U., 1996—, Loyola U., Chgo., 1998—. Mem. AAUP, Soc. Bibl. Lit., N.Am. Patristic Soc.

O'MEARA, JANET VIRGINIA, publisher, author; b. Seattle, Wash., Apr. 19, 1939; d. Fredrick Mortimer and Mary Elizabeth Wise. BA, U. Alaska, 1974. Tchr. Anchorage Sch. dist., 1974-76; reporter, editor Homer (Alaska) News, 1977-95; author, pub. Wizard Works, Homer, 1988—; cons. O'Meara Cons. and Support Svcs., Homer, 1995—; book distributor Alaska Sml. Press Catalog, Homer, 1994—; freelance writer Homer, 1995—; adj. prof. Kachemak Bay Br. Kenai Peninsula Coll., Homer, 1986—. Author: (book) Alaska Backyard Wines, 1988 (Best Instrnl. book award Nat. Fedn. of Press Women 1988), Alaska Dictionary and Pronunciation Guide, Flights of Fancy, Kid's Guide to Common Alaska Critters, Bed and Breakfast Alaska Style, Mt. Augustine, Cries from the Heart. Bd. dirs., pres. Homer Soc. Natural History, 1998. Mem. Alaska Ctr. for the Book, Consortium of No. Pubs., Make It Alaskan, Inc. Democrat. Avocations: hiking, reading, music, visiting art galleries and mus., solving puzzles. Home: PO Box 1125 Homer AK 99603 Office: Wizard Works PO Box 1125 Homer AK 99603

O'MORRISON, KEVIN, playwright; b. St. Louis; s. Sean E. and Dori Elizabeth (Adams) O'M. Privately educated; m. Linda Soma, Apr. 30, 1966. Author: (plays) Three Days Before Yesterday, 1965, Requiem, 1969, The Morgan Yard, 1970, The Realist, 1973, A Report to Stockholders, 1975, Ladyhouse Blues, 1975, Dark Ages, 1978, A Party for Lovers (Nat. Play award NRT 1981), 1979, Unfinished Business, 1980-81 (rewritten as a cabaret-opera titled The Old Missouri Jazz 1985, then as The Power Play 1986), Songs In A Strange Land, 1993, The Mutilaters, 1998, 50 Monologues For Men & Women, 1989;(screen play) Ladyhouse Blues, 1989, (novel) The Dead File, 1990-91, The Passion of Brian Loftus, 1992-96, The Honey, 1998; (TV plays) The House of Paper, 1959, A Sign for Autumn, 1962, And Not a Word More, 1960, Pompeii . . . February 13th, When The Dead Walk, 1988; (radio version) Ladyhouse Blues, 1977; (novel) Something Perfect; actor (film) Dear Ruth, 1947, The Set-Up, 1948, Eugene O'Neill: Journey Toward Genius, 1987, Funny Farm, Lonesome Dove, 1988, Woody Allen Film (untitled), 1990, Law & Order, Mathnet, 1991, Sleepless in Seattle, 1992, Lightning Jack, 1993, Medicine Ball, 1994, Eden, 1995; (screenplays) Next Time, Dynamite and Honey, rev. 1988, retitled The Cosmic Conection, 1990, Ladyhouse Blues, 1990; (pop song lyrics) I Need Someone, 1987, On a Thousand Mile Road, 1993, The Dark Wind of Missouri, 1995, If Money is the Root of All Evil, I Am Ready for Sin, 1997; vis. prof. U. Mo., Kansas City, 1976; artist-in-residence numerous univs. and colls. With USAAF, 1943-45. Creative Artists Pub. Svc. fellow, 1975; Nat. Endowment for Arts fellow, 1979-80. Mem. ASCAP, AFTRA, Actors Equity Assn., Dramatists Guild, Writers Guild Am., PEN Am. Ctr., Amnesty Internat. USA, Screen Actors Guild.

ONCKEN, ELLEN LORRAINE, minister, speaker; b. Dallas, Dec. 28, 1957; d. Keith Loren and Mary Helen (Games) Riffe; m. Bradley Paul Oncken, Dec. 15, 1983; children: Michael, Tiffany, Stephen. BA in Psychology, Socialogy, English, Calif. Bapt. Coll., Riverside, 1980; MDiv, Midwestern Bapt. Theology Sem., Kansas City, Mo., M in Religious Edn. Min. Glen Avon Cmty. Ch., Riverside, Calif., 1980-81; min. spl. mission ministry Northgate Bapt. Ch., Kansas City, 1982-83; missionary Ch. of the Redeemer, Birmingham, Eng., 1985, 87, 98; min., counselor Yucuipa Coll. Redlands (Calif.) U., 1988-90; tchr. John Jenkins Christian Acad., Santa Paula, Calif., 1990-91; min. Pleasant Valley Bapt. Ch., Camarillo, Calif., 1991-93; min., owner Value Power Sems. and Publs., Camarillo, 1993—; associational min. Blue River Bapt. Assn., Kansas City, 1981-84; staff mem. Midwestern Bapt. Sem., 1993—. Author: Arcade Ministry Manual, 1982, Value Power Study Bible, 1997. Mem. Am. Entrepreneurs Assn. (pres. 1994—), Phi Beta Kappa. Home and Office: 2801 Ivanhoe Ave Oxnard CA 93030-8633

O'NEAL, SHAQUILLE RASHAUN, professional basketball player; b. Newark, Mar. 6, 1972; s. Philip A. Harrison and Lucille O'Neal. Student, La. State U. Center Orlando Magic, 1992-96, L.A. Lakers, 1996—. Appeared in movie Blue Chips, 1994, Kazaam, 1996. Named to Sporting News All-American first team, 1990-91; recipient Rookie of the Yr. award NBA, 1993; mem. NBA All-Star team, 1993, 94, Dream Team II, 1994; first pick overall, 1992 draft. Office: LA Lakers 3900 W Manchester Blvd Inglewood CA 90305-2200*

O'NEIL, W. SCOTT, publishing executive. Publ. Investor's Bus. Daily, L.A., 1992—. Office: Investor's Bus Daily 12655 Beatrice St Los Angeles CA 90066-7303*

O'NEILL, BEVERLY LEWIS, mayor, former college president; b. Long Beach, Calif., Sept. 8, 1930; d. Clarence John and Flossie Rachel (Nicholson) Lewis; m. William F. O'Neill, Dec. 21, 1952. AA, Long Beach City Coll., 1950; BA, Calif. State U., Long Beach, 1952, MA, 1956; EdD, U. So. Calif., 1977. Elem. tchr. Long Beach Unified Sch. Dist., 1952-57; instr., counsellor Compton (Calif.) Coll., 1957-60; curriculum supr. Little Lake Sch. Dist., Santa Fe Springs, Calif., 1960-62; women's advisor, campus dean Long Beach City Coll., 1962-71, dir. Continuing Edn. Ctr. for Women, 1969-75, dean student affairs, 1971-77, v.p. student svcs., 1977-88, supt.-pres., 1988—, exec. dir. LBCC,, 1983—; mayor City of Long Beach, Calif., 1994—. Advisor Jr. League, Long Beach, 1976—, Nat. Coun. on Alcoholism, Long Beach, 1979—, Assistance League, Long Beach, 1982—, bd. dirs. NCCJ, Long Beach, 1976—, Meml. Hosp. Found., Long Beach, 1984-92, Met. YMCA, Long Beach, 1986-92, United Way, Long Beach, 1986-92. Named Woman of Yr., Long Beach Human Rels. Commn., 1976, to Hall of Fame, Long Beach City Coll., 1977, Disting. Alumni of Yr., Calif. State U., Long Beach, 1985, Long Beach Woman of Yr. Rick Rackers, 1987, Assistance League Aux., 1987, Woman of Yr., Calif. Legislature 54th Dist., 1995, recipient Hannah Solomon award Nat. Coun. Jewish Women, 1984, Outstanding Colleague award Long Beach City Coll., 1985, NCCJ Humanitarian award, 1991, Woman of Excellence award YWCA, 1990, Community Svc. award Community Svcs. Devel. Corp., 1991, Citizen of Yr. award Exch. Club, 1992, Pacific Regional CEO award Assn. Community Coll. Trustees, 1992. Mem. Assn. Calif. Community Coll. Adminstrs. (pres. 1988-90, Harry Buttimer award 1991), Calif. Community Colls. Chief Exec. Officers Assn., Rotary, Soroptomists (Women Helping Women award 1981, Hall of Fame award 1984). Democrat. Office: Office of the Mayor Civic Ctr Plz 333 W Ocean Blvd 14th Fl Long Beach CA 90802-4604*

O'NEILL, BRIAN, landmark administrator. Dir. Golden Gate Nat. Recreation Area, San Francisco. Office: Golden Gate Nat Rec Area Fort Mason Bldg 201 San Francisco CA 94123*

O'NEILL, MICHAEL FOY, business educator; b. Milw., Apr. 16, 1943; s. Edward James and Marcellian (Wesley) O'N.; m. Karen Lynn Shoots, June 13, 1968; children: Kristine, Brenna. BBA, Ohio State U., 1966; PhD in Bus. Adminstrn., U. Oreg., 1978. Cons. Robert E. Miller and Assocs., San Francisco, 1969-73; mem. faculty Calif. State U., Chico, 1971-73, 1980—, U. Oreg., Eugene, 1974-77, U. Ariz., Tucson, 1977-79; pres. Decision Sci. Inst., Atlanta, 1986-87, v.p., 1985-86. Contbr. articles to profl. jours. Served with U.S. Army, 1962-68. Recipient Dean's Research award Calif. State U., Chico, 1981. Avocations: golf, fly fishing. Home: 2819 North Ave Chico CA 95973-0916 Office: Calif State U Dept Fin and Mktg Chico CA 95926

O'NEILL, SALLIE BOYD, educational consultant, business owner, sculptor; b. Ft. Lauderdale, Fla., Feb. 17, 1926; d. Howard Prindle and Sarah Frances (Clark) Boyd; AA, Stephens Coll., 1945; m. Roger H. Noden, July 8, 1945; children: Stephanie Ann Ballard, Ross Hopkins Noden; m. Russell R. O'Neill, June 30, 1967. Course coord. UCLA Extension, 1960-72, specialist continuing edn. dept. human devel., acad. appointment, 1972-83; pres. Learning Adventures, Inc., 1985-86; v.p., CFO The Learning Network, Inc., 1985-86; ednl. cons., 1986—; sculptor, 1987—. Bd. dirs. Everywoman's Village, Sherman Oaks, Calif., 1988-98, v.p. 1993-95. Mem. Women in Bus. (founding mem., v.p., bd. dirs. 1976-77, 86-87), Golden State Sculpture Assn., UCLA Assn. Acad. Women. Democrat. Home and Studio: 15430 Longbow Dr Sherman Oaks CA 91403-4910

O'NEILL, YNEZ VIOLÉ, medical educator; b. L.A., Sept. 25, 1931; d. Pierre Paul and Edith Anne (Taix) Violé; m. Lawrence G. O'Neill, Oct. 4, 1958 (dec. Mar. 1962). BA, Stanford U., 1952; MA, UCLA, 1955, PhD, 1964. From asst. prof. to prof. UCLA Sch. Medicine, 1973-94, rsch. prof., 1994—; cons. Nat. Libr. Medicine, Bethesda, Md., 1980-87, Rsch. Libr. Group, Palo Alto, Calif., 1995-96, UCLA, 1992—; adv. com. City of Marino, Calif., 1970-87. Author: Speech and Speech Disorders, 1980; prodr.: (video) The Young Vesalius, 1993; editor Vesalius, 1995—. Chair test area coun. I Jr. Leagues Am., 1969-71; pres. First Century Families, L.A., 1984-85; bd. dirs. Historic L.A. Assn., 1970-89; trustee Marlborough Sch., L.A., 1980-88. NIH grantee, 1973-80, 88-91. Mem. Internat. Soc. for the History Medicine (pres. 1996—), Am. Assn. for the History Medicine, Am. Hist. Assn., History Sci. Soc., Am. Hist. Assn., Calif. Hist. Soc. (trustee 1977-81). Roman Catholic. Home: 241 S Windsor Blvd Los Angeles CA 90004-3819 Office: UCLA Sch Medicine 405 Hilgard Ave Los Angeles CA 90095-9000

ONISHI, YASUO, environmental researcher; b. Osaka, Japan, Jan. 25, 1943; came to U.S., 1969; s. Osamu and Tokiko (Domukai) O.; m. Esther Anna Stronczek, Jan 22, 1972; children: Anna Tokiko and Lisa Michiyo. BS, U. Osaka Prefecture, 1967, MS, 1969; PhD, U. Iowa, 1972. Rsch. engr. U. Iowa, Iowa City, 1972-74; sr. rsch. engr. Battelle Meml. Inst., Richland, Wash., 1974-77, staff engr., 1977—, mgr. rsch. program office, 1984-92; adj. grad. faculty Wash. State U., Tri-Cities, 1993—. Co-author: Principles of Health Risk Assessment, 1985, several other environ. books; contbr. articles to profl. jours.; featured in TV program NOVA. Recipient Best Platform Presentation award ASTM, 1979. Mem. ASCE (chmn. task com. 1986-96), IAEA (advisor on environ. issues), U.S. coord. water and soil assessment bilateral joint work on Chernobyl nuclear accident, Nat. Coun. Radiation Protection and Measurements (adj., mem. task com. 1983-96), Sigma Xi. Lutheran. Achievements include coordination of bilateral USA/former USSR joint soil and environmental assessment of Chernobyl accident. Home: 144 Spengler Rd Richland WA 99352-1971 Office: Battelle Pacific NW Labs Batelle Blvd Richland WA 99352

ONO, IRA, artist; b. N.Y.C., Mar. 15, 1964. BFA, Temple U., Phila.; postgrad. studies, Bklyn Mus. Art, 1965-67. instr. with Judith Jamison, Big Island Dance Retreat, 1982. Artist: Solo shows: Mixed Grill, The Volcano Art Ctr., Hawaii Nat. Park, 1993, The Home Show CBS-TV, 1994, KITV Evening News, 1994, Inside Out on Cable TV, 1994, Split Second 50, Contemporary Art Mus., Honolulu, 1995; selected juried exhibitions: Artist. of Hawaii, Honolulu Acad. Arts, 1975, 76, 82. 83, 90, 95, Am. Crafts Coun., Balt. and Springfield Show, 1986-91, 88 Jewels, San Francisco, 1989, Fiber Art Internat. 89, Pitts., 1989, Fun & Games, Artist Diversions, the Bruce Mus., Greenwich, Conn., 1989, Hawaii Craftsmen, Honolulu, 1981-84, 86-88, 93, Elvis and Marilyn 2 x Immortal, Honolulu Acad. Arts, 1997; collections: Hawaii State Found. on Culture and Arts, Momo Fujii, Tokyo, Judith Jamison, N.Y.C., Arthur Murray, Honolulu, Robin William, Hollywood, Mus. Contemporary Art, L.A., The Contemporary Mus., Honolulu, Art a la Carte, Oslo, Guggenheim MUs. Shop, N.Y.C., Whitney Mus. Shop, N.Y.C., Virginia Breir Gallery, San Francisco; dancer Open Hands, Happy Feet, Maui, Hawaii, 1979-80, Study, performance with Meredith Monk, Naropa Inst., Boulder, Colo., 1984, Feast or Famine Hui Noeau Visual Arts Ctr, Maui, Hawaii, 1993, (opening), Contemporary Art Mus., Honolulu, 1994 (opening), Maui Cultural and Arts Ctr., Kahului, Hawaii, 1994 (opening), featured Hawaiian Moving Co., KGMB, Honolulu, 1995, Waikiki Bandstand Honolulu, 1995 (opening Earth Day); Columnist: Ono Tips Island Craft Bull., 1995—. Volcano Flows, Honolulu Star Bull., 1997; contbr. articles to mags. and newspapers. Founder and head Hui Noeau Ceramics Dept., Maui, Hawaii, 1970-75, Lyceum Series Hawaii State Libr. System, 1987-90; gave workshops How to Start Your Own Crafts Bus. for Small Bus. Adminstrn., Hawaii, Artists in the Schs., Hawaii Dept. Edn., 1990-97, juror Art of Trash workshops, Pitts., Columbus, Ohio, Newton, Mass., Maui, Hawaii, 1969-99; pres. Big Island Dance Coun., 1995—; gave worksop Kauai Children's Discovery Mus., Kauai, Hawaii, 1995. Recipient Max Beckman scholarship Bklyn. Mus. Arts; grantee: Hawaii State Choreographic, 1978, Big Island Choreographic, 1982. Home: PO Box 112 Volcano HI 96785

ONO, ROBERT ALLEN, information security officer; b. Palo Alto, Calif., May 1, 1954; s. William R. and Frances I. Ono; m. Betty Ann R. Masuoka, Nov. 24, 1979; children: Lindsey K., Lauren M. AB in Health Care Adminstrn., U. Calif., Davis, 1976; MS in Health Care Adminstrn., Calif. State U., Long Beach, 1984. Cert. info. sys. security profl. Staff svcs. analyst Calif. Dept. of Health, Sacramento, 1976-78; program rev. analyst Calif. Dept. Fin., Sacramento, 1978-79; mgmt. analyst Calif. Dept. Mental Health, Sacramento, 1979-83; info. security officer Sacramento Mcpl. Utility Dist., 1983—; spkr. and lectr. in field. Mem. Info. Sys. Security Assn., Bay Area Top Secret Software Users Group (chairperson 1995—). Avocations: bicycling, tennis, golf. Home: 6269 Faustino Way Sacramento CA 95831-1069 Office: Sacramento Mcpl Utility Dist MS B254 6201 S St Sacramento CA 95817-1818

ONOFRIO, JOE FREDERICK, III, piano company executive; b. Denver, Nov. 26, 1955; s. Joe Frederick Jr. and Vivien C. (Piogossi) O.; m. Paula Marie Vann, Dec. 23, 1963; children: Stephania, Olivia, Angelica, Sylvana Rosa. BS in Acctg., Bus. Adminstrn., Regis U., 1981. Outfitter, horse wrangler Colo., Ariz., Colo., Mont., Ariz., 1969-77; piano tech. Onofrio Piano Co., Denver, 1977-81; mfrs. rep. J&B Importers, Denver, 1981-91; pres. Onofrio Piano Co., Denver, 1991—. Sponsor Opera Colo., Denver, Colo. Ballet, Denver, 1993—, Ctrl. City (Colo.) Opera, 1993—. Recipient Joseph A. Ryan Excellence in Bus. Adminstrn. award Regis U., 1981. Mem. Alpha Sigma Nu. Republican. Roman Catholic. Avocations: sailing, horses, cycling. Office: Joe Onofrio Piano Co 1332 S Broadway Denver CO 80210-2205

ONTEK, LOUIS S., retired utilities executive; b. Staten Island, N.Y., Mar. 7, 1935; s. Stephen and Ella O.; m. Beatrice Beard, July, 1950 (div. Nov. 1965); children: RoseAnn, Thomas, m. Barbara Bashuk, Oct. 8, 1966, children: Thomas, Cynthia, Regina, Louis Jr., Stephen. Grad. H.S., Staten Is-

land, N.Y., 1951. Welder, fitter Foster Wheeler, Cartaret, N.J., 1952-56; mech. supr., inspector Bergen PT Iron Works, Bayonne, N.J., 1956-60; timbermen various cos., N.Y., N.J., 1960-66; owner Diamond Drilling Co., Inc., Jackson, N.J., 1966-89, Ontek, Inc., Jackson, N.J., 1969-98, Catalina Trade Dollars, Avalon, Calif., 1992-98; ret. Catalina Trade Dollars, Avalon, 1998. Inventor environmental liquid sampler. Mem. Rotary (Paul Harris award). Avocations: boating, motorcycling. Home: PO Box 1316 Twentynine Palms CA 92277-0980

ONYEADOR, EMMANUEL OSITA, mathematics and computer educator; b. Okigwe, Imo, Nigeria, Mar. 4, 1957; came to U.S., 1985; s. Felix Anitche and Justina Mbokwo (Ezumah) O. BS in Physics with honors, U. Ife, Ile-Ife, Nigeria, 1982; BS in Computer Sci., San Francisco State U., 1991, MA in Edn., Computer Applications, 1993. Cert. tchr., Calif. Math. educator Oakland (Calif.) Unified Sch. Dist., 1987—, technology curriculum specialist, 1993—; exec. com. mem. Oakland Unified Sch. Dist./U. Calif. Partnership for Math., 1992-94; chmn. acad. achievement com. Comer process King Estates, Oakland, 1992—; rsch. assoc. Stanford Linear Accelerator Ctr., Palo Alto, Calif., 1992; advisor Leadership Inst. Chabot Observatory & Sci. Ctr., Oakland, 1994; physics/calculus educator Mills Coll., Oakland, 1991; curr. developer Oakland Unified Sch. Dist., 1991—; dir. Computer Sci. and Tech. Acad., 1996—; ednl. software developer King Estates, Oakland, 1991-94; curr. adviser KDOL-TV, Oakland, 1994—; instr. computer techs. in edn. U. Calif. Extension, Berkeley, 1995—; chmn. telecom. com. SMARTNET project Chabot Obs. and Sci. Ctr., 1994—. Editor/developer: (curriculum) Math A, 1991, Math B, 1991; developer: (interactive software) Algebra Project Software, 1992, (activity software) Fractals Activity for Math., 1994. Bd.dirs. East Bay Computer Using Edn., 1996—; cons. on various projects. Mem. NEA, Am. Phys. Soc., Assn. Computing Machinery, Physic and Engring. Physic Assn., Calif. Tchrs. Assn. (Educators award 1991), Oakland Edn. Assn. (Super Tchr. 1992). Roman Catholic. Avocations: tennis, reading, soccer. Home: 3030 Shane Dr Richmond CA 94806-2625 Office: Oakland Unified Sch Dist 4351 Broadway Oakland CA 94611-4612

OPEL, WILLIAM, medical research administrator. BA, Pepperdine U., 1968; MBA, U. So. Calif., 1993; PhD, Claremont Grad. Sch., 1998. Exec. dir. Huntington Med. Rsch. Inst., Pasadena, Calif., 1982—; lectr. in technology, mgmt., Pepperdine U. Mem. Beta Gamma Sigma, Phi Kappa Phi. Office: Huntington Med Rsch Inst 734 Fairmount Ave Pasadena CA 91105-3104

OPFER, NEIL DAVID, construction educator, consultant; b. Spokane, Wash., June 3, 1954; s. Gus Chris and Alice Ann (Blom) O. BS in Bldg. Theory cum laude, Wash. State U., 1976, BA in Econs. cum laude, 1977, BA in Bus. cum laude, 1977; MS in Mgmt., Purdue U., 1982. Cert. cost engr., project mgr., profl. constructor. Estimator Standard Oil (Chevron), Richmond, Calif., 1975; gen. carpenter forman Opfer Constrn. Corp., Spokane, 1976; assoc. engr. Inland Steel Corp., East Chgo., Ind., 1977-78; millwright supr. Inland Steel Corp., 1978-79, field engr., 1979-82, project engr., 1982-84, sr. engr., 1984-87; asst. prof. construction and construction mgmt. Western Mich. U., Kalamazoo, 1987-89; asst. prof. construction and construction mgmt. U. Nev., Las Vegas, 1989-95, assoc. prof. construction and construction mgmt., 1995—. Contbr. articles to profl. jours. Bd. dirs. Christmas in April, 1993-98, Habitat for Humanity, 1991—. Mem. Am. Welding Soc. (bd. dirs. 1982-87), Am. Inst. Constructors, Am. Assn. Cost Engrs. (nat. bd. dirs. 1995-97, Order of Engr. award 1989), Project Mgmt. Inst., Constrn. Mgmt. Assn., Tau Beta Pi (life), Phi Kappa Phi (life). Methodist. Avocations: biking, running, marathons, triathlons. Home: 1920 Placid Ravine St Las Vegas NV 89117-5961 Office: Univ Nev 4505 S Maryland Pkwy Las Vegas NV 89154-4015

OPITZ, JOHN MARIUS, clinical geneticist, pediatrician; b. Hamburg, Germany, Aug. 15, 1935; came to U.S., 1950, naturalized, 1957; s. Friedrich and Erica Maria (Quadt) O.; m. Susan O. Lewin; children: Lea, Teresa, John, Chrisanthi, Emma, Felix. BA, State U. Iowa, 1956, MD, 1959; DSc (hon.), Mont. State U., 1983; MD (hon.), U. Kiel, Germany, 1986. Diplomate Am. Bd. Pediatrics, Am. Bd. Med. Genetics. Intern, State U. Iowa Hosp., 1959-60, resident in pediatrics, 1960-61; resident and chief resident in pediatrics U. Wis. Hosp., Madison, 1961-62; fellow in pediatrics and med. genetics U. Wis., 1962-64, asst. prof. med. genetics and pediatrics, 1964-69, assoc. prof., 1969-72, prof., 1972-79; dir. Wis. Clin. Genetics Ctr., 1974-79; clin. prof. med. genetics and pediatrics U. Wash., Seattle, 1979—; adj. prof. medicine, biology, history and philosophy, vet. rsch. and vet. sci. Mont. State U., Bozeman, 1979-94, McKay lectr., 1992, Univ. prof. med. humanities MSU, Bozeman, 1994—; adj. prof. pediatrics, med. genetics U. Wis., Madison, 1979—, Class of 1947 Disting. prof., U. of Wis., 1992; coordinator Shodair Mont. Regional Genetic Svcs. Program, Helena, 1979-82; chmn. dept. med. genetics Shodair Children's Hosp., Helena, 1983-94; dir. Found. Devel. and Med. Genetics, Helena, Mont.; pres. Heritage Genetics P.C., Helena, 1996; Farber lectr. Soc. Pediatric Pathology, 1987; Joseph Garfunkel lectr. So. Ill. U., Springfield, 1987, McKay lectr. Mont. State U., 1992; Warren Wheeler vis. prof. Columbus (Ohio) Children's Hospital, 1987; Bea Fowlow lectr. in med. genet. U. Calgary, 1996; 1st vis. prof. Hanseatic U. Found. of Lübeck, 1996. Editor, author 14 books; founder, editor in chief Am. Jour. Med. Genetics, 1977—; mng. editor European Jour. Pediatrics, 1977-85; contbr. numerous articles on clin. genetics. Chair Mont. Com. for Humanities, 1991. Recipient Pool of Bethesda award for excellence in mental retardation rsch. Bethesda Luth. Home, 1988, Med. Alumni Citation U. Wis., 1989, Col. Harlan Sanders Lifetime Achievement award for work in the field of genetic scis. March of Dimes, Purkinje medal Czech Soc. Medicine, Mendel medal Czech Soc. Med. Genetics, 1996, Internat. prize Phoenix-Anni Verdi for Genetic Rsch., 1996. Fellow AAAS, Am. Coll. Med. Genetics (founder); mem. German Acad. Scientists Leopoldina, Am. Soc. Human Genetics, Am. Pediatric Soc., Soc. Pediatric Rsch., Am. Bd. Med. Genetics, Birth Defects Clin. Genetic Soc., Am. Inst. Biol. Scis., Am. Soc. Zoologists, Teratology Soc., Genetic Soc. Am., European Soc. Human Genetics, Soc. Study Social Biology, Am. Acad. Pediatrics, German Soc. Pediatrics (hon.), Western Soc. Pediatrics Rsch. (emeritus), Italian Soc. Med. Genetics (hon.), Israel Soc. Med. Genetics (hon.), Russian Soc. Med. Genetics (hon.), So. Africa Soc. Med. Genetics (hon.), Japanese Soc. Human Genetics (hon.), Sigma Xi. Democrat. Roman Catholic. Home: 2930 Craig Dr Salt Lake City UT 84109-3636 Office: U Utah Sch Medicine Primary Childrens Med Ctr 100 N Medical Dr Salt Lake City UT 84113

OPOTOWSKY, MAURICE LEON, newspaper editor; b. New Orleans, Dec. 13, 1931; s. Sol and Fannie (Latter) O.; m. Madeleine Duhamel, Feb. 28, 1959 (dec.); children: Didier Sol Duhamel, Joelle Duhamel, Arielle Duhamel (dec.); m. Bonnie Feibleman, May 4, 1991. Student, Tulane U., 1949-51; BA cum laude, Williams Coll., 1953. Reporter Berkshire Eagle, Pittsfield, Mass., 1951-53; pub. Sea Coast Echo, Bay St. Louis, Miss., 1953-54; reporter UPI, 1956-62; feature editor Newsday, Ronkonkoma, N.Y., 1962-64; Suffolk day editor Newsday, 1964-65, Nassau night editor, 1965-67, nat. editor, 1967-70, Suffolk editor, 1970-72; dir. L.I. Mag., 1972; day editor Press-Enterprise, Riverside, Calif., 1973-84, mng. editor features/adminstrn., 1984-87, sr. mng. editor, 1987-92, mng. editor, 1992-98, ombudsman, 1998—; chief N.Y. State Syndicate Service, 1961-74; mem. Calif. Freedom of Info. Exec. Com., sec., 1979-80, treas., 1980-81, v.p., 1981-82, pres., 1982-83; Pulitzer prize juror. Trustee Harbor Country Day Sch., 1970-72; bd. dirs. Calif. Newspaper Editor Conf. Bd., 1978-83; mem. Smithtown (N.Y.) Hunt, 1970-73, West Hills Hunt, 1976-80, Santa Fe Hunt, Whip, 1985—; co-chmn. Calif. Bench-Bar Media Com.; mem. adv. coun. dept. comm. Calif. State U., Fullerton, 1995-66, instr. dept. comms. 1998—. Served with AUS, 1954-56. Recipient Lifetime Achievement award Calif. 1st Amendment Assembly, 1997. Mem. AP News Execs. Calif. (chmn. 1986-87), Calif. 1st Amendment Coalition (pres., treas.), Calif. Soc. Newspaper Editors (bd. dirs., vice chmn. steering com. 1983), AP Mng. Editors Assn., Am. Soc. Newspaper Editors. Office: Press Enterprise Co 3512 14th St Riverside CA 92501-3878

OPPEDAHL, JOHN FREDRICK, publisher; b. Duluth, Minn., Nov. 9, 1944; s. Walter H. and Lucille (Hole) O.; m. Alison Owen, 1975 (div. 1983); m. Gillian Coyro, Feb. 14, 1987; 1 child, Max. B.A., U. Calif., Berkeley, 1967; M.S., Columbia U., 1968. Reporter San Francisco Examiner, 1967; reporter, asst. city editor Detroit Free Press, 1968-75, city editor, 1975-80, exec. city editor, 1981, exec. news editor, 1981-82, asst. mng. editor, 1983; nat. editor Dallas Times Herald, 1983-85, asst. mng. editor, 1985-87; mng. editor/news L.A. Herald Examiner, 1987-89; mng. editor Ariz. Republic, Phoenix, 1989-93; exec. editor Phoenix Newspapers, 1993-95; pub., CEO Phoenix Newspapers, Inc., 1996—. Trustee Walter Cronkite Sch. Journalism and Telecomm., Ariz. State U.; bd. dirs. Found. for Am. Comms., Downtown Phoenix Partnership, Valley of the Sun United Way, 1996-97 (campaign cabinet), Greater Phoenix Econ. Coun., Ariz. Communities in Schs., COMPAS; mem. Greater Phoenix Leadership. Mem. Am. Soc. Newspaper Editors, AP Mng. Editors, Newspaper Assn. of Am. Office: The Arizona Republic 200 E Van Buren St Phoenix AZ 85004-2238*

OPPEDAHL, PHILLIP EDWARD, computer company executive; b. Renwick, Iowa, Sept. 17, 1935; s. Edward and Isadore Hannah (Gangstead) O.; B.S. in Naval Sci., Navy Postgrad. Sch., 1963, M.S. in Nuclear Physics, 1971; M.S. in Systems Mgmt., U. S.C., 1978; m. Sharon Elaine Ree, Aug. 3, 1957 (dec. Aug. 1989); children: Gary Lynn, Tamra Sue, Sue Ann, Lisa Kay. Commd. ensign U.S. Navy, 1956, advanced through grades to capt., 1977; with Airborne Early Warning Squadron, 1957-59, Anti-Submarine Squadron, 1959-65; asst. navigator USS Coral Sea, 1965-67; basic jet flight instr., 1967-69; student Armed Forces Staff Coll., 1971; test group dir. Def. Nuclear Agy., 1972-74; weapons officer USS Oriskany, 1974-76; program mgr. for armament Naval Air Systems Command, Washington, 1977-79; test dir. Def. Nuclear Agy., Kirtland AFB, N.Mex., 1979-82, dep. comdr. Def. Nuclear Agy., 1982-83; pres., chief exec. officer Am. Systems, Albuquerque, 1983—; dir., bd. dirs. BASIS Internat., 1991—. Pres., bd. dirs. Casa Esperanza, 1990-92. Decorated Disting. Service medal. Mem. Naval Inst., Am. Nuclear Soc., Aircraft Owners and Pilots Assn., Assn. Naval Aviation Navy League. Lutheran. Author: Energy Loss of High Energy Electrons in Beryllium, 1971; Understanding Contractor Motivation and Incentive Contracts, 1977. Home and Office: 5850 Eubank Blvd NE Ste B 49 Albuquerque NM 87111-6111

OPPEL, ANDREW JOHN, computer systems consultant; b. Kerrville, Tex., Dec. 22, 1952; s. Wallace Churchill and Anne Kathryn (Smith) O.; m. Laura Lee Partridge, Aug. 26, 1972; children: Keith Andrew, Luke Andrew. BA in Computer Sci., Transylvania U., 1974. Computer programmer Johns Hopkins U., Balt., 1974-77; data base programmer Equitable Trust Co., Balt., 1977-78; sr. programmer, analyst Md. Casualty Co., Balt., 1978-79; sr. programmer, analyst Levi Strauss & Co., San Francisco, 1979-82, sr. requirements mgr., 1982-84, tech. cons., 1984-91, tech. advisor, 1991-93, mgr. database mgmt. sys., 1994-96, sr. sys. architect, 1996-97; sr. cons. Triadigm Internat., San Francisco, 1997-98; mng. prin. cons. Oracle Corp., Redwood Shores, Calif., 1998—; instr. U. Calif. Extension, Berkeley, 1983—. Ops. officer Alameda County Radio Amateur Civil Emergency Svc., San Leandro, Calif., 1980-92; cub master Boy Scouts Am., Alameda, Calif., 1991-92; referee U.S. Soccer Fedn., Alameda, 1988—, referee instr., 1996—. Democrat. Episcopalian. Avocation: amateur radio. Home: 1308 Burbank St Alameda CA 94501-3946 Office: Oracle M/S OPL-C4 500 Oracle Pkwy Redwood City CA 94065-1675

ORBACH, RAYMOND LEE, physicist, educator; b. Los Angeles, July 12, 1934; s. Morris Albert and Mary Ruth (Miller) O.; m. Eva Hannah Spiegler, Aug. 26, 1956; children: David Miller, Deborah Hedwig, Thomas Randolph. BS, Calif. Inst. Tech., 1956; PhD, U. Calif., Berkeley, 1960. NSF postdoctoral fellow Oxford U., 1960-61; asst. prof. applied physics Harvard U., 1961-63; prof. physics UCLA, 1963-92, asst. vice chancellor acad. change and curriculum devel., 1970-72, chmn. acad. senate L.A. divsn., 1976-77, provost Coll. Letters and Sci., 1982-92; chancellor U. Calif., Riverside, 1992—; mem. physics adv. panel NSF, 1970-73; mem. vis. com. Brookhaven Nat. Lab., 1970-74; mem. materials rsch. lab. adv. panel NSF, 1974-77; mem. Nat. Commn. on Rsch., 1978-80; chmn. 16th Internat. Conf. on Low Temperature Physics, 1981; Joliot Curie prof. Ecole Superieure de la Physique et Chimie Industrielle de la Ville de Paris, 1982, chmn. Gordon Rsch. Conf. on Fractals, 1986; Lorentz prof. U. Leiden, Netherlands, 1987; Raymond and Beverly Sackler lectr. Tel Aviv U., 1989; faculty rsch. lectr. UCLA, 1990; Andrew Lawson lectr. U. Calif., Riverside, 1992; mem. external rev. com. Nat. High Magnetic Fields Lab., 1994—. Author: (with A.A. Manenkov) SpinLattice Relaxation in Ionic Solids, 1966; divsn. assoc. editor Phys. Rev. Letters, 1980-83, Jour. Low Temperature Physics, 1980-90, Phys. Rev., 1983—; contbr. articles to profl. jours. Recipient Whitney M. Young Humanitarian award Urban League of Riverside and San Bernardino, 1998; Alfred P. Sloan Found. fellow, 1963-67; NSF sr. postdoctoral fellow Imperial Coll., 1967-68; Guggenheim fellow Tel Aviv U., 1973-74. Fellow Am. Phys. Soc. (chmn. nominations com. 1981-82, counselor-at-large 1987-91, chmn. divsn. condensed matter 1990-91); mem. AAAS (chairperson steering group physics sect.), NSF (mem. rsch. adv. com. divsn. materials 1992-93), Phys. Soc. (London), Univ. Rsch. Assn. (chair coun. pres. 1993), Sigma Xi, Phi Beta Kappa, Tau Beta Pi. Home: 4171 Watkins Dr Riverside CA 92507-4738 Office: U Calif Riverside Chancellor's Office 4148 Hinderaker Hall Riverside CA 92521-0101*

ORDUNO, ROBERT DANIEL, artist, painter, sculptor; b. Ventura, Calif., Sept. 5, 1933; s. Octavio and Mary G.; children: Patrice Schulman, Nicole Franco. Pvt. and group tchr., Santa Fe, 1990—, Australia, 1993; guest lectr. Australian Coun. on Adult Edn., 1993; interviewed on local radio stas., 1996. One man show include Koshore Indian Mus. Le Junta, Colo., 1998; exhibited in Great Falls Tribune, J.M. Swanson, 1985, Gazette, Cody Bur, Wyo., Tom Howard, 1987, Aurora, Great Falls, Mont., Shirley Edam Diaz, 1988, S.W. Art Mag., J.M. Swanson, 1990; featured artist Shaman's Drum, 1992, The Advocate, Tasmania, Australia, 1993, The New Mexican, Santa Fe, 1994, Wheelright Mus. Am. Indian, Santa Fe, 1995, The World Times, 1995, Seasons Quarterly, 1996; featured artist and cover image Internat. Fine Art Collector, 1992, cover and featured artist Informart Mag., 1994, Counseling and Psychotherapy, 1998, Mathbook, 1998, Ken Burns PBS Documentary film, 1998. Recipient Best Oil, Denver Indian Mkt., Pine Ridge S.D., 1985, 86, 87, 1st and 2d graphics Red Cloud Indian Sch., Best Painting artists choice Great Falls Native Am. Exhibit, James Bama award Best of Show, Best Contemporary Painting Buffalo Bill Hist. Ctr., Cody, Wyo., 1987, Best Painting Artists Choice award Great Falls Native Am. Exhibit, 1989, Best Show award, 1993, Okla. Indian Art competition, 1998. Avocations: skiing, surfing. Home: 153 Calle Don Jose Santa Fe NM 87501-2391

O'REGAN, DEBORAH, association executive, lawyer; b. New Prague, Minn., Aug. 30, 1953; d. Timothy A. and Ermalinda (Brinkman) O'R.; m. Ron Kahlenbeck, Sept. 29, 1984; children: Katherine, Ryan. BA, Coll. of St. Catherine, 1975; JD, William Mitchell Coll. of Law, 1980. Bar: Ala. 1982, Minn. 1980. Asst. city atty. City of Bloomington, Minn., 1978-81, asst. city mgr., 1981-82; CLE dir. Alaska Bar Assn., Anchorage, 1982-84, exec. dir., 1985—; mem. task force on gender equality State Fed. Joint Comm., Anchorage, 1991—; mem. selection com. U.S. Magistrate Judge, U.S. Dist of Ala., 1992; mem. adv. bd. Anchorage Daily News, 1991-93. Mem. Nat. Assn. Bar Execs. (exec. com. 1993-97). Avocations: travel, outdoors, rollerblading. Office: Alaska Bar Assn 510 L St Ste 602 Anchorage AK 99501-1959

O'REILLY, FRANCES LOUISE, academic administrator; b. Great Falls, Mont., Feb. 20, 1947; d. Francis Joseph and Bernadine Madeline (DeRose) O'R. BA in Sociology and English, Carroll Coll., 1969; MBA, U. Mont., 1977. Head Start tchr. Rocky Mountain Devel. Coun., Helena, Mont., 1969, social svc. dir. Head Start, 1970-76; rsch. asst. U. Mont., Missoula, 1976, teaching asst., 1976-77; broker, owner Manning & O'Reilly Realty Inc., Great Falls, 1977-81; dir. residence hall Carroll Coll., Helena, 1981—; dir. residential life Carroll Coll., 1992—, coord. residential life, 1991-92, adj. faculty mem. dept. bus. acctg. & econs., 1982-86, dept. communications, 1991—, dir. summer programs, 1983—, mem. adv. bd. student affairs com., 1983—; social work cons. Office Children Devel. Region #8, Denver, 1970-76; supr. social work practicums Head Start Rocky Mountain Devel. Coun., 1970-76. Vol. Diabetes Found., Helena, 1993-94, various polit. campaigns, Helena, 1993-94. Mem. Mont. Assn. Student Affairs, Beta Gamma Sigma. Avocations: reading, symphony, yoga, aerobics, theater. Office: Carroll Coll PO Box 64 Helena MT 59624-0064

ORENSTEIN, (IAN) MICHAEL, philatelic dealer, columnist; b. Bklyn., Jan. 6, 1939; s. Harry and Myra (Klein) O.; m. Linda Turer, June 28, 1964; 1 child, Paul David. BS, Clemson U., 1960; postgrad., U. Calif., Berkeley, 1960-61. Career regional mgr. Minkus Stamp & Pub. Co., Calif., 1964-70; mgr. stamp div. Superior Stamp & Coin Co., Inc., Beverly Hills, Calif., 1970-90; dir. stamp divsn. Superior Galleries, Beverly Hills, Calif., 1991-94; dir. space memorabelia Superior Stamp and Coin. Co., Inc., Beverly Hills, Calif., 1992-94; dir. stamp and space divsn. Superior Stamp & Coin an A-Mark Co., Beverly Hills, Calif., 1994-97; sr. buyer, appraiser Superior Stamp & Coin, Beverly Hills, Calif., 1997—; stamp columnist L.A. Times, 1965-93; writer The Brookman Times, Scott Stamp Monthly; bd. Adelphi U. N.Y. Inst. Philatelic and Numismatic Studies, 1978-81. Author: Stamp Collecting Is Fun, 1990; philatelic advisor/creator The Video Guide To Stamp Collecting, 1988. With AUS, 1962-64. Mem. Am. Stamp Dealers Assn., C.Z. Study Group, German Philatelic Soc., Confederate Stamp Alliance, Am. Philatelic Soc. (writers unit 1975-80, 89-93), Internat. Fedn. Stamp Dealers, Internat. Soc. Appraisers: Stamps, Space Memorabilia. Republican. Avocation: fishing. Office: Superior Stamp & Coin 9478 W Olympic Blvd Beverly Hills CA 90212-4299

ORI, JERRY ALLEN, management consultant; b. Highland Park, Ill., Aug. 20, 1944; s. Ralph and Edith Louise (Contratto) O. BS in Bus. Adminstrn., Roosevelt U., 1973, MPA, 1976; student, Pacific Western U., 1990-93. Assoc., prin. A.T. Kearney & Co., Chgo., 1970-75; pres. Belden Health Care Co., Chgo., 1975-80; CEO Ancillia Health Care, Chgo., 1980-89; mgmt. cons. Universal Life Associates, L.A., 1989—; bd. dirs. Cuneo Fin. Svcs., 1995—. Contbr. polit. cartoons, various publs., 1998-99. Chmn. Citizens Action Com., Norwalk, Calif., 1994—. Grantee State of Ill., Chgo., 1970, Roosevelt U., Chgo., 1976. Mem. Internat. City Mgrs. Assn. (pres. 1976), Am. Mgmt. Assn. (v. chair 1981-88), Am. Hosp. Assn. (treas. 1978-79), YMCA. Independent. Avocations: golf, reading, investments, cycling, teaching. Home: PO Box 2138 Norwalk CA 90651-2138

ORLEBEKE, WILLIAM RONALD, retired lawyer, writer; b. El Paso, Tex., Jan. 5, 1934; s. William Ronald and Frances Claire (Cook) O.; m. Barbara Raye Pike, Aug. 29, 1954 (div. 1988); children: Michelle, Julene, David; m. Kathie Waterson, 1989; 1 stepson, Jack D. Waterson. BA, Willamette U., 1956; MA, Kans. U., 1957; JD, Willamette U., 1966. Bar: Calif. 1966, U.S. Dist. Ct. (no. dist.) Calif. 1967, U.S. Ct. Appeals (9th cir.) 1967, U.S. Ct. Appeals (7th cir.) 1989, U.S. Dist. Ct. (no. dist.) Ill. 1989, U.S. Dist. Ct. (cen. dist.) Calif. 1989. Assoc. Eliassen & Postel, San Francisco, 1966-69; ptnr. Coll, Levy & Orlebeke, Concord, Calif., 1969-77, Orlebeke & Hutchings, Concord, 1977-86, Orlebeke, Hutchings & Pinkerton, 1986-88, Orlebeke & Hutchings, 1988-89; prin. Law Offices W. Ronald Orlebeke, 1989—; hearing officer Contra Costa County, Calif., 1981—; arbitrator Contra Costa County Superior Ct., 1977—, U.S. Dist. Ct. No. Calif., 1978—, Mt. Diablo Mcpl. Ct., 1987—; judge pro tem Mt. Diablo Mcpl. Ct., 1973-77. Author: Orlebeke Family in Europe and America, 1570 to 1990, 1988. Alumni bd. dirs. Willamette U., 1978-81, trustee, 1980-81; scholarship chmn. Concord Elks, 1977-79; del. Joint U.S/China Internat. Trade Law Conf., Beijing, Peoples Republic of China, 1987. Served with USMCR, 1952-59. Sr. scholar, Willamette U., 1955-56; Woodrow Wilson fellow, Kans. U., 1956-57; U.S. Bur. Nat. Affairs fellow, 1966, others. Mem. SAR, Sons of Confederate Vets. (Award of Merit 1989), Sons of Union Veterans Civil War, U.S. Navy League, First Marine Divsn. Assn. Republican. Lodges: Order Ea. Star (worthy patron 1980), Masons, Shriners, Elks, Rotary (charter pres. Clayton Valley/Concord Sunrise club 1987-88, chmn. dist. 5160 Calif. membership devel. 1989-90, dist. govs. liaison dist. 5160 1990-92, dist. 5160 Rotarian of Yr. 1989-90, Paul Harris fellow 1988, 1992 dist. conf. chmn. benefactor 1990, award of merit 1990).

ORLOFF, CHET, cultural organization administrator; b. Bellingham, Wash., Feb. 22, 1949; s. Monford A. and Janice (Diamond) O.; m. Wendy Lynn Lee, Sept. 20, 1970; children: Callman Labe, Hannah Katya, Michele Alison. BA, Boston U., 1971; MA, U. Oreg., 1978; postgrad., Portland State U. Tchr. Peace Corps, Afghanistan, 1972-75; asst. dir. Oreg. Hist. Soc., Portland, 1975-86, exec. dir., 1991—; dir. Ninth Cir. Hist. Soc., Pasadena, Calif., 1987-91. Editor: Western Legal History, 1987-91, Law for the Elephant, 1992; sr. editor: Oreg. Hist. Quar.; contbr. articles to profl. jours. Commr. Met. Arts Commn., Portland, 1981-84, Portland Planning Commn., 1989-92; pres. Nat. Lewis and Clark Bicentennial Coun., 1996—. Mem. Phi Alpha Theta. Avocations: reading, tennis. Office: Oregon Historical Society 1200 SW Park Ave Portland OR 97205-2483*

ORLOVSKI, STAS, artist, educator; b. Kishinev, Moldova, Sept. 28, 1969; s. Samuel Gregoravich and Ludmila (Rosenfeld) O.; m. Alise Leviah Arato, Apr. 3, 1997. BFA, York U., 1992; BEd, U. Toronto, 1994; MFA, U. So. Calif., 1996. Cert. tchr., Ont., Can. Instr. art Town of Vaughan Parks and REcreation Dept., Toronto, 1989-90, Red Cross Vets. Program Sunnybrook Med. Ctr., Toronto, 1992-93; grad. tchg. asst. U. So. Calif., L.A., 1994-96; tchr. art South Bay Lutheran H.S., L.A., 1996-97; adj. faculty mem. Long Beach City Coll., Rio Hondo Coll., L.A., 1996-97, U. So. Calif., Long Beach City Coll., Cypress Coll., L.A., 1998—; vis. prof. art Pomona Coll., 1997-98. Fellow Skowhegan (Maine) Art Program, 1996; recipient Award of Excellence Latcham Gallery, Toronto, John McKee Painting award, San Diego Art Inst., 1993. Mem. Coll. Art Assn. Office: U So Calif Sch Fine Arts Watt Hall 104 Univ Park Los Angeles CA 90089-0292

ORMAN, JOHN LEO, software engineer, writer; b. San Antonio, Mar. 19, 1949; s. Alton Woodlee and Isabel Joan (Paproski) O. BS in Physics, N.Mex. Inst. Mining & Tech., 1971, BS Math., MS Physics, 1974. Rsch. asst. N.Mex. Inst. Mining & Tech., Socorro, 1967-74; computer programmer State of N.Mex., Santa Fe, 1974-76; computer analyst Dikewood Corp., Albuquerque, 1976-83; nuclear engr. Sandia Nat. Labs., Albuquerque, 1983-88, software engr., 1988—. Author numerous poems. NSF fellow, 1971-74; recipient 2d place award N.Mex. State Postry Soc., 1987. Mem. IEEE Computer Soc., Am. Assn. Physics Tchrs., Assn. for Computing Machinery, Nat. Writer's Club (poetry award 1987), Southwest Writers Workshop (3d place award non-fiction 1987), N.Mex. Mountain Club. Avocations: photography, travel, skiing, hiking, tennis. Home: 719 Vista Abajo Dr NE Albuquerque NM 87123-2246 Office: Sandia Nat Labs MS 0974 PO Box 5800 Albuquerque NM 87185-0100

ORMASA, JOHN, retired utility executive, lawyer; b. Richmond, Calif., May 30, 1925; s. Juan Hormaza and Maria Inocencia Olondo; m. Dorothy Helen Trumble, Feb. 17, 1952; children: Newton Lee, John Trumble, Nancy Jean Davies. BA, U. Calif.-Berkeley, 1948; JD, Harvard U., 1951. Bar: Calif. 1952, U.S. Supreme Ct. 1959. Assoc. Clifford C. Anglim, 1951-52; assoc. Richmond, Carlson, Collins, Gordon & Bold, 1952-56, ptnr., 1956-59; with So. Calif. Gas Co., L.A., 1959-66, gen. atty., 1963-65, v.p., gen. counsel, 1965-66; v.p., sys. gen. counsel Pacific Lighting Service Co., Los Angeles, 1966-72; v.p., gen. counsel Pacific Lighting Corp., Los Angeles, 1973-75, v.p., sec., gen. counsel, 1975. Acting city atty., El Cerrito, Calif., 1952. Served with U.S. Navy, 1943-46. Mem. ABA, Calif. State Bar Assn., Richmond (Calif.) Bar Assn. (pres. 1959), Kiwanis (v.p. 1959). Republican. Roman Catholic.

ORO, DEBRA ANN, dentist; b. Mascoutah, Ill., May 12, 1953; d. Cyril John and Elizabeth Louise (Billhartz) Haas; m. Robert John Oro, June 17, 1979; children: Philip, Anna. BS in Biology with honors, U. Ill., 1975; postgrad., Harvard U., Boston, 1975-76; DMD, U. Pa., 1979. Lic. dentist, Pa., N.J., Ariz., N.Y. Dentist/rschr. NIH Dental Rsch., Bethesda, Md., 1977; dentist USPHS, Kotzebue, Alaska, 1978; resident Luth. Med. Ctr., Bklyn., 1979-80; attending/lectr. Brookdale Hosp. and Med. Ctr., Bklyn., 1980-81, Hudson Valley Hosp. Ctr., Cortlandt Manor, N.Y., 1982-96; pres., dentist Hudson Valley Dental Medicine, Cortlandt Manor, 1985-96; pres., co-founder Oro-Dontics, Inc., Oro Valley, Ariz., 1993—; nat. lectr. in field. Named one of Top Clinicians, Acad. Gen. Dentistry, 1997, Mrs. Tucson-USA, 1997, Mrs. Congeniality, 3rd runner up Mrs. Ariz.-USA, 1997; James scholar U. Ill., 1972, Robert Woods Johnson scholar, 1975; named Top Clinician, Ann. Meeting Gen. Dentistry, Chgo., 1997. Fellow Acad. Gen. Dentistry (Top Clinician award 1997); mem. Acad. Cosmetic Dentistry, N.Y. State Dental Soc., No. Westchester Dist. Dental Soc., So. Ariz. Dental Soc., Peekskill-Yorktown Dental Soc. (pres. 1987-88), Kappa Delta (v.p. 1973), Alpha Lambda Delta. Avocations: parenting, hiking, weight lifting, gardening, softball. Home: 991 W Wheatgrass Pl Oro Valley AZ 85737-8654

ORO, ROBERT JOHN, dentist, consultant, writer; b. Bklyn., Apr. 22, 1952; s. Philip Edward and Marie Catherine (Bruno) O.; m. Debra Ann Haas, June 17, 1979; children: Philip, Anna. BS in Econs. with honors, SUNY, Queens, 1974; DMD, U. Pa., 1979; Fellow, Acad. Gen. Dentistry, 1985, Master, 1988. Lic. dentist, N.Y., Ariz. Founder, dentist Free Dental

Clinic, Guadalajara, Mex., 1976; jr. resident Brookdale Hosp. and Med. Ctr., Bklyn., 1979-80, sr. resident, 1980-81, pres., CEO Hudson Valley Dental Medicine, Cortlandt Manor, N.Y., 1981-96, Penn Dental Consultanta, Cortlandt Manor, N.Y., 1996; v.p. Oro-Dontics, Inc., Oro Valley, Ariz., 1996—; CEO On Valley Denta Medicine, Ariz., 1998—; clin. instr. Brookdale Hosp. Med. Ctr., 1981-84; attending Hudson Valley Hosp. Ctr., 1981-96; officer Peekskill (N.Y.)-Yorktown Dental Soc., 1984-87, pres., 1988. Author: How to Choose Your Dentist: Confessions of an Adrenaline Addict, 1997. Active health fairs/fundraisers Hudson Valley Hosp., 1981-96; fundraiser Casa del los Ninos, Tucson, 1996, 97, St. Elizabeth's of Hungary, Tucson, 1996, 97; active health fairs Tucson Pks. and Recreation, 1997. Named Mr. Congeniality, Mrs. Ariz./USA Pagent, 1997; cited as one of four top clinicians Acad. Gen. Dentistry Ann. Meeting, 1997. Mem. ADA, Ariz. Dental Assn., N.Y. State Dental Soc., Pima County Dental Study Club, Peekskill Yorktown Dental Soc. (pres. 1981-96), Delta Omicron. Avocations: writing, sports, hiking, playing with my children. Office: Oro-Dontics Inc 991 W Wheatgrass Pl Tucson AZ 85737-8654

O'ROURKE, DENNIS, advertising executive. CFO, sr. v.p. Goldberg, Moser & O'Neill, San Francisco, Calif. Office: 77 Maiden Ln San Francisco CA 94108-5414

ORSI, THOMAS WILLIAM, television and film audio engineer; b. Chgo., Mar. 8, 1956; m. Kathryn Orsi, Feb. 15, 1997; children: Natalie Ann, Anne Elizabeth. Student, Am. Conservatory, 1973-76, Harper Coll., 1975-77. Freelance studio cons. L.A., 1991—; sound designer, mixer A&E Network/Discovery Channel, 1995—, E! Entertainment, 1995—, Black Ops Entertainment, 1996—; sound designer Fox TV, 1994—. Composer for 11 films, 30 comls., 47 records and CDs. Emmy Blue Ribbon panelist, 1994—. Recipient Emmy nomination, 1995, 96. Mem. NATAS, EARS, AES, SMPTE. Home: 7907 Hannum Ave Culver City CA 90230-6166

ORSINI, MYRNA J., sculptor, educator; b. Spokane, Wash., Apr. 19, 1943; d. William Joseph Finch and Barbara Jean (Hilby) Hickenbottom; m. Donald Wayne Lundquist, Mar. 31, 1962 (div. Mar. 1987); children: Laurie Jeanine Winter, Stephanie Lynne Lundquist. BA, U. Puget Sound, 1969, MA, 1974; postgrad., U. Ga., 1987. Tchr. Tacoma (Wash.) Pub. Schs., 1969-78; owner, pres. Contemporary Print Collectors, Lakewood, Wash., 1978-81, Orsini Studio, Tacoma, 1985—. Sculptor: works include Vartai symbolic gate for Ctrl. Europas Park, Vilnius, Lithuania, 1994; Menat steel and neon corp. commn. completed in Tacoma, Wash. 1995. Chair Supt.'s Supervisory Com., Tacoma, 1978-79; lobbyist Citizens for Fair Sch. Funding, Seattle, 1979; art chair Women's Pres. Coun., Tacoma, 1987-88; founder, bd. dirs. Monarch Contemporary Art Ctr., Wash.; bd. mem. Nisqually Regional Arts Coun., 1997—. Recipient 1st pl. sculpture award Pleinair Symposium Com., Ukraine, 1992, Peron Symposium Com., Kiev, Ukraine, 1993; recognized 1st Am. sculptor to exhibit work in Ukraine, 1993; prin. works include seven monumental sculptures worldwide. Mem. N.W. Stone Sculptors Assn. (coun. leader 1989—), Pacific Gallery Artists, Internat. Sculpture Ctr., Tacoma City Club. Avocations: reading, sailing, biking. Office: Orsini Studio PO Box 1125 Tenino WA 98589-1125

ORTH, BEVERLY JEAN, lawyer. BS, Harvey Mudd Coll., 1974; JD, Harvard U., 1978. Bar: Calif. 1978, Oreg. 1987. Assoc. Brawerman, Kopple & Lerner, L.A., 1978-81, Adams, Duque & Hazeltine, L.A., 1981-84; staff counsel William M. Mercer Inc., L.A., 1984-86, assoc., 1986-91; assoc. William M. Mercer Inc., Portland, 1991—; contr. Software Spectrum, Culver City, Calif., 1980-87. Trustee Harvey Mudd Coll., Claremont, Calif., 1985-88. Mem. ABA, NOW, Multnomah Bar Assn., Oreg. Women Lawyers, Harvey Mudd Coll. Alumni Assn. (gov. 1978-87), Western Pension and Benefits Conf. Democrat. Avocations: wine collecting, fund raising. Office: William M Mercer Inc 111 SW 5th Ave Ste 2800 Portland OR 97204-3631

ORTIZ, ANTONIO IGNACIO, public relations executive; b. Mexico City, Feb. 22, 1961; came to U.S., 1988; s. Antonio and Sylvia (Vega) O.; m. Socorro Chinolla, June 12, 1982. B in Bus., Universidad Autonoma de Baja Calif., Tijuana, 1984. With acctg. dept. Bank of the Atlantic, Tijuana, 1979-83; mgr. Aldaco, Tijuana, 1983-84; dir. pub. rels. Oh! Laser Club, Tijuana, 1984-88, Iguanas, Tijuana, 1988-90, Euebe, S.A., Tijuana, 1990—; cons. DDBSA Corp., Chula Vista, Calif., Calif. Alson Ltd., San Diego, Exim Trading Co., San Diego, R.P. Noble Enterprises, La Jolla, Ca.; dir. pub. rels. R. Noble Enterprises. Avocations: swimming, watching TV. Home: PO Box 431859 San Diego CA 92143-1859 Office: Exim Trading Corp PO Box 435108 San Diego CA 92143-5108

ORTMEYER, CARL EDWARD, retired demographer; b. Charles City, Iowa, Mar. 12, 1915; s. Arthur Herman and Sarah Emilie (Stoeber) O.; m. Anne Babuska O'Brien, Aug. 3, 1947 (dec. Dec. 15, 1995); 1 child, Kerry Michael; m. Ruth Forberg, Oct. 5, 1996. BA, U. Iowa, 1939; MS, Iowa State U., 1948, PhD in Rural Sociology, Demography, 1954. Rsch. assoc. bur. pub. health econs. Sch. Pub. Health U. Mich., Ann Arbor, 1954-56; demographer social security adminstrn. Libr. Congress, Washington, 1956-57; rsch. assoc. Sch. Medicine Howard U., 1958-59; demographer Nat. Ctr. Health Statistics Pub. Health Svc. U.S. Dept. HEW, 1959-68, demographer Nat. Inst. Occpl. Safety and Health CDC, 1968-80. Vol. caregiver Benedictine Nursing Ctr., Mt. Angel, Oreg., 1990-96, Wesley Homes Health Ctr., Des Moines, Wash., 1996—; mem. Wesley Found., Ams. for Democratic Action. Sgt. U.S. Army, 1941-45. Travel grantee London Sch. Econs. Rockefeller Found., 1969. Fellow Am. Pub. Health Assn., AAAS. Democrat. Mem. United Meth. Ch. Avocations: dancing. Home: 815 S 216th St Apt 203 Des Moines WA 98198-6332

ORTON, GLENN SCOTT, astronomer, research scientist; b. Fall River, Mass., July 24, 1948; s. Dwight E. and Lois M. (Miller) O.; m. Linda R. Brown, Jan. 1, 1979; children: Gregg, Sarah. BS, Brown U., 1970; PhD, Calif. Inst. Tech., 1975. Postdoct. fellow Jet Propulsion Lab., Pasadena, 1975-77, mem. tech. staff, 1977-95, sr. rsch. scientist, 1995—. Contbr. 95 articles to profl. jours. Mem. All Saints Episcopal Ch., Pasadena. Calif. State fellow; recipient Medal for Outstanding Scientific Achievement NASA, 1997. Mem. Am. Astronom. Soc. (mem. com. divsn. planetary sci. 1985-89), Am. Geophys. Union, Internat. Astronom. Union. Office: Jet Propulsion Lab MS 169-237 4800 Oak Grove Dr Pasadena CA 91109-8001

ORTON, WILLIAM H. (BILL ORTON), former congressman, lawyer; b. North Ogden, Utah, Sept. 22, 1948. BS, Brigham Young U., 1973, JD, 1979. Adj. prof. Portland (Oreg.) State U./Portland C.C., 1974-76, Brigham Young. U., Provo, Utah, 1984-85; tax auditor IRS, 1966-77; owner/lectr. Tax Tng. Inst., Inc., 1978-90; lectr. continuing edn. seminars Real Estate Tax Inst., N.W. Ctr. Profl. Edn., and Tax Tng. Inst., various locations in U.S., 1978-90; corp. counsel WI Forest Products, Inc., Portland, Oreg., 1980-81; of counsel Merritt & Tenney, Atlanta, 1986-90; tax atty. pvt. practice, Utah, 1980-90, Washington, 1986-90; atty., 1980-90; mem. 102d-104th Congresses from 3f Utah dist., 1990-97, fgn. affairs com., small bus. com., budget, banking and fin. svcs. coms.; ptnr. Jones, Waldo, Holbrook & McDonough, Washington, also Utah, 1997—. Democrat. Mormon. Office: Jones Waldo Holbrook & McDonough 1500 Wells Fargo Plz 170 S Main St Salt Lake City UT 84101-1605 also: Jones, Waldo, Holbrook & McDonough 411 Constitution Ave NE Washington DC 20002-5923

OSAKA, MICHI, artist, printmaking educator; b. Brooks, Oreg., May 15, 1927; d. Otoichi and Fumiyo (Masukawa) Umemoto; m. Tom S. Osaka, May 30, 1945; children: Janice Vinnedge, Gordon, Kurt. BA magna cum laude, U. Puget Sound, 1978; BFA, U. Wash., 1981, MFA, 1984. Artist Tacoma, Wash., 1978—; exhbn. chair Nat. Am. Pen Women Wash., Tacoma, 1983. Author, artist: Peace and Harmony, 1991 (Artist Trust 1991), Michi Osaka's Path, 1997, Best of Show 1997); 23 solo exhns., regionally and nationally, exhibited in group shows at Puget Sound Artists, Tacoma, 1981, 82, 83, Regional South Profl. Puyallup, Olympia, 1986, Pacific Gallery Artists, Tacoma, 1985, Puget Sound Sumie Artists, Tacoma and Seattle, 1975, 93 and others; exhibited in traveling exhibit N.W. Print Coun., Portland, 1982. Artist Ford Found. Grant, U. Wash., 1982; artist-chmn. Sister City of Kitakyushu, Tacoma, 1987. Nine Best of Show awards nationally and regionally N.W. Watercolor Soc., cert. excellence Internat. Art Competition, N.Y., 1988; fine arts recognition Pierce County Arts Commn., Tacoma, 1992. Mem. Sumie Soc. Am. (pres. 1985-86), Women's Painter Wash. (1st v.p. 1995-96), N.W. Print Coun. (Best of Show), Nat. Northcoast Collage Soc. (Merit award), N.W. Watercolor Soc. (1st place award), Phi Kappa Phi. Avocations: Bonsai, calligraphy, Saga floral arrangements. Home: 1115 62d Ave E Tacoma WA 98424

OSBORN, JEFFREY SCOTT, cardiologist; b. Kansas City, Mo., July 22, 1957; s. John D.. and Jean O.; m. Michelle Marie Mull, July 9, 1983 (div. Apr. 1993); children: Alex, Morgan; m. Jana Fowler, Apr. 15, 1993; children: Erin, Lauren, Jeffrey Ryan. BA, U. Mo., 1978, MD, 1981. Diplomate Nat. Bd. Med. Examiners, Am. Bd. Internal Medicine, Am. Bd. Cardiovascular Diseases. Intern. St. Luke's Hosp., Kansas City, 1981-82, res. internal med., 1982-84, fellow cardiology, 1984-86; Marion Labs. clin. cardiology rsch. fellow Mid-Am. Heart Inst., Kansas City, 1986-87; cons. cardiologist LDS Hosp. and Intermountain Heart Inst., Salt Lake City, 1987—; clin. faculty U. Utah Med. Sch., Salt Lake City, 1988—; cons. cardiologist Utah Cardiac Transplant Program, Salt Lake City, 1987—; co-dir. EP Lab. LDS Hosp., Salt Lake City, 1987—, mem. rsch. and human ethics com., 1988—. Contbr. articles to profl. jours. Advisor Nat. Rep. Senate Adv. Coun., Washington, 1997; mem. legal reform HALT, Washington, 1995—, pres's. circle Habitat for Humanity, GA, 1998. Recipient Marion Labs. rsch. travel award St. Luke's Hosp. and Mid-Am. Heart Inst., Kansas City, 1986. Fellow Am. Coll. Cardiology; mem. Utah State Med. Assn., Salt Lake County Med. Soc. Mem. LDS Ch. Office: Utah Heart Clinic 324 10th Ave Ste 206 Salt Lake City UT 84103-2886 also: 6360 S 3000 E Salt Lake City UT 84121-6923

OSBORN, JOHN FOLLETT, engineer, editor; b. Montmarte, Can., Aug. 21, 1914; came to U.S., 1940; s. Francis Follett and Maude Gibson (Little) O.; m. Eleanor Constance Stacey, 1940; children: John Michael, Eleanor Jane. BSEE, U. Manitoba, Can., 1939. Profl. engr. Ont., Calif. Mem. test course Gen. Electric, Can., 1937-39, control engr., 1940-47; supr. control engr. Gen. Electric, San Francisco, 1947-50, with mktg. dept., 1956-63; mgr. Gen. Electric, Redding, Calif., 1950-55; mktg., engring. supr. Gen. Electric, San Jose, Calif., 1963-84. Editor-in-chief Nuclear and Plasma Scis. Soc. Mag., 1975-98. Mem. IEEE (Disting. Mem. award 1994, Profl. Leadership award 1992), Calif. Writers Club. Avocation: writing. Home: 507 Elmhurst Cir Sacramento CA 95825-6659

OSBORN, SUSAN MARIE, management consultant; b. Dayton, Ohio; d. Kenneth H. and Alice M. Mason; children: Robert, Kendall. BA, U. Colo., 1960; MSW, U. Calif., Berkeley, 1963; PhD, The Fielding Inst., 1990. Cert. cmty. coll. tchr., cmty. coll. counselor, Calif. Cmty. Colls. Prin. Osborn Assocs., Washington and Calif., 1971—; tng. cons. Lockheed Missiles and Space Co., Sunnyvale, Calif., 1981-85; mgr. human resource devel. Lockheed Space Ops. Co., Vandenberg AFB, Calif., 1985-87; Socio tech. systems cons. Sun Microsystems, Mountain View, Calif., 1987-90; dir. M.S. in systems mgmt. Coll. of Notre Dame, Belmont, Calif., 1991-94; pres. Life Thread Publs., Sacramento, 1997—; co-chair Orgn. Devel. Network, Mountain View, 1987-90; presenter Tech. and Soc. Com., Mountain View, 1996, 97; program chair Bay Area Ind. Pubs. Assn., Corte Madera, Calif., 1997-98; adj. faculty mem. Nat. U., Chapman U., U. La Verne and U. of Phoenix, 1998—. Author: Assertive Training for Women, 1975, The System Made Me Do It, 1997. Mem. ASTD (membership chair 1983-84), Pubs. Mktg. Assn., Ind. Pubs. Network, New Alternatives for Pubs., Retailers and Artists, No. Calif. Book Publicity and Mktg. Assn., Small Pubs. Assn. N.Am., Sacramento Pubs. Assn., Psi Chi, Pi Lambda Theta. Avocations: jazz, hiking, dancing, reading. Email: sosborn@ix.netcom.com.

O'SCANNLAIN, DIARMUID FIONNTAIN, judge; b. N.Y.C., Mar. 28, 1937; s. Sean Leo and Moira (Hegarty) O'S.; m. Maura Nolan, Sept. 7, 1963; children: Sean, Jane, Brendan, Kevin, Megan, Christopher, Anne, Kate. BA, St. John's U., 1957; JD, Harvard U., 1963; LLM, U. Va., 1992. Bar: Oreg. 1965, N.Y. 1964. Tax atty. Standard Oil Co. (N.J.), N.Y.C., 1963-65; assoc. Davies, Biggs, Strayer, Stoel & Boley, Portland, Oreg., 1965-69; dep. atty. gen. Oreg., 1969-71; public utility commr. of Oreg., 1971-73; dir. Oreg. Dept. Environ. Quality, 1973-74; sr. ptnr. Ragen, Roberts, O'Scannlain, Robertson & Neill, Portland, 1978-86; judge, U.S. Ct. Appeals (9th cir.), San Francisco, 1986—, mem. exec. com., 1988-89, 1993-94, mem. Jud. Coun. 9th Cir., 1991-93; mem. U.S. Judicial Conf. Com. on Automation and Tech., 1990—; cons. Office of Pres.-Elect and mem. Dept. Energy Transition Team (Reagan transition), Washington, 1980-81; chmn. com. adminstrv. law Oreg. State Bar, 1980-81. Mem. council of legal advisers Rep. Nat. Com., 1981-83; mem. Rep. Nat. Com., 1983-86, chmn. Oreg. Rep. Party, 1983-86; del. Rep. Nat. Convs., 1976, 80, chmn. Oreg. del., 1984; Rep. nominee U.S. Ho. of Reps., First Congl. Dist., 1974; team leader Energy Task Force, Pres.'s Pvt. Sector Survey on Cost Control, 1982-83, trustee Jesuit High Sch.; mem. bd. visitors U. Oreg. Law Sch., 1988—; mem. citizens adv. bd. Providence Hosp., 1986-92. Maj. USAR, 1955-78. Mem. Fed. Bar Assn., ABA (sec. Apellate Judges Conf. 1989-90, exec. com. 1990—, chmn.-elect 1994—), Arlington Club, Multnomah Club. Roman Catholic. Office: US Ct Appeals 313 Pioneer Courthouse 555 SW Yamhill St Ste 104 Portland OR 97204-1370*

OSCARSON, KATHLEEN DALE, writing assessment coordinator, educator; b. Hollywood, Calif., Sept. 16, 1928; d. Chauncey Dale and Hermine Marie Rulison; m. David Knowles Leslie, June 16, 1957 (div. Aug. 1970); m. William Randolph Oscarson, Apr. 27, 1974. AB, UCLA, 1950, MA, 1952; Cert. Advanced Study, Harvard U., 1965; Diplomé Elementaire, Le Cordon Bleu U. Paris, 1972. Gen. secondary life credential, Calif. Cons. Advanced Placement English Calif. Dept. Edn., Sacramento, 1968-70; reader Calif. Assessment Program, Sacramento, 1989—; instr. individual study U. Calif. Extension, Berkeley, 1979-92; reader, leader Ednl. Testing Svc., Princeton, N.J., 1967—, Oakland, Calif., 1967—; reader San Jose (Calif.) State U., 1991—; tchr. English, counselor Palo Alto (Calif.) Unified Sch. Dist., 1954-90, H.S. writing assessment coord., 1987—; adj. lectr. English Santa Clara (Calif.) U., 1990-91; commr. Curriculum Study Commn., San Francisco Bay Area, 1978—; chair tchrs. English Spring Asilomar Conf., Pacific Grove, Calif., 1992, Asilomar 44, Pacific Grove, 1994; presenter Conf. on English Leadership, Chgo., 1996; advanced placement faculty cons. in English Collegeboard N.J., 1967-73, 91—. Mem. lang. arts assessment adv. com. Calif. State Dept. Edn., Sacramento, 1975-90; mem.-at-large exec. bd. Ctrl. Calif. Coun. Tchrs. English, Bay Area, 1969-71; mem. Medallion Soc. San Francisco Opera, 1984—; mem. ann. summer event com., membership com. Internat. Diplomacy Coun. Mem. MLA, Nat. Coun. Tchrs. English (group leader conf. San Francisco), Calif. Assn. Tchrs. English, Internat. Diplomacy Coun. San Francisco (membership and events coms. 1996), Harvard Club San Francisco, Christopher Marlowe Soc. Avocations: cuisine, voice, writing. Home: 230 Durazno Way Portola Valley CA 94028-7411

OSCHMANN, JACOBUS MARINUS, JR., optical systems engineer, consultant; b. Rochester, N.Y., Jan. 19, 1959; s. Jacobus Marinus and Carol Jean (Townsend) O. BS in Optics, U. Rochester, 1981; MS in Optical Scis., U. Ariz., 1983. Mem. tech. staff TRW, Redondo Beach, Calif., 1982-84, sect. head, 1987-88; sys. engr. Hughes Aircraft Co., El Segundo, Calif., 1984-87, Sensis Corp., DeWitt, N.Y., 1988-89; optical sys. mgr. Phase Shift Tech., Tucson, 1989-92; sys. engring. mgr. Gemini 8 telescope project AURA Inc., Tucson, 1992—; cons. Sensis Corp., DeWitt, 1993—. Contbr. articles to profl. jours. Inventor method and apparatus for non-contact reading of a relief pattern. Recipient Bausch & Lomb Sci. scholarship, U. Rochester, 1977-81, Sci. award Bausch & Lomb, 1977. Mem. Optical Soc. Am., Soc. Photo-Optical Instrumentation Engrs. Office: AURA Inc Gemini 8 Meter Telescopes 950 N Cherry Ave Tucson AZ 85719-4933

OSE, DOUGLAS, congressman; b. Sacramento, 1955; m. Lynnda ose; children: Erika, Emily. BS, U. Calif., Berkeley, 1977. Project mgr. Ose Properties, Sacramento, 1977-85; owner real estate devel. and investment co., 1986—; mem. 106th Congress from 3d Calif. dist., 1999—, mem. agr., banking and fin. svcs., and govt. reform coms. Former bd. dirs. Citrus Heights C. of C., Sacramento Housing and Redevel. Commn.; mem. Citrus Heights Incorporation Project. Office: 1508 Longworth House Office Bldg Washington DC 20515*

OSGOOD, FRANK WILLIAM, urban and economic planner, writer; b. Williamston, Mich., Sept. 3, 1931; s. Earle Victor and Blanche Mae ([illegible]) O.; children: Ann Marie, Frank William Jr. BS, Mich. State U., 1953; M in City Planning, Ga. Inst. Tech., 1960. Prin. planner Tulsa Met. Area Plnning Commn., 1958-60; sr. assoc. Hammer & Co. Assocs., Washington, 1960-64; econ. cons. Marvin Springer & Assocs., Dallas, 1964-65; sr. assoc. Gladstone Assocs., Washington, 1965-67; prof. urban planning Iowa State U., Ames, 1967-73; pres. Frank Osgood Assoc./Osgood Urban Rsch., Dallas, 1973-84; dir. mktg. studies MPSI Americas Inc., Tulsa, 1984-85, Comarc Systems/Roulac & Co., San Francisco, 1985-86; pres. Osgood Urban Rsch., Millbrae, Calif., 1986-95; freelance writer Millbrae and L.A., Calif., 1994—; VISTA vol. coord. Chrysalis, Santa Monica, Calif., 1995-96; pres. Osgood Urban Rsch., L.A., 1996—; adj. prof. U. Tulsa, 1974-76; lectr. U. Tex., Dallas, 1979, U. Tex., Arlington, 1983. Author: Control Land Uses Near Airports, 1960, Planning Small Business, 1967, Continuous Renewal Cities, 1970; contbr. articles to profl. jours. Chmn. awards Cub Scouts Am., Ames, 1971-73; deacon Calvary Presbyn. Ch., San Francisco, 1987-90. 1st lt. USAF, 1954-56. Recipient Community Leaders and Noteworthy Americans award 1976. Mem. Am. Inst. Cert. Planners (peninsula liaison 1987-89, dir. protem 1990 No. Calif. sect., edn. coord. 1991-92, Calif., dir. N. Cen. Tex. sect., Tex. chpt. 1983), Am. Planning Assn., Am. Inst. Planners (v.p. Okla. chpt. 1975-77), Okla. Soc. Planning Cons. (sec., treas. 1976-79), Urban Land Inst., So. Calif. Assn. Govts. (regional adv. coun. L.A. chpt. 1998—), Nat. Assn. Regional Couns., Writer's Bloc & Creative Writing, Cypress. Home: 5605 Nelson St Cypress CA 90630

O'SHAUGHNESSY, ELLEN CASSELS, writer; b. Columbia, S.C., Oct. 1, 1937; d. Melvin O. and Grace Ellen (Cassels) Hemphill; m. John H. Sloan (dec.); children: John H., Anne H.; m. John F. O'Shaughnessy, Dec. 8, 1979 (div. Mar. 1990). BA, Internat. Coll., L.A., 1977; MA in Counseling Psychology, Fielding Inst., Santa Barbara, Calif., 1980. Tchr.'s aide, art instr. Monterey Peninsula (Calif.) Unified Sch. Dist., 1968-74; tchr. adult sch. Pacific Grove (Calif.) Unified Sch. Dist., 1974-82, spl. edn. cons., 1984-85; sustitute tchr. Monterey County Office Edn., Salinas, Calif., 1983-84; owner, writer, pub. Synthesis, Pacific Grove, Calif., 1984—. Author: Teaching Art to Children, 1974, Synthesis, 1981, You Love to Cook Book, 1983, I Could Ride on the Carousel Longer, 1989, Somebody Called Me A Retard Today...And My Heart Felt Sad, 1992, Walker & Co., N.Y.C. Episcopalian. Home: PO Box 51063 Pacific Grove CA 93950-6063

OSHEROFF, DOUGLAS DEAN, physicist, researcher; b. Aberdeen, Wash., Aug. 1, 1945; s. William and Bessie Anne (Ondov) O.; m. Phyllis S.K. Liu, Aug. 14, 1970. B.S. in Physics, Calif. Inst. Tech., 1967; M.S., Cornell U., 1969, Ph.D. in Physics, 1973. Mem. tech. staff Bell Labs., Murray Hill, N.Y., 1972-82, head solid state and low temperature physics research dept., 1982-87; prof. Stanford (Calif.) U., 1987—, J.G. Jackson and C.J. Wood prof. physics, 1992—; chair physics, 1993-96. Researcher on properties of matter near absolute zero of temperature; co-discoverer of superfluidity in liquid 3He, 1971, nuclear antiferromagnetic resonance in solid 3He, 1980. Co-recipient Simon Meml. prize Brit. Inst. Physics, 1976, Oliver E. Buckley Solid State Physics prize, 1981, Nobel prize in physics, 1996; John D. and Catherine T. MacArthur prize fellow, 1981. Fellow Am. Phys. Soc., Am. Acad. Arts and Scis., Nat. Acad. Scis. Office: Stanford U Dept Physics Stanford CA 94305-4060

OSIFESO, GODWIN SOTILEWA, architect; b. Ibadan, Nigeria, Apr. 13, 1961; came to U.S., 1981.; s. George Sorinola and Funsho A. (Osibogun) O.; m. Veronica Theresa Petersen, Mar. 26, 1988; one child, Olatilewa Caylee. Hampton (Va.) Inst., 1985. Intern arch. T. Harris Archs., Upland, Calif., 1986; arch. WLC Archs., Rancho Cucamonga, Calif., 1987-96; arch., sr. assoc. Perkins & Will, Pasadena, Calif., 1996—; presenter in field. V.p. Bus. Ptnrs. in Edn. Ctrl. Sch. Dist., Rancho Cucamonga, 1994. Mem. AIA, Constrn. Specification Inst. Avocations: hist. restoration, antique cars, gardening. Office: Perkins & Will Archs 234 E Colorado Blvd Ste 600 Pasadena CA 91101-2210

OSMAN, HERBERT EUGENE, minister; b. Manchester, Ohio, Sept. 13, 1931; s. Estel Meredith and Sarah Elizabeth (Foster) O.; m. Rosamond Blockinger, June 23, 1957; children: Mary Osman Henderson, Mark Herbert, Michael Eugene. BS in Social Studies, Ea. Ill. U., 1957; BDiv in Pastoral Work, Christian Theol. Sem., 1961. Ordained to ministry Meth. Ch., 1957. Pastor Remington (Ind.) United Meth. Ch., Red Mountain United Meth. Ch., Mesa, Ariz.; mem. Ariz. Ecumenical Coun. Conf. Congl. Devel. Bd.; mem. Hospice Corp. bd. East Valley Hospice, Mesa, 1985—; pres. corp. bd. Family Emergency Svc. Ctr., Mesa, 1989—; mem. com. Homeless Trust Fund Oversight Com., State Ariz., 1991—. Cpl. U.S. Army, 1953-55. Office: 2936 N Power Rd Mesa AZ 85215-1677

OSMAN, RANDOLPH E., art appraiser, curator; b. Atlantic City, N.J., Aug. 10, 1940; s. Carlton Rufe O. and Alice (Elfreth) Eager. BA, Bucknell U., 1964; MA, NYU, 1970. Asst. prof. art history Portland State U., 1967-70; curator edn. Santa Barbara (Calif.) Mus. Art, 1972-75; dir. Gray Art Gallery East Carolina U., Greenville, N.C., 1979-85; curator edn./programs Ketchikan (Alaska) Mus., 1987-89; dir. Missoula (Mont.) Mus. Arts, 1989-90; prin. Osman Assocs. Fine Art Appraisal, Falls City, Oreg., 1990—. Author: Art Centers of the World New York, 1968. Chair restoration project Hist. United Meth. Ch., Falls City, 1996—. NEA grantee, 1982, 84; NEA Mus. Prof. fellow, 1980-84. Mem. Am. Assn. Mus., Am. Soc. Appraisers, Am. Crafts Coun., Coll. Art Assn. Am., Western Mus. Conf. Democrat. Episcopalian. Avocations: flyfishing, writing. Office: Osman Assocs PO Box 1 Falls City OR 97344-0001

OSMONSON, WADE LANE, fundraising executive; b. Baldwin Park, Calif., Feb. 27, 1963; s. Wayne Del Roy and Theda Jean (Canaday) O.; m. Lorrie Lynn Minyard, Nov. 19, 1988; children: Keith, Kyler. AA, Citrus C.C., Glendora, Calif., 1983; BS, Calif. Poly., 1987. Waiter Cask'n Cleaver Restaurant, San Dimas, Calif., 1983-87; med. sales rep. Home Americair Calif., Garden Grove, 1987-88; telerelations rep. World Vision U.S., Monrovia, Calif., 1988-89, mktg. rschr., 1989-96; devel. rsch. mgr. World Vision U.S., Federal Way, Wash., 1996—. Mem. Assn. Profl. Rschrs. for Advancement, Wash. Devel. Rschrs. Assn. Republican. Avocations: playing piano, singing, baseball, golf, time with family. Office: World Vision US 34834 Weyerhaeuser Way S Federal Way WA 98001-9523

OSTEEN, HEYWARD LEWIS, writer; b. Sumter, S.C., Sept. 10, 1938; s. Heyward Lewis, Jr. and Harriett O.; children: David, Gabrielle. BS, St. Louis U. Co-author: (novel) Matthew's Gospel; author: The Zodiac Cult Murders; author short fiction in numerous mags., including Jet, True, Motor Trend, Southern Living, others. Sgt. U.S. Army, 1958-60. Recipient 1st prize for adult fiction publisher's Weekly, Writer's Internat. Network Contest, 1st prize Fla. State Writing Competition; finalist Writer's Found. Poetry Contest, America's Best, 1995-96; winner grand prize Poetry Arts Project Finalist, 1993, Writer's Digest awards 1974, 76, 79, 81, 86, 87, others; finalist (essay) in Naval History, 1997.; prodr. plays.

OSTER, DAVID WAYNE, medical management executive; b. Denver, July 31, 1955; s. Elmer J. and Jeanette Viola (Brenneis) O.; m. Sharon Ellen Evans, July 1, 1978; 1 child, Stephanie Lynn. BA, U. Colo., 1977; MBA, Nat. U., San Diego, 1986. Commd. 2nd lt. U.S. Army, 1977, advanced through grades to maj., 1987; investment banker Integrated Resources Inc., N.Y.C., 1987-91; CEO West County Managed Care, Pinole, Calif., 1991-94; No. Calif. regional adminstr. Mullikin Med. Enterprises, San Bruno, Calif., 1994-96; v.p. mergers and acquisitions MedPartners Inc., Long Beach, Calif., 1996-97; regional v.p. No. Calif. br. MedPartners Inc., Pinole, 1998—; project mgr. logistics automation, 1983, 85. Avocations: auto collecting and racing, hunting, hiking, travel. Home: 327 Duperu Dr Crockett CA 94525-1571

OSTERHOFF, JAMES MARVIN, retired telecommunications company executive; b. Lafayette, Ind., May 18, 1936; s. Abel Lyman and Mildred Paulene (Post) O.; m. Marilyn Ann Morrison, Aug. 24, 1958; children—Anne Michelle Bitsie, Amy Louise Olmsted, Susan Marie. B.S.M.E., Purdue U., 1958, M.B.A., Stanford U., 1963. Staff asst. FMC Corp., San Jose, Calif., 1963-64; with Ford Motor Co., Dearborn, Mich., 1964-84; v.p. fin. Ford Motor Credit Co., Dearborn, 1973-75; controller car ops. N. Am. Automotive Ops., Ford Motor Co., Dearborn, 1975-76; asst. controller N. Am. Automotive Ops., Ford Motor Co., 1976-79; [illegible] Ford Motor Co., Troy, Mich., 1979-84; v.p. fin., CFO Digital Equipment Corp., Maynard, Mass., 1985-91; exec. v.p., CFO U.S.West Inc., Englewood, Colo., 1991-95; bd. dirs. GenCorp, Inc., FSA Holdings, Ltd., Pvt. Sector Coun., Colo. Neurol. Inst., Goodwill Industries of Denver. Served to lt.

(j.g.) USN, 1958-61. Recipient Disting. Engring. Alumnus award Purdue U.; named Outstanding Mech. Engring. Alumnus, Purdue U.

OSTERKAMP, DALENE MAY, psychology educator, artist; b. Davenport, Iowa, Dec. 1, 1932; d. James Hiram and Bernice Grace (La Grange) Simmons; m. Donald Edwin Osterkamp, Feb. 11, 1951 (dec. Sept. 1951). BA, San Jose State U., 1959, MA, 1962; PhD, Saybrook Inst., 1989. Lectr. San Jose (Calif.) State U., 1960-61, U. Santa Barbara (Calif.) Ext., 1970-76; prof. Bakersfield (Calif.) Coll., 1961-87, prof. emerita, 1987—; adj. faculty, counselor Calif. State U., Bakersfield, 1990—; gallery dir. Bakersfield Coll., 1964-72. Juried group shows include Berkeley (Calif.) Art, Ctr., 1975, Libr. of Congress, 1961, Seattle Art Mus., 1962. Founder Kern Art Edn. Assn., Bakersfield, 1962, Bakersfield Printmakers, 1976. Staff sgt. USAF, 1952-55. Recipient 1st Ann. Svc. to Women award Am. Assn. Women in C.C., 1989. Mem. APA, Assn. for Women in Psychology, Assn. for Humanistic Psychology, Calif. Soc. Printmakers. Home: PO Box 387 Glennville CA 93226-0387 Office: Calif State Univ Stockdale Ave Bakersfield CA 93309

OSTERKAMP, WAITE ROBERT, hydrologist; b. Richmont Hts., Mo., Nov. 7, 1939; s. Clifton Grover and Constance E. (Waite) O.; m. Liinda Kautz Smith, Mar. 21, 1987. BA in Geology, U. Colo., 1961, BA in Chemistry, 1963; MS in Geology, U. Ariz., 1970, PhD in Geology, 1976. Chemist U.S. Geol. Survey, Helena, Mont., 1966-68; hydrologist U.S. Geol. Survey, Tucson, 1971-74, rsch. hydrologist, 1991—; hydrologist U.S. Geol. Survey, Lawrence, Kans., 1974-80; rsch. hydrologist U.S. Geol. Survey, Reston, Va., 1980-87, Denver, 1987-91; rsch. assoc. U. Ariz., Tucson, 1969-71; adj. prof. George Mason U., Fairfax, Va., 1984-87, U. Denver, 1994—, U. Ariz., Tucson, 1995—; sci. adv. com. Internat. Union Geol. Scis., Paris, 1994—; cons. Zuni Indian Nation, St. Johns, Ariz., 1995—, Binghamton Geomorphology, steering com., 1994-97. Author: Perenniial-Streamflow Characteristics, 19882, An Analytical Treatment of Channel Geometry, 193, Magnitude and Frequency of Debris Flows, 1986; editor: Effects of Scale-Sediment and Water Quality, 1995. Sci. adv. panel Rincon Inst., Tucson, 1994—; expert witness Snake River Adjudication, Boise, Idaho, 1994—. Recipient Superior Svc. award U.S. Dept. Agrl., Washington, 1990, Cmty. Conservation award Rincon Inst., 1997. Fellow Geol. Soc. Am.; mem. Quaternary Geology & Geomorphology (mgmt. bd. 1993-95), Am. Geophys. Union, Internat. Union Geol. Scis. (sci. adv. 1994—), Internat. Assn. Hydrolog. Scis. Avocations: hiking, wildlife photography. Office: US Geol Survey 1675 W Anklam Rd Tucson AZ 85745-2633

OSTERLI, PHILIP P., agricultural educator; b. Visalia, Calif., Aug. 30, 1940; s. Victor Philip and Leona Otelia (Haugen) O.; m. Nancy Linda Graham, Sept. 2, 1966 (div. Jan. 1, 1985); children: Philip, Jr., Karin, James, Krista. BS, U. Calif., Davis, 1963, MS, 1971. Army advisor U.S. Army, various, 1966-69; staff rsch. assocs. U. Calif., Davis, 1970-72; farm advisor U. Calif. Cooperative Ext., Modesto, 1972-86, county dir., 1986—; bd. dirs. Calif. Crop Improvement Assn., Davis, 1991—; pres. U. Calif. Coop. Ext. Acad. Assembly, 1995. Bd. dirs. Calif. Aggie Alumni Assn., U. Calif. Davis, 1986-90. Col. U.S. Army Res., 1965-91. Mem. Calif. Assn. of Farm Advisors (pres. 1977—), Am. Soc. Agronomy (bd. dirs. Calif. chpt. 1972—), Nat. Assn. County Agr. Agts. (bd. dirs. 1976—). Republican. Lutheran. Avocations: boating, fishing, athletics. Office: Y Calif Coop Ext 3800 Cornucopia Way Ste A Modesto CA 95358-9492

OSTROM, PHILIP GARDNER, computer company executive; b. New Haven, Aug. 8, 1942; s. David McKellar and Barbara (Kingsbury) O.; m. Toni Hammons, Dec. 21, 1965; n. Nancy Jean Kahl, Apr. 2, 1983; children: Eric Craig, Paige Lynne. BS, U. Ariz., 1965; postgrad., U. Calif., 1992-94. Cert. sr. examiner quality control, Calif. Sales mgr. Procter & Gamble Co., Louisville, 1968-70, Dun & Bradstreet, L.A., 1970-71; internat. sales mgr. Memorex Corp., Santa Clara, Calif., 1971-82; dir. ops. Memtek Products, Campbell, Calif., 1982-86, Victor Techs., Scotts Valley, Calif., 1986-88; ops. mgr. Apple Computer, Cupertino, Calif., 1988-93; pres./CEO Ostrom & Assocs., San Jose, Calif., 1993—; ISO9000 lead assessor, 1992—. Spl. examiner CCQS, State of Calif., 1994—, presiding judge; examiner Malcolm Baldridge award, 1993-98. Capt. USMC, 1965-68. Office: Ostrom & Assocs 1099 Maraschino Dr M/S07PG0 San Jose CA 95129-3317

OSTROVSKY, LEV ARONOVICH, physicist, oceanographer, educator; b. Vologda, USSR, Dec. 10, 1934; s. Ahron L. Ostrovsky and Lidiya A. (Warshawskaya) Khvilivitskaya; children: Svetlana, Alexander. Cert. rsch. physicist in radiophysics, U. Gorky, USSR, 1957; PhD, U. Gorky, 1964; Dr Sci, Acoust. Inst., Moscow, 1973. Lead engr. Design Bureau, Gorky, 1957-59; asst. prof., then assoc. prof. physics Poly. Inst., Gorky, 1962-65; sr. researcher Radiophys. Rsch. Inst., Gorky, 1965-77; chief scientist and head lab. Inst. Applied Physics Russian Acad. Sci., Nizhni Novgorod (formerly Gorky), 1977—; assoc. prof to prof. U. Nizhni Novgorod, 1966-94; prof. sr. rsch. scientist U. Colo., Boulder, 1994—. *Lev Ostrovsky contributed to a variety of scientific areas: applied mathematics, fluid mechanics, oceanography, acoustics, laser optics. Designed and presented several new courses for graduate and undergraduate students. Discovered new types of waves and wave equations ("Ostrovsky Equation"). Has been an invited visitor in several leading universities in the U.S., Britain, Australia, France, and others. With a group of scientists and students, created a parametric generator of sound; suggested an "accoustic maser"; performed laboratory experiments on electromagnetic solitons, hydrodynamic turbulence and internal waves, and others. Dived around 1620 meters below the Indian Ocean in a submerged apparatus.* Co-author: Nonlinear Wave Processes in Acoustics, 1990, English edit., 1998, Modulated Waves, 1999; author or co-author 3 lectr. notes, numerous articles in profl. jours., patented various inventions; editor 3 book translations from English to Russian, 3 paper collection books, a topical dictionary; mem. editorial and adv. bds. Chaos, Ultrasonics, various Russian sci. jours. Recipient State Prize of USSR, 1985, USSR State Discovery Cert., 1981. Fellow Acoustical Soc. Am.; mem. Acoustical Soc. Russia (mem. governing body), European Geophys. Soc., Am. Geophys. Union. Office: LANL IGPP MS C305 Los Alanese NM 87545

OSWALD, CHRISTINA METCALF, lawyer; b. Chattanooga, Dec. 4, 1962; d. Kenneth Bertram and Isolde Elsa (Günther) Metcalf; m. Timothy John Oswald. BA in History, BFA in Music summa cum laude, Tulane U., 1985; JD, U. Calif., Berkeley, 1988. Bar: Calif. 1989, U.S. Dist. Ct. (ctrl. dist.) Calif. 1989. Assoc. Greenberg, Glusker, Fields, Claman & Machtinger, L.A., 1988-92; counsel The Walt Disney Co., Burbank, Calif., 1992-94, sr. counsel, 1994-97, exec. counsel, 1998—. Recipient scholarship German Acad. Exch., 1988, 3d Nat. prize Nathan Burkan Meml. Competition in Copyright, 1988. Mem. ABA, L.A. County Bar Assn. (intellectual property divsn. 1989—), Nat. Acad. Songwriters, L.A. Songwriters Symposium, Phi Beta Kappa. Lutheran. Avocation: music-piano and songwriting. Office: Walt Disney Co 500 S Buena Vista St Burbank CA 91521-0004

OTANEZ, ANDREA KAYE, editor; b. Salt Lake City, Feb. 23, 1963; d. Raymond (Frank) and Sylvia (Kaye) Otanez; m. Michael Steven Carter, Aug. 22, 1987; children: Ella Sofia Otanez Carter, Rosa Lucille Otanez Carter. BA in Comm., U. Utah, 1986, BA in French, 1986, MA in English, 1989; student, Publishing Inst./U. Denver, 1990. Copy editor The Salt Lake Tribune, Salt Lake City, 1983-87; tchg. asst. Chicano studies U. Utah, Salt Lake City, 1987-89; features editor McGraw-Hill, Provo, Utah, 1990; editl. intern, then acquisitions editor U. N.Mex. Press, Albuquerque, 1990-92; news editor The Salt Lake Tribune, 1992-94, columnist, 1994-96; freelance editor-at-large Andrea Otanez, Inc., Lit. Svcs., Salt Lake City, 1994-98; assigning editor The Seattle Times, 1999—; bd. dirs., publicity Writers at Work, Salt Lake City, 1996-98; bd. dirs. Voices of the West, Salt Lake City, 1995-96. Editor numerous books on Mexican-Ams., 1990—; author newspaper columns. Utah Arts Coun./Arts in Edn. Panel, Salt Lake City, 1996-98. Minority Pub. fellow Am. Assn. Univ. Presses/Met. Life Found., 1990-91. Mem. Nat. Assn. Hispanic Journalists, Nat. Assn. Chicano/Chicana Studies. Avocations: skiing, hiking, gardening.

OTAYA, MICHIKO, nurse; b. Iwakuni-City, Japan, Mar. 14, 1949. AA, L.A. City Coll.; BSN, Calif. State U., L.A., 1974, BA in Japanese Lit., 1980. RN, Calif. Nurse trainee to charge nurse ICU L.A. County/U. So. Calif. Med. Ctr., 1975-79; pub. health nurse various clinics, L.A., 1979-87; clinic coord. L.A. County, Cen. Dist. Health Ctr., 1979-92; HIV/Tb rsch. nurse Los Angeles County/U. So. Calif. Med. Ctr., 1992—; speaker in field. Contbr. to The Japanese Jour. for the Pub. Health Nurse. Mem. Calif. Thoracic Soc., Am. Lung Assn. (edn. coms.), So. Calif. Pub. Health Assn., Temple City Toastmasters. Home: PO Box 1435 San Gabriel CA 91778-1435

OTERO-SMART, INGRID AMARILLYS, advertising executive; b. Santurce, P.R., Jan. 9, 1959; d. Angel Miguel and Carmen (Prann) Otero; m. Dean Edward Smart, May 4, 1991; 1 child, Jordan. BA in Comm., U. P.R., 1981. Traffic mgr. McCann-Erickson Corp., San Juan, P.R., 1981-82, media analyst, 1982, asst. account exec., 1982-83, account exec., 1983-84, sr. account exec., 1984-85, account dir., 1985-87; account supr. Mendoza-Dillon & Assocs., Newport Beach, Calif., 1987-89, sr. v.p. client svcs., 1989-96, exec. v.p., dir. client svcs., 1996—. Mem. Youth Motivation Task Force, Santa Ana, Calif., 1989—; bd. dirs. Orange County Hispanic C. of C., Santa Ana, 1989-90, U.S. Hispanic Family of Yr.; mem. Santa Ana Project P.R.I.D.E., 1993. Mem. Assn. Hispanic Advt. Agys. (bd. dirs. 1998—). Avocations: reading, writing, antiques, music, theater. Office: Mendoza-Dillon & Assocs 4100 Newport Place Dr Ste 600 Newport Beach CA 92660-2439

O'TOOLE, ROBERT JOHN, II, telemarketing consultant; b. Binghamton, N.Y., Mar. 24, 1951; s. Robert John and Joan Ceclia (Martin) O'T.; m. Donna Sue Stevenson, Jan. 28, 1978 (div. 1984); 1 child, Irene Grace; m. Karen Irene Cady, Dec. 21, 1994. Student, Corning (N.Y.) C.C., 1969-71, SUNY, Brockport, 1970-71; BA, Wake Forest U., 1973; MBA, Southwestern Coll., 1986. Asst. dir. devel. Duvall Home for Children, DeLand, Fla., 1978-81; gen. mgr. Royale Art Advt., Odessa, Tex., 1981-82; v.p. Barnes Assocs. Advt., Odessa, 1982-84, Tex. Assn. for Blind Athletes, Austin, 1985-86; sales mgr. Los Amables Pub., Albuquerque, 1987-88; dir. devel. Albuquerque (N.Mex.) Help for the Homeless, 1988-91; chmn., CEO Advantage Ventures, Inc. (formerly Advantage Mktg., Inc.), Albuquerque, 1991—; CEO LaCourt, Medina & Sterling, Albuquerque, 1993-96; cons. Nat. Child Safety Coun., Austin, 1985, Assn. Profl. Fire Fighters, Austin, 1985, Reynolds Aluminum, Austin, 1986, N.Mex. State Legis., 1990, Children's Charity Fund, 1996, N.Am. Found. for AIDS Rsch., 1992-93, N.Am. Pediatric AIDS Found., 1995. Author: Telemarketing Tickets, 1988, Fishing Secrets of the Florida Poachers, 1993; founder, editor: (newspaper) Albuquerque Street News, 1990; publisher: (newspaper) The New Mexican, 1991; contbr. articles to jours. Founder Permian Basin Rehab. Ctr., Odessa, 1983, Albuquerque (N.Mex.) Help for the Homeless, Inc., 1988. Recipient Cert. of Merit, Small Bus. Adminstrn., Odessa, 1984. Mem. Direct Mktg. Assn., Amnesty Internat. Avocations: restoration of historic bldgs., archeo-geomantics, travel. Office: Advantage Ventures Inc 1019 2nd St SW # B Albuquerque NM 87102-4124 Address: PO Box 883 Orieon Springs FL 32724

OTOSHI, TOM YASUO, electrical engineer, consultant; b. Seattle, Sept. 4, 1931; s. Jitsuo and Shina Otoshi; m. Haruko Shirley Yumiba, Oct. 13, 1963; children: John, Kathryn. BSEE, U. Wash., 1954, MSEE, 1957. Mem. tech. staff Hughes Aircraft Co., Culver City, Calif., 1956-61; mem. tech. sr. staff Jet Propulsion Lab., Calif. Inst. Tech., Pasadena, 1961—; cons. in field. Recipient NASA New Tech. awards, Exceptional Svc. medal NASA, 1994. Mem. Foothill Master Chorale, Pasadena, Calif., L.A. Bach Festival Chorale. Fellow IEEE (life); mem. Sigma Xi, Tau Beta Pi. Contbr. articles to profl. jours; patentee in field. Home: 3551 Henrietta Ave La Crescenta CA 91214-1136 Office: Jet Propulsion Lab 4800 Oak Grove Dr Pasadena CA 91109-8001

OTT, ANDREW EDUARD, lawyer; b. Vancouver, B.C., Can., Sept. 23, 1962; s. Eduard Karl and Elfriede Marie (Petryc) O. BA in English, Seattle U., 1986, JD, 1989; D (hon.), U. Graz, Austria, 1986. Bar: Wash. 1990, U.S. Dist. Ct. (we. dist.) Wash. 1992. Contract atty. Keller Rohrback, Seattle, Lieff Cabraser Heimann & Bernstein, San Francisco, Jamin, Ebell, Schmitt & Mason, Kodiak, Alaska, 1989—; cons. OMNI Tech. Engring., Bothell, Wash., 1986-97. Actor musicals and theater, 1992, 93, 95, 96, 98; musician Cmty. Orch. and Jazz, 1990-98. Mem. ABA, ATLA, Nat. Assn. Self-Employed. Avocations: snow skiing, soccer, bike riding, running, acting. E-mail: Andrew@JESMKOD.com. Office: Jamin Ebell Schmitt & Mason 323 Carolyn Ave Kodiak AK 99615-6348

OTT, WAYNE ROBERT, environmental engineer; b. San Mateo, Calif., Feb. 2, 1940; s. Florian Funstan and Evelyn Virginia (Smith) O.; m. Patricia Faustina Bertuzzi, June 28, 1967 (div. 1983). BA in Econs., Claremont McKenna Coll., 1962; BSEE, Stanford U., 1963, MS in Engring, 1965, MA in Comm., 1966, PhD in Environ. Engring., 1971. Commd. lt. USPHS, 1966, advanced to capt., 1986; chief lab. ops. br. U.S. EPA, Washington, 1971-73, sr. systems analyst, 1973-79, sr. rsch. engr., 1981-84, chief air toxics and radiation monitoring rsch. staff, 1984-90; vis. scientist dept. stats. Stanford (Calif.) U., 1979-81, 90—; vis. scholar Ctr. for Risk Analysis and dept. stats., civil engring., 1990-93; sr. environ. engr., EPA Atmospheric Rsch. and Exposure Assessment Lab, 1993-95; consulting prof. of civil engring. Stanford (Calif.) U., 1995—; dir. field studies Calif. Environ. Tobacco Smoke Study, 1993-95. Author: Environmental Indices: Theory and Practice, 1976, Environmental Statistics and Data Analysis, 1995; contbr. articles on indoor air pollution, total human exposure to chems., stochastic models of indoor exposure, motor vehicle exposures, personal monitoring instruments, and environ. tobacco smoke to profl. jours. Decorated Commendation medal USPHS, 1977; recipient Nat. Statistician award for outstanding contribution to environ. statistics EPA, 1995, Commendable Svc. Bronze medal for assessing human exposure from motor vehicle pollution, 1996. Mem. Internat. Soc. Exposure Analysis (v.p. 1989-90, Jerome J. Weselowski Internat. award for career achievement in exposure assessmemt 1995), Am. Statis. Assn., Am. Soc. for Quality Control, Air and Waste Mgmt. Assn., Internat. Soc. Indoor Air Quality and Climate, Phi Beta Kappa, Sigma Xi, Tau Beta Pi, Kappa Mu Epsilon. Democrat. Clubs: Theater, Jazz, Sierra. Avocations: hiking, photography, model trains, jazz recording. Developer nationally uniform air pollution index, first total human exposure activity pattern models. Home: 1008 Cardiff Ln Redwood City CA 94061-3678 Office: Stanford U Dept Stats Sequoia Hall Stanford CA 94305

OTTEN, ARTHUR EDWARD, JR., lawyer, corporate executive; b. Buffalo, Oct. 11, 1930; s. Arthur Edward Sr. and Margaret (Ambrusko) O.; m. Mary Therese Torri, Oct. 1, 1960; children: Margaret, Michael, Maureen Staley, Suzanne Hoodecheck, Jennifer. BA, Hamilton Coll., 1952; JD, Yale U., 1955. Bar: N.Y. 1955, Colo. 1959. Assoc. Hodges, Silverstein, Hodges & Harrington, Denver, 1959-64; ptnr. Hodges, Kerwin, Otten & Weeks (predecessor firms), Denver, 1964-73, Davis, Graham & Stubbs, Denver, 1973-86; gen. counsel Colo. Nat. Bankshares, Inc., 1973-93; mem. Otten, Johnson, Robinson, Neff & Ragonetti, P.C., Denver, 1986—; rec. sec. Colo. Nat. Bankshares, Inc., Denver, 1983-93; gen. counsel Regis U., Denver, 1994—; mediator Denver Dist. Ct., 1998—; com. bd. Centura Health, Denver, St. Anthony Hosps., Denver. Lt. USN, 1955-59. Mem. ABA, Colo. Bar Assn., Denver Bar Assn., Am. Arbitration Assn. (panel arbitrators, large complex case panel, mediator panel), Nat. Assn. Securities Dealers (bd. arbitrators), Law club, Univ. Club, Denver Mile High Rotary (pres. 1992-93), Phi Delta Phi. Republican. Roman Catholic. Avocations: hiking, biking, church activities. Home: 3774 S Niagara Way Denver CO 80237-1248 Office: Otten Johnson Robinson Neff & Ragonetti PC 1600 Colorado National Bldg 950 17th St Ste 1600 Denver CO 80202-2828

OTTEN, THOMAS, zoological park director. Student, El Camino Coll., 1965-68, Brigham Young U., 1969. Animal keeper, aquarist Marineland, Rancho Palos Verde, Calif., 1969-70, lead dolphin trainer, 1970-73, curator of mammals, 1973; gen. curator, dep. dir. Point Defiance Zoo & Aquarium, Tacoma, Wash., 1981, zoo dir., 1985—; mem. adj. faculty U. Puget Sound, Tacoma, 1985-90. Contbr. articles to profl. jours. Mem. Am. Assn. Zool. Parks and Aquariums, Internat. Assn. Aquatic Animal Medicine, Internat. Soc. Zooculturalists, Marine Mammal Interest Group (chmn. 1990). Office: Point Defiance Zoo & Aquarium 5400 N Pearl St Tacoma WA 98407-3218*

OTTER, CLEMENT LEROY, lieutenant governor; b. Caldwell, Idaho, May 3, 1942; s. Joseph Bernard and Regina Mary (Buser) O.; m. Gay Corinne Simplot, Dec. 28, 1964; children: John Simplot, Carolyn Lee, Kimberly Dawn, Corinne Marie. BA in Polit. Sci., Coll. Idaho, 1967; PhD, Mindanao State U., 1980. Mgr. J.R. Simplot Co., Caldwell, Idaho, 1971-76, asst. to v.p. adminstrn., 1976-78, v.p. adminstrn., 1978-82, internat. pres., from 1982, now v.p.; lt. gov. State of Idaho, Boise, 1987—. Mem. Presdl. Task Force-AID, Washington, 1982-84; com. mem. invest tech. devel. State Adv. Council, Washington, 1983-84; mem. exec. council Bretton Woods Com., 1984—; mem. U.S. C. of C., Washington, 1983-84. Mem. Young Pres.' Orgn., Sales and Mktg. Execs., Idaho Assn. Commerce and Industry, Idaho Agrl. Leadership Council, Idaho Ctr. for Arts, Idaho Internat. Trade Council, Pacific N.W. Waterways Assn., N.W. Food Producers, Ducks Unltd. Republican. Roman Catholic. Clubs: Arid, Hillcrest Country. Lodge: Moose, Elks. Avocations: jogging, music, art collecting, horse training, fishing. Office: Office of the Lt Gov PO Box 83720 Boise ID 83720-0057*

OTTEVANGER, SUSAN LEE, artist; b. Detroit, June 25, 1951; d. Henry Adrian and Lynette (Olson) Vander Kaay; m. Michael John Ottevanger, Feb. 2, 1983. Student, Coll. Arch. and Design, 1969-72; B Fine Art with studies in Biology, U. Mich., 1972. Art work shown in U.S. and Can., 1967—. Mem. Am. Soc. Marine Artists (signature mem.), Internat. Registry Artists and Artworks. Avocations: sailing, marine wildlife.

OTTO, THOMAS JOSEPH, criminal investigator, educator; b. Farmingdale, N.Y., Feb. 4, 1948; s. Sylvester Joseph and Virginia Marie (DeBaun) O.; m. Mary Bayliss Schnaars, Mar. 20, 1979. BA, Mass. Coll. Liberal Arts, 1979; M of Criminal Justice, U. Colo., 1996. Cert. peace officer, Colo. Lead investigator divsn. consumer fraud Adams County Dist. Atty. Office, Brighton, Colo., 1987—; part-time instr. Aims C.C., Greeley, Colo., 1997—; adj. faculty Commonwealth U., Denver, 1998—. Author: A Career Criminal Speaks, 1997. Fundraiser Am. Cancer Soc., 1992-94. Mem. Am. Criminal Justice Assn. (Grad. Key award 1997), Met. Law Enforcement Assn., Colo. State Investigators Assn., Colo. Dist. Atty.'s Coun. Investigators Assn. (mem. tng. com. 1987—). Avocations: reading, hiking, sailing, shooting, cooking. Office: Adams County DA Office 450 S 4th Ave Brighton CO 80601-3123

OTUS, SIMONE, public relations executive; b. Walnut Creek, Calif., Jan. 10, 1960; d. Mahmut and Alexa (Artemenko) O. BA, U. Calif., Berkeley, 1981. Account exec. Marx-David Advt., San Francisco, 1981-82; freelance writer Mpls. and San Francisco, 1982-83; account exec. D'Arcy, MacManus & Masius, San Francisco, 1983; account supr. Ralph Silver Assocs., San Francisco, 1984-85; ptnr., co-founder Blanc & Otus Pub. Relations, San Francisco, 1985—. Address: Blanc & Otus Pub Rels 135 Main St Ste 1200 San Francisco CA 94105-1816

OUELLETTE, REGINALD A., oil industry executive; b. Lewiston, Maine, Apr. 18, 1917; s. Pierre and Virginia (Gosselin) O.; widowed. PhD, Edinburgh (Scotland) U., 1945; MBA, Northwestern U., Evanston, Ill., 1947; postgrad., Yale U., 1951. Pres. Lewis-Clark Coll., Lewiston, Idaho, 1951; faculty Wash. State U., Pullman, 1955; pres., CEO Petro/Excell Ltd., Spokane, 1972; sr. rsch. asst. Sacred Heart Med. Ctr., Spokane, 1992. Founder Internat. Lang. Bank Inland Empire, 1972. Col. USAF, 1952. Fulbright fellow, Spokane, Wash., 1996. Mem. BPO Elks Club (life; past exalted ruler), Spokane Country Club. Democrat. Roman Catholic. Avocations: performing arts, violinist, New England symphony, L.A. Symphony. Office: Petro Excell Ltd PO Box 2 Spokane WA 99210-0002

OUZTS, EUGENE THOMAS, minister, secondary education educator; b. Thomasville, Ga., June 7, 1930; s. John Travis and Livie Mae (Strickland) O.; m. Mary Olive Vineyard, May 31, 1956. BA, Harding U., 1956, MA, 1957; postgrad., Murray State U., U. Ark., U. Ariz., Ariz. State U., No. Ariz. U. Cert. secondary tchr., Ark., Mo., Ariz.; cert. c.c. tchr., Ariz.; ordained minister Church of Christ, 1956. Min. various chs., Ark., Mo., Tex., 1957-65; tchr. various pub. schs., Ark., Mo., Ariz., 1959-92; min. Ch. of Christ, Clifton and Morenci, Ariz., 1965—; 1st lt. CAP/USAF, 1980, advanced through grades to lt. col., 1989; chaplain CAP/USAF, Ariz., 1982—; asst. wing chaplain CAP/USAF, 1985—; adviser student activities Clifton (Ariz.) Pub. Schs., 1965-92; bd. dirs. Ariz. Ch. of Christ Bible Camp, Tucson, 1966—. Mem. airport adv. bd. Greenlee County, Clifton, Ariz., 1992—. Recipient Meritorious Svc. award, 1994, Exceptional Svc. award, 1997, Civil Air Patrol; named Ariz. Wing Chaplain of Yr, 1984, Thomas C. Casaday Unit Chaplain of Yr., 1985, Ariz. Wing Safety Officer of Yr., 1989, Ariz. Wing Sr. Mem. of Yr., 1994, Southwest Region Sr. Mem. of Yr., 1995, Civil Air Patrol. Mem. Mil. Chaplains Assn., Disabled Am. Vets., Am. Legion, Elks. Democrat. Avocations: flying, building and flying model aircraft, reading. Home and Office: HC 1 Box 557 Duncan AZ 85534-9720

OVE, ROBERT STEPHEN, clergyman, writer; b. Racine, Wis., Apr. 6, 1927; s. Vernor Herbert and Helen Evangeline (Hanson) O.; m. Doris E. Gils, Aug. 1948 (div. Mar. 1966); children: Matthew, Marcia; m. Barbara Agnes Martin, Dec., 1966 (div. May 1982); children: Karen Baxter, Christopher Ove, Peter Ove; m. Patricia Kay McCoy, Aug. 9, 1987; children: Joy Freeman, James Strikland. BA, Carthage (Ill.) Coll., 1949; student, State U. Iowa, 1951; MDiv, Wittenberg U., 1958. Ordained to ministry Luth. Ch. Pastoral asst. First Luth. Ch., Dayton, Ohio, 1958-60, Good Shepherd Luth. Ch., Pearl River, N.Y., 1960-61; pastor Good Shepherd Luth. Ch., Weehawken, N.J., 1961-66; pastoral asst. Trinity Luth. Ch., Phila., 1966-68, St. John's Luth. Ch., Helena, Mont., 1968-69; chaplain Webster State Coll., Ogden, Utah, 1969-73; pastor First Congregational Ch., Ogden, Utah, 1969-73, Ripon & Salida, Calif., 1973-76; pastor Bethlehem and Our Saviours Luth. Ch., Dalum & Hussar AB, Can., 1976-81, Christ Luth. Ch., Cheyenne, Wyo., 1981-92; seminary prof., pastor Mission Bd. Evangel. Luth. Ch. in Am., Kathmandu, Nepal, 1996-97, ret., 1997—. Author: Mafia Princess, 1996 (best story award 1996), Geronimo's Kids, 1997; editor, author Preacher Feature, 1994-97. Chaplain City Jail, Ogden, Utah, 1970-73, Laramie County Sheriffs, Cheyenne, Wyo., 1982-87. Recipient award Laramie County Cmty. Coll., 1998. Mem. Retired Evangel. Luth. Ch. in Am. Pastors, Rio Rancho Writers, German Club, Scandinavian Club. Avocations: photography, travel. Home: 6171 Roadrunner Loop NE Rio Rancho NM 87124

OVERGAARD, WILLARD MICHELE, retired political scientist, jurisprudent; b. Montpelier, Idaho, Oct. 16, 1925; s. Elias Nielsen and Myrtle LaVerne (Humphrey) O.; m. Lucia Clare Cochrane, June 14, 1946; children: Eric Willard, Mark Fredrik, Alisa Claire. B.A., U. Oreg., 1949; Fulbright scholar, U. Oslo, 1949-50; M.A. (non-resident scholar 1954-55), U. Wis., Madison, 1955; Ph.D. in Polit. Sci. (adminstrv. fellow 1955-56, research fellow 1962-64), U. Minn., 1969. Instr., Soviet and internat. affairs Intelligence Sch., U.S. Army, Europe, 1956-62; dir. intelligence rsch. tng. program Intelligence Sch., U.S. Army, 1958-61; asst. prof. internat. affairs George Washington U., 1964-67; sr. staff polit. scientist Ops. Research Inst., U.S. Army Inst. Advanced Studies, Carlisle, Pa., 1967-70; assoc. prof. polit. sci., chmn. dept., dir. Internat. Studies Inst., Westminster Coll., New Wilmington, Pa., 1970-72; prof. polit. sci. and pub. law Boise (Idaho) State U., 1972-94, chmn. dept., 1972-87, acad. dir. M.P.A. degree program, personnel adminstr., mem. humanities council interdisciplinary studies in humanities, 1976-87, prof. of pub. law emeritus, 1994—, dir. Taft Inst. Seminars for Pub. Sch. Tchrs., 1985-87, coord. Legal Asst. Program, 1990-95; mem. comml. panel Am. Arbitration Assn., 1974—; mem. Consortium for Idaho's Future, 1974-75; adv. com. Idaho Statewide Tng. Program Local Govt. Ofcls., 1974-78; adv. group Gov. Idaho Task Force Local Govt., 1977; co-dir. Idaho State Exec. Inst., Office of Gov., 1979-83; grievance hearing officer City of Boise, 1981-85; arbitrator U.S. Postal Svc., 1988-90; cons. in field. Author: The Schematic System of Soviet Totalitarianism, 3 vols, 1961, Legal Norms and Normative Bases for the Progressive Development of International Law as Defined in Soviet Treaty Relations, 1945-64, 1969; co-author: The Communist Bloc in Europe, 1959; editor: Continuity and Change in International Politics, 1972; chief editor: Idaho Jour. Politics, 1974-76. Served with USAAF, 1943-45; with AUS, 1951-54; ret. maj. USAR. Named Disting. Citizen of Idaho Idaho Statesman, 1979; named Outstanding Prof. of Sch. Social Scis. and Pub. Affairs, Boise State U., 1988. Mem. ABA (assoc.), Res. Officers Assn. (life). Home: 2023 S Five Mile Rd Boise ID 83709-2316

OVERHOLT, MILES HARVARD, cable television consultant; b. Glendale, Calif., Sept. 30, 1921; s. Miles Harvard and Alma Overholt; A.B., Harvard Coll., 1943; m. Jessie Foster, Sept. 18, 1947; children: Miles Harvard, Keith Foster. Mktg. analyst Dun & Bradstreet, Phila., 1947-48; collection mgr. Standard Oil of Calif., L.A., 1948-53; br. mgr. RCA Svc. Co., Phila., 1953-63, ops. mgr. Classified Aerospace project RCA, Riverton, N.J., 1963; pres. CPS, Inc., Paoli, Pa., 1964-67; v.p. Gen. Time Corp.; mem. pres.'s exec. com. Gen. Time Corp., Mesa, Ariz., 1970-78; gen. mgr., dir. svc. Talley Industries, Mesa, 1967-78; v.p., gen. mgr. Northwest Entertainment Network, Inc.,

Seattle, 1979-81; v.p., dir. Cable Communication Cons., 1982—; mcpl. cable cons., 1981—; pub. The Mcpl. Cable Regulator. Served with USMCR, 1943-46. Decorated Bronze Star, Purple Heart (two). Mem. Nat. Assn. TV Officers and Advisors. Home: 8320 Frederick Pl Edmonds WA 98026-5033 Office: Cable Communication Cons 502 E Main St Auburn WA 98002-5502

OVERLY, FREDERICK DEAN, civilian military employee, entrepreneur; b. Miami, Fla., Jan. 2, 1953; s. Harry Robert and Beverly Beryl (Dengler) O.; m. Cheryl Diane Battle, June 23, 1975 (div. Aug. 1976); Joanne Elizabeth Smart, Dec. 28, 1979; children: Heidi Johanna, Melissa Elizabeth Emma. AA in Forestry, Fla. Jr. Coll., Jacksonville, 1975; BS in Ethology, So. Ill. U., 1980. Pers. officer First Interstate Bank, Anchorage, Alaska, 1985; pers. mgmt. Alaska NG, Anchorage, 1986-89, mgmt. analyst, 1989-96; logistics plans Alaska NG, 1996—; cons. Kaladi Bros. Coffee Co., Inc., Anchorage, 1989—. Participant Alaska Pacific rim issue, Commonwealth North, Anchorage, 1993. Maj. USAF, 1980-84; lt. col. Alaska Air N.G., 1984—. Mem. Res. Officers Assn., Air Force Assn. (past pres. chpt. 103), Found. N.Am. Wild Sheep, Alaska NG Officer Assn., Safari Club Internat., Roll-Royce Owners Club, Rotary Internat. Lutheran. Avocations: hunting, antique automobile collecting, game bird raising, gun dogs. Office: Alaskan NG 176 Wing 5005 Raspberry Rd Anchorage AK 99502-1982

OVERSTREET, HON. KAREN A., federal bankruptcy judge. BA cum laude, Univ. of Wash., 1977; JD, Univ. of Oregon, 1982. Assoc. Duane, Morris & Heckscher, Phila., 1983-86; ptnr. Davis Wright Tremaine, Seattle, 1986-93; bankruptcy judge U.S. Bankruptcy Ct. (we. dist.) Wash., Seattle, 1994—; assoc. editor Oregon Law Review; dir. People's Law Sch.; mem. advisory com. U.S. Bankruptcy Ct. (we. dist.) Wash. Mem. Nat. Conf. of Bankruptcy Judges, Wash. State Bar Assn. (creditor-debtor sec.), Seattle-King County Bar Assn. (bankruptcy sec.), Am. Bar Assn., Wash. Women Lawyers Assn. Office: US Bankruptcy Ct Park Place Bldg 1200 6th Ave Ste 424 Seattle WA 98101-3123*

OVERSTREET, ROBERT KINNEAR, architect; b. Jackson, Miss., Oct. 9, 1924; s. Noah Webster and Mabel Bessie (Kinnear) O. BArch, U. Okla., 1954. Registered architect, Calif., Miss. Assoc. architect N.W. Overstreet & Assocs., Jackson, Miss., 1946-52; architect Architect Offices, San Francisco, 1955-58, 1958-63; ptnr., prin. Botsa, Overstreet Assocs., San Francisco, 1963-76, Overstreet, Rosenberg, Gray, San Francisco, 1976-85; architect pvt. practice, Corte Madera, Calif., 1985—. With USN, 1945-47, 52-54. Mem. AIA. Baptist. Avocations: art, construction. Office: 11101 E Turnberry Rd Scottsdale AZ 85255-8058

OVERTON, EDWIN DEAN, campus minister, educator; b. Beaver, Okla., Dec. 2, 1939; s. William Edward and Georgia Beryl (Fronk) O. BTh, Midwest Christian Coll., 1963; MA in Religion, Eastern N.Mex. U., 1969, EdS, 1978; postgrad. Fuller Theol. Sem., 1980. Ordained to ministry Christian Ch., 1978. Minister, Christian Ch., Englewood, Kans., 1962-63; youth minister First Christian Ch., Beaver, Okla., 1963-67; campus minister Central Christian Ch., Portales, N.Mex., 1967-68, Christian Campus House, Portales, N.Mex., 1968-70; tchr. religion, philosophy, counseling Eastern N.Mex. Univ., Portales, 1970—, campus minister, Christian Campus House, 1968—, dir., 1980—; farm and ranch partner, Beaver, Okla., 1963—. State dir. Beaver Jr. C. of C., 1964-65; pres. Beaver High Sch. Alumni Assn., 1964-65; elder Cen. Christian Ch., Portales, 1985-88, 1990-93; chmn. Beaver County March of Dimes, 1966; neighborhood chmn. Portales March of Dimes, 1997; pres. Portales Tennis Assn., 1977-78. Mem. U.S. Tennis Assn., Am. Assn. Christian Counselors, Ea. N.Mex. U. Faith in Life Com. Republican. Club: Lions. Home: 1129 Libra Dr Portales NM 88130-6123 Office: 223 S Avenue K Portales NM 88130-6643

OVIATT, LARRY ANDREW, retired secondary school educator; b. Boone, Iowa, Mar. 13, 1939; s. Eli Charles and T. Mae (Lathrop) O.; children: Julia, Vanessa, Dana. BA, Drake U., Des Moines, 1962; MS, San Diego State U., 1975. Tchr. art San Diego City Schs., 1969-96, mentor tchr., 1992-96; owner Perfect Travel of La Jolla, 1989—; prof. art edn. Calif. State U., Northridge. San Diego dir. Anderson for Pres., 1976; dist. coord. Hedgecock for Mayor, San Diego, 1984; dir. elder Help Corp., San Diego, 1988; v.p. Afrian Am. Mus., 1989-92; pres. Sushi Gallery, 1980-82; bd. dirs. Mingei Internat. Mus., 1983-87; pres. Cmty. Svc. Assn., 1984-88; past pres. Diversionary Theatre, African Am. Mus.; dir. AIDS Walk for Life, 1988, 89; bd. dirs. AIDS Art Alive. Named 1986 Tchr. of Yr. Urban League, 1986, Sec. Art Tchr. of Yr. Calif. Art Tchrs. Assn., 1988, Art Tchr. of Yr. Calif. Art Tchrs. Assn., 1992, Vol. of Yr. San Diego City Schs., 1993. Mem. So. Calif. Art Tchrs. Assn. (pres. 1984-89), Calif. Art Edn. Assn. (dir. 1984-89, conf. adminstr., Art Edn. Tchr. of Yr. award 1992), Nat. Art Edn. Assn. (dir. 1987-93). Avocations: reading, basketball, art. Home: 1571 E Orange Grove Pasadena CA 91104-4727

OVIEDO, TAMARA LENORE, management consultant, photojournalist; b. Scottsdale, Ariz., Jan. 14, 1966; d. Gary Lee Winebrener and Marcella Marie Mika; m. Manuel Rodrigo Oviedo, July 17, 1997. BA in Journalism and Polit. Sci.(cum laude), U. Ariz., 1988. Cert. Scuba instr. Photojournalist Phoenix Gazette, Tucson Citizen, Ariz. Daily Star, 1986-89; freelance photojournalist U.S., Africa, South Am., Caribbean, 1986-98; program mgr., legis. analyst CP Assocs., Arlington, Va., 1991-92; program mgr. Performance Assocs. Internat., Tucson, 1995-98; publs. mgr. IKON Office Solutions, Tucson, Ariz., 1998-99; cons. Cynosure Comm., Tucson, 1998—. Legis. asst. Congressman Jon Kyl, Washington, 1990-91. Recipient Newswriting award Ariz. Coun. on Aging, Spot News Reporting award Soc. Profl. Journalists. Mem. Soc. Profl. Journalists, Nat. Press Photographer's Assn., Soc. Tech. Communicators (bd. dirs. 1997-98), Profl. Assn. Dive Instrs., Divers Alert Network, Phi Beta Kappa, Kappa Tau Alpha. Avocations: scuba diving, sailing, travel, backpacking.

OVITZ, MICHAEL S., communications executive; b. 1946; m. Judy Reich, 1969; 3 children. Grad., UCLA, 1968. With William Morris Agy., 1968-75; co-founder, chmn. Creative Artists Agy., L.A., 1975-95; pres. Walt Disney Co., Burbank, Calif., 1995-97; chmn. exec. bd. dirs. UCLA Hosp. and Med. Ctr.; bd. advisors Sch. Theater, Film and TV UCLA; bd. dirs. Livent, Inc., Gulfstream Aero. Corp., J. Crew Group, Inc. Trustee St. John's Hosp. and Health Ctr., Santa Monica, Calif., Mus. Modern Art, N.Y.C.; bd. govs. Cedars-Sinai Hosp., L.A.; mem. exec. adv. bd. Pediatric AIDS Found.; bd. dirs. Calif. Inst. Arts, Sundance Inst. Mem. Coun. Fgn. Rels., Zeta Beta Tau. Avocations: contemporary art, African antiques, Chinese furniture. Office: Dreyer Edmonds & Assocs 355 S Grand Ave Ste 4150 Los Angeles CA 90071-3117

OWCZAREK, ROBERT MICHAL, physicist; b. Szczecin, Poland, Apr. 20, 1963; s. Stanislaw and Miroslawa (Galaj) O.; m. Hanna Ewa Makaruk. MS, Warsaw (Poland) U., 1988; PhD summa cum laude, Polish Acad. Scis., Warsaw, 1993. Rsch. assoc. Inst. Fundamental Tech. Rsch., 1988-94; assoc. prof. Polish Acad. Scis., Warsaw, 1994—; postdoctoral assoc. Los Alamos (N.Mex.) Nat. Lab., 1997—. Contbr. articles to profl. jours., chpts. to books in field. Fellow for outstanding rschrs., Warsaw, 1994, Internat. fellow Found. for Polish Sci., 1996, Sr. Fulbright fellow, 1997. Mem. Internat. Soc. for Interaction Between Mechanics and Math., Polish Soc. for Applied Electromagnetism, Am. Mathematical Soc. Roman Catholic. Achievements inlcude explaining role of topologically non-trivial vortices in phase transition in He4, finding string-like solution with non-zero helicity. Avocations: classical music, basketball, hiking. Office: Los Alamos Nat Lab MSB213 T13 Los Alamos NM 87545

OWEN, BRADLEY SCOTT, lieutenant governor; b. Tacoma, May 23, 1950; s. Laural Willis; m. Linda Owen; children: Shanie, Dana, Mark, Sherrie, Adam, Royce. Student pub. sch., Germany. State rep. Wash. Ho. Rep., Olympia, 1976-82; state senator Wash. State Senate, Olympia, 1983-96; lt. gov. State Wash., Olympia, 1997—. Mem. Wash. State substance abuse coun., 1997—. Mem. Elks, Kiwanis. Democrat. Office: Wash State Lt Gov PO Box 40482 Olympia WA 98504-0482*

OWEN, CAROL THOMPSON, artist, educator, writer; b. Pasadena, Calif., May 10, 1944; d. Sumner Comer and Cordelia (Whittemore) Thompson; m. James Eugene Owen, July 19, 1975; children: Kevin Christopher, Christine Celese. Student, Pasadena City Coll., 1963; BA with distinction, U. Redlands, 1966; MA, Calif. State U., L.A., 1967; MFA, Claremont Grad. Sch., 1969. Cert. community coll. instr., Calif. Head resident Pitzer Coll., Claremont, Calif., 1967-70; instr. art Mt. San Antonio Coll., Walnut, Calif., 1968-96, prof. art, 1996—, 1996-97, prof. emeritus, 1997, dir. coll. art gallery, 1972-73. Group shows include Covina Pub. Libr., 1971, U. Redlands, 1964, 65, 66, 70, 78, 88, 92, Am. Ceramic Soc., 1969, 97, Mt. San Antonio Coll., 1991, The Aesthetic Process, 1993, Separate Realities, 1995, San Bernardino County Mus., 1996, 97, 98, Tampa Fla. Black, White & Gray, Artists Unltd., 1998, Current Clay VII, La Jolla, Calif., 1998, Westmoreland Art Nats., 1998, Riverside Art Mus., 1998, Fine Art Inst. Juried Show, San Bernardino, 1998, 99, Parham Gallery, L.A., 1998, Angles Gate Cultural Ctr., San Pedro, Calif., 1998, Los Angeles County Fair, Pomona, Calif., 1998, Monrovia Arts Festival, 1998, Art for Heavens Sake Festival, 1998, Riverside Art Mus., 1998, Birger Sandzen Meml. Gallery, McPherson, Kans., 1998, Earthen Art Works Gallery, L.A., 1999, State Polytechnic U., Pomona, 1999, others; ceramic mural commd. and installed U. Redlands, 1991; represented in permanent collections Redlands Art Assn. Gallery, Parham Gallery, L.A. Recipient award San Bernardino County Mus., 1996, Hon. Mention, 1998, 99; Past Pres.'s Monetary award, 1997, Jack L. Conte Desing Cons. Purchase award Westmoreland Art Nats., 1998, others. Mem. Am. Ceramic Soc. (design divsn.), Calif. Scholarship Fedn., Coll. Art Assn. Am., Calif. Tchrs. Assn., Friends of Huntington Library, L.A. County Mus. Art, Redlands Art Assn., Heard Mus. Assn., Riverside Art Mus., Fine Arts Inst., Sigma Tau Delta. Republican. Presbyterian. Home: 534 S Hepner Ave Covina CA 91723-2921

OWEN, CHARLES THEODORE, journalist, publisher; b. Beech Grove, Ind., June 14, 1941; s. James Robert and Helen Maurine (Sayre) O.; m. Kathleen Rose Dellaria, Apr. 29, 1967. AS in Journalism, Vincennes U., 1972; BA in Social Sci., Chapman U., 1976; MBA, Nat. U. San Diego, 1984. Enlisted U.S. Marine Corps, 1959-72, commd. 2d lt., 1973, advanced through grades to capt., 1979; combat journalist/photographer, Vietnam, 1967-68; dep. dir. Joint Pub. Affairs Office, Camp Pendleton, 1976-79; dir. Pub. Affairs Office, Marine Corps Recruit Depot, San Diego, 1980-81; dir. comm. and mil. affairs div. Greater San Diego C. of C., 1981-82, v.p. 1987—, bd. dirs., 1982-87; now pres., pub. San Diego Bus. Jour., 1987—; host TV program Focus on San Diego Bus. Bd. dirs. San Diego Conv. and Visitors Bur., San Diego Econ. Devel. Corp.; econ. devel. advisor to Mayor of San Diego; presenter in field. Decorated Cross of Gallantry, Joint Svc. Commendation medal with Combat V (3 awards), medal of Honor 2d class (Vietnam); recipient Thomas Jefferson award, 1981. Republican. Pub. Newswriting Program Instruction, 1972. Office: 4909 Murphy Canyon Rd Ste 200 San Diego CA 92123-5381

OWEN, JOHN, retired newspaper editor; b. Helena, Mont., June 10, 1929; s. John Earl and Ella Jean (McMillian) O.; m. Alice Winnifred Kesler, June 9, 1951; children—David Scott, Kathy Lynn. B.A. in Journalism, U. Mont., 1951. Sports editor Bismarck (N.D.) Tribune, 1953-55; wire editor Yakima (Wash.) Herald, 1956; with Seattle Post-Intelligencer, 1956-94, sports editor, 1968-80, assoc. editor, 1980-94, columnist, 1968-94. Author: Intermediate Eater Cookbook, 1974, Gourmand Gutbusters Cookbook, 1980, Seattle Cookbook, 1983, Great Grub Hunt Cookbook, 1989, Press Pass, 1994, Gluttony Without Guilt, 1997; also short stories. Served with AUS, 1951-52. Named Top Sports Writer in Wash. Nat. Sportswriters Orgn., 1966, 68, 69, 71, 74, 85, 88. Home: 611 Bell St Apt 4 Edmonds WA 98020-3065

OWEN, THOMAS JAMES, artist, educator; b. Coca-Rockledge, Fla., Aug. 20, 1945; s. Irwin Arthor and Esther Ethel (Sensinig) O.; m. Judith Lea Pasternak, June 21, 1969 (div. Feb. 1983); m. Koreen Clay, June 26, 1986; 1 child, Gillian Clay. BS in Edn., N.W. Mo. State U., 1968. Cert. tchr., Mo., Nebr. Secondary educator Avon-Grove Sch. Dist., West Grove, Pa., 1968-69, Dist. # 60 Schs., Pueblo, Colo., 1969-72, Wymore (Nebr.) Unified Dist., 1972-73; art educator Sangre De Cristo F.A.C., Pueblo, 1981-86, Colorado Springs (Colo.) F.A.C. Bemis Art Sch., 1982-96, Cottonwood Art Acad., Colo. Springs, 1997—; pvt. practice Black Forest, Colo., 1996—; art dir. Columbine Cellers, Denver and Palisade, Colo., 1989-96; guest instr. Adams State Coll., Alamosa, Colo., 1990-95. Recipient Juror's Choice award San Diego Nat. Watermedia, 1981, Adirondack's Wilderness award, The Rouse Gold medallion, Adirondack's Nat. Exhbn. Am. Watercolors, 1995, Gold Medal New World Internat. Wine Label Competition, 1994, Dr. Martin's award Soc. Watercolor Artists, 1997, Silver Brush award 1999, New West award Watermedia IX, 1998, Meyer award Rocky Mt. Nat. Water Media Exhbn. Signature, 1998, Best Transparent Watercolor Watermedia X, 1999. Mem. Nat. Watermedia Soc. (signature mem., Rocky Mtn. br. bd. dirs. 1982—, Hariett Wexler Bartsch Meml. award 1994), Nat. Watercolor Soc., Colo. Artists Assn. (v.p. 1982-86), Nickerbocker Artists (assoc.), Pikes Peak Watercolor Soc. (v.p. 1990—), Acad. Sertoma Club. Avocations: trout fishing, skiing, model railroading. Home and Office: 11935 Vollmer Rd Colorado Springs CO 80908-4086

OWEN, WILLIAM FREDERICK, engineering and management consultant; b. Pontiac, Mich., July 27, 1947; s. Webster Jennings and Elizabeth (Hayes) W.; m. Delores T. Owen, Mar. 30, 1974 (div. Dec. 1978); m. Janice L. Pierce, July 29, 1983. BS, Mich. Tech. U., 1972; MS, U. Mich., 1973; PhD, Stanford U., 1978. Research engr. Neptune Microfloc, Corvallis, Oreg., 1973-75, process applications engr., 1975-76; process applications engr. Dr. Perry McCarty, Stanford, Calif., 1976-78; sr. engr. Culp/Wesner/Culp, Cameron Park, Calif., 1978-82; pres. Owen Engrng. and Mgmt. Cos., Denver, 1982—. Author: Energy in Wastewater Treatment, 1982, Turbo Mainenance Manager. Del. People-to-People, People's Republic China, 1986. Served with USN, 1965-68. Recipient Local Govt. Innovations award Denver Regional Council Govt., 1983, Boettcher Innovations award Denver Regional Council Govt., 1984, Energy Innovations award Colo. Council Energy Ofcls., 1983. Club: Pinehurst Country (Denver). Avocations: tennis, golf, downhill skiing. Home: PO Box 27749 Denver CO 80227-0749 Office: Owen Engrng and Mgmt Cons Inc 5353 W Dartmouth Ave Denver CO 80227-5515

OWENS, BILL, governor; m. Frances Owens; children: Monica, Mark, Brett. With Touche Ross & Co., Gates Corp.; legis. State of Colo., state treas., 1994-98; gov. State of Colo., Denver, 1999—; guest host Mike Rosen, Ken Hamblin and Chuck Baker talk shows; lectr. Russia. Contbr. more than 50 articles to profl. jours. Named One of Country's Ten Up-and-Coming leaders Robert Novak. Office: Office of Gov 136 State Capitol Bldg Denver CO 80203-1792*

OWENS, PHILLIP REBER, mechanical engineer; b. Downers Grove, Ill., Sept. 8, 1920; s. Thomas John and Georgia Anna (Snowden) O.; m. Sylvia Elizabeth Tyack-Lovegrove, July 25, 1952; stepchildren: Susan Lovegrove Graziano, Sara C. Lovegrove, Robert E. Lovegrove. BSME, Purdue U., 1943. Registered profl. engr., N.Mex. Design engr. Lockheed Aircraft Co., Burbank, Calif., 1943-44; staff mem. Sandia Corp., Albuquerque, 1946-85; owner, pres. The Vertel Co., Albuquerque, 1996—. Author: A History of the Purdue Club of New Mexico: 1950-1988, 1990, (mag.) New Mexico Professional Engineer, 1982-83, 97. Chmn. Sandia dist. Boy Scouts Am., 1956-59; arch.-engr. selection adv. com. mem. Albuquerque, 1988-91. With U.S. Army, 1944-46, Los Alamos, N.Mex. Recipient Silver Beaver award Boy Scouts Am., 1971. Mem. AIAA, ASME, NSPE (v.p. 1975-76, outstanding svc. award 1976), N.Mex. Soc. Profl. Engrs. (Engr. of Year 1974, pres. 1982-83). Republican. Methodist. Achievements include patent allowed for V/STOL aircraft. Avocation: mountain cabin. Home and Office: The Vertel Co 1417 Kirby St NE Albuquerque NM 87112-4541

OWENS, ROBERT PATRICK, lawyer; b. Spokane, Wash., Feb. 17, 1954; s. Walter Patrick and Cecile (Phillippay) O.; m. Robin Miller, Aug. 12, 1978; children: Ryan Barry, Meghan Jane. BA, Wash. State U., 1976; JD, Gonzaga U., 1981; LLM in Admiralty Law, Tulane U., 1983. Bar: Wash. 1982, Alaska 1984, U.S. Dist. Ct. (ea. dist.) Wash. 1982, U.S. Dist. Ct. Alaska 1984, U.S. Ct. Appeals (5th cir.) 1983. Assoc. Groh, Eggers & Price, Anchorage, 1983-88; mng. atty. Taylor & Hintze, Anchorage, 1988-90; [illegible] Copeland [illegible] Wolf [illegible] 1990—, bd. dirs. Cmty. Resources, Inc. Coord. supplies Insight Seminars, Anchorage, 1985-86. Mem. ABA (dist. 27 rep. young lawyers div. 1988-90), Alaska Bar Assn., Wash. State Bar Assn., Anchorage Bar Assn. (pres. 1991-92, v.p. 1990-91, pres. young lawyers sect. 1986-88), Alaska Fly Fishers, Phi Alpha Delta. Roman Catholic. Avocations: fishing, photography, skiing, softball. E-mail: rpowens@clbw.com. Office: Copeland Landye Bennett & Wolf 701 W 8th Ste 1200 Anchorage AK 99501

OWENS, WARNER BARRY, physical therapist; b. Detroit, Apr. 29, 1939; s. Wendell Lee and Flora Lucille (Maddox) O.; m. Frances Hutton, June 11, 1960 (div. May 1973); children—Jeffrey, Karen; m. Sandra Irene Olstyn, Nov. 16, 1974. B.S., UCLA, 1962. Staff phys. therapist Valley Phys. Therapy Ctr., Van Nuys, Calif., 1962-63; chief phys. therapist St. Joseph Med. Ctr., Burbank, Calif., 1963-70, dir. rehab., 1970—, bd. dirs. Credit Union, 1974-76, 83-91, pres., 1986-91; pres. Therapeutic Assocs. Inc., Sherman Oaks, 1992—; dir. Tetrad and Assocs., Sherman Oaks, 1972—; chmn. bd. dirs. Nat. Physical Rehab. Network, Inc.; mem. admissions com. phys. therapy option Calif. State U.-Northridge, 1976—. Childrens Hosp. Sch. Phys. Therapy Kate Crutcher scholar, 1961; recipient Outstanding Contbn. to Profession award Calif. State U.-Northridge, 1983. Mem. Am. Phys. Therapy Assn. (chmn. jud. com. 1981-82), Am. Coll. Sports Medicine, Phys. Therapy Dirs. Forum, Internat. Wine and Food Soc. (bd. dirs. San Fernando Valley 1979—, pres. 1980). Republican. Home: 780 Rockbridge Rd Montecito CA 93108-1127 Office: Therapeutic Assocs Inc 15060 Ventura Blvd Ste 240 Van Nuys CA 91403-2436

OWENS, WILLIAM ARTHUR, career officer; b. Bismarck, N.D., May 8, 1940; s. Earl and Ruth (Arthur) O.; m. Monika Bastian, Sept. 30, 1967; 1 child, Todd. BS, U.S. Naval Acad., 1962; BA, MA, U. Oxford, Eng., 1974; MBA, George Washington U., 1976. Registered profl. engr.. Commd. ensign USN, 1962, advanced through ranks to admiral, 1994, multiple assignments in nuclear submarines, 1962-77; comdg. officer USS Sam Houston (SSBN609), Honolulu, 1977-80, USS Corpus Christi (SSN705), New London, Conn., 1980-81, Submarine Squadron 4, Charleston, S.C., 1984-85, Submarine Group 6, Charleston, S.C., 1987-88; dir. USN Strategic Think Tank Washington, 1988, sr. mil. asst. to Sec. Def., 1988-90; comdr. 6th Fleet, Gaeta, Italy, 1990-92; dep. chief naval ops. Resources, Warfare Requirements & Assessments, Washington, 1992-94; vice-chmn. Joint Chiefs of Staff The Pentagon, Washington, 1994-96; vice chmn., pres./COO Sci. Applications Internat. Corp., 1996-98; vice chmn., CEO Teledesic Holdings, 1998—. Author: Future of the Maritime Strategy, 1988, High Seas, 1994. Mem. Submarine League, U.S. Naval Acad. Alumni Assn., Oxford Soc., Coun. Fgn. Rels. Episcopalian. Avocations: golf, tennis.

OWEN-TOWLE, CAROLYN SHEETS, clergywoman; b. Upland, Calif., July 27, 1935; d. Millard Owen and Mary (Baskerville) Sheets; m. Charles Russell Chapman, June 29, 1957 (div. 1973); children: Christopher Charles, Jennifer Anne, Russell Owen; m. Thomas Allan Owen-Towle, Nov. 16, 1973. BS in Art and Art History, Scripps Coll., 1957; postgrad. in religion, U. Iowa, 1977; DD, Meadville/Lombard Theol. Sch., Chgo., 1994. Ordained to ministry Unitarian-Universalist Ch., 1978. Minister 1st Unitarian Universalist Ch., San Diego, 1978—; pres. Ministerial Sisterhood, Unitarian Universalist Ch., 1980-82; mem. Unitarian Universalist Svc. Com., 1979-85, pres., 1983-85. Bd. dirs. Planned Parenthood, San Diego, 1980-86; mem. clergy adv. com. to Hospice, San Diego, 1980-83; mem. U.S. Rep. Jim Bates Hunger Adv. Com., San Diego, 1983-87; chaplain Interfaith AIDS Task Force, San Diego, 1988—. Mem. Unitarian Universalist Ministers Assn. (exec. com. 1988, pres. 1989-91, African Am. minister's action coun. 1995-98). Avocations: reading, walking, combating racism, promoting human rights, designing environments. Office: 1st Unitarian Universalist Ch 4190 Front St San Diego CA 92103-2030

OWINGS, DONALD HENRY, psychology educator; b. Atlanta, Dec. 7, 1943; s. Markley James and Loyce Erin (White) O.; m. Sharon Elizabeth Calhoun, Jan. 29, 1966; children: Ragon Matthew, Anna Rebekah. BA in Psychology, U. Tex., 1965; PhD, U. Wash., 1972. Asst. prof. psychology U. Calif., Davis, 1971-78, assoc. prof., 1978-83, prof., 1983—, chair dept., 1989-93. Co-editor: (with M.D. Beecher & N.S. Thompson) Perspectives in Ethology, Vol. 12: Communication, 1997; author: (with E.P. Morton) Animal Vocal Communication: A New Approach, 1998; contbr. articles to profl. jours., book chpts. NSF rsch. grantee, 1978-80, 82-84. Fellow Animal Behavior Soc.; mem. Internat. Soc. for Ecol. Psychology, Internat. Soc. for Behavioral Ecology, Internat. Soc. for Comparative Psychology. Democrat. Avocations: hiking, music, bird watching, reading. Home: 815 Oeste Dr Davis CA 95616-1856 Office: U Calif Dept Psychology 1 Shields Ave Davis CA 95616-8686

OWINGS, MARGARET WENTWORTH, conservationist, artist; b. Berkeley, Calif., Apr. 29, 1913; d. Frank W. and Jean (Pond) Wentworth; m. Malcolm Millard, 1937; 1 child, Wendy Millard Benjamin; m. Nathaniel Alexander Owings, Dec. 30, 1953. A.B., Mills Coll., 1934; postgrad., Radcliffe Coll., 1935; LHD (hon.), Mills Coll., 1993. One-woman shows include Santa Barbara (Calif.) Mus. Art, 1940, Stanford Art Gallery, 1951, stitchery exhbns. at M.H. De Young Mus., San Francisco, 1963, Internat. Folk Art Mus., Santa Fe, 1965. Commr. Calif. Parks, 1963-69, mem., Nat. Parks Found. Bd, 1968-69; bd. dirs. African Wildlife Leadership Found., 1968-80, Defenders of Wildlife, 1969-74; founder, pres. Friends of the Sea Otter, 1969-90; chmn. Calif. Mountain Lion Preservation Found., 1987; trustee Environ. Def. Fund, 1972-83; regional trustee Mills Coll., 1962-68; hon. v.p. Nat. Sierra Club, 1997—. Recipient Gold medal, Conservation Svc. award U.S. Dept. Interior, 1975, Convervation award Calif. Acad. Scis., 1979, Am. Motors Conservation award, 1980, Joseph Wood Krutch medal Humane Soc. U.S., Nat. Audubon Soc. medal, 1983, A. Starker Leopole award Calif. Nature Conservancy, 1986, Gold medal UN Environment Program, 1988, Conservation award DAR, 1990, Disting. Svc. award Sierra Club, 1991. Home: Grimes Point Big Sur CA 93920

OWINGS, SUZANN M., consultant, educator; b. L.A., Jan. 26, 1947; d. Theodore Raymond and Elizabeth Marie O'Malley. BA, Calif. State Coll., L.A., 1969; MAT, Ind. U., 1971; PhD, U. N.Mex., 1978. Adminstr. Ind. U., Bloomington, 1970-71; tchr. Compton (Calif.) Sr. High Sch., 1971-75; cons. Owings, Albuquerque, 1975-78; assoc. dir. Energy Consumers of N.Mex., Albuquerque, 1978-79; statewide comprehensive planner CES, N.Mex. State U., Albuquerque, 1979; strategic planner Bechtel Inc., San Francisco, 1979-83; dean Golden Gate U., San Francisco, 1983-84; cons. Bitn Assocs., Corrales, N.Mex. and L.A., 1984—; coord. Albuquerque Pub. Schs., 1992—; instr. mgmt. Troy State U., U. Phoenix, Chapman U.. Co-author, co-editor: Southwest Images and Trends: Factors in Community Development, 1979, numerous others. Co-organizer Rio Rancho 2000, 1992-93; mem., chmn. Sandoval County Intergovtl./Bus. Adv. Coun., Bernalillo, N.Mex., 1993—; mem. Sandoval County Econ. Devel. Com., 1991—. Mem. ASTD (pres.-elect, v.p., bd. dirs.), Am. Soc. for Pub. Adminstrn. (pres.-elect, chairperson Pub. Policy Inst.), Optimist (bd. dirs., pres. N.W. Albuquerque club). Avocations: walking, cycling, gardening. Home: PO Box 872 Placitas NM 87043-0872

OWNBEY, PAMELA JEAN, civil engineer, environmental engineer; b. Eugene, Oreg., Sept. 5, 1953; d. Jelde Gene and Irene Neva (Beshears) Meyer; m. Anthony William Ownbey, May 2, 1972; children: Jill Suzanne, David Timothy. BS in Civil Engring. with high honors, Oregon State U., 1986, MS in Civil Engring., 1987. Registered profl. envirn. and civil engr., Oreg. Assoc. engr. Brown & Caldwell, Eugene, Oreg., 1987-89; civil engr. USDA-Willamette NF, Eugene, Oreg., 1989-95; environ. engr. Cascade Group, Eugene, Oreg., 1989—; civil engr. David Evans and Assocs., Bend, Oreg., 1995—. Guest speaker Childrens Miracle Network Telethon, Eugene, 1989; vol. Childrens Relief Nursery, Buena Vista Spanish Sch., Eugene, 1990-95; asst. coach Kidsports, Eugene, 1992-94. GPOP fellow EPA, 1986. Mem. ASCE, Am. Waterworks Assn., Water and Environ. Fedn., Internat. Conf. Bldg. Ofcls. Home: PO Box 10921 Eugene OR 97440-2921

OZAKI, NANCY JUNKO, performance artist, educator; b. Denver, Feb. 14, 1951; d. Joe Motoichi and Tamiye (Saki) O.; m. Nathan Jeoffrey Inouye, May 25, 1980 (div. Aug. 1985); m. Gary Steven Tsujimoto, Nov. 12, 1989. BS in Edn., U. Colo., 1973; postgrad., U. Colo., Denver, 1977, Metro State Coll., 1982, Red Rocks C.C., 1982-83, U. No. Colo., 1982, U. N.Mex., [illegible] N.Mex., 1973-75, Aurora (Colo.) Pub. Schs., 1977-83, Albuquerque Pub. Schs., 1983-84, Denver Pub. Schs., 1984-87, Oak Grove Sch. Dist., San Jose, Calif., 1988-89, San Mateo (Calif.) City Elem. Dist., 1990-92; performing artist Japanese drums Young Audiences, San Francisco, 1992-93, Denver, 1994-97; performing artist Japanese drums Walt Disney World, Epcot Ctr.,

Orlando, Fla., 1993-97; co-dir., mgr., performer One World Taiko, Japanese Drum Troupe, Arvada, Colo., 1997—. Vol. worker with young Navajo children; co-sponsor girl's sewing and camping groups. Mem. Kappa Delta Pi (Theta chpt.). Avocations: reading, sewing, skiing, hiking, snorkeling. Home: 6713 W 53rd Ave Arvada CO 80002-3937 Office: One World Taiko PO Box 12252 Denver CO 80212-0252

OZANICH, CHARLES GEORGE, real estate broker; b. Fayette County, Pa. Aug. 11, 1933; s. Paul Anthony and Alma Bertha (Sablotne) O.; student Am. River Coll., Sierra Coll.; m. Betty Sue Carman, Feb. 20, 1955; children: Viki Lynn, Terri Sue, Charles Anthony, Nicole Lee. Owner, broker Terrace Realty, Basic Realty, Grass Valley, Calif., 1971—; compliance inspector Dept. Vets. Affairs. Mem. Grass Valley Vol. Fire Dept., 1965-93. Served with USAF, 1951-55; Korea. Decorated Bronze Star with three oak leaf clusters, Korean Presdl. citation, UN citation. Mem. Neveda County Bd. Realtors (dir. 1973-74). Lodges: Am. Legion, Masons, Shriners, Moose (charter mem.). Nat. Champion award Truck Drivers Roadeo class 5 semi-trailer 18 wheeler div., 1954. Home and Office: 15053 Chinook Ln Grass Valley CA 95945-8846

PABISCH, PETER KARL, German language educator; b. Vienna, Austria, Apr. 17, 1938; came to U.S., 1969; s. Ernst and Gertrude (Engel) P.; m. Patricia Ann Trench, Nov. 25, 1959; 1 child, Angela. MA, U. Ill., 1971, PhD, 1974. Tchr. pub. schs. Vienna, 1959-69; dir. summer children's homes Vienna Social Welfare Sys., Italy, 1964-69; co-dir. German summer sch. U. N.Mex., Albuquerque, 1976—, from asst. prof. to assoc. prof., 1972-84, prof., 1984—. Author: (books) Austrian Poet H. C. Artmann, 1978, Modern German Lyrics, 1992, also 4 poetry books; editor 5 books on German and Austrian studies, 1978-94. Decorated Order of Merit 1st Class, Fed. Republic of Germany, 1985, Gt. Order of Merit, Republic of Austria, 1986; recipient Award of Recognition, Goethe-Inst. Munich, 1995, Poetry awards, 1992, 93; named Best German Tchr., Am. Assn. Tchrs. of German, 1982. Democrat. Avocations: skiing, scuba diving, playing music, traveling. Home: 417 Jefferson St NE Albuquerque NM 87108-1279 Office: U N Mex German Program/FLL Albuquerque NM 87131

PACE, FRANK ANTHONY, television producer; b. White Plains, N.Y., Feb. 14, 1950; s. Dominick Edward and Rose T. (Papillo) P.; m. Karen Lynn Huggins, Nov. 5, 1983; 1 child, Erin Lynn. BS in Bus., Jacksonville U., 1972. Co-producer Winner Never Quits ABC, Los Angeles, 1985; producer Head of the Class, Los Angeles, 1986-90; supervising producer Head of the Class, 1991; producer Murphy Brown CBS, 1988; producer Ferris Bueller NBC, 1990, Babe Ruth NBC, 1991, Billy ABC, 1991; producer pilot & series Daddy Dearest FOX, 1993-94, Something Wilder NBC, 1994-95, Bless This House CBS, 1995-96, Suddenly Susan NBC, 1996—; producer For Your Love Warner Bros. Network, 1997—; 1st Am. producer in Moscow, 1988. Author: Rod Carew's Art and Science of Hitting, 1986. Named EMMY nominee Murphy Brown CBS, 1988. Mem. Dirs. Guild Am., Am. Acad. TV Arts and Scis. Office: Warner Bros 4000 Warner Blvd Burbank CA 91522-0002

PACHECO, CAROLE ELIZABETH, architect, educator; b. Opelika, Ala., July 28, 1953; d. Emil Retz and Louise (Cherry) Hargett; m. Peter Francis Pacheco, March 7, 1980 (div.); 1 child, Jesse de Arman Pacheco. BFA in Architecture, U. N. Mex., 1975; M in Architecture, U. Colo., 1992. Architect Gordon Herkenhoff & Assocs., Albuquerque, 1977-80, Leedshill Herkenhoff, Albuquerque, 1981-87, Albuquerque Pub. Schs., 1987; prin., owner Carole Pacheco, Architect, Albuquerque, Denver, 1987—; producer Lunarleaf Films, Denver, 1993-96; designer Legacy Unlimited, Denver, 1989-92; instr. Rocky Mountain Coll. Art & Design, Denver, 1994—. Producer (film) The Cloud Seeders, 1996; photographer, artist Las Puertas De Albuquerque, 1990. Instr. Colo. Literacy Program, Denver, 1998—; restoration fundraiser Cathedral of Immaculate Conception, Denver, 1992. Mem. Nat. Council Architects Registration Bd., Constrn. Specification Inst. (membership chmn. 1997), Denver Lighting Forum, Tau Sigma Delta. Roman Catholic. Avocations: screenplay writing, skiing, scuba diving, ballroom dancing, travel. Office: Rocky Mountain Coll Art and Design 6875 E Evans Ave Denver CO 80224-2329

PACIFIC, JOSEPH NICHOLAS, JR., educator; b. Honolulu, Oct. 27, 1950; s. Joseph Nicholas Sr. and Christine Mary (Mondelli) P.; m. Paulette Kay Miller, July 7, 1975. BA in Math., BS in Biology, BSEE, Gonzaga U., 1974; MMSc in Clin. Microbiology, Emory U., 1978. Cert. tchr., Hawaii, Wash. Rsch. specialist Ctr. Disease Control, Atlanta, 1978-82; supr. Joe Pacific Shoe Repair, Honolulu, 1983; lab. technician Mont. State U., Bozeman, 1984; sci. tchr. Hawaii Preparatory Acad., Kamuela, 1985-87; unit mgr. Hawaii Med. Service Assn., Honolulu, 1987-88; tchr. biology St. Andrew's Priory Sch., Honolulu, 1988—. Mem. Nat. Registry Microbiologists, Sigma Xi, Pi Mu Epsilon, Phi Sigma, Kappa Delta Pi, Alpha sigma Nu. Avocations: microscopy, bicycling. Office: St Andrew's Priory Sch 224 Queen Emma Sq Honolulu HI 96813-2388

PACK, PHOEBE KATHERINE FINLEY, civic worker; b. Portland, Oreg., Feb. 2, 1907; d. William Lovell and Irene (Barnhart) Finley; student U. Calif., Berkeley, 1926-27; B.A., U. Oreg., 1930; m. Arthur Newton Pack, June 11, 1936; children: Charles Lathrop, Phoebe Irene. Layman referee Pima County Juvenile Ct., Tucson, 1958-71; mem. pres.'s council Menninger Found., Topeka; mem. Alcoholism Council So. Ariz., 1960—; bd. dirs. Kress Nursing Sch., Tucson, 1957-67, Pima County Assn. for Mental Health, 1958—, Ariz. Assn. for Mental Health, Phoenix, 1963—, U. Ariz. Found., Casa de los Niños Crisis Nursery; co-founder Ariz.-Sonora Desert Mus., Tucson, 1975—, Ghost Ranch Found., N.Mex.; bd. dirs. Tucson Urban League, Tucson YMCA Youth Found. Mem. Mt. Vernon Ladies Assn. Union (state vice regent, 1962-84),Mt. Vernon One Hundred (founder), Nature Conservancy (life), Alpha Phi. Home: Villa Compana 6653 E Carondelet Dr Apt 415 Tucson AZ 85710-2153

PACKARD, ROBERT GOODALE, III, planner; b. Denver, Apr. 12, 1951; s. Robert and Mary Ann (Woodward) P.; m. Jane Ann Collins, Aug. 25, 1973; children: Jessica Nelson, Robert Gregg. BA, Willamette U., 1973; M in Urban and Regional Planning/Community Devel., U. Colo., 1976. Project mgr. Environ. Disiciplines, Inc., Portland, Oreg., 1973-75; asst. dir. planning Portland Pub. Schs., 1976-78; dir. planning Bur. of Parks, Portland, 1978-79; dir. planning and urban design Zimmer Gunsul Frasca, Portland, 1979-81, dir. project devel., 1981-84, mng. ptnr., 1984—. Co-author: The Baker Neighborhood/Denver, 1976. Contbr. articles to profl. jours. Trustee Willamette U., 1994; mem. City of Portland Waterfront Commn., 1982-83; mem. Mayor's Task Force for Joint Use of Schs., Portland, 1979-80; mem. Washington Park Master Plan Steering com., Portland, 1980-81; bd. dirs. Washington Park Zoo, 1983-86, pres. Arts Celebration Inc./Artquake, 1986—, New Rose Theatre, 1981-83; dir., pres. Grant Park Neighborhood Assn., Portland, 1981-83; pres. Pioneer Square Bd., 1997-98; bd. mem. Regional Arts and Cultural Coun.; mem. Archtl. Found. Oreg., 1992; mem. crafts bd. Oreg. Sch. Arts. Recipient Spl. Citation, Nat. Sch. Bds. Assn., 1978; Meritorious Planning Project award Am. Planning Assn., 1980, Nat. Am. Planning Assn., 1981; Meritorious Design award Am. Soc. Landscape Architects, 1981; Honor award Progressive Arch., 1983. Mem. AIA (Architecture Firm award 1991, assoc.), Am. Planning Assn., Young Pres. Assn., Racquet Club, Arlington Club, City Club, Racquet Club. Home: 3313 SW Fairmount Blvd Portland OR 97201-1478 Office: Zimmer Gunsul Frasca Partnership 320 SW Oak St Ste 500 Portland OR 97204-2737

PACKARD, RONALD C., congressman; b. Meridian, Idaho, Jan. 19, 1931; m. Jean Sorenson, 1952; children: Chris, Debbie, Jeff, Vicki, Scott, Lisa, Theresa. Student, Brigham Young U., 1948-50, Portland State U., 1952-53; D.M.D., U. Oreg., Portland, 1953-57. Gen. practice dentistry Carlsbad, Calif., 1959-82; mem. 98th-106th Congresses from 43rd (now 48th) Dist. Calif., 1983—; chmn. appropriations legis. subcom., former mem. pub. works and transp. com., sci., space, tech., also mem. appropriations fgn. ops. and transp. subcoms. Mem. Carlsbad Sch. Dist. Bd., 1962-74; bd. dirs. Carlsbad C. of C., 1972-76; mem. Carlsbad Planning Commn., 1974-76, Carlsbad City Coun., 1976-78; Carlsbad chmn. Boy Scouts Am., 1977-79; mayor City of Carlsbad, 1978-82; mem. North County Armed Svcs. YMCA, North County Transit Dist., San Diego Assn. Govts., Coastal Policy Com., Transp. Policy Com.; pres. San Diego div. Calif. League of Cities. Served with Dental Corps USN, 1957-59. Republican. Mem. Ch. LDS. Office: US Ho of Reps 2372 Rayburn HOB Washington DC 20515-0548*

PACKER, MARK BARRY, lawyer, financial consultant, foundation official; b. Phila., Sept. 18, 1944; s. Samuel and Eve (Devine) P.; m. Donna Elizabeth Ferguson (div. 1994); children: Daniel Joshua, Benjamin Dov, David Johannes; m. Helen Margaret (Jones) Klinedinst, July, 1995. AB magna cum laude, Harvard U., 1965, LLB, 1968. Bar: Wash. 1969, Mass. 1971. Assoc. Ziontz, Pirtle & Fulle, Seattle, 1968-70; pvt. practice, Bellingham, Wash., 1972—; bd. dirs., corp. sec. BMJ Holdings (formerly No. Sales Co., Inc.), 1977—; trustee No. Sales Profit Sharing Plan, 1977—; bd. dirs. Whatcom State Bank, 1995-98. Mem. Bellingham Planning and Devel. Commn., 1975-84, chmn., 1977-81, mem. shoreline subcom., 1976-82; mem. Bellingham Mcpl. Arts Commn., 1986-91, landmark rev. bd., 1987-91; chmn. Bellingham campaign United Jewish Appeal, 1979-90; bd. dirs. Whatcom Community Coll. Found., 1989-92; trustee, chmn. program com. Bellingham Pub. Sch. Found., 1991—; Heavy Culture classic lit. group, 1991—, Jewish studies group, 1993—; trustee Kenneth L. Kellar Found., 1995—; mng. trustee Bernard M. & Audrey Jaffe Found; pres., toral reader Congregation Eytz Chaim, Bellingham, 1995—. Recipient Blood Donor award ARC, 1979, 8-Gallon Pin, 1988, Mayor's Arts award City of Bellingham, 1993. Mem. Wash. State Bar Assn. (sec. environ. and land use law, sec. bus. law, sec. real property, probate and trust, com. law examiners 1992-94). Office: PO Box 1151 Bellingham WA 98227-1151

PACKWOOD, BOB, retired senator; b. Portland, Oreg., Sept. 11, 1932; s. Frederick William and Gladys (Taft) P.; children: William Henderson, Shyla. BA, Willamette U., 1954; LLB, NYU, 1957; LLB (hon.), Yeshiva U., 1982, Gallaudet Coll., 1983. Bar: Oreg. Law clerk to Justice Harold J. Warner Oreg. Supreme Ct., 1957-58; pvt. atty., 1958-68; chmn. Multnomah County Rep. Cen. Com., 1960-62; mem. Oreg. Legislature, 1963-69; U.S. senator from Oreg., 1969-95, chmn. small bus. com., 1981-84, chmn. commerce com., 1981-85, chmn. fin. com., 1985-86, ranking min. mem. fin. com., 1987-94, chmn. fin. com., 1995, resigned, 1995. Mem. Internat. Working Group of Parliamentarians on Population and Devel., 1977; mem. Pres.'s Commn. on Population Growth and the Am. Future, 1972; chmn. Nat. Rep. Senatorial Com., 1977-78, 81-82; bd. dirs. NYU, 1970; bd. overseers Lewis and Clark Coll., Portland, 1966. Named One of Three Outstanding Young Men of Oreg., 1967; Portland's Jr. 1st Citizen, 1966; Oreg. Speaker of Yr., 1968; recipient Arthur T. Vanderbilt award NYU Sch. Law, 1970; Anti-Defamation League Brotherhood award, 1971; Torch of Liberty award B'nai B'rith, 1971; Richard L. Neuberger award Oreg. Environ. Coun., 1972; Conservation award Omaha Woodmen Life Ins. Soc., 1974; Monongahela Forestry Leadership award, 1976; Solar Man of Yr., Solar Energy Industries Assn., 1980; Guardian of Small Bus. award Nat. Fedn. Ind. Bus., 1980; Forester of Yr., Western Forest Industries Assn., 1980; Am. Israel Friendship award B'nai Zion, 1982; Grover C. Cobb award Nat. Assn. Broadcasters, 1982; Religious Freedom award, Religious Coalition for Abortion Rights, 1983; 22d Ann. Conv. award, Oreg. State Bldg. and Constrn. Trade Council, 1983; United Cerebral Palsy Humanitarian award, 1984; Am. Heart Assn. Pub. Affairs award, 1985; Margaret Sanger award Planned Parenthood Assn., 1985; Worth his Weight in Gold award for leadership on tax reform Gen. Mills., 1986; Am. Assn. Homes for the Aging for Outstanding Svc. in cause of elderly, 1987; NARAL award for congrl. leadership, 1987; James Madison award Nat. Broadcast Editorial Assn., 1987; Pub. Excellence award First Ann. Jacob K. Javits, 1987; Golden Bulldog award Watchdogs of Treasury, Inc., 1988, 90; Sound Dollar award, 1989; Golden Eagle award Nurse Anesthetists, 1990; John F. Hogan Disting. Svc. award Radio-TV News Dirs. for def. of First Amendment, 1991; Nat. Conf. Soviet Jewry recognition, 1992, Space Shuttle Endeavor recognition, 1993, Spirit of Enterprise award U.S. C. of C., 1994, numerous others. Mem. Oreg. Bar Assn., D.C. Bar Assn., Beta Theta Pi. Office: Sunrise Rsch 2201 Wisconsin Ave NW Ste 120 Washington DC 20007-4117*

PADEREWSKI, CLARENCE JOSEPH (SIR), architect; b. Cleve., July 23, 1908. BArch, U. Calif., 1932. Chief draftsman Sam W. Hamill, 1939-44; with Heitschmidt-Matcham-Blanchard-Gill & Hamill (architects), 1943; then practiced as C.J. Paderewski, 1944-48; pres. Paderewski, Mitchell, Dean & Assoc., Inc. (and predecessor), San Diego, 1948-78; instr. adult edn. San Diego city schs., 1939 44, U. Calif. extension div., 1945, 56; Lectr. in field. Prin. works include Charactron Labs, Gen. Dynamics Corp., Convair, S.D., 1954, South Bay Elem. Schs., S.D., 1948-74; additions to El Cortez Hotel; including first passenger glass elevator in the world and New Travolator Motor Hotel, S.D., 1959, Palomar Coll., San Marcos, 1951-80, San Diego County U. Gen. Hosp., San Diego Internat. Airport Terminal Bldgs., Fallbrook Elem. Schs., 1948-74, Silver Strand Elem. Sch., Coronado, Tourmaline Terrace Apt. Bldg., San Diego Salvation Army Office Bldg. Mem. adv. bd. Bayside Social Service Center, 1953-75, San Diego Polonia Newspaper, 1994—; mem. San Diego Urban Design Com.; mem. adv. bd. Camp Oliver, 1963—, pres., 1975-76; bd. dirs. San Diego Symphony Orch. Assn., 1954-62, San Diego chpt. ARC, 1971-74; bd. dirs., chmn. coms., pres. San Diego Downtown Assn., 1963—; bd. dirs. Nat. Council Archtl. Registration Bds., 1958-66, bd. dirs. other offices, 1961-64, pres., 1965-66, chmn. internat. relations com., 1967-68, Salvation Army, vice chmn., 1989, life mem. adv. bd., 1993—, Copernicus Found., 1994—; mem. Calif. Bd. Archtl. Examiners, 1949-61, past pres., commr., 1961—; mem. Nat. Panel Arbitrators, 1953—, Nat. Council on Schoolhouse Constrn.; bd. dirs. Salvation Army, vice chmn., 1989, mem. coms., life mem. adv. bd., 1993—; hon. chmn. Ignacy Jan Paderewski Meml. Com., 1991; adv. bd. S.D. Balboa Park Cmty. Endowment Fund, 1995—. Decorated Knight Order Polonia Restituta, Polish govt. in exile, 1982; recipient Award of Merit for San Diego County Gen. Hosp., San Diego chpt., AIA, 1961, Honor award for San Diego Internat. Airport Terminal, Honor award Portland Cement Co., Golden Trowel award Plastering Inst., 1958-60, 4 awards Masonry Inst., 1961, award Prestressed Concrete Inst., 1976, Outstanding Community Leadership award San Diego Downtown Assn., 1963, 64, 65, 80. Fellow AIA (pres. San Diego chpt. 1948, 49, bd. dirs. 1947-53, chmn. several coms., spl. award 1977, Calif. Coun. Spl. award 1979, Calif. Coun. Disting. Svc. award 1982); mem. San Diego C. of C. (bd. dirs. 1959-62, 64-67), Am. Arbitration Assn. (San Diego adv. coun. 1969—), Sister City Soc. (bd. dirs.), Lions (past pres. Hillcrest Club, Lion of Yr. 1990, fellow internat. found. 1991), Father Serra Club (charter, past pres.), Outboard Boating Club San Diego, Chi Alpha Kappa, Delta Sigma Chi.*. Home: 2837 Kalmia Pl San Diego CA 92104-5418

PADGET, JOHN E., management professional; b. L.A., Aug. 26, 1948; s. LeRoy and Gladys (Black) P. BA, U. Kans., 1969, postgrad., 1970. Instr. bridge Am. Contract Bridge League, 1971-77; owner Hectors, Kirkland, Wash., 1978-84; producer TV show Sta. 2, Oakland, 1985-88; regional mgr. Keithwood Agy.-Am. Health Care Adv., Pleasanton, Calif., 1991—; exec. v.p. J. & J. Warren Co., Walnut Creek, Calif., 1991-97; pres. BBH Ltd., 1997—; pres. BBH Ltd. Author: Winning Style, 1977. Mem. AAAS, Mensa, Internat. Platfrom Soc. Jewish. Avocations: hiking, reading, travel, internet publishing. Office: PO Box 271403 Concord CA 94527-1403

PADILLA, PHILIP K., environmental health safety and risk specialist; b. Denver, Aug. 19, 1961; s. Victoriano Luis and Irene (Vigil) P.; m. Lisa Fiechtner, Aug. 1984; children: Zachary William, Joshua Tyler. BS, Colo. State U., 1986; M of Environ. Mgmt., U. Denver, 1994. Comml. underwriter Safco Ins. Co., Denver, 1986-90; environ. underwriter Environ. Risk Ins. Co., Denver, 1990-93; environ. health safety & risk mgmt. specialist U. Colo., Denver, 1993—; cons. in field. Contbr. articles to profl. jours. Bd. dirs. ACT- Waste Miniumization Rev., Thronton, Colo., 1995-97. Mem. Nat. Assn. Environ. Profls., Am. Soc. Safety Engrs., Am. Soc. Hosp. Engrs., Nat. Fire Protection Assn. Home: 11709 Glencoe Cir Denver CO 80233-1834

PADORR NILLES, LAILA, musician, record producer; b. Chgo., July 25, 1929; d. Abraham Leonard Ginsburg and Jeanette Padorr; m. Jack Mathias Nilles, July 8, 1957. MusB, Northwestern U., 1947, B of Music Edn., 1947, M of Music, 1949; postgrad., Julliard Sch. Music, 1950, 51, Ecoles d'Art Am. Fontainebleau, France, 1953. Founder, dir. Padorr Trio, Chgo. and Los Angeles, 1951-55, 56-72; dir. Concerts at the Mt., Los Angeles, 1958-60; mgr., dir. Concerts West, Los Angeles, 1965-75; freelance musician Los Angeles, 1975-77; asst. dir. Protone Records, Los Angeles, 1977-82, assoc. dir., 1982—; v.p. Jala Internat., Inc., Los Angeles, 1982—; dir. design for Sharing UCLA, L.A., 1984-89, Friends of Music U. So. Calif., 1984-90, Am. Youth Symphony, 1981-88. Soloist: (record) music for Flute and Piano by Four Americans, 1976; co-producer 40 records, cassettes and compact discs, 1977—. Recipient First prize Coleman Auditions, 1956, Young Artists League, 1956. Mem. Audio Engring. Soc., Nat. Acad. Recording Arts and Scis., Musicians Union Local 47. Club: Calif. Yacht (Marina Del Ray). Avocations: photography, sailing, astronomy. Home and Office: 971 Stonehill Ln Los Angeles CA 90049-1412

PADVE, MARTHA BERTONNEAU, urban planning and arts consultant, fundraiser; b. Scobey, Mont., Feb. 22; d. Henry Francis and Marie (Vaccaro) Bertonneau; m. Jacob Padve, May 9, 1954 (div. 1980). Student, Pasadena Jr. Coll., 1938-40; cert., S.W. U. Bus. Coll., L.A., 1940-41, Pasadena Inst. for Radio, 1946-47; student, Claremont Colls., 1972-74, U. So. Calif., 1983-84, Community Coll., Pasadena, 1987-88. Juvenile roles Pasadena (Calif.) Cmty. Playhouse, 1935-37; ptnr., bus. mgr. restaurant devel. ventures, Pasadena, 1940-50; club dir. Red Cross, Nfld., Can., 1944-45; leading roles Penthouse Theatre, Altadena, Calif., 1946-48; club dir. armed forces spl. svcs. Red Cross, Austria, 1949-52; head dept. publs. Henry E. Huntington Libr., San Marino, Calif., 1953-57; cons. art planning Model Cities program, Omaha, 1975; founding instr. contemporary art collecting class, 1979-80; dir. devel. Bella Lewitzky Dance Found., L.A., 1980-81; instr. Art. Ctr. Coll. Design, Pasadena, 1981-82, assoc. dir. devel., 1981-83; instr. U. So. Calif. Coll. Continuing Edn., L.A., 1983-84; urban planning and arts cons. The Arroyo Group, Pasadena, 1979-94; freelance writer, journalist, playwright, 1994—; developer edn. program Mus. Contemporary Art, L.A., 1984-86; author arts segment Pasadena Gen. Plan, 1980-83. Contbr. articles to newspapers. Trustee, v.p. Pasadena Art Mus., 1967-74; co-chair bldg. fund Norton Simon Mus. Art, Pasadena 1968-70; chair Pasadena Planning Commn., 1973-81, Pasadena Street Tree Plan, 1975-76, Pasadena High Rise Task Force, 1979, San Gabriel Valley Planning Coun., 1977-78; mem. Pasadena Downtown Urban Design Plan, 1980-83; founding mem. Arts, Pks. & Recreation Task Force, 1978-80; vice-chair Pasadena Design Review Commn., 1974-78; founding chair So. Calif. Fellows of Contemporary Art, 1976-78; adv. com. U. So. Calif. Art Galleries, 1976-82, UCLA oral history program contemporary art, 1983-94; chair audit com. L.A. County Grand Jury, 1986-87; founder Pasadena Robinson Meml., Inc., 1990-92, bd. dirs. 1992-93; curator Vroman's Art on the Stairwell, 1992—; exec. com. St. Andrew's Sch. Bd., 1993-94; co-chair restoration adv. com. St. Andrew's Ch., 1994; judge Pasadena Tournament of Roses, 1994; bd. dirs. San Juan Cmty. Theatre, 1997—, exec. com., 1999—. Named Woman of the Yr., Pasadena Women's Civic League, 1980; recipient Gold Crown award Tenth Muse, Pasadena Arts Coun., 1983, Commendation awards Pasadena City Dirs., 1975, 80, 82-83, Commendation award L.A. County Bd. Suprs., 1987, Graphic Arts award Southern Calif. Fellows Contemporary Art, 1978. Republican. Roman Catholic. Avocations: theater, music, wine, food. Home and Office: 350 Olympic View Ln Friday Harbor WA 98250-9662

PAGAN, KEITH AREATUS, music educator, academic administrator; b. Beggs, Okla., June 7, 1931; s. Areatus and Opal Gail (Facker) P.; m. Betty Lois Wallace; children: Melva Joy, Lisa Lynne, Beryl Kay. B in Music Edn., Bethany Nazarene Coll., 1952; M in Music Edn., Okla. U., 1953; D in Music Edn. with honors, Ind. U., 1970. Asst. prof. music Bethany (Okla.) Nazarene Coll., 1952-53, 55-58; prof. music Pasadena (Calif.) Coll., 1961-76; acad. dean, v.p. acad. affairs Point Loma Nazarene Coll., San Diego, 1976-88, prof. music, chair dept. music., 1989—; dir. S.W. Music Symposium, San Diego, 1991—; cons. Sch. for Creative and Performing Arts, San Diego, 1990—, Chula Vista, Calif., 1992—; mem. vis. team Western Coll. Assn., Calif., 1977-82. Arranger (choral) To God be the Glory, (brass) Keith A. Pagan Brass Quintet Series; mem. editorial bd. Christian Scholars Rev., 1986—, EverGreen Morning Music Press. Trustee Christian Scholars Rev., 1994—. With U.S. Army, 1953-55. Recipient WHO award Calif. Higher Edn. Assn., 1971, Lawrence Vredevoe Disting. Leadership award 1986, Spl. Svc. to Music award Calif. Music Educators Assn., 1991; winner 4th ann. anthem contest Choral Condrs. Guild; grantee Danforth Found., 1960. Mem. Calif. Coll. and Univ. Faculty Assn. (pres. 1969-70), Music Tchrs. Assn. Calif. (parliamentarian 1971-73), Western Assn. Schs. and Coll. (accreditation liaison 1976-88). Avocations: travel, photography. Home: 7450 Margerum Ave San Diego CA 92120-2025 Office: Point Loma Nazarene Coll 3900 Lomaland Dr San Diego CA 92106-2810

PAGE, JAKE (JAMES K. PAGE, JR.), writer, editor; b. Boston, Jan. 24, 1936; s. James Keena Page and Ellen Van Dyke (Gibson) Kunath; m. Aida de Alva Bound, Nov. 28, 1959 (div. 1974); children: Dana de Alva Page, Lea Gibson Page Kuntz, Brooke Bound Page; m. Susanne Calista Stone, Mar. 10, 1974; stepchildren: Lindsey Truitt, Sally Truitt, Kendall Barrett. BA, Princeton U., 1958; MA, NYU, 1959. Asst. sales promotion mgr. Doubleday & Co., 1959-60; editor Doubleday Anchor Books, 1960-62, Natural History Press, Doubleday, N.Y.C., 1962-69; editorial dir. Natural History Mag., N.Y.C., 1966-69; editor-in-chief Walker & Co., N.Y.C., 1969-70; sci. editor Smithsonian Mag., Washington, 1970-76; founder, dir. Smithsonian Books, Washington, 1976-80; start-up editor Smithsonian Air & Space Mag., Washington, 1985; pvt. practice as writer Waterford, Va., Corrales, N.Mex., 1980—; mag. cons. Denver Mus. Nat. History, 1989-90; contract text editor Doubleday, 1992. Author: (with Richard Saltonstall Jr.) Brown Out & Slow Down, 1972, (with Larry R. Collins) Ling-Ling & Hsing Hsing: Year of the Panda, 1973, Shoot the Moon, 1979, (with Wilson Clark) Energy, Vulnerability and War: Alternatives for America, 1981, Blood: River of Life, 1981, (with Susanne Page) Hopi, 1982, Forest, 1983, Arid Lands, 1984, Pastorale: A Natural History of Sorts, 1985, Demon State, 1985, (with Eugene S. Morton) Lords of the Air: The Smithsonian Book of Birds, 1989, Smithsonian's New Zoo, 1990, Zoo: The Modern Ark, 1990, Animal Talk: Science and the Voice of Nature, 1992, The Stolen Gods, 1993, Songs to Birds, 1993 (with Chalres B. Officer) Tales of the Earth, 1993, The Deadly Canyon, 1994 (with David Leeming) Goddess: Mythology of the Female Divine, 1994, The Knotted Strings, 1995, Smithsonian Guides to Natural America: Arizona and New Mexico, 1995, (with Susanne Page) Navajo, 1995, (with David Leeming) God: Mythology of the Male Divine, 1996, The Lethal Partner, 1996, (with Charles Officer) The Great Dinosaur Extinction Controversy, 1996, Operation Shatterhand, 1996, (with Michael Lieder) Wild Justice, 1997, A Certain Malace, 1998, Apacheria, 1998, (with Susanne Page) Field Guide to Southwest Indian Arts and Crafts, 1998, (with David Leeming) Native American Mythology, 1998; editor: (with Malcolm Baldwin) Law and the Environment, 1970; contbg. editorships Science Mag., 1980-86, Oceans Mag., 1987, Mother Earth News, 1990, National Geographic Traveler, 1990-93, TDC (Destination Discovery), 1991-95; contbg. author to numerous books and mags. Mem. nat. bd. advisors Futures for Children, Albuquerque, 1980—. Democrat. Avocation: Arab horses. Home and Office: PO Box 78 644 Dixon Rd Corrales NM 87048-7726

PAGE, LAVERTA WILLINE, television executive; b. El Morro, N.Mex., May 5, 1941; d. William Grade and Charline E. (Weishaar) Chrispens; m. Victor Wallace Page, Aug. 26, 1962; children: Vincent Wallace, Kevin Lee, Tricia Reneé. BS, Loma Linda U., 1963. Owner Page Enterprises, Riverside, Calif., 1963-99, Channel 53 TV, Hemet, Calif., 1995—; bd. trustees Weimar (Calif.) Inst., 1988—, Creston Coll., Mora, N.Mex., 1993—; mem. operating bd. The Quiet Hour, Redlands, Calif., 1991-98, Hemet (Calif.) Seventh Day Adventist Ch., 1997. Co-fonder Lithuanian Pub. House, Kaunas, 1994, HELP-Health Expo Lifestyle Programs, Weimar, 1990, LaVerta W. Chrispens Schs., India, 1994. Adventist. Avocations: organist for churches, travel. Office: Page Enterprises PO Box 5374 San Bernardino CA 92412

PAGE, LESLIE ANDREW, disinfectant manufacturing company executive; b. Mpls., June 5, 1924; s. Henry R. and Alma Kathryn (Steinmetz) P.; m. DeEtte Abernethy Griswold, July 6, 1952 (div. Sept. 1975); children: Randolph, Michael, Kathryn, Caroline; m. Mary Ellen Decker, Nov. 26, 1976. BA, U. Minn., 1949; MA, U. Calif., Berkeley, 1953; PhD, U. Calif., 1956. Asst. microbiologist, lectr. U. Calif., Davis, 1956-61; cons. San Diego Zoological Soc. Zoo Hosp., 1957-60; microbiologist, research leader Nat. Animal Disease Ctr., USDA, Ames, Iowa, 1961-79; ret., 1979, specialist in Chlamydial nomenclature and disease; med. text cons. Bay St. Louis, Miss., 1979-85; founder, pres., chmn. bd. Steri-Derm Corp., San Marcos, Calif., 1987—; cons. McCormick Distilling Co., Weston, Mo., 1994-95. Editor: Jour. Wildlife Diseases, 1965-68, Wildlife Diseases, 1976; contbr. chpts. to med. texts, over 70 articles to profl. jours.; patentee Liquid Antiseptic Composition, 1989. Pres. Garden Island Comty. Assn., Bay St. Louis, Miss., 1980-81; chief commr. East Hancock fire Protection Dist., Bay St. Louis,

1982-83; treas. Woodridge Escondido Property Owners Assn., 1986-88. Fellow Am. Acad. Microbiology (emeritus); mem. Wildlife Disease Assn. (pres. 1972-73, Disting. Svc. award 1980, Emeritus award 1984), Am. Soc. for Microbiology, Zool. Soc. San Diego, Sigma Xi, Phi Zeta (hon.). Home and Office: 1784 Deavers Dr San Marcos CA 92069-3359

PAGET, JOHN ARTHUR, mechanical engineer; b. Ft. Frances, Ont., Can., Sept. 15, 1922; s. John and Ethel (Bishop) P.; B. in Applied Sci., Toronto, 1946; m. Vicenta Herrera Nunez, Dec. 16, 1963; children: Cynthia Ellen, Kevin Arthur, Keith William. Chief draftsman Gutta Percha & Rubber, Ltd., Toronto, Ont., 1946-49; chief draftsman Viceroy Mfg. Co., Toronto, 1949-52; supr., design engr. C.D. Howe Co. Ltd., Montreal, Que., Can., 1952-58, sr. design engr. Combustion Engring., Montreal, 1958-59; sr. staff engr. Gen. Atomic, Inc., La Jolla, 1959-81. Mem. ASME, Soc. for History Tech., Inst. Mech. Engrs., Brit. Nuclear Energy Soc. Patentee in field. Home: 3183 Magellan St San Diego CA 92154-1515

PAIGE, NANCY LOUISE, genealogist; b. Waterloo, Ont., Can., Oct. 18, 1931; d. Ernest Bertram and Elva Estella (Turner) P. BA, U. Western Ont., London, 1959; BSW, U. Toronto, 1962; MLS, UCLA, 1967. Social worker Children's Aid Soc., London, 1958-64; libr. County of L.A., 1967-92; genealogist Family Finder Five-O, San Dimas, Calif., 1993—. Mem. San Dimas Coord. Coun., 1971-75; com. mem. San Dimas Woman's Club, 1972-80; fin. sec. San Dimas Hosp. Aux., 1972-73; vol. Pomona (Calif.) Pub. Libr., 1994—, German Geneal. Soc. of Am., LaVerne, Calif., 1995—. Named Woman of the Yr. San Dimas Bus. and Profl. Women's Club, 1974. Mem. Nat. Geneal. Soc., Assn. of Profl. Genealogists, Pomona Valley Geneal. Soc. (dir. 1992-96). Democrat. Unitarian. Home and Office: Family Finder Five-O 1418 W Badillo St San Dimas CA 91773-3534

PAIK, DANIEL KEEDUK, project director, adult educator; b. Seoul, Korea, Sept. 27, 1933; came to U.S., 1968; s. Hyon Moon and Sung Moon (Kil) P.; m. Myong Ja (Park) Paik, Dec. 30, 1963; children: Un Ju, Hyon Ju. BA in English, Dong-A Univ., Pusan, Korea, 1956-60; MA in English, Yonsei Univ., Seoul, Korea, 1960-61; AM, PhD in English, U. Ill., 1971-72. Adult ESL tchr. Belmont Cmty. Sch., L.A., 1978-80; advisor Office of Cmty. Network, L.A., 1980-82, ESL instrn., L.A., 1982-86; instrnl. cons. Divsn. of Adult Edn., L.A., 1986-92; project dir. Mid-Wilshire Adult Edn. Ctr., L.A., 1992—; dep. dir. Pacific Rim Inst., L.A., 1988—; chmn. Assn. of Korean Edn., L.A., 1986—; vice chmn. Asian Pacific Edn. Commn., L.A., 1987-89; chmn. CEO Korean Edn. Found., L.A., Inc., 1997—. Author: Conversational English I, II, III, 1981; Elem. English III and IV, 1997, 1998. Supt. Korean Sch. of So. Calif., L.A., 1980-82; pres. Korean Sch. Assn., L.A., 1985-86; pres. Korean Am. Edn. Assn., L.A., 1986-87. Named Min. of Edn., Seoul, Korea, 1982; recipient Nat. Medal of Honor, Seoul, Korea, 1984. Avocations: music, reading, traveling. Office: Mid-Wilshire Adult Edn Ctr 3407 W 6th St Ste 404 Los Angeles CA 90020-2551

PAIK, MISUNG, dentist; b. Mokpo, Korea, Aug. 10, 1964; d. Young Nam Yu and Jung Ae Choi; m. Seung Ho Paik, May 18, 1991; children: Philip Kisung, John Kiwook. Degree in dentistry, Kyung Hee U., Seoul, Korea, 1989. Gen. dentist Haemin Gen. Hosp., Seoul, Korea, 1989-90; owner Jung Wan Dentistry, Seoul, 1990-92; gen. dentist Experdent, Wilshire Park Dental Inst., L.A., 1998—. Mem. ADA, Calif. Dental Assn., Korea Dental Assn. Home: 2041 Conejo Ln Fullerton CA 92833

PAIK, SEUNGHO, mechanical engineer; b. Seoul, Korea, Mar. 17, 1962; came to U.S., 1983; s. Chong Soo and Choonja (Kim) P.; m. Misung Yu, May 24, 1991; children: Philip, John. BSME, Korea U., 1984; MSME, U. Minn., 1986, PhD, 1990. Staff engr. Idaho Nat. Engring. Lab., Idaho Falls, 1990—; cons. Korean Atomic Energy Rsch. Inst., Taejon, Korea, 1994—. Contbr. articles to profl. jours. Mem. ASME, Am. Nuclear Soc. Achievements include development of a computer code calculating thermal aspects on nuclear waste minimization. Avocations: swimming, tennis, golf, judo, racquetball. Home: 390 W 14th St # 3 Idaho Falls ID 83402 Office: Idaho Nat Engring Lab PO Box 1625 Idaho Falls ID 83415-0001

PAINTER, DIANA JEAN, urban designer, artist, consultant; b. Seattle, Dec. 29, 1953; d. Robert Cook and Nancy Marie (Chivers) P.; m. John Hazen McKean, Aug. 10, 1973 (div. Feb. 1975). BA, Western Wash. U., 1977; MUP, U. Wash., 1984; postgrad., U. Pa., 1987; PhD, Sheffield U., England, 1990. Cert. planner. Designer Cope Linder Assn., Phila., 1987-88, Dagit-Saylor Architects, Phila., 1988; urban designer WRT, Phila., 1989; designer Edwin Schlossberg Inc., N.Y.C., 1989-90; urban designer The SWA Group, Laguna Beach, Calif., 1990-91; assoc. planner City of Tukwila, Wash., 1993-97; project mgr. Sound Transit, Seattle, 1997—; cons. Diana J. Painter Archtl. & Cmty. History, Seattle, 1982—; instr. U. Wash., Seattle, 1986; printmaking instr. Sev Shoon Arts Ctr. Exhibited prints throughout West Coast; contbr. articles to profl. jours.; presenter in field. Mem. Allied Arts of Seattle Downtown Com., 1984-85; bd. dirs. Greystone Found., Pullman, Wash., 1992-93. Fellow Northwest Inst. Architecture & Urban Studies in Italy; mem. Am. Inst. Cert. Planners, Am. Assn. Planning (head mentoring program 1995—, vice-chmn. urban design divsn.), Am. Inst. Architects L.A. (mem. urban design com. 1990-91). Avocations: painting, rowing. Studio: 712 N 34th St Ste 205 Seattle WA 98103-8867

PAL, ANASUYA, English educator; b. Madanapalle, Andhra, India; came to U.S., 1979; d. Rangamma Reddy; m. Poorna Chandra Pal, May 28, 1972. MA, Benaras Hindu Univ., India, 1964; PhD, Ctrl. Inst. English, India, 1979. Lectr. Regional Inst. English, Bangalore, India, 1970-72; reader Ctrl. Inst. English, Hyderbad, India, 1972-79; instr. Montana Coll. Tech., 1980-82; sr. lectr. English U. Ilorin, Nigeria, 1982-86; prof. English U. Pontifica, Sao Paolo, Brazil, 1987-89; adj. instr. San Joaquin Delta Coll., Stockton, Calif., 1990-91, Modesto (Calif.) Jr. Coll., 1990-91; asst. prof. San Bernardino (Calif.) Valley Coll., 1991—; vis. scholar UCLA, 1979, 86, 99. Avocations: reading, writing, walking, handball, physical fitness. Home: 139 E Marshall Blvd San Bernardino CA 92404 Office: San Bernardino Valley Coll 701 S Mount Vernon Ave San Bernardino CA 92410-2705

PAL, PRATAPADITYA, museum curator; b. Bangladesh, Sept. 1, 1935; came to U.S., 1967; s. Gopesh Chandra and Bidyut Kana (Dam) P.; m. Chitralekha Bose, Apr. 20, 1968; children—Shalmali, Lopamudra. M.A., U. Calcutta, 1958, D.Phil., 1962; Ph.D. (U. K. Commonwealth Scholar), U. Cambridge, Eng., 1965. Research assoc. Am. Acad. of Benares, India, 1966-67; keeper Indian collections Mus. Fine Arts, Boston, 1967-69; sr. curator Indian and Southeast Asian art Los Angeles County Mus. Art, L.A., 1970-95, acting dir., 1979; vis. curator Indian and S.E. Asian art Art Inst. Chgo., 1995—; cons. curator Norton Simon Mus., Pasadena, Calif., 1995—; adj. prof. fine arts U. So. Calif., 1971-89; vis. prof. U. Calif., Santa Barbara, 1980, Irvine, 1994-95; William Cohn lectr. Oxford U., 1983; Catherine Mead meml. lectr. Pierpont Morgan Libr., N.Y.C., 1986; Ananda K. Coomaraswamy meml. lectr. Prince of Wales Mus., Bombay, 1987; D.J. Sibley prehistoric art lectr. U. Tex., Austin, 1989; Anthony Gardner meml. lectr. Victoria and Albert Mus., London, 1993, keynote spkr. 1st Internat. Conf. on Tibetan Art, 1994; mem. commr.'s art adv. panel IRS, Washington, 1986-96. Author: The Arts of Nepal, vol. 1, 1974, vol. 2, 1979, The Sensuous Immortals, 1977, The Ideal Image: Gupta Sculptures and its Influence, 1978, The Classical Tradition in Rajput Painting, 1978, Elephants and Ivories, 1981, A Buddhist Paradise: Murals of Alchi, 1982, Art of Tibet, 1983, Tibetan Painting, 1984, Art of Nepal, 1985, From Merchants to Emperors, 1986, Indian Sculpture, vol. 1, 1986, Icons of Piety, Images of Whimsey, 1987, Indian Sculpture, vol. 2, 1988, Buddhist Book Illuminations, 1988, Romance of the Taj Mahal, 1989, Art of the Himalayas, 1991, Pleasure Gardens of the Mind, 1993; Indian Painting, vol. 1, 1993, The Peaceful Liberators: Jain Art from India, 1994, On the Path to Void, 1996, A Collecting Odyssey, 1997, Divine Images, Human Visions, 1997, Tibet Change and Tradition, 1997; gen. editor: Marg mag., 1993—. Bd. dirs. Music Circle, Pasadena, Calif. John D. Rockefeller III Fund fellow, 1964, 69, fellow NEA, 1974; Getty scholar, 1995-96. Fellow Asia Soc. (Bombay, hon.); mem. Asiatic Soc. (Calcutta, B.C. Law gold medal 1993).

PALACIOS, ALANA SUE, computer programmer; b. Taylor, Tex., June 21, 1950; d. Alphonse T. and Doris Marie (Speegle) Hanzelka; m. Roberto C. Palacios, Mar. 10, 1956. BBA with honors, U. Tex., 1978; MPA, Calif. [illegible] Southwestern Bell Telephone, St. Louis, [illegible] Mountain Bell Telephone, Denver, [illegible]; asst. staff mgr. Southwestern Bell Telephone, 1981-84; project leader Hughes Aircraft, Long Beach, Calif., 1984-86; programmer, analyst City of Long Beach, 1986—. Civil svc. commr. Signal Hill, Calif., 1994—. Mem. NAFE, Phi Kappa Phi, Pi Alpha Alpha. Democrat. Episcopalian. Avocation: the Internet. Office: City of Long Beach 333 W Ocean Blvd Fl 12 Long Beach CA 90802-4664

PALACIOS, PEDRO PABLO, lawyer; b. Santo Tomas, N.Mex., June 29, 1953; s. Luis Flores and Refugio (Hernandez) P.; m. Kelle Haston, July 2, 1983; children: Pedro Pablo II, Charles Rey, Jose Luis. BA, Yale U., 1975; JD, U. N.Mex., 1979. Bar: N.Mex. 1979. Pvt. practice Las Cruces, N.Mex., 1983—. Mem. N.Mex. State Bar Assn. Democrat. Roman Catholic. Avocations: running, coin collecting. Home: PO Box 16335 Las Cruces NM 88004-6335 Office: 1980 E Lohman Ave Ste D-3 Las Cruces NM 88001-3194

PALADE, GEORGE EMIL, biologist, educator; b. Jassy, Romania, Nov. 19, 1912; came to U.S., 1946, naturalized, 1952; s. Emil and Constanta (Cantemir) P.; m. Irina Malaxa, June 12, 1941 (dec. 1969); children—Georgia Teodora, Philip Theodore; m. Marilyn G. Farquhar, 1970. Bachelor, Hasdeu Lyceum, Buzau, Romania; M.D., U. Bucharest, Romania. Instr., asst. prof., then assoc. prof. anatomy Sch. Medicine, U. Bucharest, 1935-45; vis. investigator, asst. assoc., prof. cell biology Rockefeller U., 1946-73; prof. cell biology Yale U., New Haven, 1973-83; sr. research scientist Yale U., 1983-89; prof.-in-residence, dean sci. affairs Med. Sch., U. Calif., San Diego, 1990—. Author sci. papers. Recipient Albert Lasker Basic Research award, 1966, Gairdner Spl. award, 1967, Horwitz prize, 1970, Nobel prize in Physiology or Medicine, 1974, Nat. Medal Sci., 1986. Fellow Am. Acad. Arts and Scis.; mem. Nat. Acad. Sci., Pontifical Acad. Sci., Royal Soc. (London), Leopoldina Acad. (Halle), Romanian Acad., Royal Belgian Acad. Medicine. Research interests correlated biochem. and morphological analysis cell structures. *

PALAGYI, ADDYSE LANE, educator; b. Salem, Oreg., July 3, 1927; d. Addison Winchester and Gladys A. (Derrick) L.; m. László Palagyi (dec.); children: Istvan, Sandor, Zsa, Zsa. BA, Willamette U., 1949; MA, Stanford U., 1952; PhD, U. N.Y., 1974. Actress, writer, poet; prof. SUNY, Albany, 1962-66, Calif. State U., Long Beach, 1976-80, San Jose State U., 1974-85, Western Oreg. U., Monmouth, 1987-98; actress with Shakespearean Festival, N.Y.C., Broadway, off-Broadway, nat. tours and one woman shows, 1952—; owner, publisher Pacific Books & Arts Mag., 1986-92; speaker, cons. in field. Contbr. articles to profl. jours. Vol., coord., organizer, 1987-98; active Episcopalian Diocese of Oreg. Recipient Vol. award City of Salem, 1989-94, Columnist award Arts Mag., 1992-97. Democrat. Avocations: painting, walking, poetry, world travel.

PALAO, ENRIQUE HENRY, electrical engineer; b. Arequipa, Peru, Mar. 12, 1924; came to the U.S., 1960; s. Manuel J. Palao and Carmela (Muniz) Vera; m. Cande Vargas, Feb. 14, 1954; children: Marie, Cecilia, Edmond. BSEE, Nat. U., Lima, Peru, 1947; postgrad., Carnegie-Mellon U., 1947-48. Pool mgr. Agrl. Coop. Svc., Nazca, Ica, Peru, 1948-53; asst. engr. Internat. Petroleum Co., Talara, Peru, 1953-56; svcs. chief engr. Pastobueno Mines, Ancash, Peru, 1956-59; plant engr. Pepsicola Plant, Lima, Peru, 1959-60; electrician journeyman Shipyards, Seattle, 1961-70; elec. inspector Port of Seattle, 1970-75; elec. inspector City of Seattle, 1975-89, retired, 1989; cons. Retired Srs. Vol. Program, 1995—; lectr. Seattle Deming Users Group, 1990—. Author: Thinking/Communications, 1997, System/Plan, 1998, New Basic Education, 1998, (5W's-1H) or (4W's-3H's)?, 1998. Co-chair task force Model Cities, Seattle, 1962; bd. dirs. Chicano Manpower Co., Seattle, 1970, Consejo for Spanish Speaking, Seattle, 1972, Seattle Mental Health Inst., 1982-84; vol. various orgs. in Seattle, 1990—. Mem. Svc. Corps of Retired Execs. (PINS award, counselor), Mondragon West Coops. (v.p. 1997—). Democrat. Roman Catholic. Avocations: inventing, designing, writing, thinking. E-mail: enrifact@juno.com. Home: 8827 31st Ave SW Seattle WA 98126-3718

PALAU, LUIS, evangelist; b. Ingeniero-Maschwitz, Argentina, Nov. 27, 1934; came to the U.S., 1960; s. Luis and Matilde Palau; m. Patricia M. Scofield, Aug. 5, 1961; children: Kevin, Keith, Andrew, Stephen. BA, St. Alban's Coll.; DD, Talbot Theol. Sem., 1977, Wheaton Coll., 1985, George Fox Coll., 1993. Missionary-evangelist Overseas Crusades Internat., 1961-66, pres., 1976-78; evangelist Luis Palau Evangelistic Team, 1967-76; pres., evangelist Luis Palau Evangelistic Assn., Portland, Oreg., 1978—. Author: Say Yes!, 1991, Healthy Habits for Spiritual Growth, 1994, Calling America and the Nations to Christ, 1994. Avocations: church history, theology. Office: Luis Palau Evangelistic Assn 1500 NW 167th Pl Beaverton OR 97006-7342

PALEY, ALFRED IRVING, value engineering and consulting company executive, lecturer; b. Monticello, N.Y., Apr. 12, 1927; s. Max and Dora (Gutkin) P.; m. Sylvia Tiffel, June 26, 1949; children: Maureen, Howard, Doreen. BEE, Poly. Inst. Bklyn., 1949. Cert. value specialist. Sr. engr. W.L. Maxson Corp., N.Y.C., 1950-58; chief engr. Acoustica Assocs., Mineola, N.Y., 1958-60; staff scientist in acoustics Am. Bosch Arma Corp., Garden City, N.Y., 1960-62; chief engr. in elec. acoustics Janus Products, Syosset, N.Y., 1962-63; mgr. Anti-Submarine Warfare systems Gyrodyne Co. of Am., St. James, N.Y., 1963-67; mgr. cost and value control Loral Electronic Systems, Yonkers, N.Y., 1967-80; v.p. program mgmt. FEL Corp., Farmingdale, N.J., 1980-84; pres. NRI Assocs., Ltd., 1984—; value engring. program mgr. CECOM, U.S. Army, Ft. Monmouth, N.J., 1985-95, ret. 1995; assoc. prof. Poly. Inst. Bklyn., 1955-65, Hofstra U., Hempstead, N.Y., 1974-79; lectr. Am. Mgmt. Assn., N.Y.C., 1973-80. Contbr. articles to profl. jours. Patentee in field. Bd. dirs. Suburban Temple, Wantagh, N.Y., 1964-80, Monmouth Reform Temple, Tinton Falls, N.J., 1983-91; bd. dirs. Miles Value Found., sec., 1996—. With USN, 1945-46. Recipient Outstanding Achivement Through Value Engring. award Dept. Def., 1995. Fellow Soc. Am. Value Engrs. Internat. (Value Engr. of Yr. 1985-86, 88-89, Disting. Svc. award 1991); mem. Project Mgmt. Inst., Soc. Info. Display, (sec. 1978), Nat. Mgmt. Assn. (pres. chpt. 1975-76). Democrat. Jewish. Home and Office: 5442 N Whitethorn Pl Tucson AZ 85704-2634

PALIA, ASPY PHIROZE, marketing educator, researcher, consultant; b. Bombay, Nov. 27, 1944; came to U.S., 1973; s. Phiroze E. and Homai P. (Irani) P. BE in Mech. Engring., U. Bangalore, 1966; MBA, U. Hawaii at Manoa, 1976; DBA, Kent State U., 1985. Sales engr. Larsen & Toubro Ltd., 1966-72, export sales engr., 1972-73; teaching fellow Coll. Bus. Adminstrn. Kent State U., 1977-80, instr. Coll. Bus. Adminstrn., 1982-84; asst. prof. Coll. Bus. Adminstrn. U. Hawaii, Manoa, 1984-89, assoc. prof., 1990-95, prof., 1996—, pres. faculty coun., 1995-96; senator U. Hawaii Manoa Faculty Congress, 1996-98; sr. fellow dept. mktg. U. Singapore, 1998—; vis. prof. Coll. Mgmt. Nat. Sun Yat-sen U., Kaohsiung, Taiwan, 1992, Chulalongkorn U., Bangkok, Thailand, 1992, 93, 97, U. Otago, New Zealand, 1995, Adminstrv. Staff Coll. India, Hyderabad, 1992; mem. U. Hawaii Manoa Ctr. for Teaching Excellence Faculty Adv. Group, 1991; mem. mktg. plan adv. com. U. Hawaii, Manoa, 1994, mem. honors and awards com., 1990-91, pres. faculty coun. 1995-96, mem. faculty adv. com. on acad. freedom, 1997; vis. scholar faculty bus. adminstrn. Nat. U. Singapore, 1991, Mktg. Inst. Singapore Exec. Devel. Seminars, 1991, 94-95, 97, Hong Kong Inst. Mktg. Exec. Devel. Seminar, 1996, others; sr. fellow dept. mktg. faculty of bus. adminstrn. Nat. U. Singapore, 1998—; affiliate faculty Japan Am. Inst. Mgmt. Sci., Honolulu, 1989—; vis. prof. Grad. Sch. Internat. Mgmt., Internat. U. Japan, Uhrasa, Yamato-machi, 1991, U. Internat. Bus. and Econs., Beijing, 1991, U. Kebangsaan Malaysia, Bangi-Selangor, Kuala Lumpur, Malaysia, 1991, 92, Mount Carmel Inst. Mgmt., Bangalore, India, 1997; lectr., cons., presenter in field. Editor: (with Dennis A. Rondinelli) Project Planning and Implementation in Developing Countries, 1976; contbr. conf. procs. and articles to profl. jours. and books, including Indsl. Mktg. Mgmt., Internat. Bus. Jour., Asia-Pacific Jour. Mgmt., Internat. Mktg. Rev., European Jour. Mktg., Fgn. Trade Rev., Internat. Rev. Econs. & Bus., others; contbr. to numerous confs. and symposia in field; developer various mktg. decision support systems and decision-making tools for use in strategic market planning and in marketing simulations. Mem. various program rev. coms. Pacific and Asian Mgmt. Inst., Acad. Internat. Bus., Assn. Bus. Simulation and Exptl. Learning, others; bd. examiners Nat. U. Singapore Sch. Postgrad. Mgmt. Studies, 1991; mem. adv. bd. [illegible] Coll. of Bus. Adminstrn. Alumni and Friends Exec. Com., 1991-93, adv. bd. Salvation Army Residential Treatment Facilities for Children and Youth Adv. Coun., 1989-96, vice chair, 1987-89; chair Salvation Army Family Treatment Svcs. Adv. Coun., 1997-98; mem. Salvation Army Honolulu Adv. Bd., 1997-98; treas., bd. dirs. Kings Gate Homeowners Assn., 1994-96. Univ. fellow Kent State U., 1983; East-West Ctr. scholar East-West Ctr., 1973-75; Ednl. Improvement Fund grantee, 1989, Instrl. Travel and Devel. Fund grantee Office Faculty Devel. and Acad. Support, 1991, 95, joint rsch. grants U. Kebangsaan Malaysia, Nat. U. Singapore, U. So. Queensland, Australia, U. Otago, New Zealand, Lingnan Coll., Hong Kong; recipient Internat. Agreements Fund award Office Internat. Programs and Svcs., 1990-91, 91-92, ORA travel award U. Rsch. Coun., 1986, 88, 89, 91, 92, 94, 95, 96, 97, 98. Mem. Am. Mktg. Assn. (academia editor Honolulu chpt. 1986-87), Acad. Internat. Bus. (chair Pacific Basin Region 1995, chair Pacific Basin chpt. 1996—, co-chair Asia Pacific Conf. 1997), Pacific Asian Consortium for Internat. Bus. Edn. and Rsch., Assn. for Bus. Simulation and Exptl. Learning, Pan-Pacific Bus. Assn. (charter), Mortar Bd. (Outstanding Educator award 1993, Mentor award 1995), East-West Ctr. Alumni Assn. U.S. (v.p. Hawaii chpt. 1987-89, ad campaign com. 1987-88), Beta Gamma Sigma (faculty advisor, sec.-treas. Alpha of Hawaii chpt. 1990—, Outstanding Svc. award 1992-93, Bd. Govs. Commitment to Excellence award 1997), Mu Kappa Tau, Pi Sigma Epsilon. Avocations: music, photography, swimming, reading, hiking. Home: 2724 Kahoaloha Ln Apt 1605 Honolulu HI 96826-3337 Office: U Hawaii Manoa Dept Mktg 2404 Maile Way Honolulu HI 96822-2223 also: Nat U Singapore Dept Mktg, 10 Kent Ridge Crescent, Singapore 119260, Singapore

PALILEO, HAZEL VALENCIA, videographer; b. Pila, Laguna, Philippines, May 22, 1951; came to U.S., 1971, naturalized citizen, 1979; d. Lauro Gomez and Edna (Valencia) P. BFA in Photography and Media, Wright State U., 1976; student, DeVry Inst. Tech., 1995-97, Applied Multimedia Tng. Ctrs., 1997-98. Lab. tech. Valdhere Films, Inc., Dayton, Ohio, 1973-76; news photographer Sta. WDTN-TV, Dayton, 1977-79; videographer Sta. WKEF-TV News, Dayton, 1979-86; chief videographer Sta. WKEF-TV News, 1983-86; videographer, still photographer Wycliffe Bible Translators, Calgary, Alta., Can., 1986-92, co-mgr. media prodns. dept., 1990-92; video mgr., media coord. Cornerstone Comms., Calgary, 1992-94; photographer, videographer & multi media specialist freelance, Calgary, 1994—. Videographer (TV news) Haviland Ave. Fire, 1984 (Emmy 1984). Recipient Best Video award Nat. Cath. Stewardship Conf., 1993. Mem. Anglican Ch. of Canada. Avocations: reading, photography, travelling, walking.

PALLOTTI, MARIANNE MARGUERITE, foundation administrator; b. Hartford, Conn., Apr. 23, 1937; d. Rocco D. and Marguerite (Long) P. BA, NYU, 1968, MA, 1972. Asst. to pres. Wilson, Haight & Welch, Hartford, 1964-65; exec. asst. Ford Found., N.Y.C., 1965-77; corp. sec. Hewlett Found., Menlo Park, Calif., 1977-84, v.p., 1985—. Bd. dirs. N.Y. Theatre Ballet, N.Y.C., 1986—, Austin Montessori Sch., 1993, Djerassi Resident Artists Program, 1998—; mem. women's adv. com., nat. coun.World Wildlife Fund, 1997—, nat. coun., 1998—; mem. program com. Ind. Sector, Washington, 1998—. Mem. Women in Founds., No. Calif. Grantmakers. Home: Apt 6203 532 Marine World Pky Redwood Shores CA 94065 Office: William & Flora Hewlett Found 525 Middlefield Rd Ste 200 Menlo Park CA 94025-3448

PALL-PALLANT, TERI, paleontologist, inventor, behavioral scientist, design engineer, advertising agency executive; b. Somerville, N.J., Jan. 6, 1921; d. Stanley and Milicent P.-P.; BA, Imperial Coll., London, 1948, MS, 1949; PhD, London U., 1954; postgrad. Warren Sch. Aeros., Los Angeles, 1950, Calif. Inst. Tech., 1951; PhD Columbia U., 1963, London U., 1966, ScD, London Inst. Applied Rsch., 1973; cert. rehab. counselor U. So. Calif., 1975; student UCLA, 1955. Design engr. Simmonds Aerocessories Ltd., London, 1949, dir. vocat. rehab., 1950; founder, owner Teri Pall Advt. Agy., Los Angeles, 1951—, Pall Indsl. Surveys, Pasadena, Calif., 1952—, Pall Tech. Industries, Tarzana, Calif., 1979—; chmn. bd. Pall Industries, Ltd., Taipei, Taiwan and Tarzana, Calif., 1980—; vertebrate paleontologist Am. Mus. Natural History, N.Y.C., 1965-69; leader Teri Pall Trio, L.A., 1951-69; exec. dir. Hoffman House, Long Beach, Calif., 1970-72; sr. adminstrv. analyst Econ. and Youth Opportunities, Los Angeles County, 1973-74; dep. dir. Head Start Program L.A. County, 1974-75; assoc. dir. Casa de las Amigas, Pasadena, dir. rsch. and evaluation projects Nat. Inst. Alcohol Abuse and Alcoholism, Washington, 1977; pvt. practice vocat. rehab. counseling, Beverly Hills, Calif., 1977; exec. dir. Little House L.A. County, 1978; robotics cons. Jet Propulsion Lab., Pasadena, 1974-95, NASA, 1990—. Fossil exhibit contbr. Los Angeles County Mus., 1968-77; chmn. Mayor's Commn. on Barrier-Free Architecture, 1978—; vice chmn. research and coordinating com. Gov.'s Commn. on Safe Energy Alternatives, 1979—; mem. Cancer Research Coordinating Com., 1979—; lectr. Long Beach Hosp., 1978; office bd. Inventor's Workshop Internat. Edn. Found., 1980—, Am. Guild of Inventors, 1990—; bd. dirs. Commn. Conserve Chinese Culture. Recipient Spl. Contbns. award Engring. and Grading Constructors Assn., 1968, Interkamera Gold award Cannes Art Festival, 1969, Speaker of Year award Toastmasters Calif., 1971, Woman of Year for Civic Leadership award Long Beach, 1971, Outstanding Achievement award Am. Cancer Soc., 1979, others. Mem. Statis. Quality Control Engrs. (sec. 1951—), Assoc. Bus. Publs., AAUW, Nat. Rehab. Counseling Assn., Architects and Engrs. Inst., Nat. Soc. Vertebrate Paleontologists, Phi Beta Kappa. Republican. Episcopalian. Author: (play) El Rancho Verde, 1951; (novel) With Banners Flying, 1953; Chinese and Western Worlds from 1800 B.C. to Modern Times, 1950; 4000 Years of Egyptian History, 1950; The Integrating Power Meter, 1956; About the Mammoth, 1962; Look, a Travelogue in Time, 1967; The History of Our Calendar, 1977; designer robotics exhibit Calif. Mus. of Sci. and Industry, L.A., 1990. Developer 2-mile cordless telephone, 1978, wrist chronograph calculator, 1979, Etch-A-Sketch, 1962, AC-DC multimeters, 1954, Miniaturized transcutaneous nerve stimulator, 1969, Electronic remote control system, 1972.

PALMA, JACK D., lawyer; b. N.Y.C., Sept. 15, 1946. BA, Allegheny Coll., 1968; JD with honors, U. Denver, 1974. Bar: Colo. 1975, Wyo. 1976. Ptnr. Holland & Hart, Cheyenne, Wyo., 1984—. Mem. ABA, Colo. Bar Assn., Wyo. State Bar, Order St. Ives. Office: Holland & Hart PO Box 1347 2515 Warren Ave Ste 450 Cheyenne WY 82003-3630*

PALMA, MICHAEL JOSEPH, marketing professional; b. Santa Clara, Calif., Dec. 22, 1968; s. James Joseph and Madelon L. (McKay) P. BA in Polit. Sci., U. Calif., Riverside, 1991; MA in Polit. Sci., U. Iowa, 1992. Analyst Frost & Sullivan, Mountain View, Calif., 1996-97; analyst worldwide rsch. ops. Gartner Group, Dataguest, San Jose, Calif., 1997—; mem. Bay Area Word Affairs Coun., San Francisco, 1997—. Mem. Jaycees, Soc. Competitive Intelligence Profls., Phi Kappa Sigma. Republican. Roman Catholic. Avocations: scuba diving, swimming. Home: 6590 Little Falls Dr San Jose CA 95120-4049 Office: Gartner Group/Dataguest 251 River Oaks Pkwy San Jose CA 95134-1913

PALMATIER, MALCOLM ARTHUR, editor, consultant; b. Kalamazoo, Nov. 11, 1922; s. Karl Ernest and Cecile Caroline (Chase) P.; m. Mary Elizabeth Summerfield, June 16, 1948 (dec. Oct. 1982); children: Barnabus, Timothy K., Duncan M.; m. Marie-Anne Suzanne van Werveke, Jan. 12, 1985. *Wife Marie-Anne S. Pitz-Palmatier is retired from the consular service with the title of Honorary Consul General Emeritus of Luxembourg.* BS in Math., Western Mich. U., 1945; MA in English, UCLA, 1947; MA in Econs., U. So. Calif., 1971. Instr. English Pomona Coll., Claremont, Calif., 1949-51; editor Naval Ordnance Test Sta., Pasadena, Calif., 1951-54; head editorial unit Rocketdyne, L.A., 1954-55; editor The RAND Corp., Santa Monica, Calif., 1955-87; cons. editor The RAND Corp., Santa Monica, 1987—; instr. English UCLA, L.A., summer 1950. Mng. editor, cons. editor Jour.: Studies in Comparative Communism, L.A., 1968-80; co-editor Perspectives in Economics, 1971; contbr. chpts. to book, book revs. and articles to profl. jours. Chmn. bd. New Start, West L.A., 1982-84. With USNR, 1943-45. Mem. Jonathan Club. Avocations: music, travel. Home: 516 Avondale Ave Los Angeles CA 90049-4804 Office: The RAND Corp 1700 Main St Santa Monica CA 90401-3297

PALMER, BEVERLY BLAZEY, psychologist, educator; b. Cleve., Nov. 22, 1945; d. Lawrence E. and Mildred M. Blazey; m. Richard C. Palmer, June 24, 1967; 1 child, Ryan Richard. PhD in Counseling Psychology, Ohio State U., 1972. Lic. clinical psychologist, Calif. Adminstrv. assoc. Ohio State U., Columbus, 1969-70, rsch. psychologist Health Svcs. Rsch. Ctr.

UCLA, 1971-77; commr. pub. health L.A. County, 1978-81; pvt. practice clin. psychology Torrance, Calif., 1985—; prof. psychology Calif. State U., Dominguez Hills, 1973—. Reviewer manuscripts for numerous textbook pubs; contbr. numerous articles to profl. jours. Recipient Proclamation County of L.A., 1972, Proclamation County of L.A., 1981. Mem. Am. Psychol. Assn. Office: Calif State U Dominguez Hills Dept Psychology Carson CA 90747

PALMER, CHARLES RAY, retired graphics specialist, investor; b. New Orleans, Oct. 17, 1940; s. Zack and Amy Cecilia Palmer; m. Jeanette Francis Smith, Oct. 24, 1964; 1 child, Bridgette Latrice. AA in Art, Southwest City Coll., 1975; BA in Art with honors, Calif. State U., Dominguez Hills, 1979. Binderyman System Devel. Corp., Santa Monica, Calif., 1964-66; duplicator operator System Devel. Corp., Santa Monica, 1966-73, Northrop Corp., Hawthorne, Calif., 1973-75; printing press operator Northrop Corp., Hawthorne, 1975-79, visual aid artist, 1979-83, graphics prodn. control specialist, 1983-87, graphic art service mgr., 1987-93; graphics specialist, 1994-95, ret., 1994; ltd. partnership, Crenshaw Graphics, L.A., 1979-82; pres. Palmer's Profiters Investment Club, 1996—. With USAF, 1960-64. Mem. Palmer's Profiteers Investment Club (founder, pres.), Am. Legion. Democrat. Roman Catholic. Home: 7630 Cimarron St Los Angeles CA 90047-2319 Office: Northrop Corp One Northorne Ave Orgn Zone 1553 # 87 Hawthorne CA 90250

PALMER, DOUGLAS S., JR., lawyer; b. Peoria, Ill., Mar. 15, 1945. AB cum laude, Yale U., 1966; JD cum laude, Harvard U., 1969. Bar: Wash. 1969. Mem. Foster Pepper & Shefelman PLLC, Seattle, 1974—. Office: Foster Pepper & Shefelman PLLC 1111 3rd Ave Fl 34 Seattle WA 98101-3207

PALMER, GILBERT CHARLES, insurance company executive; b. Milw., Feb. 4, 1944; s. Lawrence Edward and Helen Katarine (Szemerelo) P.; m. Susan Marie Kloehn, Aug. 26, 1966; children: Lawrence Edward, Jennifer Ann. Grad., Messmer H.S., Milw., 1963. Cert. assoc. in claims, fraud claims law specialist, fraud claims law assoc. Claim mgr. Allstate Ins., Milw., 1967-73; svc. dir. Hall Chevrolet, Milw., 1973-75; spl. projects dir. Allstate Ins., Northbrook, Ill., 1975-94; divsn. mgr. Auto Club of So. Calif., Costa Mesa, 1995—; bd. dirs. Collision Industry Electronic Comms. Assn., Detroit, 1992-93; cons. Nat. Ins. Crime Bur., Chgo., 1991-94, Am. Ins. Group, N.Y.C., 1994-95. Recipient Cert. of Achievement, Inter Industry Coun. on Auto Collision Repair, 1987. Republican. Roman Catholic. Avocation: automobile collecting. Home: 20 Alcott Pl Laguna Niguel CA 92677-4700 Office: Automobile Club So Calif 3333 Fairview Rd # P307 Costa Mesa CA 92626-1610

PALMER, JAMES DANIEL, inspector; b. Oklahoma City, Okla., Aug. 11, 1936; s. Athol Ford and Marjorie Lorraine (Ward) P.; m. Gail Dorothy Myers, June 1954 (div. Sept. 1956); 1 child, James Douglas; m. Gloria Jean West, Dec. 14, 1963; children: Diana Lorraine, Elana Louise, Sheri Francis. AB in Police Sci. with honors, San Jose (Calif.) State U., 1963, AB in Psychology, 1964; MPA, Golden Gate U., 1972. Cert. Calif. police officers standards and tng. Asst. foreman Hunts Foods, Inc., Hayward, Calif., 1959-64; spl. investigator Dept. A.B.C. State of Calif., Oakland, 1964-67; criminal inspector Contra Costa County Dist. Atty., Martinez, Calif., 1967-72, lt. of inspectors, 1972-92; ret., 1992; pres. Contra Costa County Peace Officers, Richmond, 1974-75; past v.p. Contra Costa County Dist. Atty's Inv. Assn., Martinez, 1971, tng. officer, 1990-92. Contbr. articles to profl. jours. Past pres. South Hayward (Calif.) Dem. Club, 1976, 77, San Leandro (Calif.) Dems., 1975; mem. Gov's Law Enforcement Adv. Commn., Sacramento, Calif., 1972-76, Calif. Dem. Coun., 1972-73; rev. Am. Fellowship Protestant Ch., 1990—, min., 1990—. With USAF, 1955-58. Avocations: stocks, bonds, real estate, family, church. Home: 2788 Sydney Way Castro Valley CA 94546-2738

PALMER, JAMES W., nurse; b. Weiser, Idaho, July 29, 1937; s. Harold Jasper and Delma May (Kelso) P.; m. G. Joy Palmer, Jul. 9, 1970 (div. June 1997); children: John David, Janel Raclene; m. Vicki M. Palmer, Jul. 29, 1997. BA in history, Walla Walla Coll., 1972, MEd, 1980; AD, Walla Walla Cmty Coll., 1990. Tchr. North Pacific Union Conf., Portland, Oreg., 1977-90; nurse Walla Walla, Wash., Oreg., 1990—. Contbr. articles to profl. jours. With USMC, 1954-57, Philippines, Japan. Avocations: jogging, hiking, travel. Home: 1604 Sunset Dr Walla Walla WA 99362-4440

PALMER, KATHARINE ANNE, artist; b. Oklahoma City, July 28, 1948; d. Gail Rodney and Barbara Belle (Warr) P.; m. Robert C. Habbersett, Jan. 2, 1993. Student abroad, U. East Anglia, Norwich, Eng., 1968-69; BA in English Lit., Oklahoma City U., 1970, BA in Art, 1974. Owner painting and sculptural jewelry studio, Oklahoma City, 1975-90, oil painting studio, Santa Fe, 1990—; cons. in art restoration Mabee-Gerrer Mus., Shawnee, Okla., 1985-86. One-woman shows include The Grapevine Gallery, Oklahoma City, 1980-90; exhibited in group shows at Art Ctr. at Fuller Lodge, Los Alamos, N.Mex., 1995, 97, 98 (Best of Show 1997, 1st prize 1998), The Wichita (Kans.) Ctr. for Arts, 1996 (Best of Show), Butler Inst. Am. Art, Youngstown, Ohio, 1997, others. Mem. Mus. of N.Mex. Found., Santa Fe, 1990—, Fuller Lodge Art Ctr., Los Alamos, 1995—. Recipient Ken Roberts N.Mex. Artist award N.Mex. Art League, 1995, award of Excellence, Gamblin Artists Colors award Oil Painters of Am., Taos, N.Mex., 1997. Mem. Allied Artists of Am. (Gene Magazzini Meml. award for Traditional Painting, 1996), Audubon Artists (assoc., Alfred D. Crimi Meml. award 1997, Jack Richeson award 1998), Oil Painters of Am. (assoc.), Knickerbocker Artists (signature), Women Artists of the West (signature), The Salmagundi Club (N.Y.C., Philip Isenberg award 1996, Katlan Family award for Seascape 1997, Antonio Cirini Meml. award 1998), Artists Fellowship Inc. (N.Y.C.), Catharine Lorillard Wolfe Art Club (N.Y.C., Art Times award 1998). Avocations: gardening, hiking, swimming.

PALMER, LYNNE, writer, astrologer; b. El Centro, Calif., Dec. 14, 1932; d. Clarence Lee and Paquita Mae (Hartley) Hafer; m. Bruno Cazzaniga, Mar. 13, 1964 (div. 1965); m. Sidney Latter, Nov. 29, 1997. Student, Ch. of Light, 1957-62, Calif. Sch. Escrows, L.A., 1960; theatre mgmt. degree, Mus. Arenas Theatres Assn., N.Y.C., 1963. Asst. teller Western Mortgage, L.A., 1957-58; head teller Sutro Mortgage Svc., L.A., 1958-61; freelance astrologer N.Y.C., 1961-92, Las Vegas, Nev., 1962—; owner, operator, tchr. astrology sch. N.Y.C., 1970-72; owner Star Bright Pubs., Las Vegas, 1996—; spkr. women's clubs, indsl. shows, astrol. orgns.; interviewed in N.Y. Post and other major newspapers and mags. including Life and Oggi (Italy), Veja (Brazil), Wall St. Jour., People Mag., Globe, Die Welt am Sonntag (West Germany), New Woman Mag., Forbes. Author: Signs for Success, Prosperity Signs, Nixon's Horoscope, Astrological Almanac, Astrological Compatibility (Profl. Astrologers ann. award for outstanding contbn. to art and sci. of astrology 1976), Horoscope of Billy Rose, ABC Basic Chart Reading, ABC Major Projgressions, ABC Chart Erection, Pluto Ephemeris (1900-2000), Daily Positions, Use Astrology and Change Your Name, Do-It-Yourself Publicity Directory, Your Lucky Days and Numbers, Money Magic, Astro-Guide to Nutrition and Vitamins, Gambling to Win, The Astrological Treasure Map, Dear Sun Signs; columnist mags. and newsletters including Self, House Beautiful, Gold; record album: Cast and Read Your Horoscope; TV appearances include The Johnny Carson Tonight Show, What's My Line, 60 Minutes, CBS News Night Watch, Cosmos (BBC), Sci. Series (Italian TV), Fantastico (Brazilian TV), Japan TV, News (Nippon), Do We Really Need It? (ASAHI), The World is Calling (Uranai); contbr. articles to mags. and newspapers. Mem. AFTRA, Am. Fedn. Astrologers (cert. astrologer). Avocation: travel. Home: 850 E Desert Inn Rd Apt 912 Las Vegas NV 89109-2100 Office: Star Bright Pubs 2235 E Flamingo Rd Las Vegas NV 89119-5129

PALMER, PATRICIA ANN, English language educator; b. Lake City, Minn., July 12, 1949; d. Gerold Henry and Ione Helen (Busch) Breuer; m. Curtis Lynn Palmer, Aug. 17, 1973. AA, Rochester Jr. Coll., 1969; BS, Mankato State Coll., 1971. Cert. in secondary edn., Minn., Ariz. Tchr. English Stewartville (Minn.) H.S., 1971-80, Mesa (Ariz.) Jr. H.S., 1983-87, Dobson H.S., Mesa, 1987—; volleyball coach, Stewartville, 1971-74, track coach, 1971-80; track/cross-country coach, Mesa, Ariz., 1983-87. Mem. Nat. Coun. Tchrs. English. Avocations: reading, hiking, dog training. Office: Dobson H S 1501 W Guadalupe Rd Mesa AZ 85202-7575

PALMER, PATRICIA ANN TEXTER, English language educator; b. Detroit, June 10, 1932; d. Elmer Clinton and Helen (Rotchford) Texter; m. David Jean Palmer, June 4, 1955. BA, U. Mich., 1953; MEd, Nat.-Louis U., 1958; MA, Calif. State U.-San Francisco, 1966; postgrad. Stanford U., 1968, Calif. State U.-Hayward, 1968-69. Chmn. speech dept. Grosse Pointe (Mich.) Univ. Sch., 1953-55; tchr. South Margerita Sch., Panama, 1955-56, Kipling Sch., Deerfield, Ill., 1955-56; grade level chmn. Rio San Gabriel Sch., Downey, Calif., 1957-59; tchr. newswriting and devel. reading Roosevelt High Sch., Honolulu, 1959-62; tchr. English, speech and newswriting El Camino High Sch., South San Francisco, 1962-68; chmn. ESL dept. South San Francisco Unified Sch. Dist., 1968-81; dir. ESL Inst., Millbrae, Calif., 1978—; adj. faculty New Coll. Calif., 1981—, Skyline Coll., 1990—; Calif. master tchr. ESL Calif. Coun. Adult Edn., 1979-82; cons. in field. Past chair Sister City Com. Millbrae. Recipient Concours de Francais Prix, 1947; Jeanette M. Liggett Meml. award for excellence in history, 1949. Mem. AAUW, NAFE, TESOL, ASCD, Am. Assn. of Intensive English Programs, Internat. Platform Assn., Calif. Assn. TESOL, Nat. Assn. for Fgn. Student Affairs, Computer Using Educators, Speech Commn. Assn., Faculty Assn. of Calif. C.C., U. Mich. Alumnae Assn., Nat.-Louis U. Alumnae Assn., Ninety Nines (Golden West chpt.), Cum Laude Soc., Soroptimist Internat. (dir., Millbrae-San Bruno Women Helping Women award 1993), Rotary Club (pres.-elect Millbrae), Chi Omega, Zeta Phi Eta. Home: 2917 Franciscan Ct San Carlos CA 94070-4304 Office: 450 Chadbourne Ave Millbrae CA 94030-2401

PALMER, ROBERT ARTHUR, private investigator; b. St. Augustine, Fla., May 20, 1948; m. Christine Lynn Creger, May 14, 1974. AA, Glendale C.C., 1975; BS, U. Phoenix, 1981; MA, Prescott Coll., 1993. Lic. pvt. investigator, Ariz.; bd. cert. forensic examiner. Dep. sheriff Maricopa County Sheriff's Office, Phoenix, 1971-79; owner Palmer Investigative Svcs., Prescott, Ariz., 1980-90; pres. The Magnum Corp., Prescott, 1990—. V.p. Mountain Club Homeowners, Prescott, 1986—. Mem. Internat. Assn. Chem. Testing, World Assn. Detectives, Nat. Assn. Legal Investigators, Nat. Assn. Profl. Process Servers, Am. Coll. Forensic Examiners, Ariz. Assn. Lic. Pvt. Investigators (pres. 1984), Ariz. Process Servers Assn. (pres. 1985-86), Prescott C. of C. (v.p. 1987-90). Avocations: photography, collecting western art. Office: Palmer Investigative Svcs PO Box 10760 Prescott AZ 86304-0760

PALMER, ROBERT L., lawyer; b. Bryn Mawr, Pa., Aug. 15, 1946. BA, Georgetown U., 1968; JD, Columbia U., 1971. Bar: D.C. 1972, Ariz. 1976. Law clerk to Hon. Harold Leventhal U.S. Ct. Appeals (D.C. cir.), 1971-72; with Covington & Burling, Washington, 1972-73, 75; asst. spec. prosecuter Watergate spec. prosecution force U.S. Dept. Justice, 1973-74; mem. Meyer, Hendricks, Victor, Osborn & Maledon, Phoenix, Ariz., 1976-95, Hennigan, Mercer & Bennett, L.A., 1995—; adj. prof. law U. Ariz., 1983.; bd. dirs. Ariz. Ctr. for Law in Pub. Interest, 1990-96, pres., 1990-92. Notes and comments editor Columbia Law Rev., 1970-71. Mem. ABA (assoc. editor litigation jour. sect. litigation 1979-82). Office: Hennigan Mercer & Bennett 601 S Figueroa St Ste 3300 Los Angeles CA 90017-5704*

PALMER, ROBERT NEAL, artist; b. Redlands, Calif., Sept. 18, 1956; s. Richard Lee and Geneva Lee (Russell) P.; m. Barbara Ann Wallen, Dec. 31, 1974 (div. 1978); 1 child, Robert Glen; m. Michele Lee Seagrave, Aug. 26, 1996. B in theology, St. Paul's Lyceum of EOCACG, 1982, M in metaphysics, 1983. Ordained deacon. Interior muralist, artist Houston, 1982-84; graphic artist Custom Creations Unlimited, San Bernardino, Calif., 1984-88; photographer, graphic artist Custom Creations Unlimited, Railto, Calif., 1988—; v.p., pub. Arlington Artists Guild, Riverside, Calif., 1987-89. Author: Reflections of Biblical Histories, 1998, Paintings By RN Palamer, 1995, Drawings by RN Palmer, 1993, Drawings by RN Palmer, 1996. Street outreach minister EOCACG, Houston, 1982-83. With U.S. Army, 1975-80. Mem. San Bernardino Art Assn., Fontana Art Asssn. Avocations: electronic repair, genealogy research, bicycling, Tychi, martial arts. Home: 249 W Victoria St Rialto CA 92376-5025

PALMER, ROGER CAIN, information scientist; b. Corning, N.Y., Oct. 14, 1943; s. Wilbur Clarence and Eleanor Louise (Cain) P. AA, Corning (N.Y.) C.C., 1964; BA, Hartwick Coll., 1966; MLS, SUNY, Albany, 1972; PhD, U. Mich., 1978. Tchr. Penn Yan (N.Y.) Acad., 1966-68, 70-71; dep. head, grad. libr. SUNY, Buffalo, 1972-75; asst. prof. UCLA, 1978-83; sr. tech. writer Quotron Sys., Culver City, 1984; sr. sys. analyst Getty Art History Info., Santa Monica, Calif., 1984-90, mgr. tech. devel., 1990-93; mgr. internal cons. group The J. Paul Getty Trust, Santa Monica, 1993-96; mgr. ITS Infrastructure Ops. The J. Paul Getty Trust, L.A., 1996-97; v.p. China and N.Am. Bus. Assocs., Inc., 1997—; gen. ptnr. Liu-Palmer, L.A., 1989—. Author: Online Reference and Information Retrieval, 1987, dBase II and dBase III: An Introduction, 1984, Introduction to Computer Programming, 1983. With U.S. Army, 1968-70. Mem. IEEE Computer Soc., ALA, Am. Soc. for Info. Scis., Spl. Librs. Assn., Art Librs. Soc. of N.Am., Assn. for Computing Machinery, Pi Delta Epsilon, Beta Phi Mu. Home: # 1-295 8205 Santa Monica Blvd # 1-295 Los Angeles CA 90046-5967 Office: China and N Am Bus Assn 2533 N Carson Ste 3422 Carson City NV 89706-0147

PALMER, VINCENT ALLAN, construction consultant; b. Wausa, Nebr., Feb. 18, 1913; s. Victor E. and Amy (Lindquist) P.; AA, Modesto Jr. Coll., 1933; BSCE, U. Calif., Berkeley, 1936; m. Louise V. Cramer, Mar. 12, 1938 (dec. June 1979); children: Margaret, Georgia, Vincent Allan; m. 2d, Hope Parker, Jan. 23, 1982. Constrn. engr. Kaiser Engrs., 1938-63, constrn. mgr., 1963-69, mgr. constrn., 1970-75, project mgr., 1975-76; project mgr. reef runway Universal Dredging Corp., Honolulu, 1975-76; pvt. practice constrn. cons., Walnut Creek, Calif., 1976—. Mem. ASCE (life). Home and Office: 1356 Corte Loma Walnut Creek CA 94598-2904

PALMER, WILLIAM JOSEPH, accountant; b. Lansing, Mich., Sept. 3, 1934; s. Joseph Flammin Lacchia and Henrietta (Yagerman) P.; m. Judith Pollock, Aug. 20, 1960 (div. Nov. 1980); children: William W., Kathryn E., Leslie A., Emily J.; m. Kathleen Francis Booth, June 30, 1990; stepchildren: Blair T. Manwell, Lindsay A. Manwell. BS, U. Calif., Berkeley, 1963. CPA. With Coopers & Lybrand, 1963-80; mng. ptnr. Sacramento, Calif., 1976-80; ptnr. Arthur Young & Co., San Francisco, 1980-89, Ernst & Young, San Francisco, 1989-94; prof. U. Calif., Berkeley, 1994—; bd. dirs. The Dutra Group; chair constrn. industry group Coopers & Lybrand, 1973-80, Arthur Young, 1980-89, Ernst & Young, 1989-94; guest lectr. Engring. Sch. Stanford U., 1976; lectr. Golden Gate Coll., 1975. Author: (books) Businessman's Guide to Constuction, 1981, Construction Management Book, 1984, Construction Accounting and Financial Management, 5th edit., 1994, Construction Litigation-Representing The Contractor, 1992, Construction Insurance, Bonding and Risk Management, 1996. bd. dirs. Sacramento Met. YMCA, 1976-82, V.p., 1979-82; bd. dirs. Sacramento Symphony Found., 1977-80; asst. state fin. chmn. Calif. Reagan for Pres., 1980. Lt. USN, 1953-59. Mem. AICPA (vice chmn. com. constrn. industry 1975-81), Nat. Assn. Accts. (pres. Oakland/East Bay chpt. 1972, Man of Yr. 1968), Calif. Soc. CPA's, Assn. Gen. Contractors Calif. (bd. dirs. 1971-74), World Trade Club, Commonwealth Club (San Francisco), Del Paso Country Club, Sutter Club, Lambda Chi Alpha. Roman Catholic. Avocations: antique boats, sailing, tennis, book collecting, pipe collecting. Home: 6 Heather Ln Orinda CA 94563-3508 Office: Ernst & Young 555 California St San Francisco CA 94104-1502

PALMIERI, ROBERT MICHAEL, music educator, researcher, pianist; b. Milw., Oct. 30, 1930; s. Michael D. and Nena (Marinelli) P.; m. Margaret Walsh, July 27, 1957; children: Michael, Nora, David, Christopher. MusB, Wis. Conservatory Music, 1953; MusM, Eastman Sch. Music, 1954. Instr. piano Wis. Conservatory Music, Milw., 1952-53; prof. music Sch. Music Kent (Ohio) State U., 1956-92, chmn. dir. keyboard instruments, 1956-92, prof. emeritus, 1992—; rsch. assoc. Western Wash. U., Bellingham, 1992—. Author: S. Rachmaninoff, 1985, Piano Information Guide, 1989; composer: Twenty Piano Exercises, 1971; editor: Encyclopedia of the Piano, 1996; concert pianist, Germany, Italy, Can., U.S.; reviewer Am. Ref. Books Ann. Faculty fellow Kent State U., 1969, 83, 86, 88, 91. Mem. Am. Musicological Soc., Am. Musical Instrument Soc. Roman Catholic. Avocation: travel.

PALMIERI, RODNEY AUGUST, state agency administrator, pharmacist; b. Santa Rosa, Calif., July 12, 1944; s. August John and Olga G.; m. Phyllis Scott, Aug. 14, 1965; children: Christopher August, Joshua Scott. AA, Santa Rosa Jr. Coll., 1964; B of Pharmacy, U. Colo., 1968. Pvt. practice pharmacy, Santa Rosa, 1968-71; pharm. cons. State of Calif., San Jose, 1971-75; chief pharm. cons. State of Calif., Sacramento, 1975-80, sr. mgr., 1991-95; project dir. Vital Record Improvement Project, 1991-95; gen. ptnr. Cold Springs Office Devel., Placerville, Calif., 1984-98; chief Office Vital Records, 1995—; dep. state registrar State of Calif., 1995—. Mem. El Dorado County Grand Jury, 1990; Webelos leader Boy Scouts Am., 1976-77, scoutmaster, 1977-82; referee, coach El Dorado (Calif.) Youth Soccer League, 1977-83; dir. El Dorado County Fair; chmn. City of Placerville Pers. Bd., 1995-98; cert. profl. guide and instr. for whitewater rafting. Mem. Rho Chi (pres. 1967-68), Phi Delta Chi. Avocations: gourmet cooking, collecting wine, martial arts, backpacking, golf. Office: Cold Springs Cons 2900 Cold Springs Rd Placerville CA 95667-4220

PALOLA, HARRY JOEL, international affairs executive, consultant; b. Kaukola, Viipuri, Finland, May 13, 1943; came to U.S., 1961; s. Heikki and Mary Dagmar (Ahokas) P.; m. Rita Hannele Ahokas, Sept. 15, 1968 (div. July 1992); children: Christine, Kathy, Kimberly. AA, L.A. City Coll., 1966; BS in Mech. Engring., Calif. State U., Long Beach, 1971; MA in Internat. Affairs, Calif. State U., Sacramento, 1995. Registered engr.-in-tng., Calif. Design engr. Northrop Corp., Hawthorne, Calif., 1971-77, Ford Aerospace and Comm. Corp., Newport Beach, Calif., 1977-81, B&M Assocs., San Diego, 1982; mech. engr. Raytheon Corp., Goleta, Calif., 1982-84; electronic packaging engr. LPL Tech. Svc., Seattle, 1984-86; design/test engr. Boeing Co., Seattle and Vandenberg, Calif., 1986-92; CEO Internat. Consultancy Corp., Santa Ynez, Calif., 1993—; cons. in basic and applied rsch. in human comm., 1993—. Author: International Finnish Studies: Language, History and Culture, 1995, The Karjala Question-Thoughts on Religious Directions, 1997. Econ. devel. student intern City of Sacramento, 1992-93. Sgt. USNG, 1966-72. Republican. Lutheran. Avocations: ocean sailing, private flying. Office: Internat Consultancy Corp 1041 N Refugio Rd Santa Ynez CA 93460-9316

PALOMINO, KRISTI SUZANN, elementary school educator; b. Garden Grove, Calif., Mar. 19, 1970; d. Stephen James and Jeanne Frances (Preleśnik) T.; m. Jessie Palomino Jr. BA in Liberal Studies, San Francisco State U., 1992, credentials in multiple subject edn., 1993. Cert. elem. tchr., Calif., crosscultural lang. acquisition devel. Tchg. asst. San Francisco State U., 1988-92; substitute tchr. Newark (Calif.) Unified Sch. Dist., 1992-93, New Haven Unified Sch. Dist., Union City, Calif., 1992-93; tchr. after-sch. program Milpitas (Calif.) Unified Sch. Dist., 1993, substitute tchr., tchr. 2nd grade, 1994, tchr. 4th and 5th grades, 1994-95; tchr. 1st grade Newark (Calif.) Unified Sch. Dist., 1995—; after-sch. tutor Chpt. 1 program Milpitas Unified Sch. Dist., 1994-95. Mem. Calif. Tchrs. Assn., San Mateo County Math and Sci. Coun. Democrat. Avocations: exercise, reading, gardening, theatre. Home: 6324 Lafayette Ave Newark CA 94560-2435

PALOVICH, GEORGE WESLEY, curator, artist, educator; b. Lorain, Ohio, Jan. 31, 1939; s. George Joseph and Josephine L. P.; m. Janet E. Trisler, May 2, 1961; children: Louise, Melissa, Donya, Shano. BE in Art, U. Toledo, 1960; MFA in Pottery and Ceramic Sculpture, Kent State U., 1965. Instr. San Antonio (Tex.) Art Inst., 1960-62; tchr., supr. Akron (Ohio) Art Inst., 1965-66; clay artist, painter, printmaker Ohio, Tex., Colo., Ariz., 1967—; asst. curator West Valley Art Mus., Surprise, Ariz., 1992-93; curator West Valley Art Mus., Surprise, 1993—; instr. ceramics Recreation Ctrs., Sun City and Sun City West, 1988—; mem. grant rev. panel Ariz. Commn. Arts, Phoenix, 1997—; mem. Meeting of Minds Symposium, Glendale C.C.; demonstrator pottery and sculpture Ariz. pub. schs.; juror numerous Ariz. exhbns. One-man shows include Toledo Mus. Art, Witte Mus., San Antonio, Eleven East Ashland Gallery, Phoenix; exhibited in group shows at Canton (Ohio) Art Inst., McNay Art Inst., San Antonio, Ashland (Ohio) Coll., Shemer Art Gallery, Phoenix, 1996, Sun Cities Mus. Art, Con el Corazon en Mex., Casa Grande Mus., Ariz., Mars Gallery, Phoenix, numerous others; represented in numerous pub. and pvt. collections. Recipient numerous awards area art shows. Mem. Nat. Assn. Mus. Exhibitors. Home: 2231 S Quitman Way Denver CO 80219-5138

PALOVICH, MARILYN LEE, elementary education educator; b. Trinidad, Colo., Apr. 24, 1943; d. Raymond Leon and Mary (Swigle) Swift; m. Joseph Lawrence Palovich, June 6, 1964; children: Milena Jo, Chad Michael. AA, Trinidad State Jr. Coll., 1963; BA, Adams State Coll., Alamosa, Colo., 1966. Cert. elem. edn. Tchr. grades 1-2-3-4 North Garcia Sch. Dist. No. 5, Trinidad, 1963-65; tchr. kindergarten Trinidad Sch. Dist. No. 1, 1965-68, tchrs. grades 3 and 5, 1970—; mem. adv. bd. Louden/Henritze Archaeology Mus., Trinidad, 1993—. Author: (poetry) Treasured Poems of America, 1994. Pres. Assn. Retarded Citizens, Trinidad, 1987-89; pres., v.p. So. Colo. Assn. to Aid the Handicapped, Trinidad, 1987-89—; mem. adv. bd., treas. So. Colo. Devel. Disability Svcs., Trinidad, 1987-89. Recipient Outstanding Elem. Tchr. award, 1974, 1st Pl. Nat. 5th Grade award Weekly Reader Editors, Middletown, 1994, Grand Prize Nat. 5th Grade award, 1995. Mem. NRA, Western Slavonic Assn., Colo. Fedn. Tchrs., Trinidad Fedn. Tchrs. Avocations: leather sewing and tooling, gun engraving, reading, writing poetry, handcrafts. Home: 733 Pine St Trinidad CO 81082-2314

PALS, BRIAN JOSEPH, industrial hygiene company executive; b. Belmond, Iowa, Apr. 29, 1959; s. Marvin Louis and Shirley E. (Proeger) P. B in Indsl. Tech./Occupational Safety, Iowa State U., 1982. Cert. safety profl.; cert. hazardous materials mgr. Safety specialist Honeywell, Littleton, Colo., 1986; indsl. hygienist Environ. Sci. and Engring. Inc., Englewood, Colo., 1986-89, Morrison Knudsen Corp., Englewood, 1990-97; prin. EH&S Svcs., Inc., Aurora, Colo., 1997—. CPR, first aid instr. ARC, Denver, 1986—. Mem. Am. Soc. Safety Engrs., Am. Indsl. Hygiene Assn., Colo. Safety Assn., Inst. of Hazardous Materials Mgmt. Avocations: skiing, hiking. Home and Office: 17411 E Gunnison Pl Aurora CO 80017-5204

PALUMBO-LIU, DAVID, literature educator; b. Rochester, N.Y.; s. Ch'ing Tung Liu and Pin-Pin T'an; m. Sylvie Palumbo-Liu; 1 child, Fabrice. BA in Comparative Lit., U. Calif., Berkeley, 1975, BA in Oriental Langs., 1977, PhD, 1988. Asst. prof. Georgetown U., Washington, 1989-90; assoc. prof. Stanford (Calif.) U., 1990—; mem. adv. bd. Rev. Edn., Pedagogy and Cultural Studies; mem. editl. bd. Positions: East Asia Cultural Critique. Author: Poetics of Appropriation, 1993, Asian/American: Historical Crossings of a Racial Frontier, 1999; editor: The Ethnic Canon, 1995; co-editor: Streams of Cultural Capital, 1997; series co-editor: Asian American History and Culture; contbr. articles to profl. publs. Fellow Am. Coun. Learned Socs.; mem. MLA. Office: Stanford U Dept Comparative Lit Stanford CA 94305

PAN, WILLIAM JIAWEI, import and export company executive, consultant; b. Shanghai, People's Republic of China, July 24, 1935; came to U.S., 1985; s. You-Yuan Pan and Ruth Li Tien; m. Lena Fengqiu Liu, Dec. 26, 1965; 1 child, Song. BS, Peking U., People's Republic of China, 1958. Cert. sr. engr., People's Republic of China. Engr. Beijing Radio Factory, 1958-78, Dong Feng TV Factory, Beijing, 1978-80; asst. gen. mgr. Beijing br. China Nat. Electronics Import/Export Corp., 1980-91; mgr. electronics dept. China Resource Products, N.Y.C., 1985-91; pres., chief exec. officer King Trading, Inc., San Francisco, 1987-91; pres., CEO Kings Internat., Inc., San Jose, Calif., 1991—. Avocations: photography, tennis, swimming, badminton. Office: Kings Internat Inc 467 Saratoga Ave Ste 150 San Jose CA 95129-1326

PANACCIONE, BRUCE ROY, system analyst, geographer; b. Van Nuys, Calif., Dec. 22, 1958; s. Thomas Edward and Dorothy Louise (Bogert) P.; m. Kaori Tokushiku, July 11, 1987; 1 child, Thomas Morio. AA in Photojournalism, L.A. Pierce Coll., 1987, AS, 1979; BA in Geography magna cum laude, Calif. State U., Northridge, 1990, postgrad. studies, 1990-92. Cert. gen. ins.; assoc. in ins. svcs. Exploration technician Unocal Corp., L.A., 1989-92; sr. market rsch. analyst, Geographic Info. Sys. leader Automobile Club of So. Calif., Costa Mesa, 1992—. *In the course of his career, Bruce Roy Panaccione has been engaged in applying geographic information system (GIS) technology to practical business problems. While employed at the Automobile Club of Southern California, the largest AAA club, he has performed analysis in the fields of marketing, facilities planning, property and causality insurance, and disaster management. He also has been active as a volunteer in promoting disaster preparedness, most recently with the American Red Cross. This avocation was partly a result of his experience*

as a survivor of the collapse of the Northridge Meadows apartments during the January 1994 Northridge Earthquake. Mem. Spkrs.' Bur. Orange County Chpt. ARC, 1997—. Recipient Geography Scholarship, Nat. Coun. for Geographic Edn., 1989. Mem. Assn. Am. Geographers, GeoBus. Assn. (charter). Office: Automobile Club So Calif 3333 Fairview Rd Costa Mesa CA 92626-1610

PANAJOTOVIC, ILIJA SVETISLAV, producer, director, writer; b. Belgrade, Yugoslavia, Apr. 25, 1932; came to U.S. 1962; s. Svetislav and Stanka P.; m. Elena Maria Panajotovic; children: Eric, Sonja. Diploma in piano, Mokranjac Music Sch., Belgrade, 1954; Law degree, Belgrade U., 1957; BA in Polit. Sci., UCLA, 1963. Sole practice Belgrade, 1957-62; prin. Noble Prodns., Inc., Los Angeles, 1966—. Assoc. producer: (films) Brown Eye Evil Eye, 1966, Curse of the Faithful Wife, 1968, Togetherness, 1970; producer, writer Operation Cross Eagles, 1969, Last Train to Berlin, 1973, Dirty Rebel, 1984, Wildwind, U.S., Yugoslavia, USSR co-prodn., 1986; producer Bomb at 10:10, 1967, Hell River, 1977, Cruise Missile, 1978, Day of the Assassin, 1981; U.S. and Yugoslavia coordinator Skalawag, 1972; producer, dir., author original story (film) Last Nazi at Large, 1994; co-writer, producer Massacre At Noon, 1989, Derwishes, 1995. Named Tennis Nat. Jr. Singles Champion, 1948, 49, All-Nat. Singles Champion, 1959. Mem. Acad. Motion Picture Arts and Scis., Am. Film Mktg. Assn. (worldwide film distbr. 1984), Arbitration Assn. Am. Serbian Orthodox. Club: Hollywood (Calif.) Fgn. Press. Avocation: tennis. Participated in Jr. Wimbledon semi-finals, 1948; mem. Nat. Davis-Cup Team for 11 years, Wimbledon 1/4 finals in doubles, 1958; Nat. Yugoslav champion in singles, 1959.

PANETTA, JOSEPH DANIEL, biotechnology executive; b. Syracuse, N.Y., Mar. 1, 1954; s. Salvatore and Josephine Mary (Sbardella) P.; m. Karin Ann Hoffman, Oct. 21, 1978; children: Lauren Marie, Christopher Daniel. BS, LeMoyne Coll., 1976; MPH, U. Pitts., 1979. Environ. protection specialist U.S. EPA, Washington, 1979-82, sr. policy analyst, 1982-84; project leader Schering Corp./NorAm Chem Co., Wilmington, Del., 1984-85; mgr. regulatory affairs agrchems. divsn. Pennwalt Corp., Phila., 1985-88; mgr. corp. regulatory affairs Mycogen Corp., San Diego, 1988-90; dir. corp. regulatory affairs and quality assurance Mycogen Corp., 1990-92; dir. corp. regulatory, environ. affairs Mycogen Corp., San Diego, 1992-97, v.p. govt. and pub. affair, 1998—; chmn. agr. and environment subcom. Internat. Bioindustry Forum; chmn. maneb data task force Inter-industry, Washington, 1985-88; guest lectr. biotech. U. Calif., San Diego, and Calif. Western Law Sch.; advisor bd. on agr. NAS. Contbr. articles to profl. jours. Mem. Rep. State Com. Del., 1987. Mem. Am. Coop Protection Assn. (chmn. com. biotech.), Nat. Agrl. Chems. Assn. (mem. registrations com. 1986-89), Biotech. Industy Orgn. (mem. food and agr. steering com., chmn. bipesticides com., internat. affairs com.), Calif. Indsl. Biotech. Assn. (mem. agrl. affairs com.), Am. Chem. Soc. (mem. agrl. div.), Am. Seed Trade Assn. (chmn. steering com. biotech.), Gov.'s Biotech. Coun. (Calif.). Roman Catholic. Avocations: yachting, skiing, classical piano. Home: 4324 Corte Al Fresco San Diego CA 92130-2160 Office: Mycogen Corp 5501 Oberlin Dr San Diego CA 92121-1718

PANG, HERBERT GEORGE, ophthalmologist; b. Honolulu, Dec. 23, 1922; s. See Hung and Hong Jim (Chuu) P.; student St. Louis Coll., 1941; BS, Northwestern U., 1944, MD, 1947; m. Dorothea Lopez, Dec. 27, 1953. Intern Queen's Hosp., Honolulu, 1947-48; postgraduate course ophthalmology N.Y.U., Med. Sch., 1948-49; resident ophthalmology Jersey City Med. Ctr., 1949-50, Manhattan Eye, Ear, & Throat Hosp., N.Y.C., 1950-52; practice medicine specializing in ophthalmology, Honolulu, 1952-54, 56—; mem. staffs Kuakini Hosp., Children's Hosp., Castle Meml. Hosp., Queen's Hosp., St. Francis Hosp.; asst. clin. prof. ophthalmology U. Hawaii Sch. Medicine, 1966-73, now asso. clin. prof. Cons. Bur. Crippled Children, 1952-73, Kapiolani Maternity Hosp., 1952-73, Leahi Tb. Hosp., 1952-62. Capt. M.C., AUS, 1954-56, Diplomate Am. Bd. Ophthalmology. Mem. AMA, Am. Acad. Ophthalmology and Otolaryngology, Assn. for Rsch. Ophthalmology, ACS, Hawaii Med. Soc. (gov. med. practice com. 1958-62, chmn. med. speakers com. 1957-58), Hawaii Eye, Ear, Nose and Throat Soc. (pres. 1960), Pacific Coast Oto-Ophthalmological Soc., Pan Am. Assn. Ophthalmology, Mason, Shriner, Eye Study Club (pres. 1972—). Home: 2228 Liliha St Honolulu HI 96817-1650

PANG, MICHAEL PILI, artistic director; b. Honolulu, Mar. 12, 1962; s. Sam Young and Violet Fung Kui (Lau) Pang. BA, U. Puget Sound, 1984. Youth counselor Alu Like, Kamuela, Hawaii, 1987; front office asst. mgr. Hyatt Regency Waikoloa, Hawaii, 1987-89, credit mgr./accts. receivable mgr., 1989-91; resource person Dept. Edn.-North Kohala, Kamuela, 1991-92; artistic dir. Hawai'i Arts Ensemble, Kamuela, 1994—; founder Halau Hula Ka No'eau, Kamuela, 1986—; apprentice Pulani Kanaka'ole Kanahele, Hawaii State Found. on Culture and Arts, 1987. Co-choreographer 'Ike/Body of Knowledge, 1997; composer, choreographer hula Hopoe, 1995; Kumu Hula/choreographer He Inoa No Emma-, 1997 (Helen Desha Beamer award), Huliau, 1997. Bd. dirs. Edith Kanaka'ole Found., Hilo, Hawaii, 1991—, Lymann Mus., Hilo, 1993-97. Recipient Preservation award Hawaii chpt. ASID, 1998. Mem. Hawaii State Dance Coun. Fax: (808) 885-9018. Home: PO Box 64-4249 Ke Kamuela HI 96743-2705 Office: Hawaii Arts Ensemble Halau Hula Ka No'eau PO Box 1907 Kamuela HI 96743-1907

PANGARO, DAVID LAWRENCE, theatre educator; b. Greenwich, Conn., July 19, 1951; s. Lawrence Patrick and Edith Virginia (Goddard) P.; m. Paula Louise Roberts, Oct. 8, 1976; children: Devin John, Nicholas David, Adrian Joseph. BA in communications, Univ. Vt., 1973; MFA, San Francisco State, 1996. Stage lighting tech. The Phoebus Co., San Francisco, 1980-96; adj. faculty design Univ. San Francisco, 1988—, tech. dir. of theatre, 1984—; freelance lighting design Brenda Wong Arts, San Francisco, 1989-93. Musician Mongrel Dogs, 1997, Duck's Breath Mystery Theatre, 1980. Recipient Greg Falls award Univ. Vt., 1973. Mem. U.S. Inst. Theatre Tech. Avocations: baseball coach, musician. Office: Univ San Francisco 2130 Fulton St San Francisco CA 94117-1050

PANIKKAR, RAIMON, priest; b. Barcelona, Spain, Nov. 2, 1918; came to U.S., 1967; s. Rammuni and Carmen (Alemany) P. Philosophy Licenciate, U. Barcelona, 1941, Chem. Sci. Licenciate, 1942; PhD, U. Madrid, 1946, D Chem. Scis., 1958. Ordained priest Roman Cath. Ch., 1946. Chaplain U. Madrid, 1946-50, U. Salamanca (Spain), 1950-53, U. Rome, 1950-63, Diocese Varanasi (India), 1964—; prof. U. Calif., Santa Barbara, 1971-87, prof. emeritus, 1987—. Author: Blessed Simplicity, 1982, Vedic Experience, 1989, The Silence of God, 1989, A Dwelling Place for Wisdom, 1993, Cultural Disarmament: A Way to Peace, 1995, Invisible Harmony, 1995, Intrareligious Dialogue, 1999. Mem. Teilhard de Chardin Centre (v.p.), Am. Acad. Religion, Internat. Inst. Philosophy. Office: U Calif Dept Religious Studies Santa Barbara CA 93106

PANINA, MARINA PETRONNA, Russian language educator; b. Sumgait, Azerbaijan, Feb. 11, 1958; came to U.S., 1991; d. Peter Semjonovich Chernyshov and Anna Alexandrana (Shishrina) Chernysova; m. Alexander Michailovich Panin, August 8, 1981; children: Dmitry, Maxim. BA, Music Coll., Sumgait, USSR, 1978; MA, Pedagogical Inst., Azerbaijan, 1983. Tchr., high sch. Moscow, 1983-91; instr. Brigham Young U., Provo, UT, 1991-92, Missionary Tng. Ctr., Provo, UT, 1992-94; adj. faculty Utah Valley State Coll., Orem, UT, 1994—. Singer, piano performance in concerts, 1993-98. Mem. No. UT Piano Assn.(jury, judge 1993—). Avocations: art, traveling. Home: 1753 Gold River Dr Orem UT 84057-7230 Office: UVSC 800 W 1200 S Orem UT 84058-5999

PANNER, OWEN M., federal judge; b. 1924. Student, U. Okla., 1941-43, LL.B., 1949. Atty. Panner, Johnson, Marceau, Karnopp, Kennedy & Nash, 1950-80; judge, now sr. judge U.S. Dist. Ct. Oreg., Portland, 1980—, sr. judge, 1992—. Office: US Dist Ct 1000 SW 3rd Ave Ste 1207 Portland OR 97204-2942*

PANOFSKY, WOLFGANG KURT HERMANN, physicist, educator; b. Berlin, Germany, Apr. 24, 1919; came to U.S., 1934, naturalized, 1942; m. [illegible] dren: Richard, Margaret, Edward, Carol, Steven. A.B., Princeton U., 1938, DSc (hon.), 1983; Ph.D., Calif. Inst. Tech., 1942; D.Sc. (hon.), Case Inst. Tech., 1963, U. Sask., 1964, Columbia U., 1977, U. Hamburg, Germany, 1984, Yale U., 1985, hon. degree, U. Beijing, 1987, DSc (hon.), U. Rome, 1988; hon. degree, Uppsala U., Sweden, 1991. Mem. staff mem. radiation lab U. Calif., 1945-51, asst. prof., 1946-48, asso. prof., 1948-51; prof. physics Stanford U., 1951-62, prof. Stanford Linear Accelerator Ctr., 1962-89, prof. emeritus, 1989—; dir. Stanford (High Energy Physics Lab., Stanford Linear Accelerator Center), 1962-84, dir. emeritus, 1984—; Am. del. Conf. Cessation Nuclear Tests, Geneva, 1959; mem. President's Sci. Adv. Com., 19600-65l cons. Office Sci. and Tech., Exec. Office Pres., 1965-73, U.S. ACDA, 1968-81; mem. gen. adv. com. to White House, 1977-81; mem. panel Office Sci. and Tech. Policy, 1977; with nat. def. rsch. Calif. Inst. Tech. and Los Alamos, 1942-45; mem. JASON, 1965—; chmn. bd. overseers Superconducting Supercollider Univs. Rsch. Assn., 1984-93; mem. com. to provide interim oversight Dept. Energy nuclear weapons complex NAS, 1988-89; mem. panel on nuclear materials control Dept. Energy, 1991-92; mem. Commn. on Particles and Field of Internat. Union Pure and Applied Physics, 1985-93. Decorated officier Legion of Honor; recipient Lawrence prize AEC, 1961, Nat. Medal Sci., 1969, Franklin medal, 1970, Ann. Pub. Service award Fedn. Am. Scientists, 1973, Enrico Fermi award Dept. Energy, 1979, Shoong Found. award for sci., 1983, Hilliard Roderick prize Sci. AAAS, 1991, Matteucei medal, 1997; named Calif. Scientist Yr., 1966. Fellow Am. Phys. Soc. (pres. 1974); mem. NAS (mem. com. on internat. security and arms control 1985—, chmn. com. 1985-93, mem. scis. com. on scholarly comm. with China 1987-92), AAAS, Am. Philos. Soc., French Acad. Scis. (fgn.), Russian Acad. Scis., Nat. Acad. Lincei (Italy), Phi Beta Kappa, Sigma Xi. Home: 25671 Chapin Rd Los Altos CA 94022-3413 Office: Stanford Linear Accelerator Ctr PO Box 4349 Palo Alto CA 94309-4349

PANSKY, EMIL JOHN, entrepreneur; b. Manhattan, N.Y., June 1, 1921; s. Stanislaus and Anna (Jankovic) P.; m. Billie B. Byrne, May 27, 1955; 1 adopted child, Jimmy. BME, Cooper Union Coll., 1941; MBA, Harvard U., 1949; MADE, NYU, 1950. Registered profl. engr., Mich. Chief insp. flight line Republic Aviation, Farmingdale, L.I., 1941-45, salvage engr., 1946-47; product control supr. to product control mgr. Ford Motor, Detroit, 1949-51; asst. plant mgr. Anderson Brass, Birmingham, Ala., 1951-53; asst. v.p. to v.p. mfg. Cummins Engine, Columbus, Ind., 1953-54; pvt. practice Emil J. Pansky Assoc., San Leandro, Calif., 1954—; treas. Lane Metal Finishers, 1968-80, Calif. Tech. Metal Finishers, 1988-90; pres. Calif. Mfrs. Tech. Assn., San Francisco, 1978-80; ind. tech. cons. to small bus., 1994—. Patentee die cast auto wheels, 1965. Pres. Menlo Circus Club, Menlo Park, Calif., 1974-81, Home Owners Assn., Kanuela, Hawaii, 1989-95; bd. dirs. No. Calif. Tennis Assn., San Francisco, 1984-87. Mem. ASME (life), Harvard Club San Francisco (bd. dirs. 1986-92), Harvard Bus. Sch. Club San Francisco (bd. dirs. 1970-73, cons. 1994-95). Democrat. Avocations: tennis, chess. Home: 901 Jackling Dr Hillsborough CA 94010-6127 Office: Emil J Pansky Assoc 1666 Timothy Dr San Leandro CA 94577-2312

PANTALEO, JACK, writer, composer, social worker, harpist; b. Melrose Park, Ill., Nov. 30, 1954; s. Jack Sam Pantaleo and Sophia Mannozzi Pantaleo Cicero. Psychiat. Tech., C.C., San Francisco, 1981; BA in Humanities, New Coll. Calif., San Francisco, 1986; MA in Writing, U. San Francisco, 1988. Lic. psychiat. technician. Asst. to dean U. San Francisco Sch. Nursing, 1984-88; grammar sch. tchr. St. Michael's Cath. Sch., San Francisco, 1989-91; instr. English Vista C.C., Berkeley, Calif., 1990-93; social worker City and County of San Francisco, 1991—; founder, dir. Evangelicals Concerned, San Francisco, 1978-85; co-founder, co-dir. AIDS InterFaith Network, San Francisco, 1983-88. Playwright/composer musical The Gospel According to the Angel Julius translated into German and performed in Hamburg, Germany, 1999; (one-act play): Uncle Fred's Ex-Staight Ministry, 1999; contbg. author: (collection of meditations) The Road to Emmaus, 1990; author booklet and articles. Caregiver for babies with AIDS, The Bridge, San Francisco, 1989-93. Work included in Silver Quill, The David Ross Meml. Competition, Wichita, 1996. Mem. Social Workers Union, Nat. Writers Union. Democrat. Episcopalian. Avocations: harp, lecturing. Office: Child Protection Ctr San Francisco Gen Hosp 995 Potrero Ave San Francisco CA 94110

PANTOS, WILLIAM PANTAZES, mechanical engineer, consultant; b. Ann Arbor, Mich., May 15, 1957; s. William Van and Lillian William (Skinner) P. BS in Mech. Engring., Northwestern U., Evanston, Ill., 1979; MS in Mech. Engring., San Diego State U., 1991. Registered profl. engr., Calif. Owner Signs & Symbols, Niles, Ill., 1975-80; engr. Hughes Aircraft, El Segundo, Calif., 1980-83, Gen. Dynamics, San Diego, 1983-85; staff engr. TRW, San Diego, 1985-90; pres. Tekton Industries, Carlsbad, Calif., 1990—. NROTC scholar USN, 1975. Mem. Am. Soc. Mech. Engrs., Nat. Soc. Profl. Engrs., Alpha Delta Phi. (pres. 1978). Greek Orthodox. Home: 1571 San Elijo Ave Cardiff By The Sea CA 92007-2420

PANTTAJA, DEAN, scenic design, theater design educator; b. Lawton, Okla., May 19, 1958; s. William Toivo an Mona Lee (Fields) P.; m. Micki Lee Goldthorpe, Sept. 15, 1984; children: Brayden, Shelby. MFA in Theatre, Humboldt State U., 1983; PhD in Edn., U. Idaho, 1995. Tech. dir. Humboldt State U., Arcata, Calif., 1983-86; scenic designer Idaho Theatre for Youth, Boise, 1992—; prof. design U. Idaho, Moscow, 1986—; lighting designer Tacoma Actor's Guild, 1998—. Active Boy Scouts of Am. Recipient Gov.'s award in arts, 1994, Meritorious Achievement award Kennedy Ctr., Washington, 1997, 98. Mem. U.S. Inst. Theatre Tech. (chmn. inland northwest sect. 1994-), Illuminating Engrs. Soc., U. Idaho Alumni Assn. Avocations: gardening, camping, woodworking. Office: U Idaho Dept Theater Arts Moscow ID 83844-3074

PAPAKONSTANTINO, STACY, English language educator; b. San Francisco, Feb. 27, 1967; d. Demetrios and Eugenia (Yiallely) P. AA, City. Coll. of San Francisco, 1987; BA in English Lit., San Francisco State U., 1989, MA in English Lang. Studies, 1991. Cert. in tchg. composition and postsecondary reading. English, ESL tutor City Coll. of San Francisco, 1986-87, instr. of English, 1991—; Greek instr. Holy Trinity Sch., 1988-90; chair student grade and file rev. com., City Coll. of San Francisco, 1996—, resource mem. student success com., 1997—, mem. student complaint com., 1997—, mem. composition/lit./reading com., 1996—. Mem. Nat. Coun. Tchrs. of English. Democrat. Orthodox. Avocations: reading, movies and plays, helping needy people, spiritual worship, fitness. Home: 48 Westpark Dr Daly City CA 94015-1055 Office: City Coll of San Francisco 50 Phelan Ave San Francisco CA 94112-1821

PAPE, ARNIS WESTON, minister; b. Portales, N.Mex., Dec. 24, 1950; s. Arnis Wilson and Lella Mae (Berry) P.; m. Lucena Ann Molzen, May 31, 1975; children: John Dayton, Jennifer Marie. BA in Psychology, U.N.Mex., 1974; MS in Biblical and Related Studies, Abilene Christian U., 1995. Ordained to ministry Church of Christ, 1972. Assoc. minister Ch. of Christ, Plainview, Tex., 1974-76; pulpit minister Ch. of Christ, Artesia, N.Mex., 1976-85, Ft. Collins, Colo., 1985-97; tchr. Pepperdine U., Malibu, 1991, 93. Author: A Journey of the Heart, 1998; contbr. articles to profl. jours.; author booklet: Happy Though Married, 1988, rev. edit., 1992. Co-founder Am. Children's Transplant Fund, Ft. Collins, 1987; mem. Parent Adv. Bd., Artesia, 1983-84; mem. pres.'s coun. Lubbock Christian U., 1985—. Recipient award for outstanding svc. Ch. of Christ, 1985. Avocations: photography, biking, camping, woodworking. Home: 2212 Shawnee Ct Fort Collins CO 80525-1849

PAPE, GREGORY LAURENCE, English language educator, poet; b. Eureka, Calif., Jan. 17, 1947; s. Laurence Albert and Irene Pape; m. Marnie Prange, July 23, 1988; children: Coleman Miles, Clay Bowen. BA, Fresno (Calif.) State Coll., 1970; MA, Calif. State U., Fresno, 1973; MFA, U. Ariz., 1974. Asst. prof. Hollins (Va.) Coll., 1979-80, U. Mo., Columbia, 1980-82; writer-in-residence U. Ala., Tuscaloosa, spring 1981, 83; Bingham poet-in-residence U. Louisville, 1983-84; vis. asst. prof. No. Ariz. U., Flagstaff, 1984-85; assoc. prof. Fla. Internat. U., Miami, 1985-87; prof. U. Mont., Missoula, 1987—; Coal Royalty endowed chair U. Ala., Tuscaloosa, 1993; dir. creative writing U. Mont., Missoula, 1994-95; mem. Javits grad. fellowship panelist U.S. Dept. Edn., Washington, 1990, 91, 92, 97. Author: Border Crossings, 1978, Black Branches, 1984, Storm Pattern, 1992, Sunflower Facing the Sun, 1992 (Iowa prize 1991). [illegible] Pushcart prize XIII Pushcart Press N.Y.C. 1988-89; fellow in creative writing Nat. Endowment for the Arts, 1978, 84. Mem. Acad. Am. Poets, Associated Writing Programs. Avocations: fly fishing, biking, hunting, surfing, photography. Office: U Mont English Dept Missoula MT 59812

PAPP, HARRY, science association administrator. Pres. Ariz. Zool. Soc., The Phoenix Zoo, 1995—. Office: Elroy Papp & Assoc 6225 N 24th St Ste 150 Phoenix AZ 85016 also: Phoenix Zoo 455 N Galvin Pkwy Phoenix AZ 85008-3431*

PAPPAS, JIM D., chief bankruptcy judge; b. 1952. Chief judge U.S. Bankruptcy Ct., Boise, 1993—. Office: US Bankruptcy Ct Fed Bldg and US Courthouse 550 W Fort St MSC 042 Boise ID 83724-0101*

PAPPAS, LEAH AGLAIA, civic worker, political consultant, educator; b. Ogden, Utah, Mar. 23, 1936; d. George Thomas and Maria (Harames) P. BA, Coll. St. Mary of the Wasatch, 1959. Tchr. Bishop Gorman High Sch., Las Vegas, Nev., 1959-64; with Dist. Atty.'s staff, Las Vegas, 1972-75; tchr. Weber State Coll., Las Vegas, 1985. Civic worker various orgns., including Opera Guild, Heart Fund, City of Hope, March of Dimes, also groups for prevention of blindness, sr. citizens' groups, others, Ogden and Las Vegas, 1955—; cons. numerous polit. campaigns, Ogden, Las Vegas and Boston, L.A., John F. Kennedy campaign, 1959; alt. del. Chgo. Nat. Conv.; vol. Senator Robert Kennedy Campaign, 1968; supr. Senator Edward M. Kennedy Campaign, Boston, 1970, 76, Presdl. Campaign, 1980; campaign worker Gov. Jerry Brown, L.A., 1978, Pres. Bill Clinton, 1996; officer mgr. Reagan-Bush Campaign, 1984. Greek Orthodox. Home: 1323 Marilyn Dr Ogden UT 84403-0424

PAQUETTE, RICHARD, airport executive. V.p. airport devel. Calgary Airport, AB, Can.; pres., CEO airport performance group Calgary Airport Authority Co. Mem. Alta. Aviation Coun. Mem. Am. Assn. Airport Execs., Calgary C. of C. Avocations: golf, skiing, bike riding, photography, hockey. Office: Shell Arrow Ctr PO Box 700, 1441 Aviation Park NE, Calgary, AB Canada T2E 8M7

PARALEZ, LINDA LEE, technology management consultant; b. Raton, N.Mex., Oct. 29, 1955. AS, Amarillo Coll., 1975; student West Tex. State U., 1975-77, BBA, Century U., Beverly Hills, Calif., 1984, MBA, 1987, PhD in Bus. Mgmt. and Econ. Century U. Teaching asst. Amarillo (Tex.) Coll., 1974-75; drafter natural gas div. Pioneer Corp., Amarillo, 1975-76, sr. drafter exploration div. Amarillo Oil Co. 1976-77; drafting supr., engring. svcs. supr., dir. speakers' bur. Thunder Basin Coal Co., Atlantic Richfield Co., Wright, Wyo., 1977-86; pres., ptnr., tech. and adminstrv. cons. Rose Enterprises, Inc., 1986—; prof. tech. mgmt. U. Phoenix, Utah, 1995-96; adj. prof. Weber State U., Ogden, Utah; tech. writer Eaton Corp., Riverton, Wyo., 1986-88; cons. State Wyo. Office on Family Violence and Sexual Assault, Cheyenne, 1986-89; Diamond L Industries, Inc., Gillette, Wyo., 1986-88; tech. writer, pubs. cons. Thiokol Corp., Brigham City, Utah, 1987-89, design specialist space ops., 1989-90, mgr. total quality mgmt. ctr. space ops., 1990—, cons. organizational effectiveness and quality mgmt. principles; cons. incident investigation team NASA Solid Rocket Booster Program, Huntsville, Ala.; cons. process improvement Puget Power, Seattle, Wash., Pub. Svc. Co. of Colo., W.R. White Co.; cons. process design Microsoft Corp., Seattle; mgmt. cons., consulting dir. Western Regional Water Utilities Benchmarking Group; process redesign cons. City of Seattle, 1995—. Author: (poetry) God was Here, But He Left Early, 1976, Gift of Wings, 1980, 89; columnist Wytech Digest; contbr. numerous articles to profl. jours. Vol. NASA Young Astronauts Program Adv. Com., 1991—; bd. dirs. Campbell County Drafting Adv. Coun., 1984-85; sec. bd. dir. exec. com. Am. Inst. Design and Drafting, 1984-85, tech. publ. chairperson, 1984-85; vol. educator, data specialist child abuse prevention coun. Ogden. Named Most Outstanding Woman, Beta Sigma Phi, 1980, 81; recipient Woman in the Industry recognition Internat. Reprographics Assn., 1980; grand prize winner Wyo. Art Show with painting titled Energy, 1976. Mem. AAUW, NAFE, NOW, Am. Soc. Quality Control, Am. Productivity and Quality Coun., Am. Legion Aux., Ocean Rsch. Edn. Soc., Gloucester, Mass. (grant proposal writer, 1984), Soc. Tech. Communications, 4-H Club. Home: 22259 Treefarm Ln Poulsbo WA 98370

PARAMO, PATRICIA ANN, city/county official; b. Wiesbaden, Germany, Mar. 17, 1970; came to U.S., 1974; d. John Anthony and Irmgard Elizabeth (Knab) D. BA, BS, U. Colo., 1993. Reporter/photographer Ark. Valley Pub., Leadville, Colo., 1993-95; copy/news editor Macari-Healey Pub., Littleton, Colo., 1995-96; editor/writer Harvard Bus. Sch., Denver, 1996-98; edtl. technician Career Svc. Authority, City/County of Denver, 1996-98, agy. mktg./pub. rels. rep., 1998—; part-time swim coach, waterbabies instr., water safety, lifeguard Aurora (Colo.) Pub. Schs., 1989-98. Freelance writer Highlands Ranch Herald, Littleton, 1995-97, Mentor for a Child, 1996—. Recipient Goethe Inst. award, 1992. Mem. Soc. Profl. Journalists, Colo. Press Assn. Avocations: mountain biking, hiking, swimming, skiing, travel. Home: 1460 S Osceola St Denver CO 80219-3819 Office: Career Service Authority 110 16th St Ste 450 Denver CO 80202-5203

PARDINI, SHARON KAY BROWN, architectural and interior designer; b. Grand Junction, Iowa, Apr. 15, 1938; d. Loyal Melvin Blanshan and Frances Mildred (Brown) Manen; m. Frederick Brown, Oct. 19, 1957 (div. Apr. 1963); 1 child Randal Alan; m. Joseph Leslie Pardini, Nov. 11, 1975; 1 child, Tiana Margaret. BA in Cosmetology, Lee Ann Acad., 1957; AA, U. Calif., Berkeley, 1966; BBA, U. Calif. Owner Sharon's Hair Fashions Salons, Oakland, Calif., 1958-80; v.p., sec., treas. Western Container Transp. Inc., 1978-87; pres. Par-West Inc. Design Firm, 1983—; mem. adv. bd. Bd. Cosmetology, Oakland, 1965-69; owner The Collection Designer Gallery, Lafayette, Calif., 1987-93. Mem. Republican Task Force, Washington, 1981-89; mem. svc. league Santa Catalina Sch., Monterey, Calif., 1986. Mem. Calif. Cosmetologist Assn. (v.p. 1973-75, bd. dirs. 1970-77), Mission Hills Country Club. Avocations; studying architecture and designing, horticulture, writing, furniture designing.

PARDUE, A. MICHAEL, retired plastic and reconstructive surgeon; b. Nashville, June 23, 1931; s. Andrew Peyton and Ruby (Fly) P.; m. Lilavati Sharma, Dec. 1996. BS, U. of the South, 1953; MD, U. Tenn., 1957. Resident in gen. surgery Pittsfield (Mass.) Affiliated Hosps., 1966; resident in plastic surgery N.Y. Hosp./Cornell Med. Ctr., 1968; plastic surgeon A. Michael Pardue, M.D., Thousand Oaks, Calif., 1968-98. Lt. comdr. USN, 1956-62. Fellow ACS; mem. Am. Soc. Plastic and Reconstructive Surgeons, Am. Soc. Aesthetic Plastic Surgery, Calif. Soc. Plastic Surgeons. Episcopalian. Avocations: fly fishing, skiing, golf, equestrian, African safaris.

PAREDES, BERT (NORBERT PAREDES), computer systems engineer; b. Frankfurt, Germany, Dec. 27, 1947; s. George and Elfriede (Kleebach) P.; m. Linda L. Stubblefield, July 5, 1968 (div. 1986); m. Katherine Blacklock, Feb. 4, 1989. BS in Computer Sci., SUNY, Albany, 1970; postgrad., U. Colo., 1977-78. Enlisted U.S. Army, 1970, programmer/analyst, 1970-79, resigned, 1979; staff engr. Martin Marietta, Denver, 1979-81, sr. staff engr., 1984-92; regional analyst, mgr. Gould Computer Systems, Denver, 1981-84; mgr. tech. analysis and support Denelcor, Inc., Aurora, Colo., 1984; v.p. C-Quad Systems, Inc., Littleton, Colo., 1992-94, pres., 1994—; Pres., chief exec. officer A.C.T., Inc., Denver, 1982-84. Contbr. articles to profl. jours. Nat. Merit scholar, 1966. Mem. Assn. Computing Machinery, Armed Forces Communications and Electronics Assn., Am. Rose Soc., Mensa, Denver Bot. Gardens. Lutheran. Home: 6859 N Beaver Run Littleton CO 80125-9202 Office: C-Quad Systems Inc 26 W Dry Creek Cir Ste 600 Littleton CO 80120-8066

PARENTI, KATHY ANN, sales professional; b. Gary, Ind., Sept. 24, 1957; d. Lee Everett Huddleston and Barbara Elizabeth (Daves) Tilley; m. Michael A. Parenti, Mar. 31, 1979 (div. Sept. 1990); m. S. Curtis McCoy, Sept. 6, 1996. Student, Ind. U., Gary, 1977; cert., U. Nev., Las Vegas, 1978; diploma, Interior Design Inst., Las Vegas, 1984. Supr. Circus Circus Hotel, Las Vegas, 1980-87; owner Interior Views, Las Vegas, 1984-87; sales rep. Win-Glo Window Coverings, 1987-88, owner Dimension Design, 1988-90, sales rep. Sidney Goldberg & Assoc., Las Vegas, 1990—; sales rep.. Parenti & Assocs., 1990—. Mem. NAFF, Am. Soc. Interior Designers, Internat. [illegible] Soc., Rep Network. Avocations: exercise, reading, playing piano.

PARIKH, MIHIR, executive. Chmn. CEO ASYST, Fremont, Calif. Office: 48761 Kato Rd Fremont CA 94538-7313*

PARIS, RICHARD WAYNE, forester; b. Corning, N.Y., July 22, 1956; s. Robert Lee and Ann (Seeley) P.; m. Alberta E. Blanchard, Mar. 21, 1992. BS in Forest Resource, Iowa State U., 1978; postgrad., Everett C.C., 1984. Forester Colville Tribal Forestry, Nespelem, Wash., 1979-81, U.S. Bur. Indian Affairs, Nespelem, 1986—; fire warden, forester State of Utah, Kamas, 1982; law enforcement park technician U.S. Nat. Park Svc., Coulee Dam N.R.A., Wash., 1983-85; park technician U.S. Corps Engrs., Somerset, Ky., 1985-86; instr. Inland Empire EMS Tng. Coun. EMT, ambulance dir., fire chief Grand Coulee (Wash.) Vol. Fire Dept., 1981—; first aid instr. ARC, Ephrata, Wash., 1980-94; instr.-trainer CPR, Am. Heart Assn., Grant Countym Wash., 1980—; mem. Wash. State EMS, Edn. Com.; vol. Boy Scouts Am., 1983-96. Recipient Outstanding Svc. award ARC, 1982. Mem. Soc. Am. Foresters, Am. Forestry Assn., Coulee Med. Found. (sec. 1987-88), Grant County EMS Coun. (pres. 1984-86, sec. 1987-94), North Ctrl. Wash. Regional EMS Coun. (pres. 1990—, EMS Adminstr. of Yr. 1989, 91). Baptist. Avocations: travel, outdoor activities, emergency medicine. Office: US Bur Indian Affairs Colville Indian Agy Nespelem WA 99155

PARK, CHAN HO, professional baseball player; b. Kong Ju City, Korea, June 30, 1973. Student, Hang Yan U., Seoul, Korea. Pitcher L.A. Dodgers Baseball Team, 1994—. Achievements include being the first Korean to play in Major Leagues. Address: LA Dodgers 1000 Elysian Park Ave Los Angeles CA 90012-1112*

PARK, DAVID COATES, agent, music industry consultant, educator; b. Sacramento, Sept. 15, 1967; s. David Alexander Park and Judy Carol (Estes) Kobert. Pres. Breaking Legs, Sacramento, 1988—; advisor music bus. program Sacramento City Coll., 1990—; exec. dir. River City Music Adv., Sacramento, 1996—; cons., lectr. Stairway to Stardom, Sacramento, 1997—. Journalist (monthly music industry column) Alive & Kicking, 1996—. Mem. ASCAP. Avocations: fly fishing, tournament pool. Home: 1219 17th St Sacramento CA 95814-4015 Office: Breaking Legs PO Box 277932 Sacramento CA 95827-7932

PARK, EDWARD CAHILL, JR., retired physicist; b. Wollaston, Mass., Nov. 26, 1923; s. Edward Cahill and Fentress (Kerlin) P.; m. Helen Therese O'Boyle, July 28, 1951. AB, Harvard U., 1947; postgrad., Amherst Coll., 1947-49; PhD, U. Birmingham, Eng., 1956. Instr. Amherst (Mass.) Coll., 1954-55; mem. staff Lincoln Lab., Lexington, Mass., 1955-57, Arthur D. Little, Inc., Cambridge, Mass., 1957-60; group leader electronic systems Arthur D. Little, Inc., Santa Monica, Calif., 1960-64; sr. staff engr., head laser system sect. Hughes Aircraft Co., Culver City, Calif., 1964-68; sr. scientist Hughes Aircraft Co., El Segundo, Calif., 1986-88; mgr. electro optical systems sect. Litton Guidance and Control Systems, Woodland Hills, Calif., 1968-70; sr. phys. scientist The Rand Corp., Santa Monica, 1970-72; sr. scientist R&D Assocs., Marina Del Rey, Calif., 1972-1986, cons., 1986-89; sr. tech. specialist Rockwell Internat., N.Am. Aircraft, Seal Beach, Calif., 1988-94. Contbr. articles to profl. jours.; patentee in field. Served to 1st lt. USAAF, 1943-46. Grantee Dept. Indsl. and Sci. Research, 1953. Fellow Explorers Club (sec. So. Calif. chpt. 1978-79); mem. IEEE, Optical Soc. Am., N.Y. Acad. Scis., Sigma Xi. Democrat. Clubs: 20-Ghost (Eng.), Harvard (So. Calif.). Avocations: music, art, architecture, body surfing, gardening. Home: 932 Ocean Frnt Santa Monica CA 90403-2410

PARK, FRANCIS WOOD, III, minister; b. Rochester, Pa., Aug. 15, 1932; s. Francis Wood and Regina Ruth (Rees) P.; m. Marie Suzane Jacobs, Aug. 29, 1953; children: Andrew Wood, Ann Margaret, Catherine Jane. BA, Coll. of Wooster, 1954; MDiv, Pitts. Theol. Sem., 1957. Ordained to ministry Presbyn. Ch., 1957. Pastor 1st Presbyn. Ch., Fredericktown, Ohio, 1957-60, Northminster Presbyn. Ch., North Canton, Ohio, 1960-65; pastor, head of staff 1st Presbyn. Ch., Elmira, N.Y., 1965-70, Covenant Presbyn. Ch., Columbus, Ohio, 1970-83; pastor Faith Presbyn. Ch., Sun City, Ariz., 1984—; bd. dirs. Pitts. Theol. Sem., 1989—, Austin Presbyn. Theol. Sem. Ctr. for Ministry with Older Adults, Sun City, 1989; mem. presbytery coun. Grand Canyon Presytery, Ariz., 1986—, chmn. planning, 1986—; mem. Gen. Assembly spl. com. on structure rev., 1991—. Author: Pray With Me, 1987. Chmn. adv. coun. for Urban Renewal, North Canton, 1964-65, dir. Young Citizens Found., 1964-65; chmn. County Coun. on the Aging, Elmira, 1967-70; dir. Newtown Towers, Elmira, 1969-70; mem. NW Mental Health Svcs. Bd., Columbus, 1975; v.p. Sun Cities Area Children's Found., Sun City, 1991—. Mem. Rotary (chmn. well-being com. Sun City-Lakeview club). Home: 10113 W Pine Springs Dr Sun City AZ 85373-1124 Office: Faith Presbyn Ch 16000 N Del Webb Blvd Sun City AZ 85351-1604

PARK, JOSEPH CHUL HUI, computer scientist; b. Seoul, Korea, Aug. 6, 1937; s. Don Gil and Eui Kyung (Shin) P.; m. Young Ja Yoon, Aug. 17, 1968; children: Esther Y.J., Maria Y.S., David Y.W., Jonathan Y.S. BA, Coll of Wooster, Ohio, 1959; BS, MIT, 1959; MS, U. Ill., 1961, PhD, 1967. Mem. rsch. staff Stanford Linear Accelerator Ctr Stanford U., 1969-72, 73-75; assoc. prof., then prof. computer sci. Korea Advanced Inst. of Sci., Seoul, 1975-82; head Computer Sci. Rsch. Ctr. Korea Advanced Inst. Sci., Seoul, Korea, 1980-82; mem. tech. staff Braegen Corp., Milpitas, Calif., 1982-86, Hewlett-Packard Labs., Palo Alto, Calif., 1986-92; tech mgr. compiler Advanced Processor div. Intergraph Corp., Palo Alto, 1992-93; sr. staff engr. Sun Microelectronics, Sun Microsystems Compter Corp., Mountain View, Calif., 1993—; lectr. in computer engring. Santa Clara (Calif.) U., 1987-94. Mem. IEEE, Assn. Computing Machinery. Baptist. Home: 14800 Masson Ct Saratoga CA 95070-9715

PARK (PARKLEE), LEE, artist; b. Seoul, South Korea; s. Chung-Kun Park and Mil-Hwa Kim; m. Chai Kyung Lim, June 3, 1994. MA, Fla. State U., 1986. Group shows include Shinpara Gallery, L.A., Up-Stairs Gallery, L.A., Beverly Plz. Hotel, Pacific Mus., Pasadena, Calif., Barnsdall Art Gallery, Hollywood, Calif., Brand XXII The Assn. of Brand Art Ctr., Glendale, Calif., Asia Invitation Art Exhibn., Sejong Cultural Ctr., Seoul, la Peintre Moderne Coreend '93, Paris, Korea-Japan Interchange Exhbn., Tokyo, 1994, Musee d'Art Moderne de la Commanderie d'Unet, Paris, 1994, Bridgeport U., N.Y., 1995, San Bernardino County Mus., 1995, Kong-Ja Culture Art Exhbn., China, 1995, His Majesty the King's 50th Anniversary Art Exhbn., Thailand, 1996, 1st Venice Annual Internat. Open Art Exbhn., 1998, 1st Internat. Biennial Contemporary Art, Perugia, Italy, 1998, Heukyong-gangsung Internat. Art Exhbn., China, 1998, Ting Shao-Kuang Fine Art Ctr., Beverly Hills; 2 person shows include Cosmos Gallery, Honolulu, The City of L.A. Cultural Affairs Dept.; solo exhibits include Modern Art Gallery, L.A., Olympic Gallery, L.A., Sun Space Gallery, L.A., Gallery Nuevo, Pusan, Korea; publ. artwork in American References, Art of California mag., Artweek mag., The Biweekly Art Jour., Seoul, Artprint mag., Washington, Art Exposure mag., Calif., Encyclopedia of Living Artists mag., Calif., Art 2000, Seoul. Recipient Bronze award Art of Calif., 1993, Gold award Art Addiction, Stockholm, 1997. Avocations: collecting stamps and antiques, music, reading books, jogging, playing tennis. Home: 1935 S La Salle Ave Ste 31 Los Angeles CA 90018

PARKER, ALLENE MARIE, writer, educator; b. Visalia, Calif., Oct. 23, 1959; d. Allen Wayne and Phyllis Marie (Holman) P.; m. John S. Mansell, June 5, 1982. AA in Liberal Arts, Coll. of Sequoias, 1978; BA in Religion, Chapman Coll., 1980; MA in Religion and the Arts, Sch. of Theology Claremont, 1982; MA in English and Creative Writing, San Francisco State U., 1988; DA in English, Idaho State U., 1996. Ordained min., 1986. Rsch. asst. Sch. of Theology, Claremont, Calif., 1980-82; editl. asst. Vanderbilt U., Nashville, 1982-83; asst. editor U. Calif., Berkeley, 1985-86; co-pastor Peace United Ch. of Christ, Tilden, Nebr., 1990-92; tchg. asst. Idaho State U., Pocatello, Idaho, 1993, fellow, 1994-96, vis. asst. prof., 1996—; textile artist Tumbleweeds Quilt/Arts, 1985—. Co-author: Voices Crying in the Wilderness, 1997; editor: The Funeral: A Pastor's Handbook, 1998. Rsch. grantee Huntington Libr. Idaho State U., 1995. Mem. MLA, Portneuf Valley Quilter's Guild, Ina Coolbrith Circle, Idah State U. Creative Writer's Alliance, Phi Kappa Phi, Alpha Gamma Sigma. Avocations: theater, music, languages, travel, swimming.

PARKER, BRIAN PRESCOTT, forensic scientist; b. Norfolk, Va., Aug. 31, 1929; s. Milton Ellsworth and Louise Randall (Smith) P.; BS in Quantitative Biology, M.I.T., 1953; JD, Northwestern U., 1957; M.Criminology, U. Calif., Berkeley, 1961, D.Criminology, 1967; m. Sonia Garcia Rosario, Dec. 23, 1960; children: Robin Marie, Augustin Keith. Research asst. U. P.R. Med. Sch., 1961; cons. P.R. Justice Dept., 1961-63; spl. asst. FDA, Washington, 1964; lectr., then asst. prof. criminology U. Calif., Berkeley, 1964-70; sr. criminalist, then sr. forensic scientist Stanford Research Inst., Menlo Park, Calif., 1971-73; prof. forensic sci. and criminal justice Calif. State U., Sacramento, 1973-92; prof. emeritus, 1988—; project dir. phys. evidence Dept. Justice, 1969-70; vis. fellow Nat. Police Research Unit, Australia, 1985; vis. prof. Elton Mayo Sch. Mgmt., South Australia Inst. Tech., 1985. Mem. Am. Chem. Soc. Co-author: Physical Evidence in the Administration of Criminal Justice, 1970, The Role of Criminalistics in the World of the Future, 1972; asso. editor Law, Medicine, Science—and Justice, 1964; contbr. to Ency. Crime and Justice, 1983. Home: 5117 Ridgegate Way Fair Oaks CA 95628-3603

PARKER, CATHERINE SUSANNE, psychotherapist; b. Norwood, Mass., Nov. 4, 1934; d. George Leonard and Hazel Olga (Remmer) P. BA, Bates Coll., 1956; MSW, U. Denver, 1961. Diplomate Acad. Cert. Social Workers; cert. social worker, Colo. Social worker Taunton (Mass.) State Hosp., 1956-59; social worker Ft. Logan Mental Health Ctr., Denver, 1961-66, clin. team leader, 1966-72; dir. adult services Western Inst. Human Resources, Denver, 1973-74; pvt. practice psychotherapy Denver, 1974—; workshop facilitator Arapahoe C.C., 1986-90. Mem. NASW. Avocations: tennis, skiing, fishing, antiques, gardening. Home: 6453 S Downing St Littleton CO 80121-2517 Office: Denver Mental Health 165 Cook St Ste 100 Denver CO 80206-5308

PARKER, CHARLES EDWARD, lawyer; b. Santa Ana, Calif., Sept. 9, 1927; s. George Ainsworth and Dorothy P.; m. Marilyn Esther Perrin, June 23, 1956; children—Mary, Catherine, Helen, George. Student, Santa Ana Coll., U. So. Calif.; J.D., S.W. U.-La. Bar: Calif. 1958, U.S. Dist. Ct. (cen. dist.) Calif. 1958, U.S. Supreme Ct. 1969, D.C. 1971, U.S. Dist. Ct. (no. and so. dists.) Calif. 1981. Prof. law Western State U., Fullerton, Calif., 1973-83; spl. counsel Tidelands, First Am. Title Co., 1980-82; dir. First Am. Fin. Corp., 1981-82. Served to sgt. U.S. Army, 1951-53. Author: (book) Tidelands and The Public Trust, 1991. Mem. ABA (com. improvement land records, sect. real property, mem. com. on title ins. sect. real property), Orange County Bar Assn., Calif. Bar Assn., D.C. Bar Assn. Club: Santa Ana Kiwanis, Lodge: Elks (Santa Ana). Contbr. articles in field to profl. jours. Office: 18101 Charter Rd Orange CA 92861-2638

PARKER, CHARLES OWEN, II, energy company executive, consultant; b. Denver, Apr. 10, 1931; s. Charles Owen and Florence Elizabeth (Lieser) P.; m. Clarice Eleanor Schmachtenberger, June 7, 1953; children—Mark J., Erich C. Engr. of Mines, Colo. Sch. Mines, 1953; M.B.A., Harvard U., 1958. Sr. mgmt. cons. McKinsey & Co., Los Angeles, 1964-69; v.p. fin./adminstrn. Kaiser Engrs., Oakland, Calif., 1970-74; sr. v.p. adminstrn. Fluor Mining & Metals, San Mateo, Calif., 1974-78; v.p. adminstrn. Pacific Power and Light, Portland, Oreg., 1978-82; sr. v.p. adminstrn./corp. devel. Pacific Enterprises, Los Angeles, 1982-85; vice chmn. So. Calif. Gas Co., Los Angeles, 1985-88. Trustee, v.p. Natural History Mus., L.A, 1983—; bd. dirs., vice chmn. Central City Assn. L.A., 1985-88; dir. Ind. Colls. So. Calif., 1985—; bd. dirs. Harvard U. Bus. Sch. Assn. So. Calif., 1986-89, mem. L.A. 2000 Com., 1986, Soc. Fellows Huntington Library, Art Gallery and Bot. Gardens, 1985—. Served to 1st lt. U.S. Army C.E., 1953-55. Recipient Disting. Achievement medal Colo. Sch. Mines, 1986. Mem. AIME, Soc. Am. Mil. Engrs., Soc. Mining Engrs., Calif. Club. Republican. Avocations: photography; bicycle touring; gardening. Office: Charles O Parker & Assocs Inc 13443 E Sorrel Ln Scottsdale AZ 85259-6316

PARKER, DIANA LYNNE, restaurant manager, special events director; b. Eureka, Calif., June 21, 1957; d. Carol Dean and Lynne Diane (Havemann) P. BA in English, Humboldt U., 1981, postgrad., 1982-84. Lic. real estate agent, Calif. Retail clk. Safeway, Inc., Eureka, 1977-84; caterer, owner TD Catering, Eureka, 1982-84; asst. buyer Macy's Calif., San Francisco, 1984-85; realtor Mason-McDuffie, Alameda, Calif., 1985-87; host, Rotunda Neiman Marcus, San Francisco, 1987-89, asst. mgr., rotunda, 1989—, dir. spl. events, 1989—. Mem. Mus. Modern Art, Calif. Restaurant Assn., San Francisco Visitor and Conv. Bur., Common Wealth Club Calif. Republican. Avocations: gourmet chef, artist, antique collecting. Office: Rotunda at Neiman Marcus 150 Stockton St San Francisco CA 94108-5807

PARKER, HARRY S., III, art museum administrator; b. St. Petersburg, Fla., Dec. 23, 1939; s. Harry S. Parker and Catherine (Baillie) Knapp; m. Ellen McCance, May 23, 1964; children: Elizabeth Day, Thomas Baillie, Samuel Ferguson, Catherine Allan. A.B. magna cum laude, Harvard U., 1961; M.A., NYU, 1966. Exec. asst., adminstrv. asst. to dir. Met. Mus. Art, N.Y.C., 1963-66, exec. asst. to pres., 1966-67, exec. asst. to dir., 1967, chmn. dept. edn., 1967-71, vice dir. edn., 1971-73; dir. Dallas Mus. Art, 1974-87, Fine Arts Mus. San Francisco, 1987—. Mem. Am. Assn. Mus. (v.p.) Assn. Art Mus. Dirs., Century Assn., Bohemian Club. Home: 171 San Marcos Ave San Francisco CA 94116-1462 Office: Fine Arts Mus of San Francisco Golden Gate Pk San Francisco CA 94118

PARKER, JAMES AUBREY, federal judge; b. Houston, Jan. 8, 1937; s. Lewis Almeron and Emily Helen (Stuessy) P.; m. Florence Fisher, Aug. 26, 1960; children: Roger Alan, Pamela Elizabeth. BA, Rice U., 1959; LLB, U. Tex., 1962. Bar: Tex. 1962, N.Mex. 1963. With Modrall, Sperling, Roehl, Harris & Sisk, Albuquerque, 1962-87; judge U.S. Dist. Ct. N.Mex., Albuquerque, 1987—; mem. Standing Commn. on Rules of Practice and Procedures of U.S. Cts., N.Mex. Commn. on Professionalism, 1986—; bd. visitors U. N.Mex. Law Sch., 1996—. Articles editor Tex. Law Rev., 1961-62. Mem. ABA, Fed. Judges Assn., Am. Judicature Soc., Am. Bd. Trial Advocates, Tex. Bar Assn., N.Mex. Bar Assn., Albuquerque Bar Assn., Order of Coif, Chancellors, Phi Delta Phi. Avocations: ranching, fly fishing, running, skiing. Office: US Dist Judge 333 Lomas Blvd NW Ste 760 Albuquerque NM 87102

PARKER, JOHN HOWARD, state official; b. Wash., July 16, 1950; s. Lewis and Kathleen Parker. AA, Butte Coll., Pentz, Calif., 1970; BA, Calif. State U., Chico, 1976. Program review analyst Calif. Dept. Fin., Sacramento, 1977-84; microcomputer resource coordinator State Tchrs. Retirement Sys., Sacramento, 1985-87, chief mgmt. and cons. svcs., 1987-89; ptnr. Investors Retirement Info. Svc., Sacramento, 1987-88; info. security officer State Tchrs. Retirement Sys., 1989-97, Calif. Dept. Transp., Sacramento, 1997—. Contbg. analyst, author, editor Pub. Departmental. Reports, 1977-84. Dept. chmn. State Employee's United Way campaign, Sacramento, 1987; charter mem. Monterey Bay (Calif.) Aquarium, 1985—; assoc. Smithsonian Instn., Wash. D.C., 1982. Served with U.S. Army, 1970-72. Mem. Acad. Polit. Sci., Ctr. for Study of Presidency. Avocations: boating, swimming, scuba, golf.

PARKER, JOHN MARCHBANK, consulting geologist; b. Manhattan, Kans., Sept. 13, 1920; s. John Huntington and Marjorie Elizabeth (Marchbank) P.; m. Agnes Elizabeth Potts, Mar. 17, 1978; m. Jan Goble, July 18, 1941 (div. 1968); children—Susan Kelly, Elizabeth Douglass, Deirdre Parker, John Eric; m. Nancy Booth, Jan. 24, 1970 (div. 1974). Student U. Minn., 1937, U. Wyo., 1938; B.S., Kans. State U., 1941. Cert. petroleum geologist Am. Inst. Profl. Geologists. Geologist, U.S. Pub. Roads Adminstrn., Alaska Hwy., Can., 1942-43; Field geologist Imperial Oil Ltd., Northwest Ter., Can., 1943-44; dist. geologist Stanolind Oil & Gas Co., Casper, Wyo., 1944-52; v.p. exploration Kirby Petroleum Co., Houston, 1952-74; v.p. exploration Northwest Exploration Co., Denver, 1974-75; cons. geologist Denver, 1975—. Contbr. articles to profl. jours. Recipient Disting. Service in Geology award Kans. State U., 1983. Fellow AAAS, Geol. Soc. Am.; mem. Am. Assn. Petroleum Geologists (pres. 1982-83, adv. council Tulsa 1983-84, Hon. Mem. award), Rocky Mountain Assn. Geologists (explorer of yr. 1979; pres. 1980-81). Home: 2615 Oak Dr # 32 Lakewood CO 80215-7182

PARKER, JOHN WILLIAM, pathology educator, investigator; b. Clifton, Ariz., Jan. 5, 1931; m. Barbara A. Atkinson; children: Ann Elizabeth, Joy Noelle, John David, Heidi Susan. BS, U. Ariz., 1953; MD, Harvard U., 1957. Diplomate Am. Bd. Pathology. Clin. instr. pathology U. Calif. Sch. Medicine, San Francisco, 1962-64; asst. prof. U. So. Calif. Sch. Medicine, L.A., 1964-68, assoc. prof., 1968-75, prof., 1975-98, prof. emeritus, 1998—, dir. clin. labs., 1974-94, vice chmn. dept. pathology, 1985-97, dir. pathology reference labs., 1991-94; assoc. dean sci. affairs U. So. Calif. Sch. Medicine, 1987-89, prof. emeritus, 1998—; co-chmn. 15th Internat. Leucocyte Culture Conf., Asilomar, Calif., 1982; chmn. 2d Internat. Lymphoma Conf., Athens, Greece, 1981; v.p. faculty senate U. So. Calif., 1991-92; bd. dirs. ann. meeting Clin. Applications of Cytometry, Charleston, S.C., 1988-97. Founding editor (jour.) Hematological Oncology, 1982-93; assoc. editor Jour. Clin. Lab. Analysis, 1985-98; co-editor: Intercellular Communication in Leucocyte Function, 1983; founding co-editor (jour.) Communications in Clin. Cytometry, 1993-97; contbr. over 180 articles to profl. jours., chpts. to books. Named sr. oncology fellow Am. Cancer Soc., U. So. Calif. Sch. Medicine, 1964-69, Nat. Cancer Inst. vis. fellow Walter and Eliza Hall Inst. for Med. Research, Melbourne, Australia, 1972-73. Fellow Coll. Am. Pathologists, Am. Soc. Clin. Pathologists; mem. Am. Assn. Pathologists, Am. Soc. Hematology, Internat. Acad. Pathology, Clin. Cytometry Soc. (v.p. 1994-95, pres. 1995-97), Phi Beta Kappa, Phi Kappa Phi. Avocations: gardening, reading, hiking. Office: U So Calif Sch Medicine CSC 108 2250 Alcazar St Los Angeles CA 90033-1004

PARKER, LEA JANE, communications educator; b. Moline, Ill., Nov. 17, 1947; d. James Elden and Margaret Lorraine Mecum; m. Gary Allen Lundburg, June 10, 1967 (div. Nov. 1983); children: Jessica Ann, Jaina Lorraine; m. Richard Anthony Parker, June 3, 1985. BA, Ariz. State U., 1972; MA, No. Ariz. U., 1983. Science tchr. Deer Valley Jr. H.S., Phoenix, 1972-75; pub. rels. specialist Marifarms, Inc., Panama City, Fla., 1969-70; from staff reporter to Cmty. News editor The Ariz. Daily Sun, Flagstaff, 1985-89; from lectr. to asst. prof. environ. comm. & journalism No. Ariz. U., Flagstaff, 1989—. Author: Kidnapped in Canyonlands, 1994, (textbook) Environmental Communication: Messages, Media & Methods, 1995, 97; regional editor, columnist Ariz. Living Mag., 1979-84; freelance writer, photographer Spirit Eagle Studio, Flagstaff, 1978—. Recipient Facilitator Svc. award Women's Polit. Caucus & NAV Leadership Program, 1993, Cmty. Svc. Reporting award Citizen's Against Substance Abuse, 1988. Mem. Nat. League of Am. Pen Women (treas. Flagstaff chpt.), Nat. Comm. Assn. Avocations: camping, hiking, photography, water sports. Office: No Ariz U Sch Comm PO Box 5619 Flagstaff AZ 86011

PARKER, NORMAN, actor; b. Bklyn.; s. Theodore and Betty (Wormser) P.; children: Jonathan, Brandon. BA, CCNY, 1966. Films include Prince of the City, 1981, Daniel, 1983, Bonfire of the Vanities, 1991, Up Close & Personal, 1997; appeared in Broadway play Chapter Two, 1985; appeared in Basic Training of Pavlo Hummel, 1977, The Transfiguration of Benno Blimpie, 1979, Something Different, Disappearance of the Jews, 1983, The Normal Heart, 1985; TV appearances include Family Ties, 1982-87, Beverly Hills 90210, Touched By An Angel, Falcon Crest, Party of Five, JAG, St. Elsewhere, Miami Vice; author (play) Feynman Lives, 1997. Recipient Best Performance award Drama-Logue, L.A., 1997. Mem. Venture West Theatre Co. (trustee 1996—).

PARKER, P. KEVIN, English educator; b. Hawthorne, Calif., Apr. 30, 1963; s. Peter Lyle and Sandra Sue (Mason) P.; m. Suzanne Therese Allard, July 21, 1990; children: Stephanie Taylor, Paige Kelsey. AA, Saddleback C.C., 1983; AS, Saddlebrook C.C., 1987; BA, U. Calif., 1990; MA, U. Mo., 1992. Asst. lectr. U. So. Calif., L.A., 1992-96; instr. English Orange Coast Coll., Costa Mesa, Calif., 1996—. Editl. bd. Teaching English in the Two-Year Coll., Urbana, Ill., 1998—, The Writing Instr., L.A., 1992-98; editor Inside English, 1998—. Mem. English Coun. of Calif. Two-Yr. Colls. (bd. dirs.), Nat. Coun. of Tchrs. of English, Coast Fedn. of Educators/Am. Fedn. of Tchrs. Democrat. Avocation: computers. E-mail: kparker@occ.ccd.edu. Office: Orange Coast Coll 2701 Fairview Rd Costa Mesa CA 92626-5563

PARKER, ROY ALFRED, transportation engineer, planner; b. Conway, Ark., Apr. 6, 1930; s. Walter Lane and Harriett Mae (Diffee) P.; m. Dixie Anna Dean, June 9, 1953; children: Walter Lane II, David Dean, Shauna Amyr. BS, U. Idaho, 1953; cert. in hwy. traffic, Yale U., 1958. Registered profl. traffic engr., Calif. Asst. planning programming engr. Bur. Pub. Roads (now Fed. Hwy. Adminstrn.), Sacramento, 1958-59; asst. city traffic engr. City of Phoenix, 1959-62; city traffic engr. Palo Alto, Calif., 1962-66; sr. transp. engr. Wilbur Smith & Assocs., London, 1966-68; project mgr. Wilbur Smith & Assocs., Sacramento, 1980; sr. transp. engr. F.R. Harris Engring. Corp., São Paulo, Brazil, 1968-69; prin. assoc. R.W. Crommelin & Assocs., Los Angeles, 1969-70; dep. transp. dir. City and County of Honolulu, 1970-75, dir. dept. transp. services, 1981-83; exec. dir. Oahu Met. Planning Orgn., Honolulu, 1975-79; sr. traffic engr. Lyon Assocs., Inc., Damascus, Syrian Arab Republic, 1979; pres. Roy A. Parker and Assocs., La Jolla, Calif., 1980; transp. engr. City of Concord, Calif., 1983-84, dep. pub. works dir., 1984-88; transp. adminstr. City San Leandro (Calif.), Calif., 1988-90, 91-93; acting dir. dept. engring. and transp. City San Leandro (Calif.), 1990-91; pres. Roy A. Parker and Assocs., Pismo Beach, Calif., 1994—; lectr. dept. civil engring. Coll. Engring., U. Hawaii, 1971-75; lectr. Inst. Transp. Studies, U. Calif., Berkeley, 1983-91. Served with USAF, 1953-57. Fellow Inst. Transp. Engrs. (pres. western dist. 1975-76, pres. San Francisco Bay Area sect. 1991-92); mem. Phi Eta Sigma, Sigma Tau. Democrat. Home and Office: 64 La Garza Pismo Beach CA 93449-2838

PARKER, THEODORE CLIFFORD, electronics engineer; b. Dallas, Oreg., Sept. 25, 1929; s. Theodore Clifford and Virginia Bernice (Rumsey) P.; BSEE magna cum laude, U. So. Calif., 1960; m. Jannet Ruby Barnes, Nov. 28, 1970; children: Sally Odette, Peggy Claudette. V.p. engring. Telemetrics, Inc., Gardena, Calif., 1963-65; chief info. systems Northrop-Nortronics, Anaheim, Calif., 1966-70; pres. AVTEL Corp., Covina, Calif., 1970-74, Aragon, Inc., Sunnyvale, Calif., 1975-78; v.p. Teledyne McCormick Selph, Hollister, Calif., 1978-82; sr. staff engr. FMC Corp., San Jose, Calif., 1982-85; pres. Power One Switching Products, Camarillo, Calif., 1985-86; pres. Condor D.C. Power Supplies, Inc., 1987-88, pres. Intelligence Power Tech. Inc., Camarillo, 1988—. Mem. IEEE (chmn. autotestcon '87), NRA (life), Am. Prodn. and Inventory Control Soc., Am. Def. Preparedness Assn., Armed Forces Communications and Electronics Assn., Tau Beta Pi, Eta Kappa Nu. Home: 250 E Telegraph Rd Spc 47 Fillmore CA 93015-2145 Office: Intelligence Power Tech Inc PO Box 3158 Camarillo CA 93011-3158

PARKER, WALTER BRUCE, arctic research specialist, consultant; b. Spokane, Wash., Aug. 11, 1926; s. Bruce Velorus and Lucille Kathryn (Chessman) P.; m. Patricia Isabelle Ertman, Jan. 28, 1946; children: Sandra Wassilie, Patrick B., Jeffrey K., Douglas S., Lisa M. BA in History, U. Alaska, Fairbanks, 1964; DSc, U. Alaska, Anchorage, 1998. Air traffic controller FAA, 1946-64; evaluation officer FAA, Anchorage, 1964-66; analyst FAA, Washington, 1966-68; planner FAA, Anchorage, 1968-70; sr. planner Fed. Field Com. for Alaska, Anchorage, 1970-71; rsch. assoc. U. Alaska, Anchorage, 1971-74; commr. Alaska Dept. Hwys., Juneau, 1974-76; chmn. Alaska Fed./State Land Use Planning Commn., 1976-79, Alaska Oil Spill Commn., Anchorage, 1990-91; pres., cons. transp. and telecom. sys. Parker Assocs., Inc., Anchorage, 1971—; commr. U.S. Arctic Rsch. Commn., Anchorage; mem. marine bd., com. on advances in pilotage and navigation NRC, 1991-94. Author: Alaska and The Law of the Sea, 1974, Alaska People's and Alaska Lands, 1977; contbr. reports to profl. publs. Chmn. Alaska Conservation Soc., Anchorage, 1969-71, Alaska Humanties Forum, Anchorage, 1987-93; active Alaska Bd. Fish and Game, Juneau, 1971-74; bd. dirs. Prince William Sound Sci. Ctr., 1996—; assemblyman Anchorage Borough, 1971-74. With USN, 1944-46. Democrat. Avocations: skiing, dog mushing and breeding, gardening. Home: 3724 Campbell Airstrip Rd Anchorage AK 99504-4422

PARKER, WILLIAM ELBRIDGE, consulting civil engineer; b. Seattle, Mar. 18, 1913; s. Charles Elbridge and Florence E. (Plumb) P.; m. Dorris Laurie Freeman, June 15, 1935; children—Dorris Laurie, Jane Elizabeth. B.S., U.S. Naval Acad., 1935. Party chief King County Engrs., 1935-39; exec. sec., cons. engr. State Wash., 1946-49; city engr., chmn. Bd. Pub. Works, City of Seattle, 1953-57; cons. City of San Diego, 1957; ptnr. Parker-Fisher & Assocs., 1958-66; cons. engr. Minish & Webb Engrs., Seattle, 1966-70; city engr. City of Bremerton (Wash.), 1970-76; owner Parker & Assocs., Seattle, 1976—. Served to capt. C.E.C., USNR, 1939-45, 51-53. Named to Broadway Hall of Fame. Registered profl. engr., Wash. Mem. Am. Pub. Works Assn., U.S. Naval Inst., Pioneers of State Wash. (pres.), U.S. Naval Acad. Alumni Assn. (chpt. pres.), College Club (Seattle). Lodges: Masons, Shriners.

PARKER, WILLIAM HAYES, JR., film director, writer, photographer; b. Mt. Vernon, N.Y., May 2, 1947; s. William Hayes and Rhoda Mae (Williams) P.; m. Bernice Lofton, June 26, 1966 (div. May 1970); children: Eric

Hayes, Stephen Lee; m. Yvonne Kelly, Mar. 5, 1978; 1 child, Stella Cailan. Student, U. Cin., 1965-66, L.A. City Coll., 1973-75. Trainee Cin. Milling, 1965-66; jet mechanic Gruman Aerospace, Point Maga, Calif., 1971-82; prodr. Rick Polack Prodn., L.A., 1973-75; unit prodn. mgr. E.U.E. Screen Genus, L.A., 1977-78; prodr., dir. Bill Parker Prodns., L.A., 1976-86; dir. Remge Films, L.A., 1986-94; pres., dir. Ali/Parker Pictures, L.A., 1994—; Dir. (music video) Part Time Liver by Stevie Wonder, 1985 (Am. Music award 1986), (comml.) Cherry Coke, 1987 (CEBA award 1987), (film) KlA$H, 1994 (Sundance award 1995). Creative vol. Youth First/Theater of Hearts, L.A., 1987—; founding mem. Children Def. Fund Awards, L.A., 1990—. With USAF, 1966-70. Avocation: flying (private pilot). Office: Ali Parker Pictures 627 N Rossmore Ave Apt 316 Los Angeles CA 90004-1240

PARKER-FAIRBANKS, DIXIE, artist; b. Cedar Rapids, Iowa, Aug. 1, 1936; d. James N. and Mary Louise (Mussell) Parker; m. Richard Fairbanks, Aug. 26, 1966 (dec. Mar. 1989). BFA, Drake U., 1958, MFA, 1959. Craft instr. State of Wis., Waukesha, 1960-61; asst. dir. dept. edn. Des Moines Art Ctr., 1961-66; art lectr. Ctrl. Wash. U., Ellensburg, 1967-69; coord./dir. Richard Fairbanks Project, Ellensburg, 1991-95. Prodr./editor: (biography) Richard Fairbanks, American Potter, 1993; exhibited in one-person shows, 1962-96, two-person shows, 1970-95; gallery affiliations include Galerie Pelin, Helsinki, Finland, City of Sanda, Japan, Galerie Prisma, Vienna, C.G. Rein, Scottsdale, Ariz., Maxwell Galleries, Inc., San Francisco, Des Moines Art Ctr., Percival Galleries, Inc., Des Moines, Greenwood Galleries, Seattle, PANACA, Bellevue, Wash., Louise Matzke Gallery, Seattle, N.W. Craft Ctr., Bellevue, Lynn McAllister Gallery, Seattle, Seattle Art Mus., Richard White Gallery, Seattle, Gallery One, Ellensburg, Allied Arts, Yakima, Wash., Oak Hollow Gallery, Yakima, Larson Gallery, Yakima. Home and Office: 1011 E 1st Ave Ellensburg WA 98926-3514

PARKHURST, VIOLET KINNEY, artist; b. Derby Line, Vt., Apr. 26, 1926; d. Edson Frank and Rosa (Beauchiene) Kinney; student Sch. Practical Arts, Boston, 1941-42, Baylor U., Waco, Tex., 1943, Calif. State U., Los Angeles, 1950-51; m. Donald Winters Parkhurst, Apr. 10, 1948. Fgn. corr. 5 Brazilian mags., 1946-53; tech. illustrator, 1954-55; owner five galleries including Ports of Call, San Pedro, Calif.; artist, specializing in seascapes; work included in permanent collection of Stockholm Mus., many pvt. collections including Presidents Richard M. Nixon, Ford, Reagan, Bush, Gov. Wilson, Mayor of Kobe, Japan, Mayor Yorty of L.A., Rory Calhoun, Barbara Rush, Jim Arness, David Rose; one-shows shows at prominent galleries; numerous paintings published. Winner 30 blue ribbons for art. Fellow Am. Inst. Fine Arts. Mem. Ch. of Religious Sci. Author: How to Paint Books, 1966; Parkhurst on Seascapes, 1972. Paintings reproduced on covers South West Art, Arizona Living; ltd. edit. prints published, also ltd. edit. plates. Office: Parkhurst Gallery Ports of Call Village San Pedro CA 90731

PARKINSON, BRADFORD WELLS, astronautical engineer, educator; b. Madison, Wis., Feb. 16, 1935; s. Herbert and Metta Tisdale (Smith) P.; m. Virginia Pinkham Wier, Nov. 26, 1977; children: Leslie, Bradford II, Eric, Ian, Bruce, Jared Bradford. BS, U.S. Naval Acad., 1957; MS, MIT, 1961; PhD, Stanford U., 1966. Commd. 2d lt. USAF, 1957, advanced through grades to col., 1972; divsn. chief AF Test Pilot Sch., 1966-68; chair dept. astronautics and computer sci. USAF Acad., 1969-71; dir. engring. ABRES, 1972; program mgr. NAVSTAR GPS, 1972-78; ret. USAF, 1978; prof. mech. engring. Colo. State U., Ft. Collins, 1978-79; v.p. advanced engring. Rockwell Internat., Downey, Calif., 1979-80; gen. mgr., v.p. Intermetrics, Inc., Cambridge, Mass., 1980-84; prof., dir. gravity probe-B Stanford (Calif.) U., 1984—; CEO, pres. Trimble Navigation Ltd., 1998—; chair adv. coun. NASA; dir. Trimble Navigation Ltd., Sunnyvale, Calif., Draper Lab., Cambridge, Integrinautics, Palo Alto, Calif., Aerospace Corp., El Segundo, Calif. Decorated Def. Superior Svc. medal, AF Commendation medal with oak leaf cluster, Meritorius Svc. medal, Presdl. Unit citation, Bronze Star, Legion of Merit, Air medal with oak leaf cluster; recipient Thurlow award Inst. Navigation, 1986, Kepler award, 1991, von Karman Lectureship Am. Inst. of Aeronautics and Astronautics, 1996, Magellan Premium, Am. Philos. Soc., 1997, Gold medal Space Tech. Hall of Fame of U.S. Space Found., 1998. Fellow AIAA (Sperry award), Royal Inst. Navigation (Gold medal 1983); mem. IEEE (Pioneer award 1994, Sperry award), AAS, NAE, Internat. Acad. Astronautics, Sigma Xi, Tau Beta Pi. Avocations: hiking, skiing, running. Home: 817 Santa Rita Ave Los Altos CA 94022-1131 Office: Stanford U HEPL Stanford CA 94305

PARKINSON, THOMAS BRIAN, marketing executive; b. Lytham-St. Annes, Lancashire, Eng., Oct. 14, 1935; came to U.S., 1966; s. Alfred and Marjorie (Wright) P.; m. Margaret Moore, Oct. 12, 1957; children: Karen, Lynn, Stephen David. Cert. Mech. Engring., Harris Coll. Further Edn., Preston, Lancashire, Eng., 1962. Apprentice tool maker English Electric Co. Ltd., Preston, Lancashire, Eng., 1951-57; designer aircraft structure British Aircraft Corp., Warton, Lancashire, Eng., 1957-63, stress engr. aircraft, 1963-66; stress engr. aircraft Douglas Aircraft Co., Long Beach, Calif., 1966-76, sales engr. commercial mktg., 1976-78, project mgr. commercial mktg., 1978-85, sales mgr. comml. mktg. Pacific and Asia, 1985-89, exec. asst. comml. mktg. Pacific and Asia, 1989-91, sr. prin. specialist analyst mkt. devel., 1991-94; ret., 1994; cons. aircraft mktg. and performance field. Commr. Planning Commn., City of Huntington Beach (Calif.), 1975-77, Underground Utilities Commn., Huntington Beach, 1975-77; chmn. City Charter Revision Com., Huntington Beach, 1977; campaign mgr. Com. to Re-Elect Jerry Matney, Huntington Beach, 1973; fire chief Kellogg Vol. Fire Dept., 1996—; bd. dirs. Kellogg Vol. Fire Dist., 1997—. With Royal Navy, 1953-55. Mem. Instn. Engring. Designers (assoc.), Pacific Area Travel Assn. (chmn. rsch. authority, bd. dirs. 1983-85, award of merit 1985). Episcopalian. Avocations: computer activity, cycling. Home: 756 Osprey Dr Umpqua OR 97486-9738

PARKS, DEBORA ANN, private school director; b. Homestead, Fla., July 23, 1954; d. Jack Wesley and Blanche Margaret (Shawver) Hardin; m. Lewis O'Dell Parks, Apr. 12, 1970 (div. May 1980); 1 child, Kerri Shane. BS in Early Childhood Edn., U. Ala., Tuscaloosa, 1983, MA in Spl. Edn., 1984, MA in Early Childhood Edn., 1987, PhD in Elem. Edn., 1991. Kindergarten tchr. Martin Luther King Jr. Elem. Sch., Tuscaloosa, 1983-85; tchr. gifted grades 2-5 Martin Luther King Jr. Elem. Sch. and Univ. Place Elem. Sch., Tuscaloosa, 1985-86; early childhood edn. instr. Shelton State C.C., Tuscaloosa, 1985-88; instr. U. Ala., Tuscaloosa, 1987; elem. tchr. 1st grade Martin Luther King Jr. Elem. Sch., Tuscaloosa, 1988-89; tchr. gifted grades 3-6 Carthay Elem. Sch., L.A. Unified Sch. Dist., 1991; faculty-in-residence Sunset Village Residence Halls and Hitch Stes. UCLA, 1991-95; tchr. gifted grades K-8 Maimonides Acad., L.A., 1992-94; asst. rschr. So. Calif. Injury Prevention Rsch. Ctr. Sch. Pub. Health, UCLA, 1993-95; facuty liaison on campus housing com.'s darkroom UCLA, 1993-95, instr. dept. edn., 1994, 95, instr., rschr., 1989-95; tchr. gifted grades 2-8 Maimonides Acad., L.A., 1995—, gen. studies prin., 1995—; grad. tchg. asst. elem. edn. U. Ala., Tuscaloosa, 1986-87; field coord., instr. Tchr. Edn. Lab., Grad. Sch. Edn., UCLA, 1989-93; enrichment tchr. grades 3-5 The Buckley Sch., Sherman Oaks, Calif., summer, 1991, 92, 93; evaluation coach/cons. Stanford Rsch. Inst., SB 620 Statewide Healthy Start Initiative Program, L.A., 1993-95; spl. faculty advisor UCLA Photographic Soc., 1993-95; evaluator lang. arts program, curriculum and tchrs. Maimonides Acad., L.A., 1994; enrichment tchr. grades 4-5 Buckley Sch., Sherman Oaks, Calif., summer 1994, enrichment tchr., summer 1995; evaluation coach, cons. Stanford Rsch. Inst., L.A., 1993-95; mem. governing bd. Nat. Assn. Creative Children and Adults, Ohio, 1992-94; rsch. adviser Phi Delta Kappa, UCLA chpt., 1992-94; mem. Adopt-A-Sch. Coun., L.A. Unified Sch. Dist., 1990-95; chairperson Tuscaloosa City Sch.'s Kindergarten Math. Com., 1984; presenter confs. and workshops. Author: The Newspaper Workbook, 1983, Pedestrian and Bicyclist Safety Curriculum for Grades K-5, 1994, Adopt-A-School Programs: A Guide for Pre-Service Teachers, 1995; manuscript asst. editor Am. Mid. Sch. Edn., 1986-87; asst. editor Adopt-A-School Newsletter, 1993; contbr. articles to profl. jours. Vol. Rebuild L.A., 1992-93. Recipient award NEA and Kodak, N.Y. and Ala., 1985, scholarships Am. Bus. Women's Assn., Ala., 1988, Beta Chi of Delta Kappa [illegible] 1993 [illegible] Thompson Endowed Scholarship, 1988, designee Ala. Tchr. of Yr. Program, 1984-85, 85-86. Mem. Phi Delta Kappa. Democrat. Avocations: photography, calligraphy, graphic arts. Home: 311 Westbourne Dr West Hollywood CA 90048-1909 Office: Maimonides Acad 310 N Huntley Dr Los Angeles CA 90048-1919

PARKS, DONALD LEE, mechanical engineer, human factors engineer; b. Delphos, Kans., Feb. 23, 1931; s. George Delbert and Erma Josephine (Boucek) P.; student Kans. Wesleyan U., 1948-50; BSME, Kans. State U., 1957, BS in Bus. Adminstrn., 1957, MS in Psychology, 1959; cert. profl. Ergonomist; m. Bessie Lou Schur, Dec. 24, 1952; children: Elizabeth Parks Anderson, Patricia Parks-Holbrook, Donna, Charles, Sandra. Elem. tchr., 1950-51; with Kans. State U. Placement Svc., 1957-59; human factors engr., systems engr. Boeing Co., Seattle, 1959-90, sr. specialist engr., 1972-74, sr. engring. supr., 1974-90; pres. D-Square Assocs. Engring. Cons., 1990-95; pres. Venture Worlds, 1995—; adj. lectr. UCLA Engring. Extension, 1989—; cons., lectr. in field; participant workshops on guidelines in profl. areas, NATO, NSF, Nat. Acad. Sci., NRC. Mem. Derby (Kans.) Planning Commn., 1961-62, chmn., 1962; del. King County (Wash.) Republican Conv., 1972. With AUS, 1952-54. Mem. Human Factors Soc. (Puget Sound Pres.'s award 1969), ASME, Am. Psychol. Assn., Elks. Presbyterian. Contbr. over 80 articles to publs., chpts. to 8 books. Home: 6232 127th Ave SE Bellevue WA 98006-3943

PARKS, HAROLD RAYMOND, mathematician, educator; b. Wilmington, Del., May 22, 1949; s. Lytle Raymond Jr. and Marjorie Ruth (Chambers) P.; m. Paula Sue Beaulieu, Aug. 21, 1971 (div. 1984); children: Paul Raymond, David Austin; m. Susan Irene Taylor, June 6, 1985; 1 stepchild, Kathryn McLaughlin. AB, Dartmouth Coll., 1971; PhD, Princeton U., 1974. Tamarkin instr. Brown U., Providence, 1974-77; asst. prof. Oreg. State U., Corvallis, 1977-82, assoc. prof., 1982-89, prof. math., 1989—; vis. assoc. prof. Ind. U., Bloomington, 1982-83. Author: Explicit Determination of Area Minimizing Hypersurfaces, vol. II, 1986, (with Steven G. Krantz) A Primer of Real Analytic Functions, 1992, (with G. Musser, R. Burton, W. Siebler) Mathematics in Life, Society and the World, 1997, (with Steven G. Krantz) The Geometry of Domains in Space, 1999; contbr. articles to profl. publs. Cubmaster Oregon Trail Coun. Boy Scouts Am., 1990-92. NSF fellow, 1971-74. Mem. Am. Math. Soc., Math. Assn. Am., Soc. Indsl. and Applied Math., Phi Beta Kappa. Republican. Mem. Soc. of Friends. Home: 33194 Dorset Ln Philomath OR 97370-9555 Office: Oreg State U Dept Math Corvallis OR 97331-4605

PARKS, MICHAEL CHRISTOPHER, journalist; b. Detroit, Nov. 17, 1943; s. Robert James and Rosalind (Smith) P.; m. Linda Katherine Durocher, Dec. 26, 1964; children: Danielle Anne, Christopher, Matthew. AB, U. Windsor, Ont., Can., 1965. Reporter Detroit News, 1962-65; corr. Time-Life News Service, N.Y.C., 1965-66; asst. city editor Suffolk Sun, Long Island, N.Y., 1966-68; polit. reporter, foreign corr. The Balt. Sun, Saigon, Singapore, Moscow, Cairo, Hong Kong, Peking, 1968-80; fgn. corr. L.A. Times, L.A., Peking, Johannesburg, Moscow, Jerusalem, 1980-95, dpty. fgn. editor, 1995-96; mng. editor L.A. Times, 1996-97, editor, 1997—, v.p., 1996-97, sr. v.p., 1997-98, exec. v.p., 1998—; v.p. Times Mirror Co., 1998—. Recipient Pulitzer Prize, 1987. Mem. Am. Soc. Newspaper Editors, Pacific Coun. on Internat. Policy, AP Mng. Editors, Royal Commonwealth Soc. London, Soc. Profl. Journalists, Fgn. Corr. Club (Hong Kong), City Club (L.A.), Coun. on Fgn. Rels. Office: L A Times Times Mirror Sq Los Angeles CA 90012

PARKS, NEAL STUART, artist; b. Howell, Mich., Jan. 13, 1962; s. Roger Parks and Sandra Hoover; m. Leta Gwen Herman, May 14, 1988; 1 child, Dunan Herman. BFA, Pratt Inst., 1984; MFA, Cranbrook Acad. Art, 1993. Artist, prin. Neal Parks Fine Art, Alameda, Calif., 1993—. Exhibited in group shows at Eden Gallery, 1996, Korean Cultural Ctr., 1996, Alameda Mus., 1997, Oakland Mus.'s Collector's Gallery, 1997-98. Recipient grant Nat. Endowment for Arts and Humanities, 1989. Office: Neal Parks Fine Art 2424 Blanding Ave Ste 303 Alameda CA 94501-1592

PARKS, RICHARD KEITH, clinical social worker; b. Rock Springs, Wyo., Oct. 13, 1947; s. Keith Andrew and Mildred Ann (Matkovich) P.; m. Debra D. Thomas, Sept. 21, 1968 (div. Nov. 1971); m. Alberta Dea Henderson, Feb. 26, 1974; children: Heather, Richell. AA, Western Wyo. Coll., 1969; BSW, U. Wyo., 1985; MSW, Denver U., 1988. Lic. social worker. Owner, mgr. Rich's Britches, Rock Springs, 1974-77; asst. mgr. Wyo. Bearing, Rock Springs, 1976-82; residential counselor Southwest Wyo. Rehab. Ctr., Rock Springs, 1983-85; community care worker, therapist Southwest Counseling Svc., Rock Springs, 1985-89; sch. social worker Sch. Dist. #1, Rock Springs, 1989-90; mental health counselor State of Nev. Rural Clinics, Fernley, 1990-92; inpatient clin. social worker Nev. Mental Health Inst., Reno, 1992-93; social work cons. Pershing Gen. Hosp., Lovelock, Nev., 1991-93; clin. social worker Human Affaire Internat.-Aetna, Salt Lake City, 1993—; program mgr. Transitional Living Ctr., 1985-87; workshop presenter in field, 1986. Vol. counselor Sweetwater Crisis Intervention Ctr., Rock Springs, 1973-83, bd. dirs., 1979-83; v.p. Downtown Mchts. Assn., 1975. Mem. NASW, Alumni Assn. U. Wyo. Congregationalist. Avocations: camping, fishing, snowmobiling, video production, travel.

PARLANTE, DIANE GOULLARD, interpreter, translator; b. Verdun, Que., Can.; came to U.S., 1979; BA in Music, U. Montreal, Que., 1979; paralegal cert., St. Mary's Coll., Moraga, Calif., 1984. Registered interpreter of non-designated langs. Calif. Jud. Coun., 1996. Legal sec., logistics coord. Honeywell, Inc., San Francisco, Brisbane, Calif., 1984-96; interpreter, translator French and English Communication Svcs., Calif. and Ariz., 1984—; paralegal Levine Newton & Irvine, L.A., Law Offices James Thierney, Santa Monica, Calif., Pillsbury Madison & Sutro, San Francisco, Aguiree & Eckmann, San Diego, 1984-91; real estate saleswoman Century 21, Fallbrook, 1991. Mem. Ariz. Prodns. Assn., etc. Avocations: ham radio (gen. lic.), handicrafts, music, walking, reading. E-Mail: frenchandenglish@worldnet.att.net.

PARMA, FLORENCE VIRGINIA, magazine editor; b. Kenilworth, N.J., Aug. 30, 1940; d. Howard Frank and Mildred Faye (Lister) von Finkel; m. Wilson Henry Parma, June 15, 1973 (div. Aug. 1986). Studies with pvt. tutor, Chaumont, France, 1961-62; student, NYU, 1962-63. Copywriter Schless & Co., N.Y.C., 1963-65; editor, researcher Barchas Lab., Stanford, Calif., 1969-73; adminstrv. exec. Crater Inc., Honolulu, 1974-79; mgr., editor Off Duty mag., Honolulu, 1979—; v.p. Mapasa, Inc. (dba The Prides of New Zealand), 1992—. Editor: Welcome to Hawaii Guide, 1985—; co-editor: Serotonin and Behavior, 1972; freelance columnist. Republican. Episcopalian. Avocations: scuba diving, stained glass, hiking. Home and Office: Off Duty Hawaii 3771 Anuhea St Honolulu HI 96816-3849

PARNELL, GARY LESTER, humanities educator, consultant; b. Loop City, Nebr., Apr. 12, 1943; s. Lester Fergeson and Dora Ann (Jonak) P.; m. Kathryn Farrer, May 21, 1971; children: Jennifer, Mark, Jacob, Margaret, Elizabeth, Mary. BA in History, Brigham Young U., 1967; MA in English, San Jose State U., 1973; PhD in Edn., U. Utah, 1984. Missionary L.D.S. Ch., Santiago, Chile, 1962-65; peace corps. vol. St. James Secondary Sch., Mokhotlong, Lesotho, South Africa, 1968-70; tchr. St. Joseph's Sch., San Jose, Calif., 1970-73, Jordan H.S., Sandy, Utah, 1973-78; prof. Snow Coll., Ephraim, Utah, 1978-98, faculty devel. dir., 1992-98; dir. studies Centro de Idiomas, Cartagena, Spain, 1986-87; Fulbright exchg. prof. Nat. U. Rio Cuarto, Argentina, 1994; instr., cons. Joint Lang. Tng. Ctr., Ogden, Utah, 1995-98; cons. Harvard Inst. for Internat. Devel., La Paz, Bolivia, 1997. Councilman Spring City, Utah, 1992-98; county chair Dem. party, Sampete County, Utah, 1994-98. Mem. Profl. and Orgn. Devel. Mem. LDS Ch. Avocations: gardening, traveling, reading, writing. Office: Snow Coll 150 E College Ave Ephraim UT 84627-1203

PARONI, GENEVIEVE MARIE SWICK, retired secondary education educator; b. Eureka, Nev., July 27, 1926; d. William Jackson and Myrtle Rose (Smith) S.; m. Walter Andrew Paroni, Dec. 26, 1954; 1 child, Andrea Marie. BA, U. Nev., Reno, 1948; MEd, U. Idaho, 1978; postgrad., MIT, Oreg. State U., U. Oreg., U. Wash., Ft. Wright Coll., U. Portland. Cert. elem. and secondary sect., Nev. Tchr., vice prin. Eureka County H.S., 1948-66; coast geodetic U.S. Govt., Eureka, 1950's; tchr. biol. and phys. scis., facilitator Pub. Schs. Dist. # 393, Wallace, Idaho, 1968-91; ret., 1991; [illegible] Dept. Edn., Boise, Idaho, 1980-83, mem. state sci. commn., 1981-82, mem. Idaho Sci. Curriculum Guide Com., 1987, Univ. Idaho Commn. on Math/Sci. Edn., 1988-89, Inland Empire Physics Alliance, 1989-90, Idaho Sci. Alliance Com., 1990. Contbr. history articles to profl. jours. Active Wallace City Coun., 1970-80; bd. dirs. Wallace Pub. Libr., 1983—, chmn., 1995—; bd. dirs. Silver Valley Arts and Crafts Assn., 1991, Greater Wallace, 1980-93, Wallace Dist. Arts Coun., 1993—, mem. citizen's adv. bd. Idaho Nat. Engring. Lab., 1994-96; facilitator Panhandle Area Ecolab., 1995; Rep. precinct chairperson, Wallace, 1970-80; bishop's warden area Episc. Ch., 1990-94; mem. coun. Episc. Diocese Spokane, 1992-96. Grantee Idaho Power, 1985; named Outstanding Tchr., Dist. #393. 1975; finalist Presdl. awards in High Sch. Sci. Teaching. Mem. NEA, AAUW (pres. 1970s), Wallace Edn. Assn. (sec. 1970s), Bus. and Profl. Women Assn. (v.p. Nev. chpt. 1953-55), Pythian Sisters (Grand Guard 1950), Order Ea. Star (matron Nev. chpt.), Delta Kappa Gamma (pres. 1980-82), Phi Delta Kappa. Avocations: playing church organ, oil and water color painting, silver jewelry. Home: PO Box 229 Wallace ID 83873-0229

PARR, JAMES ALLAN, literature professor; b. Ritchie County, W.Va., Oct. 7, 1936; s. James William and Virginia Alice (Bragg) P.; m. Franciszka Duda, May 4, 1957 (div. 1967): 1 child, Jacqueline; m. Carmen Salazar, Aug. 19, 1968 (div. 1980); m. Patricia Catherine Brinck, June 28, 1985. BA, Ohio U., 1959, MA, 1961; PhD, U. Pitts., 1967. Prof., chmn. Murray (Ky.) State U., 1964-70; prof. U. So. Calif., Los Angeles, 1970-90, U. Calif., Riverside, 1990—. Author: Don Quixote: An Anatomy of Subversive Discourse, 1988, Confrontaciones calladas, 1990, After Its Kind: Approaches to the Comedia, 1991; editor: Critical Essays on Juan Ruiz de Alarcon, 1972, El Burlador de Sevilla, 1991, On Cervantes: Essays for L.A. Murillo, 1991, Don Quixote, 1998; editor jour. Bull. of the Comediantes, 1973-98. Recipient Phi Beta Kappa award, Ohio U., 1960, Mellon fellowships, U. Pitts., 1961-63, Del Amo fellowship, U. So. Calif., Los Angeles, 1977, 84, 89, Fulbright, 1991. Mem. Modern Lang. Assn., Assn. Internacional Siglo de Oro, Internat. Assn. Hispanists. Avocation: travel. Home: 421 Elmwood Dr Pasadena CA 91105-1358

PARRENAS, CECILIA SALAZAR, secondary school educator; b. San Jose de Buenavista, Antique, Philippines, July 17, 1945; came to U.S., 1983; d. Angel Xavier Salazar and Lourdes Quibing (Jabile); m. Florante Y. Parrenas, Dec. 24, 1964; children: Rolf, Celine, Rhacel, Rhanee, Cerissa, Rheana, Margarita, Cecille. BS in Elem. Edn., Philippine Normal Coll., Manila, 1966; MA in Adminstrn., Nat. Tchrs. Coll., Manila, 1971, EdD in Edn. Mgmt., 1977; postgrad., Boston U., 1979. Faculty mem. Internat. Sch., Inc., Metro Manila, 1967-81; dept. head English and art Woodrose, Pvt. Sch. for Girls, Metro Manila, 1981-83; assoc. prof. De LaSalle U., Manila, 1983-84; program asst. sr. edn. programs MIT Sloan Sch., Cambridge, 1984-85; resource tchr. San Bernardino (Calif.) City Unified Sch. Dist., 1986-91; bilingual tchr., unit leader Pomona (Calif.) Unified Sch. Dist., 1991—; cons. Boston Pub. Schs. and Boston U. Bilingual Resource Tng. Ctr., 1978-79; presenter 20th Internat. Conf. on Bilingual/Bicultural Edn., 1991. One-woman painting and brushworks shows Brush, Ink and Color, Manila, 1981, Touchen and Calligrafen, Innsbruck, Austria, 1981, Seasons, Manila, 1982. Philippine Normal Coll. Alumni Assn. grantee, Manila, 1962-66, grantee Curso para profesores Agencia de Cooperacion Internacional, Madrid, 1991; postdoctoral fellow Boston U., 1978-79. Mem. Nat. Assn. Bilingual Edn. Avocations: painting, piano playing, writing. Home: 3784 Canyon Terrace Dr San Bernardino CA 92407-4167 Office: Pomona Unified Sch Dist Vejar Elem Sch 1381 S White Ave Pomona CA 91766-4449

PARRENT, JOANNE ELIZABETH, screenwriter, filmmaker, writer; b. Detroit, July 22, 1948; d. Elton Laverne and Geraldine Elizabeth (Racine) P. Student, U. Mich., 1966-69; BA in Communications, UCLA, 1982. Founder, dir. Feminist Fed. Credit Union, Detroit, 1973-76; editor Chrysalis Mag., L.A., 1977; program developer Women's Community, Inc., L.A., 1978; asst. to pres. Screen Actors Guild, L.A., 1979-80; freelance writer, producer, dir. L.A., 1980—. Author: (documentaries) The Workplace Hustle, 1980 (San Francisco Film Festival award, N.Y. Film Festival award), Sexual Shakedown, 1980, The Healing Force, 1983 (also dir.), Little Arkansas, 1985, 1988, (novel adaptation) Big Doc's Girl, 1987, (dramatic series) Susan B., 1989, (comedy/drama) Elizabeth and Will, 1991, (drama) The Star of Tibet, 1992, Witch-Hunt, 1993, You'll Never Make Love in This Town Again: The Movie, 1996, Once More With Feeling, 1996; co-author: Life After Johnnie Cochran, 1995; co-author, editor You'll Never Make Love in This Town Again, 1995; writer, producer, dir.: (short films) Growing Healthy, 1986, AIDS, 1986, The Childhood Of Susan B. Anthony, 1987, Love is Feeding Everyone, 1988; co-writer (series) Alice & The Rainbow Rider, The Prophecy, 1981, (drama) Changes, 1991, (episodes) Dr. Quinn, Medicine Woman, 1992, 94; contbr. Ms. Mag., 1991;. Bd. dirs. Love Is Feeding Everyone (L.I.F.E.), Los Angeles, 1983—. Recipient Minority Bus. award Detroit Minority Bus. Assn., 1975; named Feminist of Yr. NOW, 1976. Mem. PEN, Writers Guild Am.-West, Creative Collection, Veteran Feminists of Am. Democrat. Avocations: reading, tennis. Office: Feigen Parrent Lit Mgmt 10158 Hollow Glen Cir Los Angeles CA 90077-2112

PARRICK, GERALD HATHAWAY, communication and marketing executive; b. Cushing, Okla., Oct. 27, 1924; s. Gerald H. and Phyllis A. (Sheppard) P. BJ, U. Mo., 1948; m. Gail V. Straney, Dec. 5, 1984; children: Gerald Hathaway III, Candace Anne. Creative account exec. George Knox & Assoc., Oklahoma City, 1948-51; account exec. Batten, Barton, Durstine & Osborn, San Francisco, 1952-60; account dir. McCann-Erickson, Los Angeles, 1960-67, v.p., Portland, Oreg., 1967-72; dir. communications Pacific Power Co., Portland, 1972-77, spl. asst. to chmn. bd., 1977-79; pres. Entreepublic Communications, West Linn, Oreg., 1979—, Bailey/Parrick, Inc., Portland, 1981-84, Parrick/Milpacher, Inc., Portland, 1984-85, The Laugh Clinic, Inc., Portland, 1984-90, K-KOR, Inc., 1990-93. Author: A 20th Century Miracle, 1981, Touched by a Miracle, 1997. Mem. Oreg. Advt. Rev. Bd., 1974-75. Served to capt. AUS, 1943-45, 51-52, ETO. Named Oreg. Advt. Man of Yr., Oreg. Advt. Club, 1971. Mem. Am. Advt. Fedn. (chmn. edn. western region 1973-74), Portland Advt. Fedn. (pres. 1974-75), Toastmasters (pres. 1966-67) (Encino, Calif.), Kappa Tau Alpha. Home: 3950 Elmran Dr West Linn OR 97068-1509

PARRO, JON GEORGE, university administrator; b. Cleve., Oct. 7, 1959; s. Eugene Zoltan and Doris Margaret (Keller) P.; m. Diane Kekumi Watanabe, June 12, 1983; children: Joshua, Cameron. BA, Pitzer Coll., 1981; MA, Claremont Coll., 1989; EdM, Harvard U., 1989, EdD, 1997. Admissions counselor Pitzer Coll., Claremont, Calif., 1982-84, asst. dir. admissions, 1984-86, assoc. dir. admissions, 1986-88, dir. of admissions, 1987-88; grad. asst., tchg. asst. Grad. Sch. Edn. Harvard U., Cambridge, Mass., 1988-91; assoc. dir. devel. Sch. of Medicine U. So. Calif., L.A., 1991-96; dir. devel. Grad. Sch. Edn. and Info. UCLA, 1996—. Office: Grad Sch Edn Info Studies UCLA 415 Hilgard Ave Los Angeles CA 90024-2595

PARROTT, DENNIS BEECHER, sales executive; b. St. Louis, June 13, 1929; s. Maurice Ray and Mai Ledgerwood (Beecher) P.; m. Vivian Cleveland Miller, Mar. 24, 1952; children: Constance Beecher, Dennis Beecher, Anne Cleveland. BS in Econs., Fla. State U., Tallahassee, 1954; postgrad. Princeton U., 1964; MBA, Pepperdine U., 1982. With Prudential Ins. Co. Am., 1954-74, v.p. group mktg., L.A., 1971-74; sr. v.p. Frank B. Hall Cons. Co., L.A., 1974-83; v.p. Johnson & Higgins, L. A., 1983-95; exec. v.p. Arthur J. Gallagher & Co., L.A., 1995—; speaker in field. Chmn. Weekend with the Stars Telethon, 1976-80; chmn. bd. dirs. United Cerebral Palsy/Spastic Children's Found. Los Angeles County, 1979-82, chmn. bd. govs., 1982-83; bd. dirs. Nat. United Cerebral Palsy Assn., 1977-82, pres., 1977-79; bd. dirs. L.A. Emergency Task Force, 1992; mem. community adv. council Birmingham High Sch., Van Nuys, Calif., 1982-85 ; sect. chmn. United Way, Los Angeles, 1983-84; bd. dirs. The Betty Clooney Found. for Brain Injured, 1986-88; mem. com. to fund an endowed chair in cardiology at Cedars-Sinai Med. Ctr., 1986-88; adv. council Family Health Program Inc., 1986-88; bd. Deacons Bel Air Presbyn. Ch., 1990-92, chmn. 1991-92; elder Bel Air Presbyn. Ch. 1993-96; mem. adv. coun. Blue Cross Calif., 1996—; chmn. Danny Arnold Meml. Golf Classic at Riviera Country Club benefitting John Wayne Cancer Inst., 1997. Served to 1st lt. AUS, 1951-53. C.L.U. Mem. Am. Soc. C.L.U.s, Internat. Found. Employee Benefits, Merchants and Mfrs. Assns. 44th Annual Mgmt. Conf. (chmn. 1986), Employee Benefits Planning Assn. So. Calif. Republican. Presbyterian. Clubs: Los Angeles, Woodland Hills Country [illegible] Woodland Hills CA 91367-4330

PARROTT, JOEL, zoo director; b. Lake George, N.Y., Aug. 21, 1952; [illegible] Intern Denver Zoo, 1979; veterinarian in pvt. practice Castro Valley, Calif.,

1980-84; asst. dir. Oakland (Calif.) Zoo, 1984, exec. dir., 1985—. Office: The Oakland Zoo PO Box 5238 9777 Golf Links Rd Oakland CA 94605-4925*

PARROTT, SHARON LEE, retired elementary educator; b. Ostrander, Ohio, Oct. 15, 1949; d. Fay Llewellyn and Thelma Irene (Reed) P. BS in Elem. Edn., Ind. Wesleyan U., 1975. From kindergarten assoc. tchr. to asst. tchr. Columbus (Ohio) Children's Coll., 1975; 1st grade tchr. Kayenta (Ariz.) Unified Sch. Dist. 27, 1975-84, presch. tchr., 1986-95, 1st grade tchr., 1995-97; substitute tchr. Delaware and Union County Schs., Ohio, 1984-86. Tchr. Kayenta Bible Ch., 1981-92, recorder, 1991-93. Avocations: cooking, reading, outdoor activities. Home: 4375 Canyon Trail #2 Cottonwood AZ 86326-5900

PARRUCK, BIDYUT, electrical engineer; b. Calcutta, W. Bengal, India, Oct. 31, 1958; came to U.S., 1981; s. Birendra Singh and Jyotsna (Kothari) P. B in Tech., Indian Inst. Tech., Kharagpur, 1981; MS in Elec. Engring., Va. Poly. Inst., 1983. Mem. tech. staff ITT Advanced Tech. Ctr., Shelton, Conn., 1983-86; R & D engr. Contel Fin. Systems, Stamford, Conn., 1987-89; sr. design engr. TranSwitch Corp., Shelton, 1989-93; sect. head II Farinon divsn. Harris Corp., San carlos, Calif., 1993; prin. engr. Network Equipment Techs., Redwood City, Calif., 1993-94; v.p. asynchronous transfer mode sonet CorEl MicroSystems, Fremont, Calif., 1994—, also bd. dirs.; founder, advisor Next Generation Systems, Matawan, N.J., 1986—; advisor, cons. OSS Corp., Shelton, Conn., 1988—. Contbr. articles to profl. jours.; patentee in field. Vol. Ourhouse-North, Daly City, Calif., 1993-94, Holiday Project, San Francisco, 1995-96. Mem. IEEE. Avocaitons: ballroom dancing, sculpting, sailing, hiking, photography. Home: 2321 Edsel Dr Milpitas CA 95035-6144

PARRY, ROBERT WALTER, chemistry educator; b. Ogden, Utah, Oct. 1, 1917; s. Walter and Jeanette (Petterson) P.; m. Marjorie J. Nelson, July 6, 1945; children: Robert Bryce, Mark Nelson. BS, Utah State Agr. Coll., 1940; MS, Cornell U., 1942; PhD, U. Ill., 1946; DSc (hon.), Utah State U., 1985, U. Utah, 1997. Research asst. NDRC Munitions Devel. Lab., U. Ill. at Urbana, 1943-45, teaching fellow 1945-46; mem. faculty U. Mich., 1946-69, prof. chemistry, 1958-69; Distinguished prof. chemistry U. Utah, 1969-97, prof. emeritus, 1997; indsl. cons., 1952—; chmn. bd. trustees Gordon Rsch. Conf., 1967-68. Chmn. com. teaching chemistry Internat. Union Pure and Applied Chemistry 1968-74. Recipient Mfg. Chemists award for coll. teaching, 1972, Sr. U.S. Scientist award Alexander Von Humboldt-Stiftung (W. Ger.), 1980, First Govs. medal of Sci. State Utah, 1987. Mem. Am. Chem. Soc. (Utah award Utah Sect. 1978, past chmn. inorganic div. and div. chem. edn., award for distinguished service to inorganic chemistry 1965, for chem. edn., 1977, dir. 1973-83, bd. editors jour. 1969-80, pres.-elect 1981-82, pres. 1982-83, Priestly medal 1993), Internat. Union Pure and Applied Chemistry (chmn. U.S. nat. com.), AAAS (chmn. chemistry sec. 1983), Sigma Xi. Founding editor Inorganic Chemistry, 1960-63. Research, publs. on some structural problems of inorganic chemistry, and incorporation results into theoretical models; chemistry of phosphorus, boron and fluorine. Home: 5002 Fairbrook Ln Salt Lake City UT 84117-6205 Office: U Utah Dept Chemistry 315 S 1400 E Rm Dock Salt Lake City UT 84112-8948

PARRY, STANLEY WARREN, lawyer; b. Cedar City, Utah, May 7, 1949; s. Dixon C. Parry and Majorie (Miller) Dubois; m. Carol Lynne Wright; children: Heidi, John, Mathis, Joseph, Tyler. BA, So. Utah U., 1974; JD, Brigham Young U., 1977. Bar: Nev. 1977. Dep. dist. atty. County of Clark, Las Vegas, 1977-83; trial atty. U.S. Dept. Justice Strike Force, Las Vegas, 1983-89; pvt. practice Las Vegas, 1989—; ptnr. K. Michael Leavitt, Las Vegas, 1991-94, Curran & Parry, Las Vegas, 1994—; pres. Grand West Devel., Las Vegas, 1992-96. Chmn. Las Vegas Ethics Rev. Bd., 1992-95. Mem. Keystone Club (bd. dirs. 1995-97). Mem. LDS Ch. Office: Curran & Parry 601 S Rancho Dr Ste C-23 Las Vegas NV 89106-4825

PARRY, THAD B., process engineer; b. Salt Lake City, July 12, 1965; s. Karnell G. and Barbara (Batt) P. BSEE, U. Utah, 1992; M Engring. Mgmt., Brigham Young U., 1993. Researcher TransEra Corp., Orem, Utah, 1994; staff engr. SCP Global Techs., Boise, 1994—. Contbr. articles to profl. jours. Mem. IEEE. Mem. LDS Ch. Office: SCP Global Techs 400 Benjamin Ln Boise ID 83704-8333

PARSA, FEREYDOUN DON, plastic surgeon; b. Tehran, Iran, May 20, 1942; came to U.S., 1970; s. Issa and Zahra (Bismark) P.; m. Touri Akhlaghi, June 17, 1972; children: Natalie, Alan, Sean. MD, Lausanne U., Switzerland, 1969. Diplomate Am. Soc. Plastic Surgery. Chif of plastic surgery, prof. surgery U. Hawaii, Honolulu, 1981—. Contbr. articles to profl. jours. Mem. Am. Cancer Soc. Avocations: painting. Office: U Hawaii Sch Med Surg 1356 Lusitana St Honolulu HI 96813-2421 Office: U Hawaii 1329 Lusitana St Honolulu HI 96813-2429

PARSONS, DONALD D., bishop. Bishop of Alaska Evang. Luth. Ch. in Am., Anchorage, 1987. Office: Synod of Alaska 1847 W Northern Lights Blvd # 2 Anchorage AK 99517-3343

PARSONS, ELMER EARL, retired clergyman; b. Cloverland, Wash., Oct. 4, 1919; s. Claud Solomon and Bessie Lillian (Campbell) P.; m. Marjorie Emma Carlson, Aug. 29, 1942; children—Karl Elmer, James Myron, Helen Joy, Ann Elizabeth, Lois Marie, Louise Melba. B.A., Seattle Pacific U., 1942; S.T.B., N.Y. Theol. Sem., 1945; S.T.M., Asbury Theol. Sem., Wilmore, Ky., 1955; D.D. (hon.), Greenville (Ill.) Coll., 1958. Ordained to ministry Free Methodist Ch., 1944; acad. dean Wessington Springs (S.D.) Coll., 1945-47; missionary to China, 1947-49, missionary to Japan, 1949-54; supt. Japan Free Meth. Mission, 1950-54; pres. Central Coll., McPherson, Kans., 1955-64, Osaka (Japan) Christian Coll., 1964-74; Asia area sec., Free Meth. Ch., 1964-74; bishop Free Meth. Ch. N.Am., 1974-85. Author: Witness to the Resurrection, 1967. Chmn. Free Meth. Study Commn. on Doctrine, 1990-95. Named Alumnus of Year Seattle Pacific U., 1976. Mem. Wesleyan Theol. Soc.

PARTRIDGE, ERNEST, environmental philosopher, educator; b. N.Y.C., May 14, 1935; s. Ernest DeAlton and Nell (Clark) P.; m. Elinore Helen Hughes, Dec. 21, 1957. BS with honors, U. Utah, 1957, MS, 1961, PhD, 1976. Instr. Weber State Coll., Ogden, Utah, 1968-70, assoc. prof. philosophy, 1976-79; assoc. prof. environ. studies U. Calif., Santa Barbara, 1980-82; rsch. assoc. U. Colo., Boulder, 1982-86; assoc. prof. philosophy Calif. State U., Fullerton, 1989-92, U. Calif., Riverside, 1984-93; Hulings prof. humanities and environ. ethics Northland Coll., Ashland, Wis., 1993-97; rsch. assoc. U. Calif., Riverside, 1997—; advisor Lake Superior Binat. Forum, U.S. Forest Svc., Ont. Ministry of Natural Resources; mem. internat. adv. bd. Ctr. for Ecol. Protection of Baikal Region, Ulan-Ulde, Buryat Republic, SSR; advisor Comprehensive Land Use Policy and Allocation program Lake Baikal Watershed, Davis Assocs., Ctr. for U.S.-USSR Initiatives, Russian Acad. Scis., 1991. Editor: (anthology) Responsibilities to Future Generations: Environmental Ethics, 1981; mem. editl. bd.: Environ. Ethics, Jour. Environ. Edn.; contbr. numerous scholarly papers to profl. jours. and publs. Mem. pub. adv. panel Chem. Mfrs. Assn., Washington, 1994—. Recipient Interdisciplinary award NSF, 1984-86; Rockefeller Found. fellow in environ. affairs, 1978, rsch. fellow Calif. State U., Fullerton, 1991. Mem. AAAS, Internat. Soc. Environ. Ethics (treas.), Am. Philos. Assn., Am. Soc. for Polit. and Legal Philosophy, Am. Soc. for Value Inquiry, Soc. for Philosophy and Pub. Affairs, The Wilderness Soc., Inst. for Global Comms., Union of Concerned Scientists, Concerned Philosophers for Peace, Sierra Club, St. Petersburg Soc. Naturalists. Avocations: hiking, canoeing, skiing.

PASCOTTO, ALVARO, lawyer; b. Rome, Mar. 8, 1949; came to U.S., 1984; s. Antonio and Anna Ludovica (Habig) P.; m. Linda Haldan, July 20, 1985. JD, U. Rome, 1973. Bar: Italy 1976, Calif. 1987, U.S. Dist. Ct. (cen. dist.) Calif. 1987, U.S. Ct. Appeals (9th cir.) 1987. Ptnr. Studio Legale Pascotto, Rome, 1976-86, Pascotto, Gallavotti & Gardner, L.A. and Rome, 1986-90, Pascotto & Gallavotti, L.A., 1990—; of counsel Irell & Manella LLP, L.A., 1994—; counsel, cons. Quantum Inc., Reno, Nev., 1980-87, Execucorp Mgmt. Cons., Miami, Fla., 1980-85; official counsel Consulate Gen. Italy, L.A., 1987—. Mem. ABA, Calif. Bar Assn., Italian-Am. Bar Assn., Am. Mgmt. Assn., Consiglio dell'Ordine Degli Avvocati e Procuratori di Roma. Clubs: Circolo del Golf (Rome); Malibu (Calif.) Racquet Club, Regency Club (L.A.). Home: 6116 Merritt Dr Malibu CA 90265-3847 Office: Pascotto & Gallavotti Ste 900 1800 Avenue Of The Stars Los Angeles CA 90067-4212

PASHGIAN, MARGARET HELEN, artist; b. Pasadena, Calif., Nov. 7, 1934; d. Aram John and Margaret (Howell) P. BA, Pomona Coll., 1956; MA in Fine Arts, Boston Univ., 1958; student, Columbia U., 1957. Art instr. Harvard-Newton Program Occidental Coll., 1977-78; artist in residence Calif. Inst. Tech., 1970-71; grants panelist Calif. Arts Coun., Sacramento, 1993. Artist: solo shows include Rex Evans Gallery, L.A., 1965, 67, Occidental Coll., 1967, Kornblee Gallery, N.Y.C., 1969-72, U. Calif., Irvine, 1975, U. Calif. Santa Barbara, 1976, Stella Polaries Gallery, L.A., 1981, 82, Kaufman Galleries, Houston, 1982, Modernism Gallery, San Francisco, 1983, Works Gallery, Long Beach, Costa Mesa, Calif., 1986, 87, 88, 89, 90, 91, 92, Malka Gallery, L.A., 1997; group exhibitions include Pasadena Art Mus., 1965, Carson Pirie Scott, Chgo., 1965, Calif. Palace of Legion of Honor, San Francisco, 1967, Esther Bear Gallery, Santa Barbara, 1967, 69, Lytton Ctr. of the Visual Arts, L.A., 1968, Salt Lake Art Inst., Salt Lake City, 1968, Mus. Contemporary Crafts, Internat. Plastics Exhibition, 1969, Second Flint (Mich.) Invitational, 1969, Milw. Art Ctr., 1969, U.S.I.S. Mus., N.Y.C., Mus. Contemporary Art, Chgo., 1970, Studio Merconi, Milan, 1970, Calif. Inst. Tech., Baxter Art Galley, 1971, 1980, Calif. Innovations, Palm Springs Dessert Mus., 1981, Calif. Internat. Arts Found. Mus. of Modern Art, Paris, 1982, L.A. Artists in Seoul, Donsangbang Gallery, 1982, An Artistic Conversation, 1931-82, Poland, USA, Ulster Mus., Belfast, Ireland, 1983, Madison (Wis.) Art Ctr., 1994, Calif. State U., Fullerton, 1995, Oakland (Calif.) Mus., 1995; represented in pub. collections at River Forest (Ill.) State Bank, Atlantic Richfield Co., Dallas, Frederic Weisman Collection, L.A., Security Pacific Bank, L.A., Singapore, Andrew Dickson White Mus. of Art, Cornell U., Ithaca, N.Y., L.A. County Mus. of Art, Santa Barbara Art Mus., Laguna Beach Mus. of Art. Trustee, Pomona Coll, Claremont, Calif., 1987—; parade judge Tournament of RosesCentennial Parade, Pasadena, 1987; bd. dirs. L.A. Master Chorale, 1992—. NEA grantee, 1986. Home and Studio: 731 S Grand Ave Pasadena CA 91105-2424

PASHOLK, PAUL DOUGLAS, retail executive, government official; b. Columbus, Ohio, Mar. 24, 1968; s. Jerome Joseph and Norma Anne (Weigand) P.; m. Rebecca Jean Eaton, June 10, 1995; 1 child, Rachel Marie. BA in History, Ohio State U., 1990, BA in Polit. Sci., 1990. Dept. supr. Kohl's Dept. Stores, Columbus, 1991-96; market news reporter U.S. Dept. of Agriculture, Fruit and Vegetable Division, Phoenix, 1996—. Author: The Columbus Public Schools and 75 Years of School Board Elections, 1990, King of the Hill - U.S. Presidential Elections, 1992, (with Rebecca Pasholk) U.S. Senate Elections: The Numbers, and the Story Behind Them. Vol., rschr. Bill Moss for Columbus Sch. Bd., 1985, 89, 91, 97, Bill Buckel for Columbus Sch. Bd., 1987, treas. 1989, 91, 93; presdl. elector cand. Eugene McCarthy for Pres., Columbus, 1988; vol. Bruce Babbitt for Pres., Cedar Rapids, Iowa, 1988, Jesse Jackson for Pres., Columbus, 1988, Richard Letts for Judge, Columbus, 1989, Jerry Brown for Pres., Columbus, 1992; local organizer Hands Across Am., Columbus, 1986; vol. recruiter AFL-CIO support group Frontlash, Columbus, 1988-90; mem. Indsl. Workers of the World, San Francisco/ Ypsilanti, 1991—; organizer, chmn. West H.S. Class Reunion, Columbus, 1991; Ohio state campaign chmn. Ray Rollinson for Pres., Columbus, 1992; non-voting del. Libertarian Nat. Conv., Salt Lake City, 1993, Nat. Market News Assn. conf., Austin, Tex., 1997; contbr. Kirtland (Ohio) Reorganized LDS Ch. Temple Restoration, 1996; mem. Friends of Freedom & Justice, Columbus, 1998—. Libertarian. Mem. LDS Ch. Avocations: collecting buffalos, political election statistics, public speaking, editorial letters, NASCAR memorabilia. Home: 6060 W Royal Palm Rd Apt 144 Glendale AZ 85302-6745 Office: 522 N Central Ave Ste 106 Phoenix AZ 85004-2168

PASICH, KIRK ALAN, lawyer; b. La Jolla, Calif., May 26, 1955; s. Chris Nick and Iva Mae (Tormey) P.; m. Pamela Mary Woods, July 30, 1983; children: Christopher Thomas, Kelly Elizabeth, Connor Woods. BA in Polit. Sci., UCLA, 1977; JD, Loyola Law Sch., L.A., 1980. Bar: Calif. 1980, U.S. Dist. Ct. (no., so., ea. and cen. dists.) Calif. 1981, U.S. Ct. Appeals (9th cir.) 1982, U.S. Ct. Appeals (1st cir.) 1992. Assoc. Paul, Hastings, Janofsky & Walker, L.A., 1980-88, ptnr., 1988-89; ptnr. Troop Steuber Pasich Reddick & Tobey, LLP, L.A., 1989—. Author: Casualty and Liability Insurance, 1990, 96; co-author: Officers and Directors: Liabilities and Protections, 1996; contbg. editor: West's California Litigation Forms: Civil Procedure Before Trial, 1996; entertainment law columnist, ins. law columnist L.A. and San Francisco Daily Jour., 1989—; contbr. articles to profl. jours. Active bd. dirs. Nat. Acad. Jazz, L.A., 1988-89, chmn. bd. dirs. Woody Herman Found., L.A., 1989-92, active L.A. City Atty's. Task Force for Econ. Recovery, 1992-93. Named to Calif's. Legal Dream Team as 1 of state's top 25 litigators, Calif. Law Bus., 1992, as one of the nation's top 45 lawyers under age 45, The Am. Lawyer, 1995. Mem. ABA (mem. Task Force on Complex Insurance Coverage Litigation). Office: 2029 Century Park E Los Angeles CA 90067-3010

PASKALOV, GEORGE Z., plasmaphysicist; b. Tvarditca, Russia, Mar. 10, 1958; s. Zakhari G. and Anna N. Paskalov; m. Svetlana Yu Kopylova, Sept. 16, 1979; 1 child, Julia G. MS, Polytech. Inst., 1982; PhD, Tech. U., 1986. Registered prof. engr. Sr. engr. Tech. U., St. Petersburg, 1982-85, rschr., 1985-87, sr. rschr., 1987-94; pres., chief scientist Plasma Plus Inc., Van Nuys, Calif., 1992—; founder, gen. mgr. Plasma Plus Inc., Van Nuys, 1992—, Plasma Product Man. Plasma S., St. Petersburg, 1991-94. Co-author: RF and MW Plasmatorches, 1992, Plasmachemical Processes, 1991. Mem. Am. Powder Metallurgy Inst. Achievements include patent on gas plasma treatment of materials, 1993-94. Office: Plasma Plus Inc 14715 Arminta St Van Nuys CA 91402-5903

PASQUA, THOMAS MARIO, JR., journalism educator; b. L.A., Aug. 13, 1938; s. Thomas Mario and Ann Ione (Anderson) P.; m. Sandra Mae Liddell; children: Bruce Burks, Julie Burks, Geoffrey, Alexis. BA, Whittier (Calif.) Coll., 1960; MA, UCLA, 1961; PhD, U. Tex., 1973. Cert. secondary tchr. Reporter, photographer Whittier Daily News, 1954-65; tchr. LaSerna High Sch., Whittier, 1961-63, 64-65; lectr. Calif. State U., Fullerton, 1973-75, Mesa Coll., San Diego, 1978-83, U. San Diego, 1979-80, San Diego State U., 1985; prof. Southwestern Coll., Chula Vista, Calif., 1965—; staff writer San Diego Mag., 1997. Co-author: Excellence in College Journalism, 1983, Mass Media in the Information Age, 1990, Historical Perspectives in Popular Music, 1993; editor C.C. Journalist, 1983—; bibliographer Journalism Quar., 1974-92; contbr. articles to profl. jours. Mem. ch. coun. St. Andrew Luth. Ch., Whittier, 1965; mem. Chula Vista Bd. of Ethics, 1978-86; mem. Chula Vista Charter Rev. Com., 1969; mem. adv. bd. Bay Gen. Hosp., Chula Vista, 1985-87; mem. ch. coun. Victory Luth. Ch., Chula Vista, 1989-90; adv. com. Otay Valley Regional Park, 1990—. Wall St. Jour. Newspaper Fund fellow U. Wash., 1962; recipient Nat. Teaching award Poynter Inst. Media Studies, 1987. Mem. C.C. Journalism Assn. (archivist 1989—, charter inductee Hall of Fame, 1994), Journalism Assn. C.C.'s (exec. sec. 1975-81), Assn. for Edn. in Journalism and Mass Comm. (Markham prize 1974), Internat. Comm. Assn., Coll. Media Advisers, Am. Fedn. Tchrs. (pres. Southwestern Coll. 1977-78, 81-87), Phi Kappa Phi, Kappa Tau Alpha, Pi Sigma Alpha. Democrat. Avocations: gardening, cats, reading mysteries. Home: 760 Monterey Ave Chula Vista CA 91910-6318 Office: Southwestern Coll 900 Otay Lakes Rd Chula Vista CA 91910-7223

PASSALACQUA, KRISTINE GAY, interior designer; b. Phoenix, July 30, 1955; d. Richard Elmer and Doris Helen (Emerick) Anderson; m. Glenn Allen Frank, Aug. 7, 1976 (dec. Apr. 1980), m. David Passalacqua, July 7, 1984; 1 child, Jennifer Lynn. AA with honors, Mt. San Antonio Coll., 1976. Design asst. Debby's Interiors, Upland, Calif., 1979-80; prin. Kristine Gay Interiors, Ontario, Calif., 1980-84, Benicia, Calif., 1981—; prin. Kristine Passalacqua Studio of Interior Design, Benicia, 1984—. Mem. Am. Soc. Interior Designers. Republican. Avocations: snow and water skiing, parisailing, camping, gardening, cooking. Home: 1453 Sherman Dr Benicia CA 94510-2624 Office: 919 W 2nd St Benicia CA 94510-3110

PASSANANTE, JOY CATHEY, English language educator; b. St. Louis, Apr. 18, 1947; d. Bart Michael and Alberta (Rosenbloom) P.; m. Gary Williams, June 13, 1970; children: Liza Bryn Williams, Emily Caterina Williams. Student, Sarah Lawrence Coll., 1965-67; AB, Washington U., St. Louis, 1969; MA in Tchg., Cornell U., 1971. Tchr. English Homer (N.Y.) H.S., 1971-73; freelance writer, editor, 1975—; mem. faculty dept. English U. Idaho, Moscow, 1977-83, 88—, comm. specialist Coll. Bus. and Econs., 1983-90; faculty cons. Ednl. Testing Svc., Princeton, N.J., 1991—; judge nat. lit. contest Golden Key Honor Soc., 1995; acad. advisor Alpha Phi, Moscow, 1997—. Author: (book) Writing Guidelines, 1991, Sinning in Italy, 1999; contbr. poetry, stories, and essays to publs.; adv. editor: Frontiers: A Jour. of Women Studies, 1996—. Mentor Moscow H.S., 1992—. Recipient Outstanding Faculty award U. Idaho Interfraternity Coun., 1993; fellow in fiction Idaho Commn. on Arts, 1990, QuickArts grantee for poetry, 1997. Mem. No. Idaho Coun. on English, Athena, Phi Beta Kappa (v.p. Alpha of Idaho 1994-95, pres. 1995-97). Avocation: writing. Office: U of Idaho Dept of English Moscow ID 83844-0001

PASSLACK, MATTHIAS, electrical engineer, researcher; b. Dippoldiswalde, Saxony, Germany, May 24, 1959; came to U.S., 1993; s. Guenter and Christa (Klemm) P.; m. Gudrun Schwartz, Feb. 16, 1985; children: Katrin, Jessica. MS in engring., Tech. U. Dresden, Germany, 1984, D. in Engring., 1988. Asst. prof. U. Dresden, 1989-91; vis. scientist U. Ulm, Germany, 1992, AT&T Bell Labs., Murray Hill, N.J., 1993-95; sr. staff engr. Motorola PCRL, Tempe, Ariz., 1995—. Contbr. articles to IEEE Trans., Applied Physics Letters. Grantee German Rsch. Assn., 1992. Mem. IEEE (sr.), Am. Phys. Soc. Achievements include patents and patents pending in field; pioneer in field of GaAs metal-oxide-semiconductor technology. Office: Motorola Semiconductor Products Sector 2100 E Elliot Rd # 720 Tempe AZ 85284-1806

PASSMAN, STEPHEN LEE, theoretical mechanics scientist; b. Suffolk, Va., Sept. 3, 1942; s. Milton Lawrence and Jean (Lehrman) P.; children: Michael, Rebecca, Sara, Rachel. BSEM, Ga. Inst. Tech., 1964, MSEM, 1966, PhD, 1968. Instr. U.S Naval Acad., Annapolis, Md., 1968-70; postdoctoral fellow Johns Hopkins U., Balt., 1970-71; from asst. to assoc. prof. Ga. Inst. Tech., Atlanta, 1971-78; sr. mem. tech. staff Sandia Nat. Labs., Albuquerque, 1978—; lectr. George Washington U., Washington, 1969-70; vis. mem. Math. Rsch. Ctr., U. Wis., Madison, 1972, Inst. Math. and Its Applications, U. Minn., Mpls., 1984, 89, Math. Sci. Inst., Cornell U., 1987-90; cons. Bell Labs., Norcross, Ga., 1975-78; vis. scientist Pitts. Energy Tech. Ctr., 1988-90, cons., 1990-96; vis. scientist U.S. Dept. Energy, Washington, 1995—; vis. scholar Carnegie Mellon U., 1988-90; adj. prof. engring. U. Pitts., 1990-96; U.S. rep. multiphase flow com., Internat. Energy Agy., 1992-96; U.S. rep. G-7 Nuclear Experts Meeting, Paris, 1996; mem. steering com. U.S.-Russian Plutonium Disposition Program, 1995—. Contbr. articles to profl. jours. Served to capt. U.S. Army, 1968-70. Recipient Monie A. Ferst Rsch. award, 1968; scholar Johns Hopkins U., 1990. Mem. ASME (elasticity com. 1987—, multiphase flow com. 1990-96), Soc. Natural Philosophy (treas. 1977-78, dir. 1978-96, chmn. bd. dirs. 1985-86), Soc. Engring. Sci. (bd. dirs. 1986-96, treas. 1987-96), Am. Acad. Mechanics, Am. Phys. Soc., Soc. Rheology, Sigma Xi. Office: Sandia Nat Labs PO Box 5800 Albuquerque NM 87185-0100

PASTEGA, RICHARD LOUIS, retail specialist; b. Klamath Falls, Oreg., Mar. 25, 1936; s. Louie and Jennie (Borgialli) P. BS, So. Oreg. State Coll., 1960; MS, Mont. State U., Bozeman, 1961. Tchr. social studies Henley High Sch., Klamath Falls, Oreg., 1962-63, Juneau (Alaska) Douglas High Sch., 1964-67, Thessaloniki (Greece) Internat. High Sch., 1967-69; editor, pub. Breakdown Newspaper, Klamath Falls, Oreg., 1971-73; mgr. Pastega's Market, Klamath Falls, 1975—. Del. Dem. Nat. Conv., N.Y.C., 1976, Oreg. Dem. Platform conv., Eugene, Beaverton and Ashland, 1978-80, 82; councilor City of Klamath Falls, 1986-88; bd. dirs. Basin Transit Svc., Klamath Falls, 1981-87; chair Klamath County Dem. Ctrl. Com., 1983-86, sec. 1992-94; Klamath County alt. del. Oreg. Dem. State Ctrl. Com., 1998—. Mem. Sons of Italy, Klamath Solar Assn. (bd. dirs. 1998—). Democrat. E-mail: pasteqa@cdsnet.net. Home: 428 S 9th St Klamath Falls OR 97601-6126

PASTEN, LAURA JEAN, veterinarian; b. Tacoma, May 25, 1952; d. Frank Larry and Jean Mary (Slavich) Brajkovich; student Stanford U., 1970; BA in Physiology, U. Calif., Davis, 1970, DVM (regents scholar), 1974; postgrad. Cornell U., 1975. Veterinarian, Nevada County Vet. Hosp., Grass Valley Calif., 1975-80; pvt. practice vet. medicine, owner Mother Lode Vet. Hosp. (cert. wildlife rehab. ctr.), Grass Valley, 1980—. Veterinarian for Morris the 9-Lives cat (of TV comml. fame) 1985—; lect. in field; spokesperson Nat. Cat Health Month; affiliate staff Sierra Nevada Meml. Hosp.; syndicated TV show on vet. medicine, guest on Today Show re. wildlife. Author: Malignant, Tarantula Whisperer; pub. video: How to Tell a Puppy's I.Q. Bd. dirs. Sierra Svcs. for Blind. Mem. AVMA (ethics com.), AOPA, Calif. Vet. Med. Assn. (exec. com., del., Don Low fellowship selection com.), Mother Lode Vet. Assn., Am. Animal Hosp. Assn. (Mother Lode Vet. Hosp. cited for excellence), Nat. Ophthal. Soc., Nat. Pygmy Goat Assn., Nat. Llama Assn., Internat. Assn. for Arabians., Nat. Assn. Underwater Instrs., Denver Area Med. Soc., Internat. Vet. Assn. Am., Nevada County C. of C. (bd. dirs.), Ninety-Niners Pilot Assn., Mensa, Endurance Riding Soc. Republican. Lutheran. Club: Grass Valley Bus. Women. Author: (with Dr Muller) Canine Dermatology, 1970; contbr. articles to profl. jours. Home: 5125 Paso Venado Carmel CA 93923 Office: 11509 La Barr Meadows Rd Grass Valley CA 95949-7722

PASTERNACK, ROBERT HARRY, school psychologist; b. Bklyn., Nov. 30, 1949; s. William and Lillian Ruth (Levine) P.; m. Jeanelle Livingston, Apr. 10, 1980; children: Shayla, Rachel. BA, U. South Fla., 1970; MA, N.Mex. Highlands U., 1972; PhD, U. N.Mex., 1980. Dir. Eddy County Drug Abuse Program, Carlsbad, N.Mex., 1972-73; adminstrv. intern U.S. Office Edn., Washington, 1975-76; exec. dir. Villa Santa maria, Cedar Crest, N.Mex., 1976-78; clin. dir. Ranchos Treatment Ctr., Taos, N.Mex., 1978-79; sch. psychologist N.Mex. Boys Sch., Springer, 1980—, supt., 1991; pres. Ensenar Health svcs., Inc., Taos, 1980—; CEO Casa de Corazon, Taos, N.Mex., 1994-98; state dir. spl. edn. N.Mex. State Dept. Edn., Santa Fe, 1998—; instr. N.Mex. Highlands U., Las Vegas, 1980—, U. N.Mex., Albuquerque, 1980—; cons. N.Mex. Youth Authority, Santa Fe, 1988—, N.Mex. Devel. Disabilities Bur., Santa Fe, 1986—, various sch. dists.; state dir. spl. edn., N.Mex., 1998—. Author: Growing Up: The First Five Years, 1986; contbr. articles to profl. publs. Pres., bd. dirs. Children's Lobby, N.Mex., 1978, N.Mex. Spl. Olympics, 1986-88, Child-Rite, Inc., Taos, 1990; mem. Gov.'s Mental Health Task Force, Albuquerque, 1988—. Mem. Nat. Assn. Sch. Psychologists, Correctional Edn. Assn., Nat. Alliance Mentally Ill, N.Mex. Coun. on Crime and Delinquency. Avocations: tennis, racquetball, skiing, cooking. Home and Office: Enseñar Inc PO Box 3126 Taos NM 87571-3126 Office: NMex State Dept Edn Spl Edn Office 300 Don Gaspar Ave Santa Fe NM 87501-2752

PASTERNACKI, LINDA LEA, critical care nurse; b. Green Bay, Wis., May 26, 1947; d. Paul John and Marion M. (Zagzebski) P.; (div.); children: Sam, Dan, Rachel Marie. Nursing diploma, St. Francis Sch. Nursing, Wichita, Kans., 1968; BS, Coll. St. Francis, Joliet, Ill., 1981, MS in Health Adminstrn., 1986. Cert. ACLS. RN med.-surg., geriatrics, psychiatry St. Francis Hosp., Wichita, 1968-70; RN ICU-critical care unit Sunrise Hosp., Las Vegas, Nev., 1970-72; RN critical care unit Presbyn. Hosp., Albuquerque, 1972-75; RN med. ICU, surg. ICU VA Hosp., Albuquerque, 1976-81; RN emergency rm. Univ. Heights Hosp., Albuquerque, 1981-82; RN ICU, critical care unit Lovelace Med. Ctr., Albuquerque, 1982-86; RN ICU, emergency rm., surg. cornary care, intensive recovery room Presbyn. Hosp., Albuquerque, 1986-94; RN emergency rm., ICU, critical care unit St. Joseph Med. Ctr., Albuquerque, 1992-94; RN ICU, med.-surg. unit Transitional Hosp. Corp., Albuquerque, 1994-97, admissions coord., 1995; nurse Health-South, Albuquerque, 1997-98, Bernalillo County Juvenile Detention Ctr., 1997—; hyperbaric therapy instr. Presbyn. Hosp., Albuquerque, 1975; clin. instr. U. N.Mex. EMT Sch., Albuquerque, 1980. Mem. AACN, N.Mex. Nurses Assn. Home: 10605 Central Park Dr NE Albuquerque NM 87123-4844

PASTOR, EDWARD, congressman; b. Claypool, Ariz., June 28, 1943; m. Verna Mendez; children: Yvonne, Laura. BA, Ariz. State U., 1966. Mem. Maricopa County Bd. Suprs., Phoenix, Ariz., 1976-91; mem. 102nd-106th Congresses from Ariz. 2nd dist., 1991—; mem. appropriations com. Office: House of Reps 2465 Rayburn Bldg Washington DC 20515-0302*

PASTORE, THOMAS MICHAEL, telecommunications sales executive; b. Bronx, N.Y., Jan. 25, 1959; s. Philip J. and Olga E. (DeGenito) P.; m. Kimberly A. Coppersmith, Dec. 13, 1986; children: Gabriela Maria, Thomas John. BA in Bus., Western State Coll., 1981. Sales rep. Victor Technologies Inc., Denver, 1981-84; account mgr. No. Telecom Inc., Denver, 1984-87, v.p. sales coun., 1985—, sales engr., 1987-92, dist. sales mgr., 1992—. Mem. Better Air Campaign, 1990—; sec. Warren Sq. Homeowners Assn., Denver, 1987-92; player, contbr. Dale Tooley Tennis Tournament, 1991-92; fundraiser Am. Cancer Soc., Denver, 1991—; mem. Denver Art Mus., 1991-92. Republican. Roman Catholic. Avocations: skiing, tennis, biking. Home and Office: No Telecom Inc 16095 Quarry Hill Dr Parker CO 80134-9553

PASTREICH, PETER, orchestra executive director; b. Bklyn., Sept. 13, 1938; s. Ben and Hortense (Davis) P.; m. Jamie Garrard Whittington; children by previous marriages: Anna, Milena, Emanuel, Michael. A.B. magna cum laude, Yale Coll., 1959; postgrad., N.Y. U. Sch. Medicine, 1959-60; studied trumpet, with Robert Nagle at Yale U., with Raymond Sabarich, Paris. Asst. mgr. Denver Symphony, Balt. Symphony; mgr. Greenwich Village Symphony, N.Y.C., 1960-63; gen. mgr. Nashville Symphony, 1963-65, Kansas City Philharmonic, 1965-66; asst. mgr., mgr. St. Louis Symphony, 1966-78, exec. dir., 1966-78; exec. dir. San Francisco Symphony, 1978—; instr. orch. mgmt. Am. Symphony Orch. League; bd. dirs. Nat. Com. for Symphony Orch. Support; founder San Francisco Youth Orch.; rep. planning and constrn. Davies Symphony Hall, San Francisco Symphony, 1980. Author: TV comml., 1969 (CLIO award); contbr. articles to various newspapers. Mem. recommendation bd. of the Avery Fisher Artist Program, Yale U. Council com. on music; past mem. adv. panel Nat. Endowment for the Arts, co-chmn. music panel, 1985; founding mem. bd. dirs. St. Louis Conservatory, mem. policy com. Maj. Orch. Mgrs. Conf., chmn., 1980; bd. dirs. Laumeier Sculpture Park, St. Louis, Stern Grove Festival, San Francisco Conv. and Visitors Bur.; chmn. fund campaign French-Am. Internat. Sch., San Francisco. Served with U.S. Army, 1960. Recipient First Disting. Alumnus award Yale U. Band, 1977, cert. Merit Yale Sch. Music, 1984. Mem. Am. Symphony Orch. League (dir., chmn., former chmn. task force on mgmt. tng.; mem. exec. and long-range planning com., chmn. standing com. on adminstrv. policy), Assn. Calif. Symphony Orchs. (dir.), Bankers Club of San Francisco. Club: Yale (N.Y.C.). Office: San Francisco Symphony Davies Symphony Hall San Francisco CA 94102*

PASTRONE, PAUL NICOLAS, production manager; b. Van Nuys, Calif., July 23, 1966; s. John Fredric and Jill Loreen (Parker) P.; m. Melody Lynn Maurin, Sept. 3, 1994; children: O'Keefe Maurin, Caruso George. Student, U. R.I., 1984-85, Gettysburg Coll., 1985-87; BA, U. Md., 1990. Park maintenance supr. Nat. Zoo, Washington, 1990-93; custodian supr. Phoenix (Ariz.) Zoo, 1993-96; prodn. mgr. Tahoe Specialty Door, Phoenix, 1996—. Contbr. poetry and stories to anthologies. Mem. Am. Acad. Poets, Ariz. Author's Assn. Avocation: owner of five dogs. Home: 354 N Hartford St Chandler AZ 85224-4551 Office: Tahoe Specialty Door 3702 W Buckeye Rd Phoenix AZ 85009-5433

PATAKI-SCHWEIZER, KERRY JOSEF, behavioral scientist, medical anthropologist; b. Peekskill, N.Y., Nov. 1, 1935; s. John Josef and Helen Ida (Schweizer) Pataki; S.B., U. Chgo., 1960; M.A., U. Wash., Seattle, 1965, Ph.D., 1968; m. Lalitha Shirin Harben, Nov. 16, 1973; children: Nicholas Josef, Kiran Sarah, Christopher Halim. Asst. prof. anthropology and humanities Reed Coll., Portland, Oreg., 1967-69; research asso. Inst. Behavioral Sci., vis. lectr. U. Colo., 1970; asst. research anthropologist U. Calif., San Francisco, 1971-73, research asso. dept. epidemiology and internat. health, 1979—; sr. lectr. community medicine U. Papua New Guinea, 1974-82, assoc. prof. behavioral sci. and med. anthropology, 1983—; guest prof. Max-Planck-Institut, Fed. Republic of Germany, 1987-88; cons. WHO, World Bank, USAID, Papua New Guinea Dept. Health. Served with AUS, 1955-56. Woodrow Wilson fellow, 1961; NIMH fellow, 1965-66; recipient French Govt. award for translation, 1960. Fellow Am. Anthrop. Assn., Internat. Coll. Psychosomatic Medicine, Royal Anthrop. Soc., Soc. Applied Athropology, World Assn. Social Psychiatry; mem. Am. Assn. Acad. Psychiatry. Malaysian Soc. Parasitology and Tropical Medicine, Papua New Guinea Med. Soc., Soc. Med. Anthropology, Soc. Psychol. Anthropology. Clubs: S. Pacific Aero, Royal Port Moresby Yacht, PNG Petroleum Club, Aviat Club, Returned Servicemen's League. Author: A New Guinea Landscape: Community, Space and Time of the Eastern Highlands, 1980, The Ethics of Development, 1987; also articles. Home: Box 5623, Boroko Papua New Guinea

PATANO, PATRICIA ANN, marketing and public relations specialist; b. Chgo., June 14, 1950; d. Thomas Vincent and Gladys Estelle (Olejniczak) P. Student, Los Angeles Pierce Coll., 1968-70, UCLA, 1974-84; BS in Bus. and Mgmt. summa cum laude, U. Redlands, 1995. Pub. relations mgr. Motel 6, Inc., Century City, Calif., 1974-77; mgr. corp. communications 1st Travel Corp., Van Nuys, Calif., 1977-79; mktg. pub. relations mgr. Unitours, Inc., Los Angeles, 1979-81; asst. v.p. pub. relations Los Angeles Olympic Com., 1981-84; pres., co-owner PaVage Fitness Innovations, Playa del Rey, Calif., 1984-88; ptnr. J.D. Power and Assocs., Agoura Hills, Calif., 1988—; trustee Nat. Injury Prevention Found., San Diego, 1983—; cons. Dick Clark Productions, Burbank, Calif., 1985, Reebok USA Ltd., Boston, 1983—. Coauthor: MuscleAerobics, 1985; contbr. articles to profl. jours. Vol. Motion Picture Hosp., Woodland Hills, Calif., 1968-70; bd. dirs. Los Angeles Boys and Girls Club, 1984—; mem. council San Fernando Natural History Mus., 1987-89; big sister Pride House, Van Nuys, 1987-89; active juvenile delinquent program Pride House. Recipient Corp. award Pres.'s Council Phys. Fitness, 1983; fellow Alfred North Whitehead Leaderships Soc.-U. Redlands, 1995. Mem. L.A. Advt. Club, Nat. Injury Prevention Found. (trustee 1984-87), Child Shelter Homes: A Rescue Effort (bd. dirs.), Marina City Club (Marina del Rey, Calif.). Republican. Presbyterian. Office: JD Power & Assocs 30401 Agoura Rd Agoura Hills CA 91301-2084

PATEL, BIPINCHANDRA KANTILAL, clergy member, restauranteur; b. Kampala, Uganda, Sept. 2, 1961; came to U.S., 1986; s. Kantilal Dayabhai and Manjulaben P. Ordained Friends We. Buddhist Order, 1982. Resident minister Friends We. Buddhist Order-Aryaloka Buddhist Retreat Ctr., Newmarket, N.H., 1986-95; minister Rocky Mountain Friends We. Buddhist Order, Missoula, Mont., 1995—; owner Tipu's Tiger. Office: FWBO Rocky Mountain 540 S 2nd St W Missoula MT 59801-1833

PATEL, CHANDRA KUMAR NARANBHAI, communications company executive, educator, researcher; b. Baramati, India, July 2, 1938; came to U.S., 1958, naturalized, 1970; s. Naranbhai Chaturbhai and Maniben P.; m. Shela Dixit, Aug. 20, 1961; children: Neela, Meena. B.Engring., Poona U., 1958; M.S., Stanford U., 1959, Ph.D., 1961. Mem. tech. staff Bell Telephone Labs., Murray Hill, N.J., 1961-93, head infrared physics and electronics rsch. dept., 1967-70, dir. electronics rsch. dept., 1970-76, dir. phys. rsch. lab., 1976-81, exec. dir. rsch. physics and acad. affairs div., 1981-87, exec. dir. rsch., materials sci., engring. and acad. affairs div., 1987-93; trustee Aerospace Corp., L.A., 1979-88; vice chancellor rsch. UCLA, 1993—; mem. governing bd. NRC, 1990-91; bd. dirs. Accuwave Corp., Santa Monica, Calif., chmn. bd. Contbr. articles to tech. jours. Chmn. Calif. Biomed. Found., 1994—; mem. exec. bd. Calif. Healthcare Inst., 1995—; mem. L.A. Regional Tech. Alliance, 1997—. Recipient Ballantine medal Franklin Inst., 1968, Coblentz award Am. Chem. Soc., 1974, Honor award Assn. Indians in Am., 1975, Founders prize Tex. Instruments Found., 1978, award N.Y. sect. Soc. Applied Spectroscopy, 1982, Schawlow medal Laser Inst. Am., 1984, Thomas Alva Edison Sci. award N.J. Gov., 1987, William T. Ennor Manufacturing Technology award ASME, 1995, Nat. Medal of Sci., 1996. Fellow AAAS, IEEE (Lamme medal 1976, medal of honor 1989), Am. Acad. Arts and Scis., Am. Phys. Soc. (coun. 1987-91, exec. com. 1987-90, George E. Pake prize 1988, pres. 1995), Optical Soc. Am. (Adolph Lomb medal 1966, Townes medal 1982, Ives medal 1989), Indian Nat. Sci. Acad. (fng.); mem. NAS (coun. 1988-91, exec. com. 1989-91), NAE (Zworykin award 1976), Gynecol. Laser Surgery Soc. (hon.), Am. Soc. for Laser [illegible] omed. Found. (pres. 1994—), Calif. Healthcare Inst. (exec. com. 1995—), Sigma Xi (pres. 1994-96). Home: 1171 Roberto Ln Los Angeles CA 90077-2302 Office: UCLA Vice Chancellor Rsch PO Box 951405 Los Angeles CA [illegible]

PATEL, JASMIN RAMBHAI, medicinal chemist, consultant, researcher; b. Nadiad, India, Apr. 25, 1964; came to U.S., 1984; s. Rambhai G. and Smruti R. Patel; m. Rena Patel, Nov. 10, 1988. B in Pharm. with hons., Bombay U., India, 1984; PhD, Duquesne U., 1991. PPG post doctoral fellow The Scripps Rsch. Inst., La Jolla, Calif., 1990-92; rsch. scientist Gen-Probe, Inc., San Diego, 1992-95; sr. rsch. scientist Chugai Biopharmaceuticals, Inc., San Diego, 1995—; pres. Soc. of Fellows Scripps Rsch. Inst., La Jolla, Calif., 1991-92. Author: (book chpt.) Chemistry and Biology of Pteridines, 1990; contbr. articles to profl. jours. including Internat. Jour. Cancer, Anticancer Rsch., Cancer Jour., Jour. Medicinal Chemistry. Recipient Bombay U. Gold medal, 1984, G.P. Nair award Indian Drug Mfrs. Assn., 1984, J.N. Tata scholarship J.N. Tata Endowment; Nat. Merit scholar Indian Ministry Edn. and Culture. Mem. Am. Chem. Soc. (chair publicity com. We. region 1995), Am. Assn. Pharm. Scientists (chair short courses com. 1996, chair-elect medicinal and natural products chemistry sect. 1997), Am. Assn. Cancer Rsch., Rho Chi. Achievements include 7 filed U.S. and foreign Patent Applications; first synthesis of 5, 10-methylene-tetrahydro-5-deaza folate. Home: 10030 Scripps Vista Way San Diego CA 92131-2737 Office: Chugai Biopharmaceuticals 6275 Nancy Ridge Dr San Diego CA 92121-2245

PATEL, MARILYN HALL, judge; b. Amsterdam, N.Y., Sept. 2, 1938; d. Lloyd Manning and Nina J. (Thorpe) Hall; m. Magan C. Patel, Sept. 2, 1966; children: Brian, Gian. B.A., Wheaton Coll., 1959; J.D., Fordham U., 1963. Bar: N.Y. 1963, Calif. 1970. Mng. atty. Benson & Morris, Esq., N.Y.C., 1962-64; sole practice N.Y.C., 1964-67; atty. U.S. Immigration and Naturalization Svc., San Francisco, 1967-71; sole practive San Francisco, 1971-76; judge Alameda County Mcpl. Ct., Oakland, Calif., 1976-80, U.S. Dist. Ct. (no. dist.) Calif., San Francisco, 1980—; now chief judge U.S. Dist. Ct. for No. Dist. Calif., San Francisco, 1998—; adj. prof. law Hastings Coll. of Law, San Francisco, 1974-76. Author: Immigration and Nationality Law, 1974; also numerous articles. Mem. bd. visitors Fordham U. Sch. Law. Mem. ABA (litigation sect., jud. adminstrn. sect.), ACLU (former bd. dirs.), NOW (former bd. dirs.), Am. law Inst., Am. Judicature Soc. (bd. dirs.), Calif Conf. Judges, Nat. Assn. Women Judges (founding mem.), Internat. Inst. (bd. dirs.), Advs. for Women (co-founder), Assn. Bus. Trial Lawyers (bd. dirs.). Democrat. Avocations: piano playing; travel. Office: US Dist Ct Rm 19-5356 450 Golden Gate Ave San Francisco CA 94102-3661*

PATEL, SUDHIR, service executive; b. Haripura, Gujarat, India, Dec. 11, 1961; came to U.S., 1979; s. Nagin Khushal and Lalita (Mangubhai) P.; m. Rita Kantilal, May 29, 1985. BS in Biochemistry, Purdue U., 1984, MS in Indsl. Mgmt., 1985. Desk clk. Sagamore Inn, Lafayette, Ind., 1982-83, gen. mgr., 1984-86; asst. mgr. Wendys Restaurant, Seymour, Ind., 1986; fin. cons. First Investors Corp., N.Y.C., 1986-87; mgr. Westminster (Calif.) Motor Inn, 1987-88; owner Arco AM/PM, Bonita, Calif., 1988—; rsch. asst. Purdue U., West Lafayette, Ind., 1983-84. Mem. Internat. Soc. Financiers. Republican. Hindu. Home: 3174 Jamacha View Dr El Cajon CA 92019-5141 Office: Arco AM/PM 4498 Bonita Rd Bonita CA 91902-1425

PATINO, ISIDRO FRANK, law enforcement educator; b. San Antonio, Mar. 10, 1943; s. Isidro F. and Maria (Narro) P.; children: Michael, Rebecca, Karleen. BS, Calif. State U., L.A., 1973; MBA, U. Redlands, 1995. Records comdr. Placentia (Calif.) Police Dept., 1980-85; asst. dean Criminal Justice Tng. Ctr. Golden West Coll., Huntington Beach, Calif., 1986-89, assoc. dean instrn., 1989-92; divsn. dean dept. pub. svc. Rio Hondo Coll., Whittier, Calif., 1992—; pres., mem. State Chancellors Adv. Com. Pub. Safety Edn., 1991—, chmn., 1998—; chmn. So. Calif. Pub. Safety Tng. Consortium, 1994—, active, 1993—; bd. suprs. L.A. County Spl. Task Force on Pub. Safety Tng., 1995—; mem. Hispanic male adv. com. Dept. Edn. Connections Project. Kellogg C.C. Diversity Leadership fellow, 1996-97. Mem. Calif. Law Enforcement Assn. Records Suprs. (pres. so. chpt. 1985-87, state pres. 1986-87), Calif. Acad. Dirs. Assn. (chmn. 1988-89), Am. Soc. Criminologists, Acad. Criminal Justice Scis., Western and Pacific Assn. Criminal Justice Educators, Calif. Assn. Adminstrn. of Justice Educators (v.p. 1996-97, state pres. 1997-99), Calif. Peace Officers Stds. and Tng. Basic Course Consortium (chmn. instrn. com. 1987-88),World Future Soc. (pres. Orange County-Long Beach chpt. 1988- 92), Nat. Assn. Field Tng. Officers (nat. pres. 1992-93), Nat. Assn. Chiefs of Police, Internat. Assn. Chiefs of Police, Soc. Law Enforcement Trainers. Roman Catholic.

PATKAU, JOHN, architect; b. Winnipeg, Man., Can., Aug. 18, 1947; s. Abe John and Bertha (Klassen) P.; m. Patricia Frances Gargett, Aug. 10, 1974. BA, U. Manitoba, 1969, BA in Environ. Studies, 1969, MArch, 1972. Registered architect, B.C., Ont. Prin. John Patkau Architect Ltd., Edmonton, Can., 1977-83; ptnr. Patkau Archs. Inc., Vancouver, B.C., Can., 1984—; chmn. edn. com. Alta. Assn. Architects, 1981; vis. critic U. Calgary, 1981, 92, U. Waterloo, 1987, 89, U. Pa., 1987, Tech. U. N.S., 1987, U. B.C., 1988, 89, UCLA, 1989; design critic U. B.C., 1985-86; urban design panel Vancouver, 1990-92; vis. prof. William Lyon Somerville Lectureship U. Calgary, 1994; Eliot Noyes vis. design critic Harvard U., 1995. Recipient Progressive Architecture citation, 1981, 99, Progressive Architecture award, 1993, 95, Can. Architects award, 1983, 84, 86, 87, 89, 90, 92, 94, 98, 99, Wood Coun. First award, 1984, Gov. Gen. medal, 1986, 90, 92, 94, 97, Gov. Gen. award, 1990, 97, Lt. Gov. Archtl. medal, 1992, Honor award, 1992. Fellow Royal Archtl. Inst. Can. (chmn. design com. 1987); mem. Archtl. Inst. B.C., Royal Can. Coll. Art, Ont. Assn. Architects. Office: Patkau Archs, 560 Beatty St Ste L110, Vancouver, BC Canada V6B 2L3

PATKAU, PATRICIA, architect, architecture educator; b. Winnipeg, Manitoba, Can., Feb. 25, 1950; d. John Frederick and Aileen Constance (Emmett) Gargett; m. John Robert Patkau, Aug. 10, 1974. BA in Interior Design, U. Manitoba, 1973; MA in Architecture, Yale, New Haven, Conn., 1978. Ptnr. Patkau Archs., Vancouver, B.C., Can., 1983—; asst. prof. Sch. Architecture UCLA, U.S.A., 1988-90; assoc. prof. Sch. Architecture U. B.C., Can., 1992—; vis. critic U. Calgary, 1981, 87, U. Waterloo, 1987, U. Pa., U.S.A., 1987, U. Toronto, 1988, Southern Calif. Inst. Architecture, U.S.A., 1990, UCLA, 1991, U. Oreg., U.S.A., 1992, MIT, U.S.A., 1993, Yale U., 1993; design critic U. B.C., 1984-87; vis. prof. Harvard U., 1993, Eliot Noyes prof., 1995; vis. prof. U. Calgary, 1994; mem. archtl. commn. U. Wash., 1996—. Ctrl. Mortgage and Housing fellow, 1977, 78; recipient Manitoba Gold medal, 1973, Progressive Architecture citation, 1981, 93, Can. Architect Excellence award, 1983, 86, 87, 89, 90, 92, 94, Can. Wood Coun. First award, 1984, Honor award, 1992, Gov. Gen. Architecture medal, 1986, 90, 92, 94, 97, Gov. Gen. Architecture award, 1990, 97, Lt. Gov. Architecture medal, 1992, Can. Wood Coun. award, 1991. Fellow Royal Archtl. Inst. Can.; mem. Archtl. Inst. B.C. (Honor award 1988). Office: Patkau Archs, 560 Beatty St Ste L110, Vancouver, BC Canada V6B 2L3

PATRICK, LESLIE DAYLE, hydrologist; b. Grand Island, Nebr., Nov. 20, 1951; d. Robert Norman and Charlotte Ruth (Thomas) Mayfield; m. Jeffrey Rogan Patrick, July 1, 1972 (div. Feb. 1996). BA in Geology, U. Alaska, Anchorage, 1975, MS in Mgmt., 1991. Data base mgr. U.S. Geol. Survey, Anchorage, 1975-78, with digital modeling, 1980-85, with water use studies, 1978-91, chief computer sect., systems analyst, 1985-91, asst. dist. chief mgmt. ops., 1991-97, asst. dist. chief programs, 1997—. Mem. NAFE, Am. Mgmt. Assn., Am. Soc. Quality Control, Alaska Groundwater Assn. (sec., treas. 1980). Office: US Geol Survey Water Resources Div 4230 University Dr Ste 201 Anchorage AK 99508-4626

PATRICK, STEPHEN ADAM, non profit organization administrator; b. N.Y.C., Apr. 3, 1968; s. David W. and Ellen (Goldman) P.; m. Suzanne Carlson, Feb. 15, 1998. BA, Colo. Coll., Colorado Springs, 1990. Founder, dir. N.Mex. Pueblo Soccer Start, Taos, 1990-93; dir. youth programs San Juan Pueblo (N.Mex.) Tribe, 1992-96; co-founder, exec. dir. Rocky Mountain Youth Corps, Taos, 1996—; fellow Rockefeller Found., N.Y.C. and Taos; mem., pres. San Juan Pueblo Bd. Edn., 1995—. Bd. dirs. N.Mex. Cmty. Found., Santa Fe; mem. stering com. N.Mex. Human Needs Coordination Coun., Albuquerque. Avocations: back country travel, American politics and government. Office: Rocky Mountain Youth Corps PO Box 1960 Ranchos De Taos NM 87557-1960

[illegible] Sept. 3, 1913; d. Newton Felix and Mattie Priscilla (Whitson) Harrison; m. Carl Thomas Patten, Oct. 23, 1935; children: Priscilla Carla and Bebe Rebecca (twins), Carl Thomas. D.D., McKinley-Roosevelt Coll., 1941; [illegible]

Assn. of Evangelism, 1935; evangelist in various cities of U.S., 1933-50; founder, pres. Christian Evang. Chs. Am., Inc., Oakland, Calif., 1944—, Patten Acad. Christian Edn., Oakland, 1944—, Patten Bible Coll., Oakland, 1944-83; chancellor Patten Coll., Oakland, 1983—; founder, pastor Christian Cathedral of Oakland, 1950—; held pvt. interviews with David Ben-Gurion, 1972, Menachim Begin, 1977, Yitzhak Shamir, 1991; condr. Sta. KUSW world-wide radio ministry, 70 countries around the world, 1989-90, Stas. WHRI and WWCR world coverage short wave, 1990—. Founder, condr.: radio program The Shepherd Hour, 1934—; daily TV, 1976—, nationwide telecast, 1979—; Author: Give Me Back My Soul, 1973; Editor: Trumpet Call, 1953—; composer 20 gospel and religious songs, 1945—. Mem. exec. bd. Bar-Ilan U. Assn., Israel, 1983; mem. global bd. trustees Bar-Ilan U., 1991. Recipient numerous awards including medallion Ministry of Religious Affairs, Israel, 1969; medal Govt. Press Office, Jerusalem, 1971; Christian honoree of yr. Jewish Nat. Fund of No. Calif., 1975; Hidden Heroine award San Francisco Bay coun. Girl Scouts U.S.A., 1976, Golden State award Who's Who Hist. Soc., 1988; Ben-Gurion medallion Ben-Gurion Rsch. Inst., 1977; Resolutions of Commendation, Calif. Senate Rules Com., 1978, 94, Disting. Leadership award Ch. of God Sch. of Theology, 1996; hon. fellow Bar-Ilan U., Israel, 1981; Dr. Bebe Patten Social Action chair established Bar-Ilan U., 1982. Mem. Am. Assn. for Higher Edn., Religious Edn. Assn., Am. Acad. Religion and Soc. Bibl. Lit., Zionist Orgn. Am., Am. Assn. Pres. of Ind. Colls. and Univs., Am. Jewish Hist. Soc., Am.-Isreal Pub. Affairs Com. Address: 2433 Coolidge Ave Oakland CA 94601-2630

PATTEN, RICHARD E., personnel company owner; b. Seattle, May 17, 1953; s. Donald Wesley and Lorraine Louise (Kienholz) P.; m. Monica Rose Bourg, Mar. 20, 1976; children: Richard Douglas, Wesley Bourg, Melinda Rose. BA, U. Wash., 1976. Exec. v.p. Microfilm Svc. Co., Seattle, 1976-84, gen. mgr., 1985-87, chmn. bd., 1988-90; pres. Express Svcs. Temporary and Permanent Pers., Seattle, 1990—. Candidate for U.S. Ho. of Reps., 1982; deacon Bethany Bapt. Ch., Seattle, 1983-86; co-chmn. fin. com. Wash. State Billy Graham Crusade, 1990-91. Mem. Nat. Micrographics Assn. (pres. N.W. chpt. 1979-80, bd. dirs. 1978-79), Assn. Image and Info. Mgmt. (chmn. svc. co. 1987), Assn. Records Mgrs. and Adminstrs., Wash. Athletic Club, Rotary (bd. dirs. 1996-98). Republican. Baptist. Home: 7012 NE 161st St Kenmore WA 98028-4265 Office: Express Pers Svcs Ste 101 1201 4th Ave Seattle WA 98134-1531

PATTERSON, BEVERLY ANN GROSS, fund raising consultant, grant writer, federal grants administrator, social services administrator, poet; b. Pauls Valley, Okla., Aug. 5, 1938; d. Wilburn G. Jack and Mildred E. (Steward) Gross; m. Kenneth Dean Patterson, June 18, 1960 (div. 1976); children: Tracy Dean, Nancy Ann Patterson-McArthur, Beverly Jeanne Patterson-Wertman. AA, Modesto (Calif.) Jr. Coll., 1958; BA in Social Sci., Fresno (Calif.) State U., 1960; M in Community Counseling, Coll. Idaho; postgrad., Stanislaus State Coll., Turlock, Calif., U. Idaho, Boise (Idaho) State U. Cert. secondary tchr., Calif., Idaho, lic. real estate agt., Idaho. Secondary tchr. Ceres and Modesto Calif., Payette and Weiser Idaho, Ontario Oreg., 1960-67; dir. vol. svcs. mental retardation and child devel. State of Idaho, 1967-70, cons. dir. vol. svcs. health and welfare, 1970-72; dir. Ret. Sr. Vol. Program, Boise, 1972-74; exec. dir. Idaho Nurses Assn., Boise, 1974-76; community svcs. adminstr. City of Davis, Calif., 1976-78; dir. devel. and fundraising Mercy Med. Ctr., Nampa, Idaho, 1978-85; exec. dir. St. Alphonsus Med. Ctr. Found., Boise, 1985-87; dir. devel. and gift planning Idaho Youth Ranch, Boise, 1989-94; fund devel. cons. Mercy Housing, Nampa, Idaho, 1994-96, Pratt Ranch Boys Home, Emmett, Idaho, 1994-96, Northwest Childrens Home, Lewiston, Idaho, 1994-96, Idaho Spl. Olympics, Boise, 1994-95, Idaho Found. for Parks and Lands, Boise, 1994-95, St. Vincent de Paul, Inc., Boise, 1995-96, Nampa Shelter Found., Inc., 1994-95, Turning Point Inc., Nampa, 1994-95, Port of Hope Treatment Ctr. Inc., Boise, 1994-97, Idaho Theater for Youth, Inc., Boise, 1995-96, Boise Tennis Coalition, Inc., 1995—, El Ada Cmty. Action Ctr., Boise, 1995, Hemophilia Found. Idaho, 1995-96, Boise YWCA, 1996, Marsing (Idaho) Sch. Dist., 1996-98; and many more; founder Fellowship Christian Adult Singles, Boise, 1974; cons., exec. dir. Boise Hotline, 1988-90; co-dir. ACOA workshop leader Child Within Concepts, Inc., Boise, 1987—; cons. coord. Rural Hosp. Edn. Consortium, 1988; cons. hosp. fund devel. and cmty. resources Gritman Meml. Hosp., Moscow, Idaho, 1987-88; cons., conf. coord. State of Idaho, 1987-88; counsel Adult Children of Alcoholics, 1991; pres. Nonprofit Solutions, Inc., Boise, 1995—; co-dir. Child Within Concepts, Inc., Meridian, 1996—; pres. Q&A Distbg. and Cons., Meridian, Idaho, 1994-95; 501 coord. CellNet of Idaho, Boise, 1996-97; cmty. resource devel. specialist Idaho Dept. Health and Welfare, 1997—; pres. NonProfit Solutions, Inc., 1997—. Contbr. articles to profl. jours. Coord. Idaho Golf Angels Open Pro-Am Tournament, Boise, 1989-91; founding exec. v.p. Coll. Fund for Students Surviving Cancer, 1993-96; bd. dirs. Arthritis Found., Idaho, 1984-86, Idaho Mental Health Assn., 1978-97; founder Ctrl. Vol. Bur., Boise, 1971. Named Idaho Statesman Disting. Citizen, 1985. Mem. Nat. Assn. for Hosp. Devel. (accredited, treas. 1980, accreditation chmn. 1984-86, conf. chmn. 1982, 85), Assn. Healthcare in Philanthrophy (accredited), Nat. Soc. Fund Raising Execs., Idaho Devel. Network, Choices in Giving, Inc., Nationwide Auto Club (fleet dir. 1997—). Mem. Community Christian Ch. Avocations: golf, family activities. Home and Office: Child Within Concepts & NonProfit Solutions Inc RR 1 Box 1277A Homedale ID 83628-9701

PATTERSON, DANIEL WILLIAM, dentist; b. Minot, N.D., Aug. 12, 1948; s. Girdell William and Fern Lemay (Sullivan) P. DDS, Northwestern U., 1972; Alumnus degree (hon.), U. Colo., 1977; BS in Biology, U.N.Y., 1993; M in Healthcare, U. Denver, 1994. Cert. health industry orgn., ops. U.Denver, 1993, cert. gerontology, 1996. Dentist Dan L. Hansen, DDS, P.C., Lakewood, Colo., 1974-75; pvt. practice dentistry Littleton, Colo., 1975-88; clin. instr. dept. applied dentistry U. Colo., Denver, 1981-83, lectr., 1983, clin. asst. prof. depts. restorative and applied dentistry, 1989-91, dir. advanced dentistry program, 1989-90, asst. prof. clin. track dept. restorative dentistry, 1991—. Mem. editorial adv. panel Dental Econs. Jour., 1981; also articles. Active Chatfield Jaycees, Littleton, 1976-81; vocal soloist, mem. Denver Concert Chorale, 1978-82. Lt. USN, 1968-74. Fellow Acad. Gen. Dentistry; bd. eligible Am. Bd. Gen. Dentistry; mem. ADA, Met. Denver Dental Soc., Colo. Dental Assn. (Pres.'s Honor Roll 1982-84), Mensa, Sedalia Wild Game Club. Lutheran. Avocations: reading, fishing, photography. Home: 6984 N Fargo Trl Littleton CO 80125-9270 Office: U Colo Health Scis Ctr Sch Dentistry Box C-284 4200 E 9th Ave Denver CO 80262-0284

PATTERSON, JAMES, mayor; b. San Mateo, Calif., Feb. 18, 1948; m. Sharon LeTourneau, 1968; children: B.J., Jason, Lindsay. BA in Polit. Sci. summa cum laude, Calif. State U., Fresno, 1992. Radio broadcasting exec. Sta. KIRV-AM, Fresno, Calif., 1968—; mayor City of Fresno, 1993—. Mem. San Joaquin River Conservancy, Calif. Ten Largest Cities Mayor's Coalition, 1993—; vice chair Fresno County Transp. Authority; bd. mem. Fresno County Coun. Govts.; chmn. NO on Measure H Com., 1989, Criminal Justice and Law Enforcement Commn., 1990-91; vice chmn. YES on Measure E Com., 1988; mem. Human Rels. Commn., City of Fresno, 1987-91; bd. dirs. Leadership Fresno Alumni Assn., 1989-91, Fresno County YFC/Campus Life, 1984-88. Mem. Fresno City and County C. of C. (chmn. local govt. affairs com. 1990-91, bd. dirs. FRESPAC 1990-91, city budget rev. com. 1989-91, privatization task force 1988-89, charter sect. 809 rev. task force 1987-88). Office: Office of the Mayor 2600 City Hall Fresno CA 93721-3600*

PATTERSON, LLOYD CLIFFORD, psychiatrist; b. Toronto, Ont., Can., Jan. 16, 1917; came to U.S., 1942; s. William Henry and Florence May (Sonley) P.; m. Gloria May Patterson, Nov. 12, 1943; children: Diane Meisenheimer, Pamela DeBarr. MD, U. Western Ont., London, 1942. Diplomate Am. Bd. Psychiatry; cert. Am. Psychoanalytic Assn. Intern Hollywood Presybn. Hosp., L.A., 1942-43; fellow in intern medicine U. Calif. Hosp., San Francisco, 1943-44; resident in psychiatry Langley Porter Neuropsychiat. Inst., San Francisco, 1944-48; cons. psychiatrist student health U. Calif., Berkeley, 1960-70, assoc. clin. prof. U. Calif. Med. Sch., San Francisco, 1972—; dir. med. edn. Alta Bates Med. Ctr., Berkeley, 1988-97; program chair Western Divisional Psychoanalytic meetings, San Francisco, [illegible] Assn. (pres. 1968-69), San Francisco Psychoanalytic Soc. (pres. 1972-73), Am. Psychiat. Soc., Am. Psychoanalytic Soc., Calif. Med. Assn. (hosp. surveyor, mem. continuing med. edn. com. 1985-91, cons. CME com. 1992), [illegible]

Cola Ballena Alameda CA 94501-3608 Office: 3021 Telegraph Ave Berkeley CA 94705-2013

PATTERSON, MARK JEROME, computer software designer; b. Inglewood, Calif., July 23, 1960; s. Jerry Lee Patterson and Robin Helen McCracken Steely; m. Jenny Anne Lynn, Dec. 31, 1995. Programmer Green & Assocs., L.A., 1985-87; systems analyst The Software Works, Glendale, Calif., 1987-90; programmer Snow Software, Clearwater, Fla., 1990; pres. Atomic Software, Altadena, Calif., 1990-94; sr. mgr., chief technologist customer mgmt. practice divsn. KPMG Peat Marwick, L.A., Calif., 1994—; design cons. Prestige Station, Inc., 1990-93, Petro-Can., Inc., Calgary, Alta., 1988-90. Author computer programs: Set of Dataflex Macros, 1990, Ultimate File Viewer, 1992, Data Communications and Client/Server Systems, 1993-97. Libertarian. Scientologist. Achievements include 1 patent pending for data reporting technology; rschr. Worldwide Web based sales automation and retail franchise applications and electronic software distribution technology. Avocations: running, bicycling. Home: 814 N Mentor Ave Pasadena CA 91104-4625

PATTERSON, PAUL EDWARD, minister; b. Columbus, Ohio, Sept. 10, 1946; s. George William and Janice Rae (Mueller) P. AA, Miami U., Oxford, Ohio, 1981; BS, SUNY, Albany, 1996. Ordained to ministry Unity Ch., 1991; cert. vocat. and elem. tchr., authority in delinquent youth and dysfunctional family. Victim's advocate, victim's awareness tchr. State of Calif., Calif. Youth Authority, 1985—; min. Unity Ch., Sonora, Calif., 1992; founder, min. Motherlode Cmty. Ch., Sonora, 1996, group leader inner child workshops Survivors of Sexual Abuse. Past bd. dirs. Parents United of Stanislaus County. Sgt. U.S. Army, 1966-69. Pioneer in development of restorative justice in youth correctional facilities. Avocations: theology, history, psychology. Office: Motherlode Cmty Ch PO Box 4074 Sonora CA 95370-4074

PATTILLO, JAMES LOUIS, retired judge; b. Denison, Tex., July 20, 1920; s. George Pitts and Lula Elizabeth (O'Hara) P.; m. Helen Goodart, Nov. 22, 1942; children: James G., Samuel S. BA, North Tex. U., 1950; LLB, George Washington U., 1964. Bar: Va. 1964, Calif. 1965. Commd. 2d lt. Army Air Force (USAF), 1941; advanced through grades to col. USAF, 1951, ret., 1966; justice ct. judge Carpinteria (Calif.) Jud. Dist., 1967-82; judge Santa Barbara (Calif.) Mcpl. Ct., 1982-86; ret., 1986; dir. Earl Warren Showgrounds, 19th Agrl. Dist. Calif., Santa Barbara, 1994-98. Decorated D.F.C. with 2 oak leaf clusters, Air medal with 2 oak leaf clusters, Bronze Star. Mem. 20th Air Force Assn. (pres. 1995-98), Masons. Avocations: travel, reading, tennis. Home: 1143 Glenview Rd Santa Barbara CA 93108-2001

PATTISON, FRED LEWIS, minister, academic administrator; b. N.Y.C., Sept. 14, 1932; s. George Wilson and Florence Augusta (Cross) P. Ordained to ministry, 1955. Pastor Bethel Bible Christian Ch., Garden City Park, N.Y., 1954-58, Faith Bapt. Ch., Tucson, Ariz., 1958-70, Casa De Cristo Evang. Ch., Phoenix, 1976-96; pres. Phoenix Evang. Bible Inst., 1981-94; presiding bishop Anglican Gospel Chs., Pine, Ariz. Democrat. Home: 5119 N Strawberry Dr Strawberry AZ 85544 Office: PO Box 2301 Pine AZ 85544-2301

PATTON, LYNETTE ANNE, nursing educator, consultant; b. Vallejo, Calif., Oct. 6, 1941; d. Titus Neale and Cassie Jane (Davis) Carr; m. Jack Thomas Patton, Sept. 2, 1960; children: Robert Thomas, John Neale, Mark Keaka, Christopher James. BSN, Calif. State U., Long Beach, 1969; MS in Nursing, Calif. State U., Fresno, 1979; EdD, U. San Diego, 1987. RN, Calif., Hawaii; cert. pub. health nurse, Calif., Hawaii. Instr. Nazarene Coll. Nursing, Papua New Guinea, 1973-80; asst. prof. Pt. Loma Nazarene U., San Diego, 1981-84, Calif. State U., San Diego, 1984-86; dir. home health svcs. Twilight Haven, Fresno, Calif., 1986-88; faculty, dir. health svcs. Fresno Pacific U., Fresno, 1987-93; edn. cons. Summer Inst. Linguistics, Papua New Guinea, 1993-94; pvt. practice edn. and health cons. Fresno, 1995—; lectr. San Jose (Calif.) Christian Coll., 1998—; health edn. cons. WHO, Papua New Guinea, 1979-81; edn. cons. ARC, Honolulu, 1971-73; mem. adv. bd. Fresno Christian Schs., 1989-93. Author: Modular Instruction for the Community Health Nursing Care of Common Pediatric Illnesses in Papua New Guinea, 1980. Chairperson Bd. of Christian Edn., Butler Mennonite Brethren Ch., 1990-93. Home: 1566 S Adler Ave Fresno CA 93727-5101

PATTON, STUART, biochemist, educator; b. Ebenezer, N.Y., Nov. 2, 1920; s. George and Ina (Neher) P.; m. Colleen Cecelia Lavelle, May 17, 1945; children—John, Richard, Gail, Thomas, Mary Catherine, Patricia, Joseph. B.S., Pa. State U., 1943; M.S., Ohio State U., 1947, Ph.D., 1948. Chemist Borden Co., 1943-44; research fellow Ohio State U., Columbus, 1946-48; mem. faculty Pa. State U., University Park, 1949-80, prof., 1959-80; Evan Pugh rsch. prof. agr. Pa. State U., 1966-80; adj. prof. neuroscis. Sch. Medicine U. Calif., San Diego, 1981—; vis. scientist Scripps Instn. Oceanography; cons. in field, 1950—. Author: (with Robert Jenness) Principles of Dairy Chemistry, 1959, (with Robert G. Jensen) Biomedical Aspects of Lactation, 1975. Served to lt. (j.g.) USNR, 1944-46. Recipient Borden award chemistry milk Am. Chem. Soc., 1957, Agrl. and Food Chemistry award, 1975; Alexander von Humboldt sr. scientist award, 1981, Macy-Gyorgy award Internat. Soc. for Rsch. on Human Milk and Lactation, 1997. Fellow Am. Dairy Sci. Assn.; mem. Am. Chem. Soc., Am. Soc. Biochemistry and Molecular Biology, Am. Soc. Cell Biology. Home: 6208 Avenida Cresta La Jolla CA 92037-6510 Office: U Calif San Diego Ctr Molecular Genetics 0634-J La Jolla CA 92093

PAUL, BENJAMIN DAVID, anthropologist, educator; b. N.Y.C., Jan. 25, 1911; s. Phillip and Esther (Kranz) P.; m. Lois Fleischman, Jan. 4, 1936; children: Robert Allen, Janice Carol. Student, U. Wis., 1928-29; AB, U. Chgo., 1938, PhD in Anthropology, 1942. Lectr., rsch. dir. Yale U., 1942-44; community orgn. expert Inter-Am. Ednl. Found., 1946; from lectr. to assoc. prof. anthropology Harvard U., 1946-62, dir. social sci. program Sch. Pub. Health, 1951-62; prof. anthropology Stanford (Calif.) U., 1963—, chmn. dept., 1967-71, dir. program in medicine and behavioral sci., 1963-70; cons. NIH, 1957—. Editor: Health, Culture and Community: Case Studies of Public Reactions to Health Programs, 1955, Changing Marriage Patterns in a Highland Guatemalan Community, 1963, The Maya Midwife as Sacred Professional, 1975, Mayan Migrants in Guatemala City, 1981, The Operation of a Death Squad in San Pedro la Laguna, 1988. 2d lt. AUS, 1944-46. Travelling fellow Social Sci. Rsch. Coun., 1940-41, Ctr. Advanced Study Behavioral Scis. fellow, 1962-63. Mem. Am. Anthropol. Assn. (Disting. Svc. award 1994), Phi Beta Kappa, Sigma Xi. Ethnographic field rsch. in Guatemala, 1941, 62, 64-65, 68-69, 73-79, 83-95, 97-98. Home: 622 Salvatierra St Palo Alto CA 94305-8538 Office: Stanford U Dept Anthropology Stanford CA 94305

PAUL, FLORENCE JOSEPH, writer; b. N.Y.C.; d. Solomon and Stella (Kass) Joseph; m. Les Baer Paul, Nov. 4, 1939; children: Glenn Scott Paul, Kenneth Dean Paul. Student, Rancho Santiago Coll., Santa Ana, Calif. Clk. N.Y. State Unemployment Svc., N.Y.C., 1962—; writer, 1976—. Author: A Dream Betrayed, 1995, He Never Pulled the Trigger, 1996; contbr. over 50 mag. articles. Vol. Children's Hosp., 1967—; active one mile pk. constrn. Bd. Supt. Recipient 4 certs. Calif. Press Women, 1990, 95, 96, 97, bronze plaque for constrn. one mile pk. Mem. New Horizons, Hadassah (v.p. edn.). Avocations: golf, travel. Home: 13222 Eton Pl Santa Ana CA 92705-2148

PAUL, LAURENCE EDWARD, investment company executive; b. Chgo., Nov. 16, 1964; s. Robert Arthur and Donna Rae (Berkman) P. AB, Harvard Coll., 1986; MD, Harvard Med. Sch., 1990; MBA, Stanford U., 1992. Investment banker James D. Wolfensohn, Inc., N.Y.C., 1992-94; investment banker Donaldson, Lufkin & Jenrette, N.Y.C., 1994-97, L.A., 1997—; co-mgr. Harvard Med. Sch. Capital Campaign, 1996—; adv. bd. Clarity Healthcorp, 1997—; presenter in field. Bd. dirs. Keimei Fund for Edn., 1995—. Mem. Ampco Pittsburgh Corp. (bd. dirs.), 1998—. Office: Donaldson Lufkin & Jenrette 2121 Avenue Of The Stars Los Angeles CA 90067-5010

PAULOS, DANIEL THOMAS, artist, writer, college program director; b. Sioux City, Iowa, Dec. 16, 1949; s. Thomas George and Frances Mary (Saccony) P. Studied with Sister Mary Jean Dorcy, studied with Robert Lentz, studied with Paul Canfield, studied with Grieg Chapian, studied with Sister DeLourdes Bragg. Artist various locations; writer; dir. St. Bernadette Inst., Albuquerque, 1993—; has appeared in several documentary videos on various artists and their exhbns.; commd. to illustrate several record and cassette covers. One-man shows include Paul VI Inst. Arts, Washington, Most Holy Redeemer AIDS Benefit Exhibit, San Francisco, Marian Libr., Dayton, Ohio, Roesch Libr. Exhibit, Dayton, Biblical Arts Mus., Dallas, Eastbrook Gallery, Milw., Marion Ctr. Sioux City, Santuario de Guadalupe, Sante Fe, Butler Inst. Am. Art, Youngstown, Ohio, The Laredo (Tex.) Ctr. Arts; exhibited in group shows at Billy Graham Sacred Arts Mus., Wheaton, Ill., Sacred Arts Mus., Phila., Madonna & Creche Ann. Exhbn., L.A., Placitas (N.Mex.) Artist Series, KIMO Gallery, Albuquerque, Cath. Artists 90's, N.Y.C., St. John's U., Jamaica, N.Y., Villanova (Pa.) U. Art Gallery, Nabisco Brands Gallery, East Hanover, N.J., Cath. Fine Arts Soc. Ann. Exhbns., N.Y., West Bend (Ind.) Gallery Fine Art, St. Xavier U. Fine Arts Gallery, Chgo., Fontbonne Coll. Fine Arts Gallery, St. Louis, N.Mex. State Fair Art Exhibit, N.Mex. State Fair Fine Arts Gallery, Aura Nat. Exhbns., Villanova, Cath. Mus. Art. History, N.Y., Rejoice Arts Gallery, Lake Oswego, Ore., Rall Gallery, Crete, Nebr., Faces Our Lady Guadelupe, Santa Fe;represented in permanent collections Marian Ctr., Internat. Marian Libr., Dayton, Mallinckrodt Coll. Wilmette, Ill., Sacred Heart Convent, Wilmette, The Hermitage, Eureka Springs, Ark., Eternal Word TV Network, Birmingham, Ala., St. John's Abbey, Collegeville, Minn., La Salle U. Art Mus., Phila., Nat. Shrine Immaculate Conception, Washington, Hawthorne Dominican Sisters, St. Paul, Vatican Libr., Italy, Yad Vashem Holocaust Mus., Jerusalem, Sisters Christian Charity, Germany, Sisters Charity Nevers, France, others. V.p. in charge exhbns. Cath. Artists 90's, Cath. Fine Arts Soc., 1989-92; pres., dir. St. Bernadette Inst. Sacred Art. Recipient numerous awards for paintings and printings. Mem. Cath. Artists 90's, Cath. Fine Arts Soc., Assn. Uniting Religion and Art, Christians Visual Art, Calligraphy Soc. N.Mex. Democrat. Roman Catholic. Office: St Bernadette Art Institute PO Box 8249 Albuquerque NM 87198-8249

PAULSEN, VIVIAN, magazine editor; b. Salt Lake City, May 10, 1942; d. Paul Herman and Martha Oline (Blattman) P. B.A., Brigham Young U., 1964, postgrad., 1965; postgrad., U. Grenoble, France, 1966. Cert. tchr., Utah. Tchr. French Granite Sch. Dist., Salt Lake City, 1966-67; assoc. editor New Era mag., Salt Lake City, 1970-82; mng. editor Friend mag., Salt Lake City, 1982—. Am. Field Service scholar, 1959; grad. fellow Brigham Young U., 1964-66. Mem. Soc. Children's Book Writers. Republican. Mem. Ch. of Jesus Christ of Latter-day Saints. Office: The Friend 50 E North Temple F23 Salt Lake City UT 84150-3226*

PAULSON, LARRY A., protective services official. Chief of police Boise. Office: 7200 Barrister Dr Boise ID 83704-9265*

PAULSON, RICHARD GUY, retail executive; b. Portland, Oreg., Sept. 30, 1921; s. Guy W. and Bess (Spinning) P.; student Oreg. State U., 1939-41, U. Oreg., 1941-42; B.A., U. Wash., 1943; m. Norma Lee Cunningham, Apr. 29, 1944; children—Lawrance Lee, Donald Guy, Richard Guy, Jr., Beverly Sue, David William. With G.W. Paulson Co., Portland, 1946—, v.p., 1946-57, pres., 1957-88, chmn. bd. 1988—, gen. ptnr. Paulson LLP, 1992—. Served to capt. AUS, 1943-46. Mem. Portland Retail Trade Bur. (pres., chmn. bd. 1956-60), Portland C. of C. (dir., exec. com. 1956-60), Gideons, Phi Gamma Delta. Republican. Baptist. Home: 1511 NE 150th Ave Portland OR 97230-8610 Office: GW Paulson Co 3040 NE Sandy Blvd Portland OR 97232-2459

PAULSON-EHRHARDT, PATRICIA HELEN, sales executive; b. Moses Lake, Wash., June 10, 1956; d. Luther Roanoke and Helen Jane (Baird) Paulson; m. Terry Lee Ehrhardt, Mar. 12, 1983. Student, Pacific Luth. U., 1974-76; BS in Med. Tech., U. Wash., 1976; BS in Biology, MS in Biology, Eastern Wash. U., 1982. Med. technologist Samaritan Hosp., Moses Lake, 1979-81; lab. supr. Moses Lake Clinic, Kalispell (Mont.) Regional Hosp., 1982-88; med. technologist Kalispell Regional Hosp., 1987; sales mgr. Pathology Assocs. Med. Lab., Spokane, Wash., 1988—; mem. med. lab. tech. adv. com. Wenatchee (Wash.) Valley Coll., 1984-85, chmn., 1985-86; spkr. in field. Mem. Flathead Valley Community Band, 1987-90. Mem. Am. Soc. Clin. Lab. Scientists, Clin. Lab. Mgmt. Assn. (pres. Inland N.W. chpt. 1993-94, bd. dirs. 1994-95), Am. Soc. Clin. Pathologists (cert.), Pan Players Flute Soc., Flathead Tennis Assn., Sigma Xi, Kappa Delta (pledge class pres. 1976). Republican. Lutheran. Avocations: tennis, volleyball, flying, fishing, playing flute. Home: 26 Cub Dr Great Falls MT 59404-6425

PAULUS, NORMA JEAN PETERSEN, lawyer, state school system administrator; b. Belgrade, Nebr., Mar. 13, 1933; d. Paul Emil and Ella Marie (Hellbusch) Petersen; LL.B., Willamette Law Sch., 1962; LL.D. (hon.), Linfield Coll., 1985; LittD (hon.), Whitman Coll., 1990; LHD (hon.), Lewis & Clark Coll., 1996; m. William G. Paulus, Aug. 16, 1958; children: Elizabeth, William Frederick. Sec. to Harney County Dist. Atty., 1950-53; legal sec., Salem, Oreg., 1953-55; sec. to chief justice Oreg. Supreme Ct., 1955-61; admitted to Oreg. bar, 1962; of counsel Paulus and Callaghan, Salem, mem. Oreg. Ho. of Reps., 1971-77; sec. state State of Oreg., Salem, 1977-85; of counsel firm Paulus, Rhoten & Lien, 1985-86; supt. pub. instrn. State of Oreg., 1990-99; Oreg. exec. bd. US West, 1985-97; adj. prof. Willamette U. Grad. Sch. 1985; mem. N.W. Power Planning Com., 1986-89. Fellow Eagleton Inst. Politics, 1971; mem. Pacific NW Power Planning Council, 1987-89; adv. com. Defense Adv. Com. for Women in the Service, 1986, Nat. Trust for Hist. Preservation, 1988—; trustee Willamette U., 1978—; bd. dirs. Benedictine Found. of Oreg., 1980—, Oreg. Grade. Instn. Sci. and Tech., 1985—, Mid Willamette Valley coun. Camp Fire Girls, 1985-87, Edn. Commn. States, 1991-99, Coun. Chief State Sch. Officers, 1995-98, Nat. Assessment Governing Bd., 1996—, Oreg. Garden Found., 1997—; bd. dirs., adv. bd. World Affairs Coun. Oreg., 1997—; overseer Whitman Coll., 1985—; bd. cons. Goodwill Industries of Oreg.; mem. Salem Human Relations Commn., 1967-70, Marion-Polk Boundary Commn., 1970-71; mem. Presdl. Commn. to Monitor Philippines Election, 1986, Nat. Assessment Governing Bd. .Recipient Distinguished Service award City of Salem, 1971, LWV, 1995; Path Breaker award Oreg. Women's Polit. Caucus, 1976; named One of 10 Women of Future, Ladies Home Jour., 1979. Woman of Yr., Oreg. Inst Managerial and Profl. Women, 1982, Oreg. Women Lawyers, 1982, Woman Who Made a Difference award Nat. Women's Forum, 1985. Mem. Oreg. State Bar, Nat. Order Women Legislators, Women Execs. in State Govt., Women's Polit. Caucus Bus. and Profl. Women's Club (Golden Torch award 1971), Zonta Internat., Delta Kappa Gamma.

PAUP, MARTIN ARNOLD, real estate and securities investor; b. Seattle, Aug. 30, 1930; s. Clarence Jacob and Emaline Ethel (Lodestein) P.; m. Mary Jean Iske, Apr. 4, 1959; children: Barbara Ann Paup Soriano, Jennifer Marie, Elizabeth Paup Gail. BS, U. Wash., 1952. Indsl. engr. Boeing Airplane Co., Seattle, 1954-60; owner Coopers Unfinished Furniture, Seattle, 1960-63; claims rep. Unigard Ins., Seattle, 1963-66; asst. benefits mgr. Equitable Life Assurance, Seattle, 1966-85; owner Paup Ventures, Seattle, 1974--, Paup Investment Co., Seattle, 1963--, Ella Paup Properties, Seattle, 1963--. Bd. dirs. Denny Regrade Property Owners' Assn., Seattle, Denny Regrade Bus. Assn., Seattle, First Ave. Assn., Seattle. Seattle Dept. Community Devel. grantee, 1980. Mem. Greenwood C. of C., Seattle Opera Guild. Democrat. Roman Catholic. Avocations: opera, travel, lit., history. Office: Paup Co 2021 1st Ave # 4G Seattle WA 98121-2135

PAUPP, TERRENCE EDWARD, legal research associate, educator; b. Joliet, Ill., Aug. 10, 1952; s. Edward Theodore and Mary Alice (Combs) P. BA in Social Scis., San Diego State U., 1974; ThM, Luth. Sch. Theology, 1978; JD, U. San Diego, 1990. Instr. philosophy San Diego City Coll., 1983-86, Southwestern Coll., Chula Vista, Calif., 1980-83; law clerk Sch. Law U. San Diego, 1987-88; law clerk Office of Atty. Gen., San Diego, 1988-89; rsch. assoc. Frank & Milchen, San Diego, 1989, Dougherty & Hildre, San Diego, 1990-95; sr. rsch.-assoc. Inst. for Ctrl. and Ea. European Studies, San Diego State U., 1996—; cons. Cmty. Reinvestment Act, San Diego, 1993-95; sr. rsch. assoc. Inst. Ctrl. and Ea. European Studies San Diego State U., 1994-95; adj. faculty in criminal justice and polit. sci. Nat. U. Contbr. articles to law jours. Cons. Neighborhood House 5th Ave., 1994-95, Bethel Baptist Ch., 1994-95, PBS Frontline documentary The Nicotine Wars, 1994. Mem. ATLA, N.Y. Acad. Scis. Democrat. Lutheran. Avocation: tennis. Office: San Diego State University Inst Ctrl and Ea Europ Stud 4430 North Ave Apt 9 San Diego CA 92116-3980

PAVA, ESTHER SHUB, artist, educator; b. Hartford, Conn., June 29, 1921; d. Jacob H. and Rose (Rietkop) Shub; m. Jacob Pava, June 16, 1946; children: David Lauren, Jonathan Michael, Daniel Seth, Nathaniel Alexander. BFA, R.I. Sch. of Design, 1944; MA, San Francisco State U., 1971. Artist New Eng. Roto Engraving Co., Holyoke, Mass., 1944-46, Wyckoff Advt. Agy., San Francisco, 1947-48; tchr. San Francisco Unified Sch. Dist., 1963-66, Laguna Salada Sch. Dist., Pacifica, Calif., 1966-83; artist, educator Belmont, Calif., 1983—; tchr. pvt. students Manor House, Belmont, Caif. Bd. dirs. Belmont Arts Commn. Recipient numerous awards for artwork. Mem. AAUW, Burlingame Art Soc. (pres. 1983-84), Thirty and One Artists (pres. 1992-93), Soc. Western Artists (signature mem. and juror, 2d v.p. and program chmn. 1997-98, pres. 1999—), Calif. Watercolor Assn., Nat. League Am. Pen Women, Belmont Arts. Commn. Avocations: world travel, book discussion groups, sketching on location, painting in studio. Home: 2318 Hastings Dr Belmont CA 94002-3318 Studio: Manor House 1219 Ralston Ave Belmont CA 94002-1902

PAVICEVIC, GORAN, cinematographer; b. Belgrade, Yugoslavia, Feb. 13, 1961; s. Ljubomir and Radmila (Dimitrijevic) P. BFA in Film, Univ. of Arts, Belgrade, 1987; MFA in Cinematography, Am. Film Inst., L.A., 1994. Freelance cinematographer L.A., 1991—; asst. prof. Univ. of Arts, Belgrade, 1989-91. Dir. of photography: (feature film) Strangeland, 1998, (short feature films) Pereat, 1983 (1st prize Belgrade Festival 1983), Laura Sobers, 1994 (2d Pl. Turin Festival 1995), Night Train, 1995 (Golden Camera Chgo. award 1996). Joseph & Olga Auerbach scholar Am. Film Inst., 1992. Fellow Am. Film Inst. (alumni); mem. Soc. Film and TV Artists of Serbia-Yugoslavia (v.p. cinematography sect. 1989-91), Ind. Feature Project West, Am. Film Inst. Home: 823 Kodak Dr Los Angeles CA 90026

PAVLIK, NANCY, convention services executive; b. Hamtramck, Mich., July 18, 1935; d. Frank and Helen (Vorobjoff) Phillips; m. G. Edward Pavlik, June 30, 1956; children: Kathleen, Christine, Laureen, Michael, Bonnie Jean. Student, U. Ariz., 1956-80. Exec. sec. Mich. Bell, Detroit, 1951-56, RCA, Camden, N.J., 1956-58; owner S.W. Events Etc., Scottsdale, Ariz., 1969—. Chmn. hospitality industry com. Scottsdale City Coun., 1989-95; bd. dirs. Scottsdale Curatorial Bd., 1987-89. Mem. Soc. Incentive Travel Execs., Meeting Planners Internat., Am. Soc. Assn. Execs., Indian Arts and Crafts Assn., Scottsdale C. of C. (bd. dirs., tourism steering com. 1984-97), Contemporary Watercolorists Club. Democrat. Roman Catholic. Avocations: watercoloring, Indian arts, crafts. Home: 15417 E Richwood Ave Fountain Hills AZ 85268-1432 Office: SW Events Etc 3200 N Hayden Rd Ste 100 Scottsdale AZ 85251-6653

PAVLISH, DANIEL VINCENT, poet, novelist; b. Billings, Mont., Oct. 20, 1966; s. Donald Charles and Mary Regina (Tobin) P.; m. Sheila Follingstad, Oct. 1, 1994. BA in Mass Comm., Eastern Mont. Coll., Billings, 1990; student, May Tech. Coll., Billings, 1990. Various positions Billings, also Eugene, Oreg., 1990-94; floor clk. Bi-Mart, Eugene, 1995—; ambassador of poetry Internat. Soc. Poets, Washington, 1995—; emcee Voices of Paradise, Eugene, 1996-97. Author: (spy novel) PAV, 1987, (spy novel series) Crusader I-IV, 1987-92, (spiritual sci. fiction) The New Apostles, 1994, (poetry) Cafe Jones, 1994. Recipient Editor's Choice awards Nat. Libr. of Poetry, 1993-98, Larry Cook Meml. award Eastern Mont. Coll., 1986; named Poet of Merit, Internat. Soc. Poets, 1994-95; inducted into Internat. Poetry Hall of Fame, Owings Mills, Md., 1996. Mem. SCRABBLE. Democrat. Roman Catholic. Avocations: writing, bicycling, collecting, puzzles, volleyball. Home: 735 Hughes St Eugene OR 97402-2116

PAWULA, KENNETH JOHN, artist, educator; b. Chgo., Feb. 4, 1935; s. John and Clara (Brzezinski) P.; student Northwestern U., 1956, Art Inst. Chgo., 1956; B.F.A., U. Ill., 1959; M.A. in Painting, U. Calif., Berkeley, 1962. Graphic designer Motorola, Inc., Chgo., 1959-60; grad. asst. printmaking U. Calif., Berkeley, 1961-62, asso. in art, 1962-63; archaeol. delineator for Islamic excavation Am. Research Center, Egypt, 1964-65; instr. Sch. of Art, U. Wash., Seattle, 1965-67, asst. prof., 1967-73, asso. prof., 1974—; participant artist-in-residence program of Ecole Superieure Des Beaux-Arts D'Athenes at Rhodos Art Center, Greece, 1978; cons. to Wydawnictwo Interpress, Warsaw, Poland, 1978; mem. art jury ann. painting, drawing and sculpture show Art Mus. of Greater Victoria, Can., 1971, Unitarian Art Gallery, Seattle, 1968, Cellar Gallery, Kirkland, Wash., 1968, Lakewood Artist's Outdoor Exhibit, Tacoma, Wash., 1968; participant Painting Symposium, Janow Podlaski, Poland, 1977. One-man shows of paintings include: Univ. Unitarian Fine Arts Gallery, Seattle, 1970, Polly Friedlander Gallery, Seattle, 1970, Lynn Kottler Galleries, N.Y.C., 1971, U. Minn. Art Gallery, Mpls., 1971, Art Mus. of Greater Victoria, Can., 1972, Second Story Gallery, Seattle, 1972, Yuuhigaoka Gallery Osaka, Japan, Universidade Federal Fluminense Niteroi, Rio de Janiero, Brazil, 1990, Pyramid Gallery, N.Y.C., 1991; group shows include: Worth Ryder Gallery, U. Calif., Berkeley, 1962, Seattle Art Mus., 1964, 70, 65, 66, Frye Art Mus., Seattle, 1966, San Francisco Art Ins., 1966, Henry Gallery, U. Wash., Seattle, 1966, 67, 70, State Capitol Mus., Olympia, Wash., 1967, Attica Gallery, Seattle, 1967, 69, Sec. of State's Office, Olympia, 1968, Eastern Mich. U., Ypsilanti, 1968, Rogue Gallery, Medford, Oreg., 1968, Marylhurst Coll., Oreg., 1968, Spokane Art Mus., 1968, Cheney Cowles Mus., Spokane, 1969, Jade Gallery, Richland, Wash., 1969, Alaska U., 1970, Polly Friedlander Gallery, Mpls., 1971, Anchorage Art Mus., 1972, U. Nev. Art Gallery, 1972, Juneau (Alaska) Art Mus., 1972, Springfield (Mo.) Art Mus., 1973, U. N.D., Grand Forks, 1974, Washington and Jefferson Coll., Washington, Pa., 1975, MacMurray Coll., Jacksonville, Ill., 1976, Gallery of Fine Arts, Eastern Mont. Coll., 1976, Inst. of Culture, Janow Podlaski, Poland, 1977, Seattle Arts Commn., 1978, Polish Cultural Center, Buffalo, 1979, Cabo Frio Internat. Print Biennial, Brazil, 1983, Sunderland (Eng.) Poly. U. Faculty Exchange Exhbn., 1984, Internat Art Biennial Mus. Hosio Capranica-Viterbo, Italy, 1985; represented in permanent collections: San Francisco Art Mus., Seattle Art Mus., Henry Gallery, U. Wash., Seattle, Highline Coll., Midway, Wash., Marylhurst Coll., Art Mus., Janow Podlaski, Poland, Tacoma Nat. Bank, Fine Arts Gallery of San Diego. Mem. Coll. Art Assn., AAUP. Home: 2242 NE 177th St Seattle WA 98155-5241 Office: U Wash Coll Arts & Scis Sch Art Dm # 10 Seattle WA 98195

PAXTON, LAURA BELLE-KENT, English language educator, management professional; b. Lake Charles, La., Feb. 8, 1942; d. George Ira and Gladys Lillian (Barrett) Kent.; m. Kenneth Robert Paxton Jr., Jan. 2, 1962. BA, McNeese U., Lake Charles, 1963, MA in English, 1972; EdD, East Tex. U., 1983. cert. English, social studies instr., prin., supt., ednl. adminstr., Ariz. Tchr. Darrington (Wash.) High Sch., 1966-70; English instr. Maricopa C.C., Phoenix, 1974-92; migrant program instr. Phoenix Union High Sch., 1984-88; English instr. Embry-Riddle Aeronautical U., Luke AFB, Ariz., 1985-87; sales rep. Merrill Lynch Realty, Phoenix, 1985-88; co-owner Paxton Mgmt. Co., Phoenix, 1985-92; assoc. prof., chair gen. edn. Western Internat. U., Phoenix, 1992—; author Ariz. corr. courses, 1987-88; presenter migrant worker program confs., 1987—; reviewer Prentice-Hall, 1985. Author: Handbook for Middle Eastern Dancers, 1978, The Kent Family History From 1787-1981, 1981, A Handbook of Home Remedies, 1981, Elements of Effective Writing: A Composition Guidesheet, 1994, Documentation for Business Papers: A Guidesheet, 1995, (textbook) Writing Power, 1998. Mem. Everett, Wash. Opera Guild, 1966-70, Ariz. State U. Opera Guild, Tempe, 1978-80; mem. City of Darrington Council, 1969-70; ESL instr. Friendly House, Phoenix, 1978-79. Mem. Ariz. English Assn., Phi Delta Kappa.

PAXTON, RONALD BRENT, aerospace engineer; b. Salt Lake City, Feb. 7, 1947; s. Baker James and Vauna Mae (Leany) P.; m. Lynda Mihlberger, Mar. 19, 1974 (div. Jan. 1990); children: Adam, Tami, Jason, Brett, Amy; m. Karen Rae Richardson Rousselle, Nov. 19, 1993. BS in Mech. Engring., U. Utah, 1976. Lic. profl. engr., bldg. insulation contractor, Utah. Insulation specialist Baker Insulation, Salt Lake City, 1965-69, 71-75, Suprior Insulation Co., Salt Lake City, 1975-76; supr. Propellant and Adhesive Structures Thiokol Corp. Space Divsn., Brigham City, Utah, 1986; with Thiokol Corp., 1976; sr. scientist Grain Structures Thiokol Corp., Utah Tactical Divsn., Brigham City, Utah, 1987-92; grain structural analyst Thiokol Corp. Sci. and Engring., Brigham City, Utah, 1992—. Contbr. propellant grain design and structural analysis of high performance solid rocket motors, publs. in field. Missionary to Navajo Indians, LDS Ch., 1969-71; explorer scout advisor Boy Scouts Am., Brigham City, Utah, 1979-83; FAA lic. pilot, search and rescue pilot for CAP (USAF aux.), Brigham City, Utah, 1985—. Recipient

Franklin award Thiokol Corp., 1984, Trailblazer award USN, 1984. Mem. NSPE, Aircraft Owners and Pilots Assn., Exptl. Aircraft Assn., Utah Pilots Assn., NRA, Am. Mensa. Republican. Mem. LDS Ch. Avocations: flying, model building, shooting. Home: 2585 S Tess Pl Perry UT 84302-4142 Office: Thiokol Corp Brigham City UT 84302

PAYACK, PAUL JJ, marketing executive. BA in Comparative Lit., Harvard U., 1974, C.A.G.S. in Fine Arts, 1983. Tech. writer Newbury Coll., Boston, 1975-78; sr. tech. writer Digital Equipment Corp., Maenad, Mass., 1978-79; mktg. mgr., sales promotion Wang Labs., Lowell, Mass., 1980-82; corp. dir., mktg. comm. Apollo Computer Inc. (now Hewlett-Packard Workstations), Chelmsford, Mass., 1982-87; v.p., global comm. Unisys Corp., Blue Bell, Pa., 1987-90; dir., corp. comm. A.C. Nielsen, Northbrook, Ill., 1990-93; dir., worldwide network mktg. programs The Network Systems Corp.(acquired by StorageTek 1995), Mpls., 1994-95; v.p. corp. mktg. Intersolv, Rockville, Md., 1995-96; sr. v.p. strategic mktg. Intelliguard Software, Dublin, Calif., 1996—; cons. Babson Coll., GM/Hughes, Fed. Res. Bank of N.Y., Shandwick; adjuct prof. Babson Coll., Harvard U., Mass State Coll., Univ. of Tex. Contr. articles to profl. jours. Office: Intelliguard Software 6200 Village Pkwy Dublin CA 94568-3004

PAYNE, ANCIL HORACE, retired broadcasting executive; b. Mitchell, Oreg., Sept. 5, 1921; s. Leslie L. and Pearl A. (Brown) P.; m. Valerie Dorrance Davies, Apr. 6, 1959; children: Anne Sparrow, Alison Louise, Lucinda Catherine. Student, Willamette U., 1939-41, U. Oreg., 1941, U. Notre Dame, Ohio State U., 1943; B.A., U. Wash., 1947; postgrad., Am. U., 1950-51; hon. PhD, Willamette Univ., 1991. Adminstrv. asst. to congressman, Washington, 1949-52; gen. mgr. Martin Van Lines, Anchorage, 1952-56; mgr. Frontiers-Oreg. Ltd., Portland, Oreg., 1956-59; asst. v.p. bus. div. King Broadcasting Co., Seattle, 1959-63, v.p., 1963-70, exec. v.p., 1970-71, pres., 1971-87; chmn. bd. affiliates NBC, 1975-80. Mem. Oreg. Bd. Higher Edn., 1966-70; bd. trustees Whitman Coll., 1985-90; bd. dirs. Ceasefire. Lt. (j.g.) USNR, 1942-45, PTO. Mem. Monday Club, Rainier Club, Columbia Tower Club, Phi Beta Kappa Assocs., Alpha Delta Sigma. Episcopalian. Office: Ancil H Payne & Assocs 1107 1st Ave Apt 606 Seattle WA 98101-2944

PAYNE, BOYD ALAN, marketing professional; b. Granger, Utah, May 19, 1971; s. Marty Kent and Sandra Faye (Dunn) P.; m. Rachel K. McAllister, Mar. 26, 1993; 1 child, Kylaya Rae. Student, Salt Lake C.C., 1989-90, 93. Sales mgr. Signature Books, Salt Lake City, 1993—; v.p. Payne Claims Svcs., South Jordan, Utah, 1997—; bd. dirs. Payne Claims Svcs. Author: Utah Celebrities, 1995; editor (CD-ROM) New Mormon Studies, 1998. Office: Signature Books 564 W 400 N Salt Lake City UT 84116-3411

PAYNE, JACK WELLESLEY, author, publisher; b. Racine, Wis., Jan. 15, 1926; s. Ernest Wellesley and Lillian Dagmar (Koski) P.; m. Joan Natalie Jensen, Sept. 29, 1950; children: David, Ronald, Jeffrey. Student, Kent State Univ., 1948-49, Univ. Wis., 1946; BBA, Spencerian Coll., 1952. Editor Massey-Harris Co., Racine, 1952; rsch. dir. Patterson Publ. Co., Chgo., 1953-57; bus. mgr., v.p. Clissold Publ. Co., Chgo., 1957-63; editor/publ. Bus. Opportunities Digest, Racine, Wis., Farmington, N.Mex., 1963-76. Author: The Encyclopedia of Little-Known Highly Profitable Business Opportunities, 1971, How To Make A Fortune in Finder's Fees, 1973. Mem. Elks Lodge, Moose Lodge, Eagles Lodge (chaplain, 1978, treas. 1979-82, trustee 1983-84). Avocations: computer, motor vehicles, travel. Home: 6409 Parkwood Way Paradise CA 95969-2626

PAYNE, (ORVILLE) THOMAS, political scientist, educator; b. Fulton, Mo., Apr. 11, 1920; s. Rufus Thomas and Addie (Kemp) P.; m. Helen Kate Ritchie, Oct. 2, 1943 (dec. June 1974); children: David Thomas, Joseph Ritchie; m. Mora Christine MacKinnon Skari, July 10, 1975; stepchildren: Tala, Lisa Skari. A.B., Westminster Coll., 1941; A.M., U. Chgo., 1948, Ph.D., 1951. Instr. U. Tenn., 1948-50; from instr. to asso. prof. U. Mont., 1951-59, prof. polit. sci., 1959-85, emeritus, 1985-98, chmn. dept., 1959-66, 84-85; vis. prof. Inst. Adminstrn., Ahmadu Bello U., Zaria, Nigeria, 1979-80; Mem. Mont. Commn. on Local Govt., 1974-77; Nat. commn. study jurisdiction system Meth. Ch., 1956-60. Trustee elementary sch. Dist. No. 1, Missoula, Mont., 1958-64, chmn., 1962-64; trustee Rocky Mountain Coll., Billings, Mont., 1969-76. Served from pvt. to 1st. lt. USAAF, 1942-46. Mem. Am. Polit. Sci. Assn., Western Polit. Sci. Assn. (exec. council 1968-70, pres. 1973-74), Pacific N.W. Polit. Sci. Assn. (pres. 1964-65), AAUP. Republican. Mem. United Ch. of Christ. Club: Kiwanis. Home: 3929 Timberlane St Missoula MT 59802-3062 *Died Nov. 23, 1998.*

PAYTON, GARY DWAYNE, professional basketball player; b. Oakland, Calif., July 23, 1968; m. Monique Payton; children: Raquel, Gary Dwayne. Grad., Oreg. State U., 1990. Drafted NBA, 1990; guard Seattle Supersonics, 1990—. Named mem. All-Am. First Team, The Sporting News, 1990, Pacific-10 Conf. Player of Yr., 1990, NBA All-Star, 1994, 95, NBA Player of the Week; named to NBA All-Def. 1st Team, 1994, 95. Office: Seattle Supersonics 190 Queen Anne Ave N Ste 200 Seattle WA 98109-9711*

PAYTON, RALPH REED, photographer; b. Baker, Oreg., Apr. 29, 1926; s. William Miles and Bernice Irene (McCord) P.; Student, U. Oreg., 1948-49, Monterey Peninsula Coll., 1973; D.Hum., London Insts., 1973. With, Dept. Army, Cristobal, Panama, 1953-54, CIA, Washington, 1954-57, Am. Embassy, Cairo, 1957-59; free lance photographer, Carmel Valley, Calif., 1963—, represented by Sierra Artists Gallery, Mariposa, Calif.; horticulturist, inventor. Exhibitor: one-man and group shows including Internat. Platform Assn., Internat. Art Show, Washington (award), 1976; author: Western Poems & Short Stories; founder, pres. Black Raven Mining & Refining Inc., 1977-87. Patentee: plant growing process. Served with USNR, 1944-46, 50-52. Charter alumnus Eisenhower Coll., 1967; elector Photog. Hall of Fame, 1969—; recipient over 30 art show ribbons. Mem. Sierra Artists. Home: PO Box 126 Carmel Valley CA 93924-0126

PEABODY, DEBBIE KAY, elementary school educator; b. Wooster, Ohio, Apr. 9, 1954; d. Walter L. and Carolyn E. (Lee) Mussatto; m. David Leslie Peabody, Jan. 6, 1973; children: Dawn Kathleen, Lesli Kay. BS in Elem. Edn., Southwestern Adventist Coll., Keene, Tex., 1986. Cert. tchr. K-8, Ariz. Head tchr. SDA Elem. Sch., Camp Verde, Ariz., 1986-89; tchr. 6th grade Roosevelt Sch. Dist., Phoenix, 1989-93, jr. high reading tchr., 1993-94, collaborative peer tchr., 1994-96, 2d grade tchr., 1996-97, 3d grade tchr. Cologne model, 1997—; dist. assessment plan co-chair Roosevelt Sch. Dist., 1993—; mem. Greater Phoenix Curriculum Coun. Dist. Assessment Plan Writing Team, 1994—; CHAMPS coord. Sunland Elem. Sch., Phoenix, 1991-94. Co-author: (activity book) Explosion of ASAP Activities, 1994. Recipient Edn. of Merit award Southwestern Union Coll., 1985, 86. Mem. ASCD, NEA, Ariz. Edn. Assn., Roosevelt Edn. Assn., Nat. Coun. Tchrs. Math. Avocations: quilting, embroidery, biking, hiking, canoeing. Office: Southwest School 1111 W Dobson Phoenix AZ 85041

PEAR, CHARLES E., JR., lawyer; b. Macon, Ga., June 18, 1950; s. Charles Edward and Barbara Jane P.; m. Linda Sue King; children: Jennifer Sue, Charles Edward III, Stephanie Sue. BA, U. Hawaii, 1972 with honors; JD, U. Calif., Berkeley, 1975. Bar: Hawaii 1976, Fla. 1977, Colo. 1994, U.S. Ct. of Appeals (9th cir.). Assoc. Rush, Moore, Craven, Sutton, Morry & Beh, Honolulu, 1976-77, counsel, 1987-90; assoc., ptnr. Carlsmith & Dwyer, Honolulu, 1977-82; ptnr. Burke, Sakai, McPheeters, Bordner & Gilardy, Honolulu, 1983-87; vis. prof. law and computers U. British Columbia, 1990-93; counsel Holland & Hart, Denver, 1993-96, McCorriston, Miho, Miller& Mukai, Honolulu, 1996—; mem. Hawaii Real Estate Commn. com. on condominium and resort real estate legis., 1978-79; spl. counsel to consumer protection com. Hawaii State Ho. of Reps., 1981-82; chair real property and fin. svcs. sect. Hawaii State Bar Assn., Expert Sys. Interest Group, Hypermedia Interest Group. Editor-in-Chief Hawaii Conveyance Manual II, 1987; editor Hawaii Commercial Real Estate Manual, 1988; bd. editors Hawaii Inst. of Continuing Legal Edn.; co-author Nat. Assn. of Real Estate Licensing Law Officials and Nat. Timesharing Coun. Model Timesharing Act, 1981-82; contbg. author: Winning With Computers, 1992, Hawaii Real Estate Manual, 1997; lectr. in field, 1981—. Mem. ABA (document assembly interest group)

PEARCE, DRUE, state legislator; b. Fairfield, Ill., Apr. 2, 1951; d. H. Phil and Julia Detroy (Bannister) P.; m. Michael F.G. Williams; 1 child, Tate Hanna Pearce-Williams. BA in Biol. Scis., Ind. U., 1973; MPA, Harvard U., 1984; cert. exec. program Darden Sch. Bus., U. Va., 1989. Sch. tchr. Clark County, Ind., 1973-74; curator of edn. Louisville Zoo, 1974-77; dir. Summerscene, Louisville, 1974-77; asst. v.p., br. mgr. Ala. Nat. Bank N., 1977-82; legis. aide to Rep. John Ringstad Ala. Ho. of Reps., Juneau, 1983; mem. Ala. Ho. of Reps., 1984-88, minority whip, 1986; state senator State of Ala., 1988—, chmn. com. oil and gas, mem. exec. com. energy coun., 1989-90, chmn. com. labor and commerce, mem. exec. coms. western state conf., coun. state govts., energy coun., 1991-92, co-chmn. senate fin., chmn. energy coun., vice chmn. com. energy, nat. coun. state govts., 1993-94, mem. select com. legis. ethics and legis. coun., 1993—, pres. senate, mem. exec. com. energy coun., vice chmn. senate coms. resources and rules, 1995-96, co-chmn. com. senate fin., mem. exec. com. energy coun., vice chmn. com. senate judiciary, 1997—; fin. cons. Bowman and Miller, Anchorage, 1983; ptnr. 4150 Co., Anchorage and Kotzebue, Ala., 1983—, Cloverland N., Anchorage, 1993—; investor, bd. dirs. Wave Energy Corp., Anchorage; resources cons. Artic Slope Regional Corp., Anchorage, 1987-91, 95-96. Bd. dirs. Ala. Women's Aid in Crisis, Anchorage Econ. Devel. Coun., Ala. Aerospace Devel. Corp., Ala. Spl. Olympics, Gov.'s Bd.; mem. Ala. Resource Devel. Coun., Ala. Women's Polit. Caucus. Mem. DAR, Alaska C. of C. Republican. Home: 716 W 4th Ave Ste 500 Anchorage AK 99501-2107 Office: Office of the State Senate State Capitol St Juneau AK 99801-1182*

PEARCE, JOAN DELAP, research company executive; b. Oakland, Calif., June 13, 1930; d. Robert Jerome and Wilhelmina (Reaume) DeLap; m. Gerald Allan Pearce, June 18, 1953; 1 child, Scott Ford. Student, U. Oreg., 1948-55. Rsch. assoc. deForest Rsch., L.A., 1966-78, assoc. dir., 1978-92; dir. rsch. Walt Disney Prodns., Burbank, Calif., 1978; pres., bd. dirs. Joan Pearce Rsch. Assocs., 1992—; lighting dir. Wilcoxen Players, Beverly Hills, Calif., 1955-60, Theatre 40, L.A., 1960-66. Bd. advisors Living History Ctr., Marin County, Calif., 1982-89, bd. dirs., 1989-94. Mem. Am. Film Inst. Democrat. Avocations: photography; travel; theater; swimming. Home: 2621 Rutherford Dr Los Angeles CA 90068-3042 Office: Joan Pearce Rsch Assocs 8111 Beverly Blvd Ste 308 Los Angeles CA 90048-4525

PEARL, JUDEA, computer scientist, educator; b. Tel-Aviv, Sept. 4, 1936; U.S. citizen; married; 3 children. BSc, Israel Inst. Tech., 1960; MSc, Newark Coll. Engring., 1961; PhD in Elec. Engring., Poly. Inst. Bklyn., 1965. Rsch. engr. Dental Sch., NYU, 1960-61; mem. tech. staff RCA Rsch. Labs., 1961-65; dir. advanced memory devices Electronic Memories, Inc., Calif., 1966-69; prof. Sch. of Engring./Dept. Computer Scis. UCLA, 1969—; instr. Newark Coll. Engring., 1961; cons. Rand Corp., 1972, Integrated Sci. Corp., 1975, Hughes Aircraft, 1989. Recipient Outstanding Achievement award RCA Labs., 1965. Fellow IEEE, Am. Assn. Artificial Intelligence; mem. Nat. Acad. Engring. Office: UCLA Dept Computer Sci 4532 Boelter Hall Los Angeles CA 90095-1596

PEARLMAN, MITZI ANN, elementary education educator; b. Houston, July 21, 1951; d. Bernard Joseph and Annie Mae (Gollob) P. BA in Sociology, U. Colo., Boulder, 1975; MA in Elem. Edn., U. Colo., Denver, 1988. Cert. elem. tchr., Colo. Tchr. 2d grade Cherry Creek Schs., Englewood, Colo., 1987-88; tchr. 2d, 3rd grades Douglas County Schs., Castle Rock, Colo., 1988—. Vol. Denver Zoo. Recipient Douglas County NOVA awards for Creative Excellence in Teaching, 1988, 89, 90, 91, 92, Innovative Instrn. award Bus. Week mag., 1990, Douglas County Edn. Found. grants, 1993, 97, 98, Pub. Svc. Intergenerational grant, 1993, Classroom Connection Disseminator grants, 1992, 93, Classroom Connection Adaptor grants, 1992, 93, 94, 95, 96, 97, 98, Douglas County mini grant, 1989; named Channel 7 Tchr. of the Week, 1993. Mem. ASCD, Internat. Reading Assn., Douglas County Reading Assn. (treas. 1992-94), Colo. Assn. Sci. Tchrs., Phi Delta Kappa. Avocations: reading, pets, relaxing. Office: Acres Green Elem Sch 13524 Acres Green Dr Littleton CO 80124-2701

PEARSON, APRIL VIRGINIA, lawyer; b. Martinsville, Ind., Aug. 11, 1960; d. Clare Grill and Sheila Rosemary (Finch) Rayner; m. Randall Keith Pearson, Dec. 10, 1988; children: Randall Kyle, Austin Finch, Autumn Virginia. BA, Calif. State U., Long Beach, 1982; JD, Pepperdine U., 1987. Bar: Calif. 1987, Idaho 1993, D.C. 1989; cert. indsl. fire brigade, HAZWOPER Tex. A&M U. Assoc. counsel Union Oil Co. of Calif., L.A., 1988—; v.p. Pa's Bier, Long Beach, Calif., 1988—; bd. dirs. Unocal Chems. Internat., The Hague, The Netherlands, 1993-95, Ammonia Safety Tng. Inst., 1995—, sec., gen. counsel, 1997—. Mem. Women Lawyers of Long Beach (v.p. 1990-93), Am. Corp. Counsel Assn., Chem. Industry Coun. Calif. (chair regulatory affairs com. 1995). Avocations: running, tae kwon do. Office: Union Oil Co of Calif 376 Valencia Ave Brea CA 92823-6356

PEARSON, CONRAD E., financial services executive; b. Edmonton, Alta., Can., Sept. 1, 1951; came to U.S., 1960; s. Hilding A. and Elva Rose (Land) P.; m. Barbara Anne Schroeder; children: Cameron, Nicole, Morgan, Everett. Cert. in Mid. East Studies, Portland State U., 1973, BA in Polit. Sci., 1973; MA in Internat. Affairs, Johns Hopkins U., 1975. Polit. risk analyst Shell Oil, Houston, 1977-78; mgr. Chase Manhattan Bank, N.Y.C., 1979-80; pres. Risk Insights, N.Y.C., 1980-82; co-owner Pearson Fin. Group, Portland, Oreg., 1982—. Pres. Tigard (Oreg.) Coalition Chs., 1983—. Mem. Tigard C. of C. (chmn. bd. dirs. 1994-95), Rotary (pres. Tigard club 1992). Lutheran. Avocation: poetry writing. Home: 33660 SW Firdale Rd Cornelius OR 97113-6215 Office: Pearson Fin Group 5665 SW Meadows Rd Ste 120 Lake Oswego OR 97035-3130

PEARSON, JOHN, mechanical engineer; b. Leyburn, Yorkshire, U.K., Apr. 24, 1923; came to U.S., 1930, naturalized, 1944; s. William and Nellie Pearson; m. Ruth Ann Billhardt, July 10, 1944 (wid. Nov. 1984); children: John, Armin, Roger; m. Sharoll L. Chisolm, Sept. 8, 1993. B.S.M.E., Northwestern U., 1949, M.S., 1951. Registered profl. engr., Calif. Rsch. engr. Naval Ordnance Test Sta., China Lake, Calif., 1951-55, head warhead rsch. br., 1955-58, head solid dynamics br., 1958-59, head detonation physics group, 1959-67; head detonation physics div. Naval Weapons Ctr., China Lake, Calif., 1967-83, sr. rsch. scientist, 1983—; cons., lectr. in field; founding mem. adv. bd. Ctr. for High Energy Forming, U. Denver; mem. bd. examiners Sambalpur U., India, 1982-83. Author: Explosive Working of Metals, 1963; Behavior of Metals Under Impulsive Loads, 1954; contbr. articles to profl. publs; patentee impulsive loading, explosives applications. Charter mem. Sr. Exec. Svc. U.S., 1979. With C.E., U.S. Army, 1943-46, ETO. Recipient L.T.E. Thompson medal, 1965, William B. McLean medal, 1979, Superior Civilian Svc. medal USN, 1984, Haskell G. Wilson award, 1985, cert. of recognition Sec. Navy, 1975, merit award Dept. Navy, 1979, cert. of commendation Sec. Navy, 1981, Career Svcs. award Sec. Navy, 1988, John A. Ulrich award Am. Def. Preparedness Assn., 1991; 1st disting. fellow award Naval Weapons Ctr., 1989. Fellow ASME; mem. Am. Soc. Metals, Am. Phys. Soc., AIME, Fed. Exec. League, Sigma Xi, Tau Beta Pi, Pi Tau Sigma, Triangle. Home and Office: PO Box 1390 858 N Primavera St Ridgecrest CA 93555-7907

PEARSON, KEITH LAURENCE, retired environmental scientist; b. Chgo., Apr. 1, 1929; s. Victor R. and Ingeborg E. (Olson) P.; m. Ellen M. O'Dell, May 28, 1955; 1 child, Brian V. BA, Augustana Coll., 1951; MA, U. Ariz., 1965, PhD, 1969. Asst. prof. U. Wis., Superior, 1967-68; assoc. prof. No. Ariz. U., Flagstaff, 1968-76; environ. analyst Bur. Land Mgmt., Washington, 1976-78; environ. planner Bur. Land Mgmt., Phoenix, 1979-95, ret., 1995. Author: The Indian in American History, 1973; contbg. author: A Slice of Life, 1975; contbr. articles to profl. jours. Fellow Am. Anthropol. Assn.; mem. Soc. for Applied Anthropology. Democrat. Episcopalian. Avocation: computer programming. Home: 6370 W Donald Dr Glendale AZ 85310-4251

PEARSON, RICHARD JOSEPH, archaeologist, educator; b. Kitchener, Ont., Can., May 2, 1938; s. John Cecil and Henrietta Anne (Wallwin) P.; m. Kazue Miyazaki, Dec. 12, 1964; 1 child, Sarina Riye. B.A. in Anthropology with honours, U. Toronto, 1960; Ph.D., Yale U., 1966. Asst. prof., then assoc. prof. archaeology U. Hawaii, 1966-71; mem. faculty U. B.C., Vancouver, 1971—; now prof. archaeology U. B.C. Author: The Archaeology of the Ryukyu Islands, 1969, Higashi Ajia no Kodai Shakai to Kokogaku, 1984, Windows on the Japanese Past, Studies in Archaeology and [illegible] genheim fellow. Office: U BC, Dept Anthropology-Sociology, Vancouver, BC Canada V6T 1Z1

PEARSON, SUSAN ROSE, psychotherapist, fine arts educator, artist; b. Elmhurst, Ill., June 14, 1950; d. Ernest Elliott and Helen Julia (Drogoi) P. BA in Psychology, Calif. State U., 1992, MS in Ednl. Psychology & Counseling, 1995. Cert. pupil pers. svcs., cert. hypnotherapists. Art tchr., master artist Susan Rose Fine Art Gallery, Santa Rosa, Calif., 1979—; therapist Lifestyle with Dignity, Canoga Park, Calif., 1985-93; author, speaker, cons., inventor. *Susan Rose Pearson, MS, author, speaker and consultant has earned several prestigious awards from associations and organizations. Susan conducts exceptional national and international lectures on fears and phobias. She has contributed numerous articles to publications on the fear of flying. Susan is the author of the successful book, "21 Secrets to Stop Your Fear of Flying", now available as a 6-cassette home study course. She conducts a continuously demanding lecture circuit and maintains a busy private practice. Susan is also a fine arts educator, master artist and owner of Susan Rose Fine Art Gallery. Original and lithograph Southwestern prints are available for sale.* Mem. ACA, Am. Sch. Counselor Assn., Calif. Assn. Marriage and Family Therapists, Nat. Bd. for Cert. Clin. Hypnotherapists (cert. diplomate), Internat. Soc. Speakers, Authors and Cons., Am. Hypnosis Assn., Internat. Platform Assn., Psi Chi (life). Home and Office: PO Box 15235 Santa Rosa CA 95402-7235

PEARSON, WALTER HOWARD, marine biologist, researcher; b. Troy, N.Y., Mar. 25, 1946; s. Howard Stevenson and Mazel Mott (Brownhill) P.; m.. Cynthia-Ruth Egan, June 16, 1972 (div. Oct. 1989); children: Kristin Turnbull, Jeffrey Mott; m. Terri L. Sumner, Nov. 28, 1992. BS in Biology, Bates Coll., 1967; MS in Biology, U. Alaska, 1970; PhD in Oceanography, Oreg. State U., 1977. Fishery biologist, rschr. Nat. Marine Fisheries Svc., Sandy Hook Lab., Highlands, N.J., 1975-78; sr. rsch. scientist Battelle Marine Rsch. Lab., Sequim, Wash., 1978-88, tech. group leader marine scis. lab., 1988-91, mgr. tech. devel. program, 1991-93, sr. rsch. scientist, 1993-95, staff rsch. scientist, 1995—; program dir. environ. studies program Western Wash. U., Port Angeles Ctr., 1993—; tech. leader large multidisciplinary studies of oil spill effect. Contbr. articles on behavior of marine organisms and effects of pollution and human activity to jours. Sgt. U.S. Army, 1969-71. NSF grantee, 1967-69. Mem. Assn. Chemoreception Scis. (charter), AAAS, N.Y. Acad. Sci., Animal Behavior Soc., Crustacean Soc., Western Soc. Naturalists. Episcopalian. Avocations: hiking, aidiko, canoeing. Home: 136 E 8th St # 171 Port Angeles WA 98362-6129 Office: Battelle Marine Scis Lab 1529 W Sequim Bay Rd Sequim WA 98382-8415

PEASE, RON DEAN, artist, builder; b. Palo Alto, Calif., Sept. 12, 1949; s. Doyce Chapman and Amelia Martha (Kukay) P.; m. Dawn Anne Schmidt, Oct. 27, 1987. Student, Cabrilla Coll., 1971-72, U. Calif., Santa Cruz, 1973-74. Artist, mem. Center Street Gallery, Santa Cruz, 1980-82; co-founder, owner West Chaco Gallery, Aztec, N.Mex., 1994-98, co-juror Nat. Print & Drawings Exhbn., 1996, 97. One man shows include Ti Bldg., Santa Cruz, 1980, Valencia Coll., Orlando, Fla., 1997; exhibited in group shows at U. Calif., Santa Cruz, 1990, Sacramento Fine Arts Ctr., 1992, Bradley U., Peoria, Ill., 1993, Okla. State U., 1993, Coll. William and Mary, Va., 1994, Del Mar (Tex.) Coll., 1994, West Chaco Gallery, Aztec, N.Mex., 1996, San Juan (N.Mex.) Coll., 1996, Columbia (Mo.) Coll., 1998, Md. Fedn. of Arts, 1998, St. John's U., N.Y.C., 1998. Recipient De Mille scholarship Pastel Soc.-West Coast, Sacramento, Calif., 1992, Purchase/Merit award Bradley U., Peoria, Ill., 1993, Honorable Mention award Okla. State u., Stillwater, 1993, Silver award Calif. Art Inst., Napa, 1993. Mem. N.Y. Artist's Equity Assn.

PEASE-PRETTY ON TOP, JANINE B., community college administrator; b. Nespelern, Wash., Sept. 17, 1949; d. Benjamin and Margery Louise (Jordan) Pease; m. Sam Vernon Windy Boy, July 30, 1975 (div. Jan. 1983); children: Rosella L. Windy Boy, Sam Vernon Windy Boy; m. John Joseph Pretty On Top, Sept. 15, 1991. BA in Sociology, Anthropology, Ctrl. Wash. U., 1970; MEd, Mont. State U., 1987, EdD, 1994; HHD (hon.), Hood Coll., 1990; LLD (hon.), Gonzaga U., 1991; DHL (hon.), Teikyo/Marycrest U., 1992; EdD (hon.), Whitman Coll., 1993; HHD (hon.), Rocky Mountain Coll., 1998. Dep. dir. Wash. State Youth Commn., Olympia, 1971; tutor student svcs. Big Bend C.C., Moses Lake, Wash., 1971-72, upward bound dir., 1972-75; women's counselor Navajo C.C., Many Farms, Ariz., 1972; dir. adult & continuing edn. Crow Ctrl. Edn. Commn., Crow Agy., Mont., 1975-79; ednl. cons. Box Elder, Mont., 1979-81; dir. Indian career svc. Ea. Mont. Coll., Billings, 1981-82; pres. Little Big Horn Coll., Crow Agency, 1982—; exec. com. Am. Indian Higher Ednl. Consortium, Washington, 1983—; bd. dirs. Am. Indian Coll. Fund, N.Y.C., 1988—; sec. Indian Nations at Risk U.S. Dept. Edn., Washington, 1990-91, collaborator task force, 1990-91; 2d vice chmn. Nat. Adv. Coun. Indian Edn., Washington, 1994—. Chmn. Bighorn County Dem. Ctrl. Com., Hardin, Mont., 1983-88; mem. coun. First Crow Indian Bapt. Ch., 1989—; bd. dirs. Ctr. for Rocky Mountain West, 1998—. MacArthur fellow John D. & Catharine MacArthur Found., 1994. Mem. Nat. Indian Edn. Assn. (Indian educator of yr. 1990), Mont. Assn. Chs. (bd. dirs. 1997—), Crow Tribe Nighthawk Dance Soc. Office: Little Big Horn Coll PO Box 370 Crow Agency MT 59022-0370

PEASLAND, BRUCE RANDALL, financial executive; b. Buffalo, N.Y., Mar. 24, 1945; s. Kenneth Arthur and Edith Grace (Bristow) P.; m. Debra Myers Peasland, June 13, 1981; children: Michael John, Timothy Scott, Amanda Jean. BS, U. So. Calif., 1971, MBA in Fin., 1978; JD, Western St. U., 1983. Price and cost analyst McDonnell Douglas Corp., Long Beach, Calif., 1966-70; cost mgr. The Gillette Co., Santa Monica, Calif., 1971-78; controller Lear Siegler Inc., Santa Ana, Calif., 1978-85, British Petroleum, Hitco, Newport Beach, Calif., 1986-87; v.p. fin., dir. Control Components Inc., Rancho Santa Margarita, Calif., 1987-90; chief fin. officer MacGillivray Freeman Films, Laguna Beach, Calif., 1990-91; exec. v.p., chief fin. officer Intervest Industries Inc, Carlsbad, Calif., 1992—. Youth advisor YMCA, Dana Point, Calif., 1985—. With USMC, 1963-69. Recipient of Mgr. of Yr. award Nat. Mgmt. Assn., 1984. Fellow U. So. Calif. MBA Assn.; mem. Nat. Assn. of Accts., Nat. Mgmt. Assn. (dir. 1978-85), U. So. Calif. Trojan Club, U. So. Calif. Alumni Club. Republican. Episcopalian. Avocations: sailing, snow skiing. Home: 25211 Yacht Dr Dana Point CA 92629-1439 Office: Intervest Industries Inc 7720B El Camino Real Ste 201 Carlsbad CA 92009-8506

PEAT, RAYMOND FRANKLIN, endocrinologist, reseracher, consultant; b. Santee, Calif., Oct. 12, 1936; s. Sidney Howe and Lou Ella Vernelia (Osborn) P. BS, So. Oreg. Coll., 1956; MA, U. Oreg., 1960, PhD, 1972; DLitt, San Gabriel Coll., 1961. Founder, pres. Blake Coll., Internat. U., Mexico City, 1960-65; instr. Nat. Coll. Naturopathic Medicine, Portland, Oreg., 1976-79; prof. biology U. Veracruz, Jalapa, Mex., 1979-80; dir. rsch. Kenogen, Inc., Eugene, Oreg., 1982—; cons. alternative coll. programs, 1963-68, med. and psychiat. continuing edn. programs, Calif., Oreg., Wash., 1974-94. Author: Mind and Tissue, 1975, Generative Energy, 1991; patentee progesterone composition and treatment, DHEA arthritis treatment. Avocations: painting, sculpture. Home: PO Box 5764 Eugene OR 97405-0764

PECK, CHRISTOPHER, editor; b. Wyo., Aug. 2, 1950; m. Kate Duignan Peck; children: Sarah, Cody. Degree in Comms., Standord U., 1972. Editor The Wood River Jour., Sun Valley, Idaho; city editor, edtl. oage editor, mng. editor Times-News, Twin Falls, Idaho, 1975-79; columnist, 1979; editor Spokane (Wash.) Rev., 1982—; dir. Nat. Assn. Press Mng. Editors Assn.; mem. Soc. Am. Soc. Newspaper Editors; Pulitzer prize nominating judge. Office: The Spokane Review/Cowles Pub Co Western Farmer Stockman PO Box 2160 Spokane WA 99210-2160

PECK, DONALD HARVEY, chiropractor; b. Oak Park, Ill., July 18, 1945; s. Donald Ray and Dorothy Sylvia (LaFlamme) P.; m. Mary Evelyn Lamb, June 15, 1964 (div. 1971); children: Donald Lee, Nancy Ellen; m. Cheryl Jean Cox, July 7, 1973; children: Richard Krom Watkins Jr., Bradley Alan, Steven Edward. AA, Mt. San Antonio Coll., 1966; DC, Palmer Coll. of Chiropractic, 1970. Diplomate Nat. Bd. Chiropractic Examiners. Engring. technician Besteel Corp., Industry, Calif., 1965-66, City of Ontario, Calif., 1966-67; supr. Mercy Hosp., Davenport, Iowa, 1967-70; pvt. practice chiropractor San Bernardino and Redlands, Calif., 1971-81; pvt. practice Cottonwood, Ariz., 1981—; instr. Yavapai Coll. Clarkdale, Ariz., 1982-88 [illegible]

Canyon coun. Boy Scouts Am., 1981—; active Am. Youth Soccer Orgn., Cottonwood, 1977-92, regional commr., 1984-88; asst. varsity soccer coach Mingus Union High Sch., 1989-93; instr. trainer, chief instr. Ariz. Game and Fish Dept., Cottonwood, 1983—. Recipient Award of Merit Boy Scouts Am., 1980, Silver Beaver award, 1988; named Vol. of Yr. Verde Valley C. of C., 1987. Mem. Kiwanis (bd. dirs. 1985-87), Order of Arrow (vigil honor mem., Cert. Merit Boy Scout Am. Nat. Ct. of Honor 1990). Republican. Office: 703 S Main St #10 Cottonwood AZ 86326-4615

PECK, ELLIE ENRIQUEZ, retired state administrator; b. Sacramento, Oct. 21, 1934; d. Rafael Enriquez and Eloisa Garcia Rivera; m. Raymond Charles Peck, Sept. 5, 1957; children: Reginaldo, Enrico, Francisca Guerrero, Teresa, Linda, Margaret, Raymond Charles, Christina. Student polit. sci. Sacramento State U., 1974. Tng. services coord. Calif. Div. Hwys., Sacramento, 1963-67; tech. and mgmt. cons., Sacramento, 1968-78; expert examiner Calif. Pers. Bd., 1976-78; tng. cons. Calif. Pers. Devel. Ctr., Sacramento, 1978; spl. cons. Calif. Commn. on Fair Employment and Housing, 1978; cmty. svcs. rep. U.S. Bur. of Census, No. Calif. counties, 1978-80; spl. cons. Calif. Dept. Consumer Affairs, Sacramento, 1980-83, project dir. Golden State Sr. Discount Program, 1980-83; dir. spl. programs for Calif. Lt. Gov., 1983-90, ret., 1990; pvt. cons., 1990—; project dir. SSI/QMB Outreach Project, 1993-94; cons., project dir. nat. sr. health issues summit Congress Calif. Srs. Edn. and Rsch. Fund, 1995; project dir. various post-White House Conf. on Aging seminars and roundtables, 1995-97, program dir. SMART Coalition Calif., 1997—; coord. Calif. Sr. Legis., 1995-97. Author Calif. Dept. Consumer Affairs publ., 1981, U.S. Office Consumer Edn. publ., 1982. Bd. dirs Sacramento/Sierra Am. Diabetes Assn., 1989-90. Author: Diabetes and Ethnic Minorities: A Community at Risk. Trustee, Stanford Settlement, Inc., Sacramento, 1975-79; bd. dirs. Sacramento Emergency Housing Ctr., 1974-77, Sacramento Cmty. Svcs. Planning Coun., 1987-90, Calif. Advs. for Nursing Home Reform, 1990-96, Calif. Human Devel. Corp., 1995—; campaign workshop dir. Chicano/Latino Youth Leadership Conf., 1982—; v.p. Comision Femenil Nacional, Inc., 1987-90; del. Dem. Nat. Conv., 1976; mem. exec. bd. Calif. Dem. Cen. Com., 1977-89, mem., 1997—; chairperson ethnic minority task force Am. Diabetes Assn., 1988-90; steering com. Calif. Self-Esteem Minority Task Force, 1990-93; del. White House Conf. Aging, 1995. Recipient numerous awards including Outstanding Cmty. Svc. award Comuicaciones Unidos de Norte Atzlan, 1975, 77, Outstanding Svc. award, Chicano/Hispanic Dem. Caucus, 1979, Vol. Svc. award Calif. Human Devel. Corp., 1981, 98, Dem. of Yr. award Sacramento County Dem. Com., 1987, Outstanding Advocate award Calif. Sr. Legis., 1988, 89, Calif. Assn. of Homes for Aging, Advocacy award, 1989, Resolution of Advocacy award, League Latin-Ams. Citizens, 1989, Meritorious Svc. to Hispanic Cmty. award Comite Patriotico, 1989, Meritorious Svc. Resolution award Lt. Gov. of Calif., 1989, Cert. Recognition award Sacramento County Human Rights Commn., 1991, Tish Sommers award Older Women's League/Joint Resolution Calif. Legislature, 1993, Latino Eagle award in govt. Tomas Lopez Meml. Found., 1994; named Outstanding Advocate on Aging Issues, Calif. State Senate, 1998. Mem. Hispanic C. of C., Older Women's League, CongressCalif. Srs., Sacramento Gray Panthers, Latino Issues Forum, Latino Dem. Club Sacramento County (v.p. 1982-83). Home and Office: 2667 Coleman Way Sacramento CA 95818-4459

PECK, GAILLARD RAY, JR., defense contractor, aerospace and business consultant, business owner; b. San Antonio, Oct. 31, 1940; s. Gaillard Ray and Lois (Manning) P.; 1 child, Scott; m. Jean Adair Hilger, Dec. 23, 1962 (div. Oct. 1969); children: Gaillard III, Katherine Adair; m. Peggy Ann Lundt, July 3, 1975; children: Jennifer Caroline, Elizabeth Ann. BS, Air Force Acad., 1962; MA, Cen. Mich. U., 1976; postgrad., Nat. War Coll., Washington, 1982-83; MBA, U. Nev., Las Vegas, 1990. Lic. comml. pilot, flight instr. Commd. 2d lt. USAF, 1962, advanced through grades to col., 1983, ret., 1988, air force instr. pilot, fighter pilot, 1963-72; instr. Fighter Weapons Sch. USAF, Nellis AFB, 1972-75; fighter tactics officer Pentagon, Washington, 1975-78; aggressor pilot, comdr. 4477th Test & Evaluation Squadron, Nellis AFB, Nev., 1978-80; mil. advisor Royal Saudi Air Force, Saudi Arabia, 1980-82; dir. ops., vice comdr. Kadena Air Base, Japan, 1983-85; wing comdr. Zweibrucken Air Base, Germany, 1985-87; dep. dir. aerospace safety directorate USAF, Norton AFB, Calif., 1987-88; rsch. asst. U. Nev., Las Vegas, 1988-90; mktg. cons. Ctr. for Bus. & Econ. Rsch. U. Nev., Las Vegas, 1990; adminstr. Lung Ctr. of Nev., Las Vegas, 1991-93; bus. owner, cons. Las Vegas, 1993—; owner Great Western Aircraft Parts, LLC; acad. instr. USAF. Author: The Enemy, 1973, As Best I Recall, 1994. Recipient Silver Star, Legion of Merit (2), DFC (3), Air Medal (11). Mem. Phi Kappa Phi Nat. Honor Soc., Order of Daedalians, Red River Fighter Pilots Assn., Air Force Assn., Ky. Col., U. Nev. Las Vegas and Air Force Acad. Alumni Assn., The Ret. Officers Assn. Avocations: flying, auto restoration, computer sci., hiking, camping, family activities. Home: 1775 Sheree Cir Las Vegas NV 89119-2716

PECK, GEORGE HOLMES, public relations executive; b. Altoona, Pa., May 11, 1946; s. George Heckler and Regina (Jackson) P.; m. Barbara Ann Izydorczak, Feb. 21, 1970; children: Mark David, Heather Anne. BA, U. Montana, 1968; MA, Ball State U., 1978. Staff announcer KDRG Radio, Deer Lodge, Mont., 1963-66; staff announcer, producer KUFM Radio-TV, Missoula, Mont., 1965-68; commd. 2d lt. USAF, 1968; info. officer 4621st Air Base Group, Niagara Falls, N.Y., 1968-70; film writer, editor Aerospace Def. Command, Colorado Springs, 1970-72; chief info. Incirlik Common Def. Inst., Adana, Turkey, 1973-75; sr. pub. affairs rep. Camp New Amsterdam, Soesterberg, The Netherlands, 1975-78; dir. pub. affairs Wurtsmith AFB, Oscoda, Mich., 1978-80; spl. asst. pub. affairs Strategic Sys./B-1B Sys. Program, Dayton, Ohio, 1980-84; asst. to vice cmdr. HQ Air Force Sys. Command, Washington, 1984-86; dir. pub. affairs Aeronautical Sys. Divsn., Dayton, Ohio, 1986-88; chief media and civil affairs Hqrs. Strategic Air Command, Omaha, 1988-91; dep. pub. affairs officer UN Command, Seoul, South Korea, 1991-92; dir. pub. affairs Lowry Tng. Ctr., Denver, 1992-94; dir. pub. rels. Lowry Redevel. Authority, Denver, 1994-96; dir. cmty. rels. Columbia Presbyn./St. Luke's Med. Ctr., Denver, 1996-98; dir. pub. affairs and mktg. The Med. Ctr. of Aurora, Aurora, Colo., 1998—. Author: Understanding the Media, 1991. Bd. dirs. Aurora (Colo.) Edn. Found., 1991—, Leadership Aurora, 1991-98; bd. mgrs. Aurora YMCA, 1992-96. Mem. Pub. Rels. Soc. Am. (accredited), Air Force Assn., Soc. Strategic Air Command, Colo. Healthcare Communicators, Aurora Rotary, Aurora C. of C. Roman Catholic. Avocations: jogging, hiking, skiing. Home: 13250 E Center Ave Aurora CO 80012-3514 Office: Med Ctr of Aurora 1501 S Potomac St Aurora CO 80012-5411

PECK, JOAN KAY, systems engineer; b. Cedar Rapids, Iowa, Sept. 22, 1959; d. Leonard Allen and Mildred Jane (Keller) P. BS in Indsl. Engring., Iowa State U., 1983; MS in Space Tech., Fla. Inst. Tech., 1986. Student intern Rockwell-Collins, Cedar Rapids, 1979; coop. student Amana (Iowa) Refrigeration, 1981; sr. engr. Harris Govt. Aerospace Systems, Palm Bay, Fla., 1983-88; sr. systems engr. McDonnell Douglas Space Systems Co., Kennedy Space Ctr., Fla., 1988-94; clergy intern River City Met. Cmty. Ch., Sacramento, 1993—. Editor: Imago Dei. V.p. programming Inst. Indsl. Engrs., Ames, 1982-83; victim advocate Sexual Assault Victims Svcs., Fla. State Attys. Office, Brevard County, 1991-92. Recipient Outstanding Achievement award NASA, 1991.

PECK, PAUL LACHLAN, minister; b. Glens Falls, N.Y., Sept. 11, 1928; s. Paul Lee and Caroline Jeannette (Stanton) P.; children: Paul Barrett, Kathryn Elizabeth Peck, Gretchen. BS, U. Conn., 1952; ThD, Bernadean U., 1976; MEd, Westfield State Coll., 1983. Ordained to ministry Truth Ctr., 1972. With Proctor and Gamble Co., Watertown, N.Y., 1956-60; dir. deferred giving programs Syracuse (N.Y.) U., 1960-68, v.p., 1968-70; v.p. Fairleigh-Dickinson U., N.J., 1970-71, Manhattan Coll., Bronx, N.Y., 1971-75; founder, pastor Arete' Truth Ctr., San Diego, 1975—. Author: Footsteps Along the Path, 1978, Inherit the Kingdom, 1978, Milestones of the Way, 1978, Freeway to Health, 1980, Freeway to Work and Wealth, 1981, Freeway to Human Love, 1982, Freeway to Personal Growth, 1982, Your Dreams Count, 1990, Heroic Love Poems, 1990. Bd. dirs. Girl Scouts U.S.A., Syracuse, 1967-70; trustee, bd. dirs. Erickson Ednl. Found., 1970-75; vol. chaplain Auburn (N.Y.) State Prison, 1967-68; mem. chaplains' coun. Syracuse U., 1960-70; co-founder suicide and drug abuse prevention program Syracuse U., 1968-71, Fairleigh-Dickinson U., 1970-71, Manhattan Coll., 1971-75. Staff sgt. USNG, 1947-50. Mem. Internat. New Thought Alliance, SAR, Rotary, Knights of Malta (svc. award 1973), Masons, Shriners, Spiritual Frontiers Fellowship. Avocations: golf, book collecting. Home and Office: 3621 Vista Campana S Unit 3 Oceanside CA 92057-8203

PECK, RAYMOND CHARLES, SR., driver behavior research specialist and research administrator; b. Sacramento, Nov. 18, 1937; s. Emory Earl and Margaret Helen (Fiebiger) P.; m. Ellie Ruth Enriquez, Sept. 5, 1957; children: Teresa M. Peck Montijo, Linda M. Peck Heisler, Margaret V. Peck Henley, Raymond C., Christina M. Peck Reich. BA in Exptl. Psychology, Calif. State U., Sacramento, 1961, MA in Exptl. Psychology, 1968. Rsch. analyst Calif. Dept. Motor Vehicles, Sacramento, 1962-71, sr. rsch. analyst, program mgr., 1971-80, rsch. program specialist II, 1980, acting, chief rsch., 1980-81, rsch. program specialist II, 1981-84, chief of rsch., 1984—; statis. cons. to pvt. and pub. orgns., 1970—. Chmn. com. on operator regulation Transp. Rsch. Bd., Nat. Acad. Scis., 1976-82; past mem. editl. adv. bd. Traffic Safety Evaluation Rsch. Review; mem. editl. bd. Jour. Safety Rsch., Accident Analysis and Prevention; contbr. articles to profl. jours. Recipient Met. Life award of Hon., Nat. Safety Council, 1970, Met. Life Cert. of Commendation, 1972, A.R. Lauer award Human Factor Soc., 1981, award of Hon., award of Merit Traffic Safety Evaluation Rsch. Rev., 1983. Mem. APHA, AAAS, Am. Statis. Assn., Am. Assn. Automotive Medicine, Internat. Coun. Alcohol, Drugs and Traffic Safety, Human Factors Soc., N.Y. Acad. Sci., Soc. Epidemiologic Rsch. Democrat. Home: 2667 Coleman Way Sacramento CA 95818-4459 Office: Calif Dept Motor Vehicles 2415 1st Ave Sacramento CA 95818-2606

PECK, RICHARD EARL, academic administrator, playwright, novelist; b. Milw., Aug. 3, 1936; s. Earl Mason and Mary Amanda (Fry) P.; m. Donna Joy Krippner, Aug. 13, 1960; children: Mason, Laura. AB magna cum laude, Carroll Coll., Waukesha, Wis., 1961; MS, U. Wis., 1962, PhD, 1964. Asst. prof. U. Va., Charlottesville, 1964-67; assoc. dean, prof. Temple U., Phila., 1967-84; dean arts and scis. U. Ala., 1984-88; provost, v.p. academic affairs Ariz. State U., Tempe, 1988-89, interim pres., 1989-90; pres. U. N.Mex., Albuquerque, 1990—. Editor: Poems/Nathaniel Hawthorne, 1967, Poems/Floyd Stovall, 1967; author: (books) Final Solution, 1973 (nominated for John W. Campbell award as Best Sci. Fiction Novel of 1973 by Sci. Fiction Rsch. Assn.), Something for Joey, 1978, Passing Through, 1982, (plays) Sarah Bernhardt and the Bank, 1972, Don't Trip over the Money Pail, 1976, The Cubs Are in fourth Place and Fading, 1977, Phonecall, 1978, Bathnight, 1978, Prodigal Father, 1978, Lovers, Wives and Tennis Players, 1979, Curtains, 1980, A Party for Wally Pruett, 1982, Allergy Tests, 1982, Your Place or Mine, 1987, (films) Starting over Again, 1982, What Tangled Webs, 1974, Tutte le Strade Portanno a Roma, 1974, Il Diritto, 1974; contbr. numerous scholarly articles to lit. jours., book revs., travel articles and humor columns to newspapers and mags., papers to univ. orgns. and writers' confs. Bd. dirs. East Valley Partnership (Econ. Devel. Orgn.), Sci. and Tech., Samaritan Health Svcs.; gubernatorial appointee, bd. dirs. Ala. Humanities Found.; mem. Nat. Found. for Post-Secondary Edn.; bd. dirs. Phila. Alliance for Teaching Humanities in the Schs., Dela. Valley Faculty Exch.; adv. bd. Ea. Pa. Theater Coun.; chmn. Temple U. Bicentennial Festival of Am. Arts, 1976; mem. Univ. Negotiating Team in re: Temple-AAUP faculty contract. Capt. USMC, 1954-59. Recipient Whitman Pub. scholarship, 1959-63, Woodrow Wilson fellowship, 1961-62, Knapp Found. fellowship, 1962-63, C. Brooks Fry award Theater Americana, Altadena, Calif., 1979. Mem. MLA, Northeast MLA. Conf. Univs. and Colls. Arts, Letters and Scis., Coun. Colls. Arts and Scis., Nat. Assn. State Univs. and Land-Grant Colls. Home: 1901 Roma Ave NE Albuquerque NM 87106-3824 Office: U NMex Office of Pres Scholes Hall Rm 160 Albuquerque NM 87131*

PECK, ROBERT DAVID, educational foundation administrator; b. Devil's Lake, N.D., June 1, 1929; s. Lester David and Bernice Marie (Peterson) P.; m. Lylia June Smith, Sept. 6, 1953; children: David Allan, Kathleen Marie. BA, Whitworth Coll., 1951; MDiv, Berkeley (Calif.) Bapt. Div. Sch., 1958; ThD, Pacific Sch. Religion, 1964; postgrad., U. Calif., Berkeley, 1959-60, 62-63, Wadham Coll., Oxford U., Eng., 1963. Music tchr. pub. schs. Bridgeport, Wash., 1954-55; prof., registrar Linfield Coll., McMinnville, Oreg., 1963-69; asst. dir. Ednl. Coordinating Coun., Salem, Oreg., 1969-75; assoc. prof. Pacific Luth. U., Tacoma, 1976-79, U. Puget Sound, Tacoma, 1977; v.p. John Minter Assocs., Boulder, Colo., 1979-81, Coun. Ind. Colls., Washington, 1981-84; adminstrv. v.p. Alaska Pacific U., Anchorage, 1984-88; pres. Phillips U., Enid, Okla., 1988-94, chancellor, 1994-95; chmn. The Pres. Found. for Support of Higher Edn., Washington, 1995—; sr. assoc. InterEd, Phoenix, 1998—; pres. Phillips U. Ednl. Enterprises Inc., 1994-95; cons. Higher Edn. Exec. Assocs., Denver, 1984—; owner Tyee Marina, Tacoma, 1975-77; yacht broker Seattle, 1977-79. Author: Future Focusing: An Alternative to Strategic Planning, 1983, also articles. Dem. county chmn., McMinnville, 1968, Dem. candidate for state Ho. of Reps., McMinnville, 1969; pres. McMinnville Kiwanis, 1965-69. Cpl. Signal Corps, U.S. Army, 1952-54. Carnegie Corp. grantee, 1982, 84. Mem. Okla. Ind. Coll. Assn. (sec. 1989—). Mem. Christian Ch. Avocation: sailing, sculpting.

PECK, WILLIAM TRUMAN, retired court clerk, actor; b. Arenzville, Ill., Dec. 31, 1929; s. Lyman and Julia Matilda (Meyer) P.; m. Nancy June Watts, June 27, 1952; children: Julia, Wesley, Martha, Douglas, Kevin, Rose, Margaret. Student, San Diego C.C., 1967-69. Detention supr. Sheriff's Dept., San Diego, 1979-89; actor San Diego, 1981—; superior ct. clk. County of San Diego, 1989-97; instrnl. expert San Diego Sch. Dist., 1998—. Portrayed Lincoln in schs., chs. others, 1981—. With USMC, 1947-50. Mem. Assn. Lincoln Presenters (bd. dirs. 1998—), Civil War Round Table (pres. 1996-97), Lincoln Shrine, Living Legends. Republican. Avocations: golf, fishing, bicycling. Office: A Lincoln PO Box 124971 San Diego CA 92112-4971

PECKOL, JAMES KENNETH, consulting engineer; b. Cleve., Oct. 24, 1944; s. William John and Elinor Elizabeth (Bustard) P.; children: Erin, Robyn. BS Engring., Case Inst. Tech., 1966; MSEE, U. Wash., 1975, PhDEE, 1985. Cons. GE, Raytheon, Ling Temco Vought, RCA, Boeing Co., 1966-72; sr. staff engr. indsl. products bus. unit John Fluke Mfg. Co., Seattle, 1972-83, sr. staff engr. automated systems bus. unit, 1983-86, sr. staff engr. MR&D Bus. unit, 1986-93; founder Oxford Cons., Edmonds, Wash., 1987—; affiliate asst. prof. dept. elec. engring., affiliate asst. prof. dept. computers and software sys. U. Wash., Seattle, 1984-87, 95—, prof. dept. elec. engring., 1997—; sr. lectr., assoc. prof. dept. elec. engring. U. Aberdeen, Scotland, 1987; lectr. dept. math. and sci. Shoreline C.C., Seattle, 1989—; lectr. dept. computer sci. Edmonds (Wash.) C.C., 1992—; assoc. prof. dept. engring./computer sci. U. Nantes, Frances, 1993, 96; mem. computer sci. and elec. engring. curriculum adv. bd. Wash. State U., 1990—; lectr. various confs. and univs. Contbr. articles to profl. jours.; patentee in field. Mem. IEEE, Am. Assn. Artificial Intelligence, Assn. Computing Machinery, Tau Beta Pi. Home and Office: Oxford Cons Ltd 859 14th St SW Edmonds WA 98020-6611

PECORA, VINCENT PITT, English educator; b. Balt., Sept. 7, 1953; s. Pitt and Delores (Kowalski) P.; m. Karen A. McCauley, June 13, 1992; children: Ava, Olivia. BA, Brown U., 1975; PhD, Columbia U., 1983. Asst. prof. U. Ark., Fayetteville, 1984-85; asst. prof. U. Calif., L.A., 1985-90, assoc. prof., 1990-95, prof., dir. Ctr. for Modern and Contemporary Studies, 1995—, dir. Humanities Consortium, 1998—. Author: Self and Form in Modern Narrative, 1989, Households of the Soul, 1997. Office: U Calif 405 Hilgard Ave Los Angeles CA 90095-1530

PEDDER, NANCY SHANK, artist, writer; b. Indpls., Feb. 4, 1942; d. William Mullen and Mary Anne (Sheridan) S.; m. William Robert Pedder, Feb. 24, 1968; children: Shannon, Brendan. BS in Consumer and Family Scis., Purdue U., 1964. Group chief operator Ind. Bell Telephone, Indpls., South Bend, 1964-65; sr. personnel clk. Varian Assocs., Palo Alto, Calif., 1966-68; personnel staffing specialist U.S. Govt., Washington, 1968-69; freelance artist, writer Oakland, Calif., 1969—; inspirational pub. spkr. Author: A Matter of Heart, 1998. Vol. Oakland Mus., 1996—. Avocations: swimming, reading, travel.

PEDDY, JULIE ANN, admininstrative officer. MPA, Ind. U., Gary, 1984. Benefit authorizer trainee U.S. HHS, Chgo., 1979-80; investigator U.S. Office of Personnel Mgmt., Chgo., 1980-81, Def. Investigative Svc., Chgo., 1981-83; investigator, sr. resident agt. Def. Investigative Svc., Hammond, Ind., 1983-84; supervisory investigator, team chief Def. Investigative Svc., Chgo., 1984-89; spl. agt. in charge Def. Security Svc. (formerly Def. Investigative Svc.), Seattle, 1989-98; adminstr. officer Northwest Fisheries Sci. Ctr., Seattle, Wash., 1998—; mem. Seattle Fed. Exec. Bd., 1990-98, chairwoman, 1995-96. Bd. dirs. Lynwood (Ill.) Terr. Condominium Assn., 1982-89, Civic Light Opera, Seattle, 1996—, treas., CFO, 1997-98. Mem. ASPA, Ind. U. Alumni Assn. (life), Pi Alpha Alpha. Protestant. Avocations: fishing, cooking, quilting, music, crafts. E-mail: peddyj0l@sprynet.com. Office: Northwest Fisheries Sci Ctr 2775 Montlake Blvd E Seattle WA 98112-2013

PEDEN, LYNN ELLEN, marketing executive; b. L.A., Mar. 1, 1946; d. Orlan Sidney and Erna Lou (Harris) Friedman; m. Ernest Peden, Aug. 1994. Student UCLA, 1963-65, 71-72, Willis Bus. Coll., 1965-66, Fin. Schs. Am., 1982, Viewpoints Inst., 1970-71. Office mgr. Harleigh Sandler Co., L.A., 1965-67; customer svc. Investors Diversified Svcs., West L.A., Calif., 1968-76; exec. sec. McCulloch Oil Corp., West L.A., 1976; mgr. publs. Security 1st Group, Century City, Calif., 1976-80; office mgr. Morehead & Co., Century City, 1980-81; dir. mktg., mgr. customer svc. Ins. Mktg. Services, Santa Monica, Calif., 1981-82; v.p. Decatur Petroleum Corp., Santa Monica, 1982-83; asst. v.p., broker svcs., dir. Angeles Corp., L.A., 1984-87; asst. to pres. Pacific Ventures, Santa Monica, 1988-90; asst. to pres. La Grange Group, West L.A., 1990-95; property mgmt. asst. Desert Resort Mgmt., Palm Desert, Calif., 1997—. Mem. Migi Car Am. Club (sec., newsletter editor). Fin. and ins. writer; contbr. poetry to UCLA Literary Mag., 1964. Home: 78580 Villeta Dr La Quinta CA 92253-3856

PEDERSEN, GAYLEN, genealogy organization administrator; b. Salt Lake City, Mar. 4, 1934; s. Oliver Cowdery and Phoebe Gold (Gedge) P.; m. Mary Ann Hunter, Sept. 13, 1957; children: Mark Alan, Gordon Hunter, Gay Lynn, Eric David, Scott Douglas, Julie Ann, Dale Ryan. BS in Physics, Brigham Young U., 1959. Missionary Ch. of Jesus Christ of Latter-day Saints, New England states, 1954-56; instr. math. Cen. Utah Vocat. Sch., Provo, Utah, 1958-59; assoc., design engr. Boeing Co., Seattle, Washington, 1959-62; gen. mgr. Ogden Air Logistics Ctr., Hill Air Force Base (Utah), 1962-87; sr. instr. Shipley Assocs., Bountiful, Utah, 1987-89; pres., CEO Pedersen Pub., Bountiful, 1987-89; pres., chmn. bd. Gaylen Pedersen Family Orgn., Bountiful, 1976—; dir. mktg. Redcon-Resource Data Consultants, Bountiful, 1989-90; USAF sr. mgmt. staff Ogden Air Logistics Ctr., Hill Air Force Base, 1983-87, USAF mid. mgr., 1976-83; pvt. cons., 1990—. Author: System Level, Post Production Support: Tendencies, Conditions and Principles, 1988; editor: Nutritional Herbology, Vol. I, 1987, Vol. II, 1988. Instl. rep. Boy Scouts Am., Bountiful, 1965-67, basketball coach Explorer Scouts, 1980-87; bishop Ch. Jesus Christ Latter-day Saints, 1969-73. With U.S. Army, 1956-58. Republican. Avocations: gardening, genealogical research, basketball, reading. Office: Gaylen Pedersen Family Orgn 1311 Indian Trail Cir Bountiful UT 84010-1461

PEDERSEN, KNUD GEORGE, economics educator, academic administrator; b. Three Creeks, Alta., Can., June 13, 1931; s. Hjalmar Neilsen and Anna Marie (Jensen) P.; m. Joan Elaine Vanderwarker, Aug. 15, 1953 (dec. 1988); children: Greg, Lisa; m. Penny Ann Jones, Dec. 31, 1988. Diploma in Edn., Provincial Normal U., 1952; BA, U. B.C., 1959; MA, U. Wash., 1964; PhD, U. Chgo., 1969; LLD (hon.), McMaster U., 1996. Asst. prof. econs. of edn. U. Toronto; asst. prof. econs. of edn., assoc. dir. U. Chgo., 1970-72; dean, assoc. prof., then prof. U. Victoria, B.C., 1972-75; acad. v.p., prof. U. Victoria, 1975-79; pres., vice-chancellor, prof. Simon Fraser U., Vancouver, B.C., 1979-83; pres., prof. U. B.C., Vancouver, 1983-85; pres., vice-chancellor U. Western Ont., London, Can., 1985-94, prof. econs. of edn., 1985-96; interim pres. U. No. B.C., 1995; founding pres., vice-chancellor Royal Roads U., 1995-96; chancellor U. No. B.C., 1998—; bd. dirs. Assn. Univs. and Colls., Can., 1979-84, chmn., 1989-91; bd. dirs. Vancouver Bd. Trade, 1983-85; pres. Can. Club Vancouver, 1983-84; mem. coun. trustees Inst. for Rsch. on Pub. Policy, Ottawa, Ont., Can., 1983-89; chmn. Coun. Ont. Univs., 1989-91. Author: The Itinerant Schoolmaster, 1972; contbr. chpts. to books, numerous articles to profl. jours. Apptd. officer Order of Can., Order of Ont.; recipient 125th Anniversary of Confcdn. of Can. medal; fellow Ford Found., 1965-68, Can. Coll. Tchrs., 1977, Royal Soc. for Encouragement of Arts, 1984; also 11 major scholarships. Mem. Semiahmoo Golf and Country Club. Avocations: golf, fishing, gardening.

PEDERSEN, MARTIN ALBERT, consulting land surveyor; b. Rawlins, Wyo., Dec. 2, 1946; s. Rasmus and Ella (Rasmussen) P.; m. Karen Louise Bond, Aug. 26, 1967 (div. 1978); children: David Frank, Jennifer Louise; m. Patricia Ann Smith, Mar. 1, 1980; 1 child, Hans Rasmus. Student, U. Wyo., 1965. Registered land surveyor, Wyo., Mont., Idaho, Nev., Ariz., N.Mex., N.D., S.D., Colo., Calif., U.S. mineral surveyor. Surveyor Robert Jack Smith & Assocs., Rawlins, 1966-75, prin., 1975—. Scoutmaster Boy Scouts Am., Rawlins, 1969-75, dist. chmn., 1975-81; active Rawlins Search and Rescue Dive Team; mem. Christ Luth. Ch., Rotary. Mem. Wyo. Assn. Cons. Engrs. and Surveyors (pres. 1978), Wyo. State Bd. for Registration for Profl. Engrs. & Profl. Land Surveyors, Profl. Land Surveyors Wyo. (pres. 1980-81), Am. Congress Surveying and Mapping, Wyo. Engring. Soc. (sec.-treas. 1988-96), Ducks Unltd., Elks. Avocations: scuba diving, photography, hunting, fishing, flying. Home: 207 E Heath St Rawlins WY 82301-4307 Office: Robert Jack Smith Assocs Inc PO Box 1104 1015 Harshman St Rawlins WY 82301-4918

PEDERSON, CARRIE ANN, systems engineer, product trainer; b. Port Townsend, Wash., Dec. 12, 1957; d. Joe Dell and Shirley Ann (Harris) Wall; m. Joseph Allen Bauer, May 5, 1979 (div. 1986); m. Roald Leif Pederson, May 23, 1987. AS in Computer Programming, So. Ohio Coll., 1981; cert. in data processing, Live Oaks Joint Vocat. Sch., Milford, Ohio, 1976; BBA in Info. Systems, Dallas Bapt. U., 1993. Programmer Procter & Gamble Co., Cin., 1976-87; systems analyst AMP Inc., Harrisburg, Pa., 1987-89; computer sys. cons. James Rich Computing, Corsicana, Tex., 1989-91; programmer/analyst Guardian Industries, Corsicana, 1991-93; project mgr. Intrix Systems Group, Sacramento, 1993-94; sys. engr., product trainer Objective Sys. Integrators, Folsom, Calif., 1994—; prof. Navarro Coll., Corsicana, 1989-93. Vol. Updowntowners, Cin., 1986-87; sponsor Ind. Order Odd Fellows Children's Home, Corsicana, 1989-90. Mem. Newcomers Club (corr. sec. 1990). Republican. Mem. Christian Ch. Avocation: community activities. Home: 110 Kershaw Ct Folsom CA 95630-8611

PEDESKY, GERALDINE GOLICK, design project professional; b. Hayward, Calif., Oct. 27, 1935; d. Charles Anthony and Dolores Irene (Lemon) Golick; m. Charles Francis Pedesky, Nov. 10, 1960. BA, San Jose State Coll., 1957. Flight attendant Trans Continental Airlines, Burbank, Calif., 1958-62; office mgr. The Hertz Corp., L.A., 1964-77; v.p. adminstr. Vitousek Real Estate Sch., Honolulu, 1977-94; project mgr. Philpotts & Assoc., Honolulu, 1994—; mem. sec. Hawaii Assn. Real Estate Schs., Honolulu, 1977-93. Trustee Bernice Pauahi Bishop Mus., Honolulu, 1988-94, mem. exec. com., 1994; mem. Bishop Mus. Assn., Honolulu, 1983-87 (past pres.), Bishop Mus. Svc. League, Honolulu, 1977-83 (pres. 1982); bd. dirs. Outrigger Duke Kahanamoku Found., Honollulu, 1986-94 (pres.1989). Mem. Outrigger Canoe Club (bd. dirs., sec.-treas., v.p. ops.), Honolulu Acad. Arts, Contemporary Mus. Art, Nature Conservancy, Bishop Mus. Assn. Avocations: outrigger canoe paddling (state champion, 1980, 83, 85-91, 93), hiking, runnning. Office: Philpotts & Assocs 925 Bethel St Ste 200 Honolulu HI 96813-4307

PEDOLSKY, ALAN ROBERT, revenue officer; b. Bronx, N.Y., Aug. 14, 1946; s. Hyman and Hannah (Wiesner) P.; m. Joan Kathleen Anderson, July 21, 1979; stepchildren: Stacie L. Shalvay, Michael Warwas. BA, Long Island U., 1968. Tchr. Blkyn. Sch. Spl. Children, 1969-70; vol. U.S. Peace Corps., Kabul, Afghanistan, 1970-71; revenue officer IRS, N.Y.C., 1972-73, New Rochelle, N.Y., 1973-74, Tucson, 1974—; instr. IRS, Phoenix, 1983—, IRS Speakers Bur., 1988. Jewish. Avocations: photography, collectibles, travel, fishing. Office: IRS 300 W Congress St Ste 46 Tucson AZ 85701-1395

PEEBLES, CAROL LYNN, immunology researcher; b. Wellington, Kans., Jan. 20, 1941; d. Harry Alexander and Phyllis Dorothy (Pyle) P. BA, Kans. State Coll. of Pittsburg, 1962, MS, 1964; cert. med. technology, St. Francis Hosp., Wichita, Kans., 1965. Med. technologist St. Francis Hosp., Wichita, 1965-74; lab. supr. allergy and immunology Scripps Clinic and Rsch. Found., La Jolla, Calif., 1974-77; sr. rsch. asst. Autoimmune Disease Ctr. Scripps Clinic and Rsch. Found., La Jolla, 1982—; lab. supr. rheumatology lab. U.

Colo. Health Scis. Ctr., Denver, 1977-82. Author workshop manual; contbr. articles to sci. publs. Mem. Am. Coll. Rheumatology, AAAS, Am. Soc. Microbiology, Am. Soc. Med. Tech., Am. Soc. Clin. Pathology. Avocation: photography. Office: Scripps Rsch Inst Rm SBR 6 10550 N Torrey Pines Rd La Jolla CA 92037-1000

PEEL, JOHN MILTON, composer, educator; b. Ft. Worth, Oct. 7, 1946; s. Joe Howard and Lamora Alma (Garret) P.; m. Ellen Tolles, Dec. 15, 1990 (div. Mar. 1997). BA, U. Tex., Arlington, 1969; MA, Princeton U., 1972, PhD, 1982. Vis. prof. Swarthmore (Pa.) Coll., 1975-76; asst. prof. Boston U., 1977-78; assoc. prof. U. Pitts., 1980-89; prof. music, Irene Gerlinger Swindells chair Willamette U., Salem, Oreg., 1990—; artistic dir. New Music at Willamette, 1990—. Composer: (orch. and voice) Three French Texts, 1976 (NEA award 1976), The Pythia, 1980, (orch.) Diptych, 1985, (string quartet) Novellette, 1995, (opera oratorio) Voces Vergilianae, 1998. Music Competition grantee Martha Baird Rockefeller, 1979, NEA, 1980, Pa. Coun. on Arts, 1980, 87, Jerome Found., 1985. Mem. Am. Music Ctr., Coll. Music Soc. Office: Willamette U Music Dept 900 State St Salem OR 97301-3931

PEEPLES, MAIJA WOOF, artist; b. Riga, Latvia, Nov. 21, 1942; d. Herberts Amandus and Biruta (Slavcitajs) Gegeris; came to U.S., 1950, naturalized, 1955; student San Francisco Art Inst., 1963; B.A., U. Calif. at Davis, 1964, M.A., 1965; m. Earl Peeples, July 29, 1972. Artist; one-woman shows at Candy Store Gallery, Calif., annually 1965-91, Nelson Gallery, U. Calif. at Davis, 1972, Crocker Art Mus., Sacramento, 1980, Meml. Union Gallery, 1976, Solano Community Coll., 1972, Matthews Art Center, Tempe, Ariz., 1971, "World of Woof" toured Ariz., 1971-72, Sigi Krauss Gallery, London, Eng., 1970, Hansen-Fuller Gallery, San Francisco, 1969, LaJolla (Calif.) Mus. Art, 1967, Works Gallery, San Jose, Calif., 1984, Rubicon Gallery, Los Altos, Calif., 1983, J'Nette Gardens Gallery, Oakland, Calif., 1986-88, Head-Royce Gallery, Oakland, 1988, Nev. Mus. Art, Reno, 1991, Anya Horvath Gallery, Sacramento, Calif., 1991-94, Solomon/DuBrick Gallery, Sacramento, Calif., 1995-98; exhibited in group shows: Sea of Japan 1973-74, San Francisco Mus., 1973, Sacramento Sampler-Crocker Art Gallery, Sacramento and Sau Paulo, Brazil, 1972, Am. River Coll., 1976, Calif. Sec. State's Office, 1976, De Saisset Art Gallery, U. Santa Clara (Calif.), 1980, Susan Whitney Gallery, Regina, Sask., Can., 1980, Crocker Art Mus., Sacramento, 1982, Gallery Imago, San Francisco, 1986-88, James/Schubert Gallery Houston, 1988, V.C. Davis, 1992, J. Maddux-Parker, Sacramento, 1992, Sherry Frumkin Gallery, L.A., 1993, I. Wolk Gallery, St. Helena, Calif., 1993-94, (ceramic show) Natsoulas Gallery, Davis, 1995; represented in permanent collections at LaJolla Mus., Crocker Art Gallery, Sacramento, Matthews Art Center, Tempe, Candy Store Gallery, Folsom, Nev. Mus. Art, Reno, San Francisco Mus. Art. Teaching, Laney Coll., Oakland, 1968-69, Sierra Coll., Rocklin, Calif., 1970-72, U. Calif. at Davis Extension, 1972; lectr. Calif. Art Assn., 1983. Recipient Ceramics Excellence Prize Calif. State Fair Art Show, 1974, others. Mem. Artists Stable of Solomon/Dubnick Gallery, Sacramento. Home: 2586 King Richard Dr El Dorado Hills CA 95762

PEET, PHYLLIS IRENE, women's studies educator; b. Winnipeg, Man., Can., Mar. 3, 1943; came to the U.S., 1948; d. Harold Parsons and Gladys Mae (Riley) Harrison; m. Thomas Peter Richman, June 14, 1963 (div. 1969); m. Charles Francis Peet, Sept. 9, 1972. BA in Art, Calif. State U., Northridge, 1972; MA in Art History, U. Calif., L.A., 1976, PhD in Art History, 1987. Sec. L.A. County Supr. Kenneth Hahn, 1960-68; assoc. in art history L.A. County Mus. Art, 1974-75; asst. dir., curator Grunwald Ctr. for the Graphic Arts, U. Calif., L.A., 1975-78; Am. art scholar High Mus. Art, Atlanta, 1984-90; instr. women's studies Monterey (Calif.) Peninsula Coll., 1986—, dir., instr. women's programs/women's studies, 1989—; dirs.' adv. com. The Art Mus. of Santa Cruz County, 1981-84, 89-94; vis. lectr. Calif. State U., Fresno, fall 1984; program coord. conf. Inst. for Hist. Study, San Francisco, 1987; lectr. bd. studies in art U. Calif. Santa Cruz, 1991-95. Author, co-curator, editor, compiler: (book and exhbn.) The American Personality: The Artist Illustrator of Life in the United States, 1860-1930, 1976; author, curator: (book and exhbn.) American Women of the Etching Revival, 1988; co-author: American Paintings in the High Museum of Art, 1994; contbr. articles to profl. pubis. including Am. Nat. Biography, Fitzroy Dict. of Women Artists, 1997, Dict. of Literary Biography, 1998. Vol., activist Dem. Party, L.A., 1960-66, Peace and Freedom Party, L.A., 1967-71; vol. Dem. Party Candidates, Santa Cruz, Calif., 1979-96, Santa Cruz Action Network, 1980-85; mem. nominating com. Girl Scouts of Am., Monterey Bay, 1991-93. Rockefeller Found. fellow U. Calif. L.A., 1978-79, 79-80, Dickson grantee U. Calif. L.A., 1981-82; recipient Women Helping Women award Soroptimists, Monterey and Carmel, Calif., 1991, 95, Allen Griffin for Excellence in Edn. award Cmty. Found. of Monterey County, 1993, Quality of Life award Econ. Devel. Corp., Monterey, 1994. Mem. NOW, AAUW, Nat. Women's Studies Assn., Inst. for Hist. Study, Western Assn. Women Historians, Women's Internat. League for Peace and Freedom, Monterey Bay Women's Caucus for Art (founder, bd. dirs. 1988-93). Avocations: print collecting, photography. Office: Womens Programs Monterey Peninsula Coll 980 Fremont St Monterey CA 93940-4704

PEIRANO, LAWRENCE EDWARD, civil engineer; b. Stockton, Calif., May 13, 1929; s. Frank Lloyd and Esther Marie (Carigiet) P.; m. Mary Ellen Alabaster, July 26, 1952; children: Thomas Lawrence, Ellen Marie. BSCE, U. Calif., Berkeley, 1951, MSCE, 1952. Registered profl. engr., Calif.; diplomate Am. Acad. Environ. Engrs. Assoc. civil engr. Calif. Div. Water Resources, 1952-53; with Kennedy Engrs., Inc., San Francisco, 1955-94, project mgr., 1960-79, v.p., chief environ. engr., 1974-79; dir. ops. Kennedy/Jenks Engrs., Inc., San Francisco, 1979-86; sr. v.p., regional mgr. Kennedy/Jenks/Chilton, Inc., San Francisco, 1986-90; exec. v.p., chief tech. officer Kennedy/Jenks Cons., Inc. (formerly Kennedy Engrs., Inc.), San Francisco, 1990-94, also bd. dirs., chmn. bd., 1972-94; ret., 1994; spl. lectr. san. engring. U. Calif., Berkeley, 1976. Served in U.S. Army, 1953-55, Korea, Okinawa. James Monroe McDonald scholar, 1950-51; recipient Trustees' citation U. Calif., Berkeley, 1996. Fellow ASCE (life); mem. Water Environ. Fedn., U. Calif. Alumni Assn., Sierra Club, Tau Beta Pi, Chi Epsilon. Republican. Roman Catholic. Home: 3435 Black Hawk Rd Lafayette CA 94549-2326

PEIRSON, GEORGE EWELL, film producer, writer, art director, educator; b. L.A., May 16, 1957; s. Malcolm Alan and Beth (Wanlass) P. BFA, Art Ctr. Coll. of Design, Pasadena, Calif., 1986. Photographer Griffith Park Observatory, L.A., 1981-84; owner, art dir. Peirson to Peirson Studio, Winnetka, Calif., 1983—; pres. Anubis Prodns., Inc., Las Vegas, 1997—; instr. Art Workshops, L.A., 1988-89, Learning Tree U., Chatsworth, Calif., 1990-93. Art dir., films include Valentine's Day, 1986, Private Demons, 1986, The Courtyard, 1987, Hope of the Future, Escape from Lethargia, 1988, Time Scrambler, 1988, Star Quest, 1988, Star Runner, 1989, The World of Early Bird, 1989, The Deadly Avenger, 1991, Hell Comes to Frogtown II, 1991, The Minister's Wife, 1991, Eye of the Stranger, 1992, Star Runners, 1992, Monty, 1992, Guyver, Dark Hero, 1993, Tiger Mask, The Star, 1994, Dragon Fury, 1994, Arizona Werewolf, 1994, Drifting School, 1994; prodr., films include Jurassic Women, 1994, Wolves Carnival, 1995, King of Hearts, 1995, Rollergator, 1995, Lord Protector, 1996, Lancelot: Guardian of Time, 1997, The Gift, 1998; writer, films include Shalakan, 1997, Final Game, 1997. Mem. Assn. for Astron. Arts (bd. mem., v.p. 1987-89), Costumers Guild West, Assn. of Sci. Fiction and Fantasy Artists. Republican. Avocations: computers, skiing, running, bicycling, scuba diving. Office: Peirson to Peirson Studio 7657 Winnetka Ave Ste 301 Canoga Park CA 91306-2677 Corp Office: Anubis Prodns Inc 3305 Spring Mountain Rd # 60A Las Vegas NV 89102-8609

PEJZA, JOHN PHILIP, priest, academic administrator; b. Neshkoro, Wis., Aug. 5, 1934; s. Philip Peter and Regina Rosalie (Dombrowski) P. BA, Villanova U., 1957, MA, 1961, M of Secondary Sch. Sci., 1964; MA, U. San Francisco, 1981; EdD, U. San Diego, 1987. Joined Order of St. Augustine, Roman Cath. Ch., 1952; ordained priest, 1961; cert. tchr. and adminstr., Calif. Tchr. Malvern (Pa.) Prep Sch., 1961-63; tchr. St. Augustine High Sch., San Diego, 1963-64, 70-75, prin., 1983-88; tchr., asst. prin. Villanova Prep. Sch., Ojai, Calif., 1964-70, pres., 1988—, prin. Cen. Cath. High Sch., Modesto, Calif., 1975-80, Marian High Sch., San Diego, 1981-83; secondary cons. Diocese of Stockton, Calif., 1977-80; exec. sec. province planning commn., Province of St. Augustine, Order of St. Augustine, L.A., 1975-79; mem. priests' senate Diocese of San Diego, 1981-85, province dir. edn., 1994—. Contbr. articles to profl. jours. Bd. dirs. St. Augustine H.S., San Diego, 1994—, Ojai chpt. Am. Heart Assn., 1994. Mem. Nat. Cath. Ednl. Assn. (regional assoc. secondary divsn. 1987—), Augustinian Secondary Edn. Assn. (exec. sec. 1989-97), Coun. Advancement and Support of Edn., Internat. Radio Club Am. (pres. 1977-79), Rotary (bd. dirs. Ojai West 1994-98, pres. 1995-96, dist. 5240 interact chmn. 1996-99), Phi Delta Kappa. Avocations: reading, photography, genealogy. Office: Villanova Prep Sch 12096 N Ventura Ave Ojai CA 93023-3909

PELINE, VAL P., engineering executive; b. Hooversville, Pa., July 12, 1930. BS, U. Pitts., 1952, MS, 1954; PhD, Ohio State U., 1958. From rsch. specialist to mgr. Lockheed Missile & Space Co., 1958-66, mgr. space sys. tech., 1966-78, v.p., 1978-84, v.p., gen. mgr. Space Sys. Div., 1984-86, pres. Space Sys. Div., 1986-87, group pres. Electronic Sys., 1987-95; pres., CEO Stanford Telecomm., 1995—; bd. dirs. Stanford Telecomm. Inc. & Electronics Industry Assn. Mem. Nat. Acad. Engrs., Nat. Space Club, Am. Inst. Aeronautics & Astronauts; fellow Am. Astronaut Soc. Office: Stanford Telecommunications 1221 Crossman Ave Sunnyvale CA 94089-1103*

PELKY, LANCE A., financial planner, educator; b. San Diego, Jan. 10, 1960; s. Robert and Joan P.; m. Eileen; children: Mara, Madison. Prin. Lance Pelky & Assocs., San Diego. Author: The Retiree's Complete Guide to the Secrets to a Secure and Peaceful Retirement. Office: Lance Pelky & Assocs 9171 Towne Centre Dr Ste 435 San Diego CA 92122-1238

PELOSI, NANCY, congresswoman; b. Balt., Mar. 26, 1941; d. Thomas J. D'Alesandro Jr.; m. Paul Pelosi; children: Nancy Corinne, Christine, Jacqueline, Paul, Alexandra. Grad., Trinity Coll. Former chmn. Calif. State Dem. Com., 1981; committeewoman Dem. Nat. Com., 1976, 80, 84; fin. chmn. Dem. Senatorial Campaign Com., 1987; mem. 99th-102d Congresses from 5th Calif. dist., 1987-1992, 106th Congress from 8th Calif. dist., 1993—; mem. appropriations com., subcoms. on labor, HHS and edn., fgn. ops., mem. intelligence select com. Office: US House of Rep 2457 Rayburn Bldg Washington DC 20515-0508*

PELOTTE, DONALD EDMOND, bishop; b. Waterville, Maine, Apr. 13, 1945; s. Norris Albert and Margaret Yvonne (LaBrie) P. AA, Eymard Sem. and Jr. Coll., Hyde Park, N.Y., 1965; BA, John Carroll U., 1969; MA, Fordham U., 1971, PhD, 1975. Ordained priest Roman Cath. Ch., 1972. Provincial superior Blessed Sacrament, Cleve., from 1978; ordained coadjutor bishop Diocese of Gallup, N.Mex., 1986-90, bishop, 1990—; nat. bd. dirs. Maj. Superiors of Men, Silver Spring, Md., 1981-86, Tekakwitha Conf., Great Falls, Mont., 1981—. Author: John Courtney Murray: Theologian in Conflict, 1976. 1st native Am. bishop. Mem. Cath. Theol. Soc. Am., Am. Cath. Hist. Soc. *

PELTASON, JACK WALTER, foundation executive, educator; b. St. Louis, Aug. 29, 1923; s. Walter B. and Emma (Hartman) P.; m. Suzanne Toll, Dec. 21,1946; children: Nancy Hartman, Timothy Walter H., Jill K. BA, U. Mo., 1943, MA, 1944, LLD (hon.), 1978; AM, Princeton U., 1946, PhD, 1947; LLD (hon.), U. Md., 1979, Ill. Coll., 1979, Gannon U., 1980, U. Maine, 1980, Union Coll., 1981, Moorehead (N.D.) State U., 1980; LHD (hon.), 1980, Ohio State U., 1980, Mont. Coll. Mineral Scis. and Tech., 1982, Buena Vista Coll., 1982, Assumption Coll., 1983, Chapman Coll., 1986, U. Ill., 1989. Asst. prof. Smith Coll., Mass., 1947-51; asst. prof. polit. sci. U. Ill., Urbana, 1951-52, assoc. prof., 1953-59, dean Coll. Liberal Arts and Scis., 1960-64, chancellor, 1967-77; vice chancellor acad. affairs U. Calif., Irvine, 1964-67, chancellor, 1984-92; pres. U. Calif. System, Oakland, 1992-95, Am. Coun. Edn., Washington, 1977-84; prof. emeritus dept. politics and soc. U. Calif., Irvine, 1995—; pres. Bren Found., 1997—; Cons. Mass. Little Hoover Commn., 1950. Author: The Missouri Plan for the Selection of Judges, 1947, Federal Courts and the Political Process, 1957, Fifty-eight Lonely Men, 1961, Understanding the Constitution, 14th edit., 1997, orig. edition, 1949, (with James M. Burns) Government By the People, 17th edit., 1997, orig. edit., 1952; contbr. articles and revs. to profl. jours. Recipient James Madison medal Princeton U., 1982. Fellow Am. Acad. Arts and Scis.; mem. Am. Polit. Sci. Assn. (council 1952-54), Phi Beta Kappa, Phi Kappa Phi, Omicron Delta Kappa, Alpha Phi Omega, Beta Gamma Sigma. Home: 18 Whistler Ct Irvine CA 92612-4069 Office: U Calif Dept Politics and Society Social Sci Plaza Irvine CA 92697

PELTON, HAROLD MARCEL, mortgage broker; b. Montreal, Que., Can., Jan. 24, 1922; s. Grover Cleveland and Denise (Pigeon) P.; m. Frances Farley, June 1947 (div. 1968); children: Mary Virginia Joyner, Diane Jean Slagowski; m. Virginia L. King, July 11, 1970. Student, L.A. City Coll., 1948-49, Anthony Schs., Van Nuys, Calif., 1966. Lic. real estate real broker, Calif. Stockbroker, agt. Mitchum, Jones, Templeton Assurance Co., L.A., 1957-60; owner Assurance Investment Co., Van Nuys, Calif., 1960-65; sales syndicator TSI Investment Co., L.A., 1965-69; pres., owner Univest Co., Beverly Hills, Calif., 1970-72, Am. Oil Recovery, L.A., 1973-79; v.p. Newport Pacific Funding Co., Newport Beach, Calif., 1979-81; chmn. bd. dirs. TD Publs., El Toro, Calif., 1981-83; pres., broker HP Fin., Inc., Laguna Hills, Calif., 1983—. Contbg. editor Am. Oil Recovery newspaper, 1973-79; editor Trust Deed Jour., 1981-83. Served with U.S. Army, 1942-46, PTO. Mem. L. A. Mus. Art, Laguna Hills C. of C., Kiwanis, Toastmasters. Republican. Avocations: photography, travel, reading, computers. Office: HP Fin Inc 24942 Georgia Sue Laguna Hills CA 92653-4323

PELTZER, ERIC THOMAS, sculptor; b. Lancaster, Calif., Feb. 4, 1963; s. Thomas Wayne and Marsha Vickers (Hodgson) P. BA cum laude, Occidental Coll., 1985. adj. prof. sculpture Occidental Coll., L.A., 1993-95. One-man shows include Art Barn Gallery, L.A., 1992, 93, Kings Art Ctr., Hanford, Calif., 1994, Coll. of the Sequoias, Visalia, Calif., 1994; works exhibited at Roland Am. Corp., Commerce, Calif., Harbor View Hotel, Hong Kong, Facey Med. Clinic, Northridge, Calif., Yamamoto Eye Clinic, Saijo, Japan, MK Bldg., Boise, Gottschalks Corp., Visalia, Calif. Mem. Internat. Sculpture Ctr. E-mail: epeltzer@oxy.edu. Home and Office: 2857 Reposa Ln Altadena CA 91001-1732

PENA, ANTONIA MURILLO, physician, radiologist; b. San Diego, July 18, 1946; d. Blas and Elvira (Murillo) Pena. B.A., Loma Linda U., Riverside, Calif., 1968; M.D., 1973. Diplomate Nat. Bd. Radiology. Intern, White Meml. Med. Ctr., Los Angeles, 1973-74, resident, 1974-77; radiologist Paradise Valley Hosp., National City, Calif., 1978-79; neuroradiology fellow Los Angeles County-U.So. Calif. Med. Ctr., 1977-78, 79-80; radiologist Arlington Radiology Med. Group, Riverside, Calif., 1980—; attending staff Riverside Gen. Hosp. U. Med. Ctr., 1980—; assoc. staff Parkview Community Hosp., 1980—; med. dir. Magnetic Resonance Imaging Ctr., Parkview Community Hosp., 1985—; cons. radiologist Computerized Diagnostic Med. Group of Riverside, 1980—; cons. Veitch Student Health Ctr., Riverside, 1980—. Mem. Radiol. Soc. N.Am., Am. Coll. Radiology, Calif. Radiol. Soc., AMA, Calif. Med. Assn., Am. Assn. Women Radiologists, Inland Radiology Soc., Am. Soc. Neuroradiology (sr.), Riverside County Med. Soc. Republican. Seventh-Day Adventist. Office: 9851 Magnolia Ave Riverside CA 92503-3528 Address: PO Box 2191 Sun City CA 92586-1191

PEÑA, FEDERICO FABIAN, retired federal official; b. Laredo, Tex., Mar. 15, 1947; s. Gustavo J. and Lucille P.; m. Ellen Hart, May 1988. BA, U. Tex., Austin, 1969, JD, 1972. Bar: Colo. 1973. Ptnr. Pena & Pena, Denver, 1973-83; mayor City and County of Denver, 1983-91; pres. Peña Investment Advisors, Inc., Denver, 1991-93; sec. U.S. Dept. of Energy, Washington, 1993-98; sr. advisor Vestar Capital Ptnrs., Denver, 1998—; assoc. Harvard U. Ctr. for Law and Edn., Cambridge, Mass.; mem. Colo. Bd. Law Examiners. Mem. Colo. Ho. of Reps., 1979-83, Dem. leader, 1981. Named Outstanding House Dem. Legislator, Colo. Gen. Assembly, 1981. Roman Catholic.

PEÑA, JUAN JOSÉ, interpreter; b. Hagerman, N.Mex., Dec. 13, 1945; s. Rosa Peña; m. Petra Cervantes, Dec. 22, 1974 (div. 1982); children: Federico Ezequiel, Margarita María Blea. BA, N.Mex. Highlands U., 1968, MA, 1972, postgrad. With Albert Garcia Gen. Contr., Las Vegas, N.Mex., 1955-67; teaching asst. N.Mex. Highlands U., Las Vegas, 1971-72, prof. Spanish, Chicano studies, 1972--78; teaching asst. U. N.Mex., Albuquerque, 1978-79; attendant N.Mex. State Mental Hosp., Las Vegas, 1982-83; staff and supervisory interpreter U.S. Dist. Ct. N.Mex., Albuquerque, 1983—; head Raza Unida del to PLO in Lebanon, 1981, head negotiator with Iranians for release of 2 Chicanos and 1 Indian; supr ct. interpreters and reporters sect. U.S. Dist. Ct. N.Mex.; co-chmn. Cuatro-Centennial Com., Inc.; mem. exec. com. N.Mex. Human Rights Coalition. Author collection of poetry: Angustias y Remembranzas; contbr. articles to profl. jours.; author play: Canto a La Raza, 1978. Pres. Dads Against Discrimination, Albuquerque, 1993—; chmn. bd. trustees No. N.Mex. Legal Svcs., Las Vegas, 1972-81; mem. exec. com. Ind. Socialist Parties of Latin Am.; exec. commn. N.Mex. Human Rights Coalition; vice chmn. Barelas Cmty. Devel. Corp.; mem. cmty. coun. on equity Albuquerque Pub. Schs.; mem. N.Mex. Cmty. Loan Fund. Decorated Bronze Star medal. Mem. N.Mex. Translator and Interpreters Assn. (pres. 1984-86), Nat. Assn. Judiciary Interpreters (sec. 1986-88), Nat. Partido Raza Unida (pres. 1976-81), N.Mex. Partido Raza Unida (pres. 1972-75, 77-78), Vietnam Vets. Am. (vice chmn. chpt. 1993—), Vietnam Vets. N.Mex., Am. GI Forum (Albuquerque chpt. 1 comdr. 1993—, vice comdr. 1997-98), N.Mex. GI Forum (comdr. 1996), Nat. Assn. Chicano Studies (founding mem.), N.Mex. Chicano Studies Assn. (pres. 1972-78), Hispanic Round Table of N.Mex. (chmn. 1995, 98), Barelas Neighborhood Assn. (pres.), Phi Sigma Iota. Democrat. Roman Catholic. Avocations: weight lifting, swimming, ice skating, hiking, camping. Home: 1115 9th St SW Albuquerque NM 87102-4027 Office: US Dist Ct Dist of NM 333 Lomas Blvd NW Albuquerque NM 87102-3254

PENA, MARIA GEGES, academic services administrator; b. Torrance, Calif., Nov. 27, 1964; d. Nicholas John and Dina Connie (Vengel) Geges; m. Vicente Gregorio Pena, June 22, 1991. AA, El Camino Coll., 1985; BA, U. Calif., San Diego, 1987; MS, San Diego State U., 1989, postgrad.; postgrad., Claremont Grad. Sch., 1990—, Western State U., 1995—. Peer counselor El Camino Coll., Torrance, Calif., 1982-85; peer advisor U. Calif., San Diego, 1985-87, vice chancellor student affirmative action rsch. intern, 1986-87, outreach asst. disabled student svcs., 1986-89; coord. student svcs. Mira Costa Coll., Oceanside, Calif., 1989—. Contbr. articles to profl. jours. Mem. Calif. Assn. Postsecondary Educators of Disabled. Democrat. Greek Orthodox. Avocations: law, education, CD collecting, collecting Beatles memorabilia. Office: Mira Costa Coll 1 Barnard Dr Oceanside CA 92056-3820

PENCE, JAMES ROY, pastor; b. Hamilton, Ohio, Dec. 1, 1940; s. Roy Harley Pence and Ethel Netty Wyatt. A in Bibl. rsch., Logos, Houston, 1988; DD in Theology, South Calif. Grad. Sch. Theol., Fresno, 1992. Republican. Pentecostal. Home: PO Box 10004 Prescott AZ 86304-0004

PENCE, MARTIN, federal judge; b. Sterling, Kans., Nov. 18, 1904; m. Eleanor Fisher, Apr. 12, 1975. Bar: Calif. 1928, Hawaii 1933. Practice law Hilo, Hawaii, 1936-45, 50-61; judge 3d Circuit Ct., Hawaii, 1945-50; chief judge U.S. Dist. Ct., Hawaii, 1961-74; sr. judge U.S. Dist. Ct., 1974—. Office: US Dist Ct 300 Alamonana Blvd Rm C423 Honolulu HI 96850-0423*

PENDERGHAST, THOMAS FREDERICK, business educator; b. Cin., Apr. 23, 1936; s. Elmer T. and Dolores C. (Huber) P.; BS, Marquette U., 1958; MBA, Calif. State U., Long Beach, 1967; D in Bus. Adminstrn. Nova U., 1987; m. Marjorie Craig, Aug. 12, 1983; children: Brian, Shawna, Steven, Dean, Maria. Sci. programmer Autonetics, Inc., Anaheim, Calif., 1960-64; bus. programmer Douglas Missile & Space Ctr., Huntington Beach, Calif., 1964-66; computer specialist N.Am. Rockwell Co., 1966-69; asst. prof. Calif. State U., Long Beach, 1969-72; prof. Sch. Bus. and Mgmt., Pepperdine U., Los Angeles, 1972—; spl. adviser Commn. on Engring. Edn., 1968; v.p. Visual Computing Co., 1969-71; founder, pres. Scoreboard Animation Systems, 1971-77; exec. v.p. Microfilm Identification Systems, 1977-79; pres. Data Processing Auditors, Inc., 1981—; data processing cons. designing computer system for fin. health and mfg. orgns., 1972—. Mem. Orange County Blue Ribbon Com. on Data Processing, 1973; mem. Orange County TEC Policy Bd., 1982-87; mgmt. and organization devel. cons. Assn. Psychological Type, 1993—. Served to lt. USNR, 1958-60. Cert. in data processing. Mem. Users of Automatic Info. Display Equipment (pres. 1966). Author: Entrepreneurial Simulation Program, 1988, Journey to Couples' Conflict Resolution Using Game Theory, 1998. Home: 17867 Bay St Fountain Valley CA 92708-4443

PENDLETON, OTHNIEL ALSOP, fundraiser, clergyman; b. Washington, Aug. 22, 1911; s. Othniel Alsop and Ingeborg (Berg) P.; m. Flordora Mellquist, May 15, 1935; children: John, James (dec.), Thomas, Ann, Susan. AB, Union Coll., Schenectady, N.Y., 1933; BD, Eastern Bapt. Theol. Sem., 1936; MA, U. Pa., 1936, PhD, 1945; postgrad., Columbia U., 1937-38. Ordained to ministry Bapt. Ch., 1936. Pastor chs. Jersey City, 1935-39, Phila., 1939-43; dean Sioux Falls Coll., S.D., 1943-45; fund raiser Am. Bapt. Ch., N.Y.C., 1945-47; fund-raiser Mass. Bapt. Ch., Boston, 1947-54; fundraiser Seattle, Chgo., Boston, Washington, N.Y.C. and Paris, France, 1955-64, Westwood, Mass., 1971-84; staff mem. Marts & Lundy, Inc., N.Y.C., 1964-71; lectr. Andover-Newton (Mass.) Sem., 1958, Boston U. Sch. Theology, 1958, Harvard U., Cambridge, Mass., 1977-84; cons. Grant MacEwan Coll., Edmonton, Alta., Can. Author: New Techniques for Church Fund Raising, 1955, Fund Raising: A Guide to Non-Profit Organizations, 1981; contbr. articles in field to profl. jours. Address: 627 Leyden Ln Claremont CA 91711-4236

PENG, ZHONG, electrical engineer; b. Tianjin, China, May 20, 1946; came to U.S., 1981; s. Shichang and Rungeng (Bu) P. BSEE, Tianjin U., 1968; MSEE, Purdue U., 1982; MS in Computer Engring., U. So. Calif., 1984. Registered profl. engr., Calif. Elec. engr. Henan Power Adminstrn., Anyang, China, 1968-78; rsch. assoc. Electric Power Rsch. Inst., Beijing, 1980-81; lectr. Calif. State U., L.A., 1985; power system analyst CAE Electronics, Montreal, Que., Can., 1987-89; power system engr. Pacific Gas & Electric, San Francisco, 1985-87, elec. engr., 1989-94; utility engr. Nev. Pub. Svc. Commn., Las Vegas, 1994—. Contbr. articles to profl. jours. Coord. alumni svcs. Grad. Sch. Chinese Acad. Scis., 1991—. Mem. IEEE (sr., prize paper award 1987, 88). Office: State Nev Pub Svc Commn 555 E Washington Ave Ste 4600 Las Vegas NV 89101-1073

PENINGTON, GARY THOMAS, concert hall manager, video producer; b. Monte Vista, Colo., Nov. 24, 1955; s. Fred Thomas and Marcie Jean (Miller) P.; 1 child, Amanda Jean. Student, Adams State Coll., 1974-75; degree in Broadcasting, Browar Inst., 1976. Program dir. KFTM, Fort Morgan, Colo., 1976-77; account exec. RIUP, Durango, Colo., 1977-80; disc jockey ADGO, Durango, Colo., 1980-84; prin., owner Penington Adv. Pub. Rels., Durango, Colo., 1980-84, S.W. Video Prodns., Durango, Colo., 1980—; media prodn. specialist Fort Lewis Coll., Durango, Colo., 1984-96, concert hall mgr., 1996—; bd. dirs. Durango Arts Council. Dir., prodr. (videos): Bar & Country Majesty, 1988, Colorado's Campus In The Sky, 1992, Durango's Living History, 1993, Day Nothing Happened, 1993. Bd. dirs. KDUR-FM, Durango, 1984-90. Mem. Internat. Assn. Assembly Mgrs. Democrat. Methodist. Avocations: scuba diving instr. Office: FLC Concert Hall 1000 Rim Dr Durango CO 81301-3911

PENN, GENEVA I., artist; b. Louisville, Mar. 10, 1959; d. Marion and Marie Hensley, Robert and Alberta Lawson; m. Robert C. Penn, Feb. 14, 1978 (div.); children: Beverly Anne, Jonathan Robert, Christopher Lee. Student, Computerized Learning Ctr., 1992, Sawyer Coll., 1994, Lumbleau Real Estate Sch., 1995. Receptionist The Printers, Sunnyvale, Calif., 1997-99; adminstr., owner Play Penn Presch., Sunnyvale, 1998. Author of childrens stories, including Jelly Bee: Ready Reading by Computers. Baptist. Avocations: writing, sewing. Home: 1055 E Evelyn Ave # 24C Sunnyvale CA 94086-6776

PENNY, TODD, company administrator, consultant; b. Windsor, Ont., Can., Oct. 13, 1967; s. Nickolas Paul Penny and Frances (Pennell) Hope; m. Nadine Wendy Sharland, Sept. 3, 1994. BS in Physics with honors, U. London, 1989. Tech. analyst Royal Bank Scotland, London, 1989-91; tech. analyst Galileo Internat., Swindon, Eng., 1991-92, sr. tech. analyst, 1992-93; project mgr. Galileo Internat., Denver, 1993-95, systems engr., 1995—; dir. Compusulting, Inc., Denver, 1996—. Avocations: hiking, skiing, reading, travelling. Office: Compusulting Inc 8910 W Portland Ave Littleton CO 80128-8011

PENWELL, DONNA CAROL, museum director; b. Waltham, Mass., Oct. 22, 1954. BA in Am. History and Art History, U. N.C., 1976; MA in Mus. Adminstrn., SUNY, 1977. Curator art Mus. Collection Mgmt. Unit Calif. Dept. Parks and Recreation, Sacramento, 1977-78, chief curator, 1978-79; historic cons. Pine Lodge, Ehrman Manson, Lake Tahoe, Tahoma, Calif., 1979-80; exhibit designer State Capitol Restoration Project, Sacramento, 1980-82; exhibit designer mus. devel. unit Calif. Dept. Parks and Recreation, Sacramento, 1982-84; mus. dir., cultural arts mgr. Colton Hall Mus. of City of Monterey, Calif., 1984-90; mus. dir. Maritime Mus. Monterey, 1990—. Bd. mem. Monterey County Hospitality Assn., 1993—, Monterey County Cultural History Assn., 1994—. Nat. Mus. Art scholar, 1977. Mem. Am. Assn. Museums, Calif. Assn. Museums, Coun. Maritime Museums. Avocations: scuba diving, river rafting, hiking, writing. Home: 704 Granite St Pacific Grove CA 93950-4017

PENWELL, JONES CLARK, real estate appraiser, consultant; b. Crisp, Tex., Dec. 19, 1921; s. Clark Moses and Sarah Lucille (Jones) P.; BS, Colo. State U., 1949; m. A. Jerry Jones, July 1, 1967; children: Dale Maria, Alan Lee, John Steven, Laurel Anne, Tracy Lynn. Farm mgmt. supr. Farmers Home Adminstrn., Dept. Agr., 1949-58; rancher 1958-61; real estate appraiser/realty officer Dept. Interior, Tex., Calif., Ariz., Colo., Washington, 1961-78, chief appraiser Bur. Reclamation, Lakewood, Colo., 1978-80; ind. fee appraiser, cons., 1980-94; ret., 1995. Served with USN, 1940-46. Accredited rural appraiser; cert. review appraiser, gen. appraiser; recipient Outstanding Performance awards U.S. Bur. Reclamation, 1964, 75, 80. Mem. Am. Soc. Farm Mgns. and Rural Appraisers, Internat. Right-of-Way Assn., Nat. Assn. Rev. Appraisers (regional v.p. 1978-79), Jefferson County Bd. Realtors. Democrat. Presbyterian. Clubs: Elks, Rotary, Mt. Vernon Country. Author: Reviewing Condemnation Appraisal Reports, 1980; The Valuation of Easements, 1980. Home and office: 10100 W 21st Pl Lakewood CO 80215-1406

PEOPLES, DONALD R., research scientist; b. 1939. Athletic dir. Butte (Mont.) Ctrl. High Sch., 1967-69; dir. info. and evaluation Butte Model Cities Program, 1969-70; dir. pub. works, model cities and cmty. devel. Butte, 1970-77; dir. pub. works dept. Butte-Silver Bow City-County Govt., 1977-79, CEO, 1979-89; with Mont. Tech. Cos., Butte, 1989—, now pres., CEO. Office: Montana Tech Companies 220 N Alaska St Butte MT 59701-9212*

PEPLAU, HILDEGARD ELIZABETH, nursing educator; b. Reading, Pa., Sept. 1, 1909; d. Gustav and Ottylie (Elgert) P. Diploma, Pottstown Hosp. Sch. Nursing, 1931; BA, Bennington Coll., 1943; MA, Columbia U., 1947, EdD, 1953, DSc (hon.), 1983; cert., William Alanson White Inst., 1953; DSc (hon.), Alfred U., 1970, Duke U., 1974, Rutgers U., 1985, Ind. U., 1994, U. Ulster, No. Ireland, 1994; D of Nursing Sci. (hon.), Boston Coll., 1972; LHD (hon.), U. Indpls., 1987, Ohio State U., 1990. RN, N.J., Calif. Exec. officer Coll. Health Svc., Bennington (Vt.) Coll., 1938-43; dir. grad. program psychiatric nursing Tchrs. Coll., Columbia U., N.Y.C., 1948-53; exec. dir. ANA, Washington, 1969-70; dir. grad. program psychiatric nursing Rutgers U., New Brunswick, N.J., 1955-74, prof. emerita, 1974—. Author: Interpersonal Relations in Nursing, 1952; contbr. numerous articles to profl. publs. and jours., 1942—. 1st lt. Nurse Corps, U.S. Army, 1943-45. Recipient Leadership award N.Am. Nursing Diagnosis Assn., 1998. Mem. ANA (Hall of Fame 1998), Am. Nurses Found. (internat. svc. award 1997), Am. Acad. Nursing (designated Living Legend 1994), Internat. Coun. Nurses (3d v.p. 1977-81, bd. dirs. 1973-77, Christiane Reimann prize 1997), Nat. League Nursing. Democrat. Lutheran. Home: 14024 Otsego St Sherman Oaks CA 91423-1225

PEPPER, DAVID M., physicist, educator, author, inventor; b. L.A., Mar. 9, 1949; s. Harold and Edith (Kleinplatz) P.; m. Denise Danyelle Koster, Mar. 19, 1992. BS in Physics summa cum laude, UCLA, 1971; MS in Applied Physics, Calif. Inst. Tech., 1974, PhD in Applied Physics, 1980. Mem. tech. staff Hughes Rsch. Labs., Malibu, Calif., 1973-87, sr. staff physicist, 1987-91, head nonlinear and electro-optic devices sect., 1989-91, sr. scientist, 1991-94; sr. rsch. scientist HRL Labs. (formerly Hughes Rsch. Labs.), Malibu, 1994—; adj prof math and physics Pepperdine U., Malibu, 1981—; mem. adv. panel NSF, Washington, 1997. co-author: Optical Phase Conjugation, 1983, Laser Handbook, Vol. 4, 1985, Optical Phase Conjugation, 1995, Spatial Light Modulator Technology, 1995, CRC Handbook of Laser Science and Technology, 1995; tech. referee profl. jours.; contbr. articles to tech. jours. including Sci. Am.; holder 22 patents. Mem. Sons and Daughters of 1939 Club, 2d Generation of Martyrs Meml., Mus. Holocaust. Recipient Rudolf Kingslake award Soc. Photo-Optical Instrumentation Engrs., 1982, Publ. of Yr. award Hughes Rsch. Lab., 1986, Patent award of excellence HRL Labs., 1997; NSF trainee Calif. Inst. Tech., 1971; Howard Hughes fellow Hughes Aircraft Co., 1973-80. Fellow Optical Soc. Am. (conf. session chair 1996, 97, 98, 99, mem. adv. bd. topical conf. on nonlinear optics, Hawaii 1996, 98); mem. AAAS, IEEE (guest editor, assoc. editor, mem. program com. lasers and electro-optics 1997, 98, 99), SPIE (guest editor, conf. co-chmn. 1998, 99), N.Y. Acad. Scis., Am. Phys. Soc., Laser Inst. Am., Internat. Coun. Sci. Unions (com. on sci. and tech. in developing countries), Sigma Xi (v.p. 1986-87, chpt. pres. 1987-88, 90-91, 91-92), Sigma Pi Sigma. Jewish. Avocations: classical music, travel, sports, astronomy, nature. Office: HRL Labs 3011 Malibu Canyon Rd Malibu CA 90265-4737

PEPPER, JOHN ROY, oil and gas executive; b. Denver, Feb. 24, 1937; s. Wesley Wayne and Lucille (Stith) P.; m. Sallie K. Force, Dec. 13, 1958 (div. July 1970); m. Judithea Lawrence Douglas, Sept. 24, 1977; stepchildren: Sarah Douglas-Broten, Kenneth R. Douglas. BBA, U. Denver, 1961; postgrad., UCLA, 1962, U. Denver, 1965. Analyst Texaco, Inc., L.A., 1962-63; landman Texaco, Inc., Bakersfield, Calif., 1963-65; prin. John Pepper, Landman, Denver, 1965-75; owner, operator John R. Pepper Oil & Gas Co., Denver, 1975—; bd. dirs. Trans-Telecom, Miami, Fla.; cons. in field. Organizer Friends of Bob Crider campaign, Denver, 1985. Mem. Ind. Petroleum Assn. Mountain States, Ind. Petroleum Assn. of Ams. (pub. lands com. 1968-74). Republican. Lutheran. Avocations: sailing, fishing, bird hunting. Home: Unit 101 9400 E Iliff Ave Apt 101 Denver CO 80231-3485 Office: John R Pepper Oil & Gas Co 1800 Glenarm Pl Ste 200 Denver CO 80202-3829

PEPPER, NORMA JEAN, mental health nurse; b. Ellington, Iowa, Nov. 7, 1931; d. Victor F. and Grace Mae (Tate) Shadle; m. Bob Joseph Pepper, Dec. 28, 1956 (dec. Oct. 4, 1985); children: Joseph Victor, Barbara Jean, Susan Claire (dec.). Diploma in Nursing, Broadlawns Polk County Hosp., 1950-53; BSN, U. Iowa, 1953-55; MSN, U. Colo., 1955-60. Cert. mental health nurse. Head nurse Colo. Psychiatric Hosp., Denver, 1956; head nurse, Psychiatry Denver General Hosp., 1958-60; with Nurses Official Registry, Denver, 1960-73; staff nurse VA Med. Ctr., Denver, 1974-94; counselor VA Hosp. Employee Assistance Com., Denver, 1987-94. Mem. Colo. Nurses Assn. Home: 4836 W Tennessee Ave Denver CO 80219-3130

PERAGINE, MICHAEL, writer, engineer; b. L.I., May 19, 1963. BS in Engring. Mgmt., York Coll. of Pa. Engr. L.I. Lighting Co., 1983, RCA Gov. Systems, AT&T Bell Labs, 1986, Morrison-Knudson, N.Y. Transit Authority, 1988, U.S. Army Corp of Engrs., EDC Project, 1990; purchasing mgr., film and classical music archives Tower Records - Video, Hollywood, Calif., 1992—. Artist: painted murals; author: (books) Poetry and Prose, 1992, Pantheism, 1996; co-author: From Metal to Mozart, 1994; editor: UFO Intelligence Report, 1998. Mem. Fedn. Am. Scientists. Avocations: screenwriter. Office: 8801 W Sunset Blvd West Hollywood CA 90069-2104

PERAKH, MARK, physicst; b. Kiev, Russia, Nov. 2, 1924; came to U.S., 1978; s. Yakov and Paula (Elman) Popereka; m. Valentina Lebedeva, June 30, 1970; children: Nina, Vadim, Irena, Alik. PhD, Odessa Inst. Tech., 1946; DSc, Kazan U., 1967. Prof. physics Dushanbe (USSR) U., 1950-55, Alma-Ata (USSR) U., 1955-58, Krasnoyarsk (USSR) Poly. U., 1960-63, Novosibirsk (USSR) Inst. Edn., 1963-66, Kalinin (USSR) U., 1966-73, Hebrew U., Jerusalem, 1973-78; vis. scientist IBM Rsch. Ctr., Yorktown Heights, N.Y., 1978-80; sr. rsch. scientist Arco Solar Inc., Chatsworth, Calif., 1980-84; prof. physics Calif. State U., Fullerton, 1985—. Author: Internal Stress in Films, 1966, Man in a Wire Cage, 1988; contbr. articles to profl. jours.; mem. editl. bd. Surface Technology, 1974-82. Recipient award USSR Acad. Scis., 1965, DAAD, 1976, Royal Soc., 1978. Republican. Achievements include 23 patents; discovery of a new effect, photodeposition of semiconductor films, which has become a foundation of a rapidly expanding new area of research. Home: 10106 Sage Hill Way Escondido CA 92026-6607 Office: Calif State U Fullerton CA 92634

PERALTA, RICHARD CARL, groundwater engineer; b. Enid, Okla., Nov. 8, 1949; s. John Francis and Christina Margareta (Reinl) P.; m. Ann Wilson Blanchard, Mar. 27, 1972; children: Dia, Samantha, Nancy, Hugh. BS, U. S.C., 1971; MS, Utah State U., 1977; PhD, Okla. State U., 1979. Registered profl. engr., Ark., Utah. Grad. rsch. assoc. Oklahoma State U., Stillwater, 1977-79; from asst. prof. to assoc. prof. agrl. engring. U. Ark., Fayetteville, 1980-88; assoc. prof. dept. biol. and irrigation engring. Utah State U., Logan, 1988-91, prof., 1991—; cons. hydrologist U.S. Geol. Survey, Fayetteville, 1985-87; cons. engr. Mid-Am. Internat. Agrl. Consortium, Lima, Peru, 1986-87; cons. engr. ARD, FAO, 1989-98; cons. groundwater engr., 1996—. Contbr. articles to sci. jours. Co-dir. Citizens for Responsible Legis., Stillwater, 1979; elders quorum, pres., exec. sec., fin. asst. clk., activities com. chmn. LDS Ch., 1979—, elders quorum, counsellor, 1992-94; scoutmaster Boy Scouts Am., 1988-89, cubmaster, 1989-91, 94-95. 1st lt. USAF, 1971-75; col. Res. Mem. ASCE, Am. Soc. of Agrl. Engrs., Am. Water Resources Assn., Gamma Sigma Delta. Avocations: jogging, swimming, camping. Home: 522 N 350 E Hyde Park UT 84318-3353 Office: Utah State U Dept Biol/Irrig Engring 4105 Old Main Hl # Ec-216 Logan UT 84322-4105

PERCONTI, WILLIAM JOHN, music educator, musician; b. Cleve., July 23, 1953; s. Joseph and Lenore Perconti; m. Ellen S. Perconti, May 22, 1983; children: Lenore, Don. MusB, Bowling Green State U., 1975, MusM, 1977; MusD, U. Iowa, 1986. Instr. Ctrl. Mo. State U., Warrensburg, 1977-78, Coe Coll., Cedar Rapids, Iowa, 1979-86, St. Cloud (Mo.) State U., 1985-86; prof. Lewis-Clark State Coll., Lewiston, Idaho, 1986—. Appearances include 9th World Sax Congress, Tokyo, 1988, N.W. on Tour, Arts Northwest, 1995-97, (TV) Palouse Performances, 1993, Lionel Hampton Jazz Festival, 1996, 97, (outstanding band award 1996, 97), (radio) Classic NW; recording artist, prodr. (compact disc) Duo 1 point 5, 1994, Related Characters, 1998; founder, prodr. (TV) ann. Holiday Music Festival, 1988—; arranger 5 music works. Nat. Endow Arts grantee, Washington, 1995, Washington Artists Trust grantee, Seattle, 1996; recipient Individual Artist award Bossak and Heilbron Found., White Plaines, N.Y., 1998. Mem. Music Edn. Nat. Conf., N.Am. Saxophone Alliance, Idaho Music Educators Assn., Wash. Music Educators Assn. Avocations: coaching, fishing. Home: 2561 Florence Ln Clarkston WA 99403-1216 Office: Lewis-Clark State Coll 500 8th Ave Lewiston ID 83501-2691

PEREL, MICHAEL JOSEPH, dermatologist, inventor; b. Memphis, Oct. 29, 1947; s. Philip Alexander and Dorothy Louise (Dansby) P.; m. Georgia Chris Roberts, Nov. 20, 1973; 1 child, Eric. BS, Tulane U., 1969; MD, U. Tenn., Memphis, 1972. Diplomate Am. Bd. Dermatology. Pvt. practice dermatology Oxnard, Calif., 1977-89; dermatologist Riverside (Calif.) Med. Clinic, 1989—. Inventor electronic med. record, 1993, Dr. Perel's hair regrowth formula, 1995. Mem. Inland Counties Dermatologic Soc., Calif. Med. Soc. Libertarian. Avocations: skiing, tennis. Home: 2328 Caserta Ct Henderson NV 89014-5316

PERENCHIO, ANDREW JERROLD, film and television executive; b. Fresno, Calif., Dec. 20, 1930; s. Andrew Joseph and Dorothea (Harvey) P.; m. Robin Green, July 16, 1954 (div.); children: Candace L., Catherine M., John Gardner; m. Jacquelyn Claire, Nov. 14, 1969. BS, UCLA, 1954. V.p. Music Corp. Am., 1958-62, Gen. Artists Corp., 1962-64; pres., owner theatrical agy. Chartwell Artists, Ltd., L.A., from 1964; chmn. bd. Tandem Prodns., Inc. and TAT Communications Co., L.A., 1973-83; pres., CEO Embassy Pictures, L.A., from 1983; now pres. Chartwell Partnerships Group, L.A. Promoter Muhammad Ali-Joe Frazier heavyweight fight, 1971, Bobby Riggs-Billie Jean King tennis match, 1973. Served to 1st lt. USAF, 1954-57. Clubs: Bel-Air Country (Los Angeles); Westchester (N.Y.) Country; Friars (N.Y.C.). Office: Chartwell Partnerships Group 1999 Ave Of Stars Ste 3050 Los Angeles CA 90067-6022*

PEREY, RON, lawyer; b. Cleve., Feb. 2, 1943; s. John Perecinsky and Anne (Nagy) Disman; 1 child, Page Suzanne; m. Janice Ash, Aug. 19, 1995. BA in Polit. Sci., Miami U., Oxford, Ohio, 1965; JD cum laude, Ohio State U., 1968. Bar: Wash. 1968, U.S. Dist. Ct. (wc. dist.) Wash. 1968, U.S. Ct. Appeals (9th cir.) 1973, U.S. Supreme Ct. 1985. Assoc. Reed McClure, Seattle, 1968-71, ptnr., 1971-82; ptnr. Perey & Smith, Seattle, 1982-86, Perey Langley, Seattle, 1986-92; owner Law Offices of Ron Perey, Seattle, 1992—; lectr. in field of personal injury and trial practice. Contbr. articles to profl jours. Roscoe Pound Found. fellow. Fellow Roscoe Pound Found.; mem. ATLA (state del. 1989-90), ABA (litigation sect.), King County Bar Assn. (chmn. med.-legal com. 1989-90), Wash. State Trial Lawyers Assn. (bd. govs. 1983-85, 89-91), Am. Bd. Trial Advs. (diplomate; nat. bd. rep. 1996—), Wash. State Bar Assn. (bd. govs. 1994—), Damage Attys. Round Table. Democrat. Avocations: travel, reading, weight lifting, tennis, hiking, jogging. Office: Market Place Tower 2025 1st Ave Ste 250 Seattle WA 98121-2147

PEREYRA-SUAREZ, CHARLES ALBERT, lawyer; b. Paysandu, Uruguay, Sept. 7, 1947; came to U.S., 1954, naturalized, 1962; s. Hector and Esther (Enriquez-Sarano) P.-S.; m. Susan H. Cross, Dec. 30, 1983. BA in History magna cum laude, Pacific Union Coll., 1970; postgrad., UCLA, 1970-71; JD, U. Calif., Berkeley, 1975. Bar: Calif. 1975, D.C. 1980. Staff atty. Western Ctr. Law and Poverty, Inc., Los Angeles, L.A., 1976; trial atty. civil rights div. U.S. Dept. Justice, Washington, 1976-79; asst. U.S. atty., criminal div. U.S. Dept. Justice, Los Angeles, L.A., 1979-82; sr. litigation assoc. Gibson, Dunn & Crutcher, Los Angeles, L.A., 1982-84; sole practice Los Angeles, L.A., 1984-86; ptnr. McKenna & Cuneo, Los Angeles, L.A., 1986-95, Davis Wright Tremaine, L.A., 1995—. Democrat. Avocations: tennis, jogging, travel.

PEREZ, MARY ANGELICA, bilingual specialist, educational administrator; b. San Benito, Tex., Sept. 3; d. Refugio P. and Maria G. (Guerra) P. AA, Tex. Southmonost Coll., Brownsville, Tex., 1955; BS in Elem. Edn., Tex. A&I U. (now Tex. A&M U.), 1959. Cert. elem. tchr., Tex., Calif. Substitute tchr. Bassett Unified Sch. Dist., La Puente, Calif.; tchr. kindergarten West Covina (Calif.) Unified Sch. Dist., ret.; tchr. ESL Tulane U., New Orleans; tchr. bilingual kindergarten San Benito (Tex.) Consolidated Sch. Dist.; tchr. bilingual 4th grade Brownsville (Tex.) Consolidated Sch. Dist.; tchr., head coord. Headstart St. Benedict Ch., San Benito, Tex. Mem. L.A. World Affairs Coun., Nat. Dem. Club. Delta Kappa Gamma scholar, 1953; grantee NDEA, 1963, EEOC, 1969, U. Madrid, 1991; Congl. Recognition for 27 Yrs. of Tchrs. Calif. Mem. NEA, Nat. Assn. Bilingual Edn., Calif. Tchrs. Assn., Calif. Assn. Bilingual Educators, Tex. Tchrs. Assn. (pres. 1966), Calif. State Sheriff's Assn., Catholic Tchrs. Guild (pres. Brownsville Diocese 1965), Hispanic Women's Coun., L.A. World Affairs Coun. Democrat. Roman Catholic. Avocation: making and selling crafts. Home: 1829 S Lark Ellen Ave West Covina CA 91792-1104

PEREZ, REINALDO JOSEPH, electrical engineer; b. Palm River, Cuba, July 25, 1957; came to U.S., 1975; s. Reinaldo I. and Palminia Ulloa (Rodriguez) P.; m. Madeline Kelly Reilly, Mar. 11, 1989; children: Alexander, Laura-Marie, Richard Kelly, Ella-Dean. BSc in Physics, U. Fla., 1979, MSc in Physics, 1981; MScEE, Fla. Atlantic U., 1983, PhD, 1989. Comms. engr. Kennedy Space Ctr., NASA, Cape Canaveral, Fla., 1983-84; chief reliability engr. jet propulsion lab. JPL Calif. Inst. Tech., Pasadena, 1988—, chief engr. Mars surveyor program, 1994—; instr. engring. UCLA, 1990-94. Author, editor: Handbook of Electromagnetic Compatibility, Noise and Interference Issues in Wireless Communications, 3 vols., Wireless Communications Handbook; contbr. articles to profl. publs. Mem. AAAS, IEEE (sr. mem., book rev. editor 1990—), NSPE, Electromagnetic Compatibility Soc. (assoc. editor jour.), Am. Soc. Physics Tchrs., N.Y. Acad. Scis., Applied Computational Electromagnetic Soc. (assoc. editor jour., chief editor newsletter, bd. dirs.), Phi Kappa Phi. Republican. Baptist. Avocations: flying, skiing, fishing. Office: JPL Calif Inst Tech 4800 Oak Grove Dr # 301460 Pasadena CA 91109-8099

PEREZ, RICHARD LEE, lawyer; b. L.A., Nov. 17, 1946; s. Salvador Navarro and Shirley Mae (Selbrede) P.; m. Yvonne Perez; children: Kristina, Kevin, Ryan. BA, UCLA, 1968; JD, U. Calif., Berkeley, 1971. Bar: U.S. Dist. Ct. (no. dist.) Calif. 1974, U.S. Ct. Appeals (9th cir.) 1974, U.S. Dist. Ct. (ea. dist.) Calif. 1982, U.S. Dist. Ct. (no. dist.) Tex. 1984, U.S. Dist. Ct. (so. dist.) Calif. 1991. Assoc. McCutchen, Doyle, Brown & Enersen, San Francisco, 1972-74, John R. Hetland, Orinda, Calif., 1974-75; ptnr. Lempres & Wulsfberg, Oakland, Calif., 1975-82, Perez & McNabb, Orinda, 1982—; speaker real estate brokerage and computer groups and seminars; mem. adv. bd. Computer Litigation Reporter, Washington, 1982-85, Boalt Hall High Tech. Law Jour., 1984-90. Assoc. editor U. Calif. Law Rev., 1970-71. Served to capt. U.S. Army, 1968-79. Mem. ABA, Alameda County Bar Assn., Contra Costa County Bar Assn. Office: Perez & McNabb 140 Brookwood Rd Orinda CA 94563-3035

PEREZ, TOM, film director, writer; b. Oceanside, N.Y., Sept. 24, 1973; s. Raymond and Marilyn (Grispin) P. BA in Broadcasting, Ariz. State U., 1996. Prin., owner Dreamgate Filmed Entertainment, Tempe, Ariz., 1996—.

PEREZ-CASTRO, ANA VERONICA, developmental biology researcher; b. Lima, Peru, Jan. 27, 1962; came to U.S., 1986; d. Cesar Antonio and Ines Gladys (Marquina) P.; m. Alonso Castro, June 11, 1988. BS, Cayetano Heredia U., Lima, 1984, licentiate in chemistry and biology, 1985; MA, Columbia U., 1988, MPhil, 1990, PhD in Microbiology, 1992. Jr. prof. dept. chemistry Cayetano Heredia U., 1985-86; teaching asst. dept. microbiology U. Ga., Athens, 1987, Columbia U., N.Y.C., 1989; postdoctoral fellow life scis. div. Los Alamos (N.Mex.) Nat. Lab., 1992-95; rsch. assoc. dept. biology U. N.Mex., Albuquerque, 1996—; speaker Fedn. Am. Socs. for Exptl. Biology, 1992, Baylor Coll. Medicine, Houston, 1992, Mexican Soc. Genetics, Guanajuato, 1993, Mexico City 1994. Contbr. articles to sci. jours. Recipient young scientist award Fedn. Am Socs. for Exptl. Biology, 1992; Nat. Coun. Sci. and Tech. grad. fellow Cayetano Heredia U., 1985-86; Fieger predoctoral scholar Norris Comprehensive Cancer Ctr., U. So. Calif., 1991-92. Mem. AAAS, Am. Soc. Microbiology, Am. Soc. Human Genetics. Home: 3036 Pueblo Puye Santa Fe NM 87505-2564 Office: Univ NMex Dept Biology Castetter Hall Albuquerque NM 87131

PERHAM, LEN, executive. Pres., CEO IDT, Santa Clara, Calif.; bd. dirs. IDT. Office: 2975 Stender Way Santa Clara CA 95054-3214*

PERINGTON, PHILIP, management investment company executive. BA, U. Colo., 1976, cert. paralegal, 1989. Pres. Restaurant Devel. Corp., Denver, 1968-73, Harrington-Miller Co., Denver, 1973—. Regional task officer Clinton-Gore Regional Issues, 1996; chmn. Colo. State Dem. Party. Recipient Gov.'s award State of Wyo., 1991. Mem. Assn. State Dem. Chairs (chmn. 1996—). Office: Harrington-Miller Co 770 Grant St Denver CO 80203*

PERITO, JOSEPH GERALD, JR., educator, musician, counselor, consultant; b. Denver, Feb. 9, 1927; s. Joseph and Rose (Comnillo) P.; B.A. in Music Edn., Denver U., 1950, M.A., 1955; Ed.D., U. No. Colo., 1967. Tchr. music, instrumental, vocal, theory Jefferson County (Colo.) Pub. Schs. Dist. R-1, Lakewood, 1950-57, supr. music, 1957-64, rsch. specialist, 1964-65; prin. Carmody Jr. High Sch., Lakewood, 1965-78; adminstr., counselor Fundamental Mid. Alternative Sch., Lakewood, 1976-78, adminstrv. asst. in ctrl. adminstrn., 1978-81; adminstr., cons., counselor 1983—. Mem. NEA, Am. Ednl. Rsch. Assn., Am. Acad. Polit. and Social Scis., Nat., Colo. Assns. Secondary Sch. Prins., Music Edn. Nat. Conf., Am. Choral Dirs. Assn., Am. String Tchrs. Assn., Colo. Edn. Assn., Kappa Delta Pi, Phi Delta Kappa. Home: 430 N Garrison St Lakewood CO 80226

PERITORE, LAURA, law librarian; b. San Francisco, Nov. 28, 1945; d. Attilio and Anita (Firenzi) Marcenaro; children: Victor Anthony, Phillip Michael. BA, U. Calif., Santa Barbara, 1967, MA, 1970; MLS, U. Mo., 1974. Asst. libr. Mo. Hist. Soc., Columbia, 1971-74, 77-79; asst. libr. Hastings Law Libr., San Francisco, 1980-86, assoc. libr., 1986—; part-time tchr. legal rsch. City Coll., San Francisco, 1990-91. Author: Guide to California County Probate and Vital Records, 1994; contbr. articles and monographs to profl. jours. Mem. Am. Assn. Law Librs., No. Calif. Assn. Law Librs. (asst. editor newsletter 1984-86, workshop com. 1988, advt. editor 1990-91, sec. 1993-94, grantee 1984). Avocations: piano, yoga, cooking. Office: Hastings Law Libr 200 McAllister St San Francisco CA 94102-4707

PERKINS, FLOYD JERRY, retired theology educator; b. Bertha, Minn., May 9, 1924; s. Ray Lester and Nancy Emily (Kelley) P.; m. Mary Elizabeth Owen, Sept. 21, 1947 (dec. June 1982); children: Douglas Jerry, David Floyd, Sheryl Pauline; m. Phyllis Genevra Hartley, July 14, 1984. AB, BTh, N.W. Nazarene Coll., 1949; MA, U. Mo., 1952; MDiv, Nazarene Theol. Sem., 1952; ThM, Burton Sem., 1964; PhD, U. Witwatersrand, Johannesburg, South Africa, 1974; ThD, Internat. Sem., 1994. Ordained to Christian ministry, 1951. Pres. South African Nazarene Theol. Sem., Florida Transvaal, Africa, 1955-67; pres. Nazarene Bible Sem., Lourenzo Marques, Mozambique, 1967-73, Campinas, Brazil, 1974-76; prof. missions N.W. Nazarene Coll., Nampa, Idaho, 1976; prof. theology Nazarene Bible Coll., Colorado Springs, Colo., 1976-97; chmn., founder com. higher theol. edn. Ch. of Nazarene in Africa, 1967-74; sec. All African Nazarene Mission Exec., 1967-74; ofcl. Christian Council Mozambique, 1952-74. Author: A History of the Christian Church in Swaziland, 1974. Served with USN, 1944-46. Mem. Soc. Christian Philosophers, Evang. Theol. Soc., Am. Schs. Orientan Rsch., Am. Soc. Missiology, Assn. Evang. Missions Profs. Republican. Avocation: golf. Home: 6355 Oak Ave Apt 21 Temple City CA 91780-1300

PERKINS, GLADYS PATRICIA, retired aerospace engineer; b. Crenshaw, Miss., Oct. 30, 1921; d. Douglas and Zula Francis (Crenshaw) Franklin; m. Benjamin Franklin Walker, Sept. 26, 1952 (dec.); m. William Silas Perkins, Sept. 16, 1956 (dec.). BS in Math., Le Moyne Coll., 1943; postgrad., U. Mich., 1949, U. Calif., L.A., 1955-62. Mathematician Nat. Adv. Com. for Aeronautics (now NASA), Hampton, Va., 1944-49, Nat. Bur. of Standards, L.A., 1950-53, Aberdeen Bombing Mission, L.A., 1953-55; assoc. engr. Lockheed Missiles Systems Div., Van Nuys, Calif., 1955-57; staff engr. Hughes Aircraft Co., El Segundo, Calif., 1957-80; engring. specialist Rockwell Internat., Downey, Calif., 1980-87, ret., 1987. Contbr. articles to profl. publs. Named Alumnus of Yr. Le Moyne-Owen Coll., 1952; recipient Nat. Assn. for Equal Opportunity in Higher Edn. award Le Moyne-Owen Coll. Mem. Soc. of Women Engrs., Assn. of Computing Machinery, Le Moyne-Owen Alumni Assn. (pres. 1984), U. Mich. Alumni Club, Alpha Kappa Alpha. Democrat. Congregationalist. Home: 4001 W 22d Pl Los Angeles CA 90018-1029

PERKINS, LILY LEIALOHA, humanities educator; b. Lahaina Maui, Hawaii, Mar. 5, 1930; d. Samuel Umi and Margaret Malia (Kaa'a) Apo; m. Stephen G. Mark, 1954 (1966); m. Roland Francis Perkins, 1971; children: Mark 'Umi, Kele Douglas. AB in English Lit. cum laude, Boston U., 1957; MS in Libr. Sci., Simmons Coll., 1959; MA in English Lit., Mt. Holyoke Coll., 1966; PhD in Folklore, U. Pa., 1978. Catalogue libr. Mus. Fine Arts, Boston, 1959-61, Smith Coll., Northampton, Mass., 1965-66; instr. English Northeastern U., Boston, 1966-68; libr. Boston Psychoanalytic Inst., 1973-74; assoc. prof. English Atenisi U., Nuku'alofa, Tonga, 1980-86; instr. Hawaiian studies U. Hawaii-Leeward, Pearl City, 1989-94; asst. prof. Hawaiian studies U. Hawaii-West Oahu, Pearl City, 1994—; coord. Internat. Oral Traditions Program, Honolulu, 1994; exec. bd. mem. Hawaii Literary Arts Coun., Honolulu, 1995—. Author: Natural, 1979, Kingdoms of the Heart, 1980, Cyclone Country, 1997, Other Places, 1987, The Firemakers, 1987, The Oxridge Woman, 1998; founder, editor Jour. Hawaiian and Pacific Folklore and Folklife Studies, 1990—. Recipient Funding award for initiating Jour. HawnPac Folklore Folklife Studies, Hawai'i State Legis., 1984-86; named First Joint Doctoral Interne in Culture Learning Inst., U. Pa. to East-West Ctr., 1974-76; grantee for oral tradition studies Nat. Endowment for the Humanities, 1994. Mem. Assn. Social Anthropology Oceania, Assn. Literary Scholars and Critics, Soc. for Hawaiian Archaeology, Assn. Asian Am. Studies, Pacific Arts Assn., U. Pa. Alumni Assn. (Hawaii chpt.), Mt. Holyoke Alumni Assn. (Hawaii chpt.). Democrat. Avocations: music playing violin, swimming, walking, traveling, meeting people. Home: 85-175 Farrington Hwy Apt A334 Waianae HI 96792-2140 Office: Univ Hawaii W Oahu 96-129 Ala Ike St Pearl City HI 96782-3626

PERKINS, THOMAS JAMES, venture capital company executive; b. Oak Park, Ill., Jan. 7, 1932; s. Harry H. and Elizabeth P.; m. Gerd Thune-Ellefsen, Dec. 9, 1961; children: Tor Kristian, Elizabeth Siri. B.S.E.E.,

M.I.T., 1953; M.B.A., Harvard U., 1957. Gen. mgr. computer div. Hewlett Packard Co., Cupertino, Calif., 1965-70, dir. corp. devel., 1970-72; gen. partner Kleiner & Perkins, San Francisco, 1972-80; sr. ptnr. Kleiner Perkins Caufield & Byers, San Francisco, from 1980; chmn. bd. Tandem Computers, Inc., Cupertino, Calif.; chmn. bd. Tandem Computers, Genentech; dir. Spectra Physics., Corning Glass Works, Collagen Corp., LSI Logic Corp., Hybritech Inc., Econics Corp., Vitalink Communications Corp. Author: Classic Supercharged Sports Cars, 1984. Trustee San Francisco Ballet, 1980—. Mem. Nat. Venture Capital Assn. (chmn. 1981-82, pres. 1980-81). Clubs: N.Y. Yacht, Links, Am. Bugatti (pres. 1983—). also: Genentech Inc 460 Point San Bruno Blvd South San Francisco CA 94080-4918

PERKINS, WILLIAM CLINTON, company executive; b. Decatur, Ill., Mar. 7, 1920; s. Glen Rupert and Frances Lola (Clinton) P.; m. Eunice Cagle, Sept. 7, 1939 (div. 1954); stepchildren: William Rea Cagle, Howard Christy Cagle; 1 child, Clinton Colcord; m. Lillian Wuollet, Sept. 7, 1955 (div. 1965); m. Shirley Thomas, Oct. 24, 1969. BS Mil. Sci. and Meteorology, U. Md., 1954; MS in Bus. and Pub. Adminstrn., Sussex Coll., Eng., 1975. Commd. USAF, 1943-73, advanced through grades to col.; with Ship Systems div. Litton Ind., Culver City, Calif., 1973-75; dir. material Hughes Aircraft Co., Tehran, Iran, 1974-78; mgr. internat. s/c Northrop Corp., Dahran, Saudi Arabia, 1978-81; dir. materiel CRS, Riyadh, Saudi Arabia, 1981-83; head major subcontracts Lear Ziegler Corp., Santa Monica, Calif., 1984-88; pres., chmn. bd., CEO Snowtech, Inc., L.A., 1984—; bd. dirs. Ice Village Ctrs., Inc., L.A., Forefront Industries, Maywood, Calif. Bd. dirs. World Children's Transplant Fund, L.A., 1987-95; mem. Mayor's Space Adv. Com., L.A., 1970-74; mem. aerospace hist. com. Mus. Sci. and Industry, L.A., 1988-98, Mus. of Flying, 1998—. Mem. AIAA (sec. chmn. 1970), Ret. Officers Assn. (pres. 1992-95), Soc. for Non-destructive Testing (program chmn. 1973), Aerospace Hist. Soc., Am. Soc. Quality Control, Am. Meterol. Soc., Sigma Alpha Epsilon (alumni chpt. pres. 1974-76). Avocations: golf, scuba diving, sailing, flying, gardening. Home: 8027 Hollywood Blvd Los Angeles CA 90046-2510

PERKOWSKI, MAREK ANDRZEJ, electrical engineering educator; b. Warsaw, Poland, Oct. 6, 1946; came to U.S., 1981; s. Adam Perkowski and Hanna (Zielinska) Mystkowska; m. Ewa Kaja Wilkowska, Oct. 26, 1974; 1 child, Mateusz Jan. MS in Electronics with distinction, Tech. U. Warsaw, 1970, PhD in Automatics with distinction, 1980. Sr. asst. Inst. Automatics, Tech. U. Warsaw, 1973-80, asst. prof., 1980-81; vis. asst. prof. dept. elec. engring. U. Minn., Mpls., 1981-83; assoc. prof. elec. engring. Portland (Oreg.) State U., 1983-94, prof., 1994—. Co-author: Theory of Automata, 3d edit., 1976, Problems in Theory of Logic Circuits, 4th edit., 1986, Theory of Logic Circuits-Selected Problems, 3d edit., 1984; contbr. 134 articles to profl. jours., 11 chpts. to books. Mem. Solidarity, Warsaw, 1980-81. Recipient Design Automation award SIGDA/ACM/DATC IEEE, 1986-91; Rsch. grantee NSF, 1991, 94, Commn. for Familites Roman Cath. Ch., Vatican, 1981, Air Force Office Sci. Rsch., 1995. Mem. IEEE (Computer Soc.), Polish Nat. Alliance, Assn. for Computing Machinery, Am. Soc. for Engring. Edn. Roman Catholic. Avocations: tourism, philosophy, woodcarving. Home: 15720 NW Perimeter Dr Beaverton OR 97006-5391 Office: Portland State U Dept Elec & Comp Engring PO Box 751 Portland OR 97207-0751

PERLEGOS, GEORGE, electronic executive. Pres., CEO, chmn. Atmel Inc., San Jose. Office: Atmel Inc 2325 Orchard Pkwy San Jose CA 95131-1034*

PERLMAN, SETH JOSEPH, political risk analyst; b. Newark, Dec. 4, 1960; s. Preston Leonard and Evelyn Ann (Binder) P.; m. Lisette Antonia Quinones, 1990 (div. May 1992); 1 child, Rachel Aleeza; m. Alexandria Melissa Molyneaux, Apr. 2, 1993; children: Grant, Rachel. BA in Internat. Rels., George Washington U., 1985; MA in Internat. Rels., Am. U., 1988; MPhil in Polit. Sci. 1st class honors, London Sch. Econs./Polit. Sci., 1986; PhD in Internat. Security Policies, U. Md., 1990. Cert. Spanish lang. translator U.S. Dept. of State. Rsch. analyst mid.-east program U.S. Dept. State, Washington, 1984-86; legis. asst. fgn. affairs U.S. Rep. Edward F. Feighan, Washington, 1986-88; sr. writer Def. & Fgn. Affairs mag. Internat. Media, Inc., Alexandria, Va., 1988-90; S.W. editor Pacific Shipper Mag., Long Beach, Calif., 1990-91; mng. dir. Polecon Resources, Inc., Huntington Beach, Calif., 1991—; contbr. Knight-Ridder, Inc., El Segundo, Calif., 1990-91, Reuter's News Svc., L.A., 1990-91. Contbr. articles to profl. jours., periodicals, mags. Congl. Rsch. Svc. Def. and Fgn. Affairs rsch. grantee Libr. of Congress, 1988; Ctr. for Rsch. and Documentation of European Community grantee, 1989. Mem. Am. U. Alumni Assn. (v.p. 1989-90). Avocations: travel, woodworking, reading, skiing. Office: 6113 Flaming Arrow Rd North Las Vegas NV 89031

PERLMAN, SUSAN GAIL, organization executive; b. N.Y.C., Dec. 29, 1950; d. Philip and Pearl Perlman; ed. Hunter Coll., N.Y.C., 1967-71. Copywriter, Blaine Thompson Advt., N.Y.C., 1968-71; copywriter J.C. Penney Co., N.Y.C., 1971-72; assoc. exec. dir. Jews for Jesus, San Francisco, 1972—, bd. dirs., also editor Issues mag.; speaker, cons. in field; steering com. mem. Lausanne Consultation on Jewish Evangelism, Copenhagen, Denmark; del. Bapt. Gen. Conf. Mem. editorial bd. Evang. Missions Quar. Mem. Am. Jewish Congress, Interdenominational Fgn. Missions Assn. (pres.). Democrat. Baptist. Office: 60 Haight St San Francisco CA 94102-5802

PERNELL, ROBERT, municipal official. Mem. bd. dirs. Sacramento (Calif.) Mcpl. Utility Dist. Office: Sacramento Utility Dist MS B407 PO Box 15830 Sacramento CA 95852-1830*

PERNG, JESSICA, interior designer; b. Taiwan, May 1969; d. John and Vicki Perng. BA, Calif. State U., Long Beach, 1994. Receptionist, sec. Yamaha, Cypress, Calif., 1990; interior design intern Green St. Interiors, Los Alamitos, Calif., 1993; accounts receivable rep., sec. Med. Office, Oxnard, Calif., 1993-95; accounts receivables rep. Apria Pharmacy Network, Oxnard, 1995-98; CAD designer Creative Design Cons., Inc., Costa Mesa, Calif., 1998—. Mem. Am. Soc. Interior Design. Office: JessInteriors 10401 Slater Ave Apt 205 Fountain Valley CA 92708-7701

PERRIS, ANDREW ARTHUR, real estate company official; b. San Gabriel, Calif., June 28, 1968; s. Andres Flores and Lydia (Guajardo) P. Student, U. San Diego, 1986—; real estate lic., Anthony's Real estate Sch., L.A., 1987. Agt. Century 21 Advantage Real Estate, Alhambra, Calif., 1987—. Campaigner Citizens for Almquist for Congress, Alhambra, 1986, Calif. for Pete Wilson, San Diego, 1988. Mem. Calif. Assn. Realtors, Century 21 Real Estate Million Dollar Sales Club. Republican. Baptist. Avocations: skiing, racquetball, sailing. Home: 2035 Clover Dr Monterey Park CA 91755-6715 Office: Century 21 Advantage RE 115 S Garfield Ave Alhambra CA 91801-3832

PERRIZO, JAMES DAVID, art and sculpture educator, forestry pilot; b. L.A., Dec. 10, 1938; s. Francis John and Mary Ellen Perrizo; m. Helen Martin, Aug. 1, 1964; children: Teva Vaea, Rano Darian, Melia Tiare. AB, U. Calif., Berkeley, 1967, MA, 1969, MFA, 1974. Cert. airline transport pilot, DC-3, BH-47. Prof. art Calif. State U., Hayward, 1970—; forestry pilot Calif. Dept. Forestry, Sacramento, 1983-87; charter capt. Temsco Helicopters, Alaska, 1988-89, Horizon Helicopters, Calif., 1991; forestry pilot Reeder Flying Svc., Twin Falls, Idaho, 1995-96, Landells Aviation, Desert Hot Springs, Calif., 1997-98; news gatering helicopter capt. Helinet, Inc., Oakland Airport, 1998—; prin./capt. Air Charter West, Oakland, Calif., 1969-70; chair dept. art Calif. State U., Haward, 1987-91, 96-97; pres. Z-Enterprises, Hayward, 1996—. Sculptor First and Last Men, 1974, Five Moon Prairie, 1982, Overhand, 1989, Paradise, 1997. Rep.-at-large Calif. Faculty Assn., Calif. State U., Hayward, 1995-97; treas. Sun Gallery, Hayward, 1995-96. Lt. comdr. USNR, 1957-70, naval aviator, 1960-70. Mem. Pacific Rim Sculptors Group, Aircraft Owners and Pilots Assn. Democrat. Roman Catholic. Avocations: sailing, skiing, skin diving. [illegible]

PERRY, CARLA LESLIE, writer, editor; b. N.Y.C., Sept. 23, 1948; d. Saul and Bella (Feuerman) Nesbitt; m. Thom Perry, [illegible] (div. 1983); 1 child, Zachariah Raz. BA in Poetry, U. Iowa, 1970. Mgr. publs. dept. Intel Corp., Hillsboro, Oreg., 1979-85, software tech. writer, 1985-86; freelance writer, editor Oreg., 1986—; editor Talus and Scree (internat. lit. jour.), 1996—; pub., editor Dancing Moon Press, Newport, Oreg., 1998—; bd. dirs. Oreg. Coast Coun. for Arts, Newport, 1998. Author: No Questions Asked, No Answers Given, 1971, Laughing Like Dogs, 1996; coord. (monthly) Yachats Writers' Series, 1997-98; coord. NYE Beach Writers Series, 1999—,. Mem. Oreg. Coast Coun. for the Arts. Recipient Award of Excellence, Soc. Tech. Comm., 1989. Mem. N.W. Writers, Inc. Avocations: writing, illustration, photography, adventure. Office: Dancing Moon Press Talus and Scree PO Box 832 Newport OR 97365

PERRY, DAVID NILES, public relations executive; b. Utica, N.Y., Mar. 7, 1940; s. Francis N. and Marion H. P.; B.S., Utica Coll. Syracuse U., 1962; m. Jacqueline J. Adams, Dec. 21, 1962. Pub. affairs rep. Allstate Ins. Co., Pasadena, Calif., 1966-67; dir. press rrels. L.A. C. of C., 1968; rep. pub. rels. Lockheed Propulsion Co., Redlands, Calif., 1968-70; mgr. pub. rels. Bozell & Jacobs Inc., L.A., 1970-73, Phoenix, 1974; pres. David Perry Pub. Rels. Inc., Scottsdale, Ariz.; exec. dir. Ariz. Water Quality Assn. Served with USNR, 1962-65. Office: 6819 E Diamond St Scottsdale AZ 85257-3233

PERRY, DONALD LESTER, II, venture capitalist; b. Culver City, Calif., Jan. 21, 1958; s. Donald Lester Sr. and Joyce Estella (Kirklin) P.; m. Michael Albert Behn, July 24, 1982. BA in Econs. and Polit. Sci., Williams Coll., 1979; MBA in Strategic Mgmt., Claremont (Calif.) Grad. Sch., 1990. Fgn. exch. trader Morgan Guaranty Trust Co., N.Y.C., 1979-80; exec. recruiter Benson-McBride & Assoc., Beverly Hills, Calif., 1980-82; asst. v.p. money markets divsn. Nat. Australia Bank, L.A., 1982-86; v.p., eurodollar trader Sanwa Bank of Calif., L.A., 1986-88; v.p. comml. loans Union Bank, L.A., 1989-90; mng. ptnr. Pine Cobble Ptnrs., L.A., 1990—; speaker Pacific Coast Regional SBDC, L.A., 1989—, Nat. Assn. Black MBAs, L.A., 1990—, So. Calif. Edison/Joint Coun., L.A., 1990—. Contbr. articles to mags. Mem. Town Hall of Calif., L.A., 1990. Recipient Outstanding Entrepreneur of Yr., Peter F. Drucker Ctr. at Claremont Grad. Sch., 1995; named Positive Black Role Model, Assn. Black Women Entrepreneurs, 1993. Mem. L.A. Venture Assn., L.A. Urban Bankers, Pacific Coast Regional Small Bus. Devel. Corp. (mem. loan com. 1990-94), L.A. World Affairs Coun. Republican. Avocations: reading, golf, travel. Office: 3941 Veselich Ave Apt 130 Los Angeles CA 90039-1436 Address: 3941 Veselich Ave Apt 130 Los Angeles CA 90039-1436

PERRY, GLEN JOSEPH, educator; b. Oakland, Calif., May 3, 1953; s. Joseph and Lucille (Piccarelli) P.; m. Audre Lee MacDonald, Aug. 4, 1990; children: Glen Jr., Nicholas. AA, Chabot Coll., 1973; BS, Calif. State Univ., 1975. Police officer, detective City of San Leandro, San Leandro, Calif., 1975-81, City of Woodland, Woodland, Calif., 1981-85; tchr. Woodland Unified Sch. Dist., Woodland, Calif., 1988-92, discipline coord., 1992—; chair dept. math. Woodland Unified Sch. Dist., 1990-92, discipline behavior assigns, 1988—; discipline seminars, 1997—. Author: Contractual Accountability System, 1996. Elder Victory Family Fellowship, Woodland, Calif., 1997; Bible tchr., Sacramento, Woodland, Calif., 1987—. Named Outstanding Law Enforcement Officer of Yr. Woodland C. of C., 1981, Resolution of Appreciation award Woodland City Coun., 1981, Tchr. of Yr. award Douglass Jr. H.S., 1989. Mem. Woodland Profl. Tchrs. Assn., Calif. Tchrs. Assn. Office: Douglas Jr H S 525 Granada Dr Woodland CA 95695

PERRY, JAMES GREGORY, sales and marketing executive; b. Missoula, Mont., Oct. 4, 1952; s. Joseph Tarsisus and Mary Cathrine (Schneider) P.; m. Diana Sue Coen, May 24, 1974; 1 child, Natalie Shureé. Student, Yuba Coll., Marysville, Calif., 1970-72. Credit supr. CBS Mus. Instruments, Fullerton, Calif., 1975-76, mktg. rep., 1976-80, sales rep., 1980-82; mktg. rep. Paiste Am., Inc., Brea, Calif., 1982-85, nat. sales mgr., 1985-91; field sales mgr. Am. Med. Sales, 1991-93; dir. sales and mktg., 1993—; caption chief percussion So. Calif. Judges Assn., 1983—; percussion judge So. Calif. Sch. Band Orch. Assn., 1985-93. With USN, 1972-75. Mem. Mu Sigma Kappa (pres. 1972), Jaycees (pres. Castleton, Ind. chpt. 1981), Am. Drum Line Assn. (v.p. 1994—). Avocations: music, racquetball, water skiing, golf, photography. Office: Am Med Sales Inc 4928 W Rosecrans Ave Hawthorne CA 90250-6616

PERRY, JEANNE ELYCE, principal; b. Ft. Collins, Colo., Jan. 23, 1953; d. Franklin Clyde and Ruth Caroline (Skoglund) Stewart; m. William Kay Perry, Dec. 28, 1974; children: Belinda Eve, Angela Marie. BA in Elem. Edn., Western State Coll., 1975; MA in Ednl. Leadership, U. No. Colo., 1992. Tchr. elem. sch. Soroco Sch. Dist., Oak Creek, Colo., 1977-86, L.A. Unified Sch. Dist., 1986-88; coord. elem. computer Weld RE-1 Sch. Dist., Gilcrest, Colo., 1988-93; prin. Delta (Colo.) Coun. Sch. Dist., 1993—. Leader Girl Scouts Am., Yampa, Colo., 1984-86, Platteville, Colo., 1988-89; precinct committeewoman Rep. Party, Platteville, 1991-93. Colo. Gov.'s grantee, 1990, 91. Mem. ASCD, NAESP. Baptist. Avocations: hiking, skiing, gardening, crafts. Office: Hotchkiss Elem Sch PO Box 309 Hotchkiss CO 81419-0309

PERRY, JOHN RICHARD, philosophy educator; b. Lincoln, Nebr., Jan. 16, 1943; s. Ralph Robert and Ann (Roscow) P.; m. Louise Elizabeth French, Mar. 31, 1962; children: James Merton, Sarah Louise, Joseph Glenn. BA, Doane Coll., Crete, Nebr., 1964; PhD, Cornell U., Ithaca, N.Y., 1968; DLitt (hon.), Doane Coll., 1982. Asst. prof. philosophy UCLA, 1968-72; vis. asst. prof. U. Mich., Ann Arbor, 1971-72; assoc. prof. UCLA, 1972-74, Stanford (Calif.) U., 1974-77; prof. Stanford U., 1977-85, Henry Waldgrave Stuart prof., 1985—, chmn. dept. philosophy, 1976-82, 90-91, dir. ctr. study lang. and info., 1985-86, 93—, resident fellow Soto House, 1985-91. Author: Dialogue on Identity and Immortality, 1978, (with Jon Barwise) Situations and Attitudes, 1983, The Problem of the Essential Indexical, 1993. Pres. Santa Monica Dem. Club, Calif., 1972-74. Woodrow Wilson fellow, 1964-65, Danforth fellow, 1964-68, Guggenheim fellow, 1975-76, NEH fellow, 1980-81. Mem. Am. Philos. Assn. (v.p. Pacific divsn. 1992-93, pres. 1993-94). Office: Stanford U Ctr Study Lang & Info 220 Panama St Stanford CA 94305-4101

PERRY, JOSEPHINE, screen writer, playwright, educator; b. Weymouth, Mass., Aug. 20, 1950; d. John Frederick and Maria Rose (Folino) P.; m. Paul Remmele. BA, U. Mass., 1981; MFA, Ohio U., 1983; MA, Calif. State U., Long Beach, 1988. Cert. C.C. instr., Calif. Tchr. Long Beach (Calif.) Unified Sch. Dist., 1983-87, Sedona (Ariz.) Unified Sch. Dist., 1989-91; instr. English, mythology and lit. Cerritos C.C., Norwalk, Calif., 1987-89; instr. English, Lit. Los Medanos Coll., Pittsburg, Calif., 1991—; reader, script cons. L.A. Theatre Ctr., 1983-85; asst. lit. mgr. Pa. State Co., Allentown, 1982-83. Prodr. film God Talk, 1996; author: (screenplays) Blueberry Hill, 1995, Presumed Dead, 1996, Amazing Grace, 1997 (play) My Movie Star, 1995. Recipient Excellent award for Entertainment Bay Area Cable award, 1998; finalist Telly award, 1998.

PERRY, LEE ROWAN, retired lawyer; b. Chgo., Sept. 23, 1933; s. Watson Bishop and Helen (Rowan) P.; m. Barbara Ashcraft Mitchell, July 2, 1955; children: Christopher, Constance, Geoffrey. BA, U. Ariz., 1955, LLB, 1961. Bar: Ariz. 1961. Since practiced in Phoenix; clk. Udall & Udall, Tucson, 1960-61; mem. firm Carson, Messinger, Elliott, Laughlin & Ragan, 1961-99. Mem. law rev. staff, U. Ariz., 1959-61. Mem. bd. edn. Paradise Valley Elementary and High Sch. Dists., Phoenix, 1964-68, pres., 1968; treas. troop Boy Scouts Am., 1970-72; mem. Ariz. adv. bd. Girl Scouts U.S.A., 1972-74, mem. nominating bd., 1978-79; bd. dirs. Florence Crittenton Services Ariz., 1967-72, pres., 1970-72; bd. dirs. U. Ariz. Alumni, Phoenix, 1968-72, pres., 1969-70; bd. dirs. Family Service Phoenix, 1974-75; bd. dirs. Travelers Aid Assn. Am., 1985-89; bd. dirs. Vol. Bur. Maricopa County, 1975-81, 83-86, pres., 1984-85; bd. dirs. Ariz. div. Am. Cancer Soc., 1978-80, Florence Crittenton div. Child Welfare League Am., 1976-81; bd. dirs. Crisis Nursery for Prevention of Child Abuse, 1978-81, pres., 1978-80; Ariz. dir. Devereux Found., 1996—, vice chmn. 1996-98. 1st lt. USAF, 1955-58. Mem. State Bar Ariz. (conv. chmn. 1972), Rotary (dir. 1971-77, 95-96, pres. 1975-76, West Leadership award 1989), Ariz. Club (bd. dirs. 1994—, pres.-elect 1997-98, pres. 1998-99), Phoenix Country Club, Phi Delta Phi, Phi Delta Theta (pres. 1954). Republican. Episcopalian. Office: Carson Messinger Elliott Laughlin & Ragan Norwest Bank Tower PO Box 33907 Phoenix AZ 85067-3907

PERRY, LOIS WANDA, safety and health administrator; b. Seattle, Dec. 29, 1937; d. William and Ethel Lenora (Benson) Abrahamson; m. S. Peter Perry, Jan. 12, 1991; stepchildren: Christopher, Tony. BA, Pacific Luth. U., 1962; postgrad., Gonzaga U., 1984. Cert. vocat. rehabilitaton counselor. Claims rep. Social Security Adminstrn., Calif. and Oreg., 1962-69; field rep. Oreg. Dept. of Labor and Industries, Salem, Oreg., 1969-72; safety cons. and trainer, regional safety coord. Wash. Dept. of Labor and Industries, Spokane, 1987—. Guardian Ad Litem Spokane County Juvenile Ct., 1989—. Mem. AAUW (pres. Spokane Valley Br., membership v.p. Valley br. 1992-94, program v.p., co-chair 1994—, com. chair Downtown br. 1989-90, bd. dirs. 1989-90), ASTD (bd. dirs. Spokane-Inland N.W. chpt. 1992), Spokane Tng. Consortium. Democrat. Lutheran. Avocations: gardening, traveling, textile design. Home: 914 S Mckinzie Rd Liberty Lake WA 99019-9685 Office: Wash State Dept Labor & Industries 901 N Monroe St Ste 100 Spokane WA 99201-2148

PERRY, RICHARD JOHN, book publisher; b. Portland, Oreg., Nov. 4, 1960; s. Norman Lee and Carol Janet (Ashcraft) P.; m. Lisa Marlene Doescher, Sept. 10, 1988. Diploma of Culinary of Arts, Western Culinary Inst., Portland, 1985; AA, Portland C.C., 1986. Exec. chef Mt. Bachelor, Bend, Oreg., 1984-85; chef Riccardo's, Lake Oswego, Oreg., 1985-87, Hall St. Bar and Grille, Beaverton, Oreg., 1987-89; antiques dealer Portland, 1989-92; chef Stanfords Restaurant, Portland, 1990-92; pub./owner Starbound Pub., Portland, 1997—, Collectors Press, Inc., Portland, 1992—; cons. in field, 1995—. Author: (book) Maxfield Parrish, 1992. Avocations: guitar, skiing, trekking, writing, bicycling. Office: Collectors Press Inc 15655 SW 74th Ave Ste 200 Portland OR 97224-7989

PERRY, ROBERT TERRELL, JR., nuclear engineer, consultant; b. Paris, Tex., July 19, 1938; s. Robert Terrell and Eleanor Cordia (Endsley) P.; m. Elisabeth Irmina Scherf, July 1, 1976. BS, Tex. A&M U., 1961, MS, 1967, PhD, 1974. Registered prof. engr., Wis. Sr. engr. EG&G Inc., Las Vegas, 1976-78; scientist Interatom Gmbh, Bensberg, Germany, 1972-75; sr. engr. Battelle Lab, Richland, Wash., 1976-79; scientist U. Wis., Madison, 1979-81; asst. prof. Tex. A&M and Pa. State U., Coll. Sta., Univ. Park, 1981-86; tech. staff Los Alamos (N.Mex.) Nat. Lab., 1987—; vis. sci. Princeton (N.J.) U., 1975-76, Max Plank Inst., Garching, Germany, 1975; adj. prof. nuclear engring. Tex. A&M U., College Station, 1998—. Contbr. over 200 articles to profl. mags., jours., reports. 1st Lt. U.S. Army, 1961-63, Korea. Recipient Best Tech. Article award Tex. A&M U., 1979. Mem. NRA, Nat. Soc. Profl. Engrs., Am. Nuclear Soc. (co-chair RP&S tech. program com. 1996—, chair stds. com. 1996—, pres.), Los Alamos Soc. Profl. Engrs., Internat. Radiation Physics Soc., Am. Legion, Masonic Lodge. Libertarian. Mem. Universal Life. Avocations: sailing, exploration. Home: 394 Catherine Ave White Rock NM 87544 Office: Los Alamos Nat Lab MSE 541 Los Alamos NM 87545

PESCOSOLIDO, PAMELA JANE, legal research service owner, graphic designer; b. Chgo., Dec. 28, 1960; d. Carl Albert Jr. and Linda Clark (Austin) P.; m. Larry Carl Vangroningen, Mar. 5, 1994 (div.); 1 child, Harley Austin. BA, Scripps Coll., 1983; JD, Vt. Law Sch., 1990. Bar: Maine 1990. Office mgr., asst. chef The Elegant Picnic, Stockbridge, Mass., 1983; receptionist, sec. Sequoia Orange County, Exeter, Calif., 1983-84; A/R clk. Tropicana Energy Co., Euless, Tex., 1984-85; owner, calligrapher Calligraphic Arts, Great Barrington, Mass., 1986-87; legal intern Pine Tree Legal Assistance, Augusta, Maine, 1989, Office of the Juvenile Defender, Montpelier, Vt., 1990; bookkeeper Badger Farming Co., Exeter, 1991—; owner, legal drafter and researcher Legal Rsch. Svc., Visalia, Calif., 1990—; owner, graphc designer Hourglass Prodns., Visalia, 1995—; rsch. editor Vt. Law Rev., Vt. Law Sch., South Royalton, 1989-90. Designer, graphic artist polit. propaganda for Libertarian Party of Calif.; contbr. poetry to Nat. Coll. Poetry Rev. Mem. county cen. com., chair Valley Libertarians, Libertarian Party of Calif., Visalia, 1996—; candidate Libertarian Party Dist. 19, Calif. U.S. Congress, 1996. Chase scholar Vt. Law Sch., 1989. Mem. ACLU, AAUW (newsletter editor 1994—), ABA. Avocations: calligraphy, cooking, music production. Office: Sequoia Orange Co 150 W Pine St Exeter CA 93221-1699

PESHKIN, SAMUEL DAVID, lawyer; b. Des Moines, Oct. 6, 1925; s. Louis and Mary (Grund) P.; m. Shirley R. Isenberg, Aug. 17, 1947; children—Lawrence Allen, Linda Ann. BA, State U. Iowa, 1948, JD, 1951. Bar: Iowa 1951. Ptnr. Bridges & Peshkin, Des Moines, 1953-66, Peshkin & Robinson, Des Moines, 1966-82; Mem. Iowa Bd. Law Examiners, 1970—. Bd. dirs. State U. Iowa Found., 1957—, Old Gold Devel. Fund, 1956—, Sch. Religion U. Iowa, 1966—. Fellow Am. Bar Found., Internat. Soc. Barristers; mem. ABA (chmn. standing com. membership 1959—, ho. of dels. 1968—, bd. govs. 1973—), Iowa Bar Assn. (bd. govs. 1958—, pres. jr. bar sect. 1958-59, award of merit 1974), Inter-Am. Bar Assn., Internat. Bar Assn., Am. Judicature Soc., State U. Iowa Alumni Assn. (dir., pres. 1957). Home: 6445 E Winchcomb Dr Scottsdale AZ 85254-3356

PETCHENEV, ALEX, scientist; b. St. Petersburg, Russia, May 3, 1956; arrived in the U.S., 1993; BS, Poly. U., St. Petersburg, 1977, MS, 1979, PhD, 1987. Engr. Mekhanobr-Tekhnika, St. Petersburg, 1978-85, scientist, 1985-92; engr. Bently Nevada Corp., Minden, Nev., 1993-94; scientist Bently Nevada Corp., Minden, 1994—. Mem. ASME, Russian Engring. Acad. (fgn.). E-mail: alex.petchenev@bently.com. Office: Bently Nevada Corp 1711 Orbit Way Bldg 1 Minden NV 89423-4114

PETER, ARNOLD PHILIMON, lawyer, business executive; b. Karachi, Pakistan, Apr. 3, 1957; came to U.S., 1968; s. Kundan Lal and Irene Primrose (Mall) P. BS, Calif. State U., Long Beach, 1981; JD, Loyola U., L.A., 1984; MS, Calif. State U., Fresno, 1991. Bar: Calif. 1985, U.S. Dist. Ct. (ea., so., no. and cen. dists.) Calif. 1986, U.S. Ct. Appeals (9th cir.) 1989, U.S. Ct. Appeals (11th cir.) 1990. Law clk. appellate dept. Superior Ct., L.A., 1984-85, U.S. Dist. Ct. (ea. dist.) Calif., Fresno, 1986-88; assoc. Pepper, Hamilton & Scheetz, L.A., 1988-89, McDermott, Will & Emery, P.A., L.A., 1989-90, Cadwalader, Wickersham & Taft, L.A., 1990-91; labor and employment counsel City of Fresno, Calif., 1991-94; v.p. legal and bus. affairs Universal Studios, Hollywood, Calif.; adj. prof. law San Joaquin (Calif.) Sch. Law, 1993—; adj. prof. law Calif. State U., Fresno, 1993—, acad. inquiry officer, 1993—. Contbr. articles to profl. jours. Mem. ABA, L.A. County Bar Assn. (mem. conf. of dels., com. on fed. cts.), Calif. State Bar Assn. (chmn. com. on fed. cts., chmn. exec. com. labor and employment law sect.), L.A. Athletic Club. Friars Club. Office: Universal Studios 100 Universal City Plz Universal City CA 91608-1002

PETER, KENNETH SHANNON, elementary school educator; b. Chgo., Apr. 2, 1945; s. Joseph Francis and Kathleen Daley (Shannon) P.; m. Susan Ann Richardson, Aug. 27, 1977; children: Megan Elyse, Evan Michael. BA in Elem. Edn., Occidental Coll., L.A., 1967; MA in Phys. Edn., U. Laverne, Calif., 1978; MA in Ednl. Adminstrn., Calif. State U., L.A., 1988. Cert. in elem. edn., gifted and talented, ednl. adminstrn., Calif. Elem. tchr. L.A. Unified Sch. Dist., 1968; elem. tchr. Pasadena (Calif.) Unified Sch. Dist., 1969-77, phys. edn. specialist, 1978-90, project tchr., 1990—; cons. in phys. edn.; mem. program quality rev. Pasadena Unified Sch. Dist., 1990—; bd. dirs., presenter Calif. Poly Elem. Workshop Com., 1981-89. Author monographs: Characteristics of Elementary Physical Education Specialists, 1978, Comparison of Specialist and Non-Specialist Taught Studies, 1988. Mem. nat. sch. site com. Am. Heart Assn., Dallas, 1994-97, mem. Jump for Heart task force, So. Calif., 1978-89; area dir. Dem. Party, Calif., 1963-74; mem. sch. site coun. Washington Sch., Glendora, Calif., 1993-95. Named Outstanding Vol., Am. Heart Assn., 1994, Tchr. of the Yr., Pasadena Unified Schs., 1985; recipient Award of Distinction, Calif. Dept. Health Svcs., 1992. Mem. Calif. Acad. Phys. Edn. (sr. assoc.), Calif. Assn. Health, Phys. Edn., Recreation and Dance (elem. phys. edn. chair 1978—), Phi Kappa Phi, Phi Alpha Theta, Delta Phi Epsilon. Democrat. Roman Catholic. Avocations: tennis, fitness. Home: 1665 S Calmgrove Ave Glendora CA 91740-3907 Office: Pasadena Unified Sch Dist 351 S Hudson Ave Pasadena CA 91101-3599

PETERNAL, NANCY FARRELL, museum director; b. Lynn, Mass., Aug. 26, 1929; d. John Bernard and Mary Ellen (Tonry) Farrell; m. William W. Peternal, Nov. 7, 1953; children: John Farrell, Kelly Ann Peternal Thoman. AB, Emmanuel Coll., 1950; postgrad., Boston U., U. Utah, U. Wyo. Tchr. Sch. Dist. # 1, Kemmerer, Wyo., 1950-70; legislator Wyo. Ho.

of Reps., Cheyenne, 1971-75; county commr. Lincoln County, Wyo., 1980-88; mus. dir. Fossil Country Mus., Kemmerer, 1989—. Contbg. author First Ladies of Wyoming, 1990. Chair Dem. Ctrl. Com., Lincoln County; mem. Dem. State Ctrl. Com., 1970—; del. Dem. Nat. Conv., Miami, N.Y.C., Phila., 1974, 76, Disting. Delegation, USSR, Romania, Bulgaria, 1971, Internat. Women's Yr., Houston, 1978; mem. Wyo. Indsl. Siting Coun., 1991-97. Recipient Outstanding Citizen award C. of C., Kemmerer, Woman of Yr. award Bus. and Profl. Women, 1990, Nellie Tayloe Ross award, 1985. Mem. AARP (mem. legis. com.), Fossil Country Futures, Inc. (pres.), Wyo. Sr. Citizens, Inc., Wyo. commn. for Women, Nat. Com. on Status of Women (dir. 1978-82), Wyo. Coun. Devel. Disabilities (chair 1976-82). Roman Catholic. Avocation: historical research. Home: 1001 Park Dr Kemmerer WY 83101-3433

PETERS, ANDREW DAVID, artist; b. Fort Smith, Ark., Nov. 8, 1954; s. Peter Jerold and Jane Elizabeth (Savidge) P. BS, Iowa State U., 1978. One-man shows include Joselyn Art Mus., 1984, Denver Mus. Natural History, 1984, Contemporary Southwest Galleries, Santa Fe, 1992-95, Great Am. Artists, Cin., 1996-98, Artists of Am., Denver, 1998, Anderson O'brien Gallery, Omaha, 1998, Trailside Galleries, Scottsdale, Ariz., 1998. Dir. Hummel Day Camp, City of Omaha, 1976, 77. Recipient Hornaday medal Boy Scouts Am., 1970, Iowa Duck Stamp, State of Iowa, 1978, Iowa Habitat Stamp, State of Iowa, 1979. Fellow The Explorers Club; mem. Great Am. Artists, Artists of Am., Cheyenne Frontier Day Exhbn. Republican. Episcopalian. Avocations: fly fishing, riding, hunting, golf, gardening. Home: 31836 N 65th St Cave Creek AZ 85331-5736

PETERS, BARBARA HUMBIRD, writer, editor; b. Santa Monica, Calif., Sept. 26, 1948; d. Philip Rising and Caroline Jean (Dickason) P. AA, Santa Monica Coll., 1971; BS, San Diego State U., 1976; postgrad. UCLA, 1981-82, 84. Ptnr. Signet Properties, L.A., 1971-85; tech. editor C. Brewer & Co., Hilo, Hawaii, 1975; editor The Aztec Engineer mag., San Diego, 1976-77; regional publicist YWCA, San Diego, 1977-78; campaign cons. Rep. Congl. and Assembly Candidates San Diego; pollster L.A. Times, 1983; pres., dir. Humbird Hopkins Inc., San Clemente, Calif., 1978-91; pub. rels. cons. ASCE, San Diego, 1975-76, Am. Soc. Mag. Photographers, San Diego, 1980. Author: The Layman's Guide to Raising Cane: A Guide to the Hawaiian Sugar Industry, 1975, The Students' Survival Guide, 1976, 2d edit. 1977. Mem. Mayor's Coun. on Librs., L.A., 1969; mem. Wilshire Blvd. Property Owners Assn., Santa Monica, 1972-78; docent Mus. Sci. and Industry, L.A., 1970; founding mem. Comml. and Indsl. Properties Assn., Santa Monica, 1982-89. Recipient Acting award Santa Monica Coll., 1970. Mem. NAFE, Internat. Assn. Bus. Communicators, Sales and Mktg. Execs. Assn. Avocations: travel, opera, puns.

PETERS, DOROTHY MARIE, writer, consultant; b. Sutton, Nebr., Oct. 23, 1913; d. Sylvester and Anna (Olander) Peters; AB with high distinction, Nebr. Wesleyan U., 1941; MA, Northwestern U., 1957; EdD, Ind. U., 1968. Tchr. Nebr. pub. schs., 1931-38; caseworker Douglas County Assistance Bur., Omaha, 1941; hosp. field dir., gen. field rep. ARC, 1941-50; social worker Urban League, Meth. Ch., Washington, 1951-53; asst. prin., dir. guidance, Manlius (Ill.) Community High Sch., 1953-58; dean of girls, guidance dir. Woodruff High Sch., Peoria, Ill., 1958-66; vis. prof. edn. Bradley U., Peoria, 1959-77; coord., dir. Title I programs Peoria Pub. Sch. System, 1966-68, dir. pupil services, 1968-72; dir. counseling and evaluation Title I Programs, 1972-73; vol. dir. youth service programs, vol. program cons. Cen. Ill. chpt. and Heart of Ill. div. ARC, Peoria, 1973-77; owner, operator Ability-Achievement Unlimited Cons. Services, Saratoga Springs, N.Y., 1978-81; spl. cons. Courage Center, Golden Valley, Minn., 1981-84, mem. pub. policy com., bd. dirs., 1985-87; mem. sr. adv. bd. F&M Marquette Nat. Bank, 1981-85; cons. Sister Kenny Inst., Mpls., 1984-86; freelance writer, 1984—; prin. Dorothy M. Peters & Assocs., Roseville, Minn., 1985-87. Bd. dirs, home service com. disaster com. Peoria chpt. ARC, 1958-73; pres., bd. dirs. Ct. Counselor Program; mem. Mayor's Human Resources Coun., City of Peoria; chmn. met. adv. com. transp. for handicapped; ednl. dir., prin., bd. dirs. Catalyst High Sch., 1975-77; hon. life bd. mem. Am. Nat. Red Cross; mem. Saratoga Springs Hosp. Bldg. Rehab. Com.; founder, steering com. Open Sesame, Saratoga Springs, 1978-81; appointee N.Y. State Employment and Tng. Council, 1979-81, Saratoga County Employment and Tng. Com., 1979-81; bd. dirs. Unlimited Potential, 1979-81; mem. Metro Mobility Adv. Task Force, Mpls., 1981-85, mem. policy com., 1984-85 ; mem. vol. action com. United Way, Mpls., 1982-85 ; mem. Minn. State Planning Coun. for Developmentally Disabled and liason to U. Mo. Affiliated Program, 1983-89 (appreciation award 1990); mem. Gov.'s Task Force on Needs of Adults with Brain Impairment, 1985-87; chmn., bd. dirs. Met. Ctr. for Ind. Living, 1986— (svc. appreciation award 1989); mem. sr. ministries coun. United Meth. Ch., 1984-88; mem. dept. rehab. svcs. Minn. Coun. Ind. Living, 1989—; gov.'s appointee Minn. Bd. on Aging, 1989-94; mem. gov.'s sr. agenda for Ind. Living in the 1990's, 1989-94; mem. Nebr. Wesleyan U. Nat. Caucus, Mpls., 1989—; mem. United Way Older Adults Vision Coun., 1993—. Recipient Spl. Congl. Recognition cert., 1994. Mem. Peoria Edn. Assn. (v.p. 1962-64), Ill. Guidance and Pers. Assn. (v.p. Area 8, 1963-64), NEA, Ill. Edn. Assn. (del. 1962-64), Am. Pers. and Guidance Assn., Am. Sch. Counselors Assn., Nat. Assn. Women Deans and Counselors (K-12 task force chmn. 1974—, editorial bd. Jour.), Ill. Vocat. Guidance Assn. (dir.), Minn. Head Injury Found., Nat. Head Injury Found., Ill. Assn. Women Deans and Counselors, Phi Kappa Phi, Psi Chi, Pi Gamma Mu, Pi Lambda Theta, Delta Kappa Gamma, Alpha Gamma Delta. Home: 5483 S Nucla Ct Aurora CO 80015-4008

PETERS, DOUGLAS CAMERON, mining engineer, geologist; b. Pitts., June 19, 1955; s. Donald Cameron and Twila (Bingel) P. BS in Earth and Planetary Sci., U. Pitts., 1977; MS in Geology, Colo. Sch. Mines, 1981, MS in Mining Engring., 1983. Technician, inspector Engring. Mechanics Inc., Pitts., 1973-77. Rsch. asst. Potential Gas Agy., Golden, Colo., 1977-78; geologist U.S. Geol. Survey, Denver, 1978-80; cons. Climax Molybdenum Co., Golden, 1981-82; cons., Golden, 1982-84; mining engr., prin. investigator U.S. Bur. Mines, Denver, 1984-96; owner Peters Geoscis., 1996—; bur. rep. to Geosat Com., 1984-95; program chmn. GeoTech Conf., Denver, 1984-88, mem. long. range planning subcom., 1989-92, gen. chmn., 1991; engr. in tng. #11800, Colo., profl. geologist, Wyo., #367, Pa., 2365. Author: Physical Modeling of Draw of Broken Rock in Caving, 1984, Bur. Mines Articles and Reports; editor COGS Computer Contbns., 1986-90, Geology in Coal Resource Utilization, 1988-91; assoc. editor Computers & Geosciences, 1991—; contbr. articles to profl. jours.; guest editor various jours. Am. Inst. Profl. Geologists, 1984, 85, 86, Appreciation award, 87, Spl. award Denver Geotech Com., 1988, Appreciation award, 1989. Mem. Computer Oriented Geol. Soc. (charter, com. chmn. 1983-95, pres. 1985, dir. 1986, contbg. editor newsletter 1985-96), Geol. Soc. Am., Rocky Mountain Assn. Geologists, Am. Inst. Profl. Geologists (cert. profl. geologist #8274, sec. Colo. sect. 1997, pres. elect 1998, pres. 1999), Soc. Mining Metallurgy and Exploration, Am. Assn. Petroleum Geologists (astrogeology com., 1984—, pubs. com. 1995—, remote sensing com. 1990-95, Energy Mineral divsn. v.p. 1990-91, pres. 1991-92, chmn. pubs. com. 1990-98, Cert. of Merit award 1992, 93, Pres.'s award 1993, Disting. Svc. award 1995), publications com. chmn., 1990—, Am. Soc. Photogrammetry and Remote Sensing, Assn. Exploration Geochemists, Nat. Space Soc., Colo. Mining Assn., Pitts. Geol. Soc., Planetary Soc., Space Studies Inst., Soc. Exploration Geochemists, Denver Mining Club. Republican.

PETERS, EVELYN JOAN, artist; b. Anchorage, Alaska, Mar. 25, 1927; d. Algernon Sidney Jones and R. Lee (Bartholf) Jones-Lange; m. Curtis Gordon Chezem, Sept. 29, 1945 (div. Oct. 1956); children: Joanne Lee Chezem, David Gordon Chezem; m. Frederick William Peters Jr., May 30, 1958. *Evelyn Joan Jones can trace her roots back to paternal and maternal ancestors who came into the Carolinas and New Amsterdam in the early 1600's. Evelyn's great-grandfather, mother's side, Frank G. Bartholf, owned most of downtown Loveland, Colorado. On mother's maternal side, Evelyn descended from Josiah Bartlett, a Declaration of Independence signer. Evelyn's mother, R. Lee Bartholf, was graduate nurse at Railroad Hospital in Anchorage where she met Al Jones. They married June 19, 1924. At the time of his death landing a plane in Bethel, Al owned Al Jones Airways. The Alaska Aviation Heritage Museum, Anchorage, owns Evelyn's painting of her father in his plane.* Student, U. Oreg., 1945-50, Oreg. State Coll., 1955-56. Pvt. sec. Pub. Svc. Commn., Las Vegas, Nev., 1957-58; tech. sec. Los Alamos (N.Mex.) Nat. Lab., 1958-70; sr. sec. EG&G, Los Alamos, 1970-71; chmn. bd. dirs. Buchanan Arts and Crafts, Inc., Buchanan Dam, Tex., 1980-86. One woman show at Frame Corner Gallery, Farmington, 1996, San Juan Coll., Farmington, 1998; exhibited in shows at Inn of Loretto, Santa Fe, 1982, Capital Rotunda, Austin, Tex., 1983, Golub Gallery, Steamboat Springs, Colo., 1985, Sefari Park Hotel, Nairobi, Kenya, 1990 (Artistic Expressions award 1990, Gold medal 1990, St. John's Coll., Cambridge, Eng., 1992 (Bronze medal 1992), Western N.Mex. U., Silver City, 1993, Sixth Bear River Western Hist. Art Exhbn., Craig, Colo., 1994, Fed. Hall Mus., N.Y.C., 1994, 97, Ann. COGAP Exhbn., Governor's Island, N.Y., 1994 (George Gray Award, 1993), St. Francis Newman Ctr., Silver City, 1994, Apples, Aspen and Art, Cedaredge, Colo., 1995 (Most Popular Painting), Western and Wildlife Art Show, Estes Park, Colo., 1995, Sheraton-on-the Park Hotel, Sydney, Australia, 1995, Colo. Indian Market, Denver, 1995, Art Concepts Gallery, Tacoma, Wash., 1997, Keble Coll., Oxford, Eng., 1997, Sunwest Bank, Farmington, 1997, Rotunda Canon Office Bldg., U.S. Ho. of Reps., Washington, 1997; represented in permanent collections at Aviation Heritage Mus., Anchorage, Daystar Found., Oklahoma City, Golub Gallery, Steamboat Springs, Colo., Marble Falls Depot Mus., Mus. N.W. Colo., Craig, Nat. Gallery Rural Art, Bonner Springs, Kans., Pioneer and R.R. Mus., Temple, Tex.; paintings appeared in numerous mags., books, calendars and catalogs. Pres. Highland Arts Guild, Marble Falls, Tex., 1977, 90, 2d v.p., 1989; sec. Highland Lakes Arts Coun., Marble Falls, 1986. Recipient Marine Safety award Olin-Matheson, 1968, cert. of appreciation USCG Aux., 1969, 70, 1st and purchase award Kiwanis Art Competition, Granbury, Tex., 1983, 2d Pl. award Tex. Women Western Artists Show, Cresson, Tex., 1983, 2d and 3d pl. awards Llano Rodeo Art Show, 1986, 1st pl. award 9th Nat. Small Painting Western Show, 1987, 1st and purchase award Gt. Am. Art Competition, 1988, Most Popular Painter award 3d Ann. Invitational Art Show, Waco, Tex., 1988, Best of Show award Bear Valley Hist. Art Show, Craig, 1989, Highland Lakes Arts Competition, Kingsland, Tex., 1991, Internat. Woman of Yr. in art Internat. Biog. Ctr., 1991-92, Most Popular Painting award Western Colo. Ctr. for Arts, 1996, Purchase award NWNMAC, Farmington, 1997, numerous others. Mem. N.Mex. Arts Coun., signature mem. Nat. Acrylic Painters Assn. (US/UK), official Coast Guard Artist, 1987—, Salmagundi Club, 1989-95, World Found. of Successful Women (charter mem.), Am. Biog. Inst. Rsch. Assn. (life, dep. gov. 1989, Gold Cup 1993, Medal of Honor 1992, Woman of Yr. 1994, 95), World Inst. of Achievement (life, Excellence as Painter award 1988). Avocations: gardening, photography, reading, travel. Studio: Evelyn's Studio 3706 San Medina Ave Farmington NM 87401-2328

PETERS, JOSEPH DONALD, filmmaker; b. Montebello, Calif., Mar. 7, 1958; s. Donald Harry and Anna Lucia (Suarez) P. BA in Comm., U. So. Calif., L.A., 1982. Tech. support staff Xerox Corp., La Palma, Calif., 1985—; filmmaker Renaissance Prodns., Ltd., San Dimas, Calif., 1986—. Writer, prodr., dir. films, TV Seniors and Alcohol Abuse, 1986, Eskimo Ice Cream Shoes, 1990 (Gold award 1991), Rachel, 1994 (Silver and Bronze award 1995), Emotions, 1999, Sam & Kathy-Time Travelers, 1998. Mem. Am. Film Inst., Ind. Feature Project, Cinewomen. Avocations: reading film books, collecting videos, sporting events. Office: Renaissance Prodns Ltd Ste 48 301 N San Dimas Canyon Rd San Dimas CA 91773-2734

PETERS, LEROY RICHARD, materials management consulting company executive; b. Milw., June 26, 1943; s. LeRoy Edwin and Eleanor Hedwig (Bensing) Peters; m. Barbara Jean Hackney, Nov. 18, 1964 (div. July 1970); 1 child, Neal; m. Nancy Elizabeth Till, July 17, 1971; children: Richard, Brenda, Eric, Linda. BS, U. Wis., 1966; Grad., U.S. Army/Command and, Gen. Staff Coll., Ft. Leavenworth, Kans., 1977. Cert. fellow in prodn. and inventory mgmt. Inventory supr. Bucyrus Erie, Erie, Pa. and Pocatello, Idaho, ach3-76; inventory mgr. Am. Microsystems, Pocatello, 1976-78; prodn. mgr. Worthington Compressor, Buffalo, N.Y., 1978-80; mfg. mgr. St. Regis WPM Div., Denver, 1980-82; materials mgr. Robinson Brick Co., Denver, 1982-86; prodn. mgr. Merritt Equipment Co., Denver, 1986-89; instructional designer Martin Marietta, Denver, 1989-90; sr. cons. J.D. Edwards, Denver, 1990-93; sr. cons. mgr. AMX Internat., 1993-97; v.p. The Thompson Group, 1997-98; CEO, Enterprise Resource Mgmt., Inc., 1998—. Editorial com.: Aerospace and Defense Dictionary, 1990; contbr. articles to profl. jours. Scoutmaster Boy Scouts Am., Denver, 1989, cubmaster, 1988, outdoor chmn., Denver, 1990; dist. capt. Adams County Colo. Reps., Denver, 1986. Col. U.S. Army, 1966-94, Vietnam, Desert Storm. Decorated Legion of Merit, Bronze Star, Meritorious Svc. medal, Army Commendation medal. Fellow Am. Prodn. and Inventory Control Soc. (bd. dirs. region VI 1990—, pres. Colo. chpt. 1989-90); mem. Am. Def. Preparedness Assn., Moose. Lutheran. Avocations: fishing, reading, music, photography, geology. Home: 1468 W 111th Ave Northglenn CO 80234-3397

PETERS, RAYMOND EUGENE, computer systems company executive; b. New Haven, Aug. 24, 1933; s. Raymond and Doris Winthrop (Smith) P.; m. Millie Mather, July 14, 1978 (div. Nov. 1983). Student, San Diego City Coll., 1956-6l; cert., Lumbleau Real Estate Sch., 1973, Southwestern Coll., Chula Vista, Calif., 1980. Cert. quality assurance engr. Founder, pub. Silhouette Pub. Co., San Diego, 1960-75; co-founder, news dir. Sta. XEGM, San Diego, 1964-68; news dir. Sta. XERB, Tijuana, Mex., 1973-74; founder, chief exec. officer New World Airways, Inc., San Diego, 1968-77; co-founder, exec. vice chmn. bd. San Cal Rail, Inc.-San Diego Trolley, San Diego, 1974-77; founder, pres., CEO Ansonia Sta., micro systems, San Diego, 1986—; cons. on multimedia and electronic commerce sys., 1995—; co-founder, dir. S.E. Cmty. Theatre, San Diego, 1960-68; commr. New World Aviation Acad., Otay Mesa, Calif., 1971-77; co-founder New World Internat. Trade and Commerce Commn., Inc., 1991-94, New World Airways Inc, 1968-77. Author: Black Americans in Aviation, 197l, Profiles in Black American History, 1974, Eagles Don't Cry, 1988; founder, pub., editor Oceanside Lighthouse, 1958-60, San Diego Herald Dispatch, 1959-60. Co-founder, bd. dirs. San Diego County Econ. Opportunity Commn., 1964-67; co-founder Edn. Cultural Complex, San Diego, 1966-75; co-founder, exec. dir. S.E. Anti-Poverty Planning Coun., Inc., 1964-67; mem. U.S. Rep. Senatorial Inner Circle Com., Washington, 1990—; mem. bus. adv. bd. Value Add Reseller, 1995. With U.S. Army, 1950-53, Korea. Decorated (2) Bronze Svc. stars, UN medal. Mem. Am. Soc. Quality Control, Nat. City C. of C., Afro-Am. Micro Sys. Soc. (exec. dir. 1987—), Negro Airmen Internat. (Calif. pres. 1970-75, nat. v.p. 1975-77), Tuskegee Airmen (charter, bd. dirs. Benjamin O. Davis San Diego chpt. 1995—), Internat. Platform Assn., U.S. C. of C., Greater San Diego Minority C. of C. (bd. dirs. 1974—, past chmn. bd.), Masons (most worshipful grand master, supreme coun.), Shriners (Al Kadosh Disting. Cmty. Svc. award 1975). Republican. Avocations: creative writing, golf, world history. Home: Meadowbrook Estates # 245 8301 Mission Gorge Rd Santee CA 92071-3500

PETERS, RAYMOND ROBERT, bank executive; b. Concord, Calif., Sept. 14, 1942; s. Robert V. and Pegi M. (Carr) P.; m. Nancy Tsai; children: Angel, Ray, Matthew. BBA, U. Oreg., 1964. Head customer securities Bank of Am., San Francisco, 1969-71, Eurocurrency and fgn. exchange mgr., London, 1971-72, San Francisco, 1972-76, sr. v.p., head offshore funds, 1976-85, sr. v.p. head treasury, 1985-86, exec. v.p., 1987-92; group exec. v.p., treas. Bank Am. Corp., 1992—; mem. fgn. exchange com. N.Y. Fed. Res. Bank, 1978-87, chmn., 1984-85; mem. Chgo. Merc. Exchange, 1987—; mem. Chgo. Bd. Trade, 1987—; cons. on internat. interest rate risk mgmt., fgn. currency, offshore banking matters U.S. regulators, fgn. central banks, on pension or investment funds mgmt. for govts. and corps. Served to lt. USN, 1964-68. Mem. Nat. Assn. Corp. Treas. (bd. dirs. 1996—). Office: BankAm Treasury Divsn 555 California St Ste 3170 San Francisco CA 94104-1502

PETERS, ROBERT WAYNE, direct mail and catalog sales specialist; b. LaPorte, Ind., Jan. 2, 1950; s. Harry Carl and Dorothy May (Fischer) P.; m. Frances Kay Cooley, Aug. 21, 1971; children: Carolyn Marie, Angela Lynn. BA, Purdue U., 1972. CLU. Mgr. pension adminstrn. Gen. Life Ins. Corp., Milw., 1973-75; dir. qualified plan devel. Cen. Life Assurance Co., Des Moines, 1976-84; v.p. individual ops. First Farwest Ins. Co., Portland, Oreg., 1984-90; pres. CAF Enterprises, Inc., Portland, 1990—; lectr. various govt. agys. Contbr. articles to profl. jours. Mem. N.W. Vintage Thunderbird (v.p. 1988, pres. 1989-90, exec. bd. 1991, sec. 1992-93, 97-98, treas. 1995-96), Optimists (treas. West Des Moines chpt. Iowa Club 1983-84). Avocations: reading, woodworking, vintage Thunderbirds, gourmet cooking. Office: CAF Enterprises Inc 9997 SW Avery St Tualatin OR 97062-9517

PETERS, ROBERT WOOLSEY, architect; b. Mpls., Mar. 24, 1935; s. John Eugene and Adelaide Elizabeth (Woolsey) P. BArch., U. Minn., 1958; MArch., Yale U., 1961. Registered architect, N.Mex., Ariz. Dir. design Schaefer & Assocs., Wichita, Kans., 1975-76; participating assoc. Skidmore Owings & Merrill, Chgo., 1961-74; ptnr. Addy & Peters, Albuquerque, 1979-82; owner Robert W. Peters AIA Architect, Albuquerque, 1982—. Exhibited work Centre Georges Pompidou, Paris, 1980; Univ. Art Mus., Albuquerque, 1982, 92, Albuquerque Mus., 1988. Bd. dirs. Contemporary Art Soc. N.Mex. Contbr. articles to Century Mag., Progressive Architecture, House & Garden, House Beautiful, also others. Recipient honor awards N.Mex. Soc. Architects, 1980-83, 86, 87, 92; honor award HUD, 1980, 5th Nat. Passive Solar Conf., Amherst, Mass., 1981. Fellow AIA. Democrat. Roman Catholic. Club: Yale of N.Mex.

PETERS, ROXANNE LEIGH, nurse practitioner, consultant; b. Gillette, Wyo., Sept. 11, 1954; d. Leonard Andrew and Margaret Rose (DeGering) McCullough; m. Michael James Thiry, Dec. 27, 1975 (div. Aug. 1978); m. John Peters, Oct. 28, 1978; 1 child, Mandi. BA in Nursing, Augustana Coll., Sioux Falls, S.D., 1976; BS in Bus. Adminstrn., Black Hills State U., 1995. RN, Wyo.; cert. nurse practitioner, physicians asst. Nurse Crook County Meml. Hosp., Sundance, Wyo., 1976-77; nurse practitioner So. Nev. Meml. Hosp., Las Vegas, 1978, Advanced Health Systems, Sundance, 1978-82; v.p. Med. Emergency Rescue Cons., Sundance, 1981—; bus. mgr., patient edn. coordinator N.W. Wyo. Med. Ctr., Sundance, 1986-88; assoc. prof. Eastern Wyo. Coll. Outreach Program, 1994—; cons. Parachute Med. Ruscue Service, Kalamazoo, Mich., 1981, Refugee Relief Internat., Boulder, Colo., 1983—. Treas., trustee Crook County Sch. Dist., Sundance, 1982-85; chmn. Crook County unit Am. Cancer Soc., Cheyenne, Wyo., 1983-88; trustee Bd. Coop. Ednl. Services, Gillette, 1982-85, vice chmn., 1984-85; bd. dirs. Crook County Family Violence and Sexual Assault Services, 1985-92, also vice chmn., vol. trainer; commr. Wyo. Commn. for Women, 1983-89; speaker Adolescent Drug/Alcohol Community Group, 1987-94; co-presenter Bush Faculty Devel. Conf.; presenter Midcontinent Inst. Undergrad. Rsch. Conf.; rechr., author Local Bank Rsch. project. Kellogg Found. grantee, 1977; S.D. Small Bus. Inst. Project winner, 1992. Fellow Wyo. Assn. Physician Assts. (bd. dirs. 1978); mem. Am. Acad. Physicians Assts. Republican. Home: PO Box 20142 Cheyenne WY 82003-7003 Office: 18 Valley Rd Sundance WY 82729

PETERS, WILLIAM FRANK, art educator; b. Oakland, Calif., Nov. 8, 1934; s. Clifford Leslie and Gladys Fay (Parrish) P.; m. Patricia Ann Redgwick, June 3, 1956 (div. 1973); 1 child, David William. B. Art Edn. with honors, Calif. Coll. Arts & Crafts, 1961; postgrad., various schools, various locations. Cert. spl. secondary art edn. life, gen. jr. high life. Summer campus art dir., instr. Richmond (Calif.) Unified Sch. Dist., 1961-66, Sch. of Fine Arts, Mt. Diablo Unified Sch. Dist., Concord, Calif., 1967-74; instr. Liberty Union H.S. Dist., Brentwood, Calif., 1961—, chmn. arts & crafts dept., 1976-91; dist. rep. Pacific Art Assn., East Contra Costa County, Calif., 1967-70, Calif. Art Assn., East Contra Costa County, 1970-74; accreditation team mem. Western Assn. Schs. and Colls., Albany, Calif., 1981; film evaluator Contra Costa County Schs., 1965-84; art cons. Exhibited in group shows at Contra Costa County Fair (oil painting Best of Show 1968, watercolor Best of Show 1990, 1st pl. photography 1987-95, 98), Delta Art Show, Antioch, Calif. (1st pl. jewelry 1979), Festival of Color, Concord, Calif. (1st pl. ceramic 1963);. Fundraiser United Crusade, Brentwood, Calif., 1980-83; publicity vol. East Contra Costa County Soroptimist Club, East County Rape/Crisis Ctr., Kappa Beta, John Marsh Meml. Assn., Knightsen 4-H, Delta Rotary Club, Delta Recreation Dept., Oakley Women's Club, Town of Byron, others. Named Contra Costa County Tchr. of Yr. AAUW, 1981, postgrad scholar Calif. Coll. of Arts and Crafts, 1962-63. Mem. NEA, Calif. Tchrs. Assn., Liberty Edn. Assn. (chmn. salary com., past v.p., chmn. evaluation com., chmn. pers. policies com., chmn. scholarship com.), Delta Art Assn. (past bd. dirs.), Brentwood C. of C. (dir. Brentwood Christmas decorations 1968-94). Democrat. Avocations: painting, photography, reading, writing, sports. Office: Liberty Union HS Dist 929 2d St Brentwood CA 94513-1335

PETERSEN, ANN NEVIN, computer systems administrator, consultant; b. Mexico City, Aug. 7, 1937; parents Am. citizens; d. Thomas Marshall and Gerry (Cox) Nevin; m. Norman William Petersen, Aug. 24, 1956; children: Richard, Robert, Thomas, Anita, David. AS in Electronics, Monterey Peninsula Coll., Monterey, Calif., 1962; student, U. N.Mex., 1956, Las Positas Coll., Livermore, Calif., 1992. Cert. computer profl. CAD mgr. Naval Air Rework Facility, Alameda, Calif., 1979-80; computer systems analyst Space and Naval Warfare System Command, Washington, 1980-84, Facilities Computer Systems Office, Port Hueneme, Calif., 1984-86; systems mgr. Lawrence Livermore Nat. Lab., Livermore, 1986-89; data base mgr. Clayton Environ. Cons., Pleasanton, Calif., 1989-90; computer systems mgr. Waltrip & Assocs., Sacramento, 1990-94; dir. computer systems, CFO Innovative Techs. Inc., Pleasanton, 1992—. Author databases. Bd. dirs. Am. Field Svc., Port Hueneme, 1976-78; mem. various adv. bds. U.S. Navy, 1957-86; mem. adv. bd. Calif. Deaf/Blind Regional Ctr., Sacramento, 1976-80; bd. dirs. ARC Alameda County, Hayward, Calif., 1992—. Recipient Superior Performance award U.S. Navy, 1980, Speaker of Month award Toastmsters, 1985. Mem. Data Processing Mgmt. Assn., bd. dirs., sec.), Assn. for Computing Machinery, Tri Valley MacIntosh Users Group, Inst. for Cert. of Computer Profls. Avocations: astronomy, rockhounding, sewing, tennis, painting. Office: Innovative Techs Inc 5238 Riverdale Ct Pleasanton CA 94588-3759

PETERSEN, ARNE JOAQUIN, chemist; b. L.A., Jan. 27, 1932; s. Hans Marie Theodore and Astrid Maria (Pedersen) P.; m. Sandra Joyce Sharp, Aug. 12, 1961; children: Christina Lynn, Kurt Arne. AA, Compton Coll., 1957; BS, Calif. State U., Long Beach, 1959; BA, U. Calif., Irvine, 1975. Comml. pilots lic. Chemist/scientist Beckman Instruments, Inc., Fullerton, Calif., 1959-62, engr., scientist, 1962-65, project, sr. project engr., 1965-74; project/program mgr. Beckman Clin. Ops., Fullerton/Brea, Calif., 1974-80; ops. mgr. Graphic Controls Corp., Irvine, 1980-82; engr./rsch. and devel. mgr. Carle Instruments Chromatography, Anaheim, Calif., 1982-84; ops. mgr. Magnaflux/X-Ray Devel., L.A., 1984-85; rsch. and devel. dir., new products Am. Chem. Systems, Irvine, Calif., 1985-86; rsch. assoc. U. Calif., Irvine, 1987-88; ind. cons., contractor, sales real estate investment, 1989—; career guidance counselor U. Calif., Irvine, 1976. Author scientific papers in field; patentee in field. Vol. F.I.S.H., Costa Mesa and Newport Beach, Calif.; basketball coach Boys-Girls Club, Newport Beach, 1975-78, baseball coach Newport Beach Parks, 1975-78; adv. com. Newport/Costa Mesa Sch. Bd., 1974-75; exec. svc. with AID, Internat. Exec. Svc. Corps, Egypt, 1993-94. Mem. Biomed. Engring. Soc., U. Calif. Irvine Club (bd. dirs.), Kappa Sigma (founder Calif. State. U., Long Beach chpt.). Avocations: flying, photography, swimming, travel, bridge.

PETERSEN, DONALD FELIX, consultant; b. Centralia, Wash., Nov. 16, 1928; s. Otto Anders and Martha Hilda (Peck) P.; m. Norma Ingeborg Wise, Jan. 17, 1954; children: Marilyn, Ronald, Kenneth. BBA, U. Wash., 1950. Transp. rate analyst Pub. Utility Commr., Salem, Oreg., 1953-57; mgmt. effectiveness analyst Dept. of Fin. and Adminstrn., Salem, 1958, mgmt. analyst, 1958-61, supr., fiscal analyst, 1962-67; prin. fiscal analyst Legis. Budget Com., Olympia, Wash., 1967-79, legis. auditor, 1980-85; program analysis mgr. Dept. Social and Health Svcs., Olympia, 1986-91; cons. on state, fed. and local govt. Olympia, 1991—; mem. state career exec. program dept. pers. State of Wash., Olympia, 1986-89; team mem. Price-Waterhouse, Olympia, 1987. Freeholder Thurston County Bd. Freeholders, 1978-79; chmn. Tanglewilde Park and Recreation Dist., Lacey, 1987, 89-90, vice-chmn., 1988; active Dem. Party, Thurston County, 1987-94; vol. RSVP, 1988-92. Cert. of Appreciation, North Thurston Kiwanis, 1988, State of Wash., 1988, Dept. Social and Health Svcs., 1989, ACTION, 1990, RSVP Wash. State Dirs. Assn., 1994. Mem. AARP (3d congl. dist. coord. Vote Program 1990-94, mem. state legis. com. Wash. 1994—, Capital City task force coord. 1995-96, vice-chair 1996-97, 98-99), Nature Conservancy, Masons, Kiwanis (North Thurston chpt. pres. 1973-74, sec. 1970-71). Avocations: history, geography, public service volunteer, railroads. Home and Office: 423 Ranger Dr SE Olympia WA 98503-6728

PETERSEN, FINN BO, oncologist, educator; b. Copenhagen, Mar. 26, 1951; came to U.S., 1983; s. Jorgen and Ebba Gjeding (Jorgensen) P.; m. Merete Secher Lund, Mar. 7, 1979; children: Lars Secher, Thomas Secher,

Andreas Secher. BA, Niels Steensen, Copenhagen, 1971; MD, U. Copenhagen, 1978. Intern U. Copenhagen, Copenhagen, 1978-79, resident in hematology, 1980-83; fellow oncology Fred Hutchinson Cancer Rsch. Ctr. U. Wash., Seattle, 1983-85, assoc. rschr. oncology, 1985-87, asst. mem. in clin. rsch., 1987-91, asst. prof., 1988-91, prof. medicine, 1992—; clin. dir. bone marrow transplant program U. Utah Sch. Medicine, 1992—; med. dir. bone marrow transplant program LDS Hosp., 1997—. Author: Hematology, 1977; contbr. articles to profl. jours. Mem. AMA, AAAS, Internat. Soc. Exptl. Hematology, Am. Soc. Clin. Oncology, Am. Soc. Hematology, Assn. Gnotobiology. Office: U Utah Bone Marrow Transplant Program Div of Hematology and Oncology Salt Lake City UT 84132

PETERSEN, KURT EDWARD, electrical engineer, researcher, entrepreneur; b. San Francisco, Feb. 13, 1948; s. William Ernest and Shirley Ann (Bailey) P.; m. Ann Carpenter, Oct. 10, 1970; children: Scott Edward, Brett William. BSEE cum laude, U. Calif., Berkeley, 1970; MS, MIT, 1972, PhD, 1975. Mem. rsch. staff IBM, San Jose, Calif., 1975-82; founder, v.p. tech. Transensory Devices, Inc., Fremont, Calif., 1982-85, NovaSensor, Fremont, Calif., 1985-95; founder, pres. Cepheid, Sunnyvale, Calif., 1996—; cons. prof. Stanford (Calif.) U., 1994—; head tech. adv. bd. Karl Suss Corp., Germany, 1997—. Fellow IEEE (gen. chmn. solid state sensors workshop 1986). Achievements include patents in micromachining tech. Avocations: skiing, travelling. Office: Cepheid 1190 Borregas Ave Sunnyvale CA 94089-1302

PETERSEN, MARTIN EUGENE, museum curator; b. Grafton, Iowa, Apr. 21, 1931; s. Martin S. and Martha Dorothea (Paulsen) P. B.A., State U. Iowa, 1951, M.A., 1957; postgrad., The Hague (Netherlands), 1964. Curator San Diego Mus. Art, 1957-96; advisor Olaf Wieghorst Mus., El Cajon, Calif., 1996—; extension instr. U. Calif., 1958, lectr., 1960. Author art catalogues, books, articles in field. Served with AUS, 1952-54. Mem. So. Calif. Art Historians. Home: 4571 Narragansett Ave San Diego CA 92107-2915

PETERSEN, RICHARD CRAIG, dentist; b. Ft. Lewis, Wash., Mar. 24, 1950; s. Robert William and Patricia Ann (Youll) Brown; m. Edwina Vivian Peterson, Jan. 10, 1979 (div. Jan. 1983); children: Chelsea Ann, Shawn Leif. Student, Stanford Univ., 1968-69, Univ. Calif., 1969-71; D in dental surgery, Univ. Calif., 1975; MS in Biol. Materials, Northwestern U., 1998. Joint cert. rschr. critical, tech. data U.S. Dept. Def. and Can. Govt. Dentist Public Health, Hawaii, 1975, Bridgeport, Laguna Beach, Calif., 1976-84; pres. R&D Faculty Dun & Bradstreet, Balboa Island, Calif., 1984—. Liaison to past Majority Whip Alan K. Simpson, Los Alamos Nat. Lab., N.Mex., 1993-96; state chair person Am. Assn. for Cancer Rsch., Phila., 1993-96; gov. rels. Am. Inst. of Chemical Engrs., Washington, 1996-97. Recipient Mosby scholarship Book award, 1971-75, Univ. Calif. regent's Scholar award, 1971-75, Mosby Publ. award, 1975, Letter of Appreciation, Pres. Bill Clinton, 1994, Cert. of Appreciation award NASA Outreach Space Exporation Initiative, 1990. Mem. Joint Assn. Advancement of Supercritical Tech., Pentagon Advanced Rsch. Projects Agy., Am. Dental Assn. (life). Republican. Episcopalian. Achievements include testing and devised prinicpal of close blood oxygen monitoring for comatose patients with respiratory collapse. Avocations: surfing, skiing, golf, tennis, jogging. Home: PO Box 25156 Jackson WY 83001

PETERSEN, ROBERT E., publisher; b. Los Angeles, Calif., Sept. 10, 1926; s. Einar and Bertha (Putera) P.; m. Margie McNally, Jan. 26, 1963. Founder, chmn. bd. emeritus Petersen Pub. Co. (pubs. Hot Rod, Motor Trend, Car Craft, Motorcyclist, Photog., Skin Diver, Teen, Hunting, Guns & Ammo, Circle Track, Dirt Rider, Los Angeles, 1948—; owner, chmn. bd. Petersen Properties, L.A., 1996—; owner Petersen Aviation, Van Nuys, Calif., 1996—. Mem. Los Angeles Library Commn., 1963-64; Bd. dirs. Boys Club Am., past pres. Hollywood br.; bd. dirs. Thalians; founder Petersen Automotive Mus., L.A. Served with USAF. Clubs: So. Calif Safari, Chevaliers de la Chaine des Rotisseurs, Chevaliers du Tastevin. Office: Petersen Pub Co 6420 Wilshire Blvd Los Angeles CA 90048-5502*

PETERSEN, VERNON LEROY, communications and engineering corporation executive; b. Mason, Nev., Nov. 3, 1926; s. Vernon and Lenora Eloise (Dickson) P.; children: Anne C., Ruth F. Cert. naval architecture, U. Calif., 1944, cert. in plant engring., adminstrn. and supervision UCLA, 1977; cert. in real estate exchanging Orange Coast Coll., 1978. Philippines Real Estate Office, U.S. C.E., 1950-55; pres., gen. mgr. Mason Merc. Co., 1956-62; pres., gen. mgr. Mason Water Co., 1956-62; pres. Petersen Enterprises, Cons. Engrs., Nev. and Calif., Downey, 1962-79, Vernon L. Peterson, Inc., 1980—; pres., chief exec. officer Castle Communications Co. Inc., 1985—; Sta. KCCD-TV, 1985-89; installation mgr. Pacific Architects & Engrs., L.A. and South Vietnam, 1969-72, facilities engr., ops. supr., acting contract mgr. L.A. and Saudi Arabia, 1979-82; bldg. engr. Purex Co., Inc., Lakewood, Calif., 1975-79; lectr. plant engring., various colls. in Calif., 1975—. Candidate for U.S. Congress, 1956, del. Rep. State Conv., 1960-64; candidate for U.S. Presidency, 1980. With AUS, 1944-47. Inducted into the Order of the Engrs. Fellow Soc. Am. Mil. Engrs. (life mem., named Orange County Post's Engr. of Year 1977, founder Da Nang Post 1969, Orange County Post 1977, pres. 1978-79, Red Sea Post, Jeddah, Saudi Arabia 1980), Internat. Platform Assn., Orange County Engr. Coun. (pres. 1978-79), Am. Inst. Plant Engrs. (chpt. 38 Engring. Merit award 1977-78), Soc. Women Engrs. (assoc.), AIAA. Mormon. Office: Castle Comm PO Box 787 Temecula CA 92593-0787

PETERSON, ANDREA LENORE, law educator; b. L.A., July 21, 1952; d. Vincent Zetterberg and Elisabeth (Karlsson) P.; m. Michael Rubin, May 29, 1983; children: Peter Rubin, Eric Rubin, Emily Rubin. AB, Stanford U., 1974; JD, U. Calif., Berkeley, 1978. Bar: Calif., 1979, U.S. Dist. Ct. (no. dist.) Calif., 1979. Law clk. to Judge Charles B. Renfrew U.S. Dist. Ct. (no. dist.) Calif., San Francisco, 1978-79; lawyer Cooley, Godward, Castro, Huddleson & Tatum, San Francisco, 1979-80; law clk. to Justice Byron R. White U.S. Supreme Ct., Washington, 1980-81; lawyer Heller, Ehrman, White & McAuliffe, San Francisco, 1981-83; prof. law Boalt Hall U. Calif., Berkeley, 1983—. Contbr. articles to profl. jours. Office: U Calif Sch Law Boalt Hall Berkeley CA 94720

PETERSON, BARBARA ANN BENNETT, history educator, television personality; b. Portland, Oreg., Sept. 6, 1942; d. George Wright and Hope (Chatfield) Bennett; m. Frank Lynn Peterson, July 1, 1967. BA, BS, Oreg. State U., 1964; MA, Stanford U., 1965; PhD, U. Hawaii, 1978; PhD (hon.), London Inst. Applied Rsch., 1991, Australian Inst. Coordinated R, 1995. Prof. history U. Hawaii, Honolulu, 1967-96; prof. emeritus history, 1996—; chmn. social scis. dept. U. Hawaii, Honolulu, 1971-73, 75-76, asst. dean, 1973-74; prof. Asian history and European colonial history and world problems Chapman Coll. World Campus Afloat, 1974, European overseas exploration, expansion and colonialism U. Colo., Boulder, 1978; assoc. prof. U. Hawaii-Manoa Coll. Continuing Edn., 1981; Fulbright prof. history Wuhan (China) U., 1988-89; Fulbright rsch. prof. Sophia U., Japan, 1978; rsch. assoc. Bishop Mus., 1995—; lectr. Capital Spkrs., Washington, 1987—; tchr. Hawaii State Ednl. Channel, 1993—. Co-author: Women's Place is in the History Books, Her Story, 1962-1980: A Curriculum Guide for American History Teachers, 1980; author: America in British Eyes, 1988; editor: Notable Women of Hawaii, 1984, (with W. Solheim) The Pacific Region, 1990, 91, American History: 17th, 18th and 19th Centuries, 1993, America: 19th and 20th Centuries, 1993, John Bull's Eye on America, 1995; assoc. editor Am. Nat. Biography; contbr. articles to profl. publs. Participant People-to-People Program, Eng., 1964, Expt. in Internat. Living Program, Nigeria, 1966; chmn. 1st Nat. Women's History Week, Hawaii, 1982; pres. Bishop Mus. Coun., 1993-94; active Hawaii Commn. on Status of Women. Fulbright scholar, Japan, 1967, China, 1988-89; NEH-Woodrow Wilson fellow Princeton U., 1980; recipient state proclamations Gov. of Hawaii, 1982, City of Honolulu, 1982, Outstanding Tchr. of Yr. award Wuhan (China), U., 1988, Medallion of Excellence award Am. Biog. Assn., 1989, Woman of Yr. award, 1991; inducted into the Women's Hall of Fame, Seneca Falls, N.Y., 1991; named Hawaii State Mixed Doubles Tennis Champion, 1985. Fellow World Literary Acad. (Eng.), Internat. Biog. Assn. (Cambridge, Eng. chpt.); mem. AAUW, Am. Hist. Assn. (mem. numerous coms.), Am. Studies Assn. (pres. 1984-85), Fulbright Alumni Assn. (founding pres. Hawaii chpt. 1984-88, mem. nat. steering com. chairwomen Fulbright Assn. ann. conf. 1990), Am. Coun. on Edn., Maison Internat. des Intellectuals, France, Hawaii Found. History and Humanities (mem. editl. bd. 1972-73), Hawaii Found. Women's History, Hawaii Hist. Assn., Nat. League Am. Pen Women (contest chairperson 1986), Women in Acad. Adminstrn., Phi Beta Phi, Phi Kappa Phi. Avocation: tennis. Office: Hawaii Pacific Univ 1188 Fort Street Mall Fl 4th Honolulu HI 96813-2784

PETERSON, CHASE N., university president; b. Logan, Utah, Dec. 27, 1929; s. E.G. and Phebe (Nebeker) P.; m. Grethe Ballif, 1956; children: Erika Elizabeth, Stuart Ballif, Edward Chase. A.B., Harvard U., 1952, M.D., 1956. Diplomate: Am. Bd. Internal Medicine. Asst. prof. medicine U. Utah Med. Sch., 1965-67; assoc. Salt Lake Clinic; dean admissions and fin. aids to students Harvard U., 1967-72, v.p. univ., 1972-78; v.p. health scis. U. Utah, Salt Lake City, 1978-83, prof. medicine, 1983—, pres., 1983-91, clin. prof. medicine, 1991—; pres. emeritus U. Utah, Salt Lake City, 1992—; bd. dirs. First Security Corp., Utah Power & Light Co., D.C. Tanner Co., OEC Med. Systems. Mem. Nat. Assn. State Univs. and Land-Grant Colls. (chmn. 1988-89, chair U.S. Ofc. Tech. Assessment adv. bd. 1990-92). Home: 66 Thaynes Canyon Dr Park City UT 84060-6711 Office: U Utah Sch Medicine 50 N Medical Dr Rm 1C26 Salt Lake City UT 84132

PETERSON, CLAUDETTE MAY, chemistry educator; b. Kingston, Jamaica, W.I., Nov. 3, 1939; came to U.S., 1969; d. William and Ivy (Lee) Chong Fook; m. Wayne L. Peterson; children: Gregory, Kevin. BA, Edgecliff Coll., 1964; MS, L.I. U., 1973. Biology and math. tchr. Mt. St. Joseph Acad., Mandeville, Jamaica; biology tchr. All Sts. H.S., Bklyn.; sci. and math. tchr. St. James Sch., Glen Ellyn, Ill.; math. tchr. Irvin Jr. H.S., Colorado Springs, Colo.; chemistry tchr. Kingman (Ariz.) H.S. Recipient Andy Devine Tchr. of Yr. award, 1994, Women Making History Edn. award, 1996. Mem. AAUW. Avocations: reading, camping. Home: 285 Greenway Dr Kingman AZ 86401-3981

PETERSON, CRAIG ANTON, former state senator; b. Salt Lake City, May 23, 1947; m. Annette Langford, Nov. 15, 1972; 5 children. BS Mfg. Engring. Tech., Weber State U., 1966; postgrad., Tex. A&M U., Corpus Christi, 1968-72. Pres. Craig A. Peterson Cons. LLC, Orem, Utah; mem. Utah Ho. of Reps., 1986-88; mem. Utah State Senate, 1988-98, majority whip, 1993-94, majority leader, 1995-98; owner Craig Peterson Cons., Orem, Utah, 1998—; mem. various coms. including mgmt., retirement, and human svcs. Republican. Office: Craig Peterson Cons 1687 N 200 W Orem UT 84057-8505*

PETERSON, DOROTHY HAWKINS, artist, educator; b. Albuquerque, Mar. 14, 1932; d. Ernest Lee and Ethel Dawn (Allen) Hawkins; m. John W. Peterson, July 9, 1954; children: John Richard, Dorothy Anne. BS in Edn., U. N.Mex., Albuquerque, 1953; MA, U. Tex., 1979. Freelance artist, 1960—; educator, instr. Carlsbad (N.Mex.) Ind. Elem. Sch. Dist., 1953-54; instr. Charleston (S.C.) County Schs., 1955-56; instr. in painting Midland (Tex.) Coll., 1971-76, Roswell (N.Mex.) Mus. Sch., 1981-83, 91—; instr. in art history Ea. N.Mex. U., Roswell, 1989—; instr. painting N.Mex. Mil. Inst., Roswell, 1992—; bd. dirs. N.Mex. Arts Commn., Santa Fe; cons. Casa de Amigos Craft Guild, Midland, Tex., 1971-73. One woman shows include Art Inst., Permian Basin, Odessa, Tex., 1994. Tutor Roswell Literacy Coun., 1988-89; bd. dirs. N.Mex. Arts & Crafts Fair, Albuquerque, 1983-85. Named Best of Show, Mus. of the S.W., 1967, 69; recipient Top award, 1973, 75, Juror award N.Mex. Arts & Crafts Fair, 1986, 1st pl. award Profl. Watercolor N.Mex. State Fair, 1988; Talens-d' Arches award, Tex. Watercolor Soc., 1998; Bd. Dirs. award, San Diego Watercolor Soc., 1998, N. Mex. Watercolor Soc., 1998. Mem. N.Mex. Watercolor Soc. (2d pl. award 1981, San Diego Watercolor Soc. award 1988, 1st pl. award state fair 1988, Grumbacher award 1993, Wingspread award 1994, 1st pl. award 1995, 1st, 3rd and Graham award 1997). Office: Dorothy Peterson Studio PO Box 915 Roswell NM 88202-0915

PETERSON, EDWIN J., retired supreme court justice, law educator; b. Gilmanton, Wis., Mar. 30, 1930; s. Edwin A. and Leora Grace (Kitelinger) P.; m. Anna Chadwick, Feb. 7, 1971; children: Patricia, Andrew, Sherry. B.S., U. Oreg., 1951, LL.B., 1957. Bar: Oreg. 1957. Assoc. firm Tooze, Kerr, Peterson, Marshall & Shenker, Portland, 1957-61; mem. firm Tooze, Kerr, Peterson, Marshall & Shenker, 1961-79; assoc. justice Supreme Ct. Oreg., Salem, 1979-83, 91-93, chief justice, 1983-91; ret., 1993; disting. jurist-in-residence, adj. instr. Willamette Coll. of Law, Salem, Oreg., 1994—; chmn. Supreme Ct. Task Force on Racial Issues, 1992-94; mem. standing com. on fed. rules of practice and procedure, 1987-93; bd. dirs. Conf. Chief Justices, 1985-87, 88-91. Chmn. Portland Citizens Sch. Com., 1968-70; vice chmn. Young Republican Fedn. Orgn., 1951; bd. visitors U. Oreg. Law Sch., 1978-83, 87-93, chmn. bd. visitors, 1981-83. Served to 1st lt. USAF, 1952-54. Mem. Oreg. State Bar (bd. examiners 1963-66, gov. 1973-76, vice chmn. profl. liability fund 1977-78), Multnomah County Bar Assn. (pres. 1972-73), Phi Alpha Delta, Lambda Chi Alpha. Episcopalian. Home: 3365 Sunridge Dr S Salem OR 97302-5950 Office: Willamette Univ Coll Law 245 Winter St SE Salem OR 97301-3916

PETERSON, ERLE VIDAILLET, retired metallurgical engineer; b. Idaho Falls, Idaho, Apr. 29, 1915; s. Vier P. and Marie (Vidaillet) P.; m. Rosemary Sherwood, June 3, 1955; children: Kent Sherwood, Pamela Jo. BS in Mining Engring., U. Idaho, 1940; MS in Mining Engring., U. Utah, 1941. Tech. advisor Remington Arms Co., Salt Lake City, 1941-43; constrn. engr. plutonium plant duPont, Hanford, Wash., 1943-44; R & D engr. exptl. sta. duPont, Wilmington, Del., 1944-51; plant metallurgist heavy water plant duPont, Newport, Ind., 1951-57; rsch. metallurgist metals program duPont, Balt., 1957-62, prin. project engr. USAF contracts, 1962-68; devel. engr. duPont, Wilmington, 1969-80; ret., 1980. Patentee in field; contbr. articles to profl. jours. Candidate for State Senate-Am. Party, Wilmington, 1974; com. chmn. Boy Scouts Am., Wilmington, 1975-78; treas. Local Civic Assn., Wilmington, 1977-79. Rsch. fellow U. Utah, 1940. Mem. Am. Soc. Metallurgists Internat., Del. Assn. Profl. Engrs. Republican. Avocations: lapidary, jewelry making, photography, prospecting, gardening. Home: PO Box 74 Rigby ID 83442-0074

PETERSON, ERLEND DEAN, dean; b. St. George, Utah, Nov. 24, 1940; s. Dean Andrew and Lyle (Evans) P.; m. Colleen Dawn Keith, Dec. 4, 1968; children: Kristin, Sheri, Deborah, Deanne, Rebecca, Andrew. BS, Brigham Young U., 1967, MS, 1971, EdD, 1985. From registration officer to dean admissions and records Brigham Young U., Provo, Utah, 1968-90, dean admissions and records, 1990—; bd. dirs. Utah Higher Edn. Assistance Authority, Salt Lake City, Am.-Norwegian Historical Soc., Northfield, Minn.; lectr. in field; cons. in field. Contbr. articles to profl. jours. Chair, bd. dirs. United Way Utah County, Provo, 1991-94 (chair fund raising campaign 1994-95); coord. Utah Statehood Centennial Ambassadorial Visits Program, Utah, 1995-96. Recipient Norwegian Order Merit and Knight First Class award King Harald of Norway, Oslo, 1997. Mem. Am. Assn. Collegiate Registrars Admissions Officers (Utah chpt., Pacific chpt.). Republican. Mem. LDS Ch. Home: 1121 S 350 W Orem UT 84058-6769 Office: Brigham Young U PO Box 21111 Provo UT 84602-1111

PETERSON, GERALD JOSEPH, aerospace executive, consultant; b. Decatur, Ill., Oct. 27, 1947; s. Raymond Gerald and Mary Louise (Johnson) P. AA, Lincolnland Community Coll., Springfield, Ill., 1969; student, Schiller Coll., Heidelberg, Germany, 1971, Sangamon State U., Springfield, 1972, U. Minn., 1976. Cert. aircraft pilot, engring. tech. Author LOGIC IV commodities futures trading program, 1996; patentee in field. Served with USAF, 1965, French Foreign Legion, 1979. Mem. U.S. Naval Inst. (life). Office: Peterson Aerospace Corp PO Box 1294 Mountain View HI 96771-9999

PETERSON, GWEN ENTZ, artist; b. Newton, Kans., Mar. 8, 1938. BA, No. Colo. U., 1959. Art tchr. pub. schs. Colby, Kans., 1959-61, Denver, 1961-62, Lake Bluff, Ill., 1964-66; studio artist Albuquerque, 1968—. One-woman shows include Jonson Gallery, U. N. Mex., 1975, 77, 79, 81, Thompson Gallery U. N. Mex., 1984, Magnifico's Art of Albuquerque show, 1993, 95; represented in permanent collections Mt. Sinai Med. Ctr., N.Y.C., La Familia Med. Ctr., Santa Fe, U. N. Mex., Albuquerque, Eastern N. Mex. U., Fortunes, IBM, AT&T, Albuquerque. Recipient Calendar Page award Hist. Soc., Albuquerque, 1975, Poster award N.Mex. Arts & Crafts Fair, 1982, Banner Design award Nat. Presbyn. Mariners, 1997. Mem. Nat. PEN Women, Christians in the Visual Arts. Avocations: hiking, mountain climbing, reading. Studio: 3717 General Patch NE Albuquerque NM 87111

PETERSON, HARRIES-CLICHY, financial adviser; b. Boston, Sept. 7, 1924; s. Edwin William and Annekathe (Lieske) P. AB, Harvard U., 1946, MBA, 1950; MA in Edn., San Francisco State U., 1993. Sci. officer Ronne Antarctic Expdn., 1947-48; staff asst. Kidder Peabody & Co., N.Y.C., 1952-53, Devel. and Resources Corp., N.Y.C., 1959-61; dir. indsl. devel. W.R. Grace & Co., Lima, Peru, 1953-57; staff asst. Devel. & Resources Corp., N.Y.C., 1959-61; bus. cons. Lima, 1961-65; v.p. internat. div. Foremost Dairies, Inc. (now McKesson Corp.), San Francisco, 1965-67; v.p. H.K. Porter Co., Inc., Pitts., 1967-68; also chmn. and dir. overseas affiliates H.K. Porter Co., Inc., 1967-68; independent fin. adviser San Francisco and Los Angeles, 1968—; cons. investment banking projects for 3d world countries, Brazil, 1981, 82, 84, Nepal, 1987, Ecuador, 1988, Kenya, 1989, Indonesia, 1989, Peru, 1989, 90, 92, 93, 95, 96, 98, Hungary, 1992, Argentina, 1993, Bolivia, 1993; ind. cons. in field. Author: Development of Titanium Metals Industry, 1950, Che Guevara on Guerrilla Warfare, 1961, Petróleo: Hora Cero, 1964, Islamic Banking, 1979; contbr. articles gen. interest, bus., mil. publs. Served to col. USMCR, 1943-45, 51-52, 57-59. Decorated Silver Star. Mem. Colegio de Economistas del Peru (co-founder, past dir.), Am. Mgmt. Assn. (conf. chmn.). Address: PO Box 190002 San Francisco CA 94119-0002 also: Donatello 131, San Borja, Lima 41, Peru

PETERSON, HOWARD COOPER, lawyer, accountant; b. Decatur, Ill., Oct. 12, 1939; s. Howard and Lorraine (Cooper) P.; BEE, U. Ill., 1963; MEE, San Diego State Coll., 1967; MBA, Columbia U., 1969; JD, Calif. Western Sch. Law, 1983; LLM in Taxation NYU, 1985. Bar: Calif., cert. fin. planner.; CPA, Tex.; registered profl. Engr., Calif.; cert. neuro-linguistic profl. Elec. engr. Convair divsn. Gen. Dynamics Corp., San Diego, 1963-67, sr. electronics engr., 1967-68; gen. ptnr. Costumes Characters & Classics Co., San Diego, 1979-86; v.p., dir. Equity Programs Corp., San Diego, 1973-83; pres., dir. Coastal Properties Trust, San Diego, 1979-89, Juno Securities, Inc., 1983-96, Juno Real Estate Inc., 1974—, Scripps Mortgage Corp., 1987-90, Juno Transport Inc., 1988—; CFO, dir. Imperial Screens of San Diego, 1977-96, Heritage Transp. Mgmt. Inc., 1989-91, A.S.A.P. Ins. Svcs. Inc., 1983-85. Mem. ABA, Interam. Bar Assn., Nat. Soc. Public Accts., Internat. Assn. Fin. Planning, Assn. Enrolled Agts.

PETERSON, JAN ERIC, lawyer; b. Seattle, Apr. 28, 1944; s. Theodore Dare and Dorothy Elizabeth (Spofford) P.; children: Nels Andrew, Anne Elizabeth; m. Marguerite Victoria Caggiano, Mar. 31, 1984. AB in History, Stanford U., 1966; JD, U. Wash., 1969. Bar: Wash. 1969, U.S. Dist. Ct. (we. and ea. dists.) Wash. 1970, U.S. Ct. Appeals (9th cir.) 1970. Gen. counsel ACLU, Seattle, 1969-71; assoc. Daniel F. Sullivan, Seattle, 1972-73; sr. ptnr. Peterson, Young, Putra, Fletcher and Zeder, Seattle, 1973—. Drafter (state statute) Tap Water Regulation Act, 1983. Mem. ABA (editor assoc. 1976-78), Damages Attys. Round Table (founding, pres. 1997-98), ATLA (del. 1985-86), Wash. State Trial Lawyers Assn. (bd. 1973-85, pres. 1982-83), Wash. State Bar Assn. (jud. selection 1985-87, bd. govs. 1992-95), Am. Bd. Trial Adv. (diplomate, pres. Wash. chpt. 1990), ACLU. Democrat. Avocations: piano, baseball, basketball, golf. Office: Peterson Young Putra Fletcher & Zedra 1501 4th Ave Ste 2800 Seattle WA 98101-1664

PETERSON, JOHN EDWARD, artist, consultant; b. San Francisco, May 13, 1948; s. John Alfred and Lois Dorothy (Rima) P.; m. Susan Jane Kaplan, May 1, 1980 (div. May 7, 1987); 1 child, Aaron Charles. Artist, carpenter Calif., 1970-80; artist, designer Prescott, Ariz., 1980-88; theater carpenter Gaslight Theater, Tucson, 1988-92; exhibits dir. Tucson Children's Mus., 1992-96; artist, designer San Francisco, 1996—. Designer, builder Ecol. Design Earth house, 1980-87, Interactive exhibits recyc led materials, Tucson Children's Mus., 1992-96. V.p. Cmty. Coun., Dewey, Ariz., 1984-85. With U.S. Army, 1996-70. Recipient Best of Show, Southwestern Artists Assn., Ariz., 1986, judges choice, Tucson Home Show, 1995, Tu Ch Mu, Tucson Children's Mus., 1996. Avocations: medaphysics, natural medicine, appropriate design. Home: 1055 Sanchez St San Francisco CA 94114-3360

PETERSON, JOHN WILLARD, composer, music publisher; b. Lindsborg, Kans., Nov. 1, 1921; s. Peter Ephraim and Adlina Mary (Nelson) P.; m. Marie Alta Addis (Feb. 11, 1944); children: Sandra Lynn Peterson Catzere, Candace Kay Peterson Strader, Pamela Lee Peterson Cruse. Student, Moody Bible Inst., 1947-48; MusB, Am. Conservatory Music, 1952; MusD (hon.), John Brown U., 1967; DD (hon.), West Bapt. Sem., 1970; DFA (hon.), Grand Canyon U., 1979. Radio broadcaster Sta. WMBI, Chgo., 1950-55; editor in chief, pres. Singspiration, Inc., Grand Rapids, Mich., 1955-71; exec. composer Singspiration, Inc., Carefree, Ariz., 1977-83; pres. John W. Peterson Music Co., Scottsdale, Ariz., 1983—; pres. Good Life Prodns., Scottsdale, 1977-83; bd. dirs. Gospel Films, Inc., Muskegon, Mich., Family Life Radio. Co-author: (autobiography) The Miracle Goes On, 1976; composer works include numerous cantatas, musicals, gospel songs, hymns and anthems. 1st lt. USAAF 1942-45, CBI. Decorated Air medal; recipient Sacred Music award Nat. Evang. Film Found., 1966, Music Achievement award Christian Artists, 1985; Honor Cert. Freedoms Found., 1975; winner Internat. Gospel Composition of Yr., Soc. European Stage, Authors and Composers, 1986. Mem. ASCAP, Hump Pilots Assn. Inductee Gospel Music Hall of Fame, 1986. Home: 11668 N 80th Pl Scottsdale AZ 85260-5650

PETERSON, KEVIN BRUCE, newspaper editor, publishing executive; b. Kitchener, Ont., Can., Feb. 11, 1948; s. Bruce Russell and Marguerite Elizabeth (Hammond) P.; m. Constance Maureen Bailey, Feb. 11, 1975 (dec. May 1975); m. Sheila Helen O'Brien, Jan. 9, 1981. B.A., U. Calgary, Alta., Can., 1968. Chief bur. Calgary Herald, 1972-75, city editor, 1976-77, news editor, 1977-78, bus. editor, 1978, mng. editor, 1978-86, editor, asst. pub., 1986-87, gen. mgr., 1987-88, pub., 1989-96; pres. Canadian Univ. Press, Ottawa, Ont., Can., 1968-69; dir. New Directions for News. Harry Brittain Meml. fellow Commonwealth Press Union, London, 1979. Mem. Can. Mng. Editors (bd. dirs. 1983-87), Am. Soc. Newspaper Editors, Horsemen's Benevolent and Protective Assn., Alta. Legis. Press Gallery Assn. (v.p. 1971-76), Can. Daily Newspaper Assn. (bd. dirs. 1990-96, vice chmn. , treas 1992, chmn. 1993-96), Calgary Petroleum Club, Ranchmen's Club, 100-t-1 Club, (Arcadia, Calif.). Avocations: thoroughbred horse racing; art collecting.

PETERSON, LEROY, retired secondary education educator; b. Fairfield, Ala., Feb. 15, 1930; s. Leroy and Ludie Pearl (Henderson) P.; m. Theresa Petite, Apr. 6, 1968 (div. Oct. 1984); children: Leroy III, Monica Teresa; m. Ruby Willodine Hopkins, July 21, 1985 (div. Mar. 1996). Cert. in piano, Bavarian State Acad., Wuerzburg, Fed. Republic Germany, 1954; BS in Music Edn., Miami U., Oxford, Ohio, 1957. Life credential music tchr., Calif. Tchr. music Cleve. Pub. Schs., 1957-62, L.A. Unified Schs., 1963-94; retired, 1994. Song composer. With U.S. Army, 1952-54. Mem. Alpha Phi Alpha, Phi Mu Alpha Sinfonia. Republican. Avocations: amateur concert pianist, composing, photography. Home: 13005 Spelman Dr Victorville CA 92392

PETERSON, LOWELL, cinematographer; b. L.A., Feb. 1, 1950; s. Lowell Stanley and Catherine Linda (Hess) P.; m. Deanna Rae Terry, Aug. 2, 1981. Student, Yale U., 1968; BA in Theater Arts, UCLA, 1973. Asst. cinematographer, Hollywood, Calif., 1973-83; camera operator Hollywood, 1983-92, dir. photography, 1992—. Asst. cinematographer various prodns. including Blind Ambition, 1979, Hawaii Five-O, 1979-80, White Shadow, 1980-81, Lou Grant, 1981-82, Two of a Kind, 1982, Remington Steele, 1982-83, Something About Amelia, 1983; camera operator various prodns. including Tourist Trap, 1979, Newhart, 1983, Scarecrow and Mrs. King, 1983-85, Children in the Crossfire, 1984, Stranded, 1986, Knots Landing, 1986-87, 89-92, Like Father Like Son, 1987, Star Trek: The Next Generation, 1987-89, Coupe de Ville, 1990, Show of Force, 1990; dir. photography Knots Landing, 1992-93, Second Chances, 1993-94 (Am. Soc. Cinematographers award nomination), Galaxy Beat, 1994, Hotel Malibu, 1994, Lois and Clark, 1995, The Client, 1995-96, Moloney, 1996-97, Four Corners, 1998, Profiler, 1998—; contbr. articles to Film Comment, 1974, Internat. Photographer, 1984—. Mem. Soc. Motion Picture and TV Engrs., Internat. Photographers Guild, L.A. Music Ctr. Opera League, Friends of UCLA Film Archive, Am. Cinematheque, U.S. Chess Fedn., Acad. TV Arts & Scis. Home and Office:

PETERSON, MARK LEO, anthropologist; b. Mpls., Apr. 14, 1958; s. Laurence Elmer and Mimi Katherine (La Brea) P.; m. Patricia Annette Montoya, Sept. 14, 1992. BA in Cultural Anthropology, U. Calif., Irvine,

1986, MA in Social Ecology, 1993. Asst. dir. Trosby Galleries, La Jolla, Calif., 1978-81; field archaeologist RECON, ASM, Wirth & Assocs., San Diego, 1979-82; lab. archaeologist WESTEC, Heritage Svcs., San Diego, 1979-82; rsch. archaeologist Sci. Resource, Surveys, Inc., Huntington Beach, Calif., 1983-86; mng. archaeologist SRS, Macko Archaeol. Consulting, Huntington Beach, 1983-86; grad. rsch. tchr. U. Calif., Irvine, 1987-92; expdn. archaeologist U. Calif.-Irvine, UCLA, Internat. Inst. Mesopotamian Studies, 1989-92; environ. rschr. dept. social ecology U. Calif., Irvine, 1988-93; pres. Peterson & Assocs., Irvine, 1988—; consulting archaeologist Keith Internat., Costa Mesa, Calif., 1992-94; data analyst, quantitative archaeologist Chambers Group, Inc., Irvine, 1994-97; rschr., contbr. Pesticide Action Network, San Francisco, 1988—; spkr. INV Assoc. Geology Students, 1997—; hon. educator Lakota Indian-St. Josephs Indian Sch., 1997—. Art scholar Sch. of Art Design, 1976; rsch. grantee Lawrence Livermoore Nat. Lab., 1990. Mem. Internat. Inst. Mesopotamia Area Studies (rsch. staff 1988-98), INV Assn. Geology Students (spkr. 1997—), Am. Statis. Assn. (spkr., presenter 1995—). Democrat. Hindu/. Avocations: writing, painting, drawing, art, antique collecting. Home: # 21-C 5232 Michelson Dr Irvine CA 92612 Office: Peterson & Assocs # 371 5319 University Dr Irvine CA 92612

PETERSON, RALPH R., engineering executive; b. 1944. BS in Civil Engring., Oreg. State U., 1969; MS in Environ. Engring., Stanford U., 1970; AMP, Harvard Bus. Sch., 1991. Engring. aide Johnson, Underkofler & Briggs, Boise, 1962-63; surveyor Smith, Keyes & Blakely, Caldwell, Idaho, 1963-64; with Chronic & Assocs., Boise, 1964-65; with CH2M Hill Cos., Ltd., 1965—, sr. v.p., dir. tech., 1988, pres., CEO, 1990. Office: CH2M Hill Cos Ltd 6060 S Willow Dr Greenwood Village CO 80111-5142*

PETERSON, RICHARD HERMANN, history educator, retired; b. Berkeley, Calif., Jan. 16, 1942; s. William Martin and Dorothy Jean (Heyne) P.; m. Nora Ann Lorenzo, June 21, 1970; 1 child, Nina Elizabeth. AB, U. Calif., Berkeley, 1963; MA, San Francisco State U., 1966; PhD, U. Calif., Davis, 1971. Calif. community coll. teaching credential. Asst. prof. history Ind. U., Kokomo, 1971-76; instr. social studies Coll. of Redwoods, Ft. Bragg, Calif., 1976-78; assoc. prof. history San Diego State U., 1978-82, prof. history, 1982-96, prof. emeritus, 1996—; freelance writer, 1996—. Author: Manifest Destiny in the Mines, 1975, The Bonanza Kings, 1977, 91, Bonanza Rich, 1991; book rev. editor Jour. of San Diego History, 1978-82, editorial cons., 1980-82; contbr. articles to profl. jours. Judge for papers Internat. History Fair, San Diego, Tijuana, Mex., 1983-88. Faculty Summer fellow Ind. U., 1975, 76, San Diego State U., 1980; rsch. grantee Sourisseau Acad., 1977, Am. Assn. State/Local History, 1988; named Golden Poet of Yr., World of Poetry, 1987-89. Mem. Am. Hist. Assn., Calif. Hist. Soc., Western History Assn., Calif. Studies Assn. Avocations: golf, gardening, writing poetry, travel. Home: 7956 Lake Adlon Dr San Diego CA 92119-3117

PETERSON, STANLEY LEE, artist; b. Viborg, S.D., Mar. 26, 1949; s. Norman and Neva Jean (Harns) P.; m. Katherine Anne Burnett. BFA, U. S.D., 1971. Artist W.H. Over Museum, Vermillion, S.D., 1971-72; graphic artist S.D. Pub. TV, Brookings, 1972-76; free lance artist San Francisco, 1976-77; engring. technician City of Tracy, Calif., 1977-85; artist Stanley Peterson Graphics, Los Banos, Calif., 1985—; contract engring. technician, system mgr. City of Tracy, 1985-89, system mgr., 1989-90; engring. technician IV County of Sacramento, 1991, prin. engring. technician, 1991—; cons. in field. Artist/designer Nat. History Diorama, W.H. Over Museum, 1972. Democrat. Avocations: bicycling, walking, photography, travel, painting. Home: 427 N Santa Monica St Los Banos CA 93635-3223

PETERSON, THOMAS CHARLES, minister, pastoral counselor and therapist; b. San Francisco, Mar. 16, 1955; s. Roy Joseph and Grace Jeannette (Burns) P.; m. Melody Rose Clarkson, Aug. 17, 1985; children: Shannon Nicole, Chad Michael. BA, Living Word Sem., Maryland Heights, Mo., 1986; MS, Carolina Christian U., Linwood, N.C., 1990; postgrad., U. Bibl. Studies, Bethany, Okla., 1990; PhD in Counseling Psychology, Carolina U. Theology, Charlotte, N.C., 1995. Ordained to ministry Full Gospel Assemblies, 1984, Internat. Conf. Faith Ministries, 1986, Assn. Evang. Assemblies, 1989; lic. pastoral counselor and temperament therapist, Wash. Elder, tchr. Joy of Lord Fellowship, Buckley, Wash., 1980-81, By His Word Christian Ctr., Tacoma, 1982-88; assoc. pastor Valley Christian Ctr., Sumner, 1988-89; founder, pres. Joyful Life Ministries, Tacoma, 1985-92; pastoral staff Victory Bible Ch., Tacoma, 1992-96; dir., chancellor, acad. dean Tacoma Christian Life Sch. of Theology, Tacoma, 1993-96; pastor Resurrection Christian Life Ctr., Tacoma, 1996—; chaplain Tacoma Police Dept., 1988-90, Tacoma Gen. Hosp., 1988—; dir. Inst. for Personal Devel., Tacoma, 1991. Mem. Critical Incident Stress Mgmt. Team, Tacoma Gen. Hosp., 1997—. Sgt. USAF, 1973-77. Mem. Nat. Christian Counselors Assn. (profl. clin. mem.), Am. Assn. Christian Counselors (founding mem.), Internat. Assn. Christian Clin. Counselors, U.S. Chaplaincy Assn., United Assn. Christian Counselors. Republican. Home: 5615 S Verde St Tacoma WA 98409-1745 Office: Resurrection Life Ministries Internat PO Box 98198 Tacoma WA 98498-0198

PETERSON, WAYNE TURNER, composer, pianist; b. Albert Sea, Minn., Sept. 3, 1927; s. Leslie Jules and Irma Thelma (Turner) P.; m. Harriet Christiansen, 1948 (div. 1978); children: Alan, Craig, Drew, Grant. BA, U. Minn., 1951, MA, 1953; postgrad., Royal Acad. Music, London, 1953-54; PhD, U. Minn. Instr. music U. Minn., 1955-59; asst. prof. music Chico (Calif.) State U., 1959-60; prof. music San Francisco State U., 1960-91, prof. emeritus, 1991—; vis. prof. composition U. Ind., Bloomington, 1992, Stanford U., 1992-94; artist in residence Briarcombe Found., Bolinas, Calif., 1983; vis. artist Am. Acad. in Rome, 1990. Composer: Allegro for String Quartet, 1952, Introduction and Allegro, 1953, Free Variations for Orch., 1954-58, Can Death Be Sleep, 1955, Earth, Sweet Earth, 1956, (cappella chorus) Cape Ann, 1957, Three Songs for Soprano and Piano, 1957, (cappella chorus) Psalm 56, 1959, Exultation, Dithyramb and Caprice, full orchestra, 1959-60, (cappella chorus) An e e Cummings Triptych, 1962, Tangents for flute, clarinet, horn and violin, 1963, An e e Cummings Cantata, 1964, Fantasy Concertante for violin and piano, 1965, Reflections, ballet, full orchestra, 1965, Metamorphosis for Wind Quintet, 1967, Phantasmagoria for flute, clarinet, double bass, 1968, Cataclysms, full orchestra, 1968, Clusters and Fragments for string orch., 1969, Ceremony After a Fire Raid, Soprano and piano, 1969, Sinfonia and Canticle for baritone voice and organ, 1969, Capriccio for Flute and Piano, 1973, Transformations for String Quartet, 1974, Trialogue for violin, cello and piano, 1975, Diatribe for violin and piano, 1975, Encounters mixed ensemble of mini instrument, 1976, Rhapsody for Cello and Piano, 1976, An Interrupted Serenade for flute, harp and cello, 1978, Dark Reflections (cycle of four songs for high voice, violin and piano), 1980, Mallets Aforethought (symphony for percussion ensemble), 1981, Sextet for flute, clarinet, percussion, harp, violin and cello, 1982, Doubles for 2 flutes and 2 clarinets, 1982, Debussy Song Cycle transcribe for voice and small orchestra, 1983, String Quartet, 1983-84, Ariadne's Thread for harp, flute, clarinet, horn, percussion and violin, 1985, Transformations for chamber orch., 1986, Duo for violin and cello, 1986-87, Trilogy for Orch., 1987, Labyrinth for flute, clarinet, violin and piano, 1987, The Widening Gyre for full orch., 1991, The Face of the Night, the Heart of the Dark for full orch., 1991 (Pulitzer prize for music 1992), Mallets Aforthought percussion symphony revision, 1991, String Quartet # 2, 1992, Diptych, fl, cl, pec., po, rn,vc, 1992, Janus, mixed ensemble of ten instrument, 1993, Duo for Violin and Piano, 1993, And the Winds Shall Blow, a fantasy for saxophone quartet, symphony winds, brass and percussion, 1994; Theseus for smaller orchestra, Vicissiyude (fl, cl, perc, po, vn, vc, 1995, A Robert Herrick Motley (five a capella Choruses) Windup Saxophone Quartet, Peregrinations (solo clarinet) 1996; recs. with Mercury Records, Desto Records, Arch Records, Grenadilla Records, Koch Internat. CRI, Innova, Foghorn, Centur, San Francisco Chamber Singers; Recordings commd. Am. Music Ctr., 1959, Virtuosi of San Francisco, 1968, Unitarian Ch., 1969, Paul Mason, Inc., 1974, 87, NEA Consortium Commn., 1982, Charles Wuorinen and San Francisco Symphony, 1985, Am. Composers Symphony, Inc., 1987, San Francisco Symphony, 1991, Gerbode Found., 1990, Koussevitzky Found., 1990, Fromm Music Found., 1992, Philharmonic Orch. of Freiburg in Breisgau, Germany, 1993, U. Minn., 1995, Neel the Composer (Consortium, Comm.) 1996, Allen Blustine, 1996. Recipient 11th Ann. Norman Fromm Composer's award, 1982, Meritorious Svc. award Calif. State U. System, 1984, Top award Am. Harp Soc., 1985, Composer's award Am. Acad. and Inst. Arts and Letters, 1986, Pulitzer Prize for music, 1992; Fulbright scholar, Royal Acad. Music, 1953-54; NEA grantee, 1976; Guggenheim fellow, 1989-90, Djerassi Found. fellow, 1989-91. Home: 140 S Lake Merced Hls San Francisco CA 94132-2935

PETICOLAS, WARNER LELAND, retired physical chemistry educator; b. Lubbock, Tex., July 29, 1929; s. Warner Marion and Beulah Francis (Lowe) P.; m. Virginia Marie Wolf, June 30, 1969; children—Laura M., Alicia B.; children by previous marriage—Cynthia M., Nina P., Phillip W. B.S., Tex. Technol. Coll., 1950; Ph.D., Northwestern U., 1954; D (honoris causa), U. Lille, France, 1997. Research asso. DuPont Co., Wilmington, Del., 1954-60; research div. IBM, San Jose, Calif., 1960-67; cons. IBM, 1967-69, mgr. chem. physics group, 1965-67; prof. phys. chemistry U. Oreg., 1967-98; ret., 1998; vis. prof. U. Paris-Pierre and Marie Curie, 1980-81; vis. prof. Weizmann Inst. Sci., Rahovat, Israel, 1991, vis. prof. U. Reims, 1996. Committeeman Democratic party, Eugene, Oreg., 1967-70. Served with USPHS, 1955-57. Recipient Alexander von Humboldt award, W. Ger., 1984-85. Guggenheim fellow Max von Laue-Paul Langevin Inst., Grenoble, France, 1973-74. Fellow Am. Phys. Soc.; mem. Am. Chem. Soc., Am. Phys. Soc., Sigma Xi, Alpha Chi Sigma, Tau Beta Pi. Episcopalian. Home: 2829 Arline Way Eugene OR 97403-2527

PETIT, ELLEN JAYNE, sales executive; b. Jersey City, N.J., Nov. 9, 1956; d. William Henry and Margene Emma (Garrison) Scheurle; m. Joseph Edward Scarlatella, June 9, 1979 (div. 1987); children: Amy Jo, Joseph William, David Gene; m. Kim Alan Petit, May 18, 1997. Grad. h.s., Ventura, Calif. Owner, operator Joe's Mountain Copy, Running Springs, Calif., 1983-88; gaming dealer Sam's Town Goldriver, Laughlin, Nev., 1988-90; dual rate floor person Flamingo Hilton, Laughlin, 1990-95; supr. casino pit Avi Hotel & Casino, Laughlin, 1995-97; sales assoc. ULTRA Gold & Diamond Outlet, Laughlin, 1997—; instr. Mohave C.C., Bullhead City, Ariz., 1994-96. Leader Girl Scouts Am., Needles, Calif., 1988; founder Sheriff's Safety Kids, Needles, 1989. Lutheran. Avocations: dancing, reading, bowling, sewing, yard sales. Home: PO Box 3276 Needles CA 92363-2054

PETRELLA, BEN VINCENT, sales executive; b. Bklyn.; s. Louis Frank and Julie (D'Auria) P.; m. Carolyn Tracy Banninga; children: Sarah, Jessic, Louis. BA in English, San Diego State U., 1987. Sales Am. Graphics, Encinitas, Calif., 1987—; musician/songwriter drive-ins, Neptune, Wally World, Encinitas. Author: (screenplay) The Pen Men, 1998, Throw the Bum Out, 1988. Vol. Fresh Start Surg. Gifts, Encinitas, 1996-97, 1998. K.C. (dep. grand knight 1997—). Roman Catholic.

PETREVAN, CHARLES CARL, artist, educator; b. Aljmas, Yugoslavia, Nov. 24, 1919; arrived in Canada, 1930; s. Jerry Jerko and Mara Maria (Gurasin) P.; m. Linda Petrevan. Student, Ont. Coll. Art, Toronto, Canada, 1956. in charge restorer on murals Rialto Theatre, Tucson, 1995—; art educator, Tucson. Group exbns. include Arts Club, Can., 1952, Art Gallery Hamilton, 1957, 58 (named to Nat. Gallery Art Ottowa, Can.), toured with Cooperative Artists of Ont., Can., N.Mex. Art League, 1988 (3d place in oils); permanent collections Rochester's Meml. Art Gallery, Leslie Levy Fine Art, Scottsdale, Ariz. (prize 1992), U.S. Dept. Interior, Nat. Pk. Svc., Tumacacori Nat. Monument, others. Recipient award Best and Brightest Art Show, 1990. Mem. Assn. Am. Portrait ARtists, Am. Portrait Inst. (charter), Am. Portrait Soc. Democrat. Avocations: sport cars, reading Greek and Roman history. Home: 8077 N Streamside Ave Tucson AZ 85741-4614

PETROCHILOS, ELIZABETH A., writer, publisher; b. Blytheville, Ark., Aug. 11, 1943; d. James Alfred Clark and Macie Lee Burris; m. Cleomenis Matheos Petrochilos, Oct. 26, 1961 (div. Mar. 1966); children: Matthew C., Raquel D. Grad., Fresno H.S. Cashier Family Owned Markets, Fresno, 1961-64; med. receptionist Dr. Floyd E. Lee, Lemoore, Calif., 1964-65; pub., author E.A. Prodns., Fresno, 1965—; Author: (poetry) Stone the Poet, 1964. Avocations: books, music, antiques, swimming. Home: 1155 E Bullard Ave Apt 206 Fresno CA 93710-5527

PETROSINO, JAMES MICHAEL, media consultant; b. Phoenix, July 29, 1969; s. Joseph Orland and Ruth Eleanor (Seiffert) P. AAS in Computer Aided Design, CAD Inst., Phoenix. Audio engr. United Sound Svcs., San Diego, 1986-90; audio/lighting engr. Roxy, Phoenix, 1990-95; nightclub design cons. Phoenix, 1993-95; website architect Property Line, Las Vegas, 1995-96; voice/video, data network engr. ORIX Global Comm., Las Vegas, 1996—; A/V cons., Phoenix, 1993-95; website cons., Las Vegas, 1995-96. Artist (book cover) Cardinal Quest, 1984; designer, editor: (website) Property Line, 1996. Mem. HTML Writer's Guild. Avocations: fishkeeping, jet skiing, USENET News, WWW Browsing, breeding/raising dendorbatidae. Office: ORIX Global Comm 1771 E Flamingo Rd Ste B200 Las Vegas NV 89119-5154

PETRUZZI, CHRISTOPHER ROBERT, business educator, consultant; b. Peoria, Ill., July 28, 1951; s. Benjamin Robert and Mary Katherine (Urban) P.; m. Therese Michele Vaughan, Aug. 21, 1982 (div.1987); m. Georgina Sailer, June 20, 1992; 1 child, Lillian Caroline. BA, Wabash Coll., 1972; MBA, U. Chgo., 1974; PhD, U. Southern Calif., 1983. Lectr. bus. U. Wis., Milw., 1975-77; cons. H.C. Wainwright, Boston, 1978-79; lectr. U. So. Calif., 1978-81; prof. bus. U. Pa., Phila., 1981-84; prof. acctg. NYU, 1984-89, Calif. State U., Fullerton, 1989—; pres. ECON, San Clemente, Calif., 1987—. Earhart fellow, 1972-73; U. Chgo. fellow, 1974-76. Libertarian. Christian. Home: 1527 Via Tulipan San Clemente CA 92673-3717

PETTERSEN, THOMAS MORGAN, accountant, finance executive; b. Poughkeepsie, N.Y., Nov. 9, 1950; s. Olsen Thomas and Reva Frances (Palmer) P. BS, U. Albany, 1973. CPA, N.Y. Sr. acct. Arthur Andersen and Co., N.Y.C., 1973-76; sr. ops. auditor Gulf and Western Inc., N.Y.C., 1977, fin. analyst, 1978; adminstr. auditing NBC, N.Y.C., 1979; mgr. auditing NBC, Burbank, Calif., 1980, dir. auditing, 1981-88, dir. acctg. systems and ops. analysis, 1988-90; v.p. fin. and adminstrn. Data Dimensions, Inc., Culver City, Calif., 1991-92; cons. Westwood One, Inc., Culver City, 1992-93; CFO Computer Image Sys., Inc., Torrance, Calif., 1993-97; dir. corp. acctg. DeCrane Aircraft Holdings, Inc., El Segundo, Calif., 1997—. Mem. AICPA, Fin. Execs. Inst. Republican. Roman Catholic. Avocations: sports, travel. Home: 217 1st Pl Manhattan Beach CA 90266-6503 Office: DeCrane Aircraft Holdings Inc 2361 Rosecrans Ave El Segundo CA 90245-4916

PETTERSON, KENNETH CHARLES, foundation director of development; b. Billings, Mont., Jan. 8, 1966; s. Scott Charles Petterson and Marianne Wesbrook; m. Jennifer Elizabeth Kane, June 22, 1996. BA in Interpersonal Comms., U. Mont., 1989. Passenger sales promoter, intern Royal Jordanian Airlines, Vienna, Va., 1989; profl. caddie, pvt. dining supr., asst. wine steward The Coeur d'Alene (Idaho) Resort, 1990-95; travel dir. Maritz Travel Co., St. Louis, 1995-96; dir., Idaho Sports Authority Sports Sales Mgr. Boise Conv. and Visitors Bur., 1996-97; dir. devel. Spl. Olympics Idaho, Boise, 1997—. Co-chmn. Women's Elite Wheelchair Divsn. Idaho Womens Fitness Celebration, Boise, 1997; jr. and sr. high youth leader Hillview United Methodist Ch., 1997—; chmn. supervisory com. Boise Telco Fed. Credit Union, 1998; ptnr. Unified Sports Spl. Olympics. Methodist. Avocations: traveling, tennis, running, computers, fly fishing. E-mail: kpetters@micron.net. Office: Spl Olympics Idaho 8426 Fairview Boise ID 83704

PETTIGREW, EDWARD W., lawyer; b. Aurora, Ill., July 16, 1943. AB, Kenyon Coll., 1965; JD, U. Mich., 1968. Bar: Wash. 1970, Mich. 1971, U.S. Ct. Appeals (9th cir.) 1971, U.S. Dist. Ct. (we. and ea. dists.) Wash. 1971. Shareholder Graham & Dunn, Seattle, 1970—. Mem. Fed. Bar Assn. (pres. western dist. Wash. 1987-88). Office: Graham & Dunn 1420 5th Ave Fl 33 Seattle WA 98101-2333*

PETTIGREW, STEVEN LEE, healthcare management consultant; b. Colorado Springs, May 8, 1949; s. Wesley N. and Mary Ellen (Howard) P.; m. Elise Woodcock, Dec. 12, 1987. BS in Mech. Engring., Colo. State U., 1972. Regional dir. Mgmt. Engring. Svcs. Assn. Program, Inc., Phoenix, 1972-76; v.p. Ariz. Hosp. Assn., Phoenix, 1976-79; corp. exec. dir. Samaritan Health Svc., Phoenix, 1979-96; prin. Ragan Pettigrew LLC, 1996—; lectr. Ariz. State U., Tempe, 1976-78, 93-94. Contbr. articles to tech. publs. Bd. dirs. Hospice of Valley, Phoenix, 1981-88, pres., 1986-88, trustee endowment fund, 1983—; Valley Leadership Class XII, 1990-91; mem. adv. bd. Chandler Hist. Mus., 1994-98, vice-chair, 1995-96, chair, 1996-97. NSF rsch. grantee, 1971-72. Fellow Healthcare Info. and Mgmt. Sys. Soc. (bd. dirs. 1980-81); mem. Instn. Indsl. Engrs. (sr.), Sigma Tau, Kiwanis (bd. dirs. Phoenix chpt. 1985-86, 94-95, treas. 1994-95, Spl. Svc. award 1986, 92, 93, 94, 96). Methodist. Avocations: golf, hiking, travel.

PETTIS-ROBERSON, SHIRLEY MCCUMBER, former congresswoman; b. Mountain View, Calif.; d. Harold Oliver and Dorothy Susan (O'Neil) McCumber; m. John J. McNulty (dec.); m. Jerry L. Pettis (dec. Feb. 1975); m. Ben Roberson, Feb. 6, 1988; children: Peter Dwight Pettis, Deborah Neil Pettis Moyer. Student, Andrews U., U. Calif., Berkeley. Mgr. Audio-Digest Found., L.A., Glendale; sec.-treas. Pettis, Inc., Hollywood, 1958-68; mem. 94th-95th Congresses from 37th Calif. Dist., mem. coms. on interior, internat. rels., edn. and labor; pres. Women's Rsch. and Edn. Inst., 1979-80; bd. dirs. Kemper Nat. Ins. Cos., 1979-97, Lumbermens Mut. Ins. Co. Mem. Pres.'s Commn. on Arms Control and Disarmament, 1980-83, Commn. on Presdl. Scholars, 1990-93; trustee U. Redlands, Calif., 1980-83, Loma Linda (Calif.) U. and Med. Ctr., 1990-95; chair Loma Linda U. Children's Hosp. Found.; mem. Former Mems. Congress, 1988—. Mem. Morningside Country Club (Rancho Mirage, Calif.).

PETTIT, CLAUD MARTIN, religious organization administrator; b. Okemah, Okla., Sept. 19, 1926; s. Frank Martin and Ruby May (Thompson) P.; m. Margaret Esta Cain, July 30, 1948; children: Ruth Elaine Maenpaa, Paul Martin. Degree, Denver Bible Inst., 1948; BS, Rockmont Coll., 1952; postgrad., Bill Ogden Engring./Radio Sch., 1961; DD, Pioneer Sem., 1954. Ordained pastor Conservative Bapt. Assn., 1952. Pastor First Bapt. Ch., Arvada, Colo., 1952-60, Coal Creek Canyon, Colo., 1960; ceo, owner Radio Sta. KEOS, Flagstaff, Ariz., 1960-61; pastor Elmwood Bapt. Ch., Brighton, Colo., 1962-65; ceo, owner Radio Sta. KWIV, Douglas, Wyo., 1965-74; pastor Bethany Bapt. Ch., North Fed. Bapt. Ch., Denver, 1973-95; ceo, owner Radio Sta. KCMP, Brush, Colo., 1976-87; gen. dir. Better Life Ministries, Arvada, 1992—. Trustee Colo. Christian U., Lakewood, 1967—, advisor radio network, 1971—; chmn. bd. Am. Indian Crusade, Oklahoma City, 1987—; dir. Compa Food Ministries, Denver, 1981-91. Mem. Radio Hist. Soc., Broadcast Pioneers of Colo., Broadcasters Found., Model T Ford Club Am. (Mile High chpt. 1969—). Avocations: collecting and restoring antique automobiles, collecting big band music. Home: 8320 W 66th Ave Arvada CO 80004-3327

PETTIT, GHERY DEWITT, retired veterinary medicine educator; b. Oakland, Calif., Sept. 6, 1926; s. Hermon DeWitt Pettit and Marion Esther (St. John) Menzies; m. Frances Marie Seitz, July 5, 1948; children: Ghery St. John, Paul Michael. BS in Animal Sci., U. Calif., Davis, 1948, BS in Vet. Sci., 1951, DVM, 1953. Diplomate Am. Coll. Vet. Surgeons (recorder 1970-77, pres., chmn. bd. dirs. 1978-80). Asst. prof. vet. surgery U. Calif., Davis, 1953-61; prof. vet. surgery Wash. State U., Pullman, 1961-91, prof. emeritus, 1991—; mem. Wash. State Vet. Bd. Govs., 1981-88, chmn., 1987; vis. fellow Sydney (Australia) U., 1977. Author/editor: Intervertebral Disc Protrusion in the Dog, 1966; cons. editoral bd. Jour. Small Animal Practice, Eng., 1970-88; mem. editoral bd. Compendium on C.E., Lawrenceville, N.J., 1983-86, editoral rev. bd. Jour. Vet. Surgery, Phila., 1984-86, editor 1987-92; contbr. articles to profl. jours., chpts. to books. Elder Presbyn. Ch., Pullman, 1967—. Served with USN, 1944-46. Recipient Norden Disting. Tchr. award Wash. State U. Class 1971, Faculty of Yr. award Wash. State U. Student Com., 1985. Mem. AVMA, Am. Legion, Kiwanis Internat., Sigma Xi, Phi Zeta, Phi Kappa Sigma (chpt. advisor 1981-93, 2d v.p. 1993-98, internat. pres., 1998—). Republican. Avocations: camping, small boat sailing.

PETTITE, WILLIAM CLINTON, public affairs consultant; b. Reno, Nev.; s. Sidney Clinton and Wilma (Stibal) P.; m. Charlotte Denise Fryer; children: Patrick Keane, William Ellis, Joseph Clinton. Owner, Market Lake Citizen & Clark County Enterprise Newspapers, Roberts, Idaho, 1959-70, pub., 1959-61; publicity dir. Golden Days World Boxing Champs, Reno, 1970; pub. Virginia City (Nev.) Legend newspaper, 1970; public affairs cons., Fair Oaks, Calif., 1966—, owner PT Cattle Co., Firth, Idaho; cons. in Ireland, Wales, Korea, Japan, France, Czech Republic, Scotland, Alberta, British Columbia, New Brunswick, Prince Edward Island, Nova Scotia, Can., Channel Islands, Costa Rica, Macau, Hong Kong, 1984—. County probate judge, Idaho, 1959-61; acting County coroner, 1960-61; sec., trustee Fair Oaks Cemetery Dist., 1963-72; bd. dir. Fair Oaks Water Dist., 1964-72, v.p., 1967-68, pres., 1968-70; dir., v.p. San Juan Cmty. Svcs. Dist., 1962-66, 68-72; exec. sec. Calif. Bd. Landscape Archs., 1976-78, Calif. Assn. Collectors, 1966-68. Cons. Senate-Assembly Joint Audit Com. Calif. Legislature, 1971-73; exec. officer Occupational Safety and Health Appeals Bd., 1981-83; mem. regulatory rev. commn. Calif. FabricCare Bd., 1981-82; mem. Sacramento County Grand Jury, 1973-74, 1981-82, cons. bd. supvs. Sacramento County, 1985-87; chmn. bus. adv. bd. East Lawn Corp, 1991—; devel. coord. Sacramento Diocese Cath. Cemeteries, 1996—. Election campaign coord. for E.S. Wright, majority leader Idaho Senate, 1968, Henry Dworshak, U.S. Senator, 1960, Hamer Budge, U.S. Rep., 1960, Charles C. Gossett, former Gov. Idaho, 1959-74; asst. sgt. at arms Rep. Nat. Conv., 1956; chmn. Rep. County Cen. Com., 1959-61; del. Rep. State Conv., 1960. Chmn. Idaho County Centennial Commn., 1959-61. Recipient Idaho Centennial award, 1968, 69, Promotion of History award Sacramento County Hist. Soc., 1999. Mem. Assn. Sacramento County Water Dists. (bd. dir. 1967-72, pres. 1970-72), No. Calif. Peace Officers Assn., Nat. Coun. Juvenile Ct. Judges (com. 1959-61), Antelope/Highlands C. of C. (bd. dirs.). Club. Author: Memories of Market Lake, Vol. I, 1965; A History of Southeastern Idaho, Vol. II, 1977, Vol. III, 1983, Vol. IV, 1990; contbr. articles to newspapers, profl. jours. Home: PO Box 2127 Fair Oaks CA 95628-2127 Office: 2631 K St Sacramento CA 95816-5103

PEUS, JOSEPH CARL, orthopedic surgeon; b. Berlin, Germany, Oct. 9, 1936; came to U.S., 1950; s. Carl Joseph and Gerda Eva (Fischer) P.; m. Karen Elaine Peus, Aug. 22, 1964; children: Eric, Brent, Craig, Kristina. BS, U. So. Calif., 1959, MD, 1963. Diplomate Am. Bd. Orthopedic Surgery. Intern L.A. County USC Med. Ctr., 1963-64; pvt. practice family physician L.A., 1964-67; resident L.A. County USC Med. Ctr., 1967-71; total hip surgery fellowship Wrightington, Eng., 1971; orthopedic surgeon Peus, Smith, Birch, Kahmann & Gallivan, Santa Barbara, Calif., 1971—; bd. dirs. Casa Dorinda Retirement Home, Santa Barbara, 1982-90; mem. dir. orthopedic dept. Santa Barbara Cottage Hosp., 1998. Contbr. articles to profl. jours. Maj. U.S. Army, 1964-70. Mem. Am. Acad. Orthopedic Surgeons, Calif. Orthop. Assn. Avocations: golf, skiing. Office: 2324 Bath St Santa Barbara CA 93105-4330

PEVEHOUSE, DOLORES FERRELL, educator, consultant, publisher, writer, artist; b. Corsicana, Tex., Sept. 15, 1928; d. David Frank and Lorena Mae (Ferris) P.; children: Ben Ferrell, Jr., Holly Michele Norton. BA, Baylor U., 1948; JD, Western State U., 1976. Cert. elem. tchr., permanent high sch. teaching credential, Tex.; cert. elem. tchr., Calif.; ordained to ministry First Christians (Essenes) Ch., 1988. Tchr. various pub. schs., Tex., Calif., 1949-53, 68-70; exec. dir. Woman's Law Ctrs., Inc., Orange County, Calif., 1974-76; pres., CEO Woman's Law Ctrs., Inc., Dallas, 1977-79, Pevehouse Prodns., New London, Tex., 1980-87; project dir. Peacemakers, Inc., Dallas, 1987-88, also bd. dirs.; project dir. Global Peace Project, Dallas, 1987-88; pub. The London Times, New London, 1989—; cons., Dallas, 1986-87; founder Women's Law Ctrs., Inc., Calif., Tex., 1974, 76; organizer Home Sch., 1993; developer Russian River Sch. Art, Guernewood Park, Calif., 1998; owner art studio in Studio 116 Galleries, Guernewood Park, 1997-98. Author: I, The Christ, 1984, The Beloved Disciple, 1986, Dyslexic Program, 1982, Single Parenting, 1981. Advisor Hawaii Arts Coun., Honolulu, 1962; founder Sawdust Festival Corp., Laguna Beach, Calif., 1965, bd. dirs., 1967-70; organizer London Rsch. Ctr. for survivors 1937 New London Sch. disaster, 1990— (to merge with London Mus. 1993). Recipient Contbn. to Women award Dallas Times Herald, 1977. Avocation: painting seascapes. Home: 900 S Main New London TX 75682 also: 19123 F St Monte Rio CA 95462 Office: PO Box 1595 Guerneville CA 95446-1595

PEZESHKI, KAMBIZ A., metallurgical engineer; b. Tabriz, Iran, Sept. 30, 1949; came to U.S., 1970, naturalized; s. Amir Aziz and Azam (Mazi) P.; m. Shiron Cashmir Wisenbaker, Apr. 7, 1976; children: Shahene A., Shahla J. BS in Metall. Engring., U. Utah, 1977; MBA in Mktg. and Human Rels., U. Phoenix, 1983. Cert. tchr., Ariz. Process metallurgist Amax, Inc., Golden, Colo., 1977-79; process, rsch. engr. Cities Svcs. Co./Oxidental,

Miami, Ariz., 1979-84; tech. svcs. engr. Am. Cyanamid, Wayne, N.J., 1984-87; mgr. western mining Rhone-Poulenc, Inc., Salt Lake City, 1987-93; nat. sales engr. Hychem, Inc., Salt Lake City, 1993—; polymerization cons. RTZ/Kennecott Copper, Salt Lake City, 1989—. Fund raiser Jake Garn for Senate, Salt Lake City, 1976; fund raiser, motivator Barry Goldwater for Senate re-election, 1980-81; vol. Ted Wilson for Gov., Salt Lake City, 1988. Mem. Am. Mining Engrs. Soc. Republican. Presbyterian. Avocations: wind surfing, running, racquetball, tennis, total fitness.

PFAELZER, MARIANA R., federal judge; b. L.A., Feb. 4, 1926. AB, U. Calif., 1947; LLB, UCLA, 1957. Bar: Calif. 1958. Assoc. Wyman, Bautzer, Rothman & Kuchel, 1957-69, ptnr., 1969-78; judge U.S. Dist. Ct. (ctrl. dist.) Calif., 1978—; mem. Jud. Conf. Adv. Com. on Fed. Rules of Civil Procedure. pres., v.p., dir. Bd. Police Commrs. City of L.A., 1974-78. UCLA Alumnus award for Profl. Achievement, 1979, named Alumna of Yr., UCLA Law Sch., 1980, U. Calif. Santa Barbara Disting. Alumnus award, 1983. Mem. ABA, Calif. Bar Assn. (local adminstrv. com., spl. com. study rules procedure 1972, joint subcom. profl. ethics and computers and the law coms. 1972, profl. ethics com. 1972-74, spl. com. juvenile justice, women's rights subcom. human rights sect.), L.A. County Bar Assn. (spl. com. study rules procedure state bar 1974). Office: US Dist Ct 312 N Spring St Ste 152 Los Angeles CA 90012-4703*

PFEIFFENBERGER, SELMA, art historian; b. N.Y.C., May 31, 1917; widowed; 1 child, Andrea. BA, Queens Coll., 1956; MA, Inst. Fine Arts, 1958; PhD, Bryn Mawr Coll., 1966. Art historian Queens Coll., N.Y.C., 1956-58, Colo. Coll., Colorado Springs, 1966, Conn. Coll., New London, 1966-76. Contbr. articles to profl. jours. Home: 683 Callecita Jicarilla Santa Fe NM 87505-4940

PFEIFFER, GERALD G., human resources specialist; b. Bowling Green, Ohio, Oct. 23, 1939; s. Harry A. and Velma C. (Morrow) P. BS, George Washington U., 1962; MBA, Wayne State U., Detroit, 1970. CLU. With FBI, Washington, Detroit, 1960-63, Am. Std. Corp., Detroit, 1963-70; labor rels. supr. to dir. personnel ITT Corp., various cities, 1970-76; labor rels. and safety advisor to sr. e.r. cons. various cities Mobil Oil Corp., 1976-85; exec. v.p., gen. mgr. HAP Ent., Inc., San Diego, 1985-90; human resources cons. Merit Resource Group, San Francisco, 1991-93; v.p. human resources Nat. Refractories and Minerals Corp., Livermore, Calif., 1993-96; v.p. human resources and adminstrv. svcs. Xing Tech. Corp., San Luis Obispo, Calif., 1996-98, dir. human resources and adminstrv. svcs., 1998—. Contbr. articles to profl. jours. Advisor Jr. Achievement, 1967-84; human resources cons. Joan Kroc Homeless Ctr., San Diego, 1989-92, United Way, San Diego, 1989-92. Capt. USAF, 1962. W.I.N. grantee, 1968. Mem. Rotary. Avocations: sailing, golf, home computers. Home: 501 Clearview Dr Los Gatos CA 95032-1742

PFEIFFER, ROBERT JOHN, business executive; b. Suva, Fiji Islands, Mar. 7, 1920; came to U.S., 1921, naturalized, 1927; s. William Albert and Nina (MacDonald) P.; m. Mary Elizabeth Worts, Nov. 29, 1945; children—Elizabeth Pfeiffer Tumbas, Margaret Pfeiffer Hughes, George, Kathleen. Grad. high sch., Honolulu, 1937; DSc (hon.), Maine Maritime Acad.; HHD (hon.), U. Hawaii; DHL (hon.), Hawaii Loa Coll. With Inter-Island Steam Navigation Co., Ltd., Honolulu, (re-organized to Overseas Terminal Ltd. 1950); with (merged into Oahu Ry. & Land Co. 1954), 1937-55, v.p., gen. mgr., 1950-54, mgr. ship agy. dept., 1954-55; v.p., gen. mgr. Pacific Cut Stone & Granite Co., Inc., Alhambra, Calif., 1955-56, Matcinal Corp., Alameda, Calif., 1956-58; mgr. div. Pacific Far East Line, Inc., San Francisco, 1958-60; with Matson Nav. Co., San Francisco, 1960—, v.p., 1966-70, sr. v.p., 1970-71, exec. v.p., 1971-73, pres., 1973-79, 84-85, 89-90, CEO, 1973-92, chmn. bd., bd.dirs., 1978-95, chmn. emeritus, 1995—; v.p. The Matson Co., San Francisco, 1968-70; pres. The Matson Co., 1970-82; v.p., gen. mgr. Matson Terminals, Inc., San Francisco, 1960-62; pres. Matson Terminals, Inc., 1962-70, chmn. bd., 1970-79; chmn. bd. Matson Svcs. Co., 1973-79, Matson Agys., Inc., 1973-78; sr. v.p. Alexander & Baldwin, Inc., Honolulu, 1973-77; exec. v.p. Alexander & Baldwin, Inc., 1977-79, chmn. bd., 1980-95; chmn. emeritus Alexander & Baldwin, Inc., Honolulu, 1995-98; CEO Alexander & Baldwin, Inc., 1980-92, pres., 1979-84, 89-91; chmn. bd., pres., dir. A&B-Hawaii, Inc., 1988-89, chmn. bd., 1989-95; chmn. emeritus A&B-Hawaii, Inc., Honolulu, 1995—; former mem. Gov.'s commn. on exec. salaries State of Hawaii, com. on jud. salaries. Past chmn. maritime transp. rsch. bd. NAS; former mem. select com. for Am. Mcht. Marine Seamanship Trophy Award; mem. commn. sociotech. systems NRC; mem. adv. com. Joint Maritime Congress; Pacific Aerospace Mus., also bd. dirs.; vice-chmn. Hawaii Maritime Ctr.; former chmn. A. Com. on Excellence (ACE), Hawaii; bd. govs. Japanese Cultural Ctr. Hawaii; hon. co-chmn. McKinley H.S. Found. Lt. USNR, WWII; comdr. Res. ret. Mem. VFW (life), Nat. Assn. Stevedores (past pres.), Internat. Cargo Handling Coord. Assn. (past pres. U.S. Com.), Propeller Club U.S. (past pres. Honolulu chpt.), Nat. Def. Transp. Assn., Containerization & Intermodal Inst. (hon. bd. advisors), 200 Club, Aircraft Owners and Pilots Assn., Pacific Club, Outrigger Club, Oahu Country Club, Maui Country Club, Pacific Union Club, Bohemian Club, World Trade Club (San Francisco), Masons, Shriners. Republican. Home: 535 Miner Rd Orinda CA 94563-1429 Office: Alexander & Baldwin Inc 822 Bishop St Honolulu HI 96813-3925

PFORZHEIMER, HARRY, JR., oil consultant; b. Manila, Nov. 19, 1915; s. Harry and Mary Ann (Horan) P.; BS in Chem. Engring., Purdue U., 1938; postgrad. Case Inst. Tech., Law Sch., George Washington U., Case Western Res. U.; m. Jean Lois Barnard, June 2, 1945; children: Harry, Thomas. with Standard Oil Co. (Ohio), various locations, 1938-80, pres. White River Shale Oil Corp., 1974-76, v.p. Sohio Natural Resources Co., 1971-80, program dir. Paraho oil shale demonstration, Grand Junction, 1974-80; pres., chmn. bd., chief exec. officer Paraho Devel. Corp., 1980-82, sr. mgmt. advisor and dir., 1982-85, cons., 1985—; pres. Harry Pforzheimer Jr. and Assocs., 1983—, Ind. Colo. West Fin., Inc.; dir. IntraWest Bank Grand Junction; adj. prof. chem. engring. Cleve. State U. Contbr. articles to tech. and trade jours. Mem. planning adv. bd. St. Mary's Hosp. and Med. Ctr.; long-range planning com. Immaculate Heart of Mary Ch.; bd. dirs. Colo. Sch. Mines Research Inst.; mem. Petroleum Adminstrn. for War, Washington, 1942-45, Purdue U. Pres.'s Coun.; chmn. Wayne N. Aspinall Found.; mem. long range planning com. Immaculate Heart Mary Ch. Mem. Am. Inst. Chem. Engrs. (chmn. Cleve. 1955, gen. chmn. internat. meeting, Cleve. 1961), Am. Petroleum Inst., Am. Mining Congress, Colo. Mining Assn., Rocky Mountain Oil and Gas Assn., Denver Petroleum Club, Purdue Alumni Assn., Sigma Alpha Epsilon. Clubs: Army and Navy (Washington), Bookcliff Country, Rio Verde Country. Lodge: Kiwanis. Home: 2700 G Rd # 1-c Grand Junction CO 81506-1408 Office: 743 Horizon Ct Grand Junction CO 81506-8701

PFUND, EDWARD THEODORE, JR., electronics company executive; b. Methuen, Mass., Dec. 10, 1923; s. Edward Theodore and Mary Elizabeth (Banning) P.; BS magna cum laude, Tufts Coll., 1950; postgrad U. So. Calif., 1950, Columbia U., 1953, U. Calif., L.A., 1956, 58; m. Marga Emmi Andre, Nov. 10, 1954 (div. 1978); children: Angela M., Gloria I., Edward Theodore III; m. Ann Lorenne Dille, Jan. 10, 1988 (div. 1990). *Great-grandparents Theodore and Katherine Pan Becker left Germany (Hanover and Hessendamstead) for New York and marriage circa 1850. Sister Ruth Kokko recently completed a genealogical study. Father Edward Sr., according to a 1908 issue of the Spaulding Baseball Guide, was once the manager of the Hartford (Conn.) Crusaders. He started in the newspaper business with the Hartford Courant and ended his career as a linotype operator with the Lawrence Evening Tribune and the Boston Globe. Son Edward III, MS 1994, teaches English at Hanyang University, Ansan, Korea. Daughter Angela has two children: Leah Rosin, born 1981, and Christofer, born 1983. Daughter Gloria lives with her mother in Alpaugh, California* Radio engr., WLAW, Lawrence-Boston, 1942-50; fgn. svc. staff officer Voice of Am., Tangier, Munich, 1950-54; project. engr. Crusade for Freedom, Munich, Ger., 1955; project mgr., materials specialist United Electrodynamics Inc., Pasadena, Calif., 1956-59; cons. H.I. Thompson Fiber Glass Co., L.A., Andrew Corp., Chgo., 1959, Satellite Broadcast Assocs., Encino, Calif., 1982; [illegible] Electronics Specialty Co., L.A. and Thomaston, Conn., 1959-61; with Hughes Aircraft Co., various locations, 1955, 61-89, mgr. Middle East programs, also Far East, Latin Am. and African market devel., L.A., 1971-[illegible]; dir. internat. programs devel., Hughes Comm. Internat., 1985-89; [illegible]

dir. E.T. Satellite Assocs. Internat., Rolling Hills Estates, Calif., 1989—; dir. programs devel. Asia-Pacific TRW Space and Tech. Group, Redondo Beach, Calif., 1990-93, Pacific Telecom. Coun., Honolulu, 1993—. With AUS, 1942-46. Mem. AIAA, Phi Beta Kappa, Sigma Pi Sigma. Contbr. articles to profl. jours. Home: 25 Silver Saddle Ln Palos Verdes Peninsula CA 90274-2437

PFUNTNER, ALLAN ROBERT, entomologist; b. Buffalo, May 19, 1946; s. Robert James and Verna May (Colton) P.; m. Sri Hartini Hartono, Aug. 23, 1970; children: Nicolis Dean, Erin Tristina. BA in Biology, San Jose State U., 1969, MA in Biology, 1977. Cert. entomologist. Sanitarian Monterey County Health Dept., Salinas, Calif., 1972-73; vector control asst. Santa Clara County Health Dept., San Jose, Calif., 1973-75; entomologist Northwest Mosquito Abatement Dist., Riverside, Calif., 1975-84; asst. mgr. West Valley Mosquito and Vector Control Dist., Chino, Calif., 1984-89; mgr. West Valley Vector Control Dist., Chino, Calif., 1989—. Contbr. articles to jours. Served with U.S. Army, 1969-72. Mem. Entomol. Soc. Am., Am. Mosquito Control Assn., Soc. for Vector Ecology. Avocations: golf, skiing, cycling. Office: West Valley Vector Control Dist 13355 Elliot Ave Chino CA 91710-5255

PHAM, KINH DINH, electrical engineer, educator, administrator; b. Saigon, Republic of Vietnam, Oct. 6, 1956; came to U.S., 1974; s. Nhuong D. and Phuong T. (Tran) P.; m. Ngan-Lien T. Nguyen, May 27, 1985; children: Larissa, Galen. BS with honors, Portland State U., 1979; MSEE, U. Portland, 1982; postgrad., Portland State U., 1988—. Registered profl. engr., Oreg., Calif., Ariz., Fla., Wash., Mass., Conn., R.I. Elec. engr. Irvington-Moore, Tigard, Oreg., 1979-80; elec. engr. Elcon Assocs., Inc., Beaverton, Oreg., 1980-87, from sr. elec. engr., assoc. ptnr., 1987-96, v.p., 1996—; adj. prof. Portland (Oreg.) Community Coll., 1982—; mem. adv. bd. Mass Transit System Compatibility, 1994. Contbr. articles to profl. jours. Recipient Cert. Appreciation Am. Pub. Transit Assn. and Transit Industry, 1987. Mem. IEEE, N.Y. Acad. Scis., Mass Transit Sys. Compatibility Adv. Bd, Eta Kappa Nu. Buddhist. Avocations: reading, teaching; profl. interests include traction power systems simulation, analysis and design, computer systems simulations, other computer-related systems. Office: Elcon Assocs Inc 12670 NW Barnes Rd Portland OR 97229-9001

PHEBUS, MICHAEL FRANCIS, communications sales executive; b. Chandler, Ariz., Sept. 19, 1952; s. John R. Phebus and Diane Marie McNulty; m. Therese B. Jezior, Nov. 22, 1953; children: James, Diane, Mary. Various positions Ind. Cablevision Corp., Mishawaka, 1974-79; sales rep. Cable TV Supply, Addison, Ill., 1979-81; regional sales mgr. Tele-Wire Supply, Three Rivers, Mich., 1981-82; sales assoc. Peter A. Kechick and Assocs., Elk Grove, Ill., 1982; customer svc. rep. CWY Electronics, Lafayette, Ind., 1982-86; sales rep. Midwest CATV, Kenosha, Wis., 1986-91; sales exec. Midwest CATV, Englewood, Colo., 1991-93; Rocky Mountain sales rep. Times Fiber Comm., Littleton, Colo., 1993—. Chmn. Kenosha County Reps., 1989. Recipient of Hardware Suppliers award Rocky Moutain Cable TV Assn., 1996. Mem. Soc. Telecom. Engrs. (mem. scholarship subcommittee 1996—), Soc. Cable Telecom. Engrs. (sec. Rocky Mountain chpt. 1995—, pres. 1998—), Utah Cable TV Assn. (bd. dirs. 1996—). Home and Office: 7867 S Logan Dr Littleton CO 80122-2817

PHELPS, BARTON CHASE, architect, educator; b. Bklyn., June 27, 1946; s. Julian Orville and Elizabeth Willis (Faulk) P.; m. Karen Joy Simonson; 1 child, Charlotte Simonson Phelps. BA in Art with honors, Williams Coll., 1968; MArch, Yale U., 1973. Registered architect, Calif. With Colin St. John Wilson & Ptnrs., London, 1972-73, Frank O. Gehry and Assocs., Inc., Santa Monica, Calif., 1973-76, Charles Moore/Urban Innovations Group, L.A., 1976-78; dir. architecture Urban Innovations Group, L.A., 1980-84; prin. Barton Phelps & Assocs., L.A., 1984—; asst. prof. architecture Rice U. Sch. of Architecture, Houston, 1977-79; asst. dean Grad. Sch. Architecture and Urban Planning, UCLA, 1980-83; prof. architecture Sch. Arts and Architecture UCLA; faculty mem. Nat. Endowment Arts, Mayors Inst. for City Design, 1990, 92. Author, editor: Architecture California, 1988-92, 98; editor: Views From the River, 1998; mem. editl. bd. Archtl. Record, 1998—. Fellow Graham Found. for Advanced Studies in the Fine Arts, 1989, 96, Nat. Endowment for the Arts, 1990, 98. Mem. AIA (Coll. of Fellows, chair nat. com. on design, recipient design awards for Royce Hall at UCLA, Arroyo House, Kranz House, North Range Clark Libr. UCLA, L.A. Dept. Water and Power Ctrl. Dist. Hdqrs., No. Hollywood Pump Sta., East Bldg. Seeds U. Elem. Sch., UCLA, Inst. Honor for Collaborative Design, Games XXIII Olympiad L.A. 1984), L.A. Conservancy. Democrat. Home: 10256 Lelia Ln Los Angeles CA 90077-3144 Office: Barton Phelps & Assocs 5514 Wilshire Blvd Los Angeles CA 90036-3829*

PHELPS, MICHAEL EVERETT JOSEPH, energy company executive; b. Montreal, Que., Can., June 27, 1947; s. Arthur A. and Hendrina (Von De Roer) P.; m. Joy Slimmon, Aug. 8, 1970; children: Erica, Julia, Lindsay. BA, U. Manitoba, 1967, LLB, 1970; LLM, London Sch. Econs., 1971. Crown atty. Province of Man., Winnipeg, 1971-72; ptnr. Christie, Degraves, Winnipeg, 1973-76; spl. advisor, exec. asst. Minister of Justice, Ottawa, Ont., 1976-79; exec. asst. Minister of Energy, Mines & Resources, Ottawa, 1980-82; sr. advisor to pres. & chief exec. officer Westcoast Transmission Co. Ltd., Vancouver, B.C., 1982-83; v.p. strategic planning Westcoast Transmission Co. Ltd., Vancouver, 1983-87, sr. v.p., 1987, exec. v.p., chief fin. officer, 1987-88; pres., chief exec. officer Westcoast Energy, Inc. (formerly Westcoast Transmission Co Ltd.), Vancouver, 1988-92, now chmn., CEO, also bd. dirs.; bd. dirs. Canadian Imperial Bank Commerce, Canfor Corp., Canadian Pacific, Westcoast Energy Internat., Inc.; dep. chmn. bd. dirs. Foothills Pipe Lines, Ltd.; mem. adv. coun. faculty commerce and bus. adminstrn. U. B.C.; mem. adv. bd. Team Can., Inc. Chmn. bd. dirs. Asia Pacific Found. Can.; trustee Simon fraser U. Found.; chmn. com. to nominate Can. Pension Plan Investment Bd. Mem. Interstate Natural Gas Assn. Am. (bd. dirs.), The Vancouver, Hollyburn Country, Vancouver Club, Hollyburn Country Club. Office: Westcoast Energy Inc, 1333 W Georgia St, Vancouver, BC Canada V6E 3K9

PHELPS, VADA JO, town official; b. Laramie, Wyo., Aug. 30, 1943; d. Joseph Marion and Zula Alsetta (Curtis) Thronebury; m. Bobby Eugene Andrews, Feb. 11, 1962 (dec. Feb. 1976); children: Terri Lynelle, Joel Douglas; m. Robert Lee Phelps, Sept. 20, 1979. BBA, U. Denver, 1986, MBA, 1988. Office mgr. Prudential Nat. Co., Denver, 1961-64; policy clk. Conn. Mut. Life Ins. Co., Denver, 1964-68; computer operator Genuine Auto Parts Co., Denver, 1969-70; bookkeeper Summit County Schs., Frisco, Colo., 1970-71; office mgr. B.D.F. Constrn. Co., Frisco, 1972-76; town clk.-treas. Town of Frisco, 1976—; exec. dir. Cochise Private Industry Coun., Inc., Sierra Vista, Ariz., 1988—. Mem. accountability com. Summit Schs., Frisco, 1973-75, Cochise Coll. Pres. Adv. Coun., oversight bd. Cochise Commn. Mem. Internat. Inst. Mcpl. Clks. (cert. mcpl. clk.), Colo. City Clks. Assn. (2d v.p. 1986-87, 1st v.p. 1987—), Colo. Mcpl. Fin. Officers Assn., Mcpl. Treas. Assn., Ariz. juvenile justice commn., Ariz. workforce developers (sec.-treas., bd. dirs), YFC/YOU Nat. Youth Coun. (bd. dirs.), U. Denver M.E.C. Alumnae, Epsilon Sigma Alpha Internat. (Woman of Yr. award 1980). Republican. Mem. Church of Christ. Club: TOPS (Frisco). Avocations: travel, reading, education. Home: 1320 E Buckhorn Dr Sierra Vista AZ 85635-1358 Office: Town of Frisco PO Box 4100 Frisco CO 80443-4100

PHILIP, NIXON BALDWIN, JR., chemist; b. New Orleans, Apr. 16, 1943; s. Philip Nixon and Irene (Love) B.; m. Janet Clare Wimmer, June 12, 1965 (div. Oct. 1984); children: Dawn Angela, Philip III; m. Adalene Elizabeth Broussard, May 25, 1987. BS in Chemistry, Notre Dame U., 1965; MBA, U. Akron, 1967. Staff rsch. chemist Goodyear Tire & Rubber, Akron, Ohio, 1965-67; indsl. sales Jefferson Chem. Divsn., Texaco Chem., Chgo., 1968—, dist. sales mgr., 1969-73; pres., CEO PNB Corp./Memphis Oil, 1973-84; v.p. sales Chemfix Techs., Inc., Metairie, La., 1990-92, v.p. tech. devel., 1992-93; pres. CeTech Resources, Inc., Metairie, La., 1992-93; v.p. tech. ICFL, Inc., Las Vegas, 1992—; sr. v.p. tech. Pell Resources, Inc., Las Vegas, 1995-97; [illegible] field. Mem. ASTM, Am. Chem. Soc., Water Environment Fedn. Republican. Roman Catholic. Avocations: skiing, golf. E-mail: icfl@juno.com. Office: ICFL Inc 3305 Spring Mountain Rd Ste 60 Las Vegas NV 89102-[illegible]

PHILIPOSSIAN, ARA, engineer, semiconductor process technologist; b. Tehran, Iran, Feb. 22, 1961; came to U.S., 1978; s. Vigen and Ella (Babayan) P.; children: Remy, Ricky. BSChE magna cum laude, Tufts U., 1983, MSChE, 1985, PhD in Chem Engring., 1992. Process engr. BTU Internat. Inc., North Billerica, Mass., 1983-85; mfg. process engr. Analog Devices Inc., Wilmington, Mass., 1985-86; prin. engr. Digital Equipment Corp., Hudson, Mass., 1986-92; technology mgr. Intel Corp., Santa Clara, Calif., 1992—; spkr. in field. Contbr. some 80 articles to profl. jours. Mem. Electrochem. Soc., Ultra Clean Soc., Materials Rsch. Soc. Achievements include 12 patents in field. Avocations: tennis, soccer, classical music. Office: Intel Corp 2200 Mission College Blvd Santa Clara CA 95054-1549

PHILIPPI, ERVIN WILLIAM, mortician; b. Lodi, Calif., June 4, 1922; s. William and Rebecca (Steinert) P.; m. Emma Grace Mosely, May 8, 1958 (div. Mar. 1979); m. Helen Jo Hunt, June 3, 1979. Grad., Calif. Coll. Motuary Sci., 1948. Embalmer, mortician, mgr. Salas Bros. Chapel, Modesto, Calif., 1946-92; dep. coroner Stanislaus County, Calif., 1955-75. With U.S. Army, 1942-46. Avocations: old car restoration, travel.

PHILIPSBORN, JOHN TIMOTHY, lawyer, author; b. Paris, Oct. 19, 1949; s. John David and Helen (Worth) P. AB, Bowdoin Coll., 1971; MEd, Antioch Coll., 1975; JD, U. Calif., Davis, 1978. Bar: Calif. 1978, U.S. Dist. Ct. (no. and ea. dists.) Calif. 1978, U.S. Ct. Appeals (9th cir.) 1985, U.S. Supreme Ct. 1985; cert-specialist in criminal law State of Calif., 1985. VISTA vol. Office of Gov. State of Mont., Helena, 1972-73; cons. U.S. Govt., Denver, 1974; lectr. Antioch New Eng. Grad. Sch., Keene, N.H., 1973-75, U. N.H., Durham, 1973-75; ptnr. Philipsborn & Cohn, San Jose, Calif., 1978-80; atty., supr. Defenders Inc., San Diego, 1980-83; assoc. Garry, Dreyfus & McTernan, San Francisco, 1983-87; pvt. practice, San Diego and San Francisco, 1987—; cons. Nicaraguan ct. evaluation projects, 1987-88, UN Internat. Tribunal, 1995—; coord. Internat. Conf. Adversarial Sys., Lisbon, Portugal, 1990; mem. adj. faculty New Coll. Law, San Francisco, 1991—; legal asst. project refugee camps S.E. Asia, 1992—, legal edn. projects, Cambodia, 1995—; cons. on continuing edn. of bar, 1995—. Bd. editors Champion, Forum; contbr. articles to profl. jours., chpts. to book. Founder trial program San Francisco Schs., 1986; bd. dirs. Calif. Indian Legal Svcs., 1990-96. Fulbright scholar, Portugal, 1989. Mem. Nat. Assn. Criminal Def. Lawyers (assoc., co-chmn. death penalty impact litigation group 1989, co-chmn. govtl. misconduct com. 1990-92, vice chmn. task force on emerging democracies 1990-91), Calif. State Bar (evaluation panel criminal law specialists 1986—, com. on continuing edn. of bar 1991-94, criminal law subcom. state bd. legal specialists 1995-96), Calif. Attys. for Criminal Justice (bd. govs. 1989-94, assoc. editor jour. 1987—, chmn. Amicus Curiae com. 1992—, co-chmn. govtl. misconduct com. 1989-92), World Affairs Coun. Office: Civic Ctr Bldg 507 Polk St Ste 250 San Francisco CA 94102-3344

PHILLIPS, ANNA, publisher, editor-in-chief newspaper; b. Oakalla, Tex., Nov. 19, 1936; d. Edward C. and Barbara W. (Roberts) Spinks; 1 child, Kenny E. Phillips. Asst. sales mgr. Am. Legion Newspaper, San Antonio, 1961-68; sales profl. Sta. KLRN-TV Ednl. Broadcasting, San Antonio, 1969-73; sales mgr. Victor Bloom Advt. Agy., L.A., 1973-77, Non-Commd. Officers Assn., Oceanside, Calif., 1977-80; asst. sales mgr. Marshals Assn., San Diego, 1978-81; editor-in-chief, founder World of Entertainment, 1981-90; founder, pub. Associated News of So. Calif., San Bernardino, 1985-93; pub. Sheriff & Police News Southern Calif., 1987—; news editor, publ. films, Hollywood and Las Vegas, Nev., 1980-94; pub. for Hollywood celebrities and major stage productions, 1984—. Mgr. pub. rels. dept. Student Coun., Trinity U. for world famous celebrities, jazz musicians, concert news and public relations; news and pub. rels. coord. for Native Am. Indians; fund-draiser scholarships for American Indian students, 1989-98. Recipient Nat. Pub. award Nat. Fedn. of Fed. Employees, 1966, Golden Halo Trophy Motion Picture Coun. So. Calif., 1996, Star Sapphire award Motion Picture Coun. So. Calif., 1996. Mem. Associated Press (recipient Hon. Charter Mem. Plaque award, 1997, lifetime charter mem.). Avocations: jogging, bicycling, dancing, playing piano. Office: Associated News PO Box 336 Yucaipa CA 92399-0336

PHILLIPS, BILLY SAXTON, artist, designer, painter; b. Louisville, Nebr., June 20, 1915; d. Charles William and Georgia Hazel (de le Zene) Tremblay; m. John Henry Phillips, Sept. 3, 1937; 1 dau., Terry. Grad., Art Ctr. Coll. of Design, 1950. Free-lance artist L.A., 1951—; package designer Wilson Paper-Disneyland, Anaheim, Calif., 1952-56; inventor Vernon (Calif.) Container Corp., 1952-56; instr. Clatsop C.C., Astoria, Oreg., 1990-92; painter Reva-Reva Gallery, Papeete, French Polynesia, 1972-92, Royal Gallery, Lahaina, Maui, Hawaii, 1993-94; artist P.M. Prodns., L.A., 1951-90; instr., motivator Maoridom, New Zealand, 1980—; instr. Art Ctr. Coll. Design, 1952-53. Designer, patentee Ukili, 1967, packages, 1960 (Zipper openings on cardboard containers); designer Disneyland's Tinkerbell; group shows include Royal Art Gallery, Met. Gallery, Lahanina, Maui, Hawaii, 1994, Kona, Hawaii, 1995. Developer Cultural Exchange Program First Ams.-Maori, S.W. Am. Indians and New Zealand Maoris, 1986. Mem. Art Ctr. Alumni (charter, life), Trail's End Art Assn., Lady Elk, Inventors and Scientists Am. Avocations: travel, graphoanalysis, theatre.

PHILLIPS, CRAIG STEWART, artist; b. Huntington Park, Calif., Jan. 17, 1954; s. Tom Edward and Carol Ann (Stewart) P.; m. Linda Lee Myers, Oct. 8, 1977; children: Justin Craig, Cody Lee. AA, Shasta Jr. Coll., Redding, Calif., 1974; BA, Calif. State U., Chico, 1977. Profl. artist Mont. Illustrator informative signs State of Mont., Mont. Power Co.; judge Mont. Jr. Duck Stamp Competition, 1998; one man shows at Corning, Calif., 1988, 90, 92, 94, 96, 98, Plains, Mont., 1989, Chico, 1998. Mem. citizen's adv. com. Mont. Dept. Fish and Game, 1996-98. Recipient 2d Pl. award Mont. State Duck Stamp Competition, 1991, 1st Pl. award, 19922, New Brunswick Conservation Stamp award, 1998. Mem. Found. for N.Am. Wild Sheep, Rocky Mountain Elk Found. Republican. Avocations: photography, hunting, fishing, camping, hiking. Home: PO Box 1272 Thompson Falls MT 59873-1272

PHILLIPS, DARRELL, retail executive; b. Hamilton, Ohio, Oct. 7, 1956; s. Bill L. and Lois J. (Marcum) P. Student, Western State Coll., Gunnison, Colo., 1974-77; BSBA, U. No. Colo., Greeley, 1979. Sales rep. Econ. Lab., White Plains, N.Y., 1979, Color Tile, Inc., Denver, 1980-81; store mgr. Color Tile, Inc., Lake Charles, La., 1981-82; v.p. Phillips Stationers, Inc., Denver, 1982-87; pres. Pro-Dispatch Office Supply, Denver, 1988-95; pres., CEO BDLS & Assocs., Inc., 1994—. Mem. Family Firm Inst. Republican. Avocations: skiing, golf, tennis, racquetball, reading.

PHILLIPS, DAVID BRUCE, writer, planetary link; b. L.A., May 22, 1962. BS in Engring., UCLA, 1985. Engr. Rockwell MS2, Downey, Calif.; explorer L.A. Author: When Will Man Learn?, 1995. Home: PO Box 8134 Inglewood CA 90308-8134

PHILLIPS, DEMETRIA NICKOLE, graphic designer; b. Dublin, Ga., Nov. 5, 1971; George and Elizabeth Hersha (Yeomans) Hatchett. BFA, Auburn U., 1995. Graphic designer Auburn U., Ala., 1985-96, Roadmaster, Opelika, Ala., 1996-97; designer Paul T. Gant Art and Design, Nashville, 1997; graphic designer freelance, Beaverton, Oreg., 1998—. Exhibited in group show: photograph (2nd place), 1995, advertisements (best in show), 1995. Avocations: photography, painting. E-Mail: meekap@earthlink.net.

PHILLIPS, DOROTHY LOWE, nursing educator; b. Jacksonville, Fla., June 3, 1939; d. Clifford E. and Dorothy (MacFeeley) Lowe; m. Dale Bernard Phillips, Feb. 14, 1973; children: Francis D., Sean E., Dorothy F. AA in Nursing, Ventura Coll., 1969; BSN, Calif. State U. Consortium, San Diego, 1984; M. Nursing, UCLA, 1987; EdD, Nova Southeastern U., 1995. Cert. community colls. tchr., Calif.; RN, Calif., pub. health nurse, Calif., clin. nurse specialist maternal/child. Staff nurse Community Meml. Hosp., Ventura, Calif., 1969-70; charge nurse women and children's clinic Ventura County Regional Med. Ctr., Ventura, 1974-76; staff nurse, RN II Pleasant Valley Hosp., Camarillo, Calif., 1978-85; lead instr. cert. nursing [illegible] 89; staff rsch. assoc. UCLA, 1988; clin. instr. Sch. of Nursing Ventura Community Coll., 1988, college nurse, 1989; lectr. Sch. of Nursing UCLA, 1989, lectr., coord. maternity nursing Sch. of Nursing, 1989-90, 90-91; vocat. nursing dir. health occup. coord. Oxnard Union High Sch. Dist., 1990—; [illegible]

educator Health Careers unit Calif. Dept. Edn., 1992-94; cons. Oxnard Adult Sch.; mem. adv. com. nursing asst./home health aide program Ventura County Regional Occupational Program; presenter in field. Competitive events judge !st Annual Leadership Conf., Health Occupations Students of Am., Anaheim, Calif.; active St. John's Regional Med. Ctr. Health Fair, 1991, Pleasant Valley Hosp. Health Fair, 1991; seminar leader "Babies and You", March of Dimes, 1988. Grad. Div. Rsch. grantee UCLA, 1986; Calif. State PTA scholar UCLA, 1986, Ventura County Med. Secs. scholar, 1967. Mem. Calif. Assn. Health Career Educators (pres. 1994), So. Calif. Dirs. Vocat. Nursing Programs (rec. sec. 1996—), So. Calif. Vocat. Nurse Educators, Sigma Theta Tau. Republican. Lutheran. Avocations: skiing, reading, exercise, travel, backpacking. Home: 321 Bayview Ave Ventura CA 93003-2052 Office: Oxnard Adult Sch 935 W 5th St Oxnard CA 93030-5271

PHILLIPS, FLORENCE TSU, choreographer, dance educator, lawyer; b. Taipei, Republic of China, May 2, 1949; came to U.S., 1957; d. Victor Z.M. and Dulcie (Ling) Tsu; m. Patrick J. Phillips; 1 child, Roderick James. Student, NYU, 1967-69; BA summa cum laude, UCLA, 1971, JD, 1974. Bar: Calif. 1974. Dancer Imperial Japanese Dancers, N.Y.C., 1965-70, Ballet de Paris, Paris and Montreal, Que., Can., 1967-68, Grands Ballets Canadiens, Montreal, 1968-69; atty. HUD, Washington, 1974, L.A. Pub. Defender's Office, 1975-77; owner, dir. Danceworks Studio, L.A., 1978—; atty. Minami, Lew & Tamaki, LLP, San Francisco, 1997—; pvt. practice, 1998—; choreographer, dir. Sinay Ballet, L.A., 1979—. Choreographed over 30 ballets, 1979—. Mem. Bar Assn. San Francisco, Phi Beta Kappa, Pi Gamma Mu. Avocations: pets, gardening, needle crafts.

PHILLIPS, GAIL, state legislator; b. Juneau, Alaska; m. Walt Phillips; children: Robin, Kim. BA in Bus. Edn., U. Alaska. Mem. Homer (Alaska) City Coun., 1981-84, Kenai Peninsula Borough Assembly, 1986-87; chmn. legis. com. Alaska Mcpl. League; mem. Alaska Ho. of Reps., 1991-99, house majority leader, 1993-94, spkr., 1995-98; former owner, mgr. Quiet Sports; ptnr. Lindphil Mining Co.; pub. rels. cons. Active Homer United Meth. Ch., Rep. Ctrl. Com. Alaska, Kenai Peninsula Coll. Coun.; past mem. com. bd. and race coord. Iditarod Trail Dog Sled Race. Mem. Western States Legis. Coun. (exec. com.), Am. Legis Exch. Coun. (former state chmn.), Resource Devel. Coun. Alaska, Western Legis. Conf. (exec. bd.), Western States Coalition (exec. bd.), The Energy Coun. Home: PO Box 3304 Homer AK 99603-3304 Office: 345 W Sterling Hwy Ste 102B Homer AK 99603-7820 also: Alaska Ho of Reps State Capitol Juneau AK 99801-1182

PHILLIPS, GENEVA FICKER, editor; b. Staunton, Ill., Aug. 1, 1920; d. Arthur Edwin and Lillian Agnes (Woods) Ficker; m. James Emerson Phillips, Jr., June 6, 1955 (dec. 1979). BS in Journalism, U. Ill., 1942; MA in English Lit., UCLA, 1953. Copy desk Chgo. Jour. Commerce, 1942-43; editl. asst. patents Radio Rsch. Lab., Harvard U., Cambridge, Mass., 1943-45; asst. editor adminstrv. publs. U. Ill., Urbana, 1946-47; editorial asst. Quar. of Film, Radio and TV, UCLA, 1952-53; mng. editor The Works of John Dryden, Dept. English, UCLA, 1964—. Bd. dirs. Univ. Religious Conf., L.A., 1979—. UCLA teaching fellow, 1950-53, grad. fellow 1954-55. Mem. Assn. Acad. Women UCLA, Dean's Coun., Coll. Letters and Scis. UCLA, Friends of Huntington Libr., Friends of UCLA Libr., Friends of Ctr. for Medieval and Renaissance Studies, Samuel Johnson Soc. of So. Calif., Assocs. of U. Calif. Press., Conf. Christianity and Lit., Soc. Mayflower Descs. Lutheran. Home: 213 1st Anita Dr Los Angeles CA 90049-3815 Office: UCLA Dept English 2225 Rolfe Hall Los Angeles CA 90024

PHILLIPS, JANE BANNING, aviatrix, pilot examiner and flight instructor. BA, U. Calif., Irvine, 1972; AAS in Flight Tech., Lane C.C., Eugene, Oreg., 1988. Cert. multi-engine airline transport pilot, DC-3 Type Rating; FAA designated pilot examiner. Flight instr. Lane C.C., 1988-90; pilot McKenzie Flying Svc., Eugene, 1990-93; asst. chief flight instr. Lane C.C., 1990—; FAA pilot examiner Eugene, 1992—; guest lectr. C. of C., AAUW, sch. and ch. groups, Eugene, 1990—. ESL instr. Lane County Literacy Coun., Eugene, 1993. Amelia Earhart scholar, 1993; Santa Rosa Ninety-Nines scholar, 1987. Mem. Internat. Ninety-Nines, Willamette Valley Ninety-Nines (treas. 1990-91, chmn. 1993-94), Nat. Assn. Flight Instrs., Assn. Ind. Airmen, Airplane Operators and Pilots Assn., Exptl. Aircraft Assn. Avocations: restoration of antique airplanes, including 1941 Interstate Cadet S1A; gardening, camping, travel. Office: PO Box 40635 Eugene OR 97404-0104

PHILLIPS, JILL META, novelist, critic, astrologer; b. Detroit, Oct. 22, 1952; d. Leyson Kirk and Leona Anna (Rasmussen) P. Student pub. schs., Calif. Lit. counselor Book Builders, Charter Oak, Calif., 1966-77; pres. Moon Dance Astro Graphics, Covina, Calif., 1994—. Author: (with Leona Phillips) A Directory of American Film Scholars, 1975, The Good Morning Cookbook, 1976, G.B. Shaw: A Review of the Literature, 1976, T.E. Lawrence: Portrait of the Artist as Hero, 1977, The Archaeology of the Collective East, 1977, The Occult, 1977, D.H. Lawrence: A Review of the Literature and Biographies, 1978, Film Appreciation: A College Guide Book, 1979, Annus Mirabilis: Europe in the Dark and Middle Centuries, 1979, (with Leona Rasmussen Phillips) The Dark Frame: Occult Cinema, 1979, Misfit: The Films of Montgomery Clift, 1979, Butterflies in the Mind: A Précis of Dreams and Dreamers, 1980; The Rain Maiden: A Novel of History, 1987, Walford's Oak: A Novel, 1990, The Fate Weaver: A Novel in Two Centuries, 1991, Saturn Falls: A Novel of the Apocalypse, 1993; columnist Horoscope Guide Monthly; contbr. book revs. to New Guard mag., 1974-76; contbr. numerous articles to profl. jours. including Dell Horoscope, Midnight Horoscope, Astrology-Your Daily Horoscope, Am. Astrology. Mem. Young Ams. for Freedom, Am. Conservative Union, Elmer Bernstein's Film Music Collection, Ghost Club London, Count Dracula Soc., Dracula Soc. London, Richard III Soc. Republican. Home: 515 Claraday St Apt 8 Glendora CA 91740-6043 Office: Moon Dancer Astro Graphics 425 E Arrow Hwy Ste 252 Glendora CA 91740-5607

PHILLIPS, JOHN CHESTER, sociology educator; b. Oakland, Calif., Nov. 6, 1941; s. Chester and G. Frances (Kremer) P.; m. Kay Louise Logsdon, Dec. 19, 1964; children: John Stephen, David Solon. BA, San Jose State U., 1963, MA, 1965; PhD, U. Oreg., 1974. Prof. SUNY, Cortland, 1971-76; prof. U. of the Pacific, Stockton, Calif., 1976—. Author: Sociology of Sport, 1994; contbr. articles to profl. jours. Chair Bd. of Parole Commrs., San Joaquin County, 1987-91; bd. dirs. Anderson YMCA, 1992-98 (pres. 1993-96). Recipient commendation San Joaquin County sheriff, 1991. Democrat. Methodist. Avocations: running, tutoring/mentoring youth. Office: U of the Pacific Sociology Dept 3601 Pacific Ave Stockton CA 95211-0110

PHILLIPS, JOHN P(AUL), retired neurosurgeon; b. Danville, Ark., Oct. 14, 1932; s. Brewer William Ashley and Wave Audrey (Page) P.; AB cum laude, Hendrix Coll., 1953; MD, U. Tenn., 1956; m. June Helen Dunbar, Dec. 14, 1963; children: Todd Eustace, Timothy John Colin, Tyler William Ashley. Intern, Charity Hosp. La., New Orleans, 1957; resident in surgery U. Tenn. Hosps., 1958; resident in neurol. surgery U. Tenn. Med. Units, 1958-62; practice medicine, specializing in neurol. surgery, Salinas, Calif., 1962-93; retired 1993; chief of staff, chief of surgery Salinas Valley Meml. Hosp.; mem. staffs Community Hosp. Monterey Peninsula, U. Calif. Hosp., San Francisco; asst. clin. prof. U. Calif., 1962—. Commd. Ky. col. Diplomate Am. Bd. Neurol. Surgeons. Mem. ACS, Internat. Coll. Surgery, Harvey Cushing Soc., Congress Neurol. Surgery, Western Neurosurg. Assn., AMA, San Francisco Neurol. Soc., Pan Pacific Surg. Assn., Alpha Omega Alpha, Phi Chi, Alpha Chi. Home: 6 Mesa Del Sol Salinas CA 93908-9324

PHILLIPS, KEITH WENDALL, minister; b. Portland, Oreg., Oct. 21, 1946; s. Frank Clark and Velma Georgina (Black) P.; m. Mary Katherine Garland, July 16, 1973; children: Joshua, Paul, David. BA, UCLA, 1968; MDiv, Fuller Theology Sem., 1971, D. of Ministries, 1972; LHD (hon.), John Brown U., 1990. Dir. Youth For Christ Clubs, L.A., 1965-71; pres. World Impact, L.A., 1971—; commencement speaker Tabor Coll., 1969, 91, John Brown U., 1990. Author: Everybody's Afraid in the Ghetto, 1973, They Dare to Love the Ghetto, 1975, The Making of a Disciple, 1981, No Quick Fix, 1985, Out of Ashes, 1996. Chmn. L.A. Mayor's Prayer Breakfast Com., 1985—; bd. dirs. Christian Cmty. Devel. Assn., 1992—; spkr. Promise Keeper. Named Disting. Staley lectr., 1969. Mem. Evangelistic Com. of Newark (pres. 1976—), World Impact of Can. (pres. 1978—), The Oaks (pres. 1985—), Faith Works (pres. 1987—). Baptist. Office: World Impact 2001 S Vermont Ave Los Angeles CA 90007-1279

PHILLIPS, ROBERT LEE, editor, freelance writer; b. Detroit, 1931; s. Harry Neil and Ruth Mary (Lee) P.; m. Maryann Katherine Kohnekamp, Dec. 27, 1952; children: Daniel, Kathryn, Thomas. BA, Miami U., Oxford, Ohio, 1952; MS, U. Ill., 1954; PhD, U. Oregon, 1966. From asst. prof. to prof. Oregon State U., Corvallis, 1957-90; freelance writer Sunriver, Oreg., 1970-95; editor Sunriver (Oreg.) Scene, 1995—; chmn., dir., asst. to pres., Oreg. State U., Corvallis, 1963-78, 85-87; acting v.p. 1984-85. Lt.Comdr. USNR, 1953-73. Mem. Am. Soc. Journalists and Authors. Avocations: aviation, writing. Home and Office: PO Box 4412 Sunriver OR 97707-1412

PHILLIPS, ROGER, steel company executive; b. Ottawa, Ont., Can., Dec. 17, 1939; s. Norman William Frederick and Elizabeth (Marshall) P.; m. Katherine Ann Wilson, June 9, 1962; 1 child, Andrée Claire. B.Sc., McGill U., Montreal, 1960. Vice pres. mill products Alcan Can. Products Ltd., Toronto, Ont., Can., 1969-70, exec. v.p., 1971-75; pres. Alcan Smelters and Chems. Ltd., Montreal, Que., Can., 1976-79; v.p. tech. Alcan Aluminium Ltd., Montreal, Que., Can., 1980-81; pres. Alcan Internat. Ltd., Montreal, Que., Can., 1980-81; pres., chief exec. officer IPSCO Inc., Regina, Sask., Can., 1982—; sr. mem. Conf. Bd. Inc., N.Y., 1987—; bd. dirs. Toronto Dominion Bank. Bd. govs. Coun. for Can. Unity, Montreal, 1987—; bd. dirs. Conf. Bd. of Can., 1984-87. Fellow Inst. of Physics U.K. (chartered physicist); mem. Can. Assn. Physicists, Bus. Coun. on Nat. Issues, Am. Iron and Steel Inst. (bd. dirs. 1984—), Sask. C. of C. (bd. dirs. 1984—), Que. C. of C. (pres. 1981), Collegium of Work and Learning (bd. dirs.), Assiniboia Club (Regina), St. Denis Club, Univ. Club (Montreal). Home: 3220 Albert St, Regina, SK Canada S4S 3N9 Office: IPSCO Inc, Armour Rd, Regina, SK Canada S4P 3C7

PHILLIPS, RONNIE JACK, economics educator; b. Levelland, Tex.; s. Lester Damon and Sidney (Goza) P. BA, U. Okla., 1973; PhD, U. Tex., Austin, 1980. Asst. prof. econs. Colo. State U., Ft. Collins, 1983-87; assoc. prof. econs. Colo. State U., 1987-92, prof., 1992—; vis. scholar Comptr. Currency, Washington, 1996-97, FDIC, Washington, 1997. Author: The Chicago Plan and New Deal Banking Reform, 1995; editor: Economic Mavericks: The Texas Institutionalists; contbr. articles to profl. jours. Mem. Am. Econ. Assn., Assn. Evolutionary Econs. Avocation: guitar. Office: Colo State U Econs Dept Fort Collins CO 80523

PHILLIPS, TED RAY, advertising agency executive; b. American Falls, Idaho, Oct. 27, 1948; s. Virn E. and Jessie N. (Aldous) P.; m. Dianne Jacqulynne Walker, May 28, 1971; children: Scott, Russell, Stephen, Michael. BA, Brigham Young U., 1972, MA, 1975. Account exec. David W. Evans, Inc., Salt Lake City, 1972-75; dir. advt. Div. Continuing Edn., U. Utah, Salt Lake City, 1975-78; sr. v.p. Evans/Lowe & Stevens, Inc., Atlanta, 1978, exec. v.p., 1979; pres., CEO David W. Evans/Atlanta, Inc., 1979-80; dir. advt. O.C. Tanner Co., Salt Lake City, 1980-82; pres. Thomas/Phillips/Clawson Advt., Inc., Salt Lake City, 1982-86; pres. Hurst & Phillips, Salt Lake City, 1986-94; CEO, chmn. The Phillips Agy., Salt Lake City, 1994—; advt. instr. div. continuing edn. Brigham Young U., 1983-85. Dir. publicity, promotion Western States Republican Con., 1976. Recipient Silver Beaver award Boy Scouts Am., 1994, Spurgeon award, 1995. Mem. Am. Advt. Fedn. (8 Best-in-West awards, 2 nat. Addy awards, Clio finalist 1984, Telly award 1991, 92), Utah Advt. Fedn. (bd. dirs. 1976-78, 80-87, pres. 1984-85). Mormon. Home: 1792 Cornwall Ct Sandy UT 84092-5436 Office: The Phillips Agy 70 N Main St Midvale UT 84047-2447

PHILLIPS, TERESA RAE, elementary education educator, researcher; b. Burley, Idaho, Aug. 2, 1950; d. Perry Molan and Neta (McLean) Fenstermaker; m. H. Blaine Phillips II, Jan. 7, 1972; children: Neta A., Thomas B. BA in Edn., Idaho State U., 1972; postgrad., U. Nev., Reno, 1973-76, Brigham Young U., U. Utah, Utah State U., 1981—. Cert. tchr., Utah. Tchr. Sch. Dist. 25, Pocatello, Idaho, 1972-73; dep. clk. Washoe County, Reno, 1973-76; tchr. Uintah Sch. Dist., Vernal, Utah, 1983—. Editor annotation: Truth IS Stranger Than Fiction: My Life Story, 1996. Mem. AAUW (br. pres.). Mormon. Avocations: quilting, crafting, writing, genealogical research, gardening. Home: PO Box 794 Vernal UT 84078-0794 Office: Uintah Sch Dist Maeser Elem Sch 2670 W 1000 N Vernal UT 84078-8224

PHILLIPS, THOMAS H., JR., rector; b. Chester, Pa., Nov. 23, 1946; s. Thomas H. and Lena P.; m. Elizabeth Ruth Symons, May 24, 1975; children: Benjamin Thomas Symons, Jonathan David Packer. BCTS, Trinity, 1975; MDiv, Gen. Theol., N.Y.C., 1997; D in Ministry, Fuller, 1997. Campus min. The Coalition for Christian Outreach, Pitts., 1970-73, 76-77; asst. rector St. Paul's Episcopal Ch., Akron, Ohio, 1977-80; rector St. Albans, Wilmington, Del., 1980-89, St. Paul's Episcopal Ch., Yuma, Ariz., 1989—. Founder, chair The Youth Forum, Yuma, Ariz., 1994—; founder Marriage Savers of Yuma, 1996; missionary Ukraine, Russia, 1990-93; appt. to com. Gov.'s Task Force on the Homeless Trust Fund, Phoenix, 1994-95; mem. Yuma Food Bank, 1994; invitee Ariz. Town Hall, Grand Canyon, 1993. Mem. Yuma Rotary. Republican. Avocations: reading, swimming, speed walking, hiking, music. Home: St Paul's Episcopal Ch 1550 14th Ave Yuma AZ 85364

PHILLIPSON, DONALD E., lawyer; b. Denver, July 22, 1942. BS, Stanford U., 1964, JD, 1968; MS, U. Calif., Berkeley, 1965. Former mem. Davis, Graham & Stubbs, Denver; now cons., writer. Mem. Nat. Soccer Hall of Fame (adminstr.). Office: 14325 Braun Rd Golden CO 80401-1431

PHILPOT, DENNIS CRAIG, mechanical engineer; b. Silverton, Oreg., Feb. 1, 1958; s. Gerald Lee and Lois Carol (Fredrickson) P.; m. Kerry Louise Lawrence, June 18, 1983; children: Emily, Craig. BSME, Oreg. State U., 1983; MS in Applied Mechanics, Calif. State U., Northridge, 1990. Registered profl. engr., Calif. Mech. engr. Rockwell Internat., Canoga Park, Calif., 1983-96, Northrop Grumman, El Segundo, Calif., 1996—; cons. Craig Engring., Winnetka, Calif., 1995-96. Author NASA tech. briefs. Comdr. Approved Workman are not Ashamed, Canoga Park, 1990-96. Named Outstanding Young Man of Am., 1984. Mem. ASME. Republican. Avocations: guitar, golf. Home: 6531 Neddy Ave West Hills CA 91307-2833 Office: Northrop Grumman Corp One Hornet Way El Segundo CA 90245

PHILPOTT, LARRY LA FAYETTE, horn player; b. Alma, Ark., Apr. 5, 1937; s. Lester and Rena (Owens) P.; m. Elise Robichaud, Nov. 24, 1962 (div. June 1975); children: Daniel, Stacy; m. Anne Sokol, Feb. 14, 1976. B.S., Ga. So. Coll., 1962; Mus.M., Butler U., 1972. Instr. in horn Butler U., De Pauw U.; dir. music Cedarcrest Sch., Marysville, Wash., 1991—; instr. horn Western Wash. U., Dept Music, Bellingham, 1995-98. Mem., N.C. Symphony, 1960, Savannah (Ga.) Symphony, L'Orchestre Symphonique de Quebec, Que., Can., 1962-64, prin. horn player, Indpls. Symphony Orch., 1964-89, Flagstaff Summer Festival, 1968—; artist in-residence Ind.-Purdue Indpls.; appeared with, Am. Shakespeare Theatre, summer 1965, Charlottetown Festival, summers 1967-68, Flagstaff Summer Festival, 1968-85, Marrowstone Music Festival, 1985—. Served with USN, 1956-60. Mem. Music Educators Nat. Conf., Am. Fedn. Musicians, Internat. Conf. Symphony and Opera Musicians, Internat. Horn Soc., Coll. Music Soc., Phi Mu Alpha Sinfonia. Home: 14925 63d Ave SE Snohomish WA 98296-5277 also: Western Wash U Dept Music Bellingham WA 98225-9107

PHILPOTT, LINDSEY, civil engineer, researcher, educator; b. Bridestowe, Devonshire, Eng., Aug. 2, 1948; came to U.S., 1983; s. George Anthony and Joyce Thirza (Teeling) P.; m. Christine May Pembury, Aug. 20, 1974 (div.); children: David, Elizabeth; m. Kathleen Linda Matson, Feb. 17, 1982 (div.); children: Nicholas, Benjamin; m. Kim Elaine Moore, Nov. 24, 1991. Higher Nat. Cert. in Civil Engring., Bristol (Eng.) Poly., 1973; BSCE, U. Ariz., 1986, MSCE, 1987. Registered profl. engr., Calif.; lic. water treatment plant operator, Calif.; USCG lic. operator 100 ton master. Area structural engr. Dept. Environment (Property Svcs. Agy.), Bristol, 1971-73; civil engr. Webco Civil Engring., Exeter, Eng., 1973-75; tech. mgr. Devon & Cornwall Housing Assn., Plymouth, Eng., 1975-79; prin., architect S.W. Design, Plymouth, 1979-81; archtl. engr. United Bldg. Factories, Bahrain, 1981-83; jr. engr. Cheyne Owen, Tucson, 1983-87; civil engr. Engring. Sci. Inc., Pasadena, Calif., 1987-89; project engr. Black & Veatch, Santa Ana, Calif., 1989-90; sr. engr. Brown & Caldwell, Irvine, Calif., 1990-91; environ. engr. Met. Water Dist. So. Calif., San Dimas, 1991—; adj. prof. hydraulics and instrumentation, San Antonio Coll., Walnut, Calif., 1995—. Foster parent Foster Parents Plan, Tucson, 1985-87; vol. reader tech. books Recording for the Blind, Hollywood, Calif., 1988-89, South Bay, Calif., 1990-91, Pomona, Calif., 1991—; vol. sailor/tchr. L.A. Maritime Inst. Topsail Youth Program, 1994—, Orange County Marine Inst., 1998—. Mem. ASCE, Am. Water Works Assn., Am. Water Resources Assn. (water quality com. 1990—), Water Environment Fedn., Engrs. Soc. (pres. 1985-96), Mensa, South Bay Yacht Racing Club (Marina del Rey, Calif., commodore 1996), Marina Venice Yacht Club (Marina del Rey, commodore 1999), Internat. Guild of Knot Tyers (treas. Pacific Am. br. 1997). Avocations: hiking, cycling, sailing, crosswords, knot-tying. Office: Met Water Dist Environ Compliance Divsn PO Box 54153 Los Angeles CA 90054-0153

PHIPPS, CLAUDE RAYMOND, research scientist; b. Ponca City, Okla., Mar. 15, 1940; s. Claude Raymond Louis and Deva Pauline (DeWitt) P.; m. Lynn Malarney, Dec. 1, 1962 (div. Feb. 1989); 1 child, David Andrew; life ptnr. Shanti E. Bannwart. BS, MIT, 1961, MS, 1963; PhD, Stanford U., 1972. Rsch. staff Lawrence Livermore (Calif.) Nat. Lab., 1972-74; rsch. staff Los Alamos (N.Mex.) Nat. Lab., 1974-95, project leader engine support sys. tech. program, 1993; assoc. dir. Alliance for Photonic Tech., Albuquerque, 1992-95; pres. Photonic Assocs., Santa Fe, 1995—; co-instr. "Pairs" Relationship Tng., Santa Fe, N.Mex., 1990—; dir. Santa Fe Investment Conf., 1987; program com. MIT Workshop on High Temperature Superconductors, Cambridge, 1988; mem. Instl. R & D Com., Los Alamos Nat. Lab., 1990-92, project leader laser effects, 1982-87, mem. internat. rsch. tour, Australia, Japan, Scotland, 1988-89; invited discussion leader Gordon Conf. on Laser Particle Interactions, N.H., 1992; organizer, chmn. 1st Santa Fe High Power Laser Ablation Conf., 1998, Osaka High Power Laser Ablation Conf., 1999. spkr. in field. Co-author: Laser Ionization Mass Analysis, 1993; author internat. lecture series on laser surface interactions, Berlin, Antwerp, Marseilles, Xiamen, Cape Town, Durban, 1987—; contbr. articles to profl. jours. Lt. USN, 1963-65. Grad. fellow W. Alton Jones Found., N.Y.C., 1962-63. Avocations: writing poetry, reading, travel, photography. Home and Office: Photonic Assocs 200A Ojo De La Vaca Rd Santa Fe NM 87505-8808

PI, WEN-YI SHIH, aircraft company engineer, researcher; b. Beijing, Feb. 28, 1935; came to U.S., 1959; d. Chih-Chuan and Hsiu-Yun (Yang) Shih; m. William Shu-Jong Pi, July 2, 1961; 1 child, Wilfred. BS, Nat. Taiwan U., Taipei, Republic of China, 1956; MS, Stanford U., 1961, PhD, 1963. Rsch. assoc. Stanford (Calif.) U., 1963-64; engring. specialist Northrop-Grumman Corp., Hawthorne, Calif., 1965-83, sr. tech. specialist, 1983-97. Contbr. articles to profl. jours. Recipient Silver Achievement award Los Angeles YWCA, 1983; Amelia Earhart Scholar Zonta Internat., 1961-62. Fellow: AIAA (assoc.); mem. Sigma Xi.

PIAZZA, DUANE EUGENE, biomedical researcher; b. San Jose, Calif., June 5, 1954; s. Salvador Richard and Mary Bernice (Mirassou) P.; m. Sandra Patrignani, Sept. 19, 1992. BS in Biology, U. San Francisco, 1976; MA in Biology, San Francisco State U., 1986. Staff rsch. assoc. I U. Calif., San Francisco, 1975-81; sr. rsch. technician XOMA Corp., San Francisco, 1981-82; biologist II Syntex USA Inc., Palo Alto, Calif., 1982-85; pres., cons. Ryte For You, Oakland, Calif., 1985—; rsch. assoc. I Cetus Corp., Emeryville, Calif., 1986-90; rsch. assoc. II John Muir Cancer and Aging Rsch. Inst., Walnut Creek, Calif., 1991-92; rsch. assoc. Pharmagenesis, Palo Alto, Calif., 1993-96; asst. lab. mgr. DeAnza C.C., Cupertino, Calif., 1996—. CPR & first aid instr. ARC, 1980-92, vol. 1st aid sta. instr., Santa Cruz, 1985-86, vol. 1st aid sta. disaster action team, Oakland, 1986—, br. chmn. disaster action team, 1987-88; treas. Reganti Homeowner Assn., 1990-92. Mem. AAAS, Am. Soc. Microbiology, N.Y. Acad. Scis., Astron. Soc. Pacific, Planetary Soc., Mt. Diablo Astronomy Soc. Republican. Roman Catholic. Avocations: scuba diving, swimming, backpacking, photography, astronomy. Home: 1055 Rebecca Dr Boulder Creek CA 95006-9442

PICCOLO, RICHARD ANDREW, artist, educator; b. Hartford, Conn., Sept. 17, 1943; S. John D. and Lenore (Pasqual) P. BID, Pratt Inst., 1966; MFA, Bklyn. Coll., 1968. Instr. Pratt Inst., Bklyn., 1966-68, Rome, 1969—; dir. Pratt Inst., 1980—; instr. U. Notre Dame Rome Program, 1984—. Artist: solo exhibitions include: Robert Schoelkopf Gallery, N.Y.C., 1975, 79, 83, 89, Suffolk C.C., Long Island, N.Y., 1976, Am. Acad. in Rome, 1977, Galleria Temple, Rome 1979, Galleria Il Gabbiano, Rome. 1985, Contemporary Realist Gallery, San Francisco, 1989, 95; exhibited in group shows Six Americans in Italy, 1973, Metaphor in Painting, Fed. Hall Meml., N.Y., 1978, Realism and Metaphor, U. S. Fla. (traveling), 1980, Contemporary Figure Drawings, Robert Schoelkopf Gallery, 1981, Contemporary Arcadian Painting, 1982, Moravian Coll. Invitational, Bethlehem, Pa., 1981, Art on Paper , Weatherspoon Gallery of Art, N.C., 1981, Out of N.Y., Hamilton Coll., Clinton, N.Y., 1981, Galleria Gabbiano, Rome, FIAC, Paris, 1982, Contemporary Arts Mus., Houston, 1984, Umbria: Americans Painting in Italy, Gallery North, Setauket, N.Y., 1985, Storytellers, Contemporary Realist Gallery, San Francisco, Painted from Life, Bayly Mus., Charlottesville, Va., 1987; work in permanent collections Crown Am. Corp., Johnstown, Pa., Grosvenor Internat., Sacramento, Calif., Mrs. Lillian Cole, Sherman Oaks, Calif., Mr and Mrs. Robert Emery, San Francisco, Mr. Graham Gund, Boston, Dr. Robert Gutterman, San Francisco, Mr and Mrs. Joseph Jennings, San Francisco, Dr. and Mrs. Donald Innes, Jr., Charlottesville, Va., Mr. and Mrs. Alan Ovson, San Francisco, Mr. Frank Pasquerilla, Johnstown, Pa., Mr. Jon Roberts and Mr. John Boccardo, L.A. Recipient E. A. Abbey Meml. scholarship for mural painting, 1973-75; grantee NEA, 1989; mural comm. Simplicity Inspiring Invention: An Allegory of the Arts, Crown Am. Corp., Johnstown, Pa., 1989, Aer, Ignis, Terra, Aqua, U.S. Bank Plaz., Sacramento, Calif., 1991-94. Home: Piazza S Apollonia 3, Rome 00153, Italy Office: Hacket-Freedman Gallery 250 Sutter St Fl 4 San Francisco CA 94108-4451

PICK, JAMES BLOCK, management and sociology educator; b. Chgo., July 29, 1943; s. Grant Julius and Helen (Block) P. BA, Northwestern U., 1966; MS in Edn., No. Ill. U., 1969; PhD, U. Calif., Irvine, 1974. Cert. computer profl. Asst. rsch. statistician, lectr. Grad. Sch. Mgmt. U. Calif., Riverside, 1975-91, dir. computing, 1984-91; co-dir. U.S.-Mex. Database Project, 1988-91; assoc. prof. mgmt. and bus., dir. info. mgmt. program U. Redlands, Calif., 1995—, prof. mgmt. and bus., 1995—, chair dept. mgmt. and bus., 1995-97, 98-99; vis. prof. U. Iberoam., Mexico City, 1997; cons. U.S. Census Bur. Internat. Div., 1978; mem. Univ. Commons Bd., 1982-86; nat. curriculum task force IS 97; mem. U. Commn. Future of Bus. Programs, 1998; pres. Orange County chpt. Assn. Systems Mgmt., 1978-79; mem. bd. govs. PCCLAS, Assn. Borderlands Studies, 1989-92. Trustee Newport Harbor Art Mus., 1981-87, 88-96, chmn. permanent collection com., 1987-91, v.p., 1991-96; trustee Orange County Mus. Art, 1996—, chmn. collection com., 1996—. Recipient Thunderbird award Bus. Assn. Latin Am. Studies, 1993; Ford Found. grantee, 1998-99. Mem. AAAS, Assn. Computing Machinery, Assn. Info. Systems, Am. Soc. Assn., Am. Statis. Assn., Population Assn. Am., Internat. Union for Sci. Study of Population, Sociedad de Demografia Mexicana, Standard (Chgo.). Author: Geothermal Energy Development, 1982, Computer Systems in Business, 1986, Atlas of Mexico, 1989, The Mexico Handbook, 1994, Mexico Megacity, 1997; condr. rsch. in info. systems, population, environ. studies; contbr. sci. articles to publs. in fields.

PICKARD, DEAN, philosophy and humanities educator; b. Geneva, N.Y., Mar. 12, 1947; s. William Otis and Frances (Dean) P.; children: Justin Matthew, Christopher Dean. BA cum laude, U. Calif., Riverside, 1973; MA, Calif. State U., Long Beach, 1976-77; PhD, Claremont (Calif.) Grad. Sch., 1992. Instr. phys. edn. Pomona Coll., Claremont, 1975-82; instr. philosophy, humanities, and phys. edn. Moorpark (Calif.) Coll., 1978-82; assoc. prof. philosophy, humanities, and phys. edn. Mission Coll., Sylmar, Calif., 1979-83; instr. philosophy Calif. State U., Northridge, 1988-94; prof. philosophy and humanities Pierce Coll., Woodland Hills, Calif., 1983—. Author: Nietzsche, Transformation and Postmodernism; contbr. articles to profl. jours. Marious De Brabent & Henry Carter scholar, 1973; fellow Claremont Grad. Sch., 1988-89; grantee NEH, 1995. Mem. Am. Philos. Assn., Am. Fedn. Tchrs., N.Am. Nietzsche Soc., L.A. Area Nietzsche Soc. (bd. dirs. 1994-97), Phi Beta Kappa. Avocations: guitar, snow skiing, wind

surfing, golfing, martial arts (5th degree black belt). Office: Pierce Coll 6201 Winnetka Ave Woodland Hills CA 91371-0001

PICKENS, ALEXANDER LEGRAND, education educator; b. Waco, Tex., Aug. 31, 1921; s. Alex LeGrand and Elma L. (Johnson) P.; m. Frances M. Jenkins, Aug. 20, 1955. BA, So. Meth. U., 1950; MA, North Tex. U., Denton, 1952; EdD, Columbia U., 1959. Tchr. art public schs. Dallas, 1950-53, Elizabeth, N.J., 1953-54; instr. Coll. Architecture and Design U. Mich., 1954-59; assoc. prof. dept. art U. Ga. Athens, 1959-62; assoc. prof. Coll. Edn. U. Hawaii, Honolulu, 1962-68, prof. edn., 1968—; U. Hawaii; chmn. doctoral studies curriculum instrn. Coll. Edn. U. Hawaii, Honolulu, 1984-89, asst. to dean for coll. devel., 1989—; dir. children's classes Ft. Worth Children's Mus., 1951-53; head art Nat. Music Camp, Interlochen, Mich., summers, 1957-58, U. Oreg., Portland, summers 1959-60, 62; cons. youth art activities Foremost Dairies, 1964-74; cons. art films United World Films, 1970-75; art edn. cons. Honolulu Paper Co., 1970-76, Kamehameha Sch., Bishop Estate, 1978-95. Exhibited ceramics, Wichita Internat. Exhbn., Syracuse (N.Y.) Nat. Exhbn., St. Louis Mus., Dallas Mus., San Antonio Mus., Detroit Art Inst., Hawaii Craftsmen, also others; editorial bd.: Arts and Activities mag, 1955-82; editor: U. Hawaii Ednl. Perspectives, 1964—; contbr. articles to profl. jours. Memm. adult com. Dallas County chpt. Jr. ARC, 1951-53; exec. com. Dallas Crafts Guild, 1950-53; v.p., publicity chmn. U. Ga. Community Concert Assn., 1960-62, mem., program chmn. Gov.'s Commn. Observing 150 Yrs. Pub. Edn. in Hawaii, 1990-91; bd. dirs. Honolulu Theatre for Youth, 1997—, Honolulu Symphony, 1998—. Served with USAAF. Recipient award merit, Tex. State Fair, 1957, All-Am. award, Ednl. Press Assn. Am., 1968, 70, 72, 75, 79, Regents' medal for excellence in teaching, U. Hawaii, 1989, Gov.'s Commn. Observance of 150 Yrs. Pub. Edn., 1990-91. Mem. AAUP, NEA, Internat. Soc. Edn., Nat. Art Edn. Assn., Coun. for Advancement and Support of Edn., Nat. Soc. Fundraising Execs., Nat. Planned Giving Coun., Hawaii Planned Giving Coun., Phi Delta Kappa, Kappa Delta Pi. Address: 1471 Kalaepohaku St Honolulu HI 96816-1804

PICKENS, WILLIAM H., educational administrator, consultant; b. Albuquerque, June 24, 1946; s. William Hickman Pickens II and Sammie Bratton; m. Monica Neville, May 1, 1993; children: Rena, Brian. BA, U. N. Mex., 1968, MA, 1971; PhD, U. Calif., Davis, 1976; AA, Austin C.C., 1987. Deputy dir. Calif. Postsecondary Edn. Commn., 1978-86; exec. dir. Calif. Post Secondary Edn. Commn., 1986-88; assoc. v.p. adminstrn. Calif. State U., Sacramento, 1988-94; sr. mgr. MGT of Am. Cons., Sacramento, 1994-96; dir. Calif. Citizens Commn. Higher Edn., 1996—; bd. dirs. Exec. Leadership Inst. Stanford U.; exec. com. Western Assn. Coll. Univ. Bus. Affairs, 1993—. Author of books in field; contbr. articles to profl. jours. Bd. dirs. Davis (Calif.) Cmty. Housing Corp., 1989-93. Recipient Bone Marrow Donor award Sacramento (Calif.) Blood Bank, 1990. Mem. Assn. Practical Applied Ethics, Phi Beta Kappa. Presby. Avocations: running, music, politics. Office: Ctr for Govt Studies 10951 W Pico Blvd Ste 120 Los Angeles CA 90064-2126

PICKERING, AVAJANE, specialized education facility executive; b. New Castle, Ind., Nov. 5, 1951; d. George Willard and Elsie Jean (Wicker) P. BA, Purdue U., 1974; MS in Spl. Edn., U. Utah, 1983, PhD, 1991. Cert. spl. edn. Co-dir. presch. for gifted students, 1970-74; tchr. Granite Community Sch. Salt Lake City, 1974-79; tchr. coordinator Salt Lake City Schs., 1975-85; adminstrv. dir., owner Specialized Ednl. Programming Svc., Inc. Salt Lake City, 1976—; mem. Utah Profl. Adv. Bd.; adj. instr. U. Utah, Salt Lake City, 1985—; instr. Brigham Young U., 1993—. Rep. del. Utah State Conv., also county conv.; vol. tour guide, hostess Temple Square, Ch. Jesus Christ of Latter-Day Saints, 1983-88. Mem. Coun. for Exceptional Children, Coun. for Learning Disabilities, Learning Disability Assn., Ednl. Therapy Assn. Profl., Learning Disabilities Assn. Utah (profl. adv. bd.), Attention Deficit Coalition Utah (treas.), Hadassah, Delta Kappa Gamma, Phi Kappa Phi. Home: 1595 S 2100 E Salt Lake City UT 84108-2750 Office: Specialized Ednl Programming Svcs 1760 S 1100 E Salt Lake City UT 84105-3430

PICKETT, A(LBERT) DEAN, lawyer; b. Casper, Wyo., June 25, 1949; s. A. Foy and Esther Laurine (Nieman) P.; m. Lucinda Marie Wayne, July 3, 1971; children: Amanda Marie, Gregory Dean. BA, No. Ariz. U., 1971; JD with distinction, U. Ariz., 1974. Bar: Ariz. 1974, Wash. 1975. Assoc. Holesapple, Conner, Jones & Johnson, Tucson, 1978-79; Assoc. Mangum, Wall, Stoops & Warden, Flagstaff, Ariz., 1980-83; ptnr. Mangum, Wall, Stoops & Warden, P.L.L.C., 1984—; legal counsel No. Ariz. U., 1982—; lectr. edn. law Ariz. Sch. Bds. Assn., 1983—; judge Pro Tem Ariz. Ct. Appeals, 1992. Chmn. Coconino County Rep. Com., 1986-88; trustee Mus. No. Ariz., 1983-91, 92—, chmn., 1998—; bd. dirs. Flagstaff Federated Cmty. Ch., 1987. Lt. USN, 1974-77. Mem. State Bar Ariz., Wash. State Bar Assn., Nat. Assn. Coll. and Univ. Attys., Nat. Sch. Bds. Assn. Coun. Sch. Attys., Coconino County Bar Assn., Malpais Kiwanis (pres. 1982-83). Presbyterian. Avocations: skiing, camping,hiking. Home: 515 W Fir Ave Flagstaff AZ 86001-1308 Office: Mangum Wall Stoops & Warden PLLC 100 N Elden St Flagstaff AZ 86001-5295

PICKETT, DONN PHILIP, lawyer; b. Chgo., May 3, 1952; s. Philip Gordon and Gloria Joan (Hansen) P.; m. Janet Benson, Aug. 25, 1973; children: Jessica Kelly, William Benson. BA, Carleton Coll., Minn., 1973; JD, Yale U., 1976. Bar: Calif. 1976, U.S. Dist. Ct. (no. dist.) Calif. 1976, (ctrl. dist.) Calif. 1980, (ea. dist.) Calif. 1983, U.S. Ct. Appeals (9th cir.) Calif. 1979, U.S. Ct. Appeals (5th cir.) Tex. 1994, U.S. Supreme Ct. 1991, U.S. Dist. Ct. Ariz. 1997, U.S. Dist. Ct. Colo. 1997, U.S. Ct. Appeals (fed. cir.) 1997, U.S. Ct. Appeals (11th cir.) 1998. Assoc. McCutchen, Doyle, Brown & Enersen, San Francisco, 1976-83, ptnr., 1983—; mem. U.S. Dist. Ct. Civil Justice Reform Act adv. group, 1995—). Mem. ABA (vice chmn. civil practice com. antitrust sect. 1998), State Bar Calif. (com. on adminstrn. of justice 1988-91, vice chmn. 1992-93, chmn. 1993-94, legis. chmn. 1994-96), San Francisco Bar Assn. (judiciary com. 1988-92, exec. com. conf. of dels. 1993-96, bd. dirs. 1997—), Phi Beta Kappa. Home: 25 Meadow Hill Dr Tiburon CA 94920-1638 Office: McCutchen Doyle Brown & Enersen Three Embarcadero Ctr San Francisco CA 94111

PICKLE, JOSEPH WESLEY, JR., religion educator; b. Denver, Apr. 8, 1935; s. Joseph Wesley and Wilhelmina (Blacketor) P.; m. Judith Ann Siebert, June 28, 1958; children: David E., Kathryn E., Steven J. BA, Carleton Coll., 1957; B.D., Chgo. Theol. Sem., 1961; MA, U. Chgo., 1962, PhD, 1969. Ordained to ministry Am. Bapt. Conv., 1962. Asst. pastor Judson Meml. Ch., N.Y.C., 1959-60; acting dean summer session Colo. Coll., Colorado Springs, 1969-70, from asst. prof. to prof. religion, 1964—, faculty dir. internat. studies, 1994-98; vis. prof. theology Iliff Sch. Theology, Denver, 1984; vis. prof. religious studies U. Zimbabwe, Harare, 1989; cons. Colo. Humanities Program, Denver, 1975-89; coord. Sheffer Meml. Fund, Colo. Coll., Colorado Springs, 1983—. Co-editor Papers of the 19th Century Theology Group, 1978, 88, 93. Pres. bd. dirs Pikes Peak Mental Health Ctr., Colorado Springs, 1975; chmn. Colo. Health Facilities Rev. Coun., Denver, 1979-84; mem. Colo. Health Facilities Rev. Coun., Denver, 1976-84, Colo. Bd. Health, Denver, 1986-91; bd. dirs. Marson Found., Colorado Springs, 1994—. Am. Bapt. Conv. scholar, 1953-59; Fulbright Hays Grad. fellow U. Tübingen, Fed. Republic Germany, 1963-64, Danforth fellow, 1957-63, Joseph Malone fellow, 1987. Fellow Soc. for Values in Higher Edn.; mem. Am. Theol. Soc. (pres. 1996-97), Am. Acad. Religion (regional pres. 1983-84, 92-93), Cath. Theol. Soc. Am., Fulbright Assn., Phi Beta Kappa. Democrat. Home: 20 W Caramillo St Colorado Springs CO 80907-7314 Office: Colo Coll 14 E Cache La Poudre St Colorado Springs CO 80903-3298

PICKRELL-TAKATA, LINDA, artist; b. Misawa, Japan, Jan. 6, 1960; came to U.S., 1963; d. Jack Evon and Reiko (Washizu) P.; m. Wayne Takata, Jul. 18, 1986. Graphic artist United Cable, Denver, 1981-83; pub. cartoonist, 1982—; artist Denver, 1983—; curator/artist Internat. Art Show and Event, 1997. Mem. Core New Art Space, Colored Pencil Soc. Am., Alternative Arts Alliance, The Elvis Connection, Japanese Am. Nat. Mus. Democrat. Avocations: gardening, gambling, walking, bird watching, book reading.

PIEPER, DAROLD D., lawyer; b. Vallejo, Calif., Dec. 30, 1944; s. Walter A. H. and Vera Mae (Ellis) P.; m. Barbara Gille, Dec. 20, 1969. J. child Christopher Radcliffe. AB, UCLA, 1967; JD, USC, 1970. Bar: Calif. 1971.

Ops. rsch. analyst Naval Weapons Ctr., China Lake, Calif., 1966-69; assoc. Richards, Watson & Gershon, L.A., 1970-76, ptnr., 1976 ; spl. counsel L.A. County Transp. Commn., 1984-93, L.A. County Met. Transp. Authority, 1993-94; commr. L.A. County Delinquency and Crime Commn., 1983-94, pres., 1987-94; chmn. L.A. County Delinquency Prevention Planning Coun., 1987-90. Contbr. articles to profl. jours. Peace officer Pasadena (Calif.) Police Res. Unit, 1972-87, dep. comdr., 1979-81, comdr., 1982-84; chmn. pub. safety commn. City of La Canada Flintridge, Calif., 1977-82, commr 1977-88; bd. dirs La Canada Flintridge Coordinating Council, 1975-82, pres. 1977-78; exec. dir. Cityhood Action Com., 1975-76; active Calif. Rep. Party, Appellate Circle of Legion Lex U. So. Calif.; chmn. Youth Opportunities United, Inc., 1990-96, vice-chmn. 1988-89, bd. dirs. 1988-96; mem. L.A. County Justice Systems Adv. Group, 1987-92; trustee Lanterman Hist. Mus. Found., 1989-94, Calif. City Mgmt. Found., 1992—. Recipient commendation for Community Service, L.A. County Bd. Suprs., 1978, Commendation for Svc. to Youth, 1996. Mem. La Canada Flintridge C. of C. and Cmty. Assn. (pres. 1981, bd. dirs 1976-83), Navy League U.S., Pacific Legal Found., Peace Officers Assn., L.A. County, UCLA Alumni Assn. (life), U. So. Calif. Alumni Assn. (life), L.A. County Bar Assn., Calif. Bar Assn., ABA, U. So. Calif. Law Alumni Assn. Office: Richards Watson & Gershon 333 S Hope St Fl 38 Los Angeles CA 90071-1406

PIERCE, DEBORAH MARY, educational administrator; b. Charleston, W. Va.; d. Edward Ernest and Elizabeth Anne (Trent) P.; m. Henry M. Armetta, Sept. 1, 1967 (div. 1981); children: Rosse Matthew Armetta, Stacey Elizabeth Pierce. Student. U. Tenn., 1956-59, Broward Jr. Coll., 1968-69; BA, San Francisco State U., 1977. Cert. elem. tchr., Calif. Pub. relations assoc. San Francisco Internat. Film Festival, 1965-66; account exec. Stover & Assocs., San Francisco, 1966-67; tchr. San Francisco Archdiocese Office of Cath. Schs., 1980-87; part-time tchr. The Calif. Study, Inc. (formerly Tchr's. Registry), Tiburon, Calif., 1988—; pvt. practice as paralegal San Francisco, 1989—; tchr. Jefferson Sch. Dist., Daly City, Calif., 1989-91. Author: (with Frances Spatz Leighton) I Prayed Myself Slim, 1960. Pres. Mothers Alone Working, San Francisco, 1966, PTA, San Francisco, 1979, Parent Tchr. Student Assn., San Francisco, 1984; apptd. Calif. State Bd. Welfare Cmty. Rels. Com., 1964-66; block organizer SAFE, 1996; active feminist movement. Named Model of the Yr. Modeling Assn. Am., 1962. Mem. People Med. Soc., Assn. for Rsch. and Enlightenment, A Course in Miracles, Commonwealth Club Calif., Angel Club San Francisco. Democrat. Mem. Unity Christ Ch. Avocations: chess, horseback riding. Home: # 204 4960 Clairemont Mesa Blvd San Diego CA 92117

PIERCE, DIANE JEAN, artist; b. Evanston, Ill., Apr. 9, 1952; d. Kenneth William and Marjorie J. (Hansen) P.; m. William Carry Reuling, Sept. 8, 1991 (div. July 1992). BFA in Drawing and Painting, U. Utah, 1976. Illustrator Ensign Mag., Salt Lake City, 1977-79, Scott Foresman & Co. Pubs., Glenview, Ill., 1980, Children's Press, Chgo., 1981-82; mansion artist Adnan-Khoshagi's Devereaux Mansion, Salt Lake City, 1984-87; illustrator Friend Mag./Era Mag., Salt Lake City, 1978-80; artist-painter Lido Gallery, Park City, Utah, 1990-93, Thomas Charles Gallery, Las Vegas, Nev., 1994, Art Dimensions Gallery, Hollywood, Calif., 1994-96, Meyer Gallery, Park City, Utah, 1996-98, Southam Gallery, Salt Lake City, 1998; apprentice photographer Reynel Salgado Mirando, 1980 Elections, Acapulco, Mexico; 1980; juror exhbn. com. Alliance Gallery, Salt Lake Art Ctr., 1984, 85. Exhibited in group shows New Genre, 1985, 5 Star Auction Invitational, 1985, Springville Nat. Salon, 1985, Utah Women Artists, 1985, Chase Mansion Guthrie shows, 1986, Guthrie Artists, 1986, NAD, 1986, 95, Eccles Art Ctr., 1986, 87, Women's Show, 1987, 89, 91, 93, Park City Open Painting Competition, 1989-90, 93, Mus. Art, Alliance Gallery, Eccles Art Ctr., Chase Mansion, Salt Lake Art Ctr., Tivoli Gallery, Cliff Lodge Gallery, U. Utah Mus. Art, Devereaux Mansion, 1984-87, Utah divsn. Assn. Women Artists traveling show, 1989, 90, 100 Yrs.-100 Women traveling show, N.Y.C., 1989-91, Springville Mus. Art, 1992, Nat. Assn. Women ann. competition, 1993, Janet Dumbar Interiors, Sun Valley, Idaho, 1991-93, Lido Gallery, 1990-93, Elouises' Interiors, Park City, Utah, 1993-98, Thomas Charles Gallery, 1994, Art Dimensions Gallery, 1994-96, Springville Mus. Art nat. competition, Art Space, 1995, Gallery Stroll, 1995, Nat. Assn. Women Artists ann., Soho, N.Y., 1995, Nat. Assn. Women Artists, Athens, Greece, 1996; represented in permanent collections Girl Scouts Hdqs., Salt Lake City, Profl. Figure Skaters Hdqs., Sun Valley, Springville Mus. Art, Moonie & O'Conner, Cin., Van Cott, Bagley, Cornwall & McCarthy, Salt Lake City, Rasmussen & Miner, Salt Lake City, Stoel Rives LLP Attys., Salt Lake City, also pvt. collections; contbr. color plates Utah Painting and Sculptors; contbr. articles to profl. jours. Recipient Art Dirs. award Era Mag., 1979, Dirs. award U. Utah Statewide Women's Competition, Springville Mus. Fine Art, 1987, 1st pl. Best of Show, Eccles Statewide Competition, Ogden, Utah, 1987, Best Traditional Painting nat. Assn. U. Women, Utah divsn., Ogden, 1989, Best of Show, Open Painting Exhbn., Kimball Art Ctr., Park City, Utah, 1989, 3rd pl. open painting competition Kimball Art Ctr., 1990, award Artists Fellowship Inc., N.Y.C., 1993, Best of Show open painting exhbn. Kimball Art Ctr., Park City, 1993, award of merit Springville Mus. Fine Art, 1995, grant Artists Fellowship, Inc., N.Y.C., 1993. Mem. Nat. Assn. Women Artists (Susan Kahn award 1987), Nat. Mus. Women in Arts, Salt Lake Art Ctr. Home: 331 Rio Grande St Ste 307 Salt Lake City UT 84101-1131 Office: Southam Gallery 50 E Broadway Salt Lake City UT 84111-2202

PIERCE, GEORGE ADAMS, university administrator, educator; b. Carlsbad, N.Mex., May 21, 1943; s. Jack Colwell and Shirley (Adams) P.; m. Margaret Mary Brakel, Feb. 10, 1980; children: Christopher, Catherine Rose. BA in Polit. Sci., Fairleigh Dickinson U., 1969; MA in Polit. Sci., New Sch. Social Rsch., 1971; PhD in Higher Edn., Claremont Grad. Sch., 1976. Asst. dir. promotion Afco, N.Y.C., 1969-71; dir. spl. programs U. Calif., Riverside, 1971-73; asst. to pres. Claremont (Calif.) Grad. Sch., 1973-75; asst. to pres. Seattle U., 1975-78, dir. planning, 1978-83, v.p. adminstrn., 1983-87, v.p. planning, 1987-89; v.p. bus. and fin. affairs Western Wash. U., Bellingham, 1989—, adj. prof. adult and higher edn., 1998—; chmn. regional rev. panel Truman Scholarship Found., 1977-90. Chmn. Seattle Ctr. Adv. Commn., 1977-83; bd. dirs. Truman Scholarship Found., Seattle, 1986—, YMCA, Bellingham, 1990—; chmn. pack 41 Boy Scouts Am., Bellingham, 1992-94, chmn. troop 7, 1995-98. With USAF, 1963-65. Recipient Cert. Merit Riverside County Comprehensive Health Planning, 1972, Cert. Appreciation Office Mayor City of Seattle, 1983, Nat. Truman Scholarship Found., 1986. Mem. Am. Assn. Higher Edn., Assn. Instnl. Rsch. (regional pres. 1977), Nat. Assn. Coll. and Univ. Bus. Officers (chmn. pers. and benefits com. 1992-94), Rotary. Democrat. Roman Catholic. Avocations: backpacking, canoeing, swimming, tennis. Home: 421 Morey Ave Bellingham WA 98225-6344 Office: Western Wash U Old Main 300 Bellingham WA 98225

PIERCE, HILDA (HILDA HERTA HARMEL), painter; b. Vienna, Austria; came to U.S., 1940; 1 child, Diana Rubin Daly. Student, Art Inst. of Chgo.; studied with Oskar Kokoschka, Salzburg, Austria. Art tchr. Highland Park (Ill.) Art Ctr.; Sandburg Village Art Workshop, Chgo., Old Town Art Center, Chgo.; owner, operator Hilda Pierce Art Gallery, Laguna Beach, Calif., 1981-85; guest lectr. major art mus. and Art Tours in France, Switzerland, Austria, Italy; guest lectr. Russian river cruise and major art mus. St. Petersburg and Moscow, 1994. One-woman shows include Fairweather Hardin Gallery, Chgo., Sherman Art Gallery, Chgo., Marshall Field Gallery , Chgo.; exhibited in group shows at Old Orchard Art Festival, Skokie, Ill., Union League Club (awards), North Shore Art League (awards), ARS Gallery of Art Inst. of Chgo.; represented in numerous private and corporate collections; commissioned for all art work including monoprints, oils, and murals for Carnival Cruise Lines megaliner M.S. Fantasy, 1990, 17 murals consisting of 49 paintings for megaliner M.S. Imagination, 1995; contbr. articles to Chgo. Tribune Mag., American Artist Mag., Southwest Art Mag., SRA publs., others; featured in video Survivors of the Shoa, Stephen Spielberg Foundation, 1996. Recipient Outstanding Achievement award in Field of Art for Citizen Foreign Birth Chgo. Immigrant's Svc. League. E-mail: Hildaherm@aol.com.

PIERCE, LESTER LAURIN, retired aviation consultant; b. Merlin, Oreg., Apr. 7, 1904; s. Harry Lester and Bertha Ida (Mullen) P.; m. Mildred Thornton, Mar. 22, 1931. Grad. of St. Adrienne C. Freeman; Nancy L. Johnson. Grad. high sch., 1925. Theatre mgr. Redwood Theatres, Inc., Fortuna and Eureka, Calif., 1927-28; salesman, bookkeeper Thomas Furniture House, Eureka, 1930-32; pilot, mgr. Pierce Bros Flying Svc, Eureka, 1934-41; aerial photographer Pierce Flying Svc., Eureka, 1934-75; chief flight instr. Govt.

Approved Flight Sch., Eureka, 1947-60; aerial seeder, mgr., pres., salesman Pierce Flying Svc., Inc., Eureka, 1946-68; flight examiner FAA, Eureka, 1948-68, aircraft maintenance insp., 1950-68; mapping pilot Stand Aerial Surveys, Newark, 1938. Lt., flight tng., safety officer USNR, 1942, comdr., 1950. Mem. Soc. Aircraft Safety Investigators Aviation Cons., Elks. Home and office: 3428 Jacoby Creek Rd Bayside CA 95524-9304

PIERCE, THRESIA (TISH), primary school educator; b. Maize, Kans.; d. Herman and Marie Adeline (Lubbers) Korte; children: Judith, John, Mark. BS, Friends U., 1955; MS, U. Nev., Las Vegas, 1978. Cert. tchr., Nev., Nev. Life Ins. lic. Office worker Internat. Trust Co., Denver, Colo., 1951, Motor Equipment Co., Wichita, Kans., 1952-53; tchr. Wichita Pub. Schs., 1960-69, Clark County Sch. Dist., Las Vegas, Nev., 1970—. Author numerous short stories; contbr. acticles to profl. jours. Senator Clark County Edn. assn., Clark County Classroom Tchrs. Mem. NEA, Epsilon Sigma Delta (v.p. 1962). Home: 3105 Cardinal Dr Las Vegas NV 89121 Office: Will Buckley Sch 3223 S Glenhurst Dr Las Vegas NV 89121

PIERCE, WILLIAM A., financial consultant, career officer; b. Corona, Calif., Oct. 31, 1955; s. George William and Mary Ann (Skaggs) P.; m. Roswitha M. (Heift) Pierce, June 24, 1982; children: George, Ashley. BA, Calif. Poly. U., 1977. Reg. investment advisor, SEC broker and dealer, health and life ins., Nev. Transp. officer U.S. Army, 1977-93; lt. col. Nev. Army Nat. Guard, Carson City, 1993-98; cmdr. Troop Command Battalion Nev. Army Nat. Guard, 1998; dist. exec. Boy Scouts Am., Las Vegas, Nev., 1993-96; fin. cons. Merrill Lynch, Las Vegas, Nev., 1996—. Asst. Scoutmaster, Troop 903, Henderson Nev., 1998, active endowment task force, Boy Scouts Am., Las Vegas, 1998. Nominated Top 100 Fin. Advisors in U.S., Worth Mag., 1998. Mem. Nat. Def. Transp. Assn. (life mem., pres. 1983, chmn. 1986), Rotary Internat. (pres. 1993, Paul Harris fellow 1996), Nat. Guard Assn., Las Vegas U. Rotary, Boy Scouts Am. (pres. Eagle 1963-69), Order of the Arrow (pres. Vigel 1967-97). Avocations: hiking, camping, sailing, computers. Home: 275 Adorno Dr Henderson NV 89014 Office: Merrill Lynch 2300 W Sahara Ave Ste 1200 Las Vegas NV 89102-4352

PIERCY, GORDON CLAYTON, bank executive; b. Takoma Park, Md., Nov. 23, 1944; s. Gordon Clayton and Dorothy Florence (Brummer) P.; m. Roberta Margaret Walton, 1985; children: Elizabeth Anne, Kenneth Charles, Virginia Walton, Zachary Taylor Walton. BS, Syracuse U., 1966; MBA, Pace U., 1973. Mgmt. trainee Suburban Bank, Bethesda, Md., 1962-66; mktg. planning assoc. Chem. Bank, N.Y.C., 1966-70; sr. market devel. officer Seattle-First Nat. Bank, 1970-74; product expansion adminstr., mktg. planning mgr. VISA, Inc. San Francisco, 1974-76; v.p. mktg. dir. First Interstate Bank of Wash. N.A., 1983-86; sr. v.p. mktg., dir. Puget Sound Nat. Bank, Tacoma, 1986-92; sr. v.p., dir. mktg. and sales Key Bank, 1993-94, dir. corp. sales Kiro Inc., 1994; sr. v.p., dir. mktg. sales and facilities InterWest Bancorp, Oak Harbor, Wash., 1994—. Mem. Am. Mktg. Assn., Bank Mktg. Assn., Mktg. Communications Execs. Internat., Seattle Advt. Fedn., Ctrl. Whidbey Lions, Northwest Railcar, Island County EDC (exec. com.), Sigma Nu, Alpha Kappa Psi, Delta Mu Delta. Episcopalian. Home: 750 N Snowberry Ln Coupeville WA 98239-3110 Office: InterWest Bancorp PO Box 1649 Oak Harbor WA 98277-1649

PIERIK, MARILYN ANNE, retired librarian; b. Bellingham, Wash., Nov. 12, 1939; d. Estell Leslie and Anna Margarethe (Onigkeit) Bowers; m. Robert Vincent Pierik, July 25, 1964; children: David Vincent, Donald Lesley. AA, Chaffey Jr. Coll., Ontario, Calif., 1959; BA, Upland (Calif.) Coll., 1962; cert. in teaching, Claremont (Calif.) Coll., 1963; MSLS, U. So. Calif., L.A., 1973. Tchr. elem. Christ Episcopal Day Sch., Ontario, 1959-60; tchr. Bonita High Sch., La Verne, Calif., 1962-63; tchr., libr. Kettle Valley Sch. Dist. 14, Greenwood, Can., 1963-64; libr. asst. Monrovia (Calif.) Pub. Libr., 1964-67; with Mt. Hood C.C., Gresham, Oreg., 1972-98, reference libr. 1983-98, chair faculty scholarship com., 1987-98; campus archivist Mt. Hood C.C., Gresham, 1994-98; ret., 1998; mem. site selection com. Multnomah County (Oreg.) Libr., New Gresham br., 1987, adv. com. Multnomah County Libr., Portland, Oreg., 1988-89; bd. dirs. Oreg. Episcopal Conf. of Deaf, 1985-92. Bd. dirs. East County Arts Alliance, Gresham, 1987-91; vestry person, jr. warden St. Luke's Episc. Ch., 1989-92; founding pres. Mt. Hood Pops, 1983-88, orch. mgr.; 1983-91, 93—, bd. dirs., 1983-89, 1991—. Recipient Jeanette Parkhill Meml. award Chaffey Jr. Coll., 1959, Svc. award St. Luke's Episcopal Ch., 1983, 87, Edn. Svc. award Soroptimists, 1989. Mem. AAUW, NEA, Oreg. Edn. Assn., Oreg. Libr. Assn., ALA, Gresham Hist. Soc. Avocations: music, reading. E-mail: pierikm@teleport.com.

PIERRE, JOSEPH HORACE, JR., commercial artist; b. Salem, Oreg., Oct. 3, 1929; s. Joseph Horace and Miriam Elisabeth (Holder) P.; m. June Anne Rice, Dec. 20, 1952; children: Joseph Horace III, Thomas E., Laurie E., Mark R., Ruth A. Grad. Advt. Art Sch., Portland, Oreg., 1954, Inst. Comml. Art, 1951-52. Lithographic printer Your Town Press, Inc., Salem, Oreg., 1955-58; correctional officer Oreg. State Correctional Instn., 1958-60; owner Illustrators Workshop, Inc., Salem, 1960-61; advt. mgr. North Pacific Lumber Co., Portland, 1961-63; vocat. instr. graphic arts Oreg. Correctional Instn., 1963-70; lithographic printer Lloyd's Printing, Monterey, Calif., 1971-72; illustrator McGraw Hill, 1972-73; owner Publishers Art Svc., Monterey, 1972-81; correctional officer Oreg. State Penitentiary, 1982-90; ret.; owner Northwest Syndicate, 1991—. Editor/publisher: The Pro Cartoonist & Gagwriter; author: The Road to Damascus, 1981, The Descendants of Thomas Pier, 1992, The Origin and History of the Callaway and Holder Families, 1992; author numerous OpEd cols. in Salem, Oreg. Statesman Jour., others; pub. cartoons nat. mags.; mural Mardi Gras Restaurant, Salem; cartoon strip Fabu, Oreg. Agr. mo. Mem. Rep. Nat. Com., Citizens Com. for Right to Keep and Bear Arms. Served with USN, 1946-51. Decorated victory medal WWII, China svc. medal, Korea medal, Navy occupation medal. Mem. U.S. Power Squadron, Nat. Rifle Assn., Acad. of Model Aeronautics, Oreg. Correctional Officers Assn. (co-founder, hon. mem.), Four Corners Rod and Gun Club. Republican. Avocations: sailing, flying, scuba, model aircraft building and flying. Home: 4822 Oak Park Dr NE Salem OR 97305-2931

PIERSKALLA, WILLIAM PETER, university dean, management-engineering educator; b. St. Cloud, Minn., Oct. 22, 1934; s. Aloys R. and Hilda A. P.; m. Carol Spargo, Children: Nicholas, William, Michael. AB in Econs., Harvard U., 1956, MBA, 1958; MS in Math., U. Pitts., 1962; PhD in Ops. Rsch., Stanford U., 1965; MA, U. Pa., 1978. Assoc. prof. Case Western Res. U., Cleve., 1965-68, So. Meth. U., Dallas, 1968-70; prof. dept. indsl. engring. and mgmt. scis. Northwestern U., Evanston, Ill., 1970-78; exec. dir. Leonard Davis Inst., U. Pa., Phila., 1978-83; prof., chmn. health care sys. dept. U. Pa., Phila., 1982-90, prof. decision sci. and systems engring., dep. dean acad. affairs Wharton Sch., 1983-89, Ronald A. Rosenfield prof., 1986-93; dir. Huntsman Ctr. Global Competition and Leadership U. Pa. Wharton Sch., 1989-91; John E. Anderson prof. UCLA, 1993—, dean John E. Anderson Grad Sch. Mgmt., 1993-97; cons. HHS, Bethesda, Md., 1974-87, MDAX, Chgo., 1985-91, MEDICUS, Evanston, 1970-75, Sisters of Charity, Dayton, Ohio, 1982-83, Project Hope, 1990—; bd. dirs. Huntsman Ctr. for Global Competition and Leadership, 1989-93, No. Wilderness Adventures, Griffin Funds, Inc., 1993-95, No. Trust Corp. Calif., The Bush Found., The Gerald Loeb Found., Grad. Mgmt. Edn. Coun., 1996-97. Contbr. articles to various publs. Mem. advis. bd. Lehigh U., 1986-93, U. So. Calif. Bus. Sch., 1987-93; regent St. Mary's Coll., 1998—. Recipient Harold Larnder Meml. prize Can. Oper. Rsch. Soc. 1993; grantee NSF, 1970-83, HHS, Washington, 1973-82. Office: Naval Rsch., Arlington, Va., 1974-77. Mem. Ops. Rsch. Soc. Am. (pres. 1982-83, editor 1979-82, Kimball Disting. Svc. medal 1989), Inst. Mgmt. Scis. (assoc. editor 1970-77), Internat. Fedn. Operational Rsch. Soc. Am. (pres. 1987-89), Omega Rho (hon.). Office: UCLA Anderson Grad Sch Mgmt 110 Westwood Plz Box 951481 Los Angeles CA 90095-1481

PIERSON, WILLIAM STOFFEL, communications executive; b. Elkview, W.Va., May 16, 1929; s. C.H. and Mary Bertha (SToffel) P.; m. Ann Denver, 1952. Broadcast news reporter, editor, commentator various radio and TV stas. Tex., Okla. Colo., 1948-91; radio sta. owner, operator Sta. KBPI-FM, Denver, 1963-72; broadcaster radio and TV news Sta. KOA-AM/KOA-TV, Denver, 1972-75; radio news editor, commentator, Armstrong Broadcasting, Denver, 1975-78; dir. comm. Colo. Med. Soc., Denver,

1979—. Editor, author (monthly jour.) Colorado Medicine, 1979—. Mem. exec. coun. Hall of Life Health Edn., Denver, 1977—; chmn., sec. Colo. Code of Coop., Denver, 1977—; bd. dirs. Hist. Georgetown (Colo.) Inc., 1985—. Sgt. U.S. Army, 1952-54. Mem. Colo. Broadcasters Assn., Colo. Press Assn., City Club Denver (2 term pres.). Avocations: Colorado history, hiking, military vehicle restoration. Home: 10000 E Yale Ave Apt 51 Denver CO 80231-5960 Office: Colo Med Soc 7800 E Dorado Pl Englewood CO 80111-2306

PIES, RONALD E., retired city official; b. Rochester, N.Y., Mar. 21, 1940; s. Herman S. and Sylvia P.; m. Bernita Orloff, Aug. 27, 1964; children: Cara Jean Tracy, David Paul. BS, Ariz. State U., 1963. Recreation leader City of Phoenix, Ariz., 1962-64; head recreation div. City of Scottsdale (Ariz.) Parks and Recreation Dept., 1964-69; dir. parks and recreation, City of Tempe, Ariz., 1969-84, community services dir., 1984-98; club sales rep., Club Disney, 1999—; guest lectr. Ariz. State U. Mem., pres. Kyrene Sch. Dist. Governing Bd., 1979-82. Chmn., bd. regents Pacific Revenue Sources Mgmt. Sch. NRPA; gen. chmn. Fiesta Bowl Soccer Classic, 1982-98; founding mem. Tempe YMCA bd. mgrs.; apptd. mem. Ariz. State Parks Bd., 1987-93, chair, 1991. Named Outstanding Young Man, Jaycees; recipient Superior Svc. Mgmt. award ASPA, Ariz. chpt., 1988; named to Hall of Fame, Ariz. State U. Alumni for Coll. Pub. Programs, 1996, Hall of Fame, Tempe Elem. Sch. Dist., 1996. Mem. Tempe C. of C., Ariz. Parks and Recreation Assn. (bd. dirs. 1986-98, pres. adminstrs., Disting. Fellow award 1983, Life Mem. award, 1998), Nat. Recreation and Parks Assn. (Outstanding Profl. 1991), Cactus League Baseball Assn. (pres. 1993-94, appointed mem. of Ariz. baseball commn. by Gov. Symington, 1994—, chair 1995—), Sigma Alpha Epsilon. Club: Tempe Diablos.

PIETZSCH, MICHAEL EDWARD, lawyer; b. Burlington, Iowa, Aug. 1, 1949; s. Walter E. and Leanna (Moore) P.; m. K. Susan Phillips, June 17, 1978; children: Christine E., Catherine M. AB, Stanford U., 1971; JD, U. Chgo., 1974. Bar: Ill. 1974, Ariz. 1976. Assoc. Schwartz & Freeman, Chgo., 1974-75; ptnr. McCabe & Pietzsch, Phoenix, 1975-90, Pietzsch & Williams, Phoenix, 1990-95, Polese, Pietzsch, Williams & Nolan, Phoenix, 1995—. Contbr. articles to profl. jours.; speaker at profl. confs. Del. White House Conf. Small Bus., Washington, 1986, Nat. Saver Summit, 1998; chmn. bd. trustees Ariz. Sci. Ctr., 1994—; pres. The Group, Inc., 1995—. Fellow Am. Coll. Tax Counsel, Am. Coun. on Tax Policy; mem. ABA (chmn. personal svc. orgns. com. tax sect. 1986-90), Stanford Phoenix Club (pres. 1982-84). Republican. Episcopalian. Home: 6339 N 48th Pl Paradise Valley AZ 85253-4018 Office: 2702 N 3d St Ste 3000 Phoenix AZ 85004-4607

PIGOTT, CHARLES MCGEE, transportation equipment manufacturing executive; b. Seattle, Apr. 21, 1929; s. Paul and Theiline (McGee) P.; m. Yvonne Flood, Apr. 18, 1953. B.S., Stanford U., 1951. With PACCAR Inc, Seattle, 1959—, exec. v.p., 1962-65, pres., 1965-86, chmn., pres., 1986-87, chmn., chief exec. officer, 1987-97, also bd. dirs., chmn. emeritus, 1997—; dir. The Seattle Times, Chevron Corp., The Boeing Co. Pres. Nat. Boy Scouts Am., 1986-88, mem. exec. bd. Mem. Bus. Council. Office: Paccar Inc 777 106th Ave NE Ste B Bellevue WA 98004-5017

PIGOTT, MARK C., automotive executive. CEO PACCAR, Bellevue, Wash., 1997—. Office: PACCAR 777 106th Ave NE Bellevue WA 98004*

PIIRTO, DOUGLAS DONALD, forester, educator; b. Reno, Nev., Sept. 25, 1948; s. Rueben Arvid and Martha Hilma (Giebel) P.; BS, U. Nev., 1970; MS, Colo. State U., 1971; PhD, U. Calif., Berkeley, 1977; m. Mary Louise Cruz, Oct. 28, 1978. Rsch. asst. Colo. State U., 1970-71, U. Calif., Berkeley, 1972-77; forester, silviculturist U.S. Dept. Agr., Forest Svc., Sierra Nat. Forest, Trimmer and Shaver Lake, Calif., 1977-85; assoc. prof. natural resources mgmt. dept. Calif. Poly. State U., San Luis Obispo, 1985-90, prof. 1990—; researcher in field; instr. part-time Kings River Community Coll., Reedley, Calif.; forestry cons.; expert witness. Registered profl. forester, Calif.; cert. silviculturist USDA Forest Svc. Recipient Meritorious Performance and Profl. Promise awards CalPoly, 1989, 96, 97, 98, CalPoly Coll. Agr. Outstanding Tchg. award Dole Food Co., 1995. Mem. Soc. Am. Foresters, Am. Forestry Assn., Forest Products Rsch. Soc., Soc. Wood Sci. and Tech., Alpha Zeta, Xi Sigma Pi, Sigma Xi, Beta Beta Beta, Phi Sigma Kappa. Lutheran. Contbr. articles to sci. and forestry jours. E-mail: dougúpiirto@nrm.calpoly.edu. Home: 115 Eagle Creek Ct Atascadero CA 93422-5957 Office: Calif Poly State U Dept Nat Resources Mgmt San Luis Obispo CA 93407

PIKE, BRIAN, agent; b. Bklyn., June 21, 1954; m. Randis Dee Schmidt; 1 child, Justin. BA, UCLA. V.p. Prime Time Drama NBC, Burbank, Calif., 1990-93; exec. prodr. Brian Pike Prodns., L.A., 1993-97; agt. Creative Artists Agy., Beverly Hills, Calif., 1997—. Exec. prodr. (TV movies) Tonya & Nancy, 1994, Born Into Exile, 1996, (TV mini-series) Seduced By Madness, 1996. Mem. Acad. TV Arts and Scis., Hollywood Radio and TV Soc. Office: Creative Artists Agy 9830 Wilshire Blvd Beverly Hills CA 90212-1825

PIKE, DIANE KENNEDY, writer, educator; b. Norfolk, Nebr., Jan. 24, 1938; d. G. Edward and Arlene Alice (Wyant) Kennedy; m. James Albert Pike, Dec. 20, 1968 (dec. Sept. 1969). BA with distinction, Stanford U., 1959; MA, Columbia U., 1964. Tchr. Crandon Inst., Montevideo, Uruguay, 1960-62, Willow Glen H.S., San Jose, Calif., 1964-65; dir. youth and children's work First United Meth. Ch., Palo Alto, Calif., 1965-67; exec. dir. New Focus Found., Santa Barbara, Calif., 1967-69, Bishop Pike Found., Santa Barbara, 1969-72, The Love Project, San Diego, 1972-89; exec. dir. Teleos Inst., San Diego, 1989-93, Scottsdale, Ariz., 1993—. Co-author: The Other Side, 1968, The Wilderness Revolt, 1972, Channeling Love Energy, 1974, The Love Project Way, 1980; author: Search, 1971, Cosmic Unfoldment: The Individualizing Process as Mirrored in the Life of Jesus, 1976, Life is Victorious! How to Grow Through Grief, 1976, The Process of Awakening, 1985, Life As A Waking Dream, 1997. Avocations: tennis, swimming, travel.

PILAR, L. PRUDENCIO R., financial services executive; b. Bacarra, Philippines, Sept. 12, 1943; came to U.S., 1977; s. Francisco and Maria (Raralio) P.; m. Vivien Ruth Narciso, Aug. 20, 1967; children: Prudencio Rex Jr., Diogene Ruthard, Keith N., Xydia Vida Ruth N., Benedict. BS in Edn., No. Luzon Tchrs. Coll., Laoag City, Philippines, 1964; MA in Adminstrn. and Supervision, No. Luzon Tchrs. Coll., 1972. CLU, ChFC. Prin., tchr. Bur. of Pub. Schs., Solsona, Philippines, 1964-77; agt. The Equitable, Honolulu, 1978-95; pres. Pilar Fin. & Tax Strategies, Inc., Honolulu, 1995—. Pres. St. Anthony Sch. Parent-Tchrs. Guild, Honolulu, 1987, 88, 89, 94. Fellow Life Underwriter Tng. Coun.; mem. Internat. Assn. for Fin. Planning, Nat. Assn. Life Underwriters, Diocesan Congress of Filipino Cath. Clubs, Oahu Coun. Filipino Cath. Clubs, KC. Democrat. Roman Catholic. Avocation: giving seminars. Office: Pilar Fin & Tax Strategies 33 S King St Ste 108 Honolulu HI 96813-4319

PILCHER, ELLEN LOUISE, rehabilitation counselor; b. Washington, Feb. 5, 1949; d. Donald Everett and Edna Lois (Walker) P. BA in Psychology, So. Ill. U., 1971, MA in Rehab. Counseling, 1973. Social svcs. asst. Dept. Army, Ft. Huachuca, Ariz., 1973-74, New Ulm, Germany, 1974-75, Ft. Sill, Okla., 1977-87; counselor Goodwill Industries, Lawton, Okla., 1976-77; ind. living specialist Ariz. Bridge to Ind. Living, Phoenix, 1984-87; disability specialist Samaritan Rehab. Inst., Phoenix, 1987-89; disability cons. Peoria, Ariz., 1989—; founder Problems of Architecture and Transp. to Handicapped, Lawton, Okla., 1976-79; founder, past pres. Polio Echo Support Group, Phoenix, 1985—; co-founder, bd. mem. Disability Network of Ariz., Phoenix, 1986—; disability speaker Easter Seal Soc. and free lance, Phoenix, 1984—; producer, 1st known wheelchair user local TV talk show host in country, Glendale, Ariz., 1987-91; mem. nat. adv. bd. Polio Support Groups, St. Louis, 1987. Vol. work includes work with homeless, animal welfare, adoption programs, polit. lobbying for civil rights, gay rights, women's rights, disability rights; advocate, spkr. on child abuse issues. Named Ms. Wheelchair Ariz. Good Samaritan Med. Ctr., Phoenix, 1986, Second Runner-Up Ms. Wheelchair Am., Ms. Wheelchair Am. Assn., Richmond, Va., 1986, Outstanding Bus. Person Ariz. Parks/Recreation, 1987; recipient Celebration of Success award Impact for Enterprising Women, Phoenix, 1989, Extraordinary Personal Achievement award Lions Club Found., Phoenix, 1987. Mem. NOW (co-founder Lawton chpt. 1982, Glendale, Ariz. chpt. 1984), Nat. Rehab. Assn., Nat. Rehab. Counselors Assn., Ariz. Rehab. Assn., Ariz. Rehab. Counselors Assn. Democrat. Unitarian. Avocations: animal rescue and welfare, community activities, writing biography.

PILLAR, CHARLES LITTLEFIELD, retired mining consultant; b. Denver, May 25, 1911; s. Charles and Alice May (Littlefield) P.; m. Elizabeth Reed Broadhead, Sept. 10, 1932 (div. May 1939); m. Gwendola Elizabeth Lotz, Sept. 16, 1939; children: Ann, Catherine, Pamela. Engr. mines, Colo. Sch. Mines, 1935. Registered profl. engr., B.C., Ariz. Various positions in field, 1935-75; mine cons. Pillar, Lowell & Assocs., Tucson, Ariz., 1976-83; cons. Bechtel Corp., San Francisco, 1976-79, Fluor Corp., Redwood City, Calif., 1979-83; mem. Colo. Sch. Mines Rsch. Inst., Golden, 1975-83, pvt. practice Tucson, 1985-89; bd. dir. Internat. Geosystems Corp., Vancouver, B.C.; mem. pres.'s coun. Colo. Sch. Mines. Contbr. articles to profl. jours. Mem. Nat. Rep. Senatorial com.; rep. Presdl. Task Force. Capt. USAF, 1942-45; maj. USAF Res. 1946-54. Recipient Achievement in the Mining Field award Colo. Sch. Mines, 1995, Medal of Merit award Am. Mining Hall of Fame, 1996. Mem. AIME (William Saunders Gold Medal award, Disting. mem. award), Can. Inst. Mining and Metallurgy, Profl. Engrs. B.C., Heritage Found., Smithsonian Assocs., Mining Found. S.W., Nat. Exch. Club, U.S. Senatorial Club (presdl. task force), Vancouver Club, Tucson Nat. Country Club. Republican. Episcopalian. Home: 7131 N Via Assisi Tucson AZ 85704-4315

PIMBLE, TONI, artistic director, choreographer, educator. Student, Elmhurst Sch. Ballet and Dramatic Arts, Royal Acad. Dancing, London. Resident choreographer Dance Aspen Co. Project; artistic dir., resident choreographer Eugene (Oreg.) Ballet Co., 1978—; past mem. faculty Dance Aspen Summer Dance Sch. Choreographer (festival) Carlisle Choreographer's Showcase, Pa. and Colo., (ballets) Two's Company, N.Y.C., Common Ground, Atlanta, 1994, Playing Field, Indlps., Borderline, Alice in Wonderland, Nebr., 1994, Wash., 1996, Quartet in Blue, Oreg., 1994, Petrushka, Nev., 1994, 95, Children of the Raven, India, Bangladesh, Sri Lanka, Syria, Jordan, Tunisia, 1995, 96, A Midsummer Night's Dream, Nev., 1997, numerous tours and sch. performances; choreographer, tchr. U. Iowa, Interlochen Sch. Arts; resident choreographer Dance On Tour Nat. Endowment Arts; artistic dir. Ballet Idaho. Active outreach programs Young Audiences Oreg., Wash. State Cultural Enrichment Program. Oreg. Arts Commn. artist fellow, Nat. Endowment Arts grantee; co-recipient Gov.'s Arts award, Oreg., 1996. Office: Ballet Idaho 501 S Eighth St Ste A Boise ID 83702*

PINATARO, JEAN ELEANOR, artist; b. L.A.; d. Pasqual and Anna (Maresca) P. Student, UCLA, 1960-70; BA in Fine Arts, Calif. State U., Long Beach, 1988. Tech. artist, designer, illustrator N.Am. Aviation Inc. (now Boeing); designer Apollo/Soyuz Patch NASA, 1974; artist in residence Villa Montalvo Ctr. Arts, Saratoga, Calif., 1984. Author, editor: Pinataro, 1976, Live From the Pyramids, 1979, Names Have Been Changed to Protect the Guilty, 1989; exhibitions include Calif. State U., Long Beach, 1987, System M Gallery, Long Beach, 1988, Palos Verdes Art Ctr. (Calif.), 1990, Graham Horstman Gallery, Denton, Tex., 1990, The Gate Gallery, San Pedro, Calif., 1991, Sasama Gallery, Chgo., 1992, The Bridge Gallery, L.A., 1992, Muckenthaler Cultural Ctr., Fullerton, Calif., 1992, Artspace Gallery, Woodland Hills, Calif., 1993, Downey Mus. Art, 1993, 94, 96, Gallery 57, Fullerton, 1995 (Gallery Choice), Borders Books, Long Beach, Calif., 1997, Center Gallery, Long Beach, 1997, Lincoln Heights Jail, L.A., 1998. Mem. Nat. Watercolor Soc., Artists Support Group. Avocations: singing, playing guitar.

PINE, CHARLES JOSEPH, clinical psychologist; b. Excelsior Springs, Mo., July 13, 1951; s. Charles E. and LaVern (Upton) P.; m. Mary Day, Dec. 30, 1979 (div. 1996); children: Charles Andrew, Joseph Scott, Carolyn Marie; m. Inga Marie Talbert, Feb. 11, 1998. BA in Psychology, U. Redlands, 1973; MA, Calif. State U.-L.A., 1975; PhD, U. Wash., 1979; postdoctoral UCLA, 1980-81. Diplomate in Clinical Psych. Am. Bd. Profl. Psych. Lic. psychologist, Calif., Fla. Psychology technician Seattle Indian Health Bd., USPHS Hosp., 1977-78; psychology intern VA Outpatient Clinic, L.A., 1978-79; instr. psychology Okla. State U., 1979-80, asst. prof., 1980; asst. prof. psychology and native Am. studies program Wash. State U., 1981-82; dir. behavioral health services Riverside-San Bernardino County Indian Health Inc., Banning, Calif., 1982-84; clin. psychologist, clin. co-dir. Inland Empire Behavioral Assocs., Colton, Calif., 1982-84; clin. psychologist VA Med. Ctr., Long Beach, Calif., 1984-85; clin. psychologist, psychology coordinator Psychiatry div. VA Med. Ctr., Sepulveda, Calif., 1985-93; clin. dir. Traumatic Stress Treatment Ctr., Thousand Oaks, Calif., 1985-93; assoc. clin. prof. UCLA Sch. Medicine, 1985-93, Fuller Grad. Sch. Psychology, Pasadena, Calif., 1985-93, indep. practitioner Orlando, 1993-94; adj. assoc. prof. Calif. Sch. Profl. Psychology, L.A., 1989-95; mem. adj. faculty, psychologist, administv. coord. alcohol and drug abuse U. Ctrl. Fla., mem. faculty 1993-94; rsch. assoc. Nat. Ctr. for Am. Indian and Alaska Native Mental Health Rsch., U. Col. Health Sci. Ctr., Denver, 1989—; psychologist and adminstrv. coord. alcohol and drug abuse treatment program, Orlando VA Outpatient divsn. Tampa VA Med. Ctr., 1993-94; cons. NIH, 1993—; psychologist stress treatment programs Bay Pines (Fla.) VA Med. Ctr., 1994-96; psychologist Vets. Counseling Ctr., San Bernardino, Calif., 1997—; mem. L.A. County Am. Indian Mental Health task force, 1987-92. Editorial cons. White Cloud Jour., 1982-85; cons. Dept. Health and Human Services, USPHS, NIMH, 1980. Vol. worker Variety Boys Clubs Am., 1973-75; coach Rialto Jr. All-Am. Football League, 1974, Conejo Youth Flag Football Assn., pres., 1990, coach, bd. dirs. Westlake Youth Football, 1991-92; coach, Conejo Valley Little League, Dr. Phillips Little League, 1993—; co-commr., coach Dr. Phillips Pop Warner Football, 1993—. U. Wash. Inst. Indian Studies grantee, 1975-76, UCLA Inst. Am. Cultures grantee, 1981-82. Fellow Am. Psychol. Assn. (chair task force on service delivery to ethnic minority populations bd. ethnic minority affairs 1988, bd. ethnic minority affairs 1985-87); mem. Soc. Indian Psychologists (pres. 1981-83), Nat. Register Health Svc. Providers in Psychology, Calif. Psychol. Assn. Found. (bd. dirs. 1990-92), Soc. for Psychol. Study Ethnic Minority Issues (exec. com. 1987-88, pres. 1995-96), Sigma Alpha Epsilon. Republican. Roman Catholic. Contbr. psychol. articles to profl. lit.

PINE, WILLIAM CHARLES, foundation executive; b. Canton, Ill., Nov. 4, 1912; s. William Charles and Katherine Pauline (Prichard) P.; m. Virginia Rae Keeley, June 14, 1945; children: William Charles, Barry Scott, Nancy Katherine Pine McMahon. BS, Monmouth Coll., Ill., 1939; DHL (hon.), Southwestern at Memphis, 1961; Dr.Laws (hon.), Mercy Coll. Detroit, 1966. Asst. dir. admissions Monmouth Coll., 1939-42; spl. agt. FBI, 1942-45; assoc. dir. Am. City Bur., N.Y.C. and Chgo., 1945-47; dir. pub. relations Lake Forest (Ill.) Coll., 1947-48, v.p., 1948-51; dir. scholarship prog. Ford Motor Co. Fund., Dearborn, Mich., 1951-72; asst. dir. Ford Motor Co. Fund., 1972-75; prog. dir. The Collins Found., Portland, Oreg., 1976-79; exec. v.p. The Collins Found., 1979—. Contbr. articles to profl. jours. Mem. Historic Records Adv. Bd., Salem, Oreg., 1984-87. Mem. Soc. Former Spl. Agts. of FBI. Avocations: reading, mail order bus. Office: 1618 SW 1st Ave Ste 305 Portland OR 97201-5708

PINEDO, MYRNA ELAINE, psychotherapist, educator; b. Riverton, Wyo., Apr. 28, 1944; d. Pedro Berumen and Ruth Jama (Kuriyama) P.; m. Alan P. Schiesel, Sept. 9, 1964 (div. July 1973); 1 child, Elaine Marie (Schiesel) Thompson; m. Wallace Vern Calkins, Aug. 31, 1990. BA in Psychology, Calif. State U., Northridge, 1980; MA in Cmty. Clin. Psychology, Calif. Sch. Profl. Psychology, 1982; PhD in Cmty. Clin. Psychology, Calif. Sch. Profl. Psychiatry, 1987. Lic. marriage, family and child counselor, Calif.; cert. mental health counselor, Wash.; cert. marriage and family therapist, Wash. Pychiat. asst. William Newton, M.D., Marine del Rey, Calif., 1983-84; psychologist forensic svcs. dept. Kern County Mental Health, Bakersfield, Calif., 1984-88; alcohol counselor Spl. Treatment Edn. Program Svcs., Bakersfield, 1985-87; marriage and family therapist Jay Fisher & Assocs., Bakersfield, 1986-87; therapist program devel. Correctional Specialties, Bellevue, Wash., 1988-90; pvt. practice HAP Counseling Svcs., Bellevue, 1990—; adj. faculty Calif. State U., Bakersfield, 1986, Kern County Mental Health, 1987, Bellevue C.C., 1989, Antioch U., 1992, 93; instituted various treatment programs for adolescents, Spanish speaking adults and Spanish speaking sex offenders; spkr. in field; expert witness in ct. Panelist EastSide Domestic Violence Com., 1991-93; bd. dirs. Kern County Child Abuse Coun., 1986-88; mem. treatment com. Kern County Child Abuse Task Force, 1985-88; mem. Stop-Abuse by Counselors, 1993—. Mem. Am. Counseling Assn., Am. Assn. Christian Counselors, Assn. Orthopsychiatry, Wash. Assn. Mental Health Counselors, Assn. Marriage and Family Therapists. Avocations: gardening, hiking, cooking. Office: HAP Counseling Svcs 515 116th Ave NE Ste 101 Bellevue WA 98004-5204

PINGS, ANTHONY CLAUDE, architect; b. Fresno, Calif., Dec. 16, 1951; s. Clarence Hubert and Mary (Murray) P.; m. Carole Clements, June 25, 1983; children, Adam Reed, Rebecca Mary. AA, Fresno City Coll., 1972; BArch, Calif. Poly. State U., San Luis Obispo, 1976. Lic. architect, Calif.; cert. Nat. Council Archtl. Registration Bds. Architect Aubrey Moore Jr., Fresno, 1976-81; architect, prin. Pings & Assocs., Fresno, 1981-83, 86—, Pings-Taylor Assocs., Fresno, 1983-85. Prin. works include Gollaher Profl. Office (Masonry Merit award 1985, Best Office Bldg. award 1986), Fresno Imaging Ctr. (Best Instnl. Project award 1986, Nat. Healthcare award Modern Health Care mag. 1986), Orthopedic Facility (award of honor Masonry Inst. 1987, award of merit San Joaquin chpt. AIA 1987), Modesto Imaging Ctr. (award of merit San Joaquin chpt. AIA 1991), Peachwood Med. Ctr. (award of merit San Joaquin chpt. AIA). Mem. Calif. Indsl. Tech. Edn. Consortium Calif. State Dept. Edn., 1983, 84. Mem. AIA (bd. dirs. Calif. chpt. 1983-84, v.p. San Joaquin chpt. 1982, pres. 1983, Calif. Coun. evaluation team 1983, team leader Coalinga Emergency Design Assistance team), Fresno Arts (bd. dirs., counsel 1989—, pres. 1990-93), Fig Gardens Home Owners Assn. (bd. dir. 1991—, pres. 1994—). Republican. Home: 4350 N Safford Ave Fresno CA 93704-3509 Office: 1640 W Shaw Ave Ste 107 Fresno CA 93711-3506

PINIELLA, LOUIS VICTOR, professional baseball team manager; b. Tampa, Fla., Aug. 28, 1943; m. Anita Garcia, Apr. 12, 1967; children: Lou, Kristi, Derrick. Student, U. Tampa. Baseball player various minor-league teams, 1962-68, Cleve. Indians, 1968, Kansas City Royals, 1969-73; baseball player N.Y. Yankees, 1974-84, coach, 1984-85, mgr., 1985-87, 1988, gen. mgr., 1987-88, spl. advisor, TV announcer, 1989; mgr. Cin. Reds, 1990-92, Seattle Mariners, 1992—. Named to Am. League All-Star Team, 1972; recipient Ellis Island Medal of Honor, 1990; Named A.L. Rookie of the Yr Baseball Writers Assoc of Amer, 1969, Named A.L. Manager of the Yr, 1995. Office: Seattle Mariners PO Box 4100 83 X King St 3d Fl Seattle WA 98104*

PINKERTON, DANIEL WALTER, financial planner; b. Anchorage, Jan. 14, 1965; s. Frank W. and Carol J. (Moore) P.; m. Kathryn Elaine Ballard, Nov. 11, 1989; children: Daniel W. II, Sarah K., Rachael C., David M. BA, Stanford U., 1987. CFP. Regional coord. Cal Fed Bank, San Jose, Calif., 1988-91; pres. Pinkerton Retirement Specialists LLC, Anchorage, 1991—, Coeur d'Alene, Idaho, 1997—; br. mgr. Linsco/Pvt. Ledger. Author: Getting the Most Out of Your Mortgage, 1991. Nat. Honor Soc. grantee, 1983, Arco Alaska, 1983, Anchorage Rotary Club, 1983, Anchorage Elks, Anchorage Zonta, 1983; scholar Whitman Coll., 1983. Mem. NASD/SIPC, Internat. Assn. Fin. Planning, Inst. Cert. Fin. Planning, Top of Table, Stanford Alumni Assn, Million Dollar Roundtable, Estate Planning Coun., Nat. Assn. Life Underwriters, LPL's Patriots Club. Office: 2201 Ironwood Ste 100 Coeur D Alene ID 83814

PINKERTON, RICHARD LADOYT, management educator; b. Huron, S.D., Mar. 5, 1933; s. Abner Pyle and Orral Claudine (Arneson) P.; m. Sandra Louise Lee, Aug. 28, 1965 (div. 1992); children—Elizabeth, Patricia. B.A. (La Verne Noyes scholar 1952-55), U. Mich., 1955; M.B.A., Case Western Res. U., 1962; Ph.D. (Nat. Assn. Purchasing Mgmt. fellow 1967-68), U. Wis., 1969. Sr. market research analyst Harris-Intertype Corp., Cleve., 1957-61; mgr. sales devel. Triax Corp., Cleve., 1962-64; coordinator mktg. program Mgmt. Inst., U. Wis., 1964-67; dir. exec. programs Mgmt. Inst., U. Wis. (Grad. Sch. Bus.), also asst. prof. mktg., 1969-74; prof. mgmt., dean Grad. Sch. Adminstrn., Capital U., Columbus, Ohio, 1974-86; prof. mgmt., dir. Univ. Bus. Ctr., Craig Sch. of Bus. Calif. State U., Fresno, 1986-89, prof. mktg., 1989—, chair mktg. and logistics dept., 1996—; trustee Ohio Coun. Econ. Edn., 1976-87; bd. dirs. Univ. Bus. Ctr.; cons. to govt. and industry, 1960—. Co-author: The Purchasing Manager's Guide to Strategic Proactive Procurement, 1996; contbr. articles to profl. jours. Bd. dirs. The Fresno Townhouse Assn., bd. govs. Hannah Neil Home for Children, Columbus, 1975-78. Served as officer USAF, 1955-57, lt. col. USAFR, 1957-78. Mem. Nat. Assn. Contract Mgmt. (chmn. validation cert. com. 1990), Nat. Assn. Purchasing Mgmt. (chmn. acad. planning 1979-84, rsch. symposium 1992), Am. Mktg. Assn. (chpt. pres. 1972-73), Res. Officers Assn., Air Forces Assn., Ft. Washington Golf and Country Club, Beta Gamma Sigma, Alpha Kappa Psi, Phi Gamma Delta, Rotary (Paul Harris fellow). Home: 4721 N Cedar Ave Apt 111 Fresno CA 93726-1007 Office: Calif State U Dept of Mktg Fresno CA 93740-0007

PINSKER, ESSIE LEVINE, sculptor, former advertising and public relations executive; b. N.Y.C.; d. Harris and Sophia (Feldman) Levine; m. Sidney Pinsker (dec.); children: Susan Harris, Seth Howard. BA, Bklyn. Coll.; postgrad., Art Students League, 1955, Columbia U., 1958, NYU, 1959, New Sch. for Social Research, Mus. Modern Art, 1970-71, Cambridge (Eng.) U., 1985, Oxford (Eng.) U., 1991. Former buyer Ohrbach's, N.Y.C., Arkwright, N.Y.C.; fashion model; former editor Woman's Wear Daily, N.Y.C.; fashion cons. Claire Lang Assocs., N.Y.C.; former press. dir. Am. Symphony Orch., N.Y.C.; pres. Essie Pinsker Advt. Assocs., Inc., N.Y.C., 1960-82; guest editor Teen Merchandiser mag., Infant's and Children's Rev.; editor travel, beauty and fashion Woman Golfer mag.; lectr., instr. Fashion Inst. of Tech.; contbg. journalist N.Y. Times. One-woman shows include Las Vegas (Nev.) Art Mus., Vorpal Gallery, N.Y.C., Bodley Gallery, N.Y.C., Ross Watkins Gallery, Palm Desert, Calif., Left Bank Gallery, Laguna Beach, Calif.; exhibited in group shows Met. Life, N.Y.C., N. Shore Arts Ctr., Manhasset, N.Y., Huntington (N.Y.) Art League, Cadme Gallery, Phila., Allied Artists Am., N.Y.C., Susan Street Fine Art, Solana Beach, Calif., Galerie Ilse Lommel, Leverkusen, Germany, Stedman Art Gallery Rutgers U., Camden, N.J., Sandra Higgins Fine Arts, London, LK Gallery, Anaheim, Calif., Art Inst. So. Calif., Laguna Beach, Galerie Atrium, Marbella, Spain, Feingarten Galleries, L.A., Galleri Atrium, Stockholm, Arco Internat. Art Fair, Madrid, Spain; represented in permanent collections Nat. Portrait Gallery, Smithsonian Inst., Washington, Everson Mus., Syracuse, N.Y., Las Vegas Art Museum, Art Inst. So. Calif., Laguna Beach, Aldrich Mus. Contemporary Art, Ridgefield, Conn., Okla. Art Ctr., Oklahoma City, Minn. Mus. Art, St. Paul, Mus. Arts and Scis., Daytona Beach, Fla., Orange County Mus. Art, Newport Beach, Calif., UCLA Med. Ctr. L.A., City of Brea, Calif., Ctr. for Arts, Vero Beach, Okeanos Ocean Rsch. Found., Hampton Bays, N.Y., Vassar Mus., Poughkeepsie, N.Y., Mus. Modern Art, Warsaw, Poland, New Sch., N.Y.C., Pace U., N.Y.C., Necca Mus., Brooklyn, Conn., Lincoln Ctr. Fordham U., N.Y.C., Hinkhouse Collection, Eureka (Ill.) Coll., War Meml., Yehud, Israel, 1989, Rutgers Collection of Art, Camden, N.J.; represented in corp. collections Enterprise Corp. Towers, Shelton, CT, Devon, Inc., N.Y.C., Judy Bond, Inc., N.Y.C., Regina Porter, Inc., N.Y.C., Paramount Group, Los Angeles, Joseph P. Day Realty Corp., N.Y.C., Rubenstein Planning Corp., N.Y.C., Queensboro Steel Corp., Wilmington, N.C., Southerland Tours, St. Croix, V.I., Marriott Hotel, Minnetonka, Minn., Granard Communications Ltd., London, Tauck Tours, Westport, Conn., Internat. Fashion Group N.Y.C.; exec. producer film Pupae (Cine Eagle award 1973). Recipient Knickerbocker Artist's 24th ann. exhbn. sculpture award, Met. Life sculpture award. Mem. Nat. Mus. Women in the Arts, Internat. Sculpture Ctr., Fashion Group N.Y. Home: 3110 Park Newport Apt 210 Newport Beach CA 92660-5843

PINTER, JOSEPH KALMAN, mathematician; b. Janoshalma, Hungary, Jan. 12, 1953; arrived in Can., 1981; s. József and Teréz (Hoványi) P.; m. Mary Tan, Oct. 12, 1985; children: Kálmán Bonaventure, Elizabeth Anne. MS in Elec. Engring., Tech. U. Budapest, Hungary, 1976, PhD in Elec. Engring., 1979; MS in Pure Math., U. Calgary, Can., 1986, MS in Applied Math., 1996. Researcher Sefel Geophys., Calgary, Alta., Can., 1981-82; exploration geophysicist Sci. and Exploration Computer Applications, Dome Pete Ltd., Calgary, Alta., Can., 1982-87, sr. applied geophysicist, 1987-88; sr. staff geophysicist Amoco Can., Ltd., Calgary, Alta., 1988-92. Author: Propositions on the Geophysical Applications of the Radon Integral, 1990; inventor fully automated interpreter for refraction data, direct and inverse scattering in the Radon domain. Mem. Am. Math. Soc., Soc. for Indsl. and Applied Math., Assn. of Profl. Engrs. Geologists and Ge-

ophysicists of Alta. Roman Catholic. Avocations: cross country skiing, music. Home: # 864 Lake Lucerne Dr SE, Calgary, AB Canada T2J 3H4

PIPER, GLORIA NADINE, freelance writer; b. Orland, Calif., May 24, 1939; d. Lloyd Vernon and Edith Ellen (McMurphy) P. MA in Biology, Chico (Calif.) State Coll., 1968; MA in Art, Calif. State U., 1985. Cert. tchr. C.C., gen. secondary sch., Calif. Tchr. Red Bluff (Calif.) H.S., 1965-68; chemistry stockroom technician Chico State Coll., 1968-70; founder, dir. River House Global Youth Evangelism, Chico, Calif., 1970-73; receptionist Traditional Acupuncture, Chico, Calif., 1990—; tchr. City Art Ctrs., Orland, Chico, Paradise, Calif., 1982-84; contbg. writer Orland Press Register, 1995-98. Author: (manual) S.O.P. for rearing insects; contbr. rsch. articles to Mosquito News, 1976; co-founder, publisher (mag.) Along the Path, 1995. Founder, tchr. Judo Acad. Red Bluff, Calif., 1965-68; singer Glenn County Chorale, Orland, Calif., 1983—; vol. med. driver Glenn County Transp., Willows, Calif., 1997—. With U.S. Army, 1974-80. Mem. Writers Pending. Democrat. Methodist. Avocations: bell ringing, birding, walking, tai-chai, piano. Home: 4957 Road M Orland CA 95963

PIPER, LLOYD LLEWELLYN, II, engineer, government and service industry executive; b. Wareham, Mass., Apr. 28, 1944; s. Lloyd Llewellyn and Mary Elizabeth (Brown) P.; m. Jane Melonie Scruggs, Apr. 30, 1965; 1 child, Michael Wayne. *The original Piper ancestor, Nathaniel, arrived in Ipswich, Massachusetts around 1653. The original Scruggs ancestor, Richard, arrived in James City County, Virginia around 1655. The "Scruggs Piper Connections", a book published by J. Melonie Scruggs Piper, documents the genealogies of both families and allied lines. Son Michael W. Piper is an intellectual property attorney in Dallas with the firm of Locke, Pernell, Rain and Harrell. He married Tamara G. Lovell, who is an attorney in Dallas, specializing in business matters.* BSEE, Tex. A&M U., 1966; MS in Indsl. Engring, U. Houston, 1973. Registered profl. engr., Tex.; diplomate hazardous waste mgmt. Am. Acad. Environ. Engrs. With Houston Lighting & Power Co., 1965-74; project mgr. Dow Chem. Engring. & Constrn Svcs., Houston, 1974-78; project mgr. Ortloff Corp., Houston, 1978, mgr. engring., 1979-80, v.p., 1980-83; pres., chief exec. officer Plantech Engrs. & Constructors, Inc. subs. Dillingham Constrn. Corp., Houston, 1983-86; pres. The Delta Plantech Co., Houston, 1985-86; dir. on-site tech. devel. Chem. Waste Mgmt., Inc., Oak Brook, Ill., 1986-88; mgr. projects Chem. Waste Mgmt., Inc., Houston, 1988-94, dir. facility devel., 1994-95; asst. mgr. Richland (Wa.) Ops. U.S. Dept. Energy, 1995-96, dep. mgr., 1996—; bd. dirs., pres. Harris County Water Control and Improvement Dist., 1973-83; bd. dirs. Environ. Sci. and Tech. Found., 1997—; bd. dirs. United Way, 1998—, exec. com., 1998—; Ponderosa Joint Powers Agy. Harris County, 1977-83, pres., 1977-83; pres. bus. and industry adv. coun. North Harris Montgomery C. C. Dist., 1991-92. Contbr. articles to profl. jours. Recipient Disting. Svc. award Engrs. Coun. Houston, 1970, Outstanding Svc. award Houston sect. IEEE, 1974; named Tex. Young Engr. of Yr., 1976, Nat. Young Engr. of Yr., 1976. Mem. IEEE, Nat. Soc. Profl. Engrs. (chpt. pres. 1978, nat. chmn. engrs. in industry div. 1977, nat. v.p. 1977, chmn. nat. polit. action com. 1979-82, vice chmn. nat. engrs. week 1988-92, nat. trustee edn. found. 1988-90), Nat. Wildlife Fedn., Nature Conservancy, Audubon Soc., Project Mgmt. Inst., Phi Kappa Phi, Tau Beta Pi. Home: 129 Mountain View Ln Richland WA 99352-7652 Office: Dept of Energy PO Box 550 Richland WA 99352-0550

PIPERNO, SHERRY LYNN, psychotherapist; b. La Crosse, Wis., Sept. 22, 1953; d. Morris and Leona Jennie (Shelmadine-Hanson) Piperno. BA in Fine Arts, U. N.Mex., 1981; MA in Counseling, 1989. Nat. cert. counselor; lic. clin. mental health counselor; cert. criminal justice specialist. Mental health counselor Bernalillo County Detention Ctr., Albuquerque, 1990—; group facilitator and youth authority Juveinile Probation dept. 2d Jud. Dist. Ct., Albuquerque, 1990-92; program therapist Heights Psychiatric Hosp., Albuquerque, 1990-91; cons. Albuquerque Fire Dept. Mem. ACA, Nat. Assn. Forensic Counselors, Am. Mental Health Counselors Assn., Internat. Assn. Addictions and Offender Counseling, Fraternal Order of Police. Democrat. Lutheran. Avocations: rock climbing, nordic skiing, horse-back riding, animal rescue.

PIPPIN, DONALD FERRELL, musician, director, conductor; b. Raleigh, N.C., Dec. 8, 1925; s. Raymond Edward and Dorothy (Law) Pippin. Pianist, producer Sunday Night Concerts, San Francisco, 1954-78; artistic dir. Pocket Opera, San Francisco, 1978. Translator, condr. over 60 operas including Marriage of Figaro, 1981, Belle Helene, 1981, Merry Wives, 1983, Merry Widow, 1987, Barber of Seville, 1991 among others. Democrat. Home: 39 Romain St San Francisco CA 94114-2733 Office: Pocket Opera 44 Page St Ste 404A San Francisco CA 94102-5975

PIROLO, PHILIP DARRELL, graphic designer; b. L.A., Oct. 21, 1963; s. Philip Angelo and Bennie Redyne (Barker) P. BA in Music Composition & Humanities, U. So. Calif., 1986; BFA in Painting, Art Ctr Coll. Design, 1992. Graphic designer Brad Braverman Studio, L.A., 1992-93; art dir. Allivial Entertainment, Hollywood, Calif., 1993-95; creative dir. Provocateur Mag., West Hollywood, Calif., 1995—. Merit scholar Art Ctr., 1990-92l U. Soc. Calif. scholar, 1984-86. Avocations: photography, music, composition, piano. Home: 337 N Arden Blvd Los Angeles CA 90004-3021

PISCIOTTA, SAMUEL JAMES, small business owner; b. Pueblo, Colo., Dec. 10, 1938; s. Sam Jr. and Eva May (Padula) P.; m. Cynthia Diane Garrett, Aug. 8, 1961; children: Samuel, Pamela, Richard, Michael. BA, Western State Coll., 1967. Pres., mgr. Pueblo (Colo.) Bus. Men's Club, Inc., DBA Capt. Sam's Family Athletic Club, Inc., 1961—. Composer symphonic music. Co-founder, v.p. Pueblo Performing Arts Guild, 1986—; founder, co-organizer Pueblo Office So. Colo. Better Bus. Bur., 1985—, chmn. bd. 1987-88). Recipient Order of Arrow, Boy Scouts Am., 1972; named Small Bus. Man of Yr., Colo. C. of C., 1988. Mem. Nat. Swim and Recreation Assn. (pres. 1976-77), Greater Pueblo Sports Assn. and Hall of Fame (co-founder 1972), Pueblo Jaycees (state bd. dirs. 1973-75), Pueblo Bus. Exch. (co-founder 1982, pres. 1984), Kiwanis (bd. dirs. 1986), Elks, Masons, Knight Templar, Jesters, Southern Colo. Consistory, Shriners (potentate 1992), Dante Alighieri Soc., Royal Order Scotland, Order of Quetzalcoatl (charter camaxtli 1992), Tau Kappa Epsilon. Republican. Avocations: golf, swimming, fishing, fast walking, tennis. Home: 27 Pedregal Ln Pueblo CO 81005-2917 Office: Capt Sam's Family Athletic Club Inc 1500 W 4th St Pueblo CO 81004-1207

PISCIOTTA, VIVIAN VIRGINIA, psychotherapist; b. Chgo., Dec. 7, 1929; d. Vito and Mary Lamia; m. Vincent Diago Pisciotta, Apr. 1, 1951; children: E. Christopher, Vittorio, V. Charles, Mary A. Pisciotta Higley, Thomas Sansone. BA in Clin. Psychology, Antioch U., 1974; MSW, George Williams Coll., 1984; postgrad., Erickson Inst. of No. Ill., 1990. Lic. clin. social worker, Ill., Ariz.; diplomate in clin. social work; cert. ind. social worker, Ariz. Short-term therapist Woman Line, Dayton, Ohio, 1976-79; psychotherapist Cicero (Ill.) Family Svcs., 1982-83, Maywood (Ill.) - Proviso Family Svcs., 1983-84, Maple Ave. Med. Ctr., Brookfield, Ill., 1985-88, Met. Med. Clinic, Naperville, Ill., 1986-88; allied staff Riveredge Psychiat. Hosp., Forest Park, Ill., 1986-97; psychotherapist, pvt. practice Oakbrook, Ill., 1988-96; psychotherapist, co-founder Archer Austin Counseling Ctr., Chgo., 1988-89; founder Archer Counseling Ctr., Chgo., Ill., 1989-97; psychotherapist Columbia Hospitals' Columbia Riveredge Hosp., Forest Park, Ill., 1997; allied staff Linden Oaks Psychiat. Hosp., Naperville, 1990-97; psychotherapist pvt. practice, 1997—; founder Archer Ctr., Ariz., 1997—; substitute tchr. Chgo. Pub. High Sch., 1981. Author treatment prog., workshops in field. Co-founder Co-op Nursery Sch., Rockford, Ill., 1956; leader Great Books of the Western World series, Piqua, Ohio, 1977, Rockford, 1960-65; leader Girl Scouts U.S., St. Bridget Sch., Rockford, 1968-71. Mem. Assn. Labor-Mgmt. and Cons. on Alcoholism, Soc. Clin. Exptl. Hypnosis, Nat. Assn. Social Workers, Acad. Cert. Social Workers, Nat. Social Work Register (cert.), Antioch Univ. Alumnus Assn. Rockford Coll. Alumnae Orgn. (newsletter contbr. 1972-73), Soc. for Clin. and Exptl. Hypnosis (associ. mem.), Internat. Soc. for Clin. and Exptl. Hypnosis (assoc. mem.). Republican. Roman Catholic. Avocations: reading, travel, study/rsch., music, religion.

PISTER, KARL STARK, engineering educator; b. Stockton, Calif., June 27, 1925; s. Edwin LeRoy and Mary Kimball (Smith) P.; m. Rita Olsen, Nov. 18, 1950; children: [illegible] Kristofer. BS with honors, U. Calif., Berkeley, 1945, MS, 1948; PhD, U. Ill., 1952. Instr. theoretical and applied mechanics U. Ill., 1949-52; mem. faculty U. Calif., Berkeley, 1952-91, prof. engring. scis., 1962-96, Roy W. Carlson prof. engring., 1985-90, dean Coll. Engring., 1980-90; emeritus U. Calif., Berkeley, 1996—; chancellor U. Calif., Santa Cruz, 1991-96, now pres., chancellor emeritus; Roy W. Carlson prof. emeritus U. Calif., Berkeley; sr. assoc. to pres. U. Calif., Oakland, 1997—; Richard Merton guest prof. U. Stuttgart, W. Ger., 1978; cons. to govt. and industry; bd. dirs. Monterey Bay Aquarium Rsch. Inst.; trustee Monterey Inst. Internat. Studies, Am. U. of Armenia; chmn. bd. Calif. Coun. Sci. and Tech. Author research papers in field; assoc. editor: Computer Methods in Applied Mechanics and Engring, 1972, Jour. Optimization Theory and Applications, 1982; editorial adv. bd. Encyclopedia Phys. Sci. and Tech. Served with USNR, World War II. Recipient Wason rsch. medal Am. Concrete Inst., 1960, Vincent Bendix Minorities in Engring. award Am. Soc. for Engring. Edn., 1988, Lamme medal, 1993, Alumni Honor award U. Ill. Coll. Engring., 1982, Disting. Engring. Alumnus award U. Calif. Berkeley Coll. Engring., 1992, Berkeley medal, 1996. Fellow ASME, AAAS, Am. Acad. Mechanics, Am. Acad. Arts and Scis., Calif. Acad. Scis. (hon.); mem. NAE, ASCE, Soc. Engring. Sci. Office: U Calif Office of Pres 1111 Franklin St Oakland CA 94607-5200

PITCHER, HELEN IONE, advertising director; b. Colorado Springs, Colo., Aug. 6, 1931; d. William Forest Medlock and Frankie La Vone (Hamilton) Tweed; m. Richard Edwin Pitcher, Sept. 16, 1949; children: Dushka Myers, Suzanne, Marc. Student, U. Colo., 1962-64, Ariz. State U., 1966, Maricopa Tech. Coll., 1967, Scottsdale C.C., 1979-81. Design draftsman Sundstrand Aviation, Denver, 1962-65; tech. illustrator Sperry, Phoenix, 1966-68; art dir. Integrated Circuit Engring., Scottsdale, Ariz., 1968-71, dir. advt., 1981-92; advt. artist Motorola Inc., Phoenix, 1971-74; pres. Pitcher Tech. Pubs., Scottsdale, 1974-81; retired, 1996. Profl. advisor Paradise Valley Sch. Dist., Phoenix, 1984—; mem. bd. advisors graphic arts dept. Ariz. State U., Tempe. mem. Nat. Audio Visual Assn., Bus. Profl. Advt. Assn. (treas. 1982-86), Direct Mktg. Club. Democrat. Mem. Ch. Christ. Avocations: raising and showing Arabian horses and Hackney ponies. Home: 13681 N 88th Pl Scottsdale AZ 85260-4105

PITRONE, MARGO RAE, minister; b. Toronto, Ont., Can., Nov. 22, 1960; came to U.S., 1965; d. Henry Floyd and Frieda Jo (Baethke) Mattson; m. Lawrence R. Pitrone, Apr. 25, 1984. BSW, Andrews U., 1983; MDiv, Princeton Theol. Sem., 1988. Assoc. pastor Tierrasanta Seventh-day Adventist Ch., San Diego, 1988-89; v.p. North Pk. Christian Svc. Agy., San Diego, 1989, pres., 1990; chair Ministerial Adv. Com., Riverside, 1990-91. Contbr. articles to profl. jours. Vol. chaplain Paradise Valley Hosp., San Diego, 1988—; pres. Women Mins. of Southeastern Conf. of Seventh-day Adventists, Riverside, 1989-90, mem. Justice Commn., 1991. Mem. Adventist Assn. of Women, Adventist Women's Inst., San Diego Seventh-day Adventist Ministerial Assn., Tierrasanta Ministerial Assn. Home: 532 Canyon Dr PO Box 941 Bonita CA 91908-0941

PITT, WILLIAM ALEXANDER, cardiologist; b. Vancouver, B.C., Can., July 17, 1942; came to U.S., 1970; s. Reginald William and Una Sylvia (Alexander) P.; m. Judith Mae Wilson, May 21, 1965; children: William Matthew, Joanne Katharine. MD, U. B.C., Vancouver, 1967. Diplomate Royal Coll. Physicians Can. Intern, Mercy Hosp., San Diego, 1967-68, resident, 1970-71; resident Vancouver Gen. Hosp., 1968-70, U. Calif., San Diego, 1971-72; assoc. dir. cardiology Mercy Hosp., San Diego, 1972-92; with So. Calif. Cardiology Med. Group, San Diego, 1984—; pvt. practice Clin. Cons. Cardiology; bd. trustees San Diego Found. for Med. Care, 1983-89, 91—, pres., chmn. bd. trustees, 1986-88, med. dir., 1991-96; trustee Pacific Found. for Med. Care, 1996—, med. dir., 1996—; bd. dirs. Mut. Assn. for Profl. Services, Phila., 1984-92; pres. Alternet Med. Svcs., Inc., 1992-95, San Diego IPA, 1996—. Fellow Royal Coll. Physicians Can., Am. Coll. Cardiology (assoc.); mem. AMA, Am. Heart Assn., Calif. Med. Assn., San Diego County Med. Soc., San Diego County Heart Assn. (bd. dirs. 1982-88). Episcopalian. Office: So Calif Cardiology Med Group 6386 Alvarado Ct Ste 101 San Diego CA 92120-4906

PITTS, FERRIS NEWCOMB, physician, psychiatry educator; b. St. Louis, Feb. 11, 1931; s. Ferris Newcomb and Florence A. (Morris) P.; m. Jocelyn Millner, May 14, 1955; children: Andrew Ferris, Jonathan Millner, Amy Pitts Buckner. BA, Washington U., St. Louis, 1952, MD, 1955. Diplomate Am. Bd. Pediats., Am. Bd. Psychology and Neurology. Intern Wash U., St Louis Children's Hosp, 1955-56; resident pediats. Washington U., St. Louis, 1955-56, resident psychiatry, 1959-62, assoc. prof. psychiatry, 1963-76; prof. psychiatry U. So. Calif., L.A., 1976—; pres. med. staffs several hosps., 1970—, Am. Assn. Advancement Electrotherapy, 1986. Editor-in-chief Jour. Clin. Psychiatry, 1980-88; patentee in field of hyperimmunization therapy for AIDS and other viral disorders; contbr. over 100 articles to profl. jours. Lt. comdr. USN, 1957-62. Career Rsch. Devel. award, NIMH. Fellow Am. Psychiat. Assn. (life); mem. Psychiat. Rsch. Soc. (founding mem.), Internat. Soc. Neurochemistry (founding mem.), Am. Soc. Neurochemistry (founding mem.), West Coast Coll. Psychiat. Rsch. (founding mem.). Avocations: ice hockey, tennis. Home and Office: 3500 E California Blvd Pasadena CA 91107-5653

PITTS, SADIE TURNER, retired educator; b. Tucson; d. Joe and Sadie (Osborne) Turner; m. William E. Pitts, July 4, 1956; children: William E. II, Allen B., Melissa A. BA in Elem. Edn., U. Ariz., 1955; MA in Elem. Edn., Calif. State Poly., Pomona, 1975. Elem. tchr. Tucson Unified Schs., 1955-62; elem. tchr. Pomona Unified Schs., 1964-72, 90-92, reading tchr., 1972-75, lang. arts specialist, 1975-90; adv. bd. title I, Claremont (Calif.) Unified Sch. Dist., 1976-78; coord. tutorial reading program Alpha Kappa Alpha, Pomona, 1977-79. Author: Sparkle, 1989 (Lorraine Hansberry award 1990), The Tri Bros, 1995 (Pomona Alliance Black Sch. Educators award 1996); (poems) Sons on the Wind, 1995. Spkr. Pomona Schs. Career Day, 1990—; vol. lang. arts activities Convalescent Care Nursing Home; mem. com. Inland Valley Coun. Chs.; vacation bible sch. coord. South Hills Presbyn. Ch., Pomona; supt. South Hills Presbyn. Sunday Sch., 1998. Mem. NAACP, Nat. Coun. Negro Women, Soc. Children's Book Writers and Illustrators, Internat. Soc. Poets, Calif. Ret. Tchrs. Assn., Delta Kappa Gamma (pres. 1982-84, Nat. Women's History Mo. award 1995), Alpha Kappa Alpha (treas. 1960—). Home: 395 Guilford Ave Claremont CA 91711-5147

PITTS, WILLIAM CLARENCE, physicist; b. Seattle, Apr. 19, 1929; s. Clarence H. and Emily B. (Kepp) P.; m. Joanne R. Lawson, May 18, 1952 (dec. Jan. 1978); children: Starr R., Nancy H.; m. Patricia A. (Kirkland) Adams, May 1, 1981. BS in Physics, U. Wash., 1951; postgrad., Stanford U., 1951-58. Rsch. scientist NACA/NASA, Moffett Field, Calif., 1951-86, Eloret Inst., Moffett Field, 1986-95; cons. Steve Miller and Assocs., Flagstaff, Ariz., 1995—. Contbr. numerous articles to profl. pubs.; inventor multilayer infrared radiation barrier for re-entry spacecraft; combined flexible blanket insulation for re-entry spacecraft; others. Avocations: golf, bridge, cosmology. Home and Office: 7753 Beltane Dr San Jose CA 95135-2138

PIZZORNO, JOSEPH EGIDIO, JR., college president; b. San Gabriel, Calif., Dec. 7, 1947; s. Joseph Egidio Sr. and Mary (Carmela) P.; m. Mavis Bonnar (div. Oct. 1983); 1 child, Raven Muir; m. Lara Elise Udell, Sept. 28, 1985; 1 child, Galen Udell. BS with Distinction, Harvey Mudd Coll., Claremont, Calif., 1969; Naturopathic Doctor with honors, Nat. Coll. Naturopathic Medicine, Portland, Oreg., 1975. Rsch. asst. Lockheed Aircraft, Ontario, Calif., 1968; rsch. technologist U. Wash., Seattle, 1970-75; practice naturopathic medicine Seattle, 1975-82, practice midwifery, 1978-82; pres. Bastyr U., Seattle, 1978—; pres. Coun. on Naturopathic Med. Edn., Portland, Oreg., 1985-87; apptd. adv. panel safety and efficacy of dietary supplements U.S. Office of Tech. Assessment, 1993-95; sr. med. advisor Alternative and Complementary Therapies, 1995-97. Author: Total Wellness, 1996; co-author: A Textbook of Natural Medicine, 1985, Encyclopedia of Natural Medicine, 1990, 2d edit., 1998; contbg. editor Let's Live mag., Los Angeles, 1987—; contbr. articles to profl. jours. Mem. Seattle/King County Bd. Health, 1996—. Mem. Am. Assn. Naturopathic Physicians (bd. dirs. 1981—), Wash. Assn. Naturopathic Physicians (edn. dir. 1976), Seattle Midwifery Sch. (edn. com. 1978-91). Libertarian. Avocations: microcomputers, basketball, ultimate frisbie. Home: 4220 NE 135th St Seattle WA 98125-3836 Office: Bastyr Univ 14500 Juanita Dr NE Kenmore WA 98028-4300

PLASTOW, JOHN ROBERT, religion writer, publisher, musician; b. Blue Island, Ill., June 22, 1958; s. Robert Lewis and Dorothea Isabel (Kidwell) P.; m. Karen Marie Andrews, June 23, 1979; children: John Robert II, Melody Elizabeth. BA in Music and Theatre, U. Redlands, 1979. Dir. theatre Crystal Cathedral Music Ministry, Garden Grove, Calif., 1979-82; dir. Family Arts Ctr. Grace United Meth. Ch., Long Beach, Calif., 1982-83; exec. dir. Plastow Ministries/Prodns., Orange City, Calif., 1985—, Plastow Publs., Orange, Calif., 1988—, The Drama Store, Orange, 1989—; cons. various chs. and pubs., 1980—, including Crystal Cathedral, Garden Grove, 1986-88, Alexandria House, Nashville, 1988-91, Sparrow, Nashville, 1990-91; speaker, clinician MusiCalif., Music Minn., Music Tex., Mus. Fla., other nat. confs. Author: Football, Pizza and Success!, 1987; script writer over 50 dramas, 1988-91, musicals Can't Say It Loud Enough, 1991, The Majesty and Glory of Christmas, 1991; contbr. articles to religious and musical publs. Republican. Mem. Evang. Free Ch. Am. Avocations: cooking, animals, baseball.

PLATA, ARMANDO LUIS CARLOS, Spanish voiceover artist and translator; b. Bogota, July 27, 1949; s. Plata Luis and Rosa (Camacho) P.; m. Miryam Guevara, May 25, 1978 (div. Oct. 1990); m. Ines Echeverria, Jan. 18, 1997; children: Juanita, Catalina, Christian. BS, Rufino J. Cuervo, Choconta, Colombia; student, Mil. Acad., Bogota; postgrad., UCLA, Loyola Marymount,, Javeriana U. Spanish voiceover, journalist Armando Plata Prodns., L.A., 1966—; radio and TV dir. J. Walter Thompson Advt., Bogota, 1969-75; dir., anchor Caracol Radio Network, 1969-74; dir. Todelar Radio Network, Bogota, 1974-80; artistic dir. and anchor Cromavision TV, Bogota, 1980-87; news dir., artistic dir. Caracol Radio Network, Bogota, 1984-89; news dir. Radio Klaridad, Miami, 1990, WQBA Radio La Cubanissima, Miami, 1991; Spanish announcer TNT Latinoamerica, Atlanta, 1991-93; news anchor and dir. CNN-Radio Noticias, Atlanta, 1993-96. Dir./anchor: Passport to the World, 1985-88. Active YMCA Colombia, Bogota, 1964-70; mem. Ga. Reading Svc., Atlanta, 1991-94. Sgt. Colombia Mil., 1965-67. Recipient Best Talk Show award ACL colombia Assn., Bogota, 1974, Best News Cast and Dir., Image, Miami, 1990, Emmy Best Pronds., Miami, 1993, Best News Anchor award ACL Colombian Voice Over Assn., 1995. Mem. Internat. TV Assn., Colombian Announcer Assn. Republican. Roman Catholic. Avocations: golf, squash, tennis, jogging, theater. Home: 3336 Stephens Cir Glendale CA 91208-1169

PLATEK, GARY JOSEPH, special effects expert; b. L.A., Sept. 10, 1956; s. Joseph and Lorraine (Staley) P.; m. Terry Brauer, July 25, 1981. BFA, Calif. Inst. Arts, 1978. Special effects asst. W.E.D. Enterprises, Glendale, Calif., 1977-78; special projects Indsl. Light & Magic, San Rafael, Calif., 1979-82; supr. visual effects JEX FX, San Rafael, Calif., 1982-83, pres., 1984—; dir. special projects Boss Film Corp., Marina Del Ray, Calif., 1983-84. Motion picture visual effects include Raiders of the Lost Ark, 1981, The Right Stuff, 1982, Amityville 3-D, 1983, 2010, 1984, Look Who's Talking, 1988, Total Recall, 1989, Pagemaster, 1993, Frankenstein, 1994, The Mask, 1994, Apollo 13, 1995, James and the Giant Peach, 1995, Flubber, 1996, Contact, 1997, others; contbr. special effects to commercials; designed and fabricated many computer operated units to be used for various special projects including Gremlins, 1982, Top Gun, 1985, Felix the Cat, 1992, Jurassic Park, 1992, Robot Wars, 1994, others. Mem. Acad. Motion Pictures Arts and Scis., Visual Effects Soc. Avocations: tropical fish. Office: JEX FX 47 Paul Dr Ste 9 San Rafael CA 94903-2118

PLATT, JAMES ROBERT, business executive; b. Batavia, N.Y., Oct. 23, 1948; s. Robert John and Mildred J. (Foote) P.; m. Shelly A. Tunis, May 24, 1980; children: Shane Christopher, Tristan Robert. BS, SUNY, Brockport, 1970; MA, Ariz. State U., 1982. Cert. tchr., N.Y. Inside sales supr. Mallco Distbrs., Phoenix, 1972-77; grad. teaching asst. Ariz. State U., Tempe, 1978-79; sales rep. Wisco Equipment Co., Inc., Phoenix, 1979-82, sales mgr., 1984-88; sales rep. Clyde Hardware Co., Tucson, 1982-84; v.p. Wistech Controls, Phoenix, 1988—. Mem. Ariz. Coun. Excellence; youth sports coach YMCA. Regents scholar SUNY, 1966-70. Mem. Instrument Soc. Am., Young Execs.-Fluid Power Distbrs. Assn., Am. Soc. Environ. History, Soc. Mfg. Engrs., Phi Alpha Theta. Office: Wistech Controls 4810 S 36th St Phoenix AZ 85040-2970

PLATT, JOSEPH BEAVEN, former college president; b. Portland, Oreg., Aug. 12, 1915; s. William Bradbury and Mary (Beaven) P.; m. Jean Ferguson Rusk, Feb. 9, 1946; children: Ann Ferguson Walker, Elizabeth Beaven Garrow. BA, U. Rochester, 1937; PhD, Cornell U., 1942; LLD, U. So. Calif., 1969, Claremont McKenna Coll., 1982; DSc, Harvey Mudd Coll., 1981. Instr. physics U. Rochester, N.Y., 1941-43, from asst. prof. to prof., 1946-56, assoc. chmn. dept. physics, 1954-56; staff mem. radiation lab. MIT, Cambridge, 1943-46; pres. Harvey Mudd Coll., Claremont, Calif., 1956-76, now part-time sr. prof. physics; pres. Claremont U. Ctr., 1976-81; trustee Aerospace Corp., 1972-85, Consortium for Advancement of Pvt. Higher Edn., 1985-92; chief physics br. AEC, 1949-51; cons. U.S. Office Ordnance Rsch., NSF, 1953-56; mem. com. on sci. in UNESCO, NAS-NRC, 1960-62, mem. com. on internat. orgns. and programs, 1962-64, sci. advisor U.S. Del., UNESCO Gen. Conf., Paris, 1960, alt. del., 1962, chmn. Subcom. on Sino-Am. Sci. Cooperation, 1965-79; mem. panel on internat. sci. Pres.'s Sci. Adv. Com., 1961; trustee Analytic Svcs., Inc., 1958-89, chmn., 1961-89; mem. adv. com. on sci. edn. NSF, 1965-70, 72-76, chmn., 1969-70, 73-74, 74-75; bd. dirs. Lincoln Found., 1979-85, Bell & Howell Corp., 1978-88, Am. Mut. Fund, 1981-88, DeVry, Inc., 1984-87, Sigma Rsch., 1983-87, Jacobs Engring. Co., 1978-86. Author: Harvey Mudd College: The First Twenty YEars, 1994. Trustee China Found. for Promotion of Edn. and Culture, 1966—, Carnegie Found. for Advancement Tchg., 1970-78, Ancient Biblical Manuscript Ctr., 1980—, Ancient Bibl. Manuscript Ctr., 1980—; chmn. select com. Master Plan for Higher Edn. Calif., 1971-73; mem. Carnegie Coun. for Policy Studies in Higher Edn., 1975-80. Fellow Am. Phys. Soc.; mem. IEEE, Automobile Club So. Calif. (bd. dirs. 1973-90, chmn. bd. dirs. 1986-87), Calif. Club, Sunset Club, Twilight Club, Cosmos Club, Bohemian Club, Phi Beta Kappa, Sigma Xi, Phi Kappa Phi. Home: 452 W 11th St Claremont CA 91711-3833

PLATT, LEWIS EMMETT, electronics company executive; b. Johnson City, N.Y., Apr. 11, 1941; s. Norval Lewis and Margaret Dora (Williams) P.; m. Joan Ellen Redmund, Jan. 15, 1983; children: Caryn, Laura, Amanda, Hillary. BME, Cornell U., 1964; MBA, U. Pa., 1966. With Hewlett Packard, Waltham, Mass., 1966-71, engring. mgr., 1971-74, ops. mgr., 1974-77, div. gen. mgr., 1974-80, group gen. mgr., Palo Alto, Calif., 1980-84, v.p., 1983-85, exec. v.p., 1987-92, pres., CEO, chmn., 1993—; Trustee Waltham Hosp., 1978-80, Wharton Sch. Bd. Overseers, 1993; mem. Mid-Peninsula YMCA, 1980—, bd. couns. YMCA-USA, 1993—, Cornell U. Coun., 1992—, Computer Sys. Policy Project, 1993—, Calif. Bus. Roundtable, 1993-95, Bus. Coun., 1993—, Bay Area Coun., 1993—, Bus. Roundtable, 1993—; vice chmn. Y Coun., 1989, mem. bd. dirs. Joint Venture, Silicon Valley, 1996. Recipient Red Triangle award Min-Peninsula YMCA, 1992, Internat. Citizens award World Forum Silicon Valley, San Jose, Calif., 1994, outstanding alumnus, Wharton Alumni Honor Roll, Wharton Schl. Business, Univ. Pa., 1994-95, award for bus. excellence U. Calif. Sch. Bus. Adminstrn., 1996, Tree of Life award Jewish Nat. Fund, 1996, Leadership and Vision award San Francisco Chpt. French-Am. C. of C., 1997. Mem. IEEE, Sci. Apparatus Mfg. Assn. (dir. 1978-80).*

PLATT, RANDALL BETH, writer; b. Seattle, Jan. 14, 1948; d. Charles M. and Alta F. (Melendy) Lechner; m. Jonathan H. Platt; children: Elkan Wollenberg, Skye Wollenberg. Student, Portland (Oreg.) State U., 1966, 67, Oreg. State U., 1967. Supr. data processing Eddie Bauer, Inc., Seattle, 1968-73; asst. membership dir. YMCA, Tacoma, Wash., 1978-83. Author: Out of a Forest Clearing, 1991, The Four Arrows Fe-As-Ko, 1991, Reiterhof Seahorse, 1992, The Royalscope Fe-As-Ko, 1997, Honor Bright, 1997, The Cornerstone, 1998. Vol. fundraiser Tacoma-Pierce City YMCA, 1983-93; camp counselor Diabetes Assn. of Pierce County, Tacoma, 1992-97. Mem. Soc. Children's Book Writers and Illustrators, Women Writing the West, Western Writers of Am., Pacific N.W. Writers Conf. Avocations: handball, running, slang research. Fax: (253) 851-9062. E-mail: royal@harbornet.com

PLATT, WARREN E., lawyer; b. McNary, Ariz., Aug. 5, 1943. BA, Mich. State U., 1965; JD, U. Ariz., 1969. Bar: Ariz. 1969, Calif. 1991, Texas 1993. Atty. Snell & Wilmer, Phoenix. Mng. editor: Ariz. Law Rev., 1968-69.

Fellow Am. Coll. Trial Lawyers; mem. Blue Key, Order of Coif, Phi Alpha Delta. Office: Snell & Wilmer One Arizona Ctr Phoenix AZ 85004-0001

PLAYER, GERALDINE (JERI PLAYER), small business executive; b. Cleve., Mar. 26, 1952; d. Cornelius Millsape and Ola Mae (Maxie) Fisher; m. Van O. Player, Aug. 27, 1970 (dec. Mar. 1975); children—Ricardo T., Van O., Michelle. Student Sawyer Coll. Bus., Mayfield, Ohio, Virginia Marti Sch. Design, Lakewood, Ohio, Inst. Children's Lit., Conn., Case Western Res. U., Fall 1988. Owner, Jeri's Designs, Inc., Cleve., 1970—, Success Writers, Cleve., 1986—; freelance scriptwriter, 1990—; fashion cons. Active adoptive parenting orgn. Mem. Nat. Assn. Female Execs. Club: Back Wall (Beachwood, Ohio). Lodge: Brotherhood (Bklyn.). Avocations: aerobics; photography; theatre; speech. Home: 1314 Sofia Ct Jacksonville NC 28540-3353 Office: 1605 N Cahuenga Blvd Ste 211 Los Angeles CA 90028-6281

PLETSCH, MARIE ELEANOR, plastic surgeon; b. Walkerton, Ont., Can., May 3, 1938; came to U.S. 1962; d. Ernest John and Olive Wilhemina (Hossfeld) P.; m. Ludwig Philip Breiling, Aug. 25, 1967; children: John, Michael, Anne. Dr. Med., U. Toronto, 1962. Diplomate Am. Bd. Plastic Surgery. Intern Cook County Hosp., Chgo., 1962-63, resident, gen. surgery, 1963-64; resident, gen. surgery St. Mary's Hosp., San Francisco, 1964-66; resident in plastic surgery St. Francis Hosp., San Francisco, 1966-69; practice med. specializing in plastic surgery Santa Cruz, Calif., 1969—; Monterey, Calif., 1990—; adminstr. Plasticenter, Inc., Santa Cruz, 1976-88, med. dir., 1987-88. Mem. AMA, Am. Soc. Plastic and Reconstructive Surgeons, Calif. Soc. Plastic Surgeons (mem. coun. 1986-89, sec. 1989-93, v.p. 1994-95, pres. elect 1995-96, pres. 1996-97), Am. Soc. Anesthetic Plastic Surgeons, Calif. Med. Assn., Assn. Calif. Surgery Ctrs. (pres. 1988-92), Santa Cruz County Med. Soc. (bd. govs. 1983-88, 1992-94), Santa Cruz Surgery Ctr. (bd. dirs. 1988-93). Roman Catholic. Office: Santa Cruz Can-Am Med Group 1669 Dominican Way Santa Cruz CA 95065-1523

PLOMP, TEUNIS (TONY PLOMP), minister; b. Rotterdam, The Netherlands, Jan. 28, 1938; arrived in Can., 1951; s. Teunis and Cornelia (Pietersma) P.; m. Margaret Louise Bone, July 21, 1962; children: Jennifer Anne, Deborah Adele. BA, U. B.C. (Can.), Vancouver, 1960; BD, Knox Coll., Toronto, Ont., Can., 1963, DD (hon.), 1988. Ordained to ministry Presbyn. Ch., 1963. Minister Goforth Meml. Presbyn. Ch., Saskatoon, Sask., Can., 1963-68, Richmond (B.C.) Presbyn. Ch., 1968—; clerk Presbytery of Westminster, Vancouver, 1969—; moderator 113th Gen. Assembly Presbyn. Ch. Can., 1987-88, dep. clk., 1987—; chaplain New Haven Correctional Centre, Burnaby, B.C. Contbr. mag. column You Were Asking, 1982-89. Avocations: record collecting, audiophile, biking, swimming. Office: Richmond Presbyn Ch, 7111 # 2 Rd, Richmond, BC Canada V7C 3L7*

PLORDE, JAMES JOSEPH, physician, educator; b. Brewster, Minn., Feb. 16, 1934; s. James Arthur and Mary Jeanette (Lutz) P.; m. Diane Sylvia Koenigs, Aug. 28, 1964 (div. July 1974); children: Lisa Marie, Michele Louise, James Joshua; m. Jo Ann Gates, Dec. 22, 1986. BA, U. Minn., 1956, BS, 1957, MD, 1959. Diplomate Am. Bd. Internal Medicine, Am. Bd. Pathology. Vol. leader Peace Corps, Gondar, Ethiopia, 1964-66; intern King County Hosp., Seattle, 1959-60; resident U. Wash., Seattle, 1960-62, asst. prof. medicine, 1967-69, assoc. prof., 1971-78, prof. medicine, lab. medicine, 1978-98 (ret.), prof. emeritus medicine, lab. medicine, 1998—; head clin. investigation U.S. Naval Med. Research, Addis Ababa, Ethiopia, 1968-71; chief infectious diseases, microbiology VA Hosp., Seattle, 1973-98; ret., 1998; cons. WHO, 1975, Suez Canal U. Faculty of Medicine, Ismailia, Arab Republic of Egypt, 1981-85. Contbr. numerous articles to profl. jours., chpts. to books. Fellow Infectious Disease Soc., ACP; mem. AAAS, Am. Soc. Microbiology, Acad. Clin. Lab. Physicians and Scientists. Home: 3164 W Laurelhurst Dr NE Seattle WA 98105-5346 Office: Vets Med Ctr 1660 S Columbian Way Seattle WA 98108-1532

PLOTKIN, STACY JO, lawyer; b. Bklyn., Apr. 18, 1967; d. Robert Louis and Gerry Etta (Fishman) P. BA, U. Calif., Irvine, 1989, U. Calif., Irvine, 1989; JD magna cum laude, Gonzaga U., 1994. Bar: Calif. 1994, U.S. Dist. Ct. (so. dist) Calif. 1994, Washington 1995. Law clk. Calif. Dept. Justice, San Diego, 1993; assoc. Philabaum, Ledlin & Matthews, Spokane, Wash., 1995; owner Stacy Plotkin & Assocs., San Diego, 1996-97; assoc. Trichak & Redman, Seattle, 1997 . Editor: Calif. Appelate Practice Handbook, 1998. Mem. Washington Women Lawyers Assn., San Diego County Bar Assn., King County Bar Assn. Avocations: theater, river rafting, travel. Office: Trichak & Redman 400 Mercer St Ste 308 Seattle WA 98109-4641

PLOUGH, CHARLES TOBIAS, JR., retired electronics engineering executive; b. Oakland, Calif., Sept. 7, 1926; s. Charles Tobias Sr. and Miriam Lucille (Miller) P.; m. Jean Elizabeth Rose, June 13, 1950 (div. May 1969); children: Charles III, Cathleen, Mark, Barbara; m. Janet Mary Ansell Lumley, July 5, 1969; children: Mark Ansell Lumley, Simon John Lumley. AB with honors, Amherst Coll., 1950; BSEE with honors, U. Calif., Berkeley, 1953. Mgr. tech. devel. Fairchild Semiconductor, Palo Alto, Calif., 1958-71; v.p. Multi-State Devices, Montreal, Can., 1971-78; mgr. research and devel. Dale Electronics, Norfolk, Nebr., 1978-89, ret., 1989. Patentee in field. Treas. First Unitarian Ch., 1996-99. Mem. Lions (sec. Norfolk 1982-86); Leader Albuquerque Interfaith 1993—. Avocation: golf. Home: 2030 Quail Run Dr NE Albuquerque NM 87122-1100

PLUMMER, STEVEN TSOSIE, SR., bishop; b. Coalmine, N. Mex., Aug. 14, 1944; m. Catherine B. Tso; children: Brian Tso, Byron Tso, Steven, Jr., Cathlena. Student, San Juan Community Coll., Farmington, N. Mex., Phoenix (Ariz.) Jr. Coll., Ch. Divinity Sch. of the Pacific, San Francisco, Cook Christian Tng. Sch., Tempe, Ariz., 1966-68. Ordained deacon, The Episc. Ch., 1975, priest, 1976. Deacon, priest Good Shepherd Mission, Fort Defiance, Ariz., 1976-77; vicar St. John the Baptizer, Montezuma Creek, Utah, 1977-83; regional vicar for Utah Bluff, Utah, from 1983; consecrated bishop Episc. Ch. in Navajoland, Window Rock, Ariz., 1990; mem. Episc. Counc. Indian Ministries, N.Y.C. Office: The Episcopal Ch Navajoland Area Mission PO Box 720 Farmington NM 87499-0720 Address: The Episcopal Ch Navajoland Area Mission PO Box 40 Bluff UT 84512-0040

PLUMMER COBB, JEWEL, biologist, minority education advocate; b. Chgo., Jan. 17, 1924; d. Frank Victor and Carriebel (Cole) Plummer; m. Roy Raul Cobb, 1954; 1 child, Roy Jonathan. BA, Talladega Coll., 1944; MS, NYU, 1947, PhD, 1950; LLD (hon.), Wheaton Coll., 1971; LD (hon.), Rutgers U., 1982; DSc (hon.), CUNY, 1984, Northeastern U., 1990, Conn. Coll., 1994, Rensselaer Poly. Inst., 1994. Postdoctoral fellow Nat. Cancer Inst., Bethesda, Md., 1950-52; instr. anatomy, dir. tissue culture lab. U. Ill. Coll. Medicine, 1952-54; from instr. to asst. prof. rsch. surgery NYU, 1955-60; prof. biology Sarah Lawrence Coll., Bronxville, N.Y., 1960-69; dean, prof. zoology Conn. Coll., 1969-76; dean, prof. biol. scis. Douglass Coll., 1976-81; prof. Calif. State U., Fullerton, 1981-90; prin. investigator So. Calif. Sci. & Engring. ACCESS Ctr., L.A., 1991—. Mem. AAAS, AAUW, Assn. Women in Sci., N.Y. Acad. Scis., Tissue Culture Assn., Sigma Delta Epsilon, Sigma Xi. Office: Student Health Ctr 205 5151 State University Dr Los Angeles CA 90032-4226

PLUNKETT, LYNDA LEIGH, pediatrics nurse; b. Van Nuys, Calif., Apr. 17, 1959; d. Jack Thomas and June Lee (Smith) Strayer; m. Ramon A. Cardenas, Jan. 21, 1988 (div. 1991); m. Patrick Plunkett, July 4, 1997. Diploma in med. assisting, Western Tech. Coll., 1983; lic. vocat. nurse, Simi Valley Adult Edn., 1991. LVN, Calif. Med. asst. La Serena Retirement Village, Thousand Oaks, Calif., 1982-84, Registry/Pvt. Geriatrics, Simi Valley, Calif., 1984-88; nurse, staff cond. Valley Children's Home, Inc., Simi Valley, 1988-97; LVN managed care svcs. Blue Cross of Calif., 1997—.

PLUNKETT, MARVIN WAYNE, data processing company executive; b. Roseburg, Oreg., Mar. 16, 1952; s. Kenneth V. and Minnie E. (Bible) P. Student, Umpqua C.C., 1978-79. Founder, owner Profit Systems Software, Roseburg, 1979—. Mem. Roseburg Optimist Club (bd. dirs. 1993-95). Office: Profit Sys Software 1641 NW Rutter Ln Roseburg OR 97470-1949

PLUNKETT, MICHAEL C., psychotherapist; b. Nyack, N.Y., Feb. 23, 1953; s. Stephen J. Jr. and Naomi M. (Davies) P.; 1 child, Joshua E. BSBA, St. Thomas Aquinas Coll., 1975; MA in Psychology, U. No. Colo., 1986. Lic. profl. counselor, Colo.; cert. addiction counselor, Colo., instr. in prevention of HIV disease among substance abusers, Nat. Inst. Drug Abuse, instr. in outreach and retention of methadone clients. Diagnostic coord. El Paso County Dept. Health and Environ./McMaster Ctr., Colorado Springs, 1987-95, prevention & outreach supr. Prevention HIV/HEPC among IDUs, 1995—; instr. psychology Pikes Peak C.C., Colorado Springs, 1988-96, SCAP-Client Svcs. Com., 1996—, SCAP-Prevention Com., 1997—; mem. Colorado Springs HIV Edn. and Prevention Consortium; mem. EPCDHE Epidemiology Commn. Bd. dirs. So. Colo. AIDS Project, HIV Edn. and Prevention Consortium, Colorado Springs, 1995; mem. ad hoc com. HIV Prevention Cmty. Planning Com., 1994; bd. dirs. Pikes Peak region Nat. Coun. Alcoholism and Drug Dependency, 1988-91, vice-chmn., 1990; mem. subcom. on needle exch. Gov.'s AIDS Coun., 1995-98; active Coloradans Working Together (CWT) Core Planning Com., 1996—, Parity, Inclusion, and Representation Com., Combined Intervention Com., 1996-98, Prevention Case Mgmt. Working Group, 1996-98, IDU Working Group, Urban Planning Com., 1999—, Definition and Stds. Com., 1999—, Safety Network Project, 1996; mem. Violence Data Exch. Team Pike Peak region; active Pub. Cmty. Identification Process of Injecting Drug Users, El Paso County, Colo., 1997—. Mem. Harm Reduction Coalition, Nat. Assn. Preventions Profls. Avocations: hiking, bicycling, poetry, gardening, C.G. Jung Soc. Office: El Paso County Health and Environ 301 S Union Blvd Colorado Springs CO 80910-3123

POCHINI, JUDY HAY, interior designer; b. Phoenix, Mar. 16, 1932; d. Cecil Clifford and Nadine Mary (Larimer) Cook; m. Gordon Eugene Hay, June 5, 1971 (dec. 1974); m. Robert Frank Pochini, Sept. 18, 1983. BA, U. Calif., Santa Barbara, 1953; MA in Journalism, U. Calif., Berkeley, 1965. Exec. sec. Mobil Oil Corp., Mpls., 1958-60, Kaiser Aluminum & Chem. Corp., Oakland, Calif., 1960-64; asst. trade publ. editor Sunset mag., Menlo Park, Calif., 1966-68, trade publ. editor, 1968-73; owner, home furnishings editor Lifestyle West, Walnut Creek, Calif., 1974-79; interior designer Berman's Drexel-Heritage, Oakland, 1979-85, Suburban House Drexel-Heritage, Concord, Calif., 1986-87; ptnr., interior designer Judy Hay Interiors, Lafayette and Santa Barbara, Calif., 1987-95, owner, 1995—; mem. nat. consumer action panel Carpet & Rug Industry, Dalton, Ga., 1973-75; cons. in field. Contbr. articles to profl. jours. Mem. Am. Soc. Interior Designers (allied), Internat. Furnishings & Design Assn., Women in Communications Inc., Am. Assn. of U. Women, Chi Omega. Democrat. Mem. Unity Ch. Office: Judy Hay Interiors J173 1324 State St Santa Barbara CA 93101

PODBOY, JOHN WATTS, clinical, forensic psychologist; b. York, Pa., Sept. 27, 1943; s. August John and Harriett Virginia (Watts) P.; 1 son, Matthew John. B.A., Dickinson Coll., 1966; M.S., San Diego State Coll., 1971; Ph.D., U. Ariz., 1973. Dir., Vets. Counseling Center, U. Ariz., Tucson, 1972-73; project dir. San Mateo County (Calif.) Human Relations Dept., Redwood City, 1974; staff psychologist Sonoma State Hosp., Eldridge, Calif., 1975-81; cons. clin. psychologist Comprehensive Care Corp., Newport Beach, Calif., 1974-75, Sonoma County (Calif.) Probation Dept., 1976-88; pvt. practice, Kenwood, Calif., 1982—; cons. to No. Calif. Superior Cts., 1983-85; asst. prof. Sonoma State U., 1977-81; dir. Sonoma Diagnostic and Remedial Center, 1979-82. Chmn. San Mateo County Diabetes Assn., 1975. Served to lt. USNR, 1966-69. Fellow Am. Coll. Forensic Psychology, Am. Bd. Med. Psychotherapists (fellow); mem. APA, Western Psychol. Assn., Redwood Psychol. Assn. (pres. 1983), Nat. Council Alcoholism, Nat. Rehab. Assn. Home: PO Box 488 Kenwood CA 95452-0488

PODESTO, GARY, mayor; b. 1941. Mayor City of Stockton, Calif., 1996—. Office: Office of Mayor and City Coun 425 N El Dorado St Stockton CA 95202*

POE, LENORA MADISON, psychotherapist and author; b. New Bern, Ala., Jan. 3, 1934; d. Tommy and Carrie (Norfleet) Madison; m. Levi Mathis Poe, June 21, 1957; children: Michael DeWayne, Michaelle DaNita Burke. BS, Stillman Coll., Tuscaloosa, Ala., 1956; MA, Calif. State U., Hayward, 1972, MS, 1980; PhD, Ctr. for Psychol. Studies, Albany, Calif., 1991. Lic. marriage, family and child therapist. Classroom tchr. Perry County Schs., Uniontown, Ala., 1956-59, Richmond (Calif.) Unified Schs., 1962-69; guidance counselor Berkeley (Calif.) Unified Schs., 1969-79; psychotherapist in pvt. practice Berkeley, 1982—, West Coast Children's Ctr., El Cerrito, Calif., 1982—; lectr. Grandparents as Parents, 1992—; part-time prof. J.F.K. U., Orinda, Calif., 1993; del. White House Conf. on Aging, Washington, 1995; cons. in field; staff cons. Cmty. Adult Day Health Svcs., Highland Gen. Hosp., Oakland. Author: Black Grandparents as Parents, 1992. Pres. nat. bd. dirs. Stillman Coll., 1992—; mentor cons. Black Women Organized for Ednl. Devel., Oakland, Calif., 1994—; mem. adv. bd. Nat. Black Aging Network, Oakland, 1992—; founding mem., advisor Realmindcas Civic Club, Richmond, 1976—; mem. Families United Against Crack Cocaine, Oakland; bd. dirs. Ctr. for Elders for Independence, Oakland; trustee Ctr. for Psychol. Studies, Albany; chairperson Grandparents Caregivers Advocacy Task Force, Oakland, Calif.; mem. bd. edn. Ministry of Ch. by Side of Road, Berkeley; also others. Recipient cert. of Appreciation African Am. Hist. and Cultural Soc., San Francisco, 1992, President's citation for Excellence Nat. Assn. for Equal Opportunity in Higher Edn., 1993, award Excellence in Edn. Nat. Coun. Negro Women, 1993, S award Stillman Coll., Appreciation award for Excellence Nystrom Elem. Sch., Richmond, 1994, Outstanding Alumna of the Yr. award Ctr. for Psychological Studies, 1995. Mem. Nat. Coalition Grandparents as Parents (adv. com. 1992—), No. Coalition Grandparents as Parents (co-chmn. 1991-93), Stillman Coll. Nat. Alumni Assn. (pres.), Calif. Coalition Grandparent/Relative Caregivers (co-chair), Nat. Coalition Grandparent/Relative Caregivers (advisor). Home: 940 Arlington Ave Berkeley CA 94707-1929 Office: 2034 Blake St Ste 1 Berkeley CA 94704-2604

POE, ROBERT ALAN, lawyer; b. Bracken County, Ky., Apr. 25, 1951. Student, U. Ky.; BA, Centre Coll., 1973; JD, U. Va., 1976. Bar: Colo. 1976. Mem. Holland & Hart, Denver, 1976—; adj. prof. taxation U. Denver, 1986-88. Articles editor Va. Law Review, 1974-76. Mem. ABA, Order Coif, Phi Beta Kappa. Office: Holland & Hart 8390 E Crescent Pkwy Ste 400 Greenwood Village CO 80111-2822

POEDTKE, CARL HENRY GEORGE, JR., management consultant; b. Chgo., Jan. 12, 1938; s. Carl H. Sr. and Irene F. (Eskilson) P.; m. Marie-Paule M. Thiriet, Mar. 10, 1962 (dec.); children: Gislaine Canavan, Carl Henry George III; m. Janice M. Barron, Aug. 26, 1991. BS, MIT, 1959. Mgr. value engring. Chgo. Rawhide Mfg. Co., Chgo., 1962-66; ptnr. Price Waterhouse, Chgo., Paris, N.Y.C., 1966-91; ret. Price Waterhouse, Chgo., 1991. Author: Managing and Accounting for Inventories, 1980; contbr. articles to profl. jours. Bd. dir. Guild Bd. Lyric Opera, Chgo., 1984-92; mem. vis. adv. com. sch. acctg. De Paul U., Chgo., 1986-91. 1st lt. U.S. Army, 1959-62. Fellow Am. Prodn. and Inventory Control Soc.; mem. AIIE (sr., cert.) Inst. Mgmt. Cons. (bd. dirs. 1987-90, life mem.), Coun. Cons. Orgns. (bd. dirs. 1989-90), Union League Club, Masons. Home: PO Box 677 Tesuque NM 87574-0677

POGUE, CHARLES EDWARD, JR., screenwriter; b. Cin., Jan. 18, 1950; s. Charles Edward and Ruth Elizabeth (Hick) P.; m. Julieanne Beasley, Sept. 14, 1987. BA in Theater Arts, U. Ky., 1972. Co-founder, artistic dir. Mercury II Theatre, Ft. Thomas, Ky., 1969-71; artist-in-residence Globe of the Great Southwest, Odessa, Tex., 1972-73; actor with various theaters, 1973-81; screenwriter with various producers and studios, 1982—. Screenwriter: The Hound of the Baskervilles, 1983, The Sign of Four, 1983 (1st prize Cattolica Mystery Film Festival), Psycho III, 1986, The Fly, 1986 (Oscar award, Saturn award), DOA, 1988, Hands of a Murderer, 1990, Dragonheart, 1996, Kull the Conqueror, 1997; playwright: Whodunnit, Darling? (Studio Players Playwriting Competition winner), 1983, The Ebony Ape, 1987. Recipient Best of Cin. award Cin. mag., 1986, Realm of the Imagination award Psychotherapy Screening Guild, L.A., 1987, Disting. Alumni award U. Ky. Coll. Fine Arts, 1995. Mem. AFTRA, Writers Guild Am. West (bd. dirs. 1997—), Dramatists Guild, Actors Equity Assn., Screen Actors Guild. Democrat. Avocations: book collecting, walking, film and theater historian, cane collecting. Office: care Braunstein Co Bldg 269 1901 Avenue Of The Stars Los Angeles CA 90067-6001

POHL, JOHN HENNING, chemical engineering educator; b. Ft. Riley, Kans., May 29, 1944; s. Herbert Otto and Ellen Irene (Henning) P.; m. Judith Lynn Sykes, Aug. 10, 1968; children: J. Otto, Clint. AA, Sacramento City Coll., 1964; BS, U. Calif., Berkeley, 1966; SM, MIT, 1973, DSci, 1976. Inspector constrn. C.O. Henning Cons. Engrs., Sacramento, 1965; engr. E.I. du Pont Nemours, Wilmington, Del., 1966-70; rsch. asst. MIT, Cambridge, 1971-75, lectr., 1975-76; mem. tech. staff Sandia Nat. Labs., Livermore, Calif., 1976-81; dir. fossil fuels Energy and Environ. Rsch., Irvine, Calif., 1981-86; dir. R & D Energy Systems Assocs., Tustin, Calif., 1986-89; sr. scientist energy W.J. Schafer Assocs., Irvine, 1989-91; pres. Energy Internat., Laguna Hills, Calif., 1988—; sr. cons. ESA Engring., Laguna Hills, 1989-97; v.p. Advanced Combustion Tech. Co., Hsinchu, Taiwan, 1993-95; v.p. tech. Energeo, Inc., San Mateo, Calif., 1995-96; black coal utilization prof. chem. engring., dir., coord., mem. advanced characterization CRC Black Coal Utilization Rsch. Unit U. Queensland, Brisbane, Australia, 1996—. Contbr. articles to profl. jours.; patentee in field. Treas. Headstart, Cambridge, 1975-76. Recipient Sci. and Tech. Achievement award U.S. EPA, 1987, Best Energy Projects award Energy Commn., Taiwan, coal evaluation, 1989, Low NOx Burner, 1992. Fellow Australian Inst. Energy (bd. dirs. 1996—); mem. ASME (advisor corrosion and deposits com. 1989—, rsch. project subcom. 1994—), AIChE (combustion advisor 1988-92), Am. Flame Rsch. Com., Am. Chem. Soc., Combustion Inst. Western States (mem. exec. com. 1988-95), Combustion Inst. (mem. program subcom. 1976—), Engring. Found. (mem. steering com. on ash deposits 1989—). Home: 16 Foxton St Unit 3, Indooroopilly QLD 4068, Australia

POHLMAN, DAVID LAWRENCE, training systems consultant; b. Detroit, May 17, 1944; s. Lawrence Luther and Lois Betty (Huffcut) P.; m. Diane Lee Ewing, Dec. 27, 1967 (div. 1980); children: Scott David, Anne Kiersten; m. Katherine Margaret Wattigney, Dec. 11, 1981; children: Ann Margaret Williams, David Joseph Williams. BS in Edn., Ohio U., 1967; MA in Psychology, U. No. Colo., 1977. Commd. officer USAF, 1967, advanced through grades to lt. col.; instr. pilot USAF, Chandler, Ariz., 1975-78, rsch. pilot., 1978-82; div. chief USAF, San Antonio, 1982-87; ret., 1987; tng. div. mgr. Gallegos Rsch. Group, Wheatridge, Colo., 1987-88; mgr. fed. systems div. Andersen Consulting, Denver, 1988-90; pres. Dave Pohlman Assocs., Aurora, 1990—; com. chmn. Dept. Def., Washington, 1982-87, subcom. chmn. industry panel, 1988-92; subcom. mem. Intersvc.-Industry Tng. Sys., Orlando, Fla., 1987; industry co-chmn. Computer-Aided Acquisition and Logistics Human Sys. Components Com., 1987-92; vice-chair Aurora Vets. Affairs Commn., 1993-96; mem. 6th Congrl. Dist. Vets. Adv. Coun., 1993. Contbr. articles to profl. publs. Mem. Am. Ednl. Rsch. Assn., Am. Def. Preparedness Assn., Nat. Security Indsl. Assn., Air Force Assn. Roman Catholic. Avocation: outdoor activities. Home: 15350 E Arizona Ave Unit 202 Aurora CO 80017-4733 Office: 15200 E Girard Ave Ste 4400 Aurora CO 80014-5053

POLAKOFF, KEITH IAN, historian, university administrator; b. N.Y.C., Dec. 12, 1941; s. Irwin L. and Edna (Sopkin) P.; m. Carol J. Gershuny, June 21, 1964; children: Amy Ellen, Adam Matthew. BA magna cum laude, Clark U., 1963; MA, Northwestern U., Evanston, Ill., 1966, PhD, 1968. Lectr. Herbert H. Lehman Coll., CUNY, 1967-69; asst. prof. history Calif. State U., Long Beach, 1969-73, assoc. prof. 1973-78, prof., 1978—, assoc. dean instrnl. support Sch. Social and Behavioral Scis., 1980-81, assoc. dean ednl. policy, 1981-84, dean, 1985-86; dean Sch. Fine Arts, 1984-85, asst. v.p. acad. affairs, dean grad. studies, 1986-90, assoc. v.p. acad. affairs, dean grad. studies, 1991-96, assoc. v.p. instrnl. programs & rsch., 1996—; co-chair Calif. Minority Grad. Edn. Forum, 1990—; mem. coun. Big West Conf. (formerly Pacific Coast Athletic Assn.), 1982-90, Western Collegiate Athletic Assn., 1982-85. Author: The Politics of Inertia, 1973, (with others) Generations of Americans, 1976, Political Parties in American History, 1981; contbg. author: The Presidents: A Reference History, 1984, 2d edit., 1996; editor: The History Tchr., 1972-77, prodn. mgr., 1977-80. Mem., clk. bd. trustees Los Alamitos Sch. Dist., 1980-81; mem. Los Alamitos Unified Sch. Dist. Bd. Edn., 1990-94, pres. 1992-93; chmn. adv. com. on facilities, Los Alamitos Sch. Dist., 1989, chair steering com. for measure K for kids, 1990; bd. dirs. Long Beach Opera Assn., 1981-89, pres. 1982-83, treas., 1987-88; bd. dirs. Los Alamitos Jr. Baseball, 1988-90, Los Alamitos Basball, 1990-92. Avocations: travel, photography. Home: 2971 Druid Ln Los Alamitos CA 90720-4948 Office: Calif State U 1250 N Bellflower Blvd Long Beach CA 90840-0001

POLANCO, J. MARTIN, field service technician, pastry artist; b. Oakland, Calif., May 3, 1968; s. Jose B. and Oliva (Duarte) P.; m. Rosana Lim, Sept. 8, 1993; children: Jonathan M., Stephanie A. AS in Culinary Arts, Laney Coll., 1994. Head cake decorator Merritt Bakery, Oakland, Calif., 1989—; field svc. technician Danka Omnifax, Hayward, Calif., 1998—. Author: DeMartino's Guide to Cake Decorating, 1993. Home: 1470 Thrush Ave Apt 21 San Leandro CA 94578-5501

POLK, EMILY DESPAIN, conservationist, writer, designer; b. Aberdeen, Wash., July 6, 1910; d. John Dove Isaacs and Constance Ashley (DeSpain) Van Norden; m. Benjamin Kauffman Polk, Aug. 23, 1946. *Emily Polk's youngest days were in Eastern Oregon with grandmother Nancy Howard deSpain. Grandfather Jeremiah walked there from Kentucky in 1846, age 12, and became an "Empire Builder", giving settlers free land. In New York with grandparents Emily Collins Isaacs and John Dove Isaacs of Virginia and California, chief engineer war-time Nationalized Railways, called "Father of Motion Pictures", he invented alternating-current film. Emily danced for Isadora Duncan, was accepted - Emily's mother refused. Emily's complex ancestry is typically American: Druidical Celt, Briton, Norse, Saxon, Visigoth, Hessian, Norman, Spanish Sephard; the Castile, Navarre, and Valois Families.* Student, U. Oreg., 1928-29, Oreg. State U., 1929-31, Rudolph Shaefer Sch. of Art, San Francisco, 1931-32. Head display & design V.C. Morris, San Francisco, 1931-37; founder, CEO DeSpain Design, L.A. and N.Y.C., 1937-44, 63-64; ornamental & interior design arch. Benjamin Polk Arch., Calcutta and New Delhi, 1952-63; owner Galeria de San Luis, San Luis Obispo, Calif., 1966-68; founder, CEO Small Wilderness Area Preservation, Los Osos, Calif., 1969-79. *India, like other Asian countries, often brings out the "reformer" in Western professionals. Emily Polk and her architect husband, Benjamin Polk, knew India as an inspirational source. Ben's architectural skills and vision produced masterpieces truly Indian, truly contemporary. India clearly influenced his musical compositions. Emily architecturally collaborated in ornament and interior design using Indian motifs, materials and craftsmen. Later in California, realizing that communities cherished their nearby natural land, Emily founded Small Wilderness Area Preservation to preserve these wild places. By invitation, she drove all over California for nine years helping to save thousands of acres near these communities.* Author: Poems and Epigrams, 1959 (All India Book award 1959), Rockpool Trilogy, 1995, Shadows: A Giant Tree, Vols. I-II, 1995-96, A Moment in the Mind, 1997; co-author: (with B. Polk) India Notebook, 1987, (with others) Sri Lanka Buddhist Shrines, 1991; editor (poetry): Calcuttan Magazine, 1961-63; contbr. articles to jours.; designer interior and exhibits Internat. Wool Secretariat, World Trade Fair, New Delhi, 1955; hon. interior designer Pres. of India, New Delhi, 1955, Maharanee of Tripura, Calcutta, India, 1962-63, King of Nepal, Kathmandu, 1962-63, Princess Pema Choki, Gantok, Sikkim, 1963; solo exhbns. paintings India, 1963, U.S., 1963, 75, 89, 91, Eng., 1987, jewelry, U.S., 1948, fashion, India, 1955. Mem. coun. Nat. Mus. Women in the Arts, Washington, 1991-93; del., spkr. Pan Asian Cultural Conf., Calcutta, 1963. Recipient Golden Bear Conservation award Calif. Pks. and Recreation, Sacramento, 1972, Nat. Conservation award Am. Motors, 1972. Mem. Soc. Women Geographers (Calif. del., spkr. 50th Anniversary Celebrations 1972, Libr. of Congress Oral History Women of Achievement Program 1995), Small Wilderness Area Preservation, Calif. Hist. Soc., Calif. Oaks Found., Am. Women's Club (pres. 1962), Nat. Indian Assn. Women (pres.), English Speaking Union (bd. dirs.), Gyan Chakra Literary Gp. (founder). Home: 2361 Claranita Ave Los Osos CA 93402-4013

POLLACK, PHYLLIS ADDISON, ballerina; b. Victoria, B.C., Can., Aug. 31, 1919; d. Horace Nowell and Claire Melanie (Morris) Addison; m. Robert Seymour Pollack, Sept. 6, 1941; children: Robert Addison, Gwenda Joyce, Victoria Jean, Phyllis Anne. Student, SUNY, 1941-42, San Mateo Tech. Coll., 1958-62, U. Calif., San Francisco, 1962. Owner, dir. Phyllis Addison Dance Studio, Victoria, 1936-38; ballerina Taynton Dancers/Marcus Show Ballet Troupe, 1939-41, Ballet Russe, 1941; x-ray therapy tech. Meml. Hosp., N.Y.C., 1943-45; corr. fgn. tellers dept. N.C.B., N.Y.C., 1945-46; owner,

designer The Dancing Branch Studio, Sonoma, Calif., 1988—; floral designer J. Noblett Gallery, Sonoma, 1988-94. Pres. PTA, 1955-56, 62-63; mem. Assistance League San Mateo, Calif., 1960-70. Mem. Metro. Club, Bay Area Arrangers Guild, Ikebana Internat., San Francisco Garden Club. Democrat. Unitarian. Avocations: dancing, choreography, fashion modelling, photography, reading. Home: 384 Avenida Barbera Sonoma CA 95476-8069

POLLACK, REGINALD MURRAY, painter, sculptor; b. Middle Village, L.I., N.Y., July 29, 1924; m. Kerstin Birgitta Soederlund; m. Naomi Newman (div.); children: Jane Olivia, Maia Jaquine. m. Hanna Ben Dov (div). Grad. H.S., High Sch. Music and Art, N.Y.C., 1941; student with, Wallace Harrison, Moses Soyer, Boardman Robinson; student, Academie de la Grande Chaumiere, 1948-52. Occasional asst. to Constantin Brancusi; vis. critic Yale U., 1962-63, Cooper Union, 1963-64; vis. lectr. Coll. of Desert, Palm Springs, Calif., 1998; mem. staff Human Rels. Tng. Ctr., UCLA, 1966; artistic dir. The Gallery, Greater Washington Collection Fine Art, Leesburg, Va., 1991-94; chmn. artists adv. com. Loudon Arts Coun., Va., 1990-93, vis. lectr. Coll. of Desert, 1998. One-man shows include Charles Fourth Gallery, N.Y.C., 1948, Peridot Gallery, 1949, 52, 55-57, 59, 60, 62, 63, 65, 67, 69, Galerie Saint-Placide, Paris, 1952, Dwan Gallery, 1960, Jefferson Gallery, LaJolla, Calif., 1963, 68, 69, Goldwach Gallery, Chgo., 1964, 65, 66, Felix Landau Gallery, Hollywood, 1963, 65, 67, David Alexander Gallery, 1974, Washington Gallery Arts, 1974, Cosmos Club, Washington, 1976, Washington Project for Arts, 1976, Everhart Mus., Scranton, Pa., 1977, Pa. State U., 1977, Jack Rasmussen gallery, 1978, 79, 80, 81, 82, Art Washington, 1979, 81, Corcoran Mus., 1980, Zenith Gallery, Washington, 1982, Summit Gallery, N.Y., 1982, Tartt Gallery, Washington, 1986, Arctic Images Gallery, Aspen, Colo., 1987, Loudoun County Adminstrn. Bldg., 1988, 95—, Susan Conway Carroll Gallery, Washington, 1990, The Gallery, Leesburg, 1992, Loudoun Valley Vineyard, Waterford, Va., 1992—, Sordoni Art Gallery, Wilkes U., Pa., 1994, The Natural Light Art School Gallery, Leesburg, Va., 1995, George Washington U., Va. Campus, Leesburg, Merrill Lynch, Indian Wells, Calif., 1998; exhibited group shows including Whitney Mus. Am. Art, 1953, 55, 56, 58, 62, U. Nebr., 1951, 56, 57, 60, 63, Chgo. Art Inst., Carnegie, Pitts., Salon du Mai, Paris, U. Ill., Salon des Artistes Independants, Paris, 1955-58, NAS, 1990, NIH, 1990, Elaine Benson Gallery, Bridgehampton, L.I., 1991, Met. Mus. Art, 1997—, numerous others; multi-media theatrical prodns. The War of The Angels, 1974; The Twelve Gifts of Christmas, 1974; commns. include Jacob's Ladder painting, Washington Cathedral, bronze sculpture, The World Bank, awarded to King of Thailand, (TV episode Star Trek) Methuselem Returns, 1968, (laser show) The Crucible, 1996, others; represented in permanent collections, Bezalel Mus., Bklyn. Mus., Collection de L'Etat, France, U. Glasgow, Haifa, Mus. Modern Art, U. Nebr., Stanford Mus. Art, U. Calif., Santa Cruz, Newark Mus., Rockefeller Inst., Whitney Mus. Am. Art, Worcester Art Mus., Nat. Mus. Am. Art, Ft. Lauderdale (Fla.) Mus., Loew Mus. U. Miami, Fla., Met. Mus., N.Y., Hirshhorn Mus., Washington, New Orleans Mus. Art, Skirball Mus. Skidmore Coll., numerous other pub. and pvt. collections.; author and illustrator: The Magician and the Child, 1971; illustrator: Get a Horse (Steven Price), 1974, Visions from the Ramble (John Hollander), 1964, The Quest of the Gole (John Hollander), 1966, O is for Overkill, A Survival Alphabet (Merrill Pollack), 1968, The Blessed Ones (Ulla Isaksson), 1970, Oedipus (Seneca, transl. Ted Hughes), 1973, The Enjoyment of Music (Joseph Machlis). Instr. Quaker Half-way House, Los Angeles, 1968; cons. staff Lighthouse Child Guidance Center Presbyn. Hosp., 1966-69; pvt. instr., 1966-69; vis. artist Materials Research Lab., Pa. State U., 1977; trustee Washington Project for Arts, 1976-80. Served with AUS, 1941-45. Recipient Prix Neumann Paris, 1952, Prix Othon Friesz Paris, mention, 1954, 57, Prix de Peintres Etrangeres, 2d prize Paris Moderne, 1958; Ingram-Merrill Found. grantee, 1964, 70-71; Maurice Fromkis fellow, La Residence, Segovia, Spain, 1953. Address: 2283 E Smokewood Ave Palm Springs CA 92264-4967

POLLAK, NORMAN L., retired accountant; b. Chgo., Aug. 16, 1931; s. Emery and Helen P.; m. Barbara Zeff, Aug. 21, 1955 (div. 1980); children: Martin Joel, Elise Susan McNeal, Rhonda Louise Wilder; m. Sharon Levin, Nov. 12, 1995. BS, Northwestern U., 1955. CPA, Calif.; lic. real estate agt. Calif. Sr. acct., staff acct., 1952-58, pvt. practice, 1958-86; ret. acct., fin. and mgmt. cons., pres. Norman L. Pollak Accountancy Corp., Westlake Village, 1958-86; expert witness on domestic dissolution, 1984-86; lectr. profl. orgns.; bus. mgr. for Steven Martin, Nitty Gritty Dirt Band, 1967-77; acct. for Gregg and Howard Allman, 1967, Marion Ross, 1980s. Former pres. Ventura County Estate Planning Coun., 1975-78, 78-79); founder San Fernando Valley Estate Planning Coun., 1962, chpt. pres., 1964-65; founder Ventura Co. Estate Planning Coun.; chmn. Comm. Contest for Hearing Impaired Optimist Club, emergency com. Disaster Preparedness, Oak Forest Mobile Estates Assn.; compiled disaster preparedness plan; coach Braille Olympics for Blind; mem. Conejo Future Found.; bd. dirs. Oak Forest Homeowners Assn., Honokowai Palms Homeowners Assn.; bd. trustees Westlake Cultural Found.; active sponsor Code 3 for Homeless Children, 1993. Named in Internat. Biog. Ctr. Cambridge, Eng. as one of the top 2000 Outstanding People 20th Century in honor of contributions to the CPA profession, Estate Planning Couns., and Charitable orgns. Mem. AICPA (apptd. key person for legis.- polit. program Washington), Calif. Soc. CPAs (former chmn. San Fernando tech. discussion group 1960-61, former mem. com. on cooperation with credit grantors), Nat. Assn. Accts., Westlake Village C. of C., Northwestern U. Alumni Club, Delta Mu Delta. Home and Office: 143 Sherwood Dr Westlake Village CA 91361-4814

POLLARD, JANN DIANN, fine artist, graphic artist, educator; b. Mt. Pleasant, Iowa, Apr. 11, 1942; d. Donald Robert and Mary (Young) Lawrence; m. Gene A. Pollard, Apr. 25, 1970; children: Brittany, Natalie. BFA in Interior Design, U. Colo., 1963; postgrad., Coll San Mateo. Interior designer Dohrmann Co., Brisbane, Calif., 1964-68, H. Janders Design Cons., San Francisco, 1968-70, Jann Pollard Studios, Burlingame, Calif., 1970—; artist The Gallery, Burlingame, 1985—, Cottage Gallery, Carmel, Calif., 1991—. One-person shows include The Gallery, Burlingame, 1987, 88, 91, 93, 95, 97, 98, Cottage Gallery, Carmel, 1993, 95, 98; SWA Zellerbach Show, San Francisco, 1985 (hon. mention), Soc. Western Artists Ann., 1985, 91, San Diego Internat. Watercolor Show, 1990; artist for bookcovers Karen Brown Travel Books, 1991—. Active Hillsborough Aux. to Family Svc. Agy., 1983—, Nat. Kidney Found., 1994—. Recipient 2d prize Soc. Western Artists, 1973. Mem. Am. Soc. Interior Designers (profl.), Calif. Watercolor Soc. (signature mem.), Soc. Western Artists (signature mem.). Avocations: computers, genealogy. E-mail: pollardart@aol.com. Home and Studio: 105 La Mesa Dr Burlingame CA 94010-5919

POLLEY, HARVEY LEE, retired missionary and educator; b. Wapato, Wash., Aug. 14, 1924; s. Edward Prestley and Alda June Polley; m. Corinne Weber; children: Catherine, David, Corinne, Robert. BA, Whitworth Coll., Spokane, Wash., 1951; postgrad., East Wash. Coll., 1953, Berkeley Bapt. Div. Sch., 1958-59; MEd, Cen. Wash. Coll., 1958; postgrad., Ecole d'Adminstrn. des Affaires Africaines, Brussels, 1959-60. Tchr. Quincy (Wash.) Pub. Schs., 1953-57, N.W. Christian Schs., Spokane, 1958; missionary Am. Bapt. Fgn. Missionary Soc., Zaire, 1958-89; tchr. Evang. Pedagogical Inst., Kimpese, Zaire, 1961-69, asst. legal rep., dir., prin., supt., 1969-72; dir. BIM Hostel, Kinshasa, Zaire, 1972-73; mem. staff Ctr. for Agrl. Devel. Lusekele, Zaire, 1975-85, dir., 1976-79, 83-85; dir. Plateau Bateke Devel. Program, Kinshasa, 1985-89; ret., 1989. Author: Mpila Kele, a rural development guide written in the Kituba lang., 1989. Mem. Coun. Elders, Kimpese, 1969-72; pres. bd. adminstrn. Vanga (Zaire) Hosp., 1981-83; mem. exec. com. Nat. Human Nutrition Planning Coun. Govt. Zaire-USAID, Kikwit, 1983-85. With U.S. Army, 1946-47, 51-53. Home: W2405 W Johansen Rd Spokane WA 99208-9616

POLLEY, TERRY LEE, lawyer; b. Long Beach, Calif., June 2, 1947; s. Frederick F. and Geraldine E. (Davis) P.; m. Patricia Yamanoha, Aug. 4, 1973; children: Todd, Matthew. AB, UCLA, 1970; JD, Coll. William and Mary, 1973. Bar: Calif. 1973, U.S. Tax Ct. 1974, U.S. Supreme Ct. 1987. Assoc. Loeb & Loeb, L.A., 1973-78; ptnr. Ajalat, Polley & Ayoob, L.A., 1978—; lectr. taxation law U. So.Calif., 1978-94. Author (with Charles R. Ajalat) California's Water's Edge Legislation, 1987; contbr. articles to profl. [illegible] William and Mary Law Rev. Chmn. bd. dirs. Greater Long Beach Christian Schs., 1988-92, sec., 1994—; elder Grace Brethren Ch., Long Beach, 1988—. Mem. ABA (state and local tax com. 1973-92), Calif. Bar Assn. (chmn. taxation sect. 1990-91, exec. com. 1987-92, state and local tax com. 197[illegible] award 1993), L.A. County Bar Assn. (exec. com. 1980-87, chmn. exec. com. 1985-86, taxation sect.), Nat. Assn. State Bar Tax Sects. (exec. com. 1990—, chmn. 1995-96, sec. 1998—). Republican. Office: Ajalat Polley & Ayoob 643 S Olive St Ste 200 Los Angeles CA 90014-1651

POLLOCK, JOHN PHLEGER, lawyer; b. Sacramento, Apr. 28, 1920; s. George Gordon and Irma (Phleger) P.; m. Juanita Irene Gossman, Oct. 26, 1945; children: Linda Pollock Harrison, Madeline Pollock Chiotti, John, Gordon. A.B., Stanford U., 1942; J.D., Harvard U., 1948. Bar: Calif. 1949, U.S. Supreme Ct. 1954. Ptnr. Musick, Peeler & Garrett, L.A., 1953-60, Pollock, Williams & Berwanger, L.A., 1960-80; ptnr. Rodi, Pollock, Pettker, Galbraith & Cahill, L.A., 1980-89, of counsel, 1989—. Contbr. articles to profl. publs. Active Boy Scouts Am.; trustee Pitzer Coll., Claremont, Calif., 1968-76, Pacific Legal Found., 1981-91, Fletcher Jones Found., 1969—, Good Hope Med. Found., 1980—. Mem. ABA, Los Angeles County Bar Assn. (trustee 1964-66). Home: 30602 Paseo Del Valle Laguna Niguel CA 92677-2317 Office: 801 S Grand Ave Los Angeles CA 90017-4613

POLLOCK, RICHARD EDWIN, former county administrator; b. Phila., Aug. 27, 1928; s. Ernest Edwin and Evelyn Marie (Scarlett) P. Student Armstrong Coll., 1947, U. Calif., Berkeley, 1949-51, 55; BA in Recreation, San Jose State U., 1961; postgrad. San Fernando Valley State U., 1969-70, U. Calif., Davis, 1963-77, UCLA, 1964, U. Calif., Santa Barbara, 1970, U. Redlands, 1979; m. Yvonne May Graves, Oct. 11, 1952 (div. Aug. 1989); children: Colleen May, Karen Marie, Richard Irvin, Annette Yvonne, Mary Ann. Swim pool mgr. and instr. Berkley Tennis Club, 1955-56; police officer City of Berkeley, 1956; recreation and aquatic supr. Pleasant Hill (Calif.) Recreation and Park Dist., 1956-62; gen. mgr. Pleasant Valley Recreation and Park Dist., Camarillo, Calif., 1962-68; bldg. insp. Ventura County (Calif.), 1969-71; adminstr. Sacramento County-Carmichael Recreation and Park Dist., 1971-73; dir. parks and recreation Imperial County (Calif.), 1973-81; ret.; mem. faculty Imperial Valley Jr. Coll., 1974-94, aquatic cons., 1957—; real estate investor, 1984-97; chmn. San Francisco Bay Area Conf. for Cooperation in Aquatics, 1958-59. Adviser/scoutmaster Desert Trails council Boy Scouts Am.; bd. dirs., instr. ARC; work with devel. disabled and handicapped children and adults; res. dep. Sheriff, 1981-97, Served from pvt. to lt. U.S. Army, 1951-55; Korea. Recipient recognition for 52 years vol. service ARC, 1989; registered recreator and park mgr.; cert. elem., secondary and community coll. tchr., Calif.; reg. hypnotherapist. Mem. Nat. Recreation and Park Assn., AAHPER, Calif. Park and Recreation Soc., Calif. County Dirs. Parks and Recreation Assn., Calif. Boating Safety Officers Assn., Aircraft Owners and Pilots Assn., Nat. Assn. Emergency Med. Technicians. Democrat. Mormon. Author: Bibliography: A Pool of Aquatic Sources, 1960. Home: 961 S Sunshine Ave Apt 5 El Cajon CA 92020-5947

POLMANSKI, TED CHESTER, lighting director; b. Chgo., Feb. 8, 1955; s. Tadeusz and Anna (Smolin) P.; married, 1986. Student, Columbia Coll., 1973-77. Lighting dir., cameraman Catholic TV Network Chgo., 1975-77, Sears, Roebuck and Co., Chgo., 1977-78; freelance lighting dir., cameraman Los Angeles, 1978; lighting cons. Embassy TV, Los Angeles, 1987; lighting dir. NBC-TV, Burbank, Calif., 1978—. Mem. Acad. TV Arts and Scis. (Emmy cert. 1982, 11 Emmy nominations, Emmy awards Santa Barbara 1990, 91), Am. Soc. Lighting Designers (3d v.p., Outstanding Artistic Achievement award 1988, 90, Bd. Dirs. award 1989, Choice award 1992), Soc. Lighting Designers (Can.). Roman Catholic. Avocation: photography. Office: NBC 3000 W Alameda Ave Burbank CA 91523-0002

POLON, LINDA BETH, elementary school educator, writer, illustrator; b. Balt., Oct. 7, 1943; d. Harold Bernard and Edith Judith Wolff; m. Marty I. Polon, Dec. 18, 1966 (div. Aug. 1983). BA in History, UCLA, 1966. Elem. tchr. L.A. Bd. Edn., 1967—; writer-illustrator Scott Foresman Pub. Co., Glenview, Ill., 1979—, Frank Schaffer Pub. Co., Torrance, Calif., 1981-82, Learning Works, Santa Barbara, Calif., 1981-82, Harper Row Co.; editorial reviewer Prentice Hall Pub. Co., Santa Monica, Calif., 1982-83. Author: (juvenile books) Creative Teaching Games, 1974, Teaching Games for Fun, 1976, Making Kids Click, 1979, Write up a Storm, 1979, Stir Up a Story, 1981, Paragraph Production, 1981, Using Words Correctly, 3d-4th grades, 1981, 5th-6th grades, 1981, Whole Earth Holiday Book, 1983, Writing Whirlwind, 1986, Magic Story Starters, 1987, (teacher's resource guides) Just Good Books, 1991, Kid's Choice/Libraries, 1991, Write A Story Grades 1-3, 1997, Write A Story Grades 4-6, 1997, Story Starters Grades 1-3, 9999, Story Starters Grades 4-6, 1999. Mem. Soc. Children's Book Writers; writer of elem. sch. grade stories, 1997. Democrat. Home: 1308 9th St Santa Monica CA 90401-1860 Office: L A Bd of Edn 980 S Hobart Blvd Los Angeles CA 90006-1220

POLSON, DONALD ALLAN, surgeon; b. Gallup, N.Mex., May 12, 1911; s. Thomas Cress and Carrie Fern (Cantrall) P.; m. Cecily, Lady Avebury, Nov. 9, 1946; 1 child, Carolyn Kathleen. Student Stanford U.; MD, Northwestern U., 1936, MSc, 1947. Diplomate Am. Bd. Surgery. Intern, then resident in surgery St. Luke's Hosp., Chgo., 1936-38; practice medicine specializing in gen. surgery, Phoenix, 1947-83; formerly chmn. Drs. Polson, Berens & Petelin, Ltd.; chief staff Maricopa County Hosp., 1952-53, St. Joseph's Hosp., 1961; bd. dirs. Ariz. Blue Shield, 1950-55, pres., 1956. Served to col. M.C., AUS, World War II. Mem. AMA, ACS, Ariz. Med. Assn. (dir. 1955-60), Maricopa County Med. Soc. (pres. 1954), Phoenix Surg. Soc. (pres. 1959), Alpha Omega Alpha, Nu Sigma Nu. Republican. Episcopalian. Home: 7619 N Tatum Blvd Paradise Valley AZ 85253

POLSTER, LEONARD H., investment company executive; b. Columbus, Ohio, June 24, 1921; s. Max and Henrietta Polster; m. Constance L. Buderus, Mar. 20, 1948 (dec. Aug. 1967); children: Leonard M., Lance E., Lewis E.; m. Edith Motridge, Nov. 19, 1968. BA, Ohio State U., 1942. Pres. Polster, Inc., 1952-68; pres. real estate and investments co. Polster, Inc., Rancho Santa Fe, 1968—; sr. v.p. PaineWebber Inc., L.A. and Rancho Santa Fe, Calif., 1971-91. Author: Pearls Before Swine, 1994. Pres. Polster Found., Rancho Santa Fe, 1988— (awards approximately 25 univ. scholarships to needy students annually); fin. officer, bd. dirs. San Dieguito Boys Club, Solana Beach, Calif., 1991—; bd. dirs. Fairbanks Ranch Cmty. Svcs. Dist., Rancho Santa Fe, 1987-92; pres. Fairbanks Ranch Assn., Rancho Santa Fe, 1985-86, bd. dirs., 1984-86. With USAF, 1942-46. Recipient Commitment to Youth award San Dieguito Boys and Girls Club, 1989; Olympic torch bearer, Apr. 28, 1996. Mem. Fairbanks Ranch Country Club, Phi Alpha Theta. Republican. Presbyterian. Avocations: tennis, reading, music. Home and Office: PO Box 8291 Rancho Santa Fe CA 92067-8291

POLSTON, BARBARA JEAN, principal, educational psychologist; b. Litchfield, Ill., Oct. 9, 1943; d. Wilbur Lee and Frances (Leitschuh) P.; children: Charles, Beth, Ann. B of Music Edn., Webster Coll., 1965; MA, St. Louis U., 1985. Cert. elem. tchr., cert. prin., Mo., Wash., Oreg. Prin. Archdiocese of Portland, Oreg., 1997—, Archdiocese St. Louis, 1986-96, Lady of the Presentation, St. Martin de Porres, Corpus Christi, 1993-97, Archdiocese Seattle, SD, 1997-98, Cathedral Sch., Portland, 1998—; archdiocesan coord. alternative sch. practices, sch. calendars, multi media and tech., accelerative learning interventions. Mem. Mo. Lead Program, Nat. Yr. Round Edn., Danforth Found. Mem. ASCD, NCEA, Prins. Acad. Mo., Nat. Cath. Prins. Acad., Inst. Responsive Edn., Consortium Responsive Schs.

POLUMBUS, GARY M., lawyer; b. Tulsa, 1941. BS, U. Colo., 1964; JD, U. Denver, 1967. Bar: Colo. 1967, D.C. 1968. Mem. Dorsey & Whitney, Denver, 1996—. Mem. ABA, Am. Intellectual Property Law Assn. Office: Dorsey & Whitney 370 17th St Ste 4400 Denver CO 80202-5644

POLYNICE, OLDEN, basketball player; b. Nov. 21, 1964. Center Scramento Kings. Office: Sacramento Kings 1 Sports Pkwy Sacramento CA 95834-2301

POMADA, ELIZABETH L., literary agent, author; b. N.Y.C., June 12, 1940; d. Maxim Pomada and Rita Dolores (Ross) Antonio; m. Michael [illegible] BS Cornell U., 1962. Ptnr. Larsen/Pomada Literary Agts., San Francisco. Author: Daughters of Painted Ladies, 1988, America's Painted Ladies, 1992, Fun Places To Go With Children, 1997, Painted Ladies Revisited, 1998. Mem. Am. Soc. Journalists and Authors [illegible] Women's Nat. Book Assn. [illegible] Authors Guild, Calif. Press Women, PEN. Avocations: France, travel, architectural color. Office: Larsen/Pomada Literary Agts 1029 Jones St San Francisco CA 94109-5023

POMBO, RICHARD, congressman, rancher, farmer; b. Tracy, Calif., 1961; m. Annette, 1983; children: Richard Jr., Rena, Rachael. Student, Calif. State U., Pomona, 1981-83. Councilman City of Tracy, 1991-92; mayor pro-tem Tracy City Coun., 1992; mem. 103rd-105th Congresses from 11th Calif. dist., 1993—, chmn. agrl. com., subcom. on livestock, dairy and poultry; mem. Agrl. Com., Resources Com.; chmn. Pvt. Property Rights Task Force, 1993-94, Endangered Species Act Task Force, 1995-96; co-chmn. Spkr.'s Environ. Task Force, 1996. Co-founder San Joaquin County Citizen's Land Alliance, Calif., 1986—; active San Joaquin County Econ. Devel. Assn., Tracy Bus. Improvement Dist., City Coun. (vice chmn. Cmty. Devel. Agy., Cmty. Parks Com., and Waste Mgmt. Com.), San Joaquin County Rep. Ctrl. Com. Mem. Rotary Club. Roman Catholic. Office: US Ho of Reps 1519 Longworth HOB Washington DC 20515-0511

POMERANTZ, MARVIN, thoracic surgeon; b. Suffern, N.Y., June 16, 1934; s. Julius and Sophie (Luksin) P.; m. Margaret Twigg, Feb. 26, 1966; children: Ben, Julie. AB, Colgate U., 1955; MD, U. Rochester, 1959. Diplomate Nat. Bd. Med. Examiners, Am. Bd. Surgery, Am. Bd. Thoracic Surgery (bd. dirs. 1989-95). Intern Duke U. Med. Ctr., Durham, N.C., 1959-60, resident, 1960-61, 63-67, instr. surgery, 1966-67; asst. prof. surgery U. Colo. Med. Sch., Denver, 1967-71, assoc. prof. surgery, 1971-74, assoc. clin. prof. surgery, 1974-93, prof. surgery, chief gen. thoracic surgery, 1992—; chief thoracic and cardiovascular surgery Denver Gen. Hosp., 1967-73, asst. dir. surgery, 1967-70, assoc.dir. surgery, 1970-73; pvt. practice Arapahoe CV Assocs., Denver, 1974-92; clin. assoc. surgery br. Nat. Cancer Inst., 1961-63; mem.staff Univ. Hosp., Denver, Denver Gen. Hosp., Rose Med. Ctr., Denver, Denver VA Med. Ctr., Children's Hosp., Denver, U. Coll. Health Sci. Ctr., 1992—, bd. dirs., 1995-97, chmn., 1997, Am. Bd. Thoracic Surgery. Guest editor Chest Surgery Clinics N.Am., 1993; contbr. numerous articles to profl. publs., chpts. to books. Fellow ACS, Am. Coll. Chest Surgeons; mem. AMA, Western Thoracic Surg. Assn. (v.p. 1992, pres. 1993-94, counselor-at-large 1988-90), Am. Assn. Thoracic Surgeons (program com. 1991), Am. Heart Assn. (bd. dirs. Colo. chpt. 1993), Colo. Med. Soc., Denver Acad. Surgery (pres. 1980), Internat. Cardiovascular Soc., Rocky Mtn. Cardiac Surgery Soc., Rocky Mtn. Traumatologic Soc., Soc. Thoracic Surgeons (nomenclature/coding com. 1991-95, standards and ethics com., govt. rels. com., chmn. program com. 1994-95), Soc. Vascular Surgeons, Am. Bd. Thoracic Surgery (vice-chmn. 1995-97, chmn. 1997—). Office: UCHSC Divsn CTS 4200 E 9th Ave # C310 Denver CO 80220-3706

POMEROY, KENT LYTLE, physical medicine and rehabilitation physician; b. Phoenix, Apr. 21, 1935; s. Benjamin Kent and LaVerne (Hamblin) P.; m. Karen Jodelle Thomas (dec. Dec. 1962); 1 child, Charlotte Ann; m. Margo Delilah Tuttle, Mar. 27, 1964 (div. Jan. 1990); children: Benjamin Kent II, Janel Elise, Jonathan Barrett, Kimberly Eve, Kathryn M.; m. Brenda Pauline North, Sept. 1, 1990. BS in Phys. Sci., Ariz. State U., 1960; MD, U. Utah, 1963. Diplomate Am. Bd. Phys. Medicine and Rehab., Am. Bd. Pain Medicine; license homeopathic medicine, Ariz. Rotating intern Good Samaritan Hosp., Phoenix, 1963-64; resident in phys. medicine and rehab. Good Samaritan Hosp., 1966-69, asst. tng. dir. Inst. Rehab. Medicine, 1970-74, dir. residency tng., 1974-76, asst. med. dir., 1973-76; dir. Phoenix Phys. Medicine Ctr., 1980-85, Ariz. Found. on Study Pain, Phoenix, 1980-85; pvt. practice, Phoenix and Scottsdale, Ariz., 1985—; lectr. in field. Contbr. articles to med. jours. Leader Theodore Roosevelt coun. Boy Scouts Am.; mem. exec. posse Maricopa County Sheriff's Office, Phoenix, 1981—, posse comdr., 1992-94, qualified armed posseman; mem. med. adv. bd. Grand Canyon-Saguaro chpt. Nat. Found. March of Dimes, 1970-78; missionary, 1955-57. Recipient Scouter's Tng. award Theodore Roosevelt coun. Boy Scouts Am., 1984, Scouter's Woodbadge, 1985. Mem. AMA, Am. Acad. Phys. Medicine and Rehab., Internat. Rehab. Medicine Assn., Am. Assn. Orthopaedic Medicine (co-founder, sec.-treas. 1982-88, pres. 1988-90), Prolotherapy Assn. (pres. 1981-83), Am. Pain Soc., Western Pain Soc., Am. Assn. for Study Headache, Am. Acad. Pain Medicine, Nat. Eagle Scout Assn., Ariz. Soc. Phys. Medicine (pres. 1977-78), Ariz. Med. Assn., Maricopa County Med. Soc., others, Nat. Sheriff's Assn., Law Enforcement Alliance of Am., Ariz. Narcotic Officers Assn. Mem. LDS Ch. Avocations: camping, drawing, painting, writing, music.

POMPER, CATHERINE JANICE, health care administrator; b. Peckville, Pa., Jan. 29, 1940; d. Joseph Aloysius and Catherine Helen (Purcell) Hart; m. Frank Joseph Pomper, July 20, 1963; children: Patricia Ann, Robert Francis. RN, St. Joseph Hosp. Sch. Nursing, Paterson, N.J., 1960; BS in Nursing, Winston-Salem (N.C.) State U., 1980. Cert. rehab. nurse; cert. case mgr.; cert. Calif. pub. health nurse. Work compensation case mgr. Resource Opportunities, Charlottesville, Va., 1981-82; rehab. nurse, clinician A U. Va. Hosp., Charlottesville, 1982-86; work compensation case mgr. Am. Internat. Adjustmment Co., Lafayette, Calif., 1986-88; work compensation dist. mgr. Mirfak Assocs., Oakland, Calif., 1988-90; case mgr., U/R supr. Lincoln Nat. Life, Pleasanton, Calif., 1990-92; dist. mgr. Resource Opportunities, Walnut Creek, Calif., 1992-93; dist. managed care case mgr. Hillhaven, Concord, Calif., 1993-94; Medicare case mgr. Good Samaritan Med. Found., San Jose, Calif., 1994-95; Medicare case mgr., coord. Cigna for Srs., Oakland, Calif., 1995—; mem. task force Calif. Assn. of Health Plans, Oakland, 1996—; mem. rehab. adv. bd. Stanford U. Hosp., Palo Alto, Calif., 1992-94; mem. Nurse Practice Act Adv. Study, 1985; mem. Task Force Drafting Case Mgmt. Guidelines and Definition ARN and AETNA Task Force, 1986, 93. Book reviewer ARN mag., 1984—. Mem. ICMA, CMSA (mem. legis. com. 1991-94, chpt. pres. 1997-98), ARN, Continuity of Care, CIGNAnificant Spkrs. (charter mem.), Toastmasters. Avocations: sewing, oil painting, swimming, gardening. Home: 120 Pebble Pl San Ramon CA 94583-3643 Office: Cigna Health Care No Calif 1999 Harrison St Ste 1000 Oakland CA 94612-3577

PONDER, PEARLIE MAE, retired tax collector; b. Louann, Ark., Apr. 15, 1937; d. Artee and Marzella (Primm) Neal; m. Marvin Clay Ponder, Sept. 16, 1961; children: Marcus Stephon, Miguel DeLano. AA, Modesto (Calif.) Jr. Coll., 1960. Acctg. cert. and advanced acctg. cert. Cosumnes River Coll., Sacramento, Calif. Tax collector Franchise Tax Bd., Sacramento, 1980-90. Author: Links to Ancestral Ties - George Primm, Sr., 1995. Vol. calligraphy instr. Sacramento Unified Sch. Dist., Woodbine Elem. Sch., 1992. Recipient Merit award for improving efficieny in state govt. Merit Award Bd., Sacramento, 1974. Mem. Nat. Mus. Women in the Arts. Avocations: art, bicycling, skating, piano playing, cake decorating. Home: 5915 40th St Sacramento CA 95824-2617

PONDER, SUZANNE HERSKOVIC, designer, real estate consultant; b. Brussels, May 19, 1947; came to U.S., 1957; d. William and Maria Herskovic; m. Frank Ponder, Feb. 23, 1969 (div. 1988); 1 child, Danielle. Student, U. Calif., Santa Barbara, 1966, Sorbonne, 1966; BA, UCLA, 1970, interior design diploma, 1974. With sales and acctg. dept. Bel Air Camera & HiFi, L.A., 1969-73; freelance interior designer Ponder Enterprises, L.A., 1974--; set designer Interplanetary Prodns., Sherman Oaks, Calif., 1984; real estate cons. Anderson Resources, L.A., 1984—; set designer, design cons. Am. First Run, Sherman Oaks, 1988—; co-prodr. Balenciaga TV, 1990; co-founder, exec. v.p. high tech start up Infinity (3D) Multimedia, Sherman Oaks, Calif., 1994. Mem. ways and means com. Westlake Sch., Bel Air, Calif., 1987; mem. cabinet real estate div. Jewish Women's Fedn., L.A., 1988--. Avocations: snow and water skiing, karate (black belt), painting, dancing. Office: 14225 Ventura Blvd Sherman Oaks CA 91423-2758

POOLE, HENRY JOE, JR., business executive; b. Rocky Point, N.C., July 5, 1957; s. Henry Joe Sr. and Marjorie (Morse) P.; m. Loretta Lynn Scott, Sept. 12, 1981; children: Robert Howard, Amanda Lynn. AA, Cypress Coll., 1977; student, San Diego State U., 1978, Calif. State U., Fullerton, 1978-79. Pres. Poole Ventura Inc., Ventura, Calif., 1979-92; gen. mgr. W.I.C. PVI systems divsn., Ventura, Calif., 1992-94; pres. PVI, Oxnard, Calif., 1995—. Inventor in field. Mem. ASME, Soc. Mfg. Engrs., Am. Vacuum Soc., Am. Welding Soc., Soc. Vacuum Coaters. Office: PVI PO Box [illegible] Oxnard CA [illegible]

POOLE, THOMAS RICHARD, endowment capital campaign director, fund raising counsel; b. [illegible], July 1[illegible], 1947; s. Frank Baldwin and Edna Laura (Harper) Poole. [illegible]

1975. Cert. fund-raising exec., 1985. Assoc. program dir. Brakeley, John Price Jones Inc., Stamford, Conn., Newport Beach, Calif., 1976-79, program dir., 1979-81, v.p., 1981-91, sr. v.p., 1991—; assoc. campaign dir. Columbia-Presbyn. Med. Ctr., N.Y.C., 1976-79; campaign dir. Manhattan Eye, Ear and Throat Hosp., N.Y.C., 1979-82; endowment/capital campaign dir., cons. Albany (N.Y.) Med. Ctr., 1984-89; endowment/capital campaign dir. Long Beach (Calif.) Meml. Med. Ctr., 1989-95, Samaritan Health Sys., Phoenix, 1995—. Author various corporate reports and feasibility studies. Mem. Nat. Soc. Fund-Raising Execs., Assocs. Ohio Wesleyan U. Avocations: reading, sailing, hiking, swimming. Office: Brakeley John Price Jones Inc 366 San Miguel Dr Ste 300 Newport Beach CA 92660-7810

POON, PETER TIN-YAU, engineer, physicist; b. Hengyang, Hunan, China, May 31, 1944; came to U.S., 1967; s. Sam. Chak-Kwong and Lai (Yiu) P.; m. Mable Tsang, Apr. 13, 1974; children: Amy Wei-Ling, Brian Wing-Yan. BS, U. Hong Kong, 1965; MA, Calif. State U., Long Beach, 1969; PhD, U. So. Calif., L.A., 1974. Sr. engr. gasdynamics, planetary probe heat shield design, sys. simulation Jet Propulsion Lab./Calif. Inst. Tech., Pasadena, 1974-77, tech. mgr. advanced solar receiver, task leader advanced solar concentrator, 1978-80, systems engr. mission control and computing ctr. devel., 1981-83; advisor Space Sta. Ada Task, staff mem, task leader software mgmt. and assurance program NASA, 1984-85; mission control ctr. devel. telemetry systems engr. software mgmt. stds., element mgr. NASA software info. sys. Jet Propulsion Lab./Calif. Inst. Tech., Pasadena, 1986-88, systems mgr. for missions to Mars, Comet/Asteroid/Saturn, flight projects interface office, 1988-91, multimission ground systems office mgr. Mission to Mars, 1991-93, telecomm. and mission svcs. mgr. Cassini Mission to Saturn, 1993-98, radio astronomy, French and German space missions, 1998—; program com. mem. Conf. on Artificial Intelligence and ADA, 1989-90; program com. session chair Software Engring. Stds. Symposium, Brighton, Eng., 1992-93; U.S.A. chmn., program com. 2d Internat. Software Engring. Stds. Symposium, Montreal, Can., 1994-95; program mgmt. com., panel chair 3d Internat. Software Engring. Stds. Symposium, 1995-97, 4th Internat. Software Engring. Stds. Symposium, Brazil, 1998-99; session chair, mem. program com. IEEE Internat. Conf. on Engring. of Complex Computer Systems, Montreal, 1995-96, Como, Italy, 1996-97, Monterey, 1997-98; mem. Internat. Orgn. for Standardization/Internat. Electrotech. Com./Joint Tech. Com. in Info. Tech. Subcom. Working Group and U.S. Technical Adv. Group, 1995—; U.S. del., Prague, Czech Republic, 1996, Paris, 1996, Walnut Creek, U.S., 1997, Brisbane, Australia, 1997, Melbourne, Fla., 1998, Curitiba, Brazil, 1998; program chmn. Software Engring. Stds. Symposium, 1998; program chmn. 5th Internat. Software Engring. Stds. Symposium, 1999—, 2nd World Congress on Software Quality, Tokyo, 1999—. Contbr. articles to profl. jours. Recipient Group award NASA, 1977-93, Recognition cert., Inventions and Contbns. Bd. Mem. IEEE Software Engring. Stds. (exec. com. 1993—, mem. editl. bd. software quality profl. 1998—), Arcadia Music Club (pres. 1994-95, 1st v.p. 1993-94), Sigma Xi, Eta Kappa Nu, Phi Kappa Phi, Athenaeum. Avocations: music appreciation, hiking, theatre arts. Office: Jet Propulsion Lab Calif Inst Tech 4800 Oak Grove Dr Pasadena CA 91109-8001

POON, WILLIAM WAI-LIK, industrial engineer, administrator; b. Beijing, Apr. 27, 1965; came to the U.S., 1984; s. Chun Yuan and Wing Kuen (Yeung) P. BS, U. Calif., Berkeley, 1988; MBA, So. Meth. U., 1992, MS, 1998. Chartered engr. Info. sys. splst., program analyst Superconducting Super Collider Lab., 1988-94; sr. bus. sys. analyst The Union Bank Calif., 1994-96; sr. project mgr. Amdahl Corp., Sunnyvale, Calif., 1996—. Mem. NSPE, Inst. Indsl. Engrs., Inst. Cert. Mgmt. Accts., Am. Assn. Cost Engrs. Internat., Am. Prodn. and Inventory Control Soc. Office: Amdahl Corp 1250 E Arques Ave # M Sunnyvale CA 94086-4730

POONJA, MOHAMED, business reorganization, financial and management consultant; b. Mombasa, Kenya, Nov. 8, 1948; came to U.S., 1984; s. Abdulrasul and Maleksultan (Dharsee) P.; m. Zaitun Virji, Feb. 24, 1979; children: Jamil Husayn, Karim Ali. Student, Inst. Chartered Accts., Eng., Wales; MS in Mgmt. and Organizational Behavior, U.S. Internat. U. CPA. Audit supr. Ernst & Young (formerly Ernst & Whinney), Dublin, Ireland, 1966-72, Coopers & Lybrand, Dublin, 1973-76; CFO Diamond Trust of Kenya, Nairobi, 1976-78; CEO Kenya Uniforms, Ltd., Nairobi, 1978-81; sr. mgr. Coopers & Lybrand, Calgary, Alta., Can., 1981-84; ptnr. Coopers & Lybrand, San Jose, Calif., 1984 92; chpt. 7 panel bankruptcy trustee No. Dist. Calif., San Jose, Calif., 1991—; with Poonja & Co., 1992—; ptnr. Manzanita Capital Ptnrs. Ltd., 1993—; former pres. Bay Area Bankruptcy Forum; bd. dirs. Calif. Bankruptcy Forum, Los Altos Ednl. Found. Am. Youth Soccer Orgn. Mem. ABA, Am. Bankruptcy Inst., Assn. Insolvency Accts., Inst. Bus. Appraisers, Cert. Fraud Examiners, Rotary. Avocations: music, art. Home: 630 Milverton Rd Los Altos CA 94022-3930 Office: Poonja & Co 150 Giffin Rd Los Altos CA 94022-3940

POOR, CLARENCE ALEXANDER, retired physician; b. Ashland, Oreg., Oct. 29, 1911; s. Lester Clarence and Matilda Ellen (Doty) P. AB, Willamette U., 1932; MD, U. Oreg., 1936. Diplomate Am. Bd. Internal Med. Intern U. Wis., Madison, 1936-37; resident in internal med. U. Wis., 1937-40, instr. dept. pathology Med. Sch., 1940-41, clin. instr., clin. asst. dept. internal med., 1942-44; pvt. practice med. specializing in internal med. Oakland, Calif., 1944-97; mem. emeritus staff Highland Alameda County Hosp., Oakland, 1949—; mem. staff Providence Hosp., Oakland, 1947-97; pres. staff Providence Hosp., 1968-69; staff mem. Samuel Merritt Hosp., Oakland, 1947-97, Summit Med. Ctr. (merger Providence Hosp. and Samuel Merritt Hosp.), 1991-97; ret., 1997—. *Clarence Alexander Poor retired from medical practice in October, 1997, and has rejoined The Commonwealth Club of California to maintain his community service and awareness of world affairs.* Mem. Nat. Coun. on Alcoholism, 1974—, bd. dirs. Bay Area, 1977—. Mem. Am., Calif., Alameda-Contra Costa med. assns., Alameda County Heart Assn. (trustee 1955-62, 72-82, pres. 1960-61), Calif. Heart Assn. (dir. 1962-72), Soc. for Clin. and Exptl. Hypnosis, Am. Soc. Clin. Hypnosis, San Francisco Acad. Hypnosis (dir. 1966—, pres. 1973), The Commonwealth Club Calif. Home: 1241 Westview Dr Berkeley CA 94705-1650

POPE, EDWARD JOHN ANDREW, corporate executive, consultant; b. N.Y.C., July 18, 1962; s. Thomas Andrew and Barbara (McInnes) P. BS, U. Calif., L.A., 1983, MS, 1985, PhD, 1989. Engring. asst. U. Calif., 1979-83, rsch. asst., 1984-89; pres. MATECH, Westlake Village, Calif., 1989—; cons. Orion Labs., Inc., Camarillo, Calif., 1988-89, Refractory Composites, Inc., Whittier, Calif., 1989-90, ENSCI, Inc., Woodland Hills, Calif., 1990—; bd. dirs. Ventura County World Affairs Coun. Contbr. numerous articles to profl. jours. Mem. State Ctrl. Com. of Rep. Party, Calif., 1981-83; pres. UCLA Bruin Reps., L.A., 1981-82; active UCLA Chem. Adv. Coun., 1993; apptd. Ventura County Coun. on Econ. Vitality, 1993. Regent's scholar U. Calif., 1979, Chancellor's scholar, 1979; IBM Corp. fellow Watson Rsch. Ctr., 1988. Mem. Am. Ceramic Soc. (chair edn. com. 1990—), Nat. Inst. Ceramic Engrs., Materials Rsch. Soc. (acad. affairs com. 1987-89), UCLA chpt. Materials Rsch. Soc. (pres. 1982-89). Office: MATECH 31304 Via Colinas Ste 102 Thousand Oaks CA 91362-4586

POPE, JOHN WILLIAM, judge, law educator; b. San Francisco, Mar. 12, 1947; s. William W. and Florence E. (Kline) P.; m. Linda M. Marsh, Oct. 23, 1970 (div. Dec. 1996); children: Justin, Ana, Lauren. BA, U. N.Mex., 1969, JD, 1973. Bar: N.Mex. 1973, U.S. Dist. Ct. N.Mex. 1973, U.S. Ct. Appeals (10th cir.) 1976. Law clk. N.Mex. Ct. of Appeals, Santa Fe, 1973; assoc. Chavez & Cowper, Belen, N.Mex., 1974; ptnr. Cowper, Bailey & Pope, Belen, 1974-75; pvt. practice law Belen, 1976-80; ptnr. Pope, Apodaca & Conroy, Belen, 1980-85; dir. litigation City of Albuquerque, 1985-87; judge State of N.Mex., Albuquerque, 1987-92, Dist. Ct. (13th jud. dist.), N.Mex., 1992—; instr. U. N.Mex., Albuquerque, 1983—, prof. law, 1990—; lectr. in field. Mem. state cen. com. Dem. Party, N.Mex., 1971-85; state chair Common Cause N.Mex., 1980-83; pres. Valencia County Hist. Soc., Belen, 1981-83; active Supreme Ct. Jury (UJI civil instructions com., state bar hist. com., bench and bar com.). Recipient Outstanding Jud. Svc. award N.Mex. State Bar, 1996; named City of Belen Citizen of Yr. 1995, Excellence in Tchg. award 1998. Mem. Valencia County Bar, Albuquerque Bar Assn. Avocations: swimming, golf, photography, historical research. Home: 400 Godfrey Ave Belen NM 87002-6313 Office: Valencia County Courthouse PO Box 1089 Los Lunas NM 87031-1089

POPE, STEPHEN TRAVIS, composer, computer scientist; b. Ridgewood, N.J., Dec. 9, 1955; s. Philip Travis and Charlotte Edith (Thrall) P.; m. Patrice Annette Baer. BSEE, Cornell U., 1978; Cert., Vienna Music Acad., 1980. Software developer The Nomad Group, Santa Barbara, Calif., 1989—; rsch. dir. U. Calif. Santa Barbara/Music, 1996—. Author books and articles; numerous musical compositions. Mem. IEEE (adv. bd.), Internat. Computer Music Assn. (life). Office: PO Box 14043 Santa Barbara CA 93107-4043

POPKIN, RICHARD HENRY, philosophy educator, writer, editor; b. N.Y.C., Dec. 27, 1923; s. Louis and Zelda (Feinberg) P.; m. Juliet Greenstone, June 9, 1944; children: Jeremy David, Margaret Louise, Susan Judith. BA, Columbia U., 1943, MA, 1945, PhD, 1950. Instr. philosophy U. Conn., Storrs, 1946-47; from asst. to assoc. prof. U. Iowa, Iowa City, 1947-52, 57-60; vis. prof. U. Calif., Berkeley, 1953-54; prof. philosophy Harvey Mudd Coll., Claremont, Calif., 1960-63; prof., chair philosophy U. Calif., San Diego, 1963-73; Disting. prof. Lehman Coll. CUNY, 1971-72; prof. philosophy, Jewish studies Washington U., St. Louis, 1973-86, prof. emeritus, 1986—; adj. prof. U. Calif., L.A., 1986—; Woodruff prof. Emory U., Atlanta, 1982, 93-94; vis. prof. Duke U., Durham, N.C., 1967, Brandeis U., Waltham, Mass., 1968, U. Tel Aviv, 1981, 82, 84, 85. Author: History of Scepticism, 1960, 3d edit., 1979, numerous textbooks including High Road to Pyrrhonism, 1980, Third Force, 1991; editor, pres. bd. Jour. History of Philosophy, 1962—, emeritus, 1997; editor Internat. Archives of the History of Ideas Kluwer, 1960—, The Columbia History of Western Philosophy, 1999; editor, bd. dirs. Brill Series in Intellectual Netherland History; co-author, editor numerous vols. in series; contbr. articles to profl. jours. Recipient fellowship Yale U., 1945-46, Columbia U., 1947-49, Nicholas Murray Butler medal Columbia U., 1977; Fulbright scholar U. Paris, 1952-53, U. Utrecht, The Netherlands, 1957-58; Guggenheim Found. fellow, 1970, Wolfenbütte fellow, Germany, 1987, Folger fellow, 1988; grantee Nat. Endowment for Humanities, 1975. Mem. AAAS, Am. Coun. Learned Societies, Am. Soc. 18th Century Studies, Am. Philos. Assn., Phi Beta Kappa. Home: 15340 Albright St Apt 204 Pacific Palisades CA 90272-2520

PORAD, FRANCINE JOY, poet, painter; b. Seattle, Sept. 3, 1929; d. Morris H. and Gertrude (Volchok) Harvitz; m. Bernard L. Porad, June 12, 1949; children: Laurie, Bruce, Ken, Constance, Marci, Jeffrey. BFA, U. Wash., 1976. Founder, coord. Haiku NW Poets/Readers, Mercer Isle, Wash., 1988—; editor Brussels Sprout, Mercer Isle, 1988-95; co-editor Haiku Northwest Anthology, Seattle, 1996, Red Moon Press, Berryville, Va., 1996; workshop presenter Haiku Can., Toronto and Alymer, Que., Can., 1992, 95, Haiku N.Am., Calif., Toronto, 1993, 95, Haiku N.Am., Oreg., 1997, Haiku Internat., Tokyo, 1997; judge Internat. Haiku Contest New Zealand Poetry Soc., 1995, People's Haiku & Senryu Contest, Canada, 1999, San Francisco Contest for Haiku Poets of North Calif., 1992, Hawaii Edn. Assn., Honolulu, 1995, Haiku Soc. Am., 1997, Internat. People's Haiku and Senryu Contest, Can. Author: Connections, 1986, Pen and Inklings, 1986, After Autumn Rain, 1987, Blues on the Run, 1988, Free of Clouds, 1989, Without Haste, 1989 (Cicada Chapbook award 1990), Hundreds of Wishes, 1990, A Mural of Leaves, 1991, Joy is My Middle Name, 1993, The Patchwork Quilt, 1994 (Haiku Soc. Am. Merit Book 1994), Waterways, 1995 (Haiku Can. Sheet Book series 1995), All Eyes, 1995, Ladies and Jellyspoons, 1996, Extended Wings, 1996, Moon, Moon, 1997, Fog Lifting, 1997, All the Games, 1997, Let's Count The Trees, 1998 (Haiku Can. Sheet Selection 1998), Linked Haiku, 1998. Recipient 1st prize Internat. Tanka competition Poetry Soc. Japan, Tokyo, 1993, Itoen Tea award Haiku Internat., Tokyo, 1996, 98. Mem. Nat. League Am. Penwomen (treas. 1992-94, Owl award 1982, 92, 1st prize state art exhbn. Frye Mus. 1993, 1st pl. Haiku, 1995), Haiku Soc. Am. (pres. 1993, 94, Merit book 1994, judge 1997, Brady Senryu Contest H.M. award 1997), N.W. Watercolor Soc. (treas. 1980-85), Women Painters Wash. (v.p. 1987, bd. 1985-93). Avocations: computer fun, travel. Home: 6944 SE 33d St Mercer Island WA 98040-3324

PORAD, LAURIE JO, jewelry company official; b. Seattle, Dec. 19, 1951; d. Bernard L. and Francine J. (Harvitz) P. BA, U. Wash., 1974; postgrad., Seattle Pacific U., summers 1975-76. Cert. standard tchr., Wash. Substitute tchr. Issaquah (Wash.) Sch. Dist., 1974-77; with data processing dept. Ben Bridge Jeweler, Seattle, 1977-83, auditing mgr., 1983-87, systems mgr., 1987-92, MIS special project mgr., 1992—; mem. adv. bd. computer sci. dept. Highline C.C., Midway, Wash., 1985—, chmn. adv. bd., 1998 ; mem. tech. prep. leadership com., 1993-95. Tchr. religion sch. Temple de Hirsch Sinai, Seattle, 1972-76, 84—, coord. computerized Hebrew learning ctr., 1987-88, coord. of religion sch. city facility, 1988-93, coord. mentor tchr. program, 1993—; tutor Children's Home Soc. Wash., Seattle, 1976-77. Mem. Assn. for Women in Computing (life mem., chmn. chpt. workshop 1985-88, nat. chpts. v.p. 1985-88, nat. pres. 1988-90, nat. chpt. v.p., 1992-93, rep. ind. mems. 1993-97). Avocation: travel. Home: 14616 NE 44th St Apt M2 Bellevue WA 98007-7102 Office: Ben Bridge Jeweler PO Box 1908 Seattle WA 98111-1908

PORCARO, MICHAEL FRANCIS, advertising agency executive; b. N.Y.C., Apr. 3, 1948; s. Girolamo M. and Marianna (DePasquale) P.; m. Bonnie Kerr, Apr. 7, 1972; children: Sabrina, Jon. BA in English, Rockford (Ill.) Coll., 1969. Broadcaster Sta. KFQD-AM; KENI-AM/TV, Anchorage, 1970-71, Sta. KENI-AM/TV, Anchorage, 1972-73; v.p. ops. Cook Inlet Broadcasters, Anchorage, 1973-74; owner Audio Enterprises, Anchorage, 1974-75; asst. Alaska Pub. Broadcasting Commn., Anchorage, 1975-76; exec. dir. Alaska Pub. Broadcasting Commn., 1976-81; chief exec. officer, ptnr. Porcaro Blankenship Advt. Corp., Anchorage, 1981-97; CEO Porcaro Comms., Anchorage, 1997—; cons. Arco Alaska TV sta., Anchorage, 1981; expert witness U.S. Senate Subcom. on Telecom., Washington, 1978; chmn. citizens adv. com. dept. journalism U. Alaska, 1995-96. Chmn. Municipality of Anchorage Urban Design Commn., 1990-93; mem. mayor's transition team Municipality of Anchorage, 1987-88; bd. dirs. Anchorage Glacier Pilots Baseball Club, 1987-88, Anchorage Mus. History and Art, Alaska Ctr. Internat. Bus., 1996, Commonwealth North, 1996, Friends of Alaska Children's Trust, 1996-97, Anchorage Symphony Orch.; chmn. bd. dirs. Brother Francis Shelter for the Homeless, Anchorage, 1993-96; mem. mktg. com. gov.'s transition team, 1995; mem. United Way Anchorage Cabinet, 1996. Recipient Silver Mike award Billboard mag., 1974, Bronze award N.Y. Film Critics, 1981, Best of North award Ad. Fedn. Alaska, 1982—, Addy award, 1985, 91, Grand Addy award 1990, Cable TV Mktg. award 1986; Paul Harris fellow. Mem. Advt. Fedn. Alaska, Anchorage C. of C. (bd. dirs.). Republican. Roman Catholic. Avocations: softball, hockey, travel, fitness. Office: Porcaro Comm 433 W 9th Ave Anchorage AK 99501-3519

PORFILIO, JOHN CARBONE, federal judge; b. Denver, Oct. 14, 1934; s. Edward Alphonso Porfilio and Caroline (Carbone) Moore; m. Joan West, Aug. 1, 1959 (div. 1983); children: Edward Miles, Joseph Arthur, Jeanne Kathrine; m. Theresa Louise Berger, Dec. 28, 1983; 1 stepchild, Katrina Ann Smith. Student, Stanford U., 1952-54; BA, U. Denver, 1956, LLB, 1959. Bar: Colo. 1959, U.S. Supreme Ct. 1965. Asst. atty. gen. State of Colo., Denver, 1962-68, dep. atty. gen., 1968-72, atty. gen., 1972-74; U.S. bankruptcy judge Dist. of Colo., Denver, 1975-82; judge U.S. Dist. Ct. Colo., Denver, 1982-85, U.S. Ct. Appeals (10th cir.), Denver, 1985—; instr. Colo. Law Enforcement Acad., Denver, 1965-70, State Patrol Acad., Denver, 1968-70; guest lectr. U. Denver Coll. Law, 1978. Committeeman Arapahoe County Republican Com., Aurora, Colo., 1968; mgr. Dunbar for Atty. Gen., Denver, 1970. Mem. ABA. Roman Catholic. Office: US Ct Appeals Byron White US Courthouse 1823 Stout St Denver CO 80257-1823

PORPER, MARY, comptroller. V.p., comptroller Suissa Miller, L.A. Fax: (310) 392-2625. Office: Suissa Miller 11601 Wilshire Blvd 16th Fl Los Angeles CA 90025*

PORRERO, HENRY, JR., construction company executive; b. Upland, Calif., Aug. 16, 1945. AA, Chaffey Coll., 1970; BS, Calpoly Pomona U., 1973. Bus. mgr. Guy F. Atkinson Co., South San Francisco, 1973-83; controller Laird Constrn. Co., Inc., R. Cucamonga, Calif., 1983-85; pres., founder PLT Computer Systems, Inc., Upland, Calif., 1986-93; founder, pres. Porrero Constrn. Co., Upland, Calif., 1993—, Porrero Equipment Rental, 1998—. With USN, 1966-69. Mem. Nat. Assn. Home Builders, Bldg. Industry Assn., So. Calif. Contractors Assn., Am. Legion, Friends Upland Library, Calif. Sheriffs Assn. Republican. Avocations: pony league manager, soccer coach. Home: 854 Carson St Upland CA 91784-1828 Office: 902 W 9th St Ste B Upland CA 91786-4542

PORTER, BRIAN STANLEY, state legislator; b. Seattle, May 2, 1938; s. Jack D. and Margaret I. (Tuter) P.; grad. U. Alaska, 1970, Northwestern U. Traffic Inst., 1970-71, FBI Nat. Exec. Inst., 1981; m. Bette K. Schakohl, Apr. 26, 1958; children: Kelle, Kerry, Kory. With Anchorage Police Dept., 1960-87, chief of police, 1980-87; chmn. Alaska Police Stds. Coun., 1978-80; mem. Alaska Ho. of Reps., 1987—, chmn. ho. jud. com. Served with U.S. Army, 1957-58. Home: 3430 Fordham Dr Anchorage AK 99508-4556*

PORTER, DIXIE LEE, insurance executive, consultant; b. Bountiful, Utah, June 7, 1931; d. John Lloyd and Ida May (Robinson) Mathis. BS, U. Calif. at Berkeley, 1956, MBA, 1957. Personnel aide City of Berkeley (Calif.), 1957-59; employment supr. Kaiser Health Found., L.A., 1959-60; personnel analyst UCLA, 1961-63; personnel mgr. Reuben H. Donnelley, Santa Monica, Calif., 1963-64; personnel officer Good Samaritan Hosp., San Jose, Calif., 1965-67; fgn. svc. officer AID, Saigon, Vietnam, 1967-71; gen. agt. Charter Life Ins. Co., L.A., 1972-77, Kennesaw Life Ins. Co., Atlanta, from 1978, Phila. Life Ins. Co., San Francisco, from 1978; now pres. Women's Ins. Enterprises, Ltd.; cons. in field. Co-chairperson Comprehensive Health Planning Commn. Santa Clara County, Calif., 1973-76; bd. dirs. Family Care, 1978-80, Aegis Health Corp., 1977-92, U. Calif. Sch. Bus. Adminstrn., Berkeley, 1974-76; mem. task force on equal access to econ. power U.S. Nat. Women's Agenda, 1977—. Served with USMC, 1950-52. C.L.U. Mem. C.L.U. Soc., U. Calif. Alumni Assn., U. Calif. Sch. Bus. Adminstrn. Alumni Assn., AAUW, Bus. and Profl. Women, Prytanean Alumni, The Animal Soc. Los Gatos/Saratoga (pres. 1987-90), Beta Gamma Sigma, Phi Chi Theta. Republican. Episcopalian.

PORTER, DONNA JEAN, genealogist; b. Monte Vista, Colo., Aug. 20, 1931; d. George W. and Alma R. (Kile) Bishop; m. Earl Edwin Carmack, Nov. 14, 1949 (div. 1955); m. Paul W. Porter, June 4, 1955; children: LeiLonia Virginia, Paul Benjamin, Rebecca Ann. Registered profl. genealogist. Genealogist Denver, 1969—; owner Stagecoach Libr. for Geneal. Rsch., Denver; instr., lectr. in field. Co-author: Welding Lind, An Introduction to Genealogy, 1968; editor Colo. Genealogist mag., 1970-75; contbr. articles to profl. jours. and mags. Asst. libr. Family History Ctr. Libr., LDS Ch., Denver, 1966-76, mem. acquisition com., instr. spl. geneal. instrn. com.; v.p. Colo. chpt. Palatines to Am., Denver, 1985-86, pres., 1986-87, exhibitor's chair Nat. Conf., 1988. Mem. West Palm Beach Geneal. Soc. (founder, pres. 1964-66), Colo. Geneal. Soc. (corr. sec. 1968-69, pres. 1969-70, 2nd v.p., program chairperson 1971-73, seminar chairperson 1974, chairperson, judge Black Sheep contest 1988), Foothills Geneal. Soc. (pres. 1996-98, genealogist 1983-88, ednl. dir. 1992—, staff genealogist Foothills Inquirere mag. 1983—, Genie of Yr. award 1992), Colo. Coun. Geneal. Socs. (v.p. 1986-87, pres. 1987-90, chairperson Colo. State Archives Ednl. Gift Fund 1991—), Nat. Soc. DAR (Peace Pipe chpt. state lineage chairperson 1970-73, registrar 1971-77), Ind. Hist. Soc., Ind. Geneal. Soc., Nat. Geneal. Soc., Internat. Soc. for Brit. Genealogy and Family History, Ohio Geneal. Soc. (life, Colo. chpt., Champaign County chpt., Madison County chpt., Ross County chpt., Monroe County chpt.), Mo. Geneal. Soc. (life), Md. Geneal. Soc. (life), St. Andrew Soc. (life), Inst. Heraldic and Geneal. Studies, Assn. Profl. Genealogists, Assn. for Gravestone Studies, Palatines of Am. (Colo. chpt.), Lower Delmara Geneal. Soc., Baltimore County Geneal. Soc., Shockey Family Meml. Fellowship. Home: 1840 S Wolcott Ct Denver CO 80219-4309

PORTER, EDITH PRISCILLA, elementary school educator; b. Aberdeen, Wash., Mar. 1, 1941; d. Robert M. and June J. (Crown) Crawford; m. Lawrence A. Porter, June 12, 1963; children: Melanie S., Jeffrey L., Michael A. BA in Edn., Ctrl. Wash. State U., 1963; MA in Edn., Lesley Coll., 1991. Cert. tchr. Wash. 1st grade tchr. Hoquiam (Wash.) Sch. Dist., 1962-63; 1st grade tchr. Oak Harbor (Wash.) Sch. Dist., 1963-66, 3d grade tchr., 1967-68, 90—, 2d grade tchr., 1977-86, 88-90, kindergarten tchr., 1986-88. Co-author, narrator Famous Black Women of Song, 1994. Elder Whidbey Presbyn. Ch., Oak Harbor, 1995—. Recipient 2 May Carvell awards Venture Clubs Am. Mem. NEA, AAUW, Wash. Edn. Assn., Oak Harbor Edn. Assn. (rec. sec. 1994—), Delta Kappa Gamma (chpt. pres. 1977-80, state rec. sec. 1981-83, state area liaison 1983-87, state corr. sec. 1985-87). Democrat. Avocations: computers, hiking, camping, crafts, reading. Home: 904 SE 4th Ave Oak Harbor WA 98277-5219

PORTER, JAMES B., hieroglyphic specialist; b. Berkeley, Calif., June 11, 1954; s. Neil Robert and Mary Newcomb (Edwards) P. BA History of Sci., Antioch U., 1979; MA in Anthropology, U. Calif., Berkeley, 1983, PhD in Anthropology, 1989. Cert. adult tchr. Staff artist U. Calif. Berkeley Abaj Takalik Project, Guatemala, 1978-80; illustrator U Calif. Berkeley Archaeol. Rsch. Facility, 1980-88; tchng. asst. anthropology U. Calif., Berkeley, 1984, rsch. asst., 1988-89, instr. anthropology univ. ext. classes, 1989-96; tour lectr. Calif. Alumni Assn. Tours, Berkeley, 1988; instr. calligraphy Oakland (Calif.) Art Supply, 1992; instr. humanities Rose St. Sch., Berkeley, 1993; instr. anthropology Piedmont (Calif.) Adult Sch., 1993-96; instr. anthropology and archaeology Laney Coll., Oakland, Calif., 1995—; presenter, lectr. in field. Author: Exploring Maya Glyphs Vol. I Introduction, 1996; exhbns. include Escultura monumental de la costa sur; Nat. Mus., Guatemala, 1979, Berkeley Community Arts Ctr., 1989, Pro-Arts Gallery, Oakland, 1993; designer 25th anniversary artwork Berkeley Free Clinic, 1995; contbr. articles to numerous profl. jours. and publs. Recipient scholarship Studio Study Ctr., Yakima, Wash., 1972-73; Tinker Travel Fund grantee, Ctr. for Latin Am. Studies, U. Calif., Berkeley, 1983-84, Robert H. Lowie Fund grantee, 1985, Olsen scholar, 1986-89; recipient scholarship Mesoamerican Art Rsch. Inst., San Francisco, 1989. Manichaean. Avocations: handcrafts, collecting, gardening, dancing, travel.

PORTER, JEANNE SMITH, civic worker; b. Hammond, Ind., Feb. 27, 1930; d. Cyril Augustus and Mary (Mabley) Smith; m. William Harry Porter, Apr. 1, 1953; children: Wendy Alice, David William, Mary Elizabeth, Audrey Jeanne. Student, Hanover Coll., 1948-50; BA in Lit. with honors, Ind. U., 1953. Developer, area leader Recovery, Inc., Mont., 1971-82; mem. adv. bd. Mont. House Day Treatment Ctr., Helena, 1980-93; bd. dirs., libr. chmn., Mont. Alliance for Mentally Ill, Helena, 1979—; organizer, planner Columbarium garden, Episcopal Ch., Helena, 1988—; organizer T-House project Mental Health Svcs., 1983-88; developer Social Club-Mentally Ill., 1968—. Recipient Disting. Svc. award Jaycees Helena, 1974, svc. to cmty. award Carroll Coll., 1986, Electrum award Helena Arts Coun., 1988, award for long term svc. Mont. Alliance for Mentally Ill., 1989, Vol. of Yr. award Mental Health Assn. Mont., 1989. Mem. P.E.O. (philanthropic com. chpt. O 1994—). Avocations: painting, drawing, gardening, travel, reading. Home: 1425 Winne Ave Helena MT 59601-5224

PORTER, LAEL FRANCES, communication consultant, educator; b. N.Y.C., July 30, 1932; d. Ronald William Carpenter and Frances Veneranda Fernandez Carpenter; m. Ralph Emmett Porter, June 9, 1954; children: Paula Lee Porter Leggett, Sandra Lynn Livermore. BA in Comm. and Theater, U. Colo., Denver, 1982, MA in Comm. and Theater, 1986. Speech instr. Moultrie, Ga., 1954-55; owner, distributor Lael's Cosmetics & Wigs, Alexandria, Va., 1966-69; sales dept. mgr. May D & F, Denver, 1974-80; instr. comm. U. Colo., Denver, 1987-89, Red Rocks C.C., Lakewood, Colo., 1989-97; mem. coord. com. Nat. Hispana Roundtable, Denver, 1985; mem. diversity coun. and internat. dimensions Red Rocks C.C., Lakewood, Colo., 1994-96. Mem. bd. dirs., sec. Girls Count, Denver, 1991—; bd. dirs. Colo. Statewide Systemic Inc., Denver, 1994-98; mem. adv. bd. Cmty. Liberal Arts & Sci. U. Colo., Denver, 1988-93, 98—; mem. utility consumers adv. bd. State of Colo., Denver, 1989-91; mem. exec. bd. Friends Auroria Libr., 1997—; del. People to People, 1998. Recipient Founding Star award Girls Count, Cert. of Appreciation USAF, 1974, Mack Easton award U. Colo., Denver, 1990. Mem. AAUW (numerous coms. and positions including assn. pub. policy com. 1994-98, state pres. 1992-94, named gift award 1991, br. named gift award 1988, br. continuing svc. award 1994), Latin Am. Rsch. and Svc. Orgn., Nat. Comm. Assn., Leadership Lakewood, Orgn. Study Communication, Lang., and Gender. Episcopalian. Avocations: swimming, reading, internet. Home and Office: 2613 S Wadsworth Cir Lakewood CO 80227-3220

PORTER, MARIE ANN, neonatal nurse, labor and delivery nurse; b. St. Paul, June 29, 1961; d. Theodore J. Morrison and Betty Ann Verdick; 1 child, Angela. ADN, Columbia Basin Coll., 1988. RN, Wash.; cert. neonatal resusitation, Neonatal Resuscitation Program instr., ACLS. Staff RN

Kennewick (Wash.) Gen. Hosp., 1988-95; legal nurse cons. Richland, Wash., 1995—; owner, pres. Porter Med. Cons.; owner, pres. Porter Med. Cons.; legal nurse cons. Clearinghouse. Active March of Dimes. Mem. AWHONN, NAFE, Wash. State Trial Lawyers Assn., Am. Assn. of Legal Nurse Cons., Nat. Assn. Neonatal Nurses, Tri-Cities Coun. Nursing, Richland C. of C.(amb.), King County Nurses Assn.

PORTER, RICHARD KANE, audio engineer, consultant; b. Pitts., Apr. 26, 1953; s. James Albert and Dorothy Louise (Kane) P.; m. Pamela Jean Mongeon, July 6, 1990. Student, U. Pitts., 1971-74; BA, Muskingum Coll., 1977. Field engr. customer svc. divsn. Singer Bus. Machine/TRW, 1979-81; field specialist data comm. Internat. Computers Ltd., 1981-85; applications engr. Burr-Brown Corp., Tucson, 1985-88; sr. rsch. assoc. II optical scis. ctr., lunar & planetary lab. U. Ariz., Tucson, 1988-89; systems design engr. Math. Systems Design, L.A., 1989-90; field engr. Siemens Audio Inc., Hollywood, Calif., 1991-94; chief engr. Waves Sound Recorders, Hollywood, 1993-96; supervising engr. Todd-Ao Studios West, Santa Monica, Calif., 196—; composer, performer RavenWolf Music, Marina Del Rey, Calif., 1991—. Contbr. articles to profl. publs. Mem. Soc. Composers and Lyricists. Avocations: instrumental music composition, electronic music, quantum physics, sailing.

PORTER, VERNA LOUISE, lawyer; b. L.A., May 31, 1941. BA, Calif. State U., 1963; JD, Southwestern U., 1977. Bar: Calif. 1977, U.S. Dist. Ct. (ctrl. dist.) Calif. 1978, U.S. Ct. Appeals (9th cir.) 1978. Ptnr. Eisler & Porter, L.A., 1978-79, mng. ptnr., 1979-86, pvt. practice, 1986—; judge protempore L.A. Mcpl. Ct., 1983—, L.A. Superior Ct., 1989—, Beverly Hills Mcpl. Ct., 1992—; mem. state of Calif. subcom. on landlord tenant law, panelist conv., mem. real property law sect. Calif. State Bar, 1983; speaker on landlord-tenant law to real estate profls., including San Fernando Bd. Realtors; vol. atty. L.A. County Bar Dispute Resolution, mem. client rels. panel; court appointed arbitrator for civil cases, fee arbitrator. Mem. adv. coun. Freddie Mac Vendor, 1995—. Editl. asst., contbr. Apt. Owner Builder; contbr. to Apt. Bus. Outlook, Real Property News, Apt. Age; mem. World Affairs Coun. Mem. ABA, L.A. County Bar Assn. (client-rels. vol. dispute resolution and fee arbitration, 1981—), L.A. Trial Lawyers Assn., Wilshire Bar Assn., Women Lawyers' Assn., Landlord Trial Lawyers Assn. (founding mem., pres.), da Camera Soc. Republican. Office: 2500 Wilshire Blvd Ste 1226 Los Angeles CA 90057-4365

PORTNEY, JOSEPH NATHANIEL, aerospace executive; b. L.A., Aug. 15, 1927; s. Marcus and Sarah (Pilson) P.; m. Ina Mae Leibson, June 20, 1959; children: Philip, Jeffrey. BS, U.S. Naval Acad., 1952. Commd. 2d lt. USAF, 1952, advanced through grades to capt., 1956, resigned, 1960; with Litton Systems, Inc., Woodland Hills, Calif., 1960—; project engr. Litton Aero Products, 1967-68; program mgr. Litton Aero Products Litton Systems, Inc., Woodland Hills, 1968-72, advanced program mgr. Guidance and Control Sys., 1972-85, mgr. advanced programs Guidance and Control Sys., 1985-98, ret., 1998; pres. NAVSENSE cons., 1998—; navigator engr. on 3 historic inertial crossings of the North Pole. Creator solar compass, pilot and navigator calendar. Mem. Inst. of Navigation (v.p. 1988-89, pres. 1989-90), U.S. Naval Acad. Alumni Assn. (trustee 1980-83). Jewish. Avocation: classical piano. Home: 4981 Amigo Ave Tarzana CA 91356-4505 Office: NAVSENSE 4981 Amigo Ave Tarzana CA 91356-4505

PORTUESI, DONNA RAE, psychotherapist, consultant; b. Easton, Pa., Nov. 19, 1949; d. Peter and Alice Lorraine (Hull) Stagnito; m. Sebastian Portuesi, Jr., Nov. 22, 1972 (div. Sept. 1986); 1 child, Christi Noel Buck. AA, No. Seattle C.C., 1987; BA magna cum laude, Western Wash. U., 1989; MSW cum laude, U. Wash., 1992. Registered counselor, Wash. Sec. for Sen. Harry Byrd, Jr. U.S. Senate, Washington, 1970-72; founder Denver chpt. Nat. Found. for Crohn's and Colitis, 1975-79; counselor Mental Health Svcs., Everett, Wash., 1982-84; co-founder Adoption Search and Counseling Cons., Seattle, 1990-96; psychotherapist, cons. ASCC Svcs., Seattle, 1992—; press and speech asst. U.S. Senate, Washington, 1970-72; post adoption cons., Seattle, 1992-96; workshop developer, leader Adoption Search and Counseling, Seattle, 1992-96, exec. dir., 1990-96; ind. search cons. Reunite Adoptees and Birth Parents, 1991—. Contbr. articles to profl. jours. Mem. NASW, Am. Counseling Assn., Am. Adoption Congress. Democrat. Avocations: piano, travel, pets, reading. Home and Office: 12718 12th Ave NW Seattle WA 98177-4322

PORTWAY, PATRICK STEPHEN, telecommunications consulting company executive, telecommunications educator; b. June 18, 1939; s. Christopher Leo and Ceciala (King) P.; m. Malle M. Portway; children by previous marriage: Shawn, Pam, Vicki. BA, U. Cin., 1963; MA, U. Md., 1973; postgrad., Columbia U. Regional ADP coordinator GSA, Washington, 1963-68; mgr. strategic mkt. planning Xerox Corp., 1969-74; mgr. plans and programs System Devel. Corp., 1974-78; fin. indsl. mktg. exec. Satellite Bus. Systems, 1978-80; western regional mgr. Am. Satellite Co., 1980-81; CEO, Applied Bus. Telecomm., Livermore, Calif., 1981-98; prof., lectr. Golden Gate U. Grad. Sch., San Francisco, 1983—; pub. mag. Teleconference, 1981-98; pub. (newspapers) Discovery Bay, Delta Clippers; prodr. Telecon & Ioccon Confs., 1981-98, CEO ET3 Internet Edn. Co., 1998—. Author: (with others) Teleconferencing and Distance Learning, 1992, 3d edit. 1997. Presdl. elector Electoral Coll., Va., 1976; candidate Va. State Legislature from 19th Dist., 1971; mem. Discovery Bay Mcpl. Adv. Coun., 1992-96; mem adv. coun. Discovery Bay Mcpl., 1992-96, chmn. 1992. Served to 1st lt. U.S. Army, 1963-65. Recipient Internat. Rotary award for Higher Edn., Bombay, India, 1999. Mem. Internat. Teleconferencing Assn. (founder, bd. dirs. 1983-88), Nat. Univ. Teleconferencing Networdk (mem. adv. bd., bd. dirs. 1986-89), U.S. Distance Learning Assn. (founder, exec. dir. 1987—) Electronic Funds Transfer Assn. (founder, bd. dirs. 1980), Satellite Profls., Internat. Higher Edn. Acad. of Sci., Global Distance Learning Assn. (founder, exec. dir., COO 1998—), Jaycees charter pres. Chantilly, VA., Disting. Service award Dale City, VA. Club: Commonwealth. Home: 1908 Windward Pt Discovery Bay CA 94514-9510

PORZAK, GLENN E., lawyer; b. Ill., Aug. 22, 1948; m. Judy Lea McGinnis, Dec. 19, 1970; children: Lindsay and Austin. BA with distinction, U. Colo., 1970, JD, 1973. Bar: Colo. 1973. Assoc. Holme Roberts & Owen, Denver, 1973-80, ptnr., 1980-85, mng. ptnr. Boulder office, 1985-95; mng. ptnr. Porzak Browning & Johnson LLP, Boulder, 1996—; bd. dirs. Norwest Bank Boulder, 1993—. Contbr. articles to profl. jours. 1st Lt. U.S. Army, 1970-78. Named Disting. Alumnus U. Colo., 1991. Fellow Explorers Club (bd. dirs. 1995-96, Citation of Merit 1998); mem. Am. Alpine Club (pres. 1988-91), Colo. Mtn. Club (pres. 1983, hon. mem. 1983—), Colo. Outward Bound (trustee 1992—, vice chmn. 1997—), Phi Beta Kappa. Achievements include reaching summit of Mt. Everest, climbing highest peak on all seven continents. Home: 771 7th St Boulder CO 80302-7402 Office: Porzak Browning & Johnson 929 Pearl St Ste 300 Boulder CO 80302-5108

POSEY, JAMES MADISON, commissioner; b. Beaumont, Tex., June 14, 1946; s. Herbert Miles and Albertha P.; m. Cassandra Delois Holt, Nov. 20, 1976; children: Elizabeth, Cathryn, Joseph, David, Patricia. BA, Wichita State U., 1972; JD, U. Kans., 1975. Bar: Kans. 1975. Landman Atlantic Richfield Co., Dallas and Denver, 1975-77; sr. landman Atlantic Richfield Co., Anchorage, Alaska, 1979-82; oil and gas atty. Worldwide Energy Co., Denver, 1977-79; dist. landman Arco Alaska Inc., Anchorage, 1982-84, land mgr., 1984-85, issues advocacy mgr., 1985-91, mgr. fed. govt. rels., 1991-94, mgr. fed. & local govt. rels., 1994-95; mgr. bldg. safety divsn. Municipality of Anchorage, 1996; commr. Alaska Pub. Utilities, 1997—. Pres. Bayshore/Klatt Cmty. Coun., Anchorage, 1987-94; treas. Alaska Dem. Party, 1990-94; bd. dirs. Jr. Achievement of Alaska, Anchorage, 1986-92. Anchorage Youth Ct., 1996-98. Mem. ABA, Am. Assn. Blacks in Energy (bd. dirs. 1994-99), Rotary. Baptist. Avocations: skiing, fishing, reading.

POSTAER, LARRY, advertising executive; b. Chgo.. Grad., U. Mo. Sch. Journalism, 1959. Catalog copywriter Sears; with Stern, Walters & Simmons, Chgo., 1963-64, creative dir., 1964-76; [illegible] creative dir. Needham Harper & Steers, Chgo., 1976-81; exec. v.p., dir. creative svcs. Needham Harper & Steers, L.A., 1981-86; co-founder, exec. v.p., dir. creative svcs. Rubin Postaer, Santa Monica, 1986—. Named Co-leader of Yr. for [illegible] Office: 1333 2d St Santa Monica CA 90401-1100

POSTEL, MITCHELL PAUL, association administrator; b. Chgo., May 27, 1952; s. Bernard and Rosalin P.; B.A., U. Calif.-Berkeley, 1974; M.A., U. Calif.-Santa Barbara, 1977; m. Kristie McCune, Mar. 29, 1981. Devel. officer San Mateo County Hist. Mus., San Mateo, Calif., 1977-81; exec. dir. Fort Point and Army Mus. Assn., San Francisco, 1981-84, San Mateo County Hist. Assn., 1984—; faculty Coll. of San Mateo. ; Author: History of the Burlingame Country Club, 1982, Peninsula Portrait: A Pictorial History of San Mateo County, San Mateo: A Centennial History; Seventy-five Years in San Francisco, History of Rotary Club No. 2. Mem. San Mateo County Historic Resources; bd. dirs. Presidio Hist. Soc. Home: 120 Trinity Ct San Bruno CA 94066-2554 Office: San Mateo County Hist Assn 1700 W Hillside Blvd 777 Hamilton St Redwood City CA 94061*

POSTLEY, HOWARD J., interactive media executive, system architect; b. L.A., Dec. 12, 1963; s. John and Julia Ann (Colyer) P.; m. Jennifer Lee McConnell, Aug. 11, 1990; children: Colin Graeme, Tristan Michael. Lead engr. Postley Software, Inc., Van Nuys, Calif., 1982-84; v.p., tech. On Word, Inc., Santa Monica, Calif., 1984-88, Cloud 9 Interactive, L.A., 1996—; pres. Ideal Point, Inc., L.A., 1988-97; prin. cons. Price Waterhouse LLP, L.A., 1997—; cons. Wells Fargo Bank, San Francisco, 1994-95, Motorola, Schaumburg, Ill., 1993-96, AT&T, N.Y.C., 1994-95; cons., sys. architect IBM, White Plains, N.Y., 1990-93; lectr. U. So. Calif., L.A., 1994-95, UCLA, 1994. Recipient Gold Interactive Video and Multimedia awards, Assn. Visual Communicators, 1991, 93. Mem. IEEE Computer Soc., Assn. Computing Machinery. Avocations: sailing, golf, skiing. Office: Ideal Point Inc 13428 Maxella Ave Ste 236 Marina Del Rey CA 90292

POTASH, STEPHEN JON, public relations executive; b. Houston, Feb. 25, 1945; s. Melvin L. and Petrice (Edelstein) P.; m. Jeremy Warner, Oct. 19, 1969; 1 son, Aaron Warner. BA in Internat. Rels., Pomona Coll., 1967. Account exec. Charles von Loewenfeldt, Inc., San Francisco, 1969-74, v.p., 1974-80; founder, pres. Potash & Co., Pub. Rels., Oakland, Calif., 1980-87; cons. Am. Pres. Lines and APL Ltd., 1979-87, 90—,; exec. dir. Calif. Coun. Internat. Trade, 1970-87; v.p. corp. communications APL Ltd., Oakland, 1987-90; chmn. Potash & Co., Oakland, 1990—. Bd. dirs. Calif. Coun. Internat. Trade, 1987-94, Calif.-Southeast Asia Bus. Coun., 1992—, Temple Sinai, Oakland, 1979-81, mktg. com. United Way Bay Area. Mem. Pub. Rels. Soc. Am., Commonwealth Club of Calif., World Trade Club San Francisco. Office: Potash & Co Pub Rels 1946 Embarcadero Oakland CA 94606-5213

POTICHA, OTTO PAUL, architect; b. Chgo., Sept. 9, 1934; s. Charles W. and Henriette S. (Klemperer) P.; m. Sharon Scott East, Nov. 27, 1958; children: Shelley R., Corbin T. BS in architecture, U. Cin., 1958. Architect various archtl. offices, 1952-56, Perkins and Will, Chgo., 1956-58, Alden B. Dow, Midland, Mich., 1958-59, McCulloch and Bickel, Louisville, 1959-60, Lucas and Jnemijer, The Hague, The Netherlands, 1960-61, Wilmsen, Endicott & Unthank, Eugene, Oreg., 1961-62, pvt. practice, Eugene, Oreg., 1962-67, 93—; ptnr. Unthanl Seder Poticha, Eugene, Oreg., 1968-85, Unthank Poticha Waterbury, Eugene, Oreg., 1986-93; assoc. prof. U. Oreg. Sch. Architecture & Allied Arts, 1964—. Contbr. articles to profl. jours. Mem. Ferry St. Corridor Adv. Com., Eugene, 1994-95, Lane Transot Dist. Eugene Sta. Design Rev. Com., 1995-96, Eugene Design Rev. Com., 1995-96, Spl. Com. Reviewing Eugene, 1995-96, Eugene Goals Com., 1995-96, Mayor's Urban Renewal Adv. Com., 1995-96, Regional Conf./Urban Design Coun. Small Cmtys., 1964—; gov. Friends of the Mus., Eugene, 1964—. Mem. AIA, Nat. Coun. Archtl. Registration Bds., Southwestern Oreg. AIA. Avocations: flying, sailing, painting. Office: Poticha Archs 325 W 4th Ave Eugene OR 97401-2504

POTTENGER, FRANCIS MARION, III, education educator; b. Pasadena, Calif., July 19, 1928; s. Francis Marion Jr. and Elizabeth (Saxour) P.; m. Larma Jean McGuire, Dec. 24, 1950; children: Francis Jeffery, Malcolm Tyler, Mary Yvonne Pottenger Hockaday, Marcus Samuel. BS, Otterbein, 1950; MEd, Xavier U., 1957; MS, N.Mex. Highlands U., 1964; PhD, Claremont Grad. Sch., 1969. Cert. tchr. (life), Calif. Sci. tchr. Goshen (Ohio) Sch. Dist., 1955-56, Bethel (Ohio)-Tate Sch. Dist., 1956-57, Whittier (Calif.) Union High Sch. Dist., 1957-65; chemistry instr. Citrus Community Coll., Glendora, Calif., 1963-65; instr. Claremont (Calif.) Grad. Sch., 1965-66; asst. prof. edn. U. Hawaii, Honolulu, 1966-70, assoc. prof. edn., 1970-74, prof. edn., 1974—, dir. project curriculum rsch. & devel. group, 1983—, chmn. sci. sect. Curriculum Rsch. and Devel. Group (CRDG), 1966-83, 1990—, dir. Foundational Approaches in Sci. Teaching (FAST) CRDG, 1967-83, co-dir. Foundational Approaches in Sci. Teaching (FAST) CRDG, 1983—, dir. Summer Sci. Enrichment (SSE) Project CRDG, 1970-86, project mgr. individualized math. title IV project CRDG, 1972-73, dir. high sch. marine sci. study (HMSS) project CRDG, 1974-87, co-dir. marine social studies (MSS) project CRDG, 1975-76, dir. coastal zone mgmt. (CZM) project CRDG, 1976—, dir. Hawaii nutrition edn. project CRDG, 1979—; dir. fishing in the Pacific project Pacific Circle Consortium (PCC); dir. elem. exploratory computer literacy project CRDG U. Hawaii, Honolulu, 1982-83, co-dir. SCOPE math.-sci. project CRDG, 1982-83, co-dir. secondary exploratory computer literacy project CRDG, 1983-84, dir. YAP-Kosrae health project CRDG, 1983—, dir. HEAT project CRDG, 1984—, dir. politics and econs. of the coastal zone project, dir. developmental approaches in sci. and health (DASH) project CRDG, 1986—, dir. coastal zone atlas project, Hawaii Forestry project PCC, 1986—, co-dir. Hawaii marine sci. project CRDG, 1987-93, dir. Hawaii marine sci. project CRDG, 1994—, dir. The Hokule'a sci. project CRDG, 1987—, dir. high sch. edn. nutrition project CRDG, 1989—, dir. DASH dissemination project PCC, 1990—; Mem. U.S. Japan Coop. Study of Sci. Teaching Practices, NSF. Author: Developmental Approaches in Science and Health (DASH) K, 1988 (awards of excellence Nat. Diffusion Network-NDN and Pacific Region Ednl. Lab.-PREL 1993), DASH 1, 1988 (NDN and PREL awards 1993), DASH 2, 1989 (NDN and PREL awards 1993), DASH 4, 1989 (PREL award 1993), DASH 3, 1990 (NDN and PREL awards 1993), DASH 5, 1991 (PREL award 1993), DASH 6, 1992 (PREL award 1993); co-author: The Local Environment, Foundational Approaches in Science Teaching (FAST) 1, 1970 (awards of excellence NSTA 1983, NDN 1984, PREL 1993), The Flow of Matter and Energy Through the Biosphere, FAST 1, 1972 (awards NSTA 1983, PREL 1993), Change Over Time, FAST 3, 1975 (awards NSTA 1983, PREL 1993), Fundamentals of Chemistry, 1976, The Fluid Earth, 1978 (awards NSTA 1983, PREL 1993), The Living Ocean, 1978 (awards NSTA 1983, PREL 1993); mem. editorial bd. Asian and Pacific Edn. Jour., 1987—; contbr. articles to profl. jours. Fellow NSF, 1960-64; numerous grants including Hawaii State Dept. Edn., 1973, U. Hawaii, 1974, U.S.-Israel Binat. Sci. Found., 1975-77, March of Dimes, 1985, Hawaii Dept. of Planning and Econ. Devel., 1986, Eisenhower, 1990-93, NSF, 1988-93, Hawaii Dept. Bus., Econ. Devel. and Tourism, 1987-91, U.S. Info. Agy., 1996; recipient Citation for Disting. Svc. to Sci. Edn., Nat. Sci. Tchrs. Assn., 1992, Merit award U. Hawaii, 1968, 76, 81, 85, 86, Commendation of Sv. Internat. Edn., Pacific Circle Consortium, 1987, award Excellence UH-COE, 1994. Mem. AAUP, AAAS, Am. Chem. Soc. (mem. Hawaii br.), Hawaii Acad. Sci., Hawaii Nutrition Edn. Assn., Hawaii State Tchrs. Assn., Hawaii Sci. Tchrs. Assn. (bd. dirs. 1973-76, pres. elect 1983-84, pres. 1984-85), NEA, Nat. Assn. of Lab. Schs., Nat. Assn. Rsch. in Sci. Teaching, Nat. Assn. Sci. Tchrs., NAS (presenter High Sch. Biology Today and Tommorrow 1988), Pacific Circle Consortium (commendation 1985), U. Hawaii Profl. Assembly, UH adv. com. on Space Rsch., Middle Childhood Team of Nat. Bd. for Profl. Teaching Standards, Bahl Sci. Ctr. (adv. group 1987—), Phi Delta Kappa. Democrat. Avocations: painting, hiking, fishing. Home: 426 Portlock Rd Honolulu HI 96825-2024 Office: U Hawaii CRDG 1776 University Ave # Uhs2202 Honolulu HI 96822-2463

POTTENGER, MARK MCCLELLAND, computer programmer; b. Tucson, Feb. 9, 1955; s. Henry Farmer and Zipporah Herrick (Pottenger) Dobyns. BA, UCLA, 1976, DDiv (hon.), 1998. Data entry operator Astro Computing, Pelham, N.Y., 1976-77; programmer/analyst LA-CCRS, L.A., 1977-80; programmer/analyst cons. L.A., 1977—; R. Gonzalez Mgmt., L.A., 1980—; rsch. dir. Internat. Soc. for Astrol. Rsch., L.A., 1985-95. Editor: Astrological Research Methods, 1995; co-author: Tables for Aspect Research, 1986; editor The Mutable Dilemma, 1977—; author: (computer programs) CCRS Horoscope program, 1977-92, Frequencies for Aspect Rsch., 1986-92. Recipient Jansky award Aquarius Workshops, L.A., 1989. Mem. Internat. Soc. for Astrol. Rsch., Nat. Coun. for Geocosmic Rsch. [illegible] regencies. Home and Office: 838 5th Ave Los Angeles CA 90005-3522

POTTER, ANNE LOUISE, political scientist; b. Eugene, Oreg., Sept. 1, 1949; d. Daniel Oliver and Betty Louise (Harder) P.; BA, Reed Coll., 1971; MA, Stanford U., 1973, PhD, 1979. Vis. scholar Inst. Torcuato di Tella, Buenos Aires, Argentina, 1974-76; asst. prof. govt. Oberlin (Ohio) Coll., 1978-79; project mgr. Tech. Applications, Inc., Falls Church, Va., 1980-81; project mgr. Daedalean Assos., Inc., Woodbine, Md., 1981-82, Technology Applications, Inc., Falls Church, Va., 1982-84; owner Diversified Svcs. Group, 1984-88; founder, chief exec. officer Oreg. Rsch. and Cons. Group, Portland, Oreg., 1988—. Contbr. rsch. reports for U.S. Govt. and pvt. clients, articles to pub. policy, polit. sci., fin. publs. OAS rsch. fellow, 1976. AAUW dissertation fellow, 1975-76; Woodrow Wilson fellow, 1971-72; NSF grad. fellow, 1972-75. Mem. AAAS, N.Y. Inst. Sci., N.Y. Acad. Scis., Am. Polit. Sci. Assn. (Gabriel A. Almond award), Women's Caucus for Polit. Sci., World Futures Soc., Acad. Polit. Sci., Oreg. Women's Polit. Caucus, Phi Beta Kappa.

POTTER, GEORGE KENNETH, artist; b. Bakersfield, Calif., Feb. 26, 1926; s. Howard Eugene and Edythe (Keast) P.; m. Heliodora Carneiro de Mendonca, July 30, 1954 (div. July 1956); 1 child, Helen Maria Pessoa; m. Ruth Mary Griffen, Aug. 4, 1962 (div. July 1989); children: Katherine Anne Klein, Claire Lorraine, Cynthia Ann. Student, Acad. Art Coll., San Francisco, 1947-48; student Jean Metzinger, Academie Frochot, Paris, 1950-52; student, Istituto Statale dei Belli Arti, Florence, Italy, 1951; BA magna cum laude, San Francisco State U., 1974. tchr. pvt. art classes; lectr. San Francisco State U.; instr. Acad. Art Coll., San Francisco; judge Marin County Ann., 1963, Calif. State Fair Art Exhbn., 1968. One-man shows include U. Calif.-Berkeley, 1959, U. Santa Clara, Calif., 1958, Coll. Marin, Calif.,1958, Rosacrucian Mus., San Jose, Calif., 1959, Brazilian-Am. Inst., Rio de Janeiro, 1955, Frances Young Gallery, Ross, Calif., 1952, John A. Muir Gallery, Modesto, Calif., 1958, Gallerie 8, Paris, 1952, Maxwell Galleries, San Francisco, 1958, 62, Gallery 5, Santa Fe, 1960, Rotunda Gallery, San Francisco, 1949, 52, Marquoit Galleries, San Francisco, 1973, Palo Alto (Calif.) Cultural Ctr., 1977, Art Ovations Gallery, San Francisco, 1980, Kaiser Art Ctr. Gallery, Oakland, Calif., 1980, Marin County Civic Ctr., San Rafael, Calif., 1985, Northwind Gallery, Mill Valley, Calif., 1987, NutTree Gallery, Vacaville, Calif., 1987, numerous others; competitive exhibitions include Am. Watercolor Soc., 1961, 74, 76, 79, Phelan Awards Competition San Francisco Mus. Art, 1949, Calif. Palace Legion Honor, 1958, 60, San Francisco, 1958, 60, 63, 75 (San Francisco Art Festival Exhbn. award 1975), Springville (Utah) Invitational, 1963, Jack London Invitational (award 1958), Oakland, Calif., 1957-65, Calif. State Fair (awards 1958, 72) Sacramento, 1957-58, 61-68, 70-74, 76, 79, Oakland Watercolor Ann., 1948, 52, Mother Lode Ann., Sonora, Calif., 1957-58, 63, 65, Kingsley Ann., E.B. Crocker Art Mus. (award), Sacramento, 1948, 58, 61, 62, 64, 65, Marin Soc. Artists Ann., 1948-49, 58, 61, 65-73, 75, 77, 95-98, Marin County Ann. (awards 1966, 67), 1962, 65-67, 70, 71, 76, Western Assn. Mus. Shows, 1964, 67, 74, No. Calif. Arts Ann., 1961, 68, 88, 97, 98, Fukuoka (Japan) Invitational Exchange Show with Oakland, 1964, Soc. Western Artists Ann. at M.H. De Young Mus., San Francisco, 1956-64, Statewide Watercolor Show (award), Santa Cruz, 1958, Watercolor U.S.A., Springfield, Mo., 1973, 74, Royal Watercolor Soc. Invitational Exhbn., London, 1975, San Francisco Art Festival Award Exhbn., 1975, Palo Alto Cultural Ctr., 1977; executed murals Moore Bus. Forms, Inc., Oakland, Town Hall, Corte Madera, Calif., Macy's of Calif., Sacramento, San Mateo, Stockton, stained glass dome for Hale Meml., Soc. Calif. Pioneers, San Francisco, 1974, Calif. Dept. Motor Vehicles, Oakland, 1975; stained glass and resin triptych U. Calif. at San Francisco Moffitt Hosp., 1976; represented in permanent collections including HUD San Francisco regional office, San Francisco Art Commn.,; art dir. McCann-Erickson Advt. Inc., Rio de Janeiro, 1954-55, Johnson and Lewis Advt., San Francisco, 1957, Michelson Advt., Palo Alto, Calif., 1959-60; contbr. The Calif. Style-Watercolor Artists 1925-55 (McClelland and Last), 1985, The N.Y. Art Rev., 1988, Watercolors Editions Limited of San Francisco, 1990—. Served with USMCR, 1944-46, PTO. Recipient Macy's Art award, San Francisco, 1958, 1st award Watercolor Delta Ann., Antioch, Calif., 1969, 1st award Alameda County Fair, 1974, 79, 85, Santa Rosa 12th Ann., 1975, Best of Show Calif. Arts League Open Exhibition, 1988, 98, best of show Calif. Arts League, 1998, Valley Sculpture Artists 1st Ann. Exhbn. Merit award, 1998, award of excellence Opus Magnum Xi, 1998, Wash. 20th Anniversary Exhbn., 1998, numerous other awards. Mem. West Coast Water Color Soc. (pres. 1968-69), Marin Soc. Artists. Address: 4824 Skyway Dr Fair Oaks CA 95628-6510

POTTER, JAMES VINCENT, educator; b. Walla Walla, Wash., July 17, 1936; s. James Floyd and Dorothy May (Turner) P.; m. Margaret Mae Fogerson, July 4, 1954 (div. Apr. 1970); children: Deborah Ann, David Allan, Rebecca Lynn, Mary Michelle, Jonathon James; m. Paula Maureen Brutsman, Feb. 28, 1986; stepchildren: Carolyn June, Catherine Doreen, Paul Clayton, Connie Lynn. BA in Bibl. Studies, Logos Bible Coll., 1989; MA in Theology, Logos Grad. Sch., 1989; PhD, Vision Christian U., 1990, postgrad., 1991. Diplomat Nat. Assn. Forensic Counselors, Nat. Bd. Addiction Examiners; lic. clin. pastoral counselor; cert. temperament therapist, doctoral addictions counselor, domestic violence counselor, clin. hypnotherapist. Lectr., lit. evang. Seventh-day Adventist Ch., Idaho, 1956-60, Oreg., 1960-61; staff mem. U. of the Nations Family Ministries, Kailua-Kona, Hawaii, 1989; pastor Gospel of Salvation Ministries, 1989-93; dean Coll. Christian Counseling, Vision Christian U., Hilo, Hawaii, 1990-93; pres. Family Care Svcs. Internat., 1990-93; v.p. Vision Christian U., Ramona, Calif., 1991-92; adminstr., clinician Hawaii Family Care Ctrs., Hilo, 1989-93; exec. dir. Agape Family Svcs., Inc., 1995—; vice chmn. Teen Challery of Hawaii, 1991-93, govtl. apptd. mem. Hawaii Area Svc. on Mental Health and Substance Abuse, 1991-94; pres., Profl. Assn. Christian Therapists, 1989-94, Internat. Christian Counselors Assn., 1988—; lectr. western states, 1989—. Author: Soul Care, 1989, Untwisting Twisted Temperaments, 1991, (book and curriculum) Save Our Families; co-author: Family Care Center Manual, 1991, Christian Character Alinement, 1991; (newsletter) Gem-State Surveyor, 1976. Dem. nominee Idaho State Legis., House Rep., Boise, 1976, 78; vice chmn. Idaho Tech. Adv. Coun., Boise, 1976-83; pres. Idaho Assn. Land Surveyors, Boise, 1976-77; chmn. Western Fedn. Profl. Land Surveyors, 12 western states, 1979-80; nat. dir. Am. Congress Surveying Mapping, Washington, 1981-83; gov. Nat. Soc. Profl. Land Surveyors; state del. Hawaii State Rep. Conv., Turtle Bay, 1988. With USN, 1953. Am. Congress Surveying Mapping fellow, Washington, 1980. Mem. Am. Bd. Christian Psychologists, Am. Assn. Family Counselors, Am. Assn. Christian Counselors, Nat. Christian Counselors Assn (bd. dirs. 1988—), Christian Assn. Psychol. Studies. Address: 5826 Old Barn Way Redding CA 96001-4654

POTTER, J(EFFREY) STEWART, property manager; b. Ft. Worth, July 8, 1943; s. Gerald Robert Potter and Marion June (Mustain) Tombler; m. Dianne Eileen Roberb, Dec. 31, 1970 (div. Aug. 1983); 1 child, Christopher Stewart; m. Deborah Ann Blevins, Oct. 20, 1991. AA, San Diego Mesa Coll., 1967. Cert. apartment mgr., apartment property supr., housing adminstr. Sales mgr. Sta. KJLM, La Jolla, Calif., 1964-67; mgr. inflight catering Host Internat., San Diego, 1967-69; lead aircraft refueler Lockheed Co., San Diego, 1969-70; property mgr. Internat. Devel. and Fin Corp., La Jolla, 1970-72; mgr. bus. property BWY Constn. Co., San Diego, 1972-73; mgr. residents Coldwell Banker, San Diego, 1973-74; mgr. Grove Investments, Carlsbad, Calif., 1974-76, Villa Granada, Villa Seville Properties Ltd., Don Cohn, Chula Vista, Calif., 1976-83; gen. mgr. AFL-CIO Bldg. Trades Corp., National City, Calif., 1983—; instr., Cert. Apt. Mgmt. San Diego Apt. Assn. Bd. dirs. San Diego County Apt. Assn., 1995-97, Policy Panel Youth Access to Alcohal, San Diego. Fellow Internat. Platform Assn., Nat. City C. of C., Toastmasters, Founding Families San Diego Hist. Soc., Am. Assn. Retired Persons, San Diego County Apt. Assn. (bd. dirs.), La Jolla Monday Night Club (treas. 1984-89). Roman Catholic. Avocations: golf, tennis, snow skiing. Home: 8240 Caminito Modena La Jolla CA 92037-2921 Office: AFL-CIO Bldg Trades Corp 2323 D Ave National City CA 91950-6730

POTTER, KENNETH ROY, retired minister; b. Pittsfield, Mass., Dec. 29, 1919; s. Roy Wilder and Lillian Bertha (Clark) P.; m. Julia Helen Morris, June 12, 1943; children: Susan Elaine Potter Goslin, Terry LaVerne Potter Rowe, Ronald Duane. Student, Anderson (Ind.) U., 1946-48; BTh, Warner Pacific Coll., 1950. Ordained to ministry Ch. of God (Anderson, Ind.), 1950. Min. music Church of God, Couer d'Alene, Idaho, 1950-51; pastor Ch. of God, Salt Lake City, 1951-52, West Side Ch. of God, Mt. Carmel, Ill., 1952-54, First Ch. of God, Springfield, Oreg., 1954-56; pastor Ch. of God, Loton, Calif., 1957-59, Missoula, Mont., 1959-62, Gary, Ind., 1962-74; pastor

Southlake Ch. of God, Merrillville, Ind., 1974-77, Ch. of God, California City, Calif., 1977-78, Eastgate Ch. of God, Fresno, Calif., 1978-79, Ch. of God, Mt. Ayr, Ind., 1979-81, Southlake First Ch. of God, Merrillville, Ind., 1981-82, Oakview Community Ch. of God, Scio, Oreg., 1984-86, First Ch. of God, Coquille, Oreg., 1986-98; ret., 1998; pres. Laton (Calif.) Ministerial Assn., 1958-59; treas. Missoula (Mont.) Evang. Ministerial Alliance, 1961-62; counselor Gary Contact-Help, Gary-Merrillville, 1973-75; pres. Scio Ministerial Assn., 1985-86, Coquille Ministerial Assn., 1990-98; former mem. Napa, Calif. Art Assn. Crafted model automobile, Fisher Body Craftsman's Guild competition (2nd prize state award, Va.), 1937. Staff sgt. USAF, 1941-45, PTO. Mem. Coquille Valley Art Assn. Home: 845 E 14th St Coquille OR 97423-1405

POTTRUCK, DAVID STEVEN, brokerage house executive; b. 1948. BA, U. Pa., 1970, MBA, 1972. Now pres., CEO U.S. Govt., 1972-74; with Arthur Young & Co., 1974-76, sr. cons.; with Citibank N.Am., 1976-81, v.p.; with Shearson/Am. Express, 1981-84, sr. v.p. consumer mktg. and advt.; with Charles Schwab & Co., San Francisco, 1984—; exec. v.p. mktg., br. adminstr. Charles Schwab and Co., Inc.; pres., CEO The Charles Corp., Charles Schwab & Co.; pres., COO The Charles Schwab Corp. Office: Charles Schwab & Co Inc 101 Montgomery St San Francisco CA 94104*

POTTS, CHARLES AARON, management executive, writer; b. Idaho Falls, Idaho, Aug. 28, 1943; s. Verl S. and Sarah (Gray) P.; m. Judith Samimi, 1977 (div. 1986); 1 child, Emily Karen; m. Ann Weatherill, June 19, 1988; 1 child, Natalie Larise. BA in English, Idaho State U., 1965. Lic. real estate broker, Wash. Owner Palouse Mgmt., Inc., Walla Walla, Wash., 1979—; pres. Walla Walla Rental Properties, 1984-86; dir. Washington Apt. Assocs., 1984-88; founder, dir. Litmus Inc., 1967-77; founding editor COSMEP, Berkeley, Calif., 1968; host poetry radio program Oasis, NPR-KUER, Salt Lake City, 1976-77; N.W. rep. Chinese Computer Communications, Inc., Lansing, Mich., 1988; pres. Tsunami Inc. Author: Blues from Thurston County, 1966, Burning Snake, 1967, The Litmus Papers, 1969, Little Lord Shiva, 1969, Blue Up the Nile, 1972, Waiting in Blood, 1973, The Trancemigracion of Menzu, 1973, The Golden Calf, 1975, Charlie Kiot, 1976, The Opium Must Go Thru, 1976, Valga Krusa, 1977, Rocky Mountain Man, 1978, A Rite to the Body, 1989, The Dictatorship of the Environment, 1991, Loading Las Vegas, 1991, How the South Finally Won the Civil War, 1995, 100 Yrs. In Idaho, 1996; editor: Pacific Northwestern Spiritual Poetry, 1998, The Temple, 1997—; columnist (with Kyushu Gleaner) Japan's Polit. Choices, 1995—. Rep. to exec. com. 5th Congl. Dist., Wash. State Dem. Party, 1993-95. Recipient First Place Novel award Manuscript's Internat., 1991, Disting. Profl. Achievement award Idaho State U., 1994. Mem. Italian Heritage Assn. (ice cream chair 1990, award 1993), Pacific N.W. Booksellers Assn., Walla Walla Area C. of C., Downtown W2 Found., Blue Mountain Arts Alliance, Fukuoka Internat. Forum, Chinese Lang. Computer Soc., Soc. Neurolinguistic Programming (master practitioner), Toastmasters. Avocations: tennis, raspberries. Office: Palouse Mgmt 129 E Alder St Walla Walla WA 99362-1962

POTTS, DAVID BRONSON, educator in history; b. Bridgeport, Conn., Mar. 24, 1938; s. Robert and Alice Mills (Warren) P.; m. Betsy McLean Horton, June 18, 1960; children: Kenneth David, Daniel Horton, Elizabeth Warren. BA, Wesleyan U., Middletown, Conn., 1960; PhD, Harvard U., 1967. From asst. prof. to assoc. prof., assoc. dean of faculty Union Coll., Schenectady, N.Y., 1967-79; dean of the coll. Gettysburg (Pa.) Coll., 1979-86; scholar-in-residence Wesleyan U., Middletown, Conn., 1986-94; acad. v.p. U. Puget Sound, Tacoma, Wash., 1994-96; prof. history U. Puget Sound, Tacoma, 1994—; trustee Union Coll., Schenectady, N.Y., 1974-76; mem. editl. bd. History of Higher Edn. Ann., 1981—. Author: (books) Baptist Colleges, 1988, Wesleyan University, 1992 (Babbidge award 1993). Mem. Phi Beta Kappa. Office: U Puget Sound Hist Dept 1500 N Warner Tacoma WA 98416

POTWIN, JUANITA R., marketing professional, dental hygienist; b. St. Albans, Vt., Oct. 15, 1957; d. Gerald Albert Potwin and Beatrice Julia (Blake) Lamica. Cert. chemistry, N.H. Vo-Tech., Claremont, 1982; AS in Dental Assisting, Champlain Coll., 1984; AS in Dental Hygiene, N.H. Tech. Inst., 1986. Registered dental hygienist ADA. Freelance dental hygienist N.H., 1986—; New Eng. sales dir. Oxyfresh, USA, Spokane, Wash., 1993; exec. sales dir. Oxyfresh, USA, Spokane, 1994-95; N.E. sales dir. Life Sci. Products, St. George, Utah, 1995-96; Ruby sales dir. Life Sci. Products, St. George, 1996-97; exec. mktg. specialist Design 21, Santa Barbara, Calif., 1997—. Mem., supporter Am. Humane Assn., Wold Wildlife Fund, The Wilderness Soc. Scholar Dr. David S. Faigel Meml. Found., 1982. Mem. NAFE, VFW, Am. Legion Aux. Avocations: tennis, travel, golf, photography. Home: 4626 Sierra Madre Rd Santa Barbara CA 93110-1321 Office: Life Sci Products 321 N Mall Dr Saint George UT 84790-7302 Address: PO Box 61411 Santa Barbara CA 93160-1411

POULTON, CRAIG KIDD, insurance broker, consultant; b. Salt Lake City, Nov. 22, 1951; s. LaMarr Williams and Marcella (Kidd) P.; m. Diane Adamson, Dec. 28, 1973; children: Brysen, Blake, Marissa, Ashley. BA, U. Utah, 1977. Cert. ins. counselor. V.p. Poulton Insurance Agy., Inc., Salt Lake City, 1977-84, pres., 1984-90; broker Internat. Lines and Comml. Lines, Salt Lake City, 1977—; pres., chmn. Instar Corp., 1988-90, Poulton Assocs., Inc., Salt Lake City, 1990—. Mem. Rep. Presdl. Task Force, 1983—. Paul Harris fellow, 1984. Mem. Profl. Ins. Agts. Am., Ind. Ins. Agts. Assn., Rotary (bd. dirs. Holladay 1985, sec. 1987, v.p. 1987, pres. 1988). Mem. LDS Ch. Avocations: skiing, swimming, bicycling. Office: Poulton Assocs Inc 3785 S 700 E Fl 2D Salt Lake City UT 84106-1183

POUNDSTONE, WILLIAM NICHOLAS, JR., artist, author; b. Morgantown, W.Va., Sept. 29, 1955; s. William Nicholas and Doris Mae (Jamison) P. Critic N.Y. Times, N.Y.C., 1992—, The Economist, London, 1996—. Author: Big Secrets, 1983, The Recursive Universe, 1984, Labyrinths of Reason, 1988, Prisoner's Dilemma, 1992; co-producer Dave Bell Assocs., L.A., 1993-94, producer, 1994-95. Mem. PEN, Writer's Guild.

POURFARZANEH, MOHAMMAD-TAGHI (MATT), biotechnology; b. Ghazvin, Iran, Jan. 1, 1950; arrived in U.S., 1983; s. Mohammad and Zahra (karimi) P.; m. Rouhangiz Dekhi Nargessi, Jul. 21, 1971; children: Mohamad. BSC, Pars Coll., Tehran, Iran, 1976; PhD, Univ. London, 1980. Sr. biochemist St. Bartholomew's Hosp., London, 1980-83; staff scientist Internat. Diagnostic Tech., Santa Clara, Calif., 1983-85; mgr. immunochemistry Triton Biosciences Inc., Alameda, Calif., 1985-89; dir. applied tech. Microgenics Corp., Concord, Calif., 1989-93; chmn., founder Cortex Biochem Inc., San Leandro, Calif., 1993—. Contbr. numerous articles to profl. jours.; inventor and patentee in field. Mem. Harbor Bay Club. Muslem. Office: Cortex Biochem Inc 1933 Davis St San Leandro CA 94577-1260

POWELL, CHARLES WILLIAM, coach, former minister; b. Gilman, Colo., May 9, 1937; s. Harold Hayes and Rosella Charlotte (Collins) B.; m. Myrna Beth, June 11, 1995. BS Colo. State U., 1970; postgrad., Western Sem., 1982; grad., Coach U., 1998. Ordained to ministry Evang. Ch. Alliance, 1976; cert. sec. tchr., Wash. Team leader The Navigators, Colorado Springs, 1966-72; sr. pastor Albion (Wash.) Community Ch., 1972-76; hon. v.p. Am. Missionary Fellowship Portland, Oreg., 1979-81; itinerant preacher Oreg., 1976—; personal and bus. coach Port of Portland Security Dept., 1997—; field rep. Internat. Messengers, 1989-91. Contbr. articles to religious jours.; publisher Sunday Bits and Pieces, In Business for You. Res. policeman Whitman County Sheriff's Office, Colfax, Wash., 1975-76. With USN, 1956-62. Mem. Internat. Listening Assn., Internat. Coach Fedn., Am. Legion, U.S. Naval Inst., Gresham Area C. of C., Mensa, Camelopard Soc., Bus. Network Internat., Toastmasters, Shepherd Cmty. Ch. (bd. dirs.). Avocations: reading, computer science. Home and Office: 17939 SE Haig Dr Portland OR 97236-1319

POWELL, JAMES LAWRENCE, museum director; b. Berea, Ky., July 17, 1936; s. Robert Lain and Lizena (Davis) P.; m. Joan Hartmann; children: Marla, Dirk, Joanna. AB, Berea Coll., 1958; PhD, MIT, 1962; DSc (hon.), Oberlin Coll., 1983; LHD (hon.), Tohoku Gakuin U., 1986; DSc (hon.), Beaver Coll., 1992. Mem. faculty Oberlin Coll., Ohio, 1962-83, also prof. geology, asso. dean, 1973-75, v.p., provost, 1976-83; pres. Franklin and Marshall Coll., Lancaster, Pa., 1983-88, Reed Coll., Portland, Oreg., 1988-91; pres., chief exec. officer The Franklin Inst., Phila., 1991-94; pres., dir. Los Angeles County Mus. Natural History, L.A., 1994—; mem. Nat. Sci. Bd., 1986—. Author: Strontium Isotope Geology, 1972, Pathways to Leadership: Achieving and Sustaining Success: A Guide for Nonprofit Executives, 1995. Fellow Geol. Soc. Am. Home: 150 S Muirfield Rd Los Angeles CA 90004-3729 Office: LA County Mus Nat Hist 900 Exposition Blvd Los Angeles CA 90007-4057*

POWELL, LANE ALAN, editor; b. Alamogordo, N.Mex., Mar. 8, 1955; s. Cecil Lane Holmes and Janet Marie (LeRoux) Powell; m. Mari Catherine Priemesberger, July 15, 1989; children: Lane Cody, Sarah Blais, Clementine Rose. BS in Journalism, U. Fla., 1984. Info. specialist Engring. Coll. U. Fla., Gainesville, 1983-85; editor Windsor Publs., L.A., 1985-89; coord. publs. East Bay Regional Park Dist., Oakland, Calif., 1989—, firefighter, 1997—. Editor: Jacksonville and Florida's First Coast, 1989. Named Outstanding Hard Cover Pub. of Yr. Am. Chambers of Commerce Execs., 1989; recipient Best Spl. Facility Brochure in Calif. Calif. Park and Recreation Soc., 1990, Best Brochure Calif. Park and Recreation Soc., 1995. Home: 1882 N 5th St Concord CA 94519-2628 Office: E Bay Regional Park Dist 2950 Peralta Oaks Ct Oakland CA 94605-5320

POWELL, LEE GILBERT, JR., petroleum company executive; b. Portland, Oreg., Apr. 28, 1939; s. Lee Gilbert and Eva Irene (Quesnell) P.; m. Sondra Kay Powell, June 15, 1993; children: Jason Lee, Shawn, Shane, Shannon Lee. BSBA, Oreg. State U., 1961. Driver Champion Oil Co., Portland, 1959-61; with sales dept. Powell Distbg. Co., Portland, 1962-78, pres., 1978—; pres. Oreg. Oil Marketers, 1976. Chmn., Vancouver Aviation Adv. Com., 1971—. With USANG, 1961-67. Mem. Oreg. Petroleum Marketers Assn., Anturium Soc. Republican. Presbyterian. Avocations: private pilot, gardening, tennis, hunting waterfowl. Home: PO Box 2544 Vancouver WA 98668-2544

POWELL, STEPHANIE, visual effects director, supervisor; b. Dayton, Ohio, Sept. 27, 1946; d. Harley Franklin and Evelyn Luella Pence. Pres., CEO Video Assist Systems, Inc., North Hollywood, Calif., 1979—, Out of the Blue Visual Effects, 1989. Cons.: (motion pictures) Jurassic Park, 1993, Flintstones, 1994, Waterworld, 1995, Get Shorty, 1995; visual effects supr.: Blown Away, 1994, My Brother's Keeper, 1994, Powder, 1995, Mrs. Santa Claus, 1996, Devil's Advocate, 1997, various commls.; co-visual effects supr. Quantum Leap (TV); developer using 3/4-inch videotape for broadcast. Mem. Acad. TV Arts and Scis., Acad. Magical Arts and Scis. Avocations: horse showing, photography, computer graphics. Office: Video Assist Sys Inc 11030 Weddington St North Hollywood CA 91601-3212

POWER, DENNIS MICHAEL, museum director; b. Pasadena, Calif., Feb. 18, 1941; s. John Dennis and Ruth Augusta (Mott) P.; m. Kristine Moneva Fisher, Feb. 14, 1965 (div. Aug. 1984); children: Michael Lawrence, Matthew David; m. Leslie Gabrielle Baldwin, July 6, 1985; 1 stepchild, Katherine G. Petrosky. BA, Occidental Coll., 1962, MA, 1964; PhD, U. Kans., 1967. Asst. curator ornithology Royal Ont. Mus., Toronto, Can., assoc. curator, 1971-72; asst. prof. zoology U. Toronto, 1967-72; exec. dir. Santa Barbara (Calif.) Mus. Natural History, 1972-94, Oakland Mus. of Calif., 1994—; bd. dirs. Coll. Preparatory Sch., Oakland, 1997—; biol. rschr.; cons. ecology. Editor: The California Islands: Proceedings of a Multidisciplinary Symposium, 1980, Current Ornithology, vol. 6, 1989, vol. 7, 1990, vol. 8, 1991, vol. 9, 1992, vol. 10, 1993, vol. 11, 1993, vol. 12, 1995; contbr. articles to sci. jours. Bd. dirs. Univ. Club Santa Barbara, 1989-92, v.p., 1991-92; bd. dirs. Santa Barbara Chamber Orch., 1990-94, v.p., 1991-94; mem. adv. coun. Santa Cruz Island Found., 1989—; mem. discipline adv. com. for museology Coun. for Internat. Exch. of Scholars, 1991-95. NSF fellow U. Kans., 1967; NRC grantee, 1968-72, 74-78. Fellow Am. Ornithologists Union (life, sec. 1981-83, v.p. 1988-89), Am. Assn. Mus. (mem. coun. 1980-83), Calif. Acad. Scis.; mem. AAAS, Cooper Ornithol. Soc. (bd. dirs. 1976-79, pres. 1978-81, hon. mem. 1993), Calif. Assn. Mus. (bd. dirs. 1981-92, chmn. 1987-89), Western Mus. Conf. (bd. dirs. 1977-83, pres. 1981-83), Am. Soc. Naturalists, Assn. Sci. Mus. Dirs., Ecol. Soc., Am. Soc. Study of Evolution, Soc. Systematic Zoology, Bohemian Club, Sigma Xi. Office: Oakland Mus of Calif 1000 Oak St Oakland CA 94607-4820

POWERS, EDWIN MALVIN, consulting engineer; b. Denver, July 20, 1915; s. Emmett and Bertha Malvina (Guido) P.; m. Dorothy Lavane Debler, Jan. 18, 1941; children: Dennis M., Kenneth E., James M., Steven R. BS in Chem. Engring., U. Denver, 1939, MS, 1940. Registered profl. engr., N.J., Colo., Fall Out Analysts Engr., U.S. Fed. Emergency Mgmt. Agency, 1975-87. Prodn. supr. Nat. Aniline Div., Buffalo, 1940-45; engr., project supr. Merck & Co., Rahway, N.J., 1945-67, chief project coordinator, 1967-72, purchasing engr., 1972-82; ret., 1982; cons. engr., Conifer, Colo., 1982—. Capt. Air Raid Wardens, River dist., Buffalo, 1942-45. Mem., del. Conifer Home Owners Assns. Protect Our Single Homes, 1984-86, Regional Environ. Assn. Concerned Home Owners, 1985-86, task force area devel. Hwy. 285/ Conifer Area County Planning Bd. Community, 1986-88. Mem. NSPE, Am. Chem. Soc. (emeritus), Am. Inst. Chem. Engrs. (emeritus, treas. N.J. 1960, exec. com. 1961-63), Nat. Soc. Profl. Engrs. Home and Office: 26106 Amy Cir Conifer CO 80433-6102

POWERS, J. D., III, marketing executive. Pres. J.D. Powers & Assocs., Calif.; chmn. J.D. Powers & Assocs. Office: J D Powers & Assocs 30401 Agoura Rd Agoura Hills CA 91301-2084*

POWERS, RAGAN LEWIS, lawyer; b. Oakland, Calif., May 10, 1955; s. Lewis Ragan and Beverly (Neel) P.; m. Margaret Berliner, Aug. 22, 1981; children: Catherine, Andrew, Sarah. BA in Econs. and Polit. Sci., U. Calif., Davis, 1978; JD, U. Wash., 1981. Bar: Wash. 1981. Assoc. Helsell Fetterman, LLP, Seattle, 1981-88, ptnr., 1989-97; ptnr. Davis Wright Tremaine LLP, Seattle, 1997—. Vice chair Equal Justice Coalition, Wash., 1994-96, chair, 1996-98; mem. bd. trustees Law Fund, Wash., 1997-98; mem. steering com. Puget Sound Minority Leadership, Seattle, 1989-93. Recipient Pres.'s award Wash. State Bar Assn. Fellow Am. Bar Found.; mem. ABA (chair Commn. on IOLTA 1996-97), Am. Bankrupcty Inst., King County Bar Assn., Fed. Bar Assn. Office: Davis Wright Tremaine LLP 2600 Century Sq 1501 4th Ave Ste 2600 Seattle WA 98101-1688

POWERS, REBECCA ELIZABETH, educator, writer; b. Bremerton, Wash., June 25, 1947; d. Norman Francis and Joan Marie (Tatham) P.; m. Lauren Charles Bathurst, Feb. 11, 1967 (div. Dec. 1990); children: Tobias, Adrian, Suzanne, Nate. AA, Olympic Coll., 1967; BA in Sociology and Anthropology, Western Wash. U., 1970; MFA in Creative Writing, Ea. Wash. U., 1988. Registrar Whatcom Mus. History and Art, Bellingham, Wash., 1971-73; rsch. and devel. assoc. Joy Martin Assocs., Davenport, Iowa, 1975-77; dir. elderly svcs. Project N.O.W., Rock Island, Ill., 1977-78; social svcs. planner Ea. Wash. Area Agy. on Aging, Spokane, Wash., 1980-81; free-lance grant writer Spokane, Wash., 1983-85; tchr. parapsychology Spokane Community Coll., 1983-84; instr. English, creative writing Ea. Wash. U., Cheney, 1985-88; instr. composition and lit. North Idaho Coll., Coeur d' Alene, 1987-88; rsch. and devel. assoc. for exec. devel. intensive program John Scherer and Assocs., Spokane, 1990; dir. devel., radio producer KPBX Spokane Pub. Radio, 1991-92; exec. dir. Big Bend C.C. Found., Moses Lake, Wash., 1992—; judge creative writing Cen. Valley Schs., Spokane, 1988-89, Coeur d' Alene Poets, 1988. Vestrywoman Ch. of Holy Spirit, Veradale, 1987-89; chmn. evangelism and faith devel. dept. Episcopal Diocese of Spokane, 1990—; bd. dirs. United Way, Moses Lake, Spokane Diocesan Sch. Ministry. Democrat. Avocations: writing, skiing, reading, counseling.

POWERS, RUNA SKÖTTE, artist; b. Anderstorp, Sweden, Oct. 29, 1940; d. Gösta Nils Folke and Kristina Torborg (Andersson) S.; m. David Britton Powers, Mar. 13, 1965; children: Kristina, Davis. Student, Art Inst. So. Calif., 1976-83; BMA, U. So. Calif., 1986. Exhbns. include Newport Festival Arts, Newport Beach, 1980, Costa Mesa Art League, 1980, Orange County Fair, Costa Mesa, 1980, Art Inst. So. Calif., Laguna Beach, 1976-83, Studio Sem Ghelardini, Pietrasanta, Italy, 1983, Design House, Laguna, 1984, Vorpal Gallery, 1983-84, Laguna Beach Mus. Art, 1984, Gallery Sokolov, Laguna Beach, 1985-93, Margareta Sjödin Gallery, Malibu, 1988, Ana Izax Gallery, Beverly Hills, 1988, Envision Art, 1991, Gallery Slottet, Hörle, Sweden, 1990-92, J.F. Kennedy Performing Arts Ctr., Washington, 1991, Internat. Art Expn., L.A., 1985, N.Y., 1986-87, San Bernardino County Mus., 1993. Founder Found. Hörle Manor House, Värnamo, Sweden, 1987—. Avocations: music, reading, cooking, swimming. Home: 1831 Ocean Way Laguna Beach CA 92651-3235

POWERS, STEPHEN, educational researcher, consultant; b. Bakersfield, Calif., June 10, 1936; s. Robert Boyd and Mildred (Irwin) P.; m. Gail Marguerite Allen, Dec. 28, 1968; children: Rick, Joseph, Rebecca. BS in Edn., No. Ariz. U., 1959; MA, U. Ariz., Tucson, 1970, MEd, 1972, PhD, 1978. Cert. tchr., Calif.; cert. tchr., adminstr., jr. coll. tchr., Ariz. Policeman, City of Bakersfield, 1967-69; tchr. Marana (Ariz.) Pub. Schs., 1969-72; dir. Am. Sch. Belo Horizonte, Brazil, 1972-73; tchr. Nogales (Ariz.) Pub. Schs., 1973-75; rsch. specialist Tucson Unified Sch. Dist., 1975-94; prof. Walden U., U. Ariz., 1981, U. Phoenix, 1990; founder Creative Rsch. Assocs., 1991—, now pres.; bd. dirs. Manchester Coll., Oxford U.; internat. evaluator USAID, 1991. Contbr. articles to profl. jours. Nat. Inst. Edn. grantee, 1980. Mem. Am. Ednl. Rsch. Assn., Royal Statis. Soc. (U.K. chpt.), Am. Statis. Assn. Bahai. Office: 2030 E Broadway Blvd Ste 221 Tucson AZ 85719-5909

POYNTER, DAN, publishing executive, writer; b. N.Y.C., Sept. 17, 1938; s. William Frank and Josephine E. (Thompson) P. BA, Calif. State U., Chico, 1960; postgrad., San Francisco Law Sch., 1961-63. federally lic. master parachute rigger; lic. pilot. Pub., prin. Para Pub., Santa Barbara, Calif., 1969—; listed as expert witness Nat. Forensic Ctr., Tech. Adv. Service for Attys., Consultants and Consulting Organizations Directory, Lawyer's Guide to Legal Consultants, Expert Witnesses, Services, Books and Products. Author: The Parachute Manual, Parachuting, The Skydiver's Handbook, Parachuting Manual with Log, Hang Gliding, Manned Kiting, The Self-Publishing Manual, How to Write, Print & Sell Your Own Book, Publishing Short Run Books, Business Letters For Publishers, Computer Selection Guide, Word Processing and Information Processing, Publishing Forms, Parachuting Manual for Square/Piggyback Equipment, Frisbee Players' Handbook, Toobee Players' Handbook, 65 others, some translated in fgn. languages; past editor news mag. Spotter; monthly columnist Parachute mag., 1963—; contbr. over 500 tech. and popular articles and photographs to mags; patentee parachute pack, POP TOP. Recipient numerous certs. of appreciation for directing parachuting competitions. Mem. U.S. Parachute Assn. (life, chmn. bd., exec. com. 12 yrs., nat. and internat. del., achievement award, 1981, cert. 35 yr. mem., awarded Gold Parachute Wings, 1972), Parachute Industry Assn. (pres. 1985, 86), AIAA, Soc. Automotive Engrs., Nat. Aeronautic Assn., Aviation Space Writers Assn. (internat. conf. mem. 1978, 79, 82), Calistoga Skydivers (past sec.), No. Calif. Parachute Coun. (past sec.), U.S. Hang Gliding Assn. (life, past fir., del.), Internat. Assn. Ind. Pubs. (past bd. dirs., pres. Santa Barbara chpt. 1979-82), Assn. Am. Pubs., Pub. Mktg. Assn. (bd. dirs., v.p.), Book Pubs. So. Calif., Am. Booksellers Assn., Commn. Internat. de Vol Libre of Fedn. Aero. Internat. in Paris (U.S. del., past pres., lifetime Pres. d'Honneur award 1979, recipient Paul Tissander diploma, 1984), Nat. Spkrs. Assn. Home: RR 1 Santa Barbara CA 93117-9700 Office: Para Pub PO Box 8206 Santa Barbara CA 93118-8206

PRACHAR, THOMAS PATRICK, dancer, mechanic; b. Alameda, Calif., Aug. 20, 1952; s. Jefferson Cornelious and Mary Hazel (Collins) P. Student, U. Calif., Berkeley, 1971-74. Dancer Oakland (Calif.) Ballet Co., 1974—; heavy equipment mechanic Calif. Dept. Transportation, San Leandro, 1982—; mem. Caltrans Heavy Equipment Mechanic Joint Apprenticeship Com. Dancer, soloist numerous local prodns. including Nutcracker, 1974—; actor: (plays) Modrin Theater, Dinner Date, Somebunny Special. Scholar Calif. Alumni Assn. Mem. U.S. Apprenticeship Assn., Nat. Inst. for Automotive Service Excellence (cert.). Democrat. Avocations: reading, running, skiing. Home: 1660 Matheson Rd Concord CA 94521-2133 Office: Calif Dept Transp 1993 Marina Blvd San Leandro CA 94577-3246

PRACKO, BERNARD FRANCIS, II, artist, business owner; b. Ada, Okla., Jan. 17, 1945; m. Patricia Fairmont Butterfield Stone, 1967 (div. 1971); 1 child, Genevieve Suydam Stone Davis; m. Elaine Jean Nisky, 1980 (div. 1981); m. Renee Ericson Whitman, 1982 (div. 1986). AA, N.Mex. Mil. Inst., 1965; BA, U. Colo., 1970; postgrad., Ariz. State U., 1991. With Fayber Assocs., Inc., Boulder, Colo., 1974—; ednl. rschr. Tomatis Ctr., Phoenix, 1991—. One-man shows include Grand Champions, Aspen, 1992, Scottsdale Culinary Inst., 1992; exhibited in group shows at Sena Galleries, Santa Fe, 1991, Sacred Spaces, L.I., N.Y., 1991, Cultural Exch. Gallery, Scottsdale, 1992, Nelson Fine Art Mus., Tempe, Ariz., 1992, Aspen Art Mus., 1992, Sun Cities Art Mus., Sun City, ARiz., 1992, San Diego Art Inst., 1993; represented in permanent collections Scottsdale Culinary Inst., Am. West Airlines, Tempe, U. Colo., Boulder, Ariz. State U., Tempe, Sun Cities Art Mus., Sun City, Amnesty Internat., Washington. Peace awareness trainer Egypt, Israel, South Africa, Kenya, Nigeria, 1986; vol., artist coord. Amnesty Internat., U.S.A. calendar, 1990. Address: 460 S Marion Pkwy # 855 Denver CO 80209-2544 Office: Fayber Assocs Inc 460 S Marion Pkwy # 855 Denver CO 80209-2544

PRADA, GLORIA INES, mathematics and Spanish language educator; b. San Vicente de Chucuri, Colombia, Dec. 2, 1954; came to U.S., 1985; d. Roberto Gomez and Maria Celina (Serrano) Duran; m. Luis Eduardo Prada, June 19, 1975; children: Luis Ricardo, Nicholas. BS in Math., U. Indsl., Santander, Colombia, 1978. Tchr. h.s. math. Santander Sch. Dist., Bucaramanga, 1973-84; tchr. mid. sch. math., mentor tchr. Hayward (Calif.) Unified Sch. Dist., 1989—; pres. Bilingual Adv. Com., Hayward, 1986-89; mem. Gate Task Force, Hayward, 1990-93, Spanish for Educators Alameda County Office Edn., 1995—. Author: Prada's Spanish Course, 1992, Family Math, 1992, Stations on Probabilities, 1994, (math. replacement unit) Success, 1994. Office: Hayward Unified Dist Winton 119 Winton Ave Hayward CA 94544-1413

PRATKANIS, ANTHONY RICHARD, social psychologist, educator; b. Portsmouth, Va., Apr. 2, 1957; s. Tony R. and Rosemarie (Gray) P. BS summa cum laude, Ea. Mennonite Coll., 1979; MA, Ohio State U., 1981, PhD, 1984. Rsch. assoc. Ohio State U., Columbus, 1981-83; postdoctoral fellow Carnegie-Mellon U., Pitts., 1983-84; asst. prof. indsl. adminstrn. and psychology, U. Calif., Santa Cruz, 1984-87, asst. prof., then assoc. prof. psychology, 1987-95, prof., 1995—; expert legal witness; reviewer acad. jours. Author: (with E. Aronson) The Age of Propaganda, 1992; contbr. profl. papers, book chpts. J.B. Smith scholar Eastern Mennonite Coll., Harristonburg, Va., 1975-79; editor (with A. Greenwald and S. Breckler): Attitude Structure and Function. Fellow APA, Soc. for Personality and Social Psychology; mem. Midwestern Psychol. Assn., Soc. Exptl. Social Psychology. Democrat. Avocations: reading; personal computers. Research includes attitudes, persuasion, the self, consumer behavior. Home: 166 Montclair Dr Santa Cruz CA 95060-1025 Office: U Calif Bd Psychology Santa Cruz CA 95064

PRATT, ALAN JOHN, business and marketing consultant; b. Eng., July 21, 1927; s. Alan Reginald and Ellen Gwendoline (Roff) P.; m. Asako Tsuneyoshi, May 1, 1961. BA in Engring., Watford Coll., 1948; MBA, Calif. Western U., 1974, PhD, DBA, 1976. Surveyor, Air Registration Bd., Gt. Britain and Hong Kong, 1957-63; pres. Eutectic of Japan, Tokyo, 1963-66; group v.p. Alexander Industries, 1966-69; mgr. Far East, Digital Equipment Corp., Japan, 1969-72; dir. for Japan, Gen. Instrument Corp., 1972-75; exec. v.p. Klingelnberg Japan Ltd., Tokyo, 1975-79; mng. ptnr. Alan J. Pratt and Assocs., Kailua-Kona, Hawaii, 1979—; v.p. Kosei, Inc., 1979—; pres. Astra-Pacific Internat. Inc., Kailua-Kona; assoc. sr. cons. Adams-Boston Cons. Co., Tokyo, 1964-68; guest lectr. Japan-Am. Inst. Mgmt. Sci., Honolulu. pres. Kona Coffee Festival, 1984-86, Crime Stoppers West Hawaii, 1984-85, 92—, founder pres. 1964-86, 1992—; bd. dirs. Crime Stoppers Internat., chmn. conf., 1994, pres. 1997. Mem. Am. Mgmt. Assn., Inst. Quality Engrs., Soc. Mfg. Engrs., Am. C. of C. in Japan (chmn. programs com. 1972-74), Royal Aero. Soc. Gt. Britain, Brit. Inst. Mgmt., Brit. Mgmt. Assn., Kona Coast C. of C. (chmn. programs and communications com. 1980, pres. 1981-82, chmn. Japan-Asia-Australia tourist and trade relations com. 1983-86), C. of C. of Hawaii (dir.). Roman Catholic. Clubs: American, Vivi Athletic (Tokyo), Rotary. Home and Office: PO Box 5186 Kailua Kona HI 96745-5186

PRATT, BRETT LEROY, organist; b. Modesto, Calif., June 4, 1962; s. Paul Albert and Gladys Rose (Giddens) P. AA, Modesto Jr. Coll., 1984. Sales rep. Yamaha, Internat., Buena Park, Calif., 1983, 84, Baldwin Sheely Keyboards, Redding, Calif., 1980, Sherman Clay Music Co., Modesto, 1984-86; organist Unity Ch. Modesto, Modesto, 1981-91, Escalon (Calif.) Presbyn.

Ch., 1992—. Composer: There Must Be A Reason, 1986. Dean Am. Guild of Organists, 1994-96. Mem. Music Tchrs. Assn. of Calif. (bd. dirs. 1998—), Am. Guild of Organists (treas. 1996—), Am. Theatre Organ Soc. Avocations: organ recordings, swimming, cooking, camping. Office: Pratt Music Studios 2124 Hacienda Ln Modesto CA 95350-0207

PRATT, GEORGE JANES, JR., psychologist, author; b. Mpls., May 3, 1948; s. George Janes and Sally Elvina (Hanson) P.; m. Vonda Pratt; 1 child, Whitney Beth. BA cum laude, U. Minn., 1970, MA, 1973; PhD with spl. commendation for overall excellence, Calif. Sch. Profl. Psychology, San Diego, 1976. Diplomate Am. Bd. Med. Psychotherapists, Am. Acad. Pain Mgmt., Am. Coll. Forensic Examiners; lic. psychologist, Calif., 1976. Psychology trainee Ctr. for Behavior Modification, Mpls., 1971-72, U. Minn. Student Counseling Bur., 1972-73; predoctoral clin. psychology intern San Bernardino County (Calif.) Mental Health Svcs., 1973-74, San Diego County Mental Health Services, 1974-76; mem. staff San Luis Rey Hosp., 1977-78; postdoctoral clin. psychology intern Mesa Vista Hosp., San Diego, Calif., 1976; clin. psychologist, dir. Psychology and Cons. Assocs. of San Diego, 1976—; chmn. Psychology and Cons. Assocs. Press, 1977—; bd. dirs. Optimax, Inc., 1985-94; pres. George Pratt Ph.D., Psychol. Corp., 1979—; chmn. Pratt, Korn & Assocs., Inc., 1984-94; mem. staff Scripps Meml. Hosp., La Jolla, Calif., 1986—, chmn. psychology, 1993-95; founder La Jolla Profl. Workshops, 1977; clin. psychologist El Camino Psychology Ctr., San Clemente, Calif., 1977-78; grad. teaching asst. U. Minn. Psychology and Family Studies div., 1971; teaching assoc. U. Minn. Psychology and Family Studies div., Mpls., 1972-73; instr. U. Minn. Extension div., Mpls., 1971-73; faculty Calif. Sch. Profl. Psychology, 1974-83, San Diego Evening Coll., 1975-77, Nat. U., 1978-79, Chapman Coll., 1978, San Diego State U., 1979-80; vis. prof. Pepperdine U., L.A., 1976-78; cons. U. Calif. at San Diego Med. Sch., 1976-78, also instr. univ., 1978-79; psychology chmn. Workshops in Clin. Hypnosis, 1980-84; cons. Calif. Health Dept., 1974, Naval Regional Med. Ctr., 1978-82, ABC-TV; also speaker. With USAR, 1970-76. Fellow Am. Soc. Clin. Hypnosis (cert., approved cons.); mem. APA, Nat. Register of Health Svc. Providers in Psychology, Internat. Soc. Hypnosis, San Diego Psychology Law Soc. (exec. com.), Am. Assn. Sex Educators, Counselors and Therapists (cert.), San Diego Soc. Sex Therapy and Edn. (past pres.), San Diego Soc. Clin. Hypnosis (past pres.), San Diego Psychol. Assn., Soc. Clin. and Exptl. Hypnosis., U. Minn. Alumni Assn., Nat. Speakers Assn., Beta Theta Pi. Author: Sensory/Progressive Relaxation, 1979, Effective Stress Management, 1979, A Clinical Hypnosis Primer, 1984, 88, Clinical Hypnosis: Techniques and Applications, 1985, Hypnosis: Questions and Answers, 1986, HyperPerformance, 1987, Release Your Business Potential, 1988, Handbook for Hypnotic Suggestions and Metaphors, 1990, Imagery in Sports and Physical Performance, 1994, Rx for Stress, 1994; contbr. to various books. Office: Scripps Hosp Med Bldg 9834 Genesee Ave Ste 321 La Jolla CA 92037-1216

PRATT, RONALD FRANKLIN, public relations executive; b. Savannah, Ga., July 15, 1948; s. Frank Tecumseh and Lila Elizabeth (Lee) P. BA, Washington U., St. Louis, 1972. Reporter Savannah News-Press, 1972; news dir. WSOK Radio, Savannah, 1973; editor Hilton Head News, Hilton Head Island, S.C., 1974-77; account exec. Russom & Leeper, San Francisco, 1978-80; sr. account exec. Russom & Leeper, 1981-83, v.p., 1983-85; sr. v.p., prin. The Leeper Grp., San Francisco, 1985-86; pres. Ronald Pratt Pub. Rels., San Francisco, 1987-90; sr. v.p., mgmt. supr. Porter/Novelli, L.A., 1990-92, sr. v.p., group exec., 1993-94, exec. v.p., gen. mgr., 1995—; cons. Coro Found., San Francisco, 1989-90. Bd. dirs. Hilton Head Jazz Festival, 1976-77; pres. Hilton Head Inst. for the Arts, 1976-77; dir., v.p. San Francisco Coun. on Entertainment, 1985-87. Recipient Enterprise award, AP, Ga., 1973. Mem. Internat. Assn. Bus. Communicators (Gold Quill 1983), Internat. Foodsvc. Editl. Coun., Agrl. Rels. Coun., Am. Inst. Wine and Food.

PRATT, ROSALIE REBOLLO, harpist, educator; b. N.Y.C., Dec. 4, 1933; d. Antonio Ernesto and Eleanor Gertrude (Gibney) Rebollo; MusB, Manhattanville Coll., 1954; MusM, Pius XII Inst. Fine Arts, Florence, Italy, 1955; EdD, Columbia U., 1976; m. George H. Mortimer, Esquire, Apr. 22, 1987; children: Francesca Christina Rebollo-Sborgi, Alessandra Maria Pratt Jones. Prin. harpist N.J. Symphony Orch., 1963-65; soloist Mozart Haydn Festival, Avery Fisher Hall, N.Y.C., 1968; tchr. music pub. schs., Bloomfield and Montclair, N.J., 1962-73; mem. faculty Montclair State Coll., 1973-79; prof. Brigham Young U., Provo, Utah, 1984—, coord. grad. studies dept. music, 1985-87.; biofeedback and neurofeedback rsch. specialist, 1993—. U.S. chair 1st internat. arts medicine leadership conf., Tokyo Med. Coll., 1993. Co-author: Elementary Music for All Learners, 1980; editor Internat. Jour. Arts Medicine, 1991—, (procs.) 2d, 3d, 4th Internat. Symposia Music Edn. for Handicapped; contbr. articles to profl. jours. Recipient Utah Music Educator of the Yr., Utah Music Educators Assn., 1997; Fulbright grantee, 1979; Myron Taylor scholar, 1954. Mem. Am. Harp Soc. (Outstanding Svc. award 1973), AAUP (co-chmn. legis. rels. com. N.J. 1978-79), Internat. Soc. Music Edn. (chair commn. music in spl. edn., music therapy, and medicine 1985—), Internat. Soc. Music in Medicine (v.p. 1993—), Internat. Assn. of Music for the Handicapped (co-founder, exec. dir., jour. editor), Coll. Music Soc., Music Educators Nat. Conf., Soc. for Study of Neuronal Regulation, Brigham Young U. Grad. Coun., Phi Kappa Phi, Sigma Alpha Iota. Office: Brigham Young U Harris Fine Arts Ctr Provo UT 84602

PRATT, SABRINA VITTORIA, arts administrator; b. Dallas, Tex., Jan. 7, 1959; d. James Reece and Joanne Elizabeth (Henderson) P.; m. David Allen Carr, August 18, 1984; children: Wesley Allen Pratt Carr, Barret William Pratt Carr. AB, Vassar Coll., 1981; MPA, U. N. Mex., 1994. Sales coord. Santa Fe (N. Mex.) Hilton, 1984-85; adminstr. mgr. Santa Fe (N. Mex.) Convention & Visitor's Bureau, 1985-90; exec. dir. City of Santa Fe (N. Mex.) Arts Commn., 1990—; bd. dirs., treas. Northern N. Mex. Grantmakers, Santa Fe. Office: City of Santa Fe Arts Commn 200 Lincoln Ave Santa Fe NM 87501-1904

PRAUSNITZ, JOHN MICHAEL, chemical engineer, educator; b. Berlin, Jan. 7, 1928; came to U.S., 1937, naturalized, 1944; s. Paul Georg and Susi Prausnitz; m. Susan Prausnitz, June 10, 1956; children: Stephanie, Mark Robert. B Chem. Engring., Cornell U., 1950; MS, U. Rochester, 1951; Ph.D., Princeton, 1955; Dr. Ing., U. L'Aquila, 1983, Tech. U. Berlin, 1989; DSc, Princeton U., 1995. Mem. faculty U. Calif., Berkeley, 1955—, prof. chem. engring., 1963—; cons. to cryogenic, polymer, petroleum and petrochem. industries. Author: (with others) Computer Calculations for Multicomponent Vapor-Liquid Equilibria, 1967, (with P.L. Chueh) Computer Calculations for High-Pressure Vapor-Liquid Equilibria, 1968, Molecular Thermodynamics of Fluid-Phase Equilibria, 1969, 2d edit., 1986, (with others) Regular and Related Solutions, 1970, Properties of Gases and Liquids, 3d edit., 1977, 4th edit., 1987, Computer Calculations for Multicomponent Vapor-Liquid and Liquid-Liquid Equilibria, 1980; contbr. to profl. jours. Recipient Alexander von Humboldt Sr. Scientist award, 1976, Carl von Linde Gold Meml. medal German Inst. for Cryogenics, 1987, Solvay prize Solvay Found. for Chem. Scis., 1990, Corcoran award Am. Soc. for Engring. Edn., 1991, D.L. Katz award Gas Processors Assn., 1992; named W.K. Lewis lectr. MIT, 1993; Guggenheim fellow, 1962, 73, fellow Inst. Advanced Study, Berlin, 1985; Miller rsch. prof., 1966, 78; Christensen fellow St. Catherine's Coll. Oxford U., 1994, Erskine fellow U. Canterbury Christchurch, New Zealand, 1996. Mem. AIChE (Colburn award 1962, Walker award 1967, Inst. Lectr. award 1994), Am. Chem. Soc. (E.V. Murphree award 1979, Petroleum Chemistry Rsch. award 1995), NAE, NAS, Am. Acad. Arts and Scis. Office: U Calif 308 Gilman Hall Berkeley CA 94720

PRAY, RALPH EMERSON, metallurgical engineer; b. Troy, N.Y., May 12, 1926; s. George Emerson and Jansje Cornelius (Owejan) P.; student N.Mex. Inst. of Mining and Tech., 1953-56, U. N.Mex., 1956; BSMetE, U. Alaska, 1961; DScMetE. (Ideal Cement fellowship, Rsch. grant), Colo. Sch. of Mines, 1966; m. Beverley Margaret Ramsey, May 10, 1959; children: Maxwell, Ross, Leslie, Marlene. Engr.-in-charge Dept. Mines and Minerals, Ketchikan, Alaska, 1957-61; asst. mgr. mfg. rsch. Universal Atlas Cement Co., Hammond, Ind., 1966-67, owner, dir. Mineral Rsch. Lab., Monrovia, Calif., 1968—; pres., Keystone Canyon Mining Co., Inc., Pasadena, Calif., 1972-79, U.S. Western Mines, 1973—, Silveroil Rsch. Inc., 1980-85; v.p. [illegible] prime contractor def. logistics agy. U.S. Dept. Def., 1989-92; designer Vanavara Electrolytic Gold Refinery, Krasnoyarsk, Russia, 1995; owner Precision Plastics, 1973-82; bd. dirs. Bagdad-Chase Inc., 1972-75, ptnr. Mineral R&D Co., 1981-86; lectr., Purdue U., Hammond, Ind., 1966-67, Nat. Mining Seminar, Barstow (Calif.) Coll., 1969-70; guest lectr. Calif. State Poly U., 1977-81, Western Placer Mining Conf., Reno, Nev., 1983, Dredging and Placer Mining Conf., Reno, 1985, others; v.p., dir. Wilbur Foote Plastics, Pasadena, 1968-72; strategic minerals del. People to People, Republic of South Africa, 1983; vol. Monrovia Police Dept.; city coord. Neighborhood Watch, 1990—; active Citizen Patrol, 1997—. With U.S. Army, 1950-52. Fellow Geol. Mining and Metall. Soc. India (life), Am. Inst. Chemists, South African Inst. Mining and Metallurgy; mem. Soc. Mining Engrs., Am. Chem. Soc., Am. Inst. Mining, Metall. and Petroleum Engrs., NSPE, Can. Inst. Mining and Metallurgy, Geol. Soc. South Africa, Sigma Xi, Sigma Mu. Achievements include research on recovery of metals from refractory ores, beneficiation plant design, construction and operation, underground and surface mine development and operation, mine and process plant management; syndication of natural resource assets with finance sources; free-lance fiction and nonfiction writer; contbr. articles to sci. jours.; guest editor Calif. Mining Jour., 1978—; patentee chem. processing and steel manufacture. Office: 805 S Shamrock Ave Monrovia CA 91016-3651

PREDESCU, VIOREL N., electrical engineer; b. Craiova, Dolj, Romania, Sept. 14, 1950; came to U.S., 1986; naturalized, 1993; s. Nicolae I. and Constanta (Ciobanescu) P.; m. Rodica G. Apostoleanu, Sept. 14, 1974; 1 child, Dan Paul. MSEE, Poly. Inst., Bucharest, Romania, 1974. Registered profl. engr., Calif., Nev. Elec. engr. Romania, 1974-86; helper electrician CESSOP Electric Constrn., Tustin, Calif., 1986; elec. designer, drafter Sierra Pacific Tech. Svcs., Inc., Laguna Hills, Calif., 1986; asst. engr. Boyle Engring. Corp., Newport Beach, Calif., 1986-88; project engr. Hallis Engring., Inc., L.A., 1988-89; profl. engr. Elec. Bldg. Systems, Inc., North Hollywood, Calif., 1989-91; mgr. of elec. dept. William J. Yang Assocs., Inc., Burbank, Calif., 1991—. Mem. NSPE, IEEE, N.Y. Acad. Scis. Republican. Christian Orthodox. Achievements include electrical design for large variety of projects; commercial Shanghai: World Trade/Plaza Center, Far East International Building, Dong Hai Plaza Complex, So. Calif. Gas Co. Hdqrs., Torrance, Calif., industrial pump stations, water and wastewater plants, industrial buildings, medium voltage 5-35kv distribution systems, uninterruptible power systems for large computer centers, caltrans, MTA tank farms and large maintenance buildings, Calif. State U. Long Beach Sports Arena (The Pyramid), NASA facilities: JPL, Goldstone Space Center & Edwards, military facilities. Home: 12426 Lemay St North Hollywood CA 91606-1312

PREECE, NORMA, executive secretary; b. Kaysville, Utah, May 19, 1922; d. Walter and Wilma (Witt) Buhler; m. Joseph Franklin Preece, July 26, 1946 (dec. 1991); children: Terry Joe, Shannette Preece Keeler. Grad. high sch., Kaysville, 1940. Telephone operator Mountain States Telephone & Telegraph Co., Kaysville, 1940-43; clk. Civil Svc., Ogden, Utah, 1943-50; newspaper corr. Davis County Clipper, North Davis County, Utah, 1954-85; pub. communication dir. Latter-day Saints Ch., Kaysville, 1988-89; exec. sec. Kaysville Area C. of C., Kaysville, 1985-90; stake missionary Latter-Day Saints Ch., Kaysville, 1991—. Publicity chmn. Boy Scouts Am., Kaysville, 1965-69, Am. Cancer Dr., Davis County, 1967, Kaysville Civic Assn., 1960-80; mem. Utah Press Women Assn., Salt Lake City, 1973-75; active publicity Utah Congress PTA, Salt Lake City, 1977—; judge FFA, Davis County, 1968; campaign com. mem. Rep. Party, Davis County, 1990; ordinance worker LDS Temple, Ogden, Utah, 1992-94, Bountiful, Utah, 1995—; co-chmn. Kaysville City Centennial, 1950. Recipient award for outstanding contbn. Davis High Sch., Kaysville, 1979, Total Citizen award Utah C. of C., 1988, Disting. Svc. award Kaysville Arts Coun., 1981; Outstanding Svc. award Kaysville Jaycees, 1972, Disting. Svc. award, 1985, Cmty. Unsung Hero award City of Kaysville, 1994; named Citizen of Yr., City of Kaysville, 1985. Mem. Lit. Club (Athena chpt., sec. 1984, 87, v.p. 1989, pres. 1990), Fine Arts Club (pres. 1964, sec. 1994). Mem. LDS Ch. Avocations: writing, research, reading, golf, needlework. Home: 1608 S 400 E Bountiful UT 84010-4004 Office: Kaysville Area C of C 44 E 100 N Kaysville UT 84037-1910

PREGER, LESLIE, radiologist; b. Manchester, Eng., June 23, 1926; s. Harry Louis and Bertha (Mandel) P.; m. Elfriede Erika Schwara. MB ChB, Manchester U., 1953. Sr. rsch. asst. Royal Postgrad. Med. Sch., London, 1964-66; assoc., asst. prof. U. Calif. Med. Ctr., San Francisco, 1966-69; chief radiology French Hosp., San Francisco, 1969-82; chief radiologist Highland Gen. Hosp., Oakland, Calif., 1983-91; radiologist F&K Imaging, San Francisco, 1991-92, Peninsula Imaging Ctr., Burlingame, Calif., 1992—; radiology cons. Dept. Labor Black Lung Program, 1995—; clin. prof. radiology U. Calif., San Francisco, 1978—; B reader OSHA, 1977—. Co-author: Hand in Diffuse Disease, 1975; co-author, editor: Asbestos Related iseases, 1976, Induced Disease, 1980, others; contbr. articles to profl. jours. Sgt. Brit. Army, 1944-48, ETO. Decorted Meritorious Svc. medal, Army Achievement medal, Army Commendation medal; recipient medal of merit State of Calif. N.G. Fellow Royal Coll. Radiology, Royal Coll. Surgeons (Ireland), Am. Coll. Radiology. Democrat. Jewish. Avocation: hiking. Home: 166 Merced Ave San Francisco CA 94127-1028 Office: Peninsula Imaging Ctr 1825 Trousdale Dr Burlingame CA 94010-4509

PREGERSON, HARRY, federal judge; b. L.A., Oct. 13, 1923; s. Abraham and Bessie (Rubin) P.; m. Bernardine Seyma Chapkis, June 28, 1947; children: Dean Douglas, Kathryn Ann. B.A., UCLA, 1947; LL.B., U. Calif.-Berkeley, 1950. Bar: Calif. 1951. Pvt. practice Los Angeles, 1951-52; Assoc. Morris D. Coppersmith, 1952; ptnr. Pregerson & Costley, Van Nuys, 1953-65; judge Los Angeles Mcpl. Ct., 1965-66, Los Angeles Superior Ct., 1966-67, U.S. Dist. Ct. Central Dist. Calif., 1967-79, U.S. Ct. Appeals for 9th Circuit, Woodland Hills, 1979—; faculty mem., seminar for newly appointed distr. Judges Fed. Jud. Center, Washington, 1970-72; mem. faculty Am. Soc. Pub. Adminstrn., Inst. for Ct. Mgmt., Denver, 1973—; panelist Fed. Bar Assn., L.A. chpt., 1989, Calif. Continuing Edn. of Bar, 9th Ann. Fed. Practice Inst., San Francisco, 1986, Internat. Acad. Trial Lawyers, L.A., 1983; lect. seminars for newly-appointed Fed. judges, 1970-71. Author over 450 published legal opinions. Mem. Community Rels. Com., Jewish Fedn. Coun., 1984—, Temple Judea, Encino, 1955—; bd. dirs. Marine Corps Res. Toys for Tots Program, 1965—, Greater Los Angeles Partnership for the Homeless, 1988—; bd. trustees Devil Pups Inc., 1988—; adv. bd. Internat. Orphans Inc., 1966—, Jewish Big Brothers Assn., 1970—, Salvation Army, Los Angeles Met. area, 1988—; worked with U.S. Govt. Gen. Svcs. to establish the Bell Shelter for the homeless, the Child Day Care Ctr., the Food Partnership and Westwood Transitional Village, 1988. 1st lt. USMCR, 1944-46. Decorated Purple Heart, Medal of Valor Apache Tribe, 1989; recipient Promotion of Justice Civic award, City of San Fernando, 1965, award San Fernando Valley Jewish Fedn. Coun., 1966, Profl. Achievement award Los Angeles Athletic Club, 1980, Profl. Achievement award UCLA Alumni Assn., 1985, Louis D. Brandeis award Am. Friends of Hebrew U., 1987, award of merit Inner City Law Ctr., 1987, Appreciation award Navajo Nation and USMC for Toys for Tots program, 1987, Humanitarian award Los Angeles Fed. Exec. Bd., 1987-88, Grateful Acknowledgement award Bet Tzedek Legal Svcs., 1988, Commendation award Bd. Suprs. Los Angeles County, 1988, Others award Salvation Army, 1988, numerous others. Mem. ABA (vice-chmn., com. on fed. rules of criminal procedure and evidence sect. of criminal 1972—, panelist Advocacy Inst., Phoenix, 1988), L.A. County Bar Assn., San Fernando Valley Bar Assn. (program chmn. 1964-65), State Bar Calif., Marines Corps Res. Officers Assn. (pres. San Fernando Valley 1966—), DAV (Birmingham chpt.), Am. Legion (Van Nuys Post),. Office: US Ct Appeals 9th Cir 21800 Oxnard St Ste 1140 Woodland Hills CA 91367-3657*

PRELL, JOEL JAMES, medical group administrator; b. L.A., Aug. 16, 1944; s. Samuel and Mary Devorah (Schwartz) P.; m. Cheryl Prell; children: Vanessa S., Matthew. BA, U. So. Calif., L.A., 1967; cert. fin. mgmt., Ohio State U., 1979; M. Pub. Health, UCLA, 1981. Various positions, 1967-72; chief adminstrv. office sr. adminstrv. analyst L.A. County, 1972-73; dep. regional dir. for planning and community rels. L.A. County Dept. Health Svcs. Region, 1973-75; adminstr. ambulatory care L.A. County Harbro Gen. [illegible] Irvine Med. Ctr., 1976-78, asst. to the dir. rsch. and analysis unit U. Calif., Davis, 1978-80; v.p. profl. svcs. San Pedro Peninsula Hosp., 1981-84; sr. v.p. South Coast Med. Ctr., 1984-87; pres., CEO Harbor Health Systems, Inc., 1987-90; CEO Santa Monica (Calif.) [illegible] Med. Group, Inc., 1990-93; administrator Pathology Cons. Med. Group, Torrance, Calif., 1993—; spl. asst. to the contr. UCLA Hosp. and Clinics, 1980-81, adminstr. emergency medicine ctr., 1981. Mem. Hosp. Coun .So. Calif. (polit. action steering com., chmn. legis. affairs com.), Calif. Hosp. Polit. Action Com. (bd. dirs.), Health Care Execs. So. Calif., UCLA Health Svcs. Adminstrs. Alumni Assn. (pres.), Med. Group Mgmt. Assn., Am. Coll. Health Care Executives. Office: Affiliated Pathologists 20221 Hamilton Ave Torrance CA 90502-1304

PRENDERGAST, WILLIAM JOHN, ophthalmologist; b. Portland, Oreg., June 12, 1942; s. William John and Marjorie (Scott) P.; m. Carolyn Grace Perkins, Aug. 17, 1963 (div. 1990); children: William John, Scott; m. Sherryl Irene Guenther, Aug. 25, 1991. BS, U. Oreg., Eugene, 1964; MD, U. Oreg., Portland, 1967. Diplomate Am. Bd. Ophthalmology. Resident in ophthalmology U. Oreg., Portland, 1970-73; pvt. practice specializing in ophthalmology Portland, 1973-82; physician, founder, ptnr. Eye Health NW (formerly Oreg. Med. Eye Clinic), Portland, 1983—; also bd. dirs.; founder, pres. (Focus Group) Inc. Focus Group Inc., Ophthalmic Clinic Networking Venture, Portland, 1992—; clin. asst. prof. ophthalmology Oreg. Health Sci. U., 1985—; dir. Eye Health Ptnrs. Med. Optometric Managed Eye Care Venture, 1998. Vol. surgeon N.W. Med. Teams, Oaxaca, Mexico, 1989, 90. With USPHS, 1968-70. Fellow Am. Acad. Ophthalmology; mem. Met. Bus. Assn., Multnomah Athletic Club, Mazamas Mountaineering Club, Portland Yacht Club, Phi Beta Kappa, Alpha Omega Alpha. Avocations: yacht racing, mountaineering. Office: Eye Health NW 1955 NW Northrup St Portland OR 97209-1614

PRESCOTT, BARBARA LODWICH, educational administrator; b. Chgo., Aug. 15, 1951; d. Edward and Eugenia Lodwich; m. Warren Paul Prescott, Dec. 2, 1979; children: Warren Paul Jr., Ashley Elizabeth. BA, U. Ill., Chgo., 1973, MEd, 1981; MA, U. Wis., 1978; postgrad., Stanford U., 1983-87. Cert. tchr., learning handicapped specialist, cmty. coll. instr., Calif. Grad. rschr. U. Ill., Chgo., 1979-81; learning handicapped specialist St. Paulus Luth. Sch., San Francisco, 1981-83; grad. rsch. asst. Sch. Edn. Stanford (Calif.) U., 1983-87, writing cons. for law students, 1985-86; learning handicapped specialist/lead therapist Gilroy Clinic Speech-Hearing-Learning Ctr., Crippled Children's Soc., Santa Clara, Calif., 1988-89; edn. dir. Adolescent Intensive Resdl. Svc. Calif. Pacific Med. Ctr., San Francisco, 1989-95; exec. dir. Learning Profiles, South Lake Tahoe, Calif., 1995—; instr. evening San Jose City Coll., 1988-92. Contbr. articles to profl. jours.; author: Proceedings of Internat. Congress of Linguistics, 1987; editor: Proceedings - Forum for Research on Language Issues, 1986; author videotape: Making a Difference in Language and Learning, 1989. Recipient Frederick Bork Teaching Trainee award San Francisco State U., 1983; Ill. State scholar, 1973. Mem. Calif. Assn. Pvt. Specialized Edn. and Svcs., Phi Delta Kappa (v.p. 1984-86), Pi Lambda Theta (sec. 1982-83), Phi Kappa Phi, Alpha Lambda Theta. Office: Learning Profiles 2145 Harvard Ave South Lake Tahoe CA 96150-4425

PRESCOTT, LAWRENCE MALCOLM, medical and health science writer; b. Boston, July 31, 1934; s. Benjamin and Lillian (Stein) P. BA, Harvard U., 1957; MSc, George Washington U., 1959, PhD, 1966; m. Ellen Gay Kober, Feb. 19, 1961 (dec. Sept. 1981); children: Jennifer Maya, Adam Barrett; m. Sharon Lynn Kirshen, May 16, 1982; children: Gary Leon Kirshen, Marc Paul Kirshen. Nat. Acad. Scis. postdoctoral fellow U.S. Army Rsch., Ft. Detrick, Md., 1965-66; microbiologist/scientist WHO, India, 1967-70, Indonesia, 1970-72, Thailand, 1972-78; with pub. rels. Ted Klein & Co., Hill & Knowlton, Interscience, , Smith, Kline, Beecham, others, 1984—; cons. health to internat. orgns., San Diego, 1978—; author manuals; contbr. articles in diarrheal diseases and lab. scis. to profl. jours., numerous articles, stories, poems to mags., newspapers, including Living in Thailand, Jack and Jill, Strawberry, Bangkok Times, Sprint, 1977-81; mng. editor Caduceus, 1981-82; pub., editor: Teenage Scene, 1982-83; pres. Prescott Pub. Co., 1982-83; med. writer numerous journ. including Modern Medicine, Dermatology Times, Internal Medicine World Report, Drugtherapy, P&T, Clinical Cancer Letter, Hospital Formulary, Female Patient, Australian Doctor, Inpharma Weekly, American Family Physician, Ophthalmology Times, Group Practice News, Newspaper of Cardiology, Paacnotes, Genetic Engineering News, Medical Week, Medical World News, Urology Times, Gastroenterology and Endoscopy News; author: Curry Every Sunday, 1984. Home and Office: 18264 Verano Dr San Diego CA 92128-1262

PRESECAN, NICHOLAS LEE, environmental and civil engineer, consultant; b. Indpls., Sept. 4, 1940; s. Nicholas Eli and Dorothy Lee (Moore) P.; m. Joan Westin, Nov. 11, 1940; children: Julie Marie, Mary Lee, Anne Westin. BSCE, Purdue U., 1963; MS in Engring., U. Calif., Berkeley, 1967. Cert. profl. engr., 33 states. Project engr. San Bernardino County (Calif.) Flood Control, 1963, Engring. Sci. Inc., Arcadia, Calif., 1968-70; office mgr. Engring. Sci. Inc., Cleve., 1970-72, v.p., chief engr., 1972-81; v.p. internat. divsn. Engring. Sci. Inc., Arcadia, 1981-84, group v.p., 1984-87; sr. v.p. Parsons Engring. Sci. Inc., Pasadena, Calif., 1987—; mem. industry adv. bd. Sch. Engring. and Tech. Calif. State U., L.A., 1986—. Contbr. articles to profl. jours. Commr. Archtl. Commn., Claremont, Calif., 1980-86; councilman Claremont City Coun., 1986-94; mayor City of Claremont, 1989-92; mem. Pasadena Tournament of Roses Assn., 1980-96, L.A. 2000 Environ. Com., 1987-88; pres. Claremont Hills Conservation Corp., 1997—. With USMC, 1963-67. Recipient Disting. Engring. Achievement award Inst. for Advancement of Engring., 1993. Fellow ASCE (mem. internat. adv. com. 1987-90); mem. NSPE, Am. Acad. Environ. Engrs., Am. Water Works Assn. (life), Water Environ. Fedn., Soc. Am. Value Engrs., Rotary. Republican. Avocations: skiing, hiking, fishing, boating, writing. Home: 727 E Alamosa Dr Claremont CA 91711-2008 Office: Parsons Engring Sci Inc 100 W Walnut St Pasadena CA 91124-0001

PRESLEY, ARTHUR HENRY, writer, artist; b. Delano, Calif., June 1, 1953; s. James Hampton and Marjorie Joy (Quandt) P. AA, Bakersfield (Calif.) Coll., 1978; student, Brigham Young U., 1979-82, 87-89. Asst. city planner City of Lindsay, Calif., 1988-89; freelance writer, Bakersfield, 1995—. Contbr. poetry to Beneath the Harvest Moon, 1996, Best Poems of the '90s, 1996, Treasured Poems of America, 1998, CAMI Jour., 1995. Mem. Internat. Soc. Poets. Avocations: reading, music, astronomy, gardening, cooking. Home: 7500 Eloy Ave Bakersfield CA 93308-7701

PRESLEY, DAVID G., video technician; b. Santa Monica, Calif., Apr. 3, 1970; s. Bob Joe Presley and Dianne (Budden) Newcombe. BS, Tex. A&M U., 1994. Owner Mobile Techs., College Station, Tex., 1991-94. Video technician for various feature films, including Contact, The Postman, The Crow II, Dream Factory, Starship Troopers, Armageddon, Small Soldiers, The Magical Friendship, Casper III, Mask of Zorro, Deep Impact, Sometimes They Come Back, Lost Highway, also various music videos and comls. Exec. dir. Disaster Response Search and Rescue, L.A., 1997—. With U.S. Army, 1988-91. Recipient Cert. of Appreciation, Adj. Gen. State of Tex., 1990; named in Guiness Book of World Records for highest score on a video game, 1986. Mem. IATSE. Home: 4248 Whitsett Ave Apt 104 Studio City CA 91604-1678

PRESNIAKOV, ALEXANDER, painter; b. San Francisco, June 28, 1963; s. Alexander Alexandervich and Nina (Hanova) P. Student, Acad. of Art Coll., San Francisco, 1979-82. Curator Gen. Svcs. Adminstrn., Washington, 1983; artist Washington, 1984-85, San Francisco, 1986—; songwriter Hilltop Records, L.A., 1996—, Amerecord, L.A., 1996—, Premier Melodies, N.Y.C. *Published biographies of Alexander Presniakov and his works in the following International Editions: Who's Who in International Art, Switzerland; Prestige de la Peinture et de la Sculpture d'Aujourd'hui dans le Monde, Paris, France; International Biographical Center, Cambridge, England; GAL ART, Arte, Exposiciones, Artistas, Libros, Galerias, Barcelona, Spain; Le Livre d'Or des Collectionneurs et Amateurs d'Art, Paris, France; Artistas Internacionales, Barcelona, Spain.* Commd. to paint life-size portraits of Prince Charles, Princess Diana, Miss Dame Barbara Cartland, 1982, Amb. Gerald Posner Carmen, other life-size portraits for 1985 Polit. Conservative Action Conf., Sheraton Hotel, Washington; series Women in Love Cycle, 1986—; inventor Manshield Deflector, 1983; commissioned to point life-size [illegible] Press, 1995; named Prof. and Corr. Academician Dept. Arts Accademia Internazionale, Italy. Mem. Internat. Soc. Poets (disting. mem., Hall of Fame 1997-98), Legion of Honor Mus., De Young Mus., Gallery Marabella (hon.). Republican. Russian Orthodox. Achievements include creation of artistic ideal, Ultrafictorilization, utilized in all U.S. gov. Agys., 1983. Avo-

cations: tennis, golf, equestrian. Home: 775 42d Ave San Francisco CA 94121

PRESS, RICHARD H., sales executive, consultant; b. New Haven, Conn., Mar. 8, 1952; s. Herman Morse and Ruth Rhode (Voloshin) P.; m. Doreen Lynn Mautner, June 16, 1974; children: Craig Adam, Scott Eric. BS in Biomed. Engring., Northwestern U., 1974. Dist. svc. mgr. Abbott Labs. Hospital Products Divsn., Chicago, 1974-76, sr. sales rep., 1976-80, area sale mgr., 1980-84; sr. sales rep. Litton Datamedix, Phoenix, 1984-87; terr. mgr. Pharmacia Deltec, Phoenix, 1987-94; pres. SalesToolz, Inc., Scottsdale, Ariz., 1994—. Contbr. articles to profl. jours. Avocations: family, dogs, golf. Office: SalesToolz Inc 6105 E Larkspur Dr Scottsdale AZ 85254-4446

PRESSLEY, JAMES RAY, electrical engineer; b. Ft. Worth, July 14, 1946; s. Loy Dale and Dorothy Helen (Foust) P.; m. Barbara Kay McMillin, Oct. 9, 1968 (div. 1981); children: James Foust Pressley, Kreg Milam Pressley; m. Susan Marie Straw, Apr. 27, 1985 (div.); children: Shaye Eugene Straw, Rebecca Alycen Straw, Rachel Leilani Straw. BSEE, U. Tex., Arlington, 1970. Registered profl. engr., Alaska, Hawaii, Oreg., Wash., Guam. Designer/draftsman Romine & Slaughter, Ft. Worth, 1967-71; engr. Crews MacInnes & Hoffman, Anchorage, 1971-73, O'Kelly & Schoenlank, Anchorage, 1973-75, Theodore G. Creedon, Anchorage, 1975-77; v.p. Fryer, Pressley Elliott, Anchorage, 1977-80, Fryer/Pressley Engring., 1980-91, FPE Roen Engrs., Inc., 1991-98, also chmn. bd., 1991-95, v.p., bd. dirs., 1991—; v.p., bd. dirs., mgr. Anchorage ofc. PDC, Inc. Cons. Engrs., 1998—; mem. elec. constrn. and maintenance industry evaluation panel, 1982-96. Mem. IEEE, Illuminating Engring. Soc. (sustaining), Internat. Assn. Elec. Inspectors, Nat. Fire Protection Assn., Nat. Assn. Corrosion Engrs., Am. Soc. Quality. Office: PDC Inc Cons Engrs 560 E 34th Ave Ste 300 Anchorage AK 99503-4161

PRESSMAN, JACOB, rabbi; b. Phila., Oct. 26, 1919; s. Solomon David and Dora (Levin) P.; m. Marjorie Steinberg, June 14, 1942; children: Daniel Joseph, Joel David, Judith Sharon. BA, U. Pa., 1940; MHL, Jewish Theol. Sem., 1944, Dr.Hebrew Letters, 1960, Dr. Humane Letters, 1979. Ordained rabbi, 1945. Rabbi Forest Hills Jewish Ctr., N.Y.C., 1944-46, Congregation Sinai, L.A., 1946-50, Temple Beth Am, L.A., 1950—; dir. Bonds of Israel, L.A., 1988-90, city chmn., 1990-91; vice chmn. bd. govs. L.A. Jewish Fedn. Coun., 1988—; founder U. Judaism, L.A. Hebrew High Sch., Herzl Sch., Camp Ramah at Ojai, Akiba Acad., Rabbi Jacob Pressman Acad. Mem. Rabbinical Assembly Western Region (pres. 1954-56), Bd. Rabbis So. Calif. (pres. 1958-61). Office: Temple Beth Am 1039 S La Cienega Blvd Los Angeles CA 90035-2507

PRESTON, DAVID RAYMOND, lawyer; b. Harlingen, Tex., Feb. 12, 1961; s. Raymond C., Jr. and Janet (Bowman) P. BS, U. Fla., 1983, MS, 1985, PhD, 1989; JD, George Mason Sch. Law, 1996. Bar: Calif., U.S. Patent and Tradmark Office. Postdoctoral rsch. U.S. Army, Frederick, Md., 1989-90; patent examiner U.S. Patent and Trademark Office, Washington, 1990-94; tech. devel. specialist Nat. Cancer Inst., NIH, Bethesda, Md., 1994-96; intern for Judge Rader U.S. Ct. Appeals (fed. cir.), Washington, 1995; patent attorney Campbell & Flores, San Diego, 1996-97; asst. patent counsel Aurora Bioscis. Corp., San Diego, 1997-98; pres. David R. Preston & Assocs., San Diego, 1999—. Judge internat. sci. fair U.S. Patents and Trademark Office, 1991. NIH fellow, 1987, Pres.'s fellow Am. Soc. Microbiology, 1988. Mem. AAAS, ABA, Am. Intellectual Property Law Assn., Fed. Cir. Bar Assn., San Diego Intellectual Property Law Assn. Republican. Avocations: tennis, golf, skiing, surfing, windsurfing. Home: 7160 Shoreline Dr Apt 4304 San Diego CA 92122-4919 Office: Aurora Bioscis Corp 11010 Torreyana Rd San Diego CA 92121-1103

PRESTON, MICHAEL JAMES, English and folklore educator, consultant; b. Wenatchee, Wash., Sept. 5, 1943; s. Jefferson James and Rosamond Catherine (Ward) P.; m. Cathy Lynn Makin, Nov. 13, 1978; children: Theresa Maureen, Stephanie Michele. AB, Gonzaga U., 1965; MA, U. Va., 1967, U. Colo., 1972; PhD, U. Colo., 1975. Instr. English Colo. Women's Coll., Denver, 1967-75; dir. Ctr. Computer Rsch. Humanities U. Colo., Boulder, 1976-90, prof. English, 1990—; computer panel mem. Nat. Endowment Humanities, Washington, 1980. Author: The Christmas Rhyme Books, 1998; editor: Concordance to the Middle English Shorter Poem, 1975, Urban Folklore from Colorado, 1976, The Other Print Tradition, 1995. Bd. dirs. Denver chpt. Amigos de Las Ams., Denver, 1998—. Nat. Endowment Humanities fellow, 1974, rsch. grantee, 1984-86; Am. Coun. Learned Socs. rsch. grantee, N.Y., 1974. Democrat. Roman Catholic. Avocation: home remodeling. Home: 515 S 46th St Boulder CO 80303-6037 Office: U Colo Dept English Boulder CO 80309

PRESZLER, SHARON MARIE, psychiatric home health nurse; b. L.A.; d. Rudolph Edward Wirth and Bertha Marie (Thornton) Paddock; m. Alan Preszler, Aug. 31, 1966; children: Brent, Alison. BS in Nursing, Loma Linda (Calif.) U., 1963, MS in Marriage and Family Counseling, 1978. RN, Calif., Idaho; cert. pub. health nurse. Team leader med. fl. Loma Linda U. Hosp., 1963-64; office nurse Dr. Lowell Johnson, Redlands, Calif., 1964-65, Dr. H. Glenn Stevens, Loma Linda, 1965-72; team leader women's oncology Loma Linda U. Hosp., 1974-75; pub. health nurse Riverside County Pub. Health, Hemet, Calif., 1975-78; nurse, staff psychologist Dept. Health and Welfare, Idaho Falls, Idaho, 1989-91, Boise, Idaho, 1991-92; psychiat. nurse Cmty. Home Health, Boise, 1992-94, Mercy Home Health & Hospice, Nampa, Idaho, 1995—; hospice nurse, home health nurse Mercy Med. Ctr., 1995—, personal care supr. nurse for medicaid, 1996—; instr. YWCA, Bartlesville, Okla., 1984-88; tchr. Bartlesville Pub. Sch., 1984-88, Heritage Retirement, Boise, 1994. Contbr. to Focus, 1986. Mem. Am. Assn. Marriage and Family Therapy, Sigma Theta Tau. Avocations: reading, tennis.

PRETTYMAN, JANE WARDLOW, editor, writer, media critic; b. Miami, July 24, 1944; d. George Lyman and Jane (Wardlow) P.; m. John R. Sharpe Jr., June 15, 1967 (div. Oct. 1975); 1 child, Kristen Katherine. BS in Lit., Fla. State U., 1967. Assoc. editor Esquire Mag., N.Y.C., 1971-78; pub., editor Dromenon Jour., N.Y.C., 1977-83; med. editor Ind. Health, Santa Barbara, Calif., 1984—; media lectr. Santa Barbara City Coll., 1996—; moderator, founder The Media Salon, Santa Barbara, 1995—. Editor, founder internet website The Real News Page, 1995—; radio commentator, 1998—. Dade County Classroom Tchr.'s Assn., Miami, 1962-67. Mem. So. Poverty Law Ctr., The Nature Conservancy. Green Party. Avocations: gardening, walking, music, writing. Home: 1900 State St Ste I Santa Barbara CA 93101-8426

PREUSS, CHARLES F., lawyer; b. Santa Barbara, Calif., Feb. 27, 1941. BA, Dartmouth Coll., 1962; JD, Stanford U., 1969. Bar: Calif. 1970. Ptnr. Preuss Walker & Shanagher, San Francisco, 1993—. Mem. PLAC, ABOTA, IADC (pres.-elect), Def. Rsch. Inst., Mng. Counsel Group, Internat. Assn. Def. Counsel. Office: Preuss Walker & Shanagher 225 Bush St 15F1 San Francisco CA 94104-2802

PRICE, B. BYRON, historian. BS, U.S. Mil. Acad., 1970; MA in Mus. Sci., Tex. Tech. U., 1977; postgrad., Am. U., Washington, 1975. Tchg. asst. Tex. Tech. U., Lubbock, 1975, rsch. coord. Ranching Heritage Ctr./Mus., 1976-77; curator of history Panhandle-Plains Hist. Mus., Canyon, Tex., 1977-82, exec. dir., 1982-86; exec. dir. Nat. Cowboy Hall of Fame and Western Heritage Ctr., Oklahoma City, 1987-96, Buffalo Bill Hist. Ctr., Cody, Wyo., 1996—; lectr. in field; condr. seminars in field; cons. in field. Advisory editor: The Handbook of Texas, 1986-96; editl. bd. N.Mex. Hist. Rev., 1990-93, Jour. Ariz. History, 1993-95; assoc. editor The Ency. of the West, 1996; author: Cowboys of the American West, 1996, Crafting a Southwestern Masterpiece, 1986, Imagining the Open Range: Erwin E. Smith, Cowboy Photographer, 1997, Longhead: A Painter's Painter, 1991, The National Cowboy Hall of Fame Chuck Wagon Cook Book, 1995, She Doesn't Write Like a Woman: Mari Sandoz and the Cattlemen, 1996; co-author: The Golden Spread: An Illustrated History of Amarillo and the Texas Panhandle, 1986; co-editor: Cowboy Justice, 1997, Adventuring with the Old-Timers: Trails Traveled and Tales Told, 1979; contbr. articles to profl. jours. Mem. tourism task force Okla. Dept. Commerce, 1987; mem. Okla. Film Adv. Commn., 1988-90; bd. dirs. Okla. Ctr. for the Book, 1990—; judge Arts for the Parks Ann. Exhbn., 1992-93; mem. cultural opportunities work group Okla. Futures, 1993; mem. Oklahoma City Conv. and Visitors Commn., 1996—. Recipient Gov.'s Arts award State of Okla., 1994. Mem. Tex. Assn. Mus. (exec. coun. 1985-86), Okla. Mus. Assn. (v.p. 1993-95), Mus. West Consortium (pres. 1996—), Western History Assn. (mem. program com. 1997), Am. Assn. Mus., Tex. State Hist. Assn., Western Writers of Am., Panhandle Plains Hist. Soc. Home: 1338 Monument St Cody WY 82414-3407 Office: Buffalo Bill Historical Ctr 720 Sheridan Ave Cody WY 82414-3428

PRICE, BETTY JEANNE, choirchime soloist, writer; b. Long Beach, Calif., June 12, 1942; d. Grant E. and Miriam A. (Francis) Sickles; m. Harvey H. Price, Aug. 6, 1975; 1 child, Thomas Neil Gering. Degree in Acctg., Northland Pioneer Coll., Show Low, Ariz., 1977. Youth missionary Open Bible Standard Missions, Trinidad, 1958-59; typographer Joel H. Weldon & Assocs., Scottsdale, Ariz., 1980-89; exec. chief acct. Pubs. Devel. Corp., San Diego, 1991-93; coord. music and worship College Ave. Bapt. Ch., San Diego, 1994-95; ChoirChime soloist, 1986—; founder, owner Customized Funding Svcs., San Diego, 1996—. Author: 101 Ways to Fix Broccoli, 1994, ABC's of Abundant Living, 1995; co-author: God's Vitamin C for the Spirit, 1995, Bounce Back, 1997, You Can Bounce Back Too, 1998. Vol. Svc. Corps Retired Execs. Mem. Christian Writers Guild, Am. Cash Flow Assn., San Diego Cash Flow Assn. (founder, exec. bd. mem.), Nat. Entrepreneurs Assn., Bus. Incubator Alliance, Econ. Devel. Coun., Am. Soc. Notaries, Svc. Corps of Retired Execs., Soroptimist Internat. Home: PO Box 84242 La Jolla CA 92038-4242

PRICE, CLIFFORD WARREN, retired metallurgist, researcher; b. Denver, Apr. 22, 1935; s. Warren Wilson and Vivian Fredricka (Cady) P.; m. Carole Joyce Watermon, June 14, 1969; children: Carla Beth, Krista Lynn Price. MetE, Colo. Sch. Mines, 1957; MS, Ohio State U., 1970, PhD, 1975. Design engr. Sundstrand Aviation-Denver, 1957-60; materials specialist Denver Rsch. Inst., 1960-63; sr. metallurgist Rocky Flats div. Dow Chem. Co., Golden, Colo., 1963-66; staff metallurgist Battelle Columbus (Ohio) Labs., 1966-75; sr. scientist Owens-Corning Fiberglas, Granville, Ohio, 1975-80; metallurgist Lawrence Livermore (Calif.) Nat. Lab., 1980-93; retired, 1993. Contbr. articles to profl. jours. Battelle Columbus Labs. fellow, 1974-75. Mem. Metall. Soc. AIME, Microscopy Soc. Am. (treas. Denver 1961-62), Am. Soc. for Metals Internat. Achievements include research on electron, scanning probe and optical microscopy, secondary ion mass spectroscopy, deformation, fracture and recrystallization mechanisms in metals, recrystallization kinetics.

PRICE, GAIL J. GOODMAN, marriage, family and child therapist, deaf and hearing impaired specialist; b. L.A., July 17, 1950; d. David S. and Ruth M. (Eholnikoff) Goodman; children: Gregory David, Jeffrey Ranen. BA, Calif. State U., Northridge, 1972; MEd, U. Ariz., 1973; postgrad. Chapman U., 1975-77. Lic. marriage, family and child counselor. Tchr. L.A. Unified Sch. Dist., 1973-74; dir. multi-handicapped programs Ennoble Group Homes, Inglewood, Calif., 1979; deaf-blind specialist San Francisco Lighthouse for the Blind, 1979-81; supr. social svcs. Foothill Health and Rehab. Ctr., Sylmer, Calif., 1981-83; dir. counseling ctr. Planned Parenthood of Orange County, Santa Ana, Calif., 1985-88; pvt. practice marriage, family and child counselor Orange, Calif., 1984—. Mem. Nat. Disaster Med. Sys. Disaster Med. Assistance Team CA3. U. Ariz. fellow, 1972-73. Mem. Nat. Assn. Deafness, Calif. Assn. Marriage & Family Therapists, Internat. Soc. for the Study Dissociation, Greater L.A. Coun. Deafness, Kappa Delta Pi. Avocations: edible wild plants, herbal medicine. Home: 13642 Carroll Way Tustin CA 92780-1846 Office: 221 S Glassell St Orange CA 92866-1945

PRICE, GAYL BAADER, residential construction company administrator; b. Gothenburg, Sweden, Mar. 1, 1949; came to U.S., 1951; d. Harold Edgar Anderson and Jeanette Helen (Hallberg) Akeson; m. Daniel J. Baader, Nov. 27, 1971 (div. Sept. 1980); m. Leigh C. Price, Feb. 28, 1983; foster children: Heidi, Heather. BA in Fgn. Lang., U. Ill., 1971. Asst. buyer The Denver, 1971-73, buyer, 1973-75; escrow sec. Transam. Title, Evergreen, Colo., 1975-76, escrow officer, 1976-78, sr. escrow officer, 1978-79, br. mgr., 1979-84; sr. account mgr. Transam. Title, Denver, 1984-87, sales mgr., 1987-91, v.p., 1989-94; cmty. mgr. Village Homes of Colo., Littleton, Colo., 1994—. Vol. Safehouse for Battered Women, Denver, 1986—, Spl. Olympics, 1986—, Adult Learning Source, 1993—, Kids Cure for Cancer, 1994—. Mem. Nat. Assn. Homebuilders (Most Profl. award 1997), Home Builders Assn. Met. Denver (bd. dirs. 1989 93, exec. com. 1991, assoc. mem. coun. 1988-93, co-chair 1990, chair 1991, Arthur Gaeth Assoc. of Yr. 1989), Sales and Mktg. Coun. Met. Denver (bd. 1986-92, 95—, Major Achievement in Merchandising Excellence chair 1989-90, Most Profl. award 1989, 97, Sales Master award 1995, Silver MAME award 1996, Gold MAME award 1997), Douglas County Econ. Devel., Zonta Club Denver II (charter, pres. 1990, Zontian of Yr. 1988), Colo. Assn. Homebuilders (Assoc. of Yr. 1992). Avocations: cooking, volunteer work, travel. Home: 1975 Linda Ln Evergreen CO 80439 Office: Village Homes 6 W Dry Creek Cir Ste 200 Littleton CO 80120-8031

PRICE, HUMPHREY WALLACE, aerospace engineer; b. San Antonio, Sept. 25, 1954; s. Humphrey Rodes and Ruth (Wallace) P. BS in Engring., U. Tex., 1976, MS in Engring., 1978. Rsch. asst. nuclear reactor lab. U. Tex., Austin, 1976; nuclear engr. EDS Nuclear, Inc., San Francisco, 1977-78; engr. Jet Propulsion Lab., Pasadena, Calif., 1978-82; rsch. engr. SW Rsch. Inst., San Antonio, 1982-84; tech. group leader Jet Propulsion Lab., Pasadena, Calif., 1984-89; configuration engr. Cassini spacecraft NASA, 1989-93; system engr. Pluto Spacecraft, 1994-97; sys. engr. Mars Sample Return Mission, 1998—; cons. Am. Rocket Co., Camarillo, Calif., 1986-87; mem. tech. staff World Space Found., Pasadena, 1980-97. Patentee in field; contbr. to tech. papers in field. Mem. AIAA (sr.), Brit. Interplanetary Soc. Avocations: wind surfing, skiing, scuba diving. Office: HW Price Cons PO Box 454 La Canada Flintridge CA 91012-0454

PRICE, JOE (ALLEN), artist, former educator; b. Ferriday, La., Feb. 6, 1935; s. Edward Neill and Margaret (Hester) P. BS, Northwestern U., 1957; postgrad., Art Ctr. Coll., L.A., 1967-68; MA, Stanford U., 1970. Free-lance actor, artist N.Y.C., 1957-60; freelance illustrator, actor, L.A., 1960-68; free-lance comml. artist, San Carlos, Calif., 1968-69; package designer Container Corp. Am., Santa Clara, Calif., 1969; prof. studio art and filmmaking, chmn. dept. art Coll. San Mateo, Calif., 1970-94. One-man shows include Richard Sumner Gallery, Palo Alto, Calif., 1975, San Mateo County Cultural Ctr., 1976, 82, Tahir Galleries, New Orleans, 1977, 82, Kerwin Galleries, Burlingame, Calif., 1977, Edits. Gallery, Melbourne, Australia, 1977, Ankrum Gallery, Los Angeles, 1978, 84, Edits. Ltd. West Gallery, San Francisco, 1981, Miriam Perlman Gallery, Chgo., 1982, San Mateo County Arts Council Gallery, 1982, Candy Stick Gallery, Ferndale, Calif., 1984, Assoc. Am. Artists, N.Y.C. and Phila., 1984, Gallery 30, Burlingame, 1991, San Mateo, 1984, Triton Mus. Art, Santa Clara, Calif., 1986, Huntsville (Ala.) Mus. Art, 1987, Gallery 30, San Mateo, 1988-97, Concept Art Gallery, Pitts., 1991, Eleonore Austerer Gallery, San Francisco, 1995, Vault Gallery, Sonora, 1995; exhibited in groups shows at Berkeley Art Ctr., Calif., 1976, Burlingame Civic Art Gallery, 1976, Syntex Gallery, Palo Alto, Calif., 1977, Gump's Gallery, San Francisco, 1976, 77, Nat. Gallery of Australia, 1978, Sonoma County Gallery, 1979, Gov. Dummer Acad. Art, Byfield, Mass., 1979, Miss. Mus. Art, 1982, C.A.A. Galleries, Chautauqua, N.Y., 1982, Huntsville Mus. Art, 1983, Tahir Gallery, New Orleans, 1983, Hunterdon Art Ctr., N.J., 1984, Editions Galleries, Melbourne, Australia, 1988, Van Stratten Gallery, Chgo., 1988, 6th Internat. Exhbn., Carnegie-Mellon U., Pa., 1988, Forum Gallery, Jamestown, N.Y., 1988, 5th Internat. Biennale Petite Format de Papier, Belgium, 1989, 4th Internat. Biennial Print Exhibit, Taipei Fine Arts Mus., People's Republic China, 1990, Interprint, Lviv '90, USSR, 1990, New Orleans Mus. Art, 1990, Internat. Print Triennale, Cracow, Poland, 1991, 15th Ann. Nat. Invitational Drawing Exhbn. Emporia State U., Kans., 1991, Haggar U. Gallery, U. Dallas, 1991, Directions in Bay Area Printmaking: Three Decades Palo Alto Cultural Ctr., 1992, Am. Prints: Last Half 20th Century, Jane Haslem Gallery, Washington, 1992, Wenniger Graphics, Boston, 1993, Eleonore Austerer Gallery, San Francisco, 1994, Triton Mus. Art, Santa Clara, 1994, Mobile Mus. Art, 1995, Huntsville (Ala.) Mus. Art, 1995, J.J. Brookings Gallery, San Francisco, 1996, 1997, Grisham Cornell Gallery, Decatur, Ala., 1996, St. Francis Festival of the Arts Invitational, San Francisco, 1996, The Vault Gallery, Sonora, 1997, 98, Heritage Bank Gallery, San Jose, 1998, Arches Paper "Printed on Paper" Competition (touring), 1998, Kautz Internat. Vineyards Nat. Art Exhibition, Murphys CA, 1998, Audubon Artists 56th Ann. Exhibition, N.Y.C., 1998; represented in permanent collections San Francisco Mus. Modern Art, Achenbach Found. Graphic Arts, San Francisco, Phila. Mus. Art, New Orleans Mus. Art, Portland Mus. Art, Maine, The Libr. of Congress, Washington. Huntsville Mus. Art, Midwest Mus. Am. Art, Ind., Cracow Nat. Mus., Poland, Cabo Frio Mus., Brazil, Nat. Mus. Am. Art, Smithsonian Inst., Washington. Recipient Kempshall Clark award Peoria Art Guild, 1981, Paul Lindsay Sample Meml. award 25th Chautauqua Nat. Exhbn. of Am. Art, 1982, 1st Ann. Creative Achievement award Calif. State Legislature/Arts Coun. San Mateo County, 1989. Mem. Am. Color Print Soc., Audubon Artists (Louis Lozowick Meml. award 1978, Silver medal of honor award 1991), Boston Printmakers (Ture Bengtz Meml. award 1987), Calif. Soc. Printmakers (mem. council 1979-81), Los Angeles Printmaking Soc., Phila. Print Club (Lessing J. Rosenwald prize 1979), Arts Council of San Mateo County, Ctrl. Sierra Arts Coun., Theta Chi. Democrat. Studio and Office: PO Box 3305 Sonora CA 95370-3305

PRICE, JOSEPH LLEWELLYN, religious educator; b. Jackson, Miss., July 17, 1949; s. George Norman and Elizabeth Anne (Cooper) P.; m. Bonnie Louise George, Apr. 7, 1973; children: Jared Nathan, David Norman. BA, Georgetown Coll., 1971; MDiv, So. Bapt. Theol. Sem., 1974; AM, U. Chgo., 1979, PhD, 1982. Assoc. pastor First Bapt. Ch., Mt. Sterling, Ky., 1968-71; min. music Rolling Fields Bapt. Ch., Jeffersonville, Ind., 1972-74; lectr. U. Chgo., 1981-82; prof. religious studies Whittier (Calif.) Coll., 1982—; vis. lectr. U. Calif., Riverside, 1985; chair faculty Whittier Coll., 1992-94, faculty master, 1992-98; commr. So. Calif. Intercollegiate Athletic Conf., Whittier, 1990-92. Editor Religious Studies Rev., 1989-94; co-editor: New Handbook of Christian Theologians, 1996, New Handbook of Christian Theology, 1992, Whirlwind in Culture, 1988; (CD Rom) Abingdon Dictionary of Theology, 1997; mem. editl. bd. Jour. Am. Acad. Religion, 1994-98. Adult classes tchr. First Meth. Ch., Whittier, 1983-98; sponsor student chpt. Amnesty Internat., Whittier, 1994-98, Habit for Humanity, Whittier, 1996-98. Am. Coun. Edn. fellow, 1998, NEH fellow, 1985-86. Mem. Am. Acad. Religion, Am. Studies Assn., Popular Culture Assn., Soc. for the Sci. Study of Religion, Soc. for the Study of So. Lit., N.Am. Paul Tillich Soc. Avocations: singing, hiking, camping, reading. Home: 6706 Worsham Canyon Dr Whittier CA 90602 Office: Whittier Coll 13406 Philadelphia St Whittier CA 90601-4446

PRICE, KATHLEEN MCCORMICK, book editor, writer; b. Topeka, Kans., Dec. 25, 1932; d. Raymond Chesley and Kathleen (Shoffner) McCormick; m. William Faulkner Black, Aug. 25, 1956 (div. 1961); 1 child, Kathleen Serena; m. William Hillard Price, Aug. 13, 1976. BA, U. Colo., Denver, 1971. Book reviewer Denver Post, 1971-78; book editor San Diego Mag., 1978-92; cons. editor St. John's Cathedral, Denver, 1985-95. Author: There's a Dactyl Under My Foot, 1986, The Lady and the Unicorn, 1994. Dir. Colo. Episcopal Vestment Guild. Mem. PEN, Denver Women's Press Club, Denver County Club, La Garita Club, Phi Beta Kappa. Episcopalian. Home: 27 Crestmoor Dr Denver CO 80220-5853

PRICE, KEITH GLENN, accountant; b. Ft. Morgan, Colo., Nov. 24, 1941; s. George Felt and Irene Lois (Gibbs) P.; m. Norma Helen Witt, Feb. 28, 1970; children: Diana, Michael, Troy, Aaron, Christopher. BS, BA, Colo. State U., 1968. CPA. Auditor IRS, Casper, Wyo., 1968-75; ptnr. Hines, Price and Co., Cheyenne, Wyo., 1975-76, Fisher, Hines and Price, Cheyenne, Wyo., 1976-80; sole practice Cheyenne, Wyo., 1980—; co-founder, pres. High Plains Mortgage Co., 1990-91; chmn. bd. dirs. Goodwill Industries of Wyo., 1980-87. Treas. North Christian Ch., 1986-95, Salesman with a Purpose, 1980; mem. Heels, 1975—; founder Cheyenne Typing Svc. Served to sgt. USMCR, 1963-71. Mem. AICPA, Wyo. Soc. CPAs, Nat. Soc. Pub. Accts., Nat. Fedn. Ind. Bus., U.S. C. of C., Cheyenne C. of C., Nat. Soc. Tax Profls, Am. Bd. Foensic Accts. (diplomate). Republican. Mem. Ind. Ch. of Christ. Avocations: bowling, fishing, golf. Fax: 307-638-2104. E-mail: kgprice@aol.com. Home: 5333 Frederick Dr Cheyenne WY 82009 Office: 721 E 16th St Cheyenne WY 82001-4703

PRICE, LEW PAXTON, writer, engineer, scientist; b. Takoma Park, Md., Dec. 19, 1938; s. Raymond Miller and Clarene Pearl (Morris) P.; m. Sherrie Darlene Sellers, June 25, 1960 (div. Apr. 1979); children: Terilyn Ann, Heather Rae, Crystal Alene. BS, U.S. Air Force Acad., Colorado Springs, Colo., 1960. Hon. Ho-O Ryu Bushido 6th Dan Master. Electronics engr. Pacific Telephone, Sacramento, Calif., 1965-66, engring. coord., bldgs., 1966-85; pres., design engr. Condor Aeroplane Works, Ltd., Sacramento, 1983-85; engring. coord. Tuttle Engring. and Constrn. Consultants, El Dorado Hills, Calif., 1989-92; scientist, flute design cons., writer, flutemaker Fair Oaks, Garden Valley, Calif., 1977—; internat. cons. flute design, 1990—. Author: The Cosmic Stradivarius, 1974, Aquarian Anastasis, 1975, The Music of Life, 1984, Dimensions in Astrology, 1985, Native North American Flutes, 1990, Secrets of the Flute (Math, Physics & Design), 1991, Creating & Using the Native American Love Flute, 1995, Creating & Using Grandfather's Flute, The Oldest Magic (Prehistory & Influence of Music), 1995, Creating & Using Older Native American Flutes, 1995, Creating & Using Smaller Native American Flutes, 1995, Creating & Using the Native American Concert Flute, 1996, More Secrets of the Flute, 1997, Creating and Using Larger Native American Flutes, Creating and Using the Largest Native American Flutes, 1998, Creating and Using Very Small Native American Flutes, 1998; author, programmer: (computer program) Flute Design (Native American), 1996. Co-advisor Aviation Explorers, archery/space/sci. merit badge instr./examiner, Boy Scouts Am., North Highlands, Calif., 1968-70; panelist United Crusade, Sacramento, Calif., 1971; rifle/pistol/shotgun safety instr. NRA, Fair Oaks, Calif., 1970-72. Capt. USAF, 1960-65. Mem. No. Calif. Flute Circle (co-organizer 1996), Oreg. Native Am. Flute Circle (hon.). Avocations: flying, singing, flute playing, hiking, archery. Home and Office: PO Box 88 Garden Valley CA 95633-0088

PRICE, MARGARET RUTH, financial services company executive; b. Phoenix, Sept. 12, 1956; d. James John and Mavis Marie (Anderson) Knopp; m. Michael Reid Price, Sept. 15, 1979. BS in Instl. Food Svc. and Mgmt., Mont. State U., 1978. CFP. Dir. nutrition programs Human Resource Devel. Coun., Bozeman, Mont., 1979-82; investment cons. Shearson Lehman Bros., Anchorage, 1982-85; v.p., investment cons. Boettcher & Co.-Kemper Fin. Svcs., Anchorage, 1985-88; sr. v.p. investment cons., fin. planner Kemper Securities, Inc.-Kemper Fin. Svcs., Anchorage, 1988-95, Everen Securities, Anchorage, 1995—; mem. Chmns. Circle of Excellence. Chairperson Anchorage Employee Retirement Income Security Act, 1987—, Anchorage Estate Planning Coun., 1991—; bd. dirs. YWCA, 1995—; arbitrator NASD. Mem. Anchorage Nordic Ski Club. Avocations: running, hiking, bicycling, cooking, skiing. Home: 4620 Golden Spring Cir Anchorage AK 99507-4351 Office: Everen Securities 550 W 7th Ave Ste 1980 Anchorage AK 99501-3571

PRICE, MARTIN LLOYD, architect; b. San Mateo, Calif., July 12, 1958; s. Lloyd Ewart and Virginia Nancy (Schneider) P.; m. Brenda Carol Trayer, Oct. 24, 1987. AA, Santa Rosa (Calif.) Jr. Coll., 1978; BS in Architecture, U. Mich., 1981; BA in Mgmt., Sonoma State U., 1983. Lic. architect, Calif., Colo., Wyo.; lic. real estate broker, Calif.; cert. bldg. offcl.; cert. Internat. Conf. Bldg. Ofcls. in various constrn. areas, including building inspector, plans examiner, structural masonry spl. inspector, mech. inspector, plumbing inspector, accessibility specialist, housing inspector, zoning inspector. Architect Della & Hansen, Santa Rosa, 1978, 79, 83-84, Roland, Miller & Assocs., Santa Rosa, 1981, Keith, Hall & Bartley, Santa Rosa, 1982, 84-85; civil engr. Campbell & Pestell, Santa Rosa, 1985-86; architect Flewelling & Logsdon & Assoc., Santa Rosa, 1986-88; structural engr. Dennis Fagent Assoc., Santa Rosa, 1988-94; plan check engr. Morton/Phillips, Inc., 1994-98; bldg. plans examiner bldg. divsn. City of Santa Rosa, 1998—. Recipient Frank Doyle scholar Santa Rosa Jr. Coll., 1976-77, James B. Angell scholar U. Mich. 1981. Mem. Constrn. Specifications Inst. Republican. Avocations: pilot. Office: City Santa Rosa Dept Cmty Devel Bldg Divsn PO Box 1678 Santa Rosa CA 95402-1678

PRICE, RICHARD TAFT, JR., manufacturing company executive; b. San Diego, June 7, 1954; s. Richard Taft and Murial Martha (Weinhold) T. Student, Brigham Young U., 1972-76; BS, Ariz. State U., 1978. Sales mgr. Imperial Metals, L.A., 1978-83; pres. Alumatone, Inc., No. Hollywood, Calif., 1983-88; acquisitions mgr. Calif. Custom Shapes Inc., L.A., 1988-90, pres., 1990—; bd. dirs. IMCOA, Inc., L.A., Calif. Window Corp., Walnut; pres., bd. dirs. Taft Holdings, Inc., Anaheim, Calif., 1995—. Republican.

Office: Calif Custom Shapes Inc 1800 E Talbot Way Anaheim CA 92805-6727

PRICE, ROBERT OTIS, mayor; b. Abilene, Kans., Jan. 4, 1932; s. Iru Paul and Irene Isabel (Parrish) P.; m. Dorothy Faye Price, Jan. 26, 1951 (dec. 1996); m. Sondra Boyd, Mar. 28, 1997; children: Fred Dennis, Donald Eugene. BA, U. Redlands, 1978. Patrolman, sgt., lt., capt. Bakersfield Police Dept., 1956-73, chief police, 1973-88; cons., troubleshooter, various cities, 1988-92; mayor City of Bakersfield, 1993—; pres. Secret Witness Bd., 1980-83. Mem. Calif. Coun. on Criminal Justice, Sacramento, 1983-93; chmn. State Adv. Group on Juvenile Justice, Sacramento, 1988-93, Citizens Adv. Com., Fresno, Calif., 1993—, Youth Devel. Coalition, Bakersfield, 1993—, Econ. Devel. Discussion Group, Bakersfield, 1993—; chmn. western region Nat. Coalition Juvenile Justice and Delinquency Prevention, 1988-93; founder, cons. Youth Adv. Coun., Bakersfield, 1993—; founder Bakersfield Action Team, 1994. Sgt. U.S. Army, 1952-54. Recipient John W. Doubenmier award Am. Soc. Pub. Admins., 1978, Califf Morris award Calif. Probation, Parole and Corrections Officers Assn., 1982. Mem. Internat. Assn. Chiefs Police, Calif. Police Chiefs Assn., Calif. Peace Officers Assn., Calif. Council Criminal Justice, Kern County Police Chiefs Assn. (pres. 1979), Kern County Law Enforcement Admin. Assn. (pres. 1974). Republican. Avocations: photography, fishing, travel. Office: City of Bakersfield 1501 Truxtun Ave Bakersfield CA 93301-5201

PRICE, ROBERT WILLIAM, school superintendent, consultant; b. Ogden, Utah, May 13, 1950; s. William Robert and Eileen Louise (Rabe) P.; m. Sally Sandman, Sept. 20, 1975; children: Geoffrey Thomas, Caitlin Elizabeth. BS in Child Devel., Calif. State U., Hayward, 1973, MS in Sch. Adminstrn., 1986; EdD, U. Pacific, 1998. Cert. elem. tchr., Calif. Tchr. Turlock (Calif.) Sch. Dist., 1974-81; asst. prin. Monte Vista Mid. Sch., Tracy, Calif., 1981-82, prin., 1982-87; asst. supt. instrn. Tracy Pub. Schs., 1987-90, 91-93, interim supt., 1990-91; supt. Empire Union Sch. Dist., Modesto, Calif., 1993—. Cons. Campfire, Tracy, 1983; founding mem. Tracy Exch. Club, 1985; co-founder Project Bus. & Edn. Together, Tracy, 1985; bd. dirs. Boys and Girls Club of Tracy, 1987-93. Recipient Adminstrv. Leadership award Calif. Media & Libr. Educators Assn., 1994. Mem. Assn. Calif. Sch. Adminstrs. (planning com. supts. symposium 1995—, v.p. programs Region 7 1994—), Calif. League Mid. Schs. (adv. panel Region 6 1993—, chair legis. action 1994-95, Region 6 Educator of Yr. 1991). Democrat. Office: Empire Union Sch Dist 116 N Mcclure Rd Modesto CA 95357-1329

PRICE, THOMAS MUNRO, computer consultant; b. Madison, Wis., Oct. 2, 1937; s. John Edward and Georgia Winifred (Day) P.; m. Judith Ann Holm, Aug. 8, 1959; children: Scott Michael, Andrea Lynn. BS, Carroll Coll., Waukesha, Wis., 1959; MS, U. Wis., 1961, PhD, 1964. Prof. math. U. Iowa, 1964-77, U. Wyo., Laramie, 1978-79; computer user cons. U. Wyo., 1979-85, MIS prof., 1985-89; computer cons., 1989—; home rebuilder Pecos, N.Mex., 1994-97; historic home renovator Yerington, Nev., 1997—. Contbr. articles to profl. jours. Home: Nordyke House 727 State Rt 339 Yerington NV 89447

PRICE-TUMA, DIANE LYNETTE, nurse, business owner, educator; b. Burbank, Calif.; married; 2 children. AS, U. State of N.Y., N.Y.C.; BS, U. San Moritz, London, 1994, MS, 1996, PhD, 1998. RN, Calif.; cert. profl. in healthcare quality. Health and safety specialist Geometric Results Inc. a Ford subs., Escondido, Calif., 1992-93; ind. cons. Hrchitect, San Diego, 1993-95; dir. health and safety cons. Jonbar Inc., Vista, Calif., 1994-95; quality mgmt. coord. CalOptima, Orange, Calif., 1995-97; quality improvement mgr. Molina Med., Long Beach, Calif., 1994-98; pres. Ptnrs. Cons., Vista, 1996—; cons. West Moore Ins. Claims, Carlsbad, Calif., 1994-95, Grand Glass Co., San Marcos, Calif., 1992-93, 4 Squaretile Flooring, San Diego, 1992-93. Contbr. articles to Pinnacle. Mem. NAFE, Calif. Assn. Healthcare Quality, Internat. Platform Assn., Calif. Assn. Nurses. Avocations: quilting, walking, charitable activities, cooking. Office: Ptnrs Cons PO Box 2635 Vista CA 92085-2635

PRICHARD, E. DEAN, writer; b. Kansas City, Kans., Dec. 21, 1926; divorced; six children. BA, U. Ariz., 1950. Reporter Ariz. Daily Star, Kansas City Star, Detroit Free Press, 1950-56; writer, exec. J. Walter Thompson Co., Detroit, 1956-61; bur. chief Fairchild Pubs. of N.Y., Copenhagen and Moscow, 1962-67; writer The Reader's Digest, Sydney, Australia, 1968-71; instr. journalism U. Ariz., Tucson, 1975-77; instr. writing Cen. Ariz. Coll., Aravaipa, 1981-86, Pima C.C., Tucson, 1986-93; editor The San Manuel (Ariz.) Miner, 1986-94, The Tombstone (Ariz.) Epitaph, 1974—. Contbr. articles mag. and books. Bd. dirs. Ariz. Trail Assn., Phoenix, 1992—, County Line Riders, Tucson, 1994—, Pima/Pinal Regional Trails, Tucson, 1998; mem. Oracle Town Hall, Ariz., 1986—. With USN, 1944-46, ETO, PTO. Recipient numerous awards in writing, tchg. and horsemanship. Avocation: trail guide. Home: High Jinks Ranch PO Box 724 Oracle AZ 85623-0724

PRICKETT, DAVID CLINTON, physician; b. Fairmont, W.Va., Nov. 26, 1918; s. Clinton Evert and Mary Anna (Gottschalk) P.; m. Mary Ellen Holt, June 29, 1940; children: David C., Rebecca Ellen, William Radcliffe, Mary Anne, James Thomas, Sara Elizabeth; m. Pamela S. Blackstone, Nov. 17, 1991. Student Fairmont (W.Va.) State Coll., 1940-42, AB, W.Va. U., 1944; MD, U. Louisville, 1946; MPH, U. Pitts., 1955. pres. Prickett Chem. Co., 1938-43; acct. W.Va. Conservation Commn., Fed. Works Agy., 1941, 42; lab. asst., instr. chemistry, W.Va. U., 1943; intern, Louisville Gen. Hosp., 1947; surg. resident St. Joseph's Hosp., Parkersburg, W.Va., 1948-49; gen. practice, 1949-50, 55-61; physician USAF, N.Mex., 1961-62, U.S. Army, Calif., 1963-64, San Luis Obispo County Hosp., 1965-66, So. Calif. Edison Co., 1981-84; assoc. physician indsl. and gen. practice Los Angeles County, Calif., 1967—; med. dir. S. Gate plant GM, 1969-71; physician staff City of L.A., 1971-76; relief med. practice Appalachia summer seasons, 1977, 1986, 1988-97. Med. Officer USPHS, Navajo Indian Reservation, Tohatchi (N.Mex.) Health Ctr., 1953-55, surgeon, res. officer, 1957-59; pres. W.Va. Pub. Health Assn., 1951-52; local and dist. health officer, W.Va., 1951-53, sec. indsl. and pub. health sect. W.Va. Med. Assn., 1956; dist. health officer Allegheny County, Pa., 1957. Author: The Newer Epidemiology, 1962, rev., 1990, Public Health, A Science Resolvable by Mathematics, 1965, contbr. to publ. Served to 2d lt. AUS, 1943-46. Dr. Thomas Parran fellow U. Pitts. Sch. Pub. Health, 1955; named to Hon. Order Ky. Cols. Fellow Am. Pub. Health Assn.; mem. SOR (Sons of Revolution), Am. Occupational Med. Assn., Western Occupational Med. Assn., Am. Med. Assn., Calif. Med. Assn., L.A. County Med. Assn., Am. Acad. Family Physicians, Am. Legion, Elks, Phi Chi. Address: PO Box 4032 Whittier CA 90607-4032

PRIESTLEY, MICHAEL LINN, business owner executive; b. Portland, Oreg., Jan. 24, 1953; s. Chester Carroll and Darlene Blanch (Jeske) P.; m. Anna Rebecca Miller, Jan. 1, 1973; children: Benjamin Ivon, Isaac Noel, Abraham Jordan. Sales tng., Tom Hopkins and Dale Carnegie; mgmt. tng., Zig Ziglar, Portland; student, New England Christian Coll., Ellenville, N.Y., 1971-72, Portland Community Coll., 1976-79. Lic. ins. and real estate agt. Mktg. agent Oreg. Office Systems, Beaverton, Oreg., 1979-80; western region br. mgr. Ontel Corp., Portland, 1980-81; bus. account exec. Rogers Cablesystems, Portland, 1981-84; mktg. agt. A.L. Williams, Portland, 1983-85; corp. and nat. account sales engr. Sentrol, Inc., Portland, 1985-90; owner, founder AAA Oil Co., 1990—; owner Minuteman Press, Portland, 1991-96; fin. cons. in field. Pres., chmn. Richmond Neighborhood Assn., Portland, 1984-86; founder Clinton St. Coalition, 1983. Recipient Achievement award Dale Carnegie Sales Inst. L.W. Dennis & Assoc., 1981, most territory sales growth, 1986, Sentrol. Mem. Nob Hill Bus. Assn. (bd. dirs. 1992-96), Eagles Nest Club. Republican. Evang. Christian. Avocations: boating. Home: 16991 Maple Cir Lake Oswego OR 97034-5631 Office: AAA Oil Co 5418 SE Mitchell St Portland OR 97206-4842

PRINCE, DONNA JEAN, artist; b. L.A., Feb. 3, 1954; d. Robert Henry and Anna Marie (Estatico) P., m. Donald James Molyneux, Sept. 2, 1989. BA with honors, Art Ctr. Coll. of Design, 1989. Key background painter Queen of the Universe Prodn., L.A., 1990, Disney TV Animation, N. [illegible] 1991, Hanna Barbera, Hollywood, 1991-92, Rich Animation, Burbank, Calif., 1993-94; tchr. Art Ctr. Coll. Design, 1997. Mem. neighborhood activist Friends of Washington Park, Pasadena, 1991-96, workshop presenter [illegible] Pasadena Parks & Recs., 1995. Mem. Motion Picture Screen Cartoonists Guild, Friends of Washington Park (pres. 1991-94), Soc. of Illustrators (v.p. 1991). Democrat. Avocations: gardening, traveling, shopping, dancing, interior decorating. Home: 1277 N El Molino Ave Pasadena CA 91104-2839 Office: Disney TV Animation 5200 Lankershim Blvd Ste 600 North Hollywood CA 91601-3100

PRINCE, RICHARD HUDSON, film producer; b. Los Angeles, Dec. 31, 1951; s. Philip H. and Barbara (Cooper) P.; m. Julie Lynn Magnuson; children: Jennifer, Diana, Joanna. BA, UCLA, 1974, MBA, 1977. Asst. film dir. various studios, Calif., 1977-83; v.p. prodn. Point Fermin Prodns., Los Angeles, 1982-89; prodn. mgr. various film studios, Calif., 1982-98; producer, 1987—. Asst. dir. (films) Heaven Can Wait, 1977, My Bodyguard, 1979, Risky Business, 1982, Uncommon Valor, 1983; prodn. mgr. (films) Personal Best, 1982, Bluffing It, 1987, The Bedroom Window, 1986, The Lemon Sisters, 1988, Murder in Mississippi, 1989, White Fang, 1990, Only the Lonely, 1990, Distinguished Gentleman, 1992, Fatherhood, 1993, Richie Rich, 1994, Nick of Time, 1995; co-prodr. (films) Jimmy Reardon, 1987, Angels in the Outfield, 1994; exec. prodr. Gone Fishin', 1996, Rocket Man, 1997, Super Dave, 1998. Mem. Prodr. Guild Am., Dirs. Guild Am., Soc. Motion Picture and TV Engrs., Acad. TV Arts and Scis., Am. Cinemateque, Am. Film Inst. Club: Bel-Air Bay (Pacific Palisades, Calif.). Avocations: bicycling, swimming. Home and Office: 5310 Circle Dr Apt 210 Sherman Oaks CA 91401-5605

PRINCE, TERRY, organizing consultant; b. Mudeford, Dorset, Eng., Oct. 28, 1957; came to U.S., 1967; BSBA, Ithaca Coll., 1979. Owner Terry Prince, Elk Grove, Calif., 1983—. Author: Surviving and Thriving in the Home Office, 1995. Recipient Katie Maxwell Writing Achievement award Suburban Writers, 1998. Mem. Nat. Assn. of Profl. Organizers (Golden Circle award 1990), Calif. Writers, A.R. Toastmasters (pres. 1993, Disting. Toastmaster 1993), Sacramento Publishers Assn. (award chair 1994-97, chief judge 1994-99), Suburban Writers (bd. dirs., mem. at large 1996—). Home and Office: 6409 Fuego Way Elk Grove CA 95758

PRINDLE, ROBERT WILLIAM, geotechnical engineer; b. L.A., Nov. 19, 1950; s. Robert Edward and Margaret Elizabeth (Johnson) P.; m. Nancy K. Hayden, Apr. 5, 1986; children: William Robert, Amy Elizabeth. Student St. John's Coll., Camarillo, Calif., 1968-70; BSCE summa cum laude, Loyola U., L.A., 1974; MS, Calif. Inst. Tech., 1975; 40-hours hazardous waste ops. and emergency response tng.; 8-hours hazardous waste ops. supr./mgr. tng. Lic. geotechnical engr., Calif.; registered profl. civil engr., Ariz., Calif., N. Mex. Engring. aide L.A. County Sanitation Dists., 1973-74; student engr. L.A. Dept. Water and Power, 1974, 75; staff engr. Fugro, Inc., Long Beach, Calif., 1976-78; sr. staff engr. Woodward-Clyde Consultants, Orange, Calif., 1978-79; mem. tech. staff Sandia Nat. Labs., Albuquerque, 1980-89; v.p. engring. Deuel & Assocs, Inc., Albuquerque, 1989-90, pres., 1990-94; pres. Prindle-Hinds Environ., Inc., 1990-96; v.p. SVS Environ. Sys., Inc., 1996, exec. v.p., 1996-97; pres. Asgard Industries, Inc., 1997—. Regional referee Am. Youth Soccer Orgn., 1995-97, area referee, 1998—. Contbr. articles to profl. jours. Mem. N. Mex. Symphony Orch. Chorus, 1981-84. Office: Asgard Industries Inc 11024 Montgomery Blvd NE Albuquerque NM 87111-3962

PRINE, STEPHEN BRENT, publisher; b. Alton, Ill., Feb. 21, 1952; s. Virgil Earl and Isabelle (Antoinette) P.; m. Bonnie Lynn White; children: Stephen, Evan, Nicole, Jacqueline. AA with honors, Am. River Coll., Sacramento, Calif., 1971; BA, Washington U., 1973. Owner Vitrino's Pizza, St. Louis, 1972-73, S.B. Prine & Assocs., St. Louis, 1973-75, PM Petroleum, La Jolla, Calif., 1975-76, Pacific Western Imports, San Francisco, 1976-78, Prine & Assocs. Real Estate and Land Devel., Sacramento, Calif., 1978-83, Brent Oil & Gas, Houston, 1983-88, Ctrs. West Investments, Sacramento, 1987-88; pub. U.S. Realty Report, Sacramento, 1988-90, S.P. Publications, Sacramento, 1990—. Chmn. Big Hearts Internat., Sacramento, Calif. 1990—; founder, exec. dir. Missing Children Report, 1992—. Author: Foreign Investment in U.S. Real Estate, 1990. Roman Catholic. Avocations: travel, writing, reading. Address: 564 La Sierra Dr Ste 186 Sacramento CA 95864-7206

PRINGLE, EDWARD E., legal educator, former state supreme court chief justice; b. Chgo., Apr. 12, 1914; s. Abraham J. and Lena (Oher) P.; m. Pauline Judd, Aug. 17, 1941; children: Bruce, Eric. LL.B., U. Colo., 1936, LL.D., 1976; LL.D., U. Denver, 1979. Bar: Colo. Practiced in Denver, 1936-42, 47-57; with fed. govt. service Washington, 1943-47; dist. judge Colo. Dist. Ct., Denver, 1957-61; justice Supreme Ct. Colo., Denver, 1961-79; chief justice Supreme Ct. Colo., 1970-78; dir. research and writing program U. Denver Coll. Law, 1979-90, prof. emeritus, 1990—. Contbr. articles to profl. jours. Bd. dirs. Am. Med. Center, Denver; mem. Nat. Commn. for Establishment of Nat. Inst. Justice. Served with USAAF, 1942. Recipient William Lee Knous award U. Colo. Law Sch., 1975. Mem. Am., Colo., Denver bar assns., Conf. Chief Justices (chmn. 1973-74), Am. Judicature Soc. (Herbert Lincoln Harley award 1973, chmn. bd. 1974-76), Nat. Center State Cts. (pres. 1977-79). Jewish. Club: Masons (33 deg.). Office: U Denver Coll Law 1900 Olive St Denver CO 80220-1857

PRISBREY, REX PRINCE, retired insurance agent, underwriter, consultant; b. Washington, Utah, Mar. 18, 1922; s. Hyrum William and Susan (Prince) P.; m. Pinka Julieta Lucero, Nov. 16, 1943; children: Karol Sue Prisbey Lewallen, Pamela Blanche Prisbrey Ebert, Michael Rex. BA in Acctg., Denver U., 1949. CLU. Ptnr. Allen Stamm & Assocs., home builders, Farmington, N.Mex., 1949-52; acct. Linder Burke & Stevenson, Santa Fe, N.Mex., 1949-52; agt. State Farm Ins. Cos., Farmington, 1952-56; mgr. State Farm Ins. Cos., Phoenix, 1956-60; contractor, agt. State Farm Ins. Cos., Scottsdale, Ariz., 1960—; v.p., treas. Original Curio Store Inc., Santa Fe. Pres. Farmington Jr. C. of C., 1952; v.p. N.Mex. Jr. C. of C., 1953. 1st lt. USAAF, 1941-46, CBI. Decorated DFC, Air medal with oak leaf cluster; recipient Disting. Life Underwriter award Cen. Ariz. Mgrs. Assn., 1979. Mem. Am. Soc. CLU's, Scottsdale Assn. Life Underwriters (pres. 1980-81), Airplane Owners and Pilots Assn., Hump Pilots Assn. (life, speaker at meml. of Hump Flyers, Kunming, China 1993), Pinewood Country Club (bd. dirs., treas., v.p. 1985—), Civitans (pres. Scottsdale 1962-63). Avocations: flying, golf, photography. Home: 4011 N 65th St Scottsdale AZ 85251-4235

PRITCHARD, JAMES PATRICK, investment company executive; b. Buffalo, Mar. 2, 1960; s. Thomas Stanley and Marylou (Titus) P.; m. Jenny Margaret Howell, Aug. 23, 1986; children: James, Katherine, Laura. BA in Econ., Columbia U., 1982. CFP. Stockbroker Smith Barney, Scottsdale, Ariz., 1982-85; owner Pritchard Investment Mgmt., Durango, Colo., 1986—. Author: Every Boys Dream, 1998, The Gods, 1998. Pres. Chapman Hill Improvements Assn., Durango, 1993-98; v.p., bd. dirs. Medina Healthcare Found., 1990-93; actiive LaPlata Forum, Durango, 1996—. Named to Kenmore East H.S. Athletic Hall of Fame, 1996. Avocations: writing, reading, handball, ice hockey. Fax: (970) 259-8909. E-mail: jim@pritchardinvestment.com. Office: Pritchard Investment Mgmt 528 Main Ave Durango CO 81301-5434

PRIZIO, BETTY J., property manager, civic worker; b. L.A., Jan. 23, 1928; d. Harry W. and Irene L. (Connell) Campbell; divorced; children: David P., John W., Robert H., James R. AA in Social Sci., L.A. City Coll., 1949. Owner, mgr. indsl. bldgs. and condominiums Tustin, Calif., 1976—; ind. mktg. exec., Melaleuca. Bd. dirs. Founders Chpt. Aux., Providence Speech and Hearing Ctr., 1986-88, aux. pres., 1986-89; vol. Western Med. Ctr. Aux., 1985-89, chmn. gift shop com., 1987-88, 2d v.p., 1992, jr. vol. adv., mem. bd. dirs. fund raising group, mem. scholarship com., mem. Focus on Women com. 1990—; mem. adv. coun. Chapman U., Orange, Calif., 1986-87, bd. mem. Pres. Assocs., 1985-86; bd. dirs. Chapman Music Assocs., 1986—, Tustin Hist. Soc., 1988—, Santa Ana YWCA, 1976-77; mem. adv. coun. Orange County chpt. Freedoms Found. at Valley Forge, 1985—; mem. Orange County chpt. Charter 100, 1985-87; active United Meth. Ch.; others. Mem. Tustin Hist. Soc. (bd. dirs. 1988-90). Republican. Avocations: gardening, arts and crafts, travel, photography. Home: 17342 Village Dr [illegible]

PRO, PHILIP MARTIN, judge; b. Richmond, Calif., Dec. 12, 1946; s. Leo Martin and Mildred Louise (Beck) P.; m. Dori Sue Hallas, Nov. 13, 1982; 1 [illegible] 1972. Bar: Calif. 1972, Nev. 1973, U.S. Ct. Appeals (9th cir.) 1973, U.S. Dist. Ct. Nev. 1973, U.S. Supreme Ct. 1976. Pub. defender, Las Vegas, 1973-75; asst. U.S. atty., Dist. Nev., Las Vegas, 1975-78; ptnr. Semenza, Murphy & Pro, Reno, 1978-79; dep. atty. gen. State of Nev., Carson City, 1979-80; U.S. magistrate U.S. Dist. Ct. Nev., Las Vegas, 1980-87; U.S. dist. judge, 1987—; instr. Atty. Gen.'s Advocacy Inst., Nat. Inst. Trial Advocacy, 1992; chmn. com. adminstrn. of magistrate judge system Jud. Conf. U.S., 1993—. Bd. dirs. NCCJ, Las Vegas, 1982—, mem. program com. and issues in justice com. Mem. ABA, Fed. Judges Assn. (bd. dirs. 1992—), Nev. State Bar Assn., Calif. State Bar Assn., Nev. Judges Assn. (instr.), Assn. Trial Lawyers Am., Nev. Am. Inn Ct. (pres. 1989—), Ninth Cir. Jury (instructions com.), Nat. Conf. U.S. Magistrates (sec.), Nev. Am. Inn of Ct. (pres. 1989-91). Republican. Episcopalian. Office: US Dist Ct 341 Fed Bldg 300 Las Vegas Blvd S Ste 4650 Las Vegas NV 89101-5883

PROBASCO, DALE RICHARD, management consultant; b. Ogden, Utah, July 23, 1946; s. Robert Vere and Dorleen E. (Oppliger) P.; m. Joan Michele Takacs, Dec. 20, 1969 (div.); children: Todd Aaron, Brad Dillon; m. Vivian Jean Bennett, May 21, 1998. BS, Utah State U., 1975; MS, U. Phoenix, 1988. Inventory asst. Moore Bus. Form, Logan, Utah, 1973-75; systems engr. Electronic Data Systems, Dallas, 1975-76; start-up engr. Bechtel Corp., San Francisco, 1976-78; supr. project scheduling Toledo Edison Co., 1978-80; mgr. project controls Utah Power and Light Co., Salt Lake City, 1980-87, mgr. mktg. strategy, 1987-89; pres. Probasco Cons., Inc., West Jordan, Utah, 1989-90; mgr. Metzler & Assocs., Deerfield, Ill., 1990—. Contbr. articles to profl. publs. Pres. Emery County Little League, Castledale, Utah, 1981-84; coach Little League Baseball, West Jordan, Utah, 1985-86. With USN, 1965-72. Mem. Assn. Energy Svcs. Profls., Am. Pub. Power Assn., Nat. Rural Electric Coop. Assn. Lutheran. Avocations: computer programming, softball, basketball, music.

PROBERT, COLIN, advertising executive. Ptnr., pres. Goodby, Silverstein & Ptnrs., San Francisco. Office: Goodby Silverstein & Ptnrs 720 California St San Francisco CA 94108-2404*

PROBST, JOHN ELWIN, chaplain, minister; b. Klamath Falls, Oreg., Apr. 3, 1940; s. John Albert and Jocelyn Marlia (Tunnell) P.; m. Patty P. Maness, Jan. 13, 1975; children: Marla, Joni, Jessica. BTh, Internat. Bible Sem., Orlando, Fla. Ordained to ministry So. Bapt. Conv., 1969. Pastor 1st Bapt. Ch., Dorris, Calif., 1968-72; evangelist, Tex., 1972-74; youth pastor Salem Bapt. Ch., Rocky, Okla., 1974-75; pastor Retrop Bapt. Ch., Carter, Okla., 1975-79; supply pastor 1st Bapt. Ch., Hobart, Okla., 1975-79; interim pastor Mountain Heights So. Bapt. Ch., Leadville, Colo., 1979; missionary-evangelist, interim pastor Skyway Bapt. Ch., Glendale, Ariz., 1979-82; pastor 1st So. Bapt. Ch., Monrovia, Calif., 1982-85; chaplain Media Focus, Duarte, Calif., 1982—; interim pastor United Comty. Ch., Glendale, Calif., 1988-90; revival leader; former mem. evangelism and search com. Estrella Assn., Ariz.; former br. mgr. Sherwin Williams Co.; writer, casting dir., producer Seven Star Prodn.; assoc. producer, writer, casting dir. Castel Prodns.; writer Esses Films; researcher, writer, asst. producer Nunn Prodns.; telemarketer White Horse Prodns; pres. L.A. So. Bapt. Pastors Conf., 1983; ch. planter Philippine Crusade, 1983, 85; numerous others. With USAF, 1959-64. Mem. So. Calif. Motion Picture Coun. (life, Golden Halo awards 1985). Office: PO Box 618 Duarte CA 91009-0618

PROCUNIER, RICHARD WERNER, environmental scientist, administrator; b. Dallas, Tex., Oct. 27, 1936; s. Werner Richard and Dorothy (Koch) P.; m. Janet Mesing, Sept. 5, 1958 (div. Aug. 28, 1984); children: Nancy, Carol, Ellen; m. Carolyn Harris, June 25, 1988. BSEE, MIT, 1958; PhD, Univ. Coll. London, 1966. Prof. U. London, 1966-68; rsch. scientist Lockheed, Palo Alto, Calif., 1968-72; mgr. Hewlett Packard, Santa Clara, Calif., 1972-74; chief of noise control U.S. EPA, San Francisco, 1974-82, sci. advisor, 1982-83, environ. scientist, 1990—; prof. U. Calif., Davis, 1984-85; adminstr. County Health Svcs., Martinez, Calif., 1986-89; mem. Nat. Edn. Com., Nat. Environ. Health Assn., Denver, 1980-87; enforcement coord., U.S. EPA, San Francisco, 1990. Contbr. many articles to profl. jours. Proponent to incorporate Orinda, Calif., 1984. Recipient Presidential citation, Nat. Environmental Health Assn., 1981. Fellow Royal Soc. London; mem. World Affairs Coun., Commonwealth Club, Kappa Sigma (Leadership award 1958). Avocation: golf.

PRONOVE-IRREVERRE, PACITA, medical officer; b. Manila, Philippines, Oct. 12, 1919; d. Ricardo Avenido and Dolores (Laico) Pronove; m. Filadelfo Irreverre, Dec. 30, 1950. AA, U. Philippines, 1939, MD, 1944. Diplomate Am. Acad. Pediatrics. Physician Pasay City Health Dept., Philippines, 1946-52; pediatric resident Childrens Hosp., Washington, 1952-54; rsch. assoc. NIH, Bethesda, Md., 1959-61, scientist, adminstr., 1961-73. co-discoverer Bartter's Syndrome. Pres. Pasay City Jr. Women's Club, Manila, 1948, Philippine Jr. Women's Clubs, Manila, 1950. Outstanding Alumnae award U. Philippines Coll. Medicine, 1987. Avocations: travel, music, history, arts. Address: 2412 Fulton St San Francisco CA 94118-4107

PRONZINI, BILL JOHN (WILLIAM PRONZINI), author; b. Petaluma, Calif., Apr. 13, 1943; s. Joseph and Helene (Guder) P.; m. Marcia Muller. Coll. student, 2 years. Author: 50 novels (including under pseudonyms), 4 books of non-fiction, 7 collections of short stories, 1971—; first novel, The Stalker, 1971; editor 80 anthologies; contbr. numerous short stories to publs. Recipient 6 scroll awards Mystery Writers Am., Life Achievement award Pvt. Eye Writers Am., 1987. Office: PO Box 2536 Petaluma CA 94953-2536

PROPER, MARY, advertising executive. Controller Suissa Miller Advt., L.A. Office: Suissa Miller Advt 11601 Wilshire Blvd Fl 16 Los Angeles CA 90025-1770*

PROSSER, MICHAEL JOSEPH, community college staff member; b. Syracuse, N.Y., May 9, 1948; s. Palmer Adelbert and Viola Mary (Clairmont) P. AA, Riverside (Calif.) City Coll., 1971; BA in History, Calif. State Coll., San Bernardino, 1977; MSLS, U. So. Calif., L.A., 1981. Cert. cmty. coll. instr., librarian, Calif. Libr. clk. Riverside C.C., 1968-81, learning resources asst., 1981—. Author: California and the Pacific Plate: A Bibliography, 1979. Tutor, Queen of Angels Ch., Riverside, 1985—, facilitator/patrons, 1985—. With U.S. Army, 1969-71. Mem. ASCD, Internat. Soc. Poets, Calif. Media Libr. Educators Assn., Calif. Libr. Assn. Democrat. Roman Catholic. Home: 6800 Palos Dr Riverside CA 92503-1330 Office: Riverside Cmty Coll 4800 Magnolia Ave Riverside CA 92506-1242

PROTHE, MICHAEL DEAN, architect; b. Portland, Nov. 19, 1961; s. Donald Dean and Arleatha Jean (Mayer) P.; m. Janice Dell Edwards, Oct. 20, 1990. BArch, U. Oreg., 1986. Registered architect, Oreg. Draftsman, designer Barclay & Assocs., Clackamas County, Oreg., 1986; draftsman pvt. practice, Portland, 1986-87; draftsman, designer Erik Bjork, Vancouver, Wash., 1987-92, Vanlom/Edwards, Portland, 1992-95; architect pvt. practice, Portland, 1995—. Dir. mission & svc. com. Resurrection Luth. Ch., Portland, 1988-95, dir. bldg. com., 1995-96. Democrat. Lutheran. Home: 422 NE 114th Ave Portland OR 97220-2330

PROTZMAN, GRANT DALE, university administrator, state legislator; b. Ogden, Utah, May 3, 1950; s. Paul L. and Maxine E. (Nelson) P.; m. Linda Sue Gerasta, Mar. 30, 1985; children: Heather Sue, Kristen Marie, Erin Elizabeth. BA, Utah. State U., 1976; MS, Calif. Am. U., 1979; MA, U. No. Colo., 1987, EdD, 1988. Coord. student activities Weber State U., Ogden, 1976-81, coord. student govt., 1981-82, assoc. dir. student life, 1982-84, dir. co-curricular learning, 1984-87, planning and devel. officer, dir. drug and alcohol program, 1987-91, asst. to v.p., 1991—; mem., asst. minority whip Utah State Ho. of Reps., Salt Lake City, 1986-97; sr. cons. Inst. for Leadership Devel., Ogden, 1978—. Author: An Examination of Select Motivational Variables of Members in Three Different Types of Volunteer Organizations in a Collegiate Setting, 1988, An Investigation of the State of Motivation Management and Assessment in Volunteer Organizations, 1988; contbr. ar- [illegible] Emergency Planning Com., Ogden, 1988-93, critical workplace skills adv. bd. Applied Tech. Ctr., 1991—, mem. adv. bd. Pvt. Industry Coun./Local Community Coun., 1994—, State of Utah Region II Dept. Corrections,

1992—; mem. bd. dirs. Hospice No. Utah, 1994—. Named Outstanding Young Man of the Year, Jay Cees; Recipient Ptnrs. in Edn. Recognition award Weber Sch. Dist., 1987, Appreciation award Utah Vocat. Leadership Orgns., 1987, Extended Svc. award Ogden Sch. Dist., 1988, Outstanding Legislator award Utah Democratic Party Chmn's. award, 1988, Utah Sch. Employees Assn. Scroll of Honor award as Outstanding legislator, 1990, Weber State U. Student Svcs. Soar award, 1991, Utah Edn. Assn. Honor Roll award as Outstanding legislator, 1991, Utah Ednl. Libr. Media Assn. award for Outstanding Dedication and Svc. to Utah Lib. Media programs, 1992, Utah Assn. of Rehabilitative Facilities award for Svc. to Persons with disabilities, 1992, U.B.A.T.C. award for Support of Vocational Edn., 1992, Golden Key award, 1993, Utah Govt. Coun. for People with Disabilities award State Legis. Coalition, 1994. Mem. Nat. Assn. Campus Activities (regional coord. 1982-85, conf. educator 1980-83, Nat. Outstanding Unit of Yr. 1986, Regional Outstanding Unit of Yr. 1985), Utah Edn. Assn. (honor roll award 1991), Rotary, Kappa Delta Pi, Phi Sigma Alpha, Phi Delta Kappa. Democrat. Mormon. Avocations: auto restoration, waterskiing, hiking. Home: 3073 N 575 E Ogden UT 84414-2077 Office: Weber State U 3750 Harrison Blvd Ogden UT 84408-0001

PROULX, (EDNA) ANNIE, writer; b. Norwich, Conn., Aug. 22, 1935; d. George Napolean and Lois Nellie (Gill) Proulx; m. James Hamilton Lang, June 22, 1969 (div. 1990); children: Sylvia Marion Bullock Clarkson, Jonathan Edward Lang, Gillis Crowell Lang, Morgan Hamilton Lang. BA cum laude, U. Vt., 1969; MA, Sir George Williams U., Montreal, Can., 1973; DHL (hon.), U. Maine, 1994. Author: Heart Songs and Other Stories, 1988, Postcards, 1992 (PEN/Faulkner award 1993), The Shipping News, 1993 (Nat. Book award for fiction 1993, Chgo. Tribune Heartland award 1993, Irish Times Internat. Fiction award 1993, Pulitzer Prize for fiction 1994), Accordion Crimes, 1996 (Dos Passos prize for lit. 1996); contbr. more than 50 articles to mags. and jours.; editor: Best American Short Stories of 1997. Recipient Nat. Mag. award for short story Brokeback Mountain, 1998; Kress fellow Harvard U., 1974, fellow Vt. Coun. Arts, 1989, NEA, 1991, Guggenheim Found., 1992; rsch. grantee Inter.-U. Ctr., 1975; resident Ucross Found., 1990, 92. Mem. PEN Am. Ctr., Phi Beta Kappa, Phi Alpha Theta. Avocations: canoeing, reading, fishing.

PROUT, CARL WESLEY, history educator; b. Bakersfield, Calif., Apr. 19, 1941; s. George Hecla and Ruth (King) P. BA, U. Calif., Santa Barbara, 1964, MA, 1965; postgrad., U. Tenn., Knoxville, 1968-71, Am. U., Cairo, 1974, U. So. Calif., 1981, Ain Shams U., Cairo, 1981. Instr. history Santa Barbara Coll., 1965-66, U. Tenn., Knoxville, 1968-71; instr. Orange Coast Coll., Costa Mesa, 1966-68, asst. prof., 1971-73, assoc. prof., 1973-75, prof., 1975—; treas. Willmore Corp., 1980-81, sec., 1984-85, v.p., 1985-86, pres., chmn., 1988-89, also bd. dirs.; group facilitator Coastview Meml. Hosp., Long Beach, 1986-89. Research and publs. in field. Pres., chmn. bd. Alamitos Heights Improvement Assn., 1979-80, bd. dirs., 1980-82; mem. East Long Beach Joint Council, 1979-80, Local Coastal Planning Adv. Com., 1979-80 mem. preservation bd. Palm Springs Historic Site, 1994—, mem. Palm Springs Hist. Soc; founding pres. Palm Springs Hist. Site Preservation Found., 1997—. Recipient Salgo Outstanding Tchr. award, 1974-76. Mem. Am. Hist. Assn., Writers Guild Palm Springs (v.p. 1996—). Office: Orange Coast Coll 2701 Fairview Rd Costa Mesa CA 92626-5563

PROUT, RALPH EUGENE, physician; b. Los Angeles, Feb. 27, 1933; s. Ralph Byron and Fern (Taylor) P.; m. Joanne Morris, Sept. 17, 1980; children: Michael, Michelle. BA, La Sierra Coll., 1953; MD, Loma Linda U., 1957; D of Nutri-Medicine (hon.), John F. Kennedy Coll., 1987. Diplomate: Nat. Bd. Med. Examiners. Intern Los Angeles County Hosp., 1957-58; resident internal medicine White Meml. Hosp., Los Angeles, 1958-60; resident psychiatry Harding Hosp., Worthington, Ohio, 1960-61; practice medicine specializing in internal medicine Napa, Calif., 1961-63; staff internist Calif. Med. Facility, Vacaville, 1963-68, chief med. officer, 1968-84; chief med. cons. Calif. Dept. Corrections, 1977-86, chief med. services, 1983; med. cons. Wellness Cons., Placerville, Calif., 1985-96; pres. Addiction Medicine Treatment Ctr., Placerville, Calif., 1986-96; instr. Sch. Medicine, Loma Linda U., 1965-66; clin. assoc. U. Calif.-Davis Sch. Medicine, 1978-84; med. cons. Substance Abuse Pine Grove Camp, 1986—; expert witness alcoholism El Dorado (Calif.) Superior Ct., 1994—; pres. Union Am. Physicians and Dentists, Calif. State Employee chpt., 1970-72. Treas. Vacaville Republican Assembly, 1972-75; del. Republican Central Com. Solano County, 1975-78; Bd. dirs. Napa-Solano County United Crusade, Vallejo, Calif., 1969-71, v.p., 1970-71; bd. dirs., co-founder Project Clinic, Vacaville, 1974-77, Home Health Com. Inter-Community Hosp., Fairfield, 1978-80; pres. MotherLode Citizens for Drug-Free Youth, Amador County, 1985—. Named One of Outstanding Young Men of Am., 1968. Mem. AMA, Am. Assn. Sr. Physicians, Internat. Assn. New Sci., Union Concerned Scis., Am. Assn. Christian Counselors, Mother Lode Citizens for Drug-Free Youth, Native Sons of Golden West, Alpha Omega Alpha. Republican. Home and Office: 24405 Shake Ridge Rd Volcano CA 95689-9728

PROWELL, ROY WALTERS, JR., orthodontist; b. Pitts., Oct. 6, 1945; s. Roy Walters and Dorothy Jane (Forney) P.; student U. Calif., Davis, 1963-65, D.D.S. in Orthodontics (Regents scholar), U. Calif., San Francisco, 1969; m. Evelyn Joyce Morgan, Aug. 1, 1971 (div. June 1985); children: Roy Walters III, Ian Morgan; m. Gretchen Fretter, Oct. 17, 1992. Assoc., Gordon Osser, D.D.S., Castro Valley, Calif., 1970-71, Willard Collins, D.D.S., Stockton, Calif., 1971-72; practice dentistry specializing in orthodontics, Pittsburg and Antioch, Calif., 1969-76; pres. R. Walt Prowell, D.D.S., Inc., Pittsburg and Antioch, 1976-91; mem. staff Mt. Diablo Rehab. Center, Pleasant Hill, Calif., Delta Meml. Hosp., Antioch; mem. East Bay (Calif.) Cleft Palate Panel, East Bay Facial Surgery Panel. Pres., U. Calif. Orthodontic Alumni Found., 1978-81, treas., 1981-84; dist. chmn. Boy Scouts Am., 1992-95. Republican. Presbyterian. Lodge: Masons, Rotary. Office: 3107 Lone Tree Way Ste E Antioch CA 94509-4959

PROZAN, LAWRENCE IRA, financial planner; b. Albuquerque, Apr. 8, 1961; s. George and Sylvia (Simmons) P. AB, U. Calif., Berkeley, 1983. Asst. buyer Macy's, San Francisco, 1984-85; fin. planner Calvert Securities, Oakland, Calif., 1985-87, Intrust, Walnut Creek, Calif., 1987; pres. Wren Pro, Oakland, 1988—; chief fin. officer Oakland Weight Loss Corp., 1989—. Mem. Bear Backers U. Calif., 1985—, MLA founding mem. Mem. Internat. Assn. Fin. Planners. Address: 6010 Zinn Dr Oakland CA 94611-2623

PRUITT, GARY B., newspaper executive. Pres., CEO Sacramento Bee. Office: Sacramento Bee 2100 Q Street Sacramento CA 95852*

PRUNER, GARY LEE, art educator; b. Kearny, Nebr., Jan. 9, 1940; s. Lee Harold and Maxine Isabel (Cook) P.; m. Jeanette Rosalie Herrera, Apr. 13, 1960 (div. June 1980); 1 child, Michelle Russell. BA in Art, Calif. State U., Sacramento, 1964, MA in Art, 1970. Art instr. Encina H.S., Sacramento, 1964-70, Am. River Coll., Sacramento, 1970—; artist-in-residence U. of the Pacific, 1976. Recipient Artist of Yr. award Calif. State Fair, 1980. Avocations: art, computers, gardening, building, designing.

PRUNES-CARRILLO, FERNANDO, plastic surgeon, educator; b. Chihuahua, Mex.; m. Linda R. Underwood; children: Alexander, Ariadne, Anthony. MD, U. Chihuahua, Mex., 1968. Surg. intern Booth Meml. Med. Ctr., Flushing, N.Y., 1971-72; resident in gen. surgery Tucson Hosps. Med. Edn. Program, 1972-76; resident in plastic surgery Mayo Grad. Sch. Medicine, 1979-81; chief divsn. plastic surgery Kern Med. Ctr., Bakersfield, Calif., 1983—; asst. clin. prof. surgery U. Calif., San Diego, 1983—. Mem. Am. Soc. Plastic and Reconstructive Surgeons, Mayo Alumni Assn. Avocations: golf, computers. Office: Kern Med Ctr 1830 Flower St Bakersfield CA 93305-4186

PRUSA, JAMES GRAHAM, association executive; b. Cleve., Dec. 1, 1948; s. James Leonard and Mary LaVerne (Graham) P.; m. Patricia Ann Thwaits, June 20, 1971 (dec. 1975); m. Karen Beth Adamo, Nov. 30, 1980; children: Nathasha Clare, Shamus Graham. BS, Calif. State Poly. U., 1975; postgrad., U. Santa Clara, 1977-79, Stanford U., 1984. Golf course supt. China Lake NWC Golf Course, China Lake, Calif., 1975-77; golf course mgr. Pasatiempo, Inc., Santa Cruz, Calif., 1977-82; assoc. exec. dir. Golf Course Supt. Assn. Am., Lawrence, Kans., 1982-87; adminstr., chief staff exec. Nat. Office Machine Dealers Assn., Kansas City, Mo., 1987-90; gen. mgr., COO Ridgemark Golf and Country Club Resort, Hollister, Calif., 1990-93; exec. dir. Diving Equipment & Market Assn., Laguna Hills, Calif., 1993—. Contbr. articles to profl. jours.; tech. editor Golf Course Mgmt.; pubr. Spokesman mag. With USN, 1967-71, Calif. N.G. 1971-72. Decorated Air medal. Named Alumnus of the Yr., Calif. Poly. Hort. Dept., 1984. Mem. Am. Soc. Assn. Execs., Golf Writers Assn. Am., U.S. Golf Assn., Club Mgrs. Assn. of Am., Rotary Internat. Republican. Roman Catholic. Avocations: golf, writing, photography, personal computers, snow skiing. Office: Diving Equipment & Market Assn 2050 S Santa Cruz St Ste 1000 Anaheim CA 92805-6820 Address: PO Box 155 Pittsburg NH 03592-0155

PRYM, MICHAEL LEONARD, pastoral counselor; b. Chgo., Aug. 10, 1951; s. Leonard Edward and Pearl Stella (Syrtowt) P.; m. Teresa Chapp, June 24, 1996. BA in History, U. St. Thomas, 1973; MDiv., Washington Theol. U., 1979; MS in Pastoral Counseling, Loyola U., 1979; MA in Spirituality, Santa Clara U., 1990. Asst. pastor Glenmary Home Missioners, Spencer, Va., 1979-83; pastor Glenmary Home Missioners, Aberdeen, Va., 1983-88; dir. candidacy program Glenmary Home Missioners, Hartford, Ky., 1989-90; exec. dir. Threshhold for Change, Novato, Calif., 1991-93; agy. devel. dir. Moss Beach Homes, Inc., Daly City, Calif., 1993—; bd. pres. Mountaineer Foodbank, Gassaway, W.Va., 1981-83. Mem. Am. Assn. of Pastoral Counselors. Avocations: golf, model railroading, hiking. Home: 310 27th Ave San Mateo CA 94403 Office: Moss Beach Homes 333 Gellert Blvd #203 Daly City CA 94015

PSENKA, ROBERT EDWARD, real estate developer, behavioral scientist; b. Canton, Ohio, Sept. 13, 1935; s. Nicholas Charles Psenka and Julia Ella Boldizsar; children: Robert Nicholas, Eric Joseph, Rene Yvette. BA in Sociology, Kent State U., 1962, MA in Sociology, 1963; MA in Health Adminstrn., San Jacinto Coll., Pasadena, Tex., 1972. Lic. health care adminstrn. skilled nursing facilities. Planning cons. U.S. Ho. of Reps., Washington, 1962-65; dir. Health and Welfare Planning and Rsch. Coun., Youngstown, Ohio, 1965-68; CEO Health Devel. & Rsch. Assocs., Inc., Youngstown, 1968-82, Rolzcad Industries, Inc., Houston, 1983-89; adminstr. Psenka Family Investment Mgmt. Trust, Rancho Mirage, Calif., 1973—; chief exec. Conv. Mgmt. Am., Inc., Rancho Mirage, 1994—. Author: Region IX Community Mental Health Centers Guide To Development, 1964, Skilled Nursing Facilities, An Operations Guide, 1972, The Cluster Home Concept, A Guide to Devlopers, 1979 (novel) Fiction Collections, 1987, Passenger, 1986. Mem. Rep. Nat. Com., 1985; advisor Cmty. Chest, Youngstown, 1965, Child and Adult Mental Health Ctr., Youngstown, 1965; cons. Mayor Hon. Walter G. Sanders, City of West Wendover, 1996—. With JAGC, U.S. Army, 1959-61. Hosp. expansion and cmty. mental health ctr. grantee HEW, 1963. Mem. Internat. Auto Appraisers Soc. (antique automobile appraiser), Calif. Friends Native Ams., Rolls Royce Enthusiasts (London), Social Sci. Honor Soc. Republican. Mem. Ch. of Christ. Avocations: collecting and restoring antique Rolls Royce automobiles, writing poetry.. Office: City Hall West Wendover NV 80000

PTASYNSKI, HARRY, geologist, oil producer; b. Milw., May 26, 1926; s. Stanley S. and Frances V. (Stawicki) P.; m. Nola G. Whitestine, Sept. 15, 1951; children: Ross F., Lisa Joy. BS, Stanford U., 1950. Cert. profl. geologist; cert. petroleum geologist. Dist. geologist Pure Oil Co., Amarillo, Tex., 1951-55, Casper, Wyo., 1955-58; ind. geologist, Casper, 1958—. With USN, 1944-46, PTO. Mem. Am. Assn. Petroleum Geologists, Am. Inst. Profl. Geologists, Ind. Petroleum Assn. Am. (v.p., bd. dirs. 1976-85), Ind. Petroleum Assn. Mountain States (v.p., bd. dirs. 1976-80, Rocky Mountain Oil and Gas Assn. (bd. dirs., exec. com. 1980—). Republican. Episcopalian. Avocations: tennis, trout fishing, western history. Home: 1515 Brookview Dr Casper WY 82604-4895 Office: 123 W 1st St Ste 560 Casper WY 82601-2483

PTASYNSKI, ROSS FREDRICK, artist; b. Casper, Wyo., Nov. 5, 1957; s. Harry and Nola Grace (Whitestine) P. Student, U. So. Calif., 1976-80. Freelance artist Hermosa Beach, Calif., 1983-85; art dir. Pacific Screenprint, Hermosa Beach, Calif., 1985-88; jr. designer Michael Faye Assoc., Manhattan Beach, Calif., 1988-90; art dir. Bon-Vue Enterprises, Compton, Calif., 1990-92; freelance art dir., graphic designer Redondo Beach, Calif., 1992-95; art dir. AVN Mag., Van Nuys, Calif., 1995-96, 2-D Publ., Canoga Park, Calif., 1996-97. Designer Ricky Bell Meml. Found. poster, 1992; works exhibited Lifestyles Annual Sensual and Erotic Art Show. Mem. Calif. Watercolor Assn. (assoc.), Watercolor West (assoc.). Republican. Episcopalian. Avocations: watercolor painting, landscape photography, shorin-ryu karate. Office: 2401 Artesia Blvd Ste 106-146 Redondo Beach CA 90278-3260

PUCKETT, PAUL DAVID, electronics company executive; b. Atlanta, July 31, 1941; s. Jonas Levi and Ovella (Juhan) P.; m. Margaret Ann Straetz, June 29, 1974, (div. Jan. 1984); m. Catherine Marie Ryan, Apr. 5, 1984; children: Shawn Michael, Glen David. BS in Edn., Nyack Coll., 1963; MBA in Mgmt., Pace U., 1988. Mgr. quality Rockland Systems Corp., Blauvelt, N.Y., 1971-75, Electronics for Medicine, Inc., White Plains, N.Y., 1975-77; mgr. ops. Tele-Resources, Inc., Armonk, N.Y., 1977-79; mgr. quality Materials Rsch. Corp., Orangeberg, N.Y., 1979-83; mgr. quality plasma systems div. Perkin-Elmer, Wilton, Conn., 1983-84, dir. ops. plasma systems div., 1984-86, mgr. spl. studies semiconductor group, 1986-87; mgr. quality programs instrument group Perkin-Elmer, Norwalk, Conn., 1987-90; dir. ops. applied sci. div. Perkin-Elmer (sold applied sci. div. to Orbital Scis. Corp.), Pomona, Calif., 1990-93; dir. ops. Pomona (Calif.) ops. Orbital Scis. Corp., 1993—; examiner Malcolm Baldrige Nat. Quality award, Gathersberg, Md., 1989-90, Conn. State Quality award, Stamford, 1988-90, cons., trainer, 1990. Contbr. articles to profl. jours. Mem. Young Reps., New City, N.Y., 1975-76; vol. police officer Rockland County Sheriff's Dept., New City, 1974-83; coach Am. Youth Soccer Orgn., Bethel, Conn., 1984-85. Recipient Conn. State Quality award, 1989. Mem. N.Y. Acad. Sci., Am. Soc. Quality Control, Assn. for Quality and Participation, Am. Electronics Assn. Republican. Episcopalian. Avocations: golf, racing, flying. Home: 1500 Mansfield Ct Upland CA 91784-7963 Office: Orbital Scis Corp Pomona Ops 2771 N Garey Ave Pomona CA 91767-1809

PUCKETT, RICHARD EDWARD, artist, consultant, retired recreation executive; b. Klamath Falls, Oreg., Sept. 9, 1932; s. Vernon Elijah and Leona Belle (Clevenger) P.; m. Velma Faye Hamrick, Apr. 14, 1957 (dec. 1985); children: Katherine Michelle Briggs, Deborah Alison Norton, Susan Lin Rowland, Gregory Richard. Student So. Oreg. Coll. Edn., 1951-56, Lake Forest Coll., 1957-58; Hartnell Jr. Coll., 1960-70; B.A., U. San Francisco, 1978. Acting arts and crafts dir., Fort Leonard Wood, Mo., 1956-57; arts and crafts dir., asst. spl. svcs. officer, mus. dir., Fort Sheridan, Ill., 1957-59; arts and crafts dir., Fort Irwin, Calif., 1959-60, Fort Ord, Calif., 1960-86; dir. arts and crafts br. Art Gallery, Arts and Crafts Center Materials Sales Store, 1960; opening dir. Presidio Monterey Army Mus., 1968; dir. Model Army Arts and Crafts Program. Recipient First Place, Dept. Army and U.S. Army Forces Command awards for programming and publicity, 1979-81, 83-85, 1st and 3d place sculpture awards Monterey County Fair Fine Arts Exhibit, 1979, Comdrs. medal civilian svcs., 1986, other awards, Golden Acad. award, Internat. Man of Yr. award, 1991-92. Mem. Monterey Peninsula Art Assn., Salinas Fine Arts Assn., Salinas Arts Coun., Rogue Valley Art Assn., Fort Ord Alumni Assn. One-man shows: Seaside City Hall, 1975, Fort Ord Arts and Crafts Center Gallery, 1967, 73, 79, 81, 84, 86, Presidio of Monterey Art Gallery, 1979, Rogue Valley Art Assn., Salinas Valley Art Gallery; Glass on Holiday, Gatlinburg, Tenn., 1981, 82, Del Messa Gallery, Carmel, Calif., 1998; exhbns. in Mo., Ill., and pvt. collections; designed and opened first Ft. Sheridan Army Mus., Presidio of Monterey Mus. Home: 210 San Miguel Ave Salinas CA 93901-3021

PUCKETT, W. GREER, engineer; b. Oak Ridge, Tenn., Apr. 20, 1952; s. James Beverly and Jane (Greer) P. BS, U.S. Naval Acad., 1975. Design engr. Ford Motor Co., Dearborn, Mich., 1979-80; field engr. Westinghouse, Groton, Conn., 1980-84, Dunoon, Scotland, 1984-85; field engr. Westinghouse/Northrop Grumman, Groton, 1985-96; project mgr. Northrop Grumman, Sunnyvale, Calif., 1996—. Bd. dirs. Southeastern Conn. AIDS Project, New London, 1989-93, 1995-96, Concern Inc., New London, 1994-96; contbg. mem. Human Rights Campaign, Washington, 1991-98, Dem. Nat. Com., Washington, 1996—. Served U.S. Navy 1975-78. Recipient Appreciation award Southeastern Conn. AIDS Project, 1996, Westinghouse Marine Divsn. Quality Ach. award, 1989. Democrat. Presbyterian. Avocations: collecting art and antiques, playing bridge, walking, reading, doing volunteer work. Home: 6182 Oceanside Pl NE Bremerton WA 98311 Office: Northrop Grumman Marine Sys 401 E Hendy Ave Sunnyvale CA 94086-5100

PUDNEY, GARY LAURENCE, television executive; b. Mpls., July 20, 1934; s. Lawrence D. and Agnes (Hansen) P. BA, UCLA, 1956. V.p. ABC, Inc., N.Y.C., 1968—; v.p., sr. exec. in charge of spls. and talent ABC Entertainment, 1979-89; pres. The Gary L. Pudney Co., Beverly Hills, Calif., 1988—; chief oper. officer Paradigm Entertainment, Beverly Hills, 1989-92; xec. producer World Music Awards, ABC-TV, 1993, World's Greatest Magic, NBC-TV, 1994—, Grand Illusions, 1994, Caesar's World Entertainment, 1994-95, Lance Burton and Houdini, NBC-TV, 1995, Champions of Magic, ABC-TV, 1996, Hidden Secrets of Magic, NBC-TV, 1996, 30th Anniversary, Ceasars Palace-ABC, Happy Birthday Elizabeth-A Celebration of Life. Exec. producer for United Cerebral Palsy Aspen and Lake Tahoe Pro-Celebrity Tennis Festivals, 4 yrs., AIDS Project L.A. Dinner, 1985, The 25th Anniversary of the L.A. Music Ctr. Bd. dirs. nat. Cerebral Palsy Found., Ctr. Theatre Group Ahmanson Theatre, L.A., Ctr. Theatre Group of L.A. Music Ctr.; mem. bd. La Quinta Arts Found., 1991—. Recipient Helena T. Deveraux Meml. award, 1985, Humanitarian award Nat. Jewish Ctr. for Immunology and Respiratory Medicine, 1986, Gift of Love award Nat. Ctr. Hyperactive Children, 1988, Winner award Excellence The L.A. Film Adv. Bd. Mem. Hollywood Radio and TV Soc. (bd. dirs.), Acad. TV Arts and Scis. (exec. com.), Met. Mus. Art, Mus. Modern Art. Democrat. Lutheran.

PUENTE, TITO ANTHONY, orchestra leader, composer, arranger; b. N.Y.C., Apr. 20, 1923; s. Ernest Anthony and Ercilia (Ortiz) P.; m. Margaret Asencio, Oct. 19, 1963; children: Ronald, Audrey, Tito Anthony. Student, Julliard Conservatory Music, N.Y. Sch. Music, Schillinger System; MusD (hon.), SUNY, Albany, 1987. Orch. leader appearing in numerous night clubs and ballrooms, throughout U.S., 1949—; appeared in Woody Allen's Radio Days, John Candy's Armed & Dangerous, 1986-87; recorded 96 albums; appeared in concert Red Sea Jazz Festival, Israel, all major jazz festivals, including Montreaux, Monterey, Munich, North Sea, others, Tribute in P.R., 1986, Los Angeles Ford Theatre Tribute, 1987; composer Para Los Rumberos, 1960, Oye Como Va, 1962, numerous other works recorded with Dizzy Gillespie, Lionel Hampton, George Shearing, Woody Herman, other major jazz artists; sold out performance Radio City Music Hall & Apollo Theatre, 1986; appeared Madison Square Garden, N.Y.C., 1986, Los Angeles Amphitheatre, 1986, on Bill Cosby Show, 1987, Regis Philbin, Bill Boggs shows, 1987; guest artist with Bklyn. Philharmonic Symphony Orch., N.Y. and Phila., 1987. Founder T. Puente Scholarship fund, 1980. Served with USN, 1942-45. Recipient Bronze medallion City of N.Y., 1969, Key to City Los Angeles, 1976, Key to City of Chgo., 1985, Key to City of Miami, 1986; named Musician of Month on several occasions by Downbeat, Metronome, Playboy and trade mags., 1950's; named King of Latin Music, La Prensa newspaper, 1955; his band named Best Latin Am. Orch. New York Daily News, 1977; recipient 6 Grammy nominations, Grammy award, 1978, 83, 85, 90; N.Y. Music award, 1986. Office: Thomas Cassidy Inc 11761 E Speedway Blvd Tucson AZ 85748-2017*

PUETTE, ROBERT L., executive. Pres., CEO Centigram, San Jose, Calif. Office: 91 E Tasman Dr San Jose CA 95134-1618*

PUGAY, JEFFREY IBANEZ, mechanical engineer; b. San Francisco, June 26, 1958; s. Herminio Salazar and Petronila (Ibanez) P. BSME, U. Calif., Berkeley, 1981, MSME, 1982; MBA, Pepperdine U., 1986, MS in Tech. Mgmt., 1991. Registered profl. engr., Calif. Engrng. asst. Lawrence Berkeley Nat. Lab., 1978-80; assoc. tech. staff Aerospace Corp., L.A., 1981; tech. staff Hughes Space & Comm. Co., El Segundo, Calif., 1982-85, from project engr. to project mgr., 1985-95; mgr. spaceway program mktg. Hughes Comm. Inc., Long Beach, Calif., 1995-97, dir. bus. devel., 1997-99; dir. bus. devel. Hughes Network Sys, Long Beach, 1999—. Active ARC Emergency Svcs. White House Fellow regional finalist, 1991, 92. Mem. ASME, Soc. Competitor Intelligence Profls., Am. Mgmt. Assn., L.A. World Affairs Coun., Make A Wish Found., Pi Tau Sigma, Delta Mu Delta. Republican. Roman Catholic. Avocations: racquetball, scuba diving, sailing, backpacking, volleyball. Home: 8180 Manitoba St Apt 120 Playa Del Rey CA 90293-8651 Office: Hughes Comms Inc PO Box 9712 Long Beach CA 90810-0712

PUGH, KYLE MITCHELL, JR., musician, retired music educator; b. Spokane, Wash., Jan. 6, 1937; s. Kyle Mitchel, Sr. and Lenore Fae (Johnson) P.; m. Susan Deane Waite, July 16, 1961; children: Jeffray, Kari. BA in Edu., East Wash. U., 1975. Cert. tchr., Wash. Tuba player Spokane Symphony Orch., 1958-63; rec. assoc. Century Records, Spokane, 1965-73; tuba player World's Fair Expo '74, Spokane, 1974; bass player Russ Carlyle Orch., Las Vegas, 1976, Many Sounds of Nine Orch., northwest area, 1969-81; band tchr. Garry Jr. High School, Spokane, 1976-79, Elementary Band Program, Spokane, 1979-96; bass player Doug Scott Cabaret Band, Spokane, 1982-91; dept. head Elem. Band Dept., Spokane, 1984-89. Editor (newsletter) The Repeater, 1987 (Amateur Radio News Svc. award 1987); extra in movie Always, 1989. Active in communications Lilac Bloomsday Assn., Spokane, 1977. Served to E-5 USNR, 1955-63. Recipient Disting. Service award Wash. State Commn., 1974, Nev. Hollerin' Champ Carl Hayden Scribe, 1979. Mem. Am. Fedn. Musicians (life), Spokane Edn. Assn. (rec. sec. 1987), Music Educator's Nat. Conf., Am. Radio Relay League (asst. dir. 1987), Ea. Wash. Music Educator's Assn. (pres. 1978-79), Dial Twisters Club (pres. 1979-80), VHF Radio Amateurs (dir. 1980-83), Elks. Avocations: ham radio operator, model railroading, photography. Home: 5006 W Houston Ave Spokane WA 99208-3728

PUGLISI, DAVIDE FELICE, rail transportation executive, consultant; b. N.Y.C., July 15, 1963; s. Giorgio Andrea Puglisi and Arianne Carlotta (Ulmer) Cipes. AA in Digital Electronics, C.C. of the USAF, Maxwell AFB, Calif., 1985; BA in Geog., Calif. State U., Northridge, 1993; postgrad., San Jose State U., 1997—. Field telecom. repair technician Astronautics Corp. Am., Milw., 1985-87; field computer repair technician The Repair Co., Northridge, Calif., 1990; bus. operator So. Calif. Rapid Transit Dist., L.A., 1991-95; train operator L.A. County Met. Transp. Authority, 1995, adminstrn. aide, 1995-96, rail transit ops. supr., 1996—. With USAF, 1982-85. Fellow Eno Found.; mem. Nat. Assn. Railway Pass, ACLU, Orange Empire R.R. Mus., Edgar G. Ulmer Preservation Soc. (sec. 1996—), Am. Legion, Phi Kappa Phi. Avocations: rail transit history, cycling, bowling, swimming. Home: 6625 Gloria Ave Van Nuys CA 91406-5948 Office: LA County Metro Trans Authority One Gateway Plz Los Angeles CA 90012

PUGSLEY, ROBERT ADRIAN, law educator; b. Mineola, N.Y., Dec. 27, 1946; s. Irvin Harold and Mary Catherine (Brusselars) P. BA, SUNY-Stony Brook, 1968; JD, NYU, 1975, LLM in Criminal Justice, 1977. Instr. sociology New Sch. Social Rsch., N.Y.C., 1969-71; coordinator Peace Edn. programs The Christophers, N.Y.C., 1971-78; assoc. prof. law Southwestern U., L.A., 1978-81, prof., 1981—, program dir., prof. law program Vancouver, B.C., Can., 1998; adj. asst. prof. criminology and criminal justice Southampton Coll.-Long Island U., 1975-76; acting dep. dir. Criminal Law Edn. and Rsch. Ctr., NYU, 1983-86; bd. advisors Ctr. Legal Edn. CCNY-CUNY, 1978, Sta. KPFK-FM, 1985-86; founder, coordinator The Wednesday Evening Soc., L.A., 1979-86; vis. prof. Jacob D. Fuchsberg Law Ctr. Touro Coll., L.I., N.Y., summers 1988, 89; lectr. in criminal law and procedure Legal Edn. Conf. Ctr., L.A., 1982-96; lectr., dir. Comparative Criminal Law and Procedure Inst. U. B.C., Vancouver, summers 1994, 98, 99; lectr. legal profl. responsibility West Bar Rev. Faculty, Calif., 1996-98; legal analyst/commentator for print and electronic media, 1992—. Creative advisor Christopher Closeup (nationally syndicated pub. svc. TV program), 1975-83; host Earth Alert, Cable TV, 1983-87; producer, moderator (pub. affairs discussion program) Inside L.A., Sta. KPFK-FM, 1979-86, Open Jour. program, Sta. KPFK-FM, 1991-94; contbr. articles to legal jours. Founding mem. Southwestern U. Pub. Interest Law com., 1992—; mem. L.A. County Bar Assn. Adv. Com. on Alcohol & Drug Abuse, 1991-95, co-chair, 1993-95; mem. exec. com. non-govtl. orgns. UN Office of Pub. Info., 1977; mem. issues task force L.A. Conservancy, 1980-81, seminar for law tchrs. NEH UCLA, 1979; co-convener So. Calif. Coalition Against Death Penalty, 1981-83, convener, 1983-84; mem. death penalty com. Lawyer's Support Group, Amnesty Internat. U.S.A.; founding mem. Ch.-State Coun., L.A., 1984-88. Robert Marshall fellow Criminal Law Edn. and Rsch. Ctr.,

NYU Sch. Law, 1976-78; bd. dirs. Equal Rights Sentencing Found., 1983-85, Earth Alert Inc., 1984-87; mem. adv. bd. First Amendment Info. Resources Ctr., Grad. Sch. of Libr. and Info. Sci., UCLA, 1990—; mem. coun. Friends UCLA Libr., 1993—, pres., 1996—; mem. adv. bd. Children Requiring A Caring Kommunity, 1998—. Mem. Am. Legal Studies Assn., Am. Soc. Polit. and Legal Philosophy, Assn. Am. Law Schs., Inst. Soc. Ethics and Life Scis., Soc. Am. Law Tchrs., Internat. Platform Assn., Internat. Soc. Reform of Criminal Law, The Scribes. Democrat. Roman Catholic. Office: Southwestern U Sch Law 675 S Westmoreland Ave Rm 410 Los Angeles CA 90005-3905 Address: PO Box 440 East Hampton NY 11937-0440

PULCRANO, DAN MICHAEL, newspaper and online services executive; b. New Brunswick, N.J., Oct. 1, 1958; s. Charles A. and Edith (Tanner) Ostern. BA in Journalism and Newspaper Mgmt., U. Calif., Santa Cruz, 1980. Reporter Santa Barbara (Calif.) News & Rev., 1978; asst. to pub. L.A. Weekly, 1978, 79; editor, pub. Santa Cruz (Calif.) Weekly, 1981, Los Gatos (Calif.) Weekly, 1982-84; editor Metro, San Jose, Calif., 1985-93, 95—; exec. editor Los Gatos Weekly-Times, Saratoga News, Willow Glen Resident, Cupertino Courier, Sunnvale Sun, Metro Santa Cruz, San Francisco Met., Sonoma County Independent, 1990—; pres., CEO Metro Pub., Inc., San Jose, 1992—, Virtual Valley, Inc., San Jose, 1993—; pres. Boulevards New Media Inc., 1996—. Founding pres., bd. mem. San Jose Downtown Assn., 1986-95. Recipient Disting. Svc. award Oakes Coll., 1980; named Dist. Honoree City of San Jose, Dist. 3, 1989. Mem. Calif. Free Press Assn. (pres. 1991-92, bd. dirs.), Assn. Alternative Newspapers (v.p. 1993-94, bd. dirs.s 1993-95), Rotary. Avocations: gardening, bicycling, travel, photography. Home: PO Box 7 San Jose CA 95103-0007 Office: Metro Newspapers 550 S 1st St San Jose CA 95113-2806

PULIDO, MARK A., pharmaceutical and cosmetics company executive; b. 1953. McKesson Drug Co., 1975-88; Exec. v.p. FoxMeyer Drug Co., 1988-89; chmn., pres., CEO Red Line Healthcare Corp., 1989-96; pres., CEO Sandoz Pharmaceuticals Corp., 1994-95; pres., CEO, dir. McKesson Corp., 1996—. Office: McKesson Corp 1 Post St 37th Floor San Francisco CA 94104*

PULIDO, MIGUEL, mayor; b. Mexico City, Mex., 1956; m. Laura Pulido; 1 child, Miguel Robert. BSME, Calif. State U., Fullerton. Dir. computer program McCaughey & Smith Energy Assocs., v.p.; mem. Santa Ana (Calif.) City Coun., 1986—; mayor City of Santa Ana, 1994—; mem. Santa Ana Redevel. Agy., Downtown Santa Ana Bus. Assn.; mem. 1st dist. Orange County Transp. Authority. Avocations: chess, backgammon, tennis, music, guitar. Office: Office of Mayor & City Coun 20 Civic Ctr Plaza PO Box 1988 Santa Ana CA 92702-1988*

PULITZER, ROSLYN KITTY, social worker, psychotherapist; b. Bronx, N.Y., Apr. 25, 1930; d. George and Laura Eleanor (Holtz) P. BS in Human Devel. and Life Cycle, SUNY, N.Y.C., 1983; MSW, Fordham U., 1987; postgrad., Masterson Inst., N.Y.C., 1991. cert. in psychoanalytic psychotherapy of the personality disorders, Masterson Inst., N.Y.C.; lic. clin. social worker, N.Y. Clinic dir. Resources Counseling and Psychotherapy Ctr., N.Y.C., 1985-89; social worker, clin. supr. methadone maintenance treatment program Beth Israel Med. Ctr., N.Y.C., 1989-97; psychotherapist pvt. practice, 1989—; cons. therapist, clin. supr. Identity House, N.Y.C., 1980-97, exec. dir., 1985, clin. dir., 1993-94. Mem. regional adv. coun. N.Y. State Div. Human Rights, N.Y.C., 1975-76; mem. Community Bd. 6, N.Y.C., 1978-81; founder, legis. chmn. N.Y. State Women's Polit. Caucus, 1978-80. Mem. NASW, Acad. Cert. Social Workers, Soc. Masterson Inst., N.Y. Milton Erickson Soc. for Psychotherapy and Hypnosis (cert.). Avocations: photography, snorkeling. Fax: 505-438-2884; e-mail: imagesrkp@aol.com. Home: 2742 La Silla Dorada Santa Fe NM 87505-6703

PULLEN, NANCY ELLEN, marketing consultant; b. Tucson, Aug. 22, 1949; d. John Paul Pullen and Ellen Lyle (Jorgenson) Pullen Foules; m. David Lynn Preuss; Aug. 22, 1981; children: Donald, Elizabeth. BSBA, Stephen F. Austin State U., 1971; MSBA, U. Denver, 1973. Brand asst. to brand mgr. Procter & Gamble, Cin., 1973-81; mktg. mgr. Heublein Wine Divsn., San Francisco, 1981-82; account dir. Foote, Cone & Belding, S.A., Barcelona, Spain, 1981-85; sr. account dir. Addison Design Cons., San Francisco, 1985-88; exec. v.p. and prin. PSL Mktg. Resources, San Francisco, 1988—; speaker in field. Bd. dirs. Calif./Nev. United Meth. Found., San Francisco, 1993—. Mem. Roundtable for Women in Foodsvcs., Am. Mktg. Assn., San Francisco C. of C. Avocations: lay minister, cub scout leader, reading. Home: 677 Spruce St Berkeley CA 94707-1745 Office: PSL Mktg Resources Inc 10 Lombard St Ste 400 San Francisco CA 94111-1165

PULLIAM, ELIZABETH ANNE, writer, commercial; b. Richland, Wash., Aug. 28, 1963; m. William Bunker Pulliam, Apr. 5, 1997. BA in Econs. and Journalism, Pacific Lutheran U.; personal fin. planner, U. Calif., Irvine, 1997. Bus. writer Seattle Times, 1985-86; feature writer Anchorage Times, 1986-90; sr. polit. writer Anchorage Daily News, 1990-92; personal fin. writer Orange County Register, Santa Ana, Ca., 1992—. Recipient 1997 Gerald Loeb award UCLA Anderson Sch. Mgmt., 1997. Office: Orange County Register 625 N Grand Ave Santa Ana CA 92701-4347

PULLIAM, FRANCINE SARNO, real estate broker and developer; b. San Francisco, Sept. 14, 1937; d. Ralph C. Stevens and Frances I. (Wilson) Sarno; m. John Donald Pulliam, Aug. 14, 1957 (div. Mar. 1965); 1 child, Wendy; m. Terry Kent Graves, Dec. 14, 1974. Student, U. Ariz., 1955-56, U. Nev., Las Vegas, 1957. Airline stewardess Bonanza Airlines, Las Vegas, 1957; real estate agt. The Pulliam Co., Las Vegas, 1958-68, Levy Realty, Las Vegas, 1976-76; real estate broker, owner Prestige Properties, Las Vegas, 1976—; importer, exporter Exports Internat., Las Vegas, 1984—; bd. dirs. Citicorp Bank of Nev.; mem. adv. bd. to Amb. to Bahamas Chic Hect. Bd. dirs. Las Vegas Bd. Realtors, Fedn. Internat. Realtors, Nat. Kidney Found., Assistance League, Cancer Soc., Easter Seals, Econ. Rsch. Bd., Children's Discovery Mus., New Horizons Ctr. for Children with Learning Disabilities, Girl Scouts, Home of the Good Shepard, St. Jude's Ranch for Homeless Children; pres., bd. dirs. Better Bus. Bur.; chmn. Las Vegas Taxi Cab Authority; pres. Citizens for Pvt. Enterprises. Mem. Las Vegas C. of C. (bd. dirs., developer). Republican. Roman Catholic. Office: 2340 Paseo Del Prado Ste D202 Las Vegas NV 89102-4341

PUMPIAN, BETTY ANN G., advertising executive; b. Balt., Sept. 19, 1935; d. Emanuel Henry and Carlyn Rose (Freudenthal) Goldstone; m. Paul H. Pumpian, June 24, 1956. BS in Mktg., U. Balt., 1956. Network coord., asst. buyer Parkson Advt., N.Y.C., 1957-61; traffic mgr. Sta. KORK, Las Vegas, Nev., 1961; project coord., bookkeeper Art Dept., L.A., 1961-62; network and planning coord. Ogilvy & Mather, L.A., 1962-75, asst. media dir., 1975-78, assoc. media dir., 1978-80, v.p., dir. nat. broadcast and programming, 1980-89; nat./regional broadcast adminstr. Bozell, Inc., L.A., 1989-90; v.p., sr. network negotiator Western Internat. Media, L.A., 1991—; lectr. Adweek Seminars, L.A., 1989-91. Chmn. 1st Coun. Dist. Horsemen's Adv. Com., L.A., 1978-81; chmn. L.A. Equine Adv. Com., 1978-83; pres. Cal-Western Appaloosa Inc., 1981-82, bd. dirs; mem. horse drugging adv. com. Calif. Dept. Food and Agr., Sacramento, 1987—. Recipient Commendation award L.A. City Coun., 1983, Achievement cert. YWCA, L.A., 1976. Mem. Appaloosa Horse Club (dir., chmn. planning and rev. 1987-88, 93-94, chmn. rules 1988-92, chmn. mktg. 1992—, chmn. youth 1992-93, v.p. 1994-95). Republican. Avocation: breeding and racing Appaloosa horses. Office: Western Internat Media 8544 W Sunset Blvd West Hollywood CA 90069-2310

PUNCHES, HOWARD KI NEAL, physicist, retired; b. Toledo, Dec. 12, 1931; s. Howard A. and Grayce Evangeline Punches; m. Nancy Ann Cox, Jan. 19, 1957 (div. 1978); m. Linda Holm, Nov. 7, 1987; children: Howard Scott, Perry Allen. Degree in engring. physics, U. Toledo, 1957; degree in physics, Purdue U., 1959. Minuteman Boeing, Seattle, 1959-62; with Apollo Space divsn. Motorola, Scottsdale, Ariz., 1963-69, reliability physicist Fluke, Lynnwood, Wash., 1969-79, Hewlett Packard, Corvallis, Oreg., 1980-86; cons., 1986-89, ret., 1989. Author: Anchors Away, 1992; contbr. articles to profl. jours. Nat. Lead Co. scholar, 1955-58. Avocations: duplicate bridge master, sailing the West Coast. Home: PO Box 12863 Everett WA 98206-2863

PUNDT, HERMANN G., architectural historian; b. Berlin, 1928; came to U.S., 1951; BA in History of Art, Arch., U. Ill., MA in History of Art, Arch.; PhD, Harvard U. Prof. dept. arch. U. Wash., Seattle, 1968—; mem. Internat. Coun. Monuments and Sites, 1975—. Author: Frank Lloyd Wright: Vision and Legacy, Schinkel's Berlin: A Study in Environmental Planning, 1972, German edit., 1981, Japanese edit., 1985; contbr. articles to books and profl. jours. With USMC. Recipient Order of Merit 1st Class, Fed. Republic Germany, 1992. Office: Univ Wash Dept Arch PO Box 355720 Seattle WA 98195-5720

PURCELL, JOHN F., lawyer; b. Bellingham, Wash., Apr. 25, 1954. AB with honors, Stanford U., 1976; JD, Lewis and Clark Coll., 1980. Bar: Oreg. 1980. Ptnr. Miller, Nash, Wiener, Hager & Carlsen, Portland, 1987—. Mem. Oreg. State Bar. Office: Miller Nash Wiener Hager & Carlsen 111 SW 5th Ave Ste 3500 Portland OR 97204-3699

PURDOM, PAUL WAKEFIELD, public relations executive; b. Williams, Ariz., Nov. 9, 1928; s. Paul Wakefield and Mary Louise (Doran) Wallace; m. Elizabeth Chapman, Apr. 9, 1955; children: Edward, Charles. BA, U. Calif., Berkeley, 1952. Pres., founder Purdom Pub. Relations, San Francisco, 1960—; Pub. Relations Soc. of Am. Served with U.S. Army, 1954-56. Mem. Pub. Relations Soc. Am., Nat. Investor Relations Inst., Pub. Relations Exchange, Bankers Club. Office: Purdom Pub Rels 2330 Marinship Way Sausalito CA 94965-2800

PURDY, JILL, business management educator; b. Allentown, Pa., Nov. 28, 1967; d. Herbet Witts and Nancy Joyce (Kuzenski) P. BBA, Coll. William and Mary, 1988; PhD in Bus. Adminstrn., Pa. State U., 1994. Lectr. Pa. State U., University Park, 1989-93; vis. asst. prof. Bucknell U., Lewisburg, Pa., 1993-94; asst. prof. U. Wash., Tacoma, 1994—; cons. Policy Consensus Initiative, Santa Fe, 1997-98; rsch. assoc. Ctr. Rsch. Conflict and Negotiation, University Park, 1990—. Vol. Habitat for Humanity, Tacoma/Pierce County, Wash., 1994—; cons. Tacoma Empowerment Consortium, 1995; educator City of Tacoma, 1997-98. Nat. Merit scholar, 1984-88. Mem. Internat. Assn. Conflict Mgmt. (Best Paper award 1992), Orgnl. Behavior Teaching Soc., Acad. Mgmt. Avocation: musician. Fax: (253) 692-4424. E-mail: jpurdy@u.washington.edu. Home: 2340 Sunset Dr W Tacoma WA 98466-2812 Office: U Wash 1900 Commerce St # Tacoma WA 98402-3112

PURDY, TEDDY GEORGE, JR., programmer, analyst, researcher, consultant; b. Leadville, Colo., May 11, 1954; s. Teddy George and Geneva Ruth Purdy; m. Karen Ann Puleo, May 28, 1977 (div. Dec. 19, 1983); children: Christopher, Sarah. Student, Colo. U., 1972-75. Free-lance programmer/analyst Boulder, Colo., 1975-84; pres., treas. IBEX Bus. Systems, Leadville, 1984—; cons. Carlson Promotions, Mpls., 1987-91, Unidata, Inc., Denver, 1992, Household Fin., Chesapeake, Va., 1992—, Focus Tech., Dallas, 1992—. Avocations: geology, biking, hiking, books, music.

PURL, MARA CELESTE, entertainment executive, radio producer, writer; b. New Haven, Conn., Aug. 29, 1950; d. Raymond Charles Arthur and Marshelline (Patton) P.; m. Larry Brent Norfleet, July 30, 1994; stepchildren: Matthew Norfleet, Amelia Norfleet. BA, Bennington Coll., 1973. Soloist N.Y.C. Ballet, 1972—; reporter Fin. Times London, N.Y.C., 1973-77; free-lance writer Rolling Stone, AP, N.Y.C., 1977-80; pres., CEO Milford-Haven Enterprises, North Hollywood, Calif., 1987—; tchr., prodr. Student Radio Drama, L.A. and Colorado Springs, 1994—; musician, rec. artist Milford Music, L.A., 1995—; guest prof. Colo. Coll., Colorado Springs, 1997-98, U. Alaska, Fairbanks, 1998. Author: (books) What the Heart Knows, 1997, Closer Than You Think, 1998, Act Right, 1998; recurring actress: (TV show) Days of Our Lives, 1984-85. Mem. adv. bd. Haven House Shelter, L.A., 1997, 98, Comtys. in Schs., Colorado Springs, 1997, Colorado Springs Film Commn., 1997, 98, Fight Back Found., L.A., 1992. Recipient Dramatic Programming award N.Y. Internat. Radio Festivals, 1994; producing-performing grantee Kennedy Ctr. Performing Ctr., 1994, 95. Mem. SAG, AFTRA, Women in Film. Democrat. Christian Scientist. Office: Milford-Haven Enterprises 10153 1/2 Riverside Dr North Hollywood CA 91602-2561

PURSEL, HAROLD MAX, SR., mining engineer, civil engineer, architectural engineer.; b. Fruita, Colo., Sept. 15, 1921; s. Harold Maurice and Viola Pearl (Wagner) P.; m. Virginia Anna Brady, May 6, 1950; children: Harold Max, Leo William, Dawn Allen, Helen Virginia, Viola Ruth. BS in Civil Engring., U. Wyo., 1950. Asst. univ. architect U. Wyo., 1948-50; with Sharrock & Pursel, Contractors, 1951-55; owner Max Pursel, Earthwork Constrn., 1955-59; project engr. Farson (Wyo.) Irrigation Project, 1960-61; owner Wyo. Builders Service, Casper, 1962-66; head dept. home improvement Gamble Stores, Rawlins, Wyo., 1967; resident work instr. Casper (Wyo.) Job Corps Conservation Center, 1968; P.M. coordinator Lucky Mc Uranium Mine, Riverton, Wyo., 1969-80; constrn. insp. U.S. Bur. Reclamation, 1983—; cons. freelance heavy and light constrn., 1984—. Served with U.S. Army, 1942-45. Mem. Nat. Rifle Assn., Internat. Platform Assn., Mensa. Lodges: Eagles, Masons, Shriners. Exptl. research with log, timber and frame constrn. in conjunction with residential applications.; expanded experimental research to develop methods to up-date and modernize early area residences while retaining period styles, materials and general construction methods. Home: PO Box 572 Riverton WY 82501-0572

PURSGLOVE, BETTY MERLE, computer-software quality assurance tester; b. Pitts., Sept. 15, 1923; d. Earle E. and Merle A. (Smith) Baer; m. Larry A. Pursglove, June 30, 1944; children: Diana, Kathleen, Merry, Tanya, Yvonne. BS in Physics, U. Pitts., 1944; postgrad., Minn. U., 1945-47, Carnegie-Mellon U., 1947-49, W.Va. U., 1949-51, Mich. State U., 1968-69. Micro-pilot plant operator Minn. Mining and Mfg., St. Paul, 1944-46; cons. rsch. chemist Food Mach Co., Pitts., 1947-49; computer coder Dow Chem. Co., Midland, Minn., 1954; asst. entomologist pvt. collections, Midland, 1955-56; instr. chemistry Cen. Mich. U., Midland, 1958; head chem. dept. Midland Hosp., 1958-64; tchr. chemistry and physics parochial schs., Bay City, Mich., 1964; prin., chief exec. officer Crypticlear, Inc., Applegate, Oreg., 1965—. Leader Midland troup Girl Scout U.S., 1953-63. Mem. AAUW, Sigma Xi, Sigma Pi Sigma. Avocations: creative writing, performing in marching and concert bands, photography, genealogy, gardening. E-mail: lpbp@webTV.net. Home and Office: PO Box 3125 Applegate OR 97530-3125

PURVIS, JOHN ANDERSON, lawyer; b. Greeley, Colo., Aug. 31, 1942; s. Virgil J. and Emma Lou (Anderson) P.; m. Charlotte Johnson, Apr. 3, 1976; 1 child, Whitney; children by previous marriage: Jennifer, Matt. B.A. cum laude, Harvard U., 1965; J.D., U. Colo., 1968. Bar: Colo. 1968, U.S. Dist. Ct. Colo. 1968, U.S. Ct. Appeals (10th cir.) 1978. Dep. dist. atty. Boulder, Colo., 1968-69; asst. dir. and dir. legal aid U. Colo. Sch. Law, 1969; assoc. Williams, Taussig & Trine, Boulder, 1969; head Boulder office Colo. Pub. Defender System, 1970-72; assoc. and ptnr. Hutchinson, Black, Hill, Buchanan & Cook, Boulder, 1972-85; ptnr. Purvis, Gray, Schuetze and Gordon, 1985-98, ptnr. Purvis, Gray & Gordon, LLP, 1999—, acting Colo. State Pub. Defender, 1978; adj. prof. law U. Colo., 1981, 84-88, 94, others; lectr. in field. Chmn., Colo. Pub. Defender Commn., 1979-89; mem. nominating commn. Colo. Supreme Ct., 1984-90; mem. com. on conduct U.S. Dist. Ct., 1991-97, chmn., 1996-97; chmn. Boulder County Criminal Justice Com., 1975-81, Boulder County Manpower Coun., 1977-78. Recipient Ames award Harvard U., 1964; Outstanding Young Lawyer award Colo. Bar Assn., 1978, Dist. Achievement award U. Colo. Law Sch. Alumni Assn., 1997. Mem. Internat. Soc. Barristers, Internat. Acad. Trial Lawyers, Am. Bd. Trial Advocates, Am. Coll. of Trial Lawyers (state chmn. 1998—), Colo. Bar Assn. (chair litigation sect. 1994-95), Boulder County Bar Assn., Colo. Trial Lawyers Assn., Am. Trial Lawyers Assn., Trial Lawyers for Pub. Justice, Colo. Bar Found., Am. Bar Found., Supreme Ct. Hist. Soc. (state chmn. 1998—, bd. dirs. 99—), Faculty of Fed. Advocates (bd. dirs. 1999—). Democrat. Address: 1030 Walnut St Ste 301 Boulder CO 80302-5144

PURDY, GREGORY SCOTT, venture capitalist; b. Mpls., July 17, 1952; s. W. Glen and Annette L. (Livingston) P.; m. Jill J. Yager, Nov. 27, 1976; children: Christopher, Jacqueline. BS in Finance, Boston Coll., 1974. Mng. dir. Graystone Capital, Vail, Colo., 1983—; pres., CEO Livingston Capital LLC, Vail, Colo., 1985—, Cambridge Holdings LLC, Vail, Colo., 1991—, Advanced Nutraceuticals, Inc., Houston, 1997—.

PUTERBAUGH, KATHRYN ELIZABETH, retired corporate executive; b. Denver, Mar. 5, 1924; d. Fredric John and Cora (Zoph) P.; B.A., U. Colo., 1945. Acct., F.J. Puterbaugh & Co., Denver, 1946-49; sec. to Herbert Bayer artist, designer Aspen, Colo., 1950-51; acct. Himel's, New Orleans, 1951-53; asst. contr. Berol Pen Co., 1953-54; office mgr., controller Garratt-Callahan Co., Millbrae, Calif., 1955-65, corp. treas., 1966-85, also dir. Mem. com. for dedication Millbrae library, 1961; mem. steering com. People-to-People Program, Millbrae, 1962; historian Millbrae Sister City Program, 1962-63; mem. Belmont-San Carlos Human Relations Com., 1968-70; active various community fund drives; judge Bank Am. Youth Achievement Awards, 1973. Mem. LWV. Republican. Episcopalian. Clubs: Ski (Bear Valley, Calif.). Lodge: Soroptimist Millbrae-San Bruno (pres. 1965-66, various regional offices, coms.). Home: PO Box 3622 Arnold CA 95223-3622

PUTMAN, ROBERT DEAN, golf course architect; b. Wallace, Idaho, Dec. 18, 1924; m. Sally Harmon, 1945; 3 children. Grad., Fresno State Coll. Art dir. Sta. KJEO-TV, Fresno, Calif., 1950's. Prin. works include Arvin Mcpl. Golf Course, Wasco, Calif., Madera (Calif.) Mcpl. Golf Course, Rancho Canada Golf Course, Carmel Valley, Calif., La Manga Golf Course, Costa Blanca, Spain, Monterey (Calif.) Country Club Shore Course, San Joaquin Country Club, Fresno, Visalia (Calif.) Mcpl. Golf Course, River Island Golf Course, Poterville, Calif., Kings River Country Club, Kingsburg, Calif. Office: 5644 N Briarwood Ave Fresno CA 93711-2501

PUZDER, ANDREW F., lawyer; b. Cleve., July 11, 1950; s. Andrew F. and Winifried M. Puzder; m. Deanna L. Descher, Sept. 26, 1987. BA, Cleve. State U., 1975; JD, Washington U., 1978. Gen. counsel, exec. v.p. Fidelity Nat. Fin., Inc., CKE Restaurants, Inc. Editor Washington U. Law Quarterly, 1977-78. Author of law upheld by U.S. Supreme Ct. in Webster v. Reproductive Health Svcs., 1989; founding dir. Common Ground Network for Life and Choice, 1993. Mem. State Bar Nev., The Mo. Bar, State Bar Calif., Phi Alpha Theta. Address: 3916 State St # 300 Santa Barbara CA 93105-3137

PYE, DAVID THOMAS, specialty retail company executive; b. Darby, Pa., June 12, 1942; s. David and Grace Marie (Dale) P. BS, Widener U., 1964. CPA, Calif. Tax cons. Price Waterhouse & Co., Phila., 1964-70; dir. taxes Am. Instl. Devel., Inc., Phila., 1970-75; dir. tax adminstrn. Syntex Corp., Palo Alto, Calif., 1975-93; group tax mgr. Logitech Inc., Fremont, Calif., 1995-96; sr. dir. taxes West Marine, Inc., Watsonville, Calif., 1996—. Mem. AICPA, Calif. CPA Soc., Tax Execs. Inst. Home: 201 S 4th St Apt 704 San Jose CA 95112-3669 Office: 500 Westridge Dr Watsonville CA 95076-4171

PYM, BRUCE MICHAEL, lawyer; b. Alameda, Calif., Sept. 29, 1942; s. Leonard A. and Willamay (Strandberg) P. B.B.A., U. Wash., 1964, J.D., 1967. Bar: Wash. 1967, U.S. Dist. Ct. (we. dist.) Wash. 1968, U.S. Ct. Appeals (9th cir.) 1968, U.S. Tax Ct. 1969, U.S. Supreme Ct. 1971. Law clk. Wash. State Supreme Ct., Olympia, 1967-68; assoc. Graham & Dunn, Seattle, 1968-73, shareholder, 1973-92; ptnr. Heller, Ehrman, White & McAuliffe, Seattle, 1992—; mng. ptnr. Northwest Offices, 1994-99. Bd. dirs. United Way of King County, 1986-92, chmn., 1990. Mem. ABA, Wash. State Bar Assn., King County Bar Assn. (pres. 1984-85). Office: Heller Ehrman White & McAuliffe 701 5th Ave Ste 6100 Seattle WA 98104-7098

PYNE, DONALD EUGENE, priest; b. San Francisco, Dec. 24, 1929; s. Thomas Francis and Marcia Aileen (Worth) P. BA, St. Patrick's Coll., 1952, MDiv, 1977; postgrad., San Francisco Theol. Sem., 1979, Calif. State U., Dominquez Hills, 1980. Ordained priest Roman Cath. Ch., 1956. Tchr. Marin Cath. High Sch., Kentfield, Calif., 1957-66; parish priest Archdiocese of San Francisco Bay Area, 1966—; pastor St. Charles Ch., San Carlos, Calif., 1982—; dean Deanery G, So. San Mateo County, 1983—; faculty Coll. Notre Dame, Belmont, Calif., 1981-83; cons. Archdiodese San Francisco, 1983—; vice chmn. San Francisco Coun. Priests, 1984-85; mem. Com. On-Going Edn. of Priests. Address: 880 Tamarack Ave San Carlos CA 94070-3736

PYPER, JAMES WILLIAM, chemist; b. Wells, Nev., Sept. 5, 1934; s. William Jones and Wilma (Bjelke) P.; m. Phyllis Diane Henry, Aug. 30, 1957; children: Scott, Mark, Gregory, Heather, Melanie, Tara, Tammy, Wendy, Michael, Tanya, David. BS, Brigham Young U., 1958, MS, 1960; PhD, Cornell U., 1964. Ordained bishop Ch. Jesus Christ of Latter-day Saints, 1973. Research chemist Lawrence Livermore (Calif.) Nat. Lab., 1963-84, mass spectrometry group leader, 1973-75, tritium tech. group leader, 1977-78, applied phys. chemistry group leader, 1979-80, sect. leader for analytical chemistry, 1980-83, dep. sect. leader for analytical chemistry, 1983-87, assoc. div. leader condensed matter and analytical scis. div., 1987-89, quality assurance mgr., 1989-90, ret., 1990. Contbr. articles to sci. jours. Presided over local congrs., 1973-75, 87-91, 91-93; mem. stake high coun., 1976-87; missionary Ch. of Jesus Christ of Latter Saints, Thessaloniki, Greece, 1991-93, Scotland and Eng., 1994-95, Nauvoo, Ill., 1997-98. Republican.

QIAN, XUEYU, physicist; b. Wengzhou, China, Aug. 1, 1943; came to U.S., 1980; s. Peichi and Fengjuan (Huang) Q.; children: Jun, Jiang. B in Physics, Beijing U., 1968; PhD in Physics, U. Mich., 1987. Head semiconductor divsn. Wenzhou Engring. Sch., Zhejiang, 1970-74; lectr., rschr. U. Sci. and Tech., China, 1974-80; vis. scholar U. Mich., Ann Arbor, 1980-81, rsch. asst., 1981-87; rsch. assoc. U. Calif., Santa Barbara, 1987-88, Berkeley, 1988-90; tech. dir. Applied Materials, Santa Clara, Calif., 1990—. Author: (textbook) The Physics of Magnetic Recording, 1976; contbr. numerous articles to sci. publs.; patentee, inventor in field. Rsch. grantee Dept. Energy, 1981-87, Calif. Micro and Applied Materials, 1988-90. Mem. Am. Vacuum Soc. (No. Calif. chpt., editor plasma etch user's group 1996—). Office: Applied Materials 974 E Arques Ave # Ms81158 Sunnyvale CA 94086-4520

QIAN, ZIFEN, artist, researcher; b. Shanghai, Dec. 30, 1957; came to U.S., 1987; s. Mingkong and Xuan Wu (Chen) Q.; m. Li Dai, Mar. 27, 1992; 1 child, Kristin. BA, Shanghai Normal U., 1983; MFA, Portland State U., 1989. Sr. artist Carol Wilson Fine Arts, Portland, 1992—; art instr. Pacific Northwest Coll. Art, Portland, 1989-94, Portland State U., 1987-89; art editor Youth and Health mag. WHO, Shanghai, 1983-87; pres. Northwest Chinese Artists Assn., Portland, 1993-95, World Arts Pub. Co., Portland, 1997—; fine artist: (paintings, art philosophy) The Oregonian newspaper, 1987, Stepping Out Arts mag., 1988, (paintings in a book) Entertaining with Betsy Bloomingdale, 1994, (paintings prints) Carol Wilson Fine Arts, 1992—, (art experience) The Dictionary of World Chinese Artists Achievements, 1994. One-man exhbns. Denise Amato Galleries, 1989-98, Indigo Gallery, 1992, Portland State U. Gallery, 1989 (fine artist award), U.S. Bancorp Towers, 1987; paintings shows Shanghai Fine Arts Acad. Shows, 1982, 84, Across East China Nat. Art Show, 1986. Avocations: creating poetry, singing, tennis. E-mail: lzwap@aol.com.

QUACKENBUSH, JUSTIN LOWE, federal judge; b. Spokane, Wash., Oct. 3, 1929; s. Carl Clifford and Marian Huldah (Lowe) Q.; m. Marie McAtee; children: Karl Justin, Kathleen Marie, Robert Craig. BA, U. Idaho, 1951; LLB, Gonzaga U., Spokane, 1957. Bar: Wash. 1957. Dep. pros. atty. Spokane County, 1957-59; ptnr. Quackenbush, Dean, Bailey & Henderson, Spokane, 1959-80; dist. judge U.S. Dist. Ct. (ea. dist.) Wash., Spokane, 1980—, now sr. judge; part-time instr. Gonzaga U. Law Sch., 1960-67. Chmn. Spokane County Planning Commn., 1969-73. Served with USN, 1951-54. Mem. Wash. Bar Assn., Spokane County Bar Assn. (trustee 1976-78), Internat. Footprint Assn. (nat. pres. 1967), Spokane C. of C. (trustee, exec. com. 1978-79), Shriners. Episcopalian. Office: US Dist Ct PO Box 1432 Spokane WA 99210-1432

QUALLEY, CHARLES ALBERT, fine arts educator; b. Creston, Iowa, Mar. 19, 1930; s. Albert Olaf and Cleora (Dietrick) Q.; m. Betty Jean Griffith, Nov. 26, 1954; children: Janet Lynn, John Stuart. B.F.A., Drake U., 1952; M.A., U. Iowa, 1956, M.F.A., 1958; Ed.D., Ill. State U., 1967. Art tchr. Des Moines Pub. Schs., 1952, 54-55; critic art tchr. U. Iowa, 1955-57; prof. fine arts U. Colo., Boulder, 1958-90, prof. emeritus, 1990—, chmn. dept. fine arts U. Colo., 1968-71, assoc. chmn., 1981-82; vis. prof. Inst. for Shipboard Edn., semester at sea, 1979, Ill. State U., 1985. Author: Safety in the Art Room, 1986; contbg. editor Sch. Arts, 1978-85; mem. editorial adv. bd., 1985-87; author column Safetypoint, 1981-85. Served with AUS, 1952-

54, Korea. Mem. Nat. Art Edn. Assn. (v.p. 1980-82, pres. 1987-89, dir. conv. svcs. 1990—, fellow 1990—, Art Educator of Yr. 1993), Nat. Art Edn. Found. (trustee 1987—, chair bd. trustees 1996—), Colo. Art Edn. Assn. (editor 1965-67, 75, pres. 1976-78), Delta Phi Delta, Omicron Delta Kappa, Pi Kappa Delta. Home: 409 Fillmore Ct Louisville CO 80027-2273

QUATTLEBUM, DONALD LEE, minister; b. Hayward, Calif., Sept. 19, 1957; s. Chester James and Bonnie (Powers) Q.; m. Deborah Jean Stillwaggon, June 3, 1978; children: Donald Lee II, David John. Diploma of ministry, Zion Bible Inst., Barrington, R.I., 1978; BA, Southeastern Coll., Lakeland, Fla., 1989; postgrad., Liberty U., Lynchburg, Va., 1989—. Ordained to ministry Bethel Temple, 1979; lic. to preach Assemblies of God, 1983, ordained to ministry, 1988. Asst. pastor Bethel Temple, Antioch, Calif., 1978-79; assoc. pastor Calvary Temple, Klamath Falls, Oreg., 1979-82, Brentwood (Calif.) Assembly of God, 1985-86; asst. pastor 1st Assembly of God, Antioch, 1982—; youth pastor Heirborn Youth Ministries, Antioch, 1989—. Mem. Nat. Network Youth Ministries, Rotary. Office: 1st Assembly of God PO Box 2117 Antioch CA 94531-2117

QUESADA, RAMON S., JR., radiologist; b. Legaspi City, Philippines, Apr. 24, 1941; s. Ramon C. and Maria S. Quesada; m. Justa A. Quesada; children: Ramon A. III, Eryck Francis A., Monica Alysa A. MD, U. Philippines, 1966. Diplomate Am. Bd. Radiology. Intern Grace Hosp., Detroit, 1967-68; resident in radiology Georgetown U. Med. Ctr., Washington, 1968-71; fellow spl. procedures U. Calif.-Davis, Sacto. Med. Ctr., 1971-73; radiologist Serra Meml. Hosp., Sun Valley, Calif., 1973-78, Providence Holy Cross Med. Ctr., Mission Hills, Calif., 1978—; asst. clin. instr. radiology Georgetown U. Sch. Medicne, Washington, 1970-71; asst. clin prof. radiology U. Calif.-Davis., 1971-73, U. Calif. Irvine, 1973-76. Mem. Am. Coll. Radiology, Calif. Radiolog. Soc., L.A. Radiolog. Soc., Philippine Med. Assn. So. Calif. (sec. 1981-83, pres. 1983-84).e. Republican. Avocations: travel, gourmet foods, golf. Office: Providence Holy Cross Med Ctr 15031 Rinaldi St Mission Hills CA 91345-1207

QUIAT, GERALD M., lawyer; b. Denver, Jan. 9, 1924; s. Ira L. and Esther (Greenblatt) Q.; m. Roberta M. Nicholson, Sept. 26, 1962; children: James M., Audrey R., Melinda A., Daniel P., Ilana L., Leonard E. AA, U. Calif., Berkeley, 1942; AB, LLB, U. Denver, 1948, changed to JD, 1970. Bar: Colo. 1948, Fed. Ct. 1948, U.S. Dist. Ct. Colo. 1948, U.S. Ct. Appeals (10th cir.) 1948, U.S. Surpeme Ct. 1970. Dep. dist. atty. County of Denver, Colo., 1949-52; partner firm Quiat, Seeman & Quiat, Denver, 1952-67, Quiat & Quiat (later changed to Quiat, Bucholtz & Bull, P.C.), 1968; pres. Quiat, Bucholtz & Bull & Laff, P.C. (and predecessors), Denver, 1968-85; pvt. practice Denver, 1985—; bd. dirs., chmn. audit com. Guaranty Bank & Trust Co., Denver; past bd. dirs. and chmn. bd. ROMED, RMD, Inc. Past trustee Holding Co., Rose Med. Ctr., Denver, pres., chmn. bd. dirs., 1976-79; mem. Colo. Civil Rights Com., 1963-71, chmn., 1966-67, 69-70, hearing officer, 1963-71; bd. dirs. Am. Cancer Rsch. Ctr., Denver, chmn. bd., 1991-93; chmn. bd. Am. Med. Ctr., 1993-95; mem. nat. civil rights com., hon. mem. nat. exec. com., hon. nat. commr. Anti-Defamation League, B'nai B'rith, mem. exec. com., chmn. bd. Mountain States region, 1980-82. With inf. U.S. Army, 1942-45. Decorated Combat Infantry Badge, Bronze Star. Mem. ABA, Colo. Bar Assn., Colo. Trial Lawyers Assn. (pres. 1970-71), Am. Legion (comdr. Leyden-Chiles-Wickersham post 1 1955-56, past judge adv. Colo. dept.). Home: 8130 E Lt William Clark Rd Parker CO 80134-5825 Office: Penthouse Suite 1720 S Bellaire St Denver CO 80222-4304

QUICK, VALERIE ANNE, sonographer; b. Alta., Can., Feb. 14, 1952; came to U.S., 1953; d. Kenneth Conrad and Kathryn (Maller) Bjorge. Grad. high sch., Salinas, Calif. Registered adult and pediatric echocardiographer, abdomen, small parts and ob-gyn sonographer; registered cardiovasc. technician, registered diagnostic cardiac sonographer. Chief EKG technician Natividad Med. Ctr., Salinas, 1978-81, chief ultrasound dept., 1981-94, chief cardiac echo lab., 1995—. Mem. Am. Inst. Ultrasound in Medicine, Am. Soc. Echocardiography, Nat. Soc. for Cardiopulmonary Technicians, Soc. Pediat. ECHO, Soc. Diagnostic Med. Sonographers, Am. Heart Assn., Am. Registry Diagnostic Med. Sonographers. Avocations: reading, photography, travel. Office: PO Box 6694 Salinas CA 93912-6694

QUICK, WILLIAM THOMAS, author, screenwriter; b. Muncie, Ind., May 30, 1946; s. Clifford Willett and Della May (Ellis) Q. Student, Ind. U., 1964-66. Pres. Iceberg Prodns., San Francisco, 1986—. Author: Dreams of Flesh and Sand, 1988, Dreams of God and Men, 1989, Yesterday's Pawn, 1989, Systems, 1989, Singularities, 1990, (as Quentin Thomas) Chains of Light, 1992, Ascensions, 1997, (as Margaret Allan) The Mammoth Stone, 1993, Keeper of the Stone, 1994, The Last Mammoth, 1995, Spirits Walking Woman, 1997, (as W.T. Quick) Star Control: Interbellum, 1996, American Gothic: Family, 1996, Sister of the Sky, 1998, (with William Shatner) Quest for Tomorrow: Delta Search, 1997, Quest for Tomorrow: In Alien Hands, 1997, Quest for Tomorrow: Step Into Chaos, 1999, (as Sean Kiernan) Roar, 1998, Roar: The Cauldron, 1998, Roar: The Talisman, 1998. Mem. Sci. Fiction and Fantasy Writers Am., Authors Guild, Writers Guild Am., West. Home and Office: 1558 Leavenworth St San Francisco CA 94109-3220

QUIGG, RICHARD JOHN, metallurgist, lawyer; b. Bethlehem Pa., Nov. 12, 1930; s. John Paul and Frances (Gruver) Q.; m. Joan Clampett, Apr. 6, 1956 (div. 1981); children—Richard, Jr., Daniel, Laura; m. Linda Hoffman, Sept. 14, 1991; B.S. in Metall. Engring., Va. Tech., 1952; M.S. in Metall. Engring., Lehigh U., 1954; Ph.D., Case Western Res. U., 1959; J.D. Cleve. State U., 1966. Bar: Ohio 1966, Fla. 1972, N.J. 1975; registered profl. engr., Ohio. Mgr. materials and processing TRW Inc., Cleve., 1959-67; mgr. research and devel. TRW Metals div., Minerva, Ohio, 1967-70; pres. Jetshapes, Inc., Rockleigh, N.J., 1970-78; sr. materials engr. Pratt and Whitney, Hartford, Conn., 1978-80; v.p. mktg. Cannon Muskegon Corp., Muskegon, Mich., 1980-96; cons., 1996—. Contbr. articles to profl. jours. Patentee in field. Recipient W.A. Tarr award Sigma Gamma Epsilon, 1952. Fellow Am. Soc. Metals; mem. AIME, ASTM. Club: Saddle Brooke Tennis Assn. (local chpt.). Home and Office: 37547 S Canyon Side Dr Tucson AZ 85739-1317

QUIGLEY, KEVIN WALSH, state legislator, lawyer; b. Everett, Wash., Feb. 23, 1961; s. David W. Quigley and Mary (Cernetig) Thoreson; m. Suzanne Marion Bakke. BA with spl. honors, George Washington U., 1983; JD cum laude, NYU, 1986; LLM, Harvard U., 1992. Bar: Wash. 1988. Jr. fellow ctr. internat. studies NYU Law Sch., N.Y.C., 1986; assoc. Perkins Coie, Seattle, 1987-94; of counsel Perkins Coie, Seattle, 1995-97; mem. Wash. State Senate, Olympia, 1993-97; chmn. health and long-term care com., mem., vice chmn. ways and means com.; dir. bus. affairs Teledesic Corp. Grad. fellow Harvard Law Sch., 1987. Mem. Rotary, Phi Beta Kappa. Democrat. Avocations: mountain climbing, architecture, carpentry. Home: 1029 Springbrook Rd Lake Stevens WA 98258-9425*

QUIGLEY, PHILIP J., telecommunications industry executive; b. 1943. With Advanced Mobile Phone Svc. Inc., 1982-84, v.p., gen. mgr., Pacific region; with Pac Tel Mobile Access, 1984-86, pres., chief exec. officer; with Pac Tel Personal Communications, 1986-87, pres., chief exec. officer; exec. v.p., chief oper. officer Pac Tel Corp., 1987; ret. chmn., pres., chief exec. officer Pacific Telesis Group, San Francisco, 1997—; pres. Pacific Bell, 1987-94; bd. dirs. SRI Internat., Menlo Park, Calif., 1998—. Office: SRI Internat 333 Ravenswood Ave Menlo Park CA 94025-3493*

QUILLIGAN, EDWARD JAMES, obstetrician, gynecologist, educator; b. Cleve., June 18, 1925; s. James Joseph and Maude Elvira (Ryan) Q.; m. Betty Jane Cleaton, Dec. 14, 1946; children—Bruce, Jay, Carol, Christopher, Linda, Ted. B.A., Ohio State U., 1951, M.D., 1951; M.A. (hon.), Yale, 1967. Intern Ohio State U. Hosp., 1951-52, resident, 1952-54; resident Western Res. U. Hosps., 1954-56; asst. prof. obstetrics and gynecology Western Res. U., 1957-63, prof., 1963-65; prof. obstetrics and gynecology UCLA, 1965-66; prof., chmn. dept. Ob-Gyn Yale U., 1966-69; prof., chmn. dept. Ob-Gyn U. So. Calif., 1969-78, asso. v.p. med. affairs, 1978-79; prof. Ob-Gyn. U. Calif., Irvine, 1980-83, vice chancellor health affairs, dean Sch. Medicine, 1987-89; prof., chmn. ob.-gyn. dept. U. Wis., 1983-85; prof., chmn. Ob-Gyn Davis Med. Ctr. U. Calif., Sacramento, 1985-87; vice chancellor Health Scis., dean Coll. Med. U. Calif., Irvine, 1987-89, prof. ob-gyn, 1987-94, prof. emeritus ob-gyn., 1994; exec. dir. med. edn. Long Beach (Calif.) Meml. Health Svcs., 1995—. Contbr. articles to med. jours.; co-editor-in-chief: Am. Jour. Obstetrics and Gynecology. Served to 2d lt. AUS, 1944-46. Recipient Centennial award Ohio State U., 1970. Mem. Soc. Gynecologic Investigation, Am. Gynecol. Soc., Am. Coll. Obstetics and Gynecology, Sigma Xi. Home: 24 Urey Ct Irvine CA 92612-4077

QUINCY, ALPHA ELLEN BEERS, school board president; b. Olympia, Wash., Oct. 15, 1924; d. George Howard and Grace Florence (Penrose) Beers; m. John J. Quincy, Nov. 12, 1942 (dec. Feb. 1987); children: Cheri Sue, John Jay. BE in Edn., Calif. State U., Sacramento, 1960; MA in Ednl. Adminstrn., U. Calif., Berkeley, 1966, postgrad., 1996—. Life cert. adminstrn., presch., K-12 and adult, elem. sch. adminstrn., elem. tchg. Tchr., resource tchr., vice prin., prin., dist. cons. Mt. Diablo Unified Sch. Dist., 1959-83; coord. Acad. Curriculum and Instrn. Leaders Assn. Calif. Sch. Adminstrs., 1985-89; cons. edn., spkr., writer, workshop leader, 1983—; exec. dir. San Ramon Valley Sch. Age Child Care Alliance, 1992-93; mem. Contra Costa County Bd. Edn., 1988—, pres., 1992, 96; mem. Calif. Curriculum Devel. and Supplemental Materials Commn., State Bd. Edn., 1971-74; chair com. for reading and lit. Calif. Curriculum Devel. and Supplemental Materials Commn., State Bd. Edn., 1971-74, mem. English lang. arts adv. Calif. Assessment Program, 1971—. Contbr. articles to profl. jours. Bd. dirs. U. Calif. Berkeley, Inst. Sch. Adminstrs., 1979-88, Diablo Internat. Resources Ctr. Recipient Adminstr. of Yr. ann. award Assn. Calif. Sch. Adminstrs., Region 7, 1983. Mem. LWV (leader Lafayette unit 1985, edn. chairperson Diablo Valley 1987, chair nominating com. 1991, edn. chair 1989—), ASCD, Nat. Coun. Tchrs. English (writing awards com. 1990-92, ency. entry team, emeritus assembly), Calif. Assn. Tchrs. English (past bd. dirs., program chair 1990 ann. conf.), Ctrl. Coun. Tchrs. English (past bd. mem., curriculum study com. 1970—, conf. chmn. 1991, 96), Assn. Calif. Sch. Adminstrs. (past mem. mid. sch. com., C&I acad. coord. 1984-88), area VI scholarship chmn. 1990—), Calif. Sch. Bds. ASsn., Calif. County Bds. Edn. , Contra Costa Sch. Bds. Assn., Calif. Retired Tchrs. Assn., East Contra Costa County Retired Tchrs. Assn. (program chair 1992-93, pres. 1995—), Nat. Women's Polit. Caucus, U. Calif. Berkeley Alumni Assn., Internat. Reading Assn., Calif. Reading Assn., Contra Costa Reading Assn., Commonwealth Club Calif., Concord Century Club, Home Group, Phi Delta Kappa, Delta Kappa Gamma. Home: 1529 Rancho View Dr Lafayette CA 94549-2231

QUINN, ELIZABETH R., elementary education educator; b. Covina, Calif., Oct. 7, 1951; d. John Howard and Rosemary (Branine) Roberts; m. D. Whitney Quinn, July 18, 1980. BA, Ariz. State U., 1973; Marriage, Family and Child Counseling, Azuza Pacific U., 1980; BS, Calif. State U., Fullerton, 1993. Tchr. Saddleback Valley Unified Sch. Dist., Mission Viejo, Calif., 1976—, mentor tchr., 1992—; Cert. life standard elem. credential K-8, Calif. Named Tchr. of Yr. Kiwanis, Mission Viejo, 1992. Mem. Calif. Tchrs. Assn., Saddleback Valley Educators. Avocations: reading, gourmet cooking, weight lifting. Office: Del Lago Elem 27181 Entidad Mission Viejo CA 92691-1099

QUINN, FRANCIS A., bishop; b. L.A., Sept. 11, 1921. Ed., St. Joseph's Coll., Mountain View, Calif., St. Patrick's Sem., Menlo Park, Calif., Cath. U., Washington, U. Calif., Berkeley. Ordained priest Roman Cath. Ch., 1946; ordained titular bishop of Numana and aux. bishop of San Francisco, 1978; bishop Diocese of Sacramento, 1979-94, bishop emeritus, 1994—. Office: 2110 Broadway Sacramento CA 95818-2518

QUINN, KAREN TAKLE, infosystem management consultant; b. Madison, Wis., May 22, 1937; d. Carl Knutsen and Gunvor Takle; m. Francis Thomas Quinn, May 24, 1969. BS, U. Wis., 1958; cert., Oslo U., Norway, 1958; MSLS, Rutgers U., 1959; cert. mktg., U. Calif., Berkeley, 1991; MA in Orgn. Devel., The Fielding Inst., Santa Barbara, Calif., 1996, PhD in Human and Orgnl. Systems, 1996. Engring. librarian Princeton (N.J.) U., 1959-63; asst. prof. Drexel U., Phila., 1963-65; sr. librarian IBM Corp., San Jose, Calif., 1965-74; libr. dir., info. ctr. specialist STL IBM Corp., Palo Alto and San Jose, Calif., 1965-74; engr. specialist E/S IBM Corp., Palo Alto, 1983-84; product cons. IEBC IBM Corp., San Jose, 1984-87, product cons., planner PS IDE, 1987-97; pres. KTQ Assocs., Los Altos, Calif.; faculty The Fielding Inst., Santa Barbara, 1997—, Coll. Notre Dame, Belmont, 1998—; cons. Ford Found., Singapore; lectr. San Jose State U., 1971—; advisor online conf. Knowledge Mgmt., L.A., 1986-87, 89; mem. adv. bd. Internat. Sch. Info. Mgmt., Santa Barbara, 1988—, instr., 1989—. Editor: Advances in Office Automation, 1985, Info. Hotline jour., 1967-82; contbr. articles to profl. jours.; inventor. Named Disting. Alumna, Grad. Alumni Assn. Sch. Communication, Info. and Lib. Studies, Rutgers U., 1990; NSF grantee, 1963; U. Oslo scholar, 1958; recipient Centennial award Am. Soc. Engring. Edn., 1993. Fellow Inst. Info. Scientists; mem. Am. Soc. Engring. (div. chairperson 1965-68), Soc. Women Engrs., Internat. Fed. Documentation (affiliate), Am. Soc. Info. Sci. (chairperson 1983-85), Spl. Libraries Assn. (dir. San Francisco Bay Chpt. 1966-68), German Shepherd Dog Fanciers No. Calif. (bd. dirs. 1985—). Lodge: Order of Eastern Star. Office: KTQ and Assocs PO Box 277 Los Altos CA 94023-0277

QUINN, WILLIAM FRANCIS, retired government executive, writer; b. Canon City, Colo., Dec. 9, 1946; s. Eugene William and Dora B. (Roe) Q.; m. Nancy Theresa Daly, Apr. 26, 1971 (div. Nov. 1991); children: William F., Daniel J.; m. Blanca Noelia Charriez, Dec. 19, 1995. BS, Boston U., 1994. With intelligence dept. U.S. Govt., Langley, Va., 1971-95; ret. Author: PBR: The Making of a Warrior, 1996, The Dark Side of Freedom, 1997. With USN, 1963-71, Vietnam. Decorated Combat Action ribbon U.S. Govt., Vietnam, 1966, Bronze star, 1969, Gallantry Cross, 1970, Civil Action medal, 1970. Mem. VFW (life). Avocation: writing. Home: 545 Rio Grande Ave Raton NM 87740-3950

QUINT, BERT, journalist; b. N.Y.C., Sept. 22, 1930; s. George and Sadye (Slonim) Q.; m. Diane Frances Schwab, Apr. 10, 1975; children: Lara Gabrielle, Amy Frances. BS, NYU, 1952. Reporter Worcester (Mass.) Telegram, 1952-53, AP, 1953-54, N.Y. Herald Tribune, 1956-58; mag. editor, free lance corr. N.Y. Herald Tribune, Wall Street Jour., CBS News, others, Mexico City, 1958-65; corr. CBS News, 1965-93; adj. prof. broadcast journalism U. Colo., Boulder, 1993-97; journalist/anchor/writer TV Quint Colo. Inc.; writer, 1998—. Recipient Radio Reporting award Overseas Press Club, 1971. Mem. Soc. Profl. Journalists, Fgn. Corr. Assn. Mex. (pres.). Home and Office: 126 Annette Dr Portsmouth RI 02871-3704

QUINT, MARK HARLEY, art dealer; b. L.A., Feb. 13, 1953; s. J. Harley and Patricia Q.; m. Linda P., 1973 (div. Feb. 1994); 1 child, Joshua; m. Anna M. Gonzales, May 19, 1994. BA, San Francisco Art Inst., 1976. Owner Quint Contemporary Art, La Jolla, Calif., 1981—. Democrat. Office: Quint Contemporary Art 7661 Girard Ave Ste 110 La Jolla CA 92037-4435

QUINTANA, RICARDO E., pastor; b. Santa Monica, Calif., May 29, 1961; s. Carlos and Katie R. Lee (Dowell) Q.; m. Karen Ann Hendrix, July 9, 1988; children: Stephanie Nicole, Taylor Kristine. BA in Youth Ministry, Northwest Coll., 1985. Ordained to ministry Assemblies of God, 1988. Admissions rep. Northwest Coll., Kirkland, Wash., 1985-88; youth pastor Neighborhood Ch., Bellevue, Wash., 1988-93; youth, assoc. pastor Woodside New Life, Marysville, Wash., 1993-95, sr. pastor, 1995—; bd. dirs. Cedar Springs Camp, Lake Stevens, Wash. Active com. to Assess the Effects of Adult Entertainment on a Cmty., City of Marysville, Wash., 1996; camp dir. Cedar Springs Camp, Lake Stevens, Wash., 1989-95. Mem. Marysville Tulalip C. of C. (ex-officio bd. mem., chair emissary com. mktg. arm). Avocations: reading, carpentry, sports. Office: Woodside New Life Assembly 9015 44th Dr NE Marysville WA 98270-2560

QUINTERO, RUBEN DAVID, English educator; b. Montebello, Calif., May 5, 1949. BA, Calif. State U., Los Angeles, 1978, Calif. State U., Los Angeles, 1980; AM, Harvard U., 1983, PhD, 1988. Deputy sheriff L.A. County Sheriff's Dept., 1972-81; instr. Harvard U., Cambridge, Mass., 1983-88; English prof. Calif. State U., L.A., 1988—. Author: Literate Culture: Pope's Rhetorical Art, 1992 (manuscript award for eighteenth century studies U. Del. Press 1990). With U.S. Army, 1969-71, Vietnam. Recipient Purple Heart, Combat Infantry Badge, U.S. Army, 1970, commendation for selfless and humane action Commerce (Calif.) City Council, 1977, certificate of merit Am. Nat. Red Cross, 1977. Mem. Internat. Soc. History Rhetoric, Am. Soc. Eighteenth Century Studies, Assn. Literary Scholar Critics. Phi Kappa Phi. Office: English Dept Calif State U 5151 State University Dr Los Angeles CA 90032-4226

QUISENBERRY, ROBERT MAX, architect, industrial designer; b. Eugene, Oreg., Nov. 18, 1956; s. Clifford Hale and Annemaria Gertrude (Frank) Q.; m. Dawnese Elaine Tarr, Sept. 18, 1982. BArch, U. Oreg., 1982. Registered architect, Wash., Calif. Project architect Merritt & Pardini, Tacoma, 1984-87; project mgr. Lorimer-Case, San Diego, 1987-89; project design architect The Austin Hansen Group, San Diego, 1989-91; prin. Studio Q Architecture, Chula Vista, Calif., 1991-93; design dir. Exponents, Inc., San Diego, 1993-94, Powerhouse Exhibits, San Diego, 1995—. Recipient Washington State Passive Solar Design and Bldg. award, 1981, Gold and Bronze Summit Awards, 1996. Republican. Home: 644 Hartford St Chula Vista CA 91913-2456

QUON, WANDA ANN, physician; b. Los Angeles, Mar. 2, 1967; d. Bill Jack and So Fa (Ng) Q. BS, Univ. Southern Calif., 1989; DO, Univ. Health Scis., 1996. Mem. Am. Osteopathic Assn., Am. Coll. General Practitioners, Am. Coll. Osteopathic Family Physicians, Mo. Assn. Osteopathic Physicians, Phi Sigma Soc. Avocations: piano, tennis, swimming, model building, carving. Office: 808 N Hill St Los Angeles CA 90012-2321 also: 201 W Garvey Ave Monterey Park CA 91754-1602

RAAFLAUB, VERNON ARTHUR, religion educator; b. Magnetawan, Ont., Can., Apr. 30, 1938; s. Arthur Frederick and Olga Elizabeth (Hoerner) R. Diploma in electronics, Radio Electronics TV Schs., North Bay, Ont., 1959; diploma in theology, Concordia Theol. Sem., Springfield, Ill., 1965, BTh, 1972; MDiv, Concordia Theol. Sem., Ft. Wayne, Ind., 1987; addl. theol. studies, Concordia Theol. Sem., Fort Wayne, Ind.; postgrad., Wilfrid Laurier U., Waterloo, Ont., 1974-75; MA in Adminstrn., Briercrest Bible Coll., Caronport, Sask., 1985; DD (hon.), Concordia Luth. Sem., Edmonton, Alberta, Can., 1998. Ordained to ministry Luth. Ch., 1965. Pastor Nipawin (Sask.) Choiceland Luth. Parish, 1965-76; instr. Can. Luth. Bible Inst., Camrose, Alta., 1976-77, acad. dean, instr., 1977-85, prof. Old Testament studies, acad. dean, 1985—; Counsellor Luth. Ch. Mo. Synod, Carrot River Cir., 1971-75. Co-editor: The Creation Alternative, 1970; contbr. numerous articles to profl. jours. Chmn. Easter Seal Campaign, Nipawin, 1972; mem. Can. council World Mission Prayer League, 1980-85; bd. dirs. Concordia Coll., Edmonton, Alta., 1975-78. Grantee Luth. Ch. Can., Zion Found., 1975. Mem. Nat. Assn. Profs. Hebrew, Am. Schs. Oriental Rsch., Near East Archeol. Soc., Am. Sci. Affiliation (assoc.), Creation Rsch. Soc. (assoc.), Assn. Psychol. Type, Histadruth Ivrith Am., Rotary (pres. Nipawin chpt. 1972-73, bd. dirs. 1968-71). Avocations: electronics, multitrack recording, music, swimming. Fax: (780) 672-4455. E-mail: clbi@cable-lynx.net. Office: Can Luth Bible Inst, 4837 52A St, Camrose, AB Canada T4V 1W5

RABUCK, DONNA FONTANAROSE, English writing educator; b. Edison, N.J., Aug. 2, 1954; d. Arthur Thomas and Shirley Gertrude (Golub) Fontanarose; m. John Frederick Rabuck, July, 28, 1973; 1 child, Miranda Rose. BA in Eng., Rutgers U., 1976, MA in Eng. Lit., 1980, PhD in Eng. Lit., 1990. Prof. writing Pima C. C., Tucson, 1981-86; asst. dir. writing skills program U. Ariz., Tucson, 1983—; asst. dir. summer inst. writing U. Ariz., Tucson, 1985—, asst. dir. grad. writing inst., 1996—; adj. faculty Pima C. C., Tucson, 1992-95. Author: The Other Side of Silence: Performing Heroinism in the Victorian Novel, 1990, Writing Ctr. Perspectives, 1995; editor: Writing is Thinking: Collected Writings of the Summer Inst., 1985—. Founder, pres. Miles East-West Neighborhood Assn., Tucson, 1983—; dir. Ctr. for Sacred Feminine, Tucson, 1995—; program coord. U. Ariz. Arts and Scis. Minority Retention Program, 1988-93. Rutgers Alumni scholar, 1972-76; Bevier fellow Rutgers U., 1976-78. Mem. Intercollegiate Writing Com. (task force), Commn. Cultural Thinking (task force), Nat. Coun. Tchrs. Eng. Avocations: feminist scholarship, women's rituals, yoga, hiking, meditation. Home: 1115 N Camino Miraflores Tucson AZ 85745-1612 Office: Univ Ariz Writing Skills Program 1201 E Helen St Tucson AZ 85719-4407

RABUN, CLAUDE LEE, consumer products company executive, consultant; b. Berkeley, Calif., Dec. 16, 1951; s. Carl Lee and Maria Medora (Ellis) R.; children: Lanalee, Orpilla, Carl. AS, City Coll. San Francisco, 1972; BA, Golden Gate U., 1974; MPA, U. San Francisco, 1980. Security cons. Sears, Roebuck & Co., San Francisco, 1970-80; juvenile probation officer San Francisco Superior Ct., 1974-75; supervising spl. investigator Alcohol Beverage Control, Oakland, Hollywood, Calif., 1975-85; CEO, chief cons. CLR Enterprises, Inc., Hollywood, 1985—; govtl. affairs commr. Hollywood C. of C., 1991—. Active Bus. Mentors Program, First AME, L.A., 1991-94. Recipient Advanced Cert., P.O.S.T., Sacramento, 1981, Supervisory Cert., 1983. Avocations: photography, philanthropy, autophile. Office: CLR Enterprises Inc 7060 Hollywood Blvd Ste 1001 Hollywood CA 90028-6023

RABY, WILLIAM LOUIS, author; b. Chgo., July 16, 1927; s. Gustave E. and Helen (Burgess) R.; m. Norma Claire Schreiner, Sept. 8, 1956; children: Burgess, Marianne, Marlene. BSBA, Northwestern U., 1949; MBA, U. Ariz., 1961, PhD, 1971. Ptnr. VAR CPA Firms, 1950-76, Touche Ross & Co., N.Y.C., 1977-87, pres. Ariz. State Bd. Accountancy, 1993-94, mem. Ariz. State Bd. Tax Appeals, 1994—, chmn., 1997-99; prof. acctg. emeritus Ariz. State U.; columnist Tax Notes mag., Arlington, Va., 1990—; cons. on video and audio tax edn. tapes Bisk Pub. Co., 1992—. Author: The Income Tax and Business Decisions, 1964, Building and Maintaining a Successful Tax Practice, 1964, The Reluctant Taxpayer, 1970, Tax Practice Management, 1974, Introduction to Federal Taxation, annually, 1980-91, Tax Practice Management: Client Servicing, 1986; editor: Raby Report on Tax Practice, 1986-96, PPC Guide To Successful Tax Practice, 1991; mem. editorial adv. bd. Practical Tax Strategies; contbr. articles to profl. jours. Mem. AICPA (chmn. fed. tax divsn. 1980-83, v.p. 1983-84, coun. 1983-90), Tax Ct. Bar. Presbyterian (elder, chmn. adv. coun. on ch. and soc. 1979-81). Office: PO Box 26846 Tempe AZ 85285-6846

RACEK, JERRINE ANN, producer, editor; b. North Bend, Nebr., Oct. 15, 1952; d. Lorin J. and Nadine L. (Ladenburger) R. BS in Music Engring., U. Colo., 1998. Featured vocalist Paul Moorhead's Orch., Omaha, 1973-80, Dean Bushnell's Orch., Denver, 1983-98; legal sec. Otten, Johnson, Robinson, Neff & Ragonetti, P.C., Denver, 1991—; audio/video post intern Denver Ctr. Media, 1997-98; intern to mktg. prodrs. Encore Media Group, Denver, summer 1998; bd. mem. U. Colo. Denver Alumni Bd., 1998—. Vol. Colo. Symphony Orch., Denver, 1992-95, Channel 6 Pub. TV, Denver, 1992—, Opera Colo., Denver, 1992-94, World Youth Day, Denver, 1993. Dir.'s Fellowship scholar U. Colo., Denver, fall 1996, fall 1997. Mem. Golden Key Nat. Honor Soc. Democrat. Roman Catholic. Avocation: reading. Home: #304 471 S Kalispell Way Apt 304 Aurora CO 80017-2143

RACHELEFSKY, GARY S., medical educator; b. N.Y.C., 1942. Intern Bellevue Hosp. Ctr., N.Y.C., 1967-68; resident in pediatrics Johns Hopkins Hosp., 1968-70, Ctr. Disease Control, 1970-72; fellow UCLA Med. Ctr., 1972-74; clin. prof., assoc. dir. A/I Tng. Program UCLA. Mem. Am. Acad. Allergy, Asthma and Immunology (bd. dirs., pres.). Office: 11620 Wilshire Blvd Ste 200 Los Angeles CA 90025-1767

RACHFORD, MARYANN KVIETKAUSKAS, graphic designer, multimedia educator; b. Long Beach, Calif., Aug. 22, 1946; d. Anthony Joseph Kvietkauskas and Avis Josephine (Van Zante) Flowers; m. Thomas Gene Rachford, Aug. 27, 1966; 1 child, Josie Andrea Rachford Johnson. BA, Calif. State U., L.A., 1976, MA, 1978; EdD, Azusa Pacific U. Art dir. MIS Advt. Agy., Cypress, Calif., 1987-89; advt. dir. Boston Stores, Gardena, Calif., 1988-89, Nat. Stores, L.A., 1989-90; creative dir. AB&A Advt. Agy., Santa Fe Springs, Calif., 1990-92; owner, graphic designer, illustrator Pelican Prodns. Art Studio, Temple City, Calif., 1984—; prof. Azusa Pacific U., Calif., 1991—, Citrus Coll., Glendora, Calif., 1991—; mem. Citrus Coll. Future's Forum, Glendora, Calif., 1998—; mem. Ed Net Multimedia Initiative, 1997—. Artist: (watercolors) Red's Home - Pike II, 1993 (AFL-CIO Permanent Coll.), Winter Tide, 1991 (exhibit 1990), (acrylics) Pike IV, 1994 (hon. mention 1994), Land's End - Light From Within, 1990 (hon. mention 1990). Mem. All-Calif. Art Show, others. Avocations: stained glass creations, ceramics. E-mail: mrachford@citrus.cc.ca.us. or maryannsky@aol.com. Home: 9173 E Woolley St Temple City CA 91780 Office: Citrus Coll 1000 W Foothill Blvd Glendora CA 91741

RACICOT, MARC F., governor; b. Thompson Falls, Mont., July 24, 1948; s. William E. and Patricia E. (Bentley) R.; m. Theresa J. Barber, July 25, 1970; children: Ann, Timothy, Mary Catherine, Theresa, Joseph. BA, Carroll Coll., Helena, Mont., 1970; JD, U. Mont., 1973; postgrad., U. Va., 1973,

Cornell U., 1977. Bar: Mont. 1973. With U.S. Army, 1973-76; capt., 1973; legal assistance officer U.S. Army, Ft. Lewis, Wash., 1973; chief trial counsel U.S. Army, Kaiserslautern, Fed. Republic of Germany, 1975-76; resigned, 1976; dep. county atty. Missoula (Mont.) County, 1976-77; bur. chief County Prosecutor Svcs. Bur., Helena, Mont., 1977-89; asst. atty. gen. State of Mont., Helena, 1977-89; spl. prosecutor for the Atty. Gen.'s Office State of Mont., atty. gen., 1989-93, gov., 1993—. Founder Missoula Drug Treatment Program, 1977; active United Way, Helena; bd. visitors U. Mont. Sch. Law. Inducted into Basketball Hall of Fame Carroll Coll., 1982. Mem. Mont. Bar Assn. Republican. Roman Catholic. Office: State Capitol RM 204 Helena MT 59620*

RACINA, THOM (THOMAS FRANK RAUCINA), television writer, editor; b. Kenosha, Wis., June 4, 1946; s. Frank G. and Esther May (Benko) Raucina. B.F.A., Goodman Sch. Drama, Art Inst. Chgo., 1970, M.F.A. in Theatre Arts and Directing with honors, 1971. TV writer Hanna-Barbera Co., Hollywood, Calif., 1973-74, MTM Enterprises, Inc., Hollywood, 1974-76; head writer General Hospital ABC-TV, Hollywood, 1981-84; head writer Days of Our Lives NBC-TV, 1984-86, head writer Another World, 1986-88, co-head writer Generations daytime series, 1988-91, head writer syndicated Dangerous Women night-time TV series, 1991-92; assoc. head writer daytime TV series Santa Barbara, 1992-93. Author: Lifeguard, 1976, The Great Los Angeles Blizzard, 1977, Quincy, M.E., 2 vols., 1977, Kodak in San Francisco, 1977, F.M., 1978, Sweet Revenge, 1978, The Gannon Girls, 1979, Nine to Five, 1980, Tomcat, 1981, Secret Sex: Male Erotic Fantasies (as Tom Anicar), 1976, Magda (as Lisa Wells), 1981, Snow Angel, 1995, Hidden Agenda, 1997, Secret Weekend, 1999; ghost writer: non-fiction The Happy Hustler (Grant Tracy Saxon), 1976, Marilyn Chambers: My Story (Marilyn Chambers), 1976, Xaviera Meets Marilyn (Xaviera Hollander and Marilyn Chambers), 1977; musical plays A Midsummer Night's Dream, music and lyrics, 1968, Allison Wonderland, music and lyrics, 1970, The Marvelous Misadventure of Sherlock Holmes, book, music and lyrics, 1971; TV scripts Sleeping Over segment of Family, ABC, 1978, Russian Pianist segment, ABC, 1979, 1 Child of the Owl, NBC After-Sch. Spl., 1979; contbr. articles to Playboy, Cosmopolitan, Penhouse, Oui, Los Angeles, Gentleman's Quar., Westways; West Coast editor: Grosset & Dunlap, Inc., N.Y.C., 1978—; lead writer for TV: Family Passions, 1993-94, Life's A Bitch!, 1994, Friends & Lovers, 1994; theatre dir., pianist, organist, composer. Recipient Emmy award nomination 1982, 83, 84, 85, 87; U.S. Nat. Student Assn. grantee, 1965. Mem. Authors Guild Am., Writers Guild Am. West. Democrat. Roman Catholic. Home: 2851 Calle Loreto Palm Springs CA 92264-6702

RACITI, CHERIE, artist; b. Chgo., June 17, 1942; d. Russell J. and Jacque (Crimmins) R. Student, Memphis Coll. Art, 1963-65; B.A. in Art, San Francisco State U., 1968; M.F.A., Mills Coll., 1979. Assoc. prof. art San Francisco State U., 1984-89, prof., 1989—; lectr. Calif. State U., Hayward, 1974, San Francisco Art Inst., 1978; mem. artist com. San Francisco Art Inst., 1974-85, sec., 1980-81. One woman shows include U. Calif., Berkeley, 1972, Nicholas Wilder Gallery, Los Angeles, 1975, San Francisco Art Inst., 1977, Marianne Deson Gallery, Chgo., 1980, Site 375, San Francisco, 1989, Reese Bullen Gallery, Humboldt State U., Arcata, Calif., 1990, Mills Coll. Art Mus., Oakland, Calif., 1998; group shows include Whitney Mus. Art, 1975, San Francisco Sci. Fiction, The Clocktower, N.Y.C., Otis-Parsons Gallery, Los Angeles, 1984-85, San Francisco Art Inst., 1985, Artists Space, N.Y.C., 1988, Angles Gallery, Santa Monica, 1987, Terrain Gallery, San Francisco, 1992, Ctr. for the Arts, Santa Monica, 1993, Santa Monica Coll., 1998, 25/25 25th Anniversary Exhbn., So. Exposure Gallery, San Francisco, 1999. Bd. dirs. New Langton Arts, 1988-92. Eureka fellow Fleishhacker Found., San Francisco; recipient Adaline Kent award San Francisco Art Inst., 1976, Djerassi resident, 1994, Tyrone Guthrie Ctr. resident, Ireland, 1995. Office: San Francisco State U Art Dept 1600 Holloway Ave San Francisco CA 94132-1722

RACZKA, TONY MICHAEL, artist; b. Pottsville, Pa., Jan. 16, 1957; s. Albert Joseph and Rosemary Bernadette Raczka; m. Virginia Boone, 1974 (div. 1984); 1 child, Mesika; m. Patricia Martinez, June 20, 1986; 1 stepchild, Cynthia. BFA, No. Ariz. U., 1978; MFA, No. Ill. U., 1980; postgrad., U. Calif., San Diego, 1991-92. Instr. art Southwestern Coll., Chula Vista, Calif., 1981-84, No. Ariz. U., Flagstaff, Ariz., 1983; registrar Mingei Internat. Mus. World Folk Art, San Diego, 1985-86; instr. art San Diego State U., 1987; asst. dir. Quint Gallery, San Diego, 1987; sr. mus. preparator U. Art Gallery, U. Calif., San Diego, 1989-95; presenter in field. One-man shows include Quint Gallery, 1982, 83, Paris Green Gallery, La Jolla, Calif., 1987, Queens Coll. Art Ctr., 2000 CUNY, Flushing, N.Y.; two person shows include Printworks, Chgo., 1982, 84; exhibited in group shows include The Drawing Ctr., 1994, Meridian Gallery, San Francisco, 1995 (Best of Show 2d place), Carnegie Mus. Art, 1997, U. Richmond, Va., 1996, 98, San Jacinto Coll., Houston, 1998 (Merit award); author poetry. Mem. Internat. Soc. Phenomenology and Scis. of Life, San Diego Mus. Art. Home: 4430 42d St # 2 San Diego CA 92116

RADA, ALEXANDER, university official; b. Kvasy, Czechoslovakia, Mar. 28, 1923; s. Frantisek and Anna (Tonnkova) R.; came to U.S., 1954, naturalized, 1959; M.S., U. Tech. Coll. of Prague, 1948; postgrad. Va. Poly. Inst., 1956-59, St. Clara U., 1966-67; Ed.D., U. Pacific, 1975; m. Ingeborg Solveig Blakstad, Aug. 8, 1953; children: Alexander Sverre, Frank Thore, David Harald. Head prodn. planning dept. Mine & Iron Corp., Kolin, Czechoslovakia, 1941-42; mgr. experimenting and testing dept. Avia Aircraft, Prague, 1943-45; sec.-gen. Central Bldg. Office, Prague, 1948; head metal courses dept. Internat. Tech. Sch. of UN, Grafenaschau, W.Ger., 1949-50; works mgr. Igref A/S, Oslo, 1950-51; cons. engr. chief sect. machines Steel Products Ltd., Oslo, 1951-54; chief engr., plant supt. Nelson J. Pepin & Co., Lowell, Mass., 1954-55; sr. project engr., mfg. supt. Celanese Corp. Am., Narrows, Va., 1955-60; mgr. mfg., facilities and maint. FMC Corp. San Jose, Calif., 1960-62; mgr. adminstrn. Sylvania Electronic Systems, Santa Cruz, Calif., 1962-72; asst. to pres., devel. officer Napa (Calif.) Coll., 1972-88; chief exec. officer NAVCO Pacific Devel. Corp., Napa, 1984-91; pres. NAVCO Coll. Co., 1991—; prof. indsl. mgmt. Cabrillo Coll., Aptos, Calif., 1963-72; mgmt. and engring. cons., 1972—. Pres. ARC, Santa Cruz, 1965-72, bd. dirs., pres., Napa, 1977-88; mem. Nat. Def. Exec. Res., 1978-88; Commerce, Washington, 1966—, chmn. No. Calif. region 9, 1981-88; mem. President's Export Council-DEC, San Francisco, 1982—. Recipient Meritorious Service citation ARC, 1972, Etoile Civique l'Ordre de l'Etoile Civique, French Acad., 1985; registered profl. engr., Calif. Mem. NSPE, Calif. Soc. Profl. Engrs., Am. Def. Preparedness Assn., Assn. Calif. Community Coll. Adminstrs., Nat. Assn. Corp. Dirs., World Affairs Council No. Calif., Czechoslovak Foreign Inst., Praha, 1993—, Phi Delta Kappa, Editor-in-chief Our Youth, 1945-48; co-editor (with P. Boulden) Innovative Management Concepts, 1967. Home and Office: 1019 Ross Cir Napa CA 94558-2118

RADANOVICH, GEORGE P., congressman; b. Mariposa, Calif., 1955; s. Joan and George F.; m. Ethie Weaver; 1 child, George King. BS in Agr. Bus. Mgmt., Calif. State Polytechnic U., 1978. Pres. Radanovich Winery, Mariposa, Calif., 1982—; chair County Planning Comm., 1986-87, county supr., 1988-92; mem. U.S. Ho. of Reps., 104th Congress, Washington, 1995—; mem. Budget Com., Resources Com., subcoms. Water & Power Resources, Nat. Parks, Forests & Lands. U.S. Ho. of Reps., 104th Congress; mem. Resources Com. Task Force on Endangered Species U.S. Ho. of Reps., 106th Congress Calif. 19th Dist. Republican. Agrl. Leadership Program Class XXI, Rotary (Paul Harris Fellowship). Office: US Ho of Reps 213 Cannon Bldg Washington DC 20515-0519*

RADCLIFFE, ALBERT E., bankruptcy judge; b. 1947. BA in History, U. Oreg., 1969, JD, 1972. Bar: Oreg. 1972, U.S. Dist. Ct. Oreg. 1973, U.S. Ct. Appeals (9th cir.) 1983. Pvt. practice, 1973-86; judge U.S. Bankruptcy Ct. Oreg., Eugene, 1986—; vis. bankruptcy judge We. Dist. Wash., 1992; spkr. in field; mem. Fed. Bar Assn. (hon.), NW Bankruptcy Inst. Planning Com., Lane County Bar Assn. (bankruptcy subcom. chmn. 1993-94), Tau Kappa Epsilon. Office: US Bankruptcy Ct Oreg 151 W 7th Ave, Ste 300 Eugene OR 97401 2600

RADDITZ, JOAN FRANCES, landscape architect; b. Portland, Aug. 12, 1956; d. Frances Martin and Geraldine May (Wanke) R.; m. Linsey Alan Goodman, July 7, 1987; children: ...; BA in Environ. Hort. & Design, U. Calif., Davis, 1980; M of Landscape

Architecture, Calif. State Poly U., 1983. Registered landscape architect, Calif. Designer R. Bruce Shaffer, 1985, Brian Wittenkeller, 1986; part-time instr. Santa Barbara City Coll., 1990—. Author: Landscape Drafting, 1995; co-author: Inland Coastal Hills, 1983. Mem. archtl. bd. rev. City of Santa Barbara, 1990-92; co-chair Jr. League Santa Barbara, 1988-93. Recipient Exceptional Svc. award Santa Barbara chpt. AIA, 1992. Mem. Am. Soc. Landscape Architecture, Hort. Soc. Santa Barbara. Democrat. Avocations: swimming, gardening, drawing, creative memories. Home and Office: 2403 Foothill Ln Santa Barbara CA 93105-2318

RADEBAUGH, ALAN PAINE, artist; b. Boston, May 2, 1952; s. John Franklin and Dorothy (Paine) R.; m. Ann Harrison Craig, Feb. 13, 1981 (div. 1987); m. Karen Rae Olson, Dec. 3, 1991. Student, Coll. Wooster, 1970-72; BFA, U. N.Mex., 1996. Visual artist Albuquerque, 1981—; juror N.Mex. Annual Woodworkers Show, Santa Fe, 1984; cons. Albuquerque (N.Mex.) Conv. and Visitors Bur., 1992. One-man shows include Artichoke/Dartmouth St. Gallery, Albuquerque, 1991, St. Michael Episcopal. Ch., Albuquerque, 1993, 1st Unitarian Ch., Albuquerque, 1994, Firehouse Gallery, Del Rio, Tex., 1997, Peter Eller Gallery, Albuquerque, 1997, Outpost Performance Space, Albuquerque, 1998; group shows include McNeese State U., 1991, Mus. Albuquerque, 1991, Ctrl. Mo. State U., 1991, Cork Gallery, Avery Fisher Hall, Lincoln Ctr., 1992, EMU Gallery, U. Oreg., 1992, San Francisco State U., 1992, Coll. Santa Fe, 1993, 95, Museo Regional Univ., Chihuahua City, Mex., 1994, San Bernardino County Mus., 1995, Kanagawa Kenmin Gallery, Yokohama, Japan, 1995, 97, Washington & Jefferson Coll., 1996, SITE, Santa Fe 1997, U. N.Mex., 1997, Coos Art Mus., 1998; represented in permanent collections including Albuquerque Mus. Fine Arts, Mus. N.Mex., N.Mex. State Capitol Art Collection, U. N.Mex. Mus., Washington & Jefferson Coll.; prin. works include model of mus. and exhibition spaces N.Mex. Mus. Natural History, 1983, clay miniatures Archeol. Mus. Andros, Greece, 1983, graphic image Nat. Med. Assn. Dartmouth Med. Sch., 1993. Mem. U. N.Mex. Coll. Fine Arts Alumni Bd., 1998—. Artist's grantee, Vt. Studio Ctr., 1997; recipient 1st pl. in design N.Mex. Ann. Woodworkers Show, Santa Fe, 1982, Merit award Paxton Co., Albuquerque, 1983, Albuquerque United Artists, 1983, Purchase award Albuquerque Mus. Fine Arts, 1984, hon. mention award Art Ctr., Los Alamos, N.Mex., 1993, Oliver Meml. award, 1994. Mem. Albuquerque/State N.Mex. Artists Slide Registry, Maine Arts Commn. Slide Registry. Avocations: music, squash, golf.

RADER, PAUL ALEXANDER, minister, administrator; b. N.Y.C., Mar. 4, 1934; s. Lyell M. and Gladys Mina (Damon) R.; m. Kay Fuller, May 29, 1956; children: Edith Jeanne, James Paul, Jennifer Kay. BA, Asbury Coll., Wilmore, Ky., 1956; BD, Asbury Theol. Sem., 1959; LLD (hon.), Asbury Coll., Wilmore, Ky., 1984; ThM, So. Bapt. Theol. Sem. Louisville, 1961; D Missiology, Fuller Theol. Sem., 1973; DD (hon.), Asbury Theol. Sem., 1995. Ordained to ministry Salvation Army, 1961. Tng. prin. The Salvation Army, Seoul, 1973-74; edn. sec., 1974-77, chief sec., 1979-83; tng. prin. The Salvation Army, Suffern, N.Y., 1983-86; divisional comdr. for Ea. Pa. and Del. The Salvation Army, Phila., 1986-88; chief sec. ea. ter. The Salvation Army, N.Y.C., 1988; territorial comdr. U.S.A. western ter. The Salvation Army, Rancho Palos Verdes, Calif., 1989-94, gen., 1994—; adj. prof. Seoul Theol. Sem., 1980-82; trustee Asian Ctr. for Theol. Studies and Mission, 1980-83, Asbury Coll., 1988—; pres. The Salvation Army Calif. Corp., Rancho Palos Verdes, 1989—. Recipient Alumnus A award Asbury Coll., 1982, Disting. Alumni award Asbury Theol. Sem., 1989; Paul Harris fellow Rotary Internat., 1989. Mem. Am. Soc. Missiology, Internat. Assn. Mission Studies. Office: Salvation Army Internat Hdq, 101 Queen Victoria St, London EC4P 4EP, England*

RADFORD, DEIORETA LEA FUNTE, designer; b. Mason City, Iowa, Oct. 3, 1955; d. William and Beverly Funte; m. Keith Radford, Oct. 3, 1988; children: Lindsay, Chelsea. BFA, Ariz. State Univ., 1978. Retail design Entz-White, Phoenix, 1978-83; retail/trade design Shutter Shaque SSC, Phoenix, 1983-90; cons. mktg. design Architects adn Entrs. Svc., Mission Viejo, Calif., 1991-94; design DE's IGNS, Scottsdale, Ariz., 1990-95; distributer to trade/retail Dunn Edwards Corp., Tempe, Ariz., 1995—; cons. residential design, Phoenix, 1990-95; contract sales mgr. Shutter Shaque SSC, 1983-90. Active PAC mem. HBACA, 1998. Mem. Am. Soc. Interior Designers (allied practitioner). Office: Dunn Edwards Corp 1872 E Broadway Rd Tempe AZ 85282-1641

RADIN, MICHAEL ROSS, software company executive; b. Stamford, Conn., Mar. 17, 1960. BA in Bus. and Econ., Calif. State U., Fullerton, 1982; MBA, U. Calif., Irvine, 1982. CFA Assn. Investment Mgmt. and Rsch. Sr. v.p. SunGard Treasury Sys., Calabasas, Calif., 1989-97, 1997—. Mem. Treasury Mgmt. Assn. (cert. cash mgr.), L.A. Soc. Fin. Analysts. Office: ADS Assocs 23586 Calabasas Rd Ste 200 Calabasas CA 91302-1322

RADLEY, B.W., insurance claims adjuster; b. Santa Rosa, Calif., Jan. 1, 1960; s. Ray G. and Judith (Harper) R.; m. Audrey Diane Walters, Mar. 28, 1987; 1 child, Stephen C. BSBA in Fin. Mgmt., Calif. State U., Long Beach, 1982. Asst. mgr. Kinney Shoes, San Rafael, Calif., 1983-84, Longs Drugs, Inc., Hacienda Heights, Calif., 1984-87; claims adjuster Safeco Ins. Co., Fountain Valley, Calif., 1987-93; claims specialist CNA Ins. Companies, Brea, Calif., 1993—; pres. Radley Properties, West Covina, Calif., 1996—. Pres. Les Jardins Homeowners Assn., Garden Grove, Calif., 1992-94. Mem. Soc. for Am. Baseball Rsch. E-mail: bw.radley@cna.com. Home: 1024 S Holly Pl West Covina CA 91790-5211 Office: CNA Ins Cos 1800 E Imperial Hwy Brea CA 92821-6062

RADLOFF, WILLIAM HAMILTON, editor, writer; b. Milw., Mar. 5, 1914; s. Alfred Carl and Florence (Hamilton) R.; m. Mary Ellen Borgman, Nov. 10, 1940; children: Thomas M., Susan M. BA, Ripon Coll., 1936. Reporter, writer Milw. Sentinel, 1937-42; reporter, writer Milw. Jour., 1946-49, asst. city editor, 1949-60, asst. feature editor, 1960-61, feature editor, 1961-69; asst. story editor 20th Century Fox Film Corp., L.A., 1969-72; freelance writer, poet L.A., 1972—. Author: editor numerous news and feature articles. Lt. U.S. Army, Counter Intelligence, 1942-46, PTO. Recipient Letter of Commendation, Japanese Occupation. Home: 313 S Anita Ave Los Angeles CA 90049-3805

RAE, MATTHEW SANDERSON, JR., lawyer; b. Pitts., Sept. 12, 1922; s. Matthew Sanderson and Olive (Waite) R.; m. Janet Hettman, May 2, 1953; children: Mary-Anna, Margaret Rae Mallory, Janet S. Rae Dupree. AB, Duke, 1946, LLB, 1947; postgrad., Stanford U., 1951. Bar: Md. 1948, Calif. 1951. Asst. to dean Duke Sch. Law, Durham, N.C., 1947-48; assoc. Karl F. Steinmann, Balt., 1948-49, Guthrie, Darling & Shattuck, L.A., 1953-54; nat. field rep. Phi Alpha Delta Law Frat., L.A., 1949-51; research atty. Calif. Supreme Ct., San Francisco, 1951-52; ptnr. Darling, Hall & Rae (and predecessor firms), L.A., 1955—; mem. Calif. Commn. Uniform State Laws, 1985—, chmn., 1993-99; chmn. drafting com. for revision Uniform Prin. and Income Act of Nat. Conf., 1991-97, Probate and Mental Health Task Force, Jud. Coun. Calif., 1993—. Vice pres. L.A. County Rep. Assembly, 1959-64; mem. L.A. County Rep. Ctrl. Com., 1960-64, 77-90, exec. com., 1977-90; vice chmn. 17th Congl. Dist., 1962-64, 28th Congl. Dist., 1964-65; chmn. 46th Assy. Dist., 1962-64, 27th Senatorial Dist., 1977-85, 29th Senatorial Dist., 1985-90; mem. Calif. Rep. State Ctrl. Com., 1966—, exec. com., 1966-67; pres. Calif. Rep. League, 1966-67; trustee Rep. Assocs., 1979-94, pres., 1983-85, chmn. bd. dirs., 1985-87. 2d lt. USAAF, WWII. Fellow Am. Coll. Trust and Estate Counsel; academician Internat. Acad. Estate and Trust Law (exec. coun. 1974-78); mem. ABA, L.A. County Bar Assn. (chmn. probate and trust law com. 1964-66, chmn. legis. com. 1980-86, chmn. program com. 1981-82, chmn. membership retention com. 1982-83, trustee 1983-85, dir. Bar Found., 1987-93, Arthur K. Marshall award probate and trust law sect. 1984, Shattuck-Price Meml. award 1990), South Bay Bar Assn., State Bar of Calif. (chmn. state bar jour. com. 1970-71, probate com. 1974-75, exec. com. estate planning trust and probate law sect. 1977-83, chmn. legis. com. 1977-89; co-chmn. 1991-92; probate law com. group Calif. Bd. Legal Specialization 1977-88; chmn. conf. dels. resolutions com. 1987, v.p. 1982-83), Am. Legion (comdr. Almont post 1969-70), Legion Lex (bd. dirs. 1964—, pres. 1969-71), Air Force Assn., Aircraft Owners and Pilots Assn., Town Hall (gov. 1970-78, pres. 1975), World Affairs Coun., Internat. Platform Assn. (Hamilton Meml. medal for best prin.), United Commonwealth Club Chancery Club (pres. 1996-97), Rotary, Phi Beta Kappa (councilor Alpha

Assn. 1983—, pres. 1996), Omicron Delta Kappa, Phi Alpha Delta (supreme justice 1972-74, elected to Disting. Law Firm chpt. 1978), Sigma Nu. Presbyterian. Home: 600 John St Manhattan Beach CA 90266-5837 Office: Darling Hall & Rae 520 S Grand Ave Fl 7 Los Angeles CA 90071-2600

RAEBER, JOHN ARTHUR, architect, construction consultant; b. St. Louis, Nov. 24, 1947; s. Arthur William and Marie (Laux) R. AA, Jefferson Coll., 1968; AB, Washington U., 1970, MArch, 1973. Registered architect, Calif., Mo.; cert. constrn. specifier; cert. Nat. Coun. Arch. Specification writer Hellmuth, Obata & Kassabaum, St. Louis, 1973-78, constrn. administr., 1978-79; mgr. of specifications Gensler & Assocs., San Francisco, 1979-82; ind. constrn. specifier San Francisco, 1982—; adj. prof. architecture Calif. Coll. Arts and Crafts, San Francisco, 1986—; access code advisor Constrn. Industry & Owners, 1982—; spkr., instr. seminars orgns., univs., 1982—; mem. Calif. State Bldg. Standards Commn. Accessibility Adv. Panel, Sacramento, 1981, Calif. Subcom. Rights of Disabled Adv. Panel, Sacramento, 1993; cons. Nat. Inst. Bldg. Scis., 1996—. Author: CAL/ABL: Interpretative Manual to California's Access Barriers Laws, 1982; co-author: (with Peter S. Hopf) Access for the Handicapped, 1984; columnist Constrn. Specifier Mag., 1988-95. Vol. Calif. Office Emergency Svcs. Safety Assessment, Sacramento, 1991—. Fellow AIA (cert. columnist newsletter San Francisco chpt. 1984-95, Ben John Small award for Outstanding Stature as practicing specifications writer 1994, pres. St. Louis chpt. 1978-79, pres. San Francisco chpt. 1993-94, tech. com., edn. com., publs. com.), Specifications Proficiency award San Francisco chpt. 1989, Tech. Commendation award 1987); mem. Specifications Cons. in Ind. Practice (nat. pres. 1990-92, nat. sec./treas. 1988-90), Internat. Conf. Bldg. Officials, Phi Theta Kappa. Avocations: history, anthropology, sci. fiction. Home and Office: 888 Ofarrell St Apt W606 San Francisco CA 94109-9032

RAEDEKE, LINDA DISMORE, geologist; b. Great Falls, Mont., Aug. 20, 1950; d. Albert Browning and Madge (Hogan) Dismore; m. Kenneth John Raedeke, Dec. 26, 1971 (div. 1982); m. Charles Moore Swift Jr., Mar. 14, 1992. BA in History, U. Wash., 1971, MS in Geology, 1979, PhD, 1982. Geomorphologist, park planner Corporacion Nacional Forestal and U.S. Peace Corps, Punta Arenas, Chile, 1972-74; glacial geologist Empresa Nacional del Petroleo, Punta Arenas, 1972-75; geologist FAO, UN, Punta Arenas, 1974; geologist Lamont-Doherty Geol. Obs., Columbia U., Tierra del Fuego, Chile, 1974-75; Wetlands evaluation project coord. Wash. Dept. Agr., U. Wash., Seattle, 1975-76; curator Remote Sensing Applications Lab., U. Wash., 1976-77; geol. rsch. asst. U. Wash., Seattle, 1977-81; exploration geologist Chevron Resources Co., Denver, 1981-84; rsch. geologist Chevron Oil Field Rsch. Co., La Habra, Calif., 1984-89; sr. compensation analyst Chevron Corp., San Francisco, 1989-90; staff geologist Chevron Overseas Petroleum, Inc., San Ramon, Calif. 1990-91, project leader, 1991-95, new ventures coord. for the far east, 1995-96; sr. staff analyst for planning Chevron Corp., 1996-98; coord. upstream bus. Chevron Rsch. Tech. Co., 1998—; mgr. Integrated Labs., 1999—. Contbr. articles to profl. jours. Recipient Cert. of Achievement YWCA, 1988. Mem. Am. Geophys. Union, Geol. Soc. Am., Am. Assn. Petroleum Geologists (poster chmn. 1987, internat. chmn. 1996 meeting). Office: Chevron Corp 575 Market St San Francisco CA 94105-2856

RAEL, HENRY SYLVESTER, retired health administrator, financial and management consultant; b. Pueblo, Colo., Oct. 2, 1928; s. Daniel and Grace (Abeyta) R.; m. Helen Warner Loring Brace, June 30, 1956 (dec. Aug. 1980); children: Henry Sylvester Jr., Loring Victoria, Thomas Warren Bush. AB, U. So. Colo., 1955; BA in Bus Adminstrn., U. Denver, 1957, MBA, 1958. Sr. boys counselor Denver Juvenile Hall, 1955-58; adminstrv. asst. to pres. Stanley Aviation Corp., Denver, 1958-61; Titan III bd.goal and fin. control supr. Martin Marietta Corp., Denver, 1961-65; mgmt. adv. services officer U. Colo. Med. Center, Denver, 1965-72; v.p. fin., treas. Loretto Heights Coll., Denver, 1972-73; dir. fin. and adminstrn. Colo. Found. for Med. Care, 1973-86, Tri-County Health Dept., Denver, 1986-96; fin. cons., Denver, 1996—; instr. fin. mgmt., mem. fin. com. Am. Assn. Profl. Standards Rev. Orgn., 1980-85; speaker systems devel., design assns., univs., 1967-71. Mem. budget lay adv. com. Park Hill Elem. Sch., Denver, 1967-68, chmn., 1968-69; vol. worker Boy and Girl Scouts, 1967-73; bd. dirs. Community Arts Symphony, 1981-83, 85-87; controller St. John's Episcopal Cathedral, 1982-83; charter mem. Pueblo (Colo.) Coll. Young Democrats, 1954-55; block worker Republican party, Denver, 1965-68, precinct committeeman, 1977-84; trustee Van Nattan Scholarship Fund, 1974-96; bd. dirs. Vis. Nurse Assn., 1977-84, treas., 1982-84. Served with USAF, 1947-53; res. 1954-61. Recipient Disting. Service award Denver Astron. Soc., 1968, Citation Chamberlin Obs., 1985; Stanley Aviation masters scholar, 1957; Ballard scholar, 1956. Mem. Assn. Systems Mgmt. (pres. 1971-72), Hosp. Systems Mgmt. Soc., Budget Execs Inst. (v.p. chpt. 1964-65, sec. 1963-64), Colo. Pub. Employees Retirement Assn. (bd. dirs. 1993), Denver Astron. Soc. (pres. 1965-66, bd. dirs. 1982-94), Am. Assn. Founds. for Med. Care (fin. com. 1981-82), Nat. Astronomers Assn. (exec. bd. 1965-97), Brandy Chase Homeowners Assn. (bd. dir. 1997), Whispering Pines of Denver Homeowners Assn. (pres., bd. dir. 1998), Epsilon Xi, Delta Psi Omega. Episcopalian. Home: 7755 E Quincy Ave # 57 Denver CO 80237-2312

RAFAEL, RUTH KELSON, archivist, librarian, consultant; b. Wilmington, N.C., Oct. 28, 1929; d. Benjamin and Jeanette (Spicer) Kelson; m. Richard Vernon Rafael, Aug. 26, 1951; children: Barbara Martinez Yates, Brenda Elaine Derin. BA, San Francisco State U., 1953, MA, 1966; MLS, U. Calif.-Berkeley, 1968. Cert. archivist, 1989. Tchr. San Francisco Unified Sch. Dist. 1956-57; libr. Congregation Beth Sholom, San Francisco, 1965-83; archivist Western Jewish History Ctr. of Judah L. Magnes Mus., Berkeley, Calif., 1968, head archivist, libr., curator of exhibits, 1969-94; cons. NEH, Washington, NHPRC, Congregation Sherith Israel, San Francisco, Mount Zion Hosp., San Francisco, Benjamin Swig archives project, San Francisco, Koret Found., Camp Swig, Saratoga, Calif.; project dir. Ethnicity in Calif. Agriculture, 1989, San Francisco Jews of European Origin, 1880-1940, an oral history project, 1976; curator exhibits Western U.S. Jewry. Author: Continuum, San Francisco Jews of Eastern European Origin, 1880-1940, 1976, rev. edit., 1977; (with Davies and Woogmaster) poetry book Relatively Speaking, 1981; Western Jewish History Center: Archival and Oral History Collections, Judah L. Magnes Meml. Mus., 1987; contbg. editor Western States Jewish History, 1979-89. Mem. exec. bd. Bay Area Libr. Info. Network, 1986-88. NEH grantee, 1985. Mem. Calif. Libr. Assn., Soc. Am. Archivists, Acad. Cert. Archivists.

RAFEEDIE, EDWARD, SR., federal judge; b. Orange, N.J., Jan. 6, 1929; s. Fred and Nabeeha (Hishmeh) R.; m. Ruth Alice Horton, Oct. 8, 1961; children: Fredrick Alexander, Jennifer Ann. BS in Law, U. So. Calif., 1957, JD, 1959; LLD (hon.), Pepperdine U., 1978. Bar: Calif. 1960. Pvt. practice Santa Monica, Calif., 1960-69; mcpl. ct. judge Santa Monica Mun. Dist., 1969-71; judge Superior Ct. State of Calif., L.A., 1971-82; dist. judge U.S. Dist. Court (cen. dist.) Calif., L.A., 1982-96, sr. judge, 1996—. With U.S. Army, 1950-52, Korea. Office: US Dist Ct RM 244P 312 N Spring St Ste 244P Los Angeles CA 90012-4704

RAFFO, SUSAN HENNEY, elementary education educator; b. Kendallville, Ind., Feb. 14, 1945; d. Gordon Theron and Sue (Kizer) Henney; m. Lawrence Albert Raffo, Feb. 19, 1977; children: Timothy, Kathleen. BS in Elem. Edn., Ball State U., 1967; M in Spl. Edn., San Francisco State U., 1972. Cert. elem. tchr., Calif. Tchr. East Noble Sch. Corp., Kendallville, Ind., 1967-68, Burlingame (Calif.) Sch. Dist., 1968—; master tchr. San Francisco State U., 1970-95, Coll. Notre Dame, Belmont, Calif., 1980-95, instr. grad. edn. dept., 1996—. Registrar AYSO, Burlingame, 1987-94; bd. dirs. Burlingame Cmty. Edn. Found., 1989-95, sec., 1992-94. Recipient Svc. award PTA, 1989, J. Russell Kent award for innovative programs San Mateo County Bd. Edn. Assn., 1993; named Tchr. of Yr., Lions Club, 1993. Mem. Calif. Reading Assn., Alpha Delta Kappa, Phi Delta Kappa. Avocations: reading, fabric arts, golf. Office: Franklin Sch

RAFKIN, ALAN, television and film director; b. N.Y.C., July 23, 1928; s. Victor and Til (Bernstein) R.; children: Chris, Leigh Ann, Karen. Student, Syracuse U., 1950. guest lectr. Bowling Green State U., 1975. Asst. dir. Big Payoff Show, 1955, daytime shows, CBS-TV; dir. Verdict is Yours, 1960, Mary

Tyler Moore Show, 1970-71, Sanford and Son, 1972, Bob Newhart Show, 1972-73, Rhoda, 1973, Let's Switch, 1975, MASH, 1976-77, Love, American Style, 1970-71, Laverne & Shirley, 1977-83; TV movie: One Day at a Time: Barbara's Crisis, 1981-82; films include Ski Party, 1965, The Ghost and Mr. Chicken, 1966, The Ride to Hangman's Tree, 1967, Nobody's Perfect, 1968, The Shakiest Gun in the West, 1968, Angel in my Pocket, 1969, How to Frame a Figg, 1971. Served with U.S. Army, 1950-52. Democrat. Jewish. Office: Grey Entertainment 9150 Wilshire Blvd Beverly Hills CA 90212-3427*

RAFTERY, SCOTT ROBERT, secondary education educator, athletic director; b. Alhambra, Calif., June 27, 1957; s. Robert Diehm and Elane Ruth (Russell) Misner; m. Karen Rae Johnson, June 9, 1979; children: Shane Robert, Justin Bryan. BA, Azusa Pacific U., 1979, MA, 1988. Tchr. Temple City (Calif.) Unified Sch. Dist., 1980-84; varsity baseball coach Charter Oak H.S., Covina, Calif., 1982-84; tchr., varsity baseball/varsity football coach Maranatha H.S., Sierra Madre, Calif., 1984-87; dir. alumni rels. Azusa Pacific U., Azusa, Calif., 1987-89; tchr., coach, athletic dir. The Linfield Sch., Temecula, Calif., 1989—; CIF rep., coord. Christian League, So. Calif., 1990—; mem. CIF SS Softball adv. com., 1998—; NFCA H.S. State rep., 1995-98. Named Christian League Coach of Yr., 1993, 94, 95, 96, 97, 98, Calif. State Coach of Yr., Cal-Hi Sports, 1995, Calif. Coach of Yr., 1995-97. Mem. Nat. Interscholastic Athletic Adminstrs. Assn., Nat. Fast Pitch Coaches Assn., Citrus Belt Area Athletic Dirs. Assn., Calif. Athletic Dirs. Assn., Calif. Coaches Assn. Avocations: reading, walking, children's activities, hockey. Home: 31950 Pauba Rd Temecula CA 92592 Office: The Linfield Sch 31950 Pauba Rd Temecula CA 92592

RAGAN, ANN TALMADGE, media and production consultant, actor; b. Raleigh, N.C., July 6, 1951; d. Samuel Talmadge and Marjorie Lois (Usher) R.; m. L. Worth Keeter III, Aug. 22, 1992. Student, U. N.C., 1969-71, Finch Coll., 1972-73, New Sch. Social Rsch., 1973-74, Western Wash. U., 1978. Acct. estimator Benton & Bowles Inc., N.Y.C., 1971-72, media buyer, 1974-77; speechwriter, press aide Senator Robert Morgan, Wash., 1978-79; asst. producer John F. Murray Inc., N.Y.C., 1979-80; producer, sales dir. Grand Street Films, N.Y.C., 1980-84; ind. producer for various clients N.Y.C., 1984-86; asst. pub. The Pilot, Inc., Southern Pines, N.C., 1986-96; also bd. dirs. The Pilot, Inc.; prodn. mgr. Anglo Am. Media Workshops, London, 1988-90; program adminstr. profl. tng. divsn. Directing Workshop For Women, TV Writers Workshop - Am. Film Inst., L.A. Contbr. articles to newspaper and jour. Mem. Roanoke Island Hist. Assn., Moore County arts coun., 1986-89. Mem. AFTRA, SAG (conservatory com., rec. sec. 1997—), Actors Equity Assn., Internat. Platform Assn., Kings and Clowns Ednl. Shakespeare Alliance, Women in Theatre (adminstrv. dir. 1995-97, treas. 1997—, bd. dirs. 1997—), Pi Beta Phi. Democrat. Methodist. Home and Office: 10542 Bloomfield St Toluca Lake CA 91602-2813

RAGAN, BETTY SAPP, artist, educator; b. Birmingham, Ala., Mar. 15, 1937; d. Robert William and Emma Mildred (O'Neal) Sapp; m. Thaxton Drew Ragan, Apr. 1958 (div. Aug. 1986); 1 child, Robert McClearan. BA cum laude, Birmingham-So. Coll., 1958; student, Allegheny Coll., 1971-72, Auburn U., 1980-83; MFA, Pratt Inst., 1985. Teachng asst. Pratt Inst., Bklyn., 1985; vis. asst. prof. dept. art Auburn U., 1985-89; asst. prof. dept. art U. Puget Sound, 1989-91, assoc. prof. photography and printmaking, dept. art, 1992—; panel moderator Soc. for Photo Edn. N.W., Tacoma, 1993; co-curator But Is It Art, Tacoma, 1993. Exhibited photography in solo shows at Maude Kerns Gallery, Eugene, Oreg., 1995, Helen Smith Gallery, Green River C.C., Auburn, Wash., 1996, others; group shows include Hanson Gallery, New Orleans, 1980, Montgomery (Ala.) Mus. Fine Arts, 1981, Ga. State U., Atlanta, 1981, Park Ave Atrium, N.Y.C., 1985, Carnegie Art Ctr., Walla Walla, Wash., 1990, Definitive Image Gallery, Seattle, 1992, Seattle Ctr. Pavilion, 1993, San Diego Art Inst., 1993, Eagle Gallery, Murray, Ky., 1994, B St. Pier Gallery, San Diego, 1995, numerous others; artist/photographer various collage series; co-curator But Is It Art?, Tacoma, 1993. Recipient numerous awards for art including Merit award Fine Arts Mus. of the South, Mobile, 1983, Dirk Andrew Phibbs Rsch. award U. Puget Sound, Tacoma, 1994. Mem. Soc. for Photog. Edn., Soc. Photog. Edn./N.W. (sec. 1990-93), Artist Trust, Women's Caucus for Art, Coll. Art Assn., Seattle Women's Caucus for Art. Unitarian. Avocations: entomology, hiking, gardening, existential philosophy. Office: U Puget Sound Dept Art 1500 N Warner St Tacoma WA 98416-0001

RAGHAVAN, ASURI, executive. Pres., CEO Gasonics, San Jose, Calif. Office: 2730 Junction Ave San Jose CA 95134-1909

RAGHAVAN, DEREK, oncologist, medical researcher and educator; b. Buenos Aires, Aug. 11, 1949; came to U.S., 1991; m. Patricia Harrison, Jan. 4, 1979; 2 children. MB, BS with honors, Sydney U., 1974; PhD, London U., 1984. Cert. Royal Australian Coll. Physicians, Fgn. Lic. Exam Coun., Ednl. Coun. Fgn. Med. Grads., Gen. Med. Coun. (U.K.), NSW Med. Bd. (Australia). Resident, registrar Royal Prince Alfred Hosp., Sydney, 1974-77; lectr., sr. registrar Royal Marsden Hosp., London, 1978-80; rsch. fellow Ludwig Inst. Cancer Rsch., London, 1978-80; med. rsch. specialist U. Minn., Mpls., 1980-81; sr. specialist med. oncology Royal Prince Alfred Hosp., Sydney, 1981-91; prof., chief solid tumor oncology and investigational therapeutics Roswell Park Cancer Inst. and SUNY, Buffalo, 1991-97; prof. medicine and urology U. So. Calif., L.A., 1997—; chief divsn. med. oncology U. So. Calif., L.A., 1997—, assoc. dir. Norris Cancer Ctr., 1997—; pres. med. staff Roswell Park Cancer Inst., Buffalo, 1995-96; chair VA Merit Rev. Bd. in Oncology, 1996-97; mem. oncology drug adv. com. FDA, 1996—; chair cancer clin. investigations review com. Nat. Cancer Inst., 1996-97; prof. medicine SUNY, Buffalo, 1991-97, prof. urology, 1996-97; chief divsn. med. oncology U. So. Calif., 1997—, assoc. dir. U. So. Calif.-Norris Cancer Ctr., 1997—; mem. VA Merit Rev. Bd. for Prostrate Cancer, 1998; mem. scientific adv. bd. Southwest Oncology Group, 1998—, bd. of govs., 1998—, scientific program com. 2000 Am. Coll. Physicians, 1998—. Editor: The Management of Bladder Cancer, 1988, Textbook of Uncommon Cancer, 1988, 2d edit. 1999, Principles and Practice of Genitourinary Oncology, 1997; assoc. editor Urologic Oncology, 1995—, Clin. Cancer Rsch., 1996—; mem. editl. bd. Jour. Clin. Oncology, 1990-94, European Jour. Cancer, The Prostate, The Breast, Prostate Cancer, Advances in Oncology, Abstracts in Hematology and Oncology; bd. cons. Jour. Urology, 1996—; contbr. numerous articles to profl. jours. Rsch. grantee Nat. Health amd Med. Rsch. Coun., Australia, 1983-90; traveling fellow NSW Cancer Coun., Sydney, 1978; named Hospice Physician of Yr., Hospice of Buffalo, 1994. Fellow ACP, Royal Australian Coll. Physicians (chair specialist adv. com. in med. oncology 1988-90); mem. Am. Soc. Clin. Oncology, Am. Assn. Cancer Rsch., Soc. Urologic Oncology, Med. Oncology Group Australia (chmn. 1988-90), Sydney U. Med. Soc. (pres. 1974). Avocations: tennis, squash. Office: U So Calif-Norris Cancer Ctr 1441 Eastlake Ave Los Angeles CA 90033

RAGLAND, CARROLL ANN, law educator, judicial officer; b. New Orleans, Nov. 28, 1946; d. Herbert Eugene Watson and Mary May (LeCompte) Leathers; children: Robert A. Sinex, Jr., Stacie Bateman, Joy Montgomery. JD, San Francisco Law Sch., 1980. Bar: Calif. 1980, U.S. Supreme Ct. 1993. Pvt. practice Santa Rosa, Calif., 1980-85; child custody mediator Sonoma County Superior Ct., Santa Rosa, 1985-86; chief dep. county counsel Butte County Counsel, Oroville, Calif., 1986-87; chief dep. dist. atty. Butte County Dist. Atty., Oroville, 1987-95; referee Shasta County Superior Ct., Redding, Calif., 1995-96; commr. Shasta County Superior Ct., Redding, 1996—; dean faculty, law prof. Calif. No. Sch. of Law, Chico, 1987—; instr. Shasta Coll., 1996—. Commr. Yuba County Juvenile Justice and Delinquency Prevention Commn., Marysville, Calif., 1993-94. Fellow Lawyers in Mensa. Avocations: scuba diving, reading, crossword puzzles. Office: Shasta County Superior Ct 1431 Market St Redding CA 96001-1026

RAGLAND, SAMUEL CONNELLY, industrial engineer, management consultant; b. Nashville, July 12, 1946; s. Julian Potter and Stella (Thompson) R.; m. Marilyn Margaret Oppelt, July 15, 1967; children: Sherry Anne, David Michael. BSBA, Ariz. State U., 1974; MBA U. Phoenix, 1991. Indsl. engr. First Interstate Bank, Phoenix, 1966-76, Beckman Instruments, Scottsdale, Ariz., 1976-78; mgmt. analyst Ariz. Legislative Budget Com., Phoenix, 1978; indsl. engr. mgmt. systems ITT Courier Terminal Systems, Tempe, Ariz., 1978-81; project control adminstr. Gen. Host Corp., Phoenix, 1981; sr. cons. Arthur Young & Co., Phoenix, 1981-82; ops. analyst City of Phoenix, 1982-84; project leader Garrett Engine div. Allied-Signal Corp. (formerly Garrett Turbine Engine Co.), Phoenix, 1984-92, cons., program mgr., TRW, Mesa, 1992-93; prin., owner Ragland Assocs., 1994—; exec. mgmt. cons. Gov.'s Office Excellence in Govt., State of Ariz., 1995-96, mgr. quality assurance Coxreels, Inc., 1996-97; ind. engring. cons. The Boeing Co., 1997—; dir. Mary Moppets of Highland Inc., 1977-81. Mem. Inst. Indsl. Engrs. (sr. mem. cen. Ariz. chpt., dir. cmty. rels. 1983-85, dir. chpt. devel. 1985-86, v.p., pres.-elect 1986-87, 98, pres. 1987-88, 99), Inst. Indsl. Engrs. (nat. chpt. devel. com. 1988-91, chmn.), Assn. Systems Mgmt. (div. dir. 1989-92, pres. 1992-93), Phoenix Philatelic Assn. Contbr. articles to profl. publs. Address: 11319 E Jenan Dr Scottsdale AZ 85259-3121

RAHE, RICHARD HENRY, psychiatrist, educator; b. Seattle, May 28, 1936; s. Henry Joseph and Delora Lee (Laube) R.; m. Laurie Ann Davies, Nov. 24, 1960 (div. Dec. 1990); children: Richard Bradley, Annika Lee. Student, Princeton U., 1954-57; MD, U. Wash., 1961. Diplomate Am. Bd. Psychiatry and Neurology. Chief resident in psychiatry U. Wash. Sch. Medicine, Seattle, 1965; rsch. psychiatrist USN, San Diego, 1965-75; commdg. officer Naval Health Rsch. Ctr., San Diego, 1976-80; exec. officer Long Beach (Calif.) Naval Hosp., 1980-82; commdg. officer Guam Naval Hosp., Agana, 1982-84; prof. psychiatry U.S. Univ. Health Scis. Mil. Med. Sch., Bethesda, Md., 1984-86, U. Nev. Sch. Medicine, Reno, 1986—; dir. Mil. Stress Studies Ctr., Bethesda, 1984-86, Nev. Stress Ctr. Vets. Affairs Med. Ctr., Reno, 1986—. Contbr. numerous articles to sci. jours., chpts. to books; photographer prints and video. Dir. Nev. Mental Health Inst., Sparks, 1991-94. Capt. USN, 1965-86. Recipient Humanitarian award Vietnamese Refugee Com., 1974, Dept. of State award for treatment of Am. hostages held in Iran, 1981. Fellow Am. Psychiat. Assn.; mem. Am. Psychosomatic Soc. (past pres.), World Psychiat. Assn. (past. pres. mil. sect.). Avocations: hiking, skiing, swimming. Home: 638 Saint Lawrence Ave Reno NV 89509-1440 Office: VA Med Ctr Code 151-C 1000 Locust St Reno NV 89520-0102

RAHER, RICHARD RAY, minister; b. Denver, May 29, 1949; s. Ralph Gerald and Teresina M. (Jaramillo) R.; m. Robbi Louise Seagle-Simpson, Dec. 16, 1977; children: Aaron, Nathan. AS in Elec. Tech., San Diego Mesa Coll., 1977, AA in Mid. Mgmt., 1980. Elder Calvary Chapel, San Diego, Calif., 1976-80; asst. pastor Calvary Chapel, Poway, Calif., 1980-84; founder, sr. pastor Calvary Chapel, Ramona, Calif., 1984-92; co-founder, asst. pastor Calvary Chapel, Julian, Calif., 1988-90; adminstrv. pastor Calvary Chapel, Escondido, 1992—; pres. Ramona Ministerial Assn., 1988-89. Author: (booklet) Love in Action, 1989, Key Principles of Church Planting, 1993. Mem. Ramona Substance Abuse Com., 1988—; co-founder, chmn. Ramona Crisis Pregnancy Ctr., 1989-90. with USN, 1969-72, Vietnam. Grantee ADAPT Found., 1990. Mem. Calvary Chapel Outreach Fellowship. Office: Calvary Chapel 1675 Seven Oakes Rd Escondido CA 92026-2371

RAIKEN, SISU, artist; b. Glen Ridge, N.J., Nov. 26, 1951; d. Carl Albert and Barbara Jean (O'Donoghue) Peterson; 1 child, Gracie Aurora Gluchacki. BA in Music, Upsala Coll., East Orange, N.J., 1973. Faculty Nat. Shakespeare Conservatory, N.Y.C., 1982-83, Nat. Improvisational Theatre, N.Y.C., 1989-93; head dept. fine arts Lewis Carroll Acad. of Arts, Woodland Hills, Calif., 1995—; faculty dept. art Delphi Acad., La Cañada, Calif., 1997—. Author musical revues Mr. Abbott, 1997, Rodgers & Rodgers, 1998; appeared in Broadway play A Doll's Life, 1982; off-Broadway plays include Songs By Billy Solly, 1978, The Enchantress, 1978, Help!Help! The Globolinks, 1979, The Mother of Us All, 1983; performer various operas; lead singer Elegant Music, 1993—, Danny Ironstone Quartet, 1994—; co. mem. Interplay, 1984—; also commercials and voiceovers. Mem. Toastmasters. Scientologist. Avocations: film, tennis. E-mail: moonray@earthlink.net. Home: 4215 Vineland Ave Apt 10 Studio City CA 91602-3325

RAIKLEN, HAROLD, aerospace engineering consultant; b. Boston, June 7, 1920; s. Michael Isaac and Jennie Zelda (Jaffee) R.; m. Shirley Gesetz, Nov. 24, 1954; children: David R., Margery Claire. B, MIT, 1947, M, 1949. Dir. electronics and electrics Rockwell, El Segundo, Calif.; v.p. program mgr. Saturn II Rockwell, Downey and Seal Beach, Calif., 1965-70; v.p. rsch. and engring. Rockwell, Downey, Calif., 1970-72; v.p. B-1 bomber engring. Rockwell, El Segundo, Calif., 1972-80, v.p. strategic aircraft, 1980-82; amateur anthropoligist, Long Beach, Calif., 1982—. Contbr. articles to profl. jours.; co-patentee in anti-skid sys. Co-recipient Collier trophy USAF, 1976, Pub. Svc. award NASA, 1969. Fellow AIAA (assoc., Aircraft Design award 1979); mem. IEEE (life), Old Crows Assn., China Burma India Veterans Assn., Pi Tau Sigma, Tau Beta Pi, Phi Kappa Phi. Home and Office: 4300 Cerritos Ave Long Beach CA 90807-2462

RAILSBACK, SHERRIE LEE, adoption search and reunion consultant; b. Phila., Mar. 12, 1942; children: Ricky, Cindy. BBA, U. Ky., 1981. Sales mgr. Marjo Cosmetics, Ft. Wayne, Ind.; asst. dir. patient fin. svcs. Riverside Meth. Hosp., Columbus, Ohio; cons. Railsback and Assocs., Long Beach, Calif.; adoption search/reunion cons. Searchers Connection, L.A. Mem. NAFE, ASTD, Am. Adoption Congress, Book Publicists of So. Calif., Toastmasters.

RAIN, RHONDA L., performing arts executive, counselor, educator; b. Grinnell, Iowa, Feb. 28, 1952; d. Henry Garrett and Anne Lucille (Roberts) Rook. B in Univ. Studies, U. N.Mex., 1984, MA in Counseling, 1993. Lic. profl. counsel, N.Mex.; nat. cert. counselor. Tchr./counselor Rough Rock (Ariz.) Demo. Sch., 1973; acad. support staff U. N.Mex. Med. Sch., Albuquerque, 1974-84, U. N.Mex. Main Campus, Albuquerque, 1988-91; intern counselor Manzanita Ctr. U. N.Mex., Albuquerque, 1993; intern counselor Career Ctr. and Albuquerque Tech.-Vocat. Inst., 1993, career counselor, 1993—; acad. advisor and counselor, coord. advisement and testing U. N.Mex.-Valencia, Los Lunas, 1994-96, chief examiner GED, 1994-96; CEO Raindrops, 1996—; vocat. adv. com. New Futures H.S., Albuquerque, 1988-93; peer counselor U. N.Mex. Main Campus, Albuquerque, 1988-93; grad. asst. counseling dept. U. N.Mex., Albuquerque, 1991-92; vol. counselor Youth Diagnostic and Detention Ctr., Albuquerque, 1992. Neighborhood Watch capt. Crime Prevention Program, N.Mex., 1986-94; vol. musician Albuquerque Civic Light Opera Assn., 1978-83; mem. Valley cultural com. U. N.Mex.-Valencia, 1994-96. Recipient Fine Arts award Bank of Am., Huntington Beach, Calif., 1970; No. Ariz. U. music scholar, 1970-73. Mem. ACA, Nat. Acad. Advising Assn., Nat. Career Devel. Assn., N.Mex. Career Devel. Assn., Nat. Bd. Cert. Counselors (nat. cert. counselor), Internat. Platform Assn., Golden Key Internat. Honor Soc. (life), Pi Lambda Theta (v.p. 1986). Avocations: sewing, gardening, cooking, reading, swimming.

RAINEY, BARBARA ANN, sensory evaluation consultant; b. Fond du Lac, Wis., Nov. 11, 1949; d. Warren and Helen Eileen (Ginther) Bradley; m. Phillip Michael Rainey, Sept. 5, 1970; 1 child, Nicolette. BS, Kans. State U., 1971. Group leader Armour & Co. R&D Ctr., Scottsdale, Ariz., 1976-80; owner Barbara A. Rainey Cons., Manteca, Calif., 1980—. Mem. editl. bd. Jour. Sensory Studies, 1997—; contbr. articles to profl. jours. Kans. State Alumni fellow Kans. State U. Alumni Assn., 1990. Mem. ASTM, Inst. Food Technologists (profl. sensory divsn. sec. 1980-82, chmn. 1984-85, short course spkr. 1979-81, Ctrl. Valley subsect., treas. 1989-91, chmn.-elect./sec. 1991-92, chmn. 1992-93). Avocations: cooking, recipe development. Office: PO Box 622 Manteca CA 95336-1130

RAINEY, MARCELLA, sociology educator; b. Collinsville, Ill., Mar. 1, 1926; d. Wilbert and Marcella (Murphy) Bischoff; m. Thomas Rainey, Dec. 21, 1946; children: Adrienne, Ruth, Michael, Janelle. BS, Ill. State U., 1965; MA, U. Ill., 1968. Assoc. prof. sociology Lincoln (Ill.) Coll., 1965-68, prof., 1968-85. Bd. dirs. Bread for Journey, Santa Fe, N.Mex., 1995—, Children at Risk, Santa Fe, 1992—; mem. adv. com. Santa Fe C.C., 1996—. Avocation: photography.

RAINEY, RON PAUL, artist manager; b. East Stroudsburg, Pa., Feb. 3, 1946; s. Donald Elmo Rainey and Genevieve Elinore (Kwiecinski) Rushin. Concert agt. Internat. Famous Agy. (now Internat. Creative Mgmt.), N.Y.C., 1969-71; v.p. concert dept. Agy. for Performing Arts, N.Y.C. and L.A., 1971-73; chmn., CEO, Magna Artists Corp., Los Angeles, 1974-81; pres., CEO, Ron Rainey Mgmt., Inc., Beverly Hills, Calif., 1981—, Raineyville Music Pub., Beverly Hills, 1991—; pres., CEO Marshall Tucker Entertainment, Beverly Hills, 1997—; owner, pres. Am. Artists corp., Beverly Hills, 1996—. Served with USN, 1967-68. Avocation: collecting baseball cards, antique books and music memorabilia, fine wines. Office: 315 S Beverly Dr Ste 206 Beverly Hills CA 90212-4310

RAISIAN, JOHN, university institute director, economist; b. Conneaut, Ohio, July 30, 1949; s. Ernest James and Ruby Lee (Owens) R.; m. Joyce Ann Klak, Aug. 17, 1984; children: Alison Kathleen, Sarah Elizabeth. BA, Ohio U., 1971; PhD, UCLA, 1978; LLD (hon.), Albertson Coll. Idaho, 1995. Rsch. assoc. Human Resources Rsch. Ctr., U. So. Calif., L.A., 1972-73; cons. Rand Corp., Santa Monica, Calif., 1974-75, 76; vis. asst. prof. econs. U. Wash., Seattle, 1975-76; asst. prof. econs. U. Houston, 1976-80; sr. economist Office Rsch. and Evaluation, U.S. Bur. Labor Stats., Washington, 1980-81; spl. asst. for econ. policy Office Asst. Sec. for Policy, U.S. Dept. Labor, Washington, 1981-83, dir. rsch. and tech. support, 1981-84; pres. Unicon Rsch. Corp., L.A., 1984-86; sr. fellow Hoover Instn., Stanford, Calif., 1986—, assoc. dir., dep. dir., 1986-90, dir., 1990—; exec. dir. Presdl. Task Force on Food Assistance, Washington, 1983-84. Mem. editorial bd. Jour. Labor Rsch., 1983—; contbr. articles to profl. jours. Advisor Nat. Coun. on Handicapped, Washington, 1985-86, Nat. Commn. on Employment Policy, Washington, 1987-88; chmn. minimum wage bd. Calif. Indsl. Welfare Commn., 1987; mem. nat. adv.com. Student Fin. Assistance, Washington, 1987-89; corp. mem. Blue Shield Calif., 1994-96; bd. dirs. Sentinel Groups Fund, Inc., 1997—; mem. Pacific Coun. Internat. Policy, nat. adv. bd. City Innovation. Recipient Best Publ. of Yr. award Econ. Inquiry, Western Econ. Assn., 1979, Disting. Teaching award U. Houston Coll. Social Scis., 1980, Disting. Svc. award U.S. Dept. Labor, 1983; predoctoral fellow Rand Corp., 1976. Mem. Am. Econs. Assn., Western Econ. Assn. (chmn. nominating com. 1992), Commonwealth Club of Calif., World Affairs Coun., Mont Pelerin Soc., Coun. on Fgn. Rels., Nat. Assn. Scholars, Phi Beta Kappa. Republican. Avocations: wine collecting, sports enthusiast. Office: Stanford U Hoover Hoover Inst War-Revolution Stanford CA 94305-6010

RAITT, SHERRY LEE, writer, songwriter, home designer; b. Prairie City, Oreg., Oct. 4, 1949; d. Jake and Patricia (England) Raat; m. Larry Wayne Rombeck, Sept. 6, 1968 (div. 1980); 1 child, Angela Shawn. Student, Coll. Legal Arts, Portland, Oreg. Author over 20 home accessory/design books, including Magical Universe Crocheting, Prism Rainbows, Energy-Homebuilding, Hollow Center Home Designs, How to Write a Songbook. Rep. Dem. Party, Eugene, 1996-98; mem. com. Dem. Nat. Com., Washington, 1996-98; mem. Presdl. Second Term Com., Washington, 1996-98. Avocations: songwriting, singing, guitar, desigining. Home: 488 Blair Blvd Eugene OR 97402-4567

RALSTON, LENORE DALE, academic policy and program analyst; b. Oakland, Calif., Feb. 21, 1949; d. Leonard Earnest and Emily Allison (Hudnut) R. BA in Anthropology, U. Calif., Berkeley, 1971, MPH in Behavioral Sci., 1981; MA in Anthropology, Bryn Mawr Coll., 1973, PhD in Anthropology, 1980. Asst. rschr. anthropology inst. internat. studies U. Calif., Berkeley, 1979-82, rsch. assoc. Latin Am. Study Ctr., 1982-83, acad. asst. to dean Sch. of Optometry, 1990-95, prin. policy analyst, chancellor's office, 1995—; assoc. scientist, rsch. adminstr. Med. Rsch. Inst., San Francisco, 1982-85; cons. health sci. Berkeley, 1986-90; mem. fin. bd. Med. Rsch. Inst., 1983-84; speaker in field. Co-author: Voluntary Effects in Decentralized Management, 1983; contbr. articles to profl. jours. Commr. Cmty. Health Adv. Com., Berkeley, 1988-90; vice chair, commr. Cmty. Health Commn., Berkeley, 1990-93; mem. bd. safety com. Miles, Inc., Berkeley, 1992-94. Grantee Nat. Rsch. Svc. Award, WHO, NIMH, NSF. Fellow Applied Anthropology Assn.; mem. APHA, Am. Anthropology Assn., Sigma Xi. Home: 1232 Carlotta Ave Berkeley CA 94707-2707

RAMANATHAN, VEERABHADRAN, oceanographer, educator; b. Madras, India, Nov. 24, 1944; came to U.S., 1971; s. K. and J. V.; m. Girija Ramanathan, Nov. 22, 1973; children: Nithya, Dhakshin, Tara. B of Mech. Engring., Anamalai U., India, 1965; MS in Heat Transfer, All India Inst. Sci., 1970; PhD in Planetary Atmosphere, SUNY, Stony Brook, 1973. Sr. scientist Nat. Ctr. Atmospheric Rsch., Boulder, Colo., 1982-86; rsch. prof. U. Chgo., 1986-90; dir. Ctr. for Clouds, Chemistry and Climate, Scripps Inst. Oceanography, U. Calif. San Diego, La Jolla, 1991—, dir. Ctr. for Atmospheric Scis., 1996—, Alderson prof., 1990—; Bd. dirs. Tata Energy Rsch. Inst., Arilington, Va.; chmn. outreach com. NASA-Earth Observing Sys., 1997—. Contbr. articles to sci. publs. Recipient Environment prize Volvo Found., Goteborg, Sweden, 1997, Buys Ballot medal Royal Netherlands Acad. Scis., 1995; fellow Am. Acad. Arts & Scis., 1995. Fellow AAAS, Am. Meteorol. Soc., Am. Geophys. Union; mem. Acad. Europaea (fgn.). Office: UCSD-Scripps Inst Oceanog 9500 Gilman Dr La Jolla CA 92093-5003

RAMER, BRUCE M., lawyer; b. Teaneck, N.J., Aug. 2, 1933; s. Sidney and Anne S. (Strassman) R.; children: Gregg B., Marc K., Neal I. BA, Princeton U., 1955; LLB, Harvard U., 1958. Bar: Calif. 1963, N.J. 1958. Assoc., Morrison, Lloyd & Griggs, Hackensack, N.J., 1959-60; ptnr. Gang, Tyre, Ramer & Brown, Inc., L.A., 1963—. Exec. dir. Entertainment Law Inst., Law Ctr. of U. So. Calif.; bd. of councilors Law Ctr. U. So. Calif.; chmn., nat. bd. govs. Am. Jewish Com., 1995-98, nat. v.p., 1982-88, pres., 1998—, L.A. chpt., 1980-83, chair Western region, 1984-86, comty. svc. award, 1987, nat. pres., 1998—, adv. bd. Skirball Inst. on Am. Values, 1998—; chmn. Asia Pacific Rim Inst., 1989-98; trustee Loyola Marymount U., L.A. Children's Mus., 1986-89; vice chair United Way, 1991-93, corp. bd. dirs., 1981-93, chair coun. pres. 1989-90, mem. cmty. issues coun., 1989-90, chair discretionary fund distbn. com., 1987-89; bd. dirs., chair Geffen Playhouse, 1995-98, founding chair, 1998—; bd. dirs. L.A. Urban League, 1987-93, 96—, Jewish Fedn. Coun. of Greater L.A. (mem. Cmty. Rels. com., bd. dirs., exec. com.), Jewish TV Network, Sta. KCET-TV; mem., bd. dirs. Rebuild L.A., 1992-96; mem. bd. govs. Calif. Cmty. Found., 1988-98; recipient Ann. Brotherhood award NCCJs, 1990; mem. Fellows of Am. Bar Found.; mem. econ. strategy panel State Calif., 1997—; bd. dirs. Shoah Visual History Found., Righteous Persons Found., L.A. 2012 Bid Com. for the So. Calif. Olympic Games; bd. dirs. Jewish Fedn. Coun. Greater L.A., mem. exec. com., cmty. rels. com. Pvt. U.S. Army, 1958-59, 2d lt., 1961-62. Mem. ABA (mem. spl. com. jud. ind.), L.A. County Bar Assn., Calif. Bar Assn., Beverly Hills Bar Assn. (Exec. Dirs. award 1988, Entertainment Lawyer of Yr. award 1996), L.A. Copyright Soc. (pres. 1974-75), Calif. Copyright Conf. (pres. 1973-74), Princeton Club (pres. 1975-78). Office: Gang Tyre Ramer & Brown Inc 132 S Rodeo Dr Beverly Hills CA 90212-2415

RAMER, LAWRENCE JEROME, corporation executive; b. Bayonne, N.J., July 29, 1928; s. Sidney and Anne (Strassman) R.; m. Ina Lee Brown, June 30, 1957; children: Stephanie Beryl, Susan Meredith, Douglas Strassman. B.A. in Econs, Lafayette Coll., 1950; M.B.A., Harvard U., 1957; LLD (hon.), Lafayette Coll., 1992. Sales rep., then v.p. United Sheet Metal Co., Bayonne, 1953-55; with Am. Cement Corp., 1957-64; v.p. mktg. div. Riverside Cement Co., 1960-62, v.p. mktg. parent co., 1962-64; vice chmn. bd., chief exec. officer Clavier Corp., N.Y.C., 1965-66; exec. v.p., vice chmn. bd. Pacific Western Industries, Los Angeles, 1966-70; pres., chief exec. officer Nat. Portland Cement Co. Fla., 1975-89; chmn. bd. Sutro Partners, Inc., Los Angeles, 1977-89, Somerset Mgmt. Group, 1975-92, Luminall Paints Inc., Los Angeles, 1972-95; chmn. bd., chief exec. officer Bruning Paint Co., Balt., 1979—, Pacific Coast Cement Co., Los Angeles, 1979-90; pres., chief exec. officer Ramer Equities, Inc., 1990—; chmn. Lee and Lawrence J. Ramer Family Found., 1986—; bd. dirs. Orbis Internat., N.Y.C., The Music Ctr., L.A., Canyon Ranch, Tucson, Music Ctr. Found., L.A.; bd. dirs. Ctr. Theatre Group-Mark Taper Ahmanson Theatres, L.A., pres. and chmn., 1987-97. Chmn. bd. trustees Lafayette Coll., Easton, Pa.; trustee, chmn. bd. trustees Calif. Inst. Arts, Valencia, Calif.; bd. dirs. Non-Traditional Casting Project, N.Y.; nat. bd. govs. Am. Jewish Com., N.Y., assoc. chmn. bd. trustees. Office: Ramer Equities Inc 1999 Ave Of Stars Ste 1090 Los Angeles CA 90067-4612

RAMES, DOUGLAS DWIGHT, civil engineer; b. Colorado Springs, Colo., Apr. 14, 1942; s. Dwight S. and Eleanor A. (Roach) R.; m. Audrey Joan Satter, Nov. 26, 1963; children: Steven D., Wendy M., Eydee J. BSCE, S.D. Sch. Mines & Tech., 1965; postgrad., Ind./Purdue U., 1989, Harvard U., 1995. Registered profl. engr., Colo. Project engr. Colo. Dept. of Hwys., Eagle, 1970-72; resident engr. Colo. Dept. of Hwys., Grand Junction, 1972-

78; preconstrn. engr. Colo. Dept. of Hwys., Greeley, 1978-84, asst. dist. engr., 1984-88; region dir. Colo. Dept. Transp., Greeley, 1988-98, ret., 1998. Commr. urban renewal City of Greeley, 1993-98; mgr. transp. The Sear-Brown Group, 1998—. Avocations: genealogy, travel, fishing, old roadsters. Office: Sear-Brown Group 209 S Meldrum St Fort Collins CO 80521-2603

RAMEY, FELICENNE HOUSTON, dean; b. Phila.; m. Melvin R. Ramey, Sept. 5, 1964; 2 children. BS, Pa. State U., University Park, 1961; MS, Duquesne U., 1967; JD, U. Calif., Davis, 1972; MA, Calif. State U.-Sacramento, 1978. Bar: Calif. Microbiologist Pa. Dept. Labs., Phila., Walter Reed Army Med. Ctr., Washington; chemist Calgon Corp., Pitts.; instr. Carnegie-Mellon U., Pitts.; dep. atty. gen. Calif. Dept. Justice, Sacramento; clk. U.S. Dist. Ct. Calif., Sacramento; asst. prof. Calif. State U. Sch. Bus. Adminstrn., Sacramento, assoc. prof., chmn. dept. behavior and environment, assoc. dean, prof., dean, 1997—; exec. officer U. Calif., Davis; dir. litigation Human Rights Commn., Sacramento; bd. dirs. Legal Aid Soc., Sacramento mag.; vis. scholar Ga. Inst. Tech., 1981, Boston Coll., 1988. Mem. edn. com. Blacks for Effective Community Action, 1978—. ACE fellow U. Calif., Santa Cruz, 1992—. Mem. Calif. Agrl. Alumni Assn. (bd. dirs.), Western Bus. Law Assn. (pres., pres. elect, v.p., exec. sec. Calif. and Nev. chpts. 1983-89), Nat. Assn. Women Deans and Adminstrs., Sacramento Black C. of C. (edn. com. 1990—, bd. dirs. 1989—). Avocations: jogging, cross crounty skiing, reading. Office: Calif State U Coll Bus Adminstrn Sacramento CA 95819-6088

RAMIL, MARIO R., state supreme court justice; b. Quezon City, The Philippines, June 21, 1946; came to U.S. 1956; s. Quintin A. and Fausta M. (Reyes) R.; m. Judy E. Wong, Nov. 6, 1971; children: Jonathan, Bradley. BA in Polit. Sci., Calif. State U., Hayward, 1972; JD, U. Calif., San Francisco, 1975. Bar: Calif. 1976, Hawaii 1976, U.S. Dist. Ct. Hawaii, U.S. Dist. Ct. (no. dist.) Calif., U.S. Ct. Appeals (9th cir.). Law clk. San Francisco Neighborhood Legal Aid Found., 1973-75; legal counsel Sandigan-Newcomers Svcs., Inc., San Francisco, 1975-76; dep. atty. gen. Dept. Labor and Indsl. Rels., 1976-79; dep. atty. gen. gen. adminstrn. U. Hawaii, 1979-80; staff atty. house majority atty.'s office Hawaii Ho. of Reps., 1980; pvt. practice, 1980-82; dep. atty. gen. adminstrv. div. State of Hawaii, 1982-84, ins. commr., 1984-86; dir. Hawaii State Dept. Labor and Indsl. Rels., Honolulu, 1986-91; of counsel Lyons, Brandt, Cook and Hiramatsu, 1991-93; assoc. justice Hawaii Supreme Ct., Honolulu, 1993—. Bd. dirs. Hawaii Youth-At-Risk, 1989; co-chair state conv. Dem. Party State of Hawaii, 1984; mem. Adv. Coun. on Housing and Constrn., State of Hawaii, 1981; pres., bd. dirs. Hawaii Non-Profit Housing Corp.; exec. sec., chmn. adminstrv. budget com. Oahu Filipino Community Coun.; bd. dirs. legal advisor Oahu Filipino Jaycees, 1978-81. Office: Ali'iolani Hale Hawaii Supreme Ct 417 S Kinga St Honolulu HI 96813-2902 Address: PO Box 2560 Honolulu HI 96804-2560*

RAMIREZ, RICARDO, bishop; b. Bay City, Tex., Sept. 12, 1936; s. Natividad and Maria (Espinosa) R. B.A., U. St. Thomas, Houston, 1959; M.A., U. Detroit, 1968; Diploma in Pastoral Studies, East Asian Pastoral Inst., Manila, 1973-74. Ordained priest Roman Catholic Ch., 1966; missionary Basilian Fathers, Mex., 1968-76; exec. v.p. Mexican Am. Cultural Ctr., San Antonio, 1976-81; aux. bishop Archdiocese of San Antonio, 1981-82; bishop Diocese of Las Cruces, N.M., 1982—; cons. U.S. Bishop's Com. on Liturgy, from 1981; advisor U.S. Bishop's Com. on Hispanic Affairs, from 1981. Author: Fiesta, Worship and Family, 1981. Mem. N.Am. Acad. on Liturgy, Hispanic Liturgical Inst.; Padres Asociada Derechos Religiosos Educativos y Sociales. Lodges: K.C; Holy Order Knights of Holy Sepulcher. Office: Diocese of Las Cruces 1280 Med Park Dr Las Cruces NM 88005-3239*

RAMO, SIMON, engineering executive; b. Salt Lake City, May 7, 1913; s. Benjamin and Clara (Trestman) R.; m. Virginia Smith, July 25, 1937; children: James Brian, Alan Martin. BS, U. Utah, 1933, DSc (hon.), 1961; PhD, Calif. Inst. Tech., 1936; DEng (hon.), Case Western Res. U., 1960, U. Mich., 1966, Poly. Inst. N.Y., 1971; DSc (hon.), Union Coll., 1963, Worcester Polytechnic Inst., 1968, U. Akron, 1969, Case State U., 1976; LLD (hon.), Carnegie-Mellon U., 1970, U. So. Calif., 1972, Gonzaga U., 1983, Occidental Coll., 1984, Claremont U., 1985. With Gen. Electric Co., 1936-46; v.p. ops. Hughes Aircraft Co., 1946-53; with Ramo-Woolridge Corp., 1953-58, Ramo-Wooldridge Corp., 1954-58; dir. TRW Inc., 1954-85, exec. v.p., 1958-61, vice chmn. bd., 1961-78, chmn. exec. com., 1969-78, cons., 1978—; pres. The Bunker-Ramo Corp., 1964-66; chmn. bd. TRW-Fujitsu Co., 1980-83; bd. dirs. Arco Power Techs.; vice pres. mgmt. sci. Calif. Inst. Tech., 1978—; Regents lectr. UCLA, 1981-82, U. Calif. at Santa Cruz, 1978-79; chmn. Center for Study Am. Experience, U. So. Calif., 1978-80; Faculty fellow John F. Kennedy Sch. Govt., Harvard U., 1980-84; mem. White House Energy Research and Devel. Adv. Council, 1973-75; mem. adv. com. on sci. and fgn. affairs U.S. State Dept., 1973-75; chmn. Pres.'s Com. on Sci. and Tech., 1976-77; mem. adv. council to Sec. Commerce, 1976-77, Gen. Atomics Corp., 1988—, Aurora Capital Ptnrs., 1991—, Chartwell Investments, 1992—; co-chmn. Transition Task Force on Sci. and Tech. for Pres.-elect Reagan; mem. roster consultants to adminstr. ERDA, 1976-77; bd. advisors for sci. and tech. Republic of China, 1981-84; chmn. bd. Aetna, Jacobs & Ramo Venture Capital, 1987-90, Allenwood Ventures Inc., 1987—; advisor Axiom Venture Ptnrs., 1997—. Author: The Business of Science, 1988, other sci., engring. and mgmt. books. Bd. dirs. L.A. World Affairs Coun. 1973-85, Mus. Ctr. Found., L.A. L.A. Philharm. Assn., 1981-84; life trustee Calif. Inst. Tech., Nat. Symphony Orch. Assn., 1973-83; trustee emeritus Calif. State Univs.; bd. visitors UCLA Sch. Medicine, 1980—; bd. dirs. W.M. Keck Found., 1983—; bd. govs. Performing Arts Coun. Mus. Ctr. L.A., pres., 1976-77. Recipient award IAS, 1956; award Am. Inst. Elec. Engrs., 1959; award Arnold Air Soc., 1960; Am. Acad. Achievement award, 1964; award Am. Iron and Steel Inst., 1968; Disting. Svc. medal Armed Forces Communication and Electronics Assn., 1970; medal of achievement WEMA, 1970; awards U. So. Calif., 1971, 79; Kayan medal Columbia U., 1972; award Am. Cons. Engrs. Coun., 1974; medal Franklin Inst., 1978; award Harvard Bus. Sch. Assn., 1979; award Nat. Medal Sci., 1979; Disting. Alumnus award U. Utah, 1981; UCLA medal, 1982; Presdl. Medal of Freedom, 1983; named to Bus. Hall of Fame, 1984; recipient Aesculapian award UCLA, 1984, Durand medal AAIA, 1984, John Fritz medal, 1986, Henry Townley Heald award Ill. Inst. Tech., 1988, Nat. Engring. award Am. Assn. Engring. Socs., 1988, Franklin-Jefferson medal, 1988, Howard Hughes Meml. award, 1989, Air Force Space and Missile Pioneers award, 1989, Pioneer award Internat. Coun. on Sys. Engring., 1997. Fellow IEEE (Electronic Achievement award 1953, Golden Omega award 1975, Founders medal 1980, Centennial medal 1984), Am. Acad. Arts and Scis., Am. Acad. Polit. Sci.; mem. N.Y. Acad. Scis., Nat. Acad. Engring. (founder, coun. mem. Bueche award), Nat. Acad. Scis., Am. Phys. Soc., Am. Philos. Soc., Inst. Advancement Engring., Coun. Fgn. Rels., Pacific Coun. Internat. Policy, Internat. Acad. Astronautics, Eta Kappa Nu (eminent mem. award 1966), Theta Tau (Hall of Fame laureate). Office: 9200 W Sunset Blvd Ste 801 Los Angeles CA 90069-3603

RAMO, VIRGINIA M. SMITH, civic worker; b. Yonkers, N.Y.; d. Abraham Harold and Freda (Kasnetz) Smith; BS. in Edn., U. So. Calif., DHL (hon.), 1978; m. Simon Ramo; children—James Brian, Alan Martin. Nat. co-chmn. ann. giving U. So. Calif., 1968-70, vice chmn., trustee, 1971—, co-chmn. bd. councilors Sch. Performing Arts, 1975-76, co-chmn. bd. councillors Schs. Med. and Engring.; vice-chmn. bd. overseers Hebrew Union Coll., 1972-75; bd. dirs. The Muses of Calif. Mus. Sci. and industry, UCLA Affiliates, Estelle Doheny Eye Found., U. So. Calif. Sch. Medicine; adv. council Los Angeles County Heart Assn., chmn. com. to endow Chair in cardiology at U. So. Calif.; vice-chmn., bd. dirs. Friends of Library U. So. Calif.; bd. dirs., nat. pres. Achievement Rewards for Coll. Scientists Found., 1975-77; bd. dirs. Les Dames Los Angeles, Community TV So. Calif.; bd. dirs., v.p. Founders Los Angeles Music Center; v.p. Los Angeles Music Center Opera Assn.; v.p. corp. bd. United Way; v.p. Blue Ribbon-400 Performing Arts Council; chmn. com. to endow chair in gerontology U. So. Calif.; vice chmn. campaign Doheny Eye Inst., 1989. Recipient Service award Friends of Libraries, 1974, Nat. Community Service award Alpha Epsilon Phi, 1975, Disting. Service award Am. Heart Assn. 1978, Service award U. Achievement award Mannequins of Los Angeles Assistance League, 1979, Womanof Yr. award PanHellenic Assn., 1981, Disting. Service award U. So. Calif. Sch. Medicine, 1981, U. So. Calif Town and Gown Recognition award, 1986, Asa V. Call Achievement award U. So. Calif., 1986, Phi Kappa Phi scholarship award U. So. Calif., 1986, Vision award Luminaires of

Doheny Eye Inst., 1994. Mem. UCLA Med. Aux., U. So. Calif. Pres.'s Circle, Commerce Assos. U. So. Calif., Cedars of Lebanon Hosp. Women's Guild (dir. 1967-68), Blue Key, Skull and Dagger.

RAMOS, ALBERT A., electrical engineer; b. L.A., Feb. 28, 1927; s. Jesus D. and Carmen F. (Fontes) R.; B.S. in Elec. Engring., U. So. Calif., 1950, M.S. in Systems Mgmt., 1972; Ph.D., U.S. Internat. U., 1975; m. Joan C. Pailing, Sept. 23, 1950; children—Albert A., Richard R., James J., Katherine. With guided missile test group Hughes Aircraft Co., 1950-60; with TRW DSG, 1960-91, sr. staff engr. Norton AFB, San Bernardino, Calif., 1969-91, ret., 1991. Served with USNR, 1945-46. Registered profl. engr., Calif. Mem. IEEE, NSPE, Air Force Assn., Mexican-Am. Engring. Soc., Mexican-Am. Profl. Mgmt. Assn. (mem. administering commn. dept. community svcs.), Sigma Phi Delta, Eta Kappa Nu, Tau Beta Pi. Home: 8937 Napoli Dr Las Vegas NV 89117-1182

RAMOS, DOROTHY JO, information resource manager; b. Little Rock, July 8, 1949; d. Otis Joe and Dorothy Juanita (Graham) Green; m. Eddmond Virgil Mann (dec. Dec. 1979); children: Brian Eddmond, Jeremy Earl; m. Francisco Ramos Jr., Oct. 24, 1987. Student, St. Mary's Coll., 1995—. Computer specialist Naval Supply Ctr., Oakland, Calif., 1973-91, USAF, McClellan AFB, Calif., 1991-93; mgr. Defense Info. Sys. Agy., McClellan AFB, Calif., 1993-95, U.S. Treasury, San Francisco, 1995—. Mem. Greater Vallejo Lioness Club (pres. 1985). Avocations: hiking, camping, sewing, computers. Home: 130 Suncrest Way Vacaville CA 95688-8524 Office: US Treasury 390 Main St San Francisco CA 94105-2011

RAMOS, ELEANOR LACSON, transplant nephrologist; b. Quezon City, The Philippines, Mar. 26, 1956; d. Pol and Evelyn (Lacson) Ramos. BS, Tufts U., 1977; MD, Tufts Med. Sch., Boston, 1981. Diplomate Am. Bd. Internal Medicine, Am. Bd. Nephrology. Resident in internal medicine New Eng. Med. Ctr., Boston, 1981-84; fellow in nephrology Brigham and Women's Hosp., Boston, 1984-88, med. dir. renal transplant svc., 1988-90; med. dir. renal transplant svc. U. Fla., Gainesville, 1990-94; assoc. dir. immunology clin. rsch. Bristol-Myers Squibb Pharm. Rsch. Inst., Wallingford, Conn., 1994-96; asst. clin. prof. medicine Yale U., 1995-96; dir. med. rsch. Roche Global Devel., Palo Alto, Calif., 1996—. Mem. Am. Soc. Transplant Physicians (chairperson patient care and edn. com. 1994-95, clin. practice guideline com., Young Investigator award 1988), Am. Soc. Nephrology, Internat. Soc. Nephrology, Transplantation Soc., Alpha Omega Alpha, United Network for Organ Sharing (patient affairs com.).

RAMSAY, JOHN BARADA, research chemist, educator; b. Phoenix, Dec. 28, 1929; s. John A. and Helen G. Ramsay; m. Barbara Ann Hilsenhoff, Apr. 18, 1953; children: Bryan J., Kathleen L., Carol A., David A. BS in Chemistry, Tex. Western U., 1950; PhD in Analytical Chemistry, U. Wis., 1954. Mem. staff Los Alamos Nat. Lab., 1954-70, 73-95; assoc. prof. Coll. Petroleum and Minerals, Dhahran, Saudi Arabia, 1970-73; cons. U.S. Navy, USAF, 1980—; adj. prof. U. N.Mex., Los Alamos, 1980-85, Comforce 1995—. Author sci. articles. Recipient award of excellence U.S. Dept. Energy, 1984, 92. Mem. N.Mex. Acad. Sci. (pres. 1988), Am. Inst. Archeol. (chpt. pres. 1979, 96, 97), Nat. Ski Patrol (appt. 7651), Westerners Internat. (chpt. pres. 1988-90), Sigma Xi. Democrat. Home: 6 Erie Ln Los Alamos NM 87544-3810

RAMSBY, MARK DELIVAN, lighting designer and consultant; b. Portland, Oreg., Nov. 20, 1947; s. Marshall Delivan and Verna Pansy (Culver) R.; divorced; children: Aaron Delivan, Venessa Mercedes. Student, Portland (Oreg.) State U., 1966-67. With C.E.D., Portland, 1970-75; minority ptnr. The Light Source, Portland, 1975-78, pres., 1978-87; prin. Illume Lighting Design, Portland, 1987-90; ptnr. Ramsby, Dupuy & Seats, Inc., Portland, 1990-91; dir. lighting design PAE Cons. Engrs., Inc., Portland, 1991—; pvt. practice cons. Portland, 1979—. Recipient Top 100 Outstanding Achievement award Metalux Lighting, 1981-85, 100% award, 1985, Edwin F. Guth award of merit, 1990, Edison award of excellence, 1990, Edwin F. Guth award of excellence, 1993, 94, Paul Waterbury award of Merit, 1995. Mem. Illuminating Engring. Soc. Am. (sec.-treas. Oreg. sect. 1978-79, Oreg. Section and Regional and Internat. awards 1989, 90, 93, 94, Lighting Design awards). Internat. Assn. Lighting Designers. Republican. Lutheran. Avocations: lighting design, historical restoration, flyfishing, downhill skiing. Office: PAE Cons Engrs 808 SW 3d Ave Ste 300 Portland OR 97204-2426

RAMSEY, JERRY VIRGIL, educator, financial planner, radio broadcaster; b. Tacoma, July 24, 1940; s. Virgil Emory and Winifred Victoria (Carothers) R.; m. Elaine Sigrid Perdue, June 24, 1967; 1 child, Jason Perdue. BA in Elem. Edn., U. Puget Sound, 1967; MEd in Tchr. Eng. and Curriculum Devel., U. Wash., 1971; PhD in Econ. Geography Curriculum, Columbia Pacific U., 1985. Tchr. Tacoma Pub. Schs., 1967-95; fin. planner Primerica Corp., Tacoma, 1986-90, Waddell & Reed, Inc., Tacoma, 1990-93; N.Am. Mgmt., 1993-96; real estate investor, CEO Ramsey Properties, Gig Harbor, Wash., 1970-98; radio broadcaster KGHP, KJUN/The Country Gold Network, KMAS, 1990-96, KGY, 1996—; study skills specialist Sylvan Learning Ctr., 1995-98; lectr. Pacific Luth. U., Tacoma, 1972-86. Precinct committee officer Pierce County Rep. Com., Tacoma, 1968-78, 95—. With USAF, 1959-62. Recipient Golden Acorn award PTA, 1975, Meritorious Teaching award Nat. Coun. Geog. Edn., 1978, achievement award Rep. Nat. Com., 1985; grantee U.S. Office Edn., 1971. Mem. NEA (life), Fort Nisqually Assn. (chmn. mem. hist. site adv. coun. 1996—, v.p. pub. rels. 1998—), Knife and Fork Club (pres. 1983), Kiwanis (pres. Tacoma 1982) Phi Delta Kappa. Methodist. Avocation: living history interpretation, real estate investing, management and education.

RAMSEY, NANCY LOCKWOOD, nursing educator; b. L.A., Jan. 26, 1943; d. Jack Thanke and Virginia Lee (Slaughter) Lockwood; m. Gordon S. Ramsey, June 24, 1972; children: Douglas Lockwood, Kathryn Anne. BSN, Loma Linda U., 1966; MS in Nursing, Duke U., 1969; postgrad., Calif. State U., L.A., 1974. Staff nurse various hosps., 1966-82, 91-92; clin. instr. Azusa (Calif.)-Pacific U., 1966-93; instr. U. N.C., Chapel Hill, Calif. State U., L.A.; acting dir. nursing edn. Children's Hosp. L.A.; prof. nursing L.A. City Coll., East L.A. Coll., Monterey Park, Calif.; instr. pediatric nursing State Bd. Rev. Classes, L.A. and San Francisco; instr. statewide nursing program Calif. State U., Dominguez Hills. Author, editor: Child and Family Concepts of Nursing Practice, 1982, 87; contbr. articles to profl. jours. Mem. Sigma Theta Tau. Home: 1561 Berenice Dr Brea CA 92821-1802

RAMSEY, PATRICIA PRUSAK, artist; b. Cleve., Dec. 1, 1952; d. Jeffrey Kent Ramsey, Oct. 3, 1992; twins: William K. and Stephanie E. BFA, Atlanta Coll. Art, 1983. Fine artist Ramsack Studio, Atlanta, 1983-94, Roseburg, Oreg., 1994—; tchr. Callenwolde Ctr., Decatur, Ga., 1983-94, Steeplehouse Ctr., Marietta, Ga., 1984-91. Artist, photographer. Dep. dir. Ga. Vol. Lawyers for Arts, Atlanta, 1985-88; juror Mablehouse, Mableton, Ga., 1990. Recipient Best of Show award Mablehouse, 1989, 1st place award Ga. Mountain Crafts, 1992, 94, Great Mom award Grolier Books, 1998. Mem. Nat. Geog. Soc., Smithsonian Instn., Dalton Fine Arts Alliance (exhibiting artist), Fulton County Arts Coun. (artist in edn. 1992), Pinckneyville Arts Ctr. (instr. 1991), Neighborhood Art Ctr. (vis. artist 1983). Home: 1560 Echo Dr Roseburg OR 97470-8482

RAMSEY, RAY, JR., art gallery owner; b. Monterey, Calif., Sept. 23, 1935; s. Ray and Elenore (Roberta) Edsberg; m. Carla Belgrano, Oct. 3, 1954 (div. Jul. 1979); children: Ray III, Jon Frederic; m. Daniele R. Ramsey, Apr. 18, 1981. BA, General Motors Ins. 1957. Pres. Ramsey Ferrari, Monterey, San Francisco, 1958-84, Ramsey Racing, San Francisco, N.Y.C., 1958-81, Plastec Design Corp., Monterey, L.A., 1984—, Acquastrada Int. Corp., Monterey, 1984—, Ramsey Fine Art Portfolio, Carmel, Calif., 1965—, Atelier Carmel Galleries, Carmel, 1994—; builder, restorer, driver classic cars, 1958—. V.p. Alcoholics Coun. of Monterey, 1960-75; assoc. S.P.C.A. of Monterey, 1959— Pebble Beach Concourse D Elegance, 1956, 61, 67, 72. Mem. Classic Car Tennis CLub, Frick Art Rsch. Libr., Monterey Found. Art Rsch., The Smithsonian Inst., The Libr. Congress, Met Mus. Art, Carmel Found., Nat. Trust Hist. Preservation. Avocations: writing, tennis, colg. skiing, book collecting. Office: Atecier Carmel PO Box 57 Pebble Beach CA 93953-0057

RAMSEY LINES, SANDRA, forensic document examiner; b. Detroit, Dec. 8, 1940; d. Henry Alexander and Genevieve Agnes (Pilote) Habeeb; m. Richard Ramsey, Apr. 30, 1960 (div. 1965); children: Theresa L., Richard A., Renee A.; m. Ruskin R. Lines II, Sept. 11, 1998. AA, Scottdale (Ariz.) C.C., 1987; BA, U. Phoenix, 1989. Diplomate Am. Bd. Forensic Document Examiners; cert. pub. mgr. Sch. Pub. Affairs/Advanced Pub. Affairs Exec. Program Ariz. State U. Cert. peace officer, sgt. Cleve. Police Dept., 1973-82; investigator Ariz. Bd. Med. Examiners, Phoenix, 1984-84; cert. peace officer investigator Maricopa County Atty.'s Office, Phoenix, 1984-85; spl. agent cert. peace officer Office of Atty. Gen., Phoenix, 1985-96, forensic document examiner, 1991-96; forensic document examiner Bur. Alcohol, Tobacco and Firearms, Walnut Creek, Calif., 1996-99; pvt. practice as forensic document examiner, Paradise Valley, Ariz., 1999—; mem. tng. com. Ariz. Law Enforcement Coord. Com., Phoenix, 1995; asst. dir. We. States Hazardous Waste Project, Phoenix, 1987-88; presenter in field. Contbr. articles to profl. jours. Recipient Resolution for Achievements in Law Enforcement Cleve. City Coun., 1979, Committment and Support plaque Fraternal Order of Police, 1996. Fellow Am. Acad. Forensic Scis. (questioned document sect. 1996), Am. Soc. Questioned Document Examiners (provisional mem.), S.W. Assn. Forensic Document Examiners. Republican. Mem. Maronite Cath. Ch. Achievements include being one of 14 women in 1973 to be the first women in uniform patrol and later the first woman in homicide unit of Cleve. Police Dept.; establishment of forensic document lab. at Ariz. Atty. Gen.'s office; established and hosted study group meetings for Document Examiners No. Calif.

RANCE, QUENTIN E., interior designer; b. St. Albans, Eng., Mar. 22, 1935; came to U.S. 1981; s. Herbert Leonard and Irene Ann (Haynes) R.; m. India Adams, May 17, 1974. Grad., Eastbourne (Eng.) Sch. Art, 1960. Soft furnishings buyer Dickeson & French Ltd., Eastbourne, 1960-61, outside sales mgr., 1961-62; design dir. Laszlo Hoenig, Ltd., London, 1962-73; mng. dir. Quentin Rance Interiors Ltd., London, 1973-81; pres. Quentin Rance Enterprises, Inc., Encino, Calif., 1981—. Works featured in Designers West, 1983, Design House Rev., 1983, Profiles mag., 1987, Nat. Assn. Mirror Mfrs. Jour., 1988, Designer Specifier, 1990. Mem. Founders for Diabetic Research/City of Hope. Served with RAF, 1953-55. Recipient Hon. Mention award Nat. Assn. Mirror Mfrs., 1987, 1st Pl. Nat. Pub. Svc. award, Designer Specifier, 1990. Fellow Chartered Soc. Designers (Eng.); mem. Am. Soc. Interior Designers (profl., chpt. bd. dirs. 1983-87, 89-91, chmn. Avanti 1983-85, admissions chmn. 1985—, Presdl. citations 1984, 87, 91, 95, 97), Knights of Vine. Avocations: bicycling, antiques, fine wines, philately, theatre. Home and Office: 18005 Rancho St Encino CA 91316-4214

RANCK, JOHN STEVENS, human resources executive, consultant; b. Warren, Ohio, Sept. 14, 1945; s. Charles Thomas and Helen Marie (Weir) R.; m. Bibbie-Ann Rose Robertson, Dec. 25, 1975; children: James L., Edward L. BS, USAF Acad., 1971; MS in Human Resources, Gonzaga U., 1979, MBA, 1984. Cert. adminstrv. mgr.; sr. profl. in human resources mgmt. Salesman Neal's Family Shoes, Warren, 1964-65; prodn. staff Packard Elec. div. GMC, Warren, 1965-66; personnel mgr. United Paint Mfg., Inc., Greenacres, Wash., 1981-82; personnel dir. Sheraton-Spokane Hotel, 1982-83; personnel mgr. Students Book Corp., Pullman, Wash., 1984-87; personnel analyst Spokane Co., 1988-90; pres. Top Ranck Mgmt., Spokane and Loon Lake, Wash., 1990—; v.p., sec.-treas. TONGA Coffee, Co., 1993; pres. ArabiCafe, Inc., 1993-94. Active Stevens County Rep. Com. Capt. USAF, 1966-80. Paul Harris fellow, 1992. Mem. Am. Compensation Assn., Internat. Pers. Mgmt. Assn., S.W. Human Recourse Mgmt. Assn. (exec. bd. 1989-93, treas. 1993, legis. liaison 1991-92, v.p. programs 1990, coll. rels. com. 1989), Soc. Human Resource Mgmt., Mensa, Masons (Knight York Grand Cross of Honor, Order of Purple Cross, Knight Comdr. Ct. of Honor), K.T. (grand comdr. 1987-88), Red Cross Constantine, Royal Order Scotland, Shriners, Grotto, Loon Lake Health Assn. (bd. dirs. 1997—). Lutheran. Home: 40151 Morgan Rd PO Box 297 Loon Lake WA 99148-0297 Office: Top Ranck Mgmt 2400 N Wilbur Rd Apt 152 Spokane WA 99206-6663

RANDALL, (ISAAC) ERIC, real estate broker; b. N.Y.C., Nov. 6, 1933; s. Samuel and Rebekah (Stern) R.; m. Dianne Vincent, Oct. 19, 1967; children: Michelle, Michael. B of Chem. Engring., CCNY, 1956; MSChemE, Purdue U., 1957; MBA, U. So. Calif., 1975. Lic. real estate broker; registered profl. engr., Calif. Project engr. Rockwell Internat., Canoga Park, Calif., 1958-70; project mgr. Bechtel Corp., Norwalk, Calif., 1970-75, 90-96; project mgtr. CF Braun & Co., Alhambra, Calif., 1975-90; owner Randall Investments, Palos Verdes, Calif., 1978-91; real estate broker Coldwell Banker, Palos Verdes, Calif., 1995—; dir. L.A. County Bd. Realtors, 1996—. Fin. chmn. Rolling Hills United Meth. Ch., 1985-87; chmn. Rancho Palos Verdes Recreation and Pks. Com., 1988-92; dir. Palos Verdes Land Conservancy, 1996—, Pacific View Homeowners Assn., Palos Verdes, 1993-97. 1st lt. U.S. Army, 1957-63. Republican. Methodist. Avocation: hiking. Home: 6528 Madeline Cove Dr Rancho Palos Verdes CA 90275

RANDALL, HELEN AU, biologist, researcher, editor; b. Wahiawa, Hawaii, Apr. 30, 1927; d. William Wen and Kam Oi (Fong) Au; m. John Ernest Randall, Nov. 9, 1951; children: Loreen Ann, Rodney Dean. BA in Biology cum laude, Boston U., 1949, MA in Biology, 1950. Asst. in zoology U. Hawaii, Honolulu, 1950-51, grad. asst. in zoology, 1951-52, 53-55, sci. illustrator, 1952-53; rsch. asst. U. Miami, Key Biscayne, Fla., 1959-61; rsch. librarian Oceanic Inst., Waimanalo, Hawaii, 1965-66; jr. marine biologist U. Hawaii, Kaneohe, 1966-69; adminstrv. asst. Office Econ. Opportunity, Kaneohe, Hawaii, 1972-74, ICLARM, Honolulu, 1975-77; mng. editor, rsch. asst. B.P. Bishop Mus., Honolulu, 1972—. Contbr. articles to profl. jours. Office: Bernice P Bishop Mus 1525 Bernice St Honolulu HI 96817-2704

RANDALL, WILLIAM B., manufacturing company executive; b. Phila., Jan. 8, 1921; s. Albert and Ann (Fine) R.; m. Geraldine Kempson, Aug. 10, 1943; children: Robert, Erica Lynn, Lisa. Student, Rider Coll., Trenton, N.J., 1940-41. Gen. Sales mgr. Lowres Optical Mfg. Co., Newark, 1946-49; pres., founder Rand Sales Co., N.Y.C., 1949-58; gen. mgr. Sea & Ski Co. div. Botany Industries, Inc., Millbrae, Calif., 1958-61; pres., dir. Botany Industries, Inc., 1961-66, v.p., 1961-65; pres. Renauld of France, Reno, 1967-68; chmn. bd. Renauld Internat., Reading, Pa., 1963-65; pres., chief operating officer Renauld Internat., Ltd., Burlingame and Reno, 1966-67; pres., chmn. bd. Randall Internat., Ltd. 1967-68; sr. exec. v.p. Forty-two Prods. Ltd., 1969-71; pres. Exec. Products Internat. Ltd., 1969-71, New Product Devel. Ctr., Carlsbad, Calif., 1971—; pres. Internat. Concept Ctr. Exec. Products Internat. Ltd., Irvine, 1971—; pres. Sun Research Ctr., 1974—; pres. La Costa Products Internat., 1975-86; mng. dir. merchandising La Costa Hotel and Spa, 1986-88; pres., chief exec. officer Randall Internat., Carlsbad, 1989—; bd. dirs. Bank of La Costa, Garden Botanika. Served to 1st lt., navigator USAAF, 1942-45. Mem. Am. Mgmt. Assn., Nat. Wholesale Druggists Assn., Nat. Assn. Chain Drug Stores, Hon. Order Ky. Cols., Baja Beach and Tennis Club (bd. dirs.). Home: 7150 Arenal Ln Carlsbad CA 92009-6701

RANDHAWA, BIKKAR SINGH, psychologist, educator; b. Jullundur, India, June 14, 1933; came to Can., 1961, naturalized, 1966; s. Pritam S. and Sawaran K. (Basakhi) R.; m. Leona Emily Bujnowski, Oct. 8, 1966; children—Jason, Lisa. BA in Math., Panjab U., 1954, BT in Edn., 1955, MA in History, 1959; BEd, U. Alta., Can., 1963; MEd in Measurement and Evaluation, U Toronto, 1967, PhD, 1969. Registered psychologist. Tchr. secondary sch. math. Panjab, 1955-61; asst. headmaster, then headmaster, 1955-61; tchr. high sch. math. and sci. Beaver County, Riley, Alta., 1964-65, Camrose County, Alta., 1961-64; tchr. high sch. math. and sci. Edmonton (Alta.) Public Schs., 1965-67; tutor in math. for social sci. Ont. Inst. Studies in Edn., Toronto, 1968-69; mem. faculty U. Sask., Saskatoon, 1969-76, 77—; prof. edul. psychology U. Sask., 1977—; assoc. dean research and field services, 1982-87; prof., coord. Visual Scholars' Program, U. Iowa, 1976-77; cons. in field. Contbr. articles profl. jours. Fellow APA, Am. Psychol. Soc. (charter), Can. Psychol. Assn.; mem. Am. Edul. Rsch. Assn., Can. Edul. Rsch. Assn. (pres. 1997-99), Can. Soc. Study Edn., Sask. Psychol. Assn., Phi Delta Kappa (mem. Saskatoon chpt. 1971-78), Home: 510 Garrult Crescent Dr, Saskatoon, SK Canada S7N OX1

RANDISI, ELAINE MARIE, accoutant, educator, writer; b. Racine, Wis., Dec 19, 1926; d. John Dewey and Alveta Irene (Raffety) Fehd; AA,

Pasadena Jr. Coll., 1946; BS cum laude (Giannini scholar), Golden Gate U., 1978; m. John Paul Randisi, Oct. 12, 1946 (div. July 1972); children: Jeanine Randisi Manson, Martha Randisi Chaney (dec.), Joseph, Paula, Catherine Randisi Carvalho, George, Anthony (dec.); m. John R. Woodfin, June 18, 1994. With Raymond Kaiser Engrs., Inc., Oakland, Calif., 1969-75, 77-86, corp. acct., 1978-79, sr. corp. acct., 1979-82, sr. payroll acct., 1983-86, acctg. mgr., Lilli Ann Corp., San Francisco, 1986-89, Crosby, Heafey, Roach & May, Oakland, Calif., 1990-98; corp. buyer Kaiser Industries Corp., Oakland, 1975-77; lectr. on astrology Theosophical Soc., San Francisco, 1979—; mem. faculty Am. Fedn. Astrologers Internat. Conv., Chgo., 1982, 84. Mem. Speakers Bur., Calif. Assn. for Neurologically Handicapped Children, 1964-70, v.p. 1969; bd. dirs. Ravenwood Homeowners Assn., 1979-82, v.p., 1979-80, sec., 1980-81; mem. organizing com. Minority Bus. Fair, San Francisco, 1976; pres., bd. dirs. Lakewood Condominium Assn., 1984-87; mem., trustee Ch. of Religious Sci., 1992-95; treas. First Ch. Religious Sci., 1994-98. Mem. Am. Fedn. Astrologers, Calif. Scholarship Fedn. (life), Alpha Gamma Sigma (life). Mem. Ch. of Religious Sci. (lic. practioner pres. 1990-91, sec. 1989-90). Initiated Minority Vendor Purchasing Program for Kaiser Engrs., Inc., 1975-76. Home: 742 Wesley Way Apt 1C Oakland CA 94610-2339

RANDLE, ELLEN EUGENIA FOSTER, opera and classical singer, educator; b. New Haven, Conn., Oct. 2, 1948; d. Richard A.G. and Thelma Lousie (Brooks) Foster; m. Ira James William, 1967 (div. 1972); m. John Willis Randle, Dec. 24, 1983. Student, Calif. State Coll., Sonoma, 1970; studied with Boris Goldovsky, 1970; student, Grad. Sch. Fine Arts, Florence, Italy, 1974; studied with Tito Gobbi, Florence, 1974; student, U. Calif., Berkeley, 1977; BA in World History, Lone Mountain Coll., 1976, MA in Performing Arts, 1978; studied with Madam Eleanor Steber, Graz, Austria, 1979; studied with Patricia Goehl, Munich, Fed. Republic Germany, 1979; MA in Counseling and Psychology, U. San Francisco, 1990, MA in Marriage and Family Therapy, 1994, EdD, 1998. Asst. artistic dir. Opera Piccola, Oakland, Calif., 1990-92; instr. African Am. culture and humanities Mission C.C., Santa Clara, Calif.; instr. Peralta C.C. Dist., Oakland, 1996—, West Valley-Misson C.C. Dist., Saratoga, Calif.; instr. East Bay Performing Art Ctr., Richmond, Calif., 1986, Chapman Coll., 1986, Mission C.C., Santa Clara, Calif., 1997—. Singer opera prodns. Porgy & Bess, Oakland, Calif., 1980-81, LaTraviata, Oakland, Calif., 1981-82, Aida, Oakland, 1981-82, Madame Butterfly, Oakland, 1982-83, The Magic Flute, Oakland, 1984, numerous others; performances include TV specials, religous concerts, musicals; music dir. Natural Man, Berkeley, 1986; asst. artistic dir. Opera Piccola, Oakland, Calif., 1990—. Art commr. City of Richmond, Calif. Recipient Bk. Am. Achievement award. Mem. Music Tchrs. Assn., Internat. Black Writers and Artists Inc. (life mem., local #5), Nat. Coun. Negro Women, Nat. Assn. Negro Musicians, Calif. Arts Fedn., Calif. Assn. for Counseling and Devel. (mem. black caucus), Nat. Black Child Devel. Inst., The Calif.-Nebraskan Orgn., Inc., Calif. Marital & Family Therapist Assn. (San Francisco chpt.), Black Psychotherapist of San Francisco and East Bay Area, San Francisco Commonwealth Club, Gamma Phi Delta. Democrat. Mem. A.M.E. Zion Ch. Avocations: cooking, entertaining. Home: 5314 Boyd Ave Oakland CA 94618-1112

RANDOLPH, KEVIN H., marketing executive; b. Seattle, July 6, 1949; s. Howard Amos and Betty Elaine (Leahy) R.; m. Deborah Lou Newell, Sept. 18, 1976; children: Heather, Lyndsay. BA, Wash. State U., 1972. Mgr. Computers for Mktg., L.A., 1972-74; data processing mgr. Parker Rsch., Pasadena, Calif., 1974-77; prin. Randolph & Assocs., L.A., 1977-79; v.p. Bank Am. Corp., San Francisco, 1979-87, Interactive Network, Mountain View, Calif., 1987-91; sr. v.p. ICTV, Santa Clara, Calif., 1991-93; pres. Randolphs.Com., San Ramon, Calif., 1993—; v.p. U.S. West Mrg., Inc., Benicia, Calif., 1993-94; exec. v.p., COO Interactive Video Enterprises, Inc., San Ramon, 1994-95; cons. Randolph Home Ctr., Ephrata, Wash., 1972—. Mem. Am. Mktg. Assn., Am. Mgmt. Assn. Home: 170 Edinburgh Cir Danville CA 94526-2906

RANDOLPH, STEVEN, insurance and estate planner; b. Nebr., Oct. 14, 1946; m. Sherri Hamrick, 1980 (div. 1989); children: David, John, Michelle; m. Kathleen Riley, 1991. BS, U. Nebr., 1971. Registered rep. Nat. Assn. Securities Dealers, SEC; lic. in variable annuities, ins. and disabilities. Rep. Real Estate Consulting Svcs., Inc., Newport Beach, Calif., 1971-86; fin. advisor Agy. Fin. Svcs., Newport Beach, Calif., 1986—. With USMC, 1964-68, Vietnam. Mem. Nat. Assn. Securities Dealers, Nat. Assn. Life Underwriters (Nat. Sales Achievement award, Nat. Quality award), Million Dollar Round Table Club, Pres.'s Club (awards). Avocations: cooking, travel, watersports, sports cars. Fax: (949) 768-2000. Home and Office: PO Box 9612 Newport Beach CA 92658-9612

RANKIN, HELEN CROSS, cattle rancher, guest ranch executive; b. Mojave, Calif; d. John Whisman and Cleo Rebecca (Tilley) Cross; m. Leroy Rankin, Jan. 4, 1936 (dec. 1954); children—Julia Jane, Patricia Helen Denvir, William John. A.B., Calif. State U.-Fresno, 1935. Owner, operator Rankin Cattle Ranch, Caliente, Calif., 1954—; founder, pres. Rankin Ranch, Inc., Guest Ranch, 1965—; mem. sect. 15, U.S. Bur. Land Mgmt.; mem. U.S. Food and Agrl. Leaders Tour China, 1983, Australia and N.Z., 1985; dir. U.S. Bur. Land Mgmt. sect. 15. Pres., Children's Home Soc. Calif., 1945; mem. adv. bd. Camp Ronald McDonald. Recipient award Calif. Hist. Soc., 1983, Kern River Valley Hist. Soc., 1983. Mem. Am. Nat. Cattlemen's Assn., Calif. Cattlemen's Assn., Kern County Cattlemen's Assn., Kern County Cowbelles (pres. 1949, Cattlewoman of Yr. 1988), Calif. Cowbelles, Nat. Cowbelles, Bakersfield Country Club, Bakersfield Raquet Club. Republican. Baptist. Office: Rankin Ranch Caliente CA 93518

RANKIN, JAMES PATRICK, financial services company executive; b. Morris Plains, N.J., Jan. 25, 1957; s. Bernard James and Carol Joyce (Cooper) R.; m. Rebecca R. Samuel, May 11, 1989. BS, U. Calif., Davis, 1980; postgrad., U. Calif., Berkeley, 1981-83; MBA, Harvard U., 1986. Mgr. Wells Fargo Bank, San Francisco, 1979-84; asst. v.p. First Interstate Bank, L.A., 1986-88; v.p. T. Rowe Price, L.A., 1988-93; v.p., chmn. oper. com. Founders Asset Mgmt., Denver, 1993—. Active Tudor-Colo. Cmty. Ch. Whiz Kids, 1995—; bd. mem. A-T Children's Project, Boca Raton, Fla. Mem. Harvard Bus. Sch. Club Denver. Avocations: skiing, cycling, traveling. Home: 352 Paradise Rd Golden CO 80401-9455 Office: Founders Asset Mgmt Inc 2930 E 3d Ave Denver CO 80206-5002

RANKIN, JIMMIE R., neuroscience nurse; b. Auburn, Calif., May 22, 1941; s. Gilbert O. and Wilma E. (Robertson) R. MSN, U. Calif., San Francisco, 1989; BSN, USNY, 1983; BA, U. Calif., Berkeley, 1969; BS in Psychology, ASN, USNY, Albany, 1977. Staff nurse Neurol. Inst., N.Y.C.; ind. nurse, prin. Dry Bones Nursing BBS, Dry Bones Press, San Francisco; dir. nursing Pacific Coast Hosp., San Francisco. Mem. AANN. Home: 70 Yerba Buena Ave San Francisco CA 94127-1544

RANKIN, WILLIAM PARKMAN, educator, former publishing company executive; b. Boston, Feb. 6, 1917; s. George William and Bertha W. (Clowe) R.; m. Ruth E. Gerard, Sept. 12, 1942; children: Douglas W., Joan W. BS, Syracuse U., 1941; MBA, NYU, 1949, PhD, 1979. Sales exec. Redbook mag., N.Y.C., 1945-49; sales exec. This Week mag., N.Y.C., 1949-55, adminstrv. exec., 1955-60, v.p., 1957-60, v.p., dir. advt. sales, sales devel. dir., 1960-63, exec. v.p., 1963-69; gen. exec. newspaper div. Time Inc., N.Y.C., 1969-70; gen. mgr. feature svc. Newsweek, Inc., N.Y.C., 1970-74, fin. and ins. advt. mgr., 1974-81; prof., asst. to the dir. Walter Cronkite Sch. Journalism and Telecommunication, Ariz. State U., Tempe, 1981-98, prof. emeritus, also bd. dirs.; lectr. Syracuse U., NYU, Berkeley Sch. Author: Selling Retail Advertising, 1944; The Technique of Selling Magazine Advertising, 1949; Business Management of Consumer Magazines, 1980, 2 ed. 1984, The Practice of Newspaper Management, 1986. Mem. Dutch Treat Club. Home: 1220 E Krista Way Tempe AZ 85284-1545 also: PO Box 597 Rustics Rd Bomoseen VT 05732 Office: Ariz State U Walter Cronkite Sch Journalism/Telecom Tempe AZ 85287-1305

RANSOM, GAYLORD RICK, structural engineer; b. Redwood City, Calif., Feb. 3, 1953; . Gaylord Pat and Yola Grace (Old) R.; m. Linette Diane Pauls, June 25, 1984 (d ec. Sept., 1992); children: Anna, Brent, Sarah, Kimberly, Amy, Rebecca; m. Karla Jean Lauck, Feb. 7, 1993. BS in Civil Engring., Calif. State U., Fresno, 1977. Civil engr. intern III City of Fresno, Calif., 1973-75; engr. aide II City of Fresno, 1975-76, civil engineer I, 1976-78, structural engr. III, 1978-80, chief structural engr., 1980-83, dep. city engr., 1982-83, asst. dep. dir. inspections, 1980-83; prin. Ransom, Boone & Assocs., Fresno, 1976-83; assoc. William Brooks Assocs., Fresno, 1983-95; pres. Brooks, Ransom & Assocs., Fresno, 1995—. Chmn. CSUF Engring. adv. com., Fresno, 1995—. Mem. Structural Engrs. of Calif. (bd. dirs.), Calif. Soc. Profl. Engrs. (pres. 1981-82), Nat. Soc. Profl. Engrs., Internat. Conf. of Bldg. Officials. Republican. Baptist. Avocations: firearms, hunting, fishing, 4-wheel drive. Office: Brooks Ransom Assocs 100 E Shaw Ave # Ate155 Fresno CA 93710-7608

RAO, JAYANTH PEECHARA, mechanical engineer, consultant; b. Thornal, Medak, India, Apr. 15, 1941; came to U.S., 1964; s. Bapu Peechara and Venkatamma (Parvathi Neni) Rao; m. Bharathi Cheeti Rao, Aug. 13, 1964; children: Padma, Sham. BS, Osmania U., Hyderabad, India, 1964; MSME, Okla. State U., 1965. Registered mechanical engr., profl. engr., Tex. Project engr. Unit Rig & Equipment Co., Tulsa, Okla., 1968-71; engring. mgr. Clark Equipment co., Aurora, Ill., 1971-78, Armco-Baylor Co., Sugarland, Tex., 1978-85; engring. specialist Loral Defense Sys., Goodyear, Ariz., 1985-90; engr., cons. Honeywell, Phoenix, 1990-93; chief engr. Cox Reels, Tempe, Ariz., 1993-96; engr. specialist Lockheed-Martin TDS, Goodyear, Ariz., 1996—. Patentee in field. Home: 507 E Sagebrush St Litchfield Park AZ 85340-4810 Office: Lockheed Martin TDS 1300 S Litchfield Rd Goodyear AZ 85338-1528

RAO, KAMESWARA KOLLA, physicist, electrical engineer; b. Kasimkota, Andhra, India, July 28, 1944; came to U.S., 1970; s. Subbarao and Ammaji (Paluri) Kolla; m. Vasavi Namburi, Nov. 17, 1972; children: Swathi, Sandhya, Preethi, Srinivas. BS in Physics with honors, Andhra U., 1963, MSc in Physics, 1964; MS in Physics, U. Wis., 1972, PhD, 1975. Asst. prof. physics Western Mich. U., Kalamazoo, 1975-79; staff engr. Nat. Semicondr. Co., Santa Clara, Calif., 1979-81; sect. head engr. Signetics, Sunnyvale, Calif., 1981-83; project mgr. Intel., Santa Clara, Calif., 1983-86; dir. design Catalyst Semicondr. Inc., Santa Clara, 1986-94, Xilinox, San Jose, Calif., 1994—. Inventor design techniques in non-volatile memory integrated circuits. Mem. IEEE. Office: 2100 Logic Dr San Jose CA 95124-3450

RAO, SULEKHA, molecular biologist, researcher; b. Madras, India, July 30, 1962; came to U.S., 1988; d. Sreedhara and Padma R. BS, Miranda House, Delhi, 1983; MS, Indian Inst. Tech., New Delhi, 1985; PhD, U. Minn., 1994. Postdoc. rschr. dept. immunology U. Calif., Berkeley, 1996—. Contbr. articles to Protein Expression Purification, Gene, Jour. Gen. Microbiology. Biochem. Engring. Rsch. Ctr. fellow Indian Inst. Tech., New Delhi, 1985-86, Sr. Rsch. fellow, 1986-88, Blackie Floyd Cancer Rsch. fellow Hipple Cancer Rsch. Ctr., Dayton, Ohio, 1994-95. Mem. AAAS, Am. Assn. Cancer Rsch., Am. Assn. Immunologists. Avocations: art, photography. Office: U Calif 435 Life Scis Addition Berkeley CA 94720

RAPHAEL, MARTIN GEORGE, research wildlife biologist; b. Denver, Oct. 5, 1946; s. Jerome Maurice and Alys (Salmonson) R.; m. Susan Williams, August 4, 1967; 1 child, Samantha Marie. BA, Sacramento State U., 1968; BS, U. Calif., Berkeley, 1972, MS, 1976, PhD, 1980. Staff research assoc. U. Calif., Berkeley, 1974-80, assoc. specialist, 1980-84; project leader USDA Forest Svc., Laramie, 1984-89, Olympia, Wash., 1989—; adj. prof. U. Wyo., Laramie, 1986-89; cons. ecologist Pacific Gas and Electric Co., San Ramon, Calif., 1981-84. Contbr. articles to sci. jours. Mem. Ecol. Soc. Am. (editl. bd. Ecol. Applications), Soc. for Conservation Biology, Am. Ornithologists' Union, Cooper Ornithol. Soc. (chmn. membership com. 1985-90, asst. sec. 1986—, bd. dirs. 1989-92), The Wildlife Soc. (local pres. publs. com. 1983-84, assoc. editor Wildlife Soc. Bull. 1987-90), Phi Beta Kappa, Sigma Xi, Xi Sigma Pi. Avocations: sailing, skiing, photography. Home: 3224 Biscay Ct NW Olympia WA 98502-3558 Office: Pacific NW Rsch Sta 3625 93rd Ave SW Olympia WA 98512-9145

RAPIER, PASCAL MORAN, chemical engineer, physicist; b. Atlanta, Jan. 11, 1914; s. Paul Edward and Mary Clare (Moran) R.; m. Martha Elizabeth Doyle, May 19, 1945; children: Caroline Elizabeth, Paul Doyle, Mollie Clare, John Lawrence, James Andrew. BSChemE, Ga. Inst. Tech., 1939; MS in Theoretical Physics, U. Nev., 1959; postgrad., U. Calif., Berkeley, 1961. Registered profl. engr., Calif., N.J. Plant engr. Archer-Daniels-Midland, Pensacola, Fla., 1940-42; group supr. Dicalite div. Grefco, Los Angeles, 1943-54; process engr. Celatom div. Eagle Picher, Reno, Nev., 1955-57; project mgr., assoc. research engr. U. Calif. Field Sta., Richmond, 1959-62; project mgr. sea water conversion Bechtel Corp., San Francisco, 1962-66; sr. supervising chem. engr. Burns & Roe, Oradell, N.J., 1966-74; cons. engr. Kenite Corp., Scarsdale, N.Y., Rees Blowpipe, Berkeley, 1960-66; sr. cons. engr. Sanderson & Porter, N.Y.C., 1975-77; staff scientist III Lawrence Berkeley Lab., 1977-84; bd. dirs. Newtonian Sci. Found.; v.p. Calif. Rep. Assembly, 1964-65; discoverer phenomena faster than light, origin of cosmic rays and galactic red shifts. Contbr. articles to profl. jours.; patentee agts. to render non-polar solvents electrically conductive, direct-contact geothermal energy recovery devices; contbr. Marks' Standard Handbook for Mechanical Engineers, 10th edit., 1996. Mem. Am. Inst. Chem. Engrs., Gideons Internat., Lions Internat., Corvallis, Sigma Pi Sigma. Home: 8015 NW Ridgewood Dr Corvallis OR 97330-3026

RAPP, NINA BEATRICE, financial company executive; b. Copenhagen, Denmark, Sept. 3, 1958; came to the U.S., 1984; d. Sven Ove Lars Larsen and Kirsten Rung Mechik; m. Steven Douglas Rapp, July 14, 1984; 1 child, Stepanie Beatrice. BA in Econs. and Polit. Sci., Danish Royal Mil. Acad., 1982; MBA in Fin., Harvard U., 1990. Cert. explosives expert; lic. ins. and securites rep. Cons. Mei & Assocs., Waltham, Mass., 1987-88; leasing mgr. Wright Runstad & Co., Seattle, 1990-92; regional v.p. Primerica Fin. Svcs., Seattle, 1992—; ptnr. R & R Assocs., Seattle, 1990-93. Author: International Terrorism, 1982. Capt. Danish Army, 1977-82, lt., 1982-84. Mem. NAFE. Avocations: estate bldg., tchg., tng., profl. speaking. Home: 6516 163rd St SW Lynnwood WA 98037-2717 Office: Primerica Fin Svcs 21911 64th Ave W # C Mountlake Terrace WA 98043-2278

RAPPAPORT, GEORGE LEE, communications executive, retired; b. Trenton, N.J., Dec. 19, 1920; s. Morris and Gertrude (Scull) R.; m. Mary Virginia Page, June 11, 1947; children: Robert Davis, Ross Lee. Student, Pa. Acad. Fine Arts, 1939-40, Pratt Inst., 1945-46, Art Ctr. Coll. Design, 1946-47. Asst. art dir. Dozier, Graham, Eastman, L.A., 1948-49; art dir. Edward J. Robinson, L.A., 1949-50, Anderson-McConnell, L.A., 1950-53; art dir., creative dir. Calkins & Holden, N.Y.C., L.A., 1953-63; pres., owner George Rappaport Graphic Design Cons., L.A., 1963-67; head creative TV group Carson/Roberts, L.A., 1967-70; mng. dir. Lee Lacy, Ltd., London, 1970-72; founder, chmn. bd. Multi Media Presentations, Culver City, Calif., 1972-85; ret., 1985; bass player Trenton Symphony, 1937-41, MCA Orch., 1944-45. Art dir., designer (advertisements) Voice of Free Choice (Gold medal, 1964), Elizabeth Stewart Swimwear (Gold medal, 1965). Served with USAF, 1941-44. Numerous awards from Art Dirs. Clubs of N.Y.C., L.A. and Chgo. including Distinctive Merit award, Art Dirs. Club N.Y., 1943, Communications Arts Mag., 1963. Mem. L.A. Art Dirs. Club (life mem., pres. 1956-57, medal 1964, 65), Soc. Art Ctr. Coll. of Design Alumni (pres. 1962-63), Nat. Acad. Jazz (pres. 1987-88), Acad. TV Arts and Scis. Democrat. Unitarian. Avocations: tennis, playing with community symphony and small jazz combos.

RASCÓN, ARMANDO, artist; b. Calexico, Calif., Dec. 9, 1956; s. Reynoldo and Maria (Herrera) R. BFA Coll. Creative Studies, U. Calif., Santa Barbara, 1979. Owner Terrain Gallery, San Francisco, 1988—; guest faculty dept. art U. Calif., Davis, 1988, Calif. Coll. Arts and Crafts, Oakland, 1991, dept. art practice U. Calif., Berkeley, 1995; juror, panelist Artist Trust Fellowship Grants, Visual Arts, Seattle, 1994; lectr. N.Y. Mus. Modern Art, 1995; panelist LEF Found. Orgn. Grants, Cambridge, Mass., 1996, Nev. State Coun. on the Arts Grants, Carson City, 1996, 97; v.p. San Francisco Art Commn., 1996-97; presenter various lectrs., panels, workshops, confs. One-man shows include Randolph Street Gallery, Chgo., 1991, INTAR, N.Y., 1994, San Diego Mus. Contemporary Art, 1997, Blue Star Art Space, San Antonio, 1998. Bd. dirs. New Langton Arts, San Francisco, 1988-92; vice-chair Art Commn. City of San Francisco, 1997. Recipient Hazel S. Lagerson scholarship U. Calif., Santa Barbara, 1975, fellowship grant in painting Nat. Endowment for Arts, Washington, 1987, Adaline Kent award San Francisco Art Inst., 1994, Goldie award in visual art San Francisco Bay Guardian, 1994. Home & Office: 165 Jessie St Ste 2 San Francisco CA 94105-4008

RASMUSON, BRENT (JACOBSEN), photographer, graphic artist, lithographer; b. Logan, Utah, Nov. 28, 1950; s. Eleroy West and Fae (Jacobsen) R.; m. Tess Bullen, Sept. 30, 1981; children: John, Mark, Lisa. Grad. auto repair and painting sch., Utah State U. Pre-press supr. Herald Printing Co., Logan, 1969-79; profl. drummer, 1971-75; owner, builder auto racing engines Valley Automotive Specialties, 1971-76; exec. sec. Herald Printing Co., 1979-89; owner Brent Rasmuson Photography, Smithfield, Utah, 1986—, Brent Rasmuson Temple Pictures, Smithfield, 1996—. Author photo prints of LDS temples: Logan, 1987, 95, 98, Manti, 1989, Jordan River, 1989, 96, 98, Provo, 1990, Mesa, Ariz., 1990, 96, Boise, Idaho, 1990, 96, Salt Lake LDS Temple, 1990, 96, Idaho Falls, 1991, 94, St. George, 1991, 93, Portland, Oreg., 1991, 96, 97, L.A., 1991, 96, 97, Las Vegas, Nev., 1991, Seattle, 1992, Oakland, Calif., 1993, 94, Ogden, 1992; author photo print: Statue of Angel Moroni, 1994; author photos used to make neckties and watch dials of LDS temples: Salt Lake, Manti, Logan, L.A., Oakland, Seattle, Las Vegas, Mesa, Portland, St. George, Jordan River, scenic tie Mammoth Hot Springs in Yellowstone Park, 1995; landscape scenic photographs featured in Best of Photography Ann., 1987, 88, 89, also in calendars and book covers; author photo print of Harris Rsch., Inc. Internat. Hdqrs. (recipient 1st prize nat. archtl. photo competition); designer several bus. logos. Mem. Internat. Platform Assn., Assoc. Photographers Internat., Internat. Freelance Photographers Orgn., Nat. Trust Hist. Preservation. Republican. Mem. LDS Ch. Avocations: landscape design, reading, audio and video recording and mixing, music percussion, philately. Home and Office: 40 N 200 E Smithfield UT 84335-1543

RASMUSON, ELMER EDWIN, banker, former mayor; b. Yakutat, Alaska, Feb. 15, 1909; s. Edward Anton and Jenny (Olson) R.; m. Lile Vivian Bernard, Oct. 27, 1939 (dec. 1960); children: Edward Bernard, Lile Muchmore (Mrs. John Gibbons, Jr.), Judy Ann; m. Col. Mary Louise Milligan, Nov. 4, 1961. BS magna cum laude, Harvard U., 1930, AM, 1935; student, U. Grenoble, 1930; LLD, U. Alaska, 1970, Alaska Pacific U., 1993. C.P.A., N.Y., Tex., Alaska. Chief accountant Nat. Investors Corp., N.Y.C., 1933-35; prin. Arthur Andersen & Co., N.Y.C., 1935-43; pres. Nat. Bank of Alaska, 1943-65, chmn. bd., 1966-74, chmn. exec. com., 1975-82, now chmn. emeritus; mayor City of Anchorage, 1964-67, dir., emeritus and cons., 1989; civilian aide from Alaska to sec. army, 1959-67; Swedish consul Alaska, 1955-77; Chmn. Rasmuson Found.; Rep. nominee U.S. Senate from Alaska, 1968; U.S. commr. Internat. N. Pacific Fisheries Commn., 1969-84; mem. Nat. Marine Fisheries Adv. Com., 1974-77, North Pacific Fishery Mgmt. Council, 1976-77, U.S. Arctic Research Commn., 1984-92. Mem. City Coun. Anchorage, 1945, chmn. city planning commn., 1950-53; pres. Alaska coun. Boy Scouts Am., 1953; regent U. Alaska, 1950-69; trustee King's Lake Camp, Inc., 1944—, Alaska Permanent Fund Corp., 1980-82; bd. dirs. Nat. Mus. Natural History Smithsonian Inst. 1994-97. Decorated knight first class Order of Vasa, comdr. Sweden; recipient silver Antelope award Boy Scouts Am., Japanese citation Order of the Sacred Treasure, Gold and Silver Star, 1988; outstanding civilian service medal U.S. Army; Alaskan of Year award, 1976. Mem. Pioneers Alaska, Alaska Bankers Assn. (past pres.), Defense Orientation Conf. Assn., NAACP, Alaska Native Brotherhood, Explorers Club, Phi Beta Kappa. Republican. Presbyn. Clubs: Masons, Elks, Anchorage Rotary (past pres.); Harvard (N.Y.C.; Boston); Wash. Athletic (Seattle), Seattle Yacht (Seattle), Rainier (Seattle); Thunderbird Country (Palm Desert, Calif.); Bohemian (San Francisco); Eldorado Country (Indian Wells, Calif.); Boone & Crockett. Home: PO Box 100600 Anchorage AK 99510-0600

RASMUSSEN, NEIL WOODLAND, insurance agent; b. Portland, Oreg., Sept. 14, 1926; s. Ernest Roy and Lulu Mildred (Woodland) R.; m. Mary Ann Cannon, Aug. 10, 1957; children: Kirk, Sally, P. Cannon, Eric (dec.). BA, Stanford U., 1949. Registered mut. funds rep. Warehouseman Consol. Supply Co., Portland, Oreg., 1949-50, sales rep., 1955-56; sales rep. Consol. Supply Co., Eugene, Oreg., 1950-52; sales rep. Consol. Supply Co., Salem, Oreg., 1956-64, br. mgr., 1964-82; agt. life and health ins. N.Y. Life Ins. Co., Salem, 1982—. Lt. Cmdr. USN, 1952-55; officer U.S. Selective Svc. Res., 1969-73. Recipient Nat. Quality award Nat. Assn. Life Underwriters, 1986-88. Mem. Salem Assn. Life Underwriters, Res. Officers Assn. (bd. dirs. 1988-91, v.p. 1988-91), Rotary (bd. dirs. East Salem 1980-83, sr. active mem. 1990-92, Paul Harris fellow). Republican. Episcopalian. Avocations: golf, fishing, camping. Office: NY Life Ins Co 530 Center St NE Salem OR 97301-3744

RASMUSSEN, THOMAS VAL, JR., lawyer, small business owner; b. Salt Lake City, Aug. 11, 1954; s. Thomas Val and Georgia (Smedley) R.; m. Donita Gubler, Aug. 15, 1978; children: James, Katherine, Kristin. BA magna cum laude, U. Utah, 1978, JD, 1981. Bar: Utah 1981, U.S. Dist. Ct. Utah 1981, U.S. Supreme Ct. 1985. Atty. Salt Lake Legal Defender Assn., Salt Lake City, 1981-83, Utah Power and Light Co., Salt Lake City, 1983-89, Hatch, Morton & Skeen, Salt Lake City, 1989-90; ptnr. Morton, Skeen & Rasmussen, Salt Lake City, 1991-94, Skeen & Rasmussen, Salt Lake City, 1994-97; pvt. practice Salt Lake City, 1997—; co-owner, developer Handi Self-Storage, Kaysville, Utah, 1984-93; instr. bus. law Brigham Young U., Salt Lake City, 1988-90. Adminstrv. editor Jour. Contemporary Law, 1980-81, Jour. Energy Law and Policy, 1980-81. Missionary Ch. of Jesus Christ of Latter-Day Sts., Brazil, 1973-75. Mem. Utah, Salt Lake County Bar Assn., Intermountain Miniature Horse Club (pres. 1989, 2d v.p. 1990), Phi Eta Sigma, Phi Kappa Phi, Beta Gamma Sigma. Avocations: tennis, scuba diving, showing horses, travel, collecting art. Home: 3094 Whitewater Dr Salt Lake City UT 84121-1561 Office: 4659 Highland Dr Salt Lake City UT 84117-5137

RATCLIFF, MARY ELIZABETH, computer company executive; b. Memphis, Dec. 16, 1965; d. William Delbert and Stella Virginia (Talbert) R.; m. David Leonard Blake, Dec. 11, 1984 (div. Apr., 1987); 1 child, David Leonard; m. Adam Terry Retana, Jan. 13, 1989; 1 child, Amanda Stella. Grad. high sch., Wayne, W. Va., 1984. Sales exec. AT&T, Jacksonville, Fla., 1984; jr. sales rep. Laser Digital, Inc., Sunnyvale, Calif., 1988-89; mktg., sales exec. Laser Digital, Inc., Sunnyvale, 1989-90, mktg., sales dir., 1990—, also vice chmn. bd. dirs., 1990—; cons. Career Advisors, 1990—. Author: Choosing the Right PC, 1991. Mem. NAFE. Republican. Avocations: electronics hobbyist, tennis, writing. Home: 1715 Cortez St Milpitas CA 95035-2846 Office: Laser Digital Inc 1030 E Duane Ave Ste H Sunnyvale CA 94086-2624

RATLIFF, JAMES CONWAY, hospitality consultant; b. Evanston, Ill., Mar. 28, 1940; s. Harold Sugart and Marjorie (Elmore) R. BA, Mich. State U., 1967. Dir. food & beverage ops. Detroit Hilton, 1970-71; dir. food & beverage purchasing Hilton Hotels Corp., N.Y.C., 1972-77; corp. dir. procurement Hilton Hotels Corp., Beverly Hills, Calif., 1977-97; pres. James Ratliff & Assocs., 1998—; bd. dirs. Am. Inst. Food Distbn., Fair Lawn, N.J., 1985-96, treas., 1989-90, vice chmn., 1991-92, chmn., 1994-95; instr. Calif. State Poly. U., Pomona, 1987, 88. With U.S. Army, 1963-65. Mem. Food Svc. Purchasing Assn. Can. (hon.), Produce Mktg. Assn. (bd. dirs. 1986-88, v.p. 1989-90, sec.-treas. 1991, chmn. elect 1992, chmn. 1993, chmn. exec. com. 1994), Product Mktg. Assn. (chmn. foodsvc. divsn. 1989-90, bd. dirs. foodsvc. divsn. 1985-88), Nat. Restaurant Assn. Foodsvc. Purchasing Mgrs. (bd. dirs. 1977-81, chmn. 1981-83), Pacific Corinthian Yacht Club. Republican. Methodist. Avocation: tennis. Office: 3704 Surfwood Dr Malibu CA 90265-5655

RATLIFF, LEIGH ANN, pharmacist; b. Long Beach, Calif., May 20, 1961; d. Harry Warren and Verna Lee (Zwink) R. D in Pharmacy, U. Pacific, 1984. Registered pharmacist, Calif., Nev. Pharmacist intern Green Bros. Inc., Stockton, Calif., 1982-84, staff pharmacist Thrifty Corp., Long Beach, Calif., 1984-85, head pharmacist, 1986-87, pharm. buyer, 1987-92; pharmacy. mgr. Kmart Pharmacy, Long Beach, Calif., 1992-97; staff pharmacist Egyptian Pharmacy, Long Beach, Calif., 1996-97; dir. pharmacy rels. Morgan and Sampson Pacific, Los Alamitos, Calif., 1998—; mem. joint mktg. com. Calif. Pharmicist's Assn. Mem. Pacific Alumni Assocs., Nat. Trust for Hist. Preservation, Friends of Rancho Los Cerritos; treas. Bixby Knolls Ter. Homeowners Assn., 1988-92, pres. 1992-96; vol. Docent Rancho Los Cerritos Hist. Site, 1988—; vol. preceptor U. So. Calif. Sch. Pharmacy; vol. Fairfield YMCA, Long Beach. Mem. Am. Pharm. Assn., Am. Inst. History Pharmacy, Calif. Pharmacist Assn., Lambda Kappa Sigma. Republican. Methodist. Avocations: raising African cichlids, growing herbs, collecting Hull pottery, antiquing. Home: 6762 Warner Ave Apt B5 Huntington Beach

CA 92647-5317 Office: Morgan and Sampson Pacific 10572 Calle Lee Los Alamitos CA 90720-2551

RATZLAFF, VERNON PAUL, elementary education educator, consultant; b. Mt. Lake, Minn., May 16, 1925; s. Peter Benjamin and Helen (Dick) R.; m. Bonnie Lou Sommers, Dec. 17, 1955; children: Paul, Gwen, Jay, Peter. BA in Elem. Edn., German, Goshen Coll., 1954; MA, U. N.D., 1971; student, U. Minn., 1956-57, U. Oreg., 1965, U. No. Ariz., 1968. Cert. tchr. Elem. tchr. Richfield (Minn.) Pub. Schs., 1954-74; tchr. Tuba City (Ariz.) Pub. Sch., 1975—; resource person to tchrs., Grand Forks, N.C., 1970-72, resource person to upper elem. tchrs. and children, Richfield, 1967-70; adminstr. of Christian Sch. Hopi Mission, Oraibi, Ariz., 1971-75; math tchr. Nortland Pioneer Coll.; established "Look Folks-No Fail" classrooms. Author: Side by Side " Up from the Pit to Become a Shining Star" (Where Students Take Responsibility for Learning), 1990; contbr. articles to numerous jours. Mem. NEA, Ariz. Edn. Assn., Am. Assn. Retired People. Republican. Avocations: cooking, painting, writing, gardening, preaching. Home: 5743 Smoke Rise Dr Flagstaff AZ 86004-2746

RAU, RANDY J., firefighter; b. Denver, June 1, 1961; s. Robert M. and Roxanne C. (Follett) R.; m. Pamela Lynn Lubker, Aug. 14, 1984; children: Cameron, Cory. From apprentice firefighter to lt. firefighter Aurora (Colo.) Fire Dept., 1980—; tng. coord. Aurora Fire Dept., 1993-96. Bronze sculpture Fire Sta. #Z, City of Aurora, 1998. Mem. Internat. Assn. Fire Fighters, Fire Tng. Officers Assn. Avocations: outdoor, horseback riding, hunting. Home: 41575 Valley View Ct Elizabeth CO 80107-9203

RAUCINA, THOMAS FRANK See RACINA, THOM

RAUGHTON, JIMMIE LEONARD, educational foundation administrator, urban planner; b. Knoxville, Tenn., Oct. 9, 1943; s. George L. and Ann (Simotes) R. BA in Urban and Regional Planning, U. No. Colo., 1974, MA, 1976, PhD, U. Colo., 1993. Mgr., Flexitran div. Gathers, De Vilbliss Architects and Planners, 1966-68; asst. dir. planning City of Aurora, Colo., 1968-71; planner City of Lakewood, Colo., 1971-73; planner City of Boulder, Colo., 1973-74; instr. urban planning C.C. of Denver, 1974-76, div. dir. human resources and svcs., 1976-81, div. dir. sci. and tech., 1981-85; v.p. State of Colo. C.Cs., 1985—; exec. dir. Edn. Found. Colo., 1989—; coord. devel. Rocky Mountain Energy and Environ. Tech. Center, 1980. cons. Denver Regional Council of Govts. for Model Sign Code, 1973, City of Boulder Transp. Dept., 1975—; chmn. profl. advisory com. to Colo. Gov.'s Land Use Adviser, 1973; also public speaker. Mem. exec. bd. Civic Center Assn., Denver, 1973-75; supervisory com. Colo. State Employees Credit Union, 1986—;mem. bd. Support Systems Consol., 1984, Bridge Industry, 1984-85; candidate Denver City Council, 1975; bd. dirs. Plan Metro Denver, 1975-76, Four Corner Art Collection, 1973—. Recipient Citizen Award of Honor, Assn. of Beautiful Colo. Roads, 1972. Mem. Am. Inst. of Planners (mem. exec. bd. Colo. 1970-75, treas. 1972-73), Colo. City Mgrs. Assn., Am. Soc. Planning Ofcls., Am. Vocat. Assn., Am. Soc. for Tng. and Devel., Pi Alpha Alpha. Methodist. Contbr. articles to local newspapers. Home: 2501 High St Denver CO 80205-5565 Office: State of Colo CCs 1391 Speer Blvd Denver CO 80204-2508

RAUTENBERG, ROBERT FRANK, consulting statistician; b. Milw., Sept. 14, 1943; s. Raymond Clarence and Anna Josephine (Winter) R.; m. Meredith Taylor, June 2, 1965 (div. Feb. 1975); 1 child, Matthew Carl. PhD in Bus. Adminstrn., Pacific Western U., 1983; postdoctorate, Sorbonne U., Paris. Pvt. practice in acctg. Kansas City, Mo., 1975-76; pres. Seven Diamond Enterprises, Inc., San Francisco, 1976-78; CEO Assurance Sys., San Francisco, 1984-96, Probability Investigations, Honolulu, 1997—. Author: The Analytical Management Handbook, 1985, Supplement to the Analytical Management Handbook, 1991, London edit., 1996, A Bayesian Approach to Management, 1996; contbr. articles to profl. jours. and conf. proceedings. Named Internat. Man of Yr., Internat. Biog. Ctr., Cambridge, Eng., 1998. Mem. Internat. Statis. Inst., Bernoulli Soc. for Mathematical Statistics and Probability. Lutheran. Avocations: swimming, skiing, traveling, scuba diving (cert.). Office: Prob Investigations of Stats 1164 Bishop St Ste 210 Honolulu HI 96813-2810

RAVAL, RUCHIKA, regulatory affairs specialist; b. New Delhi, July 4, 1960; came to U.S., 1983; d. Raman and Rohini (Bhatt) R. MS in Microbiology, Wagner Coll., 1984. Med. technologist Jaslok Hosp., Bombay, 1980-82; rsch. scientist R & D Baxter Biotech, L.A., 1990-93, rsch. scientist quality control, 1993-94, rsch. scientist virology, 1994-96, regulatory affairs scientist, 1996—. Vol. educator M.S. U., Baroda, India, 1988-90. Mem. Am. Assn. Pharm. Scientists, Regulatory Affairs Profl. Soc., Toastmasters Club (sec. Diamond Bar chpt. 1996-97). Office: Baxter Healthcare Hyland Divsn 550 N Brand Blvd Glendale CA 91203-1900

RAVEN, ROBERT DUNBAR, lawyer; b. Cadillac, Mich., Sept. 26, 1923; s. Christian and Gladys L. (Dunbar) R.; m. Leslie Kay Erickson, June 21, 1947; children: Marta Ellen, Matt Robert, Brett Lincoln. AB with honors, Mich. State U., 1949; LLB, U. Calif., Berkeley, 1952. Bar: Calif. 1953. Assoc. Morrison & Foerster and predecessor, San Francisco, 1952-56, ptnr., 1956-94, sr. of counsel, 1994—; chmn. Morrison & Foerster (and predecessor), San Francisco, 1974-82; mem. Jud. Coun. of Calif., 1983-87. Bd. dirs. Bay Area USO, 1964-73, pres., 1968-70; mem. San Francisco Mayor's Criminal Justice Coun., 1971-72; co-chmn. San Francisco Lawyer's Com. for Urban Affairs, 1976-78; bd. dirs. Lawyers Com. for Civil Rights Under Law, 1976-96. With USAAF, 1942-45. Decorated Air medal with oak leaf cluster. Mem. ABA (pres. 1989, mem. standing com. fed. judiciary 1975-80, chmn. 1978-80, chmn. standing com. on legal aid and indigent defendants 1981-83, chair standing com. dispute resolution 1991-93, chair sect. dispute resolution 1993-94), FBA, Am. Arbitration Assn. (bd. dirs. 1988-96), CPR Inst. for Dispute Resolution (mem. exec. com.), Internat. Acad. Trial Lawyers, State Bar Calif. (gov. 1978-81, pres. 1981), Bar Assn. San Francisco (pres. 1971), Am. Law Inst., Am. Bar Found., Am. Judicature Soc., Boalt Hall Alumni Assn. (pres. 1972-73), World Trade Club (San Francisco), Order of Coif. Democrat. Home: 1064 Via Alta Lafayette CA 94549-2916 Office: Morrison & Foerster 425 Market St San Francisco CA 94105-2482*

RAVICHANDRAN, RAJAMIYER V., structural engineer; b. Karur, India, July 3, 1961; came to U.S., 1988; s. Vaidyanathan Rajamiyer and Seethalakshmi Vaidyanathan; m. Santhi Vejendla Ravichandran, Oct. 17, 1992; 1 child, Sindura. BE, Madurai (India) U., 1983; MTech, Indian Inst. Tech., Bombay, 1986; DSc, Washington U., St. Louis, 1993. Sci. asst. Indian Inst. Sci., Bangalore, 1984-85; scientist Structural Engring. Rsch. Ctr., Madras, India, 1987-88; rsch. engr. Engring. Mechs. Rsch. Corp., Troy, Mich., 1993-96; computer-aided engring. engr. Altair Engring., Inc., Troy, 1996-97, Computer Aided Design Software, Inc., San Jose, 1997—; ind. cons. in field, 1995—. Contbr. articles to profl. jours. Mem. ASCE. ASME. Hindu. Achievements include development of a local-global analytical methodology for efficient analysis of shells of revolution; development of a special nonlinear solution method for shells of revolution in the unstable equilibrium regime. Avocations: reading, classical music, photography.

RAWLINGS, ROBERT HOAG, newspaper publisher; b. Pueblo, Colo., Aug. 3, 1924; s. John W. and Dorothy (Hoag) R. Student Colo. U., 1943-44; BA, Colo. Coll., 1947; m. Mary Alexandra Graham, Oct. 18, 1947; children: Jane Louise, John Graham, Carolyn Anne, Robert Hoag II. Reporter Pueblo Chieftain and Pueblo Star-Jour., 1947-51, advt. rep. 1951-62, gen. mgr., 1962-79, pub. and editor, 1980—; sec. Star-Jour. Pub. Corp., 1962-84, pres., 1984—; Past chmn. bd. dir. Colo. Nat. Bank-Pueblo; bd. dir. U.S. Air Force Acad. Found., U. So. Colo. Found., Colo. Water Edn. Found.; pres. Robert Hoag Rawlings Found., So. Colo. Com. Found., Medal of Honor Meml. Com. Served with USNR, 1942-46. Named Colo. Newspaper Person of the Year, 1989, Disting. Univ. Fellow Pres. Club U. So. Colo., 1993, Outstanding Citizen of Yr. Pueblo C. of C., 1994, Colo. Bus. Leader of the Yr. Colo. Assn. of Commerce and Industry, 1994; recipient Outstanding Svc. to Univ. award U. So. Colo. Alumni Assn., 1993, Colo. Corp. Philanthropy award Nat. Philanthropy Assoc., 1993, Louis T. Benezet award Colo. Coll. Alumni Assn., 1996, Outstanding Am. Achievement award U. So. Colo., 1997; named Donor of Yr. Nat. Assn. Univ. Athletic Devel. Dirs., 1995, Creative Spirit award Pueblo United Way, 1998. Mem. Colo. Press Assn., (dir. 1963-66, 76-78, pres. 1985, chmn. bd. dirs. 1986, Golden Rule Makeup award 1998), Rocky Mountain Ad Mgrs. (past pres.), Colo. AP (past pres.), Colo. Forum, El Pomar Awards for Excellence Com., Colo. Mental Health Inst. Pueblo community planning com., Rotary. Presbyterian. Home: 27 Calle Del Sol Pueblo CO 81008-2047 Office: The Pueblo Cheiftain Star-Jour Pub Corp PO Box 4040 Pueblo CO 81003-0040

RAWLINS, ROBERT DANIEL, career officer; b. Bethlehem, Pa., Aug. 15, 1926; s. Daniel Thomas and Lillian Marguerite (Schwechten) R.; m. Margaret Connelley, Aug. 22, 1948 (div. July 25, 1996); 1 child, Teri Rawlins Cardell. BS, U.S. Naval Acad., 1947; MS in Electronics, U.S. Navy Postgrad. Sch., 1958. Commd. ensign USN, 1947; advanced through grades to cmdg. officer USS Triton, 1965-67; cmdg. officer USS Daniel Boone, 1967-69, USS Holland, 1969-71, U.S. Naval Submarine Base, New London, Conn., 1971-74; project planner Bechtel Inc., San Francisco, 1977-84. Editor: Naval Cover Cachet Makers Catalog, 1985, USCS Log, 1989. Bd. dirs. Healdsburg (Calif.) Mus. & Hist. Soc., 1995—. Home: 251 Almond Way Healdsburg CA 95448-4348

RAWLINSON, DENNIS PATRICK, lawyer; b. Portland, Oreg., Mar. 1, 1947; s. Thomas F. and Betty (Price) R.; m. M. Diane Schatz, Apr. 26, 1980. BA, U. Notre Dame, 1969; MBA, Cornell U., 1976, JD, 1976. Bar: Oreg. 1976, U.S. Dist. Ct. Oreg. 1976; cert. civil trial lawyer Nat. Inst. Trial Advocacy. Assoc. Miller, Nash, Wiener, Hager & Carlsen, Portland, Oreg., 1976-82, ptnr., 1982—. Contbr. articles to profl. jours. Pres., bd. dirs. Portland Opera Assn., 1990-96. 1st lt. Army Med. Svc. Corps, 1970-72, Korea. Mem. ABA (chair creditor's rights subsection and task force on discovery guidelines litigation sect.), Oreg. State Bar Assn. (mem. exec. com. debtor/creditor sect. 1988-91, chair-elect and mem. exec. com. litigation sect. 1992—, mng. editor litigation jour. 1992—, mng. editor Oreg. Comml. Practice manual 1988—), Owen Panner Inn of Ct. (master), Arlington Club Toastmasters (pres.), Rotary Club Portland (pres., bd. dirs.), Multnomah Athletic Club (pres., trustee). Avocations: running, backpacking, white water rafting, wine collecting. Office: Miller Nash Wiener Hager & Carlsen 111 SW 5th Ave Ste 3500 Portland OR 97204-3699*

RAY, BRIAN DANIEL, education and science educator; b. Vancouver, Wash., Oct. 30, 1954; s. Eugene Lamont and Nora G. (Kelleher) R.; m. Betsy Anne Briggs, Sept. 2, 1978; children: Hallie B., Rachel M., Hannah K., Daniel B., Clara A., Emma L., Abbie E., Marta A. BS, U. Puget Sound, 1976; MS, Ohio U., 1979; PhD, Oreg. State U., 1988. Tchr. sci. Sacred Heart Acad., Salem, Oreg., 1980-83; grad. teaching asst. gen. sci. dept. Oreg. State U., Corvallis, 1983-88, grad. rsch. asst. coll. liberal arts, 1986-88, supr. edn. students, 1987-88; instr. We. Oreg. State Coll., Monmouth, 1985; asst. prof. edn. Seattle Pacific U., 1988-90; pres. Nat. Home Edn. Rsch. Inst., Salem, Oreg., 1990—; assoc. prof. Western Bapt. Coll., Salem, Oreg., 1991-96; instr. anatomy and physiology Chemeketa C.C., Salem, summer 1983; instr. biology Oreg. State Penitentiary, Salem, summers 1982-84, Upward Bound, Oreg. State U., Corvallis, summers 1987-88; expert witness in ct. cases and to state legislatures on topic of home edn. Editor Home Sch. Researcher, Salem, 1985—, Jour. Rsch. in Sci. Teaching, 1991, Peabody Jour. Edn., Strengths of Their Own - Home Schoolers Across America; contbr. chpt. to book; contbr. articles to Edn. and Urban Soc., Christianity Today. Bowerman Grad. scholar Bowerman Found., 1986-88. Mem. Nat. Assn. for Rsch. in Sci. Teaching, Am. Ednl. Rsch. Assn., Oreg. Acad. Sci., NSTA, Phi Delta Theta. Republican. Avocations: running, Nordic skiing, bird watching, carpentry, gardening. Fax: 503-364-1490. E-mail: mail@nheri.org. Office: Nat Home Edn Rsch Inst PO Box 13939 Salem OR 97309-1939

RAY, JENNY, artist; b. Ontario, Oreg.; d. Thompson and Othela Jean Towell Carper; m. Gary Wayne Limbaugh, Apr. 14, 1971; children: Cindy Sue, Tina Marie, Kay Jean, Tamara Rae, Cody Wayne. Cosmetologist, Pendleton (Oreg.) Coll. Beauty, 1972; student, Blue Mountain C.C., 1979-80, Ea. Oreg. State Coll., 1991-92. Owner Butter Creek Beauty Salon, Hermiston, Oreg., 1977-80, Pretty Quick Constrn. Co., Hermiston, Oreg., 1978-93, McCord's Corner Art Gallery, Baker City, Oreg., 1986-88, Creations, Inc., Baker City, 1984-85, Western Mountain Art, Inc., Joseph, Oreg., 1982-95, Age of Bronze Art Foundry, Joseph, 1992-95, Moriah Foundry, Inc., Wallowa, Oreg., 1995—. Author: Self Esteem Repair in Recovery, 1992; artist oil portraits of famous native Americans, 1985—; one woman shows at McCords Corner Art Gallery, 1986, Klondikes of Baker City, 1987, Baker County Chamber Office, 1988, Sumpter Valley R.R. Baker, 1988. Asst. dir. Ch. of Christ Christian Sch., Hermiston, 1980, Wallowa Valley Players, Joseph, 1990-92; econ. devel. com. Wallowa Valley Arts Coun., Enterprise, Oreg., 1993—; exec. dir. Wallowa Valley Mktg. Assn., Joseph, 1994; chair Jane Jefferson Club, Pendleton, Oreg., 1975; del. Umatilla County Dem. Com., Pendleton, 1976; campaign chair Jimmy Carter Campaign, Umatilla County, 1976; mem. Dakota Sioux Tribe. Recipient Cert. of Merit Pendleton Coll. Beauty, 1980; Western Art Prodns. scholar, 1988; Ea. Oreg. Regional Arts Commn. grantee, 1996; recycle project grantee Sustainable N.W., 1996. Mem. Lakota Sioux Tribe, Nat. Mus. of the Am. Indian (charter), Nat. Mus. of Women in the Arts, Smithsonian Assocs., Grant County Art Assn., Union County Art Guild, Cross Roads Art Ctr. Avocations: fishing, hiking, raising and training Egyptian Arabian horses, camping, writing. Home: PO Box 183 Joseph OR 97846-0183 Office: Moriah Foundry Inc 101 S Storie Wallowa OR 97885

RAY, MARIANNE YURASKO, social services administrator; b. Mpls., Sept. 25, 1934; d. Andrew George and Ann (Rusinko) Yurasko; m. Raymond Robert Ray, Nov. 22, 1962 (div. July 1980); children: Joel Christopher, Angela Christine. BA, U. Utah, 1956; student, U. Wash., 1975; MA, Pacific Lutheran U., 1978. Case worker, vol. agy. liaison State of Wash. Dept. Social and Health Services, Tacoma, Wash., 1963-65, 1971-79, 1983; child placement project dir. State of Wash. Dept. Social and Health Services, Olympia, Wash., 1979-80; casework supr. Child Protective Service State of Wash. Dept. Social and Health Services, Tacoma, Wash., 1980-81, foster home recruiter and licenser, 1981-83; owner, cons. Myray Focuses, Seattle, 1983—; pres. Delta Dynamics Inc., Seattle, 1984-86; mental health therapist Children's Indsl. Home, Tacoma, 1985-86, Good Samaritan Mental Health, Puyallup, Wash., 1986-87; part-time faculty Cen. Wash. U., Ellensburg, 1985—, Highline Community Coll., Midway, Wash., 1985-87, Renton (Wash.) Vocational Tech. Inst., 1985—, Lake Washington Vocational Tech. Inst., Kirkland, Wash., 1985-96; dir. child abuse treatment Cath. Community Services, Seattle, 1987-96; cons. Tacoma Sch. Dist., 1985-86; presenter nat. conferences and workshops. Creator workshops: Humor Techniques for Stress Management in the Classroom, 1985, Humor in Stress Management: Applications in Helping Professions, 1987, Kicking the Holiday Blues, 1986, Humor for the Health of It, 1987, Laughing Matters--It Really Does!, 1984—, Relocation: What it means for the Employee and Family, 1984—, Humor in the Workplace for Higher Productivity and Team Building, 1984—, Laughter and Liberation in the Classroom to Promote Learning, 1987—, Creative Imagery in Relaxation Techniques, 1987—. Mem. Am. Psychol. Assn. (assoc.), Pacific Northwest Orgn. Devel. Network, Pacific Northwest Speakers Assn. Avocations: oil painting, cooking, writing. Office: Myray Focuses Counseling/Consulting PO Box 98570 Seattle WA 98198-0570

RAY, RICHARD STANLEY, accountant; b. Miami, Ariz., June 12, 1937; s. Milton Sevier and Anne Elizabeth (Mickelson) R.; m. Laura Ann Young, Apr. 11, 1963; children: Denise, Mark, Melanie, Laura, Jordon. AA, Ea. Ariz. Jr. Coll., 1957; BS in Acctg., Ariz. State U., 1962, MS in Acctg., 1964. CPA, Ariz. Staff acct. Deloitte, Haskins & Sells, Phoenix, 1963-65; controller AMECO, Phoenix, 1965-70, U-Haul Co., Phoenix, 1970-76; dir. audit svcs. Ariz. Pub. Service Co., Phoenix, 1976—; advisor to bd. Credit Data of Ariz., Phoenix, 1981—, chmn. bd., 1980-81; dir. Arcoa Internat., Phoenix, 1973-76. Treas., bd. mem. Big Sisters of Ariz., Phoenix, 1972-78; dist. coun. Boy Scouts Am., Phoenix, 1982-84; stake pres. Mormon Ch., Tempe, Ariz. 1987-96. Grad. rsch. fellowship, Ariz. Bankers Assn., Phoenix, 1962. Mem. Am. Inst. CPA's, Ariz. Soc. CPA's (Acctg. Achievement award 1962), Ariz. State Bd. Accountancy (continuing profl. edn. com. 1986-94), Inst. Internal Auditors (bd. dirs. Phoenix 1994—), Rotary (bd. dirs. 1997-98). Republican.

RAYE, DON, furniture finish designer; b. Louisville, Mar. 1, 1946; s. George Raymond and Melba Jean (Fowler) Irwin; m. Ellen Joan Levy, May 12, 1967 (div. 1970); m. Princella Dartey, Mar. 20, 1998. BA in Music, U. Ky., 1968. Chef Hollywood Beach Hotel Resort, Miami, Fla., 1968-69; freelance jazz drummer U.S., Can., Europe, 1969—; freelance designer, mfr. musical instruments, 1976-79; finish designer, furniture maker Reed Bros. Woodcarving, Sebastopol, Calif., 1984—; owner, mgr. Magic Touch Custom Finishes, Santa Rosa, Calif., 1991—; sales assoc. Landmark Vineyards, Kenwood, Calif., 1998—; founding ptnr. Wine Country Woodworks, Santa Rosa, 1999—; tchr. advanced yoga and meditation techniques, 1969-74. Author: Pipe Dreams, 1980. Avocations: metaphysics, photography, motorcycles, fitness, gourmet cooking. Home: 28 Pine Tree Cir Cotati CA 94931-5318 Office: Reed Bros Woodcarving 5000 Turner Rd Sebastopol CA 95472-6245

RAYGOZA, LYNETTE ROSALIND, educational administrator; b. Hanford, Calif., Sept. 16, 1953; d. King and Lupe (Vasquez) R. BA in History, St. Mary's Coll., Moraga, Calif., 1976. Adminstrv. asst. fin. aid office U. Calif., Davis, 1980-83, systems coord. fin. aid office, 1983-87; asst. dir. fin. aid office Santa Clara (Calif.) U., 1987-90, mgr. student systems and registration svcs., 1990—. Precinct capt. Dem. Party, Santa Clara, 1988; precinct worker Vasconcillos Campaign, Santa Clara, 1992; vol. Green Initiative, Palo Alto, 1990, United Farm Workers Inst., 1978. Mem. Nat. Assn. Student Fin. Aid Adminstrs., Western Assn. Student Fin. Aid Adminstrs., Calif. Assn. Student Fin. Aid Adminstrs., Nat. Assn. SIGMA Users, Am. Coun. on Edn., Nat. Idenfication Program. Roman Catholic. Avocations: swimming, baseball, reading, walking. Home: # 279 151 Buckingham Dr Apt 279 Santa Clara CA 95051-6524

RAYL, INDIA, marketing executive; b. Chateauroux, France, May 1, 1956; d. Rommie Clarence and Peggeanne (Moore) Walker; m. Robert Richard Rayl, Jr., June 19, 1982; children: Brandon Joseph, Nelia Ashley. Student, Mesa Coll., San Diego, 1982-85, U. San Diego, 1988-89; cert. in direct mktg., San Diego State Univ., Univ. San Diego, 1990. Brand mgr. Undergear Catalog, San Diego, 1983; dir. customr relations Internat. Male, San Diego, 1977-86; catalog dir. ACA Joe, San Diego, 1986-87; media mgr. Internat. Male-Hanover House Ind., San Diego, 1988; gen. mgr. Petco-Animal City, San Diego, 1988-89; mktg. mgr. More Direct Health Products, 1989-90; dir. sales and mktg. Healy and Clark, San Diego, 1991-92; mktg. promotions mgr. Road Runner Sports, San Diego, 1992-93, dir. new bus., 1993-95; dir. product devel. Entrepreneur Mag. Group, 1995-97; v.p. bus. devel. Affinity Devel. Group, San Diego, 1997—; new bus. cons. Gift Baskets, Inc., San Diego, 1988. Editor various catalogs. Mem. Nat. Assn. Female Execs., San Diego Direct Mktg. Club, Catalog Coun., We. Fulfillment Assn., Nat. Coun. Mktg. Execs. (mem. bd.). Avocations: aerobic dancing, cooking.

RAYMOND, EUGENE THOMAS, technical writer, consultant, retired aircraft engineer; b. Seattle, Apr. 17, 1923; s. Evan James and Katheryn Dorothy (Kranick) R.; m. Bette Mae Bergeson, Mar. 1, 1948; children: Joan Kay Hibbs, Patricia Lynn Adams, Robin Louise Flashman. BSME, U. Wash., 1944; postgrad., 1953-55; registered profl. engr., Tex. Rsch. engr. The Boeing Co., Seattle, 1946-59, sr. group engr., 1959-63, 66-71, sr. specialist engr., 1971-81, prin. engr. flight control tech., 1982-88; project design engr. Gen. Dynamics, Ft. Worth, 1963-66. Lt., USNR, 1943-46, 49-52; PTO. Author (book) Aircraft Flight Control Actuation System Design, 1993. Recipient prize Hydraulics and Pneumatics mag., 1958. Mem. Soc. Automotive Engrs. (cert. of appreciation, chmn. adv. bd. com. A-6 nat. com. for aerospace fluid power and control tech. 1983-88, vice-chmn. com. 1986-88, cons.), Fluid Power Soc. (dir. northwest region 1973-74), Puget Sound Fluid Power Assn., AIAA, Beta Theta Pi, Meridian Valley Country Club, Masons, Shriners. Lutheran. Aircraft editorial adv. bd. Hydraulics and Pneumatics mag., 1960-70; achievements include 5 patents in Fluid Sealing Arrangements, Quasi-Open-Loop Hydraulic Ram Incremental Actuator with Power Conserving Properties, Rotary Digital Electrohydraulic Actuator, Two-Fluid Nonflammable Hydraulic System and Load-Adaptive Hydraulic Actuator System and Method for Actuating Control Surfaces; designed and developed mechanical systems for the XB-47 and B-52 jet bombers, 707 airliner and many other aircraft, including the X-20 Dyna-Soar hypersonic space plane, the American SST, the rewinged Navy A-6 attack plane the B-2 Stealth Bomber and the Chinese XAC Y-7 commuter; contbr. over 20 technical papers and articles to profl. jours. Home and Office: 40985 Inverness Way Palm Desert CA 92211-9277

RAYMOND, LLOYD W., machinery company executive; b. Middleboro, Mass., Jan. 4, 1922; s. Millard Edgar and Ethel (Morrison) R.; m. Joyce Elaine Cox, Nov. 10, 1972. Student, N.Y.U., 1952; ThB, Christian Bible Coll., Rocky Mount, N.C., 1995, ThM, 1996, PhD in Religion, 1996; D Min., S.W. Bible Coll. and Sem., Sulphur, La., 1997. Clk. Pub. Housing Adminstrn., Washington, 1941-42; adminstrv. asst. devel. dept. Pub. Housing Adminstrn., Washington and N.Y.C., 1946-55; machinery data mgr., sales exec. Nat. Machinery Exch., Inc., Newark, 1955-76; machinery data mgr. Nat. Machinery Exch., Inc., Pico Rivera, Calif., 1976—; founder, pres., CEO, DataReports Inc., Upland, Calif., 1998—. Author: Titanic-What Went Wrong; designer computerized info. mgmt. and quote generating sys., 1991, registered trademark Infodex; writer journalistic views of environ. disasters, justice and other topics of nat. and world interest; founder Data Reports, Inc. Founder Living Pictures Programs, 1965-95. Mem. Soc. Profl. Journalists, Investigative Reporters and Editors, Titanic Hist. Soc., Brit. Titanic Soc., Am. Legion, The Mariner's Mus. Avocations: computer systems, photography, gardening, opera. Fax: 909-949-6284. E-mail: dri@datareports.com. Office: DataReports Inc PO Box 188 Upland CA 91785-0188

RAYNOLDS, DAVID ROBERT, buffalo breeder, writer; b. N.Y., Feb. 15, 1928; s. Robert Frederick and Marguerite Evelyn (Gerdau) R.; m. May (Kean) Raynolds, May 12, 1951; children: Robert, Linda, Martha, Laura, David A.F. AB, Dartmouth Coll., 1949; MA, Wesleyan U., Middletown, Conn., 1955; predoctoral, Johns Hopkins Sch. Advanced Internat. Studies, Washington, 1956; grad., Nat. War Coll., Washington, 1973. Account exec. R.H. Morris Assoc., Newtown, Conn., 1949-50; fgn. svc. officer Dept. of State, Washington, 1956-76; pres. Ranch Rangers, Inc., Lander, Wyo., 1976—; pres. Nat. Buffalo Assn., Ft. Pierre, S.D., 1987-88. Author: Rapid Development in Small Economies (Praeger); contbr. articles to profl. jours. Mem. mgmt. com. Wyo. Heritage Soc.; bd. dirs. Liberty Hall Found., Lander-Rotary Found. With U.S. Army, 1950-53. Recipient Meritorious Svc. Award, Dept. of State, Washington, 1966. Mem. The Explorers Club, Fremont County Farm Bur., Fgn. Svc. Assn., Am. Legion, Rotary, Elks. Republican. Episcopalian. Avocation: travel. Office: Table Mountain Group PO Box 1310 Lander WY 82520-1310

REA, WILLIAM J., judge; b. 1950; BA, Loyola U., 1942, LLB, U. Colo., 1949. With U.S. Census Bur., Denver, 1949-50; adjuster Farmers Ins. Group, L.A., 1950; pvt. practice law, L.A., 1950-64, Santa Ana, Calif., 1964-68; judge Superior Ct., L.A., 1968-84; judge U.S. Dist. Ct. (cen. dist.) Calif., L.A., 1984—. Past pres. L.A. chpt. Nat. Exec. Com.; chmn. Constn. and By-Laws Com. With USN, WWII. Mem. L.A. County Bar Assn. (Outstanding Jurist award 1985), So. Calif. Def. Counsel Assn. Disting. Svc. award 1982), Internat. Acad. Trial Lawyers (Trial Judge of Yr. 1982), L.A. Trial Lawyers Assn., Am. Bd. Trial Advs. (nat. pres.), L.A. County Bar Assn. (Trial Judge of Yr. 1985). Office: US Dist Ct 312 N Spring St Ste 128 Los Angeles CA 90012-4703

READ, CHARLES RAYMOND, SR., business executive; b. Clovis, N.Mex., Apr. 21, 1915; s. Charles Edward and Mary Ellen (Elder) R.; m. Elenore Littlefield, Oct. 10, 1936 (dec. July 1985); children: Charles Raymond Jr., Nancy Ann Walsh; m. Debra Rae Stutzman, Mar. 30, 1989. Baker, candymaker Peter-Paul's Candy, Clovis, 1932-34; baker Holsum Bakery, Boise, Idaho, 1934-35, Elsner's Bakery, Everett, Wash., 1935-37; head baker United Bakery, Ellensburg, Wash., 1937-40; owner, baker Read's Royal Bakery, Ellensburg, 1940-42; mgr., baker Clark's Bakery, Seattle, 1945-57; owner, baker Read's Bakery, Seattle, 1957-62; pres. Read Products, Inc., Seattle, 1962—; ptnr. Peasley-Read, Seattle, 1968—; guest TV programs KING-5, Seattle, 1950-62; distbr. Richlite, 1962—. With USN, 1942-45. Seattle Pacific U. fellow; recipient trophies, plaques for cake decorating Pacific N.W. Clinary Arts Exhibit, 1950-62. Mem. United Comml. Travelers, Smithsonian Inst., Masons (3d degree). Avocations: collecting coins, Persian art, gems, jewelry, antiques, international travel. Office: Read Products Inc 3615 15th Ave W Seattle WA 98119-1392

READ, THOMAS A., editor, retired. Assoc. editor Seattle Post-Intelligencer; ret., 1995. Office: PO Box 1909 Seattle WA 98111*

READE, C. WIGHT, physician; b. Toledo, Ohio, Sept. 25, 1923; s. Carleton Wight Reade and Margaret Catherine Bushong Wall; m. Nancy Lou Milroy, Mar. 5, 1949 (div. 1974); children: Susan, Sarah, Mary. MD, U. Mich., 1946. Diplomate Am. Bd. Pediatrics, Am. Bd. Radiology. Solo practice pediatrics, Olympia, Wash., 1950-71; ptnr. Olympia Radiologists, 1974-76; chief radiology USPHS, Seattle, 1976-84; asst. prof. radiology U. Oreg. Med. Sch., Portland, 1984-86; itinerant radiologist various locations, 1986-92; med. disability cons. Social Security, Olympia, 1955-71, Wash. Tchrs. Retirement, 1965-71. Lt. USNR, 1951-53. Mem. King County Med. Assn. Avocations: boating, flying, motorcycling, carpentry. E-mail: wightr@nwlink.com. Fax: 206-328-1486. Home: 929 Broadway East Seattle WA 98102

READE, CHRIS, recording industry executive; b. N.Y.C., Nov. 8, 1969. BS in Mktg. & Journalism, Northwestern U., 1988. Mgr. publicity.video promotion Island Records, N.Y.C., 1988-91; sr. publicist Set to Run Pub. Rels., N.Y.C., 1991-92; sr. dir. publicity Def Jam Recordings, N.Y.C., 1992-94; dir. urban publicity Interscope/Death Row Records, L.A., 1994-95; pres., owner Chris Reade Comm., L.A., 1995—; exec. dir. press & publicity Priorty Records, L.A., 1997-98; mem. adv. bd. Rad Coalition, N.Y.C., 1995—, Hip Hop Adv. Bd., L.A., 1994-97. Author: (screenplays) Macl in the Back, 1994, Hotel, Motel, Holiday Inn, 1996. Mem. Nat. Acad. Recording Arts & Scis., L.A. Music Network, Black Film Makers Found., Black Pub. Rels. Soc. Avocations: travel, reading, collecting mid-century furniture, writing for TV and film, music. E-mail: crcomm@earthlink.net. Fax: 323-227-6383. Office: Chris Reade Comm 7510 W Sunset Blvd #1426 Los Angeles CA 90046-3418

REAGAN, GARY DON, state legislator, lawyer; b. Amarillo, Tex., Aug. 23, 1941; s. Hester and Lois Irene (Marcum) R.; m. Nedra Ann Nash, Sept. 12, 1964; children: Marc, Kristi, Kari, Brent. BA, Stanford U., 1963, JD, 1965. Bar: N.Mex. 1965, U.S. Dist. Ct. N.Mex., 1965, U.S. Supreme Ct. 1986. Assoc. Smith & Ransom, Albuquerque, 1965-67; ptnr. Smith, Ransom, Deaton & Reagan, Albuquerque, 1967-68, Williams, Johnson, Houston, Reagan & Porter, Hobbs, N.Mex., 1968-77, Williams, Johnson, Reagan, Porter & Love, Hobbs, 1977-82; pvt. practice, Hobbs, 1982—; city atty. City of Hobbs, 1978-80, 97—, City of Eunice, N.M., 1980—; mem. N.Mex. State Senate, 1993-96; instr. N.Mex. Jr. Coll. and Coll. of S.W., Hobbs, 1978-84; N.Mex. commr. Nat. Conf. Commrs. Uniform State Laws, 1993-96; adv. mem. N.Mex. Constl. Revision Commn., 1993-95. Mayor, City of Hobbs, 1972-73, 76-77, city commr., 1970-78; pres., dir. Jr. Achievement of Hobbs, 1974-85; pres., trustee Landsun Homes, Inc., Carlsbad, N.Mex., 1972-84; trustee Lydia Patterson Inst., El Paso, Tex., 1972-84, N.Mex. Conf. United Meth. Ch., 1988—, Coll. of S.W., Hobbs, 1989—; chmn. County Democratic Com., 1983-85. Mem. ABA, State Bar N.Mex. (coms. 1989-96, v.p. 1992-93, pres. 1994-95), Lea County Bar Assn. (pres. 1976-77), Hobbs C. of C. (pres. 1989-90), Rotary (pres. Hobbs 1985-86), Hobbs Tennis (pres. 1974-75). Home: 200 E Eagle Dr Hobbs NM 88240-5323 Office: 501 N Linam St Hobbs NM 88240-5715

REAGAN, JANET THOMPSON, psychologist, educator; b. Monticello, Ken., Sept. 15, 1945; d. Virgil Joe and Carrie Mae (Alexander) Thompson; m. Robert Barry Reagan, Jr., Aug. 7, 1977; children: Natalia Alexandria, Robert Barry. B.A. in Psychology, Berea Coll., 1967; Ph.D. in Psychology, Vanderbilt U., 1972. Mgr. research and eval. Nashville Mental Health Center, 1971-72; mgr. eval. Family Health Found., New Orleans, 1973-74; asst. prof. dept. health systems mgmt. Tulane U., New Orleans, 1974-77; dir. eval. Project Heavy West, Los Angeles, 1977-78; asst. prof. health adminstrn. Calif. State U.-Northridge, 1978-83, assoc. prof., director health adminstrn., 1983-87, prof., dir. health adminstrn., 1987—; cons. in field. Mem. Am. Pub. Health Assn., Am. Coll. Health Care Adminstrn., Assn. Health Svcs. Rsch., Am. Coll. Health Care Execs. (com. on higher edn. 1987, chmn. 1991), Assn. Univ. Programs in Health Adminstrn. (task force on undergrad. edn. 1985-90, chmn. 1988-90, mem. bd. dirs. 1995, chmn. bd. dirs. 1998—), Psi Chi, Phi Kappa Phi. Mem. editorial adv. bd. Jour. of Long Term Care Adminstrn.; contbr. to books, articles to profl. jours., papers to profl. assns. Home: 9354 Encino Ave Northridge CA 91325-2414 Office: Calif State U Dept Health Sci Northridge CA 91330

REAGAN, NANCY DAVIS (ANNE FRANCIS ROBBINS), volunteer, wife of former President of United States; b. N.Y.C., July 6, 1923; d. Kenneth and Edith (Luckett) Robbins; step dau. Loyal Davis; m. Ronald Reagan, Mar. 4, 1952; children: Patricia Ann, Ronald Prescott; stepchildren: Maureen, Michael. BA, Smith Coll.; LLD (hon.), Pepperdine U., 1983; LHD (hon.), Georgetown U., 1987. Contract actress, MGM, 1949-56; films include The Next Voice You Hear, 1950, Donovan's Brain, 1953, Hellcats of the Navy, 1957; Author: Nancy, 1980; formerly author syndicated column on prisoner-of-war and missing-in-action soldiers and their families; author: (with Jane Wilkie) To Love a Child, (with William Novak) My Turn: The Memoirs of Nancy Reagan, 1989. Civic worker, visited wounded Viet Nam vets., sr. citizens, hosps. and schs. for physically and emotionally handicapped children, active in furthering foster grandparents for handicapped children program; hon. nat. chmn. Aid to Adoption of Spl. Kids, 1977; spl. interest in fighting alcohol and drug abuse among youth: hosted first ladies from around the world for 2d Internat. Drug Conf., 1985; hon. chmn. Just Say No Found., Nat. Fedn. of Parents for Drug-Free Youth, Nat. Child Watch Campaign, President's Com. on the Arts and Humanities, Wolf Trap Found. bd. of trustees, Nat. Trust for Historic Preservation, Cystic Fibrosis Found., Nat. Republican Women's Club; hon. pres. Girl Scouts of Am. Named one of Ten Most Admired Am. Women, Good Housekeeping mag., ranking #1 in poll, 1984, 85, 86; Woman of Yr. Los Angeles Times, 1977; permanent mem. Hall of Fame of Ten Best Dressed Women in U.S.; recipient humanitarian awards from Am. Camping Assn., Nat. Council on Alcoholism, United Cerebral Palsy Assn., Internat. Ctr. for Disabled; Boys Town Father Flanagan award; 1986 Kiwanis World Service medal; Variety Clubs Internat. Lifeline award; numerous awards for her role in fight against drug abuse. Address: 2121 Ave of the Stars 34th Fl Los Angeles CA 90067*

REAGAN, RONALD WILSON, former President of United States; b. Tampico, Ill., Feb. 6, 1911; s. John Edward and Nelle (Wilson) R.; m. Jane Wyman, Jan. 25, 1940 (div. 1948); children: Maureen E., Michael E.; m. Nancy Davis, Mar. 4, 1952; children: Patricia, Ronald. AB, Eureka Coll., 1932, MA (hon.), 1957. Actor GE Theatre, 1954-62; host TV series Death Valley Days, 1962-66; gov. State of Calif., 1967-74; businessman, rancher, commentator on public policy, 1975-80, Pres. of U.S., 1981-89. Sports announcer, motion picture and TV actor, 1932-66. Author: Where's The Rest of Me?, Speaking My Mind: Selected Speeches, 1989, An American Life: The Autobiography, 1990. Mem. Calif. State Rep. Ctrl. Com., 1964-66; del. Rep. Nat. Conv., 1968, 72; chmn. Rep. Gov. Assn., 1968-73; mem. presdl. Commn. CIA Activities Within U.S., 1975; bd. dirs. Com. Present Danger, Washington, 1977—; cand. for Rep. nomination for Pres., 1976. Served as capt. USAAF, 1942-45. Recipient Great Am. of Decade award, Va. Young Am. for Freedom, Man of Yr. Free Enterprise award, San Fernando Valley Bus. & Profl. award, 1964, Am. Legion award, 1965, Horation Alger award, 1969, George Washington Honor medal, Freedoms Found. Valley Forge award, 1971, Disting. Am. award; inducted into Nat. Football Found. Hall of Fame, Am. Patriots Hall of Fame. Mem. SAG (pres. 1947-52, 59), Am. Fedn. Radio & TV Artists, Lions, Friars, Tau Kappa Epsilon. Republican. Address: 34th Fl 2121 Ave of the Stars Los Angeles CA 90067*

REAL, MANUEL LAWRENCE, federal judge; b. San Pedro, Calif., Jan. 27, 1924; s. Francisco Jose and Maria (Mansano) R.; m. Stella Emilia Michalik, Oct. 15, 1955; children: Michael, Melanie Marie, Timothy, John Robert. B.S., U. So. Calif., 1944, student fgn. trade, 1946-48; LL.B., Loyola Sch. Law, Los Angeles, 1951. Bar: Calif. 1952. Asst. U.S. Atty.'s Office, Los Angeles, 1952-55; pvt. practice law San Pedro, Calif., 1955-64; U.S. atty. So. Dist. Calif., 1964-66; judge U.S. Dist. Ct. (cen. dist.) Calif., L.A., 1966—. Served to ensign USNR, 1943-46. Mem. Am., Fed., Los Angeles County bar assns., State Bar Calif., Am. Judicature Soc., Chief Spl. Agts. Assn., Phi Delta Phi, Sigma Chi. Roman Catholic. Club: Anchor (Los Angeles). Office: US Dist Ct 312 N Spring St Ste 217P Los Angeles CA 90012-4704*

REAM, BOB, political organization administrator. Chmn. Mont. Dem. Party, Helena. Fax: (406) 442-9534. Office: Mont Dem Party PO Box 802 Helena MT 59624*

REAM, DEBBIE LYNN, media and information publishing executive; b. Rapid City, S.D., Dec. 14, 1961; d. Edwin Anthony Romano and Sally (Labrum) Nelson; m. Kevin Gail Ream, May 21, 1988. BA, Western Wash. U., 1984. Features editor Ea. Ariz. Courier, Safford, 1984-85, editor, 1986-87; editor Parker (Ariz.) Pioneer, 1985-86; pub. affairs officer Sedgwick County, Wichita, Kans., 1987-89; comm. coord. Ontario-Pomona Assn. for Retarded Citizens, Montclair, Calif., 1989-91; pub. info. officer City of Victorville, Calif., 1991-98; mgr. corp. affairs Times Mirror Corp., L.A., 1998—. Loaned exec. Desert Cmtys. United Way, Victorville, 1992, bd. dirs., 1996-98; mem. Youth Accountability Bd., Victorville, 1993-98, Victor Valley H.S. Dist. Strategic Planning Team, Victorville, 1996-97. Named Pub. Employee of Yr., Calif. Film Commn., 1996. Mem. Soc. Profl. Journalists, Calif. Assn. Pub. Info. Ofcls. (sec. and bd. mem. 1996-98, second place award spl. events 1995), Calif. Redevelopment Assn. (pub. rels. com. 1996-98), Yosemite Assn., San Diego Zool. Soc., Victorville C. of C. (bd. dirs. 1991-98). Office: Times Mirror Times Mirror Sq Los Angeles CA 90053

REARDEN, CAROLE ANN, clinical pathologist, educator; b. Belleville, Ont., Can., June 11, 1946; d. Joseph Brady and Honora Patricia (O'Halloran) R. BSc, McGill U., 1969, MSc, MDCM, 1971. Diplomate Am. Bd. Pathology, Am. Bd. Immunohematology and Blood Banking, Am. Bd. Histocompatibility and Immunogenetics. Resident and fellow Children's Meml. Hosp., Chgo., 1971-73; resident in pediatrics U. Calif., San Diego, 1974, resident then fellow, 1975-79, asst. prof. pathology, 1979-86, dir. histocompatability and immunogenetics lab., 1979-94, assoc. prof., 1986-92, prof., 1992—, head divsn. lab. medicine, 1989-94; dir. med. ctr. U. Calif. Thornton Hosp. Clin. Labs., San Diego, 1993—; prin. investigator devel. monoclonal antibodies to erythroid antigens, recombinant autoantigens; dir. lab. exam. com. Am. Bd. Histocompatibility and Immunogenetics. Contbr. articles to profl. jours.; patentee autoantigen pinch. Mem. Mayor's Task Force on AIDS, San Diego, 1983. Recipient Young Investigator Rsch. award NIH, 1979; grantee U. Calif. Cancer Rsch. Coordinating Com., 1982, NIH, 1983; scholar Nat. Blood Found. Mem. Am. Soc. Investigative Pathology, Am. Soc. Hematology, Am. Assn. Blood Banks (com. organ transplantation and tissue typing 1982-87, tech. com. 13 edit. tech. manual 1996—), Am. Soc. Histocompatibility and Immunogenetics. Office: U Calif San Diego Dept Pathology 0612 9500 Gilman Dr Dept 612 La Jolla CA 92093-0612

REARDEN, JIM DOUGLAS, writer; b. Petaluma, Calif., Apr. 22, 1925; s. Barton Blueford and Grace Mattie (Miller) R.; m. Ursula Ruth Budde, Sept. 25, 1943 (div. Jan. 1965); children: Kathleen, Mary, Michael, Nancy, Jim K.; m. Audrey Anecia Roberts, Jan. 25, 1965; children: Terry Sagmoen, Michael Sagmoen, Tamara Sagmoen. BS in Fish and Game Mgmt., Oreg. State Coll., 1948; MS in Wildlife Conservation, U. Maine, 1950. Head dept. wildlife mgmt. U. Alaska, Fairbanks, 1950-54; freelance writer, photographer Homer, Alaska, 1954-59; area biologist, Cook Inlet Coml. Fisheries Alaska Dept. Fish and Game, Juneau, 1959-70; outdoors editor Alaska Mag., Anchorage, 1968-88; freelance writer, photographer Homer, 1988—; mem. Alaska Bd. of Fish and Game, Juneau, 1970-75, Alaska Bd. of Game, 1975-82; nat. adv. com. oceans and atmosphere, U.S. Govt., Washington, 1976-78. Field editor: Outdoor Life Mag., N.Y.C., 1976-96; author: (books) Alaska's Wolf Man, 1915-55 Wilderness Adventures of Frank Glaser, 1998, In the Shadow of Eagles, From Barnstormer to Alaska Bush Pilot, A Flyer's Story, 1994, Shadows on the Koyukuk, An Alaskan Native's Life Along the River, 1993, White Squaw, Adventures of a Lady Woodsman, 1992, Wind on the Water, The Story of a Pioneering Alaskan Couple, 1991, numerous others; contbr. more than 500 articles to fish and wildlife mags., including Nat. Geographic, Audubon, Outdoor Life, Field and Stream, Sports Afield, numerous others. With USN, 1943-45. Named Conservation Communicator of yr., nat. Wildlife Fedn. and Alaska Outdoor Coun., 1980, Disting. Alumnus, Fisheries and Wildlife Dept., U. Maine, Orono, 1987, Edn. Conservationist of Yr., Alaska Outdoor Coun., Fairbanks, 1993, Sidney Huntington Conservationist, Anchorage, 1996, Disting. Grad. Fisheries and Wildlife Dept., Oreg. State U., Corvallis, 1998. Mem. Am. Soc. Journalists and Authors. Office: Sprucewood Freelance 413 Lee Dr Homer AK 99603-7606

REAVIS, LIZA ANNE, semiconductor executive; b. N.Y.C., July 27, 1959; d. William Ralph and Juliette (Bustillo y Zelaya) Bartlett; m. Paul H. Reavis, May 25, 1985. BA in Internat. Rels., Rice U., 1981; MBA, Georgetown U., 1988. Project asst. Latham, Watkins & Hills, Washington, 1982-83; assoc. mgr. countertrade Sears World Trade, Washington, 1983-85; export asst. Weadon, Dibble & Rehm, Washington, 1985-86; assoc. cons. Vanguard Comm. Corp., Palo Alto, Calif., 1988-90; bus. mgr. Teleport Comm. Corp., San Francisco, 1990-94; sr. fin. analyst Nat. Semicondr. Corp., 1995—. Contbr. Project Open Hand, San Francisco, Calif. Wheelchair Vets. Assn., Am. Assn. for AIDS Rsch., San Francisco, 1990—; mem. Golden Gate Nat. Recreation Area, San Francisco, 1990—. Recipient Teleport Comms. Group Ann. Hero award, 1994; Presdl. scholar Dept. HEW, 1977. Mem. Women in Tech., Acad. Polit. Sci., Club des Hiboux (sec. 1979-80), Commonwealth Club, Sierra Club, Cousteau Soc., Phi Beta Kappa, Beta Gamma Sigma, Pi Delta Phi. Avocations: international cultures and politics, classical ballet, poetry, piano. Home: 2060 14th Ave San Francisco CA 94116-1310 Office: Nat Semicondr Corp 2900 Semiconductor Dr Mail Stop D3500 Santa Clara CA 95052-8090

REAVIS, SUSAN SCOTT, elementary educator; b. Tulare, Calif., Dec. 24, 1954; d. Eugene Ernest and Barbara Jane (Hyde) Scott; m. Robert Carl Reavis, June 14, 1987; stepchildren: Jaimie Rae, Peyton Ashley. BE, Northern Ariz. U., 1976; ME, U. Ariz., 1983. Cert. elem. tchr., Ariz. Tchr. Coolidge (Ariz.) Schs., 1976-78, Vail (Ariz.) Schs., 1978-85, Marana (Ariz.) Schs., 1985—. Active Red Cross Blood Program, Tucson, 1994—; mem. chancel choir Beautiful Savior Luth. Ch., Tucson, 1995—. Mem. Internat. Reading Assn., Nat. Council Tchrs. English, Marana Edn. Assn., Marana Schs. coms. Democrat. Home: 5117 W Malachite Pl Tucson AZ 85742-9402 Office: Quail Run Elementary School 4600 W Cortaro Rd Tucson AZ 85742

REBANE, ALEKSANDER, physicist, educator; b. Tartu, Estonia, Aug. 19, 1958; s. Karl and Ljubov (Shagalova) R.; m. Kaire Vaimel, Dec. 18, 1981; children: Kadri, Aleksander. MS, Tartu U., 1981; PhD, Inst. Physics Tartu, 1985. Rsch. scientist Inst. Physics, Tartu, 1984-90; asst. Swiss Fed. Inst. Tech., Zurich, 1991-96; assoc. prof. Mont. State U., Bozeman, 1996—. Inventor in field; contbr. articles to profl. jours. Recipient Internat. Commn. for Optics prize, 1993, Discover Mag. Best Invention award, 1995, Ruzicka prize, 1996. Mem. Internat. Soc. Optical Engrs., Optical Soc. Am., German Phys. Soc. Office: Mont State U Dept Physics Bozeman MT 59717-3840

REBB, KAREN MARLENE, music educator; b. Columbus, Ga.; d. Glen Percival and Vivian Irene (Williams) Loken; 1 child, Michael John-Glen. BS in Music Edn., Elem. Edn., Grand Canyon U., 1981; MA in Music Edn., No. Ariz. U., 1986. Cert. tchr., Ariz.; cert. I, II, III Levels Orff cert. Tchr. Heatherbrae Elem. Sch., Phoenix, 1981-82, Park Meadows Elem. Sch., Phoenix, 1982-95, Arrowhead Elem. Sch., Glendale, Ariz., 1995—; mem. adj. faculty Ottawa U., 1989—. Author: project Science of Music: Integrating the Arts and Technology, 1995. Mem. 1st Hist. Presbyn. Ch.; mem. site-based mgmt. team Park Meadows Sch., 1994, 95; mem. Dist. Strategic Planning Com., 1994; mem. dist. fine arts coun. writing Fine Arts Curriculum for Dist., Phoenix, 1995, 96. Recipient Ray Maben Scholar award Grand Canyon U., 1980, Ariz.; artist-in-residence grantee, 1989. Mem. NEA, Am. Orff-Schulwerk Assn., Ariz. Edn. Assn., Ariz. Orff-Schulwerk Assn. (sec., bd. dirs. 1990-92), Ariz. Music Educators Assn., Music Educators Nat. Conf. Avocations: playing piano, guitar, singing, reading, writing. Home: 19436 N 83rd Dr Peoria AZ 85382-8790

REBELEIN, DREW W., entrepreneur; b. Athens, Greece, May 2, 1967; s. Paul Richard and Elizabeth (Goldberg) Barbic; m. Annabel Horus Lee, Mar. 18, 1994; children: Speck, Burt. BS, U. Minn., 1990, MS, 1992; DSc, U.L.C., 1995. Pres. Pagan Prodn., Mpls., 1989-92; min. Ch. de Banche, Seattle, 1992-96, Universal Life Ch., San Francisco, 1996—. Author: Journals I, II, III, 1994, Up the Trang, 1998. Troop chaplain Boy Scouts Am., 1978-82. Mem. Am. Mountaineers, Order of Thelma. Office: 3288 21st St # 41 San Francisco CA 94110-2423

REBERG, ROSALIE, principal; m. Larry Alan Reberg, Aug. 16, 1975; children: Camden Ashleigh, Jacob Alan. BA, Holy Names Coll., 1971; MA with distinction, Calif. State U., Stanislaus, 1994. Elem. edn. tchr. Stanislaus Union Sch. Dist., Modesto, Calif., 1974-96; vice prin. Chrysler Elem. Sch., Modesto, Calif., 1996-97; prin. Eisenhut Elem. Sch., Modesto, Calif., 1997—; classroom mgmt. mentor tchr., Stanislaus Union Sch. Dist., 1988-89. Mem. Tchrs. English to Spkrs. of Other Langs., Assn. Calif. Sch. Adminstrs. Avocations: reading, computers. Office: Eisenjut Elem Sch 1809 Sheldon Dr Modesto CA 95350

REBHUN, JOSEPH, allergist, immunologist, medical educator; b. Przemysl, Poland, Oct. 7, 1921; came to U.S., 1950; s. Baruch and Serel R.; m. Maria Birkenhejm, Aug. 10, 1945; children: Lillian Friedland, Richard B.R., Donald. MD, U. Innsbruck, Austria, 1950; MS in Medicine, Northwestern U., 1954. Diplomate Am. Bd. Allergy and Immunology. Intern Barnert Meml. Hosp., Patterson, N.J.; resident in internal medicine Tompkins County Meml. Hosp. and Cornell U., N.Y., 1951-52; fellow in allergy Northwestern U. Med. Sch./Chidlren's Meml. Hosp., Chgo., 1952-54; fellow instr. Northwestern U. Med. Sch., 1954; asst. clin. prof. medicine Loma Linda U., 1957-93; clin. prof. medicine U. So. Calif., L.A., 1965-91, ret., 1998; chief allergy Chgo. Eye, Ear, Nose and Throat Hosp., 1953-55; cons. Pacific State Hosp., Spadra Pomona Valley Cmty. Hosp., Pomona Casa Colina Hosp. Author: SOS, 1946, The Cry of Democracy for Help, God and Man in Two Worlds, 1985, The Embers of Michael, 1993, Crisis of Morality and Reaction to the Holocaust, 1998; contbr. numerous articles to med. jours. Pres. Am. Congress Jews from Poland, 1969-70. Capt., U.S. Mil., San Francisco. Recipient honors City and County of L.A., L.A. Office Dist. Atty., Senate of State of Calif., all 1985. Fellow Am. Acad. Allergy (rsch. coun. 1960-65), Am. Coll. Allergy, Assn. Clin. Allergy and Immunology; mem. West Coast Allergy Soc., Calif. Allergy Assn., L.A. Soc. Allergy, L.A. Med. Assn., Calif. Med. Assn.

RECHARD, OTTIS WILLIAM, mathematics and computer science educator; b. Laramie, Wyo., Nov. 13, 1924; s. Ottis H. and Mary (Bird) R.; m. Dorothy Lee Duble, Nov. 19, 1943; children—Katherine L. (Mrs. Larry V. Baxter), Carol G. (Mrs. David P. Reiter), Nancy L. (Mrs. William Moore), Elizabeth A. B.A., U. Wyo., 1943; postgrad., U. Calif., Los Angeles, 1943; M.A., U. Wis., 1946, Ph.D., 1948. Instr. U. Wis., 1948; instr., asst. prof. Ohio State U., 1948-51; staff mem. Los Alamos (N.Mex.) Nat. Lab., 1951-56; prof., dir. computing ctr. Wash. State U., Pullman, 1956-68; prof., chmn. dept. computer sci. Wash. State U., 1963-76, prof., dir. systems and computing, 1968-70; prof. math. and computer scis. U. Denver, 1976-95, prof. emeritus, 1995—, dir. computing services, 1976-79; vis. prof., chmn. dept. computer sci. U. Wyo., 1986-87; cons. NSF, Idaho Nuclear Corp., Los Alamos Nat. Lab.; program dir. computer sci. program NSF, 1964-65, chmn. adv. panel on instl. computing facilities, 1969-70. Mem. Los Alamos Sch. Bd., 1954-56; mem. Pullman Sch. Bd., 1967-74; Trustee, past pres. Westminster Found., Synod Wash.-Alaska. Served to 1st lt. USAAF, 1943-45. Decorated Order of Leopold II Belgium). Fellow AAAS; mem. Assn. for Computing Machinery, Am. Math. Soc., Math. Assn. Am., IEEE Computer Soc., Soc. Indsl. and Applied Math., AAUP, Phi Beta Kappa, Sigma Xi, Phi Kappa Phi. Presbyn. (elder). Club: Rotarian. Home: RR 3 Box 369 Calder ID 83808 also: 6980 E Girard Ave Apt 405 Denver CO 80224-2915 Office: U Denver Dept Math & Comp Sci At Univ Park Denver CO 80208

REDD, SHERRILL EDNA, music educator; b. Preston, Idaho, Aug. 26, 1935; d. Reuben Merritt and Edna (Johnson) Drake; m. John Paul Redd, Dec. 21, 1954; children: John D., Jane A., Paul M., Susan E., Rebecca S., Diane M., Phillip J., Andrew H. Student, Brigham Young U., 1953-55; MusB with honors, Idaho State U., 1974, postgrad. in Voice, 1984-85, postgrad. in Composition, 1989-90. Cert. elem. sch. music tchr., Idaho. Piano accompanist Kasai Dance Studio, Pocatello, Idaho, 1947-53, Elem. Lab. Sch. Music, Provo, Utah, 1954-56, Poulsen Dance Studio, Provo, Utah, 1954; History Dept. sec. Idaho State U., Pocatello, 1978-81; gen. music specialist Sch. Dist. #25, Pocatello, 1984-91; adj. music lectr. Idaho State U., Pocatello, 1978—; vocal, choral and solo adjudicator various sch. dist. festivals, 1972—; vocal, instrumental adjudicator various music clubs, Idaho, 1990—; numerous solo soprano recitals, Idaho, Utah, Switzerland, Wales, London; invited to sing with ISU Concert Choir in Cambridge, Eng. under Sir John Aldous, 1993; soloist Hansel and Gretel, 1988, Phantom of the Opera, 1990-93; accompanist Amahl and the Night Visitors, 1989; faculty mem. Summer Music Camp, Idaho State U., 1987-89; choral, music dir. Camerata Singers, Pocatello, 1991-93; chmn., instr. Jr. Composers, Idaho Music Club, Pocatello, 1993-95; joint recitals with Dr. James Drake, Utah State U. Composer: Violin Sonatina in 3 Movements, 1985, (choral piece) What Think Ye of Christ, 1985, (choral piece) Centennial Hymn for POC, Id. LDS Stake Centennial. Recipient Cmty. Svc. award, Pocatello, 1995; named Am. Composer of Yr., Pocatello Music Club, 1987. Mem. Nat. Assn. Tchrs. Singing, Pocatello Music Club (v.p. 1998—), Pocatello Lit. Club (sec. 1998—). Mem. LDS Ch. Avocations: reading, composing, travelling, quilting, geneology. Home: 1401 Chokecherry Dr Pocatello ID 83204-5033 Office: Idaho State University Dept Music PO Box 8099 921 S 8th Ave Pocatello ID 83209-0001

REDDEL, CARL WALTER, education administration; b. Gurley, Neb., May 31, 1937; s. Walter Julius and Friedora Regina (Sorge) R.; m. Colette Marie Antoinette Mansuy, Oct. 26, 1963; children: Eric, Damien. BSED, Drake U., 1959; MA in Russian studies, Syracuse U., 1962; PhD in Russian history, Ind. U., 1973, cert. Russian studies, 1973. Lectr. U. Md., Toul-Rosieres, France, 1963-66; instr. U.S.A.F. Acad., Colo. Springs, Colo., 1967-68, 71-72, asst. prof., 1972-73, assoc. prof., 1973-80; prof., head dept. history, post-doctoral fellow U. Edinburgh, Edinburgh, Scotland, 1981-82; prof., head dept. history U.S. Air Force Acad., 1982—; nat. coord., regional World History Assn., Phila., 1990-95; bd. editors, mem. Joun. Slavic Military, London, 1988—; series editor Military Hist. Symposium Series, Colo. Springs, 1993—. Editor: Transformation in Russian and Soviet Military History, 1990; contbr. articles to profl. jours. Mem. Rotary Internat., 1994—. With U.S. Air Force, 1962—. Recipient Young Faculty exchange Internat. Rsch. Exchanges Bd., Moscow State U., 1975; Woodrow Wilson fellow, 1959-60, Danforth fellow Danforth Found., 1959-61. Mem. Am. Historical Assn., Am. Assn. Advancement of Slavic Studies, World History Assn., Rocky Mountain World History Assn., Cen. Slavic Assn. Lutheran. Home: 4504 Bell Flower Dr Colorado Springs CO 80917-1432 Office: USAF Acad Dept History Colorado Springs CO 80840

REDDEN, JAMES ANTHONY, federal judge; b. Springfield, Mass., Mar. 13, 1929; s. James A. and Alma (Cheek) R.; m. Joan Ida Johnson, July 13, 1950; children: James A., William F. Student, Boston U., 1951; LL.B., Boston Coll., 1954. Bar: Mass., 1954, Oreg., 1955. Pvt. practice Mass., 1954-55; title examiner Title & Trust Ins. Co., Oreg., 1955; claims adjuster Allstate Ins. Co., 1956; mem. firm Collins, Redden, Ferris & Velure, Medford, Oreg., 1957-73; treas. State of Oreg., 1973-77; atty. gen., 1977-80; U.S. dist. judge, now sr. judge U.S. Dist. Ct. Oreg., Portland, 1980—. Chmn. Oreg. Pub. Employee Relations Bd.; mem. Oreg. Ho. of Reps., 1963-69, minority leader, 1967-69. With AUS, 1946-48. Mem. ABA, Mass. Bar Assn., Oreg. State Bar. Office: US Dist Ct 1527 US Courthouse 1000 SW 3d Ave Portland OR 97204-2902

REDDING-LOWDER, CHRISTINE ARNITA, elementary education educator; b. Terrell County, Ga., Mar. 14, 1938; d. Otis Sr. and Fannie Mae (Roseman) Redding; m. Billy Earl Lowder, Feb. 5, 1961; children: Charles DeWayne, Penelope Darcel, Trevor Demetrius. AA, West L.A. Jr. Coll., 1970; BA in Psychology, Calif. State U.-Dominguez Hill, Carson, 1972; MS in Edn., U. So. Calif., 1975. Cert. tchr. K-8, adult edn., Calif. Telephone operator L.A. County Probation Dept., 1964-66; clk. L.A. County Assessor Dept., 1966; clk.-typist Dept. Pub. Social Svcs., L.A., 1966-67; intern L.A. Unified Sch. Dist., 1972-73, tchr., 1973—. Contbr. articles to profl. jours. Pres. Nat. Coun. Negro Women, L.A., 1994—; chair polit. subcom. 110th Anniversary 2d Bapt. Ch., L.A., 1995, mem. recruiters league, rec. sec. 1992-96; treas., v.p. Marvin Ave. Sch. PTA, L.A., 1967-69. Recipient Negotiation award Pres. United Tchrs. of L.A., 1984, Dedication/Svc. plaque United Tchrs. L.A./Black Educators, 1988, WHO award United Tchrs. L.A./NEA, 1995. Mem. AAUW, NEA (del. rep. assembly 1977—, mem. Black Caucus, Pacific region dir. Black Caucus 1996-98, sec. Black Caucus 1998—), Calif. Tchrs. Assn. (del. state coun. 1977-89, 90—, vice chair credentials and profl. devel. com. 1983-85, Assn. Better Citizenship com. Dist. J, United Tchrs.-LA 1994—), Nat. Assn. Univ. Women (regional by-laws chair 1991), Delta Sigma Theta (journalist Century City Alumnae chpt.). Democrat. Avoca-

tions: travel, reading, theater, stamp collecting, coin collecting. Office: Ralph Waldo Emerson Middle School 1650 Selby Ave Los Angeles CA 90024-5716

REDDING-STEWART, DEBORAH LYNN, psychologist; b. Miami, Fla., Feb. 16, 1953; d. Sidney Douglas and Lois May (Tily) R.; m. John Thomas Stewart, Aug. 19, 1978; children: Garrett Lorne, Tyler Douglas, Kelly Lynn. BA in Psychology, San Diego State U., 1975; MA in Psychology, U. Calif., Santa Barbara, 1980. Instr. Allan Hancock Coll., Lompoc, Calif., 1980-86; adminstr., dir. clin. svcs. Mary Lou Stewart Learning Ctr., Lompoc, Calif., 1982—; prin. Pacific Health and Fitness, Lompoc, 1994—; owner Pacific Health and Fitness. Author: The Soft Voice of the Rain, 1993. State Coun. Devel. Disabilities PDF grantee, 1990, Instructional Deve. grantee U. Calif., 1979. Avocations: aerobics, running. Home: 1019 Onstott Rd Lompoc CA 93436-2342

REDDY, MARK ANDREW, handwriting specialist, educator; b. Dodge City, Kans., Aug. 10, 1949; s. Melvin Jr. and Jean (Crane) R.; m. Diane M. Johnson, Sept. 23, 1971; children: Badi Andre, Inshallah Renee, Ma'ani Alisa, Hakim Antoin. BA, Adams State Coll., 1975; MA in Psychology of Handwriting, Prescott (Ariz.) Coll., 1997. Self-employed handwriting analyst, educator, trainer Durango, Colo., 1985—; self-employed forensic document examiner, 1995—; instr. psychology of handwriting Ft. Lewis Coll., Durango, 1997. Author: (monograph) The Empirical Study of Handwriting in Suicides, 1997, Dimensions in Handwriting Psychology. With U.S. Army, 1968-70. Mem. Nat. Assn. Document Examiners. Mem. Baha'i Faith. Office: PO Box 1573 Durango CO 81302-1573

REDELK, BONNIE MARIE, editor; b. Poplar, Mont., July 6, 1952; d. Silas Henry Clincher and Mercy Nettie (Long Dog) MacDonald; m. Herman A. Red Elk, May 11, 1987; children: Clifford Country, Cern J., Charley J., Randy L. BA, Native Am. Ednl. Svcs. Coll., Poplar, Mont., 1983. Laborer Tribal Gun Factory, Poplar, 1971; clerk FortPeck Agy., Poplar, 1971-73; reporter Worunin Wowapi, Poplar, 1975-76, editor, 1976—. Sec. Poplar Sch. Indian Edn. Com., 1993-94, Poplar Cmty. Orgn. Mem. Native Am. Journalists Assn., Poplar Sch. Indian Edn. Com. Democrat. Avocation: bead work. Home: PO Box 1476 Poplar MT 59255-1476

REDGRAVE, LYNN, actress; b. London, Mar. 8, 1943; d. Michael Scudemore and Rachel (Kempson) R.; m. John Clark, Apr. 2, 1967; children: Benjamin, Kelly, Annabel. Ed., Queensgate Sch., London, Central Sch. Speech and Drama, London. Stage debut as Helena in Midsummer Night's Dream, 1962; theatrical appearances include The Tulip Tree, Andorra, Hayfever, Much Ado About Nothing, Mother Courage, Love for Love, Zoo, Zoo, Widdershins Zoo, Edinburgh Festival, 1969, The Two of Us, London, 1970, Slag, London, 1971, A Better Place, Dublin, 1972, Born Yesterday, Greenwich, 1973, Hellzapoppin, N.Y., 1976, California Suite, 1977, Twelfth Night, Stratford Conn. Shakespeare Festival, 1978, The King and I, St. Louis, 1983, Les Liaisons Dangereuses, L.A., 1989, The Cherry Orchard, L.A., 1990, Three Sisters, London, 1990, Notebook of Trigorin, U.S., 1996; Broadway appearances include Black Comedy, 1967, My Fat Friend, 1974, Mrs. Warren's Profession (Tony award nomination), 1975, Knock, Knock, 1976, St. Joan, 1977, Sister Mary Ignatius Explains It All, 1985, Aren't We All?, 1985, Sweet Sue, 1987, A Little Hotel on the Side, 1992, The Masterbuilder, 1992, Shakespeare For My Father (Tony and Drama Desk nominations, Elliot Norton award 1993), 1993, also nat. tour, 1993, West End, 1993, Moon over Buffalo, 1996; film appearances include Tom Jones, Girl With Green Eyes, Georgy Girl (Recipient N.Y. Film Critics award, Golden Globe award, Oscar nomination for best actress 1967), The Deadly Affair, Smashing Time, The Virgin Soldiers, Last of the Mobile Hotshots, Don't Turn the Other Cheek, Every Little Crook and Nanny, Everything You Always Wanted to Know About Sex, The National Health, The Happy Hooker, The Big Bus, Sunday Lovers, Morgan Stuart's Coming Home, Getting It Right, Shine, 1996, Gods and Monsters, 1998, Strike, 1998; TV appearances include: The Turn of the Screw, Centennial, 1978, The Muppets, Gauguin the Savage, Beggarman Thief, The Seduction of Miss Leona, Rehearsal for Murder, 1982, Walking On Air, The Fainthearted Feminist (BBC-TV), 1984, My Two Loves, 1986, The Old Reliable, 1988, Jury Duty 1989, Whatever Happened to Baby Jane, 1990, Fighting Back (BBC-TV), 1992, Calling the Shots (Masterpiece Theatre), 1993, Toothless, 1997, Indefensible: The Truth About Edward Brannigan, 1997, Different, 1998, White Lies, 1998; guest appearances include Carol Burnett Show, Evening at the Improv and Steve Martin's Best show Ever, Circus of the Stars; co-host nat. TV syndication Not for Women Only, 1977—; nat. TV spokesperson Weightwatchers, 1984-92; TV series include House Calls, 1981, Teachers Only, 1982, Chicken Soup, 1989; Rude Awakening, 1998, albums: Make Mine Manhattan, 1978, Cole Porter Revisited, 1979; video: (for children) Meet Your Animal Friends, Off We Go, Off We Go Again: audio book readings include, Pride and Prejudice, The Shell Seekers, The Blue Bedroom, The Anastasia Syndrome, The Women in His Life, Snow In April, Gone With The Wind, 1994, The World of Philosophy, 1996; author: This is Living, 1990, Shakespeare For My Father, 1993. Named Runner-up Actress, All Am. Favorites, Box Office Barometer 1975; recipient Sarah Siddons award as Chgo.'s best stage actress of 1976, 94. Mem. The Players (pres. 1994). Office: care John Clark PO Box 1207 Topanga CA 90290-1207

REDING, JOHN ANTHONY, lawyer; b. Orange, Calif., May 26, 1944. AB, U. Calif., Berkeley, 1966, JD, 1969. Bar: Calif. 1970, U.S. Dist. Ct. (no., ctrl. ea. and so. dists.) Calif., U.S. Claims Ct., U.S. Supreme Ct. Formerly mem. Crosby, Heafey, Roach & May P.C., Oakland, Calif.; now ptnr. Paul, Hastings, Janofsky & Walter LLP, San Francisco. Mem. ABA (sects. on litigation, intellectual property, and natural resources, energy and eviron. law, coms. on bus. torts, internat. law, trial practice and torts and insurance), Am. Intellectual Property Law Assn., State Bar Calif. (sect. on litigation), Bar Assn. San Francisco, Assn. Bus. Trial Lawyers. Office: Paul Hastings Janofsky & Walter LLP 345 California St San Francisco CA 94104-2606

REDMAN, KEN, zoo officer. Exec. dir. Honolulu Zoo. Office: Honolulu Zoo 151 Kapahulu Ave Honolulu HI 96815-4096*

REECE, GERALDINE MAXINE, elementary education educator; b. L.A., May 13, 1917; d. Charles Kenneth and Bertha (Austin) Ballou; m. Thomas Charles Bauman, Aug. 16, 1942 (div. Oct. 1971); children: Thomas Charles Bauman, Jr., Kathleen Marie Bauman Messenger, Stephen Kenneth Bauman; m. Wilbert Wallingford Reece, Nov. 3, 1973 (dec. 1988). AA, L.A. City Coll., 1942; BA, U. So. Calif., L.A., 1966. Specialist tchr. in reading, elem. edn. Tchr. Archdiocese of L.A., Altadena, Calif., 1962-66; master tchr. Alhambra (Calif.) City and H.S., 1966-79, writer multicultural component early childhood edn. program. Author poetry. Mem. San Gabriel Child Care Task Force, 1984-86; mem. steering com. West San Gabriel Valley Cmty. Awareness Forum, 1985-87; past pres. women's divsn., bd. dirs. San Gabriel C. of C., 1989-90, publicity chair, 1994-98, incoming pres. women's divsn., 1998—; mem. sch. site and facilities com. San Gabriel, 1992-93; mem. task force Episcopal Parish/Healing Our Cities, San Gabriel, 1992-93; docent San Gabriel Mus., 1989, 92-93. Recipient Exceptional Svc. awards Am. Heart Assn., West San Gabriel Valley, 1990, 91, 93, 94, 95, Dedicated Svc. award San Gabriel C. of C., 1989, Outstanding and Dedicated Cmty. Svc. award Fedn. Cmty. Coord. Couns., San Gabriel, 1986, 87, 97-98, others, Woman of Yr. award City of San Gabriel, 1994, Diamond Homer trophy Famous Poet Soc., 1995, 96; scholarship named in her honor Divsn. 1 Calif. Ret. Tchrs. Assn. Mem. AAUW (Money Talks sect. chairperson 1981-82, corr. sec.-treas. Alhambra-San Gabriel 1982-85), Calif. Ret. Tchrs. Assn. (pres. 1989-91, Outstanding Svc. plaque 1994, divsn. one scholarship named in her honor 1998), Nat. Soc. DAR (3rd vice regent 1994—, 1st Pl. Poetry award 1996, 3d Pl. Poetry award 1998), Pasadena Women's City Club, St. Francis Guild, San Gabriel Ret. Tchrs. (pres. 1985-89, cmty. rep. 1990-97), San Gabriel Hist. Assn., San Gabriel Cmty. Coord. Coun. (pres. 1986, 1st v.p. 1997-98). Democrat. Episcopalian. Avocations: reading, Bridge, writing poetry, stitchery.

[illegible] July 10, 1935; d. Houston William and Maude Elizabeth (Martz) Hall; m. Bill Reed, Nov. 27, 1957 (div. July 1987); children: Bill, Stacy, Valerie; m. Green Clark. AB, McPherson Coll., 1957. Cert. early childhood spl. edn. Tchr. Murry Sch. Dist., Utah; head start tchr. Idaho; tchr. St. Edwards Cath. Sch., Idaho, Glenns Ferry Sch. Dist., Idaho. Author of short stories. Leader Girl Scouts Am., 1970-82. Mem. AAUW. Home: PO Box 642 Glenns Ferry ID 83623-0642

REED, CHRISTOPHER *See* **KAHAN, SHELDON JEREMIAH**

REED, DAVID GEORGE, entrepreneur; b. Alameda, Calif., July 19, 1945; s. David Francis and Anna Amelia Vangeline (Paulson) R.; m. Marianne Louise Watson, Apr. 7, 1971 (div. June 1975); m. Michele Ann Hock, June 28, 1989; 1 child, Casey Christine Michele. AA in Bus. Adminstrn., Diablo Valley Coll., Pleasant Hill, Calif., 1965; BA in Design and Industry, San Francisco State U., 1967, MBA in Mktg., 1969; cert. res. police officer, Los Medanos Coll., Pittsburg, Calif., 1977. Owner Western Furs, Ltd., Walnut Creek, Calif., 1963-72; mgmt. cons. Controlled Interval Scheduling, Rolling Hills Estates, Calif., 1972-73; owner Dave Reed's Texaco, Concord, Calif., 1973-76; mgmt. cons. Mgmt. Scheduling Systems, Houston, 1974-76, Thomas-Ross Assocs., Mercer Island, Wash., 1972-82; plant mgr. Bonner Packing, Morgan Hill, Calif., 1981; mfg. engr. Systron Donner, Concord, 1982-84, Beckman Instruments, San Ramon, Calif., 1984-90; owner Dave Reed & Co. Water Ski Sch., White Water Rafting, Chiloquin, Oreg., 1987—, Dave Reed & Co., design, market, mfg. Contender boats, Chiloquin, Oreg., 1976—; lectr. wildlife mgmt. Dave Reed & Co., Chiloquin, 1965—, lectr. mgmt. seminars, 1982—; coach Japanese Water Ski Team, Bluff Water Ski Club, Tokyo, 1984; fin. mgr. Japanese investors Dave Reed & Co., Chiloquin, 1986—, design and supply solar electric power sys., 1994—. Res. dep. sheriff Contra Costa County Sheriff's Dept., Martinez, Calif., 1977-80. With U.S. Army, 1969-71, Vietnam. Recipient Gold medal internat. freestyle wrestling Sr. Olympics, Fullerton, Calif., 1983. Mem. Am. Water Ski Assn. (Calif. state water ski champion 1977, 86, western region water ski champion 1977, silver medal nat. water ski championships 1977), Bay Area Tournament Assn. (chmn. 1968—), Diablo Water Ski Club (bd. dirs. 1968—). Republican. Avocations: water skiing, snow skiing, surfing, camping, fly fishing. Home: PO Box 336 Chiloquin OR 97624-0336

REED, EDWARD CORNELIUS, JR., federal judge; b. Mason, Nev., July 8, 1924; s. Edward Cornelius Sr. and Evelyn (Walker) R.; m. Sally Torrance, June 14, 1952; children: Edward T., William W., John A., Mary E. BA, U. Nev., 1949; JD, Harvard U., 1952. Bar: Nev. 1952, U.S. Dist Ct. Nev. 1957, U.S. Supreme Ct. 1974. Atty. Arthur Andersen & Co., 1952-53; spl. dep. atty. gen. State of Nev., 1967-79; judge U.S. Dist. Ct. Nev., Reno, 1979—, chief judge, now sr. judge. Former vol. atty. Girl Scouts Am., Sierra Nevada Council, U. Nev., Nev. Agrl. Found., Nev. State Sch. Adminstrs. Assn., Nev. Congress of Parents and Teachers; mem. Washoe County Sch. Bd., 1956-72, pres. 1959, 63, 69; chmn. Gov.'s Sch. Survey Com., 1958-61; mem. Washoe County Bd. Tax Equalization, 1957-58, Washoe County Annexation Commn., 1968-72, Washoe County Personnel Com., 1973-77, chmn. 1973; mem. citizens adv. com. Washoe County Sch. Bond Issue, 1977-78, Sun Valley, Nev., Swimming Pool Com., 1978, Washoe County Blue Ribbon Task Force Com. on Growth, Nev. PTA (life); chmn. profl. div. United Way, 1978; bd. dirs. Reno Siver Sox, 1962-65. Served as staff sgt. U.S. Army, 1943-46, ETO, PTO. Mem. ABA (jud. adminstrn. sect.), Nev. State Bar Assn. (adminstrv. com. dist. 5, 1967-79, lien law com. 1965-78, chmn. 1965-72, probate law com. 1963-66, tax law com. 1962-65), Am. Judicature Soc. Democrat. Baptist. Office: US Dist Ct 400 S Virginia St Ste 606 Reno NV 89501-2182

REED, EVA SILVER STAR, chieftain; b. Vinita, Okla., Nov. 29, 1929; d. Robert Elbert Jones and Anna Mae (Campfield) Reed; m. Johnnie Silver Eagle Reed, June 10, 1946 (dec. Sept. 1982); children: Patty Deeanne, Lorrie Ann, Billy John. Sec. United Lumbee Nation of N.C. and Am., Fall River Mills, Calif., 1979-82; nat. head chieftain United Lumbee Nation of N.C. and Am., Fall River Mills, 1982—, also bd. dirs.; bd. dirs., sec. Chapel of Our Lord Jesus, Exeter, Calif., 1974—, Native Am. Wolf Clan, Calif., 1977—; tchr. Indian beading and crafts, Calif., 1977—. Author, compiler: Over the Cooking Fires, 1982, Lumbee Indian Ceremonies, 1982, United Lumbee Deer Clan Cook Book, 1988; editor: (newspaper) United Lumbee Nation Times, 1981—. Mem. parent com. Title IV & Johnson O'Malley Indian Edn. Program, Tulare/Kings County, 1976-80, Shasta County, Calif., 1982-84. Recipient United Lumbee Nation of N.C. and Am.'s Silver Eagle award, 1991, also various awards for beadwork Intermountain Fair, Shasta County, 1982-96. Avocations: writing, Indian beadwork, basket making, Indian crafts. Office: United Lumbee Nation of NC & Am PO Box 512 Fall River Mills CA 96028-0512

REED, FRAN ANN, artist; b. La Jolla, Calif., June 12, 1943; d. Charles and Mary Alice (Colt) Williams; m. Richard MacArthur Reed, Aug. 2, 1964; children: Collin, Jocelyn. BS, U. Oreg., 1967. Dyer, finisher Musk Ox Prodr.'s Coop, Fairbanks, Alaska, 1971-75; fiber instr. Tanana Valley C.C., Fairbanks, 1971-86, artist-in-the-schs., Anchorage, Fairbanks, 1980-97; lectr. Elderhostel, Anchorage, 1987—. Pub. art selection panel Alaska State Coun. Arts, Fairbanks, 1977-86; trustee Anchorage Mus. History and Art, 1993-95; state rep. Handweavers Guild Am., Fairbanks, 1984-88. Mem. Am. Craft Coun., Friends of Fiber Arts Internat., NW Designer Craftsmen. Home: 2424 Sprucewood St Anchorage AK 99508-3975

REED, FRANK FREMONT, II, retired lawyer; b. Chgo., June 15, 1928; s. Allen Martin and Frances (Faurot) R.; m. Jaquelin Silverthorne Cox, Apr. 27, 1963; children: Elizabeth Matthiessen Mason, Laurie Matthiessen Stern, Mark Matthiessen, Jeffrey, Nancy, Sarah. Student Chgo. Latin Sch.; grad. St. Paul's Sch., 1946; A.B., U. Mich., 1952, J.D., 1957. Bar: Ill., 1958. Assoc. Byron, Hume, Groen & Clement, 1958-61, Marks & Clerk, 1961-63; pvt. practice law, Chgo., 1963-78; dir. Western Acadia (Western Felt Works), 1960-75, chmn. exec. com., 1969-71. Rep. precinct capt. 1972-78; candidate for 43d ward alderman, 1975; bd. dirs., sec. Chgo. Found. Theater Arts, 1959-64; vestryman St. Chrysostom's Ch., 1975-79, mem. ushers guild, 1964-79, chmn., 1976-78; bd. dirs. North State, Astor, Lake Shore Dr. Assn., 1975-78, pres. 1977-78; bd. dirs. Community Arts Music Assn. of Santa Barbara, 1984-93, treas. 1988-93; bd. dirs. Santa Barbara Arts Coun., 1987-89. Cpl. AUS, 1952-54. Mem. ABA, Ill. Bar Assn., Phi Alpha Delta, Racquet Club, Wausaukee Club (sec., dir. 1968-71, 92-94) (Chgo.); Birnam Wood Golf Club (Santa Barbara, Calif.). Episcopalian. Author: History of the Silverthorn Family, 4 vols., 1982, Allen Family of Allen's Grove, 1983, Goddard and Ware Ancestors, 1987, Faurot Family, 1988. Contbr. articles to The Am. Genealogist, 1972-73, 76-77. Home: 1944 E Valley Rd Santa Barbara CA 93108-1428

REED, FRANK METCALF, bank executive; b. Seattle, Dec. 22, 1912; s. Frank Ivan and Pauline B. (Hovey) R.; student U. Alaska, 1931-32; BA, U. Wash., 1937; m. Maxine Vivian McGary, June 11, 1937; children: Pauline Reed Mackay, Frank Metcalf. V.p. Anchorage Light & Power Co., 1937-42; pres. Alaska Electric & Equipment Co., Anchorage, 1946-50; sec., mgr. Turnagain, Inc., Anchorage, 1950-56; mgr. Gen. Credit Corp., Anchorage, 1957; br. mgr. Alaska SBA, Anchorage, 1958-60; sr. v.p. First Interstate Bank of Alaska, Anchorage, 1960-87, also dir., corp. sec.; dir. First Interstate Corp. of Alaska, First Nat. Bank of Fairbanks; pres., dir. Anchorage Broadcasters, Inc.; past pres., chmn. Microfast Software Corp.; dir., treas. R.M.R. Inc.; dir. Anchorage Light & Power Co., Turnagain, Inc., Alaska Fish and Farm, Inc., Life Ins. Co. Alaska. Pres., Anchorage Federated Charities, Inc., 1953-54; mem. advisory bd. Salvation Army, 1948-58; mem. Alaska adv. bd. Hugh O'Brian Youth Found., 1987-91; trustee Anchor Age Endowment Fund, 1988-96, chmn., 1991; mem. City of Anchorage Planning Commn., 1956; mem. City of Anchorage Coun., 1956-57; police commr. Ter. of Alaska, 1957-58; chmn. City Charter Commn., 1958; mem. exec. com. Greater Anchorage, Inc., 1955-65; pres. Sch. Bd., 1961-64; mem. Gov.'s Investment adv. com., 1970-72; mem. Alaska State Bd. Edn.; mem. citizens adv. com. Alaska Meth. U.; chmn. Anchorage Charter Commn., 1975; chmn. bldg. fund dr. Cmty. YMCA, 1976 director, 1976-97, hon. dir. 1998—; sec.-treas. Breakthrough, 1976-78; bd. dirs. Alaska Treatment Ctr., 1980-87, pres. 1985-86; trustee Marston Found., Inc., 1978, exec. dir. 1988. Served as lt. USNR, 1942-46. Elected to Hall Fame, Alaska Press Club, 1969; named [illegible] 1991. Mem. Am. Inst. Banking, Am. (exec. council 1971-72) Alaska (pres. 1970-71) bankers assns., Nat. Assn. State Bds. Edn. (sec.-treas. 1969-70), Anchorage C. of C. (pres. 1966-67, dir.), Pioneers of Alaska, Navy League (pres. Anchorage council 1961-62). Clubs: Tower (life), San Francisco Tennis. Lodges: Lions (sec. Anchorage, 1953-54, dir. 1988, pres., 1962-63, life), Elks (life). Home: 1361 W 12th Ave Anchorage AK 99501-4252

REED, FRANK VERN, principal; b. Basin, Wyo., Sept. 20, 1951; s. Frank Junior and Irene (McKim) R.; m. Kristine Malcolm; children: Tania, Frank. BS, U. Wyo., 1976; MA, Nova U., 1985; EdD, No. Ariz. U., 1997; BA, Ariz. State U. Cert. supt., prin., tchr., Ariz. Tchr. Apache Junction (Ariz.) Sch. Dist., 1982-85, prin., 1985-89; prin. Somerton (Ariz.) Sch. Dist., 1989—. Mem. ASCD, Ariz. Sch. Adminstrn., Phi Delta Kappa. Democrat. Methodist. Avocations: hunting, fishing, gun safety, archery, family activities. Home: 1481 W Michelle Ln Yuma AZ 85365-9629 Office: Somerton Sch Dist PO Box Bin E Somerton AZ 85350

REED, GEORGE FORD, JR., investment executive; b. Hollywood, Calif., Dec. 26, 1946; s. George Ford and Mary Anita Reed; B.A. in Econs. with honors, U. So. Calif., 1969, M.A., 1971; m. Kathryn Nixon, 1981. Analyst planning and research Larwin Group, Beverly Hills, Calif., 1971-72; with Automobile Club So. Calif., Los Angeles, 1972-76, supr. mgmt. info., research and devel., 1973-74, mgr. fin. and market analysis, 1975-81, group mgr. fin. analysis and forecasting, 1981-86; pres. Reed Asset Mgmt. Co., Inc., Los Angeles, 1986—; instr. bus. and econs. Los Angeles Community Coll. Mem. population task force Los Angeles C. of C., 1974; mem. Gov. Calif. Statewide Econ. Summit Conf., 1974. Served with U.S. Army, 1969. Mem. Assn. Corp. Real Estate Execs., Fin. Execs. Inst., Nat. Assn. Bus. Economists, Western Regional Sci. Assn., Am. Mgmt. Assn., Am. Fin. Assn., So. Calif. Planners Assn., Rotary Internat., Omicron Delta Epsilon. Home: 1001 S Westgate Ave Los Angeles CA 90049-5905 Office: 10940 Wilshire Blvd Ste 1600 Los Angeles CA 90024-3943

REED, JAMES ANTHONY, hotel industry executive, consultant; b. Marion, Ohio, June 12, 1939; s. James E. and Sue (McCurdy) R. Student, Fla. State U., 1956-59, U. N.H., 1978. Food and beverage mgr. Caneel Bay Plantation, St. John, Virgin Islands, 1960-64; mgr. Mauna Kea Beach Hotel, Kamuela, Hawaii, 1964-72; v.p. C. Brewer & Co., Ltd., Honolulu, 1972-77, Dunfey Hotel Corp., Hampton, N.H., 1977-80, Marriott Hotels & Resorts, Calif., Hawaii and Asia, 1980-89; pres. The Reed Group, Irvine, Calif., 1989; gen. mgr. La Posada de Santa Fe, 1990-91, Hotel Santa Fe, 1991-93; asst. to pres. LaJolla (Calif) Beach and Tennis Club, Inc., 1993-95; pres. The Reed Group, Santa Fe, N.M., LaJolla, 1993—; pres. Kilauea Volcano House Inc., Mackensie Hawaii Ltd., Augustine's Decor Spain; vice-chmn., bd. dirs. Picuris Pueblo Enterprises, cons. to Native Am. Tribes. Named Outstanding Young Men of Am., 1969. Mem. Calif. Thoroughbred Breeders Assn., Calif. Hotel Assn., Sch. Am. Rsch., Community Leaders of Am., Appaloosa Horse Club. Home and Office: 7550 Eads Ave La Jolla CA 92037-4800

REED, JAMES EARL, fire department commander; b. San Francisco, Mar. 21, 1957; s. Arlen Earl and Louise (Gibbs) R.; m. Jody Lynn Bales, Feb. 14, 1976 (div. Aug. 1978); 1 child, Darci Lynn; m. Donna Kaye Lewis, June 25, 1994. A in fire sci., Casper Coll., 1995. State cert. fire fighter I, II, III, state cert. fire svc. instr. I, state cert. fire prevention officer I. Shop worker, shop foreman, salesman Becker Fire Equipment, Casper, Wyo., 1975-78; safety equipment maintance Bell H2S Safety and Oilind Safety Engring., Casper, 1978-80; tchr. outreach program Casper Coll., 1988-90; owner operator J.R.'s Custom Hand Planted Signs, 1980-93; capt. Casper (Wyo.) Fire Dept., 1978-93, comdr., 1993—; artist Images Studio, Casper, 1991—; instr. CPR courses Am. Heart Soc., ARC, 1980—; instr. SCBA courses, 1983-85. Active fund raisers City/County Fire Fighters Burn Fund, 1982, 84—, fund raisers Muscular Dystrophy Assn., 1981, 82, 85-89, fund raisers March of Dimes, 1984, 85, 87, fund raisers Casper Mountain Racers Youth Olympics, 1985-87, Casper Event Ctr.'s "Spl. Christmas for Spl. Kids," 1984-87; mem. Wyo. chpt. Multiple Sclerosis Soc., 1994—. Named Firefighter of Yr. Casper Fire Dept., Casper Ladies Auxiliary, Am. Legion Regional and Post 2, 1984, Man in Blue, Casper Fire Dept., 1994. Mem. Casper Fire Fighters Assn. (entertainment com. 1980—, exec. com. 1988-90), City County Fire Fighters Burn Fund (trustee 1985-86, treas. 1986-89, sec. 1989-91, pres. 1992—). Republican. Seventh-day Adventist. Avocations: painting, alpine and water skiing, weight lifting, racquetball. Home: PO Box 2297 Casper WY 82602-2297

REED, LYNDA BERNAL, video producer, writer; b. Detroit, July 9, 1959; d. Bernard and Joyce Lydia (Gunnett) Harris; m. Ronald Daniel Bernal, June 21, 1980 (div. Oct. 1985); m. Jack Milton Reed, Nov. 4, 1993. BS in Health Sci., Ariz. State U., 1982. Audiovisual coord. Salt River Project, Phoenix, 1985-93; ind. writer/prodr. Phoenix, 1993-96; writer, prodr. Ednl. Mgmt. Group, Scottsdale, 1996-97, The Studio, Hurricane, Utah, 1997—. Writer, dir.: (videotape) Montezuma Castle: Home of the Prehistoric Sinagua, 1994 (Southwest Book award 1995, Nat. Park Svc. award of excellence 1996), Lake Powell: Heart of the Grand Circle, 1986 (Rocky Mountain Emmy award 1987, ITVA award 1986), The Wolf: A Howling in America's Parks, 1989 (CINDY award 1989), 1993 Page Promo (TELLY award 1994), Total Health: Achieving Your Personal Best (TELLY award 1998). Media cons. YWCA of Maricopa County, Phoenix, 1986-90. Mem. NATAS, Internat. TV Assn., Bus. and Profl. Women USA. Avocations: bicycling, hiking, world travel, reading.

REED, NORMAN BRUCE, real estate developer; b. Long Beach, Calif., Jan. 15, 1949; s. Eugene Cameron and Lorine Vivian (Gross) R. BS, U. So. Calif., 1971, postgrad., 1974-76. Chpt. mgmt. cons. Sigma Nu Fraternity, Lexington, Va., 1971-73; redevel. project mgr. City of Long Beach, 1973-78; project mgr. and cons. various cos., Long Beach, 1978-84; sales and mktg. dir. Island Resorts Catalina, Inc., Long Beach, 1984-87; loan and investment agt. Calif. Western Fin. Corp., Los Alamitos, Calif., 1987-88; asst. v.p. comml. and indsl. div. Chicago Title, Pasadena, Calif., 1988-89; pres. RealVest, Inc., 1989-91; v.p. Pacific Realty Group, Long Beach, Calif., 1991—; lectr. redevel. Calif. State U., Long Beach, 1977-79, Long Beach City Coll., 1977-79. Past master councilor Belmont Shore Order of DeMolay, 1964; bd. dirs. Grand Prix Com. of 300, Long Beach, 1975—, pres., 1981; bd. dirs. Pub. Corp. for Arts, Long Beach 1982-88; Cedar House Child Abuse Prevention Ctr., Long Beach, 1980-83; chmn. pub. corp. for the arts Long Beach Centennial Internat. Festival, 1988; chmn. bd. dirs. ONE in Long Beach, Inc., 1990-92; exec. com. AIDS Walk, Long Beach, 1990—; grad. and programs com. mem. Leadership Long Beach, 1991—; mem. Citizens Task Force on Effective Govt., 1992.. Recipient Small Bus. Achievement award Long Beach C. of C., 1991, Man of yr. Southland Political Action Com., 1991. Mem. Long Beach Jaycees (Disting. Svc. award, officer 1973-83), Long Beach Area C. of C. (bd. dirs. 1980-81, 90—), Long Beach Dist. Bd. Realtors, Long Beach Conv. and Visitors Coun. (mktg. com. 1984-86), Sigma Nu (Nat. Man of Yr. 1971, officer 1968-71). Avocations: civic activities, fine arts events, dancing, college football. Home: 3819 E Livingston Dr Apt 15 Long Beach CA 90803-2891 Office: Pacific Realty Group 333 W Broadway Ste 200 Long Beach CA 90802-4439

REED, RAY PAUL, engineering mechanics measurement consultant; b. Abilene, Tex., May 26, 1927; s. Raymond Roseman and Gladys Daisy (Reddell) R.; m. Mary Antoinette Wied, Oct. 7, 1950; children: Mary Kathryn, Patricia Lynn. BSME, Tex. A&M U., 1950; MS in Engring. Mechanics, U. Tex., 1958, PhD, 1966. Registered profl. engr., N.Mex., Tex. Rsch. engr. S.W. Rsch. Inst., San Antonio, 1950-54; rsch. scientist U. Tex., Austin, 1954-56; mem. tech. staff Sandia Nat. Labs., Albuquerque, 1956-61, rsch. fellow, 1961-66, disting. mem. tech. staff, 1966-94. Author: manual on the use of thermocouples; contbr. numerous reports and articles on shock measurement and thermometry to profl. jours. With USNR, 1945-46, PTO. NIH grantee U. Tex., 1962-66. Mem. ASTM (chmn. com. 1985—), ASME, Instrument Soc. Am., Am. Physics Soc., Sigma Xi. Avocations: photography, wood carving, cartooning, writing. Home and Office: Proteun Svcs 6640 Casa Loma NE Albuquerque NM 87109-3962

REED, ROSALIE, horse trainer; b. San Diego, May 5, 1954; d. Lester Woodrow Reed and Pearl (Peterson) Hampton. Trainer Fletcher Hills Ranch, San Diego, 1970-74, Willow Glen Farm, El Cajon, Calif., 1974-77, [illegible] Nat. Show, Syracuse, N.Y.., Appaloosa Horse Club. Can. Author: Handbook of Hunter Seat Equitation, 1977, Handbook of Saddle Seat Equitation, 1978; [illegible] Champions, 1978; winner 8 world championships, Appaloosa Horse Club,

1972-76, 7 nat. championships, 1972-76; demonstrator 1984 Summer Olympics, L.A. Mem. ASCAP, Am. Horse Show Assn. (judge), Internat. Arabian Horse Assn. (judge), Pacific Coast Horse Show Assn., Calif. Profl. Horsemen's Assn., Equestrian Trails Internat. Avocations: singing, songwriting, skydiving. Office: LA Equestrian Ctr 480 W Riverside Dr Burbank CA 91506-3209

REED, SANDY, magazine editor; m. Bob Ingle. B Journalism, Kans. State U. Reporting and sr. editing positions San Jose (Calif.) Mercury News, Miami (Fla.) Herald, Billings (Mont.) Gazette, Oakland (Calif.) Tribune; exec. editor news ops. InfoWorld, San Francisco, 1984-90, exec. editor Pers. Computing mag., 1985-90, editor-in-chief, 1990—, exec. editor PC/Computing, 1991—. Founding editor Macintosh Bus. Rev.; founding editl. dir. New Media Age mag. (now NewMedia mag). Named one of most influential journalists covering computer industry Mktd. Computers mag. Avocations: surfing the web, reading, travel. Office: Infoworld 155 Bovet Rd Ste 800 San Francisco CA 94402-3108*

REED, STEPHEN GREGORY, sales executive; b. Eugene, Oreg., Feb. 23, 1968; s. Gregory William and Susanne Margaret (Flynn) R.; m. Melanie Jane Fleming. BA, U. Colo., 1991. Account exec. Sta. KNBR Radio, San Francisco, 1991-95; gen. sales mgr. Sta. KFXX Radio, Portland, Oreg., 1995-97, Sta. KMTT Radio, Seattle, 1997-98. Vol. Emmanuel Hosp. Emergency, Portland, 1995—, Franciscan-Christmas in April, Portland, 1997, Christmas in April, San Francisco, 1991-93. Mem. Wash. State Assn. Broadcasters, No. Calif. Broadcasters Assn., Portland Area Radio Coun. Republican. Presbyterian. Avocations: piano, guitar, scriptwriting, basketball, family. Office: Sta KMTT Radio 1100 Olive Way Ste 1650 Seattle WA 98101-1863

REED, TODD RANDALL, electrical engineer, educator; b. Mpls., Sept. 26, 1954; s. Donald James Reed and Amy Louise (Countryman) Blume; m. Nancy Ellen Lundgren, June 18, 1977. BS, U. Minn., 1977, MS, 1986, PhD, 1988. Elec. engr. IBM, various locations, 1977-83; sr. design engr. Astrocom Corp., St. Paul, 1984-86; cons. Lincoln Lab. MIT, Lexington, 1986-88; vis. asst. prof. elec. engring. U. Minnesota, Mpls., 1988-89; asst. Swiss Fed. Inst. Tech., Lausanne, 1989-91; asst. prof. U. Calif., Davis, 1991-94, assoc. prof., 1994—; vis. rschr. Linköping (Sweden) U., 1998—. Patentee Analog Adaptive Magnitude Equalizer, 1985; contbr. articles to profl. jours. Mem. IEEE (sr.), European Assn. for Signal Processing, Assn. for Computing Machinery, Soc. for Indsl. and Applied Math., Tau Beta Pi, Eta Kappa Nu. Avocations: electronic music, bonsai. Office: U Calif Dept Elec and Computer Engring Davis CA 95616

REEDER, F. ROBERT, lawyer; b. Brigham City, Utah, Jan. 23, 1943; s. Frank O. and Helen H. (Heninger) R.; m. Joannie Anderson, May 4, 1974; children: David, Kristina, Adam. JD, U. Utah, 1967. Bar: Utah 1967, U.S. Ct. Appeals (10th cir.) 1967, U.S. Ct. Mil. Appeals 1968, U.S. Supreme Ct. 1972, U.S. Ct. Appeals (D.C. and 5th cirs.) 1979. Shareholder Parsons, Behle & Latimer, Salt Lake City, 1968—, bd. dirs., 1974-92. Bd. dirs. Holy Cross Found., 1981-90, chmn., 1987-90; bd. dirs. Holy Cross Hosp., 1990-93, treas., 1986-87, vice chmn., 1987-93; bd. dirs. Holy Cross Health Svcs. Utah, 1993-94, treas., 1993-94; bd. dirs., vice chmn. Salt Lake Regional Med. Ctr., 1995—; trustee Univ. Hosp. Found., 1995; hon. col. Salt Lake City Police, Salt Lake County Sheriff. Served with USAR, 1967-73. Mem. ABA, Utah State Bar, Salt Lake County Bar (ethic adv. com. 1989-94), Cottonwood Country Club (bd. dirs. 1978-82, 83-86, pres. 1981-82), Rotary. Office: Parsons Behle & Latimer PO Box 45898 Salt Lake City UT 84145-0898

REED-GRAHAM, LOIS L., administrator, secondary education educator; b. Muscogee, Okla., Jan. 19, 1933; d. Louis G. and Bonnie (Hill) Reed; children: Harold Gibson, Kathryn Ann Graham. RN, San Diego County Hosp., 1957; BA, Calif. State U., Sacramento, 1972, MPA, 1978; postgrad., Calif. State U., Sacremento; EdD, U. Laverne. Tchr., adminstr., job developer CETA, Sacramento, 1972-78; bus. instr. Los Rios Community Coll., Sacramento, 1978-84; tchr. grade 6 Mark Hopkins Sch., Sacramento, 1984-89; acting adminstr. Fern Bacon Sch., Sacramento; adminstr. Sacramento City Schs.; tchr. grades 7,8, mentor tchr. Fern Bacon Sch., Sacramento; asst. prin. secondary edn. Sacramento City Schs., 1989-93; elem. sch. prin. Theodore Judah Elem. Sch., Sacramento, 1993—; asst. supt. secondary, middle and K-8 schs. Sacramento City Unified Sch.; cons. Prentice Hall Pub. Co. Contbr. articles to profl. publs. Mem. Calif. State Fair Employment and Housing Commn. Mem. AAUW (bd. dirs., pres. Sacramento chpt. 1990), Nat. Assn. Univ. Women (pres.). Home: 7408 Toulon Ln Sacramento CA 95828-4641

REED-JACKSON, LEONA MAE, educational administrator; b. Crosby, Tex., Sept. 9, 1945; d. Elton Phillip and Ora Lee (Jones) Reed; m. Aaron B. Mounds Jr., Aug. 21, 1965 (div.); 1 child, Lisa Nichelle; m. Emanuel Jackson, Mar. 8, 1997. BS in Elem. Edn., Bridgewater State Coll., 1973; MA in Mental Retardation, U. Alaska, 1980. Cert. tchr. Alaska, Colo., Tex., Mass., cert. adminstrv. prin. Tchr., Sch. Dist.# 11, Colorado Springs, Colo., 1973-75; tchr. Anchorage Sch. Dist., 1976-78, 80—, mem. maths. curriculum com., reading contact tchr., mem. talent bank. Tchr. Del Valle (Tex.) Sch. Dist., 1979-80; adminstrv. prin. intern Anchorage Sch. Dist., 1989-90; asst. prin. Spring Hill Elem. Sch., Anchorage, 1990-91; elem. prin. intern.; asst. prin. Ptarmigan Elem. Sch., Anchorage, 1991-93, prin., 1993-94; with Child in Transition Homeless Project Title I Anchorage Sch. Dist., Anchorage, Alaska, 1994—. Bd. dirs. Urban League, 1974; 1st v.p. PTA, Crosby, Tex.; del. Tex. Dem. Conv., 1980; chmn. dist. 13 Dem. Party; mem. Alaska Women Polit. Caucus; bd. dirs. C.R.I.S.I.S. Inc.; tchr. religious edn., lay Eucharist minister St. Martin De Pores Roman Cath. Ch., St. Patrick's Roman Cath. Ch.; pres. Black Educators of Pike Peak Region, 1974; mem. social concerns commn. Archidiocese of Anchorage, Coun. for Exceptional Children. With USAF, 1964-66. Alaska State Tchr. Incentive grantee, 1981, Ivy Lutz scholar, 1972. Mem. NEA (human rels. coord. Alaska chpt., region 6 bd. dirs., bd dirs Alaska chpt., vice-chmn. women's caucus), NAACP, LWV, Nat. Coun. Negro Women, Anchorage Edn. Assn. (minority chmn. 1982—, mem. black caucus polit. action com., v.p. programs 1986-88), Anchorage Edn. Assn. (v.p. programs com. 1986-87, women's caucus), Assn. Supervision and Curriculum Devel., Alaska Women in Adminstrn., Prins. Assn., Alaska Women's Polit. Caucus, Alpha Kapp Alpha, Phi Delta Kappa. Office: Anchorage Sch Dist Child in Transition/Homeless Program 4600 Debarr Rd Anchorage AK 99508-3126

REES, NORMA S., academic administrator; b. N.Y.C., Dec. 27, 1929; d. Benjamin and Lottie (Schwartz) D.; m. Raymond R. Rees, Mar. 19, 1960; children—Evan Lloyd, Raymond Arthur. B.A., Queens Coll., 1952; M.A., Bklyn. Coll., 1954; Ph.D., NYU, 1959. Cert. speech-language pathology, audiology. Prof. communicative disorders Hunter Coll., N.Y.C., 1967-72; exec. officer, speech and hearing scis. grad. sch. CUNY, N.Y.C., 1972-74, assoc. dean for grad. studies, 1974-76, dean grad. studies, 1976-82; vice chancellor for acad. affairs U. Wis., Milw., 1982-85, from 1986, acting chancellor, 1985-86; vice chancellor for acad. policy and planning Mass. Bd. Regents for Higher Edn., Boston, 1987-90; pres. Calif. State U., Hayward, 1990—; chmn. Commn. Recognition of Postsecondary Accreditation, 1994-96; mem. adv. com. quality and integrity U.S. Dept. Edn. Contbr. articles to profl. jours. Trustee Citizens Govtl. Rsch. Bur., Milw., 1985-87; active Task Force on Wis. World Trade Ctr., 1985-87; bd. dirs. Am. Assn. State Colls. and Univs., 1995-97, Coun. of Postsecondary Accreditation, Washington, 1985-94, Greater Boston YWCA, 1987-90; mem. Calif. Film Commn.; mem. Calif. Sch. to Career Coun.; mem. Oakland Edn. Cabinet; mem. steering com. Econ. Devel. Adv. Bd. Alameda County, 1995—. Fellow Am. Speech-Lang-Hearing Assn. (honors); mem. Am. Coun. Edn. (com. internat. edn. 1991-93), Am. Assn. Colls. and Univs. (chair task force on quality assessment 1991-92, mem. steering com. of coun. of urban met. colls. & univs. 1992—), Nat. Assn. State Univs. and Land Grant Colls. (exec. com. divsn. urban affairs 1985-87, com. accreditation 1987-90), Hayward C. of C. (bd. dirs. 1995—), Oakland C. of C. (bd. dirs. 1997—). Office: Calif State Univ-Hayward 25800 Carlos Bee Blvd Hayward CA 94542-3001

REESE, HARRY EUGENE, artist, educator; b. Ft. Worth, Tex., Oct. 9, 1946; s. Harry Alpha and Betty Lee (Ogletree) R.; m. Sandra Liddell Paulson, Sept. 24, 1977. BA, U. Calif., Santa Barbara, 1968, MA, 1971; MA, Brown U., 1975. Artist, pub. Turkey Press, Cranston, R.I., 1974-75, Berkeley, Calif., 1975-77, Isla Vista, Calif., 1977—; lectr. art Coll. Creative Studies, U. Calif., Santa Barbara, 1978-93, asst. prof. dept. art studio, 1993-95, assoc. prof., 1995-98, prof., 1998—, chair dept., 1996—. Author, artist: Arplines, 1990; co-artist Near Goleta But Closer, 1991; artist: Funagainstawake, 1997. Bd. dirs. Contemporary Arts Forum, Santa Barbara, 1991-94. Assistance to Small Presses Orgn. grantee NEA, Washington, 1976, 77, 79, 81, Calif. Arts Coun., Sacramento, 1979, 80; Hilliard scholar in humanities, U. Nev., Reno, 1990. E-mail: reese@humanitas.ucsb.edu. Office: U Calif Dept Art Studio Santa Barbara CA 93106

REESE, JANET ISABELLA, library technician, music educator, researcher; b. Hallock, Minn., Sept. 1, 1953; d. Bernard Alden and Jennie Pearl (Hicks) R. BA in Music and French, Westmont Coll., 1975; postgrad., Calif. State U., Chico, 1976; M in Ch. Music, Golden Gate Bapt. Theol. Sem., Mill Valley, Calif., 1991. Registered tchr., Calif. Tchr. grades 7-12 Capistrano Valley Christian Sch., San Juan Capistrano, Calif., 1978-86, Trinity Christian Schs., Sacramento, 1986-87; periodicals circulation worker Golden Gate Bapt. Theol. Sem., 1989-90, grad. music tchg. asst., 1989—, adj. music prof., spring 1991, periodicals technician, 1989—, adj. prof. music rsch., 1993, adj. prof., 1993—; developer French programs, faculty advisor for speech meets Capistrano Valley Christian Sch., 1978-86. Lyricist Korean/English musical Look to the Manger, 1996. Notary pub., Calif. Mem. NASIG, Am. Diabetes Assn., Notary Assn., So. Bapt. Ch. Music. Avocations: writing, stitchery, baking bread, reading, walking. Office: Golden Gate Bapt Theol Sem Library 201 Seminary Dr Mill Valley CA 94941

REESE, JOHN ROBERT, lawyer; b. Salt Lake City, Nov. 3, 1939; s. Robert McCann and Glade (Stauffer) R.; m. Francesca Marroquin Gardner, Sept. 5, 1964 (div.); children—Jennifer Marie, Justine Francesca; m. Robin Ann Gunsul, June 18, 1988. AB cum laude, Harvard U., 1962; LLB, Stanford U., 1965. Bar: Calif. 1966, U.S. Dist. Ct. (no. dist.) Calif. 1966, U.S. Ct. Appeals (9th cir.) 1966, U.S. Dist. Ct. (cen. dist.) Calif. 1974, U.S. Supreme Ct. 1976, U.S. Dist. Ct. (ea. dist.) Calif. 1977, U.S. Ct. Appeals (6th cir.) 1982, U.S. Ct. Appeals (8th cir.) 1985, U.S. Ct. Appeals (10th cir.) 1992, U.S. Ct. Appeals (Fed. cir.) 1994. Assoc. McCutchen, Doyle, Brown & Enersen, San Francisco, 1965-74, ptnr., 1974—; adj. asst. prof. law Hastings Coll. of Law, 1991; lectr. U. Calif., Berkeley, 1987, 92. Mem. editorial, adv. bds. Antitrust Bull., Jour. Reprints for Antitrust Law and Econs. Bd. dirs. Friends of San Francisco Pub. Libr., 1981-87; bd. vis. Stanford U. Law Sch., 1983-86. Capt. U.S. Army, 1966-68. Decorated Bronze Star. Mem. ABA, State Bar Calif., San Francisco Bar Assn., U.S. Supreme Ct. Hist. Soc., Ninth Jud. Cir. Hist. Soc., Calif. Acad. Appellate Lawyers, Order of the Coif. Avocations: aviculture, gardening. Home: 9 Morning Sun Dr Petaluma CA 94952-4780 Office: McCutchen Doyle Brown & Enersen 3 Embarcadero Ctr San Francisco CA 94111-4003

REESE, KERRY DAVID, minister; b. Kennewick, Wash., Dec. 17, 1953; s. Walter Theodore and Arline Winifred (Botz) R.; m. Robin Marie Harm, Aug. 18, 1978; children: Michelle, Benjamin, Emily. AA, Concordia Coll., 1974; BA, Concordia Sr. Coll., 1976; MDiv, Concordia Sem., 1980, STM, 1987. Asst. pastor St. Peter-Immanuel Luth. Ch., Milw., 1982-83; pastor Messiah Luth. Ch., Highland, Calif., 1983-90, Shepherd of the Hills Luth. Ch., Snohomish, Washington, 1990—. Mem. Luth. Ch.-Mo. Synod (del. Wichita, Kans. conv. 1989). Office: Shepherd of the Hills Luth Ch 9225 212th St SE Snohomish WA 98296-7164

REESE, MONTE NELSON, agricultural association executive; b. Mooreland, Okla., Mar. 31, 1947; s. James Nelson and Ruby Edith (Bond) R.; m. Treisa Lou Bartow, May 25, 1968; children: Bartow Allan, Monica Lynnelle. BS in Agrl. Econs., Okla. State U., 1969. Staff asst. Wilson Cert. Foods, Oklahoma City, 1969-71; assoc. farm dir. Sta. WKY Radio and TV, Oklahoma City, 1971-73; radio-TV specialist Tex. A&M U., College Station, 1973; dir. agrl. devel. Oklahoma City C. of C., 1973-76; asst. exec. dir. Am. Morgan Horse Assn., Westmoreland, N.Y., 1976-77; v.p. pub. affairs Farm Credit Banks of Wichita, Kans., 1977-87; exec. dir. Coffey County Econ. Devel., Burlington, Kans., 1987-88; farm dir. Mid-Am. Ag Network, Wichita, 1988-89; CEO Cattlemen's Beef Promotion and Rsch. Bd., Englewood, Colo., 1989-96; exec. dir. Cattlemen's Beef Promotion & Rsch. Bd., Englewood, CO, 1996—. Lt. col. USAR, 1969—. Home: 982 S Dearborn Way Apt 2 Aurora CO 80012-3878 Office: Cattlemen's Beef Promotion and Rsch Bd PO Box 3316ec St Englewood CO 80155*

REESE, WILLIAM ALBERT, III, psychologist, clinical neuropsychologist; b. Tabor, Iowa, Nov. 23, 1932; s. William Albert and Mary-Evelyn Hope (Lundeen) R.; m. Barbara Diane Windermere, Dec. 22, 1954 (dec. Jan. 1995); children: Judy, Diane William IV, Sandra-Siobhan, Debra-Anne, Robert-Gregory, Barbara-Jaoanne; m. Ruth Alice Moller, Sept 12, 1996. *William is great-grandson of Thomas Reese who as a boy of 8 came to America from Wales, served in the Union Army in Missouri and raised 13 children with wife Mary Emmerich. William served in Vietnam, married Barbara Winder who met her untimely death, 1995, and reared 10 children. William married Dr. Ruth Moller (Reese), MD, in 1997, a board certified physician in internal medicine and a mother of three children: Ann, Alice, Jordan. Together, they promote a wellness clinic where each takes charge of their own health in order to reach their highest aspirations in life.* BA, U. Washington Reed Coll., 1955; M.Ed., U. Ariz., 1964, PhD, 1981; postgrad., Fielding Inst. Clin. Neuropsyc, 1999. Diplomate Am. Bd. Christian Psychology, Am. Bd. Forensic Psychologists; cert. in clin. neuropsychology. Clin. psychology cons. Nogales Pub. Schs., Nogales-Tucson, Ariz., 1971-79; clin. psychologist Astra-Found., N.Y.C., 1979-86, chief psychology svc., neuropsychiatry, 1980-89; chief psychologist Family Support Ctr. Community-Family Exception Mem. Svcs., Sonoita, Ariz., 1986-89, Psychol. Svc. Ctr., Mount Tabor, Iowa, 1989-95, Calif. Ctr. Health and Wellness, 1995—; dir. religious marriage and Family Life Wilderness Ctr., Berchtesgaden, W. Ger., lsummer, 1981-82; exec. sec. Astra Ednl. Found, 1975-79, bd. dirs, 1979—, EEO officer, 1978—. Author: Developing a Scale of Human Values for Adults of Diverse Cultural Backgrounds, 1981, rev. edit., 1988. Served with USAF, 1967-71, Vietnam. Decorated Bronze Star. Fellow in cons. psychology and holistic medicine Clin. Services Found., Ariz., 1979—. Fellow Am. Psychol. Soc., Am. Coll. Forensic Examiners, Clin. Neuropsychiatry and Neuropsychology, 1998; mem. APA, ACA, Internat. Neuropsychol. Assn., Calif. Psychol. Assn., Iowa Psychol. Assn., K.C., Los Padres Wilderness Ctr., Outdoor Club, Sierra Club, Skyline Estates Golf and Country Club (Tucson). Office: Psychol Service Ctr Integrated Med Ctr-Wellness Clin 225 Crossroads Blvd Ste 428 Carmel CA 93923-8649

REEVE, EDGAR GILBERT, school counselor; b. Cortlandville, N.Y., Oct. 9, 1941; s. Irving and Minnie (Belding) R.; m. Crystal, June 17, 1989; children: Michael Alan, Karin. AA, Trinidad (Colo.) Jr. Coll., 1965; BA, Adams State Coll., 1967; MEd, Ball State U., 1968. Tchr. Holly (Colo.) Sch. Dist., 1968-73; ins. sales Ohio Nat. Life, 1973-74; counselor Big Horn Sch. Dist. #4, Basin, Wyo., 1974-76, Carbon County Sch. Dist. #2, Hanna, Wyo., 1976—. Mem. Internat. Assn. Panoramic Photographers, Wyo. Counseling Assn., Am. Edn. Assn., Wyo. Edn. Assn. Avocations: travel, hiking, outdoors.

REEVE, LORRAINE ELLEN, biochemist, researcher; b. Cato, Wis., Aug. 12, 1951; d. Robert K. and Lila M. (Breneman) R.; m. Dennis L. Kiesling, July 21, 1990. BS, U. Wis., 1973, MS, 1978, PhD, 1981. Postdoctoral scholar U. Mich., Ann Arbor, 1981-86; project scientist Cleve. Clinic Found., 1986-88; sr. rsch. scientist R.P. Scherer Corp., Troy, Mich., 1988-89, Mediventures, Inc., Dearborn, Mich., 1989-92; prin. investigator Mediventures, Inc., Dearborn, 1992-94; project mgr. MDV Technologies, Inc. (formerly Mediventures, Inc.), Dearborn, 1994—. Contbr. articles to profl. jours. Mem. Founders Soc. Detroit Inst. Art, 1989—, Nat. Trust for Historic Preservation, 1991—. Mem. AAAS, N.Y. Acad. Sci. Achievements include patents for topical drug delivery, ophthalmic drug delivery, drug delivery by injection and body cavity drug delivery all with thermo-irreversible and thermoreversible gels, ablatable mask of polyoxyalkylene polymer and ionic polysaccharide gel for laser reprofiling of the cornea; European patent pending for drug delivery with thermoreversible gels. Home: PO Box 2962 Ann Arbor MI 48106-2962 Office: MDV Techs Inc 3040 Science Park Rd San Diego CA 92121-1102

REEVES, BRUCE, social worker; b. Centerville, Utah, Jan. 8, 1955; s. Leon W. and Maxine (Hodson) R. BA, U. Utah, 1979, MSW, 1983. Mental health caseworker Traveler's Aid Soc. Salt Lake, Salt Lake City, 1983-86; socialwork cons. Home Health of Utah, Bountiful, 1985-86; victim svcs. counselor Salt Lake County Atty's. Office, Salt Lake City, 1986-87; mgr., cons. AIDS and employee assistance program Aetna and Human Affairs Internat., Salt Lake City, 1987-96; dir. social work and therapies Paracelsus Home Care & Hospice, Salt Lake City, 1996-98; registrar, bus. mgr. Awakening Spirit Massage Sch., L.C., Salt Lake City, 1998-99; health educator Health Horizons, L.C., 1996-98; presenter in field. Bd. dirs. Walk-ons, Inc., Salt Lake City, 1989-98, Gay and Lesbian Cmty. Ctr. Utah, Salt Lake City, 1998—; mem. appropriations com. United Way Greater Salt Lake, Salt Lake City, 1990—, bd. assocs. Ririe-Woodbury Dance Co., Salt Lake City, 1991-95, human svcs. com. Utah Stonewall Ctr., Salt Lake City, 1992-95. Mem. NASW, APHA, Nat. Lesbian and Gay Health Assn., Gay Lesbian Student Edn. Network. Democrat. Avocations: dance, theatre, music, literature. Office: Awakening Spirit Massage Sch LLC 421 South 400 East Salt Lake City UT 84111

REEVES, DONALD BUSTER, minister; b. Seymour, Tex., Sept. 30, 1945; s. Donald Buster and Lillian Lauraine (Hughes) R.; m. June Marie Weaver, Aug. 4, 1967 (dec. 1973); 1 child, Carece Marie; m. Sandra Fay Teague, Nov. 10, 1973; children: Charity Christine, Joshua Kevin. BA, Hardin-Simmons U., Abilene, Tex., 1968; postgrad., Southwestern Sem., Ft. Worth, Tex., 1969. Ordained to ministry So. Bapt. Conv., 1967. Youth pastor Belmont Bapt. Ch., Abilene, Tex., 1965-67; youth evangelist, spreader, 1965-68; pastor various chs. various locations, 1969-73; evangelist and conf. speaker, 1970-90; pastor Temple Bapt Ch., Redlands, Calif., 1979-86, Mt. Franklin Bapt. Ch., El Paso, Tex., 1986-94; sr. pastor Rose Drive Bapt. Ch., Yorba Linda, Calif., 1994—; bd. dirs. Sta. KSCE-TV Christian TV, El Paso, 1990—; pres. Calif. State Ministers Conf., Fresno, 1985; exec. bd. Calif. So. Bapt. Con., Fresno, 1982-86; evangelism chmn. El Paso Bapt. Assn., 1989-91; chmn. Here's Hope City-Wide Crusade, El Paso, 1990; sec.-treas. Pastors Conf., Bapt. Gen. Conv. Tex., 1991-92. Mem. Com. to Re-elect Judge Jose Troche, El Paso, 1990; founding mem. Helping Other People Eat (HOPE), Redlands, 1984-86; bd. dirs. Westside YMCA, 1989-91. Mem. Rotary. Republican. Address: 5871 E Mountain Loop Trl Anaheim CA 92807-4705

REEVES, JAMES N., lawyer; b. Albert Lea, Minn., Oct. 14, 1945. AB, Dartmouth Coll., 1967; student, George Washington U.; JD, U. Minn., 1970. Bar: Minn. 1970, Alaska 1972, U.S. Ct. Appeals (9th cir.), U.S. Supreme Ct. Law clk. U.S. Dist. Ct. Minn., 1970-71; asst. atty. gen. State of Alaska, 1971-78; mem. Bogle & Gates, Anchorage. Sr. fellow East-West Ctr., Honolulu, 1977. Mem. ABA, Alaska Bar Assn. Office: Bogle & Gates 1031 W 4th Ave Ste 600 Anchorage AK 99501-1978

REGAN, SUZANNE ELIZABETH, film and television educator; b. Portland, Maine, June 23, 1949; d. Francis John and Alice Volora (Ward) R.; m. Beryl Bellman, July 20, 1990; 1 child, Sarah Alice Regan Bellman. BA, Simmons Coll., 1971; MA, UCLA, 1974; PhD, U. Mass., 1981. Prof. comm. studies Calif. State U., L.A., 1978—; presenter in field. Editor Jour. of Film & Video, 1997-02; contbr. over 30 articles to profl. jours. Sarah Orne Jewett scholar Simmons Coll., Boston, 1970-71. Mem. Internat. Comm. Assn. (Nat. chpt.), Soc. for Cinema Studies, Univ. Film & Video Assoc. (sec. 1983-84, bd. dirs. 1997-98). Office: Calif State U Dept Comm Studies 5151 State University Dr Los Angeles CA 90032-4226

REGELE, MICHAEL BRUCE, minister, information and marketing services executive; b. Corvallis, Oreg., Mar. 30, 1952; s. William and Geneva (Chapman) R.; m. Debra S. Brog, June 26,1976; children: Jonathan, Justin, Jordan, Kiersten, Elissa. BA, Seattle Pacific U., 1975; MDiv, Fuller Theol. Sem., 1986. Ordained to ministry Presbyn. Ch. U.S.A., 1987; cert. tchr., Wash. Child care worker Griffin Home for Boys, Renton, Wash., 1973-74; tchr. Grace Acad., Kent, Wash., 1975-76, Columbia Sch., Seattle, 1976-78; assoc. pastor Mariners Ch., Newport Beach, Calif., 1980-84; exec. dir. Congress on Bibl. Exposition, Irvine, Calif., 1984-86; cons. Ministry Consulting, Irvine, 1986-87; pres. Ch. Info. and Devel. Svcs. (name changed to Percept), Costa Mesa, Calif., 1987—; bd. dirs. Com. on Bibl. Exposition, Wheaton, Ill., 1983-88. Author: Your Church and Its Mission, 1988; co-author study guides. Pres., bd. dirs. Irvine Unified Sch. Dist., 1994; founding dir. Irvine Founds. for the Future. Republican. Office: Percept Group Inc 151 Kalmus Dr Ste 104A Costa Mesa CA 92626-5900

REGGIO, GODFREY, film director; b. New Orleans, 1940. Dir. (films) Koyaanisqatsi, 1983, Powaqqatsi, 1988 (Best Film, Sao Paolo Film festival), Anima Mundi, 1992, Evidence, 1995. Mem. Christian Bros., 1954-68; founder Inst. for Regional Edn., Santa Fe, N.Mex., 1972. Home: care Inst for Regional Edn PO Box 2404 Santa Fe NM 87504-2404*

REGNIER, JAMES, state supreme court justice; b. Aurora, Ill.; m. Linda Regnier; 3 children. BS, Marquette U., 1966; JD, U. Ill., 1973. Judicial Fellow ACTL, Internat. Soc. Barristers; completed atty. mediator tng., Atty.-Mediator Tng. Inst., Dallas, 1993. Lawyer pvt. practice, Rochelle, Ill., 1973-78; co-founder, ptnr. Regnier, Lewis and Boland, Great Falls, Mont., 1979-91; lawyer pvt. practice, Missoula, Mont., 1991-97; justice Mont. Supreme Ct., Helena, 1997—; appt. Mont. Supreme Ct. Commn. on Civil Jury Instrn.; appt. lawyer-rep. to 9th Cir. Judicial Confs., 1987, 88, 89, chair Mont. lawyer delegation, 1989; lectr. U. Mont. Sch. Law, numerous continuing legal edn. seminars. Contbr. Mont. Pattern Jury Instrns. for Civil Cases, 1985. Co-founder Mont. chpt. Am. Bd. Trial Advocates, 1989—, pres. Officer USN, Vietnam. Office: Montana Supreme Ct Justice Bldg 215 N Sanders St Helena MT 59620*

REGUERO, MELODIE HUBER, financial executive; b. Montebello, Calif., May 10, 1956; d. Adam W. and Helen Carolyn (Antrim) Huber; m. Edward Anthony Reguero, Oct. 3, 1987. BA in Econs. magna cum laude, UCLA, 1978; M in Bus. Taxation, U. So. Calif., 1983. CPA, Calif. Mem. tax audit staff Arthur Young & Co., Los Angeles, 1978-80; sr. mem. Singer, Lewak, Greenbaum & Goldstein, Los Angeles, 1980-82; tax supr. Coldwell Banker & Co., Los Angeles, 1983-84; fin. analyst, acquisitions specialist Coldwell Banker Residential Group, Newport Beach, Calif., 1984-86; fin. svcs. profl. The Acacia Fin. Group, Newport Beach, Calif., 1986-88; chief fin. officer, owner Fin. Engring. Concepts, Inc., Irvine, Calif., 1988—, Worldwide Investment Network, Inc., Irvine, 1989—; treas. Champions Choice, Inc., Anaheim, Calif., 1980—. Active, Center Club, Costa Mesa, 1989—, Ctr. 500 Performing Arts, Costa Mesa, 1989—. Mem. AICPA, Internat. Assn. Fin. Planning, Calif. Soc. CPAs (pres. 1980—), Irvine C. of C., Racquet Club of Irvine, Delta Gamma. Republican. Avocations: tennis, swimming, skiing, traveling, walking our two golden retrievers. Office: Worldwide Investment Network Inc 8001 Irvine Center Dr Ste 1200 Irvine CA 92618-3000

REHART, MARGARET LEE, controller; b. Van Nuys, Calif., Apr. 11, 1961; d. Ross Leo and Carolyn Lee (Stewart) R.; m. Robert Leslie Putnam, June 13, 1981 (div. July 1988); 1 child, Sabrina Nicole. Degree in bus. mgmt., LaSalle U., 1996. Gen. acct. Whittaker, ERI, Inc., Simi Valley, Calif., 1988-89; acct. ASNA, Big Bear Lake, Calif., 1990; asst. controller Splendor Tile Co., Calabasas, Calif., 1990-95; controller Wesco Sales Corp., Chatsworth, Calif., 1995—; cons. Earth & Art Landscape, Van Nuys, 1993—. Author: Accounting Procedures for the Small Construction Company, 1994. Mem. Am. Mgmt. Assn., Inst. Mgmt. Accts. Democrat. Mem. Reorganized Ch. Latter Day Saints. Avocations: music, counted cross stitch, floral arrangements. Home: 4472 Lubbock Dr Apt C Simi Valley CA 93063-1763

REHBOCK, PHILIP FREDERICK, history educator; b. Seattle, Mar. 22, 1942; s. Ralph Harold and Lillian (Fitch) R.; m. Karen Marie Smith, Apr. 18, 1970; 1 child, Maile Michelle. BA in Econs., Stanford U., 1965; PhD in History of Sci., Johns Hopkins U., 1975. Asst. prof. gen. sci. U. Hawaii, Honolulu, 1975-83, assoc. prof. gen. sci. and history, 1983-92, prof. history, 1992—; mem. Hawaii Com. for Humanities, Honolulu, 1989-96. Author: The Philosophical Naturalists, 1983; editor: At Sea With the Scientifics, 1993; co-editor: Nature in its Greatest Extent, 1988, Darwin's Laboratory, 1994. Lt. Supply Corps, USN, 1965-70. Recipient rsch. grant NSF, Eng., 1984, 86. Mem. History Sci. Soc. (editl. bd., Schuman prize 1974), Brit. Soc. History Sci., Soc. History Natural History, Pacific Cir. (editor-treas. 1985—). Avocations: piano, clarinet, saxophone. Office: Univ Hawaii Dept History 2530 Dole St Honolulu HI 96822-2303

REHFELDT, PHILLIP RICHARD, music educator; b. Burlington, Iowa, Sept. 21, 1939; s. Romiss Robert and Rachel Elizabeth (Green) R.; m. Sally Kathleen Webb, June 11, 1939; Andy, Stephen, Matthew, Douglas. B in Music Edn., U. Ariz., 1961; MusM, Mount St. Mary's Coll., 1962; D in Musical Arts, U. Mich., 1969. Tchr. elem. and jr. H.S. bands Tucson (Ariz.) Pub. Schs., 1962-65; asst. prof. clarinet No. Mich. U., 1965-68; assoc. prof., prof. clarinet and musicology U. Redlands, 1969—, chair woodwind area, dir. grad. program woodwind doubling, 1969—; part-time instr. woodwinds San Bernardino Valley Coll., 1969-74; vis. lectr. clarinet Ariz. State U., 1982-83; adj. prof. clarinet Interlochen Arts Acad., 1986-91; in charge of artists and repertory Advance Recs., 1983—; CEO MillCreek-Publications, 1983—. Performed as clarinetist and bass clarinetist with Redlands Symphony Orch., Redlands Bowl Summer Festival Orch., Riverside Chamber Orch., Faculty Wind Quintet U. Redlands, as a woodwind doubler with San Bernardino Civic Light Opera; solo performances include Cleve. Chamber Orch.; commd. and recorded over seventy-five works for various music labels; author: New Directions for Clarinet, 1978, 2nd edit., 1993, Making and Adjusting Single Reeds, 1983, Handbook for Flute Doubling, 1985, 87, Getting the Most Out of Clarinets, 1985, 87, 89, Guide to Playing Woodwind Instruments, 1989, 98, Materials for Music Research: a bibliography of essential tools and representative types, 1989, 90; music editor, compiler: (with J. Keays) The Renaissance Band Book, 1981, Study Materials for Clarinet, 1982, 85, 86, 87, White's Edition 1027, 1983, First Solo Repertory for Clarinet and Piano, 1983, Etudes for the Twenty-First Century Clarinetist, 1990, 92. Recipient Performers award for contemporary music performance Nat. Assn. Composers, 1981; grantee U. Redlands, 1970-92, Nat. Endowment for the Arts, 1982; grad. and undergrad. scholar U. Ariz. and Mount St. Mary's Coll., 1957-61; Rackham grad. fellow U. Mich., 1968-69. Mem. Internat. Clarinet Soc., Coll. Music Soc. (mem. adv. com. for performance 1986-89), Nat. Assn. Coll. Wind and Percussion Instrs., Am. Soc. Composers, Music Libr. Assn., Am. Fedn. Musicians, Pi Kappa Lambda, Phi Mu Alpha. Office: U Redlands Sch Music Redlands CA 92373

REHORN, LOIS M(ARIE), nursing administrator; b. Larned, Kans., Apr. 15, 1919; d. Charles and Ethel L. (Canaday) Williamson; m. C. Howard Smith, Feb. 15, 1946 (dec. Aug. 1980); 1 child, Cynthia A. Huddleston; m. Harlan W. Rehorn, Aug. 25, 1981. RN, Bethany Hosp. Sch. Nursing, Kansas City, Kans., 1943; BS, Ft. Hays Kans. State U., Hays, 1968, MS, 1970. RN, N.Mex.; lic. mental health technician. Office nurse, surg. asst. Dr. John H. Luke, Kansas City, Kans., 1943-47; supr. nursing unit Larned (Kans.) State Hosp., 1949-68, dir. nursing edn., 1968-71, dir. nursing, 1972-81, ret., 1981. Named Nurse of Yr. DNA-4, 1986. Mem. Am. Nurses Assn., Kans. Nurses Assn. (dist. treas.), N.Mex. Nurses Assn. (dist. chmn. 1982-86, dist. bd. dirs. 1986-88). Home: 1436 Brentwood Dr Clovis NM 88101-4602

REIBER, GREGORY DUANE, forensic pathologist; b. Loma Linda, Calif., May 25, 1955; s. Clifford D. and Anna M. (Field) R.; m. Faustina Mae Davis, Feb. 10, 1980; children: Jenessa Anne, Zachary Duane. BS magna cum laude, Andrews U., Berrien Springs, Mich., 1977; MD, Loma Linda (Calif.) U., 1981. Diplomate Am. Bd. Pathology. Resident in pathology Loma Linda U. Med. Ctr., 1981-85; fellow in forensic pathology Root Pathology Lab., San Bernardino, Calif., 1985-86; assoc. pathologist Root Pathology Lab., 1986-90, No. Calif. Forensic Pathology, Sacramento, 1990—; asst. clin. prof. pathology Loma Linda U. Sch. Medicine, 1987-90, U. Calif., Davis, 1990—; program dir. forensic pathology fellowship NCFP/U. Calif. Davis, 1994—; apptd. Calif. SIDS Autopsy Protocol Com. Contbr. articles to profl. jours. Fellow Am. Soc. Clin. Pathologists, Am. Coll. Forensic Examiners; mem. Am. Bd. Forensic Examiners, AMA, Internat. Wound Ballistics Assn., Nat. Assn. Med. Examiners, Am. Acad. Forensic Scis., Calif. Med. Assn., Sacramento-El Dorado Med. Soc., Alpha Omega Alpha. Republican. Seventh-day Adventist. Avocations: early music, biking, photography, tropical fish. Office: No Calif Forensic Pathology 2443 Fair Oaks Blvd Ste 311 Sacramento CA 95825-7684

REICHMAN, NANCI SATIN, oil company owner; b. Tulsa, July 7, 1939; d. Jack Harold and Tybie Mary (Davis) Satin; m. Louis Reichman, Dec. 25, 1960 (dec. Feb. 1972); children: David Michael, Jill Satin; life ptnr. Phillip M. Citrin. Student, Sarah Lawrence Coll., Bronxville, N.Y., 1957-59; cert. Jungian psychology, C.G. Jung Inst., Evanston, Ill., 1988. Fashion model Miss Jackson's, Tulsa, 1969-70; pres. LIR Investments, Tulsa, 1972-78; pres., dir. devel. Tymar Oil Co., Tulsa and Santa Fe, N.Mex., 1990—; owner ind. oil prodn. Chgo., 1972—; audio tape lectr for various workshops. Pres. C.G. Jung Inst., Evanston, Ill., 1980-81, 81-82, 84-85, also mem. adv. bd.; v.p. Tulsa Jr. Philharm., 1968; sec. Tulsa Ballet, 1968; mem. Women's Forum N.Mex., 1996—; bd. dirs. Found. Santa Fe Cmty. Coll., 1995—. Avocations: poetry writing, travel, reading, philanthropy. Home: 1104 Piedra Rondo Santa Fe NM 87501-8856

REID, BELMONT MERVYN, brokerage house executive; b. San Jose, Calif., May 17, 1927; s. C. Belmont and Mary Irene (Kilfoyl) R. BS in Engring., San Jose State U., 1950, postgrad.; m. Evangeline Joan Rogers, June 1, 1952. Pres., Lifetime Realty Corp., San Jose, 1969-77, Lifetime Fin. Planning Corp., San Jose, 1967-77; founder, chmn. bd. Belmont Reid & Co., Inc., San Jose, 1960-77; pres., registered investment advisor JOBEL Fin. Inc., Carson City, Nev., 1980—; pres., chmn. bd. Data-West Systems, Inc., 1984-85. County chmn. 1982-85, Carson City Rep. Cen. Com., treas., 1979-81; chmn. Carson City Dem. Mgmt. Commn., 1986-99; rural county chmn. Nev. Rep. Cen. Com., 1984-88; mem. Carson City Charter Rev. Com., 1986-91, chmn., 1988-91; bd. dirs. Carson City Coun. No. 347, Navy League of U.S., 1987—. With USN, 1945-46, 51-55. Decorated Air medals. Mem. Nat. Assn. Securities Dealers, Mcpl. Securities Rulemaking Bd., Carson City C. of C. (chpt. 1986-87, bd. dir. 1982-88), Capital Club of Carson City, Rotary (chpt. sec. 1983-84, 86-87, pres. 1988-89, Paul Harris fellow). Home: 610 Bonanza Dr Carson City NV 89706 Office: 711 E Washington St Carson City NV 89701-4063

REID, BENJAMIN FRANKLIN, bishop; b. Bklyn., Oct. 5, 1937; s. Noah W. Sr. and Viola Reid; m. Anna Pearl Batie, June 28, 1958; children: Benjamin Jr., Sylvia, Angela, Natalie. Student, U. Pitts., 1955-56, No. Bapt. Theol. Sem., 1956-58; DD, Am. Bible Inst., Kansas City, Mo., 1971; PhD, Calif. Western U., 1975; LittD (hon.), Calif. Grad. Sch. Theology, Glendale, 1981; DD (hon.), Anderson U., 1982, Pacific Christian Coll., Fullerton, Calif., 1996, Mid-Am. Bible Coll., Oklahoma City, 1997. Ordained to ministry Ch. of God (Anderson, Ind.), 1960; consecrated bishop, 1987. Pastor Adams St. Ch. of God, Springfield, Ill., 1958-59, 1st Ch. of God, Junction City, Kans., 1959-63; sr. pastor Southwestern Ch. of God, Detroit, 1963-71, 1st Ch. of God, L.A., 1971-96; presiding bishop 1st Ch. of God, Nigeria, 1981-95, Interstate Assoc. Ch. of God, Alaska, Ariz., Calif., Oreg., Wash., Nev., 1987—; pres. Nat. Assn. for the Ch. of God (U.S.A.), 1996—; pres. So. Calif. Sch. Ministry, L.A., 1985—; chmn. So. Calif. Mins.' Network, Inglewood, 1990. Author: Confessions of a Happy Preacher, 1971, Another Look at Other Tongues, 1974, rev. edit., 1981, Glory to the Spirit, 1990; contbg. editor Vital Christianity Mins. mag. Bd. dirs. L.A. Coun. Chs., 1974—, Inner City Found.-Excellence in Edn., L.A., 1987-95, Urban League, L.A., SCLC, L.A., Ecumenical Ctr.-Black Ch. Studies, L.A.; chaplain Inglewood (Calif.) Police Dept. Recipient Mayor's award City of L.A., 1981, 86, Community Svc. award U. So. Calif., 1982, Supr.'s Com. award County of L.A., 1986, Mayor's award City of Compton, Calif., 1987. Mem. NAACP (life mem. South Bay br.), Inter-Denominational Mins. Alliance (pres. 1974-76, Svc. award 1976), Concerned Clergy of L.A., Shepherd's Prayer Gathering, Fellowship Ind. Chs. (founder, pres. 1989—), L.A. Ecumenical Congress. Democrat. Office: First Ch of God 9550 Crenshaw Blvd Inglewood CA 90305-2912

REID, CONSTANCE, writer; b. St. Louis, Jan. 3, 1918; d. Ralph Bowers and Helen Marie (Hall) Bowman; m. Neil Dan Reid, June 23, 1950; children: Julia Emma, Stewart Bowman. AB, San Diego State Coll., Calif., 1938, MEd, U. Calif., Berkeley, 1949. H.s. tchr. San Diego City schs., Calif., 1939-48, Jr. Coll. tchr., 1949-50; writer freelance, 1950—. Author: From Zero to Infinity, 1955, 1992, Introduction to Higher Mathematics for the General Reader, 1959, A Long Way from Euclid, 1963, Hilbert, 1970, 1996, Courant in Goettingen and New York, 1976, (as Courant) 1996, Neyman—from life, 1982, (as Neyman) 1997, The Search for E.T. Bell, also known as John Taine, 1993, JULIA, a life in mathematics, 1996, co-author: International Mathematical Congresses/An Illustrated History 1893-1986, 1986, More Mathematical People, 1990; spkr. in field. Democrat. Avocations: contemporary art, film, reading, education.

REID, CRAIG DEREK, writer, film action coordinator; b. Reading, Mar. 30, 1956; s. James William and Kathleen Eilen Moyer (Dowie) R.; m. Silvia Nien Mei, Apr. 19, 1981. BS, Cornell U., 1979; MS, Nat. Taiwan U., Taipei, 1981; PhD, U. Ill., 1989. Rsch. asst. Cornell U., Ithaca, N.Y., 1978-79; fight choreographer various films, tv, Taipei, Hong Kong, L.A., N.Y., 1979-97; tchg. asst. U. Ill., Champaign-Urbana, 1984-90; prof. biology, microbiology U. Mo., St. Louis, 1990-91; freelance writer, 1991—; fight choreographer Universal Pictures, L.A., 1996—; tchr. English Taipei (Taiwan) Youth Ctr., 1979-81; lectr. Sch. Drama Yale U., New Haven, Conn., 1995-96; script cons. Blackburn Pictures, L.A., 1997; health cons. U. Ill. Athletic Assn., Champaign-Urbana, 1987-90. Author: (screenplay) Metamorphosis, 1996; contbr. over 112 articles to profl. jours., mags. Recipient Letter of Commendation President Reagan, 1986; named Best Husband in Am. Paramount Pictures, 1994. Avocations: martial arts, screenwriting, soccer, chess, wife. Home: #209 3770 Keystone Ave Apt 209 Los Angeles CA 90034-6340

REID, EDWARD FRASER, musician, music educator; b. Oakland, Calif., Feb. 12, 1960; s. Edward Fraser and Eleanor Irene (Ando) R.; m. Hannah Albrecht, Jan. 2, 1990; 1 child, Harrison William Albrecht. MusB, Eastman Sch. Music, 1982, MusM, 1987. Prin. trumpet Tucson Symphony, 1987—; asst. prof. trumpet U. Ariz., Tucson, 1994—; prin. trumpet Flagstaff (Ariz.) Festival Orch., 1994—; cornetist New Sousa Band Touring Group, 1997—. Mem. Internat. Trumpet Guild. Office: Univ Ariz Sch Music Tucson AZ 85721

REID, HARRY, senator; b. Searchlight, Nev., Dec. 2, 1939; s. Harry and Inez Reid; m. Landra Joy Gould; children—Lana, Rory, Leif, Josh, Key. AS, Southern Utah State U., 1959; LLD (hon.), U. So. Utah, 1984; BA, Utah State U., 1961; JD, George Washington U., 1964. Senator, co-chmn. dem. policy com. 106th Congress U.S. Senate, Washington; mem. appropriations, ethics/environment & pub. works, Indian affairs coms. *

REID, ROBERT TILDEN, medical association administrator, internist; b. Dallas, Feb. 20, 1931; s. Robert Tilden and Gldays Tressy (King) R.; divorced; children: Robert Tilden, Richard Thomas, Annette Marie, Randolph Young. BS, So. Meth. U., Dallas, 1957; MD, U. Tex.-Southwestern, Dallas, 1959. Diplomate Am. Bd. Internal Medicine, Am. Bd. Rheumatology, Am. Bd. Allergy and Immunology. Intern Parkland Meml. Hosp., Dallas, 1959-60, resident, 1960-63; with Scripps Clinic and Rsch., La Jollla, Calif., 1963-70; pvt. practice La Jollla, Calif., 1970—; chief staff Scripps Meml. Hosp., La Jollla, Calif., 1976-78; scientific dir. Erik and Ese Banck Clinical Rsch. Ctr., San Diego, 1994—. Mem. San Diego County Med. Soc. (pres. 1991), Calif. Med. Assn. (trustee 1992-95). Office: 9850 Genesee Ave Ste 860 La Jolla CA 92037-1233 also: Erik & Ese Banck Clinical Rsch 12395 El Camino Real Ste 117 San Diego CA 92130-3083

REIDY, RICHARD ROBERT, publishing company executive; b. Patchogue, N.Y., May 9, 1947; s. Joseph Robert and Irene (Jennings) R.; m. Carolyn Alyce Armstrong, Mar. 21, 1970; children: Dawn Patricia, Shawn Patrick, Christopher Keith. Student, Suffolk County Community Coll., 1966-68, L.I. Tech. Sch., 1969-70, Scottsdale Community Coll., 1983-84, 85-86. Lic. real estate agt., Ariz. Restaurant owner Reidy's, Patchogue, 1973-77; design draftsman Sverdrop & Parcel, Tempe, Ariz., 1978-79, Sullivan & Masson, Phoenix, 1979-81; pres. Success Pub. Co., Scottsdale, Ariz., 1983—; with U.S. Postal Dept., 1980—. Editor, owner, pub.: Who's Who in Arizona, 1984-85, 89-90. Chief Scottsdale YMCA, 1983-84; eucharistic minister St. Daniel the Prophet Cath. Ch., Scottsdale, 1985—; mem. World Wide Marriage Encounter, 1986—; pres. Coronado High Sch. Band Boosters, 1988-89. Mem. Scottsdale C. of C., Phoenix Better Bus. Bur. Office: Success Pub Co PO Box 3431 Scottsdale AZ 85271-3431

REIF, KARL JOSEPH, writer, editor; b. Santa Rosa, Calif., July 23, 1971; s. Karl Joseph and Jill Kathleen (tonelli) R. BA in Journalism, U. Houston, 1994, BA in Polit. Sci., 1994; postgrad., Golden Gate U. Reporter Houston Chronicle, 1993-94; reporter, editor Pierce County Herald, Puyallup, Wash., 1994; prodn. mgr. Treasured Memories, Santa Rosa, Calif., 1995-96; mng. editor World Trade Press, San Rafael, Calif., 1995-98; freelance writer Info. Sources, Inc., Berkeley, Calif., 1996, Wine Bus. Monthly, Sonoma, Calif., 1996, Uproar.com, Budapest, Hungary, 1997, John Galt Papers, San Anselmo, Calif., 1997-98. Author,m editor: Australia Business, 1997, World Trade Almanac, 1997; author: Services, 1997, Global Road Warrior, 1998. Legal vol. Marin County Family Law Ctr., San Rafael, Calif., 1997; literacy tutor Students Without Walls, Houston, 1994. Mem. Nat. Writers Union. Avocations: guitar, writing, reading, movies. E-mail: joereif@ix.netcom.com. Home and Office: PO Box 4481 Santa Rosa CA 95402-4481

REIFF, THEODORE CURTIS, construction executive; b. Cleve., Aug. 6, 1942; s. William Fred and Dorothy Louise (Knauer) R.; m. Janis Lynn Brunk, May 6, 1966 (div. Aug. 1980); m. Theresa Dolores Baranello, Oct. 30, 1982 (div. Dec. 1992). BS, Ohio State U., 1969. Lic. real estate broker, demolition contractor. Dir. adminstrv. svcs. Mgmt. Horizons, Inc., Columbus, Ohio, 1969-73; v.p. Danco Mgmt. Co., Lancaster, Ohio, 1973-74; sr. v.p. Anchor Lighting Corp., Columbus, 1974-75; ptnr. Curtis-Lee & Assocs., Delaware, Ohio, 1974-77; pres. Cartunes Corp., San Diego, Calif., 1977-91; also bd. dirs. Cartunes Corp., San Diego; facilities coord. Raytheon Co., Burlington, Mass., 1979-82; ptnr. Greenstone & Reiff, San Diego, 1982-86; pres. Creative Bus. Strategies, Inc., San Diego, 1986-94, pres., bd. dirs.; pres. Bus. Pubs. Inc., San Diego, 1989-91, also bd. dirs.; mng. dir. PM Co., Tijuana, B.C., Mex., 1991-94; co-founder, pres. The Reuse People, Inc. San Diego, 1994—; also bd. trustees Bldg. Materials Distbrs., San Diego; co-founder, treas. Materiales de Construccion de Baja California, Tijuana, Mex., 1995-97, also bd. dirs.; co-founder, ptnr. La Mas Barata, Tijuana, Mex.; bd. dirs. Integrated Ceramic Tech., San Marcos, Calif., 1986-88, Pacific Rim Interface Mems. Enterprises Inc., 1988-90, Distributed Comm. Corp., San Diego, 1990-91, Phoenix Systems & Techs., Chula Vista, Calif., 1990-91; instr. Miramar Coll., San Diego, 1984-90. Mem. Friends of San Diego Zoo, 1980—; chmn. bus. adv. com. San Diego State U. Coll. of Bus., 1979-82; mem. adv. com. Coll. Bus. Calif. State U., San Marcos, 1992-94; bd. dirs. I Love a Clean San Diego, 1997—. With Ohio N.G., 1966-72. Named Outstanding Businessman City of Columbus, Ohio, 1974; recipient Recognition award San Diego State U. Coll. of Bus., 1983, Appreciation award Am. Mktg. Assn., 1984, IEEE, 1986. Mem. Am. Electronics Assn. (chmn. small bus. com. 1988-89, chmn. fin. com. 1990-91). Avocations: tennis, skiing. Home: 3946 Murray Hill Rd La Mesa CA 91941-7649

REILLEY, KATHLEEN PATRICIA, lawyer; b. Pitts., Oct. 31, 1948; d. Edward Michael and Mary Elizabeth (Davidson) R. BA, U. Calif., Berkeley, 1976; JD, Golden Gate U., 1979. Bar: Calif. Staff atty. Fresno County Legal Svcs., Calif., 1979-85, Santa Monica (Calif.) Rent Control Bd. 1985-89; asst. city atty. City of Berkeley, 1990-91; atty. Linda DeBene Inc., Danville, Calif., 1991-94. Co-founder Calif. Housing Action & Info. Network, 1976. Mem. Calif. State Bar Assn. (real property and litigation sect.). Democrat. Episcopalian. Avocations: computers, writing, cooking, gardening. Office: 1563 Solano Ave # 528 Berkeley CA 94707-2116

REILLY, JAMES KEVIN, artist, journalist; b. Newark, N.J., Aug. 18, 1952; s. James Henry and Eileen (Moran) R. BS, U. Notre Dame, 1974, ME, U. Va., 1976; MA, Georgetown U., 1985. Engr. Babcock and Wilcox, Lynchburg, Va., 1974-75; liaison officer, engr. fed. emergency employee U.S. Dept. Energy, Washington, 1977-86; inspector IAEA UN, Vienna, Austria, 1986; cons., agt. Watson Fin. Group, N.Y.C., 1987-88; cons. Am. Quality Assurance Co., Condersport, Pa., 1987—; art news reporter. Exhibited in 5 art shows. Guard. Susan Kefauver for U.S. Senate, Pa., 1988; leader Boy Scouts Am., N.J., Pa., 1972, 84, 89-91; active Big Bros., Idaho, 1985-86. Mem. ASTM, IAATC, N.Y. Acad. Scis., Sigma Xi. Avocations: skiing.

REILLY, MICHAEL STANLEY, psychologist, educator; b. San Diego, Dec. 29, 1948; s. Richard Ernest and Barbara W. (Williams) R.; m. Theodora Reilly, Apr. 21, 1966; children: Richard Ernest II, Shawn P. BA, Union Inst., Cin., 1988; MA, Nat. U., San Diego, 1989; PhD, Walden U.,

Mpls., 1995; BA, Union Inst., Cin., 1996; postgrad., Nat. U., San Diego. Cert. sr. profl. in human resources. Pres. RPW, Inc., San Diego, 1970-78; prin. Vision Concepts, San Diego, 1978-85; dir. adminstrm. Horizon Internat., San Diego, 1985-88; prin. Reilly & Assocs., Poway, Calif., 1988—; supr. Mananatha Christian Schs., San Diego, 1990-94; asst. dir. edn. Eldorado Coll., San Diego, 1994-96; prof. Calif. U. for Profl. Studies, 1997—; instr. Advt. Arts Coll., San Diego, 1996-98, U. Phoenix, 1998—; adj. prof. Nat. U., 1998—; pres. Classical Acad., 1998—. Mem. vol. com. Rep. Nat. Conv., San Diego, 1996. Mem. AAUP, Doctoral Sssn., Friends U. Calif.-San Diego Libr., Soc. Human Resources Mgmt. (San Diego chpt.). Baptist. Avocations: sailing, golf. Office: 14781 Pomerado Rd Ste 159 Poway CA 92064-2802

REILLY, ROBERT JOSEPH, counselor; b. Spokane, Wash., Mar. 7, 1936; s. John Francis and Vivian Helen (White) R.; m. Joan Steiner, June 20, 1960; children: Sean Michael, Patrick Joseph, Bridget Colleen. BA in Psychology, Seattle U., 1985; postgrad., Infantry Officer Candidate Sch., Ft. Benning, 1960, EOAC, Ft. Belvoir, 1968, Leadership Inst. Seattle/City U., 1991-92. Ordained Congl. Ch. Practical Theology, 1992. Enlisted U.S. Army, 1953, advanced through grades to maj., 1981, ret., 1981; with U.S. Army, Korea, 1961-62, Vietnam, 1966-67, 69-70; counseling supr. Schick Shadel Hosp., Seattle, 1984-89; dir. Canyon Counseling, Puyallup, Wash., 1987-92, 95—; social worker Wash. State Employee Adv. Svc., Olympia, 1992—; v.p. Nat. Bd. for Hypnotherapy and Hypnotic Anaesthesiology, 1991-97, pres. Wash. chpt. 1991-94; exec. v.p. Coll. Therapeutic Hypnosis, Puyallup, 1989-94; mem. adj. faculty Pierce Coll., Tacoma, 1991-92; mem. Wash. State Chem. Dependency Counselor Cert. Bd., sec., 1995—. Pres. Irish Cultural Club, Tacoma, 1983-85, 93-94; sec. Tacoma chpt. Ret. Officers Assn., 1983-87, pres., 1993-96, bd. dirs., 1992-97; bd. dirs. Tacoma Mus. Playhouse Theater Co., 1997—. Decorated Vietnamese Cross of Gallantry with silver star, Bronze Star with oak leaf cluster, Meritorious Svc. medal, Army Commendation medal with 2 oak leaf clusters; named Profl. of Yr. Chem. Dependency Profls. Wash., 1994. Mem. Nat. Bd. Hypnotherapy and Hypnotic Anesthesiology (v.p. 1991-97, Mem of Yr. 1994, pres. Wash. chpt. 1991-94), Nat. Guild Hypnotists, Nat. Assn. Alcohol and Drug Abuse Counselors (mem. del. Russia & Czech Rep. 1996), Am. Congress Hypnotist Examiners, Nat. Assn. Tobacco Addiction Counselors, Army Engr. Assn., Nat. 4th Inf. Divsn. Assn. (sec.-treas. N.W. chpt. 1991—), Employee Assistance Profls. Assn. Avocations: volksmarching, symphony music, theater. Office: Wash State Employee Adv Svc PO Box 47540 Olympia WA 98504-7540

REILLY, WILLIAM KANE, former government official, educator, lawyer, conservationist; b. Decatur, Ill., Jan. 26, 1940; s. George P. and Margaret (Kane) M.; m. Elizabeth Buxton; children: Katherine, Megan. B.A. in History, Yale U., 1962; J.D., Harvard U., 1965; M.S. in Urban Planning, Columbia U., 1971. Bar: Ill., Mass. 1965. Atty. firm Ross & Hardies, Chgo., 1965; asso. dir. Urban Policy Center, Urban Am., Inc., also Nat. Urban Coalition, Washington, 1969-70; sr. staff mem. Pres.'s Council Environ. Quality, 1970-72; exec. dir. Task Force Land Use and Urban Growth, 1972-73; pres. Conservation Found., Washington, 1973-89, World Wildlife Fund, Washington, 1985-89; adminstr. U.S. EPA, Washington, 1989-93; chmn. Natural Resources Coun., Am., 1982-83; head U.S. del. Earth Summit, 1992; head U.S. del. to negotiate Amendments to Montreal Protocol on the Ozone Layer, 1990, 92; Payne vis. prof. Stanford U., 1993-94, vis. prof. 1994-97; CEO, Aqua Internat. Ptnrs., Tex. Pacific Group, San Francisco, 1997—; chmn. bd. dirs. Am. Farmland Trust; bd. dirs. E.I. DuPont de Nemours and Co., Evergreen Holdings, Inc., Nat. Geog. Soc., World Wildlife Fund, Yale U., Presidio Trust; mem. internat. adv. bd., Lafarge. Editor: The Use of Land, 1973, Environment Strategy America, 1994-96; author articles in field, chpts. in books. Served to capt., CIC U.S. Army, 1966-67. Clubs: University (Washington), Univ. (N.Y.C.). Office: Aqua Internat Ptnrs 345 California St Ste 3300 San Francisco CA 94104-2606

REIM, JOHN L., television executive; b. Salt Lake City; s. Reynold Lewis Reim and Barbara J. Mulkey, Sept. 23, 1969; children: Rebecca L., Leslie A. BA, Calif. State U., Sacramento, 1973; MBA, Brigham Young U., 1998. Various news positions Sta. KCRA-TV, Sacramento, 1973-81, mng. editor, 1981-86; sr. v.p. mktg. River City Bank, Sacramento, 1982-86; gen. mgr. Kelly News & Entertainment, Sacramento, 1987-92; exec. prodr. Sta. KIRO, Seattle, 1992-95; CEO Sta. KBYU-FM-TV, Provo, Utah, 1995—. Bd. dirs. Legis. Action Group, PBS, Wash., 1995—; bd. dirs. legis. adv. group Am.'s Pub. TV Status, 1995—. Mem. Nat. Assn. Radio and TV News Dirs., Nat. Assn. Broadcasters, Utah Assn. Broadcasters. Office: Sta KBYU-FM-TV 2000 Ironton Blvd Provo UT 84606-6203

REIM, RUTHANN, career and personal counselor, corporate trainer; b. Fresno, Calif., Oct. 4, 1943; d. F. Wayne and Charlene Marie (Young) Howd; m. Terry D. Nov. 29, 1963; children: Tracey, Brandon. BA in Sociology, San Jose State U., 1966; MA Guidance & Counseling, Pacific Luth U., 1984. Cert. counselor, nat. Tchr., elem. sch. Dupont Sch. Dist., Tacoma, 1966-67, Prince Georges Sch. Dist., Lanham, Md., 1967-68, Franklin Pierce sch. Dist., Tacoma, 1968-70; owner Rainbow Glassworks, Tacoma, 1973-76, Creative Womanlife, Tacoma, 1976-78; dir., counselor Individual Devel. Ctr., Tacoma, 1984-88; pres. Career Mgmt. Inst., Tacoma, 1989—; adj. faucltly mem. dept. edn. Pacific Luth. U., 1980-84. Author: (career booklet) Career Change Made Easy, 1990; artist 5' round stained glass window "Dogwood", 1980. Trainer Jr. League Tacoma, 1977-79. Mem. Rotary (1st woman pres. 1991-92, bd. dirs. 1988-97), Phi Kappa Phi. Avocations: world peace, hiking, raising roses. Office: Career Mgmt Inst 8404 27th St W Tacoma WA 98466-2723

REIMANN, ARLINE LYNN, artist; b. St. Louis, Nov. 25, 1937; d. Albert Robbins and Bess (Kagan) Miller; m. Hans Reimann, Feb. 24, 1957; 1 child, Robert. BA, Rutgers U., 1974; MA, Montclair State U., 1980. Exhibited in group shows at Hunterdon Nat. Print Exhbn., Hunterdon Art Ctr., Clinton, N.J., 1982, Celebration of Women's Week, Galeria San Jeronimo, San Juan, P.R., 1987, Audubon Artists Ann. Exhbn., Nat. Arts Club, N.Y.C., 1988, 90—, Celebration 89, Interch. Ctr., N.Y.C., Nat. Assn. Women Artists Traveling Printmaking Exhbn., Butler Inst. Am. Art, Youngstown, Ohio, 1989, 395 West Broadway Gallery, N.Y.C., 1994, 420 West Broadway Gallery, Soho, N.Y., 1995, Audubon Artists Invitational, Lever House Gallery, N.Y.C., 1995, Selected N.J. Mems. Nat. Assn. Women Artists, Hunterdon Art Ctr., Clinton, N.J., 1996, Art Ctr. Municipality of Athens, Greece, 1996, West Beth Gallery, Montclair in Manhattan, N.Y.C., 1996, ISE Art Found. N.Y.C., 1996. Soc. Am. Graphic Artists, New Rochelle, N.Y., 1997, Gallery Art 54, N.Y.C., 1997, Jane Voorhees Zimmerli Art Mus., New Brunswick, N.J., 1998, 99; represented in permanent collections at Jane Voorhees Zimmerli Art Mus., New Brunswick, N.J., Newark Pub. Libr. Fine Print Collection, Newark, N.J., Montclair State Univ., Upper Montclair, N.J. Recipient Best in Show award Salute to Women in Arts, Lincoln Ctr., 1981, Hon. mention award Nat. Juried Exhbn. Small Works Montclair State U., N.J., 1995. Aida Whedon Meml. award Nat. Assn. Women Artists, 1996. Mem. Nat. Assn. Women Artists (bd. dirs., chairperson traveling print exhbn. 1984-89, printmaking jury 1987-89, 95-97), Audubon Artists (bd. dirs., rec. sec. 1991-97), Soc. Am. Graphic Artists. Home: 546 Hillrise Pl Walnut Creek CA 94598-4064

REINAGLE, DAMON JOHNATHAN, artist, educator; b. Martins' Ferry, Ohio, Dec. 2, 1947; s. Charles James and Edith Eda (Nagy) R.; m. Maureen Ellen O'Grady, Nov. 14, 1970; children: Damon Jared, Grady Thomas, Lycia Anne. BS in edn., Kent State Univ., 1970. Cert. tchr. Ohio; Art Art tchr. Lakewood (Ohio) H.S., 1970-78, AJO (Ariz.) Schs., 1980-83, Mesa (Ariz.) Pub. Schs., 1983-89, St. Matthews Parish Sch., Pacific Palisades, Calif., 1989—. Author, illustrator: Draw Medieval Fantasies, 1996, Draw Alien Fantasies, 1996, Draw Sports Fantasies, 1997, Kid Centered Art, 1998. Avocations: working out writing family. Home: 18656 Collins St # 106 Tarzana CA 91356-2103

[illegible line] Lynwood, Calif., May 17, 1966; s. Robert Aarlen and Marie Antoinette (Presicci) R. AA, Riverside (Calif.) City Coll., 1989; BA, Calif. State U., San Bernardino, 1992; cert. elem. tchr., U. Calif., Riverside, 1994. Instrnl. aide Jurupa Unified Sch. Dist., Riverside, 1985, 89-93; substitute tchr. Jurupa Unified Sch. Dist., 1993—; day care worker Our Lady of Perpetual

Help, 1988-89; substitute tchr. Riverside Unified Sch. Dist., 1996—; vol. aide Jurupa Unified Sch. Dist., 1989-91; home tutor, 1987-89. Author: ABC, What's at School for Me, 1997; author children's stories Stone Soup, 1981. Little League coach, Riverside, 1980-82, scorekeeper, 1982-84; Sunday sch. tchr., supr. Hope Cmty. Ch., Riverside, 1988-98. Winner 1st pl. Lions Club speech contest, 1984; named Christian Youth of Yr. Kiwanis Club, 1985, Outstanding Young Man Am., 1992, 96. Mem. Phi Lambda Omega. Democrat. Mem. Christian Reformed Ch. Avocations: bowling, dancing, writing, acting.

REINER, ERIC ALAN, business consultant, author, lecturer, producer; b. N.Y.C., Feb. 3, 1944; s. Maury and Alice Jan (Berman) R. B.A. magna cum laude, Amherst Coll., 1966; postgrad. Oxford U., 1966-68, Grad. Inst. Film and TV, N.Y.U., 1969-70. Asst. buyer Gimbel Bros., 1966; asst. to pres. Fremantle Internat., 1968; free-lance motion picture cameraman, 1968-80; exec. dir. Celebrity Centre, N.Y.C., 1970-71, Narconon, N.Y.C., 1974-75; founder, pres. Eric Reiner Co., mgmt. cons., Los Angeles, 1974—; pres. Surg. Systems, Inc., Los Angeles, 1981—; lectr. on personal fin., interpersonal relationships, mgmt. skills. Bd. dirs. Hollywood Chorale; bd. dirs. United Pacific Credit Union, 1979-80, Pres., 1980-81. Mem. Nat. Assn. Broadcast Engrs. in TV, Am. Arbitration Assn. (mem. bd. arbitrators), Concerned Businessmen's Assn. Am. (v.p.), Phi Beta Kappa. Jeffersonian Democrat. Editor-in-chief: (poetry anthology) Golden Horses, 1975.

REINHARDT, STEPHEN ROY, federal judge; b. N.Y.C., Mar. 27, 1931; s. Gottfried and Silvia (Hanlon) R.; children: Mark, Justin, Dana. B.A. cum laude, Pomona Coll., 1951; LL.B., Yale, 1954. Bar: Calif. 1958. Law clk. to U.S. Dist. Judge Luther W. Youngdahl, Washington, 1956-57; atty. O'Melveny & Myers, L.A., 1957-59; partner Fogel Julber Reinhardt Rothschild & Feldman (L.C.), L.A., 1959-80; judge U.S. Ct. Appeals (9th cir.), L.A., 1980—; Mem. exec. com. Dem. Nat. Com., 1969-72, nat. Dem. committeeman for Calif., 1976-80; pres. L.A. Recreation an dParks Commn., 1974-75; mem. Coliseum Commn., 1974-75; mem. L.A. Police Commn., 1974-78, pres., 1978-80; sec., mem. exec. com. L.A. Olympic Organizing com., 1980-84; bd. dirs. Amateur Athletic Found. of L.A., 1984-92; adj. prof. Loyola Law Sch., L.A., 1988-90. Served to 1st lt. USAF, 1954-56. Mem. ABA (labor law coun. 1975-77). •

REINISCH, NANCY RAE, therapist, consultant; b. Chgo., Mar. 31, 1953; d. Charles Richard and Marianne (Gross) R.; m. Paul A. Salmen, June 14, 1980; children: Chas, Marcus. BA in Sociology cum laude, Colo. Coll., 1975; cert. drug and alcohol counseling, U. Minn., 1980; MSW, U. Denver, 1982. Cert. relationship therapist; lic. clin. social worker. Counselor Rampart Boys' Home, Colorado Springs, Colo., 1975; advocate bilinqual community Migrants in Action, St. Paul, 1976; therapist Chrysalis Ctr. for Women, Mpls., 1979; team leader and prevention specialist Project Charlie, Edina, Minn., 1977-80, also trainer, cons., 1985—; mental health worker Bethesda Mental Health Ctr. and Hosp., Denver, 1980-83; therapist Gateway Alcohol Recovery Ctr., Aurora, Colo., 1983-84; pvt. practice therapy, also dir. Family Practice Counseling Service, Glenwood Springs, Colo., 1984—; co-dir. Valley Sexual Abuse Ctr.; bd. dirs. Adv./Safehouse Project, Glenwood Springs; mem. Valley View Hosp. Ethics com., Glenwood Springs, 1986—. Mem. sch. accountability com. Glenwood Springs, Human Svcs. Commn., Garfield County. Recipient Countywide Humanitarian Svc. award Glenwood Post and Garfield County Human Svcs. Commn., 1995. Mem. Nat. Assn. Social Workers, NOW, Nat. Abortion Rights Action League, ACLU, Colo. Pub. Interest Research Group. Democrat. Office: Family Practice Counseling Svc 1905 Blake Ave Glenwood Springs CO 81601-4226

REINMUTH, OSCAR MACNAUGHTON, physician, educator; b. Lincoln, Nebr., Oct. 23, 1927; s. Oscar William and Catharine Anne (MacNaughton) R.; m. Patricia Dixon, June 19, 1951 (div. Jan. 1977); children—David Dixon, Diane MacNaughton, Douglas Stewart; m. Audrey Longridge Holland, June 26, 1980. B.S., U. Tex., Austin, 1948; M.D. (F.B. Hanes research fellow 1950-51), Duke U., 1952. Intern Duke Hosp., 1952-53; asst. resident in medicine Yale U. Med. Ctr., 1953-54, NIH research trainee, 1954-55; asst. resident in neurology Boston City Hosp., 1955-56, chief resident, teaching fellow in neurology Harvard U. Neurol. unit, 1956-57; NIH spl. trainee, clin. asst. Nat. Hosp., London, 1957-58; from asst. prof. to prof. neurology U. Miami (Fla.) Med. Sch., 1958-77; prof. neurology and behavioral neuroscience, chmn. dept. U. Pitts. Med. Sch., 1977-93, prof. emeritus, 1994—; prof. neurology U. Ariz. Med. Sch., Tucson, 1993—; mem. research tng. com. A and C NIH, 1966-73. Served with AUS, 1946-47. Recipient Mosby award, 1952. Fellow ACP, Am. Acad. Neurology (1st v.p. 1973-76), Am. Neurol. Assn. (1st v.p. 1977-78, 2d v.p. 1976-77), Am. Heart Assn. (fellow stroke coun., vice chmn. 1978-79, chmn. 1980-82, editor pubs. 1975-78, editor-in-chief Stroke jour. 1987-91, Award of Merit 1992). Home: 5545 N Entrada Quince Tucson AZ 85718-4709 Office: U Med Ctr Dept Neurology 1501 N Campbell Ave Tucson AZ 85724-5023

REIS, EDWARD THOMAS, JR., insurance executive, educator; b. Fresno, Calif., Aug. 27, 1948; s. Edward Thomas and Eleanor Virginia (Read) R.; m. Deborah Gerace; 1 child, Edward Thomas III. Cert., Ins. Inst. of Am., 1983; chartered, Am. Inst. for Property and Casualty Underwriters, 1986; CLU/Chartered Fin. Cons., Am. Coll., 1988. Agt. Farmers Ins., Simi Valley, Calif., 1975-82; dist. mgr. Farmers Ins., Santa Barbara, Calif., 1982-97; founder Money Seminars, 1995—; pres. Reis Fin., Santa Barbara, Calif., 1996—; pres. Reis Fin., 1996—. Mem. Farmers Pres. Coun. Mem. Nat. Assn. Life Underwriters (pres. local chpt.), Profl. Ins. Agts. Assn., Nat. Spkrs. Assn., Am. Seminar Leaders Assn., Internat. Assn. for Fin. Planning. Republican. Methodist. Avocations: golf, scuba diving. Office: Edward Reis Inc 519 W Pueblo St Santa Barbara CA 93105-4229

REIS, JEAN STEVENSON, administrative secretary; b. Wilburton, Okla., Nov. 30, 1914; d. Robert Emory and Ada (Ross) Stevenson; m. George William Reis, June 24, 1939 (dec. 1980). BA, U. Tex., El Paso, 1934; MA, So. Meth. U., 1935; postgrad., U. Chgo., 1937-38, U. Wash., 1948-49. Tchr. El Paso H.S., 1935-39; safety engr., trainer Safety and Security Divsn., Office of Chief Ordnance, Chgo., 1942-45; tchr. Lovenberg Jr. H.S., Galveston, Tex., 1946; parish sec. Trinity Parish Episcopal Ch., Seattle, 1950-65; adminstrv. sec., asst. Office Resident Bishop, United Meth. Ch., Seattle, 1965-94; observer Africa U. installation, Mutare, Zimbabwe, 1994; com. on legislation for 1996 gen. conf. Hist. Soc. of United Meth. Ch. Recipient Bishop's award, 1980. Mem. AAUW, Beta Beta Beta. Home: 9310 42nd Ave NE Seattle WA 98115-3814

REISBERG, LEON ELTON, education educator; b. Dallas, Sept. 1, 1949; s. Morris Abraham and Gertrude (Turner) R.; m. Iris Fudell, July 3, 1973 (div. 1986); children: Joshua Fudell, Leah Fudell; m. Donna Brodigan, July 11, 1993. BS in Edn., U. Tex., Austin, 1971; MEd, U. Ark., Fayetteville, 1972; EdD, U. Kans., Lawrence, 1981. Tchr. Oklahoma City Sch. Dist., 1972-75, Putnam City Sch. Dist., Oklahoma City, 1975-78, U. Kans. Med. Ctr., Kansas City, 1978-79; asst. prof. Pacific Luth. U., Tacoma, 1981-88; tchr. Tacoma (Wash.) Sch. Dist., 1989-90; assoc. prof. edn. Pacific Luth. U., 1988-94; chmn. dept. spl. edn. Pacific Luth. U., Tacoma, 1986-93, chmn. profl. edn. adv. bd., 1992-94, assoc. dean sch. edn., 1993—, prof., 1995—; project dir., Consulting Spl. Edn. Personnel Tng. Project, Tacoma, 1983-86; chmn. Profl. Edn. Adv. Bd. Cons. editor Learning Disability Quar., 1981-89, Acad. Therapy, 1988-90, Intervention, 1990—; contbr. articles to profl. pubs. Mem. Coun. Exceptional Children, Coun. Learning Disabilities (Pacific Rim region rep. 1993-96), Assn. Trainer Spl. Edn. Pers. (chmn. 1991), Phi Kappa Phi. Democrat. Jewish. Office: Pacific Luth U Sch Edn Tacoma WA 98447

REISCH, MICHAEL STEWART, social work educator; b. N.Y.C., Mar. 4, 1948; s. Joseph and Charlotte (Rosenberg) R.; m. Amy Jane Lewis, May 21, 1972; children: Jennifer, Nikki. BA in History with highest honors, NYU, 1968; PhD in History with distinction, SUNY, Binghamton, 1975; MSW with honors, CUNY, 1979. Youth worker Washington-Heights-Inwood YM-YWHA, N.Y.C., 1965-66; editor, columnist Heights Daily News, Bronx, N.Y., 1966-68; rsch./teaching asst. SUNY, Binghamton, 1970-72; unit dir., program cons. Child Study Assn.-Wel Met, Inc., N.Y.C., 1970-72; asst. dir. youth div. Mosholu-Montefiore Community Ctr., Bronx, 1972-73; project dir. Silberman Found./N.Y. Assn. Deans, N.Y.C., 1973-74; asst. dean Sch. Social Welfare, asst. prof. SUNY, Stony Brook, 1974-79; asst. prof., then assoc. prof. Sch. Social Work U. Md., Balt., 1979-86; dir. Sch. Social Work, prof. social work/pub. adminstrn. San Francisco State U., 1986-95; prof. social work U. Pa., Phila., 1995—; cons. and spkr. in field. Co-author: From Charity to Enterprise, 1989 (Social Sci. Book of Month), Social Work in the 21st Century, 1997; editor, author various books in field; contbr. articles to profl. publs., chpts. to books. Cons. to numerous local, state, and fed. polit. campaigns, 1971—; mem. Gov.'s Adv. Coun. Human Resources, Md., 1983-86; pres. Welfare Advs., Md., 1983-86; campaign mgr. Rep. Barbara Mikulski, Balt., 1982; bd. dirs. Coleman Advs. for Children and Youth, 1987-95, San Francisco Internat. Program, 1987-95, Calif. Social Work Edn. Ctr., 1991-95, Ctr. for S.E. Asian Refugee Resettlement, 1992-95, Am. Jewish Congress, N. Calif., 1994-95, Coun. Internat. Programs, 1995, Phila. Citizens for Children and Youth, 1997—; chair Children's Budget Task Force City of San Francisco, 1989-92; mem. Mayor's Adv. Coun. on Drug Abuse, San Francisco, 1988-91; mem. steering com. Poverty Action Alliance, 1993-95; mem. adv. com. Montreal Consortium for Human Rights Advocacy, 1995—. Woodrow Wilson Found. fellow, 1972-73. Mem. NASW (del. 1990-92, 94-96, chair peace and justice com. 1992-97), Coun. on Social Work Edn. (com. on status of women 1989-92, bd. dirs. 1993-97, chair commn. on ednl. policy 1994-97), Am. Hist. Assn., Bertha Capen Reynolds Soc., Soc. for Social Work Rsch., Assn. for Advancement of Social Work with Groups, Assn. Cmty. Orgns. and Social Adminstrn. Avocations: travel, hiking, cooking, swimming, creative writing.

REISDORF, EDWARD GARY, lawyer, real estate exec.; b. Milw., Mar. 8, 1941; s. Edward and Flora R.; B.S., USAF Acad., 1963; J.D., Georgetown U., 1968; m. Teresa Hermo, Dec. 4, 1975; children—Ted, Rachael, Greg, Christina. Commd. 2d lt. USAF, 1963, advanced through grades to capt., 1967, served as contracting officer, 1963-67, resigned, 1967; with Kalb, Voorhis & Co., stock brokers, Washington, 1967-68; admitted to N.J. bar, 1968; with Bourne & Noll, attys., Summit, N.J., 1968-70; pres. Reisdorf & Jaffe, P.A., attys., Springfield, N.J., 1970-74, E.G. Reisdorf P.A., attys., Springfield, 1974-80, Equity Assocs., investments, Springfield, 1980-90, N.Y. Stars, women's profl. basketball, 1978-80; CEO The Terlene Group, N.Y.C., 1983-90; pres., CEO The Resort Group, Inc., 1990—. Mem. ABA, N.J., Bar Assn. Republican. Roman Catholic. Home: 7502 N Clearwater Pkwy Paradise Vly AZ 85253-2804 Office: Ste 11 15475 N Greenway Hayden Loop Scottsdale AZ 85260-1616

REISS, JONATHAN ALLEN, filmmaker, legal and government researcher; b. N.Y.C., Aug. 12, 1956; s. Seymour and Rose (Portnoy) R. BA in Govt. and Internat. Rels. w/honors, Dartmouth Coll., 1978; MFA, NYU, 1981. Chmn. The Waterbed Gallery, N.Y.C., 1979—; dir. Motion Picture Studio, L.A., 1981—. Author: (screenplay) Heaven and Earth, 1987; author, dir. numerous short movies, including Opportunity, Room 7, Vicious Circle, Deux Ex Machina. Recipient medal of merit U.S. Congress, 1974; Tucker fellow Dartmouth Coll., 1976, Xerox award, 1977. Avocations: sports, photography, painting, writing. Office: 1355 Westwood Blvd Ste 212 Los Angeles CA 90024-4956

REISTAD, ROBERT KNUT, video production editor; b. Austin, Nov. 2, 1962; s. Knut Oluf and Berit (Vik) R.; m. Sonia Teresa Hoelle, May 22, 1993; children: Shawn, Dakota, Ciara. Degree in jazz edn., North Tex. State U., 1984. Trumpet player various big band orchs. throughout U.S., 1984-86; video editor Multi Media Prodns., Palm Springs, Calif., 1986-96, Annenberg Ctr., Rancho Mirage, Calif., 1993—; video editor, prodr. All-N-One Video, La Quinta, Calif., 1995—. Prodr., editor (promotional video) Guide Dogs of the Desert, 1993; cameraman, editor (promotional video) Angel View for the Retarded, 1994. Pres. Palm Springs Baseball League, 1997—. Home and Office: All In One Video 52-660 Avenida Martinez La Quinta CA 92253-3382

REITAN, HAROLD THEODORE, management consultant; b. Max, N.D., Nov. 3, 1928; s. Walter Rudolph and Anna Helga (Glesne) R.; m. Margaret Lucille Bonsac, Dec. 29, 1954 (div.); children: Eric, Karen, Chris, Jon. BA, St. Olaf Coll., 1950; MA in Social Psychology, U. Fla., 1962, PhD, 1967. Commd. officer U.S. Air Force, 1951, advanced through grades to col.; comdr., U.S. Air Force Spl. Treatment Ctr., Lackland, Tex., 1971-74, U.S. Air Force Corrections and Rehab. Group, Lowry, Colo., 1974-76, Tech. Tng. Wing, 1976-78, ret., 1978; mgr. health svcs. Coors Industries, Golden, Colo., 1978-84, mgr. tng. and organizational devel., 1984-89, cons. mgmt. assessment, tng. and devel., 1989—. Decorated Legion of Merit with oak leaf cluster, D.F.C. with oak leaf cluster, Bronze Star, Meritorious Svc. medal, Air medal with five oak leaf clusters. Mem. Am. Psychol. Assn., Phi Kappa Phi. Republican. Lutheran. Contbr. articles to profl. jours. Office: 116 S Nome St Aurora CO 80012-1242

REITEN, RICHARD G., natural gas industry executive; b. 1939. BA, U. Wash., 1962. With Simpson Timber Co., Seattle, 1962-64, St. Regis Paper Co., Tacoma, 1964-66, Hearin Products, Inc., Portland, Oreg., 1966-71; with Di Giorgio Corp., San Francisco, 1971-79, pres. bldg. material group; with Nicoli Co., Portland, 1979-87; dir. Oreg. Econ. Devel. Dept., Salem, 1987-89; pres. Portland Gen. Corp., 1989-92; pres. Portland Gen. Electric Co., 1992-95, pres., COO, 1996-97, pres., CEO, 1997—. Office: Northwest Natural Gas Co One Pacific Square 13th Fl 220 NW 2nd Ave Portland OR 97209

REITH, MARIANNE, retired nurse, educator, researcher; b. N.Y.C., Nov. 15, 1955; d. Edward John and Adamina (Kieliszek) R. BA in Religion, U. Fla., 1976; BS in Nursing, Cornell U., 1978; MSN, Oreg. Health Scis. U., 1988, postgrad., 1988-97. RN, N.Y., Wash., Oreg. Staff nurse Cornell U.-N.Y. Hosp. Med. Ctr., N.Y.C., 1978-79, Providence Med. Ctr., Seattle, 1979-80, U. Wash. Hosp., Seattle, 1981-84, Group Health Hosp., Seattle, 1984-85, St. Vincent Hosp. and Med. Ctr., Portland, Oreg., 1985-87; grad. asst., sr. grad. asst. Sch. Nursing Oreg. Health Scis. U., Portland, 1985-92; rsch. analyst Oreg. Health Divsn., Portland, 1992-95; dir., nurse scientist Northwest Health Rsch., Milwaukie, Oreg., 1995-98; ret., 1998. Mem. Oreg. Nurses Assn., ANA, Union Concerned Scientists, Amnesty Internat., Am. Statis. Assn., Sigma Theta Tau. Avocations: computers, bird watching, reading, choral singing.

REITZ, BRUCE ARNOLD, cardiac surgeon, educator; b. Seattle, Sept. 14, 1944; s. Arnold B. and Ruth (Stillings) R.; m. Nan Norton, Oct. 3, 1970; children: Megan, Jay. BS, Stanford U., 1966; MD, Yale U., 1970. Diplomate: Am. Bd. Surgery, Am. Bd. Thoracic Surgery. Intern Johns Hopkins Hosp., Balt., 1970-71, cardiac surgeon-in-charge, 1982-92; resident Stanford U. Hosp., (Calif.), 1971-72, 74-78; clin. assoc. Nat. Heart Lung Blood Inst., NIH, Bethesda, Md., 1972-74; asst. prof. Stanford U. Sch. Medicine, 1977-81, assoc. prof., 1981-82; prof. surgery Johns Hopkins U. Sch. Medicine, Balt., 1982-92; prof., chmn. Sch Medicine Stanford (Calif.) U., 1992—. Developer heart-lung transplant technique, 1981. Office: Stanford U Sch Medicine Dept Cardiothoracic Surgery Stanford CA 94305

REMEN, RACHEL NAOMI, pediatrician, psycho-oncologist; b. N.Y.C., Feb. 8, 1938; d. Isidore J. and Gladys Sara Remen. MD, Cornell U., 1962; PhD in Psychology (hon.), Calif. Inst. Integral Studies, San Francisco, 1996. Intern N.Y. Hosp., N.Y.C., 1962-63, resident, 1963-65; fellow Stanford U. Sch. Medicine, Palo Alto, Calif., 1965-67; asst. prof. pediat. Stanford U., Palo Alto, Calif., 1967-74, assoc. dir. pediat. clinic, 1974-77; assoc. clin. prof. family and cmty. medicine U. Calif. Sch. Medicine, San Francisco, 1996—; med. dir. Commonweal Cancer Help Program, Bolinas, Calif., 1985—; psycho-oncologist pvt. practice, 1981—; founding dir. Inst. Study of Health & Illness, 1992—. Author: Kitchen Table Wisdom, 1996; editor: (poetry book) Wounded Healers, 1995. Fellow Am. Acad. Pediats.;. Office: Commonweal PO Box 316 Bolinas CA 94924-0316

REMINGTON, ALAN, music educator; b. Chgo., Aug. 15, 1938; s. Sheppard Yvgenovich and Laura (Kalisch) Remigolskyi; m. Janet Hailparn, Aug. 8, 1961; children: Stephanie, Robert, William, Adam, Caryn. BMus, Am. Conservatory of Music, 1950, MMus in Composition, 1953. Bassoon/sax double WMAQ Radio, Chgo., 1947-50; sax/clarinet player Gene Krupa Band, Des Moines, 1947; bassoonist Houston Symphony Orch., Houston, 1953-57; condr. Myriad Prodns., N.Y.C., 1953-56; bassoon, orchestrator Paramount Pictures/Universal Pictures, Hollywood, 1957; composer, music educator Cinesound Studios, Hollywood, 1957-62; composer, contractor, conductor So. Calif., 1962-82; prof. music Orange Coast Coll., Costa Mesa, Calif., 1978—. With U.S. Army, 1951-52. Mem. Music/Entertainment Industry Educator's Assn. (dir. of student affairs 1997—, dir. membership 1990-97, nat. exec. bd.), Am. Fedn. of Musicians. Avocation: golf. Office: Orange Coast Coll 2701 Fairview Rd Costa Mesa CA 92626-5563

REMINGTON, MARY, artist, author; b. Kansas City, Mo., Jan. 15, 1930; d. Edwin Jennings and Mary Pauline (Remington) Anderson; m. Robert Alan Smith, Dec. 14, 1957 (div. 1978); 1 child, Susanah Mara Smith Malara. BA, Ottawa (Kans.) U., 1951; postgrad., U. Kans., 1951, Kansas City Art Inst. Artist animation dept. Walt Disney Prodns., Burbank, Calif., 1954-58; pvt. cartoonist Calif., 1977-92; humor and cartooning tchr. Mira Costa Coll. Extension course, Calif., 1992; tchr. So. Oreg. U., 1993; freelance cartoonist, caricaturist, Calif., Oreg. Author: Long Ago Elf, 1968, Crocodiles Have Big Teeth All Day, 1970; artist: paintings of landscapes, protraits, still lifes exhibited nationally. Mem. Grants Pass Art Museum, Rogue Gallery. Avocations: theology, interior design, reading, history, politics. Studio: 1345 A W Jones Creek Rd Grants Pass OR 97526

REMSING, DENNIS, advertising agency executive. Exec. v.p., gen. mgr. Rubin Postaer and Assocs., Santa Monica, Calif. Office: Rubin Postaer and Assocs 1333 2d St Santa Monica CA 90401*

RENARD, RONALD LEE, allergist; b. Chgo., July 31, 1949; s. Robert James and Dorothy Mae (Fruik) R.; m. Maureen Ann Gilmore, Aug. 5, 1972 (div. Mar. 1992); children: Jeffrey, Stephen, Justin, Leigh Ellen; m. Catherine L. Walker, Apr. 1, 1992; children: Morgan, Michal, Luke. 1 & 2 Degre de la Langue, U. de Montepellier, France, 1970; BS in French, U. San Francisco, 1971; MD, Creighton U., 1976. Dir. med. ICU, lt. U.S. Army Hosp., Ft. Leonard Wood, Md., 1980-81; dir. respiratory therapy, asst. chief allergy svc. Walter Reed Med. Ctr., Washington, 1981-84; staff allergist Chico (Calif.) Med. Group, 1984-86; allergist pvt. practice Redding, Calif., 1986—; dir. ACLS program Enloe Hosp., Chico, 1988-91; bd. dirs. Am. Lung Assn. Calif., 1989-91, med. dir. asthma camp, Chico, Redding, 1986-95; asst. prof. medicine USPHS, Bethesda, Md., 1982-84; asst. prof. family medicine U. Calif. Davis Med. Sch., Redding, 1990-94; Shasta County Planning Commr., 1994-95. Contbr. articles to profl. jours. Fellow Am. Acad. Allergy & Immunology, Am. Coll. Allergists; mem. Alpha Omega Alpha Nat. Honor Med. Soc., Assn. Mil. Allergists, Calif. Thoracic Soc. Republican. Roman Catholic. Avocations: hunting, biking. Office: 1950 Rosaline Ave Ste A Redding CA 96001-2543

RENDAL, CAMILLE LYNN, artist; b. San Jose, Calif., Apr. 1, 1955. Car, Otis Parsons Sch. Design, L.A., 1981. Art educator, dept. chmn. Crossroads Sch. for the Arts & Scis., Santa Monica, Calif., 1981-88; profl. artist L.A., 1984—; art educator N.Mex. State U., Las Cruces, 1993-96, Columbia Basin Coll., Pasco, Wash., 1998—. Artist posters; created commemorative postage stamp Halley's Comet, 1985. Recipient Kay Neilsen Young Talent award, L.A. County Museum of Art, 1980, Cert. for Inspired Teaching, Nat. Found. for Advancement in Arts, N.Y.C., 1989; scholarship Parsons Sch. Design, L.A., 1980, 81. Mem. Rosicrucian Order. Democrat.

RENDER, LORNE, museum director. Dir. C.M. Russell Mus., Gt. Falls, Mont. Office: CM Russell Mus 400 13th St N Great Falls MT 59401-1498*

RENETZKY, ALVIN, publisher; b. Bklyn., Aug. 2, 1940; s. Sam and Anna (Preiser) R.; m. Phyllis Ann (div.); 1 child, Davida; m. Cheryl Linden. PhD, U. Southern Calif., 1966. Publisher Academic Media, Los Angeles, 1967-70, Ready Reference Press, Santa Monica, Calif., 1974—. Editor: Directory of Career Resources for Women, 1980, Directory of Career Resources for Minorities, 1981, Career Employment Opportunities Directory, 1985, Directory of Internships; exec. prodr.: (video series) Guidance Club for Kids, 1992, Guidance Club for Teens, 1993, 94, Guidance Club for Women, 1994, Guidance Club for Parents, 1994, Career Club, 1994. Office: Ready Reference Press PO Box 5879 Santa Monica CA 90409-5879

RENGARAJAN, SEMBIAM RAJAGOPAL, electrical engineering educator, researcher, consultant; b. Mannargudi, Tamil Nadu, India, Dec. 12, 1948; came to U.S., 1980; s. Srinivasan and Rajalakshmi (Renganathan) Rajagopalan; m. Kalyani Srinivasan, June 24, 1982; children: Michelle, Sophie. BE with honors, U. Madras, India, 1971; MTech, Indian Inst. Tech., Kharagpur, 1974; PhD in Elec. Engring., U. N.B., Fredericton, Can., 1980. Tech. staff Jet Propulsion Lab., Pasadena, Calif., 1983-84; asst. prof. elec. engring. Calif. State U., Northridge, 1980-83, assoc. prof., 1984-87, prof., 1987—; vis. rschr. UCLA, 1984-93, vis. prof., 1987-88; vis. prof. U. de Santiago de Compastela, Spain, 1996, U. Pretoria, South Africa, 1997; cons. Hughes Aircraft Co., Canoga Park, Calif., 1982-87, NASA-Jet Propulsion Lab., Pasadena, 1987-90, 92-94, 96—, Ericsson Radar Electronics, Sweden, 1990-92, Martin Mariette, 1995-96; guest rschr. Chalmers U., Sweden, 1990, UN Devel. Program, 1993, Rome Lab., USAF, summer 1995. Contbr. articles to profl. jours. Recipient Outstanding Faculty award Calif. State U., Northridge, 1985, Disting. Engring. Educator of Yr. award Engrs. Coun., L.A., 1995, Meritorious Performance and Profl. Promise award, 1986, 88, Merit award San Fernando Valley Engrs., Coun., 1989, Cert. of Recognition NASA, 1991-92; Nat. Merit scholar Govt. India, 1965-71. Fellow Inst. Advancement Engrs., IEEE (L.A. chpt. sec., treas. antennas and propagation soc. 1981-82, vice-chmn. 1982-83, chmn. 1983-84), Internat. Union Radio Sci. (U.S. nat. com.), The Electromagnetics Acad. Avocations: swimming, camping, jogging, tennis. Office: Calif State U 18111 Nordhoff St Northridge CA 91330-0001

RENNE, JANICE LYNN, interior designer; b. Los Angeles, July 16, 1952; d. George Joseph and Dolly Minni (Neubaurer) R.; m. William Lee Kile, Dec. 6, 1975 (div. Sept. 1983); m. James Alan Steffen, May 31, 1998. BA, Sweet Briar Coll., 1974; AA, Interior Designers Inst., 1985. Lic. gen. contractor, Calif.; cert. interior designer, Calif. Coun. for Interior Design Certification. Exec. trainee Bullock's, Santa Ana, Calif., 1974, Pub. Fin., Inc., Huntington Beach, Calif., 1975; bookkeeper William L. Kile DDS, Inc., Santa Barbara, Calif., 1979-81, Nelson & Hamilton, Inc., Santa Barbara, 1981-82; interior designer Ultimate Designs, Irvine, Calif., 1984-85, sr. designer, 1985-86; draftsperson JBI Inc., Long Beach, Calif., 1984-85; prin. designer Janice Renne Interior Designs, Newport Beach, Calif., 1986-92, Costa Mesa, Calif., 1992—; space planner Design Pak II, Newport Beach, 1987-88; State of Calif. rep. task force for developing self-cert. process for Calif. interior designers, Internat. Soc. Interior Design, 1991. Created utility room design for Easter Seals Design House, 1985; weekly radio show host on restaurant design, 1986; work published in Orange County mag. and L.A. Times., 1988. Recipient scholarship Calif. Inst. Applied Design, Newport Beach, 1984. Mem. Am. Inst. Archs. (assoc.), Internat. Soc. Interior Designers (grad. assoc. designer butler's pantry, assoc. designer Design House powder room 1988, asst. editor Orange County chpt. 1988-89, chpt. Quar. Newsletter, chpt. gen. bd. 1991-92, chmn. licensing com. 1991-92, bd. dirs. 1991-92), Color Assn. U.S., Constrn. Specifications Inst., Nat. Exec. Women in Hospitality, Calif. Legis. Conf. in Interior Design (gen. bd. 1991-92, v.p. comm. 1992-93), Orange County and Newport Beach Letip Internat. (sec. 1987, 89-90, treas. 1991, pres. 1993), Internat. Interior Design Assn. (city ctr. dir. 1998, 99, bd. rep. Expo 1998, 99), Tall Club Internat. (editor 1998-98, merit award 1998), Tall Club Orange County (exec. v.p. 1995, co-editor High Life 1995-96, editor 1995—, Miss Congeniality award 1994, rec. sec. 1996-97, del. to conv. 1996, del. Tall Club Internat. Conv. 1996). Republican. Lutheran. Avocations: skiing, tennis, biking, photography, ballroom dancing competition. Office: 2915 Red Hill Ave Ste C101A Costa Mesa CA 92626-5932

RENNEBERGER, RAYMOND CECIL, real estate professional; b. Washington, July 19, 1932; s. Raymond cecil and Virginia Hall (Cologne) R.; m. Linda Carolyn Conover, Nov. 19, 1966; children: Deborah Lynn Weller, Martin Scott Snyder. BA, U. Md., 1957. Sales assoc. 3M Co., Washington, 1957-60; sales supr. 3M Co., San Francisco, 1960-65, dist. sales mgr., 1965-71; v.p. and gen. mgr. Ingels, Co., Colorado Springs, 1971-87; ptnr., owner, broker Fidelity Real Estate, Colorado Springs, 1987—; chmn. E.D.C. com. C. of C., Colorado Springs, 1991-96; v.p. Nat. Microfilm Assn., San Francisco, 1970-71; co-chmn. Olympathon, Nat. Olympic Com., 1979. Sgt.-at-arms Rep. Nat. Conv., San Francisco, 1964. With U.S. Army, 1953-56. Mem. Broadmoor Golf Club, El Paso Club, Garden of Gods Club, Sigma Phi Epsilon. Republican. Methodist. Avocations: golf, fishing. Home: 720 Count Pourtales Dr Colorado Springs CO 80906-4268

RENNER, ERIC PAYNE, artist; b. Phila., Nov. 6, 1941; s. Richard Louis and Josie (Wallach) R.; children Zephyr, Yarian. B.S., U. Cin., 1964; M.F.A., Cranbrook Acad. Art, 1968. Asst. prof. design SUNY-Alfred, 1968-71; adj. prof. Wright State U., Dayton, Ohio, 1974, U. Cin., 1974, Visual Studies Workshop, Rochester, N.Y., 1975; part-time instr. Coll. Santa Fe, 1976-77, Western N. Mex. U., Silver City, 1979; free-lance artist, San Lorenzo, N. Mex., 1978—; pres. Pinhole Resource; lectr., workshop participant schs. throughout U.S., Can. and Europe; represented by Visual Studies Workshop, Rochester. Author: Pinhole Photography, 1995; editor Pinhole Jour.; one-man shows include Mus. Modern Art, Mex. City, 1970, Museu de Arte de Sao Paulo, Brazil, 1976, Contemporary Arts Ctr., Cin., 1973, Tyler Sch. Art, Phila., 1982, Light Factory, Charlotte, N.C., 1981, No. Ky. U., 1981, U. N.Mex., 1980, Colo. Mountain Coll., 1979; exhibited in group shows at U. Southampton, Eng., Nat. Gallery of Can., 1980, Mus. Fine Art, Santa Fe, 1978, and others; represented in permanent collections Mus. Modern Art, N.Y.C., Bibliotheque Nationale, Paris, Mus. of Art Sao Paulo, Brazil, Inst. of Contemporary Art of Chgo., Internat. Mus. Photos George Eastman House, Rochester, N.Y., Calif. Mus. Photography, Riverside, NEA Bldg. Collection. Am.-Scandinavian Found. grantee, 1987; NEA fellow, 1976, 79. Mem. Soc. Photo Edn. Home and Studio: Route 15 Box 1355 San Lorenzo NM 88041

RENO, JOSEPH HARRY, retired orthopedic surgeon; b. Allentown, Pa., Mar. 5, 1915; s. Harvey Luther and Olive May (Wilson) R.; m. Maude Olivia Mutchler, June 27, 1942; children: Joseph David, Sally Jo, Diana Jane, Deborah Marion. Student, Temple U., 1934-37, MD, 1941. Intern. Chester (Pa.) Hosp., 1941-42; residency Tex. Scottish Rite Hosp. for Crippled Children, Dallas, 1942-43, 44-45, Robert Packer Hosp., Sayre, Pa., 1943-44; assoc. Homer Stryker, M.D., Kalamazoo, 1945-46; pvt. practice Bethlehem, Pa., 1946-71, Flagstaff, Ariz., 1971-93; team physician Lehigh U., Bethlehem, 1946-70, No. Ariz. U., Flagstaff, 1971-77, Ariz. State U., Tempe, 1977-84; chief surg. staff Flagstaff Hosp., 1975. Contbr. articles to profl. jours.; prodr. surg. films for Am. Acad. Ortho. Surgeons and others, 1952-70. Pres. Coconino County Easter Seal Soc., 1973; bd. dirs., med. advisor Ariz. Easter Seal Soc., 1974-84. Recipient Pioneer award Ariz. Med. Assn., 1981, Cert. of Appreciation, Pa. Dept. Health Crippled Children's Div., 1971; Dr. Joseph Reno Sports Medicine award named in honor, No. Ariz. State U. and Blue Cross Blue Shield, 1986. Fellow Am. Acad. Ortho. Surgeons, Am. Assn. for Surgery of Trauma, Am. Coll. Sports Med., Am. Coll. Surgeons (chmn. Lehigh Valley subcom. on trauma 1954-66, Ea. Pa. chpt. pres. 1969); mem. NRA, Am. Bd. Ortho. Surgery (cert., diplomate 1948), Coconino County Med. Soc. (pres. 1976), Western Ortho. Assn., Babcock Surg. Soc., Mason, Phi Chi, Alpha Tau Omega. Home: Apt 219 475 Jacks Canyon Rd Sedona AZ 86351

RENO, STEPHEN JEROME, academic administrator; b. Oxnard, Calif., Feb. 27, 1944; s. Warren Jerome and Marie Louise (Fischer) R.; m. Catherine Royce Motley, Sept.7, 1974; children: Matthew Stephen, Catherine Hamlen. AB, St. John's Coll., Camarillo, Calif., 1965; MA, U. Calif., Santa Barbara, 1968, PhD, 1975. Provost and dean of faculty So. Oreg. U., Ashland, 1989-94; pres. So. Oreg. U., 1994—; bd. mem. SALT Ctr. for Field Studies. Author: The Sacred Tree, 1975; author, contbr.: Penguin Dictionary of Religion, 1981; jour. editor Gen. Theol. Ctr. Maine, 1988-89; contbr. articles to religious jours. Mem. CSC, Portland, Maine, 1985-88. Recipient Rsch. awards The British Acad., London, 1976-77, 78-79. Mem. British Assn. for History of Religion, Am. Acad. Religion. Roman Catholic. Home: 610 Elkader St Ashland OR 97520-3306 Office: So Oreg U 1250 Siskiyou Blvd Ashland OR 97520-5010

RENSE, PAIGE, editor, publishing company executive; b. Iowa, May 4, 1929; m. Kenneth Noland, Apr. 10, 1994. Student, Calif. State U., L.A. Editor-in-chief Architectural Digest, L.A., 1970—. Recipient Nat. Headliner award Women in Communications, 1983, Pacifica award So. Calif. Resources Coun., 1978, editl. award Dallas Market Ctr., 1978, golden award Chgo. Design Resources Svc., 1982, Agora award, 1982, outstanding profl. incomms. award, 1982, trailblazers award, 1983, disting. svcs. award Resources Coun., Inc., 1988, Spirit of Achievement award, 1995, Pratt Inst. Founders award, 1997; named woman of yr. L.A. Times, 1976, Muses, 1986, woman of internat. accomplishment, 1991; named to Interior Design Hall of Fame. Office: Architectural Digest The Conde Nast Publ Inc 6300 Wilshire Blvd Fl 11 Los Angeles CA 90048-5204*

RENSON, JEAN FELIX, psychiatry educator; b. Liège, Belgium, Nov. 9, 1930; came to U.S., 1960; s. Louis and Laurence (Crahai) R.; m. Gisèle Bouillenne, Sept. 8, 1956; children: Marc, Dominique, Jean-Luc. MD, U. Liege, 1959; PhD in Biochemistry, George Washington U., 1971. Diplomate Am. Bd. Psychiatry. Asst. prof. U. Liège, 1957-60; rsch. fellow U. Liege, 1966-72; clin. assoc. prof. dept. psychiatry U. Calif., San Francisco, 1978—; vis. asst. prof. Stanford U., Palo Alto, Calif., 1972-77. Assoc. editor: Fundamentals of Biochemical Pharmacology, 1971. NIH fellow, 1960-66. Democrat. Avocations: neurosciences, music.

RENTZ, WILLIAM OLIPHANT, retired environmental engineer, consultant; b. Milledgeville, Ga., Dec. 10, 1932; s. Thomas Henry and Jean Gray (Oliphant) R.; m. Pamella Ann Stephens, Aug. 15, 1958 (div. July 1978); children: Cynthia Gray Rentz Rader, Craig Stephens; m. Susan Anette Johnson Tinkcom, Mar. 30, 1997. Student, Ga. Inst. Tech., 1950-51; BS, U.S. Naval Acad., 1955; postgrad., George Wash. U., 1971, MIT, 1980. Enlisted USNR, Atlanta, 1949-51; commd. ensign USN, 1955, advanced through grades to capt., 1976; evaluation mgr. INPO, Atlanta, 1985-87; cons. Williams Power Corp., Stone Mountain, Ga., 1988-91; sr. cons. United Energy Svcs. Corp., Oak Ridge, Tenn., 1991-96; v.p. Exptl. Engring. Corp., Hanford, Wash., 1996-98; chief engr. USS Enterprise, Norfolk, Va., 1960-63; commd. officer USS California, Norfolk, Va., 1976-79; ret., 1998; mgmt. cons. Lockheed Martin Energy Sys., Oak Ridge, Tenn., 1991-96; cons. in field of comm. nuclear and fossil power and environ. sampling and restoration. Active Atlanta Symphony Orch. Decorated Navy Commendation medal (Vietnam) with two gold stars, Legion of Merit with three gold stars; recipient Meritorious Svc. medal USN, 1970, Steven Decatur award Navy League U.S., 1980. Mem. U.S. Naval Inst., The Ret. Officers Assn., U.S. Naval Acad. Alumni Assn. (pres. Atlanta chpt. 1991-93, Knoxville, Tenn., chpt. 1994-96), MIT Alumni Assn., Ga. Conservancy. Democrat. Methodist. Avocations: gardening, tennis, running.

RENWICK, EDWARD RAINEY, management consultant; b. L.A., Apr. 21, 1966; s. Edward Shield and Gloria Ann (Rainey) R. AB in History with honors, Stanford U., 1988; M of Pub. Policy, Harvard U., 1995, JD cum laude, 1995. Market analyst Cushman Realty Corp., L.A., 1989; fin. analyst Goldman, Sachs & Co., L.A., 1989-91; cons. Wanli Battery Co., Chongqing, China, 1995-96, Boston Consulting Group, L.A., 1994, 96—. Founder, bd. dirs. L.A. St. Project, 1990—; advisor L.A. Tech. Coun., 1998—. Kennedy fellow Kennedy Sch.-Harvard U., 1992-95; Luce scholar Henry Luce Found., N.Y.C., 1995-96. Democrat. Roman Catholic. Avocations: jogging, reading, skiing. Home: 717 Pacific Ave Venice CA 90291-3219 Office: The Boston Cons Group Inc 355 S Grand Ave Ste 3300 Los Angeles CA 90071-1592

RENWICK, EDWARD S., lawyer; b. L.A., May 10, 1934. AB, Stanford U., 1956, LLB, 1958. Bar: Calif. 1959, U.S. Dist. Ct. (cen. dist.) Calif. 1959, U.S. Ct. Appeals (9th cir.) 1963, U.S. Dist. Ct. (so. dist.) Calif. 1973, U.S. Dist. Ct. (no. dist.) Calif. 1977, U.S. Dist. Ct. (ea. dist.) Calif. 1981, U.S. Supreme Ct. 1985. Ptnr. Hanna and Morton, L.A.; mem., bd. vis. Stanford Law Sch., 1967-69; mem. environ. and natural resources adv. bd. Stanford Law Sch. Bd. dirs. Calif. Supreme Ct. Hist. Soc. Fellow Am. Coll. Trial Lawyers, Am. Bar Found.; mem. ABA (mem. sect. on litigation, antitrust law, bus. law, chmn. sect. of nat. resources, energy and environ. law 1987-88, mem. at large coord. group energy law 1989-92, sect. rep. coord. group energy law 1995-97, Calif. del. legal com., interstate oil compact com.), Calif. Arboretum Assn. (trustee 1986-92), L.A. County Bar Assn. (chmn. natural resources law sect. 1974-75), The State Bar of Calif., Chancery Club (pres. 1992-93), Phi Delta Phi. Office: Hanna and Morton 600 Wilshire Blvd Fl 17 [illegible]

REPASS, RANDY, electrical company executive. Chmn., CEO West Marine, Watsonville, Calif. Office: West Marine PO Box 50050 Watsonville CA 95077-5050*

REQUICHA, ARISTIDES ADELINO GUALBERTO, computer scientist; b. Monte Estoril, Portugal, Mar. 18, 1939; came to U.S., 1965; s. Adelino P. and Ana (Gualberto) R.; m. Shahin A. Hakim, Sept. 5, 1970. Engring. Diploma, Univ. Lisbon, Portugal, 1962; PhD, U. Rochester, 1970. Lectr. Univ. Lisbon, 1961-63; rsch. scientist NATO Saclantcen, La Spezia, Italy, 1970-73; scientist to sr. scientist Univ. Rochester, N.Y., 1973-83; assoc. prof. Univ. Rochester, 1983-86; prof. U. So. Calif., L.A., 1986—. Editor: CVGIP-Graphic Models & Image Processing, 1989—, Springer Book Series on Computer Graphics, 1982—, Jour. Design & Mfg., 1991-95; contbr. sci. articles to profl. jours. Lt. Portuguese Air Force, 1963-65. Fellow IEEE (editor Transactions on Robotics and Automation 1991-94); mem. AAAS, Soc. Mfg. Engrs. (sr.), Assn. Computing Machinery (editor Transactions on Graphics 1984-90), Am. Assn. Artificial Intelligence, Sigma Xi. Office: U So Calif Dept Computer Sci Los Angeles CA 90089-0781

RESCH, CHARLOTTE SUSANNA, plastic surgeon; b. Charlottesville, Va., Sept. 24, 1957; d. Johann Heinrich and Eleonore Susanne (Stenzel) R.; m. John Arthur Niero, Jan. 31, 1990. Student, Dalhousie U., Halifax, Nova Scotia, Can., 1974-76; MD with distinction, Dalhousie U. Med. Sch., Halifax, Nova Scotia, Can., 1980. Diplomate Dalhousie U., Am. Bd. Plastic Surgery; licentiate Med. Coun. Can.; cert. Bd. Med. Quality Assurance Calif. Intern Ottawa Gen. Hosp., Ont., Can., 1980-81; gen. surgery resident Dalhousie U., Halifax, Nova Scotia, Can., 1981-85; plastic surgery resident Wayne State U., Detroit, 1985-87; pvt. practice San Francisco, 1988-89; pre-ptnr. Southern Calif. Permanente Physicians Group, Fontana, 1989-92, ptnr., 1992—. Contbr. articles to profl. jours. Fellow ACS; mem. Am. Soc. Plastic and Reconstructive Surgeons, Calif. Med. Soc., San Bernardino Med. Soc., Alpha Omega Alpha. Avocations: travel, skiing, bicycling, gardening, gourmet cooking. Office: Kaiser Found Hosp Dept Plastic Surgery 9985 Sierra Ave Fontana CA 92335-6720

RESNICK, JEFFREY I., plastic surgeon; b. Jersey City, Mar. 2, 1954; s. Victor and Regina (Bistritz) R.; m. Michele Gail Zinger, July 12, 1981; children: Andrew Gregory, Daniel Zachary. BS, Yale U., 1975; MD, U. Pa., 1980. Diplomate Am. Bd. Surgery, Am. Bd. Plastic Surgery. Resident in surgery Mass. Gen. Hosp., Boston, 1980-85, resident in plastic surgery, 1985-87; fellow in craniofacial surgery UCLA, 1987-88; pvt. practice plastic surgery Santa Monica, Calif., 1989—; asst. clin. prof. plastic surgery UCLA, 1987—, U. So. Calif., 1998—. Contbr. articles to profl. jours. Surgeon Interplast, Vietnam, Nepal. Mem. Am. Soc. Plastic and Reconstructive Surgeons, Am. Soc. Maxillofacial Surgeons, Am. Cleft Palate-Craniofacial Assn., Plastic Surgery Ednl. Found., Sigma Xi, Alpha Omega Alpha. Office: 1301 20th St Ste 470 Santa Monica CA 90404-2082

RESNICOFF, ETHEL, author; b. Bklyn., July 3; d. Samuel and Mildred Shirley Resnicoff. BA, Bklyn. Coll., MS. Staff writer TV show Captain Kangaroo, N.Y.C., 1969-74; freelance writer of ednl. materials for children, 1974—. Active RP Internat., Habitat for Humanity. Mem. ASCAP, Writers Guild Am. Avocations: sailing, bicycling, piano.

RETALLACK, ALEXIA ELIZABETH, editor, writer; b. Auburn, Calif., Sept. 19, 1968; d. Everett Neal and Sandra Sue (Hyde) R.; m. David M. Rutz, Sept. 27, 1992; 1 child, Anastasia Marie. BA, Calif. State Univ., 1990, MA, 1997. Editor in chief West Sacramento Press, West Sacramento, Calif., 1990-92; various Dept. of Fish & Game, Sacramento, 1992-96, info officer, editor, 1996—. Editor: Outdoor California Mag., 1996, Outdoor California, 1997. Avocations: writing, painting, gardening, cycling. Office: Dept of Fish and Game 1416 9th St Fl 12 Sacramento CA 95814-5511

REUBEN, DON HAROLD, lawyer; b. Chgo., Sept. 13, 1928; s. Michael B. and Sally (Chapman) R.; m. Evelyn Long, Aug. 27, 1948 (div.); children: Hope Reuben Boland, Michael Barrett, Timothy Don, Jeffrey Long, Howard Ellis; m. Jeannette Hurley Haywood, Dec. 13, 1971; stepchildren: Harris Hurley Haywood, Edward Gregory Haywood. BS, Northwestern U., 1949, JD, 1952. Bar: Ill. 1952, Calif. 1996. With firm Kirkland & Ellis, Chgo., 1952-78, sr. ptnr., until 1978; sr. ptnr. Reuben & Proctor, Chgo., 1978-86, Isham, Lincoln & Beale, Chgo., 1986-88; sr. counsel Winston & Strawn, 1988-94; of counsel Altheimer & Gray, Chgo., 1994—; spl. asst. atty. gen. State of Ill., 1963-64, 69, 84; gen. coun. Tribune Co., 1965-88, Chgo. Bears Football Club, 1965-88, Cath. Archdiocese of Chgo., 1975-88; coun. spl. session Ill. Ho. of Reps., 1964, for Ill. treas. for congl., state legis. and jud. reapportionment, 1963; spl. fed. ct. master, 1968-70; dir. Lake Shore Nat. Bank, 1973-93; dir. Heitman Fin., 1993-98; mem. citizens adv. bd. to sheriff County of Cook, 1962-66, mem. jury instrn. com., 1963-68; rules com. Ill. Supreme Ct., 1963-73; mem. pub. rels. com. Nat. Conf. State Trial Judges; mem. com. study caseflow mgmt. in law div. Cook County Cir. Ct., 1979-88; mem. adv. implementation com. U.S. Dist. Ct. for No. Dist. Ill., 1981-82; mem. Chgo. Better Schs. Com., 1968-69, Chgo. Crime Commn., 1970-80; mem. supervisory panel Fed. Defender Program; gen. counsel Palm Springs Air Mus., 1996—, News-Gazette, Champaign, Ill., 1997—; dir. Profl. Impressions Media Group, Inc., 1997—; lectr. on libel, slander, privacy and freedom of press. Bd. dirs. Lincoln Park Zool. Soc., 1972-84 ; trustee Northwestern U., 1977—; mem. vis. com. U. Chgo. Law Sch., 1976-79. Mem. Ill. Bar Assn., Chgo. Bar Assn. (chmn. subcom. on propriety and regulation of contingent fees com. devel. law 1966-69, subcom. on media liaison 1980-82, mem. com. on profl. info. 1980-82), ABA (standing com. on fed. judiciary 1973-79, standing com. on jud. selection, tenure and compensation 1982-85), Am. Law Inst., Am. Judicature Soc., Fellows Am. Bar Found., Am. Coll. Trial Lawyers (Rule 23 com. 1975-82, judiciary com. 1987-91), Am. Arbitration Assn. (nat. panel arbitrators), Calif. Bar Assn., Desert Bar Assn., Internat. Acad. Trial Lawyers, Union League Club (Chgo.), Tavern Club, Mid-Am. Club, Law Club, Casino Club, The Springs Club, Desert Riders of Palm Springs, The Chgo. Club, Phi Eta Sigma, Beta Alpha Psi, Beta Gamma Sigma, Order of Coif. Home: 20 Jill Ter Rancho Mirage CA 92270-2635

REUTHER, RONALD THEODORE, museum director; b. Dec. 29, 1929; s. Frederick and Grace (Roehll) R.; m. Mary B. Howard, 1956; children: Catherine Virginia, Paul Douglas, Jon Frederick, Victoria Grace. BA, U. Calif., 1951, postgrad., 1953; postgrad., U. Ariz., 1952. Mgr. Micke Grove Zoo, 1957-62; gen. curator Cleve. Zoo, 1958-62; asst. dir., 1964-66; dir. Indpls. Zoo, 1962-64, San Francisco Zoo, 1966-73; pres., exec. dir. Phila. Zoo, 1973-78; dir. corp. devel. Exploratorium, San Francisco, 1980-81; founder We. Aerospace Mus., Oakland, Calif., 1980, exec. dir., 1995—; field rep. Bell & Howell Edn. Corp./DeVry Inst. Tech., 1983-88; exec. dir. Whale Ctr., Oakland, Calif., 1988-89; edn. cons. Sierra Acad. Aerospace, Oakland, Calif., 1989-92; lectr. Golden State U., San Francisco, 1992; co-founder Pt. Reyes Bird Observatory, Calif., 1968-70; v.p. Del. Valley Mus. Coun., 1976-78. Author zoo guidebooks, Wings Over San Francisco Bay, 1997. Mem. exec. com. Greater Phila. Cultural Alliance, 1976-78. 2nd lt. USAF, 1953-57; with USARNG, 1958-66; lt. col. USAR, 1966-81, ret. Mem. The Explorers Club (chmn. No. Calif. chpt. 1990-95), Tamalpais Conservation Club (life mem.), Ox-5 Pioneers (bd. govs. Golden Gate chpt. 1996—). Office: We Aerospace Mus Oakland Airport 8260 Boeing St Oakland CA 94621-4544

REVEAL, ARLENE HADFIELD, librarian, consultant; b. Riverside, Utah, May 21, 1916; d. Job Oliver and Mabel Olive (Smith) Hadfield; children: James L., Jon A. BS with hons., Utah State U., 1938; grad. in librarianship San Diego State U., 1968; M in Libr. and Info. Sci., Brigham Young U., 1976. Social case worker Boxelder County Welfare, Brigham City, Utah, 1938-40; office mgr. Dodge Ridge Ski Corp., Long Barn, Calif., 1948-65, Strawberry (Calif.) Inn, 1950-65, Pinecrest Permittees Assn., 1955-66; adminstrv. asst. Mono County Office of Edn., Bridgeport, Calif., 1961-67; catalog libr. La Mesa (Calif.)-Spring Valley Sch. Dist., 1968-71; libr. Mono County Libr., Bridgeport, Calif., 1971-96; cmty. grandmother, 1996—; chair Mountain Valley Library System, 1987-89. Author: Mono County Courthouse, 1980. Active Devel. Disabilities Area Bd. # 12, 1974-96, chair, 1990-92. Recipient John Cotton Dana award H.W. Wilson Co., 1974; named Bridgeport Citizen of Yr., 1993, Wild Iris Woman of Yr., Mono County, 1996. Mem. Rebekah (treas. 1973-90), Delta Kappa Gamma (pres. Epsilon Alpha chpt. 1984-88), Beta Sigma Phi (treas. Xi Omicron Epsilon [illegible] 5250 W Riverside UT 84334-0156

REVER, BARBARA L., medical educator, consultant, researcher; b. Bklyn., Dec. 18, 1947. B.A., Barnard Coll., 1969; M.P.H., U. Calif.-Berkeley, 1970; M.D., N.Y. Med. Coll., 1974. Diplomate Am. Bd. Internal Medicine, Spl̄ty. Nephrology. Intern, Los Angeles County Hosp., U. So. Calif., 1974-75; resident in internal medicine, Los Angeles County Hosp., 1975-76, Kaiser Found. Hosps., Los Angeles, 1976-77; fellow in nephrology U. Calif., L.A. Sch. Medicine, 1978-80, founder and specialist in Nephrology, Salinas Valley Dialysis Services, Inc., 1982—, also chmn. bd.; spl. cons. Calif. State Dept. Pub. Health, summer 1970; research assoc. Dept. Community and Preventive Medicine, N.Y. Hosp. Coll., summer 1971; instr. biology and physiology Community Health Medic Tng. Program, Indian Health Service Hosp., N. Mex., summer 1972; asst. prof. medicine, asst. dir. renal transplantation div. nephrology UCLA, 1980-81; founder Salinas Valley Dialysis Svcs., Inc., 1983; pvt. practice nephrology, 1981—. Office: 951 Blanco Cir # D Salinas CA 93901-4451

REVLING, MICHAEL, museum administrator. Pres. Boise (Idaho) Art Mus. Office: Boise Art Mus 6705 Julia Davis Dr Boise ID 83702*

REWERTS, MILAN ALVIN, university program director; b. Princeton, Ill., Sept. 10, 1942; s. Elmer Earl and Norma Ardis (Gleason) R.; m. Carol Ann Demaree, June 20, 1964; children: Michael Allen, Michelle Ann. BS in Agrl. Sci., U. Ill., 1964; MEd in Ednl. Adminstrn., Colo. State U., 1974, postgrad., 1975-92. Extension agt. Garfield county Colo. State U. Coop Extension, Glenwood Springs, 1966-68; area extension agt. Tri River area Colo. State U. Coop Extension, Grand Junction, Colo., 1968-73; extension agt., Weld county Colo. State U. Coop Extension, Greeley, Colo., 1974-80; dist. dir., south ctrl. Colo. State U. Coop Extension, Ft. Collins, Colo., 1980-88, pers. dir., field rep., 1988-90, interim state dir., 1990-95, state dir., 1995—; Colo. state univ. rep. Colo. Rural Devel. Coun., Ft. Collins, 1993—; mem. faculty improvement com. Colo. State U. 1st lt. U.S. Army, 1964-66, USAR, 1966-93, ret. col. Contbr. articles to profl. jours. Advisor Colo. State 4-H Senate, Ft. Collins, 1977-89. Mem. Am. Mgmt. Assn., Res. Officers Assn., Nat. Assn. of County Agrl. Agts., Nat. Assn. of Extension 4-H Agts. (state pres. 1975-76, Disting. Svc. award 1976), Nat. Western Stock Show Assn., Nat. Assn. of State Univs. and Land Grant Coll. (chair nat. pers. and orgn. devel. com. 1993-94), Rotary Club of Colo., Epsilon Sigma Phi, Gamma Sigma Delta. Avocations: running, golf, basketball, reading, gardening. Office: Colo State Univ Coop Ext 1 Adminstration Bldg Fort Collins CO 80523

REYES, CARLOS, poet, educator; b. Marshfield, Mo., June 2, 1935; s. Herman Carroll King and Alice Day; m. Barbara Ann Hollingsworth (div. 1973); children: Michael Hollingsworth, Amy Sofia, Nina Heloise, Rachel Kathleen; m. Karen Ann Stoner (div. 1979); m. Elizabeth Shellin Atly, Dec. 27, 1993. BA, U. Oreg., 1961; MA, U. Ariz., 1965, ABD, 1965. Lang. instr. U. Ariz., Tucson, 1965; assoc. prof. lang. U. Maine, Orono, 1965-66, Portland (Oreg.) State U., 1967-71; lectr. Mt. Hood C.C., Gresham, Oreg., 1971-72; with Poets-in-Schs., Oreg., 1971-72; instr. English Portland Art Mus. Sch., 1972-73; pres.-pub. Trask House Books, Inc., 1973—; instr. Oreg. Writers Workshop, Portland, 1982-83; med. translator, editor CMC Rsch., Portland, 1995—; poet-in-residence Wash. Arts Commn., Nev. Arts. Commn., Regional Arts Culture Coun., 1982—. Author: Shingle Weaver's Journal, 1980, At Doolin Quay, 1982, Nightmarks, 1990, A Suitcase of Crows, 1995, Open Doors (A Translation of Edwin Madrid's Puertas Abiertas), 1999; editor Hubbub, 1982—; mem. editl. bd. Ar Mhuin Na Muice, Portland and Seattle, 1996—. Bd. dirs. Mountain Writers Series, 1996—, Portland Writers Festival, 1974-84, Gov.'s Adv. Com. on the Arts, 1971-73. With U.S. Army, 1953-56. Individual Arts fellow Oreg. Arts Commn., 1982, fellow Yaddo Corp., Saratoga Springs, N.Y., 1984, Individual fellow Fundación Valparaíso, Mojacar, Spain, 1998. Mem. PEN (co-chair 1992-94, treas. 1995-97). Home: 3222 NE Shuyler Portland OR 97212

REYES, JESS ARTHUR, telecommunications engineer; b. Stockton, Calif., Feb. 9, 1959; s. Jess Horlanda and Ile (Eclips) R. BA in Music, San Jose State U., 1983, MA in Music, 1987. Software quality engr. Apple Computers, Inc., Cupertino, Calif., 1990-95; mgr. software quality engring. Pacific Bell Video Svcs., San Ramon, Calif., 1995—; owner Sinewave Creations, Pittsburg, Calif., 1989—. Home: 44 Carroll Dr Pittsburg CA 94565-6103

REYNALDS, JEREMY GRAHAM, rescue mission administrator; b. Bath, Eng., Oct. 19, 1957; came to U.S., 1978; s. Graham John and Ruth (Bowden) R.; m. Sylvia Ellen Page, Apr. 14, 1979; children: Ben, Joshua, Jeremiah, Joel, Josiah. B Univ. Studies, U. N.Mex., 1996, postgrad., 1996—. Founder, exec. dir. His Place, Santa Fe, 1982-86, Joy Junction, Albuquerque, 1986—. Author: Homeless in America, 1994, The Walking Wounded, 1996. Recipient Jefferson award Am. Inst. for Pub. Svc., 1994. Mem. Internat. Union Gospel Missions. Mem. Calvary Chapel. Avocations: his children, reading. Office: Joy Junction PO Box 27693 4500 2d St SW Albuquerque NM 87125

REYNER, NANCY COOPER, artist; b. Norristown, Pa., Dec. 3, 1956; d. Jack Cooper and Nora (Koral) R.; m. Phillip Jonathon Cohen, Dec. 13, 1987; 1 child, Jacob. BFA in Illustration, RISD, 1978; MFA in Arts Adminstrn., Columbia U., 1986. Art retouch technician Photlettering, N.Y.C., 1979-81; co-dir. Ragabash Theater Co., N.Y.C., 1981-83; artist-in-residence N.Y. Pub. Schs., N.Y.C., 1981-85; mgr. pub. art program N.Y. Met. Transp. Authority, N.Y.C., 1986-87; co-owner Gallery 10, Santa Fe, 1987—; owner Reyner Studio, Santa Fe, 1998—; resident-in-charge Phoenix Ctr., 1995-97; panelist, juror Phoenix Arts Commn., 1989-93, N.Mex. Arts Divsn., Santa Fe, 1989-93. Bd. dirs. Ctr. for Contemporary Arts, Santa Fe, 1989-93. Recipient Disting. Grad. award Plymouth Whitemarsh (Pa.) H.S., 1998; grantee N.Y.C. Dept. Cultural Affairs, 1981-84, Phoenix Commn. on the Arts, 1996, Ariz. Commn. on the Arts, 1996. Home: 2167 Chamisos Ct Santa Fe NM 87505-5623 Office: Gallery 10 225 Canyon Rd Santa Fe NM 87501-2755

REYNOLDS, CHARLES PATRICK, pediatric oncologist, researcher; b. El Paso, Tex., Aug. 8, 1952; s. Charles Albert and Lallah Elizabeth (Munro) R.; m. Debra Dawn Adams, Feb. 3, 1979; children: Amy Elizabeth, Jennifer Ann. BA in Biology, U. Tex., 1974; MD, U. Tex. Southwestern Med. Sch., Dallas, 1979; PhD, U. Tex., 1979. Lic. Tex., Calif. Postdoctoral fellow U. Tex. Southwestern Med. Sch., Dallas, 1979-80; pediatric intern Nat. Naval Med. Ctr., Bethesda, Md., 1980-81; battalion surg. Third Marine Div., Okinawa, Japan, 1981-82; rsch. med. officer Naval Med. Rsch. Inst., Bethesda, 1982-87; asst. prof. UCLA, 1987-89; assoc. prof. U. So. Calif., L.A., 1989—; head devel. therapeutics sect. divsn. hematology-oncology Children's Hosp. L.A., L.A., 1993—; dir. Neuroblastoma Marrow Purging Lab. Childrens Cancer Group, L.A., 1988—; team physician U.S. Shooting Team, 1991—. Patentee in field; contbr. articles to profl. jours. Mem. 1992 USA Olympic Shooting Team, Barcelona, Spain. Grantee Nat. Cancer Inst., Am. Inst. Cancer Rsch., Am. Cancer Soc. Mem. Am. Soc. Clin. Oncology, Am. Assn. Cancer Rsch., Soc. Analytical Cytology. Roman Catholic. Avocations: filmmaking, guitar playing. Office: Childrens Hosp LA Div Hematology Oncology PO Box 54700 Los Angeles CA 90054-0700

REYNOLDS, CLARK WINTON, economist, educator; b. Chgo., Mar. 13, 1934; m. Nydia O'Connor Viales; children: Rebecca, C. Winton III, Matthew, Camila. AB, Claremont (Calif.) Men's Coll., 1956; student, MIT, 1956-57, 58; student divinity sch., Harvard U., 1957-58; MA, U. Calif., Berkeley, 1961, PhD in Econs., 1962. Asst. prof. Occidental Coll., L.A., 1961-62; from asst. to assoc. prof. dept. edn. and econ. growth Yale U., New Haven, 1962-67; sr. fellow The Brookings Inst., Washington, 1975-76; prof. econs., prin. investigator, founding dir. Ams. program Stanford (Calif.) U., sr. fellow Inst. Internat. Studies, 1996—, prof. emeritus econs., 1996—; vis. prof. Nat. U. Mex., Chapingo, 1966, El Colegio de Mex., Mexico City, 1964, 65, 79; vis. lectr. in econs. Stockholm U. Econs., 1968; fellow St. Antony's Coll., Oxford, 1975; vis. rsch. scholar Internat. Inst. for Applied Systems Analysis, Laxenburg, Austria, 1978. Author: The Mexican Economy, 1970; co-author: Essays on the Chilean Economy, 1965, (with C. Tello) U.S.-Mexican Relations: Economic and Social Aspects, Las Relaciones Mexico Estados Unidos, 1983, Dynamics of North American Trade, 1991, North American Labor Market Interdependence, 1992, Open Regionalism in the [illegible] Found. fellow, 1956-57, Rockefeller Found. fellow, 1957-58, Doherty Found. fellow, 1960-61, Inst. Internat. Studies fellow Stanford U., 1990—; grantee Social Sci. Rsch. Coun., Ford Found., Hewlett Found., Rockefeller Found., Mellon Found., MacArthur Found., Tinker Found. [illegible]

Cosmos Club (Washington). Office: Stanford U Inst Internat Studies Encina Hall W Rm 305/306 Stanford CA 94305-6084

REYNOLDS, JAMES FRANCIS, JR., physician; b. St. Albans, Vt., June 20, 1947; s. James F. Sr. and Eleanor (Paquette) R.; married; children: Matthew, Katelyn, Aaron. BS, U.S. Mil. Acad., West Point, N.Y., 1969; MD, U. Louisville, 1978. Diplomate Am. Bd. Pediatrics, Am. Bd. Med. Genetics. Commd. U.S. Army, 1969, advanced through grades to col., 1974; pediatrics resident U. Va., Charlottesville, 1978-81, genetics fellow, 1981-83; clin. geneticist dept. med. genetics Shodair Hosp., Helena, Mont., 1983—. Assoc. editor Am. Jour. Med. Genetics, 1983-95; editor various books on med. genetics; contbr. articles to profl. jours. Mem. health profl. adv. com. Mont. March of Dimes, 1987—; mem. Mont. Coun. for Maternal and Child Health, 1987—. Fellow Am. Acad. Pediatrics, Am. Coll. Med. Genetics; mem. Am. Soc. Human Genetics. Avocations: hiking, snow skiing, stained glass craft. Office: Shodair Hosp PO Box 5539 Helena MT 59604-5539

REYNOLDS, JOHN CURBY, sales representative; b. San Jose, Calif., Aug. 15, 1948; s. Ivan Randolph and Lillie Murrel (McBrown) R.; m. Sharon Taylor, June 12, 1982; children: Brian James, Chris John. AA, Cabrillo Jr. Coll., Aptos, Calif., 1969; student, Calif. Polytechnic U., 1969-71. Sales rep. Equitable of Iowa Ins. Co., Sacramento, 1973-79, Grand Auto Inc., Sacramento, 1979-82, Princess House, Sacramento, 1982-84; sales telemktg. Montgomery Ward, Sacramento, 1984-85; sales rep. Sanitary Supply Co., Tucson, 1986—; mem. SVEA Bus. Group, Sierra Vista, Ariz., 1986—. Mem. First So. Bapt. Ch., Sierra Vista, 1989—. Mem. Sierra Vista C. of C. (mil. affairs com.). Republican. Avocations: cooking, gardening, reading, swimming, weightlifting. Office: Sanitary Supply Co Inc 360 S 7th St Sierra Vista AZ 85635-2506

REYNOLDS, KAREN JEANNE, musician; b. Baraga, Mich., Mar. 24, 1940; d. Arthur Johannes and Ila Amanda (Björkqvist) Hill; m. Roger Lee Reynolds, Apr. 11, 1964; 1 child, Erika Lynn. MusB, U. Mich., 1962; MA, U. Calif. San Diego, La Jolla, 1975. Flute instr. San Diego State U., 1979-86, The Bishop's Sch., La Jolla, 1989—, Fairbanks Sch. Performing Arts, Rancho Santa Fe, Calif., 1998—; free-lance performer ONCE Festivals, Ann Arbor, Mich., 1961-63, Am. Wind Ensemble, Pitts., 1962, Am. Students' and Artists' Ctr., Paris, 1963-64, CROSS TALK Media Series, Tokyo, 1967-69, Orchestral Space, Tokyo, 1968, N.H. Music Festival, Plymouth, 1981; artistic coord. CROSS TALK Media Series, Tokyo, 1967-69, The Pacific Ring Festival, La Jolla, 1986; adjudicator solo and ensemble festivals, San Diego, 1980s, San Diego Flute Guild Contest, 1989—; condr. workshops San Diego Civic Youth Orch., 1979, 80, 82, 86. Rec. artist Electronic/Instrumental Music CRI SD 285. Fulbright scholar, Paris, 1963-64. Mem. Music Tchrs.' Assn., Nat. Flute Assn., Am. Fedn. Musicians, Finnish Coun. in Am., Phi Kappa Phi.

REYNOLDS, KATHLEEN DIANE FOY (KDF REYNOLDS), transportation executive; b. Chgo., Dec. 9, 1946; d. David Chancy Foy and Vivian Anne (Schwartz) R. Student, San Francisco State U., 1964-68. Taxicab medallion permit holder, City and County of San Francisco, 1995—. Studio coord. KTVU-TV, Oakland, Calif., 1968-70; assoc. prodr. KPIX-TV, San Francisco, 1970-72; music publicist Oakland, 1966-78; writer PLEXUS, West Coast Women's Press, Oakland, 1974-82, gen. mgr., 1984-86; screen writer Oakland, 1970—; gen. ptnr. Designated Driver Group, Oakland, 1990-97; assoc. owner DeSoto Cab, San Francisco, 1995-98, ptnr., 1998—; mng. ptnr. Foy Scribes, divsn. The Tallahassee Group, Oakland, Calif., 1997—; coun. mem. West Coast Women's Press, Oakland, 1975-86; founding assoc. Women's Inst. for Freedom of the Press, Washington, 1977—. Author of periodical news, reviews, features, 1974-82; author of six documentaries for comml. and PBS-TV, 1968-73. Mem. Soc. Mayflower Descendants, Casper, Wyo., 1967—. Mem. San Francisco Film Soc. Avocations: archery, reading, film festival attendance. Home: PO Box 2742 Oakland CA 94602-0042

REYNOLDS, MARGARET MAUPIN, activist, journalist; b. Frankfort, Ky., Apr. 29, 1923; d. James and Sarah (Thurmond) M.; m. Vernon Reynolds, Jul. 23, 1942 (dec. Aug. 1980); children: Christopher, John, Julia; m. Robert Barnhart, Oct. 25, 1986. BA, Univ. Long Island, 1964; MA, Beaver Coll., 1976. Radio script writer U.S. Army Signal Corps, Lexington, Ky., 1942-44; writer Holiday Mag., Phila., 1948-50; pub. rels. dir. World Affairs Coun., Phila., 1952-54; dir. Quaker Ctr., Ben Lomond, Calif., 1976-79; devel. dir. Abington Friends Sch., Jenkintown, Pa., 1964-76; ESL tchr. U.S. Peace Corp, Thailand, 1982-84; chair Alliance for Children, Santa Cruz, Calif., 1992—. Recipient Cmty. Hero award United Way, Santa Cruz, 1997, Brotherhood award Nat. Conf. Christians and Jews, 1963. Mem. United Farm Workers Union, Resource Ctr. for Nonviolence (steering com.). Home: 114 Shelter Lagoon Dr Santa Cruz CA 95060-4853 Office: Alliance for Children 515 Broadway Santa Cruz CA 95060-4621

REYNOLDS, ROBERT GARY, artist, educator; b. San Luis Obispo, Calif., Mar. 7, 1936; s. Agee Grady and Viola Elizabeth (Curran) R.; m. Sharon Ardelle Bodley, June 17, 1962 (div. 1979); children—Robert Scott, Richard Lance, Jill Elizabeth; m. Patricia Lee Smith, Oct. 5, 1981. B.P.A. with honors, Art Ctr. Coll. Design, Los Angeles, 1963; M.A., Calif. Poly. U., 1970; also various art workshops. Artist Creative Arts Studio, San Luis Obispo, 1955-56; free-lance artist/illustrator, Los Angeles and San Luis Obispo, 1957—; staff artist Calif. Poly. U., San Luis Obispo, 1964—, assoc. prof. architecture, 1970-75, prof. art and design, 1976—, dept. chair art and design dept., 1980-81, 1984-86; acting head dept. art, 1983-84; artist Ford Times mag., Dearborn, Mich., 1971-79; instr. Cuesta Coll., San Luis Obispo, 1972-76; artist, tchr., founder High Sierra Watercolor Workshop, 1975—, Asilomar Watercolor Workshop, Pacific Grove, Calif., 1980-83; free-lance illustrator for various studios, Calif., 1972—; painting instr. Robert Reynolds Workshop, High Sierra, Calif., summer, 1973-98; resident dir. London Study Program Calif. Poly Univ., London, spring, 1986, 1991; art acquisition com. mem. Calif Poly State Univ., 1997—, performing arts adv. com., 1995—, London Study Program Com., 1986—. Over-25 one-man shows including: San Luis Obispo Art Ctr., 1975, Calif. State U. Hdqrs./Gallery, 1979, Allan Hancock Coll., Santa Maria, Calif., 1981, Olive Tree Gallery, Santa Maria, 1983; group shows include: Calif. Survey Drawing and Watercolor, Humboldt, 1982, Univ. Gallery, Calif. Poly. State U., 1985; represented in permanent collections including City of Stockton, Calif., City of San Luis Obispo, Santa Barbara Mus. Natural History, Calif., Morro Bay Mus. Natural History, Calif. State U. and CSU Collection, Long Beach, Mid-State Fair Assn., also numerous pvt. collections; works include design of San Luis Obispo bicentennial symbol and coin, design of ofcl. seal of County of San Luis Obispo, ofcl. painting for 1984 Mozart Festival, San Luis Obispo; designer U.S. Commemorative Postcard Stamp, 1987; Mem. San Luis Obispo Design and Rev. Bd., 1970-73; chmn. San Luis Obispo Flag Design Competition, 1973; Author: Painting Nature's Peaceful Places, 1993. executed mural Mus. Nat. History, Calif., 1983. Served with USNR, 1955-63. Recipient Disting. Teaching award Calif. Poly State Univ., 1986, President Art award, 1993, Bronze award Nat. Painting Competition Artist Mag., 1996; Gold medal Art Inst. Calif., 1994. Mem. San Luis Obispo Art Assn. (past pres. 1970-71), Central Coast Watercolor Soc. (co-founder 1978, pres. 1980-81), Artist's Equity (mem.-at-large), San Luis Obispo Civic and Fine Arts Assn. Office: Robert Reynolds Studio 958 Skyline Dr San Luis Obispo CA 93405-1042

REYNOLDS, ROBERT HARRISON, retired export company executive; b. Mpls., Sept. 6, 1913; s. Clarence H. and Helen (Doyle) R.; m. Gladys Marie Gaster, Apr. 7, 1934 (dec.); 1 child, Shirley Anne Reynolds Potestio (dec.); m. Viola E. Shimel, June 26, 1982. Export sales mgr., rolled products sales mgr. Colo. Fuel & Iron Corp., Denver, 1938-46; pres. Rocky Mountain Export Co., Inc., Denver, 1941-93. Mem. Denver Club (life). Home: 13850 E Marina Dr Aurora CO 80014-5509 Office: 12331 E Cornell Ave Aurora CO 80014-3323

REYNOLDS, ROGER LEE, composer; b. Detroit, July 18, 1934; s. George Arthur and Katherine Adelaide (Butler) R.; m. Karen Jeanne Hill, Apr. 11, 1964; children: Erika Lynn, Wendy Claire. BSE in Physics, U. Mich., 1957, MusB in Music Lit., 1960, MusM in Composition, 1961. Assoc. prof. U. Calif. San Diego, La Jolla, 1969-73, founding dir. Ctr. Music Expt. and Related Rsch., 1972-77, prof., 1973—; George Miller prof. U. Ill., 1971—; vis. prof. Yale U., New Haven, 1981; sr. rsch. fellow ISAM, Bklyn. Coll., 1985; Valentine prof. Amherst (Mass.) Coll., 1988; Rothschild composer in residence Peabody Conservatory of Music, 1992-93. Author: MIND MODELS: New Forms of Musical Experience, 1975, A Searcher's Path: A Composer's Ways, 1987, A Jostled Silence: Contemporary Japanese Musical Thought, 1992-93; first custom-designed classical DVD, Watershed, Mode Records, 1999; contbr. numerous articles and revs. to profl. jours. Bd. dirs. Am. Music. Ctr., Meet the Composer, Fromm Found. Harvard U.; mem. bd. govs. Inst. Current World Affairs; co-founder ONCE festivals, 1960. Recipient Koussevitzky Internat. Rec. award, 1970, citation Nat. Inst. Arts and Letters, 1971, NEA awards, 1975, 78, 79, 86, Pulitzer prize for music, 1989; sr. fellow Inst. Studies in Am. Music, 1985, fellow Inst. Current World Affairs, Rockefeller Found., Guggenheim Found.; Fulbright scholar. Office: U Calif San Diego Dept Music 0326 La Jolla CA 92093

REYNOLDS, WILLIAM GEORGE, insurance company executive; b. Mpls., Feb. 6, 1961; s. Donald and Maryanne R.; m. Nicola Wood, Apr. 25, 1987; children: Chelsea, Rachel. BA, U. St. Thomas, St. Paul, Minn., 1983; MS in Fin. Svcs., Am. Coll., Bryn Mawr, Pa., 1998. CLU, ChFC, CFS. Instr. U. St. Thomas, 1983-84; tchr. Mater Dei H.S., Santa Ana, Calif., 1984-85; equity coord. Reynolds Fin., Laguna Beach, Calif., 1985-89; mktg. cons. Pacific Mut., Newport Beach, Calif., 1989-90; ins. agt. Kibble & Prentice, Seattle, 1990-95; mktg. dir. Chubb Life, Encino, Calif., 1995-98, Jefferson Pilot Fin., Westlake Village, Calif., 1998—. Mem. Am. Assn. Life Underwriters. Avocations: reading, golf, mountain biking, travel. Office: Jefferson Pilot Fin Reynolds Fin & Ins Svcs Westlake Village CA 91361

RHEIN, LEROY WALKER, ophthalmic surgeon; b. Enfield, Ill., Aug. 30, 1933; s. Leroy William and Helen Esther (Fields) R.; m. Gladys Martony, Apr. 27, 1961 (div. 1986); children: Lee Walker, Roberta Allison. BS, U. Wis., 1955, MD, 1959. Commd. 2d lt. USAF, 1958, advanced through grades to lt. col., resigned, 1969; pvt. practice ophthalmology San Diego, 1969—; chief of staff Alvarado Hosp. and Med. Ctr., San Diego, 1981, chmn. bd. dirs., 1982-87; pres. San Diego Eye Bank, 1983; chmn. bd. dirs. San Diego Found. for Med. Care, 1986—. Fellow Am. Acad. Ophthalmology, ACP; mem. Am. Soc. Cataract and Refractive Surgery. Republican. Avocations: historical building rehabilitation. Office: Alvarado Eye Assocs 5555 Reservoir Dr Ste 300 San Diego CA 92120-5194

RHEINISH, ROBERT KENT, university administrator; b. Mt. Vernon, N.Y., Oct. 27, 1934; s. Walter Washington and Doris Elizabeth (Standard) R.; m. Dorothy Ellen Steadman, May 3, 1957 (div. 1976); children: Robert Scott, Joel Nelson; m. Shirley Marie Suter, Aug. 1, 1976. BA, U. South Fla., 1963; MS, Ind. U., 1969, EdD, 1971. Staff engr. Armed Forces Radio & TV Svc., Anchorage, 1960-61; trainee Nat. Park Svc. Tng. Ctr., Grand Canyon, Ariz., 1965; historian Home of F.D.R., Nat. Historic Site, Hyde Park, N.Y., 1964-65, Sagamore Hill Nat. Hist. Site, Oyster Bay, N.Y., 1965-66; asst. coord. nat. environ. edn. devel. program Dept. of Interior, Washington, 1968; supervisory historian Lincoln Boyhood Nat. Meml., Lincoln City, Ind., 1966-68; dir. learning resources ctr. Whittier (Calif.) Coll., 1971-73; dir. media and learning resources Calif. State U., Long Beach, 1973-88; chmn. media dirs. The Calif. State Univs., Long Beach, 1975-76; radio announcer Sta. WTCX-FM, St. Petersburg, Fla., 1961-63; co-host with David Horowitz (2 broadcasts) On Campus, Sta. KNBC-TV, L.A., 1972-73; guest lectr. 6th Army Intelligence Sch., Los Alamitos Armed Forces Res. Ctr., 1987; founder Rheino Ltd., 1997. Coord. multi-media program: In Search of Yourself, 1975 (Silver award Internat. Film and TV Festival of N.Y.), The House that Memory Built, 1981 (Cindy award Info. Film Producers of Am.), The Indochinese and Their Cultures, 1985 (Silver award Internat. Film & TV Festival of N.Y.); holder 2 patents. With RCAF, 1954-55, USAF, 1957-61. U.S. Office of Edn. grad. fellow, 1969-71; recipient Learning Resources Ctr. Devel. Fund award Pepsico, Sears, Prentice-Hall, et al, 1973; Nat. Def. Edn. Act grantee, 1974-76. Mem. NRA, Am. Legion. Republican. Avocations: collecting militaria, boating, political writing. Home: 380 Long Br W Prescott AZ 86303-5306

RHOADES, FREEMAN SIDNEY, pastor; b. Lunenburg County, Va., June 13, 1947; s. Tom Sam and Roberta (Williams) R.; m. Anna Fowlkes, Aug. 12, 1967; children: Belinda Arnita Rhoades Smith, Sidney Freeman, Roberta Latreas Rhoades. BA, Va. Union Univ., 1970; M in divinity, Sch. of Theology, 1973; D in ministry, Union Theological Sem., 1974. Prof. Va. Seminary, Lynchburg, Va., 1974-75; instr. Norfolk State Univ., Norfolk, Va., 1977-79, Old Dominion Univ., Norfolk, Va., 1980-82; assoc. prof. Va. Wesleyan Coll., Norfolk, Va., 1984-85; pastor Grove Bapt. Ch., Portsmouth, Va., 1975-87, Bethlehem Bapt. Ch., Tacoma, Wash., 1987—; exec. dir. Black Dollar Task Force, Tacoma, 1990—. Author: Blacks In Every Book in the Bible, 1995, Should A Women Preach, 1996, Black Characters of Reference of the Holy Bible, 1980. Pres. Gifts Internat., 1996—. Recipient Cert. of Honor Va. Union Univ., 1969, Outstanding Leadership award Pleasant Valley Bapt. Ch., 1975. Mem. Tacoma Ministerial Alliance, Nat. Assn. for the Advancement of Colored People. Baptist. Avocations: walking, writing, traveling. Home: 3820 N Commencement Bay Dr Tacoma WA 98407-1840 Office: Bethlehem Bapt Ch 4818 E Portland Ave Tacoma WA 98404-4503

RHODES, DAISY CHUN, writer, researcher, oral historian; b. Kahuku, Hawaii, Nov. 16, 1933; d. Pyung Chan Chun and Shin Ai Park; children: Joseph, Carmella, Thomas Francese. BA in Creative Writing, Eckerd Coll., 1995. Info. specialist Reconstrn. Devel. Corp., Washington, 1970; specialist indigent funding George Washington U. Hosp., Washington, 1971-74; mgr. hosp. assistance Alexandria (Va.) Hosp., 1975-79; asst. editor Employee Futures Rsch., Luray, Va., 1980-84; editor Inside Negotiations, Rochester, N.Y., 1985-87, Educators Negotiating Svc., New Port Richey, Fla., 1987-89; novelist, writer New Port Richey, 1989-95; rschr., oral historian Honolulu, 1994; writer Colorado Springs, 1995—; rschr., cons. Donna Ladd, Writer, Colorado Springs, 1996; presenter Asian Studies Conf., Honolulu (scholarly and abstract) Korean Picture Brides, Western Asian Studies Conf., Boulder, Colo., 1997; lectr. Ctr. for Korean Studies, U. Hawaii, 1998. Author: (nonfiction) Forever Long-Never End, 1990, Wahiawa Red Dirt, 1991, At Crossroads of Inspiration, 1993, Shirley Temple Feet, 1993, Remembering the Fallen, 1994, (play) I Know About Olympus, 1993, (novel) Eye of the Dragon (finalist Hemingway 1st Novel Competition), 1994, (scholarly and abstract) How Oral History of the First Koreans in America Advances Archival Research, 1996, (non-fiction book) Passages to Paradise: Early Korean Immigrant Narratives from Hawaii, 1998. Pres. Colo. Springs Friends of Aquatics, 1997—; bd. dirs. All Souls Unitarian Ch., 1998—. Recipient Work Study award for profls. Rotary Internat. Found., South Korea, 1998-99. Mem. Assn. for Asian Studies, Korea Soc., Korean Am. Women's Soc. Greater Washington (pres. 1983-84, bd. dirs. 1984—, Commendation), West Pasco Kiwanis (pres. 1990-92). Home: 1994 Copper Creek Dr Colorado Springs CO 80910-1867

RHODES, JOHN JACOB, retired lawyer, former congressman; b. Council Grove, Kans., Sept. 18, 1916; s. John Jacob and Gladys Anne (Thomas) R.; m. Mary Elizabeth Harvey, May 24, 1942; children: John Jacob 3d, Thomas H., Elizabeth C. Rhodes Reich, James Scott. BS, Kans. State U., 1938; LLB, Harvard U., 1942. Bar: Kans. 1942, Ariz. 1945, D.C. 1965. Mem. 83d-97th congresses from 1st Dist. Ariz., chmn. Republican policy com. 89th-93d congresses, house minority leader, 1973-81; of counsel Hunton & Williams, Washington, 1985-97; mem. bd. overseers Hoover Instn., 1984-92; chmn. platform com. Nat. Rep. Conv., 1972, permanent chmn., 1976, 80. Mem. Ariz. Bd. Pub. Welfare, 1951-52. Served with AUS, World War II; Col., ret. Mem. Mesa C. of C. (pres. 1950), SAR, Am. Legion, Ariz. Club, Mesa Golf and Country Club, Capitol Hill Club, Met. Club, Burning Tree Club (Bethesda, Md.), Pinetop Country Club, Masons (33 deg., Grand Cross), KP, Elks, Moose, Rotary, Beta Theta Pi (internat. pres. 1984-87). Republican. Methodist.

RHODES, KARREN, public information officer; b. Ross, Calif., Aug. 6, 1947; d. Jack Harvey and Ruth (Barnes) R.; married: two children. Diploma in Journalism, U. Utah, 1984. Journalist Salt Lake City, 1983-85, UPI, Cheyenne, Wyo., 1985-86; journalist, editor Green River (Wyo.) Star, 1986-88; pub. info. officer Nev. Dept. Employment Security, Carson City, 1989-94, Nev. Dept. Employment, Tng. and Rehab., Carson City, 1994—; trustee Carson Access TV Found., 1996—. Photograph (recipient Best of Nat. Collegiate Photography award 1994). Mem. Dayton Hist. Soc., Nev., 1995—. Vol. of Yr. award State of Utah Gov.'s Office, Salt Lake City, 1994. Mem. Soc. Profl. Journalists. Avocations: graphic design, reading, writing books, travel. Office: State Nev Dept Employment Tng/Rehab 500 E Third St Carson City NV 89713

RHYAN, JEANETTE DELORES, physical education educator; b. Clarinda, Iowa, June 26, 1952; d. Warren DeLos and Delores Elenore (Goecker) Renander; m. James William Rhyan, Aug. 5, 1978. BS, Dana Coll., 1974. Cert. secondary tchr., Ariz. Tchr. phys. edn. and sci. Moe (Victoria) High Sch., Australia, 1974-76; tchr. phys. edn. and health and social studies Holbrook (Ariz.) Jr. High Sch., 1977—. Mem. AAHPERD, Ariz. Assn. Jr. High Student Couns. (sec. 1984-85, v.p. 1985-86, pres. 1986-87), Order Ea. Star, Delta Kappa Gamma. Republican. Lutheran. Avocations: travel, crafts, music, collecting reindeers. Office: Holbrook Sch Dist 3 PO Box 640 1001 N 8th Ave Holbrook AZ 86025-2331

RHYNE, WILLIAM J., sales management consultant, musician; b. Russell, Kans., Aug. 10, 1954; s. Francis Lewis and Elizabeth Jane (Little) R.; m. Callie Sanae Konno, Jan. 18, 1986. BA in Music, U. Hawaii-Manoa, 1977; Diploma in Internat. Bus., Erasmus U., Rotterdam, Netherlands, 1994; MBA in Mktg., U. Calif., Davis, 1995. Musician, entertainer self employed, Honolulu, 1977-82; sales rep. Med. Supplies Co. Hawaii, Honolulu, 1982-84, Profl. Med. Products, Greenwood, S.C., 1984-88, 91-93, ALM Surg. Equipment, Anaheim, Calif., 1988-91; cons. Rhyne & Assocs., Richmond, Calif., 1995—; assoc. prof. mktg. and strategy Armstrong U., Oakland, Calif., 1997—; nat. sales mgr. WildCat Canyon Software, Berkeley, Calif., 1997; band leader, guitarist The Coronados, Richmond, 1988—; v.p., sales and mktg., ptnr Rhyne Cyder, Inc., Sonoma, Calif., 1997—; owner EBC Records, San Pablo, Calif., 1992—. Producer, performer, composer mus. rec. Freedom of the Rolling Plains, 1992. Named Sales Rep. of Yr., Profl. Med. Products, 1986. Mem. Am. Mktg. Assn. Avocations: international travel, photography, music, genealogy, web page design.

RIACH, DOUGLAS ALEXANDER, marketing and sales executive, retired military officer; b. Victoria, B.C., Can., Oct. 8, 1919; s. Alex and Gladys (Provis) R.; came to U.S., 1925, naturalized, 1942; BA, UCLA, 1948; postgrad. in mktg. Fenn Coll., 1959, Grad. Sch. Sales Mgmt. and Mktg., 1960, U.S. Army Command and Gen. Staff Coll., 1966, Armed Forces Staff Coll., 1968, Indsl. Coll. of the Armed Forces, 1970-71; m. Eleanor Montague, Mar. 28, 1942; 1 child, Sandra Jean. With Gen. Foods Corp., 1948-80, terr. sales mgr., San Francisco, 1962-80; with Food Brokers, San Francisco Bay area, 1980-90; exec. v.p. Visual Market Plans Inc., Novato, Calif., 1984-87; ter. mgr. Ibbotson, Berri, DeNola Brokerage, Inc., Emeryville, Calif., 1990-96; account exec. Sales Max Inc., Richmond, Calif., 1996-97; territory mgr. Kelly Clarke, Inc., Pleasanton, Calif., 1997—. Served to capt. inf. AUS, 1941-46, ETO; to col. inf. USAR, 1946-79, from comdr. 2d inf. brigade Calif. State mil. res., 1984-87 to brigadier gen. (ret.) 1990. Decorated Legion of Merit, Bronze Star with V device and oak leaf cluster, Purple Heart, Combat Infantry Badge, Croix de Guerre avec Palme (France and Belgium), Fouragerre (Belgium), Combattant Cross-Voluntaire (France), Combattant Cross-Soldier (France), Medaille-Commemorative de la Liberee (France), Medaille-Commemorative Francais (France), Medaille-War Wounded (France), Medaille-Commemorative Belgique (Belgium), Medaille-de la Reconnaissance (Belgium), Medaille du Voluntaire (Belgium), Cross of Freedom (Poland), Virtuti Militari-Silver Cross (Poland), Royal Commemorative War Cross (Yugoslavia); named knight Order of the Compassionate Heart (internat.), knight Magnus Officialis (GOTJ), Sovereign Mil. Order, Temple of Jerusalem (knights templar), CDR Commandery of Calif. (knights templar 1992-94), comdr. Commandery of St. Francis (knights templar); knight comdr. of grace sovereign Order of St. John of Jerusalem (knights hospitaller), comdr. Commandery of St. Francis (mil., San Francisco), Sovereign Order of St. John of Jerusalem (knights hospitaller), 1997—, knight comdr. Cross with Star Polonia Restituta, knight Grand Cross Order of St. Stanislaus, comdr. Commandery of San Francisco, Order of St. Stanislas, 1996—, dep prior Priory of Calif. Order of St. Stanislas, 1997, prior, 1998—; named to U.S. Army Inf. Hall of Fame, 1982; recipient Calif. Medal of Merit and cluster, Commendation medal, Cross of Justice, Silver Cross of Merit Order of St. Stanislas, 1997. Mem. Long Beach Food Sales Assn. (pres. 1950), Assn. Grocers Mfrs. Reps. (dir. 1955), Am. Security Coun. (nat. adv. bd. 1975—), Res. Officers Assn. (San Francisco Presidio pres. 1974-76, v.p. 1977-82, v.p. dept. Calif. 1979, exec. v.p. 1980, pres. 1981, nat. councilman 1981-82), Nat. Assn. Uniformed Svcs., Exchange Club (v.p. Long Beach 1955), St. Andrews Soc. Queens Club San Francisco, Combat Infantry Assn., Assn. U.S. Army, Am. Legion, Vets. Battle of the Bulge Assn., Assn. Former Intelligence Officers, Presidio Soc., Navy League, Ret. Officers Assn., Mil. Order Purple Heart, DAV, Psychol. Ops. Assn., Nat. Guard Assn. Calif., State Def. Force Assn. Calif., Internat. Diplomacy Coun. San Francisco, Nat. Assn. Uniformed Svcs., Merchandising Execs. San Francisco (dir. 1970-75, sec. 1976-77, v.p. 1978-79, pres. 1980, bd. dirs. 1981-89), Commonwealth of Club Calif. (nat. def. sect. vice chmn. 1964-66, chmn. 1967-72), Elks, Masons (master, lodge 400, Shrine, Islam Temple, 32d degree Scottish Rite, sojouner chpt. #277). Republican. Episcopalian. Home: 2609 Trousdale Dr Burlingame CA 94010-5706

RIASANOVSKY, NICHOLAS VALENTINE, historian, educator; b. Harbin, China, Dec. 21, 1923; came to U.S., 1938, naturalized, 1943; m. Arlene Ruth Schlegel, Feb. 15, 1955; children—John, Nicholas, Maria. BA, U. Oreg., 1942; AM, Harvard U., 1947; DPhil, Oxford (Eng.) U., 1949. Mem. faculty U. Iowa, 1949-57; mem. faculty U. Calif., Berkeley, 1957—, prof. history, 1961—, Sidney Hellman Ehrman prof. European history, 1969—; trustee Nat. Council Soviet and E. European Research, 1978-82; mem. Kennan Inst. Acad. Council, 1986-89; vis. research prof. USSR Acad. Scis., Moscow, 1969, Moscow and Leningrad, 1974, 79. Author: Russia and the West in Teaching of the Slavophiles: A Study of Romantic Ideology, 1952, Nicholas I and Official Nationality in Russia, 1825-1855, 1959, A History of Russia, 1963, 5th edit., 1993, The Teaching of Charles Fourier, 1969, A Parting of Ways: Government and the Educated Public in Russia, 1801-1855, 1976, The Image of Peter the Great in Russian History and Thought, 1985, The Emergence of Romanticism, 1992, Collected Writings 1947-94, 1993; co-editor: California Slavic Studies, 1960—; editl. bd. Russian rev., Zarubezhnaia Periodicheskaia Pechat' Na Russkom Iazyke, Simvol; contbr. articles to profl. jours. Served to 2d lt. AUS, 1943-46. Decorated Bronze Star; recipient Silver medal Commonwealth Club Calif., 1964; Rhodes scholar, 1947-49; Fulbright grantee, 1954-55, 74, 79; Guggenheim fellow, 1969; sr. fellow Nat. Endowment Humanities, 1975; Fulbright sr. scholar, sr. fellow Ctr. Advanced Studies in Behavioral Scis., 1984-85; sr. fellow Woodrow Wilson Internat. Ctr. for Scholars, 1989-90. Mem. AAAS, Am. Assn. Advancement Slavic Studies (pres. 1973-76, Disting. Contbr. award 1993), Am. Hist. Assn. (award for Scholarly Distinction 1995), Internat. Acad. Arts and Scis.

RICARDO-CAMPBELL, RITA, economist, educator; b. Boston, Mar. 16, 1920; d. David and Elizabeth (Jones) Ricardo; m. Wesley Glenn Campbell, Sept. 15, 1946; children: Barbara Lee, Diane Rita, Nancy Elizabeth. BS, Simmons Coll., 1941; MA, Harvard U., 1945, PhD, 1946. Instr. Harvard U., Cambridge, Mass., 1946-48; asst. prof. Tufts U., Medford, Mass., 1948-51; labor economist U.S. Wage Stabilization Bd., 1951-53; economist Ways and Means Com. U.S. Ho. of Reps., 1953; cons. economist, 1957-60; vis. prof. San Jose State Coll., 1960-61; sr. fellow Hoover Instn. on War, Revolution, and Peace, Stanford, Calif., 1968-95, sr. fellow emerita, 1995—; lectr. health svc. adminstrn. Stanford U. Med. Sch., 1973-78; bd. dirs. Watkins-Johnson Co., Palo Alto, Calif., Gillette Co., Boston; mgmt. bd. Samaritan Med. Ctr., San Jose, Calif. Author: Voluntary Health Insurance in the U.S., 1960, Economics of Health and Public Policy, 1971, Food Safety Regulation: Use and Limitations of Cost-Benefit Analysis, 1974, Drug Lag: Federal Government Decision Making, 1976, Social Security: Promise and Reality, 1977, The Economics and Politics of Health, 1982, 2d edit., 1985; co-editor: Below-Replacement Fertility in Industrial Societies, 1987, Issues in Contemporary Retirement, 1988, Resisting Hostile Takeovers: The Gillette Company, 1997; contbr. articles to profl. jours. Commr. Western Interstate Commn. for Higher Edn. Calif., 1967-75, chmn., 1970-71; mem. Pres. Nixon's Adv. Coun. on Status Women, 1969-76; mem. task force on taxation Pres.'s Coun. on Environ. Quality, 1970-72; mem. Pres.'s Com. Health Services Industry, 1971-73, FDA Nat. Adv. Drug Com., 1972-75; mem. Econ. Policy Adv. Bd., 1981-90, Pres. Reagan's Nat. Coun. on Humanities, 1982-89, Pres. Nat. Medal of Sci. com., 1988-94; bd. dirs. Ind. Colls. No. Calif., 1971-87; mem. com. assessment of safety, benefits, risks Citizens Commn. Sci., Law and Food Supply, Rockefeller U., 1973-75; mem. adv. com. Ctr. Health Policy Rsch., Am. Enterprise Inst. Pub. Policy Rsch., Washington,

1974-80, mem. adv. coun. on social security Social Security Adminstrn., 1974-75; bd. dirs. Simmons Coll. Corp., Boston, 1975-80; mem. adv. coun. bd. assocs. Stanford Librs., 1975-78; mem. coun. SRI Internat., Menlo Park, Calif., 1977-90. Mem. Am. Econ. Assn., Mont Pelerin Soc. (bd. dirs. 1988-92, v.p. 1992-94), Harvard Grad. Soc. (coun. 1991), Phi Beta Kappa. Home: 26915 Alejandro Dr Los Altos Hills CA 94022-1932 Office: Stanford U Hoover Instn Stanford CA 94305-6010

RICCARDI, VINCENT MICHAEL, pediatrician, researcher, educator, entrepreneur; b. Bklyn., Oct. 14, 1940; s. Gabriel John and Frances Mary (Novak) R.; m. Susan Leona Bogda, July 27, 1967; children: Angela M., Ursula M., Mikah F. AB, UCLA, 1962; MD, Georgetown U., 1966; MBA, U. LaVerne, 1993. Intern, resident in medicine U. Pitts., 1966-68; fellow in genetics Harvard Med. Sch., Boston, 1968-70, 72; asst. prof. medicine U. Colo. Med. Ctr., Denver, 1973-75; assoc. prof. medicine, pediatrics Med. Coll. Wis., Milw., 1975-77; prof. medicine, pediatrics Baylor Coll. Medicine, Houston, 1977-90; med. dir. The Genetics Inst., Pasadena, Calif., 1990-92; clin. prof. pediatrics UCLA, 1991—; founder, CEO Am. Med. Consumers, La Crescenta, 1992; dir. The Neurofibromatosis Inst., La Crescenta, Calif., 1985—. Author: Genetic Approach to Human Disease, 1977, Communication and Counseling in Health Care, 1983, Neurofibromatosis, 1986, rev. edit., 1992. Maj. U.S. Army, 1970-71. Fellow ACP, AAAS, Am. Coll. Med. Genetics; mem. Am. Soc. Human Genetics, Am. Coll. Physician Execs. Avocation: writing poetry and screenplays, acting in movies. Home: 5415 Briggs Ave La Crescenta CA 91214-2205 Office: Am Med Consumers Inc 5415 Briggs Ave La Crescenta CA 91214-2205

RICCI, RON, executive. BA in Politics, Fairfield U.; M of Journalism, U. N.C. Prin. bus devel. Cunningham Co., Palo Alto, Calif. Office: Cunningham Co 1510 Page Mill Rd Palo Alto CA 94304-1125

RICCIO, THOMAS PATRICK, theater director; b. Cleve., Mar. 1, 1955; s. Anthony James and Filomena (Palmieri) R.; m. Lolita Lesheim, June 17, 1983 (div. Mar. 1990). BA, Cleve. State U., 1978; MFA, Boston U., 1982. Asst. lit. dir. Am. Repertory Theater, Cambridge, Mass., 1980-82; dramaturg Cleve. Play House, 1985-86; artistic dir. Organic Theater Co., Chgo., 1985-88; assoc. prof. theater U. Alaska, Fairbanks, 1988—; dir. Tuma Theatre, Fairbanks, Alaska; vis. prof. Korean Nat. U. of Arts, 1996. Dir. (plays) Titus Andronicus, 1987, Conduct and Life, 1988, Little Caesar, 1988, Qayaq: The Magical Man, 1991, Emandulo, 1992, Child from the Sea, 1992, Utetmun, 1992, Eagle's Gift, 1993, Makanda Mahlanu, 1993, Imipashi, 1994; playwright The Box, 1984, La Mulata, 1984, II Ronzo Del Mosche, 1984, End of the World, 1985 (Cleve. Critics award 1985), Rubber City, 1985, Betawulf, 1986, Christmas on Mars, 1986, Bosoms and Neglect, 1986, Comeback Für Elvis, 1995-96; guest dir. Natal Performing Arts Coun., South Africa, 1992, 93, Sakha Nat. Theatre (Siberia), 1993, Ctr. for the Arts, Lusaka, Zambia, 1994, XUU and Khwe Bushmen, 1994; workshop dir. Esclan Inst., Calif. Inst. Integral Studies, Helsinki Sch. Art Media, Finland, Round Festival, England; contbr. articles to profl. jours. Alaska Native Studies travel grantee, 1989, NEH, 1990. Goethe Inst. grantee, 1987, Mellon Travel grantee, 1991, 92, 93. Mem. Soc. Stage Dirs., Am. Theater in Higher Edn., Found. Shamantic Studies. Avocations: biking, hiking, kayaking, scuba diving, sports. E-mail: fftpr@aurora.alaska.edu. Office: U Alaska Theater Dept PO Box 755700 Fairbanks AK 99775-5700

RICE, BARBARA POLLAK, advertising and marketing executive; b. Ft. Scott, Kans., Nov. 11, 1937; d. Olin N. and Jeanette E. (Essen) Brigman; m. Stanley Rice, Apr. 28, 1978; 1 child, Beverly Johnson. Student N. Central Coll., 1955, Elmhurst Coll., 1956; BA in Communications, Calif. State U., Fullerton, 1982. Art dir. Gonterman & Assos., St. Louis, 1968-71; advt. mgr. Passpoint Corp., St. Louis, 1971-73; advt., pub. relations mgr. Permaneer Corp., St. Louis, 1973-74; advt. cons., advt. mgr. Hydro-Air Engring., Inc., St. Louis, 1974-76; mgr. mktg. services Hollytex Carpet Mills subs. U.S. Gypsum Co., City of Industry, Calif., 1976-79; pres. B.P. Rice & Co., Inc., Cerittos, Calif., 1979—; press affiliate Inst. Bus. Designers. Recipient Designer Best Exhibit award Nat. Farm Builders Trade Show, Creative Challenge Mead Top 60 award L.A. Bus. Profl. Advt. Assn., Top 100 L.A. Women-Owned Bus. Mem. Am. Advt. Fedn. (past nat. bd. dirs., region chmn., Silver medal), L.A. Advt. Women (pres., dir., LULU award), Bus. Profl. Advt. Assn., Calif. State U.-Fullerton Sch. Comm. Alumni Assn., Beta Sigma Phi (past pres., outstanding mem.). Author: Truss Construction Manual, 1975. Office: 13905 Equitable Rd Cerritos CA 90703-1013

RICE, CONDOLEEZZA, academic administrator, political scientist; b. Birmingham, Ala., 1955. BA cum laude, U. Denver, 1974, PhD, 1981; MA, U. Notre Dame. Asst. prof. dept. polit. sci. to assoc. prof. Stanford (Calif.) U., 1981-93, prof., 1993—, provost, 1993-99; spl. asst. to U.S. President Nat. Security Affairs, Washington, 1989-91; dir. Soviet and East European Affairs, Washington; fellow Hoover Inst., Stanford, Calif.; cons. ABC News, Washington; mem. spl. advisory panel to comdr. and chief strategic air commd.; mem. gov. ind. advisory redistricting the state of Calif.; mem. U.S. Delegation to 2+4 Talks on German Unification. Author: The Soviet Union and the Czechoslovak Army, (with Alexander Dallin) THe Gorbachev Era. Recipient Walter J. Gores award, 1984. Mem. Coun. Fgn. Rels. *

RICE, DONALD BLESSING, business executive, former secretary of air force; b. Frederick, Md., June 4, 1939; s. Donald Blessing and Mary Celia (Santangelo) R.; m. Susan Fitzgerald, Aug. 25, 1962; children: Donald Blessing III, Joseph John, Matthew Fitzgerald. BSChemE, U. Notre Dame, 1961, DEng (hon.), 1975; MS in Indsl. Adminstrn., Purdue U., 1962, PhD in Mgmt. and Econs., 1965, D. Mgmt. (hon.), 1985; LLD (hon.), Pepperdine U., 1989; LHD (hon.), West Coast U., 1993; D in Pub. Policy (hon.), Rand Grad. Sch., 1995. Dir. cost analysis Office Sec. Def., Washington, 1967-69, dep. asst. sec. def. resource analysis, 1969-70; asst. dir. Office Mgmt. and Budget, Exec. Office Pres., 1970-72; pres., CEO The Rand Corp., Calif., 1972-89; sec. USAF, 1989-93; pres., COO Teledyne, Inc., L.A., 1993-96; pres., CEO UroGenesys, Inc., Santa Monica, Calif., 1996—; bd. dirs. UroGenesys, Inc., Vulcan Materials Co., Wells Fargo & Co., Scios Inc., Pilkington Aerospace, Unocal Corp.; mem. Nat. Sci. Bd., 1974-86; chmn. Nat. Commn. Supplies and Shortages, 1975-77; mem. nat. adv. com. oceans and atmosphere Dept. Commerce, 1972-75; mem. adv. panel Office Tech. Assessment, 1976-79; adv. council Coll. Engring., U. Notre Dame, 1974-88; mem. Def. Sci. Bd., 1977-83, sr. cons., 1984-88; dir. for sec. def. and Pres. Def. Resource Mgmt. Study, 1977-79. Author articles. Served to capt. AUS, 1965-67. Recipient Sec. Def. Meritorious Civilian Service medal, 1970, Def. Exceptional Civilian Svc. medal, 1993, Forrestal award, 1992; Ford Found. fellow, 1962-65. Fellow AAAS, Nat. Acad. of Pub. Adminstrn.; mem. Inst. Mgmt. Scis. (past pres.), Tau Beta Pi. Office: UroGenesys Inc 1701 Colorado Ave Santa Monica CA 90404-3436

RICE, EARLE (WILMONT), JR., writer; b. Lynn, Mass., Oct. 21, 1928; s. Earle Wilmont and Grace Elizabeth (Nottingham) Rice; m. Georgia Joy Black Wood, Nov. 1, 1958; children: Ellen Jean, Earle Wilmont, III. Student, Sch. Practical Art, Boston, 1947, San Jose (Calif.) City Coll., 1959, Foothill Coll., Los Altos, Calif., 1971. Product engr. ISS/Sperry Univac, Cupertino, Calif., 1973-74; sr. design specialist GTE/Sylvania, Mountain View, Calif., 1974; sr. design checker Westinghouse Corp., Sunnyvale, Calif., 1974; tech. writer Nuclear Svcs. Corp., Campbell, Calif., 1974; lead checker, tech. writer ESL, Inc., Sunnyvale, 1975; sr. E/M designer Finnigan Corp., Sunnyvale, 1975-76, Advanced Devices Labs., Inc., Santa Clara, Calif., 1976, Argosys., Inc., Palo Alto, Calif., 1976; equipment designer Raytheon Co., Goleta, Calif., 1976-78; sr. staff specialist Vitro Labs./Automation Ind., Oxnard, Calif., 1978-79; engring. drawing checker Gen. Dynamics, San Diego, 1979, 87-89; sr. E/M designer GE Co., Lompoc, Calif., 1980; sr. field engr. Martin Marietta Corp., Vandenberg AFB, Calif., 1980-84; engring. pub. specialist Lockheed Austin Divsn., Austin, Tex., 1984-85; design engr. Sundstrand Turbomach, San Diego, 1985-87; sr. design engr. ROHR, INC., Chula Vista, 1989-93. Author: (fiction) Tiger, Lion, Hawk, 1977, The Animals, 1979, Fear on Ice, 1981, More Than Macho, 1981, Death Angel, 1981, The Gringo Dies at Dawn, 1993, (chpt.) The Secret of Barking Dog Bayou, 1993 (Second Place award Fla. [illegible] Writers Assn.), White Sun and Blue Sky, 1994 (Third Place award Fla. Freelance Writers Assn.), So Long, Slimeball!, 1994, (non-fiction) The Cuban Revolution, 1995, The Battle of Britain, 1996, The Battle of Midway, 1996, The French Invasion, 1996, The Battle of [illegible] Wood, 1996, The Attack on Pearl Harbor, 1996, The Tet Offensive, 1996, The Nuremberg Trials, 1996, The Salem Witch Trials, 1996, The O.J. Simpson Trial, 1996, The Final Solution, 1997, Nazi War Criminals, 1997, The Battle of the Little Bighorn, 1997, Life Among the Great Plains Indians, 1997, Life During the Crusades, 1997, Life During the Middle Ages, 1998, The Kamikazes, 1998; adaptor: Dracula, 1995, All Quiet on the Western Front, 1995, The Grapes of Wrath, 1996; contbr. articles to mags. With USMC, 1948-57. Mem. U.S. Naval Inst., Soc. Children's Book Writers and Illustrators. Republican. Avocations: reading, spectator sports. Home & Office: PO Box 2131 Julian CA 92036-2131

RICE, JERRY LEE, professional football player; b. Starkville, Miss., Oct. 13, 1962; m. Jackie Rice; children, Jaqui, Jerry Jr. Student, Miss. State Valley U. Football player San Francisco 49ers, 1985—; Sports Illustrated Player of the Year, 1986, 90, NFL MVP, 1987, AP/NFL/Sports Illustrated Offensive Player of the Year, 1993; MVP in Blue-Gray Game. Named MVP, Super Bowl XXIII, 1989, Sporting News NFL Player of Yr., 1987, 90; named to Sporting News Coll. All-Am. team, 1984, Sporting News All-Pro team, 1986-92, Pro Bowl team, 1986-96, 95, Pro Bowl MVP, 1995. Holder NFL career records for most touchdown receptions (131), most touchdowns (139); most consecutive games with one or more touchdowns (13), 1987; NFL single-season record for most touchdown receptions (22), 1987; shares NFL single-game record for most touchdown receptions (5), 1990. Office: care San Francisco 49ers 4949 Centennial Blvd Santa Clara CA 95054-1229*

RICE, JONATHAN C., retired educational television executive; b. St. Louis, Feb. 19, 1916; s. Charles M. and May R. (Goldman) R.; m. Kathleen Feiblman, Aug. 6, 1946 (dec. June 1964); children: Jefferson Charles, Kit (dec.), May Nanette. AB, Stanford U., 1938. War photographer, reporter Acme Newspix/NEA Svc., PTO of WWII, 1941-43; picture book editor Look Mag., N.Y.C., 1947-48; news/spl. events dir. Sta. KTLA-TV, L.A., 1948-53; program mgr. Sta. KQED-TV, San Francisco, 1953-67, dir. program ops., 1967-78, asst. to pres., 1978-90, bd. dirs., 1990-96, spl. advisor to the bd., 1997—, bd. dirs., 1990-96; cons. NET, PBS, Corp. for Pub. Broadcasting, Ford Found., TV Lima Peru, Sta. WGBH-TV, Boston, Sta. WNET-TV, N.Y.C., French TV, Europe Eastern Edn. TV, Dept. Justice, 1955-90; lectr. Stanford U., 1958-77. Editor: Look at America, The South, Official Picture Story of the FBI, 1947. Bd. dirs. NATAS, San Francisco, Planned Parenthood, San Francisco and Marin County, Calif. Maj. USMC, 1943-47, PTO. Recipient George Foster Peabody award, 1956, Thomas Alva Edison award for best station, N.Y.C., 1960, Gov.'s award NATAS, 1972-73, Ralph Lowell award Corp. for Pub. Broadcasting, 1972; Jonathan Rice Studio named in his honor, 1986. Avocations: rowing, cooking, photography, travel. Home: 1 Russian Hill Pl San Francisco CA 94133-3605

RICE, JULIAN CASAVANT, lawyer; b. Miami, Fla., Dec. 31, 1923; s. Sylvan J. and Maybelle (Casavant) R.; m. Dorothy Mae Haynes, Feb. 14, 1958; children—Scott B., Craig M. (dec.), Julianne C., Linda D., Janette M. Student, U. San Francisco, 1941-43; JD cum laude, Gonzaga U., 1950. Bar: Wash. 1950, Alaska 1959, U.S. Tax Ct. 1988. Pvt. practice law Spokane, 1950-56, Fairbanks, Alaska, 1959—; prin. Law Office Julian C. Rice (and predecessor firms), Fairbanks, 1959; mem. Fairbanks dist. adv. bd. Key Bank, Anchorage; founder, gen. counsel Mt. McKinley Mut. Savs. Bank, Fairbanks, 1965—, chmn. bd., 1979-80; v.p., bd. dirs., gen. counsel Skimmers, Inc., Anchorage, 1966-67; gen. counsel Alaska Carriers Assn., Anchorage, 1960-71, Alaska Transp. Conf., 1960-67. Mayor City of Fairbanks, 1970-72. Served to maj. USNG and USAR, 1943-58. Decorated Bronze Star, Combat Infantryman's Badge. Fellow Am. Bar Found. (life); mem. ABA, Wash. Bar Assn., Alaska Bar Assn., Transp. Lawyers Assn., Spokane Exchange Club (pres. 1956). E-mail: service@ptz.alaska.net. Office: PO Box 70516 Fairbanks AK 99707-0516

RICE, NANCY E., state supreme court justice; b. Boulder, Colo., June 2, 1950; 1 child. BA cum laude, Tufts U., 1972; JD, U. Utah, 1975. Law clerk U.S. Dist. Ct. of Colo., 1975-76, dep. state pub. defender, appellate divn., 1976-77; asst. U.S. atty. Dist. of Colo., 1977-87; dep. chief civil divn. U.S. Attorney's Office, 1985-87; judge Denver Dist. Ct., 1987-98; apptd. judge Colo. Supreme Ct., 1998—. Contbr. articles to profl. jours. Mem. Denver Bar Assn., Colo. Bar Assn. (bd. govs. 1990-92, exec. coun., 1991-92), Women's Bar Assn., Rhone-Brackett Inn of Ct. (master 1993-97), Women Judges Assn. (co-chair nat. conf. 1990). Office: Colo Supreme Ct Colo State Judicial Bldg 2 East 14th Ave 4th Fl Denver CO 80203-2115*

RICE, NORMAN B., bank executive, former mayor; b. Denver, May 4, 1943; m. Constance Rice; 1 child, Mian. BA in Comm., U. Wash., MPA. Past mgr. corp. contbns. and soc. policy Rainier Nat. Bank; past dir. govt. svcs. Puget Sound Coun. Govts.; past asst. dir. Seattle Urban League; past reporter KIXI Radio; past editor, writer KOMO TV; with govt. City of Seattle, 1978—, city councilman, 1978-89, mayor, 1990-97; pres., chief exec. officer Fed. Home Loan Bank of Seattle, 1999—; pres. U.S. Conf. of Mayors, 1995, chmn. super task force welfare reform. Office: Fed Home Loan Bank 1501 4th Ave Ste 1900 Seattle WA 98101*

RICE, RICHARD LEE, JR., minister, office manager; b. Hillsboro, Oreg., Mar. 29, 1967; s. Richard Lee Rice and Nanci Carol (Losli) Skriiko. AA in Biblical Studies, Multnomah Sch. of the Bible, Portland, 1988; LittD, Abilene (Kans.) Bible Coll. and Seminary, 1988. Ordained to ministry Open Bible Std. Chs., 1998. Youth dir. Rock Creek Foursquare Ch., Portland, 1984-86; assoc. pastor Valley Full Gospel Ch., Hillsboro, 1986-88; min. Congl. Bible Chs., Inc., Hillsboro, 1988-98, bishop, 1988-90; office mgr. Alliance Properties, Inc., Aloha, Oreg., 1990-96; min. Open Bible Std. Chs., 1998—; founder, pres. Pentecostal-Fire Evangelistic Assn., Hillsboro, 1986—; chmn. Gen. Presbytery, Congl. Bible Chs., Inc., 1988-90; bible tchr. Portland Foursquare Ch., 1993-96; founder, sr. pastor Ctrl. Bible Ch., Hillsboro, 1996—. Author: Our Pentecostal Heritage: A Study in Pentecostal Precursors, Promotion, Personalities and Principle, 1995, A Study in Acts, 1986, Systematic Theology, 1988, A Study in the Word: Ephesians, 1993, A Study in the Word: Minor Prophets of the Old Testament, 1994, A Study in the Word: Matthew, 1994, The Bible: How Did It Come to Us and Is It Reliable, 1995, Water Baptism: Its Meaning and History in the Christian Church, 1996, A Brief Examination of the History and Theology of the Lord's Supper, 1996, Hermeneutics: The Artful Science of Biblical Interpretation, 1996, A Commentary on Paul's Epistle to the Church in Rome, 1996; editor (newsletter) Pentecostal Fire Crusader. Committeeperson Rep. Cen. Com., Hillsboro, 1992—; mem. Oreg. Right to Life Com., Hillsboro, 1990—, Portland City Club, 1995—. Mem. NRA, Nat. Rep. Senatorial Com., Rep. Nat. Com., Rep. Presdl. Task Force, Nat. Congl. Club, Federalist Soc. Home: 23585 NW Jacobson Rd Unit 51 Hillsboro OR 97124-9389 Office: 349 SE 4th Ave Hillsboro OR 97123-4101

RICE, SHARON MARGARET, clinical psychologist; b. Detroit, Sept. 4, 1943; d. William Christopher and Sylvia Lucille (Lawecki) R.; m. Rodney John Elliot Thorpe, Nov. 13, 1997. AB, Oberlin Coll., 1965; MA, Boston U., 1968, PhD, 1977. Clin. psychologist L.A. County Juvenile Probation, 1969-75, Las Vegas (Nev.) Mental Health Ctr., 1976-81, Foothills Psychol. Assn., Upland, Calif., 1981-96; pvt. cons., Claremont, Calif., 1984—. NIMH grantee, 1967-69; recipient Good Apple award Las Vegas Tchrs. Ctr., 1978-80. Mem. APA, Calif. Psychol. Assn., Internat. Soc. for Study of Dissociation, Inst. Noetic Scis., Sigma Xi. Avocations: dog breeding and showing, sailing. Office: Foothills Psychol Assn 715 N Mountain Ave # G Upland CA 91786-4364

RICE, STEVE E., college dean; b. Mpls., Nov. 27, 1947; s. Clifford DuWayne and Beverley Joy (Andersen) R.; m. Susan Kay Lundahl, June 18, 1969; children: Joshua Andrew, David John. BA, Beloit (Wis.) Coll., 1969; MDiv, San Francisco Theol. Seminary, 1972; PhD, U. Denver, 1995. Pastor United Presbyn. Ch., Minturn, Colo., 1975-79; from asst. prof. to dean of instruction Colo. Mountain Coll., Glenwood Springs, Colo., 1979-1998, dean of acad. svcs., 1998—. Author: (with T. Clink) Breckenridge Ski Company [illegible] Assn., Steamboat Springs, Colo., 1987. Mem. U.S. Ski Assn. (nat. tech. delegate), Colo. Cmty. Coll. Chief Instructional Officers Assn. (v.p., pres.), Sunlight Ski Edn. Found. (pres. bd. trustees), United Presby. Ch. (bd. [illegible]). [illegible] Office: Colorado Mountain College 831 Grand Ave Glenwood Springs CO 81601

RICE, STEVEN DALE, electronics educator; b. Valparaiso, Ind., Aug. 11, 1947; s. Lloyd Dale and Mary Helen (Breen) R.; m. Reyanna Danti, Mar. 4, 1972; children: Joshua, Breanna. AAS, Valparaiso Tech. Inst., 1969; BS Health Sci., Ball State U., 1973; BSEE, Valparaiso Tech. Inst., 1973; MS in Vocat. Edn., No. Mont. Coll., 1991. Electronics technician Heavy Mil. Electronic Systems GE, Syracuse, N.Y., 1969-70; electronics technician Ball State U., Muncie, Ind., 1974-75; with electronic sales Tandy Corp., Valparaiso, 1976-77; electronics technician Missoula (Mont.) Community Hosp., 1977-84; instr. electronics Missoula Coll. Tech. U. Montana-Missoula, 1984-88; chmn. dept. electronics Coll. of Tech. U. Mont., Missoula, 1988—. Book reviewer Merrill Pub., 1988—, Delmar, McGraw Hill. Bd. dirs. Victor (Mont.) Sch. Bd., 1989—, chmn. bd., 1992-95. Mem. IEEE, Instrument Soc. Am., Mont. Fedn. Tchrs. Office: Coll Tech U Montana Missoula 909 South Ave W Missoula MT 59801-7910

RICE, WALLACE WILLIAM, secondary education educator; b. Basin, Wyo., May 3, 1936; s. William Peace Jr. and Emma Anne (Wahl) R.; m. Rozella Peterson, June 23, 1962 (div. 1998); children: Steven C., Kevin E. BS in Geology, U. Wyo., 1959, MS in Natural Sci., 1967. Oil well logger Anders Well Logging, Fort Collins, Colo., 1959-61; office mgr. Wyo. Hwy Dept., Cheyenne, Wyo., 1962; adminstrv. asst. Sch. Dist. #1, Cheyenne, 1962-63; sci. tchr. Johnson High Sch., Cheyenne, 1963-65; earth sci. tchr. Ctrl. H.S., Cheyenne, 1966-96; ret.; athletic ticket mgr. Ctrl. H.S., Cheyenne, 1968-96, asst. wrestling coach, 1962, 63, 67—. Sec., treas. Laramie County Rheumatic Fever Prevention Soc., Cheyenne, 1962—; leader Boy Scouts Am.; v.p. Trinity Luth. Ch., 1978, 79, King of Glory Luth. Ch., 1989, 90, 91. With USNG, 1954-62. Recipient Silver Beaver award Boy Scouts Am., 1985, Commr. award, 1988, Dist. award of Merit, 1994, Founder's award Order of Arrow, 1996. Mem. Nat. Sci. Tchr. Assn. (regional meeting dir. 1972), Wyo. Math. Sci. Assn., Am. Fedn. Tchrs. (pres. 1978, 79, 82, sec. 1982-96). Home: 222 E 2nd Ave Cheyenne WY 82001-1406

RICH, ANDREA LOUISE, museum executive. BA, UCLA, 1965, MA, 1966, PhD, 1968. Asst. prof. comms. studies UCLA, L.A., 1976; asst. dir. office learning resources UCLA, 1976, acting dir. Media Ctr., 1977, dir. office of instructional devel., 1978-80, asst. vice chancellor office of instructional devel., 1980-86, asst. exec. vice chancellor, 1986-87, vice chancellor acad. adminstrn., 1987-91, exec. vice chancellor, 1991-95; pres., CEO L.A. County Mus. of Art, L.A., 1995—. Office: L A County Mus Art 5905 Wilshire Blvd Los Angeles CA 90036-4597

RICH, BEN ARTHUR, lawyer, educator; b. Springfield, Ill., Mar. 27, 1947; s. Ben Morris and Betty Lorraine (Ingalls) R.; m. Caroline Rose Castle, Oct. 4, 1984 (div. Nov. 1988); m. Kathleen Mills, Aug. 17, 1991. Student, U. St. Andrews, Scotland, 1967-68; BA, DePauw U., 1969; JD, Washington U., 1973; PhD, U. Colo., 1995. Bar: Ill. 1973, N.C. 1975, Colo. 1984. Rsch. assoc. U. Ill. Coll. Law, Urbana, 1973-74; staff atty. Nat. Assn. Attys. Gen., Raleigh, N.C., 1974-76; prin. Hollowell, Silverstein, Rich & Brady, Raleigh, 1976-80; dep. commr. N.C. Indsl. Commn., Raleigh, 1980-81; counsel N.C. Meml. Hosp., Chapel Hill, 1981-84; assoc. univ. counsel U. Colo. Health Scis. Ctr., Denver, 1984-86; gen. counsel U. Colo., Boulder, 1986-89, spl. counsel to the regents, 1989-90; asst. clin. prof. U. Colo. Sch. Medicine, 1992-94; asst. prof. U. Colo. Health Scis. Ctr., 1995—, asst. dir. program in healthcare ethics, humanities and law, 1995—; asst. prof. attendent U. Colo. Sch. Medicine, 1986-91, adj. instr. Sch. Law, 1988-95, adj. prof., 1996—; vis. assoc. prof., 1990-91; lectr. U. Denver Coll. Law. Contbr. articles to jours., chpt. to book. Mem. Am. Coll. Legal Medicine (assoc.-in-law 1987), Am. Philos. Assn., Am. Soc. Bioethics and Humanities, Am. Soc. Law, Medicine and Ethics (health law tchrs. sect.), Toastmasters Internat. (pres. Raleigh chpt. 1978). Unitarian. Avocations: sailing, jogging, tennis. Home: 222 S Elm St Denver CO 80246-1133 Office: Univ Colo Health Scis Ctr Box B137 4200 E 9th Ave Denver CO 80220-3700

RICH, BEVERLY EILEEN, county official; b. Silverton, Colo., Dec. 8, 1950; d. Carroll Eugene and Esther Elizabeth (Richards) Orr; m. William Spencer Rich, Dec. 8, 1973. Grad. high sch., Silverton, Colo. Treas. San Juan County, Silverton, Colo. Chmn. San Juan County Hist. Soc., 1975—; mem. San Juan Regional Planning Commn., Silverton, 1985—. Democrat. Avocation: historical preservation. Office: County of San Juan PO Box 368 Silverton CO 81433-0368

RICH, BOBBY, broadcast personality, radio programmer; b. Washington; s. Howard A. and Margaret L. (Miller) Nessen; m. Debbie E. Sisco Rich, Febr. 16, 1985; children: Bryan, Jeff, Laine, Lesley. Attended, Eastern Wash. State, Cheney. Program dir. KSTT, Davenport, Iowa, 1968-73; program dir., ops. mgr. WXLO, N.Y.C., 1978-80; dir. specialized consultation Drake & Chenault, L.A., 1981; host, asst. program dir. KFI, L.A., 1982-83; host, ops. mgr. KFMB AM/FM, San Diego, 1974-78, 84-89; v.p., gen. mgr. KIXI/KMGI, Seattle, 1989-91; host, program dir. KMXZ, Tucson, 1992-; talent coach, programming advisor Rich Radio, Tucson, 1985-. Contbg. author: (book) Music Business Handbook & Career Guide, 6th Edit., 1995. Mem. bd. dirs. SIDS Found., San Diego, 1987-89; project dir. Juvenile Crisis Ctr., San Diego, 1988; steering chmn. Diaper Drive, Tucson, 1994—; lay leader St. Andrews Presbyn., Tucson, 1995-. Recipient Major Market Program Dir. & Personality of the Yr. award Billboard Mag., 1986, 87, 88, Adult Contemporary Personality of the Yr. award Gavin Report, 1988, Large Market Program Dir. of the Yr. award, 1987, 89, Dynamic Duo award Compass Health Care, 1998. Office: KMXZ 3438 N Country Club Rd Tucson AZ 85716-1257

RICH, DAVID BARRY, financial executive, accountant, entertainer; b. Bronx, N.Y., July 3, 1952; s. Steven and Gizella (Kornfeld) R.; m. Biverly Hayag, Dec. 6, 1995; 1 child, Suzanne Stephanie. BS in Health Adminstrn., Ithaca Coll., 1976; postgrad. in acctg., Bryant and Stratton Coll., Buffalo, 1977. Office mgr. Rubin Gorewitz, CPA, N.Y.C., 1977-78; auditor State of Ariz., Phoenix, 1979-83; internal auditor City of Phoenix, 1983-84; sales use tax auditor City of Mesa (Ariz.), 1984-98; sec., treas. Mascot Memorabilia, Inc.; pres. Clovis Acctg. Inc., Mesa, 1980-94; rep. H.D. Vest Investment Inc., Irving, Tex., 1984-94; owner D.B. Rich Enterprises Import/Export, Mesa, 1992—; stage name Barry Rich, Stand-up Comedy, 1994—. Treas., bd. dirs. Missing Mutts Inc., Tempe, Ariz., 1986-88. With USAF, 1971-76. Fellow Nat. Assn. Tax Preparers; mem. Toastmasters (treas. Mesa 1986-87), Phi Beta Kappa.

RICH, GARETH EDWARD, financial planner; b. Gainesville, Fla., Feb. 28, 1961. Assoc. in Bus. Adminstrn., Gainesville Coll., 1981; BBA, U. Ga., 1983; postgrad., Coll. for Fin. Planning, Denver, 1986-88. CFP; registered prin. Acct. exec. Gallo Wine Co., L.A., 1983-84; ins. and investment broker Fin. Design Group, Inc., Woodland Hills, Calif., 1984-92; ins. and investment broker, dir. equities and investments Lincoln Fin. Advisors Corp., Sherman Oaks, Calif., 1992—. Vol. City of Hope, L.A.; referee Am. Youth Soccer Orgn., Conejo Valley, Calif.; umpire Little League Baseball, Conejo Valley. Mem. San Fernando Valley Underwriters Assn., Internat. Assn. Fin. Planning. Republican. Avocations: tennis, golf, sailing, philately, softball. Home: 5626 Fairview Pl Agoura Hills CA 91301-2228 Office: Lincoln Fin Advisors Corp 15260 Ventura Blvd Ste 200 Sherman Oaks CA 91403-5325

RICH, ROBERT STEPHEN, lawyer; b. N.Y.C., Apr. 30, 1938; s. Maurice H. and Natalie (Priess) R.; m. Myra N. Lakoff, May 31, 1964; children: David, Rebecca, Sarah. AB, Cornell U., 1959; JD, Yale U., 1963. Bar: N.Y. 1964, Colo. 1973, U.S. Tax Ct. 1966, U.S. Supreme Ct. 1967, U.S. Ct. Claims 1968, U.S. Dist. Ct. (so. dist.) N.Y. 1965, U.S. Dist. Ct. (ea. dist.) N.Y. 1965, U.S. Dist. Ct. Colo. 1980, U.S. Ct. Appeals (2d cir.) 1964, U.S. Ct. Appeals (10th cir.) 1978; conseil juridique, Paris, 1968. Assoc. Shearman & Sterling, N.Y.C., Paris, London, 1963-72; ptnr. Davis, Graham & Stubbs, Denver, 1973—; adj. faculty U. Denver Law Sch., 1977—; adv. bd. U. Denver Ann. Tax Inst., 1985—; adv. bd. global bus. and culture divsn. U. Denver, 1992—, Denver World Affairs Coun., 1993—; bd. dirs. Clos du Val Wine Co. Ltd., Danskin Cattle Co., Areti Wines, Ltd., Taltarni Vineyards, Christy Sports, Copper Valley Assn., pres.; bd. dirs. several other corps.; mem. Colo. Internat. Trade Adv. Coun., 1985—, tax adv. com. U.S. Senator Hank Brown, mem. Rocky Mountain Dist. Export Coun. [illegible] Commerce, 1993—. Author treatises on internat. taxation; contbr. articles to profl. jours. Bd. dirs. Denver Internat. Film Festival, 1978-79, Alliance Francaise, 1977—, actor, musician N.Y. Shakespeare Festival, 1960; sponsor Am. Tax Policy Inst., 1991—, trustee [illegible]

adv. bd. Denver World Affairs Coun., 1993—, Anschutz Family Found. Capt., AUS, 1959-60. Fellow Am. Coll. Tax Counsel (bd. regents 10th cir. 1992—); mem. ABA, Internat. Bar Assn., Colo. Bar Assn., N.Y. State Bar Assn., Assn. of Bar of City of N.Y., Asia-Pacific Lawyers Assn., Union Internationale des Avocats, Internat. Fiscal Assn. (pres. Rocky Mt. br. 1992—, U.S. regional v.p. 1988—), Japan-Am. Soc. Colo. (bd. dirs. 1989—, pres. 1991-93), Confrerie des Chevaliers du Tastevin, Rocky Mountain Wine & Food Soc., Meadowood Club, Denver Club, Mile High Club, Cactus Club Denver, Yale Club, Denver Tennis Club. Office: Cherry Creek Sta PO Box 61429 Denver CO 80206-8429 also: Antelope Co 555 17th St Ste 2400 Denver CO 80202-3941

RICH, SUSAN ABBY, efficiency consultant; b. Bklyn., Apr. 11, 1946; d. Milton and Jeanette (Merns) Rich. BA, Bklyn. Coll., 1967, MA, 1976, advanced cert. in administrn. and supervision, 1977; cert. indsl. rels. UCLA, 1981. Tchr. speech, theater N.Y.C. Bd. Edn., 1967-77; employee rels. supr. Crocker Nat. Bank, 1977-81; plant personnel mgr. Boise Cascade Corp., 1981-82; speaker, cons., writer office efficiency and productivity Get Organized, Get Rich!, Playa del Rey, Calif. Bd. dirs. Barlow Respiratory Hosp.; bd. trustees South Bay Master Chorale. Mem. Women's Referral Svc. (Mem. of Year award 1985, Humanitarian award 1993), Nat. Speakers Assn. (Greater L.A. chpt., Bronze award 1987, Silver award 1990). Office: Get Organized Get Rich! 7777 W 91st St Ste 1154B Playa Del Rey CA 90293-8352

RICHARD, CAROLYN LEE, curator, park ranger, fire fighter; b. LaPorte, Ind., June 2, 1958; d. Arthur Stephen and Mary Lou (Boyd) Crowley; m. Ellis Edward Richard Jr., June 21, 1989. AA in natural scis., Cottey Coll., Nevada, Mo., 1978; BS in leisure studies, Ariz. State U., 1980. Fee collection pk. technician Assateague Island Nat. Seashore Pk., Berlin, Md., 1981; interpretation pk. technician Lincoln Home Nat. Hist. Site/Martin Van Buren Nat. Hist. Site, Ill., N.Y., 1982; fee collection and interpretation pk. technician Death Valley (Calif.) Nat. Monument, 1983; patrol pk. ranger Quachita River C.E., Columbia, La., 1983-84; fee collection, interpretation and mgmt. pk. ranger Death Valley Nat. Monument, 1984-85; supervisory pk. ranger Old Post Office Tower, Washington, 1985-87; curator, pk. ranger Sequoia Nat. Pk./Kings Nat. Pk., Three Rivers, Calif., 1987-88; mus. curator Grand Canyon (Ariz.) Nat. Pk., 1988—. Stain Glass Work artist, 1980—; sect. writer Nat. Pk. Svc. Manual Nat. Pk. Svc. Curator's Office, Washington, 1991; contbr. articles to profl. jours. Vol. Big Bend (Tex.) Nat. Pk., fall 1980, Recycling Drop-off Point, Grand Canyon, 1990—, Grand Canyon Community Libr., Grand Canyon, 1990—; mem. Planned Parenthood, Nature Conservancy, Western Pa. Conservancy, Philanthropic and Ednl. Organ. Mem. Pub. Broadcasting TV. Avocation: backpacking, world travel. Home: PO Box 2025 Grand Canyon AZ 86023-2025 Office: Grand Canyon Nat Pk PO Box 129 Grand Canyon AZ 86023-0129*

RICHARD, ROBERT CARTER, psychologist; b. Waterloo, Iowa, Apr. 4, 1938; s. Quentin Leroy and Adeline Pauline (Halverson) R.; student Pomona Coll., 1956-57, Westmont Coll., 1957; BA, Wheaton (Ill.) Coll., 1960; BD, Fuller Theol. Sem., 1963, PhD, 1973; STM, Andover Newton Theol. Sch., 1964; m. Shirley Ruth Jones, Aug. 25, 1962; children: David, John. Ordained to ministry Am. Bapt. Conv., 1963; pastor Peninsula Bapt. Ch., Gig Harbor, Wash., 1965-68; marriage and family counselor Glendale (Calif.) Family Service, 1970-71; psychol. asst., Oakland and Pleasant Hill, Calif., 1972-74; clin. psychologist Rafa Counseling Assos., Pleasant Hill, 1974—; mem. faculty John F. Kennedy U., Orinda, Calif., 1975-78; adj. faculty mem. New Coll., Berkeley, Calif., 1986. Co-founder, bd. dirs. New Directions Counseling Center, 1974-81. Recipient Integration of Psychology and Theology award, 1973; lic. psychologist, marriage, family and child counselor, Calif. Mem. Am., Calif., Contra Costa (past pres.) psychol. assns., Christian Assn. Psychol. Studies. Republican. Am. Baptist. Author: (with Deacon Anderson) The Way Back: A Christian's Journey to Mental Wholeness, 1989; contbr. articles to profl. publs. Researcher assertiveness tng., lay counselor tng., psychotherapy and religious experience, treatment of adults abused as children. Office: Rafa Counseling Assocs 101 Gregory Ln Ste 33 Pleasant Hill CA 94523-4915

RICHARDS, ELIZABETH LEE, knowledge engineer, researcher; b. Ft. Worth, Apr. 11, 1962; d. Charles Daniel and Martha (Latham) Bass; m. David John Richards, Dec. 29, 1990. BA in Mus. Studies, Baylor U., 1984; MLS, U. North Tex., 1987. Tech. info. specialist U.S. Gen. Acctg. Office, Dallas, 1987-90; dir. libr. St. Francis Hosp., Tulsa, Okla., 1990-94; info. specialist Nat. Rsch. Ctr. Youth Svcs., Tulsa, Okla., 1995-96; knowledge engr. eoTek, Evergreen, Colo., 1997—. Office: eoTek 27972 Meadow Dr Ste 200 Evergreen CO 80439-8343

RICHARDS, GERALD THOMAS, lawyer, consultant, educator; b. Monrovia, Calif., Mar. 17, 1933; s. Louis Jacquelyn Richards and Inez Vivian (Richardson) Hall; children: Patricia M. Richards Graul, Laura J., Dag Hammarskjold; m. Mary Lou Richards, Dec. 27, 1986. BS magna cum laude, Lafayette Coll., 1957; MS, Purdue U., 1963; JD, Golden Gate U., 1976. Bar: Calif. 1976, U.S. Dist. Ct. (no. dist.) Calif. 1977, U.S. Patent Office 1981, U.S. Ct. Appeals (9th cir.) 1984, U.S. Supreme Ct. 1984. Computational physicist Lawrence Livermore (Calif.) Nat. Lab., 1967-73, planning staff lawyer, 1979, mgr. tech. transfer office, 1980-83, asst. lab. counsel, 1984-93; sole practice, Livermore, 1976-78, Oceanside, Calif., 1994-97; emeritus atty. pro bono participant Calif. State Bar, Concord, 1998—, Contra Costa Sr. Legal Svcs., 1998—; constrn. law instr. Contrs. State License Schs., Van Nuys, Calif., 1998; mem. exec. com., policy advisor Fed. Lab. Consortium for Tech. Transfer, 1980-88; panelist, del. White House Conf. on Productivity, Washington, 1983; del. Nat. Conf. on Tech. and Aging, Wingspread, Wis., 1981. Commr. Housing Authority, City of Livermore, 1977, vice chairperson, 1978, chairperson, 1979; pres. Housing Choices, Inc., Livermore, 1980-84; bd. dirs. Valley Vol. Ctr., Pleasanton, Calif., 1983, pres., 1984-86. Recipient Engrng. award Gen. Electric Co., 1956. Maj. U.S. Army, 1959-67. Mem. ABA, Calif. State Bar (conv. alt. del. 1990-92), Alameda County Bar Assn., Eastern Alameda County Bar Assn. (sec. 1978, bd. dirs. 1991-92, chair lawyers referral com. 1992-93), Santa Barbara County Bar Assn., San Diego County Bar Assn., Bar Assn. of Northern San Diego County, San Francisco Bar Assn., Phi Beta Kappa, Tau Beta Pi, Sigma Pi Sigma. Home: 2505 Whitetail Dr Antioch CA 94509-7744

RICHARDS, JAMES WILLIAM, electromechanical engineer; b. Portland, Oreg., Oct. 24, 1921; s. Jarvis William and Thelma Helen (Eoff) R.; m. Violet Victor Ray, Oct. 9, 1946; children: Betty, Sandra, Diane, William. Student, Nat. Tech. Sch., 1942, Nat. Radio Inst., 1948, Internat. Corr. Sch., 1955; AA, Pierce Coll., 1968. Mgr. Western Design, Santa Barbara, Calif., 1948-55; sr. engr. Bendix Corp., North Hollywood, Calif., 1955-66; v.p. Talley Corp., Newbury Park, Calif., 1966-75, dir. engring., 1982-87; pvt. practice electromech. engr., Eugene, Oreg., 1975-82, 87-89; pres. Western Design, Eugene, Oreg., 1990—. Mem. Masons. Republican. Baptist. Avocation: travel. Home: PO Box 5498 Eugene OR 97405-0498 Office: Western Design PO Box 5549 Eugene OR 97405-0549

RICHARDS, MORRIS DICK, social work administrator, educator; b. L.A., Aug. 20, 1939; s. Morris Dick Richards and Annette (Fox) Briggs; m. Leslie Sondra Lefkowitz, Mar. 22, 1975. BA cum laude, Claremont Men's Coll., 1962; MA, U. Chgo., 1964; MPA, U. So. Calif., 1965; LLB, La Salle Ext. U., 1971; MS in Hygiene, PhD in Social Work, U. Pitts., 1973; MBA, Chapman Coll., 1987. Cert. social worker. Asst. dep. dir. children and youth services Orange County (Calif.) Dept. Mental Health, 1973-77; gen. mgr., indsl. therapist Paragon West, Anaheim, Calif., 1977-83; acting dir. alcohol and drug program Horizon Health Corp., Newport Beach, Calif., 1983-84; editor, pub. relations rep., sr. social worker Orange County Social Services Agy., 1983-85; staff analyst Environ. Mgmt. Agy., Orange County, 1985-90; exec. asst. to dir. planning Orange County, 1990-92; staff analyst Orange County Social Svc. Agy., 1992-95; ret., 1995, part-time health care contract adminstr., staff analyst, 1996-97; part-time staff analyst Mgmt. Svcs., 1997—; adj. clin. prof. Chapman Coll., Orange, Calif., 1974-85; instr. Calif. Grad. Inst., 1988-93; instr. U. Phoenix, 1992-95; instr. Calif. State U., Fullerton, 1997—; supervising child welfare worker, program analyst, head child welfare worker, exec. asst. L.A. County Pub. Social Svcs., 1967-71; psychiat. clin. specialist Jewish Big Bros., L.A. County, 1964-67; med. social work cons. Whittier (Calif.) Presbyn. Hosp., 1973-76; pvt. practice psychotherapy, Tustin, Calif., 1975-77; lectr. Calif. State U., Fullerton, 1997. Editor newsletter Orange County Adv., 1984-85, Planning Perspective, 1990-91, Broadmoor Cmty. News, 1992-93; contbr. articles to profl. jours. Past bd. dirs. Orange County chpt. Am. Jewish Com., 1982-88, Broadmore Cmty. Assn., Anaheim Hills, Calif., 1981-83, sec., 1990-94, treas., 1998; mem. Orange County Mental Health Adv. Bd., 1981-88, sec., bd. dirs.; mem. bd. dirs. Orange County Mental Health Assn., 1988-91; mem. Juvenile Diversion Task Force of Orange County, 1977. Served with USAR, 1958-64. Fellow U. Chgo., 1962, NIMH, 1962, 72; Haynes scholar U. So. Calif. Sch. Pub. Adminstrn., 1964; grantee Faulk Program in Urban Mental Health, U. Pitts., 1973. Mem. NASW (mental health liaison, v.p. local chpt. 1975-88, Social Worker of Yr. award Orange County chpt. 1987), Acad. Cert. Social Workers (lic. clin. social worker and marriage, family, child counselor), Registry Clin. Social Workers (past diplomate in clin. social work), Orange County Mental Health Assn. (past sec.). Avocations: karate (black belt), tennis.

RICHARDS, PAUL A., lawyer; b. Oakland, Calif., Mar. 27, 1927; s. Donnell C. and Theresa (Pasquale) R.; m. Ann Morgans, May 20, 1948 (dec. 1984); 1 child, Paul M.; m. Elise Hall, Dec. 6, 1996. Practiced law, Reno, Nev., 1953—; settlement judge settlement conf. program Supreme Ct. State of Nev., 1998—. Office: 248 S Sierra St Reno NV 89501-1908

RICHARDS, RICHARD, lawyer, political consultant; b. Ogden, Utah, May 14, 1932; s. Blaine Boyden and Violet Geneva (Williams) R.; m. Frances Annette Bott, Jan. 15, 1954; children: Julie R. Dockter, Richard Albert, Jan R. Stevenson, Amy R. Hartvigsen, Brian Lee. AS, Weber Jr. Coll., Ogden, Utah, 1959; JD, U. Utah, 1962; DHum (hon.), Coll. Boca Raton, Fla., 1982. Journeyman sign painter Richards Sign Co., Ogden, 1958-62; legis. asst. Congressman from Utah, Washington, 1962-63, adminstrv. asst., 1963-64; lawyer Froerer, Parker, Richards, Ogden, 1964-69; polit. dir. Rep. Nat. Com., Washington, 1969-70, dep. chmn., 1971; lawyer Mecham & Richards & Self, Ogden, 1972-80; pres. Commerce Cons. Internat., Washington, also Utah, 1984—; we. Presdl. coord. for Nixon, Rep. Party, Washington, 1972; we. coord. Reagan Campaign, Washington, 1980; headed transition team for Reagan Adminstrn. at Dept. Interior, 1980; Rep. nat. chmn. Rep. Nat. Com., Washington, 1981-83. Utah state chmn. Rep. Party, Salt Lake City, 1965-67, 75-77; mem. Ogden ARts Coun., 1961. 2d lt. U.S. Army, 1952-55. Named Outstanding Young Man, Ogden Jaycees, 1967, State of Utah Jaycees, 1968. Mem. Ogden Rotary Club. Republican. Mormon. Avocations: art--working in oils, water color and acrylics, golf. Home: 5273 Daybreak Dr Ogden UT 84403-3823

RICHARDS, RUTH, psychiatrist, educational psychologist; b. Lincoln, Nebr.; d. Dexter N. and Ruth (Fulton) R. BS with honors, Stanford U., 1965; MA, U. Calif., Berkeley, 1969, PhD, 1971; MD, Harvard Med. Sch., Boston, 1980. Diplomate Am. Bd. Psychiatry and Neurology; lic. psychologist, Mass.; cert. secondary edn. educator in physics, math, art, Calif. Asst. prof. ednl. psychology Boston U. Sch. Edn., 1971-75; lectr. in psychology dept. psychiatry Harvard Med. Sch., Boston, 1978—, fellow, instr., asst. clin. prof. psychiatry, 1981-94; assoc. attending psychiatrist, various appointments McLean Hosp., Belmont, Mass., 1978—, rsch. affiliate; assoc. clin. prof. U. Calif., San Francisco, 1994—; prof. psychology Saybrook Grad. Sch., San Francisco, 1995—, faculty co-chair, 1996-98; exec. adv. bd. Ency. of Creativity, 1996—; adv. bd. Manic-Depressive Illness Found., 1989—. Mem. editl. bd. Creativity Rsch. Jour., 1992—, Jour. Humanistic Psychology, 1996—; co-editor: Eminent Creativity, Everyday Creativity and Health, 1997; contbr. numerous articles to profl. jours. and chpts. to books. Adv. panel biol. application program, Office of Technol. Assessment, U.S. Congress, 1987-88; mem. Psychologists for Social Responsibility, 1996—; dir. women's leadership project in adult edn., Boston U., 1974-75, others. Sr. asst. surgeon USPHS, 1980-81. Mem. Am. Psychol. Assn., Soc. Chaos Theory in Psychology and the Life Scis., Soc. Chaos Theory in Psychology and Life Scis. Avocations: visual art, creative writing, photography, physics.

RICHARDS, WANDA JAMIE, education educator; b. Brownwood, Tex., Jan. 11, 1930; d. William Steven and Mary (Effie) Rodgers; m. Kenneth E. Graham, Mar. 29, 1949 (div. Jan. 3, 1963); 1 child, Kenneth Jr.; m. Neill Richards, Mar. 15, 1972 (dec. Dec. 2, 1982). BA, Eastern N.Mex. U., 1962; MA, Colo. State Coll., 1964; EdD, U. No. Colo., 1966. Tchr. spl. edn. Pub. Sch., Roswell, N.Mex., 1961-63; dept. head spl. edn. Eastern N.Mex. U., Portales, 1965-69; curriculum researcher N.Mex. State U., Las Cruces, 1969-71; dir. edn. Inst. of Logopedics, Wichita, Kans., 1971-72; owner W. J. Enterprises, Kans., 1973-89; pres., treas. W.J.G. Enterprise Corp., Sedona, Ariz., 1990—; pres.'s coun. on spl. edn. Fed. Govt., Washington, 1967-69; planning cons. in field. Contbr. articles to profl. jours. Mem. Citizens for Quality Edn., Sedona, 1991, C. of C., Sedona, 1990-91, Humane Soc., Sedona, 1991. Recipient Fellowship in Spl. Edn., Fed. Govt. Pub. Law 85962, 1963-65; named Faculty Woman of Yr., Eastern New Mex. U., 1967. Republican. Home: 30 Sedona St Sedona AZ 86351-7752

RICHARDSON, ALFRED, food service executive, consultant; b. Red Bluff, Calif.. D in Food Svc., Nat. Mfrs. Assn., New Orleans, 1979; D in Food Svc. Adminstrn., Dallas, Tex., 1983. Asst. food svc. dir. Folsom State Prison, Repressa, Calif., 1945-48; food adminstr. Univ. Portland, Oreg., 1948-53; food svc. dir. Oreg. State Penitentiary, Salem, 1953-57, Utah State Prison, Draper, 1957-80, Utah Tech. Coll., Salt Lake C. C., 1980-90; cons. Am. Instns. Food Svc. Assn., Salt Lake City, 1990—; tchr. Weber State Coll., Ogden, Utah, 1971; pres. Utah State Prison Employees Assn.; mem. evaluation team Am. Correctional Assn., Colo. State Prison, Canon City, 1973; founder Honor Camp One and Two, Utah State Prison, Salt Lake City; cons. Salvation Army Food Svc.; presenter in field. Author standards/goals sect. Food Svc. Accreditation Manual; compiler, pub. Am. Correctional Food Svc. Assn. Nat. Dir., 7 edit.; author, pub. Food Svc. Control Manual, 1981. Vol. Svc. Corps. Retired Execs., Cottonwood Hosp., Meals-on-Wheels. Named Boss of Yr., Beehive State Chpt. Am. Bus. Women's Assn., 1980-81, Outstanding Male Employee, Utah Pub. Employees Assn., 1983; recipient Silver Plate award Internat. Food Svc. Mfrs. Assn., 1980, Gov.'s citation, others. Mem. Am. Correctional Food Svc. Assn. (founder, past pres., past exec. dir.). Home: 7420 S 100 W Midvale UT 84047-2035

RICHARDSON, A(RTHUR) LESLIE, former medical group consultant; b. Ramsgate, Kent, Eng., Feb. 21, 1910; s. John William and Emily Lilian (Wilkins) R.; came to U.S., 1930, naturalized, 1937; student spl. courses U. So. Calif., 1933-35; m. B. Kathleen Sargent, Oct. 15, 1937. Mgr., Tower Theater, Los Angeles, 1931-33; accountant Felix-Krueper Co., Los Angeles, 1933-35; indsl. engr. Pettengill, Inc., Los Angeles, 1935-37; purchasing agt. Gen. Petroleum Corp. Los Angeles, 1937-46; adminstr. Beaver Med. Clinic, Redlands, Calif., 1946-72, exec. cons. 1972-75, 95; sec.-treas. Fern Properties, Inc., Redlands, 1955-75, Redelco, Inc., Redlands, 1960-67; pres. Buinco, Inc., Redlands, 1956-65; vice chmn. Redlands adv. bd. Bank of Am., 1973-80; exec. cons. Med. Adminstrs. Calif., 1975-83. Pres., Redlands Area Community Chest, 1953; volunteer exec. Internat. Exec. Service Corps; mem. San Bernardino County (Calif.) Grand Jury, 1952-53. Bd. dirs. Beaver Med. Clinic Found., Redlands, 1961—, sec.-treas., 1961-74, pres., 1974-75, chmn. bd. dirs. 1992—. Served to lt. Med. Adminstrv. Corps., AUS, 1942-45. Recipient Redlands Civic award Elks, 1953. Fellow Am. Coll. Med. Practice Execs. (life, disting. fellow 1980, pres. 1965-66, dir.); mem. Med. Group Mgmt. Assn. (hon. life; mem. nat. long range planning com. 1963-68, pres. western sect. 1960), Kiwanis (pres. 1951), Masons. Episcopalian. Home: 1 Verlie Dr Redlands CA 92373-6943

RICHARDSON, ARTHUR WILHELM, lawyer; b. Glendale, Calif., Apr. 3, 1963; s. Douglas Fielding and Leni (Tempelaar-Lietz) R.; m. Noriko Satake, Nov. 14, 1988; m. Noriko Satake, Nov. 14, 1998. AB, Occidental Coll., 1985; student, London Sch. Econs., 1983; JD, Harvard U., 1988. Bar: Calif. 1989. Assoc. Morgan, Lewis and Bockius, L.A., 1988-90; staff lawyer U.S. SEC, L.A., 1990-92, br. chief, 1992-96, sr. counsel, 1996—. Mem. ABA, Calif. Bar Assn., L.A. County Bar Assn., Harvard/Radcliffe Club So. Calif., Town Hall Calif., L.A. World Affairs Coun., Sierra Club, Phi Beta Kappa. Presbyterian. Home: 2615 Canada Blvd Apt 209 Glendale CA 91208-2078 Office: US SEC 11th Fl 5670 Wilshire Blvd Fl 11 Los Angeles CA 90036-5679

RICHARDSON, BERNICE DEVINE, dog groomer; b. San Diego, June 2, 1928; d. John Frank Devine and Bertha Jessie Rodriquez Keith; m. Robert Earl Richardson, Sept. 7, 1946; children: Gary M. (dec.), Kathleen A. Thomason, Marleen Thomason. Grad., San Diego H.S. Self employed dog grommer, San Diego, and Twin Falls, Idaho, 1958—; approved judge Am. Kennel Club, N.Y.C., 1987—. Mem. Bichon Frise Club Am. Inc. (corr. sec. 1973-98), Collie Club Am. Inc., San Diego Collie Club Inc. (hon. life, past pres.), Snake River Kennel Club of Idaho (founder, pres.). Avocations: ceramics, art. Home: 186 Ash St N Twin Falls ID 83301-5232

RICHARDSON, BETTY H., prosecutor; b. Oct. 3, 1953. BA, U. Idaho, 1976; JD, Hastings Coll. Law, 1982. Staff aid U.S. Senator Frank Church, 1976-77; teaching asst. Hastings Coll. Law, 1980-82, tchg. asst., 1980-82; legal rsch. asst. criminal divsn. San Francisco Superior Ct., 1982-84; jud. law clk. Chamber of Idaho Supreme Ct. Justice Robert C. Huntley Jr., 1984-86; atty. U.S. Dept. Justice, Boise, Idaho, 1993—; instr. Boise State U., 1987, 89; mem. U.S. Atty. Gen.'s Adv. Com. subcoms. on environ., juvenile justice, civil rights and native Am. issues, others; mem. hon. adv. bd. for Crime Victims Amendment in Idaho, 1994; mem. Dist. of Idaho Judges and Lawyer Reps. com., gender fairness com., Civil Justice Reform Act com. and criminal adv. com. Mem. Idaho Indsl. Commn., 1991-93, chmn., 1993; bd. dirs. Parents and Youth Against Drug Abuse; adv. bd. of the Family and Workplace Consortium. Tony Patino fellow Hastings Coll. Law, 1982. Mem. Idaho State Bar Assn. (Pro Bono Svc. award 1988—, mem. governing coun. Govt. and Pub. Sectors Lawyers sect.), Idaho State Prosecuting Attys. Assn. Office: US Attys Office PO Box 32 Boise ID 83707-0032

RICHARDSON, DONN CHARLES, business and marketing educator; b. Indpls., Mar. 3, 1940; s. George Covey and Edythe Francis (Chesterfield) R.; m. Carolyn Jean Hassan, Nov. 8, 1969; children: Bradley George, Jason Arthur, Christopher Charles. BA in Journalism and Polit. Sci., Butler U., 1962; MA in Mass Comm., Ohio State U., 1969. Staff editor Cin. Bell Mag. Cin. (Ohio) Bell, 1969-73; mgmt. newsletter editor, spl. projects mgr. US West Comms., Denver, 1973-76; Colo. pub. rels. and outreach dir. US West Comms., Boulder, 1976-84, Colo. employee comm. mgr., 1984-85, market mgr. market planning, 1986-88; fed. govt. market mgr. US West Comms., Englewood, Colo., 1989-94; pres. Richardson Info. Resources, Boulder, Colo., 1994—; cons. Northglenn (Colo.) Recreation Ctr., 1993; presenter in field. Author, pub.: The Quick Consultant's Guide to Public Speaking; contbr. articles to profl. jours. Pres. Shannon Estates Homeowners Assn., Boulder, 1978-80; pub. rels. dir. Boulder (Colo.) Mental Health Ctr. Benefit, 1980; publicity dir. FC Boulder (Colo.) Soccer Club, 1991-94. Capt. USAF, 1963-69. Mem. Internat. Assn. Bus. Communicators (dist. profl. devel. chair 1982-84, chpt. v.p. 1985, internat. pub. rels. chair 1985-86, regional conf. program chair 1996, accredited bus. communicator), Pub. Rels. Soc. Am. (accreditation judge 1989, accredited pub. rels. profl.). Avocations: youth recreation coaching, traveling. Home: 1212 Cavan St Boulder CO 80303-1602

RICHARDSON, ELAINE, state legislator. Student, Bryant Coll., Pima Coll.; U. Ariz.; D (hon.), Tucson U. Comml. real estate broker Ariz.; small bus. owner, past legis. liaison for govt. agy.; state senator Ariz. Dist. 11, Tucson, 1996—. Mem. West Univ. Neighborhood Assn., real estate rev. com. on Edn. Initiatives; precince com. person legis. dist. #11, Ariz.; mem. adv. bd. Emergency Med. Svcs. for Children, U. Ariz. Health Scis. Ctr.; bd. dirs., community substance abuse adv. coun. Altar Valley Sch. Dist.; del. Jt. Protocol Session, Ariz.-Mex. Commn. Recipient Women on the Move award, 1997. Mem. Pima County Dem. Women, Dems. of Greater Tucson, Ariz. Women's Polit. Caucus, Outdoor Confidence, Internat. Sonoran Desert Alliance, Nat. Conf. of State Legislatures (vice chair energy and transp. com.), Toastmasters, Plateau Club, Sierra Club. Office: PO Box 962 Tucson AZ 85702-0962

RICHARDSON, ERNEST RAY (ROCKY RICHARDSON), housing program supervisor; b. Dermott, Ark., Sept. 5, 1932; s. Louis Jr. and Leila Mae (Purdom) R.; m. Deloris Cobb, Mar. 25, 1955 (div. Apr. 1964); children: Victor Ray, Rodney Lynn, Regenia Ann; stepchildren, Denise Nelson, Darrin Hicks; m. Doretha Tolbert, Apr. 1964 (div. June 1978); m. Shirley Ann Johnson, June 8, 1978; 1 child, Kimberly Ann; stepchildren: Janet, Kay, and Jerome Pate. BA in Bus. Adminstrn., Franklin U., 1975; AA in Real Estate, Parkland Coll., 1980; postgrad., Lewis U., 1980-83; grad., Intergovtl. Mgmt. Tng., 1993, Leadership Modesto, 1996. Cert. real estate broker, Ill. Dir. edn. & tng. Champaign County Opportunities Industrialization Ctr., Champaign, Ill., 1968-70, exec. dir., pers. dir., 1970-73; fin. specialist City of Urbana, Ill., 1975-79; fin. specialist City of Joliet, Ill., 1979-82, dir. neighborhood svcs. divsn., 1982-87; exec. pers. dir. Aurora (Ill.) Housing Authority, 1987-89; housing program supr. City of Modesto, Calif., 1989—; mem. adv. bd. Ctrl. Valley Opportunities Ctr., Inc. Modesto, 1992-96, bd. dirs., 1996-98; vice chmn. mgmt. devel. com., City of Modesto, 1993-94, mem. mgmts. continuous improvement com., 1995, 96; alt. Stanislaus County Civil Grand Jury, 1996-97, mem., rec. sec., 1997-98; mem. nat. funds allocation rev. com. Opportunities Industrialization Ctr., 1971-72. Sgt. USAF, 1951-67. Mem. nat. Assn. Real Estate Appraisers (pres.-elect Ill. chpt. 1984-85, pres. Ill. chpt. 1985-86, Ill. chpt. Mem. of the Yr., 1988), Am. Legion, Modesto Kiwanis Club. Avocations: income tax business and real estate appraisal, walking, reading, travel. Home: 309 Yuba Ridge Ln Modesto CA 95354-3369 Office: City of Modesto Ofc Housing/Neighborhoods 940 11th St Modesto CA 95354-2319

RICHARDSON, JANE, librarian; b. Sept. 16, 1946; d. Robert Clark and Evagene (Davis) Richardson; m. Frank Velasques Martinez Jr., May 28, 1966 (div. July 1970); 1 child, Robert Louis Martinez; m. William John Lorance, Feb. 14, 1983 (div. 1996). BA in History, U. Wyo., 1971; MLibr, U. Wash., 1972. Reference and fine arts libr. Clark County Libr., 1973; dept. head Clark County Libr. Dist., 1974-77; br. supr./adminstr. Newport Beach (Calif.) Pub. Libr., 1978-82; on-call libr. Santa Ana and Newport Beach Pub. Librs., Calif. State U., Fullerton, 1984; br. adminstr. Las Vegas-Clark County Libr. Dist., 1985—. Mem. Freedom to Read Found. Mem. ALA, Popular Culture Assn., Nev. Libr. Assn., Mountain Plains Libr. Assn., So. Calif. On-Line Users Group, Newport Beach Profl. and Tech. Employees Assn. Office: Las Vegas-Clark County Libr 833 Las Vegas Blvd N Las Vegas NV 89101-2030

RICHARDSON, JOHN EDMON, marketing educator; b. Whittier, Calif., Oct. 22, 1942; s. John Edmon and Mildred Alice (Miller) R.; m. Dianne Elaine Ewald, July 15, 1967; 1 child, Sara Beth. BS, Calif. State U., Long Beach, 1964; MBA, U. So. Calif., 1966; MDiv, Fuller Theol. Sem., 1969, D of Ministry, 1981. Prof. mktg. Sch. Bus. and Mgmt. Pepperdine U., Malibu, Calif., 1969—. Author: (leader's guides) Caring Enough to Confront, 1984, The Measure of a Man, 1985; editor: Ann. Editions: Marketing, 1987—, Bus. Ethics, 1990—. Lay counselor La Canada (Calif.) Presbyn. Ch., 1978-84, mem. lay counseling task force, 1982-84. Mem. Am. Mgmt. Assn., Soc. Bus. Ethics, Christian Writers Guild, Fuller Sem. Alumni Cabinet (pres. 1982-85), Am. Mktg. Assn., Beta Gamma Sigma. Avocations: fishing, woodworking, golf, photography. Office: Pepperdine U Sch Bus and Mgmt 400 Corporate Pointe Fl 4 Culver City CA 90230-7627

RICHARDSON, JOHN FRANCIS, computer scientist; b. Bridgeport, Conn., Oct. 6, 1952; s. Francis Vincent and Lillian Mary (Alexovits) R. BA in History, Met. State Coll., Denver, 1978, BS in Math., 1983; MS in Applied Math., San Diego State U., 1997. Lic. gen. radiotelephone operator FCC. Scientist Naval Oceans Sys. Ctr., San Diego, 1985-92, NRaD (Naval Command Control & Ocean Surveillance Sys.), San Diego, 1992-97, SPAWAR Sys. Ctr. S.D., San Diego, 1997—. Author: King of Glen Ridge, 1994; contbr. articles to profl. jours. Mem. IEEE Computer Soc., Assn. Symbolic Logic, Assn. Computing Machinery, Assn. Automated Reasoning, Assn. Logic Programming. Avocations: science, science fiction, history of science. E-mail: richards@nosc.mil. Home: 1643 Rowan St San Diego CA 92105-5629 Office: SPAWAR Sys Ctr San Diego 53560 Hull St San Diego CA 92152-5001

RICHARDSON, JUDY MCEWEN, education administrator, consultant, cartoonist; b. Appleton, Wis., June 3, 1947; d. John Mitchell and Isabel Annette (Ruble) McEwen; m. Larry Leroy Richardson, Mar. 19, 1972 (div. Oct. 1983). BA in English, Stanford U., 1968, MA in Edn., 1969; PhD in Higher Edn., U. Wash., 1975. Dir. ednl. rsch. St. Olaf Coll., Northfield, Minn., 1975-79; evaluation specialist Northwest Regional Ednl. Laboratory, Portland, 1980-82; legis. rsch. analyst Ariz. State Sen., Phoenix, 1982-87; dir. sch. fin. Ariz. Dept. Edn., Phoenix, 1987-92, assoc. superintendent, 1992-94;

ednl. cons. Scottsdale, Ariz., 1994-96; exec. dir. Ariz. State Bd. for Sch. Capital Facilities, Phoenix, 1996-98; sch. fin. cons. Peacock, Hislop, Staley & Given, Phoenix, 1998—. Cartoonist for the Ariz. Capitol Times, 1995-96. Office: Peacock Hislop Staley & Given Inc 2999 N 44th St Ste 100 Phoenix AZ 85018-7261

RICHARDSON, LEATRICE JOY, artist; b. N.Y.C., Dec. 26, 1940; d. Sidney and Ottilia (Moldovan) Mayer; m. Robert John Richardson, Aug. 7, 1965; children: Todd Harper, Tiffany Jill. Student, Chouinard Art Inst., L.A., 1960-65. Group shows and exhbns. include: Akron Soc. of Artists, 1998, Houston Watercolor Soc., 1994, 97, 98, La. Watercolor Soc., 1996, Midwest Watercolor Soc., 1993, 95, 97, 98, Miss. Watercolor Soc., 1994, Nat. Assn. Women Artists, N.Y.C., Northwest Watercolor Soc., 1994, 95, San Diego Watercolor Soc., 1995, Taos Nat. Exhbn. of Watercolor II, 1996, Watercolor USA, 1996, Western Colo. Watercolor Soc., 1995, Western Fedn. of Watercolor Socs., 1996, others; publs. include People in Watercolor, 1996, Best of Watercolor: Painting Color, 1997. Recipient 2d award Houston Watercolor Soc., 1997, Jack Richeson & Co. Merit award Midwest Watercolor Soc., 1995, Art Study Club award Miss. Watercolor Soc., 1994, Northwest Watercolor Soc., Margaret Malloy Merit award, 1994, San Diego Watercolor award Watercolor West, 1992, Svoir Faire, Lana Paper Merchandise award 1992, Winsor Newton Merchandise award 1994. Mem. Watercolor West (signature), Midwest Watercolor Soc. (signature), Women Painters West (signature), Nat. Assn. Women Painters. Avocations: film, animation. Home: 3540 Ridgeford Dr Westlake Village CA 91361

RICHARDSON, RICHARD COLBY, JR., leadership and policy studies educator, researcher; b. Burlington, Vt., Sept. 10, 1933; s. Richard Colby and Florence May (Barlow) R.; m. Patricia Ann Barnhart, Dec. 21, 1954; children—Richard Colby III, Michael Donald, Christopher Robin. BS, Castleton State Coll., 1954; MA, Mich. State U., 1958; PhD, U. Tex., 1963; Litt.D. (hon.), Lafayette Coll., 1973. Instr., counselor Vt. Coll., Montpelier, 1958-61; dean instrn. Forest Park Community Coll., St. Louis, 1963-67; pres. Northampton County Area Community Coll., Bethelehem, Pa., 1967-77; chmn. dept. higher edn. and adult edn. Ariz. State U., Tempe, 1977-84, prof. edn. leadership and policy studies, 1984—. Jr. author: The Two Year College: A Social Synthesis, 1965; sr. author: Governance for the Two-Year College, 1972, Functional Literacy in the College Setting, 1981, Literacy in the Open Access College, 1983, Fostering Minority Acess and Achievement in Higher Education, 1987, Achieving Quality and Diversity, 1991, Designing State Higher Education Systems for a New Century, 1998. Bd. dirs. Easton Hosp., 1973-77, v.p., 1975-77; exec. council Minsi Trails council Boy Scouts Am., Bethelehem, 1973-77. Named Disting. Grad., Coll. Edn., U. Tex., Austin, 1982; recipient Outstanding Research Publ. award Council Univ. and Colls.-Am. Assn. Community and Jr. Colls., 1983, Disting. Service award, 1984. Mem. Am. Assn. Higher Edn. (charter life, dir. 1970-73), AAUP, Assn. for Study of Higher Edn. (bd. dirs. 1984), Am. Assn. Community and Jr. Colls. (dir. 1980-83). Democrat. Home: 5654 E Wilshire Dr Scottsdale AZ 85257-1950 Office: Ariz State U Dept Higher Edn Tempe AZ 85287-2411

RICHARDSON, TOM (EDWARD THOMPSON RICHARDSON), scenic artist; b. Upper Darby, Pa., Aug. 12, 1948; s. Edward Thompson and Elizabeth Catherine (Fredericks) R.; m. Margaret Reed Colvin, July 1, 1972; 1 child, Edward Thompson III. BFA, U. Pa., 1974, MFA, 1975. Scenic artist San Francisco Opera Assn., 1979-84, San Francisco Ballet Assn., 1982-84; scenic designer music dept. Stanford U., Calif., 1980-84; scenic designer San Jose (Calif.) Opera Assn., 1985; lead scenic artist FM Prodns., Brisbane, Calif., 1984-87, artist-in-charge, 1987-93. Scenic artist (films) James and the Giant Peach, Down Periscope, Phenomenon, A Smile Like Yours, Rainmaker, Flubber, What Dreams May Come, Mumford, (TV program) Nash Bridges. Mem. Internat. Alliance Theatrical Stage Employees (Bay area bus. rep. 1984-88, pres., 1998-99). Home: 87 Roosevelt Cir Palo Alto CA 94306-4219

RICHARDSON, WINIFRED LEE, youth counselor, writer; b. South Gate, Calif., May 7, 1963; d. J.C. and Earline (Evans) R.; 1 child, Joshua Sharp. AS, Harbor Coll., 1985. Co-editor Southwood Baptist Ch., L.A., 1984-86, word processor, 1987-89; youth counselor State of Calif., Norwalk, 1989—; prin., publisher Paramont, Calif., 1996—. Author: Balance•Balance•Balance, 1997. Mem. Writers Digest, Reader Digest. Avocations: writing, theater, tennis, piano, reading. Home: 12222 S San Pedro St Los Angeles CA 90061-2848

RICHENS, KIMBERLEE MARIE, real estate property manager, appraiser; b. Marion, Ohio, May 12, 1957; d. Rudolph Richard and Margaret Charlott (Carroll) Mucheck; m. Tim Richens, Dec. 10, 1978; 1 child, Jessica Elizabeth. Residential mgr. cert., IREM, 1984; cert., Am. Schs., Anaheim, Calif., 1992. Licensed Real Estate Appraiser. Property mgr. Forest City Mgmt. Inc., Cleveland, 1979—; real estate appraiser Grand Terrace, Calif., 1992—. Inventor sun enhancer, 1993; contbr. articles to profl. jours. Mem. Inst. Real Estate Mgmt., Nat. Assn. Real Estate Appraiser, San Bernardino Ch. of C., Grand Terrace C. of C. Democrat. Roman Catholic. Avocations: boating, Tai-Chi, hiking, dogs, gardening. Home: 12354 Pascal Ave Grand Terrace CA 92313-5635 Office: Forest City Mgmt Inc 11750 Mount Vernon Ave Grand Terrace CA 92313-8202

RICHENS, MURIEL WHITTAKER, AIDS therapist, counselor and educator; b. Prineville, Oreg.; d. John Reginald and Victoria Cecilia (Pascale) Whittaker; children: Karen, John, Candice, Stephanie, Rebecca. BS, Oreg. State U.; MA, San Francisco State U., 1962; postgrad., U. Calif., Berkeley, 1967-69, U. Birmingham, Eng., 1973, U. Soria, Spain, 1981. Lic. sch. adminstr., tchr. 7-12, pupil personnel specialist, Calif., marriage, child and family therapist, Calif. Instr. Springfield (Oreg.) High Sch., San Francisco State U.; instr., counselor Coll. San Mateo, Calif., San Mateo High Sch. Dist., 1963-86; therapist AIDS Health Project U. Calif., San Francisco, 1988—; marriage and family therapist, pvt. practice San Mateo; guest West German-European Acad. seminar, Berlin, 1975. Lifeguard, ARC. postgrad. student Ctr. for Human Communications, Los Gatos, Calif., 1974, U. P.R., 1977, U. Guadalajara (Mex.), 1978, U. Durango (Mex.), 1980, U. Guanajuato (Mex.) 1982. Mem. U. Calif. Berkeley Alumni Assn., Am. Contract Bridge League (Diamond Life Master, cert. instr., tournament dir.), Women in Comm., Computer-Using Educators, Commonwealth Club, Pi Lambda Theta, Delta Pi Epsilon. Republican. Roman Catholic. Home and Office: 847 N Humboldt St Apt 309 San Mateo CA 94401-1451

RICHEY, CANDACE, photographer; b. Long Beach, Calif., May 14, 1953; d. Wallace Charles and Colleen Adlene (Baker) Huber; m. Carl Thomas Baker, Aug. 25, 1973 (div. Sept. 1988); children: P. Gail, Jeremiah James; m. William Seth Richey, Mar. 9, 1996. Student, Grossmont Coll., 1989-91. Comml. artist Ad Svcs., Anaheim, Calif., 1967-73, Gray Pub., Anaheim, 1968-73; sec. Lee Mather Realty, Coronado, Calif., 1973-75; owner Baker Graphics, Spring Valley, Calif., 1978-90; portrait photographer United Photographic, Galion, Ohio, 1990-95; reporter, photographer Sternwheeler Pub., Castle Rock, Wash., 1994-96; owner Mt. St. Helens Photo Svcs., Castle Rock, 1995—; instr. photoshop seminar Mac Acad., Seattle, 1995; instr. web design workshop Paget Thompson, Portland, Oreg., 1998; pub. Mt. St. Helens Volcanic Quar. Firefighter Rainier (Oreg.) Fire Dept., 1995. Recipient award of excellence Profl. Photographers Am., 1990; named Photographer of Yr., United Photographic, Calif., 1991, New Club Builder, Kiwanis Internat., Washington, 1997. Mem. Kiwanis (charter, pres. Rainier Club 1996-97, pres. Mt. St. Helens Club 1997-98, lt. gov. divsn. 42 Pacific N.W. dist. 1998—). Avocations: bowling, hiking, music. Home: 2221 Spirit Lake Hwy Castle Rock WA 98611 Office: Mount St Helens Photo Svcs 2221 Spirit Lake Hwy Castle Rock WA 98611

RICHEY, EVERETT ELDON, religion educator; b. Claremont, Ill., Nov. 1, 1923; s. Hugh Arthur and Elosia Emma (Longnecker) R.; m. Mary Elizabeth Reynolds, Apr. 9, 1944; children: Eldon Arthur, Clive Everett, Loretta [illegible] Anderson, Ind., 1956; ThD, Iliff Sch. of Theology, Denver, 1960. Pastor Ch. of God, Bremen, Ind., 1946-47, Laurel, Miss., 1947-48; pastor First Ch. of God, Fordyce, Ark., 1948-52; prof. Arlington Coll., Long Beach, Calif., 1961-68; pastor Cherry Ave. Ch. of God, Long Beach, 1964-68; prof. Azusa (Calif.) Pacific U., 1968-93; mem. Christian Ministries Tng. Assn., 1968; mem., chmn. Commn. on Christian Higher Edn./Ch. of God, 1982-93; pres. Ch. Growth Investors, Inc., 1981-93. Author: cdnl. manual Church Periodical--Curriculum, 1971-83, 97. Mem. Assn. Profs. and Rschrs. Religious Edn., Christian Ministries Tng. Assn. Republican. Avocation: gardening. Home and Office: 413 N Valencia St Glendora CA 91741-2418

RICHMAN, ANTHONY E., textile rental industry association executive; b. Los Angeles, Dec. 13, 1941; s. Irving M. and Helen V. (Muchnic) R.; m. Judy Harriet Richman, Dec. 19, 1964; children: Lisa Michele, Jennifer Beth. BS, U. So. Calif., 1964. With Reliable Textile Rental Svcs., L.A., 1964—, svc. mgr., 1969, sales and svc. mgr., 1970-73, plant mgr., 1973-75, gen. mgr., bd. dirs., 1975-78, v.p., sec.-treas., 1975-82, exec. v.p., CEO, 1982-84, pres., CEO, 1984—. Bd. dirs. Guild for Children, 1979—, Valley Guild for Cystic Fibrosis, 1974—, Cystic Fibrosis Found. of L.A. and Orange Counties, 1989—; pres. Textile Rental/Svc. Assoc. Am., 1993-95; exec. dir.Western Textile Svcs. Assn., Studio City, Calif., 1996—. Office: Western Textile Svcs Assn 12444 Ventura Blvd Ste 204 Studio City CA 91604-2409

RICHMAN, MARVIN JORDAN, real estate developer, investor, educator; b. N.Y.C., July 13, 1939; s. Morris and Minnie (Graubart) R.; m. Amy Paula Rubin, July 31, 1966; children: Mark Jason, Keith Hayden, Susanne Elizabeth, Jessica Paige. BArch, MIT, 1962; M Urban Planning, NYU, 1966, postgrad., 1967-69; MBA, U. Chgo., 1977; U.S. Dept. State fellow U. Chile, 1960. Architect, planner Skidmore, Owings & Merrill, N.Y.C., 1964, Conklin & Rossant, N.Y.C., 1965-67; ptnr. Vizbaras & Ptnrs., N.Y.C., 1968-69; v.p. Urban Investment & Devel. Co., Chgo., 1969-79, sr. v.p., 1979; pres. bd. dirs. First City Devels. Corp., Beverly Hills, Calif., 1979-80; pres. Olympia & York (U.S.) Devel. (West), 1987-89, Olympia & York Calif. Equities Corp., L.A., 1981-87, Olympia & York Calif. Devel. Corp., 1981-87, Olympia & York Hope St. Mgmt. Corp., 1982-87, Olympia & York Homes Corp., 1983-89, Olympia & York Calif. Constrn. Corp., 1986-89, The Richman Co., L.A., 1989-96, pres. Richman Real Estate Group, Salt Lake City, 1995—; dean Sch. Bus. and Mgmt. Woodbury U., Burbank, Calif., 1993-97; pres. Millennium Holdings, Glendale, Calif., 1996—; lectr. NYU, 1967-69, UCLA, 1989-90, Nat. Humanities Inst., other univs. Adv. NEA. Bd. advisors UCLA Ctr. Fin. and Real Estate. With USAF, 1963-64. Registered architect; lic. real estate broker. Mem. AIA, Am Planning Assn., Internat. Coun. Shopping Ctrs., L.A. World Affairs Coun., Urban Land Inst., Nat. Assn. Office and Indsl. Parks, Chief Exec.'s Round Table, Air Force Assn., Lambda Alpha.

RICHMOND, RAY S(AM), journalist; b. Whittier, Calif., Oct. 19, 1957; s. Henry and Terri C. (Epstein) R.; m. Beth Lyn Trachman, Oct. 2, 1983 (div. Feb. 1993); children: Joshua Adam, Gabrielle Reneé; m. Heidi Merle Lieberman, May 28, 1994; 1 child, Dylan Jake. B, Calif. State U., Northridge, 1980. Feature writer L.A. Daily News, Woodland Hills, Calif., 1978-85; segment prodr. Merv Griffin Show, Hollywood, Calif., 1985-86; television writer L.A. Herald Examiner, 1986-87; television critic Orange County Reigster, Santa Ana, Calif., 1987-92, L.A. Daily News, 1992-96; television reporter Daily Variety, L.A., 1996—. Co-author: Unofficial Olympic Guide, 1984; editor: The Simpsons: A Complete Guide to our Favorite Family, 1997. Vol. AIDS Project L.A., 1993-94. Mem. Television Critics Assn. Democrat. Jewish. Avocations: exercise, reading, family, television, travel. Home: 1010 Hammond St Apt 302 West Hollywood CA 90069-3851 Office: Daily Variety 5700 Wilshire Blvd Ste 120 Los Angeles CA 90036-5804

RICHMOND, ROSALIND, clinical social worker; b. Boston, May 18, 1938; d. Leonard J. and Esther (Greenberg) R. BS, Simmons Coll., MS. Clin. social worker MGH, Boston, 1962-65; clin. social worker VA Hosp., Livermore, Calif., 1966-67, San Francisco, 1967—; lic. examiner Bd. Behavioral Scis., Sacramento, 1982; chmn. patient edn. com. San Francisco Hosp., 1983-87, social work student supr. psychiat. emergency room; co-organizer psychiatric AIDS program, 1989—; co-leader substance abuse AIDS group, 1995. Recipient Dir's. Commendation, San Francisco Hosp., 1982, 83, 85, 91. Mem. Nat. Assn. Social Workers (cert.), Simmons Coll. Alumnae Assn. (v.p. 1972-73, pres. 1973-74). Democrat. Jewish. Home: 1 Summerhill Way San Rafael CA 94903-3813 Office: VA Med Ctr 4150 Clement St San Francisco CA 94121-1598

RICHTER, BURTON, physicist, educator; b. N.Y.C., Mar. 22, 1931; s. Abraham and Fanny (Pollack) R.; m. Laurose Becker, July 1, 1960; children: Elizabeth, Matthew. B.S., MIT, 1952, Ph.D., 1956. Research assoc. Stanford U., 1956-60, asst. prof. physics, 1960-63, assoc. prof., 1963-67, prof., 1967—, Paul Pigott prof. phys. sci., 1980—, tech. dir. Linear Accelerator Ctr., 1982-84, dir. Linear Accelerator Ctr., 1984—; cons. NSF, Dept. Energy; bd. dirs. Varian Assocs., Litel Instruments; Loeb lectr. Harvard U., 1974; DeShalit lectr. Weizmann Inst., 1975; pres. designate Internat. Union of Pure and Applied Physics, 1997. Contbr. over 300 articles to profl. publs. Recipient E.O. Lawrence medal Dept. Energy, 1975; Nobel prize in physics, 1976. Fellow Am. Phys. Soc. (pres. 1994), AAAS; mem. NAS, Am. Acad. Arts and Scis. Achievements include research in elementary particle physics. Office: Stanford Linear Accel Ctr PO Box 4349 Stanford CA 94309-4349

RICHTER, HANK CHARLES, JR., artist; b. Cleve., Oct. 10, 1928; s. Henry Charles and Alvina (Cross) R.; m. Beverly Ann Loomis, June 2, 1956; children: Lélia Louise, Karin Sue, Julie Ann. Student, Phila. Sch. Art, 1949-53. Art dir. Paul Lefton, Phila., 1953-55; creative dir., art dir. Fuller Smith & Ross Inc., Cleve., 1955-56; v.p. Ptak & Richter Advt., Phoenix, 1957-60; v.p., creative dir. Phillips Ramsey, San Diego, 1960-62; v.p. Bozell-Jacobs, Phoenix, 1963-65; pres. Henry C. Richter Advt., Phoenix, 1965-70; v.p., mgr. Harwood Advt., Phoenix, 1970-72; pres. Henry C. Richter Advt., Phoenix, 1972-75; pres. Westlund Sound Inc., 1975—; tchr. sculpture Principia Coll., Elsha, Ill.; ptnr. Forever Glass Masterpieces; bd. dirs. Cafesjian Rsch.-Engring. and Tech. Enterprises, Terrasphere, Inc., Prosound. Illustrator: Gift of an Elephant, 1973. Pres. Goodwill of Cen. Ariz. Served as cpl. U.S. Army, 1946-48, Korea. Recipient Best of Festival, Gold medal Atlanta and Washington Film Festivals, 1969. Mem. Am. Indian and Cowboy Artists (pres. 1987-89), Art Group 12. Republican. Christian Scientist. Avocations: writing, research, entrepreneurship. Home and Office: 1221 W Carol Ann Way Phoenix AZ 85023-4497

RICHTER, JAMES LOWELL, plastics industry executive; b. Mpls., Sept. 21, 1955; s. Vernon Otto and Mary Lucille (Tesch) R.; m. Ligia Auxiliadora Cuadra, Jan. 4, 1987. BS in Bus., U. Minn., 1978. Sales rep. Dow Chem. Co., Walnut Creek, Calif., 1978-82; sales rep. Gen. Electric Co., Santa Clara, Calif., 1982-83, mktg. rep., 1983-87; mktg. specialist Gen. Electric Co., Pitts., Mass., 1987-89, product mgr., 1989-91; bus. mgr. Gen. Electric Co., Waterford, N.Y., 1991-94; v.p. sales & mktg. CIMCO Inc., Costa Mesa, Calif., 1995-96, Omni Plastics, Inc., Santa Fe Springs, Calif., 1996-98; dir. bus. devel. & acquisition Precise Tech., Inc., Pitts., 1998—. Vol. Elfun Soc., San Diego, 1991. Mem. Soc. Plastics Engrs. Lutheran. Avocations: backpacking, scuba diving, camping, travel, photography.

RICKARD, MARGARET LYNN, library consultant, former library director; b. Detroit, July 31, 1944; d. Frank Mathias and Betty Louise (Lee) Sieger; m. Cyriac Thannikary, Nov. 13, 1965 (div. Feb. 1973); 1 child, Luke Anthony; m. Marcos T. Perez, Mar. 1973 (dec. Oct. 1973); m. Lui Gotti, Dec. 23, 1984 (dec. Aug. 1997); m. William A. Rickard, Aug. 22, 1998. AB, U. Detroit, 1968; MLS, Pratt Inst., 1969; postgrad., NYU, 1976-77. Cert. librarian, N.Y. Sr. libr. Queens Pub. Libr., Jamaica, N.Y., 1969-77; libr. dir. El Centro (Calif.) Pub. Libr., 1977-99; ret., 1998; county libr./cons. Imperial County Free Libr., 1993-99; vice chmn., chmn. Serra Coop. Libr. Sys., San Diego, 1980-82; libr. cons., 1998—. Pres. Hist. Site Found., El Centro, 1988-99, 92, sec., 1989, trustee, 1989—, v.p., 1991—; fin. sec. St. Elizabeth Luth. Ch., El Centro, 1988; mem. Downtown El Centro Assn., mem. arches bus. improvement dist.; active numerous civic coms., fundraising events; mem. comm. and arts task force Imperial County Arts Coun.; coord. arts and culture com. City of El Centro Strategic Plan. Title IIB fellow Pratt Inst., 1968-69. Mem. ALA, AAUW (v.p. El Centro 1988), Calif. Libr. Assn., [illegible] Internat. of El Centro (v.p. El Centro 1978, corr. sec. 1990-91, 1st v.p. 1991-92, pres. 1992-93, 2d v.p. 1995-96, 98-99, recording sec. 1997-98, life mem.), Women of Moose (sr. regent El Centro 1988-89). Democrat. Lutheran. [illegible] Home and Office: PO Box 232 6008 Pony Express Trail 19 Pollock Pines CA 95726

RICKE, P. SCOTT, obstetrician, gynecologist; b. Indpls., June 28, 1948; s. Joseph and Betty (Rae) R.; divorced; 1 child. BA, Ind. U., 1970; MD, Ind. U. Sch. of Medicine, 1974. Bd. cert. ob-gyn., 1981. Intern St. Lukes Hosp., Denver, 1975; resident U. Calif. at Irvine, Orange, 1977-79; pvt. practice ob-gyn. Tucson, 1981-96; founder, dir. Inst. for Med. Weight Loss. Inventor (med. instrument) Vaginal Retractor, 1989. Bd. dirs. City of Hope, Tucson, 1981-85, Am. Cancer Soc., Tucson, 1981-83. Fellow Am. Bd. Ob-Gyn.; mem. Am. Bariatric Soc. Avocations: golfing, swimming, photography. Home: 3755 N Tanuri Dr Tucson AZ 85750-1939 Office: 3972 N Campbell Ave Tucson AZ 85719-1460

RICKS, MARY F(RANCES), archaeologist, anthropologist, consultant; b. Portland, Oreg., July 6, 1939; d. Leo and Frances Helen (Corcoran) Samuel; m. Robert Stanley Ricks, Jan. 7, 1961; children: Michael Stanley, Allen Gilbert. BA, Whitman Coll., 1961; MA, Portland State U., 1977, MPA, 1981, PhD, 1995. Asst. to dir. auxiliary services Portland State U., 1975-79, instnl. researcher, 1979-85, dir. instnl. research and planning, 1985-97, rsch. assoc. prof., 1994-97, rsch. assoc. prof. emerita, 1997—. Contbr. articles and presentations to profl. socs. Vol. archeologist BLM-USDI, Lakeview, Oreg., 1983-97. Fellow Soc. Applied Anthropology; mem. Soc. Am. Archaeology, Pacific N.W. Assn. Instnl. Rsch. and Planning (pres. 1990-91), Assn. Oreg. Archaeologists (v.p. 1988-90), Assn. Instl. Rsch., City Club of Portland, Sigma Xi. Home: 5466 SW Dover Loop Portland OR 97225-1033

RIDDELL, ROBERT JAMES, JR., retired physicist; b. Peoria, Ill., June 25, 1923; s. Robert James and Hazel (Gwathmey) R.; m. Kathryn Gamble, Aug. 12, 1950; children: Cynthia Riddell Dunham, James Duncan R. BS, Carnegie-Mellon U., 1944; MS, U. Mich., 1947, PhD, 1951. Asst. prof. physics U. Calif., Berkeley, 1951-55; sr. physicist Lawrence Berkeley Lab., 1951-82; ret., 1982; scientist AEC, Washington, 1958-60; adv. bd. Coll. Nat. Resources, U. Calif. Trustee Pacific Sch. Religion, Berkeley, 1970—, chmn. bd., 1979-84; trustee Grad. Theol. Union, Berkeley, 1982—, chmn. bd., 1990-96; trustee Coll. Prep. Sch., 1998—; pres. Friends U. Calif. Bot. Garden, 1984-95. Lt. (j.g.) USNR, 1944-46. Mem. N.Am. Rock Garden Soc. (pres. Calif. chpt. 1997—). Avocations: gardening, model building. Home: 1095 Arlington Blvd El Cerrito CA 94530-2754

RIDDLE, EARL WALDO, retired church official, small business owner; b. St. Joseph, Mo., Jan. 29, 1920; s. Roderick Edwin and Nannie Myrtle (Albertson) R.; m. Etta Kathryn McGauhey, Aug. 23, 1942; children: Martha Anne Riddle Moretty, Mary Janet Riddle Switzer, David Earl. AS, Mo. Western Coll., 1940; AB, U. Kans., 1942; MDiv, Boston U., 1945, postgrad., 1946-50; D Ministry, San Francisco Theol. Sem., 1976. Ordained to ministry United Meth. Ch. as elder, 1945; cert. leader in sex edn. for youth. Assoc. pastor College Ave. Meth. Ch., West Somerville, Mass., 1946-50; dir. Wesley Found. Oreg. State U., Corvallis, 1950-54; pastor Forest Grove (Oreg.) Meth. Ch., 1954-60; sr. pastor 1st Meth. Ch., Twin Falls, Idaho, 1960-65, Caldwell, Idaho, 1965-68; coun. dir. Oreg.-Idaho Conf., United Meth. Ch., Portland, Oreg., 1968-85; owner, operator Riddle Enterprises, Portland, 1968—; dir. youth work Morgan Meml. Ch. All Nations, Boston, 1942-45; cons. on fin. and ministerial tax; ptnr. Riddle Engring. Co.; dir. Stewardship Enterprises; mem. Nat. United Meth. Assn. Communicators, 1954—; exec. dir. local com. Gen. Conf., United Meth. Ch., Portland, 1976, mem. Gen. Conf., 1964, 66,68, 70, Western Jurisdictional Conf., 1964, 68, Gen. Bd. Edn., 1966-72; mem. Interbd. Com. on Missionary Edn., 1968-72; mem. exec. com. Conf. Program Dirs. Assn., 1968-72, Conf. Officers Assn., 1973-76; pres. Nat. Assn. Conf. Dirs., 1982-84, Nat. Assn. Stewardship Leaders, 1983-84; conf. sec. Oreg.-Idaho Ann. Conf., 1985-88; chmn. com. on correlation and edit. revision The Gen. Conf. of United Meth. Ch., 1988—. Editor: History of National Association of Conference Council Directors, 1974, Oreg.-Idaho Conf. jour., 1985-88, Tax Talk for Ministers, 1976-90; chmn. com. on correlation and editorial revision The Discipline, 1988, 92, 96; contbr. numerous articles to profl. jours. Coun. officer, scoutmaster Boy Scouts Am., 1942-45, 60-65, 68-76; exec. sec. Oreg.-Idaho United Meth. Found., 1970-85; bd. dirs., chmn. Forest Grove Union High Sch., 1955-60; mem. Oreg. Gov.'s Com. on Sexual Preference, 1976-78; mem. human rsch. com. Oreg. Health Scis. U., 1975—; bd. dirs. Planned Parenthood Assn., 1984-89, Samaritan Counseling Ctr., 1985-88; mem. fin. devel. com. Ecumenical Ministries Oreg., 1970-86, mem. Edn. Commn., 1970-85; mem. clergy com. on Oreg. Health Decisions, 1983-85; mem. health edn. curriculum development com. Oreg. Dept. Edn., 1985-88. Chaplain USNR, 1945-46. Recipient plaques and awards Boy Scouts Am., Exceptional Svc. Jason Lee award for excellence in communications, 1977, Exceptional Svc. award Parents and Friends of Lesbians and Gays, 1986, civil liberties award ACLU, 1989, spl. svc. award for Russian refugee work, 1990, Spl. Mission award United Meth. Women, 1998, Life Saver award Family Homeless Shelter, 1998. Home: 465 NW 95th Ave Portland OR 97229-6309

RIDDOCH, HILDA JOHNSON, accountant; b. Salt Lake City, July 25, 1923; d. John and Ivy Alma (Wallis) Johnson; m. Leland Asa Riddoch, Nov. 22, 1942; children: Ivy Lee (dec.), Leland Mark. Vocal student, Ben Henry Smith, Seattle; student, Art Instrn. Schs. Sales clk., marking room and sec. dist. office Sears, Roebuck & Co., Seattle, 1940-42; with billing dept., receptionist C.M. Lovsted & Co., Inc., Seattle, 1942-51; acct., exec. sec. Viking Equipment Co., Inc., Seattle, 1951-54; acct., office mgr. Charles Waynor Collection Agy., Seattle, 1955-57; pvt. practice, 1957-96; acct., office mgr. Argus Mag., Seattle, 1962-67; acct. Law Offices Krutch, Lindell, Donnelly, Dempsey & Lageschulte, Seattle, 1967-72, Law Offices Sindell, Haley, Estep, et al, Seattle, 1972-77; co-founder, acct. Bus. Svc., Inc. and Diversified Design & Mktg., Fed. Way, Auburn & Orting, Wash., 1975-96; co-founder L & H Advt. and Distbg. Co., Wash., 1992-96; sec.-treas., dir. Jim Evans Realty Inc., Seattle, 1973-87; agt. Wise Island Water Co., P.U.D., Wise Island, B.C., 1973-88, Estate Executrix, Seattle, 1987-95. Author: Ticking Time on a Metronome, 1989-90, Beloved Miss Ivy, 1996-97; writer, dir. hist. play Presidents of Relief Society Thru Ages; writer epic poetry; writer, dir. teenager activation video, 1984; pub., editor Extended Family Newsletter, 1983-96. Dir. speech and drama LDS Ch., 1983-88; ward pres. young women's orgn.; mem. ward and stake choirs, 1963-85; stake genealogy libr., Fed. Way, 1983-85; ward and stake newsletter editor various areas, West Seattle, Seattle, Renton, Auburn, 1950-90; 1st counselor in presidency, tchr. various courses Ladies' Relief Soc. Orgn., 1965-96; co-dir., organizer 1st Silver Saints Group, 1990-92; interviewer LDS Ch. Employment Svcs., 1992-93; co-resident mgr. Mountain View Estates, Orting, Wash., 1994-96. Recipient Letter of Recognition Howard W. Hunter, Pres. LDS Ch. Fellow Am. Biographical Assn. Avocations: needlework, oil painting, writing, singing, speech and drama. Home: # 4 1441 Falcon Dr Apt 4 Idaho Falls ID 83406-5840

RIDEOUT, EDNA BAKER, artist; b. Billings, Mont., Sept. 29, 1918; d. Frederick Hubbard and Edna Beers (Baker) Ballou; m. Horton Burbank Rideout, May 26, 1951; children: Douglas Burbank Rideout, Nancy Penelope Rideout, Thomas Ballou Rideout. BA, U. Wash., 1940, MA, 1949. Cert. secondary tchr., Wash. Art editor Croftonian Crofton House Sch., Vancouver, B.C., Can., 1935-36; art tchr. Neah Bay (Wash.) High Sch., 1940-41, Winlock (Wash.) High Sch., 1942-44, Seattle Pub. Schs., 1945-47, 49-51, Fish and Wildlife Svc. Pribilof Islands, St. George Island, Alaska, 1951-53; dir. Visual Art Sch., Edmonds, Wash., 1972-74; sec. Gallery North, Edmonds, 1974-76; artist, 1953—. Watercolors included in nat. juried exhbns., 8 juried mem. and regional exhbns., 36 nat. juried shows in 7 yrs., invitational exhbns. sponsored by Bellevue, Wash. Art Mus., North West Water Color Soc., Arts Olympia; works included in In Harmony with Nature, 1990; 2 ink drawings used as cover designs for Alaska Timber Econ. Studies texts. Recipient Masterfield award Fla. Soc. Exptl. Artists, 2 purchase awards Watercolor U.S.A., Ajomari/Arches/Rives award Watermedia Mont., 1st pl. award Artstravaganza Nat., 3rd pl. award Navarro Coun. of Arts, Judge's Spl. award North Coast Collage Soc. Mem. Nat. Collage Soc. (sec. 1994), Women Painters of Wash. (program dir. 1992-93), North West Watercolor Soc. (asst. program dir. 1989-91), Soc. Exptl. Artists Fla., Pa. Watercolor Soc., North West Collage Soc. (sec. 1995—), East Side Assn. Fine Arts, Gallery North (hon.), Planetary Soc. Avocations: photography, hiking, observing nature, studying outer space. Home: [illegible] 92nd Ave NE Bothell WA 98011-2207

RIDER, ANN SHERWOOD, lawyer; b. Bridgeport, Conn.; m. Anthony J. Hill; children: Laura Rider-Hill, Chelsea Rider-Hill. BS Foreign Svc., Georgetown U., 1977; JD, Southwestern U., 1984. Sr. dep. city atty. City of

Pasadena (Calif.) City Atty.'s Office, 1986—. Office: City of Pasadena City Attys Office 100 N Garfield Ave Pasadena CA 91101-1726

RIDER, FAE B., freelance writer; b. Summit Point, Utah, Mar. 1, 1932; d. Lee Collingwood and Jessie (Hammond) Blackett; m. David N. Rider, Jan. 26, 1952; children: David Lee, Lawrence Eugene. BS, No. Ariz. U., 1971, MA, 1974; postgrad., U. Nev., Las Vegas, 1985-88. Lic. tchr. in elem., reading, spl. edn. Learning specialist Las Vegas, summers 1974-76; tchr. kindergarten Indian Springs (Nev.) Pub. Schs., 1971-76; reading tchr. Las Vegas Pub. Schs., 1976-80; curriculum coord. Indian Springs Pub. Schs., 1980-91; tchr. 1st grade Las Vegas Pub. Schs., 1991-92, reading specialist, 1992-93; pvt. edn./reading cons. Las Vegas, 1993—. Author booklet: Door to Learning - A Non-Graded Approach, 1978. Bd. dirs. Jade Park, Las Vegas, 1988. Recipient Excellence in Edn. award, 1988, Outstanding Sch.and Cmty. Svc. award, 1990. Mem. Internat. Reading Assn., Ret. Tchrs. Assn., Am. Legion Aux., A.R.E study group, Delta Kappa Gamma (pres., Rose of Recognition), Kappa Delta Phi. Avocations: reading, writing, travel.

RIDER, JANE LOUISE, artist, educator; b. Brownfield, Tex., Sept. 11, 1919; d. Oscar Thomas and Florence Myrtle (Bliss) Halley; m. Rolla Wilson Rider Jr., Mar. 26, 1944 (dec. July 1992); 1 child, Dorothy Jo Neil. BA, UCLA, Westwood, 1943, tchg. diploma in secondary art; postgrad., Chgo. Art Inst., 1945, Chouinards, L.A., U. Oreg., Scripps, Claremont, Calif. Art supr., elem. and jr. high art tchr. Tulare (Calif.) City Schs. Dist., 1943-44, 44-45; art tchr. Beverly Hills (Calif.) High Sch., 1946-47; art tchr. jr. high gen. art and ceramics Santa Barbara City Schs., Goleta, Calif., 1964-66; head art dept., tchr. Morro Bay (Calif.) Jr.-Sr. High Sch. Dist., 1967-70; pvt. practice studio potter Cambria, Calif., 1961-85; artist, Santa Rosa, Calif., 1985—; founder, dir., tech. La Canada (Calif.) Youth House Art Program, 1953-60; dir. Pinedorado Art Show, Allied Arts Assn., Cambria, 1970-85. Exhibited in group shows Santa Rosa Art Guild, 1986-95, Nat. League Am. Pen Women, 1994-98, Wine Country Artist's Spring Show, 1991, 92, 93, 94, 95, 97, Gualala Art in Redwoods, 1986, 87, 88, 96, 97, 98 (merit award for watercolor), Rodney Strong Vineyards Art Guild, 1994, Oakmont Art Assn., 1985-98, revolving exhibits Berger Ctr., Chalais, Oakmont, Santa Rosa, Santa Rosa Art Guild, 1986-98; statewide art shows Spring Palettes Mumm Cuvee Winery, Napa, Calif., 1994, Luther Burbank Ctr., 1995, Summer House Gallery, Healdsberg, 1995, Armida Winery Show, 1995, Watercolor Artists of Sonoma Co., Aqua Area Shows, 1995-98, Coddingtown Mall, Audubon-Bouverie Preserve, Glen Ellen, Calif., 1996, Pedroncelli Winery, 1996, Watercolor Artists of Sonoma County, 1995-97, Marin Art Assn. Gallery, 1996, Kendall Jackson Winery, Santa Rosa, 1997-98, others. Mem. Nat. League Am. Pen Woman, Santa Rosa Art Guild (rec. sec. 1989), Ctrl. Coast Watercolor Soc. (charter 1977). Republican. Avocations: photography, gardening, listening to music, traveling, tennis. Home: 7019 Overlook Dr Santa Rosa CA 95409-6376

RIDGLEY, FRANCES AROC, principal; b. Manila, Jan. 29, 1936; came to U.S., 1966; d. Celestino Pascual and Urbana Oraliza (Velasco) Aroc; m. Ignacio Flores Rilloraza, Aug. 1, 1958 (div. July 1970); children: Ignacio Aroc Rilloraza II, Joel A. Rilloraza; m. Charles Delbert Ridgley, Jan. 29, 1983. BS, Philippine Normal Coll., 1964; MS in Edn., Ind. State U., 1967; EdD, U. Pacific, 1980. Tchr. Cubao Elem. Sch., Quezon City, Philippines, 1955-61; exec. asst. GSIS, Manila, 1961-66; grad. asst. Ind. State U. Sch. Edn., Terre Haute, 1966-67; tchr. elem. sch. Vijo County Sch. Corp., Terre Haute, 1967-68; team leader, tchr. tng. supr. Tchr. Corps New Careers, Stockton, Calif., 1968-74; coord., sch. dist. cons. Stockton Unified Sch. Dist., 1974-80; tchr. intern supr., instr. U.O.P., Stockton, 1976-80; tchr. intern supr., instr., mem. basic edn. coun. Sch. Edn. U. Pacific, 1980-82; tchr. Alum Rock Union Elem. Sch. Dist., San Jose, 1982-85, coord., vice prin., 1985-93, prin., 1993-99; guest lectr. U.O.P. Sch. Edn., 1974-80; cons. in field. Vol. ARC, San Jose, 1988; participant, mem. Poco Way Redevel. Project, San Jose, 1993—; mem. Filipino Affirmative Action, Oakland, Calif., 1995—. Recipient Disting. Educator award; Math. and Tech. grantee Santa Clara Office Edn., 1984, Global Edn. grantee Stanford U., 1978-80; Bilingual Edn. Doctoral fellow, 1976; I.D.E.A. fellow Kettering Found., 1981, 82; P.E.O. Internat. scholar, 1967. Mem. Filipino Am. Movement in Edn. (pres. 1986-88, LEadership award 1988), Filipino Am. Educators Assn. Calif. (v.p. 1987-89), Assn. Calif. Sch. Adminstrs. (pres. 1994-95), Calif. Sch. Leadership Acad., Phi Delta Kappa, Delta Kappa Gamma. Avocations: travel, golf, fitness exercise, reading, gardening. Home: 755 Tramway Dr Milpitas CA 95035-3606 Office: Alum Rock Union Elem Sch 2930 Gay Ave San Jose CA 95127-2322

RIDGWAY, MAUREEN ABBOTT, medical center administrator; b. Mt. Vernon, Wash., June 5, 1958; d. Hugh Ralph and Kathleen Marie (Conlon) R.; m. William Diaz Garcia, Aug. 8, 1987; children: William Conlon, Emma Pilar. BA in Polit. Sci., U. Wash., 1981, BA in Speech Comm., 1981; JD, Lewis & Clark Coll., Portland, Oreg., 1986. Bar: Wash. 1987. Appointments sec. Congressman Norman D. Dicks, Washington, 1981-83; dep. field dir. Ctr. for Participation in Democracy, L.A., 1988; Orange County coord. Feinstein for Gov., Victory 90, 1990, Campaign to Elect Phil Angelides, 1991; exec. dir. Democratic Found./Dem. Party Orange County, Santa Ana, Calif, 1991-93; sr. dir. devel. City of Hope Nat. Med. Ctr. and Beckman Rsch. Inst., Seattle, 1994—. Recipient Am. Jurisprudence award in family law, 1985. Mem. Wash. State Bar Assn., Seattle C. of C. Democrat. Roman Catholic. Avocations: cellist, skiing. Office: City of Hope 1309 114th Ave SE Ste 201 Bellevue WA 98004-6903

RIEDER, RICHARD WALTER, federal government official; b. Mpls., Feb. 18, 1940; s. Walter and Virginia (Lincoln) R.; m. Edelgard Lestin, May 12, 1966; children: Stephanie, Arnold. BA, Yale U., 1961; MPA, George Washington U., 1970, U. So. Calif., 1976. Budget and program analyst NASA, Washington, 1967-69, 71-81, adminstrv. officer, 1969-71, mgmt. analyst, 1982—. Elder Good Shepherd Luth. Ch., 1979-81. Served to lt. USN, 1961-66. Mem. AIAA, Am. Assn. Budget and Program Analysis, Am. Soc. Pub. Adminstrn. Club: Swiss.

RIEGEL, BYRON WILLIAM, ophthalmologist; b. Evanston, Ill., Jan. 19, 1938; s. Byron and Belle Mae (Huot) R.; BS, Stanford U., 1960; MD, Cornell U., 1964; m. Marilyn Hills, May 18, 1968; children—Marc William, Ryan Marie, Andrea Elizabeth. Intern, King County Hosp., Seattle, 1964-65; asst. resident in surgery U. Wash., Seattle, 1965; resident in ophthalmology U. Fla., 1968-71; pvt. practice medicine specializing in ophthalmology, Sierra Eye Med. Group, Inc., Visalia, Calif., 1972—; mem. staff Kaweah Delta Dist. Hosp., chief of staff, 1978-79. Bd. dirs., asst. sec. Kaweah Delta Dist. Hosp., 1983-90. Served as flight surgeon USN, 1966-68. Co-recipient Fight-for-Sight citation for research in retinal dystrophy, 1970. Diplomate Am. Bd. Ophthalmology, Nat. Bd. Med. Examiners. Fellow ACS, Am. Acad. Ophthalmology; mem. Calif. Med. Assn. (del. 1978-79), Tulare County Med. Assns., Calif. Assn. Ophthalmology (v.p. 3d party liaison 1994-96, dir. 1996-98), Am. Soc. Cataract and Refractive Surgery, Internat. Soc. Refractive Surgery, Internat. Phacoemulsification and Cataract Methodology Soc., Rotary (Visalia). Roman Catholic. Home: 3027 W Keogh Ct Visalia CA 93291-4228 Office: 2830 W Main St Visalia CA 93291-4331

RIEGELMAN, NANCY C., artist, educator; b. San Francisco, Apr. 5, 1958; d. Sid and Milli Askey. Student, U. Calif., Berkeley, UCLA, Art Ctr. Prof. Art Ctr., Pasadena, Calif., U. So. Calif., L.A., Calif. State U., Northridge, Otis, L.A. Address: No 1106 4411 Los Feliz Blvd Apt 1106 Los Angeles CA 90027-2143

RIEGER, ELAINE JUNE, nursing administrator; b. Lebanon, Pa., June 7, 1937; d. Frank and Florence (Hitz) Plasterer; m. Jere LeFever Longenecker, Sept. 13, 1958 (div. 1968); children: Julie Lyn Porto, Jere Lee Longenecker; m. Bernhard Rieger, Oct. 12, 1971. Nursing diploma, Coatesville (Pa.) Hosp. Sch. of Nursing, 1958; BA, U. Redlands, 1976; MS in Healthcare Mgmt., Calif. State U., L.A., 1984. Cert. nursing adminstr., gerontol. nurse. From staff nurse to clin. supr. to dir. of nurses St. Johns Regional Med. Ctr., Oxnard, Calif., 1966-86; dir. of nurses Motion Picture and TV Hosp., Woodland Hills, Calif., 1987-89; with Care West, Nothridge-Reseda, Calif., 1989-90; dist. nurse mgr. Hillhaven Corp., Newbury Park, Calif., 1990-91; quality mgmt. nursing cons. Beverly Enterprises, Memphis, 1991-95; DON Beverly Manor Rehab. and Nursing Ctr., Van Nuys, Calif., 1996-98; assoc. care mgr. Blue Cross of Calif., Camarillo, 1998—. Home: 1817 Shady Brook Dr Thousand Oaks CA 91362-1335 Office: Blue Cross Calif 5151 Camino Ruiz Ste A Camarillo CA 93012-8648

RIENHOFF, JOANNE WINKENWERDER, artist; b. Balt., Nov. 2, 1938; d. Walter L. and Eleanor (Zouck) Winkenwerder; m. George Sloan Oldberg, July 7, 1962 (dec. Mar. 1966); m. MacCallum Rienhoff, Dec. 17, 1966 (dec. May 1994). AB, Radcliffe Coll., 1960; MA in Tchg., Johns Hopkins U., 1963; postgrad., U. Denver, 1984-85. Tchr. Garrison (Md.) Forest Sch., 1961-62, Latin Sch. Chgo., 1963-66, Graland Country Day Sch., Denver, 1972-80; artist, 1984—. Exhibited in group shows at U. Denver, Harvard U., Sigraph Soc., Denver, Mid. Pk. Bank, Granby, Colo., others. Bd. dirs., treas. Denver Sch. Vol. Program, 1969-71; leader Jr. Gt. Books program Denver sch. sys., 1967-69; mem. women's bd. Rush Presbyn. St. Luke's Hosp., Chgo., 1965-94. Mem. Rocky Mountain Harvard U. Club, Grand County Hist. Soc., Friends of Grand County Libr. Home: Ouray Ranch Granby CO 80446

RIEPE, CHARLEINE WILLIAMS, educator; b. Lackawanna, N.Y., Oct. 24, 1924; d. Edward and Dorothy Hayd (VanAllen) Williams; B.A. cum laude, D'Youville Coll., 1945; M.A., U. Mich., 1947; postgrad. U. Hawaii, 1949, SUNY, Buffalo, 1966-70; m. Dale Maurice Riepe, May 24, 1948; children—Kathrine Leigh Herschlag, Dorothy Lorraine. Tchr., Holy Angels Acad., 1945-47, Carleton Coll., 1950-52; instr. U. S.D., 1952-54, Tsuda Women's Coll., Tokyo, 1958; Kokusai Bunka Shinkokai, Internat. House of Japan, 1957—, U. N.D., 1959-61, Tappan Middle Sch., 1960-61; tchr. Oyster Bay (N.Y.) Middle Sch., 1963; instr. SUNY, Buffalo, 1963-69; tchr. Latin, Amherst (N.Y.) Central Sr. High Sch., 1971-85, chmn. dept. fgn. langs., 1975-81; cons. N.Y. State Regents Exams, 1978-80. N.Y. Regents scholar, 1942-46; recipient Teaching Excellence award PTA Amherst, 1978. Bd. dirs. Evergreen Coll. Community Orgn. (treas. 1990-93), Wash. State Capital Mus., Friends of Evergreen State Coll. Libr. (bd. mem. 1993-99); assoc. State Capitol Mus. Mem. Archeol. Inst. Am. (treas. Western N.Y. 1977-79), Classical Assn. Western N.Y. (pres. 1974-76, exec. council 1976-85, v.p. 1972-74), Classical Assn. Empire State (exec. council 1974-78), Classical Assn. Atlantic States (regional rep. 1980-82), Am. Classical League, Classical Assn. New Eng. States, Nat. Jr. Classical League, N.Y. Assn. Fgn. Lang. Tchrs., N.Y. State Jr. Classical League, Pompeiiana, Western N.Y. Fgn. Lang. Educators Council (life), Western N.Y. Archeol. Soc. (treas. 1977-79), Wash. Ctr. Performing Arts, Palm Springs Desert Mus., Frye Art Gallery, Seattle, Henry Gallery U. Wash., Delta Kappa Gamma. Editor: Reading Selections for Latin Level III, 1973; Classical Currents, 1976-79; sec., treas., mng. editor Arethusa, 1968-71. Home: 3138 Lorne St SE Olympia WA 98501-3420 Office: Amherst Cen High Sch Main St Buffalo NY 14226

RIESE, ARTHUR CARL, environmental engineering company executive, consultant; b. St. Albans, N.Y., Jan. 2, 1955; s. Walter Herman and Katherine Ellen (Moore) R. BS in Geology, N.Mex. Inst. Mining and Tech., 1976, MS in Chemistry, 1978; PhD in Geochemistry, Colo. Sch. Mines, 1982. Lic. geologist, N.C.; registered profl. geologist, N.C., S.C., Ark., Fla., Tenn., Wyo. Asst. petroleum geologist N.Mex. Bur. Mines and Mineral Resources, Socorro, 1973-76; geologist Nord Resources, Inc., Albuquerque, 1975; rsch. asst. N.Mex. Inst. Mining and Tech., Socorro, 1976-78; vis. faculty Colo. Sch. Mines, 1978-81; rsch. geochemist Gulf R & D Co., Houston, 1982-84; sr. planning analyst/mgr. tech. planning Atlantic Richfield Co., L.A., 1984-87; sr. v.p. Harding Assocs. and Harding Lawson Assocs., Denver, 1987—; mem. affiliate faculty U. Tex., Austin, 1983—; speaker, conf. chmn. in field. Numerous patents in field. Panel participant N.Mex. First, Gallup, 1990. Recipinet Engrng. Excellence award Cons. Engrs. Coun. Colo., 1991, 95. Mem. Am. Inst. Hydrology (cert. profl. hydrogeologist 1988), Am. Inst. Profl. Geologists (cert. geol. scientist 1988). Office: Harding Lawson Assocs 2400 MCI Tower 707 17th St Denver CO 80202-3404

RIGALI, LOUIS ANTHONY, scientific instruments company executive; b. Somerville, Mass., Oct. 18, 1937; s. Anthony Louis and Emma (Marchi) R.; m. Patricia Wilson (div.); m. Julianne J. Williams; children: Susan, Denise, Anthony, Alex. BS in Chemistry, Northeastern U., 1960. Chemist Cabot Corp., Cambridge, Mass.; product mgr. Varian, Walnut Creek, Calif., LFE, Richmond, Calif.; pres. Tegal Sci., Concord, Calif.; CEO, March Instruments, Concord, Calif. Patentee in field. Mem. Am. Chem. Soc. (editor Vortex, chair-elect).

RIGBY, AMANDA YOUNG, paralegal firm executive; b. Yokosuka, Japan, Nov. 15, 1961; d. James Linton Young, Philip T. (stepfather) and Serena Margaret (Murray) Poisson; m. D'Arcy A. Rigby, Apr. 6, 1991; children: Ian A., Helen E. Cert. paralegal, U. San Diego, 1989; AA in Social Sci., Miramar Coll., 1990. Cert. domestic violence counselor, Calif. Sec. Martin & Branfman, Solana Beach, Calif., 1988-89; sr. paralegal DiGennaro & Davis, San Diego, 1989-91; owner, pres. paralegal firm AR & Co., San Diego, 1989—. Author poetry in Taking Chances mag., 1992. Vol. clinic coord. San Diego Vol. Lawyer Program, 1989-96; vol. asst. to abuse victims San Diego Police Dept., 1992—; parliamentarian Mira Mesa Town Coun., San Diego, 1992-95; founding mem. Scripps Ranch High Found., San Diego, 1992-95; sec., nat. and state rep. Pomerado Hosp. Mothers of Twins, Poway, Calif., 1994—; mem. Vista (Calif.) Unified Sch. Dist. Common Ground Task Force, 1995-97; staff paralegal San Diego Vol. Lawyer Program, 1994-95; bd. dirs. So. Calif. Mothers of Twins, Inc., 1996—; legal clinic trainer, speaker Community Resource Ctr., 1996—. Mem. ABA. Republican. Methodist. Avocations: reading, writing, sailing, exercising, working on the house. Office: AR & Co 615 Cabezon Pl Fl 2 Vista CA 92083-6309

RIGGS, BRENT DAIL, lawyer; b. Mesa, Ariz., Apr. 5, 1942; s. Morris Dail and Sylvia Lenea (Krantz) R.; m. Carla Jo Smith, 1972; children: Joseph, Ginger, John, Judy, Lyle, Hugh, Charles, Elizabeth, Cleo. AA, E. L.A. Coll., 1962; BS, Brigham Young U., 1966; JD, U. Chgo., 1969. Bar: Calif. 1970, U.S. Dist. Ct. (ctrl. dist.) Calif. 1970, U.S. Ct. Appeals (9th cir.) 1989, U.S. Supreme Ct. 1989. Dep. dist. atty. L.A. County Dist. Atty.'s Office, L.A., 1970—; panelist on recent devels. in criminal law Calif. Continuing Edn. of the Bar, 1989—. Author: (with others) California Criminal Law and Procedure, 1994. Bd. dirs. Haven House, Pasadena, Calif., 1981-85. Mem. ABA, Nat. Dist. Attys. Assn., L.A. County Bar Assn., Calif. Dist. Attys. Assn. (uniform crime charging com.). Republican. Mem. L.D.S. Office: LA County Dist Atty Appellate Divsn 849 S Broadway Ste 1100 Los Angeles CA 90014-3206

RIGGS, FRANK, congressman; b. Louisville, Ky., Sept. 5, 1950; m. Cathy Anne Maillard; three children: Ryan, Matthew, Sarah Anne. BA, Golden Gate U. With Veale Investment Properties, until 1987; co-founder (with wife) Duncan Enterprises; mem. 102nd Congress 1st Calif. Dist., 1991-92, mem. 104th and 105th Congresses, 1995—, mem. edn. and workforce transp. and infrastructure coms. With U.S. Army, 1972-75. Republican. Office: US House Reps 1714 Longworth Office Bldg Washington DC 20515-0501

RIGGS, FRED WARREN, political science educator; b. Kuling, China, July 3, 1917; (parents Am. citizens); s. Charles H. and Grace (Frederick) R.; m. Clara-Louise Mather, June 5, 1943; children: Gwendolyn, Ronald (dec.). Student, U. Nanking, China, 1934-35; BA, U. Ill., 1938; MA, Fletcher Sch. Law and Diplomacy, 1941; PhD, Columbia U., 1948. Lectr. CUNY, 1947-48; rsch. assoc. Fgn. Policy Assn., 1948-51; asst. dir. Pub. Adminstrn. Clearing House, N.Y.C., 1951-55; Arthur F. Bentley prof. govt. Ind. U., 1956-67; dir. Social Sci. Rsch. Inst. U. Hawaii, 1970-73, prof. polit. sci., 1967-87, prof. emeritus, 1987—; vis. asst. prof. Yale U., 1955-56; vis. lectr. Nat. Officials Tng. Inst., Korea, 1956; vis. prof. U. Philippines, 1958-59, MIT, 1965-66, CUNY, 1974-75; vis. scholar Inst. Soc. Studies, The Hague, 1972; sr. specialist East-West Ctr. U. Hawaii, 1962-63. Author: Pressures on Congress: A Study of the Repeal of Chinese Exclusion, 1950, reprinted, 1973, Formosa under Chinese Nationalist Rule, 1952, reprinted, 1972, The Ecology of Public Administration, 1961 (pub. in Portuguese, 1964), Administration in Developing Countries: The Theory of Prismatic Society, 1964 (pub. in Korean, 1966, Portuguese, 1968), Thailand: The Modernization of a Bureaucratic Polity, 1966, Organization Theory and International Development, 1969, Administrative Reform and Political Responsiveness: A Theory of Dynamic Balancing, 1971, Prismatic Society Revisited, 1973 (pub. in Korean, 1987), Applied Prismatics, 1978, (with Daya Krishna) Development Debate, 1987; author: (with others) Contemporary Political Systems: Classifications and Typologies, 1990, Handbook of Comparative and Development Public Administration, 1991, Terminology: Applications in Interdisciplinary Communication, 1993, Parliamentary vs. Presidential Government, 1993, Public Administration in the Global Village, 1994, Comparing Nations: Concepts, Strategies, Substance, 1994, Handbook of Bureaucracy, 1994, Standardizing and Harmonizing Terminology, 1995, Korea in the Era of Post-Development and Globalization, 1996, Viable Constitutionalism and Bureaucracy, 1996, Onomantics and Terminology, 1996, Designs for Democratic Stability, 1997, Modernity and Bureaucracy, 1997, Presidentialism vs. Parliamentarism, 1998, Public Administration in America, 1998, The Modernity of Ethnic Identity and Conflict, 1998; co-author, editor: Frontiers of Development Administration, 1971, Tower of Babel: On the Definition and Analysis of Concepts in the Social Sciences, 1975. Dir. INTERCOCTA project Internat. Social Sci. Coun., 1970-93; chair UNESCO com. INTERCONCEPT project, 1977-79; chair Comm. on Conceptual and Terminological Analysis (COCTA), Internat. Polit. Sci. Assn., Internat. Sociol. Assn. and Internat. Social Sci. Coun., 1973-79; co-chair N.A.M. roundtable on cooperation Social Sci. Info. Mpls., 1979; chair lexicographic terminology com. Dictionary Soc. N.Am., 1983-86; co-chair Com. on Viable Constitutionalism (COVICO), 1993—. Decorated Order of White Elephant, King of Thailand, 1986; fellow com. comparative politics Social Sci. Rsch. Coun., 1957-58, Ctr. Advanced Study in Behavioral Scis., 1966-67; honoree Eastern Regional Orgn. Pub. Adminstrn. Conf., 1983. Mem. Am. Soc. for Pub. Adminstrn. (chair comparative adminstrn. group 1960-71, Dwight Waldo award 1991), Am. Polit. Sci. Assn., Internat. Studies Assn. (chair comparative interdisciplinary studies sect. 1970-74, v.p. 1970-71, co-chair ethnicity, nationalism and migration sect. 1994-95), Internat. Polit. Sci. Assn., Internat. Sociol. Assn., Assn. Asian Studies (chair com. rsch. materials S.E. Asia 1969-73), Soc. for Comparative Rsch. (co-founder 1994—). Home: 3920 Lurline Dr Honolulu HI 96816-4006 Office: U Hawaii Political Science Dept 2424 Maile Way Honolulu HI 96822-2223

RIGGS, GEORGE E., newspaper publishing executive. Pub., CEO Contra Costa (Calif.) Times. *

RIGGS, HENRY EARLE, academic administrator, engineering management educator; b. Chgo., Feb. 25, 1935; s. Joseph Agnew and Gretchen (Walser) R.; m. Gayle Carson, May 17, 1958; children: Elizabeth, Peter, Catharine. BS, Stanford U., 1957; MBA, Harvard U., 1960. Indsl. economist SRI Internat., Menlo Park, Calif., 1960-63; v.p. Icore Industries, Sunnyvale, Calif., 1963-67, pres., 1967-70; v.p. fin. Measurex Corp., Cupertino, Calif., 1970-74; prof. engring. mgmt. Stanford U., Calif., 1974-88, Ford prof., 1986-88, Ford prof. emeritus, 1990—, v.p. for devel., 1983-88; pres. Harvey Mudd Coll., Claremont, Calif., 1988-97, pres. emeritus, 1997—; pres. Keck Grad. Inst., Claremont, 1997—; bd. dirs. Mutual Funds of capital Rsch. Group. Author: Accounting: A Survey, 1981, Managing High-Tech Companies, 1983, Financial and Cost Analysis, 1994; contbr. articles to Harvard Bus. Rev. Bd. dirs. Mt. Baldy Coun. Boy Scouts Am., 1993—. Baker scholar Harvard Bus. Sch., Boston, 1959; recipient Gores Teaching award Stanford U., 1980. Mem. Stanford U. Alumni Assn. (bd. dirs. 1990-94, chmn. 1993), Calif. Club, Sunset Club, Twilight Club, Phi Beta Kappa, Tau Beta Pi. Congregationalist. Office: Keck Grad Inst 1263 N Dartmouth Ave Claremont CA 91711-3941

RIGGS, LISA ANNE, elementary school educator; b. Aberdeen, Wash., July 22, 1968; d. Warner Earl and Marjorie Anne (Lindberg) Childress; m. Ronald Lon Riggs, July 30, 1994. AA, Peninsula Coll., Port Angeles, Wash., 1988; BA, Wash. State U., 1991; MEd in Curriculum, City U., Port Angeles, 1994. Tchr. 8th grade English Port Angeles Sch. Dist., 1991—; writing facilitator Port Angeles Sch. Dist., 1997-98; advisor Nat. Jr. Honor Soc., Port Angeles, 1996-98, Drama Club, Stevens Mid. Sch., Port Angeles, 1991-98. Mem. Nat. Com. Tchrs. of English, Wash. Edn. Assn. (v.p. 1996-97), Port Angeles Edn. Assn. (sec. 1995-96, v.p. 1996-97), Delta Kappa Gamma. Avocations: reading, writing, acting in local productions.

RIGGS, MEADE DAVID, clinical psychologist, priest, bishop; b. Cortland, N.Y., Sept. 6, 1923; s. Charles Morrell and Sadie (Bersson); m. Jane Elizabeth Nass Pabst, Jan. 8, 1994; 1 child, Michelle. BA, Ohio Wesleyan U., 1944; MDiv, Yale U., 1947; MEd, U. Kans., 1951; MA, Hartford Sem. Found., 1952; PhD, U. So. Calif., 1959; LHD, Newport U., 1984; DD, St. Andrews Sem., 1993. Lic. psychologist, Calif.; cert. child, marriage and family counselor, Calif. Exec. dir., chief of staff Riggs & Assoc. Psychol. Svcs. Ctr., Anaheim, Calif., 1964-80; prin. assoc., cons. Closson, Riggs & Assoc., Anaheim, Calif., 1980-94; assoc. Stanley F. Hansen, M.D., Costa Mesa, Calif., 1980-91; mem. staff Successful Living Counseling Ctr., Garden Grove, Calif., 1986—, dir., 1986-91; assoc. dir., chaplain Halfway Homes Inc., Huntington Beach, Calif., 1990-94; clin. dir. Cope Ctr., Costa Mesa, 1991—; mental health staff Universal Care Med. Group, Bellflower and Garden Grove, Calif., 1995—; cons. Rigg & Assocs., Anaheim, 1976—. Mem. Citizen's Traffic Adv. Com., Cypress, Calif., 1968, Citizen's Capital Improvement Com., Anaheim, 1977; del. mem. Orange County Health Planning Coun., 1985; consecrated bishop Philippine Ind. Cath. Ch., Los Alamitos, Calif., 1993—. Recipient 1st ann. Most Spirit award Orange County Grad. chpt. Phi Gamma Delta, 1984. Mem. Am. Assn. Clin. Counselors (diplomate), Am. Bd. Adminstrs. Psychology (diplomate), Am. B. Med. Psychotherapists and Psychodiagnosticians (diplomate), Masons. Democrat. Avocations: pipe collecting, American stamps, basketball, bridge, reading. Home: 7667 Sandalwood Way Stanton CA 90680-2321 Office: Universal Care Med Group 17660 Lakewood Blvd Bellflower CA 90706-6410

RIGGS, WILLIAM, state judge. Grad., Portland State U., 1961; JD, U. Oreg., 1968. Atty. Willner Bennet & Leonard, 1972-78; judge circuit ct. 4th Judicial Dist. Multonmah County, 1978; judge Oreg. Ct. of Appeals, 1988-98, Oreg. Supreme Ct., 1998—. Active mem. Cmty. Law Poject; founder Integra Corp. With USNR. Office: Supreme Ct Bldg 1163 State St Salem OR 97310-0260*

RIGTRUP, KENNETH, state judge, arbitrator, mediator; b. Burley, Idaho, Jan. 13, 1936; s. Robert Peter and Bessie Viola (Price) R.; m. Susanne Joan Remund, May 15, 1964; children: Mark Robert, Michael James, Scott Kenneth, Melissa Ann, Jennifer Marie. BS in Acctg., U. Utah, 1960, JD, 1962. Bar: Utah 1962; U.S. Dist. Ct. Utah, 1962. Clk. Utah Supreme Ct., Salt Lake City, 1962; ptnr. Rigtrup & Hadley, Salt Lake City, 1962-68; pvt. practice, Salt Lake City, 1968-72; admin. law judge Indsl. Commn., Salt Lake City, 1972-77; mem. Pub. Svc. Commn., Salt Lake City, 1977-80; judge 3d Dist. Ct., Salt Lake City, 1980-97; active sr. judge Utah Cts., Salt Lake City, 1997—; chmn. Bd. Sr. Judges; mem. adv. com. on rules of juvenile procedure Utah Supreme Ct., Salt Lake City, 1993-95. Copy and rsch. editor Utah Law Rev., 1961-62. Chmn. Utah White House Conf. on Handicapped Individuals, Salt Lake City, 1976-77; mem. Utah Gov.'s Com. on Employment of Handicapped, 1976-80, vice chmn. and acting chmn. 1977-80; mem. citizens evaluation and selection com. to rev. pvt. non-profit orgn. applications for urban mass transit authority grants, 1975-77, dir., vice chair. Utah Assistive Tech. Found., 1991—. Recipient Disting. Svc. award Utah Rehab. Counseling Assn., Salt Lake City, 1976-77; Nat. Citation award Nat. Rehab. counseling Assn., 1977; Maurice Warshaw Golden Key award, Utah Gov.'s Com. on Employment of Handicapped, 1975. Mem. ABA, ATLA, Utah Bar Assn. (exec. com. family sect. 1980-90, lawyers helping lawyers com., alt. dispute resolution com.), Nat. Ass. Regulatory Utility Commns. (water com. 1977-78, gas com. 1978-80), Am. Judicature Soc. Republican. Mem. LDS Ch. Home: 1961 Millbrook Rd Salt Lake City UT 84106-3853 Office: Arbitration/Mediation Svcs 3098 Highland Dr Ste 399 Salt Lake City UT 84106-3076

RILES, WILSON CAMANZA, educational consultant; b. Alexandria, La., June 27, 1917; m. Mary Louise Phillips, Nov. 13, 1941; children: Michael, Narvia Riles Bostick, Wilson, Phillip. B.A., No. Ariz. U., 1940; M.A., 1947, LL.D., 1976; LL.D., Pepperdine Coll., 1965, Claremont Grad. Sch., 1972, U. So. Calif., 1975, U. Akron, 1976, Golden Gate U., 1981; L.H.D., St. Mary's Coll., 1971, U. Pacific, 1971, U. Judaism, 1972. Tchr. elem. schs., adminstr. pub. schs. Ariz., 1940-54; exec. sec. Pacific Coast region Fellowship of Reconciliation, Los Angeles, 1954-58; with Calif. Dept. Edn., 1958-83, dep. supt. pub. instrn., 1965-70, supt. pub. instruction, 1971-83; pres. Wilson Riles & Assocs., Inc., 1983—; dir. emeritus Wells Fargo Bank, Wells Fargo Co. Past mem. editorial adv. bd.: Early Years mag. Ex-officio mem. bd. regents U. Calif., 1971-82; ex-officio trustee Calif. State Univs. and Colls., 1971-82; nat. adv. council Nat. Schs. Vol. Program; former mem. council

Stanford Research Inst.; former mem. adv. council Stanford U. Sch. Bus.; former mem. adv. bd. Calif. Congress Parents and Tchrs.; former trustee Am. Coll. Testing Program; former mem. Edn. Commn. of States; past 2d v.p. Nat. PTA.; former trustee Found. Teaching Econs.; former mem. Joint Council Econ. Edn.; former mem. Nat. Council for Children and TV. With USAF, 1943-46. Recipient Spingarn medal NAACP, 1973. Mem. Assn. Calif. Sch. Adminstrs., Cleve. Conf., NAACP (Spingarn medal 1973), Nat. Acad. Pub. Adminstrn., Phi Beta Kappa. Office: 400 Capitol Mall Ste 1540 Sacramento CA 95814-4434

RILEY, CARROLL LAVERN, anthropology educator; b. Summersville, Mo., Apr. 18, 1923; s. Benjamin F. and Minnie B. (Smith) R.; m. Brent Robinson Locke, Mar. 25, 1948; children: Benjamin Locke, Victoria Smith Evans, Cynthia Winningham. A.B., U. N.Mex., 1948, Ph.D., 1952; M.A., UCLA, 1950. Instr. U. Colo., Boulder, 1953-54; asst. prof. U. N.C., Chapel Hill, 1954-55; asst. prof. So. Ill. U., Carbondale, 1955-60, assoc. prof., 1960-67, prof., 1967-86, Disting. prof., 1986-87, Disting. prof. emeritus, 1987—, chmn. dept., 1979-82, dir. mus., 1972-74; rsch. assoc. lab. anthropology Mus. N.Mex., 1987—; rsch. collaborator Smithsonian Instn., 1988—; adj. prof. N.Mex. Highlands U., 1989—. Author: The Origins of Civilization, 1969, The Frontier People, 1982, expanded edit., 1987, Rio del Norte, 1995, Bandelier, 1996; editor: Man Across the Sea, 1971, Southwestern Journals of Adolph F. Bandelier, 4 vols., 1966, 70, 75, 84, Across the Chichimec Sea, 1978, A Zuni Life, 1998, The Casas Grandes World, 1999, others; contbr. numerous articles to profl. jours. Served in USAAF, 1942-45. Decorated 4 battle stars; grantee Social Sci. Research Council, NIH, Am. Philos. Soc., Am. Council Learned Socs., NEH, others. Home and Office: 1106 6th St Las Vegas NM 87701-4311

RILEY, GRANNAN, performing company executive. Studied with Doreen gilday, Eugene, Oreg.; BFA, U.S. Internat. U., San Diego; postgrad., Academie des Grand Ballets Canadiens, Montreal. Co-founder Eugene (Oreg.) Ballet Co, 1978—, mng. dir., 1984—; mem. dance touring panel Western States Arts Found.; mem. selection panel Arts N.W., Individual Artist Fellowship, Oreg. and Idaho. Dancer (ballets) Petrushka, the Firebird, Coppelia, others, worldwide tours. Active outreach programs Young Audiences Oreg., Wash. State Cultural Enrichment Program. co-recipient Gov.'s Arts award, 1996. Office: Eugene Ballet Co PO Box 11200 Eugene OR 97440-3400*

RILEY, JACK, actor, writer; b. Cleve., Dec. 30, 1935; s. John A. and Agnes C. (Corrigan) R.; m. Ginger Lawrence, May 18, 1975; children: Jamie, Bryan. BS in English, John Carroll U., 1961. Mem.: Rolling Along of 1960, Dept. Army Travelling Show; co-host: Baxter & Riley, Sta.-WERE, Cleve., 1961-65; numerous TV appearances, including: as Mr. Carlin on Bob Newhart Show, CBS-TV, 1972-78; Occasional Wife, 1966, Mary Tyler Moore, 1972, Barney Miller, 1979, Diff'rent Strokes, 1979, Hart to Hart, 1980, Love Boat, 1984, Night Court, 1985-91, St. Elsewhere, 1986, Babes, 1991, Evening Shade, 1992, Family Matters, 1993, Hangin' with Mr. Cooper, 1993, Dave's World, 1994, Married with Children, 1994, Coach, 1996, The Drew Carey Show, 1996, Seinfeld, 1997, numerous appearances on Tonight Show with Jay Leno, 1997-98; appeared in feature films including Catch-22, 1969, McCabe and Mrs. Miller, 1970, Long Goodbye, 1972, Calif. Split, 1974, World's Greatest Lover, 1978, High Anxiety, 1978, Butch and Sundance: The Early Years, 1979, History of the World, Part I, 1981, Frances, 1983, To Be or Not To Be, 1983, Finders Keepers, 1984, Spaceballs, 1987, Rented Lips, 1987, Gleaming the Cube, 1988, C.H.U.D. II, 1988, The Player, 1992, T-Rex, 1995, (voice) A Rugrat's Movie, 1995, Boogie Nights, 1997; plays West Coast premier of Small Craft Warnings, 1975, Los Angeles revival of 12 Angry Men, 1985, Zeitgeist, 1990, House of Blue Leaves, at Cleve. Playhouse and tour Ea. Europe, 1993; TV writer: Don Rickles Show, 1968, Mort Sahl Show, 1967; writer commls. for, Blore & Richman Inc., Los Angeles, 1966-84; numerous radio commls. and TV voice-overs, Rugrats (cartoon series), 1993. Served with U.S. Army, 1958-61. Mem. Screen Actors Guild, Actor's Equity, AFTRA, Writers Guild Am., Acad. Motion Picture Arts and Scis., Acad. TV Arts and Scis. Office: care Ho of Reps 400 S Beverly Dr Beverly Hills CA 90212-4424

RILEY, MARY JANE, computer scientist; b. Raleigh, N.C., May 26, 1946; d. Charles William and Geraldine Lucile (Adams) Hampton; m. William Walter Schubert, Dec. 30, 1967 (div. June 1979); children: Kristen, Stephen, Betsy, Kathryn; stepchildren: Lee, Scott; m. Jim Riley, Oct. 17, 1998. BA in Math., Park Coll., 1967. Programmer U. Mo. Med. Ctr., Columbia, 1968-72, City and County of Denver, 1979-80; sr. sys. programmer Citicorp Person to Person, Denver, 1980-82; sys. support rep. Software AG, NA, Denver, 1982-83; prin. info. sysm. specialist Idaho Nat. Engring. Lab., EG&G, Idaho Falls, 1983-89; adv. svcs. specialist IBM Profl. Svcs., Albuquerque, 1989-91; field mgr. IBM Svc., Boulder, Colo., 1991-93; project mgr. IBM Global Svcs., Denver, 1993—; presenter career workshop for girls No. Colo. U., Greeley, 1993. Leader Girl Scout Am., Pocatello, Idaho, Columbia, Mo., 1969-79, Idaho Falls, 1986-89, cluster leader, Rigby, Idaho, 1988-89; active Albuquerque Civic Chorus, 1990-91, Luth. Ch. Coun., 1994-96; bd. dirs. LWV, Pocatello, 1977-79, 84-85, pres., 1978-79; bd. dirs. Luth. Ch. Women, Pocatello, 1978-79; youth advisor Luth. Ch., Idaho Falls, 1984-89; tchr. Sunday sch. local ch., Albuquerque, 1990-91; youth com. chair local ch., Boulder, Colo., 1994-96; tchr. 7th and 8th grade Sunday sch., 1993-96, mem. ch. choir, 1995-96; mem. Denver Art Mus., Denver Nat. History Mus. Mem. AAUW. Episcopalian. Avocations: youth work, reading, choir, photography, skiing. Home: 5356 Morning Glory Ln Littleton CO 80123-2943

RILEY, MICHAEL (MIKE RILEY), professional football coach; b. Wallace, Idaho, July 6, 1953; m. Dee Riley; children: Matthew, Kate. BS in Soc. Sci., U. Ala., 1975; MS, Whitworth Coll., 1976. Defensive back Crimson Tide U. Ala., 1971-74; grad. asst. coach U. Calif., 1975; def. coord., secondary coach, asst. athletic dir. Linfield Coll., McMinnville, Oreg., 1977-82; secondary coach Winnipeg Blue Bombers CFL, 1983-84, winner 2 Grey Cup Winnepeg Blue Bombers, head coach Winnipeg Blue Bombers, 1987-90; defensive coord., sec. coach No. Colo. U., 1986; head coach San Antonio Riders World League Am. Football, 1991-92; asst. head coach, offensive coord./quarterbacks coach U. So. Calif., 1993-96; head coach Oreg. State U., 1997-98; head coach San Diego Chargers NFL, 1998—. Office: care San Diego Chargers PO Box 609609 San Diego CA 92160-9609*

RILEY, SHARELL DENICE, therapist, educator; b. Chattanooga, Aug. 21, 1956; d. Paul E. and Alice G. (Greenlee) Trotter; m. James E. Riley Jr., Oct. 25, 1975 (div. Apr. 1980); 1 child, Kenneth Ray. AS in Nursing, Santa Ana (Calif.) Coll., 1977. Cert. respiratory therapist, respiratory therapy instr. Ins. agt. United Ins. Co., Garden Grove, Calif., 1980-87; respiratory therapist Corona (Calif.) Regional Med. Ctr., 1989-95; respiratory therapy instr. Calif. Paramed. & Tech. Coll., Riverside, Calif., 1994-96; respiratory therapist Torrance (Calif.) Meml. Med. Ctr., 1996—. Author ednl. curriculum for continuing edn. for respiratory care practitioners, 1996. Trustee New Hope Bapt. Ch., Lake Elsinore, Calif. (fin. cons. 1996—, Musician's award, 1992). Recipient Musician's award Greater Light Bapt. Ch., Santa Ana, 1980. Avocations: music, choir director, billiards, fishing. Home: 3609 Linnet Dr Lake Elsinore CA 92530-7969

RILEY, WILLIAM L., lawyer; b. Bay Shore, N.Y., 1942. BA, Williams Coll., 1964; JD, Duke U., 1967. Bar: N.Y. 1967, Calif. 1970. Mem. Orrick, Herrington & Sutcliffe, San Francisco, 1972-95, ptr., 1975—. Contbr. to profl. jours. Office: Orrick Herrington & Sutcliffe Fed Reserve Bank Bldg 400 Sansome St San Francisco CA 94111-3143*

RIMOIN, DAVID LAWRENCE, physician, geneticist; b. Montreal, Nov. 9, 1936; s. Michael and Fay (Lecker) R.; m. Mary Ann Singleton, 1962 (div. 1979); 1 child, Anne; m. Ann Piilani Garber, July 27, 1980; children: Michael, Lauren. BSc, McGill U., Montreal, 1957, MSc, MD, CM, 1961; PhD, Johns Hopkins U., 1967; LHD (hon.), Finch U., 1997. Asst. prof. medicine, pediat. Washington U., St. Louis, 1967-70; assoc. prof. UCLA, 1970-73, prof., 1973—; chief med. genetics Harbor-UCLA Med. Ctr., 1970-86; dir. dept. pediat., dir. Med. Genetics and Birth Defects Ctr., 1986—; Steven Spielberg chmn. pediat. Cedars-Sinai Med. Ctr., L.A., 1989—; chmn. coun. Med. Genetics Orgn., 1993. Co-author: Principles and Practice of [illegible] articles to profl. jours., chpts. to books. Recipient E. Mead Johnson award Am. Acad. Pediat., 1976, Col. Harland Saunders award March of Dimes, 1997. Fellow ACP, AAAS, Am. Coll. Med. Genetics (pres. 1991-96, bd. dirs. 1996-98, pres. found. 1998—); mem. Am. Fedn. Clin. Rsch. (sec.-treas. 1972-75), Western Soc. Clin. Rsch. (pres. 1978), Western Soc. Pediat. Rsch. (pres. 1995, Ross Outstanding Young Investigator award 1976), Am. Bd. Med. Genetics (pres. 1979-83), Am. Soc. Human Genetics (pres. 1984), Am. Pediat. Soc., Soc. Pediat. Rsch., Am. Soc. Clin. Investigation, Assn. Am. Physicians, Johns Hopkins Soc. Scholars, Inst. Medicine. Office: Cedars-Sinai Med Ctr 8700 Beverly Blvd Los Angeles CA 90048-1865

RIMSZA, SKIP, mayor; b. Chgo.; m. Kim Gill; children: Brian, Jenny, Alexander, Taylor, Nicole. Mem. Phoenix City Coun., 1990-94; vice mayor City of Phoenix, 1993, mayor, 1994—; former pres. Bd. Realtors. Mem. several cmty. bds. Office: Office of the Mayor 200 W Washington St Fl 11 Phoenix AZ 85003-1611

RINAKER, SAMUEL MAYO, JR., retired utilities executive; b. Chgo., Sept. 29, 1922; s. Samuel Mayo and Marjorie (Horton) R.; m. Alice Benthey, Dec. 17, 1949 (div. 1974); children: Elizabeth Cherry, Samuel H. III, Laura Frazier, Mary Clark. Student, UCLA, 1941-42. Farmer Nebr. and Ill., 1946-49; exec. sec. to atty. gen. Olympia, Wash., 1949-52; news dir. Sta. KTNT-TV, Tacoma, Wash., 1952-57, Sta. KIRO-TV, Seattle, 1957-60; assoc. news dir., news anchor Sta. KGTV, San Diego, 1960-75; dir. pub. policy San Diego Gas & Electric Co., 1976-84; bd. dirs. 1st Nat. Bank, Beatrice, Neb., 1976-93. Maj. USAF, 1942-46, ETO. Mem. Rotary (bd. dirs. 1965-67), La Jolla Beach Tennis Club. Republican. Presbyterian. Avocations: golf. Home: 5935 Rutgers Rd La Jolla CA 92037-7834

RINDONE, JOSEPH PATRICK, clinical pharmacist, educator; b. Santa Fe, Oct. 4, 1954; s. Guido Salvatore and Elizabeth Ann (Murphy) R.; m. Diane Marie Rollins, June 11, 1991; children: Jacqueline, Alexandra. BS, U. Nebr., 1977; PharmD, Creighton U., 1978. Lic. pharmacist, Nebr., Calif. Staff pharmacist Bergan Mercy Hosp., Omaha, 1978; staff pharmacist Phoenix (Ariz.) VA Med. Ctr., 1978-81, clin. resident, 1981; clin. pharmacist Tucson VA Med. Ctr., 1982-93; asst. prof. U. Ariz., Tucson, 1982—; clin. pharmacist Prescott (Ariz.) VA Med. Ctr., 1993—, rsch. coord., 1994—. Author: Therapeutic Monitoring of Antibiotics, 1991; contbr. articles to Arch. Internal Medicine, Pharmacotherapy, Clin. Therapeutics, Am. Jour. Cardiology, Am. Jour. Therapeutics, Chest, West Jour. Medicine, Am. Jour. Health Sys. Pharm. Regents scholar U. Nebr., 1976. Mem. Ariz. Soc. Hosp. Pharmacists. Avocations: sports, photography, bridge, astronomy. Office: VA Med Ctr North Hwy 89 Prescott AZ 86313

RINEHART, CHARLES R., savings and loan association executive; b. San Francisco, Jan. 31, 1947; s. Robert Eugene and Rita Mary Rinehart; married; children: Joseph B., Kimberly D., Michael P., Scott. BS, U. San Francisco, 1968. Exec. v.p. Fireman's Fund Ins. Cos., Novato, Calif., 1969-83; pres., CEO Avco Fin. Services, Irvine, Calif., 1983-89, H.F. Ahmanson & Co., Irwindale, Calif., 1989-93; chmn., CEO Home Savs. of Am., H.F.Ahmanson & Co., Irwindale; mem. Fannie Mae Nat. Adv. Coun., Thrift Instn. Adv. Coun.; bd. dirs. Fed. Home Loan Bank San Francisco, L.A. Bus. Advisors, Kaufman and Broad Home Corp. Mem. adv. com. Drug Use is Life Abuse; mem. Tustin Pub. Sch. Found. Camp com. Served to 2d lt. U.S. Army, 1968-69. Fellow Casualty Actuarial Soc.; mem. Am. Mgmt. Assn., Am. Acad. Actuaries. Republican. Roman Catholic. Avocations: athletics, gourmet cooking, model trains. Office: Ho Savs Am/H F Ahmanson & Co 4900 Rivergrade Rd Bldg 515 Irwindale CA 91706-1404

RINESMITH, STEVEN LEE, lawyer; b. San Luis Obispo, Calif., Mar. 27, 1952; s. Paul M. and Norma J. (Mohler) R. BA, Northeast La. U., 1972; JD, U. Houston, 1977. Sr. mgr. Ernst & Young, Honolulu, 1986-88; ptnr. Deloitte & Touche, Honolulu, 1988-90; pres. Monroe & Friedlander Mgmt., Honolulu, 1990-92; atty. Case Bigelow & Lombardi, Honolulu, 1992—, also bd. dirs.; bd. dirs. St. Francis Hosp. Mem. Hawaii Bar Assn., Tex. Bar Assn., Hawaii Soc. CPA's. Avocation: travel, exercise, reading. Office: Case Bigelow & Lombardi 737 Bishop St Ste 2600 Honolulu HI 96813-3283

RINEY, HAL PATRICK, advertising executive; b. Seattle, Wash., July 17, 1932; s. Hal Patrick and Inez Marie R.; children: Benjamin Kennedy, Samantha Elizabeth; m. Edith Caldwell. BA, U. Wash., Seattle, 1954. From art dir./writer to v.p., creative dir. BBDO, Inc., San Francisco, 1956-72; exec. v.p., creative dir. Botsford Ketchum, San Francisco, 1972-76; sr. v.p., mng. dir., creative dir. Ogilvy & Mather, San Francisco, 1976-81; exec. v.p. Ogilvy & Mather West, 1981-86; chmn., CEO, Hal Riney & Ptnrs., Inc., San Francisco, 1986-98, Publicis & Hal Riney, San Francisco, 1998—. Recipient 5 Lion d'Or du Cannes awards, 18 Clio awards, 15 Addy awards, Grand Prix du Cannes; named to Creative Hall of Fame. Mem. Am. Assn. Advt. Agys., San Francisco Advt. Club, San Francisco Soc. Communicating Arts, Wild Goose Club, Meadow Club, St. Francis Yacht Club. Home: 1 Los Pinos Nicasio CA 94946-9701 Office: Publicis & Hal Riney 2001 The Embarcadero San Francisco CA 94133-5200*

RING, CHRISTOPHER LEE, software engineer; b. Akron, Ohio, Sept. 9, 1973; s. Michael Paul and Suanne Beth (Pfiefer) R.; m. Karen Wright, Aug. 17, 1996. BS, U. Calif., Santa Barbara, 1985. Software engr. Spectron Microsys., Santa Barbara, 1995-98, Dialogic Santa Barbara Labs., 1998—. Republican. Lutheran. Fax: (805) 967-1395. E-mail: c.ring@dialobic.com. Home: 64 S Patterson Ave Apt 207 Santa Barbara CA 93111-2027 Office: Dialobic Santa Barbara Labs 5385 Hollister Ave Ste 104 Santa Barbara CA 93111-2391

RING, ROBERT JOHN, sound studio executive; b. Rockville Center, N.Y., Aug. 20, 1943; s. William V. and Helen M. (Kinney) R. Student, Hofstra U., 1961-63; diploma, Radio Engring. Inst., Fredericksburg, Va., 1968; grad., Syn-Aud-Con, Tustin, Calif., 1976, 78. Cert. FCC 1st class radiotelephone operator with radar endorsement. Announcer Sta. WFYI, Mineola, N.Y., 1960; announcer, engr. Sta. WVHC-FM, Hempstead, N.Y., 1961-66; news prodn. asst. ABC Radio, N.Y.C., 1962-63; prodn. asst. Ron Cochran and the News ABC-TV, N.Y.C., 1963-64; announcer, engr. Sta. WLIR-FM, 1964-65; sound effects artist ABC Radio-TV, N.Y.C., 1964-66, 68, per diem sound effects artist, 1969—; engr. Audio Facilities, Inc., N.Y.C., 1968-74; pres. Aquarius Sound, Inc., Pacifica, Calif., 1974—. Served with USNR, 1964-70. Mem. Audio Engring. Soc., Internat. Alliance of Theatrical Stage Employees (N.Y.C. and San Francisco locals), U.S. Naval Inst., Navy League. Roman Catholic. Avocations: sailing, music. Office: Aquarius Sound Inc 270-15 Beachview Ave Pacifica CA 94044-1509 also: Aquarius Sound Inc 580F Crespi Dr Unit F Pacifica CA 94044-3422

RING, TERRY ARTJUR, engineering educator; b. Batavia, N.Y.; s. Fay Arthur and Dorothy May (Mitchie) R.; m. Susan Regina Pitcher, Dec. 5, 1983; 1 child, Brendan Arthur. BS in Chem. Engring., Clarkson Coll., 1972; MS in Chem. Engring., U. Calif., Berkeley, 1974; PhD in Chem. Engring., Cambridge U., Eng., 1980; Prof. (hon.), Fed. Inst. Tech., Lausanne, Switzerland, 1993. Rsch. engr. Kaiser Aluminum and Chem. Co., Pleasanton, Calif., 1974-76; from asst. to assoc. prof. materials sci. and engring. MIT, Cambridge, Mass., 1980-86; prof. chem. engring. U. Utah, Salt Lake City, 1986-88, 92—; chmn., 1994—; prof. powder tech. lab. Swiss Fed. Inst. Tech., Lausanne, 1988-92; bd. dirs. Power Ball Industries, Salt Lake City; dir. Tchg. Ctr. Advanced Control Tech., Salt Lake City, 1997; vis. prof. Tokyo Sci. U., 1994. Author: Fundamentals of Ceramic Powder Processing and Synthesis, 1996; contbr. more than 80 articles to profl. jours. Earl C. Anthony fellow U. Calif., Berkeley, 1973; Oliver Gatty studentship Cambridge U., 1977-80; recipient IMB Faculty Devel. award IBM Corp., 1983-85. Mem. AIChe (adv. student chpt. 1994-97), Am. Ceramics Soc., Coun. Chem. Rsch. (mem. adminstrn. com. 1996-97), Materials Rsch. Soc., Golden Hills Neighborhood Assn. (mem. exec. bd.). Avocations: skiing, mountain climbing. Fax: (801) 585-9291. Home: 8901 Kings Hill Dr Salt Lake City UT 84121-6181 Office: U Utah Dept Chem Engring Salt Lake City UT 84112

RINGO, ROBERT GRIBBLE, [illegible] Floyd V. and Claire (Williams) R.; m. Kathryn Reese, May 24, 1953; children: Molly, Robert, Charles, Julie Ann, Mary Ellen. BS, U. Oreg., 1949; LLB, N.W. Coll. Law, Portland, Oreg., 1951. Bar: Oreg. 1951, U.S. Ct. Mil Appeals 1969, U.S. Supreme Ct. 1970, U.S. Ct. Appeals (9th Cir.) 1969. Dep. dist. atty. Benton Co., Corvallis, Oreg., 1951-53; ptnr. Ringo & Walton, Corvallis, 1953-85, Ringo, Stuber, Ensor & Hadlock P.C., Corvallis, 1986—. Bd. dirs. Good Samaritan Hosp., Corvallis, 1988—. Lt. col. USAFR, 1972. Mem. ABA, Benton County Bar Assn. (pres. 1964-65), Oreg. Bar Assn. (bd. govs. 1980-83, sec. 1982-83), ATLA (bd. govs. 1982-90), Oreg. Trial Lawyers Assn. (pres. (1979-80), Am. Bd. Trial Advs. (diplomat, nat. exec. com. 1982), State of Oreg. Profl. Responsibility Bd, State of Oregon Jud. Fitness Commn., Oregon Law Found. (Pres. 1994). Democrat. Episcopalian. Office: Ringo, Stuber, Ensor & Hadlock PC PO Box 1108 Corvallis OR 97339-1108

RINI, WILLIAM ANTHONY, communications company executive, multimedia engineer; b. L.A., Sept. 14, 1967; s. William Leonard and Vonnie Lou (Stark) R. Student, Calif. State U., Northridge, L.A. Valley Coll. Registered rep. gen. securities series 7. Investment exec. Smith Barney, Beverly Hills, Calif., 1991-93, Paine Webber, Santa Monica, Calif., 1993, Cowles Sabol, Encino, Calif., 1993-94; pres. The Syndicate, Santa Monica, Calif., 1994—; dir. programming Digital Planet, Culver City, Calif., 1995-97; sr. prodr. Lightspeed Media/Asylum Inc., Culver City, 1997-98; dir. devel. eToys, Santa Monica, 1998—. Contbr. articles to profl. jours. With U.S. Army, 1987-90. Roman Catholic.

RINKER, CHARLES FREDERICK, II, surgeon; b. Washington, Aug. 29, 1945; s. Royden Carrington and Elsie Margaret (Kilroy) R.; m. Katherine Ann Bogenreif, Oct. 10, 1982; children: Neil, Brian, Lindsay, Charles. AB, Hamilton Coll., 1967; MD, Case Western Res. U., 1971. Diplomate Am. Bd. Surgery. Intern Case Western Res U. and Affiliated Hosps., Cleve., 1971-72, resident, 1972-76; ptnr. Surg. Assoc. of Bozeman, Mont., 1976—. Co-prodr. (documentary film) Trauma Care in Montana, 1994. Trustee Intermountain Opera, Bozeman, 1985-89, Mus. of the Rockies, Bozeman, 1987-93, Polit. Economy Rsch. Ctr., Bozeman, 1988-94. Fellow ACS (pres. Mont-Wyo. chpt. 1987-88, gov. at large Mont. 1992—, chair regional com. on trauma 1994—, vice-chair com. on trauma 1994—, Trauma Achievement award 1993), Southwestern Surg. Congress. Avocations: golfing, skiing, fishing, cooking. Office: Surg Assocs Bozeman 925 Highland Blvd Ste 2200 Bozeman MT 59715-6900

RINSCH, CHARLES EMIL, insurance company executive; b. Vincennes, Ind., June 28, 1932; s. Emil and Vera Pearl (White) R.; m. Maryann Elizabeth Hitchcock, June 18, 1964; children: Christopher, Daniel, Carl. BS in Stats., Ind. U., 1953; MS in Bus., Butler U., 1959; MBA, Stanford U., 1960. Budget analyst Chrysler Corp., Indpls., 1955-57; sr. fin. analyst Ford Motor Co., Indpls., 1957-59; budget dir. Nat. Forge Co., Warren, Pa., 1960-61; div. controller and asst. to v.p., fin. Norris Industries, L.A., 1961-65; v.p., treas., sec. Teledyne Inc, L.A., 1965-88; pres., chief exec. officer Argonaut Group Inc., L.A., 1988—. Cubmaster Pack 721, Boy Scouts Am., L.A., 1987-88, treas. 1981-87; mem. dean's adv. coun. Ind. U. Sch. Bus. 1st lt. U.S. Army, 1953-55. Mem. Acad. Alumni Fellows Ind. U. Sch. Bus., L.A. Treas.'s Club. Avocations: photography, travel. Home: 19849 Greenbriar Dr Tarzana CA 91356-5428 Office: Argonaut Group Inc Ste 1175 1800 Avenue Of The Stars Los Angeles CA 90067-4221

RINSCH, MARYANN ELIZABETH, occupational therapist; b. L.A., Aug. 8, 1939; d. Harry William and Thora Analine (Langlie) Hitchcock; m. Charles Emil Rinsch, June 18, 1964; children: Christopher, Daniel, Carl. BS, U. Minn., 1961. Registered occupational therapist, Calif. Staff occupational therapist Hastings (Minn.) State Hosp., 1961-62, Neuropsychiat. Inst., L.A., 1962-64; staff and sr. occupational therapist Calif. Children's Svcs., L.A., 1964-66, head occupational therapist, 1966-68; researcher A. Jean Ayres, U. So. Calif., L.A., 1968-69; pvt. practice neurodevel. and sensory integraton Tarzana, Calif., 1969-74; pediat. occupational therapist neurodevel. & sensory integration St. Johns Hosp., Santa Monica, Calif., 1991-95; pvt. practice, cons. Santa Monica-Malibu Unified Sch. Dist., 1994—. Mem. alliance bd. Natural History Mus., L.A. County, 1983—, pres., 1998-99; cub scouts den mother Boy Scouts Am., Sherman Oaks, Calif., 1986-88, advancement chair Boy Scout Troop 474, 1989-92; mem. Vol. League San Fernando Valley, Van Nuys, Calif., 1985-93; trustee Viewpoint Sch., Calabasas, Calif., 1987-90, Valley Women's Ctr., 1990-91. Mem. Am. Occupational Therapy Assn., Calif. Occupational Therapy Assn. Home: 19849 Greenbriar Dr Tarzana CA 91356-5428

RINSKY, ARTHUR C., lawyer; b. Cin., July 10, 1944. AB with honors, U. Cin., 1966; JD cum laude, U. Mich., 1969; LLM in Taxation, NYU, 1974. Bar: Fla. 1969, Calif. 1975, U.S. Tax Ct. 1974; cert. tax specialist. Ptr. Gray, Cary, Ware & Freidenrich, P.C., Palo Alto, Calif., 1975—. Mem. ABA, State Bar Calif., Phi Beta Kappa, Phi Eta Sigma. Office: Gray Cary Ware & FreidenrichPC 400 Hamilton Ave Palo Alto CA 94301-1809*

RIORDAN, RICHARD J., mayor; b. Flushing, N.Y., 1930; m. Eugenia Riordan; 6 children (2 dec.); m. Jill Riordan. Attended, U. Calif., Santa Clara; grad., Princeton U., 1952; JD, U. Mich., 1956. With O'Melveny & Myers, L.A.; owner, operator Original Pantry Cafe; founder Total Pharmaceutical Care, Tetra Tech; mayor L.A., 1993—. Co-founder LEARN, 1991; sponsor Writing to Read computer labs Riordan Found.; active Eastside Boys and Girls Club. Lt. U.S. Army, Korea. Office: Los Angeles City Hall 200 N Spring St Rm 305 Los Angeles CA 90012-4801*

RIPLEY, DAN, automotive executive, race car driver; b. Lynchburg, Va., Sept. 7, 1946; s. John Daniel Jr. and Mary Elizabeth (Anderson) R.; m. Judith Ann Gagnalius, Jan. 16, 1975 (died 1985); 1 child, Danielle Marie; m. Kathye A Post, Aug. 7, 1998. BA, U. Va., 1970. Owner, mgr. Centennial Alfa Inc., Boulder, Colo., 1974-78; owner Dan Ripley Racing, Superior, Colo., 1979—; owner, mgr. Land Rover Boulder, Superior, Colo., 1996—; owner Maxton Components Ltd., Englewood, Colo., 1988-91; dir. Colo. Grand, Englewood, 1989-95; gen. mgr. Masterdrive of Denver, Englewood, 1992-96. V.P. Assn. Driver Educator for Disabled, 1994-96. Capt. U.S. Army, 1967-70, Vietnam. Named Nat. Champion Sports Car Club Am., 1974. Mem. Internat. Motorsports Assn., Exptl. Aircraft Assn., Aircraft Owners and Pilot Assn., Monocoupe Soc., Sigma Alpha Epsilon (Va. chpt., v.p. 1969). Avocations: flying, hiking, aircraft history. Office: Land Rover Boulder PO Box 336 1500 E Coalton Rd Superior CO 80027

RIPLEY, STUART MCKINNON, real estate consultant; b. St. Louis, July 28, 1930; s. Rob Roy and Nina Pearl (Young) R.; B.A., U. Redlands, 1952; M.B.A., U. Calif., Berkeley, 1959; m. Marilyn Haerr MacDiarmid, Dec. 28, 1964; children—Jill, Bruce, Kent. Vice pres., dir. J.H. Hedrick & Co., Santa Barbara and San Diego, 1958-63; v.p. mktg. Cavanaugh Devel. Co., San Gabriel, Calif., 1963-65; v.p. mktg. dir. Calabasas Park, Bechtel Corp., Calabasas, Calif., 1967-69; v.p. mktg. Avco Community Developers, Inc., La Jolla, Calif., 1969-74; mktg. dir. U.S. Home Corp., Fla. Div., Clearwater, 1974-75; pres., dir. Howard's Camper Country, Inc., National City, Calif., 1975-77; v.p., mktg. dir. Valcas Internat. Corp., San Diego, 1976-77, pres., 1977-79; pres. Stuart M. Ripley, Inc., 1977—, Sunview Realty, Inc., a Watt Industries Co., Santa Monica, Calif., 1979-80; owner Everett Stunz Co., Ltd., La Jolla, 1981—; exec. v.p. Harriman-Ripley Co., Fallbrook, Calif.; avocado/floraculture rancher, subdivider, Fallbrook, 1978—; lectr. UCLA, 1961; pres. Century 21 Coastal, Century 21 Bajamar, Baja California, Mex., 1994-97. Served with USN, 1952-55. U. Redlands fellow, 1960—. Mem. Nat. Assn. Homebuilders, Sales and Mktg. Council, Sales and Mktg. Execs., Pi Chi. Republican. Episcopalian. Club: Elks. Home: 2085 Via Ladeta La Jolla CA 92037-6905 Office: 7624 Girard Ave La Jolla CA 92037-4420

RIPPER, RITA JO (JODY RIPPER), strategic planner, researcher; b. Goldfield, Iowa, May 8, 1950; d. Carl Phillip and Lucille Mae (Stewart) Ripper; BA, U. Iowa, 1972; MBA, NYU, 1978. Mem. planing, rsch. and analysis staff Control Data Corp., Mpls., 1974-78; regional mgr. Raytheon Corp., Irvine, Calif., 1978-83; v.p. Caljo Corp., Des Moines, Iowa, 1980-84; asst. v.p. Bank of Am., San Francisco, 1984-88; pres. The Northhaven Co., [illegible] Bank, 1998—. Am. United; vol. Cancer, Heart, Lung Assns., Edina, N.Y.C., Calif., 1974-78, 84—. Mem. Amnesty Internat., Internat. Mktg. Assn., World Trade Ctr. Assn., Acctg. Soc. (pres. 1975-76), World Trade Club, Interfel, [illegible], Beta Alpha Psi (chmn. 1977-78), Phi Gamma Nu (v.p. 1971-72) Presbyterian. Club: Corinthian Yacht.

RIPPLINGER-COSTA, VIRGINIA (GINGER) PATRICE, television executive; b. Portsmouth, Va., Jan. 12, 1959; d. Randolph Eugene and Lois Elaine (Cuthbert) Boggs; 1 child, Michael Randolph. AA in Comml. Art, Chabot Coll., 1984. Mgr. instructional TV Chabot Coll., Hayward, Calif., 1981—; graphic artist City of Hayward, Hayward, 1996-99; owner Digital Tapestry Multimedia, Castro Valley, Calif., 1996—. Contbr. articles to profl. publs. Avocations: computer graphics, web page creation, photography. Office: Chabot Coll Instrnl TV 25555 Hesperian Blvd Hayward CA 94545-2447

RIRIE, CRAIG MARTIN, periodontist; b. Lewiston, Utah, Apr. 17, 1943; s. Martin Clarence and VaLera (Dixon) R.; m. Becky Ann Ririe, Sept. 17, 1982; children: Paige, Seth, Theron, Kendall, Nathan, Derek, Brian, Amber, Kristen. AA, San Bernadino Valley Coll., 1966; DDS, Creighton U., 1972; MSD, Loma Linda U., 1978. Staff mem. Flagstaff (Ariz.) Med. Ctr., 1974—; pvt. practice dentistry specializing in periodontics Flagstaff, 1974—; assoc. prof. periodontics No. Ariz. U., Flagstaff, 1979—, chmn. dept. dental hygiene, 1980-81; med. research cons. W.L. Gore, Flagstaff, 1983—. Contbr. articles to profl. jours. Vice pres. bd. dirs. Grand Canyon coun. Boy Scouts Am., 1991—. Lt. col. USAFR. Health professions scholarship Creighton U., Omaha, 1969-71; recipient Mosby award Mosby Pub. Co., 1972; research fellowship U. Bergen, Norway, 1978-79. Mem. ADA, Am. Acad. Periodontology (cert.), Western Soc. Periodontology (chmn. com. on rsch. 1982—, bd. dirs. 1983—), No. Ariz. Dental Soc. (pres. 1994-96), Am. Acad. Oral Implantologists, Internat. Congress Oral Implantologists, Ariz. Dental Assn., Am. Cancer Soc. (bd. dirs.), Flagstaff C. of C., Rotary. Republican. Mem. LDS Ch. Avocations: skiing, tennis, golf. Home: 141 W 2600 N Pleasant Grove UT 84062-9408 Office: 1050 N San Francisco St Flagstaff AZ 86001-3259

RISCH, JAMES E., lawyer; b. Milw., May 3, 1943; s. Elroy A. and Helen B. (Levi) R.; m. Vicki L. Choborda, June 8, 1968; children—James E., Jason S., Jordan D. B.S. in Forestry, U. Idaho, 1965, J.D., 1968. Dep. pros. atty. Ada County, Idaho, 1968-69, chief dep. pros. atty., 1969-70, pros. atty., 1971-75; mem. Idaho Senate, 1974-88, 95—, majority leader, 1977-82, 97—, pres. pro tem, 1983-88, asst. majority leader, 1996; ptnr. Risch Goss & Insinger, Boise, Idaho, 1975—; prof. law Boise State U., 1972-75. Bd. dirs. Nat. Dist. Attys. Assn., 1973; pres. Idaho Prosecuting Attys., 1973; chmn. George Bush Presdl. Campaign, Idaho, 1988; gen. counsel Idaho Rep. Party, 1991—. Mem. ABA, Idaho Bar Assn., Boise Bar Assn., Ducks Unlimited, Nat. Rifle Assn., Nat. Cattlemans Assn., Idaho Cattlemans Assn., Am. Angus Assn., Idaho Angus Assn., Am. Legis. Exch. Coun., Boise Valley Angus Assn., Phi Delta Theta, Xi Sigma Pi. Republican. Roman Catholic. Avocations: hunting, fishing, skiing. Home: 5400 S Cole Rd Boise ID 83709-6401 Office: Risch Goss & Insinger 407 W Jefferson St Boise ID 83702-6012

RISLEY, TODD ROBERT, psychologist, educator; b. Palmer, Alaska, Sept. 8, 1937; s. Robert and Eva Lou (Todd) R.; 1 child, Todd Michael; m. Cheryl Thomas, Mar. 30, 1996. A.B. with distinction in Psychology, San Diego State Coll., 1960; M.S., U. Wash., 1963, Ph.D., 1966. Asst. prof. psychology Fla. State U., Tallahassee, 1964-65; research assoc. Bur. Child Research, U. Kans., Lawrence, 1965-77, sr. scientist, 1977—, asst. prof. dept. human devel., 1967-69, assoc. prof., 1969-73, prof., 1973-84; prof. psychology U. Alaska, Anchorage, 1982—; pres. Ctr. for Applied Behavior Analysis, 1970-82; dir. Johnny Cake Child Study Ctr., Mansfield, Ark., 1973-74; vis. prof. U. Auckland (N.Z.), 1978; acting dir. Western Carolina Ctr., Morgantown, N.C., 1981; dir. Alaska Div. Mental Health and Devel. Disabilities, 1988-91; cons. in field to numerous orgns. and instns. Co-author: The Infant Center, 1977, Shopping with Children: Advice for parents, 1978, The Toddler Center, 1979, Meaningful Differences, 1995; editor: Jour. Applied Behavior Analysis, 1971-74; mng. editor: Behavior Therapy, The Behavior Therapist, Behavioral Asessment, 1977-80; mem. editl. bds. of numerous profl. jours.; contbr. revs. and numerous articles. Co-chmn. Fla. task force on use of behavioral procedures in state programs for retarded, 1974—; mem. resident abuse investigating com. div. retardation Fla. Dept. Health and Rehab. Services, 1972—; mem. adv. com. Social Research Inst., U. Utah, 1977—; mem. Alaska Gov.'s Council on Handicapped and Gifted, 1983-88, NIH Mental Retardation Research Com., 1987-88, Alaska Mental Health Bd., 1988. Grantee NIMH, 1971-72, 72-73; research grantee Nat. Ctr. Health Services, 1976-79; grantee Nat. Inst. Edn., 1973, NIH, 1967—. Fellow Am. Psychol. Assn. (coun. of reps. 1982-85, pres. div. 25, 1989), Am. Psychol. Soc.; mem. AAAS, Am. Assn. Mental Deficiency, Assn. Advancement of Behavior Therapy (dir. 1975-80, pres. 1976-77, chmn. profl. rev. com. 1977—, series editor Readings in Behavior Therapy 1977—), Soc. Behavioral Medicine, Assn. Behavior Analysis, Sigma Xi. Office: U Alaska-Anchorage Dept Psychology 3211 Providence Dr Anchorage AK 99508-4614

RISSER, ARTHUR CRANE, JR., zoo administrator; b. Blackwell, Okla., July 8, 1938; s. Arthur Crane and Mary Winn (Stevenson) R.; children: Michelle W., Stephen C., Michael R. BA, Grinnell Coll., Iowa, 1960; MA, U. Ariz., Tucson, 1963; PhD, U. Calif., Davis, 1970. Mus. technician, Smithsonian Instn., Washington, 1963-64; research assoc. Sch. Medicine U. Md., Balt., 1964-65; grad. teaching asst. U. Calif., Davis, 1965-70; asst. prof. biology U. Nev.-Reno, 1970-74; asst. curator birds Zool. Soc. San Diego, 1974-76, curator birds, 1976-81, gen. curator birds, 1981-86; gen. mgr. San Diego Zoo, 1986—; co-chmn. Calif. Condor Working Group on Captive Breeding and Reintroduction, 1983-85; mem. Calif. Condor Recovery Team, 1984-86. Treas., Planned Parenthood, Reno, 1972; bd. dirs. Internat. Found. Conservation Birds, 1979-88, Conservation Rsch. Found. of Papua New Guinea, 1991—. Fellow Am. Assn. Zool. Parks and Aquariums. Office: San Diego Zoo PO Box 120551 San Diego CA 92112-0551*

RISSER, PAUL GILLAN, academic administrator, botanist; b. Blackwell, Okla., Sept. 14, 1939; s. Paul Crane and Jean (McCluskey) R.; children: David, Mark, Stephen, Scott. BA, Grinnell Coll., 1961; MS in Botany, U. Wis., 1965, PhD in Botany and Soils, 1967. From asst. prof. to prof. botany U. Okla., 1967-81, also asst. dir. biol. sta., chmn. dept. botany and microbiology, 1977-81; dir. Okla. Biol. Survey, 1971-77; chief Ill. Natural History Survey, 1981-86; program dir., ecosystem studies NSF; provost and v.p. acad. affairs U. N.Mex., 1989-92; former pres. Miami U., Oxford, Ohio; pres. Oreg. State U., 1996—. Author: (with Kathy Cornelison) Man and the Biosphere, 1979, (with others) The True Prairie Ecosystem, 1981; research, numerous publs. in field. Trustee Pioneer Multi-County Library Bd. Mem. Am. Acad. Arts and Scis., Ecol. Soc. Am. (pres.), Brit. Ecol. Soc., Soc. Range Mgmt., Southwestern Assn. Naturalists (pres.), Am. Inst. Biol. Sci. (pres.), Torrey Bot. Club. Presbyterian. Office: Oregon State University Kerr Adminstrn Bldg Office of the Pres Corvallis OR 97331-8507*

RISTINE, JEFFREY ALAN, reporter; b. Ann Arbor, Mich., Apr. 21, 1955; s. Harold G. and Amelita (Schmidt) R.; m. Karen Lin Clark, Oct. 27, 1996. BA, U. Mich., 1977. Reporter The Midland (Mich) Times, 1978-79, Johnstown (Pa.) Tribune-Dem., 1979-80, San Diego Tribune, 1980-92, San Diego Union-Tribune, 1992—. Recipient Appreciation award Am. Planning Assn., San Diego sect., 1988; named Best polit./govt. reporter San Diego Press Club, 1986. Avocations: puzzle-solving, bicycling, cat photography. Office: San Diego Union-Tribune 350 Camino De La Reina San Diego CA 92108-3003

RISTOW, BRUNNO, plastic surgeon; b. Brusque, Brazil, Oct. 18, 1940; came to U.S., 1967, naturalized, 1981; s. Arno and Ally Odette (von Buettner) R.; student Coll. Sinodal, Brazil, 1956-57, Coll. Julio de Castilhos, Brazil, 1957-58; M.D. magna cum laude, U. Brazil, 1966; m. Urannia Carrasquilla Gutierrez, Nov. 10, 1979; children by previous marriage: Christian Kilian, Trevor Roland. Intern in surgery Hosp. dos Estrangeiros, Rio de Janeiro, Brazil, 1965, Hospital Estadual Miguel Couto, Brazil, 1965-66, Instituto Aposentadoria Pensão Comerciarios Hosp. for Gen. Surgery, 1966; resident in plastic and reconstructive surgery, Dr. Ivo Pitanguy Hosp. Santa Casa de Misericordia, Rio de Janeiro, 1967; fellow Inst. of Reconstructive Plastic Surgery, N.Y. U. Med. Center, N.Y.C., 1967-68, jr. resident, 1971-72, sr. and chief resident, 1972-73; practice medicine specializing in plastic surgery, Rio de Janeiro, 1967, N.Y.C., 1968-73, San Francisco, 1973—; asst. surgeon N.Y. Hosp., Cornell Med. Center, N.Y.C., 1968-71; clin. instr. surgery N.Y. U. Sch. of Medicine, 1972-73; chmn. plastic and reconstructive surgery div. Presbyn. Hosp., Pacific Med. Center, San Francisco, 1974-92, chmn. emeritus, 1992—. Served with M.C., Brazilian Army Res., 1959-60. Decorated knight Venerable Order of St. Hubertus; Knight Order St. John of Jerusalem; fellow in surgery Cornell Med. Sch., 1968-71; diplomate Am. Bd. Plastic and Reconstructive Surgery. Fellow A.C.S., Internat. Coll. Surgeons; mem. Am. Soc. Aesthetic Plastic Surgery (chmn. edn.), Am. Soc. Plastic and Reconstructive Surgeons, Internat. Soc. Aesthetic Plastic Surgeons, Calif. Soc. Plastic Surgeons, AMA (Physician's Recognition award 1971-83), Calif. Med. Assn., San Francisco Med. Assn. Republican. Mem. Evang. Lutheran Ch. Club: San Francisco Olympic. Contbg. author: Cancer of the Hand, 1975, Current Therapy in Plastic and Reconstructive Surgery, 1988, Male Aesthetic Surgery, 1989, How They Do It: Procedures in Plastic and Reconstructive Surgery, 1990, Middle Crus: The Missing Link in Alar Cartilage Anatomy, 1991, Surgical Technology International, 1992, Aesthetic Plastic Surgery, 1993, Mastery of Surgery: Plastic and Reconstructive Surgery, 1993; Reoperative Aesthetic Plastic Surgery of the Face and Breast, 1994, 95; contbr. articles on plastic surgery to profl. publs. Office: Calif Pacific Med Ctr 2100 Webster St San Francisco CA 94115-2373

RITACCO, PATSY RICHARD, sales executive; b. Newark, Aug. 27, 1956; s. Michael Patsy and Adelaide (Caruso) R.; m. Linda La Falce, Nov. 5, 1978; children: Michael A., Patsy Richard Jr. B of History, William Paterson Coll., 1978. Notary pub., N.J., 1990—. Tchr. Belleville (N.J.) High Sch., 1978-82; bd. pneumatics Robert Tool, Saddle Brook, N.J., 1983-94; dist. sales mgr. Standard Abrasives, Simi Valley, Calif., 1994—; concert promotion dir. for edn. groups of 50s and 60s, Brooklyn Bridge, Coasters, 1980—; guest lectr. in field. Contbr. poetry to anthologies. Fellow Christ Ch. Sch. Bd., bldgs. & grounds publ rels., 1985-88; assoc. mem. Mus. Natural History; scholar bd. Unico Nat., Nutley, N.J., 1995—, treas., 1998-99. Mem. Soc. Engrs. (contbg.), Platers Assn. (contbg.), Am. Softball Assn. (assoc.). Roman Catholic. Avocations: reading, cooking, music, sports. Home: 45 Edgar Pl Nutley NJ 07110-1747 Office: Standard Abrasives 4201 Guardian St Simi Valley CA 93063-3372

RITCHEY, SAMUEL DONLEY, JR., retired retail store executive; b. Derry Twp., Pa., July 16, 1933; s. Samuel Donley and Florence Catherine (Litsch) R.; m. Sharon Marie Anderson, Apr. 6, 1956; children: Michael Donley, Tamara Louise, Shawn Christopher. BS, San Diego State U., 1955, MS, 1963; postgrad., Stanford U., 1964. With Lucky Stores Inc., 1951-61, 64-86, pres., chief operating officer, 1978-80, pres., chief exec. officer, 1980-81, chmn., chief exec. officer, 1981-85, chmn. bd., 1981-86; bd. dirs. SBC Comms. The McClatchey Co., De La Salle Inst., Liberty House, Rosenberg, FDT; grad. mgr. San Diego State U., 1961-63; lectr. in field; past chmn. Calif. Power Exchange, mem. adv. coun. Grad. Sch. Bus., Stanford U. Sloan Found. fellow. Mem. Mex. Am. Legal Def. and Edn. Fund, Western Assn. Food Chains (bd. dirs., pres.), Food Mktg. Inst. (bd. dirs., vice chmn.), Sloan Alumni Assn. (adv. bd., pres.). Office: 485 Hartz Ave Ste 105 Danville CA 94526-3803

RITCHIE, ANNE, educational administrator; b. Grants Pass, Oreg., July 1, 1944; d. William Riley Jr. and Allie Brown (Clark) R.; m. Charles James Cooper, Sept. 4, 1968 (div. 1985); children: Holly Anne, Wendy Nicole. BA in Edn. with honors, Calif. State U., Sacramento, 1981. Cert. elem. tchr., Calif. CEO El Rancho Schs., Inc., Carmichael, Calif., 1981—; citizen amb. del. People to People Internat., Russia, Lithuania, Hungary, 1993, China, 1994. Active Crocker Art Mus.; mem. Rep. Senatorial Inner Circle, Washington, 1998. Mem. AAUW, Nat. Assn. Edn. for Young Children, Profl. Assn. Childhood Educators, Nat. Child Care Assn. Episcopalian. Avocations: traveling, skiing, reading.

RITCHIE, CATHERINE D., correctional officer, deputy marshal; b. Lynwood, Calif., Aug. 22, 1954; d. Harold Francis and Betty J. (Matlock) R.; m. Walter B. Ritchie Jr., July 21, 1977; children: Jeffrey, Bradley. Bookkeeper, sec. Severy Dental Labs., Orange, Calif., 1972-74, Shell Oil Co., Santa Ana, Calif., 1974-77; owner, ptnr. Vista (Calif.) Chevron Co., 1977-78; sec.-treas. Am. Battery Corp., Escondido, Calif., 1978-85; owner, operator Sophisticated 2ds, Vista, 1983-85, Bridal Elegance, Escondido, 1984-87; sr. correctional officer Humboldt County Sheriff's Dept., Eureka, Calif., 1988—; dep. marshal North Humboldt Jud. Dist., Arcata, Calif., 1991—; sgt. correction divsn. Humboldt County Sheriff's Dept., Arcata, 1991—, jail compliance sgt., vice chmn. jail population mgmt. team, 1995—; Co-pub. How to Avoid Auto Repair Rip-offs, 1981. Mem. Nat. Bridal Service (cert., cons.), Nat. Assn. Female Execs., Escondido C. of C., Calif. Farm Bur. Republican.

RITCHIE, DANIEL LEE, academic administrator; b. Springfield, Ill., Sept. 19, 1931; s. Daniel Felix and Jessie Dee (Binney) R. B.A., Harvard U., 1954, M.B.A., 1956. Exec. v.p. MCA, Inc., Los Angeles, 1967-70; pres. Archon Pure Products Co., Los Angeles, 1970-73; exec. v.p. Westinghouse Electric Corp., Pitts., 1975-78; pres. corp. staff and strategic planning Westinghouse Broadcasting Co., 1978-79, pres., chief exec. officer, 1979-81, chmn., chief exec. officer; chmn., chief exec. officer Westinghouse Broadcasting & Cable, Inc., 1981-87; owner Grand River Ranch, Kremmling, Colo., 1977—, Rancho Cielo, Montecito, Calif., 1977—; chancellor U. Denver, 1989—. With U.S. Army, 1956-58. Office: U Denver Office of the Chancellor University Park Denver CO 80208*

RITCHIE, JOHN BENNETT, real estate executive; b. West Point, N.Y., Sept. 23, 1924; s. Isaac and Charlotte (Bennett) R.; B.A., Yale, 1946; postgrad. student George Washington U., 1946-47, U. Wash. Law Sch., 1948-50; m. Suzanne Raisin, Dec. 27, 1952; children—Randolph, Charlotte, Mark, Victoria. Pres. Ritchie & Ritchie Corp., indsl. and comml. realtors, San Francisco, Oakland, San Jose, Sacramento, Walnut Creek, Calif., Ritchie & Ritchie Ins. Brokers, Inc.; v.p. Cotton-Ritchie Corp., San Diego, Ritchie MacFarland Corp., Portland, Oreg.; owner, trustee Ritchie-Chancery Bldg., Barrett-Ritchie Block, Ritchie & Ritchie Devel. Co., Ritchie Western Mortgage Corp., Ritchie Western Equities Co.; past mem. San Francisco Planning Commn.; past mem. San Francisco Landmarks Bd.; hon. counsul Uruguay. With AUS. Mem. Soc. Indsl. Realtors, Calif. Assn. of Realtors (v.p. (1967), San Francisco (pres. 1966), Oakland, San Jose real estate bds., Calif. Hist. Soc. (pres. 1973), Japan Soc. San Francisco (pres. 1976). Republican. Mem. Ch. of Jesus Christ of Latter-day Saints (elder). Clubs: Presidio Golf (San Francisco); Tahoe Yacht (Lake Tahoe); Alta (Salt Lake City); Brook (N.Y.); Caledonian (London); Outrigger Canoe (Honolulu). Home: 1201 Greenwich St Apt 400 San Francisco CA 94109-1583 also: 209 S Meadow Rd Glenbrook NV 89413 also: 989 Rutherford Cross Rd Rutherford CA 94573 also: 247 Beach Walk Honolulu HI 96815-1995 Office: 41 Sutter St 200 Ritchie Chancery Bldg San Francisco CA 94104 also: 401 15th St Oakland CA 94612-2801 also: 34 W Santa Clara St San Jose CA 95113-1806 also: 233 A St Ste 1400 San Diego CA 92101-4010 also: 133 SW 2nd Ave Portland OR 97204-3534

RITSEMA, FREDRIC A., lawyer; b. Kansas City, Mo., Feb. 12, 1951. AB, Calvin Coll., 1973; JD, U. Colo., 1976. Bar: Colo. 1976. Ptnr. Ritsema & Lyon PC, 1993; mem. subcoms. Workers' Compensation. Mem. Denver Bar Assn., Colo. Def. Lawyers Assn. Office: Ritsema & Lyon PC 999 18th St Ste 3100 Denver CO 80202-2499

RITTER, RUSSELL JOSEPH, mayor, college official; b. Helena, Mont., July 22, 1932; s. Walter A. and SallyC. (Mellen) R.; m. Linaire Wells, Aug. 4, 1956; children—Michael, Leslie, Teresa, Gregory, Daniel. Student Carroll Coll., Helena, 1950-53; A.B. in History, U. Mont.-Missoula, 1957, M.A. in History and Polit. Sci., 1962, postgrad. in History, 1963. Salesman, Capital Ford, 1953-54, 56-57; tchr., coach Billings (Mont.) Central High Sch., 1957-58, Loyola High Sch., Missoula, 1958-62, Flathead High Sch., Kalispell, Mont., 1962-69; dir. devel. and community relations Carroll Coll., Helena, 1969-76, v.p. for coll. relations, 1976-91; dir. corp. & govt. rels. Washington Corp., 1991—; pres. Dennis & Phyllis Washington Found., Helena; commr. City of Helena, 1977-80, mayor pro-tem, 1980, mayor, 1981—; exec. sec.-treas. Carroll Coll. Found., Inc.; owner Danny's Drive In, Kalispell, 1965-69; ptnr. R-B Enterprises, Inc., Kalispell, 1967-71; bd. dirs. Brubaker & Assos., Inc., Kalispell, 1971-74; v.p. Capital Investment, Inc. (KMTX Radio), Helena, 1973-80; pres. Swinging Door Art Gallery, Inc., Helena, 1973—; bd. dirs. Norwest Bank of Helena. Bd. dirs. All Am. Indian Hall of Fame, 1972-78, Jr. Achievement, 1975-79, Mont. Physicians Service, 1984-86, Blue Cross/Blue Shield Mont., 1986—, Mont. C. of C., chmn., Mont. Community Fin. Corp., 1986; bd. govs. Mont. Spl. Olympics, 1984-86; mem. Citizen's Adv. Council, 1975-76; chmn. City-County Bldg., Inc., 1978; mem. Mont. Friendship Force; co-chmn. Mont. Centenial Celebration. Served with USMC, 1953-56. Mem. Helena C. of C. (dir. 1972-75, v.p. 1973, pres. 1974, Ambassador's Club 1976—, chmn. 1978), Mont. Ofcls. Assn., Mont. Ambassadors (Ambassador of Yr. 1986, bd. dirs. 1989, 2d v.p. 1989, pres. 1991). Club: Montana. Lodge: K.C. (4th degree).*

RITTER, SALLIE, painter, sculptor; b. Las Cruces, N.Mex., May 9, 1947; d. John Barnes Ritter and Billie Ruth (Carter) Simpson; m. Kent Frederick Jacobs, Apr. 13, 1971. Student, U. Rome Coll. Art History, 1965, Edinburgh (Scotland) Coll. Art, 1967-68; BA, Colo. Coll., 1969. One-woman shows include Lubbock (Tex.) Art Ctr., 1970, N.Mex. Arts Commn., Santa Fe, 1974, Las Cruces Cmty. Ctr., 1975, Aldridge Fine Arts, Albuquerque, 1980, Woodrow Wilson Fine Arts, Santa Fe, 1989, Adobe Patio Gallery, Mesilla, N.Mex., 1991, 93, Contemporary Southwest Galleries, Santa Fe, 1996, 97, 98, Adair Margo Gallery, 1997; exhibited in group shows at El Paso (Tex.) Mus. Art, 1988, Colorado Springs (Colo.) Fine Arts Ctr., 1995, Laguna Gloria Mus., Austin, Tex., 1979, Santa Fe Festival of the Arts, 1979, 83, The Governor's Gallery, Santa Fe, 1987, 94, Pioneer's Mus., Colo. Springs, 1985, 86, 88, N.Mex. State U., Las Cruces, 1988, 89, Dona Ana Arts Coun., Las Cruces, 1992, Tex. Commn. Arts, Austin, 1987, Tucson Mus. Art, 1995, Nat. Cowboy Hall of Fame, Oklahoma City, 1996, Autry Mus. Western Art, L.A., 1996, Albuquerque Mus. Art, 1996; represented in permanent collections U. Tex. Sch. of Law, Phelps Dodge Corp., Norwest Bank, Albuquerque, N.Mex. State U., Mus. N.Mex., Santa Fe, Nat. Mus. Women in Arts, Washington; featured in Contemporary Women Artists, 1984, Contemporary Western Artists, 1985, Houses in Time, 1997. Bd. dirs. Women's Bd., Mus. N.Mex., Santa Fe, 1987—, Dona Ana Arts Coun., Las Cruces, 1990—. Mem. Nat. Mus. of Women in the Arts. Episcopalian. Home and Studio: 3610 Southwind Rd Las Cruces NM 88005-5556 also: 1114 Main Rd Ruidoso NM 88345-6226

RITTER, WALTER ADOLF, minister, educator; b. Edmonton, Alta., Can., June 24, 1932; s. Carl and Natalie (Gliege) R.: m. Doris Pauline Elizabeth Andres, June 11, 1957; 1 child, Libby (dec. Nov. 1984). BA, Concordia Sem., 1954, BD, 1957; STM, Luth. Theol. Sem., 1985. Ordained to ministry Luth. Ch., 1957. Pastor Christ Luth. Ch., MacNutt, Sask., Can., 1957-60, Faith Luth. Ch., Winnipeg, Man., Can., 1960-67, Bethel Luth Ch., Edmonton, 1967-76; instr. Augustana Univ. Coll., Camrose, Alta., 1976-97, coord. Coll. Theology and The Arts, 1988-94, coord. for theol. lecture series, 1990-96, ret., 1996; nat. coord. coll. and univ. work for Luth. Ch. Can., 1966-70; mem. joint commn. Inter-Luth. Rels., 1961-67; chmn. Edmonton bd. control, Concordia Coll. 1973-75, chmn. master plan com., 1975-76; participant 1st Nat. Luth.-Roman Cath. ch. dialogue, 1969. Contbr. articles to religious jours. Home: 403 Park Place N, 4625-50 Street, Camrose, AB Canada T4V 4R2

RITZ, RICHARD ELLISON, architect, architectural historian, writer; b. Colfax, Wash., Dec. 8, 1919; s. Henry Clay and Katharine Fredericka (Failing) R.; m. Evelyn R. Robinson, Sept. 21, 1940; children: Margaret Karen Ritz Barss, Susan Elizabeth Ritz Williams. Student, Whitman Coll., 1936-37. Registered architect, Oreg. Draftsman, job capt. Pietro Belluschi, Architect, Portland, Oreg., 1946-51; project mgr., chief prodn. Belluschi and Skidmore, Owings & Merrill, Portland, 1951-56; project mgr., then gen. mgr. Skidmore, Owings & Merrill, Portland, 1956-82; pvt. practice architecture Portland, 1982-94; founder Greenhills Press, 1991. Author: A History of the Reed College Campus, 1990, An Architect Looks at Downtown Portland, 1991, The Central Library Portland's Crown Jewel, 1998; editor: A Guide to Portland Architecture, 1968; contbr. articles to profl. jours. Bd. dirs. Architecture Found., Portland, 1982-85; mem. Portland Hist. Landmarks Commn., 1987-98. Sgt. USAF, 1942-45. Fellow AIA (bd. dirs. Portland chpt. 1975-79, pres. 1978, mem. handbook com. Fin. Mgmt. for Architects 1980); mem. Soc. Archtl. Historians, Oreg. Coun. Architects (del. 1975-79), Portland Art Mus., Oreg. Hist. Soc., Lang Syne Soc., City Club Portland, Univ. Club (Portland), Multnomah Athletic Club. Presbyterian. Home and Office: 4550 SW Greenhills Way Portland OR 97221-3214

RIVE, SARELLE ROSELYN, retired manufacturing company executive; d. Max and Ruth Rae (Goldring) Rive; m. Norman E. Friedmann, June 22, 1952 (div. Nov. 1985); children: Marc David, Lance Alan, Keyla Ilene Treitman; m. Robert A. Suhosky, July 4, 1986 (div. July 1994); m. Steven Miller, June 7, 1998. BA with honors, Barat Coll., 1977. Owner, dir. Gallerie Sarelle, Highland Park, Ill., 1977-78, L.A., 1982-84, 86-90; owner, dir. A Neat Idea By Sarelle, L.A., 1992—; silver level exec. Quorum Internat., L.A., 1993-96; pres. Internat. Export Concepts, L.A., 1994-96; CFO Universal Diesel Products, Inc. USA subs., Vancouver, B.C., Can., 1995-96, ret., 1996. Den mother, pack leader cub scout troop Boy Scouts Am., 1959-63; day camp dir., leader Girl Scouts U.S., L.A., 1966-73; bd. dirs. YWCA, Highland Park, Ill., 1974-77; docent Mus. of Contemporary Art, L.A., 1985-88; assoc. Older People in a Caring Atmosphere (OPICA), L.A., 1981—; founding mem. Nat. Mus. Women in Arts, Washington, 1993—, Mus. Contemporary Art, L.A., 1985-93; mem. president's cir. L.A. County Mus. of Art, 1987—, mem. president's cir. of patrons. 1993-95. Mem. City of Hope (life), Kappa Gamma Pi, Delta Epsilon Sigma. Jewish. Avocations: travel, walking, jigsaw puzzles, biking, swimming. Home and Office: 811 Marguerita Ave Santa Monica CA 90402-1939

RIVERA, GEORGE, field investigator, security consultant; b. N.Y.C., Nov. 29, 1959; s. George Franco Rivera and Sara (Diaz) Perez; m. Linda Marie Donnelly, Apr. 12, 1986. AS, Mt. San Antonio Coll., 1994; BS, U. La Verne, 1996. Cert. in risk mgmt., Calif.; cert. fraud examiner. EMT Arcadia-Monrovia Amb. Svc., Monrovia, Calif., 1979-81; dep. sheriff Los Angeles County Sheriff's Dept., L.A., 1981-94; legal investigator Miramar Rsch. Group, Alta Loma, Calif., 1994—; cons. Rex Gutierrez for Congress Com., Rancho Cucamonga, Calif., 1995-96; labor rep. Assn. L.A. Dep. Sheriff's, L.A., 1982-94. Mem. Am. Soc. for Indsl. Security, Calif. Assn. Lic. Investigators, Assn. Cert. Fraud Examiners. Republican. Roman Catholic. Avocations: boating, water sports. Office: Kaiser Permanente Investigations Unit 94 S Los Robles Ave Ste 320 Pasadena CA 91101-2474

RIVERA, MILUKA, actress, journalist, writer; b. San Juan, P.R., Mar. 24, 1953; d. Francisco and Fidelina (Rabell) R.; m. Paul Navarre Matlovsky, Sept. 28, 1981; children: Élan Lixander, Miluette Nalin Matlovsky. Student, Inter-Am. U., Hato Rey, P.R., 1971-74; diploma in pub. rels., U. P.R., Rio Piedras, 1974; student in writing and journalism, UCLA, 1986. Lic. in real estate, Calif. Model Polianna/Barbizon, San Juan, 1968-74; instr. modeling, advisor, co-founder Barbizon Sch. of Modeling, San Juan, 1971-74; freelance dir., 1994—; hostess Buena Vista Cable TV, L.A., 1997—; instr. acting, modeling and etiquette Creative Arts Ctr., Burbank, Calif., 1998—. *Noted artist, awarded union leader/activist. Recently honored by Puerto Rico's House of Representatives for founding the Screen Actors Guild office in Puerto Rico. First Latina to receive SAG's "Joseph C. Riley Service Award." Co-founded/chaired many Guild's committees. Former beauty queen, lecturer, teacher, playwright and correspondent. Written hundreds of poems, children's plays and Spanish episodes, "The Extraordinary" starring Ricardo Montalban. Wrote/directed/produced with husband, Paul Navarre Matlovsky, the documentary, "Ignacio Gomez: An Artist Against All Odds." Member, Guild's Actors for Literacy. Nonviolence advocate. Her favorite quote, Joseph Campbell's "every culture's behavior is largely molded by it's myth makers and storytellers".* Appeared in T.V. shows including Kojak, Nurse and Gen. Hosp.; films include Taxi Driver, All That Jazz, Fort Apache: The Bronx; prodr. documentaries, published poem book and tribute, "Unequal Raul Julia"; author Ethnic Talent Directory, 1998; contbr. articles to profl. publs. Founder, pres. Alliance of Latin Artists, N.Y.C., 1982-84. Recipient Governor Mario Cuomo's Citation award for service, N.Y.C., 1984, Excellent Svc. award Assn. Cronistas Espectaculo, N.Y.C., 1996. Mem. AFTRA, SAG (nat. bd. dirs. 1992-93, originator, chair com., 1998—), Actors Equity Assn. Avocations: poetry, drawing, ballroom dancing, horseback riding, skiing. Office: ALAS Prodns PO Box 172 Burbank CA 91503

RIVERA, ROBERT LEROY, university administrator, educator; b. San Diego, Calif., Feb. 13, 1921; s. Reynaldo Jose and Maude (LaMain) R.; m. Barbara Ann Clark, June 23, 1963; children: Randall, Marla Baker, Caryl Blue, Clark. AB, U. So. Calif., 1945, MA in Speech Comm., 1947. Cert. gen. secondary tchr. (life), Calif., community coll. supervisory credential, Calif. Head history dept. Adolph Leutzinger H.S., Lawndale, Calif., 1947; dir. dramatics Bonita Union H.S., LaVerne, Calif., 1947, 48, San Pedro

(Calif.) H.S., 1948-53, Eagle Rock (Calif.) H.S., 1953-56; chmn. theatre arts L.A. Valley Coll., Van Nuys, Calif., 1956-70; dist. coord. instructional TV L.A. Community Coll. Dist., 1970-78; dir. forensics U. LaVerne, Calif., 1978—; cons., sales trainer Don Baxter Co., Glendale, Calif., 1957-59; speech cons. City Nat. Bank, Beverly Hills, Calif., 1960-70. Contbr. articles to profl. publs. With USMC, 1943-45. Fellow Toastmasters Internat. (gov. greater L.A. dist., 1982-83), Univ. club of Claremont Calif. (membership chmn.). Republican. Avocations: professional speaking, tennis. Home: 2319 Chapman Rd La Crescenta CA 91214-3014 Office: Univ LaVerne 1950 3rd St La Verne CA 91750-4443

RIZZI, TERESA MARIE, bilingual speech and language pathologist; b. Denver, Aug. 8, 1964; d. Theophilus Marcus and Maudie Marie (Pitts) R. BA in Speech Pathology, U. Denver, 1986, BA in Spanish, 1986; MS in Speech Pathology, Vanderbilt U., 1988. Pediatric speech-lang. pathologist Rose Med. Ctr., Denver, 1988-90; pvt. practice Denver, 1990—; Spanish tchr. Temple Emanual, Denver, 1992-95; owner, operator Niños De Colo., Denver, Talk of The Town Speech-Lang. Pathologists; Spanish tutor and interpreter, Denver, 1988—; bilingual pediatric speech-lang. pathologist The Children's Hosp., Denver, 1994-98, United Cerebral Palsy Assn., 1998-99; presenter in field. G'arin grantee Ctrl. Agy. Jewish Edn., 1993, grantee U. No. Colo. Grad. Sch., 1994. Mem. Am. Speech-Lang.-Hearing Assn. (Continuing Edn. award 1991), Colo. Speech-Lang.-Hearing Assn., Internat. Assn. Orofacial Myology, Phi Sigma Iota. Avocations: computers, chess. Office: Talk of the Town Speech-Lang Pathologists 695 S Colorado Blvd Ste 410 Denver CO 80246-8014

RIZZO, MARY ANN FRANCES, international trade executive, former educator; b. Bryn Mawr, Pa., Jan. 11, 1942; d. Joseph Franklyn and Armella Louise (Grubenhoff) R. BA magna cum laude (N.Y. State scholar), Marymount-Manhattan Coll., 1963; MA (fellow), Yale U., 1965, PhD (Lounsbury-Cross fellow), 1969; postgrad. Harvard U. Bus. Sch., 1979. Instr. Romance langs. and lit. Yale U., New Haven, 1966-70; asst. prof. Finch Coll., N.Y.C., 1971-73; v.p. Joseph F. Rizzo Co., Fla., 1969-87; owner, pres., 1987—; minister of the Word coordinator Our Lady of Perpetual Help Ch., Scottsdale, Ariz., 1986—, eucharistic min.; mem. bd. adv. Assn. Internat. des Etudiants en Sciences Economiques et Commerciales, Ariz. State U. Vice chmn., charter mem. bd. regents Cath. U. Am.; mem., coord. export counseling svc. Ariz. Dist. Export Coun.; 2d v.p. bd. advisors sch. bus. mgmt. Ariz. State U., Phoenix; bd. advisors bus. studies Paradise Valley (Ariz.) C.C. Mem. Il Circolo Italian Cultural Club (Palm Beach, Fla.), Fgn. Trade Coun. Palm Beach County (charter mem.), World Affairs Coun. of Ariz., Scottsdale C. of C. (internat. bus. devel. com.), World Trade Ctr., Alpha Chi. Republican. Roman Catholic (community coun. 1972-74). Clubs: Harvard Bus. Sch. Greater N.Y., Yale (N.Y.C. and Phoenix), Alliance Francaise (Phoenix), Ariz., Yale of Palm Beaches, Cercle Français de Palm Beach (Fla.), Ariz. Harvard Bus. Sch. Translator: From Time to Eternity, 1967; bibliographer: Italian Literature-Roots and Branches, 1976. Home: Villa Serein 2170 Ibis Isle Rd Palm Beach FL 33480-5350 Address: 5665 N 74th Pl Scottsdale AZ 85250-6416 Office: 7436 E Stetson Dr Ste 180 Scottsdale AZ 85251-3545

ROA (BURKHART), JOANN VIRGINIA, writer; b. Crookston, Minn.; d. Casper T. Roe and Andrea Quill; m. Ernest C. Burkhart, Dec. 15, 1950 (dec. Feb., 1994). AA, UCLA, 1947; student, U. So. Calif., U. Minn. Copywriter John Freiburg Agy., L.A., 1947-48; copywriter, advt. sales Guest Informant, L.A., 1948; prin., owner J. Roe Advt. Agy., L.A., 1948-52; pub. rels. mgr. IGM Comm., Bellingham, Wash., 1975-80; lectr. in field; seminar leader. Author: Castaway Cat, 1984, Fisherman Cat, 1988, Alaska Cat, 1990, The Columbia River, 1992, Samurai Cat, 1993, Seattle Uncovered, 1995, Stevens Pass, 1995, Ghost Camps & Boom Towns, 1995, Ronald MacDonald, Pacific Rim Adventurer, 1997, The North Cascades Highway, 1997, others; author: (with others) Portable Writer's Conference, 1997, Washingtonians, Buckskins, Bullets and Beans; contbr. over 500 articles to mags. Active Assistance League, Bellingham, Wash., 1977—. Recipient Gov.'s award Gov. Wash. State, 1982, Pres. award Japan-Am. Soc. Wash., 1990, 2 Mayor's awards City of Bellingham, 1988, others. Mem. Soc. Children's Book Writers & Illustrators, Soc. Am. Travel Writers, Western Writers Am., Pacific N.W. Historians Guild, Women Writing the West, Bellingham Rotary Club, Whatcom Comms. Assn. Presby. Avocations: tennis, hiking, horseback riding, golf.

ROACH, JOHN MICHAEL, gastroenterologist; b. Walla Walla, Wash., Feb. 28, 1947; s. John Francis and Johanna Patricia (Sullivan) R.; m. Nancy Marie Mudd, Mar. 31, 1973; children: Shannon, John, Luke, Patrick, William, Bartholomew, Michelle. BS, Seattle U., 1969; MD, U. Wash., 1973. Diplomate Am. Bd. Internal Medicine. Intern straight medicine Maricopa County Gen. Hosp., Phoenix, 1974, resident internal medicine, 1975-76, gastroenterology fellow, 1976-78; pvt. practice gastroenterology Kennewick, Wash., 1978—; pres. med. staff Kennewick Gen. Hosp., 1985. Contbr. articles to Gastrointestinal Endoscopy, Surgical Laparoscopy & Endoscopy, Gastroenterology. Mem. Tri-City Renaissance Com., Pasco, Wash., 1987-91. Mem. ACP, Am. Soc. Gastrointestinal Endoscopy, Am. Gastroent. Assn., Am. Coll. Gastroenterology, Benton-Franklin County Med. Soc. (chmn. continuing med. edn. 1987-88, pres. 1989), Wash. State Med. Assn., Pacific NW Endoscopy Soc. Republican. Roman Catholic. Avocations: camping, photography, electronics, elk hunting, moose hunting. E-mail: jmroach@3-cities.com. Fax: 509-586-7092. Office: 811 S Auburn St Kennewick WA 99336-5661

ROADARMEL, STANLEY BRUCE, civilian military employee; b. Albion, N.Y., May 5, 1937; s. Kenneth A. and Catherine Louise (Bobel) R.; m. Carole Ann Hayes, Nov. 26, 1959; children: Karen Marie, Oscar Pacific, Ann Catherine, William Hayes. Student, Purdue U., 1956-58; BA, Syracuse U., 1962; postgrad., Golden Gate U., 1976-78; grad., Squadron Officer Sch., 1965, Air Command Staff Coll., 1974-76, Indsl. Coll. Armed Forces, 1976. Commd. 2d lt. USAF, 1962, advanced through grades to maj.; adminstrv., security and recruiting ops. officer Air Tng. Command, Tex. and W.Va., 1962-69; chief field maintenance Titan II ICBM Strategic Air Command, Davis Monthan AFB, Ariz., 1969-71; chief 3901st Titan II maintenance evaluation team Strategic Air Command, Vandenberg AFB, Calif., 1971-74, logistics staff officer, 1974-77, contract specialist, 1977-82; contract specialist U.S. Air Forces Europe, Adana, Turkey, 1980-81; ret. USAF, 1982; launch complex constrn. contract negotiator, adminstr. NASA/USAF Space Shuttle Program, Lompoc, Calif., 1983-89, USAF Titan IV Space Booster, Vandenberg AFB, 1991-92; constrn. and maj. svcs. contract negotiator, adminstr. 30th Contracting Squadron USAF Space Command, Vandenberg AFB, 1992—; pres. Ctrl. Coast Profls., Mut. Profl. Counseling/Placement, Santa Maria, Calif., 1990-91. Author manual: Man Lifting Crane Operations, 1976 (Air Force Commendation award 1977); revision officer Air Force Manual 66-1 Maintenance Management, 1976 (Air Force Commendation award 1977); contbr. Strategic Air Command Manual 66-12 ICBM Maintenance Mgmt. Spkr. World Orgn. Ovulation Method, Calif., 1987—; pro life advocate, activist Am. Life League, Nat. Right to Life, 1980—; vol. Rep. Party, 1992—; marriage preparation instr. Cath. Archdiocese of L.A., Santa Maria, Calif., 1995—. Mem. Nat. Contract Mgmt. Assn., Air Force Assn. (life), Ret. Officers Assn. (life), Assn. Air Force Missileers (life), Am. Legion, Couple to Couple League. Avocations: aviation, music, marksmanship, travel, literature. Home: 4532 Glines Ave Santa Maria CA 93455-4313

ROARK, TERRY PAUL, astronomer, educator; b. Okeene, Okla., June 11, 1938; s. Paul J. and Erma K. (Morrison) R.; m. Beverly Brown, Sept. 7, 1963; 1 child, David. C. BA in Physics, Oklahoma City U., 1960; MS in Astronomy, Rensselaer Poly. Inst., 1962, PhD in Astronomy, 1966. Asst. provost for curricula Ohio State U., Columbus, 1977-79, assoc. provost for instrn., 1979-83; prof. physics Kent (Ohio) State U., 1983-87, v.p. acad. and student affairs, 1983-87, provost, 1985-87; pres. U. Wyo., Laramie, 1987-97, prof. physics and astronomy, 1987—; bd. dirs. Rocky Mountain Fed. Savs. Bank, chmn. audit com., 1989-93; commr. Western Interstate Commn. for Higher Edn., 1987-97, chmn., 1991; bd. dirs. Associated Western Univs., 1987-94, chmn., 1991 [illegible] Survey, 1987-97; mem. Warren AFB Civilian Adv. Coun., 1987-97; bd. dirs. First Interstate Bank of Wyo. Mem., treas. Ctr. for Pub. Edn., Columbus, 1980-83; mem. fin. adv. com. LWV, Kent, 1986; mem. long range planning com. Cleve. Urban League, 1985-86; mem. adv. com. Battelle youth sci. program Columbus and Ohio Pub. Schs., 1982; bd. dirs. Ivinson Hosp. Found., 1987—. Mem. Am. Astron. Soc., Internat. Astron. Union, Nat. Assn. State Univs. and Land Grant Colls. (bd. dirs. 1994-96, chair commn. on intenat. affairs 1995), Astron. Soc. Pacific, Sigma Xi, Phi Kappa Phi, Omicron Delta Kappa. Avocations: photography, music, hiking. Home: 1752 Edward Dr Laramie WY 82072-2331 Office: U Wyo Dept Physics and Astronomy PO Box 3905 Laramie WY 82071-3905*

ROBBINS, ANNE FRANCIS See REAGAN, NANCY DAVIS

ROBBINS, CHARLES DUDLEY, III, manufacturing executive; b. Montclair, N.J., Sept. 21, 1943; s. Charles Dudley Robbins Jr. and Elaine (Siebert) Stark; m. Rebecca Lucille Bender; children: Seth A., Evan F., Gwendolyn M., Catherine E., Christopher W. BS in Bus. Adminstrn., U. Phoenix, Irvine, Calif., 1982; MBA, U. Phoenix, Salt Lake City, 1986. Cert. mfg. engr., robotics. Project engr. Mead Paper Corp., Atlanta, 1969-73; engr. McGaw Labs., Glendale, Calif., 1973-75; mgr. tool engring. Weiser Lock Co., South Gate, Calif., 1975-77; chief engr. Bivans Corp., L.A., 1977-79; sr. project engr. Charls Wyle Engring. Corp., Torrance, Calif., 1979-80; automation specialist Mattel Toys Inc., Hawthorne, Calif., 1980-83; dir. automation engring. Deseret Med., Warner Lambert, Sandy, Utah, 1983-86, Becton Dickinson, Sandy, 1986-91; dir. Worldwide Mfg., Becton Dickinson Vascular Access, 1991—; program adv. com. Salt Lake City Cmty. Coll., 1994. Patentee in field. Mem. Sandy C. of C. (bd. dirs. 1990-92). Democrat. Episcopalian. Avocations: coin and stamp collecting. Office: 9450 State St Sandy UT 84070-3213

ROBBINS, CONRAD W., naval architect; b. N.Y.C., Oct. 11, 1921; s. Girard David and Ethyl Rae (Bergman) R.; m. Danae Gray McCartney, Jan. 8, 1923 (dec. Jan. 1971); children: Lorraine, Linton, Jennifer; m. Melissa Jahn, Apr. 15, 1971 (dec. Mar. 1992); m. Sandra Johnstone, Apr. 24, 1998. BSE, U. Mich., 1942. Estimator Pacific Electric Co., Seattle, 1946-47; pres. Straus-Duparquet, Lyons-Alpha, Albert Pick, N.Y.C. and Chgo., 1947-67, C.W. Robbins, Inc., Carefree, Ariz., 1967—; cons. in field. Capt. floating drydock USN, 1942-46. Avocations: travel, gardening, gourmet cooking. Home: 4401 E Mountain View Rd Phoenix AZ 85028-5215 Office: CW Robbins Inc 7500 Stevens Rd Carefree AZ 85377

ROBBINS, DALE ALAN, minister; b. Noblesville, Ind., Jan. 6, 1953; s. Myron Foulk and Cora Irene (Brown) R.; m. Jerri Judith Keller, Dec. 6, 1974; 1 child, Angela. Student, Ind. Christian U., 1973; BA in Bible, Spring Valley Bible Coll., 1983; MDiv, Golden State Sch. Theology, 1985; postgrad., Laney Coll., 1986; DHL (hon.), Golden State Sch. Theology, 1985. Ordained to ministry Assemblies of God Ch., 1978. Nat. evangelist Assemblies of God, Sheridan, Ind., 1973-81; sr. pastor Porter Assembly of God, Porter, Ind., 1981-82, Calvary Christian Ctr., Alameda, Calif., 1982-90, Christian Life Ctr., Grass Valley, Calif., 1990—; bd. dirs. Golden State Sch. of Theology, Oakland, Calif., 1984-86; co-chmn. Bay Area Christian TV Coalition, Alameda, Calif. 1987-88; TV personality Family Christian Broadcasting, Concord, Calif., 1985-90; founder, dir. Internat. Prayer Network, 1996; founder Pastorial Search Network, 1996. Author: Ways Toward a More Effective Prayer Life, 1985, What People Ask About the Church, 1995; TV host Pathway to Calvary, 1984-90, producer, 1984-90; TV producer Dynamic Living, 1990. Contact pastor U.S. Naval Air Sta., Alameda, 1983-90. Republican. Office: Christian Life Ctr 13010 State Highway 49 Grass Valley CA 95949-9288

ROBBINS, JAMES EDWARD, electrical engineer; b. Renovo, Pa., May 11, 1931; s. James Edward and Marguerite Neva (Cleary) R.; m. Elizabeth Anne Caton, 1959 (div. July 1971); children: James, Katherine, Ellen; m. Dorothy Raye Bell, July 23, 1971; stepchildren: Mark, Lori. BEE, Pa. State U., 1958; MS in Math., San Diego State U., 1961. Registered profl. engr., Calif., Ariz. Rsch. engr. Astronautics div. Gen. Dynamics Co., San Diego, 1961-62; sr. engr. Kearfott div. Gen. Precision Co., San Marcos, Calif., 1962-65; systems engring. specialist Teledyne Ryan Aerospace Co., San Diego, 1965-76; mgr. tech. ops. Electronics divsn. Gen. Dynamics Co., Yuma, Ariz., 1965-76; v.p. Cibola Info. Systems, Yuma, 1982-84; cons. engr. Robbins Engring. Co., Yuma, 1984-85; sr. engring. specialist Gen. Dynamics Svcs. Co., Yuma, Ariz., 1985-90; systems engr. Trimble Navigation, Sunnyvale, Calif., 1990—. Contbr. articles to profl. jours. With USN, 1951-55, Korea. Mem. Inst. Navigation, Nat. Soc. Profl. Engrs., Ariz. Soc. Profl. Engrs. (pres. western div. 1986), Am. Legion, VFW (post comdr. 1963-65), Tau Beta Pi. Home: PO Box 1728 430 Ave Portola El Granada CA 94018-1728 Office: Trimble Navigation 585 N Mary Ave Sunnyvale CA 94086-2931

ROBBINS, JEANETTE, sales and manufacturing executive; b. Portland, Oreg., July 21, 1956; d. Robert Lee and Norma Yvonne (Smith) Rassi; m. Michael Keith Robbins, May 22, 1981. A in Gen. Sci., Portland C.C., 1982. Cert. engring. aide, Oreg. With prodn. thrift Salvation Army, Portland, 1979, Goodwill Industries, Denver, 1983-87, St. Vincent De Paul, Portland, 1987-88; owner Job Devel. Rsch. Ctr., Portland, 1985—, Eye-Dea Devel. Sales & Mfg., Portland, 1988—; detective scientist, 1980—; reviewer publs. and forms IRS, 1997—, U.S. Govt., Washington, 1997—, local bus map rev., 1998. Author: (textbook) Prime Factor Pattern, 1991, Prime Pattern of (Square) Root Ends, 1994; contbr. articles and book revs. to profl. publs. and books; artist, author: (visual aid) Artrithmetic, 1982, Patricia Mae, U.S. White House, 1996, Artrithmetic-Reference, 1997. Corr., adviser, World Gov., Nat. Gov., State Gov., Local Gov., Private Citizen, Bus. Owners, 1978—, Dem. Nat. Com., Washington D.C., 1993—. With USAF, 1977. Mem. Pub. Libr. Sys. (rschr. 1978—), Nat. Geographic Soc. (corr. 1993—). Avocations: alpinist, photography, languages. Office: Eye-Dea Devel Sales & Mfg PO Box 66221 Portland OR 97290-6221

ROBBINS, JO ANN, minister; b. Ft. Dodge, Iowa, Apr. 27, 1932; d. Leland Arthur and Doris Ruby (Green) Whitted; m. Clifford Whitaker, Nov. 17, 1948 (div. Aug. 1964); m. William Vernon Robbins, Oct. 25, 1964; stepchildren: Billie Laverne Meeks, Donald Wayne Robbins, Lauri Ann Marshall. Diploma in Ministerial Studies, Berean Bible Sch., Springfield, Ill., 1983, Evangel. Ch. Alliance, Bradley, Ill., 1984. Bible study coord., counselor Aglow, Inc., Placerville, Calif., 1979; v.p. Women's Aglow, Inc., Placerville, 1979-80; pres. Calif. Gold Area, Women's Aglow, Inc., 1982-84; coord. Women's Ministries, Placerville, 1982-84; pastor, founder Feed My Sheep Ministries, Placerville, 1985—; owner JoAnn's Fashion Apparel, Placerville, 1990-91; mem. Foothill Ministerial Assn., El Dorado County, Calif., 1985-91; dir. 1st Assembly tape ministry, Placerville, 1981-83; tour host to Israel, Agape Love Tours, Placerville, 1988-89. Author: (short stories) Spiritual Warfare, 1990, Occult, 1970, (booklet) That I Might Know Him, 1981. Poll judge El Dorado Election Bd., 1988-91. Recipient Vol. Appreciation award El Dorado Convalescent Hosp., 1984-85. Mem. Evangel. Ch. Alliance, Women's Aglow. Republican. Office: Feed My Sheep Church 341 Placerville Dr Placerville CA 95667-3912

ROBBINS, KAREN DIANE, editor; b. Bloomington, Ill., Nov. 25, 1959; d. Harley Edward and Geraldine Elayne (Abell) H; m. Craig Douglas Robbins, May 25, 1992. Cert. Office Adminstrn./Info. Processing, Riverside (Calif.) C.C., 1993, Cert. Graphics Tech., 1993. Temp. Olsten Temp. Svcs., Riverside, 1982-83; inventory auditor RGIS, San Bernardino, Calif., 1984; messenger The Hammond Co., Riverside, 1984-87; data collector grocery stores INFOMAX Retail Auditing Co., Chino, Calif., 1988-90; mktg. auditor RGIS Inventory Specialists, Riverside, Calif., 1988-91. Editor Rat and Mouse Tales, AFRMA Yearbook, Rulebook and Show Regulations/Standards book. Mem. Am. Fancy Rat and Mouse Assn. (founder). Home: PO Box 2589 Winnetka CA 91396-2589 Office: Am Fancy Rat Mouse Assn 9230 64th St Riverside CA 92509-5924

ROBBINS, LYNN EILEEN, human resources specialist; b. Seattle, Aug. 13, 1958. AA, Highline C.C., 1978; BA, Seattle Pacific U., 1981. Cert. sr. profl. human resources. Receptionist Stusser Electric Co., Seattle, 1981-82, mktg. asst. Stusser Electric Co., 1982-84; adminstrv. coord. Spectrum Controls, Inc., Bellevue, Wash., 1984-89; fin. adminstr. Spectrum Controls, Inc., [illegible] human resources mgr., 1991-98. Vocalist (music/tape) Canaan, 1990. Bd. dirs. Kid's B.A.S.E., Enumclaw, Wash., 1995— (sec., 1995-97). Mem. Soc. for Human Resources Mgmt., Am. Payroll Assn., Am. Electronics Assn., Internat. Taekwon-Do Fedn., U.S. Taekwon-Do Fedn., N.W. Human Resources Mgmt. Assn. Avocations: Taekwon-Do, music, skiing. Office: Spectrum Controls PO Box 5533 Bellevue WA 98006-0033

ROBBINS, NANCY LOUISE See MANN, NANCY LOUISE

ROBBINS, RICHARD GARDNER, JR., history educator; b. Buffalo, Mar. 6, 1939; s. Richard Gardner and Anne (Jones) R.; m. Catherine Codispoti, Apr. 2, 1966; children: Carla, Nicholas. BA, Williams Coll., 1961; MA, Columbia U., 1965, cert. in Russian, 1965, PhD, 1970. Asst. prof. history U. N.Mex., Albuquerque, 1969-75, assoc. prof., 1978-89, prof., 1989—. Author: Famine in Russia, 1891-92, 1975, The Tsar's Viceroys, 1987. Mem. Am. Hist. Assn., Am. Assn. for Advancement Slavic Studies. Home: 224 12th St NW Albuquerque NM 87102-1816 Office: U NMex Dept History Albuquerque NM 87131

ROBBINS, STEPHEN J. M., lawyer; b. Seattle, Apr. 13, 1942; s. Robert Mads and Aneita Elberta (West) R.; children: Sarah E.T., Alicia S.T. AB, UCLA, 1964; JD, Yale U., 1971. Bar: D.C. 1973, U.S. Dist. Ct. D.C. 1973, U.S. Ct. Appeals (D.C. cir.) 1973, U.S. Ct. Appeals (3d cir.) 1973, U.S. Dist. Ct. (ea. and no. dists.) Calif. 1982, U.S. Dist. Ct. (cen. dist.) Calif. 1983, Supreme Ct. of Republic of Palau, 1994. Pres. U.S. Nat. Student Assn., Washington, 1964-65; dir. scheduling McGovern for Pres., Washington, 1971-72; assoc. Steptoe & Johnson, Washington, 1972-75; chief counsel spl. inquiry on food prices, com. on nutrition and human needs U.S. Senate, Washington, 1975; v.p., gen. counsel Straight Arrow Pubs., San Francisco, 1975-77; dep. dist. atty. City and County of San Francisco, 1977-78; regional counsel U.S. SBA, San Francisco, 1978-80; spl. counsel Warner-Amex Cable Communications, Sacramento, 1981-82; ptnr. McDonough, Holland and Allen, Sacramento, 1982-84; v.p. Straight Arrow Pubs., N.Y.C., 1984-86; gen. legal counsel Govt. State of Koror, Rep. of Palau, Western Caroline Islands, 1994-95; pvt. practice law, 1986—. Staff sgt. U.S. Army, 1966-68. Mem. ABA (sect. urban, state and local govt. law-land use, planning and zoning com., sect. real property, probate and trust law, sect. natural resources energy, environ. law, forum com. on affordable housing and cmty. devel.), Internat. Mcpl. Lawyers Assn., D.C. Bar, State Bar of Calif., Urban Land Inst. (mem. steering com. Sacramento dist.), Am. Hist. Assn., Am. Planning Assn. (planning and law divsn., internat. divsn.), Internat. Urban Devel., Law Assn. for Asia and the Pacific (LawAsia), Chamber Music Soc. of Sacramento, Oreg. Shakespeare Festival, Shaw Island Hist. Soc. Unitarian. Avocations: theatre, art, hiking. Office: 2150 3rd Ave Sacramento CA 95818-3102

ROBECK, MILDRED COEN, educator, writer; b. Walum, N.D., July 29, 1915; d. Archie Blain and Mary Henrietta (Hoffman) Coen; m. Martin Julius Robeck, Jr., June 2, 1936; children: Martin Jay Robeck, Donna Jayne Robeck Thompson, Bruce Wayne Robeck. BS, U. Wash., 1950, MEd, 1954, PhD, 1958. Ordnance foreman Sherman Williams, U.S. Navy, Bremerton, Wash., 1942-45; demonstration tchr. Seattle Pub. Schs., 1946-57; reading clinic dir. U. Calif., Santa Barbara, 1957-64; rsch. cons. State Dept. Edn., Sacramento, Calif., 1964-67; prof., head early childhood edn. U. Oreg., Eugene, Oreg., 1967-86; vis. scholar West Australia Inst. Tech., Perth, 1985; v.p. acad. affairs U. Santa Barbara, Calif., 1987-95; vis. prof. Victoria Coll., B.C. Can., summer 1958, Dalhousie U., Halifax, summer 1964; trainer evaluator U.S. Office of Edn. Head Start, Follow Thru, 1967-72; cons., evaluator Native Am. Edn. Programs, Sioux, Navajo, 1967-81; cons. on gifted Oreg. Task Force on Talented and Gifted, Salem, 1974-76; evaluator Early Childhood Edn., Bi-Ling. program, Petroleum and Minerology, Dhahran, Saudi Arabia, 1985. Author: Materials KELP: Kgn. Evaluation Learning Pot, 1967, Infants and Children, 1978, Psychology of Reading, 1990, Oscar: His Story, 1997, 2nd edit., 1999; contbr. articles to profl. jours. Evaluation cons. Rosenburg Found. Project, Santa Barbara, 1966-67; faculty advisor Pi Lambda Theta, Eugene, Oreg, 1969-74; guest columnist Oreg. Assn. Gifted and Talented, Salem, Oreg., 1979-81; editorial review bd. ERQ, U.S. Calif., L.A., 1981-91. Recipient Nat. Dairy award 4-H Clubs, Wis., 1934, scholarships NYA and U. Wis., Madison, 1934-35, faculty rsch. grants U. Calif., Santa barbara, 1958-64, NDEA Fellowship Retraining U.S. Office Edn., U. Oreg., 1967-70. Mem. APA, Am. Ednl. Rsch. Assn., Internat. Reading Assn., Phi Beta Kappa, Pi Lambda Theta. Democrat. Avocations: dyslexia research, historical research, duplicate bridge, writing. Home: 95999 Highway 101 S Yachats OR 97498-9714

ROBERSON, KELLEY CLEVE, health care financial executive; b. McAlester, Okla., July 11, 1950; s. Cleo Connie and Helen Frances (Sewell) R.; m. Georgia Lee Brown, Jan. 15, 1970; children: Kevin Christopher, Matthew Guy. BBA, Tex. Christian U., 1973; postgrad., U. Md., 1983-88, U. So. Calif., 1991-93. Cert. govt. fin. mgr. Commd. 2d lt. U.S. Army, 1973, advanced through grades to lt. col., 1992; exec. officer Med. Co., Ft. Carson, Colo., 1974; aviation sect. leader 377th Med. Co., Republic of Korea, 1975-76; ops. officer Aeromed. Evacuation Unit, Ft. Stewart, Ga., 1976-79; exec. officer Aeromed. Evacuation Unit, Grafenwoehr, Germany, 1980-81; comdr. Med. Co. 2nd Armored Div., Garlstedt, Germany, 1981-83; compt. Walter Reed Army Inst. Rsch., Washington, 1983-88; comdr. Aeromed. Evacuation Unit, Hickam AFB, Hawaii, 1988-90; chief manpower Tripler Army Med. Ctr., Honolulu, 1990-92; chief resource mgmt., dep. comdr. adminstrn. Letterman U.S. Army Hosp. and Health Clinic, San Francisco, 1992-94; chief resource mgmt. Tripler Army Med. Ctr., Honolulu, 1994-97; chief program and budget U.S. Army Med. Dept., 1997-98; ret. U.S. Army, 1998; v.p., CFO Hawaii Health Sys. Corp., Honolulu, 1998—. Pres. Parents Club Damien Meml. High Sch., Honolulu, 1990-91. Mem. Assn. Govt. Accts. (cert. govt. fin. mgr.), Am. Acad. of Med. Adminstrs., Order Mil. Med. Merit, Am. Soc. Mil. Comptrs. (pres. Golden Gate chpt. 1992-93), Assn. U.S. Army, Retired Officers Assn. United Methodist. Avocations: writing, running, reading. Home: 1393 Hoakoa Pl Honolulu HI 96821-1160 Office: Hawaii Health Sys Corp 3675 Kilauea Ave Honolulu HI 96816-2333

ROBERTS, ALAN SILVERMAN, orthopedic surgeon; b. N.Y.C., Apr. 20, 1939; s. Joseph William and Fannie (Margolies) S.; BA, Conn. Wesleyan U., 1960; MD, Jefferson Med. Coll., 1966; children: Michael Eric, Daniel Ian. Rotating intern, Lankenau Hosp., Phila., 1966-67; resident orthopaedics Tulane U. Med. Coll., 1967-71; pvt. practice medicine, specializing in orthopedics and hand surgery, Los Angeles, 1971—; mem. clin. faculty UCLA Med. Coll., 1971-76. Served with AUS, 1961. Recipient Riordan Hand fellowship, 1969; Boyes Hand fellowship, 1971. Mem. Riordan Hand Soc., Western Orthopaedic Assn., A.C.S., AMA, Calif., Los Angeles County Med. Assns., Am. Acad. Orthopaedic Surgeons. Republican. Jewish. Contbr. articles to profl. jours.

ROBERTS, ALICE NOREEN, educational administrator; b. Los Lunas, N.Mex., July 1, 1947; d. Earnest Lee and Lora Mae (Leatherman) Mayo; m. David Ivan Roberts, Apr. 18, 1975; children: Debra, Danielle, David II, Diana, Earnest. BA, Brescia Coll., 1970; MA, U. N.Mex., 1974. Cert. elem. tchr., adminstr., Calif. 5th and 6th grade tchr. St. John's Parochial Sch., Plattsmouth, Nebr., 1970-71; 5th grade tchr. Sacred Heart Parochial Sch., Farmington, N.Mex., 1971-72; 4th-6th grade tchr. Our Lady of Assumption Sch., Albuquerque, 1972-75; correctional officer Calif. Dept. Corrections, San Quentin, 1975-82; adult edn. tchr. Calif. Dept. Corrections, Soledad, 1983-86, San Luis Obispo, 1984; supr. acad. instrn. Calif. Dept. Corrections, Norco, 1986-90; supr. correctional edn. programs Calif. Dept. Corrections, Corcoran, 1990—, ltd. term correctional adminstr., 1996; 6th grade tchr. St. Catherine's Parochial Sch., Martinez, Calif., 1981-82; mem. curriculum adv. com. Calif. Dept. Corrections, Sacramento, 1984-86, mem. computer adv. com., 1984-88, mem. literacy adv. com., 1990-94; adj. prof. in criminology Porterville (Calif.) Jr. Coll., 1996—. Candidate for King City (Calif.) Bd. Edn., 1985; vol. Youth for Understanding rep., Hanford, 1994-96. Mem. ASCD, Am. Vocat. Assn., Correctional Edn. Assn., Calif. Literacy, Inc. (treas. region VII 1999—), Calif. Coun. for Adult Edn., Hanford Emblem Club (rec. sec. 1994-99, 1st v.p. 1999—). Roman Catholic. Avocations: computers, pencil puzzles, video games, crocheting. Office: Calif State Prison Visions Adult Sch PO Box 8800 Corcoran CA 93212-8800

ROBERTS, ARCHIBALD EDWARD, retired career officer, author; b. Cheboygan, Mich., Mar. 21, 1915; s. Archibald Lancaster and Madeline Ruth (Smith) R.; grad. Command and Gen. Staff Coll., 1952; student U.S. Armed Forces Inst., 1953, U. Md., 1958; m. Florence Snure, Sept. 25, 1940 (div. Feb. 1950); children—Michael James, John Douglas; m. 2d, Doris Elfriede White, June 23, 1951; children: Guy Archer, Charles Lancaster, Christopher Corwin. Enlisted U.S. Army, 1939, advanced through grades to lt. col., 1960; served in Far East Command, 1942, 1953-55, ETO, 1943-45,

57-60; tech. info. officer Office Surgeon Gen., Dept. Army, Washington, 1950, Ft. Campbell, Ky., 1952-53, info. officer, Camp Chicamauga, Japan, Ft. Bragg, N.C., Ft. Campbell, Ky., 1953-56, Ft. Campbell, 1956-57, Ft. Benning, Ga., Wurzburg, Germany, 1957-58, spl. projects officer Augsburg, Germany, 1959-60, U.S. Army Info. Office, N.Y.C., 1960-61; writer program precipitating Senate Armed Services Hearings, 1962; ret., 1965; mgr., salesman Nu-Enamel Stores, Ashville, N.C., 1937-38; co-owner, dir. Roberts & Roberts Advt. Agy., Denver, 1946-49; pres. Found. for Edn., Scholarship, Patriotism and Americanism, Inc.; founder, nat. bd. dirs. Com. to Restore Constn., Inc., 1965—. Recipient award of merit Am. Acad. Pub. Affairs, 1967; Good Citizenship medal SAR, 1968; Liberty award Congress of Freedom, 1969; Man of Yr. awards Women for Constl. Govt., 1970, Wis. Legislative and Research Com., 1971; medal of merit Am. Legion, 1972; Speaker of Year award We, The People, 1973; Col. Arch Roberts Week named for him City of Danville, Ill., 1974; recipient Spl. Tribute State of Mich., 1979. Mem. Res. Officers Assn., Airborne Assn., SAR, Sons Am. Colonists. Author: Rakkasan, 1955; Screaming Eagles, 1956; The Marne Division, 1957; Victory Denied, 1966; The Anatomy of a Revolution, 1968; Peace: By the Wonderful People Who Brought You Korea and Viet Nam, 1972; The Republic: Decline and Future Promise, 1975; The Crisis of Federal Regionalism: A Solution, 1976; Emerging Struggle for State Sovereignty, 1979; How to Organize for Survival, 1982; The Most Secret Science, 1984; also numerous pamphlets and articles. Home: 2218 W Prospect PO Box 986 Fort Collins CO 80522-0986

ROBERTS, ARTHUR OWEN, religion and philosophy educator, clergyman; b. Caldwell, Idaho, Jan. 7, 1923; s. Owen Lawrence and Bertha (Jansonius) R.; m. Fern Lucile Nixon, Nov. 7, 1943; children: Lloyd Owen, Patricia Mae Nielsen, Teresa Mae Rogers. BA, George Fox Coll., 1944; BD, Nazarene Theol. Sem., 1951; PhD, Boston U., 1954. Ordained to ministry Soc. of Friends, 1945. Minister Everett (Wash.) Friends Ch., 1944-48, Kansas City (Mo.) Friends Ch., 1948-51, Meth. Ch., Grasmere, N.H., Goffstown, N.H., 1951-53; prof. philosophy and religion George Fox Coll., Newberg, Oreg., 1953-87, prof. at large, 1987—; dean of faculty George Fox Coll., Newberg, 1968-76; elder NW Yearly Meeting of Friends Ch., Newberg, 1986-93; ethics commn. Christian Coll. Consortium, 1984-87; guest instr. Earlham Sch. Religion, 1960, 68, 72, Malone Coll., 1960; founding pastor Tigard Friends Ch., 1956-58; pastoral resource person Reedwood Friends Ch., Portland, Oreg., 1983-89; lectr. at various orgns. Author: Through Flaming Sword, 1959, Move Over, Elijah, 1967, Listen to the Lord, 1974, History of the Association of Evangelical Friends, 1975, Tomorrow is Growing Old: Stories of Quakers in Alaska, 1978, Sunrise and Shadow, 1984, Back to Square One: Handling Losses, 1990; co-author: (with Hugh Barbour) Early Quaker Writings, 1973; Messengers of God: The Sensuous Side of Spirituality, 1996; contbr. Beacon Dictionary of Theology, 1983, Evangelical Dictionary of Theology, 1984, Great Christian Leaders, 1987, Handbook of Church History, 1977, 2d edit., 1990, Drawn by the Light: An Autobiographical Reflection, 1993, Look Closely at the Child, 1997; editor Quaker Religious Thought, 1990—; contbr. articles to profl. jours. Mem. planning commn. City of Newberg, 1982-86; councilor City of Yachats, Oreg., 1988-93, mayor, 1997—. NEH rsch. grantee, Alaska, 1975. Mem. Am. Acad. Religion, Friends Hist. Soc. (editorial com.). Independent.

ROBERTS, DANIEL JOHN, financial advisor, educator. AA, Foothill Jr. Coll., Los Altos Hills, Calif., 1969; BS in Bus. Adminstrn., San Jose State U., 1972; MS in Fin. Svcs., The Am. Coll., Bryn Mawr, Pa., 1997. Fin. planner Cigna Fin. Svcs., San Bernardino, Calif., 1977-81, Garry Nichols and Assocs., Upland, Calif., 1993-94; fin. planner, mng. prin., owner Canyon Fin. Svcs., Corona, Calif., 1981-93; instr. ins. edn. A.D. Banker & Co., Overland Park, Kans., 1992—; personal fin. advisor Am. Express Fin. Advisors Inc., Tustin, Calif., 1996—. Fax: 714-832-6619. Office: Am Express Fin Adv Inc 14081 Yorba St Ste 240 Tustin CA 92780-2011

ROBERTS, DAVID LOWELL, journalist; b. Lusk, Wyo., Jan. 12, 1954; s. Leslie James and LaVerne Elizabeth (Johns) R. BA, U. Ariz., 1979; postgrad., U. Nebr., 1997. Founder, editor, publisher Medicine Bow (Wyo.) Post, 1977-88; journalism instr. U. Wyo., Laramie, 1987-92; adviser U. Wyo. Student Publs., Laramie, 1987-92; gen. mgr. Student Media Corp U No. Colo., Greeley, 1995-98; founder, publisher Hanna Herald, Wyo., 1979-80; exch. reporter The Washington Post, 1982; freelance reporter Casper (Wyo.) Star-Tribune, 1978-83, various publs.; founder, The Hanna Herald, 1979-80. Co-author: (book) The Wyoming Almanac, 1988, 90, 94, 96; author: (book) Sage Street, 1991; columnist Sage Street, 1989-92. Chmn. Medicine Bow Film Commn., 1984; treas. Friends of the Medicine Bow Mus., 1984-88; pres. Medicine Bow Area C. of C., 1984; dir. Habitat for Humanity of Albany County, Laramie, 1991-92. Recipient Nat. Newspaper Assn. awards, over 40 Wyo. Press. Assn. awards, Five Editorial awards U. Wyo., Citizen of Yr. award People of Medicine Bow, 1986, Student Publs. awards U. Wyo., 1990, 92. Mem. Friends of Medicine Bow Mus., Habitat for Humanity of Albany County. Democrat. Methodist. Avocations: writing, golf, visiting museums, photography. Home: Box 278 Eastlake CO 80614

ROBERTS, DAVID STONE, bishop; b. New Haven, Mar. 20, 1943; s. Harold Lucullus and Marie Ellen (Carlson) R. BA in French, United Coll. Gordon, 1966. Ordained bishop Faith Family Fellowship, 1976, Worldwide Gospel Ch., 1986. Dir. Intermountain Christian Ministries, Salt Lake City, 1984—; advisor Am./Soviet Christian Alliance, Salt Lake City, 1990-97; founder S. Salt Lake Valley Pastors Prayer Group, Sandy, Utah, 1986-93; chaplain Holy Trinity Mission, Sandy, 1990-97; founder Ch. of the Risen Christ, 1991. Editor Intermountain Christian Ministry mo. newsletter, 1978—, Russian Lang. newsletter, 1991-93. Vol. Utah State Penitentiary, Draper, 1987-90. Office: Ch of the Risen Christ PO Box 71322 Salt Lake City UT 84171-0322

ROBERTS, DENNIS WILLIAM, association executive; b. Chgo., Jan. 7, 1943; s. William Owen and Florence Harriet (Denman) R. BA in Journalism, U. N.Mex., 1968; MA in Legal Studies, Antioch U., 1982; MA, St. John's Coll., 1984. Cert. assn. exec. Gen. assignment reporter Albuquerque Pub. Co., 1964, sports writer, 1960-64, advt. and display salesman, 1967-68; dir. info. N.Mex. bldg. br. Asso. Gen. Contractors Am., Albuquerque, 1968-79, asst. exec. dir., 1979-82, dir., 1982—. Active United Way, Albuquerque, 1969-78; chmn. Albuquerque Crime Prevention Council, 1982; bd. dir. ARC (Rio Grande chpt., 1992—). Recipient Pub. Relations Achievement award Assoc. Gen. Contractors Am., 1975, 78. Mem. N.Mex. Pub. Relations Conf. (chmn. 1975, 82-83), Pub. Relations Soc. Am. (accredited, pres. N.Mex. chpt. 1981, chmn. S.W. dist. 1984, chmn. sect. 1988), Am. Soc. Assn. Execs. (cert.), Contrn. Specifications Inst. (Outstanding Industry Mem. 1974, Outstanding Com. Chmn. 1978), Sigma Delta Chi (pres. N.Mex. chpt. 1969). Republican. Lutheran. Clubs: Toastmasters (dist. gov. 1977-78, Disting. Dist. award 1978, Toastmaster of Year 1979-80), Masons, Shriners, Elks. Home: #1713 10700 Academy Rd NE Apt 1713 Albuquerque NM 87111-7335 Office: Assn Gen Contractors 1615 University Blvd NE Albuquerque NM 87102-1717

ROBERTS, DWIGHT LOREN, engineering consultant, novelist; b. San Diego, June 3, 1949; s. James Albert and Cleva Lorraine (Conn) R.; B.A., U. San Diego, 1976, M.A., 1979; m. Phyllis Ann Adair, Mar. 29, 1969; children: Aimee Renee, Michael Loren, Daniel Alexandr. Engring. aide Benton Engring. Inc., San Diego, 1968-73; pres. Robert's Tech. Research Co., also subs. Marine Technique Ltd., San Diego, 1973-76; pres. Research Technique Internat., 1978—; freelance writer, 1979—; owner Agrl. Analysis, 1985-88; constrn. mgr. Homestead Land Devel. Corp., 1988-92; sr. engr. cons. Morrison Knudson, 1992-95; sr. soils analyst Geotechnics, Inc., 1995-98; offsite field supt. coastal divsn. Kaufman and Broad, 1998—. Served with U.S. Army, 1969-71. Mem. ASTM, AAAS, Nat. Inst. Sci., N.Y. Acad. Scis., Nat. Inst. Cert. in Engring. Techs., Soil and Found. Engr. Assn., Phi Alpha Theta. Baptist. Author: Geological Exploration of Alaska, 1898-1924, Alfred Hulse Brooks, Alaskan Trailblazer, Papaveraceae of the World, Demarchism, Arid Regions Gardening, Visions of Dame Kind: Dreams, Imagination and Reality, Antal's Theory of the Solar System, Science Fair-A Teacher's Manual, Common Ground: Similarities of the World Religions, Black Sheep-Scientific Discoveries From the Fringe, After Manhattan, The Christofilos Effect; and others; contbr. articles to profl. jours. Office: 3111 E Victoria Dr Alpine CA 91901-3679

ROBERTS, GEORGE CHRISTOPHER, manufacturing executive; b. Ridley Park, Pa., May 27, 1936; s. George H. and Marion C. (Smullen) R.; m. Adriana Toribio, July 19, 1966; children: Tupac A., Capac Y. PhD, Frederico Villareal Nat. U., Lima, Peru, 1989; postdoctoral studies, Inca Garcilosa de la Vega U., Lima, Peru, 1992. Sr. engr. ITT, Paramus, N.J., 1960-65; program mgr. Arde Rsch., Mawah, N.J., 1965-67; space-life sci. program mgr. GATX rsch. divsn., 1967-69; dir. rsch. and devel. Monogram Industries, L.A., 1969-71; chmn. Inca Mfg. Corp., 1970-72; pres. Inca-One Corp., Hawthorne, Calif., 1972—; pres. Environ. Protection Ctr., Inc., L.A., 1970-76; bd. dirs., trustee Fairborn Obs.; founder Culver Nat. Bank, 1983; chmn. solar and stellar physics Mt. Wilson Rsch. Corp., 1984-87. Patentee advanced waste treatment systems. Trustee Calif. Mus. Sci. and Industry, 1988-92, Intenat. Am. Profl. Photoelectric Photmetrists, 1983—, Buckley Sch., 1984-92, Belair Prep Sch., 1992-93; bd. dirs. Peruvian Found., 1981, pres. 1986-89, chmn. 1989-91; chmn. Santa Monica Coll. Astronomy Ctr., 1993-95; chmn. adv. coun Ctr. Internat. Bus. Edn. & Studies Santa Monica Coll. 1994-97, Peruvian Govt. Cultural Commn. for L.A., Peruvian Calif. C. of C. (advisor); mem. adv. coun. dept. mech. engring. Calif. Poly State U., San Luis Obispo, 1997—. Decorated Grade of Amauta, Govt. Peru, 1989. Mem. Am. Astron. Soc., Astron. Soc. Pacific. Office: 13030 Cerise Ave Hawthorne CA 90250-5523

ROBERTS, GEORGE P., computer company executive. Chmn., CEO P-Com, Campbell, Calif. Office: P-Com 3175 Winchester Blvd Campbell CA 95008-6557*

ROBERTS, GEORGE R., investment banking company executive; married; 3 children. JD, U. Calif., San Francisco. With Bears, Stearns, New York, until 1976; founding ptnr. Kohlberg, Kravis, Roberts, San Francisco; dir. Beatrice Co., Chgo., Houdaille Industries Inc., Northbrook, Ill., Malone and Hyde, Memphis, Union Tex. Petroleum Holdings Inc., Houston. Office: Kohlberg Kravis Roberts & Co 2800 Sand Hill Rd Ste 200 Menlo Park CA 94025-7055*

ROBERTS, HELEN HOYT RANDALL, educator and writer; b. Washington, Sept. 28, 1949; d. Kenneth Lindsey and Ruth Adams (Lane) R. BA, U. Wash., 1972; MEd, U. Mass., 1973, EdD, 1975. Coord. spl. projects Nat. Coun. for Social Studies, Washington, 1976-77; dir. curriculum and evaluation N.W. Arctic Sch. Dist., Kotzebue, Alaska; adj. edn. lect. U. Alaska, 1978-80, dir. community devel. and pub. svc., 1978-80; dean for instructional improvement Calif. State U. System Office, Long Beach, 1987-94; v.p. Consortium of Universities of Wash. Metro. Area, Washington, 1994-96; v.p. acad. affairs Heritage Coll., Toppenish, WA, 1996-97; owner Roberts and Assocs., Seattle, WA, 1997—; assoc. dir. Nat. Com. on Role and Future of State Colls. and Universities, 1986-87, accreditation vis. team mem. Western Assn. Schs. and Colls., 1993-94, founder, Delaney Memorial Scholarships Cmty. Found. for Nat. Capital Region, 1996—. Editor: The Urban Funding Guide, 1983, Issues in Higher Education and Economic Development, 1986; co-editor: (book and video) Student Outcomes Assessment: What Makes It Work?, 1992; editor and co-author: Teaching From a Multicultural Perspective, 1994. Bd. dirs. Rose Towers Homeowners Assn., Long Beach, 1990-92. Recipient Disting. Svc. award Am. Assn. State Colls. and Univs., 1982, 85, 86; grantee Fund for Improvement Postsecondary Edn., Econ. Devel. Adminstrn., U.S. Dept. Edn., U.S. Dept. Labor, AID, USDA, Alaska Dept. Edn., Calif. Postsecondary Edn. Commn. Mem. Sallie Mae Higher Edn. Resource Inst., mem. Am. Assn. for Higher Edn., Am. Ednl. Rsch. Assn., Am. Anthrop. Assn., Mediation Consortium Wash. State. Independent. Office: Roberts and Assocs. 3708 SW Grayson St Seattle WA 98126-2026

ROBERTS, JAMES ALLEN, gynecologic oncologist; b. Milw., May 6, 1947; s. John A. and Florence E. (Heil) R.; m. Rosemary Frankow. BA, UCLA, 1969; MD, Med. Coll. Wis., 1973; MS, U. Mich., 1993. Diplomate Am. Bd. Ob-Gyn. Resident in ob.-gyn. UCLA, 1973-77, fellow, 1977-79, acting asst. prof. ob-gyn, 1977-79; asst. prof. U. Iowa, Iowa City, 1979-80; asst. prof. U. Mich., Ann Arbor, 1980-86, assoc. prof., 1986-93, dir. gynecol. oncology, 1986-94, prof. ob.-gyn., 1993-97; dir. gynecol. oncology Oakwood Hosp., 1987-97; med. dir. Gyn-Ob Clinic, Stanford U., 1997—, prof. gynecol. oncology, 1997—, chief (section of Gyn.), 1997—; assoc. chmn. (clin. affairs) ob-gyn, Good Samaritan Hosp., Gatos, Calif., 1998—, associate (clinical affairs) ob-gyn, 1998—; cons. Ann Arbor VA Hosp., 1981-97, Oakwood Hosp., Dearborn, Mich., 1982-97, St. Joseph Hosp., Ann Arbor, 1982-97, Chelsea (Mich.) Hosp., 1983-97, Santa Clara Valley Med. Ctr., 1997—, El Camino Hosp., Mountain View, Calif., 1997—. Contbr. articles to profl. jours.; chpts. to books. Fellow Am. Cancer Soc., 1977-79, 82-84. Fellow ACS, Am. Coll. Ob-Gyn.; mem. AMA, Soc. Gynecol. Oncologists (mng. editor newsletter 1992-95), Western Assn. Gynecologic Oncologists (pres. 1992-93, sec.-treas. 1986-91), Ctrl. Assn. Ob-Gyns., N.Y. Acad. Scis., Washtenaw Ob-Gyn. Soc. (pres. 1985-86), Mich. Med. Soc., Internat. Gynecol. Cancer Soc., Am. Soc. Colp and Cervical Pathology, Am. Soc. Clin. Oncology, Soc. Surg. Oncology, Gynecol. Laser Soc., European Soc. Gynecol. Oncology, Assn. Profl. Ob-Gyns., San Francisco Gynecol. Soc. Office: Stanford U Dept Ob-Gyn 300 Pasteur Dr # Hh333 Palo Alto CA 94304-2203

ROBERTS, KATHARINE ADAIR, retired bookkeeper; b. Columbus, Ga., June 4, 1930; d. William Lynn and Ella Miller (Adair) R. BA, U. Redlands, 1955; postgrad., San Bernardino Valley Coll., 1971-74, Calif. State U., San Bernardino, 1975-78. Bookkeeper Rettig Machine Shop, Inc., Redlands, Calif., 1970-97, ret., 1997. Pres. Dem. Study Club, San Bernardino, 1967-68, Redlands Dem. Club, 1976, Wilsonian Club, San Bernardino, 1986, World Federalist Assn., Bernardino chpt., 1987—; mem. San Bernardino County Dem. Ctrl. Com., treas. 1977-80; San Bernardino leader World Federalist Assn. Program-Ptnrs. for Global Change. Recipient Citizens of Achievement San Bernardino LWV, 1989. Mem. Dem. Luncheon Club, World Federalist Assn. (pres.), Humane Soc. of San Bernardino Valley, Redlands Humane Soc., Redlands Dem. Club, LWV. Democrat. Home: 798 W 18th St San Bernardino CA 92405-4235

ROBERTS, MARK SCOTT, lawyer; b. Fullerton, Calif., Dec. 31, 1951; s. Emil Seidel and Theda (Wymer) R.; m. Sheri Lyn Smith, Sept. 23, 1977; children: Matthew Scott, Meredith Lyn, Benjamin Price. BA in Theater, Pepperdine U., 1975; JD, Western State U., 1978; cert. civil trial advocacy program, U. Calif., San Francisco, 1985; cert. program of instrn. for lawyers, Harvard U., 1990. Bar: Calif. 1980, U.S. Dist. Ct. (cen. dist.) Calif. 1980, U.S. Supreme Ct. 1989, U.S. Ct. Mil. Appeals 1989, U.S. Tax Ct. 1990. Concert mgr. Universal Studios, Hollywood, Calif., 1973-74; tchr. Anaheim (Calif.) Union Sch Dist., 1979-80; prin. Mark Roberts & Assocs., Fullerton, Calif., 1980—; instr. bus. law Biola U., La Mirada, Calif., 1980-84; judge pro tem Orange County Superior Ct., Santa Ana, 1989—. Co-author: Legacy-Plan, Protect and Preserve Your Estate, 1996, Generations Plan Your Legacy, 1999. Mem. Calif. State Bar Assn., Orange County Bar Assn. Avocations: snow and water skiing. Office: Mark Roberts & Assocs 1440 N Harbor Blvd Ste 900 Fullerton CA 92835-4122

ROBERTS, MEL (MELVIN RICHARD KELLS), retired film editor; b. Toledo, Aug. 26, 1923; s. Paul Mickle and Letha Ellen (Mize) Kells. BA, U. So. Calif., 1950, postgrad., 1951. Film editor Graphic Films, Hollywood, Calif., 1951-52; music editor Salt of the Earth, Ind. Film Co., Hollywood, 1952-53; film editor various orgns., including Ford Found., Columbia Pictures, Hollywood, 1953-62; cinematographer and film editor Wexler Films, Hollywood, 1956-62; still photographer L.A., 1962-81, video prodr., dir., 1993-97. Photographer, pub. 14 books, including Mel Roberts Male, Rex, and others; photographs featured in 2 bound vols. from Foto Factory Press: Uniforms, Mail Bonding 2, 1998; film editor Paul Coates Confidential File; video prodr., dir. Classic Males, 1993-97; editor (TV documentary) Segregation and the South, 1957; exhibited in group show Male Bonding 2 at David Aden Gallery, Venice, Calif., 1998. Sgt. USAF, 1943-45, PTO. Avocations: collecting classic films and film publications, music. Office: 1335 N La Brea Ave # 2102 Hollywood CA 90028-7532

ROBERTS, NORMAN FRANK, English composition and linguistics educator; b. Guilford, Maine, Aug. 18, 1931; s. John Francis and Pearl Estelle (Crozier) R.; m. Shoko Kawasaki, Sept. 18, 1959; children: Norman F. Jr., Kenneth K., Kathryn M. BA, U. Hawaii, 1960, MA, 1963, cert. in linguistics, 1972. Instr. ESL, U. Hawaii, Honolulu, 1962-68; prof. English, linguistics Leeward C.C., Pearl City, Hawaii, 1968-95, prof. emeritus, 1995, chmn. divsn. lang. arts, 1975-81, 92-95; cons. Nat. Coun. Tchrs. English, 1972-94. Author: Model Essay Booklet, 1989; co-author: Community College Library Instruction, 1979; contbr. articles to profl. jours. V.p. Pacific Palisades Community Assn., Pearl City, pres., 1973-74; mem. Aloha coun. Boy Scouts Am., Honolulu, 1972—, dir wood badge course, 1985, chmn. camping promotions, 1989-92. Recipient Dist. award of Merit Boy Scouts Am., 1986. Mem. Hawaii Coun. Tchrs. English (program chmn. 1974), Am. Dialect Soc. (program chmn. Honolulu conf. 1977). Avocations: music, outdoor life. Office: Leeward Community Coll Lang Arts Div 96-045 Ala Ike St Pearl City HI 96782-3366

ROBERTS, PAUL DALE, health services administrator; b. Fresno, Calif., Jan. 17, 1955; s. Paul Marceau and Rosemarie Roberts; m. Patricia Mary Mitchell, Mar. 24, 1964; 1 child, Jason Randall Porter. AA, Sacramento City Coll., 1977; diploma in pvt. investigations, Ctrl. Investigation & Security, 1984. Office asst. I Dept. Benefit Payments, Sacramento, Calif., 1976-77; firefighter Calif. Divsn. Forestry, Colfax, 1977; key data operator Dept. Justice, Sacramento, 1977-78; intelligence analyst, spl. forces instr. U.S. Army Mil. Intelligence, Seoul, Korea, 1979-84; law libr. Employment Devel. Dept., Sacramento, 1989-92; office asst. II Dept. Health Svcs., Sacramento, 1992—; supervising program technician II Dept. Cmty. Svcs. and Devel., State Calif., Sacramento; disaster courier dept. social svcs. Gov.'s Office of Emergency Svcs., L.A., 1994; chief cert. support Dept. Health Svcs., Sacramento, 1992—. Author: Organization of D.E.A.T.H. (Destroy Evildoers and Teach Harmony), 1984, The Cosmic Bleeder, 1991, Madam Zara, Vampiress, 1993, People's Comic Book Newsletter, 1996, The Legendary Dark Silhouette, 1997, Vacationing in Dublin, Ireland and Newry, Northern Ireland, 1997, (comic book) The Legendary Dark Silhouette, 1997, Jazma Universe Online!, 1998. Sgt. U.S. Army Mil. Police, 1973-76. Democrat. Roman Catholic. Avocations: private pilot, tennis, photography, hot air balloon/glider riding, sky diving. E-mail: PROBERTS@CSD.CA.GOV. Fax: 916-327-3153. Home: 60 Parkshore Cir Sacramento CA 95831-3061 Office: Dept Cmty Svcs & Devel Rm 258 700 N 10th St Sacramento CA 95814-0338

ROBERTS, PETER CHRISTOPHER TUDOR, engineering executive; b. Georgetown, Demerara, Brit. Guiana, Oct. 12, 1945; came to U.S., 1979; s. Albert Edward and Dorothy Jean (Innis) R.; m. Julia Elizabeth Warner, Nov. 10, 1984; children: Kirsta Anne, Serena Amanda, Angelee Julia, Zephanie Elizabeth, Fiona Ann, Emrys Tudor, Peter Christopher Tudor Roberts II. BSc with honors, Southampton (Eng.) U., 1969, PhD in Microelectronics, 1975. Rsch. fellow dept. electronics Southampton U., 1974-77; prof. microcircuit dept. electronics INAOE, Tonantzintla, Mexico, 1977-79; staff scientist Honeywell Sys. & Rsch. Ctr., Mpls., 1979-84; dir. advanced tech. Q-Dot Inc. R&D, Colorado Springs, Colo., 1984-86; program mgr. Honeywell Opto-Electronics, Richardson, Tex., 1986; vis. prof. U. N.Mex. CHTM, Albuquerque, 1987; supr. engring. Loral Inc. (formerly Honeywell), Lexington, Mass., 1988-90; mgr. engring. Litton Sys. Inc., Tempe, Ariz., 1990-96; staff engr. Motorola Space and Sys. Tech. Group, Scottsdale, Ariz., 1996—; dir. Pi-Rho Technics Internat., Inc., Gilbert, Ariz., 1996—; cons. engr. Q-Dot, Inc. R&D, Colorado Springs, 1982—, pvt. stockholder, 1984—. Author: (with P.C.T. Roberts) Charge-Coupled Devices and Their Applications, 1980; contbr. articles to Boletin del INAGE, IEEE Transactions on Electron Devices, Procs. of the IEE (UK), Procs. of the INTERNEPCON, Internat. Jour. Electronics,IEEE Electron Device Letters, Electronics Letters, Solid State and Electron Devices, IEEE Jour. Solid State Circuits, others. Republican. Achievements include patent for VHSIC bipolar ROM and RAM ciruits; patents pending for GaAs 2 GHz by 16-Bit Digital Active Backplane; random access image readout, others. Home: 639 N Sunway Dr Gilbert AZ 85233-3504 Office: Motorola Space and Systems Tech Grp 8201 E Mcdowell Rd Scottsdale AZ 85257-3893

ROBERTS, PHILIP JOHN, history educator, editor; b. Lusk, Wyo., July 8, 1948; s. Leslie J. and LaVerne Elizabeth (Johns) R. BA, U. Wyo., 1973, JD, 1977; PhD, U. Wash., 1990. Bar: Wyo. 1977. Editor Lake Powell Chronicle, Page, Ariz., 1972-73; co-founder Medicine Bow (Wyo.) Post, 1977; pvt. practice in law Carbon and Laramie County, Wyo., 1977-84; historian Wyo. State Hist. Dept., Cheyenne, 1979-84; editor Annals of Wyo., Cheyenne, 1980-84, 95—; owner, pub. Capitol Times, Cheyenne, 1982-84; co-editor Wyo. History Jour., 1995-96; editor, 1996-97; owner, pub. Skyline West Press, Seattle, 1985-90; asst. prof. history U. Wyo., Laramie, 1990—; indexer Osborne-McGraw-Hill, Berkeley, 1988-95; guest lectr. media law, Dubai, United Arab Emirates, 1996; mem. editl. bd. Annals of Wyo., 1990-95. Author: Wyoming Almanac, 1989 (pub. annually), Buffalo Bones: Stories from Wyoming's Past, 1979, 82, 84, Readings in Wyoming History, 1994-96; contbr. articles to profl. jours. Cand. for gov. of Wyo., 1998. With USMC, 1970-72. Mem. Wyo. State Hist. Soc. (life), Wyo. State Bar, Pacific N.W. Historians' Guild, 9th Judicial Cir. Hist. Soc., Western History Assn., Am. Hist. Assn., Orgn. of Am. Historians. Avocations: hiking, fishing, golf, photography, travel. Office: U Wyo Univ Sta PO Box 4286 Laramie WY 82071-4286

ROBERTS, PRUDENCE FENWICK, curator, freelance; b. Phila., Jan. 8, 1948; d. Joseph Buffington and Eleanor E. (Locher) R.; m. Terry Toedtemeier, March 25, 1995. BA, Sarah Lawrence Coll., 1971; MA, Reed Coll., 1998. Assoc. editor Chilton Pub. Co., Bala-Cynwyd, Pa., 1971-75, mng. editor, 1975-76; staff editor Sunset Mag., Menlo Park, Calif., 1976-78; from educator to curator Portland (Oreg.) Art Mus., 1987-95, curator Am. Art, 1995—; bd. dirs. Crow's Shadow Inst., Pendleton, Oreg., Cooley Gallery Reed Coll., Portland, Oreg. Creator (CD Rom) Taking Art Apart, 1996. Art selection com. Federal Courthouse Bldg., Portland, 1993-96; exhibition curator Reed Coll. Women's com., Portland, 1995, 97. Recipient Jesse H. Neil award Am. Soc. Bus. Press Editors, 1976, Oreg. Art Educator of Yr. award Oreg. Art Edn. Assn., 1995. Mem. Am. Assn. Mus., Pacific N.W. Am. Studies Assn., Coll. Art Assn. Home: 8225 SE 37th Ave Portland OR 97202-8004 Office: Portland Art Museum 1219 SW Park Ave Portland OR 97205-2486

ROBERTS, ROLLIN WALTER, metallurgical engineer, executive, consultant; b. Mobile, Ala., Aug. 27, 1946; s. James Rollin and Mary (Cates) R.; m. Lynne Michelle Lee, Dec. 27, 1967 (div. Mar. 1995); Michael Rollin, Lori Michelle. BS in Metall. Engring., Tex. Coll. Mines/U. Tex., El Paso, 1970. Rsch. metallurgist ASARCO Inc., El Paso, 1970-97; shift supr. ASARCO Inc., Tucson, 1970-75; leach plant supt. ASARCO Inc., Sahuarita, Ariz., 1975-77; asst. mill supt. ASARCO Inc., Silver Bell, Ariz., 1977-89; mill supt. Freeport McMoran Copepr and Gold Co., Tembagapura, Indonesia, 1989-95; metall. cons. Metcon Rsch., Erdenet, Mongolia, 1995-96; mill mgr. Unocal-Moly Corp., Mountain Pass, Calif., 1976-97, MIM Resources, Catamarca, Argentina, 1997; mgr. bus. devel. Bateman Engring. Internat., Tucson, 1998—; pvt. cons. metall. engring. project, 1999—. Author: SME Handbook II, 1997; contbr. articles to profl. jours. Asst. scoutmaster Boy Scouts Am., El Paso, 1960-64; scoutmaster, dir. Cub Scouts Am., Tucson, 1975-78; pres. Silver Bell Fed. Credit Union, Tucson, 1970-78. Mem. Soc. Metall. and Mining Engrs. Methodist. Avocations: cameras, hiking, trout fishing, antiques, movies. Home: 3906 W Ina Rd # 308 Tucson AZ 85741-2261 Office: Bateman Engring Internat 1860 E River Rd Ste 300 Tucson AZ 85718-5836

ROBERTS, RON, county board supervisor; b. 1942. BA, San Diego State U.; MA, U. Calif., Berkeley, 1968. Chmn. county dist. 4 Office of Bd. of Suprs., San Diego, 1994—. Office: Office Bd Suprs County Adminstrn Ctr 1600 Pacific Hwy Rm 335 San Diego CA 92101*

ROBERTS, THOMAS MULVIHILL, county official, lawyer; b. San Francisco, Mar. 29, 1960; s. John Montgomery and Marie Ellen (Mulvihill) R.; m. Lorie Loeb, May 16, 1992; children: Annabelle, Paul. BA with honors in Humanities, English, Stanford U., 1982; JD, U. Calif., Berkeley, 1985. Bar: Calif. 1985. Law clk. to judge Alaska Superior Ct., Anchorage, 1985-86; acting asst. city atty. City of Berkeley, 1986; assoc. atty. Livinston & Mattesich, Sacramento, 1986-88; earthquake legal relief coord. Homeless Advocacy Project, San Francisco, 1989-90; dir. Dept. of Pro Bono Affairs N.Y. State Bar Assn., Albany, 1991-95; homeless coord., Ctr. on Homelessness, Office of Housing San Mateo County, Belmont, Calif., 1996—; mem. Bay Area Regional Homeless Initiative, 1996—, San Mateo Emergency Food & Shelter Program, 1996—, San Mateo Family Housing & Homeless Trust

Fund, 1996— Mem. Housing Calif., Sacramento, 1996—. Recipient Appreciation award N.Y. State Pro Bono Coords. Network, 1995. Mem. Berkeley Law Found. Democrat. Roman Catholic. Avocations: hiking, tennis, running. Home: 474 Cumberland Rd Burlingame CA 94010 Office: Ctr on Homelessness Office of Housing San Mateo County 262 Harbor Blvd Belmont CA 94010

ROBERTS, VIRGIL PATRICK, lawyer, business executive; b. Ventura, Calif., Jan. 4, 1947; s. Julius and Emma D. (Haley) R.; m. Eleanor Green, Aug. 28, 1973; m. Brenda Cecilia Banks, Nov. 10, 1979; children: Gisele Simone, Hayley Tasha. AA, Ventura Coll., 1966; BA, UCLA, 1968; JD, Harvard U., 1972. Bar: Calif. 1972. Assoc. Pacht, Ross, Warne Bernhardt & Sears, L.A., 1972-76; ptnr. Manning, Reynolds & Roberts, L.A., 1976-79, Manning & Roberts, 1980-81; mng. ptnr. Bobbitt & Roberts, 1995—; exec. v.p., gen. counsel Solar Records, L.A., 1981—; pres. Dick Griffey Prodns., L.A., 1982—, Solar Records, 1988—; judge pro tem L.A., Beverly Hills Mcpl. Cts., 1975—. Past bd. dirs. L.A. Black Leadership Coalition, L.A. Mus. African Am. Art, Beverly Hills Bar Assn., L.A. Legal Aid Found.; bd. dirs. Coro Found., 1984—, Calif. Cmty. Found., 1991—, L.A. Ednl. Alliance for Restructuring Now, Cmty. Build; past pres. Beverly Hills Bar Scholarship Found.; commr. Calif. Commn. for Tchr. Credentialing, 1980-83; chmn. L.A. Ednl. Partnership, 1989—, v.p. 1983-89; vice-chmn. Nat. Pub. Edn. Fund Network; chmn. bd. dirs. L.A. Annenberg Metropolitan Project. Trustee, Comm. Econ. Devel., 1991—. Recipient NAACP Legal Def. Fund Equal Justice award, 1988. Mem. Recording Industry Assn. Am., Black Entertainment and Sports Lawyers (treas., bd. dirs. 1982—). Lead atty. for NAACP in Crawford vs. Bd. Edn. desegregation case, L.A., 1979-80. Address: 4820 Vista De Oro Ave Los Angeles CA 90043-1611 Office: Bobbitt & Roberts 1620 26th St Ste 150 Santa Monica CA 90404-4067

ROBERTS, WENDY HUNTER, producer, writer, psycho-spiritual counselor; b. N.Y.C., Jan. 15, 1948; d. Charles and Jane Elinor (Cone) R. Cert., Am. Musical and Dramatic Acad., 1969; MSW, SUNY, Stonybrook, 1980; MDiv, Starr King Sch. Ministry, 1990. Freelance cons., counselor Calif., 1982—; dir. The Day Before Project, Emeryville, Calif., 1983; co-dir., media cons. Project Threads, Berkeley, Calif., 1984; fundraising cons. various organizations, Berkeley, Boston, 1985-95; liminilist, counselor E. W. Healing Arts Ctr., Oakland, Calif., 1995-97; CEO, prodr. EVOLUTION 2000, San Francisco, 1996-97; adj. faculty master's program Immaculate Heart Coll. Ctr. Feminist Spirituality. Author: (with others) Women at Worship, 1993, Celebrating Her, 1998. Bd. dirs. Soviets Meet Mid. Am., San Francisco, Russia, 1986; emcee, mem. com. After the Fire, Oakland, 1992. Mem. Am. Acad. Religion, Bay Area Entrepeneur Assn. Unitarian. Avocations: cooking, tantra, thinking, ritual celebrations. Office: EVOLUTION 2000 2 Embarcadero Ctr Ste 200 San Francisco CA 94111-3801

ROBERTS-DEGENNARO, MARIA, social work educator; b. Austin, Minn., Oct. 10, 1947; d. Clinton M. and Laura E. (DeMets) Becker; m. Paul DeGennaro, July 7, 1984; 1 child, Matthew. B of Social Work, U. Minn., 1970, MSW, 1976; PhD, U. Tex., 1981. Family counselor Hennepin County Welfare Dept., Mpls., 1970-73; coord. YMCA, Mpls., 1973-74; dist. project coord. Child Abuse and Neglect Project, Phoenix, 1976-77; prof. San Diego State U., 1980—; dir. Interdisciplinary Ctr., San Diego State U., 1987-90; dir. Interdisciplinary Program on Early Intervention San Diego State U., 1989-94. Contbr. articles to profl. jours. Mem. Assn. on Community Orgn. and Social Adminstrn., Nat. Assn. Social Workers, Coun. on Social Work Edn. Office: San Diego State U Sch Social Work San Diego CA 92182

ROBERTSHAW, THOMAS EDWARD, social worker; b. Bellevue, Pa., Nov. 7, 1963; s. Willliam Ian and Janice Lavern (Lawson) R.; m. W. Lynn Kelly, Aug. 22, 1985; children: Philip Edward, Daniel Joseph, Steven Andrew, William Aaron. BS in Social Work, Brigham Young U., 1988. LSW, Idaho. Habilitation coord. Trail Inc., Nephi, Utah, 1989-91; dialysis social worker U. Utah, Salt Lake City, 1991—. Leader Cub Scouts and Boy Scouts Am., 1989-95; vol. emergency med. technician Shelley-Firth Quick Response unit, Shelley, Idaho, 1997—. Mem. The Dye Soc. Mem. Ch. Jesus Christ LDS. Avocations: fishing, camping, geneology.

ROBERTSON, ABEL L., JR., pathologist; b. St. Andrews, Argentina, July 21, 1926; came to U.S., 1952, naturalized, 1957; s. Abel Alfred Lazzarini and Margaret Theresa (Anderson) R.; m. Irene Kirmayr Mauch, Dec. 26, 1958; children: Margaret Anne, Abel Martin, Andrew Duncan, Malcolm Alexander. BS, Coll. D.F. Sarmiento, Buenos Aires, Argentina, 1946; MD suma cum laude, U. Buenos Aires, 1951; PhD, Cornell U., 1959. Fellow tissue culture div. Inst. Histoloty and Embryology, Sch. Medicine Inst. Histology and Embryology, 1947-49; surg. intern Hosp. Ramos Mejia, Buenos Aires, 1948-50; fellow in tissue culture research Ministry of Health, Buenos Aires, 1950-51; resident Hosp. Nacional de Clinicas, Buenos Aires, 1950-51; head blood vessel bank and organ transplants Research Ctr. Ministry of Health, Buenos Aires, 1951-53; fellow dept. surgery and pathology Sch. Medicine Cornell U., N.Y.C., 1953-55; asst. vis. surgery U. Hosp. N.Y., N.Y.C., 1955-60; asst. prof. research surgery Postgrad. Med. Sch. NYU, N.Y.C., 1955-56; asst. vis. surgeon Bellevue Hosp., N.Y.C., 1955-60; assoc. prof. research surgery NYU, 1956-60, assoc. prof. pathology Sch. Medicine and Postgrad Med. Sch., 1960-63; staff mem. div. research Cleve. Clinic Found., 1963-73, prof. research, 1972-73; assoc. clin. prof. pathology Case Western Res. U. Sch. Medicine, Cleve., 1968-72, prof. pathology, 1973-82, dir. interdisciplinary cardiovascular research, 1975-82; exec. head dept. pathology Coll. Medicine, U. Ill., Chgo., 1982-88; prof. pathology Coll. Medicine U. Ill., 1982-93, prof. emeritus, 1993—; vis. prof. emeritus in cardiovascular medicine Stanford U. Coll. Medicine, 1995—; rsch. fellow N.Y. Soc. Cardiovasc. Surgery, 1957-58; mem. rsch. study subcom. of heart com. N.E. Ohio Regional Med. Program, 1969—. Mem. internat. editorial bd.: Atherosclerosis, Jour. Exptl. and Molecular Pathology, 1964—, Lab. Investigation, 1989—, Acta Pathologica Japonica, 1991—; contbr. articles to profl. jours. Recipient Research Devel. award NIH, 1961-63. Fellow AAAS, Am. Coll. Cardiology, Am. Coll. Clin. Pharmacology, Am. Heart Assn. (established investigator 1956-61, nominating com. council on arteriosclerosis 1972), Royal Microscopical Soc., Royal Soc. Promotion Health (Gt. Britain), Am. Geriatrics Soc., N.Y. Acad. Scis., Cleve. Med. Library Assn.; mem. AMA, AAUP, Am. Soc. for Investigative Pathology, Am. Inst. Biol. Scis., Am. Judicature Soc., Am. Soc. Cell Biology, Am. Soc. Pathologists, Am. Soc. Nephrology, Assn. Am. Physucuabs and Surgeons, Assn. Computing Machinery, Electron Microscopy Soc. Am., Assn. Pathology Chmn., Internat. Acad. Pathology, Soc. Cardiovascular Pathology, Internat. Cardiovascular Soc., Internat. Soc. Cardiology (sci. council on arteriosclerosis and ischemic heart disease), Internat. Fed. on Genetic Engring. and Biotechnology, Internat. Soc. for Heart Rsch., Internat. Soc. Nephrology, Internat. Soc. Stereology, Pan Am. Med. Assn. (life, councillor in angiology 1966), Ill. Registry Anatomical Pathology (treas. 1985-87), Chgo. Pathology Soc., Reticuloendothelial Soc. Leucocyte Biology, Soc. Cryobiology, Tissue Culture Assn., Ohio Soc. Pathologists, Electron Microscopy Soc. Northeastern Ohio (pres., trustee 11966-68), Heart Assn. Northeastern Ohio, N.Y. Soc. Cardiovascular Surgery, N.Y. Soc. Electron Microscopists, Cuyahoga County Med. Soc., Cleve. Soc. Pathologists, The Oxygen Soc., Sigma Xi. Fax: (650) 712-0357. E-mail: alrrob@pol.net. Home: 415 Lee Ave Half Moon Bay CA 94019-1367

ROBERTSON, CAREY JANE, musician, educator; b. Culver City, Calif., Apr. 18, 1955; d. Robert Bruce and Marjorie Ellen (Greenleaf) Coker;l m. Brian Collins Robertson, June 28, 1975 (div. July 1985); 1 child, Sean Kalen. BMus, Calif. State U., Northridge, 1977; MMus, U. So. Calif., L.A., 1979, PhD of Mus. Arts, 1987. Organist/choir dir. Village Meth. Ch., North Hollywood, Calif., 1972-75, St. Bede's Episcopal Ch., Mar Vista, Calif., 1975-79; organist interim St. Alban's Episcopal Ch., Westwood, Calif., 1985; organist Covenant Presbyn. Ch., Westchester, Calif., 1985-90; organist/choir dir. St. David's United Ch., West Vancouver, B.C., Can., 1990-91; prin. organist Claremont (Calif.) United Ch. of Christ, 1991—; prof. organ Claremont Grad. U., 1991—, Benjamin U., Buena Park, Calif.; concert or- [illegible] Theology, U. B.C., 1990. Bd. dirs. Ruth and Clarence Mader Found., Pasadena, Calif., 1993—. Recipient Music Tchrs. Nat. Assn. Wurlitzer Collegiate Artist award, 1980; Irene Robertson scholar, 1977, 79. Mem. [illegible] Pasadena chpt., 1998-99), Pi Kappa Lambda (Scholastic award 1987). Avocations: scuba diving, water skiing. Home: 7514 Pepper St Rancho Cucamonga CA 91730-2125

ROBERTSON, GERALD RANKIN, physician, internist; b. Lawton, Okla., July 12, 1944; s. Nathan Ellsworth and Lameda (Newton) R.; m. Martha Elizabeth Marvel, June 23, 1968; children: Eleanor, Rebecca, Douglas, Sharon, Stephen. AA, Cameron Coll., 1964; BS, Okla. U., 1966; MD, Tufts U., 1970. Diplomate Am. Bd. Internal Medicine. House staff officer U. N.Mex. Teaching Hosp., Albuquerque, 1970-71, 73-77; internist, pres. Cibola Med. Found., Gallup, N.Mex., 1977—. Served to capt. U.S. Army, 1971-73. Democrat. Methodist. Lodge: Rotary. Office: RMCH Clinic at Coll 2111 College Dr PO Box 1100 Gallup NM 87305-1100

ROBERTSON, HUGH DUFF, lawyer; b. Grosse Pointe, Mich., Mar. 14, 1957; s. Hugh Robertson and Louise (Grey) Bollinger; m. Mercedes Corpus Dano, May 3, 1997. BBA in Fin., U. Wis., Whitewater, 1978; JD, Whittier Coll., 1982. Bar: Calif. 1983, U.S. Tax Ct. 1984. Pres., CEO, A. Morgan Maree Jr. & Assocs., Inc., L.A., 1979—. Mem. ABA (forum com. on entertainment 1982—), State Calif., L.A. County Bar Assn., Beverly Hills Bar Assn., Acad. TV Arts and Scis., Am. Film Inst., Phi Alpha Delta. Republican. Episcopalian. Avocations: sports, swimming, reading. Office: A Morgan Maree Jr & Assocs 4727 Wilshire Blvd Ste 600 Los Angeles CA 90010-3848

ROBERTSON, MARIAN ELLA (MARIAN ELLA HALL), small business owner, handwriting analyst; b. Edmonton, Alta., Can., Mar. 3, 1920; d. Orville Arthur and Lucy Hon (Osborn) Hall; m. Howard Chester Robertson, Feb. 7, 1942; children: Elaine, Richard. *Father's family relations include American financier, statesman, and signer of the Declaration of Independence, Robert Morris of Philadelphia - Quaker. Mother's family relations include Joaquin Miller, a Quaker - lawyer, judge, publisher, poet, and prominent Oregon resident. He was well-known in Northern California, and was famous in England for his poetry and Western style. Family traveled across the plains from Indiana in 1854.* Student, Willamette U., 1937-39; BS, Western Oreg. State U., 1955. Cert. elem., jr. high. tchr., supt. (life) Oreg.; cert. graphoanalyst. Tchr. pub. schs. Mill City, Albany, Scio and Hillsboro, Oreg., 1940-72; cons. Zaner-Bloser Inc., Columbus, Ohio, 1972-85, assoc. cons., 1985-89; pres. Write-Keys, Scio, 1980-90; owner Lifelines, Jefferson, Oreg., 1991-94; tchr. Internat. Graphoanalysis Soc., Chgo., 1979; instr. Linn-Benton Community Coll., 1985-89. *Personal philosophy: Keep on learning and keep on working to make the world a better place. Marian Robertson's work included giving workshops for elementary teachers, guest lecturer in public and private colleges, and universities in Oregon and Washington. In California, she did demonstrations for teachers with students in their classrooms. She, also, had done personality profiles for companies to determine hiring of applicants, and placement in workplace. When time allows, she currently works as a speaker.* Sr. intern 5th Congl. Dist. Oreg., Washington, 1984, mem. sr. adv. coun.; precinct com. mem. Rep. Cen. Com., Linn County, 1986, alt. vice-chair, 1986, parliamentarian, 1988—; candidate Oreg. State Legis., Salem, 1986; del. Northwest Friends Yearly Meeting, Newberg, Oreg., 1990, 91, 92; master gardener vol. Marion County, Oreg. State U. Extension Svc., 1992; floriculture judge Marion County Fair, 1992; master gardener clinic Oreg. State Fair, 1992; clerk Marion Friends Monthly Meeting, 1992-93. Mem. Altrusa Internat. (internat. chmn. 1985-86, chmn. pub. rels. 1989—, corr. sec. 1990-91), Internat. Platform Assn., Knife and Fork Club. Republican. Mem. Soc. of Friends. Avocations: piano, organ, violin, gardening, writing. Home: 2757 Pheasant Ave SE Salem OR 97302-3170

ROBERTSON, RICHARD CURTIS, credit union executive; b. Portland, Oreg., Oct. 27, 1929; s. Fred Curtis and Marian Lucille (Rittenhouse) R.; m. Roberta Ann Sharrett, Oct. 14, 1950 (div. 1981); children: Robin, Rebecca. AA, Clark Coll., 1952. Acct. Reynolds Metals Co., Troutdale, Oreg., 1949-59; pres., gen. mgr. Ariz. State Savs. & Credit Union, Phoenix, 1959—; bd. dirs., past chmn. CUNA Mutual Ins. Group, Madison; bd. dirs., past pres. CUNA, Madison; chmn. Filene Rsch. Inst., Madison, 1989—; vice-chair Consumer Credit Cunseling Svcs., Phoenix. Spl. dep. supt. banks State of Ariz., Phoenix, 1970; mem. Ariz. Gov.'s Com. Interstate Banking, Phoenix, 1985. With USN, 1948-58. Recipient Disting. Svc. award World Coun. of Credit Unions, 1991. Mem. Credit Union Exec. Soc. (charter, Exec. of Yr. award 1986), Ariz. Club, Ariz. Biltmore, Fiesta Bowl Com. (life). Democrat. Avocations: golf, fishing, all sports. Office: Ariz State Savs & Credit Union 1812 W Monroe St Phoenix AZ 85007-2616

ROBERTSON, WILLIAM ABBOTT, arbitrator, mediator; b. San Francisco, Apr. 7, 1947; s. William A. Jr. and Roxana D. Robertson; m. Abigail K. Robertson; children: Sara W., Clair S.; stepchildren: Craig Harner, Geoffrey Harner, Katie Harner. BA, U. Calif., Davis, 1969; JD, U. of the Pacific, Sacramento, 1980. Bar: Calif. 1980, U.S. Dsit. Ct. (no. and ea. dists.) 1981, U.S. Ct. Appeals (9th cir.) 1981. Atty. Rodeno & Robertson, Napa, Calif., 1984-94, Robertson Law Office, Napa, 1994-96; pvt. practice mediation and arbitration, 1995—; judge pro tem Napa Consol. Cts., 1982—; assigned arbitrator Napa and Solano County Superior Cts., 1984—. Avocations: ranching, quarter horses. Office: Robertson Mediation Office PO Box 555 Saint Helena CA 94574-5055

ROBINETT, RUSH DALETH, III, robotics research manager; b. Albuquerque, July 14, 1960; s. Rush Daleth Jr. and Dorothy (Sohl) R.; m. Laurie Ellen Bowman, Dec. 28, 1993; children: Rush Daleth IV, Logan Nicholas. Student, U. Notre Dame, 1978-80; BS magna cum laude, Tex. A&M U., 1982, PhD, 1987; MS, U. Tex., 1984. Teaching asst. U. Notre Dame, South Bend, Ind., 1979-80; rsch. asst. Tex. A&M U., College Station, 1981-82, U. Tex., Austin, 1983-84; rsch. assoc. Ctr. for Strategic Tech., College Station, 1984-87; rsch. mgr. Sandia Nat. Lab., Albuquerque, 1988—, disting. mem. tech. staff, 1995; student intern NASA Hdqs. Washington, 1981; rsch. engr. Northrop Aircraft Divsn., Hawthorne, Calif., summer, 1983; adj. prof. U. N.Mex., Albuquerque, 1994—; cons. Corning, Elmira, N.Y., 1993-95, Albuquerque Pub. Schs. Budget Rev. Bd., 1990; sci. advisor Albuquerque Pub. Schs., 1990-94, sci. instr., summer, 1988-90; presenter, cons. Explora, Albuquerque, 1992. Inventor: two axis hydraulic joint, sway suppressed crane control, moving mass spacecraft attitude control system; contbr. articles to profl. jours. Mentor Valley Acad., Albuquerque, 1989-92. Fellow AIAA (assoc., tech. com. 1991-93, student v.p. 1981-82, Best Presentation award 1992); mem. N.Y. Acad. Scis., Am. Helicopter Soc., Phi Kappa Phi, Sigma Gamma Tau. Avocations: softball, volleyball, ice hockey, fishing, hunting. Home: PO Box 1661 Tijeras NM 87059-1661 Office: Sandia Nat Lab MS 1003 PO Box 5800 Albuquerque NM 87185-0100

ROBINSON, ANNETTMARIE, entrepreneur; b. Fayetteville, Ark., Jan. 31, 1940; d. Christopher Jacy and Lorena (Johnson) Simmons; m. Roy Robinson, June 17, 1966; children: Steven, Sammy, Doug, Pamela, Olen. BA, Edison Tech. U., 1958; BA in Bus., Seattle Community Coll., 1959. Dir. perss. Country Kitchen Restaurants, Inc., Anchorage, 1966-71; investor Anchorage, 1971—; cons. Pioneer Investments, Anchorage, 1983—, M'RAL, Inc. Retail Dry Goods, Anchorage, 1985. Mem. Rep. Presdl. Task Force, Washington, 1984—, Reps. of Alaska, Anchorage, 1987; mem. chmn. round table YMCA, Anchorage, 1986—; active Sta. KWN2, KQLO, Reno, Nev.; active in child abuse issues and prosecution; dir., sec. Hunter Lake Townhouse Assn., Reno, Sta. KSRU and KHOG-Radio, KIHM Cath. Radio, Reno, 1996—. Named Woman of Yr. Lions, Anchorage, 1989, marksman first class Nat. Rifle Assn., 1953. Mem. Porsche Club of Am. (racing team 1998—). Avocations: Egyptology, theology, archeology, shooting, fishing.

ROBINSON, BERNARD LEO, retired lawyer; b. Kalamazoo, Feb. 13, 1924; s. Louis Harvey and Sue Mary (Starr) R.; m. Betsy Nadell, May 30, 1947; children: Robert Bruce, Patricia Anne, Jean Carol. BS, U. Ill., 1947, MS, 1958; JD, U. N.Mex., 1973. Bar: N.Mex. 1973, U.S. Supreme Ct. 1976. Rsch. engr. Assn. Am. Railroads, 1947-49; instr. arch. Rensselaer Poly. Inst. [illegible] col., 1965, ret., 1968; engr. Nuclear Def. Rsch. Corp., Albuquerque, 1968-71; lawyer Albuquerque, 1973-85, Silver City, N.Mex., 1985-89, Green Valley, Ariz., 1989-90, Sierra Vista, Ariz., 1990-91; pres. Robinson Fin. [illegible] Dist. Com., 1968-70. Decorated Air medal. Mem. ASCE, ABA, Ret. Officers Assn., DAV, Assn. U.S. Army, VFW. Home: 11821 N Pyramid Point Dr Oro Valley AZ 85737-3726

ROBINSON, CARMEN DELORES, educator; b. Kingston, Jamaica, Jan. 15, 1954; came to the U.S., 1973; d. Alphonso Constantine and Lena Maud (Ellis) R.; 1 child, Chrystle Khalya Robinson-White. BA, Calif. State U., L.A., 1978, MS, 1981; PhD in Ednl. Adminstrn., Columbia State U., 1997. Profl. clear multiple subject credential. Tchr., instr. Hacienda La Puenta Unified Sch. Dist., L.A., 1986-88; tchr. L.A. Unified Schs., 1985-86, 88-90, SDC tchr., 1990-92, 92-94, bilingual coord., 1994-95; bilingual and curriculum resource tchr. Pasadena (Calif.) Unified Sch. Dist., 1995-97; specialist educator Lynwood (Calif.) Unified Sch. Dist., 1997—. Republican.

ROBINSON, CHARLES PAUL, nuclear physicist, diplomat, business executive; b. Detroit, Oct. 9, 1941; s. Edward Leonard and Mary Opal (Edmondson) R.; m. Barbara Thomas Woodard; children by previous marriage: Paula S., Colin C. BS in Physics, Christian Bros. U., 1963; PhD in Physics, Fla. State U., 1967. Mem. nuclear test staff Los Alamos (N.Mex.) Nat. Lab., 1967-69, chief test operator, 1969-70, mem. advanced concepts staff, 1971-72, assoc. div. leader, lasers, 1972-76, div. leader, 1976-79, assoc. dir., 1980-85; sr. v.p., bd. dirs. Ebasco Services Inc. subs. Enserch Corp., N.Y.C., 1985-88; ambass. to nuclear testing talks U.S. Dept. State, Geneva, 1988-90; v.p. Sandia Nat. Labs., Albuquerque, 1990-95, pres., 1995—; mem. sci. adv. group Def. Nuclear Agy., Washington, 1981-86; mem. nat. security bd. Los Alamos Nat. Lab., 1985-88; chmn. Presdl. Tech. Adv. Bd., 1991; mem. U.S. Strategic Command Adv. Bd. Pres. Student Concerts Inc., Los Alamos, 1972-74; instr. U. N.Mex., Los Alamos, 1974-76; exec. bd. Boy Scouts of N.Mex. Recipient Outstanding Pub. Svc. medal Joint Chiefs of Staff, 1996. Mem. Am. Phys. Soc., Am. Nuclear Soc. Avocation: choral singing. Office: Sandia Nat Labs PO Box 5800 Albuquerque NM 87185-0101*

ROBINSON, CHARLES WESLEY, energy company executive; b. Long Beach, Calif., Sept. 7, 1919; s. Franklin Willard and Anna Hope (Gould) R.; m. Tamara Lindovna, Mar. 8, 1957; children: Heather Lynne, Lisa Anne, Wendy Paige. AB cum laude in Econs., U. Calif., Berkeley, 1941; MBA, Stanford U., 1947. Asst. mgr. mfg. Golden State Dairy Products Co., San Francisco, 1947-49; v.p., then pres. Marcona Corp., San Francisco, 1952-74; undersec. of state for econ. affairs Dept. State, Washington, 1974-75, dep. sec. of state, 1976-77; sr. mng. partner Kuhn Loeb & Co., N.Y.C., 1977-78; vice chmn. Blyth Eastman Dillon & Co., N.Y.C., 1978-79; chmn. Energy Transition Corp., Santa Fe and Washington, 1979-82; pres. Robinson & Assocs., Inc., Santa Fe, 1982—; pres. Dyna-Yacht, Inc., San Diego, 1992—, Mangia Onda Co., San Diego, 1992—; bd. dirs. The Allen Telecom, Inc., NIKE, Inc. Patentee slurry transport., Brookings Instn., Washington, 1977—. Served to lt. USN, 1941-46. Recipient Disting. Honor award Dept. State, 1977. Republican. Methodist. Office: Robinson & Assocs Inc PO Box 2224 Santa Fe NM 87504-2224

ROBINSON, CLAYTON DAVID, minister, educator; b. Pasadena, Calif., Oct. 30, 1955; s. Gary Garth and Gay Elizabeth Clara (Guilmette) R.; m. Kimberly Ann Cole, June 18, 1977; children: Christina Mary, Kathleen Joy, Jonathan David. BA, So. Calif. Coll., 1975; MA, Azusa (Calif.) Pacific U., 1976; MDiv, Fuller Theol. Sem., 1978, D in Ministry, 1986. Ordained to ministry Internat. Ch. of the Foursquare Gospel, 1982. Co-pastor Foursquare Gospel Ch., Huntington Beach, Calif., 1975-82; pastor, founder Foursquare Gospel Ch., Mission Viejo, Calif., 1982-88; pastor Foursquare Gospel Ch., Arcadia, Calif., 1988-91; pastor, founder Foursquare Gospel Ch., Laguna Niguel, Calif., 1991—; mem. faculty Life Bible Coll., L.A., 1985-92; mem. adj. faculty So. Calif. Coll., Costa Mesa, 1985; dir. Pacific Pines Camp, summer 1977-82; youth dir. Orange County (Calif.) Foursquare Chs., 1974-86; founder, dir. The Net Coffee House, Huntington Beach, 1981-82; Saddleback divsn. supt. Foursquare Chs., 1994—. Author: The Revelation, 1976, 2d edit. 1991, The Antichrist, 1980, A Strategy for Church Growth and Renewal, 1986; editor, author: Church Planting, 1991; editl. advisor Ministry Advantage Mag., 1994—; contbr. numerous articles to profl. jours. Founder, pres. New Life Tng. Ctr., 1998—.

ROBINSON, CLEO PARKER, artistic director. Degree in Dance Edn. Psychology, Denver U., DFA (hon.), 1991. Founder, exec. artistic dir., choreographer Cleo Parker Robinson Dance Ensemble, Denver; mem. dance, expansion arts and inter-arts panels NEA; bd. dirs. Denver Ctr. Performing Arts; tchr. in workshops. Co-creator (documentary) African-Americans at Festae, Run Sister Run, (film) Black Women in the Arts, (music video) Borderline. Recipient Thelma Hill Ctr. for the Performing Arts award, 1986; Choreography fellow NEA; named one of Colo. 100, 1992; named to Blacks in Colo. Hall of Fame, 1994. Mem. Internat. Assn. Blacks in Dance (2nd v.p.). Office: Cleo Parker Robinson Dance Ensemble 119 Parker Ave W Denver CO 80205

ROBINSON, DAVID BROOKS, retired naval officer; b. Alexandria, La., Oct. 26, 1939; s. Donald and Marion (Holloman) R.; m. Gene Kirkpatrick, Aug. 1, 1964; children: Kirk, David. Student, Tex. A&M U., 1958-59; BS, U.S. Naval Acad., 1963; MS in Physics, Naval Postgrad. Sch., Monterey, Calif., 1969. Commd. ensign USN, 1963, advanced through grades to vice admiral, 1993; comdg. officer USS Canon and USS Ready, Guam, 1969-71; adminstrv. aide to Chmn. Joint Chiefs Staff, Washington, 1971-74; comdg. officer USS Luce, Mayport, Fla., 1976-78; surface comdr. assignment officer. and dir. fiscal mgt. and procedural control divsn. Naval Mil. Pers. Cmd., 1979-81; mem. Fgn. Service Inst. Exec. Seminar, Washington, 1982; comdg. officer USS Richmond K. Turner, Charleston, S.C., 1983-84; chief of staff, comdr. Naval Surface Force, Atlantic Fleet, Norfolk, Va., 1984; exec. asst. and sr. aide to vice chief Naval Ops., Washington, 1985, dir. Manpower and Tng. div., 1986, dir. Surface Warfare div., 1987-88; cmdr. cruiser destroyer group 8, 1988-89; vice dir. and subsequently dir. operational plans and interoperability directorate Joint Staff, Washington, 1989-91; dep., chief of staff to comdr. U.S. Pacific Fleet, 1991-93, comdr. naval surface force, 1993-96; ret. USN, 1996. Decorated Navy Cross, Def. D.S.M., D.S.M., Legion of Merit with 4 gold stars, Bronze Star, Purple Heart. Mem. Optimists (pres. Oakton, Va. 1986-87). Methodist. Avocations: golf, cycling, stamp collecting, reading.

ROBINSON, DAVID EDWARD, quality engineer, writer; b. San Antonio, Tex., May 28, 1945; s. Morris and Shirley Helen (Susnitsky) R.; m. Elizabeth Susan Wright, Jan. 23, 1973 (div. Sept. 1980); children: Jeremy David, Whitney Amber. Student, U. So. Calif., L.A., 1964. Rsch. devel. solar controls RHO Sigma/Watsco, N. Hollywood, Calif., Hialeah, Fla., 1980-83; quality control maintenance Teledyne Relays, Hawthorne, Calif., 1983-87; quality engr., tech. writer Teledyne Solid State, Hawthorne, Calif., 1988-93; quality engr./govt. liaison Teledyne Electronic Techs., L.A., 1994-98, sr. reliaiblity engr., 1998—. Author: Shards of Frozen Time, 1986, Dark Litanies, 1996. Pres., CEO Idle Hands, Inglewood, Calif., 1986-93; mem. internat. tech. stds. com. , Orlando, Fla., Newport Beach, Calif., 1996—. Mem. Libr. of Congress, Nat. Geographic Soc., Smithsonian Inst., House of Whacks (master 1986—), Order of the Golden Dawn (adeptus major 1971—). Democrat. Jewish. Avocations: musician, poet, astrologer, motorcyclist. E-mail: david e robinson@teledyne.com. & gr8ly8ed@aol.com. Home: 920 W Olive St Inglewood CA 90301-2116 Office: Teledyne Electronic Technologies 12964 Panama St Los Angeles CA 90066-6599

ROBINSON, FISHER JOSEPH, priest; b. Abbeville, La., Aug. 12, 1929; s. Fisher Joseph and Winnie (Smith) R. BA, Divine Word Coll., Epworth, Iowa, 1952; MA, Cath. U. Am., 1959. Joined Soc. of Divine Word, Roman Cath. Ch., 1950, ordained priest, 1958. Dir. formation St. Augustine Sem., Bay St. Louis, Miss., 1959-61; assoc. pastor Notre Dame Cath. Ch., St. Martinville, La., 1961-63; dir. formation Divine Word Sem., Riverside, Calif., 1963-66, instr., 1963-67; prin. Verbum Dei High Sch., L.A., 1967-80; pastor St. Malachy's Ch., L.A., 1980-89; vicar Black Caths., African-Am. Vicariate, L.A., 1986—; mem. Archdiocesan Coun. Priests, L.A., 1976-80; cons. [illegible] Ch. Studies, L.A., 1980; chair L.A. Archdiocesan Team of Nat. Black Cath. Pastoral Plan on Evangelization L.A., 1987. Co-author: Pastoral of African-American Catholics in the Archdiocese of Los Angeles, 1987. Commn. L.A. [illegible] 1978; bd. dirs. Community Care and Devel., L.A., 1983; mem. task force

Respect for Life, L.A. Archdiocese, 1987; sec., bd. dirs. St. John's Major Sem., L.A., 1988. Mem. Nat. Bd. Black Cath. Adminstrs. (bd. dirs., rep. western regional div. 1988). Home: 6028 S Victoria Ave Los Angeles CA 90043-3908 Office: African-Am Vicariate 1530 W 9th St Los Angeles CA 90015-1111

ROBINSON, GEORGE MAKENZIA LEWIS, mining services director; b. Hamilton, Ont., Can., Mar. 13, 1945; s. John F. Robinson and Barbara Holton; m. Tracey A. Murphy, Mar. 2, 1991; children: Shiloh, Amannda, Dayle. BS, Ea. N.Mex. U., 1970; MS, Kent State U., 1972. Hydrology mgr. Williams Bros. Energy Co., Tulsa, 1972-74, VTN, Denver, 1974-76; environ. mgr. Peabody Coal Co., Denver, 1976-80; hydrology mgr. Earth Tech., Denver, 1980-82, Fox Cons., Denver, 1982-84; pres., CEO Enecotech, Denver, 1984-88; v.p. Western Tech., Denver, 1988-90; gen. mgr. Chem. Waste Mgmt., Freemont, Calif., 1990-91, 1990-91; dir. mining svcs. Harding Lawson Assocs., Denver, 1991—; hydrology mgr. Earth Tech., Denver, 1980-82, UTN, Denver, 1974-76, Williams Bros. Energy Co., Tulsa, 1972-74; environ. mgr. Peabody Coal Co., Denver, 1976-80; presenter in field. Contbr. articles to profl. jours. Fellow Kent State U., 1970-72. Mem. Am. Inst. Prof. Geologists (lic.), Soc. Mining Engrs. (workshop leader 1985-86, sec. 1986-87, chmn. 1987-88), Nat. Petroleum Refinery Assn. (mem. environ. com. 1996—), Nat. Coal Assn. (com. mem. 1976-80). Avocations: golf, skiing. Office: Harding Lawson Assocs # 3400 707 17th St Ste 3400 Denver CO 80202-3434

ROBINSON, HERBERT HENRY, III, educator, psychotherapist; b. Leavenworth, Wash., Mar. 31, 1933; s. Herbert Henry II and Alberta (Sperber) R.; m. Georgia Murial Jones, Nov. 24, 1954 (div. 1974); children: Cheri Dean Asbury, David Keith, Peri Elizabeth Layton, Tanda Rene Graff, Gaila Daire. Grad. of Theology, Bapt. Bible Coll., 1959; BA in Philosophy/Greek, Whitworth Coll., 1968; MA in Coll. Teaching, Ea. Wash. U., 1976; postgrad., Gonzaga U., 1980—. Cert. psychotherapist, perpetrator treatment program supervision; nat. bd. cert. counselor. Choir dir. Twin City Bapt. Temple, Mishawaka, Ind., 1959-61; min. Inland Empire Bapt. Ch., Spokane, 1961-73; tchr. philosophy Spokane (Wash.) C.C., 1969-72; dir. Alternatives to Violence, Women in Crisis, Fairbanks, Alaska, 1985-87; tchr. pub. rels. U. Alaska, Fairbanks, 1986-87; dir. Alternatives to Violence Men Inc., Juneau, 1988-89; tchr. leadership mgmt. U. Alaska S.E., Juneau, 1988-89; min. Sci. of Mind Ctr., Sandpoint, Idaho, 1989-92; dir., therapist Tapio Counseling Ctr., Spokane, 1991—; cert. psychotherapist, supr. perpetrator treatment program Wash.; cons. Lilac Blind/Alpha Inc./Marshall Coll., Spokane, 1975-85, Alaska Placer Mining Co., Fairbanks, 1987; tchr. Spokane Falls C.C., Spokane, 1979-85; seminar, presenter Human Resource Devel., Spokane and Seattle, Wash., Pa., 1980; guest trainer United Way/Kellogg Found. Inst. for Volunteerism, Spokane, 1983. 1st trombone San Diego Marine Band, 1953-56, Spokane Symphony, 1961; bd. dirs. Tanani Learning Ctr., Fairbanks, 1987; mem. consensus bldg. team Sci. of Mind Ctr., Sandpoint, 1989-92. Cpl. USMC, 1953-56. Mem. ACA, Assn. for Humanistic Edn. and Devel., Assn. for Religious Values in Counseling, Internat. Assn. Addictions and Offender Counselors, Internat. Assn. Marriage and Family Counselors, Am. Assn. Profl. Hypnotherapists, Masterson Inst. Office: Tapio Counseling 3625 E Sprague Ave Spokane WA 99202-4840

ROBINSON, J. KENNETH, religious organization administrator, minister; b. Ft. Smith, Ark., Sept. 27, 1932; s. John B. and Jessie Mary (Ledbetter) R.; m. Addie Muriel Thompson, Nov. 22, 1956; children: J. Mark, Elizabeth Robinson Clifton, Robin Robinson Newman, Price. AA, Westark Coll., 1951; BS, Okla. Bapt. U., 1954; MRE, Southwestern Bapt. Theol. Sem., 1956. Ordained to ministry So. Bapt. Conv., 1975. Min. music/edn. San Jacinto Bapt. Ch., Amarillo, Tex., 1964-67, First Bapt. Ch., Carlsbad, N.Mex., 1967-71, Meadows Bapt. Ch., Plano, Tex., 1971-81, First Bapt. Ch., Carlsbad, N.Mex., 1981-86; dir. missions Pecos Valley Bapt. Assn., Artesia, N.Mex., 1987—; mem. com. on coms. So. Bapt. Conv., Nashville, 1971; v.p. Bapt. Conv. N.Mex., Albuquerque, 1970-71, bd. dirs., 1984-85; dir. Sunday sch. Pecos Valley Bapt. Assn., 1983-87; adj. prof. Sch. Ch. Music, Southwestern Bapt. Theol. Sem., Ft. Worth, 1979-80. Co-author: Music Making with Younger Children, 1971, Ministry of Religious Edn., 1978; contbr. articles to various jours. V.p. Plano Assn. for Retarded Citizens, 1979-81; bd. dirs. Community Concert Assn., Carlsbad, Artesia Community Concert Assn. Democrat. Home: 1407 W Cannon Ave Artesia NM 88210-1128 Office: Pecos Valley Bapt Assn PO Box 267 Artesia NM 88211-0267

ROBINSON, JULIA E., health facility administrator; b. Laramie, Wyo., Dec. 11, 1950; d. Ralph Thomas and Elinor Margaret (Sewison) R.; m. Peter Benson Kozisek; 1 child, Scott. BA, Hastings Coll., 1973; MA, Ariz. State U., 1975; PhD, U. So. Calif., 1995. Non-profit dir. Wyo. Govt. Divsn. Adminstr., Cheyenne, 1975-80; adminstr. Divsn. Pub. Assistance, Cheyenne, 1985-89; dir. Mont. Dept. Social Rehab. Svcs., Helena, 1989-92; rsch. prof. Boise State U., 1996-97; asst. prof. U. Colo., Colo. Springs, 1997-99; health cons., 1992—; cons. Idaho Commn. Nursing and Nursing Edn., Boise, 1997-98. Contbr. articles to profl. jours. Active 1st United Meth. Ch., Boise, Idaho, 1997—. Named Good Housekeeping Mag. 100 Young Women Promise, 1985; recognized for Best in the West Welfare Reform, Fed. Region VIII H.S., Helena, 1991. Mem. ASPA. Avocations: aerobics, skiing, playing piano. Home: 600 Troutner Way Boise ID 83712-7550

ROBINSON, KIT, poet, public relations director; b. Evanston, Ill., May 17, 1949; s. James Keith and Pamela Ruth (Lyne) R.; m. Andrea Barker, Aug. 9, 1984; 1 child, Ericka McConnell. BA, Yale U., 1971. San Francisco area coord. Calif. Poets in the Schs., 1976-83; dir. Tenderloin writers workshop Central City Hospitality House, San Francisco, 1982-83; mgr. comm. ComputerLand Corp., Pleasanton, Calif., 1983-93; dir. writing svcs. Blanc & Otus Pub. Rels., San Francisco, 1994-95; dir. pub. rels. PeopleSoft, Inc., Pleasanton, 1995—. Author: Ice Cubes, 1987, The Champagne of Concrete, 1991, Balance Sheet, 1993, Democracy Boulevard, 1998; translator: Ode on Visiting the Belosaraisk Spit on the Sea of Azov, 1995. Bd. mem. New Langton Arts, San Francisco, 1994-97. Recipient Artist in the Cmty. award Calif. Arts Coun., Sacramento, 1982, Poetry prize The Fund for Poetry, N.Y.C., 1995; Creative Writing fellow Nat. Endowment for the Arts, Washington, 1979. Mem. Small Press Distbn., Small Press Traffic, The Poetry Project. Avocations: basketball, music, books. Office: PeopleSoft Inc 4440 Rosewood Dr Pleasanton CA 94588-3097

ROBINSON, LARRY CLARK, professional hockey coach; b. Winchester, Ont., Can., June 2, 1951; m. Jeannette; children: Jeffery, Rachelle. With Montreal Canadians, Los Angeles Kings; head coach L.A. Kings, 1995—. Received 7 Stanley Cups. Avocations: Polo, Boating. Home: 116 29th St Manhattan Beach CA 90266-2019 Office: LA Kings Staples Ctr 3900 W Manchester Blvd Inglewood CA 90305-2200*

ROBINSON, MARK LEIGHTON, oil company executive, petroleum geologist, horse farm owner; b. San Bernardino, Calif., Aug. 4, 1927; s. Ernest Guy and Florence Iola (Lemmon) R.; m. Jean Marie Ries, Feb. 8, 1954; children: Francis Willis, Mark Ries, Paul Leighton. AB cum laude in Geology, Princeton U., 1950; postgrad. Stanford U., 1950-51. Geologist Shell Oil Co., Billings, Mont., Rapid City, S.D., Denver, Midland, Tex., 1951-56, dist. geologist, Roswell, N.Mex., 1957-60, div. mgr., Roswell, N.Mex., 1961-63, Jackson, Miss., 1964-65, Bakersfield, Calif., 1967-68, mgr. exploration econs., N.Y.C., 1969; mgmt. advisor BIPM (Royal Dutch Shell Oil Co.), The Hague, The Netherlands, 1966; pres., chmn. bd. dirs. Robinson Resource Devel. Co., Inc., Roswell, 1970—; chmn., pres. Como Petroleum Corp., Roswell, 1994—. Campaign chmn. Chaves County Rep. Com., Roswell, 1962; mem. alumni schs. com. Princeton U., 1980—. Served with USNR, 1945-46. Mem. Roswell Geol. Soc. (trustee 1972), Am. Assn. Petroleum Geologists, Stanford U. Earth Scientists Assn., Yellowstone Bighorn Research Assn., Am. Horse Shows Assn., SAR, Sigma Xi. Episcopalian. Discovered Lake Como oil field, Miss., 1971, McNeal oil field, Miss., 1973, North Deer Creek Gas Field, Mont., 1983, Bloomfield East Oil Field, Mont., 1986. Home: 1508 Oljato Rd Roswell NM 88201-9300 Office: Robinson Resource Devel Co Inc PO Box 1227 Roswell NM 88202-1227

ROBINSON, RICHARD ALLEN, JR., human resources development trainer, consultant; b. Ellensburg, Wash., Aug. 21, 1936; s. Richard Allen and Rosa Adele (Oswald) R.; m. R. Elaine Whitham, Sept. 8, 1956; children: Sharon E. Robinson Losey, Richard Allen, René L. Rivera. BA, U. Wash., 1958; postgrad. U.S. Army Command and Gen. Staff Coll., 1969-70; MA, U. Mo., 1971. Commd. 2d lt. U.S. Army, 1958, advanced through grades to lt. col., 1972, various infantry assignments including command, 1958-72, research and devel. assignments including dep. dir. test of behavioral sci., dep. commandant U.S.A. Organizational Effectiveness, 1975-77, ret., 1979; chief office orgn. and employee devel. Wash. Dept. Social and Health Services, Olympia, 1979—; pvt. practice orgn. and mgmt. devel. cons./trainer, 1979—. Decorated Legion of Merit with oak leaf cluster, Bronze Star. Mem. ASTD. Contbg. author: Games Trainers Play, vol. II, 1983. Office: DSHS Mail 8425 27th St W Tacoma WA 98466-2722

ROBINSON, THELMA MAY, pediatrics nurse, researcher, writer; b. Mahaska, Kans., June 22, 1925; d. Grant William and Della May (Dustin) Morey; m. Donald Richard Robinson, Oct. 1, 1947; children: Dennis, Mary Louise, Larry, Bruce. BSN, U. Colo., 1969, MSN, 1970. Cert. sch. nurse practitioner. Clinic coord. U. Colo., Denver, summers 1976-78; sch. nurse practitioner Boulder (Colo.) County Health Dept., 1970-79; sch. nurse practitioner instr. U. Colo., 1979-83; sch. nurse practitioner cons. Chugiak, Alaska, 1983-86; pediatric nurse specialist Pub. Health-State of Alaska, Anchorage, 1986-93; rsch. coord., editor Cadet Nurse Corps Project, Chugiak, 1993—; adj. faculty U. Alaska, Anchorage, 1984-92; presenter in field. Mem. editl. bd., writer U. Wash. N.W. Bulletin, 1992-93, Continuing Ednl. Profl. Writer, Inc., 1986. County nurse chmn., instr. ARC, Boulder, 1958, 63; host family Internat. Students, Inc., Boulder, 1979-83; vol. screener Alaska Blood Bank, Anchorage, 1992, vol. nurse Alaska Pub. Health Dept., 1998; libr. vol. Anchorage Pub. Librs., Eagle River, 1994. Served with Cadet Nurse Corps, 1944-46; Stephens minister, mission rep. to Russia, 1998. Recipient Alumni of Yr. award Lincoln Gen. Hosp. Sch. Nursing Alumni Assn., Commrs. award, 1994. Mem. ANA, Colo. Nurses Assn. (continuing edn. reviewer 1970-84, Outstanding Contbn. award 1983, Writer of Yr. award 1983, dist. 12 pres. 1983-84, Disting. Nurse of Yr. 1984), Alaska Nurses Assn. (membership com. 1985), Nat. Assn. Sch. Nurses (rsch. com. 1980-84, module writer, presenter 1980-88, Outstanding Svc. award 1984), Am. Assn. for History of Nursing (candidate elections com.); charter mem. Women in Mil. Svc. Am. (WIMSA field rep. 1996-97). Presbyterian (elder 1985-86). Avocations: quilting, hiking, nordic skiing, thimble collecting, cuisine (Great State Salad Bowl champion Alaska State Fair 1991). Home and Office: PO Box 671503 Chugiak AK 99567-1503

ROBINSON, THEODORE GOULD, golf course architect; b. Long Beach, Calif., May 17, 1923; s. Franklin Willard and Hope (Gould) R.; m. Barbara Henderson, Oct. 28, 1949; children: Theodore G. Jr., Kristine Robinson Monroe, Leigha Robinson Ramsey. BA, U. Calif., Berkeley, 1944; MS, U. So. Calif., 1948. With Gordon Whitnall & Assocs., L.A., 1941-51; prin. Robinson Golf Design, Dana Point, Calif., 1951—. Designer 170 golf courses throughout world. Ensign USN, 1943-46. Recipient awards for best new courses Golf Digest. Mem. Am Soc. Golf Course Architects (pres. 1983). Office: Robinson Golf Designs Inc 30131 Town Center Dr Ste 268 Laguna Niguel CA 92677-2082

ROBISON, JOANNE AHLEEN, elementary education educator; b. Salt Lake City, Oct. 7, 1941; d. Clarence W. and Faye (Potter) Ahleen; m. Warren S. Robison, Aug. 9, 1963; children: Sydney Bowman, Mark, Leslie Young, Stephanie Hickman, Matthew. BS, U. Utah, 1971. Cert. elem. tchr., Utah. Tchr. West Jordan (Vt.) Elem. Contbr. poetry to anthologies; exhibited paintings at shows.

ROBLES, ELIODORO GONZALES, consulting company executive, educator; b. Paniqui, Tarlac, The Philippines, July 3, 1923; s. Mariano Abraham and Lucia (Gonzales) R.; m. Rosario Palaganas Lavitoria, Oct. 30, 1964; children: Michael, Elmer, Eliodoro Jr., Marilou, Jonathan, Jay. BS in Polit. Sci., Far Eastern U., 1953; MA in Internat. Rels., Cornell U., 1954; MA in Polit. Economy, Harvard U., 1955, PhD in Polit. Economy, 1959. Cert. tchr., Calif.; cert. C.C. instr., Calif. C.C.; cert. C.C. supr., Calif. C.C. Instr. Far Eastern U., Manila, 1952-53; tech. cons., staff asst. Embassy of the Rep. of Indonesia in the Philippines, 1950-53; spl. asst. on fgn. econ. policies Program Implementation Office of the Pres. of the Philippines, 1962-64; prof. econs. and polit. sci., dean Grad. Sch. Far Eastern U., Manila, 1959-64; econ. officer, dep. dir. for econ., cultural, social affairs S.E. Asia Treaty Orgn. (SEATO), Bangkok, 1964-74; project dir. San Francisco Unified Sch. Dist., 1975-79; sr. assoc. Devel. Assocs., Inc., Walnut Creek, Calif., 1979—; evaluation specialistluding polit. economist USAID, various locations, Calif., 1984-85; ednl. adminstrn. specialist USAID, Manila and Islamabad, Pakistan, 1987; tng. specialist, Asia Narcotics Edn. Program USAID, 1988-89, polit. economist, 1992—; presenter, attendee numerous confs., seminars and workshops including Nat. Conf. on Sch. Sys. and Bilingual Edn., San Jose, Calif., 1975, Conf. on Bilingual Edn.: Asian Am. Bilingual Materials Devel. Ctr., Berkeley, Calif., 1975, Ctr. for Ednl. Devel., San Francisco, Calif., 1975, among others. Author: Economic Analysis, 1966, The Philippine in the Nineteenth Century, 1969. Lt. col. Philippine Army, 1941-46; 1st lt. inf. U.S. Army, 1946-49. Recipient scholarship Fulbright Assn., 1954; Telluride fellow Cornell U., 1954, Fletcher fellow Harvard U., 1954-55, Newberry fellow Newberry Libr., 1957-58. Mem. Fulbright Assn., Filipino Am. Tchrs. Assn., Far Eastern U. Alumni Assn. (bd. dirs., adviser 1991—), Harvard Club San Francisco. Democrat. Methodist. Avocations: general gardening, orchid growing, stamp and coin collecting. Home: 1335 Greenway Dr Richmond CA 94803 Office: Devel Assocs Inc 1475 N Broadway Walnut Creek CA 94596

ROBLES, NEOPITO DE LEON, surgeon; b. Malolos, Philippines, Jan. 20, 1932; s. Tirso Leon and Consolacion (Garcia) R.; m. Rachel Louise Mason, Oct. 4, 1959; children: Robert, Peter, James. MD, U. Santo Tomas, Manila, 1955. Intern Gen. Rose Meml. Hosp., Denver, 1955-56; resident pathology St. Lukes Hosp., Denver, 1956-57; resident gen. surgery Broaddus Hosp.-Myers Clin. Philippi, 1957-60, VA Hosp., Clarksburg, 1961-63; attending surgeon St. Mary's Hosp., 1968—, Tucson (Ariz.) Med. Ctr., 1988—; clin. asst. prof. surgery U. Ariz., 1982—. Fellow ACS, Am. Coll. Angiology, Southwestern Surg. Congress; mem. AMA, Ariz. Med. Assn. (past pres. 1983-84), Pima County Med. Soc. (pres. elect 1997). Office: Thomas-Davis Clinic 630 N Alvernon Way Tucson AZ 85711-1870

ROBSON, KENT E., philosophy educator; b. Ogden, Utah, Oct. 11, 1937; s. Ralph E. and Amy (Folkman) R.; m. Joan Soles, Aug. 18, 1961; children: Kara, Kevin, Heather, Amber. BS, U. Utah; PhD, Stanford U. Teaching asst. Stanford (Calif.) U., 1964-66, research fellow, 1966-68; research fellow U. Warsaw, Poland, 1968-69; asst. prof. philosophy Utah State U., Logan, 1969-75, assoc. prof., 1975-82, prof., head dept. langs. and philosophy, 1981—. Author, co-editor: Readings in Philosophy, 1994, The Normative Constitution, 1995; contbr. chpts. to books, articles to profl. jours. Mem. exec. com. Utah Endowment for Humanities, 1974-80; chmn. nat. screening com. Fulbright Hays Grants to Eastern Europe, 1977-78, 84; pres. Utah State U. Faculty Senate, 1992-94. Named Prof. of Yr., Utah State U., 1973; Danforth assoc., 1980. Mem. Utah Acad. Scis., Arts and Letters (chmn. philos. sect. 1974-76, 78-80, governing bd. 1982-84), Phi Beta Kappa, Phi Kappa Phi. Served to capt. U.S. Army, 1962-64. Club: Imperial Glee (Logan). Office: Utah State U Dept Langs and Philosophy Logan UT 84322

ROCHE, JOAN I., artist; b. Hamilton, Ont., Can., Jan. 21, 1935; came to U.S., 1964; d. Thomas Dick and Florence (Eaves) Bowman; m. E. Michael Roche, Jan. 23, 1954; 1 child, Wayne P. Grad., Can. Bus. Coll., 1952, Coll. of Marin, 1968, Irvine Valley Coll., 1986. Various secretarial and adminstrv. positions, 1952-70. Exhibited in numerous shows, including Coll. of Marin, 1968, Irvine Valley Coll., 1986, Pa. Watercolor Soc. (award of merit 1990), Catharine Lorrilard Art Club, N.Y., Niagara Frontier Watercolor Soc., N.Y., Rocky Mountain Nat. Watermedia Exhibit, Colo., Costa Mesa (Calif.) Fine Arts Competition (People's Choice award), Irvine Art Ctr., 1991, 92, Newport Beach Salute to Arts, Arts on the Green, Costa Mesa, Ariz. Aqueous VIII, Irvine Creative Arts Show (Best of Show), Irvine Fine Art League (1st Pl. award), Watercolor Art Soc., Tex., Art Show at the Dog Show, Kans., Brush With Nature, Newport Beach (Best of Show award), Am. Watercolor Soc., N.Y., Watercolor West, Nat. Watercolor Soc., 1995 (Watercolor West award), Nat. Watercolor Soc. Signature Mem. Show, 1996, Fallbrook Art Assn. Fall All Media Show (Best of Show), Fallbrook Art Assn. (Spring All Media Show (Best of Show), Adirondacks Nat. Exhbn., 1997, Calif. Watercolor Assn.; contbr. to books: Places in Watercolor, Painting Shapes and Edges, How To Capture Movement in Your Painting, Ency. of Flower Painting Techniques, Watercolor Planning & Painting. Recipient Winsor Newton award Am. Watercolor Soc., 1998. Mem. Nat. Watercolor Soc. (signature, 2d v.p. bd. dirs., travel show chair 1996, 97, Watercolor West award 1995), Watercolor West (juried assoc.), Fallbrook Art Assn., San Diego Watercolor Soc., Laguna Niguel Art Assn. Avocation: reading. Home: 1149 Mcdonald Rd Fallbrook CA 92028-3548

ROCK, MARY ANN, fine artist, educator, consultant; b. St. Louis, Mar. 2, 1931; d. Clobert Bernard and Mary Henrietta (Jones) Broussard; m. William Ralph Rock, Mar. 18, 1960 (div. Sept. 1967); 1 child, John Henry C. BS, Bennett Coll., 1952; postgrad., Chgo. Art Inst., 1953-54, So. Ill. U., Carbondale, 1955. Instr. arts and crafts Presidio Hill Sch., San Francisco, 1966-71; dir. gallery Cannery House Gallery, Friday Harbor, Wash., 1974-76; co-founder Island Artisans, Friday Harbor, 1980-85; gallery asst. Waterworks Gallery, Friday Harbor, 1986-95. Author, illustrator: DreamKeeper, 1995; illustrator brochures; one-woman and group shows include 13th Salon Internat. del Alpha, Lyon, France, 7th Whatcomb County Museum Bellingham, 1988, Portland C.C., 1990, Chetwynn Stapleton Gallery, Portland, 1989-98, Waterworks Gallery, Friday Harbor, 1986—. Presenter art workshops Friday Harbor Elem. Sch., 1976, 87, Portland C.C., 1989, 90; curator African art exhibit NAACP, San Francisco, 1961. Vt. Studio Ctr. fellow, Johnson, Vt., 1999. Democrat. Avocations: collecting ethnic artifacts, skiing, rock climbing, travel, reading. Office: Waterworks Gallery PO Box 28 Friday Harbor WA 98250

ROCKSTED, ELAINE MARTI, association administrator; b. Wheeling, W. Va., Oct. 7, 1944; d. Wayne and Mary Kay Marti; m. Wayne L. Dachtler, Aug. 22, 1968 (div. Nov., 1979); children: Brian K., Eric W.; m. Donald B. Rocksted, Dec. 8, 1980; 1 child, Andrea M. BA, Ohio U., 1966; MA with hons., Regis U., 1996. English instr. Arapahoe C.C., Littleton, Colo., 1991-97, Rocky Mt. Coll. of Art and Design, Denver, 1997, 98; comm. coord. Denver (Colo.) Options, 1996—. Author, editor (newsletters) Denver Options, 1997—. Mem. AAUW. Avocations: golf, bike riding, walking, reading. Office: Denver Options 5250 Leetsdale Dr Ste 200 Denver CO 80246-1451

ROCKSTROH, DENNIS JOHN, journalist, screenwriter; b. Hermosa Beach, Calif., Feb. 1, 1942; s. Philip Herman and Alicia (Rubio) R.; m. Le Thi Que Huong, May 2, 1970; children: Bryan Benjamin, Paula Kim-Mai. Student, San Luis Rey Coll., 1960-61, El Camino Coll., 1961-62, San Fernando Valley State Coll., 1965-67. Reporter Thousand Oaks (Calif.) News Chronicle, 1966-67; tchr. Girls' High Sch., Qui Nhon, Vietnam, 1967-70; instr. Dalat U./Vietnamese Mil. Acad., 1970-71, Ohlone Coll., Fremont, Calif., 1984—; freelance war corr. Dispatch News Svc., Vietnam, 1967-71; city editor Santa Paula (Calif.) Daily Chronicle, 1972-73; reporter San Jose (Calif.) Mercury News, 1973-90, columnist, 1990—; guest lectr. U. Calif., Berkeley, 1987-91. Vol. Internat. Vol. Svcs., Vietnam, 1967-71; bd. dirs. San Jose unit ARC, 1978, Hope Rehab., San Jose, 1976-77. With U.S. Army, 1962-65, Vietnam. Co-recipient Pulitzer prize for Loma Prieta earthquake coverage, 1989; decorated Army Commendation Medal for Valor, 1965. Mem. Soc. Profl. Journalists, St. Anthony's Sem. Alumni Assn., Nat. Soc. Newspaper Columnists. Roman Catholic. Home: 3573 Tankerland Ct San Jose CA 95121-1244 Office: San Jose Mercury News 39355 California St Ste 305 Fremont CA 94538-1447

ROCKWELL, DON ARTHUR, psychiatrist; b. Wheatland, Wyo., Apr. 24, 1938; s. Orson Arthur and Kathleen Emily Rockwell; m. Frances Pepitone-Arreola, Dec. 23, 1965; children: Grant, Chad. BA, Wash. U., 1959; MD, U. Okla., 1963; MA in Sociology, U. Calif., Berkeley, 1967. Diplomate Am. Bd. Psychiatry and Neurology. Intern in surgery San Francisco Gen. Hosp., 1963-64; resident in psychiatry Langley-Porter Neuropsychiatric Inst. U. Calif. Med. Ctr., San Francisco, 1964-67; instr. dept. psychiatry U. Calif. Sch. Medicine, Davis, 1969-70, asst. prof., 1970-74, assoc. prof., 1974-80, acting. assoc., dean curricular affairs, 1979-80, acting assoc. dean student affairs, 1980, assoc. dean student affairs, 1980-82, prof., 1980-84; career tchr. NIMH, 1970-72; assoc. psychiatrist Sacramento Med. Ctr.; med. dir. U. Calif. Med. Ctr., Davis, 1982-84; prof., vice chmn. dept. psychiatry and biobehavioral scis. UCLA, 1984-96; dir. UCLA NPH, 1984-95; chief profl. staff Neuropsychiat. Inst., UCLA, 1984-85, also dir. outpatient svcs.; chmn. U. Calif. Hosp. Dirs. Council, 1988-89; cons. Nat. Commn. on Marijuana, Washington, 1971-73. Co-author: Psychiatric Disorders, 1982; contbr. chpts. to books; articles to profl. jours. Bd. dirs. Bereavement Outreach, Sacramento, 1974-84, Suicide Prevention, Yolo County, 1969-84; bd. visitors U. Okla. Sch. Medicine; chmn. hosp. dirs. coun. U. Calif. Hosp.; governing coun. AHA Psychiat. Hosp. Fellow Am. Psychiat. Assn., Am. Coll. Psychiatrists, Am. Coll. Mental Health Adminstrs.; mem. AMA (gov. coun. psych. hosp.), Am. Sociologic Assn., Calif. Med. Assn. (med. staff survey com.), Cen. Calif. Psychiat. Assn. (sec.-pres. 1977-78), U. Calif. Alumni Assn. (trustee 1981-86), Alpha Omega Alpha. Home: 1816 E Las Tunas Rd Santa Barbara CA 93103-1744

ROCKWELL, ELIZABETH GOODE, dance company director, consultant, educator; b. Portland, Oreg., Sept. 10, 1920; d. Henry Walton and Elizabeth (Harmon) Goode; m. William Hearne Rockwell, Feb. 3, 1948; children: Enid, Karen, William. BA, Mills Coll., 1941; MA, NYU, 1946. Instr. dance Monticello Jr. Coll., Alton, Ill., 1941-42; dir. masters program in dance Smith Coll., Northampton, Mass., 1946-48; 1st dir. dance dept. High Sch. of Performing Arts, N.Y.C., 1948-51, 53-54; dir. Elizabeth Rockwell Sch. Dance, Bedford, N.Y., 1956-86, Rondo Dance Theater Internat. Dance Touring Co., Bedford, 1971-93; tchr. continuing dance classes CCAE, 1994—; with Martha Graham, 1944-46, with Hanya Holm, 1946-48, with José Limon, 1949-52; mem. adv. ednl. com. Calif. Ctr. for Arts, Escondido, Calif., 1993-95, dir. dance classes, 1994—. Choreographer (suite of dances) Jazz Suite, 1966, (50-minute dances) Catch the Wind, 1969, Genesis, 1972, (narrative modern ballet) The Executioner, 1974, Decathalon, 1982; dir. (subscription series) Dance-Art-Poetry-Jazz, 1978-79, (dance/music 1600-1900) Stages in Ages, 1981, (Am. dance revivals) Masterpieces of American Dance, 1982-84, Dances of the Decades, 1985-90, (revival & new choreography) Dances of Our Times, 1991; dir. dance workshops for Calif. Ctr. Arts, 1994, 95, 96; creator, founder performing group of older dancers Golden Connections Dance Ensemble of Women, CCAE, (touring San Diego area), 1996—. Bd. dirs. Coun. for Arts in Westchester, White Plains, N.Y., 1978-79, affiliate, 1978—. Recipient Medal for Performance, Israeli Army, 1966, Award for Excellence in Arts Edn. Alumnae of High Sch. of Performing Arts, 1990, various grants N.Y. State Coun. on Arts, 1971-93, Coun. Arts in Westchester, 1973-92, dance touring program grant Nat. Endowment for Arts, 1975-79. Mem. Am. Dance Guild, Westchester Dance Coun. (program dir. 1965-69), Assn. Am. Dance Cos., San Diego Area Dance Alliance (bd. dirs. 1995—). Avocations: writing, swimming, touring, reading. Home: 205 Tampico Gln Escondido CA 92025-7359

ROCKWELL, KAY ANNE, elementary education educator; b. Brighton, Mich., Feb. 12, 1952; d. Philip Oscar and Patricia Irene (Bennett) Newton; m. Lawrence Edward Rockwell, Aug. 23, 1975. BA in Social Sci. & Elem. Edn. cum laude, Spring Arbor Coll., 1974; MA in Early Childhood Edn., Ea. Mich. U., 1981. Dir. child care St. Luke's Luth. Day Care Ctr., Ann Arbor, Mich., 1980-82; tchr. 3d grade Colo. Christian Sch., Denver, 1982-94; tchr. 1st grade Front Range Christian Sch., Littleton, Colo., 1994—; chmn. Nat. Children's Book Week Colo. Christian Sch., 1993-94, chmn. ACSI spelling bee, 1991-94, chmn. ACSI speech meet, 1985-86. Spring Arbor Coll. scholar, 1972-74. Office: Front Range Christian Sch 4001 S Wadsworth Blvd Littleton CO 80123-1358

ROCKWOOD, LINDA LEE, lawyer; b. Cedar Rapids, Iowa, July 25, 1950; d. Robert Walter and Dorothy Jean (Rehberg) Sorensen; children: Holly Lynn, Christian Douglas. BA, U. Denver, 1972; JD, U. Tex., 1984. Bar: Colo. 1984, U.S. Dist. Ct. Colo., U.S. Ct. Appeals (10th cir.). Econ. and consumer research analyst May Dept. Stores, St. Louis, 1973-75; asst. dir. Ctr. for Study Am. Bus., Washington U., St. Louis, 1975-77; mgr. Mid-Columbia Symphony, Richland, Wash., 1978-79; assoc. Holland & Hart, Denver, 1984-88; shareholder, dir. Parcel, Mauro & Spaanstra, Denver, 1988-98, pres., 1996-98; ptnr. Faegre & Benson, Denver, 1998—. Author: New Mines From Old Environmental Considerations in Remining and Reprocessing of Waste Materials, 1991, The Alcan Decisions: Causation Through the Back Door, 1993, RCRA Demystified: The Professional's Guide to Hazardous Waste Law, 1996. Bd. dirs. Colo. Hazardous Waste Mgmt. Soc., 1986, 89-91, pres., 1987-88. Mem. ABA (vice chmn. environ. values com.

adminstrv. law sect. 1986-91, hard minerals com. natural resources law sect. 1987-90), Colo. Bar Assn. (exec. coun. environ. law sect. 1987-90), Order of Coif, Phi Beta Kappa. Presbyterian. E-mail: lrockwoo@faegre.com. Office: Faegre & Benson LLP 2500 Republic Plaza 370 17th St Denver CO 80202-4004

RODDICK, DAVID BRUCE, construction company executive; b. Oakland, Calif., Oct. 31, 1948; s. Bruce Ergo and Hortensia Cabo (Castedo) R.; m. Sharon Ann Belan, May 25, 1975; children: Heather Marie, Christina Dee-Ann. *Wife Sharon is an elementary school teacher for the San Jose Unified School District. She received a B.S. in Home Economics from California Polytechnic State University, San Luis Opispo in 1974 and a teaching credential from California State University, San Jose 1993. Sharon interrupted a promising career as a purchasing agent in 1980 to raise daughters Heather and Christina. Sharon changed to a teaching career after supporting an elementary school as a PTA President and member of the Site Council. Sharon also teaches adult bible study classes at Heart of the Valley Church in San Jose.* BSCE, U. Calif., Davis, 1971. Engr. Bechtel Corp., San Francisco, 1971-77, contract specialist, 1977-78; subcontract adminstr. Boecon Corp., Richland, Wash., 1978-79; constrn. mgr. BE&C Engrs., Inc., Vancouver, Wash., 1979-81; contracts mgr. Boecon Corp., Tukwila, Wash., 1981-83; sr. constrn. mgr. BE&C Engrs., Inc., Wichita, Kans., 1983-84; project mgr., v.p. ops. Carl Holvick Co., Sunnyvale, Calif., 1984-88, also sec. bd. dirs.; v.p., gen. mgr. Brookman Co. div. B.T. Mancini Co., Inc., Milpitas, Calif., 1988-92; v.p., sec., CFO B.T. Mancini Co., Inc., 1992-98, sr. v.p. ops., CFO, corp. sec., 1998—. *Over 27 years of progressively responsible experience as both a professional in the construction industry as an operational and financial manager and as a dedicated citizen-soldier in the United States Army Reserve. Contributions to the Army Engineer Regimental Corps were recently recognized by award of the Bronze de Fleury Medal from the Army Engineer Association. While working for an Engineering News-Record (ENR) Top 600 Specialty Contractor David Roddick was promoted from a position as a branch manager to Senior Vice-President Operations and CFO contributing to a reorganization of the company resulting in 115% growth in sales and record profitability.* Mem. devel. com. San Jose (Calif.) Mus. Assn., 1993-95; mem., dir. Constrn. Fin. Mgmt. Assn., 1995—, pres. elect Silicon Valley chpt., 1999—; pres. Reed Sch. PTA, San Jose, 1986-88, San Jose Coun. PTA's, 1988-89; trustee Heart of Valley Bapt. Ch.; bd. dirs. Vinehill Homeowners Assn., 1975-77. Lt. col. USAR Corps Engrs., 1969—. Decorated Army Achievement medal, 1988, Commendation medal, 1991, 96, 98, meritorious svc. medal, 1998; recipient Calif. State PTA Hon. Svc. award, 1988, Bronze de Fluery medal Army Engr. Assn., 1998. Mem. Am. Soc. Civil Engrs., Res. Officers Assn., Am. Arbitration Assn. (mem. panel arbitrators), Am. Subcontractors Assn., Engr. Regimental Assn., Calif. Aggie Alumni Assn., Ill. State Geneal. Soc., Oreg. Calif. Trails Assn., Santa Maria Valley Geneal. Soc., Army Engr. Assn. (de Fleury medal 1998), U. Calif.-Davis Century Club, Elks, Sigma Nu. Republican. Office: B T Mancini Co Inc 876 S Milpitas Blvd Milpitas CA 95035-6311

RODDY, DAVID BRUCE, college program director; b. Bozeman, Mont., May 18, 1960; s. Robert Bruce and Joanne (Dorn) R.; m. Elizabeth Ann Mittman, Sept. 10, 1994. BA, Mesa State Coll., 1985. Ops. mgr. radio sta. Rodmar Inc., Pagosa Springs, Colo., 1985-87; staff writer Leader Publ., Delta, Colo., 1987-90, News West Publ., Bullhead City, Ariz., 1990; dir. pub. info. Mohave C.C., Kingman, Ariz., 1990—. Dir. Good Shepherd Luth. Ch. Youth Group, Kingman, 1995-96. Recipient amateur phothography awards, 1987-88. Mem. Ariz. C.C. Pub. Rels. Coun. (pres. 1993-94), Nat. Coun. for Mktg. and Pub. Rels. Coun. (bd. dirs. 1993-95), Tri-State Press Club (treas. 1995—). Mem. Independent Party. Office: Mohave CC 1971 Jagerson Ave Kingman AZ 86401-1238

RODDY, MICHAEL VINCENT, construction executive; b. San Antonio, Aug. 20, 1947; s. John Vincent and Betty (Dean) R.; m. Lisa Kimberly Reynolds, Mar. 28, 1955; 1 child, Malcolm Vincent. AB, U. Calif., Berkeley, 1969. Counselor Youth Guidance Ctr., San Francisco, 1969-71; sales rep. DuBois Chems., Palo Alto, Calif., 1971-74; CEO Water Wilderness Trips, Palo Alto, 1974-77; prodn. mgr. Alten Corp., Mountain View, Calif., 1977-81; real estate developer Ashland, 1981-92; CEO Green Framing Systems, Long Beach, Calif., 1993—. Contbr. articles to profl. jours. Mem. L.A. Fgn. Affairs Coun., L.A. World Trade Orgn. Democrat. Methodist. Avocations: reading, travel, whitewater rafting. Office: Green Framing Systems 1 World Trade Ctr Ste 805 Long Beach CA 90831-0002

RODES, DAVID STUART, college program director; b. 1939. BA in Comparative Lit. summa cum laude, So. Meth. U., 1961; PhD in English, Stanford U., 1968. Asst. prof. English UCLA, 1966-74, lectr., 1974-79, sr. lectr. in English, 1980—, acting dir. Grunwald Ctr. for the Graphic Arts, 1989-92, dir. Grunwald Ctr. for the Graphic Arts, 1992—; founder chancellor's adv. com. Office of Instrnl. Devel., 1974, chair, 1980-89; acad. advisor BBC-TV Shakespeare series, 1978-84; artistic dir. Shakespeare Santa Cruz, 1981—. Gen. editor Augustan Reprint Soc. Clark Libr., 1969-91; contbr. articles to profl. jours. Mem. Phi Beta Kappa (sec. 1979-72, treas. 1978-80). Office: Armand Hammer Mus Art Culture Ctr Grunwald Ctr Graphic Arts UCLA 10899 Wilshire Blvd Los Angeles CA 90024-4201*

RODGERS, FREDERIC BARKER, judge; b. Albany, N.Y., Sept. 29, 1940; s. Prentice Johnson and Jane (Weed) R.; m. Valerie McNaughton, Oct. 8, 1988; 1 child: Gabriel Moore. AB, Amherst Coll., 1963; JD, Union U., 1966. Bar: N.Y. 1966, U.S. Ct. Mil. Appeals 1968, Colo. 1972, U.S. Supreme Ct. 1974, U.S. Ct. Appeals (10th cir.) 1981. Chief dep. dist. atty., Denver, 1972-73; commr. Denver Juvenile Ct., 1973-79; mem. Mulligan Reeves Teasley & Joyce, P.C., Denver, 1979-80; pres. Frederic B. Rodgers, P.C., Breckenridge, Colo., 1980-89; ptnr. McNaughton & Rodgers, Central City, Colo., 1989-91; county ct. judge County of Gilpin, 1987—; presiding mcpl. judge cities of Breckenridge, Blue River, Black Hawk, Central City, Edgewater, Empire, Idaho Springs, Silver Plume and Westminster, Colo., 1978-96; chmn. com. on mcpl. ct. rules of procedure Colo. Supreme Ct., 1984—; mem. gen. faculty Nat. Jud. Coll. U. Nev., Reno, 1990—, elected to faculty coun., 1993— (chair elect 1998, chair 1999). Author: (with Dilweg, Fretz, Murphy and Wicker) Modern Judicial Ethics, 1992; contbr. articles to profl. jours. Mem. Colo. Commn. on Children, 1982-85, Colo. Youth Devel. Coun., 1989-98, Colo. Family Peace Task Force, 1994-96; mem. Ho. of Dels., 1993—. Served with JAGC, U.S. Army, 1967-72; to maj. USAR, 1972-88. Decorated Bronze Star with oak leaf cluster, Air medal. Recipient Outstanding County Judge award Colo. 17th Judicial Dist. Victim Adv. Coalition, 1991; Spl. Community Service award Colo. Am. Legion, 1979. Fellow Am. Bar Found., Colo. Bar Found.; mem. ABA (jud. div. exec. coun. 1989—, vice-chair 1996-97, chair-elect 1997, chair 1998-99), Colo. Bar Assn. (bd. govs. 1986-88, 90-92, 93-99), Continental Divide Bar Assn., Denver Bar Assn. (bd. trustees 1979-82), First Jud. Dist. Bar Assn., Nat. Conf. Spl. Ct. Judges (chmn. 1989-90), Colo. County Judges Assn. (pres. 1995-96), Colo. Mcpl. Judges Assn. (pres. 1986-87), Colo. Trial Judges Coun. (v.p. 1994-95, sec. 1996-97), Denver Law Club (pres. 1981-82), Colo. Women's Bar Assn., Am. Judicature Soc., Nat. Coun. Juvenile and Family Ct. Judges, Univ. Club (Denver), Arlberg Club (Winter Park), Marines Meml. Club (San Francisco), Westminster Rotary Club (Paul Harris fellow 1996). Episcopalian. Office: Gilpin County Justice Ctr Central City CO 80427-0398

RODGERS, NANCY LUCILLE, corporate executive; b. Denver, Aug. 22, 1934; d. Francis Randolph and Irma Lucille (Budy) Baker; student public schs.; m. George J. Rodgers, Feb. 18, 1968; children by previous marriage: Kellie Rae, Joy Lynn, Timothy Francis, Thomas Francis. Mgr., Western Telearm, Inc., San Diego, 1973-93; pres. Rodgers Police Patrol, Inc., San Diego, 1973-80; br. mgr. Honeywell Inc., Protection Services div., San Diego, 1977-80; pres. Image, Inc., Image Travel Agy., Cairo, Egypt, 1981-83, Western Solar Specialties, 1979-80; founder, pres. Internat. Metaphysicians Associated for Growth through Edn., San Diego, 1979; founder, dir. Point [illegible] Breeder of Am. Bashkir Curleys; founder Zerciee Cottage Industries, 1998. Bd. dirs. Cen. City Assn. Named Woman of Achievement Cen. City Assn., 1979. Mem. Nat. Assn. for Holistic Health, Am. Bus. Women's Assn. [illegible] Scis. Democrat.

RODGERS, RONALD, sculptor, designer; b. Seattle, Feb. 6, 1949; s. Billie Jack and Elsie (Midak) R.; m. Jane Elizabeth Wiley, May 8, 1979; children: Nicholas Alexander, Ivan Thomas. AA, Chabot Coll., 1968; BA, San Francisco State Coll., 1972, MA, 1975. Foundry tech. Ohlone Coll., Fremont, Calif., 1975-76, sculpture instr., 1976-77; scultpure ceramics instr. Cerro Coso Coll., Ridgecrest, Calif., 1977; fabication designer Rodgers & Wiley, Fremont, 1977-82; sculptor cons. Ralph Goodell & Assocs., 1983-88; prin. Ron Rodgers Studio, Sebastopol, Calif., 1989—; muralist instr., San Francisco Cmty. Arts Resource Ctr., 1973; juror Sonoma County Art Trails, Sebastopol, 1992; curator Sonoma County Arts Coun., Santa Rosa, Calif; artist selection com. First Night Celebration, Santa Rosa, 1995, 96; juror pub. sculpture County Bldg., Santa Rosa, 1997; co-founder Sculpture Jam, Sebastopol, Calif., 1998. Exhibited in galleries Studio One, Gualala, Calif., Quick Silver Mining Co., Sebastopol, Calif., Magic Planter, Sausalito, Calif., Artful Eye, Healdsburg, Calif.; permanent installation commns. Heidelburg Plaza, Taichung, Taiwan, 1994, Westin Hotel Lobby, Tokyo, 1994, Westin Hotel Lobby, Surabaja, Indonesia, 1996. Mem. Internat. Sculpture Ctr., Sonoma County Cutural Arts coun. Avocations: collecting, travel, wine tasting, music, readers theater. Home: 2950 Burnside Rd Sebastopol CA 95472-9186

RODMAN, ALPINE C., arts and crafts company executive; b. Roswell, N.Mex., June 23, 1952; s. Robert Elsworth and Verna Mae (Means) R.; m. Sue Arlene Lawson, Dec. 13, 1970; 1 child, Connie Lynn. Student, Colo. State U., 1970-71, U. No. Colo. Ptnr. Pinel Silver Shop, Loveland, Colo., 1965-68, salesman, 1968-71; real estate salesman Loveland, 1971-73; mgr. Traveling Traders, Phoenix, 1974-75; co-owner Deer Track Traders, Loveland, 1975-85; pres. Deer Track Traders, Ltd., 1985—. Author: The Vanishing Indian: Fact or Fiction?, 1985. Mem. Civil Air Patrol, 1965-72, 87-92, dep. comdr. for cadets, 1988-90; cadet comdr. Ft. Collins, Colo., 1968, 70, Colo. rep. to youth tng. program, 1969, U.S. youth rep. to Japan, 1970. Mem. Bur. Wholesale Sales Reps., Western and English Salesmen's Assn. (bd. dirs. 1990), Internat. Platform Assn., Indian Arts and Crafts Assn. (bd. dirs. 1988-94, exec. com. 1989-92, v.p. 1990, pres. 1991, market chmn. 1992), Crazy Horse Grass Roots Club. Republican. Office: Deer Track Traders Ltd PO Box 448 Loveland CO 80539-0448

RODMAN, SUE A., wholesale Indian crafts company executive, artist, writer; b. Fort Collins, Colo., Oct. 1, 1951; d. Marvin F. Lawson and Barbara I. (Miller) Lawson Shue; m. Alpine C. Rodman, Dec. 13, 1970; 1 child, Connie Lynn. Student Colo. State U., 1970-73. Silversmith Pinel Silver Shop, Loveland, Colo., 1970-71; asst. mgr. Traveling Traders, Phoenix, 1974-75; co-owner, co-mgr. Deer Track Traders, Loveland, 1975-85, v.p. Deer Track Traders, Ltd., 1985—. Author: The Book of Contemporary Indian Arts and Crafts, 1985. Mem. U.S. Senatorial Club, 1982-87, Rep. Presdl. Task Force, 1984-90; mem. Civil Air Patrol, 1969-73, 87-90, pers. officer, 1988-90. Mem. Internat. Platform Assn., Indian Arts and Crafts Assn., Western and English Sales Assn., Crazy Horse Grass Roots Club. Mem. Am. Baptist Ch. Avocations: museums, piano, recreation research, fashion design. Office: Deer Track Traders Ltd PO Box 448 Loveland CO 80539-0448

RODRIGUE, CHRISTINE M(ARY), geography educator, business consultant; b. L.A., Oct. 27, 1952; d. John-Paul and Josephine Genevieve (Gorsky) R. AA in French, German, L.A. Pierce Coll., 1972; BA in Geography summa cum laude, Calif. State U., Northridge, 1973, MA in Geography, 1976; PhD in Geography, Clark U., 1987. Computer analyst Jet Propulsion Labs., Pasadena, Calif., 1977; teaching asst. Clark U., Worcester, Mass., 1976-79, rsch. asst., 1977-78; instr. geography L.A. Pierce Coll., Woodland Hills, Calif., 1981—; cons. Area Location Systems, Northridge, 1984—, tech. writer, 1990—; asst. prof. urban studies and geography Calif. State U., Northridge, 1980-89; asst. prof. geography and planning Calif. State U., Chico, 1989-94, assoc. prof., 1994—; co-dir. Ctr. for Hazards Rsch., 1994—; faculty senator Calif. State U., Chico, 1990-92, grad. geog. adviser, 1992-93, 96—, dir. rural and town planning program, grad. advisor, 1996—; ptnr. Carmel Poster Gallery and Framing, Carmel, Calif., 1989-96; owner Nomad Arabians. Exhibited in L.A. Mcpl. Art Show, 1996, 98, Faculty-Staff Art Show, Chico, 1994, 97, 98, Women's Ctr., Calif. State U., Chico, 1998; contbr. numerous articles to refereed profl. publs. Mem. bd. advisers So. Calif. Environment and History Conf., 1995—; founder, mem. bd. advisers No. Calif. Environment and History Conf., 1996—. Scholar grantee Calif. State U., summers 1990, 92, 94, 97. Mem. NOW, Am. Statis. Assn., Assn. Am. Geographers (chmn. splty. group 1983-84, councillor splty. group 1994—), Capitalism Nature Socialism (mem. editl. bd. 1991—), L.A. Geog. Soc. (v.p. 1987, pres. 1988, editor 1981-84), Planetary Soc., Internat. Arabian Horse Assn., Arabian Horse Registry. Democrat. Avocations: Arabian horses, science fiction, hiking, art, baroque music. Office: Calif State U Dept Geography and Planning Chico CA 95929-0425

RODRIGUES, ALFRED BENJAMIN KAMEEIAMOKU, marketing consultant; b. Honolulu, Jan. 23, 1947; s. Alfred Benjamin Kameeiamoku and Ruth Shiegeko (Kameda) R. BA, U. San Francisco, 1969; postgrad. U. Wis., 1977. Pub. info. mgr. Hawaiian Tel.-GTE, Honolulu, 1979-80, pub. affairs program mgr., 1980-84, dir. pub. affairs, 1984-85, dir. mktg. comms., 1986-87, dir. mktg. comms. and svcs., 1987-89 sr. v.p., Milici, Valenti and Gabriel Advt., Inc., 1989-91, exec. v.p., 1991-92; pres. Al Rodrigues & Assocs. LLC, 1992—. Bd. dirs., pub. rels. chmn. Am. Lung Assn., 1981-88; trustee, v.p. Hawaii Army Mus. Soc., 1982—; bd. dirs. ARC Hawaii, 1983-85; budget com. Aloha United Way. Maj. USAR, 1969-89. Decorated Bronze Star with three oak leaf clusters, Meritorious Svc. medal with oak leaf cluster, Army Commendation medal with 2 oak leaf clusters, Purple Heart with oak leaf cluster, Air medal with oak leaf cluster. Mem. Am. Mktg. Assn. (bd. dirs. Hawaii chpt.), Am. Advt. Fedn., Hawaii Advt. Fedn. (bd. dirs., pres., Advt. Man of Yr., 1989), Pub. Rels. Soc. Am. (pres. Hawaii, Pub. Rels. Person of Yr. 1998), Res. Officers Assn., Hawaii C. of C., Rotary (Paul Harris fellow). Republican. Roman Catholic.

RODRIGUES, MARK, financial executive, manpower consultant; b. Jhansi, India, Oct. 7, 1948; came to U.S., 1983; s. Basil and Monica (Dasgupta) R.; m. Sandra Williams, Mar. 27, 1976; children: Sarah, Daniel. BTech, Loughborough U., Leicester, Eng., 1970; MBA, Strathclyde U., Glasgow, Scotland, 1971. Cert. Acct., Eng. Fin. analyst Ford Europe, Inc., London, 1971-73; mgmt. cons., London mgr. Mann Judd Mgmt. Cons., 1973-78; pres. Bur. and Industry Svcs. Ltd., London, 1978-81; mng. dir. Indsl. Engring. Svcs., London, 1981-83; v.p. Internat. Staffing Cons., Newport Beach, Calif., 1983-88; pres. Brit. Workforce, Inc., Mission Viejo, Calif., 1988—; chmn. Euro Precision Inc., Mission Viejo, Calif., 1992—; pres. Computer Workforce, 1997—. Fellow Assn. Cert. Accts.; mem. Royal Oriental Club. Avocations: skiing, sailing, horseback riding, sail plane pilot. Office: Brit Workforce Inc 26012 Marguerite Pkwy Ste 234 Mission Viejo CA 92692-3263

RODRIGUEZ, ALEXANDER EMMANUEL, professional baseball player; b. N.Y.C., July 27, 1975. Grad. high sch., Miami. Baseball player Seattle Mariners, 1995—. Named Winner Am. League Batting Title, 1996. *

RODRIGUEZ, BENJAMIN JOHN, plastic surgeon; b. Ft. Worth, Tex., Aug. 23, 1953; s. Alexander Garcia and Marcia Marie (Orgo) R.; m. Teri Ducharme, Dec. 18, 1976; children: Mia Renee, Channing Nicole, Noelle Rafaela, Benjamin Graham, Dylan. MD, Univ. Nev., 1982. Diplomate Am. Bd. Plastic Surgery, Am. Bd. Emergency Medicine. Gen. surgery resident Univ. Colo., Denver, 1982-83; asst. dir. emer. dept. U.S. Navy, Charleston, S.C., 1983-85; assoc. dir. emer. physician Physicland Emer. Care Assocs., Dallas, 1985-87; trauma surgeon, emer. dr. Dallas, 1992-93; resident plastic surgery Univ. Mo., Kansas City, 1993-95; owner Benjamin J. Rodriguez Aesthetic & Plastic Surgery, Las Vegas, 1995—; emer. trauma adv. bd. Dallas Trauma, 1992-96; medical control physician Careflite, Dallas, 1986-93; dir. emer. dept. Charleton Meml. Hosp., Dallas, 1986-88, med. dir. Six Flags, Dallas, 1991-94. Contbr. articles to profl. jours. Scoutmaster Palmyra Ward LDS, Las Vegas, 1996—; boy scout leader, 1988-92. Fellow [illegible] State Medical Soc. Office: 3000 W Charleston Blvd #1 Las Vegas NV 89102-1940

[illegible] Peter Martin and Matilde (Guzman) R. AA, Fashion Inst., 1977; BA, San Francisco State U., 1992; MFA, Mills Coll., Oakland, Calif., 1994. Fashion designer Pacific Coast Hwy., L.A., 1980-83, Saturdays Inc., San Francisco, 1984-87; design instr. Fashion Inst., San Francisco, 1988-96, Acad. Art Coll., San Francisco, 1993-96; art instr. De Anza Coll., Cupertino, Calif., 1997—. Writer, dir. (video) Buried and Unseen, 1997, 98; exhibits include San Francisco Internat. Gay/Lesbian Film Festival, San Francisco, 1998, CineFestival, San Antonio, 1998, Turin Internat. Gay/Lesbian Film Festival, Italy, 1999, others. Office: De Anza Coll 21250 Stevens Creek Blvd Cupertino CA 95014-5702

RODRIGUEZ, FATIMA, social science researcher; b. Fresno, Calif., Mar. 2, 1967; d. N. and Susana (Fonseca) R. BSBA, Calif. State U., Fresno, 1990. Asst. office mgr. Gen Svcs. Adminstrn., U.S. Govt., Fresno, Calif., 1989-90; rsch. asst. to chair Chicano and Latin Am. studies dept. Calif. State U., Fresno, 1990—. Counselor St. Anthony Claret Youth Group, Fresno, 1984—; chaplain's aide Valley Med. Ctr., Fresno, 1988; mem. alumni bd. Calif. State U. Fresno, 1988-90; vol. actress Artes Ams., El Teatro Jalapeno, 1990—; participant 17th ann. western anthropology/sociology undergrad. rsch. conf. Santa Clara U., 1990, 15th ann. student rsch. con. Calif. State U. Social Sci. Rsch. and Instructional Coun., Cal Poly Pomona, 1990; presenter 5th ann. interuniv. symposium Calif. State U., U.S.-Mex., 1990. Recipient Latin-Am. Businessmen's award 1990, Pres.'s List award. Mem. NAFE, Soc. Human Resource Mgmt., Fresno County Hispanic C. of C., Phi Chi Theta (inter-bus. coun. rep.). Roman Catholic. Avocations: tennis, leisure writing, hosting social events, volleyball, cooking. Home: 325 S Jackson Ave Fresno CA 93702-3015

RODRIGUEZ, LEONARD, foundation administrator; b. Phoenix, Jan. 27, 1944; s. Jesus H. and Manuela (Razo) R.; m. Jo Ann Gama, Jan. 16, 1965 ; 1 child, Lena Teresa. BS in Mktg., Ariz. State U., 1981, MPA, 1995. Cert. tchr., Ariz. Adminstrv. svcs. officer Title XX Adminstrn., Phoenix, 1979-81, Block Grants Adminstrn., Phoenix, 1981-84; property mgmt. mgr. State of Ariz., Phoenix, 1984-86; pres. LTR Mgmt. Svcs., Phoenix, 1986-93; dir. PALS computer literacy program N.W. Resources and Learning Ctr., 1989-91; program cons. City of El Mirage, 1989-91; master tchr. Rio Salado C.C., 1989-91; project dir., exec. dir. Westside Coalition for Substance Abuse Prevention, 1990-91; mem. chpt. svcs. Make-A-Wish Found. of Am., 1993-97; dir. program and chpt. svcs. A Spl. Wish Found., 1997—; adj. clin. instr., faculty assoc. Ariz. State U., 1979-89; cons. Applied Econs. Curriculum, Jr. Achievement of Cen. Ariz., Inc., 1987; nat. tng. cons. Ctr. Substance Abuse Prevention, Housing & Urban Devel., Macro Internat., Washington, 1992-93. Chmn. community rels. minority recruitment program Ariz. State U., Tempe, 1985-86; bd. dirs. Concilio Latino de Salud, Inc., pres. 1993-94, Friendly House, Inc., Phoenix, 1985-87, pres., 1987; mem. community problem solving coordinating com. Valley of the Sun United Way, 1988; alliance chmn. Gov.'s Office of Drug Policy, mem. statewide exec. com., 1991; program cons. Cada Uno, Inc., 1990-91; adult literacy coord. Chandler Pub. Libr., 1992-93; tng. cons. Phoenix Fight Back Program, 1992-93; outreach coord. Hemophilia Assn., Ariz., 1992-93. Mem. Am. Soc. Public Adminstrn., Ariz. Adminstrs. Assn., Counterparts (founder 1986), Hispanic C. of C., Vesta Club (chmn. scholarship com. 1983), Rotary (pres. 1987-88, voting del. internat. conv. 1987). Avocations: painting, sculpture, late 19th century art. Home: 6225 N 30th Way Phoenix AZ 85016-2212

RODRIGUEZ, RICK, newspaper executive editor; b. Salinas, Calif.. Grad., Stanford U., 1976, Guadalajara, Mex. Newspaper intern Salinas Californian; reporter Fresno (Calif.) Bee; reporter Sacramento (Calif.) Bee, asst. mng. editor, mng. editor, 1993—; mem. Pulitzer Prize juries 1994, 95. Mem. Calif. Chicano News Media Assn. (co-founder Sacramento chpt., past bd. dirs.). Office: Sacramento Bee 2100 Q St Sacramento CA 95816-6899

ROE, CHARLES RICHARD, baritone; b. Cleve., May 24, 1940; s. Andrews Rogers and Margaret (Dalton) R.; children by previous marriage—Charles Andrews, Richard Nevins, Robert Arthur; m. Jo Ann Marie Belli, May 21, 1988. B.Mus., Baldwin-Wallace Coll., 1963; M.Mus., U. Ill., 1964. Instr. in music Tex. Tech. U., 1964-68; asst. prof. music Eastern Mich. U., 1968-74; vis. assoc. prof. U. So. Calif., L.A., 1976-77, assoc. prof. 1979-84, prof., 1984-89; prof. U. Ariz., Tucson, 1989—; vis. prof. and artist in residence Western Mich. U., 1978-79; faculty Music Acad. of the West, 1981, 82. Leading singer, N.Y.C. Opera, 1974-81; appeared in leading roles with, Mich. Opera Theater, Sacramento Opera, San Antonio Opera, Ft. Worth Opera, Ky. Opera, Conn. Opera, Utah Opera, Cleve. Opera, Miss. Opera, Lake George Opera, Shreveport Opera, Toledo Opera; appeared with, symphonies: Phila., Cleve., Detroit, Toledo, Wichita, Duluth. Mem. Am. Guild Musical Artists, Actors Equity, Nat. Assn. Tchrs. Singing (S.W. region Singer of Year 1966), AAUP. Office: U Ariz Sch Music PO Box 210004 Tucson AZ 85721*

ROEDER, STEPHEN BERNHARD WALTER, chemistry and physics educator; b. Dover, N.J., Aug. 26, 1939; s. Walter Martin and Katherine E.R. (Holz) R.; m. Phoebe E. Barber, June 28, 1969; children: Adrienne H.K., Roland K.W. B.A., Dartmouth Coll., 1961; Ph.D., U. Wis., 1965. Postdoctoral fellow Bell Telephone Labs., Murray Hill, N.J., 1965-66; lectr. physics U. Oreg., Eugene, 1966-68; asst. prof. chemistry and physics San Diego State U., 1968-72, assoc. prof., 1972-75, prof., 1975—, chmn. dept. physics, 1975-78, chmn. dept. chemistry, 1979-86, acting dir. Master of Liberal Arts Program, 1987, 89, chmn. dept. physics, 1991-94, chmn. dept. of chemistry, 1995-98, interim dean Coll. Scis., 1998—; vis. staff mem. Los Alamos Nat. Labs., 1974-92; vis. assoc. prof. chemistry U. B.C., Vancouver, Can., 1974-75; vis. prof. physics Tex. A&M U., College Station, 1982; cons. Lovelace Med. Found., 1985-90. Author: (with others) Experimental Pulse NMR, 1981. Grantee Rsch. Corp., 1968, 71, 72, NSF, 1995; recipient Excellence in Tchg. award TRW Corp., 1996, Nat. Faculty award Assn. Grad. Liberal Studies Programs, 1997. Mem. AAAS, Am. Chem. Soc., Am. Phys. Soc., Sigma Xi. Republican. Home: 6789 Alamo Way La Mesa CA 91941-5874 Office: San Diego State U Coll Scis San Diego CA 92182-4610

ROELANDTS, WILLEM P., executive. CEO Xilinx, Inc., San Jose. Office: 101 Metro Dr Ste 400 San Jose CA 95110-1343*

ROELKE, ADA (KNOCK-LEVEEN), retired psychotherapist; b. Cumberland, Md., Aug. 24, 1928; d. George William Knock and Mary Emma (Roelke) Eichelberger; children: Karen Bahnsen, Steven Leveen. BA, Syracuse U., 1950; MSW, San Diego State U., 1967; PhD, Profl. Sch. of Psychol. Studies, 1986. Bd. cert. social worker; lic. clin. social worker, Calif. Tchr. pub. schs., Syracuse, N.Y., 1960-61; social worker Dept. Pub. Welfare, San Diego, 1964-66; psychiat. social worker State of Calif., Bakersfield, 1967-68; child protection worker Dept. Social Svc., San Diego, 1968-77; pvt. practice psychotherapy La Mesa, Calif., 1969-93; field supr. Sch. of Social Wk. San Diego U., 1969-88; coord., psychotherapist chronic program Grantville Day Treatment Ctr., San Diego, 1977-81; chief social svcs. Edgemoor Geriatric Hosp., Santee, Calif., 1981-88; field supr. Grad. Sch. U. Nev., Reno, 1993-94. Recipe columnist The Nev. Appeal, 1995—. Del. State Dem. Conv.; mem. Carson City Dem. Cen. Com.; chair Carson City Dem. Womens Club; Vol. Ct.-Apptd. Spl. Advocate for Children, 1998—. Unitarian. Home: 919 Arrowhead Dr Carson City NV 89706-0620

ROEMER, CAROL KALUGA, art educator; b. Cleve., Sept. 24, 1941; d. Joseph and Helen (Belavich) Kaluga; m. William Daniel Roemer, Dec. 21, 1974 (dec. Mar. 1998). BA, Calif. State U., Long Beach, 1970, MA, 1972; PhD, Claremont (Calif.) Grad. Sch., 1992. Cert. c.c. tchr., Calif. Classroom tchr. Holy Spirit Sch., L.A., 1966-67; adj. instr. Cerritos C.C., Norwalk, Calif., 1972-81, Calif. State U., Long Beach, 1973-79, Golden West Coll., Huntington Beach, Calif., 1980-81; replacement instr. (full-time) Pasadena City Coll., 1977-80; prof. art Long Beach City Coll., 1981—. Author: The Bread of Angels: Charles Eliot Norton's Art History, 1992; multi-media [illegible] Coll. Art Assn., Mus. Latin Am. Art, Long Beach Mus. Art (guest lectr. 1990-93), L.A. County Mus. Art (guest lectr. 1997), Cairn Terrier Club of So. Calif. (bd. dirs., newsletter editor). Avocations: cairn terrior exhibitor, [illegible] Beach CA 90808

ROEMER, EDWARD PIER, neurologist; b. Milw., Feb. 10, 1908; s. John Henry and Caroline Hamilton (Pier) R.; m. Helen Ann Fraser, Mar. 28, 1935 (dec.); children: Kate Pier, Caroline Pier; m. Marion Clare Zimmer, May 24, 1980. BA, U. Wis., 1930; MD, Cornell U., 1934. Diplomate Am. Bd. Neurology. Intern Yale-New Haven Hosp., 1934-36; resident internal medicine N.Y. Hosp., 1936; resident neurology Bellevue Hosp., N.Y.C., 1936-38; instr. Med. Sch. Yale U., New Haven, 1935-36; asst. prof. neurology Cornell U., N.Y.C., 1936-41; prof. neurology U. Wis., Madison, 1946-64; chief of neurology Huntington Meml. Hosp., Pasadena, Calif., 1964-78; pvt. practice Capistrano Beach, Calif., 1978—; founder, dir. Wis. Neurol. Found., Madison, 1946-64; dir. Wis. Multiple Sclerosis Clinic, Madison, 1946-64; adv. bd. Inst. Antiquities and Christianity, Claremont Grad. Sch., 1970—; dir. found. Univ Good Hope, S.Africa. Contbr. rsch. articles on multiple sclerosis, neuropathies to profl. jours. Lt. col. med. corps U.S. Army, 1941-46, ETO. Fellow ACP, Royal Coll. Medicine, L.S.B. Leakey Found.; mem. Rotary Internat., Annandale Golf Club, El Niguel Country Club, Nu Sigma Nu, Phi Delta Theta. Republican. Achievements include significant findings in field of anthropology and archaeology in Egypt and southwest U. S. relative to prehistory and PreColumbian European influences. Home: 35651 Beach Rd Capo Beach CA 92624-1710

ROGAN, RICHARD A., lawyer; b. L.A., Sept. 6, 1950. AB with honors, Hamilton Coll., 1972; JD, U. Calif., 1975. Bar: Calif. 1975. Ptnr. Broad, Schulz, Larson & Wineberg, 1978-94, chmn., 1991-93; ptnr. Jeffer, Mangels, Butler & Marmaro, San Francisco, 1994—. Editorial assoc. Hastings Law Jour., 1974-75. Trustee Bentley Sch., 1989-92. Mem. ABA (mem. corp., banking, and bus. sect.), Bar Assn. of San Francisco (mem. comml. law and bankruptcy sect.), Delta Sigma Rho. Office: Jeffer Mangels Butler et al 12th Fl One Sansome St San Francisco CA 94104

ROGEL, STEVEN R., forest products company executive. BS in Chem. Engring., U. Wash., 1965. With St. Regis Paper Co., 1965-70; asst. mgr. St. Anne-Nackawic Pulp and Paper, Nackawic, N.B., Can., 1970-72; tech. dir. Willamette Industries, Inc., Albany, Oreg., 1972-95; pres., CEO Willamette Industries, Inc., Albany, 1995-97, Weyerhaeuser Co., Tacoma, Wash., 1997—; bd. dirs. Fred Meyer, Inc. Trustee Pacific U.; bd. dirs. Cascade Pacific coun. Boy Scouts Am. Mem. Am. Forest and Paper Assn. (bd. dirs.). Office: Weyerhaeuser Co PO Box 2999 Tacoma WA 98477-2999*

ROGERS, ALICE LOUISE, retired bank executive, writer, researcher; b. McLoud, Okla., Feb. 18, 1929; d. John Edmond and Katy McNora (Williams) Stanka; m. Jesse Ray Rogers, Apr. 18, 1948; children: Jimmy Allen, Bonnie Kay Calhoun. Student, Am. Inst. Banking, 1967-69. Clk. typist loan dept. Security Pacific Nat. Bank, L.A., 1960-64; office mgr., adminstrv. asst. to v.p. loan adminstn. divsn. City Nat. Bank, Beverly Hills, 1964-75, credit mgr. Pershing Square branch, 1975-77. Author, editor: Dance Bands and Big Bands Reference Book and Price Guide, 1986, Dance Bands, Big Bands and Swing Reference Book and Price Guide, 1993; contbr. articles to DISCoveries mag., Internat. Assn. of Jazz Record Collectors Jour., Joslin's Jazz Jour., Dancing USA mag. Mem. Internat. Assn. Jazz Record Collectors, Big Band Acad. Am., Libr. Congress Assocs. (founding nat. mem.), Smithsonian Instn. (nat. assoc. mem.). Republican. Avocations: phonograph record collection, researching jazz and dance information, postcard collection. Home: RR 1 Box 146-a Deming NM 88030-9704

ROGERS, BENJAMIN TALBOT, consulting engineer, solar energy consultant; b. Cleve., Oct. 4, 1920; s. Benjamin Talbot and Marie Aline (Miller) R.; m. Dale Hays, Sept. 11, 1961 (dec. Nov. 1975); children—Leslie, Phyllis. B.S. in Mech. Engring., U. Wis., 1944. Registered profl. engr., N.Mex., Colo., Ariz., Tex. Mech. Engr. Black & Veatch, Kansas City, Mo., 1946-49; staff mem. U. Calif., Los Alamos, N.Mex., 1949-76; cons. engring., Los Alamos, 1949-76, Embudo, N.Mex., 1976-80, 81—; vis. prof. Ariz. State U., 1980-81, 84; v.p. Barkman & Rogers Cons. Engrs., Santa Fe, N.M., 1964-70. One man shows include: Millicent Rogers Mus. Taos, N. Mex., 1994, Roller Mill Mus. Cleveland, N. Mex., 1995, Ariz. State U. Coll. Architecture, Tempe, Ariz., 1996, First State Bank Taos, N. Mex. (artist of the month, 1997), Johnson Gallery Madrid, N. Mex., 1998; contbr. articles to tech., profl. jours. Patentee in field of optics, high speed photography and explosive tech. (6). Commr., Rinconada Community Acequia, Embudo, 1961-70; v.p. adv. bd. Embudo Presbyterian Hosp., 1972; pres. Embudo Valley Health Found., 1974. Sgt. to 1st lt. Corps of Engrs., 1942-46. Recipient Solar Design award HUD, Dept. of Energy, Solar Energy Research Inst., 1978, Peter van Dresser award N.Mex. Solar Energy Assn., 1983, Maharishi award Maharishi Found., Santa Fe, 1984; grantee Graham Found. for Advanced Studies in the Fine Arts, 1992, 95. Fellow ASHRAE; mem. ASME (life), NSPE (life), Am. Soc. Materials (life). Republican. Home and Office: PO Box 2 Embudo NM 87531-0002

ROGERS, BRYAN ROSS, health care facility administrator; b. Newport Beach, Calif., May 9, 1957; s. Maurice and Patricia Mary (Ross) R.; m. Linda Lee Chase, Sept. 18, 1981. AS, Orange Coast Coll., 1978; MA in Health Sci. summa cum laude, Duke U., 1983; MS in Pub. Health, UCLA, 1985. Registered respiratory therapist; cert. physician asst. Dir. program devel. Anaheim (Calif.) Meml. Hosp., 1985-86, v.p., 1986—; pres., CEO Foothill Presbyn. Hosp., 1991—; exec. v.p. Citrus Valley Health Ptnrs., Covina, Calif., 1991—; v.p. bd. Hosp. Cen. Lab., Orange, Calif., 1986-87. Mem. Health Care Exec. Avocations: skiing, boating, rock climbing. Office: 250 S Grand Ave Glendora CA 91741-4218

ROGERS, DWANE LESLIE, management consultant; b. Maywood, Calif., Oct. 6, 1943; s. Lloyd Donald and Della (McAlister) R.; BS, Ariz. State U., 1967; MS, Bucknell U., 1968; m. Doris L. Fantel, Aug. 22, 1970; 1 child, Valerie Lynn. Successively mktg. research coordinator, customer service analyst, merchandising mgr., product planning mgr., order processing mgr. Samsonite Corp., Denver, 1968-74; dir. adminstrn. WISCO Equipment Co., Inc., Phoenix, 1974-75; dir. discontinued ops. Bowmar Instrument Corp., Phoenix, 1975-77; mgmt. cons., dir. Ariz. ops. Mariscal & Co., Phoenix, 1977-80; mgmt. cons. Ariz. Small Bus. Devel. Center, 1980-81; dir. accounts payable, accounts receivable, crude and finished product acctg. Giant Industries, Phoenix, 1981-92; instr. Maricopa County Community Coll., 1979-83; controller Hawaii Pacific Air, 1993-94; ptnr. Pacific Palms Gift World, 1994—. Mem. Am. Mktg. Assn., Mass Retailing Inst. Democrat. Episcopalian. Home: 441 Lewers St Apt 502 Honolulu HI 96815-2449

ROGERS, EARL LESLIE, artist, educator; b. Oakland, Calif., July 8, 1918; s. Robert Ray and Addie Myrtle (Dice) R.; m. Eileen Estelle MacKenzie, Apr. 9, 1945; children: Leslie Eileen, Brian Donald (dec.). Student, L.A. Valley Coll., 1949-52, Northridge State U., 1958-59, UCLA Extension, 1967, Sergei Bongart Sch. Art, 1967-68; AA, Pierce Coll., 1958. Cert. tchr., Calif. Various positions City of L.A., Van Nuys, Calif., 1948-55, Reseda, Calif., 1955-68; pvt. practice Canoga Park, Calif., 1948-68; art tchr. Mariposa (Calif.) County High Sch., 1969-70; art instr. Merced (Calif.) County Coll., 1970—; instr. Earl Rogers Studio Workshop, Mariposa, Calif., 1969—; art dir. Yosemite Nat. Park, Calif., 1973; instr. art Asilomar Conf. Grounds, Pacific Grove, Calif., 1980; juror various art orgns., 1971-95; demonstrator Clovis (Calif.) Art Guild, 1971, 89, Sierra Artists, Mariposa, 1972, 81, 82, 84, 91, Merced Art League, 1976, Yosemite Western Artists, Oakhurst, Calif., 1973, Madera (Calif.) Art Assn., 1978, Chowchilla (Calif.) Art Guild, 1983, 86, 87, 89, 91, Soc. Western Artists, 1981, 89, 93, 97. One-man shows include L.A. City Hall, 1968, Merced Coll., 1969, 95, Mariposa Title Co. Bldg., 1969, Coffee's Gallery, 1970, others; exhibited in group shows including West Valley Artists Assn., 1966-68, L.A. City Hall, 1967, Yosemite Nat. Park, 1973, Soc. Western Artists, 1977-78, Cannon Bldg. Rotunda, Washington, 1982, Mother Lode Gallery, Columbia, Calif., 1977, 78, Arbor Gallery, Merced, 1988, 98, Gold Country Gallery, 1990, 91, Merced Coll., 1969-92, 96, others; represented in permanent collections including John C. Freemont Hosp., Mariposa, Mariposa County Arts Coun., Mariposa Mus. and History Ctr. Asst. scout master Boy Scouts of Am., Canoga Park, Calif., 1956-58; art instr. L.A. Recreation Corps, L.A. Parks and Recreation Dept., 1967. Mem. Soc. Western Artists (Neva Rall Meml. award 1978), Mariposa Mus. and Hist. Ctr. (life), Pastel Soc. West Coast, Oil Painters of Am. Avocations: piano and books. Home and Office: 5323 State Highway 49 N Mariposa CA 95338-9503

ROGERS, GARTH WINFIELD, lawyer; b. Fort Collins, Colo., Nov. 4, 1938; s. Harlan Winfield and Helen Marie (Orr) R.; m. Joanne Kathleen Rapp, June 16, 1962; children: Todd Winfield, Christopher Jay, Gregory Lynn, Clay Charles. BS, U. Colo., 1958, LLB, 1962. Bar: Colo. 1962; U.S. Dist. Ct. Colo. 1962. Law clk. to presiding justice U.S. Dist. Ct., Denver, 1962-63; assoc. Allen, Stover & Mitchell, Ft. Collins, 1963-68; ptnr. Allen, Rogers & Vahrenwald, Ft. Collins, 1968-97; ret., 1997. Articles editor Rocky Mountain Law Rev., 1961-62. Bd. dirs. Salvation Army, Ft. Collins; past bd. dirs. United Way of Ft. Collins, Trinity Luth. Ch., Ft. Collins, others; bd. dirs. Poudre Sch. Dist. Bd. Edn. Mem. Ft. Collins C. of C. (past bd. dirs.), ABA, Colo. Bar Assn., Larimer County Bar Assn. Avocations: Nicaragua projects, participative sports, amateur writing, reading. Office: 215 W Oak St Ste 202 Fort Collins CO 80521-2730

ROGERS, JAMES CURTIS, movie producer, publisher, screenwriter; b. Sandston, Va., May 21, 1930; s. James Allen and Julia Pollard (Curtis) R. BA, U. Calif., Berkeley, 1961; BS, William and Mary Coll.; MA, Columbia Pacific, PhD. Sec., treas., CEO Rojet Theatre Co., Atlanta, 1954; prof. Capitol Radio and Electronics Inst., Washington, 1955; tech. writer Guided Missile Rocket dept. RCA Svc. Co., Alexandria, Va., Cherry Hill, N.J.; sec., treas., CEO Hawkeye Records, Iowa City, Iowa, 1961-63; tchr. Calvert County H.S., Prince Frederick, Md., 1964; child protective officer Social Svc. Bur., Richmond, Va., 1964-68; head master Lyceum Ednl. Com., Gloucester, Va., 1968-70; pub. Lyceum Publs., Richmond, Va., 1968-92; producer, agt. YoungStar Prodns., Richmond, 1989-91; pub., editor FutureWend Publs., Richmond, 1991—; ethics cons. The Matrism Orgn., Richmond, 1988—; publs. officer U.S. Coast GuardAux., Richmond, 1986-87. Author: Foreign Language With a Smile, 1965—, The Kidnapping, 1995; editor It's Your Choice Mag., 1993; author plays. Adminstr. Julie and Jim Rogers scholarship fund, Richmond, 1988—; scoutmaster Robert E. Lee Coun., Boy Scouts Am., Richmond, 1948-52, sea scout skipper, 1948-52; dir. Children's Theatre Project, Berkeley, 1959. Mem. Thalian Soc., Am. Inst. Hypnosis, Coll. Med. Hypnotists, Scriptwriter Network, Acad. for Polit. and Social Sci. Avocations: piano/organ public performance, foreign languages. Office: Po Box 942 Hollywood CA 90078-0942

ROGERS, JAMES STEVEN, lawyer; b. Seattle, Sept. 18, 1947; s. Fred and Frances Ruth (Teitelbaum) R.; m. Theresa M. Rosellini; children: Zoey, Sabina. BS, U. Wash., 1969; JD, U. Ariz., 1972. Bar: Wash. 1973; cert. civil trial advocate. With Law Office of Lembhard G. Howell, Seattle, 1974-75, Wolfstone Panchot & Bloch, Seattle, 1975-78, Franco, Asia, Bensussen Coe & Finegold, Seattle, 1978-81, Crane, Stamper, Dunham, Drury & Rogers, Seattle, 1981-86, Law Offices of James S. Rogers, Seattle, 1987—. Fellow Internat. Acad. Trial Lawyers; mem. ATLA (bd. govs. 1993—), Am. Bd. Trial Advocates, Wash. State Trial Lawyers Assn. (pres. 1991-92), Attys. Info. Exch. Group (bd. dirs. 1991—), Western Trial Lawyers Assn. (officer 1993—). Office: 705 2nd Ave Ste 1601 Seattle WA 98104-1711

ROGERS, JOE, state official; m. Juanita Kay; children: Trent, Jordan, Haley. Degree in bus., Colo. State U.; JD, Ariz. State U. Past law clk. to Hon. Robert Broomfield U.S. Dist. Ct.; assoc. Davis, Graham & Stubbs, Colo., 1989-93; staff counsel to Sen. Hank Brown U.S. Congress, Washington, 1993-95; lt. gov. State of Colo., 1998—. past atty. Lend-A-Lawyer Program, Colo. Mem. Denver Bar Assn. (bd. dirs. credit union 1990-93). Office: State Capitol Denver CO 80203-1792*

ROGERS, MARSHA SCOTT, secondary education educator, poet; b. Fresno, Calif., May 8, 1946; d. Thomas Henry and Elsie Mary (Myers) R. BA, Calif. State U., Fresno, 1968, tchg. credential, 1969. Tchr. Anderson Valley H.S., Boonville, Calif., 1971-73, Mineral County H.S., Hawthorne, Nev., 1978—; mem. curriculum com. Dept. Edn. Nev., Carson City. Author of poetry. Mem. Nev. English/Lang. Arts Network (v.p. 1994-96, rural chair 1996-98).

ROGERS, ROBERT REED, manufacturing company executive; b. Oak Park, Ill., Feb. 22, 1929; s. Glen Charles and Lucile (Reed) R.; m. Barbara June Fain, Feb. 22, 1951 (div.); children: Robin, Janeen, Kevin; m. Celeste Sim, Sept. 29, 1993. BS in Chemistry, Berea Coll., 1951; MBA, Ill. Inst. Tech., 1958, postgrad., 1959-62. Asst. mgr. metallurgy research dept. Armour Research Found., Ill. Inst. Tech., 1955-56, mem. faculty, econs. dept., 1956-62; cons. McKinsey & Co., Inc., 1962-64; mgr. devel. planning, profl. group Litton Industries, Inc., 1964-67; pres. N.Am. subs. Muirhead & Co., Ltd., 1967-68; group v.p. Am. Electric Inc. subs. City Investing Co., 1968-70; pres. Cleartight Corp., 1971-73; pres. Newport Internat. Metals Corp., 1973-76; pres. Kensington Assocs., Inc., Newport Beach, Calif., 1976-83; pres., chmn. bd. Proteus Group, Inc., Newport Beach, 1981-83, pres., chmn. bd. Comparator Systems Corp., Newport Beach, Calif., 1983-96; chmn. bd. UltraCard, Inc., Newport Beach, 1997-98, The Pharmakon Corp., Newport Beach, 1998—. Officer USN, 1951-55. Decorated Knight of Grace Sovereign Order St. John; Machinery and Allied Products Inst. fellow, 1956-62; Berea Coll. grantee, 1947-51. Mem. Navy League, Mensa, Intertel. Democrat. Mem. Ch. of Religious Sci. Home and Office: 565 Promontory Dr E Newport Beach CA 92660-7455 Office: Pharmakon Corp 5001 Birch St Newport Beach CA 92660-2116

ROGERS, RONALD, public relations executive. Pres. Rodgers & Assocs., L.A. Office: 1875 Century Park E Ste 300 Los Angeles CA 90067-2504*

ROGERS, SPENCER THOMAS, education company director, consultant, writer; b. Detroit, Jan. 14, 1945; s. Thomas Arthur and Mary Elizabeth (Spencer); m. Linda Lott, May 17, 1967 (div. 1975); children: Christine, Michael; m. Rosalind Marie Bienick, Mar. 13, 1985. BS in Math and Natural Sci., Ariz. State U. Math tchr. Apollo High Sch., Glendale, Ariz., 1972-90; curr. coord. Glendale Union High Sch. Dist., Glendale, Ariz., 1976-90, co-outcome based coord., 1986-90; co-founder, assoc., dir., cons. The High Success Network; co-founder, dir., sr. cons. Peal Learning Sys., Evergreen, Colo., 1994—; presenter 8 satellite broadcasts with Nat. Sch. Conf. Inst., 1997-98, 1998-99. Author: The Performance Learning and Assessment Toolbox, 1995, Quick Tips and Strategies to Increase Student Motivation and Learning (vols. 1 and 2), 1996, The High Performance Toolbox (edits. 1-3), 1997-98, Motivation and Learning, 1997. Recipient Excellence award in Teaching Mathmatics, 1985, 86, 88, 89; cert. by Ariz. State Gov. for Excellence in Teaching Math, 1985, 86, 88, 89. Mem. Assn. for Supervision and Curriculum Devel. (Colo. Chpt.), Nat. Coun. Tchrs. of Math, Am. Assn. of Educators in Pvt. Practice, Nat. Staff Devel. Coun., Am. Soc. Tng. and Devel. Avocations: hiking, skiing, learning. Home and Office: Peak Learning Sys 6784 S Olympus Dr Evergreen CO 80439-5312

ROGERS, SYLVIA GARNETTE, artist; b. Hammond, Ind., July 13, 1930; d. Kermit Thomas and Mabel Goldie (Demo) R.; m. Leonard E. Barnes, Aug. 28, 1948 (div. Feb. 1972); children: Timothy, Scott, Lenita, Bonnie. Student, Thomas Leighton Sch. of Art, 1970-74, Monterey Peninsula Coll., 1988. Cert. tchr., Calif., 1976. Portrait artist Calif., 1973—; tchr. Mt. Diablo Sch. Dist., Walnut Creek, Calif., 1974-80. Exhibited in numerous shows, including Rosicrucian Mus., San Jose, Calif., DE Young Mus., San Francisco, Hall of Flowers, San Francisco, Alameda County Art Shows, Alamo/Danville Art Shows, Soc. Western Artists, San Francisco, Las Juantas Art Shows, Contra Costa County, Calif., Faces West Art Gallery and Studio, Monterey, Calif., Simic Gallery, Carmel, Calif., Shell Fisher Gallery, Carmel, De Voux Gallery, Carmel, Who's Who in Art Gallery, Carmel, Lyon's Gallery, San Francisco, Capricorn Gallery, San Francisco, Ctr. for Visual Arts Gallery, Oakland, Calif., Gallery-on-the Sq., Oakland, Paint Palette Gallery, Walnut Creek, Diablo Scholarships Art Shows, Concord, Calif., Dudley's Restaurant, San Francisco, Sheraton Inn, Concord, Civic Ctr. Art Shows, San Francisco, Walnut Creek Golf and Country Club, Rotary Club Show, Menlo Park, Calif., Kaiser Ctr. Mall Shows, Oakland, Brookside Country Club, Stockton, Calif.; portraits commd. by St. Mary's Coll., Moraga, Calif., UCLA Sch. Law Libr., Daring Books Inc., Canton, Ohio, Ersta Sandpaper Co., Melle, Germany, five past presidents of San Joaquin Delta Coll. commd. by Delta Coll., Stockton, Calif., Concord Jazz Records/CD and cover art of headliner artists like Ray Brown, Woody Herman, Rosemary Clooney, more; commd. ofcl. portrait of former sec. of U.S. Army, John O. Marsh, Jr., U.S. Dept. Army, Washington, 1990, ofcl. portrait of Mayor of Stockton, Calif., 1997, others. Recipient numerous honors and awards from art shows. Mem. Lodi Art Ctr. Avocations: jazz, cooking, piano, grandchildren, travel. Home: 14995 Indian Springs Rd Penn Valley CA 95946

ROGERS, WALTER E., landscape architect; b. Providence, Jan. 30, 1946; s. Milton J. and Doris Elizabeth (Metevier) R.; 1 child, Tiffany Elizabeth. BS, U. Mass., 1968, M of Landscape Architecture, 1970; MBA, U. Phoenix, 1991. Landscape architect Moriele & Gray, Boston, 1971; asst. prof. SUNY, Syracuse, 1971-73; dir. coun. property devel. Girl Scouts USA, N.Y.C., 1973-76; asst. prof. U. Ariz., Tucson, 1976-81; landscape architect pvt. practice, Tucson, 1979-81; ptnr. Rogers & Gleason, Tucson, 1981-84; pres. Rogers, Gleason & Hardaway, Tucson, 1984-89, The Acacia Group, Inc., Tucson, 1989—; Author: The Professional Practice of Landscape Architecture, 1996. Mem. Am. Soc. Landscape Architects. Democrat. Avocations: skiing, fly fishing, hiking, golf. Home: 7140 N Thunderhead Dr Tucson AZ 85718-1179 Office: The Acacia Group Inc 6842 E Tanque Verde Rd Tucson AZ 85715-5328

ROGERS, WILLIAM CORDELL, financial executive; b. Louisville, Apr. 16, 1943; s. Delbert Clifton and Nelle Frances (Grimsley) R.; m. Elaine Elizabeth Nicolay, Apr. 10, 1966; children: William C. II, Erin D., Nicole M., Shannon D. AA, Lincoln Coll., 1969; BS, Ill. State U., 1971; MBA, U. Phoenix, 1993. Exec. Ill. Dept. Revenue, Springfield, 1972-74; fin. dir. Old Heritage Life Ins. Co., Lincoln, Ill., 1974-77; corp. fin. cons. DEN, Inc. CPAs, Tempe, Ariz., 1977-83; v.p., treas. Dahlberg Industries, Scottsdale, Ariz., 1983-91; cons. Act II Printed Cirs. Inc., Tempe, Ariz., 1991-93; self-employed fin. analyst Scottsdale; cons., Scottsdale, 1977—; instr. econ. Lincoln Coll., 1972-77, real estate taxation, 1978-80. With U.S. Army, 1964-67, Vietnam. Recipient Dow Jones award Dow Jones-Wall St. Jour., 1969. Mem. Rotary (bd. dirs. Scottsdale club 1986—, pres., Paul Harris fellow 1985—). Republican. Avocations: golf, reading, music. Home and Office: 8549 E Turney Ave Scottsdale AZ 85251-2831

ROGGE, RICHARD DANIEL, former government executive, security consultant, investigator; b. N.Y.C., July 5, 1926; s. Daniel Richard and Bertha (Sarner) R.; m. Josephine Mary Kowalewska, June 6, 1948 (dec. June 1995); children: Veronica Leigh Rogge-Erbeznik, Richard Daniel, Christopher Ames, Meredith Ann Rogge-Pierce. BS in Bus. Adminstrn., NYU, 1952. Cert. profl. investigator. Clerical worker FBI, N.Y.C., 1947-52, spl. agt., Phila., 1952-54, Washington, 1954-58, supr., 1958-65, asst. spl. agt. in charge, Richmond, Va., 1965-66, Phila., 1966-67, L.A., 1967-69, inspector, 1969, spl. agt. in charge, Honolulu, 1969-72, Richmond, 1972-74, Buffalo, 1974-77, now security cons., investigator, Calif.; police tng. instr.; writer, lectr. in field. With USMC, 1944-46; PTO. Recipient Order of Arrow award Boy Scouts Am., 1943, Svc. to Law Enforcement awards Va. Assn. Chiefs Police, 1975, N.Y. State Assn. Chiefs Police, 1977, others. Mem. Calif. Assn. Lic. Investigators, Calif. Peace Officers Assn., Peace Officers Assn. of Los Angeles County, World Investigators Network, Soc. Former Agts. FBI, Inc., FBI Agents Assn., Am. Legion, K.C., Elks. Republican. Roman Catholic. Home and Office: 32010 Watergate Ct Westlake Village CA 91361-4022

ROGSTAD, MARK ROLAND, secondary school educator; b. Belvidere, Ill., Mar. 1, 1957; s. Ronald Glenn and Mary Ellen (Kugath) R. BS, Ea. Ill. U., 1979, MS, 1981; EdD, U. Wyo., 1992. Grad. asst. Eastern Ill. U., Charleston, 1980-81; electronics instr. Proviso West High Sch., Hillside, Ill., 1981-85; tech. educator U. Wyo., Laramie, 1985-88, Mont. State U., Bozeman, 1988-92, Bozeman High Sch., 1992—; cons. Wyo. State Dept. Edn., Cheyenne, 1986—, Mont. Office of Pub. Instruction, 1989—. Recipient Faculty Growth award U. Wyo., Laramie, 1987, Prin. Tech. award Wyo. State Dept. Edn., Cheyenne, 1986-87, Applied Communication award Mont. Office Pub. Instrn., Helena, 1990-91. Mem. Internat. Tech. Edn. Assn. (MT Teacher Excellence Award, 1995), Coun. on Tech. Tchr. Edn., Nat. Assn. Indsl. Tech., World Future Soc., Tech. Edn. Assn. Mont., Eastern Ill. U. Alumni Assn., Epsilon Pi Tau, Phi Delta Kappa, Pather Club of Charleston. Lutheran. Avocations: photography, computing, amateur radio. Office: Mont State U 115 Cheever Hall Bozeman MT 59717

ROHDE, JAMES VINCENT, software systems company executive; b. O'Neill, Nebr., Jan. 25, 1939; s. Ambrose Vincent and Loretta Cecilia R.; m. Tatiana Rohde; children: Maria, Sonja, Daniele, Olga. BSc, Seattle U., 1962. Chmn. bd. dirs., pres. Applied Telephone Tech., Oakland, Calif., 1974; v.p. sales and mktg. Automation Electronics Corp., Oakland, 1975-82; pres., CEO. chmn. bd. dirs. Am. Telecorp, Inc., Oakland, 1982-98; founder, vice-chmn., bd. dirs. FirstTel Sys. Corp., 1998—; chmn. exec. com., chmn. emeritus Pres.'s Coun. Heritage Coll., Toppenish, Wash., 1985—; chmn. No. Calif. chpt. Coun. of Growing Cos., 1990-93. Named U.S. Dept. Commerce Export Exec. Yr. No. Calif., 1993. Mem. Am. Electronics Assn. (bd. dirs. 1992-94, vice-chmn. No. Calif. coun. 1992-93, chmn. 1993-94). Republican. Roman Catholic. Office: FirstTel Sys Corp 100 Marine Pkwy Redwood City CA 94065-1046

ROHLFING, FREDERICK WILLIAM, lawyer, travel executive, political consultant, retired judge; b. Honolulu, Nov. 2, 1928; s. Romayne Raymond and Kathryn (Coe) R.; m. Joan Halford, July 15, 1952 (div. Sept. 1982); children: Frederick W., Karl A., Brad (dec.); m. Patricia Ann Santos, Aug. 23, 1983. BA, Yale U., 1950; JD, George Washington U., 1955. Bar: Hawaii 1955, Am. Samoa 1978. Assoc. Moore, Torkildson & Rice, Honolulu, 1955-60; ptnr. Rohlfing, Nakamura & Low, Honolulu, 1963-68, Hughes, Steiner & Rohlfing, Honolulu, 1968-71, Rohlfing, Smith & Coates, Honolulu, 1981-84; sole practice Honolulu, 1960-63, 71-81, Maui County, 1988—; dep. corp. counsel County of Maui, Wailuku, Hawaii, 1984-87, corp. counsel, 1987-88; land and legal counsel Maui Open Space Trust, 1992-97, also bd. dirs.; pres. Rohlfing Cons. & Travel, Inc., 1985—; polit. cons., 1996, 98; magistrate judge U.S. Dist. Ct. Hawaii, 1991-96. Mem. Hawaii Ho. Reps., 1959-65, 80-84; Hawaii State Senate, 1966-75; U.S. alt. rep. So. Pacific Commn., Noumea, New Caledonia, 1975-77, 1982-84. Capt. USNR, 1951-87. Mem. Hawaii Bar Assn., Maui Country Club, Fed. Magistrate Judges Assn., Naval Intelligence Profls. Avocations: ocean swimming, golf. Home and Office: RR 1 Box 398 Kekaulike Ave Kula HI 96790

ROHRABACHER, DANA, congressman; b. Coronado, Calif., June 21, 1947; s. Donald and Doris Rohrabacher; m. Rhonda Carmont, Aug. 1997. Student, L.A. Harbor Coll., 1965-67; BA in History, Long Beach State Coll., 1969; MA in Am. Studies, U. So. Calif., 1976. Reporter City News Svc./Radio West, L.A., 4 yrs.; editorial writer Orange County Register, 1979-80; asst. press sec. Reagan for Pres. Campaign, 1976, 80; speechwriter, spl. asst. to Pres. Reagan White House, Washington, 1981-88; mem. 101st-102nd Congresses from Calif. dist., 1989-93, 103d-106th Congress from 45th dist. Calif., 1993—; U.S. del. Young Polit. Leaders Conf., USSR; disting. lectr. Internat. Terrorism Conf., Paris, 1985; mem. Internat. Rels. com.; chmn. sci. subcom. on space and aeronautics. Recipient Disting. Alumnus award L.A. Harbor Coll., 1987. Avocations: surfing, white water rafting. Office: US House of Reps 2338 Rayburn Bldg Washington DC 20515-0545*

ROHRER, REED BEAVER, lawyer; b. Langley AFB, Va., June 15, 1954; s. Richard L. and Elaine (Beaver) R.; m. Penny J. Pylant, June 25, 1977; children: Christopher S., Jennifer R. BBA, U. Hawaii, 1977; JD, Pepperdine U., 1980; LLM in Taxation, U. San Diego, 1981. Bar: Hawaii 1981, U.S. Dist. Ct. Hawaii 1981, U.S. Tax Ct. 1981. Tax specialist Grant Thorton (Alexander Grant), Honolulu, 1981-83; assoc. Oliver, Cuskaden & Lee, Honolulu, 1983-85; corp. counsel Bishop Trust Co. Ltd., Honolulu, 1985-89; v.p., corp. counsel Wall St. Fin. Corp., Irvine, Calif., 1989-92; prin. Law Firm of Reed B. Rohrer, Honolulu, 1992-94; ptnr. Rottenger & Rohrer, Honolulu, 1994—; bd. dirs. Rohrer Investment Corp., Coz U.S.A., Inc., Pacific Mktg. & Investments, Inc.; speaker in field. Author: (with others) Wills and Trusts Formbook, 1987; contbr. articles to profl. jours. Mem. ABA, Hawaii Bar Assn. (chmn. tax sect. 1988, estate and gift tax com.). Republican. Avocations: flying, surfing, diving, sailing. Home: 1433 Ohialoke St Honolulu HI 96821-1411 Office: Rottenger & Rohrer 841 Bishop St Ste 1710 Honolulu HI 96813-3916 also: 733 Bishop St Unit 19 Honolulu HI 96813-4019 also: 2-17-55 Akasaka, Minato-Ku, Tokyo 107, Japan

ROIZ, MYRIAM, foreign trade marketing executive; b. Managua, Nicaragua, Jan. 21, 1938; came to U.S., 1949; d. Francisco Octavio and Maria Herminia (Briones) R.; m. Nicholas M. Orphanopoulos, Jan. 21, 1957 (div.); children: Jacqueline Doggwiler, Gene E. Orphanopoulos, George A. Orphanopoulos. BA in Interdisciplinary Social Sci. cum laude, San Francisco State U., 1980. Mktg. dir. Europe/Latin Am., Allied Canners & Packers, San Francisco, 1979-83, M-C Internat., San Francisco, 1983-88; v.p. mktg.

Atlantic Brokers, Inc., Bayamon, P.R., 1988-92; owner Aquarius Enterprises Internat., San Ramon, Calif., 1992-97, advertising sales rep., Itel Publishers. Coord. Robert F. Kennedy Presdl. campaign, Millbrae, San Mateo County, local mayoral campaign, Millbrae, 1975; bd. dir. organizer fund-raising campaign for earthquake-devastated Nicaragua; active Childhelp USA, Childreach, Covenant House. Named Outstanding Employee of Yr. Hillsborough City Sch. Dist., 1973. Mem. NAFE. Democrat. Roman Catholic.

ROJANY, LISA ADRIENNE, publishing company executive; b. L.A., Feb. 14, 1964; d. Aviezer Rojany and Mary Marks. B of Comms. magna cum laude, UCLA, 1986; cert. in translation, Sorbonne U., Paris, 1987; M English and Am. Lit., Brown U., 1990. Newspaper journalist UCLA Daily Bruin, Together Newsmag., L.A., 1985-86; English tutor Paris, 1986-87; writer, reviewer TV Guide, L.A., 1987-88; freelance editor, writer, 1988—; sr. editor Intervisual Books, Santa Monica, Calif., 1991-93; editl. dir. Price Stern Sloan divsn. Penguin/Putnam Pub., L.A., 1993-97, Gateway Learning Corp., 1997; west coast publ. dir. Golden Books Family Entertainment, L.A., 1998—; proofreader MIT Univ. Press, Cambridge, Mass., 1990, Fidelity, Inc., Boston, 1990, Heinle & Heinle Pubs., Inc., Boston, 1990; correlator, proofreader Houghton Mifflin Co., Boston, 1990; spkr. in field. Author: (children's books) The Hands-on Book of Big Machines, 1992, Exploring the Human Body, 1992, King Arthur's Camelot, 1993, The Story of Hanukkah, 1993, Where's That Pig?, 1993, Santa's New Suit, 1993, Jake and Jenny on the Town, 1993, Andrews & McMeel Mini Pop-Up Quote Books, 1993, Alice in Wonderland, 1994, Token of Love and Spring Gardens, 1994, Mickey Mouse: Where's the Picnic, 1994, Winnie the Pooh: The Suprise Party, 1994, Make Your Own Valentines, 1994, 3d edit., 1996, Melvin Martian, Dumbo's Circus Train, 1995, Cinderella's Coach, 1995, The Magic Feather, 1995, Pandora's Box (CD ROM), 1995, Over in the Meadow (CD ROM), 1995, Tell Me About When I Was a Baby, 1996, Gold Diggers: The Novelization, 1996, Hanukkah Candles, 1995, Dragonheart: The Jr. Novelization, 1996, Giand Animal Fold-Outs: Big Trucks & Bigger Diggers, 1996, Giant Giants & Magic Mermaids, 1996, Dena Dinosaur, Morty Monster, Wanda Witch, 1996, Code Blue: In the Emergency Room, 1996, Code Blue: Making the Grade, 1996, Leave It to Beaver: The Novelization, 1997, I Love You Because...Love, Barbie, 1999; ghostwriter children's books: Dinotopia Pop-Up Book, 1993, Sliding Surprise Books, 1993-97, The Facts of Life, 1994, All Mixed Up, 1994, Little Merlin's Book of Magic Pets, 1994, Claverie Fairytale Theater, 1994. Vol. kids activity days Dutton's Books, Brentwood, Calif., 1996; vol. Sephardic Temple, L.A., 1996; spkr. UCLA Extension, 1993—. Recipient One of 10 Best New Parenting Books award Child Mag., 1993. Mem. PEN Ctr. U.S.A. West (editor-in-chief 1992-95), Soc. Children's Book Writers and Illustrators (manuscript reviewer 1995—), Internat. Women's Writing Guild, Author's Guild, Brown Alumni Assn. (interviewer 1995—), UCLA Alumni Assn., Phi Beta Kappa. Avocations: reading, hosting discussion salon, rollerblading, walking, mentoring. Office: Golden Books Family Entertainment 11425 Rochester Ave Ste 16 Los Angeles CA 90025-2416

ROKOSZ, RICHARD EUGENE, aerospace manager; b. Evergreen Park, Ill., Aug. 23, 1946; s. Eugene Anthony and Stephanie Bernice (Bedus) R.; m. Darlene Anne Dabney, May 19, 1973; children: Jeffrey Tyler, Bradley Alan. BSBA, Regis Coll., 1968; MS in Mgmt., Regis U., 1991. Chief adminstrv. ops. Martin Marietta, El Segundo, Calif., 1977-80; mgr. bus. ops. Martin Marietta, Houston, 1980-85, Sunnyvale, Calif., 1985-86; mgr. bus. ops. Martin Marietta, Denver, 1986-87, mgr. engring. adminstrn., 1987-92; mgr. info. sys. Lockheed Martin, Denver, 1992—; educator Regis U., Denver, 1992—, chairperson devel. com., 1992, mem. regents bd., 1996. Chairperson Douglas County (Colo.) Sch. adv. bd. Douglas County Schs., 1988-90. Decorated Bronze star. Republican. Roman Catholic. Avocations: reading, woodworking, landscaping, offroading. Home: 7968 Chaparral Rd Littleton CO 80124-3028 Office: Lockheed Martin care R E Rokosz DC 1055 PO Box 179 Denver CO 80201-0179

ROLL, JOHN MCCARTHY, judge; b. Pitts., Feb. 8, 1947; s. Paul Herbert and Esther Marie (McCarthy) R.; m. Maureen O'Connor, Jan. 24, 1970; children: Robert McCarthy, Patrick Michael, Christopher John. B.A., U. Ariz., 1969, J.D., 1972, LLM U. Va., 1990. Bar: Ariz. 1972, U.S. Dist. Ct. Ariz. 1974, U.S. Ct. Appeals (9th cir.) 1980, U.S. Supreme Ct. 1977. Asst. pros. atty. City of Tucson, 1973; dep. county atty. Pima County (Ariz.), 1973-80; asst. U.S. atty. U.S. Atty's Office, Tucson, 1980-87; judge Ariz. Ct. Appeals, 1987-91, U.S. Dist. Ct. Ariz., 1991—; lectr. Nat. Coll. Dist. Attys. U. Houston, 1976-87; mem. criminal justice mental health standards project ABA, 1980-83, mem. com. model jury instrns. 9th circuit, 1994—, chair, 1998—, mem. panel workshop criminal law CEELI program, Moscow, 1997; mem. U.S. Jud. Conf. Adv. Com. Criminal Rules, 1997—. Contbr. to Trial Techniques Compendium, 1978, 82, 84, Merit Selection: The Arizona Experience, Arizona State Law Journal, 1991, The Rules Have Changed: Amendments to the Rules of Civil Procedure, Defense Law Journal, 1994, Ninth Circuit Judges' Benchbook on Pretrial Proceedings, 1998; co-author: Manual on Jury Trial Procedures, Office of Cir. Exec., 1998. Coach, Frontier Baseball Little League, Tucson, 1979-84; mem. parish coun. Sts. Peter and Paul Roman Catholic Ch., Tucson, 1983-91, chmn., 1986-91; mem. Roman Cath. Diocese of Tucson Sch. Bd., 1986-90. Recipient Disting. Faculty award Nat. Coll. Dist. Attys., U. Houston, 1979, Outstanding Alumnus award U. Ariz. Coll. Law, 1992. Mem. Fed. Judges Assn. Republican. Lodge: K.C. (adv. coun. 10441). Office: US Dist Ct 55 E Broadway Blvd Tucson AZ 85701-1719

ROLLER, SUSAN LORRAYNE, industrial communications specialist, consultant; b. Portsmouth, Va., Sept. 13, 1954; d. Gilbert John Roller and Lois Carolyn (Moore) Logan. BS in Med. Scis., U. Wash., 1976, BA, 1980. Dir. med. programming Omnia Corp., Mpls., 1980-82; program developer Golle & Holmes, Mpls., 1982-83; dir. mktg. Santal Corp., St. Louis, 1983; pres. Fine Line, Ltd., Reno, Nev., 1984—; ind. film prodr., writer. Mem. Reno C. of C., Kappa Kappa Gamma. Republican. Episcopalian. Avocations: screenwriting, cowboy poetry, skiing, art.

ROLLINS, MICHAEL F., lawyer; b. Randolph, Vt., Jan. 5, 1953; s. Franklin D. and Eleanor F. Rollins; m. Lorraine Rasp, Sept. 1, 1978; children: Seana Kelly, Lesley Kendra. BS in Bus., U. Ariz., 1974, JD, 1978. Bar: Ariz. 1978, Calif. 1981, Mass. 1985, Colo. 1995, U.S. Ct. Appeals (9th cir.) 1978, U.S. Dist. Ct. Ariz. 1978, U.S. Dist. Ct. (so., cent. and no. dists.) 1981, Calif., U.S. Supreme Ct. 1988. Law clk. to Hon. Carl A. Muecke Chief Judge, U.S. Dist. Ct. Ariz., Phoenix, 1978-79; assoc. Craig, Greenfield, Irwin, Phoenix, 1979-80; assoc. Winston & Strawn, Phoenix, 1980-84, ptnr., 1984-86; trial specialist Law Office of Richard Grand, Tucson, 1986-88; officer Shultz & Rollins, Ltd., Tucson, 1988—. Chmn., mem. Ariz. Structural Pest Control Bd., Phoenix, 1980-85, Kino Cmty. Hosp. Bd., Tucson, 1996—; mem. Ariz. Agrl. Employment Rels. Bd., Phoenix, 1985-87; mem. Pima Health Care Sys. Commn. Mem. ATLA, Def. Rsch. Inst., Nat. Coll. Advocacy (advocate). Office: Shultz & Rollins Ltd 4280 N Campbell Ave Ste 214 Tucson AZ 85718-6594

ROLSTON, HOLMES, III, theologian, educator, philosopher; b. Staunton, Va., Nov. 19, 1932; s. Holmes and Mary Winifred (Long) R.; m. Jane Irving Wilson, June 1, 1956; children: Shonny Hunter, Giles Campbell. BS, Davidson Coll., 1953; BD, Union Theol. Sem., Richmond, Va., 1956; MA in Philosophy of Sci., U. Pitts., 1968; PhD in Theology, U. Edinburgh, Scotland, 1958. Ordained to ministry Presbyn. Ch. (USA), 1956. Asst. prof. philosophy Colo. State U., Ft. Collins, 1968-71, assoc. prof., 1971-76, prof., 1976—; vis. scholar Ctr. Study of World Religions, Harvard U., 1974-75; official observer UNCED, Rio de Janiero, 1992. Author: Religious Inquiry: Participation and Detachment, 1985, Philosophy Gone Wild, 1986, Science and Religion: A Critical Survey, 1987, Environmental Ethics, 1988, Conserving Natural Value, 1994, Genes, Genesis and God, 1999; assoc. editor Environ. Ethics, 1979—; mem. editorial bd. Oxford Series in Environ. Philosophy and Pub. Policy, Zygon: Jour. of Religion and Sci.; contbr. chpts. to books, articles to profl. jours. Recipient Oliver P. Penock Disting. Svc. award Colo. State U., 1983, Gov. award for Excellence, 1991, Disting. Lectr., Chinese Acad. of Social Scis., 1991, Disting. Lectr., Nobel Conf. XXVII, Gifford Lectr., U. Edinburgh, 1997. Mem. AAAS, Am. Acad. Religion, Soc. Bibl. Lit. (pres. Rocky Mountain Br. Phila region), Am. Philos. Assn. Internat. Soc. for Environ. Ethics (pres. 1990-94), Phi Beta

ROMAN, STAN G., lawyer; b. Athens, Ga., Dec. 31, 1954; s. Costic and Marilyn (Gracey) R.; m. Elizabeth Ann Whelan, Sept. 18, 1982; children: John, Matthew, Nicholas. BA, U. N.C., 1976; JD with honors, U. Tex., 1979. Bar: Calif. 1979, U.S. Dist. Ct. (no., so., ctrl. and ea.) Calif. 1979, U.S. Ct. Appeals (9th cir.) 1979. Congl. intern Honorable John Buchanan, Washington, 1977; summer assoc. Bradley, Arant, Rose & White, Birmingham, Ala., 1978; assoc. Bronson, Bronson & McKinnon, San Francisco, 1979-85, ptnr., 1985—; arbitrator, mediator Calif. Superior Ct., San Francisco, 1989—. Mem. ABA, Assn. Bus. Trial Lawyers, Def. Rsch. Inst., Calif. Bar Assn., San Francisco Bar Assn. San Francisco Com. Urban Affairs, Phi Beta Kappa, Phi Eta Sigma. Avocations: running, golf, skiing, swimming. Office: Krieg Keller Sloan Reilley & Roman LLP 7th Fl 114 Sansome St Fl 7 San Francisco CA 94104-3803

ROMANO, REBECCA KAY, counselor; b. Zanesville, Ohio, Mar. 26, 1958; Charles Ronald Fulkerson and Margaret Jane (Kiser) Williams; m. Richard Ralph Romano, May 24, 1986; children: Nicholas Robert, Kaitlin Kristine. BA, Walsh U., 1980; MEd, Bowling Green State U., 1981, 82. Lic. profl. counselor; nat. cert. counselor. Day program instr. Devel. Opportunities, Cañon City, Colo., 1983-85; clin. behavior specialist Pueblo Regional Ctr. Colo. Divsn. Devel. Disabilities, 1985-86; career devel. tchr. Colo. Dept. Corrections, Cañon City, 1986-87, facility mental health therapist, 1987—, devel. disabilities coord., 1991—, facility mental health coord., 1995—; therapist sex offender treatment team Colo. Dept. Corrections, 1986—, co-chair state com. to devel. lifetime supervision stds. for devel. disabled sex offenders; presenter in field. Mem. ACA, AAUW, Am. Assn. Mental Retardation (past state bd. dirs. 1987-91), Am. Correctional Assn., Nat. Assn. for Dually Diagnosed, Colo. Assn. Mental Health Counselors, Women of the Evang. Luth. Ch. Am. (exec. bd. mem., newsletter editor 1997, confirmation youth mentor, Sunday Sch. tchr. 1998-99). Lutheran. Avocations: reading, gardening, bicycling, volleyball, softball. Office: Colo Dept Corrections CTCF Mental Health PO Box 1010 Canon City CO 81215-1010

ROMANOS, NABIL ELIAS, business development manager; b. Roumie, Metn, Lebanon, June 3, 1965; came to U.S., 1982; s. Elias Rachid and Kamale (Salame) R. BA in Econs. and History magna cum laude, Georgetown U., 1986; postgrad., Hautes Etudes Commerciales, France, 1989; MBA, U. Calif., Berkeley, 1989. Rsch. assoc. Am. Fin. Svcs. Assn., Washington, 1986-87; fin. analyst Varian Assocs., Palo Alto, Calif., 1988, sr. fin. analyst, 1989-91; mgr. fin. mkt. analysis Varian Oncology Systems, Palo Alto, 1991-92; mgr. bus. devel. Varian Health Care Systems, Palo Alto, 1992-94, Zug, Switzerland, 1994-95, São Paulo, Brazil, 1996-97; mgr. internat. sales ops. and bus. devel. Varian Oncology Systems, Palo Alto, Calif., 1998—. Author: Finance Facts Yearbook, 1987. Vol. tutor for refugees Community Action Coalition, Washington, 1985-86; vol. interpreter emergency room Georgetown U., Washington, 1984-86; internat. vol. Internat. House U. Calif., Berkeley, 1987-89. Scholar Georgetown U., 1985-86, U. Calif., Berkeley, 1987-89. Mem. Phi Alpha Theta. Maronite Catholic.

ROMANOW, ROY JOHN, provincial government official, barrister, solicitor; b. 1939; s. Michael and Tekla R.; m. Eleanore Boykowich, 1967. Arts and Laws degrees, U. Sask. Mem. Sask. Legislative Assembly, 1967-82, 1986—, provincial sec., 1971-72, atty. gen. of province, 1971-82, minister of intergovernmental affairs, 1979-82, leader Sask. New Dem. Party, 1987—, leader of the opposition, 1987-91, leader of the majority, 1991—, premier, 1991—; opposition house leader for New Dem. Party Caucus, 1986. Co-author: Canada Notwithstanding, 1984. Office: Legislative Bldg, Rm 226, Regina, SK Canada S4S 0B3

ROMAN-UNFER, SUSAN, hematologist, oncologist; b. Cedar Rapids, Iowa, June 25, 1959; d. George V. Roman and Cecelia (Zieser) Roman; m. Robert Charles Unfer, June 13, 1987. BS in Microbiology, Iowa State U., 1984, MS in Molecular Biology, 1989; DO, U. Osteo. Med. & Health Scis., 1993. Rsch. asst. Nat. Animal Disease Ctr., Ames, Iowa, 1984-88; tchg. asst. in biology Iowa State U., Ames, 1988, rsch. asst., 1988-89; rsch. asst. Garst Seed Co., Slater, Iowa, 1989; resident in medicine Luth. Gen. Hosp., Park Ridge, Ill., 1993-96; fellow in hematology and oncology U. Colo., Denver, 1996—. Author: rsch. papers, abstracts in field. Recipient rsch. award Am. Leptospirosis Rsch. Com., 1985, 87, Donald E. Kahn Meml. award Am. Assn. Vet. Microbiologists, 1987. Mem. Am. Osteo. Assn., Sigma Xi. Roman Catholic. Avocations: running, golf, tennis, music. Home: 600 W County Line Rd Apt 12-3 Hghlnds Ranch CO 80126-6512 Office: Univ Colo Health Scis Ctr Box B-170 4200 E 9th Ave Denver CO 80220-3700

ROMEO, PETER, lawyer. BS, Georgetown U., 1964, JD, 1967, LLM 1969. Bar: D.C., Va.; CPA. With Securities and Exchange Commn., 1969-84; atty. Hogan and Hartson, Washington, 1984—; mem. adv. bd. NASPP. Co-author Section 16 Forms and Filings Handbook, 1996; contbr. articles to profl. jours. Office: Exec Press Section 16 Updates PO Box 21639 Concord CA 94521-0639

ROMER, ROY R., former governor; b. Garden City, Kans., Oct. 31, 1928; s. Irving Rudolph and Margaret Elizabeth (Snyder) R.; m. Beatrice Miller, June 10, 1952; children: Paul, Mark, Mary, Christopher, Timothy, Thomas, Elizabeth. B.S. in Agrl. Econs., Colo. State U., 1950; LL.B., U. Colo. 1952; postgrad., Yale U. Bar: Colo. 1952. Engaged in farming in Colo., 1942-52; ind. practice law Denver, 1955-66; mem. Colo. Ho. of Reps., 1958-62, Colo. Senate, 1962-66; owner, operator Arapahoe Aviation Co., Colo. Flying Acad., Geneva Basin Ski Area; engaged in home site devel.; owner chain farm implement and indsl. equipment stores Colo.; commr. agr. State of Colo., 1975, chief staff, exec. asst. to gov., 1975-77, 83-84, state treas., 1977-86, gov., 1987-98; chmn. Gov. Colo. Blue Ribbon Panel, Gov. Colo. Small Bus. Council; mem. agrl. adv. com. Colo. Bd. Agr. Bd. editors Colo. U. Law Rev., 1960-62. Past trustee Iliff Sch. Theology, Denver; mem., past chmn. Nat. Edn. Goals Panel; co-chmn. Nat. Coun. on Standards and Testing. With USAF, 1952-53. Mem. Gov. Gov.'s Assn. (chmn.), Nat. Gov.'s Assn. (former chmn.), Colo. Bar Assn., Order of the Coif. Democrat. Presbyterian. Office: PO Box 6949 Denver CO 80203*

ROMERO, ELIZABETH RIVERA, public health nurse; b. Manila, Jan. 10, 1958; d. Vivencio Delapaz and Erlinda (Magalona) Rivera; m. Oscar Dedios Romero; 1 child, Sherilynn R. B.S. in Nursing cum laude, San Francisco State U., 1980. R.N., Calif.; cert. profl. utilization review. Staff nurse St. Lukes Hosp., San Francisco, 1980-85; pub. health nurse St. Mary's Hosp., San Francisco, 1984-85, Kimberly Home Patient Care, Pinole, Calif., 1984-87, utilization rev. case mgr. Brookside Hosp., San Pablo, Calif., 1987-90; head nurse, utilization mgmt. case mgr. San Francisco General Hosp., 1990—; Mem. ANA, Calif. Nurses Assn., Golden Gate Nurses Assn., Am. Heart Assn. (Contra Costa chpt.), Calif. Scholarship Fedn., Interqual ISD Registry. Roman Catholic. Avocations: dancing; travel; camping; photography.

ROMERO, PHILIP JOSEPH, economic and policy advisor; b. Abington, Pa., Mar. 22, 1957; s. Joseph John and Mildred Edith (Laundis) R.; m. Lita Grace Flores, Oct. 6, 1984. BA in Econs. and Polit. Sci., Cornell U., 1979; PhD in Policy Analysts, Rand Grad. Sch., 1988. Asst. to mayor Twp. of East Brunswick, N.J., 1977-78; policy analyst Sci. Applications Internat. Corp., Washington, 1980-83; rsch. assoc. RAND Corp., Santa Monica, Calif., 1983-88, assoc. economist, 1988-90; dir. strategic planning United Technologies/Carrier, Hartford, Conn., 1990-91; chief economist Gov.'s Office, Sacramento, Calif., 1991—; dep. cabinet sec., 1993—; exec. dir. Calif. Managed Health Care Improvement Task Force, 1996-98; cons. Office of Tech. Assessment, Washington, 1989-90, RAND Corp., Washington, 1990-91, Sec. of Air Forces Sci. Adv. Bd., Washington, 1983-88, Undersec. of Def., Washington, 1985-86; adj. prof. U. So. Calif. and Calif. State U., 1987—; mem. Coun. on Fgn. Rels., 1994—; mem. adv. coun. Calif. Congl. Delegation 1997—. Coauthor: (book) The Proliferation of Nuclear Crises; 1997; author: (book) California Economic Report, 1997; Contbr. numerous reports and papers to profl. pubs. Pres. RAND Grad. Sch. Alumni Assn., Santa Monica, 1989; founder Adopt A School Honors Program Pacific Palisades Calif., 1990. Recipient Internat. Affairs Fellowship Coun. on Fgn. Rels., N.Y. award for Exemplary Civilian Svc. Sec. Def. Army, Washington 1995; sr. mem. exec. Coun. on Foreign Washington 1993; sel. Nat. Def. Univ. acting GAO Def. exec. dir. major

1989. Mem. The Planning Forum, Am. Econ. Assn., Ops. Rsch. Soc. of Am., Pacific Coun. on Internat. Policy (founding), Acad. Pub. Policy Analysts and Mgmt., Inst. Mgmt. Sci. Avocations: designer of hist. games, musical theater. Home: 1587 Barnett Cir Carmichael CA 95608-5852 Office: Gov's Office State Capitol Sacramento CA 95814-4906

ROMESBURG, KERRY D., state education administrator; b. Akron, Ohio, Mar. 12, 1945; s. Bert Lewis and Edna (Bartlett) R.; m. Judy Kaye Land, July 2, 1965; children—Rod A., Donald A. B.A., Ariz. State U., 1967, M.A., 1968, Ph.D., 1972. Tchr. math. East High Sch., Phoenix, 1969-70; asst. dir. instl. research Ariz. State U., Tempe, 1972-73; planning analyst Ariz. Bd. Regents, Phoenix, 1973-74; exec. dir. Ariz. Commn. Post Secondary Edn., Phoenix, 1974-75; exec. dir. Alaska Commn. Postsecondary Edn., Juneau, 1975—. Mem. Western Interstate Commn. on Higher Edn., Boulder, Colo., 1977—, chmn., 1981-82; mem. Western Tech. Manpower Council, 1982—; mem. Nat. Adv. Council for United Student Aid Funds, N.Y.C., 1978—. Recipient Outstanding Alumnus award Ariz. State U., 1982; NDEA fellow, 1972. Mem. State Higher Edn. Exec. Officers, Nat. Adv. Council State Postsecondary Planning Commns., Am. Assn. Higher Edn., NEA. Home: 308 Distin Ave Juneau AK 99801-1669*

ROMIG, ALTON DALE, JR., materials scientist, educator; b. Bethlehem, Pa., Oct. 6, 1953; s. Alton Dale and Christine (Groh) R.; m. Julie H. Romig. BS, Lehigh U., 1975, MS, 1977, PhD, 1979. Metallurgist, tech. staff Sandia Nat. Labs., Albuquerque, 1979-87, supr. physical metallurgy, 1987-90, mgr. metallurgy, 1990-92, dir. materials and process scis., 1992-95; dir. Microelectronics and Photonics, 1995-98, Microsystems Sci., Tech. and Components, 1998—; part time full prof. N.Mex. Inst. Mining and Tech., Socorro, 1981—; Acta/Scripta Metallurgica Lectr., 1993; Fellow Am. Soc. for Metals Internat. (trustee 1992—, v.p. 1996-97, pres. 1997-98, Outstanding Rsch. award 1992); mem. TMS, Electron Microscopy Soc. Am. (Burton Outstanding Young Sci. medal 1988), Microbeam Analysis Soc. (pres. 1990, Heinrich award for Outstanding Young Sci. 1991), Materials Rsch. Soc., Sigma Xi, Tau Beta Pi. Author: Principles of Analytical Electron Mecroscopy, 1986, Scanning Electron Microscopy, X-ray Microanalysis and Analytical Electron Microscopy, 1991, Scanning Electron Microscopy and Microanalysis, 1992; editor numerous procs. in phys. metallurgy and electron microscopy; contbr. over 160 articles to sci. jours. Home: 304 Big Horn Ridge Pl NE Albuquerque NM 87122-1446 Office: Sandia Nat Labs Sandia Nat Labs Ctr 1300 Albuquerque NM 87185

RONEY, JOHN HARVEY, lawyer, consultant; b. L.A., June 12, 1932; s. Harvey and Mildred Puckett (Cargill) R.; m. Joan Ruth Allen, Dec. 27, 1954; children: Pam Roney Peterson, J. Harvey, Karen Louise Hanke, Cynthia Allen Harmon. Student, Pomona Coll., 1950-51; B.A., Occidental Coll., 1954; LL.B., UCLA, 1959. Bar: Calif. 1960, D.C. 1976. Assoc. O'Melveny & Myers, L.A., 1959-67, ptnr., 1967-94, of counsel, 1994—; gen. counsel Pa. Co., 1970-78, Baldwin United Corp., 1983-84; dir. Coldwell Banker & Co., 1969-81, Brentwood Savs. & Loan Assn., 1968-80; spl. advisor Rehab. of Mut. Benefit Life Ins. Co., 1991-94; cons. advisor to Rehab. of Confederation Life Ins. Co., 1994-95; mem. policy adv. bd. Calif. Ins. Commn., 1991-95. Served to 1st lt. USMCR, 1954-56. Mem. ABA, Calif. Bar Assn. (ins. law com. 1991-95, chmn. 1993-94), Los Angeles County Bar Assn., D.C. Bar Assn., N.Y. Coun. Fgn. Rels., Pacific Coun. on Internat. Policy, Conf. Ins. Counsel, Calif. Club, Sky Club (N.Y.), Gainey Ranch Golf Club (Scottsdale). Republican. Home: The Strand Hermosa Beach CA 90254 Office: 400 S Hope St Ste 1600 Los Angeles CA 90071-2811

RONEY, RAYMOND G., educator; b. Phila., July 26, 1941; s. Wallace and Rosezell (Harris) R.; m. Ruth Agnes Westgaph, May 2, 1970; 1 child, Andre. BA in Polit. Sci., Cen. State U., Wilberforce, Ohio, 1963; MLS, Pratt Inst., Bklyn., 1965. Head reference dept. Howard U., Washington, 1965-66; dir. libr. and info. svcs. Nat. League of Cities/U.S. Conf. Mayors, Washington, 1967-70; dir. libr. svcs. Washington Tech. Inst., 1970-78; deputy dir. learning resources U. D.C., 1978-84; dean instrnl. svcs. El Camino Coll., Torrance, Calif., 1984—; pub. Libr. Mosaics Mag., Culver City, Calif., 1989—; pres. Yenor, Inc., Culver City, Calif., 1989—. Author: (books) Introduction to AV for Technical Assistants, 1981, AV Tech. Primer, 1988. Pres. Shepard Park Citizens Assn., Washington, 1973-83; chmn. Friends of Libr., L.A. Southwest Coll., 1993—. Recipient Adminstrv. Excellence award INTELECOM, Pasadena, Calif., 1993, Outstanding Adminstr. of Yr. award Calif. Assn. Postsecondary Adminstrs., 1997. Mem. ALA, Coun. on Libr. Media Technology (officer, bd. dirs., Outstanding Leadership award 1994), Calif. Acad. and Rsch. Librs. (program chmn.), Learning Resources Assn. of Calif. C.C. (bd. dirs.). Avocations: music, reading, travel. Office: El Camino Coll 16007 Crenshaw Blvd Torrance CA 90506

RONNING, CHARLOTTE JEAN, foreign language educator; b. Billings, Mont., Dec. 19, 1953; d. Charles and Ruth Alice (Johnson) R. BA, Mont. State U., Billings, 1978, BS, 1980; MA, U. Colo., 1995. Nat. cert. counselor. Sales/office mgr. Clint Faubions, Denver, 1980-81; office mgr. Virginia Horn Travel, Denver, 1981-82; sales, instr. R.B. Bonar & Assocs., Denver, 1982-86; fgn. lang. educator Cherry Creek Schs., Denver, 1987—; student Fgn. Study League, Europe, 1970; Dale Carnegie course instr., N.Y.C., 1982-87; sponsor Cherry Creek in Costa Rica, 1988. Mem. Fgn. Lang. Proficiency Com., Denver, 1993—; treas. Bromley Commons, Denver, 1994—. Mem. ACA, Colo. Counseling Assn., Chi Sigma Iota, Alpha Lambda Delta, Alpha Mu Gamma, Kappa Alpha Theta. Republican. Presbyterian. Avocations: piano, golf, skiing. Home: 350 Detroit St Apt 207 Denver CO 80206-4361

RONSMAN, WAYNE JOHN, insurance company executive; b. Milw., Jan. 21, 1938; s. Harry Martin and Martha Elizabeth (Popp) R.; m. Joan P. Murphy-Mays, Nov. 30, 1974; children: Allison, Alanna; children by previous marriage: Rosemary, Harry, Martha. Student Marquette U., 1955-58, U. San Francisco, 1960-66. CLU, CFP, chartered fin. cons. Acct. Otis McAllister & Co., 1960-62; acct., salesman data processing Statis. Tabulation Corp., San Francisco, 1962-66; chief acct., gen. mgr. Dillingham Bros. Ltd., Honolulu, 1966-67; ins. salesman Mut. Benefit Life Ins. Co., 1968-91, mgr. Met Life Honolulu, 1991-93, gen. agt., Hawaii, Alaska, 1991; v.p. Brenno Assos., Honolulu, 1972-80; prin. Ronsman-Brenno, Anchorage, 1980-90; owner Ronsman, Hammond & Assocs., 1991—; guest lectr. Chaminade U. Law Sch., Honolulu. Mem. Gov's Task Force Program Correctional Facilities Land, 1970-72; mem. State Bd. Paroles & Pardons, 1972-75; treas. Spl. Edn. Ctr. Oahu, 1969-78; pres. Ballet Alaska, 1986-87, Maui Ballet Co. Ltd., 1992-93; v.p. devel., chmn., trustee Make A Wish Hawaii Found., 1992—; chmn. Maui County Salary Commn., 1996-98; investment dir. Hospice, Maui, 1998-99. USMCR 1958-60. Mem. Inst. Mmt. Acct. (pres. Anchorage chpt. 1989-90), Am. Soc. CLUs, Hawaii Estate Planning Coun. (dir. 1994), Honolulu Assn. Life Underwriters (million dollar round table 1973—), Inst. Mgmt. Accts. (pres. Honolulu 1994-96), Hawaii (state editor 1970-71, nat. dir. 1972-73), Kailua (pres. 1968-69) Jaycees, Hawaii C. of C., Nat. Assn. Securities Dealers, Kailua C. of C. (pres. 1977-78). Roman Catholic. Home: Ronsman-Hammond & Assocs 1099 Alakea St Ste 1500 Honolulu HI 96813-4500 Office: PO Box 336 Honolulu HI 96809-0336

ROOK, AYESHA L, producer, writer; b. Springfield, Oreg., Dec. 15, 1967; d. Keerock and Linda Rook. BA, John Hopkins U., 1989; MJ, U. Calif., Berkeley, 1996. Radio prodr. WJHU-FM, Balt., Md., 1989-92; assoc. prodr. documentary KCTS TV/John DeGraff Prodns., Seattle, 1992-93; assoc. prodr. Am. Cmty. Found. CBS, Mill Valley, Calif., 1996—. Prodr. (radio program) The Aids Call-in, 1990 (Silver CPB Cmty. Affairs),(video documentary) And The Kings Ran No More, 1997 (Berkeley Internat. Film Festival Best ECO documentary, Second Place College Emmys), contributor: Alaska Airline Mag. 1998 (SPJ Award Second Place Arts Criticism); assoc. prodr. (documentary) Osgood Flat. Fgn. corripr. fellowship, 1995, 1996. Mem. Nat. Assn. Sci. Writers, Soc. of Prof. Journalists, Nat. Press Club.

ROOKS, CHARLES S., foundation administrator; b. Whiteville, N.C., June 29, 1937. BA in English, Wake Forest Coll., 1959; Rockefeller Brothers Sci., 1968. Rsch. assoc. Voter Edn. Project, Atlanta, 1969-70, dir. tech. assistance programs, 1970-71, dep. dir., 1971-72; exec. dir. Southeastern Coun. of Foundns. Atlanta, 1972-79; dir. nlim. Coun. on Foundns. Washington 1979-81; asst. dir. dir. acting exec. dir. exec. dir. mayor

Meml. Trust, Portland, Oreg., 1982—; instr. polit. sci. Duke U., Durham, N.C., 1963, 65-67; asst. prof. of govt. Lake Forest Coll., Ill., 1967-69; asst. prof. polit. sci. Clark Coll., Atlanta, 1969-71; bd. dirs. Pacific Northwest Grantmakers Forum, Forum of Regional Assns. of Grantmakers; mem. adv. bd. Neighborhood Partnership Fund (Oreg. Cmty. Found.); mem., adv. bd. Giving in Oreg. Coun. Contbr. articles to profl. jours. Home: 2706 SW English Ct Portland OR 97201-1622 Office: Meyer Memorial Trust 1515 SW 5th Ave Ste 500 Portland OR 97201-5450

ROONEY, PEG (MARGARET E. ROONEY), vocational education administrator; b. Pueblo, Colo., Nov. 23, 1944; d. Joseph and Margaret Pugel; children: Kate, Sean. Diploma, St. Mary Corwin Sch. Nursing, 1965; BS, U. So. Colo., 1968; MSN, Colo. U., 1975; PhD, Colo. State U., Ft. Collins, 1993. Nursing coord. Pikes Peak Community Coll., Colorado Springs, Colo.; instr. Beth El Coll. of Nursing, Colorado Springs; asst. prof. U. So. Colo., Pueblo; health programs mgr. Colo. C.C. Sys., Denver. Mem. Colo. Orgn. for ADN (pres.).

ROONEY-EWING, ELISABETH ANNE, priest; m. James E. Ewing. Student, Mt. San Antonio Coll., 1978. Ordained to ministry Evang. Episcopal Chs., 1998. Pastor, gen. overseers, CEO St. Matthew Living Cathedral, N.Y.C.; mem. Rand Rsch. Corp.; mem. diplomat cir. L.A. World Affairs Coun. Co-editor: Church History, 1996-98, The Church Visible, 1996-98, George Washington, 1996-98, Life After Death, 1996-98, Bible Lessons, 1996-98; assoc. editor Pinnacle Today Internat. Mag., St. Matthew Publs., St. Matthew Tribune. Mem. Knights of Malta (Dame). Office: St Matthew Cathedral Ste 145 10736 Jefferson Blvd Culver City CA 90230-4969

ROOP, JOSEPH MCLEOD, economist; b. Montgomery, Ala., Sept. 29, 1941; s. Joseph Ezra and Mae Elizabeth (McLeod) R.; B.S., Central Mo. State U., Warrensburg, 1963; Ph.D., Wash. State U., Pullman, 1973; m. Betty Jane Reed, Sept. 4, 1965; 1 dau., Elizabeth Rachael. Economist, Econ. Research Service, U.S. Dept. Agr., Washington, 1975-79; sr. economist Evans Econs., Inc., Washington, 1979-81; staff scientist Battelle Pacific N.W. Nat. Lab., Richland, Wash., 1981—; instr. dept. econs. Wash. State U., 1969-71; with Internat. Energy Agy., Paris, 1990-91. Contbr. tech. articles to profl. jours. Served with U.S. Army, 1966-68. Dept. Agr. Coop. State Research Service research grantee, 1971-73. Mem. Am. Econ. Assn., Econometric Soc., Internat. Assn. Energy Economics, Am. Statis. Assn. Home: 715 S Taft St Kennewick WA 99336-9587 Office: PO Box 999 MSIN K8-17 Richland WA 99352-0999

ROOS, NESTOR ROBERT, consultant; b. St. Louis, Aug. 19, 1925; s. Maurice and Fannie (Friedman) R.; m. Fay Weil, July 8, 1951; children: Marilyn Roos Hall, Eileen Roos Ruddell, Robert F. BBA, Washington U., St. Louis, 1948; MSBA, Washington U., 1949; DBA, Ind. U., 1959. Instr. bus. La. State U., Baton Rouge, 1949-51; teaching fellow Ind. U., Bloomington, 1951-53; asst. prof. Ga. State U., Atlanta, 1953-55; prof. U. Ariz., Tucson, 1955-86, prof. emeritus, 1986; chmn. Risk Mgmt. Pub. Co., Tucson, 1976-90, cons. editor, 1990—; cons., expert witness in field; bd. dirs. Blue Cross-Blue Shield Ariz., sec., 1993-95, chair, 1998—; mem. Ins. Dirs. Adv. Com., Phoenix, 1987—, Reverse Mortgage Adv. Com., Tucson, 1988-90. Author: (with others) Multiple Line Insurers, 1970, Governmental Risk Management Manual, 1976, Industrial Accident Prevention, 1980. Bd. dirs. Handmaker Geriatric Ctr., Tucson, 1987-92; pres. Temple Emanu-El, Tucson, 1981-83. With U.S. Army, 1943-45, ETO. Grantee Nat. Inst. Occupational Safety and Health, 1975. Mem. Risk and Ins. Mgmt. Soc., Western Risk and Ins. Assn. (pres. 1972-73), Public Risk and Ins. Mgmt. Assn. (dir. edn. and tng. 1982-89). Democrat. Jewish. Avocations: gardening, golf. Home: 7311 E Camino De Cima Tucson AZ 85750-2212 Office: Risk Mgmt Pub Co 2030 E Broadway Blvd Ste 106 Tucson AZ 85719-5908

ROOSEVELT, MICHAEL A., lawyer; b. L.A., Dec. 7, 1946. BA, Harvard U., 1969; JD, Columbia U., 1972. Bar: Calif. 1973. Shareholder Friedman, Olive, mcCabbin, Spalding, Bilter Roosevelt et al, San Franciso, 1996—. Mem. ABA. Office: Friedman Olive McCabbin Spalding et al 425 California St Ste 22nd San Francisco CA 94104-2207

ROOT, CHARLES JOSEPH, JR., finance executive, consultant; b. Pierre, S.D., July 26, 1940; s. Charles Joseph and Hazel Ann (Messenger) R.; 1 child from previous marriage, Roseann Marie; m. Sharon Lee, June 24, 1995; stepchildren: Nichole Marie Marcillac, Monique Marie Marcillac. Student, San Francisco Jr. Coll., 1963-65, La Salle Extension U., 1970-71, Coll. of Marin, 1971-72, Am. Coll. Life Underwriters, 1978-82. Registered investment advisor; charter fin. cons.; cert. fin. planner. Estate planner Bankers Life Co., San Francisco, 1966-78; fin. planner Planned Estates Assocs., Corte Madera, Calif., 1978-81; mng. dir. Double Eagle Fin. Corp., Santa Rosa, Calif., 1981—, investment advisor, 1983—; personal bus. mgr., 1987—. V.p. Big Bros. of Am., San Rafael, Calif., 1976-80; treas. com. to elect William Filante, San Rafael, 1978, Cmty. Health Ctrs. of Marin, Fairfax, Calif., 1982-83, Wellspring Found., Philo, Calif., 1981-85; treas., bd. dirs. Ctr. for Attitudinal Healing, Tiburon, Calif., 1989-92; bd. dirs. Pickle Family Circus, San Francisco, 1988, United Way Sonoma Lake, Mendocino Counties, 1993—; bd. dirs. Redwood Empire Estate Planning Coun., Santa Rosa, Calif., 1992—, v.p. programs, 1993, pres. 1995-96). Mem. Internat. Assn. Fin. Planners, Coll. Fin. Planning (cert. fin. planner 1988), Registry of fin. Planning, Nat. Assn. Life Underwriters, Marin County Assn. Life Underwriters (v.p. 1971-76, editor newsletter 1976-80), Rotary (Paul Harris Fellow 1980). Republican. Avocations: pilot, downhill skiing, scuba diving, golf. Office: Double Eagle Fin Corp PO Box 2790 Santa Rosa CA 95405-0790

ROOT, DORIS SMILEY, portrait artist; b. Ann Arbor, Mich., June 28, 1924; d. George O. and Hazel (Smith) Smiley. Student, Art Inst. of Chgo., 1943-45, N.Y. Sch. Design, 1976-77, Calif. Art Inst., 1984-85. Creative dir. All May Co.'s, L.A., 1962-63; advt. sales pro. dir. Seibu, L.A., 1963-64; v.p. Walgers & Assoc., L.A., 1964-70; owner, designer At The Root of Things, L.A., 1970-73; adv. sales pro. dir. Hs. of Nine, L.A., 1973-74; asst. designer MGM Grand, Reno, Nev., 1974-76; designer, office mgr. Von Hausen Studio, L.A., 1976-82; ABC libr. ABC/Cap Cities, L.A., 1982-89; portrait artist (also known as Dorian), AKA Dorian, art studio, L.A., 1982—. One-man shows include Cookeville, Tenn., 1989, Beverly Hills, Calif., 1991; artist in residence, Cookeville, 1989-90.

ROOT, GEORGE L., JR., lawyer; b. 1947. BA, Syracuse U.; JD cum laude, U. San Diego. Ptnr. Foley & Lardner, San Diego; guest lectr. Nat. U., U. Calif., San Diego; adj. prof. San Diego State U. Mem. San Diego County Bar Assn. (chmn. mental health com. 1983, task force on children at risk 1995), Assn. Calif. Hosp. Dists. (legis. com. 1995), Calif. Soc. Healthcare Attys., Healthcare Fin. Mgmt. Assn., Nat. Health Lawyers Assn. Office: Foley & Lardner 402 W Broadway Fl 23 San Diego CA 92101-3542

ROOT, GERALD EDWARD, planning and operational support administrator; b. Gridley, Calif., May 5, 1948; s. Loris Leo Root and Mary Helen (Wheeler) Murrell; m. Tricia Ann Caywood, Feb. 13, 1982; children: Jason Alexander, Melinda Ann. AA in Bus., Yuba C.C., Marysville, Calif., 1968; BA in Psychology, Calif. State U., Sonoma, 1974; MA in Social Sci., Calif. State U., Chico, 1977; postgrad., U. San Francisco, 1998—. Gen. mgr. Do-It Leisure Therapeutic Recreation, Chico, 1977-79; CETA projects coord. City of Chico, 1980-81; exec. dir. Voluntary Action Ctr., Inc., South Lake Tahoe, Calif., 1981-83; devel. dir. Work Tng. Ctr., Inc., Chico, 1983-92; exec. dir. North Valley Rehab. Found., Chico, 1986-92; dir. planning and operational support Superior Ct. of Calif., 1992—; project mgr. Juvenile Detention Alternatives Initiative, 1992-98, Feather River Industries Vocat. Tng., 1991, Creative Learning Ctr. Constrn., 1988-89, Correctional Options-Drug Ct., 1994, Violence Prevention Resource Ctr., 1995-96, Communities That Care-Juvenile Delinquency Prevention Initiative, 1995, Securing the Health and Safety of Urban Children Initiative, 1995-97, Joint Cabinets Youth Work Group/Child Welfare League Am., 1996-97, Task Force on Fairness-The Juvenile Justice Initiative, 1994-97, SacraMentor, Inc., CA Wellness Found., 1994-95, Violent Injury Prevention Coalition/Calif. Dept. Health and Human Svcs., 1995—, Domestic Violence Coordinating Coun., Sacramento County, 1995-98, Multicultural Perspectives on Family Violence Conf., 1997—, Family Violence Summit, 1997, Ptnrs. in Protection Conf. 1997 Child Abuse Prevention Coun., The Drug Store, Calif. Nat. Guard drug demand reduction program, 1996, 97, disporportionate minority confinement rsch. com. Criminal Justice Cabinet, 1997-99, Court Cmty.-Focused Strategic Plan, 1998-99. Bd. dirs. Cmty. Action Agy., Butte County, Calif., 1990-92, ARC, Butte County, 1989-90, Sunrise Recreation and Park Dist., 1996—; mem. adv. bds. Butte C.C. Dist., 1987-92, Cmty. Svcs. Planning Coun., 1994-96. Grantee Annie E. Casey Found., USDA, U.S. Dept. Justice, Robert Wood Johnson Found., Calif. Office Criminal Justice Planning, U.S. Dept. Labor, Office Juvenile Justice and Delinquency Prevention, Sacramento Criminal Justice Cabinet, CA Wellness Found. Mem. Phi Delta Kappa. Office: Supr Ct Calif County of Sacramento 720 9th St Sacramento CA 95814-3816

ROOT, LAURA LEE, personal care industry executive; b. Oxnard, Calif., Mar. 8, 1953; d. Robert James Dodge and Barbara Louise (Forest) Mickle; m. Thomas Mayfield Root, Aug. 8, 1989; children: Virginia Anne, Robert William, Sara Michelle. Grad., Internat. Esthetic/Cosmetology, Vancouver, 1997. Diplomate Internat. Com. Aesthetics. Paralegal Hughes Hubbard & Reed, L.A., 1987-89; owner, esthetician Face to Face, McMinnville, Oreg., 1994-96, Body & Soul Esthetic Retreat, McMinnville, 1997-98. Author (booklet) Professional Salon Services, 1995, (leaflet) Hip & Cellulite Reduction, 1997; editor ASEM Quarterly Report; contbr. articles to profl. jours. Mem. Aestheticians Internat. Assn., Am. Acad. Med. Esthetics, Am. Soc. Esthetic Medicine, Am. Acad. Anti-Aging Medicine, Soc. Permanent Cosmetic Profls. Republican. Avocations: Russian Classic ballet, private pilot, motorcycles. Office: Body & Soul Esthetic Retreat 5025 E Bluefield Ave Scottsdale AZ 85254

ROOT, NILE, photographer, educator; b. Denver, Dec. 11, 1926; s. Victor Nile and Ella May (Holaway) R.; student U. Denver, 1968; MS in Instructional Tech., Rochester Inst. Tech., 1978; m. Abigail Barton Brown, Feb. 5, 1960; 1 child, James Michael. Microphotographer, U.S. Dept. Commerce, Field Info. Agy. Tech., Fed. Republic Germany, 1946-48; free-lance photographer, 1949-51; pres. Photography Workshop, Inc., Denver, 1952-60; dir. dept. biophotography and med. illustration Rose Meml. Med. Ctr., Denver, 1960-70; dir. med. illustration dept. Children's Hosp., Denver, 1970-71; dir. Photography for Sci., Denver, 1971-72; prof. biomed. photog. communications Rochester Inst. Tech. (N.Y.), 1972-86 , chmn. dept., 1974-86, prof. emeritus Coll. Imaging Arts and Scis., 1986—; travel writer, photographer, Japan, China, S.E. Asia, 1986-89; writer, photographer, Tucson, 1989—. dir. HEW project for devel. of field, 1974-77. Served with USN, 1945-46. Recipient numerous awards for sci. photographs; Eisenhart Outstanding Tchr. award Rochester Inst. Tech., 1986; 1st Ann. Faculty fellow Sch. Photog. Arts and Scis., Rochester Inst. Tech., 1979. Fellow Biol. Photog. Assn. (registered, emeritus, bd. govs. 1977-79, Louis Schmidt award 1986); mem. Ctr. Creative Photography. Democrat. Contbr. illustrations to med. textbooks; represented in numerous mus. photog. exhibits and numerous pvt. collections. Home and Office: 314 N Banff Ave Tucson AZ 85748-3311

ROOT, WILLIAM DIXON, construction company executive; b. Medford, Oreg., July 27, 1951; s. Earl Merrit and Helen Edith (Dixon) R.; m. Catherine Jeanine Smiraglia, July 10, 1981; children: Stacie Marie, Shawn Dixon. BSBA, U. Nev., Reno, 1978. Contr., sec.-treas. Jensen Elec., Inc., Reno, 1977-82; v.p., sec.-treas. Clark & Sullivan, Inc., Reno, 1982—; v.p., asst. sec. G & S Gen. Inc., Reno, 1986—; v.p., sec., treas. Westech Devel., Reno, 1986—, also bd. dirs.; cons. Micro-Tech., Reno, 1984-93; bd. dirs. Sierra Schs. Credit Union, High Sierra Industries. Mem. Am. Coun. for Constrn. Edn., Assn. Sysm. Mgrs. Constrn. Fin. Mgrs. Assn. (v.p. 1986-88, exec. com. 1997—, com. chair 1997—, pres. 1988-90, chmn. 1990—, nat. bd. dirs., nat. chmn. chpt. formation com., exec. com., vice chmn. conf. planning com., chmn. liaison com. 1995—), Assn. Gen. Contractors, Sierra Nevada IBM Users, Sertoma Club (treas. 1983-88, Centurian award 1986, Tribune award 1989, Disting. Svc. award 1989), Rotary (sgt.-at-arms, treas. 1995—), Sierra Challenge Athletics Assn. (pres., past treas., bd. dirs.). Republican. Avocations: micro computers, golf, reading, sailing, racquetball. Home: 2505 Homeland Dr Reno NV 89511-9269 Office: Clark & Sullivan Inc 905 Industrial Way Sparks NV 89431-6081

ROPER, BIRDIE ALEXANDER, social sciences educator; b. New Orleans; d. Earl and Ethel (Charmer) Alexander; m. Morris F. Roper; 1 child, Andree Marie Driskell. BS, U. Dayton, 1949; MA, Azusa Pacific U., 1971, Claremont Grad. Sch., 1978; PhD, Claremont Grad. Sch., 1980. DON Flint Goodridge Hosp., New Orleans, 1954, 55; sch. nurse, health educator, classroom tchr. L.A. Unified Sch. Dist., 1963-91; extended day prof. social scis. dept. Pasadena City Coll., 1972—; clin. instr. dept. nursing Calif. State U., San Bernardino, 1993—; researcher, author, cons. in gerontology. Editor: (newsletter Calif. Nurses Assn.) Vital Signs. Mem. ANA, Am. Soc. Univ. Profs., Am. Soc. on Aging, Inst. for Rsch. on Aging, Nat. Coun. on Aging, Nat. Gerontol. Nursing Assn., Nat. Assn. Profl. Geriatric Care Mgrs., Phi Delta Kappa (bd. mem. San Antonio chpt. 1981-92), Alpha Kappa Alpha. Home and Office: 1657 W Sunnyview Dr Rialto CA 92377-3850

ROPER, LARRY LESTER, pastor, school administrator; b. England, Ark., June 10, 1948; s. Lloyd Lester and Ruth Ella (White) R.; m. Linda Lou Hornbarger, May 15, 1971; children: Larry Lester Jr., Angelica Marie. BS, So. Bible Coll., Houston, 1973. Ordained to ministry Pentecostal Ch. of God., 1974. Pastor Pentecostal Ch. of God, Clio, Mich., 1974-77; state youth dir. Pentecostal Ch. of God, St. Johns, Mich., 1977-79; pastor Pentecostal Ch. of God, Clio, 1979-80; pastor, adminstr. Pentecostal Ch. of God, Antioch, Calif., 1980-86, 91—; sec.-treas. State Yuth Pentecostal Ch. of God, Camden, Mich., 1976-77; presbyter Pentecostal Ch. of God, Citrus Heights, Calif., 1986—; advisor Women's Aglow, Antioch, 1987—. Republican. Office: Living Word Pentecostal Ch 415 W 6th St Antioch CA 94509-1602

RORER, LEONARD GEORGE, psychologist, writer; b. Dixon, Ill., Dec. 24, 1932; s. Leonard Gleason and Marion Emma (Geyer) R.; m. Gail Evans, Apr. 30, 1958 (div. May 11, 1964); children: Liat, Eric Evans; m. Nancy McKimens, Jan. 9, 1969 (div. Jan. 19, 1976); 1 child, Mya Noelani. BA, Swarthmore Coll., 1954; PhD, U. Minn., 1963 . Rsch. assoc., then assoc. dir. Oreg. Rsch. Inst., Eugene, 1963-75; prof. psychology Miami U., Oxford, Ohio, 1975-93, dir. clin. psychology tng. program, 1976-86; pres. Oreg. Psychol. Assn., 1973-75. NIMH spl. rsch. fellow U. Calif., Berkeley, 1967-68; fellow Netherlands Inst. Advanced Study, 1971-72; postdoctoral fellow Inst. for Rational-Emotive Therapy, 1982-83. Fellow APA (coun. reps. 1968-72), Am. Psychol. Soc. (charter), We. Psychol. Assn.; mem. Midwestern Psychol. Assn., Assn. Advancement Behavior Therapy, Soc. Multivariate Exptl. Psychology. Author articles in field, mem. editorial bds. profl. jours. Home: 407 High St Santa Cruz CA 95060-2613

ROSA, FREDRIC DAVID, construction company executive; b. Monroe, Wis., Oct. 31, 1946; s. Fredric Carl Rosa and Irene (Sommers) Rosa Figi; m. Melanie A. Downs, May 31, 1986; children: Mark, Katherine. BBA in Mktg., U. Wis., 1968. Dir. mktg. Swiss Colony Stores, Inc., Monroe, 1968-80; pres. Videotape Indsl. Prodns., Inc., Madison, Wis., 1980-82; agt. VR Bus. Brokers, Colorado Springs, Colo., 1982-83; sales rep. NCR Corp., Denver, 1983-85; prin. F. D. Rosa & Assocs., Denver, Aspen and Eagle, Colo., 1985-89; pres. Peak Benefit Cons., Colorado Springs, 1989-95; registered prin. Nexus Fin. Programs, Inc., Colorado Springs, Colo., 1990-92, Nutmeg Securities Ltd., Colorado Springs, 1992-94; sales staff Am. Airlines, Colorado Springs, Colo., 1993-95; cons. Kolb-Lena Cheese Co., Lena, Ill., 1983-85; instr. The Am. Coll., Bryn Mawr, Pa., 1990-91, A.D. Banker & Co., Overland Park, Kans., 1995-97; owner Fred Rosa Constrn., Colorado Springs, 1990-94, Lakewood, Colo., 1995—. Contbr. articles to trade publs. and newspapers. Mem. Am. Soc. CLU and Chartered Fin. Cons., Mensa, Internat. Legion of Intelligence, Delta Sigma Pi (life). Methodist. Avocations: big game hunting, skiing, camping, travel. Home and Office: Fred Rosa Constrn 1270 Cody St Lakewood CO 80215-4897

ROSAS, SUSAN JANE, designer, graphic artist, illustrator, art director; b. Oakland, Calif., June 30, 1937; d. Clarence Francis and Barbara Hischier Matthews; m. John Anthony Roach, July 28, 1958 (div. 1968); children: Jennifer, Adam; m. Gilbert Joseph Rosas, June28, 1975. BA, U. Calif., Santa Barbara, 1961; postgrad., Ventura Coll., 1993-94. With La Cumbre Animal Hosp., Santa Barbara, 1967-76; artist Rood Assocs., Santa Barbara, 1969-71. Designer, artist: (seasonal brochures) Ventura County Chamber Orchestra, 1994-95; designer: (nutcracker collectibles featured in Hammacher Schlemmer catalog and Collector's Mart Mag.) "Nutcracker Prince" for Adrian Taron & Sons and "Clara," 1994-95, (glass ornaments) Taron Collection. Recipient Best of Show award Fine Arts Exhibit-Acrylics U. Calif., Santa Barbara, 1961, Fine Arts Exhibit-Oils, 1961. Mem. AAUW (sec. 1961-62), Nat. Mus. Women in the Arts, U. Calif. Santa Barbara Alumni Assn., Buenaventura Art Assn., Carmel Art Assn. Avocations: painting and creating: watercolor, oils, pastel paintings, mixed media creations. Home: 1131 Windward Way Oxnard CA 93035-2459 Office: Adrian Taron & Sons 801 Linden Ave Carpinteria CA 93013-2042

ROSCH, JOHN THOMAS, lawyer; b. Council Bluffs, Iowa, Oct. 4, 1939; s. H.P. and Phebe Florence (Jamison) R.; m. Carolyn Lee, Aug. 18, 1961; children: Thomas Lee, Laura Lee. BA, Harvard U., 1961, LLB, 1965. Bar: Calif. 1966, U.S. Dist. Ct. (no. dist.) Calif. 1966, U.S. Dist. Ct. (ea. dist.) Calif. 1967, U.S. Ct. Appeals (9th cir.) 1966. Assoc. McCutchen, Doyle, Brown & Enersen, San Francisco, 1965-72, ptnr., 1972-73, 75-93; office mng. ptnr. Latham & Watkins, San Francisco, 1994—; dir. Bur. Consumer Protection, FTC, Washington, 1973-75. Contbr. articles profl. jours. Fellow Am. Bar Found., Am. Coll. Trial Lawyers; mem. ABA (past chmn. antitrust sect.), State Bar Calif., San Francisco Bar Assn., Calif. State and Antitrust and Trade Regulation Sect. (past sect. chair). Republican. Episcopalian. Office: Latham & Watkins 505 Montgomery St Fl 19th San Francisco CA 94111-2562

ROSCH, THOMAS LEE, venture capitalist; b. Cambridge, Eng., May 13, 1962; came to U.S., 1964; s. John Thomas and Carolyn Jane (Lee) R.; m. Deborah Lynne Michel, Sept. 29, 1991; children: Amelia Jameson, Catherine Michel. AB, Harvard Coll., Cambridge, 1984; JD, MBA, Stanford U., 1989. Analyst Morgan Stanley & Co., Inc., N.Y.C., 1984-85; sr. mgr. The Boston Consulting Group, L.A., 1989-96; ptnr. AT&T Ventures, Menlo Park, Calif., 1986—; dir. E-Stamp Corp., Palo Alto, Calif., 1997—, Veridicom, Inc., Santa Clara, Calif., 1998—; mem. adv. bd. Sentient Networks, Milpitas, Calif., 1997—. Mem. ABA, Nat. Venture Capital Assn., State Bar Calif., Harvard Club N.Y.C., Pacifi-Union Club. Republican. Episcopalian. Office: AT&T Ventures 3000 Sand Hill Rd Fl 1 Menlo Park CA 94025-7116

ROSE, ANN WEGENER, physician assistant; b. Portland, May 11, 1943; d. Carl William and Barbara Carolyn (Williams) Wegener; m. Bruce Alan Rose, June 28, 1965 (div. July 1986); children: David Bruce, Shannon Ann. BS, U. Oreg., 1965; cert. physician asst., Cleve. Clinic, 1981; BA, Lake Erie Coll., 1981. ordained deacon, 1993. Physician asst. N.W. Eye Ctr., Eugene, Oreg., 1984-87, Latham Flanagan MD, Eugene, 1988-93; physician asst., ind. contractor in addiction medicine Serenity Lane, Eugene, 1993—, Williamette Family Treatment Svcs., Eugene, 1998—; counselor, behavioralist McKenzie Williamette Hosp., Springfield, Oreg., 1989-90; counselor, educator pvt. practice, Eugene, 1995-97; tchr. primary level Klamath Trinity Unified Sch. Dist., Willow Creek, Calif., 1966-69; crisis counselor White Bird Clinic, Eugene, 1982-86. Deacon St. Mary's Episcopal Ch., Eugene, 1993—; campaign worker state rep. race, Eugene, 1993. Fellow Am. Acad. Physician Assts. (chief del. Ho. of Dels.), Oreg. Soc. Physician Assts. (pres., sec. chief del.); mem. Nat. Assn. for Diaconiate, Nat. Cathedral Assn., Physician Asst. Found. Avocations: travel, gardening, reading, hiking. Home and Office: 2800 Calla St Eugene OR 97404

ROSE, ARDEN ELAINE, artist, painter; b. Boston, Nov. 30, 1944. BA in Philosophy, U. Calif., Berkeley, 1966, MSW, 1968; student in oil, watercolors and pastels, De Young Mus. Art Sch., San Francisco, 1968-71; pvt. instrn. with Hilda Kidder, Acad. Fine Arts, Vienna, Austria; pvt. instrn., Royal Coll. Portrait Painters, Edinborough, Scotland. Editor: Arden Rose, The Vision of A Painter, 1992; author: Interacting Through Creative Arts Activities, 1976; one-woman shows include Louise M. Davies Symphony Hall, San Francisco, 1982, Arden Rose Art Studios, Santa Barbara, Calif. and French West Indies, 1985—; exhibited in group shows Galerie Marumo, L.A., 1982, Salon d'Automne, Paris, 1987, Music Guinet, Paris, 1988, Festivale Internat., Osaka, 1988, Companile Galleries, Inc., Chgo., 1985, others. Mem. Los Angeles County Art Museum, L.A. Recipient Cert. of Excellence, N.Y. Soho Internat. Art Competition, 1992; named Am. Artist guest of honor Fêtes des Impressionistes, French Govt., 1993, 94. Mem. L.A. County Art Mus. Home and Studio: PO Box 90625 Santa Barbara CA 93190-0625

ROSE, CAROL DENISE, orthopedic unit nurse administrator, educator; b. Las Vegas, Nev., July 31, 1960; d. Howard Elden and Sarah (Haley) Heckethorn; m. Michael Shaun Rose, June 19, 1982; 1 child, Carissa Denise. ADN, U. Nev., Las Vegas, 1981, BSN, 1985. Staff nurse orthopedic unit Univ. Med. Ctr. So. Nev., Las Vegas, 1981-84, acting head nurse, then head nurse orthopedic unit, 1984-88, asst. mgr. orthopedic unit, 1988, orthopedic unit mgr., 1988—; adj. faculty health scis. dept. Clark County C.C., North Las Vegas, Nev.; speaker at profl. confs. Mem. ANA, Nat. Assn. Orthopaedic Nurses (pres. So. Nev. chpt.), Sigma Theta Tau, Phi Kappa Phi. Democrat. Roman Catholic. Avocations: sewing, embroidery, skiing, boating, reading. Office: Univ Med Ctr So Nev 1800 W Charleston Blvd Las Vegas NV 89102-2386

ROSE, HERBERT HERMAN, rabbi; b. N.Y.C., Nov. 13, 1929; s. Morris M. and Etta (Millens) R.; m. Esther Burgin, June 5, 1955; children: Judah, Ben Zion, Eve, Regina. BA, U. Cin., 1950; BHL, Hebrew Union Coll., Cin., 1952, MHL, 1955, DHL, 1962. Ordained rabbi, 1955. Rabbi Temple Emanuel, Livingston, N.J., 1957-62, Temple Ohr Elohim, L.I., 1962-65, Beth Ohr, Bklyn., 1978-82, Congregation Har HaShem, Boulder, Colo., 1982—; pres. N.Y. Assn. Reform Rabbis, 1969-70. Author: Life and Thoughts of A.D. Gordon, 1964; contbr. articles to religious jours. Exec. bd. Interfaith Coun. of Boulder, 1989—; bd. dirs. Anti-Defamation League of Denver, 1985-91; chmn. L.I. Com. for Soviet Jewry, 1964; bd. dirs. Menorah - Adult Jewish Edn., Boulder, 1988—. Recipient State of Israel Bond award, 1967. Mem. Rocky Mt. Rabbinical Coun. (pres. 1987-88), L.I. Assn. Reform Rabbis, Rocky Mt. Am.-Israel Friendship League (bd. dirs. 1989-91), Rocky Mt. Rabbinical Coun. (bd. dirs. 1982-91). Home: 103 SE Valare Ln Crystal River FL 34429-4730 Office: Congregation Har HaShem 3950 Baseline Rd Boulder CO 80303-2502

ROSE, JOAN L., computer security specialist; b. N.Y.C., June 27, 1946; d. Vincent A. LaVertu and Joan (Mileti) Ellis; children: Robert, Lauren. BA, Bklyn. Coll./CUNY, Bklyn., 1967. Cert. Info. Sys. Security Profl. Internat. Info. Sys. Security Cert. Consortium. Programmer Met. Life Ins., N.Y.C., 1967-68; sys. analyst Western Electric, Oklahoma City, 1968-74, Pacific Intermountain Express, Oakland, Calif., 1974-78, Chevron, San Francisco, 1978-88; dep. project mgr. SHARE (IBM Users Group), Chgo., 1998—; project mgr. GUIDE (IBM Users Group), Chgo., 1983-98; dep. project mgr. SHARE (IBM Users Group). Participant Habitat for Humanity, 1995—. Mem. Info. Sys. Security Assn. (Bay Area chpt. treas. 1983—). Democrat. Home: 3299 Pine Valley Rd San Ramon CA 94583-3633 Office: Chevron H2196 6001 Bollinger Canyon Rd # H2196 San Ramon CA 94583-2398

ROSE, JOAN MARIE, medical-surgical nurse; b. Fresno, Calif., Aug. 12, 1952; d. Hobert Lee and Ila Marie (Jacobson) Hamilton; m. Steven Arthur Westenrider, May 1, 1976 (div. Dec., 1984); m. Richard Lee Rose, Aug. 6, 1994; children: John Rose, Dan Rose, Denise Haight. AS in Nursing, Fresno City Coll., 1987. RN. Nurse Valley Med Ctr., Fresno, Calif., 1988-95; RN Nancy Hinds Hospice, 1996—. Author: (book) Dreams Come True, 1996; also poetry. Avocations: writing, reading, walking, bike riding, gardening.

ROSE, ROBERT E(DGAR), state supreme court justice; b. Orange, N.J., Oct. 7, 1939. B.A., Juniata Coll., Huntingdon, Pa., 1961; LL.B., NYU, 1964. Bar: Nev. 1965. Dist. atty. Washoe County, 1971-75; lt. gov. State of Nev., 1975-79; judge Nev. Dist. Ct., 8th Jud. Dist., Las Vegas, 1986-88; justice Nev. Supreme Ct., Carson City, 1989—, chief justice, 1993-94, 99—. Office: Nev Supreme Ct Capitol Complex 201 S Carson St Carson City NV 89701-4702

ROSE, SCOTT A., lawyer; b. Flint, Mich., Feb. 10, 1953. BS with distinction, Ariz. State U., 1975, JD cum laude, 1979. Bar: Ariz. 1979. Chmn. bd. O'Connor, Cavanagh, Anderson, Killingsworth & Beshears, Phoenix, Ariz. Articles editor Ariz. State Law Jour., 1978-79. Ariz. Govt. Affairs chmn.

Internat. Coun. Shopping Ctrs. Mem. ABA, State Bar Ariz., Maricopa County Bar Assn., Downtown Phoenix Rotary Club 100 (bd. dirs.). Office: O'Connor Cavanagh Anderson Killingsworth & Beshears 1 E Camelback Rd Ste 1100 Phoenix AZ 85012-1691

ROSE, SHARON MARIE, telecommunications professional; b. Mpls., July 21, 1962; d. Thomas Kevin and Jeanette Mary (Fasnacht) Lange; m. Mark Edward Tessier, July 3, 1981 (div. Dec. 1983); 1 child, Marie Elizabeth. Grad. H.S., Elk River, Minn. Installation and testing supr. N.Am. Satellite Transmission, Chgo., 1984-85; transmission tech. Sprint Comm. Long Distance Divsn., St. Paul, 1985-86, network ops. specialist III, 1986-91; sr. network ops. specialist Sprint Comm. Long Distance Divsn., Rancho Cordova, Calif., 1994-95; telecom. technician Hewlett-Packard, Roseville, Calif., 1996—. Avocation: reading non-fiction. Home: 15825 NE Leary Way # B-115 Redmond WA 98052-4347 Office: Hewlett-Packard Mailstop 5571 8000 Foothills Blvd Roseville CA 95747-5200

ROSEBERRY, EDWIN SOUTHALL, state agency administrator; b. Roanoke, Va., July 4, 1925; s. Edwin Alexander and Gladys Edmonia (Southall) R.; m. Mary Louise Sprengel, Sept. 2, 1949 (dec. 1978); children: Edwin Jr., David, Kevin; m. Alice Proffit Boger, Dec. 27, 1980; 1 stepdaughter, Elizabeth Leigh Boger. *Paternal grandfather, Richard A. Roseberry, was a Masonic past Grandmaster, Washington D.C. 1925. Maternal grandparents, William R. and Willie Ida Southall, operated Southall's Funeral Home in Bedford, Virginia from 1922 until 1940. Brother, Colonel Robert A. Roseberry U.S.A. (deceased) was a heavily decorated career officer during World War II, the Korean War, and the war in Vietnam. First wife, Mary Lou Sprengel Roseberry, was a staff and supervisory nurse at the University of Virginia Hospital, 1948-1978. Son, Edwin S. Roseberry Jr., is a marketing executive with 3 Com Corporation, with an office in Santa Clara, California.* BS in Commerce, U. Va., 1949. Registered sanitarian, Hawaii, Va. Store mgr. Allied Arts, Charlottesville, Va., 1949-51; retail credit sales mgr. B.F. Goodrich Co., Charlottesville, 1951-53; environ. health specialist Dept. of Health, Charlottesville, 1953-84, Dept. of Labor, Honolulu, 1987—; self-employed photographer, Charlottesville, 1949-85, Honolulu, 1985—. Contbr. photographs: The Inward Eye, 1986. Election ofcl. State of Hawaii, Honolulu, 1988—. With USN, 1944-46. Recipient numerous nat. awards Eastman Kodak Co., nat. newspapers, and photography mags., 1951-69. Mem. VFW (life), Am. Indsl. Hygiene Assn., Austrian Hawaiian Club (v.p., bd. dirs. 1985), Antique Auto Assn. (pres. Piedmont region 1964), Hawaii Photo Soc. (v.p. 1989), Elks (tiler and inner guard 1985), Am. Legion, Mason (32 degree), Shriners, Pi Delta Epsilon. Episcopalian. Avocations: photography, stamp collecting, antique automobiles, figure skating. Home: 1101 Kumukumu St Apt E Honolulu HI 96825-2636 Office: State of Hawaii DLIR/DOSH 830 Punchbowl St Honolulu HI 96813-5017

ROSEHNAL, MARY ANN, educational administrator; b. Bklyn., July 25, 1943; d. Frank Joseph and Mary Anna (Corso) R.; 1 child, Scott Stoddart. BA in Sociology, San Francisco State U., 1968; M in Sch. Bus. Adminstrn., No. Ariz. U., 1985. Lic. substitute tchr., Ariz.; lic. vocat. nurse, Calif.; Ariz. Deliquency counselor, Calif., 1969-73; office mgr. Nurses Central Registry, Sun City, Ariz., 1973-75; bus. mgr. Nadaburg sch. dist., Wittmann, Ariz., 1975-78, Morristown (Ariz.) sch. dist., 1978—; served on 1st Assessment Handbook editing task force, Fair Employment Practices Handbook Task Force, 1979-80; mem. tech. adv. com. Ariz. Dept. Tech. adv. com. Ariz. Dept. Edn., 1993-94; mem. adv. com. Ariz. Auditor Gen. Uniform Sys. Fin. Records, Auditor, 1993—. Columnist Wickenburg Sun, 1975—. Clk. Morristown sch. bd., 1974-76; pres. Morristown PTA, 1977-78; sec. Wickenburg area bd., 1979; bd. dirs. Future Frontiers, 1979-81; rep. HUD block grant adv. com., 1979-85; active Wickenburg Friends of Music, 1984—, bd. dirs., 1986—, sec. bd. dirs., 1986-92, 96; sec. Wickenburg Regional Health Care Found., 1989-92, trustee, 1988-94; mem. com. Wickenburg Scenic Corridor, 1990-92. Named to Ariz. Sch. Bd. Assn. Honor Roll, 1976; named Morristown Area Vol. of Yr., 1988. Mem. AAUW, Soroptimists Internat. 1997-98, Ariz. Assn. Sch. Bus. Ofcls. (fin. dir., bd. dirs. 1985-91, v.p. 1991, pres. elect 1992-93, pres. 1993-94, immediate past pres. 1994-95, Gold award 1986-88, 90-95, 96, Silver award 1989, 97, cert. award, 1998), Assn. Sch. Bus. Ofcls. Internat. (mem. pres.'s adv. coun. 1993-94, election com. 1994-95), Morristown Federated Women's Club (edn. chmn. com. 1990-97),Theatre Guild, Wickenberg C. of C. (assoc. 1993-95). Roman Catholic. Office: PO Box 98 Morristown AZ 85342-0098

ROSELL, SHARON LYNN, physics and chemistry educator, researcher; b. Wichita, Kans., Jan. 6, 1948; d. John E. and Mildred C. (Binder) R. BA, Loretto Heights Coll., 1970; postgrad., Marshall U., 1973; MS in Edn., Ind. U., 1977; MS, U. Wash., 1988. Cert. profl. educator, Wash. Assoc. instr. Ind. U., Bloomington, 1973-74; instr. Pierce Coll. (name formerly Ft. Steilacoom (Wash.) Community Coll.), 1976-79, 82, Olympic Coll., Bremerton, Wash., 1977-78; instr. physics, math. and chemistry Tacoma (Wash.) Community Coll., 1979-89; instr. physics and chemistry Green River Community Coll., Auburn, Wash., 1983-86; researcher Nuclear Physics Lab., U. Wash., Seattle, 1986-88; asst. prof. physics Cen. Wash. U., Ellensburg, 1989—; mem. faculty senate Ctrl. Washington U., 1992-98. Lector and dir. Rite of Christian Initiation of Adults, St. Andrew's Ch., Ellensburg, Wash., 1993—, mem. parish coun., 1995—. Mem. Am. Phys. Soc., Am. Assn. Physics Tchrs. (rep. com. on physics for 2-yr. colls. Wash. chpt. 1986-87, v.p. 1987-88, 94-95, pres. 1988-89, 95-96, past pres. 1996-97), Am. Chem. Soc., Internat. Union Pure and Applied Chemistry (affiliate), Pacific Northwest Assn. Coll. Physics (bd. dirs. 1997—), Soc. Physics Students (zone councilor zone 17). Democrat. Roman Catholic. Avocations: leading scripture discussion groups, reading, writing poetry, needlework. Home: 1100 N B St Apt 2 Ellensburg WA 98926-2570 Office: Cen Wash U Physics Dept Ellensburg WA 98926

ROSELLE, CATHY COLMAN, kindergarten education, educational consultant; b. Riverside, Calif., Dec. 2, 1946; d. Carl Eugene and Elma (Skinner) Colman; m. Charles Perry Roselle, Sept. 1, 1968; children: Robert Andrew, Charles Eugene, Scott Perry. BSEE, N.Mex. State U., Las Cruces, 1977; MA, Hood Coll, 1990. Cert. tchr., reading specialist, Ariz., bilingual & ESL endorsements. Bilingual kindergarten tchr. P.T. Coe Sch., Phoenix, 1977-80; bilingual 1st grade tchr. Alta Loma Sch., Phoenix, 1981-83; Chpt. I reading tchr. Carpenter Mid. Sch., Nogales, Ariz., 1990; Chpt. I bilingual kindergarten tchr. A.J. Mitchell, Nogales, 1991-97; bilingual ESL tchr. K-2 Clark County, 1997—; ESL instr. So. Nev. C.C.; ednl. specialist S.W. Internat. Tech., Rio Rico, Ariz., 1994—; team leader Ariz. Student Assessment Profile, Nogales, 1992; mem. curriculum com. Project Wellhead, 1993-95. Co-author: Chapter I Handbook for Nogales School District, 1990. Campaign mgr. Sch. Bd Election Charles P. Roselle, Rio Rico, 1994. Mem. NEA, Ariz. Edn. Assn., Ariz. Assn. for Edn. of Young Children, Interventional Reading Assn. Avocations: reading, Scrabble, hiking, computer techonology in education. Office: Clark County Schs 6350 Juan Bautista Nogales AZ 85621

ROSEME, SHARON DAY, lawyer; b. Sacramento, Aug. 6, 1953; d. George Roseme and Alice Diane Day; m. Daniel George Glenn, June 26, 1982 (div. Nov. 1989); 1 child, Hilary. Student, San Francisco State U., 1971-72; BA, U. Calif., Santa Cruz, 1975; JD, Boalt Hall Sch. of Law, 1978. Jud. staff atty. Calif. State Ct. of Appeal, San Francisco, 1978-80; assoc. Feldman, Waldman & Kline, San Francisco, 1980-82, McDonough, Holland & Allen, Sacramento, 1982—; speaker to profl. and cmty. orgns. Contbr. articles to profl. jours. Mem. Leadership Calif. Class of 1996; bd. dirs. Am. Leadership Forum, fellow, 1998. Mem. ABA, State Bar Calif., County Bar Sacramento, County Bar Placer, Am. Arbitration Assn. (arbitrator, Sacramento adv. com.), Sacramento Area Commerce and Trade Orgn. (devel. com. 1994-97, chmn. 1996-97), Comml. Real Estate Women Sacramento (nat. del. 1998—, pres. 1997, chmn. cmty. svc. com. 1994-95, Mem. of Yr. award 1993), Order of Coif. Office: McDonough Holland & Allen 9th Fl 555 Capitol Mall Fl 9 Sacramento CA 95814-4504

ROSEMIRE, ADELINE LOUISE, writer, publisher; b. Modesto, Calif., [illegible] Mktg. profl. Blue Cross, San Jose, Calif., 1971-74; newsletter editor No. Telecom, Santa Clara, Calif., 1974-77; editor Bryan Pubs., Santa Clara, 1978-81; owner, writer The Write Stuff, San Jose, 1981—, Rosemire/Bedford-White, Santa Clara, 1983-92; owner, author Meridian Pub., Inc., San Jose, 1993—. Author: The Other Mid-Life Crisis, 1994, The 2-Ingredient Cookbook, 1996, Christmas Shortcuts, 1998. Dir. Bay Area Lupus Found., San Jose, 1994—, Crippled Children's Soc., Santa Clara, 1990-96, Bldg. Industry Assn., Dublin, Calif., 1981-89. Recipient Pres.' award Bldg. Industry Assn. Ednl. Coun., 1989. Mem. Pubs. Mktg. Assn. Office: Meridian Pub Inc PO Box 1477 Roswell NM 88202-1477

ROSEN, JACQUELINE L., flutist, music educator; b. Los Angeles, Sept. 28, 1952; d. Samuel Morris and Blanche (Seigel) R.; m. James Andrew Meckel, July 14, 1979; children: Sean Aaron, Eric Rosen. Student, Music Acad. of the West, Santa Barbara, Calif., 1973-74; BS in Music, UCLA, 1974; studies with Julius Baker, James Galway, Jean-Pierre Rampal, 1974-80. Freelance musician Los Angeles, San Francisco and Monterey, Calif., 1974—; mem. Laurel Wind Quintet, 1977-80, Allegra Trio, 1980—, Farrell/Rosen Duo, Carmel, Calif., 1978-87, Terrence Farrell Consort, Carmel, 1980—; instr. flute pvt. studio, Monterey, 1976—, Monterey Peninsula Coll., 1981-85; prin. flutist Hidden Valley Opera, Carmel Valley, Calif., 1976—; condr. master classes numerous Calif. colls., 1982—. Premiere performance (flute-guitar duo) Sonatine for Flute and Guitar, 1981; rec. artist (with Terrence Farrell) Alla Romanza, Merry Christmas; appearances with San Francisco Spring Opera, 1979, Cabrillo Music Festival, 1978-84; numerous radio broadcasts, 1977—. Benefit performances for numerous non-profit orgns., Calif. and Mass., 1980—. Recipient Southwestern Music Conf. award, 1972; Leonard Bernstein fellow, Tanglewood, 1977. Democrat. Avocation: playing jazz, gourmet cooking. Home: 15 Paseo Primero Salinas CA 93908-9110

ROSEN, MARTIN JACK, lawyer; b. L.A., Sept. 9, 1931; s. Irving and Sylvia (Savad) R.; B.A., UCLA, 1953; J.D., U. Calif.-Berkeley, 1956; m. Joan D. Meyersieck, Oct. 22, 1954; children—Dirk Rosen, Marika. Bar: Calif. 1957. Pvt. practice, Merced, Calif., 1960-62, San Francisco, 1962-82; mem. Silver, Rosen, Fischer & Stecher, P.C., San Francisco, 1964-79. Past pres. Trust for Pub. Land, 1979-97. Served with USAF, 1958-60. Fellow internat. legal studies U. Calif. Law Sch./Inst. Social Studies, The Hague, 1956-57. Fax: (415) 243-9701. E-mail: mjr@tpl.org.

ROSEN, MOISHE, religious organization founder; b. Kansas City, Mo., Apr. 12, 1932; s. Ben and Rose (Baker) R.; m. Ceil Starr, Aug. 18, 1950; children: Lyn Rosen Bond, Ruth. Diploma, Northeastern Bible Coll., 1957; DD, Western Conservative Bapt. Sem., 1986. Ordained to ministry Bapt. Ch., 1957. Missionary Am. Bd. Missions to the Jews, N.Y.C., 1956; minister in charge Beth Sar Shalom Am. Bd. Missions to the Jews, Los Angeles, 1957-67; dir. recruiting and tng. Am. Bd. Missions to the Jews, N.Y.C., 1967-70; leader Jews for Jesus Movement, San Francisco, 1970-73, exec. dir., 1973-96, founder, 1973—; speaker in field. Author: Saying of Chairman Moishe, 1972, Jews for Jesus, 1974, Share the New Life with a Jew, 1976, Christ in the Passover, 1977, Y'shua, The Jewish Way to Say Jesus, 1982, Overture to Armageddon, 1991, The Universe is Broken: Who on Earth Can Fix It?, 1991, Demystifying Personal Evangelism, 1992, Witnessing to Jews, 1998. Trustee Western Conservative Bapt. Sem., Portland, Oreg., 1979-85, 86-91, Bibl. Internat. Coun. on Bibl. Inerrancy, Oakland, Calif., 1979-89; bd. dirs. Christian Advs. Serving Evangelism, 1987-91. Named Hero of the Faith, Conservative Bapt. Assn. Am., 1997. Office: Jews for Jesus 90 Miraloma Dr San Francisco CA 94127-1641

ROSEN, STEVEN O., lawyer; b. N.Y.C., Jan. 11, 1949; s. Albert I. and Yvette (Sterenbuch) R.; m. Martha M., July 10, 1983; 1 child, Melissa L. BS Electrical Engring., SUNY, 1970; MS System and Control Engring., Case Western Reserve, 1975; JD, Lewis & Clark Coll., 1977. Bar: Ill. 1977, Oreg. 1978. Assoc. Lord, Bissell & Brook, Chgo., 1977-79; assoc. Miller, Nash, Wiener, Hager & Carlsen, Portland, Oreg., 1979-84, ptnr., 1984-98; pvt. practice Salem, Oreg., 1998—; disting. adj. prof. Lewis & Clark Law Sch., 1986. Mem. ABA (dir. divsns. sect. of litigation 1996-97, chair aviation litigation com. 1990-93), Oreg. State Bar Assn. (exec. com. aviation sect. 1984—, chair 1994-95). Avocation: skiing. Office: Rosen Law Firm 388 State St Ste 602 Salem OR 97301-3538*

ROSEN, STUART JAY, defender; b. L.A., June 26, 1941; s. Theodore W. and Sarah (Greenberg) R.; m. Joan Rosen, Aug. 4, 1968; children: Scott, Ruben, Julie. BA, UCLA, 1963, JD, 1966. Pub. defender L.A., 1967—. Democrat. Jewish. Avocations: miniatures, computing. Home: 320 S El Camino Dr Beverly Hills CA 90212-4212

ROSENAUER, ADOLF ALOIS, neurosurgeon; b. Linz, Austria, Sept. 20, 1922; came to U.S., 1951; s. Alois and Rosa (Fioriola) R.; m. Eva Moore, Nov. 25, 1954; children: Patricia, Kathleen, Michael. MD, U. Innsbruck, Austria, 1947; MS in Surgery, U. Cin., 1952. Diplomate Am. Bd. Neurol. Surgery. Instr. anatomy U. Innsbruck, 1943-47, asst. prof., 1947-50; intern Barmh. Brueder Hosp., Linz, 1950-51; fellow Rockefeller Found. Good Samaritan Hosp., Cin., 1951-52; resident in neurol. surgery U. Cin., 1951-53; resident Barmherzige Brueder Hosp., Linz, Austria, 1954-55; instr. neurosurgery U. Chgo., 1955-57; assoc. prof. Sch. Medicine U. Nev., Reno, 1957—. Contbr. articles to profl. jours. With Austrian Army, 1940-45. Decorated Iron Cross. Fellow Olympic Physicians; mem. Am. Assn. Neurol. Surgeons, Congress Neurol. Surgeons, Western Neurosurgey Soc., Order of Quiet Birdmen, Internat. Order St. Hubert (knight commdr.), Sigma Xi. Roman Catholic. Avocations: flying, sailing, scuba diving, skiing, astronomy. Home: 2150 Willow Tree Ln Reno NV 89509-8209 Office: 890 Mill St Reno NV 89502-1442

ROSENBAUM, GEORGE GENE, music educator, musician; b. Newark, Sept. 15, 1955; s. Morris Edward and Estelle Rose (Wagman) R.; m. Katherine Lynn Klink, July 2, 1989; children: Michael Aaron, David Elliot. MusB, Manhattan Sch. Music, 1980; MusM, U. North Tex., 1989, DMA, 1991. Asst. prof. music Southeastern La. U., Hammond, 1991-92, U. Memphis, 1992-94; asst. prof. music, dir. strings/orch. Mesa State Coll., Grand Junction, Colo., 1997—; adj. prof. music Tex. Christian U., Ft. Worth, 1986-91, Seminole C.C., Sanford, Fla., 1996-97. Author: (book) The Viola Sonatas of William Flakton, 1991; prin. viola Richardson (Tex.) Symphony, 1984-91, Orlando (Fla). Philharm., 1996-97, Grand Junction (Colo.) Symphony, 1997—; sect. viola Ft. Worth Symphony, 1989-91, Baton Rouge Symphony, 1991-92, Memphis Symphony, 1992-94, Orlando Philharm., 1994-96. bd. dirs. Marsha Thomas Music Found., Grand Junction, 1997—. Memb. Grand Junction Rotary Internat. Jewish. Avocations: softball, baseball, bowling, golf, bridge. E-mail: rosenbaum@wpogate.mesastate.edu. Home: 526 Pauline St Apt 3 Clifton CO 81520-7922 Office: Mesa State Coll Dept Music PO Box 2647 Grand Junction CO 81502-2647

ROSENBAUM, MICHAEL FRANCIS, securities dealer; b. N.Y.C., Feb. 9, 1959; s. Francis Fels Jr. and Joyce (Keefer) R.; m. Elika Sosnick, Mar. 8, 1986; children: Erin Sosnick, Sarah Greer, Kira Keefer. AB, Princeton U., 1981. Cert. Nat. Assn. Securities Dealers. Product mgr. Sutro & Co., Inc., San Francisco, 1981-84; v.p. sales Pacific Securities, San Francisco, 1984-89; v.p., br. mgr. Rauscher Pierce Resfnes, San Francisco, 1989-92; v.p. sales Smith Mitchell Investment Group, San Francisco, 1992-93; sr. v.p. sales Gruntal & Co., Inc., San Francisco, 1993-94; sr. v.p. taxable fixed income Coast Ptnrs. Securities, San Francisco, 1994—; bd. dirs. S.G. Rosenbaum Found., N.Y.C. Trustee Princeton U. Rowing Assn. Democrat. Jewish. Avocations: skiing, sailing, dog breeding. Home: PO Box 1104 Ross CA 94957-1104

ROSENBERG, ALEX, mathematician, educator; b. Berlin, Germany, Dec. 5, 1926; came to U.S., 1949, naturalized, 1959; s. Theodore and Rela (Banet) R.; m. Beatrice Gershenson, Aug. 24, 1952 (div. Apr. 1985); children: Theodore Joseph, David Michael, Daniel Alex; m. Brunhilde Angun, June 14, 1985. B.A., U. Toronto, 1948, M.A., 1949; Ph.D., U. Chgo., 1951. From instr. to assoc. prof. math. Northwestern U., 1952-61; prof. math. Cornell U., Ithaca, N.Y., 1961-88, prof. emeritus, 1988—, chmn. dept., 1966-69; prof. U. Calif., Santa Barbara, 1986-94, chmn. dept., 1986-87, prof. emeritus, [illegible] 1979, U. Calif., Los Angeles, 1969-70, 82, U. London, Queen Mary Coll., 1963-64, U. Munich, 1975-76, E.T.H Zurich, 1976, U. Dortmund, 1984-85; trustee Am. Math Soc., 1973-83. Editor: Proc. Am. Math. Soc., 1960-66, Am. Math. Monthly, 1974-77; Contbr. articles to profl. jours. Recipient Humboldt Stiftung Sr. U.S. Scientist award U. Munich, 1975-76, U. Dortmund, 1981. Home: Heide str 87, 58239 Schwerte Germany

ROSENBERG, DAN YALE, retired plant pathologist; b. Stockton, Calif., Jan. 8, 1922; s. Meyer and Bertha (Naliboff) R.; AA, Stockton Jr. Coll., 1942; AB, Coll. Pacific, 1949; MS, U. Calif. at Davis, 1952; m. Marilyn Kohn, Dec. 5, 1954; 1 son, Morton Karl. Jr. plant pathologist Calif. Dept. Agr., Riverside, 1952-55, asst. plant pathologist, 1955-59, assoc. plant pathologist, 1959-60, pathologist IV, 1960-63, program supr., 1963-71, chief exclusion and detection, div. plant industry, 1971-76, chief nursery and seed svcs. div. plant industry, 1976-82, spl. asst. div. plant industry, 1982-87; pres. Health, Inc., 1972-73; agrl. cons., 1988—; mem. Citrus Rsch. Adv. com. U. Calif., Riverside, 1992—; mem. Gov.'s Interagy. Task Force on Biotech., 1986—; bd. dirs. Health Inc., Sacramento, 1967, pres., 1971-72, 79-81, 81-83. Contbr. articles to profl. jours. Served with AUS, 1942-46; ETO. Mem. Am. Phytopath. Soc. (fgn. and regulatory com. 1975—, grape diseases sect. 1977-79, grape pests sect. 1979—), Calif. State Employees Assn. (pres. 1967-69), Sacramento Met. C. of C. (internat. trade com. 1993—). Home and Office: 2328 Swarthmore Dr Sacramento CA 95825-6867

ROSENBERG, MARVIN, dramatic arts educator; b. Fresno, Calif.; m. Mary Bell; 1 child, Barr. AB, MA, PhD, U. Calif., Berkeley. Sr. editor Office of War Info., 1942-45; chief, Thai sect. internat. broadcasting divn. U.S. State Dept., 1945-48; faculty U. Calif., 1949—; prof. dramatic arts U. Calif., Berkeley. Author: The Masks of Othello, The Masks of King Lear, The Masks of Macbeth, The Masks of Hamlet, The Adventures of a Shakespeare Scholar; author (with others) Shakespeare Illuminations, 1998. Office: U Calif Berkeley Dept Dramatic Art Berkeley CA 94720

ROSENBERG, PAUL HENRY, business analyst; b. San Francisco, May 14, 1945; s. Irving H. and Ruth R. (Boehm) R.; m. Sherrie Gaye Katz, Nov. 25, 1984; children: Coleman D. BA, U. Calif., 1967. Self employed prin. schedule composer San Francisco, 1960-66; jr. statistician U. Calif., Berkeley, 1967; pub. health statistician County of Alameda, Oakland, Calif., 1967-76; prin. bus. analyst City and County of San Francisco, 1976—; voting rep. Welfare Case Data Sys. Joint Com., Calif., 1980—, treas., 1981-82, chair, 1982-84, vice chair, 1995-96; lectr. Sec., pres., treas. Market St. Railway, San Francisco, 1983-94; mem. Dem. County Ctrl. Com., San Francisco, 1972-77; co-chair Citizens for Safe 6 Lane Doyle Drive, San Francisco, 1973-74. Recipient Cert. of Honor Bd. Suprs. City and County of San Francisco, 1971, Leadership award Irish-Israeli-Italian Soc. San Francisco, 1982, Life Achievement award Isaac Kalloch Centennial Soc., 1994; named Dichter (Poet) San Francisco Wagner Soc., 1995. Mem. Internat. Fedn. Profl. and Tech. Engrs. (local 21), Calif. Hist. Soc., Mechanics Inst., League of Men Voters (jr. v.p. San Francisco chpt. 1981—), Franck R. Havenner Dem. Club (grand sachem 1973—). Democrat. Jewish. Avocations: opera, San Francisco polit. history, neighborhood improvement activities. Home: 555 40th Ave San Francisco CA 94121-2522 Office: City and County of San Francisco PO Box 7988 San Francisco CA 94120-7988

ROSENBERG, RICHARD MORRIS, banker; b. Fall River, Mass., Apr. 21, 1930; s. Charles and Betty (Peck) R.; m. Barbara K. Cohen, Oct. 21, 1956; children: Michael, Peter. BS, Suffolk U., 1952; MBA, Golden Gate U., 1962; LLB, Golden Gate Coll., 1966. Publicity asst. Crocker-Anglo Bank, San Francisco, 1959-62; banking services officer Wells Fargo Bank, N.A., San Francisco, 1962-65; asst. v.p. Wells Fargo Bank, N.A., 1965-68, v.p. mktg. dept., 1968, v.p., dir. mktg., 1969, sr. v.p. mktg. and advt. div., 1970-75, exec. v.p., from 1975, vice chmn., 1980-83; vice chmn. Crocker Nat. Corp., 1983-85; pres., chief operating officer Seafirst Corp., 1986-87, also dir.; pres., chief operating officer Seattle First Nat. Bank, 1985-87; vice chmn. bd. BankAm. Corp., San Francisco, 1987-90, chmn., CEO, 1990-96; dir. Airborne Express, Potlatch Corp., Northrop Cor., SBC Comms., Pacific Mut.; past chmn. Mastercard Internat. Bd. dirs. San Francisco Symphony, United Way; trustee Calif. Inst. Tech. Jewish. Office: BankAm Corp Dept 3001-B PO Box 37000 San Francisco CA 94137-0001

ROSENBLATT, PAUL GERHARDT, judge. AB, U. Ariz., 1958, JD, 1963. Asst. atty. gen. State of Ariz., 1963-66; adminstrv. asst. to U.S. Rep., 1967-72; sole practice, Prescott, 1971-73; judge Yavapai County Superior Ct., Prescott, 1973-84; judge, U.S. Dist. Ct. Ariz., Phoenix, 1984—. Office: US Dist Ct US Courthouse Ste 7012 230 N 1st Ave Phoenix AZ 85025-0007*

ROSENBLOOM, ROBERT A., audio engineer; b. Bronxville, N.Y., Nov. 21, 1954; s. Richard and Margarita (Simon) R. BS, Calif. Poly. Inst., 1979. Co-founder Digital Video, Inc., Santa Cruz, Calif., 1984—; cons. Boulder Creek Sys., Santa Cruz, 1981—. Holder patent in field. Mem. Audio Engring. Soc., Soc. Motion Picture and TV Engrs., Exptl. Aircraft Assn. Avocation: flying. Office: Digital Video Inc 8445 Empire Grade Santa Cruz CA 95060

ROSENBLUM, RICHARD MARK, utility executive; b. N.Y.C., Apr. 28, 1950; s. Victor Sigmund and Julia (Kessler) R.; m. Michele E. Cartier, Aug. 30, 1979; children: Gialisa, Jeremy Scott. BS, MS, Rensselaer Poly. Inst., 1973. Registered profl. engr., Calif. Startup engr. Combustion Engring. Inc., Windsor, Conn., 1973-76; engr. So. Calif. Edison Co., Rosemead, 1976-82, project mgr. San Onofre Nuclear Generating Sta., 1982-83, tech. mgr., 1983-84, nuclear safety mgr., 1984-86, mgr. quality assurance, 1986-89, mgr. nuclear regulatory affairs, 1989-93, v.p. Engring. and Tech. Svcs., 1993-95, v.p. distribution, 1996-98, sr. v.p. T&D, 1998—. N.Y. State Regents scholar, 1968-73. Office: 2244 Walnut Grove Ave Rosemead CA 91770-3714

ROSENFELD, HARRY LEONARD, rabbi; b. Cleve., June 25, 1955; s. Nathan and Frances (Skrall) R.; m. Michele Lynn Hope, May 29, 1988. BS in Psychology, John Carroll U., 1976; MA in Hebrew Letters, Hebrew Union Coll., 1980. Ordained rabbi, 1981. Asst. rabbi Temple Israel, Memphis, 1981-84; rabbi Congregation Beth Sholom, Anchorage, 1984—; adj. prof. Alaska Pacific U., Anchorage, 1987—; exec. com. Alaska, Am. Israel Polit. Affairs Com., Anchorage, 1986-92. Bd. dirs. Cath. Social Svcs., Anchorage, 1991—; pres. United Way Anchorage, 1985-90; mem. Mcpl. Health and Human Svcs. Commn., Anchorage, 1986-88, Anchorage Mcpl. Equal Rights Commn., 1986; mem. Rabbinic Cabinet, United Jewish Appeal, 1994—, mem. exec. bd., 1994—, mem. exec. bd. Network of Ind. Cmtys., 1995—. Mem. Cen. Conf. Am. Rabbis (ch. state com. 1985-86), Assn. Reform Zionists. E-mail: rabbiharryrosenfeld@ibm.net. Office: Congregation Beth Sholom 7525 E Northern Lights Blvd Anchorage AK 99504-3552

ROSENFELD, SARENA MARGARET, artist; b. Elmira, N.Y., Oct. 17, 1940; d. Thomas Edward and Rosalie Ereny (Fedor) Rooney; m. Robert Steven Bach, June 1958 (div. 1963); children: Robert Steven, Daniel Thomas; m. Samson Rosenfeld III, June 5, 1976. Student, Otis/Parson Art Inst., L.A., 1994—, Idyllwild Sch. Music and Arts, 1994—. One-woman shows and group exhbns. include Robert Dana Gallery, San Francisco, Gordon Gallery, Santa Monica, Calif., Hespe Gallery, San Francisco, Gallery 444, San Francisco, Art Expressions, San Diego, Ergane Gallery, N.Y.C., Orlando Gallery, Sherman Oaks, Calif., Nat. Mus. of Women in the Arts, Washington, also in L.A., La Jolla, Calif., Aspen, Colo., New Orleans, Soho, N.Y.C., Santa Barbara, Calif., Tanglewood, Mass., Honolulu, Johannesburg, South Africa, La Sierra U., Riverside, Calif. Mem., vol., animal handler Wildlife Waysta., Angeles Nat. Forest, Calif. Recipient Best of Show award Glendale Regional Arts Coun., 1984-85, 1st pl. awards Santa Monica Art Festival, 1982, 83, 84, 85, 86, Sweepstakes award and 1st pl., 1986, Purchase prize awards L.A. West C. of C., 1986-87, Tapestry in Talent Invitational San Jose Arts Coun., 1986, 1st pl. awards Studio City and Century City Arts Couns., 1976-84, 1st award Pacific Palisades Art Affair XII, 1997, Sherman Oaks Fall Arts Festival, 1997. Mem. Nat. Mus. of Women in the Arts. Republican. Home: 6570 Kelvin Ave Canoga Park CA 91306-4021

ROSENHEIM, DANIEL EDWARD, journalist, television news director; b. Chgo., Aug. 13, 1949; s. Edward W. and Margaret Morton (Keeney) R.; m. [illegible] June 20, 1980; children: Joseph Michael, James Salans, Nicholas Edward. BA, Wesleyan U., 1971. Factory worker Pitts. and Chgo., 1972-77; reporter Sun-Jour., Lansing, Ill., 1977; bus./labor editor Hammond (Ind.) Times, 1977-80; bus. writer Chgo. Sun Times, 1980-82, spl. writer, 1982-84;

bus. writer Chgo. Tribune, 1984-85; econs. editor San Francisco Chronicle, 1985-87, city editor, 1987-94, mng. editor, 1994-96; news dir. KRON-TV, San Francisco, 1996—. Mem. Radio and TV News Dirs. Assn., San Francisco Tennis Club. Avocations: tennis, golf, fly fishing. Office: KRON-TV 1001 Van Ness Ave San Francisco CA 94109-6982

ROSENKILDE, CARL EDWARD, physicist; b. Yakima, Wash., Mar. 16, 1937; s. Elmer Edward and Doris Edith (Fitzgerald) R.; m. Bernadine Doris Blumenstine, June 22, 1963 (div. Apr. 1991); children: Karen Louise, Paul Eric; m. Wendy Maureen Ellison, May 24, 1992. BS in Physics, Wash. State Coll., 1959; MS in Physics, U. Chgo., 1960, PhD in Physics, 1966. Fellow Argonne (Ill.) Nat. Lab., 1966-68; asst. prof. math. NYU, 1968-70; asst. prof. physics Kans. State U., Manhattan, 1970-76, assoc. prof., 1976-79; physicist Lawrence Livermore (Calif.) Nat. Lab., 1979-93, lab. assoc., 1994-95, participating guest, 1995-97, cons., 1974-79; chief scientist C.R. Sci., 1993—; astronomy instr. Los Positas Coll., 1997; part-time instr. physics Bellarmine Coll. Prep., 1999. Contbr. articles to profl. jours. Woodrow Wilson fellow, 1959-60. Mem. Am. Phys. Soc., Am. Assn. Physics Tchrs., Calif. Math. Coun. C.C., Am. Coll. Forensic Examiners, Am. Astron. Soc., Soc. for Indsl. and Applied Math., Am. Geophys. Union, Acoustical Soc. Am., Math. Assn. Am., Tubists Universal Brotherhood Assn., Phi Beta Kappa, Phi Kappa Phi, Phi Eta Sigma, Sigma Xi. Republican. Presbyterian. Achievements include rsch. in nonlinear wave propagation in complex media, theoretical physics, fluid dynamics.

ROSENTHAL, JOHN DAVID, dentist; b. Portland, Oreg., Feb. 26, 1950; s. Lawrence A. and H. Bertha (Klein) R.; m. Barbara J. Loomis, Apr. 1, 1977; children: Kristin, Benjamin. BS, U. Oreg., 1973; DMD, U. Oreg. Health Sci. U., 1976. Dentist Rosenthal & Rosenthal, DMD, Portland, 1976-79; pvt. practice Portland, 1979—; ptnr. Downtown Dental Assocs., 1995—. Dental chmn. United Way of Oreg., Portland, 1985; mem. membership com. Temple Beth Israel, Portland, 1984-87; mem. adv. com. Robison Retirement Home, Portland, 1986—. Named Oreg. Denist of Yr., 1997. Fellow Am. Coll. Dentists, Acad. Gen. Dentistry, Acad. Dentistry Internat.; mem. Oreg. Soc. Dentistry for Children, Western Soc. Periodontology, Multnomah Dental Soc. (b.d dirs. 1979-81, pres. 1986), Oreg. Dental Assn. (membership chmn. 1984-88, chmn. mem. svcs. coun. 1988-91, Svc. award 1991), Oreg. Acad. Gen. Dentistry (bd. dirs. 1986-90, sec.-treas. 1990-91, pres. 1991-92, regional dir. 1995—), Oreg. Health Sci. U. Sch. Dentistry Alumni Assn. (bd. dirs. 1987-90), Theta Chi. Avocations: golf, tennis, racquetball, swimming, jogging. Home: 6565 SW 88th Pl Portland OR 97223-7273 Office: 1221 SW Yamhill St Ste 310 Portland OR 97205-2110

ROSENTHAL, SOL, lawyer; b. Balt., Oct. 17, 1934; s. Louis and Hattie (Getz) R.; m. Diane Myra Sackler, June 11, 1961; children: Karen Abby, Pamela Margaret, Robert Joel. AB, Princeton U., 1956; JD, Harvard U., 1959. Bar: Md. 1959, Calif. 1961. Law clk. to chief judge U.S. Ct. Appeals, 4th cir., Balt., 1959-60; assoc. Kaplan, Livingston, Goodwin, Berkowitz & Selvin, Beverly Hills, Calif., 1960-66, ptnr., 1966-74; ptnr. Buchalter, Nemer, Fields & Younger, L.A., 1974-96; of counsel Blanc, Williams, Johnston & Kronstadt, L.A., 1996—; bd. dirs. Playboy Enterprises, Inc., Chgo.; arbitrator Dirs. Guild Am., L.A., 1976—, Writers Guild Am., L.A., 1976—, Am. Film Mktg. Assn., 1989—; negotiator Writers Guild-Assn. Talent Agts., L.A., 1978—; mem. entertainment panel Am. Arbitration Assn., 1997—. Founder Camp Ronald McDonald for Good Times, L.A., 1985; charter founder Mus. Contemporary Art, L.A., 1988. Mem. ABA, Calif. Bar Assn., L.A. County Bar Assn. (trustee 1981-82), L.A. Copyright Soc. (pres. 1973-74), Acad. TV Arts and Scis. (bd. govs. 1990-92), Beverly Hills Bar Assn. (pres. 1982-83), Phi Beta Kappa. Office: Blanc Williams Johnston & Kronstadt 1900 Ave Of Stars Ste 1700 Los Angeles CA 90067-4408

ROSENWEIN, ANDREA LYNN, writer; b. Lynwood, Calif., Mar. 6, 1950; d. Julius Bernard and Evelyn Ethel (Brownstein) R.; divorced; 1 child, Alisha Rose. BA, UCLA, 1971; MS, Boston U., 1975. Cmty. rels. asst. Torrance (Calif.) Meml. Hosp., 1975-77; pub. info. adminstr. U. So. Calif., L.A., 1977-80; sr. writer St. Joseph Med. Ctr., Burbank, Calif., 1980-89; sr. communications exec. Jewish Fedn. Coun. of Greater L.A., 1989-92; publ. rels. dir. Silicone Dynamic Orthotics, Arcadia, Calif., 1992—; performing arts pub. rels. dir. Univ. Judaism, Bel Air, Calif., 1995-98; pub. rels. cons. Hebrew Union Coll., L.A., 1994-95; guest lectr. Univ. So. Calif., Los Angeles Valley Coll., and UCLA, 1985—. Contbr. articles to profl. jours. Bd. dirs. King Solomon Edn. Fund, 1995—; comm. liaison Jewish Cmty. Rels. Com. of Jewish Fedn. Coun., 1989-91. Recipient Bronze Quill award of Excellence Internat. Assn. Bus. Communicators, 1985, Prisms award Pub. Rels. Soc. Am., 1982 MacEachern award, 1986, Silver 6 award of Excellence Internat. Assn. Bus. Communications, 1983. Jewish. Avocation: violin. E-mail: Rosenwrite@aol.com.

ROSHONG, DEE ANN DANIELS, dean, educator; b. Kansas City, Mo., Nov. 22, 1936; d. Vernon Edmund and Doradell (Kellogg) Daniels; m. Richard Lee Roshong, Aug. 27, 1960 (div.). BMusEd., U. Kans., 1958; MA in Counseling and Guidance, Stanford U., 1960; postgrad. Fresno State U., U. Calif.; EdD, U. San Francisco, 1980. Counselor, psychometrist Fresno City Coll., 1961-65; counselor, instr. psychology Chabot Coll., Hayward, Calif., 1965-75; coord. counseling services Chabot Coll., Valley Campus, Livermore, Calif., 1975-81, asst. dir. student pers. svcs., 1981-89, Las Positas Coll., Livermore, Calif., 1989-91, assoc. dean student svcs., 1991-94, dean student svcs., 1994—; writer, coord. I, A Woman Symposium, 1974, Feeling Free to Be You and Me Symposium, 1975, All for the Family Symposium, 1976, I Celebrate Myself Symposium, 1977, Person to Person in Love and Work Symposium, 1978; The Healthy Person in Body, Mind and Spirit Symposium, 1979, Feelin' Good Symposium, 1980, Change Symposium, 1981, Sources of Strength Symposium, 1982, Love and Friendship Symposium, 1983, Self Esteem Symposium, 1984, Trust Symposium, 1985, Prime Time: Making the Most of This Time in Your Life Symposium, 1986, Symposium on Healing, 1987, How to Live in the World and Still Be Happy Symposium, 1988, Student Success is a Team Effort, Sound Mind, Sound Body Symposium, 1989, Creating Life's Best Symposium, 1990, Choices Symposium, 1991, Minding the Body, Mending the Mind Symposium, 1992, Healing through Love and Laughter Symposium, 1993, Healing Ourselves Changing the World Symposium, 1994, Finding Your Path Symposium, 1995, Build the Life You Want Symposium, 1996, Making Peace With Yourself and Your Relationships Symposium, 1997, Everyday Sacred Symposium, 1998, Wisdom of the Heart Symposium, 1999; mem. cast TV prodns. Eve and Co., Best of Our Times, Cowboy; chmn. Calif. C.C. Chancellor's Task Force on Counseling, Statewide Regional Counseling Facilitators, 1993-95, Statewide Conf. on Emotionally Disturbed Students in Calif. C.C.s, 1982—, Conf. on the Under Represented Student in California C.C.s, 1986, Conf. on High Risk Students, 1989; bd. dirs. Teleios Sinetar Ctr., Tri-Valley Unity Ch., Ctr. for Cmty. Dispute Resolution, 1998—, Pleasanton Youth Collaborative Bd., 1997-98; choir dir., 1996-98; pres. Tri-Valley Unity Ch. bd., 1998; title III activity dir. Las Positas Coll., 1995—. Mem. Assn. Humanistic Psychologists, Western Psychol. Assn., Nat. Assn. Women Deans and Counselors, Assn. for Counseling and Devel., Calif. Assn. Community Colls. (chmn. commn. on student services 1979-84), Calif. Community Colls. Counselors Assn. (Svc. award 1986, 87, award for Outstanding and Disting. Service, 1986, 87, Spl. Svc. award for outstanding svc Calif. advocated for re-entry edn., 1991), Alpha Phi. Author: Counseling Needs of Community Coll. Students, 1980. Home: 1856 Harvest Rd Pleasanton CA 94566-5456 Office: 3033 Collier Canyon Rd Livermore CA 94550-9797

ROSICA, KAREN, psychologist, psychoanalyst, writer; b. Bklyn., Dec. 5, 1944; d. Stanley Norton and Ella (German) Polan; m. Adam Rosica (div.). BS, U. Bridgeport, 1966; MSW, Rutgers U., New Brunswick, 1971; PsyD, U. Denver, 1981; cert. psychoanalysis, Colorado Ctr. Psycholanalytic Studies, 1991. Lic. clin. psychologist. Clin. social worker Childrens Psychiatric Ctr., Eatontown, N.J., 1971-72, U. Colo. Health Scis. Ctr., Denver, 1972-76; pvt. practice Denver, 1976—; bd. dirs. Colo. Ctr. Psychoanalytic Studies, Denver, pres., 1984-86. Contbr. articles to profl. jours. Mem. Am. Psychol. Assn. (bd. dirs. divsn. 39 1996-98, bd. dirs., sec. sect. IV divsn. 39 1984-88). Home: 338 Clayton St # 8 Denver CO 80206

ROSICH, RAYNER KARL, physicist; b. Joliet, Ill., Aug. 28, 1940; s. Joseph F. and Gretchen (Cox) R.; BS in Physics cum laude with distinction and honors, U. Mich., 1962, MS in Physics, 1963; PhD, U. Colo., 1977; MBA, U. Denver, 1982; m. Judy Louise Jackson, Aug. 20, 1966; children: Heidi Ann, Kimberly Ann, Dawn Ann. Teaching fellow and rsch. asst. U. Mich., Ann Arbor, 1962-67; staff, Argonne (Ill.) Nat. Lab. Applied Math. Div., summers 1961-63; physicist, project leader Inst. for Telecommunication Sci., U.S. Dept. Commerce, Boulder, Colo., 1967-80; sr. scientist and program mgr. Electro Magnetic Applications, Inc., Denver, 1980-82; applications mgr. Energy Systems Tech., Inc., Denver, 1982-83, mgr. R&D, 1983; prin. scientist, program mgr. Contel Info. Systems, Inc., Denver, 1983-84, dir. tech. audits, 1985, dir. basic and applied R&D, 1986; lab. scientist for systems engring. lab. Hughes Aircraft Co., Denver, 1986, lab. scientist for data systems lab, 1986-90, lab. scientist for systems lab., 1990-92; prin. engr., Advanced System Techs., Inc., Denver, 1992-95; project mgr. Evolving Systems, Inc., 1995; network planning engr., cons. engr./project mgr. Galileo Internat., 1996—. instr. math. Arapahoe Cmty. Coll., 1987-97. Vol. judo instr., county recreation dist., 1976-77. Recipient Spl. Achievement award U.S. Dept. Commerce, 1974, Outstanding Performance award, 1978, Sustained Superior Performance award, 1979; Libbey-Owens-Ford Glass Co./U. Mich. Phoenix Meml. fellow, 1964-66; NSF Summer fellow, 1965. Mem. Am. Phys. Soc., AAAS, IEEE (sr. mem.), Assn. Computing Machinery, Applied Computational Electromagnetics Soc., Soc. Computer Simulation, Sigma Xi, Phi Kappa Phi. Home: 7932 W Nichols Ave Littleton CO 80128-5558 Office: Galileo Internat 6061 S Willow Dr Ste 100 Englewood CO 80111-5149

ROSKY, BURTON SEYMOUR, lawyer; b. Chgo., May 28, 1927; s. David T. and Mary W. (Zelkin) R.; m. Leatrice J. Darrow, June 16, 1951; children: David Scott, Bruce Alan. Student, Ill. Inst. Tech., 1944-45; BS, UCLA, 1948; JD, Loyola U., L.A., 1953. Bar: Calif. 1954, U.S. Supreme Ct 1964, U.S. Tax Ct 1964; C.P.A., Calif. Auditor City of L.A., 1948- 51; with Beidner, Temkin & Ziskin (C.P.A.s), L.A., 1951-52; supervising auditor Army Audit Agy., 1952-53; practiced law L.A., Beverly Hills, 1954—; ptnr. Duskin & Rosky, 1972-82; s Rosky, Landau & Fox, 1982-93; ptnr. Rosky, Landau, Stahl & Sheehy, Beverly Hills, 1993; lectr. on tax and bus. problems; judge pro tem Beverly Hills Mcpl. Ct., L.A. Superior Ct.; mem. L.A. Mayor's Community Adv. Council. Contbr. profl. publs. Charter supporting mem. Los Angeles County Mus. Arts; contbg. mem. Assocs. of Smithsonian Instn.; charter mem. Air and Space Mus; mem. Am. Mus. Natural History, L.A. Zoo; supporting mem. L.A. Mus. Natural History; mem. exec. bd. So. Calif. coun. Nat. Fedn. Temple Brotherhoods, mem. nat. exec. bd.; mem. bd. govs. Loyola Sch. Law, L.A. With USNR, 1945-46. Walter Henry Cook fellow Loyola Law Sch. Bd. Govs. Fellow Jewish Chautauqua Soc. (life mem.); mem. Am. Arbitration Assn. (nat. panel arbitrators), Am. Assn. Attys.-CPAs (charter mem. pres. 1968), Calif. Assn. Attys.-CPAs (charter mem., pres. 1963), Calif. Soc. CPAs, Calif., Beverly Hills, Century City, Los Angeles County bar assns., Am. Judicature Soc., Chancellors Assocs. UCLA, Tau Delta Phi, Phi Alpha Delta.; mem. B'nai B'rith. Jewish (mem. exec. bd., pres. temple, pres. brotherhood). Club: Mason. Office: Rosky Landau Stahl & Sheehy 8383 Wilshire Blvd Beverly Hills CA 90211-2410

ROSNER, RICK, television producer; b. Englewood, N.J., May 8, 1941; s. Alfred Donald and Sylvia (Miller) R. BA, Lehigh U., 1963. Producer The Mike Douglas Show, Phila., 1964-68, Regis Philbin Show, The Della Reese Show, L.A., 1969, Steve Allen Show, 1970; exec. Warner Bros. TV, L.A., 1971-74; producer The Jerry Lewis Telethon, Las Vegas, Nev., 1974; v.p. NBC-TV, Burbank, Calif., 1976; creator, producer CHiPs NBC-TV, L.A., 1977-83; creator producer 240-Robert ABC-TV, L.A., 1979-80, creator, producer Lottery!, 1983; exec. producer New Hollywood Squares, L.A., 1985-90; creator, exec. producer "Personels" CBS Late-Night, L.A., 1991-92; creator, exec. prodr. Caesars Challenge NBC '94-95, NBC Daytime; writer, exec. prodr. Panic in the Skies! Family Chanel Movie of the Week, 1996; TV cons. v.p. Hubert Humphrey, Washington, 1968. Writer, producer (NBC movie of week) Sky Hei$t, 1975 (#1 movie of week 1974-75 season). Res. dep. sheriff L.A. County Sheriff's Dept., 1973—. Mem. Writers Guild Am., Nat. Acad. TV Arts and Scis. (Emmy award 1974). Avocations: windsurfing, swimming.

ROSNER, ROBERT ALLAN, advocate; b. Lincoln Park, N.J., Nov. 2, 1956; s. Henry and Katherine (Kravitt) R.; m. Robin Simons, May 20, 1989. BS, U. Puget Sound, 1980; MBA, U. Wash., 1992. Restaurant mgr. Eatery, Phila., 1976-78; pub. rels. mgr. Big Brothers/Sisters, Tacoma, Wash., 1979; pub. affairs dir. Sta. KNBQ, Tacoma, 1980; exec. dir. Safety Assistance from the Elderly, Seattle, 1981-82, Smoking Policy Inst., Seattle, 1982-93; dep. campaign chair United Way of King County, 1993-94; COO The Sci. Club, 1995; United Features syndicated columnist Working Wounded, 1995; chmn., shop steward Working Wounded.Com; cons. Seattle Sch. Dist., 1996; bd. dirs., chmn. bd. Giraffe Project, Langley, Wash., 1989, Coming of Age in Am., Seattle, 1989; adj. prof. Heritage Inst./Antioch, Seattle, 1988, Seattle Pacific U. Grad. Sch. Bus., 1993; radio program host KOMO radio; reporter Sta. KOMO-TV, Seattle, 1996. Author: U.S. Environmental Protection, 1990, Guide to Workplace Smoking Policies, 1990, contbr. articles to profl. jours. Bd. dirs. Salvation Army, Seattle, 1992. Recipient Gen. News Reporting award, Soc. Profl. Journalists, 1980, Emerald award Internat. TV and Video Assn., Seattle, 1986, Surgeon Gen.'s medallion, 1988. Mem. Seattle Downtown Rotary. Avocations: basketball, public relations, tennis. Office: 9187 Mandus Olson Rd NE Bainbridge Island WA 98110

ROSS, ALVIN, manufacturing executive; b. Minot, N.D., Apr. 4, 1922; s. Samuel and Goldie (Perlin) R.; m. Barbie Wechsler, Apr. 14, 1946; children: Talby W., Gelb, Elyse M. Piper, Mark W. Ross. BA, U. Wash., 1946, Master degree, 1958. Sales mgr. midwest H.D. Lee Co., Mission, Kans., 1963-72; v.p. Wrangler Boys div. Midwest Blue Bell Corp. (Wrangler Co.), Greensboro, N.C., 1972-85; v.p. mktg. Lavon Sportswear, 1985-92, 96-97; pres. Opportunity Mktg., City of Industry, Calif., 1990—; pres. Opportunity Mktg. Co. consulting Apparel Industry, Kirland, Wash., 1991; v.p. mktg. Jaime L'amour Sportswear divsn. Summit Ridge Corp., 1994-96.

ROSS, DAVID J., product manager; b. Washington, June 28, 1965; s. Harry E. and Lois Alene (Beaver) R.; m. Keiko Acakaki Ross, Feb. 10, 1989. Student, Presbyn. Coll., Clinton, S.C., 1982, U. Cin., 1984; BS in Design, Ga. Tech. U., 1987. Mech. engr. Comsat, Sterling, Va., 1989-91; product mgr. Am. Mobile Satellite, Washington, 1991-95; dir. of sales Am. Mobile Satellite, Reston, Va., 1995-96; product mgr. Qualcomm, San Diego, 1996—. Patentee in field. Lt. cpl. USMC, 1987-89. Avocations: surfing, oil painting, skiing. Office: Qualcomm 5414 Oberlin Dr Ste 300 San Diego CA 92121-4744

ROSS, DONALD HENRY, lawyer; b. Modesto, Calif., Oct. 14, 1923; s. Guy Walden Ross and Dolly Mae Brewer; m. Ruth Lorene Kitching, May 13, 1946; children: Genie Ann Kuehne, Robin Mae. BS in Indsl. Mgmt., U. So. Calif., 1953; Ms in Internat. Affairs, George Washington U., 1965; JD, U. Pacific, 1982. Bar: Nev. 1982. Sgt. pilot RAF, 1941-42; commd. 2d. lt. USAF, 1942, advanced through grades to maj. gen., retired, 1974; atty. pvt. practice, Carson City, Nev., 1982—. Republican. Avocations: flying, old car restoration, shooting. Home and Office: 4350 Meadow Wood Rd Carson City NV 89703

ROSS, JENNIFER MARIE, paralegal; b. Hays, Kans., Nov. 26, 1960; d. Richard Raymond and Armella (Pfannenstiel) R. BS in Sociology, Ft. Hays State U., 1989. Cert. paralegal ABA Denver Paralegal Inst., 1993. Case mgr. Golden West Skills Ctr., Goodland, Kans., 1989; telephone sales Olan Mills, Hays, 1991; tchr. asst. Northwest Kans. Day Care, Hays, 1990-93; telephone sales Intellisell, Victoria, Kans., 1992-93; paraprofl. Sch. Dist. # 489, Hays, 1990-93; with Hallmark, Kansas City, Mo., 1995—. Vol. Literacy Vol. of Am., Hays, 1990-93, Ct. Appt. Spl. Advocate, Hays, 1990-93, Cancer Council, Hays, 1990-91, HeadStart, Hays, 1993, Ellis County Dems. mem. AAUW (sec. 1989), NOW, Bus. and Profl. Women, Gen. Fedn. Women's Clubs, Feminist Coalition U. Kans, League of Women Voters. Roman Catholic. Avocations: aerobics, reading, cooking, travelling, crafts. Office: Sebastiens Park Meadows Town Ctr Littleton CO 80124

ROSS, JOE, poet; b. Scranton, Pa., Dec. 27, 1960; s. Joseph and Francis (Calamino) R.; m. Laura D. Wilber, Jan. 23, 1964. BA, Temple U., 1983. Rep. John F. Kennedy Ctr. for Performing Arts, Washington, 1990-97; program development coord. San Diego Commn. Arts & Culture, 1998—. Author: An American Voyage, 1993, De-elections, 1996, The Wood Series, 1997. NEA fellow, 1997, D.C. Commn. on Arts fellow, 1997. Mem. Artswire. Avocations: arts, music, sports. Home: 1266 Felspar St San Diego CA 92109-2941

ROSS, KATHLEEN ANN, editor; b. Pasadena, Calif., May 5, 1948; d. Ward Elliott and Myrtle Clara (Petersen) Drake; m. Hugh Norman Ross, July 30, 1977; children: Joel Stephen, David Michael. BA, U. So. Calif., 1971, MA, 1972. Mktg. editor L.A. Times, 1972-73; editor comm. and publs. U. So. Calif., L.A., 1973-75; instr. English Pasadena City Coll., 1975-79; freelance editor, 1979—; v.p., editor Reasons to Believe, Glendora, Calif., 1986—; editl. cons. English Lang. Inst.-China, San Dimas, Calif., 1980-93. Editor: Beyond the Cosmos, 1996, The Genesis Question, 1998; mng. editor Facts & Faith, 1986-98; script editor: (video documentary) Journey Toward Creation, 1998. Mem. site coun. Shull Sch., San Dimas, 1995-97. Avocations: mountain biking, hiking, water sports, fitness. Office: Reasons to Believe 731 E Arrow Hwy Glendora CA 91740-6504

ROSS, KATHLEEN ANNE, college president; b. Palo Alto, Calif., July 1, 1941; d. William Andrew and Mary Alberta (Wilburn) R. BA, Ft. Wright Coll., 1964; MA, Georgetown U., 1971; PhD, Claremont Grad. Sch., 1979; LLD (hon.) Alverno Coll. Milw., 1990, Dartmouth Coll., 1991, Seattle U., 1992; LHD (hon.) Whitworth Coll., 1992, LLD (hon.) Pomona Coll., 1993, LHD (hon.) Coll. of New Rochelle, 1998. Cert. tchr., Wash. Secondary tchr. Holy Names Acad., Spokane, Wash., 1964-70; dir. rsch. and planning Province Holy Names, Wash. State, 1972-73; v.p. acads. Ft. Wright Coll., Spokane, 1973-81; rsch. asst. to dean Claremont Grad. Sch., Calif., 1977-78; assoc. faculty mem. Harvard U., Cambridge, Mass., 1981; pres. Heritage Coll., Toppenish, Wash., 1981—; cons. Wash. State Holy Names Schs., 1971-73; coll. accrediting assn. evaluator N.W. Assn. Schs. and Colls., Seattle, 1975—; dir. Holy Names Coll., Oakland, Calif., 1979—; cons. Yakama Indian Nation, Toppenish, 1975—; speaker, cons. in field. Author: (with others) Multicultural Pre-School Curriculum, 1977, A Crucial Agenda: Improving Minority Student Success, 1989; Cultural Factors in Success of American Indian Students in Higher Education, 1978. Chmn. Internat. 5-Yr. Convocation of Sisters of Holy Names, Montreal, Que., Can., 1981, 96; TV Talk show host Spokane Council of Chs., 1974-76. Recipient E.K. and Lillian F. Bishop Founds. Youth Leader of Yr. award, 1986, Disting. Citizenship Alumna award Claremont Grad. Sch., 1986, Golden Aztec award Washington Human Devel., 1989, Harold W. McGraw Edn. prize, 1989, John Carroll award Georgetown U., 1991, Holy Names medal Ft. Wright Coll., 1981, Pres. medal Eastern Washington U., 1994; named Yakima Herald Rep. Person of Yr. 1987, First Annual Leadership award Region VIII Coun. Advancement and Support Edn., 1993; Wash. State Medal of Merit, 1995; MacArthur fellow, 1997; numerous grants for projects in multicultural higher edn., 1974—. Mem. Nat. Assn. Ind. Colls. and Univs., Am. Assn. Higher Edn., Soc. Intercultural Edn., Tng. and Rsch., Sisters of Holy Names of Jesus and Mary-SNJM. Roman Catholic. Office: Heritage Coll Office of Pres 3240 Fort Rd Toppenish WA 98948-9562

ROSS, LANSON CLIFFORD, JR., religion educator, author; b. Killdeer, N.D., June 23, 1936; s. Lanson Charles and Mabel (Smith) R.; children: David F., Lanson III. BA in Biblical Studies, Seattle Pacific U., 1960; M. Sacred Theology, Internat. Coll., 1984; D of Ministries, 1986. founder Planned Living Seminars; pres. Viet/Aid; pres. Barnabas Ministries. Author: Total Life Prosperity, 1983; Give Your Children a Target, 1985, Take Charge of Your Life, 1986, The Bubble Burst, 1987; producer 5 vol. video seminar A Planned Life Style, 1986, and film A Time to Grow (J.C. Mc Pheeters award 1988). Mem. Seattle Yacht Club. Office: PO Box 1354 Arizona City AZ 85223-1354

ROSS, MOLLY OWINGS, gold and silversmith, jewelry designer, small business owner; b. Ft. Worth, Feb. 5, 1954; d. James Robertson and Lucy (Owings) R. BFA, Colo. State U., 1976; postgrad., U. Denver, 1978-79. Graphic designer Amber Sky Illustrators and Sta. KCNC TV-Channel 4, Denver, 1977-79; art dir. Mercy Med. Ctr., Denver, 1979-83, Molly Ross Design, Denver, 1983-84; co-owner Deltex Royalty Co., Inc., Colorado Springs, Colo., 1981—, LMA Royalties, Ltd., Colorado Springs, 1993—; art dir., account mgr. Schwing/Walsh Advt., Mktg. and Pub. Rels., Denver, 1984-87, prodn. mgr., 1987-88; jewelry designer Molly O. Ross, Gold and Silversmith, Denver, 1988—. Pres. Four Mile Hist. Park Vol. Bd., Denver, 1985-87; bd. dirs. Four Mile Hist. Park Assn., 1985-86, Hist. Denver, Inc., 1986-87, Denver Emergency Housing Coalition, 1989-90; coun. mem. feminization of poverty critical needs area coun. Jr. League Denver, 1989-90, chmn. children in crisis/edn. critical needs area, 1990-91, chmn. project devel., 1991-92, co-chmn. Done in a Day Comty. Project 75th Anniversary Celebration, 1991-93; mem. bd. dirs., 1993-94, v.p. comty. projects, 1993-94; co-chmn. Project IMPACT, 1994-95; exec. v.p. external affairs Jr. League of Denver, 1995-96; co-chmn. Comty. Coalitions Com., 1996-98; bd. dirs. Ctr. for Ethics and Social Responsibility/PREP, 1994—, pres. bd. dirs., 1997-99; mem. steering com. Denver Urban Resources Partnership, 1995—, chmn. steering com., 1997-98; pres.-elect Jr. League of Denver, 1998-99, pres. 1999-00. Named Vol. of Month (March), Jr. League Denver, 1990, Vol. of Yr., Four Mile Hist. Pk., 1988; recipient Gold Peak Mktg. award-team design Am. Mktg. Assn., 1986, Silver Peak Mktg. award-team design Am. Mktg. Assn., 1986, Gold Pick award-art dir. Pub. Rels. Soc. Am., 1980-81. Mem. Natural Resources Def. Coun., Physicians for Social Responsibility, Am. Farmland Trust, Nat. Trust for Hist. Preservation, Environ. Def. Fund. Avocations: horseback riding, bicycling, hiking, backpacking, pastel drawing.

ROSS, MOSES JULIAN, wholesale distribution executive, publishing consultant; b. Salt Lake City, June 20, 1966; s. Galen Julian and Virginia R. DSHEA cert. Am. Nutraceutical Assn. Advt. sales The Evanston (Wyo.) Post, 1983-84; co-owner, sales mgr. Precision Printing Inc., Evanston, 1984-88; advt. sales The Daily Spectrum, St. George, Utah, 1988-89; owner, cons. The M. J. Ross Group, Inc., Portland, Ore., 1990—; pub. In Balance Mag., Portland, 1992-97; nutraceutical distbr. Mannatech, Inc., Portland, 1997—. Radio show host Sta. KKEY, 1993. Pres. Injured Workers Assistance League, Portland, 1991-93. Nominated Citizen of Yr. award Chiropractic Assn. Ore., 1993. Mem. Am. Nutraceutical Assn. Avocations: reading, sports, jazz. Office: 1017 SW Morrison St Ste 411 Portland OR 97205-2629

ROSS, STEVEN CHARLES, business administration educator, consultant; b. Salem, Oreg., Jan. 14, 1947; s. Charles Reed and Edythe Marie (Calvin) R.; m. Meredith Lynn Buholts, June 15, 1969; children: Kelly Lynn, Shannon Marie. BS, Oreg. State U., 1969; MS, U. Utah, 1976, PhD, 1980. Cons. IRS Tng. Staff, Ogden, Utah, 1977-80; asst. prof. Marquette U., Milw., 1980-88; assoc. prof. Mont. State U., Bozeman, 1988-89; assoc. prof. bus. adminstrn. Western Wash. U., Bellingham, 1989—; govt. and industry cons.; cons. editor microcomputing series West Pub. Co. Author 30 books and several articles in computer systems field. Mem. adv. com. Milwaukee County Mgmt., 1981-85, Port of Bellingham, 1990—; chmn. 1998 U.S. Sailing Jr. Championships. Capt. U.S. Army, 1969-75. Rsch. fellow U. Utah, 1977-79, Marquette U., 1981-84, Western Wash. U., 1998. Mem. Acad. Mgmt., Decision Scis. Inst., Inst. Mgmt. Scis., Assn. for Computing Machinery, Assn. Computer Educators, Bellingham Yacht Club (trustee 1992-93, sec. 1993-94, rear commodore, 1994-95, vice commodore 1995-96, commodore 1996-97). Office: Western Wash U Coll Bus and Econs Bellingham WA 98225

ROSS, TERRY D., lawyer; b. Glendale, Calif., Aug. 12, 1943. BA, U. Calif., Santa Barbara, 1965; JD, U. Calif., San Francisco, 1968. Bar: Calif. 1969. Ptnr. Gray, Cary, Ware & Freidenrich, San Diego; mem. panel arbitrators Am. Arbitration Assn. Note and comment editor Hastings Law Jour., 1967-68. Bd. dirs., mem. exec. bd., 1st v.p. Davis Grossmont YMCA. Mem. ABA (sect. litigation), State Bar Calif., San Diego County Bar Assn. (mem. arbitration panel, superior ct. com.), S.D. Marlin Club, SDMB Boat and Ski Club, Phi Delta Phi. Office: Gray Cary Ware & Freidenrich 401 B St Ste 1700 San Diego CA 92101-4240

ROSSEL, EUGENE DAVID, career officer, electrical engineer; b. Okawville, Ill., July 14, 1937; s. Anthony John and Anna Mary (Trost) R.; m. Isabel Martinez Gonzalez, June 19, 1967 (div. Feb. 1983); children: Carlos, Ana Isabel, Eugene Anthony. BSEE, St. Louis U., 1959; MS in Mgmt., Air Force Inst. Tech., 1969; Cert., Air Command and Staff Coll., 1974, Indsl. Coll. Armed Forces, 1975, Air War Coll., 1976. Registered

profl. engr., Pa. Enlisted USAF, 1954, commd. 2d lt., 1959, advanced through grades to lt. col., 1977; officer USAF, worldwide including Vietnam, Laos, Panama and Spain; radar engr. USAF, Torrejon AFB, Spain, 1972-77; space shuttle engr. USAF Space and Missile Orgn., Los Angeles Air Force Sta., 1977-80; tech. advisor to Small Bus. Adminstrn. USAF, Los Angeles Air Force Sta., 1980-83, product assurance dir. space div., 1983-84; advanced concepts dir. USAF Ballistic Missile Office, Norton AFB, Calif., 1984-87; program mgr. L'Garde, Inc., Tustin, Calif., 1987—; cons. NASA, SBA, Los Angeles, 1977-80. Author, editor: Counterinsurgency Communications Handbook, 1968; author position papers and policy studies on USAF to U.S. Army and various fgn. mil. orgns. Decorated Bronze Star, Air medal; Gallantry Cross with palm (Republic Vietnam). Mem. Soc. Profl. Engrs. (pub. relations officer 1963-66), AIAA, Air Commando Assn., Air Force Assn., Nat. Rifle Assn., Am. Legion, St. Louis U. Assn. (pres. C.Z. chpt., 1964-66). Roman Catholic. Club: Toastmasters (Madrid)(pres. 1972-74). Avocations: genealogy, amateur radio, writing. Home: 6083 Rosa Ct Chino CA 91710-4449 Office: L'Garde Inc 15181 Woodlawn Ave Tustin CA 92780-6487

ROSSER, JAMES MILTON, academic administrator; b. East St. Louis, Ill., Apr. 16, 1939; s. William M. and Mary E. (Bass) R.; 1 child, Terrence. BA, So. Ill. U., 1962, MA, 1963, PhD, 1969. Diagnostic bacteriologist Holden Hosp., Carbondale, Ill., 1961-63; rsch. bacteriologist Eli Lilly & Co., Indpls., 1963-66; coordinator Black Am. studies, instr. health edn. So. Ill. U., Carbondale, 1968-69; asst. prof. Black Am. studies dir. So. Ill. U., 1969-70, asst. to chancellor, 1970; assoc. vice chancellor for acad. affairs U. Kans., Lawrence, 1970-74; assoc. prof. edn., pharmacology and toxicology U. Kans., 1971-74; vice chancellor dept. higher edn. State of N.J., Trenton, 1974-79; acting chancellor State of N.J., 1977; pres., prof. health care mgmt. Calif. State U., Los Angeles, 1979—; tech. resource panel Ctr. for Research and Devel. in Higher Edn., U. Calif., Berkeley, 1974-76; health maintenance orgn. com. Health Planning Coun., State of N.J., 1975-79; standing com. on R & D bd. trustees Ednl. Testing Service, 1976-77; steering com. and task force on retention of minorities in engring. Assembly of Engring. NRC, 1975-78; mem. Bd. Med. Examiners, State of N.J., 1978-79; vis. faculty Inst. Mgmt. of Lifelong Edn., Grad. Sch. Edn., Harvard U., 1979; mem. Calif. State U. Trustees Spl. Long Range Fin. Planning Com., 1982-87; mem. Am. Coun. on Edn., 1979—, AFL/CIO Labor Higher Edn. Coun., 1983—, Nat. Commn. Higher Edn. Issues, 1981-82; mem. The Calif. Achievement Coun., 1983-89, strategic adv. counc. Coll. and Univs. Systems Exchange, 1988-91; bd. dirs. Am. Humanities Coun., So. Calif. Am. Humanics, Inc. Coun., Sanwa Bank Calif., Edison Internat., Fedco, Inc. Author: An Analysis of Health Care Delivery, 1977. Exec. bd., chmn. varisty scouting program L.A. area coun. Boy Scouts Am., 1980—; bd. dirs. Hispanic Urban Ctr., L.A., 1979—, L.A. Urban League, 1982-95, Cmty. TV of So. Calif., Sta. KCET, 1980-89, United Way, L.A., 1980-91, Orthopaedic Hosp., 1983-86, L.A. Philharm. Assn., 1986—, Nat. Health Found., 1990—, Calif. C. of C., 1993—; mem. Citizen's Adv. Coun. Congl. Caucus Sci. and Tech., 1983—; mem. performing arts coun./edn. coun. Music Ctr., 1984—; minority bus. task force Pacific Bell, 1985-86; bd. govs. Nat. ARC, 1986-91, Mayor's Blue Ribbon Task Force on Drugs, City of L.A., 1988, L.A. Annenberg Met. Project, 1994—; Nat. Adv. Coun. on Aging, 1989-93; bd. trustees Woodrow Wilson Nat. Fellowship Found., 1993—; bd. advisors Historically Black Colls. and Univs. and Minority Insts., Dept. Air Force, 1997—; bd. dirs. Ams. for the Arts, 1991—. NSF fellow, 1961; NDEA fellow, 1967-68; recipient award of recognition in Edn. Involvement for Young Achievers, 1981, Pioneer of Black Hist. Achievement award Brotherhood Crusade, 1981, Alumni Achievement award So. Ill. U., 1982, Friend of Youth award Am. Humanics, Inc., 1985, Leadership award Dept. Higher Edn. Ednl. Equal Opportunity Fund Program, 1989, Medal of Excellence Gold State Minority Found., 1990, Take Charge of Learning Success award Inst. for Redesign of Learning. Mem. Calif. C. of C. (bd. dirs. 1993—), Alhambra C. of C. (bd. dirs. 1979—), Los Angeles C. of C. (bd. dirs. 1985-90), Am. Assn. State Colls. and Univs., Kappa Delta Pi, Phi Kappa Phi. Roman Catholic. Office: Calif State Univ Office of the Pres 5151 State University Dr Los Angeles CA 90032-4226

ROSSI, AMADEO JOSEPH, chemist; b. Seattle, Sept. 23, 1954; s. Amadeo Joseph and Maria Asilia (Chinella) R.; m. Frances Marie Stotts, Sept. 19, 1981; children: Anthony Joseph, Matthew Christopher, Brian Michael. BS in Wood and Fiber Sci., U. Wash., 1979, MS in wood chemistry, 1987. Research aide U. Wash., Seattle, 1978-79; environ. engr. Georgia-Pacific Corp., Eugene, Oreg., 1980; v.p. hazardous waste remediation projects Foster Wheeler Environ. Corp., Seattle, 1981-98; sr. program mgr. CH2M Hill Constructors Inc., Bellevue, Wash., 1998—. Contbr. articles to profl. jours. Mem. Am. Chem. Soc., Air Pollution Control Assn., Forest Products Rsch. Soc., Xi Sigma Pi, Sigma Xi. Office: Foster Wheeler Environ Corp 10900 NE 8th St Bellevue WA 98004-4405

ROSSIN, HERBERT YALE, recreational facility executive; b. Phila., May 15, 1936; s. Jack Rossin and Edna Wolinsky; m. Meryl Ann Barsky, Nov. 15, 1965; children: Abby Rae, Shane J.P. Degree in journalism, Temple U., 1958. Gen. mgr. KIKU TV/13, Honolulu, 1968-70; br. mgr. Columbia Pictures, Las Vegas, 1970-74; pres. Internat. TV Concepts, Las Vegas, 1974-78; sta. mgr. KUAM AM/FM/TV, Agana, Guam, 1978-80; v.p. Tag Mktg. and Advt., Cherry Hill, N.J., 1981-83; gen. mgr. WLXI-TV/61, Greensboro, N.C., 1983-85; v.p., gen. mgr. WHLL-TV/27, Boston, 1986-87; v.p. Home Shopping Network, L.A., 1987-88; owner A.S.A.P. Multi-Corp., Las Vegas, 1988-97; pres. Las Vegas TV Network, 1998—; bd. chmn. Cook Race and Sports Book Lt., Cook Islands, 1998—; broadcast cons. Fashion Channel-Video Mall, L.A., 1987-88; pres. Video Music TV Stas. Am., 1984-88; network cons.; mem. Guam Gaming Commn., 1979. Prodr. motion picture Miss Conduct, 1957; creator TV shows New Millionaires, 1993, Slim Scents, 1995, Big Bucks Bingo, 1980, Sportalk, 1997, Football Weekly, 1996, Wireless Wonder, 1994, Las Vegas at Nite, 1997; editor Israel Mag., 1960. Prodr. telethon Heart Fund Am., Las Vegas, 1972. With Pa. Air Nat. Guard, 1954-59. Named Broadcaster of Yr., Video Music TV Stas. Am., 1985; recipient Edn. award Albert Einstein Acad., 1974, People Law Sch. award Nev. Trial Lawyers, 1992, others. Avocation: softball. Home and Office: ASAP Multi Corp 7704 Musical Ln Las Vegas NV 89128-4082

ROSSING, CATHERINE BARRETT SCHWAB, dental hygienist; b. San Francisco, Apr. 8, 1932; d. Richard James and Mary Ann (McAuliff) and Richard Thomas Barrett; m. Donald Theodore Schwab, Aug. 8, 1954 (div. 1965); 1 child, Carla Diane; m. Alan Robert Rossing, Mar. 31, 1989. AA, U. Calif., Berkeley, 1952, BS, 1954; MPA, Calif. State U., Long Beach, 1983. Registered dental hygienist, Calif. Preventive specialist Dr. Thomas Evans Office, Anaheim, Calif., 1968-72, 90; mem. T.E.A.M. program U. So. Calif., L.A., 1972-73; staff hygienist Dr. Joseph Berger Dental Office, Fountain Valley, Calif., 1974-88; pub. Rossing Enterprises, Pebble Beach, Calif., 1991—; co-founder Preventive Dental Care, L.A., 1985-90; co-owner Schwab/Flora Meeting Organizers, Anaheim, 1981-90. Mem. Calif. Dental Hygienists' Assn. (editor jour. 1974-76, 81-84, 89-95, Golden Pen award 1976), Am. Dental Hygienists' Assn. (trustee 1977-81, Recognition award 1981). Avocations: Monterey Bay Aquarium, gardening, orchids. Home: 1060 The Old Dr Pebble Beach CA 93953-2509

ROSSMANN, ANTONIO, lawyer, educator; b. San Francisco, Apr. 25, 1941; s. Herbert Edward and Yolanda (Sonsini) R.; m. Kathryn A. Burns, Oct. 6, 1991; children: Alice Sonsini, Maria McHale. Grad. Harvard U., 1963; JD, 1971. Bar: Calif. 1972, D.C. 1979, U.S. Supreme Ct. 1979, N.Y. 1980. Law clk., Calif. Supreme Ct., 1971-72; assoc. Tuttle & Taylor, Los Angeles, 1972-75; pub. advisor Calif. Energy Commn., 1975-76; sole practice, San Francisco, 1976-82, 85—; exec. dir. Nat. Center for Preservation Law, 1979-80; mem. McCutchen, Doyle, Brown & Enersen, San Francisco, 1982-85; adj. prof. law Hastings Coll. Law, 1981-84; vis. prof. UCLA Sch. Law, 1985-88; adj. prof. Stanford Law Sch., 1989-90, U. Calif. Sch. Law, 1991—. Bd. dirs. Planning and Conservation League, 1984—, Calif. Water Protection Council, 1982-83, San Francisco Marathon, 1982-90; pres. Western State Endurance Run, 1986-96, counselor, 1996—; pres., bd. dirs. Toward Utility Rate Normalization, 1976-79. Served to lt. comdr. USN, 1963-68. Fulbright [illegible] Bar City of N.Y., U.S. Rowing Assn., U.S. Soccer Fed. (state referee), L.A. Athletic Club, Harvard Club (San Francisco, N.Y.C.), Harvard Law Sch. Assn. of No. Calif. (pres. 1997—). Contbr. articles to legal jours.; editor Harvard U. Law Rev., 1969-71. Office: 380 Hayes St San Francisco CA 94102-4421

ROTCOP, J. KENNETH, screenwriter, producer; b. Bklyn., July 3, 1934; s. Albert and Lillian (Ragen) R.; children: Kimberly, Alison. BS, Boston U., 1956. Creative head Embassy Pictures, Los Angeles, 1968-71; head motion pictures Hanna-Barbera Prodns., Los Angeles, 1972-74; v.p. creative affairs Trans-World Prodns., Las Vegas, Nev., 1975-77; freelance writer, producer Studio City, Calif., 1978—; head Ken Rotcop Screenwriting Workshop, U. Tex., 1995—; instr. screenwriting Pierce Coll., Woodland Hills, Calif., 1985—, U. Calif., Northridge, 1988—, UCLA, 1988—. Producer, writer: (film) For Us, The Living: The Story of Medgar Evers (Writers Guild award, Image award, Neil Simon award, others), (TV series) The Magic Shop, Images and Attitudes (Unity award); screenwriter: The Arcade, Ruby and Samuel; producer (film) Bikini Shop; creator, producer TV series (with Arnold Shapiro) Couples; editor Boston U. News.

ROTELLA, SALVATORE G., college administrator; b. Barcellona, Italy, July 24, 1934; came to the U.S., 1951; s. Sebastiano and Maria (Maio) R.; m. Pilar Vives Selles, July 24, 1961; children: Sebastian, Carlo, Salvatore. BA in Internat. Rels., Hunter Coll., 1955; MA in Polit. Sci., U. Chgo., 1956, PhD in Polit. Sci., 1971; D Polit. Sci., U. Pavia, Italy, 1958. Rsch. assoc. dept. econ. rsch. AMA, Chgo., 1959-60; asst. prof. polit. sci. dept. Wright Coll., Chgo., 1960-62; chairperson dept. social sci. Loop Coll., Chgo., 1962-67, asst. dean, dir. Pub. Svc. Inst., 1967-70, v.p. career and spl. programs, 1971-74; assoc. vice chancellor Inst. for City-Wide Programs, Chgo., 1974-75; pres. Chgo. City-Wide Coll., 1976-80, Loop Coll. and Chgo. City-Wide Coll., 1980-82, Riverside (Calif.) C.C., 1992—; vice chancellor Loop Coll. and Chgo. City-Wide Coll., 1982-83; chancellor, chief exec. and ednl. officer City Colls. of Chgo., 1983-88; v.p. acad. affairs Nassau C.C., SUNY, Garden City, N.Y., 1989-92; adj. prof., dir. grad. program pub. adminstrn. Ill. Inst. Tech., Chgo., 1976-82; vis. prof. ednl. leadership and pub. policy Loyola U. Chgo., 1988-89; vis. prof. dept. French and Italian Coll. Liberal Arts SUNY, Stony Brook, 1989-92; lectr. in field. Contbr. articles to profl. jours. Mem. com. Big Bros./Big Sisters Chgo.; bd. dirs. Simon Bolivar Found.; Trustee St. Xavier Coll.; mem. arbitrators panel Am. Arbitration Assn.; former mem. edn. com. Chgo. Assn. Commerce and Industry; former mem. exec. com., long-range planning com., co-chmn. minority concerns com. Ill. C.C. Trustees Assn., Springfield; former bd. dirs. Greater State St. Coun. Recipient Order of Merit, Republic of Italy, 1985, Man of Yr. award The Gregorians, Chgo., 1985, Educator Ann. award Chgo. DC Newspaper, 1985; grant, fellow U. Chgo., Govt. of Italy, Sears Found., Inst. Internat. Edn. Mem. ASPA (pres. Chgo. chpg., mem. nat. coun., chmn. com. on pub. policy, gen. chmn. nat. conf. 1975), Am. Coun. on Edn. (commn. on nat. challenge in higher edn.), North Ctrl. Assn. Colls. and Univs. (evaluator, team chmn.), Am. Assn. Cmty. and Jr. Colls. (mem. labor/higher edn. coun., commn. on urban cmty. C.C.'s), Nat. Assn. Schs. of Pub. Adminstrn. and Pub. Affairs. Office: Riverside CC 4800 Magnolia Ave Riverside CA 92506-1242

ROTH, SUZANNE ALLEN, financial services agent; b. Santa Monica, Calif., May 31, 1963; d. Raymond A. and Ethel Allen; m. Steve Milstein Roth, Dec. 27, 1992. BA, U. Calif., Santa Cruz, 1986; MA in Edn., Calif. State U., L.A., 1989; postgrad., Art Ctr. Sch. Design, Pasadena, Calif., 1994—. Cert. tchr., Calif.; lic. real estate agt., Calif. Interviewer L.A. Times Newspaper, 1986-88; educator L.A. Unified Sch. Dist., 1987-90; educator Burbank (Calif.) Unified Sch. Dist., 1990-94, vol., 1994—; ptnr. fin. svcs. Roth & Assocs./N.Y. Life, L.A., 1993—. Model, actor, 1998—. Mem. Nat. Trust Hist. Preservation, Libr. Congress. Mem. NEA, Burbank Tchrs. Union, Nat. Soc. for Hist. Preservation, Libr. of Congress. Avocations: painting, illustrating, writing, weight training, old house renovation, wood restoration, light carpentry, landscape design.

ROTHE-BARNESON, JUNE EMMA, lay worker; b. Chico, Calif., Feb. 27, 1931; d. William Edgar and Jean Blanch (Howe) Rothe; m. John L. Barneson Jr., Apr. 26, 1953 (div. 1986); children: John L. III, Jean LaVere Barneson Ponciano. BA in Elem. Edn., Calif. State U., Chico, 1952. Cert. elem. sch. tchr. Mem. United Meth. Gen. Bd. Global Ministries, N.Y.C., 1972-80, United Meth. Gen. Commn. on Communication, Nashville, 1981-87; del. United Meth. Gen. Conf., Indpls., 1980; newsletter editor United Meth., 1980-90; trustee Glide Found., San Francisco, 1977-85, Butte County Task Force on AIDS; mem. Chico Area Interfaith Coun., 1990—, v.p., 1990-91, pres., 1991-92; co-owner Perchè No! (coffee house-ice cream shop), Chico, 1986—. Author: Cabin On Quesnel, 1969, Airspeed & Godspeed, 1976, Dogs On the Roof, 1983; contbr. articles to United Meth. mags. "Most World Minded Citizen" Douglas McArthur Scholarship Found., Chico, 1977. Democrat. Home and Office: 738 Downing Ave Chico CA 95926-2822

ROTHENBERG, HARVEY DAVID, educational administrator; b. Fort Madison, Iowa, May 31, 1937; s. Max and Cecelia Rothenberg; AA, Wentworth Mil. Acad., 1957; BBA, State U. Iowa, 1960; M.A, U. No. Colo., 1961; postgrad. Harris Tchrs. Coll., 1962-63, St. Louis U., 1962-63; PhD, Colo. State U., 1972; m. Audrey Darlynne Roseman, July 5, 1964; children: David Michael, Mark Daniel. Distributive edn. tchr. Roosevelt H.S., St. Louis, 1961-63, Proviso West High Sch., Hillside, Ill., 1963-64, Longmont (Colo.) Sr. High Sch., 1964-69, 70-71; supr. research and spl. programs St. Vrain Valley Sch. Dist., Longmont, Colo., 1971-72; chmn. bus. div. Arapahoe C.C., Littleton, Colo., 1972-75; dir. vocat., career and adult edn. Arapahoe County Sch. Dist. 6, Littleton, 1975-96; part-time instr. Met. State Coll., Denver, 1975-85, Arapahoe C.C., Littleton, 1975—, Regis U., 1996—; dir. faculty, curriculum Sch. Profl. Studies, Regis U., 1996-98, instr., facilitator, 1998—; owner HDR Bus. and Ednl. Consulting, 1988—; vis. prof. U. Ala., Tuscaloosa, summer 1972; dir. Chatfield Bank, Littleton, 1974-83, Yaak River Mines Ltd., Amusement Personified Inc.; pres. Kuytia Inc., Littleton, 1975—; co-owner Albuquerque Lasers, profl. volleyball team, owner, Rocky Mount. Thunder, Indoor Football Team, Colo. Author: Conducting Successful Business Research, 1996 . Mem. City of Longmont Long-Range Planning Commn., 1971-72, pres. Homeowners Bd., 1978-80. Recipient Outstanding Young Educator award St. Vrain Valley Sch. Dist., 1967, Outstanding Vocational Educator, Colo. 1992, We. Region U.S., 1993. Mem. Am., Colo. (mem. exec. com. 1966-68, treas. 1972-73) vocat. assns., Littleton C. of C., Colo. Assn. Vocat. Adminstrs, Colo. Educators For and About Bus., Delta Sigma Pi, Delta Pi Epsilon, Nat. Assn. Local Sch. Adminstrs., Colo. Council Local Sch. Adminstrs. Clubs: Elks, Masons, Shriners. Home: 7461 S Sheridan Ct Littleton CO 80128-7084 Office: Rocky Mt Thunder 2 N Cascade Ste 1100 Colorado Springs CO 80903

ROTHENBERGER, VICTOR CONRAD IMMANUEL, minister; b. Rhein, Sask., Can., Feb. 14, 1923; s. Conrad and Amalia (Propp) R.; m. Martha Ida Redlich, July 9, 1947; children: Sharon Rothenberger Thomson, Wayne, Deborah Rothenberger Mick, Richard. AA, Luther Coll., 1942; BA, U. Sask., 1947; ministerial diploma, Capitol U. and Sem., Columbus, Ohio, 1947; BD, Knox Coll., Toronto, Ont., Can., 1965; MA, MEd, Wright State U., 1975. Ordained to ministry Evang. Luth. Ch. in Can., 1947. Pastor various chs. in Sask., B.C. and Alta., Can., 1947-56, Sharon Luth. Ch., Pasadena, Tex., 1956-59; pastor Peace Luth. ch., Linton, N.D., 1959-62, Pickering, Ont., Can., 1962-65; pastor Christ Luth. Ch., Dayton, Ohio, 1965-74; pastor Martin Luther Ch., Vancouver, B.C., 1974-88, ret., 1988; chmn. B.C. conf. Am. Luth. Ch., Vancouver, 1952-53, mem. stewardship com. Can. dist., 1951-53; mem. campus ministry bd. Evang. Luth. Ch. in Can., Vancouver, 1981-84. Bd. dirs. Luth. Bible Sch. of B.C., 1981—. With Can. Armed Forces, 1940-43. Mem. Phi Alpha Theta. Home: 535 E 46th Ave, Vancouver, BC Canada V5W 2A2

ROTHERHAM, LARRY CHARLES, insurance executive; b. Council Bluffs, Iowa, Oct. 22, 1940; s. Charles Sylvester and Edna Mary (Sylvanus) R.; m. Florene F. Black, May 29, 1965; children: Christopher Charles, Phillip Larry, Kathleen Florene. Student, Creighton U., 1959-61; BSBA, U. Nebr., 1965; postgrad., Am. Coll., Bryn Mawr, Pa., 1985, 87. CPCU, CLU, ARM. Claims rep. and underwriter Safeco Ins. Co., Albuquerque, New Mex., 1965-69; br. mgr. Ohio Casualty Group, Albuquerque, 1969—; resident v.p. Ohio Casualty Group, Denver, 1997—; assoc. in risk mgmt. Ins. Inst. Am., [illegible] Freedom H.S., Albuquerque, 1982-86, bd. chmn. N.Mex. Property Ins. Program; mem. N.Mex. Workers compensation Appeals Bd. Mem. New Mex. Soc. Chartered Property & Casualty Underwriters (charter mem., pres. 1975-77), New Mex. Soc. Chartered Life Underwriters, New Mex. Ins. Assn. [illegible] Democrat. Roman Catholic. Avocations: race walking, swimming, hiking, camping. Home: 10677 W Parkhill Pl Littleton CO 80127-5547 Office: Ohio Casualty Group 4380 S Syracuse St Ste 600 Denver CO 80237-2607

ROTHHAMMER, CRAIG ROBERT, social worker, consultant; b. San Francisco, May 17, 1954; s. Robert Charles and Gloria Lee (Molloy) R.; m. Dawn Alicia Alvarez, 1988. BA, U. Calif., Santa Barbara, 1976; MSW, San Diego State U., 1979. Lic. clin. social worker, Calif. Social work asst. Mercy Hosp., San Diego, 1977; psychiat. social worker Lanterman State Hosp., Pomona, Calif., 1979-83, Sonoma State Hosp., Eldridge, Calif., 1983-84; children's social worker County Adoption Service, San Bernardino, Calif., 1984-86; psychiat. social worker Patton State Hosp., 1987-88; psychiat. soc. worker II Crisis Outpatient Svcs. Riverside (Calif.) County Mental Health, 1988-90; mental health svcs. supr. Interagy. Svcs. for Families, Riverside County Mental Health, 1990-95; mgr. inpatient psychiatry west/south bay sub-region Kaiser Permanente, Redwood City, Calif., 1995—; expert examiner Behavioral Sci. Examiners, Calif.; pvt. practice (part time) social work Redlands, Calif., 1986-89; field instr. MSW program Calif. State U., San Bernardino, 1989-95, marriage, family & child counselor program Loma Linda (Calif.) U., 1993. Vol. Social Advs. for Youth, Santa Barbara, Calif., 1974-76, Am. Diabetes Assn., San Diego, 1978-79, San Diego Assn. For Retarded, 1978-80; liason Adoptive Family Assn., San Bernardino, 1986. Mem. NASW, Acad. Cert. Social Workers (diplomate in clin. social work). Democrat. Avocations: scuba diving, bicycling, hiking, writing, ch. related activities. Office: Kaiser Permanente Dept Inpatient Psychiatry 900 Veterans Blvd Dept Redwood City CA 94063-2087

ROTHLISBERG, ALLEN PETER, librarian, educator, deacon; b. Jamaica, N.Y., Nov. 15, 1941; s. Allen Greenway and Agnes Clare (Donohoe) R.; m. Linda Lee Lillie, Oct. 17, 1964; children: Bethanie Lynn, Craig Allen. AB, San Diego State U., 1963; MLS, Our Lady of the Lake U., 1970. Cert. tchr., Ariz.; ordained deacon Episcopal Ch., 1989. Libr. dir. Prescott (Ariz.) Pub. Libr., 1963-75; dir. learning resources, head libr. Northland Pioneer Coll., Holbrook, Ariz., 1975-92; libr. dir. Chino Valley (Ariz.) Pub. Libr., 1992—; libr. media instr. Northland Pioneer Coll., Holbrook, Ariz., 1978—. Author: Dance to the Music of Time: Second Movement, 1972; contbr. articles to profl. publs. Recreation dir. Town of Chino Valley, 1993—, pub. access TV dir., 1993—; Episcopal deacon St. George's Ch., Holbrook, 1989-92, St. Luke's, Prescott, 1992—. Recipient Libr. of Yr. Ariz. State Libr. Assn., 1966. Mem. Elks, Masons. Democrat. Episcopalian. Avocations: reading, writing, music, theatre. Office: Chino Valley Pub Libr PO Box 1188 Chino Valley AZ 86323-1188

ROTHMAN, HOWARD MICHAEL, writer; b. Phila., Sept. 26, 1953; s. Edwin and Ida (Steinman) R.; m. Patricia Marie Myers, Apr. 20, 1975; children: Anna Leigh, Melanie Rose. BA in Journalism, Pa. State U., 1974. Sports editor Germantown (Pa.) Courier, Phila., 1976-77; editor Denver Sentinel Newspapers, 1977-79, Jackson Hole Guide, Jackson, Wyo., 1979-82; writer Littleton, Colo., 1982—. Author: (books) Future Vision, 1987, Companies with a Conscience, 1992, All That Once Was Good, 1995. Mem. Twain Accountability Com., Littleton, 1993—. Recipient Pacemaker award Wyo. Press Assn., 1981. Mem. Am. Soc. Journalists and Authors.

ROTHMAN, MICHAEL HUMPHREY, academic administrator, treasurer; b. San Francisco, Jan. 22, 1951; s. Harry D. and Helen (Stevens) R.; m. Judith Ellen Holliday, Oct. 17, 1980. BA, Claremont McKenna Coll., 1972, MBA, 1978. Exec. asst. Claremont (Calif.) McKenna Coll., 1972-74, dir. budget, 1974-76, from asst. treas. to treas., 1976-82; from v.p. to 1st v.p. planning and devel. Angeles Corp., L.A., 1982-85; CFO Humphreys & Assocs., Inc., Newport Beach, Calif., 1986-87; v.p., treas. Mills Coll., Oakland, Calif., 1987—. Home: 1121 N Sunset Ct Tacoma WA 98406-1086 Office: Mills Coll 5000 Macarthur Blvd Oakland CA 94613-1301

ROTHS, BEVERLY OWEN, organization executive; b. Kansas City, Kans., Aug. 25, 1935; d. Edward Charles and Josephine Mary (Vogel) Owen; m. Robert L. Roths, Sept. 4, 1954; children: Karen Kay, Daniel Owen, Nancy Jo. AA with honors, Antelope Valley Coll., 1975. Sec. McDonnell Aircraft Co., St. Louis, 1955-58; exec. dir. Florissant (Mo.) Valley C. of C., 1976-86; pres. Poppy Reserve/Mojave Desert Interpretive Assn., Lancaster, Calif., 1989—; pres. Soroptimist Internat., North St. Louis County, 1981-82; sec.-treas. St. Louis County League C. of C., Clayton, 1978. Prodr. Small Bus. Profiles, condr. interviews Storer Cable TV, Florissant, 1983-86. Mem. Florissant City Coun., 1968-72; bd. dirs. Mo. Mcpl. League First Woman, Florissant, 1970-71; co-chair Bicentennial, Florissant, 1985-86, Police Bldg. Bond Issue, Florissant, 1980. Recipient Woman of Achievement award Florissant Bus. and Profl. Women, 1979; Inst. Orgn. Mgmt. scholar C. of C., Jefferson City, Mo., 1980. Mem. Lancaster Woman's Club., Wildflower Preservation Found. (bd. dirs., treas. 1991—), League Calif. State Park Non-Profit Orgns. (bd. dirs., sec. 1994-98). Roman Catholic. Avocations: bird watching, gardening, golf, reading, genealogy. Office: PO Box 1408 Lancaster CA 93584-1408

ROTHSCHILD, JOHN D., art dealer; b. Chgo., June 22, 1940. BS, MIT, 1962; MBA, Columbia U., 1964. Acct. mgr. Young and Rubican, Inc., N.Y.C., 1964-77; prin., owner Rothschild Fine Arts, Inc., N.Y.C., 1977—, AZau, Paradise Valley, Ariz., 1996—, Vanier Fine Art, Ltd., Scottsdale, Ariz., 1997—. Author: (poetry) Focus on Poetry, 1996, Danger: Poets at Play, 1998. Home: 5346 E Sapphire Ln Scottsdale AZ 85253-2531

ROTHSCHILD, TOBY JAMES, lawyer; b. Los Angeles, Sept. 1, 1944; s. Otto and Sylvia (Singer) R.; m. Elena L. Hyman, Aug. 6, 1967; children: Marnie, Dana. BA, San Francisco State U., 1966; JD, UCLA, 1969. Bar: Calif. 1970, U.S. Dist. Ct. (cen. dist.) Calif. 1970, U.S. Ct. Appeals (9th cir.) 1971, U.S. Supreme Ct. 1973. Staff atty. Los Angeles Neighborhood Legal Service, 1969-71; staff atty. Legal Aid Found., Long Beach, Calif., 1971-73, exec. dir., 1973—; chmn. State Bar Com. on Adminstrn. Justice, 1986-87, vice chmn. Conf. Dels., 1995-96. Author: Automobile Transactions, 1981; contbr. articles to profl. jours. Bd. dirs., vice chmn. Western Ctr. on Law and Poverty, 1973-88; v.p. Long Beach Jewish Community Ctr., 1983-88, pres. 1989-90. Recipient Lauren Miller Legal Svcs. award State Bar Calif, 1995. Mem. Am. Arbitration Assn., Long Beach Bar Assn. (pres. 1993), L.A. County Bar Assn. (bd. govs. 1997—). Office: Legal Aid Found of Long Beach 110 Pine Ave Ste 420 Long Beach CA 90802-4421

ROTHSTEIN, BARBARA JACOBS, federal judge; b. Bklyn., Feb. 3, 1939; d. Solomon and Pauline Jacobs; m. Ted L. Rothstein, Dec. 28, 1968; 1 child, Daniel. B.A., Cornell U., 1960; LL.B., Harvard U., 1966. Bar: Mass. 1966, Wash. 1969, U.S. Ct. Appeals (9th cir.) 1977, U.S. Dist. Ct. (we. dist.) Wash. 1971, U.S. Supreme Ct. 1975. Pvt. practice law Boston, 1966-68; asst. atty. gen. State of Wash., 1968-77; judge Superior Ct., Seattle, 1977-80; judge Fed. Dist. Ct. Western Wash., Seattle, 1980—, chief judge, 1987-94; faculty Law Sch. U. Wash., 1975-77, Hastings Inst. Trial Advocacy, 1977, N.W. Inst. Trial Advocacy, 1979—; mem. state-fed. com. U.S. Jud. Conf., chair subcom. on health reform. Recipient Matrix Table Women of Yr. award Women in Communication, Judge of the Yr. award Fed. Bar Assn., 1989; King County Wash. Women Lawyers Vanguard Honor, 1995. Mem. ABA (jud. sect.), Am. Judicature Soc., Nat. Assn. Women Judges, Fellows of the Am. Bar, Wash. State Bar Assn., U.S. Jud. Conf. (state-fed. com., health reform subcom.), Phi Beta Kappa, Phi Kappa Phi. Office: US Dist Ct 705 US Courthouse 1010 5th Ave Ste 215 Seattle WA 98104-1189

ROTHSTEIN, MARJORIE HOPE, sculptor, landscape and environmental designer; b. N.Y.C., July 4, 1952; d. Nathan and Helen (Jacobs) R. BS in Fine Arts, NYU, 1974; student, Boston U., 1970-72; Cert. Environ. and Interior Design, UCLA, 1983. Solo shows include: The Sabra Soc., Beverly Hills, Calif., 1992, The Sports Club L.A., 1991, Neiman Marcus, Beverly Hills, 1991, The Regency Club, Westwood, Calif., 1991, Couturier Gallery, L.A., 1989, De Cesare Estate, Beverly Hills, 1988, Whitestone Savs. and Loan, Great Neck, L.I., 1974; group exhbns. include: The Posner Gallery, Santa Monica, Calif., 1995, Benefit for the Music Ctr., L.A., 1994, Beverly [illegible] Ranch, Montecito, Calif., Sycamore Studio Group Show, Fed. Bldg., Westwood, Calif., 1990, others; work collected in Continental Devel. of Calif., Hotels of L'Ermitage Internat., L.A., Ashkenazy Galleries, West Hol- [illegible] tinental, Yokohama, Japan, others; publs. include Calif. Art Rev., 1989-91.

ROTHWELL, ELAINE B., artist; b. Mpls., May 8, 1926; d. Frederick Roscoe and Stella Frances (LaVallee) Bartholomew; m. William Stanley Rothwell, May 10, 1946; children: Suzanne, Amy (Mrs. Donald Verrett), Wendy, Bart. BA in Fine Art, San Jose State U., 1966; pvt. study, Woodbury Graphic Studio, Los Altos, Calif., 1975-76, Amaranth Intaglio Workshop, Los Altos, 1985. *Rothwell was first known for her series of 14 etchings using chess imagery and chess positions. This series was featured in a cover story in Chess Life Magazine in March 1979. Her 1983 "Spiritus Loci" series of eight etchings forms a cartographical puzzle. In her three latest series, "Art History Mysteries"1994, "Mad Meg Amok" 1997, and "Inklings" 1998, she has arranged familiar images from art history in new settings. By means of figure ground ambiguities and enigmatic images, Rothwell's etchings baffle the viewers' eyes with games of visual discovery.* One woman shows at Triton Mus. Art, Santa Clara, Calif., 1976, Palo Alto (Calif.) Civic Ctr., 1977, Stanford (Calif.) Art Spaces, Stanford U., 1985, 88, 89, West Valley Art Mus., Surprise, Ariz., 1996; exhibited in group shows at Carnegie Art Ctr., North Tonawanda, N.Y., 1995, 96, N.J. Ctr. for Visual Arts Internat., Summit, N.J., 1997, 98, Brand Libr. and Art Ctr., Glendale, Calif., 1996, Internat. Exhbn. Art League of Manatee County, Fla., 1996 (Merit award), Nat. Soc. Artists, 1997 (Philip J. Paratore Meml. award), Am. Color Print Soc. (Hugh Hutton Meml. award for Intaglio 1997), Grand Exhbn. Nat. Competition, Akron, Ohio, 1998, Printwork'98, Barrett House, Poughkeepsie, N.Y., 1998, 73d Ann. Internat. Print Competition/The Print Ctr., Phila., 1999, others; represented in permanent collections at Newberry Libr., Chgo., Triton Mu. Art, Santa Clara, Calif., West Valley Art Mus., Brand Libr. Art Ctr., Glendale, Calif. Mem. Triton Mus. Art, Nat. Mus. Women in Arts (charter), Am. Color Print Soc., Arts Coun. Placer County, Gallery 9 (Los Altos, Calif., treas. 1973-93), Gallery II (Grass Valley, Calif.). Home: 343 S Gordon Way Los Altos CA 94022-3738 Office: Rothwell Graphic Studio 343 S Gordon Way Los Altos CA 94022-3738

ROTTER, JEROME ISRAEL, medical geneticist; b. L.A., Feb. 24, 1949; s. Leonard L. and Jeanette (Kronenfeld) R.; m. Deborah Tofield, July 14, 1970; children: Jonathan Moshe, Amy Esther, Samuel Alexander. BS, UCLA, 1969, MD, 1973. Intern Harbor-UCLA Med. Ctr., Torrance, Calif., 1973-74; fellow in med. genetics Harbor-UCLA Med. Ctr., Torrance, 1975-78, asst. research pediatrician, 1978-79, faculty div. med. genetics, 1978-86; resident in medicine Wadsworth VA Hosp., Los Angeles, 1974-75; asst. prof. medicine and pediatrics Sch. Medicine UCLA, 1979-83, assoc. prof. Sch. Medicine, 1983-87, prof. Sch. Medicine, 1987—; dir. divsn. med. genetics and co. dir. med. genetics birth defect ctr. Cedars-Sinai Med. Ctr., 1986—, assoc. dir. hypertension ctr., 1996—; key investigator Ctr. for Ulcer Rsch. and Edn., L.A., 1980-89; dir. genetic epidemiology core Ctr. for Study of Inflammatory Bowel Disease, Torrance, 1985-91; assoc. dir. Cedars-Sinai Inflammatory Bowel Disease Ctr., L.A., 1992—; dir. Stuart Found. CSMC Common Disease Risk Assessment Ctr., 1986-96; dir. genetic epidemiology core project molecular biology of arteriosclerosis UCLA, 1987—. Bd. govs. Cedars-Sinai, chair med. genetics, 1990—. Recipient Regents scholarship UCLA, 1966-73; recipient Richard Weitzman award Harbor-UCLA, 1983, Ross award Western Soc. for Pediatric Rsch., 1985. Mem. Am. Heart Assn., Am. Soc. Human Genetics, Am. Gastroent. Assn., Am. Diabetes Assn., Soc. for Pediatric Research, Western Soc. for Clin. Investigation (mem. council 1985-88), Am. Fedn. for Med. Rsch., Western Assn. Physicians, Am. Soc. for Clin. Investigation, Am. Assn. Physicians. Jewish. Avocations: reading, racquetball. Office: Cedars-Sinai Med Ctr Div Med Genetics 8700 Beverly Blvd Los Angeles CA 90048-1865

ROTZIEN, FREDERICK WILLIAM, III, marketing executive; b. Portland, Oreg., Aug. 9, 1944; s. Frederick William Jr. and Vilma E. (Brandon) R.; m. Yvonne Miller, June 12, 1975 (div. Aug. 1979). Student, Clark Coll. Mktg. pres. Rotzien and Assocs., Portland, 1970 85; mktg. exec. Heartland Farms, Portland, 1985-88; mfg./mktg. pres. Blue Ribbon Market, Portland, 1985-90; mfg. pres. Probe Electronics, Portland, 1985-90; mktg. exec. Adventure Mktg., Portland, 1990-94, Am. Elec. Motorcycle, Portland, 1994—. Author, editor: World Chart of History, 1988; author: Step by Step Tobacco Guide, 1988. Pres. Oreg. chpt. Young Am. Freedom Portland, 1962, Portland Young Reps., 1968, Oreg. Young Reps., Portland, 1969. Mem. Am. Mktg. Assn. Lutheran. Avocations: fishing, politics, reading, gardening. Home: 13005 NE Broadway St Portland OR 97230-2262

ROUSE, DELMAR LEON, school principal; b. Guthrie, Okla., June 30, 1941; s. Richard Wayne and Vera Belle (Harman) R.; m. Phyllis Evelyn Duffy, June 14, 1964; 1 child, Jeffrey Wayne. BA in Edn., Adams State Coll., 1976; MA in Edn. Leadership, U. Colo., 1993. Lic. prin., Colo. Enlisted U.S. Army, 1959, advanced through grades to maj., ret., 1991; asst. prin. Lamar (Colo.) Sch. Dist., 1994-96, Salida (Colo.) Sch. Dist., 1996—. Mem. Phi Delta Kappa. Avocations: photography, video, bow hunting, computers. Office: Longfellow Elem 350 W 8th St Salida CO 81201-1947

ROUSH, DOROTHY EVELYN, medical laboratory educator, consultant; b. Flatwoods, Ky., July 16, 1930; d. William Arch and Mary Jane (Frasure) Salyers; m. Gilbert Riley Bush, Aug. 26, 1951 (div. 1972); m. Virgil Bernard Roush, Nov. 18, 1972. Med. tech. degree, Clin. Lab., Mt. Vernon, Ohio, 1953; student, Ohio State U., 1967-72. Registered med. tech. Med. tech. Hosp. & Tb Hosp., Newark, Ohio, 1953-60; office nurse various physicians, Newark and Columbus, Ohio and Seattle, 1960-93; nursing home coord. Med. Lab., Seattle, 1980-89; sr. phlebotomist Roche BioMed. Lab., Burlington, N.C., 1990-95; nurse, phlebotomist ARC Blood Program, Columbus, Ohio, 1961-72; instr. in field; cons. in field. Contbr. articles to profl. jours. Vol. ARC, 1957-72, Boulder (Colo.) County Foster Parents, 1976, Cath. Shared Missions, Seattle, 1987. Recipient Appreciation award Gt. Brit. Red Cross Nursing Svc., 1969, Internat. Cancer Congress, 1982. Mem. Am. Assn. Med. Assts., Am. Med. Techs. (chairperson com., sci. chairperson Ariz. chpt., expert adhoc rev. com. 1994-95, Disting. Achievement award 1991), Wash. State Soc. Am. Tech. (sec., v.p., Tech. of Yr. 1989, 90), Am. Legion Aux. (pres.). Roman Catholic. Avocations: reading, writing poetry, travelling, golfing, tennis. Home and Office: 18002 N Hyacinth Dr Sun City West AZ 85375-5348

ROVEN, ALFRED NATHAN, surgeon; b. Czechoslovakia, Apr. 6, 1947; came to the U.S., 1949.; BA in Psychology, Calif. State U., Northridge, 1969; MD, U. So. Calif., 1977. Diplomate Am. Bd. Plastic and Reconstructive Surgery, Am. Bd. Otolaryngology. Resident in otolaryngology U. So. Calif., 1977-82; clin. chief plastic surgery Cedars Sinai Med. Ctr., L.A., 1989-91; resident in plastic and reconstructive surgery U. N.C., 1982-84; clin. chief burns Cedars Sinai Med. Ctr., L.A., 1990-92; clin. chief hands Cedars Sinai Med. Ctr., 1990-92; qualified med. examiner State of Calif., 1985. Contbr. articles to profl. jours. Physician L.A. Free Clinic, 1995—. Avocations: reading, computers. Office: 444 S San Vicente Blvd Ste 600 Los Angeles CA 90048-4171

ROVIRA, LUIS DARIO, state supreme court justice; b. San Juan, P.R., Sept. 8, 1923; s. Peter S. and Mae (Morris) R.; m. Lois Ann Thau, June 25, 1966; children—Douglas, Merilyn. B.A., U. Colo., 1948, LL.B., 1950. Bar: Colo. 1950. Justice Colo. Supreme Ct., Denver, 1979-95, chief justice, 1990-95, ret., 1995; mem. Pres.'s Com. on Mental Retardation, 1970-71; chmn. State Health Facilities Council, 1967-76. Bd. dirs Children's Hosp.; trustee Temple Buell Found., Denver Found., Harry S. Truman Scholarship Found. With AUS, 1943-46. Mem. ABA, Colo. Bar Assn., Denver Bar Assn. (pres. 1970-71), Colo. Assn. Retarded Children (pres. 1968-70), Alpha Tau Omega, Phi Alpha Delta. Clubs: Athletic (Denver), Country (Denver). Home: 4810 E 6th Ave Denver CO 80220-5137

ROWAN, RONALD THOMAS, lawyer; b. Bozeman, Mont., Nov. 6, 1941; s. Lawrence Eugene and Florence M.; m. Katherine Terrell Sponenberg, Sept. 4, 1964; children: Heather, Nicholaus, Matthew. BA, Wichita U., 1964; JD, U. Denver, 1969. Bar: Colo. 1969, U.S. Dist. Ct. Colo. 1969. Asst. city atty. City of Colorado Springs, Colo., 1969-71; asst. dist. atty. 4th Jud. Dist., Colorado Springs, 1971-79; gen. counsel U.S. Olympic Com., Colorado Springs, 1979—, dir. legal affairs, 1986—. Past chmn. CSC, Colorado Springs, 1975—; past chmn. Criminal Justice Adv. Bd., 1983—; past chmn. El Paso Criminal Justice Adv. Com.; bd. dirs. Crimestoppers, 1982-87, past pres. 1985-87, Internat. Anti-counterfeiting Coalition; chmn. Community Corrections Bd., 1981, 86, 87. Mem. ABA, Colo. Bar Assn., El Paso County Trial Lawyers (pres. 1972), El Paso County Bar Assn., U. Denver Law Alumni (chmn.), Colo. Trial Lawyers Assn., Pikes Peak or Bust Rodeo Assn. (Ramrod 1989). Republican. Roman Catholic. Home: 215 Ridge Rd Colorado Springs CO 80904-1460 Office: US Olympic Com One Olympic Plz Colorado Springs CO 80909

ROWE, CARL OSBORN, business consultant; b. Colorado Springs, Colo., Feb. 3, 1944; s. Prentiss Eldon and Jo Ann (Osborn) R.; m. Dale Robin Oren, Apr. 12, 1984; 1 child, Stefanie Osborn. BA in Govt. cum laude, George Mason U., 1972; M Urban Affairs, Va. Poly. Inst. and State U., 1976. Cert. pub. housing mgr. Spl. clk. FBI, Washington, 1968-71; mgmt. analyst ICC, Washington, 1972-75; dir. policy and mgmt. U.S. Bur. Reclamation, Washington, 1975-82; exec. dir. City of Las Vegas Housing Authority, 1990-94; pres. Rowe Bus. Consulting, Las Vegas, Nev., 1982-90, 94-97; exec. dir. So. Nev. Housing Corp., 1994-95; assoc. Success Strategies, Las Vegas, 1995-96; dir. orgn. and mgmt. devel. Fair, Anderson and Langerman, CPAs, Las Vegas, 1997—; bd. dirs. Flowtronics, Inc., Phoenix, Sportstech, Inc., Scottsdale, Ariz., MSP Sys., Inc., Scottsdale; interim dir. Las Vegas-Clark County Libr. Dist. Columnist Las Vegas Bus. Press, 1989-90, 94-96. Exec. dir. So. Nev. Housing Corp., So. Nev. Reinvestment and Affordable Housing Com.; founding bd. dirs., CEO Family Cabinet of So. Nev., Affordable Housing Inst. So. Nev.; bd. dirs. Opportunity Village, LLV Alumni Found.; mem. exec. bd. Nat. Assn. Housing and Redevel. Ofcls. Pacific S.W. Regional Conf., Oasis So. Nev. Cmty. Svc. Guild, Las Vegas Cmty. Empowerment Commn.; mem. adv. bd. Cmty. Food Bank Clark County, Clark County Sch. Dist. CHOICES program. Decorated USAF Commendation medal; named one of Top 50 over 50 in Las Vegas, Prime Mag. Mem. Am. Mgmt. Assn., Am. Soc. Pub. Adminstrn. (mem. governing coun., chair productivity and ptnrships. with govt. com.), Nat. Assn. Housing and Redevel. Ofcls. (mem. exec. bd.), Pub. Housing Authorities Dirs. Assn. (mem. exec. bd.), No. Calif./Nev. Exec. Dirs. Assn. (mem. exec. bd.), Leadership Las Vegas, Las Vegas C. of C. (mem. bus. a.m. com.), LLV Alumni Found. (pres.), Phi Theta Kappa. Avocations: reading, home improvement, music, cooking, physical fitness. Office: Fair Anderson and Langerman CPAs 3811 W Charleston Blvd Ste 110 Las Vegas NV 89102-1846

ROWE, DAVID MUMFORD, commercial bank officer; b. Midland, Mich., July 10, 1945; s. Loyd Harold and Olive Louisa (Mumford) R.; m. Lynne Diane Elden, June 17, 1967 (div. Dec. 27, 1995); children: Abigail Lynne, Courtney Anne, Paul David; m. Marilynn Skinner, May 4, 1996. BA, Carleton Coll., 1967; MBA, Wharton Grad. Sch. Mgmt., Phila., 1968; PhD, U. Pa., 1977. Pres., exec. dir. Wharton EFA, Inc., Phila., 1973-76, 77-79; prin. analyst Congl. Budget Office, Washington, 1976-77; exec. v.p., sr. v.p., v.p. Townsend Greenspan & Co., N.Y.C., 1979-86; chief fin. officer Security Pacific Security Inc., N.Y.C., 1989-90; v.p. Security Pacific Bank, N.Y.C., L.A., 1986-89, 90-92; from v.p. to sr. v.p. Bank of Am., San Francisco, 1992—. Treas. Episcopal Diocese L.I., Garden City, N.Y., 1988-90. Republican. Avocations: reading, history, cooking. Office: Bank of Am 555 California St # 11013 San Francisco CA 94104-1502

ROWE, ELIZABETH ANN, artist; b. Des Moines, Mar. 5, 1970; d. Walter Frank and Patricia Ann (Kroll) Kreimeyer; m. Kenneth Alan Rowe, July 10, 1993. BFA, U. No. Iowa, 1993; MFA, Syracuse U., 1996. Transition specialist Junction City (Oreg.) H.S., 1996-97; asst. prof. of art Truman State U., Kirksville, Mo., 1997-98; vis. prof. of art U. Ala., Tuscaloosa, 1996, 97. Artist: Laverne Krause Gallery, 1998, Foto Cir. Gallery, 1998.

ROWE, JAMES ARNOLD, retired education administrator, real estate agent; b. Washington, Ohio, June 14, 1924; s. David Walter and Ollie (Cook) R.; m. Gloreen Nell, June 25, 1955; children: Shelley Marie Fanning, Jeffrey James, Tuio Alph. BS, Cedarville Coll., 1949; MA, U. Redlands, 1936; EdD, U. So. Calif., 1969. Tchr. Mira Loma (Calif.) Sch. Dist., 1948-55; supt. Pedley (Calif.) Sch. Dist., 1955-64; dir. edn. Riverside (Calif.) County Schs., 1964-67; assoc. supt. Santa Barbara (Calif.) County Sch. Dist., 1962-83; lobbyist Kern County Supt., Bakersfield, Calif., 1984-95; stock broker Robert Thomas Securities, Bakersfield, Calif., 1984-98; real estate agt. Century 21, Santa Barbara, Calif., 1997-98. Vol. YMCA, Riverside (Calif.), 1952-65, ARC, Riverside, 1955-65, PTA Pedley (Calif.) Sch. Dist., 1955-65. Republican. Avocations: basketball, running, hiking, back packing, sports. Home: 5365 Vineyard Rd Santa Barbara CA 93111-1116

ROWE, MARJORIE DOUGLAS, retired social services administrator; b. Bklyn., July 29, 1912; d. Herbert Lynn and Mary Manson (Hall) Douglas; m. Richard Daniel Rowe, July 29, 1937 (dec.); 1 child, Richard Douglas. AB cum laude, Whitman Coll., 1933; MS in Social Adminstrn., Case Western Res. U., 1936. Caseworker Children's Svcs., Cleve., 1933-36, supr., 1937-39; dir. Adoption Svc. Bur., Cleve., 1940-41; social work supr., psychiat. social work cons. Ea. State Hosp., Medical Lake, Wash., 1962-67; dir. social svcs. Interlake Sch.for Developmentally Disabled, Medical Lake, 1967-74, supt., 1975-82; retired, 1982. Pres. chpt. R.P.E.O., Spokane, Wash., 1949, Spokane Alumnae chpt. Delta Delta Delta, 1955-57; chpt. mem. ARC, Orofino, Idaho, 1941-45, Orofino chpt. chmn., 1945-46, sec. Idaho state chpt. AAUW, 1945-46. Mem. Am. Assn. for Mental Deficiency (region I chmn. 1976-77, social work chmn. 1971-73), NASW (gold card mem.), P.E.O. (pres. Spokane Reciprocity 1950), Acad. Cert. Social Workers, Spokane Women of Rotary (pres. 1960-61), Phi Beta Kappa, Delta Sigma Rho, Mortar Bd. Episcopalian. Avocations: local museum volunteer, traveling, antiques, lake cabin activities. Home: 946 E Thurston Ave Spokane WA 99203-2948

ROWE, MARY SUE, accounting executive; b. Melrose, Kans., Aug. 31, 1940; d. Gene and Carmen (Glidewell) Woffard; m. Edward Rowe, Nov. 27, 1985; children from previous marriage: Denise, Dynell, Dalene, Denette. Student, MTI Bus. Coll., 1968, Calif. State U., Fullerton, 1969, Broome (N.Y.) Community Coll., 1974-76; cert. Sch. Bus. Mgmt., Calif. State U., San Bernardino, 1986. Variou bookkeeping and secretarial, 1968-76; asst. mgr., acct. RM Dean Contracting, Chenango Forks, N.Y., 1976-80; acctg. asst. Hemet (Calif.) Unified Sch. Dist., 1981-86; dir. acctg. Desert Sands Unified Sch. Dist., Indio, Calif., 1986-91; bus. svcs. cons. ednl. div. Vicenti, Lloyd & Stutzman, CPA, La Verne, Calif., 1991-97; sch. bus. cons., computer trainer Hemet, Calif., 1997—. Bd. dirs. Family Svcs. Assn., Hemet, 1982-83, PTA Officer, 1993-95. Mem. NAFE, Calif. Assn. Sch. Bus. Ofcls. (acctg. com., R*D com., vice chmn. 1988-90, chmn. 1990-91, state acctg. adv. com. 1990-92), Riverside Assn. Chief Accts. (co-chmn. 1986-88), Coalition for Adequate Sch. Housing. Republican. Home and Office: 4981 Vailwood Dr Hemet CA 92544-7819

ROWE, PATRICIA GENE, elementary education educator, recreation director; b. Elko, Nev., Feb. 2, 1941; d. William Hamilton and Evelyn Merle (Raine) Hoysted; m. James Bartell, Aug. 18, 1962; 1 child, Loralee Elaine Rowe Lynch. BS in Edn., U. Nev., Reno, 1964, MEd, 1976. Cert. reading specialist, Nev. Tchr. 2d grade Washoe County Sch. Dist., Reno, 1963-64; tchr. 1st grade Pershing County Sch. Dist., Lovelock, Nev., 1965—; mem. state bd. dirs. NV 2000, State Dept., Carson City, Nev., 1996—; mem. state and sch. panel Chpt. I Sch. Improvement Team; Mega-Skills trainer, Lovelock, 1994—; state chmn. Milken Nev. Educator awards, 1994-95. Chair tourism and recreation Silver Star Cmtys. program Office of Econ. Devel., Lovelock; co-founder, coach Lovelock Swim Team, 1975—; co-founder, mem. Lovelock Frontier Days Com., 1968—; leader, past pres. leaders coun. 4-H; founder Santa for Srs. Program, 1985—; unit pres. Cancer Soc.; co-chair Easter Seals; chmn. Pershing County Drug Task Force; pres. Altar Soc. Recipient Milken Educator awad Milken Found., 1989, Outstanding Nev. Educator Cadre award Nev. State Dept. Edn., 1997, Nat. Tchrs. Forum award State Dept. Edn., 1996; named Tchr. of Yr., Carson City, 1982-83. Mem. NEA, Nev. State Edn. Assn., Pershing County Classrm. Tchrs. (sec., v.p., pres.), Nat. State Tchrs. of Yr. (sec., v.p., pres.), Kappa Delta Pi, Beta Sigma Phi. Democrat. Roman Catholic. Avocations: children, swimming, photography, travel. Home: PO Box 102 Lovelock NV 89419-0102

ROWE, RICHARD, physician, consultant; b. Boston, Jan. 24, 1952; s. Carter and Mary Rowe; m. Jude Rowe; children: Allison, Kate. BA, U. N.C., 1974; MD, Harvard U., 1979, MPH, 1981. Diplomate Am. Bd. Anesthesiology. Physician Children's Hosp. Oakland, Calif., 1986—; cons. Nellor, Pleasantown, Calif., 1986—, HT Med., Rockville, Md., 1998. Creator computer simulation Virtual Reality Pediat. Bronchoscopy, 1998; contbr. articles to profl. jours. Office: Childrens Hosp Oakland 747 52d St Oakland CA 94611

ROWE, SANDRA MIMS, newspaper editor; b. Charlotte, N.C., May 26, 1948; d. David Lathan and Shirley (Stovall) Mims; m. Gerard Paul Rowe, June 5, 1971; children: Mims Elizabeth, Sarah Stovall. BA, East Carolina U., Greenville, N.C., 1970; postgrad., Harvard U., 1991. Reporter to asst. mng. editor The Ledger-Star, Norfolk, Va., 1971-80, mng. editor, 1980-82; mng. editor The Virginian-Pilot and The Ledger Star, Norfolk, Va., 1982-84, exec. editor, 1984-86, v.p., exec. editor, 1986-93; editor The Oregonian, Portland, 1993—; mem. Pulitzer Prize Bd., 1994—. Bd. visitors James Madison U., Harrisonburg, VA., 1991-95. Named Woman of Yr. Outstanding Profl. Women of Hampton Rds., 1987. Mem. Am. Soc. Newspaper Editors (pres., bd. dirs. 1992—), Va. Press Assn. (bd. dirs. 1985-93). Episcopalian. Office: The Oregonian 1320 SW Broadway Portland OR 97201-3499

ROWEN, MARSHALL, radiologist; b. Chgo.; s. Harry and Dorothy (Kasnow) R.; m. Helen Lee Friedman, Apr. 5, 1952; children: Eric, Scott, Mark. AB in Chemistry with highest honors, U. Ill., Urbana, 1951; MD with honors, U. Ill., Chgo., 1954, MS in Internal Medicine, 1954. Diplomate Am. Bd. Radiology. Intern Long Beach (Calif.) VA Hosp., 1955; resident in radiology Los Angeles VA Hosp., 1955-58; practice medicine specializing in radiology Orange, Calif., 1960—; chmn. bd. dirs. Moran, Rowen and Dorsey, Inc., Radiologists, 1969—; asst. radiologist L.A. Children's Hosp., 1958; assoc. radiologist Valley Presbyn. Hosp., Van Nuys, Calif., 1960; dir. dept. radiology St. Joseph Hosp., Orange, 1961—, v.p. staff, 1972; dir. dept. radiology Children's Hosp. Orange County, 1964—, chief staff, 1977-78, v.p., 1978-83, v.p., trustee, 1990-91, 92-95; asst. clin. prof. radiology U. Calif., Irvine, 1967-70, assoc. clin. prof., 1979-72, clin. prof. radiology and pediatrics, 1976-98, pres. clin. faculty assn., 1980-81; trustee Choc. Padrinos; sec. Choco Health Svcs., 1987-89, v.p., 1990-93, trustee, 1995—; trustee Found. Med. Care Orange County, 1972-76, Calif. Commn. Adminstrn. Svcs. Hosp., 1975-79, Profl. Practice Systems, 1990-92, Med. Specialty Mgrs., 1990—, St. Joseph Med. Corp., 1993-98; v.p. Found. Med. Care Children's Hosp., 1988-89; v.p., sr. v.p., bd. dirs. St. Joseph Med. Corp. IPA, 1995-98; bd. dirs. Orange Coast Managed Care Svcs., 1995-98, sr. v.p., 1995-98, Paragon Med. Imaging, 1993—, Calif. Managed Imaging, 1994—, Alliance Premier Hosps., 1995-96; chmn. bd. dirs. Children's Healthcare of Calif., 1995-99; corp. mem. Blue Shield Calif., 1995-99; mem. physician's rev. com. Blue Cross Calif., 1996-99. Mem. editorial bd. Western Jour. Medicine; contbr. articles to med. jours. Founder Orange County Performing Arts Ctr., mem. Laguna Art Mus., Laguna Festival of Arts, Opera Pacific, S. Coast Reportory, Am. Ballet Theater, World Affairs Council. Served to capt. M.C., U.S. Army, 1958-60. Recipient Rea sr. med. prize U. Ill, 1953; William Cook scholar U. Ill., 1951, Friend of Children award Children's Hosp. Guild, 1995, Charley award Children's Hosp., 1996. Fellow Am. Coll. Radiology; mem. AMA, Am. Heart Assn., Soc. Nuclear Medicine (trustee 1961-62), Orange County Radiol. Soc. (pres. 1968-69), Calif. Radiol. Soc. (pres. 1978-79), Radiol. Soc. So. Calif. (pres. 1976), Pacific Coast Pediatric Radiologists Assn. (pres. 1971), Soc. Pediatric Radiology, Calif. Med. Assn. (chmn. sect. on radiology 1978-79), Orange County Med. Assn. (chmn. UCI liaison com. 1976-78), Cardioradiology Soc. So. Calif., Radiol. Soc. N.Am., Am. Roentgen Ray Soc., Am. Coll. Physician Execs., Soc. Chmn. Radiologists Children Hosp., Center Club, Spectrum Club, Phi Beta Kappa, Phi Eta Sigma, Omega Beta Phi, Alpha Omega Alpha. Office: 1201 W La Veta Ave Orange CA 92868-4213

ROWEN, MARVIN DAVID, judge; m. Carol L. Rowen; children: Eric V. Rowen, Sheryl Elizabeth Rowen Coughlan, Rachel Rowen Karlsberg, Sarah Jean Rowen Trainin. BS, U. Calif., Los Angeles, 1953, JD, 1956. Bar: Calif. 1957, U.S. Dist. Ct. (ctrl. dist.) Calif. 1957, U.S. Tax Ct. 1976, U.S. Ct. Appeals (2nd dist.), U.S. Supreme Ct. 1984; diplomate Civil Trial Advocacy. Sr. trial deputy dist. attorney L.A. County Dist. Attorney's Office, 1957-62; mem. staff Wyman, Finnell & Rothman, Beverly Hills, Calif., 1962-64; sr. ptr. Levinson, Rowen, Miller & Jacobs, L.A., 1964-84; judge Superior Court of the State of Calif., L.A., 1984—; mem. compensation and retirement com. San Fernando Valley Legal Cmty.; mem. rules com., compensation, benefits and retirement com., bench and bar com., L.A. Superior Ct.; lectr. in field. Contbr. numerous articles to profl. jours. and publs. Adv. council The Clubhouse Children's Mus.; bd. dirs. L.A. Shriners Hosp. for Children, Jewish Home for the Aging of Greater L.A.; mem. Marines' Meml. Assn., San Francisco, L.A. Opera League, L.A. County Mus. of Art, U.S. Holocaust Meml. Mus., Washington, others. With USMCR, 1953-59. Recipient Akiba award B'nai B'rith. Mem. ABA, ATLA, Calif. State Bar Assn., L.A. County Bar Assn., UCLA Law Alumni Assn. (bd. dirs. 1985-88), Calif. Trial Lawyers Assn., Am. Arbitration Assn., Italian Am. Lawyers Assn., Calif. Judges Assn. (mem. compensation and ret. com., exec. bd. 1993-96), Anti-Defamation League (nat. commr.), Nat. Lupus Erythematosus Found. (bd. dirs.), The Marines Meml. Assn., Nat. Parks and Conservation Assn., World Jewish Congress, Internat. Assn. Jewish Lawyers and Jurists, L.A. Opera League, L.A. County Mus. Art, Al Malaikah Shrine Temple, Scottish Rite, Home Lodge, Masons.

ROWLAND, FRANK SHERWOOD, chemistry educator; b. Delaware, Ohio, June 28, 1927; m. Joan Lundberg, 1952; children: Ingrid Drake, Jeffrey Sherwood. AB, Ohio Wesleyan U., 1948; MS, U. Chgo., 1951, PhD, 1952, DSc (hon.), 1989; DSc (hon.), Duke U., 1989, Whittier Coll., 1989, Princeton U., 1990, Haverford Coll., 1992, Clark U., 1996, U. East Anglia, 1996; LLD (hon.), Ohio Wesleyan U., 1989, Simon Fraser U., 1991, U. Calgary, 1997; laurea honoris causa, U. Urbino (Italy), 1998; DSc, Carleton Coll., 1998. Instr. chemistry Princeton (N.J.) U., 1952-56; asst. prof. chemistry U. Kans., 1956-58, assoc. prof. chemistry, 1958-63, prof. chemistry, 1963-64; prof. chemistry U. Calif., Irvine, 1964—, dept. chmn., 1964-70, Aldrich prof. chemistry, 1985-89, Bren prof. chemistry, 1989-94, Bren rsch. prof., 1994—; Humboldt sr. scientist, Fed. Republic of Germany, 1981; chmn. Dahlem (Fed. Republic of Germany) Conf. on Changing Atmosphere, 1987; vis. scientist Japan Soc. for Promotion Sci., 1980; co-dir. western region Nat. Inst. Global Environ. Changes, 1989-93; del. Internat. Coun. Sci. Unions, 1993—; fgn. sec. NAS, 1994—; lectr., cons. in field. Contbr. numerous articles to profl. jours. Mem. ozone commn. Internat. Assn. Meteorology and Atmospheric Physics, 1980-88, hon. life mem., 1996, mem. commn. on atmospheric chemistry and global pollution, 1979-91; mem. acid rain peer rev. panel U.S. Office of Sci. and Tech., Exec. Office of White House, 1982-84; mem. vis. com. Max Planck Insts., Heidelberg and Mainz, Fed. Republic Germany, 1982-96; ozone trends panel mem. NASA, 1986-88; chmn. Gordon Conf. Environ. Scis.-Air, 1987; mem. Calif. Coun. Sci. Tech., 1989-95, Exec. Com. Tyler Prize, 1992—. Recipient numerous awards including John Wiley Jones award Rochester Inst. of Tech., 1975, Disting. Faculty Rsch. award U. Calif., Irvine, 1976, Profl. Achievement award U. Chgo., 1977, Billard award N.Y. Acad. Sci., 1977, Tyler World Prize in Environment Achievement, 1983, Global 500 Roll of Honor for Environ. Achievement UN Environment Program, 1988, Dana award for Pioneering Achievements in Health, 1987, Silver medal Royal Inst. Chemistry, U.K., 1989, Wadsworth award N.Y. State Dept. Health, 1989, medal U. Calif., Irvine, 1989, Japan prize in Environ. Sci., 1989, Dickson prize Carnegie-Mellon U., 1991, Albert Einstein prize of World Cultural Coun., 1994, Nobel Prize in Chemistry, 1995, Alumni medal U. Chgo., 1997, Nevada medal, 1997; Guggenheim fellow, 1962, 74. Fellow AAAS (pres. elect 1991, pres. 1992, chmn. bd. dirs. 1993), Am. Phys. Soc. (Leo Szilard award for Physics in Pub. Interest 1979), Am. Geophys. Union (Roger Revelle medal 1994); mem. NAS (bd. environ. studies and toxicology 1986-91, com. on atmospheric chemistry 1987-89, com. atmospheric scis., solar-terrestial com. 1979-83, co-DATA com. 1977-82, sci. com. on problems environment 1986-89, Infinite Voyage film com. 1988-92, Robertson Meml. lectr. 1993, chmn. com. on internat. orgns. and programs 1993—, chmn. office of internat. affairs 1994—, co-chmn. interacad. panel 1995—), Am. Acad. Arts and Scis., Am. Chem. Soc. (chmn. divsn. nuclear sci. and tech. 1973-74, chmn. divsn. phys. chemistry 1974-75, Orange County award 1975, Tolman medal 1976, Zimmerman award 1980, E.F. Smith lectureship 1980, Environ. Sci. and Tech. award 1983, Esselen award 1987, Peter Debye Phys. Chem. award 1993), Am. Meteorological Soc. (hon.), European Acad. Arts, Scis. and Humanities, Phi Beta Kappa. Home: 4807 Dorchester Rd Corona Del Mar CA 92625-2718 Office: U Calif Irvine Dept of Chemistry 571 Rowland Hall Irvine CA 92697-2025

ROWLAND, PAUL MCDONALD, education educator; b. Waverly, N.Y., Oct. 27, 1948; s. Donald Victor and Edith Irene (McDonald) R.; m. Linda S. Wackwitz (div. Dec. 1993). BA, Rutgers U., 1970, MS, 1979; PhD, N.Mex. State U., 1988. Sci. tchr. South Jefferson Ctrl. Schs., Adams, N.Y., 1973-80; edn. specialist N.Mex. Solar Energy Inst., Las Cruces, 1983-86; asst. prof. sci. edn. East Carolina U., Greenville, N.C., 1988-89; assoc. prof. curriculum

and instrn. No. Ariz. U., Flagstaff, 1989—; adv. bd. Geonauts program No. Ariz U., Flagstaff, 1994-96; dir. No. Ariz. Environ. Edn. Resources Ctr., Flagstaff, 1994—; bd. dirs. Global Network Environ. Edn. Ctrs., Knoxville. Contbr. articles to profl. jours. and books. Dir. Environ. Scis. Day Camp, Flagstaff; bd. dirs. Ariz. Nat. Hist. Assn. Mem. N.Am. Assn. for Environ. Edn., Nat. Assn. for Rsch. in Sci. Teaching, Am. Ednl. Rsch. Assn. Avocations: sea kayaking, landscape design, photography. Home: PO Box 23523 Flagstaff AZ 86002-3523 Office: No Ariz Univ PO Box 5774 Flagstaff AZ 86011

ROWLAND, RUTH GAILEY, retired hospital official; b. Salt Lake City, Dec. 7, 1922; d. Frederick George and Lucy Jane (Hill) N.; m. Joseph David Gailey, Apr. 9, 1942 (dec. July 1984); children: Sherylynne Harris-Roth, Joseph David Jr., Robert Nelson; m. Joseph Brigham Rowland, Oct. 14, 1986. Student, Felt-Tarrant Community Coll., Salt Lake City, 1941-42, U. Utah. Dir. vol. svcs., pub. rels. dir. Lakeview Hosp., Bountiful, Utah, 1961-92; now ret. Mem. Women's State Legis. Coun., Salt Lake City, 1970-92; mem. legis. com. Utah Comprehensive Planning Agy., Salt Lake City; mem. Farmington (Utah) Bd. Health, 1979-85; mem. Davis County Adv. Bd. Volunteerism; mem. social svcs. com. LDS Ch. Recipient Total Citizen award Utah C. of C., 1992. Mem. Assn. Dirs. Vol. Svcs. of Am. Hosp. Assn., Utah Assn. Vol. Auxs. (pres.). Utah Dirs. Vol. Svcs. (pres.); Salt Lake Dental Aux. (pres.), Bountiful C. of C. (bd. dirs. 1975-80), Sorompimists. Republican. Home: 871 S 750 E Bountiful UT 84010-3824

ROY, ARTHUR PUTNAM, lawyer; b. Baton Rouge, Nov. 23, 1940; s. Chalmer John and Elizabeth Putnam (Richards) R.; m. Sara Hinrichsen, Mar. 16, 1963; children: Mary Louise Manchadi, Christine Elizabeth Roy Yoder, Sara Katherine Allex. BS, Iowa State U., 1962; JD, U. Colo., 1969. Bar: Colo., 1969, U.S. Dist. Ct. Colo., 1969, U.S. Ct. Appeals (10th cir.), 1972, U.S. Supreme Ct., 1973. Pvt. practice Ft. Collins, Colo., 1969-70; assoc. counsel State Bd. Agriculture, Ft. Collins, 1970-73; dep. dist. atty. Office of Dist. Atty., Greeley, Colo., 1973-74; pvt. practice Greeley, Colo., 1974-94; judge Colo. Ct. Appeals, Denver, 1994—. Capt. USAR, 1963-74, Vietnam, 1965-66. Mem. ABA, Colo. Bar Assn. (v.p. 1984-85), Weld County Bar Assn. (pres. 1983-84), Greeley Redeye Rotary Club (pres. 1989-90). Republican. Congregational. Home: 1924 19th Ave Greeley CO 80651 Office: Colo Ct Appeals 2 E 14th Ave Denver CO 80203

ROY, CHUNILAL, psychiatrist; b. Digboi, India, Jan. 1, 1935; came to Can., 1967, naturalized, 1975; s. Atikay Bandhu and Nirupama (Devi) R.; m. Elizabeth Ainscow, Apr. 15, 1967; children: Nicholas, Phillip, Charles. MB, BS, Calcutta Med. Coll., India, 1959; diploma in psychol. medicine, Kings Coll., Newcastle-upon-Tyne, Eng., 1963. Intern Middlesborough Gen. Hosp., Eng., 1960-61; jr. hosp. officer St. Luke's Hosp., Middlesborough, Eng., 1961-64, sr. registrar, 1964; sr. hosp. med. officer Parkside Hosp., Macclesfield, Eng., 1964-66; sr. registrar Moorehaven Hosp., Ivybridge, Eng., 1966; reader, head dept. psychiatry Maulana Azad Med. Coll., New Delhi, 1966; sr. med. officer Republic of Ireland, County Louth, 1966; sr. psychiatrist Sask. Dept. Psychiat. Services, Can., 1967-68; regional dir. Swift Current, Can., 1968-71; practice medicine specializing in psychiatry Regina, Sask., Can., 1971-72; founding dir., med. dir. Regional Psychiatry. Ctr., Abbotsford, B.C., Can., 1972-82; with dept. psychiatry Vancouver Gen. Hosp., 1983—; cons. to prison adminstrs.; hon. lectr. psychology and clin. prof. dept. psychiatry U. B.C.; ex-officio mem. Nat. Adv. Com. on Health Care of Prisoners in Can.; cons. psychiatrist Vancouver Hosp.; advisor Asian chpt. Psychosomatic Medicine, World Congress of Law and Medicine, New Delhi, 1985; appointed hon. consul for Burkira Faso, 1997; appointed auditor Med. Svcs. Com. B.C., 1997. Author: (with D.J. West and F.L. Nichols) Understanding Sexual Attacks, 1978, Hopital or Prison Memories; co-author: Oath of Athens, 1979; ; assoc. editor Internat. Jour. Offender Therapy and Comparative Criminology, 1978—; field editor Jour. of Medicine and Law; corr. editor Internat. Jour. Medicine; mem. bd. Internat. Law Medicine, 1979—; mem. editl. rev. bd. Evaluation, 1977—; contbr. articles to profl. jours. Recipient merit awards Dept. Health, Republic of Ireland, 1966, Can. Penitentiary Svc., 1974, Correctional Svcs. Can., 1983, citation by pres. U. B.C., 1983, Latten Sangstand Found. prize, Holland, 1995; knighted by Order of the St. John Ecumenical Found., 1993, Awarded Order of Francisco Fajardo Gov. of Caracas, 1998, Legacy award Vancouver Trave and Conv. Ctr., 1998. Fellow Royal Coll. Psychiatry (Can.), Royal Coll. Psychiatry (Eng.), Pacific Rim Coll. Psychiatrists (founder); mem. World Psychiat. Assn. (sec., vice chmn. forensic psychiatry 1983), World Fedn. Mental Health, Internat. Coun. Prison Med. Svcs. (founding sec.-gen. 1977), Can. Med. Assn., Can. Psychiat. Assn., Internat. Acad. Legal Medicine and Social Medicine, Indian Psychiat. Assn. (life), Asian Physicians and Surgeons Who Work in Can. Prisons (founding pres. 1974), Internat. Found. for Tng. in Penitentiary Medicine and Forensic Psychiatry (founding pres. 1980), World Psychiatry Assn., Australian Acad. Forensic Sci. (corr.), Can. Physicians Interested in South Asia (v.p. 1989, pres. 1990), Internat. Coll. Psychosomatic Medicine (adv. scalian chpt.), Internat. Conf. on Health, Culture and Contemporary Soc. (chief advisor Bombay 1989), World Psyciat. Assn. (vice chmn. forensic psychiat. sect. 1989), World Assn. Health, Culture and Environ. (sec.-gen. 1995, award 1995), Order of St. John (knight 1992), Vancouver MultiCultural Soc. (bd. dirs. 1992-93), B.C. Psychiat. Assn. (pres. 1995-96). Home: 2439 Trinity St, Vancouver, BC Canada V5K 1C9 Office: 1417-750 W Broadway, Vancouver, BC Canada V5Z 1J4

ROY, PATRICK, professional hockey player; b. Quebec City, Que., Can., Oct. 5, 1965. Goaltender Montreal Canadiens, 1984-95, Colo. Avalanche, 1995—; mem. Stanley Cup Championship teams, 1986, 93, 96. Recipient Conn Smythe trophy as playoff MVP, 1986, William M. Jennings trophy 1986-89, 91-92, Trico Goaltender award, 1988-89, 89-90, Georges Vezina trophy, 1988-89, 89-90, 91-92; named to NHL All-Rookie Team, 1985-86, NHL All-Star Second Team, 1987-88, 90-91, NHL All-Star First Team, 1988-89, 89-90, 91-92., Sporting News All-Star Team, 1988-89, 89-90, 91-92. Played in Stanley Cup Championships, 1986, 93. Office: Colo Avalanche 1635 Clay St Denver CO 80204-1743

ROYBAL, DAVID D., electrical engineer; b. San Francisco, Sept. 5, 1947; s. Samuel and Gloria R.; m. Mary C. Cleese, June 27, 1970; children: Jennifer K. Roybal Andrews, Deborah L. Roybal Yong, Jonathan D. Roybal. BSEE, Santa Clara (Calif.) U., 1969. Registered profl. engr., Calif. From sales engr. to fellow application engr. Westinghouse Electric Corp., San Francisco, 1969-90, fellow application engr., 1990-94; fellow application engr. Cutler-Hammer, San Francisco, 1994—. Com. chair Boy Scouts of Am., San Mateo, Calif., 1994—. Mem. Internat. Assn. Elec. Inspectors, Nat. Soc. Profl. Engrs., Nat. Fire Protection Assn., Inst. Elec. Electronic Engrs. Democrat. Roman Catholic. Office: Cutler Hammer 3697 Mt Diablo Blvd Lafayette CA 94549-3745

ROYBAL-ALLARD, LUCILLE, congresswoman; b. Boyle Heights, Calif., June 12, 1941; d. Edward Roybal; m. Edward T. Allard; 4 children. BA, Calif. State U., L.A. Former mem. Calif. State Assembly; mem. 103rd Congress from 33rd Calif. dist., 1993—; mem. Appropriations Com. Office: Ho of Reps 2435 Rayburn Bldg Washington DC 20515-0533

ROYCE, EDWARD R. (ED ROYCE), congressman; b. Los Angeles, Oct. 12, 1951; m. Marie Porter. BA, Calif. State U. Fullerton. Tax mgr. Southwestern Portland Cement Co.; mem. Calif. Senate, 1983-93, 103rd-106th Congress from 39th dist. Calif., 1993—; mem. banking and fin. svcs. com., internat. rels. com.; vice chmn. Public Employment and Retirement Com.; mem. Bus. and Profs. com., Indsl. Rels. com.; legis. author, campaign co-chmn. Proposition 15 Crime Victims/Speedy Trial Initiative; author nation's 1st felony stalking law, bill creating Foster Family Home Ins. Fund, legis. creating foster parent recruitment and tng. program; mem. Banking and Fin. Svcs. Com., Internat. Rels. Com. Named Legis. of Yr. Orange County Rep. Com., 1986, Child Adv. of Yr. Calif. Assn. Svcs. for Children, 1987. Mem. Anaheim C. of C. Republican. Office: US Ho of Reps 1133 Longworth HOB Washington DC 20515-0539*

ROYER, KENNETH WILLIAM, food consultant, business consultant; b. Washington, Aug. 31, 1929; s. Kenneth McL and Anna Carolyn (Raver) R.; m. Joanne Feller, Oct. 2, 1954; children: Jeffrey, Lisa, Victoria, Joanne, Scott. BS, U. Wis., 1950. Pres. Purity Cheese Co., Mayville, Wis., 1966-88, Royer Brands, Mayville, Wis., 1977-87; pres. Enzo Pac, Inc., Sheboygan, Wis., 1988-92; chmn., 1992-97; cons. Phoenix, 1997—; dir. Wiley Products

Inst., Chgo., 1972-76, Newton Mut. Funds, Milw., 1972-92, Wis. Power and Light, Madison, Wis., 1972-74; pres. Nat. Cheese Inst., Chgo., 1973-74. Patentee in field. Founding pres. Lions Club, Mayville, 1958; bd. dirs. Sheboygan City YMCA, 1987-96, John Michael Kohler Art Ctr., Sheboygan, 1993-95. Mem. Ariz. Pres.'s Orgn. (edn. chair 1997-98), Rotary (Mayville pres. 1973). Republican. Methodist. Avocations: tennis, exercise, sailing. Home and Office: 5825 N Echo Canyon Cir Phoenix AZ 85018

ROYLE, ANTHONY WILLIAM, accountant; b. Corona, Calif., Dec. 22, 1956; s. William Lloyd Royle and Patricia Rae (McGahan) Magda; m. Patricia Jean Blaylock, Aug. 13, 1977 (div. Nov. 1983); m. Michell Duke, April 1998; children: Nicholas Anthony, Elizabeth Marie, Michael George. BS in Acctg., Weber State U., 1979. CPA, N.Mex. Sr. tax acct. Fox & Co. CPA, Farmington, N.Mex., 1981-83; tax mgr. Cox & Co. CPA, Farmington, 1983-85; tax supr. Arthur Young, Albuquerque, 1985-87; tax supr., tax mgr. Neff & Co., Albuquerque, 1987-95, tax ptnr., 1995—; advisor for Sound Advice C. of C., Albuquerque, 1996—. With U.S. Army, 1974-76. Mem. AICPA (tax divsn.), N.Mex. Soc. CPA, Constrn. Fin. Mgmt. Assn. (Albuquerque chpt.). Avocations: reading, weight lifting, snow skiing. Office: Neff & Co LLP 7001 Prospect Pl NE Albuquerque NM 87110-4311

ROZARIO, GWENDOLYN MICHELLE, educator; b. San Francisco, Dec. 14, 1954; children: Alicia, Alexander Jr. BA, U. San Francisco, 1976; Master's degree, Coll. Notre Dame, 1991; Doctorate, U. San Francisco, 1995. Lifetime tchg. credential. Tchr. San Francisco Unified Sch. Dist., 1977-81, Hanford (Calif.) Elem., 1981-85, Ravenswood Sch. Dist., East Palo Alto, 1985-89, San Lorenzo (Calif.) Unified Sch. Dist., 1989-92, Madera (Calif.) Unified Sch. Dist., 1992—; instr. Merced (Calif.) C.C., 1994—; grant-writing cons. Gwen's Consulting Firm, Madera. Author: (handbook) An Analysis of the Madera Unified School District New Teacher Induction Program, 1995. Recipient Comty. Svc. award Martin Luther King Found., 1992. Mem. USN Sea Cadet Corp. (ednl. svc. officer 1995—), Phi Delta Kappa. Home: 2340 W Cleveland Ave # 143 Madera CA 93637-8710

ROZGONYI, TIBOR GEORGE, mining engineer; b. Szerencs, Borsod, Hungary, July 10, 1940; arrived in U.S.A., 1977; s. Lajos and Rozalia (Zsugyel) R.; m. Agnes Somkuti; children: David, Stephan. BSc, Eger Tchrs. Coll., Hungary, 1961; BE, ME, Tech. U., Miskolc, Hungary, 1968, D of Tech., 1974. Registered profl. engr., Colo. Asst. prof. U. Tripoli, Libya, 1974-77; assoc. prof. mining engring. N.Mex. Tech., Socorro, 1978-81; prof., dir. rsch. lab. Tex. A&M U., 1981-90; prof., dean engring. U. Wollongong, NSW, Australia, 1990-95; prof., head dept. mining engring. Colo. Sch. Mines, Golden, 1995—; dir. coal & lignite rsch. lab. Tex. A&M U., 1987-90; vis. prof. U. Tex., Austin, 1985-90; bd. dirs. Coop. Rsch. Ctr. on Intelligent Mfg., Australia; cons. in field. Editor Electronic Jour Engring., 1994—. Bd. dirs. Colo. Ctr. Environ. Mgmt., 1996—. Australian Acad. Technol. Scis. & Engring. fellow, 1995. Mem. AIME, Soc. Mech. Engrs., Internat. Rock Mechanics Soc. Roman Catholic. Avocations: fishing, reading, music. Office: Colo Sch Mines 1800 Illinois St Golden CO 80401-1838

RUBELL, JOEL, interior designer; b. N.Y.C., Sept. 1, 1932; s. Albert and Molly (Altschuler) R.; children: David, Jaqueline Rubell Johnson. BS, Adelphi U., 1954. Interior designer pvt. practice, N.Y.C., 1956-76, L.A., 1976—. Columnist, editor, Interior Design, 1973. Mem. Am. Soc. Interior Designers (cert., nat. expo. chmn 1973-75, nat. by-laws com. 1975-76, nat. bd. dirs., 1973-75, N.Y. bd. dirs. 1970-76, v.p., 1975, Presidential citation, 1972, 74, 80, Disting. Svc. award 1972, 75, cert. appreciation L.A., 1978, 80). Avocations: reading, sun, movies, travel, dancing. Home and Office: 1166 Goshen Ave Apt 325 Los Angeles CA 90049

RUBENSTEIN, LEONARD SAMUEL, communications executive, ceramist, painter, sculptor, photographer; b. Rochester, N.Y., Sept. 22, 1918; s. Jacob S. and Zelda H. (Gordon) R.; m. (dec. 1983); children: Carolinda, Eric, Harley. BFA cum laude, Alfred U., 1939; student Case Western Res. U., 1938; postgrad. U. Rochester, 1940-41. Creative dir. Henry Hempstead Advt. Agy., Chgo., 1949-55; v.p., exec. art dir. Clinton E. Frank Advt. Agy., Chgo., 1955-63; v.p., nat. creative dir. Foster & Kleiser divsn. Metromedia, Inc., L.A., 1967-73, v.p. corp. creative cons., Metromedia, Inc. L.A., 1973-88; guest lectr. U. Chgo.; instr. Columbia Coll., Chgo.; past. pres. Art Dirs. Club Chgo. (spl. citation); instr. Fashion Inst., L.A.; lectr. in field. Mem. Soc. Typog. Arts (past dir.), Am. Ceramic Soc. (bd. dirs. So. Calif. chpt. 1998 design chair), Am. Craft Coun., Inst. Outdoor Advt. (mem. past plans bd.), L.A. County Mus. Art, Mus. Contemporary Art of L.A. (charter), Palos Verdes (Calif.) Art Ctr., B'nai B'rith, Phi Epsilon Pi. Author: (with Charles Hardison) Outdoor Advertising; contbr. articles to profl. publs.; one-man show at Calif. Mus. Sci. and Industry, 1970; two-person exhibition of porcelains, Palos Verdes Art Ctr., 1987; participant nat. and regional group shows; creator concept for Smithsonian exhibition Images of China: East and West, 1982; writer-prodr. (ednl. video) Paul Soldner, Thoughts on Creativity, 1989, (video documentary) High-Tech/Low-Tech: The Science and Art of Ceramics, 1994; porcelains in permanent collections. Mem. Am. Ceramic soc. (bd. dirs. So. Calif. design chpt. 1998). Home and Office: 30616 Ganado Dr Rancho Palos Verdes CA 90275-6223

RUBIN, DAVID STUART, curator, art critic; b. Los Angeles, June 18, 1949; s. Allen Morris and Ruth Elinor (Persky) R. A.B. in Philosophy, UCLA, 1972; M.A. in Art History, Harvard U., 1974. Asst. dir. Galleries of The Claremont Colls., 1977-82; asst. prof. art history Scripps Coll., 1977-82; art critic Art in America, N.Y.C., 1981-89; adj. curator San Francisco Mus. Modern Art, San Francisco, 1983-85; dir. exhbns., San Francisco Art Inst., 1983-85; dir. Freedman Gallery, Albright Coll., 1986-90; assoc. dir., chief curator Cleve. Ctr. Contemporary Art, 1990-94; curator 20th Century Art, Phoenix Art Mus., 1994—; guest curator Pacific Nat. Bank, Los Angeles, 1982. Contbg. editor Arts mag., N.Y.C., 1979-81; author exhbn. catalogues Black and White are Colors, 1979, Contemporary Triptychs, 1982, Jay De Feo, 1984, Wally Hedrick, 1985, Concerning the Spiritual, the 80's, 1985, Contemporary Hispanic Shrines, 1989, Cynthia Carlson, 1989, Donald Lipski, 1990, Cruciformed, 1991, Petah Coyne, 1992, old Glory, 1994, It's Only Rock and Roll, 1995, Phoenix Triennial, 1998; contbr. articles to Arts, 1976-80, Art in Am. mag., 1981-89, Artweek, 1978-83. Nat. Endowment Humanities Mus. fellow, 1975-76; S. R. Guggenheim Mus. summer fellow, 1976. Mem. Internat. Assn. Art Critics, Coll. Art Assn. Home: #8 5750 N 10th St Phoenix AZ 85014-2270 Office: Phoenix Art Mus 1625 N Central Ave Phoenix AZ 85004-1685

RUBIN, DIANE MARIE, accountant; b. Seattle, Oct. 26, 1951; d. Ellsworth Sydney and Betty Jane (Krause) Paulson; m. Asher Rubin, Dec. 4, 1982; children: Jacob, Shaina. BA, U. Wash., Seattle, 1973, MBA, 1975. CPA, Calif., Wash. Audit mgr. Price Waterhouse, N.Y.C. and San Francisco, 1975-81; mgr. fin. reporting Fireman's Fund Ins., Novato, Calif., 1981-84; controller Westnet Bank, San Francisco, 1984-85, Paribas Tech., San Francisco, 1985-86; v.p., controller Arthur J. Gallagher & Co., San Francisco, 1986-89; owner Diane M. Rubin, CPA, San Francisco, 1989-96; ptnr. Norogradac & Co., LLP, 1996—; bd. dirs. Audit State Bd.s Accountancy, Mt. Tamalpais Sch., Calif. Bd. Accountancy. Commr. Parks, Open Space & Cultural Svcs. Commn., Marin (Calif.) County, 1991—; bd. dirs. Florence Crittenton Svcs., San Francisco, 1980-89. Mem. AICPAs, Calif. Soc. CPAs, Jr. League of San Francisco. Office: Novogradac & Co LLP 7th Flr 425 Market St Fl 7 San Francisco CA 94105-2406

RUBIN, EDWARD, lawyer; b. Bklyn., Apr. 30, 1912; s. George and Bella (Fishman) R.; m. Nancy Cordner, 1943; children—Laurence D., Peggy Lynn Rubin Ueda. B.A., UCLA, 1933; LL.B., Duke U., 1936. Bar: Calif. 1941, U.S. Supreme Ct. 1941. Assoc. firm Proskauer, Rose, Goetz & Mendelsohn, N.Y.C., 1936-40; mem. firm Mitchell, Silberberg & Knupp, Los Angeles, 1940-42, 91—, now of counsel; mem. atty. Office of Price Adminstrn., Washington, 1942; formerly lectr. comml. law Calif. State Coll., Los Angeles, 1941; formerly lectr. entertainment law U. So. Calif.; mem. nat. panel arbitrators Am. Arbitration assn.; arbitrator Am. Film Market and L.A. County Bar Found.; mem. entertainment law panel So. Calif. ACLU; chmn. sect. on intellectual property World Peace Through Law Center; past past chmn. Los Angeles Internat. Film Festival; trustee UCLA Found.; past mem. performing arts governing body UCLA.; past mem. dean's council

History Mus. Served with Signal Corps U.S. Army, 1942-46. Recipient Profl. Achievement award UCLA, 1978; named Entertainment Lawyer of Yr. for Disting. Svc. Entertainment Field, 1987. Fellow ABA (co-chmn. Calif. fellows ABA Found., past mem. ho. of dels., past chmn. forum com. on entertainment and sports industries, chmn. standing com. on forums 1981-82); mem. Am. Judicature Soc., Los Angeles Copyright Soc., Nat. Conf. Bar Pres., Nat. Council Juvenile Ct. Judges, Nat. Juvenile Ct. Found., State Bar Calif. (pres. 1977, com. of bar examiners 1987-91), Los Angeles County Bar Assn. (trustee 1973-74, mem. sect. on intellectual property and unfair competition, past chmn., mem. 50 yrs. club), Los Angeles County Bar Found., Beverly Hills Bar Assn. (pres. 1971, past pres. found., Disting. Svc. award 1981, Contbn. to entertainment and as Pres. Bar Leadership award, 1987), Order of Coif, Phi Beta Kappa. Clubs: Bruin Hoopsters (past pres., bd. dirs.).

RUBIN, GERROLD ROBERT, advertising executive; b. Evanston, Ill., Mar. 31, 1940; s. Bennie George and Anita (Perich) R.; m. Barbara Ann Nieman, Sept. 5, 1962; children: John, Ann. B.S. in Radio, TV, Film, Northwestern U., 1962. Account exec. Leo Burnett Advt., Chgo., 1962-67; account supr. Leo Burnett Advt., Toronto, Ont., 1967-68, Needham, Harper Steers, Chgo., 1968-73; account dir. Needham, Harper Steers, Los Angeles, 1973-78; mgmt. rep. Needham, Harper & Steers, Chgo., 1978-81; pres., CEO Needham, Harper & Steers, Los Angeles, 1981-86, Rubin, Postaer & Assocs., Santa Monica, Calif., 1986—. Bd. dirs. Country Music Assn., Nashville, 1983—. Presbyterian. Office: Rubin Postaer & Assocs 1333 2nd St Santa Monica CA 90401-1100*

RUBINOFF, M. LAWRENCE, physician and surgeon; b. Detroit, Feb. 24, 1936; s. Charles and Carole Irene Hammond Saslow, June 3, 1960 (div. Apr. 1968); children: Marla Jeanette, Tamara Elise, Danita Beth; m. Virginia Leigh Innes, July 31, 1981 (dec. July 1998); 1 child, Charles Joseph. BS in Math., Wayne State U., 1956; DO, Coll. Osteo. Medicine/Surgery, Des Moines, 1960; MD, U. Calif., Irvine, 1962. Diplomate Am. Bd. Surgery, Am. Bd. Family Practice. Intern Flint (Mich.) Osteo. Hosp., 1960-61; resident in gen. surgery L.A. County Gen. Hosp., L.A., 1961-65; physician and surgeon in pvt. practice Woodland Hills/West Hills, Calif., 1965-85; physician and surgeon Your Family Med. Group, Garden Grove, Calif., 1985-97, Molina Med. Ctrs., Palmdale, Calif., 1997—. Lt. col. USAFR, 1981-91. Mem. AMA, Am. Assn. Physician Specialists, Calif. Med. Assn., L.A. County Med. Assn. Avocations: reading, skiing, movies. Office: 2279 E Palmdale Blvd Ste A Palmdale CA 93550-4909

RUBINSTEIN, ELAINE PERLE, technical writer; b. L.A., Dec. 22, 1953; d. William Crandall and Charlotte Rhoda (Streifer) R.; m. Theodore Perle, June 19, 1983. BA cum laude, Yale U., 1976. Editorial asst. Fawcett Publs., N.Y.C., 1973-74; adminstrv. asst. Japan Calif. Bank, L.A., 1977-78; word processing specialist U. Calif., Irvine, 1979-82; jr. tech. writer Burroughs Corp. (name now Unisys), Mission Viejo, Calif., 1982-85; intermediate tech. writer AST Research, Inc., Irvine, 1985-87; sr. tech. writer Emulex Corp., Costa Mesa, Calif., 1987-91, Printronix Corp., Irvine, 1993—; founder cons. firm P.C. Spectrum Services, Irvine, 1987—. Author computer user and tech. reference manuals, AST Enhanced Graphics Diagnostics Manual, 1986 (Achievement award), Emulex Performance 8000 Ethernet Terminal Server Hardware Installation Manual (Merit award), others; rsch. asst. History of Am. Women Artists, 1984 (ALA award 1982). Mem. NOW, AAUW, Soc. Tech. Communication (Orange County chpt., sec. 1983-84, co-editor newsletter 1984-85, writer 1985—, Disting. Tech. Communication Newsletter award 1985, v.p. membership 1989-90, 90-91), Orange County Yale Club. Democrat. Jewish. Avocations: bicycling, museums, theater. Address: Printronix Corp 17500 Cartwright Rd Irvine CA 92614-5846 Office: Emulex Corp 21485 Oakbrook Mission Viejo CA 92692-3044

RUBIO, ETHEL GRIÑO, architect; b. Manila, Oct. 27, 1965; came to U.S., 1986; d. Armando Lina and Norma Libre (Griño) R. BArch, U. So. Calif., L.A., 1992. Designer Siegel Diamond Architects, L.A., 1992-93; asst. project mgr. HNTB, L.A., 1993-95; planner, designer, owner Ethel G. Rubio, Assoc. AIA, L.A., 1996—; mem. Woodbury U. Archtl. Consultancy Bd., 1996—. Vol. Craft and Folk Art Mus., L.A., 1986—, UNICEF, L.A. Chpt., 1990—, Exceptional Children's Found., L.A., 1992—; assoc. Riordan Vol. Leadership Devel. Program Class 10. mem. AIA (student affairs com. chair 1991-93, assoc. pres. 1994, Landworth Meml. scholarship chair 1994—, Intern Devel. Program chair 1992, program chair 1993, pres. 1996). Democrat. Roman Catholic. Assn. for Women in Arch. (membership chair 1992, program chair 1993, pres. 1996). Democrat. Roman Catholic. Avocations: traveling, event organizing, writing, reading, volunteering.

RUCH, CHARLES P., academic administrator; b. Longbranch, N.J., Mar. 25, 1938; s. Claud C. and Marcella (Pierce) R.; m. Sally Joan Brandenburg, June 18, 1960; children: Cheryl, Charles, Christopher, Cathleen. BA, Coll. of Wooster, 1959; MA, Northwestern U., 1960, PhD, 1966. Counselor, tchr. Evanston (Ill.) Twp. High Sch., 1960-66; asst. prof. U. Pitts., 1966-70, assoc. prof., dept. chmn. 1970-74; assoc. dean sch. edn. Va. Commonwealth U., Richmond, 1974-76, dean sch. edn., 1976-85, interim provost, v.p. 1985-86, provost, v.p., 1986-93; pres. Boise (Idaho) State U., 1993—; cons. various univs., govtl. agys., ednl. founds. Author or co-author over 50 articles, revs., tech. reports. Mem. Am. Psychol. Assn., Am. Ednl. Research Assn., Phi Delta Kappa. Office: Boise State U 1910 University Dr Boise ID 83725-0399

RUCH, MARCELLA JOYCE, retired educator, biographer; b. Brutus, Mich., Sept. 20, 1937; d. Virgil Murray and Grace Milbry (Collier) Wallace; m. Robert Kirkman McMain. Aug. 29, 1956 (div. Aug. 1970); children: Melodie Froom, Kirk McMain, Nancy Hedges, Elizabeth Curran; m. Peter Jerome Ruch, Dec. 22, 1973; children: David, Dan, Michael and Justin Moore Ruch. BS, Western Mich. U., 1964; MA, U. Colo. Colorado Springs, 1973; PhD, U. Colo., Boulder, 1980. Cert. tchr., prin., counselor, Colo. Tchr. Colorado Springs Pub. Schs., 1964-69; supr. child care El Paso County Social Svcs., Colorado Springs, 1970-73; exec. dir. Antlers Day Care Ctr., Colorado Springs, 1973-77, Green Shade Schs., Colorado Springs, 1977-81, Pueblo (Colo.) Toddler Ctr., 1981-83; tchr. Penrose (Colo.) Elem. Sch., 1983-86; adminstrv. intern Cottonwood Elem. Sch., Denver, 1986-87; elem. prin. Simla (Colo.) Pub. Schs., 1987-89; tchr. Colorado Springs Pub. Schs., 1989-97; mem. adv. bd. for early childhood edn. Pikes Peak C.C., Colorado Springs, 1970-75; child care specialist Cmty. Agencies Working Together, Colorado Springs, 1970-75. Author: The Gang of One, 1998. Founder Green Shade Schs., 1977; campaign chair United Way, Canon City, Colo., 1983-84, pres., 1984-85; chair adult coun. St. Paul's United Meth. Ch., 1994-96. Mem. Delta Kappa Gamma (v.p. membership 1994-96), Phi Delta Kappa. Methodist. Avocations: gardening, hiking, reading, camping. Home and Office: 2444 Virgo Dr Colorado Springs CO 80906-0913

RUCHE, TOM, museum official. Pres. Lied Discovery Children's Mus., Las Vegas, Nev. Office: Lied Discovery Childrens Mus 833 Las Vegas Blvd Las Vegas NV 89101*

RUCKER, THOMAS DOUGLAS, purchasing executive; b. Ottumwa, Iowa, Aug. 30, 1926; s. Everett Henry and Harriett Mary (Evans) R.; A.B., Loyola U., 1951; postgrad. St. Patrick's Coll., 1950-52; m. Rita Mary Rommelfanger, Apr. 18, 1953; children—David, Theresa, Martin, Paul. Asst. purchasing agt. Radio TV Supply, Los Angeles, 1952-53; buyer Consol. Western Steel div. U.S. Steel, Commerce, Calif., 1953-64, S.W. Welding & Mfg. Co., Alhambra, Calif., 1964-70; dir. purchasing Thermal Engring. Internat. (formerly Southwestern Engring.) Commerce, Calif., 1970-87, ret. Served with USAAF, 1945-46. Office: Thermal Engring Internat 5701 S Eastern Ave Ste 300 Los Angeles CA 90040-2961

RUCKER-HUGHES, WAUDIEUR ELIZABETH, educator; b. Washington, July 30, 1947; d. Jeter and Jeannette Belle (Toomer) Rucker; B.S. D.C. Tchrs. Coll., 1969; M.A. in Edn. Admin. U. Redlands, 1974; 1 child, Teliece E.M. Tchr. history J.W. North High Sch., Riverside, Calif., 1969-76, dean students, 1976-79; lectr. Afro-Am. history Riverside City Coll., 1977-74; exec. dir. Inland Area Opportunities Industrialization Center, Riverside, 1979-90; tchr., coord. steps of success program RUSD, 1990-92; asst. prin. J.W. North High Sch., 1972-; dir. legal community relations City of Riverside, 1972-79; sec. State Inter-Group Relations Educators, 1976-77; pres. Coalition of Urban Peoples, 1978-80; lay mem. Riverside County Jud. Selection Com., 1978-84; Calif. State Bar ct. referee, 1979-84 NSF Fellow, 1970-71; C..... for Leadership Edn. grantee, 1978. Mem. NAACP

Urban League, Riverside Women's Polit. Caucus, Nat. Women's Polit. Caucus, Exec. Dirs. Assn. (sec. 1983-84, nat. historian), Officers In Charge Am. (community devel. adv. com.), Nat. Council Negro Women, Delta Kappa Gamma, Hunter Pk. C. of C. (treas., pres.), Delta Kappa Gamma. Mem. C.M.E. Ch. Club: The Thurs. Group, Phi Delta Kappa. Author: Canine Capers, 1976; A Book to Match our Diversity, 1980. Home: 590 Bruin Dr Riverside CA 92507-6074 Office: 1550 3rd St Riverside CA 92507-3404

RUDER, MELVIN HARVEY, retired newspaper editor; b. Manning, N.D., Jan. 19, 1915; s. Moris M. and Rebecca (Friedman) R.; m. Ruth Bergan, Feb. 10, 1950; 1 dau., Patricia E. Morton. BA, U. N.D., 1937, MA, 1941; postgrad., Northwestern U., 1940; LLD (hon.), U. Mont., 1998. Asst. prof. journalism U. N.D., 1940; indsl. relations specialist Westinghouse Electric Co., Sharon, Pa., 1940-41; pub. relations with Am. Machine & Foundry Co., N.Y.C., 1946; founder, editor Hungry Horse News, Columbia Falls, Mont., 1946-78; editor emeritus Hungry Horse News, 1978—. Chmn. adv. coun. Flathead Nat. Forest, Dist. 6 Sch. Bd., 1967-70; pres. Buffalo Hill Terr. Resident Coun., 1997. Served to lt. (s.g.) USNR, 1942-45. Recipient Pulitzer prize for gen. local reporting, 1965. Mem. Mont. Press Assn. (pres. 1957), Flathead Associated C. of C. (pres. 1971), Glacier Natural History Assn. (pres. 1983). Home: Buffalo Hill Terr 40 Claremont Kalispell MT 59901

RUDIN, ANNE NOTO, former mayor, nurse; b. Passaic, N.J., Jan. 27, 1924; m. Edward Rudin, June 6, 1948; 4 children. BS in Edn., Temple U., 1945, RN, 1946; MPA, U. So. Calif., 1983; LLD (hon.), Golden Gate U., 1990. RN, Calif. Mem. faculty Temple U. Sch. Nursing, Phila., 1946-48; mem. nursing faculty Mt. Zion Hosp., San Francisco, 1948-49; mem. Sacramento City Council, 1971-83; mayor City of Sacramento, 1983-92; ind. pub. policy cons. Pres. LWV, Riverside, 1957, Sacramento, 1961, Calif., 1969-71, Calif. Elected Women's Assn., 1973-97; trustee Golden Gate U., 1993-96; mem. adv. bd. U. So. Calif., Army Depot Reuse Commn., 1992-94; bd. dirs. Sacramento Theatre Co., Sacramento Symphony, 1993-96, Calif. Common Cause, 1993-96, Japan Soc. No. Calif., Sacramento Edn. Found.; v.p. Sacramento Traditional Jazz Soc. Found.; bd. dirs. Natomas Basin Conservancy. Recipient Women in Govt. award U.S. Jaycee Women, 1984, Woman of Distinction award Sacramento Area Soroptimist Clubs, 1985, Civic Contbn. award LWV Sacramento, 1989, Woman of Courage award Sacramento History Ctr., 1989, Peacemaker of Yr. award Sacramento Mediation Ctr., 1992, Regional Pride award Sacramento Mag., 1993, Humanitarian award Japanese Am. Citizen's League, 1993, Outstanding Pub. Svc. award Am. Soc. Pub. Adminstrn., 1994; named Girl Scouts Am. Role model, 1989.

RUDINSKAS, PETER JOHN, digital media executive; b. Santa Clara, Calif., Mar. 20, 1975; s. Algis and Joanne Rudinskas. Student, UCLA, 1992-95. Pres., CEO, co-founder Resonance Internet Mktg., L.A., 1995—. Avocations: public affairs, international relations, artificial intelligence, nature, chess. E-mail: prudinskas@resonance.net. Home: 10920 Wilshire Blvd # 150-9106 Los Angeles CA 90024-6502 Office: Resonance PO Box 24671 Los Angeles CA 90024-0671

RUDNICKI, STEFAN, media director, producer; b. Krakow, Poland, Jan. 1, 1945; s. Stephen J. and Danuta (Podworska) R.; m. Judith Cummings, Jan. 21, 1967. BA, Columbia Coll., 1966; MFA, Yale U., 1969. Asst. prof. U. Rochester, N.Y., 1969-77; assoc. prof. Jersey City State Coll., 1977-80; prof., chair dept. theatre L.I. U., Brookville, N.Y., 1980-87; pres. Skyboat Road Co., Inc., N.Y.C., L.A., 1979—; guest prof. NYU, 1980-82; vis. prof. Dartmouth Coll., Hanover, N.H., 1985; exec. prodr. and v.p. audio Dove Audio, L.A., 1994—. Author: (novel) Wilde, 1998; adaptor/author: (book/audio) Sun tzu's The Art of War, 1996 (Audie award 1997); co-author: (book) Colin Powell and the American Dream, 1995; compiler/author: (book) Actors Book of Monologues for Women, 1991; prodr. 200 audios, including American Pastoral, 1997 (Audie award 1998); dir.: (motion picture) ESP, 1997; dir. plays. Mem. Soc. of Stage Dirs. and Choreographers (regional board mem. 1978—), Nat. of Recording Arts and Scis. (Grammy nominee 1997, 98, 99). Home: 1532 N Hayworth Ave Apt 12A Los Angeles CA 90046-3314 Office: Dove Audio/New Star Media 8955 Beverly Blvd Los Angeles CA 90048-2420

RUDOLPH, CONRAD, medieval art history educator; b. Rock Island, Ill., Jan. 26, 1951; s. Richard C. and Mary Alice (Potter) R.; m. Roberta Peterson, Sept. 10, 1980; children: Anna Katharina, John Caspar. PhD, UCLA, 1985. Mellon postdoctoral rsch. fellow U. Pitts., 1986-87; Getty postdoctoral fellow Getty Rsch. Ctr., L.A., 1987-88; asst. prof. U. Notre Dame, Ind., 1988-91; assoc. prof. U. Calif., Riverside, 1991-97, prof., 1997—. Author: The Things of Greater Importance: Bernard of Clairvaux's Apologia and the Medieval Attitude Toward Art, 1990, Artistic Change at St.-Denis: Abbot Suger's Program and the Early Twelfth-Century Controversy Over Art, 1990, Violence and Daily Life: Reading, Art, and Polemics in the Citeaux Moralia in Job, 1997; contbr. articles to profl. jours. John Simmon Guggenheim fellow. Mem. Coll. Art Assn. (Millard Meiss Pub. fellow), Intenat. Ctr. for Medieval Art. Office: U Calif Dept History of Art Riverside CA 92521

RUDOLPH, GEORGE COOPER, lawyer; b. Butte, Mont., June 29, 1951; s. Newton Nathaniel and Delores (Losk) R. Student Mont. Coll. Mineral, Sci. and Tech., 1969-71; BA in Psychology magna cum laude, U. S.C., 1973; JD, U. Calif., San Francisco, 1976. Bar: Calif. 1976, U.S. Dist. Ct. (cen. dist.) Calif. 1977, U.S. Dist. Ct. (no. dist.) Calif. 1977, U.S. Ct. Appeals (9th cir.) 1977, U.S. Dist. Ct. (so. dist.) Calif. 1983, U.S. Supreme Ct., 1985. Assoc. Fulop, Rolston, Burns & McKittrick, Beverly Hills and Newport Beach, Calif., 1976-81, Fulop & Hardee, Newport Beach, 1981-82; ptnr. Fulop & Hardee, Newport Beach, 1982, McKittrick, Jackson, DeMarco & Peckenpaugh, Newport Beach, 1983-87, The Rudolph Law Group, Costa Mesa, Calif., 1988—; lectr. Calif. Continuing Edn. of The Bar, 1985-94, UCLA, U. Calif., Irvine, San Diego, Santa Barbara, 1985—. Mem. ABA, Assn. Trial Lawyers Am., Orange County Bar Assn., Los Angeles County Bar Assn., Beverly Hills Bar Assn. Democrat. Jewish. Lodge: B'nai B'rith. Office: The Rudolph Law Group 3200 Park Center Dr Ste 1370 Costa Mesa CA 92626-7154

RUDOLPH, JEFFREY N., museum director. Exec. dir. Calif. Sci. Ctr., L.A. Office: Calif Sci Ctr 700 State Dr Los Angeles CA 90037-1210*

RUDOLPH, RONALD ALVIN, human resources executive; b. Berwyn, Ill., May 12, 1949; s. Alvin J. and Gloria S. (Nicoletti) R. BA, U. Calif., Santa Cruz, 1971. Sr. cons. De Anza Assocs., San Jose, Calif., 1971-73; pers. adminstr. McDonnell Douglas Corp., Cupertino, Calif., 1974-75; employment rep. Fairchild Semiconductor, Mountain View, Calif., 1973-74, 75; compensation analyst Sperry Univac, Santa Clara, Calif., 1975-78; mgr. exempt compensation div. Intel Corp., Santa Clara, 1978-79, compensation mgr., 1979-82; dir. corp. compensation Intel Corp., 1982-85; v.p. human resources UNISYS Corp., San Jose, 1985-91, ASK Group Inc., Mountain View, Calif., 1991-94, 3 Com Corp., Santa Clara, 1994—; cons. Rudolph Assocs., Cupertino, 1982—; bd. dirs. Dynamic Temp. Svcs., Sunnyvale, Calif. Mem. Spl. Com. for Parolee Employment, Sacramento, 1973-75; bd. dirs. Jr. Achievement, San Jose, 1987-88. Mem. Am. Soc. Pers. Adminstrs., Am. Compensation Assn., No. Calif. Human Resources Coun. Avocations: sailing, reading, running, camping. Office: 3 Com Corp Santa Clara CA 95050

RUDOLPH, THOMAS KEITH, aerospace engineer; b. Jamestown, N.D., Oct. 4, 1961; s. Arthur John and Melinda Magdelina (Nehlich) R. BS in Aerospace Engring., Iowa State U., 1983. Registered profl. engr., Wash. Engr. Boeing Mil. Airplanes, Seattle, 1984-88, sr. engr., 1988-90; sr. engr. Boeing Comml. Airplanes, Seattle, 1990-91, specialist engr., 1991-94; specialist engr. Boeing Mil. Airplanes, Seattle, 1994—; chmn. weight improvement program Boeing B-2 Program, Seattle, 1986-88. Mem. AIAA (sr.), Soc. Allied Weight Engrs. (sr., chmn. activities com. 1985-86, treas. 1986-87, facilities chmn. internat. conf. 1987, v.p. 1987-88, pres. 1991-92), Iowa State U. Alumni Assn. (life), Marston Club (life). Republican. Methodist. Avocations: camping, skiing, golf, coins, hiking. Office: Boeing Mil Airplanes M/S 4C-45 PO Box 3707 Seattle WA 98124-2207

RUDOLPH, WALTER PAUL, engineering research company executive; b. Binghamton, N.Y., Aug. 17, 1937; s. Walter Paul and Frieda Lena (Hennemann) R.; m. Leila Ortencia Romero, Dec. 18, 1960; children: Jonathan, Jana, Catherine. BEE, Rensselaer Poly. Inst., 1959; MSBA, San Diego State U., 1964. Elec. engr. Gen. Dynamics/Astronautics, San Diego, 1959-62; ops. research analyst Navy Electronics Lab., San Diego, 1962-64; mem. profl. staff Gen. Electric Tempo, Honolulu, 1964-70, Ctr. for Naval Analysis, Arlington, Va., 1970-77; pres. La Jolla (Calif.) Rsch. Corp., 1977—. Served to Capt. USNR, 1959-92. Republican. Presbyterian. Home: 1559 El Paso Real La Jolla CA 92037-6303 Office: La Jolla Rsch Corp PO Box 1207 La Jolla CA 92038-1207

RUEBE, BAMBI LYNN, interior, environmental designer; b. Huntington Park, Calif., Nov. 13, 1957; d. Leonard John Ruebe and Vaudis Marie Powell. BS, UCLA, 1988. Millwright asst. Kaiser Steel Corp., Fontana, Calif., 1976-79; electrician Fleetwood Enterprises, Riverside, Calif., 1977; fashion model internat., 1977-85; free-lance draftsman, 1982-83; project coord. Philip J. Sicola Inc., Culver City, Calif., 1982-83; prin. designer Ruebe Inclusive Design, Highland, Calif., 1983-89, Ventura, Calif., 1990—; cons. mfg. design Burlington Homes New Eng. Inc., Oxford, Maine, 1987-90, DeRose Industries, Chambersburg, Pa., 1984, Skyline Corp., Redlands, Calif., 1982-84; cons. lighting Lightways Corp., L.A., 1984-87; mem. design rev. bd. San Bernardino (Calif.) Downtown Main St. Redevel. Com., 1987-89. Motion picture project designer, lighting design, archtl. design for the movie Deceptions, 1990. Mem. World Affairs Coun., Inland So. Calif., 1986-90; mem. Citizens adv. com. Highland Calif. Gen. Plan, 1988-90; co-chmn. civil rights com. AFL-CIO, Fontana, 1978-79. Recipient Cert. Merit Scholastic Art award Scholastic Mags. Inc., Southeastern Calif., 1974, Dirs. Incentive award for Archtl. Design City of Ventura, Calif., 1990. Mem. Nat. Trust for Hist. Preservation. Democrat. Achievements include design and specification of the first drywall system for use in the manufactured housing industry; design of first hot spa water oxygen therapy spa for people. Avocations: snow skiing, horseback riding, antique sportscar restoration, singing. Office: Ruebe Inclusive Design 50 N Oak St Ventura CA 93001-5625

RUECKER, MARTHA ENGELS, retired special education educator; b. South Gate, Calif., Sept. 22, 1931; d. Eugene and Minna (Wilhelm) Engels; m. Geert Frank Ruecker, Aug. 10, 1959 (div. 1964); 1 child, Ann. MusB, U. So. Calif., 1954, Calif. tchr. credential, 1955. Tchr. educationally handicapped Downey (Calif.) Unified Schs., 1964-92; tchr. 2d grade Lynwood (Calif.) Unified Schs., 1992-97. Recipient award for work with mentally gifted Johns Hopkins U., 1992; South Gate Kiwanis scholar U. So. Calif., 1949-54. Mem. NEA (life), Los Angeles County Art Mus. Republican. Methodist. Avocations: interior design, gardening, music, travel. Home: PO Box 630 Downey CA 90241-0630

RUGGERI, ZAVERIO MARCELLO, medical researcher; b. Bergamo, Italy, Jan. 7, 1945; came to U.S., 1978; s. Giovanni and Anna (Dolci) R.; m. Rosamaria Carrara, June 12, 1971. MD magna cum laude, U. Milan, 1970; degree in Clin. and Exptl. Hematology magna cum laude, U. Pavia, Italy, 1973, degree in Internal Medicine magna cum laude, 1981. Asst. clin. prof. hematology U. Milan, 1972-80; assoc. dir. hemophilia ctr. Policlinico Hosp., Milan, 1980-82; vis. investigator Scripps Clinic and Research Found., La Jolla, Calif., 1978-80, asst. mem., 1982-89; assoc. mem. Scripps Clinic and Rsch. Found., La Jolla, Calif., 1989-93; mem. Scripps Rsch. Inst., 1993—; dir. Roon Ctr. for Arteriosclerosis and Thrombosis, 1989—; head div. Exptl. Thrombosis and Hemostasis, 1989—; vis. investigator St. Thomas/St. Bartholomews Hosps., London, 1974-76. Editor: Clinics in Haematology, 1985; mem. editl. bds. Blood, 1988-92, Peptide Rsch., 1988—, Haematologica, 1990—, Jour. Biol. Chemistry, 1993—; assoc. editor. Jour. Clin. Investigation, 1993-96; contbr. articles to profl. jours., chpts. to books. Research scholar Italian Ministry of Edn., 1970, Italian Hemophilia Found., 1970-72. Mem. AAAS, Assn. Am. Physicians, Italian Hemophilia Found., Am. Soc. Clin. Investigation, Italian Soc. Thrombosis and Hemostasis, Internat. Soc. Thrombosis and Hemostasis, Am. Heart Assn. (council on thrombosis), World Fedn. Hemophilia, Am. Fedn. Clin. Research, N.Y. Acad. Scis., Am. Soc. Hematology. Office: Scripps Rsch Inst 10550 N Torrey Pines Rd La Jolla CA 92037-1000

RUGGLES, JOANNE BEAULE, artist, educator; b. N.Y.C., May 19, 1946; d. Robert H. and Evelyn (Corzin) Beaule; m. Philip Kent Ruggles, Aug. 31, 1968; 1 child, Lauren. B.F.A., Ohio State U., 1968, M.F.A., 1970. Lectr. art Ohio State U., Columbus, 1970-71, Allan Hancock Coll., Santa Maria, Calif., 1971-76, Cuesta Coll., San Luis Obispo, Calif., 1977-79; lectr. architecture and art Calif. Poly. State U., San Luis Obispo, 1973-80, assoc. prof. art, 1984-88, prof., 1988—; reviewer Dorland Mountain Arts Cmty. Artists Residency Grants, 1988—. Author: (with others) Darkroom Graphics, 1975. Mem. San Luis Obispo City Promotional Coordinating Com., 1978-82, chmn., 1980-82; bd. dirs. San Luis Obispo Art Assn., 1993-95, v.p., 1994-95. Recipient juror's spl. mention Cabo Frio Internat. Print Biennal, Brazil, 1983, Univ. purchase award Wesleyan 2nd Internat. Print and Drawing Exhbn., Macon, Ga., 1983, purchase award Artist's World, Somerville, N.J., 1984, Purchase award Minot State U., 1996, Jurors award Gallery Contemporary Art U. Colo., 1997; selected artist Art in Embassies program U.S. Dept. State, Washington, 1997. Mem. Nat. Assn. Women Artists, Nat. Mus. Women in Arts (founding mem.), Nat. Acrylic Painters Assn. (signature mem., Am. Artist award 1997), Nat. Oil and Acrylic Painters Soc., Am. Soc. Contemporary Artists, Calif. Soc. Printmakers, L.A. Printmaking Soc., Boston Printmakers. Home: PO Box 46 San Luis Obispo CA 93406-0046

RULEY, STANLEY EUGENE, cost analyst; b. Akron, Ohio, Jan. 24, 1934; s. Royal Lovell and Opal Lenora (McDougall) R.; m. Annie Adam Patterson, Dec. 15, 1962; children: Cheryl Ann, Janice Lynn. Student, Kent State U., 1951-53; BSBA, Ohio State U., 1955. Registered profl. engr., Calif. Indsl. engr. Gaffers & Satler Inc., Hawthorne, Calif., 1961-62; mfg. engr. data systems div. Litton Industries Inc., Van Nuys, Calif., 1962-65; contract price analyst Naval Plant Rep. Office Lockheed, Burbank, Calif., 1966-72; contract negotiator Naval Regional Procurement, Long Beach, Calif., 1972-75; cost/price analyst Def. Contract Adminstrn. Services, Van Nuys, 1975-82; chief of contract pricing, dir. contracting Air Force Flight Test Ctr., Edwards AFB, Calif., 1982-89; cons. engr., Northridge, Calif., 1971—. Served as sgt. U.S. Army, 1956-59. Recipient Sustained Superior Performance award Air Force Flight Test Ctr., 1984, Excellent Performance award Air Force Flight Test Ctr., 1982-83, Outstanding Performance award NAVPRO Lockheed, 1970. Mem. Am. Inst. Indsl. Engrs., IBM Computer User Group (Madison, Wis., Conn., San Fernando Valley), Air Force Assn. (life), Nat. Contract Mgmt. Assn. Republican. Presbyterian. Clubs: Lockheed Employee Recreation (treas. Gem and Mineral 1976, pres. 1976), Camper (Burbank) (pres. 1974). Lodge: Masons (past master, 1992). Avocations: flying, golf, camping, travel, computers. Home: 18751 Vintage St Northridge CA 91324-1529 Office: Indsl Engring Svcs 18751 Vintage St Northridge CA 91324-1529

RULIFSON, JOHNS FREDERICK, computer company executive, computer scientist; b. Bellefontaine, Ohio, Aug. 20, 1941; s. Erwin Charles and Virginia Helen (Johns) R.; m. Janet Irving, June 8, 1963; children: Eric Johns, Ingrid Catharine. BS in Math., U. Wash., 1966; PhD in Computer Sci., Stanford U., 1973. Mathematician SRI, Internat., Menlo Park, Calif., 1966-73; scientist Xerox Rsch., Palo Alto, Calif., 1973-80; mgr. ROLM, Santa Clara, Calif., 1980-85; scientist Syntelligence, Sunnyvale, Calif., 1985-87; exec. Sun Microsystems, Mountain View, Calif., 1987—. Fellow Assn. for Computing Machinery (System Software award 1990); mem. IEEE. Avocation: photography. Home: 3785 El Centro Ave Palo Alto CA 94306-2642 Office: Sun Microsystems 901 San Antonio Rd Palo Alto CA 94303-4900

RUMBAUGH, CHARLES EARL, arbitrator, mediator, educator, lawyer, speaker; b. San Bernardino, Calif., Mar. 11, 1943; s. Max Elden and Gertrude Maude (Gulker) R.; m. Christina Carol Pinder, Mar. 2, 1968; children: Eckwood, Cynthia, Aaron, Heather. BS, UCLA, 1966; JD, Calif. Western Sch. Law, 1971; cert. in advanced mgmt., U. So. Calif., 1993. Bar: Calif. 1972, U.S. Dist. Ct. (cen. dist.) Calif. U.S. Ct. Appeals (9th cir.), U.S. Supreme Ct. Engr. Westinghouse Electric Corp., Balt., 1966-68; legal counsel Calif. Dept. of Corps., L.A., 1971-77; legal counsel Hughes Aircraft Co., L.A., 1977-84, asst. to corp. dir. contracts, 1984-89, asst. to corp. v.p. contracts, 1989-95; corp. dir. contracts/pricing Lear Astronics Corp., 1995-97; pres. Ctr. for Conflict Resolution, 1998-99; arbitrator, mediator, comml., govt. contracts, internat. law, franchise, securities, real estate and constrn. panels Am. Arbitration Assn., L.A., 1989—; mem. arbitration and mediation panels ArbitrationWorks (formerly Arbitration and Mediation Internat.), 1994—, Nat. Assn. Security Dealers, Franchise Arbitration & Mediation Inc., County Superior Ct., L.A., 1993—; spkr. in field; mem. panel pvt. alt. dispute resolution neutrals U.S. Ct. Fed. Claims; mem. armed svcs. bd. of contract appeals panel of pvt. alt. dispute resolution neutrals, also settlement officer U.S. Dist. Ct. Mem. editl. bd. Nat. Contract Mgmt. Jour.; contbr. articles to profl. jours. Counselor Boy Scouts Am., L.A., 1976—; mem. City of Palos Verdes Estates (Calif.) Citizen's Planning Com., 1986-90; judge pro tem Los Angeles County Superior Ct., L.A., 1991—. Fellow Nat. Contract Mgmt. Assn. (founder, chmn. alt. dispute resolution com., cert. profl. contracts mgr., nat. bd. advisors, nat. v.p. southwestern region 1993-95, nat. dir. 1992-93, pres. L.A./South Bay chpt. 1991-92, Fellow of Yr. award 1994); mem. ABA (dispute resolution sect., forum on franchising, forum on constrn. industry, pub. contract law sect.), Nat. Assn. Purchasing Mgmt., Calif. Dispute Resolution Coun. (cons. to qualifications com. 1997—), Nat. Def. Indsl. Assn. (vice-chmn. west coast legal subcom. 1994—), Fed. Bar Assn. (pres. Beverly Hills chpt. 1992-93), State Bar Calif. (franchise law com. 1992-95, Wiley W. Manual award 1992), LA County Bar Assn., South Bay Bar Assn., Soc. Profls. in Dispute Resolution (chair internat. sector, past bd. dirs. L.A. chpt.), Aerospace Industries Assn. (chmn. procurement techniques com. 1987-88, 93-94), Christian Legal Soc. Avocations: camping, skiing, jogging, equestrian. Office: PO Box 2636 Rolling Hills CA 90274-8636

RUNDLE, JOHN BELTING, physicist, educator; b. Somerville, N.J., Aug. 31, 1950; s. David Bradford and Dorothy (Belting) R.; m. Marie Cardoza, July 27, 1974; children: Paul Belting, Daniel Edgar. Student, U. Ill., 1968-69, 74; BS in Engring., Princeton U., 1972; MS, UCLA, 1973, PhD, 1976. Postdoctoral fellow UCLA, 1976-77; research scientist Sandia Nat. Labs., Albuquerque, 1977-90; physicist Lawrence Livermore (Calif.) Nat. Lab., 1990-93; prof. physics U. Colo., 1993—; dir. Colo. Ctr. for Chaos and Complexity, 1993—; vis. assoc. Calif. Inst. Tech., Pasadena, 1981-84; cons. various govtl. agys, 1980—; mem. Nat. Acad. Scis. NRC com. on Geodesy, 1986-90, chmn., 1988-90, mem. Nat. Acad. Scis. NRC Panel on Modeling in the Earth Scis., 1989-91, NASA geophysics sci. working group, 1986—; vis. scholar dept. physics Boston U., 1988-89; chmn. evaluation panel So. Calif. Earthquake Ctr. NSF, 1990. Contbr. articles to profl. jours. Grantee NASA, NSF, Dept. Energy. Mem. Am. Geophys. Union, Seismol. Soc., Am. Phys. Soc., Am. Soc. Natural Philosophy, Princeton Club (v.p. 1985), Sigma Xi, Phi Beta Kappa, Tau Beta Pi, Phi Eta Sigma. Achievements include research in statistical mechanics of high dimensional complex nonlinear threshold systems; simulations of earthquake, neural network and other threshold systems. Avocation: golf. Fax: 303-492-5070. E-mail: rundle@cires.colorado.edu. Office: U Colo Colo Ctr Chaos Complexity Ekeley S236 Boulder CO 80309

RUNFOLA, SHEILA KAY, nurse; b. Canton, Ohio, Feb. 8, 1944; d. Benjamin and M. Suzanne (deBord) Suarez; m. Steven Joseph Runfola, Aug. 17, 1968; children: Michael, Janine, Christine; stepchildren: Stephanie Bufalini, Darlene Teran. BS in Nursing, St. John Coll. Cleve., 1966; teaching credential jr. coll. nursing, UCLA Ext., San Diego, 1973. RN, Calif.; cert. occupational health nurse, cert. pub. health nurse. Staff nurse emergency rm. Leland Meml. Hosp., Riverdale, Md., 1966-67; staff nurse/team leader med./surg. Mercy Hosp., San Diego, 1967-68; staff nurse, charge nurse emergency dept., dept. radiology U. Calif.-San Diego Med.Ctr., 1968-76; staff devel./asst. dir. nurses TLC Nursing Home, El Cajon, Calif., 1978-80; staff nurse/charge nurse emergency dept. Kaiser Permanente Hosp., San Diego, 1980-89; staff nurse emergency dept. Kaiser Permanente Hosp., Sacramento, Calif., 1989-90; house supr. Kaiser Permanente Hosp., Sacramento, 1992-94, case mgr. occupational medicine, 1995—; health svcs. nurse U.S. Automobile Assn., Sacramento, 1990-95. Contbr. articles to profl. jours. Leader Girls Scouts Am., San Diego and Sacramento, 1982-91, treas., local svc. team, 1986-89, 90; parent rep. Elk Grove (Calif.) Sch. Bd. for Elk Grove H.s., 1994, co-chair Sober Grad. Night, 1993-95. Mem. Sacramento Valley Occupational Health Nurses (v.p. 1992-95, sec. 1998—, election chair 1998), Newcomers Club, Calif. State Assn. Occupl. Health Nurse (bd. dirs. 1998—, newsletter editor). Democrat. Roman Catholic. Avocations: crafts (quilting), piano, reading, cooking, boating. Office: Kaiser Permanente Dept Occupl Med 6600 Bruceville Rd Sacramento CA 95823-4671

RUNICE, ROBERT E., retired corporate executive; b. Fargo, N.D., Aug. 20, 1929; s. E.M. and Ruth (Soule) R.; m. Geraldine Kharas, June 26, 1954; children: Michael, Christopher, Paul, Karen. B.S., N.D. State U., 1951. Sr. v.p. Northwestern Bell Tel. Co., Omaha, Nebr., 1945-81; v.p. Am. Tel. & Tel. Co.-Info. Systems, Morristown, N.J., 1981-83; v.p., pres. comml. devel. div. US West, Inc., Englewood, Colo., 1983-91; bd. dirs. Bombay Co., Ft. Worth, Tandy Brands Accessories, Arlington, Tex., Utilx Corp., Kent, Wash. Trustee Colo. Symphony Assn. Republican. Episcopalian. Home: Box 503 10940 S Parker Rd Parker CO 80134 7440 Office: 9785 S Maroon Cir Ste 332 Englewood CO 80112-5922

RUNNER, GEORGE CYRIL, JR., minister, educational administrator; b. Scotia, N.Y., Mar. 25, 1952; s. George Cyril and Kay Carol (Cooper) R.; m. Sharon Yvonne Oden, Jan. 13, 1973; children: Micah Stephen, Rebekah Kay. Student, Antelope Valley Coll., Lancaster, Calif., 1970-88; grad. mgmt. cert., Azusa Pacific U., 1988; student, U. Redlands. Lic. to ministry Am. Bapt. Chs. in USA, 1977. Exec. pastor 1st Bapt. Ch. Lancaster, 1973—; founder, exec. dir. Desert Christian Schs., Lancaster, 1977—; founder, internat. dir. Supporting Ptnrs. in Christian Edn., Lancaster, Guatemala City, Guatemala, 1989—; seminar leader Internat. Ctr. for Learning, Ventura, Calif., 1972-82; curriculum cons. Gospel Light Publs., Glendale, Calif., 1974-80; bd. dirs. Greater L.A. Sunday Sch. Assn., 1978-79. Assemblyman State of Calif., 36th Dist., Lancaster, 1996; bd. dirs. Lancaster Econ. Devel. Corp.; mem. Salvation Army, Lancaster. Mem. Internat. Fellowship Ch. Sch. Adminstrs., Assn. Christian Schs. Internat., Christian Mgmt. Assn., Lancaster Ministerial Assn. Republican. Office: Desert Christian Schs 1st Bapt Ch 44648 15th St W Lancaster CA 93534-2806*

RUNNICLES, DONALD, conductor; b. Edinburgh, Scotland, Nov. 16, 1954. Student, Edinburgh U., Cambridge U., London Opera Ctr.; DMus (hon.), U. Edinburgh, 1995. Repetiteur Mannheim, Germany, Nat. theatre, from 1980, Kapellmeister, from 1984; prin. condr. Hanover, from 1987; numerous appearances with Hamburg Staatsoper; former gen. music dir. Stadtische Buhnen, Freiburg/Breisgau; mus. dir. San Francisco Opera, 1992—; appearances with Met. Opera include Lulu, 1988, The Flying Dutchman, 1990, The Magic Flute; condr. Vienna Staatsoper, 1990-91, Sonome, 1996; debut at Glyndebourne with Don Giovanni, 1991, Salzburg Festival with Don Giovanni, 1996, also numerous symphonic engagements; condr. London Symphony Orch., La Scale Milan Freischütz, Orch. de Paris, Israel Philharm., Rotterdam Philharm., Seattle Symphony, Pitts. Symphony, St. Louis Symphony, Chgo. Symphony, San Francisco Symphony, Cleve. Orch., New World Symphony, Bavarian Radio Symphony Orch., 2 complete ring cycles with Wiener Staatsoper; rec. Hansel and Gretel (Humperdinck), Gluck's Orphée with San Francisco Opera Orch., 1995, Tannhäuser-Bayreuth Festspick, 1995, Harvey Milk with San Francisco Opera, 1996; opened Edinburgh Festival, 1994, 96. Office: San Francisco Opera War Meml Opera House 301 Van Ness Ave San Francisco CA 94102-4509

RUNYON, BRETT L., lawyer; b. Fresno, Calif., Oct. 20, 1959. AA, Fresno City Coll., 1981; BS, Calif. State U., Fresno, 1982; JD, San Joaquin Coll. Law, 1986. Atty. Marderosian, Swanson & Oren, Fresno, 1988—. Mem. Assn. Trial Lawyers of Am., Fed. Bar Assn., Fresno County Bar Assn., Delta Theta Phi (meritorious svc. award 1986). Office: Marderosian Swanson & Oren 1260 Fulton Mall Fresno CA 93721-1900

RUNYON, STEVEN CROWELL, university administrator, communications educator; b. San Rafael, Calif., June 20, 1946; s. Charles A. and Katherine C. (Pease) R.; m. Lynna Lim, Mar. 9, 1974; 1 child, Wendy Victoria. BA in Econs., U. San Francisco, 1971, postgrad., 1978—; MA in Radio and TV, San Francisco State U., 1976. Radio producer Sta. KGO, San Francisco, 1965-68; engr., announcer Stas. KSFR, KSAN, San Francisco, 1966-68; publicist Kolmar Assocs./Chuck Barris Prodns., San Francisco, 1970; instructional media technician U. San Francisco, 1968-72; technician, archivist, mgr. Wurster, Bernardi & Emmons, San Francisco,

1972-73; projectionist So. Pacific R.R., San Francisco, 1974; broadcast ops. engr. Stas. KPEN, KIOI, KIOI, San Francisco, 1968-74; public and community affairs program producer, 1971-74, AM transmitter engr., 1974; lectr. communication arts, U. San Francisco, 1974—, gen. mgr. Sta. KUSF-FM, 1974—, dir. mass media studies program, 1975-98, acting chmn. communication arts dept., 1976; TV historian; producer, engr., cons. radio and TV programs; communications and audiovisual cons. Author: A Study of the Don Lee Broadcasting Systems' Television Activities, 1930-41, 1976, Educational Broadcast Management Bibliography, 1974, (with others) Television in America, 1996, The Encyclopedia of Television, 1997, Historical Dictionary of American Radio, 1998; contbr. articles to profl. jours. Grantee Calif. Coun. Humanities in Public Policy, Rockefeller Found., Father Spieler Meml. Trust, NSF; recipient cert. of merit for documentary radio series Peninsula Press Club, 1979, Diploma of Honor, Internat. Robert Stolz Soc., 1981, Fr. Dunne award U. San Francisco, 1986, Coll. Svc. award Coll. Arts and Scis. U. San Francisco, 1988; lic. gen. class radiotelephone operator FCC. Mem. Soc. Broadcast Engrs., Broadcast Edn. Assn. (Divsnl. First Place award Refereed Paper Competition 1996), Assn. for Edn. in Journalism and Mass Communication, Assn. Recorded Sound Collections, Diamond Circle of U. San Francisco, Internat. Communication Assn. E-mail: runyon@usfca.edu. Office: U San Francisco 2130 Fulton St San Francisco CA 94117-1080

RUOTSALA, JAMES ALFRED, historian, writer; b. Juneau, Alaska, Feb. 17, 1934; s. Bert Alfred and Eva (Karppi) E.; m. Janet Ann Whelan, July 31, 1987; stepchildren: Theresa Cowden, Douglas Whelan, Peggy MacInnis, Michael Whelan, Bruce Whelan. Student, U. Md., 1960-61, Basic Officers Sch., Maxwell AFB, 1964, Air U., Maxwell AFB, 1985; AA, U. Alaska, Kenai, 1990. Asst. div. mgr. Macmillan Pub. Co., 1964-80; mgr. Denny's Restaurants, 1980-82; dir. mktg. and sales Air Alaska, 1982-89; state security supr., It. Knightwatch Security, Juneau, Alaska, 1990-96; ret., 1996; archival dir. Alaska Aviation Heritage Mus., 1987-90. Author: Lockheed Vegas in Southeast Alaska, 1980, We Stand Ready, 1986, Eielson, Father of Alaskan Aviation, 1986, Pilots of the Panhandle, The Early Years 1920-1935, 1997; Alaska's Aviation Heritage Air Alaska newspaper; contbr. articles to profl. jours. Journalist 1st cl. USN, 1951-56; sgt. U.S. Army, 1958-64; 1st sgt. USAR, 1983-94; ret. USAR, 1994; col. Alaska State Defense Force, 1985-98, ret. Decorated Korean Svc. medal with 2 combat stars, Korean Presdl. unit citation, UN Svc. medal, Nat. Def. Svc. medal, Vietnam Svc. medal, Meritorious Svc. medal with 2 oak leaf clusters, Army Commendation medal with 4 oak leaf clusters; recipient USAF Brewer Aerospace award, Grover Leoning award, Paul E. Garber award, 1984-85, State of Alaska Gov.'s Cert. Appreciation, 1983, Mayor's Pub. Svc. award, Anchorage, 1985, Commendation from Gov. of Alaska, 1993, 94, 18th Session Alaska Legis. Cert. Recognition, 1993, 94, Cert. of Appreciation, Pres. Bill Clinton, 1994. Mem. VFW (sr. vice comdr. 1995, post quartermaster 1996—), Res. Officers Assn. (pub. affairs officer 1985—), U.S. Naval Inst., Aviation and Space Writers Assn., Am. Aviation Hist. Soc., Am. Legion (historian), Pioneers of Alaska (sec. 1988, v.p. 1989, pres. 1990, Igloo 33, treas. 1994-95, Igloo 6, Cert. Appreciation 1988). Lutheran. Home: 2723 John St Juneau AK 99801-2020

RUPPEL, EDWARD THOMPSON, geologist; b. Fort Morgan, Colo., Oct. 26, 1925; s. Henry George and Gladys Myrtle (Thompson) R.; m. Phyllis Beale Tanner; children: Lisa, David, Douglas, Kristin. BA in Geology, U. Mont., 1948, Doctorate (hon.), 1996; MA in Geology, U. Wyo., 1950; PhD in Geology, Yale U., 1958. Geologist U.S. Geol. Survey, Denver, 1950-68, rsch. geologist, 1968-86; dir., state geologist Mont. Bur. Mines and Geology, Butte, 1986-94; consulting geologist Twin Bridges, Mont., 1994—. Author and co-author of approximately forty-five maps and reports; contbr. articles to profl. jours. Dir., v.p. Virginia City (Mont.) Preservation Alliance, 1997-98. Lt. (j.g.) USNR, 1943-50. Fellow Geol. Soc. Am. (sr.), Soc. Econ. Geologists; mem. Am. Inst. Profl. Geologists (cert. profl. geologist), Mont. Geol. Soc., Geol. Soc. Washington, Tobacco Root Geol. Soc. (Excellence in Field Work award 1993). Home and Office: 326 S Main St PO Box K Twin Bridges MT 59754-0402

RUSCONI, LOUIS JOSEPH, marine engineer; b. San Diego, Calif., Oct. 10, 1926; s. Louis Edward and Laura Ethelyn (Salazar) R.; m. Virginia Caroline Bruce, Jan. 1, 1972. BA in Engring. Tech., Pacific Western U., 1981, MA in Marine Engring. Tech., 1982; PhD in Marine Engring. Mgmt., Clayton U., 1986. Cert. nuclear ship propulsion plant operator, surface and submarine. Enlisted USN, 1944, electrician's mate chief, 1944-65, retired, 1965; marine electrician planner U.S. Naval Shipyard, Vallejo, Calif., 1965-72; marine elec. technician Imperial Iranian Navy, Bandar Abbas, Iran, 1974-79; marine shipyard planner Royal Saudi Navy, Al-Jubail, Saudi Arabia, 1980-86; cons. in marine engring., 1986—. Author: Shipyards Operations manual, 1980, poetry (Golden Poet award 1989, Silver Poet award 1990). Mem. Rep. Presdl. Task Force, Washington, 1989-90, trustee, 1991. Mem. IEEE, U.S. Naval Inst., Soc. of Naval Architects and Marine Engrs. (assoc. mem.), Fleet Res., Nat. Geographic Soc. Avocations: creative writing, poetry, martial arts. Home: 949 Myra Ave Chula Vista CA 91911-2315

RUSH, DOMENICA MARIE, health facilities administrator; b. Gallup, N.Mex., Apr. 10, 1937; d. Bernardo G. and Guadalupe (Milan) Iorio; m. W. E. Rush, Jan. 5, 1967. Diploma, Regina Sch. Nursing, Albuquerque, 1958. RN N.Mex.; lic. nursing home adminstr. Charge nurse, house supr. St. Joseph Hosp., Albuquerque, 1958-63; dir. nursing Cibola Hosp., Grants, 1960-64; supr. operating room, dir. med. seminars Carrie Tingley Crippled Children's Hosp., Truth or Consequences, N.Mex., 1964-73; adminstr. Sierra Vista Hosp., Truth or Consequences, 1974-88, pres., 1980-89; clin. nursing mgr. U. N.Mex. Hosp., 1989-90; adminstr. Nor-Lea Hosp., Lovington, N.Mex., 1990-94; with regional ops. divsn. Presbyn. Healthcare Svcs., Albuquerque, 1994—, regional ops., 1994—; adminstr. Sierra Vista Hosp., Truth or Consequences, N.Mex., 1995—; bd. dirs. N.Mex. Blue Cross/Blue Shield, 1977-88, chmn. hosp. relations com., 1983-85, exec. com. 1983—; bd. dirs. Region II Emergency Med. Svcs. Originating bd. SW Mental Health Ctr., Sierra County, N.Mex., 1975; chmn. Sierra County Personnel Bd., 1983—. Named Lea County Outstanding Woman, N.Mex., 1992. Mem. Am. Coll. Health Care Adminstrs., Sierra County C. of C. (bd. dirs. 1972, 75-76, svc. award 1973, Businesswoman of the Yr. 1973-74), N.Mex. Hosp. Assn. (bd. dirs., sec.-treas., pres.-elect, com. chmn. 1977-88, pres. 1980-81, exec. com., 1980-83, 84-85, recipient meritorious svc. award 1988), N.Mex. So. Hosp. Coun. (sec. 1980-81, pres. 1981-82), Am. Hosp. Assn. (N.Mex. del. 1984-88, regional adv. bd. 1984-88). Republican. Roman Catholic. Avocations: raising thoroughbred horses, cooking. Home: 1100 N Riverside Dr Truth Or Consequences NM 87901-9789 Office: 800 E 9th Ave Truth Or Consequences NM 87901-1954

RUSH, MARK TWAIN, telecommunications supervisor; b. Riverside, Calif., Feb. 9, 1951; s. John Stewart and Christine (Wenig) R. AA, Chaffey Coll., Alta Loma, Calif., 1977, AS, 1980; BS, U. Redlands, Calif., 1993. Draftsman telecomms. Volt Tech. Svcs., Pomona, Calif., 1979-80; engring. fielder GTE, Westminster, Calif., 1980-81; engr. GTE, Pomona, Calif., 1981-82; sr. engr. GTE, Covina, Calif., 1983-85; supervisor GTE, Upland, Calif., 1985-87; inspector OSP GTE, Pomona, 1987-95; sr. engr. GST-Pacific Lightwave, Rialto, Calif., 1995-96; supr. Pacific Bell, 1996—. Chmn. Worldfest Facilities Chmn., 1990; solicitor United Way, 1993. With U.S. Army, 1969-71. Mem. Sierra Club. Avocations: graphic arts, computers, tennis. Home: 7938 Montara Ave Rancho Cucamonga CA 91730-2529 Office: Pacific Bell 16816 Arrow Blvd Fontana CA 92335-3867

RUSHMER, ESTELLA VIRGINIA DIX (DIXIE RUSHMER), artist; b. Sullivan, Ind., Oct. 17, 1919; d. William Porter Jessop and Roxie Gertrude (Johnson) Dix; m. Robert Frazer Rushmer, Apr. 5, 1942; children: Donald Scott, Anne, Elizabeth. BS, Purdue U., 1940. cert. Am. Dietetic Assn. Dietetic intern St. Mary's Hosp. Mayo Clinic, Rochester, Minn., 1941-42; docent Wash. State Durke Mus., 1963-78. Author, artist: Whidbey Island Sketchbook, 1985; one-woman shows include Good Years Gallery, Edmonds, Wash., 1975, 75, 77, Stillwater Gallery, Seattle, 1979, Angeles (Wash.) Fine Arts Ctr., 1988; group shows include Bellevue (Wash.) Art Mus., 1979, 82, 84, 86-90, Peter Kirk Gallery, Kirkland, Wash., 1985-90, Frye Mus., Seattle, 1979, Frederick and Nelson Gallery, Seattle, 1980, 82,

Portico Gallery, Kobe, Japan, 1987, Meguro Mus., Tokyo, Japan, 1987, Columbia Art Ctr., Vancouver, Wash., 1990, Nat. Watercolor Soc. Show, Muckenthaler Cultural Ctr., Fullerton, Calif., 1990; represented in permanent collections at Rainier Bank, Samotomo Bank, Alpac Corp., Honeywell, Seattle; represented in pvt. collections. Pres. U. Wash. Med. Sch. Aux., Seattle, 1948; leader Girl Scouts U.S.A., Lake Forest Park, Wash., 1958-63. Mem. Northwest Watercolor Soc., U. Wash. Auxiliary, U. Wash. Med. Auxiliary, U. Wash. Retiree Assn., Women Painters of Wash. Avocations: gardening, travel, reading, genealogy, grandparenting. Home: 10901 176th Cir NE # 3526 Redmond WA 98052-7248

RUSHTON, CLIFFORD (DOUG), state water planner; b. Port Angeles, Wash., May 22, 1949; s. Carl D. Rushton and Yvonne Hunt. BS in Forestry, U. Wash., 1971, MS in Forestry, 1975. Forester U.S. Forest Svc., Idaho Falls, Idaho; wildlife area mgr. Wash. State Dept. of Game, Ferndale, Kettle Falls, Wash., 1979-81; from water and air coord. to forestry water planner Wash. State Dept. Ecology, Olympia, Wash., 1986-95, forestry water planner, 1995—; bd. of suprs. Thurston Conservation District, Olympia, Wash., 1994-98. Chair water quality com. Timber, fish, wildlife adv. group, Olympia, 1996-97, rsch. evaluation of forestry com. 1997-98; elder Victory Christian Ch., Olympia, 1987-94. Recipient Govs. Certificate of Merit Wash. State Gov., Olympia, 1995, Water Conservation award USDI Bureau of Reclamation, 1995. Mem. Soc. Am. Foresters, Wash. Agrl. Forestry Leadership Found. Avocations: old car restoration, fly-fishing, Irish history. E-mail: drus461@ecy.wa.gov.

RUSNOCK, KARL JOSEPH, computer engineer; b. Boston, Dec. 5, 1958; s. Joseph Robert and Ruth (Schlumbom) R.; m. Jo Ann Bachner, Nov. 18, 1989. BS, U. Pitts., 1980; MS, U. So. Calif., 1981. Mem. tech. staff Bell Labs., Holmdel, N.J., 1980-85; prin. staff engr. Motorola Inc., Tempe, Ariz., 1985—. Mem. IEEE, Assn. Computing Machinery. Home: 1817 S Standage Cir Mesa AZ 85202-5847 Office: Motorola Computer Group MD DW-220 2900 S Diablo Way Tempe AZ 85282-3214

RUSSEL, RICHARD ALLEN, telecommunications consultant, aerospace engineer, nuclear engineer, electrical engineer, retired naval officer; b. Shreveport, La., Jan. 24, 1958; s. Robert Lee and Gloria Jeanette (Gile) R.; m. Kathryn Joy Koehler, Dec. 30, 1983; children: Richard Allen Russel Jr., Kammie Joyce Jeanette, Jonathan Mark, Katie Jacqueline Keala, Stephen Sungmin. BSEE, U. N.Mex., 1980; AeE in Aeros. and Astronautics, Naval Postgrad. Sch., Monterey, Calif., 1994, MSc in Astron. Engring., 1994. Commd. ensign, nuclear submarine officer USN, 1980, advanced through grades to lt. comdr., 1990; main propulsion analyst USS Puffer, Pearl Harbor, Hawaii, 1981-85; antisubmarine analyst, nuclear engr., comdr. 3d fleet USN, Pearl Harbor, 1985-87; combat systems officer USS TAUTUG, Pearl Harbor, 1987-89; navigator, ops. officer USS Indpls., Pearl Harbor, 1989-92; UHF/EHF satellite navy rep. PEO-SCS, USN, El Segundo, Calif., 1994-96; project mgr. for spacecraft comms. Booz-Allen and Hamilton, Inc., San Diego, 1996-97; dir. Space and Comm. Predicate Logic Inc., San Diego, 1997—. Contbr. articles to profl. jours. Pres. congregation Christ the Cornerstone Luth. Ch.; mem. sch. bd. Our Savior Luth. Sch., Aiea, Hawaii, 1986; den leader webelos Boy Scouts Am., 1995-97; bd. dirs. Children's Angelcare Aid Internat., 1998—; chmn. bd. dirs. Christ the Cornerstone Luth. Ch. Fellow Inst. for the Advancement of Engring.; assoc. fellow AIAA (vice-chair edn. L.A. sect. 1991—; dep. dir. edn. region VI 1994-97); mem. Space Nuclear Thermal Propulsion, Eta Kappa Nu. Republican. Lutheran. Achievements include design of predictive control system for thermoacoustic refrigerator, 3D laser range and orientation measuring system, navy satellite/computer secure communications systems; asynchronous transfer mode (ATM) networks; satellite and ground system design on CYBERSTAR, EHF Communications Satellite, Global Broadcast Service, Navy UHF Follow-On Satellite, GEOSAT Follow-On satellite; digital modular radio design; submarine communications support system; wireless ethernet design and installation. E-mail: Russel@Predicate.com. Home: 2520 Brady Dr Colorado Springs CO 80917-4021

RUSSELL, BILL, coach; b. Pittsburg, Kans., Oct. 21, 1948. Head coach L.A. Dodgers. Office: c/o LA Dodgers 1000 Elysian Park Ave Los Angeles CA 90012-1112

RUSSELL, BRYON, basketball player; b. Dec. 31, 1970. Forward Utah Jazz, Salt Lake City. Office: c/o Utah Jazz 301 W South Temple Salt Lake City UT 84101-1216*

RUSSELL, CAROL ANN, personnel service company executive; b. Detroit, Dec. 14, 1943; d. Billy and Iris Koud; m. Victor Rojas (div.). BA in English, CUNY-Hunter Coll., 1993. Registered employment cons. Various positions in temp. help cos. N.Y.C., 1964-74; v.p. Wollborg-Michelson, San Francisco, 1974-82; co-owner, pres. Russell Staffing Resources, Inc., San Francisco and Sonoma, 1983-98; ret.; media guest, spkr., workshop and seminar leader in field; host/cmty. prodr. Job Net program for TCI Cable T.V. Pub. Checkpoint Newsletter; contbr. articles to profl. publs. Named to the Inc. 500, 1989, 90. Mem. Am. Women in Radio and TV, Soc. to Preserve and Encourage Radio Drama Variety and Comedy, No. Calif. Human Resources Coun., Soc. Human Resource Mgmt., Calif. Assn. Pers. Cons. (pres. Golden State chpt. 1984-85), Calif. Assn. Temp. Svcs., Bay Area Pers. Assn. (pres. 1983-84), Pers. Assn. Sonoma County, Profl. Resume Writers Am., Am. Jewish Congress.

RUSSELL, FRANCIA, ballet director, educator; b. Los Angeles, Jan. 10, 1938; d. W. Frank and Marion (Whitney) R.; m. Kent Stowell, Nov. 19, 1965; children: Christopher, Darren, Ethan. Studies with, George Balanchine, Vera Volkova, Felia Doubrouska, Antonina Tumkovsky, Benjamin Harkarvy; student, NYU, Columbia U. Dancer, soloist N.Y.C. Ballet, 1956-62, ballet mistress, 1965-70; dancer Ballets USA/Jerome Robbins, N.Y.C., 1962; tchr. ballet Sch. Am. Ballet, N.Y.C., 1963-64; co-dir. Frankfurt (Fed. Republic Germany) Opera Ballet, 1976-77; dir., co-artistic dir. Pacific N.W. Ballet, Seattle, 1977—; dir. Pacific N.W. Ballet Sch., Seattle; affiliate prof. of dance U. Wash. Dir. staging over 100 George Balanchine ballet prodns. throughout world, including the Soviet Union and People's Republic of China, 1964—. Named Woman of Achievement, Matrix Table, Women in Comm., Seattle, 1987, Gov.'s Arts award, 1989, Dance Mag. award, 1996. Mem. Internat. Women's Forum. Home: 2833 Broadway E Seattle WA 98102-3935 Office: Pacific NW Ballet 301 Mercer St Seattle WA 98109-4600

RUSSELL, IRWIN EMANUEL, lawyer; b. N.Y.C., Jan. 24, 1926; m. Suzanne Russell, Nov. 15, 1968. BS in Econs., U. Pa., 1947; JD, Harvard U., 1949. Bar: N.Y. 1949, Calif. 1971. Atty. office chief counsel Wage Stabilization bd., Washington, 1951-53; pvt. practice N.Y.C., 1954-71; founder, chmn., dir. RAI Rsch. Corp., Hauppage, N.Y., 1954-91; exec. v.p., treas., dir. The Wolper Orgn., L.A., 1971-76; pvt. practice Beverly Hills, Calif., 1977—; dir. Walt Disney Co., Burbank, Calif., The Lipper Fund, Inc. N.Y.C. With USAAF, 1944-46. Home: 10590 Wilshire Blvd Apt 1402 Los Angeles CA 90024-4563 Office: 9401 Wilshire Blvd Ste 760 Beverly Hills CA 90212-2933

RUSSELL, JOAN DELIGHT, hospital administrator, realtor, investor; b. Youngstown, Ohio, July 20, 1933; d. Jack Leonard and Pauline Frances (Cox) Burris; m. Herbert A. Cook, Dec. 12, 1964 (div. May, 1981); children—Scott, Vicki, Todd, Herbert, Jr., Tami, Susan; m. Camp Wells Russell, May 16, 1981. Student St. Paul Bible Coll., Minn., 1951-56; diploma in nursing Grant Hosp., Columbus, Ohio, 1955. Registered nurse; cert. nursing home administrator. Post-operative specialist open heart surgery various hosps., 1956-61; in-service coordinator I.V. therapist various hosps., 1962-64; owner, dir. of nurses, hosp. administr. Convalescent Hosp., Long Beach, Calif., 1964-72; v.p. Circle Convalescent Hosp., Calif., 1972-82, Leisure Convalescent Hosp., Calif., 1972-82, Hac-Con Corp., Long Beach, 1972-82; sec. Pacific Coast Convalescent Hosp. Corp., Long Beach, 1972-82; pvt. practice investments, real estate, office bldg. mgmt., Long Beach, 1972-84; [illegible] owner, operator, Calif. prises., 1987—; speaker schs. and seminars. Weekly radio broadcast, 1965-72. Del., Am. Nurses Assn., Calif. Nurses Assn.; organist West Lakewood Baptist Ch., Sunday sch. tchr.; mem. Campus Crusade, Campus Life, pres. Point

Nurses Assn., Real Estate Assn., Concerned Women Am. Republican. Club: Youth for Christ (exec. bd.). Avocations: music, boating, motor home camping. Home: PO Box 10549 Scottsdale AZ 85271-0549 Office: Calif Convalescent Hosp 3850 E Esther St Long Beach CA 90804-2009

RUSSELL, MARJORIE ROSE, manufacturing company executive; b. Welcome, Minn., Sept. 3, 1925; d. Emil Frederick and Ella Magdalene (Sothman) Wohlenhaus; m. Kenneth Kollmann Russell, Sept. 15, 1947 (div. May 1973); children: Jennie Rose, Richard Lowell, Laura Eloise, James Wesley. Student, Northwestern Sch., Mpls., 1943-45, St. Paul Bible Inst., 1946-47. Cook U. Minn., Mpls., 1943-45; maintenance person U. Farm Campus/N.W. Schs., St. Paul, 1945-46; clk. Kresge Corp., Mpls., 1945; cook, waitress, mgr. Union City Mission Bible Camp, Mpls., 1944-47; caterer for v.p. Gt. No. R.R., St. Paul, 1947; custodian Old Soldiers Home, St. Paul, 1946; nurse Sister Elizabeth Kenney Polio Hosp., St. Paul, 1946; seamstress Hirsch, Weis, White Stag, Pendleton, Mayfair, Portland, Oreg., 1960-72; owner, operator, contract mgr., creative designer The Brass Needle, Portland, 1972—; contractor Forrester's Sanderson Safety, Scotsco, Nero & Assocs., Gara Gear, Portland, 1972—; Columbia Sportswear; tchr. Indo Chinese Cultural Ctr., Portland, 1982; mfr. of protective chaps and vests for the Pacific Northwest hogging industry. Designer, producer Kisn Bridal Fair, 1969; composer: He Liveth in Me, 1968; prodr. Safety Chaps for Loggers. Sec. Model Cities Com., Portland, 1969; com. mem. Neighborhood Black Christmas Parade, Portland, 1970; custume designer Local Miss Jr. Black Beauty Contest, Portland, 1973; nominating com. Nat. Contract Mgmt. Assn., Portland, 1978; mem. nominating com. Multi-Cultural Sr. Adv. Com., 1988-91. Mem. NAFE, Urban League, Urban League Guild (historian 1991-92), Am. Assn. Ret. Persons, Nat. Contract Mgmt. Assn. Democrat. Mem. United Ch. of Christ. Avocations: music, swimming, painting, gardening, arts. Home and Office: The Brass Needle 2809 NE 12th Ave Portland OR 97212-3219

RUSSELL, MARLOU, psychologist; b. Tucson, June 2, 1956; d. William Herman and Carole Eleanor (Musgrove) McBratney; m. Jan Christopher Russell, Sept. 9, 1989. BA U. Ariz., 1981; MA Calif. Grad. Inst., 1983, PhD, 1987. Lic. psychologist; marriage, family and child counselor. Asst. to pres. Western Psychol. Svcs., L.A., 1978-81; crisis counselor Cedars-Sinai Med. Ctr., L.A., 1980-84; counselor South Bay Therapeutic Clinic, Hawthorne, Calif., 1982-84; psychotherapist PMC Treatment Systems, L.A., 1984-85, Beverly Hills Counseling Ctr., 1984-85, Comprehensive Care Corp., L.A., 1985-86; pvt. practice, L.A., 1986—; counselor Brotman Med. Ctr., L.A., 1982-83, Julia Ann Singer Ctr., L.A., 1984; bd. dirs. Los Angeles Commn. Assaults Against Women, 1987-89. Author: Adoption Wisdom: A Guide to the Issues and Feelings of Adoption, 1996. Mem. Internat. Assn. Eating Disorders Profls., Women in Health (bd. dirs. 1993-94), Women's Referral Svc., Calif. State Psychol. Assn., Calif. Assn. Marriage & Family Therapists (bd. dirs. 1993-94), Am. Adoption Congress, Westside Bus. Womens Assn. (bd. dirs. 1993-94). Democrat. Office: 1452 26th St Ste 103 Santa Monica CA 90404-3042

RUSSELL, PAMELA REDFORD, writer, film documentarian; b. Long Beach, Calif., June 11, 1950; d. George Martin and Helen Glyn (Brewen) R.; children: Caitlin, Maggie, Tess. Student, UCLA, 1970-74. Field prodr. Santa Fe Comm., L.A., 1983-84; exec. prodr. Guiding Star Prodns., L.A., 1994—. Author: The Woman Who Loved John Wilkes Booth, 1978, Wild Flowers, 1982, (screenplay) Am American Woman, 1993; writer for Mary Tyler Moore Show, 1974, Touched By An Angel, 1997, also 14 scripts for Sears and Mut. Radio Theater, 1980-81, (TV show) Touched by An Angel, 1997. Mem. Nat. Trust for Hist. Preservation, Civil War Trust., Pacific Grove Heritage Soc. Mem. Authors Guild, Writers Guild Am. West. Avocation: historic preservation. Office: Agy for Performing Arts 9000 W Sunset Blvd Ste 1200 Los Angeles CA 90069-5894

RUSSELL, PATRICK JAMES, priest; b. Boise, Idaho, May 10, 1959; s. Glenn Edward and Doralea (Trumble) R. BA, Boise U., 1982; MDiv, St. Patrick's Sem., 1986. Ordained priest Roman Catholic Ch., 1986. Assoc. pastor St. Marks Cath. Ch., Boise, 1986-91; chaplain Chateau de Boise, 1991—, Bishop Kelly H.S., 1993—. Active Nat. Cath. Office for Persons With Disabilities, 1991—, Idaho Vocations Bd., 1992-95; founder, dir. Father Russell Charity Golf Scramble for Persons with Chronic Illnesses, 1989—; apptd. tribunal advocate Office of Canonical Affairs, Idaho, 1996—. Named Idaho Handicapped Student of Yr., 1974, Best Actor, Boise Little Theatre, 1979-80, Outstanding Young Man of Am., 1983, 84, 86, 87, Outstanding Youth in Achievement, Cambridge, U.K. Personalities. Man of Yr., Cambridge, 1995. Mem. Am. Film Inst., Amnesty Internat., Nat. Theatre Comm. Group (charter), Internat. Soc. Poets (life, award), Internat. Biog. Ctr., Right to Life/Spl. Olympics, Sigma Phi Epsilon. Democrat. Avocations: writing, painting, music, public speaking, acting.

RUSSELL, THOMAS ARTHUR, lawyer; b. Corona, Calif., Aug. 2, 1953; s. Larry Arthur Russell and Patricia Helena (Collins) Heath; m. Mary Ellen Leach, June 20, 1992; children: Trevor James, Elizabeth Mary, John Thomas. BS, U. Calif., Berkeley, 1976; JD, U. So. Calif., 1982. Bar: Calif. 1983, U.S. Dist. Ct. (cen. dist.) Calif. 1983, U.S. Ct. Appeals (9th cir.) 1986, U.S. Supreme Ct. 1988. Law clk. Calif. Ct. Appeal, L.A., 1981; assoc. Graham & James, Long Beach, Calif., 1982-88; prin. Cogswell Woolley Nakazawa & Russell, Long Beach, 1988—; spkr., panelist Mat. Marine Bankers Assn., Chgo., 1987—; bd. dirs. Ctr. Internat. Comml. Arbitration, 1991—; bd. internat. Bus. Assn. So. Calif., 1989-96, pres., 1994-95. Contbg. author Benedict on Admiralty, 1995—, Recreational Boating Law, 1992, Moore's Federal Practice, Admiralty Vol., 1997—; editor Boating Briefs, 1991-96. Bd. dirs. World Trade Ctr. Assn., L.A.-Long Beach, 1996—, Long Beach Area C. of C., 1994—; hon. mem. Am. Vessel Documentation Assn., 1995. Mem. ABA (Bronze Key award 1982, maritime fin. subcom., chmn. 1994—), Maritime Law Assn. U.S. (proctor, vice chmn. 1996—), Calif. Bar Assn., L.A. County Bar Assn., Long Beach Bar Assn., Calif. Yacht Brokers Assn. (Merle Parke award 1996), Legion of Lex. Am. Inn of Ct. (barrister). Republican. Roman Catholic. Avocations: tennis, skiing. Home: 7 Mustang Rd Rancho Palos Verdes CA 90275-5250 Office: Cogswell Woolley Nakazawa & Russell 111 W Ocean Blvd Ste 2000 Long Beach CA 90802-4696

RUSSIN, ROBERT ISAIAH, sculptor, educator; b. N.Y.C., Aug. 26, 1914; s. Uriel and Olga (Winnett) R.; m. Adele Mutchnick, May 21, 1937; children: Joseph Mark, Lincoln David, Uriel Robin. BA, CCNY, 1933, MS, 1935; postgrad. (Inst. fellow), Beaux Arts Inst. Design, 1935-36. Tchr. sculpture Copper Union Art Inst., N.Y.C., 1944-47; prof. art U. Wyo., Laramie, 1947-86; prof., artist-in-residence U. Wyo., 1976-85, Disting. prof. emeritus, 1985—. One-man shows Tucson Fine Arts Ctr., 1966, Colorado Springs (Colo.) Fine Arts Ctr., 1967, Palm Springs (Calif.) Desert Mus., Chas. G. Bowers Meml. Mus., Judah L. Magnes Meml. Mus., Berkeley, Calif.; retrospective one-man exhbn. Nat. Gallery Modern Art, Santo Domingo, Dominican Republic, 1976, Tubac Ctr. of the Arts, Ariz., 1987, Old Town Gallery-Park City, Ut., Riggins Gallery, Scottsdale, Ariz., 1989, Fine Arts Mus., U. Wyo., 1991; sculpture commns. include 2 8-foot metal figures, Evanston (Ill.) Post Office, 1939, three life-size carved figures, Conshohocken (Pa.) Post Office, 1940, Benjamin Franklin Monument, U. Wyo., 1957, Bust of Lincoln, Lincoln Mus., Washington, (now in Gettysburg Mus.), 1959, Lincoln Monument atop summit Lincoln Hwy., (now U.S. Interstate 80), Wyo, 1959, monumental bas-relief bronze Cheyenne (Wyo.) Fed. Bldg, 1966, two carved wood walls, Denver Fed. Bldg., 1966, monumental fountain, City of Hope Med. Ctr., Los Angeles 1966-67, statue, Brookhaven (N.Y.) Nat. Lab., 1968, life-size bronze sculpture fountain, City of Hope, 1969, Pomona Coll., 1973, monumental bronze sculpture Prometheus Natrona County (Wyo.) Pub. Library, 1974, Man and Energy, Casper (Wyo.) C. of C., 1974, 12-foot marble carving Menorah Med. Ctr., Kansas City, Mo., 1975, Einstein and Gershwin medals Magnes Meml. Mus, Berkeley, Nat. Mus. Art, Santo Domingo, Dominican Republic, 1975, monumental fountain, Galleria d'Arte Moderna, Santo Domingo, 1977, Duarte Monument, Santo Domingo, 1977, 30 foot steel and water fountain monument City Hall, Casper, 1980, marble and bronze monument Lincoln Center, Denver, 1987, marble eagle monument, U. Wyo., Laramie, 1985, portrait head Charles Bluhdorn, chmn. Gulf & Western, 1975, portrait bust Pres. J. Balaguer of Dominican Republic, 1975, portrait head G. Wilson Knight, Shakespearean actor and scholar, 1975, 2 12-foot bronze figures The Greeting and The Gift for

Bicentennial Commn., Cheyenne, 1976, monumental marble head of Juan Pablo Duarte liberator Dominican Republic, Santo Domingo, 1976, monumental marble, Pan Am. Family, Dominican Republic, 1977, marble sculpture Trio, U. Wyo., 1985, Isaac B. Singer medal for Magnes Mus., 1983, monumental Holocaust Figure Tucson Jewish Community Ctr., 1989, granite monument Chthonodynamis, Dept. Energy Bldg., Washington, 1992, bust Hon. Milward Simpson, 1993, bust James Forest U. Wyo., 1993, bronze statue Univ. Med. Ctr., Tuscon, Head, Gov. Stanley Hathway, Cheyenne, Wy. 1995; contbr. articles to profl. jours.Head, Pres. Franklin D. Roosevelt, Rotunda (pres.hosp. Bethsda, Md.). Recipient awards sec. fine arts U.S. Treasury, 1939, 40, Lincoln medal U.S. Congress, 1959, Alfred G.B. Steel award Pa. Acad. Fine Arts, 1961, medal of Order of Duarte Sanchez y Mella, Dominican Republic, 1977; Ford Found. fellow, 1953. Mem. Nat. Sculpture Conf. (exec. bd.), Sculptors Guild, Nat. Sculpture Soc., AIA, AAUP, Coll. Art Internat. Inst. Arts and Letters, Phi Beta Kappa (hon.). Home: 61 N Fork Rd Centennial WY 82055 also: 1160 W Placita Salubre Green Valley AZ 85614-1334

RUSSO, ANGELA BROWN, assistant principal; b. Balt., Apr. 21, 1948; d. Johnny Jeff and Lavonia Vernette (Davis) Royster; m. James Elton Brown, Oct. 5, 1975 (div. Aug. 1993); 1 child, Tiffany Lavonne; m. John Russo, Nov. 26, 1993. BS in Health Edn., Morgan State U., Balt., 1971; MS in Adult Edn., Kans. State U., 1977; postgrad., Charles County C.C., LaPlata, Md., 1983. Tchr. Harlem Park Jr. H.S., Balt., 1972-73, St. Maur's Internat. Sch., Yokohama, Japan, 1973-74, Herring Run Jr. H.S., Balt., 1974-75; Homebound tchr. Geary County Unified Schs., Junction City, Kans., 1975-77; counselor/head counseling dept. Dededo (Guam) Jr. H.S., 1977-79; tchr. Walker Mill Jr. H.S., Capitol Heights, Md., 1979-82; asst. dir./instr. pre-employment tng. program Charles County C.C., LaPlata, 1982-84; ednl. dir., counselor Odyssey Alternative Sch. Utah State Employment, Salt Lake City/Clearfield, 1984-85; tchr. North Davis Jr. H.S., Ogden, Utah, 1985-87; prin. Island Paradise Sch., Honolulu, 1989-90; asst. prin. C.W. Woodbury Mid. Sch., Las Vegas, 1994—; tchr. Mahlon Brown Jr. H.S., Las Vegas, Nev., 1990-91; adminstrv. dean Green Valley H.S., Las Vegas, 1992-93, asst. prin., 1994—; asst. prin. Becker Mid. Sch., Las Vegas, 1993-94; part-time coord./counselor Sinajaha (Guam) Adult Basic Edn. Program, 1978. Foster parent; vol. Juvenile Ct. Recipient Pub. Svc. Commendation, U.S. Dept. Commerce. Mem. AAUW, ASCD, Phi Delta Gamma, Alpha Kappa Alpha, Phi Delta Kappa. Avocations: travel, community choir. Home: 1201 NE 37th St Oklahoma City OK 73111-5011 Office: CW Woodbury Mid Sch 6500 E Sahara Ave Las Vegas NV 89122-2800 Address: 3105 La Entrada St Henderson NV 89014-3606

RUSSO, LAURA, gallery director; b. Waterbury, Conn., Mar. 7, 1943; d. Lawrence and Lillian A. (Russo) Kaplan; m. John I. Lawrence, May 6, 1962 (div. 1974); children: Maia Giosi, Dylan Russo. Cert., Pacific N.W. Coll. Art, 1975. Art instr. Tucker Maxon Oral Sch., Portland, Oreg., 1970-74, Pacific N.W. Coll. Art, Portland, 1977-78; assoc. dir. Fountain Fine Arts, Seattle, 1981-82; asst. dir. Fountain Gallery of Art, Portland, 1975-86; owner, dir. Laura Russo Gallery, Portland, 1986—; lectr. Portland State Coll., 1992; juror Oreg. Sch. Design, Portland, 1988, Western Oreg. State Coll. 1992, Beaverton Arts Commn., 1992, Oreg. Hist. Soc., 1990; com. mem. Oreg. Com. for Nat. Mus. Women in Arts, 1988; guest interviewer art dept. Oreg. State Coll., 1996; mem. adv. bd. Sch. Fine and Performing Arts Portland State U., 1998—. Mem. com. awards and grants Met. Arts Commn., Portland, 1988, 89; mem. P.N.C.A.; juror Art in Pub. Schs. Program, 1990; juror ArtQuake, Portland, 1994; juror Corvallis (Oreg.) Art Ctr., 1995. Mem. Alumni Friends, Contemporary Arts Coun. (program chmn., v.p. 1989-91), Portland Art Mus. (search com. 1993-94), Oreg. Art Inst., Friends Print Soc., Oreg. Art Inst., L.A. Mus. Contemporary Art, Seattle Art Mus. (lectr. 1987), Art Table (West Coast br.). Democrat. Office: Laura Russo Gallery 805 NW 21st Ave Portland OR 97209-1408

RUSSON, LEONARD H., state supreme court justice; b. Salt Lake City, May 15, 1933. JD, Utah Coll., 1962. Pvt. practice Salt Lake City, 1962-84; judge Utah Dist. Ct. (3d dist.), Utah Ct. Appeals; justice Utah Supreme Ct., Salt Lake City; vice chair Utah Bd. Dist. Ct. Judges; mem. Jud. Conduct Commn., Utah Supreme Ct. Adv. Com. on Code of Profl. Conduct. Office: Utah Supreme Ct PO Box 140210 450 S State St Salt Lake City UT 84114-0210*

RUSTON, SHELLY SMITH, museum administrator; b. Santa Barbara, Calif.; m. Maxwell Philip Ruston, Jan. 5, 1959; children: Hilary, Max. BA, Scripps Coll.; postgrad., Harvard Univ. Dir. spl. programs Santa Barbara Mus. Art. Adv. bd. Santa Barbara Internat. Film Festival, Non-Profits in Travel. Mem. Royal Overseas League. Office: Santa Barbara Mus Art 1130 State St Santa Barbara CA 93101-2746

RUSUNEN, ROBERT LEE, purchasing manager; b. Missoula, Mont., Mar. 16, 1946; m. Sherry M. Rusunen, June 16, 1972. BS in Bus., U. Mont., 1971; MBA in Bus., Wash. State U., 1977. Cert. purchasing mgr.; cert. prodn. inventory mgmt. Buyer, merchandise mgr. Hart-Aldin Co., Billings, Mont., 1971-75; region materials mgr. GE Supply, Seattle, 1976-79; dir. purchasing Riedel Internat., Portland, Oreg., 1979-82, v.p. purchasing and pers., 1982-84; mgr. corp. purchasing Pacific Telecom, Inc., Vancouver, Wash., 1985-97; materials team mgr. Pacificorp, Portland, 1997-98; prin. cons. Price Waterhouse Coopers, Portland, 1998—. V.p. Wishing Wells Home Owners Assn., Ridgefield, Wash., 1996-97. Staff sgt., USAF, 1964-68. Mem. Nat. Assn. Purchasing Mgmt., Am. Prodn. and Inventory Control Soc., Constrn. Owners Assn. Am., Nat. Contract Mgmt. Assn. Home: 2730 S Cornett Dr Ridgefield WA 98642-8558 Office: Price Waterhouse Coopers 121 SW Morrison St Portland OR 97204

RUTES, WALTER ALAN, architect; b. N.Y.C., Sept. 21, 1928; s. Jack and Sarah (Ogur) R.; m. Helene Darville, Apr. 2, 1952; children: Daniel J., Linda Lee. B.Arch. (Sands Meml. medal 1950), Cornell U., 1950; fellow city planning, MIT, 1951; postgrad., Harvard U. Grad. Sch. Design, 1978. Cert. Nat. Council Archtl. Registration Bds. Assoc. ptnr. Skidmore, Owings & Merrill, N.Y.C., 1951-72; v.p. John Carl Warnecke & Assocs., N.Y.C., 1972-74; staff v.p. Intercontinental Hotels Corp., N.Y.C., 1974-80; dir. architecture Holiday Inns, Inc., Memphis, 1980-83; dir. design The Sheraton Corp., Boston, 1983-85; chmn 9 Tek Ltd. Devel. Cons., 1985—; chmn. adv. bd. Hult Fellowships for Constrn. Industry, 1968-75, Architects and Engrs. Com. New Bldg. Code, 1968; mem. zoning adv. com. N.Y.C. Planning Commn., 1970; lectr. in field, 1968—; mem. steering com. UNESCO Council Tall Bldgs. and Urban Habitat, 1980—; vis. prof. Cornell-Essec Grad. Program; vis. prof. Nova U. Author: Hotel Planning and Design, New Trends in Resort Design and Development; (software system) SHAPE, Megatrends and Marketecture; contbr. articles to profl. jours.; prin. works include Lincoln Center Library for Performing Arts, N.Y.C., 1967, Am. Republic Ins. Co. Nat. Hdqrs., Des Moines, 1967, HUD Apts., Jersey City, 1972, Merrill Lynch Bldg., N.Y.C., 1973, Tour Fiat, Paris, 1974, Aid Assn. for Luths. Nat. Hdqrs., Appleton, Wis., 1976, Semiramis Intercontinental Hotel, Cairo, 1985, Intercontinental, Jeddah, 1983, Embassy Suites Internat., 1985, Universal City Hotel Complex, L.A., 1986, TechWorld Conv. Hotel, Washington, 1986, Sheraton Fairplex Conv. Ctr., L.A., 1992, Orlando Conv. Ctr. Hotel, 1993, Winter Olympiad Media Complex, Norway, 1993, Ephesus Resort Complex, Turkey, 1986, Royal Christiania Hotel, Oslo, Norway, 1991, EuroFrance Leisure Park Complex, Cannes, 1993, Kuna Hills Multi Resort, Guam, 1994. Recipient Platinum Circle award Hotel Design Industry, 1988. Fellow AIA; mem. Ethical Culture Soc. Office: 8501 N 84th Pl Scottsdale AZ 85258-2419 also: 25 Richbell Rd White Plains NY 10605-4110

RUTHERFORD, JEAN, rancher; b. Gooding, Idaho, Sept. 25, 1933; d. Orval Liman and Willa Alice (Chapman) R.; m. Drew Williams Jensen, Jan. 25, 1967 (div. Mar. 1971); 1 child Bille Jensen. Vet. asst. Jerome (Idaho) Vet. Hosp., 1954-58; cattle owner Burnt River Ranch, Durkee, Oreg., 1958—; sales rep. Sports Apparel Mktg., 1982—; sec. Oreg. Cattle Women, 1964-65; cons. Western World Promotions, Denver, 1987—; queen judge Nat. H.S. Rodeo Assn., Denver, 1991, 93-94; rodeo judge, Miss., Oreg., Wash, Idaho, Ariz, 1985-92; news corres. Qtr. Horse Jour., 1959-63, Record Courier, 1963. Contbr. articles to mags. Organizer Blue Mountain Qtr. Horse Assn., Baker, Oreg., 1960, 4H Horse Club, Idaho, 1955. Named Best Dressed Westerner Gross Tailors, 1962, Best in Sales, Rodeo Am., 1992. Mem. Am. Angus Assn. (life, mfrs. rep. 1982—). Republican. Episcopalian. Avocations: rodeo, livestock events, rodeo queen judging, western wear, travel. Home and Office: RR 4 Box 4131 Hermiston OR 97838-9404

RUTHERFORD, ROBERT BARRY, surgeon; b. Edmonton, Alta., Can., July 29, 1931; s. Robert Lyon and Kathleen Emily (Gunn) R.; m. Beulah Kay Folk, Aug. 20, 1955; children: Robert Scott, Lori Jayne, Holly Anne, Trudy Kaye, Jay Wilson. BA in Biology, Johns Hopkins U., 1952, MD, 1956. Surgeon U. Colo. Health Sci. Ctr., Denver; emeritus prof. surgery U. Colo., Denver, 1996—. Editor: (texts) Management of Trauma, 1968, 4 edits., Vascular Surgery, 1978, 4 edits., An Atlas of Vascular Surgery, Vol. 1, 1993, Vol. 2, 1998; editor quar. rev. Seminars in Vascular Surgery; sr. editor Jour. Vascular Surgery. Fellow ACS, Royal Coll. Surgeons of Glasgow; mem. Internat. Soc. for Cardiovascular Surgery, Phi Beta Kappa, Alpha Omega Alpha. Republican. Unitarian. Avocations: skiing, biking, wind surfing, sailing. Office: PO Box 23159 Silverthorne CO 80498-3159

RUTSCHKE, ANNAMARIE, administrative technician; b. Santa Barbara, Calif., June 29, 1965; d. Benjamin Wiley Jordan and Jeannette Irene Rutschke; m. Robert Allan Bryant, July 31, 1988 (div. 1996). File clk. San Luis Welding Supply, San Luis Obispo, Calif., 1983; customer svc. clk. The Living Picture, Alameda, Calif., 1984, 7-11, Alameda, 1985-86; clk. Def. Subs. Reg. Pacific, Alameda, 1987-88; pers. clk. Def. Depot Tracy, Alameda, 1988-90; adminstrv. clk. Gen. Svcs. Adminstrn., San Francisco, 1990, purchasing agt., 1990-96, adminstrv. technician, 1996—. Co-coord. Fed. Recycling Coun., 1992, 93; operator Muscular Dystrophy Assn., Arroyo Grande, Calif., 1980. Democrat. Lutheran. Avocations: art, writing, computer programming. Office: Gen Svcs Adminstrn 5th Fl W 450 Golden Gate Ave San Francisco CA 94102-3661

RUYBALID, LOUIS ARTHUR, social worker, community development consultant; b. Allison, Colo., Apr. 6, 1925; s. Mike Joseph and Helen Mary (Rodriguez) R.; m. Seraphima Alexander, June 12, 1949; children: Mariana, John. BA, U. Denver, 1946-49, MSW, 1951; PhD, U. Calif., Berkeley, 1970; Professor Ad-Honorem (hon.), Nat. U., Caracas, Venezuela, 1964. Social worker Ariz., Calif., Colo., 1951-62; advisor community devel. Unitarian Service Com., Caracas, 1962-64, U.S. Agy. for Internat. Devel., Rio de Janeiro, Brazil, 1964-66; area coordinator U.S. Office Econ. Opportunity, San Francisco, 1966-68; prof., dept. head U. So. Colo., Pueblo, 1974-80; licensing analyst State of Calif., Campbell, 1984—; prof. sch. of social work Highlands U., Las Vegas, N.Mex., 1988-89; cons. UN, Caracas, 1978, Brazilian Govt., Brazilia, 1964-66, Venezuelan Govt., Caracas, 1962-64. Author: (books) Favela, 1970, Glossary for Hominology, 1978, (research instrument) The Conglomerate Hom., 1976. Mem. exec. com. Pueblo (Colo.) Regional Planning Com., 1974-79, Nat. Advisory com. The Program Agy. United Presbyn. Ch., 1978-79. Served with USN, 1944-46. Recipient Pro Mundo Beneficio medal Brazilian Acad. Human Sci., Sao Paulo, 1976; United Def. Fund fellow U. Calif., Berkeley, 1961-62, Cert. World Leadership Internat. Leaders of Achievement, 1988-89. Mem. NASW (cert.), Ethnic Minority Commn., IMAGE (nat. edn. chair), Am. Hominol. Assn. (nat. pres. 1975-79), U. Calif. Alumni Assn., AARP (minority spokesperson), Phi Beta Kappa, Phi Sigma Iota. Democrat. Avocations: tennis, boxing history. Home and Office: Ruybalid Assoc Inc 129 Calle Don Jose Santa Fe NM 87501-2364

RUYTER, NANCY LEE CHALFA, dance educator; b. Phila., May 23, 1933; d. Andrew Benedict Chalfa and Lois Elizabeth (Strode) McClary; m. Ralph Markson (div.); m. Hans C. Ruyter, Dec. 7, 1968. BA in History, U. Calif., Riverside, 1964; PhD in History, Claremont Grad. Sch., 1970. Tchr. theater dept. Pomona Coll., 1965-72; instr. dance program U. Calif., Riverside, 1972-76, acting chair dance program, 1974-75; instr. dance dept. UCLA, 1976; instr. phys. edn. dept. Orange Coast Coll., 1976-77; asst. prof. dept. phys. edn. and dance Tufts U., 1977-78; asst. prof. phys. edn. dept. Calif. State U., Northridge, 1978-82; asst. prof., then assoc. prof. dance dept. U. Calif., Irvine, 1982—, assoc. dean Sch. Fine Arts, 1984-88, 95-96, chair dept. dance, 1989-91; presenter in field. Appeared with Jasna Planina Folk Ensemble, 1972-77, 78-79, Di Falco and Co., 1955-57; choreographer, dir. numerous coll. dance prodns.; contbr. articles, revs. to profl. publs.; author: Reformers and Visionaries: The Americanization of the Art of Dance, 1979. Mem. Am. Soc. Theatre Rsch., Bulgarian Studies Assn., Congress on Rsch. in Dance (bd. dirs. 1977-80, pres. 1981-85), Folk Dance Fedn., Internat. Fedn. Theatre Rsch., Soc. Dance Rsch., Soc. Ethnomusicology, Soc. Dance History Scholars (steering com. 1980-81), Spanish Dance Soc., Theatre Libr. Assn. Office: U Calif-Irvine Dept Dance Irvine CA 92697

RYAL, DICK, scriptwriter, actor; b. Corning, N.Y., June 21, 1925; s. Richard Fuller and Jessie (Wadleigh) R. Student, Profl. Children's Sch., N.Y.C., 1942-43. Host, scriptwriter The Golden Key Sta. KTTV-TV, Hollywood, late 1950's; film, radio, TV actor N.Y.C. and Hollywood, Calif., 1960-83; writer, actor Chevron Broadcast, San Francisco, 1969-72; featured actor films, TV series Studiohouse, Hollywood, 1971-86; voice over actor Hanna-Barbera Animated Films, Hollywood, 1979; internat. in-house on camera spokesman Rockwell Internat. Corp., 1985-90. Scriptwriter: (documentary) Our Nation's Heritage, 1969-72 (Peadbody medal 1975), (drama) The Calumet, 1984 (Writers Guild Am. award), (comedy) Why Me?, 1985. Recipient Ohio State award for network documentaries, 1972, 73, 74. Mem. AFTRA, Writers Guild Am. (acad. liaison com., tellers com., spl. accolade award 1979), SAG, Pacific Pioneer Broadcasters. Office: PO Box 82 Beverly Hills CA 90213-0082

RYAN, ALLYN CAUAGAS, author, educator; b. Larena, The Philippines, June 2, 1938; came to U.S., 1957; d. Ignacio Fallorina Cauagas and Ignacia (Prudencia) Padayhag; m. James Edward Ryan, June 13, 1964; children: Monica Lynn Ryan-Border, Colleen Marie, Ryan-Spence. BA in English, UCLA, 1959, MFA in Theater, 1964. Cert. tchr. lang. arts, lit., comm. arts, theater arts, basic edn., Calif. Adj. faculty Saddleback Coll., Mission Viejo, Calif., 1983-90, Orange Coast Coll., Costa Mesa, Calif., 1986-87, Chapman U., Orange, Calif., 1987-88, Rancho Santiago Coll., Santa Ana, Calif., 1986-98. Contbr. poetry, short stories to profl. jours. Mem. legis. adv. com. Rancho Santiago Coll., 1996-97, instructional calendar group mem., 1996-97. UCI Writing Project fellow, 1989. Mem. NEA, Calif. Tchrs. Assn., C.C. Assn. (WHO award 1997), Continuing Edn. Faculty Assn. (Rancho Santiago Coll. chpt. pres. 1996-97, negotiations chmn. 1995-96), Romance Writers of Am. Avocations: oil painting, gourmet cooking. Home: 37261 Mojave Sage St Palm Desert CA 92211-1389

RYAN, BILL, executive. Ptnr. Neuhaus Ryan Wong, South San Francisco. Office: 601 Gateway Blvd Ste 900 South San Francisco CA 94080-7009

RYAN, CATHRINE SMITH, publisher; b. Calif.; d. Owen W. and Margarette D. Griffin; A.A., Bellevue Jr. Coll., Denver, 1948; grad. Barnes Sch. Commerce, Denver, 1950; student N.Y. Ballet Acad., 1954. Dir. Ballet Workshop, Enumclaw, Wash., 1958-64; dir. confs. and seminars San Francisco Theol. Sem., 1977-80; pres., dir. Cathi, Ltd., pub. and cons. office orgn. and mgmt., San Francisco, 1980—; freelance travel photographer, 1968-80; guest instr. in field; guest lectr. on German rsch. Recipient various certs. of recognition. Republican. Mormon. Author: Face Lifting Exercises, 1980, revised edit., 1997, Sullivan's Chain, 1986, Blood on the Snow, 1998; author visitor guide books; contbr. articles to procedure and policy manuals, geneal. rsch., family histories; translator old German script. Avocation: scuba diving.

RYAN, DEBBIE KAYE, financial planner; b. West Bend, Wis., Aug. 22, 1961; d. Allen August and Diann Marie (Yecke) Goldammer; m. Gregory Vincent Ryan, Aug. 12, 1991. Grad. H.S., Albuquerque. Cert. fin. paraplanner, Colo. Exec. sec. Mass Mutual Life Ins. Co., Albuquerque, 1979-82; adminstrv. asst. Mass Mutual Life Ins. Co., Phoenix, 1988-89; sec., receptionist Lyle Talbot Agy., Inc., Albuquerque, 1983-84; fin. paraplanner, adminstrv. asst. Charles Stephen & Co., Albuquerque, 1984-86; office mgr., fin. paraplanner Asset Planning Co., Inc., Albuquerque, 1986-87; brokerage rep. Monarch Life Ins. Co., Phoenix, 1988; from adminstrv. asst. to ins. agt., registered rep. Sun Life Can., Phoenix, 1990-94; mng. mem. GDR Benefits Group LLC, Phoenix, 1993—. Mem. Jr. League Phoenix (com. mem. 1994—), John C. Lincoln Guild (com. mem. 1995), Moon Valley Country Club (com. mem. 1991—). Republican. Lutheran. Avocations: community service, working out, helping friends organize, computers. Home and Office: 2 W Country Gables Dr Phoenix AZ 85023-5236

RYAN, MARY GENE, career officer, occupational health nurse; b. Corona, Calif., Sept. 11, 1953; d. Robert James and Genevieve Louise (Kubilis) Guzinski; m. Robert Eldon Ryan III, June 9, 1979; children: Michael Warren, Jessica Gene, Matthew James. BSN, So. Conn. State Coll., 1975; MPH, U. Tex., 1980. Commd. 2d lt. USAF, 1976, advanced through grades to lt. col., 1995; staff nurse obstetrics U. Conn. Med. Ctr., Farmington, 1975-76; med.-surgical staff nurse Williams AFB (Ariz.) Hosp., 1976-77; flight nurse instr. 2d Aeromed. Evacuation Squadron, Rhein Main, Fed. Republic of Germany, 1977-79; officer in charge environ. health Wilford Hall Med. Ctr., Lackland AFB, Tex., 1980-84; chief environ. health AFSC Hosp., Edwards AFB, Calif., 1984-88; dir. occupational health Peterson Med. Clinic, Oxnard, Calif., 1988-89; mgr. health and safety County of Ventura (Calif.)/Gen. Svcs. Agy., 1989-96; chief operating officer 2SCO Ltd., 1996-97; exec. dir. MG Ryan & Co., Inc., 1997—; cons. environ. health L.A. AFB, 1984-88; nurse exec. Calif. Air Nat. Guard 146 Med. Sqd., 1992—. Contbr. articles to profl. jours. Mem. choir, soloist, lay eucharistic min. Edwards AFB Cath. Chapel, 1984-88, mem. religious edn. com., 1984-85, lectr., commentator, 1986-87, marriage encounter counselor, 1991—; team mom for various sports, 1989—; AIDS educator, Edwards AFB, 1986-88. Recipient Meritorious Svc. medals USAF, Clin. award Am. Assn. Occupational Health Nurses, 1991. Mem. APHA (occupational health sect.), Am. Assn. Occupational Health Nurses, Claif. Assn. Occupational Health Nurses, Calif. Ctrl. Coast Occupational Health Nurses Assn. (pres. 1993-97, bd. dirs. 1998—), Ventura County Med. Aux. Avocations: sailing, sewing, skiing, swimming.

RYAN, MICHAEL LOUIS, controller; b. Corning, Iowa, Feb. 22, 1945; s. Leo Vincent and Elda May (Lawrence) R. AAS in Constrn. Tech., Iowa State U., 1965; BS in Acctg., Drake U., 1972. CPA, Iowa, Wyo. Acct. Ernst & Ernst, Des Moines, 1972-75, Becker, Herrick & Co., Pueblo, Colo., 1975-78; pvt. practice acctg. Gillette, Wyo., 1978-81; acct. Karen M. Moody, CPAs, Sheridan, Wyo., 1981-85; contr. T-C Investments, Inc., Sheridan, 1985—; ptnr. WHG Partnership, Sheridan, 1991—; v.p. Bosley-Ryan Constrn., Inc., Sheridan, 1993—. With spl. forces U.S. Army, 1966-68, Vietnam. Mem. AICPA (tax div.), Wyo. Soc. CPAs, Am. Legion (fin. officer 1977-81), Lodge (sec. Sheridan club 1982-90, pres. 1989), Phi Kappa Phi, Beta Alpha Psi, Beta Gamma Sigma. Democrat. Roman Catholic. Home: 735 Canby St Sheridan WY 82801-4907 Office: T-C Investments Inc 856 Coffeen Ave Sheridan WY 82801-5318

RYAN, MICHAEL THOMAS, music editor, composer; b. Chgo., Mar. 14, 1962; s. William Emmett and Patricia Alice (McKiernan) R.; m. J. Cai Hopkins, Aug. 11, 1985; 1 child, Rachel Kristine. MusB in Edn., Okla. State U., 1985. Supr. instrumental music Silver Valley H.S., Yermo, Calif., 1985-86, Temecula (Calif.) Valley H.S., 1986-88; dialogue editor West Prodns., Burbank, Calif., 1988-91; supervising music editor Segue Music, West Hollywood, Calif., 1991—. Mem. NARAS, Acad. Motion Picture Arts and Scis., Acad. TV Arts and Scis., Motion Picture Sound Editors (Golden Reel award 1995), Editors Guild, Pacific Composers Forum, Am. Fedn. Musicians, KC.

RYAN, PAUL MARTIN, lawyer; b. Portland, Oreg., Mar. 12, 1945; s. Francis B. and Catherine Aurelie (Fitzgerald) R.; m. Cynthia E. Kemp, Feb. 7, 1976; children: Jennifer, Robert F., Caroline E. BA, St. Mary's Coll., 1967; JD, Western State U., 1976. Bar: Calif. Civil servant State of Calif., L.A. and Sacramento, 1973-81; counsel Calif. Health Facilities Commn., Sacramento, 1981-84; sr. counsel Calif. Pub. Employees Retirement Sys., Sacramento, 1984—; cons. PMR Consulting, Fair Oaks, Calif., 1996-7. Author: (pamphlet) Career Guides for Entry Occupations in Electrical Utilities, 1977; contbg. author: (books) Dictionary of Occupational Titles, 1973-78, Another Place in Time, 1990, Visions, 1991, Days of Future's Past, 1991, Windows on the World, 1991, World of Poetry Anthology, 1991, (tech. report) An Evaluation of Alternative Programs for Training Beginning Typists in the Army, 1971. With U.S. Army, 1968-71, Vietnam. Decorated Bronze star. Mem. Nat. Health Lawyers Assn., Calif. Soc. for Health Care Attys., Sacramento County Bar Assn., Assn. of Calif. State Attys. and Adminstrv. Law Judges. Avocations: genealogy, comedy. Office: Calif Pub Employees Retirement Sys 400 P St Sacramento CA 95814-5345

RYAN, SYLVESTER D., bishop; b. Catalina Island, Calif., Sept. 3, 1930. Grad., St. John's Sem., Camarillo, Calif. Ordained priest Roman Cath. Ch., 1957, titular bishop of Remesiana. Aux. bishop L.A., 1990-92; bishop Monterey, Calif., 1992—. Office: Chancery Office PO Box 2048 580 Fremont St Monterey CA 93940-3216*

RYDELL, AMNELL ROY, artist, landscape architect; b. Mpls., Sept. 17, 1915; s. John S. and Josephine Henrietta (King) R.; m. Frances Cooksey, Jan. 24, 1942 (dec. May 1998). BFA, U. So. Calif., 1937; postgrad., Atelier 17, Paris, 1938, U. Calif., Berkeley, 1939-40, U. Calif., Santa Cruz, 1988. Instr. engring. Douglas Aircraft, El Segundo, Calif., 1940-46; ind. artist, designer San Francisco, 1946-48; ind. artist, designer Santa Cruz, 1948—, ind. landscape architect, 1958-91. Author, cons.: Low Maintenance Gardening, 1974; restoration design Sesnon House Garden Cabrillo Coll., 1995-98. Pres. Santa Cruz Hist. Soc., 1978-79, Rural Bonny Doon Assn., 1955-56, Santa Cruz Orgn. for Progress and Euthenics, 1977-78; mem. vision bd. City of Santa Cruz, 1991-92; mem. task force Ctr. for Art and History, 1986-94; bd. dirs. Santa Cruz Hist. Trust, 1978-94, Art Mus. Santa Cruz County, 1982-94; donor advisor Roy and Frances Rydell Visual Arts Fund, Greater Santa Cruz County Cmty. Found.; archivist pers. hist. archives, spl. collections Libr. U. Calif., Santa Cruz; mem. steering com. Pub. Art City of Santa Cruz, 1997-98; mem. Joint Cultural Coun. & Santa Cruz Cmty. Found., 1998, Art Gang Cultural Coun. Santa Cruz County, 1998. Recipient Eloise Pickard Smith award County of Santa Cruz Arts Commn., 1997. Mem. Am. Soc. Landscape Architects (emeritus), William James Assn. (vice chair bd. 1979-95, chair 1995-96), Art Forum (chair 1983-90), Art League (Disting. Artist 1996), Friends of Sesnon Gallery U. Calif., Santa Cruz. Avocation: gardening. Home: 201 Pine Flat Rd Santa Cruz CA 95060-9708

RYDER, HAL, theater educator, director; b. Evanston, Ill., Aug. 21, 1950; s. Lee Sigmund and Katherine (Philipsborn) Rosenblatt; m. Caroline Margaret Ogden, Nov. 17, 1976 (div. 1991). Student, U. Ariz., 1968-72, U. Miami, summer 1971; cert. in drama, Drama Studio London, 1973; BA in Drama, U. Wash., 1987. Drama specialist Rough Rock (Ariz.) Demonstration Sch., 1971-72; artistic dir. Mercury Theatre, London, 1973-75, Fringe Theatre, Orlando, Fla., 1976-79; dir. Drama Studio London, 1980-82, interim adminstrv. dir., 1985; artistic dir. Alaska Arts Fine Arts Camp, Sitka, 1987, Shakespeare Plus, Seattle, 1983-92; instr. Cornish Coll. Arts, Seattle, 1982-98; prof., 1998—; producer theatre Cornish Coll. Arts, Seattle, 1987-97, acting-chmn. theatre dept., 1990; artistic dir., exec. dir. Open Door Theatre, 1992-98, exec. dir., 1998—; artistic dir. Snoqualmie Falls Forest Theatre, 1992-94; founder, v.p. Ednl. Arts Resource Svcs., Inc., 1996—; creative cons. Sea World Fla., Orlando, 1979; lit. mgr. Pioneer Square Theatre, Seattle, 1983; space mgr. Seattle Mime Theatre, 1986-87. Author: Carmilla, 1976, (with others) Marvelous Christmas Mystery, 1978; editor: Will Noble Blood Die, 1987, The New Emperor's New Clothes, 1990, Hamlet & Juliet, 1997, Pirates of Penzance, 1998; dir. over 130 stage plays; appeared in over 40 prodns. Recipient Faculty Excellence award Seafirst Bank, Seattle, 1988. Mem. SAG, AFTRA, Am. Fedn. Tchrs. (Cornish chpt.), Alpha Kappa Lamda. Democrat. Jewish. Avocations: writing, cooking, gardening, travel, scuba diving. Home: 1012 NE 62nd St Seattle WA 98115-6604 Office: Cornish Coll Arts 710 E Roy St Seattle WA 98102-4604

RYGIEWICZ, PAUL THADDEUS, plant ecologist; b. Chgo., Feb. 19, 1952; s. Sigismund Thaddeus and Regina (Korpalski) R. BS in Forestry, U. Ill., 1974; MS in Wood Sci., U. Calif., Berkeley, 1976; PhD in Forest Resources, U. Wash., 1983. Research wood technologist ITT Rayonier, Inc., Shelton, Wash., 1977; research assoc. Centre National de Recherches Forestières, Nancy, France, 1983-84; research soil microbiologist U. Calif., Berkeley, 1984-85; rsch. ecologist, global climate change project leader EPA, Corvallis, Oreg., 1985—; asst. prof. dept. forest sci. Oreg. State U., 1987—. Contbr. articles to profl. jours.; rsch. on reforestation of tropical forests in Brazil, global climate changes on forests, health and function of forest ecosystems. Vol. Big Bros. of Am., Urbana, Ill., 1972-74. Fellow Regents U. Calif., Berkeley, 1973-74, Weyerhaeuser U. Calif., Berkeley, 1978-79, Inst. Nat. de la Recherche Agronomique, France, 1983-84, French Ministry of

Fgn. Affairs, 1983-84. Mem. Ecol. Soc. Am., Soil Ecology Soc., Forestry Club, Sigma Xi, Gamma Sigma Delta, Xi Sigma Pi (officer 1973-74). Avocations: bicycling, skiing, mountain climbing, camping, hiking. Office: EPA 200 SW 35th St Corvallis OR 97333-4996

RYLAARSDAM, WILLIAM F., judge; b. Haarlemmemeer, The Netherlands, Feb. 13, 1937; came to U.S., 1953; s. Daniel D. and Mary (Van Andel) R.; m. Janice E. Veneman, Sept. 7, 1957; children: Mary Jane Pike, Jennifer Vischer, Alice Jean, Daniel. BS, U. Calif., 1957; JD cum laude, Loyola U., 1964; LLM, U. Va., 1998. Bar: Calif. 1964, U.S. Supreme Ct. 1969. Ptnr. Breidenbach, Swainston, Yokaitis & Crispo, L.A., 1964-73, 78-80, Pasadena, Calif., 1974-78; mng. ptnr. Breidenbach, Swainston, Yokaitis & Crispo, Newport Beach, Calif., 1980-85; judge Superior Ct., L.A., 1985-86; judge (family law) Superior Ct., Orange County, Calif., 1986-88, supervising judge law and motion, 1988-89, supervising judge complex litigation, civil, 1990-95, presiding judge appellate panel, 1990-92; on assigment Calif. Ct. Appeals, 1994, assoc. justice, 1995—; adj. prof. ins. law Sch. Law Loyola U., 1973-79; lectr. bus. law Grad. Sch. Mgmt. U.C.I., 1990-94; lectr., panelist civil procedure and ins. law The Rutter Group, Calif. Cont. Edn. of the Bar, civil procedure, courtroom behavior Rutter Group; arbitrator L.A. Superior Ct., 1970-80. Mem. planning com. City of Pasadena, 1973-80, chmn., 1976-78. Named Judge of the Yr. litigation sect. Orange County Bar Assn. Mem. Am. Bd. Trial Advs. (Judge of the Yr. 1992), Am. Inns of Ct. (pres. Robert A. Banyard Inn 1990-92), Calif. State Bar (mem. com. maintenance profl. competence 1976-81, chmn. 1978-81, bd. legal specialization 1978-81, disciplinary com. 1973-76, bd. govs. litigation sect., jud. adv. 1991—), Calif. Judges Assn. (mem. com. civil procedure 1985-92, chair 1990-91, 94-95, jud. ethics com. 1995-98), Orange County women Lawyers Assn., Loyola Law Sch. Alumni Assn. (bd. govs. 1983-90), Pasadena Tournament of Roses Assn. Republican. Presbyterian. Avocations: bridge, history. Office: Calif Ct Appeals 925 N Spurgeon St Santa Ana CA 92701-3700

RYLANDER, ROBERT ALLAN, financial service executive; b. Bremerton, Wash., Apr. 8, 1947; s. Richard Algot and Marian Ethelyn (Peterson) R.; children: Kate, Josh, Erik, Meagan. BA in Fin., U. Wash., 1969; postgrad., U. Alaska, 1972-74. Controller Alaska USA Fed. Credit Union, Anchorage, 1974-77, mgr. ops., 1977-80, asst. gen. mgr., 1980-83, exec. v.p., chief operating officer, 1983—; chmn. Alaska Home Mortgage, Inc., Anchorage, 1992—, Alaska Option Svcs. Corp., Anchorage, 1983—, Alaska USA Trust Co., Anchorage, 1997—, EFT Alaska, Inc., Anchorage, 1998—; bd. dirs. Alaska USA Ins., Inc., Anchorage. Served to capt. USAF, 1969-74. Avocations: audio electronics, music. Home: PO Box 220587 Anchorage AK 99522-0587 Office: Alaska USA Fed Credit Union PO Box 196613 Anchorage AK 99519-6613

RYLES, GERALD FAY, private investor, business executive; b. Walla Walla, Wash., Apr. 3, 1936; s. L. F. and Janie Geraldine (Bassett) R.; m. Ann Jane Birkenmeyer, June 12, 1959; children—Grant, Mark, Kelly. B.A., U. Wash., 1958; M.B.A., Harvard U., 1962. With Gen. Foods Corp., White Plains, N.Y., 1962-65, Purex Corp., Ltd., Lakewood, Calif., 1966-68; cons. McKinsey & Co., Inc., Los Angeles, 1968-71; with Fibreboard Corp., San Francisco, 1971-79, v.p., 1973-75, group v.p., 1975-79; with Consol. Fibres, Inc., San Francisco, 1979-88, exec. v.p., 1979-81, pres., dir., 1981-86, chief exec. officer, 1986-88; cons. Orinda, Calif., 1988-90; with Interchecks Inc., 1990-92, pres., CEO, 1990-92; bus. exec., pvt. investor, 1992-94; chmn. bd., CEO Microserv, Inc., Kirkland, Wash., 1994—; bd. dirs. Sitewerks Inc., Seattle, Aculight, Bothell, WA. Mem. adv. com. entrepreneur and innovation program U. Wash. Bus. Sch. Served to capt. U.S. Army, 1958-66. Mem. Harvard Bus. Sch. Assn., Univ. Wash. Alumni Assn., World Trade Club (San Francisco), Wash. Athletic Club. Republican. Episcopalian. Home: 127 3rd Ave Apt 301 Kirkland WA 98033-6177

RYMAR, JULIAN W., manufacturing company executive; b. Grand Rapids, Mich., June 29, 1919; student Grand Rapids Jr. Coll., 1937-39, U. Mich., 1939-41, Am. Sch. Dramatic Arts, 1946-47, Wayne U., 1948-52, Rockhurst Coll., 1952-53; Naval War Coll., 1954-58; m. Margaret Macon Van Brunt, Dec. 11, 1954; children: Margaret Gibson, Gracen Macon, Ann Mackall. Entered USN as aviation cadet, 1942, advanced through grades to capt., 1964; chmn. bd., chief exec. officer, dir. Grace Co., Belton, Mo., 1955-90; chmn. bd. dirs. Shock & Vibration Research, Inc., 1956-66; chmn. bd., CEO Bedtime Story Fashions; bd. dirs. Am. Bank & Trust; comdg. officer Naval Air Res. Squadron, 1957-60, staff air bn. comdr., 1960-64. Mem. Kansas City Hist. Soc.; bd. dirs. Bros. of Mercy, St. Lukes Hosp.; adv. bd. dirs. St. Joseph Hosp.; trustee Missouri Valley Coll., 1969-74; pres. Rymar Found. Active Sch. Am. Rsch., Inst. Am. Arts, Mus. N.Mex. Found., Spanish Colonial Art Soc. Mem. Mil. Order World Wars, Navy League U.S. (pres. 1959-60, dir. 1960-70), Rockhill Homes Assn. (v.p.) Friends of Art (pres., chmn. bd. govs. 1969-70, exec. bd. 1971-74), Soc. of Fellows of Nelson Gallery Found. (exec. bd. 1972-77), Soc. Profl. Journalists, Press Club, Univ. of Mich. Club, Arts Club of Washington, Sch. of Am. Rsch., Santa Fe Symphony, Inst. Am. Indian Art, Mus. NMex. Found., Mus. Indian Arts & Culture, Mus. Internat. Folk Art, Mus. Fine Arts, Spanish Colonial Arts Soc., Quiet Birdman Club, Sigma Delta Chi. Episcopalian (dir., lay reader, lay chalice, vestryman, jr. warden, sr. warden, diocesan fin. bd., parish investment bd.).

RYMER, ILONA SUTO, artist, retired educator; b. N.Y.C., Dec. 1, 1921; d. Alexander and Elizabeth (Komaromy) Suto; m. Robert Hamilton Rymer, Mar. 27, 1944; children: Thomas Parker, Shelley Ilona. *In 1944, while she was qualifying for the WASPS, her husband, Robert, U.S. Navy photographer, invented a Gyro to stabilize an underwater camera on the prow of the USS Spadefish (submarine). His photography was later used for the opening and ending scenes of the TV series, the Silent Service. He was awarded a medal for his services.* BA, Long Beach State U., 1953, MA, 1954. Tchr., cons. Long Beach (Calif.) Sch. Dist., 1953-56; tchr. Orange (Calif.) Sch. Dist., 1956-58; tchr., cons. Brea (Calif.)-Olinda Sch. Dist., 1958-80; ind. artist, designer Graphic Ho. Studio, Santa Ynez, Calif., 1980—, Stampa-Barbara, Santa Barbara, Calif., 1990—. Author: (instrn. book) Folk Art U.S.A., 1975 (proclamation City of Brea 1975); art editor, feature writer, illustrator Arabian Connection mag., Santa Ynez, 1985-86; needlepoint designer Backstitch Store, Solvang, Calif., 1982-83; equine portrait Pres. Ronald Reagan, 1982; illustrator back cover: Khemosabi and Ruth, 1995. Co-founder, mem. Gallery los Olivos, pres., 1993—; lectr. folk art Brea Sch. Dist., 1975-80. Recipient 1st pl. Seminar award Rex Brandt, Corona del Mar, Calif., 1961, Affiliate award Laguna Art Mus., Laguna Beach, Calif., 1967, Best of Watercolor award Orange County Fair, Orange, 1969, Bicentennial trip to France, Air France, Brea, 1975, Proclamation for Tchg., City of Brea, 1980, Theme award Santa Barbara County Fair, 1991. Mem. Calif. Gold Coast Watercolor Soc. (signature), Santa Barbara Art Assn., Ctrl. Coast Art Assn., Artist Guild Santa Ynez Valley, Calif. Presbyterian. Avocation: showing family's Arabian horses. Studio: PO Box 822 Santa Ynez CA 93460-0822

RYMER, PAMELA ANN, federal judge; b. Knoxville, Tenn., Jan. 6, 1941. AB, Vassar Coll., 1961; LLB, Stanford U., 1964; LLD (hon.), Pepperdine U., 1988. Bar: Calif. 1966, U.S. Ct. Appeals (9th cir.) 1966, U.S. Ct. Appeals (10th cir.), U.S. Supreme Ct. V.p. Rus Walton & Assoc., Los Altos, Calif., 1965-66; Assoc. Lillick McHose & Charles, L.A., 1966-75, ptnr., 1973-75; ptnr. Toy and Rymer, L.A., 1975-83; judge U.S. Dist. Ct. (cen. dist.) Calif., L.A., 1983-89, U.S. Ct. Appeals (9th cir.), L.A., 1989—; faculty The Nat. Jud. Coll., 1986-88; mem. com. summer ednl. programs Fed. Jud. Ctr., 1987-88, mem. com. appellate judge edn., 1996—; chair exec. com. 9th Cir. Jud. Conf., 1990; mem. com. criminal law Jud. Conf. U.S., 1988-93, Ad Hoc com. gender-based violence, 1991-94, fed.-state jurisdiction com., 1993-96. Mem. editorial bd. The Judges' jour., 1989-91; contbr. articles to profl. jours. and newsletters. Mem. Calif. Postsecondary Edn. Commn., 1974-84, chmn., 1980-84; mem. L.A. Olympic Citizens Adv. Commn.; bd. visitors Stanford U. Law Sch., 1986—, trustee, 1991—, chair, 1993-96 exec. com., chmn. bd. trustees com. acad. policy, planning and mgmt. and its ad. hoc. com. athletics., chmn. bd. visitors Sch. Law, 1987—; bd. visitors Pepperdine U. Law Sch., 1987—; mem. Edn. Commn. of [illegible] Policy and Ind. Higher Edn., 1987-89, Carnegie Commn. Task Force Sci. and Tech. Jud. and Regulatory Decisionmaking, 1990-93, Commn. Substance Abuse Coll. and Univ. Campuses, 1992-94, commn. substance abuse [illegible] Constn. Rights Found., 1985—, Pacific Coun. Internat. Policy, 1995—, Calif. Higher Edn. Policy Ctr., 1992-97; Jud. Conf. U.S. Com. Fed.-State Jurisdiction, 1993, Com. Criminal Law, 1988-93, ad hoc com. gender based violence, 1991-94; chair exec. com. 9th cir. jud. conf., 1990-94. Recipient Outstanding Trial Jurist award L.A. County Bar Assn., 1988; named David T. Lewis Disting. Jurist-in-Residence U. Utah, 1992. Mem. ABA (task force on civil justice reform 1991-93, mem. coord. com. agenda civil justice reform in Am. 1991), State Bar Calif. (antitrust and trade regulation sect., exec. com. 1990-92), L.A. County Bar Assn. (chmn. antitrust sect. 1981-82, mem. editl. bd. The Judges Jour. 1989-91, mem. com. professionalism 1988—, numerous other coms.), Assn. of Bus. Trial Lawyers (bd. govs. 1990-92), Stanford Alumni Assn., Stanford Law Soc. Soc. Calif., Vassar Club So. Calif. (past pres.). Office: US Ct Appeals 9th Cir US Court of Appeals Bldg PO Box 91510 Pasadena CA 91109-1510

RYNEARSON, PATRICIA HEAVISIDE, elementary school educator; b. Balt., Dec. 19, 1951; d. William and Evelyn (Davis) Heaviside; m. Leo E. Rynearson, Jr., Aug. 6, 1977; children: Courtney, Cliff. BS, U. Del., 1973; MA, U. N. Mex., 1979. Cert. tchr. multiple subjects and reading, Calif. Tchr. Lavaland Sch., Albuquerque, N. Mex., 1977-78, Santo Domingo Sch., Albuquerque, 1978-79, Chapparal Sch., Albuquerque, 1979-80, Liberty Sch., Buckeye, Ariz., 1980-86, Royal Palm Sch., Phoenix, 1986-87, Juniper Sch., Fontana, Calif., 1987-89, Almeria Middle Sch., Fontana, 1989-90, Redwood Sch., Fontana, 1990-98, Truman Mid. Sch., Fontana, 1998—; mem. planning com. Environ. EXPO Calif. State Univ., San Bernardino, Calif., 1995-96. Named Inland Empire Environ. Educator of Yr., Calif. State U., San Bernardino, 1996, Conservation Tchr. of Yr., Inland Empire West Resource Conservation Dist., 1997; recipient Eleanor Roosevelt Tchg. fellowship AAUW, 1996; NORCAL model sch. grantee, 1998. Home: 2233 Drummond St Riverside CA 92506-1533 Office: Truman Mid Sch 16224 Mallory Dr Fontana CA 92335-7844

RYNERSON, S(USAN) DIANE, lawyer; b. Portland, Oreg., Dec. 20, 1952; d. Edgar Wallace and Janet Aileen (Otto) R.; m. Glendon Richard Pullen, Mar. 23, 1980; children: Margaret Aileen, Geoffrey William. BA, Portland State U., 1974; JD, Santa Clara (Calif.) U., 1985. Bar: Oreg., 1988, Calif., 1985. Exec. dir. Oreg. Women Lawyers, Portland, 1990-98, Nat. Conf. Women's Bar Assn., Portland, 1997—; treas. Profl. Svcs. Coordinating Coun. Oreg., Portland, 1995—. With U.S. Army, 1976-79. Mem. ABA, Nat. Assn. Bar Execs., Multnomah Bar Assn. Avocations: piano, gardening. Office: Nat Conf Women's Bar Assn PO Box 82366 Portland OR 97282-0366

RYNIKER, BRUCE WALTER DURLAND, industrial designer, manufacturing executive; b. Billings, Mont., Mar. 23, 1940; s. Walter Henry and Alice Margaret (Durland) R.; B. Profl. Arts in Transp. Design (Ford scholar), Art Ctr. Coll. Design, Los Angeles, 1963; grad. specialized tech. engring. program Gen. Motors Inst., 1964; m. Marilee Ann Vincent, July 8, 1961; children: Kevin Walter, Steven Durland. Automotive designer Gen. Motors Corp., Warren, Mich., 1963-66; mgmt. staff automotive designer Chrysler Corp., Highland Park, Mich., 1966-72; pres., dir. design Transform Corp., Birmingham, Mich., 1969-72; indsl. designer, art dir. James R. Powers and Assocs., Los Angeles, 1972-75; sr. design products mgr. Mattel Inc., El Segundo, Calif., 1975-95; pres., CEO Durland Prodns. and Product Devel. Co., Torrance, Calif., 1996—; dir. design and devel. Microword Industries, Inc., Los Angeles, 1977-80, also dir.; exec. mem. Modern Plastics Adv. Council, 1976-80; elegance judge LeCercle Concours D'Elegance, 1976-77; mem. nat. adv. bd. Am. Security Council, 1980; cons. automotive design, 1972— . Served with USMC, 1957-60. Mem. Soc. Art Ctr. Alumni (life), Mattel Mgmt. Assn., Second Amendment Found., Am. Def. Preparedness Assn., Nat. Rifle Assn. Designer numerous exptl. automobiles, electric powered vehicles, sports and racing cars, also med. equipment, electronic teaching machines, ride-on toys. Home: 21329 Marjorie Ave Torrance CA 90503-5443 Office: Durland Prodns Inc 21213 Hawthorne Blvd Ste B Torrance CA 90503-5522

RYPKA, EUGENE WESTON, microbiologist; b. Owatonna, Minn., May 6, 1925; s. Charles Frederick and Ethel Marie (Ellerman) R.; m. Rosemary Speeker, June 1, 1967. Student, Carleton Coll., 1946-47; BA, Stanford U., 1950, PhD, 1958. Prof. microbiology, systems, cybernetics U. N.Mex., Albuquerque, 1957-62; bacteriologist Leonard Wood Meml. Lab. Johns Hopkins U., Balt., 1962-63; sr. scientist Lovelace Med. Ctr., Albuquerque, 1963-71, chief microbiologist, 1971-93; adj. prof. U. N.Mex., 1973—; cons. Hoffmann-LaRoche Inc., 1974—, Airline Pilots Assn., Washington, 1976, Pasco Lab., Denver, 1983—; advisor Nat. Com. Clinic Lab. Standards, Pa., 1980-84. Contbr. articles to profl. jours. and chpts. in books. Served with USNR, USMC 1943-46. Fellow AAAS. Republican. Presbyterian. Avocations: martial arts, bicycle racing, pets. Home: PO Box 1637 Cedar Crest NM 87008-1637

SA, JULIE, council woman; b. Korea, Dec. 15, 1950; came to U.S., 1973, naturalized, 1982; married. Degree in Polit. Sci., Dong-A U., Korea. Owner restaurant chain; councilwoman City of Fullerton, Calif., 1992-94, 96—, mayor, 1994-95; rep. bd. Orange County Sanitation Dists.; rep. to Tri-City Park Authority, City of Fullerton. Mem. Fullerton C. of C., Orange County Korean C. of C., Orange County Chinese C. of C. Office: Office of City Council 303 W Commonwealth Ave Fullerton CA 92832-1710*

SAARI, ALBIN TOIVO, electronics engineer; b. Rochester, Wash., Mar. 16, 1930; s. Toivo Nickoli and Gertrude Johanna (Hill) S.; m. Patricia Ramona Rudig, Feb. 1, 1958; children: Kenneth, Katherine, Steven, Marlene, Bruce. Student, Centralia Community Coll., Wash., 1950-51; AS in Electronic Tech., Wash. Tech. Inst., Seattle, 1958; BA in Communications, Evergreen State Coll., Olympia, Wash., 1977. Electronic technician Boeing Co., Seattle, 1956-59; field engr. RCA, Van Nuys, Calif., 1959-61; tv engr. Gen. Dynamics, San Diego, 1961-65, Boeing Co., Seattle, 1965-70; mgr. electronic maintenance and engring. Evergreen State Coll., Olympia, Wash., 1970—; mem. adv. bd. KAOS-FM Radio, Olympia, 1979-82, New Market Vocat. Skills Ctr., Tumwater, Wash., 1985—, South Puget Sound Cmty. Coll., Olympia. Soccer coach King County Boys Club, Federal Way, Wash., 1968-70, Thurston County Youth Soccer, Olympia, 1973-78. With USAF, 1951-55. Recipient Merit award for electronic systems design Evergreen State Coll., 1978. Mem. Soc. Broadcast Engrs. (chmn. 1975-77), Soc. of Motion Picture and TV Engrs., IEEE, Audio Engring. Soc., Tele-Communications Assn., Assoc. Pub. Safety Communications Officers. Lutheran. Avocations: amateur radio, swimming. Home: 6617 Husky Way SE Olympia WA 98503-1433 Office: Evergreen State Coll Media Engring # L1309 Olympia WA 98505

SABATINI, LAWRENCE, bishop; b. Chgo., May 15, 1930; s. Dominic and Ada (Piloi) S. Ph.L., Gregorian U., Rome, 1953, S.T.L., 1957, J.C.D., 1960; M.S. in Edn., Iona Coll., 1968. Ordained priest, Roman Catholic Ch., 1957, bishop, 1978. Prof. canon law St. Charles Sem., S.I., N.Y., 1960-71; pastor St. Stephen's Parish, North Vancouver, B.C., Canada, 1970-78; provincial superior Missionaries of St. Charles, Oak Park, Ill., 1978; aux. bishop Archdiocese Vancouver, B.C., Can., 1978-82; bishop Diocese Kamloops, B.C., Can., 1982—; procurator, adviser Matrimonial Tribunal, N.Y.C., 1964-71; founder, dir. RAP Youth Counseling Service, S.I., N.Y., 1969-71; vice ofcl. Regional Matrimonial tribunal of Diocese Kamloops, 1978-82; chmn. Kamloops Cath. Pub. Schs., 1982—. Named Man of Yr. Confratellanza Italo-Canadese, 1979. Mem. Can. Canon Law Soc., Canon Law Soc. Am., Can. Conf. Cath. Bishops. Office: Diocese of Kamloops, 635A Tranquille Rd, Kamloops, BC Canada V2B 3H5*

SABATINI, WILLIAM QUINN, architect; b. Pitts.; s. William L. and Lydia M. (Contento) S.; m. Carol Anne Christoffel, Feb. 26, 1972; children: Quinn, Jay, Jillian. BA, Franklin & Marshall Coll., 1971; MArch, U. N.Mex., 1978. Registered arch., N.Mex., Nev.; cert. Nat. Coun. Archtl. Registration Bds. Intern Jess Holmes Arch., Albuquerque, 1974-78; project mgr. Jack Miller & Assocs., Las Vegas, 1978-81; sr. design arch. HNTB, Kansas City, Mo., 1981-84; prin. Holmes Sabatini Assocs. Arch., Albuquerque, 1984— [illegible] (Merit award N.Mex. Soc. Archs. 1977), Luna County Courthouse, Deming, N.Mex. (Honor award N.Mex. Hist. Preservation Soc. 1978), James R. Dickinson Libr. U. Nev., Las Vegas (Merit award AIA 1981, Honor award Nev. Soc. Arch. 1981), Reno Conv. Ctr. (Merit award Nev. Soc. Archs. 1983), Corp. Hdqs. Nev. Power Co., Las Vegas (Honor award Nev. Soc. Archs. 1983), YMCA, Las Vegas (Honor award Nev. Soc. Archs. 1983), Sanctuary Remodel St. Johns United Meth. Ch., Albuquerque (Best Interiors award N.Mex. Bus. Jour. 1986), The Presidio Office Bldg., Albuquerque (Best Bldgs. award and Best Interiors award N.Mex. Bus. Jour. 1987, Project of Yr. award Assoc. Gen. Contractors N.Mex. 1987), Suarez Residence, Albuquerque (Merit award N.Mex. Soc. Am. 1988), Fire Sta. Number 13 and Fire Marshall's Office, Albuquerque (Merit award Albuquerque Conservation Soc. 1987, Best Bldgs. award N.Mex. Bus. Jour. 1988), Santa Fe Imaging Ctr. (Citation of Excellence, Modern Health Care Mag., AIA com. on healthcare 1989, Best Bldgs. award N.Mex. Bus. Jour. 1989), Health Scis. Bldg. U. N.Mex. (Best Bldgs. award N.Mex. Bus. Jour. 1989), U.S. Port of Entry, Columbus, N.Mex. (Best Bldgs. award N.Mex. Bus. Jour. 1989, Honor award N.Mex. Soc. Archs. 1990, GSA Design award U.S. Gen. Svcs. Adminstrn. 1990), Student Svcs. Bldg., Albuquerque TVI (Best Bldgs. award N.Mex. Bus. Jour. 1989, Merit award Albuquerque Conservation Soc. 1990), Expansion and Renovation Albuquerque Conv. Ctr. (Best Bldgs. award N.Mex. Bus. Jour. 1990), Lovelace Multi-Specialty Clinic Facility, Albuquerque (Merit award N.Mex. Soc. Archs. 1991), Pete's Playground U. N.Mex. Hosp. (Honor award N.Mex. Soc. Archs. 1992, Best Bldgs. Spl. award N.Mex. Bus. Jour. 1993), Nursing Unit Remodel U. N.Mex. Hosp. (Excellence award Am. Soc. Interior Designers 1992), 3.5 Meter Telescope Kirtland AFB, N.Mex. (Honor award AIA 1993). Bd. dirs. Albuquerque Chamber Orch., 1988, Hospice Rio Grande, 1992—; mem. adv. bd. Balloon Mus., 1989—; v.p., mem. adv. bd. St. Pius High Sch., 1993—. With USAR, 1971-78. Mem. AIA (bd. dirs. Albuquerque chpt. 1986-87). Roman Catholic. Office: Holmes Sabatini Assocs Archs West Courtyard 6801 Jefferson NE Ste 100 Albuquerque NM 87109-3460*

SABERSKY, ROLF HEINRICH, mechanical engineer; b. Berlin, Germany, Oct. 20, 1920; came to U.S., 1938, naturalized, 1944; s. Fritz and Berta (Eisner) S.; m. Bettina Sofie Schuster, June 16, 1946; children—Carol, Sandra. B.S., Calif. Inst. Tech., 1942, M.S., 1943, Ph.D., 1949. Devel. engr. Aerojet Gen. Co., 1943-46, regular cons., 1949-70; asst. prof. Calif. Inst. Tech., Pasadena, 1949-55, asso. prof., 1955-61, prof. mech. engring., 1961-88, prof. emeritus, 1988—; cons. various indsl. orgns. Author: Engineering Thermodynamics, 1957, Fluid Flow, 4th edit., 1999; contbr. articles to profl. jours. Fellow ASME (Heat Transfer Meml. award 1977, 50th anniversary award Heat Transfer Div 1988); mem. Sigma Xi, Tau Beta Pi. Home: Valle Verde EG 117 900 Calle De Los Amigos Santa Barbara CA 93105-4435 Office: Calif Inst Tech Divsn Engring & Applied Sci Pasadena CA 91125

SABEY, J(OHN) WAYNE, academic administrator, consultant; b. Murray, Utah, Dec. 10, 1939; s. Alfred John and Bertha (Lind) S.; m. Marie Bringhurst, Sept. 10, 1964; children: Clark Wayne, Colleen, Carolyn, Natasha Lynne. BA in Asian Studies, Brigham Young U., 1964, MA in Asian History, 1965; PhD in East Asian History, U. Mich., 1972. Teaching asst. Brigham Young U., Provo, 1964-65, rsch. asst., 1965, adj. prof. history, 1988-89; rsch. asst. U. Mich., Ann Arbor, 1966; from instr. to asst. prof. history U. Utah, Salt Lake City, 1970-80; v.p. Western Am. Lang. Inst., Salt Lake City, 1980-84, dir., 1984-86, pres., 1986—; exec. v.p. Pacific Rim Bus. Coords., Salt Lake City, 1993—, also bd. dirs., 1993—; dir. Japan Ops. E'OLA Products, Inc., St. George, Utah, 1996—; assoc. dir. exch. program between U. Utah and Nagoya Broadcasting Network of Japan, 1973-79; lectr. in field, Superior award in extemporaneous speaking, 1956. Author essay, contbr. articles to ency. Chmn. bd. trustees Western Am. Lang. Inst., 1986—, sec. to bd. trustees, 1980-86; chmn. bd. trustees Found. for Internat. Understanding, 1982—; mem. internat. adv. coun. Salt Lake C.C., 1988-94; mem. bd. advisors Consortium for Internat. Edn., 1972-77. Horace H. Rackham Sch. grad. studies fellow, 1969-70, Fulbright-Hays rsch. fellow (Japan), 1968-69, U.S. Nat. Def. fgn. lang. fellow, 1965-68. Mem. Assn. for Asian Studies (gen. chairperson, chairperson local arrangements western conf. 1970-72), Phi Kappa Phi. Avocations: piano, hiking, basketball, stamp collecting, tennis. Home: 8710 Oakwood Park Cir Sandy UT 84094-1800

SABHARWAL, RANJIT SINGH, mathematician; b. Dhudial, India, Dec. 11, 1925; came to U.S., 1958, naturalized, 1981; s. Krishan Ch and Devti (An) S.; m. Pritam Kaur Chadha, Mar. 5, 1948; children—Rajinderpal, Amarjit, Jasbir. B.A. with honors, Punjab U., 1944, M.A., 1948; M.A. U. Calif, Berkeley, 1962; Ph.D., Wash. State U., 1966. Lectr. math. Khalsa Coll., Bombay, India, 1951-58; teaching asst. U. Calif., Berkeley, 1958-62; instr. math. Portland (Oreg.) State U., 1962-62, Wash. State U., 1963-66; asst. prof. Kans. State U., 1966-68; mem. faculty Calif. State Hayward, 1968—, prof. math., 1974—. Author papers on non-Desarguesian planes. Mem. Am. Math. Soc., Math. Assn. Am., Sigma Xi. Address: 25179 Old Fairview Ave Hayward CA 94542-1355

SABIN, JACK CHARLES, engineering and construction firm executive; b. Phoenix, June 29, 1921; s. Jack Byron and Rena (Lewis) S.; BS, U. Ariz., 1943; BSChemE, U. Minn., 1947; m. Frances Jane McIntyre, Mar. 27, 1950; children—Karen Lee, Robert William, Dorothy Ann, Tracy Ellen. With Standard Oil Co. of Calif., 1947-66, sr. engr., 1966—; pres., dir. Indsl. Control & Engring., Inc., Redondo Beach, Calif., 1966—; owner/mgr. Jack C. Sabin, Engr.-Contractor, Redondo Beach, 1968—; staff engr. Pacific Molasses Co., San Francisco, 1975-77; project mgr. E & L Assocs., Long Beach, Calif., 1977-79; dir. Alaska Pacific Petroleum, Inc., 1968—, Marlex Petroleum, Inc., 1970, 71—. Served with U.S. Army, 1942-46; capt. Chem. Corps, Res., 1949-56. Registered profl. engr., Calif., Alaska; lic. gen. engring. contractor, Ariz., Calif. Mem. Nat. Soc. Profl. Engrs., Ind. Liquid Terminals Assn., Conservative Caucus, Calif. Tax Reduction Com., Tau Beta Pi, Phi Lambda Upsilon, Phi Sigma Kappa. Republican. Clubs: Elks; Town Hall of Calif. Address: 151 Camino De Las Colinas Redondo Beach CA 90277-5828

SABIN, ROBERT EARL, lawyer; b. La Junta, Colo., Apr. 16, 1941; s. Robert Rourke and Margaret (Guthrie) S.; m. M. Kathryn Orahood, July 5, 1963; children: Robert Michael, Elizabeth Michelle. BA, U. Colo., 1963, LLB, 1966. Bar: Colo. 1966, N.Mex. 1967. Ptnr. Atwood, Malone, Turner & Sabin, Roswell, N.Mex., 1966—. Fellow Am. Coll. Trial Lawyers; mem. Am. Bd. Trial Attys., N.Mex. State Bar (chair profl. liability com. 1991—), Fedn. Ins. and Corp. Counsel. Avocations: golf, photography, computing. Office: Atwood Malone Turner Sabin 400 N Pennsylvania Ave Roswell NM 88201-4754

SABIN, SCOTT CULLEN, cultural organization administrator; b. Palo Alto, Calif., Oct. 16, 1961; s. Cullen Milo and Katherine Roberta (Kerr) S.; m. Nancy Irene Jex, July 6, 1996. BS in Polit. Sci., Oreg. State U., 1984; MA in Internat. Rels., U. San Diego, 1992. Program mgr. Floresta USA, San Diego, 1993-95, exec. dir., 1995%; bd. dirs. Los Arbolitos. Lt. USN, 1984-91. Mem. Assn. Evangelical Relief and Devel. Orgn. (exec. com. 1997—). Presbyterian. Avocation: sailing. Office: Floresta USA 4903 Morena Blvd Ste 1215 San Diego CA 92117-7352

SABRAM, STEVE, software engineer, human resources specialist; b. Pitts., Feb. 15, 1966; s. William and Mary Ann (Brown) S.; m. Mette Haahr Hansen, Mar. 20, 1998. BS in Engring., U. Pitts., 1988. Engr. Hudson Robotics, Inc., Springfield, N.J., 1988-89; software engr. Nanometrics, Inc., Sunnyvale, Calif., 1989-91; cons. Silicon Valley, Calif., 1991-97; pres. Sabuam Design, Inc., Campbell, Calif., 1998—; v.p. engring. Datastick System, Campbell, 1998—. Author: (gamebook) Chromebook Series, 1994-97, Guide to the Net, 1995, Cybergenenation, 1996; tech. mission control mem. 24 Hours in Cyberspace, 1996. Mem. Arnold Air Soc. Avocations: bodybuilding. Home: 10 Heritage Village Ln Campbell CA 95008-2034 Office: Sabram Design Inc 120 W Campbell Ave Ste D Campbell CA 95008-1044

SABSAY, DAVID, library consultant; b. Waltham, Mass., Sept. 12, 1931; s. Wiegard Isaac and Ruth (Weinstein) S.; m. Helen Glenna Tolliver, Sept. 24,1966. AB, Harvard U., 1953; BLS, U. Calif., Berkeley, 1955. Circulation dept. supr. Richmond (Calif.) Pub. Library, 1955-56; city libr. Santa Rosa (Calif.) Pub. Library, 1956-65; dir. Sonoma County Library, Santa Rosa, [illegible] Santa Rosa, 1960-64; cons. in field, Sebastopol, Calif., 1968—. Contbr. articles to profl. jours. Commendation, Calif. Assn. Library Trustees and Commrs., 1984. Mem. Calif. Library Assn. (pres. 1971, cert. appreciation [illegible]), Club: Harvard (San Francisco). Home and Office: [illegible] Montgomery Rd Sebastopol CA 95472-3020

SACCOMAN, STEFANIE ANN, secondary school educator; b. San Francisco, Dec. 13, 1953; d. Frank and Jacqueline (Collier) S. BS in Biology, Calif. Poly. U., 1976, MA in Edn., 1980; postgrad., Calif. State U., L.A., Calif. Coast U. Environ. scientist Engring.-Sci. Inc., Arcadia, Calif., 1978-83; sci. tchr. Pasadena (Calif.) H.S., 1983-90; sci. and math curriculum specialist Pomona (Calif.) Unified Sch. Dist., 1990—; instr. sci. edn. for secondary tchrs. La. State U., Baton Rouge, summer 1990, 91. Contbr. (lab. manual) Cal Poly University Institute for Cellular and Molecular Biology Experiments for Science Teachers, 1985. Spkr. on math curriculum Rotary Club, Pomona, 1993; spkr. on sci. instrn. and student self esteem Human Rights Conf., Pomona, 1994. Recipient Calif. Congress of Parents, Tchrs., Students Svc. award PTA, Pasadena, 1987, Disting. Tchr. award Verdugo Hills Hosp., Glendale, 1988; named Outstanding Young Woman of Am., 1981. Mem. ASCD, Nat. Coun. Tchrs. Math., N.Y. Acad. Sci. Avocations: traveling, gardening, nature study. Office: Pomona Unified Sch Dist 800 S Garey Ave Pomona CA 91766-3325

SACHTLEBEN, THOMAS RAY, family and sports medicine physician; b. Iowa City, Apr. 12, 1965; s. Clyde and Marilynn (Bedford) S.; m. Camille Hicks. BA, Nebr. Wesleyan U., 1987; MS, U. Nebr., 1989, MD, 1993. Physician Colorado Springs Family Practice, 1997—.

SACKMAN, DAVE, marketing executive; married; 3 children. BA in Anthropology, U. Calif. Pres., CEO Lieberman Rsch. Worldwide, L.A.; dir. rsch. Columbia Pictures; dir. mktg. Winchell's; dir. mktg. dept. group health svcs. Am. Med. Internat. Active Young Pres. Orgn. Mem. Mktg. Rsch. Assn. (mem. strategic planning com., mem. exec. com. forum on rsch. quality, mem. exec. com. nat. bd. dirs.). Avocations: basketball, tennis. Office: Liberman Rsch Worldwide 1900 Ave Of Stars Los Angeles CA 90067-4301*

SACKS, ARTHUR BRUCE, environmental and liberal arts educator; b. N.Y.C., Apr. 21, 1946; s. Fred and Lillian Pearl (Levy) S.; m. Normandy Roden, May 17, 1987; children: Rachel, Erica. BA, Bklyn. Coll., 1967; MA, U. Wis., 1968, PhD, 1975. Teaching asst. dept. English, U. Wis., Madison, 1968-72, asst. to assoc. dean for student acad. affairs, 1972-76, lectr. dept. English, 1975, sr. lectr. Inst. for Environ. Studies, 1976-90, coord. acad. programs, 1976-78, asst. to dir., asst. dir., then assoc. dir., 1983-85, acting dir., then dir., 1985-90, assoc. mem. dept. urban and regional planning, 1985-93, adminstr. acad. programs, 1978-85; sr. spl. asst. to dean grad. sch. U. Wis., 1990-93; assoc. mem. Russian and East European studies U. Wis., Madison, 1992-93, acting dir. internat. faculty and staff svcs., 1993; dir., prof. liberal arts and internat. studies Colo. Sch. Mines, Golden, 1993—; mem. adj. faculty Ohio State U., Columbus, 1992-94; prof. environ. sci. Internat. U., Moscow, 1992—. Bd. dirs. Friends of Waisman Ctr. on Mental Retardation and Human Devel., 1991-93; mem. Emergency Med. Svcs. Commn., 1992-93. Recipient blue ribbon for poetry Am. Assn. Interpretive Naturalists, 1983. Fellow Soc. of Values in Higher Edn.; mem. AAAS, Am. Assn. Higher Edn., N.Am. Assn. Environ. Edn. (adv. group internat. rels. com. 1991-94, rep. to jour. 1988—, nominating com. 1989-90, pres. 1984-85, pres.-elect 1983-84, sec. 1982-83, exec. com. 1982-86, chmn. devel. com. 1986-94, liaison to Friends of the UN Environ. Programme, chmn. participation World Decade of the Environ., 1982-92, bd. dirs., 1980-84, chmn. environ. studies sect. 1980-82, program com. confs., publs. com. 1978-83, chmn. 1981-83, polit. strategies com. 1982-83, sec.-treas. environ. studies sect. 1978-80, chmn. com. on establishing jour. environ. studies 1978, mem. spl. task force on mission, membership and orgnl. structure 1977-78, mem. planning group nat. com. environ. edn. rsch. 1979-80), Internat. Soc. Environ. Edn., World Conservation Union, Russian Acad. Edn. (fgn.). Office: Colo Sch Mines 301 Stratton Hall Golden CO 80401

SACKTON, FRANK JOSEPH, public affairs educator; b. Chgo., Aug. 11, 1912; m. June Dorothy Raymond, Sept. 21, 1940. Student, Northwestern U., 1936, Yale, 1946, U. Md., 1951-52; BS, U. Md., 1970; grad., Army Inf. Sch., 1941, Command and Gen. Staff Coll., 1942, Armed Forces Staff Coll., 1949, Nat. War Coll., 1954; MPA, Ariz. State U., 1976, DHL (hon.), 1996. Mem. 131st Inf. Regt., Ill. N.G., 1929-40; commd. 2d lt. U.S. Army, 1934, advanced through grades to lt. gen., 1967; brigade plans and ops. officer (33d Inf. Div.), 1941, PTO, 1943-45; div. signal officer, 1942-43, div. intelligence officer, 1944, div. plans and ops. officer, 1945; sec. to gen. staff for Gen. MacArthur Tokyo, 1947-48; bn. comdr. 30th Inf. Regt., 1949-50; mem. spl. staff Dept. Army, 1951; plans and ops. officer Joint Task Force 132, PTO, 1952; comdr. Joint Task Force 7, Marshall Islands, 1953; mem. gen. staff Dept. Army, 1954-55; with Office Sec. Def., 1956; comdr. 18th Inf. Regt., 1957-58; chief staff 1st Inf. Div., 1959; chief army Mil. Mission to Turkey, 1960-62; comdr. XIV Army Corps, 1963; dep. dir. plans Joint Chiefs Staff, 1964-66; army general staff mil. ops., 1966-67, comptroller of the army, 1967-70, ret., 1970; spl. asst. for fed./state relations Gov. Ariz., 1971-75; chmn. Ariz. Programming and Coordinating Com. for Fed. Programs, 1971-75; lectr. Am. Grad. Sch. Internat. Mgmt., 1973-77; vis. asst. prof., lectr. public affairs Ariz. State U., Tempe, 1976-78; founding dean Ariz. State U. Coll. Public Programs, 1979-80; prof. public affairs Ariz. State U., 1980—, finance educator, v.p. bus. affairs, 1981-83, dep. dir. intercollegiate athletics, 1984-85, dir. strategic planning, 1987-88. Contbr. articles to public affairs and mil. jours. Mem. Ariz. Steering Com. for Restoration of the State Capitol, 1974-75, Ariz. State Personnel Bd., 1978-83, Ariz. Regulatory Coun., 1981-93. Decorated D.S.M., Silver Star, also Legion of Merit with 4 oak leaf clusters, Bronze Star with 2 oak leaf clusters, Air medal, Army Commendation medal with 1 oak leaf cluster, Combat Inf. badge. Mem. Ariz. Acad. Public Adminstrn., Pi Alpha Alpha (pres. chpt. 1976-82). Clubs: Army-Navy (Washington); Arizona (Phoenix). Home: 12000 N 90th St Unit 3072 Scottsdale AZ 85260-8643 Office: Ariz State U Sch Pub Affairs Tempe AZ 85287-0603

SADILEK, VLADIMIR, architect; b. Czechoslovakia, June 27, 1933; came to U.S., 1967, naturalized, 1973; s. Oldrich and Antoine (Zlamal) S.; m. Jana Kadlec, Mar. 25, 1960; 1 child, Vladimir. PhD in City Planning summa cum laude, Tech. U. Prague, 1957. Lic. architect, 28 states. Chief architect State Office for City Planning, Prague, 1958-67; architect, designer Bank Bldg. Corp., St. Louis, 1967-70; assoc. architect Bank Bldg. Corp., San Francisco, 1970-74; owner, CEO Bank Design Cons., San Mateo, Calif., 1974-81, West Coast Devel. Co., San mateo, 1975—; pres., CEO Orbis Devel. Corp., San mateo, 1981—. Served with Inf. of Czechoslovakia, 1958. Recipient awards of excellence Bank Bldg. Corp. and AIA for planning and Design of fin. instns. in Hawaii and Calif., 1971, Ariz., N.Mex. and Tex., 1972, Colo. and Wyo., 1973, Idaho, Oreg., Wash., 1974. Republican. Roman Catholic. Home: 80 Orange Ct Burlingame CA 94010-6516 Ofifce: 1777 Borel Pl San Mateo CA 94402-3509

SADUN, ALFREDO ARRIGO, neuro-ophthalmologist, scientist, educator; b. New Orleans, Oct. 23, 1950; s. Elvio H. and Lina (Ottoleghi) S.; m. Debra Leigh Rice, Mar. 18, 1978; children: Rebecca Eli, Elvio Aaron, Benjamin Maxwell. BS, MIT, 1972; PhD, Albert Einstein Med. Sch., Bronx, N.Y., 1976, MD, 1978. Intern Huntington Meml. Hosp. U. So. Calif., Pasadena, 1978-79; resident Harvard U. Med. Sch., Boston, 1979-82, HEED Found. fellow in neuro-ophthalmology Mass. Eye and Ear Inst., 1982-83, instr. ophthalmology, 1983, asst. prof. ophthalmology, 1984; dir. residential tng. U. So. Calif. Dept. Ophthalmology, L.A., 1984-85, 90—; asst. prof. ophthalmology and neurosurgery U. So. Calif., L.A., 1984-87, assoc. prof., 1987-90; full prof. U. So. Calif., 1990—, mem. internal review bd.; prin. investigator Howe Lab. Harvard U., Boston, 1981-84, E. Doheny Eye Inst., L.A., 1984—; examiner Am. Bd. Ophthalmology; mem. Nat. Residency Rev. Com. for Accreditations, 1993—, chmn., 1998—; mem. internal rev. bd. U. So. Calif.; mem. sci. exec. bd. K. Rasmussen Found.; mem. sci. adv. bd. Internat. Found. for Optic Nerve Diseases. Author: Optics for Ophthalmologists, 1988, New Methods of Sensory Visual Testing, 1989; contbr. articles to profl. jours. and chpts. to books. James Adams scholar, 1990-91; recipient Pecan D. award, 1988-92, Rsch. to Prevent Blindness Sr. Investigator award, 1996-97, Rsch. to Prevent Blindness Sr. Investigator award, 1996. Fellow Am. Acad. Ophthalmology Neuro-Ophthalmologists; mem. NIH (Med. Scientists Tng. award 1972-78), Am. Assn. Anatomists, Assn. Univ. Prof. Ophthalmology (assoc.), Am. Bd. Ophthalmology (rep. to residency rev. com. 1994—), Soc. to Prevent Blindness, Nat. Eye Inst. (New Investigator Rsch. award 1983-86, rsch. grants 1988-91, 93—), Soc. Neurosci., Assn. Rsch. in Vision and Ophthalmology, N.Am. Neuro-Ophthal. Soc. (chmn. membership com. 1990—, v.p. 1994—). Avocation: writing. Home: 2478 Adair St San Marino CA 91108-2610

SAEGESSER, MARGUERITE M., artist; b. Bern, Switzerland, May 27, 1922; came to U.S., 1974; d. Wilhelm and Fanny (Kuepfer) Ruefenacht; m. Max Saegesser, May 27, 1952; 1 child, Francisca Marguerite; stepchildren: Anne-Marie Logan, Elisabeth, Barbara, Ursula L'Eplattenier. Solo exhbns. include De Saisset Mus., Santa Clara, Calif., 1995, Smith Andersen Gallery, Palo Alto, Calif., 1981, 85, 89, 91, 92, 95, Galerie Schindler, Bern, 1968, 90, Art Fair, Basel, Switzerland, 1990, many others; group exhbns. include Long Beach, Calif., 1971, Bienne Open Air Sculpture Show, Switzerland, 1958, 62, 66, Soc. Painters & Sculptors, Bern, 1945-46, 52, 56. Grantee Swiss Endowment Arts, 1995. Mem. South Bay Area Women's Caucus for Arts. Democrat. Home: 840 Mesa Ave Palo Alto CA 94306-3709

SAFONOV, VLADIMIR LAZAREVICH, physicist, researcher; b. Prenzlau, Germany, Aug. 25, 1955; came to U.S., 1998; s. Lazar S. and Lyudmila F. Safonov; m. Lilia V. Mushta, July 21, 1981. MSc, Moscow Inst. Physics & Tech., Dolgoprudny, USSR, 1978; PhD in Phys. and Math. Scis., Moscow Inst. Radio, Electronics and Automation, Kurchatov Inst. Atomic Energy, Russia, 1984; DSc in Phys. and Math. Scis., Russian Rsch. Ctr., Kurchatov Inst., Russia, 1992. Jr. rschr. Kurchatov Inst. Atomic Energy, Moscow, 1982-87, rschr., 1987-89; sr. rschr. Russian Rsch. Ctr. Kurchatov Inst., Moscow, 1989-95, leading rschr., 1995-96; vis. rsch. scholar Okayama (Japan) U., 1996-97; vis. faculty Info. Storage Materials Lab., Toyota Technol. Inst., Nagoya, Japan, 1997-98; vis. postgrad. rsch. physcisist Ctr. for Magnetic Rec. Rsch., U. Calif. San Diego, La Jolla, 1998—. Recipient Moscow Komsomol prize and diploma for young physicist, 1989. Mem. IEEE, Am. Phys. Soc. E-mail: safonov@sdmag4.ucsd.edu. Office: Ctr for Magnetic Rec Rsch U Calif San Diego 9500 Gilman Dr La Jolla CA 92093-0401

SAGER, MADELINE DEAN, lawyer; b. Turlock, Calif., Feb. 9, 1946; d. Paul Kenton and Jean Madeline (Ferguson) Dean; m. Gregory Warren Sager, June, 1970; children: Jeannette Carolyn, Robert Dean. BA, Sacramento State U., 1967; JD, U. Calif., Davis, 1970. Bar: Calif. 1971, U.S. Dist. Ct. (ea. dist.) Calif. 1971, U.S. Dist. Ct. (no. dist.) Calif. 1973. Atty. Blackmon, Isenberg, Moulds & Blicker, Sacramento, 1971-72, Redwood Legal Assistance, Ukiah, Calif., 1972-77, Sager & Sager, Ukiah, Willits, Calif., 1977-87, Leonard J. LaCasse, Ukiah, 1990—; dir. Law Libr. Bd., Ukiah, 1985. Sec. PTA, Calpella, Calif., 1989-90; mem. sch. site coun. Redwood Valley (Calif.) Mid. Sch., 1992-93; treas., dir. Ukiah Dolphin Swim, 1994-97; meet dir. Soroptimist Swim Meet, Ukiah, 1996. Mem. Mendocino County Bar Assn. (pres. 1986), Pacific Swimming (official 1995-98). Democrat. Presbyterian. Avocations: hiking, camping, music, travel. Home: PO Box 72 Redwood Valley CA 95470-0072 Office: Leonard J LaCasse 119 S Main St Ukiah CA 95482-4919

SAGMEISTER, EDWARD FRANK, business owner, hospitality industry executive, civic official, retired consultant, fund raiser, career officer; b. N.Y.C., Dec. 10, 1939; s. Frank and Anna (Unger) S.; m. Anne Marie Ducker, Aug. 18, 1962; children: Cynthia Anne, Laura Marie, Cheryl Suzanne, Eric Edward. BS, U. San Francisco, 1962; MBA, Syracuse U., 1968; postgrad., Air Command and Staff Coll., 1977, Air War Coll., 1981. Commd. 2d lt. USAF, 1963, advanced through grades to lt. col., pers. officer, 1963, aide-de-camp, 1965; dir. pers. sys. Alaskan Air Command, 1968; sys. design program analysis officer HQ USAF, The Pentagon, 1971; spl. asst. sec. Air Force Pers. Coun., USAF, 1975; dir. pers. programs and assignments HQUSAF Europe, 1979; Air Force dep. asst. inspector gen., 1982; ret. USAF, 1984; dir. devel. Am. Cancer Soc., Riverside, Calif., 1984-87; cons. Redlands, Calif., 1987-92; chmn. of bd., pres., CEO Hospitality Pub and Grub, Inc., San Bernardino, Calif., 1992—; instr. Am. Internat. U., L.A., 1987; program dir. Am. Radio Network, L.A., 1987; ptnr., owner Midway Med. Ctr., San Bernardino, 1990-91. Foreman pro-tem San Bernardino County Grand Jury, 1990-91; mem. Redlands 2000 Com., 1988; campaign cabinet mem. Arrowhead United Way, San Bernardino, 1986-87, loaned exec., 1985; exec. dir. Crafton hills Coll. Found., Yucaipa, Calif., 1988; vol. San Bernardino County Dept. Probation, 1985-88; mem. Redlands Cmty., Chorus, 1988-90; vice-chmn., charter mem. Redlands Human Rels. Commn., 1994—, chmn., 1996; mem. Redlands Youth Accountability Bd., San Bernardino County, 1994—, treas. 1996; mem. supt.'s human rels. adv. com., Redlands Unified Sch. Dist., 1996—. Mem. San Bernardino C. of C., Redlands C. of C., Ret. Officers Assn., Nat. Soc. Fundraising Execs., (dir., charter mem. Inland Empire chpt. 1987-88), Empire Singers (v.p. 1987). Republican. Roman Catholic. Avocations: travel, music, singing, tennis, reading. Home: 503 Sunnyside Ave Redlands CA 92373-5629 Office: Hospitality Pub and Grub Inc 1987 Diners Ct San Bernardino CA 92408-3330

SAHATJIAN, MANIK, nurse, psychologist; b. Tabris, Iran, July 24, 1921; came to U.S., 1951; d. Dicran and Shushanig (Der-Galustian) Mnatzaganian; m. George Sahatjian, Jan. 21, 1954; children: Robert, Edwin. Nursing Cert., Am. Mission Hosps.-Boston U., 1954; BA in Psychology, San Jose State U., 1974, MA in Psychology, 1979. RN, Calif., Mass. Head nurse Am. Mission Hosp., Tabris, 1945-46; charge nurse Banke-Melli Hosp., Tehran, 1946-51; vis. nurse Vis. Nurse Assn., Oakland, Calif., 1956-57; research asst. Stanford U., 1979-81, Palo Alto (Calif.) Med. Research Found., 1981-84; documentation supr. Bethesda Convalescent Ctr., Los Gatos, Calif., 1985-86; sr. outreach worker City of Fremont (Calif.) Human Svcs., 1987-90, case mgr., 1990-97; ret., 1997; guest rsch. asst. NASA Ames Lab., Mountain View, Calif., summers 1978, 79. Author (with others) psychol. research reports. Mentor elem. sch. children. Fulbright scholar, 1951; Iran Found. scholar, 1953. Mem. AAUW, Western Psychol. Assn. Democrat. Mem. St. Andrew Armenian Church. Avocations: oil painting, classic dance. Home: 339 Starlite Way Fremont CA 94539-7642

SAHO, S. BAMBA, science educator, writer; b. Banjul, Gambia, Mar. 10, 1952; came to U.S., 1969; s. Abubakarr and Jatou Saho; children: Fatma, Abubakarr, Lamin, Sulayman, Jatou. BA in Biology, Eisenhower Coll., 1975; M in Epidemiology, U. Mich., 1985. Cert. clin. bacteriology, Denmark; cert. tchr., Calif.; certn. epidemiology, Atlanta. Bacteriologist Royal Victoria Hosp., Banjul, Gambia, 1979-85, pub. health microbiologist, 1985-90; sci. tchr. Park Jr. H.S., Antioch, Calif., 1993-96; sci. tchr. Deer Valley H.S., Antioch, 1996—, club advisor, 1996-98, soccer coach, 1996-97; mem. sci. task force Antioch Unified Sch. Dist., 1996-97; pres. AATA Promotions, Banjul, 1987-91. Author: White Pelicans From Africa, 1997, Kumba-The Orphan Girl, 1997; contbr. articles to mags. Recipient 1st pl. Biol. Sci. award U.S. Army, 1971; fellow Danish Gov., 1978, U.S. Aid, 1993. Mem. NEA, Calif. Tchrs. Assn, Antioch Edn. Assn. Avocations: writing, contemporary music, sports, travel. Office: Deer Valley HS 4700 Lone Tree Way Antioch CA 94509

SAINER, ELLIOT A(RNOLD), health care executive; b. Bayshore, N.Y., Mar. 10, 1946; s. Herman L. and Janet (Salpeter) S.; m. Marcia Lisa Heim, Sept. 12, 1976; children: Todd, Diana. BA, U. Pitts., 1968; MBA, George Washington U., 1971. Assoc. adminstr. dept. psychiatry Albert Einstein Coll. Medicine, Bronx, N.Y., 1971-74; adminstr. dept. pediatrics Albert Einstein Coll. Medicine, Bronx, 1974-78; assoc. adminstr. Peachford Hosp., Atlanta, 1978-79; project dir. Charter Med. Corp., Honolulu, 1979-81; adminstr. Charter Oak Hosp., Calif., 1981-84, Charter Suburban Hosp., Paramount, Calif., 1984-86; regional dir. Charter Med. Corp., El Monte, Calif., 1986-88; pres., chief exec. officer Life Plus Found., North Hollywood, Calif., 1988-89; CEO Coll. Health Enterprises, Huntington Beach, Calif., 1989-98; pres., CEO Aspen Youth Svcs., Cerritos, Calif., 1998—; bd. govs. Fedn. Am. Health Systems, Washington, 1984—. Mem. Calif. Healthcare Assn. (bd. dirs.), Nat. Assn. Psychiat. Health Systems (bd. dirs.). Avocations: tennis, golf, reading. Home: 2000 Edgewood Dr South Pasadena CA 91030-3920 Office: Aspen Youth Svcs 17100 Pioneer Blvd Ste 300 Cerritos CA 90701-2766

ST. CHARLES, DAVID, electronics company executive. Pres., CEO Integrated Sys. Inc., Sunnyvale, Calif. Office: Integrated Sys Inc 201 Moffett Park Dr Sunnyvale CA 94089-1322*

ST. CLAIR, CARL, conductor, music director. Music dir. Pacific Symphony Orch., Santa Ana, Calif., 1990—, Ann Arbor (Mich.) Symphony Orch., 1985-92, Cayuga Chamber Orch., 1986-92. Albums include Fire Water Paper: A Vietnam Oratorio, 1995, Corigliano Piano Concerto. Recipient NEA/Seaver Condrs. award, 1990. Office: Pacific Symphony Orch 1231 E Dyer Rd Ste 200 Santa Ana CA 92705-5606*

ST. CLAIR, THOMAS MCBRYAR, mining and manufacturing company executive; b. Wilkinsburg, Pa., Sept. 26, 1935; s. Fred C. and Dorothy (Renner) St. C.; m. Sarah K. Stewart, Aug. 1, 1959; children—Janet, Susan, Carol. AB, Allegheny Coll., 1957; MS, MIT, 1958; grad. advanced mgmt. program, Harvard U. With Koppers Co., Inc., Pitts., 1958-88, asst. to gen. mgr. engring. and constrn. div., 1966-69, comptroller, asst. treas., 1969-78, pres. Engineered Metal Products Group, 1978-83, v.p., asst. to chmn., 1983-84, v.p., treas., chief fin. officer, 1984-88; sr. v.p., chief fin. officer Phelps Dodge Corp., Phoenix, 1989—; bd. dirs. Nortrust of Ariz. Trustee Allegheny Coll. Mem. Fin. Execs. Inst., Duquesne Club (Pitts.), Univ. Club (Pitts. and Phoenix). Presbyterian. Office: Phelps Dodge Corp 2600 N Central Ave Fl 14 Phoenix AZ 85004-3089

SAITO, FRANK KIYOJI, import-export firm executive; b. Tokyo, Feb. 28, 1945; s. Kaoru and Chiyoko S.; LL.B., Kokugakuin U., 1967; m. Elaine Tamami Karasawa, Feb. 22, 1975; children—Roderic Kouki, Lorine Erika. With import dept. Trois Co. Ltd., Tokyo, Japan, 1967-68; founder import/export dept. Three Bond Co., Ltd., Tokyo, 1968-71; sales mgr. Kobe Mercantile, Inc., San Diego, 1971-76; pres. K&S Internat. Corp., San Diego, 1976-97; pres. K&S Techs., Inc., 1997—. Office: 9710 Scranton Rd Ste 260 San Diego CA 92121-1744

SAITO, THEODORE T., physicist; b. Poston, Ariz., Sept. 9, 1942; s. Frank Hideo and Akiko Saito; m. Diane Gail Signorino, Aug. 31, 1968; children: Jennifer, Paul. BS, USAF Acad., 1964; SM, MIT, 1966; PhD, Pa. State U., 1970. Project officer, group leader Air Force Weapons Lab., Albuquerque, 1970-74; optics machining study leader Lawrence Livermore (Calif.) Nat. Lab., 1974-77, dep. program leader precision engring. program, 1984-87, dept. dept. head, 1987-88, group leader, 1988-92, acting leader precision engring. program, 1993-94; sci. advisor U.S. Dept. of Energy, Germantown, Md., 1994-96, ops. mgr. advanced microtechnology program, 1997-98, initiatives proliferation prevention mgr., 1998—; tech. area mgr. Air Force Materials Lab., Wright Patterson AFB, Ohio, 1979-80, dir. mgmt. tech., 1977-79; from dir. to comdr. F. J. Seiler Rsch. Lab. USAF Acad., Colo., 1980-84. Contbr. articles to profl. jours. Mem., v.p. Japanese-Am. Citizen League, Pleasanton, Calif., 1985. Fellow Optical Soc. Am., Soc. Photo-Optical Instrumentation Engrs. (sec. 1990, v.p. 1991, pres. 1992, immediate past pres. 1993); mem. Assn. Fed. Tech. Transfer Execs. (bd. dirs. 1993-95), Am. Assn. Engring. Socs. (bd. govs. 1995-96, vice chair 1997, sec./treas. 1998, chair-elect 1999). Office: Lawrence Livermore Nat Lab PO Box 808 Livermore CA 94551-0808

SAITO-FURUKAWA, JANET CHIYO, primary school educator; b. L.A., June 29, 1951; d. Shin and Nobuko Ann (Seki) Saito; m. Neil Yasuhiko Furukawa, June 30, 1990. BS, U. So. Calif., 1973; MA, Mt. St. Mary's Coll., L.A., 1990. Cert. elem. tchr. K-8, adminstrn. 1st tier, lang. devel. specialist, Calif. Tchr. grades four through six Rosemont Elem. Sch., L.A., 1973-80, psychomotor specialist, 1979-80; tchr. mid. sch. lang. arts Virgil, Parkman Mid. Schs., L.A./Woodland Hills, Calif., 1980-87, 87-90, dept. chairperson, 1974-77, 80-84, 1989-90; drama tchr. Virgil Mid. Sch., L.A., 1980-81, dance tchr., 1984-87; mid. sch. advisor L.A. Unified Sch. Dist., Encino, Calif., 1990-91; practitioner facilitator L.A. Unified Sch. Dist., Encino, 1990-97; young authors chairperson Parkman Mid. Sch., Woodland Hills, 1988-90; multicultural performance educator, Great Leap, L.A., 1988-93; mentor tchr. L.A. Unified Sch. dist., 1980-90; trainer dist. standards project, 1996—; presenter/cons. in field. Tchr./leader Psychomotor Grant, 1979; writer Level II Teamin' and Theme-in, 1994. Recipient Nancy McHugh English award English Coun. L.A., Woodland Hills, 1987, 88, 91, Outstanding Reading and Lang. Tchr. award L.A. Reading Assn., Woodland Hills, 1991, Apple award L.A. Mayor's Office, 1990, Tchr. of the Month award Phi Delta Kappa, San Fernando, Calif., 1989. Mem. ASCD, Nat. Mid. Schs. Assn. (presenter, diverse cultures com. 1996—), Nat. Coun. Tchrs. Math., Calif. Sci. Tchrs. Assn., Nat. Coun. Tchrs. English, The Learning Collaborative. Lutheran. Avocations: volleyball, fishing, reading, skiing. Office: Practitioner Ctr LA Unified Sch Dist 3010 Estara Ave Los Angeles CA 90065-2205

SAKAMOTO, KATSUYUKI, retired college chancellor, psychology educator; b. L.A., Oct. 24, 1938; m. Edna Christine Sakamoto; children: David Katsu, Bryce Yoshio. BA in Psychology, Calif. State U., Fresno, 1961, MA in Psychology, 1968; PhD in Exptl. Social Psychology, So. Ill. U., Carbondale, 1971; postgrad., Carnegie Mellon U., 1984. Acting dir. Army Edn. Ctr., Munich, 1962-63; dir. social svcs. Salvation Army, Fresno, Calif., 1964-66; assoc. prof. psychology Keuka Coll., Keyka Park, N.Y., 1971-78; prof. social psychology Ea. Oreg. State Coll., La Grande, 1978-85, assoc. dean, then acting dean, 1980-82, 84, assoc. dean acad. affairs, 1982-85; prof. psychology Ind. U. East, Richmond, 1985-91, vice chancellor for acad. affairs, 1985-90, spl. asst. to chancellor, 1990-91; prof., chancellor Calif. Sch. Profl. Psychology, Alameda, 1991-98, ret., 1998; lectr. So. Ill. U., 1970-71; vis. prof. SUNY, Binghamton, 1973; adj. prof. Alfred (N.Y.) U., 1972-76, Nazareth Coll. Rochester, N.Y., 1975-78, Eisenhower Coll., Seneca Falls, N.Y., 1975-77; evaluator Western Assn. Schs. and Colls., 1991—; commr.-at-large North Ctrl. Assn. Colls. and Schs., 1989-91, educator, cons., 1986-91; mem. exec. bd. for study ctrs. in Japan, China and Korea, campus dir. Oreg. Sys. Higher Edn., 1980-85; bd. visitors Newark (N.Y.) Devel. Ctr., 1975-77; presenter in field. Contbr. articles to profl. jours. Bd. dirs. troop 119 Boy Scouts Am., Richmond, 1986-91, Project 100001, Townsend Cmty. Ctr., Richmond, 1987-89, Alameda Girls Club, Inc., 1992—, Asian Cmty. Mental Health Svcs., 1991—, Found. for Ednl. Excellence, Alameda, 1993—; pres., bd. dirs. Whitewater Opera Co., Richmond, 1987-91, Leadership Wayne County, Richmond, 1988-91; cons. teaching mini-grant program Richmond Cmty. Schs., 1988-91; mem. citizens adv. bd. Wayne County Sheriff's Dept., 1989-91. Mem. APA, Am. Assn. for Higher Edn., Am. Assn. State Colls. and Univs., Am. Assn. Univ. Adminstrs. (nat. v.p. 1990-92, bd. dirs. Found. 1991—), Am. Assn. for Higher Edn. (founding mem. Asian Am. caucus), Asian Am. Psychol. Assn. (treas., membership officer 1983-91, pres. 1988-91), Calif. Psychol. Assn., Nat. Assn. Acad. Affairs Adminstrs., Nat. Coun. Schs. Profl. Psychology, Rotary (bd. dirs. Alameda 1993—). Home: 2837 Brown St Alameda CA 94502-7949 Office: Calif Sch Profl Psychology 1005 Atlantic Ave Alameda CA 94501-1148

SAKIC, JOSEPH STEVE, professional hockey player; b. Burnaby, B.C., Canada, July 7, 1969. Capt. Quebec Nordiques, 1991-95; with Colo. Avalanche, 1995—. Won WHL East Most Valuable Player Trophy, 1986-87, WHL Stewart (Butch) Paul Meml. Trophy, 1986-87, Four Broncos Meml. Trophy, 1987-88, Bob Clarke Trophy, 1987-88, Conn Smythe Trophy NHL, 1996; named to WHL All-Star Second Team, 1986-87, Can. Hockey League Player of Yr., 1987-88, WHL Player of Yr., 1987-88; played in NHL All-Star Game, 1990-94, 96. Office: c/o Colo Avalanche 1635 Clay St Denver CO 80204-1743*

SAKOGUCHI, BEN, artist, art educator; b. San Bernardino, Calif., 1938. Student, San Bernardino Valley Coll., 1956-58; BA, UCLA, 1960, MFA, 1964; postgrad., Calif. State U., L.A., 1982-83. Prof. art Pasadena (Calif.) City Coll., 1964-98, retired, 1998—. Solo exhbns. include Ceeje Gallery, L.A., 1964, 65, 67, La Jolla (Calif.) Mus., 1965, U. Calif. Santa Cruz, 1967, L.A. City Coll., 1968, 81, Santa Barbara (Calif.) Mus. Art, 1968, Brand Art Ctr., Glendale, Calif., 1971, Zara Gallery, San Francisco, 1973, Compton (Calif.) Coll., 1977, Works, San Jose, Calif., 1978, Mira Costa Coll., Oceanside, Calif., 1983, Roberts Gallery, Santa Monica, Calif., 1985, Mount St. Mary's Coll., L.A., 1988, Aljira Ctr. Contemporary Art, Newark, 1992, Alternative Mus., N.Y.C., Rancho Santiago Coll., Santa Ana, 1995, Space, U. Redlands (Calif.), 1995; 2 person exhbns. Santa Ana Coll., 1978, Aarnum Gallery, Pasadena, 1980, San Francisco Fine Arts Mus., 1980, Gorman Mus. U. Calif. Davis, 1984, Rancho Santiago Coll., Santa Ana, 1995; group exhbns. include Alternative Mus., 1982, 89, 91, 92, 95, NYU Stony Brook, 1983, Triton Mus., Santa Clara, 1984, ARCO Ctr. Visual Arts, L.A., 1984, L.A. Mcpl. Art Gallery, 1985, Watts Towers Art Ctr., L.A., 1986, Whatcom Mus. History and Art, Bellingham, Wash., 1989 (circulated various museums nationwide, 1992), New Mus. Contemporary Art, N.Y.C., 1990, Peace Mus., Chgo., 1995, Fort Mason Ctr., San Francisco, 1995, Mus. Modern Art, N.Y.C., 1995, others; represented permanent collections Am. Express Co., N.Y.C., Atlantic Richfield Corp., L.A., Bklyn. Mus., Chgo. Art Inst., Mus. Modern Art, N.Y.C., Phila. Mus. Art, Nat. Mus. Am. Art, Smithsonian Instn., Fogg Art Mus., Harvard U., numerous others; subject numerous articles, publs., exhbn. catalogs and revs., 1965—. NEA fellow

1980, 95; Pasadena Arts Commn. fellow 1991, Calif. Cmty. Found. J. Paul Getty Trust Fund for Visual Arts fellow, 1997. Home: 1183 Avoca Ave Pasadena CA 91105-3450 Office: Pasadena City Coll Dept Art 1570 E Colorado Blvd Pasadena CA 91106*

SALAMA, FARID, astrophysicist, spectroscopist, research scientist; b. Paris, Jan. 28, 1957; s. Aly and Marie Rose (Garroux) S.; m. Josie Bove, July 5, 1986; 1 child, Maissa. BS in Chem. Physics, U. Paris, Orsay, France, 1981; MS in Chem. Physics, U. Pierre & Marie Curie, 1983; PhD in Physical Chemistry, U. Pierre & Marie Curie, France, 1986. Postdoctoral rsch. fellow Lawrence Berkeley Lab., Berkeley, Calif., 1987-88; rsch. assoc. Nat. Rsch. Coun./NASA, Moffett Field, Calif., 1988-90; from vis. rsch. astronomer to rsch. physicist U. Calif./NASA, Berkeley, 1990-94; prin. investigator SETI Rsch. Inst./NASA, Moffett Field, Calif., 1994—; fellow Gen. Delegation Sci. Tech. Rsch., France, 1983-85; fellow NRC, 1988-90; panelist, reviewer NASA Astrophysics Rsch. & Analysis Program, 1994; speaker symposium German-Am. Frontiers Sci., 1995; reviewer Petrol. Rsch. Fund, 1996; NAS fellow German-Am. Acad. Coun., 1996. Contbr. articles to profl. jours., chpts. to books. Fellow Found. France, 1986. Mem. Internat. Soc. for Origin of Life, Astron. Soc. Pacific. Achievements include pioneering research in laboratory astrophysics in which the techniques of low temperature spectroscopy are applied to the study of interstellar and planetary material analogs. Avocations: reading, hiking, music, movies. Office: NASA-Ames Rsch Ctr Mail Stop 245-6 Moffett Field CA 94035

SALAMATI, FARSHID, environmental engineer, environmental company executive; b. Tehran, Iran, May 30, 1949; came to U.S., 1980; s. Plato and Kharman (Yezeshni) S.; m. Fariba Azari, June 19, 1978; 1 child, Behan. BSEE, U. Tehran, 1974; MS in Eviron. and Energy Mgmt., U. Calif., Berkeley, 1984; PhD in Environ. Saftey and Health, Western State U. Cert. environ. mgr., designer; cert. asbestos cons.; lic. gen., elec. and asbestos contr. Field engr. Shahin Factory, Tehran, 1968-72; supr. Irom Engring., Tehran, 1972-75; proj. mgr., pres. Techno Bond, Tehran, 1975-80; field engr. EAL Corp., Richmond, Calif., 1980-85; CFO, v.p. INOV Corp., Oakland, Calif., 1985-87; CFO, pres. Environ. Innovations Corp., Oakland, 1987—. Mem. Bldg. Owners and Mgrs. Assn., Am. Indsl. Hygiene Assn., Environ. Safety Coun. Am., Fedn. Zoroastrian Assn. N.Am., Nat. Assn. Environ. Profls., Nat. Assn. Gen. Contrs., Nat. Asbestos Coun. (qualified field instr., founding co-chmn. tech./analytical adv. com. Calif. chpt.), Calif. Energy Commn., No. Calif. Electronic Systems Contrs. Assn., Assn. Profl. Energy Mgrs., Asbestos Abatement Coun., Assoc. Bldrs. and Contrs. Inc. (Golden Gate chpt.), Environ. Assessment Assn. Avocations: swimming, tennis, surfing, snorkeling. Office: Environ Innovations Corp 8301 Edgewater Dr # 103 Oakland CA 94621-1421

SALAMON, MIKLOS DEZSO GYORGY, mining engineer, educator; b. Balkany, Hungary, May 20, 1933; came to U.S., 1986; naturalized, 1993; s. Miklos and Sarolta (Obetko) S.; m. Agota Maria Meszaros, July 11, 1953; children: Miklos, Gabor. Diploma in Engring., Polytech U., Sopron, Hungary, 1956; PhD, U. Durham, Newcastle, England, 1962; doctorem honoris causa, U. Miskolc, Hungary, 1990. Research asst. dept. mining engring. U. Durham, 1959-63; dir. research Coal Mining Research Controlling Council, Johannesburg, South Africa, 1963-66; dir. collieries research lab Chamber of Mines of South Africa, Johannesburg, 1966-74, dir. gen. research org., 1974-86; disting. prof. Colo. Sch. Mines, Golden, 1986-98, prof. emeritus, 1998, dir. Colo. Mining and Mineral Resources Rsch. Inst., 1990-94; pres. Salamon Cons. Inc., Arvada, 1995—; prof. emeritus Colo. Sch. Mines, Golden, 1998—; 22d Sir Julius Wernher Meml. lectr., 1988; hon. prof. U. Witwatersrand, Johannesburg, 1979-86; vis. prof. U. Minn., Mpls., 1981, U. Tex., Austin, 1982, U. NSW, Sydney, Australia, 1990, 91-96; mem. Presdl. Commn. of Inquiry into Safety and Health in South African Mining Industry, 1994-95. Co-author: Rock Mechanics Applied to the Study of Rockbursts, 1966, Rock Mechanics in Coal Mining, 1976; contbr. articles to profl. jours. Mem. Pres.'s Sci. Adv. Council, Cape Town, South Africa, 1984-86, Nat. Sci. Priorities Com., Pretoria, South Africa, 1984-86. Recipient Nat. award Assn. Scis. and Tech. Socs., South Africa, 1971. Fellow South African Inst. Mining and Metallurgy (hon. life, v.p. 1974-76, pres. 1976-77, gold medal 1964, 85, Stokes award 1986, silver medal 1991), Inst. Mining and Metallurgy (London), Hungarian Acad. Scis. (external), 1998; mem. AIME, Internat. Soc. Rock Mechanics. Roman Catholic.

SALAS, EDWARD ALLEN, securities trader; b. Manila, Oct. 28, 1970; came to U.S., 1986; s. Jake M. and Mila (Hilomen) S. Student, Calif. State Poly. U., 1989-94, Glendale (Calif.) C.C., 1995—. Bookkeeper Paper Chase Printing, L.A., 1989-92; stockbroker E-W Investments, San Gabriel, Calif., 1992-95; bus. banker Bank Am., Glendale, 1992-96; futures trader E.A.H. Salas, Sun Valley, Calif., 1996—. Avocations: reading fin. books, playing basketball, collecting vintage wine, gourmet cooking. Home and Office: EAH Salas 11136 Lorne St Sun Valley CA 91352-3988

SALAS, FLOYD FRANCIS, writer; b. Walsenburg, Colo., Jan. 24, 1931; s. Edward and Anita (Sanchez) S.; m. Velva Daryl (Harris) Salas, Jan. 1949 (div. 1970); 1 child, Gregory Francis Salas; m. Virginia Ann (Staley) Salas, June 25, 1979 (div. 1981). BA in English, San Francisco State Univ., 1963, MA in English, 1965. Prof. creative writing San Francisco State U., 1966-67, statewide coord., poetry in the sch., 1973-76; prof. creative writing U. Calif., 1977-78; instr., poetry San Quentin Prison, Calif., 1984-91; prof. creative writing Sonoma State U., Rohnert Park, Calif., 1985-86, Foothill Coll., Los Altos Hills, Calif., 1979—, U. San Francisco, 1995—. Author: Tattoo the Wicked Cross, 1967 (Joseph Henry Jackson award 1964), What Now My Love, 1970, Lay My Body on the Line, 1978 (Nat. Endowment for the Arts 1977), Buffalo Nickel, 1992 (CAC Lit. Fellow. 1993), State of Emergency, 1996 (PEN Oakland Lit. Censorship award 1997), Color of My Living Heart, 1996. Founder Student Peace Union, San Francisco, 1962; lit. judge Joseph H. Jackson/Phelan awards, San Francisco, 1977-78, PEN Cntr. U.S. West, L.A., 1989-90; boxing coach U. Calif. boxing team, 1975-91. Recipient scholarship El Centro Mexicano de Escritores Rockefeller found., 1958; fiction fellow Eugene F. Saxton, 1965; James P. Lynch Meml. Fellow. for outstanding tchrs., U. Calif., 1977; lit. fellow. Calif. Arts Coun., 1993; fellow Bay Area Writers Project U. Calif., 1984. Mem. No. Calif. Vet. Boxer's Assn. Ring 72. Democrat. Avocations: sculptor, painter, boxer, boxing coach, artist (line drawing). Home: 1206 Delaware St Berkeley CA 94702-1407

SALAVERRIA, HELENA CLARA, educator; b. San Francisco, May 19, 1923; d. Blas Saturnino and Eugenia Irene (Loyarte) S. AB, U. Calif., Berkeley, 1945, secondary teaching cert., 1946; MA, Stanford U., 1962. High sch. tchr., 1946-57; asst. prof. Luther Coll., Decorah, Iowa, 1959-60; prof. Spanish, Bakersfield (Calif.) Coll., 1961-84, chmn. dept., 1973-80. Vol., Hearst Castle; mem. srs. adv. group edn. Cuesta Coll. Community Svcs. Mem. AAUW (edn. com.), NEA, Calif. Fgn. Lang. Tchrs. Assn. (dir. 1976-77), Kern County Fgn. Lang. Tchrs. Assn. (pres. 1975-77), Union Concerned Scientists, Natural Resources Def. Coun., Calif. Tchrs. Assn. (chpt. sec. 1951-52), Yolo County Coun. Retarded, Soc. Basque Studies in Am., RSVP, Amnesty Internat., Common Cause, Sierra Club, Prytanean Alumnae, U. Women of Cambria, U. Calif. Alumni Assn., Stanford U. Alumni Assn., Friends of the Cambria Libr. Democrat. Presbyterian. Address: PO Box 63 Cambria CA 93428-0063

SALAZAR, ARTURO, deacon; b. L.A., May 2, 1958; s. Antonio Alvarado and Victoria (Obregon) S.; m. Margaret Lujan, Sept. 6, 1980; children: Michael, David. BSCE, U. So. Calif., 1980. Deacon 1st Fundamental Bible Ch., Monterey Park, Calif., 1982-85, 87-92, Monterey Park, 1994—; exec. bd. First Fundamental Bible Ch., Monterey Park, 1983-85, 98—, sec., 1990, chmn., deacon, 1987-89, treas., 1985, 89, 91. Alt. 60th Assembly Dist. Rep. Com., El Monte, Calif., 1989-90; mem. Caltrans Hispanic Adv. Com., L.A., 1990-92. Recipient Sustained Superior Accomplishment award, Caltrans, 1988, Cert. of Excellence, 1991. Republican. Home: 14045 Brookport St Baldwin Park CA 91706-2522

SALAZAR, KENNETH L., [illegible] and [illegible] Hope Hernandez; children: Melinda, Andrea. BA in Polit. Sci., Colo. Coll., 1977, LLD (hon.), 1993; JD, U. Mich., 1981. Bar: Colo. 1981, U.S. Dist. Ct. Colo. 1981, U.S. Ct. Appeals (10th cir.) 1981. Farmer, rancher Conejos County, Colo.; law clk. Colo. Atty. Gen., summer 1979; assoc. Sherman & Howard, Denver, 1981-86; chief legal counsel Office of Gov., Denver, 1986-90; exec. dir. Colo. Dept. Natural Resources, Denver, 1990-94; dir. Parcel, Mauro & Spaanstra, Denver, 1994-99; atty. gen. State of Colo., 1999—; gov.'s rep. State Bd. Equalization, Denver, 1990. Chair Great Outdoors Colo., Denver, 1993-94, Rio Grande Compact Commn., 1995-97, Sangre de Cristo Land Grant Commn., 1993-95; mem. Colo. Water Conservation Bd., Denver, 1990-94; mem. City and County of Denver Ethics Panel, 1993; bd. dirs. Denver Cmty. Leadership Forum, 1988; gov.'s rep. State Bd. on Property Tax Equalization, 1987-91; del. Soviet-Am. Young Leadership Dialogue, 1984; bd. dirs. Servicios de la Raza HUD 202 Project, 1985-89, chair, 1986; mem. Am. Israel Friendship League, 1986-89. mem. adv. com. Colo. U. Las Sch. Natural Resources Law Ctr., 1989-92; mem. Western Water Policy Rev. Adv. Commn., 1995-97. Juan Tienda scholar. Mem. ABA, Colo. Bar Assn. (bd. govs. 1989-90, task force to assess the legal profession 1986), Denver Bar Assn. (2d v.p. 1989, chair policy-cmty. rels. subcoms. 1982-84), Hispanic Bar Assn. (ABA task force on opptys. for minorities in legal profession, bd. dirs. 1986-87), Am. Judicature Soc. Avocations: basketball, outdoor activities, politics. Home: 5140 Chase St Denver CO 80212-2828 Office: State Colo Dept of Law 1525 Sherman 5th Flr Denver CO 80203*

SALAZAR, LUIS ADOLFO, architect; b. New Orleans, Sept. 17, 1944; s. Gustavo Adolfo and Luz Maria (Florez) S.; m. Sandra Kay Bucklew, May 30, 1969 (div. Jan. 1984); 1 child, Staci Dahnal. AA, Harbor Coll., 1966; BArch, Ariz. State U., 1971. Registered architect, Ariz., Calif. Area architect Peace Corps, Sierra Leone, 1971-73; project architect Van Sittert Assocs., Phoenix, 1973-77; pres., owner Salazar Assoc. Architects, Ltd., Phoenix, Inc., Inc., 1977—; Prin. works include bldg. design Kenema Cathedral, Kenema, Sierra Leone, West Africa, 1980, U.S. West Foothills Switching Ctr., Phoenix, Celebration Luth. Ch., Peoria, Ariz. Bd. dirs. Community Behavioral Services, Phoenix, 1983-85; Phoenix Meml. Hosp., 1984-94, Terraco Properties. mem. Subcom. on Bond Election, Phoenix, 1984; mem. Visual Improvement Awards Com., City of Phoenix, 1985-88. Mem. AIA (chmn. program com., honor award Ariz. chpt. 1984, visual improvement awards coms. 1985, 86), Inst. Architects. Roman Catholic.

SALDIN, THOMAS R., consumer products company executive, corporate lawyer; b. 1946. BA, Carleton Coll., 1968; JD, Cin. Coll. Law, 1974. Law clk. to presiding justice U.S. Dist. Ct. (so. dist.) Ohio, 1974-76; assoc. Benjamin, Faulkner & Tepe & Sach, Cin., 1976-78; asst. gen. counsel Albertson's Inc., Boise, Idaho, 1978-81, v.p., gen. counsel, 1981-83, exec. v.p., adminstrv. gen. counsel, 1983—. Office: Albertson's Inc 250 E Parkcenter Blvd Boise ID 83706-3999

SALE, GEORGE EDGAR, physician; b. Missoula, Mont., Apr. 18, 1941; s. George Goble and Ruth Edna (Polleys) S.; m. Joan M. Sutliff, 1989; children: George Gregory Colby, Teo Marie Jonsson. AB, Harvard U., 1963; MD, Stanford U., 1968. Intern U. Oreg., Portland, 1968-69; sr. asst. surgeon USPHS, Albuquerque, 1969-71; resident in pathology U. Wash., Seattle, 1971-75, instr. pathology, 1975-78, asst. prof., 1978-81, assoc. prof., 1981-88, prof., 1988—; asst. mem. faculty, dept. oncology Hutchinson Cancer Ctr., Seattle, 1975-88, assoc. mem., 1988-91, mem., 1991—. Author, editor: Pathology of Bone Marrow Transplantation, 1984, Pathology of Transplantation, 1990. Mem. AAAS, Internat. Acad. Pathology, Coll. Am. Pathologists, Am. Assn. Investigative Pathologists, Physicians for Social Responsibility. Home: 12146 Sunrise Dr NE Bainbridge Island WA 98110-4304 Office: Fred Hutchinson Cancer Rsh Ctr 1100 Fairview Ave N Seattle WA 98109-4417

SALESKY, WILLIAM JEFFREY, corporate executive; b. Boston, June 12, 1957; s. Harry Michael Salesky and Eleanor Faith (Stutman) Spater; m. Cherri Lynne DeGreek, Nov. 27, 1982; 1 child, Joshua Steven. BS, U. Calif., Davis, 1978; MS, U. Calif., Berkeley, 1980, PhD, 1982. Co-op engr. Bechtel Corp. Inc., San Francisco, 1977-78; engr. U. Calif., Davis, 1978-79; rsch. assoc. Lawrence Berkeley Lab., 1979-82; project mgr. Smith Internat., Irvine, Calif., 1982-89; dir. engring. & quality assurance Mark Controls, Long Beach, Calif., 1989-94; v.p. engring. Stamet Inc., Gardena, Calif., 1994-97; pres., founder Skytron Corp., Irvine, 1997—; cons. Printnonix Corp., Irvine, Calif., 1988, Metal Alloys Inc., Irvine, 1986-88, Ceracon Inc., Irvine, 1984-86; chmn. L.A. Conf. on Fugitive Emissions from Valves, 1993. Patentee in field. Mgr. Irvine Baseball Assn., 1990; grad. asssembly rep. U. Calif., Berkeley, 1980-81; mem. race com. Internat. Am.'s Cup Class World Championship; mem. San Diego Crew Classic Race Com., 1992-98; mem. Am.'s Cup Race Com., 1992, 95. Recipient Meritorious award Petroleum Engr. mag., 1988, award for outstanding contbns. Valve Mfrs. Assn. Am., 1993. Mem. ASTM, Am. Soc. Metals Internat. (bd. dirs. 1988-90, Earl Parker fellow 1981), Soc. Petroleum Engrs., Am. Petroleum Inst., South Shore Yacht Club (CFO 1989-91, bd. dirs. 1991-93). Avocation: yacht racing. Office: Skytron Corp 16 Technology Dr Ste 169 Irvine CA 92618-2328

SALGADO, BRENDA, news director; b. Pa'auilo, Hawaii, June 20, 1964; d. Angel Briones and Catherine (Madrona) S.; m. Darren Lee Demello, June 26, 1993; 1 child, Khyra Symone Kalalea. BA in Journalism, U. Hawaii, 1988, cert. in ethnic studies, 1988. Weekend assignment editor TV Sta. KGMB, Honolulu, 1986-87, assignment editor, 1987-96, exec. prodr., 1996-97, interim news dir., 1997, asst. news dir., 1997—. Recipient News Broadcaster of Yr. award Lee Enterprises, 1995. Mem. Nat. Acad. TV, Arts and Scis., Team Hawaii Olympic Weightlifting (sec.). Avocations: Olympic weightlifting, basketball. Home: 1430 Puanakau St Honolulu HI 96818-1933 Office: TV Sta KGMB 1534 Kapiolani Blvd Honolulu HI 96814-3715

SALIBELLO, COSMO, optometrist, medical products executive, industrial ergonomist; b. N.Y.C., Sept. 21, 1943; s. Joseph and Maria (Patalano) S.; m. Jane Susan Wilde Crawford, July 1, 1984. B Mgmt. Engring., Rensselaer Poly. Inst., 1965; BA in Biology summa cum laude, Ctrl. Wash. U., 1979; B Visual Sci., Pacific U., Forest Grove, Oreg., 1981, OD, 1983. Lic. optometrist, Oreg., Wash.; cert. indsl. ergonomist. Mgmt. devel. assoc. Bendix Corp., Elmira, N.Y., 1965-66; dep. aircrew tng. mgr. Grumman Aerospace, Tehran, Iran, 1974-76; pvt. practice Salem, Oreg., 1983-91; pres., chmn. Applied Vision Concepts, Inc., Portland, Oreg., 1991-93; v.p. tech. PRIO Corp., Lake Oswego, Oreg., 1993-97, also bd. dirs.; pres. CSE Assocs., Portland, 1997—; cons. on VDT workplace, Salem, 1983-91; mem. bd. optometry advisors Pacific U., 1986-93; founder PRIO Corp. Contbr. articles to profl. jours.; inventor VDT prescription sys.; nat. spkr. on issues of computer eye strain. Lt. comdr. USN, 1966-74, Vietnam. Fellow Am. Acad. Optometry; mem. Am. Optometric Assn., Human Factors and Ergonomics Soc., Oreg. Optometric Assn., Portland Met. Optometric Soc. Avocations: music, model airplanes, bicycle touring. Office: 9898 SW Lynwood Terr. Portland OR 97225-4341

SALISBURY, DAVID FRANCIS, science and technology writer; b. Seattle, Feb. 24, 1947; s. Vernon H. and Lurabelle (Kline) S. BS, U. Wash., 1969. Sci. editor Christian Sci. Monitor, Boston, 1972-76; correspondent Christian Sci. Monitor, Los Angeles, Boulder (Colo.) and San Francisco, 1976-85; sci. and tech. writer U. Calif., Santa Barbara, 1985-93, Stanford (Calif.) U., 1993—; mem. research adv. com. Pub. Service Electric and Gas Co., Newark, N.J., 1979-83. Author: Money Matters, 1982. contbr. many articles to popular mags. and tech. jours. Recipient sci. writing awards, NSPE, 1978, Aviation Space Writers Assn., 1981, Grand Gold medal and Bronze medal Coun. for Advancement and Support of Edn., 1988. Mem. AAAS (sci. writing award 1976), Nat. Assn. Sci. Writers (Sci-in-Soc. award 1974). Christian Scientist. Avocations: tennis, sailing. Office: Stanford U News Svc Press Courtyard Santa Teresa St Stanford CA 94305

SALISBURY, ROBERT LOUIS, lawyer, community activist; b. Livonia, Mich., Sept. 2, 1966; s. William Albert and Janice Anne (Haddad) S. BA, Mich. State U., 1989; JD, Northwestern Sch. Law, 1993. Staff atty. Met. Pub. Defender, Portland, Oreg., 1992-97; assoc. Rieke & Savage, PC, Portland, 1997—. Bd. dirs. Resolutions N.W., Portland, 1995—, chmn. bd. dirs., 1997—. Mem. Nat. Assn. Criminal Def. Lawyers, Oreg. Assn. Criminal Def. Lawyers.

SALL, JENI P., marketing executive; b. Wilmington, Del., Jan. 28, 1949; d. Bernard and Esther (Wien) Sall; m. Fritz Bettjer, Sept. 21, 1985. BA, Hofstra U., 1971; MA, U. Hawaii, 1974. Brand supr. Procter & Gamble, Cin., 1974-76; brand asst. Clorox Co., Oakland, Calif., 1976-77; acct. exec. M/A/R/C, Burlingame, Calif., 1978-81; mgr. mktg. rsch. and planning Apple Computers, Cupertino, Calif., 1982-84; gen. mgr. Western ops. Decision Rsch. Corp., Palo Alto, Calif., 1984-86; pres. Genesis Rsch. Assocs., Palo Alto, 1986—. Bd. dirs. Santa Clara Valley Vis. Nurses Assn. Mem. Am. Mktg. Assn. (v.p. Santa Clara Valley chpt. 1985, exec.), Am. Psychol. Assn. Avocations: horseback riding, scuba diving, theater. Home: 2005 Rocky Ridge Rd Morgan Hill CA 95037-9443*

SALLEY, GEORGE HENRY, III, lawyer; b. Miami, Fla., Oct. 9, 1954; s. George H. Salley and Audrey L. Stone; m. Jean Welch Salley, Dec. 28, 1979; children: Paul Ryan, Adam Keith. BS, Brigham Young U., 1977; JD, Pepperdine U., 1980. Bar: Colo. 1981, U.S. Dist. Ct. Colo. 1981. Pvt. practice Colorado Springs, Colo., 1981—. Office: 104 S Cascade Ave Ste 207 Colorado Springs CO 80903-5102

SALMON, MATT, congressman; b. Salt Lake City, Jan. 21, 1958; s. Robert James and Gloria (Aagard) S.; m. Nancy Huish, June, 1979; children: Lara, Jacob, Katie, Matthew. BA in English Lit., Ariz. State U., 1981; MA in Pub. Adminstrn., Brigham Young U., 1986. Mgr. pub. affairs U.S. West, Phoenix, 1988-94; mem. Ariz. Senate, Mesa, 1990-94; congressman, Ariz. U.S. House of Reps. 106th Congress 1st Dist., Washington, D.C., 1995—; mem. internat. rels. and sci. coms. U.S. House of Reps., Washington, D.C. Bd. dirs. Mesa United Way, 1990—, Ariz. Sci. Mus., 1992—. Recipient Outstanding Svc. award Ariz. Citizens with Disabilities, 1991, Excellence in Govt. award Tempe Ctr. for Handicapped, 1992; named Outstanding Young Phoenician, Phelps Dodge/Phoenix Jaycees, 1990, Outstanding Legislator, Mesa United Way, 1991. Republican. Mormon. Avocations: tennis, racquetball, cycling. Office: Ho of Reps 115 Cannon Washington DC 20515-0301*

SALMON, MERLYN LEIGH, laboratory executive; b. Macksville, Kans., June 24, 1924; s. Kenneth Elbert and Inez Melba (Prose) S.; student U. Kans., 1943-44; BS, U. Denver, 1951, MS, 1952; m. Flora Charlotte Sievers, Mar. 20, 1948; children: Charla Lee, Merlyn Leigh. Rsch. engr. Denver Rsch. Inst., U. Denver, 1951-56; owner-operator Fluo-X-Spec Lab., Denver, 1956-92; ret. 1992; cons. in field. With AUS, 1943-45, 45-47. Mem. Am. Chem. Soc., Am. Soc. Metals, Sigma Xi, Tau Beta Pi, Phi Lambda Upsilon. Omicron Delta Kappa. Democrat. Contbr. articles to profl. jours. Address: 718 Sherman St Denver CO 80203-3511

SALMON, SYDNEY ELIAS, medical educator, director; b. S.I., N.Y., May 8, 1936; m. Joan; children: Howard, Julia, Laura, Stewart, Russell. BA cum laude, U. Ariz., 1958; MD, Washington U., St. Louis, 1962. Intern, then resident in medicine Strong Meml. Hosp., Rochester, N.Y., 1962-64; rsch. fellow in immunology dept. pediats. Harvard U. Med. Sch., Boston, 1965-66; rsch. fellow dept. medicine Medicine and Cancer Rsch. Inst. U. Calif., San Francisco, 1966-68, asst. prof. medicine dept. medicine, 1968-72; assoc. prof. medicine U. Ariz., Tucson, 1972-74, head sect. hematology and oncology, 1972-81, prof. medicine, 1974-89, founding dir. Ariz. Cancer Ctr., 1976—, regents prof. medicine, 1989—; NIH spl. fellow Cancer Rsch. Inst., U. Calif., San Francisco, 1966-68, rsch. assoc., 1968-72; mem. nat. cancer adv. bd. Nat. Cancer Inst., 1990—; founding sci. Selectide Corp., 1990; mem. sci. adv. bds. Amplimed Corp., SUGEN Corp.; bd. dirs. Synergen Devel. Corp., Repligen Devel. Corp. Editor: Cloning of Human Tumor Cells, Human Tumor Cloning, Adjuvant Therapies of Cancer, 1982, Clinics of Haematology, 1982; mem. adv. bd. Cancer Treatment Reports, 1979-82; mem. editl. bd. Stell Cells, Jour. Clin. Oncology; patentee in field; contbr. articles to profl. jours. Surgeon USPHS, 1964-66. Recipient Lectureship award Gold Headed Cane Soc., 1979, Alumni Achievement award U. Ariz., 1986. Mem. AAAS, Am. Soc. Hematology, Am. Soc. Clin. Investigation, Am. Soc. Clin. Oncology (pres. 1984-85), Am. Cancer Soc. (bd. dirs. Ariz. divsn.), Leukemia Soc. Am., Am. Assn. Cancer Rsch., Assn. Am. Cancer Insts. (pres. 1988-89). Office: U Ariz Cancer Ctr 1515 N Campbell Ave Tucson AZ 85724-0001

SALONEN, ESA-PEKKA, conductor; b. Helsinki, Finland, June 30, 1958. Student, Sibelius Acad., Helsinki; studies with, Rautavaara and Panula. Guest condr. orchs., London, Berlin, Paris, L.A., Phila.; prin. condr. Swedish Radio Symphony Orch., 1985-95; prin guest condr. Philharmonia Orch., London, 1985-94, Oslo Philharm. Orch., 1985-90; artistic advisor Stockholm Chamber Orch., 1986—; music dir. L.A. Philharm. Orch., 1992—. Office: Columbia Artists Mgmt Inc 165 W 57th St New York NY 10019 also: Los Angeles Philharm Orch 135 N Grand Ave Los Angeles CA 90012-3013*

SALSIG, DOYEN, photographer, photography studio owner; b. San Diego, Jan. 17, 1923; d. Felix and Fay (Doyen) Johnson; m. Budd Salsig, June 11, 1943; children: Winter, Kristin, Fay, Ben. AA, San Diego City Coll., 1965; BA in Biology, U. Calif., San Diego, 1970. Owner West Wind Studio, Flagstaff, Ariz., 1972-97; photo workshop leader Mus. of No. Ariz., Flagstaff, 1978-93. Author: Parole: Quebec; Counter-sign: Ticonderoga, 1980 (grand prize Coconino County Women of the Arts 1985); contbr., photos and photographic essays to profl. jours. Bd. dirs., v.p. Grand Canyon (Ariz.) Natural History Assn., 1988-96; vice-chmn. Coconino County Rep. Com., Flagstaff, 1988-97; pres. Rep. Women's Club, Flagstaff, 1989-91; docent Mus. No. Ariz., Flagstaff, 1975-82; mem. Ariz. Humanities Coun., 1991-94; del. Rep. Nat. Conv., 1992, 96. Avocations: hiking, aerobics, swimming, camping, photography. Home and Office: 457 D Ave Coronado CA 92118-1759

SALTER, TRACY LEE, entrepreneur; b. Pasadena, Calif., Dec. 21, 1958; d. Patrick Morris and Jo Ann (Pinkham) S. Grad. H.S., Dana Point, Calif. Lab. technician Am. Edwards, Irvine, Calif., 1978-81; quality assurance supr. Mag-Media, Santa Rosa, Calif., 1982-84; field rep. Underwriters Labs., San Francisco, 1984-89; quality assurance mgr. Cellotape, Fremont, Calif., 1989-90; CEO Lighting Labels, Inc., Guerneville, Calif., 1992—; cons. Salter Consultants, Forestville, Calif., 1992—. Coach Spl. Olympics, Alameda, Pleasanton, Calif., 1992-96. Mem. NOW, ACLU, Lions. Avocations: vol. work, philosophy, mentoring, body building. Office: Lighting Labels Inc 12060B Highway 116 Guerneville CA 95446-9411

SALTZ, HOWARD JOEL, newspaper editor; b. Bronx, N.Y., Apr. 11, 1960; s. Fred Raymond and Sheila Lois (Goldberg) S. BA in Liberal Arts, SUNY, Stony Brook, 1983. Reporter Greenwich Time, So. Conn. Newspapers divsn. Times Mirror, 1983-85; with MediaNews Group, 1985—; with N.J. Advance, Dover, 1985-87, editor, 1987-88; editor Hamilton (Ohio) Jour.-News, 1988-89, Fremont (Calif.) Argus, 1989-91; editor Johnstown (Pa.) Tribune-Democrat MediaNews Group, 1991-96; dep. bus. editor Denver Post, 1996-98, dep. mng. editor features, 1998—; adv. com. dept. journalism Ohlone Coll., Fremont, Calif., 1990-91. Bd. dirs. YMCA, Fremont-Newark, Calif., 1990-91, Johnstown Area Heritage Assn., 1991-93. Mem. Greater Johnstown C. of C. (bd. dirs. 1991-96), Soc. Profl. Journalists (bd. dirs. Northern Calif. chpt. 1990-91). Avocations: skiing, travel. Address: 535 Garfield St Denver CO 80206-4513 Office: Denver Post 1560 Broadway Denver CO 80202-5177

SALUJA, SUNDAR S., international engineering consultant; b. Wasu, Punjab, India, June 23, 1927; came to U.S., 1981; s. Wadhaya Mal and Gur Devi (Bagga) S.; m. Kamla S. Grover Saluja, Oct. 12, 1953; children: Bhupinder, Urvashi, Dipender. AISM, Indian Sch. of Mines, Dhanbad, India, 1950; postgrad. diploma, U. Sheffield, United Kingdom, 1955; MS, U. Ill., 1961; PhD, U. Wis., 1963. Cert. mine surveyor and mine mgr., India. Mine engr., surveyor Mining Industry, 1950-53, mine mgr., 1953-57; prof. of coal mining Banaras Hindu U., Varanasi, India, 1957-66, head dept of mining engring., 1966-71, prin. coll. mining & met., 1966-68, dean faculty of engring. & tech., 1968-71, dir. inst. tech., 1971-81; prof. mining engring. U. N.D., Grand Forks, 1982-96, prof. emeritus, 1997—; mem. Univ. Grants, Commn. India, 1976-79; pres. assn. engring., sci. sect. Indian Sci. Congress, 1980. Co-author: Handbook on Mechanical Properties of Rocks, vol. 1, 1974, translated in Japanese, 1989. Mem. state adv. com. U.S. Commn. on Civil Rights, 1993-95; founder, pres. Gt. Plains Forum, Grand Forks, N.D., [illegible] N.D. State Pub. Svc. Commn., 1983-84; founder, pres. Global Arouse Alliance for the Reclamation of our Spiritual Environment, 1998—; vol. Kaiser Permanente Health Edn. Dept., No. Claif., 1998. Grad. fellowship, Colombo Plan, 1954-55, fellowship in Engring., Nuffield Found., 1959, Commonwealth U. Tchrs. Exch., Australia, 1960, TCM fellowship, U.S Ag. for

Int. Devel., 1961; recipient Dr. Rajendra Pasad Meml. Gold medal Inst. of Engrs., Calcutta, India, 1978. Mem. Mining, Geol. & Met. Inst. of India (coun. mem. 1966-69), Am. Soc. Engring. Edn., Am. Soc. Mining Met. & Exploration, Indian Sci. Congress Assn. (pres. en gring. 1979-80), Global Alliance for the Reclamation of Our Spiritual Environ. (founder, pres.). Achievements include pioneer rsch. on roof bolting (1954-66), blasting mechanics (1961-71), mining of thick coal seams (1964-71), airlift pumping (1976-78), Nat. Reconstruction Corps. (1972), architect of engr. clinic c prototype dev. centres (1963-78), Indian Energy Policy (1979-81), World Energy Policy (1982—), leadership role in saving the $ 3.8 billion coal gasification plant in N.D. (1984-86), rsch. in environ. of human mind to improve the quality of life and its impact on soc. (1992—). Avocations: photography, travelling and study of different cultures. Home: 885 Russet Dr Sunnyvale CA 94087-1861 Office: 467 Costa Mesa Ter Apt F Sunnyvale CA 94086-4173 also: E-343-C Greater Kailash-I, New Delhi 110048, India

SALUSSO, CAROL JOY, apparel design educator, consultant; b. Butte, Mont., Dec. 25, 1950; d. George B. and Ruth M. (Richards) S.; (div.); children: Ryan R. and Daron A. Deonier. BS, Mont. State U., 1975; MS, U. Minn., St. Paul, 1977, PhD, 1983. Grad. asst. U. Minn., St. Paul, 1975-81; asst. prof. Iowa State U., Ames, 1981-86; assoc. prof. Mont. State U., Bozeman, 1986-94, Wash. State U., Pullman, 1994—; cons. product devel., Bozeman, Mont., 1986-94. Author: (handbook) Users Guide to Fabrics, 1993. Challenge grantee USDA, Faculty grantee Sunbury Textiles. Mem. Internat. Textiles and Apparel Assn., (chair spl. events 1986-88, chair electronic comm. 1993-95, book rev. editor 1995—, co-author World Wide Web ITAA server 1995—). Avocation: apparel product devel. Home: 345 W Main St Pullman WA 99163-2829 Office: Wash State U Dept Apparel Merch Int Design White Hall 209 Pullman WA 99164-2020

SALVADOR, WENDELL CARPIO, interior designer, design educator; b. Taipei, Taiwan, Jan. 23, 1963; came to U.S., 1971; s. Benjamin Sapungan and Alfea (Carpio) S.; m. Melinda Batin, Nov. 21, 1993. BA in environ. design, Otis, Parsons Sch. Design, 1985. Cert. interior designer, Calif. Jr. designer Walker & Assocs., L.A., 1982-85; designer Intern Design, L.A., 1986-92; sr. designer Jezek & Assocs., L.A., 1990-93; project mgr., sr. designer Skidmore, Owings, & Merrill, L.A., 1994-95, Hellmuth, Obata, & Kassabaum, Santa Monica, Calif., 1996; owner, pres. Location 3, Pasadena, Calif., 1997—. Avocations: biking, skiing, golfing, skydiving, music. Office: Brooks College Dept Interior Design 4825 E Pacific Coast Long Beach CA 90804-3291

SALVATIERRA, OSCAR, JR., physician; b. Phoenix, Apr. 15, 1935; s. Oscar and Josefine S.; m. Pamela Moss; children: Mark, Lisa Marie. B.S., Georgetown U., 1957; M.D., U. So. Calif., 1961. Intern, resident in surgery and urology U. So. Calif.-Los Angeles County Med. Center, 1961-66; practice medicine Pomona, Calif., 1968-72; chief staff Casa Colina Hosp., 1972; post doctoral fellow in transplantation U. Calif.-San Francisco, 1972-73, asst. prof. surgery and urology, 1973-75, assoc. prof., 1975-81, prof., 1981-91, chmn. transplant service, 1974-91; attending surgeon and urologist Moffitt Hosp., 1973—; exec. dir. Pacific Transplant Inst., 1991-94; prof. surgery/pediatrics, dir. pediat. renal transplantation Stanford U. Med. Ctr., 1994—, attending surgeon, urologist and pediat.; mem. study sect. NIH, 1981-85, nat. adv. bd., 1986-92, chmn. nat. adv. bd. 1990-92. Contbr. over 230 articles and chpts. to med. lit.; mem. editorial bd. Transplantation and Immunology, 1984—, Transplantation, 1987—, Transplantation Procs., 1990—, Pediat. Transplantation, 1998—; assoc. editor Am. Jour. Kidney Diseases, 1987-89. Mem. nat. bd. advisors Agent Orange Class Assistance Program, 1988-96. Served with M.C., U.S. Army, Vietnam, 1966-68. Decorated Army Commendation medal; recipient Chancellor's award for pub. service U. Calif., 1986, Commendation resolution Calif. State Legislature, 1990, NIH grantee, 1974-76, 80-83, 88-90; USPHS grantee, 1986-89. Fellow ACS (bd. govs. 1986-92); mem. Am. Surg. Assn., Am. Soc. Transplant Surgeons (bd. dirs. 1977-85, pres. 1983-84, chmn. adv. com. on issues 1984-87), Soc. Univ. Surgeons, Soc. Univ. Urologists, N.Y. Acad. Scis., Am. Soc. Nephrology, Internat. Transplantation Soc. (bd. dirs. 1984—, pres.-elect 1996-98, pres. 1998—), Soc. Pediatric Urology, Am. Urol. Assn., Nat. Kidney Found., Renal Physicians Assn. (bd. dirs. 1984-87), Pacific Coast Surg. Assn., San Francisco Surg. Soc., United Network Organ Sharing (bd. dirs. 1984-88, pres. 1985-86), Internat. Soc. for Organ Sharing (bd. dirs. 1991—, pres. 1993-95), Am. Soc. for Minority Health and Transplant Profls. (pres. 1992-94), Nafziger Surg. Soc. Prin. lay figure in passage and enactment of Nat. Organ Transplant Act, 1984. Office: Stanford U Med Ctr 703 Welch Rd Ste H2 Palo Alto CA 94304-1708

SALVIN, LINDA CAROL, radio metaphysician; b. L.A., Jan. 12, 1954; d. Martin J. and Marylin H. (Zelinsky) S. Student, L.A. Valley Coll., Van Nuys, 1973; BA, San Francisco State U., 1975; MPH, U. Mich., 1977. Health educator, epidemiologist various orgns., L.A., 1977-90; pvt. practice metaphysician L.A., 1991—; host radio show Sta. KIEV, L.A., 1995; host radio show, prodr. Cable Radio Network, L.A., 1995—; cons. Kayla Prodns., L.A., 1995—; pvt. practice psychic, channeler, healer, L.A. Co-author lit. script White Butterfly, 1995. Scholar U. Mich., 1975-77. Democrat. Jewish. Avocations: singing, songwriting, exercise, comedy. Home: 2017 N Beverly Glen Bel Air CA 90077

SALZMAN, DAVID ELLIOT, entertainment industry executive; b. Bklyn., Dec. 1, 1943; s. Benjamin and Rose Harriet (Touby) S.; m. Sonia Camelia Gonsalves, Oct. 19, 1968; children: Daniel Mark, Andrea Jessica, Adam Gabriel. B.A., Bklyn. Coll., 1965; M.A., Wayne State U., 1967. Dir. TV ops. Wayne State U., 1966-67; producer Lou Gordon Program, 1967-70; program mgr. Sta. WKBD-TV, Detroit, 1970-71; program mgr. Sta. KDKA-TV, Pitts., 1971-72, gen. mgr., 1973-75; program mgr. Sta. KYW-TV, Phila., 1972-73; chmn. bd. Group W Prodns., N.Y.C and Los Angeles, 1975—; founder, pres. United Software Assocs., 1980-81; creator News Info. Weekly Service, 1981; exec. v.p. Telepictures Corp., 1980-84, vice chmn., 1984; pres. Lorimar Telepictures Corp. (merger Telepictures and Lorimar, Inc.), 1985-90, Lorimar TV, 1986-90; creator Newscope: Nat. TV News Cooperative, 1983; pres., CEO David Salzman Entertainment, Burbank, Calif., 1990-93; co-CEO Quincy Jones-David Salzman Entertainment (QDE), 1993—; exec. prodr. Jenny Jones Show, 1991—; exec. prodr. Mad-TV, In the House, 68th Ann. Acad. awards, Concert of the Americas, 1995, Vibe-TV, 1997-98, Steel, 1997; CEO David Salzman Enterprises, 1998—; co-owner QD7 Interactive, 1994, Vibe Mag., 1995—, Spin Mag., 1995—, Sta. WNOL-TV, 1995—, Sta. WATL-TV, 1995—, Sta. KCWE-TV, 1995, Sta. WGRB-TV, 1998; bd. dirs. Premiere Radio, 1994, 7th Level, Nat. Media, 1998; guest lectr. at schs.; bd. govs. Films of Coll. and Univ. Students. Contbr. articles to Variety and numerous communications trade publs. Bd. dirs. Pitts. Civic Light Opera, Am. Blood Bank, Pitts., Hebrew Inst., Jewish Community Ctr., Harrison, N.Y., Temple Etz Chaim, USC Sch. Cinema-TV, Emory U. Ctr. for Leadership, Emory Bus. Sch., Bklyn. Coll. Found. Recipient award Detroit chpt. Am. Women in Radio and TV, 1969, award Golden Quill, 1971, award Golden Gavel, 1971, local Emmy award, 1972, award AP, 1974, Gold medal Broadcast Promotion Assn., 1983, Lifetime Achievement award Bklyn. Coll., 1990, Disting. Alumnus award, Golden Plate award Am. Acad. Achievement, 1995; BPME Gold medal San Francisco Film Festival, 1984, N.Y., 1985, Chgo., 1986, Tree of Life award Jewish Nat. Fund, 1988. Mem. Acad. TV Arts and Scis., Nat. Assn. TV Program Execs., Radio-TV News Dirs. Assn., Am. Mgmt. Assn., Am. Film Inst., Brooklyn Coll. Found. Office: Mad TV Hollywood Ctr Studios 5842 W Sunset Blvd Bldg 11 Hollywood CA 90028-6607

SALZMAN, MARILYN B. WOLFSON, service company executive; b. Chgo., Dec. 25, 1943; d. Joseph and Sera (Krol) Wolfson; 1 son, Lawrence Todd. Student, U. Ill., Barat Coll., Lake Forest, Ill., U. Calif., Irvine. Cert. fundraising exec. Adminstrv. project asst. Sci. Research Assocs., Chgo., 1964-70; reporter Suburban Trib of Chgo. Tribune, 1979-80; pres. MWS Assocs., Los Angeles and Fullerton, Calif., 1980—; exec. adminstrv. dir. Crystal Tips of No. Ill., Inc., 1980-83; dir. adminstrn. Ice Dispensers, Inc., 1981-83, Sani-Serv of Ill., Inc., 1981-83; adminstrv. and organizational cons. 1140 Corp., 1980-83; adminstrv. dir. Iceman's Ico Co., Inc., 1980-83; founder, moderator DWC Workshops, 1984; dir. data processing Florence Crittenton Svs., Orange County, 1984-86, dir. MIS, 1986-88, dir. support svcs., 1988-92, bd. dirs. devel. & cmty. svcs., ways and means com., 1991—, fin. com., found. com., bd. devel. com., ann. meeting com., 1995—, dir. adminstrn. & contract compliance, 1992-94, dir. devel. & cmty. svcs., 1994—; pres. MWS Prodns., L.A. and Fullerton, Calif., 1990—; exec. producer (TV series) The State of the Child, 1990-91; panelist computers in residential treatment Child Welfare League Am. Biennial Conf. Workshop, 1986; presenter outcomes and svc. evaluation North Am. Out-of-Home Care Conf., 1991, families & children in residential treatment Calif. State U. Child Devel. Conf., Fullerton, 1994, advancing your message Child Welfare League of Am. Nat. Conf., 1995; comm. & Pub. Rels. for Profl., Child Welfare League Am. Nat. Conf., 1996, 97. Active Friends of Fullerton Library; panelist Child Welfare League Am., Bienniel Conf. Workshop; chmn. govtl., pub. affairs coms. Orange County Assn. of Children's Svcs.; mem. steering com. Orange County UN Assn. Yr. of Family, 1993-95; mem. com. Internat. Yr. of the Family Exhibit & Celebration, Bowers Mus., 1994; mem. planning com. Orange County Summit for Children, 1994-97, chair outreach com., 1996—; mem. exec. com. Anne Frank Orange County Organizing Com., 1994-97; mem. adv. com. Child Devel. & Family Life Dept., Fullerton Coll., 1994; mem. bd. mgrs. N. Orange County Family YMCA, 1995—, chmn. child care adv. com., 1995-96, mem. sr. care adv. com., exec. dir. selection com., 1996, mem. program com., 1996-98, co-chair fund devel. com., 1998—; facilitator Orange County Together, 1994-97. Mem. Calif. Assn. Svcs. for Children (rsch. and evaluation com. 1993-97, pub. rels. com. 1996-98), Soroptimist Internat. of Fullerton (TAP chmn. 1995-97, v.p. 1996, pres. elect, 1997 program chmn. 1998—, pres. 1998-99, del. internat. biennial conv. 1998), Mgmt. Forum, Fullerton C. of C. (indsl. com. 1994-96, local govt. com. 1995—), Nat. Soc. Fund Raising Execs. (Orange County chpt. 1996—), Planned Giving Coun. Contbr. articles to newspapers and indsl. jours.

SALZMAN, PAUL, social worker; b. Sioux City, Iowa, Mar. 5, 1920; s. William and Brocha (Levine) S.; m. Anne Meyersburg, Sept. 11, 1952; children: Harold, Richard. BA, UCLA, 1955, M in Social Work, 1968. Licensed clin. social worker, Calif. Clinical social worker St. John's Hosp., Santa Monica, Calif., 1968-81; pvt. practice Santa Monica, Calif., 1971—; field instr. UCLA, 1971-81. Mem. Nat. Assn. Social Workers, Am. Bd. Examiners Clinical Social Work, Acad. Certified Social Workers, Calif. Soc. Clinical Social Work, Employee Assistance Profls. Assn. (L.A. chpt., exec. bd. 1990—, co-chair edn./training com. 1990—). Democrat. Avocations: gardening, skiing, backpacking, reading. Office: 1150 Yale St Ste 1 Santa Monica CA 90403-4722

SAM, DAVID, federal judge; b. Hobart, Ind., Aug. 12, 1933; s. Andrew and Flora (Toma) S.; m. Betty Jean Brennan, Feb. 1, 1957; children: Betty Jean, David Dwight, Daniel Scott, Tamara Lynn, Pamela Rae, Daryl Paul, Angie, Sheyla. BS, Brigham Young U., 1957; JD, Utah U., 1960. Bar: Utah 1960, U.S. Dist. Ct. Utah 1966. Sole practice and ptnr. Duchesne, Utah, 1963-76; dist. judge State of Utah, 1976-85; judge U.S. Dist. Ct. Utah, Salt Lake City, 1985-97; chief judge U.S. Dist. Ct., Salt Lake City, Utah, 1997; atty. City of Duchesne, 1963-72; Duchesne County atty., 1966-72; commr. Duchesne, 1972-74; mem. adv. com. Codes of Conduct of Jud. Conf. U.S., 1987-91, Jud. Coun. of 10th Cir., 1991-93; mem. U.S. Del. to Romania, Aug. 1991. Chmn. Jud. Nomination Com. for Cir. Ct. Judge, Provo, Utah, 1983; bd. dirs. Water Resources, Salt Lake City, 1973-76. Served to capt. JAGC, USAF, 1961-63. Mem. Utah Bar Assn., Am. Judicature Soc., Supreme Ct. Hist. Soc., Am. Inns of Ct. VII (counselor 1986-89), A. Sherman Christensen Am. Inn of Ct. I (counselor 1989-98), Utah Jud. Conf. (chmn. 1982), Utah Dist. Judges Assn. (pres. 1982-83), Order of Coif (hon. Brigham Young U. chpt.). Mem. LDS Ch. Avocations: beekeeping, reading, sports, cooking chinese food. Office: US Dist Ct 148 US Courthouse 350 S Main St Ste 150 Salt Lake City UT 84101-2180

SAMANIEGO, PAMELA SUSAN, organization administrator; b. San Mateo, Calif., Nov. 29, 1952; d. Armando C. and Harriott Susan (Croot) S. Student, UCLA, 1972, Los Angeles Valley Coll., 1970-72. Asst. new accts. supr. Beverly Hills Fed. Savings, 1970-72; asst. controller Bio-Science Enterprises, Van Nuys, Calif., 1972-74; adminstr. asst. Avery/Tirce Prodns., Hollywood, Calif., 1974-78; sr. estimator N. Lee Lacy and Assocs., Hollywood, 1978-81; head of prodn. Film Consortium, Hollywood, 1981-82; exec. producer EUE/Screen Gems Ltd., Burbank, Calif., 1982-88; advt. agency dir. Barrett & Assocs., Las Vegas, Nev., 1988-90; exec. producer Laguna/Take One, Las Vegas, 1990-93; dir. Sta. KXLY-4 ABC, Spokane, Wash., 1993-94; dir. advt. and mktg. Appaloosa Horse Club, Moscow, Idaho, 1994—. Author: Millimeter & Backstage, 1982-88. Emergency room vol. San Mateo (Calif.) County Hosp., 1968-70; Sunday sch. tchr. Hillsdale Meth. Ch., San Mateo, 1968-70; vol. worker Hillsdale Meth. Ch. Outreach, San Francisco, 1967-70. Recipient CLIO award CLIO Awards, Inc., 1985, ADDY award Las Vegas Advt. Fedn., 1988. Mem. Dirs. Guild Am. (2nd asst. dir. 1987-88), Assn. Ind. Comml. Producers, Am. Horse Show Assn., Internat. Arabian Horse Assn., AHASFV (sec. 1978-79), AHASC (sec. 1978-88). Democrat. Methodist. Avocations: breed and show Arabian horses. Home: 323 E 1st St Moscow ID 83843-2810 Office: Appaloosa Horse Club 5070 Highway 8 W Moscow ID 83843-4000

SAMPLE, JOSEPH SCANLON, foundation executive; b. Chgo., Mar. 15, 1923; s. John Glen and Helen (Scanlon) S.; m. Patricia M. Law, Dec. 22, 1942 (div.); children: Michael Scanlon, David Forrest, Patrick Glen; m. Miriam Tyler Willing, Nov. 19, 1965. B.A., Yale U., 1947. Trainee, media analyst, media dir. Dancer-Fitzgerald-Sample, Inc., advt. agy., Chgo., 1947-50; v.p., media dir. Dancer-Fitzgerald-Sample, Inc., advt. agy., 1952-53; pres. Mont. Television Network KTVQ, Billings, KXLF-AM-TV, Butte, Mont., KRTV, Great Falls, Mont., KPAX-TV, Missoula, Mont., 1955-84; dir., prodr. Yellowstone Pub. Radio KEMC, Billings, 1993—. Pres. Greater Mont. Found., 1986—; chmn. Wheeler Ctr. Mont State U., 1988—. Served with AUS, 1943-46. With U.S. Army, 1950-52. Mem. Rotary, Yellowstone Country Club, Port Royal Club, Hole in The Wall Golf Club, Hilands Golf Club, Naples Yacht Club. Home: 606 Highland Park Dr Billings MT 59102-1909 Office: 14 N 24th St Billings MT 59101-2422

SAMPLE, STEVEN BROWNING, university executive; b. St. Louis, Nov. 29, 1940; s. Howard and Dorothy (Cunningham) S.; m. Kathryn Brunkow, Jan. 28, 1961; children: Michelle Sample Smith, Elizabeth Ann. BS, U. Ill., 1962, MS, 1963, PhD, 1965; DHULL (hon.), Canisius Coll., 1989; LLD (hon.), U. Sheffield, Eng., 1991; EdD (hon.), Purdue U., 1994; DHL (hon.), Hebrew Union Coll., 1994; DL (hon.), U. Nebr., 1995. Sr. scientist Melpar Inc., Falls Church, Va., 1965-66; assoc. prof. elec. engring. Purdue U., Lafayette, Ind., 1966-73; dep. dir. Ill. Bd. Higher Edn., Springfield, 1971-74; exec. v.p. acad. affairs, dean Grad. Coll., prof. elec. eng. U. Nebr., Lincoln, 1974-82; prof. elec. and computer engring. SUNY, Buffalo, 1982-91, pres., 1982-91; pres. U. So. Calif., L.A., 1991—, prof. elec. engring., 1991—; bd. dirs. Santa Catalina Island Co., UNOVA, William Wrigley Jr. Co., Presley Cos., Newport Beach, Calif.; vice chmn., bd. dirs. Western N.Y. Tech. Devel. Ctr., Buffalo, 1982-91; chmn. bd. dirs. Calspan-UB Rsch. Ctr., Inc., Buffalo, 1983-91; mem. Calif. Coun. Sci. and Tech., Irvine, Calif., L.A. Bus. Advisors, Nat. Acad. of Engring., 1998—; cons. in field. Contbr. articles to profl. jours.; patentee in field. Timpanist St. Louis Philharm. Orch., 1955-58; chmn. Western N.Y. Regional Econ. Devel. Coun., 1984-91; trustee U. at Buffalo Found., 1982-91, Studio Arena Theatre, Buffalo, 1983-91, Western N.Y. Pub. Broadcasting Assn., 1985-91; bd. dirs. Buffalo Philharm. Orch., 1982-91, Regenstrief Med. Found., Indpls., 1982—, Rsch. Found. SUNY, 1987-91; chmn. Gov.'s Conf. on Sci. and Engring. Edn., Rsch. and Devel., 1989-91; chair Calif. Bus.-Higher Edn. Forum; bd. dirs. L.A. chpt. World Affairs Coun., Hughes Galaxy Inst. Edn., L.A., 1991-94, Rebuild L.A. Com., L.A. Annenberg Metro Project, Coalition of 100 Club of L.A.; trustee L.A. Ednl. Alliance for Restructuring Now. Recipient Disting. Alumnus award Dept. Elec. Engring. U. Ill., 1980, citation award Buffalo Coun. on World Affairs, 1986, Engr. of Yr. award N.Y. State Soc. Profl. Engrs., 1985, Alumni Honor award Coll. Engring., U. Ill., 1985, Outstanding Elec. Engr. award Purdue U., 1993, Humanitarian award Nat. Conf. Christians and Jews, L.A., 1994, Hollzer Meml. award Jewish Fedn. Coun. Greater L.A., 1994; Sloan Found. fellow, 1962-63, NSF grad. fellow, 1963-65, Am. Coun. Edn. fellow Purdue U., 1970-71, NSF. Mem. AAU (chmn. com. on postdoctoral edn. 1994—), IEEE (Outstanding Paper award 1976), Nat. Assn. State Univs. and Land-Grant Colls. (ednl. telecommunications com., 1982-83, chmn. coun. of pres. 1985-86, edn. and tech. com. 1986-87, exec. com. 1987-89), Coun. on Fgn. Rels., Sigma Xi. Episcopalian. Home: 1550 Oak Grove Ave San Marino CA 91108-1108 Office: U So Calif Office of the Pres University Park ADM 110 Los Angeles CA 90089-0012

SAMPLINER, LINDA HODES, psychologist, consultant; b. Cleve., Sept. 25, 1945; d. Walter J. and Caroline Jean (Klein) Hodes; m. Richard Evan Sampliner, July 31, 1966; children: Robert David, Steven Jay. BS, Western Res. U., Cleve., 1967; EdM, Boston U., 1972, EdD, 1975. Lic. psychologist, Ariz; cert. grief therapist, cons. in clin. hypnosis. Counselor The Family Life Ctr., Columbia, Md., 1976-80; psychologist Psychology & Rehab. Assocs., Tucson, 1981-85; pvt. practice Tucson, 1985—; cons., psychologist div. econ. security Child and Family Svcs., Tucson, 1985—; psychologist Sonora Behavioral Health Assn., 1994—; cons. SHARE, Tucson, 1985, 98; trainer comm. skills for police Balt. County Dept. Mental Health, 1975-80, drub abuse adminstrn. trainer for counselors, 1975-80. Bd. dirs. Adapt Inc., Tucson, 1985-93, pres., 1990-91; bd. dirs. Mental Health Resources, 1993-95; bd. dirs. Tucson Symphony Soc., 1984-89, v.p., 1987-89; pres. bd. dirs. Tucson Mus. of Art League, 1985-86; mem. adv. bd. dept. art U. Ariz., 1993-99. Mem. APA, Assn. Death Edn. and Counseling, Ariz. Psychol. Assn., So. Ariz. Psychol. Assn. Avocations: hiking, entertaining, bicycling. Office: Sonora Behavioral Health Network 2001 W Orange Grove Rd Ste 410 Tucson AZ 85704-1141

SAMUELS, BARBARA ANN, university administrator, planner, educator, information architect; b. Montreal, Oct. 20, 1949; d. Louis and Frances Kalb; m. Keith Michael Samuels, Aug. 23, 1970; 1 child, Sumerlee Eden. BSc, U. Calgary, Alta., Can., 1969; MEd, U. Oreg., 1973, PhD, 1978. Cert. profl. tchr., Alta. Tchr., asst. prin. Calgary Bd. Edn., 1971-79, planning specialist, 1980-83; asst. v.p. svcs. U. Calgary, 1983-84, dir. planning, 1986—; exec. dir. Can. Ctr. for Learning Sys., Calgary, 1984-86; pres. B.A. Samuels & Assocs., Calgary, 1985—; treas. Knowledge @ Work Project, 1995—. Author: Understanding Culture, 1985, Multiculturalism in Canada: Images and Issues, 1996; author, rschr. rsch. studies; author mag. and CD-ROM articles. Trustee Calgary Zoo, 1990-96, Calgary Zoo Senate, 1999—, Vision of the Future Com., Jr. Achievement, Can., 1995, Akiva Acad. Sch. Bd., Calgary, 1986-87; dir. Banff-Cochrane Progressive Conservative Constituency Assn., 1989-91. F.J.C. Seymour fellow Alta. Tchrs'. Assn., 1977; recipient Women & Coop. Edn. grant Sec. of State, 1989, Centres of Excellence citation, 1984. Mem. Internat. Soc. for Planning and Strategic Mgmt., Can. Soc. for Study in Higher Edn., Pinebrook Golf and Country Club (pres. 1999), Kappa Delta Pi. Avocations: photography, tennis, golf. Office: U Calgary Office of VP, 103C Administration Bldg, Calgary, AB Canada T2N 1N4

SAMUELS, CYNTHIA KALISH, communications executive; b. Pitts., May 21, 1946; d. Emerson and Jeanne (Kalish) S.; m. Richard Norman Atkins, Sept. 12, 1971; children: Joshua Whitney Samuels Atkins, Daniel Jonathan Samuels Atkins. BA, Smith Coll., 1968. Press aide McCarthy for Pres. Campaign, Washington, 1968; assoc. prodr. Newsroom program Sta. KQED, San Francisco, 1972-73; with CBS News, 1973-80, rschr., Washington, 1969-71, documentary rschr., N.Y.C., 1973-74, asst. fgn. editor, 1973-76, asst. N.Y. bur. chief, 1976-80; writer, field prodr. Today program NBC News, N.Y.C., 1980-84, polit. prodr. Today program, 1984-89; polit. and planning prodr., 1988-89; sr. prodr. Main Street program NBC News, N.Y.C., 1987; founding exec. prodr. Channel One Program, 1989-92; exec. v.p. Whittle Comms., N.Y.C., 1989-94; internet cons., developer TV and multimedia prodn. exec., 1994—; pres., CEO Cobblestone Prodns.: Online and On TV, 1996—; cons. spl. projects iVillage.com The Women's Network, 1997—. Author: It's A Free Country!: A Young Person's Guide to Politics and Elections, 1988; editor Excite, 1995-96; contbg. editor Women's Wire, 1996-98; prodr. 3d Ann. Childrens Interactive Media Festival, 1996, Village, 1997—, Global Information Infrastructure awards, 1997-98, Education Central at Parent Soup Web site; contbr. book revs. to N.Y. Times Book Rev., Washington Post Book World; children's book editor Amazon.com, 1997-98; spl. projects cons. Village.com, 1997—; contbg. editor children's books, Barnesandnoble.com, 1998—; sr. nat. editor Washington Nat. Pub. Radio, 1999—. Recipient Emmy award No. Calif. Acad. TV Arts and Scis., 1974, Columbia DuPont citation, 1975, Media Access award Calif. Office of Handicapped, 1991, Silver award Nat. Mental Health Assn., 2 Bronze awards Nat. Assn. Edn. in Film and TV, 1993. Mem. Women in New Tech., Internat. Interactive Comms. Soc. E-mail: csamuels@earthlink.net. Office: 635 Massachusetts Ave Washington DC 20001

SAMUELS, JOSEPH, JR., police chief; b. 1949; m. Sabrina Samuels; 1 child, Joseph. BA in Psychology, Lincoln U.; MPA, Calif. State U., Hayward, 1988; student, Nat. Exec. Inst. Br. mgr. Household Fin. Corp.; with Oakland (Calif.) Police Dept., 1974-91, capt. patrol divsn., chief police, 1993—; police chief Fresno (Calif.) Police Dept., 1991-93; chair regional citizens adv. com. Calif. Youth Authority, 1986-91; former mem. Calif. State Commn. Crime, Juvenile Justice and Delinquency Prevention. Active YMCA, Oakland, East Oakland Youth Devel. Ctr., Oakland Citizens Com. Urban Renewal; mem. Fight Crime Invest in Kids, 1997. Mem. Nat. Orgn. Black Law Enforcement Execs., Calif. Peace Officers Assn., Calif. Police Chiefs Assn., Internat. Assn. Chiefs Police, Police Exec. Rsch. Forum. Office: Police Headquarters 455 7th St Oakland CA 94607-3940*

SAMUELSON, NORMA GRACIELA, architectural illustrator, artist; b. Mar del Plata, Argentina, May 29, 1957; came to U.S., 1979; d. Jose and Elsa Florinda (Camaras) Nunez; m. Jeffrey Thomas Samuelson, Oct. 9, 1982; 1 child, Taylor Sebastian. Student, Conservatory Mendelssohn, Mar del Plata, 1970-76; MFA, Superior Sch. Visual Arts, Mar del Plata, 1976. Tchr. art Domingo F. Sarmiento, Mar del Plata, 1976; graphic artist Atelier Marzoratti Munoz, Mar del Plata, 1976-79; archtl. illustrator Szabo Inc., Irvine, Calif., 1981-84; owner, archtl. illustrator Norma Samuelson Illustrations, Mission Viejo, Calif., 1985—; represented by Artreps Calif., Studio Gallery, Calif. Illustrator: Centennial of Immigration Law, 1975 (2d nat. award), Historical Buildings in Los Angeles, 1995 (ltd. edits.); art work published in Best of Colored Pencil III and Architecture in Perspective 13. Bd. dirs. Mus. Architecture, Capistrano, Calif. Mem. Color Pencil Soc. Am., Am. Soc. Archtl. Perspective. Avocations: playing piano, painting and drawing, foreign travel, French art and language. Home: 26862 Via Corta San Juan Capistrano CA 92675-5039 Office: 27001 La Paz Rd Ste 406B Mission Viejo CA 92691-5523

SANAZARO, LEONARD ROCCO, language educator, writer; b. Chgo., Oct. 29, 1949. BA, Lewis U., 1971; MA, U. Nev., 1979. Tchr. St. John the Bapt. Sch., Harvey, Ill., 1972-74; tchr. U. Nev., Reno, 1982-86, City Coll. San Francisco, 1986—. Author: (critical essays) Sylvia Plath: A Reconsideration, 1982; contbr. poetry to Antioch Rev., Seattle Rev., Denver Quar., Art and Understanding. Mem. Nat. Coun. Tchrs. English (com. mem. 1996-98), Acad. Am. Poets. Democrat. Roman Catholic. Office: City Coll San Francisco 50 Phelan Ave San Francisco CA 94112-1821

SANCHEZ, GILBERT, retired academic administrator, microbiologist, researcher; b. Belen, N.Mex., May 7, 1938; s. Macedonio C. and Josephine H. Sanchez; m. Lorena T. Tabet, Aug. 26, 1961; children—Elizabeth, Phillip, Katherine. B.S. in Biology, N.Mex. State U., 1961; Ph.D. in Microbiology, U. Kans., 1967. Research asst. U. Kans., Lawrence, 1963-67; research assoc., postdoctoral fellow Rice U., Houston, 1967-68; prof. N.Mex. Inst. Tech., Socorro, 1968-79; dean grad. studies Eastern N.Mex. U., Portales, 1979-83; v.p. acad. affairs U. So. Colo., Pueblo, 1983-85; pres. N.Mex. Highlands U., Las Vegas, 1985-95; cons. NIH, NSF, Solvex Corp., Albuquerque, 1979-83; bd. dirs. Fed. Res. Bank, Denver. Contbr. numerous articles to profl. jours. Patentee in field. Pres. Socorro Sch. Bd., 1974-79, Presbyn. Hosp. Bd., Socorro, 1977-79. Research grantee Dept. Army, 1976-79, N.Mex. Dept. Energy, 1979-83, NSF, 1979. Mem. Am. Soc. Microbiology, Am. Soc. Indsl. Microbiology, AAAS, Am. Assn. Univs. and Colls. (bd. dirs. 1988-90), Hispanic Assn. Univs. and Colls. (pres. 1986-89). Roman Catholic. Lodge: Rotary. Avocations: auto mechanics; welding; woodworking; golf.

SANCHEZ, HEATHER YVONNE, editor; b. Apple Valley, Calif., May 20, 1971; d. Wilfred Wayn and Crystal Daun (Hudson) S. AA in journalism, Orange Coast Coll., 1992; BA in journalism, Calif. State, 1994. Editor Apartment News Publ., Huntington Beach, Calif., 1995—; pub. rels., fundraising Pet Pro Life, Huntington Beach, Calif., 1997—; spokesperson Pet Pro Life, 1997—. Editor: Pet Profiles, 1998. Mem. Nat. Assn. Hispanic Jour. Avocations: running, dancing, dogs. Office: Apartment News Publ 15502 Graham St Huntington Beach CA 92649-1609

SANCHEZ, LEONEDES MONARRIZE WORTHINGTON (HIS ROYAL HIGHNESS DUKE DE LEONEDES OF SPAIN SICILY GREECE), fashion designer; b. Flagstaff, Ariz., Mar. 15, 1951; s. Rafael Leonedes and Margaret (Monarrize) S. BS, No. Ariz. U., 1974; studied, Fashion Inst. Tech., N.Y.C., 1974-75; AA, Fashion Inst. D&M, L.A., 1975; lic., La Ecole de la Chambre Syndical de la Couture Parisian, Paris, 1976-78. Lic. in designing. Contract designer/asst. to head designer House of Bonnet, Paris, 1976—; dress designer-in-residence Flagstaff, 1978—; mem. faculty No. Ariz. U., Flagstaff, 1978-80; designer Ambiance, Inc., L.A., 1985—; designer Interiors by Leonedes subs. Studio of Leonedes Couturier, Ariz., 1977, Calif., 1978, London, Paris, 1978, Rome, 1987, Milan, Spain, 1989, Palazzo de Leonedes, 1998; designer Liturgical Vesture subs. Studio of Leonedes Couturier; CEO Leonedes Internat., Design Consortium, Leonedes Internat. Ltd., 1999—; designer El Casillo de Nuevo Espana, Santa Fe, N.Mex.; owner, CEO, designer Leonedes Internat., Ltd., London, Milan, Paris, Spain, Ambian Ariz, Calif., Appolonian Costuming, Ariz., London, Milan, Paris, El Castillo de Leonedes, Sevilla, Spain, Villa Apollonian de Leonedes, Mykonos, Greece; cons. House of Bonnet, Paris, 1976—, Bob Mackie, Studio City, Calif., 1974-75; CEO, designer artistical dir., Leonedes internat.; appointee commn. on religious antiquities Congregation on the Arts, The Vatican, Italy, 1998. Bd. dirs. Roman Cath. Social Svcs., 1985-86, Northland Crisis Nursery, 1985—; bd. dirs., chmn. Pine Country Transit, 1986-88; pres. Chicanos for Edn.; active master's swim program ARC, Ariz., 1979—; eucharistic min., mem. art and environ. com., designer liturgical vesture St. Pius X Cath. Ch.; vol. art tchr., instr. St. Mary's Regional Sch., Flagstaff, 1987-90, vol. art dir.; mem. Flagstaff Parks and Recreation Commn., 1994-96, citizens' adv. com. master plan, 1994-96; mem. cmty. bd. adv. com. Flagstaff Unified Sch. Dist., 1995; active Duke de Leonedes Found. de Nuevo Espana, Santa Fe, Duke de Leonedes Found. de Neuvo Espana, Santa Fe; prin. chair Duke de Leonedes Found., The Netherlands, 1995; de neuvo espana Duke de Leuedes Found., Santa Fe, N.Mex., 1996. Decorated Duke de Leonedes (Spain), 1994, His Royal Highness (Spain, Greece, Sicily), 1998; recipient Camellian Design award 1988, Atlanta. Mem. AAU (life, chairperson swimming Ariz. 1995, vice chairperson physique, mem. citizen adv. bd. parks and recreation), Am. Film Inst., Am. Assn. Hist. Preservation, Costume Soc., Am. Nat. Physique Com., Internat. Consortium Fashion Designers, Nat. Cath. Ednl. Assn., La Legion de Honour de la Mode Parisienne, Social Register Assn., Phi Alpha Theta (historian 1972-73, pres. 1973-74), Pi Kappa Delta (pres. 1972-73, historian 1973-74). Republican. Avocations: body building, swimming. Office: El Castillo de Leonedes, Seville Spain also: El Castillo de Nuevo Espana Santa Fe NM 87501 also: Villa de Apollonian de Leonedes, Mykonos Greece

SANCHEZ, LORETTA, congresswoman; b. Anaheim, Calif., Jan. 7, 1960. BA, Chapman U., 1982; MBA, Am. U., 1984. With Orange County Transp. Authority, 1984-87, Fieldman Rolapp & Assocs., 1987-90; strategic mgmt. cons. Booz Allen & Hamilton, 1993—; owner, operator AMIGA Advisors Inc., 1993—; mem. 105th Congress from 46th Calif. dist., 1997—; mem. edn. and the workforce com., mem. armed svcs. com. 106th Congress from 46th Calif. dist. Mem. Anaheim Rotary Club. Democrat. Office: US Ho of Reps 1529 Longworth Washington DC 20515-0546*

SANCHEZ, MARLA RENA, controller; d. Tomas Guillermo and Rose Sanchez; m. Bradley D. Gaiser. BS, Stanford U., 1979, MS, 1979; MBA, Santa Clara U., 1983. Rsch. biologist Syntex, Palo Alto, Calif., 1980-81; fin. analyst Advanced Micro Devices, Sunnyvale, Calif., 1983-85; fin. mgr. ultrasound divsn. Diasonics, Inc., Milpitas, Calif., 1985-86, contr. therapeutic products divsn., 1989-93, contr. internat. divsn., 1992-93; contr. Ridge Computers, Santa Clara, Calif., 1986-88; dir. fin. VLSI Tech., Inc., San Jose, Calif., 1993-98; corp. contr. SDL, Inc., San Jose, 1999—. Avocations: dancing, backpacking, rock climbing. Home: 1234 Russell Ave Los Altos CA 94024-5541

SANCHEZ, RAYMOND G., state legislator; b. Albuquerque, Sept. 22, 1941; s. Gillie and Priscilla S.; 1 child, Raymond Michael. B.A., U. N. Mex., 1964, J.D., 1967. Bar: N. Mex. 1967. Practice law Albuquerque; mem. N.Mex. Ho. of Reps., 1970—; speaker N. Mex. Ho. of Reps., 1983-84, 87-88, 92—; mem. judiciary com., rules and order of bus. com., voters and elections com., interim mem. workers compensation, legis. reform study coms., legis. coun. Bd. dirs. New Mex. Amigos, N.Mex. Diamond Jubilee/U.S. Constl. Bicentennial Commn., New Mex. First, Albuquerque Com. Fgn. Rels., N. Valley Neighborhood Assn. Mem. Nat. Assn. Latino Elected and Apptd. Ofcls. (bd. dirs.), Alameda Optimist Club (bd. dirs., charter mem.), U. New Mex. Sch. Law Alumni Assn. (bd. dirs.), Elks Club, Sigma Xi. Democrat. Avocations: handball, scuba diving, swimming, spectator sports. Office: State Capitol Office of Speaker Santa Fe NM 87501 also: PO Box 1966 Albuquerque NM 87103-1966*

SANCHEZ, REGINA STAR, minister; b. Santa Fe, N.Mex., Mar. 7, 1951; d. Fred Paul Rodriguez and Malva Carroll (Cheusburg) Charley; m. Luis E. Tapia, Oct. 28, 1969 (div. Jan. 1980); children: Elena P. Garcia, Sergio L. Tapia; m. Joel de la Luz Sanchez, July 28, 1990. ThM, Joint Heirs Bible Coll., Albuquerque, 1991. Ordained min., Ch. of God, 1995. Mgr. Capital Copy, Santa Fe, N.Mex., 1980-89, Copy Shack, Santa Fe, 1989-90, Cheetah Copy, Albuquerque, 1990-97; co-pastor Heritage Family Fellowship, Albuquerque, 1992-94, Heritage Family Ch. of God, Albuquerque, 1994—; owner Old Town Copy, Albuquerque, 1997—; artist, N.Mex., 1975—; sec. ministerial alliance, sec. credentials com., mem. exec. bd. N.Mex. Ch. of God, Albuquerque, 1995—; sec., treas. La Cofradia de Artists, Santa Fe, 1977-80. Author: Taking it to the Streets, 1991; editor newsletter Roadrunner. Active Trumbull Com. Neighborhood Assn., Albuquerque, 1995—, Highland Mid. Sch. Initiative, Albuquerque, 1996—. Recipient award for Significant Cultural Contbn., Smithsonian Instn., Washington, 1977, 2nd pl. Spanish Market award Spanish Colonial Arts Soc., Santa Fe, 1976, 1st pl. Spanish Market award, 1977, 78, 79. Mem. Women in Ministry and Missions, Women of Ch. of God. Office: Old Town Copy and Office Supply 2314 Central Ave SW Albuquerque NM 87104-1657

SANCHEZ, RUBEN DARIO, minister, family counselor, parochial school educator, writer; b. Buenos Aires, Feb. 13, 1943; s. Ramon Jose and Maria Concepcion (Pardino) S.; m. Lina Alcira Tabuenca, Feb. 7, 1966; children: Adrian Nelson, Vivian Ethel. BA, River Plate Coll., Puiggari, Argentina, 1969; postgrad., Andrews U., 1971-72, MA, 1975; PhD, Calif. Sch. Theology, 1979; MA in counseling psychology, Nat. U., 1996. Ordained to ministry Seventh-day Adventist Ch., 1976. Pastor, tchr. River Plate Coll., Puiggari, 1969; min. lit. So. Calif. Conf., Glendale, 1970-71, Ill. Conf., Brookfield, 1972-77, Oreg. Conf., Portland, 1977-80; dir. Bible sch., assoc. speaker Voice of Prophecy, Thousand Oaks, Calif., 1980-84; dir. devel. It Is Written telecast, 1985—; founder Pacific N.W. Christian Sch., Woodburn, Oreg., 1979; founder, dir. Instituto Biblico Christiano, 1979-80; dir. Escuela Radiopostal (corr. Bible sch.), 1980-84; pres. ADVI Internat., 1990—; founder Asociacion Latino Americana para el Bienstar Familiar, 1995; dir.-spkr. daily internat. radio program Learning to Live; mem. Religious Broadcasters. Editor: Antologia Poetica, 1976; author: (textbook) Apasionante Exploration de la Biblia, 1977, Introduction to the Old Testament, 1979, (book) Back to Our Beginnings, 1996, The Danger of Loving Money, 1997, Women in the Bible, 1998, (doctrinal devotionals) Hungary Heart, 1984, The Danger of Loving Money, 1997, Take Care of Your Self-Esteem, 1997; contbr. articles to publs. Recipient Outstanding Service to Spanish Community in Oreg. award Sta. KROW, 1980; Andrews U. scholar, 1972. Mem. Assn. Christian Counselors, Christian Mgmt. Assn. Home: 24978 Avenue 208 Lindsay CA 93247-9550 Office: Lindsay Adventist Comty Ch 588 E Honolulu St Lindsay CA 93247-2144

SANCHEZ-H., JOSE, fine arts educator, producer, director, media consultant; b. Cochabamba, Bolivia, June 28, 1951; s. Victor Sanchez and Margarita Hermoso. MA, U. Mich., 1977, PhD, 1983. Camera operator NBC, WDIV/TV 4, Detroit, 1980-81; assoc. prof. Univ. del Sagrado Corazon, P.R., 1984-88; prof. Calif. State U., Long Beach, 1988—; actor Ninon Davalos Co., Cochabamba, 1969, Dept. of Fine Arts, Guadalajara, Mex., 1970-72; [illegible] U. Mich., Ann Arbor, 1984; media engr., 1982-83; photographer Mus. of Contemporary Art, L.A., 1988; cons. Loyola Marymount U., L.A., 1989. Cinematographer (film) Chautauqua: Famous American Voices of 1914, 1984; still photography (film) Secret Honor, 1984; dir. (video) Pope John Paul II, 1984; producer/dir. (videos) The Carillon Concert, 1979, Yo No Entiendo a la Gente Grande, 1986, Platinotipo, 1988, Artificial Intelligence, 1989, Partners for Success, 1990, The L.A. Mexican Dance Co., 1990, Rudolf Arnheim: A Life in Art, 1994, Ca/Rep 1995, Themes in Bicultural Education, 1991, Fue Cosa de Un Dia, 1992, (films) You and I, 1976, Who Cares About the Time?, 1977, Inside Cuba: The Next Generation, 1990; writer, producer, dir. (film) La Paz, 1994, The Delirium of Simon Bolivar, 1997; writer (play) La Paz, 1989; author: (book) The Art and Politics of Bolivian Cinema, 1999. Mem. The Long Beach Mus. of Art, Hispanic Acad. of Arts, 1987-89. Recipient Exceptional Achievement award Coun. Advancement and Support of Edn., 1982, Rackham Dissertation award U. Mich., 1982, Rackham scholarship, 1980-83. Mem. NEA, Latin Am. Found., Am. Film Inst., Profl. Photographers, Ptnrs. of the Ams., Ind. Feature Project/West. Avocations: travel, painting, music, movies, dancing. Office: Calif State U Film & Elec Arts Dept 1250 N Bellflower Blvd Long Beach CA 90840-0001

SANDAHL, BONNIE BEARDSLEY, pediatric nurse practitioner, clinical nurse specialist, nurse manager; b. Washington, Jan. 17, 1939; d. Erwin Leonard and Carol Myrtle (Collis) B.; m. Glen Emil Sandahl, Aug 17, 1963; children: Cara Lynne, Cory Glen. BSN, U. Wash., 1962, MN, 1974, cert. pediatric nurse practitioner, 1972. Dir. Wash. State Joint Practice Commn., Seattle, 1974-76; instr. pediatric nurse practitioner program U. Wash., Seattle, 1976, course coord. quality assurance, 1977-78; pediatric nurse practitioner/health coord. Snohomish County Head Start, Everett, Wash., 1975-77; clin. nurse educator (specialist), nurse manager Harborview Med. Ctr., Seattle, 1978-97, dir. child abuse prevention project, 1986-97; mgr. Children's Ctr., Providence Health Sys. Northwest, 1997—; spkr. legis. focus on children, 1987; clin. assoc. Dept. of Pediatrics, U. Wash. Sch. medicine, 1987—, clin. faculty Sch. Nursing, nurse mgr. Providence Gen. Children's Ctr., Everett, 1997—. Mem. Task Force on Pharmacotherapeutic Courses, Wash. State Bd. Nursing, 1985-86; Puget Sound Health Sys. Agy., 1975-88, pres., 1980-82; mem. child devel. project adv. bd. Mukilteo Sch. Dist., 1984-85; mem. parenting adv. com. Edmonds Sch. Dist.; chmn. hospice-home health task force Snohomish County Hospice Program, Everett, 1984-85, bd. dirs. hospice, 1985-87, adv. com. 1986-88; mem. Wash. State Health Coordinating, Coun., 1977-82, chmn. nursing home bed projection methodology task force, 1986-87; mem., interim chair Nat. Coun. Health Planning and Devel., HHS, 1980-87; mem. adv. com. on uncompensated care Wash. State Legislature, 1983-84; mem. Joint Select Com., Tech. Adv. Com. on Managed Health Care Sys., 1984-85. Pres., Alderwood Manor Cmty. Coun., 1983-85; treas. Wash. St. Women's Polit. Caucus, 1983-84; mem. com. to examine changes in Wash. State Criminal Sex Law, 1987; appointee county needs assessment com. Snohomish County Govt. United Way, 1989, 94; chair human svcs. adv. coun. Snohomish County Human Svcs. Dept., chair adv. com., 1992-96; gubernatorial appointee Western Form Health Svcs. Adv. Com. for Wash. State, 1995-97; apptd. Snohomish County Children's Commn., 1997—. Recipient Golden Acorn award Seattle-King County PTA, 1973, Katherine Rickey Vol. Participation award, 1987. Mem. Am. Nurses Assn. (chmn. pediatric nurse practitioner subcom. Com. Examiners Maternal-Child Nursing Practice, 1986-92, chair Com. Examiners Maternal-Child Nursing Practice 1988-90), Wash. State Nurses Assn. (hon. leadership award 1981, chair healthcare reform task force 1992-94), King County Nurses Assn. (Nurse of Yr. 1985, 1st v.p. 1992-96, pres. 1996—), Wash. State Soc. Pediatrics (gov. appointee State Interagency Coord. Coun., 1998—), Sigma Theta Tau. Methodist. Home: 1814 201st Pl SW Lynnwood WA 98036-7060 Office: Providence Children's Ctr Everett WA 98204

SANDDAL, NELS DODGE, foundation executive, consultant; b. Salt Lake City, Feb. 17, 1949; s. James Wesley and Charlotte Jean (Ewer) S.; m. Brenda Kay Lille Griffin, Sept. 27, 1970 (div. June 1990); m. Theresa Louise Knipe, Oct. 10, 1992; 1 child, Jami. BA in English, Carroll Coll., 1966-70; MS in Psychology, Mont. State U., 1996. In-svc. trainer Boulder (Mont.) River Sch. and Hosp., 1974-75; group home mgr. REACH, Inc., Bozeman, Mont., 1975-76; community home trainer Devel. Disabilities Tng. Inst., Helena, Mont., 1976-77; tng. coord. emergency med. svcs. bureau State Dept. Health and Environ. Scis., Helena, 1977-82; cons., lead staff Nat. Coun. State Emergency Med. Svcs. Tng. Coords., Inc., Lexington, Ky., 1981-86; account exec., lead staff Nat. Assn. Emergency Med. Techs., Clinton, Miss., 1986-87; pres., CEO Assn. Mgmt. and Cons., Inc., Boulder, 1983-89; writer, prodr., dir. North Country Media Group, Great Falls, Mont., 1990-91; chief conf. planner S.O.S. Conf. Planning Consortium, Great Falls, 1991-92; exec. dir. Critical Illness & Trauma Found., Bozeman, Mont., 1986-91; pres., CEO Critical Illness & Trauma Found., Bozeman, 1991—; season course leader Nat. Outdoor Leadership Sch., Lander, Wyo., 1966-74; mem. exec. com. Nat. Coun. State EMS Tng. Coords., 1977-82, chmn., Lexington, Ky., 1979-81; mem. adv. com. pediatric emergency med. svcs. tng. project Children's Hosp. Nat. Med. Ctr., Washington, 1985-88, pediatrics emergency instr., 1986-90; mem. grant peer rev. com. divsn. injury epidemiology Ctrs. for Disease Control, Atlanta, 1986-87; cons. Emergency Med. Svcs. Bureau, Helena, 1977, Devel. Disabilities Tng. Inst., Helena, 1977-78; mem. injury prevention profls. New Eng. Network to Prevent Childhood Injuries, Newton, Mass., 1988-95; mem. core faculty devel. trauma sys. tng. program U.S. Dept. Transp., Washington, 1989—, tech. assistance team mem. EMS, 1991-93; EMS instr. and program coord. Great Falls Vocat. Tng. Ctr., 1991-93; rsch. asst. inst. for cmty. studies U. Mo., Kansas City, 1983-95; pres. exec. com. Intermountain Regional EMS Children Coord. Coun., Salt Lake City, 1994—; site reviewer Commn. for Accreditation of Ambulance Svcs., Glenview, Ill., 1997—; firefighter/EMS trainer, Gallatin Gateway Vol. Fire Dept., Gallatin Gateway, Mont., 1998—; bd. dirs. Five Rivers chpt. ARC, Bozeman, Mont., 1998—. Editor and tech. cons.: Workbook for Prehospital Care and Crisis Intervention, 4th edit., 1992, 5th edit., 1993, Instructor Resource Manual for Prehospital Care and Crisis Intervention, 4th edit., 1992, Workbook for First Responder, 1990; contbg. editor Jour. of Prehospital Care, 1984-85, The EMT Jour., 1980-81; editl. cons. Am. Acad. Orthopaedic Surgeons, 1980-81; contbr. numerous articles to profl. jours.; video prodr. and presenter in field. Mem. Park County DUI Task Force, Livingston, 1993-96; inaugural coord. Mont. Safe Kids Coalition, Big Timber, 1988-90; adv. com. Nat. Significance Project for Respite Care, 1977-78; mem. basic life support com. of Mont., Mont. Heart Assn., 1977-82. Recipient Golden award for humanity ARC, 1976, 500 Hour award, 1976, Outstanding Svc. award Nat. Coun. State EMS Tng. Coords., 1979, Leadership award, 1981, Charter Membership award, 1984, J.D. Farrington award for excellence Nat. Assn. Emergency Med. Technicians, 1981, Jeffrey S. Harris award, 1985, Outstanding Svc. award Am. Heart Assn., 1982, Appreciation cert. for paramedic emergency care U.S. Dept. Transp., 1984, appreciation awards Colo. Trauma Inst., 1993, Healthy Mothers/Healthy Babies, Helena, Mont., 1997, Kans. Bd. of EMS, Topeka, 1996, 98, Intermountain Regional EMS-C Coordinating Coun., Inc., 1998. Mem. Nat. Registry EMTs (20 yr. recognition), Mont. Bd. Med. Examiners. Democrat. Avocations: mountaineering, hiking, sailing, golf, skiing. Home: 20 Arrowhead Trl Bozeman MT 59718-9452 Office: Critical Illness Trauma Found 300 N Willson Ave Ste 3002 Bozeman MT 59715-3572

SANDE, BARBARA, interior decorating consultant; b. Twin Falls, Idaho, May 5, 1939; d. Einar and Pearl M. (Olson) Sande; m. Ernest Reinhardt Hohener, Sept. 3, 1961 (div. Sept. 1971); children: Heidi Catherine, Eric Christian; m. Peter H. Forsham, Apr. 1990. BA, U. Idaho, 1961. Cert. interior designer. Lic. designer, Calif. Asst. mgr., buyer Home Yardage Inc., Oakland, Calif., 1972-76; cons. in antiques and antique valuation, Lafayette, Calif., 1977-78; interior designer Neighborhood Antiques and Interiors, Oakland, Calif., 1978-86; owner, Claremont Antiques and Interiors, Lafayette, Calif., 1987-94; assoc. Neiman-Marcus, San Francisco, 1994-98; interior designer The Studio, Burlingame, Calif. 1998, Benefit Boutique Inc., Lafayette, 1995-98; with Restoration Hardware, 1998—; cons., participant antique and art fair exhibits, Orinda and Piedmont, Calif., 1977—. Decorator Piedmont Christmas House Tour, 1983, 88, 89, Oakland Mus. Table Setting, 1984, 85, 86, Piedmont Showcase Family Room, 1986, Piedmont Showcase Music Room, 1986, Piedmont Kitchen House Tour, 1985, Santa Rosa Symphony Holiday Walk Benefit, 1986, Piedmont Benefit Guild Showcase Young Persons Room, 1987, Piedmont Showcase Library, 1988, Peidmont Showcase Solarium, 1989, Jr. League Table Setting, Oakland-East Bay, 1989, 90. Bd. dirs. San Leandro Coop. Nursery Sch., 1967; health coord. parent-faculty bd. Miramonte High Sch., Orinda, 1978, Acalanes Sch. Dist., Lafayette, Calif., 1978; bd. dirs. Orinda Community Ctr. Vols., 1979; originator Concerts in the Park, Orinda, 1979. Mem. Am. Soc. Interior Design (assoc.), Am. Soc. Appraisers (assoc.), Am. Decorative Arts Forum, Calif. Coun. Interior Design (cert.), De Young Mus., Nat. Trust Historic Preservation, San Francisco Opera Guild, San Francisco Symphony Guild. Democrat. Avocations: travel, hiking.

SANDER, SUSAN BERRY, environmental planning engineering corporation executive; b. Walla Walla, Wash., Aug. 26, 1953; d. Alan Robert and Elizabeth Ann (Davenport) Berry; m. Dean Edward Sander, June 3, 1978. BS in Biology with honors, Western Wash. U., 1975; MBA with honors, U. Puget Sound, 1984. Biologist, graphic artist Shapiro & Assocs., Inc., Seattle, 1975-77, office mgr., 1977-79, v.p., 1979-84, pres., owner 1984—, also bd. dirs. Merit scholar Overlake Service League, Bellevue, Wash., 1971, Western Wash. U. scholar, Bellingham, 1974-75, U. Puget Sound scholar, 1984; named Employer of Yr. Soc. Mktg. Profl. Svcs. 1988, Small Bus. of Yr. City of Seattle, Environ. Cons. of Yr., King County. Founding mem. Bellevue Children's Mus.; ; bd. dirs. Seattle Aquarium. Recipient PEMA Corp. Identity award, 1996. Mem. Seattle C. of C., Portland C. of C. , Student Conservation Assn. (dir.). Club. Avocations: swimming, hiking, traveling, painting. Office: 101 Yesler Way Ste 400 Seattle WA 98104-3425

SANDERLIN, TERRY KEITH, counselor; b. Ashland, Oreg., Aug. 5, 1950; s. Calvin Carney and Myrtle Estell (Cope) S.; m. Theresa Emma Garcia, Jan. 19, 1969 (div. Feb. 1976); 1 child, Sean Eric; m. Margaret Lillian Lutz, Dec. 26, 1987. B in Bus., U. N.Mex., 1982, M in Counseling, 1983, EdD, 1993. Diplomate Am. Psychotherapy Assn.; lic. clin. mental health, N.Mex., sch. counselor, N.Mex.; cert. hypnotherapist Internat. Assn. Counselors and Therapists; pvt. pilots lic.; keelboat cert. Unit supr. Bernalillo County Juvenile Detention Ctr., Albuquerque, 1978-80; counselor Independence Halfway House, Albuquerque, 1980-81; mental health worker Bernalillo County Mental Health Ctr., Albuquerque, 1981-82; probation parole officer N.Mex. Probation/Parole, Albuquerque, 1982-87; dist. supr. N.Mex. Probation/Parole, Gallup, 1987-88; vocat. counselor Internat. Rehab. Assn., Albuquerque, 1989-91; counseling psychologist VA, Albuquerque, 1991—; owner, dir. Counseling and Tng. Specialist, Albuquerque, 1988—; counselor Albuquerque (N.Mex.) Counseling Specialist, 1983-86; guest lectr. sociology dept. U. N.Mex., Albuquerque, 1992; presenter 5th Annual S.W. Substance Abuse Conf., Albuquerque, 1992; presenter N.Mex. Corrections Dept., Santa Fe, 1993. Author: (video tapes) Breathing Free & Good, 1991, Understanding Adolescent Satanism, 1991, (manual) Social Skills and Anger Management, 1993. Vol. counselor Adult Misdemeanor Probation, Albuquerque, 1974-76; panel mem. Cmty. Corrections Selection Panel, Albuquerque, 1987-90. With U.S. Army, 1969-72, Vietnam. Recipient Outstanding Citizenship, Albuquerque Police Dept., 1974; N.Mex. Dept. Pub. Safety rsch. grantee, 1995. Mem. ACA, Am. Corrections Assn., Am. Legion. Democrat. Avocations: scuba diving, martial arts, hiking, flying, sailing. Office: Counseling & Tng Specialist 8016 Zuni Rd SE Ste H Albuquerque NM 87108-3277

SANDERS, ADRIAN LIONEL, educational consultant; b. Paragould, Ark., Aug. 3, 1938; s. Herbert Charles and Florence Theresa (Becherer) S.; m. Molly Jean Zecher, Dec. 20, 1961. AA, Bakersfield Coll., 1959; BA, San Francisco State U., 1961; MA, San Jose State U., 1967. 7th grade tchr. Sharp Park Sch., Pacifica, Calif., 1961-62; 5th grade tchr. Mowry Sch., Fremont, Calif., 1962-64; sci. tchr. Blacow Sch., Fremont, Calif., 1964-76; 5th grade tchr. Warm Springs Sch., Fremont, 1977-87, 5th grade gifted and talented edn. tchr., 1987-94; edn. cons., 1994—. Mem. History Mus. of San Jose, 1980—, Nat. Geog. Soc., Washington, 1976—, Alzheimer's Family Relief Program, Rockville, Md., 1986; vol. 7 km. Race for Alzheimer's Disease Willow Glen Founders Day, San Jose, 1988-92. Named Outstanding Young Educator, Jr. C. of C., Fremont, Calif., 1965. Avocations: photography, travelling, visiting presidents' birthplaces, collecting license plates, collecting matchbooks worldwide. Home and Office: 1437 Stoneridge Cir Escondido CA 92029-5514

SANDERS, AUGUSTA SWANN, retired nurse; b. Alexandria, La., July 22, 1932; d. James and Elizabeth (Thompson) Swann; m. James Robert Sanders, Jan. 12, 1962 (div. 1969). Student, Morgan State U., 1956. RN. Pub. health nurse USPHS, Washington, 1963-64; mental health counselor Los Angeles County Sheriff's Dept., 1972-79; program coordinator Los Angeles County Dept. Mental Health, 1979-88; program dir. L.A. County Dept. Health Svcs., 1989-92; ret., 1992; apptd. by Calif. Gov. Jerry Brown to 11th Dist. Bd. Med. Quality Assurance, 1979-85; health cons., legal, 1994—; motivational spkr. Mem. Assemblyman Mike Roo's Commn. on Women's Issues, 1981-86, Senator Diane Watson's Commn. on Health Issues, 1979-85; chmn. Commn. Sex. Equity L.A. Unified Sch. Dist., 1984-90; bd. dirs., sec. High Desert chpt. ARC, 1998. Named Woman of Yr., Crenshaw-Latijera Local Orgn., 1988, Wilshire Local Orgn., 1990, Victor Valley Local Orgn., 1994. Mem. NAFE, Los Angeles County Employees Assn. (v.p. 1971-72), So. Calif. Black Nurses Assn. (founding mem.), Internat. Fedn. Bus. and Profl. Women (pres. L.A. Sunset dist. 1988-89, dist. officer 1982-89, Calif. v.p. membership and mktg. 1995-96), Internat. Assn. Chem. Dependency Nurses (treas. 1990-92), Victor Valley Bus. and Profl. Women (pres. 1997-98), High Desert LWV (founder), High Desert Intercoun. Women's Orgns., Nat. Coun. of Negro Women, Am. C. of C. (adminstrn.-ednl. chmn.), Victor Valley African Am. C. of C. (edn. com.), High Desert Investment Club (chmn. 1998-99), Chi Eta Phi. Democrat. Methodist. Avocations: travelling, crocheting, movies, concerts, plays.

SANDERS, DAVID CLYDE, management and marketing consultant; b. Lubbock, Tex., Oct. 8, 1946; s. Jasper Clyde and Mary Jo (Baber) S.; m. Barbara Ann Huck 1976 (div. July 1983); m. Marcia Lynn Fik, Nov. 20, 1983; children: Ashton Harrison, Geoffrey Davidson. Student, U. Tex., 1964; BA, Tex. Tech. U., 1969; postgrad., So. Meth. U., 1969-70, U. Tex., 1970-71. Exec., auditor Ch. Scientology Tex., Austin, 1971-75; exec., cons. Expansion Consultants, L.A., 1975-77; cons. pub. relations Exec. Mgmt. Specialists, L.A., 1977-80; exec. dir. Inst. for Fin. Independence, Glendale, Calif., 1980-83; mktg. dir. Michael Baybak & Co., Beverly Hills, Calif., 1983-85; sr. cons., ptnr. Mgmt. Tech. Consultants, L.A., 1985-86; sr. cons. Sterling Mgmt. Systems, Glendale, 1986-93, sr. v.p., 1988-89, exec. coun. mem., exec. establishment officer, 1988-89, advanced cons., 1989-93; workshop instr., exec. mgmt. and mktg. cons. Mgmt. Success!, Glendale, Calif., 1992-96; ptnr., sr. cons. Expansion Cons., Montrose, Calif., 1996; founder, owner David C. Sanders & Assocs., 1996—, Market Domination Specialists!, 1997—; founder Total Freedom, Inc., 1997—; spkr., ptnr. JPR & Assocs., L.A., 1985-88; pres. Prosperity Assocs., 1990—; direct distbr. 1991-93; distbr. Ruby Direct, 1993—, Founder's Direct, 1997—, Amway Corp. Author, Sanders Newsletter, 1983-88. Co-founder, pres. Bus. Adv. Bur. So. Calif., Huntington Beach, 1977-79; founder, exec. dir. Bus. Adv. Bur. Internat., 1995; mem., contbr. Citizen's Commn. on Human Rights, L.A., 1976—; co-founder Vol. Ministers L.A., 1977-78. Mem. World Inst. Scientology Enterprises (charter), Internat. Hubbard Ecclesiastical League of Pastors, Citizens for Alternative Tax Sys. (sustaining), Friends of Narconon Chilocoo New Life Ctr., Internat. Assn. Scientologists (founding mem.), Assn. for Better Living and Edn., Alpha Phi Omega (sec. Tex. Tech U. chpt. 1965-69). Republican. Avocations: dianetics and Scientology study, travel, reading, computers, purchasing, video prodn. E-mail: ConsultU@aol.com. Home: 4648 Lasheart Dr La Canada CA 91011-2125 Office: David C Sanders & Assoc Market Domination Specialists! 2529 Foothill Blvd Ste 208 La Crescenta CA 91214-3542

SANDERS, GORDON C., contractor owner; b. Spokane, Wash., Oct. 30, 1945; s. Carl and Emilia (Neuman) S.; m. Joanna Emily Atkinson, Sept. 27, 1967 (div. Jan. 1973); children: Sonja Ruddell, Angelique Sanders. Mechanics Diploma, Advanced Trade Sch., Chgo., 1976. Orchardist, owner Apple Kingdom, Green Bluff, Wash., 1967-81; supr., bldg. maintenance ABM, Spokane, Wash., 1982-87; owner, maintenance contractor Gordons Janitorial Contractors, Spokane, 1988—; owner Expanded Horizons, Spokane, Wash., 1994—. With U.S. Army, 1964-67. Mem. Freedom From Religion Found. Avocations: sculpture, quantum mechanics, cosmology, cosmogony, basketball fan.

SANDERS, JERRY, protective services official; b. San Pedro, Calif., July [illegible] Long Beach City Coll., 1970; BA in Pub. Administrn., Nat. U., [illegible]; student, San Diego State U. Cert. P.O.S.T mgmt. Police officer San Diego Police Dept., 1973-93, chief of police, 1993—. Bd. dirs. The Nat. Conf., San Diego State U. Cmty. Adv. Bd., Children's Initiative, Youth Econ. Enterprise Zones; mem. cmty.

leaders adv. bd. ElderHelp of San Diego. Recipient Headliner of Yr. award San Diego Press Club, 1984, 93, Exceptional Performance citation for SWAT leadership, 1986. Office: San Diego Police Dept 1401 Broadway San Diego CA 92101-5729*

SANDERS, JERRY WAYNE, social sciences educator; b. Brownsville, Pa., Jan. 14, 1945; m. Mercedes Elizabeth Guerrero, Dec. 23, 1965; children: Ché Jeremy, Zachariah Octavio. BA in Sociology, Ariz. State U., 1967; MA in Sociology, New Sch. for Social Rsch., 1971; PhD in Sociology, U. Calif., Berkeley, 1980. Instr. sociology Mesa (Ariz.) C.C., 1971-73; asst. prof. U. Hawaii, Hilo, 1980-82; dir. peace and world order studies World Policy Inst., N.Y.C., 1982-83, dir. security project, 1983-86; adj. assoc. prof. internat. studies CUNY, 1982-84; econ. and trade policy analyst Cuomo Com. on Trade and Competitiveness, N.Y.C., 1986-88; lectr., faculty advisor peace and conflict studies U. Calif., Berkeley, 1988—; Mem. exec. bd. Pacific Inst. for Devel., Environ. and Security, Berkeley, 1988-93; mem. exec. com. Peace Studies Assn., Boulder, Colo., 1991-93; Gaspar de Portola lectr. Colloquia in Catalonia, U. Barcelona, 1992. Author: Peddlers of Crisis: The Committee on the Present Danger and The Politics of Containment, 1983; contbr. chpt. to: Theory of Peace, 1995. Vol. Peace Corps, Cartagena, Colombia, 1967-69. Kent fellow Danforth Found., 1975-78. Sr. fellow World Policy Inst. (sr., contbg. editor World Policy jour. 1983-93, mem. editl. bd. 1993—). Office: Univ Calif Peace and Conflict Studies 101 Stephens Hall Berkeley CA 94720-2303

SANDERS, JOHN KENNETH, marketing communications executive; b. Tucson, Nov. 1, 1939; s. Autie Alfred and Ina Fae (Davis) S.; m. Diane Evelyn Nasby, Sept. 16, 1958 (div. 1981); children: John Kenneth Jr., Jeffrey Neil; m. Cathleen Victoria Watson, May 24, 1981; children: Brian Charles, Riley Scott, Julia Fae. BA, Art Ctr. Coll. Design, 1963; MA, Syracuse U., 1994. Corp. art dir., asst. advt. mgr. Southern Pacific Co., San Francisco, 1963-66; head art dir., asst. creative dir. Botsford, DeGarmo & Day, London, 1966-67; sr. art dir. Milici Advt. Inc., Honolulu, 1968-69, Lennon & Newell Pacific, Honolulu, 1970-71; pres., creative dir. Sanders & Gamlin, Honolulu, 1971-75, Sand & Printup Inc., Honolulu, 1975-82; dir. creative & mktg. svcs. Home Vue Hawaii, Honolulu, 1983-84; pres., creative dir. Sanders Mktg., Honolulu, 1984-88, 1994—; dir. mktg., pub. rels., & fin. devel. Am. Red Cross, Hi State Chpt., Honolulu, 1988-92; adv. bd. bus. banking coun. Bank Am., Honolulu, 1996—. Contbr. articles to profl. mags.; designer of numerous advt. campaigns. Bd. dirs. Kailua Urban Design Task Force, Honolulu, 1995-96, past chmn.; bd. dirs. Am. Red Cross, Honolulu, 1977-88, chmn. mktg. 1979-85; adv. Boy Scouts Am., 1977-78, coun. 1996-97; bd. dirs. Lanikai Cmty. Assn., 1988-91, chmn. playground, 1988-91; adv. com. Mental Health Assn., 1978-79, designer 1978-79; adv. com. March of Dimes Assn., 1977-78; bd. dirs. Cmty. Scholarship Assn., 1976-78. With USAR, 1957-65. Grantee State Found. Culture & Arts, 1982; recipient Pres.'s award Am. Red Cross Hawaii State chpt. 1979. Mem. Honolulu Advt. Fedn. (pres. 1971-72, lt. gov. 1972-76, gov. 1976-78, Ad Man Yr. award 1972-73), Am. Advt. Fedn. (Printer's Ink silver medal 1966), Kailua C. of C. (chmn. task force 1995-96), Hawaii Alliance Arts Edn. (pub. rels. com. 1995-97, bd. dirs.), Honolulu Symphony Soc. (chmn. fundraising 1978-83, chmn. mktg. and pub. rels. com. 1995-97, bd. dirs.), Rotary (chairman program 1996-97). Avocations: cmty. svc., architecture, building, aerobics, sports.

SANDERS, NANCY IDA, writer; b. Everett, Pa., May 17, 1960; d. Richard J. and Phyllis (Harden) Hershberger; m. Jeffrey L. Sanders, May 23, 1982; children: Daniel M., Benjamin L. Freelance writer, 1985—; editor TCC Manuscript Svc.; contbg. editor The Christian Communicator; leader Chino Hills Writers Critique Group. Author: Favorite Bible Heroes: Activities for Ages 4 and 5, 1993, Bible Crafts on a Shoestring Budget for Grades 3 and 4, 1993, Amazing Bible Puzzles: Old Testament, 1993, Amazing Bible Puzzles: New Testament, 1993, Jumbo Bible Bulletin Boards: More Bible Stories for Preschool and Primary, 1994, Jumbo Bible Bulleton Boards: Fall and Winter, Preschool and Primary, 1994, Jonah: Six Fun Surprises, 1994, Moses: Six Fun Surprises, 1994, My Book About Ben and Me, 1994, My Book About Sara and Me, 1994, Cents-ible Bible Crafts, 1995, The Fall into Sin, 1995, Jesus Walks on the Water, 1995, WA-A-A-AY COOL Bible Puzzles, 1996, Red Hot Bible Puzzles, 1996, Marshal Matt and the Slippery Snacks Mystery, 1996, Marshal Matt and the Case of the Secret Code, 1996, Marshal Matt and the Topsy-Turvy Trail Mystery, 1996, Marshal Matt and the Puzzling Prints Mystery, Marshall Matt and the Case of the Freezing Fingers, 1997, Archy's Adventures with Colors, 1998, Archy's Adventure with Numbers, 1998, Archy's Alphabet Adventure, 1998; asst. editor: Trails 'N' Treasure, Christian Magazine for Kids, 1998. Mem. Soc. Children's Book Writers and Illustrators. Home: 15212 Mariposa Ave Chino Hills CA 91709-2703

SANDERS, RICHARD BROWNING, state supreme court justice; b. Tacoma, Washington; m. Kathleen Sanders; children: Amy, Brien, Laura. BA, U. Wash., 1966, JD, 1969. Assoc. Murray, Scott, McGavick & Graves, Tacoma, Wash., 1969, Caplinger & Munn, Seattle, 1971; hearing examiner State Wash., Olympia, 1970; pvt. practice Wash., 1971-95; justice Wash. Supreme Ct., Olympia, 1995—; lectr. in field. Contbr. articles to profl. jours. Office: Supreme Court of Washington Temple of Justice PO Box 40929 Olympia WA 98504-0929*

SANDERS, TRISHA LYNN, middle school educator; b. Chowchilla, Calif., June 7, 1965; d. Kenneth L. and Karen L. (Lobo) S.; 1 child, Craig. BA in Social Sci., Calif. State U., Stanislaus, 1987; MA in Ednl. Adminstrn., Chapman U., 1992, MA in Curriculum and Instrn., 1992. Cert. tchr., Calif. 6th grade tchr. lang. arts and math. Merced (Calif.) City Sch. Dist., 1988-91, 6th grade tchr. sci. and math., 1991-94, 8th grade sci. tchr., 1994-95; 7th grade tchr. Cruickshank Mid. Sch., Merced, Calif., 1995—; mentor tchr. Merced City Schs., 1993-95, sci. cadre, 1992-95; mem. steering com. Merced High Sch., 1992-95. Mem. ASCD, CUE, Phi Delta Kappa.

SANDERS, WALTER JEREMIAH, III, electronics company executive; b. Chgo., Sept. 12, 1936. BEE, U. Ill., 1958. Design engr. Douglas Aircraft Co., Santa Monica, Calif., 1958-59; applications engr. Motorola, Inc., Phoenix, 1959-60; sales engr. Motorola, Inc., 1960-61; with Fairchild Camera & Instrument Co., 1961-69; dir. mktg. Fairchild Camera & Instrument Co., Mountain View, Calif., 1961-68, group dir. mktg. worldwide, 1968-69; pres. Advanced Micro Devices Inc., Sunnyvale, Calif., until 1987, chmn. bd., chief exec. officer, 1969—; dir. Donaldson, Lufkin & Jenrette. Mem. Semicondr. Industry Assn. (co-founder, dir.), Santa Clara County Mfg. Group (co-founder, dir.). Office: Advanced Micro Devices Inc PO Box 3453 One AMD Pl Sunnyvale CA 94086-3453

SANDERS, WILLIAM JOHN, research scientist; b. Detroit, July 10, 1940; s. John William and Charlotte Barbara (Linsday) Steele; m. Gary Roberts, Sept. 12, 1961; children: Scott David, Susan Deborah. BS, U. Mich., 1962; MSEE, U. Calif., Berkeley, 1964. Sr. rsch. scientist Stanford (Calif.) U., 1967-97; pres. Sanders Data Systems, 1991—; pres. Computers in Cardiology, 1990-93. Inventor cardiac probe; contbr. articles to profl. jours. Mem. IEEE Computer Soc., Assn. Computing Machinery. Avocations: bicycling, wind surfing. Home: 3980 Bibbits Dr Palo Alto CA 94303-4531 Office: Sanders Data Sys 3980 Bibbits Dr Palo Alto CA 94303-4531

SANDERSON, HOLLADAY WORTH, domestic violence advocate; b. Raleigh, N.C., May 17, 1950; d. Hal Venable Jr. and Mary Simmons (Andrews) W.; M. Glen Wessel Potter, Apr. 15, 1978 (div. Sept. 1980); m. Stanley McNaughton Sanderson, July 2, 1984. AB in Music and French, U. N.C., 1972; MMEd, East Carolina U., 1975; cert. advanced acctg./data processing, Kinman Bus. U., 1985; student, Va. Theol. Sem., 1997—. Orch. tchr. New Hanover County Schs., Wilmington, N.C., 1972-74, 75-78, Fairfax (Va.) County Schs., 1978-80, 86-89, Missoula (Mont.) Elem. Sch. Dist., 1983-84; musician, music tchr. Coeur d'Alene, Idaho, 1980-83, 84-86, 1989-91; adj. music faculty, violin, viola, chamber music North Idaho Coll., Coeur d'Alene, 1980-83, 84-86; organist, choir dir. St. Luke's Epsicopal ch., Coeur d'Alene, 1980-83, 84-86, St. Luke's Episcopal Ch., Coeur d'Alene, 1989-95; gen. mgr., artistic dir. Coeur d'Alene Summer Theatre, Coeur d'Alene, 1991-92; bookkeeper, adminstrv. asst. Women's Ctr., Coeur d'Alene, 1993-95, exec. dir., 1995-98. Sec. Idaho Coalition Against Sexual and Domestic Violence, 1995-98; sec.-treas. North Idaho Coalition on Domestic Violence, 1995-98; bd. dirs. Idaho Women's Network, 1997-98; mem. vestry St. Luke's Episcopal Ch., 1995-97, chair audit com., 1992-95, lay reader, chalice bearer, 1992—, parliamentarian, 1996, sr. warden, 1997; orch. dir. Pend Oreille Chamber Orch., Sandpoint, Idaho, 1994-95, North Idaho Symphony, 1991, Coeur d'Alene Summer Theatre, 1982-85; cert. QPR suicide prevention gatekeeper instr. Greentree Behavioral Ctr., Spokane, 1996—; mem. Nat. Coalition Against Domestic Violence, Washington State Coalition Against Domestic Violence; bd. dirs. Idaho Woman's Network, 1997—. Mem. Coeur d'Alene Sunrise Rotary. Democrat. Avocations: reading, cross-stitch, feminist theology. Home: 504 N 15th St Coeur D Alene ID 83814-5514 Office: Womens Ctr 2201 N Government Way Ste E Coeur D Alene ID 83814-3658

SANDFORD, MICHAEL PATRICK, poet, nurse; b. Elmhurst, Ill., Jan. 10, 1951; divorced; children: Susan, Jennifer, Stephanie, Amber (dec.). AA, Phoenix Coll., 1972; student, Ariz. State U., Tempe, 1972, 75-76; diploma, Scottsdale C.C., 1995. Cert. nursing asst. Author: History of Black Canyon City, 1998, (poetry) Michaels Sampler, 1980, 45 RPM, 1996, Knickknacks and Notions, 1998, Mad Michael's Request, 1998. Recipient Golden Poet award World of Poetry, 1985, 86. Mem. Canyon Culture Guild (prs. 1996-98).

SANDKOP, LINDA, writer; b. San Diego, Mar. 17, 1960; d. Virgil and Mildred H. (Martin) Miller. BA, San Diego State U., 1978; MA, U. San Diego, 1979; PhD, Columbia U., 1982. Film writer, prodr. Below the Ozone Layer, All in a Day's Work; author: Helen's Hallucinations, My Rainbow Bridge, 1998, The Inbetweeners. Home: 4469 White Pine Way Oceanside CA 92057-6631

SANDLER, HERBERT M., savings and loan association executive; b. N.Y.C., Nov. 16, 1931; s. William B. and Hilda (Schattan) S.; m. Marion Osher, Mar. 26, 1961. BSS, CCNY, 1951; JD, Columbia U., 1954. Bar: N.Y. 1956. Asst. counsel Waterfront Commn. N.Y. Harbor, 1956-59; partner firm Sandler & Sandler, N.Y.C., 1960-62; pres., dir., mem. exec. com. Golden West Savs. & Loan Assn. and Golden West Fin. Corp., Oakland, Calif., 1963-75; chmn. bd., co-chief exec. officer, dir., mem. exec. com. World Savs. & Loan Assn. and Golden West Fin. Corp., Oakland, 1975—; charter mem. Thrift Instns. Adv. Coun., to Fed. Res. Bd., 1980-81; former chmn. Legis. and Regulation Com. Calif. Savs. and Loan League; former mem. bd. dirs. Fed. Home Loan Bank, San Francisco. Pres., trustee Calif. Neighborhood Services Found.; chmn. Urban Housing Inst.; mem. policy adv. bd. Ctr. for Real Estate and Urban Econs. U. Calif., Berkeley. With U.S. Army, 1954-56. Office: Golden W Fin Corp 1901 Harrison St Fl 6 Oakland CA 94612-3588

SANDLER, MARION OSHER, savings and loan association executive; b. Biddeford, Maine, Oct. 17, 1930; d. Samuel and Leah (Lowe) Osher; m. Herbert M. Sandler, Mar. 26, 1961. BA, Wellesley Coll., 1952; postgrad., Harvard U.-Radcliffe Coll., 1953; MBA, NYU, 1958; LLD (hon.), Golden Gate U., 1987. Asst. buyer Bloomingdale's (dept. store), N.Y.C., 1953-55; security analyst Dominick & Dominick, N.Y.C., 1955-61; sr. fin. analyst Oppenheimer & Co., N.Y.C., 1961-63; sr. v.p., dir. Golden West Fin. Corp. and World Savs. & Loan Assn., Oakland, Calif., 1963-75, vice chmn. bd. dirs., CEO, mem. exec. com., dir., 1975-80, pres., co- chief exec. officer, dir., mem. exec. com., 1980-93, chmn. bd. dirs., CEO, mem. exec. com., 1993—; pres., chmn. bd. dirs., CEO Atlas Assets, Inc., Oakland, 1987—, Atlas Advisers, Inc., Oakland, 1987—, Atlas Securities, Inc., Oakland, 1987—; mem. adv. com. Fed. Nat. Mortgage Assn., 1983-84. Mem. Pres.'s Mgmt. Improvement Coun., 1980, Thrift Insts. Adv. Coun. to Fed. Res. Bd., 1989-91, v.p., 1990, pres., 1991; mem. policy adv. bd. Ctr. for Real Estate and Urban Econs. U. Calif., Berkeley, 1981—, mem. exec. com. policy adv. bd., 1985—; mem. ad hoc com. to rev. Schs. Bus. Adminstrn. U. Calif., 1984-85; vice chmn. industry adv. com. Fed. Savs. and Loan Ins. Corp., 1987-88, Ins. Corp., 1987-88; bd. overseers NYU Schs. Bus., 1987-89; mem. Glass Ceiling Commn., 1992-93. Mem. Phi Beta Kappa, Beta Gamma Sigma. Office: Golden W Fin Corp 1901 Harrison St Fl 6 Oakland CA 94612-3588

SANDOC, EILEEN JEAN, art director, graphic designer; b. Portsmouth, Va., July 11, 1968; d. Ernesto Lantican and Linda Estrellado S. BA in Social Scis., U. Calif., Berkeley, 1993. Mktg. asst. MetriTech, Inc., Champaign, Ill., 1992-93; ednl. events coord. ShareData, Inc., Sunnyvale, Ca., 1994-96; freelance graphic designer Precis Prodns., Milpitas, Ca., 1996-97; art dir. Creative Touch Design, Mountain View, Ca., 1997—. Mem. Nat. Assn. Female Execs., No. Calif. Chpt. Bus. Mktg. Assn. (liason Prof. Assistance Network job bank), No. Calif. Chpt. Meeting Prof. Internat. (com. chair, newsletter editor, best design award, 1996), Silcon Valley chpt. Webgrrls Internat. (steering com. mem, website adminstr.). Avocations: arts and crafts, gardening, gourmet cooking. Office: Creative Touch Design 1601 Alison Ave Mountain View CA 94040-3015

SANDOVAL, ERIC MICHAEL, architect; b. Red Bluff, Calif., s. Ernest Dominic and Lou Ann (Hawes) S.; m. Dorothy Ann, June 23, 1984; children: Stephanie Louise, Nathan Michael, Daniel Eric. BArch, U. Oreg., 1985. Drafting tech. City of Redding (Calif.), 1979-81; survey tech. CH2M-Hill, Corvallis, Oreg., 1981; teaching asst. U. Oreg., Eugene, 1982-84; project architect Nichols Melburg & Rossetto, Redding, 1985-90; architect pvt. practice, Red Bluff, Calif., 1990-91, Trilogy, Red Bluff, Calif., 1991-94; plans examiner City of Corvalis, 1994—. Starr scholar, U. Oreg., 1982-83, Nat. Hispanic scholar, 1984; recipient Centorian award, U. Oreg., 1984. Mem. AIA (scholar 1985). Democrat. Roman Catholic. Avocations: crew, flyfishing, water colors, writing, singing. Home: 2475 NW Garryanna St Corvallis OR 97330-1375 Office: City of Corvallis PO Box 1083 Corvallis OR 97339-1083

SANDOVAL, MONA LISA, daycare provider, educator; b. Wilmington, Calif., Aug. 2, 1965; d. Alfred Rudy and Lita Candelaria (Machado) S. AA, Trinidad State Jr. Coll., 1992, 1993. Tchr. asst. Trinidad (Colo.) State Jr. Coll., 1992-93; infant/toddler tchr. Alta Vista Preschool, Trinidad, 1993; preschool tchr. Headstart, Trinidad, 1994—; mem. Child Daycare Task Force, Trinidad, 1992-93; participant Workshop in Early Child Devel., Trinidad, 1993. Editor: (newspaper) Trojan Tribune, 1993, cartoonist, 1992-93. Rep. State Supervisory Adv., Denver, 1993, State Bd. for C.C.s, Denver, 1992-93. Recipient scholarship in edn., Delta Kappa Gamma, 1991, sign lang. tng., Amy Martin, Trinidad State, 1994. Mem. ASCD, Colo. Assn. for Edn. Young Children. Democrat. Roman Catholic. Avocations: sign language, spl. edn., children's book writer. Office: Headstart PO Box 42 Trinidad CO 81082-0042

SANDRICH, JAY H., television director; b. L.A., Feb. 24, 1932; s. Mark R. and Freda (Wirtschafter) S.; m. Nina Kramer, Feb. 11, 1952 (div.); children: Eric, Tony, Wendy; m. Linda Green Silverstein, Oct. 4, 1984. BA, UCLA, 1953. Producer (TV show) Get Smart, 1965; dir. (TV shows) He and She, 1967, Mary Tyler Moore Show, 1970-88, Soap, 1977-79, Cosby Show, 1984-92; dir. (films) Seems Like Old Times, 1980, For Richer, For Poorer (HBO), 1992, Neil Simon's London Suite (NBC), 1996. Served to 1st lt. Signal Corps U.S. Army, 1952-55. Mem. Dirs. Guild Am. (award 1975, 85, 86), TV Acad. Arts and Scis. (Emmy award 1971, 73, 85, 86).

SANDS, SHARON LOUISE, graphic design executive, art publisher, artist; b. Jacksonville, Fla., July 4, 1944; d. Clifford Harding Sands and Ruby May (Ray) MacDonald; m. Jonathan Michael Langford, Feb. 14, 1988. BFA, Cen. Washington U., 1968; postgrad, UCLA, 1968. Art dir. East West Network, Inc., L.A., 1973-78, Daisy Pub., L.A., 1978; prodn. dir. L.A. mag., 1979-80; owner, creative dir. Carmel Graphic Design, Carmel Valley, Calif., 1981-85; creative dir., v.p. The Video Sch. House, Monterey, Calif., 1985-88; graphic designer ConAgra, Omaha, Nebr., 1988; owner, creative dir. Esprit de Fleurs, Ltd., Carmel, Calif., 1988—; lectr. Pub. Expo, L.A., 1979, panelist Women in Mgmt., L.A., 1979; redesign of local newspaper, Carmel, Calif., 1982. Contbr. articles to profl. mags. Designer corp. ID for Carmel Valley C. of C., 1981, 90. Recipient 7 design awards Soc. Pub. Designers, 1977, 78, Maggie award, L.A., 1977, 5 design awards The Ad Club of Monterey Peninsula, 1983, 85, 87, Design awards Print Mag. N.Y., 1986, Desi awards, N.Y., 1986, 88. Mem. NAFE, Soc. for Prevention of Cruelty to Animals, Greenpeace. Democrat. Avocations: publishing art, oil painting, cactus growing, interior decorating. Home and Office: 15489 Via La Gitana Carmel Valley CA 93924-9669

SANDSTROM, MARK RAND, minister; b. Glendale, Calif., Dec. 31, 1954; s. Morris Rand and Margaret Genevive (Hogendyk) S.; m. Pamela Jean MacArthur, Sept. 4, 1976. BS with honors, Northwest Christian Coll., 1980; MDiv, Sch. Theology, Claremont, Calif., 1985. Ordained to ministry Christian Ch. (Disciples of Christ), 1985. Pastor Franklin (Oreg.) Christian Ch., 1978-80; assoc. pastor Mt. Hollywood (Calif.) Congl. Ch., 1980-82; campus min. Pasadena (Calif.) City Coll., 1982-84; youth pastor 1st Christian Ch. (Disciples), Pasadena, 1982-85; assoc. min. 1st Christian Ch. (Disciples), Torrance, Calif., 1985-88; sr. min. Covina (Calif.) Christian Ch. (Disciples), 1988—; v.p. Hollywood Mins.' Assn., 1980-82; pres. South Bay Ecumenical Cluster, Torrance, 1986-87; bd. dirs. So. Calif. Ecumenical Coun., 1986-89. Bd. dirs. Hollywood-Wilshire Fair Housing, 1980-82; Calif. Parks Ministry, 1987—, Assn. for Retarded Citizens of San Gabriel Valle, El Monte, Calif., 1989—. Mem. Order of DeMolay (master councilor 1972), Masons. Home: 239 E Juanita Ave Glendora CA 91740-5646 Office: Covina Christian Ch 240 S Grand Ave Covina CA 91724-3295

SANDSTROM, ROBERT EDWARD, physician, pathologist; b. Hull, Yorkshire, Eng., Apr. 4, 1946; came to U.S., 1946; s. Edward Joseph and Ena Joyce (Rilatt) S.; m. Regina Lois Charlebois (dec. May 1987); children: Karin, Ingrid, Erica. BSc, McGill U., Montreal, 1968; MD, U. Wash., 1971; MBA, U. Calif., Irvine, 1999. Diplomate Am. Bd. Pathology, Am. Bd. Dermatopathology. Internship Toronto (Can.) Gen. Hosp., 1971-72; resident pathologist Mass. Gen. Hosp., Boston, 1974-78; clin. fellow Harvard U. Med. Sch., Boston, 1976-78; cons. King Faisel Hosp., Riyadh, Saudi Arabia, 1978; pathologist, v.p. St. John's Med. Ctr., Longview, Wash., 1996—; v.p. Intersect Systems Inc., Longview, Wash., 1990—; chmn. bd. Cowlitz Med. Svc., Longview, 1988; participant congl. sponsored seminar on AIDS, Wash., 1987. Script writer movie Blood Donation in Saudi Arabia, 1978; contbr. articles to profl. jours. Surgeon USPHS, 1972-74. Fellow Coll. Am. Pathologists, Royal Coll. Physicians; mem. Cowlitz-Wahkiakum County Med. Soc. (past pres.). Roman Catholic. Avocations: sport fishing, mountain climbing, philately. Home: 49 View Ridge Ln Longview WA 98632-5556 Office: Lower Columbia Pathologists 1606 E Kessler Blvd Ste 100 Longview WA 98632-1841

SANER, REGINALD ANTHONY, poet, essayist, educator; b. Morgan County, Ill., Dec. 30, 1931; s. Reginald Anthony and Marie Catherine (Rexroat) S.; m. Anne Costigan, Aug. 16, 1958; children—Timothy, Nicholas. B.A., St. Norbert Coll., 1952; M.A., U. Ill., 1956, Ph.D., 1962. Freelance photographer, 1952-56; asst. prof. English lit. U. Colo., 1962-67, assoc. prof., 1967-73, prof., 1973—, disting. research lectr., spring 1983. Author: Climbing into the Roots, 1976, So This Is the Map, 1981, Essay on Air (poems), 1984, Red Letters, 1989, The Four-Cornered Falcon, 1993; contbr. to The Best American Essays, 1991; contbr. poetry to lit. jours. Recipient Poetry award Borestone Mountain, 1972, Walt Whitman award for poetry Acad. Am. Poets-Copernicus Soc. Am., 1975, Hazel Barnes award, 1992, Colo. Ctr. for the Books award, 1993; co-winner open competition Nat. Poetry Series, 1980; winner Creede Repertory Theatre Poetry Competition, 1981; Gov.'s award for excellence in the arts State of Colo., 1983, 45th Anniversary prize Quarterly Rev. Lit., 1989; Fulbright scholar, 1960-61; U. Colo. faculty fellow, 1967, 74-75, 81-84, 89-90, 94-95; Nat. Endowment for Arts fellow, 1976; Rockefeller Found. resident scholar Centro Culturale della Fondazione Rockefeller, Bellagio, 1990, Wallace Stegner award Ctr. of the Am. West, 1997. Office: U Colo Hellems 101 Campus Box 226 Boulder CO 80309-0226

SANFORD, LEROY LEONARD, rancher; b. Sanford Ranch, Wyo., June 24, 1934; s. Claude Leonard and Herminnie May (Brockmeyer) S.; m. Barbara Jo Shackleford, June 15, 1965 (dec. Oct. 1965); stepchildren: Christina Pedley, Marlena McCollum, Diana Sumners; 1 foster child, Catherine Frost. Cert. satellite geodecy, Johns Hopkins U., 1971; cert. astron. geodecy, U.S. Geol. Survey-Branch R & D, 1971. Cert. Geodesic Surveyor. Rancher Sanford Ranch, Douglas, Wyo., 1952-57; topographer, photogrametrist U.S. Geol. Survey-Topog. Divsn.-Hdqs., Denver, 1957-81; rancher Sanford Ranch, Douglas, 1981—; speaker various schs. and community orgns. Congl. Svc. medal U.S. Congress, 1972. Mem. NRA (patron), Am. Solar Energy Soc., Antarctican Soc., Wyo. Farm Bur. Republican. Avocation: photography. Home: 400 Windy Ridge Rd Douglas WY 82633-0145

SANGUINETTI, EUGENE FRANK, art museum administrator, educator; b. Yuma, Ariz., May 12, 1917; s. Eugene F. and Lilah (Balsz) S.; children: Leslie, Gregory. BA, U. Santa Clara, 1939; postgrad., U. Ariz., 1960-62. Instr. art history U. Ariz., Tucson, 1960-64; dir. Tucson Mus. and Art Ctr., 1964-67, Utah Mus. Fine Arts, Salt Lake City, 1967—; adj. prof. art history U. Utah, Salt Lake City, 1967—. Contbr. articles to profl. jours. Served with USAAF, 1942-44, to capt. M.I., U.S. Army, 1944-46. Mem. Am. Assn. Museums, Am. Assn. Mus. Dirs., Am. Fedn. of Arts, Calif. Art Assn., Western Assn. Art Museums, Salt Lake City C. of C. Home: 30 S St Salt Lake City UT 84103-4133*

SANKAR, SUBRAMANIAN VAIDYA, aerospace engineer; b. New Delhi, India, June 22, 1959; came to U.S. 1982; s. V.S.S. and Bala (Sankar) Narayanan; m. Asha Govindarajan, July 31, 1988; children: Sitara, Ankita. B.Tech., Indian Inst. Tech., Madras, 1982; MSAE, Ga. Inst. Tech., Atlanta, 1983; PhD, Ga. Inst. Tech., 1987. R & D dir. Aerometrics, Inc., Sunnyvale, Calif., 1987-09; engrng. mgr. Schlumberger ATE, San Jose, Calif., 1998—. Contbr. articles to profl. jours. J.N. Tata scholar, India. Mem. AIAA, AAAS, Nat. Geog. Soc., Inst. Liquid Atomization and Spray Sys. Home: 34211 Petard Ter Fremont CA 94555-2611 Office: Schlumberger ATE 1601 Technology Dr San Jose CA 95110-1397

SANKOVICH, JOSEPH BERNARD, cemetery management consultant; b. Johnstown, Pa., Feb. 6, 1944; s. Joseph George and Helen Mary (Kasprzyk) S. Student, St. Francis Sem., 1964-68; BA, St. Francis Coll., 1966; postgrad., St. John Provincial Sem., 1968-69; MA, U. Detroit, 1973. Cert. cemetery exec., cath. cemetery exec., profl. cons. Assoc. pastor St. Mary's Ch., Nanty Glo, Pa., 1970-71, Sacred Heart Ch., Dearborn, Mich., 1971-74; dir. Mt. Kelly Cemetery, Dearborn, 1972-84; admissions counselor U. Detroit, 1974-81; dir. religious edn. St. James Ch., Ferndale, Mich., 1981-84; exec. Diocesan Cemetery Cons., Wyoming, Pa., 1984-86; dir. cemeteries Archdiocese of Seattle, 1986-91; mgmt. cons., owner Joseph B. Sankovich & Assocs., Edmonds, Wash., 1991—, Tucson, Ariz., 1997—; cons. Archdiocese St. Paul and Mpls., 1990—, Diocese San Diego, 1991—, Archdiocese Santa Fe, 1991—, Diocese Tucson, 1991—, Diocese Toledo, 1992—, Diocese Saginaw, 1992—, Archdiocese Edmonton, Alta., Can., 1993—, Diocese Monterrey, 1993—, Diocese Fresno, Calif., 1994—, Archdiocese Anchorage, 1995, Diocese Gaylord, Mich., 1996, Trustees of St. Patrick's Cathedral, 1997, Diocese of Nashville, 1997; Diocese of London, Ont., Can., 1998; mem. Task Force on Cremation of Bishops Com. on Liturgy Nat. Conf. Cath. Bishops, 1990-92; instr. A. Cemetery Assn. Univ. Ops./Maintenance, 1994; interim dir. cemeteries Diocese of Tuscon, 1992-93, Diocese of Saginaw, 1995-96, Diocese of Springfield, Mass., 1998—. Author, editor: Directory of Western Catholic Cemeteries, 1992, 94; author mgmt. assessments, sales programs, market analyses, 1986—; contbr. articles to profl. jours. Mem. Internat. Cemetery and Funeral Assn., Nat. Cath. Cemetery Conf., Wash. Interment Assn. (bd. dirs. 1990-91), Cath. Cemeteries of the West (founder 1987, governancy com. 1987-90). Avocations: travel, reading. Address: Joseph B Sankovich & Assocs 7273 E Shoreward Loop Tucson AZ 85715-3455

SANNWALD, WILLIAM WALTER, librarian; b. Chgo., Sept. 12, 1940; s. William Frederick and Irene Virginia (Stanish) S.; children: Sara Ann, William Howard. B.A., Beloit Coll., 1963; M.A.L.S., Rosary Coll., River Forest, Ill., 1966; M.B.A., Loyola U., Chgo., 1974. Mktg. mgr. Xerox Univ. Microfilms, 1972-75; assoc. dir. Detroit Public Library, 1975-77; dir. Ventura (Calif.) County Library, 1977-79; city libr. San Diego Public Libr., 1979—; libr. design and devel. mgr. City of San Diego, 1997—; vis. instr. mktg. San Diego State U. Author: Checklist of Library Building Design Considerations, 3d edit., 1997; chairperson editorial adv. bd. Pub. Librs. Pres. Met. Libraries Sect., 1989. Recipient Outstanding Prof. award and Outstanding Mktg. Prof. award, 1985; Award of Merit AIA San Diego chpt., 1988, Irving Gill award for Architecture and Mgmt., 1995. Mem. ALA, Online Computer Libr. Ctr. (mem. users coun. 1996), Calif. Library Authority for Systems and Services (pres. congress of mems. 1980), Calif. Library Assn., Libr.

Admintrn. and Mgmt. Assn. (pres. 1995—). Roman Catholic. Home: 3538 Pasco Salamoner La Mesa CA 91941-7329 Office: San Diego Pub Libr 820 E St San Diego CA 92101-6478

SANO, EMILY JOY, museum director; b. Santa Ana, Calif., Feb. 17, 1942; d. Masao and Lois Kikue (Inokuchi) S. BA, Ind. U., 1967; MA, Columbia U., 1970, MPhil, 1976, PhD, 1983. Lectr. Oriental Art Vassar Coll., Poughkeepsie, N.Y., 1974-79; curator Asian Art, asst. dir. programs Kimbell Art Mus., Ft. Worth, 1979-89; dep. dir. collections and exhbns. Dallas Mus. Art, 1989-92; dep. dir., chief curator Asian Art Mus., San Francisco, 1993-95, dir., 1995—. Author: Great Age of Japanese Buddhist Sculpture, 1982; editor: The Blood of Kings, 1986, Weavers, Merchants and Kings, 1984, Painters of the Great Ming, 1993. Active Assn. Art Mus. Dirs.; vis. com. Harvard U. Art Mus. Woodrow Wilson Fellow, 1966-67; grantee Carnegie, 1963-64, Fulbright-Hays, 1977-78. Office: Asian Art Mus Golden Gate Park San Francisco CA 94118

SANO, ROY I., bishop. Ordained to ministry United Meth. Ch., later consecrated bishop; appointed Bishop Rocky Mountain Conf., United Meth. Ch., Denver; now bishop United Meth. Ch. in L.A. area; with Calif.-Pacific Ann. Conf., 1992—. Office: Bishop United Meth Ch LA Area PO Box 6006 Pasadena CA 91102-6006*

SANSWEET, STEPHEN JAY, journalist, author, marketing executive; b. Phila., June 14, 1945; s. Jack Morris and Fannie (Axelrod) S. BS, Temple U., 1966. Reporter Phila. Inquirer, 1966-69; reporter Wall Street Jour., Phila., 1969-71, Montreal, Que, Can., 1971-73; reporter Wall Street Jour., L.A., 1973-84, dep. bur. chief, 1984-87, bur. chief, 1987-96; dir. speciality mktg. Lucasfilm Ltd., San Rafael, Calif., 1996-97, dir. content mgmt. and fan rels., 1997—; sr. editor Star Wars Galaxy Mag., 1996—; lectr. bus. journalism U. So. Calif., L.A., 1984-87. Author: The Punishment Cure, 1976, Science Fiction Toys and Models, 1981, Star Wars: From Concept to Screen to Collectible, 1992, Tomart's Price Guide to Worldwide Star Wars Collectibles, 1994, 2d edit., 1997, The Quotable Star Wars, 1996, Star Wars Scrapbook: The Essential Collection, 1998, Star Wars Encyclopedia, 1998, Star Wars Collectibles: A Pocket Manual, 1998, Anakin Skywalker: The Story of Darth Vader, 1998, Star Wars: The Action Figure Archive, 1999; cons. editor: Star Wars Galaxy, 1993, 2d series, 1994, 3d series, 1995; editor: Star Wars Trilogy Spl. Edn. card sets, 1997. Recipient award for best fire story Phila. Fire Dept., 1968, Pub. Svc.-Team Mem. award Sigma Delta Chi, 1977; finalist Loeb award, 1990. Mem. Soc. Profl. Journalists. Avocation: collecting toys and movie memorabilia. Office: Lucasfilm Ltd PO Box 2009 San Rafael CA 94912-2009

SANTEE, DALE WILLIAM, lawyer, air force officer; b. Washington, Pa., Mar. 28, 1953; s. Robert Erwin and Elsbeth Emma (Bantleon) S.; married; 1 child, Enri De'Von; m. Junko Mori, June 2, 1992. BA, Washington & Jefferson Coll., 1975; MA, U. No. Ariz., 1982; JD, U. Pitts., 1978. Bar: Pa. 1978, U.S. Ct. Mil. Appeals 1979, Calif. 1989. Floor mgr., commn. salesman J.C. Penney Co., Washington, Pa., 1971-76; asst. mgr. Rach Enterprises, Charleroi, Pa., 1977-78; legal intern Washington County Pub. Defender commd. 2d lt. USAF, 1979, advanced through grades to lt. col.; 1996; from asst. staff judge advocate to area def. counsel Luke Air Force Base, Ariz., 1979-81; claims officer 343 Combat Support Group Judge Advocate, Eielson AFB, Alaska, 1981-83; sr. staff legal adviser Dept. Vet. Affairs, Washington, 1983-89; asst. staff judge advocate Mil. Justice div. Air Force Judge Advocate Gen.'s Office, Washington, 1986-89, 63CSG/Judge Advocate, Norton Air Force Base, Calif., 1989-91; dep. pub. defender Juvenile dir. San Diego County, 1990-93, dep. alt. pub. defender, 1993—; dep. staff judge advocate 452 AMW/Judge Advocate, March Air Res. Base, Calif., 1991-98; supervising atty. Conflict Parent-Child Office, San Diego, Calif., 1998—; v.p. Neuer Enterprises, Nanjemoy, Md., 1983-89; participant Mgmt. Devel. Seminar, 1988. Mem. San Diego County Rep. Party; pres., co-chmn. legis. com. PTA Zamorano Elem. Sch., San Diego, chmn. SITE com.; mem. San Diego County Child Abuse Coord. Coun., San Diego County Commn. on Children and Youth, San Diego County Juvenile Ct. Mental Health Task Force, San Diego County Unified Sch. Dist. Parent Adv. Coun.; bd. dirs. San Diego County Youth Ct. Program, Pub. Defenders Assn., Train Ct. Apptd. Spl. Advocates for Voices for Children, McGill Ctr. Creative Problem Solving Youth Curriculum Com. Decorated Air Force Commendation medal, 1981, 89, Air Force Meritorious Svc. medal, 1991, 96; named Outstanding Young Man of Am., U.S. Jaycees, Montgomery, Ala., 1981; acad. scholar Washington & Jefferson Coll., 1971-75, Beta scholar Washington & Jefferson Coll., 1974, Pa. Senatorial scholar Pa. Senate, 1975, 76, 77, 78; named Juvenile Justice Commn. Atty of Yr., 1997. Mem. Pa. Bar Assn., Calif. Bar Assn., San Diego County Bar Assn., San Diego County Psych-Law Soc. Avocations: swimming, softball, stamp and coin collecting, foreign travel. Home: 1156 Corrales Ln Chula Vista CA 91910-7956

SANTILLAN, ANTONIO, financial company executive; b. Buenos Aires, May 8, 1906; naturalized, 1966; s. Guillermo Spika and Raphaella L. (Abaladejo) S.; children: Andrea, Miguel, Marcos. Grad., Morgan Park Mil. Acad., Chgo., 1954; BS in Psychology, Coll. of William and Mary, 1958. Cert. real estate broker. Asst. in charge of prodn. Wilding Studios, Chgo., 1964; pres. Adams Fin. Services, Los Angeles, 1965—. Writer, producer, dir. (motion pictures) The Glass Cage, co-writer Dirty Mary/Crazy Harry, Viva Knievel; contbg. writer Once Upon a Time in America; TV panelist Window on Wall Street; contbr. articles to profl. fin. and real estate jours. Served with USNR, 1959. Recipient Am. Rep. award San Francisco Film Festival, Cork Ireland Film Fest, 1961. Mem. Writer's Guild Am., L.A. Bd. Realtors, Beverly Hills Bd. Realtors (income/investment divsn. steering com.), Westside Realty Bd. (bd. dirs.), L.A. Ventures Assn. (bd. dirs.), Jonathan Club (L.A.), Rotary, Roundtable, Toastmasters Internat. Avocations: golf, tennis, skiing. Office: Adams Fin Svcs Inc 425 N Alfred St West Hollywood CA 90048-2504

SANTOS, ERNESTO NANQUIL, electrical engineer; b. Manila, The Philippines, Aug. 31, 1954; s. Enrique Kabiling and Gloria deGuzman (Nanquil) S.; m. Lydia Regina Segovia, Mar. 27, 1981; children: Carlo Miguel, Zabrina. BSEE cum laude, U. Philippines, 1976. Registered asst. elec. engr., civil svc. First Grade. Sr. systems analyst Philips, Manila, Philippines, 1979-82; software engr., 1982-83, customer support mgr., 1983-85; sr. cons. Philips, Hong Kong, 1985-91; project mgr. AT&T Global Info. Solutions, Hong Kong, 1991-93; cons., 1993-95; project mgr. CSC Intelicom Inc., Hong Kong, 1995-97, Quintus Corp., Fremont, Calif., 1997—. Patentee data modeller. Mem. Dem. Youth Orgn., Philippines, 1971. Full scholar Dept. Sci. & Tech., Philippines, 1971-76. Mem. IEEE Computer Soc., Philippine Soc. Elec. Engrs., Phi Kappa Phi Internat. Honor Soc. Avocations: golf, hiking, running. Home: 510 Ondina Dr Fremont CA 94539-3782 Office: Quintus Corp 47212 Mission Falls Ct Fremont CA 94539-7820

SANTOS, JEFFEREY ALAN, sales executive; b. Balt., June 18, 1964; s. Raul Paez and Patricia Marie (Scott) S. Student, U. Fla., 1982-83, U. Ctrl. Fla., 1983-84. Sales mgr. Miltech Industries, Fern Park, Fla., 1985-88, Protech Industries, Sanford, Fla., 1988-92; sales rep. So. Electronic Distributors, Tucker, Ga., 1992-94; storage mktg. mgr. Avnet, Tempe, Ariz., 1994-96; bus. devel. mgr. Hamilton Hallmark, Englewood, Colo., 1996-97; account mgr. Bell Microproducts, Denver, 1997-99; mfr. sales rep. SONY Electronics Inc., Denver, 1999—; softball coach Hamilton Hallmark, Englewood, 1996-97. Author: editor (monthly newsletter) Mass Storage Media, 1995-96. Mem. Fla. Gator Softball Team, Denver, 1996—. Mem. Fla. Gator Alumni Club. Avocations: mountain biking, snowboarding, hiking, camping, music. Home: 5196 E Sydney Ave Highlands Ranch CO 80126 Office: SONY Electronics Inc 5196 E Sydney Ave Highlands Ranch CO 80126

SANTOS, JOAO MIGUEL, sales executive; b. Lisbon, Portugal, Nov. 28, 1953; came to U.S., 1974; s. Jaime Jose and Maria Isabel (Moreira Rato) S.; m. Debra Lynn Brennan, June 17, 1978; 1 child, Desiree Laree Brennan. B□ □ □ □ □ ⅢⅢⅡ 1979 □□ □ □ □ □ □ □ □ □ 1979; MBA, Pepperdine U., 1983; Grad., Naval Command Staff/Naval War Coll., Newport, R.I., 1990; M in Aerospace Engring., U. Lisbon, 1994. Sales engr. Africa McDonnell Douglas Corp., Douglas Aircraft Co., Long Beach, Calif., 1979-80, 80-82, sr. sales engr. Africa and Mid.-East, 1982-84; area mgr. airline analysis Africa and Brazil The Boeing Co., Boeing Comml. Airplanes,

Seattle, Wash., 1984-85, account mgr. sales Africa, 1985-87; mgr. sales programs Africa The Boeing Co., Boeing Comml. Airplane Group, Seattle, Wash., 1987-90, mgr. 747/767 mktg. requirements, 1990-92, regional dir. 747/767/777 product mktg. Asia/Pacific, 1992-94, regional dir. customer requirements-FX 767/747 Program, 1994-95, regional dir. airplane configuration product devel., 1995-96; dir. internat. sales The Boeing Co., Boeing Comml. Airplanes, Seattle, 1996—. Lt. comdr. USN, 1984—. Republican. Roman Catholic. Avocations: water skiing, snow skiing, flying, aviation library. Home: 28903 233rd Ave SE Black Diamond WA 98010-1222 Office: Boeing Comml Airplane Group PO Box 3707 Seattle WA 98124-2207

SANTOS, JOSE RENATO, computer scientist, researcher; b. São Paulo, Brazil, Sept. 20, 1962; came to U.S., 1992; s. Jose Wilson and Maria Luiza (Novaes) S.; m. Ana Beatriz Apolinario, Sept. 5, 1987; children: David, Aline. BSEE, U. São Paulo, 1985; MS in Computer Sci., UCLA, 1994, PhD in Computer Sci., 1998. Software engr. FOTE/USP, São Paulo, 1986-89; lectr. U. São Paulo, 1989-92; rsch. asst. dept. computer sci. UCLA, 1992-98, sys. analyst, rschr., 1998—.

SANTOS, ROBERT DAVID, health and fitness educator, consultant; b. Chalan, Pago, Guam, Jan. 1, 1952; s. Joaquin L. G. and Carmen I. (Pinaula) S.; m. Elaine Marie Pudwill, Sept. 1, 1975; children: Zane, Deylene, Makao, Shane. AAS in Gen. Studies, Pierce County C.C., Wash., 1973; EdB in Physical Edn., Ctrl. Wash. U., 1975; MPE, U. Oreg., 1979; PhD in Higher Edn. Administrn. and Adult Edn., U. North Tex., 1990; ABD in Adminstrn. in Kinesiology, Tex. Woman's U. Cert. tchr. Physical edn. tchr. George Washington H.S., Guam, 1975-76, John F. Kennedy H.S., Guam, 1978-80; math, physical edn., health tchr. Battle Mt. H.S., Battle Mt., Nev., 1981-82; math. tchr. E.C. Best Jr. H.S., Fallon, Nev., 1982-83; rsch. cons. Sitterly Mgmt. and Cons. Firm, Ft. Worth, Tex., 1986-87; health tchr. S. Sanchez H.S., Guam, 1989-91; dir., mem. gov.'s cabinet Guam Health Planning and Devel. Agy., 1991-93; lectr. divsn. health, physical edn. and athletics Western Oreg. State Coll., Monmouth, 1993—; instr. dept. physical edn. and health Linn-Benton C.C., Albany, Oreg., 1994—; pvt. personal fitness instr., 1992-95; dir. fundraiser Sports Medicine Design by Guam—A Wholistic Approach, 1992; dir. 1st Ann. Gov.'s Health Task Forces' Forum, 1992; rsch. dir. Gov.'s 21st Century Health Work Force Survey, 1991-93; wellness cons. Clark Hatch Health and Fitness Ctr., 1992-93; fitness cons. Gold's Gym, 1992-93; coaches' lectr., cons. athletic injuries Oreg. H.S., 1977-79; student teaching asst. supr. U. Nev.-Reno, 1981; wellness instr. U. North Tex., 1986-90, adj. prof. kinesiol. studies, 1986-90;. Co-author: (with John Eddy) Circle of Excellence: Basketball, 1986; contbr. articles to profl. jours. Clinic dir. Albany Boys and Girls Club, 1993; mem. fellowship com. WHO; hon. amb.-at-large Gov. Joe Ada, Guam, 1991. Recipient Coat of Arms, Mayor of Rutherford, Eng., 1991. Mem. AAHPERD, Internat. Coun. for Health, Phys. Edn., Recreation, Sport and Dance (dir. philosophy edn. and sport commn.), Am. Assn. for Wellness Edn., Counseling & Rsch., Oreg. Athletic Trainer's Soc., Nat. Athletic Trainers Assn. (cert.). Roman Catholic.

SANTUYO, RICARDO TAYTAY, business educator, deacon; b. Lauigan, Iloilo, The Philippines, Aug. 19, 1931; came to U.S., 1955; s. Cipriano Serilla and Crisanta Dangan (Taytay) S.; m. Rufina Padua Cruz, Jan. 14, 1962; 1 child, Raymond. BS in Commerce, U. San Agustin, Iloilo City, The Philippines, 1954; postgrad., U. East. Manila, The Philippines, 1971; MSA, U. Guam, 1973; EdD, Western Mich. U., 1979. Ordained Deacon Diocese of Guam, 1974. Acctg. clerk to acct. Masdelco Inc., Agana, Guam, 1955-60, analyst, transportation specialist, 1960-68; auditor, acct., supr. Government of Guam, Agana, 1968-71, 73-78; acct., office mgr. Trans-Asia Inc., Tamuning, 1972-73; auditor U.S. Naval Air Station, Fallon, Nev., 1980-81; instr. Western Mich. U., Kalamazoo, 1978-79, Long Beach (Calif.) Coll. Bus., 1981—, Long Beach City Coll., 1982—; instr. U. Guam, Mangilao, 1973-75, El Camino Coll., Torrance, Calif., 1982—, Golden State U., L.A., 1985-88. With Cursillos in Christianity, Agana, 1970-77, asst. spiritual dir., 1974-75, lay dir., 1976-77; v.p. Legion of Mary, Agana, 1975-77; deacon various dioceses Roman Cath. Ch., L.A., 1982-88, San Bernardino, Calif., 1989—, Agana, Guam, 1974-77, Kalamazoo, 1978-79. Mem. NEA, Calif. Tchrs. Assn. Republican. Roman Catholic. Avocations: hiking, cooking, reading. Home: PO Box 8592 Tamuning GU 96931-8592 Office: Long Beach Coll Dept Bus Adminstrn 455 E Artesia Blvd Long Beach CA 90805-1352

SANWICK, JAMES ARTHUR, international executive recruiter, management consultant; b. Balt., Feb. 15, 1951; s. Alfred George and Catherine Anne (von Sas) S.; m. Brenda Julia Tietz, Sept. 20, 1980; children: Luke Graham, Sierra Catherine. AS, Catonsville (Md.) C.C., 1975; BS, U. No. Colo., 1976; M in Pub. Administn., U. Alaska S.E., 1985. Lic. tchr. Dr. Edward deBono Thinking Skills Courses; cert. sr. profl. in human resources. Recreation therapist Md. Sch. for the Blind, Balt., 1974; dir. camp New Horizon United Cerebral Palsy Md., Balt., 1975; sub-dist. mgr. Nat. Park Svc., various, 1976-82; freelance mgmt. cons. Juneau, Alaska, 1982-84; regional mgr. div. labor standards Alaska Dept. Labor, Juneau, 1983-88; adj. faculty sch. bus. and pub. administrn. U. Alaska S.E., Juneau, 1985-93; mgr. Alaska Productivity Improvement Ctr., Juneau, 1989-93; mgr. human resources and pub. affairs Greens Creek Mining Co., Juneau, 1989-93; mgr. human resources, securities and pub. affairs Rawhide Mining Co., Fallon, Nev., 1993-98; founder Ctr. for Innovation and Comm., Truckee, Calif., 1997—; v.p. Mgmt. Resources Cons., Truckee, 1998—; owner Sierra Bldg. Alternatives, 1995—; bd. dirs. Gov.'s Com. on Employment Disabled persons, Alaska Acad. Decathalon Inc.; chmn. Job Svc. Employer Com., Alaska, 1989-93; bd. advisors Inst. Mine Tng. U. Alaska S.E., 1989-93. Co-author: (info. pamphlet) Blue Water Paddling in Alaska, 1980; editor: (film) Green's Creek Project, 1990; photographic editor: Inside Passage Mag., 1982, 83; photographer: (book) Death Valley, 1977. Patrolman Nat. Ski Patrol System, Juneau, 1978-83; instr., trainer ARC, Alaska, Utah, Ariz., 1979-82; v.p. bd. dirs. Alaska Acad. Decathlon; mem. Reno Exec. Roundtable, 1995—. Sgt. USMC, 1970-73. Recipient Nat. New Svc. award United Cerebral Palsy, 1975; named Candidate of Yr. Nat. Ski Patrol System, 1979. Mem. ASTD, Am. Creativity Assn., Nev. Mining Assn. (human resources com. 1993—), Soc. Human Resources Mgmt., Juneau Ski Club. Avocations: skiing, hiking, scuba diving, guitar, tennis. Office: PO Box 1793 Truckee CA 96160-1793

SAPIN, CRAIG P., lawyer; b. L.A., Aug. 5, 1956; s. Sandy Sapin and Carol (Sapin) Gold; m. Carolyn Marie Clark, June 28, 1982; children: Stephanie, Patrick. BA in Econs., U. Calif. San Diego, 1978; JD, UCLA, 1981. Bar: Calif. 1981; cert. in taxation. From assoc. to ptnr. Procopio, Cory, Hargreaves & Savitch, San Diego, 1981—. Bd. dirs. Help Disabled War Vets., San Diego, 1995—. Mem. ABA, State Bar Calif., San Diego County Bar Assn. Office: Procopio Cory Hargreaves & Savitch 530 B St Ste 2100 San Diego CA 92101-4496

SAPP, DONALD GENE, minister; b. Phoenix, Feb. 27, 1927; s. Guerry Byron and Lydia Elmeda (Snyder) S.; m. Anna Maydean Nevitt, July 10, 1952 (dec.); m. Joann Herrin Mountz, May 1, 1976; children: Gregory, Paula, Jeffrey, Mark, Melody, Cristine. AB in Edn., Ariz. State U., 1949; MDiv, Boston U., 1952, STM, 1960; D Ministry, Calif. Grad. Sch. Theology, 1975. Ordained to ministry Meth. Ch., 1950. Dir. youth activities Hyde Park (Mass.) Meth. Ch., 1950-52; minister 1st Meth. Ch., Peabody, Mass., 1952-54, Balboa Island (Calif.) Community Meth. Ch., 1954-57, Ch. of the Foothills Meth., Duarte, Calif., 1957-63; sr. minister Aldersgate United Meth. Ch., Tustin, Calif., 1963-70, Paradise Valley (Ariz.) United Meth. Ch., 1970-83; dist. supt. Cen. West Dist. of Desert S.W. Conf. United Meth. Ctr., Phoenix, 1983-89. Editor Wide Horizons, 1983-89; contbr. articles to profl. jours. Chaplain City of Hope Med. Ctr., Duarte, 1957-63; trustee Plaza Community Ctr., L.A., 1967-70; corp. mem. Sch. Theology at Claremont, Calif., 1972-80; pres. Met. Phoenix Commn., 1983-85; del. Western Jurisdictional Conf. United Meth. Ch., 1984, 88; bd. dirs. Coun. Chs., L.A., 1963-67, Orange County (Calif.) Human Rels. Coun., 1967-70, Interfaith Counseling Svc. Found., 1982-89, Wesley Community Ctr., Phoenix, 1983-89; mem. gen. conf. United Meth. Ch., 1988. With USN, 1945-46. Mem. Ariz. Ecumenical Coun. (co-chmn.), Phoenix Southside Assn., Kiwanis (pres.), Kappa Delta Pi, Tau Kappa Epsilon. Democrat. Avocations: oversee, travel. Home: 5225 E Road Runner Rd Paradise Valley AZ 85253-3306

SAPSOWITZ, SIDNEY H., entertainment and media company executive; b. N.Y.C., June 29, 1936; s. Max and Annette (Rothstein) Sapsowitz; m. Phyllis

Skopp, Nov. 27, 1957; children: Donna Dawn Chazen, Gloria Lynn Aaron, Marsha Helene Gleit. BBA summa cum laude, Paterson (N.J.) State Coll., 1980. Various fin. and oper. systems positions Metro Goldwyn Mayer, Inc., N.Y.C., 1957-68; exec. v.p. dir. Penta Computer Assoc. Inc., N.Y.C., 1968-70, Cons. Actuaries Inc., Clifton, N.J., 1970-73; exec. v.p., CFO Am. Film Theatre, N.Y.C., 1973-76, Cinema Shares Internat Distrb. Corp., N.Y.C., 1976-79; sr. cons. Solomon, Finger & Newman, N.Y.C., 1979-80; exec. v.p., chief fin. officer Metro Goldwyn Mayer, Inc., L.A., 1980-85; various positions leading to exec. v.p. fin. and adminstrn., CFO MGM/UA Entertainment Co., Culver City, Calif., 1985-86; also bd. dirs. MGM/UA Entertainment Co., L.A.; fin. v.p.; chief bus. and ops. officer, Office of Pres., dir. United Artists Corp., Beverly Hills, Calif., 1986-87; chmn. & CEO MGM/UA Telecommunications Corp., Beverly Hills, 1986-89; sr. exec. v.p., dir. mem. exec. com. MGA/UA Communications Co., 1986-89; chmn., CEO Sid Sapsowitz & Assocs., Inc. 1989—. Pres., Wayne Conservative Congregation, N.J., 1970-77. Mem. Am. Mgmt. Assn., Am. Film Inst., Acad. Motion Picture Arts and Scis., Fin. Exec. Inst., TV Acad. Arts and Scis., KP (chancellor comdr.).

SARAVANJA-FABRIS, NEDA, mechanical engineering educator; b. Sarajevo, Yugoslavia, Aug. 2, 1942; came to U.S., 1970; d. Zarko and Olga Maria (Majstorovic) Saravanja; m. Gracio Fabris, Nov. 4, 1967; children: Drazen Fabris, Nicole. Diploma in mech. engring., U. Sarajevo, 1965; MSME, Ill. Inst. Tech., 1972, PhD in Mech. Engring., 1976. Lectr. in mech. engring. U. Sarajevo, 1965-70; teaching asst. Ill. Inst. Tech., Chgo., 1970-76; lectr. U. Ill., Chgo., 1974-75; mem. tech. staff Bell Telephone Lab., Naperville, Ill., 1976-79; prof. mech. engring. Calif. State U., L.A., 1979—, chair mech. engring. dept., 1989-92; assoc. researcher Lab. for Machine Tools, Aachen, Fed. Republic Germany, 1966-67; cons. Northrop Corp., L.A., 1984; COO FAS Engring. Inc., Burbank, Calif., 1993—. Contbr. articles to profl. publs. Grantee NSF, 1986, Brown & Sharpe Co., 1989; German Acad. Exch. fellow DAAD, 1966-67, Amelia Earhart fellow Zonta Internat., 1973-74, 75-76; recipient Engring. Merit award San Fernando Valley Engring. Coun., 1990, Disting. Chair award sch. of engring. and tech. Calif. State U., L.A., 1993. Mem. AAUW, Soc. for Engring. Edn. (dir. at large mfg. divsn.), Soc. Women Engrs. (sr.), Soc. Mfg. Engrs. (sr., chpt. chmn. 1997). Home: 2039 Dublin Dr Glendale CA 91206-1006 Office: Calif State U 5151 State University Dr Los Angeles CA 90032-4226

SARICH, VINCENT M., anthropologist, educator; b. Chicago, Ill., Dec. 13, 1934; s. Matt and Manda Saric; m. Jorjan Snyder; children: Kevin, Tamsin. BS, Ill. Inst. Tech., 1955; PhD, U. Calif., Berkeley, 1967. Instr. anthropology Stanford U., Berkeley, Calif., 1965; from asst. prof. to assoc. prof. anthropology U. Calif., Berkeley, 1967-81, prof., 1981-94, prof. emeritus, 1994—; vis. faculty U. Auckland, New Zealand, 1995—. Office: U Calif Dept of Anthropology 232 Kroeber Hall Berkeley CA 94720-3710 Also: U of Auckland, Private Bag 92019, Auckland New Zealand*

SARKOWSKY, HERMAN, museum official. Chmn. bd. Seattle Art Mus. Office: Seattle Art Mus PO Box 22000 Seattle WA 98122-9700*

SARLAT, GLADYS, public relations consultant; b. Elizabeth, N.J., July 22, 1923; d. Max and Dora (Levin) S. BS, U. Wash., 1946. Asst., Kay Sullivan Assocs. N.Y.C., 1949-50; fashion dir. Warsaw & Co., N.Y.C., 1950-54; asst. fashion coord. Emporium Dept. Store, San Francisco, 1955-56; asst. prodn. mgr. Cunningham & Walsh Advt., San Francisco, 1957-58; v.p., pub. rels. dir. Harwood Advt. Inc., Tucson and Phoenix, 1959-68; v.p., dir. Waller & Sarlat Advt. Inc., Tucson, 1968-69; pres. Godwin & Sarlat Pub. Rels., Inc., Tucson, 1970-87; counsel, Godwin Sarlat Pub. Rels., 1987-88, cons., 1988—; of counsel Liess Peck & Godwin, LP&G, Tucson, 1993—; cons. in field. Mem. adv. com. Downtown Devel. Corp., 1979-85, Festival in the Sun; bd. dirs. Tucson Conv. and Visitors Bur., 1993-95. Named Woman of Yr. for Bus., Ariz. Daily Star, 1963; recipient Lulu award L.A. Woman in Advt., 1962. Mem. Pub. Rels. Soc. Am. (past bd. mem., counselors acad., mem. bd. UA presents), Fashion Group, Tucson Met. C. of C. (v.p., dir. 1976-85, chmn bd. 1986-87, Tucson Woman of Yr. 1990). Republican. Jewish. Home: 5530 N Camino Arenosa Tucson AZ 85718-5417 Office: 177 N Church Ave Ste 315 Tucson AZ 85701-1125

SARLEY, JOHN G., broadcast executive, writer; b. Cleve., Mar. 1, 1954; s. Edward James and Ann Sarley. BA, Cleve. State U., 1977. Writer, producer Marschalk Co. Advt., Cleve., 1977-80, DOCSI Corp., Hollywood, Calif., 1980—; pres. Sarley, Bigg & Bedder Inc., Hollywood, 1981—. Recipient Clio award, 1980, 84, 87, 90, 92-97, London Internat. Advt. awards Internat. Radio Festival N.Y., Radio Mercury award, The Globals, N.Y. Festival award, The Mobius award and Promax. Mem. Broadcast Promotion and Mktg. Execs., Hollywood C. of C. Office: Sarley Bigg & Bedder Inc 1644 N Stanley Ave Hollywood CA 90046-2713

SARNER, HARVEY, lawyer; b. N.Y.C., Feb. 13, 1934; s. Michael and Lillian (Greenblatt) S.: m. Lorraine C. Jelle, June 9, 1956; children: Kyra, Surah. BS, U. Minn., 1958, LLB, 1959. Atty., advisor Fed. Communications Commn., Washington, 1959-61; assoc. ho. counsel Am. Dental Assn., Chgo., 1961-71; atty. Sarner and Assocs., Chgo., 1971-87. Author: Dental Jurisprudence, 1968, Herman Wouk Checklist, 1994; editor SAA Dr.'s newsletter, 1972-87. Bd. dirs. Jewish Found. for Christian Rescuers, 1985—, Temple Isiah, Palm Springs, 1994—. With USN, 1951-55. Recipient Polish Pres. medal Polish Govt., 1994, Humanitarian award Am. Soc. Oral Surgeons, San Diego, 1993. Jewish. Avocations: book and antiquities collecting. Home: 701 W Panorama Rd Palm Springs CA 92262-2743

SAROYAN, ARAM, writer, educator, editor; b. N.Y.C., Sept. 25, 1943; s. William S. and Carol (Marcus) Matthau; m. Gailyn McClanahan, Oct. 9, 1968; children: Strawberry, Kate, Armenak. Student, U. Chgo., 1962, NYU, 1963, Columbia U., 1964. Editor, publ. Lines (mags. and books), N.Y.C., 1964-67; editor Telegraph Books, Cambridge, Mass., 1971-72; lectr. grad. writing program U. So. Calif., 1996—. Author: Trio, 1985, The Romantic, 1988, Friends of the World, 1992, Rancho Mirage, 1993, Day and Night: Bolinas Poems, 1998; editor: Selected Poems by Ted Berrigan, 1994. Recipient award for poetry NEA, 1966, 67. Mem. PEN Ctr. (pres. USA West 1992-93). Avocations: photography, jazz.

SARSON, EVELYN PATRICIA See KAYE, EVELYN PATRICIA

SARSON, JOHN CHRISTOPHER, television producer, director, writer; b. London, Jan. 19, 1935; s. Arnold Wilfred and Annie Elizabeth (Wright) S.; m. Evelyn Patricia Kaye, Mar. 25, 1963; children: Katrina May, David Arnold. BA with honors, Trinity Coll. Cambridge, Eng., 1960, MA, 1963. Dir. Granada TV, Manchester, Eng., 1960-63; producer, dir. Sta. WGBH-TV, Boston, 1963-73; pres. Blue Penguin, Inc., Boulder, Colo., 1974—; v.p. TV programming Sta. WYNC-TV, N.Y.C., 1989-90; dir. Pub. Broadcasting Assocs., Newton, Mass.; cons. to numerous pub. TV stations. Creator, producer MAsterpiece Theatre, PBS, 1970-73, Zoom, PBS, 1971-73; producer Live From the Met, PBS, 1977-79, Kid's Writes, Nickelodeon, 1982-83, American Treasure, a Smithsonian Journey, 1986, Spotlight Colorado, 1991, Parenting Works, 1995-97, Club 303, 1994. Served with Royal Navy, 1956-57. Recipient Emmy award, 1973, 74, Peabody award Ohio State U., 1978, Internat. Emmy award, 1983, Nat. Acad. TV Arts and Scis. Gov.'s award, 1991. Mem. Dirs. Guild Am., Nat. acad. TV Arts and Scis. (gov. Heartland chpt.), Windows on the Rockies User Group (pres.). Avocations: music, cooking, gardening, travel, computers. Home and Office: 3031 5th St Boulder CO 80304-2501

SARTEN, MARY ANN, health facility administrator; b. Wabash, Ind., May 20, 1938; d. David Zacharias and Golda Marie (Adams) S. Grad. h.s., Wabash, Ind., 1956. Clk., typist Dukes Meml Hosp., Peru, Ind., 1969-72; file clk. VA Hosp., Indpls., 1972-75; file clk. VA Hosp., Phoenix, 1975-78, sec., 1976-77, timekeeper, 1977—. Mem. TOPS Club Inc., Phoenix Fed. Exce. Assn. Avocations: watching professional baseball and football, studying piano. Home: 8414 N 38th Dr Phoenix AZ 85051-4723

SARVER, LINDA, mayor. Mayor City of Covina, Calif. Office: 125 E College St Covina CA 91723-2129

SARVER, LINDA KAY, costume designer, educator; b. Rockford, Ill., Apr. 19, 1953; d. Everett Charles and Ruth Irene (Wickens) S.; m. Thomas Benjamin Markus, Nov. 19, 1997. BA, Drake U., 1975; MA, Western Ill. U., 1977; MFA, Ohio U., 1979. Resident costume designer New Am. Theatre, Rockford, Ill., 1976-77, Pioneer Theatre Co., Salt Lake City, 1989—; asst. prof. Marquette U., Milw., 1979-84; assoc. prof. Fla. State U., Tallahassee, 1984-88, U. Utah, Salt Lake City, 1988—. Costumer North & South mini-series (Emmy award 1986); author, illustrator: Let's Look at Theatre, 1997; illustrator: How to Read a Play, 1996, Basic Acting, 1996; co-author, illustrator: A Novel Approach to Theatre, 1997; assoc. editor Broadside, 1994-98; publ. com. U.S. Inst. Theatre Tech., N.Y.C., 1996—; contbr. articles to profl. jours. Del. U.S. Del. Prague Quadrennial Scenography, Czech Republic, 1991, 95, 99. Mem. Nat. Theatre Conf., U.S. Inst. Theatre & Tech., Shakespeare Theatre Assn. Am., Costume Soc. Am. Office: U Utah Dept Theatre 206 Performing Arts Blvd Salt Lake City UT 84112

SARWAR, BARBARA DUCE, educational consultant; b. Mpls., Aug. 9, 1938; d. Harold Taylor and Barbara (Thayer) Duce; m. Mohammad Sarwar, Dec. 28, 1972; 1 child, Barbara Sara Depies. BS, U. Colo., 1972; M Spl. Edn., Ea. N.Mex. U., 1975, Edn. Specialist, 1979. Cert. tchr., adminstr., N.Mex. Tchr. 2d grade, English as 2d lang. Lake Arthur (N.Mex.) Mcpl. Schs., 1972-74; tchr. spl. edn. Artesia (N.Mex.) Pub. Schs., 1974-79, ednl. diagnostician, 1979-88, dir. spl. edn., 1988-97; cons. Edn. Diagnosis, Artesia, 1998—; owner Barbara's Diagnostic Svcs. Contbr. to profl. publs. Pres. Altrusa Club Artesia, 1981-82, 86-87, The Arc of Artesia, 1990-92. Named Employee of Yr. Arc of N.Mex., 1994. Mem. Artesia Edn. Assn. (pres. 1978-79), Internat. Reading Assn. (pres. Pecos Valley chpt. 1975-76, sec. N.Mex. unit 1977-78), Nat. Assn. Sch. Psychologists, Counsel Exceptional Children, Phi Kappa Phi, Phi Delta Kappa. Avocations: reading, sewing, golf. Home and Office: PO Box 1493 Artesia NM 88211-1493

SASAKI, TSUTOMU (TOM SASAKI), real estate company executive, international trading company executive, consultant; b. Tokyo, July 28, 1945; came to U.S., 1979; s. Tsuneshiro and Kimiko (Fujiwara) S.; m. Yoko Katsura, Feb. 21, 1971; children: Mari, Tomoko. BA, Sophia U., Tokyo, 1969. Plant export adminstrn. Ataka & Co., Ltd., Osaka, Japan, 1969-76; officer Seattle-First Nat. Bank, Tokyo, 1976-79, AVP bus. mgr., 1982-84; AVP Japan mgr. Seattle-First Nat. Bank, Seattle, 1979-82, v.p. Japan mgr., 1984-90; owner, pres. BBS Internat., Inc., Seattle, 1990—; bd. dirs. Java Trading Internat., Co., Ltd., Seattle, Wired, Inc., Seattle, InterPac Devel. Inc., InterPac Mgmt., Inc., Riverplace Mgmt., Inc., BBS Bus. Svc., Inc. Bd. dirs. Adopt-a-Stream Found., Everett, Wash., 1987—; bd. trustees N.W. Sch., Seattle. Am. Field Svc. scholar, 1963-64. Mem. Japan Am. Soc. Wash. (chmn. membership com. 1988, bd. dirs. 1997—), British Am. Bus. Coun., Fairwood Golf & Country Club, Wash. Athletic Club. Avocations: golf, gardening, music, photography. Home: 4761 149th Ave SE Bellevue WA 98006-3127 Office: BBS Internat Inc 720 Olive Way Ste 1025 Seattle WA 98101-1880

SASAKI, YASUNAGA TITO, engineering executive; b. Tokyo, Feb. 6, 1938; came to U.S., 1967; s. Yoshinaga and Chiyoko S.; m. Janet L. Cline; 1 child, Heather N. Diploma in Indsl. Design, Royal Coll. Art, London, 1962; MS in Ekistics, Athens (Greece) Tech. Inst., 1965. Cert. planner Am. Inst. Cert. Planners. Tech. officer London County Coun., 1962-63; sr. rschr. Inst. Battelle, Geneva, Switzerland, 1965-67; planning dir. Golden Gate Bridge, San Francisco, 1970-74; pres. Quantum Mechanics Corp., Sonoma, Calif., 1981—. Mem. ASME, AIAA, Am. Vacuum Soc., Am. Welding Soc. Achievements include co-developer of the world's most sensitive helium leak detector and the world's lowest out-gasing stainless steel. Home: PO Box 200 Vineburg CA 95487-0200 Office: PO Box 1579 21885 8th St E Sonoma CA 95476-1579

SASENICK, JOSEPH ANTHONY, healthcare company executive; b. Chgo., May 18, 1940; s. Anthony E. and Caroline E. (Smicklas) S.; m. Barbara Ellen Barr, Aug. 18, 1962; children: Richard Allen, Susan Marie, Michael Joseph. BA, DePaul U., 1962; MA, U. Okla., 1966. With Miles Labs., Inc., Elkhart, Ind., 1963-70; product mgr. Alka-Seltzer, 1966-68, dir. mktg. grocery products div., 1968-70; with Gillette Corp., Boston, 1970-79; dir. new products/new ventures, personal care div. Gillette Corp., 1977; v.p. diversified cos. and pres. Jafra Cosmetics Worldwide, 1977-79; mktg. dir. Braun AG, Kronberg, W. Ger., 1970-73; chmn. mng. dir. Braun U.K. Ltd., 1973-77; with Abbott Labs., North Chicago, 1979-84; corp. v.p., pres. consumer products div. Abbott Labs., 1979-84; pres., chief exec. officer Moxie Industries, 1984-87, Personal Monitoring Technologies, Rochester, N.Y., 1987; pres. Bioline Labs., Ft. Lauderdale, Fla., 1988; mng. dir., ptnr. Vista Resource Group, Newport Beach, Calif., 1988-90; pres., CEO, Alcide Corp., Redmond, Wash., 1991-92, CEO, 1992—. Mem. Columbia Tower Club, El Niguel Club, Wash. Athletic Club. Home: 1301 Spring St (245) Seattle WA 98104-3533 Office: Alcide Corp 8561 154th Ave NE Redmond WA 98052-3557

SASMOR, JAMES CECIL, publishing representative, educator; b. N.Y.C., July 29, 1920; s. Louis and Cecilia (Mockler) S.; 1 child from previous marriage: Elizabeth Lynn; m. Jeannette L. Fuchs, May 30, 1965. *Dr. Jeannette L. Sasmor, RNC, BS, MEd, MBA, EdD, educator, author, and founder of health organizations, is the wife of Dr. James C. Sasmor. She has had a distinguished career in nursing education. A fellow of the American Academy of Nursing, she became Full Professor and Director of Continuing Nursing Education at the University of South Florida. Following their move to Arizona, she maintained her contributions to nursing as faculty at Yavapai College and creator and director of their H.E.A.L.T.H. Institute. She has been recognized for outstanding service by the American Cancer Society and Lions International* Dr. James C. Sasmor, BS, Columbia U., 1942; MBA, Calif. Western U., 1977, PhD, 1979. Cert. Am. Bd. Med. Psychotherapists, Am. Assn. Sex Educators, Counselors and Therapists, Healthcare Risk Mgr. Am. Inst. Med. Law, diplomate Am. Bd. Sexology, AM. Bd. Disability Analysts (sr. analyst). Registered rep. Nat. Assn. Security Dealers, 1956-57; founder, owner J.C. Sasmor Assocs. Publishers' Reps., N.Y.C., 1959-89; co-founder, pres., dir. adminstrn. Continuing Edn. Cons., Inc., 1976—; pub. cons., 1959—; clin assoc., U. So. Fla. Coll. of Medicine, 1987-89; adj. faculty Coll. Nursing, 1980-89, dir. Ednl. Counseling Comprehensive Breast Cancer Ctr., U. So. Fla. Med. Ctr., 1984-89, client libm. mental health inst., 1979-89; lectr. div. Allied Health nursing and pub. svc. Yavapai Coll. Team tchr. childbirth edn. Am. Soc. Childbirth Educators; bd. dirs. Tampa chpt. ARC. pres. Am. Cancer Soc. Sedona, Ariz. Unit, 1995—, co-chmn. adult edn. com.; founder Am. Cancer Soc. edn. dept. Sedona Med. Ctr.; bd. dirs. Ariz. State Divsn., mem. pub. edn. com.; county nursing ednl. cons. ARC, chmn. instrnl. com. on nursing and health, 1979-85. With USN, 1942-58, PTO; lt. USNR ret. Recipient cert. appreciation ARC, 1979, Dept. Health and Rehab. Svcs. award for Fla. Mental Health Inst. Svc., 1980, Cert. of Appreciation Am. Fgn. Svc. Assn., 1988. Internat. Coun. of Sex Edn. and Parenthood Am. U. fellow, 1981—. Mem. NAACOG (bd. dirs. Tampa chpt.), Nat. Assn. Pubs. Reps. (pres. 1965-66), Am. Soc. Psychoprophylaxis in Obstetrics (dir. 1970-71), Am. Soc. Childbirth Educators (co-founder, dir. 1972—), Internat. Coun. Women's Health Issues (chmn. resources com.), Health Edn. Media Assn., Nursing Educators Assn. Tampa, Lions (bd. dirs. Found. Ariz., pres. Sedona club). Author: Economics of Structured Continuing Education in Selected Professional Journals'; contbr. chpts. to Childbirth Education: A Nursing Perspective; contbr. articles to profl. jours. Home: 235 Arrowhead Dr Sedona AZ 86351-8900 Office: PO Box 2282 Sedona AZ 86339-2282

SASSER, TEIKO TAKIZAWA, educator; b. Ina, Nagano, Japan; came to U.S., 1958; d. Gensuke and Yoshino (Kanazawa) Takizawa; m. Warren Joseph Sasser, Sept. 30, 1957; children: Gary, Audrey, Kay. BA, Calif. State U., Sacramento, 1982. Instr. Japanese Lang. Sch., Sacramento, Calif., 1969-81; instrl. asst. Tant. C.C., Sacramento, 1979-90; instr. Los Rios C.C., Sacramento, 1990—. Mem. AAUW. Avocations: ceramics, opera.

SASSOON, JANET, ballerina, educator; b. Sorabaya, Indonesia, Sept. 2, 1936; came to U.S., 1937; d. Edward and Flora (Bar) S.; m. John Roland Upton Jr., Aug. 7, 1983. Began training with Christensen brothers, Ruby Asquith, and Gisella Caccialanza, San Francisco; Studied with Leo Staats, Lubov Egorova, Olga Preobrajenska, Mathilde Kshessinskaya, Paris, 1951. Dancer Grand Ballet du Marquis de Cuevas, Paris, 1952-55, Chgo., Utah and San Francisco Ballets, 1955; prima ballerina Berlin Ballet, 1956; dir. Acad. of Ballet, San Francisco, 1974-89, assoc. dir., 1989-97; coach master classes in ballet, profl. dancers including Natalia Makarova, Karen Averty, Wes Chapman, Jean Charles Gil, others. Avocations: cooking, gardening, writing. Home: 1112 Pine St Calistoga CA 94515-1734

SATER, WILLIAM FREDERICK, history educator, writer; b. N.Y.C., Nov. 17, 1937; 1 child, Rachel Mayen. AB in History, Stanford U., 1959; MA, UCLA, 1964, PhD, 1968. Prof. history Calif. State U., Long Beach, 1967—; cons. Rand Corp., Calif., 1977-90, Mellon Fellowship Found., 1982-88, NEH, 1983, ABC Clio, 1985—, Libr. Congress, 1988—; book rev. editor The New World, 1984-90; guest lectr. Peace Corps, L.A., 1967, U. Chile, Santiago, 1968, UCLA, 1972, U. Concepcion, Chile, 1975, Cath. U., Santiago, 1980, U. Calgary, 1983, 87, 96, Western Can. Mil. Soc., 1983, 96; papers presented at Am. Hist. Assn., 1972, 76, Pacific Coast Conf. L.Am. History, 1972, Nat. Assn. Pvt. Schs., 1983, Conf. on Independence of Mex., U. Calif., Irvine, 1987, Can. Hist. Assn., 1990, 94, Rocky Mountain Conf. L.Am. History, Soc. for Mil. History, Ont., 1993. Editor, assoc. editor, book rev. editor The History Tchr., 1972-85; mng. editor TVI Report, 1984—; author: The Revolutionary Left and Terrorist Violence in Chile, 1986, Puerto Rican Terrorists: A Possible Threat to U.S. Energy Installations?, 1981, The Heroic Image in Chile, 1973, The History Teacher, 1981, The Research Guide to Andean History, 1981, The Southern Cone Nations, 1984, Chile and the War of the Pacific, 1986, Chile and the United States, 1990, A General History of Chile, 1996; contbr. articles to profl. jours. 1st lt. U.S. Army, 1959-60. Fellow U. Calif.-U. Chile, 1965-66, Orgn. Am. States, 1974-75; recipient Barros Arana Internat. Contest on Chilean History, Chilean Hist. Assn., 1984. Mem. Chilean Acad. History (corr.), Pacific Coast of L.Am. Studies (bd. govs., Hubert Herring award), Conf. on L.Am. History (chmn. com. teaching and teaching materials, chmn. andean studies com., acting chmn. Rio de la Plata com.), Am. Hist. Assn. Office: Calif State U Dept History Long Beach CA 90840

SATEREN, TERRY, theater technical production; b. Madison, Wis., Dec. 5, 1943; s. Leland Bernhard and Eldora (Johnson) S. BA, Augsburg Coll., 1968. Tech. prodn. dir. Guthrie Theatre, Mpls., 1974-78, dir. prodn., 1985-87; dir. exhibits Sci. Mus. Minn., St. Paul, 1978-85; tech. prodn. dir. Seattle Repertory Theatre, 1987-97; cons. acad. and community theaters and museums, 1974—, U. Minn., 1992; Master class lectr. U. Wash., Seattle, 1989-91; adj. prof. U. Wash., 1991-92. Designer: (operas) Three Penny Opera, 1972, Newest Opera in the World, 1972, Don Giovanni, 1973; commd. sculptor numerous inds., chs. and acad. instns., 1966—. Pres.'s scholar Valparaiso (Ind.) U., 1967. Mem. U.S. Inst. Theatre Tech. Avocations: scuba diving, mountain climbing, travel, museums. Home: 7341 23rd Ave NW Seattle WA 98117-5661

SATHER, SYLVIA CAROLYN, science educator, consultant; b. Morris, Minn., Feb. 27, 1944; d. Ralph Jennings and Clara Randina (Morseth) S. BA, Augusburg Coll., Mpls., 1966; MS, U. No. Colo., Greeley, 1976. Cert. elem. edn., phys. edn., gifted and talented, sci. and health endorsements. 3rd grade tchr. Mpls. Pub. Schs., 1966-68; tchr. grades 1-6 gifted/talented Denver Pub. Schs., 1968—, tchr. mid. sch. sci., math., 1987-92, tchr. biology H.S., 1992—; tchr. Denver Sch. Arts, 1997—; cons. Energy & Mans Environ., Salt Lake City, 1970-82; prof. Colo. Sch. Mines, Golden, 1975-90; grad. asst. U. Denver, 1980-81. Author: Best of Energy, 1977, Energy Man's Environment, 1971-76. Mem. Nat. Sci. Tchrs. Assn., Phi Delta Kappa. Democrat. Avocations: potter, furniture maker, naturalist, ornithologist, travel. Home: 2795 S Ingalls Way Denver CO 80227-3825

SATO, GLENN KENJI, lawyer; b. Honolulu, Jan. 6, 1952; s. Nihei and Katherine (Miwa) S.; m. Donna Mae Shiroma, Apr. 4, 1980 (dec. Aug. 1985); m. Nan Sun Oh, Mar. 27, 1987 (dec. Nov. 1997); children: Gavan, Allison, Garrett. BBA, U. Hawaii, 1975; JD, U. Calif., San Francisco, 1977. Bar: Hawaii 1978, U.S. Dist. Ct. Hawaii, 1978, U.S. Ct. Claims 1990. Assoc. Fujiyama, Duffy & Fujiyama, Honolulu, 1978-80, 83-87, ptnr., 1987-95; stockholder Law Offices of Glenn K. Sato, Honolulu, 1980-82; pres. ISL Svcs., Inc., Honolulu, 1983; ptnr. Sato & Thomas, Honolulu, 1995-98; pvt. practice Honolulu, 1998—; vice chmn. Pattern Jury Instrn. Com., State of Hawaii, Honolulu, 1993. *In twenty years of practicing trial law, Mr. Sato has tried many multi-million dollar cases. In 1990 and 1991, he tried two cases for six months and won both cases. In 1996, he formed the Asian American Publishing Group, Ltd., which publishes business news from The People's Republic of China. His publishing company has a contract with Xinhua News Agency to publish business news and conduct consulting work for foreign business and trade with China.* Treas. Polit. Action Com., Honolulu, 1993. mem. Platform Assn., Beta Gamma Sigma. Avocations: golf, hunting, target shooting, surfing. Office: 1001 Bishop St Ste 770 Honolulu HI 96813-3429

SATO, TADASHI, artist; b. Maui, Hawaii, Feb. 6, 1923. Student, Honolulu Sch. Art, Bklyn. Mus. Art Sch., New Sch. Soc. Rsch. One man shows include First Hawaiian Ctr., Honolulu, 1997-98, The Contemporary Museum at First Hawaiian Bank, 1997; exhbns. include Guggenheim Mus., N.Y.C., 1954, Honolulu Acad. Arts, 1957, Pacific Heritage Exhibit, L.A., 1963, McRoberts and Tunnard Ltd., London, 1964, White House Festival Arts, Washington, 1965, Berlin Art Festival, 1967, Japanese C. of C., Honolulu, 1993-94, Maui Cmty. and Cultural Assn., 1994; represented in permanent collections Albright-Knox Art Gallery, Buffalo, Guggenheim Mus., Whitney Mus. Am. Art, N.Y.C., Honolulu Acad. Arts, U. Art Gallery, Tucson, (mosaic) Hawaii State Capitol Bldg., State Libr. Aina Haina, Oahu, State Hosp., Kea-lakekua, Hawaii, Wailulu War Meml. Gymnasium, Maui, Krannert Art Mus., Ill., U. Nebr.; murals executed Halekulani Hotel, Honolulu, (mosaic) West Maui Recreation Ctr., (oil) Bay Club, Kapalua, Maui, (oil) ballroom of Hawaii Conv. Ctr., Honolulu; retrospective exhbn. Hui No Eau, Makawao, Maui, 1992. Office: PO Box 476 Lahaina HI 96767-0476

SATRE, RODRICK IVERSON, environmental consultant, business developer; b. Geneseo, N.Y., July 14, 1951; s. Roy Ingvold Jr. and Patricia Ruth (Holder) S.; m. Bonita Daley, Sept. 30, 1978. BS in Chem. Engring., Clarkson U., 1973; MBA in Internat. Bus., John F. Kennedy U., 1989. Plant engr., then operating asst. Chevron Chem. Co., Richmond, Calif., 1974-78, area supr., 1978-80; sr. analyst Chevron Chem. Co., San Francisco, 1980-85; group leader, then sr. rsch. engr. Chevron Chem. Co., Richmond, 1985-89; mgr. Internat. Tech. Corp., Martinez, Calif., 1990—; prin. SSD Consulting, Point Richmond, Calif., 1990-92; gen. mgr. Internat. Tech. Corp., Houston, 1992-93; mng. prin. engr. Harding Lawson Assocs., Novato, Calif., 1993-95; project dir. TRC/Environ. Solutions, Inc., Walnut Creek, Calif., 1995-96; assoc. Blasland, Bouck & Lee Inc., Novato, Calif., 1996-97; engring. mgr. ATI Engring. Svcs., San Francisco, 1997—; prin. assoc. Kertesz Internat., Inc., San Francisco, 1990—. Patentee in field. Sci. judge Richmond Unified Sch. Dist., 1985—; pres. Point Richmond Neighborhood Coun., 1996—; co-chair environ. task force Contra Costa Coun., 1996-98. Mem. AIChE, PEMA, PRNC (pres. 1996—), Contra Costa Coun. (co-chair environ. task force), Hazardous Waste Assn. Calif., Berkeley Ski Club (v.p. 1978-79, pres. 1981-82). Republican. Avocations: classic cars, sailing, skiing, travel. Office: ATI Engring Svcs Inc 944 Market St Ste 700 San Francisco CA 94102-4020

SATTLER, BRUCE WEIMER, lawyer; b. South Gate, Calif., July 30, 1944; s. LeRoy Edward and Mary Beth (Weimer) S.; m. Earle Martha Ross, July 22, 1972. BA, Stanford U., 1966, JD, 1969. Bar: Colo. 1969, U.S. Dist. Ct. Colo. 1969, U.S. Dist. Ct. Mont. 1982, U.S. Dist. Ct. (no. dist.) Tex. 1989, U.S. Ct. Appeals (10th cir.) 1969, U.S. Ct. Appeals (9th cir.) 1984, U.S. Ct. Appeals (5th cir.) 1972. Assoc. Holland & Hart, Denver, 1969-75, ptnr., 1975-87; assoc. Equal Employment Opportunity Commn., Denver, 1973, Morris, Lower & Sattler, Denver, 1987-90; ptnr. Faegre & Benson, Denver, 1990—. Bd. dirs. ACLU of Colo., Denver, 1975-80, 88-94, Legal Aid Soc. of Metro Denver, 1976—, Colo. Lawyers Com., Denver, 1990-94, Children's Legal Clinic, Denver, 1989-91, Colo. Women's Employment and Edn., Denver, 1986-89. Fellow Am. Coll. Trial Lawyers; mem. ABA, Denver Bar Assn., Colo. Bar Assn. Office: Faegre & Benson 370 17th St Ste 2400 Denver CO 80202-5665

SATTLER, JOAN LESSING, consultant; b. Hollywood, Calif., Nov. 26, 1944; d. Lessing Robert and Ruth Isabel (Chamberlain) Sattler; children: Robert Garrett, Gregory Garrett, Laura Garrett. BA, San Jose State U., 1970; postgrad., U. Calif. Cert. in non-profit orgn.mgmt., mktg. comm., human resources adminstr. and tng. Cons. to health and human svc. govtl. and non-profit orgns. Civilian Pers. Office, Fort Ord, Calif., 1993-94; ptnr. Millson, Sattler and Assocs.; bd. dirs. Growth and Opportunity, Inc, Am. Red Cross, 1990-94; cons. Saving Our Libr.'s Excellence Com. 1992-93. Pub. info. officer San Benito County (Calif.) United Way, bd. dirs., 1988-90; founding mem. San Benito County Vol. Ctr. Task Force, San Benito County Cable Access Commn., 1987-90; co-founder San Benito County Action Team; vice chair San Benito County Voluntary Orgns. Active in Disasters, 1990-91; appointed to cen. com. ARC No. Calif. Earthquake Relief and Preparedness Project, 1991; pres. Network of San Benito, 1988-90; mem. San Benito County Econ. Group, Mex. Am. Com. on Edn., 1970—, Hollister Sister Cities Assn., 1989—; sec. bd. dirs., overall econ. devel. plan com. Econ. Devel. Corp.; exec. dir. San Benito County Interfaith, 1990-91; chmn. adv. com. San Benito Health Found., 1991—; pub. rels. chair San Benito County AIDS Project, 1992-94; chair policy adv. com. San Benito Health Found.; mem. YMCA Task Force; active numerous non-profit and civic orgns.; bd. dirs ARC. Mem. AAUW, San Benito County C. of C., Phi Alpha Theta, Psi Chi, Alpha Kappa Delta. Democrat. Roman Catholic. Avocations: dancing, piano, swimming, hiking. Home: 845 Helen Dr Hollister CA 95023-6613

SAUDEK, MARTHA FOLSOM, artist, educator; b. Palo Alto, Calif., Nov. 27, 1923; d. David Morrill and Clinton Erwin (Stone) Folsom; m. William Morrison Kingsley, Dec. 3, 1943 (div. 1971); 1 child, Lucy Clinton Kingsley; m. Victor Mead Saudek, Aug. 18, 1973. BA, Pomona Coll., 1947. Tchr. Concord (Calif.) Sch. Dist., 1949-51; tchr. Hermosa Beach (Calif.) City Schs., 1966-76, adminstrv. asst. to supt., 1977-81. Contbg. artist: (books) Painting With Passion, 1994, How to Paint Trees, Flowers, and Foliage, 1995, How to Paint Water, 1996. Sch. bd. dirs. Manhattan Beach (Calif.) Sch. Dist., 1964-72, pres., 1965. Named to Top 100, Arts for the Parks, 1994, 96, One of Nat. Gold Winners, Grumbacher Hall of Fame, 1995. Fellow Am. Artists' Profl. League; mem. Calif. Art Club (signature mem.), Knickerbocker Artists USA (signature mem.). Democrat. Avocations: photography, cooking, reading, gardening. Home: 5556B Rayo Del Sol Laguna Hills CA 92653-6903

SAUER, DAVID ANDREW, writer, computer consultant; b. Urbana, Ill., Feb. 25, 1948; s. Elmer Louis and Frances (Hill) S. BA, Northwestern U., 1970; MS, Simmons Coll., 1975. Reference libr. Boston U., 1976-78, bibliographer, 1978-84, sci. bibliographer, 1984-88, head Stone Sci. Libr., 1988-94; v.p. info. svcs. CyberHelp, Inc., 1995-98; sr. tech. editor Qualcomm Inc., 1997—. Co-author: Internet for Windows, 1994, WinComm Pro: The Visual Learning Guide, 1995, ProComm Plus V2 for Windows: The Visual Learning Guide, 1995, Access for Windows 95: The Visual Learning Guide, 1995, Cruising America Online 2.5, 1995, Internet for Windows: The America Online 2.5 Edition, 1995, Internet for Windows: The Microsoft Network Edition, 1995, Cruising the Microsoft Network, 1996, Cruising CompuServe, 1996, WinFax Pro 7 for Windows: The Visual Learning Guide, 1996, Windows NT 4.0 Visual Desk Reference, 1997, Discover Internet Explorer 4, 1997, Discover Netscape Communicator, 1997. Mem. S.W. Corridor Project, Boston, 1977-87, Forest Hills Neighborhood Improvement Assn., Boston, 1977-90, Forest Hills/Woodbourne Neighborhood Group, 1991-94. Mem. ALA, Spl. Librs. Assn., San Diego Computer Soc., Highland Casitas Homeowners Assn. (chmn. 1996—). Democrat. Home and Office: 1034 La Tierra Dr San Marcos CA 92069-4617

SAUL, WALTER BIDDLE, II, music educator, composer; b. Phila., Apr. 19, 1954; s. Richard Marshall and Suzanne (Mosher) S.; m. Daphne Lois Johnson, June 28, 1980; children: Charity Elizabeth, Mary Anne. AB in Music summa cum laude, Duke U., 1976; MusM in Music Composition, Eastman Sch. Music, 1979, DMA in Music Composition, 1980. Instr. music Ea. Ill. U., Charleston, 1981; asst. prof. music Pfeiffer Coll., Misenheimer, N.C., 1982-87; assoc. prof. music Warner Pacific Coll., Portland, Oreg., 1987-94, prof. music, 1994—; adj. prof. music U. Portland, 1990—; commd. composer Oreg. Music Tchrs. Assn., 1990, N.C. Music Tchrs. Assn., 1986. Composer over 103 works. Mem. ASCAP (writing and pub. mem., Spl. Composer awards 1990-98), Music Tchrs. Nat. Assn. (cert. tchr. music in piano and composition). Republican. Methodist. Avocations: bicycling, collecting and repairing clocks, Bible study. Office: Warner Pacific Coll 2219 SE 68th Ave Portland OR 97215-4099

SAUNDERS, BRIAN KEITH, consulting company executive; b. Columbus, Ohio, June 4, 1961. BSEE, Purdue U., 1983; MBA, Dartmouth U., 1988. Asst. mgr. engring. New Eng. Telephone, Boston, 1983-85, asst. product mgr., 1985-86; assoc. Booz Allen & Hamilton, N.Y.C., 1987-90; dir. strategy and planning Pacific Bell, San Ramon, Calif., 1991-92; gen. mgr. Compus Svcs. Corp., Pleasanton, Calif., 1993-94; prin. cons., designer BKS Design, San Ramon, Calif., 1994—; sr. prin. The McKenna Group, Palo Alto, Calif., 1995-97; chief synergist The BKS Group, San Ramon, Calif., 1997—; bd. dirs. Children's Media Lab., Berkeley, Calif., 1993-97, Family Stress Ctr., Concord, Calif., 1995-97; mem. industry coun. Mt. Diablo Coll., Pleasant Hill, Calif., 1993-95; mem. exec. coun. Tuck MBEP Alumni Assn. Dartmouth Coll., Hanover, N.H., 1994—. Mem. Computer Game Developers Assn., Bay Area Video Coalition, MDG.org., World Future Soc., Armed Forces Comms. and Electronics Assn. Avocations: jazz, history, science fiction, martial arts.

SAUNDERS, DEBRA J., columnist; b. Newton, Mass., Dec. 8, 1954. BA in Latin and Greek, U. Mass., Boston, 1980. Asst. dir. Arnold Zenker Assocs., 1982-83; writer/rschr., account exec. Todd Domke Assocs., Sacramento, 1983-84, Russo Watts & Rollins, Sacramento, 1985-86; asst. to Rep. Leader Calif. Assembly, Sacramento, 1987-88; columnist, editl. writer L.A. Daily News, 1988-92; columnist San Francisco Chronicle, 1992—; leader study group on polit. speechmaking Harvard U., Cambridge, Mass., 1984; tchr. editl. and column writing UCLA Ext., 1992. Published in Wall St. Jour., Nat. Review, Weekly Std., Reason mag.; syndicated nationally via Creators Syndicate; appeared on Politically Incorrect, CNN and BBC radio. Office: San Francisco Chronicle 901 Mission St San Francisco CA 94103-2905

SAUNDERS, JAMES, management and training consultant; b. Chgo., Sept. 22, 1924; s. James Windam and Carrie Evelyn (Cox) S.; m. Gwendolyn Haithcox, Oct. 21, 1945 (dec. May 1971); children: Patricia Ann, Kathryn Lynn; m. Anita Joanne Laster, Sept. 16, 1972 (div. Oct. 1977); m. Bettye Jean Ricks, Apr. 18, 1981. BS in Math., Roosevelt U., 1953. Quality assurance rep. Dept. Army and Signal Corps., Chgo., 1945-63; dep. dir. quality assurance U.S. Naval Ordnance Plant, Forest Park, Ill., 1963-70; quality systems mgr. Gen. Foods Corp., Chgo., 1970-82; pres. Saunders and Assocs., Peoria, Ariz., 1982-91; councilman, vice mayor City of Peoria, 1985-91; examiner Ariz. Govs. Alliance for Quality, 1995. Bd. dirs., sec. Ariz. Retirement Ctrs., Peoria, 1984-85; pres., chmn., bd. dirs., founder Peoria Econ. Devel. Group, 1987-91, dir. emeritus, 1991—; mem. Peoria Personnel Bd., 1984-85, Maricopa County Pvt. Industry Coun., 1984-89, chmn., 1988-89, exec. com. Westside Transp. Coalition, Peoria, 1988-89. Recipient Black Achiever of Industry award Chgo. YMCA, 1977, Image Govt. award NAACP, 1989, also various other awards. Mem. Peoria C. of C. (v.p., bd. dirs. 1985), Westside Coalition Chambers Commerce, Lions (sec., v.p. Peoria chpt. 1983-86), Kiwanis, Masons, Alpha Phi Alpha. Avocations: travel, golf, photography, reading. Home: 18847 N 88th Dr Peoria AZ 85382-8528

SAUNDERS, JAMES HARWOOD, accountant; b. Carlsbad, N.Mex., Apr. 2, 1948; s. Eugene C. and Ruth (Powelson)S.; m. Kathleen Sue Matson, Jan. 26, 1974 (div. Apr. 1982); m. Bette Kim McCutcheon, Sept. 4, 1982 (div. Oct. 1997); children: James C., Carl J., William K. AA in Adminstrn. Justice, Glendale Coll., Glendale, Ariz., 1975; BSBA, Ariz. State U., 1978. CPA, N.M., Ariz., Colo., Nev., Utah; lic. funeral dir. and embalmer; cert. fraud examiner; lic. pvt. investigator. Embalmer Denton Funeral Home, Carlsbad, 1964-69; clk., trainee Sears & Roebuck Co., Dallas and Albu-

querque, 1969-71, Phoenix, 1971-73; police sgt. spl. ops. Phoenix Police Dept., 1973-80; staff acct. various CPA firms, Carlsbad, 1980-83; owner James H. Saunders Acctg., Carlsbad, 1983-86; pvt. practice acctg. Eagar, Ariz., 1987—; auditor, mgmt. advisor to several Ariz. municipalities, 1987—. Vol. fireman Carlsbad Fire Dept., 1965-68; reserve dep. Bermallio County Sheriff Dept., Albuquerque, 1969-70. Mem. AICPA, Ariz. Soc. CPAs, N.Mex. Soc. CPAs, N.Mex. Assn. Funeral Dirs., Lions (sec. Carlsbad chpt. 1985-87, pres. Springerville, Ariz. chpt. 1987-91). Avocations: coin collecting, hunting, fishing, old movies, reading. Office: PO Box 1270 74 N Main Eagar AZ 85925

SAUSSY, CALEB POWELL HAUN, Asian language educator; b. Nashville, Feb. 15, 1960; s. Frederick Tupper III and Lola Norwood (Haun) S.; m. Yu-Lin Wang, 1987; children: Juliana, Caleb. BA, Duke U., 1981; MPhil, Yale U., 1987, PhD, 1990. Asst. prof. UCLA, 1991-95; assoc. prof. Stanford U., Palo Alto, Calif., 1996—. Author: The Problem of Chinese Aesthetic, 1993. Office: Stanford U Dept Asian Langs Bldg 50 Stanford CA 94305

SAVAGE, CYNTHIA GAIL, business owner; b. Stuttgart, Germany, Feb. 15, 1958; d. Roscoe E. and Frances M. Savage. BS, San Jose State Univ., 1986; postgrad., Monterey Inst., 1993. Owner Honey Bears Deli Cafe, Pacific Grove, Calif., 1991-93, Imusination Music Pub., Pacific Grove, Calif., 1997—. Composer numerous songs. Mem. Eta Phi Beta, Beta Gamma (pres., 1978-81). Address: 102 S 14th St #10 San Jose CA 95112

SAVAGE, ERIC WAYNE, multimedia developer; b. San Francisco, Jan. 21, 1957; s. Hugh Allen and Beverly Nannette (Anderson) S.; m. Jennifer Sue Baker, June 13, 1992; children: Jessica, Jonathan, David, Rebecca. AA, Polk C.C., 1977; BS, Ariz. State U., 1980; MS, Colo. Tech. U., 1995. Freelance prodr. Flying S Video Svcs., Tempe, Ariz., 1980-85; graphic designer Kroy Inc., Scottsdale, Ariz., 1985-86, media svcs. mgr., 1986-90; media prodn. specialist Lockheed Tech. Ops. Co., Sunnyvale, Calif., 1990-92; sr. media prodn. specialist Lockheed Tech. Ops. Co., Colorado Springs, Colo., 1992-95; engr. instr. Lockheed Martin Tech. Ops., Denver, 1995-96, tech. instrn. specialist, 1996—. Recipient Visual Comms. Dept. of Yr. award Assn. Visual Comms., 1989. Mem. Nat. Mgmt. Assn. Home: 4631 Hotspur Dr Colorado Springs CO 80922-1715 Office: Lockheed Martin Tech Ops PO Box 31189 Aurora CO 80041-0189

SAVAGE, JOHN WILLIAM, lawyer; b. Seattle, Oct. 11, 1951; s. Stanley and Jennie Sabina (Siggstedt) S.; m. Rebecca Lee Abraham, Oct. 1, 1983; children: Bennett William, James Oliver. Student Lewis and Clark Coll., 1969-71; B.A., U. Wash., 1973; J.D., Northwestern Sch. Law, Lewis and Clark Coll., 1977. Bar: Oreg. 1977, U.S. Dist. Ct. Oreg. 1977, U.S. Ct. Appeals (9th cir.) 1977, U.S. Supreme Ct. 1985. Pvt. practice law, Portland, Oreg., 1977-79; ptnr. Bailey, Olstad, Rieke, Geil & Savage, P.C., Portland, 1979-80; ptnr., shareholder Rieke, Geil & Savage, P.C. Portland, 1980-95, shareholder Rieke & Savage, P.C., Portland, 1995—; mem. Oreg. Literacy Inc., Portland, 1979-85. Mem. standing com. City Club, Portland, 1984-88, chmn. law and pub. safety standing com. 1986-87. Mem. ABA (chairperson young lawyers sect. Nat. Community Law Week 1983-84, inmate grievance com. 1984-88), Assn. Trial Lawyers Am., Trial Lawyers for Pub. Justice, Oreg. Trial Lawyers Assn., Oreg. Bar Assn. (def. of indigent accused com. 1985-89), Oreg. Criminal Def. Lawyers Assn. (bd. dirs. 1984-86), Multnomah Bar Assn. (v.p. young lawyers sect. 1980, pres.-elect 1981, pres. 1982, Disting. Svc. award, bd. dirs. 1989-92, task force chair 1992-93, jud. selection com. 1996—, award of merit, 1994). Home: 397 Furnace St Lake Oswego OR 97034-3957 Office: Rieke & Savage PC 140 SW Yamhill St Portland OR 97204-3007

SAVAGE, TERRY RICHARD, information systems executive; b. St. Louis, Oct. 21, 1930; s. Terry Barco and Ada Vanetta (Cochran) S.; m. Gretchen Susan Wood, Sept. 26, 1964; children: Terry Curtis, Christopher William, Richard Theodore. AB, Washington U., St. Louis, 1951, MA, 1952; PhD, U. Pa., 1954. Mgr. system software IBM Rsch., Yorktown Heights, N.Y., 1956-63; dir. data processing Documentation Inc., Bethesda, Md., 1963-64; mgr. info. systems Control Data Corp., Rockville, Md., 1964-67; dir. rsch. Share Rsch. Corp., Santa Barbara, Calif., 1967-68; computer-aided acquisition and logistic support program mgr. TRW, Redondo Beach, Calif., 1968-92; ret., ind. cons. pvt. practice, 1992—; expert witness for various coms. U.S. Congress, 1981, 84, 88, 89. Contbr. articles to profl. jours. Bd. dirs. ABC-Clio Press, Santa Barbara, 1970-75, Help the Homeless Help Themselves, Rancho Palos Verdes, Calif., 1988-94, ChorusLiners, Rancho Palos Verdes, 1983—, Savage Info. Svcs., Inc., Torrance, Calif., 1992—. Mem. Cosmos Club. Home and Office: 30000 Cachan Pl Rancho Palos Verdes CA 90275-5412

SAVAGE, THOMAS WARREN, engineering manager; b. Morgantown, W.Va., Feb. 6, 1959; s. Thomas Louis Savage and Sandra Mabel (Ferguson) Crawford; m. Cydney Ellen Fry, May 8, 1981; children: Jessica Louise, Kristin Anne, Thomas Dylan. BS in Computer Engring., Santa Clara U., 1993. Electronic technician ITT North, Galion, Ohio, 1977-79; electronic test engr. Fairchild Test Systems, San Jose, Calif., 1979-82; design engr. Tandem Computers, Cupertino, Calif., 1982-94; engring. mgr. Tandem Computers, Cupertino, 1994-95; dir. Synopsys Inc., Mountain View, Calif., 1995—. Patentee in field. Mem. Order of the Engr. Avocations: archaeology, baseball, golf, skiing. Home: 1648 Capitancillos Pl San Jose CA 95120-5701 Office: Synopsys Inc PO Box 7670 Mountain View CA 94039-7670

SAVERY, MATTHEW, music conductor, director, educator; b. Berkshire County, Mass.. MusB, New Eng. Conservatory Music; MusM, U. Mich.; studied with Gustav Meier, Pascal Verrot, Frank Battisti. Music dir., conductor Symphonic Choir, 1994—, Butte Symphony Orch., 1994—, Bozeman (Mont.) Symphony Orch., 1994—; lectr. schs. Mont.; clincian Music Ekucators N.W. Conf., 1997; chmn. young artist competition Mont. Assn. Symphony Orch., 1997—. Music dir., conductor (theater) Damn Yankees, Guys and Dolls, Annie; past music dir. Comic Opera Guild, Ann Arbor, Mich., Stockbridge (Mass.) Sinfonia, Tecumseh (Mich.) Orch.; past conductor orch. festivals Mont. AA H.S.; appeared in , conductor Tchaikovsky's Nutcracker, 1995, 96, Tchaikovsky's Sleeping Beauty, The Magic Toy Shop. U. Mich. fellow; recipient Eugene and Sadie Power award for performing arts. Office: Bozeman Symphony Orch PO Box 1174 Bozeman MT 59771-1174*

SAVIN, RONALD RICHARD, chemical company executive, inventor; b. Cleve., Oct. 16, 1926; s. Samuel and Ada (Silver) S.; m. Gloria Ann Hopkins, Apr. 21, 1962; children: Danielle Elizabeth, Andrea Lianne. BA in Chemistry and Lit., U. Cin., 1944-46; BA in Chemistry and Literature, U. Mich., 1948; postgrad., Columbia U., 1948-49, Sorbonne, Paris, 1949-50; grad., Air War Coll., 1975, Indsl. Coll. Armed Forces, 1976. Pres., owner Premium Finishes, Inc., Cin., 1957-91; cons. aerospace and anti-corrosive coatings; inventor and owner Hyperseal Inc. Contbr. articles to profl. jours.; 15 patents in field. With USAF, 1948-55, World War II and Korea, col. Res. 1979, ret. 1986. Mem. Steel Structures Painting Coun., Nat. Assn. Corrosion Engrs., Fedn. Paint Techs., Fedn. Coatings Tech., Air Force Assn., Res. Officers Assn., Army Navy Club. Avocations: scientific development, photography, tennis.

SAVITRIPRIYA, SWAMI, Hindu religious leader, author; b. Apr. 1, 1930; divorced; three children. Ordained Hindu nun, Holy Order of Sannyas, 1975. Psychotherapist, 1970-75; founder, spiritual dir. Shiva-Shakti Kashmir Shaivite Hindu Ch., Ashram, Marin County, Calif., 1975-77, Shiva-Shakti Ashram, Oakland, Calif., 1978, Convent of the Divine Mother, Kona, Hawaii, 1979-80, Holy Mountain Monastery and Retreat Ctr., Groveland, Calif., 1984-92, Holy Mountain U., Groveland, Calif., 1985-92; founder, spiritual dir. Inst. for New Life, Groveland, Calif., 1990-92, Santa Cruz, Calif., 1993-95; founder, spiritual dir. Shiva-Shakti Ananda Ashram, Lake Chapala-San Juan Cosala, Jalisco, Mexico, 1995—. Author (books) [illegible] of Mystical Awakening: The Yoga Sutras, 1991, The Cloud of the [illegible] 1986, The Worlds of the Chakras, 1987, Arising Woman, 1988, Arising Man, 1988, Tantras of Personal and Spiritual Unfoldment, 1989, New World [illegible] 1989, [illegible] Bhagavad Gita, 1974, Narada Bhakti Sutras, 1976, Upanishads, 1981, Shiva Sutras, 1984, Pratyabhijnahridayam, 1987, Vijnana Bhairava, 1989, others. E-mail: savitrip@bgl.vshl.net.in. Office: Shiva-Shakti Ananda Ashram 9297 Siempre Viva Rd # 71-270 San Diego CA 92173-3601

SAVONA, MICHAEL RICHARD, physician; b. N.Y.C., Oct. 21, 1947; s. Salvatore Joseph and Diana Grace (Menditto) S.; m. Dorothy O'Neill, Oct. 18, 1975. BS summa cum laude, Siena Coll., 1969; MD, SUNY, Buffalo, 1973. Diplomate Am. Bd. Internal Medicine. Intern in internal medicine Presbyn. Hosp. Columbia U., N.Y.C., 1973-74, resident in internal medicine, 1974-76; vis. fellow internal medicine Delafield Hosp./Columbia U. Coll. Physicians and Surgeons, N.Y.C., 1974-76; practice medicine specializing in internal medicine Maui Med. Group, Wailuku, Hawaii, 1976-87, gen. practice medicine, 1987—; dir. ICU, Maui Meml. Hosp., also dir. respiratory therapy, CCU., chmn. dept. medicine, 1980—; clin. faculty John A. Burns Sch. Medicine, U. Hawaii, asst. prof. medicine, 1985—, asst. rsch. prof., 1989—. Bd. dirs. Maui Heart Assn.; dir. profl. edn. Maui chpt. Am. Cancer Soc.; mem. Maui County Hosp. Adv. Commn.; mem. coun. Community Cancer Program of Hawaii. Recipient James A. Gibson Wayne J. Atwell award, 1970, physiology award, 1970, Ernest Whitebsky award, 1971, Roche Lab. award, 1972, Pfiser Lab. award, 1973, Phillip Sang award, 1973, Hans Lowenstein M.D. Meml. award, 1973. Mem. AMA, Am. Thoracic Soc., Hawaii Thoracic Soc., Maui County Med. Assn. (past pres.), Hawaii Med. Assn., Hawaii Oncology Group, ACP, SW Oncology Coop. Group, Alpha Omega Alpha, Delta Epsilon Sigma. Office: 1830 Wells St Wailuku HI 96793-2365

SAVOY, DOUGLAS EUGENE, bishop, religion educator, explorer, writer; b. Bellingham, Wash., May 11, 1927; s. Lewis Dell and Maymie (Janett) S.; m. Elvira Clarke, Dec. 5, 1957 (div.); 1 son, Jamil Sean (dec.); m. Sylvia Ontaneda, July 7, 1971; children: Douglas Eugene, Christopher Sean, Sylvia Jamila. Student, U. Portland, 1947-8; DST, D Canon and Sacred Law, Jamilian U. of the Ordained, 1980; PhD in Theology, DD (hon.), Tech. Inst. Bibl. Studies, Nev., 1990. Ordained to ministry Internat. Community of Christ Ch., 1962, bishop, 1971. Head bishop Internat. Community of Christ Ch., 1971—; lectr. in ministerial tng. studies, 1972—; pastor Univ. Chapel, Reno, 1979—; founder Jamilian Parochial Sch., 1976; chancellor, founder Sacred Coll. of Jamilian Theology; pres., founder Jamilian U. of the Ordained, 1980; pres. Advs. for Religious Rights and Freedoms; chmn. World Coun. for Human Spiritual Rights, 1984—; head Jamilian Order of Patriarchs, 1990—; engaged in newspaper pub. West Coast, 1949-56; began explorations in jungles east of Andes in Peru to prove his theory that high civilizations of Peru may have had their origin in jungles, 1967; pres., founder Andean Explorers Found & Ocean Sailing Club, Reno; expedition dir. Grand Ophir Sea Expedition; capt. Feathered Serpent III-Ophir, 1997—. Author: Antisuyo, The Search for Lost Cities of the High Amazon, 1970, Vilcabamba, Last City of the Incas, 1970, The Cosolargy Papers, vol. 1, 1970, vol. 2-3, 1972, The Child Christ, 1973, Arabic edit., 1976, Japanese edit., 1981, The Decoded New Testament, 1974, Arabic edit., 1981, Millenium Edition, 1983, On The Trail of The Feathered Serpent, 1974, Code Book and Community Manual for Overseers, 1975, Prophecies of Jamil, First Prophecy to the Americas, vol. 1, 1976, Second Prophecy to the Americas, 1976, The Secret Sayings of Jamil, The Image and the Word, vol. 1, 1976, vol. 2, 1977, Project X—The Search For the Secrets of Immortality, 1977, Prophecy to the Races of Man, Vol. 2, 1977, Solar Cultures of The Americas, 1977, Dream Analysis, 1977, Vision Analysis, 1977, Christoanalysis, 1978, The Essaei Document: Secrets of an Eternal Race, 1978, Millennium edit., 1983, The Lost Gospel of Jesus: Hidden Teachings of Christ, 1978, Millennium edit., 1983, Secret Sayings of Jamil, vol. 3., 1978, vol. 4, 1979, Prophecy to The Christian Churches, vol. 3, 1978, The Sayings, vol. 4, 1979, Solar Cultures of Oceania, 1979, Prophecy of The End Times, vol. 4, 1980, Solar Cultures of Israel, vols. 1 and 2, 1980, Solar Cultures of China, 1980, Christotherapy, 1980, Christophysics, 1980, Christodynamics, 1980, Code Book of Prophecy, 1980, The Sayings, vol. 5, 1980, vol. 6, 1981, Solar Cultures of India, 1981, Prophecy on the Golden Age of Light and the Nation of Nations, Vol. 5, 1981, Solar Cultures of Israel, vol. 3, 1981, The Counsels, 1982, Prophecy of the Universal Theocracy, vol. 6, 1982, Prophecy of the New Covenant, vol. 7, 1982, The Book of God's Revelation, 1983, Miracle of the Second Advent, 1984, Clerical Studies in Theology, Book I, Book II, Book III, Book IV, Transformative Theology: The School of Revelation, Transformative Theology: The School of Prophecy, Liturgical Theology: Preparation for Advanced Degrees, 1993; over 400 audio tape rec. lectures, 1974—, numerous others.; dir. documentary film Adventure: Trail of the Feathered Serpent, 1970, Lost City of the Andes, 1987; wrote, dir. videos Royal Roads to Discovery, Mystery of the Essenes of Old Israel, Secrets From the High Andes of Peru, 1993, The Gran Vilaya Expeditions, 1996; contbr. articles on Peruvian cultures to mags., also articles on philosophy and religion; discoverer lost city of Incas at Vilcabamba Cuzco, numerous ancient cities in Amazonia including Gran Pajaten, Gran Vilaya, Monte Peruvia, Twelve Cities of the Condor. Trustee in Trust Head Bishop Internat. Community of Christ. Served with AS USNR, 1944-46. Decorated Order of the Grand Cross Senate of Peru, 1989; recipient Participant's medallion Seawanhaka Yacht Club, 1977; Gold medal Ministry Industry and Tourism Peru, Silver Hummingbird, 1987; Silver medal and scroll City of Ica, Peru; honored with Gene Savoy Day by City of Reno, 1996, numerous exploring awards. Mem. Geog. Soc. Lima, Andean Explorers Found., Ocean Sailing Club (Explorer of the Century 1989, Flag awards), World Coun. for Human Spiritual Rights, Advs. for Religious Rights and Freedoms, Authors Guild, Explorers Club (N.Y.C., Flag awards), L.A. Yacht Club. Home: 2025 La Fond Dr Reno NV 89509-3025 Office: 643 Ralston St Reno NV 89503-4436

SAVRUN, ENDER, engineering executive, researcher, engineer; b. Adana, Turkey, July 29, 1953; came to U.S., 1978; s. Yusuf and Nemide Savrun; m. Canan Erdamar, Oct. 23, 1979; children: Altay, Seray. BS, Istanbul (Turkey) Tech. U., 1976, MS, 1978; PhD, U. Wash., 1986. Rsch. engr. Charlton Industries, Redmond, Wash., 1984-85; rsch. scientist Flow Industries, Kent, Wash., 1985-87, Photon Scis., Bothell, Wash., 1987-88; mgr. rsch. Keramont Rsch. Corp., Tucson, 1988-89; v.p. R & D Keramont Corp., Tucson, 1989-92; founder, pres. Sienna Rsch., Inc., Tucson, 1992—. Contbr. articles to profl. jours.; patentee in field. Turkish Govt. scholar, 1979. Mem. Materials Rsch. Soc., Am. Soc. for Metals, Am. Ceramic Soc. Avocations: cross-country skiing, camping, travel.

SAWADA, IKUNE, artist; b. Hayashima, Japan, Aug. 30, 1936; arrived in U.S., 1969; s. Tomejiro and Tsurue (Kuwada) S. BA, Art Univ. Kyoto, Kyoto, Japan, 1960. Art tchr. Public Sch., Okayama, Osaka, Japan, 1960-65; antique dealer Kobe, Kyoto, Japan, 1965-69; artist Seattle, Wash., 1971-91, Walla Walla, Wash., 1991—. Recipient Lulu Fairbank award Internat. Understanding Through Students, 1970. Avocations: bonsai, music, travelling, gardening, reading. Home: 637 Pleasant Walla Walla WA 99362

SAWYER, THOMAS EDGAR, management consultant; b. Homer, La., July 7, 1932; s. Sidney Edgar and Ruth (Bickham) S.; m. Joyce Mezzanatto, Aug. 22, 1954; children: Jeffrey T., Scott A., Robert J., Julie Anne. BS, UCLA, 1959; MA, Occidental Coll., 1969; PhD, Walden U., 1990. Project engr. Garrett Corp., L.A., 1954-60; mgr. devel. ops. TRW Systems, Redondo Beach, Calif., 1960-66; spl. asst. to gov. State of Calif., Sacramento, 1967-69; prin., gen. mgr. Planning Rsch. Corp., McLean, Va., 1969-72; dep. dir. OEO, Washington, 1972-74; assoc. prof. bus. mgmt. Brigham Young U., 1974-78; pres., chmn. bd. Mesa Corp., Provo, Utah, 1978-82; pres. and dir. Sage Inst. Internat., Inc., Provo, Utah, 1982-88; chmn. bd., CEO Pvt. Telecom Networks, Inc. (name changed to Nat. Applied Computer Techs, Inc.), Orem, Utah, 1988-98; chief tech. officer GST Telecom. (formerly Greenstar Telecom., Inc.), San Francisco, 1993-98; also bd. dirs. GST Telecom. (formerly Greenstar Telecom., Inc.), Vancouver, Wash., 1995-98; chmn. bd. NeTrue Comm., Inc., Fullerton, Calif., 1998—; dir. Intechna Corp., HighTech Corp., Indian Affiliates, Inc., Greenstar USA, Inc., San Francisco, 1994-98, GST Global Comm., Inc., Vancouver, Can., 1998—, Highpoint Telecom., Inc., Vancouver, Can., 1998—, World Wide Wireless Comm., Inc., Salt Lake City, 1998—, Columbia Hosp., Orem, Utah 1998—. Author: Assimilation Versus Self-Identity: A Modern Native American Perspective, 1976, The Promise of Funding a New Educational Initiative Using the [illegible] through, Current Challenges of Welfare: A Review of Public Assitance as Distributive Justice, 1989, New Software Models for Training and Education Delivery, 1989, New Organizations: How They Deviate from Classical Models, 1989, Increasing Productivity in Organizations: [illegible] 1989, An Introduction and Assessment of Strategic Decision Making Paradigms in Complex Organizations, 1989, The Future of Technology in Education, 1989, Impact of Failure by Senior Executives to Receive Accurate Critical Feedback on Pervasive Change, 1990, The Influence of Critical Feedback and Organizational Climate on Managerial Decision Making, 1990. Chmn. Nat. Adv. Coun. Indian Affairs, Utah State Bd. Indian Affairs, So. Paiute Restoration Com.; mem. Utah Dist. Export Coun., Utah dist. SBA Coun.; mem. adv. coun. Nat. Bus. Assn.; mem. Utah Job Tng. Coordinating Coun. Served with USMC, 1950-53. Mem. ASPA, Am. Mgmt. Assn., Utah Coun. Small Bus. (dir.), Utah State Hist. Soc. (bd. dirs. 1993—), Masons. Republican. Mormon. Home: 548 W 630 S Orem UT 84058-6154 Office: 1450 E 820 N Orem UT 84097-5481

SAXE, STEVEN LOUIS, lawyer; b. San Francisco, May 28, 1942; s. Jules Irving and Marian (Adams) S.; m. Joanne Saxe, July 12, 1964; children: Julie Ann, Jeffrey Scott. BS, U. Calif., Berkeley, 1964; JD, U. San Francisco, 1967. Bar: Calif. 1967, U.S. Dist. Ct. (no. and ea. dist.) Calif. 1967. Clk. Calif. Ct. Appeals, San Francisco, 1967-68; assoc. Farella, Brown & Martel, San Francisco, 1968-69; sr. counsel Bank Am., San Francisco, 1969-80; ptnr. Boyden, Cooluris, Hauser & Saxe, San Francisco, 1980-91, Pillsbury, Madison & Sutro, San Francisco, 1991—. Dir. Ecumenical Assn. Housing, San Rafael, Calif., 1985-92; pres. Congregation Rodef Sholom, San Rafael, 1992-94; dir. Fair Housing Marin, San Rafael, 1995—. Mem. ABA, Consumer Bankers Assn., Coll. Am. Coll. Fin. Svcs. Lawyers. Office: Pillsbury Madison & Sutro 235 Montgomery St Fl 16 San Francisco CA 94104-3074

SAXENA, ARJUN NATH, physicist; b. Lucknow, India, Apr. 1, 1932; s. Sheo and Mohan (Piyari) Shanker; came to U.S., 1956, naturalized, 1976; BSc, Lucknow U., 1950, MSc, 1952, profl. cert. in German, 1954; Post MS diploma, Inst. Nuclear Physics, Calcutta, India, 1955; PhD, Stanford U., 1963; m. Veera Saxena, Feb. 9, 1956; children: Rashmi, Amol, Varsha, Ashvin. Rsch. asst. Stanford U., 1956-60; mem. tech. staff Fairchild Semicondr. Co., Palo Alto, Calif., 1960-65; dept. head Sprague Electric Co., North Adams, Mass., 1965-69; mem. tech. staff RCA Labs., Princeton, N.J., 1969-71; pres., chmn. bd. Astro-Optics, Phila., 1972; pres. Internat. Sci. Co., Princeton Junction, N.J., 1973—; disting. vis. scientist Centre de Récherches Nucléaires, Strasbourg, France, 1973, 77; sr. staff scientist, mgr. engring. Data Gen. Corp., Sunnyvale, Calif., 1975-80; mgr. process tech. Signetics Corp., Sunnyvale, 1980-81; Gould AMI scientist, dir. advanced process devel. Gould AMI Semicondrs., Santa Clara, Calif., 1981-87; dir. Ctr. for Integrated Electronics, prof. dept. elec. and computer system engring. Rensselaer Poly. Inst., Troy, N.Y., 1987-96, emeritus prof., 1996—; disting. vis. scientist Inst. Microelectronics, Stuttgart, Germany, 1993-94. Treas. Pack 66, Boy Scouts Am., W. Windsor, N.J., 1970-74. Recipient Disting. Citizen award State of N.J., 1975. Mem. IEEE (life), Stanford Alumni Assn. (life). Contbr. articles on semicondr. tech., optics, nuclear and high-energy physics to sci. jours., 1953—; patentee in field. FAX: 650-856-1794. Home: 4217 Pomona Ave Palo Alto CA 94306-4312

SAXENA, NARENDRA K., marine research educator; b. Agra, India, Oct. 15, 1936; came to U.S., 1969; s. Brijbasi Lal and Sarbati Saxena; children: Sarah Vasanti, Lorelle Sarita. Diploma Geodetic Engring., Tech. U., Hanover, Fed. Republic Germany, 1966; D in Tech Scis., Tech. U., Graz, Austria, 1972. Research assoc. geodetic sci. Ohio State U., Columbus, 1969-74; asst. prof. U. Ill., Urbana, 1974-78; asst. prof. U. Hawaii, Honolulu, 1978-81, assoc. prof., 1981-86, prof., 1986-97, dept. chmn., 1994-97; adj. research prof. Naval Postgrad. Sch., Monterey, Calif., 1984-87; co-chmn. Pacific Congresses on Marine Tech., Honolulu, 1984, 86, 88; pres. Pacon Internat. Inc., 1987—. Editor Jour. Marine Geodesy, 1976—. Mem. Neighborhood Bd., Honolulu, 1984. Fellow Marine Tech. Soc. (various offices 1974—); mem. Am. Geophys. Union, The Tsunami Soc. Office: U Hawaii Dept Civil Engring Honolulu HI 96822

SAXTON, LLOYD, psychologist, author; b. Loveland, Colo., Sept. 28, 1929; s. Oliver George and Alice Augusta (Andersen) S.; m. Nancy Alison Roberts, Dec. 17, 1955; children: Perry Brent, Jay Ronald, Barbara Jean. AB in English, U. Calif., Berkeley, 1950, BS in Psychology, 1954; MS in Psychology, San Francisco State U., 1955; PhD in Psychology, U. of the Pacific, Stockton, Calif., 1957. Diplomate Am. Bd. Forensic Examiners (cert. 1996); lic. psychologist, Calif. Intern in clin. psychology Childlren's Hosp., San Francisco, 1955-56; teaching fellow U. Pacific, San Francisco, 1955-57, instr. psychology, 1957-58, asst. prof. psychology, 1958-60; assoc. prof. psychology Am. Acad. of Asian Studies, San Francisco, 1960-62, prof. psychology, 1962-65; chmn. dept. psychology Coll. of San Mateo, Calif., 1965-75, prof. psychology, 1975-92; pvt. practice San Francisco/Larkspur, 1958—; emeritus, 1995. Author: Individual, Marriage and the Family, 1968, Individual, 9th edit., 1996; author/editor: A Marriage Reader, 1970, The American Scene, 1970. Mem. APA, AAAS, AAUP, Am. Assn. Marriage and Family Therapists, Western Psychol. Assn., Am. Coll. Forensic Examiners, Mensa, Am. Chess Fedn. Democrat. Avocations: chess, sailing, music, ballet, opera. Home and Office: 57 Hatzic Ct Larkspur CA 94939-1992

SAY, CALVIN, state official; b. Feb. 1, 1952; m. Cora Say; children: Geoffrey, Jared. BEd, U. Hawaii at Manoa. Mem. state house State of Hawaii, 1976—; mgr. Kotake Shokai Ltd.; chmn. fin. com. Staste of Hawaii, mem. labor mgmt. com. Mem. Palolo Little League, Pop Warner, Hawaii Youth Symphony, Hawaii Sports Hall of Fame and Mus., Palolo Cmty. Coun., Honolulu Symphony Soc., Gov.'s Com. Commemorating the Chinese Bicentennial,; dir. Pacific Rim Found. Democrat. Office: Hawaii Ho of Reps Hawaii State Capitol Rm 431 415 S Beretania St Honolulu HI 96813*

SAYANO, REIZO RAY, electrochemical engineer; b. Los Angeles, Dec. 15, 1937; s. George Keiichiro and Miyo (Nakao) S.; m. Tamiko Shintani, May 28, 1967; children—Kiyomi Coleen, Naomi Jennifer. A.A., Los Angeles Community Coll., 1958; B.S., UCLA, 1960, M.S., 1962, Ph.D., 1967. Research asst. electrochem. and shock tube research dept. engring. UCLA, 1961-66; mem. staff TRW Systems, corrosion and advanced battery research and devel. Redondo Beach, Calif., 1966-78; dir. engring. Intermedics Intraocular Inc., Pasadena, Calif., 1978-80, dir. research and devel., 1980-82, v.p. engring. devel. and research, 1982-84; v.p. research and devel. Interpore Internat. Inc., 1984-85; dir. research and devel., product process devel. IOLAB Corp. subs. Johnson & Johnson Co., Claremont, Calif., 1985-87, dir. new tech., research and devel., 1987-88; v.p., gen. mgr. Nidek Techs., Inc., Pasadena, Calif., 1988—. NASA predoctoral trainee, 1964-65. Mem. Electrochem. Soc., Nat. Assn. Corrosion Engrs., AAAS, Am. Mgmt. Assn., Sigma Xi. Office: 675 S Arroyo Pky Ste 330 Pasadena CA 91105-3264

SAYLOR, DENNIS ELWOOD, hospital chaplain; b. St. Louis, Sept. 22, 1933; s. Clarence Claude and Maggie Dena (Beard) S.; m. Helen Lucile Howe, Aug. 9, 1953; children: Dennis Alan, Douglas Brian. ThB, Calvary Bible Coll., 1954; BA, Taylor U., 1956; MA, Ball State U., 1957; PhD, Clayton U., 1978. Asst. prof. Calvary Bible Coll., St. Louis, 1958-60; pastor 1st Presbyn. Ch., Tilden, Ill., 1960-68; asst. prof. Ill. Coll., Jacksonville, 1968-71; chaplain Passavant Hosp., Jacksonville, 1971-74; dir. chaplaincy Presbyn. Hosp., Albuquerque, 1974-88; dir. pastoral care San Diego Hosp. Assn., 1988—; with adv. coun. Bethel Sem., San Diego, 1989—. Author: And You Visited Me, 1979, Songs in the Night, 1980, A Guide to Hospital Calling, 1983; contbr. 30 articles to jours. Bd. dirs. Consumer Credit Counseling Svc., Albuquerque, 1978-88; mem. profl. edn. com. Am. Cancer Soc., San Diego, 1988—. Recipient Teagle Found. grant, 1985. Fellow Coll. Chaplains Am. Protestant Hosp. Assn. (state rep. 1984-88); mem. Assn. for Clin. Pastoral Edn., Pastoral Care Inst. (exec. dir. 1983-88). Presbyterian. Office: Sharp HealthCare 7901 Frost St San Diego CA 92123-2701

SAYLORS, JO ANN, sculptor; b. Lewisburg, Tenn., Apr. 23, 1932; d. Benjamin Harris and Nell Inez (McConnell) Rambo; m. Cecil L. Saylors, June 30, 1956; children: Kara Lea, Matthew G. Tchr. Scottsdale (Ariz.) Artists Sch., Loveland (Colo.) Acad. of Art. Sculptor: 12-ft Centenial Bronze, 1993, 14-ft K/A Bar Found., 1990, Dallas Children's Hosp., Fayetteville Ark. Hosp., 1997.

SAYRE, EDWARD CHARLES, [illegible] 1923; s. Kenneth C. Sayre and Clare (Davis) Clingan; m. Virginia A. Hoy, June 9, 1951; children: Steven Anthony, Sabrina Karen. BA, Coll. of Gt. Falls, 1955; MA, U. Idaho, 1961; MLS, U. Md., 1968. Coordinator library

services Thomas Nelson Community Coll., Hampton, Va., 1968-69; dir. Roswell Pub. Library, N.Mex., 1969-70; cons. N.Mex. State Library, Santa Fe, 1970-72; dir. Central Colo. Library System, Denver, 1972-78, Serra Coop. Library System, San Diego, 1978-79, Los Alamos County (N.Mex.) Library System, 1979-88; county adminstr. Los Alamos County, 1988-89; cons., 1976—, ret., 1989. Contbr. articles to profl. jours. Mem. state governing coun. Common Cause N.Mex. Home: 3 Timber Ridge Rd Los Alamos NM 87544-2317

SAYRE, HENRY MARSHALL, art history educator, critic, writer; b. Boulder, Colo., May 2, 1948; s. John Marshall and Jean (Miller) S.; m. Laura Rice, June 1976 (div. Dec. 1989); children: Robert, John; m. Sandra Lee Brooke, Nov. 3, 1990. BA, Stanford U., 1971; PhD, U. Wash., 1976. Asst. prof. English Wake Forest U., Winston-Salem, N.C., 1976-79, U. Wash., Seattle, 1979-80; from asst. prof. to assoc. prof. art history Oregon State U., Corvallis, 1983-90, prof. art history, 1990—. Author: The Visual Text of William Carlos William, 1980, The Line in Postmodern Poetry, 1986, The Object of Performance, 1989, Writing About Art, 1989, 2d edit., 1994, 3rd edit., 1999, A World of Art, 1993, 2d edit., 1997, 3rd edit., 1999; exec. prodr. pub. TV program World of Art: Works in Progress, Annenberg and Corp. for Pub. Broadcasting project, 1995-97. Grantee Annenberg Found. at the Corp. for Pub. Broadcasting, 1995-97; fellow NEH, 1980, 82-83, 86, Am. Coun. Learned Socs., 1979. Mem. MLA, Coll. Art Assn. Avocations: skiing, refereeing soccer. Office: Oregon State U Dept Art Fairbanks 106 Corvallis OR 97331

SAYRE, JOHN MARSHALL, lawyer, former government official; b. Boulder, Colo., Nov. 9, 1921; s. Henry Marshall and Lulu M. (Cooper) S.; m. Jean Miller, Aug. 22, 1943; children: Henry M., Charles Franklin, John Marshall Jr., Ann Elizabeth Sayre Taggart (dec.). BA, U. Colo., 1943, JD, 1948. Bar: Colo. 1948, U.S. Dist. Ct. Colo. 1952, U.S. Ct. Appeals (10th cir.) 1964. Law clk. trust dept. Denver Nat. Bank, 1948-49; asst. cashier, trust officer Nat. State Bank of Boulder, 1949-50; ptnr. Ryan, Sayre, Martin, Brotzman, Boulder, 1950-66, Davis, Graham & Stubbs, Denver, 1966-89, of counsel Davis, Graham & Stubbs, 1993—; asst. sec. of the Interior for Water and Sci., 1989-93. Bd. dirs. Boulder Sch. Dist. 3, 1951-57; city atty. City of Boulder, 1952-55; gen. counsel Colo. Mcpl. League, 1956-63; prin. counsel No. Colo. Water Conservancy Dist. and mcpl. subdist., 1964-87, spl. counsel, 1987, bd. dirs. dist., 1960-64; former legal counsel Colo. Assn. Commerce and Industry. Lt. (j.g.) USNR, 1943-46, ret. Decorated Purple Heart. Fellow Am. Bar. Found. (life), Colo. Bar Found. (life); mem. ABA, Colo. Bar Assn., Boulder County Bar Assn. (pres. 1959), Denver Bar Assn., Nat. Water Resources Assn. (Colo. dir. 1980-89, 93-95, pres. 1984-86), Denver Country Club, Univ. Club, Mile High Club, Phi Beta Kappa, Phi Gamma Delta, Phi Delta Phi. Republican. Episcopalian. Home: 355 Ivanhoe St Denver CO 80220-5841 Office: Davis Graham & Stubbs PO Box 185 Denver CO 80201-0185

SAYWELL, WILLIAM GEORGE GABRIEL, foundation administrator; b. Regina, Sask., Can., Dec. 1, 1936; s. John Ferdinand Tupper and Vera Marguerite S.; m. Helen Jane Larmer; children: Shelley Jayne, William James Tupper, Patricia Lynn. BA, U. Toronto, 1960, MA, 1961, PhD, 1968; LLD (hon.), U. B.C., 1994, Simon Fraser U., 1997. Asst. prof. dept. East Asian studies U. Toronto, Ont., Ont., Can., 1963-69; asst. prof. U. Toronto, Ont., Can., 1969-71, assoc. prof., 1971-82, prof., 1982-83, chmn. dept., 1971-76; prof. dept. history, pres., vice chancellor Simon Fraser U., Burnaby, B.C., Can., 1983-93; pres., chief exec. officer Asia Pacific Found. of Can., Vancouver, B.C., 1993—; sinologist and 1st sec. Can. Embassy, Beijing, 1972-73; dir. U. Toronto-York U. Ctr. Modern East Asia, 1974-75; prin. Innis Coll., 1976-79; vice provost U. Toronto, 1979-83; dir. Westcoast Energy, Spar Aerospace, Western Garnet Internat., Tokyo-Mitsubishi Bank (Can.). Author articles and revs. on Chinese affairs to profl. jours. Decorated Order B.C. Office: Asia Pacific Found Can, 666-999 Canada Pl, Vancouver, BC Canada V6C 3E1

SCAGLIONE, CECIL FRANK, marketing executive, publisher; b. North Bay, Ont., Can., Dec. 2, 1934; came to U.S., 1967, naturalized, 1982; s. Frank and Rose (Aubin) S.; m. Mary Margaret Stewart, Nov. 11, 1954 (div. 1982); children: Cris Ann, Michael Andrew, Patrick Andrew; m. Beverly Louise Rahn, Mar. 25, 1983; student North Bay Coll., 1947-52, Ryerson Tech. Inst., Toronto, Ont., 1955-56, San Diego State U. Inst. World Affairs, 1979. Accredited Pub. Rels. Soc. Am. Fin. writer Toronto Telegram, 1955; reporter Sarnia (Ont.) Observer, 1956-57; reporter, editor Kitchener-Waterloo (Ont.) Record, 1957-61; reporter, editor, analyst Windsor (Ont.) Star, 1961-67; writer, editor, photo editor Detroit News, 1967-71; reporter, assoc. bus. editor San Diego Union, 1971-80; mgr. corp. communications Pacific Southwest Airlines, San Diego, 1981-83; sr. v.p. media rels. Berkman & Daniels, Inc., San Diego, 1984-87, prin. Scaglione Mktg. Comm., 1987—; pres., CEO Mature Life Features, 1990—. Mem. San Diego County Crime Commn. Recipient award B.F. Goodrich Can., Ltd., 1962, 66, San Diego Pub. Rels. Profl. of the Yr., 1995, Spl. Achievement award Nat. Assn. Recycling Industries, 1978; named Nat. Media Advocate SBA, 1980; Herbert J. Davenport fellow, 1977 U. Mo.; Can. Centennial grantee, 1966. Mem. San Diego Press Club (hon. life, past pres.) awards 1978, 80, 84, Airline Editors Forum awards 1982, 83, Soc. Profl. Journalists. Roman Catholic. Founding editor-in-chief Aeromexico mag., 1973; contbr. articles, columns and photographs to various publs.

SCAMAHORN, MARK, English writing educator, artist; b. San Francisco, July 13, 1967; s. Bruce Edward Scamahorn and Maria (Boysen) Brown. BA, San Francisco State U., 1989; MFA, U. Ariz., 1994. Instrnl. asst. U. Calif., Santa Barbara, Calif., 1990-91; writing lab. instr. U. Ariz., Tucson, 1992-94; English instr. Delgado C.C., New Orleans, 1996, Loyola U., New Orleans, 1996, Santa Barbara (Calif.) City Coll., 1994—; cons. in field. Author: On The Bus, 1992, Insomnia, 1993, A Vaccine..., 1998; co-editor: (textbook) America Now, 3d edit., 1998. Coord. vol. Childs Play--Presch., Santa Barbara, 1997. Grad. scholar U. Ariz., 1993. Mem. Santa Barbara C.C. Tchrs. Assn. Avocations: hiking, camping, music. Office: Santa Barbara City Coll 721 Cliff Dr Santa Barbara CA 93109-2312

SCANNELL, JOHN R., publishing consultant; b. Dobbs Ferry, N.Y., Dec. 23, 1947; s. John Joseph and Veronica Rose (Hannigan) S.; m. Faye Naomi Snyder, July 11, 1969; children: Michelle, Amanda, Rebecca, Benjamin. BS in Edn., Kutztown (Pa.) State Coll., 1965; MA in Speech, U. Wash., 1974. Tchr. English Nazareth (Pa.) Sch. Dist., 1969-70, Upper Dauphin Sch. Dist., Elizabethville, Pa., 1970-72; tchr. Bellevue (Wash.) Sch. Dist., 1974-85; sales rep. Macmillan Pub., Seattle, 1985-88; nat. cons. social studies and lang. arts McGraw-Hill Pub., Bothell, Wash., 1988—. Pres., Our Lady of Lake Parents Club, Seattle, 1981-83; dir. Our Lady of Lake Players, Seattle, 1980, 82, 84. Recipient Wilma Grimes award U. Wash., 1972; named DECA Tchr. of Yr., Nazareth H.S., 1970. Mem. Nat. Coun. Tchrs. English, Nat. Coun. for Social Studies, Nat. Hist. Soc. Democrat. Roman Catholic. Avocation: woodworking. Home: 22627 7th Dr SE Bothell WA 98021-8274

SCARBROUGH, MICHAEL DEAN, anesthesiologist, photographer; b. Charleston, S.C., Feb. 6, 1954; s. Hollis and Alice Scarbrough; m. Tana Scarbrough; children: Chad, Cole. BA, Andrews U., 1977; MD, Loma Linda U., 1982. Cert. Am. Bd. Anesthesiology. Intern in internal medicine Loma Linda (Calif.) U. Med. Ctr., 1982-83, resident in anesthesiology, 1983-85; fellow in cardiovasc. and pediat. anesthesiology U. Ala., Birmingham, 1985-86; staff anesthesiologist Pomona Valley Med. Ctr., Pomona, Calif., 1986-87, Alaska Native Med. Ctr., Anchorage, 1987-91, St. Joseph Hosp. and Med. Ctr., Tacoma, 1991—; dir., bd. dirs. Anesthesia Svcs. N.W., Seattle, 1997—; ctr. artist Pub. Health Svcs., Visual Arts Ctr. Alaska, Anchorage, 1990-91. Photographer: (book) Fly Patterns of Alaska, 1993; contbr. photographs to mags. including Alaska's Wildlife, 1991, Seattle Mag., 1997. Lt. commdr. USPHS, 1987-91. Mem. Am. Soc. Anesthesiologists, Internat. Anethesia Rsch. Soc. Avocations: backpacking, fly fishing, music. Office: Pacific Anesthesia PC PO Box 2197 Tacoma WA 98401-2197

SCARLETT, RANDALL H., lawyer; b. Athens, Ohio, July 12, 1957; s. John Donald and Sherry (Richards) S.; m. Mary Anne Scarlett, Sept. 21, 1991; children: Randall Alexander, Christina Marie. BA, San Francisco State U., 1982; JD, Golden Gate U., 1985. Bar: Calif. 1988, U.S. Dist. Ct. (no. dist.) Calif. 1985, U.S. Dist. Ct. (ea. dist.) Calif. 1988, U.S. Dist. Ct. (so. and ctrl. dists.) Calif. 1995, U.S. Ct. Appeals (9th cir.) 1995, U.S. Supreme Ct. 1995. Ptnr. Belli, Belli, Brown, Monzione, Fabbro & Zakaria, San Francisco, 1989-93, Brown, Monzione, Fabbro, Zakaria & Scarlett, San Francisco, 1993-96, Brown, Fabbro & Scarlett, San Francisco, 1996—; lectr. Mem. ATLA (sustaining, com. Traumatic Brain Injury Litigation Group), Consumer Attys. Calif. (sustaining), San Francisco Lawyers Assn., Bar Assn. San Francisco,. Avocations: golfing, scuba diving. Office: Brown Fabbro & Scarlett 425 Battery St Ste 400 San Francisco CA 94111-3218

SCATENA, LORRAINE BORBA, rancher, women's rights advocate; b. San Rafael, Calif., Feb. 18, 1924; d. Joseph and Eugenia (Simas) de Borba; m. Louis G. Scatena, Feb. 14, 1960; children: Louis Vincent, Eugenia Gayle. BA, Dominican Coll., San Rafael, 1945; postgrad., Calif. Sch. Fine Arts, 1948, U. Calif., Berkeley, 1956-57. Cert. elem. tchr., Calif. Tchr. Dominican Coll., 1946; tchr. of mentally handicapped San Anselmo (Calif.) Sch. Dist., 1946; tchr. Fairfax (Calif.) Pub. Elem. Sch., 1946-53; asst. to mayor Fairfax City Recreation, 1948-53; tchr., libr. U.S. Dependent Schs., Mainz am Rhine, Fed. Republic Germany, 1953-56; translator Portugal Travel Tours, Lisbon, 1954; bonding sec. Am. Fore Ins. Group, San Francisco, 1958-60; rancher, farmer Yerington, Nev., 1960—; hostess com. Caldecott and Newbury Authors' Awards, San Francisco, 1959; mem. Nev. State Legis. Commn., 1975; coord. Nevadans for Equal Rights Amendment, 1975-78, rural areas rep., 1976-78; testifier Nev. State Senate and Assembly, 1975, 77; mem. adv. com. Fleischmann Coll. Agr. U. Nev., 1977-80, 81-84; speaker Grants and Rsch. Projects, Bishop, Calif., 1977, Choices for Tomorrow's Women, Fallon, Nev., 1989. Trustee Wassuk Coll., Hawthorne, Nev., 1984-87; mem. Lyon County Friends of Libr., Yerington, 1971—, Lyon County Mus. Soc., 1978—; sec., pub. info. chmn. Lyon County Rep. Ctrl. Com., 1973-74; mem. Marin County Soc. Artists, San Anselmo, Calif., 1948-53; charter mem. Eleanor Roosevelt Edn. Fund for Women and Girls, 1990, sustaining mem., 1992—; Nev. rep. 1st White House Conf. Rural Am. Women, Washington, 1980; participant internat. reception, Washington, 1980; mem. pub. panel individual presentation Shakespeare's Treatment of Women Characters, Nev. Theatre for the Arts, Ashland, Oreg., Shakespearean Actors local performance, 1977; mem. Nev. Women's History Project, U. Nev., 1996—. Recipient Outstanding Conservation Farmer award Mason Valley Conservation Dist., 1992, Soroptimist Internat. Women Helping women award 1983, invitation to first all-women delegation to U.S.A. from People's Republic China, U.S. House Reps., 1979; Public Forum Travel grantee Edn. Title IX, Oakland, Calif., 1977; fellow World Lit. Acad., 1993. Mem. Lyon County Ret. Tchrs. Assn. (unit pres. 1979-80, 84-86, v.p. 1986-88, Nev. State Outstanding Svc. award 1981, state conv. gen. chmn. 1985), Rural Am. Women Inc., AAUW (br. pres. 1972-74, 74-76, chair edn. found. programs 1983—, state conv. gen. chmn. 1976, 87, state sec. 1970-72, state legis. program chmn. 1976-77, state chmn. internat. rels. 1979-81, state pres. 1981-83, br. travelship, discovering women in U.S. history Radcliffe Coll. 1981, State Humanities award 1975, Future Fund Nat. award 1983, Lorraine Scatena endowment gift named in her honor for significant contbns. to AAUW Ednl. Found. 1997), Mason Valley Country Club, Italian Cath. Fedn. (pres. 1986-88), Uniao Portuguesa Estado da Calif. Roman Catholic. Avocations: writing, photography. Home: PO Box 247 Yerington NV 89447-0247

SCHAAF, DOUGLAS ALLAN, lawyer; b. Green Bay, Wis., Nov. 18, 1955; s. Carlton Otto and Fern (Brunette) S.; m. Kathlyn T. Bielke, Feb. 23, 1988. BBA magna cum laude in Internat. Bus., St. Norbert Coll., DePere, Wis., 1978; JD, U. Notre Dame, 1981. Bar: Ill. 1981, Calif. 1987. Assoc. McDermott, Will & Emery, Chgo., 1981-84, Skadden, Arps, Slate, Meagher & Flom, 1984-89; ptnr. Paul Hastings, Janofsky & Walker, L.A., 1989—; adj. faculty mem. John Marshall Law Sch., 1984-87. Atty. Chgo. Vol. Legal Services, 1984-87; bd. dirs. Orange County Alzheimer's Assn. Mem. Orange County Bar Assn. (chair tax sect. 1994-96). Office: Paul Hastings Janofsky & Walker 695 Town Center Dr Ste 1700 Costa Mesa CA 92626-7191

SCHABACKER, BETTY BARCHET, artist; b. Balt., Aug. 14, 1925; d. Stephen George and Louise (Lankford) Barchet; m. Robert Bailey Schabacker, June 8, 1945; 1 child, Elizabeth S. Priest. Student, Conn. Coll. Women, 1946. Freelance artist Santa Fe, 1950—. Mem. Soc. Animal Artists, Nat. Water Color Soc., Audubon Artists, Inc., Coll. Artists Am. Home and Studio: 3 Dandelion Cir Santa Fe NM 87501-8519

SCHABOW, JOHN WILLIAM, accountant; b. Chgo., Mar. 30, 1937; s. William John and Mary V. (Brink) S.; m. Gail P. Ekren, Oct. 17, 1959; children: Robin, John R. Student, Davis Elkins Coll., 1955-58, Ariz. State U., 1972-74. Accredited tax advisor Accreditation Coun. for Accountancy & Taxation. Cost clk. G.D. Searle, Skokie, Ill., 1958-60; acct. Sugarcreek Foods, Chgo., 1960-63, Arlington Park Rack Track, Chgo., 1963-65, G. Heiss & Assocs., Chgo., 1965-69, Murray & Murray CPA's, Phoenix, 1969-70, Wm. R. Schulz & Assocs., Phoenix, 1970-73; pres., owner John W. Schabow, Ltd., Phoenix, 1973—; registered rep. H.D. Vest Investment Securities, Inc., Phoenix, 1985—, adv. bd. dirs. Mem. editorial adv. bd. Accounting Today, 1993—. Bd. dirs. Inst. for Partially Sighted, Phoenix, 1986-87, Phoenix Girl's Choir, 1995-97. With U.S. Army, 1961-62. Mem. Ariz. Soc. Practicing Accts. (pres. 1987-88, co-founder, co-chair legis. com. 1994-97), Nat. Soc. Pub. Accts. (state dir. 1983-87, bd. govs. 1988-92, chmn. nat. affairs com. 1995-97, chmn. nominating com. 1997-98). Republican. Lutheran. Avocation: golf. Home: 4440 W Bluefield Ave Glendale AZ 85308-1613 Office: 11725 N 19th Ave Phoenix AZ 85029-3500

SCHACH, BARBARA JEAN, elementary education educator; b. Bakersfield, Calif., Dec. 3, 1945; d. James Fleming and Ann (Sanderson) Meeks; m. Henry Edward, June 20, 1970; children: David Henry, Natalie Ann. Student, U. Nev., 1967, UCLA, 1973, Calif. State U., Dominguez Hills, 1974. Tchr. Redondo Beach, Calif., 1967-73; tchr. 5th grade L.A. Unified Sch. Dist., 1981—; bd. dirs. Carson (Calif.) Coord. Coun.; com. mem. Carson 2000, 1995—. Prodr.: (TV prodns.) Education Connection Quiz Kids, 1994 (Educator of Yr. award 1994), Children's News, 1995 (Educator of Yr. award 1995); coord. (TV prodn.) The Learning Hour, 1995 (Educator of Yr. award 1996). Bd. dirs. Carson Family Ctr., 1993-96; mem. Rep. Women, L.A., 1990. Healthy Start grantee State of Calif., 1993, L.A. Ednl. Partnershhip grantee, 1991, 92, 94, Polaroid grantee Polaroid Corp., 1990, Early Literacy grantee L.A. Unified Sch. Dist., 1996. Mem. AAUW, ASCD, Women in Ednl. Leadership (v.p. programs 1994—, pres. 1994—), Video Using Educators, Phi Delta Kappa, Phi Kappa Phi. Avocations: reading, sewing, gourmet cooking, art. Home: 6917 Hartcrest Dr Rancho Palos Verdes CA 90275-2933

SCHADE, WILBERT CURTIS, educational administrator; b. St. Louis, Jan. 4, 1945; s. Wilbert Curtis and Florence Mary (Allen) S.; m. Jacqueline Siewert, May 14, 1977; children: Benjamin Allen Siewert, Timothy Knorr Siewert. BA, U. Pa., 1967; AM, Washington U., St. Louis, 1970; PhD, Ind. U., 1986. Teaching asst. dept. Romance Lang. Washington U., St. Louis, 1967-68; tchr. French St. Louis Priory Sch., 1970-71; assoc. instr. Dept. French and Italian, Ind. U., Bloomington, 1972-74, 76-80; tchr. French Webster Groves (Mo.) H.S., 1975-76; asst. dir. admissions Beloit (Wis.) Coll., 1980-83, assoc. dir. admissions, 1983-84; dir. coll. placement and dir. admissions Westover Sch., Middlebury, Conn., 1984-90; head upper sch. The Key Sch., Annapolis, Md., 1990-94, interim dir. devel., 1994-95; tchr. French, head lang. dept. Wasatch Acad., Mt. Pleasant, Utah, 1995-96, asst. headmaster for acad. affairs, 1996—; lectr. in field. Co-editor: African Literature in its Social and Political Dimensions, 1983; contbr. articles to profl. jours. including World Lit. Written in English, Studies in 20th Century Lit. and articles in books. Mem. Anne Arundel County (Md.) Task Force on Year Round Edn., 1994-95; mem. Utah State Office of Edn.'s Fgn. Lang. Instrl. Materials and Texbook Adv. Com., 1996-98. NEH Summer Inst. on African Am. Lit. and Film grantee, 1994. Mem. Nat. Assn. Coll. Admission Counseling (presenter nat. conf. 1985), Rocky Mountain Assn. for Coll. Admission Counseling (exec. bd., chief assembly del. to Nat. Assn.), African Lit. Assn. (exec. com. 1979), Phi Delta Kappa. Soc. of Friends. Avocation: tennis. Home: 47 S 100 W Mount Pleasant UT 84647-1508 Office: Wasatch Acad 120 S 100 W Mount Pleasant UT 84647-1509

SCHAEFER, DAN L., congressman; b. Gutenberg, Iowa, Jan. 25, 1936; s. Alvin L. and Evelyn (Everson) S.; m. Mary Margaret Lenney, 1959; children: Danny, Darren, Joel, Jennifer. BA, Niagara U., 1961, LLD (hon.), 1986; postgrad., Potsdam State U., 1961-64. Pub. rels. cons., 1967-83; mem. Colo. Gen. Assembly, 1977-78; mem. Colo. Senate, 1979-83, pres. pro tem, 1981-82, majority whip, 1983; mem. 98th-105th Congresses from 6th dist. Colo., Washington, 1983—; mem. house small bus. com., 1983, govt. ops. com., 1983, energy and commerce com., 1984-86 (subcom. on fossil and synthetic fuels; commerce, transp. and tourism; oversight/investigations), environ. and energy study com., 1987— (subcoms. on Transp. and Hazardous materials, Telecom. and Fin.), Energy and Commerce ranking Rep Oversight and Investigations, 1993—, Rep. study com.; mem. house sci. and high tech. task force, mil. reforms caucus, congl. grace caucus; mem. adv. com., com. of concern for Soviet Jewry; mem. exec. bd. Environ. and Energy Study Conf., 1995; chmn. Subcom. on Energy and Power House Commerce Com.; mem. Subcom. on Telecom. and Fin., House Vet. Affiars Com., Subcom. on Edn., Training, Employment and Housing, 1995—; co-chmn. The Mainstream Conservative Alliance. Co-chair Nat. Retail Sales Tax Caucus, Congl. Oil and Gas Forum; mem. Spkrs. Task Force on Environ.; founder Nat. Trails Caucus, House Renewable Energy Caucus; pres. Foothills Recreation Bd., 1973-76; sec. Jefferson County Rep. Party, Colo., 1975-76. With USMCR, 1955-57. Recipient Colo. Park and Recreation citation, 1976; named Elected Ofcl. of Yr., Lakewood/South Jeffco C. of C., 1986, 88, 90, Leadership award U.S. Congl. Adv. Bd., Am. Security Coun. Found., Taxpayers Friend award Nat. Taxpayer's Union, 1985-86, 88, 90, 91, 92, 93, 94, 95, Golden Bulldog award Watchdog of Treasury, 1985-86, 87-88, 88-89, 89-90, 91-92, 93-94, 95-96, Spirit of Enterprise award U.S. C. of C., 1995, Nat. Health award Am. Assn. Nurse Anesthetists, 1996, Nat. Security Scorecare Perfect 100 award Ctr. for Security Policy, 1995, Friend of Taxpayer Perfect 100% award Ams. for Tax Reform, 1996; named Guardian of Small Bus., Nat. Fedn. Ind. Bus., 1996. Mem. C. of C., Rotary, Beta Theta Pi. Roman Catholic. Office: House of Reps 2160 Rayburn Bldg Ofc B Washington DC 20515-0005

SCHAEFFER, PETER MORITZ-FRIEDRICH, literature educator; b. Breslau, Germany, May 14, 1930; came to U.S., 1939; s. Rudolf Franz and Katharina (Krebs) S.; m. Brigitte Ehrler, Sept. 4, 1968. Lic. Theol., U. Ottawa, Ont., Can., 1959; PhD, Princeton U., 1971. Asst. prof. Princeton (N.J.) U., 1970-74; vis. lectr. U. Calif., Berkeley, 1974-76; assoc. prof. U. Calif., Davis, 1976-83, prof. German, classics, 1983—. Editor, translator: De poetica (Vadianus), 1973-77, Aethiopica (Heliodor), 1984, Two Poems (Hans Sachs), 1990, De curriculo (Hoffmanswaldau), 1992. Grantee NEH, 1989, 91, 93, 94. Mem. 16th Century Soc., Erasmus of Rotterdam Soc., Amis de la Bibliotheque Humaniste. Democrat. Jewish. Avocations: piano, Latin, Greek. Home: 1101 Alice St Davis CA 95616-2114 Office: Univ Calif Dept German Davis CA 95616

SCHAEFFER, REINER HORST, career officer, retired librarian, foreign language professional; b. Berlin, Lichterfelde, Fed. Republic Germany, Jan. 13, 1938; came to U.S., 1958; s. Immanuel Emil and Wilhelmine (Fahrni) Frei-S.; m. Cathy Anne Cormack, Apr. 6, 1966; 1 child, Brian Reiner. Nat. cert., Bus. Sch., Thun, Switzerland, 1957; BGS in Bus., U. Nebr., 1970; MPA in Orgnl. Behavior, U. Mo., 1972; PhD in Fgn. Lang. Edn., Ohio State U., 1979. Commd. officer USAF, 1958, advanced through grades to lt. col.; instr. German, French USAF Acad., Colorado Springs, Colo., 1975-77, assoc. prof., 1979-81, chmn. German, 1981, dir. librs., 1982-86, prof., 1986-92, dir. Acad. Librs., 1986—. Bd. dirs. Friends of AF Acad. Librs.; pres. Fgn. Lang. Ctr., Inc., 1999—. Named Disting. Grad. Air Force Inst. Tech, Wright-Patterson AFB, Ohio, 1979; recipient 5 Meritorious Service medals, 5 Air Force Commendation medals. Mem. Am. Assn. Tchrs. of German, Swiss Club (pres. Colorado Springs chpt. 1990-96, chmn.), Pi Alpha Alpha, Alpha Sigma Alpha. Republican. Avocations: skiing; golfing; hiking; soccer. Home: 4941 W Red Rock Dr Larkspur CO 80118-9054 Office: Fgn Lang Ctr LLC 315 E Willamette Ave Colorado Springs CO 80903-1115

SCHAFER, MARIANNE MARKS (MARIANNE MARKS), television production company executive, actress; b. Jakarta, Indonesia; m. Stanley M. Marks; m. Jerry S. Schafer, Oct. 1, 1979; 5 children. Actress more than 20 roles various internat. TV prodn. cos. and Hollywood studios,, 1977-79; actress, ops. dir. Sanford Internat. Entertainment, Inc., Malibu, Calif., Las Vegas, Nev., 1979-88; actress, ops. dir. Internat. Video Comm., Inc., Las Vegas, 1988—; t.v. spokesperson, co-prodr., narrator host documentaries Imperial Palace Hotel & Casino, Las Vegas, 1983-85, Riviera Hotel & Casino, Las Vegas, 1991-93, Desert Inn Hotel & Casino, Las Vegas, 1991-94, Sands Hotel & Casino, Las Vegas, 1993, TV spokesperson and program co-prodr. Nev. Hwy. Patrol, 1990—, Nev. Dept. Pub. Safety, 1991—, MADD, Las Vegas, 1990-93, Stop D.U.I., Las Vegas, 1993—. Host, narrator over 50 TV programs; co-prodr. over 75 TV programs; TV host, co-prodr. documentaries, ednl. programs, game and talk shows; co-prodr., narrator, host pub. svc. documentary Get M.A.D.D., 1992 (MADD appreciation award 1992); co-prodr., narrator, host documentary Inside the Nevada Highway Patrol, 1992 (USA's Best Performance, Best Narration), (TV series) Code 4: Suspect in Custody, 1998; narrator, host, spokesperson documentary The Las Vegas Academy of International Studies, Performing & Visual Arts, 1996; co-star movies Wrong Is Right, Wild Times, Adventure: The Billion Dollar Threat, lead Fists of Steel, 1988; co-prodr. 29 pub. svc. announcements; spokesperson 21 pub. svc. announcements DMV; co-prodr., spokesperson pub. svc. announcements divsn. motion picture Nev. Dept. Econ. Devel., 1994. Recipient Gov.'s Appreciation award State of Nev., 1993, Racers Against Impaired Drivers award Nev. Hwy. Patrol, 1993, Congrl. Recognition, 1993; named Hon. Constable No. Las Vegas Constables Office, 1985—. Mem. SAG, AFTRA. Avocations: cooking, aerobics, metaphysics, photography, interior design. Office: Internat Video Comm Inc PO Box 15101 Las Vegas NV 89114-5101

SCHAFF, ALFRED, mechanical engineer, consultant; b. Bogas Del Tora, Panama, June 8, 1920; s. Alfred and Juanita (Kragstadt) S.; m. Cecile Becker, 1942 (div. 1949); children: Thomas, Anita; married; 1 child, Edward. BSME, Calif. Inst. Tech., 1941; PhD, Kensington U., 1982. Lic. pilot. Maintenance supt. Pan Am.-Grace Airways, 1941-44, capt., 1946-51; large liquid, rocket test engr. Aerojet Gen., 1951-57, mgr. test and field svc. divsn., 1957-60, mgr. spl. solid rocket projects., 1960-65, engring. mgr. nuclear rocket test facility, 1965-69; v.p., gen. mgr., dir. rsch. and devel. Ametek/Micro Electronics, El Segundo, 1969-87. Contbr. articles to profl. jours.; patents in field. Mem. IEEE, ASTM, SME, ISHM, Assoc. Calif. Inst. Tech., Am. Rocket Soc., Ancient and Secret Order of Quiet Biromen (keyman 1997—), OX-S Aviation Pioneers, Red Barrows. Republican. Avocations: flying. Home: 8143 Billowvista Dr Playa Del Rey CA 90293-7805

SCHAFFER, JEFFREY L., lawyer; b. L.A., Aug. 21, 1952. AB, U. Calif., Berkeley, 1974; JD, U. Calif., 1979. Bar: Calif. 1979, U.S. Dist. Ct. (no. dist.) Calif., U.S. Ct. Appeals (9th cir.) 1985. Mem. Howard, Rice, Nemerovski, Canady, Falk & Rabkin, San Francisco, 1988—; panelist Continuing Edn. Bar, 1983-92, computer law inst. U. So. Calif., 1986. Assoc. editor Calif. Law REv., 1977-79. Mem. ABA (bus. law sect.), Am. Bankruptcy Inst., State Bar Calif. (bus. law sect., mem. debtor/creditor and bankruptcy com. 1987-90, 96-98, UCC com. 1998—), Bar Assn. San Francisco (comml. law and bankruptcy sect., co-chair barristers club's bankruptcy and comml. law com. 1984-85), Berkeley Law Found., Order of Coif, Phi Beta Kappa. Office: Howard Rice Nemerovski Canady Falk & Rabkin 3 Embarcadero Ctr Ste 7 San Francisco CA 94111-4003*

SCHAFFER, JOEL LANCE, dentist; b. Bklyn., Oct. 18, 1945; s. Martin Alter and Irene Natalie (Shore) S.; m. Susan Anne Swearingen, Feb. 14, 1980 (div.); 1 child, Jericho Katherine. BS, L.I. U., 1967; DDS, Howard U., 1971. Dental intern Eastman Dental Ctr., Rochester, N.Y., 1971-72; gen. practice dentistry, Boulder, Colo., 1973—; evaluator Clin. Rsch. Assocs.; lectr. in field, 1972—. Contbr. articles to dental jours; patentee in field. Advisor Boulder Meals on Wheels; mem. Boulder County Com. for Persons with Disabilities. Named outstanding clinician Boulder County Dental Forum, 1979. Fellow Am. Soc. Dental Aesthetics; mem. ADA, Am. Acad. Oral Implantology, Boulder County Dental Soc., Tau Epsilon Phi, Alpha Omega. Jewish. Home: 4171 S Hampton Cir Boulder CO 80301-6017 Office: 2880 Folsom St Boulder CO 80304-3739

SCHAFFNER, RIVKA ANN, art educator, artist; b. L.A., Sept. 13, 1960; d. Irving and Charlotte Elaine (Gross) S. BFA, Calif. State U., 1983, postgrad., 1989. English and art tchr. Gregg Internat. Coll., Tokyo, 1984; childrens book illustrator Alchemy II, Northridge, Calif., 1985-87; animator, color supr. DIC Animation Co., Burbank, Calif., 1987-90; art educator Simi

Valley (Calif.) Unified Schs., 1991, St. Katherines Indian Sch., Santa Fe, N.Mex., 1991-93, Viewpoint Sch., Calabasas, Calif., 1993 95, La Reina H.S., Thousand Oaks, Calif., 1995-98; mural club moderator, art edn. cross-curricular advisor La Reina H.S., Thousand Oaks, 1995-98, Agoura (Calif.) H.S., 1998—. Illustrator: Sing Along with Sarah, 1988, Passover Haggada, 1991; inventor brush rest; exhibited works in shows at Del Mono Gallery, L.A., 1983-86, Pomegranates in the Sun, Hawaii, 1981-84, Delgato St. Studio, Santa Fe, 1991-95, Tapestry Gallery, Madrid, 1994-96. Summer camp counselor art tchr. Viewpoint Sch., Calabasas, 1993-95; supr. window painting, Conejo Valley Days, Thousand Oaks, 1997-98. Recipinet 1st Place-Mixed Media award Westlake Art Guild, 1987; named Outstanding Art Educator Calif. State U., 1990. Mem. Nat. Art Edn. Assn., Calif. Art Edn. Assn. (bd. dirs. 1987-98), Conejo Valley Art Edn. Assn. (founding mem., pres. 1996-98), Cath. Educators, Conejo Valley Hist. Soc. (debutant 1977), Alpha Omicron Pi. Jewish. Avocations: rock climber, downhill skier, yoga, camping, sculpture designer.

SCHAKOSKY, LAURIE LEIGH, artist; b. Ft. Worth, Tex., Dec. 2, 1968; d. Ronald Lee Schakosky and Nancy Lauren (Dennis) Ladd; married. Student, U. North Tex., 1989; Grad. in Modeling, Kim Dawson Agy., Tex. Cert. make-up artist for 1998 Olympics, Nagano, Japan; cert. aromatherapist, esthetician. Freelance model Dallas, Tex.; freelance hair and make-up artist L.A.; Trainee Local 706 Union, L.A. Hair stylist and make-up artist for various TV shows, photo galleries and press tours, including: Drew Carey, Hard Copy, 60 Minutes (Australia), The Today Show (Australia), The Miday Show (Australia), Inside Edition, Coach, Comedy Central, Entertainment Tonight, Oprah, ABC News, Dr. Quinn Medicine Woman, Melrose Place, Am. Gladiators, Boy Meets World, Foxworthy, numerous others; stylist for commls. including Miller Beer, Dr. Pepper, Am. Express, Honda, Fraiser, Spy Game, Oldsmobile, numerous others; clients include Nicole Kidman, Dudley Moore, Elizabeth Taylor, Shirley McClaine, Michael J. Fox, Mickey Roonie, Sinbad, Barbara Eden, Shaquille O'Neil, Fabio, Henry Winkler, numerous others. Avocations: yoga, tennis, writing, travel, rsch. Home: 3321 Troy Dr Los Angeles CA 90068-1433

SCHALLER, JOANNE F., nursing consultant; b. Columbus, Ga., July 15, 1943; d. John Frank and Ethel Beatrice (Spring) Lanzendorfer; m. Robert Thomas Schaller, Jan. 22, 1977; 1 child, Amy. BS, Pacific Luth. U., 1969; M in Nursing, U. Wash., 1971. House supr. UCLA Hosp., 1971-72; outpatient supr. Harborview Hosp., Seattle, 1973-75; outpatient clinic and emergency room supr. U. Wash. Hosp., Seattle, 1975-77; nurse specialist in hypertension, 1975—; co-author, researcher with Robert Schaller MD Seattle, 1977-87; prin. Nursing Expert-Standards of Care, Seattle, 1987—; cons. Wash. State Trial Lawyers, Wash. Assn. Criminal Def. Lawyers, 1989—, Bastyr U., 1999—; founder, CEO Present Perfect, Seattle, 1991—; appt. Breast Cancer cons. UWMC, 1995—. Contbr., editor articles to profl. jours. Bd. dirs. Pacific Arts Ctr., 1992—; vol. guardian ad litem King County Juvenile Ct., 1978—; vol. Make a Wish Found. U.S. Bank, 1984—, Multiple Sclerosis Assn., 1986—, Am. Heart Assn., 1986—, Internat. Children's Festival, 1987—, Seattle Children's Festival, 1987—, Seattle Dept. Parks and Recreation Open Space Com., 1990—, Pacific N.W. Athletic Congress, 1991—, Wash. Fed. Garden Clubs Jr. Advisor, 1992—, Fred Hutchison Cancer Rsch. Ctr., 1993—; mem. parent coun. Seattle Country Day Sch., 1986-96—, volunteer, U.S. Rowing events; mem. Photo Coun. Seattle Art Mus., 1986—, Native Am. Coun., 1989—; mem. N.W. Coun. Seattle Art Mus., 1992—, mem. NAOO Coun. Seattle Art Mus., 1989—, Plestcheeff Inst. Decorative Arts, 1992—; mem. fundraiser Children's Hosp. Med. Ctr., 1977—, Breast Cancer Fund, 1994—, Susan G. Komen Breast Cancer Found., 1994—. Named 1st Migrant Health Care Nurse, State of Wash., 1969, 1st Am. nurse visiting China, 1974. Mem. AAUW, ANA, Wash. State Nurses Assn., U. Wash. Alumni Assn. Avocations: photography, writing, gardening, hiking, music. Home and Office: 914 Randolph Pl Seattle WA 98122-5267

SCHANDER, MARY LEA, police official; b. Bakersfield, Calif., June 11, 1947; d. Gerald John Lea and Marian Lea Coffman; BA (Augustana fellow) Calif. Luth. Coll., 1969; MA, UCLA, 1970; m. Edwin Schander, July 3, 1971. Staff aide City of Anaheim (Calif.) Police Dept., 1970-72, staff asst., 1972-78, sr. staff asst., 1978-80; with Resource Mgmt. Dept., City of Anaheim, 1980-82; asst. to dir. Pub. Safety Agy., City of Pasadena Police Dept., 1982-85, spl. asst. to police chief, 1985-88, adminstrv. comdr., 1988-92, police comdr., 1992—; freelance musician; publisher Australian Traditional Songs, 1985, Songs in the Air of Early California, 1994; lectr. Calif. Luth. Coll.; instr. Calif. State U., Northridge; cons. City of Lodz, Poland, Internat. Assn. Chiefs of Police; speaker, panelist League of Calif. Cities, Pasadena Commn. on Status of Women; mcpl. mgmt. asst. CLEARS. Producer (cable TV program) Traditional Music Showcase. Contbr. articles in field to profl. jours. Bd. dirs. Women At Work, Step Up Adv. Program, Southwest Chamber Music; instr. Bd. Corrections. Recipient Police Chief's Spl. award City of Pasadena, 1987, Women at Work Medal of Excellence, 1988, 2d Century Leadership award YWCA, 1998 . Mem. Pasadena Arts Coun., L.A. County Peace Officers, Internat. Assn. Chiefs of Police, Rotary (chair vocat. svc. com.), S.W. chamber Music Soc. (pres. bd. dirs.). Home: PO Box 50151 Pasadena CA 91115-0151 Office: Pasadena Police Dept 207 N Garfield Ave Pasadena CA 91101-1791

SCHANKER, HARRY H., JR., writer; b. Kansas City, Kans., Dec. 27, 1932; s. Harry H. Sr. and Anna L. (Roush) S.; m. Carol L. Schanker, Sept. 5, 1953; children: Chris S., Debra K., Kimberly A., Darin L. BS in Edn., U. Kans., 1954; MA, U. Colo., 1960; postgrad., Boston U., 1966. Lifetime tchg. credential, Colo., Kans. Tchr. Denver Pub. Schs., 1954-95; author McGraw-Hill/MacMillan, N.Y.C., 1968—; state thespian dir. Internat. Thespian Soc., Cin., 1973-75; pres. Colo. Drama and Speech Assn., 1990; drama dir., tchr. Cherry Creek Schs., Denver, 1992-95; active Stage Eleven Acting Sch., Englewood, Colo., 1992-94; theater dir. Town Hall Arts Ctr., Littleton, Colo., 1994-98. Authro: The Stage and the School, 1972-99, The Spoken Word, 1982—; editor: Dramatic Comedy, 1982—; author of play It All Began. Bd. dirs. Colo. Youth Citizenship Awards, Denver, 1973-99, pres., 1993-94; mem. devel. com. Swedish Med. Ctr., Englewood, 1974-75; bd. dirs. Town Hall Arts Ctr., Littleton, 1994-97. Recipient A for Tchrs. award KCNC-TV, Denver, 1992. Mem. NEA, Am. Alliance for Theater and Edn., Alliance for Colo. Theater (treas. 1993-94, Colo. Theater Educator of Yr. 1993), Colo. Edn. Assn., Denver Classroom Tchrs. Assn. Avocations: stamp collecting, model railroading. Home: 5937 S Pearl St Littleton CO 80121-2248

SCHAPIRA, MOREY RAEL, electronics sales executive; b. Chgo., Jan. 4, 1949; s. Julius and Rose (Schwartz) S; m. Barbara Stein, May 29, 1977; children: Rachel, Deborah, Michael. BS in Physics cum laude, Case Western Res. U., 1970; MBA, Harvard U., 1977. Rsch. scientist rsch. div. Raytheon Co., Waltham, Mass., 1970-75; cons. scientist Lincoln Labs., MIT, Lexington, 1976; product mktg. engr. microwave semicondr. div. Hewlett Packard Co., San Jose, Calif., 1977-80; domestic sales mgr. optoelectronics div. Hewlett Packard Co., Palo Alto, Calif., 1980-81, distbr. mktg. mgr. optoelectronics div., 1981-83; corp. distbn. mgr. Hewlett Packard Components, San Jose, Calif., 1983-85; nat. distbr., sales mgr. Micro Power Systems, Santa Clara, Calif., 1985-87; nat. sales mgr. Network Gen. Corp., Menlo Park, Calif., 1987-89, v.p. worldwide sales, 1989-90, gen. mgr. Asia/Ams. sales, 1991-93; v.p. mktg. Digital Link Corp., Sunnyvale, Calif., 1993-94; v.p. sales and mktg. SmartDB Corp., Palo Alto, Calif., 1994-97; nat. sales dir. NetCom Sys., Chatsworth, Calif., 1997—. Editor-in-chief, then pub. A Guide to Jewish Boston, 1974-77; pub., editor-in-chief HarBus News, 1976-77. gen. mgr. network gen. Asia, Ams. Div. chmn. United Way Campaign., 1978; nat. v.p. Union of Councils for Soviet Jews, 1979-84, nat. pres., 1984-86; pres. Bay Area Council on Soviet Jewry, San Francisco, 1980-84. Mem. Am. Mgmt. Assn., No. Calif. Venture Capital Assn., Harvard Bus. Sch. Assn. No. Calif., Am. Phys. Soc., Churchill Club. Home: 1154 Crespi Dr Sunnyvale CA 94086-7039 Office: Netcom Sys 20550 Nordhoff St Chatsworth CA 91311-6113

SCHAPP, REBECCA MARIA, museum director; b. Stuttgart, Fed. Republic Germany, Dec. 12, 1956; came to U.S., 1957; d. Randall Todd and Elfriede Carolina (Scheppan) Spradlin; m. Thomas James Schapp, May 29, 1979. AA, DeAnza Coll., 1977; BA in Art, San Jose State U., 1979, MA in Art Adminstrn., 1985. Adminstrv. dir. Union Gallery San Jose (Calif.), 1979-82; from mus. coordinator to dep. dir. de Saisset Mus. Santa Clara (Calif.) U., 1982-92, dir., 1993—. Mem. San Francisco Mus. Modern Art; bd. dirs. Works of San Jose, v.p. 1983-85. Mem. Non-Profit Gallery Assn. (bd. dirs.). Democrat. Avocations: racquetball, walking, bicycling, camping. Office: De Saisset Museum Santa Clara Univ 500 El Camino Real Santa Clara CA 95050-4345

SCHATT, PAUL, newspaper editor; b. N.Y.C., Aug. 31, 1945; divorced; children: Suzannah, Andrew. BA with distinction Polit. Sci., English, Ariz. State U., 1967. Editor Ariz. Republic, 1964-66, reporter, 1965-74, urban affairs editor, 1974-75, asst. city editor, 1975-79, chief asst. city editor, 1979-82, asst. met. editor, 1985-86, met. editor, 1986-88, editor edit. pages, 1993—; asst. editor Ariz. Mag., 1981-82, editor, 1982-85; editor edit. pages Phoenix Gazette, 1988-93; editor edit. pages The Ariz. Republic, 1993-97, assoc. editor, 1998—; vis. lectr. Pub. Affairs Journalism, Ariz. State U., 1976—, instr. Mass. Comm. Dept., 1974-76; dir. Eugene C. Pulliam Fellowship. Phoenix program, 1990—; writing coach, 1989; del. Pre White House Conf. Librs., 1991. v.p. Crisis Nursery, 1984-87, bd. dirs. 1980-87; exec. bd. Hospice of the Valley, 1980-87; pres. Friends of Phoenix Pub. Libr., 1985-86, bd. dirs. 1986—; bd. trustees 1st Amendment Congress, 1989—; bd. dirs. Camelback Hosps. 1982-89, chmn. bd. dirs. 1986-87, Cactus Pine Coun. Girl Scouts Am., 1988-89, Sun Sounds Inc., 1982-89, Valley Leadership Inc., 1991—, alum. assn., 1985-89, Ariz. Zool. Soc., 1991—, Barrow Neurol. Found., 1991—, Kids Voting, 1991-93, Barry Goldwater Inst., 1991-93, Ariz. Club, 1991—. With Ariz. Nat. Guard, 1966-79. Recipient Montgomery award Outstanding Svc. to Community Friends of Phoenix Pub. Libr., 1989; profl. Journalism fellow Stanford U., 1970-71. Mem. Am. Soc. Newspaper Editors, Soc. Profl. Journalists (pres. Valley of Sun chpt. 1974-75, 83-84, exec. bd. 1988-92), Sigma Delta Chi (co-chair nat. convention 1974). Office: The Ariz Republic Editorial Dept 200 E Van Buren St Phoenix AZ 85004-2238

SCHATZ, MONA CLAIRE STRUHSAKER, social worker, educator, consultant, researcher; b. Phila., Jan. 4, 1950; d. Milton and Josephine (Kivo) S.; m. James Fredrick Struhsaker, Dec. 31, 1979 (div.); 1 child, Thain Mackenzie. BA, Metro State Coll., 1976; postgrad., U. Minn., 1976; MSW, U. Denver, 1979; D in Social Work/Social Welfare, U. Pa., 1986. Teaching fellow U. Pa., Phila., 1981-82; asst. prof. S.W. Mo. State U., Springfield, 1982-85; assoc. prof. Colo. State U., Ft. Collins, 1985—, field coord., 1986-88, dir. non-profit agy. adminstrn. program, 1995-97, project dir. Edn. and Rsch. Inst. for Fostering Families, 1987—, dir. youth agy. adminstrn. program Am. Humanics, 1988-90; mem. coun. foster care cert. program Western Gov.'s U., 1998—; cons. Mgmt. and Behavioral Sci. Ctr., The Wharton Sch. U. Pa., 1981-82; resource specialist So. N.J. Health Sys. Agy., 1982; adj. faculty mem. U. Mo., Springfield, 1994; med. social worker Rehab. and Vis. Nurse Assn., 1985-90; mem. Colo. Child Welfare Adv. Com., Family Conservation Initiative; internat. cons. and trainer Inst. for Internat. Connections, Russia, Latvia, Albania, U.S., Hungary, Ukraine, Romania, 1992—. Contbr. articles to profl. jours. including Jour. Social Work Edn., New Social Worker, Chosen Child: Internat. Adoption Mag., others. Cons., field rep. Big Bros./Big Sisters of Am., Phila., 1979-83; acting dir., asst. dir. Big Sisters of Colo., 1971-78; owner Polit. Cons. in Colo., Denver, 1978-79; active Food Co-op, Ft. Collins, Foster Parent, Denver, Capital Hill United Neighbors, Adams County (Denver) Social Planning Coun., Co., Colo. Justice Coun., Denver, Regional Girls Shelter, Springfield; bd. dirs. Crisis Helpline and Info. Svc. Scholar Lilly Endowment, Inc., 1976, Piton Found., 1978; recipient Spl. Recognition award Big Bros./Big Sisters of Am., 1983, Recognition award Am. Humanics Mgmt. Inst., 1990. Mem. Inst. Internat. Connections (bd. dirs., mem. adv. bd.), Coun. Social Work Edn., Group for Study of Generalist Social Work, Social Welfare History Group, Nat. Assn. Social Workers (nominating com. Springfield chpt., state bd. dirs., No. Colo. rep.), Student Social Work Assn. Colo. State U. (adv. 1986-89), Permanency Planning Coun. for Children and Youth, NOW (treas. Springfield chpt. 1984-85), Student Nuclear Awareness Group (advisor), Student Social Work Assn. (advisor), Har Shalom (tchg. in youth edn. program), Alpha Delta Mu. Democrat. Avocations: cooking, traveling, reading, biking, sewing. Office: Colo State U Social Work Dept Fort Collins CO 80523

SCHAUER, RONALD L., executive. Chmn., pres. CEO HMT Tech., Fremont, Calif. Office: 1055 Page Ave Fremont CA 94538-7341*

SCHAUFLER, MARK SHERIDAN, evangelist; b. Myrtle Point, Oreg., Jan. 13, 1955; s. Paul Gerhard and Sue Lynn (Nelson) S.; m. Kristy Sue Knuth, Dec. 12, 1957; children: Amanda, Silas, Abigail. BS in environ. sci., Wash. State U., 1978; M Biblical lit., Assemblies of God Theol. Sem., Springfield, Mo., 1996. Project engr. Swift Engring., Lacey, Wash., 1978-80; custodial work Evergreen Christian Ctr., Olympia, Wash., 1981-82; assoc. pastor Faith Assembly of Lacey, 1982-92; pres. MST Ministries, Olympia, 1992—; asst. youth dir. N.W. Dist. Assemblies of God, Everett, Wash., 1994—; dir. Ambassadors in Missions N.W. Dist., 1993—. Author: He Loves, 1996, Painting the Two White Lines, 1998, Kingdom Accomplishments, 1998, Once Upon a Time, 1996. Mem. Stop the Violence com., Lacey, 1994-95. Avocations: travel, sports, music, writing. Home: PO Box 8490 Lacey WA 98509-8490 Office: MST Ministries PO Box 8490 Lacey WA 98509-8490

SCHAWLOW, ARTHUR LEONARD, physicist, educator; b. Mt. Vernon, N.Y., May 5, 1921; s. Arthur and Helen (Mason) S.; m. Aurelia Keith Townes, May 19, 1951; children: Arthur Keith, Helen Aurelia, Edith Ellen. BA, U. Toronto, Ont., Can., 1941, MA, 1942, PhD, 1949, LLD (hon.), 1970; DSc (hon.), U. Ghent, Belgium, 1968, U. Bradford, Eng., 1970, U. Ala., 1984, Trinity Coll., Dublin, Ireland, 1986; DTech (hon.), U. Lund, Sweden, 1987; DSL (hon.), Victoria U., Toronto, 1993. Postdoctoral fellow, rsch. assoc. Columbia U., 1949-51, vis. assoc. prof., 1960; rsch. physicist Bell Tel. Labs., 1951-61, cons., 1961-62; prof. physics Stanford (Calif.) U., 1961-91, also J.G. Jackson-C.J. Wood prof. physics, 1978, prof. emeritus, 1991—, exec. head dept. physics, 1966-70, acting chmn. dept., 1973-74. Author: (with C.H. Townes) Microwave Spectroscopy, 1955; Co-inventor (with C.H. Townes), optical maser or laser, 1958. Recipient Ballantine medal Franklin Inst., 1962, Thomas Young medal and prize Inst. Physics and Phys. Soc., London, 1963, Schawlow medal Laser Inst. Am., 1982, Nobel prize in physics, 1981, Nat. Medal of Sci., NSF, 1991, Arata award High Temperature Soc. Japan, 1994, Ronald H. Brown Am. Innovator award U.S. Dept. Commerce, 1996; named Calif. Scientist of Yr., 1973, Marconi Internat. fellow, 1977; named to Am. Inventors Hall of Fame, 1996. Fellow Am. Acad. Arts and Scis., Am. Phys. Soc. (coun. 1966-70, chmn. div. electron and atomic physics 1974, pres. 1981), Optical Soc. Am. (hon. mem. 1983, dir.-at-large 1966-68, pres. 1975, Frederick Ives medal 1976); mem. NAS, IEEE (Liebmann prize 1964), AAAS (chmn. physics sect. 1979), Am. Philos. Soc., Royal Irish Acad. (hon.). Office: Stanford U Dept Physics Stanford CA 94305

SCHAYE, CARMEN ESTRADA, college dean; b. Hollywood, Calif., Aug. 22, 1948; d. Ramiro Tomas Estrada Nieto and Carmen Ballesteros Von Herbold; m. Gordon Fels Schaye, May 12, 1993; children: Robert, Celeste. BA, Calif. State Univ., 1976, MA, 1979; MA, Calif. State Univ., Northridge, 1983; EdD, Pepperdine Univ., 1995. Founder, dir. career ctr. L.A. East L.A. Coll., 1984-87; founder, dir. transfer ctr. L.A. Southwest Coll., 1987-89, assoc. dean, 1989-95; assoc. dean L.A. City Coll., 1995—; dir. NE Valley Health Corp., Pocoima, Calif., 1984-90, Assn. Prof. Hisp. Edn., 1976-80; chmn. curriculum com. Work Force L.A., 1998—. Pres. Nat. Women Political Caucus, L.A. South Bay, 1997—. Recipient Art Legend award Watts Health Found., 1997, Commendation award L.A. City Coun., 1992, Commendation award U.S. Congress, 1989; named Innovator of Yr. L.A. Cmty. Coll., 1987. Democrat. Avocations: architecture and real estate. Home: 58 Portuguese Bend Rd Rolling Hills CA 90274-5070 Office: L A City Coll 855 NE Vermont Los Angeles CA 90029

SCHECHTER, JOHN MENDELL, music educator; b. Rockville Centre, N.Y., Apr. 29, 1946; s. Jennie (Woldman) S.; m. Janis O'Driscoll, June 25, 1970; 1 child, Anna. AB in Music, Hamilton Coll., 1967; MMus, Ind. U. [illegible] (N.Y.) U., 1983-84; from vis. asst. prof. music to assoc. prof. music U. Calif., Santa Cruz, 1985—. Author: The Indispensable Harp, 1992. Mem. Soc. Ethnomusicology, Phi Beta Kappa. Office: U Calif Music Dept 1156 High St Santa Cruz CA 95064-1077

SCHEDLER, GILBERT WALTER, religion educator; b. Vancouver, B.C., Can., Mar. 11, 1935; s. Oscar August and Margaret (Barth) S.; children: Christopher, Rachel, Sara. BA, Concordia Coll., St. Louis, 1957; BD, Concordia Sem., St. Louis, 1960; MA, Washington U., St. Louis, 1963; PhD, U. Chgo., 1970. Prof. U. Pacific, Stockton, Calif., 1967—. Author: (poetry) Waking Before Dawn, 1978, Making Plans, 1980, That Invisible Wall, 1985, Starting Over, 1992. NDEA fellow, 1960-64; NEH grantee, 1987. Taoist. Home: 1781 Oxford Way Stockton CA 95204-4260 Office: U Pacific 3601 Pacific Ave Stockton CA 95211-0110

SCHEER, GARY WERNER, electrical engineer; b. Rapid City, S.D., Sept. 11, 1954; s. Alfred Carl and Marcella Nadine (Caltvedt) S.; m. Karen Lynn Kradolfer, June 18, 1977; children: Nicole Rebecca, Lisette Megan. BSEE, Mont. State U., 1977. Registered profl. engr. Ind. automation cons. Bozeman, Mont., 1977; engr. project mgr., software supr. Mont. Power Co., Butte, 1977-84; mgr. tech. support and assessment Tetragenics Co., Butte, 1985-88, mktg.mgr., 1988-90; devel. engr. Schweitzer Engring. Labs., Inc., Pullman, Wash., 1990-92, engring. mgr., 1992-96, v.p. R&D, 1996-98, v.p. automation and engring. svcs., 1998—. Trustee YMCA at Wash. State U., Pullman, 1992—; candidate for Mont. State Legislature, 1984. Inducted into Mont. Inventors Hall of Fame, 1988. Mem. IEEE, IEEE Computer Soc., IEEE Power Engring. Soc., Asns. Computing Machinery, Internat. Soc. Measurement Control. Achievements include patent for model 2 coder/decoder, patent for relay to relay communications. Home: 2000 NW Friel St Pullman WA 99163-3610 Office: Schweitzer Engring Labs 2350 NE Hopkins Ct Pullman WA 99163-5600

SCHEER, JANET KATHY, mathematics educator; b. Bklyn., Apr. 22, 1947; d. Seymour and Hilda (Shoer) S. BA, Bklyn. Coll., 1968; MS, Syracuse (N.Y.) U., 1969; PhD, Ariz. State U., 1977. Cert. tchr., N.Y., Ariz.; cert. prin., Ariz. Math. tchr. Jamesville (N.Y.) DeWitt Middle Sch., 1969-72; math. tchr., middle sch. coordinator Am. Internat. Sch., Kfar Shmaryahu, Israel, 1972-74; from asst. prof. to assoc. prof. So. Ill. U., Carbondale, 1977-88; nat. product devel. specialist Scott, Foresman and Co., Glenview, Ill., 1989-90; dir. field svcs. for math. Scott, Foresman and Co., 1991; exec. dir. Create A Vision, Foster City, Calif., 1992—; cons. in field, 1977—; sr. nat. math. cons. Holt, Rinehart & Winston, N.Y.C., 1986-89, Harcourt Brace-Jovanovich/Holt, 1989. Editor Ill. Math. Tchr. jour., 1980-83; author: Manipulatives in Mathematics Unlimited, 1987; columnist Learning Mag., 1996-97; contbr. to textbooks and profl. jours. Named one of Outstanding Young Women Am., 1978, 81-85, Outstanding Tchr. Yr. So. Ill. U., 1978-79; recipient numerous grants. Mem. Nat. Council Tchrs. Math., Research Council for Diagnostic and Prescriptive Math. (charter mem., v.p. 1984-86), Ill. Council Tchrs. Math. (various offices), Phi Delta Kappa, Kappa Delta Pi. Avocations: swimming, golf, tennis. Office: Create A Vision 1175 Chess Dr #206 Foster City CA 94044

SCHEFTER, JAMES LORAN, author; b. Little Falls, Minn., Mar. 15, 1940; s. Richard Loren and Cora Geneva (Wang) S.; m. Mary Florence Ainsworth, June 3, 1967; children: Michael, William, Andrew. BA, Laverne (Calif.) U., 1975; MBA, U. Mo., Kansas City, 1978. Reporter Houston Chronicle, 1963-65; corr. Time and Life Mags., 1965-73; with pub. rels. dept. TRW, Redondo Beach, Calif., 1973-75; mgr. pub. rels. Hallmark Cards, Inc., Kansas City, 1975-76; dir. comm. Midwest Rsch. Inst., Kansas City, 1976-78, cons., 1978—; west coast editor Popular Sci. Mag., L.A., 1978-89; contbg. editor Popular Sci. Mag., 1997—; freelance author, 1989—. Author: All Corvettes Are Red, 1997, Santa Fe, 1989, Capturing Energy From the Wind, 1982, The Race, 1999. Street commr. City of El Lago, Tex., 1970-72; mem. platform com. Rep. Party of Tex., Houston, 1971-72. With U.S. Army, 1960-63. Recipient writing award Deadline Club, N.Y.C., 1976, numerous awards Aviation and Space Writers Assn., 1978-88. Mem. Nat. Assn. Sci. Writers. Republican. Avocations: skiing, computers. Fax: 435-645-7480. Home and Office: PO Box 2160 Park City UT 84060

SCHEIBER, HARRY N., law educator; b. N.Y.C., 1935. BA, Columbia U., 1955; MA, Cornell U., 1957, PhD, 1961; MA (hon.), Dartmouth Coll., 1965, JD (hon.) Uppsala U. (Sweden), 1998,. instr. to assoc. prof. history Dartmouth Coll., 1960-68, prof., 1968-71; prof. Am. history U. Calif., San Diego, 1971-80; prof. law Boalt Hall, U. Calif., Berkeley, 1980—, chmn. jurisprudence and social policy program, 1982-84, 90-93, assoc. dean, 1990-93, 96—; The Stefan Riesenfeld Prof., 1991—; vice chair Univ. Academic Senate, 1993-94. chair, 1994-95; Fulbright disting. sr. lectr., Australia, 1983, marine affairs coord. Calif. Sea Grant Coll. Program, 1989—; vis. rsch. prof. Law Inst. U. Uppsala, Sweden, 1995, hon. prof. DiTella U., Buenos Aires, 1998—. Chmn. Littleton Griswold Prize Legal History, 1985-88; pres. N.H. Civil Liberties Union, 1969-70; chmn. Project '87 Task Force on Pub. Programs, Washington, 1982-85; dir. Berkeley Seminar on Federalism, 1986-95; cons. judiciary study U.S. Adv. Commn. Intergovernmental Rels., 1985-88; dir. NEH Inst. on Constitutionalism, U. Calif., Berkeley, 1986-87, 88-91. Recipient Sea Grant Colls. award, 1981-83, 84-85, 86-98, 99—; fellow Ctr. Advanced Study in Behavioral Scis., Stanford Calif., 1967, 71; Guggenheim fellow, 1971, 88; Rockefeller Found. humanities fellow, 1979, NEH fellow, 1985-86; NSF grantee, 1979, 80, 88-89; Fellow U. Calif. Humanities Rsch. Inst., 1989. Mem. Am. Hist. Assn., Orgn. Am. Historians, Agrl. History Soc. (pres. 1978), Econ. History Assn. (trustee 1978-80), Law and Soc. Assn. (trustee 1979-81, 1996-99), Am. Soc. Legal History (dir. 1982-86, 90-93, 96-99), Nat. Assessment History and Citizenship Edn. (chmn. nat. acad. bd. 1986-87), Marine Affairs and Policy Assn. (bd. dirs. 1991-96), Ocean Governance Study Group (steering com. 1991—), Internat. Coun. Environ. Law. Author numerous books including: (with L. Friedman) American Law and the Constitutional Order, 1978, 2d edit. 1988, The State and Freedom of Contract, 1998; contbr. articles to law revs.and social sci. jours., 1963—. Office: U Calif Berkeley Law Sch Boalt Hall Berkeley CA 94720-2150

SCHELAR, VIRGINIA MAE, chemistry consultant; b. Kenosha, Wis., Nov. 26, 1924; d. William and Blanche M. (Williams) S. BS, U. Wis., 1947, MS, 1953; MEd, Harvard U., 1962; PhD, U. Wis., 1969. Instr. U. Wis., Milw., 1947-51; info. specialist Abbott Labs., North Chgo., Ill., 1953-56; instr. Wright Jr. Coll., Chgo., 1957-58; asst. prof. No. Ill. U., DeKalb, 1958-63; prof. St Petersburg (Fla.) Jr. Coll., 1965-67; asst. prof. Chgo. State Coll., 1967-68; prof. Grossmont Coll., El Cajon, Calif., 1968-80; cons. Calif., 1981—. Author: Kekule Centennial, 1965; contbr. articles to profl. jours. Active citizens adv. coun. DeKalb Consol. Sch. Bd.; voters svc. chair League Women Voters, del. to state and nat. convs., judicial chair, election laws chair. Standard Oil fellow, NSF grantee; recipient Lewis prize U. Wis. Fellow Am. Inst. Chemists; mem. Am. Chem. Soc. (membership affairs com., chmn. western councilor's caucus, exec. com., councilor, legis. counselor, chmn. edn. com., editor state and local bulletins). Avocations: swimming, folk dancing.

SCHELL, MERRY L., critical care and oncological nurse; b. Seminole, Tex., Sept. 16, 1946; d. Tiny Hollis and Mary Elizabeth (Yates) Odom; m. Thomas E. Schell, Jan. 17, 1965; children: Carrie Elizabeth, Thomas Wade. AS, Bakersfield Community Coll., 1977; BSBA, U. San Francisco, 1984. Cert. oncology nurse specialist. Dir. nursing Med. Pers. Pool, Bakersfield, Calif.; head nurse in oncology and hematology San Joaquin Community Hosp., Bakersfield; clin. dir. critical cre Delano (Calif.) Regional Med. Ctr. Mem. Oncology Nursing Soc.

SCHELL, PAUL E. S., mayor; b. Fort Dodge, Iowa, Oct. 8, 1937; m. Pam Schell. BA, U. Iowa, 1960; JD, Columbia U., 1963. Pvt. practice, 1963-74; dir. dept. cmty. devel. City of Seattle, 1974-77, mayor, 1998—; pres., founder Cornerstone Columbia Devel. Co., 1979-87; commr. Port of Seattle, 1989—, pres. commn., 1995—; dean Architecture and Urban Planning U. Wash., 1992-95. Past bd. dirs. Intiman Theatre, A Contemporary Theater; past pres. Allied Arts; founder, active Cascadia Project; bd. dirs. Trade Devel. Alliance; mem. Friends of the Pike Place Market. Office: Office of the Mayor Municipal Bldg 600 4th Ave 12th Fl Seattle WA 98104-1850*

SCHELLER, ERIN LINN, publishing company executive; b. Port Arthur, Tex., Dec. 25, 1942; d. Truman Edward Jr. and Margaret Jane (Imhoff) [illegible] Oct. 10, 1981; 1 child, Christopher Wayne Levy. Student, Barat Coll., 1960-61; BS, U. Tex., 1964. Tchr. Cath. Sch. Dist., Houston, 1965-67; owner, pres. The Pub.'s Mark, Incline Village, Nev., 1982—, pres., chmn. bd. EduVision Inc., computer software co., Incline Village, 1994—, guest lectr. [illegible]

Author: Children Are Not Paper Dolls, 1982, I Know Just How You Feel, 1986, Dear Teacher, 1988, 150 Facts About Grieving Children, 1990, Premonitions, Visitations and Dreams, 1991. Advisor Mo. Bapt. Children's Group, St. Louis, 1980-81; chpt. leader The Compassionate Friends, Denver, 1980-81, Greeley, Colo., 1981-83; 2nd v.p. Republican Women's Club, Incline Village, 1987-90; mem. AAUW, Incline Village, 1987-89; pres. Teester's Ladies Golf Assn., Incline Village, 1987-90; mem. Assn. for Death. Edn. and Counseling, 1985—, Grief Edn. Inst., 1981—, The Compassionate Friends, 1980—. Named Honored Author, Ill. Libr. Exposition, 1985. Republican. Lutheran. Avocations: golf, tennis, racketball, cross-country skiing, needlework. Home and Office: The Publishers Mark PO Box 6300 Incline Village NV 89450-6300

SCHELLING, ANDREW, poet, translator, educator; b. Washington, D.C., Jan. 14, 1953; s. Thomas C. and Corinne (Saposs) S.; m. Kristina Rose Loften, Oct. 12, 1980; (div. June 15, 1993); 1 child, Althea Rose. BA, U. Calif., Santa Cruz, 1975. Assoc. prof. Naropa Inst., Boulder, Colo., 1990—; contbg. editor Shambhala Sun, Halifax, Nova Scotia, 1995—. Author 12 books including: Dropping the Bow, 1991 (Acad. of Am. Poets award 1992), Old Growth, 1995, Cane Groves of Narmada River, 1998, The Road to Ocosingo, 1998; editor (anthology) Disembodied Poetics, 1995. Grantee: Witter Bynner Poetry Found., Santa Fe, N. Mex., 1996; contemplative fellow Am. Coun. Learned Socs., N.Y.C., 1998. Avocation: wilderness activities. Office: The NAROPA Inst 2130 Arapahoe Ave Boulder CO 80303

SCHENDEL, WINFRIED GEORGE, insurance company executive; b. Harpstedt, Germany, June 19, 1931; s. Willi Rudolf Max and Anna Margarete (Sassen) S.; came to U.S., 1952, naturalized, 1956; B.S. in Elect. and Indsl. Engring., Hannover-Stadthagen U., Hannover, W. Germany, 1952; m. Joanne Wiiest, Aug. 24, 1953; children—Victor Winfried, Bruce Lawrence, Rachelle Laureen. Elec. draftsman Houston Lighting & Power Co., 1954-57; elec. draftsman, corrosion technician Transcontinental Gas Pipeline Co., Houston, 1957-59; elec. engr. Ken R. White Cons. Engrs., Denver, 1959-61; sales engr. Weco div. Food Machinery & Chem. Corp., various locations, 1961-64; ins. field underwriter N.Y. Life Ins. Co., Denver, 1964-66, asst. mgr., 1966-70, mgmt. asst., 1970-71, gen. mgr., 1971-77, mgr., 1979-85, field underwriter, 1985—; ind. gen. agt., Denver, 1978-79; ins. broker and adviser, 1979—. Instl. rep., advancement chmn. Denver Area council Boy Scouts Am., Lakewood, Colo., 1968-72; precinct chmn. Republican Party, Jefferson County, Colo., 1976, 78; founder, mem. (life) Sister City Program, Lakewood, Colo.; chmn. adv. bd. ARC, Jefferson County, Colo., 1987-89. Recipient Centurion award, 1966; Northwestern Region Leader Manpower Devel. award N.Y. Life Ins. Co., 1968, Salesman of Yr. award Jefferson County Salesman with a Purpose Club, 1983, Top awards ARC, 1988-89. Mem. Nat. Assn. Life Underwriters, Gen. Agents and Mgrs. Assn. (recipient Conf. Nat. Mgmt. award, 1975), Colo. Life Underwriters Assn. (reg. v.p. Denver Metro area 1989-90), Mile High Assn. Life Underwriters (pres. 1986-87, nat. com. 1988, 91), Lakewood C. of C. (pres. people-to-people, Trailblazer of Yr. award 1982, 83, Trail Boss of Yr. 1983). Presbyterian (elder). Clubs: Lions, Edelweiss, Internat. Order Rocky Mountain Goats, N.Y. Life Star, Masons, Rotary (bd. dirs. Fort Collins chpt., Paul Harris award, 1995), Shriners. Home and Office: 925 Deerhurst Cir Fort Collins CO 80525-6919

SCHENKEL, FELICIA ANN, cardiothoracic transplant coordinator; b. N.Y.C., July 11, 1960; d. Richard Warren and Marcia S.; m. Mark C. Barr, Mar. 12, 1993; 1 child, Erin Rachel. ADN, Quennipiac, Hamden, Calif., 1981, BA, 1982. Cert. clin. transplant coordinator NATCO. Sr. coord. cardiothoracis transplantation U. So. Calif. U. Hosp., L.A., 1992—. Contbr. chpt. to book. Mem. United Network Organ Sharing (del. 1998—). Office: USC Univ Hosp 1510 San Pablo St Ste 619 Los Angeles CA 90033-4586

SCHENKKAN, ROBERT FREDERIC, writer, actor; b. Chapel Hill, N.C., Mar. 19, 1953; s. Robert Frederic Sr. and Jean (McKenzie) S.; children: Sarah Victoria, Joshua McHenry. BA in Theatre Arts, U. Tex., 1975; MFA in Acting, Cornell U., 1977. Author: (plays) Final Passages, 1981, The Survivalist, 1982 (best of the fringe award Edinburgh Festival 1984), Tachinoki, 1987, Tall Tales, 1988 (Playwrights Forum award 1988, Best One Act Plays 1993), Heaven on Earth, 1989 (Julie Harris Playwright award Beverly Hills Theatre Guild 1989), The Kentucky Cycle, 1991 (Pulitzer prize for drama 1992, L.A. Drama Critics Circle Best Play award 1992, Penn Ctr. West award 1993, Best Play Tony award nominee 1993, Best Play Drama Desk award nominee 1993), Conversations with the Spanish Lady and Other One-Act Plays, 1993, The Dream Thief, 1998, (films) The Long Ride Home, 1995, Crazy Horse, 1996, The Quiet American, 1997, Play for a Kingdom, 1998, The Liars' Club, 1998. Grantee Vogelstein Found., 1982, Arthur Found., 1988, Fund for New Am. Plays grantee 1990, Calif. Arts Coun. grantee, 1991. Mem. Writers Guild, Dramatists Guild, Actors Equity, SAG, Ensemble Studio Theatre.

SCHERER, ALICE E., writer, researcher; b. Ft. Devons, Mass., Apr. 25, 1953; d. Hal Norman and Louise Anita (Duso) Krogstad; m. Howard Newcomb, Jan. 1987 (div. July 1996). Student, Ball State U., 1971-72. Dir. Ctr. for the Study of Beadwork, Portland, Oreg., 1986—. Co-author: The New Beadwork, 1992. Mem. Soc. Bead Rschrs. (publs. com. 1996—), Portland Bead Soc. (founding mem.), Am. Craft Coun. Avocations: sewing, photography, travel, reading. Office: Ctr for Study of Beadwork PO Box 13719 Portland OR 97213-0719

SCHERER, CORALIE R., psychologist; b. Miami, Sept. 13, 1949; came to U.S., 1944; d. Samuel Elias and Jeannette (Rosen) S.; children: Rachel Glickman, Daniel Quigley. BA, U. Fla., 1971, MA, 1974, PhD, 1991. Lic. psychologist, Fla. Reading, English tchr. PK Yonge Lab. Sch., Gainesville, Fla., 1971-86, various middle schs., Fla.; alcohol and drug counselor New Perspectives of Marin, Larkspur, Calif., 1987-88; pvt. practice psychology Eric Cohen & Assocs., Menlo Park, Calif., 1990—, San Jose Marital and Sexuality Ctr., Santa Clara, 1990—; asst. prof. reading Coll. of San Mateo, Calif., 1989—; co-editor dept. of sexuality Self Help and Psychology mag., San Diego, 1996—. Mem. Am. Psychol. Assn., Calif. Psychol. Assn., Santa Clara County Psychol. Assn. (editor). Office: San Jose Marital & Sexuality Ctr 100 N Winchester Blvd Santa Clara CA 95050-6520

SCHERF, DIETMAR, publishing executive; b. Graz, Austria, June 12, 1961; came to U.S., 1990; s. Friedrich and Maria (Rosenberger) S.; m. Patricia Michaela Rech, Apr. 9, 1987; children: Alexander, Deborah, Daniel, David. Diploma, trade sch., Graz, 1979. CEO Handelshaus D. Scherf, Vienna, Austria, 1987-90; CEO, pres. Scherf, Inc., Las Vegas, Nev., 1990—. Author: Short Term Trading, 1990, (booklet) Ross Perot, 1992, I Love Me: Avoiding and Overcoming Depressions, 1998. Avocations: swimming, movies, reading, Bible studies. Office: Scherf Inc PO Box 80180 Las Vegas NV 89180-0180

SCHERICH, ERWIN THOMAS, civil engineer, consultant; b. Inland, Nebr., Dec. 6, 1918; s. Harry Erwin and Ella (Peterson) S.; student Hastings Coll., 1937-39, N.C. State Coll., 1943-44; B.S., U. Nebr., 1946-48; M.S., U. Colo., 1948-51; m. Jessie Mae Funk, Jan. 1, 1947; children—Janna Rae Scherich Thornton, Jerilyn Mae Scherich Dobson, Mark Thomas. Civil and design engr. U.S. Bur. Reclamation, Denver, 1948-84, chief spillways and outlets sect., 1974-75, chief dams br., div. design, 1975-78, chief tech. rev. staff, 1978-79, chief div. tech. rev. Office of Asst. Commr. Engring. and Rsch. Ctr., 1980-84; cons. civil engr., 1984—. Mem. U.S. Com. Internat. Commn. on Large Dams. Served with AUS, 1941-45. Registered profl. engr., Colo. Fellow ASCE; mem. NSPE (nat. dir. 1981-87, v.p. southwestern region 1991-93), Profl. Engrs. Colo. (pres. 1977-78), Jefferson County West C. of C. Republican. Methodist. Home and Office: 3915 Balsam St Wheat Ridge CO 80033-4449

SCHERR, RICHARD J., sales professional; b. Oceanside, Calif., Sept. 25, 1946; children: Jason R., Chris R. AA, Phoenix Coll., 1967; BS, Ariz. State U., 1971. Sales mgr. Western region Bio Compression, Irvine, Calif., 1995—. Mem. Hoag Hosp. Found., Newport Beach, Calif., 1995—. Maj. USMCR ret. Mem. Ariz. State U. Alumni Assn. (bd. dirs. 1995—). Home and Office: PO Box 8857 Newport Beach CA 92658-8857

SCHETNAN, BRENDA, nurse; b. Johnstown, Pa., Jan. 27, 1964; d. Thomas G. and Sally L. (Ream) Hampton; m. Richard Schetnan, Oct. 18, 1997. ASN, Mt. Aloysius Jr. Coll., 1988. RN N.Mex., Ark., Maine, SC, Del., VA, Fla., KY, Tex., Calif. Nurse U. Va. Hosp., Charlottesville, 1988-89; travel nurse Travel Nursing Cos., U.S.A., 1989-96; hospice nurse Quality Continuum Hospice, Albuquerque, 1996-98, Presbyn. Hospice, 1997—. Mem. Romance Writers Am. (sec. Land of Enchantment Romance Authors chpt. 1998). Methodist. Avocations: writing, yoga, sewing, needlecrafts, pets. Home: 9013 Hendrix Rd NE Albuquerque NM 87111-3111

SCHEUERELL, DOUGLAS ANDREW, musician, educator; b. Madison, Wis.; s. Orville James and Elizabeth Evelyn (Bickett) S.; m. Victoria Ann Martin, Aug. 4, 1992; 1 child, Adrian. MusB with distinction, U. Wis., 1971. Cert. tchr. K-12, Wis., Calif. Musician Madison, Wis., 1966-74; intern choral dir. Sun Prairie (Wis.) High Sch., 1970; mem. faculty East Bay Ctr. for the Performing Arts, Berkeley, Calif., 1977-78, Family Light Music Sch., Sausalito, Calif., 1978; pers. mgr. Vitamin Rsch. Products, Mountain View, Calif., 1982-83; tabla tutor Eugene, Oreg., 1988-93; mem. faculty U. Oreg. Sch. of Music, Eugene, 1993—; recording artist Stas. WHA and WHA-TV, Madison, 1973-74; musician, composer Missing Link Theater Co., Berkeley, 1977-78; accompanist U. N.Mex. Sch. of Dance, Albuquerque, 1979-1980; tabla soloist and accompanist North Indian classical music, Calif., Oreg., 1988—. Performance grantee Lane Regional Arts Coun., Eugene, 1989; Faculty Devel. grantee U. Oreg., Eugene, 1996. Avocation: golf. Home: 65 N Lawrence St Eugene OR 97401 Office: U Oreg Sch of Music Eugene OR 97403-1225

SCHICKEL, RICHARD, writer, film critic, producer; b. Milw., Feb. 10, 1933; s. Edward J. and Helen (Hendricks) S.; children: Erika Tracy, Jessica Avery. BS, U. Wis., 1955. Sr. editor Look mag., 1957-60, Show mag., 1960-63; freelance writer, 1963—; film critic Life mag., 1965-72, Time mag., 1973—; cons. Rockefeller Bros. Fund, 1964, Rockefeller Found., 1965; lectr. in history art Yale, 1972, 76; adj. prof. film, U. S. Calif., 1989; pres. Lorac Prodns., 1986—. Author: The World of Carnegie Hall, 1960, The Stars, 1962, Movies: The History of an Art and an Institution, 1964, The Gentle Knight, 1964, The Disney Version, 1968, The World of Goya, 1968, Second Sight: Notes on Some Movies, 1972, His Picture in the Papers, 1974, Harold Lloyd: The Shape of Laughter, 1974, The Men Who Made the Movies, 1975, The World of Tennis, 1975, The Fairbanks Album, 1975, Singled Out, 1981, Cary Grant, A Celebration, 1984, D.W. Griffith: An American Life, 1984, James Cagney, A Celebration, 1985, Intimate Strangers: The Culture of Celebrity, 1985, Striking Poses, 1987, Schickel on Film, 1989, Brando: A Life In Our Times, 1991, Double Indemnity, 1992, Clint Eastwood: A Biography, 1996; co-author: Lena, 1965, The Platinum Years, 1974, Hollywood at Home, 1990 (novel) Another I, Another You, 1978; co-editor: Film 67-68, 1968; producer, dir., writer (TV series) The Men Who Made the Movies, 1973; producer, writer: (TV spls.) Life Goes to the Movies, 1976, SPFX, 1980, Cary Grant, A Celebration, 1989; producer, writer, dir.: (TV spls.) Funny Business, 1978, Into the Morning: Willa Cather's America, 1978, The Horror Show, 1979, James Cagney: That Yankee Doodle Dandy, 1981, From Star Wars to Jedi: The Making of a Saga, 1983, Minnelli on Minnelli; Liza Remebers Vincent, 1987, Gary Cooper: American Life, American Legend, 1989, Myrna Loy: So Nice to Come Home To, 1990, Barbara Stanwyck: Fire and Desire, 1991, Eastwood & Co.: Making Unforgiven, 1992, Hollywood on Hollywood, 1993, Elia Kazan: A Director's Journey, 1995, The Moviemakers, 1996, Eastwood on Eastwood, 1997, The Harryhausen Chronicles, 1998; exec. producer: AFI's 100 Years 100 Movies, 1998. Recipient Book prize Brit. Film Inst., 1985; Guggenheim fellow, 1964. Mem. Nat. Soc. Film Critics, N.Y. Film Critics, Dirs. Guild Am., Writers Guild Am.

SCHICKETANZ, DALE EDWIN, educator; b. Omaha, Aug. 21, 1943; s. Lew Edwin and Carrie (Olson) S.; m. Pamela S. Scheu, Jan. 4, 1945. AA, Southwestern Coll., 1966; BA, San Diego State U., 1968; MA, Calif. State U., Fresno, 1974. Photography inst. Northland Pioneer Coll., Show Low, Ariz., 1976—. Author: Visions of the West, 1998. With U.S. Forestry Svc., White Mountains, Ariz., 1996-98. Sgt. USAF, 1968-72. Avocation: collecting pocket watches. Office: Northland Pioneer Coll PO Box 610 Holbrook AZ 86025

SCHIED, DAVID EUGENE, producer, animator, stunt-man; b. Billings, Mont., Aug. 22, 1957; s. Dale Edward Schied and Sharron Lee (Fisher) Hay; m. Barbara Ann Iserman, June 4, 1994; 1 child, Nolan David. BA (cum laude) in Cinema, TV Prodn., U. So. Calif., L.A., 1995, BA (cum laude) in Asian Lang., Culture, 1995. Stunt-actor various, 1982-96; pvt. practice Houston, L.A., 1982-89; fitness trainer YMCA, YWCA, Leisure Learning, Houston, 1982-85; karate, gymnastics tchr. Private Gyms, Houston, San Fernando Val, Calif., 1983-95; asst. dir. feature films, TV, Sun Valley, L.A., Ventura, Calif., 1993, 96; computer animator corporate videos, Ventura County, Calif., 1997—. Stunt work in films include Lone Wolf McQuade, 1982, Direct Hit, 1993, Ice, 1993; acted in Last Night of the Alamo, 1982; author: Streetwise: Self-Defense, 1986, Safe at Last!, 1989; co-producer (nat. TV commercial) Safe at Last!, 1990. Vol. U.S. Olympic Festival, Houston, 1986; bd. advisors Coalition On Victims Equal Rights, L.A., 1986-90; mem. Justice for Homicide Victims, Beverly Hills, Calif., 1997—. Ebelle scholar Ebelle of L.A., 1992-94, Gilmore Citation Award scholar U. So. Calif., L.A., 1992-95, Maskedal scholar U. So. Calif., L.A., 1993-95; grantee U. So. Calif., L.A., 1992-95. Mem. Internat. Friendship Force, Internat. Tae Kwon Do Fedn. (2nd degree black belt), Internat. Vietnamese Fighting Arts Fedn. (1st degree black belt), U.S. Judo Assn. (2nd degree black belt), Golden Key Nat. Honor Soc. Avocations: martial arts, acrobatics, hiking, camping, travel. Home and Office: 2124 Morley St Simi Valley CA 93065-3536

SCHIELDGE, JOHN PHILIP, physicist, researcher; b. Hartford, Conn., Feb. 28, 1937; s. Philip Adam and Henrietta Barbara (Uliasz) S.; m. Sandra Marshall Chassagne, Oct. 8, 1966; children: Kristy Lynne, Kurt Janek. BA, U. Calif., Santa Barbara, 1962; MS, UCLA, 1970, PhD, 1974. Postdoctoral fellow dept. atmospheric scis. UCLA, 1974-75; postdoctoral fellow, resident rsch. assoc. Nat. Rsch. Coun., Jet Propulsion Lab., Pasadena, Calif., 1976-78; rsch. scientist Calif. Inst. Tech./Jet Propulsion Lab., Pasadena, 1978—; asst. group mgr. Environ. Observations br. Climate Rsch. Group, NASA, 1981-82. Contbr. articles to profl. jours. Capt. USAF, 1963-68. Decorated Air Force Commendation medal; recipient NASA Spl. Achievement award, 1983. Mem. AIAA, Am. Meterology Soc., Am. Geophys. Union. Democrat. Office: Calif Inst Tech/Jet Propulsion Lab Terrestrial Sci Element 4800 Oak Grove Dr Pasadena CA 91109-8001

SCHIELE, PAUL ELLSWORTH, JR., educational business owner, writer; b. Phila., Nov. 20, 1924; s. Paul Ellsworth Sr. and Maud (Barclay) S.; m. Sarah Irene Knauss, Aug. 20, 1946; children: Patricia Schiele Sommers, Sandra Schiele Kicklighter, Deborah Schiele Hartigan. AT, Temple U., 1949; BA, LaVerne U., 1955; MA, Claremont Grad. U., 1961; PhD, U.S. Internat. U., San Diego, 1970. Cert. sec. tchr., Calif. 1961. Tchr. sci. and math. Lincoln High Sch., Phila., 1956-57, Ontario (Calif.) Sch. Dist., 1957-65; math. and sci. cons. Hacienda La Puente U. Sch. Dist., Calif., 1965-75; asst. prof. Calif. State U., Fullerton, 1975-83; pres., owner Creative Learning Environments and Resources, Glendora, Calif., 1983—, cons. sci. curriculum, 1985—; dir. title III project ESEA, 1974-75, cons. for project, 1975-77; cons. in field. Author: Primary Science, 1972, 2d edit., 1976, (novel) Under Cover of Night, 1995, Chasing the Wild Geese, 1996, Deceptive Appearances, 1997; editor: A Living World, 1974, 2d edit., 1986; writer 9 sound filmstrips, model units for sci. and math. activity books, 10 sci. activities for L.A. Outdoor Edn. Program, 1980; editor 21 sci. and math. activity books, 1975-76; writer, co-dir. (TV) Marine Biology Series, 1970-71; contbr. numerous articles to profl. mags., 1960-85; writer and designer of 2 sci. ednl. games; designer in field. Apptd. adv. com. Sci. and Humanities Symposium Calif. Mus. Sci. and Industry, 1974; mem. State Sci. Permit Com., Tide Pools of Calif. Coast, 1974-75; active Playhouse 90, Pasadena (Calif.) Playhouse; mem. Friends of Libr., Friends Libr. Found. Mem. Internat. Platform Assn., Glendora Hist. Soc., ABI Rsch. Assn. (bd. govs.), Calif. Elem. Edn. Assn. (hon.), Nat. PTA (hon.), Calif. Inter-Sci. Coun. (pres., chmn. 1971, 72), Elem Sch. Scis. Assn. (past pres., bd. dirs.), Paddlewheel Steamboating Soc. of Am., Phi Delta Kappa (chartered). Republican. Lutheran. Avocations: travel, etchings, art collecting, fencing. Home: 231 Catherine Park Dr Glendora CA 91741-3018

SCHIFF, GUNTHER HANS, lawyer; b. Cologne, Germany, Aug. 19, 1927; came to U.S., 1936; s. Hans and Alice (Goldstein) S.; m. Katharine MacMillan, Jan. 27, 1950 (div. 1957); children: Eric Alan, Mary Alice; m. JoAnn R. Schiff; children: Jage, Hans Judson. B.S.F.S., Georgetown U., 1949, J.D., 1952. Bar: D.C. 1952, Calif. 1953. Assoc., ptnr., of counsel various firms, Beverly Hills, Calif., 1954-94; pvt. practice Beverly Hills, Calif., 1994—; sec. Los Angeles Copyright Soc., Beverly Hills, 1975-76. Contbr. articles to profl. jours. Pres. Beverly Hills Civil Svc. Commn., 1984-85, 88-89; pres. Free Arts for Abused Children, 1993-94, dir.; chmn. Rent Control Rev. Bd., Beverly Hills, 1980-84; trustee Young Musicians Found. With USNR, 1945-46. Mem. ABA, Beverly Hills Bar Assn. (chmn. Resolutions Com. 1977-78), Los Angeles County Bar Assn., Los Angeles Copyright Soc., Calif. Yacht Club. Avocations: sailing; skiing; golfing. Office: 9430 W Olympic Blvd Beverly Hills CA 90212-4552

SCHIFFNER, CHARLES ROBERT, architect; b. Reno, Sept. 2, 1948; Robert Charles and Evelyn (Keck) S.; m. Iovanna Lloyd Wright, Nov. 1971 (div. Sept. 1981); m. Adrienne Anita McAndrews, Jan. 22, 1983. Student, Sacramento Jr. Coll., 1967-68, Frank Lloyd Wright Sch. Architecture, 1968-77. Registered architect, Ariz., Nev., Wis. Architect Taliesin Associated Architects, Scottsdale, Ariz., 1977-83; pvt. practice architecture Phoenix, 1983—; lectr. The Frank Lloyd Wright Sch. of Architecture, 1994, 95. Named one of 25 Most Promising Young Americans Under 35, U.S. mag., 1979; recipient AIA Honor award Western Mountain Region, 1993, Western Home awards Sunset Mag., 1989, 91, AIA Ariz. Merit award, 1993 and numerous others. Home: 5202 E Osborn Rd Phoenix AZ 85018-6137 Office: Camelhead Office Ctr 2600 N 44th St Ste 208 Phoenix AZ 85008-1565

SCHIFFRIN, MILTON JULIUS, physiologist; b. Rochester, N.Y., Mar. 23, 1914; s. William and Lillian (Harris) S.; m. Dorothy Euphemia Wharry, Oct. 10, 1942; children: David Wharry, Hilary Ann. AB, U. Rochester, 1937, MS, 1939; PhD cum laude, McGill U., 1941. Instr. physiology Northwestern U. Med. Sch., Chgo., 1941-45; lectr. pharmacology U. Ill. Med. Sch., 1947-57, clin. asst. prof. anesthesiology, 1957-61; with Hoffmann-La Roche, Inc., Nutley, N.J., 1946-79, dir. drug regulatory affairs, 1964-71, asst. v.p., 1971-79; pres. Wharry Rsch. Assn., Seattle, 1979—; chmn. Everglades Health Edn. Ctr., 1986-87. Author: (with E.G. Gross) Clinical Analgesics, 1955; editor: Management of Pain in Cancer, 1957. Bd. dirs. Univ. Adult Day Ctr., 1993—; mem. adv. bd. Regional Ombudsman Program, 1998—, Residents Coun. Washington, 1998—. Capt. USAAF, 1942-46. Mem. Am. Med. Writers Assn. (bd. dirs. 1967-70, pres. N.Y. chpt. 1967-68, nat. pres. 72-73), Am. Physiol. Soc., Internat. Coll. Surgeons, Am. Therapeutic Soc., Coll. Clin. Pharmacology and Therapeutics, Am. Chem. Soc. Home and Office: Unit 401 1001 2nd Ave W Seattle WA 98119-3560

SCHILBRACK, KAREN GAIL, systems analyst; b. Tomahawk, Wis., Sept. 28; d. Edward Richard and Irene Angeline (Ligman) S. Student U. Calif.-Santa Barbara, 1967-69; BA in Anthropology, U. Calif.-Davis, 1971; post-grad. in Edn. and Archeology, Calif. State Poly. U., San Luis Obispo, 1971-72. Cert. tchr., computer specialist, data processing; lic. cosmetologist. Computer specialist Facilities Systems Office, Port Hueneme, Calif., 1975-78, sr. computer specialist, 1978-80, project mgr. U.S. Naval Constrn. Bn. Ctr., 1980-89, imaging systems computer specialist Comptr. Office, 1989-92; fiscal quality specialist Dept. Def. Finance and Acctg. Svc., DAO, Port Hueneme, 1992-95; fund adminstr. Naval Constrn. Tng. Ctr., Port Hueneme, 1995—; tng. cons. FACSO, 1981, 82; curriculum cons. Ventura Community Coll., Calif., 1981-89; instr. U.S. Navy, Port Hueneme, 1983, 91, Civil Service Commn., Port Hueneme, 1978-80. Author: AMALGAMAN Run Procedures, 1976; Cobol Programming Efficiencies, 1978, Imaging System UserManual, 1991; co-author, editor: Training Manual for Direct Data Entry System, 1983. Mem. Vols. for Camarillo State Hosp., Camarillo, 1978-88, coord. Ventura County, 1981; chmn. scholarship fund drive Ventura, Santa Barbara, Los Angeles, Counties, 1980. Named Young Career Woman of Yr., Calif. Bus. and Profl. Women, 1979. Mem. Young Ladies Inst. (pres. Santa Paula, dist. dep. Ventura/Santa Barbara Counties), Am. Biog. Inst. Research Assn. (lifetime dep. gov.). Lodge: Toastmistress. Home: 6993 Wheeler Canyon Rd Santa Paula CA 93060-9759 Office: Compt Office Code 243-A USNCBC Port Hueneme CA 93042

SCHILE, WAYNE, newspaper publishing executive. Pub. Billings (Mont.) Gazette, 1984—. Adress: PO Box 36300 Billings MT 59107 Office: 401 N Broadway Billings MT 59101-1243*

SCHILLER, ANITA ROSENBAUM, librarian; b. N.Y.C., June 16, 1926; d. Aaron and Helen (Camnitz) Rosenbaum; B.A. in Econs., N.Y. U., 1949; M.L.S., Pratt Inst., 1959; m. Herbert I. Schiller, Nov. 5, 1946; children—Daniel T., P. Zachary. Reference librarian Nat. Indsl. Conf. Bd., 1960-61; instr. U. Ill. Grad. Sch. Bus. Adminstrn., 1961-62; reference librarian Pratt Inst., 1962-63; successively research asst., research asso., research asst. prof. U. Ill. Library Research Center, 1964-70; reference librarian, bibliographer U. Calif., San Diego, 1970-91, libr. emeritus, 1991—. Bd. dirs. Calif. Coun. Humanities, 1987-91. Ralph R. Shaw vis. scholar Rutgers U., 1978. Co-recipient award for mag. writing Los Angeles chpt. PEN, 1982. Fellow Council Library Resources, 1976-77. Mem. ALA (councillor 1972-76, sec.-treas. library research round table 1978-80, mem. council com. on status of women in librarianship 1980, Equality award 1985). Contbr. articles to profl. publs.; editor Aware column Am. Libraries, 1971-72; mem. editorial bds. profl. jours. Home: 7109 Monte Vista Ave La Jolla CA 92037-5326

SCHILLER, GERALD ALAN, writer; b. Phila., Feb. 13, 1936; s. Victor and Ida (Rosenbloum) S.; m. Esther Shoemaker, Aug. 24, 1957; children: Lisabeth, greg. BS in Edn., Temple U., 1957; MA in Cinema, UCLA, 1963. Cert. tchr., Calif. Tchr. Phila. Schs., 1957-58, L.A. Schs., 1960-91. Author: (novel) Deadly Dreams, 1996, Death Underground, 1999, (children's book) The Dog That Belonged to No One, 1998; script writer advt. and promotional videos and audio-visual prodns. for J.K. Lesser Prodns.; co-writer feature films The Red Fox, 1988, Wild Country, 1989; writer, dir. documentary films including The World Outside, The Great Stone Face, 1980, Chaplin-A Character is Born, 1979; writer, dir. ednl. films; author articles and revs. With U.S. Army, 1959-60. Recipient Cine Golden Eagle award The World Outside, 1st prize Calif. State Coll. Film Festival, Blue Ribbon award Am. Film Festival, Chris award Columbus Film Festival, 2d prize Nat. Ednl. Film Festival, Tchr. of Yr. award L.A. Film Tchrs. Assn., 1990, others. Mem. Ventura Writers Club (pres. 1997-99), Sisters in Crime, Small Pubs. Network. Jewish. Avocations: bicycling, book collecting.

SCHILLING, DEAN WILLIAM, manufacturing executive; b. Waverly, Iowa, Apr. 25, 1944; s. Alvin Louis and Etta Christine (Poppe) S.; m. Betty Ann (Homeister), Aug. 5, 1962; children: Angela Marie, Christine Ann. AS, Iowa State U., 1964, BS, 1969. Engr. Systems Genetics, Clarksville, Iowa, 1970-81; sr. tech. support Hewlett Packard, Sunnyvale, Calif., 1983-85; pres. Cryo Genetic Technology, Soquel, Calif., 1985—. Inventor biol. devices and methods to remedy human infertility; holder 3 patents. Mem. Am. Fertility Soc., Soc. Cryobiology, Iowa State Alumni Assn., Douglas Electric Coop. (bd. dirs. 1995), Order of Knoll (founders club 1988). Lutheran. Avocations: concertina and trumpet music.

SCHILLING, FREDERICK AUGUSTUS, JR., geologist, consultant; b. Phila., Apr. 12, 1931; s. Frederick Augustus and Emma Hope (Christoffer) S.; m. Ardis Ione Dovre, June 12, 1957 (div. 1987); children: Frederick Christopher, Jennifer Dovre. *The Schillings first settled in Pennsylvania in 1849, having been constrained to leave central Europe (Bavarian origins) during the political unrest of the time. Preachers and teachers have been the principal product with current generations getting into engineering and science. College degrees have been part of the family tradition since the early 1920's for both the men and the women. Daughter, Jennifer Geer and husband, Derek are electrical engineers and have opened their own firm in San Diego. Son, Chris, has been with Delta Airlines for the last 14 years.* BS in Geology, Wash. State U., 1953; PhD in Geology, Stanford U., 1962. Registered geologist, Calif.; registered engring. geologist, Calif.; registered environ. assessor, Calif. Computer geophysicist United Geophys. Corp., Pasadena, Calif., 1955-56; geologist various orgns., 1956-61, U.S. Geol. Survey, 1961-64; underground engr. Climax (Colo.) Molybdenum Co., 1966-68; geologist Keradamex Inc., Anaconda Co., M.P. Grace, Ranchers Exploration & Devel. Corp., Albuquerque and Grants, N.Mex., 1968-84, Hecla Mining Co., Coeur

d'Alene, Idaho, 1984-86, various engrng. and environ. firms, Calif., 1986-91; prin. F. Schilling Cons., Canyon Lake, Calif., 1991—. *Frederick Schilling is a consulting, engineering geologist with 20 early years in the mining field. At Ranchers Exploration, he was principally responsible for sifting through thousands of precious metal prospects in the western states for the purpose of selecting targets for exploration. At Hecla Mining Co., he was a member of the President's Council for long range planning to select mineral commodities with new demand potential for company attention. His current activity is focused on Southern California projects in the environmental and geotechnical fields. Adventure and exploration have been the guiding spirit. It stems from the Johnsons, London, Buck, and Tangier Smith.* Author: Bibliography of Uranium, 1976. Del. citizen amb. program People to People Internat., USSR, 1990-91. With U.S. Army, 1953-55. Fellow The Explorers Club; mem. Geol. Soc. Am., Am. Assn. Petroleum Geologists, Soc. Mining Engrs., Internat. Platform Assn., Adventurers' Club L.A., Masons, Kiwanis, Sigma Xi, Sigma Gamma Epsilon. Republican. Presbyterian. Avocation: track and field. E-mail: faschillepacbell.net. Office: F Schilling Cons 30037 Steel Head Dr Canyon Lake CA 92587-7460 also: 14661 Myford Rd Ste C Tustin CA 92980

SCHILPEROORT, SHARON ANN, secondary education educator; b. Tacoma, Wash., Apr. 25, 1947; d. Donald Earl and Ingeborg (Johnsrud) Skidmore; m. William Lester Schilperoort, Apr. 11, 1970; children: Heather Marie, Sara Ann, Andrew Michael. BS in English, Evangel Coll., Springfield, Mo., 1969; MEd in Profl. Devel., Heritage Coll., Toppenish, Wash., 1996; cert. prin., Heritage Coll., 1997. Cert. prof. educator, continuing tchr., Wash. Tchr. lang. arts grades 7 and 8 Highland Sch. Dist., Tieton, Wash., 1969-70, Mt. Adams Sch. Dist., Harrah, Wash., 1970-71; tchr. grades 6-8 Harrah Cmty. Christian, 1983-85; tchr. English grades 6-12, dept. chair West Side Christian Sch., Yakima, Wash., 1986-93; tchr. grades 6-8 OIC-Reach Mid. Sch., Yakima, 1993-94; tchr. lang. arts grade 8 Yakima Sch. Dist., 1994—. Mem. truancy bd. Yakima Sch. Dist., 1997-98; mem., bd. dirs., officer Yakima Cmty. Concert Assn., 1992-95; mem. Harrah Town Coun., 1973-80, Parent, Tchr., Student Assn. Wilson Mid. Sch.; alt. mem., bd. dirs. Yakima County Health Dept., 1979-80; mem. admission and allocations bd. Yakima County United Way, 1975-77, bd. chmn. Lower Valley admissions and allocations bd., 1973-75. Named Outstanding Young Woman of Am., 1970. Mem. NEA, ASCD, Nat. Coun. Tchrs. of English, Wash. Edn. Assn., Yakima Edn. Assn. Avocations: travel, reading, environmental issues. Home: 3621 Harrah Rd Harrah WA 98933-9730

SCHIMMELBUSCH, WERNER HELMUT, psychiatrist; b. Vienna, Austria, Nov. 16, 1937; came to U.S., 1954; s. Hans Mowgli and Anneliese Martha (Koeppe) S.; m. Faye Karina Wrangel, Dec. 29, 1958 (div. Mar. 1967); m. Jeanette Ramona Dyal, Mar. 26, 1971; children: Andre Curt, Anne Ramona. MD, U. Wash., Seattle, 1962; psychiatrist, Yale U., 1968; adult psychoanalyst, Seattle Inst. Psychoanalysis, 1977, child psychoanalyst, 1992. Instr. Dept. Psychiatry and Behavioral Sci. U. Wash., Seattle, 1968-69; pvt. practice Seattle, 1969—; clin. prof. U. Wash., Seattle, 1984—; tng. and supervising psychoanalyst Seattle Inst. Psychoanalysis, 1990—. Capt. U.S. Army, 1963-65. Mem. AMA, Am. Psychiatric Assn., Am. Psychoanalytic Assn., Seattle Psychoanalytic Soc. (pres. 1979-80, 94-96). Avocations: skiing, hiking, sailing. Office: 4033 E Madison St Seattle WA 98112-3104

SCHINDLER, RONALD IRVIN, lawyer; b. Port Angeles, Wash.; s. William I. and F. Colleen (Jenson) S.; m. Helena Onggo, June 7, 1988; children: Alexander Ong Yong Hui, Andrew Ong Yong Hsin. BA, Idaho State U., 1990; JD, U. Denver, 1993, LLM, 1998. Bar: Colo. 1994, Idaho 1996, U.S. Dist. Ct. Idaho 1996. Geologist Exploration Methods, Englewood, Colo., 1990; intern Sen. Tim Wirth, Denver, 1992; law clk. Cyprus Amax Minerals Co., Engelwood, 1992-94; atty. Bradley Campbell Carney & Madson, Golden, Colo., 1994-95; shareholder, v.p. Root & Schindler, Denver, 1995—; presenter in field. Contbr. articles to profl. jours.; editor: Colo. Water Ct. Reporter, 1991, 92. Mem. ABA, SME, Geol. Soc. Am., Colo. Bar Assn., Idaho Bar Assn., Denver Bar Assn., Rocky Mountain Assn. Mineral Landmen (pres.), Rocky Mountain Mineral Law Found. (pubs. com. 1996—). Republican. Mem. LDS Ch. Avocations: music, horsemanship. Office: Root & Schindler 410 17th St Ste 460 Denver CO 80202-4402

SCHINE, WENDY WACHTELL, foundation administrator; b. White Plains, N.Y., May 5, 1961; d. Thomas and Esther Carole (Pickard) Wachtell; m. Jonathan Mark Schine, Sept. 2, 1990; children: Jameson Myer, Bradley Thomas, Davis Berndt. BA, Wellesley Coll., 1983; MA in Journalism, U. So. Calif., L.A., 1987. Legis. asst. U.S. House Reps., Washington, 1983-85; varied positions KCBS-TV, L.A., 1986-88; v.p. Joseph Drown Found., L.A., 1988—; bd. dirs. L.A. Urban Funders, So. Calif. Assn. Philanthropy, U. So. Calif. Sch. Planning and Devel. Non Profit Studies Ctr.; advisor Psychol. Trauma Ctr., L.A., 1988-98, Ctr. for Talented Youth, Glendale, Calif., 1989-98; chair adv. bd. The Accelerated Sch. Mem. oversight com. Pathways Project, Big Sisters, L.A. Office: Joseph Drown Found Ste 1930 1999 Avenue Of The Stars Los Angeles CA 90067-4612

SCHIRM, LOUIS, IV, digital signal processing systems engineer; b. Burbank, Calif., Jan. 27, 1948; s. Louis III and Henriette F. Schirm; m. Linda Nesbit, Aug. 4, 1973; children: Kelli, Lisa. BSEE, Calif. State Poly. U., 1971. Design engr. Rockwell Internat., Anaheim, Calif., 1971-78; sr. applications engr. TRW LSI Products, San Diego, 1978-81; pres., owner DSP Systems Corp., Anaheim, 1981-90; v.p. engring. ISP Technologies, Anaheim, 1990—; assoc. instr. U. Calif. Irvine, 1987-89; corr. IPC Design Coun., Northbrook, Ill., 1993—. Contbr. papers to profl. pubs. including IEEE Jour., others. Tribal chief YMCA Indian Princess program, Yorba Linda, Calif., 1986-94; head usher St. Joseph's Ch., Placentia, Calif., 1985—. Recipient 3d place award ECN Internat. Design Award Competition, Anaheim, 1990, Pinacle Design award Harris Semiconductor, Irvine, 1994. Mem. Computer Soc. of IEEE. Achievements include patent on low power terminator for high speed digital circuits; development of 1st 1 giga-op fixed point circuit board, development of 1st 100+ MFLOP circuit board. Home: 17902 La Entrada Dr Yorba Linda CA 92886-2347 Office: ISP Tech Inc 1250 N Lakeview Ave Ste H Anaheim CA 92807-1801

SCHIRRA, WALTER MARTY, JR., business consultant, former astronaut; b. Hackensack, N.J., Mar. 12, 1923; s. Walter Marty and Florence (Leach) S.; m. Josephine Cook Fraser, Feb. 23, 1946; children: Walter Marty III, Suzanne Karen. Student, Newark Coll. Engring., 1940-42; B.S., U.S. Naval Acad., 1945; D. Astronautics (hon.), Lafayette Coll., U. So. Calif., N.J. Inst. Tech. Commd. ensign U.S. Navy, 1945, advanced through grades to capt., 1965; designated naval aviator, 1948; service aboard battle cruiser Alaska, 1945-46; service with 7th Fleet, 1946; assigned Fighter Squadron 71, 1948-51; exchange pilot 154th USAF Fighter Bomber Squadron, 1951; engaged in devel. Sidewinder missile China Lake, Calif., 1952-54; project pilot F7U-3 Cutlass; also instr. pilot F7U-3 Cutlass and FJ3 Fury, 1954-56; ops. officer Fighter Squadron 124, U.S.S. Lexington, 1956-57; assigned Naval Air Safety Officer Sch., 1957, Naval Air Test Ctr., 1958-59; engaged in suitability devel. work F4H, 1958-59; joined Project Mercury, man-in-space, NASA, 1959; pilot spacecraft Sigma 7 in 6 orbital flight, Oct. 1962; in charge operations and tng. Astronaut Office, 1964-69; command pilot Gemini 6 which made rendezvous with target, Gemini 7, Dec. 1965; comdr. 11 day flight Apollo 7, 1968; ret., 1969; pres. Regency Investors, Inc., Denver, 1969-70; chmn., chief exec. officer ECCO Corp., Englewood, Colo., 1970-73; chmn. Sernco, Inc., 1973-74; with Johns-Manville Corp., Denver, 1974-77; v.p. devel. Goodwin Cos., Inc., Littleton, Colo., 1978-79; ind. cons., 1979-80; dir. Kimberly Clark, 1983-91. Decorated D.F.C.(3), Air medal (2), Navy D.S.M.; recipient Distinguished Service medal (2) NASA, Exceptional Service medal. Fellow Am. Astronautical Soc., Soc. Exptl. Test Pilots. Home and Office: PO Box 73 Rancho Santa Fe CA 92067-0073

SCHLACHTER, GAIL ANN, publishing company executive; b. Detroit, Apr. 7, 1943; d. Lewis E. and Helen (Blitz) Goldstein; children—Eric, Sandra. B.A., U. Calif.-Berkeley, 1964; M.A. in History, Edn., U. Wis.-Madison, 1966, M.A. in Library Sci., 1967; Ph.D., in Library Sci., U. Minn., 1971; M.B.A., U. So. Calif., 1979. Asst. prof. U. So. Calif., Los Angeles, 1971-74; library dept. head Calif. State U., Long Beach, 1974-76; asst. library dir. U. Calif.-Davis, 1976-81; dir. serials ABC-Clio Info. Services, Santa Barbara, Calif., 1981-82, v.p. pubs., 1982-83, v.p. gen. mgr., 1983-85; pres. Reference Service Press, El Dorado Hills, Calif., 1985—; exec. dir. Info. Inst., Santa Barbara, 1981-82. Author: Library Science Dissertations 1925-1972, 1974; 1973-81, 83; Directory of Internships, 1975; Minorities and Women: A Guide to Reference Literature in the Social Sciences, 1976 (Choice's outstanding acad. book 1977); Directory of Financial Aids for Women, 1978; Service Imperative For Libraries, 1982; Directory of Financial Aids for Minorities, 1984; Reference Sources in Library and Information Services, 1984; How to Find Out About Financial Aid, 1987; Financial Aids for the Disabled, 1988; Financial Aid for Veterans Military and Their Dependents, 1988, Financial Aid for Study & Training Abroad, 1992, Financial Aid for Research & Creative Activities Abroad, 1992, College Students Guide to Merit & Other No-Need Funding, 1996, Money for Graduate Students in the Sciences, 1996, Money for Graduate Students in the Social Sciences, 1996, Money for Graduate Students in the Humanities, 1996, Back-to-School Money Book, 1996, Financial Aid for Native Americans, 1997, Financial Aid for Hispanic Americans, 1997, Financial Aid for Asian Americans, 1997, Financial Aid for African Americans, RPS Funding for Nursing Students & Nurses, 1998. Named Outstanding prof. Library Sch. U. So. Calif., 1973; recipient Knowledge Industry Publs. award for Library Lit.; fellow U.S. Office Edn., 1968-71, Ford Found., 1966. Mem. Calif. Library Assn. (chpt. pres. 1977-78, bd. dirs. 1980—), ALA (editor RQ 1977—, councillor 1986—, v.p., pres. reference and adult services div. 1987, Isador Gilbert Mudge award 1992, Louis Shores-Oryx Press award 1997), Assn. Library and Info. Sci. Educators. Office: Reference Service Press 5000 Windplay Dr Ste 4 El Dorado Hills CA 95762

SCHLADOR, PAUL RAYMOND, JR., insurance agent; b. Riverside, Calif., Oct. 16, 1934; s. Paul Raymond Sr. Schlador and Lois Geraldine (Burrus) Kaeding; m. Evangeline Kathern, Aug. 19, 1955; children: Debora Lynn TeSam, Cheryl Jean Bastian, Bonnie Kay Tucker. Student, San Diego City Jr. Coll., 1954-55, Ins. Industry, San Diego, 1960-62, Am. Coll., San Diego, 1970-74. CLU. Agt. Bankers Life of Nebr., San Diego, 1959-63; agt./ mgr. Southwestern Life Ins. Co., San Diego, 1959—; ind. agt. State Farm Ins. Co., San Diego, 1978—. With USNG, 1952-60. Mem. San Diego Assn. Life Underwriters (pres. 1989-90, legis. v.p. 1988), Kiwanis Club El Cajon Valley. Republican. Methodist. Avocations: tennis, camping, sr. Olympic basketball. Home: 1267 Oakdale Ave # C El Cajon CA 92021-6454 Office: State Farm Ins 7800 University Ave # 1A La Mesa CA 91941-4928 also: BPOE Lodge # 1812 El Cajon CA 92021

SCHLAHT, KIMBER LEE, childcare provider; b. San Diego; d. Ronald Victor Morfitt and Laurel Lee Smith; m. William Milo Schlaht Jr., Apr. 6, 1996; 3 children. Outdoor sch. counselor, 1977-78; mgr. Bresler's Ice Cream Parlor, 1979-80; teller, clk. I 1st Interstate Bank, 1981-84; utility III, Clackamas County Bank, 1984-87; home daycare provider, 1988—. Home: 13460 SE Richey Rd Boring OR 97009

SCHLATTER, O. EDWARD, judge; m. Patricia Schlatter; 2 children. BA, So. Ill. U., 1964; JD, U. Denver, 1970. Dist. and chief judge 11th jud. dist. U.S. Dist. Ct. State of Colo., Denver, 1981-92, magistrate judge, 1992—. Mem. Colo. Bar Assn. (exec. coun. criminal law sect 1984-86, bd. govs. 1987-92, sr. v.p. 1991-92), 11th Jud. Dist. Bar Assn. (v.p. 1985-87, pres. 1987-89). Office: US Dist Ct State of Colo 1929 Stout St Rm C-162 Denver CO 80294-0001*

SCHLEGEL, JAMES M., educational administrator; b. Kansas City, Mo., Jan. 10, 1946; s. Jack Howard and V. Irene (Hall) S.; m. Janice Ann Taylor, Sept. 2, 1965; children: Shana R. Irish, Shan S. BS in Edn., Emporia State U., 1970, MS in Edn., 1972. Cert. tchr., counselor, adminstr., Alaska. Mktg. tchr./coord. Fremont County Sch. Dist. #1, Lander, Wyo., 1972-76, pupil svcs./vocat. edn. dir., 1976-79; vocat. leadership coord. Oreg. State U., Corvallis, 1979-82; vocat. edn. adminstr. Fairbanks North Sch. Dist., 1982-91; asst. v.p. U. Alaska Sys., Fairbanks, 1991-94; edn. program mgr. Ilisagvik Coll., Barrow, Alaska, 1994-95; vocat. edn. adminstr. Lower Kuskokwim Sch. Dist., Bethel, Alaska, 1995—; owner/mgr. (JS)2 Svcs., Fairbanks, 1982—; presenter to numerous confs.; evaluator Vocat. Edn. adminstrv. Assessment Team, Lebanon, S.D., Career and Vocat. Edn. Assessment Team, Reedsport, S.D., career guidance program Edn. divsn. Singer Corp., comprehensive coop. career edn. project Windsor (Colo.) Pub. Schs., Cheyenne Ctrl. H.S.; cons. in field. Contbr. articles to profl. jours. Mem. alaska Sch.-to-Work Implementation task Force, Gov.'s Human Resources Devel. Policy Adv. Com., Alaska Sch.-to-Work Rural Delivery Strategies Com., Alaska State Tech.-Prep Initative Planning Com., Alaska Vocat. Edn. Com. of Practitioners, Alaska Workforce Preparation Conf. Exec. Planning Com., Alaska Edn. Coord. Com., Alaska Vocat. Edn. Program Stds. Task Force, Alaska Sch. Found. Formula Fin. Adv. Com., Fairbanks Pvt. Industry Coun., North Star Ctr. Adv. Coun., others; bd. dirs. Alaska Crippled Children and Adults; mem. adminstrv. mgmt. team Fairbanks North Star Borough Sch. dist., numerous coms. U.S. Congl. fellow, 1975-76. Mem. Nat. Coun. of Local Adminstrs. for Vocat. Edn., Alaska State Vocat. Assn., Am. vocat. Assn., Phi Delta Kappa. Home: 180 Humboldt Way Fairbanks AK 99709-2958

SCHLEGEL, JOHN PETER, academic administrator; b. Dubuque, Iowa, July 31, 1943; s. Aaron Joseph and Irma Joan (Hingtgen) S. BA, St. Louis U., 1969, MA, 1970; BDiv, U. London, 1973; DPhil, Oxford U., 1977. Joined Soc. of Jesus, 1963, ordained priest Roman Cath. Ch., 1973. From asst. prof. to assoc. prof. Creighton U., Omaha, 1976-79, asst. acad. v.p., 1978-82; dean Coll. Arts and Scis. Rockhurst Coll., Kansas City, Mo., 1982-84, Marquette U., Milw., 1984-88; exec. and acad. v.p. John Carroll U., Cleve., 1988-91; pres. U. San Francisco, 1991—; cons. Orgn. for Econ. Devel. and Cooperation, Paris, 1975-76. Author: Bilingualism and Canadian Policy in Africa, 1979; editor: Towards a Redefinition of Development, 1976; contbr. articles to profl. jours. Mem. Milwaukee County Arts Coun., 1986-88, Mo. Coun. on Humanities, Kansas City, 1984; trustee St. Louis U., 1985-91, Loyola U. Chgo., 1988-95, 98—, Loyola U. New Orleans, 1995-98, St. Ignatius H.S., Cleve., 1990-91, Loyola Coll. in Md., 1992-98, Xavier U., 1998—; bd. dirs. Coro Found., Commonwealth Club Calif., Calif. Coun. on World Affairs, 1997—. Oxford U. grantee, 1974-76; Govt. of Can. grantee, 1977-78. Mem. Am. Coun. on Edn., Olympic Club, Univ. Club, Bohemian Club. Avocations: racquet sports, classical music, cooking, hiking. Office: U San Francisco Office of Pres 2130 Fulton St San Francisco CA 94117-1080

SCHLEH, EDWARD CARL, business analyst; b. St. Paul, Nov. 2, 1915; s. Edward G. and Augusta (Seltz) S.; m. Myra Adelle Oberschulte, June 7, 1941; children: Jeanne, John, Richard, Elizabeth, Robert. BBA, U. Minn., 1937. Placement officer U. Minn. Employment Office, Mpls., 1937-39, Ells Employment Svc., Mpls., 1939-40; mgr. personnel rsch. 3-M Co., St. Paul, 1940-48; pres. Schleh Assocs., Inc., Mpls. and Palo Alto, Calif., 1948-95; U.S. del. to internat. mgmt. confs. in Chile, France, Germany, Australia, Japan; bd. Exec. Svc. Corps., San Francisco; adv. bd. Santa Clara U. Bus. Sch.; bd. dirs. Coun. Internat. Progress in Mgmt.; presenter seminars, speeches for profit orgns. U.S. and abroad. Author: Successful Executive Action, Management by Results, Effective Management of Personnel, The Management Tactician, How to Boost Your Return on Management; contbr. articles to profl. pubs. Mem. Soc. Advancement of Mgmt. (Frederick Taylor Key award), Am. Mgmt. Assn. (wall of fame). Home: 368 Selby Ln Menlo Park CA 94027-3933

SCHLEHUSER, TODD CHARLES, industrial engineer; b. Lafayette, Ind., Aug. 11, 1974; s. Charles Henry and Carolyn Ann S.; m. Wendy Lynn Schlehuser, May 30, 1998. BSIE, Purdue Univ., 1997. Co-op engr. Thomson Consumer Elec., Indpls., 1993-96; mfg. engr. Oregon Freeze Dry, Albany, Oreg., 1997—. Vol. Indpls. Children's Bureau, 1995. Recipient JA scholarship Jr. Achievement, 1992. Mem. IIE, Soc. Profl. Engrs., Alpha Lambda Delta Soc., Phi Eta Sigma Soc., Alpha Pi Mu, Golden Key Nat. Republican. Avocations: basketball, tennis, golf, baseball. Home: 4570 NW University Dr Apt 4 Corvallis OR 97330-1668

SCHLENKER, ERROL RICKLAND, architect; b. Jamestown, N.D., July 9, 1950; s. Jack Melvin and Lila Sulvia (Hieb) S.; m. Denise Gertrude Moos; children: Amy Elizabeth, Christopher Errol. BArch, N.D. State U., 1973. Registered architect. Architect in tng. [illegible] Fargo, N.D., 1973-77; architect Hunter Grobe Architects, Fargo, N.D., 1977-78, Richard I. Shope Architects, Helena, Mont., 1978-80; prin. E.R. Shlenker Architects, Helena, Mont., 1980-88, Schlenker & McKittrick Architects, Helena, Mont., 1988—. Mem. [illegible] (past pres.). Avocations: skiing, fishing, hunting, collecting vintage wines, hiking. Office: Schlenker & McKittrick Architects 50 S Last Chance Gulch St Helena MT 59601-4131

SCHLESINGER, DEBORAH LEE, librarian; b. Cambridge, Mass., Sept. 13, 1937; d. Edward M. and Edith D. (Schneider) Hershoff; divorced; children: Suzanne, Richard. BA, U. Mass., 1961; MS, Simmons Coll., 1974; postgrad., U. Pitts., 1983. Reference librarian Bently Coll., Waltham, Mass., 1964-65; dir. Carnegie Library, Swissvale, Pa., 1973-77, South Park Twp. Library, Library, Pa., 1977-81, Monessen (Pa.) Library, 1981-82, Lewis & Clark Library, Helena, Mont., 1983-88, 89—; state librarian Mont. State Library, Helena, Mont., 1988-89; vis. scholar Pitts. Regional Library Ctr., 1982-83. Editor Pa. Union List, 1982-83. Mem. exec. bd. Mont. Cultural Advocacy, 1983—. Mem. Mont. Library Assn. (chmn. legis. com. 1984-92, MLA lobbyist 1992—), Mont. Assn. Female Execs. (fin. com. 1986—), AAUW (exec. com. 1985-86). Democrat. Club: Montana (Helena). Avocations: flying, painting, reading, rafting, travel. Home: 2 Washington Pl Helena MT 59601-6283 Office: Lewis & Clark Libr 120 S Last Chance Gulch St Helena MT 59601-4133

SCHLESINGER, VIOLET MURRAY, biomedical consultant; b. Denver, June 14, 1929; d. Robert Robertson Ferguson and Virginia Lee (Murray) Corbin; m. Robert Alexander Schlesinger, June 14, 1953; children: Roberta Diane, William Alexander. BA, U. Colo., 1952; MA, Goddard Coll., 1967; mins. license, Bethesda Sch. Ministry, 1990; PhD, Columbia Pacific, 1993. Prof. Ecole Normale, Tours, France, 1952-53; tchr. Denver and L.A. Pub. Schs., 1953-56; exec. dir. Wilde Woode Children's Ctr., Palm Springs, Calif., 1980-87; trustee Anderson Children's Found., Palm Springs, 1987-90; pastor Candle Cross Chapel, Palm Springs, 1990-95; exec. dir. Prevention Pays, Palm Springs, 1990-95. Author: Spiritual, Mental and Physical, 1967, A Wholistic Approach to Wellness A Needed Answer to American Healthcare Crises, 1993. Pastor Candle Cross Chapel, 1990-94. Republican. Avocation: hiking. Home: 380 Pablo Dr Palm Springs CA 92262

SCHLESSINGER, PHILIP JOSEPH, educator emeritus American government and politics; b. Mpls., July 10, 1914; s. Harry H. and Margaret S.; m. Phyllis Schlessinger. BS and MA, U. Minn., 1941; PhD, U. So. Calif., 1943. Tchg. asst. U. Minn., Mpls.; rsch. asst. in pub. adminstrn. U. So. Calif., L.A.; pers. technician L.A. City Civil Svc. Commn.; market analyst Lockheed Aircraft Corp.; instr. Am. Govt. and U.S. History L.A. City Coll., prof. polit. sci.; chmn., mem. NSF rev. bds., Washington, mem. rev. bd. selecting C.C. instrs. and civil svc. pers.; speaker for C.C. Social Sci. Assn. at confs.; frequent speaker to civic and ednl. groups; lobbyist on ednl. matters, Calif. State Legis., Sacramento; ednl. advisor to State Sen. David A. Roberti, L.A. Author: (textbook) Calif. State and Local Government. Sponsor of Govt. Internships and trips to state and local legis. bodies; cand. for Calif. State Assembly; past mem. of Calif. State Ctrl. and County Ctrl. Coms. Home: 1961 Myra Ave Los Angeles CA 90027-3254

SCHLITT, WILLIAM JOSEPH, III, metallurgical engineer; b. Columbus, Ohio, June 12, 1942; s. William Joseph Jr. and Florence (McCall) S.; m. Anne Marie Ritchie, Apr. 1, 1994. BSMetE, Carnegie Inst. Tech., 1964; PhD in Metallurgy, Pa. State U., 1968. Registered profl. engr., Tex. Scientist Kennecott Minerals Co., Salt Lake City, 1968-75, sr. scientist, 1975-76, mgr. hydrometallurgy dept., 1977-81, prin. program mgr., 1981-82; process staff mgr. Brown & Root, Inc., Houston, 1982-83, mgr. tech., 1983-93, product line mgr. chems., 1993-94; mgr. process tech. Davy Nonferrous Divsn. of Kvaerner Metals, San Ramon, Calif., 1994—; mem. oversight com. soln. mining NSF, Socoro, N.Mex., 1977-79; mem. oversight com. smelter flue dust Environ. Prot. Agy., Butte, Mont., 1978-79; mem. internat. adv. bd. In Situ jour., N.Y.C., 1988—. Editor: In Situ Uranium Leaching and Ground Water Restoration, 1979, Leaching and Recovering Copper from As-Mined Materials, 1980 (Publ. Bd. Commendation 1981), Gold and Silver-Leaching, Recovery and Economics, 1981, Interfacing Technologies in Solution Mining, 1982 (Publ. Bd. Commendation 1983), Salts and Brines '85, 1985; assoc. editor: (handbook) SME Mining Engineering Handbook, 1992; contbr. more than 40 tech. articles to profl. jours., trade publs., and proc. volumes including Metall. Transactions B, AIME Transactions, In Situ, Minerals and Metall. Processing. Pres. Ft. Bend County Kennel Club, Richmond, Tex., 1988-90. Trainee NSF, 1984-88; recipient Arthur F. Taggart award Soc. for Mining, Metallurgy and Exploration, 1998. Mem. Soc. Mining Engrs. (bd. dirs. 1984-95, chmn. mining and exploration divsn. 1986-87), The Metall. Soc. (bd. dirs. 1982-83), Can. Inst. Mining and Metallurgy, Sigma Xi, Tau Beta Pi, Phi Kappa Phi. Achievements include patents in field. Avocation: licensed dog show judge. Office: Kvaerner Metals Davy Nonferrous Divsn 12657 Alcosta Blvd # 2000 San Ramon CA 94583-9026

SCHLOSE, WILLIAM TIMOTHY, health care executive; b. West Lafayette, Ind., May 16, 1948; s. William Fredrick and Dora Irene (Chitwood) S.; m. Linda Lee Fletcher, June 29, 1968 (div. 1978); children: Vanessa Janine Schlose Hubert, Stephanie Lynn; m. Kelly Marie Martin, June 6, 1987; 1 child, Taylor Jean Martin-Schlose. Student, Bowling Green State U., 1966-68, Long Beach City Coll., 1972-75. Cert. tchr., Calif. Staff respiratory therapist St. Vincent's Med. Ctr., L.A., 1972-75; cardio-pulmonary chief Temple Cmty. Hosp., L.A., 1975-76; adminstrv. dir. spl. svcs. Santa Fe Meml. Hosp., L.A., 1976-79; mktg. and pub. rels. staff Nat. Med. Homecare Corp., Orange, Calif., 1979-81, Medtech of Calif., Inc., Burbank, Calif., 1981-84; regional mgr. Mediq Health Care Group Svcs., Inc., Chatsworth, Calif., 1984-88; pres. Baby Watch Homecare, Whittier, Calif., 1988-90, Tim Schlose and Assocs., Brea, Calif., 1990—; staff instr., Montebello (Calif.) Adult Schs.; v.p. Naptime Diagnostics, Brea, 1990—. Author: Fundamental Respiratory Therapy Equipment, 1977; mem. editl. bd. RT, The Jour. Respiratory Car Practitioners, 1997—. With USN, 1968-72. Mem. Am. Assn. Respiratory Care, Calif. Soc. Respiratory Care (past officer), Nat. Bd. Respiratory Care, Nat. Assn. Apnea Profls., Am. Assn. Physicians Assts., L.A. Pediatric Soc., Calif. Perinatal Assn., Saleen Owners Enthusiasts Club, SVT Cobra Owner's Club So. Calif., Mustang Club Am., Saleen Mustang Owners Group (founder). Republican. Methodist. Avocations: boating, automobile racing, automobile restoration, wrist watch collecting, fly fishing. Office: Tim Schlose and Assocs 747 S Brea Blvd Ste 36 Brea CA 92821-5379

SCHLOTTMANN, DAVID HENRY, accountant; b. Olympia, Wash., Oct. 11, 1944; s. David Frank and Phyllis Emily (Cook) S.; Jr. Accountant, Dietz Bus. Coll., 1968; m. Carol Ann Pink, Nov. 22, 1968; children—Julianna Carol, Amy Marie, David Jesse, Caleb Tyrell Henri. Clk., Wash. State Dept. Labor and Industries, 1968, clk. typist Dept. Motor Vehicles, 1968-69, accounting asst. Dept. Hwys. 1969-70, fed. grants accountant Div. Instns., Dept. Social and Health Services, Olympia, Wash., 1970-72, welfare program accountant Div. Pub. Assistance, 1972-73, budget analyst Vets. Program, 1973-76; chief accountant Dep. Vets.' Affairs, 1976-81, budget analyst Dept. Corrections, 1981-95, ret., 1995; owner, Ookkee's Bookshop, Olympia, 1974—. Mem. 1976 Jack London Centennial Com., 1973-76; mem. Council of State Agy. Fiscal Officers, 1980-81. Bd. dirs. London NW, 1976—. Served with AUS, 1963-66. Decorated Army Commendation medal. Named Jack London Man of Year, 1973. Mem. Ch. of God (Cleve., Tenn., ch. clk. 1974-97). Editor, pub.: What's New About London, Jack?, 1971—, The Chaney Chronical (about London's father), 1972—, The Wolf, a Jack London ann., 1973—, non profit lit. jours. centering around life of Am. author Jack London; editor, pub. Sons of the Pioneers Historical Society, 1988. Home: 929 S Bay Rd NE Olympia WA 98506-4808

SCHLUETER, GEORG JOHANN, computer technology executive; b. Wilhelmishaven, Germany, Aug. 20, 1938; s. Heinrich and Lisa (Cordes) S.; m. Tosca M.L. Hempel; children: Frank H., Nicole Louise. MSME, Inst. of Tech., Aachen, Germany, 1963, MBA in Bus. Mgmt., 1966, PhD in Nuclear Physics, 1976. Registered profl. engr., Calif. Mgr. engring. Gen. Atomics, San Diego, 1976-80, dir. bus. devel., 1980-86; pres. Hull Electronics, San Diego, 1986-90, Hansa Tech., San Diego, 1990-94; v.p. Integration Ptnrs. [illegible] San Diego, 1985; mem. faculty U. Phoenix, 1994—.. Pres. Home Owners Assn., San Diego, 1990-96. Avocations: skiing, swimming, sailing, reading. Home: PO Box 2263 Rancho Santa Fe CA [illegible]

SCHMALENBERGER, JERRY LEW, pastor, seminary educator; b. Greenville, Ohio, Jan. 23, 1934; s. Harry Henry and Lima Marie (Hormel) [illegible]

Sarah Layton. BA, Wittenberg U., 1956, DDiv (hon.), 1984; MDiv, Hamma Sch. Theology, Springfield, Ohio, 1959, D of Ministry, 1976. Ordained to ministry Luth. Ch., 1959. Dir. Camp Mowana, Mansfield, Ohio, 1958-59; pastor 3d Luth. Ch., Springfield, 1959-61, 1st Luth. Ch., Bellefontaine, Ohio, 1961-66; sr. pastor 1st Luth. Ch., Tiffin, Ohio, 1966-70, Mansfield, 1970-79; sr. pastor St. John's Luth. Ch., Des Moines, 1979-88; pres. Pacific Luth. Theol. Sem., Berkeley, Calif., 1988-96, prof. parish ministry, 1988-99; co-dir. Iowa Luth. Hosp. Min. of Health Program, Des Moines, 1986-88; Roland Payne lectr. Gbarnga (Liberia) Sch. Theology, 1987; lectr. Luth. Theol. Sem., Hong Kong, 1994, The United Theol. Coll., Kingston, Jamaica, 1994, HKBP Sem., Sumatra, 1997; guest prof. The Augustana Hochschule, Germany, 1996; guest lectr. Inst. Superior Evangelical Theol. Studies, Theol. Seminary, Argentina, 1998, Ecumenical Ctr., Montevideo, Uruguay, 1998, Moravian Theol. Seminary, Paramararibo, Suriname, 1998. Author: Lutheran Christians' Beliefs Book One, 1984, Book Two, 1987, Iowa Parables and Iowa Psalms, 1984, Saints Who Shaped the Church, 1986, Stewards of Creation, 1987, Nights Worth Remembering, 1989, The Vine and the Branches, 1992, Call to Witness, 1993, Plane Thoughts on Parish Ministry, 1994, Invitation to Discipleship, 1995, The Preacher's Edge, 1996, Preparation for Discipleship, 1998, These Will Preach, 1999; columnist Rite Ideas, 1987-88. Bd. dirs. Grand View Coll., Des Moines, 1980-88, Wittenberg U., Springfield, Ohio, 1974-87, Luth. Social Services of Iowa, 1980-87, chmn. pre fund drive, 1988; bd. dirs. Planned Parenthood of Mid-Iowa, Des Moines, 1987-88; dir. Evang. Outreach/Luth. Ch. Am., 1983-85; mem. Iowa Luth. Hosp. Charitable Trust, 1986-88; chair Com. for Homeless Fund, Des Moines, 1986. Named Outstanding Alumni Wittenberg U., 1965, Young Man of Yr. Tiffin Jaycees, 1965, Man of Yr. Bellefontaine Jaycees, Disting. Alumni award Trinty Sem., Columbus, 1989. Mem. NAACP, Acad. Preachers, Acad. Evangelists (organizer 1986—), Kiwanis, Rotary. Avocations: historical research and writing, travel, boating. Home and Office: 162 Pelican Loop Pittsburg CA 94565-2004

SCHMALTZ, ROY EDGAR, JR., artist, art educator; b. Belfield, N.D., Feb. 23, 1937; s. Roy and Mercedes (Martin) S.; m. Julia Mabel Swan, Feb. 1, 1958; children: Liese Marlene, Jennifer Lynn, Gregory Jason. Student Otis Art Inst., Los Angeles, 1959-60, U. Wash., 1960-61, Akademie der Bildenden Kunste, Munich, W. Ger., 1965-66; B.F.A., San Francisco Art Inst., 1963, M.F.A., 1965. Lectr. art Coll. of Notre Dame, Belmont, Calif., 1968-70, M. H. De Young Meml. Art Mus., San Francisco, 1968-70; prof. art St. Mary's Coll. of Calif., Moraga, 1969—, chmn. dept. art; mem. artists' bd. San Francisco Art Inst., 1989-92; exhbns. include: Seattle Art Mus., 1959, M. H. De Young Meml. Art Mus., 1969, Frye Art Mus., Seattle, 1957, San Francisco Mus. Modern Art, 1971, U. Calif.-Santa Cruz, 1977, Fine Arts Mus. of San Francisco, 1978, Oakland Art Mus., 1979, Rutgers U., Camden, N.J., 1979, Springfield (Mo.) Art Mus., 1980, Butler Inst. Am. Art, Youngstown, Ohio, 1981, Huntsville (Ala.) Mus. Art, 1982, Haggin Mus., Stockton, Calif., 1982, U. Hawaii-Hilo, 1983, Alaska State Mus., Juneau, 1981, Tex. State U., San Marcos, 1980, Crocker Art Mus., Sacramento, 1982, Hearst Art Gallery, 1986; group exhbns. include San Francisco Internat. Airport Gallery, 1987, Solano Coll., Fairfield, Calif., 1988, U. Del., Newark, 1988, San Francisco Art Inst., 1989, Natsoulas Gallery, Davis, Calif., 1989, Bedford Regional Ctr. Arts, Walnut Creek, Calif., 1989, Contemporary Realist Gallery, San Francisco, 1994, Hearst Art Gallery, Moraba, Calif., 1995; represented in permanent collections: Richmond Art Ctr. (Calif.), U. Hawaii-Hilo, Las Vegas Art Mus. (Nev.), Hoyt Mus. and Inst. Fine Arts, New Castle, Pa., Frye Art Mus., San Francisco Art Inst., M. H. De Young Meml. Art Mus., Mills Coll., Oakland, Amerika-Haus, Munich, Contra Costa County Art Collection, Walnut Creek, Calif., Western Wash. U., Bellingham, Clemson U., S.C.; dir. Hearst Art Gallery, St. Mary's Coll.; vis. artist lectr. Academie Art Coll., San Francisco, 1971, grad. program Lone Mountain Coll., San Francisco, 1973-74. Coach Little League Baseball Team, Concord, Calif., 1982; mem. artist's bd. San Francisco Art Inst., 1989-93. Fulbright fellow, 1965-66; Frye Art Mus. traveling fellow, 1957; recipient Painting award All Calif. Ann., 1965; Nat. Watercolor award Chautauqua Inst., 1980; Seattle Art Assn. Painting award, 1957; San Francisco Art Inst. award, 1961; Otis Art Inst. award, 1959; Walnut Creek Civic Art Ctr. award, 1982, San Francisco Art Commn. award, 1985, Calif. State Fair Art award, 1985, Sears award for excellence in leadership, 1989-90. Mem. Coll. Art Assn., Fine Arts Mus. of San Francisco, AAUP, San Francisco Art Inst. Alumni Assn. Home: 1020 Whistler Dr Suisun City CA 94585-2929 Office: Saint Marys Coll Dept Art Moraga CA 94575

SCHMALZ, CHARLES JOSEPH, artist, photographer, creative consultant, writer, publisher; b. Indpls., Nov. 3, 1947; s. Charles Joseph and Mary Ann (Eberle) S. BFA Visual Comm., Advt. Design cum laude, Pratt Inst., Bklyn., 1971. Tchr. Sacred Heart Elem. Sch., Indpls., 1964-65; spl. projects art dir. Random House, Knopf, Inc., N.Y.C., 1970-73; art dir. Klemtner Advt., N.Y.C., 1973-76; v.p. group art dir. Medigraphics, Wm. D. McAdams, N.Y.C., 1976-79; exec. art dir. Vicom Assocs., San Francisco, 1980-81; creative dir. Rainoldi, Kerzner & Radcliffe, San Francisco, 1981-87; author, tchr. basic layout Acad. of Art Coll., San Francisco, 1989-90; prin. Charles Schmalz Creative Svcs., San Francisco, 1988—. Photographer: solo exhibitions include Galleria U. Calif. Extension, San Francisco, 1984, Davis Art Ctr. The Hallway Gallery Davis, Calif., 1993, LCR Gallery, Weed, Calif., 1994, Palos Verdes Art Ctr., Ranchos Palos Verdes, Calif., 1995, Merced (Calif.) Coll. Art Gallery, 1995, So. Vt. Art Ctr., Manchester, 1996, Cerro Coso Cmty. Fine Arts Gallery, Ridgecrest, Calif., 1996, Callery of Photography, Ea. Wash. U., Cheney, 1998; group exhibitions include Lilian Paley Ctr. for Visual Arts, Oakland, 1992, Orange County Ctr. for Contemporary Art, Santa Ana, Calif., 1993, Paris Gibson Sq. Mus. of Art, Gt. Falls, Mont., 1993, Hoyt Nat. Art Show, 1993, Univ. of Toledo Ctr. for the Visual Arts, Nat. Juried Exhibit, 1993, Alexandria (La.) Mus. of Art, 1994, Dadian Gallery, The Ctr. for Arts and Religion, Washington, 1995, Colombia (Mo.) Coll., 1995, Mus. of N.W. Colo., Craig, 1995, Downey (Calif.) Mus. of Art, 1996, San Bernadino County Mus., Redlands, Calif., 1996, Barrett House Galleries, DCAA, Poughkeepsie, N.Y., 1997, 1078 Gallery, Chico, Calif., 1997, 750 Gallery, Sacramento, Calif., 1997; pub., author: RaliaGuide, Individual, Family & Caregiver Guide, 1998. Exec. dir., founder Fresh Start reintegration process for the homeless, 1989-90. Recipient Merit award 15th Ann. N.D. Nat. Juried Exhibition U. N.D., 1992, 1st Pl. award 89th Open Juried Exhibit, Long Beach Arts, Calif., 1993, People's Choice award, 9th Ann. Photo Show, Mus. Anthropology Calif. State U., Chico, 1993, Gallery Choice award, Gallery 57, Fullerton, Calif., 1993, Purchase awards S.W. Tex. State U., San Marcos, 1994, Univ. Gallery, U. Del., 1994; 1st pl. award Mus. N.W. Colo. Mem. Amnesty Internat., Greenpeace, Artists Equity. Home and Studio: 271 Santa Rosa Ave San Francisco CA 94112-1906

SCHMID, LYNETTE SUE, child and adolescent psychiatrist; b. Tecumseh, Nebr., May 28, 1958; d. Mel Vern John and Janice Wilda (Bohling) S.; m. Vijendra Sundar, June 13, 1987; children: Jesse Christopher Mikaéle, Eric Lynn Kalani, Christina Elizabeth Ululani. BS, U. Nebr., 1979; MD, U. Nebr., Omaha, 1984; postgrad., U. Mo., 1984-89. Diplomate Am. Bd. Med. Examiners, Am. Bd. Psychiatry and Neurology. Child and adolescent psychiatrist Fulton (Mo.) State Hosp., 1990-91, Mid-Mo. Mental Health Ctr., Columbia, Mo., 1991-96; owner Fairview Motel, Kemmerer, Wyo., 1996—; clin. asst. prof. psychiatry U. Mo., Columbia, 1990-96. Contbr. articles to profl. jours. Mem. Am. Psychiat. Assn., Am. Acad. Child and Adolescent Psychiatry, Ctrl. Mo. Psychiat. Assn. (sec.-treas. 1992-93, pres.-elect 1993-94, pres. 1994-95), U. Nebr. Alumni Assn., Phi Beta Kappa, Alpha Omega Alpha. Republican. Baptist. Avocations: walking, reading, studying scripture.

SCHMIDT, BALDWIN STEPHEN, manufacturing company executive; b. Cin., Aug. 3, 1942; s. William Christian and Edna Marie (Baldwin) S. BS, U.S. Naval Acad., 1964; MA, Calif. State U., San Francisco, 1974. Lic. contractor, Calif. Commd. ensign USN, 1964; advanced through grades to lt. USN, Vietnam; resigned USN, 1969; mental health worker Ross (Calif.) Gen. Hosp., 1974-76; pres. Marin Energy Planning, San Rafael, Calif., 1976-81; sales mgr. Le Fiell Co., San Francisco, 1981-83; pres. LeFiell Co., San Francisco, 1984—, LeFiell, Ltd., Calgary, Atla., 1987-90; trustee local AFL-CIO Welfare Plan, Oakland, Calif. Marin County dir. Calif. for Nuclear Safety, San Francisco, 1974-76; mem. Dem. cen. com. Marin County, 1977-81; bd. dirs. Acad. World Studies, San Francisco, 1978-81, Golden Gate Energy Ctr., San Francisco, 1979-81, Marin Community Video, San Rafael, Calif., 1976-78. Mem. Calif. Metal Trades Assn. (bd. dirs. 1983-90), Reno-Sparks C. of C., Nev. World Trade Coun. Home: 1585 Butterfly Dr Reno NV 89523-2511 Office: Le Fiell Co Inc 5601 Echo Ave Reno NV 89506

SCHMIDT, BYRON WINFIELD, film company executive; b. Faulkton, S.D., Jan. 22, 1925; s. Irwin Henry and Elizabeth (Lambert) S. AA, City Coll., Long Beach, Calif., 1949; BS, U. So. Calif., 1951; cert., Columbia Coll., 1955. Dir. spl. promotions Trans World Airlines, Los Angeles, 1957-70; exec. dir. Travel 8, Inc., Beverly Hills, Calif., 1971-74; pres. Airline Film and TV Promotions, Pacoima, Calif., 1974—. Writer, producer: (radio shows) Clock Time, 1950, Let's Go Traveling, 1963-64. Active World Affairs Council, Beverly Hills, 1972-74. Served with USAF, 1943-45. Mem. Am. Film Inst., Hollywood C. of C. (editor Premiere 1960), Hollywood Jr. C. of C. Republican. Methodist. Avocations: photography, sports. Office: Airline Film and TV 13246 Weidner St Pacoima CA 91331-2391

SCHMIDT, FRANK BROAKER, executive recruiter; b. Shamokin, Pa., Aug. 8, 1939; s. Frank Wilhelm and Doris (Maurer) S.; children by previous marrage: Susan E., Tracie A.; m. Elizabeth Mallen, Mar. 18, 1989; children: Alexandra M., Frank W.M. BS, U. Pa., 1962; MBA, Case Western Res. U., 1969; cert. brewmaster, Siebel Inst. Brewing Tech., Chgo., 1964. With Carling Brewing Co., Cleve., 1964-69, mgr. sales and advt. div., brand mgr., 1969-70; advt. and merchandising mgr. The Pepsi-Cola Co., Purchase, N.Y., 1970-73, dir. mktg. programs, then dir. mgmt. devel., 1973-74; dir. sales and mktg. The Olga Co., Van Nuys, Calif., 1974-75; pres. F.B. Schmidt, Internat., L.A., 1975—; chmn. Mediterranean Properties, 1994—. Author: Draft Beer Manual, 1967, Assn. Nat. Advertisers Computerized Media System, 1970. Chmn. Morrison Ranch Estates Homeowners Assn., 1993-96. Mem. Calif. Exec. Recruiters Assn., Wharton Alumni Assn., Personnel Cons. Am. (region chmn. 1981-83, chmn. 92-95), Am. Mktg. Assn. Republican. Avocations: sports cars, flying, marathon bicycling. Office: 30423 Canwood St Ste 239 Agoura Hills CA 91301-4318

SCHMIDT, JEANNE LOUISE, retired sales specialist; b. Brighton, Colo., June 2, 1947; d. Virgil Ulysses and Edith Marie (Clark) Dack; m. Gerald Dean Smith, Apr. 10, 1967 (div. July 1994); m. Kenneth George Schmidt, Mar. 13, 1996. Grad., Airlines Tng. Sch., Denver, 1965; student in Computer Sci., Skagit Valley, 1988; student in Interior Design, LaSalle U., 1977; student, Coll. of the Desert, 1998—. Reservation sales Continental Airlines, Denver, 1965-83; owner, mgr. Great Western Investments, Denver, 1977-83; mktg. specialist Potlatch RV Pk., Laconner, Wash., 1988-89; activities dir. Outdoor Resorts, Palm Springs, Calif., 1991-94; social hostess Smoke Tree Ranch, Palm Springs, Calif., 1995-96; tutor recruitment Sunny Sands Sch., Cathedral City, Calif., 1996-98; concierge Esmerelda Hotel, Indian Wells, Calif., 1998. Editor (newsletter) Baby Boomers, 1984-90; contbr. articles to mags. Mem. Writer's Assn. Avocations: writing, dancing, hiking, reading, crafts. Home: 68055 Village Dr Cathedral City CA 92234

SCHMIDT, JOANNE (JOSEPHINE ANNE SCHMIDT), language educator; b. N.Y.C., June 7, 1950; d. Joseph William and Maria Esther (Morazzani) S. BA, Chestnut Hill Coll., Phila., 1972; MA, U. Va., 1974, PhD, 1980. Tchg. asst. U. Va., Charlottesville, 1973-76, Lycée Marie Curie, Sceaux, France, 1976-77; lectr. U. Va., Charlottesville, 1977-79; asst. prof. Cedar Crest Coll., Allentown, Pa., 1981-84; asst. prof. Calif. State U., Bakersfield, 1984-88, assoc. prof., 1988-94, prof., 1994—; freelance translator, Bklyn., 1979-81, Allentown, Pa., 1981-84, Bakersfield, Calif., 1984—. Author: (book) If There Are No More Heroes There Are Heroines: A Feminist Critique of Corneille's Heroines, 1987, (jour.) San Jose Studies, 1987, (poetry book) (author as Teresita Bosch) Portraits, 1991; assoc. editor: (jour.) Coll. Tchg., 1985-89. V.p. Women, Inc., Allentown, 1983-84; pub. spkr. Alliance Against Family Violence, Bakersfield, Calif., 1985-90. Fulbright Hays grantee Fed. Govt., 1976-77, Affirmative Action grantee Calif. State U., 1985, 87, 91. Mem. MLA, NOW, Am. Assn. Tchrs. of French, Nat. Women's Studies Assn., Calif. Lang. Tchrs. Assn., Delta Kappa Gamma. Democrat. Avocations: carpentry, golf, creative writing, family history, oral history. Office: Calif State U Fgn Langs Dept 9001 Stockdale Hwy Bakersfield CA 93311-1022

SCHMIDT, JOHN WESLEY, radiation health physicist, environmental scientist; b. Pendleton, Oreg., Aug. 26, 1954; s. Earl B. and Mary C. (Eaton) S.; m. Julia Anne Hampton, Nov. 23, 1988. AA, Columbia Basin Coll., 1985, AAS in Nuclear Technology, 1985; BSME, Wash. State U., 1991. Health physics technician Rockwell Hanford Co., Richland, Wash., 1985-87; health physics technician Westinghouse Hanford Co., Richland, Wash., 1987-90, sr. engr., 1990-96; sr. engr. Rust Fed. Svcs., Inc., Richland, 1996-97; health physicist Wash. State Dept. Health, Olympia, 1997—. Mem. Assn. N.W. Environ. Profls., Health Physics Soc., Tri Cities Enological Soc., Columbia Basin Health Physics Soc., Richland Rod and Gun Club. Avocations: hunting, fishing, backpacking, whitewater rafting, skiing. Office: Wash State Dept Health PO Box 47901 1300 Quince St SE Olympia WA 98501-7329

SCHMIDT, JOSEPH DAVID, urologist; b. Chgo., July 29, 1937; s. Louis and Marian (Fleigel) S.; m. Andrea Maxine Herman, Oct. 28, 1962. BS in Medicine, U. Ill., 1959, MD, 1961. Diplomate Am. Bd. Urology. Rotating intern Presbyn. St. Luke's Hosp., Chgo., 1961-62, resident in surgery, 1962-63; resident in urology The Johns Hopkins Hosp., Balt., 1963-67; faculty U. Iowa Coll. Medicine, Iowa City, 1969-76; faculty U. Calif., San Diego, 1976—, prof., head div. urology, 1976—, vice-chmn. dept. surgery, 1985-97; cons. U.S. Dept. Navy, San Diego, 1976—; attending urologist Vets. Affairs Dept., San Diego, 1976—; assoc. dir. for clin. rsch. U. Calif. San Diego Cancer Ctr., 1997-98. Author, editor: Gynecological and Obstetric Urology, 1978, 82, 93. Capt. USAF, 1967-69. Recipient Francis Senear award. U. Ill., 1961. Fellow Am. Coll. of Surgeons; mem. AMA, Am. Urol. Assn. Inc., Alpha Omega Alpha. Avocations: collecting antique medical books, manuscripts. Office: U Calif Med Ctr Divsn Urology 200 W Arbor Dr San Diego CA 92103-1911

SCHMIDT, KARL A., lawyer; b. Stockton, Calif., Sept. 18, 1947. BS, U. Calif., Berkeley, 1969, JD, 1974. Bar: Calif. 1974. Mem. Parker, Milliken, Clark, O'Hara & Samuelian, L.A. Mem. ABA. Office: Parker Milliken Clark OHara & Samuelian 333 S Hope St Ste 2700 Los Angeles CA 90071-1449

SCHMIDT, KATHRYN WAGNER, artist; b. Dubuque, Iowa, July 11, 1952; d. Joseph Francis and Monica Mary (McAndrews) Wagner; m. Anthony Jay Schmidt, Jul. 2, 1983; 1 child, Anna. BFA, Univ. Iowa, 1977. tchr. adult edn. series, Univ. Iowa, 1975-76, sculpture workshops Montana Interscholastic Arts program, 1987, vis. artist Custer County Art Ctr., Miles City, Mont., 1986; participant Mont. Artists in Schs./Cmty. program, 1993-95. Exhibited at numerous galleries including 55 Mercer Gallery, 1981, Fine Arts Gallery, 1984, Missoula Mus. of Arts, 1987, Gallery Paule Anglim, San Francisco, 1987, Arts-in-Company Gallery, Kalispell, Mont., 1988, San Francisco Mus. of Modern Art Sales and Rental Gallery, 1989, Centennial Show Custer County Art Ctr., Miles City, Mont., 1989, Mus. of the Rockies, 1990, Paris Gibson Square Great Falls, Mont., 1990, Mont. State Univ., 1991, Beall Park Art Ctr., 1993, Nicolaysen Art Mus., 1993, Yellowstone Art Ctr., 1994, Missoula Mus. of the Arts, 1994, CSPS, Cedar Rapids, Iowa, 1994, Beall Park Art Ctr., 1995, Tacoma Art Mus., 1995, Hockaday Ctr. for the Arts, Kalispell, 1996. Recipient artist fellowship Mont. Arts Coun., 1994. Home: 12789 Rose Creek Rd Bozeman MT 59715

SCHMIDT, L(AIL) WILLIAM, JR., lawyer; b. Thomas, Okla., Nov. 22, 1936; s. Lail William and Violet Kathleen (Kuper) S.; m. Diana Gail (div. May 1986); children: Kimberly Ann, Andrea Michelle; m. Marilyn Sue, Aug. 11, 1990; stepchildren: Leland Darrell Mosby, Jr., Crystal Rachelle Mosby. BA in Psychology, U. Colo., 1959; JD, U. Mich., 1962. Bar: Colo. 1962, U.S. Dist. Ct. Colo. 1964, U.S. Tax Ct. 1971, U.S. Ct. Appeals (10th cir.) 1964. Ptnr. Holland & Hart, Denver, 1962-77, Schmidt, Elrod & Wills, Denver, 1977-85, Moye, Giles, O'Keefe, Vermeire & Gorrell, Denver, 1985-90; of counsel Hill, Held, Metzger, Lofgren & Peele, Dallas, 1989—; pvt. practice law Denver, 1990—; lectr. profl. orgns. Author: How To Live-and Die-with Colorado Probate, 1985, A Practical Guide to the Revocable Living Trust, 1990; contbr. articles to legal jours. Pres. Luth. Med. Ctr. Found., Wheat Ridge, Colo., 1985-89; pres. Rocky Mountain Prison and Drug Found., Denver, 1986—; bd. dirs. Luth. Hosp., Wheat Ridge, 1988-92; bd. dirs. Bonfils Blood Ctr. Found., 1995—, Planned Giving Adv. Group of Nat. Jewish Hosp., Denver, 1996-98; planned giving advisor Aspen Valley Med. Found., 1997—; mktg. and gifts adv. com. The Denver Found., 1998—. Fellow Am. Coll. Trust and Estate Counsel (Colo. chmn. 1981-86); mem. ABA, Am. Judicature Soc., Rocky Mtn. Estate Planning Coun. (founder, pres. 1970-71), Greater Denver Tax Counsel Assn., Am. Soc. Magicians, Denver Athletic Club, Phi Delta Phi. Republican. Baptist. Avocation: magic. Office: 1050 17th St Ste 1700 Denver CO 80265-2077 also: Law Offices of Robert L Bolick Ltd 6060 Elton Ave Ste A Las Vegas NV 89107-0100

SCHMIDT, MARY MARGARET, non-profit company administrator, consultant; b. Cleve., Apr. 3, 1966; d. Albert Frank Jr. and Bonita Mae (Rudolph) S. BA, Mills Coll., 1991; MA in Bus., Calif. Inst. Integral Studies, 1995. Office mgr. Give Something Back, Oakland, Calif., 1992-94; capital campaign dir. The Women's Bldg., San Francisco, 1994-96; devel. dir. Sports Bridge, San Francisco, 1996—; mem. renovation leadership com. The Women's Bldg., San Francisco, 1996—. Ropes course leader Ft. Miley/T.R.U.E., San Francisco, 1997—. Mem. Nat. Soc. Fund Raising Execs. (bd. dirs., diversity chair 1996—). Office: Sports Bridge 965 Mission St # 600 San Francisco CA 94103

SCHMIDT, RUTH A(NNA) M(ARIE), geologist; b. Bklyn., Apr. 22, 1916; d. Edward and Anna M. (Range) S. AB, NYU, 1936; MA, Columbia U., 1939, PhD, 1948. Cert. profl. geologist. Geologist U.S. Geol. Survey, Washington, 1943-56; dist. geologist U.S. Geol. Survey, Anchorage, 1956-63; prof., chmn. geology dept. U. Alaska, Anchorage, 1959-84; cons. geologist Anchorage, 1964—; lectr. Elder Hostels, Alaska Pacific U., Anchorage, 1988-89, U. Alaska, Anchorage, 1994; coord. Engrng. Geol. Evaluating Group, Alaskan 1964 Earthquake, Anchorage, 1964; environ. cons. Trans Alaska Pipeline, Office of Gov., Anchorage, 1975-76. Editor: Alaska geology field trip guide books, 1984, 89; contbr. articles to profl. jours. Trustee, pres. Brooks Range Libr., Anchorage, 1979-91; bd. dirs., com. chmn. Anchorage Audubon Soc., 1989-98; mem. exec. bd., chmn. various coms. Alaska Cen. Environment, Anchorage. Fellow AAAS, Arctic Inst. N.Am. (bd. govs. 1983-94), Geol. Soc. Am.; mem. Am. Inst. Profl. Geologists (charter), Am. Assn. Petroleum Geologists, Internat. Geol. Congress (del.), Alaska Geol. Soc. (hon. life mem., bd. dirs. 1993-95), Sigma Xi. Avocations: photography, gardening, hiking.

SCHMIDT, STANLEY EUGENE, retired speech educator; b. Harrington, Wash., Dec. 14, 1927; s. Otto Jacob and Ella Genevieve (Wilson) S.; m. Randall Lee, Stephen Douglas. BS in Edn., U. Idaho, 1956; MEd in Adminstrn., U. Oreg., 1958; MA in Speech, Wash. State U., 1975. Supt., tchr., coach Rose Lake (Idaho) Sch. Dist. # 35, 1949-55; forensics coach, speech tchr. Jefferson H.S., Portland, Oreg., 1955-65; dir. forensics Portland C.C., 1965-93, lead speech instr., 1979-82, subject area chmn., 1986-90; adj. prof. speech U. Portland, 1987-93; parliamentarian faculty senate, 1975-80. Co-author anthology: The Literature of the Oral Tradition, 1963. Chmn., precinct committeeman Rep. Party, Kootenai County, Idaho, 1951-53; mem. Easter Seal Soc.; pres. Kootenai County Tchrs. Assn., 1953-54, North Idaho Edn. Assn., 1954-55, Oreg. Speech Assn., 1960-61, Oreg. C.C. Speech Assn., 1971-72. Recipient Excellence award U.S. Bank, Portland, 1993, Merit award N.W. Forensic Assn., 1992, Faculty Merit award Portland C.C., 1984. Mem. Portland Rose Soc., Oreg. Ret. Tchrs. Assn., Royal Rosarian, Masons (jr. grand deacon 1990-91, jr. grand steward 1991-92, grand orator, 1992-93, dist. dep. 1986-90, 33d deg. Scottish Rite, comdr. 1989-90), Cryptic Masons of Oreg. (grand orator 1994-95, illustrious master 1997), Tualatin Valley Shrine Club (pres. 1994), Red Cross of Constantine (St. Laurence Conclave, recorder 1993-97, dir. of the work 1989—). Baptist. Avocations: rose gardening, stamps, coins, fishing, sports. Home: 5460 SW Palatine St Portland OR 97219-7259

SCHMIDT, TERRY LANE, health care executive; b. Chgo., Nov. 28, 1943; s. LeRoy C. and Eunice P. Schmidt; children: Christie Anne, Terry Lane II. B.S., Bowling Green State U., 1965; M.B.A. in Health Care Adminstrn, George Washington U., 1971; postgrad., Med. U. S.C. Resident in hosp. adminstrn. U. Pitts. Med. Center, VA Hosp., Pitts., 1968-69; adminstrv. asst. Mt. Sinai Med. Center, N.Y.C., 1969-70; asst. dir. Health Facilities Planning Council of Met. Washington, 1970-71; asst. dir. dept. govtl. relations A.M.A., Washington, 1971-74; pres. Terry L. Schmidt Inc. Physician Svcs. Group, San Diego, 1974—; exec. dir., chief operating officer Emergency Health Assocs. P.C., Phoenix, 1989-91, Charleston Emergency Physicians, S.C., S.C., 1990-95, Joplin Emergency Physican Assocs., 1991-92, Big Valley Med. Group, 1991-92, Blue Ridge Emergency Physicians, P.C., 1992-93, Berkeley Emergency Physicians, P.C., 1992-95; pres. Med. Cons. Inc., 1983-84; v.p. Crisis Communications Corp. Ltd., 1982-90; pres. Washington Actions on Health, 1975-78; partner Washington counsel Medicine and Health, 1979-81; pres. Ambulance Corp. Am., La Jolla, Calif., 1984-87; chmn., pres. Univ. Inst., 1992—; lectr., part-time faculty dept. health care adminstrn. George Washington U., 1969-84, preceptor, 1971-84; adj. prof. grad. sch. Pub. Health San Diego State U., 1995-98, preceptor, 1989—, guest lectr. health care adminstrn. Nat. U. San Diego, 1992-93; adj. prof. Bus. Adminstrn. U.S. Internat. U., San Diego, 1994-95; asst. prof. Nat. Naval Sch. Health Care Adminstrn., 1971-73; faculty Civil Svc. Commn. Legis. Insts., 1972-76, Am. Assn. State Colls. and U. Health Tng. Insts.; mem. adv. com. ambulatory care standards Joint Commn. Accreditation of Hosps., 1971-72. Author: Congress and Health: An Introduction to the Legislative Process and the Key Participants, 1976, A Directory of Federal Health Resources and Services for the Disadvantaged, 1976, Health Care Reimbursement: A Glossary, 1983; mem. editl. adv. bd. Nation's Health, 1971-73; contbr. articles to profl. jours. Bd. dirs. Nat. Eye Found., 1976-78. Mem. Med. Group Mgmt. Assn., Health Care Fin. Mgmt. Assn., Assn. Venture Capital Groups (bd. dirs. 1984-89), San Diego Venture Group (chair 1984-87), U. Calif. San Diego Faculty Club, Univ. Club (life), Nat. Dem. Club (life), Nat. Rep. Club (life), Capitol Hill Club (life), Alpha Phi Omega (pres. Bowling Green alumni chpt. 1967-70, sec.-treas. alumni assn. 1968-71). Office: 7770 Regents Rd Ste 113-611 San Diego CA 92122-1937

SCHMIDT, WALDEMAR ADRIAN, pathologist, educator; b. L.A., Aug. 22, 1941; s. Waldemar Adrian and Mary Charlotte (Parker) S.; m. Karmen LaVer Bingham, Feb. 1, 1963; children: Rebecca, Sarah, Waldemar, Diedrich. BS, Oreg. State U., 1965; PhD, U. Oreg., 1969, MD, 1969. Intern U. Oreg. Hosps. and Clinics, Portland, 1969-70, resident, 1970-73; pathologist LDS Hosp., Salt Lake City, 1973-77; prof. pathology U. Tex. Med. Sch., Houston, 1977-91; prof. pathology Oreg. Health Sci. U. and VA Med. Ctr., Portland, 1991—, chief pathology and lab. medicine svc., 1997—. Author: Principles and Techniques of Surgical Pathology, 1982; editor Cytopathology Annual, 1991-94, Revs. in Pathology-Cytopathology, 1994—. Asst. scoutmaster Boy Scouts Am., Houston, 1982-91. Maj. U.S. Army, 1970-76. Mem. Coll. Am. Pathologists (program com.), Sigma Xi, Alpha Omega Alpha. Avocations: photography, silviculture. Office: VA Med Ctr 3710 SW Us Veterans Hospital R Portland OR 97201-2964

SCHMIDT, WALLACE ALAN, communications executive; b. Loma Linda, Calif., June 4, 1948; s. Elmer Alonzo and B. Irene (Wallace) S.; m. Donna Lynn Rich, June 28, 1970; children: Allison Marie, Emily Alizabeth. BS, Pacific Union Coll., 1970. TV prodn. mgr. audiovisual service Loma Linda Univ. Med. Ctr., 1974-78, dir. audiovisual service, 1978-94, asst. dir., spl. projects coord. med. records, 1994-98, dir. edn. & tng. dept., 1998—. Office: Loma Linda U Med Ctr 11234 Anderson St Loma Linda CA 92354-2804

SCHMIDTKUNZ, JAMES E., chemical company executive; b. Milw., Apr. 22, 1949; s. Donald and Florence Schmidtkunz; m. Carol Duke, Mar. 18, 1973 (div. May 14, 1998); children: Christopher, Michael, Jeanne. BA, Marquette U., 1971. Sales rep. Procter & Gamble, Cin., 1975-76, zone mgr., 1977-83; region mgr. Chemed Corp., Cin., 1984-90; nat. accounts mgr. Diversey Group, Detroit, 1991-94; divsn. mgr. Washing Sys., Inc., Cin., 1994-97, group v.p., 1997—. Lt. USN, 1971-75, Vietnam. Mem. U.S. Naval Inst., Textile Rental Svcs. Assn., Uniform Textile Svcs. Assn. Republican. Roman Catholic. Avocations: chess, theater. Office: Washing Sys Inc 4000 Barranca Pkwy Ste 250 Irvine CA 92604-1713

SCHMIEDEL, DONALD EMERSON, Spanish educator; b. Ravenna, Ohio, Nov. 21, 1939; s. Franklin Edward and Dorothy Ellen (Weldin) S.; m. Grace Arlene Baters, Aug. 21, 1965. AB, Kent State U., 1961; PhD, U. So. Calif., 1967. Assoc. prof. Spanish U. nev., Las Vegas, 1965—. Author:

(book) El Conde de Sex by Antonio Coello: A Critical Edition and Study, 1976. Mem. United Ch. of Christ. Office: Univ of Nev Las Vegas Las Vegas NV 89154-5047

SCHMIEDER, CARL, jeweler; b. Phoenix, Apr. 27, 1938; s. Otto and Ruby Mable (Harkey) S.; m. Carole Ann Roberts, June 13, 1959; children: Gail, Susan, Nancy, Amy. Student Bradley Horological Sch., Peoria, Ill., 1959-61; BA, Pomona Coll., 1961; Owner timepiece repair svc., Peoria, 1959-61; clock repairman Otto Schmieder & Son, Phoenix, 1961-65, v.p., 1965-70, pres., 1970—, chief exec. officer, 1970—. Mem. subcom. Leap Commn., 1966; area rep. Pomona Coll., 1972-76. Cert. jeweler; cert. gemologist, gemologist appraiser; recipient Design award Diamonds Internat., 1965, Cultured Pearl Design award, 1967, 68, Diamonds for Christmas award, 1970; winner Am. Diamond Jewelry Competition, 1973; bd. dirs. Lincoln Hosp., 1983—, Ariz. Mus., 1984-88; delegate White House Conf. on Small Bus., 1986, 95; chmn. Gov.'s Conf. on Small Bus., 1988-91; col. Confederate Air Force. Mem. Am. Gem. Soc. (dir. 1973-86, nat. chmn. nomenclature com. 1975-77, chmn. membership com. 1977-81, officer 1981-86), Ariz. Jewelers Assn. (Man of Yr. 1974), Jewelers Security Alliance (dir. 1974-78), Jewelers Vigilance Com. (dir. 1981-87), Jewelry Industry Council (dir. 1982-88), 24 Karat Club So. Calif., Exptl. Aircraft Assn., Warbirds of Am. (dir. 1990—), Deer Valley (Ariz.) Airport Tenants Assn. (dir. 1980-90, pres. 1983-90), Ariz. C. of C. (bd. dirs. 1985-89), Small Bus. Council (bd. dirs. 1985-89, chmn. 1988, del. to White House Conf., 1986, 95, chmn. Govs. Conf. on small bus. 1988-89), Nat. Small Bus. United (bd. dirs. 1990-94), Kiwanis (pres. Valley of Sun chpt. 1975-76), Friends of Iberia, Rotary. Republican. Methodist. Home: 1016 W Rovey Ave Phoenix AZ 85013-1445 Office: Park Ctrl Phoenix AZ 85013

SCHMITT, DIANA MAE, elementary education educator; b. Dubuque, Iowa, Jan. 19, 1950; d. Raymond J. and Marie Arlen Schmitt. BA, U. Iowa, 1972; MA, Clarke Coll., Dubuque, 1981; postgrad., U. Wyo. 6th grade tchr. Shelby County Sch. Dist., Shelby, Iowa, 1972-73; 4th and 5th grade tchr. Dist. 200, Woodstock, Ill., 1973-76; rural sch. tchr. Albany County Sch. Dist., Laramie, Wyo., 1976-83; 1st, 3d, 5th and 6th grade tchr. Albany County Sch. Dist., 1983-98; chmn. outdoor classrm. devel. Indian Paintbrush Elem., 1992—; mem. rev. com. for excellence in sci. edn., adv. com. Western Edn. Adv. Com. for Wyo., 1989; tchr. sci. methods for elem. sch. U. Wyo., 1990-91; mem. Higher Edn. Grant Reading State Com., 1994; participant Sci. Grasp, 1990, Inst. Chemical Edn. Fundamental, 1992; presenter 1st Soviet-Am. Sci. Conv., Moscow, 1991; mem. workshop on water, Nat. Geog. Soc., 1993; presenter NSTA nat. and regional convs., state Wyo. Interdisciplinary Conf. convs., No. Iowa Beginning Reading conf. Recipient Delta award, 1993; named Dist. Exemplary Sci. Tchr., 1986-87; Wyo. Game and Fish grantee, 1993-95, Nat. Geog. Soc. grantee, 1997. Mem. NEA, Internat. Reading Assn., Nat. Sci. Tchrs. Assn., Wyo. Sci. Tchrs. Assn. (sec.), Alpha Delta Kappa (pres.). Home: 5737 Southview Rd Laramie WY 82070-6801 Office: Indian Paintbrush 1653 N 28th St Laramie WY 82072-9200

SCHMITT, NANCY CAIN, public and corporate relations executive, writer; b. Fayetteville, N.C., June 12, 1942; d. Carlton White and Cleo Margaret (Parnell) Cain; m. Louis Dennis Schmitt, July 13, 1974 (div.). BA, Wake Forest U., 1960-64; postgrad., U. Alaska, 1989-90. Intern Winston-Salem (N.C.) Jour.-Sentinel, 1963-64; reporter Gastonia (N.C.) Gazette, 1964-66; copy editor, reporter Twin City Sentinel, Winston-Salem, 1966-67; entertainment editor Fayetteville Observer, 1967-78; lifestyle editor Anchorage Times, 1978-83; pub. rels. specialist Multivisions Cable TV Co., Anchorage, 1983-84; editor Alaska Jour. of Commerce, Anchorage, 1984-85; sr. comms. specialist U.S. Postal Svc., 1985—. Author: How to Care for Your Car: A Women's Guide to Car Care in Alaska, 1978 (nat. award 1979); mem. editl. bd. Episc. Diocean of Alaska, Fairbanks, 1983-86; contbr. articles to profl. jours. and nat. publs. Mem. Advocates for (Foster) Children in Alaska. Recipient Asst. Postmaster Gen.'s award for excellence, USPS Legis. Affairs Corp. Rel. Sr. VP Opportunity award, Sr. Op-Ed Writing award, Patriotic Writing award VFW. Mem. Nat. Fedn. Press Women (nat. bd. dirs. 1990-91, 97-98), Pub. Rels. Soc. Am., Alaska Press Women (pres. 1990-91, 97-98, treas., sec., communicator of achievement, recipient numerous awards), Alaska Press Club (recipient 3 awards), Rotary Internat. (bd. dirs. 1991-92). Home: 6716 E 16th Ave Apt A Anchorage AK 99504-2513 Office: U S Postal Svc Corp Rels 3201 C St Anchorage AK 99503-3934

SCHMITT, PAUL JOHN, history and geography educator; b. Pitts., Jan. 25, 1951; s. Phillip John and Adeline Marie (Barnhart) S.; m. Ruth Margaret Glass, June 20, 1987. BS, Ariz. State U., 1976, BA in Edn., 1978; MA, U. Nev., Las Vegas, 1994. Registration clk. Hermosa Inn Resort, Scottsdale, Ariz., 1978-79, asst. mgr., 1979-82; convention svc. mgr. Carefree (Ariz.) Inn Resort, 1982-84; tchr. Tonopah (Nev.) High Sch., 1984-85; reservation clk. Desert Inn Country Club and Spa, Las Vegas, Nev., 1985-92; prof. history C.C. of So. Nev., Las Vegas, 1992—. Mem. Assn. Am. Geographers, Orgn. Am. Historians, Am. Western History Assn., Orgn. Am. Historians, Phi Alpha Theta, Gamma Theta Upsilon. Avocations: reading, photography, horseback riding. Office: CC So Nev Cheyenne Campus Dept Regional Studies 3200 E Cheyenne Ave # C North Las Vegas NV 89030-4228

SCHMITT, REED REESE, television director, sports photographer; b. Madison, Wis., Sept. 10, 1965; s. David Reese and Sue Fran (Stinchcomb) S. BA in Broadcast Comms. summa cum laude, Wash. State U., 1990. Dir. Sta. KXLY-TV, Spokane, Wash., 1991—. Recipient award of Distinction, The Videographers Awards, Arlington, Tex., 1998. Avocations: sports, motorcycles, aviation, music. E-mail: reeds@kxly.com. Fax: 509-326-5344. Office: KXLY TV 500 W Boone Spokane WA 99201

SCHMITT, RICHARD GEORGE, industrial engineer; b. St. Cloud, Minn., June 18, 1948; s. George William and Viola Theresa (Mechenich) S.; m. Ligia Marie Pereira, Aug. 29, 1970; children: Christopher Michael, Scott Andrew. B in Indsl. Engring. with honors, Gen. Motors Inst., 1971. Indsl. engr. Gen. Motors, Fremont, Calif., 1966-78; sr. indsl. engr. Gen. Motors, Oklahoma City, 1978-80; indsl. engring. mgr. Shugart Assocs., Sunnyvale, Calif., 1980-81; mfg. tech. mgr. Magnex Corp., San Jose, Calif., 1981-82, prodn. mgr., 1982-83; facilities mgr. Apple Computer, Fremont, 1983, indsl. engring. mgr., 1984-85, robotics mgr., 1985-86, new product ops. mgr., 1987, Pacific logistics ops. mgr., 1988-93; Pacific phys. logistics mgr. Apple Computer, Cupertino, Calif., 1987—, Pacific ops. dir., 1993, Pacific supply chain design mgr., 1994-96, worldwide logistics strategy mgr., 1996—. Transp. chmn. Mt. Hamilton dist. Boy Scouts Am., 1984, asst. scoutmaster, 1986-92; chief YMCA Indian Guides, San Jose, 1977-83. Mem. Am. Assn. Indsl. Engrs. (sr.), Soc. Mfg. Engrs. (sr.), Coun. Logistics Mgmt., Am. Prodn. Inventory Control Soc., Lions (scholar 1966). Republican. Roman Catholic. Home: 9848 Beckenham Dr Granite Bay CA 95746-7209 Office: Apple Computer 900 E Hamilton Ave # Ms72 Campbell CA 95008-0613

SCHMITZ, CHARLES EDISON, evangelist; b. Mendota, Ill., July 18, 1919; s. Charles Francis Schmitz and Lucetta Margaret (Foulk) Schmitz Kaufmann; m. Eunice Magdalene Ewy, June 1, 1942; children: Charles Elwood, Jon Lee. Student, Wheaton Coll., 1936-37, 38, 39; BA, Wartburg Coll., Waverly, Iowa, 1940; BD, Wartburg Theol. Sem., Dubuque, Iowa, 1942, MDiv, 1977. Ordained to ministry Luth. Ch., 1942. Founding pastor Ascension Luth. Ch., L.A., 1942-48, Am. Evang. Luth. Ch., Phoenix, 1948-65; dir. intermountain missions, founding pastor 14 Evang. Luth. Parishes, Calif., Ariz., N.Mex., Fla., 1942-89; evangelist Am. Luth. Ch., Mpls., 1965-73; sr. pastor Peace Luth. Ch., Palm Bay, Fla., 1973-89; pastor-at-large Am. Evang. Luth. Ch., Phoenix, 1989—; charter mem. Navajo Luth. Mission, Rock Point, Ariz., 1960—; chmn. Greater Phoenix Evangelical Ministers Assn., 1998—; pastoral advisor Ariz. Luth. Outdoor Ministry Assn., Prescott, 1958-65, 89—; Kogudus Internat. Retreat master and chaplain, Fla., Berlin and Marbach, Germany, 1990; mem. transition team Fla. Synod, Evang. Luth. Ch. Am., 1985-89. Author: Evangelism for the Seventies, 1970; co-author: ABC's of Life, 1968; assoc. editor Good News mag., 1965-71. Founder, chmn. Ariz. Ch. Conf. on Adult and Youth Problems, 1956-65; vice chmn. synod worship & ch. music com. Am. Luth. Ch., Mpls., 1960-66; chmn. Space Coast Luth. Retirement Ctr., Palm Bay, Fla., 1985-89; [illegible] Luth. Brotherhood, 1991— Named Citizen of Yr., Palm Bay C. of C., 1979. Mem. Nat. Assn. Evangelicals, German Am. [illegible] Congress (nat. chaplain), Lions (life mem., officer Phoenix and Palm Bay clubs 1952—, Ariz. Dist. 21A chaplain 1994-95, Melvin Jones fellow 1995), Kiwanis (bd. dirs. L.A. chpt. 1942-48). Republican. Home: 12444 W Toreador Dr Sun City West AZ 85375-1926

SCHMOLDT, PEGGY SUE, cosmetology educator; b. International Falls, Minn., Apr. 11, 1959; d. John Herbert and Elizabeth Ann (Powers) Hauptli; m. Stephen Michael Schmoldt, Jan. 5, 1980 (div. Feb. 1996); children: Jillian Marie, Megan Elizabeth. Student, U. Iowa, 1977-78; diploma, Capri Cosmetology Coll., 1979; student, Regis U., 1993—. Lic. cosmetologist, Colo., Fla.; cert. pvt. cosmetology tchr., vo-tech. tchr., Colo. Hair designer Fashion Ave., Dubuque, Iowa, 1979-81, LaVonne's, Denver, 1981-83, A Unique Boutique, Destrehan, La., 1984-85, V.I.P. Salon, Boca Raton, Fla., 1987-89; sch. mgr., instr. LaVonne's Acad. of Beauty, Denver, 1981-83; nat. platform educator Anion Labs., Inc., Harvey, La., 1984-85; salon mgr., designer, publ. rels. specialist, educator Lord & Taylor Salons, Boynton Beach/Boca Raton, Fla., 1985-87; dir. edn. Cantwell/Creative Sch. Beauty, Pompano Beach, Fla., 1988-91; dir. cosmetology edn. Boca Raton Inst., 1991-92; freelance cosmetologist, educator Profl. Salon Svcs., Westminster, Colo., 1993—; mem., educator La. Hair Fashion Com., New Orleans, 1985; tchr. Le Team Styles Group, Ft. Lauderdale, Fla., 1986-87; mem. Colo. Edn. Com., Denver, 1993; educator Inter Mountain Beauty Supply, Denver, 1995; cosmetology educator Inst. Hair Design, Arvada, Colo., 1996—; mem. Nexxus Design Team, 1994, Nat. Hair Am., 1994. Pres. New Orleans Cosmetology Assn., 1984; treas., membership chair Palm Beach Cosmetology Assn., 1986-88; vol. Look Good-Feel Better program Am. Cancer Soc., Palm Beach/Broward County, Fla., 1989, Denver, 1993; mem. nat. planning com. trainer's panel LGFB, 1995; sec., mem. legislation/edn. com. Broward County Cosmetology Assn., 1990-92; mem. spkrs. bur. Planned Parenthood of Rocky Mountains, Denver, 1993. Mem. Denver Cosmetology Assn. (pres. 1993, 94), Colo. Cosmetology Assn. (3d v.p. 1993, 1st v.p. 1994, mem. legislation/by-laws com., pres. 1995=96). Roman Catholic. Avocations: swimming, ballet, skiing, hiking, biking.

SCHNACK, HAROLD CLIFFORD, lawyer; b. Honolulu, Sept. 27, 1918; s. Ferdinand J. H. and Mary (Pearson) S.; m. Gayle Hemingway Jepson, Mar. 22, 1947; children: Jerrald Jay, Georgina Schnack Hankinson, Roberta Schnack Poulin, Michael Clifford. BA, Stanford, 1940, LLB, 1947. Bar: Hawaii, 1947. Dep. prosecutor City and County Honolulu, 1947-48; gen. practice with father F. Schnack, 1948-60; pvt. practice, Honolulu, 1960-86; pres. Harcliff Corp., 1961—, Schnack Indsl. Corp., 1969-73, Instant Printers, Inc., 1971-81, Koa Corp., 1964—, Nutmeg Corp., 1963-89, Global Answer System, Inc., 1972-78. Pres. Goodwill Industries of Honolulu, 1971-72. Mem. ABA, Hawaii Bar Assn., Internat. Platform Soc., Nat. Fedn. Ind. Bus. Coun. of 100, Outrigger Canoe Club, Pacific Club, Phi Alpha Delta, Alpha Sigma Phi. Office: 817 A Cedar St PO Box 3077 Honolulu HI 96802-3077

SCHNAPP, ROGER HERBERT, lawyer; b. N.Y.C., Mar. 17, 1946; s. Michael Jay and Beatrice Joan (Becker) S.; m. Candice Jacqueline Larson, Sept. 15, 1979; 1 child, Monica Alexis. *Father Michael Jay Schnapp was a respected entrepreneur and businessman on the East Coast until his retirement. He introduced innovative approaches in each of the industries in which he held leadership positions. Daughter Monica Alexis Schnapp attends the Pegasus School, a school which specializes in the education of intellectually gifted children.* BS, Cornell U., 1966; JD, Harvard U., 1969; postgrad. Pub. Utility Mgmt. Program, U. Mich., 1978. Bar: N.Y. 1970, U.S. Ct. Appeals (2d cir.) 1970, U.S. Supreme, 1974, U.S. Dist. Ct. (so. dist.) N.Y. 1975, U.S. Ct. Appeals (4th and 6th cirs.) 1976, U.S. Ct. Appeals (7th cir.) 1977, U.S. Dist. Ct. (so. dist.) N.Y. 1975, U.S. Dist. Ct. (no. dist.) Calif. 1980, U.S. Ct. Appeals (8th cir.) 1980, Calif., 1982, U.S. Dist. Ct. (cen. dist.) Calif. 1982, U.S. Ct. Dist. Ct. (ea. dist.) Calif., 1984. Atty. CAB, Washington, 1969-70; labor atty. Western Electric Co., N.Y.C., 1970-71; mgr. employee rels. Am. Airlines, N.Y.C., 1971-74; labor counsel Am. Electric Power Svc. Corp., N.Y.C., 1974-78, sr. labor counsel, 1978-80; indsl. rels. counsel Trans World Airlines, N.Y.C., 1980-81; sr. assoc. Parker, Milliken, Clark & O'Hara, L.A., 1981-82; ptnr. Rutan & Tucker, Costa Mesa, Calif., 1983-84, Memel, Jacobs, Pierno, Gersh & Ellsworth, Newport Beach, Calif., 1985-86, Memel, Jacobs & Ellsworth, Newport Beach, 1986-87; pvt. practice Newport Beach, 1987—; bd. dirs. Dynamic Constrn., Inc., Laguna Hills, Calif., 1986—; commentator labor rels. Fin. News Network; commentator Sta. KOCN Radio, 1990-91; lectr. Calif. Western Law Sch., Calif. State U.-Fullerton, Calif. State Conf. Small Bus.; lectr. collective bargaining Pace U., N.Y.C.; lectr. on labor law Coun. on Edn. in Mgmt.; N.E. regional coord. Pressler for Pres., 1979-80. Author: Arbitration Issues for the 1980s, 1981, A Look at Three Companies, 1982; editor-in-chief Indsl. and Labor Rels. Forum, 1964-66; columnist Orange County Bus. Jour., 1989-91; contbr. articles to profl. publs. Mem. Bus. Rsch. Adv. Coun. U.S. Dept. Labor; trustee Chapman U., 1991-95. Mem. Calif. Bar Assn. (chmn.), Labor Law Consulting Group, Calif. Bd. of Legal Specialization, Balboa Bay Club, The Ctr. Club, Club 33. Republican. Jewish. Office: PO Box 9049 Newport Beach CA 92658-1049

SCHNEBELEN, PIERRE, resort planner and developer, consultant; b. Mulhouse, Alsace, France, June 10, 1935; s. Emile and Renee (Gingelwein) S.; children: Stephanie, Mathieu; m. Francois E. Roetynck, June 1, 1985; children: Yvan, Sophie, Wendy, Thomas. Diploma in engring., Ecole Nat. d'Arts et Metiers, Paris, 1958; MS, MIT, 1960. With Mobil Oil Internat., N.Y.C., 1961; founder, chief exec. officer SEFCO, 1965-73, Soc. des Telepheriques de la Grande Motte, 1967-87, SEGMO, 1974-88; founder, pres. SEPARFI, SEGMO IMMOBILIER; founder, dir. Soc. de reprentacoes et de participacoes, Sao Paulo, Brazil, 1977—; pres., chief exec. officer Piersen SA, 1989—; founder, pres. P.S.I. Resorts, Paris, 1988—; founder, pres. Soc. des telepheriques de Valfrejus, 1983-88, societa delle Funivie del Frejus, 1983-88; founder, dir. SEGMO Vacances; CEO Westbrock Assocs. LLC, Boise, Idaho, 1998—; pres., CEO Athlon Fin. Corp., L.A., 1995—. Avocations: skiing, tennis, squash. Home: 18134 Kingsport Dr Malibu CA 90265-5634 Office: Athlon Resorts 1801 Ave Of Stars Los Angeles CA 90067-5902

SCHNEBLY, F(RANCIS) DAVID, aerospace and electronics company executive; b. San Francisco, May 1, 1926; s. Frederick Dorsey and Mary Florence (Blake) S.; m. Miriam Louise Ford, Aug. 27, 1949; children: Mary Diane, Linda Marie, Anne Louise, David Albert, Kathleen Marie. BE in Areo. Engring., U. So. Calif., 1950; cert. advanced mgmt., Harvard U., 1970. Project engr. Hiller Aircraft Corp., Palo Alto, Calif., 1950-55, mgr. ops. rsch., 1955-58; mgr. ops. analysis Lockheed Missiles & Space Co., Sunnyvale, Calif., 1958-63, mgr. mil. programs, 1963-65, asst. dir. advanced programs, 1965-67, project mgr. advanced aircraft, 1967-70, dir. airborne systems, 1970-76, dir. remotely piloted vehicles, 1976-83; pres. F. David Assocs., Inc., Santa Rosa, Calif., 1983—; v.p. devel., bd. dirs. Command Systems Group, Inc., Torrance, Calif.; mem. panel U.S. Army Sci. Adv. Bd., Washington, 1965-66; presenter seminars in field. Author: Helicopter Performance Analysis Method, 1955. Pres. Hiller Mgmt. Club, Palo Alto, 1957; capt. Mounted Patrol San Mateo County, Woodside, Calif., 1976. Recipient award U.S. Army Aviation Rsch. and Tech. Labs. Mem. Am. Unmanned Systems Orgn., Am. Assn. Profl. Mgrs., Shack Riders (bd. dirs. 1983-87), Alpha Eta Rho (pres. Iota chpt. 1949). Republican. Avocations: horseback riding, woodworking, yachting. Home and Office: 1160 Pine St Apt B Menlo Park CA 94025-3456

SCHNEIBEL, VICKI DARLENE, public relations administrator; b. Astoria, Oreg., Mar. 11, 1946; d. Howard Stanley and Sally (Thompson) Brandt; m. Lawrence Walter Schneibel, Mar. 18, 1967. AAS, Anchorage Community Coll., 1986; BA, Alaska Pacific U., 1991, MAT, 1994. Cert. profl. sec. Clk. typist The Oregonian, Portland, Oreg., 1964-67; statis. typist Rader Pneumatics, Inc., Portland, Oreg., 1967-71; sec., bookkeeper Larry's Custom Remodeling, Portland, Oreg., 1971-73; bookkeeper Tualatin Hills Pk. & Recreation Dist., Portland, Oreg., 1973-74; pvt. sec. Aloha (Oreg.) Community Bapt. Ch., 1974-79; exec. sec. Hyster Sales Co., Tigard, Oreg., 1979-83, 1st Nat. Bank of Anchorage, 1983-84; office mgr. Control Data Alaska, Anchorage, 1984-86; human resource adminstr. Westmark Hotels, Inc., Anchorage, 1986—; cmty. adv. bd. mgr. Holland Am. Line (parent co. Westmark Hotels, Inc.), 1996—; Cmty. Advisory Bd. Mgr. for Holland America Line (parent co. of Westmark Hotels, Inc.). Author: Let Sleeping Moose Lie, Good Dog!, 1994. Active Anchorage Women's Commn., [illegible] Am. Mgmt. Assn., Soc. For Human Resource Mgmt. Lutheran. Avocations: reading, tennis, walking, writing, camping. Home: 1341 W 70th Ave Anchorage AK 99518-2010 Office: Holland Am Lines 510 L St Ste 400 Anchorage AK 99501-1956

SCHNEIDER, CALVIN, physician; b. N.Y.C., Oct. 23, 1924; s. Harry and Bertha (Green) S.; A.B., U. So. Calif., 1951, M.D., 1955; J.D., LaVerne (Calif.) Coll., 1973; m. Elizabeth Gayle Thomas, Dec. 27, 1967. Intern Los Angeles County Gen. Hosp., 1955-56, staff physician, 1956-57; practice medicine West Covina, Calif., 1957—; staff Inter-Community Med. Ctr., Covina, Calif. Cons. physician Charter Oak Hosp., Covina, 1960—. With USNR, 1943-47. Mem. AMA, Calif., L.A. County med. assns. Republican. Lutheran. Office: 224 W College St Covina CA 91723-1902

SCHNEIDER, CHARLES I., newspaper executive; b. Chgo., Apr. 6, 1923; s. Samuel Hiram and Eva (Smith) S.; m. Barbara Anne Krause, Oct. 27, 1963; children: Susan, Charles I. Jr., Kim, Karen, Traci. BS, Northwestern U., 1944. Indsl. engr., sales mgr., v.p. mktg. and sales Curtis-Electro Lighting Corp., Chgo., 1945-54, pres., 1954-62; pres. Jefferson Electronics, Inc., Santa Barbara, Calif., 1962-64; pres. 3 sub., v.p., asst. to pres. Am. Bldg. Maintenance Industries, Los Angeles, 1964-66; group v.p. Times Mirror Co., Los Angeles, 1966-88, ret.; pvt. investor and cons., 1988—; bd. dirs. Jeppesen Sanderson, Inc., Denver, Graphic Controls Corp., Buffalo, Regional Airports Improvement Corp. Bd. regents Northwestern U., Evanston, Ill.; trustee, past pres. Reiss-Davis Child Study Center, L.A.; bd. govs., past pres. The Music Ctr.; trustee the Menninger Found.; pres. St. John's Hosp. and Health Ctr. Found., Santa Monica, Calif. Served with AUS, 1942-44. Mem. Chief Execs. Orgn. (past pres., bd. dirs.). Clubs: Standard (Chgo.); Beverly Hills Tennis (Calif.); Big. Ten of So. Calif. Avocations: tennis, squash, music, reading. Home: 522 N Beverly Dr Beverly Hills CA 90210-3318

SCHNEIDER, CHRISTIAN IMMO, German language and literature educator; b. Dresden, Saxony, Germany, Jan. 27, 1935; came to U.S., 1964; s. Helmut Richard and Irmgard (Goldfriedrich) S.; m. Sylvia A. Lambert, Nov. 27, 1964; 1 child, Brent Lorin. PhD in German, U. Calif. at Santa Barbara, 1968; MA in Music, Ctrl. Wash. U., 1978. German asst. Antioch U., Yellow Springs, Ohio, 1964-65; instr. German U. Calif., Santa Barbara, 1964-68; prof. German Ctrl. Wash. U., Ellensburg, Wash., 1968—. Author, concert organist, composer: Das Todesproblem bei H. Hesse, 1973, Vignetten zu Weihnachtsliedern, 1988, Twelve Short Organ Pieces, 1991, Hermann Hesse Autorenbuch, 1991. Named Disting. Prof. for Rsch. and Creativity, Ctrl. Wash. U., 1991, Scholar of Yr. Ctrl. Wash. U. chpt. Phi Kappa Phi, 1994-95. Office: Ctrl Wash U 400 E 8th Ave Ellensburg WA 98926-7502

SCHNEIDER, EDWARD LEE, botanic garden administrator; b. Portland, Oreg., Sept. 14, 1947; s. Edward John and Elizabeth (Mathews) S.; m. Sandra Lee Alfarone, Aug. 2, 1968; children: Kenneth L., Cassandra L. BA, Ctrl. Wash. U., 1969, MS, 1971; PhD, U. Calif., Santa Barbara, 1974. From asst. to assoc. prof. botany S.W. Tex. State U., San Marcos, 1974-84, prof., 1984-94, chmn. biology dept., 1984-89, dean sci., 1989-92; exec. dir. Santa Barbara (Calif.) Botanic Garden, 1992—. Author: The Botanical World, CEOs and Trustees--Building Working Partnerships; contbr. articles to profl. jours. Recipient Presdl. Rsch. award S.W. Tex. State U., 1986, Disting. Alumnus award Ctrl. Wash. U., 1996; grantee NSF, 1980, 90. Fellow Tex. Acad. Sci. (pres. 1992-93); mem. Internat. Water Lily Soc. (bd. dirs., sec. 1989-96, inducted into Hall of Fame, Award of Appreciation 1997), Internat. Pollination Congress, Nat. Coun. Deans. Home: 1140 Tunnel Rd Santa Barbara CA 93105-2134 Office: Santa Barbara Botanic Garden 1212 Mission Canyon Rd Santa Barbara CA 93105-2126

SCHNEIDER, EDWARD LEWIS, medicine educator, research administrator; b. N.Y.C., June 22, 1940; s. Samuel and Ann (Soskin) S. BS, Rensselaer Poly. Inst., 1961; MD, Boston U., 1966. Intern and resident N.Y. Hosp.-Cornell U., N.Y.C., 1966-68; staff fellow Nat. Inst. Allergy and Infectious Diseases, Bethesda, Md., 1968-70; research fellow U. Calif., San Francisco, 1970-73; chief, sect. on cell aging Nat. Inst. Aging, Balt., 1973-79, assoc. dir., 1980-84, dep. dir., 1984-87; prof. medicine, dir. Davis Inst. on Aging U. Colo., Denver, 1979-80; dean Leonard Davis Sch. Gerontology U. So. Calif., L.A., 1986—, exec. dir. Ethel Percy Andrus Gerontology Ctr., 1986—, prof. medicine, 1987—, William and Sylvia Kugel prof. gerontology, 1989—; sci. dir. Buck Ctr. for Rsch. in Aging, 1989-98; cons. MacArthur Found., Chgo., 1985-93, R.W. Johnson Found., Princeton, N.J., 1982-87, Brookdale Found., N.Y.C., 1985-89. Editor: The Genetics of Aging, 1978, The Aging Reproductive System, 1978, Biological Markers of Aging, 1982, Handbook of the Biology of Aging, 1985, 95, 96, Interrelationship Among Aging Cancer and Differentiation, 1985, Teaching Nursing Home, 1985, Modern Biological Theories of Aging, 1987, The Black American Elderly, 1988, Elder Care and the Work Force, 1990, A Secure Old Age: Financing Long-Term Care, 1998. Med. dir. USPHS, 1968—. Recipient Roche award, 1964. Fellow Gerontology Soc., Am. Soc. Clin. Investigation; mem. Am. Assn. Retired Persons, U.S. Naval Acad. Sailing Squadron (coach 1980-86). Office: U So Calif Andrus Gerontology Ctr Los Angeles CA 90089-0191

SCHNEIDER, EUGENE SAUL, microbiologist, laboratory administrator; b. N.Y.C., Apr. 28, 1920; s. Isreal and Gertrude (Mendelsohn) S.; m. Bertha Gollan, Feb. 18, 1945; 1 child, Myles Gordon. BS in Microbiology, Cornell U., 1942. Cert. med. technologist, microbiologist. Microbiologist 50th Gen. Hosp., 1942-45, Morrisania City Hosp., Bronx, N.Y., 1946; rsch. microbiologist Coll. Phys. and Surg., N.Y.C., 1946; microbiologist Tacoma Gen. Hosp., 1946-48; lab. dir. Pierce County Hosp., Tacoma, 1948-52, St. Helens Med. Labs., Tacoma, 1952-68, Nat. Health Labs., Kent, Wash., 1985-92, Meridian Valley Lab., Kent, 1992—; founding pres. Wash. State Soc. Med. Tch., 1947-48, Wash. Soc. AMTs, 1963-66; mem. Stae Commn. on Alcoholism. Contbr. articles to profl. jours.; presenter in field. Mem. Tacoma Coun. on Alcoholism, 1961-75. 1st lt. U.S. Army, 1949-52. Recipient Disting. Citizen award, Olympia, Wash., 1972, Order of Golden Microscope, AMT, 1963. Mem. Anaerobic Soc. of the Ams. Democrat. Jewish. Avocations: painting, model railroading. Home: 6810 Opal Ln SW Tacoma WA 98498-6410 Office: Meridian Valley Clin Lab 515 W Harrison St Kent WA 98032-4403

SCHNEIDER, GERALD L., plastic surgeon; b. Mechanicsburg, Pa., Oct. 25, 1945; s. Gordon Henry and Pauline Emma (Rife) S.; m. Patricia Davis, July 15, 1978; 1 child, Ross Roberts. BS, No. Ariz. U., 1968; MD, U. Ariz., 1973. Intern Naval Regional Med. Ctr., San Diego, 1973-74; resident in gen. surgery U.S. Naval Hosp., San Diego, 1974-78; resident in plastic surgery U.S. Naval Hosp., Portsmouth, Va., 1978-80; staff surgeon divsn. plastic surgery U.S. Naval Hosp., San Diego, 1981-83, chief divsn. plastic surgery, 1983-84; pvt. practice Flagstaff, Ariz., 1984-90; staff surgeon La Jolla (Calif.) Cosmetic Surgery Ctr., 1990-91; surgeon Scripps Clinic & Rsch. Found., La Jolla, 1991—. Capt. USNR. Fellow ACS; mem. Am. Soc. Plastic and Reconstructive Surgeons, Lipoplasty Soc. North Am. Avocation: golf. Office: Scripps Clinic & Rsch Found 10666 N Torrey Pines Rd La Jolla CA 92037-1092*

SCHNEIDER, KENNY, artist, educator; b. Ellenville, N.Y., Jan. 3, 1939; s. Herbert Eli and Ruth Lillian (Star) S.; m. Judith Sara Oliver, 1960 (div. 1980); children: Janice Marion, Lisa Marie; m. Nella Maria Barriga, Oct. 5, 1985; children: Rachel, Gina, Sofia. BA in Art, U. Miami, 1960. With Children & Youth Devel. Svcs.,, Bklyn.; videotape instr. Western Conn. State Coll., video technician; film lectr. CCNY; art instr. Trinidad State Jr. Coll., 1996—; guest panelist Internat. Continuing Ednl. Inst., SUNY; mem. constrn. staff Flowering of Am. Folk Art, Whitney Mus. Am. Art, Am. Pop Art; artist-in-residence MPO Videotronics; videotape technician, cameraman Rimyth Ednl. Program, Bklyn. One person shows include Ground Zero Gallery, Miami Beach, Fla., 1988, Fiona Whitney Gallery, L.A., 1991; exhibited in group shows at 80 Washington Square East Galleries, NYU, N.Y.C., 1979, 84, Zaner Gallery, Rochester, N.Y., 1982, 84, Provincetown Art Assn., 1983, Allied Arts Coun., Las Vegas, 1984, Woodstock (N.Y.) Sch. Art, 1984, Temari-Book Art, Honolulu, 1984, Shreveport Art Guild, 1984, Fla. Gulfcoast Art Ctr., Bellaire, Fla., 1985, Francis Wolfson Art Gallery, Miami, 1985, Lowe Art Gallery, U. Miami, Coral Gables, Fla., 1985, Brea Gallery, Fullerton, Calif., 1985, Southeastern Ctr. Contemporary Art, Winston-Salem, N.C., 1985, Mus. Contemporary Art, Miami, 1986, Gloria Luria Gallery, Bay Harbor Island, Fla., 1986, Helander Gallery, Palm Beach, Fla., 1986, Southwest Tex. State U., San Marcos, 1986, Mus. Art, Ft. Lauderdale, Fla., [illegible] Palm Beach, 1987, Orange County Ctr. Contemporary Art, Santa Ana, Calif., 1995; commd. by Caribbean Cruise Lines, 1987, Seattle Arts Commn., 1987, Miami-Site/Crandon Gardens, 1987, Palm Beach Internat. Airport Project,

1988, Hollywood Blvd. Project, 1993, NOHO Sculpture Project, 1994, Selma Park Project, 1994, Miami Beach Transp. Mgmt. Assn., 1996; represented in pvt. collections Senator and Mrs. Howard Metzenbaum, Mel Brooks and Ann Bancroft, Mr. and Mrs. Milton Sidley, Mr. and Mrs. Gerald Robins, Mr. and Mrs. Joel Friedland, Mr. and Mrs. Steven Muss, Ms. Meryle Samuels, Ms. Ann Rachlin, Gloria Luria, Mr. and Mrs. Alan Greenwald, Joy Moos, Dr. Paul Dermer, Mr. And Mrs. Larry Samson, Mr. and Mrs. Ron Seiden, Mr. and Mrs. Eugene Massin, Mr. and Mrs. Neal Amdur, Mr. and Mrs. Barry Sugarman, Tony Goldman, Raymond Zimmerman, Gen. and Mrs. Charles Burson, Mr. and Mrs. Barry Massin, and Mr. and Mrs. Michael Shapiro, Ms. Michelle Isenburg, Ms. Barbara Marcus, (pub. collections) David W. Bermant Found., Santa Barbara, Calif., Cmty. Redevel. Agy., L.A., Seattle Arts Commn., Palm Beach Internat. Airport, The Miami-Dade Arts in Pub. Places Trust, Holiday Inn Corp., AT&T Transtec, The Miami-Dade Pub. Libr. Sys., Walter Annenburg collction, Caribbean Cruise Lines, La Cinematique Francaise, Musee de Cinema, Paris, N.Y. Pub. Libr., Bklyn. Pub. Libr., Bklyn. Coll. Film Libr., Nassau and Suffolk County Librs., L.I., N.Y., Colo. State Libr., Denver, U. Calif., Berkeley, Boston Pub. Libr., Rochester Pub. Libr.; film festivals: Chgo. Internat. Film Festival, 1969, Antioch Film Festival, 1969, Rochester Internat. Film Festival, 1970, Sorrento (Italy) Internat. Film Festival, San Francisco Internat. Film Festival, 1970, Festival de Film Underground, Paris, 1971, Festivale di Popoli, Florence, Italy, 1972, Yale Film Festival, 1968, 70, 72, Ann Arbor Film Festival, 1972-73, Tampere (Finland) Internat. Film Festival, 1973, among others; films shown at Bklyn. Coll., 1968, Millenium Workshop, N.Y.C., 1969, Robert Flaherty Film Seminar, 1970, Whitney Mus. Am. Art, 1971, Temple U., 1973, 74, Art Dirs. Club, N.Y.C., 1975. Art advisor, pub. art Hist. Ark. River Project, Pueblo, Colo., 1996—; arts commr. Arts Commn. of Ojai, 1994-95; bd. dirs. La Clinica, Inc., Gardner, Colo., 1996—, Huerfano Med. Ctr., Walsenburg, Colo., 1997. With USAR, 1959-67. Recipient Cert. of Appreciation Cmty. Redevel. Agy. City of L.A., City Capital Projects Design awards Seattle Design Commn., 1987-88, 24th Ann. Small Painting Exhibit hon. mention, Art in Cauly Sq. award, N.Y. State Coun. on the Arts award, N.Y. Film Festival award, award of merit Tampere Film Festival, Chgo. Internat. Film Festival, awards Yale Film Festival, Oskar Kokoschka prize Sommer Akademic fur Bildende Kunst. Home: PO Box 8 Gardner CO 81040-0008

SCHNEIDER, MARGARET PERRIN, writer; b. N.Y.C., Dec. 31, 1923; d. Sam and Peggy (Flood) Perrin; m. Paul Schneider, Apr. 10, 1950; children: Peggy Lee, Peter-Lincoln, Ann Rose. BA in Psychology and Edn., UCLA, 1949. Gen. elem. tchg. credential, Calif. Tchr. L.A. City Schs., North Hollywood, 1944-55; script writer MGM Studios, 1957-75; staff wrtier Universal Studios, 1957-75; head writer CBS Studios, N.Y.C., 1975-76; participant Women in Film, L.A., 1975; chmn. Writers Craft Conf., Arrowhead, Calif., 1975. Mem. Writers Guild Am. (freelance writers com. 1985), Dems. for Action. Avocations: wild flower photography, birding, gardening, traveling. Home: PO Box 65 54386 Village View Idyllwild CA 92549

SCHNEIDER, PAUL, writer; b. Passaic, N.J., Aug. 4, 1923; s. Solomon Peter and Rose (Levine) S.; m. Margaret Flood Perrin, Apr. 10, 1951; children: Peggy Lee, Peter Lincoln, Ann. BA, Harvard U., 1945. Writer N.Y.C., Hollywood, Calif., 1954-91; staff writer Universal City Studios, North Hollywood, Calif., 1967-74; head writer Love of Life CBS Studios, N.Y.C., 1974-76. Writer: (TV) Star Trek, 1954-85, Bonanza, 1954-85, Marcus Welby, M.D., 1954-85, (movies) The Looters, 1957, Ride the Wind, 1966, (plays) Effigy, 1983, Acrimonious, 1962. Mem. Writers Guild Am. (chmn. violence com. 1980-81), Harvard Alumni Assn., Dems. for Action. Avocations: hiking, mountain trails, travel, Zen. Home: PO Box 65 Idyllwild CA 92549-0065

SCHNEIDER, SOLOMON See MARIN, PAUL

SCHNEIDER, THOMAS, retired administrative law judge, mediator; b. Vienna, Austria, May 3, 1931; came to the U.S., 1939; s. Ernst and Hedy (Latzko) S.; m. Elaine J. Smith, Dec. 19, 1959; children: Ellen, David. BA, Harvard Coll., 1952; LLB, Columbia U., 1955. Bar: N.Y. 1956, Calif. 1958, U.S. Supreme Ct. 1968. Law clk. Justice Roger J. Traynor Calif. Supreme Ct., San Francisco, 1957-58; lawyer Legal Aid Soc., Oakland, Calif., 1966-75; adminstrv. law judge U.S. Dept. Labor, San Francisco, 1977-97, ret., 1997; pvt. practice mediator Berkeley, Calif., 1998—; mem. mediation panel U.S. Dist. Ct. (no. dist.) Calif., 1998. With U.S. Army, 1955-57. Mem. ABA (dispute resolution sect.). Democrat. Avocations: hiking, carpentry, folk dancing. Office: PO Box 9601 Berkeley CA 94709-0601

SCHNEIDLER, JON GORDON, lawyer; b. Seattle, Oct. 22, 1938; s. J. Gordon and Mary Louise (Bartholomew) S.; m. Linda Gilmore White, June 27, 1964 (div. June 1988); children: Kristina Richards, Jolie Wolcott, Andrew Schneidler, Peter Schneidler; m. Elizabeth Ann Nairn, Apr. 2, 1989; 1 stepdaughter: Jessica Albright. BA, U. Wash., 1962, JD, 1968. Bar: Wash.; U.S. Ct. Appeals (9th Cir.), U.S. Dist. Ct. (we. dist.) Wash. CEO Schneidler Industries, Inc., Seattle, 1968-70; ptnr. Cartano, Botzer & Chapman, Seattle, 1970-86; with 4100 Assocs., Ltd., Seattle, 1986—; dir., CEO 4100 Assocs., Seattle, 1989—; sec. Transiplex Internat., Inc., Seattle; mem. adv. bd. Pacific Legal Found., Sacramento; trustee Ehrlich Donnan Found., Seattle. Co-author: (book) Real Property Deskbook, 1981, 2d edit. 1986; patentee Air Structure Systems, 1969. Bd. dirs. North Kitsap Sch. Bd., Poulsbo, Wash., 1984, Friends of Youth, Renton, Wash., 1974; founder, dir. Tchr. of Yr. Found., Poulsbo, 1988—. 1st lt. USAF, 1962-66. Decorated Air Force Commendation medal; recipient Baker scholar George F. Baker Foun., 1957-60. Fellow Paul Harris Found.; mem. Wash. State Bar Assn., King County Bar Assn., Coll. Club (trustee 1998—), Rotary. Avocations: fly fishing, competitive bridge, sailing, gardening. Office: 999 3rd Ave Ste 4100 Seattle WA 98104-4084

SCHNEITER, GEORGE MALAN, golfer, development company executive; b. Ogden, Utah, Aug. 12, 1931; s. George Henery and Bernice Slade (Malan) S.; B in Banking and Fin., U. Utah, 1955; m. JoAnn Deakin, Jan. 19, 1954; children: George, Gary, Dan, Steve, Elizabeth Ann, Michael. With 5th Army Championship Golf Team U.S. Army, 1955-56; assoc. golf pro Hidden Valley Golf Club, Salt Lake City, 1957; golf pro Lake Hills Golf Club, Billings, Mont., 1957-61, sec., 1957-61, pres., 1964-90; pres. Schneiter Enterprises, Sandy, Utah, 1974—; developer Schneiter's golf course, 1973—, and subdiv., 1961—; player PGA tour 1958-78; sr. player PGA tour, 1981—. Missionary So. State Mission, LDS Ch., 1951-52. Eagle Scout, 1944. With U.S. Army, 1955-56. Winner Utah sect. Sr. Championship, Wyo. Open Super Sr. Championship, Salt Lake City Parks Tournament, Vernal Brigham Payson Open, Yuma Open, Ariz.; named U.S. Army Ft. Carson Post Golf Champ, 5th Army Championship Golf Team, 1955-56. Mem. PGA, Salt Lake City C. of C., Intermountain Golf Course Supertaints Assn. Office: 2009 Brassy Dr Las Vegas NV 89122-2033

SCHNELL, ROGER THOMAS, business owner, state official, retired career officer; b. Wabasha, Minn., Dec. 11, 1936; s. Donald William and Eva Louise (Barton) S.; m. Barbara Ann McDonald, Dec. 18, 1959 (div. Mar. 1968); children: Thomas Allen, Scott Douglas. A in Mil. Sci., Command and Gen. Staff Coll., 1975; A in Bus. Administn., Wayland Bapt. U., 1987. Commd. 2d lt. Alaska N.G., 1959, advanced through grades to col., 1975; shop supt. Alaska N.G., Anchorage, 1965-71, personnel mgr., 1972-74, chief of staff, 1974-87, dir. logistics, 1987; electrician Alaska R.R., Anchorage, 1955-61, elec. foreman, 1962-64; dir. support personnel mgmt. Joint Staff Alaska N.G., 1988-92, ret.; personnel mgr. State of Alaska, 1992; asst. commr. dept. mil. and vets. affairs State of Alaska, Ft. Richardson, 1992-95, dep. commr. dept. mil. and vets. affairs, 1995-99; owner, ind. distbr. for an internat. health and preventative medicine corp. RTS Enterprises, 1999—. *Roger Schnell has over 25 years of progressively responsible experience in state and federal government key decision making roles at the senior management and executive levels. While serving as Chief of Staff, Alaska Army National Guard, Col. Schnell directed staff expansion of the organization from 2,200 members and employees to over 3,000. From 1988 through 1991 while serving as director of personnel management of the Alaska National Guard, Col. Schnell administered the expansion of the full time work force from 850 to over 1,350. In late 1992, Roger was appointed Chief of Staff, Department of Military and Veterans Affairs. In 1995, Roger was promoted to Deputy Commissioner and is currently responsible to the commissioner for the day-to-day operations of 8 divisions with over 4,500 personnel and a $150 million budget. Personal philosophy: Success is built on honesty, hard work, determination, committment and the ability to make personal sacrfices to strive for high professional goals. Always keep a positive attitude and treat each person as you would like to be treated.* Bd. dirs. Meth. Trust Fund. Mem. Fed. Profl. Labor Relations Execs. (sec. 1974-75), Alaska N.G. Officers Assn. (pres. 1976-78, bd. dirs. 1988—), NG Assn. U.S. (life, rep. from Alaska 1993—), Am. Legion, Amvets. Republican. Methodist. Lodge: Elks. Avocations: traveling, photography. Home and Office: Huntwood Park Estates 6817 Queens View Cir Anchorage AK 99504-5203

SCHNELL, RUSSELL CLIFFORD, atmospheric scientist, researcher; b. Castor, Alta., Can., Dec. 12, 1944; s. Henry Emmanuel and Anna (Traudt) S.; m. Suan Neo Tan, May 25, 1974; children: Alicia, Ryan. BSc with distinction, U. Alta. (Can.), Edmonton, 1967; BSc, Meml. U., St. John's, Nfld., Can., 1968; MSc, U. Wyo., 1971, PhD, 1974. Research scientist U. Wyo., Laramie, 1971-74, Nat. Ctr. Atmospheric Research and NOAA, Boulder, Colo., 1974-76; dir. Mt. Kenya study World Meteorol. Orgn. div. UN, Nairobi, Kenya, 1976-78; research scientist U. Colo., Boulder, 1979-82, dir. Arctic Gas and Aerosol Sampling Program, 1982-91, fellow Coop. Inst. Research in Environ. Scis., 1985-92; dir. Mauna Loa Observatory, Hilo, Hawaii, 1992-98, NOAA Observatory Ops., Boulder, Colo., 1998—; mem. aerobiology com. Nat. Acad. Sci., 1976-79; cons. UN, Geneva, 1977-80, Shell Devel., Modesto, Calif., 1978-79, Holme, Roberts & Owen, 1990-92; mem. adv. bd. Frost Tech., Norwalk, Conn., 1983-85; bd. dirs. TRI-S Inc., Louisville, Colo., Magee Sci.. Editor Geophys. Research Letters, Arctic Haze Edit., 1983-84; discovered bacteria ice nuclei, 1969; patentee in field; contbr. articles to profl. jours. Bd. dirs. Boulder Valley Christian Ch., 1978-91; chmn. Boulder Council Internat. Visitors, 1983-85. Rotary Internat. fellow, 1968-69. Mem. Am. Geophys. Union, AAAS, Am. Meteorol. Soc. (cert. cons. meteorologist), Internat. Assn. Aerobiology, Soc. Cryobiology, Sigma Xi, Sigma Tau. Avocations: travel (63 countries), real estate investing, public speaking, flying. Office: NOAA/CMDL R/E/CG 325 Broadway St Boulder CO 80303-3337

SCHNEPF, CARRIE BIGGS, sales and marketing professional; b. Mesa, Ariz., Sept. 3, 1960; d. Robert Darrel and Carolyn Sarah (Cox) Biggs; m. Mark Edward Schnepf, Apr. 13, 1991. Degree in Comm., Brigham Young U., 1979-85. Anchor Sta. KIVI-TV, Boise, Idaho, 1985-87; reporter, anchor Sta. KPHO-TV, Phoenix, 1987-89; sales and mktg. profl. Ariz. Escrowq & Title, Phoenix, 1989-91; mktg. dir. country store, festival site, tours Schnepf Farms, Queen Creek, AZ, 1995—; comml. spokesperson Robert Black Agy., Phoenix, 1989—; with promotions dept. Country Thunder USA, Queen Creek, 1993—; pres. The Regal Group, Phoenix, 1992—. Chmn. spl. event Ariz. Spl. Olympics, Phoenix, 1991—;, bd. dirs. Am. Heart Assn., Phoenix, 1993—, chmn. spl. event, 1993—; mem. fundraising com. PreHab of Ariz., Mesa, 1991—; founding mem., chmn. Project B.E.S.T., Queen Creek. Recipient chmn.'s award Ariz. Spl. Olympics, 1993. Mem. Desert Club (publicity com. 1992—). Republican. Avocations: musical theatre, piano playing, travel, all outdoor sports, cooking. Home and Office: 22601 E Cloud Rd Queen Creek AZ 85242-9556

SCHNITZER, ARLENE DIRECTOR, art dealer; b. Salem, Oreg., Jan. 10, 1929; d. Simon M. and Helen (Holtzman) Director; m. Harold J. Schnitzer, Sept. 11, 1949; 1 child, Jordan. Student, U. Wash., 1947-48; BFA (hon.) Pacific NW Coll. Art., 1988. Founder, pres. Fountain Gallery of Art, Portland, Oreg., 1951-86; exec. v.p. Harsch Investment Corp., 1951—. Apptd. to Oreg. State Bd. Higher Edn., 1987-88; former bd. dirs. Oreg. Symphony Assn., v.p. Oreg. Symphony; former bd. dirs. U.S. Dist. Ct. Hist. Soc.; former bd. dirs. Boys and Girls Club, 1988—; mem. Gov.'s Expo '86 Commn., Oreg.; mem. exec. com., former bd. dirs. Artquake; former mem. adv. bd. Our New Beginnings; past bd. dirs. Artists Initiative for a Contemporary Art Collection; former trustee Reed Coll., 1982-88; mem. exec. com. bd. dirs. N.W. Bus. Com. for Arts., 1992-97; former trustee, mem. exec. com. Oreg. Health Scis. Univ. Found.; mem. arts acquisition and collections com. Portland Art Mus.; mem. Nat. Com. for the Performing Arts, Kennedy Ctr., 1995—; adv. bd. Svcs. to Children and Families, Orgn., 1995-97; bd. trustees Oreg. Jewish Cmty. Found., 1996-97; mem. Nat. Coun. Fine Arts Mus. San Francisco, 1995—; bd. dirs. Oregon Hist. Soc., 1998—. Recipient Aubrey Watzek award Lewis and Clark Coll., 1981, Pioneer award U. Oreg., 1985, Met. Arts Commn. award, 1985, White Rose award March of Dimes, 1987, Disting. Svc. award Western Oreg. State Coll. 1988, Oreg. Urban League Equal Opportunity award 1988, Gov's. award for Arts, 1987, Woman of Achievement award YWCA, 1987, Disting. Svc. award U. Oreg., 1991, SAFECO Art Leadership award ArtFair/Seattle, 1994, Portland First Citizen award Portland Met. Assn. Realtors, 1995, Tom McCall Leadership award, 1995; honored by Portland Art Assn., 1979, Northwest Bus. Com. for the Arts, 1997, Arts Champions, 1997. Mem. Univ. Club, Multnomah Athletic Club, Portland Golf Club. Office: Harsch Investment Corp 1121 SW Salmon St Ste 400 Portland OR 97205-2092

SCHOBER, ROBERT CHARLES, electrical engineer; b. Phila., Sept. 20, 1940; s. Rudolph Ernst and Kathryn Elizabeth (Ehrisman) S.; m. Mary Eve Kanuika, Jan. 14, 1961; children: Robert Charles, Stephen Scott, Susan Marya. BS in Engring. (Scott Award scholar), Widner U., 1965; postgrad., Bklyn. Poly. Extension at Gen. Electric Co., Valley Forge, Pa., 1965-67, U. Colo., 1968-69, Calif. State U.-Long Beach, 1969-75, U. So. Calif., 1983-84. Engr. Gen. Electric Co., Valley Forge, 1965-68, Martin Marietta Corp., Denver, 1968-69; sr. engr. Jet Propulsion Lab., Pasadena, Calif., 1969-73, sr. staff, 1986—; mem. tech. staff Hughes Semiconductor Co., Newport Beach, Calif., 1973-75; prin. engr. Am. Hosp. Supply Corp., Irvine, Calif., 1975-83; sr. staff engr. TRW Systems, Redondo Beach, Calif., 1983-84; cons. Biomed. LSI, Huntington Beach, Calif. Mem. IEEE (student br. pres. 1963-65), Soc. for Indsl. and Applied Math., Assn. for computing Machinery, Tau Bea Pi. Republican. Patentee cardiac pacemakers. Current Work: Develop large scale integrated circuits for computer, spacecraft, and military, as well as commercial applications; design high speed signal processing integrated circuits; instrumental in starting the quest for low power integrated circuits; actively persuing the advancment of ultra low power technology; provides dissemination through public domain distribution of a low power MOSIS cell library, workshops and publications. Subspecialties: application specific microprocessor architecture design; ultra low power analog and digital systems and integrated circuits; integrated circuit design; focal plane electronic signal processing arrays, neural networks; synchro converter electronics; sigma-delta analog to digital converters and signal processing electronics; implantable medical devices including cardiac pacemakers, defibulators and hearing aids. Office: Jet Propulsion Lab 4800 Oak Grove Dr Pasadena CA 91109-8001

SCHOEBEL, HENRY LEO, artist, educator; b. Rockville Centre, N.Y., Aug. 15, 1955; s. Henry Russell and Jeanne Elizabeth (Kiley) S. BFA magna cum laude, Syracuse U., 1977; MFA, U. Md., 1980. Instr. Cath. U., Washington, 1983-86, Pace U., N.Y.C., 1987, U. R.I., Kingston, 1987, The New Sch. Social Rsch., N.Y.C., 1986-90; lectr. Princeton (N.J.) U., 1992; assoc. prof. Ariz. State U., Tempe, 1990—; vis. artist Towson (Md.) State U., 1988-89. One-man shows include McIntosh/Dryside Gallery, Houston, 1982, White Columns Gallery, N.Y.C., 1983, Osuna Gallery, Washington, 1984, 86, Am. Ctr. Galleries, Pakistan, Karachi, Lahore, Islamabad, 1985, Holzman Gallery, Towson, 1989, Scottsdale Ctr. for Arts, Ariz., 1991, Brody's Gallery, Washington, 1993, Bentley Gallery, Scottsdale, 1997; grouop shows include Foundry Gallery, Washington, 1979, Cramer Gallery, Washington, 1980, Corcoran Gallery Art, Washington, 1981, Alma Thomas Gallery, Washington, 1982, Gallery K, Washington, 1983, Anderson Gallery, Va., 1984, Jehinger Art Gallery, Bombay, India, 1985, Jane Haslem Gallery, Washington, 1986, The Bklyn. Mus., 1987, David Adamson Gallery, Washington, 1988, BEI Gallery, Bklyn., 1990, U. Ariz. Art Mus., 1993, Brody's Gallery, 1994, Scottsdale Ctr. Arts, 1995, Finch Gallery, Phoenix, 1996, Phoenix Art Mus., 1998, others; represented in permanent collections Freddie Mac, Washington, Deutsche Bank, N.Y.C., R.J. Reynolds.Nabisco, Washington, Mr. Joseph Hirshhorn, Washington, Netzwerk, Rostock, Germany, Artery Orgn., Chevy Chase, Md., Crowne Plz, Holidan Inn, Rockville, Md., Scottsdale Ctr. for Arts, Ariz. State U. W., Phoenix, Towson State U., Phoenix Art Mus. Office: Ariz Stae U Sch Art PO Box 871505 Tempe AZ 85287-1505

SCHOENBORN, BENNO P., biophysicist, educator; b. Basel, Switzerland, May 2, 1936; came to U.S., 1955; s. Wilhelm and Maria (Dobler) S.; m. Catherine Cowie Kay, Oct. 26, 1962. BA, UCLA, 1958; PhD, U. New South Wales, Australia, 1962; DSc (hon.), N.J. Inst. Tech., 1982. Teaching fellow U. New South Wales, Sydney, 1958-61; postdoctoral fellow U. Calif., San Francisco, 1962-63, asst. prof. dept. pharmacology, 1966-67, assoc. prof. dept. pharmacology and biochemistry, 1967; biophysicist dept. biology Brookhaven Lab., Upton, N.Y., 1968-74, sr. biophysicist dept. biology, 1974-92, assoc. chmn. dept. biology, 1984-90; head ctr. structural biology, 1984-91; sr. fellow Los Alamos (N.Mex.) Nat. Lab., 1992—; adj. prof. biochemistry Columbia U., N.Y.C., 1978-93; vis. scientist Molecular Biology Lab., Cambridge, Eng., 1966-67; adj. scientist biophysics SUNY, Stony Brook, 1988-92; mem. editorial bd. Biophys. Jour., 1977-80; mem. Reactor Safety Com., 1972-79. Editor: Neutrons in Biology, 1976, 84, 96; contbr. articles to profl. jours.; patent in multilager monochromator, 1975. Recipient E.O. Lawrence award Dept. of Energy, 1980. Mem. Nat. Com. for Crystallography, Biophys. Soc. (coun. mem. 1976-79). Republican. Avocation: sailing. Home: 816 Stagecoach Dr Santa Fe NM 87501-1144

SCHOENDORF, JUDSON RAYMOND, allergist; b. New Orleans, Jan. 13, 1942; s. John Adam and Thelma Elizabeth (Verges) S. BA, Tulane U., 1962; MD, La. State U., 1966; MBA, Pepperdine U., 1992. Lic. physician, La., Calif.; cert. Am. Bd. Med. Mgmt. Intern Charity Hosp. of La., New Orleans, 1966-67; resident in pediatrics L.A. County/U. So. Calif. Med. Ctr., 1969-70; fellow UCLA/Harbor Gen. Hosp., 1970-72; allergist Russell T. Spears, M.D., Long Beach, 1972-76, The Harriman Jones Med. Group, Long Beach, 1976—; chief exec. officer The Harriman Jones Med. Group, 1989-91; pres., CEO, The Harriman Jones Med. Found., 1992-94; staff Kaiser Hosp. Bellflower, 1970-72, Children's Hosp., Long Beach, 1972—, Bauer/St. Mary's Hosp., Long Beach, 1972—, UCLA Hosp., 1972—, Community Hosp., Long Beach, 1977—; faculty UCLA, 1972—, Harbor Gen. Hosp., 1972—, others; prin. investigator Clin. Drug Study Abbott Labs., 1996-97. Contbr. articles to profl. jours. Bd. dirs. Long Beach Children's Clinic, 1976-81, pres., 1978-81; bd. dirs. Long Beach Symphony Orch., 1985-89; bd. dirs. Am. Lung Assn. Calif., 1985—, exec. com., 1988—; adv. coun. phys. edn. dept. Calif. State U., Long Beach, 1985—; mem. Civil Svc. Commn., City of Long Beach, 1981-89, pres., 1982-83, 85-86; bd. dirs. Long Beach Civic Light Opera, 1986-88; mem. Redevel. Agy., City of Long Beach, 1989—; chair, RDA, 1993—; mem. cultural steering com. Pub. Corp. Arts, Long Beach; bd dirs. Adv. Com. Pub. Art, 1992—; mem. Mayor's Econ. Coun., 1994—, Joint Powers Authority Spring St. Corridor-Long Beach/Singal Hill, 1994—. Lt. USN, 1967-69, capt. USNR, 1985—. Decorated Navy Commendation medal, also others; recipient Katherine White Humanitarian award Long Beach Kiwanis Club, 1995. Mem. Calif. Med. Assn., L.A. County Med. Assn., Long Beach Med. Assn., Acad. Allergy, L.A. Soc. Allergy and Immunology, Am. Coll. Physician Execs. Avocations: gardening, bagpipes, parrot breeding. Office: Harriman Jones Med Group 2600 Redondo Ave Long Beach CA 90806-2325

SCHOENFELD, JIM, professional hockey coach; b. Galt, Ont., Can., 1954; m. Theresa Schoenfeld; children: Justin, Katie, Adam, Nathan. Head coach Washington Capitols, 1994-97, Phoenix Coyotes, 1997—. Office: Phoenix Coyotes Cellular One Ice Den 9375 East Bell Rd Scottsdale AZ 85260*

SCHOENFELD, LAWRENCE JON, real estate developer, asset lender; b. L.A., Nov. 30, 1945; s. Donald and Trudy (Libizer) S.; Carol Sue Gard, Aug. 24, 1969. AA, L.A. Valley Coll., Van Nuys, Calif., 1963; BBA, Wichita State U., 1969, MSBA, 1970; grad., Army Med. Acad., 1976, US Army Command/Gen Staff Coll., Ft. Leavenworth, Kans., 1988. Cert. tchr., Calif.; life lic. jr. coll. tchg. credential, Calif.; lic. real estate developer, Calif. Asst. treas. Advance Mortgage, Los Angeles, 1970-72; v.p. ops. Unigem Internat., Los Angeles, 1972-98; pres. C. & L. Schoenfeld Investments Inc., 1998—; bd. dirs. The Schoenfeld Constrn. Co., South Star Wours, Uniorr Corp., Execucentre-West, Schoenfeld & Co., Customer Ground Handling Svc. Corp.; co-developer Los Osos Mini Storage Co., Los Osos, Calif., Bay Osos,, 1984, Bay Osos Mini Storage Co., 1984, El Mercadero World Trade Show, Guatemala, 1986, 97, Santiago, 1987, Bahai, 1988, Paraguay, 1989, El Mercado, Costa Rica, 1990, Panama City, 1995, Manaus, 1996, Guayaquil, 1998, Los Osos Mini Storage Co., Quito, 1991, Santa Cruz, 1993, Equador, 1998; pres. Accents on Beverly Hills, 1991, Accents at the Biltmore, Santa Barbara, 1995, Accents on Newport Beach, 1996. Mem. Improvement Commn., Hermosa Beach., Calif. 1976-78. Served to maj. Med. Svc. Corps, U.S. Army, 1970-72; lt. col. USAR, 1972-98. Mem. South Am. Travel Assn., World Trade Assn. (assoc.), Town Hall, Wichita State U. Alumni Assn. (nat. dist. rep., mem. coun. 1992—), Res. Officers Assn., Brit. Am. C. of C. Jewish. Fax: 310-289-9200. Office: Unigem Internat 350 S Beverly Dr Ste 350 Beverly Hills CA 90212-4800

SCHOENKE, MARILYN LEILANI, foundation administrator; b. Wahiawa, Hawaii; m. Donald N. Basham; children: Neil, Steven, Leilani. BB, Corpus Christi State U. Exec. dir. Moanalua Gardens Found., Hawaii, 1994—. Exec. dir. Lawyer's Care; vol. Am. Cancer Soc. Mem. Alzheimer's Assn. (support svcs. coord., vol.), Manu O Ke Kai Canoe Club, Native Hawaiian C. of C., U.S. Tennis Assn., Hawaii Pacific Tennis Assn. Office: Moanalua Gardens Found 1352 Pineapple Pl Honolulu HI 96819-1754*

SCHOESLER, MARK GERALD, state legislator, farmer; b. Ritzville, Wash., Feb. 16, 1957; s. Gerald E. and Dorothy (Heinemann) S.; m. Ginger J. Van Aelst, Apr. 8, 1978; children: Veronica, Cody. AA, Spokane (Wash.) C.C., 1977. Mem. Wash. Ho. of Reps., Olympia, 1992—; house majority whip, mem. rules, agr. and ecology, fin. chair joint adminstrv. rules rev. coms., 1995-96. Pres. Wash. Friends Farms and Forests, 1991-92; mem. Cmty. Econ. Revitalization Bd. Mem. Wash. Assn. Wheat Growers (dir. 1990-92). Republican. Mem. United. Ch. Christ. Home: 1588 E Rosenoff Rd Ritzville WA 99169-8710

SCHOETTLER, GAIL SINTON, former state official; b. Los Angeles, Oct. 21, 1943; d. James and Norma (McLellan) Sinton; children: Lee, Thomas, James; m. Donald L. Stevens, June 23, 1990. BA in Econs., Stanford U., 1965; MA in History, U. Calif., Santa Barbara, 1969, PhD in History, 1975. Businesswoman Denver, 1975-83; exec. dir. Colo. Dept. of Personnel, Denver, 1983-86; treas. State of Colo., Denver, 1987-94, lt. gov., 1995-99; bd. dirs. Nat. Jewish Hosp.; mem. bd. trustees U. No. Colo., 1981-87. Mem. Douglas County Bd. Edn., Colo., 1979-87, pres., 1983-87; trustee U. No. Colo., Greeley, 1981-87; pres. Denver Children's Mus., 1975-85. Decorated Chevalier, French Legion of Honor, 1998; recipient Disting. Alumna award U. Calif. at Santa Barbara, 1987, Trailblazer award AAUW, 1997, Childrens Advocacy award Colo. Soc. Sch. Psychologists, 1997. Mem. Nat. Women's Forum (bd. dirs. 1981-89, pres. 1983-85), Internat. Women's Forum (mem. bd. dirs. 1981-89, pres. 83-85), Women Execs. in State Govt. (bd. dirs. 1981-87, chmn. 1988), Leadership Denver Assn. (bd. dirs. 1987, named Outstanding Alumna 1985), Nat. Congress Lt. Govs., Stanford Alumni Assn. Democrat.

SCHOFIELD, JAMES ROY, computer programmer; b. Reedsburg, Wis., Aug. 16, 1953; s. G. C. Schofield and Margaret (Collies) Tverberg. BA, Carleton Coll., 1976. Programmer Brandon Applied Systems, San Francisco, 1977-78, Rand Info. Systems, San Francisco, 1979-83; systems programmer IBM, San Jose, Calif., 1983-91; programmer Office of Instnl. Rsch./U. Calif., Berkeley, 1991-94, Datis Corp., San Mateo, Calif., 1994-95, Compuware Corp., Los Gatos, Calif., 1995-96, Pacific Bell, San Ramon, Calif., 1996—. Mem. Assn. for Computing Machinery, Assn. for Computing Machinery Spl. Interest Group in Computers and Soc., Phi Beta Kappa. Avocations: guitar, reading, swimming. Home: PO Box 25143 San Mateo CA 94402-5143 Office: Pacific Bell 2600 Camino Ramon San Ramon CA 94583-5099

SCHOLTEN, PAUL, obstetrician, gynecologist, educator; b. San Francisco, Oct. 14, 1921; s. Henry Francis and Gladys (Lamborn) S.; m. Marion Lucy O'Neil, Feb. 7, 1948; children: Catherine Mary (dec.), Anne Marie, Pauline Marie, Joseph, Stephen, John. AB, San Francisco State U., 1943; postgrad., Stanford U., 1946-47; MD, U. Calif., San Francisco, 1951. Diplomate Am. Bd. Ob-Gyn. Intern San Francisco Gen. Hosp., 1951-52; resident in ob-gyn U. Calif., San Francisco, 1952-55; pvt. practice specializing in ob-gyn San Francisco, 1955-80; coll. physician Student Health Svc. San Francisco State U., 1956-80, dir. women's svcs. Student Health Svc., 1980-91; pvt. practice

San Francisco, 1991—; part-time ship's surgeon Delta Lines, 1980-84; assoc. clin. prof. Med. Sch., U. Calif., San Francisco, 1955 , assoc. clin prof. Nursing Sch., 1987—; preceptor Med. Sch., Stanford U., 1989-91; lectr. on health and wine at numerous univs., profl. groups. Contbr. articles to profl. publs., chpts. to books. Cons. U.S. Wine Inst.; sci. advisor Calif. State Adv. Bd. on Alcohol-Related Problems, 1980-86; bd. dirs. A.W.A.R.E., Century Coun. Sgt. U.S. Army, 1944-46. Mem. AMA, Calif. Med. Assn., Pan Am. Med. Assn., San Francisco Med. Soc. (editor 1971—, historian, past pres.), San Francisco Gynecol. Soc., Am. Coll. Ob-Gyn., Soc. Med. Friends of Wine (bd. dirs. 1955—, past pres.), San Francisco Wine and Food Soc. (bd. dirs. 1960—, past pres.), Internat. Wine and Food Soc. (gov. 1989—, Bronze medal 1989), San Francisco State U. Alumni Assn. (bd. dirs. 1962—), German Wine Soc., Sierra Club. Republican. Roman Catholic. Home and Office: 121 Granville Way San Francisco CA 94127-1133

SCHOMBERG, A. THOMAS, sculptor; b. Sioux City, Iowa, Apr. 25, 1943; s. Ludwig and Esther (Bojens) S.; m. Cynthia Anne Cush, July 11, 1949 (div.); 1 child, Robin Anne. BFA, Wayne State Coll., 1964; MA, U. Denver, 1970, MFA, 1972. Instr. Omaha Pub. Schs., 1964-70; from assoc. to prof. Brookdale C.C., Lincroft, N.Y., 1972-76; advisor Nat. Art Mus. Sport, Indpls., 1988—. Sculptures include Rocky, 1980, Down but Not Out...Lost But Not Forgotten, 1984, Athletics of Race—Modern and Primitive, 1988, Veteran's Memorial, 1986. Fellow Nat. Sculpture Soc. (bronze award 1982, silver award 1984); mem. Lotos Club. Home: 4923 Snowberry Ln Evergreen CO 80439-5622

SCHOMER, HOWARD, retired clergyman, educator, social policy consultant; b. Chgo., June 9, 1915; s. Frank Michael and Daisy (Aline) S.; m. Elsie Pauline Swenson, Mar. 23, 1942 (dec. Nov. 1996); children: Karine, Mark, Paul, Ellen. B.S. summa cum laude, Harvard U., 1937, postgrad., 1939-40; student, Chgo. Theol. Sem., 1938-39, 40-41, D.D., 1954; LL.D., Olivet Coll., 1966. Ordained to ministry Congl. Ch., 1941. Student pastor Fitzwilliam, N.H., Oak Park, Ill.; asst. dean U. Chgo. Chapel., 1940-41; counsellor Am. history Harvard U., 1939-40; civilian pub. service Am. Friends Service Com., 1941-45; Am. Bd. Mission fellow to chs. of Europe Chambon-sur-Lignon, France, 1946-55; history tchr., work camp dir. Coll. Cevenol; founder internat. conf. center Accueil Fraternel, Permanent Conf. Protestant Chs. in Latin Countries of Europe; asst. to rapporteur UN Commn. on Human Rights, UN Econ. and Social Council, 1947-48; inter-church aid sec. for Europe World Council Chs., Geneva, 1955-58; pres., prof. ch. history Chgo. Theol. Sem., 1959-66; exec. dir. dept. specialized ministries Div. Overseas Ministries, Nat. Council Chs., N.Y.C., 1967-70; participant integration demonstrations in Ala., Ga., Washington, Chgo., SCLC, 1960-66; world issues sec. United Ch. Bd. World Ministries, 1971-80; Indochina liaison officer World Council of Chs., 1970-71; United Ch. of Christ officer for social responsibility in investments, 1972-81; founder, dir. Corp. Adv. Services, 1980-90; founder, mem. United Ch. Christ Working Group with United Ch. in German Democratic Rep. and Fed. Rep. of Germany, 1977-86; vis. prof. religion and society Andover Newton Theol. Sch., 1981; vis. lectr. Manchester Coll., St. John's U.; Woodrow Wilson vis. fellow Drew U., 1981; pres. Internat. Fellowship of Reconciliation, 1959-63, v.p., 1963-65; participant 1st-3d assemblies World Council Chs., Amsterdam, 1948, Evanston, 1954, New Delhi, 1961; rep. UN non-govt. orgn. UNIAPAC, 1979-85; pastoral assoc. First Congl. Ch. (United Ch. Christ), Montclair, N.J., 1983-89; delegated observer Vatican Council II, 1963; v.p. Am. Friends Coll. Cevenol., 1981-89; bd. dirs. Interfaith Center for Corp. Responsibility, 1973-81; chmn. exec. com. Freedom of Faith - A Christian Com. for Religious Rights, 1978-81; mem. nat. adv. bd. N.Y. State Martin Luther King Jr. Inst. for Nonviolence, 1989-92. Translator: The Prayer of the Church Universal (Marc Boegner), 1954; editor: The Oppression of Protestants in Spain, 1955, the Role of Transnational Business in Mass Economic Development, 1975; editor-at-large Christian Century, 1959-70; contbr.; Business, Religion and Ethics-Inquiry and Encounter, 1982, Aspects of Hope, 1993; articles to religious and interdisciplinary publs.; corr. in U.S. for Évangile et Liberté, 1988—. Past co-chmn. Chgo. Com. for Sane Nuclear Policy; bd. dirs. World Conf. on Religion and Peace, 1974-84, sec. for Kampuchea issues, 1979-81; former trustee Am. Waldensian Aid Soc.; mem. internat. council Internat. Ctr. Integrative Studies, 1984-91, bd. dirs., 1987-91; trustee Internat. Inst. for Effective Communication, 1987-93; bd. dirs. Alternative Lifelong Learning, 1992-97, Cambodian Found. for Justice, Peace and Devel., 1993—. Mem. ACLU, Wider Quaker Fellowship, Fellowship Reconciliation, Ctr. for Theology and the Natural Scis., Outlook Club (Berkeley), Harvard Club San Francisco, Phi Beta Kappa. Home: 110 41st St Apt 512 Oakland CA 94611-5240

SCHONBERGER, CLAYTON JAMES, artist; b. Guantanamo Bay, Cuba, Apr. 2, 1964; s. Richard John and Nancy Louise (Sell) S.; m. Leslie Lou Holmes-Schonberger, oct. 12, 1996. BA, Seattle U., 1990. Ptnr. Schonberger and Assocs., Seattle, 1982—; co-owner Organic Minds Exch. Web Gallery, Denver, 1997—. Author: (collections) Molten Clouds, 1998, Molten Treads, 1997; artist: CORE New Art Space, 1998. Avocations: poetry readings, music, art history, travel. Office: Organic Minds Exch PO Box 620664 Littleton CO 80162

SCHOOLEY, JENNIFER LYNN, broadcasting executive; b. Oakdale, Calif., Sept. 22, 1957; d. Irwin Ross and Elvira Janet (Brown) Hickman; m. Bruce O. Schooley, Apr. 21, 1991; 1 child, James Bruce. BS in Communications, Pacific Union Coll., 1981. On-air commentator Sta. KCDS, Angwin, Calif., 1983—, talk show host, 1986-88, script writer for Step Aside (formerly Mellow Majesty), 1988-92, host Step Aside, 1989-94; gen. mgr. Sta. KCDS, Angwin, 1993-96. Seventh-day Adventist. Avocations: computer design, quilting, writing, photography, family.

SCHOOLEY, OTIS BRYSON, III, commercial airport executive. BA in Bus. Adminstrn./Acctg., Calif. State U.; cert. in exec. mgmt., U. Calif., Irvine. Asst. dir. John Wayne Airport, Orange County, Calif., 1991-95, dir., 1995—; chmn. Calif. Transp. Commn.'s Tech. Adv. Com. on Aviation. Mem. So. Calif. Assn. of Govt. (aviation tech. adv. com.), Calif. Assn. of Airport Execs., Am. Assn. of Airport Execs. Office: John Wayne Airport Orange County 3160 Airway Ave Costa Mesa CA 92626-4608

SCHOONOVER, MARGARET See LEFRANC, MARGARET

SCHOPF, JAMES WILLIAM, paleobiologist; b. Urbana, Ill., Sept. 27, 1941; s. James Morton and Esther Julie (Nissen) S.; m. Julie Morgan, Aug. 7, 1965 (div. 1979); 1 child, James Christopher; m. Jane Shen, Jan. 16, 1980. A.B. with high honors, Oberlin Coll., 1963; A.M., Harvard U., 1965, Ph.D. (Harvard fellow, NSF fellow), 1968. Research chemist NASA, Ames Research Center, Calif., 1967; mem. lunar sample preliminary exam. team Manned Spacecraft Center, Tex., 1968-71; asst. prof. dept. earth and space scis. UCLA, 1968-70, assoc. prof., 1970-73, prof., 1973—, mem. Inst. Evolutionary and Environ. Biology, 1970-76, mem. Inst. Geophysics and Planetary Physics, 1973—, dean honors div. Coll. Letters and Sci., 1983-85, dir. Ctr. for Study Evolution and Origin of Life, 1985—, Sigma Xi Disting. lectr., 1976, Rubey lectr., 1976, Golden Yr. Disting. lectr., 1980, Faculty Research lectr., 1984; Sigma Xi Disting. lectr. U. Cin., 1980; Disting. lectr. Buffalo Mus. Sci., 1982; J.A. Bownocker lectr. Ohio State U., 1982; vis. lectr. Am. Inst. Biol. Scis. Vis. Biologists Program, 1969-72; M.W. Haas vis. disting. prof. geology U. Kans., 1979; extraordinary vis. prof. exobiology U. Nijmegen, Netherlands, 1980-81; C. O'Neal lectr. Ohio Wesleyan U., 1982; Sandia disting. lectr. U. N.Mex., 1985; Sigma Xi disting. lectr. U. Oreg., 1985; Du Pont disting. lectr. U. Ill., 1985; R. Stanier disting. lectr. U. Calif.-Berkeley, 1987; H.P. Mangelsdorf disting. lectr. U. N.C., 1987; mem. Bot. Soc. Am. del., People's Republic China, 1978; Academia Sinica vis. research scientist, People's Republic China, 1981, 82; mem. NASA Terrestrial Bodies Sci. Working Group, 1975-76, space program adv. council NASA Life Scis. Com., 1976-78, NASA Working Group on Origins of Life, 1978-79, NASA Space Sci. Adv. Com., 1979-82, mem. NASA Life Scis. Strategic Planning Study Com., 1985—; Alan T. Waterman Award com. NSF, 1978-81; mem. working group on precambrian biostratigraphy Internat. Geol. Correlation Program, UNESCO, [illegible] Working Group on Cambrian-Precamb-rian Boundary, 1976—; mem. adv. com. USSR and Eastern Europe, Commn. Internat. Relations NRC, 1981-85, mem. bd. earth sci. Commn. Phys. Scis., Math. and Resources, 1982-85, mem. space sci. bd., 1983-86; mem . com. on guidelines for paleontol. collecting, 1984-86, sub.-com. on evolution and diversity Commn. on Life Scis., 1986; mem. com. space research Internat. Council Sci. Unions. Mem. editorial bd.: Origins of Life, 1973—, Precambrian Research, 1973—, Evolutionary Theory, 1973—, U. Calif. Press, 1973-82, Paleobiology, 1974-83, Geomicrobiology Jour., 1977—, Evolutionary Monographs, 1977—; contbr. articles to profl. jours. Bd. dirs. Brentwood Glen (Calif.) Assn., 1972-75; trustee UCLA Found., 1983-85. Recipient N.Y. Bot. Garden award Bot. Soc. Am., 1966; Group Achievement award NASA, 1969; Outstanding Paper award Jour. Paleontology, 1971; Charles Schuchert award Paleontol. Soc., 1974; Disting. Teaching award UCLA, 1977; Alan T. Waterman award NSF, 1977; G. Hawk award U. Kans., 1979; spl. recognition diploma NASA, 1979; Outstanding Vol. in Phys. Scis. award Am. Assn. Pubs., 1983; Mark Clark Thompson medal Nat. Acad. Scis., 1986; Guggenheim fellow, 1973; U.S. Nat. Acad. Scis. exchange scientist USSR, 1975. Fellow Geol. Soc. Am. (vice-chmn. Cordilleran sect. 1983-84, chmn. 1984-85); mem. Bot. Soc. Am. (com. on sci. liaison with People's Republic China 1978—), Paleontol. Soc. (mem. Schuchert Award com. 1978-82), Internat. Soc. Study of Origin of Life (treas. 1977-83, nat. meeting adv. com. 1980, 83, 86, councilor, 1983—), Geochem. Soc. (nominating com. 1980-82), Soc. Study of Evolution (edn. com. 1980-83), Am. Philos. Soc., Sigma Xi (treas. UCLA chpt. 1972-74, chpt. v.p. 1984-84, pres. 1984-85). Office: U Calif LA Geology Bldg Dept Earth And Scis Los Angeles CA 90095*

SCHOR, SUZI, lawyer, psychologist; b. Chgo., Feb. 1, 1947; d. Samuel S. and Dorothy Helen (Hineline); 1 child, Kate. BSBA, Ind. U., 1964; MBA Mktg., Northwestern U., 1967, JD, 1970; PhD in Fine Arts (hon.), U. Nev., PhD in Clin. Psychology, 1989. Bar: Ill., 1971. Pvt. practice L.A., 1971-80; v.p. legal affairs Little Gypzy Mgmt., Inc., Beverly Hills, Calif., 1980—; mem. Pres.'s Coun. on Alcoholism. Author: 13th Step to Death, 1995; contbg. author Wine and Dine Mag.; contbr. articles to profl. jours. Bd. dirs. Nat. Ctr. for Hyperactive Children, L.A., 1989-91, sec. Rainbow Guild Cancer Charity, L.A., 1985-89, ind. cons. Jewish Legal Aid, L.A., 1988—; campaign coord. advisor Dem. Nat. Campaign, L.A., 1990, 94; donor mem. L.A. Coun. on World Affairs. Recipient Poet of Yr. award Nat. Libr. and Assn. of Poetry, 1995, 98. Mem. ABA (criminal justice com. 1994), AAUW, NAADAC, CAADAC, L.A. Breakfast Club (chmn. entertainment 1988-90), Rotary, Mensa. Jewish. Avocations: singing, skiing, writing.

SCHORR, ALAN EDWARD, librarian, publisher; b. N.Y.C., Jan. 7, 1945; s. Herbert and Regina (Fingerman) S.; m. Debra Genner, June 11, 1967; 1 son, Zebediah. BA, CUNY, 1966; MA, Syracuse U., 1967; postgrad., U. Iowa, 1967-71; MLS, U. Tex., 1973. Tchr., rsch. asst. dept. history U. Iowa, 1967-70; govt. publs. and map libr., asst. prof. Elmer E. Rasmuson Libr., U. Alaska, 1973-78; assoc. prof., dir. libr. U. Alaska, Juneau, 1978-84; prof., dean univ. libr. Calif. State U., Fullerton, 1984-86; pres. The Denali Press, Juneau, 1986—; freelance indexer and bibliographer; vis. lectr. Birmingham (Eng.) Poly., 1981; mem. Alaska Ednl. Del. to China, 1975. Author: Alaska Place Names, 1974, 4th edit., 1991, Directory of Special Libraries in Alaska, 1975, Government Reference Books, 1974-75, 1976, 1976-77, 1978, Government Documents in the Library Literature 1909-1974, 1976, ALA RSBRC Manual, 1979, Federal Documents Librarianship 1879-1987, 1988, Hispanic Resource Directory, 1988, 3d edit., 1996, Refugee and Immigrant Resource Directory, 1990, 92, 94; editor: The Sourdough, 1974-75, Directory of Services for Refugees and Immigrants, 1987, 3d edit., 1993, Guide to Smithsonian serial publs., 1987 ; book reviewer, columnist: S.E. Alaska Empire, 1979-82, L.A. Times; contbr. articles to profl. jours. Mem. Auke Bay (Alaska) Vol. Fire Dept.; mem. Juneau Borough Cemetery Adv. Com., 1980-81, Juneau Borough Libr. Adv. Com., 1981-82, Am. Book Awards Com., 1980; mem. strategic com. Juneau Sch. Bd., Juneau Bd. Edn., 1991—, chmn. facilities com., 1994-96, chmn. policy com., 1996—. Mem. ALA (mem. reference and subscription books rev. com. 1975-86, mem. reference and adult svcs. divsn. publs. com. 1975-77, Nat. Assn. Hispanic Publs., Mudge citation commn. 1977-79, 84-86, Dartmouth Coll. Medal Commn., Governing Coun. 1977-84, mem. Dewey medal com. 1984-85, Denali Press award), Alaska Libr. Assn. (mem. exec. bd. 1974-75, mem. nominating com. 1977-79), Pacific N.W. Libr. Assn. (rep. publs. com. 1973-75), Assn. Coll. and Rsch. Librs. (mem. publ. com. 1976-80), Spl. Librs. Assn. (assoc. editor geography and map divsn. bull. 1975-76), Soc. for Scholarly Pub., Internat. Assn. Ind. Pubs (bd. dirs. 1990-92, 95—), Pub. Mktg. Assn., Alaska State Employees Fed. Credit Union (bd. dirs. 1997—), PEN Ctr. USA West, Amnesty Internat., Explorers Club N.Y., No. Pub. Consortium (regional rep. 1993-96). Office: Denali Press PO Box 1535 Juneau AK 99802

SCHORR, MARTIN MARK, forensic examiner, psychologist, educator, screenwriter; b. Sept. 16, 1923; m. Dolores Gene Tyson, June 14, 1952; 1 child, Jeanne Ann. Student, Oxford (Eng.) U., 1945-46; AB cum laude, Adelphi U., 1949; postgrad., U. Tex., 1949-50; MS, Purdue U., 1953; PhD, U. Denver, 1960; postgrad., U. Tex. Diplomate in psychology, Am. Bd. Profl. Disability Cons., Am. Bd. Forensic Examiners, Am. Bd. Forensic Medicine; lic. clin. psychologist. Chief clin. psychol. svcs. San Diego County Mental Hosp., 1963-67; clin. dir. human services San Diego County, 1963-76; pvt. practice San Diego, 1962—; forensic examiner superior, fed. and mil. cts., San Diego, 1962—; prof. abnormal psychology San Diego State U., 1965-68; chief dept. psychology Center City (Calif.) Hosp., 1976-79; cons. Dept. Corrections State of Calif., Minnewawa, 1970-73, Disability Evaluation Dept. Health, 1972-75, Calif. State Indsl. Accident Commn., 1972-78, Calif. Criminal Justice Adminstrn., 1975-77, Vista Hill Found., Mercy Hosp. Mental Health, Foodmaker Corp., Convent Sacred Heart, El Cajon, FAA Examiner; screenwriter KT Entertainment, 4-Sq. Prodns. of San Diego. *Personal philosophy: Some wag once said that the hardest thing one learns in life is which bridge to cross and which to burn! Dr. Schorr has been called as an expert witness in over 800 homicide investigations covering California and three other states of the Union. In addition, he participated in the investigation of the Jay Sebring, Sharon Tate and La Bianca slayings which led to the capture of the Charles Manson gang. Schorr is the only forensic examiner to be consulted by attorneys in both Kennedy assassinations. He led off the defense team of Sirhan B. Sirhan in 1969. Schorr's primary role, however, has been as a witness for the prosecution. Dr. Schorr is now a screenwriter developing projects in association with KT Entertainment of San Diego.* Author: Death by Prescription, 1988; dir. Alpha Centauri Prodns., San Diego. Recipient award for aid in developing Whistle Blower Law Calif. Assembly, 1986, Man of Yr. award, 1995. Fellow Internat. Assn. Social Psychiatry, Am. Coll. Forensic Examiners (life); mem. AAAS, PEN, APA, Am. Acad. Forensic Scis. (qualified med. evaluator), Internat. Platform Assn., World Mental Health Assn., Mystery Writers Am., Nat. Writers Club, Mensa. Home: University City 2970 Arnoldson Ave San Diego CA 92122-2114

SCHOTT, MARVIN ARTHUR, military officer; b. Santa Fe, N.Mex., Apr. 30, 1945; s. Lucian Charles and Ruth Charolette (Johnson) S.; m. Sally Kay Braun, Dec. 7, 1973 (div. July 1986); m. Pamela Anne Combs, Aug. 14, 1993; children: Katrina, Amanda, Walter, Mary. BS in Aerospace Engring., Iowa State U., 1969; MS Systems Mgmt., U. So. Calif., 1978. Commd. 2d lt. USAF, 1969, advanced through grades to col., 1991, flight squadron comdr., 1986-90, flight test ctr. comdr., 1990-94, test mgr., 1994—. Mem. Order of Daedalions. Home: 1112 Oro Real Dr NE Albuquerque NM 87123-1939

SCHOVILLE, DENNIS A(RNOLD), lawyer; b. Richland Ctr., Wis., May 31, 1945. BS, U. Wis., 1967; JD with Distinction, Ill. Inst. Tech., 1973; LLM, Northwestern U., 1974. Bar: Wis. 1973, Ill. 1973, U.S. Dist. Ct. (no. dist.) Ill. 1973, Calif. 1974, U.S. Dist. Ct. (so. dist.) Calif. 1974, U.S. Ct. Appeals (9th cir.) 1985, U.S. Ct. Claims. Ptnr. Schoville & Arnell, LLP, San Diego. Capt. U.S. Army, 1968-73. Recipient Broderick award for professionalism, integrity and ethics, 1996; named Consumer Attys. San Diego Trial Lawyer of the Yr., 1995. Mem. ABA, ATLA, Am. Coll. Trial Lawyers, Am. Bd. Trial Advocates, Ill. State Bar Assn., State Bar Wis., State Bar Calif., San Diego County Bar Assn., San Diego Trial Lawyers Assn. (Outstanding Trial Advocacy award-civil 1984, 89, 94), Am. Inns of Ct. (master), Dist. Flying Cross Soc. Office: Schoville & Arnell 600 W Broadway Ste 2800 San Diego CA 92101-3360

SCHOW, TERRY D., state official; b. Ogden, Utah, Dec. 14, 1948; s. Hugh Stuart Sloan and Minnie [illegible]; m. [illegible], 1973; children: Amy, Jason. AD, Honolulu C.C., 1975; BA, Chaminade U., 1975. Cert. in mgmt., Utah. Spl. and criminal investigator State of Utah, Ogden, 1976-83, lead investigator, 1984-92; investigator Fed. Govt., Salt Lake City, Denver, 1983-84; mgr. State of Utah, Ogden, 1992—. Mem. Gov.'s Coun. on Vets. Issues, 1989—, chmn., 1990—; mem. State of Utah Privatization Policy Bd., 1989-92; chmn. 1st Congressional Dist. Utah Rep. Party, 1982-83, mem. state exec. com., 1982-83; chmn. legis. dist Weber County Rep. Party, Ogden, 1987-91, 93—; trustee Utah's Vietnam Meml., Salt Lake City, 1988—; leader Boy Scouts Am., Ogden, 1985—; mem. citizens' adv. com. Ogden City Neighborhood Redevel., 1996—. Sgt. U.S. Army, 1967-70, 72-76; Vietnam. Decorated Bronze Star, 1970, Combat Inf. Badge, 1970; recipient Championship Team Trophy Pistol U.S. Army, 1975. Mem. DAV (life Weber chpt. 4, comdr. 1994, state comdr. 1995—), NRA (life), VFW, AL (comdr. Ogden post 9 1996-97, area comdr. 1997-98, dept. vice chmn. 1998—, state comdr. 1999—), Utah Peace Officers Assn., Utah Pub. Employees Assn. (bd. dirs. 1988-89, v.p. 1989-92, pres. 1992-93, chmn. Ogden Valley dist.), Kiwanis (Ogden chpt. pres. 1992-93, pres. Layton chpt. 1985-86, named Kiwanian of Yr. 1982-83, lt. gov. divsn. 3 ut/Id dist. Kiwanis internat. 1995—, homeless vets. fellow Ogden 1992—, Weber County vets. meml. com. 1994—). Republican. Mormon. Avocations: woodworking, photography, scouting. Home: 4045 Bona Villa Dr Ogden UT 84403-3203 Office: State of Utah Office Recoveries 2540 Washington Blvd Fl 4 Ogden UT 84401-3112

SCHRADER, BARRY WALTER, composer, educator; b. Johnstown, Pa., June 26, 1945; s. Walter John and Gladys Adelaide (Smith) S. BA in English, U. Pitts., 1967, MA in Musicology, 1970; MFA in Composition, Calif. Inst. of the Arts, 1971. Mem. faculty Calif. Inst. of the Arts, L.A., 1971—, Calif. State U., L.A., 1975-78, U. Calif., Santa Barbara, 1996. Composer numerous electro-acoustic works including Celebration, 1971, Bestiary, 1972-74 (GMEB award 1974), Trinity, 1976, Classical Studies, 1977, Lost Atlantis, 1977, Electronic Suite from Moon-Whales and Other Moon Songs, 1982-83, California Dream, 1986-87, Bachahama, 1987, Triptych, 1987 (Urban-15 award 1987), Dance Suite for Harp and Computer, 1987, Love in Memoriam, 1989, Night, 1990, Two Square Flowers Red: Songs for Choir and Electronics, 1990, Excavations for Harpsichord and Electronics, 1992, 816, 1997, (film scores) How To Make a Woman, 1972, Death of the Red Planet, 1973, Heavy-Light, 1973, Exploratorium, 1975, The Glory Road West, 1976, Mobiles, 1978, Along the Way, 1980, Galaxy of Terror, 1982, Gallery 3, 1988, (video) California Dream, 1921-89, 1989; author: Introduction To Electro-Acoustic Music, 1982; contbr. articles to profl. jours. Mem. Soc. for Electro-Acoustic Music in the U.S. (pres. 1984-87), ASCAP (numerous awards 1979—), So. Calif. Resource for Electro-Acoustic Music (founder). Democrat. Avocations: computers, cooking, gardening, reading. Office: Calif Inst of the Arts Sch Music Valencia CA 91355

SCHRADER, ROBERT WESLEY, judge; b. Cheyenne, Wyo., Feb. 3, 1944; s. Marvin Glen and Bertha Lorene (Winingar) S.; m. Betty Ann Pruter, June 14, 1964; children: Christina Lynn, Tashana Dee. AA in Mortuary Sci., San Francisco Mortuary Sci., 1965; BSBA, U. Wyo., 1967, JD, 1979. Bar: Wyo., 1978, U.S. Dist. Ct. Wyo., 1978 U.S. Ct. Appeals (10th cir.), 1979, U.S. Supreme Ct., 1991. Assoc. Omohundro & O'Brien, Buffalo, Wyo., 1978-80; pvt. practice Schrader Law Office, Buffalo, 1980-84; ins. commr. State Wyo., Cheyenne, 1984-86; pvt. practice Schrader Law Office, Cheyenne, 1986-92; dist. ct. commr. 1st Jud. Dist., Cheyenne, 1987—; justice of the peace, Johnson County, Wyo., 1980-84; dist. ct. commr. 4th Jud. Dist., Johnson County, 1981-84; pres., bd. mem. Attention Homes, Inc., Cheyenne, 1983-98; pres. Scottish Rite Found., Cheyenne, 1992—. Heels, Cheyenne Frontier Days, 1979—; Wyo. races officer Wyo. Emergency Mgmt. Agy., Cheyenne, 1991-97. Capt. U.S. Army, 1967-70, Vietnam, lt. col. USAFR ret. 1994. Decorated three Meritorious Svc. medals USAF, Combat Med. badge U.S. Army, Vietnam, 1968. Mem. VFW Post 11454 (adv.), Burns Lodge 41 AF&AM (past master), Scottish Rite Bodies, York Rite Bodies, Korein Shrine (chief clown), Shrine Circus (sec.-treas.), Phi Epsilon Phi, Sigma Phi Epsilon. Republican. Episcopalian. Avocations: flying, raising quarter horses, clowning, hunting, amateur radio. Home: 607 Monte Carlo Dr Cheyenne WY 82009-2050 Office: First Jud Dist Ct Dist Ct 309 W 20th St Cheyenne WY 82001-3601

SCHRADER, WILLIAM P., organization executive, farmer; b. Phoenix; m. Bondena; children: Alissa Schrader Urshel, William P. Jr., Larry, Travis. Student, Ariz. State U. Bd. dirs. Salt River Project, Phoenix, 1964-90, v.p. bd., 1990-94, pres., 1994—; pres. Schrader Farms, Inc. Bd. dirs. Greater Phoenix Econ. Coun., Groundwater Users Adv. Coun.; mem. Maricopa C.C.'s Found., East Valley Partnership, Scottsdale (Ariz.) Mcpl. Corp.; former mayor and mem. city coun. City of Scottsdale; 1st chmn. Parada del Sol, Scottsdale Rodeo. Named to Scottsdale Hall of Fame; named Citizen of Yr., City of Scottsdale. Mem. Am. Pub. Power Assn., Am. Mgmt. Assn., Nat. Water Resources Assn., Colorado River Water Users Assn., Scottsdale C. of C., Scottsdale Jr. C. of C. (life, Disting. Svc. award), Scottsdale Charros (life), White Mountain Country Club, Ariz. Club, Mesa Country Club (Ariz.). Methodist. Home: 5611 E Calle Camelia Phoenix AZ 85018-4663 Office: Salt River Project PO Box 52025 Phoenix AZ 85072-2025*

SCHRAG, PETER, editor, writer; b. Karlsruhe, Germany, July 24, 1931; came to U.S., 1941, naturalized, 1953; s. Otto and Judith (Haas) S.; m. Melissa Jane Mowrer, June 9, 1953 (div. 1969); children: Mitzi, Erin Andrew; m. Diane Divoky, May 24, 1969 (div. 1981); children: David Divoky, Benaiah Divoky; m. Patricia Ternahan, Jan. 1, 1988. A.B. cum laude, Amherst Coll., 1953. Reporter El Paso (Tex.) Herald Post, 1953-55; asst. sec., asst. dir. publs. Amherst Coll., 1955-66, instr. Am. Studies, 1960-64; asso. edn. editor Sat. Rev., 1966-68, exec. editor, 1968-69; editor Change mag., 1969-70; editor at large Saturday Rev., 1969-72; contbg. editor Saturday Review/Education, 1972-73; editorial adv. bd. The Columbia Forum, 1972-75; editorial bd. Social Policy, 1971—; contbg. editor More, 1974-78, Inquiry, 1977-80, The Am. Prospect, 1995—; editorial page editor Sacramento Bee and McClatchy Newspapers, 1978-96, contbg. editor, 1996—; vis. lectr. U. Mass. Sch. Edn., 1970-72; fellow in profl. journalism Stanford U., Palo Alto, Calif., 1973-74; lectr. U. Calif. at Berkeley, 1974-78, 90—; Pulitzer Prize juror, 1988-89. Author: Voices in the Classroom, 1965, Village School Downtown, 1967, Out of Place in America, 1971, The Decline of the Wasp, 1972, The End of the American Future, 1973, Test of Loyalty, 1974, (with Diane Divoky) The Myth of the Hyperactive Child, 1975, Mind Control, 1978, Paradise Lost: California's Experience, America's Future, 1998; contbr. articles. Mem. adv. com. Student Rights Project, N.Y. Civil Liberties Union, 1970-72; mem. Com. Study History, 1958-72; trustee Emma Willard Sch., 1967-69; bd. dirs. Park Sch., Oakland, Calif., 1976-77, Ctr. for Investigative Reporting, 1979-81, Ed Source, 1998—; bd. visitors Claremont Grad. Sch.; mem. bd. advisors Pub. Policy Inst. Calif. Guggenheim fellow, 1971-72; Nat. Endowment for Arts fellow, 1976-77. Office: 5835 Colton Blvd Oakland CA 94611-2204

SCHRANK, SHIRLEY ANN, artist; b. Nunda, N.Y., Jan. 30, 1933; d. Ward Donald and Norma Mae (Kelley) Crane; m. John Roberts McKalip Jr., Oct. 8, 1966 (dec. May 1974); children: Catherine, William Ward; m. William Thomas Schrank, Nov. 24, 1976 (dec. Aug. 1993). Degree in nursing, U. Rochester, 1954, BSN, 1960, MS in Nursing Edn., 1961. Staff nurse dept. psychiatry U. Rochester, N.Y., 1954-56; team leader dept. medicine U. Rochester, 1956-60; instr. in pediatric nursing Genesee Hosp., Rochester, 1960-61; nurse pvt. duty surg. patients Presbyn. Med. Ctr., San Francisco, 1962; instr. medicine, surg. and ICU nursing Samuel Merritt Hosp. Sch. Nursing, Oakland, Calif., 1963-67, ret., 1967; with The Sculpture Group Gallery, Danville, Calif., 1995-99, East Bay Women Artists, Oakland, Calif., 1993—. Stephen min., Stephen tchg. leader. Mem. AAUW. Republican. Presbyterian. Avocations: camping, traveling, singing, needlepoint. Home: 609 Maureen Ln Pleasant Hill CA 94523

SCHREIBER, ANDREW, psychotherapist; b. Budapest, Hungary, Aug. 1, 1918; s. Alexander and Bella (Gruen) S.; m. Mona Schreiber, Aug. 6, 1950; children: Julie, Brad, Robin. BA, CCNY, 1941, MEd, 1943; MSW, Columbia U., 1949; PhD, Heed U., 1972. Diplomate Am. Bd. Sexology; lic. psychotherapist, Calif. Pvt. practice Belmont, Calif., 1970—; sales mgr. vibro ceramics dir. Gulton Industries, Metuchen, N.J., 1949-57; mktg. mgr. Weldotron Corp., Newark, 1957-63; head dept. spl. edn. San Mateo (Calif.) High Sch. Dist., 1964-70; mem. faculty Heed U., 1970-71, advisor to [illegible] West Coast, 1971; lectr. spl. edn. U. Calif.-Berkeley, 1973; cons. on hypnotherapy Psoriasis Rsch. Inst., Palo Alto, Calif., 1987—. Art Students League of N.Y. scholar, 1933-35, San Francisco State U. grantee. Fellow Am. Acad. Clin. Sexology; mem. NEA, AACD, Learning Disabilities Assn., Am. Assn. Sex Educators, Counselors and Therapists,

Calif. Assn. Marriage and Family Therapists, Calif. Tchrs. Assn. Home: 2817 San Ardo Way Belmont CA 94002-1341

SCHREIBER, DAVID M., lawyer, judge; b. Kansas City, Mo., Aug. 13, 1937; s. William and Hinda Gold Schreiber; m. Adrienne Rennie Ehre, May 31, 1959; children: Beth F., Kathy L. JD, U. Ariz., 1962, LLB, 1962; cert. jud. devel. adminstrv. law, Nat. Jud. Coll., 1997. Bar: Ariz., 1962, Nev., 1968, U.S. Ct. Appeals (9th cir.), 1978, U.S. Dist. Ct., 1968, U.S. Supreme Ct., 1972. Pvt. practice Tucson, Ariz., 1962-64; hearings officer, referee Indsl. Commn. Ariz., Phoenix, 1964-67; asst. v.p., house counsel First Western Savings & Loan, Las Vegas, Nev., 1967-69; chief dep. pub. defender Clark County Pub. Defenders Office, Las Vegas, 1969-71; chief dep. dist. atty., counsel Nev. Juvenile Ct., Las Vegas, 1971-76; pvt. practice Las Vegas, 1976-92; adminstrv. law judge State of Nev., Dept. Motor Vechiles and Pub. Safety, Las Vegas, 1992—. Chmn. Cmty. Devel. Adv. com., Clark County, Nev., 1995-96. Recipient Law Enforcement Commendation medal Nat. Soc. Sons Am. Revolution, 1995. Mem. Nat. Assn. Adminstrv. Law Judges. Avocations: classical music, collecting art, politics. Home: 3310 Brookfield Dr Las Vegas NV 89120-1969 Office: State of Nev Dept Motor Vechiles 2701 E Sahara Ave Las Vegas NV 89104-4119

SCHREIBER, JOHN T., lawyer; b. N.Y.C., Mar. 30, 1960; s. Toby Schreiber and Morley Ann (Perrish) Clark; m. Theresa Ann Sawyer, Aug. 11, 1984; children: Zoe Cassandra Bloch Schreiber, Alana Nichole Perrish Schreiber. BA Politics, Brandeis U., 1982; JD, Santa Clara U., 1986. Bar: Calif. 1987; U.S. Dist. Ct. (no. dist.) Calif. 1987; U.S. Dist. Ct. (ea. dist.) Calif. 1990; U.S. Ct. Appeals (9th cir.) 1989. Assoc. Law Offices of Wm. D. McHugh, San Jose, Calif., 1987-88, Hallgrimson, McNichols, McCann & Inderbitzen, Pleasanton, Calif., 1989-92; pvt. practice Walnut Creek, Calif., 1993—; bd. dirs. East Bay Depot for Creative Re-use, Oakland. Field coord. Cen. Contra Costa County, Tom Bradley Campaign for Govs., Concord, Calif., 1982, Clinton-Gore Campaign, Walnut Creek, Calif., 1992; mem. Ask-A-Lawyer Program Contra Costa Legal Svcs. Found., Richmond, Calif., 1992—; co-chair Clinton-Gore Contra Costa County, 1996. Mem. ABA, Contra Costa Bar Assn. (program dir. appellate sect. 1993-95, pres. appellate sect. 1995-96), MCLE com. 1995—), Bar Assn. San Francisco (appellate sect. 1993—), Santa Clara Bar Assn., Am. Israeli Polit. Action Com. Avocations: reading, golf, softball, movies, exercising. Office: 961 Ygnacio Valley Rd Walnut Creek CA 94596-3825

SCHREMPF, DETLEF, professional basketball player; b. Leverkusen, Germany, Jan. 21, 1963. Student, U. Washington. Forward Dallas Mavericks, 1985-89, Indiana Pacers, 1989-93, Seattle Supersonics, 1993—; player West German Olympic Team, 1984, 92. Recipient Sixth Man award NBA, 1991, 92; mem. NBA All-Star team, 1993. *

SCHRENK, GARY DALE, foundation executive; b. San Jose, Calif., Apr. 29, 1949; s. Robert Shepard and Katherine Mildred (Grant) S.; m. Rhonda Lynn King, Oct. 9, 1981 (div. Jan. 1989); children: Stephen, Kristen, James. BA in Communication, Am. U., 1970; postgrad., Regis U., 1990—. TV dir. WTOP (now WUSA), Washington, 1971-73, KBTV (now KUSA), Denver, 1973-75; with Denver Area Boy Scouts Am., 1975-80; regional dir. St. Jude Children's Rsch. Hosp., Memphis, 1980-83; dir. devel. Denver Art Mus., 1983-85; asst. dir. devel. The Children's Hosp., Denver, 1985-87; pres. North Colo. Med. Ctr. Found., Greeley, 1987—; dir., instr. Fast Start Course, 1985—; pres. Monfort Children's Clinic, Greeley, 1994—. Pres. Vision Together, Weld County, Colo., 1994-95; chair, founding dir. Weld Citizen Action Network, 1995-98; founding dir., v.p. First Steps Weld County, 1993—; chair Weld Cmty. Health Coalition, 1992—; chair pub. support com. Team Colo. ARC, 1997—. Recipient Disting. Citizen award Highlanders, Denver, 1974; named Eagle Scout. Mem. Nat. Soc. Fund Raising Execs. (mem. nat. found. bd. 1998—, nat. assembly 1994-98, bd. dirs. Colo. chpt. 1979—, pres. 1984), Colo. Assn. Nonprofit Orgns. (founding dir. 1987-92), Greeley Rotary, Greeley Country Club, Tahosa Alumni Assn. (past pres., past chair). Methodist. Avocation: golf. Home: 4956 13th St Greeley CO 80634-2215 Office: North Colo Med Ctr Found 1801 16th St Greeley CO 80631-5154

SCHRIER, RUTH, artist, educator; b. Bklyn., May 20, 1924; d. Morris And Bella (Balopole) Feinman; m. Aaron Schrier, Feb. 20, 1963; children: Tina, Paul. BA, Calif. State U., Northridge, 1962; MFA, U. So. Calif., 1970. Art tchr. Clark Jr. High, Glendale, Calif., 1962-63, Glendale C.C., 1963-70; prof. Calif. State U., Northridge, 1970-95. One-woman shows include Mcpl. Art Gallery, L.A., 1976, Faculty Ctr., Calif. State U., Northridge, 1978, Oviatt Libr., 1982, Gallery II, 1984, N. Gallery, 1993, Homestead Savings, Sausalito, Calif., 1978, Glendale C.C., 1979, Office Chancellor, Long Beach, Calif., 1979, Orlando Gallery, 1999, Sherman Oaks, Calif., 1996; exhibited in group shows at Fine Arts Main Gallery, Calif. State U., Carnegie Mus., 1998, Northridge, 1979, Ariz. Show, 1983, Descanso Gardens Hospitality Ho., La Canada, Calif., 1984, Encino (Calif.) Ter. Ctr., 1987, Creative Arts Ctr., Burbank, Calif., 1993. Home: 7127 Goodland Ave North Hollywood CA 91605-5028

SCHROCK, BARBARA JEAN, clinical neuropsychologist; b. Odessa, Tex., July 16, 1952; d. Clarence and Lillian Bernice (Howard) S.; m. Kevin David Gerhart, Aug. 20, 1977; children: David Adam Gerhart, Kathryn Margaret Gerhart. BA, U. Redlands, 1975; MA, U. Houston, 1983, PhD, 1985. Cert. clin. neuropsychologist. Clin. co-dir. Transitional Learning Community, Galveston, Tex., 1982-84; assoc. dir. U. Houston Neuropsychology Cons., 1984-86; staff neuropsychologist Santa Clara Valley Med Ctr., San Jose, Calif., 1986-89; pvt. practice, consultation San Jose, 1989-90; pvt. practice San Diego, 1990—; head dept. rehab. psychology svcs. Sharp Rehab. Ctr., San Diego, 1991—, clin. dir. disability assessment program, 1992—; asst. clin. prof. dept. psychiatry U. Calif., San Diego, 1993—; rehab. cons. Stepping Stones, San Jose, 1988-90; neuropsychology cons. Saratoga (Calif.) Sub-Acute, 1989-90. Mem. APA, Internat. Neuropsychol. Soc., Calif. Psychol. Assn. Office: Sharp Rehab Ctr 2999 Health Center Dr San Diego CA 92123-2762

SCHRODER, STEPHANIE MARIE, government relations specialist; b. Moline, Ill., Nov. 3, 1966; d. Stanley David and Andrea Ruth (Lundeen) S. BBA, Iowa State U., 1988. Staff asst. Office of U.S. Senator Charles Grassley, Washington, 1989; mem. minority staff Ho. Adminstrn. Com. U.S. Ho. of Reps., Washington, 1989-90; various positions Office of Gov. Pete Wilson, Sacramento, Calif., 1990-94; chief of staff Office of Vice Mayor Jeff Kellogg, Long Beach, 1994; dir. govt. rels. St. Francis Med. Ctr., Lynwood, Calif., 1994-95; dir. civic action program Atlantic Richfield Co., L.A., 1995—. Bd. dirs. Queen of Angels-Hollywood Presbyn. Med. Ctr. Found., L.A., 1997; co-chair steering com. Venice Family Clinic Young Profl. Support Group, L.A., 1998; chair com. Jr. League L.A., 1998. Mem. Young Execs. Am. (bd. dirs. 1998), Pub. Affairs Coun., Town Hall L.A., Women in Health Care Adminstrn. Republican. Lutheran. Fax: (213) 486-2284. E-mail: sschrod@mail.arco.com. Home: 1021 Lincoln Blvd Apt 115 Santa Monica CA 90403-4021 Office: ARCO 515 S Flower St # 4649 Los Angeles CA 90071-2201

SCHROEDER, ARNOLD LEON, mathematics educator; b. Honolulu, May 27, 1935; s. Arnold Leon and Wynelle (Russell) S.; BS in Math., Oreg. State U., 1960, MS in Stats., 1962; NSF Insts. at UCLA, 1964, U. So. Calif., 1965; m. Maybelle Ruth Walker, Nov. 9, 1956; children: Steven, Michael, Wendy. Assoc. prof. math. Long Beach (Calif.) C.C., 1962—; computer cons. McDonnell-Douglas Corp., 1966-74, statis. researcher in med. and social sci., 1976-80; cons. statis. software including SPSS, BMDP, and Fortran, 1980—; dir. Schroeder's Statis. Svcs. Author: Statistics/Math Note's for Colleges, 1986—. Chmn. bd. elders Grace Bible Ch., South Gate, Calif., 1985-92. Served with USAF, 1953-57. Mem. Faculty Assn. Calif. C.C., C.C. Assn., Am. Bowlers Tour (life). Home: 5481 E Hill St Long Beach CA 90815-1923 Office: 4901 E Carson St Long Beach CA 90808-1706

SCHROEDER, GERALD F., state supreme court justice; b. Boise, Idaho, Sept. 13, 1939; s. Frank Frederick and Josephine Ivy (Lucas) S.; m. Carole Ann McKenna, 1967; children: Karl Casteel, Erich Frank. BA magna cum laude, Coll. of Idaho (now Albertson Coll. of Idaho), 1961; JD, Harvard U., 1964. Bar: Idaho 1965. Assoc. Moffatt, Thomas, Barrett & Blanton, Boise, 1965-66; pvt. practice Boise, 1966-67; asst. U.S. atty. Dept. Justice, Boise, 1967-69; judge Ada County Probate Ct., Boise, 1969-71; magistrate State of Idaho, Boise, 1971-75; dist. judge U.S. Dist. Ct. (4th dist.) Idaho, 1975-95; justice Idaho Supreme Ct., 1995—; instr. Boise Bar Rev., 1973—; adj. faculty law Boise State U., 1986-95; former mem. Gov. Coun. on Crime and Delinquency. Author: Idaho Probate Procedure, 1971; (novel) Triangle of the Sons-Phenomena, 1983; contbr. chpt. to history text. Bd. dirs. Boise Philharm. Assn., 1978-81; adminstrv. and dist. judge 4th dist. State of Idaho, 1985-95. Toll fellow Nat. Coun. State Govt., 1990. Mem. Idaho Bar Assn., Boise Racquet and Swim Club (pres. bd. dirs. 1991-93).

SCHROEDER, JERRY M., architect; b. Spokane, Wash., Jan. 29, 1941; s. Myron A. and Roberta G. S.; m. Linda L., Jan. 29, 1979; children: Phil, Aubrey, Sara. BArch, Wash. State U., 1964. Drafter W.C. Heylman & Assocs., Spokane, Wash., 1964-65; designer Environ. Concern, Inc., Spokane, Wash., 1965-75; owner, architect Schroeder Assocs., Sacramento, Calif., 1976-87, SH2A, Inc., Sacramento, Calif., 1987—. Avocation: sailing. Home: 3922 Oak Hurst Cir Fair Oaks CA 95628-7408 Office: SH2A Inc 1718 3d St Sacramento CA 95814

SCHROEDER, MARY MURPHY, federal judge; b. Boulder, Colo., Dec. 4, 1940; d. Richard and Theresa (Kahn) Murphy; m. Milton R. Schroeder, Oct. 15, 1965; children: Caroline Theresa, Katherine Emily. B.A., Swarthmore Coll., 1962; J.D., U. Chgo., 1965. Bar: Ill. 1966, D.C. 1966, Ariz. 1970. Trial atty. Dept. Justice, Washington, 1965-69; law clk. Hon. Jesse Udall, Ariz. Supreme Ct., 1970; mem. firm Lewis and Roca, Phoenix, 1971-75; judge Ariz. Ct. Appeals, Phoenix, 1975-79, U.S. Ct. Appeals (9th cir.), Phoenix, 1979—; vis. instr. Ariz. State U. Coll. Law, 1976, 77, 78. Contbr. articles to profl. jours. Mem. ABA, Nat. Assn. Women Judges (pres. 1998-99), Ariz. Bar Assn., Fed. Bar Assn., Am. Law Inst. (coun. mem.), Am. Judicature Soc., Nat. Assn. Women Judges, Soroptimists. Office: US Ct Appeals 9th Cir 6421 Courthouse-Fed Bldg 230 N 1st Ave Phoenix AZ 85025-0230

SCHROEDER, MICHAEL CRAIG, architect; b. Virogua, Wis., Sept. 19, 1946; s. Cleo Matthew and Agnes Marion S.; divorced; children: Jon, Geoffrey. MArch, Iowa State U., 1970. Architect's advocate Vista, Nashville, 1970-71; project designer Fariburn Assocs., 1972-74, Skidmore Owings & Merrill, 1974-76, Welton Becket, 1976-78; ptnr. Lendrum Assocs., Phoenix, 1978-86; ptnr.-in-charge Langdon Wilson, Phoenix, 1986—. Prin. works include U.S. Fed. Cthse., 1996, Phoenix City Hall, 1995, Phoenix Mus. History, 1995. Pres. contemporary forum Phoenix Art Mus., 1990-91; nominating chair Phoenix Body positive, 1995-98; mem. Phoenix Cmty. Alliance; commr. Phoenix Hist. Preservation Commn., 1994-97, Phoenix Arts Commn., 1990-93; bd. dirs. Phoenix Symphony, 1985-87. Mem. AIA. Democrat. Home: 7027 N Barbados Pl Phoenix AZ 85021-8761 Office: Langdon Wilson 455 N 3d St Ste 333 Phoenix AZ 85004

SCHROEDER, MICHAEL JOHN, lawyer; b. Grosse Pointe, Mich., Mar. 29, 1956; s. Paul James and Dessa Marie (Cheyovich) S.; 1 child, Sara. BA, Calif. State U., Fullerton, 1979; JD, U. So. Calif., Los Angeles, 1982. Bar: Calif. 1982, Hawaii 1987, U.S. Dist. Ct. (cen., ea., no. and so. dists.) Calif. 1987, U.S. Ct. Appeals (9th cir.) 1987, U.S. Dist. Ct. Hawaii 1990, U.S. Supreme Ct. 1990. Assoc. Wyman, Bautzer, Christensen, Kuchel & Silberg, Newport Beach, Calif., 1982-87; ptnr. Case, Schroeder, Knowlson, Mobley & Burnett, Newport Beach, Calif., 1987-90; of counsel Hart, King & Coldren, Santa Ana, Calif., 1991—; bd. dirs. Legion Lex., U. So. Calif. Law Sch., Los Angeles, 1983—; gen. counsel Calif. Chiropractic Assn., Sacramento, 1983-91. Editor in chief Jour. Major Tax Planning, 1980-82, Jour. Computer/Law, 1980-82. Del. White Ho. Conf. on Productivity, San Diego, 1983; mem. George Deukmejian's Govt. Efficiency Team, Sacramento, 1982, pres. Calif. Rep. Assembly, 1991-93; mem. exec. com. Calif. Rep. Party, treas., 1993-95, vice-chmn., 1995-97, chmn., 1997-99. Mem. Calif. Bar Assn., Hawaii Bar Assn., Orange County Bar Assn. Republican. Roman Catholic. Avocations: traveling, photography, white water rafting. Office: Hart King & Coldren Fl 4 200 E Sandpointe Ave Santa Ana CA 92707-5751*

SCHROEDER, PATRICIA SCOTT (MRS. JAMES WHITE SCHROEDER), former congresswoman; b. Portland, Oreg., July 30, 1940; d. Lee Combs and Bernice (Lemoin) Scott; m. James White Schroeder, Aug. 18, 1962; children: Scott William, Jamie Christine. B.A. magna cum laude, U. Minn., 1961; J.D., Harvard U., 1964. Bar: Colo. 1964. Field atty. NLRB, Denver, 1964-66; practiced in Denver, 1966-72; hearing officer Colo. Dept. Personnel, 1971-72; mem. faculty U. Colo., 1969-72, Community Coll., Denver, 1969-70, Regis Coll., Denver, 1970-72; mem. 93d-104th Congresses from 1st Colo. dist., 1973-96; co-chmn. Congl. Caucus for Women's Issues, 1976-96; dir. New Solutions for a New Century, Inst. for a Civil Soc.; prof. Princeton U.; pres., CEO Assn. Am. Pubs., Washington, 1997—; mem. Ho. of Reps., ranking minority mem. judiciary subcom. on the Constitution, mem. Nat. Security Com. Inducted, National Women's Hall of Fame, 1995. Congregationalist. Office: Assn Am Publisher's 1718 Connecticut Ave NW Ste 700 Washington DC 20009-1162

SCHROEDER, RITA MOLTHEN, retired chiropractor; b. Savanna, Ill., Oct. 25, 1922; d. Frank J. and Ruth J. (McKenzie) Molthen; m. Richard H. Schroeder, Apr. 23, 1948 (div.); children—Richard, Andrew, Barbara, Thomas, Paul, Madeline. Student, Chem. Engring., Immaculate Heart Coll., 1940-41, UCLA, 1941, Palmer Sch. of Chiropractic, 1947-49; D. Chiropractic, Cleve. Coll. of Chiropractic, 1961. Engring.-tooling design data coordinator Douglas Aircraft Co., El Segundo, Santa Monica and Long Beach, Calif., 1941-47; pres. Schroeder Chiropractic, Inc., 1982-93; dir. Pacific States Chiropractic Coll., 1978-80, pres. 1980-81. Recipient Palmer Coll. Ambassador award, 1973. Parker Chiropractic Research Found. Ambassador award, 1976, Coll. Ambassador award Life West Chiropractic Coll. Mem. Internat. Chiropractic Assn., Calif. Chiropractic Assn., Internat. Chiropractic Assn. Calif., Assn. Am. Chiropractic Coll. Presidents, Council Chiropractic Edn. (Pacific State Coll. rep.), Am. Pub. Health Assn., Royal Chiropractic Knights of the Round Table. Home: 8701 N State Highway 41 Spc 18 Fresno CA 93720-1010 Office: Schroeder Chiropractic Inc 2535 N Fresno St Fresno CA 93703-1831

SCHROEDER, WILLIAM JOHN, electronics executive; b. Havre de Grace, Md., June 9, 1944; s. William Martin and Dorothy Jeanne (McLaughlin) S.; m. Marilee Jane Alne, May 28, 1966; children: Kristen, Kari Britt, Kimberley. BSEE, Marquette U., 1967, MSEE, 1968; MBA, Harvard U., 1972. Devel. engr. Honeywell Inc., Mpls., 1968-70; mgmt. cons. McKinsey & Co., Los Angeles, 1972-76; mgr. product planning Memorex Corp., Santa Clara, Calif., 1976-78; pres. Priam Corp., San Jose, Calif., 1978-85, chmn., 1985-86; pres. Conner Peripherals, Inc., San Jose, 1986-89, vice chmn., 1989-94; CEO Arcada Software Inc., a Conner Co., 1993-94; pres., CEO Diamond Multimedia Systems, Inc., San Jose, Calif., 1994—; bd. dirs. Xircom Corp., Thousand Oaks, Calif., ShareWave Inc., El Dorado Hills, Calif., CNF Transp., Inc., Palo Alto, Calif., Sync Rsch., Inc., Irvine, Calif. Office: Diamond Multimedia Systems Inc 2880 Junction Ave San Jose CA 95134-1922

SCHROEDER, WILLIAM ROBERT, actor, graphic designer, linguist; b. L.A., July 9, 1941; s. Robert Manville and Miriam Ruth (Sloop) S.; m. Marie Paule Fautrel, Sept. 7, 1963. BA, UCLA, 1964; BFA, Art Ctr. Coll. Design, Pasadena, Calif., 1971. Mailman U.S. Post Office, Santa Monica, Calif., 1967-71; art dir., producer N.W. Ayer/West, Los Angeles, 1971-75; pres., gen. mgr. Advt. Ctr., Los Angeles, 1976-77, Alouette Internat., Santa Monica, Calif., 1972—; free-lance woodcarver, Santa Monica, 1981—; free-lance actor, Hollywood, Calif., 1983—; appeared in feature films King of the Streets, 1983, The Forbidden Tome, 1984, The End of Innocence, 1985, Poltergeist II, 1986. Producer TV commercials, 1972-75; author, creator computerized lang. courses Mattel Intellivision, 1980-82; real estate developer, 1989—. Publicity mgr. Concerned Homeowners of Santa Monica, 1981-82. Recipient 1st Pl. award Belding award for Excellence in Advt., Los Angeles, 1974; Cert. of Merit, Art Dirs. Club Los Angeles, 1972. Mem. Am. Fedn. Radio and TV Artists, Santa Monica C. of C., Mensa (Los Angeles), Combat Pilots Assn., Orange County Squadron, Internat. Plastic Modelers Soc., The Planetary Soc., The Found. Brain Rsch., Astronomical Soc. Pacific, Internat. Soc. Philosophical Inquiry, Internat. Legion of Intelligence, Santa Monica Theatre Guild, The Air Mus. Libertarian. Office: Alouette Internat 1626 Montana Ave Santa Monica CA 90403-1808

SCHRUMPF, ROBYN LYNN, dentist; b. San Francisco, July 15, 1959; d. Walter Fred and Donna De Ella (Rogelstad) S. BS, U. Calif., Davis, 1981; DDS, Creighton U., 1985; cert. gen. practice residency, VA Med. Ctr., Palo Alto, Calif., 1986. With dental staff VA Med. Ctr., Palo Alto, 1985-86; with dental staff VA Med. Ctr., Menlo Park, Calif., 1985-86, respite team cons. dentist, 1986; assoc. Milpitas (Calif.) Dental Ctr., 1987—, Sunnyvale (Calif.) Dental Group, 1987-89; pvt. practice Sunnyvale, 1989—; dir. dentistry Idylwood Care Ctr., Sunnyvale, Calif., 1991—; dentist Macy (Nebr.) Indian Reservation, 1984, Spinal Cord Injury Ctr., Palo Alto, 1985-86, Blind Rehab. Ctr., Palo Alto, 1985-86; instr. preventive dental care Girl Scouts U.S., Sunnyvale, 1987. Regents scholar U. Calif., Davis, 1977-78, Albert Bijou Meml. scholar U. Calif., Davis, 1978-79; Lonney White scholar Creighton U., 1984. Mem. ADA, Am. Soc. Dentistry for Children (pres. Creighton U. chpt. 1982-85, merit award 1985), Calif. Dental Assn., Calif. Soc. Dentistry for Children, Calif. Scholarship Fedn. (pres. 1977), U.S. Gymnastics Fedn., Omicron Kappa Upsilon. Lutheran. Avocations: dance, singing, community theater, swimming, aerobics.

SCHRYVER, BRUCE JOHN, safety engineer; b. Newark, Aug. 14, 1944; s. Francis Henry and Ann Laura (Hart) S.; m. Lorraine Patricia Simodis, Oct. 8, 1966 (div.); children: Holly Lynn, Wendy Marie. BA in Occupational Safety and Health, Western States U., 1984, MS in Safety Mgmt., 1989, PhD in Safety Mgmt., 1989. Cert. safety profl.; cert. products safety mgr.; cert. hazard control mgr.; cert. hazardous materials mgr.; cert. healthcare safety profl. Inspector Lansing B. Warner Inc., Chgo., 1968-69; engring. rep. Glens Falls Ins. Co., Newark, 1969; safety dir. Hillside Metal Products, Newark, 1969-70; loss prevention specialist Warner Ins. Group, Chgo., 1970-79, regional loss control mgr., 1979-82, nat. loss control coordinator, 1982-85; mgr., asst. v.p. loss control svcs. Ins. Co. of the West, San Diego, 1985-90; v.p. loss control svcs. Ins. Co. of the West, 1990—; v.p. mcpl. law enforcement svcs. Ins. Co. of the West, San Diego, 1992—. Inventor Emergency Light Mount, 1971. Mem. Town of Clay (N.Y.) Pub. Safety Com., 1976-78, Beacon Woods East Homeowners Assn., Hudson, Fla., 1979-85, Meadowridge Homeowners Assn., La Costa, Calif., 1986-98; cons. Town of Clay Police Dept., 1975-78. With USCG, 1964-68. Recipient letter of appreciation Town of Clay, 1977, cert. of appreciation DAV, 1968, Golden State award, 1990. Mem. Am. Soc. Safety Engrs., Soc. Fire Protection Engrs., Nat. Safety Mgmt. Soc., Vets. Safety, Nat. Fire Protection Assn., San Diego Safety Coun., Calif. Conf. Arson Investigators. Republican. Roman Catholic. Avocations: auto racing, boating, photography, electronics. Home: 974 Mariner St Carlsbad CA 92009-1108 Office: Ins Co of the West 11455 El Camino Real San Diego CA 92130-2088

SCHUDT, ALICIA MARIE, scriptwriter; b. Mineola, N.Y.; d. William Arthur and Eugenia Marie (Richards) S.; m. Robert Schechter, Nov. 21, 1982; 1 child, Ashley Marie. AA, Centenary Coll., 1970; BA, Upsala Coll., 1972. Freelance writer L.A., 1985—; instr. UCLA Extension, 1990—; co-chair Women in Film. Story editor ALF (animated), The Chipmunks (animated), 1988, 227, 1989-90, Nutt House, 1989; freelance script writer Alf, Brothers, Different World, Duet, It's A Living, Sledge Hammer, The Hogan Family, Zazoo U., Doug, Dream Patrol, Ace Ventura, Pet Detective, Sylvester & Tweety Mysteries. Mem. Writers Guild Am., Aerobics and Fitness Assn. Am. (cert.), Acad. TV, Arts and Scis., Price Club. Presbyterian. Avocations: aerobics, cartooning, computers. Home and Office: 19143 Kenya St Northridge CA 91326-2307

SCHUELEIN, STEVEN HARRY, freelance writer; b. N.Y.C., Feb. 26, 1946; s. Robert and Rosa (Simon) S. BA, U. Buffalo, 1967; MA, Syracuse U., 1969. Sportswriter Herald-Jour., Syracuse, 1969-77; sportswriter Buffalo Evening News, 1977-81; publicity writer Hollywood Park, Inglewood, Calif., 1982-84, Santa Anita, Arcadia, Calif., 1984-90; writer Racing Times, N.Y.C., 1991; columnist Daily Racing Form, Hightstown, N.J., 1992-94; freelance writer, 1995—; dir. racing Premier Horse Network, Burbank, Calif., 1994-97. With USAR, 1969-75. Named N.Y. State Wrestling Writer of Yr. N.Y. State H.S. Coaches Assn., 1980; recipient Regents scholarship N.Y. State Bd. of Regents, 1963, assistantship Newhouse Sch. of Comm., Syracuse, 1967-69, John Hervey award Harness Mag., 1983, 84. Mem. Soc. Profl. Journalists, U.S. Harness Writers Assn. (pres. Vernon chpt. 1978, Calif. chpt. 1989), Nat. Turf Writers Assn. Avocations: golf, tennis, swimming, movies, travel. Home: PO Box 6011 Playa Del Rey CA 90296

SCHUETZ, JOHN MICHAEL, sales executive; b. Chgo., Apr. 16, 1947; s. Henry Albert and Ann Delores (Kunst) S.; m. Jacqueline Claire Furneaux, Apr. 22, 1972; children: Michael Richard, Sean David. BS in Advt., Marquette U., Milw., 1969. Gen. field mgr. Ford Motor Co., San Jose, 1972-85; v.p. we. region IVECO Trucks of N.Am., Huntington Beach, Calif., 1985-91; nat. dealer mgr. Wynnoil Co., 1992-94; v.p., CEO Ben's Oil, Inc., Toro, Calif., 1994-95; nat. sales ops. mgr. KIA Motors America, Inc., 1995—; bd. dirs. Forsyte Rsch. Group, Santa Rosa, Calif., 1988-94. Leader Boy Scouts Am., El Toro, Calif., 1988—; coach Am. Youth Soccer Orgn., Saddleback Valley. Lt. USN, 1969-72. Mem. Sun and Sail Club, Phi Theta Psi. Republican. Roman Catholic. Avocations: sailing, boating, golf. Home: 2 Cromwell Irvine CA 92618-1816

SCHULMAN, ELIZABETH WEINER, financial consultant; b. Tucson, Nov. 17, 1950; d. Leonard and Doris (Goldman) Weiner; m. Steven Andrew Schulman, Aug. 15, 1981. BA, Brandeis U., 1972; postgrad., U. Ariz., 1976-78. Office mgr. Assocs. in Periodontics and Endodontics, Tucson, 1973-78; campaign cons. various polit. campaigns Tucson, 1978-79; v.p., sr. fin. cons. Merrill Lynch Pvt. Client Group, Tucson, 1979—. Bd. dirs. Catalina coun. Boy Scouts of Am., Tucson, 1987-90, adv. coun., 1990-92; bd. dirs. Jewish Community Found., Tucson, 1989-91, Jewish Fedn. So. Ariz., 1998-99, Jewish Family and Children Svcs., 1998-99; mem. alumni admissions coun. Brandeis U., 1990-95; mem. Angel Charities Children, 1996-98. Mem. Investment Mgmt. Cons. Assn. (bd. dirs. 1991—, chmn. cert. com. 1989—, treas. 1993-94, v.p. 1994-96, pres. 1997-98), Jr. League of Tucson (coun. sec. 1989-90), Hadassah (spl. gifts. chmn. 1989-91). Avocations: bicycling. Office: Merrill Lynch 5210 E Williams Cir Ste 900 Tucson AZ 85711-3750

SCHULMAN, MARK HAROLD, university president; b. Washington, Aug. 18, 1945; s. Sol and Eveline (Dolin) S.; children: Susannah, Saranella, Saul, Sophia; m. Sheila Diane Collins, May 1, 1993; 1 stepchild, Alicia. BA, Antioch Coll., 1969; MS, Ind. U., 1971; PhD, The Union Inst., 1985. Asst. prof. Mt. Vernon Coll., Washington, 1972-76, Antioch Coll., Yellow Springs, Ohio, 1976-79; assoc. prof. St. Mary's Coll., Moraga, Calif., 1979-84, CUNY, N.Y.C., 1984-90; chair comm. dept. New Sch. Social Rsch., N.Y.C., 1990-94; acad. dean Pacific Oaks Coll., Pasadena, Calif., 1994-97; acad. v.p. Pacific Oaks Coll., Pasadena, 1997-98; pres. Antioch. U. of S. Calif., Marina del Rey, Santa Barbara, Calif., 1998—; lectr. & spkr. in field. Contbr. articles to profl. jours., chpts. to books. Office: Antioch Univ 13274 Fiji Way Marina Del Rey CA 90292

SCHULTE, HENRY GUSTAVE, university administrator; b. Seattle, Oct. 14, 1920; s. John Henry and Alma (Winter) S.; m. Joan Noel Burton, Aug. 20, 1949; children—Steven Craig, Scott John, Jane Martha. B.A. in Econs. and Bus., U. Wash., 1948. With D.K. MacDonald & Co., Seattle, 1952-67, asst. treas., 1957-60, treas., 1960-67; bus. mgr. legal firm Bogle, Gates, Dobrin, Wakefield & Long, Seattle, 1967; adminstr. Child Devel. and Mental Retardation Ctr. U. Wash., Seattle, 1968-86; mem. steering com. mental retardation research ctrs. group Nat. Inst. Child Health and Human Devel., 1971-85. Mem. exec. bd., treas. Assn. Univ. Affiliated Facilities, 1974-77. Served with AUS, 1940-45. Mem. Soc. Research Adminstrs. (mem. exec. com. 1971-72), Am. Assn. Mental Deficiency. Office: U Wash PO Box 357920 Seattle WA 98195-7920

SCHULTHEIS, PATRICK JOSEPH, lawyer; b. Spokane, Wash., Sept. 3, 1964; s. John Arthur and Catherine Christina (McCann) S. AB, Stanford U., 1986; JD, U. Chgo., 1989. Bar: Calif. 1989, Wash. 1998. Assoc. Wilson, Sonsini, Goodrich & Rosati, Palo Alto, Calif., 1989-96; mem. Wilson, Sonsini, Goodrich & Rosati, Palo Alto, 1997—. Mem. ABA (bus. law sect.), Federalist Soc., Buck Club, Kappa Sigma. Republican. Roman Catholic. Office: Wilson Sonsini Goodrich & Rosati 5300 Carillon Point Kirkland WA 98033

SCHULTZ, PAUL W., music educator, conductor; b. Mt. Clemens, Mich., July 26, 1938; s. Wilburn H. and Irene M. (Bauer) S.; m. Donnna M.

Gartman, Dec. 25, 1971; 1 child, David P. MusB, Ctrl. Mich. U., 1961, MA, 1964; PhD, Mich. State U., 1974. Choral dir. Chelsea (Mich.) Pub. Schs., 1964-66, Mt. Pleasant (Mich.) Pub. Schs., 1966-70, East Lansing (Mich.) H.S., 1970-82; condr. Mich. State Men's Glee Club, East Lansing, 1977-82; dir. choral activities U. Puget Sound, Tacoma, Wash., 1982—; condr. Tacoma Symphony Chorus, 1997—; resident artist condr. Tacoma City Ballet, 1997—. 1st lt. U.S. Army, 1961-63. Mem. Am. Choral Dirs. Assn. (pres. 1984-86, First Leadership award Wash. chpt. 1990). Avocations: gardening, hiking. Office: U Puget Sound Sch Music 1500 N Warner St Tacoma WA 98416-0001

SCHULTZ, RICHARD DALE, national athletic organizations executive; b. Grinnell, Iowa, Sept. 5, 1929; s. August Henry and Marjorie Ruth (Turner) S.; m. Jacquilyn Lu Duistermars, June 26, 1949; children: Robert Dale, William Joel, Kim Marie. BS, Ctrl. Coll., Pella, Iowa, 1950; EdD (hon.), Ctrl. Coll., 1987; LLD (hon.), Wartburg Coll., 1988, Alma Coll., 1989, Luther Coll., 1991; PhD (hon.), U.S. Sports Acad., 1993; LLD (hon.), Daniel Webster Coll., 1997, Gettysburg Coll., 1998. Head basketball coach, athletic dir. Humboldt (Iowa) High Sch., 1950-60; freshman basketball coach U. Iowa, Iowa City, 1960-62; head baseball coach, assoc. basketball coach U. Iowa, 1962-70, head basketball coach, 1970-74, asst. v.p., 1974-76; dir. athletics and phys. edn. Cornell U., Ithaca, N.Y., 1976-81; dir. athletics U. Va., Charlottesville, 1981-87; exec. dir. NCAA, Mission, Kans., 1987-94; pres. Global Sports Enterprises, 1994-95; exec. dir. U.S. Olympic Com., Colorado Springs, Colo., 1995—; mem. honors ct. Nat. Football Found. and Hall of Fame, Nat. Basketball Hall of Fame, 1992; chmn. bd. NCAA Found., 1989; organizer Iowa Steel Mill, Inc.; bd. trustees Gettysburg Coll., 1996—. Author: A Course of Study for the Coaching of Baseball, 1964, The Theory and Techniques of Coaching Basketball, 1970; Contbr. articles to mags. Bd. dirs. Fellowship of Christian Athletes, 1986, chmn., 1990; chmn. Multiple Sclerosis, 1974-75; mem. Knight Found. Commn. on Intercollegiate Athletics, 1990—; mem. adv. com. on svc. acad. athletic programs Def. Dept. Recipient Disting. Alumni award Ctrl. Coll., Pella, 1970, 98, Lifetime Svc. award U. Iowa, 1994, Corbett award Nat. Assn. Collegiate Dirs. Athletics, 1994, medal of honor Ellis Island, 1997, Disting. Alumni award Ctrl. Coll., 1998; mem. Basketball Hall of Fame Honor Ct., 1992, Sportsman of Yr. award Marine Corp., 1997; inducted into Iowa Baseball Hall of Fame, 1993. Mem. Nat. Assn. Coll. Basketball Coaches, Ea. Coll. Athletic Assn. (mem. exec. com. 1980-81), Am. Basketball Coaches Assn. (Award of Honor 1994), Am. Football Coaches Assn. (lifetime membership award 1995). Home: 3670 Twisted Oak Cir Colorado Springs CO 80904-4720 Office: US Olympic Com One Olympic Plz Colorado Springs CO 80909

SCHULTZE, ERNST EUGENE, marketing communications executive; b. Columbia, Mo., Jan. 20, 1944; s. Andrew Byron and Jeanne V. (Homsley) S.; m. Marlene Diane Finke, June 7, 1964 (div. 1981); 1 child, Nicole Johanna Dove; m. Shea C. Schultze. BA, Nebr. Wesleyan U., 1968; MBA, San Diego State U., 1975; lifetime teaching credential, Calif. Community Colls. Mktg. coord. Ektelon Corp., San Diego, 1976-79, ops. project mgr., 1979-80; exec. v.p. Mktg. Group, San Diego, 1980-83; v.p. Jack Lewis Agy., San Diego, 1983-84; mktg. strategist Gable Agy., San Diego, 1984-85; pres. Schultze & Wilson, San Diego, 1985-97; sr. v.p. mktg. IWC, Carlsbad, Calif.,, 1997—; investor, pres. Nat. Mgmt. Assn., 1979; mktg. com. Gaslamp Quarter Coun., San Diego, 1988-98; bd. dirs. MedEquip Ams., Inc. Author: Carry That Weight, 1998; contbr. articles to profl. jours. Counsel Schulze City Coun. campaign, San Diego, 1975, Killea City Coun. campagin, San Diego, 1981. Recipient Golden State award, 1989; named Big Hitter in Bus. City San Diego. Mem. Am. Mktg. Assn., Phi Kappa Tau. Republican. Avocations: reading, running, bicycling, travel, mountain climbing.

SCHULZ, JASON DOUGLAS, film maker; b. Elgin, Ill., Jan. 29, 1969; s. Dennis William and Deborah Jeanne (Naslund) S. Assocs. Degree, McHenry County Coll., 1992; Bachelors Degree, Calif. State U., Fullerton, 1993. Audio/visual tech. Photo and Sound, Costa Mesa, Calif., 1992-94; script coord. Peter Matthew Prodn., L.A., 1994. Author: Everything You Need To Know As A Motion Picture Extra, 1993. Republican. Avocations: sports, model aviation. E-mail: JASONúSCHULZ@WARNER-BROS.COM. Fax: 818-954-4183. Home: 10880 Valley Dr Riverside CA 92505-2002 Office: Warner Bros 4000 Warner Blvd Burbank CA 91522-0002

SCHULZ, LAURA JANET, writer, retired secretary; b. Alba, Tex., Aug. 12, 1931; d. Joseph Clifton and Laura Oza (Carruth) English; m. Gordon Robert Schulz, Dec. 4, 1953; children: LeAnn Clarinda Schulz Barclay, Peggy Gaynell Schulz Lingbloom. Grad. H.S., Denison, Tex. Sec. history dept. Tex. Christian U., Ft. Worth, 1948-49; continuity editor Sta. KDSX, Denison, 1949-51; clk., typist Perrin AFB, Sherman, Tex., 1951-55; acctg. clk. England AFB, Alexandria, La., 1955; sec. Emile R. Jardine, CPA, Stockton, Calif., 1957-59, Heather, Sanguinetti, Caminata & Sakai, CPAs, Stockton, 1983-92; sec., feature writer, photographer Lodi (Calif.) Dist. C. of C., 1993-97. Author: Katy's Children, 1990, Little Rocky's True Adventures, 1991, Katy's Children, Too, 1999. Hon. life mem. Wesleyan Svc. Guild Trinity Meth. Ch., Denison, 1955—, Calif. Congress of PTA, 1984—; pres. PTA Needham Sch., Lodi, 1968-69, 69-70; leader Camp Fire, Lodi, 1974-82; vol. advisor, tchr. Grapevine Newspaper Vinewood Sch., Lodi, 1974-82; mem. First United Meth. Ch. Recipient Appreciation award Vinewood Sch., Lodi Unified Sch. Dist., 1974-82. Mem. Nat. League Am. Pen Women, Sierra Club. Democrat. Methodist. Avocations: photography, reading, walking, camping, nature. Home: 1910 W Tokay St Lodi CA 95242-3440

SCHULZ, RAYMOND ALEXANDER, medical marketing professional, consultant; b. Paris, June 2, 1946; s. Helmut W. and Colette (Prieur) S.; m. Dixie Lee Suzanne Specht, Apr. 9, 1977 (div. Dec. 1990); children: Christopher, William; m. Casey Elizabeth Watson, Apr. 10, 1999. BA in Physics, W.Va. U., 1970; MS in Computer Sci., Columbia U., N.Y.C., 1975. Sr. programmer Meml. Sloan Kettering Cancer Ctr., N.Y.C., 1972-74; program coord. Neurol. Inst. Columbia Presbyn. Hosp., N.Y.C., 1974-76; engring. mgr. EMI Med. Systems, Northbrook, Ill., 1976-78; product mgr. Johnson & Johnson (Technicare), Solon, Ohio, 1978-80; group product mgr. Siemens Corp., Iselin, N.J., 1980-82; mktg. mgr. Toshiba Am. Med. Systems (formerly Diasonics MRI), South San Francisco, 1983-92; dir. mktg. Voxel, Laguna Hills, Calif., 1992—; presenter in field. Contbr. articles to Life mag. and profl. jours. Recipient first prize Roentgen Centenary Congress, 1995. Mem. Am. Assn. Physicists in Medicine, N.Y. Acad. Scis., Internat. Soc. Magnetic Rsch. in Medicine, Larchmont Yacht Club, Commonwealth Club Calif., Eta Kappa Nu. Avocations: skiing, running, hiking, swimming, mountainbiking. Office: Voxel 26081 Merit Cir Ste 117 Laguna Hills CA 92653-7017

SCHULZ, ROBERT ADOLPH, management educator, management consultant; b. Long Branch, N.J., Aug. 20, 1943; s. Robert Adolph and Anna Elizabeth (Fuga) S. BA in Math., St. Vincent Coll., Latrobe, Pa., 1965; BS in Mech. Engring., U. Notre Dame, 1966; MBA, U. Pitts., 1967; PhD in Bus. Adminstrn., Ohio State U., 1971. Rsch. asst. Tech. and Bus. Svcs., Ohio State U., Columbus, 1967-68; teaching asst. dept. mktg. Ohio State U., 1968-70; sr. assoc. Mgmt. Horizons, Inc., Columbus, 1970-71; dir. tech. edn. Mgmt. Horizons Data Systems, Columbus, 1971-72, dir. edn., 1972-73; assoc. prof., Faculty of Mgmt. U. Calgary, Alta., Can., 1973-88, acad. dir. petroleum land mgmt., 1983—, prof. mgmt., 1988—, univ. coord. teaching devel. office, 1991—; pres. Myosymmetries Internat., 1996—; pres. Scenario Mgmt. Cons. Ltd., Calgary, 1987—. Chmn. Align to 21st Century Task Force, Calgary Econ. Devel. Authority, 1989-92, bd. govs., 1994-96; chmn. coord. com. Calgary Cath. Diocese Synod, 1990-94, co-chmn. Synod implementation com., 1994—; bd. dirs. Calgary Sponsor and Refugee Soc., 1981-83. Recipient awards for teaching and coaching acad. teams, Hon. Life Mem. award U. Calgary Students' Union, 1991, Order of U. Calgary, 1994, City of Calgary award for edn., 1995. Mem. Soc. for Teaching and Learning in Higher Edn., Can. Assn. Petroleum Landmen (hon.), Order of the U. of Calgary, Beta Gamma Sigma. Roman Catholic. Avocations: golf, basketball, jogging. Home: 24-1815 Varsity Estates Dr NW, Calgary, AB Canada T3B 3Y7 Office: U Calgary, Faculty of Mgmt, Calgary, AB Canada [illegible]

SCHULZ, SUZON LOUISE, fine artist; b. Chgo., Sept. 2, 1946; d. Carl George and Ruth Ada (Eberhardt) S. BFA, R.I. Sch. Design, 1968. Studio [illegible]

Idaho Com. on the Arts, 1980—, Wash. State Arts Com., 1980-82, Mississippi County C.C. Libr., Blytheville, Ark., 1984-85, various art couns., Oreg., 1983—; tchr. elem. art seminar Ea. Oreg. Coll. Bend Br., Bend, 1996; owner Flying Shoes Studio, Bend, 1982—; cartoonist, writer, illustrator NOW News, Bend, 1991-94; represented by Artworks West, Sisters, Oreg. Painter: (series) In the Home, 1982—, The World Beyond, 1984—, Living With a Man, 1986—, Tipi Now, 1988—. Mem. Nat. Mus. Women in Arts, Cen. Oreg. Arts Assn. Avocations: walking, hiking, reading, writing, cross-country skiing. Home and Studio: 16881 Varco Rd Bend OR 97701-9135

SCHULZE, MARK LEVON, video producer, communications executive; b. Joliet, Ill., Oct. 30, 1958; s. Rolf and Evonne (Seron) S.; m. Patricia Kathryn Mooney, July 23, 1987. BA in Telecomm., Sociology, U. Calif., San Diego, 1981. Owner, operator New & Unique Videos, San Diego, 1979—, Crystal Pyramid Prodns., San Diego, 1985—. Visual cons.: Cheech and Chong's Next Movie, 1979; rschr., interviewer: Why in the World?, 1980; founder: Video Cooperative, 1981, Compupac Co., 1982-84; producer, dir.: Cheryl Carroll & Co., 1982-84, Cox Cable Pub. Access TV, 1983; producer: Massage for Relaxation, 1987, Common Sense Self-Defense for Women, Soaring in a Sailplane, 1985, Anti-Terrorism: Weapons & Tactics, 1987, The Great Mountain Biking Video, 1988, Ultimate Mountain Biking, 1989, Battle at Durango: The 1st World Mountain Biking Championships, 1990, Lessons In Cycling, 1991, Full Cycle: World Odyssey, 1995, Steppin Out, 1994; producer pub. svc. announcements. Active George McGovern for U.S. Pres., Colleen O'Connor, King Golden and John French for U.S. Congress, others. Recipient Featured Speaker award Bus. Profl. Advt. Assn., San Diego, 1985, Silver and Bronze Telly awards, 1990-91, Internat. Film TV Festival N.Y. award, 1990, Internat. Film TV Festival Houston award, 1995, Silver Hugo, 1995, Charleston Worldfest award, 1995, 2 bronze CINDY awards, 1996, Gold Aurora award, 1996, Excellence award Aegis, 1998; named to Top 100 Prodrs., 1997, Internatl. Sports Video and Film Fest., 1998. Mem. Video Producers Assn. Am. (v.p. promotions and pub. rels. 1984-85), Internat. TV Assn. (3 awards 1985), Cousteau Soc., Greenpeace, Smithsonian Inst., Natural Resources Def. Coun., San Diego Ad Club. Avocations: world travel, scuba diving, mountain bicycling, body surfing, hiking. Office: New & Unique Videos 2336 Sumac Dr San Diego CA 92105-4651

SCHUMACHER, HENRY JEROLD, museum administrator, former career officer, business executive; b. Torrance, Calif., June 17, 1934; s. Henry John and Rene (Wilcox) S.; m. Barbara Howell, Aug. 24, 1958; children: Sheri Lynn, Henry Jerold II. Student, Stanford U., 1953; B.S., U.S. Mil. Acad., 1957; M.S., Northeastern U., Boston, 1965; M.B.A., Auburn U., 1977. Commd. lt. U.S. Army, 1958, advanced through grades to maj. gen., 1982; army attaché Moscow, 1969-71; chief communications ops. Vietnam, 1971-72; exec. officer Office Chief of Staff, 1972-75; comdr. U.S. Army Communications Command, Panama, 1977-79; dir. network integration, Office Asst. Chief of Staff Automation and Communications, Dept. Army, 1979-81; comdr. The White House Communications Agy., Washington, 1981-82; chief U.S. Army Signal Corps, 1981-83; ret., 1983; sr. v.p. Visa Internat., 1983-86; chief oper. officer Fuel Tech., Inc., Stamford, Conn., 1986-87; pres. IMM Systems, Phila., 1987-89; exec. v.p. Cylink Corp., Sunnyvale, Calif., 1990-95; exec. dir. Hiller Mus. of No. Calif. Aviation History, Redwood City, 1995-98. Decorated Def. D.S.M., D.S.M., Legion of Merit. Home: 156 Normandy Ct San Carlos CA 94070-1519

SCHUMACHER, SUZANNE LYNNE, artist, art educator; b. San Francisco, Apr. 20, 1951; d. Martin John and Evelyn Lucinda (Andrews) S.; m. Timothy Van Ert, June 24, 1983 (div. Aug. 1988). BA, St. Marys Coll., 1972; MFA, San Francisco Art Inst., 1983. Instr. art Coll. Marin (Calif.), 1984-90; tchr. Montera Jr. High Sch., Oakland, Calif., 1989-92; prof. art St. Marys Coll., Moraga, Calif., 1990—; developer, dir. Myrtle Street Art Studios, Oakland, 1978—. Avocations: ballet, tennis, languages. Home: 3037 Myrtle St Oakland CA 94608-4526 Office: St Mary's Coll Dept Art St Mary's Rd Moraga CA 94575

SCHUMACK, MAXINE LYNNE, community college counselor; b. N.Y.C., Jan. 6, 1951; d. Selig-David and Ruth-Helen (Weinstock) S. AA, L.A. Valley Coll., Van Nuys, Calif., 1974; BA, Calif. State U., Northridge, 1976; MA, Pepperdine U., Malibu, Calif., 1983. Cert. mental health counselor; lifetime counselor credential Calif. C.C. Case aide, social work assoc. United Way Agy., Van Nuys, 1976-78; pers. asst. L.A. Unified Sch. Dist., West Los Angeles, 1979-80; psychol. asst. Vera Wayman, MD, Glendale, Calif., 1980-84; entrepreneur Seminars for Industry, Sherman Oaks, Calif., 1984-89; resources specialist Ind. Living Ctrs. So. Calif., Van Nuys, 1989-92; cultural diversity specialist ARC, Van Nuys, 1991-92; litigation specialist, advocate Protection and Advocacy, Glendale, 1992-93; counselor Calif. Cmty. Colls., Sacramento, 1993—. Recipient Vol. award MADD of L.A., 1992, Cert. of Appreciation, ARC, 1991. Mem. AAUW, Calif. State Psychol. Assn., Calif. Assn. Marriage and Family Counselors, Psi Chi. Home: 13621 Addison St Sherman Oaks CA 91423-1411

SCHUNKE, HILDEGARD HEIDEL, accountant; b. Indpls., Nov. 24, 1948; d. Edwin Carl and Hildegard Adelheid (Baumbach) S. BA, Ball State U., Muncie, Ind., 1971, MA in German/English, 1973, MA in Acctg., 1975. CPA, Ind., Calif. Exch. tchg. grad. asst. Padagogische Hochschule, Germany, 1971-72; tchg.ing grad. asst. in German and acctg. Ball State U., 1972, 74-75, asst. prof. acctg., 1975-78; investing rschr. Family Partnership, Muncie, 1977-83; staff acct. Am. Lawn Mower Co., Muncie, 1984-88, G&J Seiberlich, CPAs, St. Helena, Calif., 1988-89, R.A. Gullotta, MBA, CPA, Sonoma, Calif., 1989-90; plant acct. Napa (Calif.) Pipe Corp., 1990—. ESOL instr. Napa County Project Upgrade, 1988-92; ticketing and refreshments com. North Bay Philharm. Orch., Napa, 1988—, North Bay Wind Ensemble, Napa, 1988— ; mem. TC 207 Tag Team. Mem. AICPA, Calif. Soc. CPAs (continuing edn. instr. Redwood City 1990, bd. dirs. East Bay chpt. 1998—), Ind. Soc. CPAs, Inst. Internal Auditors, Environ. Auditing Roundtable, Am. Soc. for Quality, TC 207 TAG Team. Avocations: gardening, transcribing, translating and reading German. Home: 1117 Devonshire Ct Suisun City CA 94585-3343 Office: Napa Pipe Corp 1025 Kaiser Rd Napa CA 94558-6257

SCHUSSEL, ALAN LEWIS, rehabilitation counselor; b. Bklyn., Oct. 27, 1963; s. Erwin Marvin and Suellen (Kleppel) S.; m. Clarice Ann West, June 9, 1991; children: Zachary Terence, Marni Amber. BA, Gallaudet U., 1989; MA, U. Ariz., 1994. Cert. rehab. counselor, cmty. coll. tchr., Ariz. Resident advisor Rochester (N.Y.) Inst. Tech., 1983-87; resident advisor Gallaudet U., Washington, 1987-89, tutor, 1987-92; residential counselor Family Svcs. Found., Landover, Md., 1989; case mgr. People Encouraging People, Balt., 1990-92; rehab. counselor dept. econ. security State of Ariz., Tucson, 1993-96, 97; project assoc. Pima Prevention Partnership, Tucson, 1996; adj. faculty Am. sign lang. Pima C.C., Tucson, 1995—; chmn. bd. dirs. Cmty. Outreach Program for Deaf, 1997—; bd. dirs. Rehab. Counselor Dir. Search, Ariz. Coun. for Hearing Impaired, 1994—, mem. rules writing com. 1996; mem. preconf. com. Am. Deafness and Rehab. Assn., San Francisco, 1992-93; mem. Statewide Interpreter Planning Com., Phoenix, 1993-98, chair subcom. interpreter preparation planning, 1994-97; mem. Com. on Real Time Captioning Project, 1995-97; dir. New Agy. Planning Project, 1995-97; chair Sign-Out Com. Project, 1997—, exec. dir. search com., 1997-98; mem. annual clients awards ceremony com. Dept. Econ. Security, 1997—; mem. Ariz. Coun. for Hearing Impaired Task Force Com., 1998—. Active Silent Protest, U. Ariz., 1993, Deaf Pres. Now, Gallaudet U., Washington, 1988, Empowerment for the Deaf, Phoenix, 1994, Project Pride Cmty. Outreach, Tucson, 1992-93; com. mem. Christopher City Elections, Tucson, 1992. Recipient Pres. Recognition award Ariz. Assn. of Deaf, 1996, Proclamation Pima County Bd. Suprs., 1996. Mem. ACA, Nat. Rehab. Assn., Ariz. Rehab. Assn., Am. Sign Lang. Club (treas. 1992-93), Ariz. Assn. of the Deaf (rep. to bd. 1995-96, v.p. 1996-97, sec. 1997—, panelist on deaf culture 1992—, Recognition award 1996, 97), Kappa Sigma. Democrat. Jewish. Avocation: coin collection. Home: 16960 W Falcon Ln Marana AZ 85653-9199 Office: Vocat Rehab 7225 N Mona Lisa Rd Ste 259 Tucson AZ 85741-2350

SCHUSTER, DONALD, insurance agency executive; b. Portland, Oreg., May 31, 1946; s. Charles A. Schuster and [illegible]; m. bonnie G. Schuster, Dec. 26, 1989; 1 child, Angie Dawn. BS in Econs. and Gen. Studies, Portland State U., 1989. Store mgr. Fred Meyer, Portland, [illegible] Nibbles N' More, Portland, 1986-95; registered rep. Am. Express, Portland, 1995-96, Fin. Ptnrs., Portland, 1996-97; sr. mem. RH Ins. Group, Salem, Oreg., 1997—; fin. cons. Capital Ins., Salem, Cascade Ski club, Portland, Oreg. Motor Car Co., Portland; instr. Mt. Hood Meadows. Mentor children at Risk, Portland, 1995. Mem. Cascade Ski Club (pres. 1995—). Avocations: skiing, golf, hiking, running. Home: 17352 SW 128th Ave Tigard OR 97224-1818 Office: RH Ins Group 3962 Center St NE Salem OR 97301-2948

SCHUSTER, PHILIP FREDERICK, II, lawyer, writer; b. Denver, Aug. 26, 1945; s. Philip Frederick and Ruth Elizabeth (Robar) S.; m. Barbara Lynn Nordquist, June 7, 1975; children: Philip Christian, Matthew Dale. BA, U. Wash., 1967; JD, Willamette U., 1972. Bar: Oreg. 1972, U.S. Dist. Ct. Oreg. 1974, U.S. Ct. Appeals (9th cir.) 1986, U.S. Supreme Ct. 1986. Dep. dist. atty. Multnomah County, Portland, Oreg., 1972; title examiner Pioneer Nat. Title Co., Portland, 1973-74; assoc. Buss, Leichner et al, Portland, 1975-76; from assoc. to ptnr. Kitson & Bond, Portland, 1976-77; pvt. practice Portland, 1977-95; ptnr. Dierking and Schuster, Portland, 1996—; arbitrator Multnomah County Arbitration Program, 1985—; student mentor Portland Pub. Schs., 1988—. Contbg. author OSB CLE Publ., Family Law; contbr. articles to profl. jours. Organizer Legal Aid Svcs. for Community Clinics, Salem, Oreg. and Seattle, 1969-73; Dem. committeeman, Seattle, 1965-70; judge Oreg. State Bar and Classroom Law Project, H.S. Mock Trial Competition, 1988—. Mem. ABA, ATLA, NAACP (exec. bd. Portland, Oreg. chpt. 1979-98), ACLU, Multnomah Bar Assn. (Vol. Lawyers Project), Internat. Platform Assn., Alpha Phi Alpha. Avocations: river drifting, camping, swimming, walking, writing. Office: 1500 NE Irving St Ste 540 Portland OR 97232-4209

SCHUSTER, ROBERT PARKS, lawyer; b. St. Louis, Oct. 25, 1945; s. William Thomas Schuster and Carolyn Cornforth (Daugherty) Hathaway; 1 child, Susan Michele. AB, Yale U., 1967; JD with honors, U. of Wyo., 1970; LLM, Harvard U., 1971. Bar: Wyo. 1971, U.S. Ct. Appeals (10th cir.) 1979, U.S. Supreme Ct. 1984, Utah 1990. Dep. county atty. County of Natrona, Casper, Wyo., 1971-73; pvt. practice law, Casper, 1973-76; assoc. Spence & Moriarity, Casper, 1976-78; ptnr. Spence, Moriarity & Schuster, Jackson, Wyo., 1978—. Trustee U. Wyo., 1985-89; Wyo. Dem. nominee for U.S. House of Reps., 1994; polit. columnist Casper Star Tribune, 1987-94. Ford Found. Urban Law fellow, 1970-71; pres. United Way of Natrona County, 1974; bd. dirs. Dancers Workshop, 1981-83; chair Wyo. selection com. Rhodes Scholarship, 1989-98; mem. bd. visitors Coll. Arts and Scis., U. Wyo., 1991—; mem. Dem. Nat. Com., 1992—; chair Wyo. Public Policy Forum, 1992-98; mem. Wind River Reservation Econ. Adv. Coun., 1998—. Mem. ABA, ATLA, Wyo. Trial Lawyers Assn. Home: PO Box 548 Jackson WY 83001-0548 Office: Spence Moriarity & Schuster 15 S Jackson St Jackson WY 83001

SCHÜTRUMPF, ECKART ERNST, classical languages and philosophy educator; b. Marburg, Hesse, Germany, Feb. 3, 1939; came to U.S., 1987; s. Hans Justus and Margarethe (Wetz) S.; m. MaryAnne Leaver, Dec. 21, 1971; children: Fleming, Caroline, Helen, Justin. PhD, Philipps U., Marburg, 1966, Habilitation, 1976. Lectr. Philipps U., Marburg, 1966-81; pvt. docent Philips U., Marburg, 1979-83; sr. lectr. U. Cape Town, 1983-85, prof., 1985-87; prof. classics U. Colo., Boulder, 1987—. Author: Die Bedeutung des Wortes ethos in der Poetik des Aristoteles, 1970, Die Analyse der polis durch Aristoteles, 1980, Xenophon Poroi, Vorschläge zur Beschaffung von Geldmitteln, 1982, Aristoteles Politik Buch I-III (2 vols.), 1991, (with H.J. Gehlke) vol. 3, 1995; contbr. 40 articles to profl. jours. Rsch. scholar Deutsche Forschungsgemeinschaft, 1973-75, Exch. scholar British Coun., 1979, Rsch. scholar Volkswagenwerk Found., 1981-83. Mem. APA, Classical Assn. Mid West and South, Mommsen Gesellschaft. Avocations: classical music, hiking. Office: U Colo Classics Dept PO Box 348 Boulder CO 80309-0348

SCHUTZ, JOHN ADOLPH, historian, educator, former university dean; b. L.A., Apr. 10, 1919; s. Adolph J. and Augusta K. (Gluecker) S. AA, Bakersfield Coll., 1940; BA, UCLA, 1942, MA, 1943, PhD, 1945. Asst. prof. history Calif. Inst. Tech., Pasadena, 1945-53; assoc. prof. history Whittier (Calif.) Coll., 1953-56, prof., 1956-65; prof. Am. history U. So. Calif., L.A., 1965-91; chmn. dept. history U. So. Calif., 1974-76, dean social scis. and communication, 1976-82. Author: William Shirley: King's Governor of Massachusetts, 1961, Peter Oliver's Origin and Progress of the American Rebellion, 1967, The Promise of America, 1970, The American Republic, 1978, Dawning of America, 1981, Spur of Fame: Dialogues of John Adams and Benjamin Rush, 1980, A Noble Pursuit: A Sesquicentennial History of the New England Historic Genealogical Society, 1995, Legislators of the Massachusetts General Court, 1691-1780, 1997; joint editor: Golden State Series; contbg. author: Spain's Colonial Outpost, 1985, Generations and Change: Genealogical Perspectives in Social History, 1986, Making of America: Society and Culture of the United States, 1990, rev. edit., 1992. Trustee Citizens Rsch. Found., 1985—. NEH grantee, 1971; Sr. Faculty grantee, 1971-74. Mem. Am. Hist. Assn. (pres. Pacific Coast br. 1972-73, sec.-treas. 1995-96), Am. Studies Assn. (pres. 1974-75), Mass. Hist. Soc. (corr.), New Eng. Hist. Geneal. Soc. (trustee 1988—, editor, author intro. book Boston Merchant Census of 1789, 1989, rec. sec. 1995—), Colonial Soc. Mass. (corr.). Home and Office: 1100 White Knoll Dr Los Angeles CA 90012-1353

SCHUTZKY, MARILYN HORSLEY, artist; b. Soda Springs, Idaho, July 13, 1936; d. Earl James and Alta (Bollwinkel) Horsley; m. Victor Sergay Schutzky, Oct. 11, 1957; children: Allen Victor, Sandra Kristin. Student, U. Calif., Berkeley, 1954-55, U. Utah, 1955-57. Free-lance artist, 1957—. One-woman shows include Design Concepts, Alamo, Calif., 1991, Harbor Studio Gallery, Gig Harbor, 1991, Back Bay Gardens Gallery, Corte Madera, Calif., 1988, St. Paul Towers, Oakland, Calif., 1988, Marin Arts Guild, Larkspur, Calif., 1986, Two Birds, Forest Knolls, Calif., 1983, Avoir Gallery, Kirkland, Wash., 1993, 94, Andrea Schwartz Gallery, San Francisco, 1996, Glendale (Ariz.) C.C., 1997, Sun Cities Mus. Art, 1997, Ch. of Beatitudes, Phoenix, 1998; exhibited in groups shows at Waterworks '92, '93, '94, '95, Seattle Conv. Ctr., Grand Exhbn. '92, Akron (Ohio) Soc. of Artists, Howard Mandeville Gallery, Kirkland, 1992, The Nut Tree, 1991, Kaiser Gallery, 1991, Ariz. Aqueous, Tubac, 1993, 95, 96, 97, Suncities Mus., Phoenix, 1994, 97, Western Fedn. Watercolor Socs., Phoenix, 1994, others; Basic Flower Painting--Techniques in Watercolor, 1996, The Artistic Touch II-Chris Unwin, 1996. Recipient 1st award Frye Art Mus., 1990, James Copley Purchase award San Diego Watercolor Soc., 1988, 2d Pl. award The Artist's Mag., 1993, Excellence award Western Fedn. Watercolor Socs., 1993, award San Diego Internat. Watercolor Exhbn., 1998. Mem. N.W. Watercolor Soc. (Past Pres.'s award 1992, Signature award 1992, Merit award 1993), Marin Soc. Artists, Ariz. Watercolor Assn. (awarded Coatimundi Soc. membership, Royal Scorpion membership), Calif. Watercolor Soc. (Signature award 1989), Fedn. Can. Artists, Marin County Watercolor Soc., Watercolor West (Barr award 1995, Signature award 1995). Home and Studio: 7340 E Turquoise Ave Scottsdale AZ 85258-1220 also: Marilyn Schutzky Studio 8915 N Harborview Dr Apt 103 Gig Harbor WA 98332-2179

SCHUYLER, ROB RENE, lawyer; b. Larchmont, N.Y., Aug. 13, 1932; s. William and Margaret S.; children: Marc Philip, Clifford Robert, Paul Frederick. Student, U. Paris, 1950-52; Bachelors, U. So. Calif., 1955; JD, U. Mich., 1958. Bar: Calif. 1958, U.S. Dist. Ct. 1958, U.S. Supreme Ct. 1962. Dep. city atty. L.A. City Atty.'s Office, 1959-62; ptnr. Maury & Schuyler, L.A., 1962-65; pvt. practice, L.A., 1965-73; ptnr. Mihaly, Schuyler & Mitchell (formerly Mihaly, Schuyler & Burton), L.A., 1973—. Mem. L.A. County Bar Assn. (chmn. internat. law sect. 1972-73), Wilshire Bar Assn. (pres. 1970). Republican. Fax: 310-284-7982. E-mail: robrschuyler@earthlink.net. Office: Mihaly Schuyler & Mitchell 1888 Century Park E Ste 1500 Los Angeles CA 90067-1719

SCHUYLER, ROBERT LEN, investment company executive; b. Burwell, Nebr., Mar. 4, 1936; s. Norman S. and Ilva M. (Hoppes) S.; m. Mary Carol Huston, June 13, 1958; children: Kylie Anne, Nina Leigh, Melynn Kae, Gwyer Lenn. BS, U. Nebr., 1958; MBA, Harvard U., 1960. Asst. to treas. Potlatch Forests, Inc., Lewiston, Idaho, 1962-64; dir. corp. planning Potlatch Forests, Inc., San Francisco, 1964-66; mgr. fin. analysis Weyerhaeuser Co., Tacoma, 1966-68; mgr. investment evaluation dept. Weyerhaeuser Co., 1968-70, v.p. fin. and planning, 1970-72, sr. v.p. fin. and planning, [illegible] v.p., chief fin. officer, 1985-91; mng. ptnr. Nisqually Ptnrs., Tacoma, 1991-95, bd. dirs. Grande Alberta Paper, Ltd., 1992—; past mem. nat. adv. bd.

Chem. Bank, U. Wash. MBA program, coun. fin. exec. Conf. Bd., Pvt. Sector Coun., exec. com. Am. Paper Inst.; bd. dirs. Paragon Trade Brands Inc., Montrail, Inc. Chmn. Santa Fe County Bd. Econ. Advs.; vice chmn. Santa Fe Bus. Incubators; trustee Santa Fe Chamber Music Festival. Mem. Anglers Club, Sangre de Cristo Flyfishers, Las Campanas Golf & Country Club, Quixote Club. Home and Office: 46 Hollyhock Cir Santa Fe NM 87501-8595

SCHWAB, CHARLES R., brokerage house executive; b. Sacramento, 1937; m. Helen O'Neill; 5 children. Stanford U., 1959, Postgrad., 1961. Formerly mut. fund mgr. Marin County, Calif.; founder brokerage San Francisco, 1971; now chmn., CEO Charles Schwab & Co., Inc. Author: How to be Your Own Stockbroker, 1984. Republican. Office: Charles Schwab & Co Inc 101 Montgomery St Ste 200 San Francisco CA 94104-4175*

SCHWALBERG, CAROL, writer, editor; b. N.Y.C., Feb. 11, 1930; d. Arthur Stein and Madeline Schoenberg Stein Ullman; m. Robert M. Schwalberg, Aug. 24, 1952 (div. Mar. 1958); m. Eugene F. Schoerluke, June 23, 1985. BA, NYU, 1950. Copy chief McCall's Needlework, N.Y.C., 1955-56; editor-in-chief Scholastic Roto, N.Y.C., 1963-65; editor-in-chief Sch. Bank News East N.Y. Savs. Bank, Bklyn., 1971-73; text editor Alfred Van Der Marck Edits., N.Y.C., 1984; contbg. editor Kessler Exch., L.A., 1988; instr. Calif. State U., Long Beach, 1979, 84-85. Author: From Cattle to Credit Cards, 1969, Light and Shadow, 1972, Doing It, or How to give the Perfect Orgy, 1973; author of short stories; contbr. poetry to Black River Rev., New Voices Anthology West, others; writer features for newspapers; contbr. articles and revs. to various publs. County committeewoman Dem. Party, N.Y.C., 1970-71. Helene A. Wurlitzer Found. fellow, Taos, N.Mex., 1972. Mem. PEN, Authors Guild, Nat. Writers Union. Home and Office: 629 Palisades Ave Santa Monica CA 90402

SCHWANTES, CARLOS ARNALDO, history educator, consultant; b. Wilmington, N.C., Mar. 7, 1945; s. Arnaldo and Frances (Casteen) S.; m. Mary Alice Dassenko, Sept. 4, 1966; children: Benjamin, Matthew. BA, Andrews U., 1967; MA, U. Mich., 1968, PhD, 1976. From instr. to prof. Walla Walla Coll., College Place, Wash., 1969-85; prof. history U. Idaho, Moscow, 1984—; cons. TV History of Idaho, 1988. Author: Coxey's Army: An American Odyssey, 1985, The Pacific Northwest: An Interpretive History, 1989, In Mountain Shadows: A History of Idaho, 1991, Railroad Signatures Across the Pacific Northwest, 1993; also author or editor 7 other books; mem. editl. bd. Pacific N.W. Quar., 1982-97, Idaho Yesterdays, 1987—, Forest and Conservation History, 1988-95, Pacific Hist. Rev., 1991-95; contbr. articles to profl. jours. NEH fellow, 1982-83, rsch. fellow Idaho Humanities Coun., 1989-90; Idaho State Bd. Edn. rsch. grantee, 1990-91. Mem. Orgn. Am. Historians, Western History Assn., Mining History Assn. (coun. 1990-94), Lexington Soc., Idaho State Hist. Soc. Republican. Seventh-day Adventist. Avocations: photography, backpacking, travel. Office: U Idaho Dept History Moscow ID 83844

SCHWANZ, KATHLEEN ANN, librarian; b. Spokane, Wash., Mar. 3, 1957; d. Michael Vincent Jr. and Carol Joy (Miller) Walsh; m. Daniel Carl Schwanz, Aug. 22, 1980. BS in Social Work, Ea. Wash. U., 1979; MLS in Libr. and Info. Sci., U. Wash., 1989. Lic. libr., Wash. Ref. libr. Carroll Coll., Helena, Mont., 1989-91; hosp. libr. Ballard Cmty. Hosp., Seattle, 1992; ref. libr. Highline C.C., Des Moines, Wash., 1992-93; br. campus libr. Wash. State U., Spokane, 1995—; mem. local arrangements com. for Gov.'s Conf., Helena, 1991; acad. libr. rep. Wash. State Adv. Coun. Librs., Olympia, 1998—. Mem. ALA, Assn. Coll. and Rsch. Librs., Distance Edn. Sect. Democrat. Office: Wash State Univ 668 N Riverpoint Blvd Spokane WA 99202-1677

SCHWARTZ, BERNARD JULIAN, lawyer; b. Edmonton, Alberta, Can., July 29, 1960; came to U.S., 1982; s. Sol and Anne (Motkovich) S. BA, U. Alberta, 1981; JD, McGeorge Sch. Law, 1986. Bar: U.S. Supreme Ct. 1991. Atty. Ropers, Majeski, San Francisco, 1987-88, Riverside County Pub. Defenders, Riverside, Calif., 1988-89; pvt. practice Riverside, 1990—. Coach Riverside County H.S. Mock Trial Team, 1990, 96, 97. Mem. Calif. Attys. Criminal Justice, Calif. Pub. Defenders Assn., Riverside County Bar Assn. Home: 6157 Hillary Ct Riverside CA 92506-2139

SCHWARTZ, CHERIE ANNE KARO, storyteller, writer; b. Miami, Fla., Feb. 24, 1951; d. William Howard and Dorothy (Olesh) Karo; m. Lawrence Schwartz, Aug. 12, 1979. BA in Lit., The Colo. Coll., 1973; MA in Devel. Theater, U. Colo., 1977. Tchr. English, drame, mime, creative writing, speech coach South High Sch., Pueblo, Colo., 1973-76; tchr. English and drama Rocky Mountain Hebrew Acad., Denver, 1981-83; full-time profl. storyteller throughout N.Am., 1982—; storyteller, docent, tchr. tng., mus. outreach Denver Mus. Natural History, 1982—; trainer, cons., performer, lectr, keynote speaker various orgns., synagogues, instns., agys., confs. throughout the country, 1982—; co-founder, chairperson Omanim b'Yachad: Artists Together, Nat. Conf. Celebrating Storytelling, Drama, Music and Dance in Jewish Edn., Denver, 1993. Storyteller: (audio cassette tapes) Cherie Karo Schwartz Tells Stories of Hanukkah from Kar-Ben Books, 1986, Cherie Karo Schwartz Tells Stories of Passover From Kar-Ben Books, 1986, Miriam's Trambourine, 1988, Worldwide Jewish Stories of Wishes and Wisdom, 1988; storyteller, actor: (video tape) The Wonderful World of Recycle, 1989; author: (book) My Lucky Dreidel: Hanukkah Stories, Songs, Crafts, Recipes and Fun for Kids, 1994; author numerous stories in anthologies of Jewish lit., including Chosen Tales, Because G-d Loves Stories, Reading Between the Lines. Title III grantee State of Colo. Edn., Pueblo, 1975-76. Mem. Coalition for Advancement of Jewish Edn. (coord. Jewish Storytelling Conf. 1989-98, coord. Nat. Jewish Storytelling Network 1994-97), Nat. Assn. for Preservation and Perpetuation of Storytelling, Nat. Storytelling Assn. (Colo. state rep. and liaison), Rocky Mountain Storytelling Guild, Rocky Mountain Storyteller's Conf. (bd. mem., performer, tchr.). Democrat. Jewish. Home: 996 S Florence St Denver CO 80231-1952

SCHWARTZ, JOHN LEONARD, publishing executive, psychiatrist; b. Washington, Jan. 2, 1946; s. Harry and Ruth (Blumner) S.; divorced; children: David, Mark. Student, MIT, 1962-64; BA, Columbia Coll., 1966; MD, N.Y. U., 1970. Diplomate Am. Bd. Psychiatry. Chmn., psychiatry Children's Hosp., Orange, Calif., 1976-84; chmn., psychiatry Western Med. Ctr., Santa Ana, Calif., 1975-86, pres., med. staff, 1980-82; psychiatrist-in-chief Western Med. Ctr., Anaheim, Calif., 1981-84, United Western Med. Ctr., Santa Ana, 1980-86; chief exec. officer Continuing Med. Edn., Inc., Santa Ana, 1978—; editor-in-chief The Psychiatric Times, Santa Ana, 1984—. Fellow Am. Psychiat. Assn., Am. Assn. for Social Psychiatry, Am. Acad. Child Psychiatrists. Republican. Jewish. Avocations: jogging, bike riding, automobile collecting. Office: CME Inc 2801 McGraw Ave Irvine CA 92614

SCHWARTZ, MICHAEL LEE, financial planner, consultant; b. Chgo., Dec. 8, 1945; s. Harry and Charlotte (Rose) S.; m. Patricia Helen Chapman, Jan. 15, 1972; children: Scott Daniel, Michelle Lynn. CFP, CFS, RFC, CFdC; Certified Benefits Instr. Field engr. Storage Tech. Corp., Chgo., 1973-76; v.p. AMS Life Ins. Co., Bridgeview, Ill., 1976-81; pres. Wealth Masters Inc., Rolling Meadows, Ill., 1981—; instr. Morraine Valley Community Coll., Worth, Ill., 1985-87, St. Xavier Coll., Chgo., 1986-87, Prairie State U., Chicago Heights, Ill., 1987. Mem. Nat. Coun. on the Aging, 1991-93. Mem. Inst. CFPs, Internat. Assn. of Registered Fin. Consultants, Internat. Assn. Fin. Planning, Inst. Cert. Fund Specialists, Colorado Assn. of Chartered Fid. Cons. Avocations: amateur radio, racquet ball, traveling. Office: Wealth Masters Inc 7500 E Arapahoe Rd Ste 101 Englewood CO 80112-1276

SCHWARTZ, ROBERT JOHN, landscape contractor, landscape designer; b. Elkhorn, Wis., June 14, 1954; s. Robert Knilans and Mary Cosella (Fleming) S. 2 BS degrees cum laude, U. Wis., Stevens Point, 1976; AA in Landscape Design ad hoc, U. Minn., 1985; AA, Calif. Poly. Inst., Pomona. Lic. landscape contractor, Calif., Nev. Real estate broker, salesman McKy-Ellis Realtors Madison Wis., Janesville, Wis., 1979-80; sole proprietor Tetonic Landscapes Co., Milw., 1982-85, Rialto, Calif., 1985—. Supporter St. Joseph's Indian Sch., Chamberlain, S.D., 1986—, Mercy Home for Boys and Girls, Chgo., 1986—, Asian Relief, Inc., Riverdale, Md., 1986—, So. Poverty Law Ctr., Montgomery, Ala., 1991-93; active The Heritage Found., Washington, 1992—, The Wall of Liberty Nat. Found., Washington, 1993—, Am. Conservative Union, Washington, 1993—. Recipient City Hall Coun. citations City of Claremont, Calif., 1986-87, City of Upland, Calif., 1989. Republican. Avocations: para-sailing, traveling, ancient and medieval European Armaments collecting, teutonic landscapes. Home and Office: 9709 Double Rock Dr Las Vegas NV 89134-6409

SCHWARTZ, ROBERT LEWIS, law educator; b. Los Angeles, June 22, 1948; s. Jerome W. and Selma (Meyers) S.; m. Jane Zwisohn, Dec. 23, 1973; children: Mirra, Elana. BA, Stanford U., 1966; JD, Harvard U., 1975. Bar: Am. Samoa 1973, N.Mex. 1975, N.Y. 1982, U.S. Dist. Ct. N.Mex., U.S. Ct. Appeals (10th cir.) 1975, U.S. Supreme Ct. 1982. Legal rsch. assoc. High Ct. Am. Samoa, Pago Pago, 1973-74; assoc. law firm Rodey, Dickason, SLoan, Akin & Robb, Albuquerque, 1974-75; gen. counsel N.M. Dept. Human Svcs., Santa Fe, 1986; vis. prof. U. Delhi, India, 1985; prof. law U. N.M., Albuquerque, 1977—; postdoctoral fellow Hastings Ctr., 1980-81; vis. scholar Wolfson Coll., Cambridge (Eng.) U., 1984-85, Grayson disting. vos. prof. SIU Carbondale, 1996-97. Author/editor: Health Law, 3d edit., 1997; contbr. articles to profl. jours. Chair N.Mex. Health Policy Commn., 1991-92. Democrat. Jewish. Office: Univ of New Mexico Albuquerque NM 87131

SCHWARTZ, STEPHEN ALFRED, historian, journalist; b. Columbus, Ohio, Sept. 9, 1948; s. Horace Osman and Mayme Eileene (McKinney) S.; m. Mary Uhren, July 7, 1969 (div. 1974); 1 child, Matthew. AA, City Coll., San Francisco, 1972; student, U. Calif., Berkeley, 1972, 76, 89-90. Freelance writer San Francisco, 1966-81; sr. editor Internat. Thomson Bus. Press, San Francisco, 1981-84; historian Sailors Union Pacific, AFL-CIO, San Francisco, 1983-86; fellow Inst. for Contemporary Studies, San Francisco, 1984-89; writer San Francisco Chronicle, 1989—; cons. U.S. Inst. for Peace, Washington, 1988, U.S. Info. Agy.; steward publicist Brotherhood By Clks., AFL-CIO, San Francisco, 1973-81; publicist Fomento Obrero, San Francisco, 1977-83; sec. No. Calif. Media Workers Guild Typographical Union, AFL-CIO, 1996—; guest speaker Am. Assn. for Advancement Slavic Studies, Phoenix, 1992, Mont Pelerin Soc., Indpls., 1987, Inst. Catalan Studies, Barcelona, 1986; publicist ARDE/Nicaraguense, San Francisco, 1983-85; cons. author Hoover Inst., 1989-91. Author: From West to East, 1998, A Strange Silence, 1992, Brotherhood of the Sea, 1986; co-authro: Spanish Marxism vs. Soviet Communism, 1988; editor: The Transition, 1987; N.Am. editor: Arguments & Facts Internat., 1989—; translator: What is Surrealism?, 1978; editor The Albanian Cath. Newsletter, 1998—. Earhart Found. fellow, 1987, 89; rsch. fellow Olin Found., 1988-89. Mem. No. Calif. Newspaper Guild, AFL-CIO (sec. 1996—). Jewish. Avocations: poetry, modern art, lang. studies. Office: San Francisco Chronicle San Francisco CA 94119

SCHWARTZ, STEVEN, author, English language educator; b. Chester, Pa., May 3, 1950; s. Benjamin and Jeannette (Pearlmutter) S.; m. Emily Moore Hammond, May 25, 1985; children: Zachary, Elena. BA in Psychology, U. Colo., 1973; MFA in Creative Writing, U. Ariz., 1981. Instr. U. New Orleans, 1982-84; assoc. prof. dept. English, Colo. State U., Ft. Collins, 1984—. Author: To Leningrad in Winter, 1985, Therapy, 1994, A Good Doctor's Son, 1998, Lives of the Fathers (short story collection), 1991. Recipient Nelson Algren award Chgo. Tribune, 1988, O.Henry award, Doubleday and Co., 1983, 91; grantee NEA, Washington, 1993. Office: Colo State U Dept English Fort Collins CO 80523

SCHWARTZMAN, GLENDA JOY, artist; b. L.A., Dec. 24, 1939; d. Morton and Thelma Lorrain (Bryer) S.; m. Leonard I. Schwartzman, June 21, 1961 (div. Sept. 1973); children: James Elliot, Eric Bennett. Student, Otis Art Inst., Calif., 1958, Chouinard Art Inst., Calif., 1959-60. One-woman shows include: Angeles Press, L.A., 1990, Boringer Gallery, Dallas, 1988, Krieger Gallery, Santa Barbara, Calif., 1987, SOMA Exhbns., Denver, 1986, De Vorsan Gallery, 1987, Inamori, Beverly Hills, Calif., 1982, Lelia Ivy Gallery, Santa Monica, Calif., 1982, others; group shows include TransAmerica Bldg., San Francisco, 1990, Wells Fargo Bank, L.A., 1990, La Jolla (Calif.) Mus., 1990, 1989, Col.-Jems Studios, others; work in pub. and pvt. collections; author: (book) Art in California, 1990. Mem. Dems., Calif., Benedict Canyon. Recipient fine art scholarship Otist Art Inst. Mem. Calif. Yacht Club, So. Calif. Women's Caucas for Art. Jewish. Avocations: chess, bridge, boating. Office: Glenda Schwartzman Studio 807 Hampton Dr Venice CA 90291-3020

SCHWARZ, GERARD, conductor, musician; b. Weehawken, N.J., Aug. 19, 1947; s. John and Gerta (Weiss) S.; m. Jody Greitzer, June 23, 1984; children: Alysandra, Daniel, Gabriella, Julian. BS, Juilliard Sch., 1972, MA, 1972; DFA (hon.), Fairleigh Dickinson U., Seattle U.; DMus (hon.), U. Puget Sound. Trumpet player Am. Symphony Orch., 1965-72, Am. Brass Quintet, 1965-73, N.Y. Philharm., 1973-77; trumpet player, guest condr. Aspen Music Festival, 1969-75, bd. dirs., 1973-75; music dir. Erick Hawkins Dance Co., 1967-72, SoHo Ensemble, 1969-75, Eliot Feld Ballet Co., N.Y.C., 1972-78; Music Sch. Princeton (N.J.) U.; music dir. N.Y. Chamber Symphony, 1977—, L.A. Chamber Orch., 1978-86, White Mountains (N.H.) Music Festival, 1978-80, Music Today at Merkin Concert Hall, N.Y.C., 1988-89; music advisor Mostly Mozart Festival, Lincoln Ctr., N.Y.C., 1982-84, music dir., 1984—; music advisor Seattle Symphony, 1983-84, prin. condr., 1984-85, music dir., 1985—; artistic advisor Tokyu Bunkamura's Orchard Hall, Japan, 1994—; mem. faculty Juilliard Sch., N.Y.C., 1975-83, Mannes Coll. Music, 1973-79, Montclair (N.J.) State Coll., 1975-80; guest condr. various orchs. including Phila. Orch., L.A. Philharmonic, St. Louis, Buffalo, Detroit, San Francisco, Atlanta, Houston, Pitts., Minn., Jerusalem Symphony, Israel Chamber Orch., Moscow Philharmonic, Moscow Radio Orch., Orch. Nat. de France, Paris, London Symphony Orch., Frankfurt Radio, Stockholm Radio, Helsinki Philharm., Ensemble InterContemporain, Monte Carlo Philharm., Nat. Orch. Spain, English Chamber Orch., London Symphony, Scottish Chamber Orch., City of Birmingham (Eng.) Symphony, Nouvel Orchestre Philharmonique, Sydney (Australia) Symphony, Melbourne (Australia) Symphony, Orchestre National de Lyon, France, Orchestre Philharm. de Montpellier, France, Washington Opera, Da Capo Chamber Players, 20th Century Chamber Orch., Chamber Music Soc. Lincoln Ctr., San Francisco Opera, Seattle Opera, Tokyu Bunkamura, Japan, Residentie Orch. of The Hague, The Netherlands, St. Louis Symphony, London Mozart Players, Kirov Orch., St. Petersburg, Russia, Tokyo Philharm., Royal Liverpool (Eng.) Philharm., Vancouver (Can.) Symphony Orch., City of London Symphonia, Evian Festival in France, 1994; also numerous appearances on TV; rec. artist Columbia, Nonesuch, Vox, MMO, Desto, Angel, Delos records; record: Seattle Symphony 1994-95 Season, 1995, New Orch. of Japan, 1998. Bd. dirs. Naumburg Found., 1975—. Recipient award for concert artists Ford Found., 1973, Grammy award nominee, Mumms Ovation award, Record of Yr. awards, Ditson Condrs. award Columbia U., 1989; named Condr. of Yr., Musical Am. Internat. Directory of Performing Arts, 1994.

SCHWARZ, GLENN VERNON, editor; b. Chgo., Nov. 24, 1947; s. Vernon Edward and LaVerne Louise (Schuster) S.; m. Cynthia Frances Meisenhoelder, June 17, 1984; 1 child, Chloe. BA, San Francisco State U., 1970. Sports writer San Francisco Examiner, 1970-87, sports editor, 1988—. Fundraiser San Francisco Zoological Soc., 1987—. Mem. AP Sports Editors, Baseball Writers Assn. Am. (bd. dirs. 1986-87). Avocation: nature travel. Office: San Francisco Examiner 110 5th St San Francisco CA 94103-2918*

SCHWARZ, JOSEPH RICHARD, engineering manager; b. Pomona, Calif., Dec. 7, 1954; s. Robert Joseph and Edith M. (Varian) S.; m. Pamela Anne Galligan, Apr. 8, 1978 (div. June 1983); m. Kathleen Linda Varder, Aug. 23, 1996. BSEE magna cum laude, Calif. State Polytech. U., Pomona, 1977. Digital systems engr. Metron Corp., Upland, Calif., 1977-78; installation mgr. Hughes Aircraft, Denmark, Hawaii and Fed. Republic Germany, 1978-88; co-owner Penrose Gallery, Big Bear Lake, Calif., 1988-90; system engr. Gen. Dynamics, Pomona, Calif., 1989-91; ops. mgr. Amacron/Cycad Corp., Rancho Cucamonga, Calif., 1991-94; sr. system engr. Sysecca Inc., Marina del Rey, Calif., 1995—; installation mgr. Chgo. Transit Authority Supervisory Control Sys., Balt. Transit Authority. Telephone counselor Garden Grove (Calif.) Community Ch., 1984-90. Mem. ACLU, L.A. Music Ctr., Sierra Club, Toastmasters, Eta Kappa Nu, Tau Beta Pi. Republican. Avocations: skiing, classic automobiles. Home: 7903 Appaloosa Ct Alta Loma CA 91701-1202

SCHWARZ, MICHAEL, lawyer; b. Brookline, Mass., Oct. 19, 1952; s. Jules Lewis and Estelle (Kosberg) S.; m. Rebecca Handy; 1 child, Patrick Joshua Charles. BA magna cum laude, U. No. Colo., 1975; postgrad. U. N.Mex., 1977, JD, 1980; Rsch. reader in Negligence Law, Oxford U., 1978; diploma in Legal Studies, Cambridge U., 1981. Bar: N.Mex. 1980, U.S. Dist. Ct. N.Mex. 1980, U.S. Ct. Appeals (10th, D.C., and Fed. cirs.) 1982, U.S. Ct. Internat. Trade, 1982, U.S. Tax Ct. 1982, U.S. Supreme Ct. 1983, N.Y. 1987. VISTA vol., Albuquerque, 1975-77; rsch. fellow N.Mex. Legal Support Project, Albuquerque, 1978-79; supr. law Cambridge (Eng.) U., 1980-81; law clk. to chief justice Supreme Ct. N.Mex., Santa Fe, 1981-82; pvt. practice law, Santa Fe, 1982—; spl. prosecutor City of Santa Fe, 1985; spl. asst. atty. gen., 1986-88; mem. editorial adv. com. Social Security Reporting Svc., 1983-95. Author: New Mexico Appellate Manual, 1990, 2nd. edit., 1996; contbr. articles to profl. jours. Vice dir. Colo. Pub. Interest Rsch. Group, 1974; scoutmaster Great S.W. Area coun. Boy Scouts Am., 1977-79; mem. N.Mex. Acupuncture Licensing Bd., 1983. Recipient Cert. of Appreciation Cambridge U., 1981, Nathan Burkan Meml. award, 1980, N.Mex. Supreme Ct. Cert. Recognition, 1992, 93, 95. Mem. ABA (litigation com. on profl. responsibility, litigation com. on pretrial practice and discovery, TIPS, appelate sect., 10th cir. editor 1998), ATLA, Am. Arbit. Assn., Bar Assn. U.S. Dist. Ct. Dist. N.Mex., State Bar N.Y., N.Mex. State Bar (bd. dirs. employment law sect. 1990-96, chair employment law sect. 1991-92, bd/ dirs. family law sect., 1998—), N.Y. Bar Assn., First Jud. Dist. Bar Assn. (treas. 1987-88, sec. 1988-89, v.p. 1989-1990, pres. 1990-91, local rules com. mem. 1989-92), U.S. Dist. Ct. N.Mex. (local civil rules com. 1997—), N.Mex. Supreme Ct. (standing com. on profl. conduct 1990—, chmn. 1998), Am. Inns. of Ct. N.Mex. (barrister), Nat. Employment Lawyers Assn. (Nat. chpt., N.Mex. chpt.), Defenders of Wildlife, Amnesty Internat., Internat Wolf Ctr. Home and Office: PO Box 1656 Santa Fe NM 87504-1656

SCHWARZER, WILLIAM W, federal judge; b. Berlin, Apr. 30, 1925; came to U.S., 1938, naturalized, 1944; s. John F. and Edith M. (Daniel) S.; m. Anne Halbersleben, Feb. 2, 1951; children: Jane Elizabeth, Andrew William. AB cum laude, U. So. Calif., 1948; LLB cum laude, Harvard U., 1951. Bar: Calif. 1953, U.S. Supreme Ct. 1967. Teaching fellow Harvard U. Law Sch., 1951-52; asso. firm McCutchen, Doyle, Brown & Enersen, San Francisco, 1952-60; ptnr. McCutchen, Doyle, Brown & Enersen, 1960-76; judge U.S. Dist. Ct (no. dist.) Calif., San Francisco, 1976—; dir. Fed. Jud. Ctr., Washington, 1990-95; sr. counsel Pres.'s Commn. on CIA Activities Within the U.S., 1975; chmn. U.S. Jud. Conf. Com. Fed.-State Jurisdiction, 1987-90; mem. faculty Nat. Inst. Trial Advocacy, Fed. Jud. Ctr., All-ABA, U.S.-Can. Legal Exch., 1987, Anglo-U.S. Jud. Exch., 1994-95, Salzburg Seminar on Am. Studies; disting. prof. Hastings Coll. Law U. Calif. Author: Managing Antitrust and Other Complex Litigation, 1982, Civil Discovery and Manadatory Disclosure, 1994, Federal Civil Procedure Before Trial, 1994; contbr. articles to legal publs., aviation jours. Trustee World Affairs Coun. No. Calif., 1961-88; chmn. bd. trustees Marin Country Day Sch., 1963-66; mem. Marin County Aviation Commn., 1969-76; mem. vis. com. Harvard Law Sch., 1981-86. Served with Intelligence, U.S. Army, 1943-46. Fellow Am. Coll. Trial Lawyers (S. Gates award 1992), Am. Bar Found.; mem. ABA (Meador Rosenberg award 1995), Am. Law Inst., San Francisco Bar Assn., State Bar Calif., Coun. Fgn. Rels. Office: 450 Golden Gate Ave San Francisco CA 94102-3661

SCHWEIGERT, BYRON FREDERICK, health services administrator; b. Orange, Ca., Feb. 20, 1947; s. Frederick Albert and Alma (Helgasom) S.; m. Katherine Elise Yeager Schweigert, Aug. 20, 1969; children: Tracie Lynn, Robin Elise. Pharm. D., San Francisco Sch. Pharm., 1970. Registered pharmacist Ca., Nev. Asst. dir. pharmacy svs. Meml. Med. Ctr., Long Beach, Ca., 1971-77; v.p. Pharmacy Consulting Svcs., Inc., Huntington Beach, Ca., 1975-81; assoc. dir. pharm. svcs. Long Beach Meml. Med. Ctr., Long Beach, 1977-91; dir. pharm. svcs. Long Beach Meml. Med. Ctr., 1991, v.p. pharm. svcs., 1991-96; spl. asst. to the pres. Meml. Health Svcs., Long Beach, 1996—; adj. asst. prof. pharm. practice U. So. Calif. Sch. Pharm., L.A., 1991—; asst. clin. prof. Dept. Clin. Pharm., U. Calif. San Francisco Sch. of Pharm., 1980—. Contbr. artiles to prof. jours. Del. Am. Soc. Hosp. Pharmacists representing CSHP, 1989-91, 1994, 1995; bd. dirs. Calif. Soc. Hosp. Pharmacists, 1985-88 (Hosp. Pharmacist of the Year award, 1988); doping control coord. Games of the XXIIIrd Olympiad, L.A., 1984. Recipient Hosps. Pharmacist of the Year award Orange Count Soc. Hosp. Pharmacist, 1985. Mem. Voluntary Hosps. Am. (chmn. clin. svcs. com. 1992-93), Pharm. Practice TaskForce, Voluntary Hosps. Am. Nat. Pharm. Adv. Com. Republican. Avocations: golf, backpacking, gardening, cycling. Office: Meml Health Svcs 9900 Talbert Ave Fl 3 Fountain Valley CA 92708-5153

SCHWEIKART, DEBORA ELLEN, lawyer; b. Belfonte, Pa., Apr. 14, 1971; d. Kenneth Earl and Catherine Joyce (Seaman) S. BA in Russian Lang. and Lit., U. Pitts., 1992, JD, 1996. Bar: Pa. Rsch. asst. U. Pitts. Sch. Law, 1994-96, teaching asst., 1994-95; teaching asst. Pa. Govs. Sch. Internat. Studies, Pitts., 1994-96; atty. Peterson Cons., Pitts., 1997; jud. clk. N.Mex. Ct. Appeals, 1997-99. Contbr. articles to profl. publs. Scholar Internat. Christian Youth Exch., Ronde, Denmark, 1989, Am. Coun. Tchrs. Russian, 1992, Internat. Women's Club, 1992, U. Pitts., 1996. Mem. Dona Anna County Bar Assn. (treas.), Tonali Women's Legal Alliance, Am. Inns of Ct., Kappa Alpha Theta (house dir. 1996-97). Avocations: photography, horseback riding, dance, horseback riding. Home: Apt 302C 3333 Majestic Ridge Las Cruces NM 88011 Office: 201 W Picacho Ave Ste C Las Cruces NM 88005-1833

SCHWEIZER, EDWARD SOWERS, television network executive; b. Houston, May 6, 1938; s. John Mel Jr. and Alicia Lucille (Sowers) S.; m. Suzan Lee Peterson, June 20, 1964; children: Edward Jr., Sally, Elizabeth. Degre superieur, U. Paris, 1957; BA, Occidental Coll., 1961; MA, Pepperdine U., 1978. Cert. surface warfare officer USN. Owner ESS Ins. Svcs., Mission Viejo, Calif., 1989—; exec. The Peoples Network, Dallas, 1996—; mem. bd. Laguna Beach Pageant of the Masters; mem. adv. bd. San Diego Found., 1998-99, Orange County Register, Santa Ana, Calif., 1998-99. Commr. City of Mission Viejo, 1990-92, 97—. Capt. USN, 1962-88. Decorated Meritorious Svc. medal. Mem. Ret. Officers Assn., Res. Officers Assn., Naval Res. Assn., KC (Brother Knight, Grand Knight 1989-90), Navy League of the U.S. Republican. Roman Catholic. Avocations: civic affairs, fine art, international traveling, running, ocean swimming, skiing.

SCHWENNESEN, CAROL ANN, artist, educator; b. Orange, Calif., Aug. 28, 1945; d. Jarvis Larson and Marie Theresa (Riedel) S.; children: Aaron, Molly, Leslie. BA in Art History magna cum laude, Western Wash. U., Bellingham, 1984, BFA, 1984; MFA, Claremont (Calif.) Grad. U., 1987. Cert. tchr., Calif. Lectr. art Cypress (Calif.) Coll., 1987, Mt. San Antonio Coll., Walnut, Calif., 1987-89, Chaffey Coll., Alta Loma, Calif., 1988-90; asst. prof. Scripps Coll., Claremont, Calif., 1988-90; instr. Blue Heron Art Ctr., Vashon Island, Wash., 1990-96; adj. faculty Crafton Hills Coll., Yucaipa, Calif., 1997—; cons. ABC-TV, N.Y., Calif., 1990, Fortune 500, Washington, 1996; juror Art in Pub. Places, King County/Metro Seattle, 1993, King County Work-Study Acad. Tng. Program, Vashon H.S., Seattle, Tacoma, Vashon Island, Wash., 1994-97. Artist paintings, drawings in Beetlejuice, 1988; group shows include Silverwood Gallery, Vashon Island, Wash., Art Works Gallery, Riverside, Calif. Recipient merit scholarship Swedish Club L.A., 1985, travel grant Coll. Art Assn., N.Y., 1994. Mem. Coll. Art Assn. Avocations: physics, psychoneuroimmunology, systems of teaching/learning. Home and Office: 16939 Westside Hwy SW Vashon WA 98070-4405

SCHWERTFEGER, FRANK DENNIS, lawyer; b. Chgo., Nov. 25, 1960; s. Thomas Leo and Frances Grace (Vacarro) S.; m. Kathy McCuskey, Jul. 8, 1995; children: Alexandra, Thomas. BA, Northwestern Univ., 1983; JD, Georgetown Law Ctr., 1986. Bar: Calif. Assoc. Urrick, Herrington & Sutcliffe, L.A., 1986-88, Riordan & McKinzie, L.A., 1988-95; v.p., gen. coun. Coast Asset Mgmt. Corp., L.A., 1995—; dir. Coast Fund L.P., Cayman Islands, 1995—. Office: Coast Asset Mgmt Corp 725 Arizona Ave Ste 400 Santa Monica CA 90401-1723

SCHWICHTENBERG, DARYL ROBERT, drilling engineer; b. nr. Tulare, S.D., Nov. 8, 1929; s. Robert Carl and Lillian Rose (Hardie) S.; m. Helen M. Spencer, 1955 (div. Jan. 1971); children: Helayne, Randall, Hyalyn, Halcyon, Rustan; m. Helen Elizabeth Doehring, Nov. 11, 1971 (div. May 1982); 1

child, Suzanne. Student, U. Wyo., 1954-55; BSME, S.D. Sch. Mines and Tech., 1957; postgrad., Alexander Hamilton Inst., N.Y.C., 1962-63. Lic. pilot, rated AMEL. Office engr. Ingersoll-Rand Co., Mpls., 1957-58; sub br. mgr. Ingersoll-Rand Co., Duluth, Minn., 1959-60; product engr. Ingersoll-Rand Co., N.Y.C., 1960-63, devel. engr., 1964; sales mgr. Ingersoll-Rand Co., Phillipsburg, N.J., 1965; pres., founder Daryl Drilling Co., Inc., Flagstaff, Ariz., 1965-82; pres. Silent Rose Mining Co., Fallon, Nev., 1982-85; sr. design engr. Nev. Test Site Fenix & Scisson, 1985-90; prin. project engr. Raytheon Svcs. Nev., 1990-95; project mgr. Raytheon Svcs. Nev., Nev. Test Site, 1995-96; asst.project mgr. Bechtel Nev., Las Vegas, 1996—; co-owner, mgr. Dead Shot Ranch, Bondurant, Wyo., 1977-82. Inventor electronic subtitling for opera patrons. 1st lt. U.S. Army, 1950-54, Korea. Decorated Bronze Star. Mem. ASME, NRA, VFW, Inst. Shaft Drilling Tech. (speaker, instr. 1986-96), Am. Legion, Mensa. Republican. Avocations: hunting, raising and training horses, flying, prospecting. Office: Bechtel Nev M/S NTS-330 PO Box 98521 Las Vegas NV 89193-8521

SCHWIND, DAVID ALAN, historical researcher, writer; b. Arcadia, Calif., Oct. 2, 1975; s. Rodger Anthony and Barbara Jean (Skaer) S. BS, Regents Coll., 1998. English instr. Moscow Dept. Edn., 1993; team leader Air Land Emergency Resource Team, Watersmeet, Mich., 1994; asst. project mgr. Hopkins Constrn., Bridgeville, Del., 1995; dir. distbn. Moscow (Russia) News, 1996; English editor Russian Info. Agy., Moscow, 1996. At-Risk youth counselor, Indpls. Juvenile Justice Dept., 1993. Ensign USN, 1998. Recipient Conspicuous Svc. award City of Indpls., 1993, Disting. Svc. award Moscow Dept. Edn., 1994, City of Knoxville, 1995, U.S. Congress commendation on Congl. record, 1992, 93, 94. Mem. Navy League of U.S., United States Naval Inst. (assoc.). Avocations: polit. studies, internat. travel, playing bagpipes, running. Home: 2335 S 3rd Ave Arcadia CA 91006-5304

SCHWINKENDORF, KEVIN NEIL, nuclear engineer; b. Newberg, Oreg., Mar. 11, 1959; s. Waldemar Adolf and Hattie Bertha (Baumgarten) S. BS, Oreg. State U., 1981, MS, 1983; PhD, U. Wash., 1996. Reg. profl. engr., Wash. Advanced engr. UNC Nuclear Industries, Richland, Wash., 1983-84, engr., 1986-87; sr. engr. Westinghouse Hanford Co., Richland, 1987-96, Fluor Daniel Northwest, Richland, 1996—; ptnr. Three Rivers Techs., 1998—; v.p. numerical methods, Analyst Devel. Corp., Scappoose, Oreg., 1990—. Designer: (ballistics software) PC-Bullet-ADCs, 1990 (Best Paper award 1992); author tech. publ. in field; co-patentee of rifle barrel vibration control; co-patentee in rifle barrel vibration control. Participant March of Dimes Walk-a-Thon, Richland, 1989, 90. Mem. Am. Nuclear Soc., NSPE, NRA, Soc. Computer Simulation, Safari Club Internat., Tau Beta Pi. Republican. Avocations: hunting, target shooting, personal computing, model building, bicycling. Home: 1121 Pine St Richland WA 99352-2135 Office: FDNW Criticality & Shielding MSIN B4-44 PO Box 1050 Richland WA 99352-1050

SCHWYN, CHARLES EDWARD, accountant; b. Muncie, Ind., Oct. 12, 1932; s. John and Lela Mae (Oliver) S.; m. Mary Helen Nickey, May 25, 1952 (dec.); children: Douglas, Craig, Beth; m. Madelyn Steinmetz, June 26, 1993. BS, Ball State U., 1957. CPA, Calif., D.C. With Haskins, Sells & Orlando, Chgo., Orlando, Fla., 1958-67; mgr. Deloitte, Haskins & Sells, Milan, Italy, 1967-70, San Francisco, 1970-80; with Deloitte, Haskins & Sells (now Deloitte & Touche), Oakland, Calif., ptnr. in charge, 1980-92, ret., 1992. Bd. dirs. Jr. Ctr. Art and Sci., 1982-89, pres., 1987-88; bd. dirs., trustee Oakland Symphony, 1982-86, 89-91; bd. dirs. Oakland Met. YMCA, 1984-89, Oakland Police Activities League, 1981-91, Joe Morgan Youth Found., 1982-91, Summit Med. Ctr., 1989-94, 96—, Marcus A. Foster Ednl. Inst., 1986-95, pres., 1991-93; bd. dirs. Greater Oakland Internat. Trade Ctr., 1996; mem. adv. bd. Festival of Lake, 1984-89, U. Oakland Met. Forum, 1991—; co-chmn. Commn. for Positive Change in Oakland Pub. Schs., 1989-91; mem. campaign cabinet United Way Bay Area, 1989; bd. regents Samuel Merritt Coll., 1993—; chmn., bd. regents, 1996—; chief of protocol, City of Oakland, 1996-97; mem. Calif. Coun. of the Oakland Mus. of Calif. Found., 1997—. With USN, 1952-56. Recipient Cmty. Svc. award Kiwanis Club, Cert. Recognition Calif. Legis. Assembly, 1988, Ctr. for Ind. Living award, Oakland Bus. Arts award for outstanding bus. leader Oakland C. of C., 1992, Schwyn Endowment fund for cancer rsch. Bay Area Tumor Inst., 1998; honoree Bay Area Tumor Inst., Schwin Endowment Fund for Cancer Rsch.; date of job retirement honored in his name by Oakland mayor; named Knight Order of St. John of Jerusalem Knights Hospitaller. Mem. AICPA (coun. 1987-90), Oakland C. of C. (chmn. bd. dirs. 1987-88, exec. com. 1982-89), Oakland Met. C. of C., pres., 1996, Calif. Soc. CPAs (bd. dirs. 1979-81, 83-84, 85-87, pres. San Francisco chpt. 1983-84), Nat. Assn. Accts. (pres. Fla. chpt. 1967), Claremont Country Club (treas., bd. dirs. 1989-97), Lakeview Club (bd. govs. 1987-92), Oakland 100 Club (pres. 1994), Rotary (bd. dirs. Oakland club 1986-88, 91-92, treas. 1984-86, pres. 1991-92).

SCHY, GAY, artist, investor; b. Greenwich, Conn., July 10, 1937; d. Ralph Morrel and Dorothy (Abrams) Griswold; m. John Craver (div. 1974); 1 child, Linda Craver; m. Charles W. Torrey, July 22, 1979. BS, U. Chgo., 1959, MSW, 1964; MA, San Jose State U., 1989, MFA, 1990. Social worker Santa Clara County, San Jose, Calif., 1970-80, pvt. practice, Los Gatos, Calif., 1980-86; artist Santa Cruz, Calif., 1986—; represented by Fredrick Spratt Gallery, San Jose, Calif.; bd. dirs. San Jose State Sch. Art and Design, 1988-92; advisor, bd. dirs. San Jose Inst. for Contemporary Art, 1990—. Vol. Habitat for Humanities, Santa Cruz, 1991—, U. Calif. Santa Cruze Arboratum, 1996—. Avocations: gardening, bicycling, reading, travel, swimming. Home: 3040 Pleasant Valley Rd Aptos CA 95003-9716

SCIAME, DONALD RICHARD, computer systems analyst, dentist, magician, locksmith; b. Bklyn., Sept. 10, 1945; s. Mario and Ruth Marie (Kozell) S.; m. Kathy Ann Thamann, Mar. 17, 1987. AB, Rutgers U., 1967; DMD, N.J. Coll. Medicine & Dentistry, 1971; MAPA, U. N.Mex., 1984; cert. locksmith, electronic security, NRI Schs., 1988. Dep. chief svc. unit dental program USPHS Indian Hosp., Whiteriver, Ariz., 1971-73; chief svc. unit dental program USPHS Indian Hosp., Sacaton, Ariz., 1973-76, Santa Fe, 1976-88; systems analyst USPHS Area Office, Albuquerque, 1988-90; dir. div. info. mgmt. svcs. USPHS-IHS Area Office, Albuquerque, 1990—. Contbr. articles to profl. jours. Mem. IHS Dental Profl. Specialty Group, IHS Dental Computer Users Group, ADA, Internat. Coll. Dentists, Psi Omega Dental Fraternity, N.J. Dental Sch. Alumni Assn., USPHS Commn. Officers Assn., Albuquerque Area Dental Soc. Indian Health Svcs., M Tech. Assoc., Soc. Am. Magicians. Home: 1914 Conejo Dr Santa Fe NM 87505-6108 Office: IHS Area Office 5338 Montgomery Blvd NE Rm 123 Albuquerque NM 87109-1311

SCIARONI, LINDA GILLINGHAM, high school educator; b. Torrance, Calif., Feb. 15, 1962; d. Robert Edward and Dorathea Ellenor (Dixon) Gillingham; m. Daniel Martin Sciaroni, Feb. 14, 1987. BA, Whitworth Coll., Spokane, Wash., 1983; MA in Spl. Edn.: Gifted, Calif. State U., L.A., 1996. Sci. cert. Nat. Bd. Profl. Tchg. Standards, 1998. Tchr. Franklin H.S. L.A. Unified Sch. Dist., 1984—, chair dept. sci., 1992-94, gifted coord., 1986-94, Title IX coord., 1993-94, sci. advisor LAUSD divsn. instrn., 1995-96. Named Outstanding Tchr., Rotary Club L.A., 1995; Sci-Mat fellow Coun. Basic Edn., 1993, Eleanor Roosevelt fellow AAUW, 1990, May V. Seagoe scholar Calif. Assn. for Gifted, 1993. Mem. AAUW, AAAS, Nat. Sci. Tchr. Assn., Calif. Sci. Tchr. Assn., Greater L.A. Sci. Tchrs. Assn., Calif. Assn. for the Gifted, Phi Delta Kappa. Avocations: ethnobotany, textiles, swimming.

SCIGLIANO, ERIC ROBERT, writer, newspaper editor; b. Chgo., Feb. 25, 1953; s. Robert George and June Genevieve (Buerge) S.; 1 child, Kathryn Alma. Student, St. John's Coll., Annapolis, Md., 1970-71, St. John's Coll., Santa Fe, 1972-74, Boston Coll., 1971-72. Feature writer Santa Fe Reporter, 1977-79; mng. editor Argus, Seattle, 1980-81; editor Puget Sound, Seattle, 1984; staff writer, staff writer, news editor Seattle Weekly, 1982-83, 85—; ptnr. Ad Lib Graphics, Santa Fe, 1975-78; instr. writer's program U. Wash., Seattle, 1993-95. Contbr. articles to N.Y. Times, Technology Review, Outside, others; translator poems Yale U. Viet Nam Forum, 1995. Recipient [illegible] award AAAS, Washington, 1987, Livingston award [illegible] Washington, 1982, Lowell Mellett award Free Press Found., 1984; Telluride summer scholar Deep Springs (Calif.) Coll., 1969. Mem. Nat. Writer's Union, Telluride Assn. (assoc.). Office: Seattle Weekly 1008 Western Ave Ste 300 Seattle WA 98104

SCOFIELD, NORMAN WILLIAM, civil engineer; b. Palo Alto, Calif., Jan. 16, 1956; s. William and Bernice (Benz) S. BSCE, San Jose State U., 1979; MBA, U. Hawaii, 1985. Constrn. engr. Dillingham Constrn., Honolulu, 1980-81, project engr., 1981-85, project mgr., San Jose, Calif., 1985-87; engr. IV Hawaiian Dredging Constrn., Honolulu, 1987-89, sr. project engr., 1989—. Democrat. Avocation: woodworking. Office: Hawaiian Dredging Constrn 614 Kapahulu Ave Honolulu HI 96815-3891

SCOGGIN, DANIEL PAUL, English educator; b. Phoenix, Jan. 18, 1969; s. James Vivian and Janet Phyllis (Huntman) S.; m. Andrea Marla Pankowski, Mar. 14, 1998. BA, Santa Clara U., 1991, Claremont Grad. U., 1992; PhD, Claremont Grad. U., 1998. Basketball coach Pomona Coll., Claremont, Calif., 1991-94; English instr. Harvey Mudd Coll., Claremont, Calif., 1992-97, Mesa (Calif.) C.C., 1996-98, Tempe (Ariz.) Prep. Acad., 1998—. Mem. MLA. Home: 13646 S 41st Pl Phoenix AZ 85044-4668

SCOLEDES, ARISTOTLE GEORGIUS MICHALE, retired science and technology educator, research consultant; b. N.Y.C., Feb. 22, 1929; s. Michael George and Soultanitsa (Hadtzifoca) S.; m. Anne-Marie Furchtenicht, Sept. 7, 1957 (dec. Nov. 1970); children: Alexander Michael, Alexandra Anne; m. Barbara Lynn Sterling, Aug. 14, 1977; 1 child, Dylan. AB, Syracuse U., 1951; MSE, Johns Hopkins U., 1953; ScD, MIT, 1957; PhD, Stanford U., 1965. Rsch. assoc. Johns Hopkins U., Balt., 1951-53; rsch. fellow U. Chgo., 1953-54, MIT, Cambridge, Mass., 1955-59; exec. engr., project coord. Apollo Mission program Philco Western Devel. Labs./Ford-Aerospace, Sunnyvale, Calif., 1960-62; asst. prof. philosophy of sci. Alfred (N.Y.) U., 1962-63; assoc. prof. philosophy of sci. and theoretical biology SUNY, Buffalo, 1963-68; prof. philosophy sci. and tech. Ga. Inst. Tech., 1968-72; sr. cons. sponsored minorities program Econ. Opportunity Atlanta/CETA, U.S. Govt., Atlanta, 1972-77; project mgr., dir. Consulting Consortium U.S./Stanford/MIT, Stanford, 1977-95; mem. MIT/Stanford Venture Lab. Contbr. articles to profl. jours. Recipient Rsch. Svcs. Recognition award Offices of Naval Rsch. and Chief of Naval Ops., 1984; hon. fellow AIAA, 1971. Mem. Nat. Space Soc., The Planetary Soc., Am. Assn. Univ. Profs., Democritus Soc., History of Sci. Soc., Air Force Assn., Philosophy of Sci. Assn., Am. Philos. Assn., Sigma Xi (hon.), Tau Beta Pi. Avocations: public speaking, drawing, philately, numismatics. Home: 3609 S Court Palo Alto CA 94306-4258

SCOLES, EUGENE FRANCIS, law educator, lawyer; b. Shelby, Iowa, June 12, 1921; s. Sam and Nola E. (Leslie) S.; m. R. Helen Glawson, Sept. 6, 1942; children—Kathleen Elizabeth, Janene Helen. A.B., U. Iowa, 1943, J.D., 1945; LL.M., Harvard U., 1949; J.S.D., Columbia U., 1955. Bar: Iowa 1945, Ill. 1946. Assoc. Seyfarth-Shaw & Fairweather, Chgo., 1945-46; asst. prof. law Northeastern U., 1946-48, assoc. prof., 1948-49; assoc. prof. U. Fla., 1949-51, prof., 1951-56; prof. U. Ill., Champaign, 1956-68; Max Rowe prof. law U. Ill., 1982-89, prof. emeritus, 1989—; vis. prof. McGeorge Law Sch. U. Pacific, Sacramento, 1989-92; prof. U. Oreg., 1968-82, dean Sch. Law, 1968-74, disting. prof. emeritus, 1982—; vis. prof. Khartoum U., Sudan, 1964-65. Author: (with H.F. Goodrich) Conflict of Laws, 4th edit., 1964, (with R.J. Weintraub) Cases and Materials on Conflict of Laws, 2d edit., 1972, (with E.C. Halbach, Jr.) Problems and Materials on Decedents' Estates and Trusts, 5th edit., 1993, Problems and Materials on Future Interests, 1977, (with P. Hay) Conflict of Laws, 2d edit., 1992; contbr. articles to profl. jours.; notes and legislation editor Iowa Law Rev., 1945; reporter Uniform Probate Code Project, 1966-70; mem. joint editorial bd. Uniform Probate Code, 1972—. Mem. ABA, Soc. Pub. Tchrs. Law, Am. Law Inst., Ill. Bar Assn., Assn. Am. Law Schs. (pres. 1978), Order of Coif. Home: 1931 Kimberly Dr Eugene OR 97405-5849 Office: U Oreg Sch of Law 11th and Kincaid Eugene OR 97403-1221

SCORSINE, JOHN MAGNUS, lawyer; b. Rochester, N.Y., Dec. 3, 1957; s. Frank and Karin (Frennby) S.; m. Susan Nauss, May 31, 1980 (div.); m. Theresa A. Burke, Dec. 17, 1988; 1 child, Jennifer E. BS, Rochester Inst. Tech., 1980; JD, U. Wyo., 1984. Bar: Wyo. 1984, U.S. Dist. Ct. Wyo. 1984, U.S. Ct. Appeals (10th cir.) 1989, U.S. Army Ct. Criminal Appeals 1995. Part-time deputy sheriff Monroe County (N.Y.), 1978-80; police officer Casper (Wyo.) Police Dept., 1980-81; intern U.S. Atty. Office, Cheyenne, Wyo., 1983-84; pvt. practice Rock Springs, Wyo., 1984-85; ptnr. Scorsine and Flynn, Rock Springs, 1986; prin. Scorsine Law Office, Rock Springs, 1986-95; commr. Dist. and County Court, 1986-95; dep. chief of staff for mil. support Wyo. Nat. Guard, 1995—; ptnr. Sunset Advt., 1987-89; chmn. bd. dirs. Youth Home Inc., Rock Springs, 1987-88; treas. Sweetwater County Cmty. Corrections Bd., 1990-95; mem. Nat. Ski Patrol, 1976—, Wyo. Bd. of Parole, 1998—. Leader Medicine Bow Ski Patrol, Laramie, Wyo., 1983; legal advisor Rocky Mountain divsn. Nat. Ski Patrol, 1984; asst. patrol leader White Pine Ski Area, Pinedale, Wyo., 1986; avalanche advisor Jackson Hole Snow King Ski Patrol, 1987-96, avalanche instr. 1993—; sect. chief Teton sect. nat. Ski Patrol, 1991-94, mem. Eldore Ski Patrol, 1996—; mem. Sweetwater County Search and Rescue, 1989-95, tng. officer, 1993-95; mem. Sweetwater County Emergency Dive Team, 1990-95, mem. Sweetwater County Fire Dept., 1992-94, Reliance Vol. Fire Dept., 1994-95; lt.k, training officer Laramie Cmty. Fire Dist. #6 and Burns Ambulance Svc., 1995-98, treas./sec. bd. dirs. 1997-98, Am. N. Peary Land expdn., 1989; scoutmaster Boy Scouts Am., 1987-93, 96-98, 4H leader, 1997—; pres. Sweetwater County Vol. Fire Assn., 1993-94; mem. Laramie County Sch. Dist. #2 accreditation panel; dir. emergency svcs. Wyo. Civil Air Patrol, 1998—. Maj. JAG, USAR, 1991—; bd. dirs., sec. Burns Cmty. Ambulance, 1997—. Recipient Yellow Merit star Nat. Ski Patrol, 1993, Fritch Volunteerism award, 1993, Armed Forces Outstanding Vol. Svc. medal. Mem. ABA, Wyo. State Bar, Wyo. Trial Lawyers Assn., Assn. Am. Trial Lawyers, Rock Springs C. of C., Res. Officers Assn. (nat. councilman 1993—, state pres. 1994), Rotary. Democrat. Lutheran. Avocations: rock climbing, backpacking, hunting, scuba, karate. Home: 1090 State Hwy 214 Burns WY 82093 Office: Wyo Nat Guard 5500 Bishop Blvd Cheyenne WY 82009-3320

SCOTT, AMY LYNNE, engineer; b. Ellensburg, Wash., Dec. 9, 1970; d. Howard Lewis and Patrica Louise (Anderson) S. BFA, Wash. State U., 1994, MFA, 1997. Graphic artist Wash. State U., Pullman, 1991-97, mktg. analyst, 1991-97, instr. electronic imaging technologies dept. fine arts, 1994-97; applications integrations specialist Advance Computing Applications Lab., Pullman, 1994-97; QA engr. Adobe Sys., San Jose, Calif., 1997—. Mem. Women's Caucus for the Arts, Coll. Art Assn. Avocations: printmaking, painting, graphic design, web design. E-mail: ascott@adobe.com. Home: 5002 20th Ave NE Seattle WA 98105 Office: 801 N 34th St Seattle WA 98103

SCOTT, BRIAN DAVID, lawyer; b. Spokane, Wash., Sept. 30, 1946; s. Dick E. and Helene L. (Johnson) S.; m. Lynita G. Muzzall, Sept. 9, 1972; children: D. Alexander, Rachel E., S. Andrew. BA, U. Wash., 1968; JD, U. Wis., 1972. Bar: Wis. 1972, Wash. 1972, U.S. Dist. Ct. (we. dist.) Wash. 1972, U.S. Dist. Ct. (we. dist.) Wis. 1972. Asst. atty. gen. Wash. State Atty. Gen.'s Office, Seattle, 1972-74; assoc. Jackson, Ulvestad, Goodwin, Grutz, Seattle, 1974-81; ptnr. Goodwin, Grutz & Scott, Seattle, 1981-96, Grutz, Scott & Kinney, Seattle, 1996—. Mem. ATLA, Wash. Trial Lawyers Assn., Wash. Athletic Club. Democrat. Avocations: boating, skiing, travel. Home: 158 Prospect St Seattle WA 98109-3750 Office: Grutz Scott & Kinney 600 University St Ste 1928 Seattle WA 98101-4115

SCOTT, BYRON ALTON, professional basketball player; b. Ogden, Utah, Mar. 28, 1961; m. Anita Scott; children: Thomas, Londen. Student, Ariz. State U., 1979-85. With L.A. Lakers, 1983-93, 96-97; shooting guard Indiana Pacers, Indpls., 1993-95, Vancouver Grizzlies, 1995-96; asst. coach Sacramento Kings, Sacramento, 1998—; mem. NBA Championship Team, 1985, 87, 88. Office: Sacramento Kings ARCO Arena 1 Sports Pky Sacramento CA 95834*

SCOTT, DAGNY, editor-in-chief; b. Chgo., Oct. 9, 1962. BA in Polit. Sci., Northwestern U., 1983, M in Journalism, 1988. Freelance features writer Chgo. Tribune, 1988, 89; copy editor The Santa Fe New Mex., 1990-91, asst. news editor, 1991-93, news editor, 1993-96; editor Running Times Mag., [illegible] editor-in-chief Women's Sports & Fitness, [illegible] Colo., 1996—; spkr., cons. on women's sports issues; asst. dir. Susquehanna Cross Country & Track and Field Camp; former v.p. Team Endurance, Albuquerque and Santa Fe. Recipient Front Section Design award AP Mng. Editors, 1991, Overall Design and Typography award [illegible] 1992, Page Editing award N.Mex. Press Women, 1993, Headlines, 1993, 94, 95, Page Design, 1993, 94, 95, Headlines award Nat. Press Women, 1993, 95, Page One Design award Soc. Newspaper Design, 1995, Page One Portfolio award, 1996; Santa Fe New Mexican named as one of 20 World's Best Designed Newspapers, Soc. Newspaper Design, 1996; N.Mex. women's Grand Prix Road Racing champion USA Track & Field, 1994, 95. Fax: 303-545-0906. Office: Womens Sports & Fitness Editor-in-chief PO Box 1682 Boulder CO 80306

SCOTT, DONALD MICHAEL, educational association administrator, educator; b. L.A., Sept. 26, 1943; s. Bernard Hendry and Barbara (Lannin) S.; m. Patricia Ilene Pancoast, Oct. 24, 1964 (div. June 1971); children: William Bernard, Kenneth George. BA, San Francisco State U., 1965, MA, 1986. Cert. tchr. Calif. Tchr. Mercy High Sch., San Francisco, 1968-71; park ranger Calif. State Park System, Half Moon Bay, 1968-77; tchr. adult div. Jefferson Union High Sch. Dist., Daly City, Calif., 1973-87; dir. NASA-NPS Project Wider Focus, Daly City, 1983-90; dir. Geo.S. Spl. Projects Wider Focus, San Francisco, 1990—; also bd. dirs. Wider Focus, Daly City; nat. park ranger/naturalist Grant-Kohrs Ranch Nat. Hist. Site, Deer Lodge, Mont., 1987-88; nat. park ranger pub. affairs fire team Yellowstone Nat. Park, 1988; nat. park ranger Golden Gate Recreation Area, 1988-92; rsch. subject NASA, Mountain View, Calif., 1986-90; guest artist Yosemite (Calif.) Nat. Park, 1986; nat. park ranger Golden Gate Nat. Recreation Area, Nat. Park Svc., San Francisco, 1986, nat. park svc. history cons. to Bay Dist., 1988-94; adj. asst. prof. Skyline Coll., 1989-94, Coll. San Mateo, 1992-94; aerospace edn. specialist NASA/OSU/AESP, 1994—; cons. Friends of Ea. State Penitentiary Project, Phila., 1993. Contbr. articles, photographs to profl. jours., mags., chpts. to books. Pres. Youth for Kennedy, Lafayette, Calif., 1960; panelist Community Bds. of San Francisco, 1978-87; city chair Yes on A com., So. San Francisco, San Mateo County, Calif., 1986; active CONTACT Orgn., 1991—, bd. dirs. 1995—; chair edn. working group Case for Mars VI, Boulder, 1996. Mem. Nat. Assn. for Interpretation (founder), Yosemite Assn. (life), Wider Focus, Friends of George R. Stewart, Nat. Sci. Tchrs. Assn., Nat. Coun. of Tchrs. of Math., Internat. Tech. Edn. Assn., Smithsonian Air and Space (charter mem.), Planetary Soc. (charter mem.), Mars Soc., Indep. Scholar, 1982—, Geol. Soc. Am., Orange County Space Soc. Avocations: photography, hiking, camping, travel. Home and Office: NASA Ames Rsch Ctr MS 253-2 Moffett Field CA 94035-1000

SCOTT, EDWARD WILLIAM, software engineer; b. Glendale, Calif., May 28, 1947; m. Ruey Mei Phan, 1975. BFA, Art Ctr. Coll. Design, 1977; BSEE, Calif. Poly. Inst., 1981. Sr. software engr. Hughes Aircraft, 1984-92, Sony Transcom, 1992-93, Hughes Avicom, 1993-95, Walt Disney Co., Anaheim, Calif., 1997—. Achievements include research in digital imaging techniques involving the use of selected portions of spectrum, error detection and correction techniques, image formats supporting runtime image compositing on the Web; 12 U.S. patents. Office: 6797 E Swarthmore Dr Anaheim CA 92807-5040

SCOTT, GREGORY KELLAM, state supreme court justice; b. San Francisco, CA, July 30, 1943; s. Robert and Althea Delores Scott; m. Carolyn Weatherly, Apr. 10, 1971; children: Joshua Weatherly, Elijah Kellam. BS in Environ. Sci., Rutgers U., 1970, EdM in Urban Studies, 1971; JD cum laude, Ind. U., Indpls., 1977. Asst. dean resident instrn. Cook Coll. Rutgers U., 1972-75; trial atty. U.S. SEC, Denver, 1977-79; gen. counsel Blinder, Robinson & Co., Inc., Denver, 1979-80; asst. prof. coll. law U. Denver, 1980-85, assoc. prof., 1985-93, prof. emeritus, 1993—, chair bus. planning program, 1986-89, 92-93; justice Colo. Supreme Ct., Denver, 1993—; of counsel Moore, Smith & Bryant, Indpls., 1987-90; v.p., gen. counsel Comml. Energies, Inc., 1990-91; presenter in field. Author: (with others) Structuring Mergers and Acquisitions in Colorado, 1985, Airport Law and Regulation, 1991, Racism and Underclass in America, 1991; contbr. articles to profl. jours. Mem. ABA, Nat. Bar Assn., Nat. Assn. Securities Dealers, Inc., Nat. Arbitration Panel (arbitrator), Colo. Bar Found., Sam Cary Bar Assn., Am. Inn Ct. (founding mem. Judge Alfred A. Arraj inn). Avocations: golfing, reading, traveling. Office: Supreme Ct Colo Judicial Bldg 2 E 14th Ave Denver CO 80203-2115*

SCOTT, HARLAN NOEL, tree farmer, writer; b. Joseph, Oreg., Feb. 16, 1931; s. Noel Sebert and Ethel Mary (Halsey) S.; m. Mollie Mensinger Williams, Mar. 3, 1960 (div. July 1976); children: Rick, Juliana, Joy, Brett; m. Rebecca Ann Holliday, Apr. 7, 1979. BA, Oreg. State U., 1959. Farmer Elgin, Oreg., 1952-53; wildlife biologist Oreg. Dept. Fish and Wildlife, Pendleton, Troy, Corvallis, Scoppoose, Prineville, 1959-89; tree farmer Elgin, 1989—. Author: Through the Eyes of a Boy, 1997. Mem. Kiwans Club, Scappoose, 1970-74, pres.; mem. sch. bd. Crooh County Schs., Prineville, 1982-87; bd. dirs. Elgin TV Assn., 1997—. Democrat. Methodist. Avocations: fishing, hunting, fly tying, writing poems, wildlife viewing. Home: PO Box 247 Elgin OR 97827-0247

SCOTT, HOWARD WINFIELD, JR., temporary help services company executive; b. Greenwich, Conn., Feb. 24, 1935; s. Howard Winfield and Janet (Lewis) S.; B.S., Northwestern U., 1957; m. Joan Ann MacDonald, Aug. 12, 1961; children: Howard Winfield III, Thomas MacDonald, Ann Elizabeth. With R.H. Donnelly Corp., Chgo., 1958-59; sales rep. Masonite Corp., Chgo. also Madison, Wis., 1959-61; sales rep. Manpower Inc., Chgo., 1961-63, br. mgr., Kansas City, Mo., 1963-65, area mgr., Mo. and Kans., 1964-65, regional mgr. Salespower div., Phila., 1965-66; asst. advt. mgr. soups Campbell Soup Co., Camden, N.J., 1966-68; pres. PARTIME, Inc., Paoli, Pa., 1968-74; dir. marketing Kelly Services Inc., Southfield, Mich., 1974-78; pres. CDI Temporary Services, Inc., 1978-91; pres. Dunhill Pers. System, Inc., Woodbury, N.Y., 1991-94; v.p. SOS Temporary Svcs., Salt Lake City, 1994; pres., chief operating officer SOS Staffing Svcs., Salt Lake City, 1995-97, CEO, 1997. Served with AUS, 1957-58. Mem. Nat. Assn. Temporary Services (sec. 1970-71, pres. 1971-73, bd. dirs. 1982-91), Kappa Sigma. Republican. Home: PO Box 980142 Park City UT 84098-0142 also: 1204 Annapolis Sea Colony E Bethany Beach DE 19930 Office: SOS Staffing Svcs 1415 S Main St Salt Lake City UT 84115-5313

SCOTT, JOHN CARLYLE, retired gynecologist, oncologist; b. Mpls., Sept. 24, 1933; s. Horace Golden and Grace (Melges) S.; m. Beth Krause, 1958 (div. 1977); m. Paola Maria Martini, Feb. 8, 1986; children: Jeff, David, Suzanne, Danielle. AB, Princeton U., 1956; BS, MD, U. Minn., 1961. Diplomate Am. Coll. Ob-gyn., Pan Am. Ob-gyn. Soc. Intern Sch. Medicine Marquette U., Milw., 1961-62, resident Sch. Medicine, 1962-66; resident Harvard Med. Sch., Boston, 1965; Am. Cancer fellow Marquette Med. Sch., Milw., 1966-67, instr. ob-gyn., 1966-67; clin. instr. ob-gyn. U. Wash. Med. Sch., Seattle, 1968-75, clin. asst. prof., 1975-85, clin. assoc. prof., 1985—, ret., 1998; mem. faculty adv. com. dept. ob-gyn. U. Wash., Seattle, 1973-97. Author: First Aid for N.W. Boaters, 1977; author Am. Jour. Ob-Gyn., 1970, 75, 77, 97, Jour. Neurologic and Orthopedic Surgery. Bd. dirs. Renton (Wash.) Handicapped Ctr., 1968-70, March of Dimes, 1974-79; bd. dirs. enabling sys. U. Hawaii, Honolulu, 1977-80. Capt. U.S. Army, 1950-52, Korea. Decorated U.S. Senate Medal of Freedom, Bronze and Silver Stars, Pres. Ronald Reagan's Task Force Medal of Merit and Eternal Flame of Freedom. Fellow Royal Soc. Medicine (gynecology and oncology sects.), Am. Coll. Ob-Gyn, Internat. Coll. Surgeons (v.p. 1997—, pres. 1999—); mem. Seattle Gynecol. Soc. (pres. 1978), Baker Channing Soc., Sigma Xi. Avocations: photography, constrn., ornithology, sailing, skiing. Home: 726 16th Ave E Seattle WA 98112-3916

SCOTT, JOHN NATHANIEL, foundation administrator; b. Sanford, N.C., May 9, 1961; s. Lassfe Lucian Sr. and Margaret Irene (Hardy) S. BA in Psychology, N.C. State U., 1983. Mortgage officer 1st Union Nat. Bank, Charlotte, N.C., 1984-86, Dunwoody (Ga.) Savings, 1986-89; real estate developer Atlanta Gemini, 1990-92; pres., exec. dir. Elton John AIDS Found., Beverly Hills, Calif., 1992—; co-founder, dir. Elton John AIDS Found., London, 1993—. Fed. club mem. Human Rights Campaign, Washington, 1990—; bd. dirs. Nat. AIDS Fund, Washington, 1992—. Mem. Lambda Chi Alpha. Avocations: photography, running, horses, motorcycles. Office: Elton John AIDS Found 9744 Wilshire Blvd Ste 301 Beverly Hills CA [illegible]

SCOTT, JOHN WAYNE, state manager; b. Flint, Mich., June 16, 1951; s. John William Scott and Dorothy Anne (Neldon) Scruggs; m. Lana Lynn, [illegible]

Macomb C.C., 1976; BS in Edn., Wayne State U., 1981; MS in Human Resources Mgmt., Kennedy-Western U., 1996, student, 1996—. Cons. employment, training Dept. Labor, West Branch, Mich., 1988-90; employment security specialist Dept. Labor, Homer, Ala., 1991-93; employment svc. mgr. Dept. Labor, Sitka, Alaska, 1993-97; balance of state operations mgr. Dept. Labor, Anchorage, Alaska, 1997-1998, south ctrl. operations mgr., 1998—; tchr. Whittemore (Mich.) Prescott Sch. District, 1983-89. Author: The Magic Hat, 1982, One-Stop in Job Service-Common Elements, 1996; author: (poetry) Chasing Rainbows, 1987. With USN, 1969-73, Viet Nam. Grantee City of Sitka, 1996. Mem. Internat. Assn. Personnel Employment Security. Avocations: fly fishing, writing. Home: 2052 Paxson Dr Anchorage AK 99504-3432

SCOTT, KELLY, newspaper editor. Sunday Calendar editor The L.A. Times. Office: LA Times Times Mirror Sq Los Angeles CA 90053

SCOTT, LARRY, electronics engineer; b. Des Moines, May 18, 1935; s. Glenn Filmore and Helen Marie (Mann) S.; m. Ursula Deiss, June 21, 1959 (div. June 1971); children: Ulrike, Barbara; m. Caroline Patricia Driver, Dec. 21, 1972; adopted children: Robert, Michael, Dhyana, Leah, Ananda. AA, Los Angeles City Coll., 1955; BS in Engring with honors, U. Calif., Berkeley, 1957, MS in Elec. Engring., 1959; Dr sc techn, Swiss Fed. Inst. Tech., 1966. Instrumentation engr. Lawrence Radiation Lab., Berkeley, 1959-62; teaching asst. Swiss Fed. Inst. Tech., Zurich, 1962-66; design engr. Hewlett Packard Co., Boeblingen, Fed. Republic Germany, 1966-67; program mgr. TRW Systems, Redondo Beach, Calif., 1967-69; scientist Systems Sci. and Software Co., San Diego, 1969-71; ind. cons. Del Mar, Calif., 1971-72; sr. scientist Sci. Applications Internat. Corp., La Jolla, Calif., 1972-77; chief scientist Def. Tech. Group, La Jolla, Calif., 1980—; sr. scientist JAYCOR, Del Mar, Calif., 1977-80; instrumentation advisor Def. Nuclear Agy., Washington, 1976-96; cons. and spkr. in field. Contbr. articles to tech. pubs; Patentee Pulse Stretching Network, Planar MOS Transistor with Dielectric Isolation. Mem. IEEE (sr.), Sigma Xi, Tau Beta Pi, Eta Kappa Nu. Republican. Buddhist. Avocations: philosophy, language, bicycling. Home: PO Box 99 Warner Springs CA 92086-0099

SCOTT, PARTICIA JEAN, educational telecommunications administrator; b. Tacoma, Wash., Oct. 30, 1946; d. Donald Matthew and Gladys Myrtle (Olson) Gregurich; m. George Larkham Scott IV, Aug. 1, 1969; 1 child, Matthew Larkham. BA, Wash. State U., 1968; MA in Instrl. TV, Gonzaga U., 1975; PhD in Ednl. Policy and Mgmt., U. Oreg., 1994. Cert. secondary tchr., Wash. Tchr. secondary Moses Lake (Wash.) Schs., 1968-70; project dir. Wash. Commn. for Humanities, Spokane, 1975-77; adminstrv. asst. for telecourses Spokane Falls C.C., 1977; office mgr. Oreg. C.C. Telecom. Consortium, Portland, 1983-89; intern to dir. of edn. policy and planning, govs. office State Oreg.; intern to commr. for cmty. colls. State Dept. of Edn., Salem, 1988; ednl. cons. pvt. practice, 1997—; grant writer Riggs Inst., Beaverton, Oreg., 1986-88; tchr. adult literacy, Portland, 1986—. Fundraiser St. Mary of the Valley Cath. Sch., Beaverton, 1982-83; precinct com. person Spokane County, 1976-80; mem. Catlin Gabel Sch. Auction com., Portland, 1983-86. Mem. AAUW, NAFE, Women in Comms. Internat. Avocations: reading, gourmet cooking. Home: 3848 N 3rd Ave Apt 1084 Phoenix AZ 85013-3459

SCOTT, PATRICIA M., educator; b. La Grande, Oreg., Mar. 12, 1962; d. A. Warren and Louise E. (Larrow) S. BSc, U. Oreg., 1984; MA, Bowling Green State U., 1986; student, Oreg. State U., 1995—. Asst. dir. student activities Lorain County C.C., Elyvia, Ohio, 1984-85; student life coord. Terra Tech. Coll., Fremont, Ohio, 1985-86; asst. dir. career svcs. Roger Williams U., Bristol, R.I., 1986-89; asst. prof. U. Oreg., Eugene, 1989-93; dir. student support S.W. Oreg. C.C., Coos Bay, Oreg., 1993—; test supr. Ednl. Testing Svc., Trenton, N.J., 1995—. Co-chair Leadership Coos, Coos Bay, Oreg., 1996—. Mem. Nat. Assn. Special Programs (conference chair 1995, 96), Soroptimist Internat. (scholarship chair 1994—), Habitat for Humanity (partner com. 1995-98). Avocations: fitness, crafts, golf, sailing, border collie dogs.

SCOTT, PETER BRYAN, lawyer; b. St. Louis, Nov. 11, 1947; s. Gilbert Franklin and Besse Jean (Fudge) S.; children: Lindsay W., Sarah W., Peter B. Jr. AB, Drury Coll., 1969; JD, Washington U., St. Louis, 1972, LLM, 1980. Bar: Mo. 1972, Colo. 1980, diplomate Ct. Practice Inst.; accredited estate planner. Pvt. practice, St. Louis, 1972-80; assoc. McKie and Assocs., Denver, 1980-81; ptnr. Scott and Chesteen, P.C., Denver, 1981-84, Veto & Scott, Denver, 1984-92; pvt. practice, Denver, 1992—; tchr. Denver Paralegal Inst., Red Rocks C.C. Mem. Evergreen Christian Ch., Disciples of Christ. Capt. USAR, 1971-79. Mem. ABA, Mo. Bar Assn., Colo. Bar Assn., Denver Bar Assn. Republican. Home: 6305 W 6th Ave C-18 Lakewood CO 80215 Office: Peter B Scott PC 6595 W 14th Ave Denver CO 80214-1998

SCOTT, SHIRLEY, city council; married; four children. BA, Drew U., 1965; MA Germanic Langs., U. Cin., 1968. Operator Scott Supply Svc. Inc.; city coun. Tucson City Coun., 1995—; bd. dirs. Tucson Clean and Beautiful. Office: Tucson City Coun 7575 E Speedway Blvd Tucson AZ 85710-8809*

SCOTT, WILLIAM CORYELL, medical executive; b. Sterling, Colo., Nov. 22, 1920; s. James Franklin and Edna Ann (Schillig) S.; m. Jean Marie English, Dec. 23, 1944 (div. 1975); children: Kathryn, James, Margaret; m. Carolyn Florence Hill, June 21, 1975; children: Scott, Amy Jo, Robert. AB, Dartmouth Coll., 1942; MD, U. Colo., 1944, MS in OB/GYN, 1951. Cert. Am. Bd. Ob-Gyn., 1956, 79, Am. Bd. Med. Mgmt., 1991. Intern USN Hosp., Great Lakes, Ill., 1945-46, Denver Gen. Hosp., 1946-47; resident Ob-Gyn St. Joseph's Hosp., Colo. Gen. Hosp., Denver, 1946-51; practice medicine specializing in Ob-Gyn Tucson, 1951-71; assoc. prof. emeritus U. Ariz. Med. Sch., Tucson, 1971-94, 1994; v.p. med. affairs U. Med. Ctr., Tucson, 1984-94. Contbr. articles to med. jours. and chpt. to book. Pres. United Way, Tucson, 1979-80, HSA of Southeastern Ariz., Tucson, 1985-87; chmn. Ariz. Health Facilities Authority, Phoenix, 1974-83. Served to capt. USNR, 1956-58. Recipient Man of Yr. award, Tucson, 1975. Fellow ACS, Am. Coll. Ob-Gyn, Pacific Coast Ob-Gyn Soc., Ctrl. Assn. of Ob-Gyn; mem. AMA (coun. on sci. affairs 1984-93, chmn. 1989-91), Am. Coll. Physician Execs., Am. Coll. Health Care Execs., Ariz. Med. Assn., La Paloma Country Club. Republican. Episcopalian. Avocations: golf, gardening, photography. Home: PO Box 805 Sonoita AZ 85637-0805

SCOUTEN, WILLIAM HENRY, chemistry educator, academic administrator; b. Corning, N.Y., Feb. 12, 1942; s. Henry and M. Anna (Kimble) S.; m. Nancy Jane Coombs, July 16, 1965; children: Lisa, Linda, Michael, William Jr., Thomas, David. BA, Houghton Coll., 1964; PhD, U. Pitts., 1969. NIH postdoctoral fellow SUNY, Stony Brook, 1969-71; asst. prof. Bucknell U., Lewisburg, Pa., 1971-77; assoc. prof. Bucknell U., Lewisburg, 1977-83, prof., 1983-84; prof., chmn. dept. chemistry Baylor U., Waco, Tex., 1984-93; dir. biotech. ctr. Utah State U., Logan, 1993—; vis. scientist for minority inst. Fedn. Am. Socs. Exptl. Biology, Washington; adj. prof. U. of Utah, 1996, mem. Ctr. for Biopolymers at Interfaces, 1996; chmn. Coun. of Biotech. Ctrs., 1998; mem. govt. rels. coms. Coun. Chem. Rsch., 1996; bd. dirs. emerging cos. sect. Biotechnology Industry Orgn., 1997; mem. Nat. Adv. Bd. Agrl. Rsch. Author: Affinity Chromatography, 1981; editor: Solid Phase Biochem., 1983; assoc. editor Internat. Jour. Bio-Chromatography, 1994—; mem. editl. bd. Bioconjugate Chemistry, 1994—, Jour. Molecular Recognition, 1994—, Bioseparation, 1995—. Fulbright fellow, 1976; Dreyfus Tchr. scholar, Dreyfus Found., 1976; NSF Sci. Devel. NSF, 1978; Lindbach Disting. Tchr. Bucknell U., 1975. Mem. Am. Soc. Biol. Chemists, Am. Chem. Soc., Internat. Soc. for Biorecognition Tech., Coun. for Biotech. Ctrs. (bd. dirs. 1996—), Internat. Soc. for Molecular Recognition (pres. 1990-93), Assn. for Internat. Practical Tng. (bd. dirs. 1991—). Republican. Baptist. Office: Utah State U 4700 Old Main Hl Logan UT 84322-4700

SCOZZARI, ALBERT, portfolio manager; b. Chgo.. BA, Northeastern Ill. U., 1973; MPA, Ill. Inst. Tech., 1974; PhD, Columbia Pacific U., 1986. Cons. World Bank Group. Author: Mass Communications in Politics, 1978, Managing for Effectiveness, 1986, Management in the 90s, 1990, Vietnam Faces, 1995, Field Cross, 1996, The Mountain, 1997, The Trail, 1997, A Collection of Verses and Poems, 1997. Pres. Homeowners Assn., Phoenix, 1992-96, Scozzari Meml. Scholarship Found., 1991—. With USNR, 1961-66, ret. ANG, 1979-87. Mem. Am. Mensa Assn. (life), Vietnam Vets. of Am. (life). Home: PO Box 7445 Chula Vista CA 91912-7445

SCRITSMIER, JEROME LORENZO, manufacturing company executive; b. Eau Claire, Wis., July 1, 1925; s. Fredrick Lorenzo and Alvera Mary (Schwab) S.; B.S., Northwestern U., 1950; m. Mildred Joan Lloyd, June 27, 1947; children—Dawn, Lloyd, Janet. Salesman, Sylvania Elec. Products, Los Angeles, 1951-69; chmn. Cameron Properties Inc.; chief fin. officer Environ. Lighting for Architecture Co., Los Angeles, 1973—. Served with USAAF, 1943-46. Mem. Apt. Assn. (pres., dir. Los Angeles County). Republican. Club: Jonathan (Los Angeles). Home: 2454 Cameron Ave Covina CA 91724-3921 Office: 17891 Arenth Ave City Of Industry CA 91748

SCRIVER, ROBERT MACFIE, sculptor; b. Browning, Mont., Aug. 15, 1914; s. Thaddeus Emery and Ellison Scriver; m. Mary Helen Strachan, Nov. 27, 1966 (div. Nov. 1970); m. Lorraine, Aug. 15, 1972. Student, Dickinson State Tchr's Coll., N.D., 2 years; Bachelor's degree, Vandercook Sch. Music, Chgo., 1935, Master's degree, 1941; postgrad., Northwestern Univ., summer 1937, U. Wash., summer 1938; D.Arts hon., Carroll Coll. mem. C.M. Russell Adv. Bd., Great Falls, Mont., 1983—. Group of works includes No More Buffalo, 1983 (gold medals 1983), An Honest Try (gold medals), Bob Scriver Hall of Bronze Mus. Mont. Wildlife, 1989; author: No More Buffalo, 1983 (pub. awards 1983), An Honest Try (pub. awards), The Blackfeet, Artists of the Northern Plains, 1990 (pub. awards). Justice of the peace Glacer County, Mont.; city magistrate City of Browning. Served to sgt. USAAF, 1940. Recipient Gold and Silver medals Cowboy Artists Am., Phoenix, Gold and Silver medals Nat. Acad. Western Arts, Oklahoma City, Mont. State Gov.'s award, 1990; honoree Bob Scriver Day State Mont., Helena. Mem. Nat. Sculpture Soc., Nat. Acad. Western Art, Soc. Animal Artists, Browning C. of C. (pres.); mem. emeritus Cowboy Artists Am. Republican. Native American. Lodge: Masons. Office: Mus Mont Wildlife Junction Hwys 2 & 89 Browning MT 59417

SCRUGGS, ELAINE M., mayor; m. Larry Scruggs; 1 child, Jenny. Former mgmt. specialist various cos., various cities; elected mem. Glendale (Ariz.) City Coun., 1990-93; apptd., then elected mayor City of Glendale, 1993-96, re-elected, 1996—; chmn. Maricopa (Ariz.) Assn. Govts., chair youth policy adv. com., immediate past chmn. Regional Pub. Transp. Authority, vice chmn. Ariz. Mcpl. Water Users Assn., chair Maricopa Assn. Govt. Regional Aviation Systems policy com. Dir. Glendale Leadership Program, 1984-89; mem. Ariz. Coalition for Tomorrow, Ariz. Women in Mcpl. Govt.; mem. youth adv. commn., Mayor's Alliance Against Drugs and Gangs. Mem. Glendale C. of C. Office: Office of Mayor 5850 W Glendale Ave Glendale AZ 85301-2563*

SEABOLT, RICHARD L., lawyer; b. Chgo., Aug. 28, 1949. *Wife, Kathleen Hallissy, also graduated with a Juris Doctor from Hastings College of Law, University of California, in 1975, and was a deputy district attorney from 1975 to 1993. Sons Jack Seabolt and Will Seabolt are students at Wildwood Elementary School, Piedmont, California. Father, Lee Seabolt, before retirement was President and Chairman of Selz Seabolt Associates, a Chicago based public relations firm.* BGS with distinction, U. Mich., 1971; JD, U. Calif., Hastings, 1975. Bar: Calif. 1975. With Hancock, Rothert & Bunshoft, San Francisco, 1975—, ptnr., 1981—; pres. Def. Seminar Assocs., 1992—. *Hancock, Robert & Bunshoft has offices in San Francisco, Los Angles, Tahoe City, and London, England and focuses its practice on complex business and insurance litigation. Lead defense lawyer, representing certain Underwriters' at Lloyd's of London in an environmental insurance coverage trial between Aerojet-General Corporation and 54 insurers. After a ten month trial, the jury rendered a verdict for the defendants. The defense verdict in that case was featured in 1992 articles in California Law Business and the National Law Journal as among the largest cases tried to a defense verdict in California and in the United States for that year. In 1997 California Supreme Court Affirmed that verdict.* Frequent speaker and author profl. journs., pres. Defense Seminar Assoc., 1992, AAA Large Complex Case Panel-Construction (Arbitration). Mem. ABA, Am. Arbitration Assn.(large complex case panel, construction), State Bar Calif., Bar Assn. San Francisco. Fax: 415-955-2599. Office: Hancock Rothert & Bunshoft 10th Flr 4 Embarcadero Ctr Fl 10 San Francisco CA 94111-4106

SEABORG, GLENN THEODORE, chemistry educator; b. Ishpeming, Mich., Apr. 19, 1912; s. H. Theodore and Selma (Erickson) S.; m. Helen Griggs, June 6, 1942; children: Peter, Lynne Seaborg Cobb, David, Stephen, John Eric, Dianne. AB, UCLA, 1934; PhD, U. Calif.-Berkeley, 1937; numerous hon. degrees; LLD, U. Mich., 1958, Rutgers U., 1970; DSc, Northwestern U., 1954, U. Notre Dame, 1961, John Carroll U., Duquesne U., 1968, Ind. State U., 1969, U. Utah, 1970, Rockford Coll., 1975, Kent State U., 1975; LHD, No. Mich. Coll., 1962; DPS, George Washington U., 1962; DPA, U. Puget Sound, 1963; LittD, Lafayette Coll., 1966; DEng, Mich. Technol. U., 1970; ScD, U. Bucharest, 1971, Manhattan Coll., 1976, U. Pa., 1983; PhD, U. Paris S., 1996. Rsch. chemist U. Calif., Berkeley, 1937-39, instr. dept. chemistry, 1939-41, asst. prof., 1941-45, prof., 1945-71, univ. prof., 1971—, leave of absence, 1942-46, 61-71, dir. nuclear chem. divsn., 1946-58, 72-75, assoc. dir. Lawrence Berkeley Lab., 1954-61, 72—; chancellor Univ. (U. Calif.-Berkeley), Berkeley, 1958-61; dir. Lawrence Hall of Sci. U. Calif., Berkeley, 1982-84, chmn. Lawrence Hall of Sci., 1984-98; sect. chief metall. lab. U. Chgo., 1942-46; chmn. AEC, 1961-71, gen. adv. com., 1946-50; research nuclear chemistry and physics, transuranium elements.; chmn. bd. Kevex Corp., Burlingame, Calif., 1972-87, Advanced Physics Corp., Irvine, Calif., 1988-94; mem. Pres.'s Sci. Adv. Com., 1959-61; mem. nat. sci. bd. NSF, 1960-61; mem. Pres.'s Com. on Equal Employment Opportunity, 1961-65, Fed. Radiation Council, 1961-69, Nat. Aeros. and Space Council, 1961-71, Fed. Council Sci. and Tech., 1961-71, Nat. Com. Am.'s Goals and Resources, 1962-64, Pres.'s Com. Manpower, 1964-69, Nat. Council Marine Resources and Engring. Devel., 1966-71; chmn. Chem. Edn. Material Study, 1959-74, Nat. Programming Council for Pub. TV, 1970-72; dir. Ednl. TV and Radio Center, Ann Arbor, Mich., 1958-64, 67-70; pres. 4th UN Internat. Conf. Peaceful Uses Atomic Energy, Geneva, 1971, also chmn. U.S. del., 1964, 71; U.S. rep. 5th-15th gen. confs. IAEA, chmn., 1961-71; chmn. U.S. del. to USSR for signing Memorandum Cooperation Field Utilization Atomic Energy Peaceful Purposes, 1963; mem. U.S. del. for signing Limited Test Ban Treaty, 1963; mem. commn. on humanities Am. Council Learned Socs., 1962-65; mem. sci. adv. bd. Robert A. Welch Found., 1957—; mem. Internat. Orgn. for Chem. Scis. in Devel., UNESCO, 1981-92, pres., 1981-92, pres. emeritus, 1992—; mem. Nat. Commn. on Excellence in Edn., Dept. Edn., 1981-83; co-discoverer elements 94-102 and 106: plutonium, 1940, americium, 1944-45, curium, 1944, berkelium, 1949, californium, 1950, einsteinium, 1952, fermium, 1953, mendelevium, 1955, nobelium, 1958, seaborgium, 1974; co-discoverer nuclear energy isotopes Pu-239, U-233, Np-237, other isotopes including I-131, Fe-59, Te-99m, Co-60; originator actinide concept for placing heaviest elements in periodic system. Author: (with Joseph J. Katz) The Actinide Elements, 1954, The Chemistry of the Actinide Elements, 1957, (with Joseph J. Katz and Lester R. Morse) 2d ed. Vols. I & II, 1986, The Transuranium Elements, 1958, (with E.G. Valens) Elements of the Universe, 1958 (winner Thomas Alva Edison Found. award), Man-Made Transuranium Elements, 1963, (with D.M. Wilkes) Education and the Atom, 1964, (with E.K. Hyde, I. Perlman) Nuclear Properties of the Heavy Elements, 1964, (with others) Oppenheimer, 1969, (with Ben Loeb) Stemming the Tide, 1987, (with W.R. Corliss) Man and Atom, 1971, Nuclear Milestones, 1972, (with Ben Loeb) Kennedy, Khruschev and the Test Ban, 1981, (with Walt Loveland) Elements beyond Uranium, 1990, (with Ben Loeb) The Atomic Energy Commission Under Nixon: Adjusting to Troubled Times, 1993, (with Ray C. Colvig) Chancellor at Berkeley, 1994, (with Ronald L. Kathren, Jerry B. Gough, Gary T. Benefiel) The Plutonium Story: The Journals of Professor Glenn T. Seaborg 1939-1946, 1994; editor: Transuranium Elements: Products of Modern Alchemy, 1978, (with W. Loveland) Nuclear Chemistry, 1982, Modern Alchemy: The Selected Papers of Glenn T. Seaborg, 1994, A Scientist Speaks Out: A Personal Perspective on Science, Society and Change, 1996, A Chemist in the White House: From the Manhattan Project to the End of the Cold War, 1998; assoc. editor Jour. Chem. Physics, 1948-50; mem. editorial adv. bd. Jour. Inorganic and Nuclear Chemistry, 1954-82, Indsl. Rsch., Inc, 1967-75; mem. adv. bd. Chem. and Engring. News, 1957-59; mem. editorial bd. Jour. Am. Chem. Soc., 1950-59, Ency. Chem. Tech., 1975—, Revs. in Inorganic Chemistry, 1977—; mem. hon. editorial adv. bd. Internat. Ency. Phys. Chemistry and Chem. Physics, 1957—, Nuclear Sci. and Techniques, Chinese Nuclear Soc., 1989—; mem. panel Golden Picture Ency. for Children, 1957-61; mem. cons. and adv. bd. Funk and Wagnalls Universal Standard Ency, 1957-61; mem. Am. Heritage Dictionary Panel Usage Cons., 1964; contbr. articles to profl. jours. Trustee Pacific Sci. Ctr. Found., 1962-77, Sci. Svc., 1965, pres., 1966-88, chmn., 1988-95; trustee Am.-Scandinavian Found., 1968—, Ednl. Broadcasting Corp., 1970-72; bd. dirs. Swedish Coun. Am., 1976—, chmn. bd. dirs., 1978-82; bd. dirs. World Future Soc., 1969—, Calif. Coun. for Environ. and Econ. Balance, 1974-83; bd. govs. Am. Swedish Hist. Found. 1972—; sr. tech. rev. group Amarillo Nat. Resource Ctr. for Plutonium, 1995—. Decorated officier Legion of Honor (France), 1973; recipient John Ericsson Gold medal Am. Soc. Swedish Engrs., 1948; Nobel prize for Chemistry (with E.M. McMillan), 1951, John Scott award and medal City of Phila., 1953, Perkin medal Am. sect. Soc. Chem. Industry, 1957, U.S. AEC Enrico Fermi award, 1959, Joseph Priestley Meml. award Dickinson Coll., 1960, Sci. and Engring. award Fedn. Engring. Socs., Drexel Inst. Tech., Phila., 1962; named Swedish Am. of Year, Vasa Order of Am., 1962; Franklin medal Franklin Inst., 1963; 1st Spirit of St. Louis award, 1964; Leif Erikson Found. award, 1964; Washington award Western Soc. Engrs., 1965; Arches of Sci. award Pacific Sci. Center, 1968; Internat. Platform Assn. award, 1969; Prometheus award Nat. Elec. Mfrs. Assn., 1969; Nuclear Pioneer award Soc. Nuclear Medicine, 1971; Oliver Townsend award Atomic Indsl. Forum, 1971; Disting. Honor award U.S. Dept. State, 1971; Golden Plate award Am. Acad. Achievement, 1972, Daniel Webster medal, 1976, John R. Kuebler award Alpha Chi Sigma, 1978; Founders medal Hebrew U. Jerusalem, 1981; Great Swedish Heritage award, Swedish Coun. Am., 1984, Ellis Island Medal of Honor, 1986, Swedish Coun. Am. Seaborg medal UCLA, 1987, Vannevar Bush award NSF, 1988, Nat. Medal of Sci. NSF, 1991, Royal Order of the Polar Star Sweden, 1992, Profl. Fraternity Assn. Career Achievement award, 1993; Minor Planet 4856-Asteroid Seaborg named in his honor, 1995; atomic element 106 named seaborgium (symbol Sg) in his honor, 1997. Fellow Am. Phys. Soc., Am. Inst. Chemists (Pioneer award 1968, Gold medal award 1973), Chem. Soc. London (hon.), Royal Soc. Edinburgh (hon.), Am. Nuclear Soc. (hon. chair Spl. Panel on Protection and Mgmt. of Plutonium 1994-95, Henry DeWolf-Smyth award 1982, Seaborg award 1984), Am. Nuclear Soc., Calif. Acad. Scis., N.Y. Acad. Scis., Washington Acad. Scis., AAAS (pres. 1972, chmn. bd. 1973), Royal Soc. Arts (Eng.); mem. Am. Chem. Soc. (award in pure chemistry 1947, William H. Nichols medal N.Y. sect. 1948, Charles L. Parsons award 1964, Gibbs medal Chgo. sect. 1966, Madison Marshall award No. Ala. sect. 1972, Priestley medal 1979, pres. 1976, George C. Pimentel award in chem. edn., 1994), Am. Philos. Soc., Royal Swedish Acad. Engring. Scis. (adv. council 1980), Am. Nat., Argentine Nat., Bavarian, Polish, Royal Swedish, USSR acads. scis., Royal Acad. Exact, Phys. and Natural Scis. Spain (acad. fgn. corr.), Soc. Nuclear Medicine (hon.), World Assn. World Federalists (v.p. 1980), Fedn. Am. Scis. (bd. sponsors 1980—), Deutsche Akademie der Naturforscher Leopoldina (East Germany), Nat. Acad. Pub. Adminstrn., Internat. Platform Assn. (pres. 1981-86), Am. Hiking Soc. (bd. dirs. 1979-84, v.p. 1980, adv. com. 1984—), Royal Soc. of Edinburgh, Phi Beta Kappa, Sigma Xi, Pi Mu Epsilon, Alpha Chi Sigma (John R. Kuebler award 1978), Phi Lambda Upsilon (hon.); fgn. mem. Royal Soc. London, Chem. Soc. Japan, Serbian Acad. Sci. and Arts. Clubs: Bohemian (San Francisco); Chemists (N.Y.C.); Cosmos (Washington), Faculty (Berkeley). Office: Lawrence Berkeley Nat Lab Mailstop 70A-3307 1 Cyclotron Rd 70A-3307 Berkeley CA 94720*

SEAGER, DAUNA GAYLE OLSON-STOKES, speech therapist; b. Logan, Utah, Sept. 22, 1925; d. Helmar Alexander and La Rena Barnes (Jones) Olson; m. Arch Jr. Stokes, Aug. 5, 1943 (dec. April 1970); children: Jeffrey David, John Phillip, Jeannette; m. Floyd W. Seager, July 7, 1973 (dec.). AS, Weber State U., 1964; BS, Utah State U., 1969, MS in Audiology Speech Pathology, 1969. X-ray ech., physician asst. Robins X-Ray, Ogden, Utah, 1946-52; asst. to supt. Lyman (Wyo.) Pub. Schs., 1952-60; clinic supr. Utah State U., Logan, 1965-69; speech, language, hearing therapist Weber/Davis Sch. District, Ogden, Farmington, Utah, 1969-73, various, Utah, 1970-90; coord. Clinic at O.R.M., Ogden, Utah, 1988—; bd. dirs. Weber County DUP Mus., Ogden. Author: Pioneer Settlers, 1990; contbr. articles to profl. jours. Co-founder Seager Indigent Clinic, Ogden Mission, Utah, 1988—; organized Stroke Club for Families of CVA Support Group, Ogden, 1972-74, Stroke Unit St. Benedict's Hosp., Ogden, 1972-74, Parent Child Tchr. Group, Ogden, 1970-73; co-chmn. Ogden Sesquicentennial com.; mem. Ogden Mayor's Cemetery Enhancement Commn. Fellow Utah State U., Logan, 1967-68, 68-69. Mem. Aglaia Club, Altrusa Internat., Weber Far South Ctr. Co., Weber County Women's Legislative Council and Rep. Women, Ogden Bus. Profl. Women, Daus. of Utah Pioneers. Mem. LDS Ch. Avocations: historian/lecturer, writer, golfer, bridge, swimmer, ballroom dance instr. Home and Office: 4046 South 895 East Ogden UT 84403-2416

SEAGRAVE, JANET LEE, economic developer; b. Okinawa, Japan, Dec. 31, 1951; (parents Am. citizens); d. Rodman Gamble and Patricia Jane (McDonald) S. Student, Maple Woods Coll., 1974-78, Del Mar Coll., 1978-79. Cert. econ. developer. Exec. sec. Am. Indsl. Devel. Coun., Kansas City, Mo., 1973-78; dir. western sales Indsl. Properties Report, Corpus Christi, Tex., 1978-79; indsl. devel. location cons. Amarillo (Tex.) Bd. Devel., 1979-81; dir. econ. devel. divsn. Roswell (N.Mex.) C. of C., 1981-86; exec. dir. Sheridan (Wyo.) County Econ. Devel. Coun., 1986-90, High Plains Devel. Authority, Great Falls, Mont., 1990-94, Indsl. Devel. Corp. of Lea County, Hobbs, N.Mex., 1994—; mem. faculty Ariz. Basic Econ. Devel. course, U. Ariz., Tucson, 1983-94. Bd. regents Am. Indsl. Devel. Coun., 1981-83, bd. dirs., 1984-88; chmn., bd. dirs., mediator, treas. Great Falls Area Labor/Mgmt. Com., 1991-94; mem. Pres.'s coun. Coll. of Great Falls, 1991-94. 9th woman in N.Am. to obtain Cert. Econ. Developer designation, 1982. Mem. Mont. Profl. Econ. Devel. Assn. (bd. dirs. 1993-94), Am. Devel. Coun. (bd. dirs. 1982-86, bd. regents 1982-84), N.Mex. Indsl. Devel. Execs. (bd. dirs. 1994—), N.Mex. Commerce and Industry Assn., Hobbs Rotary, Order of Eastern Star. Republican. Baptist. Avocations: gardening, walking, working with children, church activity. Home: PO Box 294 Hobbs NM 88241-0294 Office: 2702 N Grimes St # B Hobbs NM 88240-1804

SEAL, TEDDY ALLEN, police officer; b. Winchester, Va., June 4, 1956; s. Elmer Woodrow and Helen Maxine (Pappas) S.; m. Bonnie Lou Feltner, Sept. 7, 1977; 1 child, Brandon. BA, Columbia Pacific U., 1988, MA, 1989. Dep. sheriff Frederick County Sheriff's Dept., Winchester, 1978-79; police officer Middletown (Va.) Police Dept., 1979-80, Front Royal (Va.) Police Dept., 1980-82, City of Mannassas, Va., 1982, Paradise Valley (Ariz.) Police Dept., 1983—; adv. bd. Ariz. Law Enforcement/Prosecution Adv. Bd., Phoenix, 1993—. Author: The Police Investigative Function, 1987, Equal Employment Opportunity and the Police, 1987. Recipient commendation U.S. Senate, Washington, 1996. Mem. SW Assn. Tech. Accident Investigators, Masons, Scottish Rite. Republican. Roman Catholic. Avocation: cattle ranching. Office: Paradise Valley Police Dept 6433 E Lincoln Dr Paradise Valley AZ 85253

SEALE, ROBERT L., state treasurer; b. Inglewood, Calif., Oct. 4, 1941; m. Judy Seale (dec.). BSA, Calif. Poly. U. Former contr. and sr. fin. officer Rockwell Internat.; sr. accountant Ernst & Ernst, L.A.; mng. ptnr. Pangborn & Co., Ltd. CPA's, 1985-88; now state treas. State of Nev. Former treas. Nev. Rep. Com. Mem. Nat. Assn. State Treas. (past pres.). Office: Office of State Treas Capitol Bldg 101 N Carson St Ste 4 Carson City NV 89701-4786

SEALE, ROBERT MCMILLAN, office services company executive; b. Birmingham, Ala., Feb. 1, 1938; s. Robert McMillan and Margaret Sutherland (Miller) S.; B.A., Emory U., 1959. With N.Y. Life Ins. Co., San Francisco, 1960-67; with Dictaphone Office Services div. Dictaphone Corp., San Francisco, 1967-69; pres. Am. Profl. Service, Inc., Dictation West, Miss Jones' Word Processing, San Francisco, Pleasant Hill, South San Francisco, Calif., Los Angeles, Beverly Hills, Riverside, Portland, Phoenix, Las Vegas, Orange County, Calif. and Denver, 1969-93, Environments West, 1980-86, Los Arcos Properties, 1980—; founder Seale Orgn., 1993; bd. dirs. The Rose Resnic Ctr. for Blind and Handicapped, Computer Based Patient Record Inst.; med. word processing cons. to hosps., health care insts., office equipment mfrs.; lectr. in field. Contbr. articles in field to profl. jours. Chmn. San Francisco Mayor's Com. for Employment of Handicapped, 1971-73; mem. Calif. Gov.'s Planning and Adv. Com. for Vocat. Rehab. Planning, 1968-69; pres. Calif. League for Handicapped, 1968-70, bd. dirs., 1966-73, 84-89, adv. council, 1973-77; v.p. Stebbins Found., 1980—89; pres Stebbins Housing Corp., 1980-89; assoc. St. Francis Hosp. Found., 1990—. Recipient Spoke and Spark award U.S. Jr. C. of C., 1967; KABL Outstanding Citizen's award, 1965, 71. Mem. Am. Health Info. Mgmt. Assn., Adminstrv. Mgmt. Soc., Sales and Mktg. Execs. Assn., Am. Assn. Med. Transcription (Disting. Service award 1985), Med. Transcription Industry Alliance, Emory U. Alumni Assn., Emory Lamplighters Soc., U.S. C. of C., Las Palmas Alliance

(chmn.), Delta Tau Delta. Republican. Office: 280 W Camino Sur Palm Springs CA 92262-4303

SEALING, JEFFERY ALAN, security officer, writer; b. Grand Junction, Colo., Oct. 3, 1968; s. Clee Ellis and Roberta Lee (Edlin) S.; m. Tonya Lynn Stark, July 23, 1988 (div. Mar. 1990); m. Terri Lynn Grant, Aug. 18, 1995; 1 child, Andrew John. Student, Applied Tech. Sys., Virginia Beach, Va., 1992-93, Tidewater C.C., Portsmouth, Va., 1994-95. Security officer Pinkerton Security and Investigations Svcs., Inc., Colorado Springs, Colo., 1995-98, Mitsui Advanced Multi Media, Inc., Colorado Springs, 1998—. Author: The Dark, 1994, Legacy, 1995, Liquefied Natural Gas, 1995, Los Angeles: 2020, 1996. With USN, 1987-95. Roman Catholic. Avocations: fishing, target shooting, camping, backpacking, model trains.

SEAMAN, ARLENE ANNA, musician, educator; b. Pontiac, Mich., Jan. 21, 1918; d. Roy Russell and Mabel Louise (Heffron) S. BS, life cert., Ea. Mich. U., 1939; MMus, Wayne State U., 1951; postgrad., Colo. Coll., 1951-52, Acad. Music, Zermatt Switzerland, 1954, 58, U. Mich. guest conductor Shepherds and Angels, Symphonie Concertante, 1951; asst. conductor Detroit Women's Symphony, 1960-68; adjudicator Mich. State Band and Orch. Festivals, Solo and Ensemble Festivals, 1950-70, Detroit Fiddler's Band Auditions, 1948-52, Mich. Fedn. Music Clubs, 1948-55; tchr. Ea. Mich. U., 1939-42, Hartland Sch. Music, 1939-42, Pontiac (Mich.) Pub. Schs., 1942-45, Detroit Pub. Schs., 1945-73, pvt. studio, 1973-90. Performer cello South Oakland Symphony, 1958-65, Detroit Women's Symphony, 1951-68, Riviera Theatre Orch., 1959, 60, Masonic Auditorium Opera, Ballet Seasons, 1959-65, Toledo Ohio Symphony, 1963-70, others; performer trumpet Detroit Brass Quartet, 1974-78; piano accompanist various auditions, recitals, solo and ensemble festivals; composer: Let There Be Music, 1949, Fantasy for French Horn and Symphonic Band, 1951. Mem. Quota Internat., Delta Omicron. Home: 14650 N Alamo Canyon Dr Tucson AZ 85737-8812

SEAMAN, LYNN, research engineer, investor; b. DeQueen, Ark., Aug. 1933; s. Harvard lake and Bessie S.; m. Elisabeth Rosenthal, May 21, 1957 (div. May 1987); children: Peggy, Ellen, Mark, Tanya; m. Renate Cords, Dec. 26, 1989. BSc, U. Calif., Berkeley, 1959; PhD, MIT, 1961. Registered civil engr., Calif. Sr. rsch. engr. SRI Internat., Menlo Park, Calif., 1961—; vis. scientist Inst. Applied Mechanics, Bremen, Germany, 1990, Ecole Nat. Supérieure de Mécanique et d'Aérotechnique, Poitiers, France, 1995-96, Ecole Nat. Superiear, Cachan, France, 1997; lectr. Beijing Inst. Tech., 1983. Contbr. 96 articles to profl. jours. Corp. U.S. Army, 1953-55. Alfred E. Sloan scholar Sloan Found., Berkeley, Calif., 1957-59; fellow General Electric, Mass., 1959-61. Mem. Am. Physical Soc. (meeting chmn. 1981), Am. Soc. Civil Engrs. Avocations: sculpture, psychology, travel, language. Office: SRI International 333 Ravenswood Ave Menlo Park CA 94025-3453

SEAMOUNT, PHILIP JAMES, retired machine operator; b. Rifle, Colo., May 24, 1927; s. Daniel and Flossie Mabel (Taylor) S. Avocations: writing poetry, oil painting. Home: 1213 Lafayette St Alameda CA 94501-4171

SEARIGHT, MARY DELL (MRS. PAUL JAMES SEARIGHT), nursing educator; b. Cordell, Okla., Jan. 4, 1918; d. John Quitman and Grace Jewel (Giles) Williams; diploma St. Francis Hosp. Sch. Nursing, 1940; B.S. with honors, U. Calif. at Berkeley, 1960; M.S., U. Calif. at San Francisco, 1961; Ed.D., U. San Francisco, 1980; m. Paul James Searight, June 12, 1953; children—Gregory Newton, Sara Ann. Clin. nursing in various hosps., clinics, industries, drs. offices, 1940-59; instr. nursing Merritt Coll., Oakland, Calif., 1961-66; lectr. U. Calif. at San Francisco Sch. Nursing, 1966-68; nursing cons. regional med. programs, lectr. U. Minn., Mpls., 1968-71; chmn. dept. Sonoma State U., 1971-77, prof. nursing, 1971-87, prof. emeritus, 1987—; mem. acad. senate, 1972-75, cons. nursing edn., 1972-77; project dir. Nat. 2d Step Project, 1978-81; cons. Bur. Health Resources Devel., San Francisco, 1973-75; mem. chancellor's liaison com. nursing edn. Calif. State U. and Colls. Office of Chancellor, Los Angeles, 1973-76; chmn. Sonoma County Health Facilities Planning Com., Santa Rosa, Calif., 1970-72; mem. planning com. Sonoma Health Services/Edn. Activities, Santa Rosa, 1972; mem. exec. com., bd. dirs. Sonoma County Comprehensive Health Planning Com., 1970-72. Mem. Nat. League Nursing, Am. Assn. Colls. Nursing, Am., Calif. (Lulu Hassenplug award 1975) Nurses Assns., Santa Rosa Symphony League, Sigma Theta Tau. Author: Your Career in Nursing, 1970, 2d edit., 1977; editor, contbg. author: The Second Step, Baccalaureate Education for Registered Nurses (Book of Year, Am. Jour. Nursing), 1976; contbr. articles to profl. jours. Address: 5555 Montgomery Dr Apt C-1 Santa Rosa CA 95409-8805

SEARIGHT, PATRICIA ADELAIDE, retired radio and television executive; b. Rochester, N.Y.; d. William Hammond and Irma (Winters) S. BA, Ohio State U. Program dir. Radio Sta. WTOP, Washington, 1952-63, gen. mgr. info., 1964; radio and TV cons., 1964-84; ret., 1984; producer, dir. many radio and TV programs; spl. fgn. news corr. French Govt., 1956; v.p. Micro Beads, Inc., 1955-59; sec., dir. Dennis-Inches, Corp., 1955-59; exec. dir. Am. Women in Radio and TV, 1969-74; fgn. service officer U.S. Dept. State, ret., AEC, ret. Mem. pres.'s coun. Toledo Mus. Art. Recipient Kappa Kappa Gamma Alumna achievement award. Mem. Am. Women in Radio and TV (program chmn.; corrs. sec.; dir. Washington chpt.; pres. 1958-60, nat. membership chmn. 1962-63, nat. chmn. Industry Info. Digest 1963-64, Mid-Eastern v.p. 1964-66), Soc. Am. Travel Writers (treas. 1957-58, v.p. 1958-59), Nat. Acad. TV Arts and Scis., Women's Advt. Club (Washington, pres. 1959-60), Nat. Press Club, Soroptimist, Kappa Kappa Gamma. Episcopalian. Home: 9498 E Via Montoya Scottsdale AZ 85255-5074

SEARLES, QUENTIN, artist; b. Dunn Center, N.D., Feb. 20, 1919; s. Leland Day and Bertha Marie (Schmidt) S.; m. Barbara Hoskins, Nov. 10, 1956; 1 child: Susan Searles Nielsen. BFA, Ctrl. Wash. U., 1948; cert. in secondary tchg., U. Wash., 1949; postgrad., U. Oreg. Social case worker State Dept. Social and Health Svcs., Yakima, Wash., 1953-61; art instr. Yakima Valley (Wash.) C.C., 1964-67; painter Orchard Garden, Naches, Washington, 1961—. *Included in juried group showings at the Seattle Art Museum eight times receiving an honorable mention. Exhibited in group showings in the Frye Museum in Seattle, Denver Art Museum, Salt Lake City Art Museum, Tacoma Art Museum, Olympia Capitol Museum and the Cheney Cowles Memorial Museum in Spokane.* With U.S. Army, 1941, CBI. Recipient 1st place Parnassus award U. Wash., 1947, Festival of Arts Columbia Basin Coll., Pasco, Wash., Artists Ctrl. Wash. Larson Gallery: grantee Wash. State Art Commn., 1978. Avocation: book collecting. Home: 8252 Us Highway 12 Naches WA 98937-8789

SEARS, ALAN EDWARD, lawyer; b. Chattanooga, Oct. 31, 1951; s. Edward Lee and Anna Maria (Shepperd) S.; m. Paula Scott Lebeau, Nov. 11, 1988; children: Kelley, Shelby, Anna Marie, Rebecca, Isaiah, Isabella. BA, U. Ky., 1974; JD, U. Louisville, 1977. Bar: Ky. 1977, U.S. Supreme Ct. 1980, Ariz. 1987, D.C. 1989, Calif. 1990, U.S. Dist. Ct. (we. and ea. dists.) Ky., U.S. Dist. Ct. Ariz., U.S. Dist. Ct. D.C., U.S. Ct. Appeals (D.C., 4th, 5th, 6th, 7th, 9th, 11th and D.C. cirs.), U.S. Tax Ct., U.S. Dist. Ct. (ctrl. & so. dists.) Calif. Asst. corp. counsel City of Ashland, Ky., 1977-78; assoc. Johnson, Dunnagan & Martin, Ashland, 1977-79, Amshoff & Amshoff, Louisville, 1979-81; chief criminal div., asst. U.S. atty. U.S. Dept. Justice, Louisville, 1981-85; exec. dir. atty. gens. commn. on pornography U.S. Dept. Justice, Washington, 1985-86; assoc. solicitor U.S. Dept. Interior, Washington, 1986-87; exec. dir. Children's Legal Found., Phoenix, 1987-90; assoc. Snell & Wilmer, Phoenix, 1990; exec. dir., gen. counsel Nat. Family Legal Found., Phoenix, 1990-91; asst. U.S. atty. U.S. Dept. Justice, 1991-93; pres., gen. counsel Alliance Def. Fund, 1993—; cons. and pub. speaker to numerous organizations. Co-author: Time, Place & Manner Regulation, 1989, Prosecution & Trial of Obscenity Case, 1988; contbr. chpts. to books. Bd. dirs. Ariz. Family Rsch. Inst. Phoenix, 1988-92, Lincoln Caucus Ednl. Corp., Phoenix, 1990—, Nat. Family Legal Found., Phoenix, 1991—; precinct capt. Rep. Party, 1979-81, legis. dist. chmn., 1980-81; mem. campaign staff Gov. Louie Nunn, 1979, and Senator Cook for U.S. Senate, 1974, other party activities. Mem. ABA, Ariz. Lawyers Div. Federalist Soc. (dir. 1988—), Calif. Bar Assn., Ariz. Bar Assn., Ky. Bar Assn., D.C. Bar [illegible] 85260-1622

SEARS, STEVEN LEE, [illegible]; b. Ft. Gordon, Ga., Dec. 23, 1957; s. Richard Bruce Sr. and Marian (Dean) S. AA, U. Fla., 1976; BA in Theater cum laude, Fla. State U., 1980. Writer Stephen J. Cannell Prodns., Hollywood, Calif., 1984-88, story editor, 1987-88; story editor VI-ACOM/Hargrove/Silverman Prodns., 1988; writer A. Shane Prodns., Superboy Prodns., 1989; exec. story cons. Highwayman Glen Larson/New West Prodns., Universal City, Calif., 1988; writer TV pilots Columbia Pictures TV, 1990. Writer (TV shows) Riptide, 1984-86, Hadcastle & McCormick, 1985, The A-Team, 1986-87, Stingray, 1987, Jesse Hawkes, 1989, Superboy, 1989, Grand Slam, 1989, Hardball, 1989, Who Gets Harry?, 1989, Robin's Hoods, 1994, Walker, Texas Ranger, 1994, (TV pilots) Harry O'Fell-Detective from Hell, 1990, The Inquisitor, 1990, (screenplay) Endangered Species, (interactive movie) Dreadnought, 1995, (TV show) Itsy Bitsy Spider, 1995; story editor TV shows J.J. Starbuck, 1987-88, The Father Dowling Mysteries, 1988; co-producer (TV show) Swamp Thing, 1991; producer (TV show) Raven, 1992-93; supervising prodr. (TV show) Xena Warrior Princess, 1995-97, co-exec. prodr., 1997—; exec. prodr. (feature) The Last Perfect Wave, 1995. Mem. AFTRA, SAG, Writers Guild Am. Democrat. Avocations: traveling, computers, karate.

SEASTRAND, ANDREA H., former congresswoman; b. Chgo., Aug. 5, 1941; m. Eric Seastrand (dec.); children: Kurt, Heidi. BA in Edn., DePaul U., 1963. Prof. religion U. Santa Barbara; mem. Calif. Assembly, 1990-94, U.S. Ho. of Reps., 1995-96; exec. dir. Calif. Space and Tech. Alliance, Calif. Space Port Authority; asst. Rep. leader; mem. Rep. caucus; mem. edn. com., agr. com., consumer protection com., new tech. com., govtl. efficiency com., and ways and means com.; mem. rural caucus and select com. on marine resources. Mem. Calif. Fedn. Rep. Women (past pres.).

SEAU, JUNIOR (TIANA SEAU, JR.), professional football player; b. Samoa, Jan. 19, 1969. Student, U. So. Calif. Linebacker San Diego Chargers, 1990—; player Super Bowl XXVIV, 1994. Named to Sporting News Coll. All-Am. Team, 1989, to Pro Bowl Team, 1991-93, 96, to Sporting News NFL All Pro Team, 1992, 93. Office: San Diego Chargers PO Box 609609 San Diego CA 92160-9609*

SEBRIS, ROBERT, JR., lawyer; b. N.Y.C., May 20, 1950; s. Robert and Ruth (Kagis) S.; m. S. Lawson Hollweg, Sept. 8, 1973; children: Jared Matthew, Bryan Taylor. BS in Indsl. Labor Rels., Cornell U., 1972; JD, George Washington U., 1978. Bar: D.C. 1978, Wash. 1980. Labor rels. specialist Onondaya County Office labor rels., Syracuse, N.Y., 1973-74, U.S. Dept. Labor, Washington, 1972-75; labor rels. mgr. U.S. Treasury Dept., Washington, 1975-78; employee rels. mgr. Washington, 1978-80; assoc. Davis, Wright, Todd, Riese & Jones, Seattle, 1980-84; ptnr. Davis, Wright, Tremain, Bellevue, Wash., 1985-92, Sebris Busto, P.S., Bellvue, Wash., 1992—; expert witness T.E.A.M. Act Amendments NLRA U.S. Senate hearing, 1997. Co-Author: Employer's Guide to Strike Planning, 1985; contbr. articles to profl. jours. Mem. Bellevue C.C. Found., 1988-95, pres., 1995-96; chair employment law cert. program U. Wash. Law Sch., 1996-97. Mem. ABA (health law forum, labor and employment law sect., com. on employee rights), Wash. Bar Assn., D.C. Bar Assn., Seattle/King County Bar Assn. (chmn. labor law sect. 1991-92), Pacific Coast Labor Law Conf. (planning com. 1980-93, chmn. 1991-92), Nat. Acad. Hosp. Attys., Soc. Human Resource Mgmt. Avocations: golf, soccer, coaching youth sports. Home: 16301 Mink Rd NE Woodinville WA 98072-9463 Office: Sebris Busto PS 1500 Plz Ctr 10900 NE 8th St Bellevue WA 98004-4405*

SECOR, ROBERT JOHN, writer; b. Pasadena, Calif., Sept. 1, 1956; s. John Paul and Leta Adine (Chapin) S. AA, Pasadena City Coll., 1976; BA, U. Puget Sound, 1978; M Internat. Studies, Claremont (Calif.) Grad. U., 1984. Prin. Gorak Books, Pasadena, 1984—. Author: Mexico's Volcanoes: A Climbing Guide, 1981, The High Sierra: Peaks, Passes and Trails, 1992, Aconcagua: A Climbing Guide, 1994, Denali Climbing Guide, 1998. Mem. Sierra Club, Am. Alpine Club, So. Calif. Mountaineers Assn., Calif. Mountaineering Club (pres. 1990-91). Republican. Lutheran. Avocations: skiing, sailing, mountaineering. Home and Office: 2366 Las Lunas St Pasadena CA 91107-2510

SEDLAK, CARL M., program manager; b. New London, Conn., Nov. 17, 1950; s. Richard K. Sedlak and Virginia L. Drittel; m. Gwendolyn Sadleir, March 30, 1974; children: David, Deborah, Laura. BA in Math, San Diego State U., 1974. Software engr. various, San Diego, 1972-78; cons. General Dynamics, San Diego, 1978-82; program mgr. SAIC, San Diego, 1982—; pres. Found. for Animation and Creative Tech., San Diego, 1996—. Mem. central com. Republican Party of San Diego, 1990-94. Mem. U.S. Soccer Fedn. (referee 1988, nat. licensed coach 1990—). Mem. LDS Ch. Home: 13021 Entreken Ave San Diego CA 92129-2208 Office: SAIC 10260 Campus Point Dr San Diego CA 92121-1522

SEDLOCK, JOY, psychiatric social worker; b. Memphis, Jan. 23, 1958; d. George Rudolph Sedlock and Mary Robson; m. Thomas Robert Jones, Aug. 8, 1983. AA, Ventura (Calif.) Jr. Coll., 1978; BS in Psychology, Calif. Luth. U., 1980; MS in Counseling and Psychology, U. LaVerne, 1983; MSW, Calif. State U., Sacramento, 1986. Research asst. Camarillo (Calif.) State Hosp., 1981, tchr.'s aide, 1982; sub. tchr. asst. Ventura County Sch. Dist., 1981; teaching asst. Ventura Jr. Coll., 1980-82, tchr. adult edn., 1980-84; psychiatric social worker Yolo County Day Treatment Ctr., Broderick, Calif., 1986, Napa (Calif.) State Hosp., 1986—. Bd. dirs. Napa County Humane Soc. Home: PO Box 1095 Yountville CA 94599-1095 Office: Napa State Hosp Napa/Vallejo Hwy Napa CA 49558

SEE, CAROLYN, English language educator, novelist, book critic; b. Pasadena, Calif., Jan. 13, 1934; d. George Newton Laws and Kate Louise (Sullivan) Daly; m. Richard Edward See, Feb. 18, 1955 (div. June 1959); 1 child, Lisa Lenine; m. Tom Sturak, June 11, 1959; 1 child, Clara Elizabeth Marya. BA, Calif. State U., L.A., 1958; PhD, UCLA, 1963. Prof. English, Loyola Marymount Coll., L.A., 1970-85, UCLA, L.A., 1985—; book critic L.A. Times, 1981-93, Washington Post, 1993—. Author: (novels) Rhine Maidens, 1980, Golden Days, 1986, Making History, 1991, Dreaming: Hard Luck and Good Times In America, 1995, The Handyman, 1999, also 3 others. Bd. dirs. Calif. Arts Coun., L.A., 1987-91, Day Break, for homeless, Santa Monica, Calif., 1989—, Friends of English, UCLA, 1990—; buddy for life AIDS Project Los Angeles, AIDS relief, L.A., 1990—. Recipient award Sidney Hillman Found., 1972, Robert Kirsch award L.A. Times, 1994; PEN Ctr. USA West Lifetime Achievement award 1998; grantee Nat. Endowment for Arts, 1980, Guggenheim fellow, 1990-91. Mem. Writers Guild Am., Libr. Found. Calif., PEN Ctr. USA West (pres. 1990-91), Nat. Book Critics Cir. (bd. dirs. 1986-90). Democrat. Avocations: gardening, sailing, dancing, brush clearing. Home: 17339 Tramonto Dr Pacific Palisades CA 90272-3124 Office: UCLA Dept English 405 Hilgard Ave Los Angeles CA 90095-9000

SEEBACH, LINDA ANNE, journalist; b. Rockville Centre, N.Y., Dec. 6, 1939; d. Ferdinand Anthony and Edythe Jane Perissi; m. J. Arthur Seebach Jr., Aug. 23, 1959 (div. Aug. 1992); 1 child, A. Peter. BA, Gettysburg (Pa.) Coll., 1960; MA, Northwestern U., 1962. Asst. prof. St. Olaf Coll., Northfield, Minn., 1965-71; pres. Small World Press, Northfield, 1972-87; fgn. expert East China Normal U., Shanghai, 1987-88; journalist Minn. Daily, Mpls., 1988-92; editl. writer L.A. Daily News, 1992-95; editl. page editor Valley Times, Pleasanton, Calif., 1995-97; editl. writer Rocky Mountain News, Denver, 1997—. Editor: The Chinese Intellectual, 1987. Mem. Soc. Profl. Journalists (Region 11 dir. 1993-97), Nat. Conf. Editl. Writers, Nat. Soc. Newspaper Columnists, Investigative Reporters and Editors, Mensa. Office: Rocky Mountain News 400 W Colfax Ave Denver CO 80204-2694

SEED, JOHN ALBERT, art and art history educator; b. Santa Monica, Calif., July 18, 1957; s. Albert Bracwell and Lois (Condee) S.; m. Jane Marie Mitchell, Aug. 9, 1992; children: April, Sky, Brian. BA with distinction, Stanford U., 1979; MA in Art, U. Calif., Berkeley, 1982. Prof. art and art history, chair art dept. Mt. San Jacinto (Calif.) Coll., 1986—. Mem. Mt. San Jacinto Coll. Faculty Assn. (pres. 1997-98), Stanford Alumni Assn. (life). Democrat. Home: 860 S State St Hemet CA 92543-7102 Office: Mt San [illegible]

SEEGALL, MANFRED ISMAR LUDWIG, retired physicist, educator; b. Berlin, Germany, Dec. 23, 1929; s. Leonhard and Vera Antonie (Vodackova) S.; came to U.S., 1952, naturalized, 1957; m. Alma R. Sterner Clarke; 2 stepchildren: James, Mark. BS magna cum laude, Loyola Coll., 1957; MS, Brown U., 1960; PhD, Stuttgart (Germany) Tech. U., 1965. Research engr. Autonetics Corp. div. N.Am. Aviation, Downey, Calif., 1959-61; physicist Astronautics div. Gen. Dynamics, Inc., San Diego, 1961-62; research scientist Max Planck Inst., Stuttgart, 1962-65; instr. stats. and algebra San Diego City Coll., 1966; sr. research engr. Solar div. Internat. Harvester Co., San Diego, 1967-73; research cons. in energy and pollution, San Diego, 1974-83; part-time evening instr. Mesa Coll., San Diego, 1980-81; instr. Grossmont Coll., El Cajon, Calif., 1981; sr. scientist Evaluation Research Corp., San Diego, 1981-82, RCS analyst Teledyne Micronetics, San Diego, 1983-84, sr. design specialist Alcoa Defense Systems, San Diego, 1984-87, cons. phys scis., 1987-89; ind. contractor in tech. writing, engring. rsch. and real estate, 1990-92, freelance writer, 1993—. Mem. IEEE (sr.), Internat. Platform Assn., Calif. Parapsychology Found. (pres. 1994-96), Cottage of Czechoslovakia of House of Pacific Rels., Rosicrucian Order, Loyola Coll., Brown U. alumni assns. Republican. Club: San Diego Lodge AMORC. Contbr. articles on acoustics, pollution and temp. measurement methods to tech. jours.; patentee in field. Address: 8735 Blue Lake Dr San Diego CA 92119-3512

SEEGER, SONDRA JOAN, artist; b. L.A., May 27, 1942; d. Reinhold Josheph and Bertha Catherine (Monese) S.; m. Richard John Pahl, Aug. 18, 1961 (div. 1974); children: Catherine Marie, Douglas Richard, Angela Gay, Susan Joan; m. David Ernest Matteson, Apr. 25, 1990. Student, Marylhurst Coll., 1960. Pvt. practice musician various locations, 1973-81; security guard MGM Hotel, Las Vegas, 1981-82; real estate salesperson Century 21, Kent, Wash., 1983-85; mgr. Viera Land & Cattle, Inc., La Grande, Oreg., 1984-92; freelance artist, Casper, Wyo., 1991—; ptnr. Old West Saddle Shop, Casper, 1989-93, Casper, Wyo., 1993—; com. mem. Oreg. State Forest Practices Com., N.E. Region, 1990-91. Named Union Co. Tree Farmer of Yr., Am. Tree Farm System, 1987. Mem. NRA, Nat. Soc. Artists, Women Artists of the West, Allied Artists, Cider Painters of Am., Australian Soc. of Miniature Art, Small Woodlands Assn., Knickerbocker Artists (assoc.), United Pastelists of Am. (signature), Nat. Soc. Artists (signature), Women Artists of the West, Pacific Art League, The Art League of Alexandria, Va., Miniature Art Soc. Fla., Oil Painters Am., Wyo. Artists Assn., Cody Country Art Guild, Am. Soc. Classical Realism, Gen. Artist Mem., Internat. Platform Assn., Oreg. Forest Resources Inst., Am. Artists' Profl. League. Republican. Avocations: dog obedience tng., hunting, wildlife habitat enhancement. Home and Office: Old West Saddle Shop RR 3 Box 248 Espanola NM 87532-9615

SEELENFREUND, ALAN, distribution company executive; b. N.Y.C., Oct. 22, 1936; s. Max and Gertrude (Roth) S.; m. Ellyn Bolt; 1 child, Eric. BME, Cornell U., 1959, M. in Indsl. Engring., 1960; PhD in Mgmt. Sci., Stanford U., 1967. Asst. prof. bus. adminstrn. Grad. Sch. Bus. Stanford U., Palo Alto, Calif., 1966-71; mgmt. cons. Strong, Wishart and Assocs., San Francisco, 1971-75; various mgmt. positions McKesson Corp., San Francisco, 1975-84, v.p., chief fin. officer, 1984-86, exec. v.p., chief fin. officer, 1986-89, chmn., CEO, 1989-97, chmn., 1997-99, also bd. dirs., chmn., 1997—; bd. dirs. Pacific Gas and Electric Co. Bd. dir. Golden Gate Nat. Park Assn. Mem. World Affairs Coun. No. Calif., Bay Area Coun., Nature Conservancy, World Wildlife Fund, Bankers Club, St. Francis Yacht Club, Villa Taverna Club, Pacific Union Club. Avocations: sailing, skiing. Office: McKesson Corp 1 Post St Ste 3275 San Francisco CA 94104-5292

SEELY, ALICE WARDER, artist; b. Cheyenne, Wyo., Jan. 31, 1943; d. William Warder and Sylvia Ann (Shipley) Abeyta; m. George Seely, Jan. 28, 1961 (div. Mar. 1993); children: Kathryn, Chris, Tristan. Gallery artist N.Mex., 1967—; pres. Urban Fetishes Jewelry Inc., Hondo, N.Mex., 1993—; cons. on explosive art N.Mex. Sch. of Mining and Tech., Socorro, 1986-86. Author, illustrator: (book) Echoes on the Rocks, 1998; co-artist: (mural) Petroglyphs, 1997. Named Selected Artist, N.Mex. Arts Divsn. Mural, 1996, N.Mex. Arts Divsn. Painting, 1997, Ctr. for Explosive Rsch., 1986; recipient Introduction 76 award Albuquerque Mus., 1976. Home and Office: PO Box 166 Hwy 70 MM 284 Hondo NM 88336-0166

SEETHALER, WILLIAM CHARLES, international business executive, consultant; b. N.Y.C., Dec. 4, 1937; s. William Charles and Catherine Frances (Flaherty) S. Student, Quinnipiac Coll., Conn., 1955-56, Ohio State U., 1956-58; BSBA, U. San Francisco, 1977; MBA, Pepperdine U., 1982. Asst. to v.p. sales T. Sendzimir, Inc., Waterbury, Conn. and Paris, 1960-66; mgr. internat. ops. Dempsey Indsl. Furnace Co., East Longmeadow, Mass., 1966-67; mgr. internat. sales Yoder Co., Cleve., 1967-74; mng. dir., owner Seethaler & Assocs., Palo Alto, Calif.; owner, chief exec. officer Seethaler Internat. Ltd., Palo Alto, Calif., 1974—; ptnr. DFS Computer Assocs., San Jose, Calif., 1976-87. Bd. dirs. Palo Alto Fund, 1979-93, chmn., 1986-88; comty. rels. advisor Stanford U., 1986—. Mem. Inst. Indsl. Engrs. (sr., v.p. profl. rels. Peninsula chpt. 1988-90, del. to Silicon Valley Engring. Coun. 1991-97, bd. dirs.), Joint Venture: Silicon Valley (bd. dirs. 1992-95), Assn. Iron and Steel Engrs. (life), Assn. MBA Execs., Palo Alto C. of C. (v.p. orgn. affairs 1976-77, pres. 1977-78, bd. dirs. 1975-79), U. San Francisco Alumni Assn., Stanford U. Alumni Assn., Pepperdine U. Alumni Assn., Stanford Diamond Club. Office: 701 Welch Rd Ste D100 Palo Alto CA 94304

SEGAL, VLADIMIR M., metallurgist, researcher; b. Barashi, USSR, Oct. 3, 1936; came to U.S., 1989; s. Miron S. and Rahei N. (Volfovich) S.; m. Galina M. Freidlina, Feb. 20, 1962; children: Svetlana, Leonid. MSME, Tech. U., 1959, Phd in Metallurgy, 1965; ScD in Metallurgy, Acad. Scis., 1974. Devel. engr. Minsk Tractor Plant, Minsk, Buelorussia, 1959-65; sr. scientist Acad. Scis., Minsk, Buelorussia, 1965-86; prof. Engring. Inst., Lygansk, Ukraine, 1986-89; design engr. Interstate Forging Industry, Navasota, Tex., 1990-92; rsch. engr. Texas A&M U., College Station, Tex., 1992-95; principal rsch. scientist Johnson Matthey Electronics, Spokane, Wash., 1996—. Author: 8 books in Russian, 1966-95. Achievements include invention of new metalworking techniques for materials processing for properties; over 50 patents in field. Home: 1906 S Sonora Dr Veradale WA 99037-8011 Office: Johnson Matthey Electronics 15128 E Euclid Ave Spokane WA 99216-1895

SEGEL, KAREN LYNN JOSEPH, lawyer; b. Youngstown, Ohio, Jan. 15, 1947; d. Samuel Dennis and Helen Anita Joseph; m. Alvin Gerald Segel, June 9, 1968 (div. Sept. 1976); 1 child, Adam James. BA in Soviet and East European Studies, Boston U., 1968; JD, Southwestern U., 1975. Bar: Calif., 1996, U.S. Tax Ct., 1996, U.S. Dist. Ct. (cen. dist.) Calif., 1996, U.S. Ct. Appeals (9th cir.), 1997. Adminstrv. asst. Olds Brunel & Co., N.Y.C., 1968-69, U.S. Banknote Corp., N.Y.C., 1969-70; tax acct. S.N. Chilkov & Co. CPA's, Beverly Hills, Calif., 1971-74; intern Calif. Corps. Commr., 1975; tax. sr. Oppenheim Appel & Dixon CPA's, L.A., 1978, Fox, Westheimer & Co. CPA's, L.A., 1978, Zebrak, Levine & Mepos CPA's, L.A., 1979; ind. cons. acctg., taxation specialist Beverly Hills, 1980—; bd. dirs. World Wide Motion Pictures Corp., L.A.; law student mentor Southwestern U., 1996-99, tax moot ct. judge, 1997. Editorial adv. bd. Am. Biog. Inst. High sch. amb. to Europe People-to-People Orgn., 1963. Named 1991, 93 Woman of Yr., Am. Biog. Inst. Mem. Nat. Soc. Tax Profls., Nat. Assn. Tax Practitioners, Nat. Trust for Hist. Preservation, Calif. State Bar, Winterthur Guild, Women's Inner Circle of Achievement, Consumer Lawyers of L.A., Calif. Young Lawyers Assn., Beverly Hills Bar Assn., Santa Monica Bar Assn., Complex Litigation Inns of Ct., L.A. County Bar Assn, Beverly Hills Tinseltown Rose Soc. Avocations: collecting seashells, lhasa apso dog breeding, art, traveling, music.

SEGER, LINDA SUE, script consultant, lecturer, writer; b. Peshtigo, Wisc., Aug. 27, 1945; d. Linus Vauld and Agnes Katherine Seger; m. Theodore Newton Youngblood, Jr., Aug. 28, 1968 (div. Jan. 1970); m. Peter Hazen LeVar, April 12, 1987. BA in English, Colo. Coll., Colorado Springs, 1967; MA in theatre arts, Northwestern U., Evanston, 1968; MA in religion and arts, Pacific Sch. of Religion, Berkeley, 1973; ThD in drama and theology, Graduate Theological U., Berkeley, 1976; postgrad., Immaculate Heart Coll. Ctr., L.A., 1994. Instr. drama Grand Canyon Coll., Phoenix, 1969-71; instr. drama and theology McPherson (Kans.) Coll., 1976-77; instr. drama and humanities LaVerne (Calif.) U., 1977-79; asst. Provisional Theatre, L.A., [illegible] 83; pvt. practice script cons. L.A., 1981—, pvt. practice lectr., author, 1984—. Author: Making a Good Script Great, 1988, Creating Unforgettable Characters, 1990, The Art of Adaptation, 1992, When Women Call the Shots, 1996, Making A Good Writer Great, 1999; co-author: From Script to

Screen, 1994. Mem. NOW, Women in Film, Acad. of TV Arts and Scis. Democrat. Mem. Soc. of Friends. Avocations: horseback riding, piano, travel. Home and Office: 2038 Louella Ave Venice CA 90291-4015

SEGO, SEAN P., safety advisor; b. Terre Haute, Ind., June 28, 1969; s. Lewis P. and Kathleen Sego; m. Michelle Mealey, June 19, 1993. BA in Health and Safety Mgmt., Ind. State U., 1993. Cert. safety profl. Safety engr. Cherne, Mpls., 1992-96; safety advisor Arco, L.A., 1996—. Editor: (newsletter) Lartimes, 1996—. Mem. Am. Soc. Safety Engrs. Democrat. Roman Catholic. Avocations: equities/market, tennis, biking. Home: 14317 Utica Ave Savage MN 55378-2801 Office: Arco 1801 E Sepulveda Blvd Carson CA 90745-6121

SEGUR, WINTHROP HUBBARD, JR., management and busineses educator; b. Hartford, Conn., May 21, 1936; s. Winthrop Hubbard and Althea (Rosen) S. BS in Math., Trinity Coll., Hartford, Conn., 1958; MA in Math., Bowdoin Coll., 1965; PhD in Agrl. Econs., U. Calif., Davis, 1980. Instr. math. Thacher Sch., Ojai, Calif., 1961-68; cmty. organizer United Farm Workers, Delano, Calif., 1968-73; asst. prof. econs. U. of the Pacific, Stockton, Calif., 1979-85; lectr. econs. and bus. Calif. State U., Chico, 1985-87; staff economist United Farm Workers, Keene, Calif., 1987-89; prof. bus. and mgmt. U. Redlands, Calif., 1989—, chair dept., 1989-95; mem. agrl. adv. com. Calif. State Assembly, Stockton, 1983-85; mem. com. on long range planing Calif. State Senate, Stockton, 1985-87; mem. Farm Labor Estimation project U.S. Dept. Labor, Washington, 1988-91; bd. dirs. Calif. Inst. for Rural Studies, Davis, 1992—. Contbr. articles to profl. jours. Chair rural econs. alternatives project com. Am. Friends Svc. Com., Stockton, 1983-85. Mem. AAUP, 1996—, Indsl. Rels. Rsch. Assn. (chpt. pres. 1994, 97), S.W. Labor Studies Assn. (conf. cir. 1992), Am. Agrl. Econs. Assn., Am. Econ. Assn. Avocations: sping training, Shelby Am., Calif. Hwy 99, Brautigan, Bauer. Office: U Redlands Mgmt and Bus/ANWC E Colton Ave Redlands CA 92373

SEIBEL, ERWIN, oceanographer, educator; BS, CCNY, 1965; MS, U. Mich., 1966, PhD, 1972. Asst. research oceanographer U. Mich., Ann Arbor, 1972-75, assoc. research oceanographer, 1975-78, asst. dir. sea grant, 1975-78; environ. lab dir. San Francisco State U., 1978-81, chmn. dept. geoscis., 1981-88, dean undergraduate studies, 1988—. commr. Calif. Commn. on Tchr. Credentialing; sr. scientist cruises U. Mich., 1971-78; mem. sea grant site rev. teams Nat. Sea Grant Program, Washington, 1978—; bd. govs. Moss Landing Marine Labs., Calif., 1981—; mem. adv. com. Ctr. Advancement Mercantile Spacefaring; coord. Biology Forum Calif. Acad. Scis., 1988-89; exec. sec. Oceans 83 Marine Tech. Soc., IEEE, San Francisco, 1982-83; coord. Symposium for Pacific AAAS El Nino Effect, 1983-84; dir. environ. monitoring nuclear power plant, 1972-78; mem. sci. adv. panel Calif. Commn. Tchr. Credentialing, 1988-93; mem. steering com. Pacific Basin Studies Ctr., 1990-93; commr. Calif. Commn. on Teaching Credentialing, 1993—, fiscal planning & policy com., 1994—, performance stds. com., 1995—, appeals & waivers com., 1996—. Contbr. articles to profl. jours.; developer photogrammetric technique for continuous shoreline monitoring. Advisor MESA program for Minority Students, San Francisco area, 1981-88; vol. San Francisco Bay Area council Girl Scouts U.S., 1982-86. Served to capt. U.S. Army, 1967-71, Vietnam. Grantee Am. Electric Power Co., 1972-78, Gt. Lakes Basin Commn., 1975-76, Calif. Div. Mines and Geology, 1986-88, Am. Coun. Edn. and Ford Found., 1990-94. Recipient Exceptional Merit Service award San Francisco State U., 1984. Fellow AAAS, Calif. Acad. Scis., Geol. Soc. Am.; mem. N.Y. Acad. Scis., Am. Geophys. Union, Marine Tech. Soc. (pres. San Francisco Bay chpt. 1982-83), Western Assn. Schs. and Colls. (mem. student learning and teaching effectiveness task force 1994-95), U. Mich. Alumni Assn., Gold Key (hon.), Sigma XI (pres. San Francisco State U. chpt. 1982-84, 90-92, Chautauqua coord, 1989-96, faculty athletic rep. NCAA, NCAC, 1991-93). Office: San Francisco State U Dean of Undergrad Studies 1600 Holloway Ave San Francisco CA 94132-1722

SEIDEL, GEORGE ELIAS, JR., animal scientist, educator; b. Reading, Pa., July 13, 1943; s. George E. Sr. and Grace Esther (Heinly) S.; m. Sarah Beth Moore, May 28, 1970; 1 child, Andrew. BS, Pa. State U., 1965; MS, Cornell U., 1968, PhD, 1970; postgrad., Harvard U. Med. Sch., Boston, 1970-71. Asst. prof. physiology Colo. State U., Ft. Collins, 1971-75, assoc. prof., 1975-83, prof., 1983-93, univ. disting. prof., 1993—; vis. scientist Yale U., 1978-79, MIT, 1986-87; mem. bd. on agr. NRC. Co-editor: New Technologies in Animal Breeding, 1981; contbr. articles to profl. jours. Recipient Alexander Von Humboldt award, N.Y.C., 1983, Animal Breeding Research award Nat. Assn. Animal Breeders, Columbia, Mo., 1983, Clark award Colo. State U., 1982, Upjohn Physiology award, 1986; Gov's. award for Sci. and Tech., Colo., 1986. Mem. AAAS, NAS, Am. Dairy Sci. Assn., Am. Soc. Animal Sci. (Young Animal Scientist award 1983), Soc. for Study of Reprodn., Internat. Embryo Transfer Soc. (pres. 1979). Home: 3101 Arrowhead Rd Laporte CO 80535-9374 Office: Colo State U Animal Repro Biotech Lab Fort Collins CO 80523

SEIDEL, SALLY CAROL, physicist, educator; b. Cleve., Jan. 8, 1958; d. Rudolf and Margaret Seidel.; m. Gordon Joseph Zwartz, Mar. 11, 1995. BS in Physics, Yale U., 1980; MS in Physics, U. Mich., 1983, PhD in Physics, 1987. Tchg. asst. in physics U. Mich., 1980-82, rsch. asst., 1982-87; rsch. assoc. in physics U. Toronto, 1987-91; asst. prof. physics U. N.Mex., Albuquerque, 1991-97, assoc. prof., 1997—; Mem. Fermilab Users Exec. Com., 1992-94, CDF Collaboration Exec. Bd., others; co-chair ATLAS Collaboration Pixel Sensor Group, 1996—, instnl. rep., mem. collaboration bd. ATLAS; mem. collaboration pixel detector steering group, invited session chair IEEE Nuclear Sci. Symposium, 1997; invited speaker various workshops and confs. Editor: DPF '94 Procs., 1995; contbr. articles to sci. publs. NSF Travel grantee, 1984, Natural Scis. and Engring. Rsch. Coun. Travel grantee, 1991, U.S. Dept. of Energy grantee, 1992—, NSF grantee, 1995-96, 99—, Sandia Univs. Rsch. Program grantee Sandia Nat. Labs., 1992, 93. Mem. Am. Phys. Soc. (co-recipient Bruno Rossi prize 1989), Am. Assn. Physics Tchrs. Office: U NMex Dept Physics & Astronomy 800 Yale Blvd NE Albuquerque NM 87131

SEIDELMAN, ARTHUR ALLAN, director; b. N.Y.C.; s. Theodore and Jeanne (Greenberg) S. BA, Whittier (Calif.) Coll., 1958; MA, UCLA, 1960. Adminstr. Forum Theater, Lincoln Ctr., N.Y.C., 1970-72; pres. LSV Prodns., N.Y.C., 1972-76; v.p. Golden Eagle Prodns., N.Y.C., 1977-79; pres. Entertainment Profls., Inc., L.A., 1980-92, Entpro, Inc., L.A., 1992—. Dir.: (feature films) Walking Across Egypt, Rescue Me, Hercules in New York, The Caller, Children of Rage, Echoes; (TV episodes) Hill Street Blues (Emmy, Humanitas awards for "Doris in Wonderland"), Murder She Wrote, Magnum, P.I., Knots Landing, Trapper John, M.D., Fame, A Year in the Life, L.A. Law, Capital News, WIOU, F.B.I. The Untold Stories, Sweet Justice, Amazing Grace, others; (TV movies) Which Mother is Mine? (Emmy award, Christopher award, Golden Halo award), I Love Liberty (Writer's Guild award), Schoolboy Father, Having a Baby, Look Away (Emmy nomination), Macbeth, Matter of Time (Emmy award, Chgo. Film Festival Silver plaque, N.Y. Internat. Film Festival Silver plaque), She Drinks a Little (Emmy award, Golden Halo award), Strange Voices, A Place at the Table, An Enemy Among Us (Nancy Susan Reynolds award), Poker Alice, Sin of Innocence, Kate's Secret, A Friendship in Vienna (Grand prize N.Y. Internat. Film Festival), The People Across the Lake, Addicted to His Love, The Glory Years, False Witness, The Kid Who Loved Christmas, Body Language, Dying to Remember, Trapped in Space, The Secrets of Lake Success, Amazing Grace (pilot), Harvest of Fire (Movie Guide award), The Summer of Ben Tyler, Deep Family Secrets, Miracle in the Woods, Grace and Glorie; dir. broadway and off-broadway plays Hamp. Ceremony of Innocence, Awake and Sing, Billy, Inherit the Wind, Justice Box, Vieux Carrè, The Most Happy Fella for the N.Y.C. Opera, Gypsy Princess for Opera Pacific, The Sisters at the Pasadena Playhouse and Hatlen Theater, Of Thee I Sing for Reprise, others; host TV series Actors on Acting (Emmy award). Bd. dirs. ACLU So. Calif., L.A., 1986-94. Democrat. Office: Entpro, Inc 1015 Gayley Ave # 1149 Los Angeles CA 90024-3424

SEIDEN, SANDRA MAE, artist; b. San Diego, Jan. 26, 1949; d. Edward Irvin and Ruth Margaret (Schmidt) Seiden; 1 child, Shayne Magic McIntyre. Exhibited in numerous shows; artist oil on canvas in Ency. of the Living Artist, 11th edit., 1999.

SEIDENSTICKER, EDWARD GEORGE, Japanese language and literature educator; b. Castle Rock, Colo., Feb. 11, 1921; s. Edward George and Mary Elizabeth (Dillon) S. B.A., U. Colo., 1942; M.A., Columbia U., 1947; postgrad., Harvard U., 1947-48; LittD (hon.), U. Md., 1991. With U.S. Fgn. Service, Dept. State, Japan, 1947-50; mem. faculty Stanford U., 1962-66, prof., 1964-66; prof. dept. Far Eastern langs. and lit. U. Mich., Ann Arbor, 1966-77; prof. Japanese Columbia U., 1977-85, prof. emeritus, 1986—. Author: Kafu the Scribbler, 1965, Japan, 1961, Low City, High City, 1983, Tokyo Rising, 1990, Very Few People Come This Way, 1994; transl.: (by Murasaki Shikibu) The Tale of Genji, 1976. Served with USMCR, 1942-46. Decorated Order of Rising Sun Japan; recipient Nat. Book award, 1970; citation Japanese Ministry Edn., 1971; Kikuchi Kan prize, 1977; Goto Miyoko prize, 1982; Japan Found. prize, 1984; Tokyo Cultural award, 1985; Yamagata Banto prize, 1992. Home: 1350 Ala Moana Blvd Apt 3103 Honolulu HI 96814-4229

SEIFF, GLORIA LOUISE, volunteer; b. Denver, Apr. 3, 1929; d. Edward Hyatt and Lilliian Pearl (Blend) Holtzman; m. Stephen S. Seiff, Apr. 16, 1950; children: Stuart R., Sherri P. Seiff Sloane, Karen E. Seiff Sacks. Student, Washington U., 1947-48. Commr. Pub. Works Commn., Beverly Hills, Calif., 1990-98, bd. pres. 1993, 96; pres. Beverly Vista Elem. Sch. PTA, Beverly Hills, lif.,968-69, PTA Coun., Beverly Hills, 1972-73; bd. dirs. Beverly Hills S.W. Homeowners Assn., 1985—, Braille Inst. Aux., L.A., 1998—; founding mem., bd. dirs., trustee Beverly Hills Edn. Found., 1975-79; v.p. devel. Assistance League So. Calif., L.A., 1994-98, bd. dirs., 1994—; trustee L.A. County Mosquito Abatement Dist., 1984-92, bd. pres. 1988; pres. LWV, Beverly Hills, 1985-87. Recipient Hon. Svc. award PTA, Beverly Hills, 1972, Outstanding Cmty. Svc. award, Beverly Hills City Coun., 1986-87, Resolution Cmty. Svc. award Beverly Bd. Edn., 1986. Mem. Calif. Yacht Club. Avocation: sailing.

SEIFF, STEPHEN S., ophthalmologist; b. L.A., Sept. 30, 1925; s. Max and Minnie F. (Feldman) S.; m. Gloria Louise Holtzman, Apr. 16, 1950; children: Stuart R., Sherri Seiff Sloane, Karen Seiff Sacks. AA, UCLA, 1945; AB, U. Calif., Berkeley, 1946; MD, U. Calif., San Francisco, 1949. Diplomate Am. Bd. Ophthalmology. Intern County Gen. Hosp., L.A., 1949-50; fellow in anesthesiology Lahey Clinic, Boston, 1950-51; resident in ophthalmology U. Calif., San Francisco, 1952-55; clin. prof. dept. ophthalmology UCLA, 1956—; pvt. practice Beverly Hills, Calif., 1955—; clin. chief divsn. ophthalmology Cedars/Sinai Med. Ctr., L.A., 1957—; attending ophthalmologist Children's Hosp., L.A., 1956-94; lectr. in field; assoc. examiner Am. Bd. Ophthalmology. Collaborating author: Clinical Anticoagulant Therapy, 1965; contbr. articles to profl. jours. Bd. dirs. That Man May See Inc., San Francisco; former exec. com. mem. UCLA Hosp. Lt. M.C. USNR, 1950-52. Recipient Sr. Honor award UCLA Dept. Ophthalmology, 1994. Fellow ACS, Am. Acad. Ophthalmology; mem. L.A. Soc. Ophthalmology (past pres.), Frederick Cordes Eye Soc. (past nat. pres.), L.A. County Med. Assn., Calif. Med. Assn., Am. Soc. Cataract and Refractive Surgery (founding mem.). Avocation: sailing. Office: 435 N Roxbury Dr Ste 107 Beverly Hills CA 90210-5003

SEILER, KAREN PEAKE, psychologist; b. Seattle, Jan. 31, 1952; d. Louis Joseph and Donna Mae (Waters) Tomaso; m. Arthur J. Seiler; children from previous marriage: Jeremy S. Peake, Anthony K. Peake. BA/BSW magna cum laude, Carroll Coll., 1987; postgrad., MIT, 1994. Cert. strategic planning Pacific Inst.; cert. orgnl. cons. Covey Learning Ctr., 1993. Admissions counselor Shodair Children's Hosp., Helena, Mont., 1984-86; asst. dir., counselor Career Tng. Inst., Helena, 1986-90; pres. Corp. Cons., Helena, 1990—; apptd. amb. Mont. Ambs., 1990—; active Gov.'s Task Force on Econ. Devel., 1991-94; chairperson Mont. Dist. Export Coun./U.S. Dept. Commerce, 1992—; exec. com. mem. Mont. World Trade Ctr., Missoula, 1995—;. Mem. YWCA, 1986-90, pres., 1989; mem. Bus. and Profl. Women's Orgn., 1987-93, sec., 1990; pres. Helena Area Econ. Devel. Coun., 1989-92; exec. com. Leadership Helena, 1990-91; monitoring chair Concentrated Employment Program Pvt. Industry Coun., Mont., 1990—; bd. dirs., exec. com. Mont. Women's Capital Fund, 1990-95; exec. com. Mont. Race for the Cure, 1994—. Mem. NAFE, Partnership for Employment and Tng., Delta Epsilon Sigma (Outstanding Citizen award). Roman Catholic. Avocations: sailing, river rafting, 4-wheeling, reading, traveling. Home and Office: 315 N Park Ave Helena MT 59601-5056

SEILER, STEVEN LAWRENCE, health facility administrator; b. Chgo., Dec. 30, 1941; married. B, U. Ariz., 1963; M, U. Iowa, 1965. Adminstrv. resident Rush-Presbyn.-St. Luke's Med. Ctr., Chgo., 1965, adminstrv. asst., 1965-68; asst. adminstr. Lake Forest (Ill.) Hosp., 1968-71, adminstr., 1971-73, pres., 1973-86; exec. v.p Voluntary Hosps. Am., Park Ridge, Ill., 1987-89, sr. v.p., 1986-92; CEO Good Samaritan Regional Med. Ctr., Phoenix, 1992—; adj. prof. Contbr. articles to profl. jours. Mem. AHA (svc. com.)., Ill. Hosp. Assn. (chair 1980-81). Home: 3930 E Rancho Dr Paradise Vly AZ 85253-5025 Office: Good Samaritan Regional Med Ctr 1111 E Mcdowell Rd Phoenix AZ 85006-2612

SEITZ, WALTER STANLEY, cardiovascular research consultant; b. L.A., May 10, 1937; s. Walter and Frances Janette (Schleef) S. BS in Physics and Math., U. Calif., Berkeley, 1959; PhD in Biophysics, U. Vienna, 1981, MD, 1982. Health physicist U. Calif. Radiation Lab., 1959-61; rsch. assoc. NIH at Pacific Union Coll., 1961-63; physicist Lockheed Rsch. Labs., Palo Alto, Calif., 1961-63; staff scientist Xerox Corp., Pasadena, Calif., 1963-66; sr, scientist Applied Physics Cons., Palo Alto, 1966-75; instr. clin. sci. U. Ill Coll. Medicine, Urbana, 1983-84; cons. cardiology Cardiovascular Rsch. Inst. U. Calif. Sch. Medicine, San Francisco, 1987—; sr. scientist Inst. Med. Analysis and Rsch., Berkeley, 1987—. Contbr. articles to profl. jours. Postdoctoral Rsch. fellow, U. Calif. San Francisco, 1984. Fellow Am. Coll. Angiography; mem. AAAS, Royal Soc. Medicine London, N.Y. Acad. Scis., Physicians for Social Responsibility. Avocations: reading, music, hiking. Office: IMAR Cons Inc 38 Panoramic Way Berkeley CA 94704-1828

SEKINE, DEBORAH KEIKO, systems analyst, programmer; b. Honolulu, Dec. 1, 1952; d. Yoshiteru and Yaeko (Matsuda) Isa; m. Andrew K. Sekine, May 8, 1993. BA in Math. with distinction, U. Hawaii, 1974, BEd with distinction, 1974, MS in Computer Sci., 1976, MBA, 1987. Data analyst, engr. in-charge Kentron, Honolulu, 1977-81; sys. analyst Am. Savs., Honolulu, 1981-82; analyst, programmer City and County of Honolulu, 1982—; cons. Am. Savs., Honolulu, 1982. Contbr. articles to profl. jours. Vol. Hawaii Dem. Conv., Honolulu, 1984, Mayoral campaign, 1988, 92; com. co-chair Hui Makaala, Honolulu, 1989—; caregiver Makiki Christian Ch., Honolulu, 1991—. Mem. IEEE, Assn. for Computing Machinery, Am. Fedn. State County Mcpl. Employees, U. Hawaii MBA Alumni Assn., Phi Kappa Phi. Mem. United Ch. of Christ. Avocations: jogging, reading, writing, tennis, listening to gospel music. Home: 3322 George St Honolulu HI 96815-4319

SEKLECKI, EUGENE WALTER, retired oral surgeon; b. Chgo., Apr. 28, 1943; s. Anthony Vincent and Eugenia S.; m. Renee Paula Ring, May 17, 1969; children: Derek Eugene, Mariette Theresa, Kara Renee. BS in Biology, Loyola U., 1966, DDS, 1970. Diplomate Am. Bd. Oral, Maxillofacial Surgery. Commd. gen. dental officer USN, 1970-73; resident Loyola U. Medical Ctr., Chgo., 1973-76, Hines V.A. Hosp., Chgo., 1973-76; pvt. practice Tucson, 1976-98; retired Tucson, 1998; oral surgeon Ariz. C.C., 1993-94; surgeon Ariz. Correctional System, 1979-98; adj. prof. Pima Cmty. Coll., 1993—. Fellow Internat. Coll. Dentists, Am. Coll. Dentists, Am. Soc. Oral Maxillofacial Surgns (Ariz. chpt., Western chpt.), Pierre Fauchard Soc.; mem. ADA (delegate, Ariz. chpt. past pres., spkr. of the house, trustee), Am. Assn. Dental Anesthesia, Southern Ariz. Dental Soc. Office: Eugene W Seklecki DDS PC 3945 N Pantano Rd Tucson AZ 85750-2352

SELANNE, TEEMU, hockey player; b. Helsinki, Finland, July 3, 1970. Hockey player Winnipeg Jets Nat. Hockey League, 1992-95, hockey player Phoenix Coyotes, 1995-97, hockey player Anaheim Mighty Ducks, 1997—; played in All-Star Game, 1996, 94, 93. Named Rookie of Yr. Sporting News, 1992-93, All Rookie team, 1992-93; Recipient Calder Meml. Trophy, 1992-93. Office: Mighty Ducks PO Box 61077 2695 E Katella Ave Anaheim CA 92803

SELBY, JEROME M., mayor; b. Wheatland, Wyo., Sept. 4, 1948; s. John Franklin and Claudia Meredith (Hudson) S.; m. Gloria Jean Nelson, June 14, 1969; children: Tyan, Cameronn, Kalen. BS in Math., Coll. Idaho, 1969, MA in Ednl. Adminstrn., 1974; MPA, Boise State U., 1978. Assoc. engr. Boeing Co., Seattle, 1969-71; dir. evaluation WICHE Mountain States Regional Med. Program, Boise, 1971-74; dir. rsch., evaluation Mountain States Health Corp., Boise, 1974-76, with health policy analysis and accountability, 1976-78; dir. health Kodiak (Alaska) Area Native Assn., 1978-83; mgr. Kodiak Island Borough, 1984-85, mayor, 1985-98, bus., mcpl. and fisheries cons., 1998—; regional dir. planning and devel. Providence Health System, 1998—; proprietor Kodiak Tax Svc., 1978—, Registered Guide, Kodiak, 1987—; cons. Nat. Cancer Inst., Washington, 1973-78, others. Contbr. articles to profl. jours. Treas. ARC, Kodiak, 1978-93, bd. dirs., 1978-95, chmn., 1989-90, mem. western ops. hdqrs. adv. bd., 1986-92, mem. group IV and V nat. adv. coj., 1986-89, nat. bd. govs., 1989-95, chmn. chpt. rels. com., 1994-95; pres. S.W. Alaska Mcpl. Conf., Anchorage, 1988-89, v.p., 1986-87, treas., 1996-98, bd. dirs., 1986-98; pres. Alaska Mcpl. League Investment Pool, Inc., 1992-98; v.p. Alaska Mcpl. League, 1988-90, pres., 1990-91, bd. dirs., 1988-98; bd. dirs. Alaska Mcpl. League Jt. Ins. Assn. Bd., 1995—, v.p., 1996-98, pres., 1998—; mem. Alaska Resource Devel. Coun., 1987—, exec. com., 1989—; mem. policy com. of outer continental shelf adv. bd. U.S. Dept. Interior, 1990—, vice chair, 1996-98, chair, 1998—; co-chair Alaska Task Force, 1995—; mem. Com. on Oil Pollution Act, 1995s; mem. Nat. Assn. Counties, Cmty. and Econ. Devel. Steering Com., 1990-98, Alaska govtl. roles task force, 1991-92; mem. Alaska state/local govt. task force, 1996-98; chmn. Kodiak Island Exxon Valdez Restoration Com., 1991-95; dir. Kodiak Health Care Found., 1992—, v.p. 1992—; co-chmn. Arctic Power, 1993—; bd. dirs. Western Interstate Region Nat. Assn. of Counties, 1993-98; bd. dirs. Alaska Oceans, Seas, Fisheries Rsch. Found., 1998—, pres., 1998—; mem. environment, energy and land use steering com. Nat. Assn. Counties., 1997-98. Paul Harris fellow, 1987, 88, 91, 92, 96; recipient Outstanding Contbn. award Alaska Mcpl. League, 1994, Disting. Alumni award Albertson Coll. of Idaho, 1997, Lifetime Achievement award Alaska Mcpl. League, 1998. Mem. Alaska Conf. Mayors, Nat. Soc. Tax Profls., Acad. Polit. Sci., Alaska Mcpl. Mgrs. Assn., Kodiak C. of C. (dir. 1983—), Rotary (bd. dirs. 1989-97, treas. 1989-93, v.p. 1993-94, pres.-elect 1994-95, pres. 1995-96). Office: Providence Health Systems PO Box 196604 3200 Providence Dr Anchorage AK 99519-6604

SELDNER, BETTY JANE, environmental engineer, consultant, aerospace company executive; b. Balt., Dec. 11, 1923; d. David D. and Miriam M. (Mendes) Miller; m. Warren E. Gray, June 20, 1945 (div. 1965); children: Patricia, Deborah; m. Alvin Seldner, Nov. 15, 1965; children: Jack, Barbara. BA in Journalism, Calif. State U., Northridge, 1975, MA in Communications, 1977. Dir. pub. info. United Way, Van Nuys, Calif., 1958-63; dir. edn. United Way, Los Angeles, 1963-68; dir. pub. relations, fin. San Fernando Valley Girl Scout Council, Reseda, Calif., 1968-73; asst. dir. pub. info. Calif. State U., Northridge, 1973-75; dir. environ. mgmt. HR Textron Corp., Valencia, Calif., 1975-87; environ. engr. Northrop Aircraft, Hawthorne, Calif., 1987-88, EMCON Assocs., Burbank, Calif., 1988-92, Atkins Environ., 1992-93, Seldner Environ., Valencia, Calif., 1993—; prin. Seldner Environ. Svcs., 1993—. Author non-fiction. Mem. Santa Clarita Valley Environ. Mgrs. Soc. (chmn. bd. dirs. 1984), San Fernando Valley Round Table (pres. 1971-72), Hazardous Materials Mgrs.' Assn., Zonta Internat., Valencia Indsl. Assn. (environ. chair). Republican. Jewish. Avocation: sailing.

SELDON, MERVYN W. ADAMS, artist, editor; b. Chgo., May 9, 1930; d. Robert McCormick and Janet (Lawrence) Adams; m. M. Robert Seldon, Mar. 25, 1973 (dec. Mar. 1982). Student, Smith Coll., 1947-50, U. Chgo., 1950-51; MA, Columbia U., 1964; MFA, Calif. State U., 1997. Adminstrv. asst. East Asian Inst. Columbia U., N.Y.C., 1964-68; editor Praeger Publs., N.Y.C., 1968-73; cons. editor, series editor Westview Press, Boulder, Colo., 1975-90; dir. found. and corp. relations Claremont (Calif.) McKenna Coll., 1981-85; program officer W.M. Keck Found., Los Angeles, 1985-86; dir. devel. Performing Tree, Los Angeles, 1986-90; sec. L.A Artcore; treas. Gallery 57. Democrat. Roman Catholic. Clubs: Claremont. Avocation: tennis.

SELFRIDGE-FIELD, ELEANOR, educator; b. New Orleans, June 29, 1940. BA magna cum laude, Drew U., 1962; MSc, Columbia U., 1963; PhD, Oxford (Eng.) U., 1969. Tchr. U. Pitts., Drew U.; sr. rsch. assoc. CCARH, 1984—; cons. prof. Stanford (Calif.) U., 1995—; cons. in field. Author: Venetian Institute Music, 1974, 80, 94, Pallade Veneta, 1985, The Music of B. and A. Marcells, 1990, Beyond MIDI, 1997; co-editor: Computing in Musicology, 1985. Office: CCARH Stanford U Braun #128 Stanford CA 94305-3076

SELIGMAN, ADAM WARD, writer, publisher; b. L.A., Dec. 21, 1961; s. Selig Jacob and Muriel B. (Bienstock) S.; m. Julie Ann Furger, Aug. 14, 1993. Freelance journalist various music mags., 1983-96; CEO, AWS Publicity, Santa Monica, Calif., 1985-93, Echolalia Press, Santa Rosa, Calif., 1995—; dir. publicity Soundwings Records, Santa Monica, 1985-89; adminstrv. asst. Sch. of Optometry, Berkeley, Calif., 1985-89. Author: Echolalia, 1991, (poetry) Requiem for Orpheus, 1997; editor: Don't Think About Monkeys: Extraordinary Stories Written by People With Tourette Syndrome, 1992. Fund-raising assoc. Disability Rights Edn. and Def. Fund, Berkeley, 1992; bd. dirs. Nat. Orgn. Rare Diseases, Hartford, Conn., 1981-85; testified in front of Ho. of Reps., Washington, 1980, U.S. Congress, 1981, Congress, L.A., 1984. Mem. AFTRA, Writers Guild of Am. West, Inc. (chmn. com. of disabled writers 1981-87, negotiation com. 1988). Democrat. Wiccan. Avocations: Star Trek, science fiction, music. E-mail: seligman@sonic.net. Office: Echolalia Press 1055 W College Ave Ste 119 Santa Rosa CA 95401-5036

SELINGER, ANDREW JOSEPH, ice and roller rink development company executive; b. Seattle, Oct. 3, 1966; s. Edward and Nancy S. BA, Harvard U., 1988; JD, UCLA, 1991. Airline exec. Trans Con., Orlando, Fla., 1991-94; developer Hockey World, Marina Del Ray, Calif., 1994—. : Office: Hockey World 333 Washington Blvd Ste 235 Marina Del Rey CA 90292

SELK, ELEANOR HUTTON, artist; b. Duboise, Nebr., Oct. 21, 1918; d. Anderson Henry and Florence (Young) Hutton; R.N., St. Elizabeth Hosp., Lincoln, Nebr., 1938; m. Harold Frederick Selk, Aug. 3, 1940; children: Honey Lou, Katherine Florence. Nurse, Lincoln, 1938-40, Denver, 1940-50; with Colo. Bd. Realtors, 1956-66; owner, mgr. The Pen Point, graphic art studio, Colorado Springs, 1974-94; instr. history and oil painting, 1994—; one-woman shows: Colo. Coll., 1970, 72, Nazarene Bible Coll., 1973, 1st Meth. Ch., 1971 (all Colorado Springs); exhibited in group shows: U. So. Colo., 1969, 70, 71, 72, Colorado Springs Art Guild, 1969-72, Pike's Peak Artists Assn., 1969-73, Mozart Art Festival, Pueblo, Colo., 1969-74, numerous others; represented in permanent collection U.S. Postal Service, Pen-Arts Bldg., Washington, Medic Alert Found. Internat. Hdqrs., Turlock, Calif., Colorado Springs Music Co. Piano Gallery. Rec. sec. Colo. chpt. Medic Alert Found. Internat., 1980-90, chairperson El Paso County and Colorado Springs chpt., 1980-90, Colo. bd. dirs., 1980-89, rec. sec., 1980-89. Recipient 3d pl. award Nat. Tb and Respiratory Disease and Christmas Seal Art Competition, 1969, finalist award Benedictine Art competition Hanover Trust Bank, N.Y.C., 1970, numerous awards and certs. for pub. service and art, award Music of the Baroque, 1991, Editors Choice award Nat. Libr. Poetry, 1993. Mem. Nat. League Am. Pen Women (rec. sec. 1972-74, travelling art slide collection 1974—, designer jewelry, awards for book cover art, numerous Gold Bangle awards). Contbr. med. articles, short stories, poetry to newspapers. Home and Studio: 518 Warren Ave Colorado Springs CO 80906-2343

SELL, ROBERT EMERSON, electrical engineer; b. Freeport, Ill., Apr. 23, 1929; s. Cecil Leroy and Ona Arletta (Stevens) S.; m. Ora Lucile Colton, Nov. 7, 1970. B.S., U. Nebr., 1962. Registered profl. engr., Nebr., Mo., Ill., Ind., Ohio, W.Va., Ky., Ark., Tex., Oreg., Wash., Calif. Chief draftsman Dempster Mill Mfg. Co., Beatrice, Nebr., 1949-53; designer-engr. U. Neb., Lincoln, 1955-65; elec. design engr. Kirkham, Michael & Assos., Omaha, 1965-67; elec. design engr. Leo A. Daly Co., Omaha, St. Louis, 1967-69; mech. design engr. Hellmuth, Obata, Kassabaum, St. Louis, 1969-70; chief elec. engr. Biagi-Hannan & Assos., Inc., Evansville, Ind., 1971-74; elec. project engr. H.L. Yoh Co., under contract to Monsanto Co., Creve Coeur, Mo., 1974-77; elec. project engr. Dhillon Engrs., Inc., Portland, Oreg., 1978-85; project coordinator Brown-Zammit-Enyeart Engring., Inc., San Diego,

1985-88; elec. engr. Morgen Design, Inc., San Diego, 1988; lead elec. engr. Popov Engrs., Inc., San Diego, 1988-89; mech. and elect. specialist Am. Engring. Labs., Inc. div. Prof. Svc. Industries, Inc., San Diego, 1990—; instr. Basic Inst. Tech., St. Louis, 1971. Mem. ASHRAE, IEEE. Home and Office: PO Box 261578 San Diego CA 92196-1578

SELLER, GREGORY EROL, marketing executive, writer; b. Denver, Oct. 4, 1953; s. Otto Gustave and Dolores Louise (Crawford) S. BBA, U. Colo., 1975. Account exec. Gt.-West Life, L.A., 1975-79; asst. v.p. group devel. Gt.-West Life, Denver, 1980-84; v.p. govt. mkts. and nat. accts. Great-West Life, L.A., 1988—; pres., chief exec. officer Benefits Communication Corp., Denver, 1985-87; bd. dirs. Benefits Communication Co. Editor newsletter Focus on 457, 1988—. Mem. vestry, treas. St. Thomas Episc. Ch., Hollywood, Calif., 1989-93. Mem. Delta Upsilon. Democrat. Home: 37 New York Ct Monarch Beach CA 92629-4524 Office: Great-West Life 18101 Von Karman Ave Ste 1460 Irvine CA 92612-1043

SELLS, KEVIN DWAYNE, marine engineer; b. Bridgeport, Conn., Sept. 20, 1958; m. Ketruthai Houngsatjakul, July 14, 1986; children: Corey A., David H. III, Vidhya Sarah. AS in Quality Assurance, Ft. Steilacoom C.C., Tacoma, 1984; BS in Marine Engring., Pierce Coll., 1987. Nuc. shipfitter elec. boat divsn. Gen. Dynamics, Groton, Conn., 1976-79; quality assurance surveyor Tacoma Boatbuilding Co., 1979-81, marine constrn. planner, 1981-84; sr. logistics engr. F.E. Basil, Washington, 1984-86; ship repair engr. C. Long Assocs., Bangkok, Thailand, 1987-89; sr. logistics analyst C. Long Assocs., Tucson, 1989—. Mem. Soc. Naval Architects, Am. Archeology Soc., Smithsonian Inst., Libr. Congress. Achievements include research and implementation of modular shipbuilding techniques; revamped Saudi Arabian naval supply system. Avocations: auto mechanics, photography, hiking, archeology. Office: C Long Assocs 718 W Hatfield St Tucson AZ 85706-7606

SELVIN, NEIL, computer company executive. Pres., CEO Global Village, Sunnyvale, Calif. Office: Global Village 1146 E Arques Ave Sunnyvale CA 94086-4602*

SELYEM, BRUCE JADE, photographer; b. Cleve., Aug. 24, 1953; s. Edwin Joseph and Ursula Anna (Neustadt) S.; m. Leslie Ann Smith Shaw, Aug. 25, 1975 (div. Mar. 1982). m. Barbara Jean Krupp, 1998. BS in Photography, Mont. State U. Color photo lab. technician Mont. State U., Bozeman, 1986-88, plant pathology lab. asst., 1987-88, tchg. asst., 1989, staff photographer Mus. of the Rockies, 1989—; trail crew leader Chugach Nat. Forest, Seward, Alaska, 1989; mem. Historic Preservation Bd. Gallatin County, Bozeman, 1992-98, chmn., 1995-98; founder, pres. Country Grain Elevator Hist. Soc., Bozeman, 1996—. Photog. contbr.: Glacier Country, Montana's Indians, Montana Almanac, Digging Up Tyrannosaurus Rex, Tyrannosaurus Rex, also numerous other books, mags., reports, catalogs and profl. jours. Asst. fire chief East Glacier Park (Mont.) Vol. Fire Dept., 1979-83. Recipient Program Spkr. award Mont. Com. for the Humanities, 1996—. Avocations: hiking, backpacking, cross country skiing, canoeing, traveling. Home: 155 Prospector Trl Bozeman MT 59718-7988

SEMEL, GEORGE HERBERT, plastic surgeon; b. N.Y.C., Apr. 20, 1938; s. Louis Bennett and Sara Sonja (Eutis) S. AB, Columbia U., 1959; MD, Boston U., 1963. Diplomate Am. Bd. Plastic Surgery. Intern L.A. County Gen. Hosp., 1963-64; resident gen. surgery Long Beach (Calif.) VA Hosp., 1964-67; residency in plastic surgery Mayo Clinic, Rochester, Minn., 1967-69; chief resident plastic surgery Med. U. S.C., Charleston, 1969-70; pvt. practice L.A., 1970—; staff Cedars Sinai Hosp., L.A. Founder L.A. Music Ctr., 1978, Mus. Contemporary Art, 1980. With Calif. NG, 1964-69, USNG, 1969-73. Mem. AMA, Am. Soc. Plastic Surgery, Am. Lipoplasty Soc., L.A. Soc. Plastic Surgeons, L.A. County Med. Soc., Phi Gamma Delta. Office: 450 S Beverly Dr Beverly Hills CA 90212*

SEMILIAN, JULIAN ANDREI, film editor, poet, translator; b. Bucharest, Romania, May 28, 1948; s. David and Gisele Semilian; m. Liz Cairo, June 2, 1991 (div. Sept. 1993). Grad., U. Minn. Film editor: The Force, 1993-94, The Secretary, 1994, Serial Killer, 1994-95, Daddy's Girl, 1995-96, The Nurse, 1996, Cupid, 1996, The Fiance, 1996-97, Killing Grounds, 1997, Night Caller, 1997, Landlady, 1997, Captured, 1997-98; author: (poems) Arshile, 1998; translator: (Romanian poems) Mr. Knife & Miss Fork, 1998, Ribbot, 1998; poet, translator: (poems) Suitcase, 199-98, Exquisite Corpse, 1993-98, World Letter, 1998.

SEN, SHUSMITA, English educator, researcher; b. Faizabad, India, Apr. 7, 1952; came to U.S., 1981; d. Sudhindra Nath and Monica (Dasgupta) Chanda. BA in English with honors, St. Xavier's Coll., India, 1972; MA in English, Visva Bharti U., Santiniketan, India, 1976, Okla. State U., 1984, Ea. Wash. U., 1988. Grad. tchg. asst. Okla. State U., Stillwater, 1981-84, Wash. State U., Pullman, 1984-86; grad. tchg. asst. Ea. Wash. U., Cheney, 1984-86, adj. faculty, 1986-90; instr. in English, fgn. lang. Spokane (Wash.) C.C., 1990—; module coord. English 201, Okla. State U., 1983-84; computer lab. supr. Ea. Wash. U., 1988-90; student outcomes liaison Spokane C.C., 1996-97. Mem. Am. Assn. Women C.C. Hindu. Avocations: reading, photography, music, cinema. Home: 451 Annie Pl Cheney WA 99004-2140 Office: Spokane CC 1810 N Greene St Spokane WA 99217-5320

SENA, ROBERT STEPHEN, planner; b. N.Y.C., Mar. 18, 1943; s. Ralph and Dorothy S.; m. Maureen Dalton Armbruster, June 19, 1976; 1 child, Mariel. B in Landscape Architecture, State U. N.Y., 1964; M in Regional Planning, Cornell U., 1966; PhD in Urban Planning, U. Wisc., 1976. Licensed landscape architect, Calif. Assoc. project mgr. Royston Hanamoto Alley & Abey, Mill Valley, Calif., 1970-80, prin., 1988-93; cons. dir. planning Summa Corp., L.A., 1981-83; prin., owner Roberts Assocs., San Francisco, 1983-88; dir. planning POD/Sasaki, San Francisco, 1988, Moore Iacofano Goltsman, Inc., Berkeley, Calif., 1993—; project coord. Golden Gate Nat. Recreation Area, 1975, Playa Vista Master Plan, L.A., 1981-83, U. Calif., Riverside Long Range Plan, 1991; cons. USAID, Washington, Tallinn Bot. Garden, Estonia, 1994, Shanghai (China) Jiao Tong U., 1996-97; vis. prof. Cornell U., 1993; planner 2002 Olympic Village Concept, 1997-98; Ohio State U. Coll. Sociology and Behavioral Sci. Facilities Plan. Photographer (book): The Wilderness Next Door, 1982. Bd. dirs. Environ. Design Found. N. Calif., San Francisco, 1986-89, San Francisco Tree Adv. Bd. Recipient First Place Civic Ctr. Design Competition City of Palo Alto, Calif., 1986, Distinguished Svc. to City of San Francisco award City of San Francisco, 1990. Mem. Am. Soc. Landscape Architects (pres. N. Calif. chpt. 1987-89, Merit award 1976), Am. Inst. Cert. Planners, Soc. Coll. Univ. Planning (mem. west regional coun.). Avocations: photography, gardening, landscape architecture, cooking. E-mail: bob@migcom.com. Fax: 510-845-8750. Office: Moore Iacofano Goltsman 800 Hearst Ave Berkeley CA 94710-2018

SENN, GREGORY PAUL, artist, educator; b. Racine, Wis., Jan. 31, 1956; s. Charles G. and Jeanette E. (Neumann) S.; m. Barbara G. Klapperich, Sept. 12, 1981; children: Jennifer, Jacob. AS, U. Wis. Marathon County, Wausau; BS, U. Wis., Platteville, 1982; MFA, West Tex. State U., 1985. Asst. prof. art Ea. N.Mex. U., Portales, 1986-91, assoc. prof., 1991—. Jewelry works include chainmaille belt (2d place award 1997), necklace and earring set (1st place award 1995); creator sculptures Kokopelli, 1997 (1st place award 1997), Belligoni Eagle, 1996 (1st place award 1996). Mem. Portales Mainstreet Com., 1996—, Parents and Children Together, Portales, 1991—, Friends of the Library, Portales, 1998—, Clovis, N.Mex., 1998; advisor Kappa Pi Art Fraternity. Recipient Aegis award for Tchg. Excellence, Kappa Pi, 1997, Best of Show award, Roosevelt County, Portales, 1994; Instrnl. Equipment Fund grantee Associated Students Activity Bd., 1998, Tchg. Tech. Initiative grantee, Ea. N.Mex. U., 1998. Mem. High Plains Art Coun. (v.p. 1995-98), Ampgard (referee). Avocations: gardening, fishing, reading, flint knapping. E-mail: Greg.Senn@enmu.edu. Office: ENMU Sta 19 Portales NM 88130

SENUNGETUK, VIVIAN RUTH, lawyer; b. Syracuse, N.Y., Sept. 27, [illegible] George Moore, William Guugzhuk Senungetuk. BA, SUNY, Binghamton, 1968; MAT, U. Alaska, 1972; JD, Boston U., 1984. Bar: Alaska 1985, Mass. 1985, U.S. Dist. Ct. Alaska 1985, N.Y. 1996, U.S. Dist. Ct. (no. dist.) N.Y. 1996. Adminstr. Indian Edn., Sitka, Alaska, 1974-76, Cook Inlet Native Assn., Anchorage, 1977-80; assoc. Erwin, Smith & Garnett, Anchorage, 1984-86; sole practice Anchorage, 1986—; adj. prof. constitutional law U. Alaska, Anchorage, 1986-88. Author: A Place for Winter, 1987. Mem. ABA, Alaska Acad. Trial Lawyers. Democrat. Pentecostal. Avocations: creative writing, aerobics.. Office: 880 N St Ste 203 Anchorage AK 99501-3276

SEPEHRI, RON MEHRAN, materials engineer; b. Kerman, Iran, June 17, 1956; came to U.S., 1978; s. Sorosh Sepehri and Dolat Ghazigari. PhD, Stanford U., 1981. Reg. engr. Tech. staff Oracle Corp., Redwood Shoras, Calif., 1993-95; program mgr. Applied Materials, Santa Clara, 1995—. Fellow Indsl. Engrs. Soc.; mem. Am. Soc. Quality Assurance. Home: 18408 Swarthmore Dr Saratoga CA 95070-4717

SEPETYS, KRISTINA M., economic and management consultant; b. Detroit, July 24, 1962; d. George N. and Phyllis J. Sepetys; m. William Barrows Peale, Sept. 21, 1996. BA, Smith Coll., 1984; MTS, Harvard U., 1988; postgrad., U. So. Calif. Anlayst ICF Karsby Internat., Boston, 1989; rsch. assoc. Putnam, Hayes & Bartlett, L.A., 1989-92; experienced mgr. Arthur Andersen Econ. Consulting, L.A., 1992-97; sr. cons. Nat. Econ. Rsch. Assn., San Francisco, 1997—. Co-author: Electricity Restructuring, 1996; contbr. articles to profl. jours. Recipient Energy Efficiency Study grant Rockefeller Found., 1993. Office: Nat Econ Rsch Assocs 444 Market St San Francisco CA 94111-5325

SEPETYS, RUTA ELIZABETH, entertainment company executive; b. Detroit, Nov. 19, 1967; d. George N. and Phyllis Jean (Schefsky) S. BS, Hillsdale (Mich.) Coll.; M. Internat. Mgmt., ICN, Paris. Mgr. Deston Entertainment, Santa Monica, Calif., 1990-94; pres. Sepetys Entertainment Group, Santa Monica, 1994—; vis. faculty Musician's Inst., Hollywood, Calif., 1994-97; guest spkr. Full Sail Music Sch., Orlando, Fla., 1997. Staff mem. Grammys in the Schs., L.A., 1996—. Mem. Nat. Acad. Rec. Arts and Scis., Rec. Industry Assn. Am., L.A. Music Network. Office: Sepetys Entertainment Group 1223 Wilshire Blvd # 804 Santa Monica CA 90403-5400

SEQUEIRA, JOHN EDWARD, deacon; b. San Francisco, Feb. 13, 1940; s. Edward Charles and Mary Josephine (McCarty) S.; m. Barbara Carol Coughlan, Aug. 22, 1964; children: Margaret Mary, Carol Louise. BA, U. San Francisco, 1964. Ordained deacon Roman Cath. Ch., 1990. Pastoral min. Roman Cath. Ch., 1964-90; risk mgr. Fritz Cos., San Francisco, 1988—; permanent deacon Archdiocese San Francisco, 1990—. Mem. Serra Club San Francisco (pres. 1987-88). Home: 2602 Monte Cresta Dr Belmont CA 94002-1333

SER, RANDY JAY, production designer, director. AA in Theater, Miami-Dade Community Coll., 1973; BA in Theater, Fla. State U., 1975, MFA in Theater, 1977. Freelance prodn. designer Los Angeles, 1980—; freelance 2d unit dir., 1994—. Prodn. designer: (feature films) Dutch Treat, 1986, Casual Sex?, 1987, FEDS, 1988, Darkman, 1989, Wild Hearts Can't Be Broken, 1990, The Mighty Ducks, 1991, (TV show) Rags to Riches, 1986, L.A. Firefighters, 1996, Ghost of a Chance, 1997, Ghosts of Fear Street, 1997, The Burning Zone, 1997, Martial Law, 1998, (TV film) Bridesmaids, 1988, Rodgers and Hammerstein's Cinderella, 1997 (1997 Emmy for outstanding art direction, variety/musical spl., recipient Excellence in Prodn. Design award for a variety or music spl., Soc. Motion Picture and TV Art Dirs., 1997); art dir.: (feature films) 40 Days of Musa Dagh, 1980, Mortuary, 1981, Tomboy, 1984, Jocks, 1985, (TV shows) Southern California Easter Seal Telethon, 1981, The Mask Wraparound, 1982, Robot Monster Wraparound, 1982, Hollywood Ballyhoo, 1983, Fantastic Voyage Series, 1985, First and Ten, 1985, Strictly Confidential, 1986, (rock videos) Steve Miller Band/Shangri-La, 1984, Harlem Globetrotters/Sweet Georgia Brown, 1985, also numerous commls.; asst. art dir.: (films) My Champion, 1980, My Tutor, 1982, The Check is in the Mail, 1983; set decorator: (films) Dreamscape, 1983, Exterminator II, 1984; property master: (films) Weekend Pass, 1983, Lies, 1983; scenic artist: (films) Android, 1982, Love Letters, 1982; 2d unit dir. (TV shows) Against the Grain, 1994, L.A. Firefighters, 1996, The Burning Zone, 1997, (feature film) Family Portrait, 1995. Mem. Acad. TV Arts and Scis., Dirs. Guild of Am., Soc. of Motion Picture and TV Art Dirs. Avocations: Western riding, general aviation, camping, Nordic skiing, mountain biking.

SERAFIN, ROBERT JOSEPH, science center administrator, electrical engineer; b. Chgo., Apr. 22, 1936; s. Joseph Albert and Antoinette (Gazda) S.; m. Betsy Furgerson, Mar. 4, 1961; children: Katherine, Jenifer, Robert Joseph Jr., Elizabeth. BSEE, U. Notre Dame, 1958; MSEE, Northwestern U., 1961; PhDEE, Ill. Inst. Tech., 1972. Engr. Hazeltine Rsch. Corp. Ill. Inst. Tech. Rsch. Inst., 1960-62; assoc. engr., rsch. engr., sr. rsch. engr. Nat. Ctr. for Atmospheric Rsch., Boulder, Colo., 1962-73, mgr. field observing facility, 1973-80; dir. atmospheric tech. div. Nat. Ctr. for Atmospheric Rsch., Bouulder, Colo., 1981-89, dir. ctr., 1989—; chair Nat. Weather Svc. Modernization Com. Author: Revised Radar Handbook, 1989; contbr. numerous articles to profl. jours.; editl. bd./com. Acta Meteorologica Sinica; editl. founder Jour. Atmospheric and Oceanic Tech.; patentee in field. Speaker various civic groups in U.S. and internationally. Fellow Am. Meteorol. Soc. (mem. exec. com.); Mem. IEEE (sr.), NAE, NAS (human rights com.), Boulder C. of C., Sigma Xi. Avocations: golf, fishing, skiing. Office: Nat Ctr Atmospheric Rsch 1850 Table Mesa Dr PO Box 3000 Boulder CO 80303-3000*

SERAFINE, MARY LOUISE, psychologist, educator, lawyer; b. Rochester, N.Y., July 2, 1948. B.A. with honors in music, Rutgers U., 1970; Ph.D., U. Fla., 1975; JD, Yale U., 1991. Bar: Calif., D.C.; U.S. Tax Ct. Teaching and research fellow U. Fla., Gainesville, 1970-76; vis. asst. prof. U. Tex.-San Antonio, 1976-77; asst. prof. U. Tex.-Austin, 1977-79; postdoctoral fellow dept psychology Yale U., New Haven, 1979-83, lectr., 1981-83; asst. prof. dept. psychology Vassar Coll. Poughkeepsie, N.Y., 1983-88; with O'Melveny & Myers, L.A., 1988-96, Chadbourne & Parke, L.A. Author: Music as Cognition: The Development of Thought in Sound, 1988. Contbr. articles to profl. jours. Editorial reviewer Child Devel., Devel. Psychology, Am. Scientist, Jour. Experimental Child Psychology, Jour. Applied Developmental Psychology, Yale Law Jour. Grantee State of Fla., 1974-75, U. Tex.-Austin, 1977, Spencer Found., 1979-85. Office: Fried Frank Harris Shriver & Jacobson 350 S Grand Ave Ste 3200 Los Angeles CA 90071-3474

SERAFINI, VICTOR RENATO, aerospace engineer; b. Chgo., June 9, 1934; s. Renato Victor and Stella (Koch) S.; m. Donetta Werre. BS in Aero. Engring., U. Ill., 1957, postgrad., 1957-65; postgrad., UCLA, 1957-65. Rsch. and project engr. Rocketdyne Div. N.Am. Aviation, Canoga Park, Calif., 1957-67; program/project mgr. TRW Inc., Redondo Beach, Calif., 1967-78; dir. spacecraft engring. Comms. Satellite Corp. (now Comsat Corp.), El Segundo, Calif., 1978-94; aerospace cons., pres. S.T.D. Assocs., Rancho Palos Verdes, Calif., 1995—; bd. dirs., cont. Autobahn West, Westlake Village, Calif.; mgmt. cons. Westoaks Realty, Westlake Village, 1975—; pres. STD Assocs., Rancho Palos Verdes, Calif., 1965—. Recipient award of recognition TRW Inc., 1965, Recognition of Outstanding Effort award NASA and TRW, 1963-64, Outstanding Contbn. award to recovery stranded Intelsat VI 603 satellite Intelsat Orgn., 1992. Mem. AIAA (liquid rocket tech. com. 1985-86). Mem. Christian Ch. Avocations: flying, sailing, swimming, mountain climbing, toy collecting. Home and Office: STD Assocs PO Box 2665 Rancho Palos Verdes CA 90275-8665

SERBEIN, OSCAR NICHOLAS, business educator, consultant; b. Collins, Iowa, Mar. 31, 1919; s. Oscar Nicholas and Clara Matilda (Shearer) S.; m. Alice Marie Bigger, Sept. 16, 1952; children: Mary Llewellyn Serbein Parker, John Gregory. BA with highest distinction, U. Iowa, 1940, MS, 1941; PhD, Columbia U., 1951. Grad. asst. math. U. Iowa, Iowa City, 1940-41; clk. Met. Life Ins. Co., N.Y.C., 1941-42; lectr. U. Calif., Berkeley, summer 1948, 50; lectr., asst. prof., assoc. prof. Columbia U., N.Y.C., 1947-59; prof. ins. Stanford (Calif.) U., 1959-89, dir. doctoral program Grad. Sch. Bus., 1960-64, prof. emeritus ins., 1989—; cons. Ins. Info. Inst., N.Y.C., 1971-78, [illegible] Menlo Park, Calif., 1980-81, other bus.; cons., expert witness various law firms. Author: Paying for Medical Care in the U.S., 1953, Educational Activities of Business, 1961; co-author: Property and Liability Insurance, 4 ed., 1967, Risk Management: Text and Cases, 2 ed., 1983; also articles. Bd. dirs. Sr. Citizens Coord. Coun., Palo Alto, 1986-89, dir. emeritus, 1990—. Maj. USAF, WWII. Decorated Bronze Star, 1944. Mem. Am. Risk and Ins. Assn., Western Risk and Ins. Assn., Phi Beta Kappa, Sigma Xi, Beta Gamma Sigma. Democrat. Methodist. Club: Stanford Faculty. Avocation: gardening. Home: 731 San Rafael Pl Stanford CA 94305-1007 Office: Stanford U Grad Sch Business Stanford CA 94305

SERLING, CAROLYN K., editor; b. Columbus, Ohio; d. Warren A. and Anne (Caldwell) Kramer; m. Rod E. Serling, June 1948 (dec. 1975); children: Jodi Suzanne, Anne Caldwell. BA, Antioch Coll., 1950. Editor T.Z. Mag., N.Y.C., 1981-89, Daw Books, Inc., N.Y.C., 1991-94; cons. entertainment bus. L.A., 1995—. Author, editor: Grace in the Afternoon, 1999. Trustee Ithaca Coll., N.Y., 1988—, Antioch U., Ohio, 1985-91.

SERNA, JOE, JR., mayor; b. Stockton, Calif.; m. Isabel Serna; children: Phillip, Lisa. BA in Social Sci., Govt., Sacramento State Coll., 1966; postgrad., U. Calif., Davis. Vol. Peace Corps., Guatemala, 1966; edn. advisor Lt.-Gov. Mervyn Dymally, 1975-77; prof. govt. Calif State U., Sacramento, 1969—; mayor City of Sacramento, 1992—; bd. dirs. Freddie Mac, McLean, Va. Mem. Sacramento City Coun. 5th Dist., 1981-92, law and legis. com., 1989-92, Housing & Devel. Commn., Sacramento, chmn. budget and fin. com., 1981-89, transp. and cmty. devel. com., 1989-92; dir. United Farmworkers Am.'s Support Com. in Sacramento County, 1970-75; co-trustee Crocker Art Mus. Assn.; founder Thursday Night Market, Mayor's Summer Reading Camp; mem. Sacramento Housing & Devel. Commn.; bd. dirs. Regional Transit. Office: Office of the Mayor 915 I St Sacramento CA 95814-2608

SERNA, PATRICIO, state supreme court justice; b. Reserve, N.Mex., Aug. 26, 1939; m. Eloise Serna; 1 stepchild, John Herrera; children: Elena Patricia, Anna Alicia. BSBA with honors, U. Albuquerque, 1962; JD, U. Denver, 1970; LLM, Harvard U., 1971; postgrad., Nat. Jud. Coll., 1985, 90, 92, 94. Bar: N.Mex., Colo., U.S. Dist. Ct. N.Mex. Probation and parole officer State of N.Mex., Santa Fe, Las Cruces, 1966-67; spl. asst. to commn. mem. Equal Opportunity Commn., Washington, 1971-75; asst. atty. gen. State of N.Mex., Santa Fe, 1975-79; pvt. practice Santa Fe, 1979-85; dist. judge First Jud. Dist., Santa Fe, 1985-96; supreme ct. justice N.Mex. Supreme Ct., Santa Fe, 1996—; adj. prof. law Georgetown U., Washington, 1973, Cath. U., Washington, 1974-75; faculty advisor Nat. Jud. Coll., Reno, 1987. Exhibited at N.Mex. Mus. Fine Arts, Gov.'s Gallery, Santa Fe. Active Citizens Organized for Real Edn., Santa Fe, No. N.Mex. Martin Luther King Jr. State Holiday Commn., Santa Fe; past bd. dirs. Santa Fe Group Homes Inc. With U.S. Army, 1963-65. Mem. N.Mex. Bar Assn., N.Mex. Hispanic Bar Assn., Nat. Hispanic Bar Assn., Nat. Coun. Juvenile and Family Ct. Judges, No. N.Mex. Am. Inns of Ct., Santa Fe Bar Assn., Elks, Fraternal Order of Eagles, Fraternal Order of Police, Phi Alpha Delta. Avocations: hiking, fishing, ping pong, chess, painting. Office: NMex Supreme Ct PO Box 848 Santa Fe NM 87504-0848

SERONDE, ADELE HERTER, artist; b. Manchester, Mass., June 17, 1925; d. Christian A. and Mary Caroline (Pratt) Herter; m. Joseph Seronde, Aug. 26, 1945; children: Antoine, Jacques, Pierre, Dorée, Jeanne. Student, Bennington Coll., 1943-45. One-woman show DeCordova Mus., Lincoln, Mass., 1956, Nova Gallery, Boston, 1958, Galleria Vigna Nuova and Gallerie Santa Croce, Florence, Italy, 1964, 66, Herbert Benevy Gallery, N.Y.C., 1976; 2-person show Art Directions Gallery, N.Y.C., 1966, S.W. Symphony Gallery, Sedona, 1985; exhibited in group shows Sedona (Ariz.) Arts Ctr., 1988, 92; one-woman show and group shows Wingspread Gallery, Gallery 68, Belfast, Maine, 1969, 73, 76, 80, 83, 88, 90, 93; also others; represented in permanent collections Phillips Mus., Washington, also numerous pub. and pvt. instns. Co-coord. visual arts Summerthing, neighborhood arts program, Boston, 1968-71; pres. Christian Herter Ctr.; mem. Sedona Cultural Arts Commn., 1989-90; sec., v.p., bd. dirs. Internat. Friends of Transformative Art, Phoenix, 1989-95; organizer show Sedona Art Mus., 1993. Avocations: poetry, gardening, teaching. Home and Studio: 345 Longwood Dr Sedona AZ 86351-7208

SERY, GIL, reporter; b. Johanessburg, South Africa, Dec. 11, 1972; s. Joe and Estee P. Sery. BS in Journalism, Calif. Poly. State U., 1998. Staff writer Moorpark (Calif.) Coll. Reporter, 1993-94, Mesa Coll. Mesa Press, San Diego, 1994-95, Cal Poly. Mustang Daily, San Luis Obispo, 1997; freelancer Carmel Valley News, San Diego, 1997, Rancho Santa Fe (Calif.) Rev., 1997, New Times, San Luis Obispo. Mem. Soc. Profl. Journalists (Outstanding Grad. 1998, sec.-treas. Calif. Poly. chpt. 1996-97, pres. Calif. Poly. chpt. 1997-98). Avocations: writing, computers, movies.

SESLAR, PATRICK GEORGE, writer, artist; b. Ft. Wayne, Ind., Sept. 20, 1947; s. Dale Milton and Alice Georgiana (Lincoln) S.; m. Lin L. Coleman, Sept. 20, 1968. BS in Psychology, Purdue U., 1969. Contbg. editor The Artist's Mag., Cin., 1985—; columnist Trailer Life Mag., Agoura, Calif., 1988-90. Author: Painting Seascapes in Sharp Focus, 1987, Wildlife Painting Step by Step, 1995; co-author: Painting Nature's Peaceful Places, 1993; exhibiting artist Art Sales and Rental Gallery, Phila., 1996—, Phila. Mus. Art, 1996—, painting From Photographs, 1999. Recipient Award of Merit, Winter Pk. Art Festival, 1995, 3d pl. (painting) Coconut Grove Arts Festival, 1996, Juror's award (painting) Cherry Creek Arts Festival; 1997. Mem. Nat. Assn. Ind. Artists. Avocations: backpacking, mountain biking, hiking. Home and Office: 5580 La Jolla Blvd # 334 La Jolla CA 92037-7651

SESTANOVICH, MOLLY BROWN, writer; b. Denver, Nov. 30, 1921; d. Ben Miller and Mary (McCord) Brown; m. Stephen Nicholas Sestanovich, July 9, 1949; children: Stephen, Mary, Robert Benjamin. Student, Fairmont Jr. Coll., 1939-41. Radio comml. writer Young & Rubicam Advt., N.Y.C. and Hollywood, Calif., 1941-47; radio scriptwriter Korean Broadcasting Co., Seoul, 1947-48; substitute tchr. County Sch. Bd., Montgomery County, Md., 1956-58; syndicated polit. columnist Lesher Newspapers, various locations, 1971-91; freelance polit. writer Moraga, Calif., 1991—; active internat. women's orgns., Italy, Thailand, Singapore, Finland, Venezuela, 1949-70. Writer LWV, Diablo Valley, Calif., 1970, 91. Recipient prize for contbn. to cause of peace and justice Mt. Diablo Peace Ctr., 1989. Mem. Am. Fgn. Svc. Assn., Lamorinda Dem. Club (program chmn. 1985). Unitarian. Avocations: genealogy, gardening. Home: 15 Idlewood Ct Moraga CA 94556-1107

SESTINI, VIRGIL ANDREW, retired biology educator; b. Las Vegas, Nov. 24, 1936; s. Santi and Merceda Francesca (Borla) S. BS in Edn., U. Nev., 1959; postgrad., Oreg. State U., 1963-64; MNS, U. Idaho, 1965; postgrad., Ariz. State U., 1967, No. Ariz. U., 1969; cert. tchr., Nev. Tchr. biology Rancho High Sch., 1960-76; sci. chmn., tchr. biology Bonanza High Sch., Las Vegas, 1976-90; ret., 1990; co-founder, curator exhibits Meadows Mus. Nat. History, 1993-94; part-time tchr. Meadows Sch., 1987-94; ret., 1994; edn. specialist, cell biologist SAGE Rsch., Las Vegas, 1993, ret., 1998; founder Da Vinci Enterprises, Las Vegas, 1995. Served with USAR, 1959-65. Recipient Rotary Internat. Honor Tchr. award, 1965, Region VIII Outstanding Biology Tchr. award, 1970, Nev. Outstanding Biology Tchr. award Nat. Assn. Biology Tchrs., 1970, Nat. Assn. Sci. Tchrs., Am. Gas Assn. Sci. Teaching Achievement Recognition award, 1976, 1980, Gustov Ohaus award, 1980, Presdl. Honor Sci. Tchr. award, 1983; Excellence in Edn. award Nev. Dept. Edn., 1983; Presdl. award excellence in math. and sci. teaching, 1984, Celebration of Excellence award Nev. Com. on Excellence in Edn., 1986, Hall of Fame award Clark County Sch. Dist., 1988, Excellence in Edn. award, Clark County Sch. Dist., 1987, 88, Spl. Edn. award Clark County Sch. Dist., 1988, NSEA Mini-grants, 1988, 89, 92, World Decoration of Excellence medallion World Inst. Achievement, 1989, Cert. Spl. Congl. Recognition, 1989, Senatorial Recognition , 1989, mini-grant Jr. League Las Vegas., 1989, Excellence in Edn. award, Clark Country Sch. Dist., 1989; named Nev. Educator of Yr., Milken Family Found./Nev. State Dept. Edn., 1989; grantee Nev. State Bd. Edn., 1988, 89, Nev. State Edn. Assn., 1988-89. Author: Lab Investigations For High School Honors Biology, 1989, Microbiology: A Manual for High School Biology, 1992, Laboratory Inves- [illegible] 1995, Science Laboratory Report Data Book, 1995, Field and Museum Techniques for the Classroom Teacher, 1995, Selected Lab Investigations and Projects for Honors and AP Biology, Vol. I Microbiology, 1995, Telecommunications: A Simulation for Biology Using the Internet, 1995; co-author:

A Biology Lab Manual For Cooperative Learning, 1989, Metrics and Science Methods: A Manual of Lab Experiments for Home Schoolers, 1990, Experimental Designs in Biology I: Botany and Zoology, 1993, Designs in Biology: A Lab Manual, 1993, Integrated Science Lab Manual, 1994; contbr. articles to profl. jours. Mem. AAAS, NEA, Nat. Assn. Taxidermists, Nat. Sci. Tchrs. Assn. (life, Nev. State chpt. 1968-70), Nat. Assn. Biology Tchrs. (life, OBTA dir. Nev. State 1991-93), Am. Soc. Microbiology, Coun. for Exceptional Children, Am. Biographic Inst. (rsch. bd. advisors 1988), Nat. Audubon Assn., Nat. Sci. Suprs. Assn., Am. Inst. Biol. Scis., Internat. Plastic Modelers Soc., So. Nev. Scale Modelers (Las Vegas coord. Modeloberfest, 1995). Avocations: scale models, military figures, scale model circus, photography, chess.

SETCHKO, EDWARD STEPHEN, minister, theology educator; b. Yonkers, N.Y., Apr. 27, 1926; s. Stephen John and Mary Elizabeth (Dulak) S.; m. Penelope Sayre, Nov. 18, 1950; children—Marc Edward, Kip Sherman, Robin Elizabeth, Jan Sayre, Dirk Stephen. B.S., Union Coll., 1948; M.Div. cum laude, Andover Newton Theol. Sch., 1953, S.T.M., 1954; Th.D., Pacific Sch. Religion, 1962. Ordained to ministry United Ch. of Christ, 1954; cert. profl. hosp. chaplain. Psychometrician, Union Coll. Character Research Project, Schenectady, N.Y., 1947-50; asst. pastor Eliot Ch., Newton, Mass., 1950-54; clin. tng. supr. Boston City Hosp., 1951-54; intern, chaplain Boston State Mental Hosp., 1953-54; univ. campus minister U. Wash., Seattle, 1954-58; Danforth grantee, 1958-59; grad. fellow in psychotherapy Pacific Sch. Religion, Berkeley, Calif., 1959-60, instr. dept. pastoral psychology, 1960-61, grad. fellow, lectr. theology and psychology, 1961-62, asst. prof. psychology and counseling, 1962-63, dir. continuing theol. edn., 1962-63; clin. psychologist Calif. Correctional Facility, Vacaville, Calif., 1961-62; field research sec. laity div. United Ch. Christ, Berkeley, Calif. and N.Y.C., 1963-68; vis. prof. psychology and sociology Starr King Ctr. for Religious Leadership, Berkeley, 1967-69; assoc. prof. religion and soc. Starr King Ctr., Grad. Theol. Union, Berkeley, Calif., 1969-71, prof., 1971-83; career counselor The Ctr. for Ministry, Oakland, Calif., 1986-89; mem. faculty, chmn. curriculum and faculty com. Layman's Sch. Religion, Berkeley, 1960-67; cons. and lectr. in field. Del. voter registration delegation, Miss., 1965; mem. peace del., Mid-East, 1983; lectr. Internat. Conf. on the Holocaust and Genocide, Tel Aviv, 1982, Nuclear Disarmament Conf., W.Ger., 1980, 81, 82, Internat. Ctr. for Peace in the Middle East, Resource Ctr. for Non-Violence, Clergy & Laity Concerned, Ecumenical Peace Inst., Internat. Peace Acad.; World Policy Inst., Inst. Peace and World Order, Am. Friends Service Com. (bd. dirs.), Berkeley Ctr. for Human Interaction, Ristad Found., Am. Friends Golan Heights, Pacific Inst. of Criminal Justice; dir. The Project for Peace and Reconciliation in the Middle East (non-profit Calif. Found. 1983-89); vol. South Berkeley Cmty. Ch. hunger project Alta Bates Hospice. Lt. (j.g.) USNR, 1944-46, WW II. Mem. Am. Psychol. Assn. (cert.), Calif. State Psychol. Assn., Assn. Clin. Pastoral Edn., World Future Soc., Soc. Sci. Study of Religion, Inst. Noetic Scis., Com. for Protection Human Subjects (U. Calif.-Berkeley). Democrat. Contbr. articles to profl. jours.; condr. seminars: Futurology; Intricacies of Being Human, Images of Women and Men; Changing Values in Roles Between the Sexes in a Technological Society, Cybernetics and Humanization of Man; developer curriculum: Peace and Conflict Studies (U. Calif., Berkeley).

SETEROFF, SVIATOSLAV STEVE, management and logistics company executive; b. Shanghai, People's Republic of China, Oct. 6, 1937; came to U.S., 1949; s. Leo G. and Olga D. (Pankova) S.; m. Deanna Catherine Rogers (div. 1964); children: Steven James, Richard Aubrey; m. Joyce Eileen Schieldge, Feb. 22, 1965; children: Barbara Lynn Seteroff Anderson, Leanne Marie Seteroff DeBroeck. AA, Chapman Coll., 1974, BA cum laude, 1975; MBA, U. Puget Sound, 1983; D of Bus. Adminstrn., Nova Southeastern U., 1997. Enlisted USN, 1955-75, commd. warrant officer, 1976-85; sr. analyst McDonnell Douglas Astronautics Co., Rockville, Md., 1985-87; program mgr. Anadac, Inc., Arlington, Va., 1987; v.p. Systems Mgmt. Am. Corp., San Diego, 1987-89; project mgr. info. systems, logistics, sr. ops. analyst MERIT Systems, Inc., Bremerton, Wash., 1989-91; pres., CEO Mgmt. and Logistics Assocs., Inc., Poulsbo, Wash., 1990—; adj. assoc. prof. Residence Edn. Ctr., Chapman U., Bangor, Wash., 1985—; adj. instr. City U., 1996—; conf. presenter IEEE North Conf., 1994, 96, 98. Developer Scrivener Masonic Lodge Mgmt. Program, 1992. Mem. Am. Soc. Naval Engrs. (nat. chmn. logistics symposium 1991-93, conf. presenter logistics conf. 1992, 94, Pres. award 1993), Am. Soc. Logistics Engrs. (symposium presenter, chmn. advanced tech. steering group 1994-98, gen. chmn. internat. logistics conf. 1998, Sole Pres. award 1998), Ret. Officers Assn., Masons. Office: 12890 Old Military Rd NE Poulsbo WA 98370-7985

SETTGAST, LELAND G., religion educator, minister; b. Columbus, Nebr., June 6, 1939; s. George E. and Dena (Henke) S.; m. Eunice Wurdeman, Apr. 29, 1964; children: Bradford Lee, Christine Renee. Student, U. Nebr., 1956-57, St. Paul's Coll., 1958-59; BTh, Concordia Sem., Ft. Wayne, Ind., 1964; MA in Psychology, Calif. Coast U., 1977; DD, So. Calif. Theol. Sem., 1990. Ordained to ministry Luth. Ch.-Mo. Synod, 1964. Pastor Immanuel Luth. Ch., Osceola, Iowa, 1964-66, Highland Park Luth. Ch., L.A., 1966-68; sr. pastor Christ Luth. Ch., Norfolk, Nebr., 1968-73; exec. dir. Luth. Bible Translators, Orange, Calif., 1974-75; dir. chaplains Christian Jail Workers, Inc., L.A., 1976—, Los Angeles County Sheriff and Probation Depts., L.A., 1976—; dir. pub. rels. English dist. Luth. Ch.-Mo.Synod, Detroit, 1978—; chaplain Calif. Instn. for Women, 1988-89; prof. So. Calif. Theol. Sem., 1990—; dir. vol. edn., Gleaners, Inc., 1991—; panelist radio talk show Religion on the Line, L.A., 1983—; participant TV talk shows, L.A., 1980—; official chaplain Al-impics Internat., Castaic, Calif., 1987-89; participant Nat. Prayer Breakfast, Washington, 1988, Nat. Leadership Conf., Washington, 1988; U.S. dir. Philippine Prison Ministry, Bohol, The Philippines, 1988—; cons. Intentional Interim Ministry, 1993—; prof. Vision Internat. U., 1998—. Producer, dir. filmstrip Victory Is Sobriety, 1983 (award of merit 1984), radio broadcast Beyond Prison Walls, 1977-79; editor Broken Shackles newspaper, 1976-83; actor TV and motion pictures, 1989—. Bd. dirs. Highland Park Symphony, L.A., 1967-68, Big Bros. Am., Norfolk, 1972-73; v.p., sec. Nat. Found. for Rehab., San Clemente, Calif., 1987—; bd. dirs. Friends Christ Coll., Irvine, Calif., 1980-81. Mem. Am. Protestant Correctionnal Assn., Am. Film Inst., Religion in Media, So. Calif. Broadcasters Assn., Kiwanis. Republican. Home: 2875 E Virginia Ave Anaheim CA 92806-4443

SETZEKORN, WILLIAM DAVID, retired architect, consultant, author; b. Mt. Vernon, Ill., Mar. 12, 1935; s. Merrett Everet and Audrey (Ferguson) S.; m. Georgia Sue Brown, Feb. 4, 1958 (div. 1968); children: Jeffrey Merle, Timothy Michael. BArch, Kans. State U., 1957; cert. in computer graphics, Harvard U., 1968; BA with MA equivalency in Humanities, Western Ill. U., 1982. Registered arch., Calif. Coord. design and constrn. Cal-Expo, Sacramento, 1968; pvt. practice, Los Altos and Redding, Calif., Seattle, 1968-85; cons. Contra Costa County, Martinez, Calif., 1985-89, El Dorado County, Placerville, Calif., 1985-89, Somerset, Calif., 1989—; cons. Fed. Emergency Mgmt. Agy., The Presidio, San Francisco, 1989-95, Gov. Keating's task force for disaster recovery, Oklahoma City, 1995; apptd. Calif. State Grand Jury, 1996—. Author: Formerly British Honduras: A Profile of the New Nation of Belize, 1975, 4 other titles; contbr. articles to mags. Recipient Ofcl. Commendation, State of Calif., 1968, U.S. Presdl. Medal of Merit, Ronald Reagan, 1988. Fellow Augustan Soc. (bd. dirs. 1994-96); mem. Noble Co. of the Rose (knight 1979, lt. magister rosae 1995—), Mil. and Hospitaller Order of St. Lazarus (comdr.), numerous other internat. orders of chivalry, Family Setzekorn Assn. (prin. officer 1979—), San Leandro (Calif.) Yacht Club (founding), Kiwanis. Republican. Unitarian. Avocations. Genealogy, medieval history, heraldry, travel. Home and Office: PO Box 706 Somerset CA 95684-0706

SEVALSTAD, SUZANNE ADA, accounting educator; b. Butte, Mont., Mar. 26, 1948; d. John Cornelius and Ivy Jeanette (Cloke) Pilling; m. Nels Sevalstad, Jr., Mar. 11, 1975. BS in Bus. with high distinction, Mont. State U., 1970, MS in Bus., 1972. CPA, Mont. Internal auditor Anaconda Co., Butte, 1970-71; mgr. Wise River (Mont.) Club, 1976-79; instr. acctg. Bozeman (Mont.) Vocat./Tech. Ctr., 1970-72, Ea. Mont. Coll., Billings, 1972-73, Mont. State U., Bozeman, 1973-76, U. Nev., Las Vegas, 1979—. Recipient Women of Month award Freshman Class Women, 1976, Disting. Tchr. Coll. Bus. U. Nev., 1983, 86, 89, 93, Prof. of Yr. award Student Acctg. Assn. U. Nev., 1984, 87, 88, 90, 91, Outstanding Acctg. Prof. award Acctg. Students of U. Nev., 1987, 88, 89, Spanos Disting. Teaching award, 1989, 94, U. Nev. Disting. Tchg. award, 1998. Mem. AICPA, Am. Acctg. Assn., Nat. Inst. Mgmt. Acctg. (campus coord. 1988—), Inst. Mgmt. Accts., Assn. for Female Execs., Golden Key Soc. (hon.). Avocations: horseback riding, hiking, tennis, golf. Office: U Nev Dept Acctg 4505 S Maryland Pky Las Vegas NV 89154-9900

SEVERINSEN, DOC (CARL H. SEVERINSEN), conductor, musician; b. Arlington, Oreg., July 7, 1927; m. Emily Marshall, 1980; children—Nancy, Judy, Cindy, Robin, Allen. Ptnr. Severinsen-Akwright Co.; pops condr. The Phoenix (Ariz.) Symphony Orchestra; prin. pops condr. Minn. Orch., 1993. Mem. Ted Fio Rito Band, 1945, Charlie Barnet Band, 1947-49, then with, Tommy Dorsey, Benny Goodman, Norro Morales, Vaughn Monroe; soloist network band: Steven Allen Show, NBC-TV, 1954-55; mem. NBC Orch. Tonight Show, 1962-67, music dir., 1967-92; past host of: NBC-TV show The Midnight Special; recs., RCA Records, including; albums: Brass Roots, 1971, Facets, 1988, The Tonight Show Band, Night Journey. Address: Minn Orch 1111 Nicollet Mall Minneapolis MN 55403-2406 also: care William Morris Agency 151 S El Camino Dr Beverly Hills CA 90212-2704 also: care The Phoenix Symphony Orch 455 N 3rd St Ste 390 Phoenix AZ 85004-3942*

SEVIER, ERNEST YOULE, lawyer; b. Sacramento, June 20, 1932; s. Ernest and Helen Faye (McDonald) S.; m. Constance McKenna, Apr. 12, 1969; children: Carolyn Stewart, Katherine Danielle. A.B., Stanford U., 1954, J.D., 1956. Bar: Calif. 1956, U.S. Supreme Ct. 1965. Asso. mem. firm Sedgwick, Detert, Moran & Arnold, San Francisco, 1958-62; mem. firm Severson & Werson, San Francisco, 1962—. Served with USAF, 1956-57. Fellow Am. Bar Found.; mem. ABA (chmn. tort and ins. practice sect. 1982-83, exec. coun. 1976-84, chmn. standing com. on assoc. comms. 1988-90, chmn. coord. com. on Outreach to Pub. 1989-90, chmn. standing com. on lawyers responsibility for client protection 1991-94, commn. on non-lawyer practice 1992-95), Calif. Bar Assn., Internat. Assn. Def. Counsel, Fedn. Ins. and Corp. Counsel. Office: Severson & Werson 26th Flr 1 Embarcadero Ctr San Francisco CA 94111-3628

SEVILLA, CARLOS A., bishop; b. San Francisco, Aug. 9, 1935. Ed., Gonzaga U., Santa Clara U., Jesuiten Kolleg, Innsbruck, Austria, Cath. Inst. Paris. Ordained priest Roman Cath. Ch., 1966, bishop, 1989. Titular bishop Mina, 1989—; aux. bishop San Francisco, 1989—. Office: Archdiocese San Francisco 445 Church St San Francisco CA 94114*

SEVILLA, ENID N., production company executive; b. Davao City, The Philippines, June 12, 1953; d. Victor J. and Emerita N. Sevilla. Student, U. Santo Tomas, Manila, 1973, Sisters Formation Inst., Quezon City, The Philippines, 1981. Cert. legal sec., cert. notary pub., Calif. Comm. rschr., writer Nat. Office Mass Media, Manila, 1973-76; fin. officer, tchr. Religious of the Assumption, Manila, 1977-85; sec. Craig Printing, L.A., 1986-88; legal sec. S. Roger Rombro, ALC, L.A., 1988-93; gen. mgr., fin. officer Paulist Prodns., Inc., L.A., 1995—. Office: Paulist Prodns Inc 17575 Pacific Coast Hwy Pacific Palisades CA 90272-4148

SEWARD, GRACE EVANGELINE, retired librarian; b. L.A., Feb. 2, 1914; d. William Henry and Maud Leuty (Elphingstone) S. BA, Calif. State, L.A., 1959; MLS, U. So. Calif., L.A., 1961. Cert. tchr., Calif. Page L.A. County Pub. Library, San Gabriel, Calif., 1927-37, asst. branch librarian, 1938-40; various clerical positions Zoss Const./Consolidated, San Diego, 1941-42; time keeper Cal Ship Constrn., Wilmington, Calif., 1942-45; turkey ranch mgr. Bagnard Turkey Ranch, Baldwin Park, Calif., 1945-47; filing clerk Union Hardware, L.A., 1947-49; library asst. Rosemead (Calif.) H.S., 1949-60; librarian Anaheim (Calif.) Union H.S., 1960-61; catalog head librarian Pasadena (Calif.) City Coll., 1961-79; library classifier Pasadena City Coll., 1979-81. Author: (bibliographies) Man and Environment, 1970, Black America, 1978, (index) American Rose Mag., 1989-91; editor: Bulletin Rose Soc. Rose Parade, 1974-87. Mem. Am. Rose Soc. (life, life judge, cons. 1978—, elected dist. dir. Pacific S.W. 1985-88, Pacific S.W. Dist. Silver Honor medal 1991, Outstanding Dist. Judge award 1995), L.A. Rose Soc. (life, Bronze Honor medal 1994), Pacific Rose Soc. (life), Royal Nat. Rose Soc. (life), Calif. Garden Clubs (life, pres. Rancho De Duarte 1991-96), Calif. Libr. Assn., Beta Phi Mu (hon.). Avocations: rosarian, gardener, book collector. Home: 2397 Morslay Rd Altadena CA 91001-2715

SEWELL, BEVERLY JEAN, financial executive; b. Oklahoma City, July 10, 1942; d. Benjamin B. Bainbridge and Faith Marie (Mosier) Allision; m. Ralph Byron Sewell, Jan. 23, 1962; children: M. Timothy, Pamela J. Student, U. Okla., 1960-61, Jackson C.C., 1973-77; BA in Bus., Mesa Coll., 1982; cert., Coll. Fin. Planning, 1984, MS in Fin. Planning, 1994. Sole practice fin. planning Grand Junction, Colo., 1985-87; fin. planner, broker Interpacific Investors Services, Grand Junction, 1987-88; investment broker A.G. Edwards & Sons, Inc., Grand Junction, 1988-92, v.p., 1992—. Mem. ctrl. com. Grand Junction Rep. Orgn., 1988; mem. Grand Junction Planning Commn., 1987-89; bd. dirs. Grand Junction Symphony, 1991-94, Downtown Devel. Authority, St. Mary's Hosp. Mem. Inst. Cert. Fin. Planners, Internat. Assn. Fin. Planning. Avocations: tennis, jogging. Home: 717 Wedge Dr Grand Junction CO 81506-1866 Office: A G Edwards & Sons Inc 501 Main St Grand Junction CO 81501-2607

SEWELL, CHARLES ROBERTSON, geologist, exploration company executive, investor; b. Malvern, Ark., Feb. 7, 1927; s. Charles Louis and Elizabeth (Robertson) S.; m. Margaret Helen Wilson, Dec. 26, 1953 (dec. July 1985); children: Michael Stuart, Charles Wilson, Marion Elizabeth; m. Louise T. Worthington, Nov. 29, 1985; 1 child, Ginger B. BS, U. Ark.-Fayetteville, 1950; MA, U. Tex.-Austin, 1955, postgrad., 1961-64. Registered geologist, Ariz. Well logging engr. Baroid, Houston, 1950; asst. metallurgist Magcobar, Malvern, Ark., 1951; geologist Socony-Mobil Petroleum Co., Roswell, N.Mex., 1955; sr. geologist Dow Chem. Co., Freeport, Tex., 1956-61; spl. instr. U. Tex., Austin, 1962-65; pvt. practice cons. geologist, Austin, 1962-65; dist. geologist, mgr. Callahan Mining Corp., Tucson, 1965-68; owner, cons. geologist Sewell Mineral Exploration, worldwide, 1968—, extensive work USSR-CIS, 1988—. Contbr. articles to profl. jours. Elder, Presbyn. Ch., Tucson, 1973—. With USN, 1944-46, 51-53. NSF grantee, 1962-64, 63. Mem. AIME, Ariz. Geol. Soc., Mining Found. Southwest (bd. govs. 1982-86, 90—, pres. 1984), Masons. Republican. Achievements include discovery/co-discovery of numerous metallic and non-metallic ore deposits; extensive work on gold/silver systems in western U.S., Mexico, Costa Rica and Kazakhstan. Home and Office: 260 S Sewell Pl Tucson AZ 85748-6700

SEWELL, RALPH BYRON, investment broker, financial planner, manager; b. Oklahoma City, May 24, 1940; s. Ralph Llewellyn and Amy (Taylor) S.; m. Beverly Jean Bainbridge, Jan. 23, 1962; children: Michael Timothy, Pamela Jean. BS in Engring. Physics, U. Okla., 1963; MS in Fin. Planning, Coll. for Fin. Planning, 1994. Cert. fin. planner. Project engr. Kerr McGee Corp., Oklahoma City, 1969; sr. engr. Consumers Power Co., Charlevoix, Mich., 1969-70; nuclear licensing adminstr. Consumers Power Co., Jackson, Mich., 1970-77; ops. mgr. Plateau Resources Ltd., Grand Junction, Colo., 1977-80; investment broker Boettcher & Co., Grand Junction, 1980-83, spl. ptnr., 1983-87; v.p. investments A.G. Edwards & Sons, Inc., Grand Junction, 1987-90, assoc. v.p., 1990-94, v.p., 1994—. Lt. USN, 1963-68. Recipient Appreciation award Bus. Partnership Program Bd. Edn. Sch. Dist. #51, 1989, 90. Mem. Inst. of Cert. Fin. Planners, Lions. Republican. Avocations: tennis, fishing, cross country skiing. Home: 717 Wedge Dr Grand Junction CO 81506-1866 Office: AG Edwards & Sons Inc 501 Main St Grand Junction CO 81501-2607

SEXTON, JERRY LEE, multimedia company executive, consultant; b. Malden, Mo., Aug. 4, 1954; s. Jack and Ann (Yater) S.; m. Pamela Sue Mischler, May 20, 1984; children: Christopher James, Jennifer Nicole. BS in Mass. Comm., Fla. State U., 1976; MS in Pub. Rels., Am. U., 1984; postgrad., Air Command and Staff Coll., Maxwell AFB, Ala., 1990. Commd. 2d lt. USAF, 1976, advanced through grades to lt. col., 1991; comdr. Det. 13 1369 audiovisual squadron USAF, L.A., 1980-81; mem. pub. rels. staff Office Sec. Def. USAF, Washington, 1981-84; dep. dir. ops. 1352 audiovisual squadron USAF, San Bernardino, Calif., 1984-87; dir. ops. 1363 audiovisual squadron USAF, Honolulu, 1987-90; comdr. Def. Visual Info. Sch. USAF, Denver, 1991-95; dir. ops. Media Lab Inc., Louisville, Colo., 1995-96; CEO Digital Metropolis Inc., Denver, 1996—; instr. Leeward C.C., Honolulu, 1988-90; mem. faculty Denver U., 1995—; mem. adv. coun. Fed. Imaging Expositions, Washington, 1993-95, U. Colo., Denver, 1996—. Prodr. (multimedia CD) Hewlett-Packard HPVEE, 1997, (motion picture) Internment of the Unknown Soldier, 1985 (award 1985), (videotape) Armed Forces Day Nat. TV Spots, 1984, (multimedia prodn.) Mil. Airlift Command Briefing, 1987. Mem. Colo. Film and Video Assn., Nat. Press Photographers Assn. (conv. com. 1993-95), Denver Advt. Fedn., Air Force Assn., South Metro Denver C. of C. Republican. Baptist. Avocations: hiking, soccer, biking, computers, photography. Office: Digital Metropolis Inc 5359 S Flanders Way Aurora CO 80015-3747

SEXTON ATKINS, JANNAH, artist; b. Frankfurt, Germany, Sept. 10, 1951; d. Thomas Logan Sexton and Wanda Jean (Spurlock) Ingram; m. Charles E. Atkins, Apr. 13, 1985. AA, Kauai C.C., Hawaii, 1975; studied sculptural clay with Toshiko Takaezu, 1975; cert., Windtree Sch. Drawing and Illustration, 1990; studied with David Passalacqua, studied monoprints with Rodney Konopaki, 1990, studied with David Passalacqua; BFA cum laude, U. Alaska, Anchorage, 1990, BA cum laude, 1992. Art educator various Alaskan arts orgns., Alaska, 1990—; art dir. ARCA Murals, 1993-94; dir. and owner Earthwind Studio, Anchorage, 1994—; curator of exhibits Alaska Pacific U., Anchorage, 1995—; curator Alaska Contemporary Art Bank Alaska State Coun. on Arts, 1997—; leader various art workshops, 1991-94; bd. dirs. Visual Arts Ctr. Alaska, 1992-94, exhbn. coord., 1992; vol. juror asst. Anchorage Mus. History and Art, 1993; exhbn. coord. Grandview Gardens Cultural Ctr., Alaska, 1994; art juror reflections program Nat. PTA, 1995; display asst. Nordstroms, 1995-96; scenic artist Anchorage Opera, 1995-96; mural asst. Blaines Art Supply, 1996, 97, 98; adj. prof. art history Alaska Pacific U., Anchorage, 1996—. Exhibitions include Callanetics Studio, Anchorage, 1995, Stonington Gallery, Anchorage, 1995, Pratt Mus., Homer, 1996, Alaska Pacific U., Anchorage, 1996, Fireweed Gallery, Homer, 1996, Blaines Art and Frame, Homer, 1996, Toast Gallery, Anchorage, 1997, Bunnell St. Gallery, Homer, Alaska, 1997; represented in permanent collections Pratt Mus.; represented in pvt. collections. Pol. advocacy advisor People First, Anchorage, 1993-95; rep. arts adv. commn. Municipality of Anchorage, 1994—. Recipient Ceramic award Kauai C.C. Arts Festival, 1975, Hon. Mention U. Alaska, Anchorage, 1988, 1989, Best Graphic Design/Illustration, 1990, hon. mention Am. Coll. Theatre Festival and Northwest Drama Competition, 1989, XXIV all Alaska juried, 1992; Alaska Found. scholar, 1984, 85, 86, 87; Chancellor's scholar, 1986, 87; Saradell Ard scholar, 1989, 90. Avocations: art, skiing, mountain biking. Home and Office: 1747 Talkeetna St Anchorage AK 99508-3244

SEYFERT, HOWARD BENTLEY, JR., podiatrist; b. Clifton Heights, Pa., July 10, 1918; s. Howard Bentley and Mabel (Ashenbach) S.; m. Anna Mary van Roden, June 26, 1942; 1 child, Joanna Mary Irwin. D of Podiatric Medicine, Temple U., 1940. Cert. Nat. Bd. Podiatry Examiners (past pres.), Ariz. State Bd. Podiatry Examiners (past pres.). Pvt. practice podiatry Phoenix, 1950-82, Sedona, Ariz., 1982—; mem. med. staff Marcus J. Lawrence Meml. Hosp., Cottonwood, Ariz. Served to capt. USAAF, 1942-46, ETO, lt. col. Res. ret. Decorated Bronze Star. Fellow Acad. Ambulatory Foot Surgery, Am. Coll. Foot Surgeons; mem. Ariz. Podiatric Med. Assn. (past pres.), Am. Podiatric Med. Assn., Gen. Old Golf Club. Republican. Presbyterian. Clubs: OakCreek Country (Sedona); Fairfield Flagstaff Country (Flagstaff, Ariz.). Avocations: golf, gardening, landscaping. Home: Air Force Village W 21364 Westover Cir Riverside CA 92518-2923

SEYMOUR, JEFFREY ALAN, governmental relations consultant; b. L.A., Aug. 31, 1950; s. Daniel and Evelyn (Schwartz) S.; m. Valerie Joan Parker, Dec. 2, 1973; 1 child, Jessica Lynne. AA in Social Sci., Santa Monica Coll., 1971; BA in Polit. Sci., UCLA, 1973, MPA, , 1977. Councilmanic aide L.A. City Coun., 1972-74; county supr.'s sr. dep. L.A. Bd. Suprs., 1974-82; v.p. Bank of L.A., 1982-83; prin. Jeffrey Seymour & Assocs., L.A., 1983-84; ptnr. Morey/Seymour & Assocs., 1984—; mem. comml. panel Am. Arbitration Assn., 1984—. Chmn. West Hollywood Parking Adv. Com., L.A., 1983-84; chmn. social action com. Temple Emanuel of Beverly Hills, 1986-89, bd. dirs. 1988-93, v.p., 1990-93; v.p. Congregation N'vay Shalom, 1994-95; mem. Pan Pacific Park Citizens Adv. Com., L.A., 1982-85; bd. dirs. William O'Douglas Outdoor Classroom, L.A., 1981-88, exec. sec. Calif. Fedn. Young Dems., 1971; mem. Calif. Dem. Cen. Com., 1979-82; pres. Beverlywood-Cheviot Hills Dem. Club, L.A., 1978-81; co-chmn. Westside Chancellor's Assocs. UCLA, 1986-88; mem. L.A. Olympic Citizens Adv. Com.; mem. liaison adv. commn. with city and county govt. for 1984 Olympics, 1984; v.p. cmty. rels. metro region, Jewish Fedn. Coun. of L.A., 1985-87, co-chmn. urban affairs commn., 1987-89, vice chmn., 1989-90, subcom. chmn. local govt. law and legislation commn., 1990—, chmn. campus outreach task force, 1994—; mem. adv. bd. Nat. Jewish Ctr. for Immunology & Respiratory Medicine, 1991—; bd. dirs. Hillel Coun. of L.A., 1991—; mem. platform on world peace and internat. rels. Calif. Dems., 1983; pres. 43d Assembly Dist. Dem. Coun., 1975-79; arbitrator BBB, 1984—; trustee UCLA Found., 1989—; pres. UCLA Jewish Alumni, 1992-95; mem. Santa Monica Mountains Conservancy, 1995-96, adv. com., 1996—; mem. cabinet Jewish Cmty. Rels. Com. Greater L.A., 1994—, chair campus outreach task force, 1994-95, govtl. rels. commn., 1995-96, v. chair Jewish Cmty. Relations Com. Jewish Federation. Coun. Greater L.A., 1998—; mem. adv. bd. L.A. Peace Now. Recipient Plaques for services rendered Beverlywood Cheviot Hills Dem. Club, L.A., 1981, Jewish Fedn. Coun. Greater L.A., 1983; Certs. of Appreciation, L.A. Olympic Organizing Com., 1984, County of L.A., 1984, City of L.A., 1987; commendatory resolutions, rules com. Calif. State Senate, 1987, Calif. State Assembly, 1987, 96, County of L.A., 1987, City of L.A., 1987. Mem. Am. Soc. Pub. Adminstrn., Am. Acad. Polit. and Social Scis., Town Hall of Calif., So. Calif. Planning Congress, Urban Land Inst., UCLA Alumni Assn. (mem. govtl. steering com. 1983—, bd. dirs. 1995—, chair bd. dirs. 1995-97, pres. 1998—). Office: Morey/Seymour and Assocs 233 Wilshire Blvd Ste 290 Santa Monica CA 90401-1217

SEYMOUR, LISA, museum director; b. Oct. 30, 1962; m. E. David Seymour. BA in Mass Comms., U. Denver, 1984; MA in Mass Comms., 1985. Grad. teaching asst. U. Denver, 1985; records clk. typist Kingman (Ariz.) Police Dept., 1985-86; sec. First Presbyn. Ch., Elko, Nev., 1986-87; exec. dir. Elko (Nev.) County Against Domestic Violence, 1987; exec. dir. of found. Elko (Nev.) Gen. Hosp. Found., 1989-90; mgr. cmty. rels. Elko (Nev.) Gen. Hosp., 1987-90; adtg. mgr. Elko (Nev.) Ind., 1990-91, newspaper editor, reporter, photographer, 1991-94; archivist and oral historian Northeastern Nev. Mus., Elko, 1994-95; interim mus. adminstr., 1995, mus. dir., 1996—. Grantee Newmont Gold Co., E.L. Cord Found., E.L. Wiegard Found., 1996. Office: Northeastern Nev Mus 1515 Idaho St Elko NV 89801-4021

SHABOT, MYRON MICHAEL, surgeon, critical care educator, informaticist; b. Houston, Aug. 5, 1945; s. Sam and Mona Doris (Stalarow) S.; 1 child, Samuel Laib. Student, Tulane U., 1963-64; BA, U. Tex., Austin, 1966; MD, U. Tex., Dallas, 1970. Lectr. surgery UCLA Sch. Medicine, 1977-78, asst. prof., 1978-82, clin. assoc. prof. surgery and anesthesiology, 1983-97, prof. surgery, 1997—; dir. surg. ICU, Los Angeles County Harbor Med. Ctr.-UCLA Sch. Medicine, 1980-82; dir. surg. ICU, Cedars-Sinai Med. Ctr., L.A., 1982—, med. dir. Enterprise Info. Svcs.; sec. Cedars-Sinai Med. Ctr. Attending Staff, 1999—. Contbr. articles to profl. jours. Served to lt. comdr. USPHS, 1971-73. Fellow ACS (So. Calif. chpt. bd. dirs. 1988—, pres. 1992-93, gov., 1992—); mem. Western Surg. Assn., Pacific Coast Surg. Assn., Soc. Critical Care Medicine, Am. Assn. Surgery of Trauma, Soc. Computers in Critical Care and Pulmonary Medicine (bd. dirs. 1988—, treas. 1989—, pres., 1993-94), Soc. Clin. Data Mgmt. Systems (pres. 1985-86), L.A. Surg. Soc. (pres. 1997-98), Phi Eta Sigma. Jewish. Office: Cedars-Sinai Med Ctr 8700 Beverly Blvd Ste 8215 Los Angeles CA 90048-1865

SHABOY, BENNY, editor, writer; b. Benicia, Calif.. Prin., owner Art PR, San Francisco, Benicia, Calif., 1981-94; editor studioNOTES, Benicia, Calif., 1993—; cons. in field; juror for various shows and public art installations. Author: Getting a Gallery, 1998; editor studioNOTES, 1993—,. Co-founder, organizer Benicia (Calif.) Open Studios, 1982, 1988-90. Avocations: visual art, computer programming. Office: studioNOTES PO Box 502 Benicia CA 94510-0502

SHABTAI, JACOB, artist, art dealer, antique dealer; b. Tehran, Iran, Dec. 31, 1947; came to U.S., 1972; s. Abraham and Sarrah S.; m. Roya Shabtai, Jan. 5, 1980; childrne: Jubin, Jasmine, Jennifer. BA, BS, U. Jerusalem, 1969. Owner, artist Art Gallery, Iran, 1970-72; owner Oriental Rug Exch., L.A., 1972—. Artist portraits, realism, Old Master style. Mem. Rug Dealers

Assn. L.A. Office: Oriental Rug Exch 339 N La Cienega Blvd Los Angeles CA 90048-1924

SHACKELFORD, GORDON LEE, JR., physics educator; b. South Bend, Ind., Apr. 7, 1948; s. Gordon Lee and Leatha Mae Shackelford; m. Janis Elizabeth Mead, Apr. 6, 1974. BS in Physics, San Diego State U., 1970, MS in Radiol. Physics, 1974. Electronic designer for physics dept. San Diego State U., 1969-70; electronic engr. Naval Electronics Lab., Point Loma, Calif., 1970; electronic engr. product design Info. Machine Corps., Santee, Calif., 1970-71; lectr. physics San Diego State U., 1971—, asst. dir. alumni and devel. Coll. of Scis., 1980-81, assoc. dean scis., external rels., 1981-98, project mgr. Biomass Power Plant, 1984-87, 89—; project mgr. SDSU 100 Telescope, 1989-97, Tijuana River Tidal Wetlands Restoration Project, chmn. faculty senate athletic sub-com. Mem. quality life bd. City of San Diego, 1989-90; chmn. Lakeside Community Planning Group; chmn. senate com. on acad. resources and planning. Home: 9716 Red Pony Ln El Cajon CA 92021-2343 Office: San Diego State U Physics Dept San Diego CA 92182

SHACKLEY, MICHAEL STEVEN, archaeologist, geochemist; b. San Diego, May 13, 1949; s. Guy Bates and Norma Luella (Jones) S.; m. Dianna Lee Bennett Hoff, Sept. 15, 1973 (div. Oct. 1980); 1 child, Eroica Dawn Shackley Saiz; m. Kathleen Lois Butler, June 24, 1995. BA in Anthropology, Geology, San Diego State U., 1979, MA in Anthropology, 1981; PhD in Anthropology, Ariz. State U., 1990. Registered profl. archaeologist. Sr. archaeologist Wirth Assocs., San Diego, 1979-82, Ariz. State U., Tempe, 1985-88, Dames & Moore, San Diego, 1988-89, Brian Mooney Assocs., San Diego, 1989-90; lectr. Calif. State U., Fullerton, 1987-91; adj. asst. prof. San Diego State U., 1989-90; from asst. prof. rsch. to assoc. prof. rsch. U. Calif., Berkeley, 1990—; assoc. dir. archaeol. collections and rsch. P.A. Hearst Mus. Anthropology, 1990—; dir. Archaeol. XRF Lab. Author: (3 vols.) Archaeological Investigations in the Western Colorado Desert: A Sociological Approach, 1984; (with others) Early Formative Adaptations in the Southern Southwest, 1996; (ency. entry) Archaeology of Prehistoric North America: An Encyclopedia, 1998; author/editor: Archaeological Obsidian Studies: Theory and Method, 1998; author, co-editor: Prehistoric Hunter-Gatherers of South Central Arizona: The Picacho Reservoir Archaic Project, 1986; assoc. editor: Archaeometry, 1999-2004; contbr. articles to profl. jours.; presenter in field. Recipient faculty mentor award U. Calif., 1994; achievement awards for Coll. Scientists fellow, 1984-85; AZ Archeol. & Hist. Soc. grantee U.S. S.W., 1992, 94, NSF grantee US S.W., 1992-94, Stahl Endowment grantee U.S. S.W., 1993-94, 95-96, N.Mex., 1994-95, 98-99. Mem. AAAS, Internat. Assn. for Obsidian Studies (pres. 1993-94), Soc. Archaeological Scis. (v.p. 1992—), Soc. for Am. Archaeology (program com. pres. 1979), Geol. Soc. Am., Soc. Calif. Archaeology, Ariz. Archaeol. and Hist. Soc., Phi Beta Kappa. Democrat. Achievements include pioneer in systematic acad. study of prehistoric obsidian and its use in the Greater Am. S.W. Home: 17 Carmel Ave El Cerrito CA 94530-4112 Office: U Calif P A Hearst Mus Anthropology 103 Kroeber Hall Berkeley CA 94720-3712

SHACTER, DAVID MERVYN, lawyer; b. Toronto, Ont., Can., Jan. 17, 1941; s. Nathan and Tillie Anne (Schwartz) S. BA, U. Toronto, 1963; JD, Southwestern U., 1967. Bar: Calif. 1968, U.S. Ct. Appeals (9th cir.) 1969, U.S. Supreme Ct. 1982. Law clk., staff atty. Legal Aid Found., Long Beach, Calif., 1967-70; asst. city atty. City of Beverly Hills, Calif., 1970; ptnr. Shacter & Berg, Beverly Hills, 1971-83, Selwyn, Capalbo, Lowenthal & Shacter Profl. Law Corp., 1984—; del. State Bar Conf. Dels., 1976—; lectr. Calif. Continuing Edn. of Bar, 1977, 82, 83, 86; judge pro tem L.A. and Beverly Hills mcpl. cts.; arbitrator L.A. Superior Ct., 1983—, also judge pro tem; disciplinary examiner Calif. State Bar, 1986. Bd. dirs. and pres. Los Angeles Soc. Prevention Cruelty to Animals, 1979-89. Mem. Beverly Hills Bar Assn. (bd. govs. 1985—, editor-in-chief jour., sec. 1987-88, treas. 1988-89, v.p. 1989-90, pres.-elect 1990-91, pres. 1991-92), Am. Arbitration Assn. (nat. panel arbitrators, NASD arbitration panel), City of Hope Med. Ctr. Aux., Wilshire C. of C. (bd. dirs., gen. counsel 1985-87). Office: Selwyn Capalbo Lowenthal & Shacter Profl Law Corp 8383 Wilshire Blvd Ste 510 Beverly Hills CA 90211-2404

SHADDOCK, PAUL FRANKLIN, SR., human resources director; b. Buffalo, Apr. 7, 1950; s. William Edmund and Rhea (Riester) S.; m. Linda Jeannine Bauer, July 19, 1980; children: Paul Jr., Jessica. BS, State U. Coll. N.Y., Buffalo, 1973; MBA, SUNY, Binghamton, 1975 Warehouse mgr. Ralston Purina Co., Denver, 1976-77; prodn. supr. Samsonite Corp., Denver, 1978-79, labor rels. rep., 1979-83; dir. human resources NBI, Inc., Denver, 1984-89, United Techs. Corp., Colorado Springs, Colo., 1990-95, Rockwell Semiconductor Sys., Newport Beach, Calif., 1995-96; v.p. human resources CSG, Systems, Inc., Denver, Colo., 1996—. Mem. Colo. Alliance of Bus., Denver, 1983-85, 90—, exec. com. U. Colo., Colorado Springs, 1990—. Mem. Assn. of Quality Participation, Am. Personnel Assn., Colo. Human Resource Assn., Human Resource Electroncis Group, Mountain States Employers Coun., Rocky Mountain Human Resources Group, Colorado Springs C. of C. Republican. Roman Catholic. Avocations: swimming, tennis, skiing. Home: 5744 S Lima St Englewood CO 80111-4145

SHADE, LINDA BUNNELL, university chancellor. BA in English and Comm., Baylor U., 1964; MA in English Lang. and Lit., U. Colo., 1967, PhD in English Lit., 1970. Asst. prof. English, acting assoc. dean Coll. Humanities U. Calif., Riverside, 1970-77; dean acad. programs and policy studies Calif. State U. Sys., 1977-87; vice chancellor acad. affairs Minn. State U. Sys., St. Paul, 1987-93; chancellor U. Colo., Colorado Springs, 1993—; active Minn. Women's Econ. Round Table, 1989-93; mem. exec. com. Nat. Coun. for Accreditation Tchr. Edn., 1996-99. Mem. St. Paul chpt. ARC; mem. cmty. bd. Norwest Bank, Colorado Springs, 1997—, mem. El Pomar awards for Excellence com., 1997—; mem. leadership commn. ACE, 1997—; mem. subcom. ROTC; mem. edn. com. U.S. Army. Recipient Disting. Alumni award Baylor U., 1995; Woodrow Wilson dissertation fellow, Univ. Colo. Avocations: gardening, baseball, cooking, Sable Burmese cats. Office: U Colo 1420 Austin Bluffs Pkwy Colorado Springs CO 80918*

SHADEGG, JOHN B., congressman; b. Phoenix, Oct. 22, 1950; s. Stephen and Eugenia Shadegg; m. Shirley Shadegg; children: Courtney, Stephen. BA, U. Ariz., 1972, JD, 1975. Advisor U.S. Sentencing Commn.; spl. asst. atty. gen. State of Ariz., 1983-90; spl. counsel Ariz. Ho. Rep. Caucus, 1991-92; pvt. practice; mem. 104th-106th Congresses from 4th Ariz. dist., 1995—; mem. budget com., govt. reform and oversight com.; asst. whip 104th Congress from 4th Ariz. dist., mem. resources com.; mem. Victims Bill of Rights Task Force, 1989-90; mem. Fiscal Accountability and Reform Efforts Com., 1991-92; counsel Arizonian's for Wildlife Conservation, 1992; chmn. Proposition 108-Two-Thirds Tax Limitation Initiative, 1992. Rep. Party Ballot Security chmn., 1982; active Corbin for Atty. Gen., 1982-86; Rep. Precinct committeeman; chmn. Ariz. Rep. Caucus, 1985-87; chmn. Ariz. Lawyers for Bush-Quayle, 1988; mem. steering com., surrogate spkr. Jon Kyl for Congress, 1988-92; former pres. Crime Victim Found.; founding dir. Goldwater Inst. Pub. Policy; chmn. Ariz. Juvenile Justice Adv. Coun.; mem. adv. bd. Salvation Army; mem. vestry Christ Ch. of Ascension, 1989-91; mem. class II Valley Leadership; bd. dirs. Ariz. State U. Law Soc. Office: US House Reps 430 Cannon Office Bldg Washington DC 20515-0304*

SHADZI, BAHRAM, engineering executive; b. Esfahan, Iran, Dec. 22, 1948; came to U.S., 1967; s. Javad and Robab (Emadolsadati) S.; m. Judith I. Shadzi, Sept. 18, 1971; children: Javad, Taraneh, Peymon. BSChemE, U. Minn., 1972, MSChemE, 1976. Chem. process engr. 3M Co., St. Paul, 1973-76; supt. pulp mill Iran Wood & Paper Ind., Gilan, Iran, 1976-81; prin. scientist Control Data Corp., Mpls., 1981-84, process devel. mgr., 1984-86; mgr. advanced media devel. Control Data Corp., Omaha, 1986-89; process engring. mgr. Seagate Tech. Corp., Omaha, 1989-92; engring. mgr. HMT Tech. Corp., Fremont, Calif., 1992—; pres. mgmt. club Seagate Tech. Corp., 1987-89. Contbr. articles to profl. jours. Mem. AIChE. Achievements include patents (with others) for the development and innovation related to magnetic computer disks and the application of spin coating technology for manufacture of computer disks. Home: 10187 Byrne Ave Cupertino CA 95014-2843

SHAEFFER, THELMA JEAN, primary school educator; b. Ft. Collins, Colo., Feb. 1, 1949; d. Harold H. and Gladys June (Ruff) [illegible]; m. Charles [illegible] 1971; 1 child, Shannon [illegible]. BA, U. No. Colo., 1970, MA, 1972. Cert. profl. tchr., type B, Colo. Primary tchr. Adams County Dist #12 Five Star Schs., Northglenn, Colo., 1970-84; title I (lang. arts) tchr. Adams County Dist #12 Five Star Schs., Northglenn, 1984-97, title I, read succed tchr., 1992-97; mem. policy coun. Adams County Dist. # 12 Five Star Schs., Northglenn, 1975-79, dist. sch. improvement team, 1987-89; presenter Nat. Coun. Tchrs. of English, 1990. Vol. 1992 election, Denver, alumni advisor for Career Connections U. No. Colo., 1993-97. Mem. Colo. Tchrs. Assn. (del. 1992), Dist. Tchrs. Edn. Assn. (exec. bd. mem. 1991-93), Internat. Reading Assn. (pres. Colo. coun. 1988), Internat. Order of Job's Daughters (coun. mem.), Order of Eastern Star, Delta Omicron. Episcopalian. Home: 6502 Perry St Arvada CO 80003-6400 Office: Hulstrom Elem Sch 10604 Grant Dr Northglenn CO 80233-4117

SHAEUMIN, MINAYA, claims representative; b. San Francisco, July 11, 1928; d. John Jesse and Helen Elizabeth (Forsyth) McNeil; m. Maurice Loren Turner, July 28, 1949 (div. Nov. 1955); 1 child, Colleen Ann; m. Rayee Shaeumin, Feb. 13, 1973. Student, Santa Rosa (Calif.) Jr. Coll., 1958-60; AA, Tanana Valley C.C., Fairbanks, Ark., 1987; BS in Anthropology, Oreg. State U., 1992. Lic. life ins. agt., health and accident agt. Intern tchr. 2d grade Primrose Elem. Sch., Santa Rosa, 1961-62; floor clk. surg. wing Santa Rosa Meml. Hosp., 1962; lab. technician Optical Coating Labs., Santa Rosa, 1962-63; live-in practical nurse, housekeeper, sch. tchr. Healsburg, Calif., 1963-65; saleslady, mgr. cosmetic dept. Empire Drug Store, Santa Rosa, 1965-67; cmty. ctr. aide, coord. Cmty. Ctr., Ukiah, Calif., 1968-69; picture framer New Horizons Art Gallery, Fairbanks, Alaska, 1985; seed analyst Oreg. State U. Seed Lab., Corvallis, 1988; owner, operator Best Publs., 1991-92; customer svc. rep. Prequest Co., 1993-95; security officer Am. Protective Svcs., Inc., 1995-96. Inventor matchbook holder-dispensor; inventor-designer free standing mag. rack; writer songs. Active mem. Pro-Choice Orgn., 1991—; mem. The Planetary Soc., 1989-91, Nat. Space Soc., 1990-91; mem. gold club North Shore Animal League, N.Y., 1985—. Recipient Benefactor award North Shore Animal League, 1991, Cert. of Appreciation, Nat. Cm. to Preserve Social Security and Medicare, 1991. Mem. Amnesty Internat. USA, Ams. to Limit Congl. Terms, Am. Policy Inst. "We the People", LWV, Srs. Coalition, So. Poverty law Ctr., Nat. Com. to Preserve Social Security and Medicare. Avocations: painting in oil and water colors, designing furniture/floor plans, writing, collecting limited editions plates and leather bound classic books. Home: 205 NW 11th St Apt 2 Corvallis OR 97330-6048

SHAFER, ELIZABETH JANE, writer; b. Colorado Springs, Colo., Jan. 18, 1924; d. Ira Elmer and Grace Leota (Groves) S. Student, Colo. Coll., 1942-45. Mem. advt. staff Colorado Springs News, 1944; continuity writer KVOR, Colorado Springs, 1944-46; reporter Western Advt., L.A., 1958-59; CS reporter Fairchild Publs., N.Y.C., 1959-70; reporter Religious News Svc., N.Y.C., 1961-73, USIA, Washington, 1969—; asst. editor Earth Sci. Mag., Colorado Springs, 1973-80. Co-author: 7 Keys to the Rocky Mountains, 1968; author: The Ellen T. Brinley Guild, 1992; editor, ghostwriter numerous regional books, 1980—; contbr. numerous articles, fiction and poems to profl. publs. Mem. Nat. League Am. Pen Women (pres. 1958-60, cert. appreciation 1984), Colo. Authors League (Top Hand awards 1968-88), Poetry Soc. Colo. (Colorado Springs workshop dir. 1966-97), Colorado Springs Poetry Fellowship (pres. 1960-62, life mem.). Democrat. Avocations: gardening, photography, book collecting, regional history. Home and Office: 215 Custer Ave Colorado Springs CO 80903-3523

SHAFER, JACK DOUGLAS, writer, dog breeder; b. Loma Linda, Calif., Jan. 14, 1927; s. Frederick Franklin and Florence Ruth (Drengberg) S. Student pub. schs., Sacramento. Chief page Calif. State Legislature; actor MGM, 20th Century Fox Studios; champion dog breeder Tustin Calif.; author, 1994, columnist. Author dog breeding book, 1994 (number one best seller, 1994-98). Recipient Presidential Commendation from former Pres. George Bush. Avocations: raising, breeding animals, fine food, wine. Home: 17300 17th St # J126 Tustin CA 92780-1955

SHAFER, JAMES ALBERT, health care administrator; b. Chgo., Aug. 26, 1924; s. James Earl and Kathleen (Sutterland) S.; m. Irene Jeanne Yurcega, June 20, 1948; children: Kathleen Mary, Patricia Ann. Technician Zenith Radio Corp., Chgo., 1946-47; owner, operator Eastgate Electronics, Chgo., 1947-61; applications engr. Perfection Mica Co., Bensenville, Ill., 1961-71; pres. Electronics Unltd., Northbrook, Ill., 1972-73, Ariz. Geriatric Enterprises Inc., Safford, 1974-86; sec.-treas. Saguaro Care Inc., 1988—; bd. dirs. Mt. Graham Community Hosp., Safford. Republican. Roman Catholic. Avocations: computers, photography. Home: PO Drawer H 10729 W Cottonwood Rd Pima AZ 85543-0630 Office: Saguaro Care Inc PO Drawer H Pima AZ 85543

SHAFF, BEVERLY GERARD, educational administrator; b. Oak Park, Ill., Aug. 16, 1925; d. Carl Tanner and Mary Frances (Gerard) Wilson; m. Maurice A. Shaff, Jr., Dec. 20, 1951 (dec. June 1967); children: Carol Maureen, David Gerrard, Mark Albert. MA, U. Ill., 1951; postgrad., Colo. Coll., 1966, 73, Lewis and Clark Coll., 1982, Portland State U., 1975-82. Tchr. Haley Sch., Berwyn, Ill., 1948-51; assoc. prof. English, Huntingdon Coll., Montgomery, Ala., 1961-62; tchr. English, William Palmer High Sch., Colorado Springs, Colo., 1964-67, 72-76, dir., 1967-72; tchr. English, Burns (Oreg.) High Sch., 1976-78; tchr. English as 2d lang. Multnomah County Ednl. Svc. Dist., Portland, Oreg., 1979-85; coord. gen. studies Portland Jewish Acad., 1984-90; with Indian Edn. Prog./Student Tng. Edn. Prog. (STEP) Portland Pub. Schs., 1990-92, 95—; tchr. St. Thomas More Sch., Portland, 1992-95; tchr. Indian Edn. Act Program Portland Pub. Schs., 1995—. Del. Colorado Springs Dem. Com., 1968, 72; active Rainbow Coalition, Portland; ct. apptd. spl. adv. CASA; mem. Lake Oswego Libr. Bd., Citizens Rev. Bd. Mem. Nat. Assn. Admnstrs., Nat. Assn. Schs. and Colls., Nat. Coun. Tchrs. Math., Nat. Coun. Tchrs. English. Home: 1925 NE 19th #6A Portland OR 97212

SHAFFER, SHERRILL LYNN, economist; b. Tyler, Tex., Aug. 1, 1952; s. Douglas Marsene and Ethel Elizabeth (Green) S.; m. Margaret Jane Ahrens, Jun 20, 1987; 1 child, David Carsten. BA, Rice U., 1974; MA, Stanford U., 1978, PhD, 1981. Rsch. asst. Stanford (Calif.) U., 1976-79, instr., 1979-80; from economist to chief Fed. Res. Bank N.Y., N.Y.C., 1980-88; from rsch. officer, economist to asst. v.p./discount officer Fed. Res. Bank Phila., 1988-97; John A. Guthrie disting. prof. banking and fin. svcs. U. Wyo., Laramie, 1997—; violinist solo and with orchs., Calif., N.Y., 1976-88; cons. asst. Rosse & Olszewski, Palo Alto, Calif., 1978-80. Assoc. editor to editor Jour. Econs. and Bus., 1993—; contbr. articles to profl. jours. Sec. bd. dirs. N.Y. Arts Group, N.Y.C., 1982-83; mem. program com. So. Fin. Assn., 1996; exec. adv. coun. mem. dept. fin. Temple U., 1996-97; bd. dirs. artist selection com. Tri-County Concerts Assn., 1996-98; mem. fin. com. St. Matthew's Cathedral, Laramie, Wyo., 1998—, mem. vestry, 1999—. Recipient Messier cert. Astronomical League, 1993. Mem. AAAS, Am. Econ. Assn., Am. Math. Soc., Math. Assn. Am., N.Am. Econs. and Fin. Assn., Indsl. Orgn. Soc., N.Y. Acad. Scis., Fin. Mgmt. Assn. (program com. 1991), So. Fin. Assn. (program com. 1996), Delaware Valley Amateur Astronomers (observing chmn. 1993, publicity chmn. 1994-96), Chamber Music Am. Episcopalian. Avocations: hiking, theology, number theory, astronomy, computer programming. Home: 30 Silver Spur Rd Laramie WY 82072-9563 Office: U Wyo Dept Econs and Fin PO Box 3985 Laramie WY 82071-3985

SHAGAM, MARVIN HÜCKEL-BERRI, private school educator; b. Monongalia, W.Va.; s. Lewis and Clara (Shagam) S. AB magna cum laude, Washington and Jefferson Coll., 1947; postgrad., Harvard Law Sch., 1947-48, Oxford (Eng.) U., 1948-51. Tchr. Mount House Sch., Tavistock, Eng., 1951-53, Williston Jr. Sch., Easthampton, Mass., 1953-55, Westtown (Pa.) Sch., 1955-58, The Thacher Sch., Ojai, Calif., 1958—; English dept. head Kurasini Internat. Edn. Centre, Dar-es-Salaam, Tanzania, 1966-67; dept. head Nkumbi Internat. Coll., Kabwe, Zambia, 1967-68; vol. visitor Prisons in Calif., 1980-95, Calif. Youth Authority, 1982-92; sr. youth crisis counsellor InterFace, 1984-94. With U.S. Army, 1942-46; 1st lt. M.I. [illegible] 1946-57. Danforth Found. fellow, 1942; Coun. for the Humanities fellow, Tufts U., 1983. Mem. Western Assn. Schs. and Colls. (accreditation com.), Great Teaching (Cooke chair 1977—), Phi Beta Kappa, Delta Sigma Rho, Cum Laude Soc. Republican. Avocations: hiking, camping, travel.

SHAH, AJAY, electronics company executive. Chmn., pres., CEO Smart Modular Tech., Fremont, Calif. Office: Smart Modular Tech 4305 Cushing Pkwy Fremont CA 94538-6408*

SHAH, DEVANG KUNDANLAL, software engineer; b. Mombasa, Kenya, Oct. 2, 1963; s. Kundan B. and Saryu K. (Mehta) S. B Tech Electronics Engring. with honors, Inst. Tech. Banaras Hindu U., Varanasi, India, 1985; MA in Computer Sci., U. Tex., 1989; MBA, U. Calif., 1995. Software engr. Tata Consultancy Svcs., Bombay, India, 1985-86; staff engr. SunSoft, Inc. subs. Sun Microsystems, Inc., Mountain View, Calif., 1990—; Sun Microsystems rep. to Unix Internat. multiprocessor working group, Parsippany, N.J., 1990. Co-author: Programming with Threads, 1996; author tech. papers in field. Mem. IEEE (tech. com. on oper. systems & stds. 1990-91, stds. com. on threads ext. for portable oper. systems), Assn. for Computing Machinery. Avocations: reading, windsurfing, sailing, swimming, tennis. Home: 1023 Foster City Blvd Apt B Foster City CA 94404-2335 Office: SunSoft Inc M/S MPK17-301 901 San Antonio Rd Palo Alto CA 94303-4900

SHAH, GIRISH POPATLAL, data processing services company executive; b. Junagadh, India, Apr. 11, 1942; came to U.S., 1963; s. Popatlal Gulabchand and Lalitaben Popatlas (Kamdar) S.; m. Devmani Manilal Jhaveri, June 18, 1968; children: Nivisha, Munjal, Bhavin. B in Tech., Indian Inst. Tech., Bombay, 1963; MS, U. Calif., Berkeley, 1965. Project analyst IBM Corp., Palo Alto, Calif., 1965-67; v.p. Optimun Systems, Inc., Palo Alto, 1967-72; pres. Banking Systems Internat. Corp., Jakarta, Indonesia and Campbell, Calif., 1972-76; dir. software services Tymshare Transactions Services, San Francisco, 1980-83; sr. scientist McDonnell Douglas Corp., Fremont, Calif., 1984-86; dir. corp. devel. Sysorex Internat., Inc., Cupertino, Calif., 1986-87; v.p. Sysorex Internat., Inc., Mountain View, Calif., 1987-96; sr. v.p. Sysorex Info. Systems Inc., Mountain View, 1987-91; exec. cons. IBM Corp., Mountain View, 1996—. Mem. adv. bd. Goodwill Industries, San Francisco, 1980-82; bd. dirs. Gujarate Cultural Assn., 1982; chmn. temple bd. Jain Ctr., 1990-94; co-chmn. Jaina Conv., 1991-94; city gov. Fedn. Indo-Am. Assns., Fremont, Calif., 1991—; pres.'s coun. Fedn. Jain Assoc. N.Am., 1995—; mem. Jaina charitable trust, 1995—; bd. dirs. Jain Ctr. No. Calif., 1996—. J.N. Tata Trust nat. scholar, 1963. Mem. Assn. Indians in Am. (v.p. 1980). Democrat. Home: 4048 Twyla Ln Campbell CA 95008-3721 Office: IBM Corp 1055 Joaquin Rd Mountain View CA 94043-1243

SHAHIDI, PARISIMA, school psychologist; b. Tehran, Iran, June 14, 1951; came to U.S., 1966; d. Emil and Victoria (Dadras) Shahidi; m. Abbas Behbehani, Aug. 24, 1979; 1 child, Sara. BS, Queens Coll./CUNY, 1973, MS, 1976, MFA, 1978; EdD, U. So. Calif., L.A., 1996. Cert. sch. psychologist, pupil pers. credential, resource specialist, learning handicapped credential, severely handicapped credential, art edn. credential, all Calif. Art instr. Met. Mus. Art, N.Y.C., 1976-79; spl. edn. tchr. Dorothy Brown Sch., L.A., 1980-82; resource specialist Alhambra (Calif.) Sch. Dist., 1982-84; resource specialist Long Beach (Calif.) Unified Sch. Dist., 1984-87, sch. counselor, 1987-92, sch. psychologist, 1992—. Mem. Assn. Long Beach Ednl. Mgrs., Calif. Assn. Sch. Psychologists, Long Beach Pupil Pers. Assn., Phi Delta Kappa. Avocation: hypno-therapy. Office: Long Beach Unified Sch Dist Fremont Sch 4000 E 4th St Long Beach CA 90814-2818

SHAHIN, THOMAS JOHN, dry cleaning wholesale supply company executive; b. Buffalo, July 30, 1943; s. Thomas Mark and Marie (Colletto) S.; m. Laraine Edna Clements, Feb. 25, 1967; 1 child, Lori Lynn. BSBA, Calif. State U., L.A., 1966. Asst. v.p. stock brokerage div. United Calif. Bank, L.A., 1969-76; v.p., gen. mgr., treas. Newhouse Splty. Co. Inc., Santa Ana, Calif., 1976—, also bd. dirs. Patentee belt buckle. Officer USN, 1966-69, Vietnam. Mem. Textile Care Allied Trade Assn., Laundry and Drycleaners Suppliers, Fabricare Inst., Internat. Drycleaners Congress, Calif. Fabricare Inst., Beta Gamma Sigma. Republican. Roman Catholic. Avocations: new product research, reading, travel, golf, tennis. Office: Newhouse Splty Co Inc 2619 Oak St Santa Ana CA 92707-3720

SHAKELY, JOHN BOWER (JACK SHAKELY), foundation executive; b. Hays, Kans., Jan. 9, 1940; s. John B. and Martha Jean (Gaston) S.; 1 child, Benton. BA, U. Okla., 1962. Vol. Peace Corps., Costa Rica, 1963-64; editor publs. Dept. Def., 1967-68; dir. devel. U. Okla., 1968-70, Resthaven Mental Health Ctr., L.A., 1970-74; pres. Jack Shakely Assocs., L.A., 1974-75; sr. adv. Grantsmanship Ctr., L.A., 1975-79, Coun. on Founds., Washington, 1979; pres. Calif. Community Found., L.A., 1980—; lectr. in field. Bd. dirs. Emergency Loan and Assistance Fund, 1985—, chair bd. dirs., 1988-93; mem., vice chair L.A. Am. Indian Commn.; bd. dirs. So. Calif. Assn. Philanthropy, 1980—, Comic Relief, 1987—; chmn. bd. dirs. Nonprofit Channel. Served to 1st lt. U.S. Army, 1965-68. Decorated Army Commendation medal; named Nat. Philanthropy Day Outstanding Exec., L.A. Com. Nat. Philanthropy Day, 1989.

SHAKLEE, KIMBERLY LORRAINE, sculptor; b. Denver, Nov. 6, 1956; d. Theron Morgan and Lorraine Nell (Mock) Holland; m. Elwin Eugene Shaklee, Jul. 27, 1975. Student, Colo. State Univ., 1974-75. Locksmith Accurate Lock & Key Co., Denver, 1975—; sculptor Nature in Bronze, Denver, 1991—; adv. dir. Women Artists of the West, 1994-97; adv. cons. Signature 16 Artist Soc., 1997—. Represented in permanent collection Nat. Zoo, Washington, 1999. Recipient Marine Environ. Wildlife award Mystic Maritime Mus., 1994, 95, Publs. award Coast Mag., 1997, Pub. award Art of the West Mag., 1998, Anna Hyatt Huntington Bronze medal Catharine Lorillard Wolfe Art Club Nat. Arts Club, 1994, Leila Gardin Sawyer Meml., Helen G. Oehler Meml. Awd. Amer. Artists Profl. League, 1998. Fellow Am. Artists Profl. League (Leila Gardin Sawyer Meml. award 1997, 95); mem., Am. Soc. Marine Artists, Allied Artists of Am., Pen & Brush Inc., Women Artists of the West (Gold medal 1997). Republican. Methodist. Avocations: horse activities, music, bird watching, travel, antiques. Home: 14599 Picadilly Rd Brighton CO 80601-8705 Office: Nature In Bronze 14599 Picadilly Rd Brighton CO 80601-8705

SHALLENBERGER, GARVIN F., lawyer; b. Beloit, Wis., Jan. 7, 1921; s. Garvin D. and Grace (Hubbell) S.; m. Mary L., May 5, 1945; children: Diane, Dennis Clark. BA in Pre-law, U. Mont., 1942; JD, U. Calif., Berkeley, 1949; LLD (hon.), Western State U., Fullerton, Calif., 1988. Bar: Calif. 1949, U.S. Dist. Ct. (cent. dist.) Calif. 1949, U.S. Ct. Appeals (9th cir.) 1949, U.S. Supreme Ct. 1961, U.S. Dist. Ct. (no. and so. dists.) Calif. 1963. Rutan & Tucker, Costa Mesa, Calif.; chmn. spl. adv. com. state bar legal svcs. program, 1979-89, pub. law ctr Orange County, 1979-90. Recipient distinguished svc. award Boalt Hall (U. Calif. Berkeley); Judge Learned Hand Human Rel. award Nat. Jewish Com., 1990. Fellow Am. Coll. Trial Lawyers; mem. Am. Bd. Trial Advs. (a founder and 1st sec.),Calif. Bar Assn. (bd. govs. 1975-76, pres. 1977-78; mem. com. on jud. nominees 1978-79, pres. 1980), mem. Orange County Bar Assn. (bd. dirs. 1970-71, pres. 1972, Franklin West award 1979). Democrat. Avocations: tennis, writing. Office: Rutan & Tucker PO Box 1950 Costa Mesa CA 92628-1950

SHAMBAUGH, STEPHEN WARD, lawyer; b. South Bend, Ind., Aug. 4, 1920; s. Marion Clyde and Anna Violet (Stephens) S.; m. Marilyn Louise Pyle; children: Susan Wynne Shambaugh Hinkle, Kathleen Louise Shambaugh Thompson. Student San Jose State Tchrs. Coll., 1938-40, U. Ark., 1951; LLB, U. Tulsa, 1954. Bar: Okla. 1954, Colo. 1964. Mem. staff Reading & Bates, Inc., Tulsa, 1951-54; v.p., gen. mgr., legal counsel Reading & Bates Drilling Co. Ltd., Calgary, Alta., Can., 1954-61; sr. ptnr. Bowman, Shambaugh, Geissinger & Wright, Denver, 1964-81; sole practice, Denver, 1981-97, now ret.; dir., fin. counsel various corps. Col. USAF ret. Mem. ABA, Fed. Bar Assn., Colo. Bar Assn., Okla. Bar Assn., Denver Bar Assn., P-51 Mustang Pilots Assn., Masons, Shriners, Elks, Spokane Club, Petroleum Club of Bakersfield, Phi Alpha Delta.

SHAMLIAN, BARBARA SUE, religion educator, biblical researcher; b. Wewoka, Okla., Dec. 16, 1936; d. John Timothy and Myrtle Esther (Bruce) Davisson; m. Paul Little Shamlian, Mar. 1, 1958; children: Paul Little Jr., Anthony Ray, Frank Bruce, Richard Mahabad. ThD, Cal. Bible Theology, San Jacinto, Calif., 1992. Pres. Christian Warriors Ministries and Corr. Bible Sch., Reno, 1993—. Author: Record of the Boal Family, 1987, Tithing: A Religious Fraud, 1989, New Testament [illegible], 1993, Old Testament Tabernacle, 1993. Republican. Avocations: genealogical researcher, promoting

non-contemporary Reformation information. Home: 3865 Sandpiper Dr Reno NV 89506-8841

SHANAFELT, NANCY SUE, quality consultant, career consultant; b. Northampton, Mass., Nov. 21, 1947; m. John D. Shanafelt; children: Amy, Nicholas. BS, U. Mass., 1969; MA in Human Resources/Orgnl. Devel., U. San Francisco, 1991. Tchr. Southwick (Mass.) Pub. Schs., 1969-70; acctg. asst. Maricopa County Schs., Phoenix, Ariz., 1973-74; tax auditor to br. chief IRS, San Jose, 1974-89; enrolled agt., 1984-85; OD specialist IRS, San Jose, 1991-93; creator IRS Women's Network, San Francisco, 1981—. Leader Girl Scouts U.S., Santa Clara, 1980-96, Golden Valley, 1996—, cons., 1981-82, 96—, svc. mgr., 1982-84, trainer, 1982-84; leader Boy Scouts Am., 1992-96; facilitator Unwed Parents Anonymous, 1992—; master catechist Diocese of San Jose, 1992-96. Recipient Disting. Performance award IRS, 1993, 95. Mem. AAUW, NAFE, ASTD, Calif. Assn. for Counseling and Devel., Federally Employed Women, Commonwealth Club Am., Italian Cath. Fedn. (sec. 1991—), Bay Area Orgnl. Devel. Network, Medugorje PGL. Avocations: antique cars, travel. Office: Mail Stop FR4300 821 M St Fresno CA 93721-2716

SHANAHAN, MICHAEL GEORGE, police officer; b. Seattle, Oct. 14, 1940; s. Raymond Roderick and Carletta (Anderson) S.; m. Jo-Anne Genevieve David, Sept. 16, 1961; children: Patrick, Matthew, Raymond. BA in Psychology, Stanford U., 1962. Asst. police chief U. Wash., Seattle, 1971-75, vol. police cons. and mgmt. pvt. sector issues, 1995—; mem. law enforcement task force interim mcpl. com. Wash. State Legis., 1970-71, campus law enforcement task force-higher edn. com., 1970-71; co-chmn. Wash. Law Enforcement Standards Task Force; founding chmn. Washington Law Enforcement Exec. Forum, 1981, Operation Bootstrap, 1985, others. Author: Private Enterprise and the Public Police: The Professionalizing Effects of a New Partnership, 1985; contbr. articles to profl. jours. Mem. nat. exploring com. Boy Scouts Am., 1977, exec. bd., chief Seattle council, 1984-88; mem. Blanchet High Sch. Bd., Seattle, 1978-79, Gov.'s Coun. on Criminal Justice, 1980-81, Gov.'s Coun. Food Assistance, 1983-86. Major U.S. Army, 1963-70, Vietnam. Decorated Bronze Star; recipient award for pub. svc. U.S. Dept. Transp., 1984, Humanitarian award Seattle chpt. NCCJ, 1985, Silver Beaver award Boy Scouts Am., 1986, St. Matthew award Northwest Harvest, 1987, Paul J. Breslin award Internat. Security Mgrs. Assn., 1990, Criminal Justice award of excellence Wash. State U., 1989, Service Above Self awd. Rotary Intl., 1998. Mem. FBI Nat. Acad. Assocs., Nat. Inst. Justice (peer rev. program), Internat. Assn. Chiefs of Police (life, bd. officers 1983-84, gen. chmn. divsn. state assns. 1983-84, co-chmn. pvt. sector liaison com.), Police Exec. Rsch. Forum, Wash. Assn. Sheriffs and Police Chiefs, Rotary Internat. (Svc. Above Self award 1998, pres. Univ. Rotary Club Seattle 1985-86, Svc. Above Self award 1988, founding chmn. Rotary Op. First Harvest), Univ. Dist. Club (local award). Roman Catholic. Avocations: fishing, gardening.

SHANAHAN, MIKE, professional football coach; b. Oak Park, Ill., Aug. 24, 1952; m. Peggy; children: Kyle, Krystal. BS Phys. Edn., Eastern Illinois U., Charleston, Ill., 1974; MS Phys. Edn., 1975. Student coach Eastern Illinois U.; asst. coach U. Oklahoma, 1975-76; offensive coord., No. Ariz. U., 1976-77, Ea. Ill. U., 1977-78, U. Minn., 1979-80, offensive coord., U. Fla., 1980-84, asst. head coach, 1983-84; receivers coach Denver Broncos, 1984-87; head coach Los Angeles Raiders, 1988-89; asst. coach Denver Broncos, NFL, 1989-91; offensive coordinator San Francisco 49ers, 1992-94; head coach Denver Broncos, 1995—. Golf, travel. Office: Denver Broncos 13655 Broncos Pkwy Englewood CO 80112-4150*

SHANE, WILLIAM WHITNEY, astronomer; b. Berkeley, Calif., June 3, 1928; s. Charles Donald and Mary Lea (Heger) S.; BA, U. Calif., Berkeley, 1951, postgrad., 1953-58; ScD, Leiden (The Netherlands) U., 1971; m. Clasina van der Molen, Apr. 22, 1964; children: Johan Jacob, Charles Donald. rsch. assoc. Leiden U., 1961-71, sr. scientist, 1971-79; prof. astronomy, dir. Astron. Inst., Cath. U. Nijmegen, The Netherlands, 1979-88; guest prof. astronomy Leiden U., 1988-93; C.H. Adams fellow Monterey (Calif.) Inst. Rsch. Astronomy, 1994—. With USN, 1951-53. Fellow AAAS; mem. Internat. Astron. Union (commns. 33, 34), Am. Astron. Soc., Astron. Soc. Netherlands, Astron. Soc. of the Pacific, Phi Beta Kappa. Achievements include research on structure and dynamics of galaxies, observational astronomy. Home: 9095 Coker Rd Prunedale CA 93907-1401 Office: Monterey Inst Rsch Astronomy 200 8th St Marina CA 93933-6002

SHANK, CHARLES VERNON, science administrator, educator; b. Mt. Holly, N.J., July 12, 1943; s. Augustus Jacob and Lillian (Peterson) S.; m. Brenda Buckhold, June 16, 1969. BS, U. Calif., Berkeley, 1965, MS, PhD, 1969. Mem. tech. staff AT&T Bell Labs., Holmdel, N.J., 1969-76, head quantum physics and electronics dept., 1976-83, dir. Electronics Rsch. Lab., 1983-89; dir. Lawrence Berkeley Lab., faculty mem. chemistry, physics, elec. engring. and computer scis. U. Calif., Berkeley, 1989—. Numerous patents in field. Recipient E. Longstreth medal Franklin Inst., Phila., 1982, Morris E. Leeds award IEEE, 1982, David Sarnoff award IEEE, 1989. R.W. Wood prize. Fellow AAAS, Am. Phys. Soc. (George E. Pake prize 1996, Arthur L. Schawlow prize 1997), Optical Soc. Am. (R. W. Wood prize 1981); mem. NAS, NAE, Am. Acad. Arts and Scis. Home: 9 Ajax Pl Berkeley CA 94708-2119 Office: U Calif Lawrence Berkeley Lab 50A-4119 1 Cyclotron Rd Berkeley CA 94720-0001*

SHANK, GREGORY LLOYD, journal editor; b. Vallejo, Calif., Dec. 5, 1948; s. Clifford Lewis Shank and Barbara Lee (Metzger) Finstrom; m. Jennifer Suzanne Dod, Oct. 28, 1977 (div. 1987); 1 child, Renee Andrea. BA in Sociology, U. Calif., Berkeley, 1974, BA in Criminology, 1974, MA in Sociology and Edn., 1977. Mng. editor Crime and Social Justice, Berkeley, 1974-85, Social Justice, San Francisco, 1986—; dir. rsch. Ctr. for Study of Crime and Social Justice, San Francisco, 1984-88; CEO, pres., bd. dirs. Global Options, San Francisco, 1987—. Mem. editl. adv. bd.: Law in Context, Victoria, Australia, 1986—; editor: Power, Politics and Order in the 1990s, 1992, South Africa in Transition, 1991, Japan Enters the 21st Century, 1994; contbr. articles to profl. jours. Participant Friends of Urban Forest project, San Francisco, 1992. Mem. ACLU, Criminal Justice Editors Rsch. Group, East-West Project, World Affairs Coun., Phi Beta Kappa. Avocations: microcomputers, guitar, travel, sports. Home: 2766 23rd St San Francisco CA 94110-3442 Office: Social Justice PO Box 40601 San Francisco CA 94140-0601

SHANK, THOM LEWIS, real estate executive, entertainment consultant, author; b. Butler, Pa., Apr. 23, 1953; s. Berdyne Delmont and Florence Elizabeth (Glasser) S. BA in Sociology, U. Pa., 1974; MBA, Pepperdine U., 1981. Negotiator Worldmark Travel, N.Y.C. and Phila., 1971-76; retail ops. mgr. Just Plants, Inc., Roxborough, Pa., 1973-79; founder, mgr. The Best-direct mail sales, Edgemoor, Del., 1974-79; property mgr. Moss and Co., Westwood, Calif., 1977-82; talent mgr. Thom Shank Assocs., Brentwood, Calif., 1979-84; pres., founder The Great Am. Amusement Co., Palm Desert, Calif., 1979-84; sales exec. Fred Sands Realtors, Brentwood, 1981-85; sales and mktg. dir. Coldwell Banker, Newport Beach, Calif., 1985-86, Great Western Ranches, Burbank, Calif., 1988-95; dist. and regional mgr. E.R.A. Real Estate, Pasadena, Calif., 1986; owner Century 21 Realtors, Tarzana, Calif., 1987-89; resorts dir. Prudential Jon Douglas Co., Beverly Hills, Calif., 1996—. Lutheran. Avocations: tennis, flying, reading, film, photography. Office: 301 N Canon Dr Beverly Hills CA 90210-4722

SHANKLAND, KENNETH CARL, engineer; b. Topeka, Kans., Dec. 13, 1972; s. KEvin Steves and Brooke Eileen (Teasley) S. AA, Univ. Phoenix, 1997; grad., Naval Nuclear Power Sch., 1994, Naval Nuclear Prototype, 1995. Transition clerk U.S. Postal Svc., Topeka, 1992-93; nuclear mech., engr. tech. U.S. Navy, Orlando, Idaho Falls,, 1993—; crew mem. U.S. Hawkbill, Honolulu, 1995-99. Recipient Kansas State scholar Kans. Bd. of Regents, 1991, 92. Mem. Nat. Assn. of Corrosion Engrs. Avocations: reading. Home: PO Box 2791 Aiea HI 96701-8279 Office: 14552 N Cedar Rd Valley Falls KS 66088-5138

SHANNON, CYNTHIA JEAN, biology educator; b. Phila., Feb. 19, 1961; d. Foster Lloyd and Nancy Ellen (Chapman) S.; m. Gerald Thomas Braden, Dec. 21, 1997. AA, Fullerton (Calif.) Coll., 1981; BA in Psychology, Calif. State U., Fullerton, 1986; BS in Zoology, Calif. Poly. State U., 1985, MS in Biology, 1991. Biology instr. Calif. State Poly. U., Pomona, Calif., 1986-91, Mt. San Antonio Coll., Walnut, Calif., 1986—; chair biology dept. Mt. San Antonio Coll., Walnut, 1996-97. Mem. AAAS, Ornithological Soc. N.Am., So. Assn. Naturalists, Golden Key, Phi Kappa Phi. Democrat. Avocations: bird watching, hiking, dogs, food and wine, reading. Office: Mt San Antonio Coll 1100 N Grand Ave Walnut CA 91789-1341

SHANNON, MICHAEL THOMAS, priest; b. Ireland, 1911. Pastor Cath. chs. Home: 1107 N Astor St Spokane WA 99202-1724

SHANNON, RICHARD STOLL, III, financial executive; b. N.Y.C., Mar. 22, 1943; s. Richard Stoll Jr. and Margaret (Cather) S.; m. Ann Wright Schmidt, June 14, 1965; children: Clea Cather, Kathryne Baltzelle, Arianna Wright. BA, Stanford U., 1966, MA, 1969; PhD, Harvard U., 1973. Asst. prof. U. Mich., Ann Arbor, 1973-78; mgr., trustee, gen. ptnr. various family trusts, partnerships and corps. Englewood, Colo., 1978-84; pres. Shannon Mgmt. Corp., Englewood, 1985—. Author: The Arms of Achilles, 1975; editor (with others) Oral Literature and The Formula, 1976. Bd. dirs. Cherryvale Sanitation Dist., Englewood, 1984—, pres., 1986-93; regional chmn. Stanford Ann. Fund/Keystone Project, 1985—; mem. Rackham Advancement Coun., U. Mich., 1992-97. Teaching fellow Harvard U., 1970-73. Mem. Am. Philol. Assn., Denver C. of C., Cherry Creek Commerce Assn., Cherry Hills Country Club, Denver Petroleum Club, Phi Beta Kappa. Avocations: golf, fishing, reading, research. Office: Shannon Mgmt Corp 3098 S Pennsylvania St Englewood CO 80110-1649

SHANNON, ROBERT RENNIE, optical sciences center administrator, educator; b. Mt. Vernon, N.Y., Oct. 3, 1932; s. Howard A. and Harriebell S.; m. Helen Lang, Feb. 13, 1954; children: Elizabeth, Barbara, Jennifer, Amy, John, Robert. B.S., U. Rochester, 1954, M.A., 1957. Dir. Optics Lab., ITEK Corp., Lexington, Mass., 1959-69; prof. Optical Scis. Ctr., U. Ariz., 1969—, dir., 1983-92, prof. emeritus, 1992—; cons. Lawrence Livermore Lab., 1980-90; trustee Aerospace Corp., 1985-94, 96—; mem. Air Force Sci. Adv. Bd., 1986-90; mem. NRC Commn. on Next Generation Currency, 1992-94, NRC Commn. on Optical Sci. and Engring., 1996-97; mem. com. on def. space tech. Air Force Studies Bd., 1989-93, com. on optical sci. and engring, 1996-97, Hubble Telescope recovery panel, 1990; bd. dirs. Precision Optics Corp. Editor: Applied Optics and Optical Engineering, Vol. 7, 1980, Vol. 8, 1981, Vol. 9, 1983, Vol. 10, 1987, Vol. 11, 1992, Art and Science of Optical Design, 1997; editor Engring. and Lab. Notes, 1995-98. Fellow Optical Soc. Am. (pres. 1985, mem. engring. coun. 1989-91), Soc. Photo-Optical Instrumentation Engrs. (pres. 1979-80, mem. SPIE/OSA joint task force 1998, recipient Goddard award 1982, Gold medal, 1996); mem. NAE, Tucson Soaring Club (past pres.), Sigma Xi. Home: 7040 E Taos Pl Tucson AZ 85715-3344 Office: U Ariz Optical Scis Ctr Tucson AZ 85721

SHANNON, THOMAS FREDERIC, German language educator; b. Cambridge, Mass., Mar. 16, 1948; m. Christine D. Höner. BA in German summa cum laude, Boston Coll., 1969; MA in German Lit., SUNY, Albany, 1973; MA in Theoretical Linguistics, Ind. U., 1975, PhD in Germanic Linguistics, 1982. Instr. in German Boston Coll., 1969-70; teaching fellow in German SUNY, Albany, 1971-73; univ. fellow Ind. U., Bloomington, 1973-74, assoc. instr., 1974-76, 79-80; acting asst. prof. in Germanic linguistics U. Calif., Berkeley, 1980-82, asst. prof., 1982-87, assoc. prof., 1987-94, prof., 1994—, dir. lang. lab., 1989-92, assoc. dir. Berkeley Lang. Ctr., 1994-95; co-organizer Berkeley Confs. on Dutch Lang. and Lit., 1987, 89, 91, 93, 95, 97; econs. presenter and spkr. in field. Contbr. articles to profl. jours. With USAR, 1970-76. Grantee Fulbright Found., 1976-78, U. Calif. Berkeley, 1983-84, 94-95, ACLS, 1987, Internat. Assn. Netherlandic Studies, 1988, 91, 94, 97, German Acad. Exch. Svc., summer 1996; NDEA fellow, 1969; Fulbright rsch./lectr. grantee Rijksuniversiteit Groningen, Netherlands, 1992-93; Inst. fuer deutsche Sprache summer rsch. grantee, Mannheim, Germany, 1997. Mem. MLA (exec. com. discussion group in Germanic philology 1989-94, discussion group for Netherlandic Studies 1995-99, divsn. on lang. change 1995-99), Am. Assn. Netherlandic Studies (exec. com. 1988—, editor newsletter 1989-95, series editor publs. 1994—), Am. Assn. Tchrs. German, Internat. Assn. Netherlandic Studies, Internat. Assn. Germanstik, Internat. Soc. Hist. Lingusitics, Linguistic Soc. Am., Netherlands Am. U. League, Pacific Ancient & Modern Lang. Assn., European Linguistic Soc., Soc. Germanic Philology (v.p. 1991-92, 95—), Interna. Cognitive Linguistics Soc., Alpha Sigma Nu. Home: 770 Rose Dr Benicia CA 94510-3709 Office: U Calif Dept German 5319 Dwinelle Hall Berkeley CA 94720-3244

SHANSTROM, JACK D., federal judge; b. Hewitt, Minn., Nov. 30, 1932; s. Harold A. and Willian (Wendorf) S.; m. June 22, 1957; children: Scott S., Susan K. BA in Law, U. Mont., 1956, BS in Bus., 1957, LLB, 1957. Atty. Park County, Livingston, Mont., 1960-65; judge 6th Jud. Dist. Livingston, 1965-82; U.S. magistrate Billings, Mont., 1983-90, U.S. Dist. judge, 1990-96; chief judge U.S. Dist. Ct., Mont., 1996—. Capt. USAF, 1957-60. Office: US Dist Ct Fed Bldg PO Box 985 316 N 26th St Ste 5405 Billings MT 59103*

SHAPERO, HARRIS JOEL, pediatrician; b. Winona, Minn., Nov. 22, 1930; s. Charles and Minnie Sara (Ehrlichman) S.; m. Byong Soon Yu, Nov. 6, 1983; children by previous marriage: Laura, Bradley, James, Charles. AA, UCLA, 1953; BS, Northwestern U., 1954, MD, 1957. Diplomate and cert. specialist occupational medicine Am. Bd. Preventive Medicine; qualified med. evaluator, Indsl. Med. Coun.; ind. med. examiner, Calif.; cert. aviation medicine FAA. Intern, L.A. County Harbor Gen. Hosp., 1957-58, resident in pediatrics, 1958-60, staff physician, 1960-64; attending physician Perceptually Handicapped Children's Clinic, 1960-63; disease control officer for tuberculosis, L.A. County Health Dept., 1962-64; pvt. practice medicine specializing in pediatrics and occupational medicine, Cypress, Calif., 1965-85; pediatric cons. L.A. Health Dept., 1983-85, disease control officer sexually transmitted diseases, 1968-78; emergency room dir. AMI, Anaheim, Calif., 1968-85; mem. med. staff Anaheim Gen. Hosp., Beach Cmty. Hosp., Norwalk Cmty. Hosp.; courtesy staff Palm Harbor Gen. Hosp., Bellflower City Hosp.; pediatric staff Hosp. de General, Ensenada, Mex., 1978—; primary care clinician Sacramento County Health, 1987-88; pvt. practice medico-legal evaluation, 1986-92; founder Calif. Legal Evaluation Med. Group; apptd. med. examiner in preventive and occupational medicine State of Calif. Dept. of Indsl. Rels., 1989; health care provider, advisor City of Anaheim, City of Buena Park, City of Cypress, City of Garden Grove, Cypress Sch. Dist., Magnolia Sch. Dist., Savanna Sch. Dist., Anaheim Unified Sch. Dist., Orange County Dept. Edn.; pediatric and tuberculosis cons. numerous other orgns.; FAA med. examiner, founder Pan Am. Childrens Mission. Author: The Silent Epidemic, 1979. Named Headliner in Medicine Orange County Press Club, 1978. Fellow Am. Coll. Preventive Medicine; mem. L.A. County Med. Assn., L.A. County Indsl. Med. Assn., Am. Pub. Health Assn., Mex.-Am. Border Health Assn. Republican. Jewish. Avocations: antique books and manuscripts, photography, graphics, beekeeper. E-mail: hjswilton@aol.com. Home: PO Box 228 Wilton CA 95693-0228 Office: 5411 Madison Ave Ste 1 Sacramento CA 95841-3151

SHAPIRO, DAVID, newspaper editor; b. Culver City, Calif., Sept. 1, 1948; m. Maggie Shapiro; children: Treena, Jared. BA in Am. History, U. Hawaii. Editorial asst. Star-Bulletin, Hilo, Hawaii, 1968-87; mng. editor Star-Bulletin, Honolulu, 1987—. Office: Star Bulletin 605 Kapiolani Blvd Honolulu HI 96813*

SHAPIRO, ISADORE, materials scientist, consultant; b. Mpls., Apr. 25, 1916; s. Jacob and Bessie (Goldman) S.; m. Mae Hirsch, Sept. 4, 1938; children: Stanley Harris, Jerald Steven. BChemE. summa cum laude, U. Minn., 1938, PhD, 1944. Asst. instr. chemistry U. Minn., 1938-41, rsch. fellow, 1944-45; rsch. chemist E. I. duPont de Nemours and Co., Phila., 1946; head chem. lab. U.S. Naval Ordnance Test Sta., Pasadena, Calif., 1947-52; dir. rsch. lab. Olin-Mathieson Chem. Corp., 1952-59; head chemistry Hughes Tool Co., Aircraft div., Culver City, Calif., 1959-62; pres. Universal Chem. Systems Inc. 1962—, Aerospace Chem. Systems, Inc., 1964-66; dir. contract rsch. HITCO, Gardena, Calif., 1966-67; prin. scientist Douglas Aircraft Co. of McDonnell Douglas Corp., Santa Monica, Calif., 1967; prin. scientist McDonnell Douglas Astronautics Co., 1967-70; head materials and processes AiResearch Mfg. Co., Torrance, Calif., 1971-82, cons., 1982—; inaugurated dep. gov. Am. Biog. Inst. Rsch. Assn., 1988; dep. dir. gen. Internat. Biog. Ctr., 1989, Eng. Rater U.S. Civil Svc. Bd. Exam., 1948-52. Served 1st lt. AUS, 1941-44. Registered profl. engr., Calif. Fellow Am. Inst. Chemists, Am. Inst. Aeros and Astronautics (assoc.); mem. AAAS, Am. Ordnance Assn., Am. Chem. Soc., Soc. Rheology, Soc. Advancement Materials and Process Engring., Am. Inst. Physics, AIM, Am. Phys. Soc., N.Y. Acad. Sci., Am. Assn. Contamination Control, Am. Ceramic Soc., Nat. Inst. Ceramic Engrs., Am. Powder Metallurgy Inst., Internat. Plansee Soc. for Powder Metallurgy, Sigma Xi, Tau Beta Pi, Phi Lambda Upsilon. Author articles in tech. publs. Patentee, discoverer series of carborane compounds; created term carborane; formulator of universal compaction equation for powders (metals, ceramics, polymers, chemicals). Home: 5624 W 62nd St Los Angeles CA 90056-2009

SHAPIRO, LARRY JAY, pediatrician, scientist, educator; b. Chgo., July 6, 1946; s. Philip and Phyllis (Krause) S.; m. Carol-Ann Uetake; children: Jennifer, Jessica, Brian. A.B., Washington U., St. Louis, 1968, M.D., 1971. Diplomate Am. Bd. Pediatrics, Am. Bd. Med. Examiners, Am. Bd. Med. Genetics. Intern St. Louis Children's Hosp., 1971-72, resident, 1971-73; research assoc. NIH, Bethesda, Md., 1973-75; asst. prof. Sch. Medicine, UCLA, 1975-79, assoc. prof., 1979-83, prof. pediatrics and biol. chemistry, 1983-91; investigator Howard Hughes Med. Inst., 1987-91, W.H. and marie Wattis Disting. Prof.; prof., chmn. dept. pediat. U. Calif.-San Francisco Sch. Medicine, 1991—, chief pediat. svcs. U. Calif. San Francisco Med. Ctr., 1991—. Contbr. numerous articles to profl. publs. Served to lt. comdr. USPHS, 1973-75. Fellow AAAS, Am. Acad. Pediatrics (E. Mead Johnson award in rsch. 1982); mem. Inst. Medicine-NAS, Soc. Pediatric Rsch. (coun. 1984-87, pres. 1991-92), Western Soc. for Pediatric Rsch. (coun. 1983-87, Ross award in rsch. 1981, pres. 1989-90), Soc. for Inherited Metabolic Disease (coun. 1983-88, pres. 1986-87), Assn. Am. Physicians, Am. Soc. Human Genetics (council 1985-88, pres. elect 1995, pres. 1997), Am. Soc. Clin. Investigation, Am. Pediatric Soc., Am. Acad. Arts & Scis. Office: U Calif Third Ave & Parnassus San Francisco CA 94143

SHAPIRO, MARGARET GOODWIN, astronomy educator; b. Maxton, N.C., Sept. 3, 1944; d. Harold and Marion Edna (Goodwin) S. BA, San Francisco State U., 1967, MA, 1971; Cert. Achievement, Simpson Coll., Modesto, Calif., 1976. C.C. lifetime credential, Calif. Instr. astronomy, phys. sci. San Francisco State U., 1968-71, 84; instr. astronomy, phy. sci. Modesto Jr. Coll., 1971-73; instr. geology Merritt Coll., Oakland, Calif., 1977; instr. astronomy Chabot Coll., Hayward, Calif., 1981-83, Los Medanos Coll., Pittsburg, Calif., 1982-84; instr. astronomy, phys. sci., physics Ohlone Coll., Fremont, Calif., 1982-91; instr. physics Calif. State U., Hayward, 1986; instr. astronomy, phys. sci. West Valley Coll., Saratoga, Calif., 1989-90; instr. astronomy City Coll. San Francisco, 1991—; advisor to astronomy club S.T.A.R.S., City Coll. San Francisco, 1994, advisor to bible study, 1995; paraprofl. San Francisco City Schs., 1970-71; instr. Coll. for Kids, Ohlone, Chabot colls., Fremont and Hayward, 1982-83, 85. Author 14 planetarium shows, 1982-86. Adv. Campus Girl Scouts, 1997. Mem. Astron. Soc. Pacific, San Francisco Amateur Astronomers (sec. 1960, editor monthly bull. 1962), Pacific Planetarium Assn., 1981-85. Democrat. Jewish. Avocations: books, ceramics, weaving, interior decorating, gardening. Office: City Coll San Francisco 50 Phelan Ave San Francisco CA 94112-1821

SHAPIRO, PHILIP ALAN, lawyer; b. Chgo., May 14, 1940; s. Joe and Nettie (Costin) S.; A.A., Wilson Coll., 1960; BS in Fin., So. Ill. U., 1965; MBA with distinction in Mktg., Nat. U., San Diego, Calif., 1976; MBA with distinction, San Diego State U., 1977; JD Western State U. Coll. Law, 1985; Bar: Calif. 1988; m. Joyce Barbara Chapnick, May 29, 1966; children: David Ian, Russell Scott, Mindi Jennifer. Bar: Calif. Spl. Agt. U.S. Secret Svc., Washington, 1965-67, Chgo., 1967-77; mgr. div. sales Roche Labs. div. Hoffmann-La Roche, Inc., Chgo.; with Complete Communications, San Diego, 1983—; account exec. Cellular Communications, Inc., San Diego, 1985; assoc. Law Office Jeffrey S. Schwartz, 1988-91; pvt. practice, 1991—; chair gen. and solo practice section State Bar of Calif.; editor law rev. Western State U. Coll. Law. Mem. Spreckes Elem. Sch. Advisory Bd., San Diego, 1976-77; mem. University City Town Council, San Diego, 1977; pres. Congregation Beth El, La Jolla, Calif., 1976-79. Served with USMC, 1958-60. Recipient Award of Merit, U.S. Treasury Dept., 1965, Israel Solidarity award, 1977, U. of Judiasm award, 1978, Wiley W. Manuel award State Bar Calif., 1990, 91. Mem. ABA (vice chmn. gen. practice sect.), Calif. Trial Lawyers Assn., San Diego County Bar Assn., San Diego Trial Lawyers Assn., State Bar Calif. (exec. com. gen. practice sect.), San Diego Bus. Referrals (pres. 1998-99). Fax: 619-239-1533. E-mail: Pshaplaw@aol.com. Office: 225 Broadway Ste 1210 San Diego CA 92101-5028

SHAPIRO, RICHARD STANLEY, physician; b. Moline, Ill., June 11, 1925; s. Herbert and Esther Dian (Grant) S.; BS, St. Ambrose Coll., 1947; BS in Pharmacy, U. Iowa, 1951, MS in Preventive Medicine and Environ. Health, 1951, M.D., 1957; m. Arlene Blum, June 12, 1949; children: Michele Pamela, Bruce Grant, Gary Lawrence; m. Merry Lou Cook, Oct. 11, 1971. Pharmacist, Rock Island, Ill., 1951-53; research asst. U. Iowa Coll. Medicine, Iowa City, 1950-51, 53-57; practice medicine specializing in allergy, Beverly Hills, Calif., 1958-62, Lynwood, Calif., 1962—; attending physician Good Hope Found. Allergy Clinic, Los Angeles, 1958-62, Cedars of Lebanon Hosp., Hollywood, Calif., 1959-68, U. So. Calif.-Los Angeles County Med. Center, 1962—; physician St. Francis Hosp., Lynwood, 1962—; assoc. clin. prof. medicine U. So. Calif., 1978-84, emeritus, 1984—. Bd. dirs. Westside Jewish Community Center, 1961-65, Camp JCA, 1964-65. Served with USNR, 1943-45; PTO. Diplomate Am. Bd. Allergy and Immunology. Fellow Am. Geriatric Soc., Am. Coll. Allergy, Am. Assn. Clin. Immunology and Allergy; mem. Am. Soc. Tropical Medicine and Hygiene, Am. Acad. Allergy, Los Angeles Allergy Soc., AMA, Calif., Los Angeles County med. assns., West Coast Allergy Soc., AAAS, Am., Calif. socs. internal medicine, Calif. Soc. Allergy, Am. Heart Assn., Sierra Club, Sigma Xi. Jewish. Mason; mem. B'nai B'rith. Contbr. articles to profl. jours. Office: 8301 Florence Ave Ste 104 Downey CA 90240-3946

SHAPIRO, ROBERT JOSEPH, trance channel, writer; b. St. Paul, Minn., Dec. 12, 1943; s. Robert Joseph and Lorraine (Shalett) S. Pvt. practice Sedona, Ariz., 1979—, Honolulu, Hi., 1998—. Author: The Explorer Race Series Books 1-6, 1996-98, Shining the Light Series Books I-V, 1994-98; author: (with others), Sedona Vortex Guidebook, Sedona Jour. of Emergence, 1990—. Avocations: reading, good restaurants. Office: Sedona Jour of Emergence 2020 Contractors Rd 4 Sedona AZ 86336

SHARAN, FARIDA JEANNINE, writer, natural medicine professional; b. Vancouver, B.C., May 28, 1942; came to U.S., 1963; d. Albert William and Doris Marguerite (Wilson) Sewell; m. Tony Melendy, Feb. 12, 1963 (div.); children: Galon, Casel Lowe, Chalice Collier; m. John Davidson, Feb. 12, 1977 (div. Feb. 1987). Registered naturopath, British Nat. Coun., London, 1978; cert. master herbalist, Sch. of Natural Healing, Orem, Utah, 1981; hon. doctorate, Medicine Alternativa, Amsterdam, 1986. Founder, dir. British Sch. of Iridology, Cambridge, Eng., 1977-88; founder, dir. Sch. Natural Medicine, Cambridge, 1977—, Boulder, Colo., 1988—; internat. lectr. in field; naturopath cons.; bd. dirs. Wisdome Press. Author: (textbook) Iridology-A Complete Guide, 1988, Herbs of Grace, 1994, Creative Menopause, 1994. Bd. dirs. Pure Health Found. Scholar Santa Monica (Calif.) Coll., 1971. Fellow British Register of Iridologists (founder), Internat. Guild of Naturopathic Iridologists; mem. Am. Herbalists Guild (profl.), Col. Soc. Holistic and Naturopathic Physicians. Mem. Radha Soami Ch. Avocations: dance, snorkling, travel. Office: Sch of Natural Medicine 2888 Bluff St Ste 403 Boulder CO 80301

SHARE, MARK LOWELL, lawyer; b. L.A., Apr. 4, 1964; s. Richard Hudson Share and Adrienne (Perlin) Marchang; m. Susan Beth Poltun, June 28, 1987; 1 child, Matthew David. BA, Reed Coll., 1986; JD, Northwestern Sch. Law, Portland, Oreg., 1990. Jud. extern 9th Cir. Ct. Appeals, Portland, 1989; atty. Brown, Winfield & Canzonie, L.A., 1990-94, Lipofsky & Ruben, Beverly Hills, Calif., 1994—; spkr. Beverly Hills Bar, 1997; judge pro tem L.A. Mcpl. County, 1997. Office: Lipofsky and Ruben 8383 Wilshire Blvd Ste 708 Beverly Hills CA 90211-2406

SHARE, RICHARD HUDSON, lawyer; b. Mpls., Sept. 6, 1938; s. Jerome and Millicent S.; m. Carolee Martin, 1970; children: Mark Lowell, Gregory Martin, Jennifer Hillary, Ashley. BS, UCLA, 1960; JD, U. So. Calif., 1963. Bar: Calif. Sup. Ct. 1964, U.S. Dist. Ct. (cen. and so. dists.) Calif., U.S. Supreme Ct. 1974. Field agt. IRS, 1960-63; mem. law divsn., asst. sec. Avco Fin. Svcs., 1963-72; founder Frandzel and Share, L.A., 1972—; lectr. Nat. Bus. Inst. Mem. Calif. Bankers Assn., Cmty. Bankers of So. Calif., Rivera Tennis Club, Pacific Palisades. Office: 17th Fl 6500 Wilshire Blvd Fl 17 Los

Angeles CA 90048-4920 also: 26th Fl 100 Pine St Fl 26 San Francisco CA 94111-5102

SHARIFF, ASGHAR J., geologist; b. Haft Kel, Iran, July 28, 1941; came to U.S., 1964, naturalized, 1978; s. Abdulwahab and Sakineh (Kamiab) S.; m. Kay L. Schoenwald, Aug. 9, 1969; 1 child, Shaun. B.Sc., Calif. State U., Northridge, 1971, M.Sc., 1983. Cert. profl. geologist, Wyo. Petroleum geologist Iranian Oil Exploration and Producing Co., Ahwaz, 1971-74; geol. cons. D.R.L., Inc., Bakersfield, Calif., 1974-76, Strata-log, Inc., 1976-79, Energy Log, Inc., Sacramento, 1979-80; geologist U.S. Dept. Energy, Washington, 1980-81, Bur. Land Mgmt. Dept. Interior, Washington, 1981-89, asst. dist. mgr., Rawlins, Wyo., 1989-93, chief reservoir mgmt. group, Casper, Wyo., 1993—. Contbr. articles to profl. jours. Mem. Am. Assn. Petroleum Geologists, Soc. Petroleum Engrs.

SHARKEY, RICHARD DAVID, architectural artisan, inventor, musician; b. Columbus, Ohio, May 8, 1957; s. John David and Beatrice Diane (Ziesler) S.; m. Melissa Duke Smith, Dec. 21, 1980 (div. 1995); children: Flax Allistair Linden, Ambrosia Rose Ashley. Student, U. No. Colo., 1975-77, Emporia State U., 1977-78, U. Denver, 1978-81. Music tchr., pvt. studio, piano, cello, composition theory Evergreen, Colo., 1978-82; pvt. bus., period residential restoration Sharkey and Assocs., Evergreen and Denver, 1978-86; stair apprentice Denver Stair Co., 1985-86; stair master Heidelberg Stair Co., Evergreen, 1986; pvt. bus., designer period staircases, millwork O'Searcaigh, Ltd., Evergreen and Denver, 1986-90; with Archtl. Artworks, Englewood, Colo., 1993-95, Form & Structure Ltd., Denver, 1995-96; prin. Adobe Homes, Denver, 1996—, Archtl. Artisans, Questa, N.Mex., 1997—; cons. archtl. product design and devel. Heidelberg Stair, Evergreen, Frank's Woodworking, Lyons, Colo., Pierce Segerberg & Spaeh Architects, Vail, Colo., Charles Cunnifree & Assoc., Apsen, Colo., numerous manufacturers, contractor, architecture, design firms, 1987—; cons. archtl. design period features. Composer numerous piano compositions, 1972—; designer, inventor numerous archtl. products, machines, tools and accessories. Recipient scholarship Outward Bound Colo., Optimist Club of Evergreen, 1973, music grant, U. No. Colo., Greeley, 1975-76, Emporia (Kans.) U., 1977; scholar U. No. Colo., 1976. Mem. Internat. Soc. Archtl. Artisans (pres., founder 1988—), Denver Cherry Creek Club (charter mem.), Rotary. Mem. Christian Science Ch. Avocations: art history, architecture history, collecting and designing of architectural products, musician, ballroom dancing. Home and Office: PO Box 980 Questa NM 87556-0980

SHARMA, ARJUN DUTTA, cardiologist; b. Bombay, June 2, 1953; came to U.S., 1981; s. Hari D. and Gudrun (Axelsson) S.; m. Carolyn D. Burleigh, May 9, 1981; children: Allira, Eric, Harisson. BSc, U. Waterloo, Ont., Can., 1972; MD, U. Toronto, Ont., 1976. Intern Toronto Gen. Hosp., 1976-77, resident in medicine, 1978-80; resident in medicine St. Michael's Hosp., Toronto, 1980-81; residency medicine Toronto Gen. Hosp., 1977-78; Rsch. assoc. Washington U., St. Louis, 1981-83; asst. prof. pharmacy and toxicology U. Western Ont., London, 1985-89, asst. prof. medicine, 1983-89, assoc. prof. medicine, 1989-90; dir. interventional electrophysiology Sutter Meml. Hosp., Sacramento, 1990-95; abstract reviewer, faculty of ann. sci. sessions N.Am. Soc. for Pacing and Electrophysiology, 1993-97; assoc. clin. prof. U. Calif., Davis, 1990-96, clin. prof. medicine, 1997—; cons. Medtronic Inc., Mpls., 1985—, Telectronics Pacing Sys., Inc., 1990-94; mem. rsch. com. Sutter Inst. Med. Rsch., 1991—; mem. exec. com. Sutter Heart Inst., 1992; program dir. Update in Tachyarhythmia Mgmt., Palm Springs, 1996, Pacing Defibrillation and Electrophysiology, Squaw Valley, 1997. Reviewer profl. jours., including Circulation, Am. Jour. Cardiology; contbr. articles to profl. publs. Mem. coun. for basic sci. Am. Heart Assn., chmn. ann. sci. session, 1989. Recipient John Melady award, 1972, Dr. C.S. Wainwright award, 1973-75, Rsch. prize Toronto Gen. Hosp., 1979, 80, Ont. Career Scientist award Ont. Ministry of Health, 1983-89; Med. Rsch. Coun. Can. fellow, 1981-83. Fellow ACP, Am. Coll. Cardiology; mem. Am. Fedn. Clin. Rsch., Canadian Cardiovasc. Soc., N.Y. Acad. Scis., Sacramento Eldorado Med. Soc. Avocations: skiing, tennis, philately. Office: 3941 J St Ste 260 Sacramento CA 95819-3633

SHARMA, PETER, III, actor, clergyman; b. L.A., June 11, 1959. BFA, U. Colo., 1981; PhD, Universal Life Ch., Modesto, Calif., 1991. Pres. Sirius, Inc., L.A., 1991—; founder Sirius Encounters Couples Therapy, 1995. Actor: Danger Bay (CTV network). Office: Sirius Inc 10416 Irene St Apt 15 Los Angeles CA 90034-3681

SHARMA, RENU, educator, researcher; b. Rohtak, India, July 15, 1952; came to U.S., 1985; s. Banwarilal and Sharwan (Devi) S.; m. Shri Niwas Bhardwaj; children: Manu, Mona. BSc, Panjab U., Chandigarh, India, 1970, BEd, 1971; PhD, Stockholm U., 1985. Tchr. Govt. Girls Higher Secondary Sch., Delhi, India, 1972-78; rsch. asst. Stockholm U., 1978-85; postdoctoral fellow Ariz. State U., Tempe, 1985-89, rsch. scientist, 1989—; rsch. asst. Swedish Inst. Stockholm U., 1980. Editor: In Situ Electron and Tunnelling Microscopy of Dynamic Process,1995; contbr. more than 60 articles to profl. jours.; spkr. in field. Mem. Microscopy Soc. Am., Materials Rsch. Soc. Avocations: reading, travel. Office: Ariz State U Ctr for Solid State Sci Tempe AZ 85287-1704

SHARMAN, WILLIAM, professional basketball team executive; b. Abilene, Tex., May 25, 1926; m. Joyce Sharman; children from previous marriage: Jerry, Nancy, Janice, Tom. Student, U. So. Calif. Basketball player Washington Capitols, 1950-51, Boston Celtics, 1951-61; coach L.A./Utah Stars, 1968-71; coach L.A. Lakers, 1971-76, gen. mgr., 1976-82, pres., 1982-88, spl. cons., 1991—. Author: Sharman on Basketball Shooting, 1965. Named to All Star 1st Team, NBA, 1956-59, 2d Team, 1953, 55 (game MVP), 60, All League Team, 7 times, named Coach of Yr., 1972, One of Top Players in NBA History, league 50th anniversary, 1997, league leader free-throw percentage, 7 times; named to Basketball Hall of Fame, 1975, Naismith Basketball Hall of Fame, 1976; named All-Am., twice; inductee U. So. Calif. Hall of Fame, 1994; Porterville H.S. gymnasium renamed in his honor, 1997. Home: 27996 Palos Verdes Dr E Rancho Palos Verdes CA 90275 Office: LA Lakers PO Box 10 3900 W Manchester Blvd Inglewood CA 90305-2200

SHARON, TIMOTHY MICHAEL, physicist; b. Portsmouth, Va., Aug. 21, 1948; s. Lester Clark and Ruth May (Banister) S.; student Santa Ana Coll., 1966-68; B.A., U. Calif.-Irvine 1970, M.A., 1972, Ph.D., 1976; m. Carla Deon Colley, Dec. 17, 1977. Jr. specialist solid state theory U. Calif.-Irvine, 1976, research asst. radiation physics Med. Center and Sch. Medicine, 1976-77, cons. to attending staff Research and Edn. Found., 1976-77; mktg. physicist Varian Assos., Irvine, 1977-78; prin. engr., program mgr. Spectra Research Systems, Newport Beach, Calif., 1977-82; v.p. Brewer-Sharon Corp., Newport Beach, 1981-86, Micor Instruments, Inc., Irvine, Calif., 1983-86; pres., chief exec. officer Medelec Instruments Co., Inc., Newport Beach, 1986-88; pres. Pacific Crest Enterprises, El Toro, Calif., 1988-91; pres., chief exec. officer Novus Group NA, El Toro, Calif., 1991-96; pres. Instafil, Irvine, 1995—; adj. faculty physics and engring. Columbia Pacific U., San Rafael, Calif., 1981-87; dean Sch. Engring., Newport U., Newport Beach, Calif., 1983-87; mem. adv. panel on pub. Am. Inst. Physics, 1974-75. Brython P. Davis univ. fellow, 1973-74. Mem. AAAS, Am. Phys. Soc., Brit. Interplanetary Soc. (asso. fellow), Am. Assn. Physicists in Medicine, IEEE, Assn. Advancement Med. Instrumentation, Smithsonian Instn., Am. Film Inst., Nat. Hist. Soc., Nat. Geog. Soc., Festival of Arts Laguna Beach, Mensa, Intertel, Sigma Pi Sigma, Phi Theta Kappa, Alpha Gamma Sigma. Clubs: Acad. Magical Arts, Club 33. Contbr. articles to profl. jours.

SHARP, LEWIS I., museum director. Dir. Denver Art Mus. Office: Denver Art Mus 100 W 14th Ave Pkwy Denver CO 80204-2749*

SHARP, PAMELA ANN, quality assurance engineer; b. Pullman, Wash., Dec. 20, 1950; d. Robert Melvin and Vivian Lois (Steele) Olson; m. David William Sharp, June 16, 1973; children: Jaime David, Erik Scott. Student, Big Bend C.C., Moses Lake, Wash., 1969-70; BS in Zoology, Wash. State U., 1973; postgrad., Portland State U., 1976. Lab. technician The Carter Mining Co., Gillette, Wyo., 1977-79, lab. supr., 1979-80, quality control supr., 1980-81, engring. analyst, 1982-88; engr. quality control The Carter Mining Co., Gillette, 1988-89; owner Sharp Consulting, Gillette, 1989—, Landscape Design, 1993—; leader auditor tng. ISO 9000; owner Prairie Skullpture; obedience dog tng. instr., 1990 [illegible] Supt. Campbell County Fair, Gillette, [illegible]

on-line analysis com., apptd. U.S.A. expert on on-line analysis to ISO), Am. Water Ski Assn. (regular judge 1974-91, ea. regional water ski trick record 1975, 3d nat. trick title 1962, state champion in tricks Wash., Idaho, Mont. 1961-73, 2d 1987 Western region women's III tricks). Republican. Presbyterian. Avocations: handball, photography, water skiing. Office: Sharp Consulting/Prairie Skullpture 2406 Hillcrest Dr Gillette WY 82718-5641

SHARPE, KATHRYN PECK, artist; b. Chgo., Nov. 21, 1942; d. Charles John and Kathryn (Assman) Peck; m. Richard Lammerding, Sept. 10, 1966 (div. Jan. 1976); children: Erik Wesley, Kiersten Lea; m. William Forsyth Sharpe, Apr. 5, 1986. Student, Colo. Woman's Coll., 1962; degree in design, N.Y. Sch. Interior Design, 1964. Interior designer Morton Textile, Chgo., 1964, Richardson's, Menlo Park, 1964-65; office mgr. Cutler-Hammer, Menlo Park, 1977-79; faculty sec./adminstr. Stanford (Calif.) U., 1979-86; v.p., adminstr. William F. Sharpe Assocs., Los Altos, Calif., 1986-93; profl. fine artist Los Altos, 1993—; mem. com. Filoli-Arts Program, Woodside, Calif., 1998, Open Studios of Santa Clara County, 1998. Mem. Oil Painters of Am., Santa Clara Valley Watercolor Soc., Calif. Watercolor Soc., Pacific Art League (cmty. site dir. 1986—, com. mem. 1998), Calif. Art Club. Democrat. Home and Office: 25 Doud Dr Los Altos CA 94022-2323

SHARPE, ROLAND LEONARD, engineering company executive, earthquake and structural engineering consultant; b. Shakopee, Minn., Dec. 18, 1923; s. Alfred Leonard and Ruth Helen (Carter) S.; m. Jane Esther Steele, Dec. 28, 1946; children: Douglas Rolfe, Deborah Lynn, Sheryl Anne. BS in Civil Engring., U. Mich., 1947, MSE, 1949. Registered civil engr. and structural engr., Calif. Designer, Cummins & Barnard, Inc., Ann Arbor, Mich., 1947-48; instr. engring. U. Mich., 1948-50; exec. v.p. John A. Blume & Assocs., engrs., San Francisco, 1950-73; chmn., founder Engring. Decision Analysis Co., Inc., Cupertino, 1974-87; cons. earthquake engr., 1987—; mng. dir. EDAC, GmbH, Frankfurt, Germany, 1974-82; dir. EDAC; pres. Calif. Devel. & Engring. Co., Inc., Las Vegas, Nev., 1973-81; mem. nat. earthquake hazard reduction program adv. com. overviewing Fed. Emergency Mgmt. Agy., U.S. Geol. Survey, NSF and Nat. Inst. Stds. and Tech., 1990-93. Author: (with J. Blume, E.G. Kost) Earthquake Engineering for Nuclear Facilities, 1971. Mem. Planning Commn., Palo Alto, 1955-60; mng. dir. Applied Tech. Coun., Palo Alto, 1973-83; dir. Earthquake Engring. Rsch. Inst., 1972-75, now mem.; project dir., editor Tentative Provisions for Devel. of Seismic Regulations for Buildings, 1978; tech. mgr., contbr., editor Data Processing Facilities: Guidelines for Earthquake Hazard Mitigation, 1987. Served with USMC, 1942-46. Author, co-author over 200 engring. papers and reports; author of 3 chpts.: DOE Seismic Safety Manual, 1996. Fellow ASCE (hon. mem. 1994, chmn. dynamic effects com., 1978-80, exec. com. structural div. 1980-84, 89-93, chmn. 1983, mgmt. group B 1989-93, Earnest E. Howard award 1994); mem. Japan Structural Cons. Assn. (hon. mem. 1992), Structural Engrs. Assn. Calif. (dir. 1971-73, chmn. seismology com. 1972-74), Structural Engrs. No. Calif. (dir. 1969-71, life mem.), Am. Concrete Inst. (life), Structural Engrs. World Congress (pres. 1995—, chair 1998). Recipient citation for contbn. to constrn. industry Engring. News Record, 1978-79, 86-87; chmn. U.S. Joint Com. on Earthquake Engring., 1982-88. Home: 10320 Rolly Rd Los Altos CA 94024-6568 Office: Sharpe Struct Engrs 10320 Rolly Rd Ste 1 Los Altos CA 94024-6568

SHARPE, SHANNON, professional football player; b. Chgo., June 26, 1968. Student, Savannah State U. Tight end Denver Broncos, 1990—; player AFC Championship Game, 1991. Named to Pro Bowl Team, 1992, 93, 96, Sporting News NFL All-Pro Team, 1993. Office: Denver Broncos 13655 Broncos Pkwy Englewood CO 80112-4150*

SHARPE, WILLIAM FORSYTH, economics educator; b. Cambridge, Mass., June 16, 1934; s. Russell Thornley Sharpe and Evelyn Forsyth (Jillson) Maloy; m. Roberta Ruth Branton, July 2, 1954 (div. Feb. 1986); children: Deborah Ann, Jonathan Forsyth; m. Kathryn Dorothy Peck, Apr. 5, 1986. AB, UCLA, 1955, MA, 1956, PhD, 1961; DHL honoris causa, DePaul U., 1997. Economist Rand Corp., 1957-61; asst. prof. econs. U. Wash., 1961-63, assoc. prof., 1963-67, prof., 1967-68; prof. U. Calif., Irvine, 1968-70; Timken prof. fin. Stanford U., 1970-89, Timken prof. emeritus, 1989-92; prin. William F. Sharpe Assocs., 1986-92; prof.fin. Stanford U., 1993-95, STANCO 25 prof. of fin., 1995—; chmn. Financial Engines, Inc., 1996—; chmn. Fin. Engines, Inc., 1996—. Author: The Economics of Computers, 1969, Portfolio Theory and Capital Markets, 1970; co-author: Fundamentals of Investments, 1989, 2d edit., 1993, Investments, 6th edit., 1999. With U.S. Army, 1956-57. Recipient Graham and Dodd award Fin Analysts' Fedn., 1972, '73, '86-88. Nicholas Molodovsky award, 1989. Nobel prize in econ. scis., 1990, UCLA medal, 1998. Mem. Am. Fin. Assn. (v.p. 1979, pres. 1980), Western Fin. Assn. (Enduring Contbn. award 1989), Ea. Fin. Assn. (Disting. Scholar award 1991), Am. Econ. Assn., Phi Beta Kappa.

SHARPLES, THOMAS DAVY, retired mechanical engineer; b. West Chester, Pa., Sept. 3, 1916; s. Philip M. and Jean Watt (Davy) S.; m. Renate Adele Backhausen, Sept. 20, 1948; children: Thomas D. Jr., Hendrik W. Student, Calif. Inst. Tech., 1935-37, Swarthmore Coll., 1937-39. Owner Art Tech. Studio and Sch. of Photography, South Pasadena, Calif., 1939-42; dir. rsch. Sharples Corp., Phila., 1948-51, mgr. product design, 1952-65; chief mech. engr. Beckman Instruments, Inc., Palo Alto, Calif., 1966-74; mgr. product design Beckman Instruments, Inc., Palo Alto, 1974-84, engring. staff specialist, 1985-88, mgr. engring. rsch., 1988-91; owner Sharples Engring., Junction City, Oreg., 1991—. Patentee in field. Capt. U.S. Army, 1942-46, North Africa, ETO. Named Beckman fellow, 1991. Mem. Photographic Soc. of Am., Soc. Mfg. Engineers, Am. AAAS, History of Science Soc. Republican. Soc. of Friends. Avocations: antique scientific books and instruments, microscopy, glass blowing, machine shop. E-mail: TDSENG@aol.com. Home: 128 Heather Dr Atherton CA 94027-2120 Office: Sharples Engring 91448 Steinmetz Rd Junction City OR 97448-9540

SHARPLES, THOMAS DAVY, JR., engineering executive; b. Phila., Aug. 8, 1951; s. Thomas Davy and Renate (Bachausen) S.; m. Shirley A. Hamada Torp; 1 child, Andrea Tomoe. Student, Menlo Coll., 1970-72, U. Munich, 1972-74. Founder, tech. dir. The Hyde Street Studios, San Francisco, 1979-82; engr. mgr. R&D facility Otari Corp., 1982-85; founder, sr. v.p. of engring. Personics Corp., Menlo Park, Calif., 1985-90; co-founder, vice-chmn., chief tech. officer Telescan Corp., Burlingame, Calif., 1991—; cons. Otari, Teac, Wilson, Sonsini, Goodrich & Rosati. Patentee time-code and synchronizer designs, high -speed optical data storage and retrieval, multi-user wireless info. systems; contbr. articles to profl. jours. and mags. Co-recipient Smithsonian-Computerworld award for innovation, 1990, Gold & Silver awards for technical achievement Pop Advt. Inst., 1998. Mem. Audio Engrs. Soc. (lectr.), Aircraft Owners and Pilots Assn., Am. Radio Relay League (Newington, Conn.), Technology Network, Calif. Hist. Radio Soc. Mem. Am. Soc. of Friends. Avocations: aviation, antique auto restoration, music, amateur radio. Office: Telescan Corp 828 Mahler Rd Burlingame CA 94010-1604

SHARPTON, THOMAS, physician; b. Augusta, Ga., July 15, 1949; s. Thomas and Elizabeth (Dozier) S. BA, Northwestern U., 1971; MS, Stanford U., 1973, MD, 1977. Intern Martinez (Calif.) VAMC, 1977-78, resident, 1978-80; mem. staff Kaiser Permanente Med. Group, Oakland, Calif., 1980—; asst. clin. prof. medicine U. Calif., San Francisco, 1994—; cons. Berkeley (Calif.) Free Clinic, 1977—; chmn. peer review Kaiser Permanente Med. Group, Oakland, 1985-86; clin. mem. faculty U. Calif., San Francisco, 1992, asst. clin. prof., 1994; chair AIDS therapeutics com. No. Calif. Kaiser Hosps., 1996—. Mem. Alameda County Profl. Adv. Com., Oakland, 1984-88, Alameda County AIDS Task Force, Oakland, 1985-88. Fellow ACP; mem. Calif. Med. Assn., Alameda-Contra Costa Med. Assn., Mensa, Sigma Pi Sigma, Phi Beta Kappa. Republican. Club: Phi Beta Kappa of No. Calif. Avocations: classical piano. Office: Kaiser PMG 280 W Macarthur Blvd Piedmont CA 94611-5642

SHARTIN, STACY D., lawyer; b. Mpls., Mar. 10, 1949. AB cum laude, U. Calif., L.A., 1970, JD, 1973. Bar: Calif. 1973. Ptr. Seyfarth, Shaw, Fairweather & Geraldson, L.A., 1980—. Mem. ABA, Calif. State Bar (exec. com. labor and employment sect.), Los Angeles County Bar Assn. Office: Seyfarth Shaw Fairweather & Geraldson 2029 Century Park E Ste 3300 Los Angeles CA [illegible]

SHATNER, CANDY M., writer, actress, lobbyist; b. L.A., Feb. 11, 1955; d. William Shatner. Student, Tri-County Tech., 1984, Northwestern U., Sacramento, 1994. Prodr. Am. Radio Network, L.A., 1991-93; actress Film Industry Work, L.A., 1996—; prodr. Shatner Prodn., L.A., 1998; exec. The Conservative Action Lobby, L.A., 1988-98, L.I.C.K., 1998—; mem. The Seneca Network, Inc. Author: (polit. satires) Zen II. Game, 1997, The Dusty Eagle, 1998; editor: (newsletter) The Econ. Watch, 1988-98. Fundraiser Rep. Nat. Com., Washington, 1986-88, also environ. and profl. groups, L.A., 1994-95. Avocations: tennis, karate, weight-lifting, swimming, horseback riding. Home and Office: PO Box 931602 Los Angeles CA 90093-1602

SHATNEY, CLAYTON HENRY, surgeon; b. Bangor, Maine, Nov. 4, 1943; s. Clayton Lewis and Regina (Cossette) S.; m. Consuelo Perez Santibañez; children: Tony, Andy. BA, Bowdoin Coll., 1965; MD, Tufts U., 1969. Asst. prof. surgery U. Md. Hosp., Balt., 1979-82; assoc. prof. U. Fla. Sch. Medicine, 1982-87; clin. assoc. prof. Stanford (Calif.) U. Sch. Medicine, 1987—; dir. traumatology Md. Inst. Emergency Med. Svcs., Balt., 1979-82; dir. trauma U. Hosp., Jacksonville, 1982-85; assoc. dir. trauma Santa Clara Valley Med. Ctr., 1992—; cons. VA Coop. Studies Program, Washington, 1980—. Mem. editl. bd. Circulatory Shock, 1989-94, Panam Jour. Trauma, 1995—. Maj. U.S. Army, 1977-79. State of Maine scholar Bowdoin Coll., 1961-65. Fellow ACS, Southeastern Surg. Congress, Southwestern Surg. Congress, Soc. Surg. Alimentary Tract, Am. Assn. Surg. Trauma, Soc. Critical Care Medicine, Soc. Internat. de Chirurgie, Western Surg. Assn., Pacific Coast Surg. Assn., Phi Kappa Phi. Home: 900 Larsen Rd Aptos CA 95003-2640 Office: Valley Med Ctr Dept Surgery 751 S Bascom Ave Dept Surgery San Jose CA 95128-2604

SHAW, ARTHUR E., conductor. Studied with, Sidney Harth; degree, Wichita State U.; postgrad. in Conducting, U. Mich., 1982-85. Asst. condr. Ark. Symphony Orch., 1977-79; music dir., condr. Adrian (Mich.) Symphony Orch., 1979-87, Rogue Valley Symphony, Ashland, Oreg., 1987—; condr. Rogue Opera, 1987-89; founding dir., guest condr. Youth Symphony So. Oreg.; guest condr. Little Rock Cmty. Theatre, 1979, Summer Music Camp No. Ariz. U., 1988, Ota (Japan) Jr. Symphony, 1990, Jalisco Philharm., Mex., 1992, Ctrl. Oreg. Symphony, 1994, Britt Festivals, 1996. James Robertson Meml. Conducting scholar, 1976-77. Office: Rogue Valley Symphony SOSC Music Hall 1250 Siskiyou Blvd Ashland OR 97520-5010*

SHAW, CHARLES ALDEN, engineering executive; b. Detroit, June 8, 1925; s. Fred Alden and Amy (Ellis) S.; m. Barbara Loveland, Mar. 9, 1963 (div. 1979); children: Amy Elizabeth, Polly Nicole; m. Jeanne Steves Partridge, Apr. 22, 1989. BS, Harvard U., 1945; MSEE, Syracuse U., 1958. Test and design engr. G.E., Syracuse-Schenectady, N.Y., 1947-51; chief engr. Onondaga Pottery Co., Syracuse, 1951-60; mgr. semiconductor div. G.E., Syracuse-Schenectady, 1960-66; cons. to gen. dir. Bull-G.E., Paris, 1966-69; mgr. CAD sect. integrated cir. product dept. G.E., Syracuse, 1969-71, mgr. CAD ctr. solid state applied ops., 1971-78, mgr. computer support solid state applied ops., 1978-81; dir. CAD G.E. Intersil, Cupertino, Calif., 1981-88; cons. in field Cupertino, 1988-89; mgr. tech. program Cadence Design Systems, Santa Clara, Calif., 1989—. Trustee Hidden Villa, Los Altos Hills, Calif., 1986-92; vol. tech. KTEH Channel 54 pub. TV, 1984—. With USN, 1942-45, PTO. Mem. IEEE, Assn. Computing Machinery (chmn. spl. interest group SIGDA 1986-91), Design Automation Conf. (exec. bd. 1985-95), Harvard Club of Peninsula. Democrat. Unitarian. Avocations: skiing, scuba diving, music. Home: 4925 Monaco Dr Pleasanton CA 94566-7671 Office: 555 River Oaks Pky San Jose CA 95134-1917

SHAW, DAVID LYLE, journalist, author; b. Dayton, Ohio, Jan. 4, 1943; s. Harry and Lillian (Walton) S.; m. Alice Louise Eck, Apr. 11, 1965 (div. Sept. 1974); m. Ellen Torgerson, July 17, 1979 (dec.); stepchildren: Christopher, Jordan; m. Lucy Stille, Apr. 14, 1988; 1 child, Lucas. BA in English, UCLA, 1965. Reporter Huntington Park Signal (Calif.), 1963-66, Long Beach Independent (Calif.), 1966-68; reporter L.A. Times, 1968-74, media critic, 1974—. Author: WILT: Just Like Any Other 7-Foot, Black Millionare Who Lives Next Door, 1973, The Levy Caper, 1974, Journalism Today, 1977, Press Watch, 1984, The Pleasure Police, 1996; contbr. numerous articles to mags. including Gentlemen's Quar., Cigar Aficionado, Esquire, TV Guide, Bon Appetit, Food & Wine. Recipient Mellet Fund Nat. award, 1983, PEN West award, 1990, Calif. Bar Assn. Gold Medallion, 1990, Pulitzer Prize for disting. criticism, 1991. Office: LA Times Times Mirror Sq Los Angeles CA 90012

SHAW, KURT, artist; b. Pitts., July 21, 1967; s. Jere Adrian and Lois Ann (Schlieper) S.; m. Holly Sue Besanceney, Dec. 5, 1992, (div. 1998). BFA with honors, Carnegie Mellon U., 1989; GMAW Cert., Hobart Inst. Welding, Technology, Troy, Ohio, 1995. Artist Pitts., 1989—. Exhbns. include Susquehanna Art Mus., Harrisburg, Pa., 1997, Hoyt Inst. of Fine Arts, New Castle, Pa., 1993, 94, 98, Erie Art Mus., Pa., 1994; creator/designer numerous wall sculptures placed in corporate settings including: four pieces in Windjammer Restaurant on Royal Caribbean Cruises Ltd. Ship "Sovereign of the Seas", 1996, Miami, three pieces in the atrium of Bayview Corp. Ctr., Toms River, N.J., 1996. Mem. Internat. Sculpture Ctr., Calif. Lawyers Arts. Office: 1400 Marsten Rd Ste D Burlingame CA 94010-2422

SHAW, LILLIE MARIE KING, vocalist; b. Indpls., Nov. 27, 1915; d. Earl William and Bertha Louise (Groth) King; m. Philip Harlow Shaw, June 26, 1940 (dec. 1985). *Husband, Philip Harlow Shaw (1912-1985) was well-known as a Tenor Soloist and Assistant Director of the Orpheus Male chorus of Phoenix in their appearances in Europe as well as the US. His high school choruses were known for their radio and concert appearances state-wide and he held a church soloist position for many years in Phoenix. Some of his vocal and choral compositions are in use in the church and schools in Arizona and Indiana.He received his Bachelor's degree from Indiana University and his Master's degree from Arizona State University.* Student, Jordan Conservatory Music, Indpls., 1940-43; BA, Ariz. State U., 1959; MA, Denver U., 1962; pvt. vocal study, 1944-70. Educator, libr. Glendale (Ariz.) Schs., 1959-67; lectr. libr. sci. Ariz. State U., Tempe, 1962-68. Concertizing, oratorio, symphonic soloist, light opera, 1965-82; soloist First Ch. of Christ Scientist, Sun City West, Ariz., 1980—. Monthly lectr. Christian Women's Fellowship, Phoenix, 1989-96; World Conf. del. Soc. of Friends, 1967. Mem. Nat. Soc. Arts and Letters (sec. 1990-94, nat. del. 1992), Am. Philatelic Assn. (life), Am. Topical Assn., Phoenix Philatelic Soc., Auditions Guild Ariz. (sec. 1989-92), Phoenix Opera League, Phoenix Symphony Guild, Sigma Alpha Iota Alumnae (Phoenix chpt., life, treas. 1988-96, Sword of Honor 1972, Rose of Honor 1982, Rose of Dedication 1995). Republican. Avocations: philately, gardening. Home: 6802 N 37th Ave Phoenix AZ 85019-1103

SHAW, MARK HOWARD, lawyer, business owner, entrepreneur; b. Albuquerque, Aug. 26, 1944; s. Brad Oliver and Barbara Rae (Mencke) S.; m. Ann Marie Brookreson, June 29, 1968 (div. 1976); adopted children: Daniel Paul, Kathleen Ann, Brian Andrew; m. Roslyn Jane Ashton, Oct. 9, 1976; children: Rebecca Rae, Amanda Leith. BA, U. N.Mex., 1967, JD, 1969. Bar, N.Mex. 1969. Law clk. to presiding justice N.Mex. Supreme Ct., Santa Fe, 1969-70; ptnr. Gallagher & Ruud, Albuquerque, 1970-74, Schmidt & Shaw, Albuquerque, 1974-75; sr. mem. Shaw, Thompson & Sullivan P.A., Albuquerque, 1975-82; chief exec. officer United Ch. Religious Sci. and Sci. Mind Publs., L.A., 1982-91; bus. owner, entrepreneur Santa Fe, N.Mex., 1991-94; mem. Coppler & Mannick, P.C., Santa Fe, N.Mex., 1994-98; pvt. practice Santa Fe, 1998—. Trustee 1st Ch. Religious Sci., Albuquerque, 1974-77, pres. 1977; trustee Sandia Ch. Religious Sci., Albuquerque, 1980-82, pres. 1981-82; trustee United Ch. Religious Sci., Los Angeles, 1981-82, chmn. 1982; trustee Long Beach (Calif.) Ch. Religious Sci., 1983-86, chmn. 1983-86; chmn. Bernalillo County Bd. Ethics, Albuquerque, 1979-82, v.p. Santa Fe Rape Crisis Ctr., 1997—. Served as sgt. USMCR, 1961-69. Mem. N.Mex. Bar Assn. Avocations: sailing, fly fishing. Home: 2724 Puerto Bonito Santa Fe NM 87505-6534 Office: 529 W San Francisco St Santa Fe NM 87501-1838

SHAW, RICHARD EUGENE, cardiovascular researcher; b. Springfield, Ohio, Jan. 20, 1950; s. Eugene Russell and Marjorie Caroline Shaw; m. Nov. 26, 1976; 2 children. BA, Duquesne U., 1972; MA, U.S. Internat. U., San Diego, 1977; PhD, U. Calif., San Francisco, 198[illegible] [illegible]

technologist. Nuclear Medicine Tech. Cert. Bd. Staff nuc. med. technologist Scripps Meml. Hosp., La Jolla, Calif., 1975-79; rsch. asst. U. Calif. San Francisco Sch. Medicine, 1980-85; mgr. rsch. programs San Francisco Heart Inst., Daly City, Calif., 1985-87, dir. rsch., 1988-90, dir. rsch. and ops., 1991—; sr. advisor steering com. for databases Daus. of Charity Nat. Health Sys., St. Louis, 1993—; cons. comm. informatics project HealthLink SmartPhone, San Francisco, 1992—. Editor-in-chief Jour. Invasive Cardiology, King of Prussia, Pa., 1989—; contbr. more than 200 articles and book chpts. to med. lit. Coach Am. Youth Soccer Orgn. and Youth Baseball Assn. (bd. dirs.), Burlingame, Calif., 1990—. Fellow Am. Coll. Cardiology; mem. Am. Heart Assn., Soc. for Clin. Trials, N.Y. Acad. Scis., Am. Statis. Assn., Am. Med. Informatics Assn., Soc. Behavioral Medicine. Avocation: music. Office: San Francisco Heart Inst Seton Med Ctr 1900 Sullivan Ave Daly City CA 94015-2200

SHAW, VALEEN JONES, special education educator, elementary school educator; b. Coalville, Utah, June 19, 1930; d. G. Allen and Mabel Leon (Clark) Jones; m. Melvin Francis Shaw, June 21, 1948; children: C. Allene Shaw Fuhriman, Denise Ellen Shaw Call, Sharon Marie Shaw Williams. BS, Weber State U., Ogden, Utah, 1966; postgrad., U. Utah, Utah State U., Brigham Young U. Cert. tchr. elem. edn., early childhood edn., spl. edn. Tchr. 3rd grade Morgan (Utah) Sch. Dist., 1965-66; tchr. 6th grades N. Summit Sch. Dist., Coalville, Utah, 1966-67, tchr. 2d grades, 1967-82, tchr. resource, spl. edn., 1982-92, teaching specialist elem. summer sch. prog., 1967-92; elementary resource and spl. edn. tchr. North Summit Sch. Dist., Coalville, 1982-92; mentor N. Summit Elementary Sch., 1988-89. Tchr./trainer Coalville Ch. of Jesus Christ of Latter-day Saints. &D. Mem. NEA, ASCD Inst., Utah Edn. Assn., Morgan Edn. Assn., North Summit Edn. Asssn, Utah Fedn. Coun. for Exceptional Children.

SHAY, ROSHANI CARI, political science educator; b. Milw., Oct. 5, 1942; d. Walter John and Dorothee May (Dahnke) O'Donnell; 1 child, Mark Sather. Student, Willamette U., 1960-63; BA, U. Oreg., 1968, MA, 1971, PhD, 1974. Adminstrv. asst. Dept. of Youth Svcs., Lubbock, Tex., 1963; teaching asst., instr. U. Oreg., Eugene, 1969-72; vis. asst. prof. Oreg. State U., Corvallis, 1973-74, Willamette U., Salem, Oreg., 1973-79, Lewis and Clark Coll., Portland, Oreg., 1976, 78; from asst. prof. to prof. Western Oreg. U., Monmouth, 1979—, chair history, polit. sci., pub. adminstrn. dept., 1991-94, chair social sci. divsn., 1994—. Author: (with others) The People of Rajneeshpuram, 1990, Religion and the Social Order, vol. 5, 1995, (simulation) European Unity Project, 1982. Co-founder, v.p., sec.-treas Ind. Opportunities Unltd., Salem, 1986—; co-founder, sec. Inst. for Justice and Human Rights, San Francisco, 1988-94; bd. dirs. Oreg. UN Assn., Portland, 1982—, Salem UN Assn., 1982-91; v.p., pres., bd. dirs. Garten Svcs. Inc. for Disabled, Salem, 1989—; pres. Assn. Oreg. Faculties, 1989-91; mem. adv. bd. Connections Program for Disabled Deaf, Salem, 1989—; pres., bd. dirs. Model UN of the Far West, San Diego, 1981-84, 86-88, 95—; mem. Oreg. Women's Polit. Caucus. Danforth Found. fellow, 1968-74; named Woman of Achievement YWCA Tribute, Salem, 1990, Mem. of Yr., Oreg. Rehab. Assn., 1995. Mem. Am. Fedn. Tchrs. (v.p., legis. officer local 2278 1982-88), Western Polit. Sci. Assn., Communal Studies Assn., Mental Health Assn. Oreg., Oreg. Acad. Sci., Oreg. Internat. Coun., Phi Kappa Phi (hon.). Democrat. Avocations: volunteer work with multiply disabled deaf, reading, meditation. Home: 348 S Main St Falls City OR 97344-9763 Office: Western Oreg U 345 Monmouth Ave N Monmouth OR 97361-1314

SHCOLNIK, ROBERT MILTON, insurance company executive; b. South Bend, Ind., Aug. 21, 1938; s. Harry and Esther (Baim) S.; m. Linda K. Egleberry, Aug. 10, 1972; children: Scott, Keith, Carin, Patricia. BS in Bus., Ariz. State U., 1960; grad., Am. Savings & Loan Inst., 1961; diploma in ins., Hartford Ins. Group Ins. Group, 1965. Loan officer, branch mgr., asst. to the pres. Home Savings & Loan Assn., 1959-61; pres. Harris/Shcolnik & Assocs., Inc., Phoenix, 1961—; ptnr. Harris/Shcolnik Properties; guest lectr. in ins. Phoenix Coll.; speaker Ind. Ins. Agts. Am. Contbr. articles to profl. jours.; designer interface mini-computer concept. Mem. nat. presidents circle Ctrl. Mutual Ins. Co., inter-circle, 1975, 76, 94, Ariz. Jonathan Trumbull Coun., Hartford Ins., 1979-80, Nat. Product Devel. Com. Hartford Inst., 1993-94, Nat. Great Am. Ins. Agts. Adv. Coun., 1979-81, chmn., 1979, Pacer (agts. coun., chmn. regional comml. lines, nat. coun. lines com. 1990-93), CNA group, agts. coun. Cigna Inst.; mem. Key Club, Continetnatl Assurance Co., 1970-75; past pres. Am. Savs. and Loan Inst., Ariz.; bd. dirs. Jewish Cmty. Ctr., 1980-86, v.p., exec. com., 1983-85; mem. combined ops. coun. Jewish Ctrs. Greater Phoenix, 1987-88; mem. Mauor's Task Force on Graffiti, 1993-95; chmn. Anti-GRFFTI Hotline Maricopa County. Named Outstanding Agt. of Yr. Maricopa County Assn. Independent Ins. Agts., 1973, 76-78; recipient Jewish Community Ctr. Disting. Svc. award, 1981, 83, 85. Mem. Ind. Ins. Agts. Ariz. (pres. 1985), Phoenix Cmty. Alliance (bd. dirs., exec. com. 1992-97). Republican. Jewish. Office: Harris Shcolnik & Assocs 1750 E Glendale Ave # 100 Phoenix AZ 85020-5505

SHEA, JOHN DWANE, communications executive; b. Chgo., Sept. 28, 1939; s. John Stephen and Dorthy (Moryer) S.; m. Beverly M. Kehoe, July 22, 1993; children: Eric, April. MSMT, Transumer Coll., Rome, 1960; BS in Electronic Tech., Phoenix Coll., 1961; MS of Strategic Intellegence, Def. Intelligenc Inst., 1978. V.p. Intergrated Circuit Engring. Corp., Scottsdale, Ariz., 1974-80; pres. Tech. Analysis Group, San Jose, 1980-84, Sierra Tech. Group, Lake Taho, Calif., 1984-86, Shea Tech. Group, Saratoga, Calif., 1986—. Author: Electrical Engineering Automatic Wafer FHB Manufacturing, 1982, Electronic Intelligence, 1984, Japan Technology for Computing, 1985. Recipient Intelligence Achievement award Ministry of Def., 1989, Global Intelligence award, 1989. Fellow Assn. Former Intelligence Officers; mem. Armed Forces Communications and Electronics Assn., Assn. Old Crows, Am. Def. Preparedness Assn. Republican. Roman Catholic. Avocations: military history, flying jet fighters. Home: PO Box 3226 Saratoga CA 95070-1226 Office: Shea Tech Group Inc 51 E Campbell Ave Ste 1082 Campbell CA 95008-2047

SHEAFFER, RICHARD ALLEN, electrical engineer; b. Bronxville, N.Y., May 30, 1950; s. Harold Aumond and Carol Lois (Henry) Sweet; children: Alan Michael Sheaffer, Russell Logan Sheaffer, Neil Andrew Sheaffer. BSEE, Pa. State U., 1972; MSEE, U. So. Calif., 1975; MBA, Pepperdine U., 1996. Registered profl. engr., Calif., Fla. Elec. engr. So. Calif. Edison Co., Rosemead, 1973-79, 80-90, Harris Controls div., Melbourne, Fla., 1979-80; cons. to elec. utility industry, 1990-91; sr. transmission planner San Diego Gas & Electric, 1991—; project leader nomogram study for Pacific and S.W. transfer subcom. Western Systems Coordinating Coun., 1988, 91; project leader Ariz.-Calif. 7550 NW Path Rating, 1994-97. Author: 1984 West-of-the-River Operating Study, 1985, December 22, 1982 Disturbance Study, 1983. Mem. IEEE (Power Engring. Soc., Engring. Mgmt. Soc.), Phi Eta Sigma. Episcopalian. Avocations: running, bicycling, playing guitar, golf, fitness. Office: 8316 Century Park Ct San Diego CA 92123-1530

SHEARER, KAREN MARIE, writer, producer, director; b. San Diego; m. Roger H. Mayer. BA, San Diego State U.; ESL teaching credential, London U. Copywriter Weidenfeld and Nicolson, Ltd., London, MCA-Universal Pictures, Universal City, Calif.; dir. pub. rels. MCA Records, Universal City; dir. music affairs Billy Jack Enterprises, Inc., Culver City, Calif.; ind. writer, producer L.A. Writer, dir., producer Casey's Top 40, The Rolling Stones 25th Anniversary Spl., 1989-90, (internat. radio spls.) Elvis Presley, A Golden Celebration With Pete Townshend, 1985; writer, prodr. various TV programs, including How'd They Do That?, Modern marvels, Biography, wildlife features. Mem. Nat. Assn. Rec. Arts and Scis. E-mail: rhinoprod@aol.com.

SHEARING, MIRIAM, state supreme court justice; b. Waverly, N.Y., Feb. 24, 1935. BA, Cornell U., 1956; JD, Boston Coll., 1964. Bar: Calif. 1965, Nev. 1969. Justice of peace Las Vegas Justice Ct., 1977-81; judge Nev. Dist. Ct., 1983-92, chief judge, 1986; justice Nevada Supreme Ct., Carson City, 1993-97, chief justice, 1997—. Mem. ABA (mem. exec. com.), Am. Judicature Soc., Nev. Judges Assn. (sec. 1978), Nev. Dist. Ct. Judges Assn. (sec. 1984-85, pres. 1986-87), State Bar Nev., State Bar Calif., Clark County Bar Assn. Democrat.

SHEBL, JAMES MICHAEL, communications executive; b. Tacoma, July 1, 1942; s. Joseph James and Mary Ellen (Hurley) S.; m. Patricia Ann Pedroni, Aug. 22, 1965; children: Bonnie Marie Peartree, Catherine Teresa. BA, Creighton U., Omaha, 1965; MA, U. Nebr., 1969; PhD, U. Pacific, 1972. Administr., prof. U. Pacific, Stockton, Calif., 1969-83; dir. corp. comm. St. Joseph's Regional Health Sys., Stockton, 1984-97; pub. affairs officer Calif. Gov.'s Office Emergency Svcs., Sacramento, 1998—, Fed. Emergency Mgmt. Agy., 1998—. Author: King, of the Mountains, 1974, In This Wild Water, 1976, Weber!, 1993; editor: The Tulebreakers, 1983. Pres. San Joaquin AIDS Found., Su Salud Health Edn. Fair; chmn. Cultural Heritage Bd., St. Joseph's Helping Hands. NEH publs. fellow. Mem. Jebediah Smith Soc. (pres.). Republican. Roman Catholic. Avocations: horsepacking, backpacking, swimming, exploring, fly fishing. Home: 3517 Stone River Cir Stockton CA 95219-3144

SHEEHAN, MICHAEL JARBOE, archbishop; b. Wichita, Kans., July 9, 1939; s. John Edward and Mildred (Jarboe) S. MST, Gregorian U., Rome, 1965; D of Canon Law, Lateran U., Rome, 1971. Ordained priest Roman Cath. Ch., 1964. Asst. gen. sec. Nat. Coun. Cath. Bishops, Washington, 1971-76; rector Holy Trinity Sem., Dallas, 1976-82; pastor Immaculate Conception Ch., Grand Prairie, Tex., 1982-83; bishop Diocese of Lubbock, Tex., 1983-93; archbishop Archdiocese of Santa Fe, Albuquerque, N.Mex., 1993—; past chmn. Am. Bd. Cath. Missions, 1989-91; trustee Cath. Relief Svcs., 1992—. Contbr. articles to New Cath. Ency. Trustee St. Mary Hosp., Lubbock, 1983-89; bd. dirs. Tex. Conf. of Chs. Mem. Serra Club (chaplain 1983-93). Avocations: snow skiing, racquetball. Office: Archdiocese of Santa Fe 4000 St Josephs Pl NW Albuquerque NM 87120-1714

SHEELEY, ELLEN R., marketing consultant, finance consultant; b. Charles City, Iowa, Oct. 15, 1956. BA in Psychology, Wright State U., 1978; MBA, Colo. State U., Ft. Collins, 1982. Mgr. Ctrl. Bank of Denver, 1982-83; sr. mktg. cons. Devel. Bank of We. Samoa, Apia, 1983-86; sr. mgr. Bank of Am., San Francisco, 1986-89; test mktg. mgr. First Deposit Corp., San Francisco, 1989; pres. Nob Hill Consulting, San Francisco, 1989—; sr. cons. Alex Sheshunoff Mgmt. Svcs., Inc., Austin, 1995. Contbr. numerous articles to profl. jours. Mem. Alliance Francaise, World Affairs Coun., Commonwealth Club Calif. Avocations: travel, tennis, reading, fine and performing arts. Fax: (415) 986-2346. E-mail: nhconsult@earthlink.net. Home: 655 Powell St Ste 303 San Francisco CA 94108-3026 Office: Nob Hill Consulting 655 Powell St Apt 303 San Francisco CA 94108-3026

SHEEN, PORTIA YUNN-LING, retired physician; b. Republic of China, Jan. 13, 1919; came to U.S., 1988; d. Y. C. and A. Y. (Chow) Sheen; m. Kuo, 1944 (dec. 1970); children: William, Ida, Alexander, David, Mimi. MD, Nat. Med. Coll. Shanghai, 1943. Intern, then resident Cen. Hosp., Chungking, Szechuan, China, 1943; with Hong Kong Govt. Med. and Health Dept., 1948-76; med. supt. Kowloon (Hong Kong) Hosp., 1948-63, Queen Elizabeth Hosp., Kowloon, 1963-73, Med. and Health Hdqrs. and Health Ctr., Kowloon, 1973-76, Yan Chai Hosp., New Territories, Hong Kong, 1976-87. Fellow Hong Kong Coll. Family Physicians; mem. AAAS, British Med. Assn., Hong Kong Med. Assn., Hong Kong Pediatric Soc., N.Y. Acad. Sci. Methodist. Avocations: reading, music. Home: Entry 1 1408 Golden Rain Rd Apt 7 Walnut Creek CA 94595-2442

SHEERAN, MICHAEL JOHN LEO, priest, college administrator; b. N.Y.C., Jan. 24, 1940; s. Leo John and Glenna Marie (Wright) S. AB, St. Louis U., 1963, PhL, 1964, AM in Polit. Sci., 1967, AM in Theology, 1971, STL, 1971; PhD, Princeton U., 1977. Joined Soc. Jesus, 1957; ordained priest Roman Catholic Ch., 1970. Exec. editor Catholic Mind, N.Y.C., 1971-72; assoc. editor Am. mag., N.Y.C., 1971-72; assoc. chaplain Aquinas Inst., Princeton, N.J., 1972-75; asst. dean Regis Coll., Denver, 1975-77, dean of Coll., 1977-82, v.p. acad. affairs, 1982-92, acting pres., 1987-88, pres., 1993—; retreat dir., cons. on governance for religious communities, 1970—. Author: Beyond Majority Rule, 1984. Contbr. articles and editorials to publs. Trustee Rockhurst Coll., Kansas City, Mo., 1982-91, Creighton U., Omaha, 1985-95, U. San Francisco, 1985-94, Loyola U., New Orleans, 1994-96, Rocky Mountain Coll. of Art and Design, 1994—, Regis Jesuit H.S., 1999—; chmn. bd. Mile High United Way, 1999—. Ford Found. scholar, 1963. Democrat. Home: 3333 Regis Blvd Denver CO 80221-1154 Office: Regis U 3333 Regis Blvd Denver CO 80221-1099

SHEETS, GARY BRUCE, information systems manager, educator; b. L.A., Apr. 4, 1944; s. Lester B. and Irene M. (Larson) S.; m. Maria Luisa Sheets, Sept. 18, 1993; children: Steven A., Sheryl Lynn. BS in Bus., U. Antioch, 1985, MS in Orgnl. Mgmt., 1988. Info. sys. mgr. L.A. Dept. Water & Power, 1968-98, ret., 1998. 1st vice chmn. bd. L.A. Fed. Credit Union, 1994-98, chmn. bd., 1997-98. Roman Catholic. Avocations: writing, inventing, computers, electronics. Home: 4450 Richard Cir Los Angeles CA 90032

SHEFFIELD, SIMONE, business executive; m. Ronald Divincintio, Mar. 19, 1971 (dec. May 1979); children: Mary, Sharon, Samantha, Mark, Luke, Erica. Student, Ramapo Coll., 1973, So. Coll., 1974, St. Monica Coll., 1991. Asst. dist. mgr. United Artist Theatre Corp., N.Y.C., 1972-77, v.p. creative affairs Motown Records, Calif., 1977-81; CEO Canyon Entertainment, Calif., 1981—; prodr. music videos, feature films and live prodns.; talent cons. Am. Music Awards, M.T.V. awards, Billboard awards, Grammy awards, Soul Train awards, Essence awards, Golden Globe awards, Peoples Choice awards, ESPN Sports awards, many others. Inventor tuck-a-way tissue. Democrat. Roman Catholic. Avocations: travel, rare coins, movie memorabilia, music. Office: Canyon Entertainment PO Box 256 Palm Springs CA 92263-0256

SHEKTER, WILLIAM BERNARD, ophthalmologist; b. Jamaica, N.Y., Jan. 20, 1928; s. Adela Breakstone (Fisher) S. BA, Tufts U., 1947; MD, NYU, 1950. Diplomate Am. Bd. Ophthalmology. Chief dept. ophthalmology Kaiser-Permanente Med. Ctr., San Francisco, 1960-93; mem. exec. com. ophthalmology dept. Calif. Pacific Med. Ctr., San Francisco, 1980-93, assoc. prof. ophthalmology , co-chair. Bd. dirs. Baphr Found., San Francisco, 1991-97, Lighthouse for the Blind & Visually Disabled, San Francisco, 1988—. Lt. comdr. USNR, 1955-60, PTO. Fellow Am. Acad. Ophthalmology, ACS; mem. Pacific Coast Oto-Ophthalmol. Soc. Avocations: photography, travel.

SHELDON, DEENA LYNN, television camera operator; b. Groveland, Mass., Mar. 10, 1962; d. Frederic J. and Penny Margolis. BS, Boston U., 1984. Youth counselor. Co. mem. Body Lang. Dancers, 1986; mem. Michael Macchio's Jazz Co., 1980-85, Danny Sloan's Repertory, 1980-82, Celtic's Green Gang, 1980-82, Dean Brittenham's Shiley Elite Athletic Program. Camera operator Redsox and Bruins, Sta. WSBK-TV, Boston, 1985, Am.'s Cup, Major League Baseball and postseason play, Homerun Derby, Boston Marathon, Extreme Games, ESPN, 1986—; N.Y. Mets and N.Y. Islanders, Sportschannel, 1987-92; N.Y. Mets, Sta. WWOR-TV, 1987-92; Monday Night Football, Ky. Derby, Triple Crown, Indy 500, Rose Bowl, Probowl, NFL Hall of Fame game, Superbowl XXIX halftime show, Dem. and Rep. convs., ABC, 1992—; Late Night with David Letterman, NBC, 1996; NFL, Olympics, Phil Donahue Show, Macy's Day Parade, NBC, 1986—; NFL and championship games, Daytona 500, Joan Rivers Show, Major League Baseball and postseason play, CBS, 1987—; Superbowl, World Series, NFL, NHL, Fox Sports, 1994—; robotic camera operator Met. Life and Fuji blimps, NFL championship and playoff games, Daytona 500, Indy 500, 1989—. Youth counselor and instr. athleticism. Recipient Emmy awards for CBS's Postseason Major League Baseball, 1990, CBS's Daytona 500, 1993, ESPN's Extreme Games, 1995, 96, 97; N.Y. Emmy for N.Y. Mets, 1992-93, 93-94; Emmy nominee for ESPN's Am.'s Cup, 1995. Mem. NAFE, Nat. Assn. Broadcast Employees and Technicians, Internat. Brotherhood Elec. Workers. Avocations: trail running, dancing, sunshine, instructing in athleticism. Home: 955 Harbor Island Dr Ste 145 Box 103 B San Diego CA 92101

SHELDON, GARY, conductor, music director; b. Bay Shore, N.Y., Jan. 21, 1953. Student, Wash. U., St. Louis, 1972; BMus, Juilliard Sch. Music, 1974; diploma, Inst. Hautes Etudes Musicales, Montreux, Switzerland, 1975. Prin. condr. Opera Theater, Syracuse, 1976-77; asst. condr. Syracuse Symphony Orch., 1976-77, New Orleans Symphony Orch., 1977-80; assoc. condr. Columbus (Ohio) Symphony Orch., 1982-89; music dir. Lancaster (Ohio) Festival, 1988—, Marin Symphony Orch., San Rafael, Calif., 1990—. Composer: Variations on a Theme of Handel, 1984, Mississippi River (for documentary film Miss. River Mus.), Memphis; rec. performances include Beauty and the Beast (with Frank DiGiacomo), 1977, Ballet Class with Karen Hebert, 1982. Recipient New Orleans Music and Drama Found. award, 1982, 3d prize Rupert BBC Symphony Found., London, 1982, 4th prize Leopold Stokowski Conducting Competition, 1986. Mem. Am. Symphony Orch. League (youth orch. div. bd. dirs. 1980—). Office: Marin Symphony Orch 4340 Redwood Hwy San Rafael CA 94903-2121*

SHELDON, MARK SCOTT, research engineer; b. Orange, Calif., May 19, 1959; s. Howard Lezurn and Vida Louise (Winegar) S.; m. Marti Reisman, Aug. 8, 1986. BS in Engring. and Applied Sci., Calif. Inst. Tech., 1981; MSME, Cornell U., 1985. Rsch. engr. Energy and Environ. Rsch. Corp., Irvine, Calif., 1985-91, sr. rsch. engr., 1991—. Mem. ASME (assoc.). Mem. Reorganized LDS Ch. Office: Energy and Environ Rsch Corp 18 Mason Irvine CA 92618-2706

SHELLAN, RONALD A., lawyer; b. Everett, Wash., Oct. 17, 1949; s. Henry and Sondra Ilsa (Hess) S.; m. Rebecca Rae, March 24, 1972; children: Elisabeth S., David W. BA magna cum laude, U. Wash., 1972; LLM, Willamette U., 1975. Bar: Oreg. 1975, U.S. Dist. Ct. Oreg. 1979, U.S. Tax Ct. 1982; CPA, Oreg. 1978. Law clk. Oreg. Tax Ct., Salem, 1976; tax sr. Coopers & Lybrand, Portland, 1977-79; atty. Sussman, Shank, Wapnick, Caplan & Stiles, Portland, 1979-91, Weiss, Jensen, Ellis & Botteri, Portland, 1991; ptnr. Miller, Nash, Wiener, Hager & Carlsen, Portland, 1991—. Author: G Reorganization Tax Free Acquisition of Financially Distressed Corporations; assoc. editor Willamette Law Jour., 1974-75. V.p. Nat. Multiple Sclerosis Soc. Oreg. Chapter, 1989-96, Robison Jewish Home, Portland, 1990-96. Mem. Oreg. State Bar (chair tax section), Oreg. Soc. CPA's (dir. 1978), Portland Tax Forum (pres.). Avocations: racquetball, skiing. Office: Miller Nash Wiener Hager Carlsen 111 SW 5th Ave Ste 3500 Portland OR 97204-3699*

SHELLEDY, JAMES EDWIN, III, editor; b. Spencer, Iowa, Nov. 11, 1942; s. James E. Jr. and Patricia L. (Cornwall) S.; m. Susan Emily Thomas, Mar. 7, 1986; 1 child, Ian Whittaker. BA, Gonzaga U., 1966. Reporter Spkesman-Rev., Spokane, Wash., 1963-66; tchr., coach Kootenai High Sch., Harrison, Idaho, 1967-71; reporter AP, Boise, Idaho, 1971-72; reporter, editor Lewiston (Idaho) Morning Tribune, 1973-80; editor, pub. Idahonian, Moscow, Idaho, 1981-91, Daily News, Pullman, Wash., 1981-90; editor The Salt Lake Tribune, Salt Lake City, 1991—; juror Pulitzer Prize Com., Columbia U., 1987-88; dir. Investigative Reporters and Editors, 1978-82; bd. dirs. New Directions for News, 1989-96, Newspaper Agy. Corp., 1994—; mem. AP audit com., N.Y.C., 1982-91. Dir. Idaho Parks Found., Boise, 1976-78, Idaho-Washington Symphony, Pullman, Wash., 1986-89; commr. Idaho Lottery Commn., Boise, 1990-91; adv. bd. Utah YWCA, 1992-97. Roman Catholic. Avocations: golf, sailing. Office: The Salt Lake Tribune 143 S Main St Ste 400 Salt Lake City UT 84111-1945*

SHELLHORN, RUTH PATRICIA, landscape architect; b. L.A., Sept. 21, 1909; d. Arthur Lemon and Lodema (Gould) S.; m. Harry Alexander Kueser, Nov. 21, 1940. Student dept. landscape architecture, Oreg. State Coll., 1927-30; grad. landscape architecture program, Cornell U. Coll. Architecture, 1933. Pvt. practice landscape architecture, various cities Calif., 1933—; exec. cons. landscape architect Bullocks Stores, Calif., 1945-78, Fashion Sqs. Shopping Ctrs., Calif., 1958-78, Marlborough Sch., L.A., 1968-93, El Camino Coll., Torrance, Calif., 1970-78, Harvard Sch., North Hollywood, Calif., 1974-90; cons. landscape architect, site planner Disneyland, Anaheim, Calif., 1955, U. Calif., Riverside Campus, 1956-64, numerous others, also numerous gardens and estates; landscape architect Torrance (Calif.) City Goals Com., 1969-70; cons. landscape architect City of Rolling Hills (Calif.) Community Assn., 1973-93. Contbr. articles to garden and profl. publs.; subject of Oct. 1967 issue Landscape Design & Constrn. mag. Named Woman of Year, Los Angeles Times, 1955, Woman of Year, South Pasadena-San Marino (Calif.) Bus. Profl. Women, 1955; recipient Charles Goodwin Sands medal, 1930-33, Landscape Architecture award of merit Calif. State Garden Clubs, 1984, 86, Horticulturist of the Yr. award So. Calif. Hort. Inst., numerous nat., state, local awards for excellence. Fellow Am. Soc. Landscape Architects (past pres. So. Calif. chpt.), Phi Kappa Phi, Kappa Kappa Gamma (Alumni Achievement award 1960). Projects subject of Oct. 1967 issue of Landscape Design and Constrn. Mag. Home and Office: 362 Camino De Las Colinas Redondo Beach CA 90277-6435

SHELTON, CONNIE LEE, writer, publisher; b. Albuquerque, Nov. 9, 1951; d. Harold E. and Marilyn June (Sanford) Tidenberg; m. Carl Daniel Shelton, July 24, 1993; children: Stephanie J. Quigley, Brandon S. March. Collections supr. Pitney Bowes, Albuquerque, 1971-72; ptnr. The March Co., Albuquerque, 1974-90; pres. Columbine Pub. Group In., Angel Fire, N. Mex., 1994—. Author: Deadly Gamble, 1995, Vacations Can Be Murder, 1996, Partnerships Can Kill, 1997, Small Towns Can Be Murder, 1998. Sec. Angel Fire (N. Mex.) Search and Rescue, 1995; sec., treas. Moreno Valley Arts Council, Angel Fire, 1995-96. Mem. Mystery Writers Am. (Rocky Mountain chpt., treas. 1998), Small Pub. Assn. North Am. (dir. 1998), Moreno Valley Writers Guild (bd. dirs., pres. 1995-96, first place short story award 1994), Sisters in Crime, Publishers Mktg. Assn. Office: Columbine Publishing Group Inc PO Box 456 Angel Fire NM 87710-0456

SHELTON, JERRELL WILSON, information company executive; b. Dickson, Tenn., Aug. 12, 1945; s. James Ellison and Helen Elizabeth (Spann) S.; m. Helen Hawk, June 3, 1995; 1 child, Julianne. B in Fin. and Bus. Adminstrn. cum laude, U. Tenn., 1970; MBA, Harvard U., 1973. Tooling inspector AVCO Aerostructures, Nashville, 1965-1967, v.p., COO, 1979-80; asst. to v.p. Aladdin Electronics, Nashville, 1970-71; mgr. prodn. ops. Berkline Corp., Morristown, Tenn., 1973-74; mgr. gen. mdse. Reed Wallcovering Div., Toronto, Ont., Can., 1974-76; gen. mgr. Wholesale Bldg. Products, Nashville, 1976-78; pres., chief exec. officer Tridon Internat., Nashville, 1980-83, Cherokee Forest Products, Paris, Tenn., 1983-84; pres., chief exec. officer Advantage Cos. Inc., Nashville, 1984-91, also bd. dirs.; pres., CEO Thomson Bus. Info., Stamford, Conn., 1991-96, Continental Graphics Holdings, Inc., L.A., 1996—; chmn. NDC Holdings II, Inc., Tustin, Calif., 1998—; bd. dirs. Continental Graphics Holdings Inc., Continental Graphics Corp. Mem. Pres.'s (Reagan) Coun., 1984-85, Amb. for Tenn., 1982-84, Jr. Achievement, Vanderbilt Grad. Sch. Bus. Adminstrn. Steering Com. Mem. Nat. Assn. Corp. Dirs., Am. Mgmt. Assn., U. Tenn. Alumni Assn., Harvard Alumni Assn., Nashville C. of C., Rotary. Republican. Episcopalian. Home: 980 Overton Lea Rd Nashville TN 37220-1503 Office: NDC Holdings II Inc 2552 Walnut Ave Tustin CA 92780-6935

SHELTON, JOEL EDWARD, clinical psychologist; b. Havre, Mont., Feb. 7, 1928; s. John Granvil and Roselma Fahy (Ervin) S.; m. Maybelle Platzek, Dec. 17, 1949; 1 child, Sophia. AB, Chico (Calif.) State Coll., 1951; MA, Ohio State U., 1958, PhD, 1960. Psychologist Sutter County Schs., Yuba City, Calif., 1952-53; tchr., vice prin. Lassen View Sch., Los Molinos, Calif., 1953-55; tchr. S.W. Licking Schs., Pataskala, Ohio, 1955-56; child psychologist Franklin Village, Grove City, Ohio, 1957; clin. psychologist Marion (Ohio) Health Clinic, 1958; intern Children's Mental Health Ctr., Columbus, Ohio, 1958-59; acting chief research psychologist Children's Psychiat. Hosp., Columbus, 1959-60; cons. to supt. schs. Sacramento County, Calif., 1960-63; mem. faculty Sacramento State Coll., 1961-69; clin. psychologist DeWitt State Hosp., Auburn, Calif., 1965; exec. dir. Children's Ctr. Sacramento, Citrus Heights, Calif., 1963-64, Gold Bar Ranch, Garden Valley, Calif., 1964-72; clin. psychologist El Dorado County Mental Health Ctr., Placerville, Calif., 1968-70, Butte County Mental Health Dept., Oroville, Calif., 1970-94; dir. dept. consultation, edn. and community services Butte County Mental Health Ctr., Chico, 1974-85, outpatient supr., 1986-94; mgmt. cons., 1972-94; advisor to pres. Protaca Industries, Chico, 1974-80; exec. sec. Protaca Agrl. Rsch., 1974-80; small bus. cons., 1983—; cons. on coll. scholarships and funding, 1991-92, computer cons., 1994—; freelance photographer, 1995—. With U.S. Army, 1946-47. Mem. APA, Western Psychol. Assn. Home: 1845 Veatch St Oroville CA 95965-4787

SHEN, EDWARD NIN-DA, cardiologist, educator; b. Hong Kong, July 3, 1950; came to U.S., 1979; s. Han-Ting and Yay-Wen (Tsu) S.; m. MaryRose Yung-Yung Wong, June 19, 1983; children: Erin Pey-Juan, Dylan Hua-Juan. BSc in Biochemistry with 1st class honors, McGill U., Montreal, Que., Can., 1972, MD, CM, 1976. Diplomate Am. Bd. Internal Medicine, Am. Bd. Cardiovascular Disease, Am. Bd. Clin. Cardiac Electrophysiology. Resident in internal medicine McGill U., 1976-79; cardiology fellow U.

Calif., San Francisco, 1979-81, electrophysiology fellow Cardiovascular Rsch. Inst., 1981-82, instr. in medicine Moffitt Hosp., 1982-83; assoc. chief cardiology Santa Clara Valley Med. Ctr., San Jose, Calif., 1983-85; clin. asst. prof. U. Calif., San Francisco, Stanford, 1983-85; dir. clin. electrophysiology Straub Clinic, Honolulu, 1986-93, chief of medicine, 1991-93; assoc. prof. medicine U. Hawaii, Honolulu, 1988-93, chief cardiology, 1993—, prof. medicine, 1994—; attending physician Moffit-Long Hosps., 1982-83; dir. electrocardiography, co-dir. noninvasive cardiac lab. Santa Clara Valley Med. Ctr., 1983-85; attending cardiologist Queen's Heart Inst., Straub Clinic & Hosp., St. Francis Hosp., Kuakini Hosp., 1993—; fellow Med. Rsch. Coun. Can., 1981-83; presenter in field. Contbr. over 90 articles to profl. jours. Bd. dirs. Am. Heart Assn., 1987-89, mem. peer rev. bd. for grant-in-aid applicants, 1987-89. Univ. scholar, 1968-75; recipient Charles E. Frosst prize and medal, Cushing Meml. prize Montreal Children's Hosp., John C. Milnor Profl. and Grey Champion Activities award Straub Found., 1990; Edward N. Shen scholar award in his honor U. Hawaii. Fellow ACP, Royal Coll. Physicians and Surgeons of Can. (specialist cert.), Am. Coll. Cardiology (gov. 1989-92), Am. Coll. Chest Physicians, Am. Heart Assn. Coun. Clin. Cardiology (Hawaii rep. 1991—); mem. N.Am. Soc. Pacing and Electrophysiology, Assn. Profs. of Cardiology, Mensa. Roman Catholic. Achievements include performance of first percutaneous transaluminal coronary angioplasty in Hong Kong, the first cases of automatic implantable cardiovertor-defibrillator, catheter ablation of arrhythmic circuits, coronary atherectomy, intracoronary stenting in Hawaii. Avocations: golf, classical guitar, Chinese poetry and literature. Office: 1380 Lusitana St Ste 701 Honolulu HI 96813-2443

SHEN, JUN, scientist; b. Wuhan, Hubei, People's Republic of China, Jan. 26, 1959; came to U.S., 1982; s. Yi Li Shen and Guo Ying Liu; m. Jennie Si, July 27, 1988. BS, South China Inst. Tech., Guangzhou, 1982; MS, Tex. Tech U., 1984; PhD, U. Notre Dame, 1990. Prin. staff scientist Motorola Inc., Tempe, Ariz., 1990-96; assoc. prof. dept. elec. engring. Ariz. State U., Tempe, 1996—; grad. teaching, rsch. asst. Tex. Tech U., Lubbock, 1982-84; grad. rsch. asst. U. Notre Dame, Ind., 1984-90. Inventor/co-inventor more than 20 U.S./fgn. patents; contbr. numerous articles to profl. jours. Mem. IEEE (sr.), Am. Phys. Soc. Avocations: volleyball, hiking.

SHEN, MASON MING-SUN, medical center administrator; b. Shanghai, Jiang Su, China, Mar. 30, 1945; came to U.S., 1969; s. John Kaung-Hao and Mai-Chu (Sun) S.; m. Nancy Hsia-Hsian Shieh, Aug. 7, 1976; children: Teresa Tao-Yee, Darren Tao-Ru. BS in Chemistry, Taiwan Normal U., 1963-67; MS in Chemistry, S.D. State U., 1971; PhD in Biochemistry, Cornell U., 1977; postgrad., U. Calif., Berkeley, 1977-79; MS in Chinese Medicine, China Acad., Taipei, Taiwan, 1982; OMD, San Francisco Coll Acupuncture, 1984; D Acupuncture Medicine (hon.), Asian Am. Acupuncture Coll., San Diego, 1985; MD (Medicina Alternativa), Internat. U., Colombo, Sri Lanka, 1988. Diplomate Nat. Commn. for Cert. of Acupuncturists; lic. acupuncturist, clin. chemist technologist, Calif. Rsch. assoc. Lawrence Livermore (Calif.) Lab., 1979-80; assoc. prof. Nat. Def. Med. Coll., Taipei, 1980-82; prof. Inst. of Chinese Medicine China Acad., Taipei, 1981-82, San Francisco Coll. Acupuncture, 1983-85, Acad. Chinese Culture and Health Scis., Oakland, Calif., 1985-86; pres. Florescent Inst. Traditional Chinese Medicine, Oakland, 1995—; adminstr. Am. Ea. Med. Inst., Pleasanton, 1993—; chmn. adminstrn. subcom., 1991-92, acupuncture com. State of Calif., 1988-92; dir. United Calif. Practitioners of Chinese Medicine, San Francisco, 1985-98; chief acupuncturist Acupuncture Ctr. Pleasanton, 1993—, Acupuncture Ctr. Tracy, 1995-98, Ea. Med. Ctr. Danville, Calif., 1996— ; v.p. Modern Medicine, Hayward, Calif., 1997-98, U. Health Sci., Honolulu, 1997—; adminstrv. officer Rsch. Inst. Chinese Medicine, San Francisco, 1998—; bd. dirs. Am. Inst. Acupuncture Orthopedics and Traumatology, San Francisco. Contbr. over 50 articles to profl. jours. Mem. Danville Rep. Com., 1988-93; bd. dirs. Asian Rep. Assembly, 1989-98; mem. presdnl. adv. com. Republican Presdl. Task Force, 1992-99; mem. chmn's. adv. bd. Republican Nat. Com., 1993—; pres. Internat. Congress Chinese Medicine, Danville, 1987—. Recipient Nat. Rsch. Svc. award NIH, 1977, Presdl. Order of Merit, Pres. of the U.S., 1991. Mem. AAAOM (pres.), N.Y. Acad. Scis., Calif. Cert. Acupuncturists Assn. (bd. dirs. 1984-88, pres. 1984-85, mem. polit. action com. 1995—), Acupuncture Assn. Am. (bd. dirs. 1986-90, v.p. 1987-89), Am. Assn. Acupuncture and Oriental Medicine (bd. dirs. 1987-92, pres. 1989-90, Acupuncturist of Yr. 1998), Nat. Acupuncture Detoxification Assn. (cons. 1987—), Am. Assn. Traditional Chinese Medicine (exec. dir. 1997—), Presdl. Round Table (presdl. adv. com.), Hong Kong and Kowloon Chinese Med. Assn. (hon. life pres. 1985), Internat. Congress Chinese Medicine (pres. 1997—), United Calif. Practitioners Chinese Medicine (bd. dirs. 1995—),. Republican. Avocations: travel, horse back riding, rifles. Home: 3240 Touriga Dr Pleasanton CA 94566-6966 Office: Eastern Med Ctr 450 Old Santa Rita Rd Ste D Pleasanton CA 94588-3466 also: 400 El Cerro Blvd Ste 105 Danville CA 94526-1731

SHEN, YONGRONG, research scientist; b. Hefei, Anhui, China, Sept. 23, 1952; s. Guangbing Shen and Shihua Hu; m. Liyun Cao, May 14, 1980; 1 child, Tao. MS, Chanhchun Inst. Physics, Chinese Acad. Scis., People's Republic of China, 1983, U. Paderborn (Nordrhein-Westfalen, Germany), 1990; PhD, U. Paderborn (Nordrhein-Westfalen, Germany), 1994. Rsch. asst. Changchun (Jilin, People's Republic of China) Inst. Physics, Chinese Acad. Scis., 1977-83, rsch. assoc., 1983-88; rsch. asst. U. Paderborn (Nordrhein-Westfalen, Germany), 1988-94, rsch. assoc., 1994-95; rsch. assoc. U. Wis., Madison, 1995-97; rsch. assoc. Wash. State U., Pullman, 1998, sr. rsch. assoc., 1998—; vis. rsch. advisor Lab. Excited State Processes, Chinese Acad. Scis., Changchun, Jilin, 1995-96; referee Jour. Physics, 1997—. Mem. Am. Soc. Physics, German Soc. Physics. E-mail: yrshen@wsu.edu. Home: 1650 NE Valley Rd Pullman WA 99163-4373 Office: Wash State U Fulmer Hall Pullman WA 99164

SHENKER, ARDEN EARL, lawyer; b. Portland, Oreg., Oct. 28, 1938; s. William S. and Elizabeth (Myerson) S.; m. Lois M. Sussman, July, 3, 1960; children: Joel Isaac, Diana Beth, Jordan Benjamin. BA, Stanford U., 1959; JD, Yale U., 1962. Bar: Oreg. 1962, U.S. Dist. Ct. Oreg., 1962, U.S. Ct. Appeals (9th cir.) 1965, U.S. Supreme Ct. 1967. Law clk. to chief judge Gus J. Solomon U.S. Dist. Ct. Oreg., Portland, 1962; assoc. Tooze Shenker Duden Creamer Frank & Hutchinson and predecessor firm, Portland, 1963-65; ptnr. Tooze Shenker Duden Creamer Frank and Hutchison, Portland, 1966-96; atty. pvt. practice, Portland, 1996—; fed. mediator; adj. prof. law Lewis and Clark Coll., 1982—; mem. Oreg. Bd. Bar Examiners, 1968-71, Bd. Rev. Examiners, 1981-83; chair Oreg. del. 9th Cir. Jud. Conf. Bd. dirs. Coun. Jewish Fedns., 1975-93, Hebrew Imigrant Aid Soc., 1989—; mem. exec. com. World Coun. on Soviet Jewry, 1989-92; chair Nat. Jewish Comm. Rels. Adv. Coun., 1989-92; Presdl. appointee M.L. King, Jr., Nat. Commn. Recipient Young Leadership award Jewish Fedn. Portland, 1967, Torch of Liberty award Anti-Defamation League, N.Y.C., 1977, Disting. Svc. award U. Judaism, L.A., 1981. Mem. Inns of Ct. (founding master, pres. 1993-94), Am. Leadership Forum (founder), Order of Coif, Phi Beta Kappa. Republican. Office: 1 World Trade Ctr 121 SW Salmon St Ste 1480 Portland OR 97204-2925

SHEP, ROBERT LEE, editor, publisher, textile book researcher; b. Los Angeles, Feb. 27, 1933; s. Milton and Ruth (Miller) Polen S. BA, U. Calif.-Berkeley, 1955; student Royal Acad. Dramatic Art, London, 1956; BFgn Trade, Am. Inst. Fgn. Trade, 1960. Asst. area mgr. fgn. dept. Max Factor, Hollywood, Calif., 1960-65; editor, pub. The Textile Booklist, Lopez Island, Wash., 1980-84; free-lance writer, book reviewer, library appraiser, book repairer; sponsor Triannual R. L. Shep Symposium, L.A. County Mus. Art. Author: Cleaning and Repairing Books, 1980, Cleaning and Care for Books, 1983, Bhutan - Fibre Forum, 1984, Civil War Gentleman, 1994, Late Victorian Women's Tailoring, 1997, Regency Etiquette, 1997; co-author: (annotated edit.) The Costume or Annals of Fashion, 1986, Dress and Cloak Cutter: Womens Costume 1877-1882, 1987; editor: The Handbook of Practical Cutting, 2d rev. edit., 1986, RAGS: Quarterly Revs. Cosume, Clothing & Ethnic Textile Books; pub. Ladies' Guide to Needle Work, 1986, Edwardian Ladies' Tailoring, 1990. Art of Cutting and History of English Costume, 1987; editor, pub. Tailoring of the Belle Epoque, 1991, Late Georgian Costume, 1991, Civil War Cooking, 1992, Art in Dress, 1993, Minister's Complete Guide to Practical Cutting, 1993, Freaks of Fashion, 1993; pub. Civil War Era Etiquette, 1988, Ladies Self Instr., 1988; mem. editl. rev. bd. The Cutter's Rsch. Jour. Bd. dirs. [illegible] Pacific Textiles. Mem. Costume Soc. (London), Costume Soc. Am. (bd. dirs. 1985-87), Costume Soc. Ont., Mendocino County HIV Consortium (mem. steering com.), Australian Costume and Textile Soc., U.S. Inst. Theatre Tech.

SHEPARD, ROBERT CARLTON, English language educator; b. Akron, Ohio, Dec. 20, 1933; s. Robert and Mildred Lucille (Stewart) S.; m. Marjorie Alma Mackey, June 9, 1956; children: Robert Lincoln, Donald Ward. BA, U. Oreg., 1970, MA, 1971; postgrad., England, 1979, 1991. Prof. English Southwestern Oreg. C.C., Coos Bay, 1971-94, chair divsn. English, 1976-78, prof. emeritus, 1994—; liaison Oreg. Com. for Humanities, 1985-86; judge statewide writing contests Nat. Coun. Tchrs. English, Urbana, Ill., 1987-88; founder Willamette Valley Vineyards, Turner, Oreg., 1991; co-founder Nor 'Wester Brewing Co., Portland, 1993, Breweries Across Am., Portland, 1994. Author, photographer, producer: (multi-image show) Christmas Fiestas of Oaxaca (Mexico), 1985; editl. cons., 1996—; developer ednl. software, 1993—. With USMCR, 1954-58. Grad. Teaching fellow U. Oreg., 1970-71. Democrat. Avocations: bicycling, photography, music appreciation, world travel. Home: 3280 Sheridan Ave North Bend OR 97459-3043

SHEPARD, ROBERT HENRY, retired oil company executive; b. N.Y.C., Dec. 6, 1926; s. Henry Joseph and Elfrieda (Allerhand) S.; m. Gloria June Caraway, July 16, 1950; children: Steven Douglas, Roger Neal, John Kirby. Cert. of Engring., Cornell U., 1944; BSc, Bklyn. Coll., 1949; Diploma Basico, U. Salamanca, Spain, 1995. Geologist U.S. Geol. Survey, Roswell, N.Mex., 1949, So. Petroleum Exploration/Malco, Roswell, 1950; field geologist Superior Oil Co., Midland, Tex., 1950-51; divsn. geologist Standard Oil Co. Tx., Houston, 1951-69; exploration mgr. Chevron Overseas Petroleum, Madrid, 1969-73; sr. staff geologist Chevron Overseas Petroleum, San Francisco, 1973-82; petroleum ops. mgr. Chevron Overseas Petroleum, Zagreb, Yugoslavia, 1982-89. Pres. sch. bd. Am. Sch. of Madrid, Spain, 1972-73. With USAF, 1943-44. Fellow Geol. Soc. Am.; mem. Am. Assn. Petroleum Geologists, Am. Geophys. Union, No. Calif. Geol. Soc., Soc. Exploration Geophysicists, Quintocentenario Toastmasters (pres. 1994-98). Methodist. Avocations: Spanish, music, art. Home: 2 Blanket Flower Cir Santa Fe NM 87501-8512

SHEPERSKY, MIMI, probate examiner; b. Portland, Oreg., Oct. 12, 1964; d. Sigman Roe and June Kim; m. Douglas M. Shepersky; children: Matthew Aaron, Katherine Ann, Grace Lee. Grad. high sch., Rancho Palos Verdes, Calif.; cert. legal asst. with honors, U. San Diego, 1989. Paralegal, office mgr. Law Offices Thomas Kagy, L.A., 1983, Law Office Tong S. Suhr, L.A., 1983-84; head litigation sect., paralegal def. litigation Wells Fargo Bank, N.A., L.A., 1984-85; paralegal bankruptcy and fed. litigation Pachulski, Stang & Ziehl, P.C., L.A., 1985-88; paralegal, office mgr. Law Offices Donald H. Glaser, San Diego, 1989—; paralegal probate, computer cons. Village Law Ctr., San Marcos, 1990-91; paralegal, probate, trust adminstrn. Law Offices Arthur S. Brown, Carlsbad, Calif., 1992-93, Higgs, Fletcher & Mack, San Diego, 1993-94. Editor newsletter Noteworthy, 1984-85. Sec.-elect Korean Am. Coalition, L.A., 1983-84; counselor Korean Am. Youth Found., 1974-82. Mem. San Diego Assn. Legal Assts., Nat. Notary Assn. (founding co-chair North County com.). Republican. Presbyterian. Avocations: piano, ch. vol., artist, photography, gutiar. Home: 1503 Sundale Rd El Cajon CA 92019-3725 Office: Superior Ct County San Diego 201 W Broadway San Diego CA 92101

SHEPHERD, JOHN MICHAEL, lawyer; b. St. Louis, Aug. 1, 1955; s. John Calvin and Bernice Florence (Hines) S.; m. Deborah Tremaine Fenton, Oct. 10, 1981; children: Elizabeth White, Katherine Tremaine. BA, Stanford U., 1977; JD, U. Mich., 1980. Bar: Calif. 1981, D.C. 1991, U.S. Dist. Ct. (no. dist.) Calif. 1981. Assoc. McCutchen, Doyle, Brown & Enersen, San Francisco, 1980-82; spl. asst. to asst. atty. gen. U.S. Dept. Justice, Washington, 1982-84, dep. asst. atty gen., 1984-86; assoc. counsel to The President The White House, Washington, 1986-87; sr. dep. comptroller of the currency Dept. Treasury, Washington, 1987-91; spl. counsel Sullivan & Cromwell, N.Y.C., 1991-93, Washington, 1993; exec. v.p., gen. counsel Shawmut Nat. Corp., Boston, 1993-95; ptnr. Brobeck, Phleger & Harrison LLP, San Francisco, 1995—; chmn. fin. svcs. and insolvency group, 1996-97, mem. policy com., 1997—. Contbr. articles to profl. jours. Asst. dir. policy Reagan-Bush Presdl. Transition Team, Washington, 1980-81; bd. dirs. Reagan Dep. Asst. Secs., Washington, 1985-90; trustee New Eng. Aquarium, 1994-96. Named one of Outstanding Young Men Am., U.S. Jaycees, 1984; Wardack Research fellow Washington U., 1976. Mem. ABA (chmn. fin. markets and ins. com., antitrust law sect. 1992-95, mem. banking law com. 1983—, vice chair 1998—, chmn. bank holding co. acquisitions subcom. 1995-98, bus. law sect., standing com. on law and nat. security 1984-96), D.C. Bar Assn., New Eng. Legal Found. (bd. dirs. 1994-96), Pacific Coun. Internat. Policy, Chevy Chase Club, Univ. Club, Met. Club, Olympic Club. Home: 2699 Filbert St San Francisco CA 94123-3215 Office: Brobeck Phleger & Harrison LLP 1 Market St San Francisco CA 94105-1420

SHEPHERD, KAREN, finance executive, former congresswoman; b. Silver City, N.Mex., July 5, 1940; m. Vincent P. Shepherd. BA, U. Utah, 1962; MA, Brigham Young U., 1963. Former instr. Brigham Young U., Am. U., Cairo; former pres. Webster Pub. Co.; former adminstr. David Eccles Sch. Bus., U. Utah; former dir. Salt Lake County Social Svcs., Utah; former dir. continuing edn. Westminster Coll.; former mem. Utah Senate; mem. 103d Congress from 2d Utah dist., Washington, 1993-95, Nat. Common Cause Governing Bd., Washington, 1995—; exec. dir., U.S. rep. European Bank for Reconstruction Devel., 1996—; founding mem. Utah Women's Polit. Caucus, Project 2000; mem. Internat. Delegation to Monitor Elections in West Bank and Gaza, Israel. Former mem. United Way, Pvt. Industry Coun.; former mem. adv. bd. U.S. West Grad. Sch. Social Work; trustee Westminster Coll. Recipient Women in Bus. award U.S. Small Bus. Assn., Woman of Achievement award, Pathfinder award, YWCA Leadership award, 1st place award Nat. Assn. Journalists, Disting. Alumni award U. Utah Coll. Humanities. Fellow Inst. Politics Kennedy Sch Govt., Internat. Women's Forum; Salt Lake Area C. of C. (pub. rels. com.). Home: PO Box 1049 Salt Lake City UT 84110-1049 Office: 21 G St Salt Lake City UT 84103-2949

SHEPPARD, JACK W., retired career officer; b. Parkersburg, W.Va., Aug. 8, 1931; s. James Lee and Audrey Irene (Heiney) S.; m. Norma Ann Stutler, Sept. 4, 1953; children—Bradley, Gregory. BAC, U. Akron, Ohio, 1955; MA in Pub. Adminstrn., George Washington U., 1965. Commd. lt. U.S. Air Force, 1955, advanced through grades to maj. gen.; vice comdr. 60 Mil. Airlift Wing, USAF, Travis AFB, Calif., 1977-79; comdr. 1606 Air Base Wing, USAF, Kirtland AFB, N.Mex., 1979-81; dir. internat. staff Inter Am. Def. Bd., USAF, Washington, 1981-82; dep. chief staff for personnel USAF Mil. Airlift Command, Scott AFB, Ill., 1982-83, chief of staff, 1983-85; comdr. Twenty First Air Force, McGuire AFB, N.J., 1985-87; asst. dep. chief staff programs and resources Hdqrs. USAF, Washington, 1987-88, ret., 1988. Mem. Kirtland partnership com., pres. Albuquerque Armed Forces Adv. Assn. Mem. Order of Daedalians, Air Force Assn., Airlift Assn., Armed Forces Adv. Assn., Theta Chi. Presbyterian. Home: PO Box 908 21 Beaver Ln Cedar Crest NM 87008-9433

SHERBERT, SHARON DEBRA, financial services executive; b. Bklyn., Aug. 18, 1953; d. Joseph George and Leah (Katzman) Goldstein; m. Robert Fisher, Oct. 20, 1973 (div. Nov. 1981); 1 child, Meredith Audra Fisher; m. Michael Sherbert, Apr. 4, 1982; 1 child, Jared Alan. Grad. high sch., Bklyn. Cert. fin. planner; registered fin. cons. Real estate agent Century 21 R.E., Sepulveda, Calif., 1976-80; life ins. agt. Prudential Life Ins., North Hollywood, Calif., 1980-82; sr. v.p. Profl. Planning, Encino, Calif., 1982-90; exec. v.p. Comprehensive Fin. Svcs., Burbank, Calif., 1992—; columnist on Internet Web site Women in Tech., Inc., Van Nuys, Calif., 1996—. Co-host: (TV show) You and Your Money, 1993—. Mem. NAFE, Nat. Assn. Women Bus. Owners, Internat. Assn. for Fin. Planners, Inst. Cert. Fin. Planners, Zonta Club of Santa Clarita Valley (sunshine sec. 1992-93). Office: Comprehensive Fin Svcs 3811 W Burbank Blvd Burbank CA 91505-2116

SHERICK, MICHAEL JACK, publisher, editor; b. L.A., May 8, 1957; s. Jack Sherick and Joanne Elaine [illegible]; 1 son, Henry Burr. BA in Lit., U. Calif., Santa Barbara, 1981. Publisher Table Talk Press, Santa Barbara, Calif., 1984-95; publisher, editor Times Change Press, Ojai, Sebastopol, Calif., 1996—. Office: Times Change Press 8453 Blackney Rd Sebastopol CA 95472-4608

SHERIDAN, GEORGE EDWARD, manufacturing company executive; b. Emporia, Kans., July 4, 1915; s. George and Josephine Frances (Benson) S.; m. Edith Joye Card, July 4, 1940; 1 dau., Phyllis Lynne. Liberal arts student Coll. of Emporia, 1934-36; engring. student Nat. Schs., 1936-37, Los Angeles City Jr. Coll., 1937-38. Cert. mfg. engr.; registered profl. engr., Calif. With Douglas Aircraft, Santa Monica, Calif., 1939-40, Northrop Aircraft, Hawthorn, Calif., 1940-45; pres. Sheridan Products, Inc., Inglewood, Calif., 1940-87; ret., 1987. Active, YMCA, Inglewood, 1960—. Mem. Soc. Mfg. Engrs. (life, award 1979-80, Industrialist of Yr. 1982 past chmn.), U.S. Power Squadron, Am. Ordnance Def. Preparedness Assn., Nat. Rifle Assn., Smithsonian Assos., Cutting Tool Mfg. Assn., Nat. Fedn. Ind. Bus., Mech. Bank Collectors Am., Antique Toy Collectors Am. Republican. Quaker. Patentee double edge scraper. Home: 27692 Via Rodrigo Mission Viejo CA 92692-2019

SHERIDAN, GUY MITCHELL, retired journalist; b. Butte, Mont., July 29, 1911; s. Guy Emerson and Anna Irene (LeSage) S.; m. Jacqueline Chabane, July 31, 1946. BA in Journalism, U. Mont., 1933. Reporter Flathead Monitor, Kalispell, Mont., 1936, Butte Daily Post, 1936-42; mem. staff copy desk Sacramento Bee, 1946-60, editor, 1960-75, asst. to mng. editor, 1975-76, ret., 1976. Bd. dirs. Cmty. Concert Assn., Sacramento, 1989—. Capt. inf., U.S. Army, 1942-46. Mem. Soc. Profl. Journalists, Rio Oro Racquet Club. Republican. Roman Catholic. Avocations: photography, tennis.

SHERIDAN, JANETTE, management specialist; b. Euclid, Ohio, Apr. 17, 1962; d. John Edward and Bernice Elizabeth (Reschke) S. Grad., West Covina (Calif.) H.S., 1979. Publicity dept. Columbia Records, L.A., 1979, Elektra Records, L.A., 1979-80; assoc. booking agt. ICM, L.A., 1980-85; mktg. mgr. Direct Mgmt., L.A., 1985-89; personal mgr. L.A., 1989-91; with legal dept. Largo Pictures, L.A., 1989-91, Tri-Star Pictures, L.A., 1989-91; personal mgr. Direct Mgmt., L.A., 1992—. Office: Direct Mgmt 947 N LaCrenega Los Angeles CA 90068

SHERK, KENNETH JOHN, lawyer; b. Ida Grove, Iowa, Feb. 27, 1933; s. John and Dorothy (Myers) Sherk; m. Virginia Kay Taylor, June 28, 1958; children: Karin Fulton, Katrina, Keith, Kyle. BSC, U. Iowa, 1955; JD, George Washington U., 1961. Bar: Ariz. 1962, U.S. Dist. Ct. Ariz. 1962, U.S. Ct. Appeals (9th cir.) 1966, U.S. Supreme Ct. 1974. Assoc. Moore & Romley, Phoenix, 1962-67, ptnr., 1967-79; ptnr. Romley & Sherk, Phoenix, 1979-85; dir. Fennemore Craig, Phoenix, 1985—. 1st lt. U.S. Army, 1955-58, Korea. Recipient Profl. Achievement Svcs. award George Washington Law Assn., 1986, Ariz. Judges Assn., 1989, Disting. Svc. award Phoenix Assn. Def. Counsel, 1990; named Mem. of Yr. State Bar of Ariz., 1994. Fellow Am. Coll. Trial Lawyers, Am. Acad. Appellate Lawyers, Am. Bar Found., Ariz. Bar Found.; mem. ABA (ho. of dels. 1990-93), Ariz. Bar Assn. (pres. 1985-86), Maricopa County Bar Assn. (pres. 1978-79). Republican. Congregational. Avocations: fishing, hiking, bicycling. Home: 1554 W Las Palmaritas Dr Phoenix AZ 85021-5429 Office: Fennemore Craig 3003 N Central Ave Ste 2600 Phoenix AZ 85012-2913

SHERLIN, JERRY MICHAEL, retired hydro meteorological technician; b. Chattanooga, Oct. 8, 1938; s. Chester Wallace and Eva Pearl (Scruggs) S; m. Susan Loxie Doenhoefer, July 22, 1993. BGS, U. Nebr., 1971; MA, Ball State U., 1976. Advanced through grades to master sgt. USAF, 1959, ret., 1981; rsch. asst. Sacramento Peak Solar Observatory, Sunspot, N.Mex., 1981-82; meteorological technician Nat. Weather Svc., Sioux City, Iowa, 1982-89; coop. program mgr. Nat. Weather Svc., Denver, 1989-94, hydrometeorological technician, 1994-99. Co-editor: Observe-and-Understand the Sun, 1976; contbr. articles to profl. jours. Vol. Denver Mus. of Natural History, Denver, 1990—; chmn. Astronomical League 50th Ann. Nat. Conv., Copper Mountain, Colo., 1997. Recipient G. R. Wright Svc. award Astronomical League, 1992; decorated Air Force Commendation medal with 2 oak leaf clusters, 1974, 79, 81. Fellow Royal Astron. Soc.; mem. AAAS, Am. Astron. Soc., Am. Assn. Variable Star Observers, Astron. Soc. of the Pacific. Home: 17002 E Prentice Dr Aurora CO 80015-2412 Office: Nat Weather Svc 10230 Smith Rd Denver CO 80239-3238

SHERMAN, DONALD H., civil engineer; b. Jackson, Wyo., May 14, 1932; s. Howard M. and Dorothy (Turner) S.; children: D. John, Cynthia Lynn Pierceall, Richard L., Sheila L. Bufmack; m. Patricia A. Hoffman, June 26, 1993. AA in Engring., Fullerton Jr. Coll., 1953; diploma in surveying and mapping, I.C.S., 1955; BS in Geology, U. Wyo., 1960, BS in Civil Engring., 1968. Registered profl. engr., Wyo., Colo. Geophysicist Texaco Geophysical, Casper, Wyo. and Billings, Mont., 1960-63; surveyor Wyo. Hwy. Dept., Jackson, 1963-64; engring. geologist Wyo. Hwy. Dept., Cheyenne, 1964-66, hydraulics engr., 1968-72; civil engr., rotation trainee U.S. Bur. Reclamation, Denver, 1972-73; civil engr. D.M.J.M.-Phillips-Reister-Haley, Denver, 1973-79, Stearns Roger, Inc., Glendale, Colo., 1980-82, Centennial Engring., Arvada, Colo., 1983-85; civil engr. land devel. York Assocs., Denver, 1986-87; civil engr. City of Colo. Springs, 1987—; owner Valley View Trailer Park, Jackson, 1965-96; advisor to U.S. Senator Clifford Hansen on Black 14 incident, 1969. Recipient Presdl. Legion of Merit Rep. Nat. Com., 1992-96, Presdl. Commn., Rep. Nat. Com., 1992-96, Cert. of Award Presdl. Adv. Commn., 1991-92, 94, 96. Mem. Citizens Against Govt. Waste (charter), Concerned Women of Am., Nat. Right to Life, Nat. Republican Congressional Com., Nat. Republican Senatorial Com., Reublican Presdl. Task Force, Rebublican Presdl. Trust, Nat. Taxpayers Union, Am. Conservation Union. Republican. Avocations: photography, hiking, writing government leaders, genealogy. Home: 131 N Roosevelt St Colorado Springs CO 80909-6547 Office: City Engring 30 S Nevada Ave Rm 403 Colorado Springs CO 80903-1825

SHERMAN, ERIC, director, writer, educator; b. Santa Monica, Calif., June 29, 1947; s. Vincent and Hedda (Comorau) S.; m. Eugenia Blackiston Dillard, Apr. 1, 1978; children: Cosimo, Rocky. BA cum laude, Yale U., 1968. Film producer, dir., writer, photographer and editor; films include: Charles Lloyd-Journey Within, 1968; Paul Weiss-a Philosopher in Process, 1972; Waltz, 1980; Inside Out, 1982; Measure of America, 1983; Michael Reagan's Assault on Great Lakes, 1983, Futures, 1990 (Peabody Broadcast award 1990); represented in film festivals N.Y.C. Cine Golden Eagle, Melbourne, Australia, Bilbao, Spain, others; books include: (with others) The Director's Event, 1970; Directing the Film, 1976; Frame by Frame, 1987, Selling Your Film, 1990; pres. Film Transform; film tchr. Art Ctr. Coll. Design, Cal Arts, Pepperdine U., UCLA; guest lectr. Yale, Calif. Inst. Tech., U. So. Calif.; Andrew Mellon lectr. on arts Calif. Inst. Tech., 1977; chief cons. (motion picture industry) Gallup Orgn.; contbr. numerous articles to film publs. and distbn. catalogues, book dedication; works include three oral histories for Am. Film Inst. under Louis B. Mayer Found. grant. Trustee Am. Cinematheque; bd. dir. Film Forum. Mem. Soc. Motion Picture and TV Engrs. (asso.), Assn. Ind. Video and Filmmakers, Univ. Film Assn., Assn. Visual Communicators, Nat. Alliance Media Arts Ctrs. Home and Office: 4421 Dundee Dr Los Angeles CA 90027-1211

SHERMAN, FRIEDA FRANCES, writer; b. N.Y.C., Oct. 21, 1929; d. Benjamin and Anna (Brown) Jeffe; m. Alan Morton Sherman, Feb. 21, 1952; children: Steven, Daniel, Elizabeth, Richard. BA, Hunter Coll., 1951. Market researcher Am. Broadcasting Co., N.Y.C., 1953-55, Am. Inst. Mgmt., N.Y.C., 1955-56; tchr. dance Palo Alto (Calif.), 1960-70; co-founder Workshop Unltd., Palo Alto, 1970-74; dir. client support Prognostics, Palo Alto, 1982-85; dance therapist pvt. practice, Palo Alto, 1975-90; cons. Market Intelligence Rsch., Palo Alto, 1985. Author of poems and short stories. Coord. cmty. outreach Lively Arts Stanford (Calif.) U., 1990-92; bd. dirs. SPCA, Santa Cruz, Calif., 1994; judge Nat. Poetry Contest, Santa Cruz, 1994. Mem. Nat. Writers Union, Phi Beta Kappa. Avocations: dancing, hiking, music. Home: 900 Glen Canyon Rd Santa Cruz CA 95060-1619

SHERMAN, MARTIN PETER, lawyer; b. N.Y.C., May 2, 1940; m. Susan Randall, Feb. 16, 1969; children: David, Timothy, Peter. BA, UCLA, 1961; JD, U. Chgo., 1964; LLM, U. So. Calif., 1969. Bar: Calif. 1965, Pa. 1972. Law clk. L.A. Superior Ct., 1964-65; dep. county counsel L.A. County, 1965-66; [illegible] Ventura, San Francisco and L.A., 1966-69; counsel Atlantic Richfield Co., L.A. and Phila., 1969-72; asst. gen. counsel Ampex Corp., Redwood City, Calif., 1973-87, corp. counsel Amgen, Inc., Thousand Oaks, Calif., 1987-88; sr. atty., Intel Corp., Santa Clara, 1988-95; spl. counsel Tomlinson, Zisko, Morosoli & Maser, Palo Alto, Calif.,

1995-97. Mem. ABA. Contbr. articles to law jour. Office: 1131 Stanley Way Palo Alto CA 94303-2915

SHERMAN, RANDOLPH, plastic and reconstructive surgeon, educator; b. St. Louis, May 27, 1951; s. Leon and Pearl (Lichtenfeld) S.; m. Sandra Lee Wackerman, May 3, 1992; 1 child, Max Lassen. BA, U. Rochester, 1973; MD, U. Mo., 1977. Diplomate Am. Bd. Surgery, Am. Bd. Plastic Surgery (cert. added qualification in hand surgery 1989). Intern in gen. medicine U. Wis., Madison, 1978; intern in surgery U. Calif., San Francisco, 1978-79, resident in surgery, 1979-81; resident in surgery SUNY, Syracuse, 1981-83; fellow in plastic and reconstructive surgery U. So. Calif., 1983-85; asst. prof. surger and orthopedics U. So. Calif., L.A., 1985-91, assoc. prof. clin. surgery and orthopaedics, 1991-92, assoc. prof. clin. surgery, orthopaedics and neurol. surgery, 1992-96, chmn. divsn. plastic and reconstructive surgery, 1994—, prof. clin. surgery, orthopaedics and neurol. surgery, 1996—; mem. cons. staff City of Hope Nat. Med. Ctr., Duarte, Calif., 1985-91, 94—, St. John's Hosp., Santa Monica, 1989—; mem. staff, med. dir. Microsurg. Ctr. Hosp. Good Samaritan, L.A., 1985-93; mem. plastic and reconstructive surgery staff Kenneth Norris Jr. Cancer Hosp., L.A., 1985—, L.A. County/U. So. Calif. Med. Ctr., L.A., 1985—; mem. staff St. Vincent Med. Ctr., L.A., 1986-92, Orthop. Hosp., L.A., 1986—; Shriner's Hosp. for Crippled Children, L.A., 1987-92, Children's Hosp. L.A., 1987—, Cedars Sinai Med. Ctr., L.A., 1987—, Estelle Doheny Eye Hosp., L.A., 1994—, numerous others; chief plastic and reconstructive surgery divsn. U. So. Calif. U. Hosp., L.A., 1991—; lectr., rschr. in field. Editor: Orthopedic Clinics, 1993; assoc. editor Surg. Rounds, 1989—, Jour. Hand Surgery, 1992-96, Am. Jour. Reconstructive Microsurgery, 1995—; contbr. articles to profl. jours., chpts. to books. Founder L.A. chpt. Operation Smile Internat., 1993—. Recipient L.A. Humanitarian award Calif. Hosp., 1994; Microsurg. Devel. grantee Hosp. Good Samaritan, 1987-92, U. So. Calif. U. Hosp., 1992—; grantee Searle R&D, 1995-97, Cohesion Corp., 1997. Fellow ACS, Am. Assn. Plastic Surgeons, Am. Assn. Hand Surgeons (bd. dirs. 1991-95), Am. Soc. Hand Surgery, Am. Soc. Reconstructive Microsurgery, Calif. Soc. Plastic Surgery; mem. Am. Soc. Plastic and Reconstructive Surgery, Am. Soc. Peripheral Nerve, Internat. Soc. Reconstructive Microsurgery, Calif. Med. Assn., Calif. Soc. Plastic Surgery, Assn. Acad. Chmn. Plastic Surgery, Plastic Surgery Rsch. Coun., Musculoskeletal Infection Soc., Undersea Med. Soc., Flying Physicians Assn., Wound Healing Soc. Avocations: flying, mountain climbing, scuba diving, jazz piano, gardening. Office: U So Calif Divsn Plastic Surgery 1450 San Pablo St Los Angeles CA 90033-1042*

SHERMAN, RICHARD S., record and video company executive; b. N.Y.C.; s. Milton H. and Sally (Seymour) S.; m. Vivian Cacciatori (div.); m. Linda Jordan; children: Andrea Marie, Robert Anthony. BS in Econs., L.I. U., 1948; LLB, NYU, 1950; LLM, N.Y. Law Sch., 1951. Nat. sales rep., product mgr. Mercury Records Corp., Chgo., 1962-67; nat. sales mgr. Warner Bros. Records, Los Angeles, 1967-71; product mgr., sales mgr. Motown Record Corp., Los Angeles, 1971-74; exec. v.p. sales Hollywood, Calif., 1981-85; dir. West Coast Ops. Bell Records, Los Angeles, 1974-75; sr. v.p. sales, distbn. exec. Casablanca Records, Los Angeles, 1975-81; sr. v.p. sales, distbn., mktg. Motown Records Corp., Los Angeles, 1981-85; sr. v.p. sales, distbn. exec. JCI, Agoura Hills, Calif., 1985-87; pres. August Moon Prodns., 1987—. Mem. NARAS. Home: 6461 Zuma View Pl Malibu CA 90265-4470

SHERMAN, ROBERT B(ERNARD), composer, lyricist, screenwriter; b. N.Y.C., Dec. 19, 1925; s. Al and Rosa (Dancis) S.; student UCLA, 1943; BA, Bard Coll., 1949; MusD (hon.) Lincoln U., 1990; m. Joyce Ruth Sasner, Sept. 27, 1953; children: Laurie Shane, Jeffrey Craig, Andrea Tracy, Robert Jason. Popular songwriter, 1950-60, including Tall Paul, Pineapple Princess, You're Sixteen (Gold Record); songwriter Walt Disney Prodns., Beverly Hills, Calif., 1960-68, for 29 films including The Parent Trap, 1961, Summer Magic, 1963, Mary Poppins, 1964, That Darn Cat, 1965, Winnie The Pooh, 1965, Jungle Book, 1967, Bedknobs and Broomsticks, 1971; co-composer song It's A Small World, theme of Disneyland and Walt Disney World, Fla.; composer, lyricist United Artists, Beverly Hills, 1969—, songs for film Chitty, Chitty, Bang, Bang, 1969, Snoopy, Come Home!, 1972; song scores Charlotte's Web, 1972, Cabbage Patch Kids, 1974, Little Nemo, 1992, The Mighty Kong, 1996; composer for Walt Disney's Wonderful World of Color, TV, 1961—; co-producer NBC-TV spl. Goldilocks, 1970, v.p. Musi-Classics, Inc.; co-producer, composer, lyricist stage musical Victory Canteen, 1971; composer-lyricist Broadway show Over Here, 1975, Busker Alley, 1995; screenplay and song score Tom Sawyer, United Artists, 1972, Huckleberry Finn, 1974, The Slipper and the Rose, 1977, The Magic of Lassie, 1978. Served with inf. AUS, 1943-45; ETO. Decorated Purple Heart; recipient 2 Acad. awards best score for Mary Poppins, 1964, best song for Chim Chim Cheree, 1964; Grammy award, 1965; Christopher medal, 1965, 74; nine Acad. award nominations; Acad. award nomination for song score Bedknobs and Broomsticks, 1971, for best song The Age of Not Believing, 1971, others; 16 golden, 4 platinum and one diamond record album, 1965-83; first prize best composer song score Tom Sawyer, Moscow Film Festival, 1973, B.M.I. Pioneer award, 1977; Golden Cassette awards for Mary Poppins, Jungle Book, Bed Knobs and Broomsticks, 1983, Mouscar award Disney Studios, Disney Legend award, 1990, BMI Richard Kirk Achievment award, 1991. Mem. Acad. Motion Picture Arts and Scis. (exec. bd. music br. 12 yrs.), AFTRA, Nat. Acad. Rec. Arts and Scis., Composers and Lyricists Guild (exec. bd.), Dramatists Guild, Authors League. Office: 9030 Harratt St West Hollywood CA 90069-3858

SHERMAN, SIGNE LIDFELDT, portfolio manager, former research chemist; b. Rochester, N.Y., Nov. 11, 1913; d. Carl Leonard Broström and Herta Elvira Maria (Tern) Lidfeldt; m. Joseph V. Sherman, Nov. 18, 1944 (dec. Oct. 1984). BA, U. Rochester, 1935, MS, 1937. Chief chemist Lab. Indsl. Medicine and Toxicology Eastman Kodak Co., Rochester, 1937-43; chief rsch. chemist Chesebrough-Pond's Inc., Clinton, Conn., 1943-44; ptnr. Joseph V. Sherman Cons., N.Y.C., 1944-84; portfolio strategist Sherman Holdings, Troy, Mont., 1984—. Author: The New Fibers, 1946. Fellow Am. Inst. Chemists; mem. AAAS, AAUW (life), Am. Chem. Soc., Am. Econ. Assn., Am. Assn. Ind. Investors (life), Fedn. Am. Scientists (life), Union Concerned Scientists (life), Western Econ. Assn. Internat., Earthquake Engring. Rsch. Inst., Nat. Ctr. for Earthquake Engring. Rsch., N.Y. Acad. Scis. (life), Internat. Platform Assn., Cabinet View Country Club. Office: Sherman Holdings Angel Island 648 Halo Dr Troy MT 59935-9415

SHERRARD, RAYMOND HENRY, retired government official; b. Chgo., Mar. 8, 1944; s. Henry Loren and Minnie Valeria (Elrod) S.; m. Marsha L. McDermid, 1967 (div. 1971). AA, Long Beach City Coll., 1965; BA, Calif. State U., 1967; grad., Treasury Dept. Law Enforcement, Washington, 1970. Spl. dep. U.S. Marshal, L.A., 1970; pres. RHS Enterprises, Cypress, Calif., 1981—; criminal investigator criminal investigation div. IRS, Santa Ana, Calif., 1969-94; story cons. Charles Fries Prodns., Hollywood, Calif., 1976—; instr. Fed. Law Enforcement Tng. Ctr., Glynco, Ga., 1977—; screenwriter Orion TV, Century City, Calif., 1984—; tech. advisor Paramount Pictures, Hollywood, 1987—; dir. speaker panel IRS, Laguna Niguel, Calif., 1984-92. Author: Federal Law Enforcement Patches, 1983, vol. 2, 1987, About Badges, 1987, Badges of the United Marshals, 1990, The Centurions Shield-A History of the Los Angeles Police Department, Its Badges and Insignia, 1996; columnist Police Colector News; contbr. articles to profl. jours. Recipient Presidential Commendation, Pres. U.S.A., Washington, 1980, Spl. Act award U.S. Treasury Dept., L.A., 1978, 87. Mem. Nat. Assn. Treasury Agts. (v.p. 1995-98), Fed. Criminal Investigators Assn. (life, regional v.p. 1978-80), Assn. Fed. Investigators, Fed. Law Enforcement Officers Assn., Calif. Narcotic Officers Assn. (life, sec. 1974). Republican. Avocations: Korean Tae Kwon Do, screenwriting, film and TV cons./tech. Home: PO Box 5779 Garden Grove CA 92846-0779

SHERRIFFS, ALEXANDER CARLTON, higher education administrator; b. San Jose, Dec. 14, 1917; s. Alexander and Ruth Irene (Turner) S.; m. Bette Sansome Meredith, July 4, 1998. BA in Econs., Stanford U., 1939, MA in Psychology, 1941, PhD in Psychology, 1946; LLD, Pepperdine U., 1974. Lic. psychologist, Calif. Prof. psychology U. Calif., Berkeley, 1944-67, rsch. assoc. Inst. Human Devel., 1949-50, vice chancellor student affairs, 1958-65; edn. advisor to gov. State of Calif., Sacramento, 1967-73; statewide vice chancellor acad. affairs Calif. State U., Long Beach, 1973-83; cons., writer, 1983—; lectr. in field. Contbr. articles to profl. jours. Democrat. Avocations: fly fishing, photography, gardening, reading, grape growing and wine making. Home and Office: 3607 Windspun Dr Huntington Beach CA 92649

SHERRIFFS, RONALD EVERETT, communication and film educator; b. Salem, Oreg., Apr. 10, 1934; s. Robert William and Margaret Kathleen (Tutt) S.; m. Mary Lona West, July 9, 1960; children: Ellen, Matthew. BA, San Jose State U., 1955, MA, 1957; PhD, U. So. Calif., 1964. Instr. theater Mich. State U., East Lansing, 1960-61; asst. prof. broadcasting Tex. Tech U., Lubbock, 1964-65; asst. prof. speech U. Oreg., Eugene, 1965-70, assoc. prof., 1970-79, prof. telecomm. and film, 1979-92, chmn. dept. speech, 1978-84, 88-90, prof. journalism and comm., 1993—. Author: (with others) Speech Communication via Radio and TV, 1971, TV Lighting Handbook, 1977, Small Format TV Production, 1985, 3d edit., Video Field Production and Editing, 1994, 4th edit., 1996; prodr., dir. TV programs, 1965—. Mem. Oreg. Pub. Broadcasting Policy Adv. Bd., 1980-88. Served to lt. comdr. USNR, 1957-68, PTO. Faculty enrichment program grantee Can., 1984, 91. Mem. Nat. Communication Assn., AAUP, We. States Communication Assn. Clubs: Oreg. Track; McKenzie Flyfishers (Eugene). E-mail: sherriffs@ballmer.uoregon.edu. Office: Univ Oreg Journalism Sch Eugene OR 97403

SHERWOOD, ALLEN JOSEPH, lawyer; b. Salt Lake City, Sept. 26, 1909; s. Charles Samuel and Sarah (Abramson) Shapiro; m. Edith Ziff, Jan. 19, 1941; children—Mary (Mrs. John Marshall), Arthur Lawrence. Student, UCLA, 1927-30; AB, U. So. Calif., 1933, LLB, 1933. Bar: Calif. 1933, U.S. Supreme Ct. 1944. Pvt. practice law L.A., 1933-54, Beverly Hills, 1954-95; legal counsel Internat. Family Planning Rsch. Assn., Inc., 1970-76; bd. dirs. Family Planning Ctrs. Greater L.A., Inc., 1968-84, pres., 1973-76. Mem. editorial bd. So. Calif. Law Rev., 1932-33. Contbr. articles to profl. jours. Mem. Calif. Atty. Gen.'s Vol. Adv. Coun. and its legis. subcom., 1972-78. Mem. Med.-Legal Soc. So. Calif. (bd. dirs. 1966-74), ABA, L.A. County Bar Assn., Beverly Hills Bar Assn., State Bar of Calif., Am. Arbitration Assn. (nat. panel arbitrators 1965—), Order of Coif, Tau Delta Phi, Brentwood Country Club (L.A.), Masons. Home: 575 Moreno Ave Los Angeles CA 90049-4840

SHERWOOD, GRETCHEN WIETING, financial consultant, cosmetics company executive; b. Birmingham, Mich., May 13, 1953; d. Harry Nye III and Jean Kathryn (Wyckoff) Wieting; m. Roderick Mackenzie Sherwood III, Aug. 27, 1983; children: Roderick MacKenzie IV, Hunter Cameron Wieting, Harry Wieting. Student, U. Ariz., 1971-73, Oakland U., Rochester, Mich, 1974-76; BA, U. Mich., 1977, MA in Communication, 1977. Fin. cons. Merrill Lynch, Ann Arbor, Mich., 1978-83, sr. fin. cons., 1984-87; pres. Trimetiques, Inc., Ann Arbor, Mich., 1986—; instr. Mich. Inst. Tech., Ann Arbor, 1979-80, Washtenaw Community Coll., Ann Arbor, 1982-83. Pres. Huron Svcs. for Youth, Ann Arbor, 1984-87; founder, past pres. Ronald McDonald House, Ann Arbor, 1982-86; past pres., active mem. Jr. League, Ann Arbor, 1983—, bd. dirs., 1989-90, chair pub. affairs, del. state pub. affairs com.; active Lucille B. Congor Alumnae Group, Ann Arbor, 1984—; bd. dirs. Jazz for Life, 1988—. Recipient Vol. Commendation award William Beaumont Hosp., 1969. Mem. Internat. Assn. Reg. Reps., Nat. Assn. Bank Women, Mich. Fedn. Pvt. Child and Family Agys. (named Bd. Mem. of Yr. 1986), Barton Hills Country Club, Ann Arbor Women's City Club, Sigma Gamma. Republican. Episcopalian. Avocations: reading, sports, needle work, interior design, travel.

SHERWOOD, JOHN MARTIN, rabbi; b. N.Y.C., Apr. 15, 1936; s. Lew and Rosalind Stella (Eckstein) S.; m. Dolores G. Singer, Apr. 5, 1983; children: Bruce, June, Jay, Robert, Wendy. BA, Calif. State U., Northridge, 1963; BHL, Hebrew Union Coll., L.A., 1964; MAHL, Hebrew Union Coll., 1967, DD, 1992. Ordained rabbi 1967. Founding rabbi Temple Sholom, Vancouver, B.C., 1967-69; rabbi Temple Beth Ohr, La Mirada, Calif., 1969-71; rabbi Temple Emet of Woodland Hills (Calif.), 1971-93, rabbi emeritus, 1993—; adj. prof. St. John's Cath. Sem., Camarillo, Calif., 1987—; dir. Hillel Found., Vancouver, 1967-68; lectr. U. B.C., Religious Studies Dept., 1968-69; chaplain L.A. Police Dept., 1981—. Author: High Holy Day Prayers, 1986. Active in past various charitable orgns.; 1st Jewish chaplain Ventura County (Calif.) Fire and Rescue Dept. With U.S. Army, 1957-59. Recipient Walter S. Hilborn award, Hebrew Union Coll. 1963. Mem. San Fernando Valley Interfaith Coun. (past pres.), W. San Fernando Valley Clergy Assn., Cen. Conf. Am. Rabbis, Bd. Rabbis of So. Calif., Masons. E-mail: rabjms@earthlink.net.

SHEU, BING JAY, electrical engineering educator; b. Hsin-Chu City, Taiwan, Oct. 26, 1955; came to U.S., 1980; s. So Paul and Da (Wang) S.; m. Shelley Amy Liao, Dec. 12, 1985; children: Jennifer C., Roger J. BS in Elec. Engring., Nat. Taiwan U., Taipei, 1978; MS in Elec. Engring., U. Calif., Berkeley, 1983, PhD in Elec. Engring., 1985. Registered profl. engr., Taiwan. Tchg. asst. dept. elec. engring. and computer sci. U. Calif., Berkeley, 1981-82, rsch. asst. Electronics Rsch. Lab., 1982-85; profl. cons. Palo Alto Rsch. Ctr. Xerox Corp., Palo Alto, Calif., 1983-84; asst. prof. U. So. Calif., L.A., 1985-91, assoc. prof. elec. engring. dept., 1991—, assoc. prof. biomed. engring. dept., 1994—; dir. VLSI Signal Processing Lab., U. So. Calif., L.A., 1989—; hon. cons. prof. Nat. Chiao Tung U., Hsin-Chu, Taiwan, 1992—. Author: Neural Information Processing and VLSI, 1995. Recipient Cert. of Recognition NASA/Jet Propulsion lab., Pasadena, Calif., 1995. Fellow IEEE (bd. govs. Circuits and Systems Soc. 1996—, editor-in-chief Trans. on VLSI Systems 1997—, tech. program chair Internat. Conf. on Computer Design 1997, Best Presenter award 1995), Internat. Neural Network Soc. (Best Poster Paper award 1995). Achievements include invention of popular computer-based model for silicon transistor; patent pending for one-dimensional signal processor with optimized solution capability, VLSI neural processor based on optimization neural networks; avocations: reading, watching TV programs, science fiction, tennis, swimming. Office: U So Calif Dept Elec Engring Powell Hall-604 Los Angeles CA 90089

SHI, SHAN-RONG, research pathology educator; b. Jiangan, Sichuan, China, Feb. 6, 1936; came to U.S., 1989; s. Sheng-Zhi and Xing-Rui (Liu) S.; m. Shou-Xian Wang, Feb. 15, 1969 (div. Oct. 1991); 1 child, Yan Shi. MD, West China U. Med. Scis., Chengdu, Sichuan, 1957. Attending physician ear, nose, and throat Sichuan Med. Coll., Chengdu, 1967-75, instr. ear, nose, and throat pathology, 1976-79; rsch. fellow pathology Harvard U. Med. Sch., Boston, 1982-84; assoc. prof. ear, nose, and throat Sichuan Med. Coll., 1980-87; asst. prof. pathology U. So. Calif., L.A., 1992—. Mem. editl. bd.: Jour. Histochemistry & Cytochemistry, 1993—; contbr. articles to profl. jours. Recipient Chinese Sci. award Chinese Govtl. Rsch. Found., 1986. Mem. Internat. Otopathology Soc., Histochem. Soc., Nat. Soc. Histotech. Taoist. Achievements include patent for heating antigen retrieval (AR) technique, first inventor for nonheating AR technique. Avocations: swimming, ballroom dancing, music, movies. E-mail: sshi@hsc.usc.edu. Office: U So Calif Sch Medicine Dept Pathology HMR 310A 2011 Zonal Ave Los Angeles CA 90033-1034

SHI, WENYUAN, microbiologist; b. Hangzhou, Zhejiang, China, June 26, 1962; came to U.S., 1985; s. Zhuxian Shi; m. Hanjing Yang, Sept. 3, 1987; 1 child, Jamie Young. BS in Genetics, Fudan U., Shanghai, China, 1984; PhD in Genetics, U. Wis., 1992. Rsch. asst. U. Wis., Madison, 1985-92; rsch. scientist U. Calif., Berkeley, 1992-95; prof. UCLA, 1995—. Author: Methods in Molecular Microbiology, 1994; contbr. articles to profl. jours. Pres. SOS China Edn. Fund, Calif., 1992-93, gen. sec., 1994; pres. Smargen Hitechland, Calif., 1994—. Mem. Am. Soc. Microbiology. Home: 7011 Kentwood Ave Los Angeles CA 90045-1253 Office: Sch Medicine and Dentistry Ctr for Health Scis 10833 Le Conte Ave Los Angeles CA 90095-3075

SHIBATA, GEORGE EISHIN, minister; b. Fukuoka-ken, Japan, Apr. 13, 1938; came to U.S., 1939, naturalized, 1963; s. Tesshin and Haruko (Fukuyoshi) S.; m. Yasuko Kawasaki, Oct. 27, 1973. Student, U. Wash., 1957-62; BA, Ryukoku U., Japan, 1966; MA, Ryukoka U., Japan, 1969. Ordained to ministry Jodo Shinshu Honganji Sect Buddhist Chs. Am., 1964. Asst. min. Gardena (Calif.) Buddhist Ch., 1970-73; asst. dir. Bur. Buddhist Edn., Buddhist Chs. Am. Hdqrs., San Francisco, 1974; resident min. Reedley (Calif.) Buddhist Ch., 1975—; overseer min. Buddhist Ch. Parlier, 1987-89; mem. literary propagation com. Buddhist Chs. Am., 1975-81, exec. com. Sunday sch. dept., 1976-78, 81-85, recording sec., 1980-81, chmn. Sunday sch. dept., 1982-85, mem. ministerial affairs com., 1980—, mem. Buddhist edn. com., 1986-89, trustee dept. Buddhist edn., 1986-87, interim dir. dept. Buddhist edn., 1987-89. Author: Buddhist Holidays, 1974. Trustee Inst. Buddhist Studies, 1982-83. Mem. Buddhist Chs. of Am. Mins. Assn. (English lang. recording sec. 1981-83, 89-90, vice chmn. 1986-87), Cen. Calif. Buddhist Ministerial Assn. (treas. 1975-77, 83-86, 90—, chmn. 1978-80, 86-87, 89-90, vice chmn. 1981-82, 87-88, auditor 1988-89). Home: PO Box 24 1459 J St Reedley CA 93654-3325 Office: 2035 15th St Reedley CA 93654-3351

SHIERSHKE, NANCY FAY, artist, educator, property manager; b. St. Helens, Oreg., May 10, 1935; d. David Cline and Matilda Ruth (Pearce) Morrison; m. H. McNeal Kavanagh, Sept. 4, 1955 (dec. Dec. 1978); children: Marjorie L. Wood, David M. Kavanagh, Katherine F. Fiske; m. Richard M. Shiershke, Nov. 29, 1980. AA, Pasadena (Calif.) City Coll., 1956; BA, UCLA, 1965. Substitute elem. sch. tchr. Buena Park, Calif., 1967-69; property mgr. Pky. Cts., Arcadia, Calif., 1977—; libr. Reading Rm., Arcadia, 1979-87; freelance artist Kavanagh-Shiershke Art St., San Gabriel, Arcadia, Calif., 1985—; art gallery hostess Descanso Gardens, La Canada, Flintridge, Calif., 1990—; display and sales person Village Fine Arts Gallery, Arcadia, 1991-92; art instr. Tri Cmty. Adult Edn., Covina, Calif., 1994—, Claremont (Calif.) Art Edn., 1998—; art instr. Claremont (Claif.) Adult Edn. Group shows include Pasadena Presbyn. Ch., 1985—, Hillcrest Ch., 1992—, Descanso Gardens, 1994—, San Gabriel Fine Arts, 1994—. Named Artist of the Yr. Mid Valley art League, 1990; Recipient Best of Show San Gabriel Fine Arts, 1991, Hulsebus award Pasadena Prebyn. Ch., 1996. Mem. Nat. Watercolor Soc., San Gabriel Fine Arts, Mid Valley Arts League (Artist of Yr. 1998), East Valley Art Assn., Valley Watercolor Soc., Foothill Creative Arts Group, Water Color West. Home: 505 Vaquero Rd Arcadia CA 91007-6045 Office: 614 E Vine Ave West Covina CA 91790-5103

SHIFFER, JAMES DAVID, retired utility executive; b. San Diego, Mar. 24, 1938; s. Kenneth Frederick and Thelma Lucille (Good) S.; m. Margaret Edith Rightmyer, Sept. 5, 1959 (div. July 1986); children: James II, Elizabeth Gonzales, Russell; m. Esther Zamora, Sept. 13, 1986; stepchildren: Bryan Boots, Jeremy Hellier, Marisol Boots. BS ChemE, Stanford U., 1960, MS ChemE, 1961. Registered profl. engr., Calif. Nuclear engr. Pacific Gas & Electric Co., Humboldt Bay Power Plant, Eureka, Calif., 1961-71; tech. mgr. Pacific Gas & Electric. Co., Diablo Canyon Power Plant, Avila Beach, Calif., 1971-80; mgr. nuclear ops. Pacific Gas & Electric Co., San Francisco, 1980-84, v.p. nuclear power generation, 1984-90, sr. v.p., gen. mgr. nuclear power generation bus. unit, 1990-91; exec. v.p. Pacific Gas & Electric, San Francisco, 1991-97; ret., 1997; pres., CEO PG&E Enterprises, San Francisco, 1994-95, also bd. dirs.; bd. dirs. Nuclear Energy Inst., U.S. Oper. Svcs. Co., Math., Engring., Sci. Achievement. Mem. AIChE, Commonwealth Club of Calif. (bd. govs. 1992-97). Republican. Episcopalian. Avocations: golf, music. Home: 2550 Royal Oaks Dr Alamo CA 94507-2227

SHIFFMAN, LESLIE BROWN, management executive; b. Fresno, Calif., Dec. 9, 1936; d. Albert Brown and Marion Jean (Riese) Brown-Propp; married, Jan. 20, 1957 (div. 1972); m. Sydney Shiffman, July 4, 1993; children: Susan, Steven, David, Thomas. BS, U. So. Calif., 1958. Office mgr. pvt. practice physician, Long Beach, Calif., 1971-73; cost acct. Panavision, Inc., Tarzana, Calif., 1974-76; exec. sec. Hartman Galleries, Beverly Hills, Calif., 1976-78; adminstrv. exec., corp. treas. Galanos Originals, L.A., 1978-98; membership and adult edn. sec. Sinai Temple, L.A., 1998—. Named L.A. Alumnae Panhellenic Assn. Women of Yr., 1977. Mem. Alpha Epsilon Phi (nat. pres. 1985-89, trustee, sec. Found. Inc. 1990-91, pres. 1991-95, treas. 1996-98, Woman of Distinction award 1993), Order of Omega. Republican. Jewish. Avocation: designing and hand knitting sweaters. Home: 1745 S Bentley Ave Apt 1 Los Angeles CA 90025-4323 Office: Sinai Temple PO Box 240099 Los Angeles CA 90024-9199

SHIFFMAN, MICHAEL A., lawyer; b. Newark, July 23, 1941. LLB magna cum laude, Lincoln U., 1973. Bar: Calif. 1973, U.S. Dist. Ct. (no. dist.) Calif. 1973; lic. real estate broker. Atty. Lanahan & Reilley, San Francisco. Editor: Lincoln U. Law Rev., 1972-73. Mem. ABA, Internat. Bar Assn., State Bar Calif. Office: Lanahan & Reilley 500 Sansome St Ste 301 San Francisco CA 94111-3217

SHIGEMOTO, APRIL FUMIE, English educator secondary school; b. Lihue, Hawaii, Apr. 22, 1948; d. Warren Itaru and Edith Yuriko (Y-oshimura) Tanaka; m. Tom Hideo Shigemoto, July 21, 1973; children: Taylor, Tyron, Tryson, Thomas-Jay. BA in English, U. Hawaii Manoa, 1970, profl. diploma secondary, 1971. English tchr. Kapaa (Hawaii) H.S. and Intermediate Sch., 1971-81, Kauai H.S. and Intermediate Sch., Lihue, Hawaii, 1981-90; core curriculum coord. Kauai H.S. and Intermediate Sch., 1990—. Leader Boy Scouts of Am., Lihue, Hawaii, 1982—. Recipient one of seven Status of Women awards, Kauai, Lihue, Hawaii, 1988, Den Leader of the Yr. award Boy Scouts of Am., 1988, Milken Educator's award, Milken Found., L.A., 1992; named Outstanding Working Mother, Garden Island Newspaper, Lihue, Hawaii, 1989, Kauai Dist. Tchr. of Yr., State Dept. Edn., Hawaii, 1990, State Tchr. of Yr., Scottish Rite Order of Free Masons, Honolulu, 1991, one of Kauai's Outstanding Families, Garden Island Newspaper, Hawaii, 1992. Mem. Nat. Coun. Tchrs. of English, Assn. for Supervision and Curriculum Devel., Phi Delta Kappa, Delta Kappa Gamma. Democrat. Avocations: traveling, reading, golfing. Office: Kauai HS & Intermediate Sch 3577 Lala Rd Lihue HI 96766-9520

SHIGETOMI, KEITH SHIGEO, lawyer; b. Honolulu, Oct. 16, 1956; s. Samson Shigeru and Doris (Ogawa) S.; m. Ann Keiko Furutomo, Oct. 29, 1985; children: Samson Shigeru II, Marisa Mae. BSBA magna cum laude, Drake U., 1978; JD, U. Hawaii, 1983. Bar: Hawaii, 1983, U.S. Dist. Ct. Hawaii 1983, U.S. Ct. Appeals (9th cir.) 1986. Dep. pub. defender Office of Pub. Defender, Honolulu, 1983-88; pvt. practice Honolulu, 1988-90, 94—; ptnr. Shigetomi & Thompson, Honolulu, 1990-94; ind. grand jury counsel Cir. Ct., State of Hawaii, Honolulu, 1988-89. Finalist Three Outstanding Young Persons Hawaii Jaycees, 1994; named Criminal Def. Lawyer of Yr. Consumer Bus. Rev., 1996, 1997. Mem. Hawaii State Bar Assn., Nat. Asian Pacific Bar Assn., Beta Gamma Sigma, Beta Alpha Psi, Phi Eta Sigma. Office: 711 Kapiolani Blvd Ste 1440 Honolulu HI 96813-5238

SHIH, ANDREW HAN-TING, marketing executive; b. Taipei, Taiwain, Sept. 12, 1968; s. Albert Ping-Ling and Emily Lu-Yun (Hwang) S. BA in Physics, U. Calif., Berkeley, 1990. Applications engr. Watkins-Johnson Co., Scotts Valley, Calif., 1990-94; engr. Xerox Parc, Palo Alto, Calif., 1994-95; mktg. mgr. Lam Rsch. Corp., Fremont, Calif., 1995—; product mgr. LAM Rsch. Corp., Fremont, Calif., 1998—. Contbr. articles to profl. jours. Mem. Soc. for Info. Display. Avocations: opera, classical music, choral singing, skiing, fencing. Home: 1347 Ocaso Camino Fremont CA 94539-5641 Office: Lam Rsch Corp 47131 Bayside Pkwy Fremont CA 94538-6517

SHIH, HSIENCHENG, medicinal chemist; b. Pingtung, Taiwan, Feb. 13, 1947; came to U.S., 1975; s. Ching-nan and Ching-Jui (Wang) S.; m. Weiyung Yoko Chan, Nov. 26, 1983; children: Renshy Alexis, Renshuay Justin. BS in Pharmacy, Kaohsiung Med. Coll., 1969; MS in Medicinal Chemistry, U. R.I., 1977; PhD in Medicinal Chemistry, SUNY, Buffalo, 1982. Postdoctoral fellow M.D. Anderson Hosp. & Tumor Inst., Houston, 1982; group leader Food & Drug Bur., Taipei, Taiwan, 1983; postdoctoral fellow Med. U. S.C., Charleston, Taiwan, 1984; rsch. fellow Naylor Dana Inst. Am. Health Found., Valhalla, N.Y., 1984-86; rsch. assoc. Marshall U., Huntington, W.Va., 1986-89; asst. mem. The Whittier Inst., La Jolla, Calif., 1989-90; rsch. staff U. Calif., San Diego, 1991—. Patentee in field. Mem. Am. Chem. Soc., Am. Assn. Pharm. Scientists. Achievements include developments of anticancer drugs and the fully automated solid-phase synthesis of cystine-peptide hormones. Home: 10735 Passerine Way San Diego CA 92121-4216 Office: U Calif 9500 Gilman Dr La Jolla CA 92093-5003

SHIMASAKI, CHRISTINE, sales executive; b. Sept. 4, 1956; d. Tom Toshimi and Mitsuye (Uyeda) S. BS, UCLA, 1978. With Atari, Inc., Santa Clara, 1978-83; account exec. Marriott's, Santa Clara, 1983-85; sales mgr. Marine del Rey Hotel, 1985-86, Marriott's, Santa Barbara, 1986-87; dir. sales Marriott's, Rancho Mirage, Calif., 1987-89, San Diego Marriott's, 1990-93; dir. sales San Diego, 1993-96, v.p., 1996—. Avocations: golf, snow skiing. Office: San Diego Convention & Visitors Ctr 111 W Harbor Dr San Diego CA 92101-7822

SHIMAZAKI, TATSUO, physicist; b. Tokyo, June 28, 1925; s. Gentaro and Kise (Mikame) S.; m. Michiyo Tachibana, Apr. 4, 1955; children: Naoki, Junji, Shozo. PhD, U. Tokyo, 1949, DSc, 1959. Rsch. asst. Nagoya (Japan) U., 1949-50; rsch. fellow Radio Rsch. Lab., Tokyo, 1950-63; postdoc. fellow NRC, Ottawa, Ont., 1960-62; physicist NOAA, Boulder, Colo., 1963-74; physicist NASA, Mountain View, Calif., 1974-90, rsch. assoc., 1990—; tchr. Japanese Lang. Sch., San Francisco, 1991—; vis. prof. U. Ill., Urbana, 1970-71, Inst. Space and Astron. Sci., Kanagawa, Japan, 1988-89; cons. Pa. State U., University Park, 1972-74. Author: The Stratospheric Ozone, 1979, Minor Constituents in the Middle Atmosphere, 1985, The Stratospheric Ozone, Why it Decreases and What Happens if it Decreases, 1989, Mars and Mankind, 1999; contbr. over 80 articles to sci. jours. U.S. Dept. Transp. grantee, Washington, 1971-74; recipient Tanakadate prize Soc. Geomagnetism and Geoelectricity, Tokyo, 1959. Mem. Am. Geophys. Union, Nat. Space Soc., Planetary Soc., Internat. Ho. Japan. Avocations: hiking, music. Home: 19723 Elisa Ave Saratoga CA 95070-3337

SHIMEK, JOHN ANTON, legal investigation business owner, educator; b. Chgo., Sept. 1, 1925; s. John Anton Sr. and Florence Marie (Redman) S.; m. Corinne Gladys Hornburg, Mar. 1, 1947 (div. June 1988); m. Janet Lea Inghram Snyder, Sept. 10, 1988; children: Ronald Wayne, Scott Anthony, Brian Dean Snyder. AA, Phoenix Coll., 1963; BS, Grand Canyon Coll., 1967; M of Phys. Edn., Sussex (Eng.) Coll., 1974. Cert. sch. adminstr. Am. Police Acad.; cert. aquatic dir.; lic. pvt. investigator; lic. ins. agt. Patrolman Chgo. Police Dept., 1946-51; agt. Met. Life Ins., Colorado Springs/Phoenix, 1951-61; owner, head coach Ariz. Swim Devils, Phoenix, 1967-80; phys. dir., assoc. dir. Phoenix YMCA, 1957-67; sch. adminstr. Cartwright Sch. Dist., Phoenix, 1967-88; pres., owner Shimek & Assocs., Inc., Glendale, Ariz., 1988—; adj. prof. Grand Canyon Coll., Phoenix, 1963-83; spl. agt Internat. Intelligence and Organized Crime Investigations Assn., Washington, 1981-83; mem. AAU Regional Swimming Com., 1967-68; mem. coach AAU State Swim Com., chmn., 1966-67. Author: Physical Education Handbook, 1979, 80, Shimek Heritage, 1998, Swimming Today, 1998; co-author: An Annotated Bibliography of Experimental Research Concerning Competitive Swimming, 1970, (video) Desert Survival, 1983; contbr. articles to mags. Commdr., instr. search and rescue team Maricopa County Sheriff's Office, Ariz., 1980-89; counselor police acad. Ariz. Dept. Pub. Safety, Tucson, 1982. With USN, 1942-47, WWII. Named to Swimming Hall of Fame, Internat. Swimming Hall of Fame, 1971-72. Mem. Am. Legion (comdr. 1980—, Americanism citation 1980-81), Fraternal Order of Police (trustee 1980—), Arrowhead Country Club. Republican. Methodist. Home: 7827 W Julie Dr Glendale AZ 85308-5908

SHIMODA, JERRY YASUTAKA, retired national historic park superintendent; b. Haleiwa, Hawaii, Mar. 21, 1930; s. Tamotsu and Sasai Shimoda; m. Clara H. Segawa, Aug. 7, 1954; children: Karen Marie K., Randall T., Shaun T., Teri Ellen H., Jacqueline Y., David Y. BA in Govt., U. Hawaii, 1952, MA in Far Ea. Area Studies, 1957; postgrad., St. Louis U., 1957-59. Historian Jefferson Nat. Expansion Meml. Nat. Hist. Site, St. Louis, 1957-60; chief historian, in charge hist. rsch. and visitor svcs. Saratoga Nat. Hist. Park, Stillwater, N.Y., 1960-66; chief historian Home of Franklin D. Roosevelt Nat. Hist. Site and, Frederick Vanderbilt Nat. Hist. Site, Hyde Park, N.Y., 1966-69; instr. Nat. Park Svc. Stephen T. Mather Tng. Ctr., Harpers Ferry, W.Va., 1969-72; supt. Pu'uhonua o Honaunau (Hawaii) Nat. Hist. Park, 1972-96, Puukohola Heiau Nat. Hist. Site, Kawaihae, 1972-96; ret., 1996; lectr. environ. edn. Pa. State U., U. W.Va., Shepherd Coll., 1969-72; acting supr. Kaloko-Honokohau Nat. Hist. Park, 1988-90; instr. environ. edn., interpretive and basic instructing techniques U. Hawaii, Hilo, Kapiolani C.C.; instr. Japanese culture U. Hawaii, Hilo, 1994; U.S. del. U.S.-Japan Panel on Nat. Parks and Equivalent Res., 1968-97, World Conf. on Marine Parks, Tokyo, 1975; Japanese translator U.S. Nat. Park Svc.; mem. internat. bd. dirs. Heritage Interpretation Internat., 1989-98; numerous presentations at confs. and tng. courses. Author booklets on nat. parks, mgmt. and history; contbr. numerous articles to profl. publs., mags. and newspapers. Bd. dirs. Volcano Art Ctr.; mem. adv. com. Wailoa State Ctr.; mem. Hawaii Gov.'s Task Force on Ocean and Recreation; chmn. restoration com. St. Benedict's Ch., Honaunau, 1982-95; chmn. bd. dirs. Kahua Na'au 'Ao, 1996-97. Recipient spl. achievement award Nat. Park Svc., 1964, 68, 70, resolution W.Va. Senate, 1971, Hawaii Ho. of Reps., 1982, sec.'s cert. Dept. Interior, 1971, Exec. of Yr. award West Hawaii chpt. Profl. Secs. Internat., 1981, cert. Govt. of Japan, 1981, staff plaque Pu'uhonua o Honaunau Nat. Hist. Park, Puukohola Heiau Nat. Hist. Site and Kaloko-Honokohau Nat. Hist. Park, 1988, cert. Japan Nat. Parks Assn., 1989, cert. of appreciation South Kona Aloha Lions Club, 1990, Meritorious Svc. award Sec. Interior, 1996, also others. Mem. Hawaii Mus. Assn. (bd. dirs. 1988-92), Kona Hist. Soc. (bd. dirs. 1988-92), Big Island Ocean Recreation and Tourism Assn. (exec. com.), Kona Judo Club (pres. 1977—), Rotary (pres. Kona Mauka 1978-79, Paul Harris fellow 1991, Disting. Svc. award 1992). Avocations: writing, reading, travel, teaching.

SHIMOKAWA, COLIN H., architect; b. Honolulu, May 12, 1952; m. Janice M.; children: Rosos, Ryan. BFA in Pre-Architecture, U. Hawaii, 1974; MArch, U. Colo., 1977. Designer, drafter Wimberly Whisbrand, Allison, Torg & Goo Archs., Honolulu, 1974-75, 77-78; ptnr. Lawton Umemura & Yamamoto, Honolulu, 1978-88; sr. v.p. Hemmeter Design Group, Honolulu, 1988-90; ptnr. Projects Internat., Honolulu, 1991—. Mem. Waialaeiki 5 Cmty. Assn. (chmn, archtl. adv. bd 1995—, dir. 1997—). Office: Shimokawa Archs Suite 1050 1580 Makaloa St Ste 1050 Honolulu HI 96814-3240

SHIMPFKY, RICHARD LESTER, bishop; b. Albuquerque, Oct. 18, 1940; m. Jamel Shimpfky, 1966; children: Trevor, Allison, Joshua. Grad., U. Colo., 1963, Va. Theol. Seminary, 1970. Ordained to diaconate Episc. Ch., 1970. With William L. Philips Found., Richmond, Va., 1963-67; curate St. Peter's Ch., Arlington, 1970-72; vicar All Saints' Sharon Chapel, Alexandria, Va., 1972-73, rector, 1973-77; rector Christ Ch., Ridgewood, N.J., 1977-90; bishop Diocese El Camino Real, Monterey, Calif., 1990—. Avocations: reading, traveling. Office: Diocese of El Camino Real PO Box 1903 Monterey CA 93942-1903*

SHIN, HELEN HYUN, academic administrator, educator; b. Seoul, Korea, July 28, 1942; came to U.S., 1967; d. Young Ki and On Sun (Yun) S.; m. Jin Chung Song, Feb. 21, 1964; children: Pual Chung, Kwang Scout, Elia Song. BFA, Seoul U., 1959; MA, San Diego U., 1972; PhD, NYU, 1976. Art instr. Hon-Ik U., Seoul, 1978-80, U. So. Calif., 1984-86, U. Hawaii, Honolulu, 1983-87; pres. Hyun's Art Sch., Honolulu, 1980-88, San Jose Art Acad., Santa Clara, Calif., 1988—; presenter in field. Author: Child Art Education, 1979, Exploring Nature, 1988; exhibited in groups shows at Honolulu Assn., 1976, 79, 81, 84, 88, 91, 93, 96; artist Olympic poster, Seoul, 1988; author (series) History through Religion of Art, 1997—. Dir. San Jose Am. Cmty. Svc., 1983-97; trustee Nat. Woman's Club, Honolulu, 1983-88; mem. coun. Korean Immigration Svc., 1985-88. Recipient 1st place award Asian Artists Exhbn., Japan, 1976, grant Am. Art Watercolor Soc., 1993, 1st place award Santa Clara County Art Exhbn., 1995. Mem. Nat. Art Multicultural Artists, Nat. Art Edn. Assn., Am. Korean. Artist Assn. (chairperson 1984-97), Santa Clara Watercolor Assn. Home: 954 Eton Way Sunnyvale CA 94087-4926 Office: San Jose Art Acad 890 Pomeroy Ave Ste 1104 Santa Clara CA 95051-5235

SHIN, ILSOON, foreign language educator; b. Kunsan, South Korea, July 18, 1939; s. Hyonjwa and Bong Hak (Ahn) S.; m. Kyecha Shin; children: Judy, Tong, Philip. PhD, Columbia Pacific U., 1987, Walden U., 1998; EdD, U. Sarasota, 1998. Pub. sch. tchr. Kunsan Bd. of Edn., 1957-72; prof. Kunsan Chonmun Coll., 1973-78; fgn. lang. prof. Def. Lang. Inst., Presidio of Monterey, Calif., 1985—. Author: Sweeping the Darkness, 1992. Home: 1101 David Ave Pacific Grove CA 93950-5407

SHINN, DUANE K., music publisher; b. Auburn, Calif., Nov. 13, 1938; s. Archie W. and Iola E. (Eisley) S.; m. Beverly J. Luman; children: Kurt, Kendra, Garin, Garth. BS, So. Oreg. State Coll., 1970, MS, 1977. Prin. [illegible] pub. instructional audio and video cassettes on piano playing, including: Piano Improvising, 1985, How to Dress Up Naked Music, 1988, Keyboard by Chords, 1982, Piano Tricks; author: Will Hugh Go to Hell for Biting the [illegible] Make on Any Keyboard, 1998. E-mail: pianoman@playpiano.com. Office: Duane Shinn Publs PO Box 700 Medford OR 97501-0047

SHINSTINE, DRUCELLA GAYLE, artist; b. Clinton, Okla., Jan. 17, 1943; d. William Ernest and Oleeta Merle (Drake) Cathey; m. Douglas Arthur Shinstine, Nov. 4, 1961; children: Kelly A. Berch, D. Reid, Wendy J. Smith, W. Morgan. Grad. high sch., Sumner, Wash., 1961. Exhibited in group shows at St. of Dreams, Puyallup, Wash., 1992, Art Concepts, Tacoma, 1992, Ellensburg (Wash.) Art Gallery, 1988, 91, Eileen Enck Gallery, Bellevue, Wash., 1990, Avoir Gallery, Kirkland, Wash., 1990, Annie Wright gallery, Tacoma, 1988, 90, Sidney Mus. and arts Assn., Port Orchard, Wash., 1989, Silverdale (Wash.) Hotel, 1988, Tolles Gallery, Mercer Island, Wash., 1998, Issaquah Art Gallery, Issaquah, Wash., 1998, North Valley Art League Nat. Show, Redding, Calif., 1999. Recipient 1st place Pacific Gallery Artists, Pacific Luth. U., Tacoma, 1990, 91, 1st place Western Wash. State Fair, 1991, 1st place, 4th place, honorable mention Western Wash. State Fair, 1990, 1st place Renton (Wash.) Creative Arts Show, 1989, 90, 1st place Lakewood Artists, Tacoma, 1989, 2d place Sydney Gallery, Port Orchard, 1989, 2d place Eastside Assn. of Fine Arts, Kirkland, Wash., 1988, Best of Show, North Valley Art League Nat. Show, Redding, Calif., 1990, others, 2d place Pacific Gallery Artists, 4th place oils and watercolor, Western Wash. State Fair, 1998. Mem. Pacific Gallery Artists (pres. 1990-91, show chmn. 1989), Eastside Assn. Fine Artists, Northwest Ten, Northwest Pastel Soc., Puget Sound Art League, Women's Painters of Wash. N.W. Watercolor Soc. Home: 3815 Forest Beach Dr NW Gig Harbor WA 98335-5845

SHIPLEY, NANCY LOUISE, health science association executive; b. Wilkinsburg, Pa., June 26, 1950. BS, Slippery Rock (Pa.) State Coll., 1972, MEd, 1974. Tchr. phys. edn. Monroeville (Pa.) Jr. High Sch., 1972-77; rep. sales Knoll Pharms., Whippany, N.J., 1978-80; N.Y. regional rep. med. sales Surgidev Corp., Morristown, N.J., 1980-82; regional rep. med. sales Ioptex, Morristown, 1982-84; pres. surg. custom trays Surg. Services and Supplies, Inc., Montvale, N.J., 1984-85; sales med. instruments Allergan Humphrey Corp., New Eng., 1985-87; exec. adminstr. Eye Inst. Essex, Belleville, N.J., 1987-89; sr. sales exec. Allergan Med. Optics, Detroit, 1989-90; N.Y. regional sales mgr. Allergan Med. Optics, Scotch Plains, N.J., 1990-91; mgr. med. bus. mgmt. group programs Allergan Med. Optics, Irvine, Calif., 1991-93; v.p. BSM Consulting Group, Incline Village, Nev., 1993-95; sole gen. ptnr. and pres. Nat. Healthcare Bus. Solutions L.P., Laguna Hills, Calif., 1996—. Contbr. articles to profl. jours. Republican. Avocations: golf, swimming. Home: 28092 Morro Ct Laguna Niguel CA 92677-7017 Office: Nat Healthcare Business Solutions LP 27071 Cabot Rd Ste 103 Laguna Hills CA 92653-7025

SHIPMAN, KEITH BRYAN, sportscaster; b. Puyallup, Wash., Apr. 26, 1961; s. Richard James and Carol Esther (Christianson) S.; m. Julie Anne Poppe, June 30, 1984; children, Alicia Bryanne, Gregory Dane. BA in Comms., Wash. State U., 1983. Sportscaster/producer KOMO Radio/TV, Seattle, 1983-85; sports/pub. affairs dir. KCPQ TV, Tacoma-Seattle, 1986—; AM drive sports host KJR Radio, Seattle, 1991-93; play by play announcer RayCom Sports, Charlotte, N.C., 1992-95; disc jockey KPUG AM/KNWR FM Radio, Belligham, Wash., 1978-81; play-by-play annoucer Turner Broadcasting System, Atlanta, 1990; host/prodr. "The Chuck Knox Show", Anderson/Baer Prodns., Bainbridge Island, Wash., 1987-88; host "The Chuck Knox Show", Andersen Ent., Bellevue, Wash., 1985-88, various other free-lance work; Edward R. Murrow Sch. of Comms. profl. adv. bd. Wash. State U., 1996—. Pres. bd. dirs. Plaza Hall, Tacoma, Wash., 1989-94; exec. com. Muscular Dystrophy Assn., Seattle, 1989-91; vol. Boys and Girls Club of King County, Seattle and Whatcom County, Bellingham, 1988—, Children's Hosp., Seattle, 1992—. Named Sportscaster of the Yr. for Wash., Nat. Sportscasters and Sportswriters Assn., 1986, 87, 88; recipient Emmy award NATAS, 1990, 92, 94. Mem. Nat. Sportscasters and Sportswriters Assn. (bd. dirs. 1989-96), NATAS, Radio TV News Dirs. Assn. Office: KCPQ TV 1813 Westlake Ave N Seattle WA 98109-2706

SHIPPER, TODD JEFFREY, communications executive; b. Detroit, Nov. 18, 1946; s. Norman N. Shipper and Evaline (Spring) Krasner; m. Sherry E. Brown, May 30, 1968 (div. 1969). AA, L.A. Valley Coll., 1970; student, Calif. State U., Northridge, 1970-72. Announcer various radio stas., 1967-73; salesman, mgr. Standard Shoes, Encino, Calif., 1973-76; asst. mgr. K-Mart, Westminster, Calif., 1976-77; salesman Contractors Lic. Sch., Van Nuys, Calif., 1977-80; dir. mktg. Columbia Sch. Broadcasting, Hollywood, Calif., 1980-84; owner, operator Nat. Broadcasting Sch., Sacramento, Portland, Seattle, 1984-92, Las Vegas, 1984-94; owner, operator NBS Travel Tng. Sch., 1989-92, Nat. Career Tng. Ctr., Las Vegas, 1992-94; prin. Sound Ideas, Inc., Las Vegas, 1994—; operations mgr. Waiters on Wheels, Las Vegas, 1998—; prin. Nat. Advt. Agy., Las Vegas, 1986—, Nat. Ednl. Cons., Las Vegas, 1986—. With USAF, 1965-67. Mem. Nat. Assn. Trade and Tech. Schs., Assn. Broadcasters. Democrat. Jewish. Office: Sound Ideas PO Box 29063 Las Vegas NV 89126-3063

SHIRAI, SCOTT, communications executive; b. Honolulu, June 5, 1942; s. George Yoshio and Thelma Takeko (Tominaga) S.; m. Michelle M.; children: Todd, Kimberly, Lance, Lyle. MusB, U. Hawaii, 1983; exec. dir. news, reporter Sta. KHON-TV, Honolulu, 1974-81; asst. gen. mgr. Vanguard Investments, Berkeley, Calif., 1976-79; newscaster Sta. KPOI, Honolulu, 1979-80; news dir. Sta. KGU, Honolulu, 1981-82; owner Visual Perspectives, 1981—; dir. pub. rels. Hawaiian Electric Co., Honolulu, 1982-90; dir. cmty. rels., Hawaiian Electric Industries, 1990—; instr. U. Hawaii, 1984—; pres. Hawaii Cmty. TV, 1993—; dir. BBB of Hawaii, 1995, Hawaii Pub. Broadcasting, 1996—, chair, dir. Hawaii Pub. TV Found., 1997—. Author: Karaoke: Sing Along Guide to Fun & Confidence, 1997. Bd. dirs., sec. Hawaii Com. For Freedom of Press, 1982—; bd. dirs. Mental Health Assn. in Hawaii, 1981—, Moanalua Gardens Found., 1981-84, Health and Cmty. Svcs. Coun., 1982-86, Friends of Father Damien, 1986; v.p. Mele Nani Singers, 1986—; mem. Mayors Adv. Com. on Mcpl. TV, 1987, Office of Hawaiian Affairs Pub. Rels. Adv. Com., 1987, (all Honolulu); sec., dir. Pro Geothermal Alliance, 1990-91. Recipient Jefferson award Honolulu Advertiser, 1985, Gold award Audio-Visual Producers Assn. Am., 1985, Audio-Visual Dept. of Yr. award Videography mag., 1986, Award of Excellence Nat. Hospice Orgn., 1987, Intre award Inst. Teleradial Atica Puerto Rico, Inc., 1988. Mem. ASTD, Internat. TV Assn. (pres. 1983—), Am. Film Inst., AFTRA (bd. dirs. 1980-83), Pub. Rels. Soc. Am. (past pres. and nat. del. 1995—), Hawaii Speakers Assn., Hawaii Film Bd., Honolulu Cmty. Media Council, Hawaii Cmty. TV Assn. (pres. 1990—). Clubs: Honolulu Press (bd. dirs. 1984—), Hui Luna (bd. dirs. 1986-90) (Honolulu). Avocations: martial arts, singing. Office: Hawaiian Electric Industries PO Box 730 Honolulu HI 96808-0730

SHIRE, HAROLD RAYMOND, law educator, author, scientist; b. Denver, Nov. 23, 1910; s. Samuel Newport and Rose Betty (Herman) S.; m. Cecilia Goldhaar, May 9, 1973; children: David, Darcy, Esti. MBA, Pepperdine U., 1972; LLD (hon.), 1975; JD, Southwestern U., L.A., 1974; M in Liberal Arts, U. So. Calif., 1977; PhD in Human Behavior, U.S. Internat. U., San Diego, 1980. Bar: Calif. 1937, U.S. Dist. Ct. (so. dist.) Calif. 1939, U.S. Supreme Ct. 1978. Dep. dist. atty. L.A. County, Calif., 1937-38; asst. U.S. atty. So. Dist. Calif., L.A. and San Diego, 1939-42; pvt. practice, L.A., 1946-56; pres., chmn. bd. Gen. Connectors Corp., U.S. and Eng., 1956-73; prof. mgmt. and law Pepperdine U., Malibu, Calif., 1974-75, U.S. Internat. U., San Diego, 1980-83; dir. Bestobell Aviation, Eng., 1970-74. Advisor U. S.C. Gerentology, Andrus Ctr., pre-retirement tng., 1976-80; bd. dirs. Pepperdine U., 1974-80; nat. bd. govs. Union Orthodox Jewish Congregations Am., 1973—. Mem. Rep. Nat. Com. With U.S. Army, 1942-46. Author: Cha No Yu and Symbolic Interactionism: Method of Predicting Japanese Behavior, 1980; The Tea Ceremony, 1984. Patentee aerospace pneumatics; invented flexible connectors; designed, manufactured flexible integrity systems. Pres. Jewish Nat. Fund Legion of Honor, 1991—; mem. Presdl. Roundtable, Washington, 1989-97. Decorated chevalier du vieux moulin (France); companion Royal Aero. Soc. (U.K.), recipient Tea Name Grand Master Soshitsu Sen XV Urasenke Sch., Kyoto, Japan, 1976, Medal of Honor Jewish Nat. Fund, Legion of Honor, 1991. Mem. Am. Legion (svc. officer China #1 [illegible] Legion of Honor Jewish Nat. Fund (chmn. 1998), Calif. Smphony Soc. (pres. 1998—). Achievements include designing and mfg. fluidic sys. flexible integrity for Saturn IV and welding in Apollo XI Landing on moon, 1969. Office: [illegible]

SHIREMAN, JOAN FOSTER, social work educator; b. Cleve., Oct. 28, 1933; d. Louis Omar and Genevieve (Duguid) Foster; m. Charles Howard Shireman, Mar. 18, 1967; 1 child, David Louis. BA, Radcliffe Coll., 1956; MA, U. Chgo., 1959, PhD, 1968. Caseworker N.H. Children's Aid Soc., Manchester, 1959-61; dir. research Chgo. Child Care Soc., 1968-72; assoc. prof. U. Ill., Chgo., 1972-85; prof. Portland (Oreg.) State U., 1985—, dir. PhD program, 1992—; interim exec. dir. Partnership for Rsch., Tng. and Grad. Edn. in Child Welfare, 1994; research cons. child welfare orgns., Ill., 1968-85, Oreg. 1985—; lectr. U. Chgo., 1968-72. Co-author: Care and Commitment: Foster Parent Adoption Decisions, 1985, Adoption: Theory, Policy and Practice, 1997; mem. editl. bd. Jour. Sch. Social Work, 1978-81, Social Work Rsch. and Abstracts, 1990-93, Children and Youth Svcs. Rev., 1990-95, Jour. Social Work Edn., 1990-95; contbr. articles to profl. jours., chpts. to books. Bd. dirs. Oreg. chpt. Nat. Assn. for Prevention Child Abuse, 1985-87; bd. dirs. Friendly House, Portland, 1991-97, pres., 1995-96; mem. adv. com. children's svcs. divsn. State of Oreg., 1985-95. Grantee HEW, 1980-82, Chgo. Community Trust, 1982-86, Oreg. Children's Trust Fund, 1991-96. Mem. NASW, AAUP, Acad. Cert. Social Workers, Coun. on Social Work Edn., Phi Beta Kappa. Home: 2535 SW Sherwood Dr Portland OR 97201-1679 Office: Portland State U Grad Sch Social Work PO Box 751 Portland OR 97207-0751

SHIRLEY, COURTNEY DYMALLY, nurse; b. Trinidad, July 17, 1937; came to U.S., 1960; d. Andrew Hamid Dymally; m. Adolph Shirley, Apr. 8, 1960; children: Ingrid, Robyne, Andrea, Kirk, Sandra. Cert. mgmt./adminstrn. health facilities, UCLA, 1978; BBA, Calif. Coast U., 1980, MBA, 1983. Cert. critical care nurse, advanced critical care nurse, nursing home adminstr. Head nurse med. unit Prince of Wales Gen. Hosp., London, 1959-60; asst. head nurse, CCU staff nurse Cedars-Sinai Hosp., L.A., 1962-73; asst. dir. nursing, dir. in-svc. edn., staff nurse Beverly Glen Hosp., 1973-75; supr. ICU/CCU/house Imperial Hosp., 1975-76; house supr. Med. Ctr. of North Hollywood, 1976-77; dir. nursing Crenshaw Ctr. Hosp., 1977-78, Mid-Wilshire Convalescent, 1978-79; supr. ICU/CCU, coord. utilization rev. Temple U., 1979-80; house supr. East L.A. Doctors' Hosp., 1980-81; pvt. nurse various hosps. and homes, 1981-86; utilization rev. coord. Managed Care Resources, L.A., 1986-88; prof. rev. sys. utilization rev. coord., case mgr. Nat. Med. Enterprises, Santa Monica, Calif., 1988—, cert. case mgr., 1993-97; adminstr. Tri-Med Home Care, Inc., Thousand Oaks, Calif., 1997—. Mem. AACN, Internat. Case Mgmt. Assn., Sci. of Mind, Toastmasters (sgt. at arms 1990). Avocations: reading, scrabble, dominoes, entertaining, blackjack. Office: Tri-Med Home Care Inc 299 W Hillcrest Dr Thousand Oaks CA 91360-4264

SHIRLEY, ROBERT CLARK, retired university president, strategic planning consultant, educator; b. Jacksonville, Tex., July 1, 1943; s. James Cullen and Mary Jim (Clark) S.; m. Terrie Thomas, June 17, 1967; children: Robin, Deron. B.B.A., U. Houston, 1965, M.B.A., 1967; Ph.D., Northwestern U., 1972. Asst. dean faculties U. Houston, 1974-76; asst. to pres. SUNY-Albany, 1976-77, assoc. v.p. acad. affairs, 1977-79; assoc. prof. Central U. Iowa, Pella, 1979-81; prof. Trinity U., San Antonio, 1981-84; pres. U. So. Colo., Pueblo, 1984-96, pres. emeritus, 1997—; cons. on strategic planning and mgmt. to numerous colls. and univs. Author: Strategy and Policy Formation, 1981; contbr. articles to profl. publs. Mem. Pueblo Econ. Devel. Bd. Bill Laufman Meml. scholar U. Houston, 1965-66; Northwestern U. fellow, 1969-71; HEW research asst. grantee, 1971, 72; La. State U. Found. grantee, 1972, 73. Mem. Acad. Mgmt., Soc. Coll. and Univ. Planning, Pueblo C. of C. Presbyterian. Lodge: Rotary. Office: U So Colo 2200 Bonforte Blvd Pueblo CO 81001-4901

SHIRTCLIFF, JOHN DELZELL, business owner, oil jobber; b. Roseburg, Oreg., Mar. 2, 1948; s. Henry Marion and Sheila Nell (Delzell) S.; m. Connie Lee Cantrell, June 13, 1975; children: Darcie, Danielle, Andrew. BS, Oregon State U., 1970. Pres. Shirtcliff Oil Co., Myrtle Creek, Oreg., 1971—. Engr. Myrtle Creek (Oreg.) Vol. Fire Dept., 1971—, emergency technician, 1981—; mem. Rep. Cen. Com., Roseburg, Oreg., 1982-88; chmn. Umpqua Community Coll. Budget Com., Roseburg, 1983-96; bd. dirs. Mercy Hospice, Roseburg, 1988-96. 2nd lt. U.S. Army, 1970-71. Named Citizen of Year, Myrtle Creek City, 1986, Vol. of Year, Douglas County C. of C., 1987. Mem. Petroleum Marketers Assn. Am. (dir. Oreg. 1988), Oreg. Petroleum Marketers Assn. (v.p. legis. chmn. 1986, pres. 1987, PMAA dir. 1988), Pacific Oil Conf. (bd. dirs., v.p. 1995, gen. chmn. 1997), Lions, Elks, Masons, Shriners. Republican. Avocations: landscaping, jogging, racquetball. Office: Shirtcliff Oil Co 283 SW Western Ave PO Box 6003 Myrtle Creek OR 97457-0051

SHISHIM, FRANCIS G., artist, performer; b. Santa Monica, Calif., May 8, 1953; s. Francis A. and Margaret W. (Addes) Shishim. BFA in Painting, Art Ctr. Coll., 1975. lectr. Art Ctr. Coll. Design, Pasadena, Calif., Otis/Parson Sch. Design, Los Angeles, Calif. Inst. Arts, Valencia, U. Calif.-Berkeley Art Mus., San Francisco Art Inst., Trinity Coll., Hartford, Conn., 1986, Mus. Art, San Jose, 1985. Exhibitions with Paul Velick (The Light Bob) include Ruth S. Schaffner Gallery, Los Angeles, 1978, Swope Gallery/Art Garden, Venice, Calif., 1979, Los Angeles Inst. Contemporary Art, Los Angeles, 1979, Vanguard Gallery, Los Angeles, 1980, Espace Gallery, Los Angeles, 1981, Upstairs Gallery, Tryon, N.C., 1981, WPA Gallery, Washington, 1981, Marianne Deson Gallery, Chgo., 1982; exhibited in group shows at Los Angeles Inst. Contemporary Art, 1976, 81, Craft and Folk Art Mus., Los Angeles, 1980, Long Beach (Calif.) Mus. Art, San Francisco Internat. Video Festival, 1980, Mus. Contemporary Art, Chgo., 1981, Downtown Gallery, Los Angeles, 1981, Tortue Gallery, Santa Monica, 1981, Am. Gallery, Los Angeles, 1982, UCLA, 1982, WPA Gallery, 1982, Phila. Mus. Art, 1998; solo exhibits as The Dark Bob Calif. State U., Long Beach, 1983, U. Colo., Boulder, 1988, U. Calif., Irvine, 1998, traveling exhibitions, Los Angeles, Buffalo, 1983, Cochise Fine Arts Gallery, Bisbee, Ariz., Kansas City (Mo.) Art Inst., Spaces Art Ctr. Cleve. State U., Film in the Cities Jerome Hill Theatre, St. Paul, Randolf St. Gallery, Chgo., Chgo. Art Inst., Inst. Contemporary Art, Boston, Painted Bride Art Ctr., Phila,. Swain Sch. Design, New Bedford, Mass., Portland (Oreg.) Ctr. Visual Arts, L.A.C.E. Gallery, Los Angeles, New Langton Gallery, San Francisco, Inst. Contemporary Art, San Jose, Calif., Contemporary Arts Forum, Santa Barbara, Calif., Calif. State U., Long Beach., Sushi Art Gallery, San Diego, The Roxy, Hollywood, Calif., 1987, Diverse Works, Houston, 1987, D-Arts Gallery, Dallas, 1987, Utah Media Ctr, Salt Lake City, 1988, D.C. Spaces, Washington, 1988, Main Arts Festival, Portland, Minn., 1988, Barnsdall Gallery Theatre, L.A., 1988; exhibited with Rachel Rosenthal Mus. Contemporary Art, L.A., 1984; albums: One Bob Job, 1982, On Pico, 1983, Kabbalamobile (with Rachel Rosenthal) 1984, Uncontrollable Love, 1987, An Ever Ominous Dream, 1995, Kingdom Come, 1998; films: The Fossil Dig, 1983, A Day and A Night in The Life and The Death, 1984, Good Morning Balcony, 1986, The Untold Origin of The Super The Dark Bob, 1987, Mister Whisker, 1988, Parfectije (for Everyone) 1993, Valerie, 1998; appeared in numerous performances, radio interviews, recordings and videos, 1975—. E-mail: darkbob@#clarkbob.com. Office: PO Box 6461 Beverly Hills CA 90212-1461

SHIVELY, JUDITH CAROLYN (JUDY SHIVELY), contract administrator; b. Wilkinsburg, Pa., Jan. 30, 1962; d. John Allen and Edith (Crowell) S. BA in English, U. Nev., Las Vegas, 1984. Circulation aide Charleston Heights Libr., Las Vegas, 1979-86; asst. food editor Las Vegas Sun Newspaper, 1985-88, asst. horse racing editor, 1985-90, features writer, page editor, 1988-89, editor youth activities sect., 1989-90; racebook ticket writer, cashier Palace Sta. Hotel Racebook, Las Vegas, 1989-92; contract adminstr. nat. accts. Loomis, Fargo & Co., Las Vegas, 1992—; propr. Creative Computing, Las Vegas, 1996—; horse racing historian, rschr., Las Vegas, 1985—; vol. rsch. asst. Dictionary of Gambling and Gaming, 1982-84; part-time clk. Hometown News, Las Vegas, 1994-96. Staff writer horse race handicaps, columns, articles, feature stories Las Vegas Sun Newspaper, 1985-90; freelance writer for monthly horse racing publ. Inside Track, 1992-94. Mem. Phi Beta Kappa. Republican. Avocations: collecting horse racing books, clippings, materials for personal library of horse racing, computers. Home: PO Box 26426 Las Vegas NV 89126-0426

SHKURKIN, EKATERINA VLADIMIROVNA (KATIA SHKURKIN), social worker; b. Berkeley, Calif., Nov. 20, 1955; d. Vladimir Vladimirovich and Olga Ivanovna (Lisenko) S. Student, U. San Francisco, 1972-73; BA, U. [illegible]

Grad. Sch., 1986, Calif. Coast U., 1994—. Cert. police instr. domestic violence, Alaska. Social worker Tolstoy Found., N.Y.C., 1978-79, adminstr., 1979-80; program supr. Rehab. Mental Health Ctr., San Jose, Calif., 1980-81; dir. svc. counselor Kodiak (Alaska) Crisis Ctr., 1981-82; domestic violence counselor Abused Women's Aid in Crisis, Anchorage, 1982-85; pvt. practice social work Susitna Therapy Ctr., Anchorage, 1985-96; pvt. practice, 1985-89; field instr. Abused Women's Aid in Crisis, Anchorage, 1983-88, Divsn. Family and Youth Svcs., State of Alaska, 1989-91, South Ctrl. Found.-Dena A. Coy Prematernal Alcohol Treatment Ctr., 1991-92; expert witness Anchorage Mcpl. Cts., 1982-96; interim faculty U. Alaska, Anchorage, summer 1985, fall 1988-95, LaVerne U., Anchorage, 1986-96; family therapist Anchorage Ctr. for Families, 1994-96; clin. supr., dir. New Parent Support Program, Ft. Lewis, Wash., 1997—. Coordinator Orthodox Christian Fellowship, San Francisco, 1972-76; pub. speaker Abused Women's Aid in Crisis, Anchorage, 1982-95; active nat. and local election campaigns, 1968—. Mem. NASW (cert.). Democrat. Russian Orthodox. Avocations: organic gardening, reading, crocheting, soccer. Home and Office: 7643 10th Way SE Lacey WA 98503-1800

SHMAVONIAN, GERALD S., entertainment executive; b. L.A., June 26, 1945; s. Sarkis Neshan and Berje-Lucia (der Hareutunyan) S. Student, U. Calif., Berkeley, 1964-70. Leader archaeol. excavation team Guatemala, Turkey, 1970-75; pub. City Mags., 1975-80; special advisor Bicentennial Commission, Washington, D.C., 1987; chmn. Am. Nationalities Coun., Stanford U., 1983-86; pres. L.A. Talent, 1986—. Recipient Intercollegiate Boxing Championship, 1965. Mem. Calif. Scholarship Fedn. (life, pres. 1963), Nat. Forensic League (pres. 1963, degree of honor). Home: 6219 N Prospect Ave Fresno CA 93711-1658

SHNEOUR, ELIE ALEXIS, biochemist; b. Neuilly-sur-Seine, France, Dec. 11, 1925; came to U.S., 1941, naturalized, 1944; s. Zalman and Salomea (Landau) S.; m. Polly H. Henderson, Sept. 7, 1990; children from previous marriage: Mark Zalman, Alan Brewster. BA, Columbia U., 1947; DSc (hon.), Bard Coll., 1969; MA, U. Calif., Berkeley, 1955; PhD, UCLA, 1958. Tchr. and rsch. fellow U. Calif., Berkeley, 1953-55, Am. Heart Assn. rsch. fellow, 1958-62; tchg. and rsch. fellow U. Calif., L.A., 1958; rsch. fellow Nat. Cancer Inst., 1956-57; Am. Heart Assn. rsch. fellow NYU, 1958-59; rsch. assoc. genetics Stanford U., 1962-65; assoc. prof. biology and neuroscis. U. Utah, 1965-69; rsch. neurochemist City of Hope Nat. Med. Ctr., Duarte, Calif., 1969-71; dir. rsch. Calbiochem., 1971-75; pres. Biosystems Insts., Inc., 1975—; dir. Biosystems Rsch. Inst., 1979—; mem. exec. com. Nat. Acad. Sci. Study Group on Biology and the Exploration of Mars, 1964; chmn. Western Regional coun. Rsch. in Basic Bioscis. for Manned Orbiting Missions, Am. Inst. Biol. Scis., NASA, 1966-69; fellow Com. Sci. Investigation Claims of Paranormal, 1996—. Author: Extraterrestrial Life, 1965, (with Eric A. Ottesen) National Academy of Sciences, National Rsch. Coun., 1966, (with S. Moffat) Life Beyond the Earth, 1966, The Malnourished Mind, 1974; contbr. numerous articles to sci. and lay jours. Chmn. citizens adv. coun. San Diego Pub. Schs., 1971-72; mem. adv. coun. Cousteau Soc., 1977-98; bd. dirs. Am.-Ukraine Trade Coun., 1991-96, Lunar Power System Coalition, 1993—, Transinnova S.A. France, 1990—; chmn. sci. adv. bd. County of San Diego, 1995—. With U.S. Army, 1944-45. Recipient William Lockwood prize, 1947. Mem. IEEE, AAAS (chmn. So. Calif. Skeptics soc. Pacific divsn. 1988-90), Am. Chem. Soc., N.Y. Acad. Scis., Am. Inst. Biol. Scis., Am. Soc. for Biochemistry and Molecular Biology (chmn. sci. advisors program 1973-75, mem. com. on pub. policy 1974-76, congl. liaison 1992—), Am. Soc. Neurochemistry (mem. coun. 1971-73), Soc. Neurosci., Internat. Soc. Neurochemistry, U.S. C. of C. (bd. dirs. 1993—), La Jolla Chamber Music Soc. (bd. dirs. 1994-97), Internat. Coun. for Global Health Progress (N.Am. adv. bd. 1996—), Sigma Xi, Phi Sigma. Office: Biosyss Insts Inc/Biosyss Rsch Inst 700 Front St Ste CDM-608 San Diego CA 92101-6009

SHOBE, NANCY, fundraising consultant, small business owner; b. Detroit, Oct. 3, 1961; d. Richard William and Barbara Ann (Williams) S.; 1 child, Allison Elizabeth Stelyn; m. William Wright Watling, Aug. 23, 1996. BA, Mich. State U., 1983. Copywriter Wickes Lumber Hdqr., Vernon Hills, Ill., 1983-85; asst. to prodr. Music Ctr. of L.A., 1985, mercado coord., 1985-86; dir. comms. Candlelight Pavilion, Claremont, Calif., 1987-88, corp. dir. mktg., 1988; asst. dir. devel. The Webb Schs., Claremont, Calif., 1988-90; dir. devel. Crane Sch., Santa Barbara, Calif., 1991-96; owner Shobe Comm., Santa Barbara, Calif., 1996—. Contbr. chpts. to books. Mem. Coun. Advancement and Support of Edn. (heavy hitter spkr. 1993, cir. of excellence award for ednl. fund raising 1995). Democrat. Episcopalian. Avocations: antiques, travel, walking, swimming, reading. Office: Shobe Comm PO Box 41334 Santa Barbara CA 93140-1334

SHOCKEY, GARY LEE, lawyer; b. Casper, Wyo., Sept. 25, 1950; s. Bernis L. and Shirley E. (Diehl) S.; m. Dona K. Galles, June 1, 1979; children: Amber, Jeremy, Kimberly. AB in Polit. Sci. and Sociology, Yale U., 1973; JD, U. Wyo., 1976. Bar: Wyo. 1976, U.S. Dist. Ct. Wyo. 1976, U.S. Ct. Appeals (10th cir.) 1984, U.S. Ct. Appeals (9th cir.) 1988, U.S. Claims Ct. 1989, U.S. Supreme Ct. 1989, U.S. Ct. Appeals (fed. cir.) 1993, U.S. Dist. Ct. Ariz. 1994. Pub. defender State of Wyo. and City of Casper, 1976-78; sole practice, Casper, 1976-79; assoc. Spence, Moriarity & Schuster, Casper and Jackson, Wyo., 1978-82, ptnr., Jackson, 1982—. Mem. ABA, Wyo. State Bar (continuing legal edn. com. 1984-85, law and legis. reform com. 1986-88), Assn. Trial Lawyers Am., Wyo. Trial Lawyer's Assn. (bd. dirs. 1984-90). Office: Spence Moriarity & Schuster PO Box 548 Jackson WY 83001-0548

SHOCKEY, GEORGANNE MICHELLE, sales manager; b. St. Marys, Ohio, July 1, 1958; d. George Michael and Clover B. (Werner) Apelian; m. Gregory L. Shockey, June 22, 1985. BS in Home Econs., Ohio State U., 1980. Asst. dir. food svc. Meml. Hosp. Marriott Corp., Houston, 1981-84; assoc. dir. food svc. Cedars Med. Ctr. Marriott Corp., Miami, Fla., 1984-85; dir. food and nutrition svc. Children's Hosp. Stanford Sodexho USA, Calif., 1985-89; dir. food and nutrition Torrance (Calif.) Meml. Med. Ctr. Sodexho USA, 1989-92; regional sales mgr. Sodexho USA, Inc., Alameda, Calif., 1992—. Participant Shell Oil/L.A. Marathon Wheelchair Race, 1993-96, Children's Miracle Network, L.A. area, 1994, 95, Real Women Cook to Fight Breast Cancer, L.A., 1995. Recipient award Real Women Cook to Fight Breast Cancer, 1995, Salesperson of Yr. Sodexho USA, 1993, 95. Mem. NAFE, Am. Soc. Hosp. Food Svc. Assocs., Roundtable for Women in Food Svc., Phi Mu (past officer, nat. adv. dir. 1981-84, area coord.). Avocations: travel, golf. Office: Sodexho USA Inc # 400 2300 Contra Costa Blvd Ste 275 Pleasant Hill CA 94523-3955

SHOCKLEY, JAMES THOMAS, physics educator; b. Topaz, Mo., Sept. 16, 1925; s. William Ervin and Minnie Catherine (Turnbull) S.; m. Joan Elsie Griess, June 17, 1950 (div. Aug. 1968); 1 child, John William; m. Betty Jean Truitt, July 28, 1989. BA, Calif. State U., Fresno, 1951, MA, 1953; postgrad., Claremont Grad. Sch., 1955; PhD, U. So. Calif., 1961. Cert. secondary tchr., Calif.; cert. community coll. tchr., Calif. Aerodynamicist N.Am. Aviation, Los Angeles, 1953; instr. Calif. State U., Fresno, 1954-55, asst. prof. physics, 1956-63, instr. workshop in phys. sci. for elem. tchrs., 1961, credential advisor, supr. student teaching, 1956-86, assoc. prof., 1963-68, prof., 1968-90, prof. emeritus physics, 1990—; cons. Fresno County Schs., 1971, USAF, Fresno, 1971, 72; validity cons. Commn. Tchr. Preparation and Licensing, San Francisco, 1977; instr. NSF Inst. for high sch. physics tchrs., 1962-63. Author: Physics and Astronomy for Liberal Arts Students, 1970; creator 7 Univ. Courses, 1958-85; textbook reviewer, 1965-77. Active mem. Civil Def., Fresno, 1952; mem. City-Univ. Edn. Liaison Com., Fresno, 1963-64; judge Bullard High Sch. Sci. Fair, Fresno, 1964-66; sponser Physics Club, Fresno, 1953-55. Recipient I Dare You award Danforth Found., Sanger, Calif., 1944, Tchr. grant Danforth Found., Fresno, 1958; Congress of Parents and Tchrs. scholar, San Diego, 1960. Mem. Am. Inst. Physics, Planetary Soc., Astron. Soc. Pacific, Aero Club, Phi Delta Kappa. Mem. Christian Ch. Avocations: flying, oil painting, internat. travel, reading, photography.

SHOEMAKER, BILL (WILLIAM LEE SHOEMAKER), retired jockey, horse trainer; b. Fabens, Tex., Aug. 19, 1931; s. B. B. and Ruby (Call) S.; 1 child, Amanda Elisabeth. Jockey, 1949-90, ret., 1990, trainer, 1990-97. Author: Stalking Horse, 1994, Fire Horse, 1995, Dark Horse, 1996. Winner Ky. Derby, 1955, 59, 65, 86, Belmont Stakes, 1957, 59, 62, 67, 75, Preakness Stakes, 1963, 67; ret. with 8,833 wins, including over 1000 Stakes wins. Office: care Vincent Andrews Mgmt 315 S Beverly Dr Ste 208 Beverly Hills CA 90212-4310*

SHOEMAKER, CAMERON DAVID JAMES, dean, educator; b. Honolulu, Dec. 15, 1940; s. John James and Belle Bird (Kellogg) S.; m. Catherine LaMoyne Prevost, May 23, 1966 (div. 1969); 1 child, David James; m. Leona Martha Wohlwend, May 18, 1972; 1 child, Jennifer Lee. BA in Polit. Sci., The Citadel, 1963; MA in History, San Jose State U., 1973; EdD, U. San Francisco, 1990. Commd. 2d lt. U.S. Army, 1963, advanced through grades to maj., 1971; fgn. area officer U.S. Army, U.S., Korea, Germany and Vietnam, 1972-84; ret. U.S. Army, 1984; mgmt. analyst Def. Lang. Inst., Monterey, Calif., 1985; ednl. tech. project mgr. Def. Lang. Inst., Monterey, 1985-86, dir. info. resources mgmt., 1986-90; evening coll. adminstr., instnl. researcher Monterey Peninsula Coll., 1990-92; dean of bus. Sacramento (Calif.) City Coll., 1992-98; coll. dean Vista Coll., Berkeley, Calif., 1999—; instr., Chapman Coll., Monterey, 1982-84, Monterey Inst., 1987; chmn. Asian Employment Program Com., Monterey, 1983-84; guest lectr., Naval Postgrad. Sch., Monterey, 1986-87; mem. Handicapped Individual Program Com., Monterey, 1986-90, treas., 1989-90. Contbr. articles to various publs. Pres., Creekside Community Assn., Salinas, Calif., 1985-86; mem. County Svc. Area Adv. Bd., Salinas, 1985-87, Flood Control Dist. Planning Com., Salinas, 1986-87; active Leadership Monterey Peninsula, grad., 1992. Decorated Silver Star medal; recipient Comdrs. award for Civilian Svc. Dept. of Army, 1990; Carl D. Perkins fellow, 1993. Mem. Royal Asiatic Soc., Monterey Peninsula Scottish Soc. (treas. 1986-92), Los Rios Mgmt. Assn. (pres. 1995-96), Caledonian Club of Sacramento (treas. 1994-97, chief 1997-99). Republican. Roman Catholic. Home: 11577 Melones Cir Gold River CA 95670-7738 Office: Vista Coll 2020 Milvia St Berkeley CA 94704

SHOEMAKER, HAROLD LLOYD, infosystem specialist; b. Danville, Ky., Jan. 3, 1923; s. Eugene Clay and Amy (Wilson) S.; A.B., Berea Coll., 1944; postgrad. State U. Ia., 1943-44, George Washington U., 1949-50, N.Y. U., 1950-52; m. Dorothy M. Maddox, May 11, 1947 (dec. Feb. 1991). Research physicist State U., Ia., 1944-45, Frankford Arsenal, Pa., 1945-47; research engr. N.Am. Aviation, Los Angeles, 1947-49, Jacobs Instrument Co., Bethesda, 1949-50; asso. head systems devel. group The Teleregister Corp., N.Y.C., 1950-53; mgr. electronic equipment devel. sect., head planning for indsl. systems div. Hughes Aircraft Co., Los Angeles, 1953-58; dir. command and control systems lab. Bunker-Ramo Corp., Los Angeles, 1958-68, v.p. Data Systems, 1968-69, corp. dir. data processing, 1969-75; tech. staff R & D Assocs., Marina Del Rey, Calif., 1975-85; info. systems cons., 1985—. Served with AUS, 1945-46. Mem. IEEE. Patentee elec. digital computer. Home: PO Box 3385 Granada Hills CA 91394-0385

SHOEMAKER, MELVIN HUGH, religious educator; b. Bryant, Ind., Feb. 11, 1940; s. H. Vaughn S. and Thelora Shoemaker (Avey) Mason; m. Glenna Joan Cockrell, Dec. 29, 1961; children: David Wesley, Diana Marie Thornton, Daniel Luther. BA, Ind. Wesleyan U., 1962; MDiv with honors, Asbury Theol. Sem., Wilmore, Ky., 1967; postgrad., U. Wis., 1966; MPhil, Drew U., 1988; D of Ministry, Fuller Theol. Sem., 1997. Ordained to ministry Wesleyan Ch. as elder, 1964. Instr. Ind. Wesleyan U., Marion, 1966-67; prof. Bartlesville (Okla.) Wesleyan Coll., 1979-84; prof. New Testament, dir. honors program Azusa (Calif.) Pacific U., 1986—; mem. adv. coun. for Oxford (Eng.) U. honors semester Coalition for Christian Colls. and Univs.; sr. min. Hillside Wesleyan Ch., Marion, Ind., 1967-70, Houghton (N.Y.) Coll. Wesleyan Ch., 1970-73, Dearborn (Mich.) Free Meth. Ch., 1973-79, Calvary Wesleyan Ch., Bartlesville, Okla., 1980-82, 84-86; interim sr. min. Brethren in Christ Ch., Upland, Calif., 1989; asst. dist. supt. Tri-State Dist. Wesleyan Ch., Ark., Mo., Okla., 1985-86; mem. N.T. adv. bd. Baker Book House, 1990-93. Author: Eerdmans Bible Dictionary, 1987 (Gold medal 1988), Evangelical Dictionary of Biblical Theology, 1996. Youth affairs commr. City of Dearborn, 1976-78; pres. Dearborn Area Clergy, 1975-76; min.'s adv. coun. Youth for Christ of Greater Detroit, 1974-79. Mem. Soc. Bibl. Lit., Wesleyan Theol. Soc., Theta Phi. Home: 208 Calle Concordia San Dimas CA 91773-3987 Office: Azusa Pacific U 901 E Alosta Ave Azusa CA 91702-2769

SHOGREN, JASON FREDRICK, economics educator; b. Cloquet, Minn., Sept. 29, 1958; s. Travis L. and Lou Ann (Prevost) S.; m. Deborah Riley, June 16, 1984; children: Maija Liisa, Riley Travis. BA, U. Minn., Duluth, 1980; PhD, U. Wyo., 1986. Asst. prof. Appalachian State U., Boone, N.C., 1986-90; assoc. prof. econs. Iowa State U., Ames, 1990-95; mem. coun. econ. adviser Exec. Office of Pres. of U.S., 1997; Stroock Disting. prof. natural resource conservation/mgmt. U. Wyo., Laramie, 1995—; head resoure environ. policy Ctr. for Agrl. and Rural Devel. Iowa State U., Ames, 1990-92; vis. prof. Yale U., 1993. Author/editor 7 books on environ. econs.; contbr. articles to profl. jours. Trustee Albany County Sch. Dist. 1, Laramie, 1997—. Mem. Assn. Environ. Resource Econs. (editor newsletter 1992—). Office: U Wyo Dept Econs Laramie WY 82071

SHOLTIS, JOSEPH ARNOLD, JR., business owner, nuclear and aerospace engineer, consultant; b. Monongahela, Pa., Nov. 28, 1948; s. Joseph and Gladys (Frye) S.; m. Cheryl Anita Senchur, Dec. 19, 1970; children: Christian Joseph, Carole Lynne. BS in Nuc. Engring. (Disting. Mil. Grad.), Pa. State U., 1970; diplomas Air Univ., 1975, 78; MS in Nuclear Engring., U. N.Mex., 1977, postgrad., 1978-80. Lic. sr. reactor operator NRC, 1980-84. Mathematician, statistician, mine safety analyst U.S. Bur. Mines, Pitts., 1968-70; commd. 2d lt. USAF, 1970, advanced through grades to lt. col. 1988, ret., 1993; nuclear rsch. officer Fgn. Tech. Div., USAF, Wright-Patterson AFB, Ohio, 1971-74; chief space nucl. sys. safety branch Air Force Weapons Lab., Kirtland AFB, N.Mex., 1974-78; mil. mem. tech. staff, project officer Sandia Nat. Labs., Albuquerque, 1978-80; chief radiation sources div., reactor facility dir. Armed Forces Radiobiology Rsch. Inst., Bethesda, Md., 1980-84; program mgr. SP-100 space reactor power sys. tech. devel. program Air Force Element U.S. Dept. Energy, Germantown, Md., 1984-87; chief analysis and evaluation br. Air Force Safety Agy., Kirtland AFB, N.Mex., 1988-91, chief nuc. power and sources div., 1991-92, chief nuc. energy systems, 1992-93; dir. rsch. and engring., gen. mgr. N.Mex. ops. Oakton Internat. Corp., Va., 1993-96; cons. in field, 1993—; owner, chief exec.,prin. cons. Sholtis Engring and Safety Consulting, 1996—; space shuttle nuclear payload safety assessment officer Air Force Weapons Lab., Kirtland AFB, 1976-78; instr. med. effects nuc. weapons Armed Forces Radiobiology Rsch. Inst., Bethesda, 1980-85, mem. reactor and radiation facility safety com., 1980-85; faculty, lectr. Uniformed Svcs. Univ. Health Scis., Bethesda, 1982-87; chmn. Power System Subpanel Interagency Nuclear Safety Rev. Panel risk assessments of Galileo and Ulysses nuclear-powered space missions, 1987-92; Dept. of Def. chmn. Interagency Nuclear Safety Rev. Panel Evaluation of Ulysses and Cassini nuclear-powered space missions for the office of the pres., 1989-93; mem. power system subpanel Interagency Nuclear Safety Rev. Panel for evaluation of Mars Pathfinder and Cassini nuclear-powered space missions, 1993-98, mem. Southwest Regional Spacecraft Commn. Coord. Com., 1998—; instr., Inst. for Space Nuclear Power Studies U. N.Mex., 1987-91; U.S. del., tech. advisor UN Sci. and Tech. Subcom. and Legal Subcom. Working Group on Nuclear Power Sources in Outer Space, 1984-88; mem. U.S. contingent U.S. and U.S.S.R. discussions on nuclear space power system safety, 1989-90; mem. adv. com., tech. program com., outstanding paper award com., Space Tech. Applications Internat. Forum, U. N.Mex., 1989—; mem. Multimegawatt Space Reactor Power Project safety working group, 1988-91; mem. SP-100 Space Reactor Project safety adv. com., 1990-93; mem. space exploration initiative Nuclear Safety Policy Working Group, 1990-91; mem. Air Force Thermionic Space Power Program Safety com., 1990-93; mem. Strategic Def. Initiative Orgn. Ind. Evaluation Group, 1991-93; mem., ind. advisor U.S. Dept. Energy Ind. Safety Assessment of TOPAZ-II space reactor power system, 1993; mem. Ind. Rev. Team recert. evaluation Cassini space mission, 1994; mem. program com. Reactor Safety Divsn. Am. Nuclear Soc., 1992-94; lectr. N.Mex. Acad. of Sci. Vis. Scientist Program, 1991—. Author: (with others) LMFBR Accident Delineation, 1980, Military Radiobiology, 1987, Power Systems Subpanel Reports for Galileo, Ulysses, Mars Pathfinder, and Cassini Space Missions, 1989-97, Safety Evaluation Report for Ulysses Space Mission, 1990, A Critical Review of Space Nuclear Power and Propulsion 1984-1993, 1994; contbr. over 85 articles to profl. jours., chpts. to books. Charter mem. N.Mex. Edn. Outreach Com., 1989-93; USGA sectional affairs com. mem. for N.Mex., 1996—, USGA rules and course rating ofcl., mem. bd. dir., Sun Country Amateur Golf Assn., N.Mex., 1996—; edn. officer, career enhancement officer, Albuquerque sect. AIAA, 1997—. vice pres., Engrg. Alumni Assn., Univ. of New Mex., 1998—, pres., Tijeras Arroyo Golf Assn., Kirkland AFB, Mex., 1998—. Decorated Def. Meritorious Svc. Medal (2), Air Force Meritorious Svc. medal (2) Air Force Commendation medal (3), Nat. Def. Svc. medal (2), U.S. Army Reactor Comdr. Badge, U.S. Air Force Missileman Badge, Air Force Master Space Systems Badge, Nat. Aeronautics and Space Administration Achievement awards (4); recipient White House citation. Assoc. fellow AIAA; mem. Am. Nuclear Soc. (Best Paper 1977), ASME, AAAS, Planetary Soc., Nat. Space Soc., Nat. Orgn. Test, Rsch., and Tng. Reactors, Profl. Aerospace Contractors Assn. N.Mex., Sigma Xi. Republican. Achievements include origination of idea to develop coated particle fuels and fuel forms to enhance the safety, specific mass & volume, and performance of radioisotopic heaters and power systems for future space use, 1997. Avocations: hunting, fishing, camping, golfing, motorcycle touring. Office: Sholtis Engring & Safety Cons PO Box 910 Tijeras NM 87059-0910

SHONK, ALBERT DAVENPORT, JR., advertising executive; b. L.A., May 23, 1932; s. Albert Davenport and Jean Spence (Stannard) S.; BS in Bus. Adminstrn., U. So. Calif., 1954. Field rep. mktg. div. Los Angeles Examiner, 1954-55, asst. mgr. mktg. and field supr. mktg. div. 1955-56, mgr. mktg. div., 1956-57; account exec. Hearst Advt. Svc., Los Angeles, 1957-59; account exec., mgr. Keith H. Evans & Assos., San Francisco, 1959-65; owner, pres. Albert D. Shonk Co., L.A., 1965-97; gen. ptnr. Shonk Land Co. LTD, Charleston, W.Va., 1989—; pres. Signet Circle Corp., Inc., 1977-81, dir., 1962-81, hon. life dir., 1981—, treas., 1989—. Bd. dirs. Florence Crittenton Ctr., sec., 1978, 1st v.p., 1978-79, exec. v.p., 1979-81, pres., 1981-83, chmn. bd., 1983-85, hon. life dir., 1986—, treas., 1997, pres., 1997—; co-chair centennial com., founding chmn. Crittenton Assocs. Recipient Medallion of Merit Phi Sigma Kappa, 1976, Founders award, 1961, NIC Interfraternal award, 1989 . Mem. Advt. Club Los Angeles, Pubs. Rep. Assn. of So. Calif., Nat. Assn. Pubs. Reps. (past v.p. West Coast 1981-83), Jr. Advt. Club L.A. (hon. life, dir., treas., 1st v.p.), Trojan Club, Skull and Dagger, U. So. Calif., U. S.C. Marshall Sch. Bus. Alumni Assn. (nat. bd. 1991-, treas. 1995—), U. S.C. Assocs., Inter-Greek Soc. (co-founder, hon. life mem. and dir., v.p. 1976-79, pres. 1984-86), Rotary (Paul Harris Fellow), Phi Sigma Kappa (dir. grand council 1962-70, 77-79, grand pres. 1979-83, chancellor 1983-87, 90-91, recorder 1995—, v.p. meml. found. 1979-84, pres. 1984, trustee pres. Phi Sigma Kappa found. 1984-95, trustee emeritus 1995—), World Affairs Coun., Alpha Kappa Psi, Town Hall. Home: 225 Sapphire Ave Newport Beach CA 92662-1148

SHOPTAW, SHAUNA LYNN, middle school educator; b. Hayward, Calif., Oct. 23, 1966; d. Larken Clarence III and Loranne Jean (Long) S. BA in English Lit., Calif. State U., Hayward, 1987. Summer sch. tchr. San Lorenzo (Calif.) H.S., 1988; summer sch. h.s. and middle sch. tchr. Castro Valley (Calif.) Unified Sch. Dist., 1989—; tchr. 8th grade English and drama Canyon Mid. Sch., Castro Valley, 1988—. Summer youth concert condr. Jenny Lin Found., Castro Valley, 1995—; workshop leader Kids Turn, East Bay San Francisco, 1992-97; choir mem., soloist Calif. Singing Churchwomen, East Bay Area, Calif., 1989—; youth leader First So. Bapt. Ch., San Lorenzo, 1988-98, music dir., 1997—. Mem. Nat. Educator's Assn., Nat. Coun. Tchrs. English, Calif. Tchrs. Assn., Calif. Assn. Tchrs. English, Castro Valley Tchrs. Assn. Democrat. Southern Baptist. Avocations: music, reading, computers. Office: Canyon Mid Sch 19600 Cull Canyon Rd Castro Valley CA 94552-3715

SHORENSTEIN, WALTER HERBERT, commercial real estate development company executive; b. Glen Cove, N.Y., Feb. 23, 1915; m. Phyllis J. Finley, Aug. 8, 1945 (dec.); children: Joan (Dec.), Carole, Douglas. Student, Pa. State U., 1933-34, U. Pa., 1934-36; D in Econs. (hon.), HanYang U., Seoul, Republic of Korea, 1988. With property sales mgmt. depts. Milton Meyer & Co., San Francisco, 1946-51, ptnr., 1951-60, owner, chmn. bd. dirs., 1960—; owner, chmn. bd. dirs. Shorenstein Group, San Francisco, Shorenstein Co., San Francisco, 1960—. Past chmn. bd. trustees Hastings Law Ctr., U. Calif., San Francisco; founding mem. exec. adv. com. Hubert H. Humphrey Inst. Pub. Affairs, U. Minn.; founder Joan Shorenstein Barone Ctr. on Press, Politics and Pub. Policy, Harvard U. Kennedy Sch. Govt.; past pres., hon. life bd. dirs. San Francisco Park and Recreation Commn.; chmn. Vietnam Orphans Airlift; bd. dirs. San Francisco Performing Arts Ctr.; trustee Asia Found.; fin. chmn. Dem. Nat. Conv., 1984; apptd. by Pres. Clinton to Nat. Svc. Commn., 1994; chmn. San Francisco UN50 nat. com., 1995, also numerous polit. activities. Maj. USAF, 1940-45. Named Leader of Tomorrow, Time mag., 1953, Calif. Dem. of Yr., 1985; recipient Nat. Brotherhood award NCCJ, 1982, Disting. Svc. award Dem. Nat. Com., 1983, Golden Plate award Am. Acad. Achievement, 1991, Lifetime Achievement award Dem. Party, 1997; inducted Real Estate Legends Hall of Fame, 1997, Bay Area Coun. Bay Area Bus. Hall of Fame, 1998. Mem. Calif. C. of C. (bd. dirs.), San Francisco C. of C. (past chmn. bd. dirs., life bd. dirs. Office: Shorenstein Co 555 California St Ste 4900 San Francisco CA 94104-1714

SHORT, GREGORY NORMAN, composer, musician, educator; b. Toppenish, Wash., Aug. 14, 1938; s. Ralph Orling S. and Norma Marie (Alexander) Spence; m. Harriet Adele Nixon, Sept. 1958 (div. 1962); children: Kemberly Shiobhan; m. Grace Marie Wertman, Dec. 1968 (div. 1974); 1 child, Aric Grayson; m. Bonnie Jean Threkeld, July 1, 1978 (div. 1992). BM, U. Oreg., 1971, D in Musical Arts, 1995. Instr. piano Cornish Sch. Allied Arts, Seattle, 1965-69; pvt. instr. piano, composition Seattle and Whidbey Is., Wash., 1958—, Eugene, Oreg., 1969-74; instr. class piano, theory Highline C.C., Midway, Wash., 1967-69; music dir., 1977-82; tchg. asst. class piano U. Oreg., 1971-74, 91-93, grad. tchg. fellow history, 1991-92, grad. tchg. fellow theory, 1992-93; instr. theory, piano Judgendmusikschule, Hagen, Germany, 1974-76; instr. music history and lit. Skagit Valley Coll., Whidbey Is., 1993—; Co-founder Seattle Classical Music Supporters, 1968; co-organizer N.W. Composers Festival, 1973-74; music advisor Composers and Artists Support Assn., 1988-90; music dir. Skid Row Theater, Seattle, 1986, Carco Theater, Renton, Wash., 1987, St. Francis Episcopal Ch., Mill Creek, Wash., 1988-90; adjudicator Wash. Solo and Ensemble Contest, 1966-69, San Francisco Opera Auditions, Seattle, 1969, young composers project Wash. State Mus. Tchrs.' Assn., 1987-88, 94-97, East Side Music Festival, Bellevue, Wash., 1994-98, Seattle Fedn. Music Tchrs., 1995, 97; lect. Seattle Symphony, 1965-69; originator, writer, performer The American Composer KCTS-TV, Seattle, 1968-69; spkr., lectr. in field. Author: More About Music, Vol. 1, 1968-69, 94-98, A Book of Musical Lists, 1995-97; composer: Symphony No. 1 for Orchestra, 1956-68, American Concerto No. 1 for piano, 1965-68, Symphony No. 2 for Brass and Percussion, 1972, 76, Salute to the American Armed Forces, 1976, Bicentennial Sonata No. 4, 1976, Tehame Suite for band, 1982, 6 preludes for orch. on The Hobbit and Fellowship of the Ring, Farewell Duet for orch., 1982, Spirituals Sonata No. 5, 1982, Women Out West Sonata No. 6, 1985, Symphony No. 3 for Symphonic Wind Ensemble, 1985-86, Ghost Dance Sonata No. 7, 1987, Sequoia Concerto No. 2 for piano, 1987, Centennial Sonata No. 9 for piano, 1989, (video music) Clean Air for U.S. Forestry Svc., 1989, Northwest Tetrology: The Raven Speaks, 1987, Mount Takhoma, 1965, 91, Pahto-The Warrior Who Became A Mountain, 1992, 95, Chief Seathl, 1992, 96, Fog Woman, 1997, Mountain Sonata No. 8, 1988, Vistas for 4 euphonium, 4 trombone and 4 tuba, 1992, Tears of Heaven for organ, 1996, numerous others; chamber music includes (series) Sonatas in Tribute, Duo Sonata for flute and piano, 1989, Blue Dawn for violin, clarinet, piano, 1991, I Heard the Owl for solo flute, 1991, A Passing of the Sun for solo viola, 1991, Rhapsody for solo cello, 1991, Soliloquy for solo contrabass, 1991, Duets for brass, 1991, Dance Panels, 1991, Duo Sonata for violin and vibraphone/marimba, 1991, In Praise of Darkness for tuba and piano, 1992, Metaphors (string quartet), 1992, Crimson Moon for flute, viola, piano, 1992, others; vocal music includes Silver, Silent Moon for tenor and piano, 1992, Summer Dawn for soprano and piano, A Line in Winter for soprano, horn, piano, 1993; concert performances include Wash. State Centennial Artist, 1989, Recital of Washington Composers, 1989, others; numerous piano and composition recordings; appeared on Nat. Pub. Radio. Nat. Def. and Edn. Act fellow U. Oreg., 1971-74, Ruth Lorraine Close fellow U. Oreg., 1993; accompaniment scholar Eugene Womens' Choral Soc., 1970-71; recipient Best Composition 1970 Eugene Women's Choral Soc.; named Composer of Yr. Wash. Music Tchrs.'s Assn., 1989, Centennial Artist Wash. State, 1989. Mem. Am. Music Scv., BMI, Pi Kappa Lambda (Beta Theta chpt.). Episcopalian. Avocations: family, friends, reading, astronomy, art. Home: 6056 Robinson Rd Freeland WA 98249-9556

SHORTLIFFE, EDWARD HANCE, internist, medical informatics educator; b. Edmonton, Alta., Can., Aug. 28, 1947; s. Ernest Carl and Elizabeth

Joan (Rankin) S. AB, Harvard U., 1970; PhD, Stanford U., 1975, MD, 1976. Diplomate Am. Bd. Internal Medicine. Trainee NIH, 1971-76; intern Mass. Gen. Hosp., Boston, 1976-77; resident Stanford Hosp., Palo Alto, Calif., 1977-79; asst. prof. medicine Stanford U. Sch. Medicine, Palo Alto, 1979-85, assoc. prof., 1985-90, prof., 1990—, chief div. gen. internal medicine, 1988-95; assoc. dean info. resources and tech. Stanford U. Sch. Medicine, 1995—; pres. SCAMC, Inc. (Symposium on Computer Applications in Med. Care), Washington, 1988-89; assoc. chair medicine Primary Care, 1993-95; bd. dirs. Smart Valley, Inc.; advisor Nat. Bd. Med. Examiners, Phila., 1987-93; mem. Nat. Fed. Networking Adv. Coun., NSF, 1991-93; mem. computer sci. and telecomm. bd. NRC, 1991-96; bd. regents ACP, 1996—; mem. Presdl. Info. Tech. Adv. Com., 1997—. Editor: Rule-Based Expert Systems, 1984, Readings in Medical Artificial Intelligence, 1984, Medical Informatics: Computer Applications in Health Care, 1990; developer several medical computer programs including MYCIN, 1976 (Grace M. Hopper award Assn. Computing Machinery). Recipient Young Investigator award Western Soc. Clin. Investigation, 1987, rsch. career award Nat. Libr. of Medicine, 1979-84; scholar Kaiser Family Found., 1983-88. Fellow Am. Assn. Artificial Intelligence, Am. Coll. Med. Informatics (pres. 1992-94); mem. Soc. for Med. Decisionmaking (pres. 1989-90), Inst. Medicine, Am. Soc. for Clin. Investigation, Am. Med. Informatics Assn., Assn. Am. Physicians, Am. Clin. and Climatol. Assn. Avocation: skiing. Office: Stanford U Sch Medicine Stanford Med Informatics Msob X201 251 Campus Dr Stanford CA 94305

SHOUSHA, ANNETTE GENTRY, critical care nurse; b. Nashville, May 25, 1936; d. Thurman and Laura (Pugh) Gentry; m. Alfred Shousha, May 29, 1959; children: Mark André, Anne, Mary, Melanie. Diploma, St. Thomas Hosp., Nashville, 1957; student, Belmont Coll., Nashville, 1958, No. State U., Aberdeen, S.D., 1973; BSN, S.D. State U., 1985. Cert. coronary care. Instr. med. nursing Nashville Gen. Hosp., 1958-59, ob-gyn. nurse, 1959-60; insvc. educator Tri County Hosp., Ft. Oglethorpe, Ga., 1960-61; clin. mgr., office nurse Britton, S.D., 1962-90; med. nursing Nashville VA Hosp., 1990-92, gastrointestinal nurse, 1992-94, critical care nurse ICU, 1994-95. Contbr. essays to S.D. Jour. Medicine. Del., S.D. Dem. Conv. Recipient Gov.'s Recognition award for outstanding vol. svc. Mem. ANA, AMA Aux. (state pres.), Nat. Hospice Assn., Nurses Orgn. VA, Donelson/Hermitage C. of C. Home: 3632 S Agave Way Chandler AZ 85248-4155

SHOWALTER, BUCK (WILLIAM NATHANIEL SHOWALTER, III), major league baseball team manager; b. DeFuniak Springs, Fla., May 23, 1956. Student, Chipola Jr. Coll., Fla., Miss. State U. Player various minor league teams N.Y. Yankee orgn., 1977-83, minor league coach, 1984, minor league mgr., 1985-89; coach N.Y. Yankees, 1990-91, mgr., 1992-95; with Ariz. Diamondbacks, 1996—. Named N.Y.-Pa. League Mgr. of Yr., 1985, Eastern League Mgr. of Yr., 1989, Am. League Mgr. of Yr., 1994. Office: Arizona Diamondbacks Bank One Ball Park 401 East Jefferson St Phoenix AZ 85004*

SHREEVE, JEAN'NE MARIE, chemist, educator; b. Deer Lodge, Mont., July 2, 1933; d. Charles William and Maryfrances (Briggeman) S. BA, U. Mont., 1953, DSc (hon.), 1982; MS, U. Minn., 1956; PhD, U. Wash., 1961; NSF postdoctoral fellow, U. Cambridge, Eng., 1967-68. Asst. prof. chemistry U. Idaho, Moscow, 1961-65; assoc. prof. U. Idaho, 1965-67, prof., 1967-73, acting chmn. dept. chemistry, 1969-70, 1973, head dept., and prof., 1973-87, v.p. rsch. and grad. studies, prof. chemistry, 1987—; Lucy W. Pickett lectr. Mt. Holyoke Coll., 1976, George H. Cady lectr. U. Wash., 1993; mem. Nat. Com. Standards in Higher Edn., 1965-67, 69-73. Mem. editl. bd. Jour. Fluorine Chemistry, 1970—, Jour. Heteroatom Chemistry, 1988-95, Accounts Chem. Rsch., 1973-75, Inorganic Synthesis, 1976—; contbr. articles to sci. jours. Mem. bd. govs. Argonne (Ill.) Nat. Lab., 1992-98. Recipient Disting. Alumni award U. Mont., 1970; named Hon. Alumnus, U. Idaho, 1972; recipient Outstanding Achievement award U. Minn., 1975, Sr. U.S. Scientist award Alexander Von Humboldt Found., 1978, Excellence in Teaching award Chem. Mfrs. Assn., 1980; U.S. hon. Ramsay fellow, 1967-68, Alfred P. Sloan fellow, 1970-72. Mem. AAAS (bd. dirs. 1991-95), AAUW (officer Moscow chpt. 1962-69), Am. Chem. Soc. (bd. dirs. 1985-93, chmn. fluorine divsn. 1979-81, Petroleum Rsch. Fund adv. bd. 1975-77, women chemists com. 1972-77, Fluorine award 1978, Garvan medal 1972, Harry and Carol Mosher award Santa Clara Valley sect. 1992), Göttingen (Germany) Acad. Scis. (corr. mem.), Phi Beta Kappa. Office: U Idaho Rsch Office 111 Morrill Hall Moscow ID 83844

SHREIBMAN, HENRY M., religious educator; b. Phila., Jan. 21, 1952; s. Oscar and S. June (Snyder) S.; m. Barbara Miller, Apr. 3, 1981; children: Jesse Oscar, David Benjamin. BA, Dickinson Coll., Carlisle, Pa., 1974; MA, Columbia U., 1976, MPhil, 1978, PhD, 1988. Rabbi, 1981. Rabbi Congregation Am Haskalah, Allentown, Pa., 1978-83; instr. Gratz Coll., Phila., 1978-85; lectr. Hebrew U., Jerusalem, 1984-86; adj. asst. prof. Spertus Coll., Chgo., 1988-93; dir. Bd. Jewish Edn. Met. Chgo., 1986-93; head of sch. Brandeis Hillel Day Sch., San Francisco and Marin; lectr. Phila. Coll. Performing Arts, 1979-83, Limmud Conf., 1989, 97; bd. dirs. Broadcast Commn., Chgo., 1988-97; cons. Spertus Mus., 1987-93, Field Mus. exhibits, Chgo., 1989-90. Creator, writer TV programs, Seacher/Arts Alive, 1988—; performer, writer pantomime Everyman, 1968—; author: (childrens prayer book series) Siddur Mikor-Hayyim. Recipient Outstanding Svc. award, Theater for Children, Blvd. Arts Ctr., Chgo., 1990, Exemplary Teaching award, Kohl Internat. Found., 1987; fellow, Columbia U. Ctr. for Israel and Jewish Studies, 1977-78, 76, Jerusalem Fellows, 1983-86. Mem. No. Calif. Bd. of Rabbis, Reconstructionist Rabbinical Assn. Office: Brandeis Hillel Day Sch 655 Brotherhood Way San Francisco CA 94132-2901

SHREVE, THEODORE NORRIS, construction company executive; b. St. Louis, Feb. 14, 1919; s. Truxtun Benbridge and Beulah (Dyer) S.; m. Caroline Prouty, Jan. 7, 1943; children: Sara Ann Caile, Suzanne Shreve Foster, Theo Carol. BS, U. Colo., 1942. Sec., treas. Trautman & Shreve, Inc., Denver, 1946-68, pres., 1965-86, chmn. bd., 1984—; pres. 4030 Corp., 1984—. Mem. Colo. U. Found. Bd., 1988—; Rep. County Assembly, 1962. Served with USNR, 1942-45. Registered profl. engr., Colo. Mem. Mech. Contractors Assn., Colo. Soc. Profl. Engrs., Rotary, Gyro Club, Denver Country Club, Sigma Phi Epsilon. Republican. Episcopalian. Home: 420 S Marion Pkwy Apt 1403 Denver CO 80209-2549 Office: Trautman & Shreve 4406 Race St Denver CO 80216-3818

SHRIVASTAVA, VINAY KUMAR, communication arts educator, film and video producer; b. Allahabad, Up, India, July 1, 1954; came to U.S., 1980; parents Rajeshwar Prasad and Suman Bala; m. Rajrekha, Jan. 1, 1985; children: Rinay Kumar, Tanay Kumar. Diploma in Cinema, Film and TV Inst. India, 1976; MA, U. Tex., 1982; PhD, U. So. Calif., 1990. Asst. prof. communication arts Loyola Marymount U., Los Angeles, 1985-88; asst. prof. broadcast and electronic communication arts San Francisco State U., San Francisco, 1990—; tchr. radio-TV-film Calif. State U., Long Beach, 1988-90; dean academic affairs U. of Sound Arts, 1988—; co-producer films; ind. sound engr. 1976-80. Developed rec. arts program Loyola Marymount U. Mem. Univ. Film and Video Assn., Soc. Cinema Studies, Cinema Sound Assn., Broadcast Edn. Assn. Avocations: photography, palmistry. Home: 2216 Placer Dr Bay Point CA 94565-3340

SHRONTZ, FRANK ANDERSON, airplane manufacturing executive; b. Boise, Idaho, Dec. 14, 1931; s. Thurlyn Howard and Florence Elizabeth (Anderson) S.; m. Harriet Ann Houghton, June 12, 1954; children: Craig Howard, Richard Whitaker, David Anderson. Student, George Washington U., 1953; LLB, U. Idaho, 1954; MBA, Harvard U., 1958; postgrad., Stanford U., 1969-70. Asst. contracts coordinator Boeing Co., Seattle, 1958-65, asst. dir. contract adminstrn., 1965-67, asst. to v.p. comml. airplane group, 1967-69, asst. dir. new airplane program, 1969-70, dir. comml. sales operations, 1970-73, v.p. planning and contracts, 1977-78; asst. sec. Dept. Air Force, Washington, 1973-76, Dept. Def., Washington, 1976-77; v.p., gen. mgr. 707/727/737 div. Boeing Comml. Airplane Co., Seattle, 1978-82, v.p. sales and mktg., 1982-84, pres., 1985-86; pres., chief exec. officer The Boeing Co., Seattle, 1986-96, chmn., 1988-97, chmn. emeritus, 1997—; bd. dirs. Boise Cascade Corp., 3M Co., Chevron, mem. Boeing bd., 1985-97, vice chmn. New Am. Schs. Devel. Corp. Regent Smithsonian Instn. 1st lt. AUS, 1954-56. Mem. Phi Alpha Delta, Beta Theta Pi. Clubs: Overlake Golf and Country, Columbia Tower. Office: The Boeing Co PO Box 3707 Seattle WA [illegible]

SHROPSHIRE, DONALD GRAY, hospital executive; b. Winston-Salem, N.C., Aug. 6, 1927; s. John Lee and Bess L. (Shouse) S.; m. Mary Ruth Bodenheimer, Aug. 19, 1950; children: Melanie Shropshire David, John Devin. B.S., U. N.C., 1950; Erickson fellow postgrad., U. Chgo., 1958-59; LLD (hon.), U. Ariz., 1992; EdD (hon.), Tucson U., 1994. Personnel asst. Nat. Biscuit Co., Atlanta, 1950-52; asst. personnel mgr. Nat. Biscuit Co., Chgo., 1952-54; adminstr. Eastern State Hosp., Lexington, Ky., 1954-62; assoc. dir. U. Md. Hosp., Balt., 1962-67; adminstr. Tucson Med. Ctr., 1967-82, pres., 1982-92, pres. emeritus, 1992—, bd. dirs., 1995; pres. Tucson Hosps. Med. Edn. Program, 1970-71, sec., 1971-86; pres. So. Ariz. Hosp. Council, 1968-69; bd. dirs. Ariz. Blue Cross, 1967-76, chmn. provider standards com., 1972-76; chmn. Healthways Inc., 1985-92; chmn. bd. La Posada at Park Centre, Inc., Green Valley, Ariz., 1996—. Bd. dirs. Health Planning Coun. Tucson, mem. exec. com., 1969-74; chmn. profl. divsn. United Way, Tucson, 1969-70, vice chmn. campaign, 1988, Ariz. Health Facilities Authority, bd. dirs., 1992—; chmn. dietary svcs. com., vice chmn., 1988, Md. Hosp. Coun., 1966-67; bd. dirs. Ky. Hosp. Assn., 1961-62, chmn. coun. profl. practice, 1960-61; past pres. Blue Grass Hosp. Coun.; trustee Assn. Western Hosps., 1974-81, pres., 1979-80; mem. accreditation Coun. for Continuing Med. Edn., 1982-87, chair, 1986; bd. govs. Pima C.C., 1970-76, sec., 1973-74, chmn., 1975-76, bd. dirs. Found., 1978-82, Ariz. Bd. Regents, 1982-90, sec., 1983-86, pres., 1987-88; mem. Tucson Airport Authority, 1987—, bd. dirs., 1990-95, pres., 1995; v.p. Tucson Econ. Devel. Corp., 1977-82; bd. dirs. Vol. Hosps. Am., 1977-88, treas., 1979-82; mem. Ariz. Adv. Health Coun. Dirs., 1976-78; bd. dirs. Tucson Tomorrow, 1983-87, Tucson Downtown Devel. Corp., 1988-95, Rincon Inst., 1992-97, Sonoran Inst., 1992-97; dir. Mus. No. Ariz., 1988—; nat. bd. advisors Coll. Bus. U. Ariz., 1990—, mem. Dean's Bd. Coll. Fine Arts, 1992—, chmn., 1992-96, pres. Ariz. Coun. Econ. Edn., 1993-95; vis. panel Sch. Health Adminstrn. and Policy Ariz. State U., 1990-92; bd. dirs. Tucson Cmty. Found., 1996—; mem. adv. bd. Steele Meml. Rsch. Ctr., U. Ariz. Coll. Medicine, 1996—. Named to Hon. Order Ky. Cols.; named Tucson Man of Yr. 1987, Tucson Father of Yr. 1997; recipient Disting. Svc. award Anti-Defamation League B'nai B'rith, 1989. Mem. Am. Hosp. Assn. (nominating com. 1983-86, trustee 1975-78, ho. dels. 1972-78, chmn. coun. profl. svc. 1973-74, regional adv. bd. 1969-78, chmn. joint com. with NASW 1963-64, Disting. Svc. award 1989), Ariz. Hosp. Assn. (Salisbury award 1982, bd. dirs. 1967-72, pres. 1970-71), Ariz. C. of C. (bd. dirs. 1988-93), Assn. Am. Med. Colls. (mem. assembly 1974-77), Tucson C. of C. (bd. dirs. 1968-69), United Comml. Travelers, Nat. League for Nursing, Ariz. Town Hall (bd. dirs. 1982-92, chmn. 1990-92, treas. 1985), Pima County Acad. Decathlon Assn. (dir. 1983-85), The Rotary Club of Tucson (pres. 1993-94), U. Ariz. Alumni Assn. Coll. Nursing (hon. alumnus 1998). Baptist (ch. moderator, chmn. finance com., deacon, ch. sch. supt., trustee, bd. dirs. ch. found.). Home: 6734 N Chapultepec Cir Tucson AZ 85750-1001 Office: Tucson Med Ctr 555 N Wilmot Rd Ste 201 Tucson AZ 85711

SHROPSHIRE, HELEN MAE, retired historian; b. Prosser, Nebr., May 7, 1909; d. William Pearl and Dicy Belle (Myer) Stafford. Grad., Rogers Bus. Coll., Everett, Wash., 1928. Co-owner Camera Exchange, Pacific Grove, Calif., 1947-62; co-owner, photographer, writer Shropshire Film Prodns., Pacific Grove, 1950-76; pilot, co-owner Monarch Aviation, Monterey, Calif., 1962-63; co-founder, mgr. Calif. Heritage Guides, Monterey, Calif., 1971-98. Mem. Ninety Nines Inc. (life), Nat. Aviation Hall of Fame (bd. nominations 1996—). Republican. Avocations: golf, flying. Home: 1623 Josselyn Canyon Rd Monterey CA 93940-5273

SHTENGOLD, YEFIM SHELICHOVICH, medical educator, researcher; b. Novograd Volinsk, Russia, Apr. 16, 1927; came to U.S., 1996; s. Shelik David and Basya (Grushko) S.; m. Liliya Nikitichna Vasilevskaya, Feb. 16, 1961; children: Ekaterina Gribanova. MD, Med. Inst., Kishinew, Moldova, 1954. Intern in oncology Regional Med. Ctr., Grodno, Belarus, 1954-58; surgeon Regional Med. Ctr. Oncology, Moscow, 1958-62; anesthesiologist Inst. Child Surgery, Moscow, 1962-64; head Organ Preservation Lab., Inst. Clin. and Exptl. Surgery, Moscow, 1964-74; head Artificial Heart Lab., Inst. Transplantology and Artificial Organs, Moscow, 1974-80; head dept. biophysics, biomechanics and biomed. engring. Inst. Problems in Mechanics-Russian Acad. Sci., Moscow, 1980-96, prof., 1992—. Author: Mathematical Simulation of the Physiological Systems, 1971, Organ Preservation, 1975, Biomechanics of the Myocardial Muscle, 1981, Stress-Deformed Cardiovascular System and Hypertension, 1990; contbr. over 300 articles to sci. publs.; patentee in field. Home: 7549 Lexington Ave Los Angeles CA 90046

SHUBART, DOROTHY LOUISE TEPFER, artist, educator; b. Ft. Collins, Colo., Mar. 1, 1923; d. Adam Christian and Rose Virginia (Ayers) Tepfer; m. Robert Franz Shubart, Apr. 22, 1950; children: Richard, Lorenne. AA, Colo. Women's Coll., 1944; grad., Cleve. Inst. Art, 1946; student, Western Res. U., 1947-48; BA, St. Thomas Aquinas Coll., 1974; MA, Coll. New Rochelle, 1978. Art tchr. Denver Mus., 1942-44, Cleve. Recreation Dept., 1944-50; adult edn. art tchr. Nanuet (N.Y.) Pub. Schs., 1950-65, Pearl River (N.Y.) Adult Edn., 1950-51; rec. sec. Van Houten Fields Assn., West Nyack, N.Y., 1969-74. Exhibited in group shows at Hopper House, Rockland Ctr. for Arts, CWC, Cleve. Inst. Art, Coll. New Rochelle, Rockland County Ann. Art Fair, Gonzalez Sr. Ctr.; co-author: Windmills & Dreams, 1997. Leader 4-H Club, Nanuet, 1960-80, Girls Scouts U.S., Nanuet, 1961-68; mem. scholarship com., gen. com. PTA, Nanuet, 1964-68; rec. sec. Van Houten Fields assn., West Nyack, N.Y., 1969-74; com. mem. Eldorado (Santa Fe) Cmty. Improvement Assn.-Arterial Rd. Planning Com., 1992-94, Environ. Def. Fund, Union of Concerned Scientists, Nat. Com. to Preserve Social Security and Medicare; capt. Neighborhood Watch, local organizer Eldorado chpt. security com.; mem. Eldorado Conservation Greenbelt Com., 1996-97; campaign vol. Jim Baca for Gov., N.Mex., 1996, Eric Serna for Congress, 1996, Tom Udall for Congress, 1998; mem. Eldorado Hist. Com., 1995-97, Shakespeare in Santa Fe Guild, 1998. Gund scholar Cleve. Inst. Art, 1946. Mem. AAUW, NOW, Audubon Soc., Ams. for Dem. Action, Environ. Def. Fund, Union Concerned Scientists, Action on Smoking and Health, Wilderness Club, Delta Tau Kappa, Phi Delta Kappa. Democrat. Avocations: books, gardening, photography, bicycling, writing. Home: 8 Hidalgo Ct Santa Fe NM 87505-8898

SHUBB, WILLIAM BARNET, judge; b. Oakland, Calif., May 28, 1938; s. Ben and Nellie Bernice (Fruechtenicht) S.; m. Sandra Ann Talarico, July 29, 1962; children: Alisa Marie, Carissa Ann, Victoria Ann. AB, U. Calif., Berkeley, 1960, JD, 1963. Bar: Calif., 1964, U.S. Ct. Internat. Trade 1981, U.S. Customs Ct. 1980, U.S. Ct. Appeals (9th cir.) 1964, U.S. Supreme Ct. 1972. Law clk. U.S. Dist. Ct., Sacramento, 1963-65; asst. U.S. atty., Sacramento, 1965-71; chief asst. U.S. atty. (ea. dist.) Calif., 1971-74; assoc. Diepenbrock, Wulff, Plant & Hannegan, Sacramento, 1974-77, ptnr., 1977-80, 81-90; U.S. atty. Eastern Dist. Calif., 1980-81; judge U.S. Dist. Ct. (ea. dist.) Calif., 1990-96, sr. judge, 1996—; chmn. com. drafting of local criminal rules U.S. Dist. Ct. (ea. dist.) Calif., 1974, mem. speedy trial planning com., 1974-80; lawyer rep. 9th Cir. U.S. Jud. Conf., 1975-78; mem. faculty Fed. Practice Inst., 1978-80; instr. McGeorge Sch. Law, U. Pacific, 1964-66. Mem. ABA, Fed. Bar Assn. (pres. Sacramento chpt. 1977), Calif. Bar Assn., Assn. Def. Counsel, Am. Bd. Trial Advs., Sacramento County Bar Council.*

SHUGARD, OWEN STEPHEN, fine arts and antiques dealer; b. Corpus Christi, Tex., Sept. 9, 1955; s. Owen James and Mary Anna (Moss) S.; m. Leslee Kay Phillips, Nov. 5, 1994. BA in Art History, Am. U., Washington, 1985. Propr. Owen Shugard Antiques, Santa Fe, 1993—. Office: Owen Shugar Antiques 418 Cerrillos Rd Santa Fe NM 87501-2661

SHUGART, ALAN F., retired electronic computing equipment company executive; b. L.A., Sept. 27, 1930. BS in Engring. and Physics, U. Redlands, 1951. Dir. engring. IBM, San Jose, Calif., 1952-69; v.p. Memorex Corp., Sunnyvale, Calif., 1969-73; pres. Shugart Assocs., 1973-78; chmn., pres., chief exec. officer, coo Seagate Tech., Scotts Valley, Calif., 1978-98, also bd. dirs. Office: care Seagate Tech 920 Disc Dr Scotts Valley CA 95066-4544

SHUKLA, PRADIP KANTILAL, academic administrator, educator, consultant; b. Ahmedabad, Gujarat, India, Sept. 7, 1956; came to U.S., 1961; s. Kantilal T. and Manju K. (Vyas) S.; m. [illegible]; children: Monica, Amy. BSc in Bus. Adminstrn., Calif. State U., Long Beach, 1978, BA in Econs., 1978, MBA, 1979; MSc in Bus. Adminstrn., U. So. Calif., 1983; MEd, UCLA, 1983, PhD in Ednl. Adminstrn., 1990. Cert [illegible] (Calif.) Coll. 1976, instr. bus. and law, 1980-86, adminstrv. analyst, 1982-83, dir. instnl. rsch., 1986-88, asst. to pres., 1990—; night libr. Lynwood (Calif.) Adult Sch., 1974-78, lectr. in mgmt. Calif. State U., Long Beach, L.A., Northridge, 1978-91; mgmt. cons. P.K. Shukla & Assocs., Orange, Calif., 1979—; assoc. prof. mktg. and mgmt. Chapman U., Orange, 1985—; cons. various corps. and colls., Calif., 1979—; internat. cons. and speaker import/export ventures. Adv. bd. St. Francis Med. Ctr., Lynwood, Calif., 1979-81, Santa Ana (Calif) Zoo, 1988—; community breakfast chairperson City Lynwood, 1980; polit. cons. various candidates local and statewide, Calif., 1979—. Scholar Bank of Am., Soc. Calif. Edison Co., UCLA Grad. Sch. Mgmt.; grantee U.S. Dept. Edn., Compton Coll., Chapman U. Mem. Internat. Acad. Mgmt. Mktg., Internat. Acad. Bus. & Soc. (charter), Computer Using Instrs., Western Acad. Mgmt. (program reviewer, arrangements com., program com.), Western Mktg. Educators Assn. (program reviewer, session chmn.), Am. Mktg. Assn., Acad. Mgmt. (program reviewer). Republican. Avocations: photography, poetry. Home: 10492 Park Villa Cir Villa Park CA 92861-5318 Office: Chapman U 333 N Glassell St Orange CA 92866-1099

SHULER, SALLY ANN SMITH, telecommunications, computer services and software company executive; b. Mt. Olive, N.C., June 11, 1934; d. Leon Joseph and Ludia Irene (Montague) Simmons; m. Henry Ralph Smith Jr., Mar. 1, 1957 (div. Jan. 1976); children: Molly Montague, Barbara Ellen, Sara Ann, Mary Kathryn; m. Harold Robert Shuler, Aug. 2, 1987 (div. Mar. 1997). BA in Math., Duke U., 1956; spl. studies, U. Liège, Belgium, 1956-57; postgrad. in bus. econs., Claremont Grad Sch., 1970-72. Mgr. fed. systems GE Info. Svcs. Co., Washington, 1976-78; mgr. mktg. support GE Info. Svcs. Co., Rockville, Md., 1978-81; dir. bus. devel. info. tech. group Electronic Data Systems, Bethesda, Md., 1981-82; v.p. mktg. optimum systems div. Electronic Data Systems, Rockville, 1982-83; v.p. planning and communications Electronic Data Systems, Dallas, 1983-84; exec. dir. comml. devel. U.S. West Inc., Englewood, Colo., 1984-90; v.p. mktg. devel. Cin. Bell Info. Systems Inc., 1990-92; mgmt. cons. in mergers and acquisitions Denver, 1992-93; v.p. major accounts U.S. Computer Svcs., Denver, 1993-95; mgmt. cons. in mergers and acquisitions Mktg., Telecom., Denver, 1995—. Recipient GE Centennial award, Rockville, 1978. Mem. Women in Telecommunications, Rotary (Found. fellow, pres. Denver Tech. Ctr., amb. scholar 1956-57), Phi Beta Kappa, Tau Psi Omega, Pi Mu Epsilon. Democrat. Presbyterian. Office: 1626 S Syracuse St Denver CO 80231-2691

SHULTZ, GEORGE PRATT, former government executive, economics educator; b. N.Y.C., Dec. 13, 1920; s. Birl E. and Margaret Lennox (Pratt) S.; children: Margaret Ann Shultz Tilsworth, Kathleen Pratt Shultz Jorgensen, Peter Milton, Barbara Lennox Shultz White, Alexander George; m. Charlotte Mailliard, Aug. 15, 1997. BA in Econs., Princeton U., 1942; PhD in Indsl. Econs., MIT, 1949; Hon. degree, Yeshiva U., U. Tel Aviv, Technion-Israel Inst. Tech., Keio U., Tokyo, Brandeis U., U. Notre Dame, Princeton U., Loyola U., U. Pa., U. Rochester, Carnegie-Mellon U., Baruch Coll., Northwestern U., Tblisi State U. Mem. faculty M.I.T., 1949-57; assoc. prof. indsl. relations MIT, 1955-57; prof. indsl. relations Grad. Sch. Bus., U. Chgo., 1957-68, dean sch., 1962-68; fellow Ctr. for Advanced Study in Behavioral Scis., 1968-69; U.S. sec. labor, 1969-70; dir. Office Mgmt. and Budget, 1970-72; U.S. sec. treasury, also asst. to Pres., 1972-74; chmn. Council on Econ. Policy, East-West Trade Policy com.; exec. v.p. Bechtel Corp., San Francisco, 1974-75, pres., 1975-77; vice chmn. Bechtel Corp., 1977-81; also dir.; pres. Bechtel Group, Inc., 1981-82; prof. mgmt. and pub. policy Stanford U., 1974-82, prof. internat. econs., 1989-91, prof. emeritus, 1991—; chmn. Pres. Reagan's Econ. Policy Adv. Bd., 1981-82; U.S. sec. of state, 1982-89; disting. fellow Hoover Instn., Stanford, 1989—; bd. dirs. Charles Schwab & Co., Bechtel Group, Inc., Gulfstream Aerospace Corp., AirTouch Comm.; mem. GM Corp. Adv. Coun.; mem. Gilead Scis. Bd.; chmn. J.P. Morgan Internat. Coun.; chmn. adv. coun. Inst. Internat. Studies, Calif. Gov.'s Econ. Policy Adv. Bd. Author: Pressures on Wage Decisions, 1951, (with Charles A. Myers) The Dynamics of a Labor Market, 1951, (with John R. Coleman) Labor Problems: Cases and Readings, 1953, (with T.L. Whisler) Management Organization and the Computer, 1960, (with Arnold R. Weber) Strategies for the Displaced Worker, 1966, (with Robert Z. Aliber) Guidelines, Informal Controls and the Market Place, 1966, (with Albert Rees) Workers and Wages in the Urban Labor Market, 1970, Leaders and Followers in an Age of Ambiguity, 1975, (with Kenneth W. Dam) Economic Policy Beyond the Headlines, 1977, 2d edition, 1998, Turmoil and Triumph: My Years as Secetary of State, 1993; also articles, chpts. in books, reports, and essays. Served to capt. USMCR, 1942-45. Mem. Am. Econ. Assn., Indsl. Relations Research Assn. (pres. 1968), Nat. Acad. Arbitrators. Office: Stanford U Hoover Instn Stanford CA 94305-6010

SHULTZ, SUSAN KENT FRIED, executive search and international business consultant; b. N.Y.C., Mar. 25, 1943; d. L. Richard and Jane (Kent) Fried; BA in Govt. and Econs., U. Ariz., 1964; postgrad. in internat. affairs George Washington U., 1965-67; congl. legis. asst.Rep. Wm. E. Brock, 1964-68; campaign and press dir. various polit. campaigns, 1968-78; public relations cons., 1974-81; contbr. editor Phoenix mag., 1973-89; pres. exec. search and internat. svcs. SSA Exec. Search Internat., Phoenix, 1981—; U.S. ptnr. Morgan & Ptnrs. Exec. Search, Europe; writer Beverly Hills Diet and sequel, 1981-82, How to Adopt the Child You Want, 1990. Republic Nat. Conv., 1964, 68, 80, 92; dir. Acad. Bus. Coll.; charter mem. Charter 100, 1980; charter class Valley Leadership, 1980; Pacific Coun. Internat. Policy; membership chmn. Village 5 Phoenix Planning Com., 1980; del. White House Conf. Small Bus., 1986; mem. adv. Ariz. State U. Sch. Agribus. and Environ. Resources; past bd. dirs. Ariz. Bd. Trade and Tourism; past nat. adv. bd. SBA's Small Bus. Devel. Ctrs. Mem. Ariz. Bus. Leadership Assn. (past pres.), Phoenix Com. Fgn. Rels. (pres.), Nat. Assn. Corp. Dirs., Jr. League of Phoenix. Episcopalian. Address: 6001 E Cactus Wren Rd Paradise Valley AZ 85253-4239

SHUMAN, R(OBERT) BAIRD, academic program director, writer, English language educator, educational consultant; b. Paterson, N.J., June 20, 1929; s. George William and Elizabeth (Evans) S. A.B. (Trustees scholar), Lehigh U., 1951; M.Ed., Temple U., 1953; Ph.D. (Univ. scholar), U. Pa., 1961; cert. in philology, U. Vienna, Austria, 1954. Tchr. Phila. Pub. Schs., 1953-55; asst. instr. English U. Pa., 1955-57; instr. humanities Drexel U., Phila., 1957-59; asst. prof. English San José (Calif.) State U., 1959-62; asst. prof. English, edn. Duke U., 1962-63, assoc. prof., 1963-66, prof. edn., 1966-77; prof. English, dir. English edn. U. Ill., Urbana-Champaign, 1977-85; dir. freshman rhetoric U. Ill., 1979-84, coord. Univ. Associates in Rhetoric Program, 1978-84, dir. devel., 1988-93, acting dir. Ctr. for Study of Writing, 1989-90, prof. emeritus, 1993—; vis. prof. Moore Inst. Art, 1958, Phila. Conservatory Music, 1958-59, Lynchburg Coll., 1965, King Faisal U., Saudi Arabia, 1978, 81, Bread Loaf Sch. English, Middlebury Coll., 1980, East Tenn. State U., Johnson City, 1980, Olivet Nazarene Coll., 1984, 86, 88, U. Tenn., Knoxville, 1987; cons. Ednl. Testing Svc., 1970—, Am. Coll. Testing Svc., 1975-82; cons. in lang. and lit. Coll. Engring., U. Ill., 1980-97, Worldwide Youth in Sci. and Engring., 1995-97; mem. William Inge Nat. Festival Com., 1989—. Author: Clifford Odets, 1962, Robert E. Sherwood, 1964, William Inge, 1965, rev. edit., 1989, Strategies in Teaching Reading: Secondary, 1978, (with Robert J. Krajewski) The Beginning Teacher: A Guide to Problem Solving, 1979, Elements of Early Reading Instruction, 1979, The First R: Strategies in Early Reading Instruction, 1987, rev. edit., 1989, Classroom Encounters: Problems, Case Studies, Solutions, 1989, (with Eric Hobson) Reading and Writing in High School, (with Denny T. Wolfe Jr.) Teaching English Through the Arts, 1990, Resources for Writers, 1992, American drama 1918-1960, 1992, Georgia O'Keeffe, 1993; editor: Nine Black Poets, 1968, An Eye for an Eye, 1969, A Galaxy of Black Writing, 1970, Creative Approaches to the Teaching of English: Secondary, 1974, Questions English Teachers Ask, 1977, Educational Drama for Today's Schools, 1978, Education in the 80's—English, 1980, The Clearing House: A Closer Look, 1984, 70th anniversary issue The Clearing House, 1995; exec. editor The Clearing House jour., 1976—; cons. editor Poet Lore, 1977-90, Cygnus, 1978—, Jour. Aesthetic Edn., 1978-82; contbg. editor Reading Horizons, 1975-85; editor quar. column Reading Horizons, 1975-85; editor Trends in English column Ednl. Leadership, 1989-96. Active Nat. Trust Hist. Preservation. NEH researcher Trinity Coll., Dublin, Ireland, 1985. Mem. MLA, Nat. Coun. Tchrs. English [illegible] profls.), Internat. Fedn. Tchrs. English, Internat. Coun. Edn. of tchrs., Nev. Coun. Tchrs. English, Conf. English Edn. (exec. com. 1976-79), Internat. Reading Assn (coord. symposium on cultural literacy, Queensland, Australia 1988), Internat. Assn. Univ. Profs. English, Nat. Soc. Study Edn., Am.

Fedn. Tchrs., Union Profl. Employees (editor newsletter 1988-92, exec. com. 1988-92). Democrat. Home: PO Box 27647 Las Vegas NV 89126-1647

SHUMAN, THOMAS ALAN, correctional operations executive, consultant; b. Fairmont, W.Va., Dec. 31, 1946. BA, N.Mex. State U., 1969, 73; post-grad., U. N.Mex., 1988. Mgr. Drum Appliance, Inc., Las Cruces, N.Mex., 1971-75; classification supr. N.Mex. Corrections Dept., Santa Fe, 1976-80, mgmt. analyst supr., 1981-83, dir. classification, 1983-84, dep. sec., 1984-87; pres. Correctional Data Systems, Santa Fe, 1987—; owner Desktop Publ. Co., Santa Fe, 1988—; dir. N.Mex. Corrections Tng. Acad., 1991-95, probation, parole dir., 1995—; pres. Silicon Wizard Corp., 1989—; cons. Nat. Inst. Corrections, Washington, 1988, Am. Correctional Assn., Md., 1987—. Mem. Smithsonian Inst., U.S. Naval Inst. Served to lt. U.S. Army, 1969-71, Vietnam. Decorated Bronze Star, Presdl. Commendation. Mem. NRA, N.Mex. State U. Alumni Assn. Republican. Presbyterian. Avocations: fishing, painting, photography, writing.

SHUMATE, CHARLES ALBERT, retired dermatologist; b. San Francisco, Aug. 11, 1904; s. Thomas E. and Freda (Ortmann) S.; B.S., U. San Francisco, 1927, H.H.D., 1976; M.D., Creighton U., 1931. Pvt. practice dermatology, San Francisco, 1933-73, ret., 1973; asst. clin. prof. dermatology Stanford U., 1956-62; pres. E Clampus Vitus, Inc., 1963-64; hon. mem. staff St. Mary's Hosp. Mem. San Francisco Art Commn., 1964-67, Calif. Heritage Preservation Commn., 1963-67; regent Notre Dame Coll. at Belmont, 1965-78, trustee, 1977-93; pres. Conf. Calif. Hist. Socs., 1967; mem. San Francisco Landmarks Preservation Bd., 1967-78, pres., 1967-69; trustee St. Patrick's Coll. and Sem., 1970-86; dir. U.S. Catholic Hist. Soc., 1988—. Served as maj. USPHS, 1942-46. Decorated knight comdr. Order of Isabella (Spain); knight Order of the Holy Sepulchre, knight of St. Gregory, knight of Malta. Fellow Am. Acad. Dermatology; mem. U. San Francisco Alumni Assn. (pres. 1955), Calif. Book Club (pres. 1969-71), Calif. Hist. Soc. (trustee 1958-67, 68-78, pres. 1962-64), Soc. Calif. Pioneers (dir. 1979—), Drum Found. (v.p. 1986—). Clubs: Bohemian, Olympic, Roxburghe (pres. 1958-59) (San Francisco); Zamorano (Los Angeles). Author: Life of George Henry Goddard; The California of George Gordon, 1976, Jas. F. Curtis, Vigilante, 1988, Francisco Pacheco of Pacheco Pass, 1977; Life of Mariano Malarin, 1980; Boyhood Days: Y. Villegas Reminiscences of California 1850s, 1983, The Notorious I.C. Woods of the Adams Express, 1986, Rincon Hill and South Park, 1988, Captain A.A. Ritchie, Pioneer, 1991, Stormy Life of Major William Gouverneur Morris, 1993, Lord Sholto Douglas, Clamper, 1996. Mem. St. Andrew Soc. (hon. mem.). Home: 1901 Scott St San Francisco CA 94115-2613 Office: 490 Post St San Francisco CA 94102-1401

SHUR, EDWARD H., newspaper editor; b. N.Y.C., Apr. 12, 1953; s. Ira Shur and Harriet (Schechter) Steiner. BA, U. R.I., 1978. Night editor Carroll County Times, Westminster, Md., 1983-84; bureau chief The Baltimore (Md.) Sun, 1984-93; exec. editor, gen. mgr. Minn. Sun Publications, Bloomington, Minn., 1993-96; sunday, projects editor Reno (Nev.) Gazette-Journal, 1996—; CEO Shurshots Publishing, Sparks, Nev., 1978—. Recipient Special Section award Suburban Newspapers of Am., 1995, Enterprise award Nev. Press Assn., 1997, Best of Gannett award Gannett Co., Inc., 1997, 98. Mem. Am. Soc. Newspaper Editors, Soc. Profl. Journalists, Newspaper Assn. Am., Investigative Reporters & Editors. Avocations: reading, travelling, computers. E-mail: shurshots@aol.com. Fax: (702) 788-6458. Home: 926 Lionel Ct Sparks NV 89434-8899 Office: Reno Gazette Jour 955 Kuenzli St Reno NV 89502-1179

SHURTLEFF, AKIKO AOYAGI, artist, consultant; b. Tokyo, Jan. 24, 1950; d. Kinjiro and Fumiyo (Sugata) Aoyagi; m. William Roy Shurtleff, Mar. 10, 1977 (div. 1995); 1 child, Joseph Aoyagi. Grad., Women's Coll. Art, Tokyo, 1971; student, Acad. Art, San Francisco, 1991-92. Fashion designer, illustrator Marimura Co. and Hayakawa Shoji, Inc., Tokyo, 1970-72; co-founder, art dir. Soyfoods Ctr. consulting svcs., Lafayette, Calif., 1976-94; freelance illustrator, graphic designer; lectr. U.S. Internat. Christian U., Tokyo, 1977, Japanese Tofu Mfrs. Conv., Osaka, 1978; presenter cooking demonstrations, tchr. cooking classes. Co-author, illustrator: The Book of Tofu, 1975, The Book of Miso, 1975, The Book of Kudzu, 1977, Tofu and Soymilk Prodduction, 1979, The Book of Tempeh, 1979, Miso Production, 1979, Tempeh Production, 1980; illustrator: Spirulina (L. Switzer), 1982, The Book of Shiatsu-The Healing Art of Finger Pressure (S. Goodman), 1990, Staying Healthy with Nutrition (E. Haas), 1992, Culinary Treasures of Japan (by John and Jan Belleme), 1992, Yookoso, An Invitation to Contemporary Japanese, Vols. 1 and 2 (Hasu-Hiko Tohsaku), 1994-95, Blue Collar and Beyond (Yana Parker), 1995, Damn Good Ready to Go Resumes, 1995, Homework (Peter Jeswald), 1995, Vegetarian's A to Z Guide to Fruits and Vegetables (Kathleen Robinson with Pete Luckett), 1996, Hubert Keller's Cuisine, 1996, Doctor Generic Will See You Now (Oscar London), 1996, Everyday Pediatrics for Parents (Elmer R. Grossman, M.D.), 1996, Angels in My Kitchen-Devine Dessert Recipes (Caryl Westwood), 1997. Avocations: walking, designing greeting cards, running, dancing. Office: PO Box 443 Lafayette CA 94549-0443

SHURTLEFF, WILLIAM ROY, food products executive; b. Oakland, Calif., Apr. 28, 1941; s. Lawton Lothrop and Barbara Anne (Reinhardt) S.; m. Akiko Aoyagi, Mar. 10, 1977 (div. May 1995); 1 child: Joseph Aoyagi. BS in Indsl. Engring. and Physics, Stanford U., 1962, MEd, 1966. Indsl. engr. U.S. Steel Corp., Pittsburg, Calif., 1963; with Peace Corps, Nigeria, 1964-66; founder, dir. Esalen program in human awareness Stanford (Calif.) U., 1967-68; founder, dir. Soyfoods Ctr., Lafayette, Calif., 1976—, SoyaScan, 1998—; speaker in field. Author: The Book of Tofu, 1975, The Book of Miso, 1976, Miso Production, 1981, The Book of Tempeh, 1985, Tofu and Soymilk Production, 1984, Tempeh Production, 1986, Soyfoods Industry and Market: Directory and Databook, 1984, Soymilk Industry and Market: Worldwide and Country-by-Country Analysis, 1984, History of Tempeh, 1985, Tofutti and Other Soy Ice Creams: Non-dairy Frozen Dessert Industry and Market, 1985, Thesaurus for SoyaScan, 1999, and others; compiler over 45 bibliographies on soybeans and soyfoods; prodr. computerized bibliographic database SoyaScan. Mem. Soyfoods Assn. Am. (bd. dirs.), Tofu Standards Com. (co-chair 1984-86), Earthsave Found. (bd. dirs.), Tau Beta Pi. Home and Office: 1021 Dolores Dr Lafayette CA 94549-2907 also: PO Box 234 Lafayette CA 94549-0234

SHURY, VERA, security services company executive, insurance agency executive; b. Bremen, Ger., Dec. 7, 1939; came to U.S., 1951; d. Werner Voigt and Lisa Mali Magda Karla (Stege) Vujovic; m. Donald Shury, June 9, 1962 (div. Jan. 1984); children—Lisa, Donald. Student Fenn Coll., 1959-62, Ursuline Coll., 1977-81, Pima C.C., 1995-98, U. Ariz., 1996-98. Gen. agt. A-1 Bonding, Cleve., 1963-83; pres. State Alarm Systems, 1979-84, A-Aalavera Surety, Inc., Cleve., 1983—; pres. Liberty Sci., Inc., 1984—; chair gov. affairs Sun City Assn., 1994-95. Lobbyist Cleve. Growth Assn., 1982. Recipient Sr. Olympics medals. Mem. No. Ohio Bail Assn. (pres. 1979-83), Beta Sigma Phi, Phi Theta Kappa. Republican. Office: 12995 N Oracle Rd #141 Tucson AZ 85739

SHUSHKEWICH, KENNETH WAYNE, structural engineer; b. Winnipeg, Man., Sept. 22, 1952; m. Valdine Cuffe, Sept. 28, 1980. BSCE, U. Man., Winnipeg, 1974; MS in Structural Engring., U. Calif., Berkeley, 1975; PhD in Structural Engring., U. Alta., Edmonton, Can., 1985. Engr. Wardrop and Assocs., Winnipeg, 1974-78, Preconsult Can., Montreal, Que., 1978-80; prof. U. Alta., 1981-85, U. Man., 1985-87; engr. T.Y. Lin Internat., San Francisco, 1988-90, H.J. Degenkolb Assocs., San Francisco, 1990-92, Ben C. Gerwick, Inc., San Francisco, 1993-94, J. Muller Internat., Chgo., 1994-95, T.Y. Lin Internat., San Francisco, 1995—; mem. bridge design com., prestressed concrete com. ASCE-Am. Concrete Inst. Prin. works include design of prestressed concrete segmental bridges, seismic strengthening of San Francisco Ferry Building damaged in Loma Prieta earthquake, seismic retrofit of Presidio Viaduct in San Francisco; design mgr. for long-span west approach bridge of Northumberland Strait Crossing in Can.; contbr. articles to profl. jours. Recipient award for design of Vierendeel truss bridge, Man. Design Inst., 1977. Mem. ASCE, Am. Concrete Inst., Prestressed Concrete Inst., Internat. Assn. Bridge and Structural Engrs. Office: PO Box 2590 San Francisco CA 94126-2590

SHUSS, JANE MARGARET, artist; b. Ost, Kans., Feb. 15, 1936; d. Leo and Mary Catharine (Thimesch) Nett; m. Robert Hamilton Shuss, Feb. 19, 1954; children: Patrick, Andrea, Matt, Lisa, Robert, Eric. Student, Otis Art Inst., L.A. sec. Found. for Plein Air Painting, Avalon, Calif., 1995-97. One woman shows include Challis Galleries, Laguna Beach, Calif., 1981, 82, 83, Esther Wells Gallery, 1984, 85, 86, 87, 94; exhibited in group shows at Plein Air Painters of Am., 1985, 86, 87, 88, 89, 90, 91, 92, 93, 94, 95, 96, 97, 98—, Western Acad. Women Artists, 1996, O'Brien's Gallery, Scottsdale, Ariz., 1996, Desert Caballeros Mus., 1997, City of Avalon, Santa Catalina Island Co., 1998. Mem. Am. Acad. Women Artists (signature mem.), Soc. Am. Impressionists, Plein Air Painters Am. (treas. 1996-97, signature mem.), Calif. Art Club. Republican. Office: Shuss Design 15222 1/2 Pipeline Ln Huntington Beach CA 92649-1136

SHUSTER, MARGUERITE, minister, educator; b. Oxnard, Calif., Sept. 10, 1947; d. Carroll Lloyd and Grace Margaret (Hornbeck) S. BA (great distinction), Stanford U., 1968; MDiv, Fuller Sem., Pasadena, Calif., 1975; PhD, Fuller Grad. Sch. Psychology, Pasadena, Calif., 1977. Ordained to ministry Presbyn. Ch. (U.S.A.), 1980. From asst. to assoc. pastor Arcadia (Calif.) Presbyn. Ch., 1980-86; pastor Knox Presbyn. Ch., Pasadena, Calif., 1987-92; adjunct asst. prof. of preaching Fuller Sem., Pasadena, Calif., 1988-90; assoc. prof. preaching Fuller Theol. Sem., Pasadena, Calif., 1992—; del. Gen. Assembly Mission Consultation Planning Team, 1984-85, Inst. Ecumenical and Cultural Rsch., Collegeville, Minn., 1985, 86, Gen. Assembly (com. chair), 1988; editorial bd. mem. Theology, News and Notes, Pasadena, 1986—. Author: Power, Pathology, Paradox, 1987, numerous articles, sermons, and reviews in religious jours. and books.; editor and contbr. Perspectives on Christology, 1991, Who We Are: Our Dignity as Human, 1996. Named one of Outstanding Young Women in Am., 1979, 83. Mem. Presbytery of San Gabriel (chair, com. on ministry 1991, moderator, permenent jud. commn. 1993-95, moderator Presbytery 1996), Phi Beta Kappa. Home: 675 Mount Wilson Trl Sierra Madre CA 91024-1232 Office: Fuller Theol Sem 135 N Oakland Ave Pasadena CA 91182-0001

SHUSTERMAN, MELISSA LYNN, television producer, educator; b. Augusta, Ga., Sept. 8, 1967; d. Richard Melvin and Joan Ann (Meszaros) S.; m. Garyfallos Garyfallov, Sept. 12, 1998. BA in Liberal Arts, Lafayette Coll., 1989; MA in Film and Video, Am. U., Washington, 1993. Assoc. prodr. MTV, N.Y.C.; field prodr. Extra, N.Y.C.; prodr. VH1, N.Y.C., Food TV Gourmet Getaways with Robin Leach, N.Y.C.; adj. prof. U. Colo., Denver, Red Rocks C.C., Colo. Avocations: cycling, rowing, travelling, cooking.

SHUTTS, PETER GEOFFREY, architect; b. New Orleans, Oct. 26, 1946; s. Hamilton and Elizabeth (Chowins) S.; m. Katherine Elisabeth Small, Feb. 5, 1977; 1 child, Monica Elisabeth. BArch, U. Oreg., 1970. Architect pvt. practice, Pleasanton, Calif., 1976—; retired profl. race car driver. Chmn. Design Rev. Bd., Pleasanton. With U.S. Army Res., 1970-76. Mem. AIA (bd. dirs. Santa Clara chpt. 1985). Home: 4169 Alba Ct Pleasanton CA 94588-3088 Office: 4133 Mohr Ave Ste G Pleasanton CA 94566-4750

SHVIDLER, MARK JOSEPH, mathematician; b. Khmelnitsky, Ukraine, USSR, Mar. 25, 1931; s. Joseph Zuss and Lea Gersh (Gleyzer); m. Mariam Moses Mendelson, July 24, 1959; children: Irene, Eugene. MS in Applied Mechanics, Kiev State U., USSR, 1953; PhD, All-Union Rsch. Sci. Oil and Gas Inst., Moscow, 1958, DS, 1964. Scientist Sci. Rsch. Oil Inst., Ufa, USSR, 1953-58, dept. head, 1958-67; scientist All-Union Rsch.-Sci. Natural Gas Inst., Moscow, 1967-70; scientist, prof., dept. head All-Union Rsch.-Sci. Oil and Gas Inst., Moscow, 1970-91; scientist Lawrence Berkeley Nat. Lab., Berkeley, Calif., 1991-92; vis. scientist Atomic Energy of Can. Ltd., Chalk River, Ont., Can., 1993, Lawrence Berkeley Nat. Lab., Berkeley, 1994-99. Author: (books) Filtration Flow in Heterogeneous Media, 1964, One-Dimensional, Immiscible Flow Through Porous Media, 1970, Statistical Hydrodynamics of Porous Media, 1985; contbr. 150 articles to profl. jours. Mem. Am. Geophys. Union, Internat. Acad. Edn. Science Arts & Industry. Achievements include pioneer rsch. studies on statis. hydrodynamics of porous media and devel. of the theory. Avocations: chess, swimming. Home: 2951 Derby St Apt 228 Berkeley CA 94705-1350

SI, JENNIE, engineering educator; b. Changchun, Jilin, China, Mar. 16, 1963; d. Quanyou Si and Baolin Jiao; m. Jun Shen, July 27, 1988. BS, Tsinghua U., Beijing, 1985, MS, 1988; PhD, U. Notre Dame, 1992. Rsch. asst. U. Notre Dame, South Bend, Ind., 1988-91; asst. prof. Ariz. State U., Tempe, 1991-96, assoc. prof., 1996—; cons. Intel Corp., Chandler, Ariz., 1996, Ariz. Pub. Svc., Palo Verde, 1997; proposal panelist/reviewer NSF/NRC, Washington, 1995—; adviser Assn. Chinese Sci. Engr., Tempe, 1996—; adv. com. Social, Behavioral and Econs. Scis. divsn. NSF. Assoc. editor IEEE Transaction on Automatic Control, IEEE Transaction on Semiconductor Mfg. Presdl. Faculty fellow The White House/NSF, Washington, 1995-2000; recipient Rsch. Initiation award NSF, Washington, 1993-96, Motorola Excellence award Motorola, Semicon. Prod. Sector, Tempe, 1995. Mem. IEEE (voting mem. neural network coun. 1995—). Avocation: skiing. Office: Ariz State U Dept Elec Engring Tempe AZ 85287

SIBBETT, GENE, small business owner; b. Soda Springs, Idaho, Nov. 25, 1958; s. Glade G. and Eliza L. (Call) S.; m. Terri M. Lester, Sept. 1, 1979; children: Kuulei, Keli, Kanani, Kealoha, Melinda, Eugene, Ricky. Student, Brigham Young U.-Hawaii Campus, Laie, 1977-79; cert., Coll. for Recording Arts, San Francisco, 1980. Musician, sound technician Dolly Parton, Roy Clark, Vince Gill, others, Nashville, 1981-95; owner E-Tech Sys., Soda Springs, 1992-95; corp. advisor Kokua, Inc., Olympia, Wash., 1995-98; CEO, founder Buyers Edge, Inc., Elma, Wash., 1996—. Coord. 1992 Presdl. Campaign, Grays Lake, Idaho. Mem. LDS Ch. Avocations: golf, music recording, computers, basketball. E-mail: buyersedge@olynet.com. Office: Buyers Edge Inc PO Box 2035 Elma WA 98541-2035

SIBLEY, PETER EDWARD, lawyer; b. Ft. Walton Beach, Fla., June 12, 1944. Student, St. Mary's Coll.; BA, U. Calif., Santa Barbara, 1966; JD, U. Calif., 1970. Bar: Calif. 1970. Ptnr. Cooper, White & Cooper, San Francisco, 1986—. Office: Cooper White & Cooper 201 California St Fl 17 San Francisco CA 94111-5002*

SICHOL, SISTER MARCIA WINIFRED (SISTER), nun, fund administrator; b. Lewiston, Maine, Oct. 17, 1940; d. Adam Bernard and Ruth Winifred (Beck) S. BA in Humanities magna cum laude, Villanova U., 1969; MA in Philosophy, Georgetown U., 1977, PhD in Philosophy, 1984. Cert. tchr., Pa. Tchr. Sch. of the Holy Child, Rosemont, Pa., 1964-75, prin., 1970-75; prin. Sch. of the Holy Child, Drexel Hill, Pa., 1977-79; asst. dean Rosemont (Pa.) Coll., 1979-80; asst. prof. philosophy Xavier U., Cin., 1984-85, Neumann Coll., Aston, Pa., 1985-89; mem. leadership team Soc. of the Holy Child, Drexel Hill, 1989-96; exec. dir. Conrad N. Hilton Fund for Sisters, L.A., 1996—. Author: The Making of a Nuclear Peace, 1990. Trustee Rosemont Coll., 1989-96, Cornelia Connely Sch., 1998—. Hubert Humphrey fellow in disarmament State Dept., 1983-84. Office: 10100 Santa Monica Blvd Los Angeles CA 90067-4003

SICILIAN, JAMES MICHAEL, research engineer; b. Bronx, N.Y., May 25, 1947; s. Leonard James and Veronica Patricia (Reinwald) S. BS, MIT, 1969; MS, Stanford U., 1970, PhD, 1973. Tech. editor C.S. Draper Lab., Cambridge, Mass., 1968-69; research analyst Savannah River Lab., Aiken, S.C., 1973-76; staff Los Alamos (N.Mex) Scientific Lab, 1976-79, asst. group leader, 1979-80; sr. scientist Flow Science, Inc., Los Alamos, 1980-96, sec. of corp., 1980-96, v.p., 1990-96; cons., 1996—. Mem. Cultural Ctr. adv. com., Los Alamos, 1987-89; vice chmn. Park and Recreation Bd., Los Alamos, 1989-90; treas. N.Mex. Theater Assn., 1983-85; pres. Los Alamos Little Theater, 1978-79, v.p., 1997—; sec. Los Alamos Light Opera, 1990-91. Recipient AEC spl. fellowship, U.S. AEC, 1969-72. Mem. AIAA, ASME, Sigma Xi. Avocations: theatrical productions, skiing. Office: Remolinos 1345 Los Pueblos St Los Alamos NM 87544-2663

SICKEL, JOAN SOTTILARE, foundation administrator; b. Jersey City, Dec. 29, 1941; d. Peter S. and Rose M. (Maresca) Sottilare; m. Walter F. Sickel Jr., Jan. 4, 1964 (div. July 1979); children: Walter F. III (dec.), Linda Hilaire. AB, Georgian Ct. Coll., 1963. Dir. ann. giving Tucson Med. Ctr. Found., 1980-87; dir. devel. and pub. rels. Ariz. Children's Home, Tucson, 1987-93; exec. dir. Ariz. Children's Home Found., Tucson, 1993-94; curator edn. program devel. Ariz. Aerospace Found., Tucson, 1995-96; cons. Postal History Found., Tucson, 1996; ann. giving officer Nature Conservancy, Tucson, 1996; tchr. Amphitheater Pub. Schs., Tucson, Ariz., 1997—. Mem. women's studies adv. coun. U. Ariz. Mem. Nat. Soc. Fund Raising Execs., Nat. Assn. for Hosp. Devel., Pub. Rels. Soc. Am., Planned Giving Round Table of So. Ariz., AAUW, Ariz. Assn. for Hosp. Devel. (treas. 1986-88), U. Ariz. Presidents Club, U. Ariz. Wildcat Club, Soroptimists Internat. (chair fin. com. 1985). Home: 4151 N Camino Ferreo Tucson AZ 85750-6358 Office: Nature Conservancy 4151 N Camino Ferreo Tucson AZ 85750-6358

SIDDIQI, TOUFIQ ALIUDDIN, science administrator, researcher, educator; b. Hyderabad, India, Sept. 6, 1937; came to U.S., 1967; s. Raziuddin and Khurshid S.; m. Ulrike Wetzel, Dec. 9, 1966. BA with honors, Cambridge U., England, 1959; D in Nuclear Physics, Johann Wolfgang Goethe U., Frankfurt, Fed. Republic of Germany, 1966. Research assoc. Ind. U., Bloomington, 1967-69, 70-72, from asst. to assoc. prof., 1972-77; research assoc. East-West Ctr., Honolulu, 1977-92, spl. asst. to pres., 1984-87, sr. fellow environment program, 1992-97; pres. Global Environ. & Energy in the 21st Century, 1997—; regional adviser on energy UN Econ. and Social Commn. Asia and the Pacific, 1995-97; pres. Hawaiian Acad. Scis., 1990-91. Author: World Energy, 1976; co-editor: Coal Transportation in Asia and the Pacific, 1985, Newer Coal Technologies, 1986, Energy Policies and Global Climate Change, 1991; contbr. articles to profl. jours. Mem. Am. Phys. Soc., AAAS, Sigma Xi. Avocations: tennis, photography, reading, computers. Home: 250 Kawaihae St Apt 17F Honolulu HI 96825-1930 Office: Global Environ & Energy in 21st Century PO Box 25248 Honolulu HI 96825-0248

SIDES, ELIZABETH M., artist, educator; b. Cin., Apr. 12, 1937; d. John W. and Agnes (Hales) Blackford; m. Alfred B. Sides, Dec. 24, 1956; children: Leisa, Alan, Rebecca. B in Behavioral Sci., Nat. Lewis U., 1982; postgrad. studies, Claremont (Calif.) Grad. Sch., 1984; MA in Tchg., Nat. Lewis U., 1989. Cert. tchr., Calif. Tchr. Claremont Unified Sch. Dist., 1991—; instr. Dale Carnegie Inc. of Inland Empire, Calif., 1993—; facilitator J. Paul Getty Inst., 1994-96; owner A&E Enterprises, Claremont, Calif., 1995-98, Elizabeth's Art Studio, 1997—. Artist: works include: (oil) Resurrection, 1996 (2d pl. award), (water color) Elizabeth's Mountain, 1997 (hon. mention), (mural) El Ranchero Memories, 1998; illustrator: (book) Skipper and the Princess, 1996. Judge America's Kids, L.A. County Fair, Pomona, Calif., 1997, Reflections Competition, Upland, Calif., 1998. Grantee Best Bet Grant, C. of C., Claremont, Calif., 1996; finalist Bravo award Dorothy Chandler Music Ctr. Edn. Guild, 1996; (with others) Faculty Disting Sch., State of Calif., 1998. Mem. Associated Artists Assn., Pomona Valley Art Assn., Claremont Lions Club. Office: Elizabeth's Art Studio 226 W Foothill Blvd Ste J Claremont CA 91711-2740

SIDNEY, WILLIAM WRIGHT, retired aerospace company executive; b. Anaconda, Mont., Dec. 31, 1929; s. Paul and Lily Maud (Wright) S.; divorced; children: Kay Elise, Paul Daniel. Student U. Calif., Berkeley, 1953-56. Supr. prodn. Kaiser Aerospace, San Leandro, Calif., 1953-57, project engr., 1957-67, chief engr., 1967-69, gen. mgr., 1969-77; pres. Kaiser Aerotech, San Leandro, Calif., 1977-95, Kaiser Space Products, Pueblo, Colo., 1988-95, ret., 1995. With USN, 1948-52. Recipient NASA Pub. Svc. medal 1981. Home: 6025 Ridgemont Dr Oakland CA 94619-3721

SIEBEL, THOMAS M., executive. Chmn., CEO Siebel System, San Mateo, Calif. Office: 1855 S Grant St San Mateo CA 94402-7016*

SIEGEL, CHARLES NEIL, writer; b. N.Y.C., Feb. 14, 1947; s. Milton and Ethel (Navasky) S.; m. Jeanne Marie Miller, Oct. 29, 1980; 1 child, Benedict Siegel-Miller. AB, Columbia U., 1967; MA, Rutgers U., 1971. Freelance writer Berkeley, Calif., 1985—; dir. Preservation Inst., Berkeley, 1996—. Author: The ABCs of Paradox, 1989, Teach Yourself C, 1989, Mastering FoxPro, 1990, Teach Yourself dBASE IV, 1991, Practical Approach, 1993, Teach Yourself Access, 1993, Teach Yourself dBASE for Windows, 1994, The Power of Approach, 1995, Mastering Visual FoxPro, 1996, Teach Yourself Access for Windows, 1996, The Preservationist Manifesto, 1996; editor: The Original Book of Ecclesiastes, 1997. Transp. commr. City of Berkeley, 1986-87; transp. chair Sierra Club San Francisco Bay Chpt., Oakland, Calif., 1993-94; spokesperson Urban Ecology, Oakland, 1995—; bd. mem. Bicycle Friendly Berkeley Coalition, 1997—. Office: Preservation Inst 2140 Shattuck Ave # 2122 Berkeley CA 94704-1210

SIEGEL, DAVID AARON, accountant; b. Brizdowicz, Poland, June 10, 1913; came to U.S., 1920; s. Isaac and Malka (Pickholtz) S.; m. Rose Minsky, June 20, 1937; children: Stanley, Ira Theodore. BBA, St. Johns U., 1934; MBA, NYU, 1939. CPA, N.Y., Calif. Pvt. practice N.Y.C., 1929-49, L.A., 1974—; chmn. bus. City of N.Y., 1950-73. Co-author (with Stanley Siegel): Accounting and Financial Disclosure. Bd. govs., fin. sec. Ketubah Unit B'nai B'rith, L.A., 1980—, pres., 1986-87; chmn. audit com. Congregation Mogen David, L.A., 1990—. Recipient award for svc. B'nai Brith, L.A., 1990, 150th Anniv. Cert. of Appreciation, 1993, Plaque for Svc. N.Y. State Soc. CPA's, 1993-94; named Man of Yr. Congregation Mogen David, L.A., 1995. Mem. Knights of Pythias (chancellor comdr. 1981, chmn. fin. com. 1985). Avocations: swimming, theater, music. Home: 2175 S Beverly Glen Blvd Los Angeles CA 90025-6050

SIEGEL, MICHAEL ELLIOT, nuclear medicine physician, educator; b. N.Y.C., May 13, 1942; s. Benjamin and Rose (Gilbert) S.; m. Marsha Rose Snower, Mar. 20, 1966; children: Herrick Jove, Meridith Ann. AB, Cornell U., 1964; MD, Chgo. Med. Sch., 1968. Diplomate Nat. Bd. Med. Examiners. Intern Cedars-Sinai Med. Ctr., L.A., 1968-69; resident in radiology, 1969-70; NIH fellow in radiology Temple U. Med. Ctr., Phila., 1970-71; NIH fellow in nuclear medicine Johns Hopkins U. Sch. Medicine, Balt., 1971-73, asst. prof. radiology, 1972-76; assoc. prof. radiology, medicine U. So. Calif., L.A., 1976—; prof. radiology, 1989—, dir. divsn. nuclear medicine, 1982—; dir. Sch. Nuclear Medicine, L.A. County-U. So. Calif. Med. Ctr., 1976—; dir. divsn. nuclear medicine Kenneth Norris Cancer Hosp. and Rsch. Ctr., L.A., 1983—; dir. dept. nuclear medicine Orthopaedic Hosp., L.A., 1981—, Intercommunity Hosp., Covina, Calif., 1981—, U. So. Calif. Univ. Hosp., L.A., 1993—; cons. dept. nuclear medicine Rancho Los Amigos Hosp., Downey, Calif., 1976—. Author: Textbook of Nuclear Medicine, 1978, Vascular Surgery, 1983, 88, and numerous others textbooks; editor: Nuclear Cardiology, 1981, Vascular Disease: Nuclear Medicine, 1983. Mem. Maple Ctr., Beverly Hills. Served as maj. USAF, 1974-76. Recipient Outstanding Alumnus award Chgo. Med. Sch., 1991. Fellow Am. Coll. Nuclear Medicine (sci. investigator 1974, 76, nominations com. 1980, program com. 1983, bd. trustees 1993, disting. fellow, 1993, bd. reps., 1993—, bd. dirs. 1994—, treas. 1996—, ann. sci. program chmn. 1996—, pres.'s award 1997, v.p. 1997-98, pres.-elect 1998, pres., 1999); mem. Soc. Nuclear Medicine (sci. exhbn. com. 1978-79, program com. 1979-80, Silver medal 1975), Calif. Med. Assn. (sci. adv. bd. 1987—), Radiol. Soc. N.Am., Soc. Nuclear Magnetic Resonance Imaging, Alpha Omega Alpha. Lodge: Friars So. Calif. Research on devel. of nuclear medicine techniques to: evaluate cardiovascular disease and diagnose and treat cancer, clinical utilization of video digital displays in nuclear medicine development; inventor pneumatic radiologic pressure system. Office: U So Calif Med Ctr PO Box 693 1200 N State St Los Angeles CA 90033-1029

SIEGEL, PATRICIA ANN, association management specialist; b. Louisville, Mar. 29, 1955; d. Roy John and Theresa (Preate) S. BS in Human Svcs., U. Scranton, 1977; M Psychosocial Sci., Pa. State U., 1982, cert. cmty. psychologist, 1982. Field rep. Am. Cancer Soc., Bethlehem, Pa., 1978-80; teen dir. YWCA, Harrisburg, Pa., 1980-82; mgr. membership devel. AAUW, Washington, 1982-85; mgr. membership Boat Owners Assn. U.S. (BOAT/US), Alexandria, Va., 1985-88; asst. v.p. leadership and membership devel. Nat. Assn. Home Builders, Washington, 1988-95; prin. Siegel & Assocs. Internat., San Francisco, 1995—; founder, pres. Ctr. for Excellence in Assn. Leadership; cons. to membership-based assns., San Francisco, 1995—. Contbg. author: The National-Chapter Partnership, 1993; contbr. articles to profl. publs. Mem. Am. Soc. Assn. Execs. (cert., trainer, presenter confs. and meetings 1990-95, bd. dirs. 1993-95, edn. com. 1995, charter chmn. chpt. rels. sect. 1993-95, award of membership excellence in membership 1992, cert. assn. exec. 1990). Avocations: fitness walking, reading, travel. Office: 236 W Portal Ave # 136 San Francisco CA 94127-1423

SIEGEL, PETER HOWARD, millimeter-wave engineer, researcher; b. N.Y.C., Aug. 9, 1954; s. Bernard and Dorothy Eve (Kaplan) S.; m. Ronnie Ann Swire, July 4, 1976; 1 child, Alexander Rigel. BA, Colgate U., 1976;

MS, Columbia U., 1978, PhD in Elec. Engring., 1983. Mem. staff Sigma Data Corp., N.Y.C., 1976; rsch. asst. Columbia U. Radiation Lab., N.Y.C., 1977-83; with Nat. Rsch. Coun. Assn. Goddard Inst. Space Studies, N.Y.C., 1983-84; mem. tech. staff Nat. Radio Astronomy Observatory, Charlottesville, Va., 1984-87; from mem. staff to tech. group supr. Calif. Inst. Tech., Pasadena, Calif., 1987-93, tech. group supr., 1993—; mem. sci. adv. bd. U. Mich. Ctr. for Space Tech., Ann Arbor, 1995-97. Contbr. articles to profl. jours. Nat. Rsch. Council fellow NASA, 1983. Mem. IEEE (sr.), Union of Radio Sci. Commission D. Democrat. E-mail: phs@merlin.jpl.nasa.gov. Fax: 818-393-4683. Office: Calif Inst Tech Jet Propulsion Lab 4800 Oak Grove Dr Pasadena CA 91109

SIEGEL, ROBERT IRVING ALLEN, minister, writer; b. Miami Beach, Fla., Dec. 3, 1953; s. Seymour and Muriel (Burkas) S.; m. Laura Gay Grahm, Jan. 8, 1977; children: Elizabeth Charity, Nathanael Robert Mark. BA in Theater Arts, San Jose State U., 1977; MA in Campus Ministry, Denver Sem., Englewood, Colo., 1982. Ordained to ministry Goleta (Calif.) Bapt. Ch., 1981; min.'s lic. 1st Bapt. Ch., San Jose. Campus min. Mission to the Ams., Tempe, Ariz., 1977-79, Goleta, 1979-84; pastor of the ch. Sojourner's Christian Fellowship, San Diego, 1984-88; itinerant evangelist Mission to the Ams., San Diego, 1988—; regional dir. for Ariz. and Calif. Mission to the Ams., 1993—; creative dir. Warehouse Theater, Christian Cmty. Theater, El Cajon, Calif., 1997—. Author 12 plays, (mus.) All in One Night, 1996, (nonfiction) A Call to Radical Discipleship, 1997; co-editor: (mag.) The Areopagus, 1994—. Recipient honors for feature article U. Calif.-San Diego Guardian, 1986, Daily Californian, 1997, for outstanding drama rev., 1997. Mem. Conservative Bapt. Assn. So. Calif. (voting mem.). Democrat. Avocations: playwriting, music composition, nonfiction writing, acting, debating. Office: 2621 Denver St Ste A5 San Diego CA 92110-3355

SIEGEL, SHELDON C., physician; b. Mpls., Jan. 30, 1922; s. Carl S.; m. Priscilla Rikess, Mar. 3, 1946; children—Linda, Nancy. A.A., Va. Jr. Coll., 1940; B.A., B.S., U. Minn., 1942, M.D., 1945. Intern U. Minn. Hosp., 1946, resident in pediatrics, 1947-48; fellow in pediatric allergy Rochester, N.Y., 1949-50; practice medicine specializing in pediatric allergy and pediatrics St. Paul, 1950-52, San Antonio, 1952-54, Los Angeles, 1954—; clin. instr. pediatrics U. Rochester, 1949-50, U. Minn., 1950-51; asst. prof. pediatrics U. Tex., 1952-54; asst. clin. prof. U. Calif. at Los Angeles Med. Sch., 1955, clin. asso. prof., 1957-62, clin. prof., 1963—, co-chief pediatric allergy clinic, 1957—; mem. staff Harbor Gen. Hosp., Torrance, Calif., Daniel Freeman Hosp., Inglewood, Calif., Centinela Valley Community Hosp., Inglewood, Hawthorne (Calif.) Community Hosp. Editorial bd.: Jour. Allergy, 1973-75; contbr. articles to med. jours. Fellow Am. Acad. Allergy (pres. 1974), Am. Coll. Allergists, Am. Acad. Pediatrics; mem. AMA, Allergy Found. Am. (pres. 1976), Calif., Los Angeles County med. assns., Los Angeles Pediatric Soc., Calif., Los Angeles socs. allergy, Western Pediatric Research Soc., Am. Bd. Med. Specialists, Sigma Xi. Office: 11620 Wilshire Blvd Los Angeles CA 90025-1706

SIEGESMUND, RICHARD EVANS, art educator, consultant; b. Washington, Jan. 10, 1951; s. John Conrad and Marjorie Ann (Evans) S.; m. Sharon Rei Lumho, June 24, 1975 (div. Jan. 1996); children: Evan, Emily; m. Brigitta M. Hangartner, July 6, 1996. BA in Studio Art, Trinity Coll., 1973; postgrad., U. Hawaii, 1973-75; MA in Edn., Stanford U., 1995. Program coord. Mayor's Adv. Com. on Art and Culture, Balt., 1977-79; program dir. crafts, visual arts, mus. Pa. Coun. on the Arts, Harrisburg, 1982-86; assoc. dir. Washington Project for the Arts, 1986-89; dir. The Fabric Workshop, Phila., 1989-91; dep. dir. for curatorial affairs San Francisco Mus. Modern Art, 1991-92; tchg. asst. Stanford (Calif.) U., 1995—; arts orgnl./ednl. cons., Berkeley, Calif., 1983—; mem. adv. com. Nat. Endowment for the Arts, Washington, 1990; mem. visual arts adv. bd. Nat. Air and Space Mus., Washington, 1988-89. Author: (with others) An Industrious Art, 1991; contbr. articles to profl. jours. Arts Mgmt. fellow Nat. Endowment for the Arts, 1981. Mem. Am. Ednl. Rsch. Assn., Nat. Art Edn. Assn., Am. Assn. Mus., Coll. Art Assn. Home and Office: 3010 Benvenue Ave Berkeley CA 94705-2510

SIEGMUND, MARK ALAN, editor, publisher, business consultant, design scientist; b. Mpls., Oct. 19, 1942; s. Lucian Albert and Jeanette Katherine (Hayhoe) S.; m. Barbara Ann Cedergren, June 27, 1965 (div. Aug. 1971). BS, Sierra U., Santa Monica, Calif., 1985; PhD, World Peace Univ., Escazu, Costa Rica, 1989. Internat. bus. cons. Wanigatunga, Siegmund & Assocs., L.A., 1975-77; lang. tchr. Bilingual Inst., Mexico City, 1978-81; program coord. Univ. Without Walls, Santa Monica, 1981-84, faculty mem., 1984-86; asst. to pres. Sierra U., 1986-87; prof., vice chancellor for external affairs World Peace Univ., 1988-89; co-founder, dir. U. of Air, Radio for Peace Internat. UN Univ. for Peace, Costa Rica, 1989; assoc. editor, mem. bd. Internat. Jour. Humanities and Peace, Flagstaff, Ariz., 1990—; dir. Tetworld Peace Through Devel. Project, 1998—; cons. Min. Edn., Belize, Ctrl. Am., 1987-88; cons. Belize Nat. Libr., 1987-88; mem. adv. coun. for global edn., Calif. State U., L.A., 1982-85. Contbr. various articles to profl. jours. Co-chair fund distbn. com. Morongo Basin United Way, Yucca Valley, Calif., 1996, bd. dirs. 1996—, pres. 1997—; appointed county commr. CSA-70M San Bernardino County Bd. Suprs., 1997—. Recipient Cert. of Appreciation City of L.A. Dept. Aging, 1990. Mem. Humane Soc. Am., Calif. State Grange (environ. com. 1992-96), Wonder Valley Grange (exec. com. 1993-96), Wonder Valley TV Assn. (co-founder, chmn.), Wonder Valley Hiking Club. Avocations: systems design, aquaculture, travel, global design and planning, writing. Home: HC 2 Box 434-h2 Twentynine Palms CA 92277-9802 Office: Internat Jour Humanities & Peace 1436 Evergreen Dr Flagstaff AZ 86001-1416

SIEMON-BURGESON, MARILYN M., education administrator; b. Whittier, Calif., Nov. 15, 1934; d. John Roscoe and Louise Christina (Secoy) Mason; m. Carl J. Siemon, Aug. 18, 1956 (div. Oct. 1984); children: Timothy G., Melanie A. Siemon Imes; Troy M.; m. James K. Burgeson, Jan. 24, 1987. BA, U. Redlands, 1956; MA, Pacific Oaks Coll., 1975; postgrad., Point Loma Coll., 1979-80. Cert. adminstr., elem. and early childhood tchr. Tchr. Sierra Madre (Calif.) Cmty. Nursery Sch., 1970-77; tchr. parent edn. and music Pasadena (Calif.) Unified Schs., 1977-79, project coord., 1980-82, tchr. curriculum resource dept., 1982-83, adminstr. Washington Children's Ctr., 1983—; endorsed trainer High Scope Found. Register, 1990—; trainer Program for Infant/Toddler Caregivers; instr. Citrus Coll., 1996—; conf. chair Calif. High Scope Educators, 1995—. Active Arcadia (Calif.) Bicentennial Commn., 1974-76; mem. policy coun. for cmty. housing svcs. Pasadena Head Start, 1992-95; life mem. Sierra Madre Sch. PTA; mem. Child Care Coalition, Pasadena; lay Eucharistic minister St. Edmunds, San Marino, Calif. Ednl. Professions Devel. fellow Pacific Oaks Coll., Pasadena, 1969. Mem. AAUW (past pres., co-chair Math.-Sci. Conf. 1983, chair Coll./Univ. Rels. 1988—, v.p. ednl. found. 1996-98, grantee 1982, 83), Nat. Assn. Edn. Young Children (grantee 1970), Child Care Info. Svc. (bd. dirs., chair parent edn. and family affairs 1986—), Women Ednl. Leadership (asst. program v.p.), Calif. Child Devel. Adminstrs. Assn. (bd. dirs. 1994—), Coun. Women's Clubs (pres. 1995-97), Delta Kappa Gamma (pres. Omicron chpt. 1986-88, 92-94). Republican. Episcopalian. Avocation: music. Home: 2266 Kinclair Dr Pasadena CA 91107-1022 Office: Washington Children's Ctr 130 E Penn St Pasadena CA 91103-1828

SIEVEKE-PEARSON, STARLA JEAN, language educator; b. Deadwood, S.D., Nov. 10, 1963; d. Alfred Frank and Ivis Irene (Zirbel) S.; m. Darin L. Pearson, Feb. 14, 1988; children: Drew, Kaitlyn. BS, Black Hills State Univ., 1986; MA, Univ. No. Colo., 1994; postgrad., Univ. Colo., 1998—. Eng. tchr. White Pine H.S., Ely, Nev., 1987-90; secondary edn. faculty Metro State Coll., Denver, 1994—; eng., arts tchr. Flood Middle Sch., Englewood, Colo., 1990—. Pres. Nev. State Coun. Tchrs., 1988-90; exec. bd. Blue Spruce Awards Com., 1997—. Mem. Nat. Coun. Tchr. Eng., Assn. Secondary Curriculum & Devel., Colo. Lang. Arts Soc. of Eng. (exec. bd. 1997—). Lutheran. Avocations: reading, playing piano, interior decorating, traveling Home: 448 Benton St Castle Rock CO 80104-8593 Office: Flood Mid Sch 3695 S Lincoln St Englewood CO 80110-3657

SIEWERT, THOMAS ALLEN, metallurgist; b. Kenosha, Wis., Oct. 30, 1947; s. William F. and Gladys E. Siewert; m. Betsy A. Siewert, May 21, 1977; children: Peter, John, Jill. MS, U. Wis., Milw., 1969; U. Wis., Madison, 1974; PhD, U. Wis. Madison, 1976. Registered profl. engr., Pa. Supervising rsch. engr. Chemetron Corp., Hanover, Pa., 1976-80; mgr. R&D Alloy Rods, Hanover, 1980-84; metallurgist Nat. Inst. Standards & Tech., Boulder, Colo., 1984-88, supr. metallurgist, 1988-93, dep. chief materials reliability divsn., 1993—; adj. prof. Colo. Sch. Mines, Golden, 1986—; lectr. R.D. Thomas, Jr. Internat. Lecture, 1995. Author: Computerization of Welding Information-A Workshop Report, 1988; editor (with others) Nondestructive Evaluation: NDE Planning and Application, vol. V, 1989, Computerization of Welding Data- Proceedings of the Conference and Workshop October 19 to 21, 1988, 1990, Computerization of Welding Information-III, 1992, International Conference on Computerization of Welding Information-IV, 1993, Metals Handbook, vol. 6 - Welding, 1993, Pendulum Impact Machines: Procedures and Specimens for Verification, 1995, Fifth International Welding Computerization Conference, 1995, Seventh International Conference on Computer Technology in Welding, 1997; contbr. articles to profl. jours. Trustee Calvary Bible Ch., Boulder, 1996—. Recipient Bronze medal U.S. Dept. Commerce, 1991, Excellence in Tech. Transfer awards Fed. Lab. Consortium, 1994, 98. Fellow Am. Welding Soc.; mem. ASTM, Am. Materials Soc., Internat. Inst. Welding (Am. coun., chmn. 1996—, commn. chmn. 1994—, rep. gen. assembly 1996—), Am. Welding Soc. (bd. dirs. 1991-94), Phi Kappa Phi, Alpha Sigma Mu, Sigma Xi. Evangelical Free Ch. Achievements include 3 patents in field. Office: NIST 325 Broadway St Boulder CO 80303-3337

SIFFORD, BENTON ALEXANDER, III, energy consultant; b. Evanston, Ill., Sept. 20, 1955; s. Benton Alexander Jr. and Gail Byrd (Sollender) S.; m. Saralynn Baker, Nov. 6, 1982. BA in Geography, U. Calif., Santa Barbara, 1978; MS in Geography, U. Idaho, 1984. Mgr. Oak Tree Antiques, London, 1978-80; geothermal specialist Idaho Office Energy, Boise, 1980; sr. assoc. Eliot Allen & Assocs., Salem, Oreg., 1981-84; program mgr. Oreg. Dept. Energy, Salem, 1984-94; pvt. practice Sifford Energy Svcs., Neskowin, Oreg., 1995—; pres. Wood Energy Coordination Group, Portland, 1988-90. Author: Geothermal Resources Council Transactions, Vol. 7, 1984, Vol. 14, 1990, Bioenergy Conversion Opportunities, 1988; also articles. Pres. Neskowin (Oreg.) Cmty. Assn., 1989-94; commr. Neskowin Regional Water Dist., 1993—. Recipient cert. of appreciation USDA Forest Svc., 1988, 89, Lions Internat., Salem, 1990. Mem. Geothermal Resources Coun. (pres. Pacific N.W. sect. 1985-88, bd. dirs. 1988-90), Assn. Pacific Coast Geographers, Internat. Dist. Heating Assn. Avocations: winemaking, rafting, skiing. Home: PO Box 760 Neskowin OR 97149-0760 Office: Sifford Energy Svcs PO Box 760 Neskowin OR 97149-0760

SIGLER, MARJORIE DIANE, computer programming executive, analyst; b. Fullerton, Calif., Sept. 19, 1943; d. Earl Lawrence Whipple and Ruth Juanita (Long) Purcell; children: Stephen, Deborah; m. William A. Sigler, June 10, 1995; Grad computer programming LaSalle U., Chgo., 1973; BSBA U. Phoenix, 1994; MS CIS U. Phoenix, 1997. Computer programmer Los Alamos (N.Mex.) Nat. Lab., 1972-81, cons. control data, 1984-89, computer technician, 1989—; contract programmer Computer Assistance, Inc., Tulsa, 1981-82; profl. svcs. analyst Control Data Corp., Denver, 1982-84, Los Alamos, 1984-89. Mem. Order Eastern Star (past matron). Home: 90 Aspen Grv Jemez Springs NM 87025-9683

SIGMAN, MELVIN MONROE, psychiatrist; b. N.Y.C., Dec. 15, 1935; s. Irving and Lillian (Pearlman) S. BA, Columbia U., 1956; MD, SUNY, N.Y.C., 1960; postgrad., William Alanson White Analytic Inst., N.Y.C., 1969. Staff psychiatrist Hawthorne (N.Y.) Cedar Knolls Sch., 1966-68; pvt. practice psychiatry N.Y.C., 1966-72, Fresno, Calif., 1974-87; staff psychiatrist Fresno County Dept. of Health, 1974-87, Psychol. Svcs. for Adults, L.A., 1987-93; psychiatrist pvt. practice, L.A., 1993—; attending staff psychiatry Bellevue Hosp., N.Y.C., 1966-68; cons. N.Y. Foundling Hosp., N.Y.C., 1966-72; assoc. attending staff Roosevelt Hosp., N.Y.C., 1967-72; asst. clin. prof U. Calif. San Francisco, Fresno, 1977; chmn. Ctrl. Calif. com. Columbia Coll. Nat. Alumni Secondary Schs. Served to capt. USAF, 1961-63. Fellow Royal Soc. Health, Am. Orthopsychiat. Assn.; mem. Holiday Spa Clf., Fresno Racquet Club. Avocations: piano, tennis. Office: 10780 Santa Monica Blvd Ste 250 Los Angeles CA 90025-4749

SIGNOROVITCH, DENNIS JAMES, communications executive; b. Norristown, Pa., July 23, 1945; s. James and Regina S.; m. Susan E. McLaughlin, 1968; children: James Edward, Sarah Elizabeth. BS in Fgn. Svc., Georgetown U., 1967; MA, Old Dominion U., 1972; postgrad., U. Toledo., 1972. Instr. U. Toledo, 1972-77; writer/editor Doehler Jarvis div. NL Industries, Toledo, 1977-78; mgr. pub. rels. Eltra Corp., N.Y.C., 1979, mgr. planning, 1980; various assignments AlliedSignal Corp., Morristown, N.J., 1980-92; v.p. pub. affairs AlliedSignal Inc., Torrance, Calif., 1992-98; v.p. mktg. and comm. AlliedSignal Aerospace MS & S, Torrance, 1998—; mem. Exec. Comm. Forum. With U.S. Army, 1967-70. Decorated Bronze Star with oak leaf cluster. Mem. The Conf. Bd. (corp. comm. coun. 1991), Vol. Ctr. of South Bay (bd. dirs. 1994), L.A. Music Ctr. Unified Fund (aerospace com. mem. 1992, 93, 96, vice chmn. corp. campaign 1997, chair aerospace industry 1998), Arthur W. Page Soc., San Francisco Acad. (trustee). Office: Allied Signal Inc. 2525 W 190th St Torrance CA 90504-6002

SIKES, CYNTHIA LEE, actress, singer; b. Coffeyville, Kans., Jan. 2, 1954; d. Neil and Pat (Scott) S.; m. Alan Bud Yorkin, June 24, 1989. Student, Am. Conservatory Theater, San Francisco, 1977-79. Appeared in TV series St. Elsewhere, 1981-83, L.A. Law, 1989; TV movies include His Mistress, 1990; films include Man Who Loved Women, That's Life, Arthur On The Rocks, Love Hurts, 1988; producer, actress (television) Sins of Silence, 1996; also Broadway musical Into The Woods, 1988-89. Active Hollywood Women's Polit. Com. Recipient Gov.'s Medal of Merit, Kans., 1986. Democrat. Avocations: hiking, writing, reading.

SIKORA, JAMES ROBERT, educational business consultant; b. Sacramento, July 8, 1945; s. George Robert and Marian Frances (Fears) S.; m. Marie Lynore Nyarady, June 22, 1968. BEE, U. Santa Clara, 1967; postgrad., U. Calif., Santa Cruz, 1979—, personal fin. planning cert., 1998. Electronic engr. GTE-Sylvania, Santa Cruz, 1967-69; sys. analyst GTE-Sylvania, 1969-71; sr. support analyst GTE-Sylvania, Mt. View, Calif., 1971-73; coord. bus. sys. Santa Clara County Office Edn., San Jose, Calif., 1973-76, dir. dist. payroll, pers. svcs., 1976-85, dir. dist. bus. svcs., 1985-95; self-employed sch. bus. cons. Omniserve, Ben Lomond, Calif., 1995—; cons. records mgmt. County Santa Clara, San Jose, 1982; con. Sonoma County Office of Edn., Santa Rosa, 1995, Union Sch. Dist., San Jose, 1996—, San Jose Unified Sch. Dist., 1997, Santa Clara County Office of Edn., San Jose, 1997, 98—; Milpitas Unified Sch. Dist., 1995-97, Los Altos Sch. Dist., 1998—; interim asst. supt. bus. svcs. Mountain-View/Los Altos Union H.S. Dist., Mountain View, 1997; interim asst. supt. fiscal svcs. Cupertino Union Sch. Dist., 1997-98; interim CFO Union Sch. Dist., San Jose, 1998; spl. asst. Milpitas Unified Sch. Dist., 1998—; interim bus. mgr. Los Gatos Sch. Dist., 1997; vice-chmn. Edn. Mandated Cost Network Exec. Bd., 1991-95; mem. Schs. Fin. Svcs. subcom. 1987-94; mem. Maui Arts and Cultural Ctr. Ilima Club, U. Calif. San Francisco Dean's Assoc.; life mem. Napa Valley Wine Libr. Assn. Author, co-editor Howdy Rowdy Memorial, 1979. Mem. Corps De Ballet Circle, San Jose/Cleveland Ballet; sponsor Dixieland Monterey; patrons cir. Monterey Bay Aquarium; actor's circle, seat donor San Jose Repertory Theater; patron Second Harvest Food Bank; friend Schs. Plus; vol. Mountain Pks. Found.; active Ctr. Photog. Arts, Long Marine Lab.; mem. Team Shakespeare, Shakespeare Santa Cruz; bd. dirs., treas. Mountain Parks Found., 1997—; mem. dean's assocs. U. Calif. San Francisco Sch. Medicine. Mem. Pub. Agy. Risk Mgmt. Assn., Am. Diabetes Assn., Calif. Assn. Sch. Bus. Ofcls. (subsect. pres. 1984-85, sect. bd. dirs. 1987-93, sect. pres. 1991-92, state bd. dirs. 1991-92, state legis. com. 1989—, state risk mgmt. com. 1985-87, 96-97, state schs. employer adv. com. rep. 1991—, state strategic planning com. 1994), Norwegian Elkhound Assn. (pres. 1977-79), Golden Gate Nat. Park Assn., Santa Cruz Fly Fisherman, Wine Investigation for Novices and Oenephiles, Amnesty Internat., Calif. Trout, Trout Unltd., Calif. State Parks Found., Point Lobos Natural History Assn., Waddell Creek Assn. (sponsor), Monterey Hot Jazz Soc., Planned Parenthood, Felton Cmty. Hall (supporter), Americans for Hope, Growth and Opportunity, Nature Conservancy, Friends of Santa Cruz Pub. Librs., Am. Assn. Ret. Persons, Redwood Coast Brewers Assn., Am. Assn. Individual Investors (life), Am. Dog Owners Assn., Sierra Club (life), Cabrillo Music Festival New Century Club, Montalvo Assn. (patron), San Jose Mus. Art (educator mem.), Golden Gate Nat. Park Assn., Santa Cruz Fly Fisherman, Santa Cruz Mus. Art and History. Libertarian. Roman Catholic. Avocations: photography, travel, oenophilia, fishing, snorkelling. Home and Office: 400 Coon Heights Rd Ben Lomond CA 95005-9711

SILAK, CATHY R., state supreme court justice; b. Astoria, N.Y., May 25, 1950; d. Michael John and Rose Marie (Janor) S.; m. Nicholas G. Miller, Aug. 9, 1980; 3 children. BA, NYU, 1971; M in City Planning, Harvard U., 1973; JD, U. Calif., 1976. Bar: Calif. 1977, U.S. Dist. Ct. (no. dist.) Calif. 1977, D.C. 1979, U.S. Ct. Appeals (D.C. cir.) 1979, U.S. Dist. Ct. (so. dist.) N.Y. 1980, Idaho 1983, U.S. Dist. Ct. Idaho 1983, U.S. Ct. Appeals (2nd cir.) 1983, U.S. Ct. Appeals (9th cir.) 1985. Law clk. to Hon. William W. Schwarzer U.S. Dist. Ct. (no dist.), Calif., 1976-77; pvt. practice San Francisco, 1977-79, Washington, 1979-80; asst. U.S. atty. So. Dist. of N.Y., 1980-83; spl. asst. U.S. atty. Dist. of Idaho, 1983-84; pvt. practice Boise, Idaho, 1984-90; judge Idaho Ct. Appeals, 1990-93; justice Idaho Supreme Ct., Boise, 1993—; assoc. gen. counsel Morrison Knudsen Corp., 1989-90; mem. fairness com. Idaho Supreme Ct. and Gov.'s Task Force on Alternative Dispute Resolution; instr. and lectr. in field. Assoc. note and comment editor Calif. Law Rev., 1975-76. Land use planner Mass. Dept. Natural Resources, 1973; founder Idaho Coalition for Adult Literacy; bd. dirs. Literacy Lab., Inc.; mem. adv. bd. Boise State U. Legal Asst. Program. Recipient Jouce Stein award Boise YWCA, 1992, Women Helping Women award Soroptimist, Boise, 1993. Fellow Idaho Law Found (ann., lectr.); mem. ABA (nat. conf. state trial judges jud. adminstrn. divsn.), Nat. Assn. Women Judges, Idaho State Bar (corp./securities sect., instr.), Am. Law Inst., Fellows of the Am. Bar Found. Office: Idaho Supreme Ct Supreme Ct Bldg PO Box 83720 Boise ID 83720-3720*

SILBERGELD, ARTHUR F., lawyer; b. St. Louis, June 1, 1942; s. David and Sabina (Silbergeld) S.; m. Carol Ann Schwartz, May 1, 1970; children: Diana Lauren, Julia Kay. BA, U. Mich., 1968; M City Planning, U. Pa., 1971; JD, Temple U., 1975. Bar: N.Y. 1976, Calif. 1978, D.C. 1983, U.S. Ct. Appeals (2d, 9th and D.C. cirs.). Assoc. Vladeck, Elias, Vladeck & Lewis, N.Y.C., 1975-77; field atty. NLRB, Los Angeles, 1977-78; ptnr., head employment law practice group McKenna, Conner & Cuneo, L.A., 1978-89; ptnr., head labor and employment law practice group Graham & James, L.A., 1990-96; labor ptnr. Sonnenschein Nath & Rosenthal, L.A., 1996—; instr. extension divsn. UCLA, 1981-89. Author: Doing Business in California: An Employment Law Handbook, 2d edit. 1997, Advising California Employers, 1990, 91, 93, 94, 95 supplements; contbr. numerous articles to profl. jours. Founding mem. L.A. Mus. Contemporary Art; mem. Mus. Modern Art, N.Y., Art Inst. Chgo.; bd. dirs. Bay Cities unit Am. Cancer Soc., Calif., 1981-85, Jewish Family Svc. L.A., 1981-85, So. Calif. Employment Round Table, 1990-96, Leadership Coun., So. Poverty Law Ctr., L.A. Child Devel. Ctr., 1998—, Leadership Task Force, Drs. Without Borders. Mem. L.A. County Bar Assn. (vice chair labor and employment law sect. 1998—). Office: Sonnenschein Nath & Rosenthal 601 S Figueroa St Fl 15 Los Angeles CA 90017-5704

SILBERMAN, IRWIN ALAN, retired public health physician; b. Newport News, Va., Sept. 1, 1932; s. Henry and Toby (Weiss) S.; m. Lynne Sussman, Feb. 1954 (div. 1961); children: Denise, Donn; m. Mitsue Fukuyama, May 1964 (div. 1984); children: Daniel, Dean, Dana; m. Andrea Z. George, Nov. 1993. BA, U. Calif., Berkeley, 1953; MD, U. Calif., San Francisco, 1956; MS, U. No. Colo., 1980. Intern L.A. County Harbor Gen. Hosp., Torrance, Calif., 1956-57; resident ob-gyn. Harbor/UCLA Med. Ctr., Torrance, 1957-61; commd. USAF, 1961, advanced through grades to col., 1973; staff obstetrician-gynecologist Tachikawa (Japan) Air Base, 1963-65; chief ob-gyn. Mather Air Force Base, Sacramento, 1965-66; chief aeromed. services Yokota Air Base, Tokyo, 1966-68; dir. base med. services Itazuke Air Base, Fukuoka, Japan, 1968-70, Kirtland Air Force Base, Albuquerque, 1970-72; chief hosp. services USAF Hosp. Davis-Monthan, Tucson, 1972-81; ret. USAF, 1981; med. dir. CIGNA Healthplan of Fla., Tampa, 1981-83; chief women's clinic H.C. Hudson Comprehensive Health Ctr., L.A., 1983-85; dir. maternal health and family planning programs Los Angeles County Dept. Health Svcs., L.A., 1985-91, dir. family health programs, maternal and child health, 1991-98; ret., 1998; mil. cons. to surgeon-gen. USAF, 1980-81; bd. dirs. L.A. Regional Family Planning Coun.; clin. prof. ob-gyn. U. So. Calif., Sch. Medicine, 1992—; pres. Perinatal Adv. Coun. of L.A. Comtys., 1993-94, Calif. Conf. of Local Dirs. of Maternal, Child and Adolescent Health, 1997-98. Chmn. health profls. adv. com. March of Dimes, Los Angeles, 1988; camp physician Boy Scouts Nat. Jamboree, Fort Hill, Va., 1985. Recipient Meritorious Service medal, USAF, 1972, 81, Air Force Commendation medal, 1980, Air medal, 1969. Fellow Am. Coll. Obstetricians and Gynecologists, Am. Coll. Physician Execs., Am. Coll. Preventive Medicine; mem. APHA, Am. Acad. Med. Dirs., So. Calif. Pub. Health Assn. Avocations: skiing, photography. Home: 3716 Beverly Ridge Dr Sherman Oaks CA 91423-4509

SILBERT, AMY FOXMAN, clinical art therapist; b. Augusta, Ga., July 11, 1953; d. Elliott and Anita Foxman; m. Philip Silbert, Sept. 6, 1987; children: Sean Kenneth, Karen Debra, Samantha Danielle. BA in Design, UCLA, 1976; MA, Loyola Marymount U., 1990. Art dir., advt. mgr. Unico Am. Corp., L.A., 1976-78; freelance graphic artist, art specialist, tchr., 1979-82; vol. coord., tchr. Craft and Folk Art Mus., L.A., 1983-86; art specialist Art Reach, UCLA Calif. Arts Coun., 1983-84; editor in chief Grad. Achievement Preparation Svc., Santa Monica, Calif., 1985-87; tchr. coordinator art exhibit Hebrew Union Coll., Los Angeles, 1984; guest children's TV programs, 1970-84. Gov. intern U.S. Congress, Washington, 1973. Recipient 1st Place award traffic light design City Monterey, Calif., 1973. Democrat. Jewish. Home: 760 Briercliff Ln Lake Oswego OR 97034-1642

SILLER, GARRETT FRANK, wood craftsman; b. Henderson, Nev., May 8, 1964; s. Frank Pete and Dorothy Regina (Stiener) S.; m. Julia Leona Robinson, Apr. 27, 1988; children: Michelle, Robinson, Ciarra. Auto mechanic Joe VW Svc., Henderson, Nev., 1979-81; auto body repair Henderson Auto Bldy, 1981-82; head welder Star Stove, Henderson, 1982-83; constrn. worker Phoenix, 1983-84; warehouseman Kerr McGee, Henderson, 1987-94; owner Treeco Fine Furniture & Repair, Boulder City, Nev., 1994—. With U.S. Army, 1984-87. Mem. Elks. Avocations: boating, hiking, skiing. Home: 621 Kings Pl Boulder City NV 89005-2914

SILLS, DEBORAH R., religious studies educator; b. L.A., Apr. 28, 1949; d. Irvin and Dolly S.; m. Giles B. Gunn, July 9, 1983; children: Adam, Abigail. BA, U. Calif., Santa Barbara, 1975, MA, 1980, PhD, 1984. Lectr. relig. studies U. Calif., Santa Barbara, 1985-89; prof. religion Calif. Luth. U., Thousand Oaks, 1990—; adj. asst. prof. U. Colo., Boulder, 1989; vis. prof. Am. studies U. Munich, Germany, 1994. Mem. Am. Acad. Religion, Santa Barbara Women's Polit. Commn. (founding), Women's Environ. Watch (founding), Soc. Biblical Literature. Office: Calif Luth U 2744 Macadamia Ln Santa Barbara CA 93108-1658

SILVA, ROBERT OWEN, retired protective service official; b. La Junta, Colo., Sept. 5, 1935; s. Owen Delbert and Gertrude H. (Kerr) S.; m. Meredith Ann Ginn, Dec. 18, 1953; children—Edward, Andrew, Colleen. Student Pueblo Jr. Coll., 1953, FBI Nat. Acad., 1975, Police Found. Exec. Program, 1979-80. Cert. peace officer, Colo. Police officer Pueblo Police Dept., Colo., 1958-66, sgt., 1966-72, capt., 1972-77, chief of police, 1977-92, ret. dir. Colo. Police Officers Standards and Tng. Bd. dirs. Salvation Army, Pueblo, Easter Seals Soc., Pueblo, Community Corrections Bd., Pueblo, Served with U.S. Army, 1955-57; apptd. by gov. Colo. Crim. Justice Comsn., 1990. Mem. Pueblo Community Coll. Criminal Justice Adv. Bd., Leadership Pueblo Steering Com., Pikes Peak Community Coll. Criminal Justice Program (chmn. adv. bd. 1981), Organized Crime Strike Force (bd. dirs. 1977-84, chmn. 1982, 83, 84); Colo. Assn. Chiefs of Police (pres. 1984-85), Rocky Mountain Info. Network (chmn. bd. dirs. 1986—), Presbyterian (elder). Lodges: Kiwanis (bd. dirs. 1982-84), Elks.

SILVER, BARNARD JOSEPH STEWART, mechanical and chemical engineer, consultant, inventor; b. Salt Lake City, Mar. 9, 1933; s. Harold Farnes and Madelyn Cannon (Stewart) S.; m. Cherry Bushman, Aug. 12, 1963; children: Madelyn Stewart Palmer, Cannon Farnes, Brenda Picketts Call. BS in Mech. Engring., MIT, 1957; MS in Engring. Mechanics, Stanford U., 1958; grad. Advanced Mgmt. Program, Harvard U., 1977. Registered profl. engr., Colo. Engr. aircraft nuclear propulsion div. Gen. Electric Co., Evandale, Ohio, 1957; engr. Silver Engring. Works, Denver, 1959-66, mgr. sales and tech. svcs., 1966-71; chief engr. Union Sugar div. Consol. Foods

Co., Santa Maria, Calif., 1971-74; directeur du complexe SODESUCRE, Abidjan, Côte d'Ivoire, 1974-76; supt. engring. and maintenance U and I, Inc., Moses Lake, Wash., 1976-79; pres. Silver Enterprises Denver, Moses Lake, 1971—, Silver Energy Systems Corp., Moses Lake, 1980—; pres., gen. mgr. Silver Chief Corp., 1983—; pres. Silver Corp., 1984—; chmn. bd. Silver Pubs., Inc., 1986-87, 89—; chmn. bd. Agronomics Internat., McLean, Va., 1994—; mgr. Cascadian Inulin L.L.C., Sedro-Wooley, Wash., 1996—; mgr. Silver Inulin L.L.C., Moses Lake, 1996—; v.p. Barnard J. Stewart Cousins Land Co., 1987-88, 92—; dir. Isle Piquant Sugar Found., 1993-94; mem. steering com. World Botanical Inst., 1993—; instr. engring. Big Bend C.C., 1980-81. Explorer adviser Boy Scouts Am., 1965-66, 89-90, chmn. cub pack com., 1968-74, 94-96, chmn. scout troop com., 1968-74, vice chmn. Columbia Basin Dist., 1986-87; pres. Silver Found., 1971-87, v.p., 1987—; endl. counselor MIT, 1971-89; pres. Chief Moses Jr. H.S. Parent Tchr. Student Assn., 1978-79; missionary Ch. of Jesus Christ of Latter-day Saints, Can., 1953-55, Hawaii, Puerto Rico, Central & South America, Asia, 1959-68, West Africa, 1988, Côte d'Ivoire, 1988-89, Zaire, 1989, Holladay North Stake, 1991, 95—, dist. pres. No. B.C., No. Alberta, Yukon and N.W. Ters., 1955; stake high counselor, Santa Maria, Calif., 1971-72, Moses Lake Wash., 1977-79; presiding elder Côte d'Ivoire, 1974-76, 88; 2d counselor Moses Lake Stake Presidency, 1980-88; bd. dirs. Columbia Basin Allied Arts, 1986-88; mem. Health Sci. Coun. U. Utah, 1991—; mem. Sunday sch. gen. bd. Ch. of Jesus Christ of Latter-Day Saints, 1991-93, com. for mems. with Disabilities, 1992-93, CHOICE adv. bd., 1993-95; emergency preparedness dir. Holladay North Stake, 1993—. Served with Ordnance Corps, U.S. Army, 1958-59. Decorated chevalier Ordre National (Republic of Côte d'Ivoire). Patentee in field, including patent for extracting liquids soluable substances from subdivided solids, 1995. Mem. ASME, Assn. Energy Engrs., AAAS, Am. Soc. Sugar Beet Technologists, Internat. Soc. Sugar Cane Technologists, Am. Soc. Sugar Cane Technologists, Environ. Engrs. & Mgrs. Inst., Sugar Industry Technicians, Nat. Fedn. Ind. Bus.; Utah State Hist. Soc. (life), Mormon Hist. Assn., G.P. Chowder and Marching Soc., Western Hist. Assn., Sons of Utah Pioneers, Univ. Archeol. Soc. (life), Kiwanis, Cannon-Hinckley Study Group, Sigma Xi (life, sec., treas. Utah chpt. 1994—), Pi Tau Sigma, Sigma Chi, Alpha Phi Omega. Republican. Mormon. E-mail: cbsilver@worldnet.att.net. Home: 4391 Carol Jane Dr Salt Lake City UT 84124-3601 Office: Silver Energy Systems Corp 13184 Road 3 SE Ste B Moses Lake WA 98837-9483 also: Silver Enterprises 4391 South 2275 E Carol Jane Dr Salt Lake City UT 84124-3601 also: Silver Corporation 4391 Carol Jane Dr Salt Lake City UT 84124-3601 also: Silver Chief Corp 1433 S Skyline Dr Moses Lake WA 98837-2417 also: Agronomics Internat 6928 Butternut Ct Mc Lean VA 22101-1506 also: Silver Pubs Inc 4390 S 2300 E Salt Lake City UT 84124-3501

SILVER, BEN(JAMIN), broadcast journalist, journalism educator; b. N.Y.C., Mar. 25, 1927; s. Samuel and Rosa (Sokolovsky) S.; m. Joan Ida Jackson (div.); children: Donald M., James D., Julie S.; m. Linda Louise Rude, Apr. 6, 1968; children: Scott A., Kurt B., Beth L. BA, U. Iowa, 1950, MA, 1955. Reporter, writer Sta. KTIV-TV, Sioux City, Iowa, 1955-57; news reporter Sta. WCKT-TV (now Sta. WSVN-TV), Miami, Fla., 1957-66; news reporter, assignment editor CBS-TV News, N.Y.C., 1966-71; assoc. prof. Walter Cronkite Sch. Journalism, Ariz. State U., Tempe, 1971-91, prof. emeritus, 1991—; cons. in field. Contbr. articles to profl. jours. With U.S. Army, 1945-46. Mem. Soc. Profl. Journalists, Radio-TV News Dirs. Assn., Assn. Edn. in Journalism (nat. awards Outstanding TV News Story RTNDA 1955, Peabody award 1961). Major participant Sta. WCKT-TV coverage of Castro's Cuba. Fax: 602 655 1097. Home: 1713 N Alamo Cir Mesa AZ 85213-3409

SILVER, DAVID LAWRENCE, art dealer; b. L.A., Oct. 20, 1957; s. Alan Jerome and Ruth (Caplan) S. BA, Calif. State Univ., 1979. Pres. David Lawrence Editions, Beverly Hills, Calif., 1980—, Lawrence Gallery, Beverly Hills, Calif., 1996—. Publisher numerous fine art prints, 1987—. Office: Lawrence Gallery PO Box 3702 Beverly Hills CA 90212-0702

SILVER, STEPHEN HAL, stockbroker, financial planner; b. Indpls., Oct. 7, 1949; s. C. Hal and Betty (Jean) S.; m. Mary Starr Wilson, Oct. 22, 1977; children: Marisa, Scott, Stephanie. BA, Hanover (Ind.) Coll., 1972. Cert. fin. planner. Buyer men's sportswear Meier & Frank, Portland, Oreg., 1974-80, mdse. mgr., 1980-81; v.p. investments Dean Witter, Portland, 1981—. Deacon, St. Andrews Presbyn. Ch., Portland, 1984; leader Cub Scouts troop Boy Scouts Am., Tigard, Oreg., 1992; coach Tigard Little League, 1989. Recipient Pres.'s Merit award, 1983. Mem. Director's Club. Republican. Avocations: golf, skiing, collecting antique swords. Home: 9595 SW Ventura Ct Tigard OR 97223-9167 Office: Dean Witter 10260 SW Greenburg Rd Ste 300 Portland OR 97223-5478

SILVERBERG, STUART OWEN, obstetrician, gynecologist; b. Denver, Oct. 14, 1931; s. Edward M. and Sara (Morris) S.; BA, U. Colo., 1952, MD, 1955; m. Joan E. Snyderman, June 19, 1954 (div. Apr. 1970); children: Debra Sue Dackert, Eric Owen, Alan Kent; m. 2d, Kay Ellen Conklin, Oct. 18, 1970 (div. Apr. 1982); 1 son, Cris S.; m. 3d, Sandra Kay Miller, Jan., 1983. Intern Women's Hosp. Phila., 1955-56; resident Kings County Hosp., Bklyn., 1958-62; practice medicine specializing in obstetrics and gynecology, Denver, 1962—; mem. staff Rose Med. Ctr., N. Suburban Med. Ctr., U. Hosp., St. Anthony Hosp.; med. exec. bd., chmn. dept. obstetrics and gynecology, 1976-77, 86-87, dir. Laser Ctr., 1994-95; clin. instr. U. Colo. Sch. Medicine, Denver, 1962-72, asst. clin. prof., 1972-88, assoc. clin. prof., 1989—, dir. gynecol. endoscopy and laser surgery, 1988-90; v.p. Productos Alimenticos, La Ponderosa, S.A.; dir., chmn. bd. Wicker Works Video Prodns., Inc., 1983-91; cons. Ft. Logan Mental Health Ctr., Denver, 1964-70; mem. Gov.'s Panel Mental Retardation, 1966; med. adv. bd. Colo. Planned Parenthood, 1966-68, Am. Med. Ctr., Spivak, Colo., 1967-70. Mem. Colo. Emergency Resources Bd., Denver, 1965—. Served to maj. AUS, 1956-58; Germany. Diplomate Am. Bd. Obstetrics and Gynecology, Am. Bd. Laser Surgery. Fellow Am. Coll. Obstetricians and Gynecologists, Am. Soc. Laser Medicine and Surgery, ACS; mem. Am. Internat. fertility socs., Colo. Gynecologists and Obstetricians Soc., Hellman Obstet. and Gynecol. Soc., Colo. Med. Soc. (bd. dirs. 1987-95, speaker of the house 1989-95), Clear Creek Valley Med. Soc. (trustee 1978, 80, 87, 93—, pres. 1995), Phi Sigma Delta, Flying Physicians Assn., Aircraft Owners and Pilots Assn., Nu Sigma Nu, Alpha Epsilon Delta. Jewish. Mem. editorial rev. bd. Colo. Women's Mag.; editor in chief First Image, Physicians Video Jour., 1984-86.

SILVERMAN, ALAN HENRY, lawyer; b. N.Y.C., Feb. 18, 1954; s. Melvin H. and Florence (Green) S.; m. Gretchen E. Freeman, May 25, 1986; children: Willa C.F., Gordon H.F. BA summa cum laude, Hamilton Coll., 1976; MBA, U. Pa., 1980, JD, 1980. Bar: N.Y. 1981, U.S. Dist. Ct. (so. and ea. dist.) N.Y. 1981, U.S. Ct. Internat. Trade 1981, D.C. 1986, U.S. Supreme Ct. 1990. Assoc. Hughes, Hubbard & Reed, N.Y.C., 1980-84; asst. counsel Newsweek, Inc., N.Y.C., 1984-86; v.p., gen. counsel, sec., dir. adminstrn. Cable One, Inc., Phoenix, 1986—. Contbr. articles to profl. jours. Mem. prevention adv. com. Gov. Pa. Justice Commn., 1975-79; bd. dirs. Lawyers' Alliance for N.Y., 1982-85, N.Y. Lawyers Pub. Interest, 1983-85, Nat. Assn. JD-MBA Profls., 1983-85, Bus. Vols. for Arts, Inc., Phoenix, 1989-93, Ariz. Vol. Lawyers for the Arts, Inc., 1994-97, First Amendment Coalition Ariz., Inc., 1991—; mem. Maricopa County Citizens Jud. Adv. Coun., 1990-93. Mem. ABA, Assn. of Bar of City of N.Y., D.C. Bar Assn., Phi Beta Kappa. Home: 5833 N 30th St Phoenix AZ 85016-2401 Office: Cable One Inc 1314 N 3d St Phoenix AZ 85004

SILVERMAN, SHERRI LYNN, artist, educator; b. Atlanta, Apr. 19, 1951; d. Sigmund J. and Faye (Bloshtein) S. BA in English/Am. Lit., Emory U., 1971; MA in English/Am. Lit., Brandeis U., 1974; PhD in Art History and Humanities, The Union Inst., 1996. adj. faculty fine arts, humanities and English Fla. C.C., Jacksonville, 1993, lang. and lit. dept. U. North Fla., Jacksonville, 1993-94, art history and humanities depts. TVI C.C., Albuquerque, 1997-98; vis. faculty honors program U. North Fla., Jacksonville, 1994, U. N.Mex., Albuquerque, 1996; vis. faculty N.Mex. Highlands U., Las Vegas, 1997, adj. faculty Coll. Santa Fe, humanities dept., 1999; seminar coconvener The Union Inst., Cin., 1996, 97; founder Women Artists and Art on the Move (WAAM), 1998, co-founder, pres. Santa Fe Sch. Art and Enlightenment, 1998; instr. of Sahaj Samadhi meditation and art of living basic course Internat. Art of Living Found. One woman shows include TVI C.C. Chambers Gallery, 1998, Bank of Santa Fe Gallery, 1997, Heaven on Earth, Atlantic Beach, Fla., 1994, The Book Mark, Atlantic Beach, 1994, Vandroff Gallery, Jacksonville, 1993, Santa Fe East, 1992; exhibited in group shows at North Moon Gallery, Telluride, Colo., 1997, Pensacola Mus. of Art, 1996, Ctr. for Contemporary Arts, Santa Fe, 1995, Santuario de Guadalupe, Santa Fe, 1995, Jacksonville Coalition for the Visual Arts Gallery 88, Ponte Vedra Beach, Fla., 1993, 25th Ann. Mandarin Arts Festival, Jacksonville (2d Pl. award), 1993, First Nat. Bank, Santa Fe, 1992, others; represented in numerous pub. and pvt. collections; contbr. poetry to various publs. Mem. Citywide Women's History Month Planning com., Jacksonville, 1993-94. Mem. Assn. for Asian Studies, Coll. Art Assn., Am. Coun. for So. Asian Art. E-mail: shrisilver@aol.com. Home: PO Box 66 Santa Fe NM 87504-0066

SILVERMAN, TREVA, writer, producer, consultant; b. N.Y.C.; d. Nathan and Janno (Harra) S. Student, U. Chgo., 1956; BA, Bennington Coll., 1958. Staff writer: (TV) The Entertainers, 1964, The Monkees, 1966, 67, 68, Captain Nice, 1968, Room 222, 1969, The Mary Tyler Moore Show, 1970-75 (Emmy award Best Comedy Writer 1974, Writer of Yr. 1974); episode writer He and She, 1968, Get Smart, 1968; writer: (TV pilots) Dates from Hell, 1991, Boy, Girl, Boy, 1991, Home Again, 1992, Ladies Night, 1992, The Rev, 1995, San Diego Presents, 1996; (features) A Nice Girl, 1980, Going All the Way, 1986, Act One, 1987; writer, prodr. children's musicals Theatre East, N.Y.C., 1960-63, Scandal, 1985, Hearts' Desire: Out of Town, 1992; contbg. writer: Julius Monk's Upstairs at the Downstairs, 1962-64; cons. Columbia pictures TV comedy programming, 1985-86, MTM Prodns., 1986, Just in Time, ABC-TV, 1987. Named one of TV Women of Yr., Ladies Home Jour., 1975. Mem. Writers Guild Am. (Best Spl./Variety Writer award 1969), Dramatists Guild, Acad. TV Arts and Scis. Democrat. Office: Tudor Entertainment Inc 9437 Santa Monica Blvd Beverly Hills CA 90210-4604

SILVERN, LEONARD CHARLES, retired engineering executive; b. N.Y.C., May 20, 1919; s. Ralph and Augusta (Thaler) S.; m. Gloria Marantz, June 1948 (div. Jan. 1968); 1 child, Ronald; m. Elisabeth Beeny, Aug. 1969 (div. Oct. 1972); m. Gwen Taylor, Nov. 1985. BS in Physics, L.I. U., 1946; MA, Columbia U., 1948, EdD, 1952. Registered profl. consulting engr., Calif. Tng. supr. U.S. Dept. Navy, N.Y.C., 1939-49; tng. dir. exec. dept. N.Y. Div. Safety, Albany, 1949-55; resident engring. psychologist Lincoln Lab. MIT for Rand Corp., Lexington, 1955-56; engr., dir. edn., tng., rsch. labs. Hughes Aircraft Co., Culver City, Calif., 1956-62; dir. human performance engring. lab., cons. engring. psychologist to v.p. tech. Northrop Norair, Hawthorne, Calif., 1962-64; prin. sci., v.p., pres. Edn. and Tng. Cons. Co., 1964—, Sedona, Ariz., 1980, pres. Systems Engring. Labs. div., 1980—; cons. hdqrs. Air Tng. Command USAF, Randolph AFB, Tex., 1964-68, Electronic Industries Assn., Washington, 1963-69, Edn. R and D Ctr., U. Hawaii, 1970-74, Ctr. Vocat. and Tech. Edn., Ohio State U., 1972-73, Coun. for Exceptional Children, 1973-74, Canadore Coll. Applied Arts and Tech., Ont., Can., 1974-76, Centro Nacional de Productividad, Mexico City, 1973-75, N.S. Dept. Edn., Halifax, 1975-79, Aeronutronic Ford-Ford Motor Co., 1975-76, Nat. Tng. Systems Inc., 1976-81, Nfld. Pub. Svc. Commn., 1978, Legis. Affairs Office USDA, 1980, Rocky Point Techs., 1986; adj. prof. edn., pub. adminstrn. U. So. Calif. Grad. Sch., 1957-65; vis. prof. computer scis. U. Calif. Extension Div., L.A., 1963-72. Dist. ops. officer, disaster communications svc. L.A. County Sheriff's Dept., 1973-75, dist. communications officer, 1975-76; bd. dirs. SEARCH, 1976—; mem. adv. com. West Sedona Community Plan of Yavapai County, 1986-88; councilman City of Sedona, 1988-92; rep. COCOPAI, 1988-89; vol. earth team Soil Conservation Svc., U.S. Dept Agr., 1989-92; Verde Resource Assn., 1988-90, Group on Water Logistics, 1989-90; chair publs. com. Ariz. Rural Recycling Conf., 1990. With USN, 1944-46. Mem. IEEE (sr.), APA, Am. Radio Relay League (life), Nat. Solid Waste Mgmt. Symposium (chmn. publs. com. 1988-89), Ariz. Rural Recycling Conf. (chair publs. com. 1990), Friendship Vets. Fire Engine Co. (hon.), Soc. Wireless Pioneers (life), Quarter Century Wireless Assn. (life), Sierra Club (treas. Sedona-Verde Valley Group 1991-93), Assn. Bldg. Coms., Vox Pop (chmn. bd. dirs. Sedona, 1983-93, dir. 1993-95), Nat. Parks and Conservation Assn., Wilderness Soc., Ariz. Ctr. Law in Pub. Interest, Old Old Timers Club. Contbg. editor Ednl. Tech., 1968-73, 81-85; reviewer ACM Computing Revs., 1962-92. Contbr. numerous articles to profl. jours. Office: PO Box 2085 Sedona AZ 86339-2085

SILVERSTEIN, DAVID, cantor, educator; b. L.A., Apr. 29, 1955; s. Merrill Saunders and Edith Esther (Krentzman) S.; m. Barbara Jean Prather, Jan. 11, 1981; 1 child, Joshua Adam. BA, UCLA, 1977, JD, 1980; postgrad., U. Judaism, 1985-87, 90—. Cantor Temple Emanu El, Burbank, Calif., 1975-79, Temple Aliyah, Woodland Hills, Calif., 1979-85, Adat Ari El, North Hollywood, Calif., 1985—; mem. exec. coun. Cantors Assembly, N.Y.C., 1986—; chmn. Conv. of Cantor Assembly, N.Y.C., L.A., 1989-91; bd. dirs. SVF Fedn. Coun., L.A., 1982-84. Producer rec. Windows of the Soul, 1988. Vol. Jewish Homes for the Aging, L.A., 1988-91; mem. Guardians for the Jewish Homes, 1989—. Democrat. Avocations: biking, camping, organ, opera, computing. Office: Adat Ari El 12020 Burbank Blvd North Hollywood CA 91607-2198

SILVERSTEIN, JOSEPH HARRY, conductor, musician; b. Detroit, Mar. 21, 1932; s. Bernard and Ida (Katz) S.; m. Adrienne Shufro, Apr. 27; children—Bernice, Deborah, Marc. Student Curtis Inst. Music, 1945-50; hon. doctoral degrees Tufts U., 1971, Rhode Island U., 1980, Boston Coll., 1981, New Eng. Conservatory, 1986, Susquehanna. Violinist, Houston Symphony Orch., Phila. Orch.; concertmaster Denver Symphony Orch., Boston Symphony Orch.; formerly chmn. string dept. New Eng. Conservatory Music; also chmn. faculty Berkshire Music Sch.; mem. faculty Boston U. Sch. Music, Yale U. Sch. Music; music dir. Boston Symphony Chamber Players, Boston U. Symphony Orch., Chautauqua (N.Y.) Instn., 1987—; interim music dir. Toledo Symphony Orch.; prin. guest condr. Balt. Symphony Orch., 1981; condr. Utah Symphony, music dir., 1983—; mus. dir. Worcester Orch., Mass., until 1987. Recipient Silver medal Queen Elizabeth of Belgium Internat. contest, 1959, Naumberg found. award, 1960; named one of ten outstanding young men, Boston C. of C., 1962. Fellow Am. Acad. Arts and Scis. Office: care Utah Symphony Orch 123 W South Temple Salt Lake City UT 84101-1403*

SILVERSTEIN, RICHARD, advertising agency executive. Grad., Parsons Sch. of Design. Co-chmn., creative dir. Goodby, Silverstein & Ptnrs., San Francisco, 1983—. Office: Goodby Silverstein & Ptnrs 720 California St San Francisco CA 94111-1426*

SILVERSTEIN, STEVEN B., railroad executive; b. Cleve., Sept. 21, 1951; s. Fred R. and Norma (Gillett) S.; m. Mary C. Straley, Aug. 6, 1988; children: Zachariah, Alisha. Student, Syracuse U., 1969-70, U. Rochester, 1972-73. Purchasing and warehouse mgr. Arctic Catering, Anchorage, 1979-80, field supr., 1980-82; freight auditor, then dir. in-bound logistics JB Gottstein Co., Anchorage, 1982-86; sr. logistics specialist, sr. supply mgmt. specialist ARCO Alaska, Inc., Anchorage, 1986-96; sr. dir. freight svcs. Alaska R.R. Corp., Anchorage, 1996—; speaker Atlanta Internat. Intermodal Expo, 1989, 91. Bd. dirs. Anchorage Ctr. for Performing Arts, 1993—. Mem. Am. Soc. Transp. and Logistics (cert., pres. 1982-88, Best Small Chpt. award 1986), Anchorage Concert Assn. (v.p., treas., bd. dirs. 1980—, now pres.), Coun. Logistics Mgmt. Jewish. Home: 1210 N St Anchorage AK 99501-4272

SILVESTRI, PATTI MARIE, elementary education educator; b. L.A.; d. William and Irene (Chavira) Ayala; m. David M. Silvestri, Oct. 12, 1991. BA in Child Devel., Calif. State U., L.A., 1992, MA in Edn. with honors, 1998. Cert. elem. tchr., reading specialist, Calif. Tchr. asst. B. Dawson Edn. Ctr., La Mirada, Calif., 1990-91; tchr. Oakwood Acad., Long Beach, Calif., 1992-94, New Horizon, Pasadena, Calif., 1994-96, South Whittier (Calif.) Sch. Dist., 1996—; reading tutor, La Mirada, 1997—; part-time prof., mentor Calif. State U., L.A. Author: (children's book) Laila's Leaving, 1996. Vol. cheer/dance coach Nativity elem. sch., El Monte, Calif., 1981-88; religion tchr. Beatitudes Ch., La Mirada, 1994-95. Mem. Golden Key Nat. Honor Soc. Roman Catholic. Avocations: writing, gourmet cooking, water sports, cheer/dance, sign language. Home: 14681 Sunnymead Dr La Mirada CA 90638-1051 Office: South Whittier Sch Dist Los Altos Sch 12001 Bonavista Ln Whittier CA 90604-2702

SILVIA, RAYMOND ALAN, librarian; b. Gustine, Calif., Apr. 10, 1950; s. Antonio and Mary (Viveiros) S.; m. Doris Elizabeth Newcomb, Jan. 9, 1972; children: Mary, Paul, Hilary, Dominic, Elizabeth. AA in English, Modesto (Calif.) Jr. Coll., 1970; BA in English summa cum laude, Calif. State U., Fresno, 1972, MA in English with distinction, 1982; MLS, San Jose State U., 1985. Cert. cmty. coll. tchr., Calif. Lectr. Calif. State U., Fresno, 1980-82; investor Clovis, Calif., 1982—; ref. libr./supr. King's County Libr., Hanford, Calif., 1986-90; libr./sr. libr. Calif. State Dept. Corrections, Sacramento, 1990-94; supervising libr. Calif. State Dept. Justice, Sacramento, 1994—; spkr./trainer, mem. statewide correctional law libr. task Calif. State Dept. Corrections, Sacramento, 1994; spkr. in field. Contbr. articles to profl. jours. Chmn. ref. com. San Joaquin Valley Libr. Sys., Fresno, 1989-90; mem. Secular Franciscan Order, Fresno, 1975—, novice master, 1984. Mem. MLA, Spl. Librs. Assn., Calif. State U. Fresno Alumni Assn., Phi Kappa Phi. Republican. Roman Catholic. Avocations: reading, music, hiking, travel.

SILZER, MARK MITCHELL, educational technology executive, consultant; b. Chgo., Apr. 9, 1947; s. Richard F. and Jennie F. (Banfield) S.; m. Barbara E. Luke, Aug. 9, 1969; children: Stephanie, Alison, Ashley. BA, Concordia Coll., River Forest, Ill., 1969; MS, No. Ill. U., 1972; PhD, U. Ill., 1981. Cert. supt., adminstr., Ill. Tchr. St. Peter's Luth. Sch., Schaumburg, Ill., 1969-71, prin., 1971-72; media dir. Hong Kong Internat. Sch., 1972-73, mid. sch. prin., 1973-78; adminstrv. asst. U. Ill., Urbana, 1978-80; sr. cons. EPIE Inst., Watermill, N.Y., 1980-81; exec. dir. Valley Luth. High Sch., Phoenix, 1981-84; prin. Our Redeemer Sch., Honolulu, 1984-87; pres. Menehune Data Systems, Honolulu, 1985-88; sr. mgr. Jostens Learning Corp., San Diego, 1987-91; v.p. The Edison Project, 1991-94; mng. dir. Acad. Systems, Mtn. View, Calif., 1994—; talk show host KGO Radio, Honolulu, 1984-85. Bd. dirs. Phoenix Boys Choir, 1982-85, Pleasanton Ptnrs. in Edn., Calif., 1990—; v.p. St. Philip Ch., Dublin, Calif., 1990-92; choir dir. St. Philip Ch., Dublin, 1991—; pres. Valley Luth. Sch., 1992—. B. L. Dodds fellow U. Ill., 1980. Mem. ASCD, Phi Delta Kappa (pres. Beta Tau chpt. 1983-86), Phi Kappa Psi. Avocations: reading, running, sailing, music. Home: 2810 Camino Segura Pleasanton CA 94566-8645 Office: 333 Hegenberger Rd Oakland CA 94621-1420

SIM, JOHN KIM-CHYE, minister; b. Singapore, Feb. 28, 1957; came to U.S., 1981; s. Hai Yong Sim and Ah Soon Quek; m. Ammelia Beng-Geok Tan, Sept. 4, 1978; 1 child, Samuel. Diploma in Bible with high distinction, Tung Ling Bible Sch., Singapore, 1980; AA in Practical Theology, Christ for the Nations, 1982; BA with high honors, Life Bible Coll., 1984; diploma in teaching, Evang. Teacher Tng. Assn., 1984; MDiv, Alliance Theol. Sem., 1990; ThM, Princeton Sem., 1993; postgrad., Fuller Theol. Sem., 1994—. Ordained to ministry Christian and Missionary Alliance, 1991. Asst. pastor Ch. of Our Savior (Anglican), Singapore, 1980-81, Chapel of the Resurrection (Anglican), Singapore, 1984-87; pastor Toledo Chinese Alliance Ch., 1990-93; asst. pastor Vineyard of Hope, 1997—. Home: 456 Via De Leon Placentia CA 92870-3226 Office: Vineyard of Hope PO Box 5252 Hacienda Heights CA 91745-0252

SIMAS, EDWARD ALFRED, chairman county board supervisors; b. Ripon, May 26, 1944; children: John, Gina. BBA, U. Pacific, 1966. Chmn. county seat Office of Bd. County Supervisors, Stockton, Calif., 1988—; vice-chmn. bd. suprs. Office of Bd. County Suprs., Stockton, 1991, 96, chmn. bd. suprs., 1992, 97. Office: Bd of County Suprs Courthouse 222 E Weber Ave Rm 701 Stockton CA 95202-2709

SIMBURG, MELVYN JAY, lawyer; b. San Francisco, June 15, 1946; s. Earl J. and Pearl Estelle (Garmaise) S.; m. Barbara Sherri Frost, Jan. 1, 1981; 2 children. AB, U. Calif., Berkeley, 1968; JD, Columbia U., 1972, M in Internat. Affairs, 1972. Bar: Wash. 1972, U.S. Ct. Appeals (9th cir.) 1972. Assoc. Perkins Coie, Seattle, 1972-76; pvt. practice, Seattle, 1976-81; pres. Melvyn Jay Simburg, P.S., A Profl. Svc. Corp., Seattle, 1981-83, Simburg, Ketter, Sheppard & Purdy, LLP, Seattle, 1983—; adj. prof. Law Sch., U. Puget Sound (now Seattle U.), Tacoma, 1972-74; chmn. ann. seminar on U.S. Can. bus. trans. of Bar Assn. B.C. and Wash. State. Former pres. Leschi Improvement Council, Seattle; active Seattle Film Soc., Seattle Art Mus. Mem. ABA (com. on internat. intellectual property rights, sect. internat. law and practice, com. on internat. bus. law, sect. bus. law), Wash. State Bar Assn. (chmn. sect. internat. law and practice 1986-87), Seattle-King County Bar Assn. (past chmn. sect. internat. and comparative law), World Trade Club Seattle (bd. dirs. 1983-86), World Affairs Council Seattle, Seattle C. of C. (vice chmn. internat. trade and devel. com. 1984-86). Contbr. articles to profl. jours. Fax: 206-223-3929. Home: 235 Lake Dell Ave Seattle WA 98122-6310 Office: Simburg Ketter Sheppard & Purdy LLP 2525 1st Interstate Ctr 999 3d Ave Seattle WA 98104-4089

SIMEON, ESTRELLA BALBAS, educator; b. Tarlac, The Philippines, Nov. 18, 1932; d. Braulio Lafrades and Laurcana Ventura (Blas) Balbas; m. Ernani Guerrero Simeon, Dec. 22, 1958 (dec. Mar. 1981); children: Maria Teresa, Guia, Violeta. BS in Edn., MA in Edn., U. of The Philippines, Manila, 1974. Profl. edn. permit Office of Profl. Certification. Classroom tchr. Divsn. of City Schs., Manila, 1968-74; prof. III The Philippine Women's U., Quezon City, 1983-87; classroom tchr. Wash. Sch. Dist., Renton, 1991-92; English and sci. coord., supr. La Consolacion Sch., Caloocan, The Philippines, 1983-87. Author: (nonfiction) How to Survive the Aging-Parent Problem, 1998; mem. editl. staff, columnist The Torch, 1953. Recipient Leadership/Vol. award Philippine Nat. Red Cross, 1980, Leadership award Girl Scouts of The Philippines, 1979-80. Roman Catholic. Avocations: poetry, fiction and nonfiction writing. Home: 1513 21st Ave S Seattle WA 98144-3605

SIMEROTH, DEAN CONRAD, chemical engineer; b. Marysville, Calif., Mar. 21, 1946; s. Raphael Conrad and Mary Beatrice (Watson) S.; m. Phyllis Deborah Minakowski, Feb. 7, 1971 (div. Nov. 1994); 1 child, Brian Conrad. BS in Chem. Engring., U. Calif., Davis, 1968. From air pollution specialist to chief engr. evaluation br. Calif. Air Resources Bd., Sacramento, 1969-87; chief criteria pollutant br. Calif. Air Resources Bd., 1987—. Served in U.S. Army, 1969-71, Korea. Mem. AIChE, Air Waste Mgmt. Assn., Kiwanis (treas. Woodland, Calif. chpt. 1988-96). Democrat. Roman Catholic. Avocations: hunting, fishing, tennis, history. Office: Calif Air Resources Bd PO Box 2815 2020 L St Sacramento CA 95814-4219

SIMIEN, OCTAVIA RUBEN, reporter, former educator, principal; b. Beaumont, Tex., Feb. 23, 1928; d. Bud and Emily (Cormier) Ruben; m. Joseph Warren Simien, Dec. 26, 1959. Cert., Lincoln Bus. Coll., Beaumont, Tex., 1946; BA, Sophia U., Tokyo, 1967; MA, Chapman U., 1973. Elem. sch. tchr. Blessed Sacrament Sch., Beaumont, 1948, asst. music tchr., 1956; tchr. North Sacramento Sch. Dist., 1969-70, spl. edn. counselor, 1970, 73, asst. prin., 1973-78, prin., 1978-80; social and ednl. corr. Sacramento Observer Newspaper, 1997—; owner greeting card bus. Simien & Simien Personally Yours. Contbr. book chpts. to: God is Able, 1995, My Mother Mary, 1995; freelance writer Profiles for Caths. Herald. Bd. dirs. Sacramento Black Cath. Coun., 1980—; cmty. concerns chairperson Sacramento Diocese Coun. Cath. Women, 1997—; pres. Sacramento Deanery, 1997-99; legis. city planning reporter Calif. Women's Coun., Sacramento, 1992-98; Grand Lady ladies aux. Knights of St. Peter Claven. Mem. NAACP, Nat. League Am. Pen Women (v.p. 1998), Calif. Writers Club, Cath. Daus. of Ams. (regent 1991—, Woman of Yr. 1992). Avocations: writing, poetry, reading. Home: 8518 Bennington Way Sacramento CA 95826-3155

SIMKHOVICH, BORIS ZALMAN, biochemist, researcher; b. Riga, Latvia, July 26, 1947; came to U.S., 1989; s. Zalman Israel and Sofia (Lipkina) S.; m. Mara Turets, May 30, 1991. MD, Riga Med. Inst., 1971, PhD, 1974; DMS, Inst. for Gen. Pathology, Moscow, 1988. Rsch. assoc. Inst. of Organic Synthesis, Riga, 1975-85, head rsch. lab., 1985-89; rsch. assoc. U. So. Calif., L.A., 1989-90; dir. biochemistry Heart Inst. Good Samaritan Hosp., L.A., 1990—; asst. prof. rsch. medicine U. So. Calif. Sch. Medicine, L.A., 1995—. Contbr. scientific papers to profl. jours.; reviewer for rsch. jours. in the field of cardiology. Recipient 1st prize Annual Scientific award Latvian Acad. of Scis., 1985. Mem. Internat. Soc. for Heart Rsch. (Am. sect.), Am. Heart Assn. Avocations: classical music, literature, travel. Office: Good Samaritan Hosp 1225 Wilshire Blvd Los Angeles CA 90017-1901

SIMMONS, GEOFFREY STUART, physician; b. Camp Gordon, Ga., July 28, 1943; s. Ted R. and Jane A. (Lavander) S.; m. Sherry Simmons, Sept. 7, 1985; children: Bradley, Anais. BS, U. Ill., 1965, MD, 1969. Intern U. So. Calif., L.A., 1969-70, resident, 1971-74; pvt. practice Astoria, Oreg., 1974-77, Eugene, Oreg., 1977—; chmn. internal medicine dept. Peace Health Med. Group, 1996—; bd. dirs. Lane County Med. Soc.; med. correspondent KUGN Radio, 1993-95. Author: The Z Papers, 1977, The Adam Experiment, 1978, Pandemic, 1980, Murdock, 1982, The Glue Factory, 1995, To Glue Or Not To Glue, 1997; med. commentator KABC Radio, 1970. Avocation: writing.

SIMMONS, GEORGE MICHAEL, educational administrator; b. Portland, Oreg., June 26, 1943; s. Vernon L. and Petra K. (Svenddal) S.; m. Mary Katherine Walker, June 27, 1970; 1 child, Alex George. BS in Chem. Engring., U. Idaho, 1965, MS in Chem. Engring., 1966; PhD in Chem. Engring., Stanford U., 1970. Registered profl. engr., Idaho. NASA postdoctoral trainee, then sr. engr. Jet Propulsion Lab., Pasadena, Calif., 1970-74; prof. chem. engring. U. Idaho, Moscow, 1975-98, chmn. dept. chem. engring., 1982-85, dean Sch. Art and Architecture, 1990-92, assoc. v.p., 1985-91, vice provost, 1991-95, interim provost, 1995-97, asst. v.p. rsch., 1997-98; dean sci. & engring. Seattle U., 1998—; coll. div. chmn. U. Idaho Centennial Campaign, 1985-89; adv. bd. North Idaho Bus. Technology Incubator, Moscow, 1989—. Contbr. articles to chem. engring. publs. Bd. dirs. Associated Western U., 1994-97. Kellogg Found. fellow, 1987-90. Avocations: piano, Renaissance music. Office: Seattle U 900 Broadway Seattle WA 98122-4340

SIMMONS, HOWARD LEE, education educator; b. Mobile, Ala.. BS in Secondary Edn., Spring Hill Coll., 1960; MAT in Slavic langs. and Lit., Ind. U., 1965; PhD in Design and Mgmt. of Postsecondary Edn., Fla. State U., 1975; LHD (hon.), Sojourner-Douglass Coll., 1995; HHD (hon.), King's Coll., 1998. Assoc. dir. , asst. exec. sec. Commn. on Higher Edn. Middle States Assn. of Colls. & Schs., Phila., 1974-95, exec. dir., 1988-95; prof., coord. edn. leadership in higher edn. Ariz. State U., Tempe, 1996—, assoc. dean, 1996-97; vis. lectr. in Russian Lafayette Coll., Easton, Pa., 1970-71; part-time Russian/Spanish instr. Clayton (Mo.) High Sch., 1965-67; dean instructional svcs. Northampton Community Coll., Bethlehem, Pa., 1969-74; chmn. dept. fgn. lang. Forest Park Community Coll., Mo., 1964-69; sr. researcher Ariz. State U., nat. Ctr. for Postsecondary Governance and Fin., 1986-87; cons. in field including cons./evaluator North Cen. Assn. of Colls. and Schs., 1997—; keynote speaker in field; researcher on accreditation and blacks in higher edn. Contbr. articles to profl. jours. NDEA grantee Spring Hill Coll., 1958-60, grantee Japan-U.S. Friendship Commn., 1993-94; NDEA fellow Ind. U., 1963-64, Edn. Professions Devel. Act fellow Fla. State U., 1973-75, fellow Am. Coun. Edn., 1972-73; USIA Acad. Specialist grantee, Quito, Ecuador, 1996. Mem. Am. Ednl. Rsch. Assn., Am. Assn. for Community and Jr. Colls. (assoc.), Assn. for the Study of Higher Edn., Assn. of Tchrs. of Slavic and East European Langs., Assn. Caribbean Tertiary Instn., Internat. Accreditation Specialist, 1996—, Am. Assn. for Higher Edn. (exec. bd. black caucus, nat. cultural diversity award by caucuses 1992), Lang. Labs. and Faculty Assn. Pres. (dir.), Phi Delta Kappa, Kappa Delta Pi. Home: 2008 N Squire Ave Tempe AZ 85281-1330 Office: Ariz State U Coll Edn PO Box 872411 Tempe AZ 85287-2411

SIMMONS, JANET BRYANT, writer, publisher; b. Oakland, Calif., Apr. 22, 1925; d. Howard Pelton and Janet Horn (McNab) Bryant; m. William Ellis Simmons, May 17, 1944 (div. 1979); children: William Howard, Janet Margaret Simmons McAlpine. BA, San Jose State U., 1965; MA, U. San Francisco, 1979. Social worker Santa Clara County Social Svcs., San Jose, Calif., 1965-91; editor, pub. Enlightenment Press, Santa Clara, 1994—. Author: The Mystical Child, 1996. Mem. AAUW, Am. Booksellers Assn., Pubs. Mktg. Assn., Bay Area Ind. Pubs. Assn., Audubon Soc., Jacques Cousteau Soc. Avocations: playing piano, swimming, Tai Chi, travel, gardening. Office: Enlightenment Press PO Box 3314 Santa Clara CA 95055-3314

SIMMONS, JOY LOUISE, activist; b. Torrington, Wyo., Sept. 9, 1946; d. Jack Mervin and Betty Case Thompson; foster parents William R. and Ruth Martin; m. Richard L. Simmons, Sept. 9, 1971; children: Cheleen L. Simmons-Morgan, Michael L. Grad. H.S., Cheyenne, Wyo. Cocktail waitress Las Vegas, Nev., 1967-78; casino dealer Laughlin, Nev., 1979-85; owner Trifles of Arizona, 1985-92. Author: This of Joy, Celestial Arts, 1975. Activist Civil Rights, Wyo, Colo., Nev., 1962—, Feminist Movement ERA, Comty. Action Against Rape, Nev., 1969—, Worker's Rights, Nev., 1985-87, Silicone, 1991-92, Anti-Nuke; spearheaded class action suit against Dow Chem. for liquid injections of silicone. Mem. ACLU, Common Cause, Halt, Pub. Citizen. Democrat. Home: 3129 Palo Verde Dr Laughlin NV 89029-0118

SIMMONS, KAREN ELAINE, artist; b. Bremerton, Wash., Feb. 2, 1937; d. Arthur William Hardy and Marjorie Jollie; m. George Carroll Simmons, Sept. 4, 1972; children: Kristan Dodge, Kerryn Araiza. BBA, U. Ark., Fayetteville, 1962; BS in Social Sci., U. Ark., 1973. Chief dep., assesor, recorder, clk. County of San Diego, 1974-96; adv. bd. Regional Urban Info. Sys., San Diego, 1985-96. One-woman shows include The Gathering, 1995, Point Loma Cultural Ctr., 1995, Paige Hardy & Assocs., 1996, Southwestern Coll., 1996, 97, 98, County Libr., 1996, San Diego County Adminstrn. Ctr., 1997, San Diego City Info. Ctr., 1998, Little Italy Assn., 1998, Sony Artwalk, 1998, Galeria Del Centro Cultural De La Raza, 1998. Bd. dirs. City Hosp., Siloam Springs, Ark., 1960-71. Recipient Achievement awards Nat. Assn. Counties, 1980-96; grantee Campbell Soup Co., Inc., 1960, First Nat. Bank, Dale Carnagie & Assocs., 1962, Am. Banker's Assn., 1964-65, U.S. Law Enforcement Adminstrn., 1973; scholar Whitman Coll., 1955, Outstanding Freshman scholar U. Ark., 1956, Baldwin Piano Co. scholar, 1957-58, Urrutia Green scholar, 1997. Mem. Nat. Assn. Fine Artists, San Diego Mus. Art, Nat. Mus. Women in the Arts, The Athenaeum. Avocations: travel, skiing, scuba diving, horses, dogs. Office: San Diego County 1600 Pacific Hwy Ste 103 San Diego CA 92101-2422

SIMMONS, MARC STEVEN, historian; b. Dallas, May 15, 1937; s. Julian Marion and Lois Judson (Skielvig) S. BA, U. Tex., 1958; MA, U. N.Mex., 1960, PhD, 1965. Prof. history U. N.Mex., Albuquerque, 1965-66, 70-71, 83-84, Colo. Coll., Colorado Springs, 1975, 78. Author 35 books; contbr. over 150 articles to popular and profl. jours. Recipient Woodrow Wilson fellow, 1958, Nat. Endowment for Humanities fellow, 1979, Guggenheim fellow Guggenheim Found., 1980; knighthood with rank of Comendador, Order of Isabela la Católica, King of Spain, 1993. Mem. Santa Fe Trail Assn. (pres. 1986-89), Western Writers Am. (Golden Spur award for best western non-fiction book 1982), Author's Guild.

SIMMONS, MARCIA ANN, reporter; b. Topeka, Kans., Oct. 29, 1954; d. William Eugene Simmons and Ruth Mae (Engle) Shaw; m. George Z. Guzowski, Mar. 20, 1982 (dec. Nov. 1987); children: Kevin King, Stefan Guzowski, William Lindstedt. BA, U. N.Mex., 1977. Anchor, reporter KUNM Radio, Albuquerque, 1975-76; anchor reporter KNWZ Radio, Albuquerque, 1976-77, KOAT-TV, Albuquerque, 1981-88, KOA, Denver, 1991—; reporter, editor Old Town Times, Albuquerque, 1976; assignments editor, anchor KGGM-TV, Albuquerque, 1977-81; reporter KOB-TV, Albuquerque, 1990; media advisor N.Mex. Games, Albuquerque, 1988. Writer, reporter Nativity Newspaper, Broomfield, Colo., 1994. Bd. dirs. Gov.'s Task Force on Developmentally Disabled, Santa Fe, N.Mex., 1988-89, N.Mex. Animal Humane Assn., Albuquerque, 1986; media advisor Bob Schwartz for Dist. Atty. Campaign, Albuquerque, 1988. Recipient Nat. Gavel award ABA, 1982, Reporting award AP, 1985. Mem. Am. Women in Radio and TV. Democrat. Roman Catholic. Avocations: skiing, writing, camping, reading. Home: 1162 Clubhouse Dr Broomfield CO 80020-1240

SIMMONS, NEWTON LESTER, aircraft company executive; b. Spokane, Wash., Nov. 15, 1947; s. John Newton and Emily Martha (Polson) S.; m. Astrid Schmidt, Feb. 10, 1986; 1 child, Jonathan. BA, U. Wash., 1973, MBA, 1977. Product mgr. Conrail, Phila., 1980-83; gen. mgr. Hafnia Inc., Copenhagen, Denmark, 1984-85; mgr. ops. planning Danish Nat. Rwy., Copenhagen, 1985-88; mgr. strategic planning The Boeing Co., Seattle, 1977-79, 89—. Mem. The Mountaineers, Seattle, 1990-92; chair pub. rels. com. Salvation Army, Seattle, 1992-94; cons. adv. bd. Harborview Hosp., Seattle, 1994—. Mem. World Affairs Coun., 1990—. Avocations: hiking, tennis, museums, skiing, piano. Home: 2006 29th Ave S Seattle WA 98144-4855 Office: The Boeing Co Lynnwood Seattle WA 98124

SIMMONS, RICHARD J., lawyer; b. Brockton, Mass., Nov. 26, 1951. BA summa cum laude, U. Mass., 1973; JD, U. Calif., Berkeley, 1976. Bar: Calif. 1976. Ptnr. Sheppard, Mullin, Richter & Hampton, L.A., 1995—; lectr. State of Calif., 1977-88; instr. UCLA, 1980-87; appointed to bd. Calif. Minimum Wage Bds. 1982, 84, 87; adv. bd. U. Calif. Boalt Hall Law Sch. Indsl. Relations Law Journal, 1985—. Reviews editor, editor in chief: Indsl. Relations Law Jour. 1975-76; Author: Wrongful Discharge and Employment Practices Manual, 1989, Employee Handbook and Personnel Policies Manual, 1983, 87, 92, Wage and Hour Manual for California Employers, 1982, 86, 88, 89, 91, Employment Discrimination and EEO Practice Manual for California Employers, 1982, 85,91, Employer's Guide to the American with Disabilities Act, 1990, 91, 92, The Employer's Guide to the California Family Rights Act of 1991, 1992, Employer Obligations Under the Federal Plant Closing Law, 1989, 90, The New Federal Polygraph Law, 1989, The New Federal Immigration Law: The Immigration Reform and Control Act of 1986, 1987, COBRA: The Federal Health Insurance Rules for the 1990's, 1987,90. contbr. to profl mags. and jours. Commonwealth scholar. Mem. ABA (labor, employment law, tax sect.), L.A. County Bar Assn. (tax, labor sect.), The State Bar Calif., Calif. Soc. Health Care Attys., Am. Soc. Health Care Attys., Phi Kappa Phi. Office: Sheppard Mullin Richter & Hampton 333 S Hope St 43rd 7L Los Angeles CA 90071*

SIMMONS, ROY WILLIAM, banker; b. Portland, Oreg., Jan. 24, 1916; s. Henry Clay and Ida (Mudd) S.; m. Elizabeth Ellison, Oct. 28, 1938; children—Julia Simmons Watkins, Matthew R., Laurence E., Elizabeth Jane Simmons Hoke, Harris H., David E. Asst. cashier First Nat. Bank Layton, Utah, 1944-49; Utah bank commr., 1949-51; exec. v.p. Bank of Utah, Ogden, 1951-53; pres. Lockhart Co., Salt Lake City, 1953-64, Zion's First Nat. Bank, Salt Lake City, 1964-81; chmn. bd. Zion's First Nat. Bank, 1965-98; chmn., CEO Zion's Bancorp, 1965-91, chmn. bd., 1991—; chmn. bd. Zion's Savs. & Loan Assn., 1961-69; pres. Lockhart Co., 1964-87; bd. dirs. Beneficial Life Ins. Co., Ellison Ranching Co. Chmn. Utah Bus. Devel. Corp., 1969-80; Mem. Utah State Bd. Regents, 1969-81. Mem. Salt Lake City C. of C. (treas. 1964-65), Sigma Pi. Republican. Mem. Ch. of Jesus Christ of Latter Day Saints. Home: 817 E Crestwood Rd Kaysville UT 84037-1712 Office: Zions Bancorp 10 E South Temple Ste 1000 Salt Lake City UT 84133-1112

SIMMONS, SARAH R., lawyer; b. Ducktown, Tenn., Jan. 23, 1948. BA magna cum laude, U. Ariz., 1970, postgrad.; JD magna cum laude, U. Denver, 1973. Bar: Colo. 1974, Ariz. 1975. Mem. Molloy, Jones & Donahue, Tucson, Brown & Bain, P.A., Tucson. Trustee Tohono Club Park, 1995—, sec., 1997-99, v.p. 1999—; trustee Tucson Airport Authority, 1996—; mem. Law Coll. Assn. Bd., 1996—, sec. 1998—; 4th R bd. Tucson Unified Sch., 1996—; bd. dirs. United Way of Tucson, 1995—, Family Advocacy Resource and Wellness Ctrs., Resources for Women, 1995—; bd. dirs. Ariz. Town Hall, 1998—; mem. adv. bd. Ariz. for a Drug Free Workplace, 1991—, So. Ariz. Sports Devel. Corp., U. Ariz. Social and Behavioral Scis., 1994-96; sec. So. Ariz. Minutemen, 1996—. Recipient Tucson Woman of Yr. C. of C., 1994, Women on the Move award YWCA, 1995, Outstanding Alumni award U. Ariz. Coll. of Law, 1993. Fellow ABA, Ariz. Bar Assn.; mem. Nat. Assn. Bond Lawyers, State Bar Ariz. (bd. govs. 1987-95, sec.-treas. 1989-90, 2d v.p. 1990-91, 1st v.p. 1991-92, pres.-elect 1992-93, pres. 1993-94, employment law sect., profl. conduct com., fee arbitration com.), Ariz. Women Lawyers Assn. (charter), Colo. Bar Assn., Pima County Bar Assn. (bd. dirs. 1985-94), Am. Judicature Soc., So. Ariz. Legal Aid (bd. dirs. 1990—), Lawyers Against Hunger (bd. dirs., v.p. D-M 50 1996-98, pres. 1998—), Order St. Ives, Phi Beta Kappa, Phi Kappa Phi, Phi Alpha Theta, Kappa Beta Pi, MOrrisk Edall Inn of Ct. Office: Brown & Bain PA 19th Fl 1 S Church Ave # Tucson AZ 85701-1612

SIMMONS, TED CONRAD, writer; b. Seattle, Sept. 1, 1916; s. Conrad and Clara Evelyn (Beaudry) S.; m. Dorothy Pauline Maltese, June 1, 1942; children: Lynn, Juliet. Student U. Wash., 1938-41, UCLA and Los Angeles State U., 1952-54, Oxford (Eng.) U., 1980. Drama critic Seattle Daily Times, 1942; indsl. writer, reporter-editor L.A. Daily News, 1948-51; contbr. Steel, Western Metals, Western Industry, 1951—; past poetry dir. Watts Writers Workshop; instr. Westside Poetry Center; asst. dir. Pacific Coast Writers Conf., Calif. State Coll. Los Angeles. Served with USAAF, 1942-46. Author: (poetry) Deadended, 1966; (novel) Middlearth, 1975; (drama) Greenhouse, 1977, Durable Chaucer, 1978, Rabelais and other plays, 1980, Dickeybird, 1981 (nominated TCG Plays-in-Progress award 1985), Alice and Eve, 1983, Deja Vu, Deja Vu, 1986, The Box, 1987, Ingrid Superstar, 1988, Three Quarks for Mr. Marks, 1989, Ingrid: Skier on the Slopes of Stromboli, 1990, A Midsummer's Hamlet, 1991, Hamlet Nintendo, After Hours, Dueling Banjoes, Viva el Presidente, Climate of the Sun, 1992, Nude Descending Jacob's Ladder, 1993, Almost an Opera, 1994, Landscape with Inverted Tree and Fred Astaire Dancing, 1995, O.J. Othello, Fast Track, Searching for Alice Liddell, Mr. Blue of Freaky Animals, Inc., 1997, Rosenstern & Guildencrantz II, 1997, Rosa/Rosa of the Centuries/Rosa of the Thorns, 1997, Joyce, 1997, Joyce-After Hours, 1997, Amadeus & da Cultchur Club, 1997, Wonderland: Alice's New Adventures, 1998, The Brilliant Life of an Intelligent Orchid-A Play about Ingrid Bergman, 1998, Chekhov Off-Broadway, The Premiere, Good Night Sweet Prince; writer short story, radio verse; book reviewer Los Angeles Times; contbr. poetry to The Am. Poet, Prairie Wings, Antioch Rev., Year Two Anthology; editor: Venice Poetry Company Presents, 1972. Grantee Art Commn. King County, 1993.

SIMMONS, TIMOTHY DONALD, fire service; b. Oklahoma City, May 10, 1954; s. Donald George and BetteRuth (Reeder) S.; m. Jean (Kashitsina) Simmons, Aug. 8, 1997; 1 child, Helena. AA, Phoenix Coll., 1975; BA in Journalism, Ariz. State U., 1978. With Phoenix Fire Dept., 1985—. Author: Up From the Ashes, 1986, Brothers of the Pine, 1995; contbr. articles to profl. publs. Vol. capt. Nogales (Sonora, Mex.) Fire Dept., 1988—. Mem. Nat. Writers Assn., Soc. Profl. Journalists, Western Writers Am. Home: 3946 W Sierra Vista Dr Phoenix AZ 85019-1232

SIMMS, MARIA ESTER, health services administrator; b. Bahia Blanca, Argentina; came to U.S., 1963; d. Jose and Esther (Guays) Barberio Esandi; m. Michael Simms, July 15, 1973 (Aug. 1993); children: Michelle Bonnie Lee Carla, Michael London Valentine, Matthew Brandon. Degree medicine, Facultad del Centenario, Rosario, Argentina, 1962; Physician Asst. Cert. (hon.), U. So. Calif., 1977. Medical diplomate. Pres. Midtown Svcs. Inc., L.A., 1973—; dir. internat. affairs, speaker Gov. of Papua, New Guinea, 1996—; dir., CFO, pres. World Film Inst., 1996—; dir. internat. affairs, speaker on humanitarian, cultural and econ. matters Govt. of Papua New Guinea; advocate, internat. spkr. for women, children and animal rights. Chmn. bd. Am.'s Film Inst., Washington; chmn. bd. trustees World Film Inst, Dir. Intl. Affairs, speaker-Humanitarian, Economic and Cultural Consulate of Papua New Guinea, Los Angeles, Calif. Nominated chairwoman of bd. trustees World Film Inst., nominated pres. 1997. Fellow Am. Acad. Physicians' Assts.; mem. Bus. for Law Enforcement (northeast divsn.), Physicians for Social Responsibility, Mercy Crusade Inc., Internat. Found. for Survival Rsch., Noetic Scis. Soc., Inst. Noetic Scis., So. Calif. Alliance for Survival, Supreme Emblem Club of U.S., Order Eastern Star, Flying Samaritans, Shriners. Avocations: coin collecting, designing, writing, oil painting, flying.

SIMMS, MARIA KAY, writer, non-profit organization executive; b. Princeton, Ill., Nov. 18, 1940; d. Frank B. and Anna (Haurberg) S.; m. Neil F. Michelsen, Oct. 2, 1987 (dec. 1990); children: Shannon Sullivan Stillings, Molly A. Sullivan, Elizabeth Maria Jossick; m. James l. Jossick, July 12, 1998. BFA, Ill. Wesleyan U., 1962. Cert. cons. profl. astrologer; ordained min. L.A. Cmty. Ch. of Religious Sci. Elder priestess Covenant of the Goddess; art tchr. elem. and jr. high pub. schs., Dundee, Northbrook, Ill., 1962-65; H.S. art tchr. Danbury, Conn., 1975-76; freelance gallery painter various cities, 1962-77, free-lance comml. illustrator, 1972-74, 86-87; shop, gallery café owner Conn., 1976-79; art dir. ACS Pubs., Inc., San Diego, Calif., 1987-90; pres. Astro Comm. Svcs., Inc. (formerly ACS Pubs.), San Diego, 1990-98, dir., 1990—, acquisitions editor, 1998—; bd. dirs. Omni Techs. Corp.; conf. lectr. Author: Twelve Wings of the Eagle, 1988, Dial Detective, 1989; co-author: Search for the Christmas Star, 1989, Circle of the Cosmic Muse, 1994, Your Magical Child, 1994, Future Signs, 1996, The Witch's Circle, 1996, Millenium: Fears, Fantasies and Facts, 1998; contbr. articles to popular mags. High priestess Cir. of the Cosmic Muse; elder priestess Covenant of the Goddess, 2d officer Calafia Local Coun., 1995-96, pub. info. officer, 1996-98; mem. adv. bd. Kepler Coll., 1998—. Recipient numerous art awards. Mem. Nat. Coun. Geocosmic Rsch. Inc. (dir., pubs. dir. 1981-92, editor jour. 1984-92, chairperson bd. 1999—), Am. Fedn. Astrologers, Internat. Soc. Astrol. Rsch., New Age Pubs. Assn., Alpha Gamma Delta. Office: Astro Comm Svcs Inc 5521 Ruffin Rd San Diego CA 92123-1314

SIMMS, THOMAS HASKELL, police chief; b. Yuma, Ariz., Sept. 3, 1945; s. Jessie Lee and Mary Elizabeth (Servos) S.; divorced; m. Ginny Lee David, Mar. 26, 1988; children: Thomas Haskell Jr., Julie Marie. BA, St. Mary's Coll., Moraga, Calif., 1981; MS, Calif. Poly., Pomona, 1991. Officer Mountain View (Calif.) Police Dept., 1972-76; police sgt. East Bay Parks, Oakland, Calif., 1976-79; police lt. Town of Moraga, Calif., 1979-84, chief police, 1984-87; chief police City of Piedmont, Calif., 1987-91; chief of police City of Roseville, Calif., 1991—; mem. U. Calif.-Davis Med. Ctr. Leadership Coun.; bd. dirs. Child Abuse Prevention Coun. of Placer County, Sierra Family Svcs. Bd. dirs. Piedmont coun. Boy Scouts Am., 1988-89. Maj. U.S. Army, 1967-71, Vietnam. Mem. Calif. Chiefs Police Assn. (bd. dirs.), Calif. Peace Officers Assn., Calif. Peace Officers Meml. Found. (bd. dirs.), Rotary, Kiwanis (pres. Moraga 1982-83, Kiwanian of Yr. award 1983). Presbyterian. Avocations: hiking, photography, travel, golf, fly fishing. Office: Roseville Police Dept 311 Vernon St Roseville CA 95678-2649*

SIMON, DIANE MEYER, environmental company executive; b. South Bend, Ind., Apr. 2, 1946; d. Orlando Lott Meyer and Irene Elizabeth (Speheger) Best; m. N. Stuart Grauel, Aug. 2, 1969 (div. Nov. 1976); m. Herbert Simon, Nov. 25, 1981; children: Sarah, Rachel, Asher Benjamin. BA in Psychology, Butler U., 1968; postgrad., IUPUI. Press/media staff U.S. Senator Robert F. Kennedy, 1968; adminstr. U.S. Senator Birch Bayh, Washington and Indpls., 1968-79; pres. Meyer Simon Group, Indpls., 1981-89; prin. ECO Ptnrs., Inc., Indpls., 1990—, ECO Educators, Indpls., 1990-94; founder, pres. emeritus Global Green USA, Venice, Calif. and Washington, 1993—; exec. bd. Green Cross Internat., Geneva, 1993—. Bd. dirs. Hollywood Policy Ctr. Found., Calif., Sadat Peace Found., N.Y., Sundance Inst., Indpls. Children's Mus., Indpls. Symphony Orch., United Way Indpls., WFYI Channel 20 (PBS); co-founder Dialogue Today (Coalition of Black and Jewish Women); bd. sponsors Ind. Planned Parenthood; mem. Ind. U. Found., Indpls. Clean City Com., Indpls. Human Rels. Task Force; capital campaign co-chair Madame C.J. Walker Urban Life-Ctr.; bd. govs. Orchard Country Day Sch.; trustee YMCA; fin. chair Baron Hill for U.S. Senate, Ind.; mem. fin. com. Evan Bayh for Gov., Ind.; mem. pres. adv. com. JFK Ctr. for Performing Arts; committeewoman Dem. Nat. Com. Recipient Ind. State award for design ASID, Ind., 1986, Mary Mcleod Bethune award Nat. Coun. Negro Women, Ind., 1986, Wilma Rudolph Found. award, Indpls., 1988, King, Walker, Wilkins, Young award, Indpls., 1989, Millennium award Green Cross Internat., Geneva, 1997, Founders award Global Green USA, Venice and Washington, 1997; named Woman of Yr., City of Indpls., 1985, Soroptimist Internat. Woman of Distinction for Environment, Indpls., 1988. Mem. Internat. Womens Forum. Jewish. Home: 665 Buena Vista Dr Montecito CA 93108-1407 Office: Global Green USA 1600 Main St Venice CA 90291-3626

SIMON, JOEL ARTHUR, physician, medical educator; b. Bklyn., Sept. 16, 1948; s. Sidney Jack and Esther (Rubin); m. Sarah Ellan Samuels, Dec. 31, 1983; 1 child, Jeremy. BA cum laude, SUNY, Binghamton, 1970; MD, SUNY, Buffalo, 1974; MPH, U. Calif., Berkeley, 1990. Diplomat Am. Bd. Internal Medicine. Intern, resident and chief resident internal medicine SUNY Downstate Med. Ctr., Bklyn., 1974-78; staff physician Kaiser-Permanente, Inc., Hayward and Fremont, Calif., 1978-90; postdoct. rsch. fellow U. Calif., San Francisco, 1990-92, asst. clin. prof., 1992-94, asst. prof., 1994—; mem. scientific adv. coun. Calif. Walnut Mktg. Bd., Sacramento, 1995—; coord. preventive medicine program San Francisco VA Med. Ctr., 1996—. Contbr. over 21 articles, 11 commentaries, editls. to profl. jours. Fellow ACP, Am. Coll. Nutrition, AHA (assoc. fellow Coun. on Epidemiology 1995). Office: SFVAMC Gen Internal Medicine 4150 Clement St San Francisco CA 94121-1545

SIMON, WILLIAM LEONARD, film and television writer and producer, author; b. Washington, Dec. 3, 1930; s. Isaac B. and Marjorie (Felsteiner) S.; m. Arynne Lucy Abeles, Sept. 18, 1966; 1 child, Victoria Marie; 1 stepson, Sheldon M. Bermont. BEE, Cornell U., 1954; MA in Ednl. Psychology, Golden State U., 1982, PhD in Comm., 1983. Writer features and TV movies, documentary and indsl. films, TV programs, 1958—; lectr. George Washington U., Washington, 1968-70; juror Coun. on Nontheatrical Events Film Festival, 1975-90, Cindy Festival Blue Ribbon Panel, 1985—; jury chmn., bd. dirs. CINE film festival, 1990—. Writer more than 600 produced works for motion pictures and TV, including (screenplays) Fair Woman Without Discretion, Majorca, Swindle, A Touch of Love, (teleplays and documentaries) From Information to Wisdom, Flight of Freedom II, Missing You, (home video) Star of India, Combat Vietnam series; writer, prodr.: The Star of India: Setting Sail; co-author: Profit from Experience-The Story of Transformation Management (best seller, nominee Global book awards), 1995, Lasting Change, 1997; author: Beyond the Numbers, 1996; co-author: On the Firing Line, My 500 Days at Apple Computer, 1998 (Best Seller), High Velocity Leadership--The Mars Pathfinder Approach to Faster, Better, Cheaper, 1999. Pres. Foggy Bottom Citizens Assn., 1963-65, mem. exec. bd., 1965-69; v.p. Shakespeare Summer Festival, 1966-67, trustee, 1965-70; mem. interview com. Cornell U., 1987-88. Lt. USN, 1954-58. Recipient 12 Golden Eagle awards Cine Film Festival, gold medal N.Y. Internat. Festival, gold medal Freedoms Found., IFPA Gold Cindy; awards Berlin, Belgrade and Venice film Festivals, numerous others. Mem. Nat. Acad. TV Arts and Scis. (gov. D.C. chpt. 1970-73, gov. San Diego chpt. 1998—), Writers Guild Am., Am. Film Inst., Internat. Documentary Assn., Rotary (bd. dirs., program chmn.), Eta Kappa Nu (chpt. pres. 1953-54), Tau Beta Pi. Republican. Avocations: crew member square-rigged brig Pilgrim, San Diego Museum ship Star of India, tennis. Home: 6151 Paseo Delicias PO Box 2048 Rancho Santa Fe CA 92067-2048

SIMONDS, JOHN EDWARD, newspaper editor; b. Boston, July 4, 1935; s. Alvin E. and Ruth Angeline (Rankin) S.; m. Rose B. Muller, Nov. 16, 1968; children—Maximillian P., Malia G.; children by previous marriage—Rachel F., John B. B.A., Bowdoin Coll., 1957. Reporter Daily Tribune, Seymour, Ind., 1957-58, UPI, Columbus, Ohio, 1958-60; reporter, asst. city editor Providence Jour. Bull., 1960-65, Washington Evening Star, 1965-66; corr. Gannett News Svc., Washington, 1966-75; mng. editor Honolulu Star Bull., 1975-80, exec. editor, 1980-87, sr. editor, editorial page editor, 1987-93; exec. Hawaii Newspaper Agy., Honolulu, 1993—. Served with U.S. Army, 1958. Mem. Am. Soc. Newspaper Editors, AP Mng. Editors, Soc. Profl. Journalists, Nat. Conf. Editorial Writers. Home: 5316 Nehu Pl Honolulu HI 96821-1941 Office: Hawaii Newspaper Agy 605 Kapiolani Blvd Honolulu HI 96813-5195

SIMONDS, MARTHA MUÑOZ, musician, educator; b. Washington, Nov. 26, 1960; d. Roger Tyrell and Peggy (Muñoz) S.; m. David Robert Teeters, May 5, 1996. MusB, Juilliard Sch., 1982; MusM, Eastman Sch. Music, 1984. Tchg. asst. Eastman Sch. Music, Rochester, N.Y., 1984; violinist Santa Fe Opera Orch., 1984; assoc. prin. 2d violin San Francisco Ballet Orch., 1984—; 1st violin San Francisco Opera Orch., 1985—; assoc. concertmaster New Century Chamber Orch., San Francisco, 1993—; violinist Due Voci Duo, San Francisco, 1993—; pvt. music tchr., Oakland, Calif., 1985—; performer Earplay, San Francisco, 1985—, Berkeley (Calif.) Contemporary Players, 1998—. Cmty. activist Cmty. Action Network, Oakland, 1991—. Touring grantee Calif. Arts Coun., 1992. Mem. Musicians Union Local 6. Democrat. Avocations: gardening, rescues animals, improvisational acting, Qi Gong, salsa dancing. Home: 5464 El Camile Ave Oakland CA 94619

SIMONS, STEVE, executive. Pres. Rock Shox, San Jose, Calif. Office: 401 Charcot Ave San Jose CA 95131-1192*

SIMONSON, MICHAEL, lawyer, judge; b. Franklin, N.J., Feb. 5, 1950; s. Robert and Eleanor (Weiss) S. BA, U. Ariz., 1973; JD, Southwestern U., Los Angeles, 1976; LLM in Taxation, Washington U., St. Louis, 1978. Bar:

Ariz. 1977, U.S. Dist. Ct. Ariz. 1979, U.S. Tax Ct. 1978. Bailiff, law clk. Superior Ct. Maricopa County Div. 2, Phoenix, 1976-77; sole practice, Scottsdale, Ariz., 1978-79; ptnr. Simonson, Groh, & Lindteigen, Scottsdale, 1979-81, Simonson & Preston, Phoenix, 1984-86, Simonson, Preston & Arbetman, 1986-87, Simonson & Arbetman, 1987-89; judge pro tempore Mcpl. Ct., City of Phoenix, 1984—, City of Mesa, 1990—; judge pro tempore Maricopa County Superior Ct., 1991—; adj. prof. Ariz. State U Coll. Bus., Tempe, 1984—, Coll. for Fin. Planning, Denver, 1984—, Maricopa County Community Colls., 1984—, Western Internat. U., Phoenix, 1984—, Ottawa U., 1987—; prof. law Univ. Phoenix, 1985—, area chmn. legal studies, 1986-90, Keller Grad. Sch. Mgmt., 1990—. Mem. Maricopa County Foster Child Care Rev. Bd. No. 17, 1978-81; pres. Camelback Mountainview Estates Homeowners Assn., 1980-81, Congregation Tiphereth Israel, 1979-81; dir., sec. Fifth Ave Area Property Owners Assn., 1988-92. Co-author: Buying and Selling Closely Held Businesses in Arizona, 1986, 89, Commercial Real Estate Transactions, 1986. Fellow Ariz. Bar Found.; mem. ABA (taxation sect., various coms.), State Bar Ariz. (cert. specialist in tax law), Maricopa County Bar Assn., Cen. Ariz. Estate Planning Coun., Nucleus Club, Mensa, Shriner, Masons. Democrat. Jewish. Office: 6925 E 5th Ave Ste O Scottsdale AZ 85251-3804

SIMONSON, SUSAN KAY, hospital administrator; b. La Porte, Ind., Dec. 5, 1946; d. George Randolph and Myrtle Lucille (Opfel) Menkes; m. Richard Bruce Simonson, Aug. 25, 1973. BA with honors, Ind. U., 1969; MA, Washington U., St. Louis, 1972. Perinatal social worker Yakima Valley Meml. Hosp., Yakima, Wash., 1979-81, dir. patient support program, 1981—, dir. social svc., 1982—; instr. Spanish, ethnic studies, sociology Yakima Valley Coll., Yakima, Wash., 1981—; pres. Yakima Child Abuse Council, 1983-85; developer nat. patient support program, 1981. Contbr. articles to profl. jours. Mem. Jr. League, Yakima; mem. adv. council Robert Wood Johnson Found. Rural Infant Health Care Project, Yakima, 1980, Pregnancy Loss and Compassionate Friends Support Groups, Yakima, 1982—, Teen Outreach Program, Yakima, 1984—. Recipient NSF award, 1967, discharge planning program of yr. regional award Nat. Glasrock Home Health Care Discharge Planning Program, 1987; research grantee Ind. U., 1968, Fulbright grantee U.S. Dept. State, 1969-70; Nat. Def. Edn. Act fellowship, 1970-73. Mem. AAUW, Soc. Med. Anthropology, Soc. Hosp. Social Work Dirs. of Am. Hosp. Assn. (regional award 1989), Nat. Assn. Social Workers, Phi Beta Kappa. Office: Yakima Valley Meml Hosp 2811 Tieton Dr Yakima WA 98902-3799

SIMONTACCHI, CAROL NADINE, nutritionist, retail store executive; b. Bellingham, Wash., July 6, 1947; d. Ralph Eugene and Sylvia Arleta (Tyler) Walmer; m. Bob Simontacchi, Oct. 3, 1981; children: Caryl Anne, Bobbie Anne, Melissa Anne, Laurie Anne. BS in Social Sci., Columbia Pacific U., 1996, MS in Social Sci., 1997. Cert. clin. nutritionist, Wash. CEO The Health Haus, Inc., Vancouver, Wash., 1985-98; host radio program Back to the Beginning, Vancouver, 1990-97; CEO The Natural Physician Ctr., Beaverton, Oreg., 1995-97, Enique Internat., 1995-97; chair bd. dirs. Enique Internat., 1996—. Author: Your Fat is Not Your Fault, 1994, 97, The Sun Rise Book: Living Beyond Depression, 1996, All About Clitosan, 1999, All About Evening Primrose Oil, 1999; host. Your Personal Health, 1997—. Mem. Soc. Cert. Nutritionists (pres. bd. 1992-93), Nat. Nutritional Foods Assn. (chair edn. com. 1996—), Internat. Assn. Clin. Nutritionists, Am. Assn. Clin. Nutritionists, Autograph Soc. (chair 1999—). Republican. Christian Ch. Office: The Health Haus Inc 101 E 8th St Ste 250 Vancouver WA 98660-3294

SIMPSON, ALAN KOOI, former senator; b. Cody, Wyo., Sept. 2, 1931; s. Milward Lee and Lorna (Kooi) S.; m. Ann Schroll, June 21, 1954; children—William Lloyd, Colin Mackenzie, Susan Lorna. BS, U. Wyo., 1954, JD, 1958; LLD (hon.), Calif. Western Sch. of Law, 1983, Colo. Coll., 1986, Notre Dame U., 1987; JD (hon.), Am. U., 1989, Rocky Mountain Coll., 1996. Bar: Wyo. 1958, U.S. Supreme Ct. 1964. Asst. atty. gen. State of Wyo., 1959; city atty. City of Cody, 1959-69; ptnr. Simpson, Kepler, and Simpson, Cody, Wyo., 1959-78; mem. Wyo. Ho. of Reps., 1964-77, majority whip, 1973-75, majority floor leader, 1975-77, speaker pro tem, 1977; mem. U.S. Senate from Wyo., 1978-96, asst. majority or minority leader, 1984-94, chmn. vets. affairs com., chmn. fin. subcom. on Social Security and Family Policy, chmn. subcom. on immigration and refugee policy; mem. Sen. Rep. Policy Com. Spec. Com. on Aging; guest lectr. London exchange program Regent's Coll., London, 1987; vis. lectr. Lombard chair Shorenstein Ctr. for Press, Politics and Pub. Policy, Kennedy Sch. Govt., Harvard U.; bd. dirs. I.D.S.-Am. Express, PacifiCorp, Biogen. Chmn. bd. trustees Buffalo Bill Hist. Ctr., Cody, Grand Teton Music Festival; del. Nat. Triennial Episcopal Ch. Conv., 1973-76; mem. Smithsonian Nat. Bd., Washington; bd. trustees Folger Shakespeare Libr., Washington; dir. Inst. of Politics of the Kennedy Sch. Harvard Univ., Cambridge, Mass. Recipient Nat. Assn. Land Grant Colls. Centennial Alumni award U. Wyo., 1987, Lifetime Svc. award Vietnam Vets. Am., 1993, Thomas Jefferson award in law U. Va., 1998. Mem. Wyo. Bar Assn., Park County Bar Assn., U Wyo Alumni Assn. (pres. 1962, 63, Disting. Alumnus award 1985), VFW (life), Am. Legion, Amvets. (Silver Helmet award). Lodges: Eagles, Elks, Masons (33 deg.), Shriners, Rotary (pres. local club 1972-73).

SIMPSON, BILLY FRANCIS, JR., systems engineering analyst; b. San Diego, Aug. 30, 1954; s. Billy Francis and Edith Leora (Fengler) S.; m. Laura Ann Wilcox, Oct. 7, 1975 (div. July 1983); 1 child, Stephenie Ann; m. Linda Sue Phelps, July 12, 1986; 1 child, Jennifer Kay. AA in Sys. Programming, Southwestern Coll., Chula Vista, Calif., 1989. Enlisted U.S. Army, 1972, advanced through grades to staff sgt., 1982, resigned, 1983; inventory control supr. C.W.O. Distbn., San Diego, 1989-94; engring. analyst Continental Engring. Svcs., San Diego, 1994—. Author: Changing Spirits, 1997. Councilor substance abuse orgns., San Diego, 1994—; pres. St. James Luth. Ch., Imperial Beach, Calif., 1996—. Decorated Purple Heart. Mem. MADD, Southwestern Bus. Club (pres. 1987-88, Man of Yr. 1987), Chi Epsilon (Man of Yr. 1986). Democrat. Lutheran. Avocations: fishing, camping, swimming, horseback riding. Home: 1981 Dunning Cir San Diego CA 92154-2009 Office: Continental Engring Svcs 7630 Carroll Rd San Diego CA 92121-2428

SIMPSON, BOB G., retired quality assurance professional; b. DeWitt, Ark., Feb. 20, 1932; s. Fearmon Lambert Simpson and Myrtle Elsie (Lowrance) Simpson Palmer. BS in Physics., U. Ctrl. Ark., 1962. Quality/reliabilty engr. Motorola Inc., Phoenix, 1963-70; reliability engr. Motorola Inc., Mesa, Ariz., 1973-74; component engr. Control Data Corp., Tucson, 1971-73; mgr., supr. quality assurance Engineered Sys. Inc., Tempe, 1976-97, plant facilities mgr., 1996-97. Mem. Greater Phoenix Ch. of God; former chmn. coun. Phoenix Ch. of God Internat.With USN, 1951-55; with AEC Contractor, 1957-59.

SIMPSON, CHARLES ROBERT, marketing professional. BS in Bus. Adminstrn., U. Tenn., 1971; MBA in Mktg., Bloomfield Coll., 1973. Gen. ptnr. Simpson Constrn. and Restoration, Paterson, N.J., 1972-79; v.p. sales and mktg. The Jim Walter Corp., Tampa, Fla., 1979-83; v.p. franchise mktg. Comml. Credit/Control Data, Mpls., 1983-84; v.p. acquisitions Equity Program Investment Corp., Falls Church, Va., 1984-85; pres., gen. mgr. Simpson Mktg. Group, Chandler, Ariz., 1985-87; v.p. mktg. and sales Hooker U.S.A., L.J. Hooker Homes, L.J. Hooker Internat., Phoenix, Atlanta, Dallas, 1987-91; cons. Resolution Trust Corp.-Oversight Bd., Phoenix, Denver, 1991—; lectr. Ariz. State U., Tempe, Harvard U. Grad. Sch. Bus. Contbg. editor of rsch. recommendations in weekly publs. Mem. Habitat for Humanities; adv. bd. Resolution Trust Corp.; mem. Greenspeace; past mem. bd. dirs. Verde Valley Sch., Sedona, Ariz. Recipient Pacesetter award Nat. Assn. Homebuilders, 1989, MIRM designation, 1988, MAME award in a career total of 21 categories, 1987-90, Nat. MIRM award, 1988. Mem. Nat. Trust for Hist. Preservation, Nat. Park and Wildlife Fedn., Benevolent Protective Order of Elks, Univ. Club, Essex County Hist. Soc. (past pres.). Office: PO Box 31203 Phoenix AZ 85046-1203

SIMPSON, GARY LAVERN, public health medical executive; b. St. Louis, Jan. 3, 1947; m. Sandra Cheryl Lapham; children: Cassandra Alyn, Courtney Meredith. BS, U. Ill., 1969, MS, 1970, PhD, 1973; MD, Rush Med. Coll., Chgo., 1974; MSc in Clin. Medicine, U. Oxford, Eng., 1977; MPH in Tropical Pub. Health, Harvard U., 1978. Diplomate Mass. Bd. Med. Examiners, Am. Bd. Internal Medicine, Calif. Bd. Med. Examiners, N.Mex. Bd. Med. Examiners. Intern Peter Bent Brigham Hosp., Boston, 1974-75, resident, 1975-76; sr. registrar in internal medicine/infectious diseases U. Oxford, Clin. Med. Sch., Radcliffe Infirmary, Eng., 1976-77; fellow infectious diseases divsn. infectious diseases Stanford (Calif.) U., 1978-79; asst. prof. medicine divsn. infectious diseases U. N.Mex., Albuquerque, 1979-83, clin. assoc. prof. medicine, 1983-88; attending physician Presbyn. Healthcare Svcs., Albuquerque, 1987-89; med. dir. infectious diseases Pub. Health divsn. Dept. Health, State of N.Mex., Santa Fe, 1992—; teaching asst. U. Ill., Champaign-Urbana, 1969-70, rsch. assoc., 1970-72; rsch. cons. U. N.Mex., Albuquerque, 1973-74, adj. assoc. prof. dept. biology, 1986-87; rsch. prof. dept. biology U. N.Mex., 1996—; rsch. scientist Rush Med. Sch., 1973-74; clin. fellow Harvard Med. Sch., Boston, 1974-76; dir., chief medicine Raymond Hosp., Wrentham, Mass., 1976; staff physician Children's Hosp. Med. Ctr., Boston, 1976; vis. prof. Instituto Nacional de Salud, Bogota, Colombia, 1979-80; attending physician U. N.Mex. Hosp., 1979-87, VA Med. Ctr., Albuquerque, 1980-87; assoc. scientist Lovelace Med. Found., Albuquerque, 1983-86; med. dir. Cottonwood de Albuquerque, Residential Treatment Ctr., Los Lunas, N.Mex., 1983-84, Jim Kelly Counseling Assocs., Albuquerque, 1984-86, Presbyn. Alcohol and Drug Treatment Ctr., Northside Presbyn. Hosp., Albuquerque, 1987-89; sr. cons. bur. communicable diseases AID, Dept. State, Washington, 1984—; cons. Am. Inst. Biol. Scis., Washington, 1984—; Eagleson lectr. Am. Biol. Safety Assn. 36th Annual Conf., Albuquerque, lectr. in field; vis. prof. dept. med. microbiology and sec. of infectious diseases Faculty of Medicine U. Man., Winnipeg, Can.; adj. prof. dept. biology U. M.Mex., Albuquerque, 1996—. Contbr. articles to profl. jours. Recipient Cert. award U.S. Indian Health Svc., 1995; Robert Wood Johnson fellow, 1977, Agy. for Internat. Devel. Edn. fellow, 1978, Palo Alto Med. Rsch. Found. fellow, 1979; hon. I award U. Ill. Fellow ACP, Am. Soc. Addiction Medicine (cert.); mem. AAAS, Oxford Med. Soc., Royal Soc. Tropical Medicine and Hygiene, Am. Soc. Microbiology, Am. Soc. Tropical Medicine and Hygiene, Am. Fedn. Clin. Rsch., Infectious Diseases Soc. Am. Home: 18 Senda Aliento Dr Placitas NM 87043-9530

SIMPSON, JOHN BERCHMAN, JR., clergy member, chaplain, retired law enforcement officer, retired newspaper editor; b. Hartford, Conn., July 18, 1938; s. John Berchman Simpson and Gertrude Elizabeth; m. Yvonne Elaine McGruder, July 2, 1958 (div. May 1978); children: John B. III, Joan B. Gupton, Jeffery Brian, James Bryant, Jason Brent; m. Donna Jean Hadra, Dec. 27, 1978; children: Cheri Lynn DeBolt, Byrl Arthur Gibson, Michele Renee Thacker. BA in Journalism, Bklyn. Coll., 1963; BS in Divinity, Houston Divinity Coll., 1984, DD, 1989. Cert. protection profl., Ariz. Editor USAF, 1956-65; mng. editor Enfield (Conn.) Press, 1967; bur. chief, state editor The Hartford (Conn.) Times, 1965-67; publs. editor Aetna Life & Casualty Co., 1968-69, The Hartford Ins. Co., 1969-70; rewrite editor The New Haven Register, 1970-73; dir. pub. affairs U.S. Coast Guard Res., New London, Conn., 1970-89; pres. Loss Prevention Inst., Houston, 1980-84; asst. pastor Chapel of Prayer, Houston, 1982-84; officer, chaplain Maricopa County Sheriff's Office, Phoenix, 1985-96; pastor Chapel of Divine Faith, Scottsdale, Ariz., 1996-98; sr. chaplain Ariz. State Vets. Home, Phoenix, 1998—. Author: Retail Loss Prevention, 1983; editor The Deputy, 1986. Mem. Ariz. Sci. Ctr., Am. Diabetes Assn., Rep. Presdl. Task Force 2000; merit award sponsor U.S. Olympic Shooting Team; bd. dirs. Maricopa County Dep. Sheriff's Assn., Phoenix, 1986-93, Coun. of Chs., Houston, 1984, Phoenix, 1996; chaplain VA Hosp., Houston, 1980-84. Comdr. U.S. Coast Guard Res., 1989. Named to Hon. Order of Ky. Cols., Editor of Yr., Sigma Delta Chi, Hartford, 1966; recipient Medal of Valor, New Haven (Conn.) Police Dept., 1972, Disting. Svc. award VA Hosp., Houston, 1984. Mem. NRA, DAV (life), Res. Officers Assn. (life, chaplain 1993-94), U.S. Naval Inst. (life), Soc. Profl. Journalists (Pres.'s Club), Elks (Lodge 2656), Fraternal Order of Police Lodge 5, Am. Legion (Post 83, chaplain 1993-96, svc. officer 1998—, life), Ret. Officers Assn., U.S. Navy League, Disabled Am. Vets. (dep. chaplain 1998—). Republican. Avocations: photography, reading. Home: 6226 E Anaheim St Mesa AZ 85205-8333

SIMPSON, JOHN DOUGLAS, landscape architect; b. Glendale, Calif., June 3, 1951; s. Floyd Robert and Mildred (Orlebeke) S. BS, U. Oreg., 1973, MA, 1977. Registered landscape architect, Oreg. Planner City of Bellevue (Wash.), 1978-79, park planner Hawaii Cmty. Devel. Authority, Honolulu, 1979-80; dir. planning and info. Hawaii Housing Authority, Honolulu, 1980-83; prin. Pacific Upcountry Design, Bend, Oreg., 1982-93; landscape architect John Simpson & Assocs., Bend, Oreg., 1994—; dir. parks & devel. Bend Met. Parks & Recreation Dist., 1995—; vis. lectr., landscape architect U. Oreg., Eugene, 1978; television commentator KTVZ Television, Bend, 1994, 95. contbr. to periodical publs. and books. Recipient Design of Yr. award Oreg. Park and Recreation Assn., Design award Internat. Park and Recreation Assn. Mem. Am. Soc. Landscape Architects. Avocations: painting, skiing, squash, sculpture, gardening. Home and office: 1546 NW Awbrey Rd Bend OR 97701-1831

SIMPSON, LINDA ANN, English language educator; b. Omaha, Sept. 4, 1947; d. W.R. Elton and Margie Ruth (Pollard) Newman; m. Kenneth Richard Simpson, June 26, 1970; children: Scott Richard, David Kenneth. BA in English, U. Utah, 1969. Tchr. English Cerro Villa Jr. H.S., Villa Park, Calif., 1969-70, El Modena H.S., Orange, Calif., 1970-74, Mt. Jordan Jr. H.S., Sandy, Utah, 1974, Bonneville Jr. H.S., Salt Lake City, Utah, 1974-77; tchr. libr. J.E. Cosgriff Meml. Sch., Salt Lake City, 1986-93; tchr. English Judge Meml. Cath. H.S., Salt Lake City, 1993—. Elder Presbyn. Ch. Recipient Tchr. of the Yr. award Judge Memorial, 1994, Alumni-Alliance award, 1997. Mem. Presbyn. Women Utah (hon. life), Wasatch Community Symphony SLC (concert master 1994—). Presbyterian. Avocations: violin, theatre, travel, reading. Home: 4279 Shirley Ln Salt Lake City UT 84124-3056 Office: Judge Meml Cath H S 650 S 1100 E Salt Lake City UT 84102-3902

SIMPSON, LINDA ANNE, retired police detective, municipal official; b. Greensburg, Pa., Oct. 23, 1953; d. Henry Theodore and Marceline (Krempasky) S.; m. Gail Montgomery, Jan. 10, 1977 (div. May 1981); m. Jeri Anne Sheely, July 10, 1981; children: Jessica Ann, Alexander Richard, Allison Dawn. BA, Calif. U. Pa., 1976, 78; cert., Pa. Police Acad., 1978. Asst. security supt. Rouse Svc. Co., Greensburg, 1971-77; asst. police chief Ellsworth (Pa.) Borough Police Dept., 1977-78; police officer Fallowfield Twp. Police Dept., Charleroi, Pa., 1978-80; police detective, trainer, instr., coord. field tng., supr. sex crimes unit Rock Springs (Wyo.) Police Dept., 1980-96, ret., 1996; security officer ACSS Microsoft Co., Redmond, Wash., 1997—; rsch. asst. centennial com. Rock Springs Police Dept.; police instr. State of Wyo., 1982—; instr. Women's Inst., Western Wyo. Coll., Rock Springs, 1996—, actor, cons. tng. film series theater dept., 1987-88. Editor quar. newsletter Blue Knights News Wyo., 1986-92. Asst. basketball coach Spl. Olympics, Rock Springs, 1987; mem. Sweetwater County Child Protection Team, 1995-96; mem. Domestic Violence Coun., 1995-96, Harry Benjamin Internat. Genoce Dysphoria Assn., 1997—, City of Seattle Sexual Minorities Commn., 1996-98. Recipient numerous commedations Rock Springs Police Dept., 1980-96, Outstanding Law Enforcement Officer award, 1985, Disting. Svc. medal, 1987, Svc. medal 1988. Mem. Internat. Found. for Gender Edn., Nat. Assn. Field Tng. Officers, Police Protective Assn. (v.p. 1984-85, treas. 1990-94), Western Alliance Police Officers (v.p. 1985-87), Calif. U. Pa. Alumni Assn., Intermountain World War II Reenactment Assn., Shooting Stars Motorcycle Club (pres. 1980-84), Blue Knights Internat. Law Enforcement Motorcycle Club (pres. Wyo. chpts. 1985-92, bd. dirs. Wyo. chpt. 1 1992-96), High Desert Riders, Motorcycle Club (legis. officer 1991-94), Salt Lake Gender Consortium (mem. bd. protectors 1995-96). Avocations: camping, reading, gender studies. Home: 4306 156th Ave NE # FF120 Redmond WA 98052 Office: ACSS Microsoft Corp 1 Microsoft Way Redmond WA 98052-8300

SIMPSON, MARY KATHLEEN, lawyer; b. Pomona, Calif., Aug. 2, 1952; d. Ernest Peter and Opal Petunia (Frederiksen) Hanks; m. Sidney Lawrence Simpson, Nov. 17, 1976 (div. Aug. 1980). BS in Chemistry, La Verne Coll., 1974; JD, U. Calif. Berkeley, 1980. Bar: Calif. 1980, D.C. 1982, U.S. Dist. Ct. (no. dist.) Calif. 1985, U.S. Ct. Appeals (6th cir.) 1986; cert. family law specialist Calif. State Bar Assn., 1993. Law clk. U.S. Ct. Appeals 6th Cir., Memphis, 1980-81; assoc. Howrey & Simon, Washington, 1981-82; counsel Enforcement divsn. SEC, Washington, 1982-84; assoc. Hogan & Hartson, Washington, 1984-85, McCutcheon, Doyle et al, San Jose, Calif., 1985; pvt. practice San Jose, 1986—. 2d v.p. Santa Clara Valley Audubon Soc., Cupertino, Calif., 1994—; chair conservation com.-south, chair rare plants-south Santa Clara chpt. Calif. Native Plant Soc., 1996—. Recipient Am. Jurisprudence award for torts and civil procedure Bancroft-Whitney, 1978. Avocations: amateur naturalist, birding. Home: 640 Millich Dr # B San Jose CA 95117-3631 Office: 1550 The Alameda Ste 305 San Jose CA 95126-2304

SIMPSON, PETER KOOI, university official; b. Sheridan, Wyo., July 31, 1930; s. Milward Lee and Lorna Helen (Kooi) S.; m. Lynne Alice Livingston, June 18, 1960; children: Milward Allen, Margaret Ann, Peter Kooi Jr. BA, U. Wyo., 1953, MA, 1962; PhD, U. Oreg., 1973. Pres. Western Hills, Inc., Billings, Cody, Wyo., 1959-61; asst. prof. history Ea. Oreg. Coll., La Grande, Oreg., 1962-65, Lane Community Coll., Eugene, Oreg., 1968-69, 70-72; instr. U. Oreg., Eugene, 1969-70; asst. to pres. Casper (Wyo.) Coll., 1974-77, coord. U.Wyo.-Casper Coll. upper div., 1976-77; dean instrn. Sheridan Coll., 1977-83, asst. to pres. for devel., dean instrn., 1983-84; v.p. for devel., alumni and univ. rels., exec. dir. Found., U. Wyo., Laramie, 1984-89, v.p. for institutional advancement, 1989-97, v.p. emeritus, 1997—, disting. Simpson prof.of polit. sci., 1998; bd. dirs. Bank of Laramie, U. Wyo. Found. Author: The Community of Cattlemen, 1987; also articles. Mem. Wyo. Ho. of Reps., 1980-84; Rep. nominee for gov. of Wyo., 1986; bd. dirs. Wyo. Vol. Assistance Corp., Laramie, 1985-89, Casper Troopers Found., 1988—, Ivinson Meml. Hosp. Found., 1993—; mem. libr. adv. com. Buffalo Bill Hist. Ctr., 1997—. Lt. USNR, 1954-60. Recipient award for signal contbn. to hist. preservation Wyo. Conservation Com., 1989; grantee Oreg. Edn. Coordinating Coun., 1971; named outstanding educator Am. Fuller and Dees, 1975, exemplary alumni U. Wyo. Coll. Arts & Scis., 1993. Mem. SAG, Wyo. Hist. Soc., Cowboy Joe Club (exec. com. 1984-97), Rotary (chmn. Found. 1990-92), Masons (33 degree), Shriners, Jesters. Episcopalian. Avocations: community theater, astronomy, running, reading, madrigal singing. Home: 812 Grand Ave Laramie WY 82070-3942 Office: U Wyo Found PO Box 3924 Laramie WY 82071-3924

SIMPSON, WARREN CARL, information brokerage executive; b. Waukegan, Ill., Apr. 5, 1954; s. Barton Oliver and Irene Susan (Brockway) S.; m. Tina Marie Barney, Nov. 25, 1981 (div. Feb. 1989); children: Sara, Robert, Shawn; m. Debra Jeanne Graves, Sept. 30, 1990; 1 child, Harmony. Student, Tucson Bus. Coll., 1985; A. in Computer Scis., Pima Coll., 1987; postgrad., U. Ariz., 1988-90. With retail sales various cos. Waukegan, 1968-72; with mgmt. Donovan's Inc., Chgo., 1972-74; owner Master Photographers, Tucson, 1975-79; with mgmt. various cos. Tucson, 1979-84; records clk. State of Ariz., Tucson, 1985-90; pres., founder C.S. Svcs., Tucson, 1990—, chmn. bd. dirs., 1990—. Author: The New Power-Information, 1991, (handbook) Speaking to Hold, 1988. Pub. activist, Tucson, 1978—; coach Little League baseball, Tucson, 1986-87; ordained minister non-denominational ch. Mem. Toastmasters Internat. (Tucson, hon. life, pres. 1987, 88, Competent Toastmaster 1986, Parliamentarian 1987, Most New Mem. Drive 1987, Best Entertaining Speech 1989). Avocations: reading textbooks, studying business trends, computers, swimming, photography. Home: 2954 S Kolb Rd Tucson AZ 85730-1748 Office: C S Svcs/Admiral Vinyl 1800 S Pantano Rd Apt 3137 Tucson AZ 85710-6733

SIMS, MARCIE LYNNE, English language educator, writer; b. Monrovia, Calif., Feb. 22, 1963; d. Charles Eugene and Delores May (Wonert) S.; m. Douglas Todd Cole; 1 child, Marcus Anthony Cole. BA in English, Calif. State Poly., 1986; MA in English, San Diego State U., 1990. Page U.S. Senate, Washington, 1979; instr. Calif. Conservation Corps, San Diego, 1990; instr. in English Shoreline C.C., Seattle, 1990-94, Seattle Ctrl. C.C., 1990-94; instr. in English, chmn. divsn. English Green River C.C., Auburn, Wash., 1994—; founder Wild Mind Women Writers Workshop, Seattle, 1992—. Author: Soul-Making: John Keats and the Stages of Death, 1990; contbg. author Moms on Line, 1996—; co-editor: The Great Tchrs. Almanac, 1988-90. Vol. cons. Camp Fire, Wash., 1994-96. Mem. Am. Fedn. Tchrs., The Keats-Shelley Orgn., Wash. Fed. Tchrs. (exec. bd. mem. 1993-94), Phi Kappa Phi, Sigma Tau Delta. Democrat. Avocations: cooking, tennis. Office: Green River CC 12401 SE 320th St Auburn WA 98092-3622

SIMUNICH, MARY ELIZABETH HEDRICK (MRS. WILLIAM A. SIMUNICH), public relations executive; b. Chgo.; d. Tubman Keene and Mary (McCamish) Hedrick; m. William A. Simunich, Dec. 6, 1941. Student Phoenix Coll., 1967-69, Met. Bus. Coll., 1938-40. Exec. sec. sales mgr. Sta. KPHO radio, 1950-53; exec. sec. mgr. Sta. KPHO-TV, 1953-54; account exec. Tom Rippey & Assos., 1955-56; pub. rels. dir. Phoenix Symphony, 1956-62; co-founder, v.p. Paul J. Hughes Pub. Rels., Inc., 1960-65; owner Mary Simunich Pub. Rels., Phoenix, 1966-77; pub. rels. dir. Walter O. Boswell Meml. Hosp., Sun City, Ariz., 1969-85; pub. rels. cons., 1985—; pres. DARCI PR, Phoenix, 1994—, Cityscape, Inc. (formerly Citynet, Inc.), 1994—; instr. pub. rels. Phoenix Coll. Evening Sch., 1973-78. Bd. dirs. Anytown, Ariz., 1969-72; founder, sec. Friends Am. Geriatrics, 1977-86. Named Phoenix Advt. Woman of Year, Phoenix Jr. Advt. Club, 1962; recipient award Blue Cross, 1963; 1st Pl. award Ariz. Press Women, 1966. Mem. NAFE, Women in Comm., Internat. Assn. Bus. Communicators (pres. Ariz. chpt. 1970-71, dir.), Pub. Rels. Soc. Am. (sec., dir. 1976-78), Am. Soc. Hosp. Pub. Rels. (dir. Ariz. chpt. 1976-78), Nat., Ariz. Press Women. Home: 4133 N 34th Pl Phoenix AZ 85018-4771 Office: DARCI Group 2425 E Camelback Rd Ste 450 Phoenix AZ 85016-4236

SIN, TOMMY KA-KEUNG, engineering/business executive; b. Hong Kong, May 16, 1965; came to the U.S., 1995; s. Kwai-Sang Sin and Man-Chun Ng; m. Rose Wai-Tak Leung, Aug. 3, 1989; children: Fionna, Cecilia. Diploma in engring., Dalhousie U., Halifax, N.S., Can., 1985; cert. bus. mgmt., Dalhousie U., 1994; B in Engring., Tech. U. N.S., Halifax, 1988; diploma in mktg. and internat. bus., St. Mary's U., N.S., 1994; MBA, San Jose State U., 1998. Component engr. GE Consumer Electronics, Hong Kong, 1988; sr. tech. officer Hong Kong Tel. Co. Ltd., 1988-89; engring. mgr. Seagate Tech., Inc., Singapore, 1989-92; mgmt. exec. STD Tech. Inc., Toronto, Ont., Can., 1992; v.p. ops. STD Tech. Inc., Halifax, 1993, exec. v.p., 1993-95; mfg. project cons. Seagate Tech. Inc., San Jose, Calif., 1995—; part-time tchr. Maryknoll Tech. Coll., Hong Kong, 1988-89; part-time lectr. Hong Kong Coll. Tech., 1989; coun. mem., v.p. Santa Teresa Sch. Site Coun., 1998—; bd. dirs. Calif. Grove San Jose Homeowners Assn., 1998—. Recipient Outstanding Bus. Grad. Student award, San Jose State U., 1998. Mem. AACE Internat., Inst. Elec. Engrs. (assoc.), Hong Kong Instn. Engrs., Internat. Assn. for Mgmt. Edn. (life), Beta Gamma Sigma, San Jose State U. Alumni Assn. (scholar 1998). Avocations: management training, writing management books, world economics. E-mail: tommyksin@yahoo.com. and tommyksin@notes.seagate.com. Fax: 408-456-3292. Home: 6228 Tibouchina Ln San Jose CA 95119 Office: Seagate Tech Inc 2720 Orchard Pkwy San Jose CA 95134

SINBERG, STAN, columnist, radio commentator; b. N.Y.C., Feb. 25, 1952; s. Norman Sinberg and Terry (Trachtenberg) Legrange. BA, Queens Coll., 1976. Radio commentator KFOG, San Francisco, 1977—; columnist Pacific Sun, Mill Valley, Calif., 1994—; radio commentator KFOG, San Francisco, 1997—. Co-author (musical) For Whom the Bridge Tolls, 1994. Jewish. Avocations: traveling, hiking, dancing. E-mail: ssinberg@yahoo.com. Home: 39 Roque Moraes Mill Valley CA 94941

SINCLAIR, SARA VORIS, health facility administrator, nurse; b. Kansas City, Mo., Apr. 13, 1942; d. Franklin Defenbaugh and Inez Estelle (Figenbaum) Voris; m. James W. Sinclair, June 13, 1964; children: Thomas James, Elizabeth Kathleen, Joan Sara. BSN, UCLA, 1965. RN, Utah; lic. health care facility adminstr.; cert. health care adminstr. Staff nurse UCLA Med. Ctr. Hosp., 1964-65; charge nurse Boulder (Colo.) Meml. Hosp., 1966, Boulder (Colo.) Manor Nursing Home, 1974-75, Four Seasons Nursing Home, Joliet, Ill., 1975-76; dir. nursing Home Health Agy of Olympia Fields, Joliet, Ill., 1977-79; dir. nursing Sunshine Terr. Found., Inc., Logan, Utah, 1980, asst. adminstr., 1980-81, adminstr., 1981-93; dir. divsn. health systems improvement Utah Dept. Health, Salt Lake City, 1993—; mem. long term care profl. and tech. adv. com. Joint Commn. on Accreditation Healthcare Orgns., Chgo., 1987-91, chmn., 1990-91; adj. lectr. Utah State u., 1991-93; mem. adj. clin. faculty Weber State U., Ogden, Utah; moderator radio program Healthwise Sta. KUSU-FM, 1985-93; spkr. Nat. Coun. Aging, 1993, Alzheimers Disease Assn. Ann. Conf., 1993; del. White House Conf. on Aging, 1995; chmn. Utah Dept. of Health's Ethics, Instnl. Rev. Bd. Com., 1995—, Utah Dept. Health Risk Mgmt. Com., 1995—; mem. Utah Long Term Care Coalition (exec. com. 1995, chmn. 1997), oversight com. and long term care tech. adv. group Utah Health Policy Commn., 1996—;

Health Insight Utah State Coun, 1996—; presenter in field. Contbg. author: Associate Degree Nursing and The Nursing Home, 1988. Mem. dean's adv. coun. Coll. Bus. Utah State U., Logan, 1989-91, mem. presdl. search com., 1991-92; chmn., co-founder Cache Comty. Health Coun., Logan, 1985; chmn. bd. Hospice of Cache Valley, Logan, 1986; mem. Utah State Adv. Coun. on Aging, 1986-93; apptd. chmn. Utah Health Facilities Com., 1989-91; chmn. Bear River Dist. Adv. Coun. on Aging, 1989-91; chmn. health and human svcs. subcom. Cache 2010, 1992-93; mem. long term care tech. adv. group, oversight com. Utah Health Policy Commn., 1997; dir. Health Insight, 1996. Recipient Disting. Svc. award Utah State U., 1989. Fellow Am. Coll. Health Care Adminstrs. (presenter 1992-93, 95, 1996 ann. convocations, v.p. Utah chpt. 1992-94, convocation and edn. coms. 1992-93, region IX vice gov. 1994-96, bylaws com. 1996—); mem. Am. Health Care Assn. (non-proprietary v.p. 1986-87, region v.p. 1987-89, presenter workshop conv. 1990-93, exec. com. 1993, presenter ann. convocation 1995), Utah Health Care Assn. (pres. 1983-85, treas. 1991-93, Disting. Svc. award 1991, Svc. award for long term care 1996), Utah Gerontol. Soc. (bd. dirs. 1992-93, 95—, chmn. nominating com. 1993-94, chmn. ann. conf. 1996, pres. 1997), Cache C. of C. (pres. 1991), Logan bus. and Profl. Women's Club (pres. 1989, Woman of Achievement award 1982, Woman of Yr. 1982), Rotary (Logan chpt., chair cmty. svc. com. 1989-90); hon. mem. Golden Key Nat. Honor Soc. Avocations: walking, reading. Office: Utah Dept Health Div Health Sys Improvement 288 N 1460 W Box 142851 Salt Lake City UT 84114-2851

SINCLAIR, WILLIAM DONALD, church official, fundraising consultant, political activist; b. L.A., Dec. 27, 1924; s. Arthur Livingston and Lillian May (Holt) S.; m. Barbara Jean Hughes, Aug. 9, 1952; children: Paul Scott, Victoria Sharon. BA cum laude, St. Martin's Coll., Olympia, Wash., 1975; postgrad. Emory U., 1978-79. Commd. 2d lt. USAAF, 1944, advanced through grades to col., USAF, 1970; served as pilot and navigator in Italy, Korea, Vietnam and Japan; ret., 1975; bus. adminstr. First United Methodist Ch., Colorado Springs, Colo., 1976-85; bus. adminstr. Village Seven Presbyn. Ch., 1985-87; bus. adminstr. Sunrise United Meth. Ch., 1987-89; vice-chmn. council fin. and adminstrn. Rocky Mountain conf. United Meth. Ch., U.S.A., 1979-83. Bd. dirs. Chins-Up Colorado Springs, 1983-86; chmn. bd. dirs. Pikes Peak Performing Arts Ctr., 1985-92; pres. Pioneers Mus. Found., 1985—; Rep. candidate for Colo. State Chmn., 1992-93, mem. Ho. of Reps., Colo., 1996—. Decorated Legion of Merit with oak leaf cluster, D.F.C., Air medal with 6 oak leaf cluster, Dept. Def. Meritorious Service medal, Vietnam Cross of Gallantry with Palms. Fellow Nat. Assn. Ch. Bus. Adminstrs. (nat. dir., regional v.p., v.p. 1983-85, pres. 1985-87; Ch. Bus. Adminstr. of Yr. award 1983, inducted hall of fame 1995), Colo. Assn. Ch. Bus. Adminstrs. (past pres.), United Meth., Assn. Ch. Bus. Admins. Adminstrs. (nat. sec. 1978-81), Christian Ministries Mgmt. Assn. (dir. 1983-85), USAF Acad. Athletic Assn. Clubs: Colorado Springs Country, Garden of the Gods, Met. (Denver), Winter Night Club. Lodge: Rotary (pres. Downtown Colorado Springs club 1985-86), Order of Daedalians. Home: 3007 Chelton Dr Colorado Springs CO 80909-1008

SINCLITICO, DENNIS J., lawyer; b. St. Louis, Mo., Jan. 9, 1947. BA, U. San Diego, 1968; JD cum laude, U. Wis., 1971. Bar: Wis. 1971, Calif. 1972, U.S. Dist. Ct. (cen. and so. dists.) Calif. 1972. Prof. Calif. Coll. Law, 1972; ptnr. La Follette, Johnson, De Haas, Fesler & Ames, P.C., L.A.; arbitrator spl. arbitration plan Los Angeles County Superior Ct., 1975—. Mem. Am. Bd. Trial Advocates (nat. exec. com. 1978—, pres. L.A. chpt., editor newsletter), State Bar Wis., State Bar Calif., Assn. So. Calif. Def. Counsel (program chmn. 1980-81, bd. dirs. 1980—), Cal-Abota (chair 1994), Phi Alpha Delta. Office: La Follette Johnson De Haas Fesler & Ames PC 865 S Figueroa St Ste 3100 Los Angeles CA 90017-2578

SINCOFF, STEVEN LAWRENCE, science administrator, scientist; b. N.Y.C., Apr. 17, 1948; s. Murray B. and Lillian (Goldberg) S.; m. Marcella Seay, June 12, 1993; children by previous marriage: Kristina Lynne, Carolyn Suzanne. BSChemE, N.J. Inst. Tech., 1969, MSChemE, 1972; PhD in Analytical Chemistry, Ohio State U., 1980. Commd. 2d lt. USAF, 1969, advanced through grades to lt. col., 1987, retired, 1991; fuels mgmt. officer USAF, Albuquerque and Galena, Alaska, 1970-74; chem. engr. Aero. Systems Div., Wright-Patterson AFB, Ohio, 1974-77; assoc. prof. chemistry USAF Acad., Colorado Springs, Colo., 1980-84, dir. continuing edn. dept. chemistry, 1982-84; chief gas analysis lab. McClellan (AFB) Cen. Lab., Calif., 1984-88; exec. officer to comdr. Tech. Ops. Div. McClellan AFB, Calif., 1988-89, chief info. officer, 1989-91; gen. mgr. ChemWest Analytical Lab., Sacramento, 1991-92; dir. ops. Barringer Labs., Inc., Golden, Colo., 1992-94; instr. chemistry C.C. Aurora, Colo., 1995-98, Butte Coll., Oroville, Calif., 1998—; reviewer chemistry textbooks Saunders Pub., Phila., 1983-84. Mem. Am. Chem. Soc., Air Force Assn. Jewish. Avocations: microcomputers, sports, motorcycling. Home and Office: 14574 Carnegie Rd Magalia CA 95954-9647

SINEGAL, JAMES D., variety store wholesale business executive; b. 1936. With Fed-Mart Corp., 1954-77, exec. v.p.; v.p. Builders Enporium, 1977-78; exec. v.p. Price Co., 1978-79; with Sinegal/Chamberlin & Assocs., 1979-83; pres., chief oper. officer Costco Wholesale Corp., 1983—, chief exec. officer, 1988—, bd. dirs. Address: Costco Wholesale PO Box 34331 999 Lake Dr Issaquah WA 98027*

SINES, RANDY DWAIN, business executive; b. Spokane, Jan. 16, 1948; s. Myron Jones and Paula Inez (Walls) S.; student Wash. State U., 1966-67, U. Wash., 1968-69; m. Irene Cheng, Mar. 18, 1981. With Boeing Co., 1967; with Winchell's Donut House, Inc. , Seattle, 1968-71; owner, mgr. bakeries, Wash. and Mont., 1972-78; owner, mgr. Sonsine Inc., Great Falls, Mont., 1976-79; pres. Gardian Port Corp., Oxnard, Calif., 1980-82; pres., chmn. SNS Motor Imports, Inc., Oxnard, 1982-86; chmn. Karakal Corp. of Ams., Ventura, Calif., 1986-89; chief exec. officer, chmn. Steel Stix, U.S.A., 1990—; chmn. Mitt USA Corp., 1991—; mng. ptnr. Sharps Internat., 1993—; CEO Casinovations Inc., 1995-96; founder, CEO Inven Corp., Spokane, Wash., 1996-97; chmn. Digideal Corp., Las Vegas, 1998—. Recipient alumni grant Wash. State U., 1967; lic. water well contractor, Wash., Mont. Patentee sports apparatus, over 30 patents worldwide. Home: 4056 S Madelia St Spokane WA 99203-4227

SINGARAJU, BHARADWAJA KESHAVA, electronics engineer; b. Secunderabad, Andhra Pradesh, India, June 20, 1945; came to the U.S., 1965; s. Subbarao and Subbamma (Gattupalli) S.; m. Camille H. Hamilton, Nov. 25, 1972; children: Raj, Ravi. BS, N.Mex. State U., 1968, MS, 1971, PhD, 1973. Rsch. engr. Dike Wood Corp., Albuquerque, 1976-78; electronics engr. Air Force Weapons Lab., Kirtland AFB, N.Mex., 1978-82, chief applications br., 1982-91; tech. dir. space electronics/software divsn. Phillips Lab., Kirtland AFB, N.Mex., 1991-93, chief space electronics divsn., 1993-96, chief space mission tech. divsn., 1996-97, tech. dir. surveillance and control divsn., 1997—; tech. and program chmn. various nat. and internat. confs. Contbr. chpt. to book and articles to profl. jours. Recipient Nat. Rsch. Coun. associateship NSF, 1974-76. Fellow AIAA (assoc.); mem. IEEE (sr.), Sigma Xi, Eta Kappa Nu. Avocations: skiing, bicycling, hiking, wood working. Office: Phillips Lab/VTM 3550 Aberdeen Ave SE Kirtland AFB NM 87117-5776

SINGER, GEORGE MILTON, clinical psychologist; b. Phila., Oct. 13, 1924; s. Benjamin and Bessie (Podlisker) S.; m. Carol Ann Horton, June 15, 1977; children: Elizabeth Carol, Susan Theresa, Sonnet Marie-Anne. BA, Temple U., 1950, AM, 1952, PhD, 1958. Grad. asst. exptl. psychology lab. Temple U., Phila., 1950-51, grad. asst. psychol. clinic, 1951-53, lectr., 1953-54; chief psychologist Phila. State Hosp., 1953-56; dir. psychol. services Pennhurst State Hosp., Spring City, Pa., 1958-61; clin. psychologist Kern County Mental Health Dept., Bakersfield, Calif., 1961-68; project dir., coordinator Kernview Community Mental Health Ctr., Bakersfield, 1968-70; pvt. practice clin. psychology Bakersfield, 1953—; mem. med. staff Kern View Mental Health Ctr. and Hosp., Bakersfield, Calif., 1988-92; mem. med. staff Meml. Ctr. for Behavioral Health, Bakersfield, 1992-97; affiliated med. staff Hoag Meml. Hosp., Newport Beach, Calif., 1972-73; cons. psychologist [illegible] Bd., 1976-83, adv. bd. Patton State Hosp., 1979-85; bd. dirs. Orange County Child Guidance Clinic, 1973-74. Served with USAAF, 1943-46, ETO, MTO. Recipient Service award Psi Chi, 1952, Cert. of Achievement Southeast Pa. Mental Health Assn., 1956. Mem. AAAS, APA, Calif. Psychol. Assn., Am. Soc. Clin. Hypnosis, Kern County Soc. Clin. Psychologists (pres. 1993-94), Kern County Psychol. Assn. (pres. 1968-69), Internat. Soc. Hypnosis, Rotary of Spring City (pres. 1960-61). Home: 1805 Ridgewood Dr Bakersfield CA 93306-3829 Office: 1712 19th St Ste 202 Bakersfield CA 93301-4324

SINGER, HERSH, marketing executive. Chmn. SMS Rsch. & Mktg. Svcs. Office: SMS Rsch & Mktg Svcs 1042 Fort St Mall Ste 200 Honolulu HI 96813-5601*

SINGER, JEFFREY ALAN, surgeon; b. Bklyn., Feb. 2, 1952; s. Harold and Hilda (Ginsburg) S.; m. Margaret Sue Gordon, May 23, 1976; children: Deborah Suzanne, Pamela Michelle. BA cum laude, Bklyn. Coll., 1973; MD, N.Y. Med. Coll., 1976. Diplomate Am. Bd. Surgery. Intern Maricopa County Gen. Hosp., Phoenix, 1976-77, resident, 1977-81, mem. teaching faculty, 1981-96; trauma cons. John C. Lincoln Hosp., Phoenix, 1981-83; pvt. practice Phoenix, 1981-87; group pvt. practice Valley Surg. Clinics, Ltd., Phoenix, 1987—, S.W. Surg. Clinics, P.C., Phoenix, 1996-97; adj. clin. faculty, Ariz. Coll. of Osteopathic Med., sec.-treas. med. staff Humana Desert Valley Hosp., Phoenix, 1987-89, chief surgery, 1985-87, 91-93, exec. com., 1993-95. Assoc. editor Ariz. Medicine. Rep. precinct committeeman, Phoenix, 1986—; bd. dirs. Goldwater Inst. for Pub. Policy Rsch. Fellow ACS, Internat. Coll. Surgeons, Southwestern Surg. Congress, Am. Soc. Abdominal Surgeons; mem. Ariz. Med. Assn. (bd. dirs. polit. com. 1985, chmn. bd. dirs. polit. com. 1991-93, legis. com. 1986—), Maricopa County Med. Soc. (v.p. 1998, bd. dirs. 1998—). Avocations: philosophy, politics, history, travel, underwater sports, writing. Office: Valley Surg Clinics Ltd 16601 N 40th St Ste 105 Phoenix AZ 85032-3353

SINGER, KURT DEUTSCH, news commentator, author, publisher; b. Vienna, Austria, Aug. 10, 1911; came to U.S., 1940, naturalized, 1951; s. Ignaz Deutsch and Irene (Singer) S.; m. Hilda Tradelius, Dec. 23, 1932 (div. 1954); children: Marian Alice Birgit, Kenneth Walt; m. Jane Sherrod, Apr. 9, 1955 (dec. Jan. 1985); m. Katherine Han, Apr. 8, 1989. Student, U. Zürich, Switzerland, 1930, Labor Coll., Stockholm, Sweden, 1936; Ph.D., Div. Coll. Metaphysics, Indpls., 1951. Escaped to Sweden, 1934; founder Ossietzky Com. (successful in release Ossietzky from concentration camp); corr. Swedish mag. Folket i Bild, 1935-40; founder Niemöller Com.; pub. biography Göring in Eng. (confiscated in Sweden), 1940; co-founder pro-Allied newspaper Trots Allt, 1939; corr. Swedish newspapers in, U.S., 1940; editor News Background, 1942; lectr. U. Minn., U. Kans., U. Wis., 1945-49; radio commentator WKAT, 1950; corr. N.Am. Newspaper Alliance, N.Y.C., 1953—; pres. Singer Media Corp., 1987—; dir. Oceanic Press Service, San Clemente, Calif. Author, editor: underground weekly Mitteilungsblätter, Berlin, Germany, 1933; author: The Coming War, 1934, (biog.) Carl von Ossietzky, 1936 (Nobel Peace prize), Germany's Secret Service in Central America, 1943, Spies and Saboteurs in Argentina, 1943, Duel for the Northland, 1943, White Book of the Church of Norway, 1944, Spies and Traitors of World War II, 1945, Who are the Communists in America, 1948, 3000 Years of Espionage, 1951, World's Greatest Women Spies, 1952, Kippie the Cow; juvenile, 1952, Gentlemen Spies, 1953, The Man in the Trojan Horse, 1954, World's Best Spy Stories, 1954, Charles Laughton Story; adapted TV, motion pictures, 1954, Spies Over Asia, 1955, More Spy Stories, 1955, My Greatest Crime Story, 1956, My Most Famous Case, 1957, The Danny Kaye Saga; My Strangest Case, 1958, Spy Omnibus, 1959, Spies for Democracy, 1960, Crime Omnibus Spies Who Changed History, 1961, Hemmingway-Life and Death of a Giant, 1961, True Adventures in Crime, Dr. Albert Schweitzer, Medical Missionary, 1962, Lyndon Baines Johnson-Man of Reason, 1964, Ho-i-man; juveniles, 1965; Kurt Singer's Ghost Omnibus, 1965; juvenile Kurt Singer's Horror Omnibus; The World's Greatest Stories of the Occult, The Unearthly, 1965, Mata Hari-Goddess of Sin, 1965, Lyndon Johnson-From Kennedy to Vietnam, 1966, Weird Tales Anthology, 1966, I Can't Sleep at Night, 1966, Weird Tales of Supernatural, 1967, Tales of Terror, 1967, Famous Short Stories, 1967, Folktales of the South Pacific, 1967, Tales of The Uncanny, 1968, Gothic Reader, 1968, Bloch and Bradbury, 1969, Folktales of Mexico, 1969, Tales of the Unknown, 1970, The House in the Valley, 1970, Hablan Los Artistas, 1970, Tales of the Macabre, 1971, Three Thousand Years of Espionage, 1971, El Mundo de Hoy, 1971, Cuentos Fantasticos del Mas, 1971, Aldous Huxley, El Camino al Infierno, 1971, Ghouls and Ghosts, 1972, The Unearthly, 1972, The Gothic Reader, 1972, Satanic Omnibus, 1973, The Plague of the Living Dead, 1973, Gothic Horror Omnibus, 1974, Dictionary of Household Hints and Help, 1974, Supernatural, 1974, They are Possessed, 1976, True Adventures into the Unknown, 1980, I Spied-And Survived, 1980, Great Adventures in Crime, 1982, The Oblong Box, 1982, Shriek, 1984, First Target Book of Horror, 1984, 2d, 1984, 3d, 1985, 4th, 1985, Solve A Crime, 1994, The Ultimate Quiz Book, 1994, The Complete Guide to Career Advancement, 1994, The Sex Quiz Book, 1994, The Marriage Quiz Book, The Psychology Quiz Book, The Teenage Quiz Book, Success Secrets, 1995, Conozcase Mejor y Triunfe, 1995, The Joy of Practical Parenting, 1995; editor: UN Calendar, 1959-58; contbr. articles to newspapers, popular mags., U.S., fgn. countries, all his books and papers in Boston U. Library-Spl. Collections, Awd Literatur Haus, Vienna, Austria. Mem. UN Speakers Research Com., UN Children's Emergency Fund, Menninger Found. Mem. Nat. Geog. Soc., Smithsonian Assos., Internat. Platform Assn. (v.p.), United Sch. Assemblies (pres.). Address: Singer Media Corp Seaview Business Pk 1030 Calle Cordillera # 106 San Clemente CA 92673-6234

SINGER, MICHAEL HOWARD, lawyer; b. N.Y.C., Nov. 22, 1941; s. Jack and Etta (Appelbaum) S.; m. Saundra Jean Kupperman, June 1, 1962; children: Allison Jill, Pamela Faith. BS in Econs., U. Pa., 1962; JD, NYU, 1965, LLM in Taxation, 1968. Bar: N.Y. 1965, U.S. Ct. Claims 1968, U.S. Supreme Ct. 1969, U.S. Ct. Appeals (6th cir.) 1970, D.C. 1972, U.S. Tax Ct. 1972, Nev. 1973, U.S. Ct. Appeals (9th cir.) 1973. Law asst. Appellate Term Supreme Ct., N.Y.C., 1965-68; trial lawyer Ct. Claims Tax Div., Washington, 1968-72; tax lawyer Beckley, DeLanoy & Jemison, Las Vegas, 1972-74; ptnr. Oshins, Singer, Segal & Morris, Las Vegas, 1974-87; pvt. practice Las Vegas, 1987; ptnr. Michael H. Singer Ltd., Las Vegas, 1987-96, Singer, Brown, and Barringer, LLC, Las Vegas, 1996—; settlement judge Nev. Supreme Ct., 1997-99. Pres. Las Vegas chpt. NCCJ, 1980-82. Mem. ABA, ABI, Nev. Bar Assn., Las Vegas Country Club (bd. dirs. 1999—). Democrat. Jewish. Avocations: golf, tennis. Home: 4458 Los Reyes Ct Las Vegas NV 89121-5341 Office: Singer Brown and Barringer LLC 520 S 4th St Fl 2 Las Vegas NV 89101-6524

SINGER, OSCAR, author; b. Chgo., Sept. 20, 1920; s. Max and Esther Singer. BS in Meteorology, U. Chgo., 1941. Served to maj. USAF, 1940-53; editor, pub. periodical The Bible of Weather Forecasting, Singer Press, L.A., 1984-85. Author, pub.: The Revolution in Understanding Weather, 1983. Avocation: organic gardening. Home: 1540 Rollins Dr Los Angeles CA 90063-1030

SINGER, ROBERT, plastic surgeon; b. Buffalo, Oct. 22, 1942; s. Murray and Fay Singer; m. Judith Harris. Student, SUNY, Buffalo, 1960-63; MD, SUNY, 1967. Lic. physician, Calif.; diplomate Am. Bd. Plastic and Reconstructive Surgery. Resident in gen. surgery Stanford Med. Ctr., Palo Alto, Calif., 1967-69, Santa Barbara Cottage and Gen. Hosp., 1972-74; resident in plastic surgery Vanderbilt U., 1974-76; pvt. practice specializing in emergency and trauma San Diego, 1971-72; pvt. practice plastic, reconstructive and aesthetic surgery La Jolla, Calif., 1976—; prior asst. clin. prof. plastic surgery U. Calif., San Diego; sr. staff, chief plastic surgery Scripps Meml. Hosp., La Jolla, 1980-86, vice chmn. dept. surgery, 1989-91. Contbr. articles to profl. jours. Active San Diego Opera, San Diego Mus. of Man, La Jolla Playhouse, Voices for Children, San Diego Zoo, Mus. Photog. Arts, KPBS, others; mem. exec. com. Anti-Defamation League. Fellow ACS; mem. AMA, Calif. Med. Assn., San Diego County Med. Soc., San Diego Internat. Soc. Plastic Surgeons (pres. 1988-89), Calif. Soc. Plastic Surgeons (pres. 1995), Am. Soc. Aesthetic Plastic Surgeons (pres. 1994-95), Internat. Soc. Clin. Plastic Surgeons, Am. Soc. Plastic and Reconstructive Surgeons (trustee 1996—), J.B. Lynch Soc., Royal Soc. Medicine, Am. Assn. for Accreditation of Ambulatory Surgery Facilities (v.p. 1994), San Diego Plastic Surgery Soc. (pres. 1989-90), Aesthetic Surgery Edn. and Rsch. Found. [illegible] 9834 Genesee Ave Ste 100 La Jolla CA 92037-1214

SINGH, LOREN CHAN, technical writing specialist; b. Palo Alto, Calif., Sept. 10, 1943; s. Shau Wing and Anna Mae Chan; m. Frances Anastasia Chow, Apr. 19, 1975 (div. Jan. 1988); children: Karen Monique Chan, Pierre Benedict Chan, Marc Henri Chan. AB, Stanford U., 1965, AM, 1966; MS, Golden Gate U., 1988; PhD, UCLA, 1971. Teaching asst. UCLA, 1968-69, teaching assoc., 1969-70; lectr. in history Calif. State U., Northridge, 1970-71; lectr. in history San Jose (Calif.) State U., 1971-72, asst. prof. history, 1972-76, assoc. prof. history, 1976-80; lectr. history Calif. State U., Hayward, 1980-81; prodn. test technician Nicolet Paratronics Corp., Fremont, Calif., 1982; computer svc. technician Bell-Northern Rsch., Mountain View, Calif., 1982-83; rsch. analyst Bell-No. Rsch., Mountain View, 1984-85, tech. writer, 1985-87; sr. tech. writer StrataCom, Inc., Campbell, Calif., 1987-88; tech. writer Sun Microsystems, Mountain View, 1988-90, sr. tech. writer, 1990—. Author: Sagebrush Statesman, 1973, SPARCstation 1 Installation Guide, 1989, Collected Technical Support Notes, 1988, SPARCstation 2 Installation Guide, 1990, Desktop Storage Pack Installation Guide, 1989-90, SPARCstation 10 Installation Guide, 1992, SPARCstation 10 Networking and Communication Guide, 1993, SPARCstation 10SX VSIMMs Installation, 1993, SPARCstation 20 HyperSPARC Module Upgrade, 1995, SPARCstation 20 SuperSPARC-II Module Upgrade, 1995, Sun Ultra 1 Reference Manual, 1995-96, Sun Ultra 2 Reference Manual, 1996, Sun Ultra 30 Installation Guide, 1997, Sun Ultra 30 Reference Manual, 1997, SPARCstorage Flex-iPack Removable Storage Tray Installation Guide, 1997; editor: Chinese-American History Reader, 1976; contbr. articles to profl. jours. Radio sta. trustee ARC, Menlo Park, Calif., 1975-80. Recipient Presdl. Sports award Pres.'s Coun. on Phys. Fitness and Sports, 1973. Mem. Nat. Geog. Soc., Underwater Soc. Am., Am. Radio Relay League, Confederate Stamp Alliance, Almaden Masters Swim Club. Democrat. Sikh. Avocations: masters swimming, amateur radio, philately. Home: 5719 Makati Cir Apt D San Jose CA 95123-6211

SINGLETON, HENRY EARL, retired industrialist; b. Haslet, Tex., Nov. 27, 1916; s. John Bartholomew and Victoria (Flores) S.; m. Caroline A. Wood, Nov. 30, 1942; children: Christina, John, William, James, Diana. S.B., S.M., Mass. Inst. Tech., 1940, Sc.D., 1950. V.p. Litton Industries, Inc., Beverly Hills, Calif., 1954-60; CEO Teledyne Inc., Los Angeles, 1960-86; chmn. Teledyne Inc., 1960-91, Singleton Group, Beverly Hills, Calif., 1991-96; chmn. exec. com. Teledyne, Inc., L.A., 1991-96, retired; bd. dirs. Argonaut Group Inc., L.A. *

SINGLETON, JAMES KEITH, federal judge; b. Oakland, Calif., Jan. 27, 1939; s. James K. and Irene Elisabeth (Lilly) S.; m. Sandra Claire Hoskins, Oct. 15, 1966; children: Matthew David, Michael Keith. Student, U. Santa Clara, 1957-58; AB in Polit. Sci., U. Calif., Berkeley, 1961, LLB, 1964. Bar: Calif. 1965, Alaska, 1965. Assoc. Delaney Wiles Moore and Hayes, Anchorage, 1963, 65-68, Law Offices Roger Cremo, Anchorage, 1968-70; judge Alaska Superior Ct., Anchorage, 1970-80, Alaska Ct. Appeals, Anchorage, 1980-90; judge U.S. Dist. Ct. for Alaska, Anchorage, 1990-95, chief judge, 1995—; chmn. Alaska Local Boundary Commn., Anchorage, 1966-69. Chmn. 3d Dist. Rep. Com., Anchorage, 1969-70. Mem. ABA, Alaska Bar Assn., Phi Delta Phi, Tau Kappa Epsilon. Office: US Dist Ct 222 W 7th Ave Unit 41 Anchorage AK 99513-7504

SINHA-MOREY, BOBBI ANN, poetry editor, researcher, poet; b. Oakland, Calif., Mar. 13, 1962; d. Arthur Robert and Barbara Jane (Edwards) Jensen; m. Arvind Sinha, June 15, 1982 (div. Jan., 1992); m. Joseph Scott Morey, Aug. 13, 1994. BA in Comm. with hons., Wright State U., 1987. Poetry editor Midnight Zoo, Walnut Creek, Calif., 1991-94, Aberations, Walnut Creek, 1991-94; contbg. writer The Orinda (Calif.) News, 1992-93; editorial assoc. Aberrations, San Francisco, 1994-97; poetry editor Dark Regions, Concord, Calif., 1992—; poetry reviewer Small Press Writers and Artists Orgn., Concord, Calif.; editor, reviewer The Genre Writer's News, Orinda, Calif., 1996-98; contbg. editor Horror Mag., Concord, Calif., 1995-98, editor, 1998—. Author: (poetry books) The Lighter Side of the Writing Life, 1990, Serendipity, 1994, The Sixth Vision, 1995, The Lilac-Bleeding Star, 1996; editor: (book) Sensuous Debris by Bruce Boston, 1995; editor (chapbooks) Antepenult, W. Gregory Stewart, 1994, The Crow's Companion, Jacie Ragan, 1994, Moon Canoes, Wendy Rathbone, 1994, The Conspiracy Unmasked, David Kopaska-Merkel, 1994, Eonian Variations, Marge Simon, 1995, The 1995 Small Press Genre Assn. Showcase, 1996, Variations of Sleeping Alone, Herb Kauderer, 1996, Speaking Bones, Denise Dumars, 1996, Writhing in Darkness I & II, Michael Arnzen, 1997, Anubis on Guard, Don Webb, 1998, Poking the Gun, John Grey, 1998. Recipient cert. of merit Nexus Mag., 1987, award of merit Iliad Literary Awards Program, 1989, blue ribbon Hourglass Poetry Competition, 1990, 1st place cert. N. Tex. Profl. Writers' Assn., 1996, LLC Poet's award Cedar Bay Press, 1997; named Best Poet Small Press Genre Assn., 1994, Best Mag. Poetry Editor, 1995. Mem. Horror Writers' Assn., Sci. Fiction Poetry Assn. Avocations: cooking, aerobics, horseback riding, swimming, chess. Home: 30 Canyon View Dr Orinda CA 94563 Office: Dark Regions Press PO Box 6301 Concord CA 94524-1301

SINISCALCO, GARY RICHARD, lawyer; b. N.Y.C., Aug. 14, 1943. BA in Econs., Le Moyne Coll., 1965; JD, Georgetown U., 1969. Bar: Calif. Regional counsel, sr. trial atty. EEOC, San Francisco, 1969-78; ptnr. in charge of client rels. Orrick, Herrington & Sutcliffe, San Francisco, 1978—, co-chairperson employment law dept.; mem. adv. bd. Nat. Employment Law Inst.; lectr. in field. Co-author: Manager's Guide to Lawful Terminations, 1991; author: (with others) Employment Discrimination Law, 1979, 3rd edit., 1996; contbr. articles to profl. jours. Mem. ABA (mem. com. on internat. labor rels. and equal employment opportunity, mgmt. co-chairperson equal employment opportunity com. 1996—), State Bar Calif., Bar Commonwealth Va., Am. Employment Law Coun. (founder). Office: Orrick Herrington 400 Sansome St San Francisco CA 94111-3143*

SIPOS, EVA MAGDALENA, pharmacist; b. Prague, Czech Republic, Aug. 12, 1954; came to the U.S., 1965; d. Frank and Magdalena (Neumann) S. BA summa cum laude, Western Mich. U., 1976; BS, U. Ariz., 1981, PharmD, 1981. Registered pharmacist. Pharmacist Auburn (Wash.) Gen. Hosp., 1982-83, Waldo Hosp., Seattle, 1983, Payless/Osco/Skaggs, Wash., 1983-88, Evergreen Pharm., Kirkland, Wash., 1988—, Pacific Med. Ctr., Seattle, 1997—. Exhibited photographs Squibb Gallery, Princeton, N.J., 1975, Ray Manley Gallery, Tucson, 1977. Mem. Rho Chi, Gold Key. Republican. Avocations: fishing, photography, gardening, cooking.

SIPUS, RONALD G., school administrator; b. Snowflake, Ariz., Oct. 10, 1944; s. George Sipus and Nancy Alice Malone; m. Carol Lynn Greene, June 2, 1966; children: Kimberly Tara Sipus Sitts, Healther Leann Sipus Bunce. BS, Grand Canyon Coll., 1966; MA, Ariz. State U., 1971, PhD, 1977. Cert. secondary tchr., prin., supt., Ariz. English and biology tchr. Cortez H.S., Phoenix, 1966-67; epidemiologist USPHS, Phoenix, 1967; tchr., coach Peoria (Ariz.) Unified Sch. Dist., 1969-70; tchr., coach Cortez H.S., Phoenix, 1970-73, dean of students, 1973-74; asst. prin. Thunderbird H.S., Phoenix, 1974-78; prin. Camelback H.S., Phoenix, 1978-79; supt. Scottsdale Christian Acad., Phoenix, 1979-90, Payson (Ariz.) Unified Sch. Dist., 1990-92, Village Christian Schs., Sun Valley, Calif., 1992—; seminar cons., spkr. in field; cons., instr. Phoenix Aoclhol Safety Action project Ariz. State U. and City of Phoenix, 1971-74. Mem. Christian Sch. Trust Fund; bd. dirs. Spalding Edn. Found., Phoenix; former mem. Grand Canyon U. Devel. Coun., Ariz. Gov.'s Office for Child Phys. and Sexual Abuse Prevention Task Force; former trustee Grand Canyon U.; former bd. dirs. Ariz. Bus. and Edn. Partnership. With U.S. Army, 1967-69. Mem. North Ctrl. Accrediting Assn. (evaluation mem.), Assn. Christian Schs. Internat. (accreditation team mem.), Ariz. Interscholastic Assn. (evaluation mem.), Assn. Christian Schs. Internat., Ariz. Secondary Prins. Assn. Home: 29313 Begonias Ln Canyon Cntry CA 91351-5909 Office: Village Christian Schs 8930 Village Ave Sun Valley CA 91352-2199

SIRDOFSKY, KATRINA, personal manager, recording studio owner; b. San Francisco, Apr. 22, 1964; d. Murray Sirdofsky and Margaret Morrison Haffner. Propr. Rebel Mgmt., San Francisco, 1986—; personal mgr. Death Angel (Enigma/Capitol Records, 1985-88), Vain (Island Records, 1987-91, 4 Non Blondes (Interscope Records), 1990-94, Lamb (N.Am. Mercury [illegible] 1991. Office: Rebel Mgmt PO Box 170545 San Francisco CA 94117-0545

SIRIGNANO, WILLIAM ALFONSO, aerospace and mechanical engineer, educator; b. Bronx, N.Y., Apr. 14, 1938; s. Anthony P. and Lucy (Caruso)

S.; m. Lynn Haisfield, Nov. 26, 1977; children: Monica Ann, Jacqueline Hope, Justin Anthony. B.Aero.Engring., Rensselaer Poly. Inst., 1959; Ph.D., Princeton U., 1964. Mem. research staff Guggenheim Labs., aerospace, mech. scis. dept. Princeton U., 1964-67, asst. prof. aerospace and mech. scis., 1967-69, assoc. prof., 1969-73, prof., 1973-79, dept. dir. grad. studies, 1974-78; George Tallman Ladd prof., head dept. mech. engring. Carnegie-Mellon U., 1979-85; dean Sch. Engring., U. Calif.-Irvine, 1985-94, prof., 1994—; cons. indsutry and govt., 1966—; lectr. and cons. NATO adv. group on aero. rsch. and devel., 1967, 75, 80; chmn. nat. and internat. tech. congs.; chmn. acad. adv. coun. Indsl. Rsch. Inst., 1985-88; mem. space sci. applications adv. com. NASA, 1985-90, chmn. combustion sci. microgravity disciplinary working group, 1987-90; chmn. com. on microgravity rsch. space studies bd. NRC, 1991-94. Assoc. editor: Combustion Sci. and Tech., 1969-70; assoc. tech. editor Jour. Heat Transfer, 1986-92; contbr. articles to nat. and internat. profl. jours., also rsch. monographs. United Aircraft research fellow, 1973-74; Disting. Alumni Rsch. award U. Calif. Irvine, 1992. Fellow AIAA (Pendray Aerospace Lit. award 1991, Propellants and Combustion award 1992), ASME (Freeman scholar 1992), AAAS; mem. Inst. Dynamics of Explosives and Reactive Systems (v.p. 1991-95, pres. 1995—, Oppenheim award 1993), Combustion Inst. (treas. internat. orgn., chmn. ea. sect., Alfred C. Egerton Gold medal 1996), Soc. Indsl. and Applied Math., Orange County Engring. Coun. (Excellence award 1994), Am. Electronics Assn. (recognition 1994). Office: U Calif Sch Engring S 3202 Engring Gateway Irvine CA 92697

SISEMORE, CLAUDIA, educational films and videos producer, director; b. Salt Lake City, Sept. 16, 1937; d. Darrell Daniel and Alice Larril (Barton) S. BS in English, Brigham Young U., 1959; MFA in Filmmaking, U. Utah, 1976. Cert. secondary tchr., Utah. Tchr. English, drama and writing Salt Lake Sch. Dist., Salt Lake City, 1959-66; tchr. English Davis Sch. Dist., Bountiful, Utah, 1966-68; ind. filmmaker Salt Lake City, 1972—; filmmaker-in-residence Wyo. Coun. for Arts and Nat. Endowment for Arts, Dubois, Wyo., 1977-78; prodr., dir. ednl. films Utah Office Edn., Salt Lake City, 1979-93, Canyon Video, 1993—. Prodr., dir. Beginning of Winning, 1984 (film festival award 1984), Dancing through the Magic Eye, 1986, Se Hable Espanol, 1986-87; writer, dir., editor (film) Building on a Legacy, 1988, (videos) Energy Conservation, 1990, Alternative Energy Sources, 1990, Restructuring Learning, 1991, Kidsercise, 1991, Traditional Energy Sources, 1992, A State Government Team, 1992, Problem Solving Using Math Manipulative, 1993, Canyon Video, 1993—; videos Western Mountains and Basins, 1994, Ramps and Rails, 1994, Fitness After 50, 1995, Timescape, 1996, Splash of Color, 1996, A Winter's Hush: Understanding Depression, 1996, Your Guide to the Internet, 1997; exhibited (abstract paintings) in group show Phillips Gallery; represented in numerous pvt. and pub. collections. Juror Park City (Utah) Arts Festival, 1982, Utah Arts Festival, Salt Lake City, 1982, Am. Film Festival, 1985-86, Best of West Film Festival, 1985-86; bd. dirs. Utah Media Ctr., Salt Lake City, 1981-87; mem. multi-disciplinary program Utah Arts Coun., Salt Lake City, 1983-87. Recipient award Utah Media Ctr., 1984, 85; Nat. Endowment for Arts grantee, 1978, Utah Arts Coun. grantee, 1980. Mormon. Avocations: writing, reading, music.

SITRICK, MICHAEL STEVEN, communications executive; b. Davenport, Iowa, June 8, 1947; s. J. Herman and Marcia B. (Bofman) S.; m. Nancy Elaine Eiseman, July 1, 1969; children: Julie, Sheri, Alison. BS in Bus. Adminstrn. and Journalism, U. Md., 1969. Coordinator press services Western Electric, Chgo., 1969-70; asst. dir. program services City of Chgo., 1970-72; asst. v.p. Selz, Seabolt & Assocs., Chgo., 1972-74; dir. communications and pub. affairs Nat. Can Corp., Chgo., 1974-81; dir. communications Wickes Cos., Inc., San Diego, 1981-82; v.p. communications Wickes Cos., Inc., Santa Monica, Calif., 1982-84, sr. v.p. communications, 1984-89; chmn., chief exec. officer Sitrick and Co., L.A. and N.Y.C., 1989—. Office: Sitrick and Co 2029 Century Park E Ste 1750 Los Angeles CA 90067-3003

SIYAN, KARANJIT SAINT GERMAIN SINGH, software engineer; b. Mauranipur, India, Oct. 16, 1954; came to U.S., 1978; s. Ahal Singh and Tejinder Kaur (Virdi) S.; m. Dei Gayle Cooper, Apr. 8, 1987. B in Tech. Electronics, Indian Inst. Tech., 1976, M in Tech. Computer Sci., 1978; MS in Engring., U. Calif., Berkeley, 1980; PhD of Computer Sci., Kennedy-Western U., Berkeley, 1994. Cert. enterprise netware engr.; cert. microsoft profl.; cert. master novell engr. Sr. mem. tech. staff Rolm Corp., San Jose, Calif., 1980-84; cons. Siyan Cons. Svcs., L.A., 1985-86, Emigrant, Mont., 1987—. Author, sr. instr. Learning Tree Internat., 1985—; author: Internet Firewalls and Network Security, Inside Java, Inside TCP/IP, Inside TCP/IP for Windows NT, Inside Visual J Netware-The Professional Reference, Windows NT Server: The Professional Reference, Netware Training Guide-Network 4 Update, Building Intranets with Netware Web Server, Netware Training Guide-Network 4 Update, Netware 4 Training Guide-Netware 4 Adminstration, CNE Training Guide-TCP/IP and NFS, Internetworking with Netware TCP/IP; co-author: Downsizing Netware, Implementing Internet Security, LAN Connectivity, Netware 4 for Professionals, Banyan Vines-The Professional Reference; author seminars on Novell Networking, TCP/IP Networks, Windows NT, Solaris-PC Network Integration. Mem. IEEE, Assn. for Computing Machinery, Enterprise, Network Profl. Assn., Kappa Omicron Phi.

SIZEMORE, HERMAN MASON, JR., newspaper executive; b. Halifax, Va., Apr. 15, 1941; s. Herman Mason and Hazel (Johnson) S.; m. Connie Catterton, June 22, 1963; children: Jill, Jennifer. AB in History, Coll. William and Mary, 1963; postgrad., U. Mo., 1965; MBA, U. Wash., 1985. Reporter Norfolk (Va.) Ledger-Star, summers 1961, 62, 63; copy editor Seattle Times, 1965-70, copy-desk chief, 1970-75, asst. mng. editor, 1975-77, mng. editor, 1977-81, prodn. dir., 1981-83, asst. gen. mgr., 1984, v.p., gen. mgr., 1985, pres., chief operating officer, 1985—; vis. instr. Sch. Comms. U. Wash., 1972-78; bd. dirs. Times Comms. Co., Walla Walla Union-Bull, Inc., Yakima Herald-Republic, Blethen Maine Newspapers, Northwestern Mut. Life Ins. Co., 1993—, mem. policyowner examining com., 1985, chmn., 1986. Bd. dirs. Ctrl. Puget Sound Campfire Coun., 1985-91, pres., 1989-90; bd. dirs. Ptnrs. in Pub. Edn., 1987-88, United Way of King County, 1994—, Downtown Seattle Assn.; adv. coun. Puget Sound Blood Ctr. and Program; adv. bd. USO-Puget Sound Area, U. Wash. Sch. Bus. Named Seattle Newsmaker of Tomorrow, 1978; recipient Alumni medallion Coll. William and Mary, 1998. Mem. AP Mng. Editors, Soc. Profl. Journalists, Pacific N.W. Newspaper Assn. (bd. dirs.), Newspaper Assn of Am. (vice-chair newsprint com.), Allied Daily Newspapers Washington (bd. dirs.), Coll. William and Mary Alumni Assn., Greater Seattle C. of C. (bd. dirs.), U. Wash. Exec. MBA Alumni Assn. (pres. 1988), Wash. Athletic Club (bd. dirs.), Rainier Club, Rotary. Methodist. Office: Seattle Times PO Box 70 Seattle WA 98111-0070

SIZEMORE, NICKY LEE, computer scientist; b. N.Y.C., Feb. 13, 1946; s. Ralph Lee and Edith Ann (Wangler) S.; m. Frauke Julika Hoffmann, Oct. 31, 1974; 1 child, Jennifer Lee Sizemore; 1 stepchild, Mark Anthony Miracle. BS in Computer Sci., SUNY, 1989. Sgt. first class U.S. Army, 1964-68, 70-86; computer operator UNIVAC, Washington, 1968-69, programmer, 1969-70; programmer/analyst Ultra Systems, Inc., Sierra Vista, Ariz., 1986-87; computer scientist Comarco, Inc., Sierra Vista, 1987-92, ARC, Profl. Svcs. Group, Sierra Vista, 1992-93, Computer Scis. Corp., Ft. Huachuca, Ariz., 1994; sr. cons. Inference Corp., 1995; subject matter expert Northrop Corp., Sierra Vista, Ariz., 1995—; sr. info. sys. engr. Harris Corp., Sierra Vista, Ariz., 1996—; speaker numerous confs., seminars, symposia; tech. columnist Sierra vista Herald. Mem. Computer Soc. IEEE, Am. Assn. for Artificial Intelligence (co-dir. workshop on verification, validation, and test of knowledge-based sys. 1988), Assn. for Computing Machinery, Armed Forces Comms.-Electronics Assn. Avocations: chess, jogging/aerobics, karate. Home: 880 E Charles Dr Sierra Vista AZ 85635-1611 Office: Harris Tech Svcs Corp 101 E Wilcox Dr Sierra Vista AZ 85635-2540

SJOBERG, JÖRGEN CARL, business owner; b. Los Gatos, Calif., Apr. 14, 1963; s. Carl Magnus-Johann and Astrid Olga-Marie (Lauren) S.; m. Diane Elizabeth Thomas, June 11, 1988 (div. Mar. 1991). Cert., Foothill Coll., 1991. Shipping and receiving supr. So. Lumber Co., San Jose, Calif., 1979-82, Blackburn Designs, Inc., Campbell, Calif., 1982-84; with quality assurance documentation and test dept. Internat. Microcircuits, Inc., Santa Clara, Calif., 1984-86; purchasing/warehouse mgr. Blackburn Designs, Inc., Campbell, Calif., 1986-91; purchasing mgr. Spectre Industries, San Jose, Calif., 1991-92; sales assoc. Century 21, Auburn, Calif., 1992-94; owner, mgr. The Booksmith, Grass Valley, Calif., 1994—. Avocations: camping, reading, travel, theatre. Office: The Booksmith 10021 Wolf Rd Grass Valley CA 95949-8147

SJOLANDER, GARY WALFRED, physicist; b. Bagley, Minn., Dec. 5, 1942; s. Tage Walfred and Evelyn Mildred (Kaehn) S.; m. Joann Lorraine Tressler, June 18, 1966; 1 child, Toby Ryan. BS in Physics, U. Minn., 1970, MS in Physics, 1974, PhD in Physics, 1975. Rsch. assoc. U. Minn., Mpls., 1975-76; rsch. scientist Johns Hopkins U., Balt., 1977-78, sr. physicist, 1978-82; sr. engr. Westinghouse Electric Corp., Annapolis, Md., 1982-85; sr. staff engr. Lockheed Martin Astronautics, Denver, 1985-95; engring. scientist data techs. divsn. TRW, Aurora, Colo., 1996—; pres. Cypress Improvement Assn., Inc., Severna Park, Md., 1984-85; advisor Inroads/Denver, Inc., 1986-88. Author numerous articles in field. With USAF, 1960-64. Mem. AIAA, Internat. Soc. for Optical Engring., Am. Geophys. Union, The Planetary Soc. Lutheran. Avocations: tennis, motorcycling, wooden-ship models, piano, woodworking. Home: 811 W Kettle Ave Littleton CO 80120-4443

SKAGGS, BEBE REBECCA PATTEN, college dean, clergywoman; b. Berkeley, Calif., Jan. 30, 1950; d. Carl Thomas and Bebe (Harrison) P. BS in Bible, Patten Coll., 1969; BA in Philosophy, Holy Names Coll., 1970; MA in Bibl. Studies New Testament, Wheaton Coll., 1972; PhD in Bibl. Studies New Testament, Drew U., 1976; MA in Philosophy, Dominican Sch. Philosophy & Theology, 1990; postgrad., U. Calif., Berkeley, 1991-92. Ordained to ministry Christian Evang. Ch., 1963. Co-pastor Christian Cathedral, Christian Evang. Chs. Am., Inc., 1964—; assoc. prof. Patten Coll., Oakland, Calif., 1975-82, dean, 1977—, prof. N.T., 1982—; presenter in field. Author: Before the Times, 1980, The World of the Early Church, 1990; contbg. author: Internat. Standard Bibl. Ency., rev. edit., 1983, Women's Study Bible, Pneuma faculty dialogue. Active Wheaton Coll. Symphony, 1971-72, Drew U. Ensemble, 1971-75, Young Artists Symphony, N.J., 1972-75, Somerset Hill Symphony, N.J., 1973-74, Peninsula Symphony, 1977, 80-81, Madison Chamber Trio, N.J., 1973-75. Named one of Outstanding Young Women of Am., 1976, 77, 80-81, 82; St. Olaf's Coll. fellow, 1990. Mem. AAUP, Am. Acad. Religion, Soc. Bibl. Lit., Internat. Biographical Assn., Christian Evang. Chs. of Am., Inc. (bd. dirs. 1964—), Christian Assn. for Student Affairs, Assn. for Christians in Student Devel., Inst. for Bibl. Rsch., Soc. for Pentecostal Studies (pres. 1998—), Phi Delta Kappa.

SKAGGS, DAVID E., association administrator, lawyer, educator; b. Cin., Feb. 22, 1943; s. Charles and Juanita Skaggs; m. Laura Locher, Jan. 3, 1987; 1 child, Matthew; stepchildren: Clare, Will. BA in Philosophy, Wesleyan U., 1964; student law, U. Va., 1964-65; LLB, Yale U., 1967. Bar: N.Y. 1968, Colo. 1971. Assoc. Patterson, Belknap & Webb, N.Y.C., 1967-68, Newcomer & Douglass, Boulder, Colo., 1971-74, 77-78; chief of staff, congressman Tim Wirth, Washington, 1974-77; ptnr. Skaggs, Stone & Sheehy, Boulder, 1978-86; mem. 100th-105th Congresses from 2d Colo. dist., Washington, 1987-99; mem. Appropriations com. Commerce and Justice, Interior, 1991-98; various subcoms., 1991-98; exec. dir. Democracy and Citizenship program The Aspen Inst., Washington, 1999—; mem. Ho. Permanent Select Com. on Intelligence; mem. Colo. Ho. of Reps., Denver, 1980-86; minority leader, 1982-85, subcom. tech. and tactical intelligence, ranking minority mem.; adj. prof. U. Colo. Former bd. dirs. Rocky Mountain Planned Parenthood, Mental Health Assn. Colo., Boulder County United Way, Boulder Civic Opera. Served to capt. USMC, 1968-71, Vietnam; maj. USMCR, 1971-77. Mem. Colo. Bar Assn., Boulder County Bar Assn., Boulder C. of C. Democrat. Congregationalist. Office: US House of Reps 1124 Longworth Bldg Washington DC 20515-0602 also: 9101 Harlan St Unit 130 Westminster CO 80030-2961

SKALAGARD, HANS MARTIN, artist; b. Skuo, Faroe Islands, Feb. 7, 1924; s. Ole Johannes and Hanna Elisa (Fredriksen) S.; came to U.S., 1942, naturalized, 1955. Pupil Anton Otto Fisher, 1947; m. Mignon Diana Haack Haegland, Mar. 31, 1955; 1 child, Karen Solveig Sikes. Joined U.S. Mcht. Marine, 1942, advanced through grades to chief mate, 1945, ret., 1965; owner, operator Skalagard Sq., Rigger Art Gallery, Carmel, 1966—; libr. Mayo Hays O'Donnel Libr., Monterey, Calif., 1971-73; painter U.S. Naval Heritage series, 1973—; exhibited in numerous one-man shows including Palace Legion of Honor, San Francisco, 1960, J.F. Howland, 1963-65, Fairmont Hotel, San Francisco, 1963, Galerie de Tours, 1969, 72-73, Pebble Beach Gallery, 1968, Laguna Beach (Calif.) Gallery, 1969, Arden Gallery, Atlanta, 1970, Gilbert Gallery, San Francisco, Maritine Mus. of Monterey, Calif., 1993, Rigger Art Gallery, Carmel, Calif., Stanton Ctr., Monterey, 1993, St. Francis Yacht Club, San Francisco, 1995, Monterey Nat. Mus., 1993; group shows: Am. Artists, Eugene, Oreg., Robert Louis Stevenson Exhibit, Carmel Valley Gallery, Biarritz and Paris, France, David Findley Galleries, N.Y.C. and Faroe Island, Europe, Martime Mus., Calif, 1993, 94, 95, Pacific Coast Lumber Schooners, 1994, numerous others; represented in permanent collections; Naval Post Grad. Sch. and Libr., Allen Knight Maritime Mus., Salvation Army Bldg., Monterey, Calif., Robert Louis Stevenson Sch., Pebble Beach, Anenberg Art Galleries, Chestlibrook Ltd., Skalagard Art Gallery, Carmel, 1984; work represented in numerous book including Modern Masters of Marine Art, 1993; profiled in profl. jours.; lectr. Bd. dirs. Allen Knight Maritime Mus., 1973—, mem. adv. and acquisition coms., 1973-77; founder Skalagard Square Rigger Gallery; chairperson Mayor's Choice Exhibit Carmel, Calif., 1995; co founder Carmel Gallery Alliance. Recipient Silver medal Tommaso Campanella Internat. Acad. Arts, Letters and Scis., Rome, 1970, Gold medal, 1972, Gold medal and hon. life membership Academia Italia del Arti e del Honoro, 1980, Gold medal for artistic merit Academia d'Italia. Mem. Navy League (bd. dir. Monterey), Internat. Platform Assn., Sons of Norway (cultural dir. 1974-75, 76-77). Subject of cover and article Palette Talk, 1980, Compass mag., 1980. Home: 602 Stony Point Rd Petaluma CA 94952-1048 Office: PO Box 6611 Carmel CA 93921-6611 also: Dolores At 5th St Carmel CA 93921

SKARDA, RICHARD JOSEPH, clinical social worker; b. Santa Monica, Calif., Jan. 2, 1952; s. Robert Ralph and Cathryn Marie (Tourek) S. AA, Los Angeles Valley Coll., Van Nuys, Calif., 1976; BA, U. Calif., Berkeley, 1978; MSW, UCLA, 1980. Lic. clin. social worker, Calif. Children's svcs. worker L.A. County Dept. Children's Svcs., Panorama City, Calif., 1980-82; children's services worker Ventura (Calif.) County Pub. Social Svcs. Agy., 1983-85; head social work dept. Naval Med. Clinic, Port Hueneme, Calif., 1985-94; pvt. practice, 1996—. With USN, 1970-74. Mem. NASW, Acad. Cert. Social Workers. Avocations: traveling, music.

SKEELS, H(ARRY) WILBUR, clergyman, composer; b. Dunedin, Otago, New Zealand, May 25, 1938; came to U.S., 1960; s. Arthur Lennard and Leida (Hammer) S.; m. Delia Peña, June 23, 1962; children: Andrew, Mark, David. MA, U. New Zealand, 1959; MDiv, Fuller Theol. Sem., Pasadena, Calif., 1963; DMin, Am. Bapt. Sem. of the West, Berkeley, Calif., 1973. Recognized by Am. Bapt. Chs. in U.S.A.; cert. cmty. coll. tchr., Calif. Concert accompanist Los Robles Master Chorale, Moorpark, Calif., 1980—; owner, pub. Cantus Quercus Press, Thousand Oaks, Calif., 1994—; pastor Raumati Bapt. Ch., Raumati Beach, New Zealand, 1963-67, First Bapt. Ch., Twentynine Palms, Calif., 1968-74, Conejo Valley Bapt. Ch., Thousand Oaks, 1974-80; min. of music Pleasant Valley Bapt. Ch., Camarillo, Calif., 1980-90; pastor First Bapt Ch., Ojai, Calif., 1990—; founding pres. Morongo Basin Mental Health Assn., Twentynine Palms, 1970-74, Hospice of the Conejo, Thousand Oaks, 1977-79, Ojai Valley Family Shelter, Ojai, 1993—;dir. Choral Condrs. Guild, L.A., 1976-81. Composer and/or arranger more than 60 pub. choral compositions, including translations from Latin, German, French, Spanish and Portuguese. Fulbright Exch. grantee, Ky. and Calif., 1960-63. Mem. Am. Choral Dirs. Assn., Am. Bapt. Mins. Coun. Avocations: travel, baseball, handbells, internet, foreign languages. Home: 1275 Hendrix Ave Thousand Oaks CA 91360-3559 Office: Cantus Quercus Press 1275 Hendrix Ave Thousand Oaks CA 91360-3559

SKEELS, STEPHEN GLENN, civil engineer; b. Salem, Oreg., Mar. 8, 1951; s. Glenn Arthur and Shirley Belle (Brown) S. BS in Math., Oreg. Coll. Edn., Monmouth, 1974; cert., Computer Career Inst., Portland, Oreg., 1978. Profl. civil engr., 1994. Engring. aide Oreg. State Hwy. Dept., Coquille, 1974-76; programmer, analyst Northwest Area Sys., Inc., Salem, 1978-81, Interstate Fin. Svcs., Salem, 1981; engring. aide Oreg. Dept. Transp., Portland, 1983-84, engring. tech., 1985-86, assoc. transp. engr., 1986—. Active Rep. Presdl. Legion of Merit, 1992. Mem. ASCE, Math. Assn. Am. Libertarian. Avocations: chess, guitar.

SKEEN, JOSEPH RICHARD, congressman; b. Roswell, N.Mex., June 30, 1927; s. Thomas Dudley and Ilah (Adamson) S.; m. Mary Helen Jones, Nov. 17, 1945; children: Mary Elisa, Mikell Lee. B.S., Tex. A&M U., 1950. Soil and water engr. Ramah Navajo and Zuni Indians, 1951; rancher Lincoln County, N.Mex., 1952—; mem. N.Mex. Senate, 1960-70, 97th-103rd Congresses from 2nd N.Mex. dist., Washington, D.C., 1981—; mem. appropriations com., subcom. agr., chmn. appropriations com., subcom. def., mem. subcom. interior. Chmn. N.Mex. Republican Party, 1963-66. Served with USN, 1945-46; Served with USAFR, 1949-52. Mem. Nat. Woolgrowers Assn., Nat. Cattle Growers Assn., N.Mex. Woolgrowers Assn., N.Mex. Cattle Growers Assn., N.Mex. Farm and Livestock Bur. Republican. Club: Elks. Office: House of Reps Washington DC 20515

SKEFF, KELLEY MICHAEL, health facility administrator; b. Center, Colo., 1944. MD, U. Chgo., 1970. Diplomate Am. Bd. Internal Medicine. Intern Harbor Gen. Hosp., Torrance, Calif., 1970-71; resident in internal medicine U. Colo. Med. Ctr., Denver, 1974-75; resident in internal medicine Stanford (Calif.) U. Hosps., 1975-76, fellow in internal medicine, 1976; resident in internal medicine Stanford U., 1989—, assoc. prof. medicine. Recipient Alpha Omega Alpha award Assocs. Am. Med. Coll., 1994. Office: Stanford U Dept Med 300 Pasteur Dr Palo Alto CA 94304-2203*

SKEITH, GEORGE GLENN, environmental health specialist, technologist; b. Henrietta, Okla.; s. George S. and Edna Glenn (Harmon) S.; m. Jeneviv N. Campbell, Apr. 23, 1939; children: George, James. AA, U.S. Armed Forces Inst., 1954. Registered environ. health specialist, Calif. Chief warrant officer USN, 1946-58; supervising environ. health specialist Orange County Health Dept., Santa Ana, Calif., 1958-79; Cons. Practitioner of Infection Control, Calif., Food Svc. Adv. Bd., Salem, Oreg. Mem. Masons, Scottish Rite, Shriners, Elks. Republican. Avocation: golf. Home: 6626 Continental Cir SE Salem OR 97306-1437

SKELLY, JOHN JOSHUA, clergyman, fundraiser; b. Central Falls, R.I., Oct. 25, 1932; s. Joshua Essa and Catherine (Hermiz) S.; m. Una C. Meadowcroft, June 21, 1959 (div.); children: Timothy John, Joan Louise, Steven Allan. BSBA, Pepperdine U., 1956; BD, San Francisco Theol. Sem., 1959, DS in Theology, 1981; DD, Tarkio Coll., 1971. Asst. pastor First Presbyn. Ch., Granada Hill, Calif., 1959-61; pastor Port Hueneme (Calif.) Presbyn. Ch., 1961-65; v.p. devel. Pikeville (Ky.) Coll., 1967-69; sr. pastor Westminster Presbyn. Ch., Topeka, 1969-72; v.p. seminary rels. San Francisco Theol. Sem., 1972-83; pres. Pacific Homes Found., Woodland Hills, Calif., 1988—; area counselor The Fifty Million Fund, United Presbyn. Ch., Kans.-Mo., 1965-67; mission devel. cons., 1967—; cons. Model Cities Program, Pikeville, 1968; campaign cons. United Way, L.A., 1986-87. V.p. student body Pepperdine U., L.A., 1955-56; pres. Hueneme-Oxnard Ministerial Assn., Port Hueneme, 1962; chmn. law enforcement com. Ventura County Grand Jury, 1964-65; chaplain of the day Ho. of Reps., State of Kans., 1970. Staff sgt. U.S. Army, 1950-52. Named Most Inspirational Player, Pepperdine Rugby Club, L.A., 1955, Outstanding Young Men of Am., U.S. Jr. C. of C., Port Hueneme, 1964. Democrat. Avocations: gardening, cooking Middle Eastern food, swimming, biking, golfing. Home: 850 E Ocean Blvd Unit 206 Long Beach CA 90802-5446 Office: Pacific Homes 2835 N Naomi St # 300 Burbank CA 91504-2024

SKELTON, DOUGLAS H., architect; b. Cottage Grove, Oreg., Apr. 17, 1939; s. Harry Edward and Mary Jane (Caldwell) S.; m. Bonita L. Baker, June 17, 1961; children: Paul D., Cynthia J., Justin D. Student, Oreg. State U., 1957-59; degree in architecture, U. Oreg., 1963. Registered architect, Oreg. Draftsman Payne & Struble Architecture, Medford, Oreg., 1965-66; intern architect Wayne Struble Architect, Medford, Oreg., 1966-70, assoc., 1973-78; project architect William Seibert Architect, Medford, Oreg., 1970-73; ptnr. Struble & Skelton Architects, Medford, Oreg., 1978-83; owner Douglas Skelton Architect, Medford, Oreg., 1983-89; ptnr. Skelton, Straus & Seibert Architects, Medford, Oreg., 1989—; mem. law rev. com. State Bd. Architects, Oreg., 1991. Design bldg. renovation (911 Mag. award 1991, Excellence in Sch. Architecture AS&U mag. 1987). Bd. dirs. Rogue Valley Christian Ch., 1994. Recipient Outstanding Sch. Bldg. award Am. Sch. and Univ. mag., 1987. Mem. AIA (v.p. So. Oreg. chpt. 1972, pres. 1973), Architects Coun. Oreg. (del., treas. 1989), Rotary (v.p., bd. dirs. Jacksonville/Applegate chpt. 1994). Avocations: camping, fishing, boating, bicycling, cross-country skiing. Office: Skelton Straus & Seibert 26 Hawthorne Ave Medford OR 97504-7114*

SKELTON, RAY BECK, agriculture company administrator, consultant; b. Lewiston, Idaho, July 9, 1966; s. William Joseph and Darlene Belle (Smith) S.; m. Patti Delynn MacDowell, Apr. 1, 1989; children: Jacob William, Adam. Student in agri-bus., U. Idaho, 1985-86. Cost engr. Goodfellow Bros., Inc., Maui, Hawaii, 1989-90, project mgr., 1990-93, ops. mgr., 1993—; irregation cons. Maui Rsch. & Tech., Kihei, Hawaii, 1991—. Participant Cmty. Clean-up, Kihei, 1989—. Recipient Cmty. Appreciation award County of Maui, 1992. Mem. Ka Lima O Maui (bd. dirs. 1997—). Catholic. Avocations: golf, family. Office: PO Box 220 Kihei HI 96753-0220

SKENANDORE, RODNEY CURTIS, artist; b. Crow Agency, Mont., June 9, 1939; s. Reginald Curtis Skenandore (dec.) and Regina Mahala (Parker) Pease; m. Barbara Ann Malanga, Aug. 17, 987; children: Sam, James, Amanda, Jean, Blue, Jess, Tria, Wris, Chey, Tosa-Ry. A in Elec., Mech. Engring, Colo. U., 1961. Sub-contractor Aerospace industry, Pasadena, Huntington Beac, Calif., 1961-66; Resident Medicine Man St. Joseph's Hosp., Denver, 1970—, cons., advisor Bd. Indian Mental Health, Denver, 1973, 74; Reiki master, 1996—. Author: Peace and Non-Violence, 1973; contbr. articles to profl. jours. Co-founder, chmn. bd. Am. Indian Movement, Denver, 1969-74, dir. ct. svcs., 1970-74; exec. chmn. Nat. Indian Adv., Denver, 1974—, developed Indian Jr. C. of C., 1966. With U.S. Army Airborne, 1956-60, 62, 66, 72. Mem. Internat. Medicine Man, Leader Clan, Tobacco Soc., Skull Draggers Soc., Touch the Heart Sun Dance Soc. (Sun Dance chief). Avocations: bicycling, backpacking, jewelry design, music. Home: PO Box 3224 Cody WY 82414-5913

SKIDMORE, DONALD EARL, JR., government official; b. Tacoma, Apr. 27, 1944; s. Donald E. and Ingeborg (Johnsrud) S.; BSc, Evangel Coll., 1968. With Dept. Social and Health Svcs., State of Wash., Yakima, 1967-74; quality rev. specialist Social Security Adminstrn., Seattle, 1974-76, program analyst, Balt., 1976-79, Seattle, 1979-81, quality assurance officer, mgr. Satellite office, Spokane, Wash., 1981-84, program analyst, Seattle, 1984-90, mgmt. analyst, 1990—. Pres., bd. dirs. Compton Court Condo Assn., 1980-81; v.p., trustee Norwood Village, 1987-90; vice chair ops. subcom., mem. citizen's adv. com. METRO, 1987-89; mem. citizen's adv. com. land use planning, Bellevue, Wash., 1988-90. Grad. Bellevue Police Citizen's Acad., 1992. Office: Ste 1000 M/S 103 701 Fifth Ave Seattle WA 98104

SKIELLER, CHRISTIAN, manufacturing executive; b. Copenhagen, Mar. 23, 1948; came to U.S., 1979; s. Erik C. and Vibeke (Tvilstegaard) S.; m. Kathleen E. Christman, Jan. 11, 1986; children: Claudia Christman, Christina Christman. MSc, Tech. U. Denmark, Copenhagen, 1971; MBA, Stanford U., Calif., 1981. Mgr. mfg. ops. Schou Mfg., Copenhagen, 1972-76; systems engr. IBM, Copenhagen, 1976-79; partner, gen. mgr. CSMC, Menlo Park, Calif., 1982-84; mfg. mgr. Oximetrix/Abbott Labs., Mountain View, Calif., 1984-87; prin. cons. Christian Skieller Cons., Menlo Park, 1987-90; v.p. ops. ABAXIS, Mountain View, 1990-91; v.p. mfg. Medtronic Cardio-Rhythm, San Jose, Calif., 1992-96; v.p. ops. Cardio Thoracic Systems, Cupertino, CA, 1996—. Mem. Am. Prodn. and Inventory Control Soc. Home: 55 Black Fox Way Woodside CA 94062-4103

SKILLIN, THERESE JENO, elementary school educator; b. San Jose, Calif., Feb. 16, 1956; d. Joseph John and Eloise Martha (Holden) Jeno; m. Robert Hance Skillin, Sept. 28, 1985;; children: Paul Holden, Julia Rose, Anna Katherine. BA, San Francisco State U., 1978, MA, 1983. Cert. Calif. multiple subject life tchr. Tchr. Lost Hills (Calif.) Union Sch., 1979-81, Panama Unified Sch. Dist., Bakersfield, Calif., 1981-85, Santa Paula (Calif.) Sch. Dist., 1985-90; adult literacy tutor Family Literacy Aid to Reading

Program, Bakersfield, 1986, 87; cons. Ventura (Calif.) County Farm Bus., 1987-88, Ventura County Supt. County Schs.; sci. specialist, chair Ventura County Environ. and Energy Edn. Coun., 1990; originator, presenter Farm Day, Kern and Ventura Counties; presenter Ventura County Creative Arts Seminar, 1990, Calif. Kindergarten Conf., San Francisco, 1995; tchr. agrl. seminar, Ker County, 1992-96. Author children's books. Recipient award of appreciation Kern Co. Farm Bur., 1996. Mem. AAUW (mem. Camarillo Creative Arts Workshop 1988), Ventura County Reading Assn., Northern Calif. Kindergarten Assn., So. Calif. Assn. Sci. Specialists, Wasco Jr. Woman's Club (sec. 1982-83, v.p. 1983-84, dir. Annual Fun Run, named Woman of Yr. 1982), Santa Barbara Cactus and Succulent Soc. (cons.), Petroleum Wives Assn. (com. chairperson 1993-94). Democrat. Roman Catholic. Avocations: hiking, skiing, sewing, crafts. Home and Office: 2901 22nd St Bakersfield CA 93301-3237

SKINNER, HOWARD MORSE, college dean, educator; b. Montgomery, Ala., July 19, 1930; s. Howard Morse and Ada Emma (Rupp) S.; m. Beverley Mae Erickson, June 8, 1951; children: Teresa Kay, Kent Howard, Diane Lee. BA, Sterling Coll., 1951; MusB, MacPhail Coll. Music, 1953, MusM, 1954; MusD, Northwestern U., 1961. Asst. prof. music Taylor U., Upland, Ind., 1954-56; assoc. prof. music Tex. Wesleyan Coll., Ft. Worth, Tex., 1956-63; from prof. music to pres. U. Northern Colo., Greeley, Colo., 1963-96, pres., 1996-98. Conductor, dir. Greeley (Colo.) Philharmonic Orchestra, 1970—. Recipient Choral Conductor of Yr. award Colo. Music Educators Assn., 1995. Mem. Am. Choral Dirs. Assn., Music Educators Nat. Conference. Avocations: reading, jogging. Home: 1357 43rd Ave Greeley CO 80634-2449 Office: U No Colo Frasier Hall Greeley CO 80639

SKINNER, KNUTE RUMSEY, poet, English educator; b. St. Louis, Apr. 25, 1929; s. George Rumsey and Lidi (Skjoldvig) S.; m. Jeanne Pratt; 1953; divorced 1954; 1 child, Frank; m. Linda Kuhn, Mar. 30, 1961 (div. Sept. 1977); children: Dunstan, Morgan; m. Edna Kiel, Mar. 25, 1978. Student, Culver-Stockton Coll., 1947-49; BA, U. No. Colo., 1951; MA, Middlebury Coll., 1954; PhD, U. Iowa, 1958. Instr. English U. Iowa, Iowa City, 1955-56, 57-58, 60-61; asst. prof. English Okla. Coll. for Women, 1961-62; lectr. creative writing Western Wash. U., Bellingham, 1962-71; asso. prof. English Western Wash. U., 1971-73, prof. English, 1973-97; pres. Signpost Press Inc., nonprofit corp., 1983-95. Author: Stranger with a Watch, 1965, A Close Sky Over Killaspuglonane, 1968, 75, In Dinosaur Country, 1969, The Sorcerers: A Laotian Tale, 1972, Hearing of the Hard Times, 1981, The Flame Room, 1983, Selected Poems, 1985, Learning to Spell "Zucchini," 1988, The Bears and Other Poems, 1991, What Trudy Knows and Other Poems, 1994, The Cold Irish Earth: New and Selected Poems of Ireland, 1965-1995, 1996, An Afternoon Quiet and Other Poems, 1998; editor: Bellingham Rev., 1977-83, 93-95; contbr. poetry, short stories to anthologies, textbooks, periodicals. Nat. Endowment for the Arts fellow, 1975. Mem. Am. Conf. Irish Studies, Wash. Poets Assn.

SKLADAL, ELIZABETH LEE, retired elementary school educator; b. N.Y.C., May 23, 1937; d. Angier Joseph and Julia May (Roberts) Gallo; m. George Wayne Skladal, Dec. 26, 1956; children: George Wayne Jr., Joseph Lee. BA, Sweet Briar Coll., 1958; EdM, U. Alaska, 1976. Choir dir. Main Chapel, Camp Zama, Japan, 1958-59, Ft. Lee, Va., 1963-65; choir dir. Main Chapel and Snowhawk, Ft. Richardson, Alaska, 1968-70; tchr. Anchorage (Alaska) Sch. Dist., 1970-98. Active Citizen's Adv. Com. for Gifted and Talented, Anchorage, 1981-83; mem. music com. Anchorage Sch. Dist., 1983-86; soloist Anchorage Opera Chorus, 1969-80, Cmty. Chorus, Anchorage, 1968-80; mem. choir First Presbyn. Ch., Anchorage, 1971—, deacon, 1988—, elder, 1996—, mission com. chair, 1996—; participant 1st cultural exch. from Anchorage to Magadan, Russia with Alaska Chamber Singers, 1992; participant mission trip to Swaziland, Africa with First Presbyn. Ch., Anchorage, summer 1995. Named Am. Coll. Theater Festival winner Amoco Oil Co., 1974; recipient Cmty. Svc. award Anchorage U. Alaska Alumni Assn., 1994-95. Mem. AAUW, Anchorage Concert Assn. Patron Soc. (assocs. coun. of dirs.), Alaska Chamber Singers, Am. Guild Organists (former dean, former treas., mem.-at-large). Republican. Presbyterian. Avocations: camping, travel, cycling, fishing, cross-country skiing, gardening. Home: 1841 S Salem Dr Anchorage AK 99508-5156

SKLAR, LOUISE MARGARET, service executive; b. L.A., Aug. 12, 1934; d. Samuel Baldwin Smith and Judith LeRoy (Boughton) Nelson; m. Edwynn Edgar Schroeder, Mar. 20, 1955 (div. July 1975); children: Neil Nelson, Leslie Louise Schroeder Grandclaudon, Samuel George; m. Martin Sklar, Oct. 17, 1983. Student, U. So. Calif., 1952-54, UCLA, 1977-79. Acct. Valentine Assocs., Northridge, Calif., 1976-78, programmer, 1978-79; contr. Western Monetary, Encino, Calif., 1979-81; pres. Automated Computer Composition, Chatsworth, Calif., 1984—. Mem. Am. Contract Bridge League (bd. govs. 1993—, mem. nat. charity com. 1982, mem. nat. goodwill com. 1994—), Assn. Los Angeles County Bridge Units (bd. dirs. 1990—, sec. 1984-86), DAR, Conn. Soc. Genealogists, Ky. Hist. Soc., So. Calif. Assistance League, Heart of Am. Geneal. Soc., Chatsworth C. of C., Greater L.A. Zoo Assn., Safari Club Internat., Zeta Tau Alpha. Republican. Avocations: tournament bridge, travel. Office: Automated Computer Composition Inc 21356 Nordhoff St Chatsworth CA 91311-6917

SKLAR, RICHARD LAWRENCE, political science educator; b. N.Y.C., Mar. 22, 1930; s. Kalman and Sophie (Laub) S.; m. Eva Molineux, July 14, 1962; children: Judith Anne, Katherine Elizabeth. A.B., U. Utah, 1952; M.A., Princeton U., 1957, Ph.D., 1961. Mem. faculty Brandeis U., U. Ibadan, Nigeria, U. Zambia, SUNY-Stony Brook, UCLA; now prof. emeritus polit. sci. UCLA; mem. fgn. area fellowship program Africa Nat. Com., 1970-73; Simon vis. prof. U. Manchester, Eng., 1975, Fulbright vis. prof. U. Zimbabwe, 1984; Lester Martin fellow Harry S. Truman Rsch. Inst., Hebrew U. Jerusalem, 1979; fellow Africa Inst. of South Africa, 1994—. Author: Nigerian Political Parties: Power in an Emergent African Nation, 1963, Corporate Power in an African State, 1975; co-author: Postimperialism: International Capitalism and Development, 1987, African Politics and Problems in Development, 1991; co-editor: Postimperialism and World Politics, 1999; contbr. articles to profl. jours. Served with U.S. Army, 1952-54. Rockefeller Found. grantee, 1967. Mem. Am. Polit. Sci. Assn., African Studies Assn. (dir. 1976-78, 80-83, v.p. 1980-81, pres. 1981-82), AAUP (pres. Calif. Conf. 1980-81). Home: 1951 Holmby Ave Los Angeles CA 90025-5905

SKLAREWITZ, NORMAN, journalist; b. Chgo., Feb. 1, 1924; s. Max and Anne Rae (Datnow) S.; m. Esther Louise Bohn, July 18, 1948. BA, Ind. U., 1948; MLA, U. So. Calif., 1978. Civilian reporter Stars & Stripes, Tokyo, 1956-59; corr. Wall St. Jour., Tokyo, N.Y.C., 1963-70, San Francisco, 1963-70; bur. chief U.S. News & World Report, L.A., 1970-74; freelance journalist Beverly Hills, Calif., 1974—. With AUS, 1943-46, ETO. Mem. Am. Soc. Journalists and Authors, Soc. Am. Travel Writers. Office: PO Box 5385 Beverly Hills CA 90209-5385

SKLOVSKY, ROBERT JOEL, naturopathic physician, pharmacist, educator; b. Bronx, N.Y., Nov. 19, 1952; s. Nathan and Esther (Steinberg) S. BS, Bklyn. Coll., 1975; MA in Sci. Edn., Columbia U., 1976; PharmD, U. of Pacific, 1977; D in Naturopathic Medicine, Nat. Coll. Naturopathic Medicine, 1983. Intern Tripler Army Med. Ctr., Honolulu, 1977; prof. pharmacology Nat. Coll. Naturopathic Medicine, Portland, Oreg., 1982-85; pvt. practice Milwaukie, Oreg., 1983—; cons. State Bd. Naturopathic Examiners, Oreg., Hawaii, Clackamas County Sherriff's Dept., Internat. Drug Info. Ctr., N.Y.C., 1983—, Albert Roy Davis Scientific Rsch. Lab, Orange Park, Fla. 1986. Recipient Bristol Labs. award, 1983. Mem. Am. Assn. Naturopathic Physicians, Oreg. Assn. Naturopathic Physicians, N.Y. Acad. Sci. Avocations: classical and jazz music, tap dance, art, botany, acting. Office: 6910 SE Lake Rd Portland OR 97267-2101

SKOGEN, HAVEN SHERMAN, investment company executive; b. Rochester, Minn., May 8, 1927; s. Joseph Harold and Elpha (Hemphill) S.; m. Beverly R. Baker, Feb. 19, 1949; 1 child, Scott H. BS, Iowa State U., 1950; MS, Rutgers U., 1954, PhD, 1955; MBA, U. Chgo., 1970. Registered [illegible] Elmhurst (Ill.) Coll., 1957-58; chief engr. Stackpole, St. Marys, Pa., 1958-62; plant mgr. Magnatronics, Elizabethtown, Ky., 1962-65; mgr. Allen-Bradley, Milw., 1965-70; v.p. Dill-Clithrow, Chgo., 1970-74, oil co. exec. Occidental [illegible]

1992—. Author: Synthetic Fuel Combustion, 1984; inventor radioactive retort doping, locus retorting zone. Naval Rsch. fellow, 1951-55. Fellow Am. Inst. Chemists; mem. Internat. Platform Assn., Masons, Elks, Sigma Xi, Phi Beta Kappa, Phi Lambda Upsilon. Republican. Avocations: fly fishing, travel, reading, teaching. Home: 3152 Primrose Ct Grand Junction CO 81506-4147

SKOMAL, EDWARD NELSON, aerospace company executive, consultant; b. Kansas City, Mo., Apr. 15, 1926; s. Edward Albert and Ruth (Bangs) S.; m. Elizabeth Birkbeck, Mar. 4, 1951; children: Susan Beth, Catherine Anne, Margaret Elaine; m. Joan Kerner, Apr. 9, 1988. BA, Rice U., Houston, 1947, MA, 1949. Engr., Socony Rsch. Labs., Dallas, 1949-51; asst. sect. head Nat. Bur. Standards, Washington, 1951-56; project engr. Sylvania Research Lab., Palo Alto, Calif., 1956-59; mgr. applications engrng., chief applications engr. Motorola Solid State Systems Div., Phoenix, 1959-63; dir. communications dept. Aerospace Corp., El Segundo, Calif., 1963-86, ret., 1986; mem. Presdl. Joint Tech. Adv. Com. on Electromagnetic Compatibility, Washington, 1965-70, 71-75. Author: Man Made Radio Noise, 1978, Automatic Vehicle Locating Systems, 1980; Measuring the Radio Frequency Environment, 1985; contbr. articles to profl. jours. Patentee in field of radio systems, solid state devices, radar cross sect. reduction of ballistic rentry vehicles and solid state microwave components. Elder Riverside Presbytery. With USN, 1944-6. Fellow IEEE (asst. editor Trans. Electromatic Compatibility 1978-86, chmn. tech. adv. com. 1982-86, chmn. tech. com. electromagnetic environments 1976-82, standards com. 1980-86, nat. com. standards coordinating com. on definitions 1986—, Richard A. Stoddart award 1980, cert. of Achievement 1971, Paper of Yr. award 1970); mem. IEEE Electromagnetic Soc. (life), Am. Phys. Soc., Internat. Union Radio Scientists, Sigma Xi. Republican. Presbyterian. Home: 1831 Valle Vista Dr Redlands CA 92373-7246

SKOOG, WILLIAM ARTHUR, former oncologist; b. Culver City, Calif., Apr. 10, 1925; s. John Lundeen and Allis Rose (Gatz) S.; m. Ann Douglas, Sept. 17, 1949; children: Karen, William Arthur, James Douglas, Allison. AA, UCLA, 1944; BA with gt. distinction, Stanford U., 1946, MD, 1949. Intern in medicine Stanford Hosp., San Francisco, 1948-49, asst. resident medicine, 1949-50; asst. resident medicine N.Y. Hosp., N.Y.C., 1950-51; sr. resident medicine Wadsworth VA Hosp., Los Angeles, 1951, attending specialist internal medicine, 1962-68; practice medicine specializing in internal medicine, Los Altos, Calif., 1959-61; pvt. practice hematology and oncology Calif. Oncologic and Surg. Med. Group, Inc., Santa Monica, Calif., 1971-72; pvt. practice med. oncology, San Bernardino, Calif., 1972-94; assoc. staff Palo Alto-Stanford (Calif.) Hosp. Center, 1959-61, U. Calif. Med. Center, San Francisco, 1959-61; asso. attending physician U. Calif. at Los Angeles Hosp. and Clinics, 1961-78; vis. physician internal medicine Harbor Gen. Hosp., Torrance, Calif., 1962-65, attending physician, 1965-71; cons. chemistry Clin. Lab., UCLA Hosp., 1963-68; affiliate cons. staff St. John's Hosp., Santa Monica, Calif., 1967-71, courtesy staff, 1971-72; courtesy attending med. staff Santa Monica Hosp., 1967-72; staff physician St. Bernardine (Calif.) Hosp., 1972-94, hon. staff, 1994—; staff physician San Bernardino Cmty. Hosp., 1972-90, courtesy staff, 1990-94; chief sect. oncology San Bernardino County Hosp., 1972-76; cons. staff Redlands (Calif.) Cmty. Hosp., 1972-83, courtesy staff, 1983-94, hon. staff, 1994—; asst. in medicine Cornell Med. Coll., N.Y.C., 1950-51; jr. rsch. physician UCLA Atomic Energy Project, 1954-55; instr. medicine, asst. rsch. physician dept. medicine UCLA Med. Center, 1955-56, asst. prof. medicine, asst. rsch. physician, 1956-59; clin. asso. hematology VA Center, Los Angeles, 1956-59; co-dir. metabolic rsch. unit UCLA Center for Health Scis., 1955-59, 61-65; co-dir. Health Scis. Clin. Rsch. Ctr., 1965-68, dir., 1968-72; clin. instr. medicine Stanford, 1959-61; asst. clin. prof. medicine, assoc. rsch. physician U. Calif. Med. Center, San Francisco, 1959-61; lectr. medicine UCLA Sch. Medicine, 1961-62, assoc. prof. medicine, 1962-73, assoc. clin. prof. medicine, 1973—. Served with USNR, 1943-46, lt. M.C., 1951-53. Fellow ACP; mem. Am., Calif. med. assns., So. Calif. Acad. Clin. Oncology, Western Soc. Clin. Research, Am. Fedn. Clin. Research, Los Angeles Acad. Medicine, San Bernardino County Med. Soc., Am. Soc. Clin. Oncology, Am. Soc. Internal Medicine, Calif. Soc. Internal Medicine, Inland Soc. Internal Medicine, Phi Beta Kappa, Alpha Omega Alpha, Sigma Xi, Alpha Kappa Kappa. Episcopalian (vestryman 1965-70). Club: Redlands Country. Contbr. articles to profl. jours. Home: 1119 Kimberly Pl Redlands CA 92373-6786

SKRAPEC, CANDICE ANN, criminological psychologist, consultant; b. Kamsack, Sask., Can., June 29, 1952; came to U.S., 1984; d. Albert and Martha Anne (Loucks) S. BSc, U. Calgary, Alta., Can., 1976, MSc, 1980; MPhil, CUNY, 1988, PhD in Criminal Justice, 1997. Cert. and chartered psychologist, Alta. Coord. Police Crisis Unit Calgary Police Svc., 1981-83; psychologist in pvt. practice, 1980-84; rsch. assoc. Am. Correctional Assn./Nat. Ctr. Pub. Productivity, N.Y.C., 1986-87; coord. Diagnostic Ctr. N.Y.C. Dept. Correction/John Jay Coll. Criminal Justice, 1987-90; criminological psychologist N.Y.C., 1985—; psychol. cons./trainer N.Y.C. Police, N.Y.C. Transit Police, N.Y.C. Health and Hosps. Corp., Police Acad., N.Y.C. Dept. Mental Hygiene; adj. faculty in criminology John Jay Coll. Criminal Justice, 1988-92; vis. prof. SUNY, 1992-93; mem. faculty U. Windsor, Can., 1993-94, Calif. State U., Fresno, 1994—; cons. on serial murder and investigative profiling of crime scenes to police, authors, film makers, others, 1986—. Author: Introduction to The Sadist, 1992; contbr. chpts. to books. Grad. Sch. CUNY disting. scholar and dissertation fellow, 1989-90. Mem. Psychologists Assn. Alta. (chartered), Can. Psychol. Assn., Am. Soc. Criminology, Acad. Criminal Justice Scis., N.Y. Acad. Scis, Centre Internat. de Scis. Criminelles (scientific com., hon. mem.). Office: Calif State U Dept Criminology 2225 E San Ramon Ave Fresno CA 93740-8029

SKROCKI, EDMUND STANLEY, II, health fair promoter, executive; b. Schenectady, N.Y., Sept. 6, 1953; s. Edmund Stanley I and Lorraine (Nocian) S.; m. Diane Carolyn Sittig, Sept. 6, 1976 (div. 1992); children: Carolyn, Michelle, Edmund III, Johnathan Edmund; m. Deborrah Anne Allen, June 4, 1998. AA, LaValley Coll., 1981; BA, Sonoma State U., 1982, MA, 1987; postgrad., Am. Inst. Hypnotherapy. Pres. Skrocki's Philos. Svc., Lakeview Terrace, Calif., 1971-81, Redding, Calif., 1982—; pres., CEO Skrocki's Superior Svc., Lakeview Terrace, 1971-76, Redding, Calif., 1976—; pres., CEO, promoter, prodr. Realife Expositions, 1991—; producer Realife Expo Stars Over Hollywood, 1997. Bd. govs., deacon Ch. of Universal Knowledge, 1991—. Named one of Outstanding Young Men Am., 1980. Mem. Shasta Submarine Soc. (pres. 1984—). Avocations: chess, basketball, reading, health, fitness.

SKUJINŠ, JOHN JANIS, soil biochemist, environmental consultant; b. Liepaja, Latvia, Apr. 13, 1926; s. Janis and Zelma (Silinš) S.; m. Irena Vizulis, 1955 (div. 1978); children: Andrejs, Juris. BA in Biochemistry, U. Calif., Berkeley, 1957, PhD in Agrl. Chemistry, 1963. Rsch. biochemist Cornell U., Ithaca, N.Y., 1962-64; rsch. biochemist U. Calif., Berkeley, 1964-69, lectr., 1966-67; assoc. prof. Utah State U., Logan, 1969-76, prof., 1976-89, prof. emeritus, 1989—; vis. scientist, cons. U. Helsinki, Finland, 1977-83, Swedish U. Agr., Uppsala, 1984-86; cons. U.S.-USSR Environ. Agreement Team, U.S. EPA, Moscow, 1976. Editor: Semiarid Lands and Deserts, 1991; co-editor: Soil Biochemistry, 1971, Nitrogen in Desert Ecosystems, 1978; editor-in-chief Arid Soil Rsch. and Rehab., 1987—; contbr. over 60 articles to profl. jours. Pres. Calif. Latvian Assn., San Francisco, 1956-59. Sgt. U.S. Army, 1950-54. Recipient Cert. of Appreciation, U. Helsinki, 1980. Mem. Internat. Symposia on Environ. Biogeochemistry (pres. 1973-89, pres. emeritus 1989—, Cert. of Appreciation 1993), Latvian Acad. Scis., Internat. Soil Sci. Soc. Lutheran. Office: Utah State U Dept Biology 5305 Old Main Hill Logan UT 84322-5305

SKWARA, ERICH WOLFGANG, novelist, poet, educator, literary critic; b. Salzburg, Austria, Nov. 4, 1948; came to U.S., 1975, naturalized, 1981.; s. Alois Gaigg and Hermine Maria Skwara; m. Victoria Anne Dufresne, July 10, 1974 (div. Mar. 1978); m. Gloria Elaine Winniski, June 8, 1978; children: Gabriella Maria, Alexandra Felicitas. BA, U. Paris VII, 1970, MA, Salzburg U., 1972; PhD, N.Y. State U., Albany, 1985. Instr. U. Md., Balt., 1975-77; freelance author Balt. and Paris, 1977-82; vis. lectr. Georgetown U., [illegible] humanities, comparative lit. and German San Diego State U., 1986—; dep. editor-in-chief for cultural affairs Die Welt, Berlin, 1993; cultural and lit. corr. for a number of German and Austrian newspapers and media, 1979—. [illegible]

Island, 1992, Die Heimlichen Könige, 1995, Plague in Siena, 1994, 95, Ice on the Bridge, 1997, Versuch einer Heimkehr, 1998, Nach dem Norden, 1998, The Angel of Death, 1998, Zwischengeschichte, 1999, others; translated (from English and French to German) works by T. Williams, Thomas Wolfe, J.J. Rousseau, Gustave Flaubert, others; own works translated into English, French, Japanese, Arabic, others. Mem. Internat. PEN Club, PEN Ctr. of German Speaking Authors Abroad (bd. dirs. 1985—), PEN Ctr. of Austria, PEN Ctr. of France. Roman Catholic. Avocations: fine wines, travel, walking. Office: San Diego State U Dept Classics/Humanities San Diego CA 92182 also: Suhrkamp Verlag, Linden Str 29-35, D60325 Frankfurt am Main Germany

SKYLSTAD, WILLIAM S., bishop; b. Omak, Wash., Mar. 2, 1934; s. Stephen Martin and Reneldes Elizzbeth (Danzl) S. Student, Pontifical Coll., Josephinum, Worthington, Ohio; M.Ed., Gonzaga U. Ordained priest Roman Catholic Ch., 1960; asst. pastor Pullman, Wash., 1960-62; tchr. Mater Cleri Sem., 1961-68, rector, 1968-74; pastor Assumption Parish, Spokane, 1974-76; chancellor Diocese of Spokane, 1976-77; ordained bishop, 1977; bishop of Yakima, Wash., 1977-90, Spokane, Wash., 1990—. Office: Diocese of Spokane PO Box 1453 1023 W Riverside Ave Spokane WA 99201-1103 Home: 1025 W Cleveland Ave Spokane WA 99205-3320*

SLACK, DONALD CARL, agricultural engineer, educator; b. Cody, Wyo., June 25, 1942; s. Clarence Ralbon and Clara May (Beightol) S.; m. Marion Arline Kimball, Dec. 19, 1964; children: Jonel Marie, Jennifer Michelle. BS in Agrl. Engring., U. Wyo., 1965; MS in Agrl. Engring., U. Ky., 1968, PhD in Agrl. Engring., 1975. Registered profl. engr., Ky., Ariz. Asst. civil engr. City of Los Angeles, 1965; research specialist U. Ky., Lexington, 1966-70; agrl. engring. advisor U. Ky., Tha Phra, Thailand, 1970-73; research asst. U. Ky., Lexington, 1973-75; from asst. prof. to assoc. prof. agrl. engring. U. Minn., St. Paul, 1975-84; prof. U. Ariz., Tucson, 1984—, head dept. agrl. and biosystems engring., 1991—; vis. prof. dept. atmospheric scis. Fed. U. Paraiba, Campina Grande, Brazil, 1997; tech. advisor Ariz. Dept. Water Resources, Phoenix, 1985—, Tucson active mgmt. area, 1996—; cons. Winrock Internat., Morrilton, Ark., 1984, Water Mgmt. Synthesis II, Logan, Utah, 1985, Desert Agrl. Tech. Systems, Tucson, 1985—, Portek Hermosillo, Mex., 1989—, World Bank, Washington, 1992—, Malawi Environ. Monitoring Project, 1996, Mex. Inst. for Water Tech., 1997, Nat. Agrl. Rsch. Inst. La Serema, Chile, 1997; dep. program support mgr. Rsch. Irrigation Support Project for Asia and the Near East, Arlington, Va., 1987-94; mem. adv. team Cearan Found. for Meteorology and Hydrology, Fortaleza, Brazil, 1995—; mem. internat. adv. panel Matrou Resources Mgmt. Project, World Bank, Egypt, 1996—. Contbr. articles to profl. jours. Fellow ASCE (Outstanding Jour. Paper award 1988), Am. Soc. Agrl. Engrs. (Ariz. sect. Engr. of Yr. 1993); mem. Am. Geophys. Union, Am. Soc. Agronomy, Soil Sci. Soc. Am., Am. Soc. Engring. Edn., SAR, Brotherhood of Knights of the Vine (master knight), Sigma Xi, Tau Beta Pi, Alpha Epsilon, Gamma Sigma Delta. Democrat. Lutheran. Achievements include 3 patents pending; developer of infrared based irrigation scheduling device. Avocations: hunting, camping, hiking, model railroading. Home: 9230 E Visco Pl Tucson AZ 85710-3167 Office: U Ariz Agrl Biosystems Engring Tucson AZ 85721

SLADOJE, GEORGE, business executive; b. Duncanwood, Ohio, Apr. 19, 1942; s. Marko and Jovanka (Tepavcevic) S.; m. Susan Mueller Sladoje, July 20, 1968; children: Steven Thomas, Julie Anne, Kathryn Jane. BS, Ohio State U., 1965; MBA, Northwestern U., 1973. CPA, Ill. Staff acct. Am. Hosp. Supply, Evanston, 1967-69; audit, cons. mgr. Peat, Marwick, Mitchell & Co., Chgo., 1969-76; asst. to corp. contr. McGraw-Edison Co., Elgin, Ill., 1976-78; exec. v.p. Chgo. Bd. of Trade, Chgo., 1978-93; exec. v.p., CFO Chgo. Stock Exch., 1993-97; pres., CEO Calif. Power Exch., Pasadena, 1998—; cons., Chgo., 1997; adv. bd. Max Fisher Coll. of Bus. Ohio State U., 1992—, Kellogg Alumni adv. bd. Kellogg Sch. of Bus., Evanston, Ill., 1996—. Chmn. screening com. Glenbrook H.S. #225 Caucus, Glenview, Ill., 1992; chmn. Gleenbrook South Booster Club, 1991. Mem. AICPA, L.A. World Affairs Coun., Fin. Execs. Inst., (exec. com. 1988-92), Econ. Club of Chgo. (greeting com. 1982—), Futures Industry Assn., Pres. Club Ohio State U., Ohio State U. Alumni Assn. (chmn. alumni adv. coun. 1996-98). Home: 462 Ida May Ln Sierra Madre CA 91024 Office: Calif Power Exch Corp 1000 S Fremont Ave Alhambra CA 91803

SLAGLE, KENNETH A., engineering manager; b. Oakland, Calif., July 12, 1945; s. Edward A. and Effie B. (Briley) S.; m. Deanna S. Mason, Sept. 9, 1967; children: Shelly, Kevin. BS in Engring., UCLA, 1967; MS in Civil Engring., Calif. State U., Long Beach, 1969; MBA, U. So. Calif., L.A., 1975. Registered profl. engr., Calif. Startup supr. So. Calif. Edison San Onofre Nuc. Sta., San Clemente, 1980-82, maintenance mgr., 1982-83, project mgr., 1983-85, adminstrv. svcs. mgr., 1985-89, outage mgr., 1989-94, quality mgr., 1994—. Mem. Am. Soc. Civil Engrs., Am. Nuclear Soc. Office: So Calif Edison PO Box 128 San Clemente CA 92674-0128

SLATER, DON AUSTIN, shipyard executive, consultant; b. Bay City, Mich., May 27, 1938; s. William Stuart and Inez Fern (Hagen) S.; m. Sara Belva Sanford, Feb. 3, 1962; children: Shandra Sanford, Nathan Dorman. BS in Naval Architecture and Marine Engring., U. Mich. Naval architect Western Boat Bldg. Corp., Tacoma, 1964; exec. v.p. and gen. mgr. Star Marine Industries, Tacoma; gen. mgr. Shipyard div. Marine Iron Works, Tacoma; pres., CEO Marine Industry N.W., Inc., Tacoma, 1976—; cons. to various law firms, Wash. and N.J., 1975—; arbitrator Am. Arbitration Assn., 1985—. 1st v.p. Va. V Found., Seattlem 1986; bd. dirs. Puget Sound Marine Hist. Soc., 1978-80. Mem. Soc. Naval Architects and Marine Engrs. Avocations: boating, wood carving, collecting antique boats. Fax: (253) 627-1094. E-mail: dslater@mininw.com. Home: 30720 43rd Ave SW Federal Way WA 98023-2164 Office: Marine Industries NW Inc PO Box 1275 Tacoma WA 98401-1275

SLATER, KEN G., motion picture executive; s. Jerry Lee and June Elisabeth (Plum) S.; m. Victoria Jeannette Wilson, July 13, 1996; 1 child, Diane Kristen. BS in Motion Pictures, Mont. State U., 1973. Prodr./dir. YWAM, Switzerland, 1973-77; pres. Western Am. Films, Bozeman, Mont., San Diego, Calif., 1978-90; prodr. effects Video It, L.A., 1991-96; playback graphics cons. Dreamworks, L.A., 1997; pres. Moving Pictures, L.A., 1998—; chmn. Premise, L.A., 1996-98. Cons.: (movie) Deep Impact, 1997. Recipient 18 Addy awards, Mont. Advt. Assn., 1980-88, 13 Telly awards Nat. Telly awards, Cin., 1984-92, 8 Houston Internat. Film Festival awards HIFF, Houston, 1985-94. Mem. Rotary. Avocation: mountain biking.

SLATER, SHELLEY, telecommunications company administrator; b. Ogden, Utah, June 26, 1959; d. Lynn Russell and Darlene (Allen) Slater; m. Dale Thomas Hansen, Jan. 26, 1977 (div. Feb. 1979); 1 child, Thomas Arthur; m. Eugene Allan DuVall, Mar. 8, 1981 (div. Dec. 1985); 1 child, Gregory Allan; m. Steven Blake Allender, June 9, 1990 (div. May 1993). BBA cum laude, Regis U., 1992, MS in Mgmt., 1997. Installation, repair technician MT Bell, Clearfield, Utah, 1977-81; ctrl. office technician MT Bell, Salt Lake City, 1981-83, engring. specialist, 1983-86; engring. specialist U.S. West Comm., Englewood, Colo., 1986-93; network analyst, documentation and tng. mgr. Time Warner Comm., Englewood, Colo., 1993-97; ops. process mgr. Time Warner Connect, Englewood, Colo., 1997; sr. process mgr. ICG Comms., Englewood, 1997-98; level 3 mgr. Louisville Enterprize Arch., Louisville, 1998—; bus. cons. Jr. Achievement, Denver, 1988-89. Day capt. AZTEC Denver Mus. of Natural History, 1992; loaned exec. Mile High United Way, 1993. Mem. Soc. Cable Telecomms. Engrs., Women in Cable and Telecomms. Democrat. Avocations: snow skiing, biking, softball, golf. Office: Level 3 1450 Infinite Dr Louisville CO 80027-9440

SLATKIN, WENDY, art historian, educator, researcher, writer; b. N.Y.C., June 20, 1950; d. Robert and Helen (Gleischman) S.; m. Fred R. Cohen, June 19, 1984 (dec. Apr. 1990); children: Joshua I., Sara Gail. BA, Barnard Coll., 1970; MA, Villa Schifanoia, Florence, Italy, 1971; PhD, U. Pa., 1976. Asst. prof. Rutgers U., Camden, N.J., 1976-83; lectr. art history U. Calif., [illegible] Poly. U., Pomona, 198—; dir. devel., guest curator Riverside Art Mus., 1998—. Author: Aristide Maillol in the 1890s, 1982; Women Artists in History. From Antiquity to the 20th Century, 1985, 2d edit., 1990, 3d edit., [illegible]

SLATON, STEVEN CHARLES, radio announcer; b. Tacoma, Jan. 16, 1953; s. Walter Charles Slaton and Patricia Anne (Murphy) Jones; m. Cindy Lee Gwinn, Nov. 20, 1976 (div. 1981); 1 child, Allison Patricia; m. Catherine Sutthoff, Apr. 11, 1986; children: Rosemary Frances, Emma Pearl. Grad. high sch., Tacoma. All night disc jockey Sta. KISW-FM, Seattle, 1973-76, mid-day music dir., 1976-78, early evening music dir., 1978-86, asst. program dir. "Afternoon Drive", 1986-92; asst. program dir. "Afternoon Drive" Sta. KZOK-FM, Seattle, 1992—, program dir., 1994-98; music dir., 1998—. Named "Regent" of Seattle Disc Jockeys by Time Mag., 1992. Avocation: collecting antique juke boxes, 1950's baseball cards. Office: Sta KZOK-FM 113 Dexter Ave N Seattle WA 98109-5103

SLAUGHTER, JOHN BROOKS, university administrator; b. Topeka, Mar. 16, 1934; s. Reuben Brooks and Dora (Reeves) S.; m. Ida Bernice Johnson, Aug. 31, 1956; children: John Brooks, Jacqueline Michelle. Student, Washburn U., 1951-53; BSEE, Kans. State U., 1956, DSc (hon.), 1988; MS in Engring., UCLA, 1961; PhD in Engring. Scis, U. Calif., San Diego, 1971; D Engring. (hon.), Rensselaer Poly. Inst., 1981; DSc (hon.), U. So. Calif., 1981, Tuskegee Inst., 1981, U. Md., 1982, U. Notre Dame, 1982, U. Miami, 1983, U. Mass., 1983, Tex. So. U., 1984, U. Toledo, 1985, U. Ill., 1986, SUNY, 1986; LHD (hon.), Bowie State Coll., 1987; DSc (hon.), Morehouse Coll., 1988, Kans. State U., 1988; LLD (hon.), U. Pacific, 1989; DSc (hon.), Pomona Coll., 1989; LHD (hon.), Alfred U., 1991, Calif. Luth. U., 1991, Washburn U., 1992. Registered profl. engr., Wash. Electronics engr. Gen. Dynamics Convair, San Diego, 1956-60; with Naval Electronics Lab. Center, San Diego, 1960-75, div. head, 1965-71, dept. head, 1971-75; dir. applied physics lab. U. Wash., 1975-77; asst. dir. NSF, Washington, 1977-79; dir. NSF, 1980-82; acad. v.p., provost Wash. State U., 1979-80; chancellor U. Md., College Park, 1982-88; pres. Occidental Coll., Los Angeles, 1988—; bd. dirs., vice chmn. San Diego Transit Corp., 1968-75; mem. com. on minorities in engring. Nat. Rsch. Coun., 1976-79; mem. Commn. on Pre-Coll. Edn. in Math., Sci. and Tech. Nat. Sci. Bd., 1982-83; bd. dirs. Monsanto Co., ARCO, Avery Dennison Corp., IBM, Northrop Grumman Corp.; chmn. advancement com. Music Ctr. of L.A. County, 1989-93. Editor: Jour. Computers and Elec. Engring, 1972—. Bd. dirs. San Diego Urban League, 1962-66, pres., 1964-66; mem. Pres.'s Com. on Nat. Medal Sci., 1979-80; trustee Rensselaer Poly. Inst., 1982; chmn. Pres.'s Com. Nat. Collegiate Athletic Assn., 1986-88; bd. govs. Town Hall of Calif., 1990; bd. dirs. L.A. World Affairs Coun., 1990. Recipient Engring. Disting. Alumnus of Yr. award UCLA, 1978, UCLA medal, 1989, Roger Revelle award U. Calif.-San Diego, 1991, Disting. Svc. award NSF, 1979, Svc. in Engring. award Kans. State U., 1981, Disting. Alumnus of Yr. award U. Calif.-San Diego, 1982, Martin Luther King Jr. Nat. award, 1997; Naval Electronics Lab. Ctr. fellow, 1969-70; elected to Topeka High Sch. Hall of Fame, 1983, Hall of Fame of Am. Soc. Engring. Edn., 1993; named Kansan of Yr. by Kans. Native Sons and Daus., 1994. Fellow IEEE (chmn. com. on minority affairs 1976-80), Am. Acad. Arts and Scis.; mem. NAE, Nat. Collegiate Athletic Assn. (chmn. pres. commn.), Am. Soc. for Engring. Edn. (inducted into Hall of Fame 1993), Phi Beta Kappa (hon.), Tau Beta Pi, Eta Kappa Nu. Office: Occidental Coll 1600 Campus Rd Los Angeles CA 90041-3314

SLAUGHTER, RODNEY ALLEN, firefighter, training consultant; b. Inglewood, Calif., Jan. 16, 1954; s. Matthew LaVern and Barbara Jean (Daniels) S.; m. Shirley Mae Barton, Aug. 27, 1975; 1 child, Clinton. Student, Honolulu C.C.; BA in Anthropology, Calif. State U., Sacramento, 1983; postgrad., Calif. State U., Chico. Cert. instr. Calif. State Fire Marshal. Engr. Mather & McClelland AFB Fire Depts., Sacramento, 1978-88; dep. state fire marshal Calif. State Fire Marshal's Office, Chico, 1988-98; sole propr. Dragonfly Comms. Network, Chico, 1998—; cons. Calif. Energy Commn., Sacramento; program cons. Calif. Integrated Waste Mgmt. Bd., Sacramento. Author, editor: (text, video, instr.'s guide) Rings of Fire: Fire Prevention and Suppression of Scrap Tire Piles, 1992, California's I-Zone: Fire Prevention and Mitigation of the Urban/Wildland Interface, 1995, A Solution to Oil Pollution: Fire Prevention for Used Oil Collection Centers, 1996, Emergency Response to Electric Vehicles, 1997, The Fire Service Guide to Proposal Writing, 1998. With USAF, 1974-78. Mem. Internat. Assn. Fire Chiefs (found. scholar 1994), Calif. State Firefighters Assn. Avocations: gardening, bonsai, antique furniture. Fax: (530) 894-5227. E-mail: DragonFly@DragonFlyNet.com. Home: 528 Oak Mill Ct Chico CA 95926 Office: Dragonfly Comms Network PO Box 6476 Chico CA 95927-6476

SLEETER, JOHN WILLIAM HIGGS, physician, health service administrator; b. Toledo, Iowa, Feb. 16, 1917; s. Charles Elmer and Meta DeLad (Higgs) S.; m. Betti Deming, Aug. 28, 1943 (div. Mar. 1963); m. Patricia C. Parker, July 1963 (dec. Oct. 1986); m. Patricia Catherine Parrillo, July 8, 1989; children: John William, Marilee Ann, Thomas David. BA, Cornell Coll., Mt. Vernon, Iowa, 1942; MD, U. Iowa, 1945. Pres. San Gabriel Primary Care, Arcadia, Calif., 1952-62, L.A. County Acad. GP, Calif., 1965-66; inst. paramedic care St. Terisita Hosp., Duarte, Calif., 1970-75; pres., chief operating officer Profsnl. Rev. Area 21, 1970-75; 1st pres. L.A. County Paramedic Commn., 1974-75; pres., CEO, dir. pvt. practice assn., Arcadia, 1984—. Capt. AUS, 1945-49. Mem. Balboa Bay Club, San Gabriel Country Club, Masons (32d degree). Republican. Avocation: golf. Office: 1041 W Huntington Dr Arcadia CA 91007-6536

SLEIGH, EMILY SMITH, artist, writer; b. Hopkinsville, Ky., June 1, 1947; d. James William and Fannie Summers (Stewart) Smith; m. Donald Thornton Gill (div. May 1985); children: Erin Alexandra, Emily Catherine; m. Howard Thomas Sleigh, Jr., Feb. 18, 1995. BS in Art History, Murray State U., 1971; MA in Art History, U. Del., 1981; ABD in Art History, U. Mich., 1984; grad. level sec. tchr. cert. in soc. studies, Austin Peay State U., 1989. Tchg. asst. in art and art history Murray State U., 1971; new accts. mgr. Fort Hood Nat. Bank, 1972-74; tchr. German art and art history Germany, 1974-77; asst. curator Del. Art Mus., 1980; art workshop dir., instr. for children and seniors Pennyroyal Art Coun., Hopkinsville, Ky., 1990-95; writer Oro Valley Times/Desert Eye Pubs., 1996-98; acting chair, instr. art and art history U. Ky., Hopkinsville C.C., 1984-86; adj. art history instr. Austin Peay State U., 1988, U. Ky. C.C. Sys., Fort Campbell Extended Campus, 1994-96; pres. Hopkinsville Art Guild, 1986; juror Tenth Ann. Artist Show, Princeton, Ky., 1986, Sixth Ann. U.S. Recreation Svcs. Art Contest, Aschaffenburg, Germany; mem. Oro Valley Art Adv. Bd., Ariz., 1996—; sec., grant writer Greater Oro Valley Arts Coun., 1996-97. Editor: The School Lady, 1978-79; photographer, reporter: Aberdeen Proving Ground News, 1978-79; author poetry; one woman shows include Sunrisre Art Gallery, Page, Ariz., 1998; represented in permanent collections Murray (Ky.) State U., 1970, Wertheim (Germany) Officers Club, 1976, Adsmore Gallery and Gift Shop, Princeton, Ky., 1992-96, Cappuccino's, Tucson, 1997, Oro Valley (Ariz.) Town Hall Gallery, 1997, Oro Vallery Magistrates Ct., 1997, Oro Valley Pub. Workds Bldg., 1998, El Conquistador Country Club, 1998, others; group exhbns. include Hopkinsville Art Guild Ann. Exhibit, 1967, Bel Air (Md.) Art Gallery, 1978, Hopinsville Dogwood Festival, 1992, The Art Co., 1996, 97, Tucson/Pima County Rural Arts Exhibit, 1998, Tubac Ctr. Arts Gallery, 1998, Tubac Resort and Golf Club, 1999, Tubac Ctr. Arts, 1999; lithographs and watercolors, Europe and U.S.; contbr. articles to profl. jours. Sec. Girl Scout Neighborhood Bd., Aschaffenburg, 1975-77; campaign treas. Co. to Elect W. Bryant, 1999. Recipient Vol. award for cmty. svc. Town of Oro Valley, 1997. Mem. Ariz. Pastel Artists Assn., Nat. Mus. Women in Arts, Aqual-Ariz. Groundwater Users Assn., Coll. Art Assn., Tubac Ctr. for the Arts, Com. Valley's Future. Avocations: photography, freelance reporter, writer. Home and Studio: 12717 N Copper Queen Way Tucson AZ 85737

SLIDE, ANTHONY CLIFFORD, film historian, writer; b. Birmingham, Eng., Nov. 7, 1944; came to U.S., 1971; s. Frederic Clifford and Mary Florence (Eaton) S. LitD (hon.), Bowling Green U., 1990. Editor, pub. The Silent Picture, Eng. and U.S.A., 1968-74; rsch. assoc. Am. Film Inst., Beverly Hills, Calif., 1971-72; assoc. film archivist Am. Film Inst., Washington, 1972-75; film historian Acad. Motion Picture Arts and Scis., Beverly Hills, 1975-80; pvt. practice Studio City, Calif., 1980—; cons. Acad. Motion Picture Arts and Scis., Beverly Hills, 1980-86, That's Hollywood TV series, 1981-82, Lillian Gish: The Actor's Life for Me, PBS, 1988; appraiser of memorabilia; expert witness L.A. Superior Court. Author: over 60 books including Directing: Learn From The Masters, 1996, DeToth On DeToth: Put the Drama in Front of the Camera, 1997, Before, In and After Hollywood: The Autobiography of Joseph Henabery, 1997, Ravished Armenia and the Story of Aurora Mardiganian, 1997, The New Historical Dictionary of the American Film Industry, 1998, Banned in the U.S.A., 1998; editor Filmmakers Series, 1982—; book review editor Classic Images, 1989—; mem. editorial bd. Film History, Am. Film Inst. Catalog; prodr., dir. Portrait of Blanche Sweet and The Silent Feminists: America's First Women Directors, others; creator over 50 film tributes including Groucho Marx, Mary Pickford, W.C. Fields; presentor of film programs at various film festivals; contbr. articles to profl. jours. Organized Britain's first silent film festival; founder The Silent Picture jour., 1968-74. Recipient James R. Quirk Meml. award 1984, Soc. Cinephiles award 1986, Outstanding Reference Source of Yr. award Am. Libr. Assn., 1986, 94, Outstanding Academic Book of Yr. award Choice Mag., 1989, 94. Mem. Internat. Dictionary Films and Filmmakers (adv. bd.), Sinking Creek Film Celebration (adv. bd.), Dorothy and Lillian Gish Film Theatre (nat. adv. com.). Home and Office: 4118 Rhodes Ave Studio City CA 91604-1629

SLIDER, MARGARET ELIZABETH, elementary education educator; b. Spanish Fork, Utah, Nov. 27, 1945; d. Ira Elmo and Aurelia May (Peterson) Johnson; m. Richard Keith Slider, Oct. 25, 1968; children: Thomas Richard, Christopher Alan. AA, Chaffey Coll., 1966; BA, Calif. State U., San Bernardino, 1968, MEd in English as Second Lang., 1993. Cert. elem. tchr., Calif. Tchr. Colton (Calif.) Unified Sch. Dist., 1968—; lead sci. tchr. McKinley Sch., 1994-96; mem. sci. steering com. Colton Joint Unified Sch. Dist., 1996—; mem. kindergarten assessment com. Colton Joint Unified Sch. Dist., Colton, 1988-90, dist. math. curriculum com., 1992-94; trainer Calif. State Dept. Edn. Early Intervention for Sch. Success, 1993—, demonstrator on-site classroom, 1994. Treas. McKinley Sch. PTA, Colton, 1989-91. Mem. NEA, ASCD, AAUW, Calif. Tchrs. Assn., Calif. Elem. Edn. Assn., Calif. Assn. of Tchrs. of English to Students of Other Langs., Calif. Mathematics Coun., Assn. Colton Educators, Pi Lambda Theta. Avocations: needlework, reading, bicycling. Home: 1628 Waterford Ave Redlands CA 92374-3967 Office: Colton Unified Sch Dist 1212 Valencia Dr Colton CA 92324-1731

SLINKER, JOHN MICHAEL, academic director; b. Lafayette, Ind., Jan. 8, 1952; s. William Guy Mahan and Betty Lucille (Utterback) and Richard Earl Slinker; m. Pamela Jo Pickering, Mar. 15, 1975; two children. BS, Ea. N.Mex. U., 1974, MA, 1979; EdD, No. Ariz. U., 1988. Cert. specialist in planned giving; cert. fund-raising exec. Asst. sports infor. dir., news writer Ea. N.Mex. U., Portales, 1970-74, news svcs. dir., sports info. dir., 1974-82; dir. univ. news and publs. No. Ariz. U., Flagstaff, 1982-86; dir. pub. affairs Humboldt State U., Arcata, Calif., 1988-92, dir. univ. rels., 1992—; cons. Calif. Dept. Parks and Recreation, Sacramento, 1989-90. Vol. Boy Scouts Am., Eureka, Calif., 1991-93, dist. commr., 1991-92. Mem. Coun. for Advancement and Support of Edn. (Bronze medal), Sigma Nu (div. comdr. 1976-81, chpt. advisor, Outstanding Alumnus 1976, 79, 81, 82). Republican. Methodist. Avocations: sports, travel, woodworking, stained glass, genealogy. Home: 1971 Gwin Rd McKinleyville CA 95519-3961 Office: Humboldt State U Office Univ Rels Arcata CA 95521

SLOAN, JERRY (GERALD EUGENE SLOAN), professional basketball coach; b. McLeansboro, Ill., Mar. 28, 1942; m. Bobbye; 3 children: Kathy, Brian, Holly. Student, Evansville (Ind.) Coll., 1965. Professional basketball player, Baltimore, 1965-66, Chicago Bulls, NBA, 1966-76; head coach Chicago Bulls, 1979-82; scout Utah Jazz, NBA, Salt Lake City, 1983-84, asst. coach, 1984-88, head coach, 1988—; player 2 NBA All-Star games; named to NBA All-Defensive First Team, 1969, 72, 74, 75. Office: care Utah Jazz Delta Ctr 301 W South Temple Salt Lake City UT 84101-1216*

SLOAN, LANNY GENE, municipal official; b. Denver, Aug. 30, 1945; s. Vincent Eugene and Leta Velma (Atwood) S.; m. Janet Cellen, July 5, 1968 (div. 1973); m. Patti Stucker, 1990. Student, U. Utah, 1963-68; BA in Bus. Mgmt., Lewis-Clark State Coll., 1990. Registered land surveyor, Idaho. Engr.'s technician Idaho Dept. Transp., Jerome, 1970-77; land surveyor Edwards-Howard-Martens, Engrs., Twin Falls, Idaho, 1977-80; project supt. J. Holley Constrn., Wells, Nev., 1981—; dir. pub. works City of Jerome, 1982-90, City of Coos Bay (Oreg.), 1990-93; city adminstr. City of Salmon, Idaho, 1993—; mem. adv. bd. N.W. Tech. Transfer Ctr., Olympia, Wash. Chmn. bd. dirs. Jerome City Libr., 1986-90; bd. trustees Coos Bay Libr., 1991—; bd. dirs. Jerome City Airport, 1986-90, Bay Area Rehab., 1990—. Mem. Am. Pub. Works Assn., Am. Water Works Assn. (trustee intermountain sect. 1987—), Pacific N.W. Pollution Control Assn., Green Drake Soc. Avocations: pvt. pilot, skiing, camping, fishing. Office: City of Salmon 200 Main St Salmon ID 83467-4111

SLOAN, MICHAEL DANA, information systems specialist; b. Santa Monica, Calif., Sept. 30, 1960; s. Avery and Beverly Rae (Krantz) S.; m. Barbara Rogers; 1 child, Ashley Harrison. BS in Bus. Adminstrn., Calif. State U., Northridge, 1983; MBA, Pepperdine U., 1987. Programmer/analyst TICOR, Inc., L.A., 1979-80; data processing analyst Deluxe Check Printers, Inc., Chatsworth, Calif., 1980-83; fin. systems analyst Wismer & Assocs., Inc., Canoga Park, Calif., 1983-84; sr. systems analyst Coast Savs. & Loan, Granada Hills, Calif., 1984-86; microcomputer systems specialist Litton Industries, Woodland Hills, Calif., 1986-87; systems mgr., info. resources mgr. TRW, Inc.- Space and Def., Redondo Beach, Calif., 1987-93; project mgr. Health Net, Woodland Hills, 1993-95; mgr. fin. and sales systems Merisel Ams. Inc., El Segundo, Calif., 1995-97; cons. Data Most, Inc., Chatsworth, 1982-83, Home Savs. & Loan, North Hollywood, Calif., 1987, Micro Tech., L.A., 1987, TRW, Inc.-Space and Def., Redondo Beach, Calif., 1993—, Pacificare Health Systems, Inc., 1997, Nissan Motor Corp., USA., 1998—. Mem. IEEE Computer Soc., Salle Gascon Fencing Club, U.S. Fencing Assn., Delta Sigma Pi. Republican. Avocations: fencing, softball, tennis, volleyball, travel, sailing. Office: 18501 S Figueroa St Gardena CA 90248-4504

SLOAN, PATRICE S., artist; b. Banner Elk, N.C., Jan. 14, 1955; d. George Wallace and Edna Earle (Heaton) Shook; m. Michael L. Sloan, July 1, 1988; 1 child, George Walter Shook. BA in History, U. S.C., 1977, BA in English, 1977. Artist Myrtle Beach, S.C., 1980-88, Juneau, Alaska, 1988-94; artist, gallery owner Dutch Harbor, Alaska, 1994—; graphic cons. Aleutian-Pribilof Islands Assn., Unalaska, Alaska, 1996. Contbg. artist Dutch Harbor Fisherman, 1996; prin. works include pastels Still Water, 1996, The Law, 1996, acrylic Arctic Squirrel, 1996, oil Life in the Arctic, 1996. Mem. Nat. Assn. Fine Arts, Arts for Healthy Alaska, Bering Sea Exch. Home: PO Box 1543 Nome AK 99762-1543

SLOANE, BEVERLY LEBOV, writer, consultant; b. N.Y.C., May 26, 1936; d. Benjamin S. and Anne (Weinberg) LeBov; m. Robert Malcolm Sloane, Sept. 27, 1959; 1 child, Alison Lori Sloane Gaylin. AB, Vassar Coll., 1958; MA, Claremont Grad. U., 1975, doctoral study, 1975-76; cert. in exec. mgmt., UCLA Grad. Sch. Mgmt., 1982, grad. exec. mgmt. program, 1982; grad. intensive bioethics course Kennedy Inst. Ethics, Georgetown U., 1987, advanced bioethics course, 1988; grad. sem. in Health Care Ethics, U. Wash. Sch. Medicine, Seattle, summer 1988-90, 94; grad. Summer Bioethics Inst., Loyola Marymount U., summer 1990; grad. Annual Summer Inst. on Teaching of Writing, Columbia U. Tchrs. Coll., summer 1990; grad. Annual Summer Inst. on Advanced Teaching of Writing, Columbia Tchrs. Coll., summer 1993; grad. Annual Inst. Pub. Health and Human Rights, Harvard U. Sch. Pub. Health, 1994; grad. pub. course profl. pub., Stanford U., 1982; cert. clin. intensive biomedical ethics, Loma Linda U. Med. Ctr., 1989, cert. Ethics Fellow, 1989, cert. clin. intensive biomedical ethics, 1989; grad. exec. refresher course profl. pub., Stanford U., 1994; cert Exec. Mgmt. Inst. in Health Care, U. So. Calif., 1995; cert. in ethics corps tng. program, Josephson Inst. of Ethics, 1991; cert. advanced exec. program Grad. Sch. Mgmt., UCLA, 1995; grad. Women's Campaign Sch., Yale U., 1998. Circulation libr. Harvard Med. Libr., Boston, 1958-59; social worker Conn. State Welfare, New Haven, 1960-61; tchr. English Hebrew Day Sch., New Haven, 1961-64; instr. creative writing and English lit. Monmouth Coll., West Long Branch, N.J., 1967-69; v.p. council grad. students, Claremont Grad. U., 1971-72, adj. dir. Writing Ctr. Speaker Series, 1993—, spkr., 1996, 97, 98; mem. adv. coun. tech. and profl. writing Dept. English, Calif. State U., Long Beach, 1980-82 ; mem. adv. bd. Calif. Health Rev., 1982-83; mem. Foothill Health Dist. Adv. Coun. L.A. County Dept. Health Svcs., 1987-93, pres., 1989-91, immediate past pres., 1991-92; vis. scholar Hastings Ctr., 1996; spkr. N.Y. State Task Force on Life and the Law, 1996; panel spkr. ann. conf. Am. Assn. Suicidology, 1998. Author: From Vassar to Kitchen, 1967, A Guide to Health Facilities: Personnel and Management, 1971, 2nd edit., 1977, 3d edit., 1992. Mem. pub. relations bd. Monmouth County Mental Health Assn., 1968-69; chmn. creative writing group Calif. Inst. Tech. Woman's Club, 1975-79; mem. ethics com., human subjects protection com. Jewish Home for the Aging, Reseda, Calif., 1994-97; mem. task force edn. and cultural activities, City of Duarte, 1987-88; mem. strategic planning task force com., campaign com. for pre-eminence Claremont Grad. U., 1986-87, mem. alumni coun., 1993-96, bd. dirs., governing bd. alumni assn., 1993-96, mem. vol. devel. com., 1994-96, alumnae awards com. 1993-96; Vassar Coll. Class rep. to Alumnae Assn. Fall Coun. Meeting, 1989, class corr. Vassar Coll. Quarterly Alumnae Mag., 1993-98; mem. gift com. class of 1958 40th reunion Vassar Coll., 1997-98, program chmn., 1998, v.p., 1998—; co-chmn. Vassar Christmas Showcase New Haven Vassar Club, 1965-66, rep. to Vassar Coll. Alumnae Assn. Fall Coun. Meeting, 1965-66; co-chmn. Vassar Club So. Calif. Annual Book Fair, 1970-71; chmn. creative writing group Yale U. Newcomers, 1965-66; dir. creative writing group Yale U. Women's Orgn., 1966-67; grad. AMA Ann. Health Reporting Conf., 1992, 93; mem. exec. program network UCLA Grad. Sch. Mgmt., 1987—; trustee Ctr. for Improvement of Child Caring, 1981-83; mem. League Crippled Children, 1982—, bd. dirs., 1988-91, treas. for gen. meetings., 1990-91, chair hostesses com., 1988-89, pub. rels. com., 1990-91; bd. dirs. L.A. Commn. on Assaults Against Women, 1983-84; chmn. 1st ann. Rabbi Camillus Angel Interfaith Svc. Temple Beth David, 1978, v.p., 1983-86, spkr., 1997; mem. cmty. rels. com. Jewish Fedn. Council Greater L.A., 1985-87; del. Task Force on Minorities in Newspaper Bus., 1987-89; cmty. rep. County Health Ctrs. Network Tobacco Control Program, 1991; mem. N.Y. Citizens Com. Health Care Decisions. Recipient cert. of appreciation City of Duarte, 1988, County of L.A., 1988, Ann. Key Mem. award L.A. Dept. Health Svcs., 1990; recipient cert of appreciation Alumni Coun. Claremont Grad Sch., 1996; Coro Found. fellow, 1979; named Calif. Communicator of Achievement, Woman of Yr. Calif. Press Women, 1992. Fellow Am. Med. Writers Assn. (pres. Pacific Southwest chpt. 1987-89, dir. 1980-93, Pacific S.W. del to nat. bd. 1980-87, 89-91, chmn. various conv. coms., chmn . nat. book awards trade category 1982-83, chmn. Nat. Conv. Networking Luncheon 1983-, 84, chmn. freelance sect. 1984-85, gen. chmn. 1985, Asilomar Western Regional Conf., gen chmn. 1985, workshop leader 1985, program co-chmn. 1987, speaker 1985, 88-89, program co-chmn. 1989, nat. exec. bd. dirs. 1985-86, nat. adminstr. sects. 1985-86, pres.-elect Pacific S.W. chpt. 1985-87, pres. 1987-89, immediate past pres. 1989-91, bd. dirs. 1991-93, moderator gen. session nat. conf. 1987, chair gen. session nat. conf. 1986-87, workshop leader Nat. Ann. Conf. 1984-89, 90-92, 95, chair Walter C. Alvarez Meml. Found. award 1986-87, appreciation award for outstanding leadership 1989, named to Workshop Leaders Honor Roll 1991); mem. Women in Comm. (dir. 1980-82, 89-90, v.p. cmty. affairs 1981-82, N.E. area rep. 1980-81, chmn. awards banquet 1982, sem. leader, speaker ann. nat. profl. conf., 1985, program adv. com. L.A. chpt. 1987, v.p. activities 1989-90, chmn. L.A. chpt. 1st ann. Agnes Underwood Freedom of Info. Awards Banquet 1982, recognition award 1983, nominating com. 1982, 83, com. Women of the Press Awards luncheon 1988, Women in comm. awards luncheon 1988), Am. Assn. for Higher Edn., AAUW (legis. chmn. Arcadia br. 1976-77, books and plays chmn. Arcadia br. 1973-74, creative writing chmn. 1969-70, 1st v.p. program dir. 1975-76, networking chmn. 1981-82, speaker 1987, Cert. of appreciation 1987, chmn task force promoting individual liberties 1987-88, named Woman of Yr., Woman of Achievement award 1986, cert. of appreciation 1987, pres.-elect 1998—, edn. equity chmn. 1998—, chmn. Tech Trek Sci. Camp Scholarship for Girls 1999, Career Day 1999), Coll. English Assn., APHA, Am. Soc. Law, Medicine and Ethics, Calif. Press Women (v.p. programs L.A. chpt. 1982-85, pres. 1985-87, state pres. 1987-89, past immediate past state pres. 1989-91, chmn. state speakers bur. 1989—, del nat. bd. 1989—, moderator ann. spring conv., 1990, 92, chmn. nominating com. 1990-91, Calif. lit. dir. 1990-92, dir. state lit. com. 1990-92, dir. family literacy day Calif., 1990, Cert. of Appreciation, 1991, named Calif. Communicator of Achievement 1992), AAUP, N.Y. Acad. Scis., Ind. Writers So. Calif. (bd. dirs. 1989-90, dir. Specialiazed Groups 1989-90, dir. at large 1989-90, bd. dirs. corp. 1988-89, dir. Speech Writing Group 1991-92), Hastings Ctr. (vis. scholar 1996), AAAS, Nat. Fedn. Press Women (bd. dirs. 1987-93, nat. co-chmn. task force recruitment of minorities 1987-89, del. 1987-89, nat. dir. of speakers bur. 1989-93, editor of speakers bur. directory 1991, cert. of appreciation, 1991, 93, Plenary of Past Pres. state 1989—, workshop leader-speaker ann. nat. conf. 1990, chair state women of achievement com. 1986-87, editor Speakers Bur. Addendum Directory, 1992, editor Speakers Bur. Directory, 1991, 92, named 1st runner up Nat. Communicator of Achievement 1992), Internat. Assn. Bus. Communicators, Soc. for Tech. Comm. (workshop leader 1985, 86), Kennedy Inst. Ethics, Soc. Health and Human Values, Assoc. Writing Programs, Authors Guild, Women's City (Pasadena), Claremont Colls. Faculty House, Pasadena Athletic, Town Hall of Calif. (vice chair cmty. affairs sect. 1982-87, speaker 1986, faculty-instr. Exec. Breakfast Inst. 1985-86, mem. study sect. coun. 1986-88), Rotary (chair Duarte Rotary mag. 1988-89, mem. internat. svc. com. 1989-90, info. svc. com. 1989-90). Home and Office: 1301 N Santa Anita Ave Arcadia CA 91006-2419

SLOANE, ROBERT MALCOLM, university administrator; b. Boston, Feb. 11, 1933; s. Alvin and Florence (Goldberg) S.; m. Beverly LeBov, Sept. 27, 1959; 1 child, Alison Sloane Gaylin. A.B., Brown U., 1954; M.S., Columbia U., 1958. Adminstrv. resident Mt. Auburn Hosp., Cambridge, Mass., 1957-58; med. adminstr. AT&T, N.Y.C., 1959-60; asst. dir. Yale New Haven Hosp., 1961-67; assoc. adminstr. Monmouth Med. Center, Long Branch, N.J., 1967-69; adminstr. City of Hope Nat. Med. Center, Duarte, Calif., 1969-80; pres. Los Angeles Orthopedic Hosp., Los Angeles Orthopedic Found., 1980-86; pres., CEO Anaheim (Calif.) Meml. Hosp., 1986-94; pres. Vol. Hosp. Am. West, Inc., L.A., 1995; healthcare cons. Monrovia, Calif., 1996-98; v.p. Rudolph Dew and Assocs., Torrance, Calif., 1997-98; dir. health adminstrn. program U. So. Calif., L.A., 1998—; mem. faculty Columbia U. Sch. Medicine, 1958-59, Yale U. Sch. Medicine, 1963-67, Quinnipac Coll., 1963-67, Pasadena City Coll., 1972-73, Calif. Inst. Tech., 1973-85, U. So. Calif., 1976-96, clin. prof. 1987-95, 98—, UCLA, 1985-87; chmn. bd. Health Data Net, 1971-73; bd. dirs. Intervalley Health Plan, 1995—; pres. Anaheim Meml. Devel. Found., 1986-94; pres., CEO InTech Health Sys., Inc., 1996—; sr. cons. APM, Inc., 1996-97. Author: (with B. L. Sloane) An Introduction to Health Care Delivery, Organization, Functions and Management, 1971, 2d edit., 1977, 3d edit., 1992, 4th edit., 1999; mem. editl. and adv. bd. Health Devices, 1972-90; contbr. articles to hosp. jours. Bd. dirs. Health Systems Agy. Los Angeles County, 1977-78, Vol. Hosps. of Am., 1986-95, chmn., 1993-94, pres., 1995; bd. dirs. Calif. Hosp. Polit. Action Com., 1979-87, vice chmn., 1980-83, chmn., 1983-85. Served to lt. (j.g.) USNR, 1954-56. Fellow Am. Coll. Healthcare Execs. (regent 1989-93, nominations com. 1994-97); mem. Am. Hosp. Assn., Healthcare Assn. So. Calif. (bd. dirs. , sec. 1982, treas. 1983, chmn. elect 1984, chmn. 1985, past chmn. 1986, 89), Calif. Healthcare Assn. (bd. dirs. exec. com. 1984-86, 89), Anaheim C. of C. (bd. dirs. 1994). Home: 1301 N Santa Anita Ave Arcadia CA 91006-2419 Office: U So Calif VKC373E University Park Los Angeles CA 90089

SLOAN PINK, ANDREA, lawyer, writer; b. Pasadena, Calif., Sept. 15, 1962; d. Peter O'Neil and Anne Marie (Bárczay) Sloan; m. Jonathan Stuart Pink, May 17, 1961; 1 child, Alexandra Hélène Bárczay P. BA, UCLA, 1984, MFA, 1993, JD, 1996. Bar: Calif. 1997. Assoc. Cooley Godward LLP, San Diego, Calif., 1997-98, Gibson, Dunn & Crutcher LLP, Irvine, Calif., 1998—. Contbr. short stories to anthologies. Recipient Ruth Brill scholarship, UCLA, 1992, Internat. Student and Scholars Essay award, 1992. Avocations: gardening, travel, collecting art and antiques. E-mail: asloanpink@gdclaw.com. Office: Gibson Dunn & Crutcher LLP 4 Park Plz Irvine CA 92614

SLOMANSON, WILLIAM REED, law educator, legal writer; b. Johnstown, Pa., May 1, 1945; s. Aaron Jacob and Mary Jane (Reed) S.; m. Anna Maria Valladolid, June 24, 1972; children: Lorena, Michael, Paul, Christina. BA, U. Pitts., 1967; JD, Calif. Western U., 1974; LLM, Columbia U., N.Y.C., 1975. Bar: Calif. 1975. Assoc. Booth, Mitchel, Strange & Smith, L.A., 1975-77; prof. law Western State U., San Diego and Fullerton, Calif., 1977-95; prof. Thomas Jefferson Sch. of Law, 1996—; judge Provisional Dist. World Ct., L.A., 1990—. Author: (reference book) International Business Bibliography, 1989, (textbooks) Fundamental Perspectives on International Law, 1990, 2nd edit., 1995, 3rd edit., 1999, California Civil Procedure, 1991, California Civil Procedure in a Nutshell, 1992, (practitioner's treatise) The Choice Between State and Federal Courts in California, 1994, supplement, 1996. Lt. USN, 1967-71, Vietnam. Mem. Am. Soc. Internat. Law (chair,

editor newsletter on UN decade of internat. law), San Diego County Bar Assn. (co-chair internat law sect 1988-92). Office: Thomas Jefferson Sch Law 2121 San Diego Ave San Diego CA 92110-2928

SLUSSER, ROBERT WYMAN, aerospace company executive; b. Mineola, N.Y., May 10, 1938; s. John Leonard and Margaret McKenzie (Wyman) S.; BS, MIT, 1960; MBA, Wharton, 1962; ERC, Ft. Belvior Def. Systems Mgmt. Sch., 1977; AMP, Claremont, 1982; m. Linda Killeas, Aug. 3, 1968; children: Jonathan, Adam, Robert, Mariah. Assoc. adminstr.'s staff NASA Hdqrs., Washington, 1964-65; with Northrop Corp., Hawthorne, Calif., 1965-96, adminstr. Space Labs., 1965-68, mgr. bus. and fin. Warnecke Electron Tubes Div., Chgo., 1968-71, mgr. bus. and fin. Aircraft Systems Div., 1971-75, mgr. adminstrn. F-18/Cobra programs, also mgr. F-18 design to cost program, 1975-79, mgr. engring. adminstrn., 1980-82, acting v.p. engring., 1982, v.p. info. resources, 1983-91, mgr. long range planning, 1991-93; program mgr.-bus. F/A-18E/F program, 1994-96, cons. 1996—. CFO, bd. dirs. So. Calif. Hist. Aviation Found., 1987-90, chmn. of bd., pres., 1990-97; treas. Flight Path Learning Ctr. of So. Calif., 1996—; bd. dirs., contracting officer, PDES, 1988-91; mem. dirs. adv. bd. S.C. Rsch. Authority, 1991-95. Grumman Aircraft Engring. scholar, 1956-60. Fellow AIAA (assoc., membership chmn. L.A. sect. 1996-98); mem. So. Calif. Soc. Info. Mgnt., (mem. exec. com. 1987-91), Northrop Mgmt. Club (bd. dirs. 1992-93, Man of Yr. 1991-92). Home: 7270 Berry Hill Dr Rancho Palos Verdes CA 90275-4402

SMALLIE, PAUL (DONALD), author, editor and publisher; b. Madera, Calif., Aug. 22, 1913; s. Robert Samuel and Lillie (Kelly) S.; m. Margret Lloyds, Feb. 8, 1952; children: Marlies Diane Smallie Wickham, Donald David, Dennis Robert. Doctor of Chiropractic, Ratledge Chiropractic Coll., 1935; HHD (hon.), Columbia U., 1972. Mem. faculty San Francisco Chiropractic Coll., 1946-47; editor/publisher WORLD-WIDE REPORT, Stockton, Calif., 1958—. Author: Chiropractic Encyclopedia, 1972, 2d edit. 1980, Scientific Chiropractic, 1985, Happy Healthy Way to Life, 1985, Opening of Chiropractic Mind, 1988. Served with U.S. Army, 1941-42. Mem. Internat. Chiropractors Assn. (exec. sec. 1972-77), Chiropractic Press Guild (pres. 1968-72), Am. Chiropractic Assn., Calif. Chiropractic Assn. (editor 1964-69). Lodge: Lions (pres. 1960-61). Home: 1056 Friar St Stockton CA 95209-1947 Office: 2027 Grand Canal Blvd Stockton CA 95207-6650

SMARANDACHE, FLORENTIN, mathematics researcher, writer; b. Balcesti-Vilcea, Romania, Dec. 10, 1954; came to U.S., 1990; s. Gheorghe and Maria (Mitroiescu) S.; m. Eleonora Niculescu; children: Mihai-Liviu, Silviu-Gabriel. MS in Computer Sci., U. Craiova, 1979; postgrad., Ariz. State U., 1991, U. Phoenix, 1996; PhD in Math., Kishinev U., 1997. Mathematician I.U.G. Craiova, Romania, 1979-81; math. prof. Romanian Coll., 1981-82, 1984-86, 1988; math. tchr. Coop. Ministry, Morocco, 1982-84; French tutor pvt. practice, Turkey, 1988-90; software engr. Honeywell, Phoenix, 1991-95; prof. math. Pima C.C., Tucson, 1995-97; asst. prof. U. N.Mex., 1997—. Author: Nonpoems, 1990, Only Problems, Not Solutions, 1991, numerous other books; contbr. articles to profl. jours. Mem. U.S. Math. Assn., Romania Math. Assn. Zentralblatt fur Math. (reviewer). Achievements include development of Smarandache function, numbers, quotients, double factorials, consecutive sequence, reverse sequence, mirror sequence, destructive sequence, symmetric sequence, permutable sequence, consecutive sieve, prime base, cubic base, square base, class of paradoxes, multi-structure and multi-space, paradoxical geometry, anti-geometry, inconsistent systems of axioms. Office: U N Mex Dept Math Gallup NM 87301

SMART, JOHN MARSHALL, university administrator, educational consultant; b. Santa Barbara, Calif., Aug. 9, 1934; s. John Walter Jr. and Pauline Louise (Hazzard) S.; m. Wiebke von Buch, Nov. 28, 1956 (dec. Oct. 1988); children: Conrad L., Marshall C.; m. Pamela Zamora, Oct. 24, 1992. BA, U. So. Calif., L.A., 1955, MA, 1958, PhD, 1968. Asst. dir., higher edn. specialist Calif. Coord. Coun. for Higher Edn., Sacramento, 1961-70; various adminstrv. positions Calif. State U. Sys., Long Beach, 1970-78, asst. vice chancellor, 1978-83, dep. provost, 1983-87, vice chancellor univ. affairs, 1987-91; spl. asst. to pres. Calif. State U., L.A., 1991—, vice chancellor emeritus, 1991—; sr. cons. Calif. Edn. Round Table, Sacramento, 1991-97; pers. reviewer various univs., 1991—. Contbr. articles to profl. jours. Mem. sch.-to-work program Unite L.A., 1996—. With U.S. Army, 1959-64. Calif. legis. fellow Calif. State Assembly, 1958-59, Coro fellow, 1956-57. Mem. Am. Assn. for Higher Edn., Art Inst. So. Calif. (bd. trustees 1995—), Ctr. for Calif. Studies (adv. bd. 1991—), L.A. Area C. of C. (rep. for Calif. State U. 1985-91), Phi Beta Kappa, Phi Kappa Phi. Democrat. Avocations: traveling, reading, running. Home: 16671 Baruna Ln Huntington Beach CA 92649-3015

SMARTT, RICHARD A., museum director. Dir., sci. chmn. N.Mex. Mus. Natural History, Albuquerque. Office: New Mexico Mus Natural History and Science 1801 Mountain Rd NW Albuquerque NM 87104-1375*

SMEGAL, THOMAS FRANK, JR., lawyer; b. Eveleth, Minn., June 15, 1935; s. Thomas Frank and Genevieve (Andreachi) S.; m. Susan Jane Stanton, May 28, 1966; children: Thomas Frank, Elizabeth Jane. BS in Chem. Engring., Mich. Technol. U., 1957; JD, George Washington U., 1961. Bar: Va. 1961, D.C. 1961, Calif. 1964, U.S. Supreme Ct. 1976. Patent examiner U.S. Patent Office, Washington, 1957-61; staff patent atty. Shell Devel. Co., San Francisco, 1962-65; patent atty. Townsend and Townsend, San Francisco, 1965-91, mng. ptnr. 1974-89; sr. ptnr. Graham and James, San Francisco, 1992-97; pres., ptnr. Knobbe, Martins, Olson & Bear, San Francisco, 1997—; mem. U.S. del. to Paris Conv. for Protection of Indsl. Property. Pres. bd. dirs. Legal Aid Soc. San Francisco, 1982-84, Youth Law Ctr., 1973-84; bd. dirs. Nat. Ctr. for Youth Law, 1978-84, San Francisco Lawyers Com. for Urban Affairs, 1972—, Legal Svcs. for Children, 1980-88; bd. dirs., presdl. nom., Legal Svcs. Corp., 1984-90, 93—. Capt. Chem. Corps, U.S. Army, 1961-62. Recipient St. Thomas More award, 1982. Mem. Ct. of Appeals for Federal Ct. (adv. com. 1992-96), ABA (chmn. PTC sect. 1990-91, ho. of dels. 1988—, mem. standing com. Legal Aid and Indigent Defendants, 1991-94, chair sect. officer conf., 1992-94, mem. bd. govs., 1994-97), standing com. on Pro Bono and Pub. Svc., Nat. Coun. Intellectual Property Law (chmn. 1989), Nat. Inventors Hall Fame (pres. 1988), Calif. Bar Assn. (v.p. bd. govs. 1986-87), Am. Patent Law Assn. (pres. 1986), Internat. Assn. Intellectual Property Lawyers (pres. 1995—), Bar Assn. San Francisco (pres. 1978), Patent Law Assn. San Francisco (pres. 1974). Republican. Roman Catholic. Clubs: World Trade, Olympic, Golden Gate Breakfast (San Francisco); Claremont (Berkeley). Contbr. articles to publs. in field. Office: Knobbe Martens Olson & Bear 275 Battery St Ste 1840 San Francisco CA 94111-3335

SMELICK, ROBERT MALCOLM, investment bank executive; b. Phoenix, Mar. 27, 1942; s. Valentine and Mary Helen (McDonald) S.; m. Gail Paine Sterling, Dec. 10, 1979; children: Christopher Paine, Alexandra McBryde, Gillian Sterling. Ba, Stanford U., 1964; MBA, Harvard U., 1968; postgrad. U. Melbourne (Australia), 1965-66. v.p. Kidder Peabody & Co., Inc., N.Y.C. and San Francisco, 1968-79; mng. dir. First Boston Corp., San Francisco, 1979-89; mng. prin., founder Sterling Payot Company, San Francisco, 1989—; bd. dirs. Willamette Industries, Portland, Oreg., Accrue Software, Inc., Sunnyvale, Calif. Republican. Episcopalian. Office: 222 Sutter St Fl 8 San Francisco CA 94108-4445

SMILANIC, MICHAEL JEROME, art director; b. Denver, Sept. 30, 1957; s. Wallace Joseph and Carmel Josephine S.; m. Rae Marie Pepe, Aug. 16, 1980; children: Max, Minni. BFA, Met. State Coll., 1978. Art dir. Lance Jackson & Associates., Denver; art dir. Brock/Cook Advt., Denver, assoc. creative dir.; art dir. Barnhard Advt., Denver, Karsh & Hagan Advt., Denver; creative dir. Kinzley-Hughes, Denver; sr. art dir. Thomas & Perkins, Denver. Work pub. in Print Mag. Regional Ann., Communication Arts Mag. Advertising Ann. Recipient Gold Clio, 1993, Denver Gold Lion 1991, Silver Athena, 1998. Mem. Denver Advt. Fedn., Art Dirs. Club Denver. Avocations: writing poetry, performing & composing acoustic guitar music.

SMIRNOY, IGOR VASILEVICH, artist; b. St. Petersburg, Russia, Apr. 1, Krilosky, June 25, 1975; as Vasily A. and Alexandra V. Br in Irina B.

Russia, 1971; MA in Engring. Design, Naval Acad., St. Petersburg, Russia, 1975; MA in Psychology, St. Petersburg U., 1986. Restorator Russian Mus., St. Petersburg, Russia, 1976-79; restorator, supr. Mus. Urban Sculpture, St. Petersburg, Russia, 1980-82; designer Mali Balet Theater, St. Petersburg, Russia, 1982-85. Contbr. articles to profl. jours. Avocations: herbal medicine, psychological influence of art. Home and office: 3375 Calle Odessa Carlsbad CA 92009-8623

SMITH, ALAN JAY, computer science educator, consultant; b. N.Y.C., Apr. 10, 1949; s. Harry and Elsie Smith. SB, MIT, 1971; MS, Stanford (Calif.) U., 1973, PhD in Computer Sci., 1974. From asst. prof. to full prof. U. Calif., Berkeley, 1974—; assoc. editor ACM Trans. on Computers Systems, 1982-93; vice-chmn. elec. engring. & computer sci. dept. U. Calif., Berkeley, 1982-84; nat. lectr. ACM, 1985-86; mem. editorial bd. Jour. Microprocessors and Microsystems, 1988—; subject area editor Jour. Parallel and Distbn. Computing, 1989—; mem. IFIP working group 7.3.; program chmn. Sigmetrics 89, Performance 1989, Hot Chips Symposium, 1990, 94, 97. Fellow IEEE (disting. visitor 1986-87); mem. Assn. for Computing Machinery (chmn. spl. interest group on computer architecture 1991-93, chmn. spl. interest group on ops. systems 1983-87, bd. dirs. spl. interest group on performance evaluation 1985-89, bd. dirs. spl. interest group on computer architecture 1993—, nat. lectr. 1985-86), Computer Measurement Group. Office: U Calif Dept of Computer Sci Berkeley CA 94720

SMITH, ALBERT CROMWELL, JR., investments consultant; b. Norfolk, Va., Dec. 6, 1925; s. Albert Cromwell and Georgie (Foreman) S.; m. Laura Thaxton, Oct. 25, 1952; children: Albert, Elizabeth, Laura. BS in Civil Engring., Va. Mil. Inst., 1949; MS in Govtl. Adminstrn., George Washington U., 1965; MBA, Pepperdine U., 1975; PhD in Bus. Adminstrn. LaSalle U., 1994. Enlisted USMC, 1944, commd. 2d lt., 1949, advanced through grades to col., 1970; comdr. inf. platoons, companies, landing force; variously assigned staffs U.K. Joint Forces, U.S. Sec. Navy, Brit. Staff Coll., Marine Staff Coll., U.K. Staff Coll., U.K. Latimer Staff Coll.; adviser, analyst amphibious systems; ret., 1974; pres. A. Cromwell-Smith, Ltd., Charlottesville, Va., 1973, head broker, cons. A. Cromwell Smith, Investments, La Jolla and Coronado, Calif., 1975—. Bd. dirs. Reps. La Jolla, 1975-76; vestryman St. Martin's Episcopal Ch., 1971-73. Decorated Legion of Merit with oak leaf cluster with V device, Bronze Star with V device with oak leaf cluster, Air medal with 2 oak leaf clusters, Purple Heart, Vietnamese Galantry cross with gold star. Mem. ASCE, SAR, Nat. Assn. Realtors, Calif. Assn. Realtors, San Diego Bd. Realtors, Coronado Bd. Realtors, Stockbrokers Soc., So. Calif. Options Soc., Mil. Order Purple Heart. Author: The Individual Investor in Tomorrow's Stock Market, 1977, The Little Guy's Stock Market Survival Guide, 1979, Wake Up Detroit! The EVs Are Coming, 1982, The Little Guy's Tax Survival Guide, 1984, The Little Guy's Sailboat Success, 1996, The Little Guy's Business Success, 1997, Little Guy's Real Estate Success Guide, 1990, Little Guy's Stock Market Success Guide, 1992, Little Guy's Stock Market Future Effectiveness, 1994, Semper Fidelis in Peace and War, 1995, Sailboat Success, 1996, Business Success, 1997, Real Estate Success, 1997, Stock Market Success, 1998, Tax Survival Guide, 1998; contbr. articles to civilian and mil. publs. Office: PO Box 180192 Coronado CA 92178-0192

SMITH, ANDREW VAUGHN, telephone company executive; b. Roseburg, Oreg., July 17, 1924; s. Andrew Britt and Ella Mae (Vaughn) S.; m. Dorothy LaVonne Crabtree, Apr. 25, 1943; children: Janet L., James A. B.S. in Elec. Engring. Oreg. State U., 1950. Registered profl. engr., Oreg. With Pacific N.W. Bell Tel. Co., 1951-89; asst. v.p. ops. Pacific N.W. Bell Tel. Co., Seattle, 1965, v.p. ops., 1970-78; v.p., gen. mgr. Pacific N.W. Bell Tel. Co., Portland, Oreg., 1965-70; v.p. ops. Pacific N.W. Bell Tel. Co., 1970-78; pres. Pacific N.W. Bell Tel. Co., Seattle, 1978-88; pres. ops. U.S. West Communications, 1988-89; exec. v.p. U.S. West Inc., 1989; pres. Telephone Pioneers of Am., 1989-90; ret. U.S. West Inc., 1989; bd. dirs. Bell Commns. Rsch., N.J., Bellevue Prime Source, U.S. Bancorp. Hon. trustee Oreg. State U. Found.; trustee U. Wash. Grad. Sch. Bus., 1985, chmn. bd. trustees, 1984-85; gen. chmn. United Way of King County, 1980-81; mem. Wash. State Investment Com., Olympia, 1989-92; mem. bd. regents U. Wash., 1989-95; trustee Horizon House, Seattle. With USNR, 1943-46. Mem. Seattle C. of C. (chmn. 1985-86). Mem. Wash. Athletic Club (pres. 1982-83), Seattle Yacht Club, Rainier Club, Overlake Golf and Country Club, Columbia Tower Club (Seattle), Desert Island Country Club (Palm Desert, Calif.), The Palm Springs (Calif.) Club. Episcopalian. Office: 1600 Bell Plz Rm 1802 Seattle WA 98191

SMITH, ANITA BINGHAM, accountant, tax preparer; b. Charlotte, N.C., July 11, 1919; d. Irving Westerman and Lula Vernon (McGregor) Bingham; m. Charles Marsden Smith Sr., Sept. 9, 1944; children: Anita Dempsey, Thomas, Charles M. Jr., Martha. Cert., Queens Coll., 1936. Lic. tax preparer, Calif. Acct. B. R. Sharp & Co., Riverside, Calif., 1953-59; asst. office mgr. Crail Fuller Co., Vandenberg AFB, Calif., 1959-61; tchr. Govt. Guam (Mich.), 1961-62; pvt. practice acct. and tax preparer Riverside, 1965—. Treas. Riverside County Rep. Ctrl. Com., 1973-83; v.p. and pres. Rubidoux Cmty. Svcs. Dist., Riverside, 1978—; treas. Riverside Art Mus., 1980-84; pres. Riverside Art Alliance, 1986-87; treas. Legislator and Senator, Calif. State Legislature, Riverside, 1987—; chairperson and vice chairperson bd. dirs. Calif. State Water, Riverside, 1983-95;. Anita B. Smith Treatment Facility named in her honor Rubidoux Cmty. Svcs. Dist., 1995; floral design chosen for floral arrangement calender Nat. Coun. State Garden Clubs Inc., 1997. Presbyterian. Avocations: orchid hobbyist, floral arranger, political activist, community service. Home: 5881 Sandoval Ave Riverside CA 92509-6343

SMITH, BARBARA BARNARD, music educator; b. Ventura, Calif., June 10, 1920; d. Fred W. and Grace (Hobson) S. B.A., Pomona Coll., 1942; Mus.M., U. Rochester, 1943, performer's cert., 1945. Mem. faculty piano and theory Eastman Sch. Music, U. Rochester, 1943-49; mem. faculty U. Hawaii, Honolulu, 1949—; assoc. prof. music U. Hawaii, 1953-62, prof., 1962-82, prof. emeritus, 1982—; sr. fellow East-West Center, 1973; lectr. recitals in Hawaiian and Asian music, U.S., Europe and Asia, 1956—; field researcher Asia, 1956, 60, 66, 71, 80, Micronesia, 1963, 70, 87, 88, 90, 91, Solomon Islands, 1976. Author publs. on ethnomusicology. Mem. Internat. Soc. Music Edn., Internat. Musicol. Soc., Am. Musicol. Soc., Soc. Ethnomusicology, Internat. Coun. for Traditional Music, Asia Soc., Am. Mus. Instrument Soc., Coll. Music Soc., Soc. for Asian Music, Music Educators Nat. Conf., Pacific Sci. Assn., Assn. for Chinese Music Rsch., Phi Beta Kappa, Mu Phi Epsilon. Home: 1314 Kalakaua Ave Apt 1403 Honolulu HI 96826-1929

SMITH, BERNARD JOSEPH CONNOLLY, civil engineer; b. Elizabeth, N.J., Mar. 11, 1930; s. Bernard Joseph and Julia Susan (Connolly) S.; BS, U. Notre Dame, 1951; BS in Civil Engring., Tex. A&M U., 1957; MBA in Fin., U. Calif.-Berkeley, 1976; m. Josephine Kerley, Dec. 20, 1971; children: Julia Susan Alice Birmingham, Teresa Mary Josephine, Anne Marie Kathleen. Asst. Bernard J. Smith, cons. engr. office, Dallas, 1947-57; hydraulic engr. C.E. U.S. Army, San Francisco, 1957-59, St. Paul dist., 1959-60, Kansas City (Mo.) dist., 1960-63, Sacramento dist., 1963-65; engr. Fed. Energy Regulatory Commn., San Francisco Regional Office, 1965— Served with U.S. Army, 1952-54. Registered profl. engr., Calif.; Mo.; lic. real estate broker, Calif. Mem. ASCE, Soc. Am. Mil. Engrs., Res. Officers Assn. (chpt. pres. 1973). Club: Commonwealth of Calif. Home: 247 28th Ave San Francisco CA 94121-1001 Office: Fed Energy Regulatory Commn 901 Market St Ste 350 San Francisco CA 94103-1778

SMITH, BETTY DENNY, county official, administrator, fashion executive; b. Centralia, Ill., Nov. 12, 1932; d. Otto and Ferne Elizabeth (Beier) Hasenfuss; m. Peter S. Smith, Dec. 5, 1964; children: Carla Kip, Bruce Kimball. Student, U. Ill., 1950-52; student, LA. City Coll., 1953-57, UCLA, 1965, U. San Francisco, 1982-84. Freelance fashion coordinator L.A., N.Y.C., 1933-58, tchr. fashion Rita LeRoy Internat. Graduion 1959 60; mgr. No Nadler Fashion, L.A., 1961-64; showroom dir. Jean of Calif. Fashions, L.A., 1965—; freelance polit. book reviewer for community news Assistance Found., 1969-76; founder, pres., dir. Volce Services to Animals L.A., 1972-76; mem. County Com. To Discuss Animals in Rsch. 1973-74; mem May 4th ran on animal control L.A. County 1973-74; dir. L.A. County Animal Care and Control Dept 1987—

Technician Exam. Com., 1975-82, chmn., 1979; bd. dirs. L.A. Soc. for Prevention Cruelty to Animals, 1984-94, Calif. Coun. Companion Animal Advocates, 1993-97, dir. West Coast Regional Office, Am. Humane Assn. 1988-97; CFO Coalition for Pet Population Control, 1987-92; trustee Gladys W. Sargent Found., 1997, Coalition to End Pet Overpopulation, 1998; cons. Jungle Book II, Disney Studios, 1997; mem. Coalition to Protect Calif. Wildlife, 1996—; mem. Calif. Rep. Cen. Com., 1964-72, mem. exec. com., 1971-73; mem. L.A. County Rep. Cen. Com. 1964-70, mem. exec. com. 1966-70; chmn. 29th Congl. Cen. Com., 1969-70; sec. 28th Senatorial Cen. Com., 1967-68, 45th Assembly Dist. Cen. Com., 1965-68; mem. speakers bur. George Murphy for U.S. Senate, 1970; campaign mgr. Los Angeles County for Spencer Williams for Atty. Gen., 1966; mem. adv. com. Moorpark Coll., 1988—; mem. adv. bd. Wishbone Prodn., 1995—; mem. Coalition to End Pet Overpopulation, 1998. Mem. Internat. Platform Assn., Mannequins Assn. (bd. dirs. 1967-68), Motion Picture and TV Industry Assn. (govt. rels. and pub. affairs com. 1992-97), Lawyer's Wives San Gabriel Valley (bd. dirs. 1971-74, pres. 1972-73), L.A. Athletic Club, Town Hall. Home: 1766 Bluffhill Dr Monterey Park CA 91754-4533

SMITH, C. JAY, radio talk show host, marketing professional; b. Port Washington, N.Y., Oct. 3, 1947; s. Charles and Helen (Manning) S.; m. Ramona Smith, Dec. 31, 1992; 1 child, Lisa. BA, C.W. Post, Bethpage, N.Y., 1968. Pres. Telmark Assocs., Hicksville, N.Y., 1975-90, Omega Mktg., Seattle, 1990-93; sr. v.p. Cancall Cellular Comms., Las Vegas, 1993—; cons. N.P.M., Seattle, 1990-93, Cancall Cellular, Las Vegas, 1993-97. Editor: Small Cap Review Newsletter, 1995-97, As We See It Newsletter, 1990-95. With U.S. Army, 1968-71, Vietnam. Recipient Bronze Star U.S. Army, Vietnam, 1969; named Sales Mgr. of Yr. Mansfield Rubber, N.Y.C., 1972-75. Mem. VFW, Kiwanis Club. Avocations: golf, skiing, reading.

SMITH, CARTER BLAKEMORE, broadcaster; b. San Francisco, Jan. 1, 1937; s. Donald V. and Charlotte M. (Nichols) S.; children: Carter Blakemore, Clayton M. AA, City Coll. San Francisco, 1958; BA, San Francisco State U., 1960; postgrad. N.Y. Inst. Finance, 1969-70; Assoc. in Fin. PLanning, Coll. for Fin. Planning, 1984. Announcer, Sta. KBLF, Red Bluff, Calif., 1954-56; personality Sta. KRE-KRE FM, Berkeley, Calif., 1958-63, Sta. KSFO, San Francisco, 1963-72, Sta. KNBR, San Francisco, 1972-83, Sta. KSFO, San Francisco, 1983-86, Sta. KFRC, San Francisco, 1986-91, 93-94, Sta. KABL, San Francisco, 1996—; mem. faculty radio-TV dept. San Francisco State U., 1960-61. Mem. adv. bd. Little Jim Club Children's Hosp., 1968-71; bd. dirs. Marin County Humane Soc., 1968-73, San Francisco Zool. Soc., 1980-90; trustee Family Svc. Agy. Marin, 1976-85; mem. alumni bd. Lowell High Sch. Recipient award San Francisco Press Club, 1965; named one of Outstanding Young Men in Am. U.S. Jaycees, 1972. Mem. Amateur Radio Relay League (life), Quarter Century Wireless Assn., Alpha Epsilon Rho.

SMITH, CHARLES ANTHONY, businessman; b. Santa Fe, Sept. 16, 1939; s. Frances (Mier) Vigil. Student various adminstrv. and law courses; m. Paula Ann Thomas, June 26, 1965; 1 dau., Charlene Danielle. Circulation mgr. Daily Alaska Empire, 1960-63; agt. Mut. of N.Y. Life Ins. Co., Juneau, Alaska, 1964-65; mng. partner Future Investors in Alaska and Cinema Alaska, Juneau, 1961-62; SE Alaska rep. K & L Distbrs., 1966-68; mgr. Alaska Airlines Newspapers, SE Alaska, 1969; dev. Alaska Retirement System, Juneau, 1970-71; apptd. dir. hwy. safety, gov.'s hwy. safety rep., Juneau, 1971-83; pres. Valley Service Ctr., Inc., 1984-94; pres. 3-S Corp., 1995—; apptd. chmn. S.E. Alaska for ESGR, 1995; apptd. state dir. Selective Svc., 1996—. Alaska pres. Muscular Dystrophy Assn. Am.; pres. SE Alaska Emergency Med. Services Council, 1965-72; state dir. Selective Svc., 1996. Served to major Army N.G., 1964-88. Named Alaska Safety Man of Yr., 1977. Mem. Am. Assn. Motor Vehicle Adminstrs., Alaska Peace Officers Assn., Nat. Assn. Gov.s' Hwy. Safety Reps., N.G. Assn., Internat. Platform Assn. Roman Catholic. Club: Elks (Juneau). Author various hwy. safety manuals and plans, 1971—. Home: PO Box 32856 Juneau AK 99803-2856

SMITH, CHARLES LEWIS, retired career officer and association executive; b. Clarkston, Ga., Oct. 27, 1920; s. Robert Clyde and Emelyn (Bloodworth) S.; m. Mildred Lee Stilley, Sept. 5, 1947; children: Jan, Robert Eugene. Student, Ga. Sch. Tech., 1938-39. Enlisted USN, 1937, advanced through grades to comdr., 1968; various assignments including comdg. officer USS Chickasaw (ATF 83), 1962-64; leadership devel. officer Amphibious Force U.S. Pacific Fleet, 1964-66; comdg. officer USS Tioga County (LST 1158), 1966-68; dept. head Amphibious Sch. U.S. Naval Amhibious Base, Coronado, Calif., 1968-70, ret., 1970; dir. pub. rels. and fin. San Diego County Coun. Boy Scouts Am. 1971-80, dir. pub. rels., 1980-82, dir. planned giving, 1982-85, ret., 1985; mem. nat. adv. bd. Am. Security Coun., 1994-97. Trustee God Bless Am. Week, Inc., 1972-80, pres., 1977-78, co-chmn. San Diego Bicentennial Pageant, 1976; mem. adv. bd. Commd. Officers Mess (Oper.) U.S. Naval Sta., 1973-89; bd. dirs. Boys Club Chula Vista, Calif., 1985-87; devel. com. Alvarado Health Found., Alvarado Hosp. Med. Ctr., 1986-87; charter rev. com. City of Chula Vista, 1986-88; mem. accolades com. City of San Diego, 1988-90; rsch. bd. advisors Am. Biog. Inst., 1988—; vol. Boy Scouts Am. 1935-71, 85—; scout commr. San Diego County coun. 1969-71, mem. internat. rels. com. 1985-92, bd. dirs., 1995-97, scoutmaster 7th Nat. Jamboree, Farragut State park, Idaho, 1969, 13th World Jamboree, Japan, 1971, mem. local staff Nat. Jamboree, Ft. A.P. Hill, Va., 1986, mem. nat. staff, 1997. Recipient svc. award Civitan Internat., 1968, Cmty. Svc. resolution Calif. Senate, 1970, Southwestern Coll., 1973, Silver Beaver award Boy Scouts Am., 1965, Svc. to Youth resolution Calif. Senate, 1985, award Armed Forces YMCA Century Club, 1988, Appreciation award United Way San Diego, 1974-82, citation for heroism Sheriff of San Diego, 1991, Recognition award San Diego Rotary Club, 1991, citation for svc. City of San Diego Accolades Com., 1992, Disting. Svc. award U.S.S. Chickasaw (ATF) 83 Assn., 1993, Svc. award U.S.S. Wickes (DD578), 1995, Cert. of Appreciation, USN Meml. Found., 1997, Cert. of Appreciation, Warrant Officers Assn., 1998; Scouter Chuck Smith Day proclaimed by City of San Diego, 1985; flagpole dedicated to Scouter Chuck Smith San Diego County Coun. Boy Scouts Am., 1992; named to Hon. Order Ky. Cols., 1985, bd. dirs., 1987—, pres., 1996. Mem. VFW (Cert. of Appreciation 1995, 96, 97), Nat. Soc. Fund Raising Execs. (bd. dirs. San Diego chpt. 1975-80, 84-85, hosp. com. 1984-85), UN Assn. (bd. dirs. San Diego chpt. 1972-85), Ret. Officers Assn. (life, bd. dirs. Sweetwater chpt. 1972-92, pres. 1975, 81), Navy League U.S. (bd. dirs. 1984—), greeters 1983—, Appreciation award 1985, Cert. of Merit 1991), Mil. Order World Wars (comdr. 1989-90, nat. citations 1987, 91, 92, Outstanding Chpt. Comdr. award Dept. So. Calif. 1990, Patrick Henry medallion and medal 1996), Am. Legion, Crazy Horse Meml. Found., Clarkston Civitan Club (founding bd. dirs.), Eagle Scout Alumni Assn. (founder 1973, bd. dirs. 1986-88, life mem. 1985—), Hammer Club San Diego, Kiwanis (bd. dirs. 1984-88, chmn. fellowship com. 1983-84, boys and girls com. 1984-85, planned giving com. 1988-89), Order of the Arrow (vigil, Cross Feathers award 1968), Masons, Shriners, Order of Ea. Star (life), Nat. Sojourners. Methodist.

SMITH, CHARLES RICHARD, high technology marketing executive; b. Covington, Ohio, Nov. 5, 1932; s. Richard Weller and Harriet Rosalind (Minton) S.; m. Margaret Jean Porter, Aug. 7, 1954; children: David Paul, Kevin Richard, Jennifer Perlee, Melinda Jean. BA, Ohio Wesleyan U., Delaware, 1954; B Chem. Engring., Ohio State U., 1960. Product engr. Dow Corning Corp., Midland, Mich., 1960-63; tech. rels. mgr. Clyde W. Williams & Co., Columbus, Ohio, 1963-66; dir. pub. rels. Chem. Abstracts Svc., Columbus, 1966-68; v.p. sales/mktg. Ventron Corp., materials div., Bradford, Pa., 1968-73; v.p. sales/mktg. Applied Materials, Inc., Santa Clara, Calif., 1973-78; gen. mgr. Gyrex Corp., Santa Barbara, Calif., 1977-81; pres., CEO Auto/Recognition Systems, Santa Barbara, 1982-84; v.p. mktg./sales Tylan Corp., Torrance, Calif., 1984-85, Benzing Tech., Santa Clara, Calif., 1985-88; v.p. sales High Yield Tech., Sunnyvale, Calif., 1988-91; cons. Internat. Remote Imaging Systems, Chatsworth, Calif., 1981-82, Hakuto Co. Ltd., Tokyo, 1989—; dir. Micropulse Systems, Santa Barbara, Benzing Tech., Santa Clara founder, Action Pro Tem internat bur cons co. Author: Plasma Jet Technology. 1962; contbr. articles to profl. jours. Mem. U.S. Internat., Washington, Citizens Against Waste, Washington. With USAF, 1973-93. mem. Democratic national and financial committees 1989-91. sales exec. com. 1988-90, W.C. Benzing award 1993, Marines Memit. Assn., Churchill Club. Republican. Avocations: skiing, soaring, choral music. Home: 7933 Caledonia Dr San Jose CA 95135-2112 Office: Action Pro Tem

SMITH, CHARLES Z., state supreme court justice; b. Lakeland, Fla., Feb. 23, 1927; s. John R. and Eva (Love) S.; m. Eleanor Jane Martinez, Aug. 20, 1955; children: Carlos M., Michael O., Stephen P., Felica L. BS, Temple U., 1952; JD, U. Wash., 1955. Bar: Wash. 1955. Law clk. Wash. Supreme Ct., Olympia, 1955-56; dep. pros. atty., asst. chief criminal div. King County, Seattle, 1956-60; ptnr. Bianchi, Smith & Tobin, Seattle, 1960-61; spl. asst. to atty. gen. criminal div. U.S. Dept. Justice, Washington, 1961-64; judge criminal dept. Seattle Mcpl. Ct., 1965-66; judge Superior Ct. King County, 1966-73; former assoc. dean, prof. law U. Wash., 1973; now justice Wash. Supreme Ct., Olympia. Mem. adv. bd. NAACP, Seattle Urban League, Wash. State Literacy Coun., Boys Club, Wash. Citizens for Migrant Affairs, Medina Children's Svc., Children's Home Soc. Wash., Seattle Better Bus. Bur., Seattle Foundation, Seattle Symphony Orch., Seattle Opera Assn., Community Svc. Ctr. for Deaf and Hard of Hearing, Seattle U., Seattle Sexual Assault Ctr., Seattle Psychoanalytic Inst., The Little Sch., Linfield Coll., Japanese Am. Citizens League, Kawabe Meml. Hous, Puget Counseling Ctr, Am. Cancer Soc., Hutchinson Cancer Rsch. Ctr., Robert Chinn Found.; pres. Am. Bapt. Chs. U.S.A., 1976-77, lt. col. ret. USMCR. Mem. ABA, Am. Judicature Soc., Washington Bar Assn., Seattle-King County Bar Assn., Order of Coif., Phi Alpha Delta, Alpha Phi Alpha. Office: Wash Supreme Ct Temple of Justice PO Box 40929 Olympia WA 98504-0929

SMITH, CHESTER, broadcasting executive; b. Wade, Okla., Mar. 29, 1930; s. Louis L. and Effie (Brown) S.; m. Naomi L. Crenshaw, July 19, 1959; children: Lauri, Lorna, Roxanne. Country western performer on Capitol records, TV and radio, 1947-61; owner, mgr. Sta. KLOC, Ceres-Modesto, Calif., 1963-81, Sta. KCBA-TV, Salinas-Monterey, Calif.7; owner, gen. ptnr. Sta. KCSO-TV, Modesto-Stockton-Sacramento, 1966-97, Sta. KCVU-TV, Paradise-Chico-Redding, Calif., 1986—, Sta.; owner Sta. KBVU-TV, Eureka, Calif., 1990—, Sta. KNSO-TV, Merced-Fresno, 1996—, Calif., KCSO-TV (formerly KES-TV), Sacramento, 1996—, KFWU-TV, 1996-97, Fort Bragg, Calif., 1996-97, KRVU-TV, Redding, 1997—, Univision 28, Chico, Calif. Mem. Calif. Broadcasters Assn. Republican. Mem. Christian Ch. Original rec. Wait A Little Longer Please Jesus in Country Music Hall of Fame, Nashville, 1955, inductee Western Swing Hall of Fame, Sacramento, 1988; recipient cert. of recognition for 50 years of cmty. svc. Calif. Assembly, 1997.

SMITH, CLIFFORD NEAL, business educator, writer; b. Wakita, Okla., May 30, 1923; s. Jesse Newton and Inez Lane (Jones) S.; m. Anna Piszczan-Czaja, Sept. 3, 1951; children: Helen Inez Smith Barrette. BS, Okla. State U., 1943; AM, U. Chgo., 1948; postgrad. Columbia U., 1960. Selector, U.S. Displaced Persons Commn., Washington and Munich, Germany, 1948-51; auditor Phillips Petroleum Co., Caracas, Venezuela, 1951-58; planning analyst Mobil Internat. Oil Co., N.Y.C., 1960, 65-66, Mobil Oil A.G., Deutschland, Hamburg, Germany, 1961-63; asst. to v.p. for Germany, Mobil Inner Europe, Inc., Geneva, 1963-65; asst. prof. No. Ill. U. Sch. Bus., DeKalb, 1966-69, part-time prof. internat. bus., 1970—; owner Westland Publs.; lectr. in field. Author: Federal Land Series, vol. 1, 1972, vol. 2, 1973, vol. 3, 1980, vol. 4, part 1, 1982, vol. 4, part 2, 1986, Encyclopedia of German-American Genealogical Research, American Genealogical Resources in German Archives, 1977, numerous monographs in German-Am., Brit.-Am., French-Am. geneal. research series, German and Central European Emigration Series, Selections from the American State Papers; contbg. editor Nat. Geog. Soc. Quar., Geneal. jour. (Utah); contbr. articles to profl. jours. Mem. at large exec. com. Friends Com. on Nat. Legis., 1968-75; mem. regional exec. com. Am. Friends Service Com., 1969-76; v.p. Riverside Dem., N.Y.C., 1959-61; precinct committeeman, 1984—; mem. Ariz. State Central Com. of Dem. Party, 1984—; sec. Dem. Cen. Com. of Cochise County; mem. com. to Re-Elect Clinton for Pres. Recipient Distinguished Service medal Ill. Geneal. Soc., 1973, award for outstanding service to sci. genealogy Am. Soc. Genealogists, 1973; court appointed arbitrator for civil cases, 1992. Fellow Geneal. Soc. of Utah; mem. S.R., SAR, Soc. Descs. Colonial Clergy, Soc. Advancement Mgmt., Ill. Genealogic Soc. (dir. 1968-69), Phi Eta Sigma, Beta Alpha Psi, Sigma Iota Epsilon. Mem. Soc. of Friends. Club: American of Hamburg (v.p. 1962-63); contbr. articles to profl. jours.

SMITH, CONRAD GLENN PAGE, communications educator; b. Lawrence, Kans., Feb. 14, 1940; s. Harold Theodor Uhr and Althea (Page) S.; m. Sophronia Suzanne Albright, Jan. 21, 1963; children: Melisande, Deirdre. BS, Ohio State U., 1969, MA, 1971; PhD, Temple U., 1981. Postal clk. U.S. Postal Svc., Columbus, Ohio, 1965-67, film dir. KWSU-TV, Pullman, Wash., 1971-75; instr., then asst. prof. Idaho State U., Pocatello, 1977-81; asst. prof. Colo. State U., Ft. Collins, 1981-83; asst. prof., then assoc. prof. Ohio State U., Columbus, 1983-96; prof., chair dept. comm. and mass media U. Wyo., Laramie, 1996—; expert witness, cons. KHQ-TV, Spokane, 1978; lectr. media rels. U.S. Forest Svc., Marana, Ariz., 1992-98. Author: Media and Apocalypse, 1992; prodr. documentary Against the Flow of Eime, 1974, animated film Mathematical Integration, 1968. With U.S. Army, 1963-65. Mem. Sierra Club (chmn. svc. trip subcom. 1998—). E-mail: cgsmith@uwyo.edu. Home: 1458 Wyman Ct Laramie WY 82072-2993 Office: U Wyo Dept Comm and Mass Media PO Box 3904 Laramie WY 82071-3904

SMITH, D. ADAM, congressman; b. Washington, June 15, 1965; m. Sara Bickle-Eldridge, 1993. BA, Fordham U., 1987; JD, U. Wash., 1990. Driver United Parcel Svc., 1985-87; mem. Wash. State Senate, 1990-96; atty. Cromwell Mendoza Belur, 1992-93; asst. prosecuting atty. City of Seattle, 1993-96; mem. 105th Congress from 9th dist. Wash., 1997—. Democrat. Office: 1505 Longworth Washington DC 20515-4709*

SMITH, DAVID ELVIN, physician; b. Bakersfield, Calif., Feb. 7, 1939; s. Elvin W. and Dorothy (McGinnis) S.; m. Millicent Buxton; children: Julia, Suzanne, Christopher Buxton-Smith, Sabree Hill. Intern San Francisco Gen. Hosp., 1965; fellow pharmacology and toxicology U. Calif., San Francisco, 1965-67, assoc. clin. prof. occupl. medicine, clin. toxicology, 1967—, dir. psychopharmacology study group, dir. Inst. of Health, 1966-70, assoc. clin. prof., rsch. physician Med. Sch.; practice specializing in toxicology/addiction medicine San Francisco, 1965—; physician Presbyn. Alcoholic Clinic, 1965-67, Contra Cost Alcoholic Clinic, 1965-67; dir. alcohol and drug abuse screening unit San Francisco Gen. Hosp., 1967-68; co-dir. Calif. drug abuse info. project U. Calif. Med. Ctr., 1967-72; founder, med. dir. Haight-Ashbury Free Med. Clinic, San Francisco, 1967—; rsch. dir. Merritt Peralta Chem. Dependency Hosp., Oakland, Calif., 1984—; med. dir. Calif. State Substance Abuse Svcs.; chmn. Nat. Drug Abuse Conf., 1977; mem. Calif. Gov.'s Commn. on Narcotics and Drug Abuse, 1977—; nat. health adviser to former U.S. Pres. Jimmy Carter; mem. Pres. Clinton's Health Care Task Force on Addiction and Nat. Health Reform, 1993; with Office Drug Abuse Policy, White House Task Force Physicians for Drug Abuse Prevention; dir. Benzodiazepine Rsch. and Tng. Project, Substance Abuse and Sexual Concerns Project, PCP Rsch. and Tng. Project; vis. assoc. prof. U. Nev. Med. Sch., 1975—; cons. numerous fed. drug abuse agys. Author: Love Needs Care, 1970, The New Social Drug: Cultural, Medical and Legal Perspectives on Marijuana, 1971, The Free Clinic: Community Approaches to Health Care and Drug Abuse, 1971, Treating the Cocaine Abuser, 1985, The Benzodiazepines: Current Standard Medical Practice, 1986, Physicians' Guide to Drug Abuse, 1987; co-author: It's So Good, Don't Even Try it Once: Heroin in Perspective, 1972, Uppers and Downers, 1973, Drugs in the Classroom, 1973, Barbiturate Use and Abuse, 1977, A Multicultural View of Drug Abuse, 1978, Amphetamine Use, Misuse and Abuse, 1979, PCP: Problems and Prevention, 1981, Sexological Aspects of Substance Use and Abuse, Treatment of the Cocaine Abuser, 1985, The Haight Ashbury Free Medical Clinic: Still Free After All These Years, Drug Free: Alternatives to Drug Abuse, 1987, Treatment of Opiate Dependence, Designer Drugs, 1988, Treatment of Cocaine Dependence, 1988, Treatment of Opiate Dependence, 1988, The New Drugs, 1989, Crack and Ice in the Era of Smokeable Drugs, 1992, others; also drug edn. films; founder, editor Jour. Psychedelic Drugs (now Jour. Psychoactive Drugs), 1967—; contbr. over 300 articles to profl. jours. Mem. Physicians for Prevention White House Office Drug Abuse Policy, 1995; pres. Youth Projects, Inc.; founder, chmn. bd., pres. Nat. Free Clin. Coun., 1968-72. Recipient Rsch. award Borden Found., 1964, AMA Rsch. award, 1977, Cmty. Svc. award U. Calif., San Francisco, 1974, Calif. State Drug Abuse Treatment award, 1984, Vernelle Fox Drug Abuse Treatment award, 1985, UCLA Sidney Cohen Addiction Medicine award, 1989, U. Calif. San Francisco medal of honor, 1995; named one of Best Doctors in U.S., 1995, 96, 97. Mem. AMA (alt. del.), CMA (alt. del.), Am. Soc. on Addiction Medicine (bd. dirs., pres. 1995), San Francisco Med. Soc., Am. Pub. Health Assn., Calif. Soc. on Addiction Medicine (pres., bd. dirs.), Am. Soc. Addiction Medicine, Sigma Xi, Phi Beta Kappa. Methodist. Home: 289 Frederick St San Francisco CA 94117-4051 Office: Haight Ashbury Free Clinics 612 Clayton St San Francisco CA 94117-2927

SMITH, DAVID MICHAEL, financial planner; b. Fresno, Calif., Dec. 29, 1944; s. Ralph S. and Verla Fern (Tharp) S.; m. Barbara J. Bryson, June 27, 1964; children: Brandon, Eric. AA, Fresno City Coll., 1964; AB, Calif. State U., Fresno, 1966. Tchr. English Fresno Unified Sch. Dist., 1967-79; registered rep. TMI Equities, Inc., Fresno, 1979-82; regional mgr. TMI Equities, Inc., Camarillo, Calif., 1982-85; fin. planner Associated Planners Securities Corp., Camarillo, 1985-89, David M. Smith & Assocs., Camarillo, 1989—; mayor City of Camarillo, 1991, 95. Council mem. City of Camarillo, 1988-95; pres. Fresno Dem. Coaltion, 1979. Mem. Inst. Cert. Fin. Planners, Internat. Assn. Fin. Planning, Camarillo Noontime Optimists Club. Office: David M Smith & Assocs 1200 Paseo Camarillo Ste 190 Camarillo CA 93010-6085

SMITH, DAVID MITCHELL, fire and explosion consultant; b. San Bernardino, Calif., Feb. 2, 1947; s. Harry Arnold and Norma Deanne (Miles) S.; m. Linda Sue McCormick, Apr. 9, 1994; children: Sean David Kimble, Jennifer Laura Thacker. Cert. fire investigator Internat. Assn. of Arson Investigators. Patrolman Tucson (Ariz.) Police Dept., 1968-70, detective, 1970-81; president Associated Fire Consultants, Tucson, 1981—. Co-author: (manual) National Fire Protection Association 921, 1995; contbr. articles to profl. jours. Chair Catalina Village Coun., Tucson, 1995—; bd. dirs. Catalina Family Med. Ctr., Tucson, 1996—, Pima Youth Partnership, 1996—. Sgt E-5, USMCR, 1966-72. Recipient Appreciation award Bur. Alcohol, Tobbaco and Fireamrs, Dearborn, Mich., 1990. Mem. Internat. Assn. Arson Investigators (bd. dirs. St. Louis sect. 1982-87, pres. 1989-90, Disting. Svc. award 1993, life mem.), Nat. Fire Protection Assn. (com. mem. 1991—), Congl. Fire Svcs. Inst. (bd. dirs. 1989-90), Internat. Fire Svc. Tng. Assn. (com. mem.). Office: Associated Fire Cons Inc 7493 N Oracle Rd Ste 103 Tucson AZ 85704-6328

SMITH, DAVID WAYNE, psychologist, educator; b. Ind., Apr. 16, 1927; s. Lowell Wayne and Ruth Elizabeth (Westphal) S.; m. Marcene B. Leever, Oct. 20, 1948; children: David Wayne, Laurreen Lea. B.S., Purdue U., 1949; M.S., Ind. U., 1953, Ph.D., 1955. Diplomate Am. Bd. Psychol. Specialities. Prof. rehab., dir. Rehab. Center; asso. dean, later asst. v.p. acad. affairs Ariz. Health Scis. Center, U. Ariz., Tucson, 1955-80; research prof. rehab., adj. prof. medicine, cons. in research S.W. Arthritis Center, Coll. Medicine, 1980-87; prof. rehab. and rheumatology, dept. medicine U. Ariz., 1987—, also dir. disability assessment program; pres. allied health professions sect. Nat. Arthritis Found.; bd. dirs. Nat. Arthritis Found. (S.W. chpt.); nat. vice chmn. bd. dirs.; mem. NIH Nat. Arthritis Adv. Bd., 1977-84; also chmn. subcom. community programs and rehab.; mem. staff Ariz. Legislature Health Welfare, 1972-73; Mem. Gov.'s Council Dept. Econ. Security, 1978-85; pres., bd. dirs. Tucson Assn. for Blind, 1974-86; chmn. Gov.'s Council on Blind and Visually Impaired, 1987—; active Gov.'s Coun. on Arthritis and Musculoskeletal Disease, 1987—. Author: Worksamples; contbr. chpts. to books and articles to profl. jours. Mem. Gov.'s State Rehab. Coun., 1998. Recipient Gov.'s awards for leadership in rehab., 1966, 69, 72, 73; awards for sci. and vol. services Nat. Arthritis Found., 1973, 75; 1st nat. Addie Thomas award Nat. Arthritis Found., 1983, Benson award, 1989, Govt. Affairs award, 1989; Arthritis Found. fellow, 1983. Mem. Am. Psychol. Assn. (div. 17 counseling psychology), Am. Coll. Forensics, Assn. Schs. Allied Health Professions, Nat. Rehab. Assn., Ariz. Psychol. Assn. Home: 5765 N Camino Real Tucson AZ 85718-4213 Office: U Ariz Arizona Health Scis Ctr Tucson AZ 85724

SMITH, DICK MARTIN, oil field service company executive, owner; b. Alamosa, Colo., Nov. 20, 1946; s. Jack and Mary (Turnbull) S.; m. Janyce Wood Smith, Jan. 5, 1971 (div. May 1975); 1 child, DAnna Marie; m. Patricia Ann Connors, June 5, 1987; stepchildren: Shawna Parker, Scott Parker. Student, U. Md., 1969-72, U. York, Harrogate, Eng., 1969-72, U. N.Mex., 1975-79. With spl. ops. Nat. Security Agy., U.S. Govt., Ft. Meade, Md., 1969-74; with engring. rsch. U. N.Mex., Albuquerque, 1974-78; engr. fluids Internat. Mineral and Chem. Co., Houston, 1978-82; owner, pres., CEO Corrosions Monitoring Svcs. Inc., Capser, Wyo., 1981—; bd. dirs. Trenching Svcs., Casper, CMS Farms, Alamosa, Colo. With USN, 1964-68. Decorated Navy Unit Citation. Mem. Soc. Petroleum Engrs., Casper Wildcatters, Aircraft Owners Pilots Assn., DAV. Republican. Avocations: golf, flying, gardening, music. Home: 4471 E 12th St Casper WY 82609-3247 Office: CMS Inc PO Box 9826 Casper WY 82609-0826

SMITH, DONALD E., broadcast engineer, manager; b. Salt Lake City, Sept. 10, 1930; s. Thurman A. and Louise (Cardall) S.; B.A. Columbia, 1955; B.S.; U. Utah, 1970; postgrad. U. So. Calif., U. Utah, Harvard PhD (hon.), Columbia, 1985; m. Helen B. Lacy, 1978. Engr., Iowa State U., (WOI-TV), 1955-56; asst. chief engr. KLRJ-TV, Las Vegas, 1956-60; studio field engr. ABC, Hollywood, Cal., 1960; chief engr. Teletape, Inc., Salt Lake City, 1961; engring. supr. KUER, U. Utah, Salt Lake City, 1962-74, gen. mgr., 1975-85. Freelance cinematographer, 1950—; cons. radio TV (mgmt. engr. and prodn.), 1965—. Mem. Soc. Motion Pictures and TV Engrs., Lambda Chi Alpha. Home: 963 Hollywood Ave Salt Lake City UT 84105-3347

SMITH, DONALD EVANS, library consultant; b. Shanendoah, Iowa, Dec. 2, 1915; s. William Wesley and Bess Alice (Evans) S.; student Ricks Coll., 1939-40; BA, Hastings Coll., 1946; MLS, U. Wash., 1964. Tchr. English, librarian Tenino (Wash.) High Sch., 1950-51, Rochester (Wash.) High Sch., 1954-59; librarian North Thurston High Sch., Lacey, Wash., 1959-67; head librarian, coord. instructional materials Lakes High Sch., Lakewood Ctr., Wash., 1959-80; library cons., 1980—. Mem. awards com. Wash. Library Commn., 1964-66. With Signal Corps, AUS, 1942-45; to 1st lt., M.I., U.S. Army, 1951-54; to col. Wash. State Guard, 1971-80, now ret. Mem. VFW, Disabled Am. Vets., Wash. Assn. Sch. Librarians (com. chmn.), Clover Park Edn. Assn. (com. chmn. 1970-71), Am. Legion, Phi Delta Kappa (del. nat. confs.). Home and Office: 4530 26th Ave SE Lacey WA 98503-3218

SMITH, DONALD RICHARD, editor, publisher; b. Stockton, Calif., Aug. 20, 1932; s. Robert Gordon and Gertrude (Schweitzer) S.; m. Darlene Ruth Thomas, May 7, 1961; children: Douglas Robert, Deborah Renae. Student, Coll. Pacific, 1951, Delta Coll., 1951-52. Editor, pub. Calif. Odd Fellow & Rebekah, Linden, 1950—; editor Elk Grove (Calif.) Citizen, 1953-55; asst. dir. U.N. Pilgrimage for Youth, N.Y.C., 1956-59; editor, pub. Linden (Calif.) Herald, 1959-86, Lockeford (Calif.)-Clements Post, 1960-62, Internat. Rebekah News, Linden, 1963-86, Internat. Odd Fellow & Rebekah, Linden, 1986-97; dir. communications Sovereign Grand Lodge, Linden, 1990-92. Author: From Stagestop to Friendly Community, 1976, Leadership Manual, 1980, The Three Link Fraternity, 1993, Six Links of Fellowship, 1995. Bd. dirs. Odd Fellow-Rebekah Youth Camp, Inc., Long Barn, Calif., 1959-61; bd. dirs. The Meadows of Napa Valley, 1995—, pres. bd., 1998—; bd. dirs., chmn., S.J. County 4-H Found., 1986—; chmn. Linden Rep. Com., 1962-66, Linden Centennial Observance, 1963, Linden Mcpl. Coun., 1981-90. Recipient Legion of Honor Order of Demolay, 1961, John Williams award S.J. Tchrs. Assn., 1963, 87, Golden Key award Stockton Tchrs. Assn., 1971, Achievement award County Bd. Suprs., 1970, Grand Decoration of Chivalry, 1969, Citizen of Yr. award Lions Internat., 1982. Mem. IOOF Internat. Press Assn. (pres. 1962-63), Desktop Pub. Assn., Berkeley Macintosh Users Assn., Linden Peters C. of C. (pres. 1968-69), S.J. Hist. Soc. (trustee 1986-90). Methodist. Lodges: Lions, Odd Fellows (Calif.) (grand master 1958-59), Odd Fellows Internat. (sovereign grand master 1969-70), Internat. Coun. IOOF (sec. 1990—). Avocations: collecting Lionel trains, stamps, coins, historical books, research. Home: 5350 Harrison St Linden CA 95236-9630 Office: Linden Publ 19033 E Main PO Box 129 Linden CA 95236-0129

SMITH, DOROTHY OTTINGER, jewelry designer, civic worker; b. Indpls.; d. Albert Ellsworth and Leona Aurelia (Waller) Ottinger; student Herron Art Sch. of Purdue U. and Ind. U., 1941-42; m. James Emory Smith, June 25, 1943 (div. 1984); children: Michael Ottinger, Sarah Anne, Theodore Arnold, Lisa Marie. Comml. artist William H. Block Co., Indpls., 1942-43, H.P. Wasson Co., 1943-44; dir. Riverside (Calif.) Art Center, 1963-64; jewelry designer, Riverside, 1970—; numerous design commns. Adviser Riverside chpt. Freedom's Found. of Valley Forge; co-chmn. fund raising com. Riverside Art Ctr. and Mus., 1966-67, bd. dirs. Art Alliance, 1980-81, Art Mus.; mem. Riverside City Hall sculpture selection panel Nat. Endowment Arts, 1974-75; chmn. fund raising benefit Riverside Art Ctr. and Mus., 1973-74, trustee, 1980-84, chmn. permanent collection, 1981-84, co-chmn. fund drive, 1982-84, trustee, 1998—; chmn. Riverside Mcpl. Arts Commn., 1974-76, Silver Anniversary Gala, 1992; juror Riverside Civic Ctr. Purchase Prize Art Show, 1975; mem. pub. bldgs. and grounds subcom., gen. plan citizens com. City of Riverside, 1965-66; mem. Mayor's Commn. on Civic Beauty, Mayor's Commn. on Sister City Sendai, 1965-66; bd. dirs., chmn. spl. events Children's League of Riverside Community Hosp., 1952-53; bd. dirs. Crippled Children's Soc. of Riverside, spl. events chmn., 1952-53, bd. dirs. Jr. League of Riverside, rec. sec., 1960-61; bd. dirs. Nat. Charity League, pres. Riverside chpt., 1965-66; mem. exec. com. of bd. trustees Riverside Arts Found., 1977-91, fund drive chmn., 1978-79, project rev. chmn., 1978-79, advisor Evening for the Arts, 1998; juror Gemco Charitable and Scholarship Found., 1977-85; mem. bd. women deacons Calvary Presbyn. Ch., 1978-80, elder, 1989-92; mem. incorporating bd. Inland Empire United Fund for Arts, 1980-81; bd. dirs. Hospice Orgn. Riverside County, 1982-84; trustee Riverside Art Mus., 1998—; mem. Calif. Coun. Humanities, 1982-86. Recipient cert. Riverside City Coun., 1977, plaque Mayor of Riverside, 1977. Mem. Riverside Art Assn. (pres. 1961-63, 1st v.p. 1964-65, 67-68, trustee 1959-70, 80-84, 87-92), Art Alliance of Riverside Art Ctr. and Museum (founder 1964, pres. 1969-70). Recipient Spl. Recognition Riverside Cultural Arts Coun., 1981, Disting. Service plaque Riverside Art Ctr. and Mus., Jr. League Silver Raincross Community Svc. award, 1989, Cert. Appreciation Outstanding Svc. to the Arts Community Riverside Arts Found., 1990. Address: 3979 Chapman Pl Riverside CA 92506-1150

SMITH, DUNBAR WALLACE, retired physician, clergyman; b. Dunbar, Nebr., Oct. 17, 1910; s. Clarence Dunbar and Marie Christine (Eden) S.; m. Kathryn Avis Johnson, May 2, 1935; children: Dunbar Wesley, John Wallace. BSc, La Sierra Coll., Riverside, Calif., 1949; MD, Loma Linda U., 1950; DTM and Hygiene, Sch. of Tropical Med. London U., 1951; MPH, Columbia U., 1967. Diplomate Nat. Bd. Med. Examiners. Pastor 7th-day Adventist Chs., San Diego, Omaha, N.Y., India, Ceylon, 1935-44; med. dir. 7th-Day Adventist Mission Hosps., India, 1951-056; adminstr. Battle Creek (Mich.) Sanitarium, 1957-62; med. dir. Bates Meml. Hosp., Yonkers, N.Y., 1962-67; dep. commr. health Nassau County, N.Y., 1967-69; dir. dept. health for Africa, 7th-day Adventist Ch., 1969-76; dir. dept. health for Far East, 7th-day Adventist Ch., Singapore, 1976-80; adj. asst. prof. internat. health Loma Linda (Calif.) U., 1980-90; v.p. Emerald Health and Edn. Found., Loma Linda, 1986-91. Author: Report of CME (now Loma Linda U. Sch. Medicine) Rsch. to Date, 1946, (textbook) Home Health Aide, 1960, Autobiography of Dunbar W. Smith, 1994, American Family, 1997, (booklet) The Cold Turkey Way to Stop Smoking, 1967, The Smiths and Their Kinship with over 400 Doctors of Medicine and Dentistry, 1997; contbg. author: The Dunbar Pedigree, 1996; contbr. numerous articles to various publs. V.p. Emerald Health and Edn. Found., 1991—. Recipient Honored Alumnus award Loma Linda U. Sch. Medicine, 1975, Golden award La Sierra U. Alumni Soc., 1992. Fellow AMA, SAR, Am. Coll. Nutrition, Royal Soc. Tropical Medicine, Royal Soc. Health, Internat. Med. Assn. (bd. dirs. 1987—); mem. N.Y. Acad. Scis. Republican. Avocations: photography, travel. Home and Office: 217 Bellevue Ave Redlands CA 92373-4907

SMITH, DWIGHT MORRELL, chemistry educator; b. Hudson, N.Y., Oct. 10, 1931; s. Elliott Monroe and Edith Helen (Hall) S.; m. Alice Beverly Bond, Aug. 27, 1955 (dec. 1990); children—Karen Elizabeth, Susan Allison, Jonathan Aaron; m. Elfi Nelson, Dec. 28, 1991. BA, Ctrl. Coll., Pella, Iowa, 1953; PhD, Pa. State U., 1957; ScD (hon.), Cen. Coll., 1986; LittD (hon.), U. Denver, 1990. Postdoctoral fellow, instr. Calif. Inst. Tech., 1957-59; sr. chemist Texaco Rsch. Ctr., Beacon, N.Y., 1959-61; asst. prof. chemistry Wesleyan U., Middletown, Conn., 1961-66; assoc. prof. Hope Coll., Holland, Mich., 1966-69, prof., 1969-72; prof. chemistry U. Denver, 1972 , chmn. dept., 1972-83, vice chancellor for acad. affairs, 1983-84, chancellor, 1984-89; pres., bd. trustees Hawaii Loa Coll., Kaneohe, 1990-92; bd. dirs. Aina Inst., Hawaii; mem. Registry for Interim Coll. and Univ. Pres.; mem. adv. bd. Solar Energy Rsch. Inst., 1989-91; mem. vis. com. Zettlemoyer Ctr. for Surface Studies Lehigh U., 1990-96, dept. chemistry and geochemistry Colo. Sch. Mines; mem. sci. adv. bd. Denver Rsch. Inst. Editor Revs. on Petroleum Chemistry, 1975-78; editl. adv. bd. Recent Rsch. Devels. in Applied Spectroscopy, 1998—; contbr. articles to profl. jours.; patentee selective hydrogenation. Chmn. Chs. United for Social Action, Holland, 1968-69; mem. adv. com. Holland Sch. Bd., 1969-70; bd. commrs. Colo. Adv. Tech. Inst., 1984-88, Univ. Senate, United Meth. Ch., Nashville, 1987-88, 91-93; mem. adv. bd. United Way, Inst. Internat. Edn., Japan Am. Soc. Colo., Denver Winter Games Olympics Com.; mem. ch. bds. or consistories Ref. Ch. Am., N.Y., Conn., Mich., United Meth. Ch., Colo. DuPont fellow, 1956-57, NSF fellow Scripps Inst., 1971-72; recipient grants Research Corp., Petroleum Research Fund, NSF, Solar Energy Research Inst. Mem. AAAS, Am. Chem. Soc. (chmn. Colo. 1976, sec. western Mich. 1970-71, joint coun. and bd. com. on sci. 1997-98, award Colo. sect. 1986), Catalysis Soc., Soc. Applied Spectroscopy, Mile High Club, Pinehurst Country Club, Sigma Xi. Home: 1931 W Sanibel Ct Littleton CO 80120-8133 Office: U Denver Dept Chem U Pk 1 Univ Denver Denver CO 80208

SMITH, ELDRED GEE, church leader; b. Lehi, Utah, Jan. 9, 1907; s. Hyrum Gibbs and Martha E. (Gee) S.; m. Jeanne A. Ness, Aug. 17, 1932 (dec. June 1977); children: Miriam Smith Skeen, Eldred Gary, Audrey Gay Smith Vance, Gordon Raynor, Sylvia Dawn Smith Isom; m. Hortense H. Child, May 18, 1978; stepchildren: Carol Jane Child Burdette (dec.), Thomas Robert Child. Employed with sales div. Bennett Glass & Paint Co., Salt Lake City, 6 years; mech. design engr. Remington Arms Co., 2 years; design engr., prodn. equipment design Tenn. Eastman Corp., Oak Ridge, Tenn., 3 years; now presiding patriarch Ch. Jesus Christ of Latter-day Saints. Home: 2942 Devonshire Cir Salt Lake City UT 84108-2526 Office: 47 E South Temple Salt Lake City UT 84150-1005

SMITH, EPHRAIM PHILIP, academic administrator, former university dean, educator; b. Fall River, Mass., Sept. 19, 1942; s. Jacob Max and Bertha (Horvitz) S.; m. Linda Sue Katz, Sept. 3, 1967; children—Benjamin, Rachel, Leah. B.S., Providence Coll., 1964; M.S., U. Mass., 1965; Ph.D., U. Ill., 1968. Chmn. dept. acctg. U. R.I., Kingston, 1972-73; dean Sch. Bus. Shippensburg State Coll., Pa., 1973-75; dean Coll. Bus. Adminstrn. Cleve. State U., 1975-90; dean Sch. Bus. Adminstrn. and Econ. Calif. State U., Fullerton, 1990-98, v.p. acad. affairs, 1998—. co-author: Principles of Supervision: FIrst and Second Level Management, 1984, Federal Taxation-Advanced Topics, 1995, Federal Taxation-Basic Principles, 1999, Federal Taxation Comprehensive Topics, 1999; contbr. articles to profl. jours. Mem. Am. Acctg. Assn., Am. Taxation Assn., Am. Inst. for Decision Scis., Fin. Execs. Inst., Beta Gamma Sigma, Beta Alpha Psi. Office: U Fullerton VPAA Office MH-133 800 N State College Blvd Fullerton CA 92831-3547

SMITH, FERN M., judge; b. San Francisco, Nov. 7, 1933. AA, Foothill Coll., 1970; BA, Stanford U., 1972, JD, 1975. Bar: Calif. 1975. children: Susan Morgan, Julie. Assoc. firm Bronson, Bronson & McKinnon, San Francisco, 1975-81, ptnr., 1982-86; judge San Francisco County Superior Ct., 1986-88, U.S. Dist. Ct. for Northern Dist. Calif., 1988—; mem. U.S. Jud. Conf., Adv. Com. Rules of Evidence, 1993-96, chair, 1996—; mem. hiring, mgmt. and pers. coms., active recruiting various law schs. Contbr. articles to legal publ. Apptd. by Chief Justice Malcolm Lucas to the Calif. Jud. Coun.'s Adv. Task Force on Gender Bias in the Cts., 1987-89; bd. visitors Law Sch. Stanford U. Mem. ABA, Queen's Bench, Nat. Assn. Women Judges, Calif. Women Lawyers, Bar Assn. of San Francisco, Fed. Judges Assn., 9th Cir. Dist. Judges Assn., Am. Judicature Soc., Calif. State Fed. Judicial Coun., Phi Beta Kappa.*

SMITH, GARY CHESTER, meat scientist, researcher; b. Ft. Cobb, Okla., Oct. 25, 1938; s. William Chester and Aneta Laura (Lisk) S.; m. Carol Ann Jackson (div. 1965); children: Todd, Toni; m. Kay Joy Camp, Feb. 12, 1965; children: Leaneta, Stephanie, Kristl, Leland. BS, Calif. State U., Fresno, 1960; PhD, Tex. A&M U., 1968. Asst. prof. dept. animal sci. Wash. State U., Pullman, 1968-69; from assoc. prof. to prof. dept. animal sci. Tex. A&M U., College Station, 1969-82, head dept. animal sci., 1982-90; prof. Nat. Meat Inspection Tng. Ctr., College Station, 1987-90; Monfort Endowed prof. dept. animal sci. Colo. State U., Ft. Collins, 1990—, univ. disting. prof., 1993—; chmn. irradiation com. NAS, 1977-79, mem. packaging com. Office Tech. Assessment, 1973-74. Author: Laboratory Exercises in Meat Science;

contbr. numerous articles to profl. jours. including Jour. Animal Sci., Jour. Food Sci., Meat Sci. Bd. dirs. Internat. Stockmen's Edn. Found., Houston, 1983-91. Recipient Disting. Svc. award Nat. Livestock Grading and Mktg. Assn., 1989, 92, 96, Svc. award Am. Meat Inst., 1997, Secretariat Agr. of Argentina, 1998, Nat. Meat Assn., 1999. Fellow Am. Soc. Animal Sci. (Meat Rsch. award 1974, Disting. Tchg. award 1980); mem. Am. Meat Sci. Assn. (pres. 1976-77, Disting. Rsch. award 1982, Disting. Teaching award 1984, Signal Svc. award 1993, Meat Judging award 1997), Inst. Food Technologists, Coun. Agrl. Sci. and Tech. Republican. Baptist. Achievements include development of USDA grading standards for beef, pork, lamb carcasses; process for electrical-stimulation tenderization of beef carcasses; discovery of relationship between fat-cover insulation and tenderness of beef and lamb; research on first shipments of chilled beef to Europe and Japan; research on chemical residues in, and bacteria on, beef, pork and lamb carcasses, variety meats, primal/retail cuts and ground products. Home: 1102 Seton St Fort Collins CO 80525-9498 Office: Colo State U Dept Animal Scis Fort Collins CO 80523

SMITH, GEORGE LARRY, analytical and environmental chemist; b. Beloit, Kans., Oct. 11, 1951; s. Richard Bailey and Vonda Ellene (Cox) S.; m. Charlene Janell Musgrove, Sept. 4, 1973; 1 child, Brian Lawrence. BA, Augustana Coll., 1973. Cert. grade 3 water treatment operator, Calif. Lab. technician Sanitary Dist. of Hammond, Ind., 1973; chemist Federated Metals Corp., Whiting, Ind., 1973-77; rsch. technician Air Pollution Technology, Inc., San Diego, 1978-80, environ. chemist, 1980-81, sr. tech. asst., 1981; staff chemist I Occidental Research Corp., Irvine, Calif., 1981-82, receiving chemist, 1982-84; processing chemist Chem. Waste Mgmt., Inc., Kettleman City, Calif., 1984-87, analytical chemist, 1987-89, wet analytical chemistry group leader, 1989-90, inorganic lab. supr., 1990-94, quality assurance/quality control specialist, 1994-96; lab. mgr. Bolsa Rsch. Assocs., Inc., Hollister, Calif., 1996—; lab. analyst for published article in environ. sci. and tech., 1981. bd. dirs. Apostolic Christian Missions, Inc., San Diego, 1978-82. Mem. Am. Chem. Soc., Nat. Geog. Soc., Internat. Union Pure and Applied Chemistry, Assn. Ofcl. Analytical Chemists Internat., N.Y. Acad. Scis., Planetary Soc., Commonwealth Club Calif. Avocations: coin collecting, drawing, photography, reading about science, history and religion. Home: 991 Meridian St Hollister CA 95023-4130 Office: Bolsa Rsch Assocs Inc 8770 Hwy 25 Hollister CA 95024

SMITH, GLENN A., lawyer; b. Oakland, Calif., July 11, 1946. BA, Pomona Coll., 1968; JD, U. Calif., Berkeley, 1971; LLM in Taxation, NYU, 1973. Bar: Calif. 1972, D.C. 1975. Law clerk to Hon. William M. Drennen U.S. Tax Ct., 1973-75; ptnr. Heller, Ehrman, White & McAuliffe, Palo Alto, San Francisco, Calif., 1977—. Office: Heller Ehrman White & McAuliffe 525 University Ave Ste 1100 Palo Alto CA 94301-1908*

SMITH, GORDON EUGENE, pilot; b. Corpus Christi, Tex., Nov. 22, 1953; s. Orvis Alvin and Helen Lucille (Lockhart) A.; m. Crisanta Lacson Oqueriza, Jan. 5, 1979; children: Pia Marie, Helena Irita. AAS in Electronics, Riverside City Coll., 1985; BSEE, Calif. Polytech., 1987. Electronics technician Lear Siegler, Inc., Ontario, Calif., 1981-86, Rockwell Internat., Palmdale, Calif., 1986-87; pilot Orion Air Inc., Raleigh, N.C., 1987-90; pilot, dir. maintenance, asst. dir. ops. Nat. Air, Riverside, Calif., 1990-93; pilot MGM Grand Air, 1993-96, Sun Pacific Internat., Tucson, 1996—. With USAF, 1972-79, with Res. 1979—. Mem. Aircraft Owners and Pilots Assn., Team One (v.p. 1980—). Republican. Dunkard Brethren. Avocations: flying, golf, bowling, baseball, computers. Office: Sun Pacific Intl 2502 E Benson Hwy Tucson AZ 85706-1702

SMITH, GORDON HAROLD, senator; b. Pendleton, Oreg., May 25, 1952; s. Milan Dale and Jessica (Udall) S.; m. Sharon Lankford; children: Brittany, Garrett, Morgan. BA in History, Brigham Young U., 1976; JD, Southwestern U., 1979. Law clk. to Justice H. Vern Payne N.Mex. Supreme Ct.; pvt. practice Ariz.; owner Smith Frozen Foods; mem. Oreg. State Senate, 1992-95, pres., 1995-96; U.S. senator from Oreg., 1997—; mem. Budget com. U.S. Senate; vice chair subcom. water and power, subcom. forests and pub. land mgmt., subcom. energy rsch., devel., prodn. and regulation Energy and Natural Resource com.; chair subcom. European affairs, subcom. Near Eastern and South Asian affairs, subcom. internat. ops. Fgn. Rels. com. Office: SD-359 Dirksen Senate Offic Washington DC 20510-3701

SMITH, GORDON PAUL, management consulting company executive; b. Salem, Mass., Dec. 25, 1916; s. Gordon and May (Vaughan) S.; m. Daphne Miller, Nov. 23, 1943 (div. 1968); m. Ramona Chamberlain, Sept. 27, 1969; children: Randall B., Roderick F. BS in Econs, U. Mass., 1947; M.S. in Govt. Mgmt, U. Denver (Sloan fellow), 1948; postgrad. in polit. sci, NYU, 1948-50; DHL (hon.), Monterey Inst. Internat. Studies, 1994. Economist Tax Found., Inc., N.Y.C., 1948-50; with Booz, Allen & Hamilton, 1951-70; partner Booz, Allen & Hamilton, San Francisco, 1959-62, v.p., 1962-67, mng. pntr. Western U.S., 1968-70; partner Harrod, Williams and Smith (real estate devel.), San Francisco, 1962-69; state dir. fin. State of Calif., 1967-68; pres. Gordon Paul Smith & Co., Mgmt. Cons., 1968—; pres., chief exec. officer Golconda Corp., 1972-74, chmn. bd., 1974-85; pres. Cermetek Corp., 1978-80; bd. dirs., exec. com. First Calif. Co., 1970-72, Groman Corp., 1976-85; bd. dirs. Madison Venture Capital Corp.; adviser task force def. procurement and contracting Hoover Commn., 1954-55; spl. asst. to pres. Republic Aviation Corp., 1954-55; cons., Hawaii, 1960-61, Alaska, 1963; cons. Wash. Hwy. Adminstrn., 1964, also 10 states and fed. agys., 1951-70, Am. Baseball League and Calif. Angels, 1960-62; bd. dirs. Monterey Coll. Law; chmn. Ft. Ord Econ. Devel. Adv. Group, 1991; chmn. Coalition on Rsch. and Edn., 1993—; bd. dirs. Monterey Bay Futures Project; adv. bd. Ctr. for Non-Proliferation Studies, 1997—; over 750 TV, radio and speaking appearances on econs., mgmt. and public issues. Author articles on govt., econs. and edn. Mem. 24 bds. and commns. State of Calif., 1967-72, sr. advisor to pres., 1998—; mem. Calif. Select Com. on Master Plan for Edn., 1971-73; mem. alumni council U. Mass., 1950-54, bd. dirs. alumni assn., 1964-70; bd. dirs. Alumni Assn. Mt. Hermon Prep. Sch., 1963; bd. dirs. Stanford Med. Ctr., 1960-62, pres., chmn., 1962-66; chmn. West Coast Cancer Found., 1976-87, Coalition Rsch. and Edn., 1993—, Jim Tunney Youth Fund, 1994—; trustee, chmn. Monterey Inst. Internat. Studies, 1978-92, trustee emeritus, 1995—; trustee Northfield Mt. Hermon Sch., 1983-93, Robert Louis Stevenson Sch., 1993—; mem. devel. council Community Hosp. of Monterey Peninsula, 1983-84; bd. dirs. Friends of the Performing Arts, 1985—; bd. dirs. Monterey County Symphony Orch., 1991-96, Monterey Bay Futures Project, 1992—. Recipient spl. commendation Hoover Commn., 1955, Alumni of Yr. award U. Mass., 1963, Trustee of Yr. award Monterey-Peninsula, 1991, Monterey-Peninsula Outstanding Citizen of Yr. award, 1992, Laura Bride Powers Heritage award, 1991, U.S. Congl. award, 1992, Calif. Senate and Assembly Outstanding Citizen award, 1992, Wisdom award of honor Wisdom Soc., 1992; permanent Gordon Paul Smith Disting. Chair for Internat. Studies established at Monterey Inst. Internat. Studies; Gordon Paul Smith Scholarship Fund named in his honor Northfield Mt. Hermon Sch.; named to Honorable Order of Ky. Cols. Mem. Monterey History and Art Assn. (bd. dirs. 1987-92, pres. 1985-87, chmn. 1987-92, hon. lifetime dir. 1992—), The Stanton Heritage Ctr. (chmn. 1987-92, chmn. emeritus 1992—), Salvation Army (bd. dirs., chmn. hon. cabinet), Monterey Peninsula Mus. Art, Carmel Valley (Calif.) Country Club, Monterey Peninsula Country Club, Old Capitol Club. Home: 253 Del Mesa Carmel CA 93923

SMITH, GREGORY R., lawyer; b. Chgo., Jan. 9, 1944. BA summa cum laude, Claremont Men's Coll., 1965; JD magna cum laude, Harvard U., 1968; MS, London Sch. Econs., 1969. Bar: Calif. 1969. Ptnr. Irell & Manella, L.A., 25 yrs.; vis. prof. U. Kansas Sch. Law, 1975. Mem. bd. editors Harvard Law Review, 1966-68. Mem. State Bar Calif., Phi Alpha Delta. Office: Irell & Manella Ste 900 1800 Avenue Of The Stars Los Angeles CA 90067-4276*

SMITH, HARRY MENDELL, JR., science educator; b. Wichita, Kans., Aug. 19, 1943; s. H. Mendell and Sevilla Mae (Cooper) S.; m. Cecile Marie Adams, Sept. 19, 1964; children: Jeff, Shauna, Noelle. AA, Pasadena Coll., 1966; BA, Calif. State U., L.A., 1970; Vocat. Credential, UCLA, 1979. Tchr. Glendora (Calif.) Unified Schs., 1970-80; instr. Citrus Coll., Azusa, Calif., 1978-82; mgr. Christian Chapel, Walnut, Calif., 1980-82; pres. Whitmore Printing, Inc., La Puente, Calif., 1981-83, mgr. Evang. Free Ch., Fullerton, Calif., 1985-87; prof. Mt. San Antonio Coll., Walnut, 1985—, chair divsn. applied sci. and tech., 1993—; prof. physics Biola U., La Mirada, Calif., 1998—; dir. Faculty Senate, Mt. San Antonio Coll., 1989-91. Author: Electronic Devices and Circuits Lab Book, 1994, Experiments in DC/AC Circuits, 1998. Treas. Sojourner Evangelical Free Ch., Fullerton, 1996-98. Chancellor's Office Electronic Tech. grantee, 1990. Mem. Nat. Assn. Radio and Telecommunications Engrs., Home Bldrs. Fellowship (pres. 1990-92), Calif. Indsl. Arts and Edn. Assn., Calif. Coun. Electronics (bd. sec. 1998—), Vocat. Indsl. Clubs Am. (region 3 coord. post secondary 1997—). Republican. Avocations: music, numismatics, electronics, physical fitness, sailing. Home: 951 S Idaho St Apt 70 La Habra CA 90631-6649 Office: Mt San Antonio Coll 1100 N Grand Ave Walnut CA 91789-1341

SMITH, HELEN ELIZABETH, retired career officer; b. San Rafael, Calif., Aug. 11, 1946; d. Jack Dillard and Marian Elizabeth (Miller) S. BA in Geography, Calif. State U., Northridge, 1968; MA in Internat. Rels., Salve Regina, Newport, R.I., 1983; MS in Tech. Comm., Rensselaer Poly. Inst., 1988; postgrad., Naval War Coll., 1982-83. Commd. ensign USN, 1968, advanced through grades to capt., 1989; adminstrv. asst. USN Fighter Squadron 101, Key West, Fla., 1969-70; adminstrv. officer Fleet Operational Tng. Group, Mountain View, Calif., 1970-72; leader human resource team Human Resource Ctr., Rota, Spain, 1977-79; adminstrv. officer Pearl Harbor (Hawaii) Naval Sta., 1979-80; dir. Family Svc. Ctr., Pearl Harbor, 1980-82; officer-in-charge R&D lab. Naval Ocean Systems Ctr., Kaneohe, Hawaii, 1983-85; exec. officer Naval ROTC, assoc. prof. Rensselaer Poly. Inst., Troy, N.Y., 1985-88; comdg. officer Navy Alcohol Rehab. Ctr., Norfolk, Va., 1988-90; faculty mem., commanding officer Naval Adminstrv. Command, dean adminstrv. support, comptr. Armed Forces Staff Coll., Norfolk, Va., 1990-93; ret., 1993; exec. dir. Calif. for Drug-Free Youth, 1995-96. Author: (walking tour) Albany's Historic Pastures, 1987; composer (cantata) Night of Wonder, 1983. Chair Hawaii State Childcare Com., Honolulu, 1981-82; coun. mem. Hist. Pastures Neighborhood Assn., Albany, N.Y., 1985-88; mem. working group Mayors Task Force on Drugs, Norfolk, 1989-90; chair, bd. dirs. Va. Coun. on Alcoholism, 1989-92, Calif. for Drug Free Youth, 1995-96; singer North County Baroque Ensemble; assoc. Westar Inst. Avocation: writing. Home: 952 Frederico Blvd Belen NM 87002

SMITH, IRBY JAY, film producer; b. San Antonio, Apr. 17, 1938; s. Irby Jay and Virginia Lee (Algee) S.; m. Elaine Nicholson, June 8, 1956; children: Kimberly, Carrie, Jay. Student, Occidental Coll., 1955-56; BA summa cum laude, U. Calif., Berkeley, 1960. Pub. info. spcialist, tv interview host, writer U.S. Dept. Health, Edn. and Welfare, L.A., 1960-66; writer, dir. CRM/McGraw-Hill Films, L.A., 1969-70; pvt. practice asst. dir., prodn. mgr., prodr., dir., 1966—. Prodr. City Slickers, Prefontaine, Wild America, Rookie of the Year, Angels in the Outfield, Enemies a Love Story, Major League, Young Guns I and II. Recipient ALA award for writing and directing ednl. films, 1970, 2 Cine Golden Eagle awards for writing and directing ednl. films, 1970. Mem. Dirs. Guild Am., Phi Beta Kappa. Democrat. Avocation: thought.

SMITH, JAMES ALEXANDER, metal processing executive; b. Harvey, N.D., Jan. 16, 1926; s. James Kay MacKenzie and Palma Theresa (Johnson) S.; m. Cleo Lorraine, Sept. 1, 1948 (div. 1962); children: Deborah Kay Smith Hooper, Daryl Lynn Smith O'Neill, Darcey Amelia Smith Ryan; m. Louise Mae Hammer, July 21, 1979. BS, U. Minn., 1951. Ptnr., v.p. VIP, Phoenix, 1960-78; founder Therm-O-Low Inc., Phoenix, 1978-84; v.p., gen. mgr., pres. 3XKryogenics, Phoenix, 1984-86; founder, pres. Cryogenics Internat., Inc., Tempe, Ariz., 1987-90; lectr. and speaker on cryogenics. Patentee (U.S. and fgn.) in field. Staff sgt. U.S. Army, 1943-46. Decorated Bronze star, Combat Infantryman Badge with 2 battle stars. Mem. Soc. Mfg. Engrs. (Ariz. chpt. chmn. 1983, chmn. western states zone 1985, Pres.'s award 1984), Cryogenic Soc. Am., Am. Soc. Metals, VFW (life mem.). Republican. Lutheran.

SMITH, JAMES MICHEAL, marketing executive; b. Ft. Carson, Colo., July 14, 1951; s. Richard Allen Smith and Cathrine Clare (Kehl) Ryan; m. Amelia Joann Carr, June 7, 1973; children: Peter Micheal, Lisa Danielle. BS in Basic Scis., USAF Acad., 1973; MA in Bus. Mgmt., Ctrl. Mich. U., 1977. Sr. cons. Strategic Mktg. Group, Inc., Denver, 1986-87; dir. ops. U.S.A. Direct, Inc., Englewood, Colo., 1987; mktg. rep. Martin Marietta Corp., Denver, 1988-90, sr. mktg. rep., 1990-92, mgr. bus. devel., 1992-95; dir. mktg. Hughes Info. Tech. Corp., Aurora, Colo., 1995-97; dir. bus. devel. Electronic Data Systems, Plano, Tex., 1997—. Patroller Nat. Ski Patrol, 1985—; cub scout leader Boy Scouts Am., 1993—. Maj. USAF, 1973-86, col. USAFR, ret. Recipient Purple Merit Star for life saving Nat. Ski Patrol, 1990. Mem. AIAA, Air Force Assn. (life), Res. Officer Assn. (life). Republican. Mem. LDS Ch. Avocations: skiing, racquetball, biking, hiking. Home: 1362 Meadow Trl Franktown CO 80116-7912 Office: EDS PO Box 1034 Franktown CO 80116-1034

SMITH, JANET HUGIE, lawyer; b. Logan, Utah, Aug. 1, 1945. BA cum laude, Utah State U., 1967; MA cum laude, Stanford U., 1969; JD, U. Utah, 1976. Bar: Utah 1976, U.S. Ct. Appeals (10th cir.) 1977. Shareholder, exec. com. Ray, Quinney & Nebeker, Salt Lake City, 1983—. Mem. ABA, Utah State Bar (labor and employment law sect.), CUE/NAM (labor lawyers adv. coun.). Office: Ray Quinney & Nebeker Deseret Bldg 79 S Main St Ste 400 Salt Lake City UT 84111-1996

SMITH, JANICE ALFREDA, secondary school educator; b. San Pedro, CA, Jan. 4, 1938; d. Willis Alfred and Elsie Ann (Moser) S. AA, Compton (Calif) Jr. Coll., 1957; BA, Calif. State U., Long Beach, 1960. Tchr. Mayfair H.S., Lakewood, Calif., 1960-85, Redmond (Oreg.) H.S., Sch. Dist. 2J, 1985-98; drill team instr. Mayfair H.S. Athletic Dept., Lakewood, Calif., 1962-71, coach volleyball, basketball, softball, 1974-85. Coach 10 league championship teams, Mayfair H.S., Lakewood, Calif., 1974-82, 1 Calif. Interscholastic Fedn. So. Divsn. League Champion, 1979; recipient Youth Sports award Lakewood (Calif.) Youth Hall of Fame, 1983. Mem. NEA, Redmond Edn. Assn. (bargaining chmn. 1996-97, co-pres. 1997-98). Avocations: travel, devel. lang. arts curricula, golf, dogs. Home: 666 NE Basalt Ave Terrebonne OR 97760-9733

SMITH, JEAN, interior design firm executive; b. Oklahoma City; d. A. H. and Goldy K. (Engle) Hearn; m. W. D. Smith; children: Kaye Smith Hunt, Sidney P. Student Chgo. Sch. Interior Design, 1970. v.p. Billco-Aladdin Wholesale, Albuquerque, 1950-92, v.p. Billco Carpet One of Am, 1970. Pres. Opera Southwest, 1979-83, advisor to bd. dirs.; active Civic Chorus, 1st Meth. Ch.; pres. Inez PTA, 1954-55, life mem.; hon. life mem. Albuquerque Little Theater, bd. dirs. Republican. Clubs: Albuquerque County, Four Hills Country, Daus. of the Nile (soloist Yucca Temple). Home: 1009 Santa Ana Ave SE Albuquerque NM 87123-4232 Office: Billco-Aladdin Wholesale 7617 Menaul Blvd NE Albuquerque NM 87110-4647

SMITH, JEFFREY JOHN, writer, publisher; b. Winchester, Mass., Apr. 28, 1951; s. Charles E. and Anne Marie (Overman) S.; m. Shaun Lea Gant, Aug. 20, 1988; children: Nathaniel Owen, Julia Colleen, Maximilian Robert. BA in English, Holy Cross Coll., 1973; MEd, U. Mass., 1976. Tchr. English St. Sebastian's Prep. Sch., Newton, Mass., 1973-75, Falmouth (Mass.) High Sch., 1975-76; counselor Sun Valley Ranch/Adolescents, Missoula, Mont., 1976-78; sawyer Champion Internat., Missoula, 1978-80; community coord. Five Valleys Health Care, Missoula, 1981-83; project dir. Inst. Rockies, Missoula, 1984; freelance writer Missoula, 1983—; pub. info. coord. St. Patrick Hosp., Missoula, 1986-94, writing cons., 1987—; owner Historic Mont. Pub., 1998—; owner Montana 2000 Writing and Pub., 1994—. Author: K. Ross Toole's Montana, 1985, (screenplay) The Great Montana Road Race, 1995, Wild Child, 1996; editor Missoula Muse, Northwest Mileposts, Pathos Mag., 1999—; ; contbr. numerous articles to profl. jours. Bd. dirs. Genesis House, Stevensville, Mont., 1979-80, Inst. of the Rockies, Missoula, 1984-85, Citizens Adv. Com. on Cable TV, 1983-89, 92-94, Internat. Wildlife Film Festival, 1997-98, The Virginia City Preservation Alliance, 1997—. Recipient Book of Yr. award Mont. Inst. of Arts, Billings, 1986. Democrat. Avocations: fly fishing, wilderness backpacking, skiing, hunting, gardening. Home and Office: 216 Woodford St Missoula MT 59801-4041

SMITH, JEFFRY ALAN, health administrator, physician, consultant; b. L.A., Dec. 8, 1945; s. Stanley W. and Marjorie E. S.; m. Jo Anne Hague. BA in Philosophy, UCLA, 1967, MPH, 1972; BA in Biology, Calif. State U., Northridge, 1971; MD, UACJ, 1977. Diplomate Am. Bd. Family Practice. Resident in family practice WAH, Takoma Park, Md., NIH, Bethesda, Md., Walter Reed Army Hosp., Washington, Children's Hosp. Nat. Med. Ctr., Washington, 1977-80; occupational physician Nev. Test Site, U.S. Dept. Energy, Las Vegas, 1981-82; dir. occupational medicine and environ. health Pacific Missile Test Ctr., Point Mugu, Calif., 1982-84; dist. health officer State Hawaii Dept. Health, Kauai, 1984-86; asst. dir. health County of Riverside (Calif.) Dept. Health, 1986-87; regional med. dir. Calif. Forensic Med. Group, Monterey, Calif., 1987-94; med. dir. Cmty. Human Svcs., Monterey, Calif., 1987-94, Colstrip (Mont.) Med. Ctr., 1994-97; cons. San Bernadino County, Riverside County, Calif., 1998—; regional med. dir. Point Loma Healthcare Med. Group, Inc., San Diego, 1997-99; med. dir., CEO So. Calif. Mobile Physician Svcs., 1999—. Fellow Am. Acad. Family Physicians; mem. AMA, Am. Occupational Medicine Assn., Flying Physicians, Am. Pub. Health Assn. Avocations: pvt. pilot. Home: 1417 14th St W Ste 250 Billings MT 59102-3137 Office: 5225 Canyon Crest Dr Ste 71-448 Riverside CA 92507-6301

SMITH, JEREMY, computer programmer; b. London, June 14, 1954; came to U.S., 1978; s. John Bernhard and Marion Elaine (Reynolds) S. BSc in Botany and Chemistry, London U., 1976. Rsch. assoc. Henry Doubleday Rsch. Assn., Bocking Braintree, Essex, Eng., 1977, 33 Energies, Irvine, Calif., 1978; landscape artist Capability Brown Landscapes, Corona Del Mar, Calif., 1979; computer programmer Bostram Bergen Metal Products, Oakland, Calif., 1980-82, AMF Sci. Drilling, Irvine, 1982-85; scientist U.S. EPA, Corvallis, Oreg., 1986-96; release engr. Rogue Wave Software, Corvallis, 1997—. Author: HP-41 Synthetic Quick Reference Guide, 1983, American-British/British-American Dictionary, 1992. Flight sgt. RAF, 1968-72. Mem. Personal Programming Ctr. Avocations: gardening, programming, reading. E-mail: Jeremy@peak.org. Address: Code Smith 301 NE Byron Pl Corvallis OR 97330-6233

SMITH, JOEY SPAULS, mental health nurse, home health nurse, biofeedback therapist, consultant, educator, bodyworker, hypnotist; b. Washington, Oct. 9, 1944; d. Walter Jr. and Marian (Och) Spauls; children: Kelly, Sean. BSN, Med. Coll. Va., 1966; MA in Edn., U. Nebr., Lincoln, 1975. RNC, ANA; cert. psychiat. and mental health nurse; cert. zero balancer, cert. hypnotist, cert. biofeedback therapist; cert. perineometry cons.; ANA cert. home health nurse. 1st lt. U.S. Army Nurse Corps, 1965-67; staff nurse Booth Meml. Hosp., Omaha, 1969-71; asst. house supr. Nebr. Meth. Hosp., Omaha, 1971-72; head nurse, clin. instr. U. Calif., Davis, 1976-78; staff nurse Atascadero State Hosp., Calif. Dept. Mental Health, 1978-79; nurse instr. psychiat. technician Atascadero State Hosp., 1979-84, insvc. tng. coord., 1984-86; nursing coord. chem. dependency recovery program French Hosp. Med. Ctr., San Luis Obispo, Calif., 1986-87; relief house supr. San Luis Obispo County Gen. Hosp., 1982-88; regional program assoc. statewide nursing program Consortium Calif. Sate U., 1986-88; nurse instr., health svcs. staff devel. coord. Calif. Men's Colony, Dept. Corrections, San Luis Obispo, 1987-92; pvt. practice San Luis Obispo, Calif., 1990—; clin. instr. nursing divsn. Cuesta Coll., 1988—. Fellow Biofeedback Certification Inst. of Am.; mem. Assn. Applied Psychophysiology and Biofeedback, Biofeedback Soc. of Calif., Zero Balancing Assn. (cert.), Esalen Massage and Bodyworkers Assn., Soc. Urol. Nurses and Assocs., Ctrl. Coast Nurses Coop. Coun., Biofeedback Cert. Inst. Am., Alpha Sigma Chi, Phi Delta Kappa. Home: 8345 Curbaril Ave Atascadero CA 93422-5173 Office: PO Box 4823 San Luis Obispo CA 93403-4823

SMITH, JOHN KERWIN, lawyer; b. Oakland, Calif., Oct. 18, 1926; 1 dau., Cynthia. BA, Stanford U.; LLB, Hastings Coll. Law, San Francisco. Ptnr., Haley, Purchio, Sakai & Smith, Hayward, Calif.; bd. dirs. Berkeley Asphalt, Mission Valley Ready-Mix; gen. ptnr. Oak Hill Apts., City Ctr. Commercial, Creekwood I and Creekwood II Apts. Road Parks Commn., 1957, mem. city coun., 1959-66, mayor, 1966-70; chmn. Alameda County Mayors Conf., 1968; chmn. revenue taxation com. League Calif. Cities, 1968; vice-chmn. Oakland-Alameda County Coliseum Bd. Dirs.; bd. dirs. Coliseum Found., Mission Valley Rock, Rowell Ranch Rodeo; former pres. Hastings 1066 Found. (Vol. Svc. award 1990), Martin Kauffman 100 Club. Recipient Alumnus of Yr. award Hastings Coll. Law, 1989. Mem. ABA, Calif. Bar Assn., Alameda County Bar Assn., Am. Judicature Soc., Rotary. Office: 22320 Foothill Blvd Ste 620 Hayward CA 94541-2700

SMITH, JOHN LEROY, mathematics educator; b. Cooper, Tex., July 15, 1944; s. John Jr. and Annie (West) S.; m. Barbara Ann Frazier, Dec. 27, 1965 (div. Apr. 1972); m. Mary Anne Anthony, June 17, 1978; children: Alexander Anthony, Annastasia Marie, Jeannette Joy. BS in Math., U. Wash., 1966; MA in Math., San Diego State U., 1971; BS in Info. & Computer Sci., U. Calif., Irvine, 1986. Computer operator U. Wash., Seattle, 1964-66; tchr. math., sci., English, 1966-70; tchr. math., sci. Highline, Wash., 1971-73; tchr. math. & computer scis. Kwajalein (Marshall Islands) Jr./Sr. H.S., 1973-75; instr. scuba diving Santa Ana (Calif.) Coll., 1978-91; prof. math., computer sci. Rancho Santiago C.C. Dist., Santa Ana, 1975—; math dept. chair Santiago Canyon Coll., Orange, Calif., 1998—; mem. adv. bd. govs. Faculty Assn. Calif. C.C., Sacramento, 1991—; treas. Faculty Assn. Rancho Santa Ana Coll., 1988—. Editor (newsletter) FARSIGHT, 1989—; editor Dive Boat Calender, 1987-91. Choir mem. St. Paul's Greek Orthodox Ch., Irvine, 1993—, mem. parish coun., 1987-89; asst. scoutmaster Boy Scouts Am., Irvine, 1994—. Mem. NEA, Nat. Assn. Underwater Instrs., Nat. Coun. Tchrs. Math., Am. Math Assn. Two Yr. Colls., Profl. Assn. Diving Instrs. Avocations: scuba diving, camping, hiking, running. Home: 1 Caraway Irvine CA 92604-3211 Office: Santiago Canyon Coll Orange CA 92869

SMITH, JON DAVID, advertising executive; b. Pomona, Calif., Nov. 11, 1960; s. Joseph Samuel and Grace Ellenora (Gothard) S.; m. Linda Anne Esslinger, June 2, 1984; children: Cheyne, Chad, Caitlyn. Student, Calif. Poly. Inst., Pomona, 1978-81. Prodr., dir. Trinity Broadcasting, Tustin, Calif., 1980-86, Roever Comms., Ft. Worth, 1986-87; assoc. dir., editor The Edit Bay, Orange, Calif., 1987-95; prodr. Hendry Lindman & Assoc., Irvine, Calif., 1995-98, asst. creative dir., 1998—; owner, prodr. Jon D. Smith Prodns., Mission Viejo, Calif., 1984—; freelance dir. Promise Keepers, Denver, 1996—; freelance dir. Roever Ednl. Assistance Program. Ft. Worth, 1995—; dir., editor Billy Graham-Mission World, Hong Kong, Buenos Aires, Essen, Germany and San Juan, P.R., 1990-95. Candidate for City Coun., Lake Forest, Calif., 1991; pres. bd. dirs. Willowglen Homeowners Assn., Lake Forest, 1990-93; v.p. bd. dirs. Serrano Highlands Homeowners Assn., Lake Forest, 1990-93; v.p. bd. dirs. Acts for Children, 1995—. Recipient Silver Angel award Religion in Media, 1984, 95. Office: Hendry Lindman & Assoc 17992 Mitchell S Irvine CA 92614-6813

SMITH, KAY PRIDGEN, art museum officer. Pres. Nicolaysen Art Mus., Casper, Wyo. Office: Nicolaysen Art Mus 400 E Collins Dr Casper WY 82601-2815*

SMITH, KEITH LARUE, research company executive; b. Salida, Colo., Dec. 15, 1917; s. Leroy Holt and Verna Lea (Tunnell) S.; student Marion Coll., 1935-38; A.B. in Math., Ind. U., 1946; postgrad. DePauw U., 1946-47; M.A. in Internat. Affairs, Harvard U., 1955; M.P.A., Calif. State U.-Fullerton, 1979; m. Evelyn May De Bruler, Aug. 29, 1943; 1 son, Eric Douglas. Mil. intelligence research specialist Dept. of Army, Washington, 1951-60; staff engr. Librascope div. Gen. Precision, Inc., Glendale, Cal., 1960-61; sr. operations research analyst Space div. N.Am. Rockwell Corp., Downey, Cal., 1961-71; dir. research Am. Research Corp., Paramount, Calif., 1972-80; instr. math. and polit. sci. DePauw U., 1946-47; cons. model bldg. and gaming techniques, 1960—; mgmt. cons., 1970—; instr. math. and sci. Verbum Dei High Sch., 1974-85; CEO K.L. Smith and Assocs., 1988—. Adult leader Boy Scouts Am., Long Beach, Calif., 1961-75. Treas., UN Council Harvard, 1947-49, Young Democratic Club, Arlington, Mass., 1949-50. Served to capt. USAAF, 1941-46; ETO. Recipient scholarship award Inst. World Affairs, 1947, Outstanding Efficiency award Dept. Army, 1960, Apollo 8 and Apollo 11 medallions, NASA, 1969, 70. Mem. Am. Mus. Natural History, Nat. Geog. Soc., Harvard Alumni Assn., Pi Sigma Alpha. Mason. Research on mil. operations research and war game model bldg., tech. mgmt. techniques. Home: 666 E Memory Ln Apt 310 Santa Ana CA 92706-1702

SMITH, LANE JEFFREY, automotive journalist, technical consultant; b. Honolulu, May 17, 1954; s. Gerald Hague and JoEllen (Lane) S.; m. Susan Elizabeth Gumm, May 24, 1980 (div. 1997); children: Amber Elizabeth, Graham Hague. BS in Journalism, Iowa State U., 1978. Feature editor Car Craft mag. Peterson Pub., L.A., 1979—, tech. editor, sr. editor, editor Hot Rod Mag., 1987-93, exec. editor, 1993—; speaker in field. Avocations: military history, aviation, building and racing high performance automobiles. Home: 18320 Citronia St Northridge CA 91325-1717 Office: Hot Rod Mag 6420 Wilshire Blvd Fl 11 Los Angeles CA 90048-5502*

SMITH, LAWRENCE RONALD, lawyer; b. Santa Monica, Calif., July 26, 1966; s. Lawrence Horton Camp and Joan Marie (Keating) S.; m. Constance Amanda Sullivan, Oct. 18, 1997. BA in Polit. Sci., UCLA, 1988; JD, Whittier Coll., 1993. Bar: Calif. Internal clk. U.S. Dist. Ct., L.A., 1992-93; assoc. Bonne, Bridges, Mueller, O'Keefe & Nichols, L.A., 1994-96; v.p., gen. counsel AZ3, Inc. d.b.a. B.C.B.G., Vernon, Calif., 1996—. Mem. Am. Corp. Coun. Assn. (chmn. So. Calif. small legal depts. com. 1996—, chmn. 1996—), Calif. State Bar Assn., Whittier Law Sch. Alumni (bd. dirs. 1994—). Avocations: golf, soccer. Office: AZ3 Inc d.b.a. B.C.B.G 2761 Fruitland Ave Vernon CA 90058-3607

SMITH, LE ROI MATTHEW-PIERRE, III, municipal administrator; b. Chgo., Jan. 11, 1946; s. Le Roy Matthew and Norma Buckner (McCamey) S.; 1 son, Le Roi Matthew Pierre. B.A. in Psychology, Idaho State U., 1969; Ph.D. in Psychology, Wash. State U., 1977. Instr. psychology Idaho State U., Pocatello, 1969-70, Wash. State U., Pullman, 1970-71; mem. faculty dept. psychology Evergreen State Coll., Olympia, 1971-81; dir. diversity program Port of Seattle, 1981—; cons. in field. Bd. dirs. Thurston-Mason County Community Mental Health Ctr., Olympia; v.p., Idaho State Human Rights Commn., Bannock County, Idaho, 1968-70. Office Edn. fellow, 1969-70; U.S. Dept. Labor grantee, 1968; NSF grantee, 1972; Lilly Found. fellow, 1980. Mem. Am. Psychol. Assn., Am. Personnel and Guidance Assn., Wash. State Black Econs. and Edn. Conf., Assn. Black Psychologists, Am. Assn. of Affirmative Action Officers, Phi Delta Kappa. Democrat. Roman Catholic. Home: PO Box 2903 Blaine WA 98231-2903 Office: PO Box 1209 Seattle WA 98111-1209

SMITH, LEE L., hotel executive; b. Long Beach, Calif., Oct. 15, 1936; s. Lowell Llake and Violet Margaret (Chrissman) S.; m. Sharon M.C. Lanahan, (div. 1977). AA, Long Beach City Coll., 1958; BA in Music, Chapman Coll., 1965; postgrad., Calif. State U., Long Beach, 1966-67, U. Calif., Santa Barbara, 1974. Cert. tchr. Calif.; lic. ins. agt., Calif. Owner, mgr. Lee's Land Cattle Ranch, Cuyama Valley, Calif., 1960—; tchr. Cuyama Valley Schs., New Cuyama, Calif., 1967-79; owner, mgr. Cuyama Buckhorn Restaurant & Motel, New Cuyama, 1979-83; owner Allstate Ins. Agy., Desert Hot Springs, Calif., 1987-91; owner, mgr. Caravan Resort Spa, Desert Hot Springs, 1983-91; owner S & S Printing, 1990—, Lee's Land Bed & Breakfast, 1992—. Violinist Bakersfield (Calif.) Symphony, 1967—, Brook String Quartet, Palm Springs, Calif., 1984-91; dir. Planning Commn., Desert Hot Springs, 1985-87; chmn. Environ. Rev., Desert Hot Springs, 1986-88; mem. Redevel. Com., Desert Hot Springs, 1983-88; mem. exec. bd. growth and devel. Boys and Girls Club; bd. dirs. Food Now Program, 1988-91. Mem. Am. Fedn. Musicians, Desert Hot Springs C. of C. (Bus. Person Yr. 1987), Taft C. of C. (pres. 1997), Breakfast Rotary (pres. 1987-88), Taft Rotary, Elks. Republican. Avocations: hiking, flying. Home: HC 1 Box 185B Maricopa CA 93252-9629 Office: S & S Printing 606 Center St Taft CA 93268-3125

SMITH, LEONORE RAE, artist; b. Chgo.; d. Leon and Rose (Hershfield) Goodman; m. Paul Carl Smith, Apr. 17, 1943; children: Jill Henderson, Laurie Christman. Student, Chgo. Art Inst., 1935-40, U. Chgo., 1939—. performer in many Broadway shows, with Met. Opera Quartet, Carnegie Hall, nat. concerts; portrait, landscape painter; signature artist Oil Painters of Am., Chgo., 1992-98, Am. Acad. of Women Artists, 1997-98; ofcl. artist U.S. Coast Guard, Washington, 1989-98; cert. artist Am. Portrait Soc., Huntington Harbor, Calif., 1985; nat. adv. bd. The Portrait Club, N.Y.C., 1983. Pres. Pacific Palisades Rep. Women, Calif. Recipient Best of Show awards Salamagundi U.S. Coast Guard, N.Y.C., 1989, Pacific Palisades Art Assn., 1987, 1st prize in oils Greater L.A. Art Competition, Santa Monica, Calif., 1995, prize The Artist's Mag., 1995, Internat. Soc. Artists, 1977; named One of Master Artists of World Internat. Artists Mag., 1996. Mem. Am. Acad. Women Artists (signature mem.), Salmagundi Club, Pacific Palisades Art Assn. (past pres.), Calif. Art Club, Oil Painters of Am. (signature mem.), Am. Portrait Soc. Avocations: singing, acting, poetry.

SMITH, LINDA WASMER, writer; b. West Memphis, Ark., Nov. 9, 1957; d. Frederick Lark and Nettie Belle (Pittman) Wasmer; m. David Alan Smith, May 28, 1977 (div. 1998); children: Amanda Lark, Michael David. BA, U. N.Mex., 1979. Freelance writer Albuquerque, 1982—; webmaster Health Writer Website, 1997—. Author: Of Mind and Body, 1997, Louis Pasteur=Disease Fighter, 1997; contbr. numerous chpts. to books, articles to mags. Ct.-appointed spl. adv., Bernalillo County, N.Mex., 1998—. Mem. Am. Med. Writers Assn., Nat. Assn. Sci. Writers, Am. Soc. Journalists and Authors.

SMITH, LINDA ZIMBALIST, investment research executive; b. St. Louis, Jan. 27, 1953; d. Sidney Eli and Blanka M. (Wassermann) Zimbalist; m. William Martin Smith, May 27, 1979; children: Brian Alexander, Tyler Scott. BA, Pitzer Coll., Claremont, Calif., 1978; MBA, U. Chgo., 1978. Research asst. Stein Roe & Farnham, Chgo., 1975-76, Chgo. Bd. Options Exchange, 1976-79; arbitrage analyst First Boston, N.Y.C., 1980-82; gen. ptnr. Zimbalist Smith Investments, Bend, Oreg., 1982—. Avocation: tennis. Office: Zimbalist Smith 2955 N Highway 97 Bend OR 97701-7509

SMITH, LOUIS JOHN, retired gynecologist; b. Helena, Mont., Nov. 9, 1924; s. Louis and Jennie (Kovacic) S.; married, Aug. 9, 1947; children: Kevin, Karen, Lisa, Michelle, Christopher, Robert. MD, Oreg. Health Scis. U., Portland, 1952. Diplomate Am. Bd. Ob-Gyn. Intern, resident Queen of Angels Hosp., L.A., 1952-56; pvt. practice obstetrics and gynecology Burbank, Calif., 1956-93; ret., 1993. With USN, 1943-46. Home: 4006 Longridge Ave Sherman Oaks CA 91423-4926

SMITH, MARK LEE, architect; b. L.A., Nov. 16, 1957; s. Selma (Moidel) Smith. BA in History of Architecture, UCLA, 1978, MA in Architecture, 1980. Registered architect Calif., Nev., Oreg., Wash., Tenn., Colo., N.Y., Ohio. Designer, drafter John B. Ferguson and Assocs., L.A., 1976-83, architect, 1983; pvt. practice architecture L.A., 1984—; mem. Los Angeles County Archtl. Evaluation Bd., 1990—; spkr. Western Pool and Spa Show, 1997, 98, 99. Essay columnist AIA/SFV monthly, 1997—; contbr. articles to profl. jours. Bd. govs. UCLA John Wooden Ctr., 1978-80; judge Bank Am. Achievement Awards, 1998. Regents scholar, U. Calif., Berkeley, UCLA, 1975-78; UCLA Grad. Sch. Architecture Rsch. fellow, 1979-80. Mem. AIA (treas. San Fernando Valley chpt. 1986, bd. dirs. 1986—, v.p. 1987, pres. 1988, Design award 1988, 89, 90, 91, 99, chmn. Design awards 1994, bd. dirs. Calif. coun. 1989-94, v.p. 1991-94, chmn. continuing edn. 1991-93, chmn. 1992 conf.), Phi Beta Kappa. Office: 18340 Ventura Blvd Ste 225 Tarzana CA 91356-4278

SMITH, MARTIN BERNHARD, journalist; b. San Francisco, Apr. 20, 1930; s. John Edgar and Anna Sophie (Thorsen) S.; m. Joan Louvat Muller, Apr. 25, 1953; children: Catherine Joan, Karen Anne. AB, U. Calif., Berkeley, 1952, M Journalism, 1968. Reporter, city editor Modesto (Calif.) Bee, 1957-64; reporter, mng. editor Sacramento Bee, 1964-75; polit. editor, columnist McClatchy Newspapers, Sacramento, 1975-92; ret., 1992. Episcopalian.

SMITH, MAUREEN MCBRIDE, laboratory administrator; b. Santa Monica, Calif., Mar. 4, 1952; d. Clayton Laird McBride and Luella (Sullivan) Boudreau; step-father Henry A Boudreau; m. Gary Howard Cothran, July 27, 1974 (div. Apr. 1982); m. Guy Gordon Smith, Feb. 12, 1983; stepchildren: Keri Lynn, Scott Allen. BS magna cum laude, Calif. State Coll., San Bernardino, 1978, MS, 1993. Analytical chemist Chalco Engring., Edwards AFB, Calif., 1978-79, 82; microbiol. lab. tech. AVEK Water Agy., Quartz Hill, Calif., 1979-81, chemist, lab. mgr., 1982—; instr. Antelope Valley Coll., Lancaster Calif., 1980-82. Mem. AAAS, Am. Chem. Soc. Avocations: skiing, photography, training and showing golden retrievers. Address: 6500 W Avenue N Palmdale CA 93551-2855

SMITH, MAYNARD DWIGHT, minister; b. Milo, Iowa, Feb. 22, 1921; s. Foster Clayton and Myrtle May (Nutting) S.; m. Betty Luella Vander Wal; children: Todd Allen, Timothy Ray. BA, Cen. Coll., Pella, Iowa, 1943; BD, McCormick Theol. Sem., Chgo., 1950; D of Ministry, McCormick Theol. Sem., 1976; MA, Wayne State U., 1966; ThM, San Francisco Theol. Sem., 1967. Ordained to ministry Presbyn. Ch., 1950. Pastor Douglas Ave. Presbyn. Ch., Des Moines, 1950-58, Highland Park Presbyn. Ch., Detroit, 1958-66, Deerhurst Presbyn. Ch., Kenmore, N.Y., 1967-71, St. John's Presbyn. Ch., Houston, 1971-86; tchr. world religions Sierra Nev. Coll., Incline Village, Nev., 1987-91; clergy v.p. The Met. Orgn., Houston, 1979-85; moderator Gen. Coun. New Covenant Presbytery, Houston, 1983-85. Contbr. prayers and short story to periodicals. Pres. Human Rels. Coun., Highland Park, Mich., 1964-65; bd. dirs. ACLU, Western N.Y., 1968-71. 1st lt. USMC, 1943-46, PTO. Home and Office: 498 Equity Ct Windsor CA 95492-7969

SMITH, MICHAEL, biochemistry educator; b. Blackpool, Eng., Apr. 26, 1932. BSc, U. Manchester, Eng., 1953, PhD, 1956. Fellow B.C. Rsch. Coun., 1956-60; rsch. assoc. Inst. Enzyme Rsch., U. Wis., 1960-61; head chem. sect. Vancouver Lab. Fisheries Rsch. Bd. Can., 1961-66; med. rsch. assoc. Med. Rsch. Coun. Can., 1966-71, career investigator, 1971—; assoc. prof. biochem. U. B.C., Vancouver, 1966-70, prof., 1970—, Peter Wall disting. prof. biotech., 1994—. Recipient Gairdner Found. Internat. award, 1986, Nobel Prize in Chemistry, 1993. Fellow Chem Inst. Can., Royal Soc. (London), Royal Soc. Can., Royal Soc. Chemistry; mem. NAS (fgn. assoc.), Sigma Xi, Order of British Columbia, Companion of the Order of Can. Achievements include research in nucleic acid and nucleotide chemistry and biochemistry using in-vitro mutagenesis gene expression. Office: U BC Biotech Lab, 6174 University Blvd 237, Vancouver, BC Canada V6T 1Z3

SMITH, MICHAEL ROBERT, electro-optical engineer, physicist; b. Tela, Honduras, Aug. 24, 1937; s. Ike Morgan and Edith Helen (Hudson) S.; m. Suzanne Ruth Hudgins, Aug. 20, 1960; children: Stephen, Monica, Meryl. BME, Ga. Inst. Tech., 1959, MS in Nuclear Engring., 1961; PhD, Case Inst. Tech., 1965. Mem. tech. staff Hughes Rsch. Labs., Malibu, Calif., 1965-68; v.p., dir. rsch. Britt Corp., L.A., 1968-73; sr. staff engr. Singer/Librascope divsn., Glendale, Calif., 1973-78; pres. Exocor Tech., Newbury Park, Calif., 1978-95; asst. prof., head physics program Calif. Luth. U., Thousand Oaks, 1990-96; design leader LIGO project Calif. Inst. Tech., Pasadena, 1996—. Contbr. articles to profl. jours.; inventor emergency vehicle warning and traffic control sys., emergency vehicle warning sign, flat electro-optic display panel, high power mirror, laser recording film with opaque coating, pulsed gas laser with radiation cooling, infrared laser photocautery device; 8 U.S. patents; 9 fgn. patents. Greek folk dance tchr. Arts Coun., Thousand Oaks, Calif., 1991-97. Mem. IEEE, Laser Electro-Optic Soc. (chair 1995-97), Sigma Xi, Pi Tau Sigma. Republican. Home: 680 S Marengo Ave Apt 9 Pasadena CA 91106-3659

SMITH, NATHAN MCKAY, JR., university administrator; b. Riverside, Calif., Sept. 22, 1954; s. Nathan McKay and Joyce Annette (Carmen) S.; m. Phyllis Anne Stewart, Aug. 18, 1977; children: Nathan Blair, Rachael, Sarah, Jeremiah, Seth, Peter, Hannah. BS, Brigham Young U., 1980; MS, Utah State U., 1990. Cert. tchr., Utah. Tchr. elem. sch. Washington County Schs., St. George, Utah, 1980-92; dir. ednl. resources & tech. NASA Regional Tchr. Resource Ct Utah State U., Logan, 1992—. Author: (website) Teacher Link, 1995; co-author: (multimedia instrn.) Project FORE, 1989. Scout leader LDS Ch. coun. Boy Scouts Am., Utah, 1984— Phi Kappa Phi, Phi Delta Kappa. Avocations: computers, art. Office: Utah State U 170 EDUC-UMC 2845 Logan UT 84322

SMITH, PAMELA IRIS, consulting company executive; b. Pitts., Aug. 23, 1958; d. Robert Edward and Rae R. Kline; m. Robert T. Smith; 1 child, Elise Kristin. Cert., U. Paris, Sorbonne, 1979; AB magna cum laude, Harvard U., 1980, MBA, 1984. Asst. staff mgr. Bell of Pa., Phila., 1980-82; product mgr. Visa Internat., San Francisco, 1983; v.p. Prognostics, Palo Alto, Calif., 1984-91; dir. Diefenbach/Elkins, San Francisco, 1991-92; ptnr. The McKenna Group, 1992—. Vol. San Jose Civic Lights, 1987; dir. Harvard/Radcliffe Fundraising, Boston, 1980—; chmn. Harvard/Radcliffe Schs. com., San Mateo County, 1985—. Recipient TWIN award YWCA. Mem. Young Profl. Woman Assn., Radcliffe Club (dir. 1987—), Harvard Club. Republican. Avocations: swimming, jogging, scuba, tennis, reading. Home: 50 Los Altos Rd Los Altos CA 94022 Office: The McKenna Group 1755 Embarcadero Rd Palo Alto CA 94303-3309

SMITH, PATRICIA JACQUELINE, marketing executive; b. Orange, N.J., June 13, 1944; d. Michael Joseph and Helen Francis (Costello) S. BS, U. Md., 1967. Field dir. Colgate Palmolive Co., N.Y.C., 1967-71; account exec. Foote Cone & Belding, N.Y.C., 1971-72; dir. regional sales, dir. ARA Services, Inc., Phila., 1973-76; dir. federally funded programs Ogden Food Service, Boston, 1976-79; v.p. Smith Tool Co., Manesquan, N.J., 1979-84; chmn., CEO Hygolet Metro, Inc., New Canaan, Conn., 1984-87; mktg. cons. Smith Mktg. Svcs., La Jolla, Calif., 1988-94; pres. Tea for Two Inc., Laguna Beach, Calif., 1995—; ptnr. La Jolla Playhouse. Bd. dirs., treas. Big Sister League, San Diego; mem. exec. com. Multiple Sclerosis Brunch Soc.; ptnr. La Jolla Playhouse. Mem. Women in Sales, Nat. Assn. Profl. Saleswomen, Bus. and Profl. Women's Club (N.Y.), Victorian Tea Soc., The Discovery Mus., Women's Club Laguna Beach, AAUW, Laguna Beach C. of C. Republican. Home: PO Box 4994 Laguna Beach CA 92652-4994

SMITH, PAUL JAY, interior designer; b. Bronx, N.Y., Jan. 16, 1948; s. Julius and Florence Sarah (Springer) S.; m. Paulette Sandra Fink, Feb. 16, 1969; children: Mindy Nadine, Hayley Alexis. Tech. Cardian Electronics, Woodbury, N.Y., 1969-70; prin., owner Paul Smith Stationary, Floral Park, N.Y., 1970-73; pres. Country Club Market, Inc., Tucson, 1972-77; partner S&S Handyman Svcs., Tucson, 1977-79; prin., pres. P. Smith & Co., Inc., Tucson, 1979—; bd. dirs. Interiors wiht Imagination, Strictly Blinds. Mem. Nat. Assn. Home Builders, Am. Soc. Interior Designers, Southern Ariz. Home Builders Assn., Tucson Metropolitan C. of C., Phoenix C. of C., Tucson Better Bus. Bureau, Knights of Pythias. Democrat. Jewish. Avocations: travel, music, cooking, woodworking. Fax: (520) 885-4135. Home: 8950 E 3rd St Tucson AZ 85710-2672 Office: P Smith & Co Inc 8950 E 3rd St Tucson AZ 85710-2672

SMITH, PHYLLIS MAE, healthcare consultant, educator; b. Coeur d'Alene, Idaho, May 2, 1935; d. Elmer Lee Smith and Kathryn Alice (Newell) Wilson. Diploma, Lutheran Bible Inst., Seattle, 1956, Emanuel Hosp. Sch. Nursing, Portland, Oreg., 1959; student Coll. San Mateo, Calif., 1971. Staff nurse in surgery Emanuel Hosp., Portland, 1959-61, St. Vincent's Hosp., Portland, 1962-63; head nurse central service Sacred Heart Hosp., Eugene, Oreg., 1964-69; dir. central services Peninsula Hosp., Burlingame, Calif., 1969-74; pres. Phyllis Smith Assocs., Inc., Lewiston, Idaho, 1975-88; sr. tech. advisor, dir. ednl. programs, Parkside Material Mgmt. Services, Park Ridge, Ill., 1988-90; AIDS coord. Asotin County Health Dist., 1989—; lectr., cons. in field in over 11 countries. Contbr. to manuals, profl. jours. Mem. Internat. Assn. Hosp. Central Service Mgmt. (dir. edn. 1973-88, chmn. technician edn. and affairs com. 1978-88, John Perkins award, 1977, Chesire award 1977), Assn. for Advancement Med. Instrumentation, Nat. Assn. Female Execs. Episcopalian. Lodge: Eagles Aux. Avocations: fishing, walking, photography, chess, reading. Home and Office: 3730 11th St Lewiston ID 83501-5484

SMITH, RALPH EARL, virologist; b. Yuma, Colo., May 10, 1940; s. Robert C. and Esther C. (Schwarz) S.; m. Sheila L. Kondy, Aug. 29, 1961 (div. 1986); 1 child, Andrea Denise; m. Janet M. Keller, 1988. BS, Colo. State U., 1961; PhD, U. Colo., 1968. Registered microbiologist Am. Soc. Clin. Pathologists. Fellow Duke U. Med. Ctr., Durham, N.C., 1968-70, asst. prof., 1970-74, assoc. prof., 1974-80, prof. virology, 1980-82; prof., head dept. microbiology Colo. State U., Ft. Collins, 1983-88, prof. microbiology, assoc. v.p. rsch., 1989—, interim v.p. rsch., 1990-91, prof. microbiology, assoc. v.p. rsch., 1991—; cons. Bellco Glass Co., Vineland, N.J., 1976-80, Proctor & Gamble Co., Cin., 1985-86, Schering Plough Corp., Bloomfield, N.J., 1987-89. Contbr. articles to profl. jours.; patentee in field. Bd. dirs. Colo. Ctr. for Environ. Mgmt., v.p. for rsch.; mem. pollution prevention adv. bd. Colo. Dept. Pub. Health and Environment; mem. Rocky Mountain U. Consortium on Environ. Restoration, Environ. Inst. Rocky Flats; asst. scoutmaster Boy Scouts Am., Durham, 1972-82, com. mem., Ft. Collins, 1986-91; mem. adminstrv. bd. 1st United Meth. Ch., Ft. Collins. Eleanor Roosevelt fellow Internat. Union Against Cancer 1978-79. Mem. AAAS, Am. Soc. Microbiology, N.Y. Acad. Scis., Am. Soc. Virology, Gamma Sigma Delta. Democrat. Methodist. Avocations: photography, hiking. Home: 2406 Creekwood Dr Fort Collins CO 80525-2034 Office: Colo State U VP Rsch Fort Collins CO 80523

SMITH, RAYMOND EDWARD, retired health care administrator; b. Freeport, N.Y., June 17, 1932; s. Jerry Edward and Madelyn Holman (Jones) S.; BS in Edn., Temple U., 1953; MHA, Baylor U., 1966; m. Lena Kathryn Jernigan Hughes, Oct. 28, 1983; children: Douglas, Ronald, Kevin, Doris Jean, Raymond. Commd. 2d lt. U.S. Army, 1953, advanced through grades to lt. col., 1973; helicopter ambulance pilot, 1953-63; comdr. helicopter ambulance units, Korea, 1955, Fed. Republic of Germany, 1961; various hosp. adminstrv. assignments, 1963-73; pers. dir. Valley Forge (Pa.) Gen. Hosp., 1966; adminstr. evacuation hosp., Vietnam, 1967; dep. insp. Walter Reed Gen. Hosp., Washington, 1970; dir. personnel divsn. Office of Army Surgeon Gen., Washington, 1971-73, ret., 1973; adminstr. Health Care Ctrs., Phila. Coll. Osteo. Medicine, 1974-76; dir. bur. hosps. Pa. Dept. Health, Harrisburg, 1976-79; contract mgr. Blue Cross of Calif., San Diego, 1979-88, Cmty. Care Network, San Diego, 1989-95, ret. 1995. Decorated Bronze Star, Legion of Merit. Mem. Am. Hosp. Assn., Am. Legion, Ret. Officers Assn., Kappa Alpha Psi. Episcopalian. Club: Masons. Home: 7630 Lake Adlon Dr San Diego CA 92119-2518

SMITH, RICHARD ALAN, neurologist, medical association administrator. Student, Brandeis U., 1958-61; grad., U. Miami, 1965. Intern in medicine Jackson Meml. Hosp., Miami, Fla., 1965-66; resident in neurology Stanford U. Hosp., Palo Alto, Calif., 1966-69; head neurology br. Navy Neuropsychiatric Rsch. Unit, San Diego, 1969-71; mem. assoc. staff microbiology Scripps Clinic and Rsch. Found., La Jolla, Calif., 1972-79, mem. assoc. staff neurology, 1972-82; dir. Ctr. Neurologic Study, San Diego, 1979—; mem. sr. staff Scripps Meml. Hosp., La Jolla, 1982—; mem. med. adv. bd. Multiple Sclerosis Soc., San Diego; founder neurosci. network Affil. Rsch. Ctrs., Gurnee, Ill., 1995—; pres. Coordinated Clin. Rsch. Corp., San Diego, 1996—. Editor: Interferon Treatment for Neurologic Disorders, 1988, Handbook of Amyotrophic Lateral Sclerosis, 1992; contbr. articles to profl. jours. Recipient Henry Newman award San Francisco Neurologic Soc., 1968; NIH STTR grantee, 1996-97; Skaggs Clin. scholar Scripps Rsch. Inst., 1998-99. Mem. AAAS, Am. Acad. Neurology (assoc.). Achievements include 5 U.S. patents; work on methodology for enhancing the systemic delivery of Dextromethorphan for the treatment of neurological and medical disorders, including emotional lability, pain and cough. Office: 9850 Genesee Ave Ste 320 La Jolla CA 92037-1208

SMITH, ROBERT BRUCE, former security consultant, retired career officer; b. De Quincy, La., Apr. 22, 1920; s. Malcolm Monard and Jewell (Perkins) S.; m. Gladys Opal Borel, Feb. 22, 1941; children: Susan, Richard, Bruce. B.J., La. State U., 1941; grad., Command and Gen. Staff Coll., 1951-52, Army War Coll., 1958-59. Commd. 2d lt. U.S. Army, 1941, advanced through grades to maj. gen., 1969; plans and ops. officer 83d Div. Arty., Europe, 1943-45; personnel officer Philippine-Ryukyus Command, Manila, 1947-49; prof. mil. sci. and tactics ROTC, Lanier High Sch., Macon, Ga., 1949-51; chief res. officers sect., procurement br. Dept. Army, 1952-55; chief troop info. Office Chief Info., Dept. Army, 1962-63, dep. chief info., 1968-69; comdg. officer 8th F.A. Bn., 25th Inf. Div., Hawaii, 1955-56; G-1 25th Inf. Div. and U.S. Army Hawaii, Hawaii, 1956-58; mem. staff, faculty Command and Gen. Staff Coll., Fort Leavenworth, Kans., 1959-62; chief Alt. Nat. Mil. Command Center, Fort Ritchie, Md., 1963-64; dep. dir. ops. Office Joint Chiefs of Staff, 1964-65; asst. div. comdr. 7th Inf. Div., Korea, 1965-66; dep. comdt. Army War Coll., Carlisle, Pa., 1966-68; dep. comdg. gen. Ryukyus Islands, 1969-72, 6th U.S. Army, Presidio of San Francisco, 1972-73; ret. active duty, 1973; reporter, news editor Lake Charles (La.), 1946-47; region adminstrv. mgr. Burns Security Service, Oakland, Calif., 1974-76; ptnr. constrn. co. Napa, Calif., 1976-77, Burns Security Service, 1978-81; now ret.; dir. 1st Am. Title Co., Napa, Calif., 1988-92. Trustee Queen of Valley Hosp. Found., 1987-89; mem. Nat. coun. Boy Scouts Am., 1969-70; pres. Silverado Property Owners Assn., Inc., 1990-95. Decorated D.S.M. with oak leaf cluster, Legion of Merit with 2 oak leaf clusters, Bronze Star with oak leaf cluster; inducted into La. State U.'s Manship Sch. of Mass Communication Hall of Fame, 1996, Disting. Leadership Cadets Ole War Skule Hall of Honor, 1998. Club: Silverado Country (Napa, Calif.). Home: 350 St Andrews Dr Napa CA 94558-1544

SMITH, ROBERT HAMIL, author, fund raiser; b. Oak Park, Ill., Nov. 8, 1927; s. Henry Garfield and Mary Ellen (Hamil) S.; student U. Denver, 1946-48, LLB, 1953, JD, 1960; m. Mary Helen Kingsley, Dec. 29, 1948; children: David H., Mark K., Steven H., Rebecca Anne. Dep. clk. County Ct., City and County of Denver, 1948-53; with Colo. Ins. Group, 1953-59; mgr. claims dept. R.H. Smith & Assos., 1959-64; cons. Am. Bapt. Home Mission Soc., 1964-68; assoc. dir. devel. Ill. Wesleyan U., 1968-69; asst. to chancellor U. Calif., San Diego, 1969-77; exec. dir. devel. Scripps Clinic and Research Found., La Jolla, Calif., 1977-82, v.p. devel., 1982-88; pres. Cartographic Enterprises, 1981—; owner C Books, 1981; bd. dirs. Nat. Com. on Planned Giving, 1990-94; fund raising cons. deferred giving. Served with USNR, 1945. Mem. Nat. Soc. Fund Raising Execs., Internat. Yachting Fellowship of Rotarians (San Diego fleet comdr. 1979-81). Baptist. Author: Guide to Harbors, Anchorages and Marinas So. and No. California edits., 1983, The Physician as a Fundraiser, 1984, Naval Inst. Guide to Maritime Museums in U.S./Canada, 1991, Smith's Guide to Maritime Museums U.S./Canada, 1993; pub.: Maritime Museums of North America Including Canada, 1998. Home: PO Box 176 Del Mar CA 92014-0176

SMITH, ROBERT LONDON, SR., commissioner, retired air force officer, political scientist, educator; b. Alexandria, La., Oct. 13, 1919; s. Daniel Charleston and Lillie (Roberts) S.; m. Jewel Busch, Feb. 5, 1949; children: Jewel Diane, Robert London, Karl Busch. B.A., Coll. St. Joseph, 1954; M.A., U. Okla., 1955; Ph.D., Am. U., 1964. Commd. 2d lt. USAAF, 1941; advanced through grades to lt. col. USAF, 1961; various assignments in aircraft engring., command and logistics, 1941-60; rsch. logistics Hdqs. Office Aerospace Rsch., 1960-63; project sci., adminstr. postdoctoral rsch. program, asst. dir. NAS, Hdqs. Office Sci. Rsch., 1963-65; ret., 1965; asso. prof. polit. sci., head dept. eve. classes and corr. study U. Alaska, College, 1966-68, dean Coll. Bus., Econs. and Govt., 1966-70, prof., head dept. polit. sci., 1966-84, prof. emeritus, 1984—; commr. Alaska Dept. Health and Social Services, 1983—; mem. govt. panels and planning groups; dir. Arctic 1st Fed. Savs. & Loan Assn.; corporator Mt. McKinley Mut. Savs. Bank. Author: (with others) Squadron Adminstration, 1951; also publs. on nat. security and nat. def.; Contbr. to: (with others) The United Nations Peace University, 1965. Committeeman Western region Boy Scouts Am., 1968-73; mem. exec. bd. Midnight Sun council, 1973-74, committeeman-at-large nat. council, 1968—; mem. Alaska Gov.'s Employment Commn.; pres. United Service Orgn. Council, Fairbanks, Alaska; mem. active corps execs. SBA. Recipient Silver Beaver award Boy Scouts Am.; named Outstanding Prof. U. Alaska, 1975. Mem. Nat. Acad. Econs. and Polit. Sci., AAAS, Air Force Hist. Found., Nat. Inst. Social and Behavioral Scis., Nat. Inst. U.S. in World Affairs, Am. Polit. Sci. Assn., Assn. U.S. Army (bd. dirs. Polar Bear chpt.), Alaska C. of C. (edn. com.), Pi Gamma Mu, Pi Sigma Alpha. Roman Catholic. Club: Rotary. Home: Smithhaven 100 Goldizen Ave Fairbanks AK 99709-3634 also: Smithawaii Nani Kai Hale 73 N Kihei Rd Apt 607 Kihei HI 96753-8823 also: Costa Vida Unit #920-921, Puerto Vallarta Jalisco, Mexico

SMITH, SALLY ELAINE, association executive; b. Salinas, Calif., Aug. 25, 1958; d. William Charles and Audrey Mae (Sarmento) S.; m. Dennis Lynn Thompson, Mar. 8, 1986 (div. Aug. 1989); 1 child, Morgan. BA in Psychology with honors, U. Calif., Santa Cruz, 1980. Legis. asst. ACLU, Sacramento, 1981-84; adminstrv. asst. Lobby for Ind. Freedom and Equality, Sacramento, 1987-88; exec. dir. Nat. Assn. to Advance Fat Acceptance, Inc., Sacramento, 1988—; spkr. Obesitas, Antwerp, Belgium, 1993, Soc. for Nutrition Edn., Portland, Oreg., 1994, Harvard Med. Sch., Cambridge, Mass., 1994, Stanford Med. Sch., Palo Alto, Calif., 1996. Contbr. articles to profl. jours. Pub. rels. specialist, svc. unit specialist, troop leader Tierra Del Oro

Girl Scout Coun., Sacramento, 1981-84, 87-89; mem. legis. adv. com. Calif. Orgn. for Women, Sacramento, 1990-92. Recipient Achievement award Assn. for Health Enrichment of Large Peopole, 1995. Mem. ACLU, Am. Soc. Assn. Execs. Democrat. Avocations: Star Trek, reading. Office: Nat Assn to Advance Fat Acceptance Inc PO Box 188620 Sacramento CA 95818-8620

SMITH, SALLY LYON, portrait artist; b. Pitts., Oct. 31, 1919; d. Prescott Langworthy and Mary Louise (Steele) Lyon; m. Robert E. Smith, Jan. 5, 1942 (dec. 1992); children: Prescott Lyon, Robert E., Samuel Thayer. Grad. h.s., Phila. Cert. Am. Portrait Soc. Portrait artist Old Sacramento, Calif., 1974-77, Sacramento, 1977-80, Folsom, Calif., 1980-95, Carmichael, Calif., 1995—. One woman shows Casa de Los Ninos, 1985, 88, 89, 92, Midtown Gallery-Sacramento, 1995, 96, Dr. Patrick McMenamin-Sacramento Office Complex, 1995; groups exhibitions include Calif. Arts League, 1980-96, Soc. of Western Artists, 1980, 91, 95, Pastels Soc. of the West Coast, 1987, 88, 89, 91, 93, 95; represented in permanent collections. Bd. dirs. Gateway Ho., Sacramento, 1965-75, guild mem. 1975-85, founder 1965. Recipient numerous awards. Mem. Pastel Soc. of West Coast (sec. 1986-87), Soc. of Western Artists, Calif. Arts League. Republican. Episcopalian. Avocations: painting, sketching. Home and Studio: 5156 Sugar Pine Loop Roseville CA 95747-8629

SMITH, SAM CORRY, retired foundation executive, consultant; b. Enid, Okla., July 3, 1922; s. Chester Hubbert and Nelle Kate (Corry) S.; m. Dorothy Jean Bank, Sept. 21, 1945; children: Linda Jean, Nancy Kay, Susan Diane. Student, Phillips U., 1940-43; BS in Chemistry, U. Okla., 1947, MS in Chemistry, 1948; PhD in Biochemistry, U. Wis., 1951. Asst. and assoc. prof. Med. Sch. U. Okla. Med. Sch., Oklahoma City, 1951-55; assoc. dir. grants Research Corp., N.Y.C., 1957-65, dir., 1965-68, v.p. grants, 1968-75; exec. dir. M.J. Murdock Charitable Trust, Vancouver, Wash., 1975-88; foundation cons., 1988—; pres. Pacific Northwest Grantmakers Forum, 1983-84. Contbr. sci. articles to profl. jours. Trustee Nutrition Found., Washington, 1976-84, Internat. Life Scis. Inst., Washington, 1984-86; bd. councilors U. So. Calif. Med. Sch., L.A., 1977-82; mem. adv. com. Coll. Natural Scis. Colo. State U., 1977-80; pres. Cardiopulmonary Rehab. Programs Oreg., 1990-91; bd. dirs. Clark Coll. Found., 1992-98. Named Boss of Yr., Am. Bus. Women's Assn., 1982, Bus. Assoc. of Yr., 1983. Fellow AAAS; mem. Am. Chem. Soc. Avocations: tennis, photography, gardening. Home: 5204 Dubois Dr Vancouver WA 98661-6617

SMITH, SAMUEL DAVID, artist, educator; b. Thorndale, Tex., Feb. 11, 1918; s. Otto Frank and Jeanette (Joyce) S.; m. Elizabeth Marie Smith; children: Cezanne, Rembrandt, Michelangelo. Ed. pub. schs. Prof. art U. N.Mex., 1956-84, prof. art emeritus, 1984—. Illustrator: Roots in Adobe, 1967, Cowboy's Christmas Tree, 1956; also: Coronet mag; one man exhbns. include, Corcoran Gallery Art, Washington, 1949, Santa Fe Mus. Art, 1947, Roswell (N.Mex.) Mus. Fine Art, 1953, 64, Goodwell (Okla.) Hist. Mus., 1964, Panhandle Plains Mus., Canyon City, Tex., 1964, Biltomore Galleries, Los Angeles, 1946, First Nat. Bank, Los Alamos, 1968, group exhbns. include, Baker Galleries, Lubbock, Tex., 1964-73, Met. Mus., N.Y.C., 1944, Blue Door Gallery, Taos, N.Mex., 1946-53, Galeria del Sol, Albuquerque, 1968-73, Brandywine Galleries, 1972-73, Watercolor Workshop, Telluride, Colo., 1984; one-man show includes Retrospective Exhbn. U. of N.Mex., Albuquerque, 1986, World War II War Art Exibit, Nat. Bldg. Mus., 1995. Served as combat artist AUS, 1942-45. Hon. life mem. N.Mex. Art League. Mem. Artist Equity Assn. (pres. N.Mex. chpt. 1957-58, 66-67, 70-71), Elks. Gallery: PO Box 2006 Telluride CO 81435-2006

SMITH, SAMUEL HOWARD, academic administrator, plant pathologist; b. Salinas, Calif., Feb. 4, 1940; s. Adrian Reed and Elsa (Jacop) S.; m. Patricia Ann Walter, July 8, 1960; children: Samuel, Linda Kjelgaard. BS in Plant Pathology, U. Calif., Berkeley, 1961, PhD, 1964; D (hon.), Nihon U., Tokyo, 1989, Far Eastern State U., Vladivostok, Russia, 1997. NATO fellow Glasshouse Crops Research Inst., Sussex, Eng., 1964-65; asst. prof. plant pathology U. Calif., Berkeley, 1965-69; assoc. prof. Pa. State U., Arendtsville, 1969-71; assoc. prof. Pa. State U., University Park, 1971-74, prof., 1974-85, head dept. plant pathology, 1976-81, dean Coll. Agr., dir. Pa. Agrl. Expt. Sta. and Coop. Extension Service, 1981-85; pres. Wash. State U., 1985—; bd. dirs. Assoc. Western Univs.; adv. com. Wash. Sch. Employees Credit Union, 1993-95; mem. adv. com. Battelle Pacific N.W. Lab., 1993—; chair Pacific-10 Conf. CEOs, 1993-94; bd. dirs. All-Nations Alliance for Minority Participation; mem. pres.' commn. NCAA, 1994—, divsn. I chair, 1995-96; chair Pres.'s Commn., 1996—. Bd. dirs. Forward Wash., 1986-95, The Technology Alliance, 1996—, China Rels. Coun.; mem. Wash. Coun. Internat. Trade, Western Interstate Commn. Higher Edn.; bd. dirs. Assn. Western Univs., 1993—. Mem. AAAS, Am. Phytopath. Soc., Nat. Assn. State Univs. and Land-Grand Colls. (bd. dirs. 1994—, chair commn. info. tech. 1994-96), Gamma Sigma Delta, Alpha Zeta, Epsilon Sigma Phi, Sigma Xi, Omicron Delta Kappa, Golden Key, Pi Kappa Alpha (hon.). Home: 755 NE Campus St Pullman WA 99163-4223 Office: Wash State U French Adminstrn Bldg Pullman WA 99164-1048

SMITH, SARAH KIM HUEY, training and development consultant; b. Wichita Falls, Tex., Nov. 5, 1952; d. John Thomas Huey and Dovie Maurine (Nash) Huey Murphy; m. Robert Lynn Smith, Apr. 22, 1982. BA summa cum laude, Midwestern State U., 1975; MA, Tex. Tech U., 1976. Prodn. coord. Tex. Instruments, Inc., Lubbock, Tex., 1976-77, tng. mgr., 1977-80, br. tng. mgr., 1980-82; sr. cons. Action Systems, Inc., Dallas, 1982-84; tng. mgr. Aviall, Inc., Dallas, 1984-86; dist. mgr. Devel. Dimensions Internat., Dallas, 1986-90; v.p. DDI Pitts., 1990-91; v.p., gen. mgr. DDI Can., Toronto, 1991-92; v.p. DDI L.A., 1992—; presentor seminars, papers at convs. Vol. tchr. Operation L.I.F.T. (Literacy Instrn. for Texans), Dallas, 1983-84, Big Bros./Big Sisters, 1988-89; mem. Foster Parents Plan, Amnesty Internat., World Wildlife Fund, People for the Ethical Treatment of Animals. Mem. Am. Soc. Tng. and Devel., Alpha Chi Omega, Alpha Psi Omega. Democrat. Avocations: running, music, reading. Office: DDI 3150 Bristol St Ste 300 Costa Mesa CA 92626-3052

SMITH, SELMA MOIDEL, lawyer, composer; b. Warren, Ohio, Apr. 3, 1919; d. Louis and Mary (Oyer) Moidel; 1 child, Mark Lee. Student UCLA, 1936-39; student in law U. So. Calif., 1939-41; JD, Pacific Coast U., 1942. Bar: Calif. 1943, U.S. Dist. Ct. 1943, U.S. Supreme Ct. 1958. Gen. practice law; mem. firm Moidel, Moidel, Moidel & Smith. Field dir. civilian adv. com. WAC, 1943; mem. nat. bd. Med. Coll. Pa. (formerly Woman's Med. Coll. Pa.), 1953—, exec. bd., 1976-80, pres., 1980-82, chmn. past pres. com., 1990-92. Decorated La Orden del Merito Juan Pablo Duarte (Dominican Republic). Mem. ABA (sr. lawyers divsn.) vice chair editl. bd. Experience mag. 1997—, chair, Arts Com., 1998—, chair arts com., 1998—, State Bar Calif. (servicemen's legal aid com., conf. com. on unauthorized practice of medicine, 1964, Disting. Svc. award 1993), L.A. Bar Assn. (psychopathic ct. com., Outstanding Svc. award 1993), L.A. Lawyers Club (pub. defenders com.), Nat. Assn. Women Lawyers (chmn. com. unauthorized practice of law, social commn. UN, regional dir. western states, Hawaii 1949-51, mem. jud. adminstrn. com. 1960, nat. chmn. world peace through law com. 1966-67, liaison to ABA sr. lawyers divsn. 1996—, chmn. bd. elections 1997, 98, mem. centennial com. 1997—), League of Ams. (dir.), Inter-Am. Bar Assn., So.Calif. Women Lawyers Assn. (pres. 1947, 48), Women Lawyers Assn. L.A. (chmn. Law Day com. 1966, subject of oral hist. project, 1986, hon. life mem., 1998), Coun. Bar Assns. L.A. County (charter sec. 1950), Calif. Bus. Women's Coun. (dir. 1951), L.A. Bus. Women's Coun. (pres. 1952), Calif. Pres.'s Coun. (1st v.p.), Nat. Assn. Composers U.S.A. (dir. 1974-79, ann. luncheon chmn. 1975), Nat. Fedn. Music Clubs (nat. vice chmn. for Western region, 1973-78), Calif. Fedn. Music Clubs (state chmn. Am. Music 1971-75, state conv. chmn. 1972), Docents of L.A. Philharm. (v.p. 1973-83, chmn. Latin Am. community rels. 1972-75, press and pub. rels. 1972-75, cons. coord. 1973-75), Assn. Learning in Retirement Orgns. in West (pres. 1993-94, exec. com. 1994-95, Disting. Svc. award 1995), Euterpe Opera Club (v.p. 1974-75, chmn. auditions 1972, chmn. awards 1973-75), ASCAP, Iota Tau Tau (dean L.A., supreme treas.), Plato Soc. of UCLA (Toga editor, 1990-93, [illegible] Constitution Bicentennial Project, 1985-87, moderator UCLA extension lecture series 1990, Exceptional Leadership award 1994). Composer of numerous works including Espressivo-Four Piano Pieces (orchestral premiere 198[illegible]), performance Nat. Mus. Women in the Arts 19[illegible]), author: A Century

of Achievement: The National Association of Women Lawyers, 1998. Home: 5272 Lindley Ave Encino CA 91316-3518

SMITH, SHEILA ANNE, nursing administrator, lecturer; b. La Jolla, Calif.; d. Rex Hoe and Ola Vivian (Baxter) S. BA in Health Sci. and Environ. Health, Calif. State U., Fresno, 1974; diploma in nursing, U. So. Calif., 1980; M Health Adminstrn., U. La Verne, 1996. RN, Calif.; cert. perioperative nurse. Staff nurse LAC/U. So. Calif. Med. Ctr., L.A., 1980-81, Huntington Meml. Hosp., Pasadena, Calif., 1981—; ENT specialty coord. Hungington Outpatient Surgery Ctr., Pasadena, 1989-97, insvc. edn. coord., 1990-96; clin. supr. operating rm. perioperative svcs. Friendly Hills Health Care Network, La Habra, Calif., 1996-97; asst. dept. adminstr. perioperative svcs. Kaiser Permanente, L.A., 1997—. Contbr. articles to profl. jours; award winning poet. Religious restoration worker Ch. of Ascension, Sierra Madre, 1982—. Mem. Am. Assn. Managed Care Nurses, Assn. Oper. Rm. Nurses (bd. dirs. 1987-90, 96-97, edn. chairperson 1996-98, bd. dirs. 1998-00), Soc. Otorhinolaryngology and Head-Neck Nurses, Inc. (v.p. So. Calif. region 1992-96), Nat. Assn. Managed Care Physicians, Inc., Operating Rm. Nursing Coun. Calif., Sierra Madre Woman's Club (nurse cons., healthcare lectr. 1988—), Delta Zeta (pres. Alumni chpt. 1974-75). Avocatons: painting, writing, sewing, hiking, religious restoration work. Home: 4195 Chino Hills Pkwy Apt 156 Chino Hills CA 91709-2618 Office: Kaiser Permanente Nursing Adminstrn 4867 W Sunset Blvd Los Angeles CA 90027-5969

SMITH, SHERWOOD PAUL, plastic surgeon; b. Sault St. Marie, Ont., Can., May 25, 1941; came to U.S., 1972; s. Irwin and Sophie Edith (Freeman) S.; m. Judith Ann Gebhard, Jan. 24, 1966; 1 child, Stephen Barclay. MD, U. Toronto, 1965; MSc, McGill U., 1969. Diplomate Am. Bd. Plastic Surgery. Plastic surgeon Olympia (Wash.) Plastic Surgeons Inc. PS, 1972—. Vol. plastic surgeon Gen. Hosp. Columbo, Sri Lanka, 1985—. Fellow ACS, Royal Coll. Physicians and Surgeons of Can.; mem. Olympia Yacht Club, South Sound Sailing Soc. Avocations: sailing, bicycling, hiking, mountaineering. Office: Olympia Plastic Surg Inc PS 300 Lilly Rd NE # B Olympia WA 98506-5032*

SMITH, STANFORD SIDNEY, state treasurer; b. Denver, Oct. 20, 1923; s. Frank Jay and Lelah (Beamer) S.; m. Harriet Holdrege, Feb. 7, 1947; children: Monta Smith Ramirez, Franklin Stanley. Student, Calif. Inst. Tech., 1941-42, Stanford U., 1942-43; BS, U.S. Naval Acad., 1946. Pres. Vebar Livestock Co., Thermopolis, Wyo., 1961—; mem. Wyo. Senate, 1974-76; pres. Wyo. Wool GrowersAssn., 1976-78; mem. Wyo. Ho. of Reps., Cheyenne, 1978-82; treas. State Wyo., Cheyenne, 1983-99; dir. Coun. of State Govts., 1990-92; v.p. Wyo. Wool Growers, dir., 1976-82. County commr. Hot Springs County, Wyo, 1966-74. Lt. USN, 1943-54. Decorated Bronze Star. Mem. Nat. Assn. State Treas. (pres. 1990-91). Republican. Methodist. Office: State of Wyoming State Capital Cheyenne WY 82002*

SMITH, STEPHEN RANDOLPH, aerospace executive; b. Des Moines, Apr. 17, 1928; s. Norvin Ellis and Helen (Heberling) S.; m. Margaret Anne Graves, Dec. 20, 1950; children: Stephen Randolph Jr., Susan Canning, Sara Kutler, Anne Barrette, Julia Carroll. BSME, Stanford U., 1951, MSME, 1952; MBA Advanced Mgmt. Program, Harvard U., 1974. Registered profl. engr., Calif. Sr. analyst, preliminary design engr. Northrop & Garrett Corps., L.A. and Hawthorne, Calif., 1952-55; propulsion lead design engr. Northrop Corp., Hawthorne, 1955-59; engrng. rep. ea. dist. Northrop Corp., Washington, 1959-60; T-38/F-5/F-20 program mgr. Northrop Corp., Hawthorne, 1960-75; v.p. Iran ops. Northrop Corp., Tehran, 1975-78; v.p. advanced stealth projects Northrop Corp., Hawthorne, 1978-83, v.p. engrng. and advanced devel., 1983-86, v.p., program mgr. F-20/YF-23A, 1986-88, corp. v.p., gen. mgr. aircraft divsn., 1988-92; cons. tech. mgmt. Palos Verdes, Calif., 1992—; bd. mem. Quarterdeck Ptnrs., Inc., L.A. and Washington, 1992—, NASA Advanced Aeronautics Com., 1984-86; invited lectr. aircraft design USAF Acad., 1983. Author, designer, patentee in field. Bd. dirs. Boy Scouts Am., L.A. coun., 1986—, charter comm. chmn., 1996; pres. Penn Srs., Palos Verdes, Calif., 1996. Sgt. U.S. Army, 1946-48. Recipient Disting. Civilian Svc. medal for Tacit Blue, U.S. Dept. Def., Washington, 1983. Fellow AIAA (chmn. L.A. sect. 1985-86, adv. bd. 1988—, Spl. Citation 1994), Inst. Advancement Engrng.; mem. Soc. Automotive Engrs. (chmn. aerotech. 1986-87, honors 1987), Sierra Club, Trailfinders Conservation Coun. (life, coun. chief 1940). Republican. Episcopalian. Avocations: competitive sailing, tennis, backpacking, skiing, running. Home and Office: 2249 Via Guadalana Palos Verdes Estates CA 90274-1617

SMITH, STEVEN A., newspaper editor. Editor Gazette Telegraph. Office: The Gazette 30 S Prospect St Colorado Springs CO 80903*

SMITH, STEVEN COLE, engineering process consultant; b. Idaho Falls, Idaho, Oct. 3, 1952; s. Merrell Cordon and Myrtle Jean (McArthur) S.; m. Gay Lynn Pendleton, May 2, 1975; children: Jennifer, Melinda, Gregory, Aimilee. BS, Brigham Young U., 1977; MS, West Coast U., 1992. Engr. Gen. Dynamics, San Diego, 1978-81, Hughes Aircraft, L.A., 1981-82; cons. CAD/CAM Splty., L.A., 1982-83; system mgr. Solar Turbines, San Diego, 1983-87; mktg. support Evans and Sutherland, Costa Mesa, Calif., 1987-88; mktg. mgr. Computervision, San Diego, 1988-98, Divsn., Inc., San Diego, 1998—; instr. Southwestern C.C., San Diego, 1986-87. Mem. AIAA. Mormon. Office: Objectlogic 5850 Oberlin Dr Ste 310 San Diego CA 92121-4712

SMITH, STEVEN SIDNEY, molecular biologist; b. Idaho Falls, Idaho, Feb. 11, 1946; s. Sidney Ervin and Hermie Phyllis (Robertson) S.; m. Nancy Louise Turner, Dec. 20, 1974. BS, U. Idaho, 1968; PhD, UCLA, 1974. Asst. research scientist Beckman Research Inst. City of Hope Nat. Med. Ctr., Duarte, Calif., 1982-84, staff Cancer Ctr., 1983—, asst. research scientist depts. Thoracic Surgery and Molecular Biology, 1985-87, assoc. research scientist, 1987-95; rsch. scientist City of Hope Nat. Med. Ctr., Duarte, 1995—; dir. dept. cell and tumor biology Beckman Research Inst. of the City of Hope, Duarte, Calif., 1990—; Wellcome vis. prof. in basic med. scis. Okla. State U., 1995-96; cons. Molecular Biosystems Inc., San Diego, 1981-84, Am. Inst. Biol. Scis., Washington, 1994. Mem. editl. bd. Analytical Biochemistry, 1997—; contbr. articles to profl. jours. Swiss Nat. Sci. Found. fellow U. Bern, 1974-77, fellow Scripps Clinic and Rsch. Found., La. Jolla, Calif., 1978-82, NIH fellow Scripps Clinic, 1979-81. Mem. Am. Soc. Cell Biology, Am. Assn. Cancer Rsch., Am. Chem. Soc., Phi Beta Kappa. Avocation: backpacking. Office: Beckman Rsch Inst of the City of Hope 1450 Duarte Rd Duarte CA 91010-3011

SMITH, STUART ROBERT, foundation executive; b. South Amboy, N.J., Aug. 14, 1942; s. Stuart Conroy and Elizabeth Beatrice (Keenan) S.; m. Nancy Jo Roberts, Apr. 24, 1965; children: Mark Christopher, Melissa Jo. BA in Psychology, St. Vincent Coll., Latrobe, Pa., 1964; postgrad., Stanford U., 1986. Dist. exec. Raritan coun. Boy Scouts Am., Perth Amboy, N.J., 1965-68, Greater Niagara Frontier Coun., Buffalo, 1968-69; assoc. dir. devel. Canisius Coll., Buffalo, 1969-70; dir. devel. Kenmore (N.Y.) Mercy Hosp., 1971-74; dir. community rels. and devel. United Hosp., Port Chester, N.Y., 1974-77; exec. dir. Shadyside Hosp. Found., Pitts., 1977-79; exec. v.p. Samaritan Found., Phoenix, 1979-87, pres., chief exec. officer, 1988—; cons. fundraising and found. mgmt.; founding bd. mem. Cert. Fund Raising Exec. (CFRE) Profl. Cert. Bd., 1996—. Contbr. articles to profl. jours., newsletters. Founding mem. bd. govs. LPGA Std. Register Ping Golf Tournament, 1983—; pres., bd. dirs. Crisis Nursery, Phoenix, 1990-91, v.p., 1987, 88, found. sec., 1993—; chmn. Fiesta Bowl Golf Classic, Phoenix, 1988, 89; life mem. com. Fiesta Bowl, Phoenix, 1986—; bd. dirs. Palms Clinic & Hosp. Found., Phoenix, 1993, exec. com., v.p.; vol. com. chmn. Super Bowl XXX. Fellow Assn. for Healthcare Philanthropy (nat. v.p. 1977-80, bd. accreditation 1986—); mem. Ariz. Assn. Hosp. Devel. (pres. 1990, exec. com. 1989—), Nat. Soc. Fund Raising Execs. (cert. various offices local chpts., Outstanding Fundraising Exec. award Ariz. chpt. 1989), LPGA (sponsors bd., treas. 1988-92), Moon Valley Country Club. Republican. Roman Catholic. Avocations: golf, fishing, water sports, skiing. Office: The Samaritan Found 1441 N 12th St Phoenix AZ 85006-2837

SMITH, SUSAN KIMSEY, lawyer; b. Phoenix, Jan. 15, 1947; d. William Lewis and Margaret (Bowes) Kimsey; m. Alfred Jon Olsen, Apr. 15, 1979. Student U. Ariz., 1965-66; BA, Principia Coll., 1969; MA, U. Va., 1970; JD, [illegible]

Atty. trust dept. Valley Nat. Bank Ariz., Phoenix, 1976-77; assoc. Lane & Smith, Ltd., Phoenix, 1977-78; mem. Olsen-Smith, Ltd., Phoenix, 1979—, pres., 1979—; mem. Phoenix Tax Workshop, 1976—, Tax Study Group, 1979—, 401 Com., 1982—; chmn. taxation sect. State Bar Ariz., 1985-86, mem. tax. adv. commn.; lectr. profl. confs. and univs., 1977, 80—. Author: Estate Planning Practice Manual, 1984; editorial adv. bd. Practical Tax Lawyer, 1985—; contbr. writings to profl. publs. Bd. dirs. Ariz. Community Found., Samaritan Found.; chair legal adv. com. Ariz. Community Found.; chair Samaritan Gift Planning adv. com. Samaritan Found. Recipient J.P. Walker Am. History award, Principia Coll., 1969, Ethics award, State Bar Ariz., 1974. Fellow Am. Coll. Trust and Estate Counsel Regent (Ariz. chmn. 1992-97), Am. Coll. Tax Counsel; mem. ABA (chmn. com. econs. of tax practice 1983-84, chmn. com. liaison with other ABA sects. and coms., sect. econs. of law practice 1983—, selection com. appts. to U.S. Tax Ct., com. mem. sect. taxation 1976—, com. mem. sect. real property probate and trust law 1982—, chmn. taxation task force on family partnerships, editorial bd. Practical Tax Lawyer), Internat. Acad. of Estate and Trust Law, State Bar Ariz. (chmn. taxation sect. 1985-86, mem. tax adv. commn., cert. tax specialist, cert. estate and trust specialist), Maricopa County Bar Assn., Fed. Bar Assn. (vice chmn. estate and gift taxation com., taxation council 1979-80), Valley Estate Planners (pres., elected first life time mem.), Central Ariz. Estate Planning Council (bd. dirs. 1986-88), The Group, Alpha Lambda Delta, Phi Alpha Eta. Republican. Office: Olsen-Smith Ltd 301 E Virginia Ave Ste 3300 Phoenix AZ 85004-1218

SMITH, V. ROY, neurosurgeon; b. N.Y.C., Feb. 12, 1943; s. Leslie Ewart and Vera (Dhlosh) S.; m. Elizabeth Kay Bartlett, June 12, 1971; children: Rebecca L., Adam L., Andrew R. BA, Ohio State U., 1964, MD, 1967. Diplomate Am. Bd. Neurol. Surgeons. Ptnr. Fresno Neurol. Med. Group, Calif., 1975—; pres. med. staff St. Agnes Hosp., Fresno, Calif., 1987-89, chief of surgery, 1983-85, chmn. div. neurosurgery, 1993-95. Lt. U.S. Navy, 1969-71, Vietnam. Fellow Am. Coll. Surgeons; mem. AMA, Am. Coll. Surgeons, Am. Assn. Neurol. Surgeons. Home: 2627 E Birch Ave Clovis CA 93611-9167 Office: Fresno Neurosurg Med Group 6137 N Thesta St Ste 103 Fresno CA 93710-5266

SMITH, VERNON LOMAX, economist, researcher; b. Wichita, Kans., Jan. 1, 1927; s. Vernon Chessman and Lula Belle (Lomax) S.; m. Joyce Harkleroad, June 6, 1950 (div. Aug. 1975); m. Carol Breckner, Jan. 1, 1980. BSEE, Calif. Inst. Tech., 1949; MA in Econs., U. Kans., 1952; PhD in Econs., Harvard U., 1955; D of Mgmt. (hon.), Purdue U., 1990. Asst. prof. econs. Purdue U., West Lafayette, Ind., 1955-58, assoc. prof., 1958-61, prof., 1961-65, Krannert prof., 1965-67; prof. Brown U., Providence, 1967-68, U. Mass., Amherst, 1968-75; prof. U. Ariz., Tucson, 1975—, Regents' prof.; Contbr. articles to profl. jours. Fellow Ctr. for Advanced Study in Behavioral Scis., Stanford, Calif., 1972-73; Sherman Fairchild Disting. Scholar Calif. Inst. Tech., Pasadena, 1973-74; adj. scholar CATO Inst., Washington, 1983—. Fellow AAAS, Am. Acad. Arts and Scis., Econometric Soc., Am. Econ. Assn. (Disting. fellow); me. Pvt. Enterprise Edn. Assn. (Adam Smith award), Nat. Acad. Sci. Home: 6020 N Pontatoc Rd Tucson AZ 85718-4323 Office: U Ariz Econ Sci Lab Tucson AZ 85718

SMITH, VIN, sports editor, business owner, novelist; b. Whittier, Calif., May 19, 1944; s. M. Clifford and Anna Eugenia (Hill) S.; m. Marthea Karen Callaham, May 15, 1969 (div. 1979); children: Jayare Smith, Eric Smith; m. Ginger Hammon, Oct. 20, 1984; children: Amy Michelle, Stacey Erin, Kellie Rae. Student, Columbia Sch. Broadcasting, San Francisco, 1967; AA, Cuesta Coll., 1974; grad., Am. Sch. of Piano Tuning, 1978. Sales mgr. Sta. KTAT, Frederick, Okla., 1967-69; announcer KOCY, Oklahoma City, 1969; owner Melmart Markets, San Luis Obispo, Calif., 1971-73, Am. Direct Sales, Grover City, Calif., 1973-79; instr. piano Valley View Acad., Arroyo Grande, Calif., 1977-78; instr. piano Long Piano Co., San Luis Obispo, 1977-79, piano technician, 1978-79; owner Chocolate Piano, Yreka, Calif., 1979—; instr. piano Makah Indian Tribe, Neah Bay, Wash., 1981-82; sports editor New Words Digest, Bakersfield, Calif., 1988—; cons., stress evaluator seminar Yreka Stress Therapy Clinic, 1986-87; founder Vinco Distbrs. (formerly Vinco Enhancement Sys.), 1998. Sports columnist New Words Digest, 1987-91; guest columnist Siskiyou Daily News, 1991-94; nat publicist chamber music concerts So. Oreg. State Coll., 1993—; contbr. articles to profl. jours. Chmn. heart fund Tillman County Okla., 1968; pub. co-chmn. Siskiyou County No-Prop 174, 1994; campaign worker Ken Jourdan for sheriff, Yreka, 1986; publicity dir. Gene Breceda for supr., 1993-94. Recipient Cert. of Appreciation, Siskiyou County, 1988, Achievement award, 1988; winner Golden Poet award World of Poetry, 1989. Mem. Nat. Writers Club (chmn. student com. Yreka chpt. 1988), Author's Guild, Inc., Author's League of Am., Mystery Writers Am., Soc. Children's Book Writers, Jr. C. of C. (sgt.-at-arms Frederick chpt. 1967-69), Kiwanis, Moose. Avocations: horse shoe pitching, photography, reading. Home: 710 Knapp St Yreka CA 96097-2343 Office: Chocolate Piano Svcs PO Box 447 Yreka CA 96097-0447

SMITH, WALDO GREGORIUS, former government official; b. Bklyn., July 29, 1911; s. John Henry and Margaret (Gregorius) S.; m. Mildred Pearl Prescott, July 30, 1935 (dec. Jan. 1992); 1 dau., Carole Elizabeth Smith Levin. Student CCNY, N.Y., 1928-29; BS in Forestry, Cornell U., 1933. Registered prof. engr., Colo. Forester Forest Svc., U.S. Dept. Agr., Atlanta, 1933-41, Ala. Div. Forestry, Brewton, 1941-42; engr., civil engring. technician Geol. Survey, U.S. Dept. Interior, 1942-71, cartographic technician, 1972-75; chmn. Public Transp. Council, 1975-89; legislator aide to individuals Colo. State Legis. Internship Program, 1987-95. Recipient 40 Yr. Civil Service award pin and scroll; 42 Yr. Govt. Service award plaque. Fellow Am. Congress Surveying and Mapping (life, sec.-treas. Colo. chpt. 1961, program chmn. 1962, reporter 1969, mem. nat. membership devel. com. 1973-74, rep. to Colo. Engrng. Council 1976-77); mem. AAAS (emeritus), Denver Fed. Center Profl. Engrs. Group (U.S. Geol. Survey rep. 1973-76, Engr. of Yr. award 1975), Nat. Soc. Profl. Engrs. (pre-coll. guidance com. 1986-91, life 92—), Profl. Engrs. Colo. (chpt. scholarship chmn. 1979-96, advt. corr., service award 1983), Cornell U. Alumni Assn. (alumni secondary schs. com. Quadrangle Club), Common Cause, Colo. Engring. Council (chmn. library com. 1970—, spl. rep. Regional Transp. Dist., 1974-75; mem. sci. fair com. 1970-71; rep. ex officio Denver Pub. Library Found. Bd. Trustees 1975-80, mem. historic agreement with Denver Pub. Libr. 1993, Pres.'s Outstanding Service award 1987), Environ. Concerns (chmn. com. 1988—, treas. 1989-91, Rocky Mountain Arsenal Cleanup, 1994—, mem. site specific adv. bd., restoration adv. bd.), Fedn. Am. Scientists, Am. Soc. Engring. Edn., People for Am. Way. Contbr. articles to profl. jours. Home: 3821 W 25th Ave Denver CO 80211-4417

SMITH, WALTER J., engineering consultant; b. Climax, Kans., Feb. 8, 1921; s. Jacob Walter and Thelma Christina (Stark) S.; m. Wanda Jean Sandys, Apr. 20, 1944 (div. 1965); children: Walter Brooke, Judith Jean; m. Evadean Louise Smith, Sept. 21, 1965; stepchildren: Stephen Henslee, Kimberly Ann; 1 adopted child, Nancy Louise. BEE, Cleve. State U., 1948; postgrad., UCLA, 1955-58, Western State U. Law, Anaheim, Calif., 1970-71. Lic. profl. engr., Ohio, Calif. Field tech. rep. to Air Force Jack & Heintz, Inc., Maple Hts., Ohio, 1942-44; rsch. engr. Jack & Heintz, Inc., 1948-50, N. Am. Aviation Inc., Downey, Calif., 1950-54; asst. chief engr. Ala. Engring. & Tool Co., Huntsville, Ala., 1954-55; rsch. specialist to dir. prodn. ops. N. Am. Aviation Inc./Rockwell Internat., Anaheim, 1955-86; engring. mgmt. cons. Anaheim, 1986-93; engring. mgmt. cons., Palm Desert, Calif., 1993-98. Contbr. articles to profl. jours. Mem. Anaheim Indsl. Devel. Bd., 1982-86, Anaheim Pub. Utilities Bd., 1987-92; bd. dirs. Rep. Ctrl. Com. of Orange County, 1976-78; pres., bd. dirs. Galerie Homeowners Assn., 1987-93; bd. dirs. Coun. on Environ. Edn. and Econ. Through Devel., Inc., 1974-86, Action Com. to Inform Orange Now, Inc. Mem. Anaheim C. of C. (bd. dirs. 1983-90, pres. 1983-84), Gladhanders Acad. Hospitality Internat. (bd. dirs. 1989-95, Man of Yr. 1989). Republican. Religious Science. Avocations: golf, jewelry design, gardening, dancing. Home and Office: 78615 Purple Sagebrush Ave Palm Desert CA 92211-1444

SMITH, WILLARD GRANT, psychologist; b. Sidney, N.Y., June 29, 1934; s. Frank Charles and Myrtle Belle (Empet) S.; m. Ruth Ann Dissly, Sept. 14, [illegible] Richards, John Charles. BS, U. Md., 1976; MS, U. Utah, 1978, PhD, 1981. lic. psychologist, Utah; cert. sch. psychologist, sch. adminstr., tchr., Utah, nat. cert. sch. psychologist; diplomate Am. Bd. Forensic Examiners, Am. Bd. [illegible] Med. Ctr. U. Utah, 1977, teaching asst.

dept. ednl. psychology, 1976-78, rsch. cons. dept. edn., 1977; program evaluator Salt Lake City Sch. Dist.; program evaluator and auditor Utah State Bd. Edn., 1978; sch. psychologist Jordan Sch. Dist., Sandy, Utah, 1978-82, tchr., 1979-80; exec. dir. Utah Ind. Living Ctr., Salt Lake City, 1982-83; spl. edn. cons. Southeastern Edn. Svc. Ctr., 1983-85; sch. psychologist Jordan Sch. Dist., Sandy, 1985-96; assoc. psychologist Don W. McBride & Assocs., Bountiful, Utah, 1989-91; pvt. practice Sandy, Utah, 1991—. Master sgt. USAF, 1953-76. Decorated Air Force Commendation medal with 2 clusters. Mem. APA, Am. Coll. Forensic Examiners, Nat. Assn. Sch. Psychologists, Air Force Sgts. Assn., Ret. Enlisted Assn., Phi Kappa Phi, Alpha Sigma Lambda. Home: 8955 Quail Hollow Dr Sandy UT 84093-1903

SMITH, WILLIAM RAY, retired biophysicist, engineer; b. Lyman, Okla., June 26, 1925; s. Harry Wait and Daisy Belle (Hull) S. BA, Bethany Nazarene Coll., 1948; MA, Wichita State U., 1950; PhD, UCLA, 1967. Engr., Beech Aircraft Corp., Wichita, Kans., 1951-53; sr. group engr. McDonnell Aircraft Corp., St. Louis, 1953-60; sr. engr. Lockheed Aircraft Corp., Burbank, Calif., 1961-63; sr. engr. scientist McDonnell Douglas Corp., Long Beach, Calif., 1966-71; mem. tech. staff Rockwell Internat., L.A., 1973-86, CDI Corp.-West, Costa Mesa, Calif., 1986-88, McDonnell Douglas Aircraft Corp., Long Beach, 1988-93; ret., 1993. tchr. math. Pasadena Nazarene Coll. (now Point Loma Nazarene Coll., San Diego), 1960-62, Glendale Coll., Calif., 1972; asst. prof. math. Mt. St. Mary's Coll., L.A., 1972-73; math. cons. L.A. Union Rescue Mission Bank of Am. Learning Ctr., 1995—, Wayfarer's Ministry 1997—; deacon Presbyn. Ch. Recipient Recognition certificate NASA, 1982. Mem. Town Hall Calif., Yosemite Assocs., UCLA Faculty Club, Sigma Xi, Pi Mu Epsilon. Republican. Avocations: sailing, photography, teaching Sunday sch. first grade. Home: 2405 Roscomare Rd Los Angeles CA 90077-1839

SMITH, ZACHARY ALDEN, political science and public administration educator; b. Stanford, Calif., Aug. 8, 1953; s. Alden Wallace and Lelia (Anderson) S. BA, Calif. State U., Fullerton, 1975; MA, U. Calif., Santa Barbara, 1979, PhD, 1984. Adj. lectr. polit. sci. U. Calif., Santa Barbara, 1981-82; asst. prof., dir. Ctr. for Island and Ocean Resources Mgmt. U. Hawaii, Hilo, 1982-87, assoc. prof., 1987-89; assoc. prof. No. Ariz. U., Flagstaff, 1989-93, prof., 1993—. Author: Groundwater and the Future of the Southwest, 1984, Groundwater Policy in the Southwest, 1985, Groundwater in the West, 1989, The Environmental Policy Paradox, 3rd edit., 1995, 4th edit., 1999, Hawaii State and Local Government, 1992, Politics and Public Policy in Arizona, 1993, 2d edit., 1995, Environmental Politics and Policy in the West, 1993, Groundwater Management in the West, 1999. Active campaign for various state propositions, 1970, 74, 76; elected to Orange County (Calif.) Dem. Cen. Com., 1976-78; councilman City of Flagstaff, 1996—. Rsch. grantee U. Calif., Los Alamos (N.Mex.) Sci. Lab., Water Resources Ctr., Davis, Calif., U.S. Dept. HUD. Mem. ASPA, Am. Water Resources Assn., Am. Polit. Sci. Assn., Southwestern Social Sci. Assn., Western Polit. Sci. Assn., Western Social Scis. Assn. (exec. coun. 1995—). Office: No Ariz U Dept Polit Sci Box 15036 Flagstaff AZ 86011

SMITHER, JAMES CUMMING, landscape architect; b. Richmond, Va., May 26, 1963; s. Bryan Mercer Jr. and Louise Bray (Cumming) S.; m. Susan Reed, Feb. 27, 1969. BA in Urban Studies, Roanoke Coll., 1985; M of Urban & Regional Planning, George Washington U., 1991; M of Landscape Architecture, U. Va., 1993. Intern landscape architect Calton Abbott & Ptnrs., Williamsburg, Va., 1994-95; assoc. planner City of Forest Grove (Oreg.), 1995-97; urban designer, assoc. planner Malcolm Carpenter Assocs., Colma, Calif., 1997—. Mem. Am. Planning Assn., Am. Soc. Landscape Architects. Episcopalian. Avocations: watercolor & oil painting, sailing, drums, guitar, skiing. Home: 1408 Giltspur Rd Richmond VA 23233-4818 Office: Malcolm carpenter Assocs. 1190 El Camino Real Colma CA 94014-3212

SMITH-FARNSWORTH, SHARON ANNE, elementary education educator; b. San Francisco, Aug. 6, 1945; d. Donald Franklin and Maxine Anna (Alterman) Steiner; m. Edward Earl Smith III, Nov. 7, 1968 (div. Dec. 1987); 1 child, Edward Earl IV; m. Matthew Lee Farnsworth, Jan. 15, 1988;. BA in History, U. Calif., Berkeley, 1967; cert. in gifted and talented in edn., U. Calif., Riverside, 1986. Cert. elem. tchr., Calif. Tchr. Manhattan Beach (Calif.) City Sch., 1968-78, Moreno Valley (Calif.) Unified Sch. Dist., 1984—. Mem. ASCD, NEA, NAACP, Calif. Leadership Acad., Calif. Tchrs. Assn., Moreno Valley Educators Assn. (rep. 1984-91, v.p. 1991-94), Smithsonian Inst., Phi Sigma Sigma. Republican. Avocations: reading, writing poetry, traveling. Home: 10689 Willow Creek Rd Moreno Valley CA 92557-2953 Office: Badger Springs Mid Sch 24750 Delphinium Ave Moreno Valley CA 92553-5812

SMITHSON, DAVID MATTHEW, lawyer; b. Chgo., Jan. 14, 1957; s. Paul Stanley and Barbara Jane (Sherman) S.; m. Susan Marie Bletcher, Aug. 11, 1984; 1 child, Rachel Carmella. BS, U. Oreg., 1980; JD, Boston Coll., 1984. Bar: Calif. 1985, Conn. 1997, U.S. Dist. Ct. (ctrl. dist.) Calif. 1985, U.S. Dist. Ct. (so. dist.) Calif. 1987. Atty. Parker & Stanbury, L.A., 1984-89, Shield & Smith, L.A., 1989-91, Hornberger & Criswell, L.A., 1991-93, Chapman & Glucksman, L.A., 1993-95, Cummins & White, L.A., 1995—. Avocations: tennis, golf, travel, museums. Office: Cummins & White LLP 865 S Figueroa St Fl 24 Los Angeles CA 90017-2543

SMOLKA, JAMES WILLIAM, aerospace research pilot; b. Mt. Clemens, Mich., July 31, 1950; s. Joseph William and Patricia Joan (Righetti) S. BS in Astronautics, USAF Acad., 1972; MS in Aero., Astronautics, MIT, 1980; engineers degree in aero. & astronautics, Stanford U., 1994. Commd. 2d lt. USAF, 1972, advanced through grades to col., 1996; served as pilot 3d Tactical Fighter Squadron, Korat RT AFB, Thailand, 1974, 21 Tactical Air Support Squadron, Shaw AFBSC, 1975-77; test pilot 6510 Test Wing, Edwards AFB CA, 1981-83; exptl. test pilot Ft. Worth div. Gen. Dynamics, Edwards AFB, 1984-85; aerospace rsch. pilot N.A.S.A. Dryden FRC, Edwards AFB, 1985—; officer USAF, 1972-83, USAFR, 1983—; adj. prof. Calif. State U., Fresno, 1984—. Author: Analysis and Testing of Aircraft Flight Control Systems, 1982. Mem. Soc. Exptl. Test Pilots. Home: PO Box 2123 Lancaster CA 93539-2123 Office: NASA Dryden Flight Rsch Ctr PO Box 273 Edwards CA 93523-0273

SMYER, MYRNA RUTH, drama educator; b. Albuquerque, June 10, 1946; d. Paul Anthony and Ruth Kelly (Klein) S.; m. Carlton Weaver Canaday, July 5, 1980. BFA, U. N.Mex., 1969; MA, Northwestern U., 1971. Pvt. practice drama instr. Albuquerque, 1974-78; dir. drama Sandia Preparatory Sch., Albuquerque, 1977-98, chmn. dept. fine arts, 1980-98; exec./artistic dir. Once Upon A Theatre, 1998—; dialect coach, dir. Chgo. Acting Ensemble, 1969-71; lectr., performer Albuquerque Pub. Schs. and various civic orgns., Albuquerque, 1974—; writer, dir., performer Arts in the Pks., Albuquerque, 1977-80; performer, crew various indsl. videos, 1981-86; instr. workshops and continuing edn. U. N.Mex. 1977-80; exec. artistic dir. Once Upon a Theatre (A Touring Theatre for Children), 1998—. Writer, dir., designer children's plays including May The Best Mammal (Or Whatever) Win, 1977, A Holiday Celebration, 1977, Puppets on Parade, 1978, A Witch's Historical Switches, 1979, Once Upon a Rhyme, 1987— (Outstanding Contbn. Arts in Edn. Bravo award Albuquerque Arts Alliance 1995), Little Red Riding Hood, 1987, Goldilocks and The Three Bears, 1988, Cinderella, 1989, Hansel and Gretel, 1990, Rumpelstiltskin, 1991, The Dancing Princesses, 1992, The Three Pigs, 1994, Sleeping Beauty, 1996, (melodrama) A Governess Wronged or He Betrayed Her Trust, 1999; dir. numerous other children and adult plays. Instr., writer, dir. various community theatres including Albuquerque Little Theatre, Corrales Adobe Theatre, Kimo Theatre, Albuquerque Civic Light Opera, Now We Are Theatre; mem. Albuquerque Cable TV Adv. Bd.; mem. task force on the arts for children Albuquerque Little Theatre. Recipient Helen and Doug Bridges award for Outstanding Instr., 1990, Albuquerque Acad. grant (children theatre), 1993, 95, 97, Neighborhood Appreciation award Four Hills, 1993, Helen and Doug Bridges award for Outstanding Instr., 1990. Mem. Am. Alliance for Theatre and Edn., Theater N.Mex., Albuquerque Arts Alliance. Avocations: travel, reading, hiking, dancing. Office: Once Upon a Theatre 13170-B Central Ave SE #130 Albuquerque NM 87123

SMYTH, CORNELIUS EDMONSTON, retired hotel executive; b. N.Y.C., Aug. 20, 1926; s. Cornelius Joseph and Roberta Ernestine (Anderson) S.; m. Jeanne Laura Dillingham, Nov. 25, 1950 (dec. Oct. 1996); m. Jeanette M. Hubbard, Apr. 18, 1998; children: Cornelius E. Jr., Loretta M., William D., James B., Laura I., Robert B. BS in Econs., U. Pa., Phila., 1946. Cert. Hospitality Acct. Exec. Contr. Caesars Palace Hotel and Casino, Las Vegas, Nev., 1970-73, fin. v.p., 1974, adminstrv. v.p., 1975-77, exec. v.p., 1977-81; pres. Sands Hotel and Casino, Las Vegas, Nev., 1981-83; exec. v.p. Latin Am. ops. Caesars World Internat., L.A., 1983-89, pres. Mexican ops., 1989-90; bd. dirs. Inland Entertainment Corp., San Diego; cons., Coronado, Calif., 1994-97. Co-author: A Uniform System of Accounts for Hotels, 7th rev. edit., 1977. Comdr. USNR, 1944-70. Named to U.S. Table Tennis Hall of Fame, 1996. Mem. Pi Gamma Mu, Sigma Chi. Republican. Roman Catholic. Avocations: table tennis, body surfing.

SMYTH, DAVID SHANNON, real estate investor, commercial and retail builder and developer; b. Denver, May 13, 1943; s. William James and Constance Ruth (Sherman) S.; student Regis Coll., 1967-69, USAF Acad., 1961-65, U. No. Colo., 1965-67; m. Sharon Kaye Swiderski, Jan. 3, 1980; children: Julia Caitlin, Alexander Jeremiah, Matthew Davis; 1 son by previous marriage, Shannon David. Accountant, Colo. Nat. Bank, 1966-69; bus. analyst Dun & Bradstreet, 1969-70; pres., dir. Georgetown Valley Water & Sanitation Dist., 1973-74, Realists, Inc., 1973-74, Silver Queen Constrn. Co., 1973-74; v.p., sec., dir. Georgetown Assocs., Inc. (Colo.), 1970-74; pres., chief ops. officer Lincoln Cos., Denver, 1975-76; project mgr., sales mgr., prin. Brooks-Morris Homes, Fox Ridge, Colo., 1976-77; project mgr. U.S. West Homes, Denver, 1977-78; pres., dir. Denver Venture Capital, 1978-81; prin., dir., exec. v.p. Shelter Equities, Inc., 1982-87; prin., dir., exec. v.p. Comml. Constrn. Mgmt. Services, Inc., 1987-88, Shelter Equities, Inc., 1984-87; owner, dir., exec. v.p. Maple Leaf Realty Corp.; v.p., dir. Gibraltar Devel. Corp., Dominion Properties Ltd., 1978-82; investment dir. Van Schaack & Co., 1987-91; prin. investor, head devel. The Farkas Group, 1991-92; sr. residential loan officer, Freedom Mortgage Co., 1992-93; sr. loan officer, dir. builder mktg. NVR Mortgage Co., Englewood, Colo., 1994-96; sr. loan officer Market St. Mortgage, 1996-97; dist. builder account mgr. N.Am. Mortgage Co., Denver, 1997-98; v.p. 1st United Bank, Englewood, Colo., 1998—. Served with USAF, 1961-65. Lic. real estate broker. Home: 9618 S Timber Hawk Cir Apt 22 Hghlnds Ranch CO 80126-7126 Office: MegaBank 8100 E Arapahoe Rd Englewood CO 80112

SMYTH, JAMES ALLEN, artist, art educator; b. Tribune, Kans., Dec. 28, 1938. BA, U. Calif., Berkeley, 1972; Fine Arts Credential, Calif. C.C.; student of art and artists, various instns. and artists, worldwide. Master printer Appletree Etchers, San Mateo, Calif.; tchr. anatomy for artists Foothill Coll., Los Altos Hills, Calif.; art tchr. Pacific Art League, Palo Alto Cultural Ctr., Palo Alto, Calif., 1972—; tchr. linear perspective and color theory Fashion Inst. of Design, San Francisco, 1997—; instr. Canada Coll., Redwood City, Calif., 1999—; lectr., workshop demonstrator, juror various western U.S. art groups. Artist: exhbns. include Coll. San Mateo, Foothill Coll., Appletree Etchers, San Mateo, Pacific Art League, Palo Alto, Canyon Gallery, Monterey, Calif., Lighthouse Gallery, Monterey, Gallery of Foster City, Calif., Royal Coll. of Art, London, Art Rise, San Bruno, Calif., N.Y. Acad., N.Y.C., Art Students League, N.Y.C., Union League Club, N.Y.C., Oil Painters Am. Representational Ann., Santa Barbara, Calif. With USAF, 1962-65. Recipient Paul Emerson award, 1993, Salies de Bearn 9th Internat. Competition award, France, 1996. Mem. Internat. Visual Arts Found. (founding dir. 1998), Appletree Etchers (founding mem., master printer), Pacific Art League Palo Alto (Kenneth Washburn award 1988), Calif. Acad. Painters (founding mem.). Office: 3790 El Camino Real Ste 195 Palo Alto CA 94306

SMYTH, THEODORE HILTON, real estate developer; b. New London, Conn., Apr. 3, 1915; s. Joseph H. and Ida Mae (Towson) S.; m. Elizabeth Norton McBride, Apr. 2, 1949; children: Elizabeth Towson, Theodore Hilton Jr. BA, Bard Coll., 1937, PhD, 1973; D of Bus. Adminstrn. (hon.), Hillsdale Coll., 1997. Shoe buyer Melville Shoe Corp., 1937-40; commercial aviator Am. Overseas Airlines, N.Y., 1946-50; investment counselor Lakeside Co., Seattle, 1950-52; real estate developer Hawaii, 1952—; ltd. ptnr. Conversion Project, Atlanta, 1980. Pres. Santa Barbara (Calif.) Symphony, 1960-62, dir., 1958-68; dir. United Way, Santa Barbara, 1970-74, Calif. Tech. Assocs., Pasadena, 1980-85; chmn. Info Genesis, Santa Barbara, 1985—; former trustee Bard Coll.; mem. bd. vistors and govs. St. John's Coll., 1990-96. Lt. Comdr. USNR, 1940-45. Republican. Avocations: tennis umpiring, swimming, tennis. Home: 4234 Cresta Ave Santa Barbara CA 93110-2410

SNARE, CARL LAWRENCE, JR., business executive; b. Chgo., Oct. 25, 1936; s. Carl Lawrence and Lillian Marie (Luoma) S.; BBA, Northwestern U., 1968; BS, SUNY, 1995; postgrad. Roosevelt U.; postgrad. in econs. San Francisco State U., 1976-77, Coll. Fin. Planning. Cert. fin. planner. Asst. sec., controller Bache Halsey Stuart & Shields Inc. (now Prudential Securities), Chgo., 1968-73; controller Innisfree Corp. div. Hyatt Corp., Burlingame, Calif., 1973-76; cash mgr. Portland (Oreg.) Gen. Electric Co., 1976-79; chief fin. officer, controller Vistar Fin. Inc., Marina del Rey, Calif., 1979-82, v.p., treas. Carson Estate Co., Rancho Dominguez, Calif., 1988-96; pres. Snare Properties Co., Long Beach, Calif., 1984-96, Snare Fin. Services Corp., Rialto, Calif., 1985-89, Carl Snare & Assocs., Long Beach. CPA, cert. fin. planner, Calif.; pres., CEO Glenshire Homes Inc., Phoenix, 1996—, Glenshire Tech., Boulder, Colo., 1997—. Mem. AICPA, Calif. Soc. CPAs. Founder Cash Mgmt. Assn., Portland, Oreg. Home: 1094 E 17th Ave Broomfield CO 80020-1308 Office: 11024 N 28th Dr Ste 200 Phoenix AZ 85029-4336

SNASDELL, SUSAN KATHLEEN, computer company executive; b. St. Louis, July 17, 1948; d. Russell John and Gertrude Burnett (Gassman) S. BA, So. Nazarene U., 1972. Office adminstr. Lake, Van Dyke & Browne Med. Group, Pasadena, Calif., 1972-83; founder, ptnr., adminstr. ComputerEase, Oxnard, Calif., 1984—. Contbr. articles to profl. jours. Mem. Better Bus. Bur., Oxnard C. of C. Avocations: gardening, photography, cooking. Office: ComputerEase 2361 Fairway Ct Oxnard CA 93030-7774

SNELL, NED COLWELL, financial planner; b. Cowley, Wyo., May 16, 1944; s. Jay Hatton and Freda Hope (Colwell) S.; m. Barbara Anne Frandsen, Apr. 24, 1969; children: Taylor Anthony, Trevor Cameron. BA, U. Utah, 1969; CLU, Am. Coll., 1983, ChFC, 1985. English tchr. Granite Sch. Dist., Salt Lake City, 1969-71; ins. agt. Prudential Ins. Co., Salt Lake City, 1971-76; pres. Snell Fin. Corp., Salt Lake City, 1976—. Bd. dirs. Utah chpt. Arthritis Found., Salt Lake City, 1980-82, pres. 1982-83; missionary Mormon Ch. 1963-66; chmn. voting dist. 2604 Rep. Nominating Convs., 1986, 90. Recipient Golden Key Soc. Devel. award, 1990. Mem. NALU (Nat. Sales Achievement award 1971-89, Nat. Quality award), Am. Soc. CLU and ChFC (bd. dirs. Utah chpt. 1990-93, treas. 1993-94, v.p. 1994-96, pres. 1996-97), Million Dollar Round Table (knight 1988—), Salt Lake Assn. Life Underwriters (bd. dirs. 1974-76, 80-82). Republican. Avocations: creative writing, fly tying, fishing, basketball, tennis. Home: 1101 S 2000 E Salt Lake City UT 84108-1971 Office: 1800 S West Temple Ste 416 Salt Lake City UT 84115-1851

SNELL, PATRICIA POLDERVAART, librarian, consultant; b. Santa Fe, Apr. 11, 1943; d. Arie and Edna Beryl (Kerchmar) Poldervaart; m. Charles Eliot Snell, June 7, 1966. BA in Edn., U. N.M., 1965; MSLS, U. So. Calif., 1966. Asst. edn. libr. U. So. Calif., L.A., 1966-68; med. libr. Bedford (Mass.) VA Hosp., 1968-69; asst. law libr. U. Miami, Coral Gables, Fla., 1970-71; acquistions libr. U. N.Mex. Law Sch. Libr., Albuquerque, 1971-72; order libr. Los Angeles County Law Libr., 1972-76, cataloger, 1976-90; libr. Parks Coll., Albuquerque, 1990-92; records technician Technadyne Engring. Cons. to Sandia Nat. Labs., 1992-93; libr. Tireman Learning Materials Ctr. U. N.Mex., Albuquerque, 1993-96, instr. libr. sci. program Coll. Edn., 1991—; rsch. technician City of Albuquerque, 1996—. Ch. libr.. Beverly Hills Presbyn. Ch., 1974-90, ch. choir libr., 1976-90. Southwestern Library Assn. scholar 1965. Mem. ALA, N.Mex. Libr. Assn., Pi Lambda Theta. Avocations: travel, reading. Office: U N Mex Coll Edn EM/LS Program Ed Admin B 29 Albuquerque NM 87131

SNELL, RICHARD, holding company executive; b. Phoenix, Nov. 26, 1930; s. Frank L. and Elizabeth (Berlin) S.; m. Alice Cosette Wiley, Aug. 1, 1954. BA, Stanford U., 1952, JD, 1954. Bar: Ariz. Ptnr. firm Snell & Wilmer, Phoenix, 1956-81; pres., chmn., chief exec. officer Ramada Inc., Phoenix, 1981-89; chmn., chief exec. officer Aztar Corp., 1989-90, chmn., bd. dirs., 1990-92; chmn., chief exec. officer, pres. Pinnacle West Capital Corp., Phoenix, 1990—, bd. dirs.; bd. dirs. Bank One Ariz. Corp., Bank One Ariz. NA, Aztar Corp., Ctrl. Newspapers Inc.; bd. dirs., chmn. Ariz. Pub. Svc. Co. Trustee Am. Grad. Sch. Internat. Mgmt., Phoenix; past pres. YMCA Met. Phoenix and Valley of Sun. With U.S. Army, 1954-56. Mem. ABA, Ariz. Bar Assn., Paradise Valley Country Club, Phoenix Country Club. Republican. Lutheran. Office: Pinnacle West Capital Corp 400 E Van Buren St Phoenix AZ 85004-2223 also: Arizona Public Service Co PO Box 53999 # 9960 Phoenix AZ 85072-3999

SNIDER, KAREN CECILE, artist; b. Eugene, Oreg., Sept. 25, 1938; d. Ralph Otis and Kathryn (Schwind) Hodges; m. Fred L. Snider, Apr. 26, 1959; children: Julie Lynn, Steven Fredrick. Student, Eugene Sch. Art, 1972-74. Art instr. Lane Cmty. Coll., Eugene, 1974-88, Linn, Benton Cmty. Coll., Sweet Home, Oreg., 1986-88; artist for reproduction Leanin Tree Inc., Colo., 1990-97, Oracle Publ., Chico, Calif., 1997—; pres. Gallery 30, Eugene, 1982-83; bd. dirs. Emerald Empire Arts Assn., Springfield, Oreg., 1985-86, Nestucca Valley Artisans, Pacific City, Oreg., 1994-97. Exhibited at numerous galleries. Den mother Cub Scouts, Marcola, Oreg., 1971-74; tchr. sunday sch., 1969-74, vacation Bible sch., 1969-74. Home: 2044 SW 21st St Redmond OR 97756-9554 Office: Oracle Publ 702 Mangrove Ave # 305 Chico CA 95926-3948

SNIDER, PAUL NORMAN, psychiatrist; b. Worcester, Mass., Oct. 14, 1943; s. Abraham and Betty (Simon) S.; m. Ellen Vera Karell, Aug. 27, 1967; children: Rebecca, Jessica, Seth. BA, Tufts Coll., 1965, MD, 1969. Diplomate Am. Bd. Psychiatry and Neurology. Intern Mt. Auburn Hosp., Cambridge, Mass., 1969-70; resident in psychiatry Stron Meml. Hosp., Rochester, N.Y., 1970-73; pvt. practice Mountain View, Calif., 1973—; mem. staff El Camino Hosp., Mountain View, Calif., 1973—; chief psychiatry El Camino Hosp., Mountain View, 1978-79. With USAR, 1971-77. Mem. Am. Psychiat. Assn., Santa Clara County Med. Soc. Office: 515 South Dr Ste 11 Mountain View CA 94040-4209

SNIDER, RONALD ALBERT, minister; b. Detroit Lakes, Minn., May 31, 1931; s. George Albert and Mabel Scmidt (Warren) S.; m. Ida Jane Mettling, June 8, 1950; children: Brian, Craig, Robin, Kevin. BA, North Cen. Coll., 1953; ThB, Internat. Sem., 1980, ThM, 1981, DDiv (hon.), 1981. Ordained to ministry Assemblies of God, 1952. Founding pastor Assembly of God Ch., Staples, Minn., 1952-55, West Covina, Calif., 1955-57; pastor Assembly of God Ch., Spring Valley, Minn., 1957-61, Baywood Park, Calif., 1961-69; pastor Fallbrook (Calif.) Assembly of God, 1969—; chaplain Calif. Dept. Corrections, Rainbow, 1970-82; youth dir. North Coast sect. Assembly of God, Baywood Park, 1965-70, chmn. ministerial ethics com. So. Calif. dist. coun., Cosa Mesa, 1982. Contbr. articles to religious jours.; speaker in field. Office: Fallbrook Assembly of God 2000 Reche Rd Fallbrook CA 92028-3627

SNIEZEK, PATRICK WILLIAM, real estate loan officer; b. Zainesville, Ohio, Apr. 25, 1964; s. Richard Anton and Wanda Lee (Sir) S. BSBA in Mktg., U. Ariz., 1987. Customer svc. rep. Great Am. Bank, Tucson, 1983-85, customer svc. rep. II, 1985-87, real estate loan officer, 1987-91; real estate loan officer Waterfield Fin. Corp., Tucson, 1991-93; asst. v.p., br. mgr. Norwest Mortgage Inc., Tucson, 1993-96; br. mgr. The Bank of Ariz., Tucson, 1996-98; sr. v.p. Sun Cmty. Mortgage Co., 1998—. Bd. mem. So. Ariz. Kidney Found., Tucson, 1987-88; bus. cons. Jr. Achievement, Tucson, 1987—; treas. Active 20/30 Club, Tucson, 1987-88, sec. 1988-89, bd. dirs., 1989-90. Named Outstanding Young Man of Yr., Outstanding Young Men of Am., Montgomery, Ala., 1988, Future Bus. Leader of Yr., Future Bus. Leaders of Am., Phoenix, 1988. Republican. Roman Catholic. Avocations: running, tennis, golf, racquetball. Home: 3725 N Calle Perdiz Tucson AZ 85718-7215 Office: Sun Community Mortgage Co 4400 E Broadway Blvd # 610 Tucson AZ 87511-3579

SNODGRASS, LYNN, small business owner, state legislator; married; children: Jenne, Megan. BS in Elem. Edn., Oreg. State U., 1973; degree, Portland State U., 1975. Owner Drake's 7 Dees Nursery & Landscape Co., Oreg.; mem. Oreg. Ho. of Reps., 1995—; dep. majority leader, 1995-97, majority leader, 1997—; speaker of the house Oregon House of Reps, Salem, 1998; Mem. Damascus (Oreg.) Sch. Dist. Budget Com., 1985-88, Damascus Sch. Bd., 1991-94; mem. Oreg. Ho. of Reps. Human Resources and Edn. Com. (Edn. sub-com.), 1995-97, Labor Com., 1995-97, Commerce Com. (Bus. sub-com.), 1995-97, Children and Families Com., 1995-97, Emergency Bd. Com. (Edn. sub-com.), 1995-97, Interim Edn. Com., 1995-97, Legis. Adminstrn. Com., 1995—, Rules and Election Com., 1997—. Mem., past pres. Mt. Hood Med. Ctr. Found.; bd. dirs. Specialized Housing, Inc., Metro Home Builder; mem. Good Shepherd Cmty. Ch.; tchr. Jr. Achievement; classroom vol. Avocations: racquetball, reading, singing, camping, cooking. Fax: 503-986-1347. Office: Oreg Ho of Dels 269 State Capitol Salem OR 97310*

SNOOK, QUINTON, construction company executive; b. Atlanta, July 15, 1925; s. John Wilson and Charlotte Louise (Clayson) S.; student U. Idaho, 1949-51; m. Lois Mullen, Jan. 19, 1947; children: Lois Ann Snook Matteson, Quinton A., Edward M., Clayson S., Charlotte T. Rancher, Lemhi Valley, Idaho, 1942—; owner, mgr. Snook Constrn., Salmon, Idaho, 1952—; owner Snook Trucking, 1967—, Lemhi Posts and Poles, 1980—. Mem. Lemhi County Commn., Dist. 2, 1980-93. Named to Idaho Agrl. Hall of Fame, 1996. Mem. Am. Quarter Horse Assn., Farm Bur., Nat. Rifleman's Assn., Idaho Assn. Commrs. and Clerks (sec. 1986, v.p. 1987, pres. 1988), Am. Hereford Assn., Idaho Cattlemen's Assn., Elks. Republican. Episcopalian. Home: RR 1 Box 49 Salmon ID 83467-9701

SNOW, ALAN ALBERT, religious studies writer; b. Van Nuys, Calif., July 20, 1946; s. Perry William and Virginia (Show) S. BA, Pepperdine U., L.A., 1969; MA, Sch. of Theology, Claremont, Calif., 1974; ThD, Andersonville Bapt. Sem., 1994. mem. Jesus seminar Weststar Inst. Contbg. author to anthologies: The Book Your Church Does Not Want You to Read, 3d edit., 1997, Sydney Omarr's Astrol. Guides for Your, 1994, 95, 96, 97, (poetry) The Long and Winding Road, 1997. Mem. Am. Assn. Christian Counselors, Assn. Ind. Clergy, Dead Sea Scroll Rsch. Coun., Bibl. Archaeology Soc. Democrat. Home: 518 S Bay Front Newport Beach CA 92662-1040

SNOW, MARYLY ANN, librarian, artist; b. Oakland, Calif., Dec. 1, 1944; d. John Condit Snow and Mary Aileen (Lawler) Cauchois. BA in Social Welfare, U. Calif., Berkeley, 1966, M in Libr. and Info. Studies, 1974. Libr. asst. reference and interlibr. loan depts. McHenry Libr., U. Calif., Santa Cruz, 1970-72; libr. asst. Ctr. for Libr. Rsch. U. Calif., Berkeley, 1972-74, ctr. libr. Ctr. for Study of Law and Soc., 1973-75, asst. libr. map rom., 1974-75, lectr. Sch. Libr. and Info. Studies, 1974-76, 78, head arch. slide and photograph libr., 1979—; cons. Calif. State U., Long Beach, 1976, N.J. Inst. Tech., 1994, Harold Stump Archtl. Found., 1995—, Denver Pub. Libr., 1993, 97; presenter in field. One-person shows include Sun Gallery, Hayward, Calif., 1977, Van Doren Gallery, San Francisco, 1977, Nathan Hart Gallery, San Francisco, 1985; exhibited in group shows Concourse Gallery, Bank of Am. World Hdqs., San Francisco, 1976, Crown Zellerbach Exhbn., San Francisco, 1981, Creative Growth Gallery, Oakland, Calif., 1984, Los Medanos Coll., Martinez, Calif., 1987, Kala Inst., Berkeley, 1990, Internat. Print Biennial, Sapporo, Japan, 1991, Sebastopol (Calif.) Art Ctr., 1995, Tex. Art Assn. traveling exhbn., 1996-98, Inst. Franco-Am., Renne, France, 1997; represented in collections 3M Corp., Minn., ITEL Corp., San Francisco, Claire Carlevaro, El Cerrito, Calif., Wells Fargo Bank, San Francisco, others; represented in permanent collections Achenbach Found. Prints and Drawings, Fine Arts Mus. San Francisco; author: (book chpts.) Beyond the Book, 1991; contbr. articles to profl. jours. Libr. fellow Townsend Ctr. for the Humanities, U. Calif., Berkeley, 1997-98; grantee Libr.'s Assn. of U. of Calif., 1997-98, Librs.'s Assembly, U. of Calif., Berkeley, 1988, U. Calif., Berkeley, Office of Ednl. Devel., 1989, 96. Mem. Art Librs. Soc. N.Am. (visual resources divsn. task force on authorities 1986-90, art and arch. adv. com. 1989-92, liaison to Visual Resources Assn. data stds. com. 1995-96, sec. 1995-97, mem. awards com. 1997-98, mem. visual resources adv. com. 1997-98), Visual Resources Assn. (MARC format com. 1989-93, data stds. com. 1993-95, intellectual property rights com. 1995-97), Calif. Soc. Printmakers. E-mail: slides@socrates.berkeley.edu. Office: U Calif Berkeley Arch Slide Libr 232 Wurster Hall Berkeley CA 94720-1802

SNOW, RICHARD ERIC, education educator; b. Newark, June 6, 1936; s. Howard Bartley and Thelma Eleanor (Johnson) S.; m. Alice Alexandra Niedzinski, Aug. 16, 1958 (div. June 1980); children: Erich, Shenandoan, Alec, September; m. Joan Ethel Talbert, Mar. 15, 1981; 1 child, Ryan. BA, U. Va., 1958; MS, Purdue U., 1960, PhD, 1963; PhD (hon.), U. Leuven, Belgium, 1992, Goteborg (Sweden) U., 1993. Instr. Audio Visual Ctr. Purdue U., Lafayette, Ind., 1960-62, asst. prof. Audio Visual Ctr., 1962-65, assoc. prof. Audio Visual Ctr., 1965-66; asst. prof. edn. Stanford (Calif.) U., 1967-69, assoc. prof. edn., 1969-75, prof. edn. and psychology, 1975-97, Watkins U. prof., 1992-97; cons. U.S. Govt. Dept. Edn., Washington, WHO, Geneva, 1975-80; liaison scientist for psychology Office of Naval Rsch., London, 1983-85; adv. Nat. Assess of Ednl. Progress, Washington, 1985-95. Author: Pygmalion Reconsidered, 1971, Aptitudes and Instruction, 1977; editor: Aptitude Learning Instruction, 3 vols., 1980-87; contbr. articles to profl. jours. Fellow APA (divsn. 15 pres. 1981-82), Am. Psychol. Soc.; mem. AAAS, Am. Ednl. Rsch. Assn. (divsn. C v.p. 1982-84), European Assn. Rsch. on Learning Instrn. Avocations: history, music. Home: 675 Alvarado Row Stanford CA 94305-8507 Office: Stanford Univ Sch Edn Stanford CA 94305

SNOW, W. STERLING, education educator, sports coach, science educator; b. Devils Lake, N.D., Feb. 14, 1947; s. Morgan Williams and Josephine Elizabeth Ann (Erickstad) S.; m. Barbara Kay Jolley, Aug. 29, 1976; 1 child, Michelle Rene. AB, U. Calif., Santa Cruz, 1970; postgrad., U. Calif., Santa Barbara, 1970-71; MA, Chapman Coll., 1976. Cert. secondary sch. tchr., Calif., Alaska, Ariz.; cert. in adminstrn., Calif., Ariz.; cert. cmty. coll. instr., Ariz. Tchr., coach Monterey (Calif.) Peninsula Unified Sch. Dist., 1972-76; tchr., coach Anchorage (Alaska) Sch. Dist., 1976-96, athletic dir., 1987-92, tchr., 1992-96; sabbatical, 1996—; conf. asst. U. Calif., Santa Cruz, 1971-78. Bd. dirs. Dimond Alumni Found., Anchorage, 1987-92. Recipient Merit award for outstanding athletic program Alaska Dept. Edn., 1990, Appreciation award Dimond Alumni Found., 1990, Appreciation award Dimond High Sch. Activities and Athletics, 1993, Hall of Fame award, 1995. Mem. AAAS, ASCD, NSTA, Nat. Assn. Biology Tchrs. (life), Nat. Interscholastic Athletic Adminstrs. Assn. (life), Soc. Coll. Sci. Tchrs., Alaska Athletic Adminstrs. Interscholastic Assn. (Athletic Dir. of Yr. 1990), N.Y. Acad. Scis., Kappa Delta Pi. Lutheran.

SNOWDEN, DAVID L., protective services official. Chief of police Costa Mesa, Calif. Office: 99 Fair Dr Costa Mesa CA 92628-6520*

SNYDER, ALLEGRA FULLER, dance educator; b. Chgo., Aug. 28, 1927; d. R. Buckminster and Anne (Hewlett) Fuller; m. Robert Snyder, June 30, 1951 (div. Apr. 1975, remarried Sept. 1980); children: Alexandra, Jaime. BA in Dance, Bennington Coll., 1951; MA in Dance, UCLA, 1967. Asst. to curator, dance archives Mus. Modern Art, N.Y.C., 1945-47; dancer Ballet Soc. of N.Y.C. Ballet Co., 1945-47; mem. office and prodn. staff Internat. Film Found., N.Y.C., 1950-52; editor, dance films Film News mag., N.Y.C., 1966-72; lectr. dance and film adv., dept. dance UCLA, 1967-73, chmn. dept. dance, 1974-80, 90-91, acting chair, spring 1985, chair of faculty Sch. of the Arts, 1989-91, prof. dance and dance ethnology, 1973-91, prof. emeritus, 1991—; pres. Buckminster Fuller Inst., Santa Barbara, Calif.; chairwoman bd. dirs. Buckminster Fuller Inst., 1984; vis. lectr. Calif. Inst. Arts, Valencia, 1972; co-dir. dance and TV workshop Am. Dance Festival, Conn. Coll., New London, 1973; dir. NEH summer seminar for coll. tchrs. Asian Performing Arts, 1978, 81; coord. Ethnic Arts Intercoll. Interdisciplinary Program, 1974-73, acting chmn., 1986; vis. prof. performance studies NYU, 1982-83; hon. vis. prof. U. Surrey, Guildford, Eng., 1983-84; cons. Thyodia Found., Salt Lake City, 1973-74; mem. dance adv. panel Nat. Endowment Arts, 1968-72, Calif. Arts Commn., 1974-91; mem. adv. screening com. Coun. Internat. Exch. of Scholars, 1979-82; mem. various panels NEH, 1979-85; core cons. for Dancing, Sta. WNET-TV, 1988—. Dir. film Baroque Dance 1625-1725, in 1977; co-dir. film Gods of Bali, 1952; dir. and wrote film Bayanihan, 1962 (named Best Folkloric Documentary at Bilboa Film Festival, winner Golden Eagle award); asst. dir. and asst. editor film The Bennington Story, 1952; created films Gestures of Sand, 1968, Reflections on Choreography, 1973, When the Fire Dances Between Two Poles, 1982; created film, video loop and text Celebration: A World of Art and Ritual, 1982-83; supr. post-prodn. film Erick Hawkins, 1964, in 1973. Also contbr. articles to profl. jours. and mags. Adv. com. Pacific Asia Mus., 1980-84, Festival of the Mask, Craft and Folk Art Mus., 1979-84; adv. panel Los Angeles Dance Currents II, Mus. Ctr. Dance Assn., 1974-75; bd. dirs. Council Grove Sch. III, Compton, Calif., 1976-81; apptd. mem. Adv. Dance Com., Pasadena (Calif.) Art Mus., 1970-71, Los Angeles Festival of Performing Arts com., Studio Watts, 1970; mem. Technology and Cultural Transformation com., UNESCO, 1977. Fulbright research fellow, 1983-84; grantee Nat. Endowment Arts, 1981, Nat. Endowment Humanities, 1977, 79, 81, UCLA, 1968, 77, 80, 82, 85; recipient Amer. Dance Guild Award for Outstanding Achievement in Dance, 1992. Mem. Am. Dance Therapy Assn., Congress on Rsch. in Dance (bd. dirs. 1970-76, chmn. 1975-77, nat. conf. chmn. 1972), Coun. Dance Adminstrs., Am. Dance Guild (chmn. com. awards 1972), Soc. for Ethnomusicology, Am. Anthrop. Assn., Am. Folklore Soc., Soc. Anthropology of Visual Comm., Soc. Humanistic Anthropology, Calif. Dance Educators Assn. (conf. chmn. 1972), L.A. Area Dance Alliance (adv. bd. 1978-84, selection com. Dance Kaleidoscope project 1979-81), Fulbright Alumni Assn. Home: 15313 Whitfield Ave Pacific Palisades CA 90272-2548 Office: Buckminster Fuller Inst Ste 224 2040 Alameda Padre Serra Santa Barbara CA 93103-1760*

SNYDER, FRANCINE, psychotherapist, registered nurse, writer; b. Balt., Mar. 13, 1947; d. Jack and Naomi (Rapoport) S. AA, C.C. Balt., 1968; BA in Psychology, Antioch Coll. W, 1973; MA in MFCC, Azusa Pacific Coll., 1975; PhD in Clin. and Ednl. Psychology, Internat. Coll., 1981. RN, Hawaii; lic. marriage, family, and child counselor, Calif.; instr., Calif.; counselor, Calif.; credentialed cmty. coll. counselor, Calif., cmty. coll. instr. health, phys. care svcs., related techs., nursing and psychology; cert. addiction specialist, cognitive behavioral therapist; endorsed domestic violence counselor 1, 2 & 3 Nat. Bd. Cognitive Behavioral Therapists. Staff & reliefnurse, crisis counselor Midway Hosp., L.A., 1972-77; counselor So. Calif. Counseling Ctr., L.A., 1972-77; counselor, exec. bd. mem., steering com. mem. Healing Ctr. for the Whole Person, Northridge, Calif., 1974-75; counselor The Family Home, North Hollywood, Calif., 1976; pvt. practice Beverly Hills, Calif., 1975-86; counselor St. Johns Mental Health Ctr., Santa Monica, Calif., 1977-79, Calif. Family Study Ctr., Burbank, 1979-80; pvt. practice Kauai, Hawaii, 1986—; clin. dir., therapist Kauai YWCA Sex Abuse Treatment Program, Hawaii, 1989-90; clin. cons. Iniki Ohana Project, Kapaa, Hawaii, 1993; student nurse Johns Hopkins Hosp., Balt., 1965-68; head and relief nurse, team leader, 1966-70; nurse Nix Meml. Hosp., San Antonio, Tex., 1970; staff nurse, team leader Cmty. Hosp, Chandler, Ariz.; cons. Slim Bionics Med. Group, L.A., 1974-75; instr. Pierce Coll., Woodland Hills, Calif., 1977, Saint Johns Med. Ctr., Santa Monica, Calif., 1977-79, Maple Ctr., Beverly Hills, Calif., 1979-80. Speaker in field. Mem. Am. Anorexia Nervosa/Bulimia Assn., Inc., Am. Mental Affiliates for Israel (exec. bd., head of allocations com.), Am. Assn. Marriage and Family Therapists (clin.), Internat. Platform Assn., Calif. Assn. Marriage and Family Therapists (clin.), Assn. for Humanistic Psychology, Children's Coalition for TV, Ctr. for the Healing Arts, Alliance for Survival, UCLA Alumni Assn.; cons. Help Anorexia, Inc., Performance Design Syss. Home: PO Box 1303 Hanalei HI 96714-1303 Office: InnerVisions Counseling & Tng PO Box 1303 Hanalei HI 96714-1303

SNYDER, GEORGE MORRIS, JR., adult education educator, writer, consultant; b. Upper Chichester, Pa., Aug. 27, 1917; s. George Morris and Mary Alice (McGuirk) Snyder; m. Roberta Rose Riggs, Dec. 21, 1962 (div. Dec. 1973); children: Kent, Rhea; m. Anita Lince Green, Dec. 21, 1948 (dec.). BA in Edn., West Chester (Pa.) State U., 1940; MA in Sociology, Temple U., 1948; postgrad., U. So. Calif., Calif. State U., Long Beach. Cert. secondary edn. social studies, English. Tchr. West Phila. H.S., 1945-46, Redondo Union Dist. H.S., Redondo Beach, Calif., 1946-71, So. Bay Adult Sch., 1977—; asst. prof. Northrop U., Inglewood, Calif., 1972-78. Author: Freshly Remember'd, 1978. Chmn. Dem. Party Club, 1960. Mem. So. Bay [illegible] writing, reading. Home: 3504 Blossom Ln Redondo Beach CA 90278-1411

SNYDER, JOHN HENRY, computer science educator, consultant; b. [illegible]

S.; m. Patricia Reilly, Mar. 11, 1984; children: Matthew Melvin George, Mark John Joseph. BA, U. Kans., 1970; MS, Nova U., Ft. Lauderdale, Fla., 1984. Cert. tchr. Nev., N.D. Computer sci. tchr. Hyde Park Jr. High Sch., Las Vegas, Nev., 1981-86, Chapparal High sch., Las Vegas, 1986-91, Cimarron Meml. High Sch., Las Vegas, 1991-94; chair dept. sci. & tech. Advanced Tech. Acad., Las Vegas, 1994—; copywriter pub. info. office CCSD, Las Vegas, 1982-84; chmn. gifted children spl. interest group, Am. Mensa, 1984; mem. tech. com. Nev. 2000 Task Force, 1994-95, Nev. State Network Internet Com., 1994-95; mem. sch. dist. tech. coord. task force, 1994-95; cons. Office Supt. Clark County Sch. dist., Las Vegas, 1984, 85, IBM Corp., Atlanta, 1991-96; systems analyst Homes & Narver, 1988 (summer); adminstrv. aide EG&G Energy Measurements, Las Vegas, 1989 (summer); adj. instr. computer sci. Nova U., 1984-93, U. Nev. Las Vegas, 1990—, The Meadows Sch., 1991-96; bd. dirs. Ctr. for Teaching Resources, The Mazer Corp., N.Y., Akron, Ohio, 1990—; treas., 1994-95; webmaster, 1998—. Newsletter editor Nat. State Tchrs. of Yr., 1991-93; contbr. articles to profl. jours. Co-chmn. Ednl. Exposition, Las Vegas, 1984; tech. cons. Harry Reid for U.S. Senate, 1986, 92; mem. Nevada 2000 Tech. Subcom., 1993, Nev. State Network Internet Com., 1993—. Named Tchr. of Yr., State of Nev., 1989-90, U. Nev., Las Vegas, Southland Tchr. of Yr., 1990, Tandy Tech. Scholar, 1991, Nev. Educator of Yr., Milliken Family Found., 1992, Nev. Tchr. of the Yr. Microsoft Corp./Technology & Learning Mag., 1995; recipient Innovative Teaching award Bus. Week Mag., 1990, Mc Caulufffe fellowship, 1994, 97, Impact Innovator grantee, 1996. Mem. NEA (Instrn. and Profl. Devel. chmn. 1979-80), ASCD, KC (sec., v.p., pres., past pres., local lodge newsletter editor), Am. Legion, Phi Delta Kappa (newsletter editor Overall Excellence award 1990). Democrat. Roman Catholic. Avocations: programming, guitar, classical music, website construction, virtual reality. Office: Advanced Tech Acad 2501 Vegas Dr Las Vegas NV 89106-1643

SNYDER, JOHN JOSEPH, optometrist; b. Wonewoc, Wis., June 30, 1908; s. Burt Frederick and Alta Lavinia (Hearn) S.; A.B., UCLA, 1931, postgrad., 1931-32; postgrad. U. Colo., 1936, 38, 40, 41, U. So. Calif., 1945-46; B.S. in Optometry, Los Angeles Coll. Optometry, 1948, O.D., 1949. Tchr., La Plata County (Colo.) Pub. Schs., 1927-28; supt. Marvel (Colo.) Pub. Schs., 1932-33; tchr. Durango (Colo.) High Sch., 1933-41; pvt. practice optometry, Los Angeles, 1952-72, Torrance, Calif., 1972-78; now retired. Former bd. dirs. Francia Boys' Club, Los Angeles; former pres. Exchange Club South Los Angeles, also sec. Mem. AAAS, Am. Inst. Biol. Scis., Am., Calif., Optometric Assn., Internat. Biog. Assn. Republican. Home: 25937 Reynolds St Loma Linda CA 92354-3962

SNYDER, RICHARD GERALD, research scientist, administrator, educator, consultant; b. Northampton, Mass., Feb. 14, 1928; s. Grant B. and Ruth (Putnam) S.; m. Phoebe Jones, Mar. 2, 1949; children: Dorinda, Sherrill, Paul, Jeff, Jon, David. Student Amherst Coll., 1946-48; BA, U. Ariz., 1956, MA, 1957, PhD, 1959. Diplomate Am. Bd. Forensic Anthropology. Teaching asst. dept. anthropology U. Ariz., Tucson, 1957-58, assoc. rsch. engr. Applied Rsch. Lab., Coll. Engring., 1958-60, mem. staff Ariz. Transp. and Traffic Inst., 1959-60, assoc. prof. systems engring., 1960; chief phys. anthropology Civil Aeromed. Rsch. Inst., FAA, Oklahoma City, 1960-66, rsch. pilot, 1962-66, acting chief Protection and Survival Labs., 1963-66; mgr. biomechanics dept. Office of Automotive Safety Rsch., Ford Motor Co., Dearborn, Mich., 1966-68, prin. rsch. scientist, 1968; assoc. prof. anthropology U. Mich., Ann Arbor, 1968-73, prof., 1973-85, rsch. scientist Hwy. Safety Rsch. Inst., 1968-85, head biomed. dept., 1969-84, dir. NASA Ctr. of Excellence in Man-Vehicle Systems, 1984-85, prof. emeritus, 1985—, rsch. scientist emeritus, 1989—; pres. Biodynamics Internat., Tucson, Ariz., 1986—; pres., bd. dirs. George Snively Rsch. Found., 1992—; adj. assoc. prof. U. Okla., 1963; rsch. assoc. Zoller Lab. U. Chgo., 1964-65, rsch. assoc. dept. anthropology, 1965-67; assoc. prof. Mich. State U., East Lansing, 1967-68; cons. USAF Aerospace Med. Rsch. Labs., Nat. Acad. Scis., U.S. Dept. Transp., adv. com. Office Naval Rsch. Dept. Navy, numerous others. Assoc. editor: Jour. of Communication, 1961-63; cons. editor: Jour. of Biomechanics, 1967-81; editorial bd. Product Safety News, 1973—; adv. bd. Aviation Space and Environ. Medicine, 1980-91, 94—; contbr. chpts. to books and numerous articles to profl. jours. Judge, Internat. Sci. Fair, Detroit, 1968; mem. coun. Explorer Scouts, Ann Arbor, 1968-70; dir. Am. Bd. Forensic Anthropology, 1978-84, 85-91; dir. Snell Meml. Found., 1990—; bd. dirs. N.Mex. Rsch. Inst., 1996—. 1st lt. USAF, 1949-54, Korea. Recipient Met. Life award, Nat. Safety Coun., 1970; Arch T. Colwell Merit award Soc. Automotive Engrs., 1973; Award for Profl. Excellence Aerospace Med. Assn., 1978; Admiral Luis de Flores Flight Safety award Flight Safety Found., 1981; named to Safety and Health Hall of Fame Internat., 1993, Ariz. Aviation Hall of Fame, 1998. Fellow Aerospace Med. Assn. (Harry G. Moseley award 1975, John Paul Stapp award in aerospace biomechanics 1994), Royal Anthrop. Inst., AAAS, Am. Anthropl. Assn., Am. Acad. Forensic Scis. (T. Dale Stewart award 1992); mem. AIAA (assoc. fellow), Am. Assn. Phys. Anthropologists, Ariz.-Nev. Acad. Sci., Soc. Automotive Engrs. (Aerospace Congress award 1982, Tech. contributions to Air Transport Safety), Internat. Soc. Aircraft Safety Investigators, Aerospace Physiologists Soc., Sigma Xi, Beta Beta Beta. Republican. Congregationalist. Avocations: aviation, aerospace medicine, forensic anthropology. Home: 3720 N Silver Dr Tucson AZ 85749-9709 Office: Biodynamics Internat Tucson AZ 85749

SNYDER, SHERRY ANN, university administrator; b. Rochester, N.Y., July 5, 1950; d. Charles Donald and Patricia (Alderman) S. BA, Ashland (Ohio) U., 1972; MS, Nazareth Coll., Pittsford, N.Y., 1976; EdS, U. Colo., 1982; PhD, Colo. State U., 1997. Cert. secondary edn. adminstrn., reading specialist K-12. Reading tchr./cons. Boches #1 Monroe County, Fairport, N.Y., 1973-78; counselor/registrar Adams #12 Schs., Northglenn, Colo., 1979-84; instr. Front Range C.C., Westminster, Colo., 1984-86; instr. Loretta Heights Coll., Denver, 1986-87, dir., 1987-88; coord. acad. skills program U. Colo., Boulder, 1988—; participant U. Colo. Fellows Program, 1992-93, Leadership for a New Century, Tempe, Ariz., 1991-92. Author: (booklet) Study Smarter, 1994. Recipient Outstanding Young Woman award Outstanding Young Women Am., 1987. Mem. Internat. Reading Assn., Colo. Coun. Adult Educators and Cmty. Educators, Nat. Inst. for Leadership Devel. in Women. Democrat. Office: U Colo C B 107 Boulder CO 80309-0107

SOBELLE, RICHARD E., lawyer; b. Cleve., Mar. 18, 1935. BA, Stanford U., 1956, JD, 1960; LLM, U. So. Calif., 1967. Bar: Calif. 1961, U.S. Supreme Ct. 1969. Exec. Tracinda Corp., Las Vegas. Mem. ABA (mem. corp., banking and bus. law sect. 1969—), State Bar Calif. (del. to conf. state bar dels. 1965-77, mem. exec. com. bus. law sect. 1977-78), L.A. County Bar Assn. (mem. exec. coun., jr. barristers 1965-68, mem. exec. com. bus. and corps. sect. 1973-75). Office: Tracinda Corp # 250 150 S Rodeo Dr Ste 250 Beverly Hills CA 90212-2417

SOBEY, EDWIN J. C., museum director, oceanographer, consultant; b. Phila., Apr. 7, 1948; s. Edwin J. and Helen (Chapin) S.; m. Barbara Lee, May 9, 1970; children: Ted Woodall, Andrew Chapin. BS, U. Richmond (Va.), 1969; MS, Oreg. State U., 1974, PhD, 1977. Rsch. scientist Sci. Applications, Inc., Boulder, Colo., 1977-79, div. mgr., 1979-81; exec. dir. Sci. Mus., West Palm Beach, Fla., 1981-88, Mus. Sci. and History, Jacksonville, Fla., 1988, Nat. Invention Ctr., Akron, Ohio, 1989-92, Fresno (Calif.) Met. Mus., 1993-95; ednl. cons., 1995—; exec. prodr. (t.v. show) Idea Factory, KFSN-30, Fresno, 1995-97; exec. dir. A.C. Gilbert's Discovery Village, Salem, Oreg., 1997-99; instr. mus. mgmt. U. Wash., 1998—. Alumni v.p. Leadership Palm Beach County; expdn. leader Expdn. Tng. Inst., S.E. Alaska, 1980; mem. U.S. Antarctic Research Program, 1974. Author: Complete Circuit Training Guide, 1980; Strength Training Book, 1981; (with others) Aerobic Weight Training Book, 1982, The Whole Backpacker's Catalog, 1988, Increasing Your Audience, 1989, Inventing Stuff, 1995, Wrapper Rockets and Trombone Straws-Science at Every Meal, 1996, Car Smarts, 1997, Just Plane Smart, 1998; mem. editorial adv. bd. Invent Mag., 1989-92. Founder, bd. dirs. Visually Impaired Sports Program, Boulder, 1978-81; fitness instr. YMCA Boulder, 1977-81; convener 1st Nat. Conf. Sports for the Blind, 1979; bd. dirs. Leadership Palm Beach; vice chmn. County Com. [illegible] pres. Leadership Akron; v.p. Ohio Mus. Assn., 1991-92, pres., 1992-93; co-host Blow the Roof Off Ednl TV show, 1992; bd. dirs. Fla. Mus. Assn., 1988-89; mem. adv. bd. Marine Sci. Inst., 1990—. Lt. USN, 1970-73. Fellow Explorers Club; mem. Marine Tech. Soc. (sect. chmn. 1982-84), Coral Reef Soc. (chpt. pres. 1982-87), Nat. Inventive Thinking Assn. (bd. dirs. 1989—). E-mail: sobey@gte.net. Home: 2420 178th Ave NE Redmond WA 98052-5820

SOBKOWSKI, NIKKI TAMINEN, executive director; b. Chgo., Nov. 22, 1943; d. Arvid Martin and Victoria (Sclavounos) Taminen; s. Stephen Leonard Sobkowski, Sept. 17, 1966 (div. Dec. 1995); children: Lydia Helen, Katherine Ann. BA, Mich. State U., 1967; MALS, Rosary Coll., 1972; MA, U. Mich., 1982. Media comm. specialist Program for Ednl. Opportunity, Ann Arbor, 1977-82; asst. dir. annual giving U. Mich., Ann Arbor, 1985-90; dir. annual giving Rollins Coll., Winter Park, Fla., 1990; adminstrv. dir. Planned Parenthood, Las Vegas, 1993-94; dir. of devel. KNPR/Nev. Public Radio, Las Vegas, 1994-97; exec. dir. Arthritis Found., Las Vegas, 1997—. Recipient Bronze quill Internat. Assn. of Bus. Communicators. Mem. AAUW, Nat. Soc. Fund Raising Execs. (pres. 1997-98), Leadership Las Vegas Alumni Assn. (pres. 1997). Avocations: reading, travel. Home: 5103 Southern Hills Ln Las Vegas NV 89113-1393 Office: Arthritis Found 2660 S Rainbow Blvd Las Vegas NV 89146-5183

SOBOLEWSKI, JOHN STEPHEN, computer scientist, consultant; b. Krakow, Poland, July 14, 1939; came to U.S., 1966; s. Jan Zygmund and Stefania (Zwolinska) S.; m. Helen Skipper, Dec. 17, 1965 (div. July 1969); m. Carole Straith, Apr. 6, 1974; children: Anne-Marie, Elisa, Martin. BE, U. Adelaide, Adelaide, South Australia, 1962, ME, 1966; PhD in Computer Sci., Wash. State U., 1971. Sci. officer Weapons Research Establishment, Salisbury, South Australia, 1964-66; asst. prof. computer sci. Wash. State U., Pullman, 1966-73; dir. research, assoc. prof. U. Wash., Seattle, 1973-80, dir. computer svcs., 1980-88; assoc. v.p. computing U. N.Mex., Albuquerque, 1988—; cons. govt. and industry, Seattle, 1973—; mem. bd. trustees Fisher Found., Seattle, 1984—. Author: Computers for the Dental Office, 1986; contbr. articles to profl. jours. Served as engr. with Royal Australian Army, 1957-60. Australian govt. scholar, 1954-60, Elec. Res. Bd. scholar CSIRO, Melbourne, Australia, 1961-64. Mem. IEEE, Computer Soc. Roman Catholic. Avocation: mineral collecting. Home: 8501 Northridge Ave NE Albuquerque NM 87111-2107 Office: U NMex CIRT 2701 Campus Ave NE Albuquerque NM 87131

SOCHYNSKY, YAROSLAV, lawyer, mediator, arbitrator; b. Feb. 5, 1946. BA in English, Colgate U., 1967; JD, Georgetown U., 1970. Bar: Calif., N.Y. Assoc. White & Case, N.Y.C., 1970-71; law clerk to Hon. William T. Sweigert U.S. Dist. Ct. (no. dist.) Calif., 1971-73; assoc. Landels, Ripley & Diamond LLP, San Francisco, 1973-76; sr. ptnr. Landels, Ripley & Diamond, San Francisco, 1976—; lectr. Calif. Continuing Edn. Bar, 1985, Equity Asset Mgr.'s Assn., 1987, Calif. Dept. Real Estate, 1986-89). Originator, co-author California ADR Practice Guide, 1992; co-author Real Property Practice and Litigation, 1990; case and notes editor, mem. editorial bd. Georgetown Law Jour.; contbr. articles and monographs to profl. jours. Fellow Chartered Inst. Arbitrators (London); mem. ABA (mem. exec. coun. sect. on real property, probate and trust, lectr. 1988, 89, 91), Am. Arbitration Assn. (cert. mediator, mem. pres.' panel of mediators, large and compley case panel, internat. panel, real property valuation panel, No. Calif. adv. coun., lectr. 1990, speaker various panels, No. Calif. Outstanding Mediator award 1991), San Francisco Bar Assn., San Francisco Lawyers Com. for Civil Rights under Law. E-mail: ys@landels.com. Office: Landels Ripley & Diamond 350 The Embarcadero San Francisco CA 94105-1250

SOCRANSKY, LISA ELLEN, lawyer; b. Montreal, Que., Can., June 15, 1965; d. Isadore Samuel and Carol (Genender) S. BA, U. Calif., Berkeley, 1987; JD, Loyola U., L.A., 1991. Bar: Calif. 1991, U.S. Dist. Ct. (fed. dist.) Calif. 1991. Assoc. Ervin Cohen & Jessup, Beverly Hills, Calif., 1991-94, King Purtich Holmes Paterno & Berliner, L.A., 1995-98; counsel Davis & Shapiro, L.A., 1998—. Office: Davis & Shapiro 1724 N Vista St Los Angeles CA 90046-2235

SOCWELL, MARGARET G., reading and language arts educator, consultant; b. Avoca, Iowa, Oct. 7, 1946; d. Fay and Mary Gertrude (Grote) Osborn; m. Richard John Socwell, Mar. 11, 1971 (div. May 1979); 1 child, Benjamin Adam. BS, Ohio State U., Columbus, 1968; MS, U. Wis., 1979. Cert. reading specialist, libr. media specialist, Spanish and French tchr., Ariz. Tchr. French Mason (Ohio) Pub. Schs., 1969-70; tchr. Spanish and French St. Matthias Cath. Girls H.S., L.A., 1970-71; tchr. French Whitewater (Wis.) Pub. Schs., 1971-72, tchr. Spanish, 1972-78; reading specialist Chilton (Wis.) Pub. Schs., 1978-79, Tolleson (Ariz.) Elem. Schs., 1979-80; tchr. reading and Spanish Deer Valley Unified Schs., Phoenix, 1980-88; tchr. reading Rio Salado C.C., Phoenix, 1987-91, tchr. lang. arts, 1989-93, tchr. social studies, 1993-96, libr. media specialist, 1996—; state forensics judge Whitewater Pub. Schs., 1974—; test designer Deer Valley Reading Curriculum Com., Phoenix, 1986-87, participant lang. arts pilot program Deer Valley Unified Sch. Dist., 1989; designer integrated social studies curriculum, Hillcrest Mid. Sch., Deer Valley Unified Pub. Schs., Phoenix, 1994-96. Creator online Ariz. Holistic Healing Directory, 1999. Recipient grant Deer Valley Edn. Found., Inc., 1992. Democrat. Avocations: reading, embroidery, cross-stitch, knitting, travel. Office: Deer Valley Pub Schs #97 20402 N 15th Ave Phoenix AZ 85027-3636

SOFAER, ABRAHAM DAVID, lawyer, legal advisor, federal judge, law educator; b. Bombay, India, May 6, 1938; came to U.S., 1948, naturalized, 1959; m. Marian Bea Scheuer, Oct. 23, 1977; children: Daniel E., Michael J., Helen R., Joseph S., Aaron R., Raphael J. BA in History magna cum laude, Yeshiva Coll., 1962; LLB cum laude, NYU, 1965. Bar: N.Y. 1965, D.C. 1988. Law clk. to Hon. J. Skelly Wright, U.S. Ct. Appeals (D.C. cir.), Washington, 1965-66; law clk. to Hon. William J. Brennan Jr. U.S. Supreme Ct., Washington, 1966-67; asst. U.S. atty. U.S. Dist Ct. (so. dist.) N.Y., N.Y.C., 1967-69; prof. law Columbia U., N.Y.C., 1969-79; judge U.S. Dist. Ct. (so. dist.) N.Y., 1979-85; legal advisor U.S. Dept. State, Washington, 1985-90; ptnr. Hughes Hubbard & Reed, Washington, 1991-94; George P. Shultz disting. scholar, sr. fellow Hoover Instn., Stanford U., 1994—; prof. law Stanford U., Calif., 1996—; hearing officer N.Y. Dept. Environ. Conservation, 1975-76. Author: War, Foreign Affairs and Constitutional Power: The Origins, 1976; contbr. articles to legal, polit., fgn. jours.; editor-in-chief: NYU Law Rev, 1964-65. Served with USAF, 1956-59. Root-Tilden scholar NYU, 1965. Mem. ABA, Fed. Bar Assn., N.Y.C. Bar Assn., N.Y. Bar Assn., Am. Law Inst. Jewish. Fax: 650-723-2103. Home: 1200 Bryant St Palo Alto CA 94301-2716 Office: Stanford Univ The Hoover Instn Stanford CA 94305-6010

SOFONIO, MARK VINCENT, plastic and reconstructive surgeon; b. L.A., May 14, 1963; s. Lawrence and Hendrika Sofonio. BS in Biomed. Sci. magna cum laude, U. Calif., Riverside, 1984; MD, UCLA, 1988. Diplomate Am. Bd. Plastic Surgery; lic. physician, Calif., Ohio, Mich., Hawaii, N.Y. Intern gen. surgery integrated surg. residency program U. Hawaii, Honolulu, 1988-89, resident, 1989-91; fellow burn surgery N.Y. Med. Coll., Westchester County Med. Ctr., Valhalla, 1991-92; resident plastic and reconstructive surgery Med. Coll. Ohio, Toledo, 1992-94; fellow cosmetic surgery Bruce Connell, MD, Santa Ana, Calif., 1994-95; pvt. practice plastic and reconstructive surgery Rancho Mirage, Calif., 1996—. Author: (with others) Plastic, Maxillofacial and Reconstructive Surgery, 3rd edt., 1997, Grabb and Smith's Plastic Surgery, 5th edt., 1997; contbr. to profl. jours. Named Palm Springs Teenager of the Year 1981; recipient Rsch. Presentation award Am. Coll. Surgeons Ann. Hawaiian Conf., 1990. Mem. ACS, AMA, Am. Soc. Laser Medicine and Surgery, Am. Soc. Plastic and Reconstructive Surgery, Calif. Med. Assn., Am. Burn Assn. Republican. Avocations: exercising, tennis, golf, weight lifting, biking. Office: Kiewit Bldg 39000 Bob Hope Dr Ste 405 Rancho Mirage CA 92270-3221

SOH, CHUNGHEE SARAH, anthropology educator; b. Taegu, Korea, May 1, 1947; came to U.S., 1970; d. Sang Yung and Ock Yun (Choi) S.; m. Jerry Dee Boucher. BA summa cum laude, Sogang U., 1971; postgrad., U. Calif., Berkeley, 1971; MA in Anthropology, U. Hawaii, 1983, PhD in Anthropology, 1987. Staff instr. English Korean Air Lines, Edn. & Tng. Ctr., Seoul, 1978-79; instr. anthropology Ewha Womans U., Seoul, 1985; asst. [illegible] Marcos, 1991-94; asst. prof. anthropology San Francisco State U., 1994-96, assoc. prof. anthropology, 1996—; guest lectr. Chaminade U. Honolulu, 1988; vis. asst. prof. anthropology U. Ariz., 1990-91, adj. prof. Intercultural Inst. Calif., 1990 [illegible]

U., The Netherlands, 1998; cons. in field. Author: Women in Korean Politics; contbr. articles to profl. jours. Grantee East-West Ctr., 1981-87, NSF, 1985-86; fellow Korea Found., 1993, Japan Found., 1997-98, vis. fellow Inst. Social Sci., U. Tokyo, 1997-98; vis. scholar Hoover Inst., 1996-97. Fellow Am. Anthrop. Assn., Inst. for Corean-Am. Studies; mem. Am. Ethnological Soc., Soc. Psychol. Anthropology, Assn. Asian Studies (exec. bd. Com. Women Asian Studies), Western Social Sci. Assn., Korean Assn. Womens Studies, Royal Asiatic Soc. Korean Br. Office: San Francisco State U Dept Anthropology 1600 Holloway Ave San Francisco CA 94132-1722

SOHNEN-MOE, CHERIE MARILYN, business consultant; b. Tucson, Jan. 2, 1956; d. D. Ralph and Angelina Helen (Spiro) Sohnen; m. James Madison Moe, Jr., May 23, 1981. BA, UCLA, 1977. Rsch. asst. UCLA, 1975-77; ind. cons. L.A., 1978-83; cons. Sohnen-Moe Assocs., Inc., Tucson, 1984—. Author: Business Mastery, 1988, 2d edit., 1991, 3d edit., 1998; contbr. to Compendium mag., 1987-90, Massage Mag., 1992-94, 96-97, Am. Massage Therapy Assn. Jour., 1989—; bus. editor Massage Therapy Jour., 1998—. Vol. Am. Cancer Soc., Tucson, 1984—; mem. Ariz. Sonora Desert Mus., Tucson; pres. Women in Tucson, 1989. Recipient Outstanding Instr. award Desert Inst. of Healing Arts, 1992. Mem. NOW, ASTD (dir. mem. svcs. 1988, dir. mktg., Disting. Svc. award 1988, Profl. Achievement award 1997), Nat. Fed. Independent Bus., Internat. Assn. Ind. Pubs., Pubs. Mktg. Assn. Avocations: reading, swimming, crossword puzzles, board games, singing. E-mail: sma@rtd.com. Office: Sohnen-Moe Assocs Inc 3906 W Ina Rd # 200-367 Tucson AZ 85741-2261

SOKOL, JAN D., lawyer; b. N.Y., May 27, 1952. BS magna cum laude, Rutgers U., 1974; JD Northwestern Sch. of Law, Lewis and Clark Coll., 1977. Bar: Oreg. 1978, U.S. Dist. Ct. (dist. Oreg.), U.S. Ct. Appeals (9th cir.) 1981, U.S. Claims Ct. 1982, U.S. Supreme Ct. 1982. Law clerk to Hon. George A. Juba U.S. Dist. Ct. (dist. Oreg.), 1978-79, law clerk to Hon. Gus J. Solomon, 1979-80, law clerk to Hon. James A. Redden, 1980; mng. mem. Stewart, Sokol & Gray, 1994. Case note and comment editor Environmental Law, 1976-77. Mem. ABA (mem. forum com. on the construction industry, fidelity and surety, forest resources com.), Multnomah County. Office: Stewart Sokol & Gray 1500 Benjamin Franklin Plz One SW Columbia Portland OR 97258*

SOKOL, STEWART, health services administrator; b. N.Y.C., Nov. 30, 1944; s. David and Sylvia (Pogolowitz) S.; children: Laura Gail, Brian Eli. BA, Queens Coll., 1967, MS, 1974. Tchr. N.Y.C. Bd. Edn., 1968-73; pres. Cuzzins Mgmt., N.Y.C., 1973-76, Sokol Entertainment Enterprises, N.Y.C., 1976-88; supr. Nat. AIDS Hotline, N.Y.C., 1987-89; tchr. of children with AIDS N.Y.C. Bd. Edn., 1989-90; mng. dir. theatre in health edn. project London Ctrl. YMCA, 1991—; dir. HIV/AIDS Program Svcs. South Bay Free Clinic, L.A., 1991-95; cons. HIV/AIDS L'Hopital Avicenne, Paris, 1993, Australian Fedn. AIDS Orgns. (West Australia, NSW, Victoria, Queenland), 1990, others; mem. adv. bd. Women's Health Care Clinic Harbor UCLA Med. Ctr., 1992-95; mem. adv. com. UCLA Women and Family Project, 1995-96; commr. L.A. Commn. on HIV Health Svcs., 1997—; program dir. Beach Cities AIDS Svcs., 1995—; co-chair L.A. Counseling and Testing Task Force. Co-author: An Introduction to Spiritual Awareness Through Meditation, 1984, Developing Channeling Abilities with Spiritual Awareness, 1985; author: Create...Joy, 1986, Harmony: A Message to YourSelf, 1987, The Light and the Height Are in Sync, 1989. Mem. South Bay AIDS Network (chair 1991—), L.A. Adolescent Consortium, L.A. HIV Coalition Network. Avocation: international travel.

SOLARI, R. C., heavy construction company executive; b. 1925; married. With Granite Construction Co., 1946—, formerly pres.; now pres., chief exec. officer, dir. Granite Construction Co., Watsonville, Calif., chmn. bd. dirs. Office: Granite Constrn Co PO Box 50085 Watsonville CA 95077-5085

SOLKOVITS, GREGG, secondary education educator; b. Mpls., Nov. 25, 1956; s. David and Judith Ann (Rakov) S.; m. Lucia Arias, Nov. 18, 1995. BS, Calif. State U., Northridge, 1979. Cert. tchr. social studies, English, Journalism, Cross-Cultural Lang. Devel., Minn. Faculty chair, tchr. Monroe H.S., North Hills, Minn., 1981—; West Valley area chair United Tchrs. L.A., 1996—, bd. dirs.; polit. cons., 1981—. Editor: Southern Sierran, 1984-97, Calif. Tchr., 1980-84, United Tchr., 1978. Mem. Am. Fedn. Tchrs. (del. convs.), NEA (del. convs.), Calif. Tchrs. Assn. (mem. state coun. 1981—), Soc. of Profl. Journalists, Sierra Club. Democrat. Avocations: photography, writing, gardening, travel. Home: 17042 Sunburst St Northridge CA 91325-2606

SOLMER, RICHARD, surgeon; b. South Bend, Ind., Feb. 11, 1947. MD, U. Mich., 1972. Diplomate Am. Bd. Plastic Surgery. Surgical intern Hosp. of the U. Pa., Phila., 1972-73; gen. surgical resident Calif. Hosp. Med. Ctr., L.A., 1976-80; plastic surgery resident Allentown (Pa.) Affiliated Hosp., 1980-82; pvt. practice Huntington Beach, Calif., 1982—. Fellow Am. Coll. Surgeons; mem. Am. Soc. Plastic and Reconstructive Surgery. Office: 17742 Beach Blvd Ste 300 Huntington Beach CA 92647-6853

SOLOFF, MORDECAI ISAAC, retired rabbi; b. Igumen, Minsk, Russia, July 2, 1901; s. Louis and Rivko Esther (Goldberg) S.; widowed; children: Rav Asher, Tamar. BS, CUNY, 1923; MA, Tchr.'s Coll., N.Y.C., 1927; DD (hon.), Hebrew Union Coll., 1965. Ordained rabbi, 1940. Tchr., prin. various Jewish schs., 1920-24; mem. staff Bur. Jewish Edn., N.Y.C., 1924-27; supr. Jewish Schs. Chgo., 1927-29; instr. Hebrew Union Coll., Cin., 1937-40; rabbi Temple Akiba, Culver City, Calif., 1952-73, now rabbi emeritus, 1973—. Author: (textbooks) When the Jewish People Was Young, 1934, How the Jewish People Grew Up, 1936, How the Jewish People Live Today, 1940, 49, 52, The Covenant People, Vols. I-III, 1973, 74, 79, (with Soloff and Brower) Sacred Hebrew Series: Jewish Life, 1981, 90, Your Siddur, 1981, 91, Torataynu I, 1982, Torataynu II, 1983, The Faithful Jew, Vols. 1-6. Mem. Cen. Conf. Am. Rabbis (B'yad Chazakah award), Pacific Assn. Reform Rabbis, Nat. Assn. Ret. Reform Rabbis. Home: 337 14th St Santa Monica CA 90402-2113

SOLOMON, AMELIA KROLL, artist; b. Zwenigorodka-Kiev, Russia, Nov. 24, 1908; d. Abraham Krugliak Kroll and Nora Pipco; m. Herman Lampert Solomon, July 31, 1931 (dec. 1989); children: Ernest, Suzon, Semyon T., Sheba S. Studied with Ralph Stackpole, 1947; attended, Patri Sch. Fine Art, 1960, Foothill Coll., 1969, San Miguel de Allenda Art Inst., 1970; student, DeAnza Coll.; BA magna cum laude, San Jose State U., 1979, MFA, 1986. lectr. in field. Solo shows include Stanford (Calif.) U., 1982, 83, Oakland (Calif.) Art Assn., 1985, Open Studio, San Jose, 1989, 90, Rosicrucian Egyptian Mus., San Jose, 1989, Metro Contemporary Art Gallery, Foster City, Calif., 1989, Koret Gallery, Palo Alto, Calif., 1992, Cooper-Molera Adobe, Monterey, Calif., 1998; group shows include Palo Alto Art Club, 1966, 69, San Mateo Floral Fiesta, 1970, Livermore (Calif.) Art Assn., 1979, San Francisco Women Artists, 1980, 81, Ana Gardner Gallery, 1980, Soma Gallery, San Francisco, 1980, Open Studio, 1986, Fenwick's Estate Art Show, Los Altos Hills, Calif., 1987, San Jose Inst. Contemporary Arts, 1987, 94, Gallery III, San Jose, 1990, Olive Hyde Gallery, Fremont, Calif., 1990, Lincoln Ctr., N.Y., 1992, San Jose Art League, 1993, Los Gatos (Calif.) Tait Mus., 1993, 94, Gallery Tanantzin, San Juan Bautista, 1993, Syntex Gallery, Palo Alto, 1993, Synopsis Gallery, Mountain View, Calif., 1993, Solomon Dubnick Gallery, Sacramento, 1994, Seippe Gallery, Palo Alto, 1994, Koret Gallery, 1995, Contract Design Ctr. Juried Show, San Francisco, 1996, Ironstone Gallery Juried Show, Sonora, Calif., 1996, Memory Park Invitational, Monterey, 1996, Merced (Calif.) Coll. Art Gallery, 1996, Anne Frank Exhibit, Mt. View (Calif.) Cultural Ctr., 1996, Works Gallery Mem. Show, San Jose, 1997, Cooper-Molera Adobe Sculpture Show, Monterey, 1997. Recipient 1st prize for sculpture De Anza Coll., 1969, 75, 76-77. Mem. San Jose State U. Sculptors Guild (treas. 1997-98), League Nat. PEN Women, Womens Caucus for Arts, Internat. Sculpture Ctr.

SOLOMON, DOROTHY JEANNE ALLRED, writer, communications executive; b. Salt Lake City, June 24, 1949; d. Rulon Clark and Mabel (Finlayson) Allred; m. Bruce Craig Solomon, Jan. 8, 1968; children: Denise, Layla, Jeffrey, Laurie. BA in Lit., Theater and Speech, U. Utah, 1971, MA in Lit. and Creative Writing, 1981. Cert. secondary edn. educator, Utah. Storyteller, libr. Salt Lake City Libr., 1971; tchr. Salt Lake Sch. Dist., 1971-74; instr. U. Utah/Columbia Coll., Salt Lake City, 1974-80; writer-in-residence Utah Arts Coun., Salt Lake City, 1980-93; human devel. trainer Lifespring, San Rafael, Calif., 1983-87; media specialist Rivendell Psychiat. Hosps., West Jordan, Utah, 1987-90; curriculum writer Positive Action Pub., Twin Falls, Idaho, 1990-96; co-founder, v.p. Rising Star Comm. and Team Resource Assocs., Salt Lake City, 1994—; bd. dirs. Rising Star Comm. Author: In My Father's House, 1984 (1st prize Biography, 1981, Pub. prize 1982), Inside Out: Creative Writing, 1989, Of Predators, Prey and Other Kin, 1996 (1st prize Non-fiction 1996); contbr. stories to anthologies Stories That Shape Us, What There Is, The Best of Writers at Work, A New Genesis, Great and Peculiar Beauty, In Our Lovely Deseret, Mormon Fictions, 1998; screenwriter: In My Father's House, 1986-87. Bd. dirs. The Children's Ctr., Salt Lake City, 1982-85, Writers at Work, Park City, Utah, 1986-89, Lifespring Found., San Rafael, Calif., 1985-89; mem. curriculum com. Salt Lake Sch. Dist., 1971-74; coord. (with Bruce Solomon) lit. arts Utah Arts Festival "Performing Word", Salt Lake City, 1982; vol. Big Sisters, Salt Lake City, 1970-71; coord. cmty. edn. Rivendell Conf., West Jordan, Utah, 1987-89. Recipient Disting. Journalism 1st prize Am. Acad. Pediat., San Francisco, 1979, 1st prize feature writing Sigma Delta Chi, Salt Lake City, 1979, 1st prize essay Utah Original Writing Contest, Salt Lake City, 1995, 1st prize Biography, 1981, 96, award of excellence Gov.'s Media Awards, Utah, 1990, Utah State Pub. prize, 1982. Mem. Associated Writing Programs. Mem. LDS Ch. Avocations: golf, reading, movies, environmental protection, child/family advocacy projects. Home: 6521 Snowview Dr Park City UT 84098-6167

SOLOMON, JULIUS OSCAR LEE, pharmacist, hypnotherapist; b. N.Y.C., Aug. 14, 1917; s. John and Jeannette (Krieger) S.; student Bklyn. Coll., 1935-36, CCNY, 1936-37; BS in Pharmacy, U. So. Calif., 1949; postgrad. Long Beach State U., 1971-72, Southwestern Colls., 1979, 81-82, San Diego State U., 1994—; PhD, Am. Inst. Hypnotherapy, 1988; postgrad. San Diego State U., 1994—. m. Sylvia Smith, June 26, 1941 (div. Jan. 1975); children: Marc Irwin, Evan Scott, Jeri Lee. Cert. hypnotherapist; cert. hypnoanaesthesia therapist. Dye maker Fred Fear & Co., Bklyn., 1935; apprentice interior decorator Dorothy Draper, 1936; various jobs, N.Y. State Police, 1940-45; rsch. asst. Union Oil Co., 1945; lighting cons. Joe Rosenberg & Co., 1946-49; owner Banner Drug, Lomita, 1949-53, Redondo Beach, Calif., 1953-72, El Prado Pharmacy, Redondo Beach, 1961-65; pres. Banner Drug, Inc., Redondo Beach, 1953-72, Thrifty Drugs, 1972-74, also Guild Drug, Longs Drug, Drug King, 1976-83; pres. Socoma, Inc. doing bus. as Lee & Ana Pharmacy, 1983-86, now Two Hearts Help Clinic, 1986—. Charter commr., founder Redondo Beach Youth Baseball Council; sponsor Little League Baseball, basketball, football, bowling; pres. Redondo Beach Boys Club; v.p. South Bay Children's Health Ctr., 1974, Redondo Beach Coordinating Coun., 1975; bd. dirs. So. Bay Assn. Little Theatres, 1972-75; actor in 8 shows; founder Redondo Beach Community Theater, 1975; actor Man of La Mancha Vangard Theatre, San Diego, 1995; active maj. gift drive YMCA, 1975; mem. SCAG Com. on Criminal Justice, 1974, League Calif. Environ. Quality Com., 1975; mem. Dem. State Cen. Com., Los Angeles County Dem. Cen. Com.; del. Dem. Nat. Conv., 1972; chmn. Redondo Beach Recreation and Parks Commn.; mem. San Diego County Parks Adv. Commn., 1982; mem. San Diego Juvenile Justice Commn., 1986-92; mem. San Diego County Adv. Com. Adult Detention, 1987-92; mem. human resource devel. com., pub. improvement com. Nat. League of Cities; v.p. Redondo Beach Coordinating Coun.; councilman, Redondo Beach, 1961-69, 73-77; treas. 46th Assembly Dist. Coun.; candidate 46 Assembly dist. 1966; nat. chmn. Pharmacists for Humphrey, 1968, 72; pres. bd. dirs. South Bay Exceptional Childrens Soc., Chapel Theatre; bd. dirs. so. div. League Calif. Cities, U.S.-Mex. Sister Cities Assn., Boy's Club Found. San Diego County, Autumn Hills Condominium Assn. (pres.), Calif. Employee Pharmacists Assn. (pres. 1985), Our House, Chula Vista, Calif., 1984-86; mem. South Bay Inter-City Hwy. Com., Redondo Beach Round Table, 1973-77; mem. State Calif. Commn. of Californias (U.S.-Mexico), 1975-78; mem. Chula Vista Safety Commn., 1978, chmn., 1980-81; chmn. San Diego County Juvenile Camp Contract Com., 1982-83; mem. San Diego County Juvenile Delinquency Prevention Commn., 1983-85, 89-91, San Diego County Juvenile Justice Commn., 1986-91, San Diego County Adv. Com. for Adult Detention, 1987-91; spl. participant Calif. Crime and Violence Workshop; mem. Montgomery Planning Commn., 1983-86; mem. Constnl. Observance Com., 1990-93, Troubled Teenagers Hypnosis Treatment Program, 1989—; vol. mentor Palomar H.S. S.D. County Sch. Dist., Chula Vista, 1998. With USCGR, 1942-45. Recipient Pop Warner Youth award, 1960, 1962, award of merit Calif. Pharm. Assn., 1962, award Am. Assn. Blood Banks, 1982. Diplomate Am. Bd. Diplomates Pharmacy Internat., 1977-81; Fellow Am. Coll. Pharmacists (pres. 1949-57); mem. South Bay Pharm. Assn. (pres.), South Bay Councilman Assn. (founder, pres.), Palos Verdes Peninsula Navy League (charter), Am. Legion, U. So. Calif. Alumni Assn. (life), Assn. Former N.Y. State Troopers (life), AFTRA, Am. Pharm. Assn., Nat. Assn. Retail Druggists, Calif. Pharmacists Assn., Calif. Employee Pharmacist Assn. (bd. dirs. 1980-81), Hon. Dep. Sheriff's Assn., San Ysidro C. of C. (bd. dirs. 1985-87), Fraternal Order of Police, San Diego County Fish and Game Assn., Rho Pi Phi (pres. alumni). Club. Trojan (life). Lodges: Elks (life), Masons (32 deg.; life), Lions (charter mem. North Redondo). Established Lee and Ana Solomon award for varsity athlete with highest scholastic average at 10 L.A. South Bay High Schs. in Los Angeles County and 3 San Diego area South Bay High Schs.

SOLOMON, MARK A., lawyer; b. Cedar Rapids, Iowa, Aug. 30, 1950. BA summa cum laude, Calif. State U., San Jose, 1972; JD magna cum laude, U. Santa Clara, 1975. Bar: Calif. 1975, Nev. 1976. Mem. Lionel Sawyer & Collins, Las Vegas, Nev., 1976—. Mem. ABA, State Bar Calif., State Bar Nev., Clark County Bar Assn. Office: Lionel Sawyer & Collins 1700 Bank Am Plz 300 S 4th St Ste 1700 Las Vegas NV 89101-6053*

SOLOVAY, MARK LIONEL, cardiologist, educator; b. N.Y.C., June 21, 1942; s. Benjamin and Irene (Lerner) S.; m. Alice Faye Rosenbluth, July 4, 1965 (div. Oct. 1994); children: Sondra, Matthew. BA with honors, Clark U., 1963; MD, SUNY, N.Y.C., 1967. Diplomate Am. Bd. Internal Medicine with subspecialty in cardiovascular disease and critical care medicine. Intern and asst. resp. USPHS Hosp., S.I., N.Y., 1967-69; assoc. resident Bellevue Hosp., N.Y.C., 1970-71; cardiology resident Mt. Sinai Hosp. and Sch. of Medicine, 1972-73; sr. cardiology fellow U. Miami, 1974; pvt. practice Hollywood, Fla., 1974-78, Yuma, Ariz., 1978-85; cardiologist, pres. Yuma Multispecialty Med. Group, 1985-89; pvt. practice Yuma, 1989-94; cardiologist, group dir. Yuma Heart Inst., 1995—; clin. faculty U. Calif.-San Diego Med. Ctr., 1980—; bd. govs. Yuma Regional Med. Ctr., 1988, 89, 97, 98; chief of staff YRMC, 1988, co-chief 1997, 98. Contbr. articles to profl. jours. Founding v.p./pres. Am. Heart Assn., Yuma, 1986-90. Lt. comdr. USPHS, 1967-70. Fellow Am. Coll. Cardiology (coun. mem., adv. com. 1986-89). Office: Yuma Heart Inst 2281 W 24th St Ste 5 Yuma AZ 85364-6162

SOLOW, HERBERT FRANKLIN, film producer, writer; b. N.Y.C., Dec. 14, 1930; s. Morris David and Frances Louise (Birnbaum) S.; children: Jody, Bonnie, Jamie; m. Yvonne Fern, 1996. AB, Dartmouth Coll., 1953. Agt. William Morris Agy., N.Y.C., 1954-58; dir., exec. NBC, N.Y.C., 1958-59, Los Angeles, 1959-60, CBS, Los Angeles, 1961-63; v.p. Desilu Studios, Los Angeles, 1964-69; v.p. prodn. Paramount TV, Los Angeles, 1969; v.p. worldwide prodn. Metro-Goldwyn-Mayer, Los Angeles, 1969-73; pres. Solow Prodn. Co., Los Angeles, 1976-79; v.p. Sherwood Prodns., Los Angeles, 1980-83; ind. producer, writer Los Angeles, 1984—. Mem. Writers Guild Am., Dirs. Guild Am., Acad. Motion Picture Arts and Scis., Acad. TV Arts and Scis.

SOLTERO, MARY ANN, elementary education educator; b. Bellingham, Wash., Feb. 25, 1949; d. Thomas Redmond and Berniece Olive (Walker) Maloney; m. Gregory Alan Soltero, Aug. 18, 1978; children: Ann Marie, Elizabeth Elaine. BS, Eastern Mont. Coll., 1971, MS, 1979. Third grade tchr. Cody (Wyo.) Pub. Schs., 1971-72; second grade tchr. Sunset Elem. Sch., Cody, Wyo., 1972-81, remedial reading tchr., 1981-89, third grade tchr., 1989—; writer lang. art curriculum com., Cody Pub. Schs., 1992-94. Recipient grant State of Wyo., 1994. Mem. NEA, Wyo. Edn. Assn., Cody Edn. Assn. (treas. 1987-88), Internat. Reading Assn., Nat. Coun. Tchrs. Eng., Delta Kappa Gamma (1st v.p. 1994). Democrat. Roman Catholic. Avocations: quilting, counted cross stitch, sewing. Home: PO Box 944 Cody WY 82414-0944 Office: Sunset Sch 1520 21st St Cody WY 82414-4412

SOLTICE, CAPRICE ANN, computer programmer; b. Reno, Nev., June 3, 1969; d. Richard Soltice and Sue (Pendarvis) Carey. CNA. Programmer, analyst Analytical Tech., San Diego, 1991-94, CIC Mktg. Rsch., San Diego, 1994-95; info. sys. mgr. No Fear, Inc., Carlsbad, Calif., 1995—; cons. in field. Mem. Am. Horse Show Assn. Office: No Fear Inc 2251 Faraday Ave Carlsbad CA 92008-7209

SOMERS, LEONORA PATIÑO, psychotherapist; b. N.Y., Mar. 28, 1927; d. Carlos Eduardo and Marie Catherine Czerwinski Patiño; m. Bernard Joseph Somers (div. 1984); children: Bianca Somers Ohle, Evan Carlos Somers. BS, M. Stewart Internat. U., 1976; MA, Goddard Coll., 1977. Lic. marriage, family and child therapist, Calif. Founding area reference person Re-Evaluation Counseling, L.A., 1970-77; guest instr. psychology L.A. County Dept. Healt Svcs., 1978-82; dimension faculty mem. Sierra U., Santa Monica, Calif., 1980-87; mental health care provider Blue Shield, L.A., 1986-96, Prunetwork, L.A., 1990-96; pvt. practice L.A., 1978—; mem. internat. reference com., Re-Evaluation Counseling, Seattle, 1971-75, regional reference person, 1973-75; mem. advisory bd. Sierra U., Santa Monica, 1980-87; guest. lectr. U. So. Calif., L.A., 1982-85. Author: (book) Emotional Freedom, 1996; contbr. articles to profl. jours. Founding area reference person Co-Counseling, L.A., 1972; pres. L.A. chpt. Nat. ParaPlegia Found., 1979-81; so. Calif. chair SANE, L.A., 1967-69; mem. Californians for Liberal Reps., L.A., 1968-70. Mem. Calif. Assn. Marriage and Family Therapists, Am. Assn. Counseling and Devel., U. Calif. L.A. Alumni Assn. Democrat. Avocations: piano playing, reading, gardening, puzzle solving, photography. Home and Office: 3565 Tilden Ave Los Angeles CA 90034-6108

SOMERSET, HAROLD RICHARD, retired business executive; b. Woodbury, Conn., Sept. 25, 1935; s. Harold Kitchener and Margaret Mary (Roche) S.; m. Marjory Deborah Ghiselin, June 22, 1957 (dec. Jan. 1984); children: Timothy Craig, Paul Alexander; m. Jean MacAlpine DesMarais, Jan. 2, 1985; stepchildren: Cheryl Lyn DesMarais, James Fenelon DesMarais. B.S., U.S. Naval Acad., 1957; B.C.E., Rensselaer Poly. Inst., Troy, N.Y., 1959; LL.B., Harvard U., 1967. Bar: Mass. 1967, Hawaii 1973. Commd. ensign U.S. Navy, 1957, advanced through grades to lt., 1961; service in U.S. and Hawaii; resigned, 1964; with firm Goodwin, Procter & Hoar, Boston, 1967-72; corp. counsel Alexander & Baldwin, Inc., Honolulu, 1972-74, v.p., gen. counsel, 1974-78, group v.p.-sugar, 1978-79, exec. v.p.-agr., 1979-84; with Calif. & Hawaiian Sugar Co., San Francisco, 1984-93, exec. v.p., chief operating officer, 1984-88, pres., chief exec. officer, 1988-93, bus. cons., 1994—; bd. dirs. Longs Drug Stores Corp., Brown and Caldwell, PLM Internat., Inc. Trustee San Francisco Nat. Maritime Mus., Carquinez Strait Preservation Trust (mgmt. com., past pres.). Mem. St. Mary's Coll. Sch. Edn. (adv. coun.). Home and Office: 19 Donald Dr Orinda CA 94563-3646

SOMERSON, PAUL, editor-in-chief. V.p., editor-in-chief P.C. Computing, San Francisco. Office: PC Computing 54 Beale St Fl 13 San Francisco CA 94105-1808*

SOMERVILLE, DIANA ELIZABETH, author; b. Lincoln, Nebr., June 12, 1942; d. Edward John and Eunice Louise (Johnson) Wagner; m. Dale Springer Johnson, Aug. 7, 1961 (div. 1971); children: Carlyle Johnson Lee, Kelmie Blake. BA in English Lit., Centenary Coll., 1967. Dir. info. office Nat. Ctr. Atmospheric Rsch., Boulder, Colo., 1969-81; mgr. info. svcs. RDD Cons., Boulder, 1981-82; sci. writer U. Colo., Boulder, 1983-87; mgr. comm. Optoelectronic Computing Sys. Ctr., Boulder, 1987-88; columnist Daily Camera, Boulder, 1992—; lectr. U. Colo., 1996—; founder Colo. Mag. Writers Inst. Editor: Optimum Utilization of Human Knowledge, 1983, Artful Meditation, 1995; contbr. numerous articles to mags. including New Scientist, Earth mag. and in World Book Ency. Mem. women's caucus AAAS, 1969-75; mem. com. on pub. info. Am. Geophys. Union, 1977-78; mem. edni. programs com. Am. Meteorol. Soc., 1978-80; mem. Turning the Wheel dance/theatre co. Recipient Exceptional Achievement award Coun. for the Advancement and Support of Edn., Gold medal, 1986, Gold Pick award Pub. Rels. Soc. Am., 1985, Gold Quill award Internat. Assn. Bus. Comms., 1985. Mem. Nat. Writers Union, Nat. Assn. Sci. Writers, Am. Soc. Journalists and Authors, Boulder Media Women. Avocations: theatre, dance, Jungian dreamwork, healing rituals, women's issues.

SOMERVILLE, VIRGINIA PAULINE WINTERS, executive assistant; b. Jo Daviess County, Ill., Jan. 14, 1936; d. Roy and Effie Winters; m. Thomas C. Somerville, June 8, 1957; children: Tod Andrew, Ian Winter. BMus magna cum laude, U. Dubuque, 1957; MMus with honors, Roosevelt U., 1964. Music tchr. pub. sch. Jessup, Iowa, 1959-60; music tchr. pvt. sch. P.R., Puerto Rico, 1960-61; prof. music St. Andrews Presbyn. Coll., Laurinburg, N.C., 1966-71; pvt. music tchr. Glendale, Calif., 1976-86; exec. asst. to sr. min. First Congl. Ch. L.A., 1986—; workshop and seminar leader Chapman Coll. Ch. Sec.'s Seminar, Orange, Calif., 1991, 92. Performer one-woman musical shows. Active PTA, Canoga Park, Calif., Glendale, 1972-84, Glendale Assistance League, 1975—. Recipient Citizen Appreciation award PTA-Verdugo Woodlands, Glendale, 1980, various music awards. Mem. Nat. Exec. Secs., Nat. Assn. Tchrs. of Singing. Avocations: concert going, reading, films, travel, theater. Office: First Congl Ch LA 540 S Commonwealth Ave Los Angeles CA 90020-1204

SOMMER, JOHN LAMBERT, retired surgeon; b. Pekin, Ill., Jan. 23, 1927; s. Oscar Julius Sommer and Norah (Mae) Lambert; m. Donna Mae Meddawgh, June 14, 1953; children: Andrew John, Matthew Harvey. PhB, U. Chgo., 1948, SB, 1950, MD, 1953. Diplomate Am. Bd. Urology. Instr. surgery urology U. Chgo., 1958, asst. prof. surgery urology, 1960, assoc. prof. surgery urology, 1965; asst. clin. prof. surgery urology Stanford (Calif.) U., 1968; chief dept. urology Kaiser Permanente Med. Ctr., Hayward, Calif., 1966-82; physician in charge Kaiser Permanente Med. Ctr., Fremont, Calif., 1982-87; chief med. legal affairs Kaiser Permanente Med. Ctr., Hayward, Calif., 1978-84, 89-90, ret., 1990. Author, editor: The Kyrgyz and Their Reed Screens, 1996. Pres. San Francisco Bay Area Rug Soc., 1991—; trustee Textile Mus., Washington, 1991—; bd. dirs. Textile Arts Coun. Fine Arts Mus. San Francisco, 1992-98; sec. gen. Internat. Conf. Oriental Carpets, 1997—. Home: 4575 Odell Ct Fremont CA 94536-6850

SOMMERS, LARRY DONALD, artist, educator; b. Battle Creek, Mich., Aug. 17, 1953; s. Donald and Jean S. BFA, Ctrl. Mich. U., 1975; MFA, U. Oreg., 1978. Instrl. technician U. Wash., Seattle, 1985—; owner, mgr. Inky Dink Press, Seattle, 1980—. Writer, dir.: (video tape) Health and Safety in Arts, 1997. Co-organizer Health and Safety Seminar, Cornish Coll. of Art, Seattle, 1995. Mem. Book Arts Guild (pres. 1995—). Democrat. Avocation: puppetry. Office: U Wash Sch of Art Rm 210A PO Box 353440 Seattle WA 98195-3440

SOMMERS, WILLIAM PAUL, management consultant, Research and development institute executive; b. Detroit, July 22, 1933; s. William August and Mary Elizabeth (Baietto) S.; m. Josephine A. Sommers; children: William F., Clare M., John C. Hughes, Joanna M. Weems, Russell L. Hughes. B.S.E. (scholar), U. Mich., 1955, M.S.E., 1956, Ph.D. (Riggs fellow, Texaco fellow, Univ. fellow), 1961. Research asso. U. Mich. Inst. Sci. and Tech., Ann Arbor, 1958-61; chief chem. propulsion space and missile systems Martin Marietta Corp., Balt., 1956-58, 61-63; v.p. Booz, Allen & Hamilton, Inc., Bethesda, Md., 1963-70; pres. Tech. Mgmt. Group Booz, Allen & Hamilton, Inc., 1973-79, sr. v.p., 1979-92; exec. v.p. Iameter, Inc., San Mateo, Calif., 1992-94; pres., CEO SRI Internat., Menlo Park, Calif., 1994-98, ret., 1998; bd. dirs. Kember Fin. Svcs., Evergreen Solar Inc., PSI Inc., Litton Inc., Nuance Comm., Evergreen Solar, Inc., Pressure Sys., Inc. Contbr. articles to profl. jours., also chpt. in book. Pres. Washington chpt. U. Mich. Alumni Club, 1970-71; v.p. Wildwood manor Citizens Assn., 1968-70; chief Adventure Guide program YMCA, 1971-72; bd. visitors Coll. Engring. U. Calif., Davis; mem. nat. adv. bd. Coll. Engring. U. Mich.; mem. conf. bd. Internat. Coun. on Innovation and Tech. Mem. Columbia Country Club, Willow Bend Country Club, Wianno Yacht Club, Marsh Landing Country Club, Marshlanding Country Club, Sigma Xi, Tau Beta Pi, Pi Tau Sigma. Republican. Roman Catholic.

SONG, SHUNFENG, economist, researcher; b. Jinhua, China, July 6, 1962; came to U.S., 1986; s. Lin Fu Song and Xiaoying He; m. Jian Ling Feng, July 9, 1985; children: Sisi, Conan A. BS in Mechanics, Beijing U., 1983; MA in Econ., U. Calif., Irvine, 1991, PhD in Econ., 1992. Instr. Xiamen

(China) U., 1983-86; asst. prof. dept. econ. U. Nev., Reno, 1992-96, assoc. prof., 1996—. Author, editor: Raising International Competitiveness, 1998; contbr. articles to profl. jours. Mem. Am. Econ. Assn., Am. Real Estate Soc., Chinese Economists Soc. (dir. 1996-98, v.p. 1997-98), Western Regional Sci. Assn., Western Econ. Assn. Internat., Regional Sci. Assn. Internat. Avocations: travel, table tennis, playing cards. Office: U Nev Dept Econ 030 Reno NV 89557

SONNTAG, MARTIN LEROY, retired software company executive; b. Toledo, May 6, 1951; s. Frank Louis Sonntag and Delila Lee (Steward) Schuette; m. Helen Kelly, Sept. 24, 1982 (div. Apr. 1991). BS, U. Mich., 1975, MS, 1980, PhD, 1991. Software mgr. Med. Data Sys., Ann Arbor, Mich., 1981-84; sys. project coord. Bus. Sch. U. Mich., Ann Arbor, 1984-86; program mgr. Microsoft Corp., Redmond, Wash., 1991-98; ret., 1998.

SONNTAG, VOLKER KARL HEINZ, neurosurgeon, educator; b. Graudenz, Germany, Nov. 23, 1944; came to U.S., 1957, naturalized, 1965; s. Heinz and Gisla Sonntag; m. Lynne Twohig, Apr. 24, 1974; children: Alissa, Christopher, Stephen. BA in Chemistry summa cum laude, Ariz. State U., 1967; MD, U. Ariz., 1971. Diplomate Am. Bd. Neurol. Surgery; cert. advanced trauma life support. Intern Ariz. Med. Ctr., U. Ariz., Tucson, 1971-72; resident in neurosurgery Tufts-New Eng. Med. Ctr., Boston, 1972-75, chief resident, 1975-77; pvt. practice, Youngstown, Ohio, 1977-78, Scottsdale, Ariz., 1978-83, Phoenix, 1978—; chmn. spine sect., vice chmn. dept. neurosurgery Barrow Neurol. Inst., Phoenix, 1984—; clin. assoc. prof. surgery U. Ariz., 1985-88, clin. prof., 1989—; numerous presentations in field; invited prof. U. Nev., 1986, Columbia-Presbyn. Neurol. Inst., 1987, U. Ala., Birmingham, 1989, Emory U., Atlanta, 1989, U. Tokyo, 1989, U. Mich., Ann Arbor, 1990, Syracuse (N.Y.) U., 1990, U. Tex. S.W. Med. Ctr., Dallas, 1990, Uniformed Svcs. U. Health Scis., Bethesda, Md., 1991, Chgo. Neurosurg. Ctr., 1991, N.J. Med. Coll., Newark, 1992, SUNY, Buffalo, 1992, U. Chgo., 1993, Johns Hopkins U., Balt., 1993, U. Ark., Little Rock, 1994, numerous others. News editor BNI Quar., 1982-86, sci. editor, 1992—; mem. editl. bd. Jour. Spinal Disorders, 1988-93, Neurosurgery, 1998—, Critical Rev. in Neurosurgery, 1993—; dep. editor Spine, 1993—; contbr. over 200 articles and abstracts to med. jours., numerous chpts. to books; editor 3 books. Fellow ACS; mem. AMA, Congress Neurol. Surgeons , Soc. for Neurosci., Am. Assn. Neurol. Surgeons, Soc. Neurol. Surgeons, Neurosurg. Soc. Am., N. Am. Spine Soc. (sec. 1996-97), Rocky Mountain Neurosurg. Soc., Ariz. Med. Assn., Ariz. Soc. for Neurosurgeons, Maricopa County Med. Soc., Alpha Omega Alpha (hon.). Office: Neurosurg Assocs Ltd Barrow Neurosurg Inst 2910 N 3rd Ave Phoenix AZ 85013-4434

SOPER, HENRY VICTOR, neuropsychologist; b. Glen Ridge, N.J., Mar. 10, 1945; s. Kenneth L. and Sylvia (Caldwell) S.; B.A., Yale U., 1966; M.A., U. Conn., 1972, Ph.D., 1974. Neurophysiologist, Brain Research Inst., UCLA, 1974-76; NIH fellow dept. psychology, 1976-78; asst. prof. Calif./ State U.-Northridge, 1978; research neuroanatomist, clin. psychologist U. Ill.-Chgo., 1978-82; clin. psychology intern Camarillo (Calif.) State Hosp., 1982-83, research scientist, neuropsychologist UCLA Neuropsychiat. Inst. Program, 1982—. Served to 1st lt. C.E., U.S. Army, 1966-68; Decorated Bronze Star; recipient Norman Hall award Yale U., 1965, Robert R. Chamberlain award, 1965; State of Conn. predoctoral fellow, 1972-74; NIH fellow, 1976-78. Mem. Am. Psychol. Assn., Soc. Neurosci., N.Y. Acad. Sci., Psychonomic Sci., Am. Assn. Primatologists, Internat. Primatol. Soc., AAAS, Sigma Xi. Club: Los Angeles Rugby. Author publs. in field; editorial cons. profl. jours. Office: 2021 Sperry Ave Ste 15 Ventura CA 93003-7418

SORBY, J(OSEPH) RICHARD, artist, educator; b. Duluth, Minn., Dec. 21, 1911; s. Joseph Austin and Lydia A. (Esterly) S.; m. P. Elizabeth Ferguson, Dec. 9, 1950. B.A., U. Northern Colo., 1937, M.A., 1952; postgrad., UCLA, 1953, U. of Americas, 1952, U. Colo., 1954. Instr. art Greeley High Sch., Colo., 1937-41; asst. prof. art U. Nebr., Lincoln, 1941-43; assoc. prof. art U. Denver, 1946-59; prof. design and painting Calif. State U., San Jose, 1959-72, prof. emeritus, 1972—; guest prof. Southern Utah U., Cedar City, June, July 1964; artist in residence Casa de las Campanas, Rancho Bernardo, Calif., 1988—. Exhibited in numerous nat. competitive exhbns. including Rocky Mountain Nat. Watermedia Exhbn. and various publ. collections. Served with USN, 1943-46, lt. comdr. USNR, ret. Recipient Purchase award Joslyn Art Mus., Omaha, Mid-Am. Annual, William Rockhill Nelson Gallery, Kansas City, Nat. Watercolor Competition, Washington, Denver Art Mus., Mus. N.Mex., Southwestern Artist's Annual; selected for U.S. nat. traveling exhbn. Mem. Fifteen Colo. Artists (pres. 1957-58), exhibited in Fifty Yr. Reunion of Fifteen Colo. Artists (Elizabeth Schlosser Fine Art 1998), Denver; Retired officers Assn., Mil. Order World Wars, East Bay Art Assn. (v.p. 1966-68), Group 21 (pres. Los Gatos, Calif. 1970-71). Home and Office: 18655 W Bernardo Dr San Diego CA 92127-3002 Studio (summer): Morningsun Studio 15 N Fork Rd Glen Haven CO 80532-3020

SORENSEN, LINDA, lawyer; b. Eureka, Calif., Mar. 3, 1945. BS, U. Wis., Madison, 1967; JD, U. Calif., 1976. Bar: Calif. 1976, U.S. Dist. Ct. (no. dist.) Calif. 1977, U.S. Ct. Appeals (9th cir.), U.S. Dist. Ct. (ea. dist.) Calif. Shareholder Feldman, Waldman & Kline, P.C., San Francisco, 1997—. Mem. ABA (mem. subcom. on avoiding powers, bus. bankruptcy com. 1983—), Bar Assn. of San Francisco (chmn. comml. law and bankruptcy sect. 1984, editor fed. cts. com., no. dist. Calif. digest 1979-82). Office: Feldman Waldman & Kline 3 Embarcadero Ctr Ste 28 San Francisco CA 94111-4003

SORENSEN, MARTHA STEWART, psychologist; b. Colusa, Calif., Jan. 3, 1956; d. Robert Philip and Ethel Lucille (Fowler) Stewart; m. Carl Eric Sorensen, May 29, 1976; children: Lisa Renée, Amy Lorraine. B in Psychology, U. Calif., Santa Cruz, 1986; M in Clin. Psychology, San Jose State U., 1988; PhD in Clin. Psychology, Calif. Sch. Profl. Psychology, 1994. Diplomate Am. Bd. Psychol. Specialties. Intern Planned Parenthood, Walnut Creek, Calif., 1987-88; trainee VA, Livermore, Calif., 1988-89; intern Residency Merrithew Meml. Hosp., Martinez, Calif., 1990-92; pvt. practice Walnut Creek, 1993-94, Longmont, Colo., 1996—; psych. fellow U. Colo. Health Sci. Ctr., Denver, 1994-95. Group leader Rocky Mountain Christian Ch., Niwot, Colo., 1995—; v.p. Creekside I Homeowners Assn., Longmont, 1996-97, pres. 1998; presenter 1st Christian Church, Longmont, 1996—; vol. Am. Cancer Soc., Longmont, 1997—. Mem. Am. Psychol. Assn., Nat. Register Healthcare Providers, Am. Coll. Forensic Examiners, Calif. Psychol. Assn., Colo. Psychol. Assn., Prescribing Privileges for Psychologists, Am. Diabetes Assn. Democrat. Avocations: camping, travelling, needlepoint, gardening, writing. Office: Ste 108 16 Mountain View Ave Longmont CO 80501-3420

SORENSEN, SHEILA, state senator; b. Chgo., Sept. 20, 1947; d. Martin Thomas Moloney and Elizabeth (Koehr) Paulus; m. Wayne B. Slaughter, May, 1969 (div. 1976); 1 child, Wayne Benjamin III; m. Dean E. Sorensen, Feb. 14, 1977; (stepchildren) Michael, Debbie, Kevin, Dean C. BS, Loretto Heights Coll., Denver, 1965; postgrad. pediatric nurse practicioner, U. Colo., Denver, 1969-70. Pediatric nurse practicioner Pub. Health Dept., Denver, 1970-71, Boise, Idaho, 1971-72; pediatric nurse practicioner Boise (Idaho) Pediatric Group, 1972-74, Pediatric Assocs., Boise, 1974-77; mem. Idaho State Ho. Reps., 1987-92; mem. Idaho Senate, 1992—, chair senate health and welfare com., 1992-94, chair senate majority caucus, 1994-96, vice chair state affairs com., 1996-98, chair state affairs com., 1998—; state chair Am. Legis. Exchange Coun. Precinct committeeman Ada County Rep. Ctrl. Com., Boise, 1982-86, dist. vice chair, 1985-88; polit. chair Idaho Med. Assn. Aux., 1984-87, Ada County Med. Assocs., 1986-87; bd. dirs. Family Practice Residency Program, 1992-94, Univ./Cmty. Health Sci. Assn., Bishop Kelly Found., 1993—; chair Senate Majority Caucus, 1995, vice chair state affairs com. Recipient AMA Nathan Davis award for Outstanding State Legislator, 1994. Mem. Nat. Conf. State Legislators, Nat. Orgn. Women Legislators (state chair), Am. Legis. Exch. Coun. (Legis of Yr. award 1999). Roman Catholic.

SORIANO, BERNARD C., engineering executive; b. Lihue, Hawaii, Oct. 16, 1962; s. Pedro G. and Juana (Cayabyab) S.; m. Bonnie Lee Billington, July 11, 1987; 1 child, Morgan Maile. BS in Mech. and Aero. Engring., U. Calif., Davis, 1985; MSME, U. So. Calif., L.A., 1988; PhD in Engring., U. Calif., Irvine, 1996. Mem. tech. staff I Hughes Space and Comm., L.A., 1985-89, mem. tech. staff II, 1989-90, tech. supr., 1990-92, tech. head, 1992-93, mgr. III, 1993-94; asst. tech. dir. USGA Rsch. and Test Ctr., Far Hills, N.J., 1994-97; chief tech. officer dept. forestry and fire protection State Calif., Sacramento, 1997—. Contbr. articles to profl. jours.; patentee in field. Vol. Habitat for Humanity, Somerset County, N.J., 1995-96. Lt. USNR, 1988—. U. Calif. GOP fellow, 1989; finalist NASA Astronaut Program. Mem. IEEE, ASME, AAAS, Am. Coll. Sports Medicine. Achievements include patents and contributions to design of satellite attitude control systems; biomechanical studies of human motion. Avocations: sports and athletics, motorcycles, fly fishing, music. Office: 1021 O St Rm 205 Sacramento CA 95814-5718

SORIANO, DEBBIE ANN, educator; b. Montebello, Calif., Dec. 10, 1963; d. Peter and Bernice (Ewing) Villescas; m. Douglas Earl Roberts, June 6, 1981 (div. Mar. 1989); 1 child, Douglas Earl II; m. Marcos Soriano III, June 27, 1992. BA, Biola U., 1982; MA, Calif. State U., L.A., 1983; MBA, Devry-Keller Bus. Sch., 1997; PhD, Azusa Pacific U., 1997. Adminstrv. credential, single subject tchg. credential, multiple subjects tchg. credential, ESL credential. Script asst. Val Prodns., Arcadia, Calif., 1979; tchr., coord. Lang. Inst., Toyko, 1980, El Monte (Calif.) Union Schs., 1983-84; tchr. English Montebello (Calif.) Schs., 1984-96; state del. Calif. Tchrs. Assn., Montebello, 1994-95. Vol. Police Dept., Arcadia, 1993-94; mem. World Affairs Coun., L.A., 1995-96, UNIFEM, N.Y.C., 1995-96, The Noel Found., L.A., 1995-97. With USNR, 1996—. Recipient Summer Inst. award NEH, Long Beach, Calif., 1994, Summer Seminar award NEH, Amherst, Mass., 1995. Mem. AAUW, DAR, Navy Wives, Clan Ewen Soc., Pi Lambda Theta. Avocations: traveling, researching world leaders. Home: PO Box 2095 Arcadia CA 91077-2095

SOROM, TERRY ALLEN, ophthalmic surgeon; b. Lanesboro, Minn., Jan. 9, 1940; s. Martin John and Elvira (Lodahl) S.; m. Suzanne A. Johnson, children: Martin, Jeb, Abraham, Theodore. BS, Luther Coll., 1962; MD, U. Minn.-Mpls., 1966. Diplomate Am. Bd. Ophthalmology. Intern. U. Oreg., Portland, 1967, resident in ophthalmology, 1969-73; ophthalmic surgeon Eye and Ear Clinic, Inc., Wenatchee, Wash., 1973—. Chmn. bd. dirs. Wash. Health Plan, 1993—. Charter trustee Wenatchee Visitor and Conv. Bur., 1980; bd. dirs. Blue Cross Wash., and Alaska, 1983-91; pres. Wenatchee Valley Coll. Found., 1986-88. Capt. M.C., USAF, 1967-69. Mem. AMA, Am. Acad. Ophthalmology, Contact Lens Assn. Ophthalmology, Am. Intraocular Implant Soc., Wash. State Acad. Ophthalmology (trustee 1978-80, pres. 1996-97), Wash. Acad. Eye Physicians and Surgeons (pres. 1997-98), Oregon Ophthalmologic Alumni Assn. (pres. 1988—), Greater Wenatchee Found. (bd. dirs.), Chelan-Douglas County Med. Assn., Ctrl. Wash. Health Plan (bd. dirs., chmn. 1996—), Rotary (pres. 1993-94). Republican. Lutheran. Office: Eye & Ear Clinic Wenatchee PO Box 3027 Wenatchee WA 98807-3027

SORRELL, ROZLYN, singer, actress; b. Bklyn.; d. Nathaniel Otis and Cupid Viola (Logan) S. BA in Theatre, CUNY, 1976, MS Edn., 1985. Cert. tchr., Calif., N.Y. Tchr. L.A. Unified Sch. Dist., 1997, Sylvan Learning Ctr., L.A., 1998; mem. Albert McNeil Jubilee Singers, L.A., 1994—; voice tchr., L.A., 1992—; bus. cons., L.A., 1989—. Actress various TV programs, commls., stage prodns. and films, 1986—; soloist Hour of Power, Glory of Christman, Glory of Easter, Garden Grove, Calif., 1994—, Honolulu Symphony, 1998. Mem. AFTRA, SAG, Actors Equity Assn. Avocations: dancing, walking, working out, theatre. Office: Double E Enterprises PO Box 2089 Hollywood CA 90078-2089

SORRELLS, AMY HUTCHINSON, book publisher; b. Mpls., Apr. 2, 1958; d. Charles Smith and Elizabeth Dunbar (Hall) Hutchinson; m. Daniel Kevin Sorrells, Sept. 12, 1981; children: Kay Elizabeth, Brian Daniel. BFA, Colo. State U., 1981. Mktg. coord. Fins and Feathers, Mpls., 1981-84; assoc. media dir. Fitzgerald Advt., New Orleans, 1984-86; rsch., dir. WWL-TV, New Orleans, 1986-87; direct mail supr. The Christian Sci. Monitor, Boston, 1988; pres. Moonlight Mktg., New Orleans and Phoenix, 1987-92; pub. dir. GeoSci. Press, Phoenix, 1990-94; mng. editor Roberts Rinehart Pubs., Niwot, Colo., 1994-96; editls. prodn. mgr. Univ. Press. of Colo., Niwot, 1996-97; pub. Velo Press, Boulder, Colo., 1997—; v.p., bd. dirs. GeoSci. Press, Tucson, 1996—. Mem. adv. bd. Downtown Devel. Dist., New Orleans, 1996-97. Mem. Rocky Mountain Book Pubs. Assn. (treas., bd. dirs. 1992-97), Advt. Club of New Orleans. Avocations: hiking, skiing, biking, reading, gardening. Office: Velo Press 1830 N 55th St Boulder CO 80301

SORRENTINO, JOSEPH NICHOLAS, prosecutor, writer; b. N.Y.C.; s. Nicholas A. and Angelina C. (Trezza) S.; 1 child, Joseph Jr. BA, U. Calif., Santa Barbara, 1963; MA, U. Calif., L.A., 1971; JD, Harvard Law Sch., 1967; doctorate, So. Vt. Coll., 1976. Bar: Calif. 1968. Prosecutor intern U.S. Dept. Justice, L.A., 1968; writer Prentice Hall, Englewood Cliffs, N.J., 1968-71; adj. prof. U. So. Calif., UCLA, U. Calif. Irvine, Pepperdine U., 1971-81; juvenile ct. judge (pro tem) L.A., 1974-76; prosecutor Office of Riverside/L.A. Dist. Atty., 1981—; lectr., nationwide, 1970-84; host, guest numerous TV programs including 60 Minutes, Newsmakers, Good Morning Am., Tonight Show, 1970-84. Author: Up From Never, 1971, 2nd edit., 1976, The Moral Revolution, 1973, The Concrete Cradle, 1975, The Gold Shield, 1980, (poems) People Who Stopped for You, 1995; contbr. numerous articles to profl. jours. and mags. Chmn. United Way mentally disabled com. L.A. Human Rights Commn., 1970-72. With USMC, 1963-64, USMCR, 1964-67. Recipient Notable Book award ALA, 1971; named Outstanding Spkr. of Yr. Nat. Authors and Celebrities Forum, 1977. Mem. Calif. Bar Assn., Calif. Assn. Dist. Attys., Calif. Consumers Activist Group (bd. dirs.), Constl. Rights Found., Sugar Ray Robinson Found. (bd. dirs.). Avocations: amateur archeology, mountain climbing, world travel. Home: 2350 Nichols Canyon Rd Los Angeles CA 90046-1733

SORRICK, SONJA H., interior designer; b. Watertown, Wis., Oct. 18, 1970; d. John W. and Sandra Lee (Schultz) Elliott; m. Gary Wayne Sorrick, Nov. 16, 1996; 1 child, Kayla Ryan. BA in Art and Interior Design, Fresno State U., 1995. Fin. svc. asst. Great Western Bank, Salinas and Clovis, Calif., 1989-94; office mgr. La-Z-Boy Showcase, Fresno, Calif., 1994-95; design asst. Linda's Final Touch, Fresno, 1994-95; designer Chambers Lorenz, Fresno, 1995—. Vol. Habitat for Humanity, Fresno and Clovis, 1993-94. Mem. Am. Soc. Interior Design, Phi Sigma Epsilon (dir. acctg. 1992-93, Outstanding Achievement award), Golden Key Nat. Honor Soc. Roman Catholic. Avocations: gardening, movies, bicycling, travel. Home: 5865 W Beechwood Ave Fresno CA 93722-2619 Office: Chambers Lorenz Design 6770 N West Ave Ste 105 Fresno CA 93711-1399

SORSTOKKE, SUSAN EILEEN, systems engineer; b. Seattle, May 2, 1955; d. Harold William and Carrol Jean (Russ) S. BS in Systems Engring., U. Ariz., 1976; MBA, U. Wash., Richland, 1983. Warehouse team mgr. Procter and Gamble Paper Products, Modesto, Calif., 1976-78; quality assurance engr. Westinghouse Hanford Co., Richland, Wash., 1978-80; supr. engring. document ctr. Westinghouse Hanford Co., Richland, 1980-81; mgr. data control and adminstrn. Westinghouse Electric Corp., Madison, Pa., 1981-82, mgr. data control and records mgmt., 1982-84; prin. engr. Westinghouse Elevator Co., Morristown, N.J., 1984-87; region adminstrn. mgr. Westinghouse Elevator Co., Arleta, Calif., 1987-90; ops. rsch. analyst Am. Honda Motor Co. Inc., Torrance, Calif., 1990-95; project leader parts sys. Am. Honda Motor Co., Inc., Torrance, Calif., 1995-96, mgr. parts systems and part number adminstrn., 1996-97, mgr. parts systems, 1997—; adj. prof. U. LaVerne, Calif., 1991-92. Advisor Jr. Achievement, 1982-83; literacy tutor Westmoreland Literacy Coun., 1983-84, host parent EF Found., Saugus, Calif., 1987-88, Am. Edn. Connection, Saugus, 1988-89, 91; instr. Excell, L.A., 1991-92; mem. Calif. Acad. Math. and Sci., 1996-97. Mem. Soc. Women Engrs., Am. Inst. Indsl. Engrs., Optimists Charities, Inc. (bd. dirs. Acton, Calif. 1991-94). Republican. Methodist. Home: 2567 Plaza Del Amo Unit 205 Torrance CA 90503-8962 Office: Am Honda Motor Co Inc Dept Parts 100-5C-2B 1919 Torrance Blvd Torrance CA 90501-2722

SORTER, BRUCE WILBUR, federal program administrator, educator, consultant; b. Willoughby, Ohio, Sept. 1, 1931; s. Wilbur David and Margaret Louisa (Palmer) S.; m. [illegible] 1 child, David Robert. BA, U. Md., 1967; MCP, Howard U., 1969; PhD, U. Md., 1972. Cert. community developer. Commd. USAFR, 1967, advanced through grades to lt. col., 1964, sr. planner, cons. Md. Nat. Capital Park and Planning Comm., [illegible]

C.C., Columbia and Largo, Md., 1971-72; cmty. resource devel. dept. Md. Coop. Extension Svc., U. Md., College Park, Md., 1972-92; coord. rural info. ctr. Md. Coop. Ext. Svc., U. Md., College Park, 1989-92; affiliate prof. U. Md., 1985-92, ret., 1996; ext. advisor USDA Internat. Programs, Washington, 1991-96; co-author, co-dir. Dept. Edn. Coun. Effectiveness Tng. Program, 1979-81; author First County Energy Conservation Plan, Prince George's County, 1978-85. Author, co-author 12 books; contbr. articles to profl. publs., chpts. to books. Developer, dir. teamwork tng. programs U.S. Dept. Edn., U.S. Dept. Agriculture, Brazil, Poland, Nat. Grange, 1972-92; cons. Fed. Power Commn. U.S., 1973-75, State Dept. Natural Resources, Md., 1978-79, Dept. Edn., Brazil, 1981-82, Nat. Grange, 1987, Edn. Ext. Svcs., Poland, 1991-92. Urban Planning fellow Howard U., 1968, Human Devel. fellow U. Md., 1970; recipient Meritorious Svc. award Dept. Def., 1983, Disting. Community Svc. award Md. Community Resource Devel. Assn., 1983, Citation for Outstanding Svc., Ptnrs. of Am., 1983, Excellence in Ednl. Programs award Am. Express, 1984, Project of Yr. award Am. Psychol. Assn., 1976, Award of Yr. Am. Vol. Assn., 1976, Achievement award Nat. Assn. of Counties, 1980. Mem. Internat. Cmty. Devel. Soc. (bd. dirs., Achievement award for outstanding contbn. to cmty. devel. 1985, Disting. Svc. award 1990), Md. Cmty. Resource Devel. Assn. (sec.-treas. 1979, pres. 1980, 88-89). Republican. Methodist. Avocations: volunteer work, tennis, sailing, skiing.

SORTLAND, TRUDITH ANN, speech and language therapist, educator; b. Butte, Mont., Dec. 3, 1940; d. Kenneth Hjalmer Sortland and Sigrid V. (Kotka) Strand. BS, Minot (N.D.) State U., 1965. Tchr. Westby (Mont.) Sch., 1960-61, Glasgow (Mont.) Southside Sch., 1962-65, Glasgow AFB, Mont., 1965-80; tchr., speech and lang. pathologist Mineral County Sch. Dist., Hawthorne, Nev., 1965-68, 78—; kindergarten tchr. Mineral County Sch. Dist., Mina, Nev., 1968-72; elem. tchr. Mineral County Sch. Dist., Mina, 1978-80; speech, language pathologist Mineral County Sch. Dist., Mina, Republic of Korea, 1980—; tchr. Dept. Def., Pusan, Republic of Kores, 1972-73, Illesheim, Fed. Republic Germany, 1973-78; tchr. Mohall (N.D.) Pub. Sch., 1964-65; cons. Mary Kay Cosmetics, tchr. Glasgow AFB, 1965-68. Supt. Sunday sch. Bethany Luth. Ch., Hawthorne, 1987—, sec. Ladies Aid, 1987—. Mem. NEA, Nev. Edn. Assn., AAUW (past sec., pres.), Pair O Dice Square Dance Club (sec. 1989—), Delta Kappa Gamma. Avocations: square and round dancing, photography. Home: PO Box 816 Hawthorne NV 89415-0816 Office: Mineral County Sch Dist A St Hawthorne NV 89415

SOTER, NICHOLAS GREGORY, advertising agency executive; b. Great Falls, Mont., Apr. 26, 1947; s. Sam Nick and Bernice (Bennett) S.; m. Kathleen Lyman, Feb. 20, 1970; children: Nichole, Erin, Samuel Scott, Kara, Stephen Andrew, Riley Kyle. BS, Brigham Young U., 1971. With McLean Assocs., Provo, Utah, 1970-75; chmn. bd., CEO Soter Assocs. Inc., Provo, 1975—; founder, pres. RS Corp., 1986-88, Plum C Corp., 1988, Due Respect LLC, 1991; owner, developer Parkside Apts., 1994—; instr. advt. Utah Valley State Coll., Orem, 1971-75, Brigham Young U., Provo, 1980-84. Publisher: Journal of Joseph, 1979, Journal of Brigham, 1980, LaVell Edwards, 1980, Amos Wright, 1981, Moments in Motherhood, 1981, What It Means to Know Christ, 1981, Mormon Fortune Builders, 1982, Utah History, 1982; contbr. articles to profl. jours. Active Utah Valley Pub. Comm. Coun. for LDS Ch., 1982-87; mem. adv. coun. Monte L. Bean Life Sci. Mus., 1987-89; Rep. dist. chmn.; v.p. exec. com. Am.'s Freedom Festival at Provo, 1990-91; jury chmn. Coun. for Advancement and Support Edn., 1989; vocalist Ralph Woodward Chorale, 1991-95, pres., 1992-94; mem. govt. rev. com., Provo, Orem, 1992-95; trustee, v.p. Greek Assn. Family History and Tradition, 1990-95; unit commr., advisor Explorer post Boy Scouts Am., 1995-98; bd. advisors Am. Cancer Soc., 1996-98. Recipient N.Y. Art Dir.'s The One Show award, Salt Lake Art Dirs. Communications Assn. of Utah Valley awards. Mem. Utah Advt. Fedn., Pub. Rels. Soc. Am., Communications Assn. Utah Valley (past pres.), Provo C. of C. (bd. dirs.), Innisbrook Network of Advt. Agys. (pres. 1986-87). Home: 1728 S 290 E Orem UT 84058-7928 Office: Soter Assocs Inc 209 N 400 W Provo UT 84601-2746

SOTOMAYOR, IVAN J., accountant, international consultant; b. Quito, Ecuador, May 28, 1951; came to U.S., 1967; s. Jaime E. and Bettina (Morejon) S.; m. Eugenia, Aug. 24, 1973; children: Yvette, Karina. BA, Calif. State U., L.A., 1978; MBA, Golden Gate U., 1984. CPA, Calif. Investment dept. Security Pacific Nat. Bank, L.A., 1974-79; v.p., mgr. Wells Fargo Bank, San Francisco, 1979-85; ptnr. Grobstein & Co. CPA's, Shermanoks, Calif., 1985-91; pres. Sotomayor & Co. CPA's, Glendale, Calif., 1991—. Contbr. articles to profl. jours. Mem. Inter-Am. Acctg. Assn. (exec. com., v.p. 1997—), Soc. Calif. CPAs (recognition award 1997), Am. Inst. CPA (chair 1996—), Latin Bus. Assn. (chair internat. com. 1997—). Avocations: jogging, tennis, reading. Office: Sotomayor & Co CPAs 541 W Colorado St Ste 201 Glendale CA 91204-1101

SOUKUP, PAUL ARTHUR, priest, educator; b. Burbank, Calif., Aug. 15, 1950; s. Frank Kermit and Jeannette Laurette (Ramsey) S. AB, St. Louis U., 1973; MDiv, Jesuit Sch. Theology, Berkeley, Calif., 1979; Phd, U. Tex., 1985. Ordained priest Roman Catholic Ch., 1979. Tchr. Loyola H.S., L.A., 1973-76; assoc. pastor St. Theresa's Ch., Austin, Tex., 1980-85; assoc. prof. Santa Clara (Calif.) U., 1985—; cons. U.S. Cath. Conf., Washington, 1983-88, 94-98, Am. Bible Soc., N.Y.C., 1995—. Author: Christian Communication, 1989; editor: Media, Culture, and Catholicism, 1996, (with P. Rossi) Mass Media and Moral Imagination, 1994, (with R. Hodgson) From One Medium to Another, 1997. Mem. Nat. Comm. Assn., Cath. Comm. Assn., Internat. Comm. Assn. Office: Santa Clara U Dept Comm 500 El Camino Real Santa Clara CA 95953

SOUSA, JOSEPH PHILIP, secondary education educator; b. Azores, Portugal, May 26, 1943; s. Agostinho and Emilia Augusta (Freitas) S.; m. Filomena Alice Castro, Apr. 1, 1967 (div. Aug. 1983); children: Yvette Marie, John Philip. BA in Math., San Jose State U., 1981. Cert. tchr., Calif., Ga.; ordained priest Cath. and Apostolic Ch. of Antioch, 1989, bishop, 1991. Tchr. math. Milpitas (Calif.) Unified Sch. Dist., 1981-93, mentor tchr., 1989-91; tchr. Cobb County Sch. Dist., 1993, South San Francisco Unified Sch. Dist., 1994—; advisor math. engring. and sci. achievement San Jose (Calif.) State U., 1982—; cons. math. Coll. Bd., 1986-88. With USAR, 1965-83. Mem. NEA, Nat. Coun. Tchrs. Math., Calif. Tchrs. Assn., Calif. Union Portuguese (pres. 1984), Irmandade Divino Espirito Santo (sec. 1982-85). Avocations: collecting stamps, soccer, meditation, Tai-Chi, Regenesis. Home: 4349 La Cosa Ave Fremont CA 94536-4721

SOUTHERN, RONALD D., diversified corporation executive; b. Calgary, Alta., Can., July 25, 1930; s. Samuel Donald and Alexandra (Cuthill) S.; m. Margaret Visser, July 30, 1954; children: Nancy, Linda. BSc, U. Alta., Edmonton, 1953; LLD (hon.), U. Calgary, 1976, U. Alberta, 1991. Pres., CEO ATCO Ltd., Calgary, 1954-85, dep. chmn., CEO, 1985-91, chmn., pres., CEO, 1985-93; chmn., CEO ATCO Ltd. and Can. Utilities Ltd., Calgary, 1994—, ATCO Ltd., Calgary, 1994—, Can. Utilities Ltd., Calgary, 1994—; chmn. Akita Drilling Ltd.; bd. dirs. Fletcher Challenge Ltd., Can. Airlines, Can. Pacific Ltd., Chrysler Can. Ltd., IMASCO Ltd., LaFarge, Royal Ins. Ltd., Xerox of Can. Inc., Southam Inc.; co-chmn. Spruce Meadows Tournaments; chmn. Spruce Meadows Round Table. Recipient Holland Trade award Gov. of The Netherlands, 1985, (with wife) Sportsmen of Yr. award Calgary Booster Club, Internat., Disting. Entrepreneur award U. Man. Faculty Mgmt., 1990; inducted into Can. Bus. Hall, 1995; named Businessman of Yr. U. Alta., 1986, to Order of Can. Brit. Empire, 1986, Comdr. Brit. Empire, 1995, CEO of the Yr. Fin. Post, 1996. Mem. Ranchmen's Club. Calgary Golf and Country Club. Office: ATCO Ltd & Can Utilities, 1600 909-11 Ave SW, Calgary, AB Canada T2R 1N6

SOUTHEY, TREVOR, visual artist; b. Gatooma, Rhodesia, Jan. 12, 1940; came to U.S., 1965; s. Trevor Desmond and Eleanor Mary (Brading) S.; m. Elaine Fish Walton, May 27, 1967 (div. Dec. 1982); children: Mary Anna, [illegible] art Brigham Young U., Provo, Utah, 1969-77. Co-author: Trevor Southey: Reconciliation, 1997. Recipient Purchase prize Beyond Boundries, Richmond Art Ctr., 1969. Mem. Calif. Soc. Printmakers. Democrat. Office: [illegible] Southey Studio 60 Belcher St San Francisco CA 94114-1107

SOUTHWICK, STANTON W., landscape architect; b. Ogden, Utah, Dec. 2, 1957; s. William S. and Jeneane (Garner) S.; m. Jill Williamsen, June 20, 1980; children: Sharlin, Skyler, Courtney, Chanelle, Clarke. B in Landscape Arch., Utah State U., 1983. Registered landscape arch., Nev., Ariz., Calif. Constrn. foreman Holt Landscaping, Salt Lake City, 1983-84, Erickson Landscaping, Salt Lake City, 1984-85; landscape designer Randolph Hlubik Assocs., Riverside, Calif., 1985-86, Whiting's, Las Vegas, 1986-88; landscape arch. Southwick & Assocs., Las Vegas, 1988-94, Poggemeyer Design Group, Las Vegas, 1994—. Scoutmaster Boy Scouts Am., Las Vegas, 1992—. Mem. Am. Soc. Landscape Archs. (sect. chmn. 1997). Avocations: golf, softball. Office: Poggemeyer Design Group 2601 N Fenaya Way Las Vegas NV 89128

SOUTHWORTH, ROD BRAND, computer science educator; b. Binghampton, N.Y., Aug. 24, 1941; s. William Tanner Southworth and Ruth Evelyn (Brabham) Woods; m. Patrice Marie Gapen, Jan. 10, 1978; children: Suzi Lynn, Judi Leigh, Megan Marie, Robin Ashley. BS in Bus., U. Ariz., 1965; MS in Mgmt. Sci. and Info Systems, Colo. State U., 1978. Mktg. rep. IBM, Denver, 1966-69; system analyst Colo. State U., Fort Collins, 1969-73, grad. teaching asst., 1978-79; project mgr. Systems and Computer Tech., Portland, Oreg., 1973-75; asst. dir. Systems and Computer Tech., Fairbanks, Alaska, 1975-77; instr. in computer info. systems Laramie County C.C., Cheyenne, Wyo., 1979—. Author: (software) PC-DOS/MS-DOS Simplified, 1st edit. 1988, 3rd edit. 1992, DOS Complete and Simplified, 1990, DOS Essentials, 1991, DOS 5 Simplified, 1992, DOS 6.2 Simplified, 1994. Mem. Civil Air Patrol, Cheyenne, 1991. Mem. Data Processing Mgmt. Assn. (mem. assoc. level model curriculum 1984-85), Assn. Computing Machinery (mem. assoc. level computer info. processing model curriculum 1991-92). Avocations: boating, water skiing, fishing, stamp collecting, tennis. Home: PO Box 5457 Cheyenne WY 82003-5457 Office: Laramie County Comm Coll 1400 E College Dr Cheyenne WY 82007-3204

SOUZA, JOAN OF ARC, educational administrator; b. Honolulu, Nov. 16, 1943; d. Peter B. and Helen Souza. AA, Maria Regina Coll., Syracuse, N.Y., 1967; BA in Theology, St. Joseph Coll., Rensselaer, Ind., 1970; MA in Adminstrn. of Religious Edn., LaSalle Coll., Phila., 1976. Joined Sisters of 3d Franciscan Order, Roman Cath. Ch., 1961. Youth minister Cath. Diocese, Syracuse, 1963-71, St. Peter's Parish, Riverside, N.J., 1971-73, IHM Parish, Liverpool, N.Y., 1984-91; tchr. St. Francis Sch., Honolulu, 1973-84, jr./sr. high sch. prin., 1991—. Author AIDS Ednl. Workshops, 1988-91, Kindergarten Religious Edn. Program, 1985. Mem. Pro-Life Com., Honolulu, 1980-84; buddy AIDS Buddy Program of Ctrl. N.Y., Syracuse, 1987-91; founder St. Francis Sch. Kaua'i Campus, 1997; mem. Malama O Manoa, Honolulu. Mem. ASCD, AAUW, Nat. Cath. Ednl. Assn., Nat. Assn. for Year-Round Edn., Nat. Assn. of Secondary Sch. Prins., Hawaii Assn. Ind. Schs. Roman Catholic. Avocations: gardening, swimming, sewing, biking, reading. Office: St Francis School 2707 Pamoa Rd Honolulu HI 96822-1838

SOVEREL, PETER WOLCOTT, conservation executive, educator; b. Portsmouth, Va., Jan. 21, 1941; s. William W. and Emily (Hoey) S.; m. Marion (Joy), June 8, 1963; children: Christine Wilson, Gregory, Camille. BS, U.S. Naval Acad., 1963; M of Pub. Adminstrn., U. Wash., 1970, postgrad., 1973. Commd. ensign USN, 1963, advanced through grades to capt., 1986; pres. Wild Salmon Ctr., Edmonds, Wash., 1987—; adj. prof. U. Wash., Seattle, 1991—; dir. Wild Steel Salmon mag., Seattle, 1992—. Contbr. author: Problems of Sea Power as We Approach the Twenty-First Century, 1977; contbr. articles to profl. jours. Chair Steelhead Com., Seattle, 1988-98; dir. Save our Wild Salmon, Seattle, 1989-97, Steelhead Soc. B.C., Vancouver, Can., 1990—. Decorated Silver Star, Bronze Star; recipient Presdl. Unit citation Pres. Johnson, 1968; named Conservationist of Yr., Fedn. Fly Fishers, 1994. Office: Wild Salmon Ctr 16430 72d Ave W Edmonds WA 98026

SOWDER, KATHLEEN ADAMS, marketing executive; b. Person County, N.C., Feb. 9, 1951; d. George W. and Mary W. (Woody) A.; BS, Radford Coll., 1976; MBA, Va. Poly. Inst., 1978; m. Angelo R. LoMascolo, Apr. 11, 1980 (div.); 1 child, Mary Jennifer. Asst. product mgr. GTE Sylvania, Waltham, Mass., 1978-79, product mgr. video products, 1979-80; comml. mktg. mgr. Am. Dist. Telegraph, N.Y.C., 1980-87; v.p. mktg. ESL, Hingham, Mass., 1987-91; exec. v.p. Falcon Detection Techs., Inc., Plymouth, Mass., 1991-94; gen. mgr. Westec Bus. Security, Irvine, Calif., 1995—. Mem. Am. Mktg. Assn., Am. Soc. Indsl. Security (past chair standing com. on phys. security). Republican. Home: 1851 Royal Oak Rd Tustin CA 92780-6667 Office: Westec 16662 Hale Ave Irvine CA 92606-5031

SOWERS, MIRIAM RUTH, painter; b. Bluffton, Ohio, Oct. 4, 1922; d. Paul S. and Edith E. (Triplehorn) Hochstettler; m. H. Frank Sowers, Apr. 15, 1944; children: Craig V., Keith A. BFA, Miami U., Oxford, Ohio, 1944; postgrad., Chgo. Art Inst., 1946, U. N.Mex., 1957. Draftsman Army Map Service, Chgo., 1945-46; owner studio Findlay, Ohio, 1949-53, Albuquerque, 1953-60; owner Old Town Gallery, Albuquerque, 1961-80; owner pvt. studio Albuquerque, 1980—. One-woman shows include Tex. Agrl. and Indsl. U., Kingville, Houston Bapt. Coll., Winblad Galleries, San Francisco, L'Atelier Gallery, Cedar Falls, Iowa, Southwestern Galleries, Dallas, Albuquerque Unitarian Ch., Am. Bible Soc., N.Y.C., Peacock Gallery, Corrales, N.Mex., 1984, U. N.Mex. Community Ctr. Arts, Las Cruces, 1985, Wharton's Gallery, Santa Fe, 1985, Aliso Gallery, Albuquerque, 1986, Statesman Club, Albuquerque, Arts Internat. Gallery, Findlay, Findlay Coll., Springfield (Ohio) Mus. Art, Provenance Gallery, Maui, Hawaii, 1988, Saint Johns Coll., Santa Fe, 1988, King Kamehameha Hotel, Kailua-Kona, Hawaii, 1989, Marine Gallery, Kona, 1990, Kona Surf Hotel, 1990, Luigi De Rossi Gallery, Kealakaua, Hawaii, Blankley Gallery, Albuquerque, Blankley Gallery, Albuquerque, 1992, Southwest Cornerhouse Gallery, 93, 94, 95, 96, 97, 98, Albuquerque, 1993; group and gallery exhibits include Dayton (Ohio) Art Inst., Butler (Ohio) Art Inst., Akron (Ohio) Art Inst., Massilon (Ohio) Art Inst., Toledo Mus. Art (prize), Sun Carnival, El Paso, Chelmont Nat., El Paso, Tucson Fiesta Show, Santa Fe Biennial, Corrales All State Show (prize), N.Mex. State Fair (prize), Ohio Tri-State Show, Ohio State Fair, I.P.A. Nat., Washington, Roswell (N.Mex.) Mus., All Albuquerque Show and Jonson Gallery (prize), Galeria de Artesanos, Albuquerque, 1985, Little Studio Gallery, N.Y.C., Ft. Smith (Ark.) Art Ctr., The Gallery, Roswell, Gallery D., Mesilla, N.Mex., Creative Endeavors, Taos, N.Mex., Smith LTD. Galleries, Ruidoso, N.Mex., Alice Moxey Gallery, Midland, Tex., Linda Lundeen Gallery, Las Cruces, Hand Made U.S.A., Albuquerque, Reynolds Gallery, Albuquerque, El Dor Gallery, Albuquerque, Weems Gallery, Albuquerque, My Place, Albuquerque, Casa Manana Gallery, Albuquerque, Preusser Gallery, Albuquerque, Argosy Arts & Artifacts Gallery, Albuquerque, Fuller Lodge, Los Alamos, Kona Arts & Crafts, Volcano House Gallery, Volcano Nat. Pk., Hawaii, Universal Ctr. for the Arts, Las Cruces, N.Mex., Milagro Gallery, Taos, N.Mex., Eloise Contemporary, Taos, Wakefield Gardens Gallery, Honaunau-Kona, Hawaii, 1992, Kona Arts & Crafts Gallery, Kailua-Kona, Hawaii, 1992, Crystal Star Gallery, Kealaka Kua, Hawaii, 1992, Ken Dewey Gallery, Albuquerque, 1994, New Mexico's Own, Bernalillo, 1994, Foxfire Gall., Albuquerque, Shephard of the Valley Church, 1988, others; works pub.: (mags.) Western Rev., 1967, N.Mex. Cultural News, 1968, Albuquerque Clubwoman, 1969, S.W. Art Mag., 1973, Art Voices South, 1980, (books) Parables from Paradise, 1975, The Suns of Man, 1981, (poetry quar.) Encore, 1979, (video) Layerist Artists, 1990; included in books Leap, Limited Edition Art Prints, 1979-80, American Artists, 1985, New York Artists, 1988, Artists of New Mexico vol. 3, 1989, Layerist Artists, 1991, Merto Plus, Albuquerque Jour., 1992. Home and Office: 3020 Glenwood Dr NW Albuquerque NM 87107-2925

SOWERWINE, ELBERT ORLA, JR., chemist, chemical engineer; b. Tooele, Utah, Mar. 15, 1915; s. Elbert Orla and Margaret Alice (Evans) S.; BS in Chemistry, Cornell U., 1937, MSChemE, 1938; m. Norma Borge; children: Sue-Ann Sowerwine Jacobson, Sandra Sowerwine Montgomery, Elbert Orla 3d, John Frederick, Avril Sowerwine Taylor, Albaro Francisco, Octavio Evans, Zaida Sowerwine Roberts. Analytical chemist Raritan Copper Works, Perth Amboy, N.J., summers 1936-37; rsch. chem. engr. Socony-Vacuum Oil Co., Paulsboro, N.J., 1938-43; prodn. supr. Merck & Co., Elkton, Va., 1943-45; asst. plant mgr. U.S. Indsl. Chems. Co., Newark, 1945-48; project engr. and rsch. dir. Wigton-Abbott Corp., Newark, 1948-50, Cody, Wyo., 1950-55; cons. engring., planning, indsl. and community devel., resource evaluation and mgmt. Wapiti, Wyo., also C.Am., Honduras, Nicaragua, 1955-98, ret. 1998. Commr. N.J., Boy Scouts Am., 1938-43; mem. Wapiti and Park County (Wyo.) Sch. Bds., 1954-58; dir. Mont. State Planning Bd., 1959-61; exec. bd. Mo. Basin Rsch. and Devel. Coun., 1959-61. Fellow Am. Inst. Chemists; mem. AIChE, Am. Planning Assn., Nicaraguan Assn. Engrs. and Architects. Libertarian. Mem. Christian Ch. Achievements include rsch. in desulfurization of petroleum products, process control, alternate energy projects; patentee in petroleum and chem. processes and equipment. Home: Broken H Ranch Wapiti WY 82450 Office: Sowerwine Cons Wapiti WY 82450

SPADE, GEORGE LAWRENCE, scientist; b. Sioux City, Iowa, Dec. 14, 1945; s. Walter Charles and LaVancha May (Green) S.; m. Carol Margaret Deaton, Mar. 14, 1966 (div. June 1985); children: Aaron Michael, Margaret. Mem. earthquake study group for China, U.S. Citizen Amb. Programs, 1989. Contbr. articles to profl. jours. Mem. AAAS, Am. Math. Soc., Math. Assn. Am., N.Y. Acad. Scis., Mensa. Avocations: poetry, painting, music. Home and Office: PO Box 2260 Columbia Falls MT 59912-2260

SPAFFORD, MICHAEL CHARLES, artist; b. Palm Springs, Calif., Nov. 6, 1935. BA, Pomona Coll., 1959; MA, Harvard U., 1960. One man shows include Seattle Art Mus., 1982, 86, Reed Coll., 1984, Whtcom county Mus., 1987, U. Puget Sound, Tacoma, Wash., 1973, Tacoma Art Mus., 1975, 86, Utah Mus. Fine Arts, Salt Lake City, 1975, Francine Seders Gallery, Seattle, 1965—, Bellevue Art Mus., 1991, Cheney-Cowles Mus., Spokane, Wash., 1994; exhibited in group shows at Wilcox Gallery, Swarthmore Coll., Pa., 1977, Seattle Art Mus., 1977, 80, 84, Am. Acad. and Inst. Arts and Letters, N.Y.C., 1980, 83, 89, 95, Kobe, Japan, 1981, Eastern Wash. U., 1982, Henry Art Gallery, 1982, 86, Bellevue Art Mus., 1987, 95, Cheney Cowles Mus., 1988, Holter Mus. of Art, Helena, Mont. Recipient Rome Prize Am. Acad. in Rome, 1967-69, award Am. Acad. and Inst. Arts and Letters, 1983; Louis Comfort Tiffany Found. grantee, 1965-66; Neddy fellow, 1996. Address: c/o Francine Seders Gallery 6701 Greenwood Ave N Seattle WA 98103*

SPAMAN, MORGAN PATRICK, fire and safety specialist; b. Springfield, Mass., Feb. 27, 1960; s. Gerald Allen and Marilyn Jean (Rouselle) S.; m. Sherry Anita Jennings, Apr. 10, 1979; children: Michael Wayne, Lisette Amanda. A in Fire Sci., Cmty. Coll. Air Force, Maxwell AFB, Ala., 1985. Cert. fire officer II, fire instr. II.; accredited, Internat. Fire Svc. Accreditation Congress. Fire protection supr. USAF, Anchorage, 1978-94; sr. fire and safety specialist Alyeska Pipline Svc. Co., Anchorage, 1994—; part-time tchr. U. Alaska, Galena, 1985-86. Sgt. USAF, 1978-94. Avocations: fishing, snowmobile riding, travel. Home: 905 Agate Ln Wasilla AK 99654-3439 Office: Alyeska Pipeline Svc Co 1835 S Bragaw St Anchorage AK 99512-0099

SPANGLER, NITA REIFSCHNEIDER, volunteer; b. Ukiah, Calif., Apr. 17, 1923; d. John Charles and Olga Augusta (Wuertz) Reifschneider; m. Raymond Luper Spangler, Sept. 22, 1946 (dec.); children: Jon Martin, Mary Raymond, Thor Raymond. BA, Univ. Nev., 1944. News reporter Redwood (Calif.) City Tribune, 1944-46, Country Almanac, Woodside, Calif., 1969-77. Mem. bd. dirs. San Mateo (Calif.) County Hist. Assn., 1961-68, pres., 1964-66; founder, 1st pres. Portolá Expedition Bicentennial Found., 1966-70; chmn. San Mateo County Scenic Rds. Com., 1967-76; mem. San Mateo County Hist. Resource Adv.; mem. commn. San Mateo County Parks and Recreation, 1983-97, past chmn.; cons. hwy. aesthetics Cal Trans., 1981-83; mem. sch. coms. Recipient Commendation, County Bd. Suprs., 1968, 1977, 92. Mem. Sierra Club, Western History Assn., Mormon History Assn., Nev. State Hist. Soc. (life), San Mateo County Hist. Assn. (life, Resolution of Thanks 1968, 76, 94), Friends Redwood City, Kappa Alpha Theta. Democrat. Episcopalian. Avocations: historic preservation. Home: 970 Edgewood Rd Redwood City CA 94062-1818

SPANGLER, SCOTT MICHAEL, retired private investor; b. Toledo, Aug. 4, 1938; s. Walter James and Martha Zoe (Hirscher) S.; m. Jean Galt Schmonsees, June 10, 1963; children—Karen Elizabeth, Scott Michael, Andrew Galt. B.M.E., U. Cin., 1961; M.B.A., Harvard U., 1963. Research asso. M.I.T., 1963-65; fin. exec. Cooper Industries, Inc., Mt. Vernon, Ohio, 1965-68; v.p. indsl. group White Motor Corp., Cleve., 1968-70; pres. Spangler and Co., Houston, 1970-73; dir., pres., chief exec. officer AZL Resources, Inc. (and affiliates), Phoenix, 1973-84; pres., chief exec. officer First Phoenix Capital, Inc., Scottsdale, Ariz., 1984-90; assoc. adminstr. AID, Washington, 1990-93; pres. First Phoenix Capital Inc., Phoenix and Washington, 1993-94, retired, 1994—; bd. dirs. First So. Capital Corp., Alamosa Nat. Bank, Cen. Ariz. Bank, New London Oil Inc. Mem. World Pres.' Orgn., Chief Execs. Orgn., Harvard Club, Paradise Valley Country Club, Met. Club. Republican. Presbyterian.

SPANOS, ALEXANDER GUS, professional football team executive; b. Stockton, Calif., Sept. 28, 1923; m. Faye Spanos; children: Dean, Dea Spanos Berberian, Alexis Spanos Ruhl, Michael. LLD (hon.), U. Pacific, 1984. Chmn. bd. dirs. A.G. Spanos Constrn. Inc., Stockton, Calif., 1960—; chmn. bd. dirs. A.G. Spanos Properties Inc., Stockton, Calif., 1960—, A.G. Spanos Mgmt. Inc., Stockton, Calif., 1967—, A.G. Spanos Enterprises Inc., Stockton, Calif., 1971—, A.G. Spanos Devel. Inc., Stockton, Calif., 1973—, A.G. Spanos Realty Inc., Stockton, Calif., 1978—, A.G. Spanos Jet Ctr. Inc., Stockton, Calif., 1980—, A.G.S. Fin. Corp., Stockton, Calif., 1980—, San Diego Chargers, 1984—; Chmn. bd. dirs. A.G.S. Spanos Land Co., Stockton, Calif., 1982—. Former trustee Children's Hosp., San Francisco, San Francisco Fine Arts Mus.; trustee Eisenhower Med. Ctr., Rancho Mirage, Calif.; hon. regent U. Pacific, Stockton, 1972-82; gov. USO, , Washington, 1982—. Served with USAF, 1942-46. Recipient Albert Gallatin award Zurich-Am. Ins. Co., 1973, Horatio Alger award Horatio Alger Found., 1982, medal of Honor Statue of Liberty-Ellis Islan Found., 1982. Mem. Am. Hellenic Ednl. Progressive Assn., Calif. C. of C. (bd. dirs. 1980-85). Republican. Greek Orthodox. Avocation: golfing. Office: San Diego Chargers Qualcomm Stadium, Jack Murphy Stadium PO Box 609609 San Diego CA 92160-9609 also: A G Spanos Constrn Co 1341 West Robin Hood Dr Stockton CA 95207-5515*

SPARER, MALCOLM MARTIN, rabbi; b. N.Y.C.; m. Erna Reichl (dec. Sept. 1990); children: Ruth, Arthur (dec.), Jennifer, Shoshana. AB, M in Hebrew Lit., Yeshiva U.; MA in Sociology, CCNY; cert. in pastoral counseling, Des Moines Coll. Osteopathic Medicine; PhD in Sociology, NYU. Ordained rabbi, 1953. Pres. Menorah Inst., San Francisco, 1981—; exec. dir. Rabbinical Coun. Calif., L.A., 1957-66; chaplain VA; adminstr. Tchr's. Coll. of West Coast, Torah U. (now Yeshiva U.), 1957-66; rabbi Beth El Jacob, Des Moines, 1966-69, Chevra Thilim, San Francisco, 1969-72; pres. No. Calif. Bd. Rabbis, 1977-96, pres. emeritus, 1996—; sr. lectr. San Francisco C.C.; liason Union of Orthodox Jewish Congregations Am., 1957-66, moderator radio series Lest We Forget, 1962, moderator TV spls. Sta. KNXT, L.A., 1964-65, Des Moines, 1967-69; instr. dept. philosophy Drake U., 1966-69; pres. San Francisco dist. Zionist Orgn. Am., 1969-82, also bd. dirs.; chmn., mem. nat. bd. San Francisco Bay Area Zionist Fedn., 1971-84; co-chmn. Jerusalem Fair, 25th Ann. State of Israel, 1973; chmn. Commn. on Soviet Jewry, Jewish Cmty. Rels. Coun., 1974-81; cons. internat. leaders, founder Menorah Inst.; cons. Commn. on Christian-Jewish and Moslem Rels. to European Parliament Nations; cons. in field; writer, lectr. colls., ch. groups on Judaica and world affairs; chmn. dept. world affairs/internat. politics C.C. San Francisco; former chaplain Letterman Army VA Hosp., San Francisco Presidio; co-founder Black and Jewish Clergy; mem. San Francisco Coun. Chs., bd. dirs. food bank program, United Jewish Appeal, chmn. rabbinic cabinet of western region; invited mem. del. bishops and ch. leaders various denominations conducting meml. svc. at Dachau on 50th ann. Reich's Kristallnacht, Fed. Republic Germany, 1988. Hon. chmn. Mayor's Commn. on Holocaust Meml., San Francisco; mem. Mayor's Task Force for Homeless; co-chmn. Gov.'s Family Task Force, San Francisco. With USN, WWII, Korean War, chaplain USAF. Annual Jerusalem Lectr. Series named in his honor, 1998. Address: PO Box 15055 San Francisco CA 94115-0055

SPARKS, CAROLYN MORLEDGE, hotel and casino executive; b. Glendale, Calif., Jan. 7, 1942; d. Frederick Leighton and Malvina Elizabeth (Walford) Morledge; m. Kenneth D. Sparks, June 27, 1964; children: Katherine, Robert, Patricia. BA, U. Calif., Berkeley, 1963. Co-owner, co-founder Internat. Ins. Svcs., Ltd., Las Vegas, Nev., 1966—; dir. Pri Merit Bank, Las Vegas, 1988-96, S.W. Gas Corp., Las Vegas, 1988—; dir. Showboat Hotel & Casino, Las Vegas, Atlantic City, N.J., Sydney and East Chicago, Ind., 1991—; mem. Pres. Inner Circle, U. Nev., Las Vegas, 1996-97, Pres. Assocs., 1992-96; mem. Fedn. Cmty. Coll. So. Nev., 1997. Regent Univ. & C.C. Sys. Nev., Reno and Las Vegas, 1984-96; chair U. Med. Ctr. Found., 1982-84, 97; com. chair bd. regents Bishop Gorman H.S., 1990-95; chair Nev. Ctr. for Children Found., 1996—; chair telethon Children's Miracle Network, 1983-85. Recipient Cmty. Svc. award, Clark County, Nev., 1982, Pres. medal U. Nev., Las Vegas, 1997; named outstanding alumna Alpha Gamma Delta, 1994. Mem. Disting. Women So. Nev., Jr. League Las Vegas. Republilcan. Roman Catholic. Office: Internat Ins Svcs Ltd 7424 W Sahara Ave Las Vegas NV 89117-2740

SPARKS, DALE BOYD, allergist, health facility administrator; b. Springfield, Mo., July 14, 1929; s. Roscoe R. and Ruby V. (Boyd) S.; m. Caroline P. Porter, Aug. 3, 1956; children: Susan L., Laura A., Lisa M., Jennifer G. AB, BS, Southwest Mo. State U., 1951; BS in Medicine, U. Mo., 1953; MD, St. Louis U., 1955. Diplomate Am. Bd. Allergy and Immunology. Intern Kansas City (Mo.) Gen. Hosp. U. Med. Ctr., 1955-56; resident U. Mo. Hosp., 1958-60; fellow in allergy and immunology Northwestern U., 1960-61; mem. cons. staff Parkview Cmty. Hosp., 1961—; mem. med. staff Riverside (Calif.) Cmty. Hosp., 1961—, dir. respiratory therapy, 1968-85; dir. respiratory therapy and diagnostic svcs. Riverside Gen. Hosp. U. Med. Ctr., 1965—, chmn. dept. medicine, 1978—, chief med. staff, 1990—; acting dir., health officer Riverside Pub. Health Dept., 1991-93; clin. prof. medicine Loma Linda U. Mem. editl. bd. Immunology and Allergy in Practice, 1980—. Lt. USNR. Fellow ACP (coun. subspecialty Socs. 1988—), Am. Coll. Allergy and Immunology (disting., bd. regents 1989-93, pres. 1990-91, chmn. fin. com./treas. 1990-93, recert. com.), Coll. Allergy, Asthma and Immunology; mem. AMA, Am. Soc. Internal Medicine, Am. Lung Assn. (bd. dirs. 1990—), Am. Heart Assn. (bd. dirs. 1964-70, pres. 1966), Joint Coun. Am. Allergy and Immunology (bd. dirs. 1985-90), Calif. Med. Assn., Calif. Soc. Allergy, Inland Soc. Internal Medicine, Riverside County Med. Assn. (bd. councilors 1980—, alt. del. CMA 1988—), Riverside County Found. Med. Care (sec., past pres.). Office: 3498 Ramona Dr Riverside CA 92506-1257

SPARKS, JACK NORMAN, college dean; b. Lebanon, Ind., Dec. 3, 1928; s. Oakley and Geraldine Ruth (Edrington) S.; m. Esther Lois Bowen, Apr. 11, 1953; children: Stephen Michael, Robert Norman, Ruth Ann, Jonathan Russell. BS, Purdue U., 1950; MA, U. Iowa, 1951, PhD, 1960. Tchr. math. Leyden Community High Sch., Franklin Park, Ill., 1954-58; rsch. asst. U. Iowa, Iowa City, 1958-60; assoc. prof. applied stats., dir. bur. of rsch. U. No. Colo., Greeley, 1960-65; assoc. prof. ednl. psychology Pa. State U., State Coll., 1965-68; dir. corr. Campus Crusade for Christ, San Bernardino, Calif., 1968-69; dir. Christian World Liberation Front, Berkeley, Calif., 1969-75; pastor, ch. overseer New Covenant Apostolic Order, Berkeley, 1975-77; dean St. Athanasius Acad. Orthodox Theology, Santa Barbara, Calif., 1977-87, St. Athanasius Coll., Santa Barbara, 1987-93, St. Athanasius Acad. of Orthodox Theology, Elk Grove, Calif., 1996—, 1996—; cons. Measurement Rsch. Ctr., Iowa City, 1959-60, Western States Small Schs. Project, Greeley, 1962-65, Colo. Coun. on Edn. Rsch., Denver, 1963-65; project dir. Orthodox Study Bible Old Testament Project, 1998—. Author: Letters to Street Christians, 1971, The Mind Benders, 1977, 79, The Resurrection Letters, 1978, The Preaching of the Apostles, 1987, Victory in the Unseen Warfare, 1993; editor: Apostolic Fathers, 1978, 88; gen. editor: The Orthodox Study Bible, 1993, Virtue in the Unseen Warfare, 1995, Prayer in the Unseen Warfare, 1996, Christ Is Our Holiness, 1996, The Coming of the Prince, 1997, Tradition in the Early Church, 1997, The Letters of St. Ignatius, 1998. Trustee Rock Mont Coll., Denver, 1962-77, Thomas Nelson Co., Nashville, 1977-78. 1st lt. U.S. Army, 1952-54. Mem. Am. Sci. Affiliation, Assn. Orthodox Theologians, Conf. on Faith and History, Phi Delta Kappa (pres. Epsilon chpt. 1959-60). Democrat. Orthodox Christian. Home: 8758 Williamson Dr Elk Grove CA 95624-1829 Office: St Athanasius Acad Orthodox Theology 10519 E Stockton Blvd Ste 170 Elk Grove CA 95624-9704

SPARR, DANIEL BEATTIE, federal judge; b. Denver, June 8, 1931; s. Daniel John and Mary Isabel (Beattie) S.; m. Virginia Sue Long Sparr, June 28, 1952; children: Stephen Glenwood, Douglas Lloyd, Michael Christopher. BSBA, U. Denver, 1952, JD, 1966. Bar: Colo. U.S. Dist. Ct. Assoc. White & Steele, Denver, 1966-70; atty. Mountain States Telephone & Telegraph Co., Denver, 1970-71; ptnr. White & Steele, Denver, 1971-74; atty. Wesley H. Doan, Lakewood, Colo., 1974-75; prin. Law Offices of Daniel B. Sparr, Denver, 1975-77; judge 2d dist. Colo. Dist. Ct., Denver, 1977-90; judge U.S. Dist. Ct. Colo., Denver, 1990—. Mem. Denver Bar Assn. (trustee 1975-78), Denver Paralegal Inst. (bd. advs. 1976-88), William E. Doyle's/Am. Inns of Ct., Am. Bd. Trial Advs., ABA, Colo. Bar Assn. Office: US Dist Ct 1929 Stout St Denver CO 80294-0001*

SPARROWK, CORA CATHERINE, lay church leader; b. Martin, Tenn., Aug. 23, 1917; d. Ernest Clark and Edna (Harris) C.; m. John Sparrowk, Jan. 19, 1937; children: Jack Ernest, Jill Ann. DD (hon.), Am. Bapt. Sem. West, 1978. Contbr. articles to profl. jours. Chmn. Commn. on Christian Ethics, Bapt. World Alliance, chmn. div. study and rsch., 1985-90, v.p., 1900—, also mem. exec. com. and gen. coun.; mem. internat. com. World Day of Prayer, 1982—; dep. v.p. Ch. Women United USA, N.Y.C., 1980-84; past trustee Am. Bapt. Sem. West; bd. dirs. Ea. Bapt. Sem. and Ea. Coll., 1981—; pres. Am. Bapt. Internat. Ministries, 1976-78, Am. Bapt. Chs. U.S.A., 1978-79. Named Layman of Yr., Berkeley Bapt. Div. Sch., 1959; recipient citation Cen. Bapt. Theol. Sem., 1978, Valiant Woman award Ch. Women United U.S.A., 1984. Mem. Round Hill Country Club. Democrat. Address: 3370 Camanche Pky N Ione CA 95640-9409

SPATZ, RONALD MARVIN, English language educator, editor, filmmaker, writer; b. N.Y.C., Apr. 10, 1949; s. Jacob John R. and Estelle (Jacobs) S.; m. Barbara L. Larlin; 1 child, Benjamin. Student, CUNY, 1967-70; BA, U. Iowa, 1971, MFA, 1973. Instr., dir. Writers Workshop Corr. Program in Fiction Writing, Iowa City, 1972-73; instr. English U. Mo., Columbia, 1973-74; instr., asst. prof. Western Mich. U., Kalamazoo, 1974-78; asst. prof. Mo. Western State Coll., St. Joseph, 1979-80; asst. prof., assoc. prof. U. Alaska, Anchorage, 1980-88, prof., 1988—, dir. Program in Creative Writing, 1984—, 1st v.p. faculty senate, 1985-87, pres. assembly, chmn. statewide assembly, 1986-87, asst. to assoc. vice chancellor for acad. affairs, 1987-88, spl. advisor to chancellor, 1994—, chair dept. creative writing and literary arts, 1996, dir. Univ. Honors Program, 1996—; founder, univ. coord. U. Alaska Anchorage/Anchorage Daily News Statewide Creative Writing Contest. Founding, exec. and fiction editor Alaska Quar. Rev., 1982—; contbr. short stories to anthologies and jours.; dir., prodr., editor film and video For the Love of Ben, 1988-89, also 9 others. Creative Writing fellow NEA, 1982, fellow Alaska Coun. for Arts, 1985; grantee Alaska Coun. for Arts, 1982—, Alaska Humanities Forum grantee, Mich. Coun. for Arts grantee, Literary Pub. grantee NEA, 1986, 93, 96, 98; recipient Disting. Tchr. of Yr. award U. Alaska Alumni Assn., 1986, resolution of appreciation U. Alaska Bd. Regents, 1987, cert. of appreciation for outstanding leadership U. Alaska Statewide Assembly, 1987, Chancellor's award for excellence in teaching U. Alaska, 1990, Special Recognition award Contbn. to Literacy in Alaska, 1994. Mem. Phi Kappa Phi. Office: U Alaska 3211 Providence Dr Anchorage AK 99508-4614

SPAULDING, JOHN PIERSON, public relations executive, marine consultant; b. N.Y.C., June 25, 1917; s. Forrest Brisbine and Genevieve Anderson (Pierson) S.; m. Eleanor Rita Bonner, Aug. 18, 1947; children: Anne Spaulding Balzhiser, John F., Mary T. Spaulding Calvert; m. 2d, Donna Alene Abrescia, May 15, 1966. Student Iowa State Coll., 1935-36, Grinnell Coll., 1936-38, U. Chgo., 1938-39. Reporter, Chgo. City News Bur., UPI, 1939-40; editor Cedar Falls (Iowa) Daily Record, 1940-41; picture editor Des Moines Register & Tribune, 1941-42, 47-50; pub. relations dir. Motor Club Iowa, Davenport, 1950-51; commd. 2d. lt. USAF, 1942, advanced through grades to maj., 1947, recalled, 1951, advanced through grades to lt. col.; ret., 1968; v.p. Vacations Hawaii, Honolulu, 1969-70; dir. pub. relations, mgr. pub. relations services Alexander & Baldwin, Inc., Honolulu, 1970-76; mgr. community relations Matson Navigation Co., Honolulu, 1976-81. Pres., Econ. Devel. Assn., Skagit County, Wash., 1983-85; pres., chmn. Fidalgo Island Ednl. Youth Found.; mem. Anacortes (Wash.) Sch. Bd., 1982-88; mem. Gov.'s Tourism Devel. Council, 1983-85; mem. adv. com. State Ferry System, 1982—, productivity coun., 1990—;

chmn. Everett chpt. S.C.O.R.E., 1984-86, Bellingham chpt., 1991—; mem. citizens adv. com. Skagit County Transit, 1995 , Decorated Air medal. Mem. Pub. Relations Soc. Am. (pres. Hawaii chpt. 1974), Hawaii Communicators (pres. 1973), Nat. Def. Transp. Assn. (pres. Aloha chpt. 1980-81, Disting. Service award 1978-79), Air Force Assn., Can. Inst. Internat. Affairs, Anacortes C. of C., Sigma Delta Chi (life). Clubs: Propeller (pres. Port of Honolulu 1979-80), Honolulu Press, Fidelgo Yacht, Hawaii Yacht, Royal Hawaiian 400 Yacht (sec. 1996-98), Rotary (sec. 1996-98). Home: 6002 Sands Way Anacortes WA 98221-4015

SPEARS, JAMES WILLIAM, systems programmer, consultant; b. Mt. Clemens, Mich., Oct. 2, 1958; s. Arthur Jackson and Margaret Elizabeth (McLeod) S. Student, Oakland C.C., 1983-85, Northwestern U., 1976-78. Computer operator, tutor Oakland C.C., Farmington Hills, Mich., 1983-84; systems programmer, application programmer Nat. Wholesale Drug Co., Detroit, 1984-85; systems programmer Domino's Pizza, Inc., Ann Arbor, Mich., 1985-86; systems engr. Computer Assocs. Internat., Inc., Dearborn, Mich., 1987; cons. JWS and Assocs., Walled Lake, Mich., 1987-90; systems programmer Alexander Hamilton Life Ins., Inc., Farmington Hills, 1990-91; cons. level 2 support staff IBM, Poughkeepsie, N.Y., 1991-94; sr. tech. support rep. Legent Corp.; Columbus, Ohio, 1994-95; lead tech. support specialist Cross Access Corp., Sunnyvale, Calif., 1995—; mem. adj. faculty Oakland C.C., Farmington Hills, 1987-88. Mem. Nat. Systems Programmer Assn. Lutheran. Home: 655 S Fairoaks Ave Apt J114 Sunnyvale CA 94086-7851

SPECCHIO, LISA ANNA, lawyer; b. Reno, May 31, 1963; d. Michael Ronald Specchio and Kathleen Christina (Baldwin) Duncan. BA, U. Nev., 1985; JD, U. Pacific, 1988. Bar: Calif. 1988. U.S. Ct. Appeals (9th cir.) 1989, U.S. Dist. Ct. (ctrl. dist.) Calif. 1989. Assoc. Barton Klugman & Oetting, L.A., 1988-89, Harry Scolinos Law Firm, Pasadena, Calif., 1989-90, Hampton & Wilson, North Hollywood, Calif., 1991-92, Bower & Weiner, Van Nuys, Calif., 1992—. Roman Catholic. Avocations: drawing, art, racquetball. Home: PO Box 276 Gold Beach OR 97444-0276

SPECTOR, PHIL, record company executive; b. Bronx, N.Y., Dec. 25, 1940; m. Veronica Bennett, 1968 (div. 1974); children: Gary Phillip and Louis Phillip (twins), Donte Phillip, Nicole and Phillip (twins). Student, UCLA. Producer with Atlantic Records, 1960-61; founder Philles Records, 1962; now pres. Warner-Spector Records, Inc.; also Mother Bertha Music. Mem. mus. group: Teddy Bears, 1958-59; producer records for Gene Pitney, Ike and Tina Turner, Ben E. King, the Beatles, Righteous Bros., Checkmates, Crystals, Ronettes, John Lennon, George Harrison, The Ramones, Yoko Ono, others; producer album A Concert for Bangladesh (Grammy award); composer songs including You've Lost That Lovin' Feelin' (7 million performances); named most performed song in U.S. broadcasting history 1997), others; appeared in films Tami, Easy Rider; prod., TV documentary film A Giant Stands 5 Ft. 7 In.; prod. film That Was Rock. Named to Rock and Roll Hall of Fame, 1989; named Country Music Song of Yr. Songwriter and Pub. for To Know Him Is To Love Him, 1989; recipient lifetime achievement award U. Calif., Berkeley, 1994, Phila. award Phila. Music Alliance, 1994 (includes star on Phila.'s Walk of Fame); inducted into Songwriters Hall of Fame, 1996. Office: care Warner-Spector Records Inc 686 S Arroyo Pky Pasadena CA 91105-3233

SPEERS, DAVID, opera company director; b. Edmonton, Alta., Can.; m. Cydney Speers; children: Robert, Cailen. BM, U. Alta., 1976, MM, 1981; postgrad., Juilliard Sch., N.Y.C., 1977. Contract opera prodn. and stage mgmt. work Can., 1974-82, conductor more than 50 profl. main stage prodns., 1980-92; gen. dir. Calgary (Can.) Opera, 1988-98; artistic dir. Ariz. Opera, Phoenix, 1998—. Conducted operas include Manon Lescaut, La Boheme, Donizetti, Don Pasquale, La Traviata, Rigoletto, Il Trovatore, Romeo and Juliette, others. NEA scholar; grantee Can. Coun. Adminstrv. Apprenticeship program, 1978; recipient award Aspen Music Festival, 197, Flore Shaw Grad. award in music, 1981. Avocations: opera, theater, golf, sports fan, computers and internet. Office: Ariz Opera Co 4600 N 12th St Phoenix AZ 85014-4005

SPELLMAN, DOUGLAS TOBY, advertising executive; b. Bronx, N.Y., May 12, 1942; s. Sydney M. and Leah B. (Rosenberg) S.; BS, Fairleigh Dickinson U., 1964; m. Ronni I. Epstein, Jan. 16, 1966 (div. Mar. 1985); children: Laurel Nicole, Daren Scott; m. Michelle Ward, Dec. 31, 1986, 1 child, Dallas Ward Spellman. Media buyer Doyle, Dane, Bernbach, Inc., N.Y.C., 1964-66; Needham, Harper & Steers, Inc., N.Y.C., 1966; media supr. Ogilvy & Mather, Inc., N.Y.C., 1966-69; media dir. Sinay Advt., L.A., 1969-70; chief ops. officer S.H.H. Creative Mktg., Inc., L.A., 1969—; assoc. media dir. Warren, Mullen, Dolobowsky, Inc., N.Y.C., 1970—; dir. West Coast ops. Ed Libov Assocs., Inc., Los Angeles, 1970-71; media supr. Carson/Roberts Advt. div. Ogilvy & Mather, Inc., L.A., 1971-72; assoc. media dir. Ogilvy & Mather, Inc., L.A., 1972-73; media dir. Vitt Media Internat., Inc., L.A., 1973-74; v.p. dir. West Coast ops. Ind. Media Svcs., Inc., L.A., 1974-75; owner Douglas T. Spellman, Inc., L.A., 1975-77, pres., chmn. bd., 1977-82; pres., chief operating officer Douglas T. Spellman Co. div. Ad Mktg., Inc., L.A., 1982-85; pres., chief exec. officer, chmn. bd. Spellbound Prodns. and Spellman Media divs. Spellbound Communications, Inc., L.A., 1984-86; gen. ptnr. Faso & Spellman, L.A., 1984-86; chief oper. officer, pres. Yacht Mgmt. Internat., Ltd., L.A., 1984-86; v.p. media Snyder, Longino Advt. div. Snyder Advt., L.A., 1985-86; advt./media cons., L.A., 1986-91; gen. ptnr., Nucleus Nuance, L.A., 1987-88; gen. ptnr. Convention Photos Unltd, Hawaii, 1988-89; v.p. mktg. Pacific Med. Products, Inc., L.A., 1990-91; media dir., Kennedy-Wilson Inc., L.A., 1991-94; dir. media and advt. svcs. Goddard & Claussen/First Tuesday, L.A., 1994-97; v.p. advt. mktg. Cosmetic Tech. Internat., Inc., L.A., 1997-98; mng. dir. Med. Mktg. and Advt., L.A., 1998—; guest lectr. sch. bus UCLA, U. So. Calif. Served with U.S. Army Res. N.G., 1964-69. Mem. Aircraft Owners and Pilots Assn., Nat. Rifle Assn., Calif. Pistol and Rifle Assn., Phi Zeta Kappa, Phi Omega Epsilon. Jewish. Clubs: Rolls Royce Owners, Mercedes Benz Am., Aston Martin Owners.

SPENCE, ANDREW MICHAEL, dean, finance educator; b. Montclair, N.J., 1943. BA in Philosophy summa cum laude, Princeton U., 1966; BA, MA in Maths., Oxford U., 1968; PhD in Econs. with honors, Harvard U., 1972. Asst. prof. polit. econ. Kennedy Sch. Govt. Harvard U., Cambridge, Mass., 1971-75, prof. econs., 1977-83, prof. bus. adminstrn., 1979-83, George Gund prof. econs. and bus. adminstrn., 1983-86, vis. prof. econs. dept., 1976-77, chmn. bus. econs. PhD program, 1981-83; chmn. econs. dept. Harvard U., 1983-84, dean Faculty Arts and Scis., 1984-90; assoc. prof. dept. econs. Stanford (Calif.), U., 1973-75, Philip H. Knight prof., dean Grad. Sch. Bus., 1990—; bd. dirs. BankAm. Corp., Gen. Mills, Inc., Nike, Inc., Siebel Syss., Sun Microsyss., VeriFone, Inc.; chmn. Nat. Rsch. Coun. Bd. on Sci., Tech. and Econ. Policy. Author: 3 books; mem. editl. bd. Am. Econs. Rev., Bell. Jour. Econs., Jour. Econ. Theory and Pub. Policy; contbr. over 50 articles to profl. jours. Mem. econs. adv. panel NSF, 1977-79; mem. econs. adv. com. Sloan Found., 1979—. Danforth fellow, 1966; Rhodes scholar, 1966; recipient J.K. Galbraith prize for excellence in tchg., 1978. Fellow AAAS, Econometric Soc.; mem. Am. Econ. Assn. (John Bates Clark medal 1981). Office: Stanford U Grad Sch Bus Bldg 350 Memorial Way Stanford CA 94305-5015

SPENCER, CAROL BROWN, association executive; b. Normal, Ill., Aug. 26, 1936; d. Fred William and Sorado (Gross) B.; m. James Calvin Spencer, Dec. 18, 1965 (div. July 1978); children: James Calvin Jr.; Anne Elizabeth. BA in English, Calif. State U., Los Angeles, 1964, MA in Pub. Adminstrn., 1986. Cert. secondary edn. tchr., Calif. Tchr. English Seneca Vocat. High Sch., Buffalo, 1966-70; pub. info. officer City of Pasadena, Calif., 1979-90, City of Mountain View, 1990-93; exec. dir. Calif. Assn. for the Gifted, 1993-95; owner PR to Go, 1994—; bd. dirs. Calif. Music Theatre, 1987-90; bd. dirs. Pasadena Beautiful Found 1984-90, Pasadena Cultural Festival Found., 1983-86, Palo Alto-Stanford Heritage, 1990-93, Mountain View Libr. Found., 1997-98, mayoral appointee Strategic Plan. Bd. Council Pasadena, 1988-90; coms. community relations Calif. Music Educators Assn., 1997-98; bd. dirs. Diridon Sta. Found., Redwood City, 1997-98. Mem. NOW; mem. Publ. Rels. Soc. Am., Calif. Assn. for the Gifted (exec. bd.), Paul Clark Achievement award 1986, award for mktg. 1990), City/County Comms. and Mktg. Assn. (bd. dirs. 1988-90, Savvy award for mktg. 1990), Nat. Assn. for Gifted Children. Democrat. Episcopalian. Home: 7915 Laurena Ave Las Vegas NV 89147-5064

SPENCER, CAROLINE, library director. BA, U. Mich., AMLS. Past pres. Hawaii Libr. Assn. Office: HI State Public Lib 478 S King St Honolulu HI 96813-2901

SPENCER, CONSTANCE MARILYN, secondary education educator; b. New York, Jan. 2, 1942; d. Edward Bennett and Blanche Lloyd (Miller) Asbury; m. Robert Michael Spencer, Dec. 30, 1966; children: Keane Thomas, Keith Lyle. BA, U. Calif., Santa Barbara, 1964; MA in English, U. West Fla., 1974. Cert. lang. devel. specialist, preliminary adminstr. Tchr. Valley Stream (N.Y.) N. H.S., Workman Jr. H.S., Pensacola, Fla., Imperial Beach (Calif.) Elem. Sch.; substitute tchr. South Bay Union Sch., Imperial Beach; mgr. Geni, Inc., Pasadena, Calif., Avon Products, Inc., Pasadena; tchr. Walnut (Calif.) H.S., 1985—; pres. Am. Computer Instrn. Inc., Upland, Calif.; grant writer Walnut Valley Unified Sch. Dist., 1986-97, mentor tchr., 1988-97; accreditation co-chair Walnut H.S., 1993-94. Mem., sec. Toastmistress, Ontario, Calif., 1977-86. Grantee Calif. Dept. Edn., 1987, Walnut Valley Unified Sch. Dist., 1988, Diamond Bar (Calif.) Rotary, 1994. Republican. Roman Catholic. Avocation: writing. Home: 2238 Coolcrest Way Upland CA 91784-1290 Office: Walnut HS 400 Pierre Rd Walnut CA 91789-2535

SPENCER, DOUGLAS LLOYD, chemist, manufacturing executive; b. Berkeley, Calif., July 19, 1952; s. Alma Glenn and Anna Lea (Lloyd) S.; m. Connie Jeanette Whitesel, Aug. 23, 1974; children: Jeanette Dawn, Jared Douglas, Jilissa Annette, Janine David, Janelle Renee, Jeffrey Brian. AA, Diablo Valley Coll., 1971; BS, Brigham Young U., 1974. Lab. instr. chemistry dept. Brigham Young U., 1973-74; rsch. chemist Dow Chem. Western div., Pittsburg, Calif., 1975-80; pres. Sunset Distbg., Inc., Brentwood, Calif., 1980-82; pres. Maier & Assocs., Inc., Brentwood, 1982-83; pres. Doug Spencer & Assocs., Placerville, 1983-94; buyer major wholesale merchandise distbr., Bacar, Inc., San Jose, 1995-97; life agt. Beneficial Life, Sacramento, 1997—. Mem. Brentwood Planning Commn., 1980-81; missionary, dist. zone leader Eastern States Mission, 1971-73; active Boy Scouts of Am.. Rossmoor residents scholar, 1969-71, Brigham Young U. scholar, 1973-74. Republican. Mormon. Avocations: camping, fishing, gardening. Home: 2010 Clearview Dr Hollister CA 95023-6239

SPENCER, RICHARD PRAIL, property management educator, job placement counselor; b. Mar. 1, 1948; s. Richard Victor and Doris Louise (Byington) S.; m. Carol J. Vassar, Apr. 16, 1981; children: Chris, Matthew, Nicholas. Lic. postsecondary tchr., Calif. Real estate assoc. Spencer Realty & Investments, Ukiah, Calif., 1975-81; resort owner Headwater's Inn, Lake Wenatchee, Wash., 1981-83; property mgr. Spencer Property Mgmt., Santa Rosa, Calif., 1983-86; property mgmt. instr., founder Agapé Sch. Property Mgmt., Forestville, Calif., 1986—; spkr., Santa Rosa. Author: Professional Development, 1987; co-author: The Complete Reference Manual for Property Owners and Managers, 1988, The Complete Maintenance Manual for Property Owners and Managers, 1988, Practical On-site Mobile Home Park Management, 1998. Founder Project Genesis for the Homeless, Forestville, Calif., 1989. Recipient SBA award Nat. Bank Score, 1993. Democrat. Avocations: fly fishing, jazz music, drums, harmonica, singing.

SPENCER, ROBERT C., retired political science educator; b. Chgo., Mar. 28, 1920; m. Edith Maxham McCarthy, Sept. 13, 1941; children: Margaret, Catherine, Anne, Thomas More. David. AB, U. Chgo., 1943, MA, 1952, PhD in Polit. Sci. (Univ. fellow 1952-53), 1955. Instr. polit. sci. and sociology St. Michaels Coll., 1949-51, asst., then assoc. prof. polit. sci., 1953-60, prof. govt., 1960-63, dir. summer sessions, 1960-61, asst. to pres., 1963-65; prof. polit. sci., chmn. dept., dean summer sessions U. R.I., 1965-67; grad. dean U. R.I. (Grad. Sch.), 1967-69; founding pres. Sangamon State U., Springfield, Ill., 1969-78; prof. govt. and public affairs Sangamon State U., 1978-88; prof. emeritus U. Ill. Springfield, 1988-93, retired, 1993—; research assoc. Indsl. Relations Center, U. Chgo., 1952-53; extension lectr. N.Y. State Sch. Indsl. and Labor Relations, Cornell U., 1956-57; vice chmn. West Central Ill. Ednl. Telecommunications Consortium, 1975-77, chmn., 1977-78; chmn. task force personnel Vt. Little Hoover Commn., 1988-90; mem. Ill. adv. com. U.S. Commn. on Civil Rights, 1979-87; bd. mgrs. Franklin Life Variable Annuity Funds, 1974—; vis. prof. polit. sci., sr. rsch. assoc. local govt. ctr. Mont. State U., Bozeman, 1985, 89, 90—. Author: (with Robert J. Huckshorn) The Politics of Defeat, 1971. Bd. dirs. City Day Sch., Springfield, 1979-83, Gt. Am. People Show Repertory Co., 1980-90; vice chmn. Petersburg Libr. Bd., 1982-88; chmn. Petersburg Zoning Bd. Appeals, 1984-90; mem. Vt. Senate, 1959-63; faculty fellow Ford Found.'s Nat. Ctr. for Edn. in Politics, rsch. dir. Dem. Nat. Com., 1962-63; mem. adv. bd. Landmark Preservation Coun. Ill., 1986-89; mem., treas. Gallatin County Coun. on Aging, 1993—. Roman Catholic. Home: 2303 S 3rd Ave Bozeman MT 59715-6009*

SPENCER, TED, museum director. Exec. dir. Alaska Aviation Heritage Mus., Anchorage. Office: Alaska Aviation Heritage Mus 4721 Aircraft Dr Anchorage AK 99502-1080*

SPENCER, TRICIA JANE, writer; b. Springfield, Ill., Dec. 8, 1952; d. Frank Edward and LaWanda (Edwards) Bell; m. Mark Edward Spencer, Aug. 21, 1982. Student pub. schs. Instr., Falcons Drum & Bugle Corps, Springfield, 1969-72; concert, stage, TV, film performer, 1970-82, part-time 1982—; guest dir. Sing out Salem, Ohio, 1973; contbg. writer Saddle Tramps Wild West Revue, 1977—; legal sec. to pvt. atty., Tustin, Calif., 1980-82; owner Am. Dream Balloons & Svcs., Orange, Calif., 1982-89; founder, corp. pres. Am. Dream Limousine Svc., Inc., Orange, 1983-90; founder, pres., designer Am. Dream Creations Co., Inc., Irvine, Calif., 1988—; founder Am. Dream Bride's Mus., 1992. Songwriter; designer greeting cards, T-shirts and wedding related gifts; one-of-a-kind automobile; producer, dir. mus. stage shows, 1974-82; author: TIPS - The Server's Guide to Bringing Home the Bacon, 1987, There's a Bunny in the House, 1992, Real Rabbitts Don't Eat Lettuce, 1992, Elysium, 1996, Miracle Man, 1997, Deviled Eggs, 1998. Performer, Up With People, 1972-73; organizer Bicentennial Com. Springfield, 1976; mediator Limousine and Chauffeur Council, Orange County, 1984—; vol. Orange County Performing Arts Soc., 1985—. Recipient Appreciation, Achievement awards Muscular Dystrophy Assn., 1977-79, Transp. Partnership award, 1988, 7 songwriting and vocal performance awards Music City Song Festival, 1989, Outstanding Booth Display award Chgo. Gift Show, 1991; named one of top 100 Bridal Companies Assn. Bridal Consultants. Mem. Am. Entrepreneurs Assn., Internat. Platform Assn., Nat. Limousine Assn., So. Calif. Limousine Owners Assn., Nat. Assn. Female Execs., Nat. Bridal Assn., Orange County C. of C., Greenpeace, Doris Day Animal League. Republican. Avocations: guitar, piano, writing, animal welfare.

SPENGEMAN, EDWIN W., real estate executive; b. Jersey City, N.J., Feb. 6, 1934; s. Edmund Spengeman and Barbara A. (Erichsen) Drake; m. Dorothy Miskovsky, May 20, 1961 (dec. Sept., 1979); children: Barbara, Cathy, Judy; m. Deanne Martin, Nov. 28, 1980 (dec. Nov., 1995); stepchildren: Bob, Jeff Martin. BBA, U. Notre Dame, 1956. Lic. real estate broker, Ariz., Fla., S.C. Resale sales mgr. Mobil Oil Corp., Phila., 1959-74; sales exec. Sea Pines Realty, Hilton Head, S.C., 1974-81; gen. mgr. Hilton Head Co. Realty, Hilton Head, S.C., 1981-84; v.p. sales, mktg. Williams Island Assocs., Miami, Fla., 1985, Harbor Ridge, Stuart, Fla., 1985-92; real estate cons. Boca Raton, Fla., 1992-96; v.p. sales, mktg. Desert Mountain Assocs., Scottsdale, Ariz., 1996—; cons. Hilton Head, S.C., 1974-84, Boca Raton, Fla., 1984-96. Mem. NAR; mem. Notre Dame Club of Ariz. Republican. Roman Catholic. Home: 5316 E Calle De Los Flores Cave Creek AZ 85331-5574 Office: Desert Mt Assocs 3770 N Desert Mt Pkwy Scottsdale AZ 85262

SPERLING, SCOTT EDWARD, software consultant; b. Tucson, Jan. 11, 1961; s. Fritz Eric and Ruth Ann S.; m. Moon Hee, March 16, 1985; children: Scott Edward, Charlotte Moon. BSc in Applied Physics, Calif. Inst. Tech., Pasadena, 1983; BSc in Info Computer Sci. U Calif. Irvine 1985. Software engr. Interstate Electronics, Anaheim, Calif., 1985-87, Hughes Aircraft, Fullerton, Calif., 1987-88; software cons. Hughes Aircraft, 1988-91; adj. prof. Calif. State U Fullerton 1990-91; software cons. Litton Guidance & Control Sys., Woodland Hills, Calif., 1993—; prin., owner Scripture Studies Inc., SSper Inc., Foothill Ranch, Calif., 1994—, 1997—. Author, editor Scripture Studies, 1994—. Avocations: music, literature. E-mail: ssper@aol.com. Home and Office: Scripture Studies Inc 20 Pastora Foothill Ranch CA 92610-1730

SPERO, DIANE FRANCES, school director; b. Glen Ridge, N.J., Sept. 4, 1949; d. Gerard Anthony and Frances Dolores (Duffy) Racioppi; m. John David Spero, Feb. 21, 1971; children: John, Lisa. BA in Elem. Edn., Trenton (N.J.) State Coll., 1971; postgrad., Ariz. State U. Tchr. Mount Laurel (N.J.) Twp. Schs., 1971-75, Chandler (Ariz.) Unified Schs., 1975-77, Madison Sch. Dist., Phoenix, 1977-78; dir., tchr. Creative Art Sch. for Youth, Scottsdale, Ariz., 1985—. Choir dir., youth choir dir. St. Patricks Ch., Scottsdale, 1986-92; vol. Am. Diebetes Assn., 1990—, Am. Cancer Soc., 1990-93. Mem. ASCD, Nat. Assn. for the Edn. of Young Children, Ariz. assn. for the Edn. of Young Children, Assn. for Childhood Edn. Internat. Roman Catholic. Avocations: writing musical shows, reading. Home: 9208 N 83rd Pl Scottsdale AZ 85258-1884 Office: CASY Country Day Sch 7214 E Jenan Dr Scottsdale AZ 85260-5416

SPICER, RONALD L., education educator; b. Louisville, Jan. 21, 1949; s. Robert Joseph and Ann (Stafford) S.; m. Joan E. Vining, Dec. 20, 1969 (div. June 1988); children: Jennifer Joan Spicer McMuller, Ronald Geoffrey; m. JoAnn F. Snyder, Feb. 18, 1989; 1 child, Veronica Michelle. BS in Sociology, Carroll Coll., 1971, BS in Psychology, 1971; MA in Orgn. Mgmt., U. Phoenix, 1997. CPCU, CLU, CHFC, ARM. V.p. sales Alexander & Alexander, Atlanta, 1982-88; exec. v.p. Powell and Co., Atlanta, 1988-89; v.p. sales Corroon and Black, Balt., 1989-90; broker, owner Profl. Ins. Brokers, York, Pa., 1990-93; sr. account exec. Hilb, Rogal and Hamilton, Denver, 1993-95; ins. program coord. Pikes Peak C.C., Colorado Springs, 1995-97; pres., CEO Peak Profl. Svcs., Inc., Colorado Springs, 1997—, owner, 1997—; adv. com. Ins. Inst. of Am., Malvern, Pa., 1995—; mem. next generation com., Life and Health Ins. Edn. Assn., N.Y.C., 1996-97. Author: (book) Colorado P&C PreLicense Course, 1998; contbr. articles to profl. jours. Mem. Soc. CPCU (pres. 1998-99), Soc. CLU/CHFC (v.p. 1998-99), Optimist (pres. Uptown Club 1979-81), Masons. Republican. Episcopal. Avocations: skiing, camping, scuba diving. Home: 953 Bayfield Way Colorado Springs CO 80906 Office: Peak Profl Svcs Inc 620 N Tejon St Ste 201 Colorado Springs CO 80903

SPIEGEL, CHARLES (LOUIS S.J. SPIEGEL), psychology educator; b. Toronto, Mar. 27, 1921; came to U.S., 1938; s. Israel and Eva (Gilbert) S.; m. Ruth Kagan, Sept. 19, 1954 (div. Oct. 1970); 1 child, Laurence. BA, U. Toronto, 1948; MSc in Edn., U. So. Calif., L.A., 1951; cert., Inst. Gen. Semantics, Conn., 1950; postgrad., Unarius Acad. Sci., El Cajon, Calif., 1975-79. Lifetime cert. counseling, instr. psychology, gen. secondary cert. Aerial photographer RCAF, Toronto, 1939-42; instr. English, 1951-53; dir. fundraising United Jewish Appeal, Toronto, 1954-56; life ins. agt. Sunlife Ins. Co., Toronto and Boston, 1957-72; h.s. instr. English/math. San Diego Secondary Schs., 1972-75; instr. ednl. psychology San Diego C.C. Dist., 1975-81; instr. psychology Unarius Acad. Sci., El Cajon, Calif., 1981-93, psychology, physics dir., 1993—, past life therapy educator, 1981-96. Author: (autobiography) Confessions of I Bonaparte, 1985; editor: Interdimensional Physics, 1984; co-author 35 books on interdimensional physics and sci. of life. Sgt. USMC, 1942-46. Mem. Am. Psychol. Soc., Am. Phys. Soc. Avocations: sailing, bird watching, flying. Office: Unarius Acad Sci 145 S Magnolia Ave El Cajon CA 92020-4522

SPIEGEL, ROBERT MOORE, publishing executive, writer; b. Pontiac, Mich., Aug. 13, 1950; s. Thomas Burdette and Phyllis (Moore) S.; m. Jean Spiegel (div. Nov. 1976); m. C. Eleanor Bravo (div. Jan. 1991); m. Jill Sullivan, 1991; children: Jesse Bravo, Mara Terese, Connie Moore. B, U. N.Mex., 1980. Dir. mktg. Access Innovations, Albuquerque, 1982-85; v.p. S.W. Press, Albuquerque, 1985-86; pres. Out West Pub., Albuquerque, 1986—; CFO Border Books, Inc., 1993—; pres. Spiegel Enterprises, 1997—. Author: (book of poems) Stepping in the Field, 1985, (books) Quit Your Day Job, 1999, The Shoestring Entrepreneur's Guide to the Best Home Businesses, 1999, The Complete Home Business Guide, 1999; pub. (mag.) The Whole Chile Pepper (now Chile Pepper Mag.), 1988-96, (newsletter) Freelancers Marketplace, 1998—. Dem. Ward chmn., Albuquerque, 1988; bd. dirs. Christ Unity Ch., 1992-96 (pres. 1995-96). Mem. Am. Mktg. Assn. (pres. N.Mex. chpt. 1987-88), Mag. Pubs. Am. (edn. com. 1992—). Home: PO Box 20130 Albuquerque NM 87154-0130

SPIEGEL, RONALD STUART, insurance company executive; b. Chgo., Sept. 12, 1942; s. Arthur I. and Elaine M. (Young); m. Carol J. Lieberthal, July 25, 1964; children: Eric, Elissa. BA, Calif. State U., Los Angeles, 1966. Pres. Newhouse Automotive, Los Angeles, 1966-78; agt. N.Y. Life Ins. Co., Santa Fe Springs, Calif., 1978-82, sales mgr., 1982-86, assoc. gen. mgr., 1986-88, gen. mgr., 1989-91; assoc. gen. mgr. N.Y. Life Ins. Co., Fullerton, Calif., 1991—; v.p. Cerritos Valley Br. Life Underwriters Assn. of Los Angeles, 1984-86, pres., 1987-88. Pres. Temple Shalom, West Covina, Calif., 1975-77, 88-89, 93-94, treas., 1978-83; pres. Temple Ami-Shalom, West Covina, 1994-95, Jewish Fedn. Coun. Ea. Region, L.A., 1986-89, v.p., 1984-85. Mem. Am. Soc. CLUs, Gen. Agts. and Mgrs. Assn., Airline Owners and Pilots Assn. Nat. Assn. Life Underwriters. Democrat. Lodge: Kiwanis. Avocation: flying, golf. Home: 5050 Coldwater Canyon Ave # 401 Sherman Oaks CA 91423-1670 Office: NY Life Ins Co 3230 E Imperial Hwy Ste 100 Brea CA 92821-6735

SPIEGELBERG, EMMA JO, business education educator, academic administrator; b. Mt. View, Wyo., Nov. 22, 1936; d. Joseph Clyde and Dorcas (Reese) Hatch; BA with honors, U. Wyo., 1958, MEd, 1985; EdD Boston U., 1990; m. James Walter Spielberg, June 22, 1957; children: William L., Emory Walter, Joseph John. Tchr. bus. edn. Laramie (Wyo.) High Sch., 1960-61, 65-93, adminstr., 1993-97; prin. McCormick Jr. H.S., Cheyenne, Wyo., 1997—. Bd. dirs. Cathedral Home for Children, Laramie, 1967-70, pres., 1985-88, Laramie Plains Mus., 1970-79. Author: Branigan's Accounting Simulation, 1986, London & Co. II, 1993; co-author: Glencoe Computerized Accounting, 1993, 2nd edit., 1995, Microcomputer Accounting: Daceasy, 1994, Microcomputer Accounting: Peachtree, 1994, Microcomputer Accounting: Accpac, 1994, Computerized Accounting with Peachtree, 1995, Glencoe Computerized Accounting: Peachtree, 1995. Named Wyo. Bus. Tchr. of Yr., 1982, Wyo. Acct. Tchr. of Yr. 1997. Mem. Am. Vocat. Assn. (policy com. region V 1984-87, region V Tchr. of Yr. 1986), Wyo. Vocat. Assn. (exec. bd. 1978-80, pres. 1981-82, Outstanding Contbns. to Vocat. Edn. award 1983, Tchr. of Yr. 1985, exec. sec. 1986-89), Nat. Bus. Edn. Assn. (bd. dirs. 1987-88, 1991-96, Sec. Tchr. of the Yr. 1991), Mt. Plains Bus. Edn. Assn. (Wyo. rep. to bd. dirs. 1982-85, pres. 1987-88, Sec. Tchr. of the Yr. 1991, Leadership award 1992), Internat. Soc. Bus. Edn., Wyo. Bus. Edn. Assn. (pres. 1979-80), NEA, Wyo. Edn. Assn., Albany County Edn. Assn. (sec. 1970-71), Nat. Assn. Secondary Sch. Prins., Wyo. Assn. Secondary Sch. Prins. (exec. bd. C. of C. (bd. dirs. 1985-88), U. Wyo. Alumni Assn. (bd. dirs. 1985-90pres. 1988-89), Kappa Delta Pi, Phi Delta Kappa, Alpha Delta Kappa (state pres. 1978-82), Chi Omega, Pi Lambda Theta, Delta Pi Epsilon. Mem. United Ch. of Christ. Club: Zonta. Home: 3310 Grays Gable Rd Laramie WY 82072-5031 Office: McCormick Jr HS 6000 Education Dr Cheyenne WY 82009

SPIELBERG, STEVEN, motion picture director, producer; b. Cin., Dec. 18, 1946; m. Amy Irving, Nov. 27, 1985 (div.); 2 children: Max Samuel, Sasha; m. Kate Capshaw; 1 dau. BA, Calif. State Coll., Long Beach; Hon. Doctorate in Creative Arts, Brandeis U., 1986. Founder Amblin Entertainment (Universal Studios), Dreamworks SKG (with Jeffrey Katzenberg and David Geffen); directed segments of TV series Columbo; dir. TV movies Night Gallery, 1969, Duel, 1971, Savage, 1972, Something Evil, 1972; exec prodr. series: Steven Spielberg's Amazing Stories, Tiny Toon Adventures, Family Dog, seaQuest DSV; films include (dir.): The Sugarland Express, 1974 (also story), Jaws, 1975, Close Encounters of the Third Kind, 1977 (also co-writer), 1941, 1979, Raiders of the Lost Ark, 1981, Indiana Jones and the Temple of Doom, 1984, Indiana Jones and the Last Crusade, 1989, Hook, 1991, Jurassic Park, 1993, Men in Black, 1996, (dir., prodr.): E.T. The Extra-Terrestrial, 1982, The Color Purple, 1985, Empire of the Sun, 1987 Always 1989, Schindler's List, 1993 (Best Drama & Best Dir. Golden Globe awards, Best Picture & Best Dir. Acad. awards), Saving Private Ryan (Golden Globe award for Best Dir. 1999, nominee Best Picture and Best Dir. 1999); (prodr.): Poltergeist, 1982 (also co-writer) An American Tail, 1986, Fievel Goes West, 1991, Casper, 1995; (exec. prodr.): I Wanna Hold Your Hand, 1978, Used Cars, 1980, Continental Divide, 1981, Gremlins, 1984, The Goonies, 1985, Back to the Future, 1985, Young Sherlock Holmes, 1985, The Money Pit, 1986, An American Tail, 1986, Innerspace, 1987, *batteries not included,

1987, Who Framed Roger Rabbit?, 1988, The Land Before Time, 1988, Dad, 1989, Back to the Future Part II, 1989, Joe Verses the Volcano, 1990, Back to the Future Part III, 1990, Gremlins 2: The New Batch, 1990, Arachnophobia, 1990, Cape Fear, 1991, We're Back!: A Dinosaur's Story, 1993, The Flintstones, 1994, The Little Rascals, 1994, Balto, 1995, Twister, 1996, The Lost World, 1997, Amistad, 1997, Deep Impact, 1998, The Mask of Zorro, 1998, The Last Days, 1998; (T.V. series) Steven Spielberg Presents Toonsylvania, 1998; (actor): The Blues Brothers, 1980. Recipient Man of Yr. award Hasty Pudding Theater, Harvard U., 1983, Outstanding Directorial Achievement award for feature films Dirs. Guild Am., 1985, Film award Brit. Acad. Film and TV Arts, 1986, Irving Thalberg Mem. award Acad. Motion Picture Arts and Scis., 1987, Golden Lion award for career achievement Venice Film Festival, 1993, Life Achievement award Am. Film Inst., 1995. Fellow Brit. Acad. Film and TV Arts. Won film contest with 40-minute war movie, Escape to Nowhere, at age 13; made film Firelight at age 16, and made 5 films while in coll.; became TV dir. at Universal Pictures at age 20. Office: CAA 9830 Wilshire Blvd Beverly Hills CA 90212-1804*

SPIER, LUISE EMMA, film editor, director; b. Laramie, Wyo., Aug. 22, 1928; d. Louis Constantine Cames and Vina Jane Cochran; m. John Spier, Sept., 1957 (div. 1962). Student, U. Wyo., 1947, U. Calif., Berkeley, 1948-53. Head news film editor Sta. KRON-TV, San Francisco, 1960-70, film editor, 1980—; freelance film editor, director San Francisco, 1970-80, 83—. Edited and directed numerous news specials and documentaries, including The Lonely Basque, Whaler, The American Way of Eating. Recipient numerous awards for film editing and directing, including Cine Golden Eagle, Best Med. Res. Film award John Muir Med. Found., Chris Statuette, Bronze and Silver Cindy awards Info. Film Producers Am.

SPIERING, NANCY JEAN, accounting executive; b. Park Ridge, Ill., Apr. 15, 1958; d. Richard Arthur and Helen Mary (Henry) S. BS, De Paul U., 1982; postgrad., U. Minn., North Ctrl. Coll., 1989-90; MBA, U. Phoenix, 1998. CPA, Ill. Staff acct. Ruzicka & Assocs., Inc., Chgo., 1980-84; supr. acctg. Cargill, Inc., Carpentersville, Ill., 1984-87, regional asst. acctg. mgr., 1988-89; sr. internat. tax acct. Cargill, Inc., Minnetonka, Minn., 1989-90; acctg. mgr. Barnant Co. divsn. Cole Parmer, Barrington, Ill, 1990-98, Matac divsn. Bemis, N. Las Vegas, 1998—; mgr. Twin Pines Janitorial Service, Elgin, Ill., 1980-89; pvt. practice tax service, Elgin, 1984-89; acctg. supr. Bonanza Materials, Inc., Henderson, Nev., 1994—. Official Michael Bakalis campaign, Chgo., 1980; vol. Disabled Am. Vets., Cin., 1987. Mem. Am. Soc. CPA's, Ill. Soc. CPA's, Chgo. Soc. Women CPA's. Roman Catholic. Club: Dundee Dart (Ill). Avocations: raising and tng. dogs, reading Gothic novels, gardening, English darts, ceramics. Home: 7521 Gilmore Ave Las Vegas NV 89129-6577 Office: Matac 4701 Mitchell St North Las Vegas NV 89031-2728

SPIES, KAREN BORNEMANN, writer, education consultant; b. Renton, Wash., Sept. 5, 1949; d. William Edward and Aina Jeanette (Johnson) Bornemann; m. Allan Roy Spies, July 18, 1970; children: Karsten, Astrid. BA, Calif. Luth. U., Thousand Oaks, 1970; MEd, U. Wash., 1974. Vice prin., tchr. Lake Washington Sch. Dist., Kirkland, Wash., 1971-79; tchr. various pub. schs. N.J., 1979-82; kindergarten tchr. Mt. Park Sch., Lake Oswego, Oreg., 1982-84; writer, seminar leader, cons. Wash., 1984-87, Oreg., 1984-87, Littleton, Colo., 1987—; lectr. Arapahoe Community Coll., Littleton, 1988—; ski instr. various locations, 1974—; curriculum writer Augsburg-Fortress Pubs.; lectr. in field. Author: Family Activities for the Christmas Season, 1988, Denver, 1988, Raffi: The Children's Voice, 1989, Visiting in the Global Village, Vol. I, 1990, Vol. II, 1991, Vol. III, 1992, Vol. IV, 1993, Vol. V, 1994, Everything You Need to Know About Grieving, 1990, Competitiveness, 1991, Barbara Bush, 1991, George Bush, 1991, Everything You Need to Know About Incest, 1992, Our National Holidays, 1992, Our Money, 1992, The American Family: Can It Survive, 1993, Everything You Need to Know About Diet Fads, 1993, Our Folk Heroes, 1994, Earthquakes, 1994, Our Presidency, 1994, Isolation vs. Intervention, 1995, Buffalo Bill Cody: Western Legend, 1998, Franklin D. Roosevelt, 1999. Organist Wooden Cross Luth. Ch., 1977-79. Title III grantee, 1974. Mem. AAUW, Soc. Children's Book Writers and Illustrators, Mensa, Profl. Ski Instrs. Am., Pi Lambda Theta. Republican. Lutheran. Avocations: tennis, reading, sewing, skiing.

SPIKES, BARBRA JEAN, claims processor; b. Chgo., Nov. 12, 1951; d. Robert Harold and Eva Mae (Shaw) Ralston; m. Nicholas Robert Barron Spikes (div.). Grad. Morgan Park H.S., Chgo.; student, Kennedy King Jr. Coll. Author of poetry. Mem. So. Christian Leadership Conf., Chgo., 1968. Home: 141 Creek Way Santa Rosa CA 95403-8081

SPINDLER, GEORGE DEARBORN, anthropologist, educator, author, editor; b. Stevens Point, Wis., Feb. 28, 1920; s. Frank Nicholas and Winifred (Hatch) S.; m. Louise Schaubel, May 29, 1942; 1 dau., Sue Carol Spindler Coleman. B.S., Central State Tchrs. Coll., Wis., 1940; M.A., U. Wis., 1947; Ph.D., U. Calif. at Los Angeles, 1952. Tchr. sch. in Wis., 1940-42; research asso. Stanford, 1950-51, mem. faculty, 1951—, prof. anthropology and edn., 1960-78, exec. head dept., 1963-67, 84; vis. prof. U. Wis., Madison, 1979, 80, 81, 82, 83, 84, 85; editor Am. Anthropologist, 1962-66; cons. editor Holt, Rinehart & Winston, 1965-91, Harcourt, Brce, 1991—; vis. prof. U. Calif., Santa Barbara, 1986-91. Author: Menomini Acculturation, 1955, (with A. Beals and L. Spindler) Culture in Process, 1967, rev. edit., 1973, Transmission of American Culture, 1959, (with L. Spindler) Dreamers Without Power, 1971, rev. edit., 1984, Burgbach: Urbanization and Identity in a German Village, 1973, (with Louise Spindler) The American Cultural Dialogue and its Transmission, 1990; editor: Education and Anthropology, 1955, (with Louise Spindler) Case Studies in Cultural Anthropology, 1960—, Methods in Cultural Anthropology, 1965—, Case Studies in Education and Culture, 1966—, Basic Units in Anthropology, 1970; editor, contbr.: Education and Culture, 1963, Being An Anthropologist, 1970, Education and Cultural Process, 1974, rev. edit., 1987, 97, The Making of Psychological Anthropology, 1978, 2nd edit., 1994, Doing the Ethnography of Schooling, 1982, Interpretive Ethnography of Schooling at Home and Abroad, 1987, Pathways to Cultural Awareness: Cultural Therapy with Students and Teachers, 1994. Pres. Peninsula Sch. Bd., Menlo Park, Calif., 1954-56. Served with AUS, 1942-45. Recipient Lloyd W. Dinkelspell award Stanford U., 1978, Disting. Svc. award Soc. Internat. Diplomacy and Third World Anthropologists, 1984, Disting. Career Contbn. award Com. on Role and Status of Minorities, Am. Edn. Rsch. Assn., Nat. Acad. Edn., 1994; fellow Ctr. Advanced Study of Behavioral Scis., 1956-57; subject of Vol. 17 Psychoanalytic Study of Soc. essays, 1992. Fellow Am. Anthrop. Assn.; mem. Southwestern Anthrop. Assn. (pres. 1962-63), Coun. for Anthropology and Edn. (pres. 1982, George and Louise Spindler award for outstanding contbns. to ednl. anthropology 1987, disting. Scholar award 1998), Nat. Acad. Edn. Home: 1274 Alice Dr Davis CA 95616 Office: Ethnographics 1247 Alice St Davis CA 95616

SPINK, DOUGLAS B., technology executive; b. Pitts., Feb. 17, 1971; s. Jack Derry and Claire (LaConte) S.; m. Judy Kathleen Forton, Oct. 10, 1995; children: Matthew, Casey, Becky, Carrie. BA in Anthropology, Reed Coll., 1993; MBA in Mktg., U. Chgo., 1994. Database mktg. cons. Leo Barnett & Col., Inc., Chgo., 1993-94; strategic cons. Basten Cons. Group, Chgo., 1994; v.p. analytic svcs. Ideon Group, Inc., Portland, 1994-96; western region dir. Tenera Enterprise Systems, Portland, 1996—. Rhodes scholar, 1993; U. Chgo. Bus. fellow, 1992. Mem. Soc. Info. Mgmt., Direct Mktg. Assn., Data Warehousing Inst. Episcopalian. Avocations: ultramarathoning, rock climbing, snowboarding. Home: 21641 NW Dairy Creek Rd Cornelius OR 97113-6115

SPINN, MARIAN ROSE, artist, retired realtor; b. St. Louis, June 29, 1926; d. Leo J. and Alvina (Luepker) Schneider; m. Robert D Spinn, Oct. 15, 1946; 1 child, Douglas R. Student, Washington U., St. Louis, 1945, U. Hawaii, 1982, 84, 87, Palomar, 1990-91. Prin. Marian Spinn Realty, Honolulu, 1976-88. One woman shows include San Diego, 1998; exhibited in group shows including Hawaii Watercolor Soc., 1975-88, Assn. Honolulu Artists, 1977-80, Nat. League Am. Pen Women, 1977-88, City & County Honolulu, 1981, Office of Lt. Gov. Hawaii, 1981, Gov.'s Office, Honolulu, 1982, Hawaii Artists League, 1985, Hawaii Women's History Week Show, 1987; represented in permanent collections including, State Hawaii Collection, Castle & Cook Collection (Dole), Hawaii, Senator Salii of Saipan, Sun Gold Investment Co., San Francisco, Russ Tummelson, Martin & MacArthur Co., Honolulu, Knish Collection, Honolulu; represented in numerous private collections; contbr. articles to profl. jours. Mem. Hawaii Watercolor Soc. (pres. 1980-81, Best of Show award 1977, 1st Pl. Ann. Dinner awards 1975, 80, 2d Pl. award 1982), Nat. League Am. Pen Women (v.p. 1985-86, 98), Assn. Honolulu Artists, San Diego Watercolor Soc., Honolulu Acad. Arts. Home: 1476 Sierra Linda Dr Escondido CA 92025-7629

SPINWEBER, CHERYL LYNN, psychologist, sleep specialist; b. Jersey City, July 26, 1950; d. Stanley A. And Evelyn M. (Pfleger) S.; m. Michael E. Bruich, June 18, 1977; children: Sean Michael Bruich, Gregory Alan Bruich. AB with distinction, Cornell U., 1972; PhD in Exptl. Psychology, Harvard U., 1977. Lic. psychologist, Calif. Asst. prof. psychiatry Tufts U. Sch. Medicine, Medford, Mass., 1977-79; asst. dir. sleep lab. Boston State Hosp., 1973-79; dep. head dept. behavioral psychopharmacology Naval Health Research Ctr., San Diego, 1978-86, head dept. behavioral psychopharmacology, 1986-89; research asst. prof. dept. psychiatry Uniformed Svcs. U. of the Health Scis., Bethesda, Md., 1985—; lectr. workshop instr. U. Calif. San Diego, La Jolla, 1979-81, vis. lectr. 1979-86; assoc. adj. prof. Dept. Psychology, 1989-94, adj. prof., 1994—; courtesy clin. staff appointee dept. psychiatry Naval Hosp., San Diego, 1984-89, clin. dir. Sleep Disorders Ctr. Mercy Hosp., San Diego, 1991—; pediatric sleep specialist Children's Hosp., San Diego, 1992-95. Contbr. articles to profl. jours. Scholar Cornell U., Ithaca, N.Y., 1968-72, West Essex Tuition, 1968-72, Cornell U. Fedn. Women, 1917-72, Harvard U., 1972-73, 74-76, NDEA Title IV, 1973-74; postdoctoral associateship Nat. Research Council, 1978-80, Outstanding Tchg. award U. Calif. San Diego, 1994. Fellow Am. Sleep Disorders Assn., Clin. Sleep Soc., We. Psychol. Assn. (sec.-treas. 1986—); mem. Am. Men and Women of Sci., Sleep Rsch. Soc. (exec. com. 1986-89), Calif. Sleep Soc., Sigma Xi.

SPIRTOS, ANDREA C., columnist; b. Freeport, Ill., May 23, 1952; d. Carl E. H. and Eldora E. (Baker) DeFrane; m. Nicholas George Spirtos, Aug. 19, 1979. BA in Psych., BA in Edn. cum laude, U. Dubuque, 1973; MA in Guidance Counseling cum laude, U. Iowa, 1974; JD, Loyola U., L.A., 1983; EdD in Instl. Mgmt., Pepperdine U., 1994. Tchr., counselor Kennedy H.S., Cedar Rapids, Iowa, 1973-74; counselor UCLA, 1974-77; youth cons. Am. Red Cross, 1977-79; dir. donor svcs. and shelter svcs. United Way, 1979-80; dir. youth svcs. Am. Heart Assn., 1980-82; pres. Comprehensive Office Sys. Technology, 1982; co-founder, corp. officer Pacific Multiple Sclerosis Rsch. Found., 1982-99; devel. dir. Junipero Serra H.S., 1987-88; v.p. Compensation Strategies, 1988; office mgr. Law Office of Nicholas G. Spirtos, 1982—; pres. Tekni-query Cons., 1990-99; account rep. Met. Life, 1996; contbr. The Desert Woman Monthly, Palm Springs, Calif., 1997—; columnist Charity Check The Desert Sun Gannet Pub., 1997—. Author: Not in My Wildest Dreams, 1995; co-editor, author: Cutting Edge Technologies: The Future of Community Colleges, 1993; columnist: Seventeen Mag., 1969-70, Freeport Jour. Standard, 1968-70, Freeport H.S. Gazette, 1967-70, Trumpeter, 1990-92; columnist, editor, layout Youth News, 1977-82. Recipient Danworth fellow, 1973-74, medallion of recognition Joint Chiefs of Staff U.S., 1993, Presdl. Order of Merit, 1991, Presdl. Legion of Merit, 1992. Mem. Am. Pen Women, Internat. Platform Assn. (gov. 1994—, author poetry newsletter 1995-96, co-editor poetry anthology 1992, 93, 94, 95), Amnesty Internat., Kappa Delta Pi. Republican. Greek Orthodox. Avocations: painting, knitting, hot rodding, organic gardening, gourment cooking. E-mail: rydnhd1@aol.com. Office: Law Office of Nicholas G Spirtos Ste D-404 44489 Town Center Way Palm Desert CA 92260

SPIRTOS, NICHOLAS GEORGE, lawyer, financial company executive; b. Youngstown, Ohio, Mar. 19, 1950; s. George Nicholas Spirtos and Tulla (Palaologos) Waldron; m. Andrea Carel DeFrane, Aug. 19, 1979. BA in Physics, Philosophy, UCLA, 1969, MA in Biochemistry, 1974, JD, 1978. Bar: Calif., 1978; cert. rape crisis counselor, Calif. Intelligence analyst, 1969-72; dir. product devel. Adolph's Food Products, Burbank, Calif., 1972-73; asst. to pres. Eckel Research and Devel., San Fernando, Calif., 1973-74; dep. State Public Defender Los Angeles, 1977-82; pvt. practice Pacific Palisades, Calif., 1982-94, Palm Desert, Calif., 1994—; co-founder Tekni-Query Cons., 1990; appellate lawyer Calif. and U.S. Supreme Ct., 1982; exec. v.p. Gen. Counsel Compensation Strategies Group, Santa Ana, Calif., 1988-89; pro bono legal counsel Junipero Serra H.S., Gardena, Calif., 1987-88; cons. to U.S. Govt., 1982—; bd. dirs. Myelin Project, Washington, 1993-95. Patentee solubilization of Sodium CMC at room temperature, 1972. Founder, fund raiser Pacific Multiple Sclerosis Research Found., Beverly Hills, Calif., 1982—, coordinator with Reed Neurology Ctr. at UCLA; bd. dirs. John F. Kennedy Ctr. Performing Arts, Very Spl. Arts for Cachella Valley, 1996—. Westinghouse Sci. scholar, 1965; recipient Gregor Mendell award in genetics, 1962; named Jr. Engr. of Yr. Am. Assn. Aero. Engrs., 1963, Outstanding Speaker U. So. Calif., 1965. Mem. State Bar Calif., Am. Pen Women (assoc.), Internat. Platform Assn., Mensa. Independent. Greek Orthodox. Avocation: classic automobiles. Office: 44489 Town Center Way # D-404 Palm Desert CA 92260-2723

SPITALERI, VERNON ROSARIO, newspaper publisher, manufacturing company executive; b. Pelham, N.Y., Aug. 2, 1922; s. Rosario S. and Martha (Landerer) S.; m. Marjorie A. Ferrar, Oct. 14, 1952; children: Marc, Eric, Kris, Lynn. B.S., Carnegie Mellon U., 1942. Mgr. mech. dept. Am. Newspaper Pubs. Assn., N.Y.C., 1946-53; research dir., gen. adminstr. Miami Herald and Knight Newspapers (Fla.), 1953-57; chmn. bd., pres. Sta-Hi Corp., Newport Beach, Calif., 1957-74; v.p. Republic Corp., 1974-76, Sun Chem. Corp., 1976-79; chmn. bd. Sta-Hi Color Service, Sta-Hi Europe, Brussels, Concrete Floats-Huntington Engring. Corp., Huntington Beach, Calif., Kamalloy Alloys Corp.; editor, pub. Laguna Beach (Calif.) News-Post, 1967-81; pres. Laguna Pub. Co., Nat. Newspaper Found.; dir. Suburban Newspapers Am.; chmn. bd. Victory Profl. Products, Mango Surfware. Pres., Boys Club, Laguna Beach; mem. citizens adv. com. Laguna Beach; pres. Laguna Beach Library Bd., Laguna Playhouse, Laguna Coordinating Council; bd. dirs. Sta-Hi Found.; dir. Opera Pacific. Served to lt. comdr. USNR, 1942-46. Decorated Purple Heart. Mem. Am. Mgmt. Assn., Nat. Newspaper Assn. (dir.), Calif. Newspaper Pubs. Assn. (dir.), Laguna Beach C. of C. (bd. dir.), Alpha Tau Omega. Republican. Roman Catholic. Club: Dana Point Yacht.

SPITZER, MATTHEW L., retired retail store executive; b. Pitts., June 20, 1929; s. Martin and Ruth G. S.; student U. Buffalo, 1948-50; children: Mark, Edward, Eric, Joseph. Lic. airline transport pilot. Product line mgr. Gen. Dynamics, Rochester, N.Y., 1962-67; dir. contracts Friden div. Singer, San Leandro, Calif., 1968-69; asst. v.p. Talcott Computer Leasing, San Francisco, 1970-71; pres. Spitzer Music Mgmt. Co., Hayward, Calif., 1972-95; pres. Spitzer Helicopter Leasing Co., Hayward, Calif.; chmn. bd. Leo's Audio and Music Techs., Oakland, Calif.; Masons, Mensa. Office: 5447 Telegraph Ave Oakland CA 94609-1921

SPIVAK, KENIN M., broadcast executive; b. N.Y.C., May 14, 1957; s. Edwin Howard and Charlotte S. AB, Columbia U., 1977, MBA, 1980, JD, 1980. V.p. Merrill Lynch Capital Markets, 1985-88; pres. Island World Group, 1991-94; COO Maniua Comm. Co., 1988-90; co-chmn., exec. com. Premiere Radio Network, L.A., 1995-97; chmn. Knowledge Exch., L.A., 1995-97; pres., CEO Archon Comm., Inc., L.A., 1995-97; vice chmn. John Paul Mitchell Systems, Beverly Hills, Calif., 1996—; chmn., CEO Spivak Sports, L.A., 1997—; chmn. Aquarius Holdings, Inc., L.A., 1997—; chmn., CEO Telemac Corp., 1998—. Editor: Knowledge Exchange Business Encyclopedia. Office: Ste 1205 9701 Wilshire Blvd Ste 1205 Beverly Hills CA 90212-2019

SPLANE, RICHARD BEVERLEY, social work educator; b. Calgary, Alta., Can., Sept. 25, 1916; s. Alfred William and Clara Jane (Allyn) S.; m. Verna Marie Huffman, Feb. 22, 1971. BA, McMaster U., 1940, LLD (hon.), 1990; cert. social sci. and adminstrn., London Sch. Econs., 1947; MA, U. Toronto, 1948, MSW, 1951, PhD, 1961; LLD (hon.), Wilfrid Laurier U., 1988, U. B.C., Can., 1996. Exec. dir. Children's Aid Soc., Cornwall, Ont., Can., 1948-50; with Health and Welfare Can., Ottawa, 1952-72; exec. asst. to dep. minister nat. welfare Health and Welfare Can., 1959-60, dir. unemployment assistance, 1960-62, dir. gen. welfare assistance and services, 1960-70, asst. dep. minister social allowances and services, 1970-72; vis. prof. U. Alta., Edmonton, 1972-73; prof. social policy Sch. Social Work, U. B.C., Vancouver, 1973—; cons. Govt. Can., Govt. Alta., UNICEF. Author: The Development of Social Welfare in Ontario, 1965; (with Verna Huffman Splane) Chief Nursing Officers in National Ministries of Health, 1994, 75 Years of Community Service to Canada: Canadian Council on Social Development, 1920-1995. Served with RCAF, 1942-45. Recipient Centennial medal Govt. Can., 1967, Charles E. Hendry award U. Toronto, 1981, Commemorative medal for 125th anniversary of Confedn. of Can., 1992, Disting. Svc. award Internat. Coun. on Social Welfare, 1996. Mem. Can. Assn. Social Workers (Outstanding Nat. Svc. award 1985), Can. Inst. Pub. Adminstrn., Can. Hist. Assn., Can. Coun. on Social Devel. (Lifetime Achievement award 1995), Internat. Assn. Schs. Social Work, Internat. Confs. Social Devel., World Federalists of Can., Vancouver Club, Order of Can. Mem. United Ch. Can.

SPOLTER, PARI DOKHT, scientific books writer; b. Teheran, Iran, Jan. 30, 1930; came to U.S., 1957; m. Herbert Spolter, Aug. 16, 1958; children: David, Deborah. Licence chimie biologique, U. Geneva, 1952; PhD in Biochemistry, U. Wis., 1961. Rsch. assoc., instr. Temple U., Phila., 1961-65; rsch. biochemist U.S. Pub. Health Svc. Hosp., San Francisco, 1965-68; writer Orb Pub. Co., Granada Hills, Calif., 1988—. Mem. AAAS, Am. Math. Soc., N.Y. Acad. Scis. Office: Orb Pub Co 11862 Balboa Blvd # 182 Granada Hills CA 91344-2753

SPOOR, JAMES EDWARD, human resouces executive, entrepreneur; b. Rockford, Ill., Feb. 19, 1936; s. Frank Kendall and Genevieve Eileen (Johnson) S.; BS in Psychology, U. Ill., 1958; m. Nancy E. Carlson, Sept. 8, 1962; children: Sybll K., Kendall P., Andrea K., Marcie K. Pers. mgr. Nat. Sugar Refining Co., N.Y.C., 1960-64, Pepsico, Inc., N.Y.C., Auburn, N.Y., 1964-67; mgr. internat. pers. Control Data Corp., Mpls., 1967-75; v.p. pers. and employee rels. Vetco, Inc., Ventura, Calif., 1975-79; v.p. employee rels. Hamilton Bros. Oil Co., Denver, 1979-84; pres., CEO Spectrum Human Resource Systems Corp., 1984—; cons., author, spkr. on human resources and entrepreneurism. Mem. adv. bd. Salvation Army, 1978-79; chmn. Spl. Commn. for Ventura County Bd. Suprs., 1978; mem. task force on human resources Colo. Sch. Mines, 1983; state chairperson Coun. Growing Cos., 1991-92, nat. pres., 1992-94; bd. dirs. Breckenridge Outdoor Edn. Ctr., 1994-98, chmn., 1996-98, Nat. Bd. dirs. Internat. Human Resource Mgmt. Assn., 1997—.

SPRAGGS, LAURENCE DALE, educator; b. Flint, Mich., July 7, 1947; s. Robert Henry and Lorena May (Smith) S. BA, Wayne State U., 1970, MSc, 1973; ArtsD, Idaho State U., 1980. Assoc. prof. North Country C.C., Saranac Lake, N.Y., 1980-86, dir. continuing edn., 1986-92; dean math and sci. Red Rocks C.C., Lakewood, Colo., 1992-96, v.p. instruction, 1996—. Mem. Colo. Alliance for Sci. (bd. govs.), Rotary. Office: Red Rocks Community Coll 13300 W 6th Ave Lakewood CO 80228-1213

SPRINCZ, KEITH STEVEN, financial services company professional; b. Whitewater, Wis., Mar. 8, 1956; s. Steven B. Sprincz and Mary Lou (Crotte) Zolli; m. Renee Michele Werner, Sept. 11, 1982; children: Nicholas, Cameron. BS in Mktg., Colo. State U., 1978; student, Am. Coll., 1985-86. CLU, ChFC. Agt. Prudential, Denver, 1978-83; ins. broker Nolen/Western, Denver, 1983-88, ptnr., 1988—; pres. Sprincz and Assoc., Inc., Englewood, Colo., 1997—; tchr. Life Underwriters Tng. Coun., Bethesda, Md., 1991-92. Chmn. bd. elders Bethlehem Luth. Ch., Lakewood, Colo., 1989; campmaster coord. Boy Scouts Am., Denver, 1989—, scoutmaster, 1983—; capt. March of Dimes, Denver, 1981, Big Bros., Denver, 1984; pres. Centennial Assn. Life Underwriters, 1986-87; sch. bd. mem., 1993—, pres., 1995—. Recipient Outstanding Family award Boy Scouts Am., 1986. Avocations: stamp collecting, fishing, softball, gardening. Office: Sprincz and Assocs Inc 5690 Dtc Blvd Ste 345 Englewood CO 80111-3232

SPRINGER, CHARLES EDWARD, retired state supreme court chief justice; b. Reno, Feb. 20, 1928; s. Edwin and Rose Mary Cecelia (Kelly) S.; m. Jacqueline Sirkegian, Mar. 17, 1951; 1 dau., Kelli Ann. BA, U. Nev., Reno, 1950; LLB, Georgetown U., 1953; LLM, U. Va., 1984; student Grad. Program for Am. Judges, Oriel Coll., Oxford (Eng.), 1984. Bar: Nev. 1953, U.S. Dist. Ct. Nev. 1953, D.C. 1954, U.S. Supreme Ct. 1962. Pvt. practice law Reno, 1953-80; atty. gen. State of Nev., 1962, legis. legal adv. to gov., 1958-62; legis. bill drafter Nev. Legislature, 1955-57; mem. faculty Nat. Coll. Juvenile Justice, Reno, 1978—; juvenile master 2d Jud. Dist. Nev., 1973-80; justice Nev. Suprem Ct., Carson City, 1981—; vice-chief justice Nev. Supreme Ct., Carson City, 1987, chief justice, 1998—, ret., 1999; mem. Jud. Selection Commn., 1981, 98, Nev. Supreme Ct. Gender Bias Task Force, 1981—; trustee Nat. Coun. Juvenile and Family Ct. Judges, 1983—; mem. faculty McGeorge Sch. Law, U. Nev., Reno, 1982—; mem. Nev. Commn. for Women, 1991-95. With AUS, 1945-47. Recipient Outstanding Contbn. to Juvenile Justice award Nat. Coun. Juvenile and Family Ct. Judges, 1989, Midby-Byron Disting. Leadership award U. Nev., 1988. Mem. ABA, Am. Judicature Soc., Am. Trial Lawyers Assn., Phi Kappa Phi. Office: Nev Supreme Ct Capitol Complex 201 S Carson St Carson City NV 89701-4702

SPRINGER, GERALD WILLIAM, sales executive; b. Amherst, Ohio, Nov. 13, 1943; s. Raymond W. and Ione J. (Myers) S.; m. Marilyn F. Gregg, Aug. 28, 1971. BBA, Kent State U., 1966. Dist. sales mgr. Flintkote Co., Kent, Ohio, 1970-72, US Gypson Co., Denver, 1972-75, Ameron Corp., Denver, 1975-79; nat. sales mgr. Blue Bird Internat. Co., Englewood, Colo., 1979-81; sales mgr. Smith & Wesson, Golden, Colo., 1981-85; pres. The West & Assocs., Inc., Hudson, Colo., 1985—. Served with Ohio N.G., 1963-67. Jeffco Posse Club. Republican. Congregationalist. Avocations: horseback riding, skiing, camping.

SPRINGER, KARL GOERGE, religious organization administrator; b. N.Y.C., Oct. 20, 1949; s. Gustave and Florence (Hacker) S.; m. Jane Anne Condon, June 10, 1978 (div. 1981). BA, Brandeis U., 1971; DD, Naropa Inst., 1977. Ordained to ministry, Vajradhatu Buddhist Assn., 1977. Dir. Karme Choling Retreat Str., Barnet, Vt., 1971-75; dir., chief exec. officer Naropa Inst., Boulder, Colo., 1975-77; v.p. Vajradhatu Internat., Boulder, 1977—; exec. dir. U.S. Com. UN Lumbini Project, Boulder, 1983—; founder, co-chmn. Am. Buddhist Congress, L.A., 1986—; bd. dirs. Karma Triyana Dharmachakra, Woodstock, N.Y., San Luis Valley Tibetan Project, Crestone, Colo., World Resources Com., Bangkok; regional dir. World Fellowship Buddhists, Bangkok. Compiler, dir. Asian Art Exhbn.. MIT, 1974; contbr. articles to to mags. Del. UN Conf. on Disarmament and Devel., N.Y.C., 1987. Mem. UN Assn., UN Assn. in India, Acad. Polit. Sci. Democrat. Avocations: skiing, swimming, walking, travel, Asian art. Home: 1214 Grandview Ave Ojai CA 93023-2018 Office: 323 E Matiuja Ste 112 Ojai CA 93023

SPRINGER, SALLY PEARL, university administrator; b. Bklyn., Mar. 19, 1947; d. Nathaniel Margulies and Fanny (Schoen) S.; m. Hakon Hope; children: Erik Jacob Hope, Mollie Liv Hope. BS, Bklyn. Coll., 1967; PhD, Stanford U., 1971. Postdoctoral fellow Stanford U. Med. Sch., Calif., 1971-73; asst. prof. SUNY-Stony Brook, 1973-78, assoc. provost, 1981-85, assoc. prof., 1978-87; exec. asst. to chancellor U. Calif., Davis, 1987-92, asst. chancellor, 1992—. Author (with others): Left Brain, Right Brain, 1981 (Am. Psychol. Found. Disting. Contbr. award 1981), 5th rev. edit., 1998, How to Succeed in College, 1982; contbr. articles to profl. jours. Mem. Internat. Neuropsychol. Soc., Psychonomic Soc. Office: U Calif Office Chancellor Davis CA 95616

SPRINKLE, RONALD LEO, counseling psychologist, UFO researcher; b. Rocky Ford, Colo., Aug. 31, 1930; s. Rex Houston and Annas (Dodson) S.; m. Marilyn Joan Nelson, June 7, 1952; children: Nelson R., Eric E., Matthew D., Kristen M. BA, U. Colo., 1952, M in Personnel Svc., 1956; PhD in Counseling Psychology, U. Mo., 1961. Lic. psychologist, Wyo. Counselor/instr. Stephens Coll., Columbia, Mo., 1956-61; asst. prof. psychology U. N.D., Grand Forks, 1961-64, dir. Counseling Ctr., 1963-64; assoc. prof. guidance edn. U. Wyo., Laramie, 1964-65, counselor, asst. prof. psychology, 1965-67, counselor, assoc. prof. psychology, 1967-70, dir. counseling and testing, assoc. prof. psychology, 1970-77, dir. counseling and testing, prof. counseling svcs., 1977-82, counseling psychologist, prof. counseling svcs., 1983-89; counseling psychologist Laramie, 1989—; cons. ABC-TV, NBC-TV; cons. UFO Rschr., 1961—. Author: Soul Samples, 1999; contbr. over 50 articles to profl. jours. Cpl. U.S. Army, 1952-54. Mem. AAAS (life), APA, Am. Assn. Counseling (life), Assn. for Past Life Rsch. and Therapies (life), Soc. Sci. Exploration, Acad. Clin. Close Encounter

Therapists (pres. 1994—). Avocation: senior Olympics-3 man basketball. Office: Trance Formations Unltd 105 S 4th St Laramie WY 82070-3103

SPROSTY, JOSEPH PATRICK, weapons specialist, producer, writer, consultant; b. Cleve., Aug. 25, 1947; s. Joseph Patrick and Anna Margret (Loucka) S.; m. Sharon Marie Blair, Sept. 29, 1993. Grad., Midpark H.S., Middleburgh, Ohio, 1965; student, San Diego City Coll., 1972-73. Class 2 firearms lic. Prop builder The Goulardi Show WJW-TV8, Cleve., 1962-65; sub-agent Internat. Artists Agy., San Diego and L.A., 1982-83; casting dir. Cinemode Films, 1982; operator, owner Actors Artists Agy., L.A., 1983-87; founder, prodr., dir. Magnum Prodns., 1985; founder Sprosty Prodns., 1990; demonstrator weapons and handling of weapons, Propmaster TV Co., Van Nuys, Calif., 1992; expert witness Laser Weapon Scam, 1984; vis. lectr. firearms safety, handling, rules and regulations governing use of firearms in motion picture, TV prodn. U. So. Calif., 1996—; animal wrangler specializing opossums. Scriprwriter: (films) Vanishing Point II, The Apartment Manager, The Big House, Rambo III (optioned), Rambo IV (revised), Boneyard, Mister Ed - Talking Again, Mister Ed - Radio Talk, Brick, Life Plus One, Gun Slave, Fixation, Last Chance (renamed Terminal Virus), numerous others; prodr., dir. (video) Break Disc, 1985; location mgr., armorer, weapons splst.: (film) Heat from Another Sun (retitled Maladiction), 1988; armorer, 2nd asst. dir., assoc. prodr., weapons splst.: (film) Provoked, 1989; weapons splst., armorer: (film) Big City, 1990; co-prodr., animal wrangler, weapons splst.: (film) Opossum de Oro, 1996; weapons splst.: (tv shows) Jake and the Fat Man, Black's Magic, Hill Street Blues, Murder, She Wrote, On the Edge of Death, Emerald Point N.A.S., (7 episodes) America's Most Wanted, (3 episodes) FBI: The Untold Stories, numerous others, (films) Revolt, Rocky IV, Streets of Fire, Walk in the Sun, Cloak & Dagger, One Man's Poison, Killing Zoe, Desert Storm, The Movie, Live Shot, Outer Heat, Zipperhead, Four Minute Warning, The Robbery, Spirit, Texas Payback, High Adventure, The Waterfront, The Philadelphia Experiment II, Opossum de Oro, Harlem Nights, Tango & Cash, Die Hard, Provoked, Beverly Hills Cop II, Big City, numerous others. Spkr. Veterans Day Calif. State U., Dominguez Hills, 1993. Served with USN, 1965-67 (hon. discharge). Mem. AFTRA, SAG (charter mem. San Diego br.). Home: 337 W Maple St Glendale CA 91204-2014

SPROUL, JOHN ALLAN, retired public utility executive; b. Oakland, Calif., Mar. 28, 1924; s. Robert Gordon and Ida Amelia (Wittschen) S.; m. Marjorie Ann Hauck, June 20, 1945; children: John Allan, Malcolm J., Richard O., Catherine E. A.B., U. Calif., Berkeley, 1947, LL.B., 1949. Bar: Calif. 1950. Atty. Pacific Gas & Electric Co., San Francisco, 1949-52, 56-62, sr. atty., 1962-70, asst. gen. counsel, 1970-71, v.p. gas supply, 1971-76, sr. v.p., 1976-77, exec. v.p., 1977-89; gen. counsel Pacific Gas Transmission Co., 1970-73, v.p., 1973-79, chmn. bd., 1979-89, also bd. dirs.; atty. Johnson & Stanton, San Francisco, 1952-56; bd. dirs. Oreg. Steel Mills, Inc. Bd. dirs. emeritus Hastings Coll. Law. Served to 1st lt. USAAF, 1943-46. Mem. Calif. Bar Assn. (inactive), Pacific Coast Gas Assn., World Trade Club, Pacific-Union Club, Orinda Country Club. Home: 8413 Buckingham Dr El Cerrito CA 94530-2531 Office: Pacific Gas and Electric Co Mail Code H17F PO Box 770000 San Francisco CA 94177-0001

SPROULE, BETTY ANN, computer industry strategic planning manager; b. Evanston, Ill., Dec. 30, 1948; d. Harold Fletcher and Lois (Reno) Mathis; m. J. Michael Sproule, Mar. 3, 1973; children: John Harold, Kevin William. BS, Ohio State U., 1969, MS, 1970, PhD, 1972. Mem. tech. staff Bell Telephone Labs., Columbus, Ohio, 1973-74; asst. prof. U. Tex., Odessa, 1974-77; analyst bus. systems Maj. Appliance Bus. div. GE, Louisville, 1977-78; dir. forecasting and analysis Brown and Williamson Tobacco, Louisville, 1978-86; strategic planning mgr. Hewlett-Packard Co., Santa Clara, Calif., 1986—. Contbr. articles to profl. jours.; patentee in field. Sr. mem. IEEE, Soc. Women Engrs. Home: 4135 Briarwood Way Palo Alto CA 94306-4610 Office: Hewlett-Packard Co 11000 N Wolfe Rd Cupertino CA 95014-0678

SPRUNG, ARNOLD, lawyer; b. N.Y.C., Apr. 18, 1926; s. David L. and Anna (Stork) S.; m. Audrey Ann Caire; children: Louise, John, Thomas, Doran, D'Wayne. AB, Darmuth Coll., 1947; JD, Columbia U., 1950. Bar: N.Y. 1950, U.S. Dist. Ct. (so. dist.) N.Y. 1950, U.S. Patent Office 1952, U.S. Dist. Ct. (we. dist.) N.Y. 1954, U.S. Ct. Appeals (2d cir.) 1958, U.S. Ct. Customs and Patent Appeals 1958, U.S. Dist. Ct. (ea. dist.) N.Y. 1962, U.S. Dist. Ct. (no. dist.) Tex. 1971, U.S. Supreme Ct. 1971, and others. Sr. ptnr. Sprung, Kramer, Schaefer & Briscoe, Westchester, N.Y., 1950—. Lt. USN, 1943-46, PTO. Mem. ABA, N.Y. Intellectual Property Assn. Avocations: skiing, wind surfing, racquetball, biking, tennis. E-mail: asprung@aol.com.

SPYROS, NICHOLAS L., JR., lawyer; b. N.Y.C., Nov. 27, 1961; s. Nicholas Leonidas and Elizabeth (Kennedy) S.; m. Elizabeth Wolfe, Feb. 18, 1989; children: Sarah, Paul. BS in Physics, Georgetown U., 1983, MBA, 1985, JD, 1994. Bar: N.C. 1995. Asst. v.p. Merrill Lynch & Co., N.Y.C., 1986-91; v.p. Global Plasma Sys./Plasmat Tech. Corp., Washington and Raleigh, N.C., 1996-97; assoc. Carr McClellan Ingersol Thompson & Horn, Burlingame, Calif., 1997—. Republican. Greek Orthodox. Avocation: scuba diving. Office: Carr McClellan Ingersol Thompson & Horn 216 Park Rd Burlingame CA 94010-4200

SRAON, HARBANS SINGH, temple executive, geneticist; b. Ludhiana, Punjab, India, Jan. 15, 1941; came to U.S., 1970; s. S. Kehar Singh and Dhan K. Sraon; m. Surinder Kaur Thind, Apr. 3, 1966; children: Dilber S., Maninder K. BS, Punjab Agrl. U., Ludhiana, 1963, MS, 1965; PhD, S.D. State U., 1974; L.I. in Biology, Inst. Biology, London, 1969. Pres. MIC, Irvine, Calif., 1989—. Co-editor: Advanced Studies of Sikhism, 1989 (Community Excellence award); contbr. papers to profl. jours. Pres. Midwest Sikh Assn., Kansas City, Kans., 1985-86, Sikh Temple, Buena Park, Calif., 1988—; coord. Sikh Community of N.Am., Irvine, 1989; founder Sikh Community Found., Irvine, 1987; mem. S.O.S. Fellow Interfaith Coun. (civic svc. award 1981); mem. Am. Acad. Religion, Kiwanis (pres. 1985-86). Home: PO Box 642 Stockton CA 95201-0642 Office: Sikh Community Found 18021 Skylark Cir # J Irvine CA 92714

SRINIVASAN, UPPILI R., software engineer; b. Madras, India, Aug. 12, 1968; came to the U.S., 1991; s. Rangarajan and Vijaya (Rajgopal) S.; m. Priya Dhilipkumar, June 8, 1995; 1 child, Arjun. B in Computer Sci., Regional Engring. Coll., Trichy, India, 1990; M in Computer Sci., U. Fla., 1993. Assoc. software engr. Unisys Corp., Mission Viejo, Calif., 1994-95; software engr. Unisys Corp., Mission Viejo, 1995-97, sr. software engr., 1997—; software R&D staff Unisys, Mission Viejo, 1994—. Patentee in field. Avocations: tennis, reading, traveling, music. Office: Unisys Corp 25725 Jeronimo Rd Mission Viejo CA 92691-2792

SRYGLEY, PAUL DEAN, marketing manager; b. Nashville, July 1, 1944; s. Hubbard Fletcher Srygley and Lyda Russell (Forsee) Jones; m. Catherine Elizabeth Woodruff, Nov. 14, 1969 (div. June 1982); m. Kathleen Anne Higgins-Srygley, Oct. 20, 1990. Comml. Design, U. Calif. San Diego, La Jolla. Graphic arts supr. Scientific-Atlanta, San Diego, 1971-83; sr. graphics designer Gen. Dynamics-Convair, San Diego, 1984-92; instr., comml. art Platt Coll., San Diego, 1983-84; instr. advt. Southwestern J.C., Chula Vista, Calif., 1979-80; internat. mktg. coord. Calbiochem, San Diego, 1993-95; mktg. mgr. Zyzatech Water Sys. Inc., Seattle, 1996-98; prod. mgr. Bankamerica Housing Svcs., San Diego, 1998—. Mem. US Jaycees (pres., v.p., dir. pub. rels.), El Cajon, Calif., 1971-75. With U.S. Army, 1964-67. Avocations: flying, outdoor activities, computers.

STACK, KEVIN J., lawyer; b. N.Y.C., Aug. 12, 1951. BA cum laude, UCLA, 1973; JD cum laude, Loyola U., L.A., 1976. Bar: Calif. 1976, U.S. Dist. Ct. (ctrl. dist.) Calif. 1977. Ptnr. Knapp, Petersen & Clarke, Glendale, Calif., 1984—. Office: Knapp Petersen & Clarke 500 N Brand Blvd Fl 20 Glendale CA 91203-1904

STACKELBERG, JOHN RODERICK, history educator; b. Munich, May 9, 1945; came to U.S. 1946; s. Curt Freiherr von Ellen (Biddle) von Stackelberg (Buddy) von Stackelberg; m. Bobbie Jean Jett, Aug. 30, 1991; children: Katherine Ellen, Nicholas Olaf, Emmet Winkle. AB, Harvard U., 1956; MA, U. Vt., 1972; PhD, U. Mass., 1974. Reading instr. Baldridge Reading Svcs., Greenwich, Conn., 1957-82; lang. instr. Harvard schule, Berlin, 1963-67; English and social studies tchr. Lake Region Union

High Sch., Orleans, Vt., 1967-70; lectr. history San Diego State U., 1974-76; asst. prof. history U. Oreg., Eugene, 1976-77, U. S.D., Vermillion, 1977-78; asst. prof. history Gonzaga U., Spokane, Wash., 1978-81, assoc. prof. history, 1981-88, prof. history, 1988—; Powers prof. of humanities Gonzaga U., Spokane, 1997—. Author: Idealism Debased, 1981, Hitler's Germany: Origins, Interpretations, Legacies, 1999; contbr. articles to profl. jours. Pres. Spokane chpt. UN Assn., 1986-90. With U.S. Army, 1958-60. Leadership Devel. fellow Ford Found., 1969-70. Avocations: chess, tennis. Home: 9708 E Maringo Dr Spokane WA 99206-4429 Office: Gonzaga U Dept History Spokane WA 99258

STAEHELIN, LUCAS ANDREW, cell biology educator; b. Sydney, Australia, Feb. 10, 1939; came to U.S., 1969; s. Lucas Eduard and Isobel (Malloch) S.; m. Margrit Weibel, Sept. 17, 1965; children: Daniel Thomas, Philip Roland, Marcel Felix. Dipl. Natw., Swiss Fed. Inst. Tech., Zurich, 1963, Ph.D. in Biology, 1966. Research scientist N.Z. Dept. Sci. and Indsl. Research, 1966-69; research fellow in cell biology Harvard U. Cambridge, Mass., 1969-70; asst. prof. cell biology U. Colo., Boulder, 1970-73, assoc. prof., 1973-79, prof., 1979—; vis. prof. U. Freiburg, 1978, Swiss Fed. Inst. Tech., 1984, 92, U. Melbourne, Australia, 1998; mem. cellular biology and physiology study sect. NIH, Bethesda, Md., 1980-84; mem. DOE panel on rsch. directions for the energy bioscis., 1988, 92; mem. NSF adv. panel for cellular orgn., 1994-96; mem. plant biology panel NASA. Editor Jour. Cell Biology, 1977-81, European Jour. Cell Biology, 1981-90, Plant Physiology, 1986-92, Plant Jour., 1991-97, Biology of the Cell, 1996-99; editor: (with C.J. Antzen) Encyclopedia of Plant Physiology, Vol. 19, Photosynthesis III, 1986; contbr. numerous articles to sci. jours. Recipient Humboldt award Humboldt Found., 1978, Sci. Tchr. award U. Colo., 1984; grantee NIH, 1971—, USDA, 1994—, NASA, 1997—. Mem. AAAS, Am. Soc. Cell Biology, Am. Soc. Plant Physiology, German Acad. Natural Scis. Leopoldina. Home: 2855 Dover Dr Boulder CO 80303-5305 Office: U Colo Dept Molecular Cell/Devel Biology PO Box 347 Boulder CO 80309-0347

STAFFORD, ELSAN HUGH, novelist, poet, retired deputy sheriff; b. Santa Ana, Calif., Sept. 29, 1913; s. Guy and Elsa (Zimmerman) S.; m. Ann Ruelle (div. May, 1961); children: Mike, Tim, Patrick, Alice. AA in English, L.A. City Coll., 1938. Planner, writer Goodyear Tire Co., L.A., 1936-40; police officer L.A. Police Dept., 1945; sherri's officer L.A. County Police, L.A., 1946-51; planner, writer Douglas Aircraft, L.A., 1954-58; mgr. Auldin Arms, Torrance, Calif., 1965-68; planner electron industry Torrance, 1969-73; apt. mgr. Goldrich & Kest Co., L.A., 1974-83; bus. cons. Creative Adminstr. Writers, L.A., 1989—; mgr. Lyric Lines Publ., Grants Pass, Oreg., 1998—. Author: (poetry) Walk On (finalist 1997), The Star and Rose (finalist 1998). Fund raiser Calif. Rep. Org., Reseda, 1980; donor, mem. Audubon Soc., Srs. Coalition. Lt. U.S. Army, 1941-45. Avocations: writing, reading, classical music, chess. E-mail: homework@cosnet.net.

STAFFORD, KIM R., humanities educator, writer; b. Portland, Oreg., Oct. 15, 1949; s. William E. and Dorothy (Frantz) S. PhD in English, U. Oreg., 1979. Oral historian Pioneer Mus., Florence, Oreg., 1975-76; printer Graywolf Press, Port Townsend, Wash., 1977-78; adj. faculty Idaho State U., Boise, 1981-82, U. Calif., Davis, 1983-84; dir. N.W. Writing Inst.-Lewis and Clark Coll., Portland, 1986—. Editor: Having Everything Right: Essays of Place, 1986. Recipient Book award Pacific N.W. Booksellers, Portland, 1987; creative writing fellow NEA, Washington, 1976, 84. Mem. Nat. Coun. Tchrs. of English.

STAFFORD, PATRICK PURCELL, poet, writer, management consultant; b. L.A., Mar. 13, 1954; s. Elsan H. Stafford and Ann (Ruelle) Lane; m. Liane Beale Stafford, Jan. 2, 1987; 1 child, David. Student, U.S. Armed Forces Inst., 1971, UCLA, 1980, 81. Head script writer Hollywood (Calif.) Radio Network, 1981-82; mgr. new bus. Harry Koff Agy., Encino, Calif., 1984-85; pres., mgr. Legal Experts, L.A., 1988-94, Creative Adminstrs., L.A., 1994—; office adminstr. Moneymaker & Kelley, L.A., 1989-90; sales rep. Now Messenger Svc., L.A., 1993-98; staff mgr. Stafford Resume Svc., L.A., 1990—. Contbr. poems, articles, short stories to profl. publs. Mem. Big Bros. of Greater L.A., 1991. With USMC, 1971-78, Vietnam. Recipient Concept/Essay award L.A. Rtd., 1990, Poetry Contest award Tradition Mag., 1991, Hon. Mention award Iliad Press, 1992, Wash. State Coll., 1990, Winner in Play-Reading Series, Altered Stage Theatre Co., 1991. Mem. The Writer's Exch. (life), Marino's of Beverly Hills (charter). Libertarian. Avocations: classical music and films, martial arts, biking, boxing. E-mail: thinksuccess@hotmail.com. Home and Office: 1775 Southgate Way Grants Pass OR 97527-5660

STAFFORD-MANN, PATRICIA ANN, library and textbook consultant, writer; b. San Francisco, Aug. 14, 1919; d. Alfonce Henry and Regina Dorothy (Flynn) Heller; m. Paris Howard Stafford, Sept. 25, 1944 (dec. 1979); children: Philip, Michael, Teresa, Marie, Stephen; m. Roy Everett Mann, Dec. 16, 1986. AA, Moorpark Coll., 1972; tchrs. credential, UCLA, 1975. Mem. sales staff May Co., Ventura, Calif., 1972; library media specialist Ventura County Supt. Schs., Camarillo, 1972-85; textbook cons. Ventura County Supt. Schs., Camarillo, 1985-94; library cons. Calif. Lutheran U., Thousand Oaks, 1986; freelance writer; cons. to textbook pubs., 1976-84. Author: People of Ventura County (with others), 1982, Your Two Brains, 1986, Dreaming and Dreams, 1991; contbr. articles to various mags.; spkr. on children's books. Cpl. USMC, 1943-44. Mem. Soc. Children's Book Writers, LWV (past pres. Monrovia chpt.), Am. Goldstar Mothers (past pres. Oxnard chpt.), Friends of Libr., San Clemente Women's Club, Kiawanis, Los Escribientes. Republican. Roman Catholic. Avocations: embroidery, oil painting, mosaics, world travel (over 80 countries), water aerobics. E-mail: rapmann@earthlink.net. Home: 23 Segovia San Clemente CA 92672-6057

STAFL, JAN H., physician; b. Prague, Czech Republic, Oct. 15, 1956; s. Adolf and Jaja (Buman) S.; m. Liba I., july 10, 1982; children: Erik, Lenka, Natalie. BSM, Northwestern U., Evanston, Ill., 1980; MD, Northwestern U., Chgo., 1981. Bd. cert. ob-gyn. Resident ob-gyn Johns Hopkins, Balt., 1982-85; pelvic surgery fellow Union meml. Hosp., Balt., 1985-86; pvt. practice ob-gyn Owatonna (Minn.) Clinic, P.A., 1986-94; assoc. clin. prof. U Minn., Mpls., 1986-94; pvt. practice ob-gyn Health Care for Women, Eugene, Oreg., 1994-96, Pacific Women's Ctr., LLC Eugene, 1996—; ob-gyn phys. Pacific Womne's Ctr., LLC, Eugene, 1996—. Fellow ACOG; mem. Am. Holistic Med. Assn., Oreg. Med. Assn., Rotary (com. chmn. 1996-97). Home: 68 Constantine Pl Eugene OR 97405-9551 Office: Pacific Womens Ctr LLC 151 W 7th Ave Ste 110 Eugene OR 97401-2676

STAGER, DONALD K., construction company executive. Chmn. Dillingham Constrn. Holdings Inc., Pleasanton, Calif.; dir. Harding Lawson Assocs., Novato, Calif. Recipient, Roebling award Am. Soc. of Civil Engineers, 1995, Golden Beaver award for Mgmt Beavers, Inc., 1998. Office: 957 Wapato Way Manson WA 98831-9595

STAHELI, LYNN TAYLOR, pediatric orthopedist, educator; b. Provo, Utah, Nov. 13, 1933; s. Harvey Roulin and Letha (Taylor) S.; m. Ann Lee Smith, June 4, 1957 (div. 1976); children: Linda Ann, Diane Kay, Todd Kent; m. Lana Ribble, June 11, 1977. BS, Brigham Young U., 1956; MD, U. Utah, 1959. Intern U. Utah, Salt Lake City, 1960; resident in orthopedic surgery U. Wash., 1964-68; dir. rsch. and edn. Children's Hosp., Seattle, 1968-77, dir. dept. orthopedics, 1977-92; prof. dept. orthopedics U. Wash., Seattle, 1968—; mem. med. exec. com. Children's Hosp. and Med. Ctr., Seattle, 1977-92; cons. Fircrest Sch., Seattle, 1968-80, Boyer Children's clinic, Seattle, 1968-80, Seattle Pub. Schs. Spl. Edn. Program, 1968-80; invited speaker for more than 1000 individual presentations in 30 countries, 1960—; founder Duncan Seminar for Cerebral Palsy, 1980. Editor: Jour. Pediatric Orthopedics, 1981—; author: Med. Writing and Speaking, 1986, Fundamentals of Pediatric Orthopedics, 1992; contbr. articles to numerous profl. jours. Founding mem. bd. N.W. Inst. Ethics and Life Scis., Seattle, 1974—; bd. dirs. Rainier Found., Seattle, 1988—; founder Internat. Scholarship for Pediatric Orthopedics Seattle, 1988-91, Cont. U.S.F., 1960-63. Mem. Pedi orthopedics com. 1980-86), Am. Acad. Pediatrics (chmn. com. on shoewear 1985—, Disting. Svc. award 1995), Am. Acad. Cerebral Palsy and Devel. Medicine (chmn. instrnl. course com. 1982—), Alpha Omega Alpha. Avocations: flying, sailing, boating, canoeing, photography. Home: 4110 48th

Ave NE Seattle WA 98105-5116 Office: Childrens Hosp Dept Orthopedics 4800 Sand Point Way NE Seattle WA 98105-3901

STAHL, JACK LELAND, real estate company executive; b. Lincoln, Ill., June 28, 1934; s. Edwin R. and Edna M. (Burns) S.; m. Carol Anne Townsend, June 23, 1956; children: Cheryl, Nancy, Kellea. BS in Edn., U. N.Mex., 1957. Tchr. Albuquerque Public Schs., 1956-59; pres. House Finders, Inc., Albuquerque, 1959-65; v.p. N.Mex. Savs. & Loan Assn., Albuquerque, 1965-67; chmn. bd. Hooten-Stahl, Inc., Albuquerque, 1967-77; mem. N.Mex. Ho. of Reps., 1969-70; pres. The Jack Stahl Co., Albuquerque, 1977—; mem. N.Mex. Senate, 1981-86; lt. gov. State of N.Mex., 1987-90. Mem. N. Mex. Ho. of Reps., 1969-70, exec. bd. Gr. S.W. Coun. Boy Scouts Am., 1982-89; bd. dirs. BBB N. Mex., 1968-82, pres. 1975-76; trustee Univ Heights. Hosp.,1980-85; vice chmn. N. Mex. Bd. Fin., 1987-90, N. Mex. Cmty. Devel. Coun., 1987-90; bd. dirs. Ctr. for Entrepreneurship and Econ. Devel., 1994-96; mem. Gov.'s Bus. Adv. Coun., 1995-97. Named Realtor of Yr., Albuquerque Bd. Realtors, 1972. Mem. Nat. Assn. Realtors, Nat. Homebuilders Assn., N.Mex. Amigos, 20-30 Club (pres. 1963-64), Rotary. Republican. Methodist. Office: 1911 Wyoming Blvd NE Albuquerque NM 87112-2865

STAHL, LOUIS A., lawyer; b. Oct. 31, 1940; s. Louis A. and Dorothy (Cox) S.; m. Mary Kathleen Quinn, Apr. 4, 1960; children: Lisa, Suzanne, Gretchen, Nicole. BA magna cum laude, Wheeling Jesuit U., 1962; postgrad., Duquesne U., 1965-66; JD summa cum laude, Notre Dame U., 1971. Bar: Ariz. 1971, U.S. Dist. Ct. Ariz. 1971, U.S. Ct. Appeals (9th cir.) 1974, U.S. Supreme Ct. 1975. Ptnr. Streich Lang P.A., Phoenix, 1971—; mem. Maricopa County Superior Ct. Rule 26.1 Study Com., 1992—; Frances Lewis lawyer in residence Washington & Lee Univ. Law Sch., 1986; seminar panelist Ariz. Bankers Assn., 1987, Profl. Ednl. Systems, Inc., 1989; mediator, arbitrator U.S. Arbitration and Mediation of Ariz., Nev. and N. Mex., 1993—. Contbg. author: Arizona Attorneys' Fees Manual, 1987, Arizona Professionalism Manual, 1992; contbr. papers to law revs. and jours. Active Phoenix and Maricopa County Young Reps., Ariz. Rep. Party's Lawyers' Ballot Security Com., 1980, Vols. for Reagan-Bush, 1980, Re-elect Rep. Ernest Baird Fin. Com., 1992, Ariz. Rep. Caucus.; founding mem., v.p., dir., legal counsel Performing Arts Combined Talent; pres., bd. dirs. Make a Wish Found. Ctrl. & So. Ariz., 1995—. Mem. ABA (vice-chmn. health ins. com., sect. ins., negligence and compensation law 1973-79, contbg. editor The Forum 1976-79), State Bar Ariz. (mem. profl. liability com. 1979-86, chmn. 1983-86, mem. com. on rules of profl. conduct ethics com. 1981-93, com. on professionalism 1989-91, discipline task force 1991-92, co-chmn. peer rev. com. 1991—), Def. Rsch. Inst., Ariz. Assn. of Def. Counsel, Ariz. Bar Found., Phoenix C. of C. (military affairs com.), Am. Numismatic Assn., Phoenix Coin Club. Office: Streich Lang PA Renaissance One 2 N Central Ave Phoenix AZ 85004-2391*

STAHL, MARGO SCHNEEBALG, marine biologist; b. Coral Gables, Fla., June 24, 1947; d. Martin and Rose (Osman) Schneebalg; m. Glenn Stahl, Aug. 17, 1969 (div. June 1988); 1 child, Shaina Flori Georgina. BS in Biology, U. Miami, 1969, MS in Marine Biology, 1973. Fish and wildlife aide Calif. Dept. Fish and Game, Long Beach, 1973; assoc. rsch. engr. So. Calif. Edison Co., Rosemead, 1973-75; rsch. assoc. in urban and regional planning U. Hawaii, Honolulu, 1975-76, Hawaii Inst. Marine Biology, Kaneohe, 1975-77, Anuenue Fisheries Rsch. Ctr., Honolulu, 1977-79; aquatic biology Hawaii Dept. Land and Natural Resources, Honolulu, 1979-83; instr. sci. U. Hawaii Windward C.C., Kaneohe, 1985-88; ecologist U.S. Army C.E., Honolulu, 1988-93; supervisory fish and wildlife biologist U.S. Fish and Wildlife Svc., Honolulu, 1993—; pres. Mermaid Aquatic Cons., Honolulu, 1979-81, 84-88; mem. Hawaii Water Quality Tng. Interagy. Com., Honolulu, 1991-93. Contbg. author: Taste of Aloha, 1983 (Jr. League award 1985); contbr. articles to profl. jours. Project mgr. Kokokahi Aquaculture Model, Kaneohe, 1978-80; mem. adv. bd. Windward C.C., 1982-83; hon. coord. RESULTS Hunger Lobby, Honolulu, 1989. Recipient Stoye award in icythyology Am. Soc. Ichtyologists and Herpetologists, 1972, Career Woman award Sierra Mar dist. Calif. Bus. and Profl. Womens Club, 1975, Comdr's award for exceptional performance U.S. Army C.E., Ft. Shafter, Hawaii, 1990. Mem. Nat. Assn. Environ. Profls. (cert. environ. profl., chmn. cert. com. 1992-93, C.E.P. award 1991), Assn. for Women in Sci. (bd. dirs. 1985), Hawaii Assn. Environ. Profls. (bd. dirs. 1991-93, pres.-elect 1993-94), World Mariculture Soc. (bd. dirs. 1981), Am. Fisheries Soc., Western Soc. Naturalists. Avocations: scuba diving, gardening, classical music, animals. Home: 46-436 Holopeki St Kaneohe HI 96744-4227 Office: US Fish and Wildlife Svc Honolulu HI 96850

STAHL, RICHARD G. C., journalist, editor; b. Chgo., Feb. 22, 1934; m. Gladys C. Weisbecker; 1 child, Laura Ann. Student, Northwestern U., U. Ill., Chgo. Editor Railway Purchases and Stores Mag., Chgo., 1960-63; editor pub. rels. dept. Sears Roebuck & Co., Chgo., 1963-68; dir. pub. rels. dept. St. Joseph's Hosp. Med. Ctr., Phoenix, 1968-72; v.p. pub. rels. Consultation Svcs., Inc., Phoenix, 1972-73; creative dir. Don Jackson and Assoc., Phoenix, 1973; editor, pub. rels. mgr. Maricopa County Med. Soc., Phoenix, 1974-76; sr. editor Ariz. Hwys. mag., Phoenix, 1977-99; ret., 1999. Regional editor: (travel guides) Budget Travel, 1985, USA, 1986, Arizona, 1986; freelance writer and editor. Mem. Soc. Profl. Journalists. Avocation: woodworking. Office: Ariz Hwys Mag 2039 W Lewis Ave Phoenix AZ 85009-2819*

STALLCOP, BRIAN KIRBY, journalist; b. Grand Forks, N.D., Sept. 12, 1963; s. Robert Harvey Stallcop and Linda Colleen Hinton; m. Shawna Lynn Cauthron, Jan. 12, 1985. BA in Latin Am. Studies, U. Mo., 1985, MA in Journalism, 1989. Designer The Commercial Appeal, Memphis, 1987-88; photo editor The Indianapolis (Ind.) News, 1988-90; from photo editor, designer to news editor The Virginian-Pilot, Norfolk, 1990-94, news editor, 1994-95; mng. editor The Sun, Bremerton, Wash., 1995-97, editor, 1998—; lectr. in field. Dir. United Way of Kitsap County, Bremerton, 1998—. Recipient 1st Editing Place award Nat. Press Photographers Assn., 1991; recognized in Presstime Mag. in 20 under 40, 1997. Mem. Am. Soc. Newspaper Editors, Soc. Profl. Journalists, Soc. News Design, Rotary Club Bremerton. Fax: (360) 479-7681. Office: The Sun 545 5th St Bremerton WA 98337-1476

STALLKNECHT-ROBERTS, CLOIS FREDA, publisher, publicist; b. Birmingham, Ala., Dec. 31, 1934; d. August and Sadie Bell (Wisener) Anton; m. Randall Scott Roberts; children: Yvonne Denise, April O'dell, Kurt William. Publicist Ms. Clois Presents, L.A., 1968—; advt. Engineered Magic, Advt., Santa Ana, Calif., 1976, 77, 81; pub. Internat. Printing, L.A., 1981—. Editor: Nostradamus, William Bartram, Apuleius, 1990-92, Metamorphoses L.A., 1996-97. Home and office: PO Box 165 Inyokern CA 93527-0165 Office: Engineered Magic 510 De La Estrella San Clemente CA 92672

STALLONE, THOMAS MICHAEL, clinical psychologist; b. N.Y.C., Dec. 5, 1952; s. Vito Joseph and Mary Ellen (Kearney) S.; m. Bonnie Elizabeth Wenk, May 30, 1982; 1 child, Thomas Lucius. B of Profl. Studies, N.Y. Inst. Tech., 1987; MA, Spalding U., 1991; D of Psychology, Pacific U., 1994. Lic. psychologist, Wash.; cert. psychol. assoc. in clin. psychology, Ky.; cert. rational emotive therapist; diplomate Am. Bd. Forensic Examiners. Internat. banker Sumitomo Bank, Ltd., N.Y.C., 1980-82, Bank of N.Y., N.Y.C., 1982-87; pvt. practice hypnosis cons. LaGrange, Ky., and N.Y.C., 1982-90; rehab. specialist Goodwill Industries Ky., Louisville, 1989; psychol. assoc. div. mental health Ky. Corrections Cabinet, La Grange, 1989-91; teaching asst. Pacific U. Forest Grove, Oreg., 1991-93; psychotherapist Portland, Oreg., 1991-95; clin. psychologist Vancouver, Wash., 1995—; Author: The Boke of Taliesyne, 1979, The Effects of Psychodrama on Inmates Within a Structured Residential Behavior Modification Program, 1993, Rational Emotive Behavior Therapy and Subpersonalities, 1997. Cons. Hist. Arms, Ltd., N.Y.C., 1983-87, N.Y. Medieval Festival, 1984; founder, chmn. Whitestone (N.Y.) Creative Arts Workshop, 1977, Ky. Shakespeare Festival, Louisville, 1987-88; treas., advisor 4H Exec. Coun., La Grange, 1988-91. Decorated Grant of Arms, Chief Herald of Ireland; named to Honorable Order of Ky. Chief Eile O'Carroll of Clan Cian. Mem. APA, Am. Soc. Group Psychotherapy and Psychodrama, Internat. Soc. for Profl. Hypnosis, Wash. State Psychol. Assn., Ancient Order Hibernians. Mem. Avocations: hypnosis, meditation, Martial Arts, Medieval history, teaching.

STAMBAUGH, ROBERT HOWARD, JR., management consultant; b. Leetonia, Ohio, Apr. 9, 1946; s. Robert Howard and Rosemary (Stevens) S. AB, Stanford U., 1969. Analyst SRI Internat., Menlo Park, Calif., 1970-79; mgr. Crocker Bank, San Francisco, 1979-80, Intel Corp., Santa Clara, Calif., 1980-82; cons. VRC Cons. Group Inc., Los Altos, Calif., 1982-83, v.p., 1983-88; v.p. The Hunter Group, Baltimore, 1988-92; pres. Kapa'a Assocs., Kekaha, Hawaii, 1992—; lectr. Golden Gate U., San Francisco, 1982—; pres. IHRIM Inc., Chicago, 1980-84, chpt. dir., San Francisco, 1980—. Editor (jour.) IHRIM Jour., 1982-84. Mem. IEEE, Am. Mgmt. Assn., Am. Compensation Assn., Australian Human Resources Inst., Am. Futures Soc., Assn. for Computing Machienry, Soc. Human Resources Mgmt. Lutheran. Office: Kapaa Associates PO Box 250 Kekaha HI 96752-0250

STAMES, WILLIAM ALEXANDER, realtor, cost management executive; b. Douglas, Ariz., Mar. 26, 1917; s. Alex Basil and Teresa (Ruis) S.; AA, Long Beach Coll., 1941; postgrad. U. Calif., Berkeley, 1962-64; cert. mgmt. practices Naval Officers CIC Sch., Glenview, Ill., 1955; grad. Real Estate Inst., Calif.; m. Marguerite Winifred Nelson, June 11, 1943; 1 child, Wynn Loraine. Owner, Stames Beverage Co., Brawley, Calif., 1945-50; liaison engr. Lockheed Missiles & Space Co., Sunnyvale, Calif., 1958-60, liaison engr. sr., 1960, adminstr., 1960-62, staff adminstr., 1962-63, liaison engr., sr., design engr. sr., 1965-76; owner, mgr. Cost Reduction Equipment Sales & Tech., Sunnyvale, 1967-76; realtor Cornish & Carey, 1988—. Dir. ret. activities office Naval Amphibious Base, Coronado, Calif. Comdr. USNR, 1941-69, ret., World War II, Korea, Vietnam. Decorated D.F.C., Air medal with four gold stars, Presdl. citation; inductee D.F.C. Soc. Honor Roll. Mem. Am. Mgmt. Assn., Mountain View Real Estate Bd. (pres.), Calif. Assn. Realtors (bd. dirs.), Tailhook Assn. Clubs: Commonwealth San Francisco, Ret. Officers (past pres. Peninsula chpt.), Lions. Author: Polaris Electrical Subsystems Design History, 1964; Poseidon Subsystem Invention, 1971. Home: 1060 Coronado Ave Coronado CA 92118-2439

STAMM, BOB, museum official. Chmn. bd. trustees Albuquerque Mus. Office: Albuquerque Mus PO Box 1293 Albuquerque NM 87103-1293*

STAMPER, EDWARD ZENE, foundations and research director; b. Great Falls, Mont., Oct. 7, 1949; s. Firm Zene and Lena Flora (Parisian) S.; m. Mel Jenkins, Sept. 1966 (div. Jan. 1969); children: Melissa Rea Kelleher, Becky Jones; children: Edward Ronald, April Dawn, Autumn Rose. Cert. in air conditioning/refrigeration, Practical Sch. Inc., L.A., 1968; BS in Elem. Edn., No. Mont. Coll., 1978; MEd in Sch. Adminstrn., Mont. State U., 1983. Tchr. aide supr. Rocky Boy Sch., Box Elder, Mont., 1978-79; environ. health technician Rocky Boy Indian Health Svc., Box Elder, summer 1979; most in need program coord. Rocky Boy Tribal Edn. Dept., Box Elder, 1981-82, adult edn. dir., 1982-84, asst. tribal edn. dir., 1984-87; student svcs. dir. Stone Child Coll., Box Elder, 1987-96, founds. and rsch. dir., 1996—; external evaluator RJS & Assocs., Box Elder, 1982-95; external evaluator, pres. Stamper & Assocs., Box Elder, 1982—; environ. health adv. bd. Rocky Boy Natural Resources Dept., Box Elder, 1997—; grant writer. Tribal mem. Chippewa Cree Tribe, Rocky Boy's Indian reservation. Bilingual Edn. scholar Office of Indian Edn., Washington, 1979-81. Mem. Nat. Indian Edn. Assn., Mont. Indian Edn. Assn. (Educator of the Yr. 1983), Mont. Adv. Coun. to Indian Edn. Democrat. Roman Catholic. Avocations: ranching, fishing, hunting, golfing, gardening. Office: Stone Child Coll RR 1 Box 1082 Box Elder MT 59521

STAMPER, MALCOLM THEODORE, publishing company executive; b. Detroit, Apr. 4, 1925; s. Fred Theodore and Lucille (Cayce) S.; m. Marion Philbin Guinan, Feb. 25, 1946; children: Geoffrey, Kevin, Jamie, David, Mary, Anne. Student, U. Richmond, Va., 1943-44; BEE, Ga. Inst. Tech., 1946; postgrad., U. Mich., 1946-49; DHumanities, Seattle U., 1994. With Gen. Motors Corp., 1949-62; with Boeing Co., Seattle, 1962-90; mgr. electronics ops., v.p., gen. mgr. turbine div. Boeing Co., 1964-66; v.p., gen. mgr. Boeing Co. (747 Airplane program), 1966-69, v.p., gen. mgr. comml. airplane group, 1969-71, corp. sr. v.p. ops., 1971-72; pres. Boeing Co., 1972-85, vice chmn., 1985-90; CEO, Storytellers Ink Pub., Seattle, 1990—, also chmn. bd. dirs.; bd. dirs. Esterline Co., Pro-Air Inc., Whittaker Corp.; trustee The Conf. Bd., 1988—. Candidate for U.S. Ho. of Reps., Detroit, 1952; trustee, chmn. Seattle Art Mus.; nat. bd. dirs. Smithsonian Assocs. With USNR, 1943-46. Named Industrialist of Year, 1967; recipient Educator's Golden Key award, 1970, Elmer A. Sperry award, 1982, AIEE award, Ga. Inst. Tech. award, Sec. Dept. Health and Human Services award, Silver Beaver award Boy Scouts Am., 1989, Literary Lions award, 1995; named to Engring. Hall of Fame. Mem. Nat. Alliance Businessmen, Phi Gamma Delta.

STAMPER, NORMAN H., police chief. BS, MS in Criminal Justice Adminstrn., San Diego State U.; PhD in Leadership and Human Behavior, U.S. Internat. U. Chief of police Seattle Police Dept., 1994—; exec. dir. Mayor Pete Wilson's Crime Control Commn.; apptd. (by U.S. Atty. Gen. and Sec. Health and Human Svcs.) Adv. Coun. Violence Against Women; mem. adv. panel on Excessive Force by Police, Police Exec. Rsch. Forum, Major Cities Chiefs; mem. steering com. Seattle Equal Justice Coalition; co-chair Ptnr's. in Pub. Edn's. Urban Scholar's Program; mem. bd. dirs. Leadership Tomorrow; trustee Ctr. for Ethical Leadership. Author: Removing Managerial Barriers to Effective Police Leadership, 1992; tchnical adv. Municipal Police Administration, 1992. Named to Alumni Hall of Fame Boys and Girls Club of Am.; recipient Katharine M. Bullitt award for Leadership Ptnrs. in Pub. Edn. Mem. Internat. Assn. Chiefs of Police. Office: Police Dept 1001 Public Safety Bldg 610 3rd Ave Seattle WA 98104-1824*

STANDAGE, BLAYNE ALLAN, surgeon; b. Lincoln, Nebr., Oct. 14, 1950. MD, Stanford U., 1980. Diplomate am. Bd. Surgery. Intern Oreg. Health Scis. U., Portland, Oreg., 1980-81, resident in surgery, 1981-86; mem. staff Legacy Portland Hosps.; clin. assoc. prof. surgery Oreg. Health Scis. U.; dir. surgical resident edn. Legacy Good Samaritan Hosp. Office: Oreg Surg Cons 1130 NW 22nd Ave Ste 300 Portland OR 97210-2970

STANDING BEAR, ZUGGUELGERES GALAFACH, criminologist, forensic scientist, educator; b. Boston, Jan. 10, 1941; m. Nancy Lee Karlovic, July 13, 1978 (div. Aug. 1985); m. Virginia Anne Red Hawk, Mar. 22, 1988. BS, U. Nebr., 1971; MS in Forensic Sci., George Washington U., 1974; postgrad. cert. in forensic medicine, Armed Forces Inst. Pathology, 1974; MSEd, U. So. Calif., 1976; MPA, Jacksonville State U., 1981; PhD in Criminology, Fla. State U., 1986. Diplomate Am. Bd. Forensic Examiners, Am. Bd. Forensic Medicine; cert. coroner, Ga., 1988-92; cert. criminal justice instr., Calif., Ga. Criminal investigator U.S. Army, 1965; dist. comdr. 7th region U.S. Army Criminal Investigation Command, Seoul, 1974-77; course mgr. U.S. Army Mil. Police Sch., Ft. McClellan, Ala., 1978-81; ret. U.S. Army, 1981; instr. Fla. State U., Tallahassee, 1981-85; asst. prof. No. Ariz. U., Flagstaff, 1985-86; program coord., prof. Valdosta (Ga.) State U., 1986-95; assoc. prof. Colo. State U., Ft. Collins, 1995—; v.p. Bearhawk Cons. Group, Ft. Collins, 1986—. Editor Jour. Contemporary Criminal Justice, 1992. Mem., task group coord. Com. for Sexual Assault Evidence Stds., ASTM, 1993— Com. Colo State U.; mem. leadership coun. Cmty. Policing Project, Valdosta, Ga., 1993-95; treas. and v.p. edn. and rsch. No. Colo. WOLF rescue, edn., and rsch. project, LaPorte, Colo., 1995—; mem. Nat. Am. lang. preservation com. Colo. State Univ. Decorated Bronze Star medal, Meritorious Svc. medal (with oak leaf cluster). Fellow Am. Acad. Forensic Scis. (gen. sec. 1987-88, gen. chmn. 1988-90, gen. program co-chair 1995-96, Gen. Sec. Meritorious Svc. award 1996), Am. Coll. Forensic Examiners, Internat. Assn. Forensic Nurses (disting. fellow, mem. exec. bd. dirs., cons. and permissions exec., chmn. ethics com.); mem. ASTM (co-coord. sexual assault evidence stds. task group), Am. Sociol. Assn., Acad. Polit. Sci., Am. Soc. Criminology, Acad. Criminal Justice Scis. (program com. 1996-97), So. Criminal Justice Assn., Am. Assn. of U. Profs., Harley Owners Group. Democrat. Haudenosaunee (Native Am.). Avocations: wolf behavior, traditional Native American religious counseling, motorcycling. Office: Colo State U Dept Sociology Fort Collins CO 80523

STANDLEY, MARK, school program administrator, consultant; b. Waco, Tex., Feb. 12, 1954; s. Troy and Julia (Crockett) S.; m. Christine Selin Standley, Dec. 31, 1986; children: Aron, Robin Joanne. BA, S.W. Tex. State U., 1976; MS, U. Oreg., 1993. Cert. tchr., adminstr. Vol. U.S. Peace Corps, South Korea, 1976-79; tchr. Northway (Ala.) Sch., 1985-90; prin. Mentasta (Ala.) Lake Sch., 1990-92; program mgr. Ala. Gateway Sch. Dist., Tok, 1993-95; account exec. Apple Computer, TOK, Alaska, 1995—; co-founder Nat. Acad. for Ednl. Tech., Eugene, Oreg., 1993; ednl. advisor Dynamix Software, Eugene, 1993—; team leader Tech. Leadership Retreats, Ala., 1992—. Co-author: Technology Advisory Councils, 1993, Teacher's Guide to the Incredible Machine, 1994. Bd. dirs. No. Ala. Environ. Ctr., Fairbanks, 1983-84; v.p. Upper Tanana Natural History Assn., Tok, 1988-89; mem. Tom Snyder Prodns. Presenters Club, 1994—. Recipient Tchr. Fellowship grant Am. Indian Soc. for Engring. and Sci., 1987, Tech. Incentive grant Apple Computer, Inc., 1989. Mem. ASCD, Internat. Soc. for Tech. in Edn., Ala. Soc. for Tech. in Edn. (bd. dirs. 1992—, pres.-elect 1994—, Pres.'s award 1994). Avocations: kayaking, snow shoe racing. Home: 19913 Kalka Cir Eagle River AK 99577-8711

STANDRING, JAMES DOUGLAS, real estate developer; b. Fresno, Calif., Dec. 2, 1951; s. James Robert Pusey and Jacquelin (Moore); m. Paula Jean Monson, Oct. 27, 1972; children: Craig Douglas, Ryan Scott, Melinda Jean, Kevin Paul. BS, Calif. State U., Fresno, 1975. Pres. Westland Industries, Inc., Portland, Oreg., 1976—; ptnr. Aloha Land and Cattle, Inc., Portland, 1982—; bd. dirs. Homebuilders Assn. Metro Portland, v.p. 1988-90, pres. 1990-91; bd. dirs. Oreg. Bldg. Industry Assn., v.p. 1993-96, pres. 1996-97; bd. dirs. Nat. Assn. Homebuilders, Washington, Oreg. trustee BUILD-PAC, 1992—, exec. com., 1994—. Bd. dirs. Tualitin Valley Econ. Devel. Corp., Portland, 1988-95; co-founder, bd. dirs. People for Washington County Charities, Beaverton, Oreg., 1985-88; mem. Tualitin Valley Econ. Devel. Commn., 1000 Friends of Oreg.; steering com. Oreg. Med. Laser Ctr., 1995—. Named Portland Metro. Builder of Yr., 1992, Oregon Builder of Yr., 1992. Mem. Multnomah Athletic Club, Portland City Club, Portland Golf Club, Sierra Club, Univ. Club, Elks. Republican. Episcopalian. Home: 5 Nansen Smt Lake Oswego OR 97035-1029 Office: Westland 12670 SW 68th Ave Ste 400 Portland OR 97223-8370

STANFILL, DENNIS CAROTHERS, business executive; b. Centerville, Tenn., Apr. 1, 1927; s. Sam Broome and Hattie (Carothers) S.; m. Therese Olivieri, June 29, 1951; children: Francesca, Sara, Dennis Carothers. BS, U.S. Naval Acad., 1949; MA (Rhodes scholar), Oxford U., 1953; LHD (hon.), U. S.C. Corporate finance specialist Lehman Bros., N.Y.C., 1959-65; v.p. finance Times Mirror Co., Los Angeles, 1965-69; exec. v.p. 20th Century-Fox Film Corp., 1969-71, pres., 1971, chmn. bd., chief exec. officer, 1971-81; pres. Stanfill, Bowen & Co., 1981-90; chmn. bd. dirs., chief exec. officer AME, Inc., 1990-91; co-chmn., co-CEO Metro-Goldwyn-Mayer, Inc., 1992-93; sr. advisor Credit Lyonnais, 1993-95; pres. Dennis Stanfill Co., 1995—. Trustee Calif. Inst. Tech.; bd. dirs. Weingart Found. Served to lt. USN, 1949-59; politico-mil. policy div. Office Chief Naval Ops., 1956-59.

STANFILL, SHELTON G., performing arts administrator; m. Brigitte. BA in History and Social Scis., Colo. State U., postgrad. Exec. dir. Hopkins Ctr. Dartmouth Coll.; dir. cultural programs Colo. State U.; dir. Nat. Arts Festival 12th Winter Olympic Games; ptnr. Brown, Stanfill & Brown; pres., CEO Wolf Trap Found. for Performing Arts, Vienna, Va.; pres. Music Ctr. L.A. County, 1994-96, R. Woodruff Arts Ctr., Atlanta, 1996—; chair panels, cons. Nat. Endowment for Arts, Lincoln. Ctr., Bklyn. Acad. Music, UCLA; advisor Telluride Film Festival. Avocations: reading, wine, dancing, film, medieval history. *

STANFORD, JOSEPH BARNEY, medical educator, physician; b. July 9, 1961; s. Kathleen Barnett; children: Matthew Joseph, Jesse Barnett, Hyrum Porter, Caleb Dean, Thomas Barnett. BA magna cum laude, Mankato State U., 1984; MD, U. Minn., 1988. Diplomate Am. Bd. Family Practice. Resident family and cmty. medicine U. Mo.-Columbia, 1988-91, chief resident family and cmty. medicine, 1990-91, academic fellow, clinical instr. dept. family and cmty. medicine, 1991-93; asst. prof. dept. family and preventive medicine U. Utah, Salt Lake City, 1993—; part time staff physician Cherchez La Femme Birth Svcs. Ltd., Columbia, Mo., 1991-93; med. cons. U. Utah BirthCare HealthCare, 1994—; physician N.E. Family Health Ctr., Salt Lake Regional Med. Ctr., U. Utah Hosp., Primary Children's Med. Ctr., 1993; invited observer Pontifical Acad. Scis. Working Group on Natural Fertility Regulation, Vatican, Italy, 1994. Contbr to prof. jours. Mem. Soc. Tchrs. of Family Medicine (mem. group family centered perinatal care 1990—), Am. Acad. Family Physicians, Am. Acad. Natural Family Planning (chairperson sci. and rsch. com. 1993—), Am. Holistic Med. Assn., Am. Soc. Clinical Hypnosis, Collegium Aesculapium, North Am. Primary Care Rsch. Group, Alpha Omega Alpha, Phi Kappa Phi. Avocations: hiking, camping, reading, writing, skiing. Office: U Utah Dept Family Preventive Med 50 N Medical Dr Salt Lake City UT 84132-0001

STANFORD, JOSEPH JAMES, computer scientist; b. Rhinebeck, N.Y., Apr. 6, 1970; s. Robert Francis and Lillian Katherine (Kobetitsch) S.; m. Oksana Piper Yurievna, May 10, 1997. BS in Computer Sci., Marist Coll., 1992; MS in Religion, ULC Seminary, 1997, PhD in Religion, 1998, DDiv (hon.), 1997. Ordained min. Universal Life Ch., 1997. Adj. prof. computer sci. Marish Adult Edn., Poughkeepsie, N.Y., 1988-92; software developer IBM, Boulder, Colo., 1991-93; project mgr. Keane, Inc., Denver, 1993-98; owner Stanford's Wildcard, Longmont, Colo., 1997—; project. mgr. IBM, Boulder, 1998—; adj. prof. computer sci. Denver Tech. Coll., 1997—. Rescue ground ops. dir. CAP, Colo., 1993—; bd. dirs. Longmont Environ. Bd. Affairs, 1997—. Mem. Project Mgmt. Inst. (project mgr. 1998—). Republican. Avocations: racing, ham radio, backpacking, travel. Fax: (303) 772-9665. E-mail: rescue-1@usa.net. Home: 3216 Lake Pkwy #202 Longmont CO 80503 Office: IBM Boulder 6300 Diagnol Hwy Boulder CO 80301

STANGELAND, ROGER EARL, retail chain store executive; b. Chgo., Oct. 4, 1929; s. Earl and Mae E. (Shaw) S.; m. Lilah Fisher, Dec. 27, 1951; children: Brett, Cyndi Stangeland Meili, Brad. Student, St. Johns Mil. Acad., 1943-47, Carleton Coll., 1947-48; B.S., U. Ill., 1949-51. With Coast to Coast Stores, Mpls., 1960-78, pres., 1972-77; sr. v.p., exec. v.p. Household Merchandising, Chgo., 1978-84; chief exec. officer, chmn. bd. Vons Grocery Co., Los Angeles, 1984-85; past CEO The Vons Cos., Inc., Arcadia, Calif., chmn., 1986—, now chmn. emeritus. Chmn. Wauconda (Ill.) Bd. Edn., 1957-60, Hopkins (Minn.) Bd. Edn., 1968-74; bd. fellows Claremont (Calif.) U. Ctr. and Grad. Sch., 1986; bd. dirs. L.A. area Boy Scouts Am.; trustee Hugh O'Brian Youth Found.; mem. CEO bd. advisors U. So. Calif. Sch. Bus. Adminstrn.; trustee St. John's Mil. Acad; bd. visitors Peter F. Drucker Grad. Mgmt. Ctr. Mem. Am. Inst. Wine and Food (bd. dirs.), Food Mktg. Inst. (chmn. bd. dirs.), Food Employers Coun. (exec. com., bd. dirs.), Mchts. & Mfrs. Assn. (bd. dirs.), L.A. Area C. of C. (bd. dirs.), Jonathan Club (L.A.), Calif. Club. Home: 842 Oxford Rd San Marino CA 91108-1214 Office: Vons Grocery Co 618 Michillinda Ave Arcadia CA 91007-6300

STANGLER, GREG FRANK, infosystems executive; b. Melrose, Minn., July 8, 1960; s. Robert Henry and Mary Ann (Hudovernik) S.; m. Sandra M. Jacobson; children: Urelle Erin, Isaac Douglas. BS in Computer Sci., N.D. State U., 1982. Sci. programmer Sperry Corp., Eagan, Minn., 1982-86; mktg. systems analyst McQuay Corp., Plymouth, Minn., 1986-87; cons., prin. Danning Co., Mpls., 1986-89; ind. subcontractor Salem Tech., Mpls., 1987-89; prin. GSTech, Mpls., 1989-95; pres. SageWorks, Castle Rock, Colo., 1996—. Tech. writer Gary Hart Campaign for Pres., St. Paul, 1984; steering com. Nat. Issues Forum Dakota County Library Systems, Eagan, 1986. Mem. Robotics Internat., Assn. Computing Machinery (chmn. 1981-82), MICOM (stock analyst 1983—, treas. 1987—). Avocations: racquetball, hiking, study in internat. relations.

STANLEY, FORREST EDWIN, fundraiser, university program director; b. Bakersfield, Calif., Sept. 6, 1942; s. James Edwin and Lucile Haworth (Sloan) S.; student UCLA, 1960-63, MS, 1970; BS, Calif. State U., Northridge, 1969; m. Suzanne Roberts, June 15, 1968 (div. 1984); children: John Forrest, Cheryl Suzanne; m. Virginia Louise Sorenson, Jan. 18, 1987. Sr. clk. So. Calif. Gas Co., 1963-65, programmer analyst, 1965-70; fin. analyst Continental Bldgs. Co., Burbank, Calif., 1970-72; fin. analyst McKinsey & Co., Inc., L.A., 1972-74; analyst Unionamerica Advisors, Beverly Hills, Calif., asst. v.p., asst. treas., 1974-75; dir. alumni and devel. Grad. Sch. Mgmt., UCLA, 1976-80; dir. spl. campaigns U. Calif., Berkeley, 1980-84; dir. devel. U. Colo., Colorado Springs, 1984-86; dir. devel. pub. affairs, Calif. State U., Bakersfield, 1987-92, asst. sec., 1989-92; v.p. U. Colo. Found., Inc., 1984-86; mgr. LH Stanley Trust, 1991—. Mem. Am. Inst. Cert. Computer Profls., Assn. for Computing Machinery, Coun. Advancement and Support of Edn., UCLA Mgmt. Alumni Assn. (v.p. 1974, pres. 1975-77), Sons Am. Colonists, Mensa, Lambda Chi Alpha (UCLA alumni chpt. pres. 1974-77, treas. 1977-80). Clubs: North Kern. Office: PO Box 917 Bakersfield CA 93302-0917

STANNARD, DAPHNE EVON, critical care nurse; b. New Haven, Oct. 12, 1963; d. Jerry Wilmert and Katherine Evon (Moore) S.; m. Bertram C.H. Simon, July 18, 1992. BSN, Vanderbilt U., 1986; MS in Critical Care Nursing, U. Calif., San Francisco, 1991; postgrad., U. Calif. San Francisco, San Francisco, 1991—. CCRN, Calif.; cert. ACLS. Critical care nurse U. Mich. Med. Ctr., Ann Arbor, 1986-87; nurse recovery room UCLA Med. Ctr., 1987; pub. health nurse Home Care Ptnrs., L.A., 1988; surg. ICU critical care nurse Cedars-Sinai Med. Ctr., L.A., 1988-89; critical care nurse med. surg. ICU U. Calif. Med. Ctr., San Francisco, 1989-91, critical care nurse, adult critical care float unit, 1992-95; recovery rm. nurse Mt. Zion Med. Ctr./Calif. at San Francisco Med. Ctr., San Francisco, 1992-96. Contbr. articles to profl. jours. Mem. ANA, AACN (mem. subject matter expert group for the study of practice 1995—, pres. San Francisco chpt. 1995-96, mem. editl. bd. Nursing SCAN' Critical Care 1994—), Soc. Critical Care Medicine (bd. dirs. Calif. chpt. 1995—), Nat. Coun. Family Rels., Sigma Theta Tau, Omicron Delta Kappa. Home: 1265 Washington St Apt 9 San Francisco CA 94108-1062 Office: Dept Psychological Nursing Box 0610 U Calif San Francisco Sch Nursing San Francisco CA 94143

STANOVSKY, ELAINE J.W., minister, church organization administrator; b. Vancouver, Wash., Oct. 12, 1953; d. Robert Byron and Edith Vernie Woodworth; m. Clinton Sebastian Stanovsky, June 11, 1977; children: Walker, Micah, C. Axel. BA, U. Puget Sound, Tacoma, 1976; MDiv, Harvard U., 1981. Ordained elder Pacific N.W. Conf. United Meth. Ch., 1983. Pastor Kennydale United Meth. Ch., Renton, Wash., 1981-88, Crown Hill United Meth. Ch., Seattle, 1988-90; pres., dir. Ch. Coun. of Greater Seattle, 1990-95; dist. supt. Puget Sound Dist. United Meth. Ch., Everett, Wash., 1995—. Co-author: Generation to Generation: Church Council of Greater Seattle, 1996. Trustee U. Puget Sound, 1995—; del. World Coun. of Chs., Canberra, Australia, 1991, Gen. Conf. United Meth. Ch., Portland, Oreg. and Denver, 1976, 96, Sister Ch. Program, Seattle and St. Petersburg, Russia, 1991; del. or alt. Consultation on Ch. Union, N.J., 1976-88; co-chair Seattle Holocaust Conf., 1982; mem. Mayor's Partnership for Homeless, Seattle, 1992. Avocations: gardening, hiking, reading. Office: Puget Sound Dist United Meth Ch PO Box 1052 Everett WA 98206-1052

STANTON, LEA KAYE, elementary school educator, counselor; b. Denver, Nov. 13, 1930; d. Edgar Malcolm and Eunice Lois (Chamberlain) Wahlberg; m. Charles M. Stanton, June 15, 1952; children: Gary Charles, Thomas Edgar, Brian Paul, Craig John, William Mayne. BS, Ea. Mich. U., 1954, MA, 1977, EdS in Counseling, 1984. 1st grade tchr. Taylor (Mich.) Pub. Schs., 1952-53; 1st-8th grade tchr., 7th-9th grade counselor Dearborn (Mich.) Pub. Schs., 1972-75; substitute tchr. grade 1-8 Estes Park (Colo.) Pub. Schs.; tutor YWCA, Dearborn and Inkster, Mich., 1956-59; mem. sch. adv. com. Salina Elem. Sch., Dearborn, 1972-80. V.p. Dearborn Ink Human Rels. Coun., 1960-75; bd. dirs. Dearborn Interfaith Action Coun., 1960-75; union rep. McDonald Pub. Sch., Dearborn, 1985-90; mem. Vanguard Voices Cmty. Chorale, Dearborn, 1993-94; den mother Boy Scouts Am., Dearborn. Mem. AAUW (new mem. chmn.), Women's Internat. League for Peace and Freedom, Mich. Group Psychotherapy Soc., Nat. Bd. Cert. Counselors. Avocations: hiking, reading, singing, writing. Home: PO Box 2383 Estes Park CO 80517-2383

STANTON, LEWIS HARRIS, software company executive; b. London, Apr. 2, 1954; came to U.S., 1980; s. Gerald and Carole (Harris) S.;divorced; children: Graham, Joshua. BS, U. Birmingham, Eng., 1976. CPA, Calif.; chartered acct., Eng. Sr. mgr. Arthur Andersen & Co., L.A., London, 1976-88; chief fin. officer Data Analysis Inc., L.A., 1988-96; CEO WorldSite Networks Inc., Beverly Hills, Calif., 1996-97; exec. v.p., COO, CFO MAI Sys. Corp., Irvine, Calif., 1997—. Chmn. L.A. Youth non-profit orgn., 1997. Fellow Inst. Chartered Accts.; mem. AICPA, Calif. Soc. CPAs (chmn. mems. in industry com. 1990-94), Assn. Western Securities Mgmt. (pres. 1989). Avocations: tennis, visual arts. Office: MAI Sys Corp 9601 Jeronimo Rd Irvine CA 92618-2025

STANTON, WILLIAM JOHN, JR., marketing educator, author; b. Chgo., Dec. 15, 1919; s. William John and Winifred (McGann) S.; m. Imma Mair, Sept. 14, 1978; children by previous marriage: Kathleen Louise, William John III. BS, Ill. Inst. Tech., 1940; MBA, Northwestern U., 1941, PhD, 1948. Mgmt. trainee Sears Roebuck & Co., 1940-41; instr. U. Ala., 1941-44; auditor Olan Mills Portrait Studios, Chattanooga, 1944-46; asst. prof., asso. prof. U. Wash., 1948-55; prof. U. Colo., Boulder, 1955-90; prof. emeritus, 1990—; head mktg. dept. U. Colo., 1955-71, acting dean, 1963-64; assoc. dean U. Colo. (Sch. Bus.), 1964-67. Author: Economic Aspects of Recreation in Alaska, 1953; (with Rosann Spiro) Management of a Sales Force, 10th edit., 1999 (also Spanish transl.), (with others) Challenge of Business, 1975, (with M. Etzel and B. Walker) Fundamentals of Marketing, 11th edit., 1997 (also Spanish, Portuguese and Indonesian transls.), (with M.S. Sommers and J.G. Barnes) Can. edit. Fundamentals of Marketing, 8th edit., 1998, (with K. Miller and R. Layton) Australian edit., 3d edit., 1994, (with R. Varaldo) Italian edit., 2d edit., 1990, (with others) South African edit., 1992; monographs on Alaska Tourist Industry, 1953-54; contbr. articles to profl. jours. Mem. Am. Mktg. Assn., Western Mktg. Assn., Beta Gamma Sigma. Roman Catholic. Home: 1445 Sierra Dr Boulder CO 80302-7846

STANWAY, PAUL WILLIAM, newspaper editor; b. Manchester, Eng., Apr. 22, 1950; arrived in Canada, 1976; s. William and Gladys (Wright) S.; m. Erina Danyluk, May 5, 1976; children: Scott, Nicole. Reporter Nottingham (Eng.) Post, 1969-72, Express and Star, Wolverhampton, Eng., 1972-76, Free Press, Winnipeg, Can., 1976-77; city editor Edmonton (Can.) Sun, 1978-80, news editor, 1980-81, mng. editor, 1981-84, assoc. editor, columnist, 1988-90; editor Calgary (Can.) Sun, 1988-90; European bur. chief Toronto Sun Pub., London, 1990-96; editor-in-chief Edmonton Sun/Sun Media Corp., 1992—. Avocations: skiing, golf, fishing, travel. Office: The Edmonton Sun/Sun Media Corp, 4990 92d Ave Ste 250, Edmonton, AB Canada T6B 3A1*

STAPLETON, JEAN, journalism educator; b. Albuquerque, June 24, 1942; d. James L. and Mary (Behrman) S.; m. John Clegg, Apr. 15, 1965 (dec. Sept. 1972); m. Richard Bright, Jan. 13, 1973 (div. 1985); children: Lynn, Paul, Bright; m. William Walter Farran, Nov. 9, 1996. BA, U. N.Mex., 1964; MS in Journalism, Northwestern U., 1968. Reporter Glenview (Ill.) Announcements, 1967-68, Angeles Mesa News Advertiser, L.A., 1968-69, City News Svc., Radio News West, L.A., 1969-71; press sec. polit. campaign, 1972; instr. journalism East L.A. Coll., 1973-75, prof., dept. chair, 1975—. Author: Equal Marriage, 1975, Equal Dating, 1979. Mem. NOW (pres. L.A. chpt. 1973-74), Assn. Women in Comm., Soc. Profl. Journalists, Ninety Nines, L.A. Poets Writers Collective. Democrat. Methodist. Home: 3232 Philo St Los Angeles CA 90064-4719 Office: East LA Coll 1301 Avenida Cesar Chavez Monterey Park CA 91754-6001

STAPLETON, KATHARINE HALL (KATIE STAPLETON), food broadcaster, author; b. Kansas City, Mo., Oct. 29, 1919; d. William Mabin and Katharine (Hall) Foster; m. Benjamin Franklin Stapleton, June 20, 1942; children: Benjamin Franklin, III, Craig Roberts, Katharine Hall. BA, Vassar Coll., 1941. Cookbook reviewer Denver Post, 1974-84; producer, writer, host On the Front Burner, daily radio program Sta. KOA-CBS, Denver, 1976-79, Cooking with Katie, live one-hour weekly, Sta. KOA, 1979-89; guest broadcaster Geneva Radio, 1974, London Broadcasting Corp., 1981, 82; tour leader culinaries to Britain, France and Switzerland, 1978-85. Eng., 1978. Chmn. women's div. United Fund, 1955-56; founder, chmn. Denver Debutante Ball, 1956, 57; hon. chmn. Nat. Travelers Aid Assn., 1952-56, 93-96; commr. Denver Centennial Authority, 1958-60; trustee Washington Cathedral, regional v.p., 1967-73; trustee, Colo. Women's Coll., 1975-80; sole trustee Harmes C. Fishback Found. Decorated Chevalier de L'Etoile Noire (France); recipient People-to-People citation, 1960, 66, Beautiful Activist award Altrusa Club, 1972, Gran Skillet award Colo.-Wyo. Restaurant Assn., 1981, Humanitarian of Yr. award Arthritis Found., 1995, Arts award Colo. Symphony, 1998; named Chevalier du Tastevin, 1989, Outstanding Vol. Fundraiser, Nat. Philanthropy Day, 1995. Mem. Denver Country Club.

Republican. Episcopalian. Author: Denver Delicious, 1980, 3d edit., 1983, High Notes, 1984. Home: 8 Village Rd Cherry Hills Village CO 80110-4908

STARING, GRAYDON SHAW, lawyer; b. Deansboro, N.Y., Apr. 9, 1923; s. William Luther and Eleanor Mary (Shaw) S.; m. Joyce Lydia Allum-Poon, Sept. 1, 1949; children: Diana Hilary Agnes, Christopher Paul Norman. A.B., Hamilton Coll., 1947; J.D., U. Calif.-Berkeley, 1951. Bar: Calif. 1952, U.S. Supreme Ct. 1958. Atty. Office Gen. Counsel, Navy Dept., San Francisco, 1952-53; atty. admiralty and shipping sect. U.S. Dept. Justice, San Francisco, 1953-60; assoc. Lillick & Charles, San Francisco, 1960-64, ptnr., 1965-95, of counsel, 1995—; titulary mem. Internat. Maritime Com.; bd. dirs. Marine Exchange at San Francisco, 1984-88, pres. 1986-88; instr. pub. speaking Hamilton Coll., 1947-48; adj. prof. Hastings Coll. Law, 1996-97. Author: Law of Reinsurance, 1993; assoc. editor Am. Maritime Cases, 1966-92, editor, 1992—; contbr. articles to legal jours. Mem. San Francisco Lawyers Com. for Urban Affairs, 1972-90; bd. dirs. Legal Aid Soc., San Francisco, 1974-90, v.p., 1975-80, pres., 1980-82. With USN, 1943-46, comdr. USNR. Fellow Am. Bar Found., Am. Coll. Trial Lawyers; mem. ABA (chmn. maritime ins. com. 1975-76, mem. standing com. admiralty law 1976-82, 86-90, chmn. 1990, ho. dels. 1986-90), Fed. Bar Assn. (pres. San Francisco chpt. 1968), Bar Assn. San Francisco (sec. 1972, treas. 1973), Calif. Acad. Appellate Lawyers, Maritime Law Assn. U.S. (exec. com. 1977-88, v.p. 1980-84, pres. 1984-86), Brit. Ins. Law Assn., Brit.-Am. C. of C. (bd. dirs. 1987—), World Trade Club San Francisco, Tulane Admiralty Inst. (permanent adv. bd.), Assocs. Maritime Mus. Libr. (dir. 1990—, pres. 1992-94). Home: 195 San Anselmo Ave San Francisco CA 94127-1513 Office: 2 Embarcadero Ctr Ste 2600 San Francisco CA 94111-3900

STARK, ALAN, sales and marketing administrator; b. Vallejo, Calif., Oct. 15, 1946; s. Loyal Paul and Zelma Enid (Travis) S.; m. Barbara Arata, June 12, 1971 (div. June 1980); m. Linda Roth Tiley, Aug. 31, 1984. BS in Journalism, U. Md., 1971. Salesman to colls. Harcourt Brace, San Diego, 1978-83; sales mgr. Westview Press, Boulder, 1984-85; mktg. mgr. Colo. Associated Univ. Press, Boulder, 1986; dir. sales and mktg. Fullrom Pub., Golden, Colo., 1986-91; owner Beal Mktg., Boulder, 1992-96; owner, pub. Travis Isse Pub., Bainbridge Island, Wash., 1993; dir. sales and mktg. The Mountaineers Books, Seattle, 1996—; exec. dir. Rocky Mountain Book Pubs. Assn., Boulder, 1986-93; mem. Colo. Ctr. fot Book, Denver, 1990-94, pres., 1992-94. Dog walker for cancer patients Friend of Colo. Friend, Seattle, 1994-95. With USAR, 1970-76. Avocations: sea kayaking, back country skiing, cooking, garden construction. Home: 3262 Old Mill Rd Bainbridge Island WA 98110 Office: The Mountaineers Books 1001 SW Klickitat Way Ste 201 Seattle WA 98134-1161

STARK, FORTNEY HILLMAN (PETE STARK), congressman; b. Milw., Nov. 11, 1931; s. Fortney Hillman Sr. and Dorothy M. (Mueller) S.; children: Jeffrey Peter, Beatrice Ann, Thekla Brumder, Sarah Gallun, Fortney Hillman Stark III; m. Deborah Roderick. BS, MIT; MBA, U. Calif. Teaching asst. MIT, Cambridge, 1953-54; prin. Skaife & Co., Berkeley, Calif., 1957-61; founder Beacon Savs. & Loan Assn., Antioch, Calif., 1961; pres., founder Security Nat. Bank, Walnut Creek, Calif., 1963-72; mem. 93d-102nd Congresses from 9th Calif. dist., 1973—; chmn. ways and means subcom. on health 93d-103d Congresses from 13th dist. Calif., 1973—; mem., chmn. D.C. com., Ways and Means com., subcom. Health, Select Revenue Measures, joint econ. com.; mem. ways and means com. 105th Congress. Bd. dirs. ACLU, 1971, Common Cause, 1971, Starr King Sch.; del. Dem. State Cen. Com.; trustee Calif. Dem. Coun. Capt. USAF, 1955-57. Mem. Delta Kappa Epsilon. Office: Ho of Reps 239 Cannon Bldg Washington DC 20515-0513*

STARK, JACK LEE, academic administrator; b. Urbana, Ind., Sept. 26, 1934; s. Lynn C. and Helen (Haley) S.; m. Jil Carolyn Harris, June 14, 1958; children: Janet, Jeffrey, Jennifer, Jonathan. BA, Claremont McKenna Coll., 1957; hon. degree, Redlands U., LDH, 1973. Asst. to pres. Claremont (Calif.) McKenna Coll., 1961-70, pres., 1970—. Active Pomona Valley Cmty. Hosp.; bd. dirs. Thacher Sch., Ojai, Calif. Capt. USMCR, 1957-60. Mem. Assn. Ind. Calif. Colls. and Univs. (chmn.), Ind. Colls. So. Calif. (bd. dirs.), Western Coll. Assn. (bd. dirs.). Club: California (Los Angeles). Home: 1679 Tulane Rd Claremont CA 91711-3426 Office: Claremont McKenna Coll Office of Pres 500 E 9th St Claremont CA 91711-5903

STARK, MILTON DALE, sports association executive; b. Fellows, Calif., Apr. 28, 1932; s. Ernest Esco and Ruth Hazel (Keeney) S.; m. Katherine Margaret Boyd, Dec. 17, 1955 (div. June 1978); children: Mark Boyd, Kimberly Kay, Matthew Scott, Martin Dean; m. Diana Lynn Mead, July 26, 1980; 1 child, Ryan. AA, Taft Coll., 1956; BA, Whittier Coll., 1958, MEd, 1963. Cert. ednl. adminstr., Calif. Sec. Western Softball Congress, Hollywood, Calif., 1962-70; commr. Internat. Softball Congress, Anaheim Hills, Calif., 1966-75, sec., 1975-83, exec. dir., 1983—; v.p. U.S. Fastpitch Assn., Colorado Springs, Colo., 1993—; mem. coun. Amateur Softball Assn., 1994—; sports cons. Whittier (Calif.) News, 1959-70. Editor-in-chief Softball Illus. mag., 1966-69; columnist The Fastpitch Chronicle, 1993—; contbg. author: FastPitch World, 1993; contbr. articles to softball mags. Served with USAF, 1951-55. Named to Internat. Softball Congress Hall of Fame, 1981, recipient Alumni Achievement award Whittier Coll. Lancer Soc., 1989. Mem. Whittier Coll. Alumni Assn. (bd. dirs. 1989-94). Republican. Avocations: theater, wine and book collecting, traveling. E-mail: mdstark@aol.com. Home and Office: Internat Softball Congress 6007 E Hillcrest Cir Anaheim CA 92807-3921

STARK, RAY, motion picture producer. Student, Rutgers U. Publicity agt., lit. agt.; talent agt. Famous Artist Agy., to 1957; co-founder Seven Arts Prodn. Co., 1957; ind. film producer, 1966—. Producer : (films) The World of Suzie Wong, 1960, The Night of the Iguana, 1964, Reflections in a Golden Eye, 1967, Funny Girl, 1968, The Owl and the Pussycat, 1970, Fat City, 1972, The Way We Were, 1973, Funny Lady, 1975, The Sunshine Boys, 1975, Murder By Death, 1976, Smokey and the Bandit, 1977, The Goodbye Girl, 1977, The Cheap Detective, 1978, California Suite, 1978, Chapter Two, 1979, The Electric Horseman, 1979, Seems Like Old Times, 1980, Annie, 1982, Blue Thunder, 1983, Nothing in Common, 1986, Peggy Sue Got Married, 1986, The Secret of My Success, 1987, Biloxi Blues, 1988. Steel Magnolias, 1989, Revenge, 1990, Lost in Yonkers, 1993, Barbarians at the Gate, 1993 (Emmy award Outstanding Made to Television Movie 1993), Mr. Jones, 1993, Dr. Jekyll and Ms. Hyde, 1995, Mariette in Ecstacy, 1996, To Gillian on Her 37th Birthday, 1996, Harriet the Spy, 1996, Random Hearts, 1998. Recipient Thalberg award Acad. Motion Picture Arts and Scis., 1980. Office: Hepburn Bldg W 10202 Washington Blvd Culver City CA 90232-3119

STARK, SUSAN MARIE, real estate agent; b. Milw., Aug. 5, 1959; d. Don Frances and Marie (Homar) S. BS in Comm., U. Tenn., 1981. Convention salesperson Peabody Hotel, Hilton Hotel, Memphis, 1981-83; salesperson, mktg. TV Syndication 20th Century Fox Film Corp., L.A., 1983-89; sr. residential assoc. Coldwell Banker, Brentwood, Calif., 1989—; previous property specialist Women's Coun. Realtors. Mem. L.A. Bd. Realtors, Beverly Hills/L.A. Assn. Realtors. E-mail: Starkers59@AOL.com. Office: Coldwell Banker Brentwood Ct 11990 San Vicente Blvd Ste 100 Los Angeles CA 90049-6608

STARKEY, DON J., museum director. Exec. dir. The Space Ctr., Alamogordo, N.Mex., 1993—. Office: The Space Ctr PO Box 533 Alamogordo NM 88311-0533*

STARKEY, HARRY CHARLES, retired geologist; b. Wheeling, W.Va., Dec. 10, 1925; s. Burtice Johannes and Mary Irene (Hilton) S.; BS, W.Va. U., 1950; m. Ruth Woods, May 16, 1964. With U.S. Geol. Survey, 1955-84, geologist specializing in clay mineralogy, Denver, 1950-84. With inf. U.S. Army, 1944-46. Methodist. Achievements include research in clay mineralogy, ion-exchange in clay and zeolites, chem. reactions involving clays; [illegible] 6754

STARKEY, MARIUS LANE, artist, educator; b. Sterling, Kans., Oct. 21, 1951; s. James and Nadra (Melvin) S.; m. Maria Mejia, May 23, 1979. BFA in Painting, Baker U., Baldwin City, Kans., 1976; MFA in Printmaking, Croydon (Eng.) Coll., 1982; student, Kansas City (Mo.) Art Inst., 1975. Artist in residence Young Audiences, Kansas City, Mo., 1986-89, Young Audiences, Bay Area, San Francisco, 1989-94, Learning Through Edn. in Arts, San Francisco, 1994-97; artist Vorpal Gallery, San Francisco, 1996-97. One and two-person shows include Art Ctr. Group, London, 1979, Kansas City Artist Coalition, 1986, Osaka (Japan) Contemporary Art Ctr., 1989, 91, 97, Kaibundo Gallery, Kobe City, Japan, 1989, 91, 94, 97, Joy Horwich Gallery, Chgo., 1990, McKesson World Hqrs., San Francisco, 1992, Gallery Chako, Tokyo, 1995, Commonwealth Club, San Francisco, 1996, Vorpal Gallery, San Francisco, 1997, 1999; exhibited in group shows at Morley Gallery, London, 1982, Nelson Atkins Mus., Kansas City, 1984, 85, Kansas City Mus., 1985, Mus. Hudson Highland, 1988, Mesa Gallery Group, San Francisco, 1990, Dupage Club, Oakbrook, Ill., 1992, Lake Onzui Wako Mus., Japan, 1992, McKesson World Hqrs., San Francisco, 1994, Kaleidoscope Bayfront Gallery, San Francisco, 1995, Kiabundo Gallery, Kobe, Japan, 1995, NUAL 12th Ann. Nat. Juried Show, Redding, Calif., 1996; represented in permanent collections at Nelson Atkins Mus. Print Collection, Kansas City, Helen Foresman Spenser Mus. Art, Lawrence, Kans., Hallmark Cards, Kansas City, Twenty-First Century Collections, Kansas City. Bd. dirs., chair arts com. San Francisco-Osaka Sister City Assn., 1995-99, del. Osaka, 1997, 40th Anniversary Celebration, Osaka I House, Japan, 1997. Recipient purchase award and best of show Art in the Woods, Overland Park, Kans., 1987, grant award Helene Warliter Found. of N. Mex. 1998. Home: 11 Dolores St Apt 15 San Francisco CA 94103-1031

STARKS, ELIZABETH VIAL, gifted/talented education educator; b. Chgo., Feb. 2, 1943; d. George McNaughton and Mary Margaret (Beatty) Vial; m. Edward Arnold Kearns, June 6, 1964 (div. 1978); m. Kevin James Starks, Aug. 4, 1979; children: Lauren Elizabeth Kearns, Jason Edward Kearns. BA, U. Ariz., 1964; MA, Denver U., 1994. Tchr. grade 6 Tucson Pub. Schs., 1965-66; gifted/talented tchr. grades 4-6 Sch. Dist Re-3(J), Keenesburg, Colo., 1988—; gifted/talented coord. RE-3(J) Sch. Dist., 1992—, social studies curriculum com., 1993—, technology com., 1993-94. Bd. dirs. A Woman's Place (safe house), Greeley, Colo., 1994—; chmn. adv. bd. South County A Woman's Place, Ft. Lupton, Colo., 1994—; bd. dirs. Weld Mental Health Ctr., Greeley, 1984-87; County Dem. chairperson, Greeley, 1976-79. Mem. ASCD, ACLU, Nat. Assn. Gifted and Talented, Colo. Assn. Gifted and Talented, Phi Delta Kappa, Kappa Kappa Gamma. Avocations: reading, golf, swimming, gourmet cooking, theatre. Office: Hudson Elem Sch PO Box 278 Hudson CO 80642-0278

STARKWEATHER, FREDERICK THOMAS, retired data processing executive; b. Sioux City, Iowa, Feb. 24, 1933; s. Fred Ervin and Gertrude Faye (Madden) S.; m. Margot Glassen, Nov. 19, 1959; children: Thomas Frederick, Jerry Russell, Michael Glassen. BA in Math. and Physics, U. Nebr., Omaha, 1955. Mathematician Flight Determination Lab., White Sands Missile Range, N.Mex., 1955-56; supervisory mathematician Analysis & Computation, White Sands Missile Range, 1956-81; chief data scis. div. Nat. Range Ops., White Sands Missile Range, 1981-98; ret.; Nat. council rep. Am. Def. Preparedness Assn., Washington, 1980—; pres. White Sands Pioneer Group, White Sands Missile Range, 1983-86; bd. dirs. Assn. U.S. Army, Washington. Author hist. and genealog. books; contbr. book reviews and articles to newspapers and mags. Chmn. El Paso (Tex.) City Planning Commn., 1980-84; bd. dirs. El Paso County Hist. Soc., 1983-87; mem. El Paso County Hist. Commn., 1983—. With USAR, 1955-63. Recipient Profl. Secs. Internat. Exec. of Yr. award, 1987, Conquistador award City of El Paso, 1980; named Disting. Alumnus U. Nebr., Omaha, 1985; named to Hon. Order of St. Barbara U.S. Field Arty. Assn., 1988; cited for svcs. to mankind El Paso chpt. Sertoma, 1985. Mem. Fed. Mgrs. Assn. (bd. dirs.), Freedom Found. at Valley Forge (pres. El Paso chpt., George Washington Hon. medal 1982), El Paso C. of C. (assoc. dir. 1984—, bd. dirs.), Toastmasters (dist. gov. 1970-71), Masons, Tau Kappa Epsilon (Hall of Fame 1986). Avocations: numismatics, genealogy, books, weaponry.

STARKWEATHER, TERESA MADERY, artist, educator; b. L.A., June 12, 1950; d. Earl and Maureen Madery; m. Lee A. Starkweather, May 29, 1977; children: Ashley, Chelsea. Student, Art Ctr. Coll. Design, L.A., 1970-72; BFA, Atlanta Coll. Art, 1973; credential, Calif. State U., Northridge, 1994-96. artist Chaleur, Torrance, Calif., 1991, Prestige Graphics, L.A., 1993-95; artist, designer Zarah Co., Topanga, Calif., 1991-95. Artistic dir. Echoes Cards, Topanga, Calif., 1991-94. Contbg. artist Am. Artist Mag., spring 1991, The Best of Watercolor, 1995, Splash 4 The Splendor of Light, 1996, Splash 5, 1997, Painting the Many Moods of Light, 1999; exhibited Lankershim Arts Ctr., Calif., 1990, L.A. City Hall, 1990, Orlando Gallery, Sherman Oaks, Calif., 1991, Watercolor West Nat. Exhbn., Calif., 1991, 95, 97, Century Gallery, L.A., 1992, L.A. Mcpl. Art Gallery, 1993, Artspace Gallery, L.A., 1993, Springfield Art Mus., Mo., 1994, Foothills Art Ctr., Colo., 1994, Orlando Gallery, Sherman Oaks, 1996, Nan Miller Gallery, Rochester, N.Y., 1998. Recipient Bronze medal Art Calif. Mag. Discovery Awards, 1992, 93, 1st pl. award Valley Watercolor Assn., Artspace Gallery, L.A., 1993, 98, Patron Purchase award Watercolor U.S.A., Springfield, Mo., 1994, 2d pl. award Nat. Watercolor Soc. Show, 1997, Best of Show award Valley Watercolor Soc. Show, 1998; finalist The Artist's Mag. Awards, 1996, 97; named Signature Mem., Watercolor West, 1997. Avocations: horseback riding, tennis.

STARR, GRIER FORSYTHE, retired pathologist; b. Jamestown, N.D., Oct. 6, 1926; s. Earl Grier and Grace (Forsythe) S.; m. Virginia Lucille Heidinger, June 25, 1948; children: William Grier, Joan Elizabeth Starr Barton. BS cum laude, Jamestown (N.D.) Coll., 1947; MD, Northwestern U., 1951; MS in Pathology, U. Minn., 1956. Diplomate Nat. Bd. Med. Examiners, 1952, Minn., Mich., Oreg. and Wash. state bds., Am. Bd. Pathology in Clin. Pathology, 1956, and in Pathol. Anatomy, 1957. Intern Evanston (Ill.) Hosp., 1951-52; sr. resident in pathology Henry Ford Hosp., Detroit, 1955-56; fellow in pathology Mayo Clinic, Rochester, Minn., 1952-55, cons. surgical pathology, 1956-59; cons., pathologist Lab. Pathology and Pathology Cons., Eugene, Oreg., 1959-91, pres., 1973-85; mem. staff McKenzie-Willamette Hosp., Springfield, Oreg., 1959-91—; mem. staff Sacred Heart Gen. Hosp., Eugene, Oreg., 1959-91, chief of staff, 1969-71, dir. labs., 1973-86, emeritus staff, 1992—; chmn. bd., chief ops. officer Oreg. Consol. Labs., Eugene, Oreg., 1986-89; bd. dirs. PeaceHealth (Sisters of St. Joseph of Peace), Bellevue, Wash.; affiliate in pathology Oreg. Health Scis. Ctr., Portland, 1972-88; assoc. prof. U. Oreg., Eugene, 1986. Contbr. articles to profl. jours. Served with USN, 1944-46. Fellow Am. Coll. Pathologists, Am. Soc. Clin. Pathologists; mem. AMA, Lane County Med. Soc. (pres. 1984-85), Am. Soc. Cytology, Internat. Acad. Pathologists, Pacific NW Soc. Pathologists (pres. 1979-80), Oreg. State Soc. Pathologists, Am. Soc. Dermatopathology (chmn. 1984, peer rev. com. 1976-91). Republican. Presbyterian. Avocation: raising, training and showing Am. Quarter Horse Assn.-registered cutting horses. Home: 2455 S Louis Ln Eugene OR 97405-1026

STARR, MELVIN LEE, counseling organization executive; b. N.Y.C., Mar. 17, 1922; s. Herman and Martha (Aberman) S.; m. Eileen Ferne Kagan, Sept. 7, 1947; children: Marianne, Lisa Caren. BBA, U. Miami, 1947; postgrad. Columbia U., 1949-53, U. Denver, 1955-56, Ariz. State U., 1956-57; MA, U. Ariz., 1950; EdD, Western Colo. U., 1974. Faculty, adminstrn. Tucson Pub. Schs., 1950—; tchr. Doolen Jr. High Sch., 1951-53, counselor high sch., 1953-62, asst. prin. Alice Vail Jr. High Sch., 1962-64, Catalina High Sch., 1964-68; prin. Rincon High Sch., 1968-71, Tucson High Sch., 1971-74; asst. supt. Tucson Pub. Schs., 1974-78, assoc. supt., 1978-82; pvt. practice family counseling; pres., CEO Psychol. Engring. for Bus. and Industry, Tucson, 1984—. Mem. Tucson Mayor's Com. on Human Relations, 1969—; mem. Ariz. state com. Anti Defamation League, 1971; Ariz. state adv. bd. Good Shepherd Sch. for Girls, 1971; mem. Dem. Cen. Com., Pima City, Ariz., 1968—; bd. dirs., Mobile Meals of Tucson, Pima County Bd. Health, So. Arix. Girl Scouts U.S. Council; chmn. Tucson Community Ctr. Commn.; bd. dirs. Amigos de los Americanos, AnyTown, Ariz., Lighthouse YMCA, Beacon Found., Big Bros., NCCJ, Jr. Achievement, Tucson Community Center, Pacific Western region Anti-Defamation League, Handmaker Nursing Home Pima County, United Way, CODAC, Planned Parenthood, Girl Scouts Am., Ariz. Mobile Meals, Epilepsy Soc. So. Ariz., Drug Abuse and Alcohol Consortium; adv. bd. Tucson Free Med. Clinic; bd. dirs. Los Ninos Crisis Ctr., 1995—. Mem. Ariz. Assn. Student Teaching (state treas.), NEA, Ariz. Interscholastic Assn. (pres. conf. 1971, legis. council), Ariz. Personnel and Guidance Assn., Nat. Assn. Secondary Sch. Prins., Am. Assn. Sch. Adminstrs., Assn. Supervision and Curriculum Devel., Ariz. Sch. Adminstrs., Phi Epsilon Pi, Phi Delta Kappa. Home: 7101 E River Canyon Rd Tucson AZ 85750-2111 Office: PO Box 30163 Tucson AZ 85751-0163

STARR, ROBERT IRVING, plant physiologist, chemist; b. Laramie, Wyo., Dec. 11, 1932; s. George Herman and Meriel Louise (Spooner) S.; m. Lavon Fabricius, June 10, 1956; children: Deborah Ann, Kenneth Irving. BS in Chemistry, U. Wyo., 1956, MS in Soil and Biochemistry, 1959, PhD in Plant Physiology and Chemistry, 1972. Ordained deacon and elder Presbyn. Ch. Chemist Shell Chem. Corp., Dominguez, Calif., 1956-57; biochemist Bur. Sport Fisheries and Wildlife, Denver, 1960-63; plant physiologist U.S. Bur. Sport Fisheries and Wildlife, Denver, 1968-74; plant physiologist Colo. State U., Ft. Collins, 1963-64, chemist toxic residue lab., 1965-68; analytical chemist FDA, Denver, 1964-65; environ. scientist coal mining U.S. Geol. Survey, Denver, 1974-77, chief environ. tech. unit, 1977-78; chief biol. and ecol. scis. br. Office of Surface Mining U.S. Dept. Interior, Denver, 1979-81, sr. tech. coord., cons. environ. chemistry, 1984-89; sr. scientist pesticide rsch. Wildlife Rsch. Ctr. USDA, Denver, 1989-93; cons. environ. chemistry Fort Collins, Colo., 1993—; pvt. practice cons. environ. chemistry, 1993—; cons. in environ. chemistry and fin. planning/real estate, 1982-84. Reviewer Jour. Agrl. Food Chemistry, 1970; editor, Reclamation Rev., 1981; contbr. articles to profl. jours. Served to 1st lt., AUS, 1957-64. Fellow Am. Inst. Chemists; mem. Am. Chem. Soc., Ft. Collins Swimming Club, Sigma Xi.

STARRATT, PATRICIA ELIZABETH, writer, actress, composer; b. Boston, Nov. 7, 1943; d. Alfred Byron and Anna (Mazur) S.; AB, Smith Coll., 1965; grad. prep. dept. Peabody Conservatory Music, 1961. Teaching asst. Harvard U. Grad. Sch. Bus. Aminstrn., 1965-67; mng. dir. INS Assocs., Washington, 1967-68; adminstrv. asst. George Washington U. Hosp., 1970-71; legal asst. Morgan, Lewis & Bockius, Washington, 1971-72; profl. staff energy analyst Nat. Fuels and Energy Policy Study, U.S. Senate Interior Com., 1972-74; cons., exec. asst. energy resource devel. Fed. Energy Adminstrn., Washington, 1974-75; sr. cons. energy policy Atlantic Richfield Co., 1975-76; energy cons., Alaska, 1977-78; govt. affairs assoc. Sohio Alaska Petroleum Co., Anchorage, 1978-85; legal asst. Hughes, Thorsness, Gantz, Powell and Brudin, Anchorage, 1989-90; writer, media specialist corp. affairs Alyeska Pipeline Svc., Co., 1990-95; legal asst. Hughes Thorsness Powell Huddleston & Bauman LLC, 1996-97, pres. Starratt Monarch Prodns., 1986—, sr. paralegal Brit. Petroleum, 1997—; Econ. Devel. Commn., Municipality of Anchorage, 1981; actress/asst. dir. Brattle St. Players, Boston, 1966-67, Washington Theater Club 1967-68, Gene Frankel, Broadway 1968-69; actress Aspen Resident Theater, Colo. 1985-86, Ranyevskya (The Cherry Orchard), Anchorage, 1994, Bonfila (SLAVS!), Frau Schmidt (The Sound of Music), Anchorage, 1995, Maria (Moonlight), Anchorage, 1997; Olga (Three Sisters), Eccentric Theatre Company, Anchorage, 1998; writer and assoc. producer Then One Night I Hit Her, 1983; screenwriter, prodr., actress, composer/pianist A Call to Live, 1995, Marmee (Little Women), 1997; appeared Off-Broadway in To Be Young, Gifted and Black; performed as Mary in Tennessee, Blanche in A Streetcar Named Desire, Stephanie Dickinson in Cactus Flower, Angela in Papa's Wine, Elizabeth Procter in The Crucible, Candida in Candida, Zeuss in J.B., Martha in Who's Afraid of Virginia Woolf, Amy in Dinny and The Witches, as Columbina in Servant of Two Masters, as Singer in Death of Morris Biederman, as Joan in Joan of Lorraine, as Mado in Amadee, as Mrs. Rowlands in Before Breakfast, as the girl in Hello Out There, as Angela in Bedtime Story, as Hannah in Night of the Iguana, as Lavinia in Androcles and the Lion, as Catherine in Great Catherine, as Julie in Lilliom, as First Nurse in Death of Bessie Smith, as Laura in Tea and Sympathy, as Amelia Earheart in Chamber Music; appeared at Detroit Summer Theatre in Oklahoma, Guys and Dolls, Carousel, Brigadoon, Kiss Me Kate, Finnian's Rainbow; asst. to dir. Broadway plays A Cry Of Players, A Way Of Life, Off-Broadway play To Be Young, Gifted, and Black; screenwriter Challenge in Alaska, 1986, Martin Poll Films; asst. dir. Dustin Hoffman, 1974; contbr. articles on natural gas and Alaskan econ. and environ. to profl. jours. Bd. dirs. Anchorage Community Theatre, Alaska Assn. Legal Assts., 1996—; industry rep. Alaska Eskimo Whaling Commn.; mem. Alaska New Music Forum. Mem. Actors' Equity. Episcopalian. Avocations: skiing, horseback riding, biking, hiking. Home: 1054 W 20th Ave Apt 4 Anchorage AK 99503-1749

STARSHAK, JAMES L., lawyer; b. Chgo., Feb. 3, 1945; s. Norbert Phillip and Enda (Reiter) S.; m. Susanne M. Smith, Oct. 25, 1969; children: Lesle M., Phillip E. BBA, U. Notre Dame, 1966, JD, 1969. Bar: Ill. 1969, Hawaii 1972, U.S. Dist. Ct. (no. dist.) Ill., U.S. Tax Ct., U.S. Supreme Ct. Atty. estate tax IRS, Chgo., 1969-71, Honolulu, 1971-77; ptnr. Steiner & Starshak, Honolulu, 1971-79; assoc. Conahan & Conahan, Honolulu, 1979-86; ptnr. Carlsmith, Ball et al, Honolulu, 1986—. Office: Carlsmith Ball et al Pacific Tower 22d Fl 1001 Bishop St Honolulu HI 96813-3429

STASHOWER, ARTHUR L., lawyer; b. Cleve., Apr. 12, 1930; s. Joseph G. and Tillie (Merlin) S.; m. Joy Schary, Sept. 1, 1957 (div. 1982); children: Keren, Saul, David; m. Barbara Hayden, Jan. 17, 1985. AB, U. Mich., 1951, JD with distinction, 1953. Bar: Ohio 1953, Mich. 1953, Calif. 1957, U.S. Dist. Ct. (mid. dist.) Calif. 1957, U.S. Ct. Appeals (9th cir.) 1962. Assoc. Kaplan Livingston Goodwin & Berkowitz, Beverly Hills, Calif., 1957-64; exec. United Artists Corp., L.A., 1964-65, Artists Agy. Corp., L.A., 1965-67; assoc. Greenberg & Glusker, Beverly Hills, 1967-68; ptnr. Swerdlow Glikbarg & Shimer, Beverly Hills, 1968-71, Sklar Coben & Stashower, L.A., 1971-84; of counsel Shea & Gould, L.A., 1985-88; ptnr. Chrystie & Berle, L.A., 1988-92, of counsel, 1993-97; of counsel Kenoff & Machtinger, L.A., 1997—; arbitrator Hughes Aircraft, E.A.S.T. Mem. Anti-Defamation League, 1961-79, exec. com. 1967-73; mem. Assn. Alternative Pub. Schs., L.A., 1973-79. Lt. USCGR, 1953-57. Mem. ABA, Am. Arbitration Assn., L.A. Bar Assn., State Bar Assn. Calif., Beverly Hills Bar Assn., L.A. Copyright Soc. (trustee 1986-90), Fed. Mediation and Conciliation Svc. Democrat. Jewish. Avocations: jogging. Office: Ste 1250 1999 Ave of the Stars Los Angeles CA 90067

STASSINOS, GAIL, lawyer; b. N.Y.C., July 6, 1949; d. John and Harriet (Katzen) S. BA in Psychology with honors, San Francisco State U., 1974; MA in Psychology with honors, Calif. State U., Sacramento, 1976; JD, U. Calif., Davis, 1987. Bar: Calif. 1987; Calif. C.C. counseling credential. Counselor Sacramento, 1976; head resident U. Wash., Pullman, 1976-78; pers. dir. Ctrl. Valley Opportunity Ctr., Merced, Calif., 1978-80; field rep. Calif. Sch. Employees Assn., Bakersfield, 1980; pers. analyst III Santa Barbara County, Calif., 1980-84; law clk. Beeson, Tayer, Badine, 1985; assoc. Canelo, Hansen & Wilson, Merced, Calif., 1987-89, Lea, Balavage & Arruti, Sacramento, 1989-90; pvt. practice Carmichael, Calif., 1990—; coord. ann. labor rels. conf. U. Calif., Davis, 1986; instr. U. Calif. Ext., Santa Cruz, 1978; pro tem judge small claims ct., Sacramento County. Author: (orgn. pers. manual) Central Valley Opportunity Center, 1979. Mem. ABA (litigation sect.), Sacramento Social Security Reps. Orgn., NOW (founding mem. Golden Gate chpt. 1968-69), Nat. Orgn. Social Security Reps., Calif. Trial Lawyers Assn., Calif. Women Lawyers, Capitol City Trial Lawyers, Women Lawyers of Sacramento, Bus. and Profl. Women (treas. 1984). Democrat. Jewish. Avocations: tri-lingual (English, Spanish, French), Karate greenbelt, agility dog shows, wine collecting, blues. Office: 5740 Windmill Way Carmichael CA 95608-1379

STATON, ANGELA RENEE, educator, counselor; b. Staunton, Va., Nov. 26, 1961; d. Cecil Brown and Virginia Lucille (Painter) S.; m. Steven Elliot Grande, June 20, 1997. BS, James Madison U., 1983, MEd, 1992; PhD, U. Va., 1997. Cert. counselor. Leadership coord. James Madison U., Harrisburg, Va., 1989-94; rsch. asst. U. Va., Charlottesville, Va., 1994-95, tchg. asst., 1995-97; asst. prof. Calif. State U., Fresno, 1997—; bd. dirs. Opportunity Plus, Fresno, Calif. Author: (with others) Feminist Family Therapy, 1998. Profl. Devel. grantee Calif. State U., Fresno, 1997. Mem. Internat. Assn. Marriage Family Counselors, Am. Counseling Assn., Assn. Counselor Edn. Supervision, Assn. Mulitcultural Counseling Devel., Food not Bombs. Avocations: travel, hiking, photography. Office: Calif State U Dept Coun-[illegible]

STATON, JACK WARREN, immigration judge; b. Mullens, W.Va., Dec. 29, 1954; s. William Robert and Marcella Joan (Sutphin) S.; m. Mary Robin Pryor, Sept. 4, 1976; children: Robert E. II, Michael A. BA in Polit. Sci., W.Va. U., 1976, JD, 1979. Bar: W.Va. 1979, U.S. Supreme Ct. 1987. Assoc.

Furbee, Amos, Webb & Critchfield, Morgantown, W.Va., 1979-84; fgn. svc. officer U.S. Dept. State, Washington, 1984-90; immigration judge U.S. Dept. Justice, El Centro, 1990—. Columnist (polit. commentary) The Mullens Advocate, 1974-76. Mem. W.Va. Rep. State Exec. Com., W.Va. 9th Senatorial Dist., 1974-82; trustee Am. Sch. Algiers, Algeria, 1985-86; mem. McCabe Sch. Bd., El Centro, Calif., 1996—. Presbyterian. Avocations: organist, pianist. Office: Immigration Ct 2409 La Brucherie Rd Imperial CA 92251

STATTIN, ERIC LAURENTIUS, retired savings and loan company executive; b. Chgo., Sept. 28, 1933; s. Eric Laurentius and Ingeborg (Rodstrom) S.; m. Martha Link, Sept. 1, 1956; children: Elizabeth, Eric III, Jonathan. BS in Acctg., U. Ill., 1956; postgrad., U. So. Calif., 1959-60. CPA. Tax mgr. Arthur Anderson & Co., Chgo. and Los Angeles, 1956-67; chief dep. savs. & loan commr. State of Calif., Los Angeles, 1967-69; dir. examinations and supervision Fed. Home Loan Bank Bd., Washington, 1969-71; ptnr. Touche Ross & Co., Los Angeles, 1972-78; pres. County Fed. Savs. & Loan, N.Y.C., 1978, also bd. dirs.; mng. dir. instl. Shearson Lehman, Los Angeles, 1979-85; chmn., pres. Fla. Fed. Savs. & Loan Assn., St. Petersburg, 1985-88; of counsel Touche Ross & Co., Los Angeles; bd. dirs. Pioneer Fed. Savs. Bank, Hawaii. Bd. dirs. Downtown Improvement Corp., St. Petersburg, 1985-88, Bayfront Ctr. Found., St. Petersburg, 1986-88; trustee Heritage Family of Mutual Friends, St. Petersburg, 1987—; mem. Golden Triangle Civic Assn., St. Petersburg, 1986-88. Served to capt. U.S. Army, 1957. Mem. Am. Inst. CPA's, Twentieth Century Econ. Roundtable, Nat. Council Savs. Instns. (chmn. tax. com. 1986-88, class III dir. 1987-88). Republican. Clubs: Los Angeles Athletic; Racquet (St. Petersburg). Avocations: running, racquetball, tennis, skiing, home remodeling.

STAVENGER, PAUL LEWIS, chemical engineer; b. La Grange, Ill., Mar. 17, 1924; s. Lewis and Clara Rose (Burdorf) S.; m. Barbara Louise Boesel, Feb. 22, 1952; children: Pamela, Nash, Derek lewis, Timothy Lewis. BS in Chem. Engring., U. Ill., 1947; MS in Chem. Engring., U. Mich., 1948. Dir. of technology Dorr-Oliver, Inc., Milford, Conn., 1948-87. Patentee in field. Chmn. bd. of Christian Mission, Saugatuck Congrl. Ch., Westport, Conn., 1965, chmn. bd. deacons, 1968, ch. moderator, 1970. With USN, 1943-45. Fellow AICE (gen. arrangements chmn. 70th ann. meeting, N.Y.C., 1977, chmn. admissions com., chmn. pubs. com., chmn. Fairfield County section, chmn. N.Y.C. section). Avocations: sailing, woodworking.

STAYTON, RICHARD JOSEPH, journalist, editor; b. Linton, Ind., Nov. 3, 1946; s. Richard Dale and Rose Margaret (Smith) S.; m. Mary McNamara, Aug. 23, 1997; 1 child, Daniel McNamara. MFA, San Francisco State U., 1973. Theatre critic L.A. Herald Examiner, 1983-89; writer, drama critic L.A. Times, 1989-94; mag. editor WESTWAYS Mag., L.A., 1996-98; comm. cons. Sheppard Assocs., Glendale, 1998-99. Author (play) After the First Death, 1985 (Goshen Peace Play prize 1985). Office: Sheppard Assocs 110 N Maryland Ave Glendale CA 91206

STEAD, JERRE L., telecommunications company executive; b. Maquoketa, Iowa, Jan. 8, 1943; s. H. Victor and Anna Catherine (Grindrod) S.; m. Mary Joy Kloppenburg, Dec. 26, 1961; children: Joel A., Jay A. BBA, U. Iowa, 1965; grad. advanced mgmt. program, Harvard U., 1982. Mgr. regional sales Honeywell Corp., Phila., 1971-73; dir. prodn. Honeywell Corp., Mpls., 1974-75, dir. distbn., 1975-76, v.p. fin. and adminstrn., Brussels, 1979-82; v.p., gen. mgr. Honeywell-Phillips Med. Electronics, Brussels, 1981-82; v.p., gen. mgr. Honeywell Corp., Mpls., 1982-85, v.p., group exec., 1986; pres., COO Sq. D Co., Palatine, Ill., 1987-88, pres., CEO, chmn. bd., 1989-91, also bd. dirs.; chmn., CEO Global Info. Solutions AT&T, N.Y.C., 1991-95; CEO Legent Corp., Vienna, Va., 1995—; bd. dirs. Eljer Industries, Plano, Tex., Ameritech, Chgo., USG, Chgo., TJ Internat., Inc. Mem. Pres.' coun. Am. Lung Assn., N.Y.C., 1986—, The Wash. Ctr. Nat. Campaign Com.; bus. adv. com. N.C. A&T U.; trustee Coe Coll., Cedar Rapids, Iowa, 1987; mem. coun. on competitiveness Ill. Bus. Roundtable; bd. visitors U. Iowa, Iowa City. Mem. Nat. Elec. Mfrs. Assn. (bd. govs. 1984—), Nat. Assn. Elec. Distbrs. (edn. com.), Chgo. Com., Elec. Mfrs. Club. Republican. Methodist. Office: TJ Internat Inc 200 E Mallard Dr Boise ID 83706-6658

STEAD LEE, POLLY JAE See **LEE, PALI JAE**

STEADMAN, ROBERT KEMPTON, oral and maxillofacial surgeon; b. Mpls., July 8, 1943; s. Henry Kempton and Helen Vivian (Berg) S.; m. Susan E. Hoffman; children: Andrea Helene, Darcy Joanne, Richard Kempton, Michael Dean. BS, U. Wash., Seattle, 1969, DDS, 1974. Diplomate Am. Bd. Oral and Maxillofacial Surgery. Residency USAF, Elgin AFB, Fla., 1974-75; resident oral and maxillofacial surgery U. Okla., 1977-80, La. State U., Shreveport, 1980-81; pvt. practice Spokane, Wash., 1981—; cons. Group Health Coop., 1989—; mem. adv. bd. Osteoporosis Awareness Resource, 1988—. Select recruiting ptnr. U. Wash. Sch. Dentistry, 1990. Fellow Am. Acad. Cosmetic Surgery, Internat. Assn. Oral and Maxillofacial Surgery, Am. Coll. Oral and Maxillofacial Surgery, Am. Soc. Oral and Maxillofacial Surgery, Acad. Gen. Dentistry; mem. Internat. Soc. Plastic, Aesthetic and Reconstructive Surgery, Am. Acad. Cosmetic Surgery, Delta Sigma Delta (pres. 1987-88). Office: 801 W 5th Ave Ste 212 Spokane WA 99204-2800

STEARNS, SUSAN TRACEY, lighting design company executive, lawyer; b. Seattle, Oct. 28, 1957; d. Arthur Thomas and Roberta Jane (Arrowood) S.; m. Ross Alan De Alessi, Aug. 11, 1990; 1 child, Chase Arthur. AA, Stephens Coll., 1977, BA, 1979; JD, U. Wash., Seattle, 1990. Bar: Calif. 1990, U.S. Ct. Appeals (9th cir.) 1990, U.S. Dist. Ct. (no. dist.) Calif 1990, U.S. Dist. Ct. (we. dist.) Wash. 1991, Wash. 1991. TV news prodr. KOMO, Seattle, 1980-86; atty. Brobeck, Phleger & Harrison, San Francisco, 1990-92; pres. Ross De Alessi Lighting Design, Seattle, 1993—. Author periodicals in field. Alumnae Assn. Coun. Stephens Coll., Columbia, Mo., 1995—. Named Nat. Order of Barristers U. Washington, Seattle, 1990. Mem. ABA (mem. state labor and employment law subcom.), Wash. State Bar Assn. (mem. bench-bar-press com.), State Bar Calif., King County Bar Assn., Bar Assn.San Francisco, Wash. Athletic Club. Avocations: travel, dance. Office: Ross De Alessi Lighting Design 2815 2nd Ave Ste 280 Seattle WA 98121-1261

STEBBINS, ELIZABETH JOSEPH HINTON, management and statistics educator, researcher; b. L.A., Sept. 14, 1923; d. James Thomas and M. Evangeline (Russell) Hinton; m. James Frederick Stebbins, July 7, 1945 (dec.); children: James Wyatt (dec.), John Russell. BA Archeology, Anthropology, Fine Arts, U. So. Calif., 1945, postgrad. in Edn.; MA in Psychology and Fine Arts, Chapman U., 1963; PhD in Human Behavior-Leadership, U.S. Internation U., 1989. Elem. tchr. L.A. Unified Sch. Dist. and Orange County Sch. Dists.; sch. administr. Covina Valley (Calif.) Sch. Dist.; cons. curriculum and evaluation L.A. County Schs., 1965-71; project mgr. for innovative sch. model State of Calif., 1971-72; v.p. The Bradford Group-Exec. Search, Newport Beach, Calif., 1978-84; commodity broker, 1975-78; prof. mgmt. and supervision Coastline C.C., 1979—; prof. mgmt., stats. and counseling U. Phoenix, Orange County, Calif., 1990—; owner, pres. profl. career advisement Hinton Cons. Recipient Nat. Inst. for Staff and Orgnl. Devel., 1992. Mem. Calif. Assn. for Measurement & Evaluation in Counseling (past-pres.), Nat. Counsel Measurement in Edn., Am. Ednl. Rsch. Assocs., Calif. Assn. Counseling and Devel., Chi Phi. Avocation: oil and water color painting. Address: 23592 Windsong Apt 41A Aliso Viejo CA 92656-1392

STECKLER, CRAIG THEODORE, law enforcement official; b. Scottsfield, Ill., Feb. 3, 1944; s. Albert George and Mary Lorene (Johnston) S.; m. Karen Capellutto, Mar. 11, 1978; children: Theresa, Rachael, Suzanne, Mark. AA, Saddleback Coll., 1973; BA, Calif. State U., L.A., 1975; postgrad., U. Va., 1982, Peace Officer Standards & Tng., Pomona, Calif., 1986. Dist. mgr. Orange County Register, Santa Ana, Calif., 1962-68; police officer, sgt., then lt. City of San Clemente, Calif., 1968-80; police chief City of Piedmont, Calif., 1980-86; dep. police chief City of Fremont, Calif., 1986-92, chief of police, 1992—; instr., Cypress (Calif.) Coll., 1975-77, Los Mondos Coll., Pittsburg, calif., 1982-83. Mem. Am. Mgmt. Assn., Calif. Peace Officers Assn., Calif. Police Chiefs Assn. (bd. dirs.), Command Coll. Grads. (bd. dirs.), Rotary. Republican. Roman Catholic. Avocation: golf. Office: Fremont Police Dept 2000 Stevenson Blvd Fremont CA 94538-2336*

STECKLER, LARRY, publisher, editor, author; b. Bklyn., Nov. 3, 1933; s. Morris and Ida (Beekman) S.; m. Catherine Coccozza, June 6, 1959; children: Gail Denise, Glenn Eric, Kerri Lynn, Adria Lauren. Student, CCNY, 1951. Assoc. editor Radio-Electronics mag., N.Y.C., 1957-62, editor, 1967-85; pub., editor in chief Radio Electronics mag., 1985-92; electronics editor Popular Mechanics mag., N.Y.C., 1962-65; assoc. editor Electronic Products mag., Garden City, N.Y., 1965-67; editorial dir. Merchandising 2-Way Radio mag., N.Y.C., 1975-77; v.p., dir. Gernsback Publs., N.Y.C., 1975-84, pres., dir., 1984—; pub., editorial dir. Spl. Projects mag., 1980-84, Radio-Electronics Ann., 1982-84; pub., editor in chief Hands-On Electronics, 1984-88, Computer Digest, 1985-90, Experimenters Handbook, 1986-96, Modern Short Stories, 1987-90, Video/Stereo Digest, 1989-91, Popular Electronics Mag., 1988—, GIZMO, 1988—, Hobbyists Handbook, 1989-96, Sci. Probe! mag., 1989-93, StoryMasters, 1989—, Electronics Shopper, 1990—, Electronics Market Ctr., 1991—, Electronics Now Mag., 1992—, Radio Craft, 1993-96, Poptronix Handbook, 1996—; pres. Claggk, Inc., 1986-97, Silicon Chip, 1993-94, Sci. Probe Inc., 1989-93, Poptronix Inc., 1997—; pub., editor-in-chief Poptronix online, 1997—; mem. electronics adv. bd. Bd. Coop. Ednl. Services, Nassau County, N.Y., 1975-77; pres. Electronics Industry Hall of Fame, 1985—; bd. dirs. Pub. Hall of Fame, 1987-89. Author books, handbooks; pub.; contbr. articles to profl. jours. Bd. dirs. Nassau County council Camp Fire Girls, 1971-72. Served with U.S. Army, 1953-56. Recipient Coop. award Nat. Alliance TV and Electronic Services Assns., 1974, 75; inducted into Electronics Industry Hall of Fame, 1985. Mem. IEEE, Internat. Soc. Cert. Electronic Technicians (chmn. 1974-76, 79-81, 93-95, Chmn.'s award 1985, dir.-at-large 1991-93, rep. to NESDA bd. 1991-93, Region 9 dir. 1995-97), Nat. Electronics Sales and Svc. Dealers Assn. (rec. sec. N.Y. state 1976-78, Man of Yr. award 1975, 85, treas. 1991-94, M.L. Finneyberg Excellence award 1994), Am. Mgmt. Assn., Radio Club Am., Internat. Underwater Explorers Soc., Am. Soc. Bus. Press Editors (sr.), Internat. Performing Magicians (exec. dir.), Soc. Profl. Journalists, L.A. Press. Home: 9072 Lawton Pine Dr Las Vegas NV 89129-7044 Office: Gernsback Pub Inc 500 BiCounty Blvd Farmingdale NY 11735-3918

STECKLER, PHYLLIS BETTY, publishing company executive; b. N.Y.C.; d. Irwin H. and Bertha (Fellner) Schwartzbard; m. Stuart J. Steckler; children: Randall, Sharon Steckler-Slotky. BA, Hunter Coll.; MA, NYU. Editorial dir. R.R. Bowker Co., N.Y.C., Crowell Collier Macmillan Info. Pub. Co., N.Y.C., Holt Rinehart & Winston Info. Systems, N.Y.C.; pres., CEO Oryx Press, Scottsdale, Ariz., 1973-76, Phoenix, 1976—; adj. prof. mktg. scholarly publs. Ariz. State U., Tempe; mem. president's corp. adv. coun. Hunter Coll.; mem. dean's coun. Coll. of Extended Edn., Ariz. State U., Phoenix. Past chmn. Info. Industry Assn.; pres. Ariz. Ctr. for the Book; v.p. Contemporary Forum of Phoenix Art Mus., Phoenix Pub. Libr. Friends; past pres. Friends of the Librs., U.S.A.; mem. Ariz. Women's Forum. Recipient Women Who Make a Difference award The Internat. Women's Forum, 1995, Excellence in Pub. award Ariz. Book Pub. Assn., 1997 ; elected to Hunter Coll. Hall of Fame. Mem. ALA, Ariz. Libr. Assn., Univ. Club of Phoenix (pres.). Home: 6446 N 28th St Phoenix AZ 85016-8946 Office: Oryx Press 4041 N Central Ave Ste 700 Phoenix AZ 85012-3397

STEEFEL, DAVID SIMON, lawyer; b. Mpls., June 27, 1951; s. Lawrence D. Jr. and Marion (Charlson) S.; m. Mary Ann Moody, May 24, 1981; children: Emily, Daniel, Katherine. BA, Carleton Coll., 1973; JD, U. Colo., 1978. Bar: Colo. 1978, U.S. Dist. Ct. Colo. 1978, U.S. Ct. Appeals (10th cir.) 1978. Assoc. Gorsuch, Kirgis, Denver, 1978-80; assoc. Holme Roberts & Owen, Denver, 1980-84, ptnr., 1984—; instr. U. Colo. Law Sch., Boulder, 1978, 91. Home: 1300 Green Oaks Dr Littleton CO 80121-1331 Office: Holme Roberts & Owen 1700 Lincoln St Ste 4100 Denver CO 80203-4541

STEEL, JON, advertising executive. Vice chmn., strategic planning dir. Goodby Silverstein & Ptnrs., San Francisco. Office: Goodby Silverstein & Ptnrs 720 California St San Francisco CA 94108-2404*

STEELE, CHARLES GLEN, retired accountant; b. Faulkton, S.D., July 24, 1925; s. Clifford D. and Emily O. (Hanson) S.; m. Shirley June Ferguson, Nov. 9, 1947; children: Richard Alan (dec.), Deborah Ann Steele Most. B.B.A., Golden Gate U., San Francisco, 1951, M.B.A., 1962. With Deloitte Haskins & Sells, 1951-86, partner, 1963-86, partner charge Chgo. office, 1973-76; partner charge personnel and adminstrn. Deloitte Haskins & Sells, N.Y.C., 1976-78; chmn., chief exec. officer Deloitte Haskins & Sells, 1978-86; instr. evening program Golden Gate U., 1952-58. Served with USNR, 1943-48. Recipient Elijah Watts Sells Gold medal for highest grade in U.S. for C.P.A. exam., 1951. Mem. Am. Inst. C.P.A.s. Home and Office: 26349 Rio Ave Carmel CA 93923-9101

STEELE, JOELLE, writer, artist, photographer; b. San Francisco, Apr. 19, 1951; d. LeRoy Basilio and Norma Elisabeth (Steele) Martelli. Ind. mgmt. cons. San Francisco, 1973-78; gen. mgr. Richard L. Segal & Assocs., Santa Monica, Calif., 1980-84; ind. mgmt. cons. L.A., 1985-89; ind. pub., editor The New Leaf Press Newsletter, L.A., 1985-90; ind. writer, artist, photographer L.A., 1989-97; ind. writer, artist Pacific Grove, Calif., 1997—. Author 17 books; contbr. over 600 articles to jours. and publs. Recipient various awards for art and poetry; certs. completion/ach. in horticulture, astrology and graphology. Avocations: philately, indoor gardening, reading, astrology, bicycling, fossils, minerals & shells.

STEELE, NANCY EDEN ROGERS, educator; b. Elgin, Ill., Aug. 18, 1946; d. Vance Donald and Barbara Marie (Yarwood) Rogers; m. James Frederick Steele, Apr. 12, 1976; children: Justin Vance Jabari, Barbara Marie Noni. BS, Centenary Coll., 1968; MA, U. Nebr., 1971. Program asst. Head Start & Follow Through, Lincoln, Nebr., 1971-74; K-12 resource tchr. Nantucket (Mass.) Pub. Schs., 1975-77; kindergarten lead tchr. Parkville Sch., Guaynabo, P.R., 1977-79; instr. in gen. psychology L.A. C.C., Sebana Seca, P.R., 1978-79; lang. arts and parent edn. tchr. Sweetwater Union H.S. Dist., Chula Vista, Calif., 1980-86; upper grade team leader Park View Elem. Sch., Chula Vista, 1986-91; upper grade tchr. Clear View Elem. Sch., Chula Vista, 1991-94; mentor tchr. Chula Vista Elem. Sch. Dist., 1990-94; acad. dir. AmeriCorps Nat. Civilian Cmty. Corps, San Diego, 1994-96; asst. prin. Harborside Elem. Sch., Chula Vista, 1996-98; prin. Burton C. Tiffany Elem. Sch., Chula Vista, 1998—; cons. in field. Author: Peace Patrol: A Guide for Creating a New Generation of Problem Solvers, 1994 (Golden Bell award 1993); co-author: Power Teaching for the 21st Century, 1991. Recipient Peacemaker of Yr. award San Diego Mediation Ctr., 1993, Champion for Children award Children's Hosp. and San Diego Office of Edn., 1994, Leadership award San Diego Channel 10, 1998. Mem. ASCD, AAUW, Nat. Coun. for Social Studies, Assn. Calif. Sch. Adminstrs., Chula Vista Aquatics Assn. (bd. dirs. 1986-96), Optimist Club. Home: 1551 Malibu Point Ct Chula Vista CA 91911-6116

STEELE, WILLIAM ARTHUR, financial analyst, public utilities executive; b. Albuquerque, Dec. 21, 1953; s. William Robert and Lois Ellen (Garvett) S. BSBA, U. No. Colo., 1976; MBA, U. Phoenix, Denver, 1987. Buyer Joslins Dept. Stores, Denver, 1978-79; transp. specialist Colo. Pub. Utilities Commn., Denver, 1979-80, fin. analyst, 1980-83, sr. fin. analyst, 1983-87, prin. fin. analyst, 1987—. Mem. Colo. State Mgr. Assn., Nat. Assn. Regulatory Commn. (staff subcom. on mgmt. analysis). Avocations: skiing, hiking, fishing, golf. Office: Pub Utilities Commn 1580 Logan St Denver CO 80203-1939

STEEN, NANCY, artist; b. Denver, Feb. 7, 1949; d. John and Petrita (Pino) Ciddio; m. Charles A. Steen, Nov. 13, 1968 (div. June 1976); children: Monica Lee Steen, Charles A. Steen III; m. Ben Q. Adams, Dec. 31, 1985. BA cum laude, Gonzaga U., 1973; postgrad., N.Mex. State U., 1973-74, U. N.Mex., 1974-76. Pub., owner New Leaf Press, Walnut Creek, Calif., 1974-79, The Leaf Press, Santa Monica, Calif., 1974-79, New Leaf Press, Albuquerque, 1974-79; rsch. adminstr. Taos Editions, Albuquerque, 1981-89; asst. dir. Western Graphics, Albuquerque, 1983—, R.C. Gorman pub., 1983-91. Author: R.C. Gorman: The Graphic Works, 1988, Who is R.C. Gorman?: An Insiders Portrait, 1996; exhibited in one-woman and group shows including Art Outdoors, Albuquerque, 1980, Mus. of Art, Albuquerque, 1980, 81, Susanne Brown, Scottsdale, Ariz., 1981, Mus. of Art, Santa Fe, 1982, Am. Design, Dallas, 1983, Phoenix Art Mus., 1983, Nabisco World Headquarters, East Hanover, N.J., 1984, Gallery One, Dallas, 1986, Gallery One, Denver, 1986, 87, Gallery Mach, Seattle, 1988, Mus. of the Permain Basin, Odessa, Tex., 1989, Silver City (N.Mex.) Mus., 1990, Santa Fe Style, Madison, Wis., 1990, Denver Art Mus., 1993, Dartmouth Street Gallery, 1994, Fiesta Del Carazon Creative Response to AIDS, Albuquerque, 1994, Live at the KIMO, Albuquerque, 1994; exhibited in numerous permant collections include L.A. County Mus. of Art, Oakland Mus. of Art, San Jose Mus. of Art, Phoenix Art Mus., U. Nev., Koofenay Sch. of Art, U. Calgary, U. Wash., N.Mex. State U., Maderia Sch., Tamarind Inst., Crocker Gallery, Western Graphics Collection, Mus. of Fine Art, Monterey Peninsula Mus. of Art, many others. Chairperson NAMES Project-Quilt Dis., Albuquerque, 1994; bd. dirs. NMAPLA-N.Mex. Assn. of People Living with AIDS, Albuquerque, 1993-94; fundraiser Make A Wish, Denver, 1994, Am. Heart Assn., Honolulu, Albuquerque, 1994-97. Grantee N.Mex. State U., 1973. Mem. Pi Beta Phi. Democrat. Roman Catholic. Avocations: gardening, reading, music. Home: PO Box 373 Corona NM 88318-0373 Office: Western Graphics Workshop PO Box 373 Corona NM 88318-0373

STEEN, PAUL JOSEPH, retired broadcasting executive; b. Williston, N.D., July 4, 1932; s. Ernest B. and Inez (Ingebrigtson) S.; m. Judith Smith; children—Michael M., Melanie. BA, Pacific Luth. U., 1954; MS, Syracuse U., 1957. Producer, dir. Sta. KNTV, San Jose, Calif., 1957-58, Sta. KVIE, Sacramento, 1958-60; asst. prof. telecommunications Pacific Luth. U., Tacoma, 1960-67; dir. ops. Sta. KPBS San Diego State U., 1967-74; gen. mgr., 1974-93, prof. telecommunications and film, 1974-93, dir. univ. telecommunications; co-chmn. Office of New Tech. Initiatives. Dir. (tel. program) Troubled Waters (winner Nat. Edn. TV award of excellence 1970). With AUS. Named Danforth Assoc. Mem. Pacific Mountain Network (bd. dirs., chmn., bd. of govs. award 1993), NATAS, Assn. Calif. Pub. TV Stas. (pres.), Pi Kappa Delta. Home: 4930 Campanile Dr San Diego CA 92115-2331

STEENSGAARD, ANTHONY HARVEY, federal agent; b. Rapid City, S.D., Mar. 21, 1963; s. Harvey Hans and Dorothy Lorraine (Hansen) S. Student, Anchorage C.C., 1983-84; BSCE, U. Alaska, 1985; AAS in Indsl. Security, C.C. Air Force, 1989; BS in Criminal Justice, Wayland U., 1989; MS in Computer Systems Engring., U. Calif., San Diego, 1996. Lic. pilot, radio operator; cert. hostage negotiator FBI; cert. in-flight security specialist FAA. Bookseller B. Dalton Bookseller, Rapid City, S.D., 1978-81, Anchorage, Alaska, 1981-83; warehouseman Sears, Roebuck & Co., Anchorage, 1983-85; security specialist Alaska Air N.G., Anchorage, 1985-88; agt., draftsman, engring. cons. U.S. Border Patrol, El Centro, Calif., 1988—; pvt. computer cons., 1994—. Author: Unit Security Manager's Guide Book, 1988. Vol. U.S. Senator George McGovern's Campaign, Rapid City, 1980, Congressman Tom Daschle's Campaign, Rapid City, 1980, Spl. Olympics, Rapid City, 1981; observer CAP, Anchorage, 1981; public affairs officer Civil Air Patrol, Rapid City, S.D., 1996. With USNR, 1980-81, USMC, 1981-85, USAFR, 1985-95. Recipient hon. sci. award Bausch and Lomb, 1984, commendation State of Alaska, 1987. Mem. HTML Writer's Guild, Am. Legion, Air Force Assn., VFW, Fraternal Order Eagles, Fraternal Order of Police. Avocations: reading, computers, aviation, history, wargaming. Office: US Border Patrol 1111 N Imperial Ave El Centro CA 92243-1795

STEENSMA, MICHAEL ERIC, controller; b. Logan, Utah, Sept. 18, 1965; s. Robert Charles and Sharon Carol (Hogge) S.; m. Ginger Hunsaker, June 30, 1989; children: Ryan Michael, Cameron Lewis. BS in Fin., U. Utah, 1989, MBA, 1993. Office asst. Triad Am. Corp., Salt Lake City, 1985-87; acct. Resolution Trust Corp., Salt Lake City, 1987-89; auditor Salt Lake County, Salt Lake City, 1989-90; plant acct. Becton Dickinson & Co., Sandy, Utah, 1991-96, plant contr., 1996—. Youth league coach Sandy City Recreation, 1998. Mem. Inst. Mgmt. Accts., U. Utah Alumni Assn. Avocations: skiing, basketball, golf, softball, reading. Office: Becton Dickinson & Co 9450 State St Sandy UT 84070-3234

STEERS, GEORGE W., lawyer; b. N.Y.C., Jan. 29, 1941. BA, Yale U., 1963; LLB cum laude, Columbia U., 1966. Bar: Wash. 1970. Law clk. U.S. Ct. Appeals (2d cir.), 1966-67; ptnr. Stoel Rives, LLP, Seattle, Wash., 1974—. Mem. ABA, Wash. State Bar Assn., Seattle-King County Bar Assn. Office: Stoel Rives LLP 600 University St Ste 3600 Seattle WA 98101-4109*

STEFAN, VLADISLAV, academic administrator; b. Feb. 5, 1948; s. Bozhidar and Rosanda Stefan; m. Svetlana Stefan, 1975 (dec. 1988); 1 child, Andrej. BEE, U. Belgrade, Russia, 1972, MS, 1975; DSc, Russian Acad. Scis., 1978. Rsch. scientist Inst. Nuclear Scis., Belgrade, 1973-81; asst. prof. U. Belgrade, 1979-81; rsch. scientist MIT, Cambridge, 1981-82, UCLA, 1982-83; rsch. scientist, prof. U. Calif., San Diego, 1984-89; pres. Inst. for Advanced Physics Studies, La Jolla, Calif., 1989-96, The Stefan U., La Jolla, Calif., 1996—; vis. rsch. physicist P.N. Lebedev Physics Inst., Russian Acad. Scis., Moscow, 1977-79; referee Physics of Fluids, Princeton, N.J., 1983—; cons. Maxwell Labs., Inc., San Diego, 1985-89; proposal referee NSF, Washington, 1987-90, NASA, Washington, 1988-90. Author: Physics and Society, 1997, Elthspeth's Wisdom, 1998; editor: Nonlinear and Relativistic Effects, 1992; series editor: Research Trends in Physics, 1990—. Recipient award Inst. Boris Kidrich, Belgrade, 1978, award Internat. Rsch. Exch., 1980. Fellow Am. Phys. Soc. mem. AAAS, Am. Optical Soc., Am. Acoustical Soc. Avocations: painting, music, rock climbing. Office: 7596 Eads Ave La Jolla CA 92037-4813

STEFANKI, JOHN X., airline pilot; b. Chgo., July 14, 1920; s. Stephen and Anastasia (Stopak) S.; m. Dorothy Lancaster, Apr. 4, 1945; children: Cathy Ann, Steve, John, Mike, Judy, Larry, Mary, Megan, Dorothy. Student, Western Ill. U., 1940-41, Northwestern U., 1942, U. Iowa, Elmhurst Coll. Capt. United Air Lines, 1946-85, ret.; aviation safety cons. Lt. USN, 1942-46. Recipient Gen. Spruance award SAFE, 1973, Pfizer award of Merit U.S. Civil Def. Coun., 1974, Outstanding Alumni Achievement award Western Ill. U., 1975, Cert. Appreciation NFPA, 1976, Silver Plate award Internat. Assn. Airport and Seaport Police, London UK, 1977, cert. Commendation State of Calif., 1981, Annual Air Safety award, Air Line Pilot Assn., 1978, Laura Taber Barbour Air Safety award Flight Safety Found., 1990, others. Mem. NFPA (former chmn. 424 airport/community emergency planning, mem. planning com.), Ret. Airline Pilots Assn. (legis. chmn., v.p. legis. com., Am. Safety award 1978), others. Democrat. Roman Catholic. Home: 26901 Beatrice Ln Los Altos CA 94022-3464

STEGENGA, PRESTON JAY, international education consultant; b. Grand Rapids, Mich., July 9, 1924; s. Miner and Dureth (Bouma) S.; m. Marcia Jean DeYoung, July 28, 1950; children: James Jay, Susan Jayne. BA, Hope Coll., 1947; MA, Columbia U., 1948; PhD, U. Mich., 1952; LHD (hon.), Northwestern Coll., Iowa, 1989. Instr. history, polit. sci. Berea Coll., Ky., 1948-50; asoc. prof. Berea Coll., 1952-55; assistantship U. Mich., 1950-52; pres. Northwestern Coll., Orange City, Iowa, 1955-66; chief Cornell U. Project, U. Liberia-U.S. AID Program, Monrovia, W. Africa, 1966-68; coordinator internat. program Calif. State U., Sacramento, 1968-71; dir. Calif. State U. (Internat. Center), 1971-88; acting v.p. acad. affairs Calif. State U., 1974-75; spl. asst. to pres. Calif. State U., Sacramento, 1988-92; mem. Calif. State Liaison Com. for Internat. Edn.; ednl. cons. to Pres., Republic of Liberia, 1973-74; cons. internat. programs Am. Assn. State Colls. and Univs., 1975-89; cons. UN Devel. Programme, 1975-88; internat. edn. cons., 1992—; v.p. Sacramento chpt. UN Assn., U.S.A., 1969-71, pres., 1971-73, bd. dirs., 1973-; mem. Calif. UN Univ. Adv. Coun., 1976-80, internat. trade com. C. of C., 1984—, chair coll.-U. com., 1995—, com. World Trade Ctr., 1996—; pres. Tri-State Coll. Conf., 1963-64; dir. Fulbright project for Chinese scholars, 1985; cons. internat. projects Calif. State Fair, 1990—. Author: Anchor of Hope, 1954; asst. to editor History of Edn. Jour.; contbr. articles to profl. jours. Trustee Western Sem., Mich., Northwestern Coll., Iowa, 1955-66, 91-96, New Brunswick Sem., N.J., 1955-66, Global Calif. Coun., 1991-93; trustee, v.p. World Affairs Coun., 1976-77, 85-90, pres., 1990-92, trustee, 1993-; mem. Task Force for Improving Am. Competence in World Affairs, 1980-89; mem. internat. bd. Los Rios Coll. Found., 1980-85; mem. Am. Coun. for UN U., 1979-85, Interfaith Svc. Bd., 1985-90; bd. dirs. New Zealand-Sacramento Sister City, 1989—. With AUS, 1942-45. Decorated Purple Heart; named hon. chief Kpelle Tribe, West Africa, 1973, hon. commodore Port of Sacramento, 1983, Multi-Cultural Educators Hall of Fame, 1996; recipient Disting. Svc. award UN Assn., 1971, Republic of Venezuela Edn. award, 1979, Outstanding Svc. award Fed. Republic of Germany, 1985, Disting. Svc. award Calif. State U. Chancellor, 1988, Citation of Achievement, Calif. Sec. of State, 1988, U.S. Congl. Register

Recognition Citation, 1988, President's Award, World Affairs Coun., 1992, Gov.'s award Calif. State Fair, 1993, Internat. award Sacramento C. of C., 1993, Disting. Svc. award Assn. Citizens & Friends of Liberia, 1995; Ministry of Edn. scholar Republic of China, 1981; German Acad. Exch. Svc. fellow U. Bonn, 1981; Hon. Legis. Resolutions, Calif. State Senate and Assembly, 1988. Mem. Assn. Iowa Coll. and Univ. Pres. (v.p. 1965-66), NEA, Calif. State Univ. Student Pers. Assn., Coun. for Internat. Visitors, Am. Acad. Polit. and Social Sci., Assn. for Advancement of Dutch-Am. Studies, Phi Delta Kappa, Phi Kappa Phi, Phi Beta Delta. Mem. Reformed Ch. Am. Home: 545 Mills Rd Sacramento CA 95864-4911

STEGMAN, CHARLES ALEXANDER (CHUCK ALEXANDER STEGMAN), marketing professional; b. Denver, Apr. 17, 1959; s. Harvey Eugene and Mary Martha (Newell) S. BSEE, U. Colo., 1981. Mktg. rep. Businessland, Oakland, Calif., 1984-86, sr. mktg. rep., 1986; systems engr. instr. Businessland of San Jose, 1986-87; mktg. mgr. of networks Businessland, San Jose, Calif., 1987-88, mgr. mktg. advanced systems div., 1988-90, dir. systems mktg., 1990-91; product mgr. Mail div. Lotus, Mountain View, Calif., 1991-93; prin. analyst Dataquest, San Jose, 1993-94, v.p., group dir. online multimedia and software, 1994-95; v.p. and Asia/Pacific mng. dir. Gartner Cons., San Jose, 1995-97, mng. v.p. bus. devel. ctr., 1997—; worldwide lectr. on Internet, multimedia, computers and software. Mem. Sigma Phi Epsilon. Home: 700 Grand View Ave San Francisco CA 94114-3510 Office: Gartner Group 251 River Oaks Pkwy San Jose CA 95134-1913

STEIDEL, YAEKO, spiritual counselor; b. Kagoshima, Japan, June 9, 1923; came to U.S., 1963; d. Tokuhei and Tamayo (Goto) Nagata; m. Jack E. Steidel, March 19, 1963; 1 child, Shizuko. BS in Psychology, Portland (Oreg.) State U., 1972, MS in Psychology, 1979, PhD in Urban Studies, 1993. Author: With My Mentally Retarded Friends, 1989, David's Tree, 1993. Instr. Yaeko's Vol. Painting Class for Mentally Retarded People, Portland, 1971—, Yaeko's Vol. Meditation Class for Citizens, Portland, 1982—. Avocations: painting, gardening, camping. Home: 8444 NW Whitney Ave Portland OR 97231-1239

STEIDER, DORIS, artist; b. Decatur, Ill., Apr. 10, 1924; d. Rudy C. and Helen (Regan) Sleeter; m. Robert E. Steider, Nov. 16, 1944 (div.); children—Kristen (Mrs. Gerald Latham), Robert S., Tim D.; m. Carroll B. McCampbell, May 19, 1972. B.S., Purdue U.; M.A., U. N.Mex., Exhibited in more than 190 maj. juried shows including Smithsonian Instn., Washington, Gilcrease Inst., Tulsa, Army Traveling Print Shows, 1963, 64, Witte Mus. Western Art, San Antonio, Mont. State Hist. Soc. Mus., Helena, Mus. N.Mex. Biennials, N.Mex. State Fair Profl. Show, Nat. Art Shows, La Junta, Colo., 1978, 81, 83, Nebraskaland Days Invitational Art Exhbns., 1976—; exhibited in over 80 one-woman shows; represented in permanent collections Holt Rinehart and Winston, Purdue U. Galleries, Time Inc., Loewen Group British Columbia, West Tex. Mus., U. N. Mex. Art Mus., N. Mex. State Fair Collection, Albuquerque Pub. Library, numerous others. Book (by Mary Carroll Nelson) A Vision of Silence: The Egg Tempera Landscapes fo Doris Steider, 1997. Doris Steider Street named in her honor Albuquerque, 1989; recipient over 80 local, regional and national awards. Mem. Albuquerque Fine Arts Adv. Bd., 1966-72; chmn. standards com. N. Mex. Arts and Crafts Bd., 1964-70; chmn. invitational rev. bd. SW Arts and Crafts Fair, 1977-78. Republican. Mem. Am. Acad. Women Artists, Soc. of Layerists in Multi-Media. Home and Office: Route 5 30 Silverhills Ln SE Albuquerque NM 87123-9617

STEIN, ARTHUR OSCAR, pediatrician; b. Bklyn., Apr. 3, 1932; s. Irving I. and Sadie (Brander) S.; AB, Harvard U., 1953; MD, Tufts U., 1957; postgrad. U. Chgo., 1963-66; BFA, San Jose State U., 1998; m. Judith Lenore Hurwitz, Aug. 27, 1955; children: Susan, Jeffrey, Benjamin. Intern U. Chgo. Hosps., 1957-58, resident, 1958-59; resident N.Y. Hosp.-Cornell U. Med. Center, 1959-61; practice medicine specializing in pediatrics, 1963-95, ret., 1995; instr. pediatrics U. Chgo., 1963-66, asst. prof. pediatrics, 1966-70; mem. Healthguard Med. Group, San Jose, Calif., 1970-72; mem. Permanente Med. Group, San Jose, 1972-95; ret. 1995; asst. chief pediatrics Santa Teresa Med. Center, 1979-87; clin. instr. Santa Clara Valley Med. Center, Stanford U., 1970-72. Served to capt., M.C., AUS, 1961-63. USPHS Postdoctoral fellow, 1963-66. Fellow Am. Acad. Pediatrics. Jewish (v.p. congregation 1969-70, pres. 1972-73), Santa Clara County Med. Assn., Calif. Med. Assn. Clubs: Light and Shadow Camera (pres. 1978-80) (San Jose); Central Coast Counties Camera (v.p. 1980-81, pres. 1981-82), Santa Clara Camera. (pres. 1991). Co-discoverer (with Glyn Dawson) genetic disease Lactosylceramidosis, 1969. Home: 956 Redmond Ave San Jose CA 95120-1831

STEIN, BEVERLY, chairperson county board supervisors. BA, U. Calif., Berkeley; JD, U. Wis. Chair county seat Office Bd. Commrs., Portland, Oreg., 1993—. Office: Bd of Commrs Portland Bldg 1120 SW 5th Ave Portland OR 97204-1914*

STEIN, ELEANOR BENSON (ELLIE STEIN), playwright; b. New Haven, Conn., Feb. 18, 1922; d. Harry Lorin and Bertha Adeline (Schwolow) Benson; m. Louis Stein; children: Eleanor Smith, Patrice Forgues, Mary Kelly, Paul Stein. Student, Rockland C.C., Suffern, N.Y., 1966-67, S.D. State U., 1969-70, Mesa Coll., 1975, S.D. City Coll., 1976. Office mgr. Thatcher & Hurst Attys., San Diego, Calif., 1968-73. Author: (plays) Squeeze, 1989, Emily Dickinson, 1996; prodr. (plays) Epitaph, Edgar Allan Poe: The Man, The Legend, Paul Revere: An American Rebel, 60 and Holding, Always, Harriet Tubman: A Woman Called Moses, Sacagawea: Indian Guide to Lewis and Clark Expedition. Bd. dirs. local theater groups; v.p. NewWorks Theatre. Recipient Roll of Honored Women Unitarian Universalist Women's Fedn., 1978, Aurelia Reinhardt Roll of Honored Women, 1983, Unitarian Universalist award for cmty. svc. First Unitarian-Universalist Ch., 1990, Woman of Achievement So. Regional Conf. Women, 1991. Mem. Nat. League Am. Pen Women, Nat. Womens Polit. Caucus, Older Women's League, Actors' Alliance San Diego, Dramatists Guild, Stripteasers, Poets in Profile, Looking Glass Mobile Theatre. Home and Office: 4870 1/2 Old Cliffs Rd San Diego CA 92120-1144

STEIN, ELLYN BETH, mental health services professional; b. Chgo.. BS, Ariz. State U., 1988, M of Counseling, 1991. Cert. profl. counselor, Ariz. Rsch. asst. Ariz. State U., Tempe, 1985, 87, practicum, 1990, grad. asst., 1990, 91; residential counselor/supr. Wayland Family Ctrs., Phoenix, Ariz., 1988-91; intern St. Luke's Behavioral Health, Phoenix, 1991, Phoenix Adolescent Recovery Ctr., 1991; intake specialist II ComCare, Phoenix, 1991-94; needs assessment and referral coord. Charter, Chandler, Ariz., 1993—; clin. case mgr. Contact, Tempe, 1994—; vol. crisis counselor Terros, Phoenix, 1989-95; vol. warm line ComCare, Phoenix, 1995—. Mem. Valley of the Sun Active 20/30 Club, Phoenix, 1993—; vol. Make-A-Wish Found., Phoenix, 1995—. Mem. Am. Counseling Assn., Am. Mental Health Counselors Assn., Phi Beta Kappa (v.p.).

STEIN, KARL N., plastic and reconstructive surgeon; b. Phila., July 1, 1940; m. Sandra Diane Segal; children: Laura, Leigh. BA in Chemistry, Temple U., 1962, MD, 1966. Diplomate Am. Bd. Plastic Surgery. Intern U. Pa. Grad. Hosp., 1966-67; resident in surgery Abington Meml. Hosp., 1967-68; resident in surgery SUNY Up-State Med. Ctr., 1970-71, instr. in surgery, 1970—; resident in plastic surgery Hosp. Albert Einstein Coll. Medicine, Bronx Mcpl. Hosp. Ctr., 1971-74, asst. instr. plastic surgery and hand surgery, 1974; pvt. practice in plastic surgery, 1974—; surgeon Sherman Oaks (Calif.) Burn Ctr., 1975—; cons. L.A. Dept. Water and Power. Author (patent) Treatment of Tar Burns, 1980. Capt. USAF, 1969-71. Fellow Am. Coll. Surgeons; mem. AMA, Am. Soc. Plastic and Reconstructive Surgeons, Am. Burn Assn., Am. Assn. Hand Surgery, Am. Soc. Aesthetic Plastic Surgery, Calif. Soc. Plastic Surgeons, Calif. Med. Assn., L.A. Soc. Plastic Surgeons, L.A. County Med. Assn. Office: 4910 Van Nuys Blvd Ste 302 Sherman Oaks CA 91403-1788

STEIN, MARY KATHERINE, writer, editor, photographer, communications executive; b. Denver, Sept. 7, 1944; d. Robert Addison and Minta [illegible] 1974); m. Donald L. Stein, Aug. 16, 1982. BS in Journalism, U. Kans., 1966. Sr. editor Am Family Physician mag., Kansas City, Mo., 1967-78; editor-in-chief Current Prescribing mag., Oradell, N.J., 1978-79; sr. editor [illegible] Medicine, Bolton, Conn., 1983-85; pres. MD Comm., Tucson, 1983—. Author: Child Abuse, 1987, Caring for the AIDS Patient, 1987, Lifetime Weight Control, 1988, Substance Abuse, 1988, An Overview of HIV Infections and AIDS, 1989, Cardiovascular Disease: Evaluation and Prevention, 1989, Substance Abuse: A Guide for Healthcare Professionals, 1997; mng. editor: Eating Disorders Rev., 1990—; editor Nutrition and the M.D., 1992-95; contbr. articles to mags. Mem. Women in Comm. (pres. Greater Kansas City chpt. 1977-78, pres. Orange County chpt. 1990-92), Am. Med. Writers Assn., Profl. Photographers Am. Democrat. Lutheran. Avocation: photography. Office: MD Comm 302 S Pinto Pl Tucson AZ 85748-6902

STEIN, M(EYER) L(EWIS), journalist, magazine editor, writer; b. Escanaba, Mich., July 30, 1920; s. Alexander and Fannie Stein; m. Romana Susan Paal, Apr. 15, 1981 (dec. Feb. 1994); children: Andrea, Jeannine; stepchildren: Adam Paal, Edith Paal. BJ, U. Mo., 1942; MA, Stanford U., 1961. Reporter, telegraph editor Daily Tribune, Royal Oak, Mich., 1946-51; reporter San Francisco Examiner, 1951-60; prof., chair dept. journalism and mass comm. NYU, 1961-74; prof., chair dept. journalism Calif. State U., Long Beach, 1974-87; west coast editor Editor & Publ. mag., Palo Alto, Calif., 1988—. Author 15 books including: Freedom of the Press, 1970, Reporting Today, 1971, How to Write Plain English, 1976, Shaping the News, 1974, When Presidents Meet the Press, 1969, Under Fire: Story of American War Correspondents, 1995, Introduction to Journalism (with Susan Paterno), 1998; contbr. over 500 articles to newspapers and mags. Sgt. U.S. Army, 1942-45, Africa, Italy. Gannett fellow, 1980. Mem. Assn. Edn. in Journalism and Mass Comm. (chmn. freedom and responsibility com. 1964), Am. Soc. Journalists and Authors. Avocation: travel. Home and Office: Editor & Publ 101 Alma St Apt 405 Palo Alto CA 94301-1005

STEIN, RICHARD ALLEN, theatre producer, director; b. Sacramento, Mar. 16, 1953; s. Bernard George and Iris (Trueheart) S.; m. Alison Archer Bly, Sept. 6, 1981. BA, Columbia U., 1976; MA, Syracuse U., 1978. Assoc. producer Contemporary Theatre, Syracuse, N.Y., 1978-81; mem. faculty Syracuse U., 1976-81; exec. dir. Oswego County Coun. on Arts, Fulton, N.Y., 1978-80; sales promotion mgr. Syracuse Symphony Orch., 1980-81; dir. mktg. and pub. rels. The Fla. Orch., Tampa Bay, 1981-82; dir. Lincoln Theater, U. Hartford (Conn.), 1982-87; mng. dir. Grove Shakespeare Festival, Garden Grove, Calif., 1987-90; exec. dir. The Laguna Playhouse Laguna Beach, Calif., 1990—; mem. panel New Eng. Found. for Arts, Cambridge, Mass., 1983-87, Western States Arts Found., Santa Fe, 1987; mem. panel, cons. Conn. Commn. on the Arts, Hartford, 1983-87; emissary Internat. Theatre Inst., Seoul, South Korea, 1988; cons. Calif. Arts Coun., 1992; participant Leadership Greater Hartford, 1985-86. Stage dir.: Teibele and Her Demon, 1986, Seascape, 1987, The Labors of Hercules, 1996, A Child's Christmas in Wales, 1996, Travels With My Aunt, 1997, Old Wicked Songs, 1999; producer: Albertine, In Five Times, 1986 (Conn State Arts award 1987); contbr. articles to profl. jours. Pres. adv. bd. WRVO-FM Pub. Radio, Oswego, N.Y., 1981-82; mem. adv. bd. Oswego County CETA, 1981-82; mem. John Wayne Airport Arts Commn., Orange County, 1990-93, chmn. 1991-93; co-chmn. Nat. Philanthropy Day Orange County, 1990, 94; mem. adv. bd. U. Calif. Irvine Program in Arts Adminstrn., 1993-94. NEH fellow, Columbia U., N.Y.C., 1984. Mem. Nat. Soc. Fund Raising Execs. (cert., sec. Orange County chpt. 1993, pres.-elect 1994, pres. 1995, del. Nat. Assembly 1994-96), Sierra Club, Garden Grove C. of C., (v.p. 1989-90), Garden Grove Sister City Assn. (v.p. 1988-90). Jewish. Avocations: tennis, hiking, sailing. Office: Laguna Playhouse PO Box 1747 Laguna Beach CA 92652-1747

STEINBERG, JACK, lawyer; b. Seattle, Jan. 6, 1915; s. Solomon Reuben and Mary (Rashall) S.; widower; children: Roosevelt, Mary Ann Steinberg Shulman, Quentin. BA, U. Wash., 1936, JD, 1938. Bar: Wash. 1938, U.S. Dist. Ct. (we. dist.) Wash. 1938, U.S. Ct. Appeals (9th cir.) 1938. Ptnr. Steinberg & Steinberg, Seattle, 1938—. Former editor and pub. The Washington Examiner; contbr. numerous articles to legal jours. Judge pro tem Seattle Mcpl. Ct., Seattle, 1952; past pres. Emanuel Congregation, Seattle, Seattle chpt. Zionist Orgn. Am. Recipient Scrolls of Honor award (3) The State of Israel. Mem. Assn. Trial Lawyers Am., Am. Judicature Soc., Wash. Bar Assn., Wash. Assn. Trial Lawyers, Seattle-King County Bar Assn. Jewish Orthodox. Avocation: outdoor activities. Office: Steinberg & Steinberg 1210 Vance Bldg Seattle WA 98101

STEINBERG, JOAN EMILY, retired middle school educator; b. San Francisco, Dec. 9, 1932; d. John Emil and Kathleen Helen (Montgomery) S. BA, U. Calif.-Berkeley, 1954; EdD, U. San Francisco, 1981. Tchr., Vallejo (Calif.) Unified Sch. Dist., 1959-61, San Francisco Unified Sch. Dist., 1961-93, elem. tchr., 1961-78, tchr. life and phys. sci. jr. high sch., 1978-85, 87-93, sci. cons., 1985-87; lectr. elem. edn. San Francisco State U., 1993-94; ind. sci. edn. cons., 1993—. Contbr. articles to zool. and edn. books and profl. jours. Fulbright scholar U. Sydney (Australia), 1955-56; recipient Calif. Educator award, 1988, Outstanding Educator in Teaching award U. San Francisco Alumni Soc., 1989. Mem. San Francisco Zool. Soc., Exploratorium, Astron. Soc. Pacific, Am. Fedn. Tchrs., Calif. Acad. Scis., Calif. Malacozool. Soc., Nat. Sci. Tchrs. Assn., Elem. Sch. Sci. Assn. (sec. 1984-85, pres. 1986-87, newsletter editor 1994—), Calif. Sci. Tchrs. Assn., Sigma Xi. Democrat.

STEINBERG, WARREN LINNINGTON, school principal; b. N.Y.C., Jan. 20, 1924; s. John M. and Gertrude (Vogel) S.; student U. So. Calif., 1943-44, UCLA, 1942-43, 46-47, BA, 1949, MEd, 1951, EdD, 1962; m. Beatrice Ruth Blass, June 29, 1947; children: Leigh William, James Robert, Donald Kenneth. Tchr., counselor, coach Jordan High Sch., Watts, Los Angeles, 1951-57; tchr. athletic coordinator Hamilton High Sch., Los Angeles, 1957-62; boys' vice prin. Univ. High Sch., Los Angeles, 1962-67, Crenshaw Hig Sch., Los Angeles, 1967-68; cons. Ctr. for Planned Change, Los Angeles City Sch., 1968-69; instr. edn. UCLA, 1965-71; boys' vice prin. LeConte Jr. High Sch., Los Angeles, 1969-71, sch. prin., 1971-77; adminstrv. cons. integration, 1977-81, adminstr. student to student interaction program, 1981-82; prin. Gage Jr. High Sch., 1982-83, Fairfax High Sch., 1983-90. Pres. Athletic Coordinators Assn., Los Angeles City Schs., 1959-60; v.p. P-3 Enterprises, Inc., Port Washington, N.Y., 1967-77, Century City (Calif.) Enterprises, 1966-88. V.p. B'nai B'rith Anti-Defamation League, 1968-70; mem. adv. com. Los Angeles City Commn. on Human Relations, 1966-71, 72-76, commr., 1976—, also chmn. edn. com.; pres. Los Angeles City Human Relations Commn., 1978-87; mem. del. assembly Community Relations Conf. of So. Calif., 1975-91; mem. citizens adv. com. for student integration Los Angeles Unified Sch. Dist., 1976-79; chmn. So. Calif. Drug Abuse Edn. Month com., 1970. Bd. dirs. DAWN, The Seedling, 1993-95, Project ECHO - Entrepreneurial Concepts, Hands-On, 1996—. Served with USMCR, 1943-46. Recipient Beverly Hills B'nai B'rith Presdl. award, 1965, Pres.'s awardCommunity Rels. Conf. So. Calif., 1990, Lifetime Achievement award L.A. City Human Rels. Commn., 1996, award Bd. Edn. L.A. Unified Sch. Dist., 1997; commended Los Angeles City Council, 1968, 88. Mem. West Los Angeles Coordinating Council (chmn. case conf., human relations), Beverly-Fairfax C. of C. (bd. dirs. 1986-88). Lodges: Lions (dir. 1960-62), Kiwanis. Contbr. articles on race relations, youth behavior to profl. jours. and newspapers. Home: 2737 Dunleer Pl Los Angeles CA 90064-4303

STEINBOCK, JOHN THOMAS, bishop; b. L.A., July 16, 1937. Student, L.A. Diocesan sems. Ordained priest Roman Cath. Ch., 1963. Aux. bishop Diocese of Orange, Calif., 1984-87; bishop Diocese of Santa Rosa, Calif., 1987-91; titular bishop of Midila, 1984; bishop Diocese of Fresno, Calif., 1991—. Office: Diocese of Fresno 1550 N Fresno St Fresno CA 93703-3788

STEINER, BETSY DAVIES, equestrian, trainer, public speaker, commentator, author; b. Cleve., Feb. 2, 1951; d. John E. and June A. (Davies) McMillan; m. Uwe Steiner, Feb. 14, 1970 (separated); children: Jessie L., Devon R. Student, Reitinstitut von Neindorff, Karlsruhe, Germany, 1969-71. Examiner for cert. instrs. U.S. Dressage Fedn. Team mem. Concours Dressur Internat. U.S. Equestrian Team, Toronto, Can., 1986, team mem. U.S. Equestrian Team, Lusanne, Switzerland, 1988; individual Am. Horse Show Assn., U.S. Equestrian Team, Aachen, Germany, 1990; U.S. Equest- [illegible] Olympic Sports Festival, L.A., 1991; coach, chef d'equipe young rider, Ill., Calif., 1991-95; mem. Athlete's Adv. Coun. to U.S. Olympic Com., 1995—. Contbr. articles to profl. jours. Recipient Tiffany award for most elegant [illegible] (bd. dirs. 1992-93, chmn. active riders com. 1992—), Am. Horse Show Assn. (bd. dirs. 1992—). Home: RR 1 Box 1230 Keswick VA 22947-9801 Office: Dressage Classic Internat 933 W Potrero Rd Thousand Oaks CA 91361-5019

STEINER, HERBERT MAX, physics educator; b. Goeppingen, Germany, Dec. 8, 1927; came to U.S., 1939, naturalized, 1944; s. Albert and Martha (Epstein) S. B.S., U. Calif., Berkeley, 1951, Ph.D., 1956. Physicist Lawrence Berkeley Lab., Berkeley, Calif., 1956—; mem. faculty U. Calif., Berkeley, 1958—, prof. physics, 1966—, William H. McAdams prof. physics, chmn. dept., 1992-95; vis. scientist European Center Nuclear Research, 1960-61, 64, 68-69, 82-83, Max Planck Inst. Physics and Astrophysics, Munich, 1976-77; vis. prof. Japanese Soc. Promotion Sci., 1978; vis. prof. physics U. Paris, 1989-90; vis. scientist Deutsches Electron Synchrotron Lab., 1995-96. Author articles in field. Served with AUS, 1946-47. Recipient Sr. Am. Scientist award Alexander von Humboldt Found., 1976-77; Guggenheim fellow, 1960-61. Fellow Am. Phys. Soc. Office: U Calif Berkeley Dept Physics #7300 Berkeley CA 94720

STEINER, KENNETH DONALD, bishop; b. David City, Nebr., Nov. 25, 1936; s. Lawrence Nicholas and Florine Marie (Pieters) S. B.A., Mt. Angel Sem., 1958; M.Div., St. Thomas Sem., 1962. Ordained priest Roman Catholic Ch., 1962, bishop, 1978; asso. pastor various parishes Portland and Coos Bay, Oreg., 1962-72; pastor Coquille Ch., Myrtle Point, Powers, Oreg., 1972-76, St. Francis Ch., Roy, Oreg., 1976-77; aux. bishop Diocese of Portland, Oreg., 1977—; pastor St. Mary's Ch., Corvallis, Oreg., 1986—; adminstr. Archdiocese Portland, 1995-96. Democrat. Office: Saint Marys Cath Ch 501 NW 25th St Corvallis OR 97330-5415*

STEINER, MARY ANN, nursing administrator, consultant; b. Spokane, Wash., Nov. 12, 1946; d. John Anthony and Mildred Ann (Costello) S.; m. Michael Moloney; 1 child, Christine Hutton. Vacat. nurse (cum laude), Coll. San Mateo, 1970; RN, NYU, 1980. Staff nurse Mills Meml. Hosp., San Mateo, Calif., 1970-73; charge nurse emergency dept. Grande Ronde Hosp., LaGrande, Oreg., 1973-76; charge nurse CCU, SCU Mills Meml. Hosp., San Mateo, 1976-90; pres. Maids, Etc., San Mateo, 1990-92; supr. advice nurse Mills-Peninsula Homecare, Burlingame, Calif., 1992-94; home health nursing educator Age Ctr. Alliance, Burlingame, 1992-94; home health nurisng educator Age Ctr. Alliance, Menlo Park, Calif., 1993—; nurse mgr. telemedicine dept. MidPeninsula Homecare & Hospice, Mountainview, Calif., 1994-96; nurse mgr. Home Health Plus, Burlingame, Calif., 1997—; pub. speaker League of Women Voters, San Mateo, 1985-95, Calif. State dir. of speakers No. On Prop. 128, Burlingame, 1990, telemedicine cons. Hosp. Consortium of San Mateo Co., Burlingame, 1993—. Bd. dirs. League of Women Voters, San Mateo, 1985-95, vice chair Libertarian party, San Mateo, 1995-97; chairwoman Libertarian Party, San Mateo. Roman Catholic. Home: 815 N Humboldt St San Mateo CA 94401-1471

STEINER, SHARI YVONNE, publisher, editor, journalist; b. Colorado Springs, Colo., Mar. 3, 1941; d. Evan Keith and Blanche Marie (Ketzner) Montgomery; m. Clyde Lionel Steiner, June 24, 1962; children: Vienna Kay, Marco Romano. BA, Adams State Coll., 1962; cert. in sociology, London Sch. Econs., 1978; postgrad., U. Calif., Berkeley, 1988—. Lic. real estate broker, Calif. Freelance journalist various publs., 1964—; owner, mgr. SREI Group, San Francisco, 1985-87; tng. design developer 1st Nationwide Bank, San Francisco, 1987-90; pub., editor Ind. Info. Publs., San Francisco, 1990—; pres. The SREI Group, San Francisco; feature writer Internat. Herald Tribune, Rome, 1964-79; acct. exec. Allen, Ingersol & Weber, Rome, 1970-72; gen. ptnr. Greenhaven Park, Sacramento, 1990—, Port Chicago Indsl., Concord, Calif., 1991-98, Star/Steiner, 1997—. Author: The Female Factor: A Report on Women in Europe, 1972, 2d edit., 1996, Steiners' Complete How to Move Handbook, 1997, Steiners' Complete How to Talk Mortgage Talk, 1998; editor The Bottom Line newsletter, 1985-92; assoc. editor The Semaphore, 1990-92. Coord. urban reforestation Friends of Urban Forest, San Francisco, 1989; co-founder New Sch. for Internat. Elem. Students, Rome, 1970. Recipient internat. journalism award Guida Monaci, 1970, award of merit Lotus Club, N.Y.C., 1975; corr. in archives Am. Heritage Ctr., U. Wyo. Mem. Nat. Assn. Realtors (multiple listing svc. selection com. 1986, 91, investment real estate group 1991), Comml. Real Estate Women (editor, bd. dirs. 1985—), Am. Soc. Journalists and Authors, PEN Internat., Employee Relocation Coun. Avocation: gardening.

STEINFELD, RAY, JR., food products executive; b. Portland, Oreg., Nov. 21, 1946; s. Ray and June Catherine (Cox) S.; children: Erik, Blair. Student, Wheaton Coll., 1964-66, Drew U., 1967; BS in Polit. Sci., Lewis and Clark Coll., 1968. Sales rep. Continental Can Co., L.A., 1969-72; co-chmn. bd., CEO, Steinfeld's Products Co., Portland, Oreg., 1972—; chmn. Oreg. Mus. Sci. in Industry, 1992-94. Treas., bd. dirs. Portland Recycling Team, 1973—; pres. exec. bd. Stop Oreg. Litter and Vandalism, 1973-92, pres., 1976; chmn., exec. com. Oreg. Landmark of Quality, 1985-87, Oreg. Ballet Theatre, 1994—, bd. dirs., 1995—, v.p. devel., 1997—, pres., 1998—; pres. exec. com. William Temple House, 1985-91; vestry mem. Trinity Episcopal Ch., 1987-90; chmn. Oregn. Strategic Plan Agrl. Dept., 1988, World Trade Week, Portland, 1989; mem. Gov. Robert's Task Force, Salem, Oreg., 1991-92; bd. dirs. Oreg. Enterprise Forum, 1992—, chmn., 1995. Mem. Pickle Packers Internat. (mem. mdse. com.), Portland C. of C. (bd. dirs. 1995—). Democrat. Espiscopalian. Avocations: tennis, golf, bridge. Office: 10001 N Rivergate Blvd Portland OR 97203-6526

STEINHARDT, HENRY, photographer; b. N.Y.C., Nov. 15, 1920; s. Maxwell and Ruth (Davis) S.; m. Elizabeth Smith, 1946 (dec. 1955); children: Elizabeth, Maxwell; m. Helene Fleck, Feb. 1, 1958; 1 child, Henry III. AB, Harvard U., 1942, MArch, 1949. Registered architect. Office mgr. R.H. Cutting, Architect, N.Y.C., 1951-53; ptnr., architect Steinhardt & Thompson, Architects, N.Y.C., 1953-61; architect The Cerny Assocs., St. Paul, 1961-63, John Graham & Co., Seattle, 1963-67, Morse/Kirk, Seattle, 1967-68, N.G. Jacobson & Assocs., Seattle, 1968-69; pvt. practice Mercer Island, Wash., 1969-75; architect USN, Bremerton, Wash., 1975-78; photographer Mercer Island, 1979—. Prin. works exhibited at Washington, Seattle and Andover, Mass.; contbr. articles to fgn. archtl. jours. 1st lt. U.S. Army, 1943-46; capt. USAF, 1950-52. Recipient Design award Progressive Architecture, 1959, Archtl. award Fifth Ave. Assn., 1960. Fellow AIA. Democrat. Home and Office: 7825 SE 63rd Pl Mercer Island WA 98040-4813

STEINHAUSER, SHELDON ELI, sociology and gerontology educator, consultant; b. N.Y.C., Aug. 11, 1930; s. Charles W. and Helen (Rosenstein) S.; m. Frances Goldfarb, June 28, 1953 (div. 1963); children: Karen, Lisa Steinhauser Hackel; m. Janice M. Glass, May 2, 1965; children: Shayle, David, Susan Hirschman. BS, L.I. U., 1963; DPS (hon.), Regis U., 1994. Community cons. Anti-Defamation League, Columbus, Ohio, 1951-57; regional dir. Anti-Defamation League, Denver, 1957-85, dir. nat. field svcs., 1977-85, dir. nat. community svcs. divsn., 1979-81, western area dir., 1975-85; exec. v.p. Allied Jewish Fedn. of Denver, 1985-91; pres. Sheldon Steinhauser & Assocs., Denver, 1991—; instr. sociology Met. State Coll., Denver, 1969-71, assoc. prof., 1994—; arbitrator Am. Arbitration Assn., Denver, 1988—; pres. Anti-Defamation League profl. Staff Assn., Agy. Orgn., Denver, 1963; past cons. EEOC. Mem. editl. bd. Sustainable Cmtys. Rev. Missions to Egypt and Israel, 1982, 83; staff dir. Mission to Israel, 1986, 87, 90; former mem. Denver Anti-Crime Coun.; chmn. Mountain States Inst. of Judaism, Denver, 1958-59; pres. Adult Edn. Coun. Met. Dever; past mem. cmty. adv. bd. Jr. League Denver; cons. U.S. Dept. Justice Cmty. Rels. Svc., 1994; mem. Colo. Martin Luther King Holiday Planning Com., Latin Am. Rsch. and Svc. Agy., founding bd. mem.; mem. adv. com. Regis U. Inst. Common Good; Equal Opportunity Adv. Coun., Met State Coll., Denver; cmty. working group Nat. Civilian Cmty. Corps.; congl. del. White House Conf. on Aging, 1995. Recipient M.L. King Jr. Humanitarian award Colo. M.L. King Commn., Denver, 1986, 1st Ann. Human Rels. award Colo. Civil Rights Commn., Denver, 1983, Humanitarian award NAACP, Denver, 1980, ADL Civil Rights Achievement award, 1989; named to Gallery of Fame, Denver Post, 1979, 80. Mem. Diversity Assocs. In- [illegible] Jewish Reconstructionist Fedn., Am. Soc. on Aging, Sociol. Practice Assn., Assn. for Gerontology in Higher Edn. (nat. pub. policy com.), Gerontol. Soc. Am., Colo. Gerontol. Soc., Am. Arbitration Assn. (Rocky Mountain adv. [illegible] cantorial music.

STEINKE, BETTINA, artist; b. Biddeford, Maine, June 25, 1913; d. William and Alice Mary (Staples) S.; m. Don Blair, Mar. 21, 1946. Student, Sch. Fine Arts, Newark, 1930, Cooper Union, 1931-33, Phoenix Art Sch., 1934-35. Represented in permanent collections Indpls. Mus., Ft. Worth Mus., Nat. Cowboy Hall of Fame and Western Heritage; artist original drawings of Toscanini, 1938, Paderewski, 1939 (both now in Smithsonian Inst.); charcoal portraits NBC book on Toscanini and Orch., 1938; many portraits of well known personalities; retrospective shows Palm Springs Desert Mus., Gilcrease Mus., Tulsa, Okla., Nat. Cowboy Hall of Fame, 1995; subject of biography Bettina. Pres. bd. dirs. Harwood Found. U. N.Mex.; exec. bd. Nat. Cowboy Hall of Fame and Western Heritage. Recipient Gold and Silver medals Nat. Cowboy Hall of Fame, Oklahoma City, 1973-89, Gold medal award for Outstanding Contbn. to Painting, 1995, N.Mex. Gov.'s award, 1996, John Singer Sargant award Portrait Soc. (East Coast), 1996, others; scholar Phoenix Art Sch., N.Y.C., 1934-35. Mem. Nat. Acad. Western Artists (Prix de West award, Cowboy Hall of Fame). Home: PO Box 2342 Santa Fe NM 87504-2342

STEINKE, GREG A, music educator, administrator, composer, oboist; b. Fremont, Mich., Sept. 2, 1942; s. Donald Ferdinand John and Ella Louise (Clute) S.; m. Karen Florence Larsen, June 5, 1971; children: Carl Asa, Kyle Alban. MusB, Oberlin Conservatory, 1964; MMus, Mich. State U., 1967, PhD, 1976; MFA, U. Iowa, 1971. Instr. music U. Idaho, Moscow, 1967-68, dir. Sch. Music, prof. music, 1983-86; chmn. dept music, prof. San Diego State U., 1986-88; instr. music U. Md., College Park, 1968-72; asst. prof. music Calif. State U., Northridge, 1973-75; mem. faculty Evergreen State Coll., Olympia, Wash., 1975-79; chmn., prof. music dept. Linfield Coll., McMinnville, Oreg., 1979-83; asst. dir. U. Ariz. Sch. Music, Tucson, 1988-91; dir., prof. Sch. Music Ball State U., Muncie, Ind., 1991-96, dean, prof., Coll. Fine Arts, Millikin U., Decatur, Ill., 1996-97, mem. faculty No. Ariz. U., Flagstaff, Ariz., 1998—; guest composer Contemporary Music Festival Western Ill. U., 1982, 90-91, Charles Ives Ctr. for Am. Music, New Milford, Conn., summer 1982, 91, 1st Ann. Festival of New Music Bowling Green State U., 1980, New Music Fest XV Memphis State U., 1987, 5th Symposium for New WWQ5 Mus. U. Ga., 1988, Biennial Festival New Music Fla. State U., 1989, 91, 93, 96, S.W. Tex. U., 1990, Birmingham So. U., 1990; composer-participant numerous music festivals, Atlantic Ctr., for Arts Assoc., 1995. Contbr. articles to profl. jours.; author music theory books; numerous compositions for voice, piano, instrumental chamber orch., wind ensemble, miscellaneous, incidental music for plays; also arrangements of music; oboe performer, 1961—. Recipient numerous awards, including: commn. Western Arts Music Festival, Laramie, Wyo., 1986, award Standards Awards Panel of ASCAP, 1979—; Phi Mu Alpha Composition Contest winner Sam Houston State U., 1975; fellow Tucson/Pima Arts Coun. Composition, 1991; grantee Ariz. Arts Commn. Special Project Grant, 1990.Bd. dirs. McMinnville Arts Assn., 1980-81; mem. com. Moscow City Arts Commn., 1984-86. Mem. Am. Fedn. Musicians, Am. Music Ctr., Soc. Composers, Inc. (past chmn. region IX, editor monograph Series, chair nat. council, 1988-97), ASCAP, Bela Bartok Soc., Alban Berg Soc., Ernest Bloch Soc., Oreg. Coast Council for the Arts, Coll. Music Soc., Internat. Double Reed Soc., Nat. Assn. Composers, U.S.A., Soc. Oreg. Composers (past pres.).

STEINLICHT, STEVEN, astrologer, minister, educator; b. Bloomington, Ill., Mar. 13, 1950; s. Henry Jr. and Mary Elizabeth (Ritter) S. Student, U. Ill., 1968; D in Metaphysics, Universal Life Ch., 1975. Lic. psychol. counselor, Universal Life Ch. Minister Temple of Truth, Universal Life Ch., Bloomington, Ill., 1977; co-founder Ascension, Bloomington, 1979; stockroom supr. Murray's Shoes, Bloomington, Ill., 1981-86; psychic Rainbow Place, Albuquerque, 1988-90; software mgr., corp. astrologer Computer Bazaar, Albuquerque, 1991-96; pres., founder Albuquerque Metaphys. Inst., 1993—; tchr., healer Gold Key Ctr., Albuquerque, 1987-88, pub. spkr. New Age Connection, Albuquerque, 1987—, psychic Metaphysical Crystal Palace, Albuquerque, 1987; detective N.M. Bur. Investigations, 1988. Author: Astarunum, The Portable Oracle, 1993; columnist Rainbow Place, 1988-90, Up Front! Mag., 1996-97; inventor. Min. Universal Life Ch., 1972—. Mem. Mensa Internat., Soc. for Creative Anachronism, S.W. Psychic Forum. Avocations: photography, hiking, role-playing games, magic tricks, calligraphy.

STEINMAN, JOHN FRANCIS, psychiatrist; b. N.Y.C., May 5, 1916; s. David Barnard and Irene Stella (Hoffman) S.; m. Helen G. Meyer (div. 1963); children: James, Judith, Jill; m. Roxane Bear (div. 1972); m. Ellen M. Sears, Nov. 16, 1985. AB with hons., Columbia U., 1936, MD, 1940. Diplomate Am. Bd. Psychiatry and Neurology. Intern Strong Meml. Hosp., Rochester, N.Y. and Cin. Gen. Hosp., 1940-43; resident psychiatry Nebr. Psychiat. Inst., 1948, 58, R.I. Med. Ctr., 1961; psychiatrist, dir. Lincoln (Nebr.) and Lancaster County Child Guidance Ctr., 1948-61; instr. pediatrics, psychiatry and neurology U. Nebr., Lincoln, 1951-52; postdoctoral fellow in psychiatry Yale U., New Haven, Conn., 1962-64; psychiatrist U. Conn., Storrs, 1964-69, Community Mental Health Services, San Francisco, 1971-79; pvt. practice psychiatry San Francisco, 1979—. Delgate, chmn. Nebr. health com. White House Conf. Children and Youth, Washington, 1960. Served to capt. M.C., AUS, 1943-46, PTO. Mem. Am. Psychiat. Assn. (life), Am. Orthopsychiat. Assn., N.Y. Acad. Scis., Phi Beta Kappa. Home and Office: 164 Otsego Ave San Francisco CA 94112-2536

STEINMANN, JOHN COLBURN, architect; b. Monroe, Wis., Oct. 24, 1941; s. John Wilbur and Irene Marie (Steil) S.; m. Susan Koslosky, Aug. 12, 1978 (div. July 1989). BArch., U. Ill., 1964; postgrad. Ill. Inst. Tech., 1970-71; Project designer C.F. Murphy Assocs., Chgo., 1968-71, Steinmann Architects, Monticello, Wis., 1971-73; design chief, chief project architect State of Alaska, Juneau, 1973-78; project designer Mithun Assocs., architects, Bellevue, Wash., 1978-80; owner, prin. John C. Steinmann Assos., Architect, Kirkland, Wash., 1980-94; supr. head facilities sect. divsn. fin. Dept. Edn. State of Alaska, Juneau, 1994-96; docs. mgr. Loschky Marquardt and Nesholm, Architects, Seattle, 1996-98; project mgr. Dept. Gen. Adminstrn., Divsn. Engring. and Archtl. Svcs., State of Wash., Olympia, 1998—; bd. dirs. Storytell Internat.; lectr. Ill. Inst. Tech., 1971-72; prin. works include: Grant Park Music Bowl, Chgo., 1971, Menomonee Falls (Wis.) Med. Clinic, 1972, Hidden Valley Office Bldg., Bellevue, 1978, Kezner Office Bldg., Bellevue, 1979, The Pines at Sunriver, Oreg., 1980, also Phase II, 1984, Phase III, 1986, The Pines at Sunriver Lodge Bldg., 1986, 2d and Lenora highrise, Seattle, 1981, Bob Hope Cardiovascular Research Inst. lab. animal facility, Seattle, 1982, Wash. Ct., Bellevue, 1982, Anchorage Bus. Park, 1982, Garden Townhouses, Anchorage, 1983, Vacation Internationale, Ltd. Corp. Hdqrs., Bellevue, 1983, Vallarta Torres III, Puerto Vallarta, Mex., 1987, Torres Mazatlan (Mex.) II, 1988, Canterwood Townhouses, Gig Harbor Wash., 1988, Inn at Ceres (Calif.), 1989, Woodard Creek Inn, Olympia, Wash., 1989, Northgate Corp. Ctr., Seattle, 1990, Icicle Creek Hotel and Restaurant, Leavenworth, Wash., 1990, Bellingham (Wash.) Market Pl., 1990, Boeing Hot Gas Test Facility, Renton, Wash., 1991, Boeing Longacres Customer Svc. Tng. Ctr. Support Facilities, Renton, 1992, Boeing Comml. Airplane Group Hdqs., Renton, 1996, U. Wash./Cascade C.C., Bothell; also pvt. residences. Served to 1st lt. C.E., USAR, 1964-66; Vietnam. Decorated Bronze Star. Registered architect, Wash., Oreg., Calif., N.Mex., Ariz., Utah, Alaska, Wis., Ill. Mem. AIA, Am. Mgmt. Assn., Nat. Council Archtl. Registration Bds., Alpha Rho Chi. Republican. Roman Catholic. Clubs: U. Wash. Yacht, Columbia Athletic. Address: 4316 106th Pl NE Kirkland WA 98033-7919

STEITZ, WILLIAM WARREN, bank executive; b. L.A., Feb. 27, 1954; s. Warren C. and Viletta (Petersen) S.; m. Linda McKibben, July 3, 1982 (div. Mar. 1987); m. Meg Jacobson, Feb. 17, 1996. Student, U. Colo., 1971-77; BS, Met. State Coll., 1979; MA cum laude, U. Colo., Denver, 1990. Mgr. Avco Fin. Svcs., Denver, 1976-78; loan officer First Nat. Bank Denver, 1978-83; v.p. Century Bank, Denver, 1983-94; v.p., area mgr. Key Bank Colo., Denver, 1994—. Mem. tech. rev. com. Mayor's Office Econ. Devel., Denver, 1990-95; bd. mem. U. Colo. Denver Alumni Assn., 1990-97, pres., 1995-96; bd. dirs. Colo. Housing Assistance Corp., Denver, 1992—, chmn., 1996—; mem. devel. com. U. Colo. Found., Denver, 1996—. Mem. Denver Pub. Libr. Friends Found., Robert Morris Assocs., Phi Alpha Theta. Presbyterian. Home: 1000 S Cove Way Denver CO 80209-5112 Office: Key Bank Colo 3300 E 1st Ave Denver CO 80206-5810

STEMMER, JAY JOHN, safety engineer, consultant; b. Wilkes-Barre, Pa., Apr. 29, 1939. BSCE, N.J. Inst. Tech., 1962; MBA, Calif. State U., Long Beach, 1969. Registered profl. engr., Calif.; cert. safety profl.; cert. hazard control mgmt. Engr. Factory Mut., N.J., 1973-77; cons. McKay & Assoc., Calif., 1977-81, Index Research, Calif., 1981-83, Fireman's Fund, Calif., 1983-85, AIG Cons., Calif., 1985-87; sr. cons. Argonaut, Calif., 1987—; assoc. prof. Sierra Coll., Los Angeles, 1979-80. Author: Medical Manual of Industrial Toxicology, 1965, Latin America, A Study of Air Transport Development and Potential in the Decade Ahead, 1970. Served to lt. USAF, 1962-65. Mem. NSPE, Calif. Soc. Profl. Engrs., Am. Soc. Safety Engrs., Am. Bd. Motion Pictures and TV Engrs., Screen Actors Guild, Actors Equity Assn., AFTRA. Avocations: graphology, duplicate bridge, photography, white water rafting, pub. speaking. Home: 1935 Alpha Rd Apt 225 Glendale CA 91208-2135

STENDER, CHARLES FREDERICK, test pilot; b. East Orange, N.J., Nov. 17, 1940; s. Robert Conrad and Ruth Warne (Cobb) S. BSCE, Pa. State U., 1962; MS in Systems Mgmt., U. So. Calif., University Park, Calif., 1982. Commd. ensign USN, 1962; advanced through grades to capt. USNR, 1983, ret., 1991; naval aviator USN, various, 1962-72; test pilot Grumman Aerospace, Point Mugu, Calif., 1972-77; airline pilot TWA, L.A., 1977-80; mgr., test pilot Hughes Aircraft Co., L.A., 1980—. Decorated Disting. Flying Cross (3), Vietnam, Air medal (13), Vietnam, Navy Commendation medal. Mem. Soc. Exptl. Test Pilots (assoc. fellow), Tailhook Assn., Air Line Pilots Assn. Address: 16551 Saticoy St Van Nuys CA 91406

STENNER, ROBERT DAVID, environmental and health research engineer, toxicologist; b. Fennimore, Wis., Mar. 12, 1946; s. Arno F. and Edna M. (Mill) S.; m. Vicki S. Muller, June 12, 1965; children: James Brian, Heidi Diane. BS in Power Mechanics with honors, U. Wis., Menomonie, 1970; MS in Nuclear Engring., Idaho State U., 1981; PhD in Toxicology, Wash. State U., 1996. Environ. engr. Gaston County Air Pollution Control, Gastonia, N.C., 1973-77; environ. engring. specialist environ. divsn. State of Idaho, Pocatello, 1977-81; chem. and radiation protection engr. Pacific Gas and Electric Co., San Francisco, Eureka, Calif., 1981-84; rsch. engr. sci. III and IV Battelle N.W. Labs., Richland, Wash., 1984—; mem. audit team Assurance Program for Remedial Action, Dept. of Energy, Washington, 1984-86; risk assessment rep. Environ. Mgmt. Ops. Cons. Selection Team, Richland, Wash., 1988-89; mem. chem. protection initiative team Battelle N.W. Labs., 1989-90, point of contact-Life Sci. Ctr., 1993—. Contbr. articles to profl. jours. Sec. Lions Club, Bessemer City, N.C., 1974-77; youth program counselor United Meth. Chs., numerous cities, 1973-95; vol. ARC, Kennewick, Wash., 1989. Recipient Merit award Menomonie Area C. of C., 1970. Mem. Am. Soc. Testing Materials, Soc. Toxicology (chair E47.14 Com., Pacific N.W. Assn. Toxicologists, Soc. Risk Analysis. Democrat. Avocations: outdoor recreation, European sports car restoration, travel, music. Home: 1238 Glenwood Ct Richland WA 99352-9404 Office: Battelle NW Labs PO Box 999 Richland WA 99352-0999

STENSETHER, JOHN ELDON, minister; b. Mpls., Feb. 28, 1944; s. John H. and Gertie Marie (Stensaas) S.; m. Barbara L. Erickson, Sept. 3, 1966; children: Julie Lyn, Kevin John. BA, U. Minn., 1966; postgrad., Fuller Theol. Sem., Pasadena, 1966-69; PhD, Calif. Grad. Sch. Theology, Glendale, 1970. Ordained to ministry Evang. Free Ch. Am., 1972. Sr. pastor Del Rey Hills Evang. Free Ch., Playa del Rey, Calif., 1968-72, Calvary Evang. Free Ch., Essex Fells, N.J., 1972-76, Trinity Evang. Free Ch., South Bend, Ind., 1976-80, Evang. Free Ch., Turlock, Calif., 1980—; vis. prof. Northeastern Bible Coll., Essex Fells, N.J., 1973-75; staley disting. Christian scholar lectr. Trinity Coll., Deerfield, Ill., 1985; speaker various Colls., sems. and confs. Fellow Evang. Free Ch. of Am. Ministerial, Turlock Evang. Assn. of Ministers. Office: Evang Free Ch 1360 N Johnson Rd Turlock CA 95380-3507

STENSRUD, MARENE HANSEN, English language educator; b. Idaho Falls, Idaho, Nov. 11, 1960; d. LaMar J. and A. Marie (Wright) H.; m. Grant H. Stensrud, July 12, 1997. BA, Brigham Young U., 1988; M in Edn., U. Utah, 1997. Spanish/English tchr. Northwest Middle Sch., Salt Lake City, 1988-94; English and gifted edn. tchr. West H.S., Salt Lake City, 1994—; contract and negotiations team Salt Lake Tchrs. Assn., 1997—; speaker in field. Avocation: gardening. Office: West H S 241 N 300 W Salt Lake City UT 84103-1120

STENSVAD, ALLAN MAURICE, minister; b. Melstone, Mont., Mar. 27, 1934; s. Arthur Leonard and Mabel Violet (Rykken) S.; m. Margaret Lillian Fountain, Aug. 21, 1954; children: Sondra Louise, Joy Lynn, Jill Linda, Janiece Lorraine, Sharla Lee. BA in History, Cascade Coll., 1956; ThM, Dallas Theol. Sem., 1960. Ordained to ministry Conservative Bapt. Assn. Am., 1962. Interim pastor Trinity Bapt. Ch., Walla Walla, Wash., 1960-61; missionary to Brazil Unevangelized Fields Mission, Bala Cynwyd, Pa., 1962-71; min. of evangelism Bible Bapt. Ch., Auburn, Wash., 1972-75; pastor 1st Bapt. Ch., Dayton, Wash., 1975-80, Berean Bapt. Ch., Eugene, Oreg., 1980-93, First Bapt. Ch., Philomath, Oreg., 1994—; dir. No. Evang. Christian Sem., Sao Luis, Brazil, 1966-71; trustee Conservative Bapt. Assn. Wash., 1976-80, Conservative Bapt. Assn. Oreg., N.W. Conservative Bapt. Assn., 1985-91; mem. consolidation com. Conservative Bapt. Assn. Oreg./Wash., 1985, ann. meeting program chmn., 1986-91; vis. lectr. Seminário Cristão Evangélico do Norte, São Luís, Brazil, 1998. Mem. Philomath Ministerial Assn. (chmn. 1995—). Republican. Home: PO Box 1078 2355 Applegate St Philomath OR 97370 Office: First Bapt Ch 335 S 26th St Philomath OR 97370-9239

STENZEL, FRANZ ROBERT, JR., insurance broker, financial consultant; b. Durham, N.C., Apr. 7, 1934; s. Franz R. (dec.) and Marion L. (Mason-Haskell) (dec.) S.; m. Margaret Ellen Manns, July 15, 1967 (div. June 1981); children: Franz III, Laura, Nicholas; m. Cecelia L. Dorminey, Dec. 6, 1997. Grad., Columbia Prep. H.S., Portland, Oreg., 1952. CLU; ChFC. Agt., mgr. Equitable N.Y., L.A., 1960-89, ret., 1989; broker, mgr., gen. agt. Trans-Am. Life, L.A., 1960-89, ret., 1989; ins. broker, mgr., gen. agt., fin. cons. Stenzel Fin. Svcs., L.A., 1960-81, Arroyo Grande, Calif., 1981—. With U.S. Army, 1953-55. Mem. Elks. Republican. Episcopalian. Avocations: travel, reading, tennis, foreign languages. Office: PO Box 800 Arroyo Grande CA 93421-0800

STEPANEK, JOSEPH EDWARD, industrial development consultant; b. Ellinwood, Kans., Oct. 29, 1917; s. Joseph August and Leona Mae (Wilson) S.; m. Antoinette Farnham, June 10, 1942; children: Joseph F., James B., Antoinette L., Debra L. BSChemE, U. Colo., 1939; DEng in Chem. Engring., Yale U., 1942. Registered profl. engr., Colo. Engr. Stearns-Roger Mfg., Denver, 1939-45; from asst. to assoc. prof. U. Colo., Boulder, 1945-47; from cons. to dir. UN, various countries, 1947-73; cons. internat. indsl devel., U.S.-China bus. relations Boulder, 1973—; bd. dirs. 12 corps., 1973—. Author 3 books on indsl. devel.; contbr. 50 articles to profl. jours. Exec. dir. Boulder Tomorrow, 1965-67. Recipient Yale Engring. award Yale Engring. Assn., 1957, Norlin award U. Colo. 1978, Annual award India League of Am., 1982. Mem. AAAS. Democrat. Unitarian. Avocation: ranching. Home: 1622 High St Boulder CO 80304-4224

STEPHANS, MICHAEL LEE, English language educator, musician, poet, author; b. Miami, Fla., June 9, 1945; s. Samuel Irwin and Ruby Mirium Stephans; m. Susan Wolfson, June 30, 1968 (div. 1998); children: Jennifer, Melissa. BA, U. Miami, 1967, MEd, 1968; PhD, U. Md., 1976. Cert. c.c. instr., Calif. Mem. faculty Merit Coll., L.A., 1975-80, Woodbury U., L.a., 1985-90; mem. English faculty Calif. State U. and U. So. Calif. Extensions, 1993—; mem. faculty student svcs. divsn. Pasadena (Calif.) City Coll., Pasadena, Calif., 1990—. Author: Bright Size Life, 1991, Mythematics, 1993, The Color of Stones, 1997. Performer AIDS Project L.A., 1990-95. Grantee Nat. Endowment Arts and Humanities, 1973, Smithsonian Instn., 1973; named Poet of Yr. Inscape Literary Anthology, 1993; winner Conejo Valley Poetry Festival, 1997. Mem. Calif. Intersegmental Articulation Coun., Phi Mu Alpha, Kappa Delta Pi. Avocations: reading, performance art, outdoor activities. Office: Pasadena City Coll 1570 E Colorado Blvd Pasadena CA 91106-2003

STEPHENS, BOB, electronic executive. Pres. Adaptec, Inc., Milpitas, Calif. Office: Adaptec Inc 691 S Milpitas Blvd Milpitas CA 95035-5484*

STEPHENS, ELISA, art college president, lawyer. Pres. Acad. Art Coll., San Francisco, 1993—. Office: Acad Art Coll Office of President 79 New Montgomery St6th Fl San Francisco CA 94105-3410*

STEPHENS, JACK, writer, photographer; b. Huntington Park, Calif., Dec. 1, 1936; s. Herman Franklin and Ruth Thekla (Burleson) S.; m. Kristi Marie Kellogg, Feb. 14, 1987. BA, Wash. State U., 1962. With D'Velco, Lawndale, Calif., 1952-54; reporter/editor Daily Evergreen, Pullman, Wash., 1959-62, Ferndale Record, Wash., 1961; morn. edit. editor Idaho Falls Post-Register, 1962; reporter Maui (Hawaii) News, 1963-67; instr. Maunaolu Coll., Makawao, Hawaii, 1967-73; reporter Pacific Bus. News, Honolulu, 1969-72; owner Aquarius Ent., Wailuku, 1968—. Author: Maui Now, 1969; contbr. articles to profl. jours.; writer/photographer Sci. Digest, 1966, Nat. Parks Mag., 1967, Ariz. Hwys. Mag., 1988-91, Trailer Life Mag., 1992-95. With USAF, 1955-58. Mem. Soc. Profl. Journalists. Avocations: backpacking, hiking, camping, swimming, nature photography. Home: 3-3400 Kuhio Hwy Apt A-103 Lihue HI 96766

STEPHENS, LAWRENCE KEITH, lawyer; b. Cleve., Aug. 7, 1959; s. Gary Baker and Emilie Mae (Abbott) S.; m. Sunee Del Smith, Jan. 9, 1982; children: Shannon Ruth, Sierra Del. BS cum laude, Tex. A&M U., 1981; JD, Santa Clara U., 1990. Bar: Calif. 1990, Tex. 1992, U.S. Patent Office, 1987. Sys. programmer IBM, Irving, Tex., 1981-83; rep. account mktg. IBM, Charlottesville, Va., 1983-86; patent agt. IBM, Santa Clara, Calif., 1987-90; corp. counsel IBM, White Plains, N.Y., 1990-91, Austin, Tex., 1991-92; dir. intellectual property Taligent, Cupertino, Calif., 1992-96; spl. counsel Cooley Godward, LLP, Palo Alto, Calif., 1996-97; dep. chief intellectual property Rockwell Internat. Corp., Costa Mesa, Calif., 1997-98; with Andersen Consulting, 1998; founding ptnr. Hickman, Stephens and Coleman, L.L.P., 1999—; bd. dirs. Hilltop Manor, Inc., San Jose, Calif., chmn. 1995-97; bd. dirs. FBC, San Jose. Patentee in field; contbr. articles to profl. jours. Deacon First Bapt. Ch., San Jose, 1989-97. Mem. Am. Intellectual Property Law Assn. (chair copyright internet 1995—). Avocations: golf, skiing, swimming, bridge, roller blading. Home: 13730 Beaumont Ave Saratoga CA 95070-4935

STEPHENS, MARTIN R., state official; b. Ogden, Utah, Mar. 26, 1954; m. Carole Stephens. BSin Bus. Administrn., Webder State U. Mayor Farr West City, Utah, 1986-88; house speaker State of Utah, 1999—; coun. mem. Farr West City, 1984-85, vice chair Weber Area Coun. of Govts., 1986-87, chair, 1988, elected Utah rep. White House Conf. Small Bus., Washington, 1986, majority leader, 1993-94, chair legis. mgmt. com., judiciary standing com., govt. ops. standing com., retirement com., exec. appropriations com. (chair 1993-94), commerce and revenue appropriations com., 1999—. Recipient Roy B. Gibson Freedom of Information award Soc. Profl. Journalists, 1991. Office: Utah Legis 318 State Capitol Salt Lake City UT 84114 also: 3159 N Higley Rd Farr West UT 84404*

STEPHENS, MICHAEL DEAN, hospital administrator; b. Salt Lake City, May 1, 1942; married. B, Columbia U., 1966, MHA, 1970. Adminstrv. resident Mt. Sinai Med. Ctr., N.Y.C., 1969-70; asst. adminstr. Greenville (S.C.) Gen. Hosp., 1970-71, assoc. adminstr., 1971-72, adminstr., 1972-75; pres., CEO Hoag Meml. Hosp.-Presbyn., Newport Beach, Calif., 1975—. Mem. Am. Coll. Healthcare Execs. Home: 900 Alder Pl Newport Beach CA 92660-4121 Office: Hoag Meml Hosp Presbyn PO Box 6100 Newport Beach CA 92658-6100

STEPHENS, STEVIE MARIE, psychotherapist; b. San Diego, Feb. 24, 1959. Student, Calif. State U., Fullerton, 1978-80; BA in Sociology with distinction, San Diego State U., 1983; M of Social Welfare, U. Calif., Berkeley, 1988. Lic. clin. social worker, Calif. Homefinder Indian Child Welfare Consortium, Escondido, Calif., 1986; alcoholism counselor, social work intern Harriet Street Ctr., San Francisco, 1986-87; social work intern psychiatry dept. San Francisco Gen. Hosp., 1988; social worker Adult Protective Svcs., Inc., San Diego, 1989 90, Naval Hosp., San Diego, 1990-91; psychotherapist, adminstr. in pvt. practice San Diego, 1993—. Vol. Learning Disabilities Assn. of Calif., San Diego, 1992-93, Battered Women's Svcs., San Diego, 1985-86; pres. coll. chpt. Am. Advt. Fedn., 1979; mem. Comms. Student Activities Coun., Fullerton, 1979. Recipient various naval awards; Kappa Kappa Gamma scholar. Mem. NASW, Calif. Soc. for Clin. Social Work, Am. Mensa, Ltd., Alpha Kappa Delta. Address: PO Box 98 La Jolla CA 92038-0098

STEPHENSON, ARTHUR EMMET, JR., corporate and investment company executive; b. Bastrop, La., Aug. 29, 1945; s. Arthur Emmet (dec.) and Edith Louise Stephenson; m. Toni Lyn Edwards, June 17, 1967; 1 child, Tessa. BS in Fin. magna cum laude, La. State U., 1967; MBA (Ralph Thomas Sayles fellow), Harvard U., 1969. Chartered fin. analyst. Adminstrv. aide to U.S. Sen. Russell Long of La., Washington, 1966; security analyst Fidelity Funds, Boston, 1968; chmn. bd., pres. Stephenson & Co., Denver, Stephenson Mcht. Banking Inc., Circle Corp.; sr. ptnr. Stephenson Ventures, Stephenson Properties; founder, chmn. StarTek, Inc., Gen. Commn., Inc., Denver; also chmn. bd. dirs. StarTek, Inc., Gen. Commn., Inc.; founder StarTek, Inc., Denver; also chmn. bd. dirs. StarTek, Inc.; Co-founder Pub. Network, Inc.; underwriting mem. Lloyd's of London, 1978-92; founder Charter Bank and Trust, chmn., 1980-91; mem. adv. bd. First Berkshire Fund, Capital Resources Ptnrs., L.P., Empower Am., Washington; former pub. Law Enforcement Product News, Colo. Book, Pub. Safety Product News, 1990-98, Colo. Book, Denver Mag., Denver Bus. Mag. Mem. assocs. coun. Templeton Coll. at Oxford U., Eng.; nat. trustee Nat. Symphony Orch. at John F. Kennedy Ctr. for Performing Arts, 1995-98; mem. nat. steering com. Norman Rockwell Mus., Stockbridge, Mass.; past mem. Colo. small bus. coun.; del. White House Conf., 1980; mem. adv. bd. Empower Am., Washington; bd. dirs. Ptnrs. in Excellence La. State U. Recipient Hall of Fame award Inc. mag., 1994; named to Hall of Distinction, La. State U. Coll. Bus. Adminstrn., 1998. Mem. Harvard U. Bus. Sch. Assn. (internat. pres. 1987-88), Chief Execs. Orgn., World Pres.'s Orgn., Colo. Investment Advisors Assn. (treas., bd. dirs. 1975-76), Fin. Analysts Fedn., Denver Soc. Security Analysts (bd. dirs. 1975-77), Colo. Press Assn., Colo. Harvard Bus. Sch. Club (pres. 1980-81, chmn. 1981-82), Thunderbird Country Club (Rancho Mirage, Calif.), Annabel's (London), Jonathan Club (L.A.), Denver Petroleum Club, Harvard Bus. Sch. Clubs (N.Y.C., So. Calif. and Boston), Harvard Clubs (N.Y. and Boston), Glenmoor Country Club, Omicron Delta Kappa, Phi Kappa Phi, Beta Gamma Sigma, Kappa Sigma, Delta Sigma Pi. Office: 100 Garfield St Denver CO 80206-5597

STEPHENSON, BARBERA WERTZ, lawyer; b. Bryan, Ohio, Dec. 10, 1938; d. Emerson D. and Beryl B. (Barber) Wertz; m. Gerard J. Stephenson Jr., June 22, 1960; 1 child, Thomas. Student, Smith Coll., 1956-57; BSEE, MIT, 1961; JD, U. N.Mex., 1981. Bar: N.Mex. 1981. Electronic engr. Digital Equipment Corp., Maynard, Mass., 1960-66; logic analyst Libroscope, Glendale, Calif., 1966; electronic engr. Md. Dept. of Def., Ft. Meade, 1966-68; mem. tech. staff Xerox Data Systems, Rockville, Md., 1968; pvt. practice cons., Silver Spring, Md., 1969-78; pvt. practice law, Albuquerque, 1981—. Author: Financing Your Home Purchase in New Mexico, 1992; patentee analog to digital converter, kitchen calculator. Mem. N.Mex. Bar Assn.

STEPHENSON, CHARLES GAYLEY, lawyer; b. San Francisco, May 18, 1935; s. John Towle and Elizabeth (Gayley) S.; m. Tracy Elizabeth Innes, Aug. 26, 1961; children: Gayley, Kate, Anthony. BA, U. Calif., Berkeley, 1957; LLB, Stanford U., 1963. Bar: Calif. 1964, U.S. Dist. Ct. (no. dist.) Calif. 1964, U.S. Ct. Appeals (9th cir.) 1964. Assoc., ptnr. Chickering & Gregory, San Francisco, 1963-73; ptnr. Jackson, Tufts, Cole & Black and predecessors, San Francisco, 1973—. 1st lt. U.S. Army, 1957-59. Fellow Am. Coll. Probate Counsel; mem. Internat. Acad. Trusts and Estates Lawyers, Lagunitas Country Club, Pacific Union Club. Democrat. Episcopalian. Avocations: sports, movies, piano. Home: 240 32d Ave San Francisco CA 94121-1014 Office: Jackson Tufts Cole & Black 650 California St Ste 3130 San Francisco CA 94108-2699

STEPHENSON, FRANK ALEX, engineer, consultant; b. Helena, Mont., May 4, 1940; s. Alex Banning and Phyllis Jean (Smith) S.; m. Lorann Marcella Berg, July 9, 1962 (div. Aug. 1970); children: Patty Jo, Scott Alex; m. Brenda Mae Vitales, June 21, 1986; 1 child, Jennifer Jean. BS in Civil Constrn. Engring., Mont. State U., 1967; MS in Sanitary Engring., Delft U.,

1973; PhD in Environ. Engring., Exeter U., 1975. Registered profl. engr., Ariz., Mont., S.D., Colo., N.Mex., Wyo., Kans. Constrn. engr. Al Johnson Co., Mpls., 1967-70; sr. engr. Stearns Roger Inc., Denver, 1975-79; ptnr. Thomas Group Inc., San Jose, Calif., 1979-85; sr. engr. CH2M Hill Inc., San Jose, Calif., 1985-87; dir. engring. western div. Dames & Moore, Phoenix, 1987-93; dir. techs. Terranext, Phoenix, 1993-97; systems engr. Sumitomo-Sitix, Phx., 1997-98; prin. engr. Harding Lawson Assoc., 1998—. Recipient Ernest Cook Rsch. fellowship Royal Acad. Sci., London, 1973. Mem. AIChE, Hazardous Waste Soc., diplomate Am. Coll. Forensic Engrs. Presbyterian. Achievements include development of technology for on-line total organic carbon analysis using ultraviolet light and resistivity changes; design and installation of first reverse osmosis unit used in a nuclear (electric power) reactor. Avocations: model railroading, fishing, swimming, bicycling. Home: 1702 E Aurelius Ave Phoenix AZ 85020-5508 Office: EOS Engring Inc 5016 S Ash Ave Ste 101 Tempe AZ 85282-6845

STEPHENSON, HERMAN HOWARD, retired banker; b. Wichita, Kans., July 15, 1929; s. Herman Horace and Edith May (Wayland) S.; m. Virginia Anne Ross, Dec. 24, 1950; children: Ross Wayland, Neal Bevan, Jann Edith. BA, U. Mich., 1950; JD with distinction, U. Mo., Kansas City, 1958, LLD (hon.), 1993. Bar: Kans. 1958. With City Nat. Bank, Kansas City, Mo., 1952-54, City Bond & Mortgage Co., Kansas City, 1954-59, Bank of Hawaii, Honolulu, 1959-94; ret. chmn. CEO, 1994; chmn., exec. com., bd. dirs. Pacific Century Fin. Corp. and Bank of Hawaii; bd. dirs. Bank of Hawaii Internat. Inc.; internat. treas., dir. Pacific Basin Econ. Coun. U.S. Mem. Com. Bd. dirs. Maunalani Found.; chmn., bd. dirs. Pacific Fleet Submarine Meml. Assn. With U.S. Army, 1950-52. Mem. Navy League of U.S., Pacific Forum/CSIS (bd. govs.), U.S.-Korea Bus. Coun., Kappa Sigma, Pi Eta Sigma, Oahu Country Club, Waialae Country Club, Rotary, Lambda Alpha Internat. Office: Bank of Hawaii PO Box 2900 Honolulu HI 96846-0001

STEPHENSON, IRENE HAMLEN, biorhythm analyst, consultant, editor, educator; b. Chgo., Oct. 7, 1923; d. Charles Martin and Carolyn Hilda (Hilgers) Hamlin; m. Edgar B. Stephenson, Sr., Aug. 16, 1941 (div. 1946); 1 child, Edgar B. Author biorhythm compatibilities column Nat. Singles Register, Norwalk, Calif., 1979-81; instr. biorhythm Learning Tree Open U., Canoga Park, Calif., 1982-83; instr. biorhythm character analysis 1980—; instr. biorhythm compatibility, 1982—; owner, pres. matchmaking svc. Pen Pals Using Biorhythm, Chatsworth, Calif., 1979—; editor newsletter The Truth, 1979-85, Mini Examiner, Chatsworth, 1985—; researcher biorhythm character and compatibility, 1974—, biorhythm columnist Psychic Astrology Horoscope, 1989-94, True Astrology Forecast, 1989-94, Psychic Astrology Predictions, 1990-94, Con Artist Types, 1995, Pedophile (child molester) Types, 1995, Personality Types, 1996, Trouble-Addict (Suicide) Types, 1997, Domineering/Nag Types, 1998, Con Artists, Sweetheart Swindlers, Super Con Artist Types, 1998; author: Learn Biorhythm Character Analysis, 1980, Do-It-Yourself Biorhythm Compatibilities, 1982; contbr. numerous articles to mags.; frequent guests clubs, radio, TV. *To be happy, you have to be what is natural for you, not what someone else wants you to be. In 1974, Irene Hamlen Stephenson discovered a character side to biorhythm. She learned no one else had yet made this discovery. She did research and found that we are born with our personality. A few of the many different character types that can be seen from just a birthdate are: con-artist, pedophile, sexual harasser, and trouble addict. She feels that anyone can learn this side of biorhythm. If her biorhythm charcteer and compatibility research were used, it could help to lessen the current 50% divorce rate. It is her greatest dream to see this research used for the bendefit of society* Office: PO Box 3893-ww Chatsworth CA 91313

STEPHENSON, LARRY KIRK, strategic planner, management and geography educator; b. Seattle, Sept. 22, 1944; s. Norman Eugene and Virginia Dare (Frost) S.; m. Margery Alsever, Aug. 15, 1992; children: Mathew Alan, Leah Anela. BS, Ariz. State U., 1966, MA, 1971; PhD, U. Cin., 1973; Manpower research analyst Employment Security Commn. of Ariz., 1969-70; asst. prof. dept. geography U. Hawaii, Hilo, 1973-76, assoc. prof., 1976-78, chmn. dept., 1975-77; vis. lectr. dept. geography Ariz. State U., 1978, adj. assoc. prof., 1979—; planner Ariz. Dept. Health Services, Phoenix, 1978-84; vis. assoc. prof. dept. geography, area devel. and urban planning U. Ariz., 1978; strategic plannner City of Glendale, Ariz., 1984-92; pub. health analyst Gila River Indian Community, 1992-98, econ. devel. planner, 1998—; mem. faculty U. Phoenix, 1979—; adj. prof. Golden Gate U., 1981—; ptnr. Urban Research Assocs., Phoenix, 1981—; adj. prof. Coll. St. Francis, 1982—; mem. faculty Troy State U., 1990—. Mem. Hawaii Island Health Planning Council, 1974-78; mem. Glendale Community Colls. Pres.'s Council, 1986-92. Served with U.S. Army, 1966-68. NDEA fellow, 1971-72. Mem. Am. Inst. Cert. Planners, Am. Planning Assn., Assn. Am. Geographers, Ariz. Planning Assn. (pres. 1987—), Southwest Profl. Geog. Assn., Lambda Alpha. Unitarian. Author books in field; contbr. chpts. to textbooks, articles to profl. jours. Home: RR 1 Box 453-f Laveen AZ 85339-9654 Office: PO Box 97 Sacaton AZ 85247-0097

STEPHERD, MICHAEL R., public relations executive; b. Anchorage, Alaska, Jan. 8, 1955; s. Jack G. Baucher and Cherie D. (Shepherd) Brownlee; m. Barbara W. Smith, Aug. 16, 1979 (div. Aug. 1982). BA, U. Wash., 1994. Mktg. dir. KTBY-TV, Anchorage, 1985-87; v.p. The Murray Group, Seattle, 1980-85, 87-90; account dir. Evans Group, Seattle, 1990-91; account supr. Delaunay/Phillips, Seattle, 1991-92; mng. ptnr. Shepherd Pub. Rels., Seattle, 1992—; adj. prof. U. Wash., Seattle, 1996—, Seattle U., 1996—. Pres., bd. trustees Childhaven, Seattle, 1996-97; bd. dirs. Seattle Fallen Fire Fighters, Seattle, 1997—; tournament co-chair Childhaven Celebrity Golf Tournament, Olympia, Wash., 1998. Recipient Best TV feature Pub. Rels. Soc. of Am., 1982, Best Multi-Media feature, 1983, Best Print feature, 1982. Mem. City Club of Seattle, Wash. Athletic Club, Mission Hills Country Club. Avocations: tennis, golf. Home: 392 E Stevens Rd Unit D13 Palm Springs CA 92262-4747 Office: Shepherd Pub Rels Coun 911 Western Ave Ste 512 Seattle WA 98104-1047

STEPP, ROBERT JOHN, physician; b. Spartanburg, S.C., Sept. 2, 1948; s. Robert George and Rose Marie (Oliveta) S.; m. Iona LaVerne Afterburn, Apr. 8, 1971. BA in Chemistry, St. Mary of Plains Coll., 1971; MD, Creighton U., 1975; MPH, U. Tex., San Antonio, 1984. Diplomate Am. Bd. Preventive Medicine. Intern in family practice Creighton U. Affiliated Hosps., Omaha, 1975-76; commd. 2d lt. USAF, 1976, advanced through grades to col.; gen. med. officer USAF Hosp., Karamursel, Turkey, 1976; chief med. svcs. USAF Med. Aid Sta., Karamursel, Turkey, 1976-78, officer in charge, 1978-79; officer in charge flight medicine USAF Clinic, McChord AFB, 1979-82, chief aeromed. svcs., 1982-83; resident in aerospace medicine USAF Sch. Aerospace Medicine, San Antonio, 1984-85; chief aeromed. svcs. 509th Strategic Hosp., Pease AFB, N.H., 1985-87, chief hosp. svcs., 1987-88; comdr. 305th Strategic Clinic, Grissom AFB, Ind., 1988-90; chief operational medicine divsn. Office of Comman Surgeon, Hdqrs. Strategic Air Command, Offutt AFB, Nebr., 1990-92; dir. installation support Wilford Hall USAF Med. Ctr., Lackland AFB, Tex., 1992-93; comdr., dean USAF Sch. Aerospace Medicine, Brooks AFB, Tex., 1993-95; comdr. surgeon USAF, Air Force Space Command, Peterson AFB, Colo., 1995-97; assoc. aeromedical advisor Airline Pilot's Assn., Aurora, Colo., 1997—. Decorated Legion of Merit, Meritorious Svc. medals, Air Force Commendation medals. Fellow Aerospace Med. Assn.; mem. Soc. USAF Flight Surgeons (bd. govs. 1994-96, pres. 1995-96). Home: 20045 Doewood Dr Monument CO 80132-8054 Office: Aviation Medicine Adv Svc 14707 E 2nd Ave Aurora CO 80011-8914

STERBICK, PETER LAWRENCE, lawyer; b. Tacoma, Nov. 12, 1917; s. Anton John and Pearl (Medak) S.; m. Rita J. Morrell, Dec. 26, 1946; children: Marilyn, Lawrence, Thomas, David, Colleen. BBA, U. Wash., 1941, LLB, 1948. Bar: Wash. 1949. Adjuster Gen. Accidenty Ins. Co., Seattle, 1948-49, Farmers Ins. Group, Tacoma, 1949-50; dep. pros. atty. Pierce County, Tacoma, 1950-51; ptnr. Sterbick and Sterbick, Tacoma, 1951-57, Sterbick, [illegible] and Sterbick, Tacoma, [illegible] and Sterbick, Tacoma, 1972—. 2d lt. USAAF, 1943-45. Mem. Wash. Bar Assn., Wash. State Trial Lawyers Assn., Tacoma-Pierce County Bar Assn., Kiwanis, KC, Elks. Roman Catholic. Home: 3143 Olympic Blvd W University Place WA 98466-1605 Office: 15 Oregon Ave Ste 303 Tacoma WA 98409-7404

STERLING, DONALD JUSTUS, JR., retired newspaper editor; b. Portland, Oreg., Sept. 27, 1927; s. Donald Justus and Adelaide (Armstrong) S.; m. Julie Ann Courteol, June 7, 1963; children: Sarah, William, John. A.B., Princeton U., 1948; postgrad. (Nieman fellow), Harvard U., 1955-56. Reporter Denver Post, 1948-52; news staff mem. Oreg. Jour., Portland, 1952-82; editor Oreg. Jour., 1972-82; asst. to pub. The Oregonian, 1982-92, ret., 1992. Pres. Tri-County Community Coun., 1972-73. Recipient Izaak Walton League Golden Beaver award, 1969, Edith Knight Hill award, 1978, Jessie Laird Brodie award Planned Parenthood Assn., 1983, McCall award Women in Communications, 1987, Roger W. Williams Freedom of Info. award Oreg. Newspaper Pubs. Assn., 1989; English-Speaking Union traveling fellow, 1959. Mem. Oreg. Hist. Soc. (pres. 1977-79), Mazamas, Lang Syne Soc., City Club (Portland pres. 1973-74), Multnomah Athletic, Dial Elm Cannon (Princeton), Phi Beta Kappa. Home: 1718 SW Myrtle St Portland OR 97201-2300

STERLING, DONALD T., professional basketball team executive; b. Chgo.. Lawyer L.A. (formerly San Diego) Clippers, Nat. Basketball Assn., owner, also chmn. bd. Office: care LA Clippers LA Meml Sports Arena 3939 S Figueroa St Los Angeles CA 90037-1200*

STERLING, HARRY MICHAEL, lawyer, educator; b. Denver, Feb. 24, 1935; s. Samuel Harry and Mildred (Reed) S.; m. Victoria Aybar, Aug. 14, 1994; children: Lauren, Elissa, Fran. BS in Bus. and LLB, U. Colo., 1958. Bar: Colo. 1958, U.S. Dist. Ct. Colo. 1958, U.S. Ct. Appeals (10th cir.) 1959, U.S. Suprmeme Ct. 1968. Ptnr. Sterling & Sterling, Denver, 1958-67, Johnson, Makris, Simon & Sterling, Denver, 1967-71, Sterling & Simon, Denver, 1971-83, Hughes & Dorsey, Denver, 1983, Sterling & Miller, Denver, 1984-89, Gelt, Fleishman & Sterling, Denver, 1989—; adj. prof. U. Colo. Law Sch., Boulder, 1979, U. Denver, 1980-88. Pres. Temple Sinai, Denver, 1972-75; bd. dirs. B'nai B'rith Internat., Washington, 1982-85; commr. Anti-Defamation League, N.Y.C., 1985—. 1st lt. USAR, 1958-66. Fellow Am. Coll. Bankruptcy; mem. ABA, Colo. Bar Assn., Denver Bar Assn., Comml. Law League, Phi Delta Phi. Democrat. Avocations: golf, travel. Office: 303 E 17th Ave Denver CO 80203-1235

STERMER, DUGALD ROBERT, designer, illustrator, writer, consultant; b. Los Angeles, Dec. 17, 1936; s. Robert Newton and Mary (Blue) S.; m. Jeanie Kortum; children: Dugald, Megan, Chris, Colin, Crystal. B.A., UCLA, 1960. Art dir., v.p. Ramparts mag., 1965-70; freelance designer, illustrator, writer, cons. San Francisco, 1970—; founder Pub. Interest Communications, San Francisco, 1974; chmn. illustration dept. Calif. Coll. Arts and Crafts, 1994—; bd. dirs. Am. Inst. Graphic Arts; mem. San Francisco Art Commn., 1997—. Cons. editor: Communication Arts mag., 1974-90; designer: Oceans mag., 1976-82; editor: The Environment, 1972, Vanishing Creatures, 1980; author: The Art of Revolution, 1970, Vanishing Creatures, 1980, Vanishing Flora, 1994, Birds and Bees, 1994; designer 1984 Olympic medals; illustration exhbn. Calif. Acad. Scis., 1986; one-man show Jernigan Wicker Gallery, San Francisco, 1996. Mem. Grand Jury City and County San Francisco, 1989; bd. dirs. Delancey St. Found., 1990—. Recipient various medals, awards for design and illustration nat. and internat. competitions. Office: 600 The Embarcadero # 204 San Francisco CA 94107-2121

STERN, ARTHUR I, architectural glass artist, sculptor, painter; b. Pitts., June 18, 1950; s. Sidney and Trudy (Garber) S.; m. Kathrin Sears, Sept. 30, 1996.. BFA in Environ. Design, Calif. Coll. Arts & Crafts, Oakland, 1973. Owner, designer Arthurn Stern Studios, Oakland, 1976-94, Benicia, Calif., 1994—. Contbr. articles and photographs to profl. jours. Recipient design awards AIA/IFRAA, 1987, 90, AIA, 1996, excellence in design and craftsmanship award CCAIA, 1983. Avocations: musician, audophine, citroenist, book and architectural remnant collector. Office: 1075 Jackson St Benicia CA 94510-2905

STERN, ARTHUR PAUL, electronics company executive; b. Budapest, Hungary, July 20, 1925; came to U.S., 1951; s. Leon and Bertha (Frankfurter) S.; m. Edith M. Samuel; children: Daniel, Claude, Jacqueline. Diploma in Elec. Engring., Swiss Fed. Inst. Tech., Zurich, 1948; MSEE, Syracuse U., 1955. Mgr. electronic devices and applications lab. GE, Syracuse, N.Y., 1957-61; dir. engring. Martin Marietta Corp., Balt., 1961-64; dir. ops. Bunker Ramo Corp., Canoga Park, Calif., 1964-66; v.p., gen. mgr. advanced products divsn. Magnavox, Torrance, Calif., 1966-79; pres. Magnavox Advanced Products and Systems Co., Torrance, 1980-90; vice chmn., bd. dirs. Magnavox Govt. and Indsl.Electronics Co., Ft. Wayne, Ind., 1987-90; pres. Ea. Beverly Hills Corp., 1991—; pres. Calif.-Israel C. of C., 1994-98, chmn. bd. 1998—; mem. governing coun. Am.-Jewish Congress, 1997—; bd. dirs. Jewish Coun. Pub. Affairs, 1996—; non-resident staff mem. MIT, 1956-59; instr. GE Bus. Mgmt., 1955-57. Author: Transistor Broadcast Receivers, 1954; co-author: Transistor Circuit Engineering, 1957, Handbook of Automation, Computation and Control, 1961; also articles; U.S., fgn. patentee in field. Chmn. engring. divsn. United Jewish Appeal, Syracuse, 1955-57; mem. adv. bd. dept. elec. engring. U. Calif., Santa Barbara, 1980-92; mem. Sch. Engring. Adv. and Devel. Coun. Calif. State U., Long Beach, 1985-90; bd. dirs. Bur. Jewish Edn., L.A., 1995—. Fellow AAAS, IEEE (pres. 1975, bd. dirs., officer 1970-77, guest editor spl. issue IEEE Trans. on Circuit Theory 1956, invited guest editor spl. issue Procs. IEEE on Integrated Electronics 1964, chmn. com. on U.S. competitiveness policy, Centennial medal 1984).

STERN, DAVID HOWARD, physician, journalist; b. Oakland, Calif., Nov. 8, 1959; s. Richard Ian and Judith Kay (Putzier) S.; m. Lan Thi Nguyen, June 29, 1996; 1 child, My Linh Saré. BS in Life Sci., U. Nebr., 1982; MD, U. Nebr., Omaha, 1986. Diplomate Am. Bd. Family Practice. Internship, resident U. Calif., L.A., 1986-89; ind. contractor So. Calif., 1988-93; assoc. Western Medical Group, Torrance, Calif., 1993-96; pvt. practice Torrance, Calif., 1996—; cons. Western Medical Group, Torrance, 1994-96; asst. dir. Centrala Hosp. Airport Medical, El Segundo, Calif., 1995-96. Contbr. articles to profl. jours.; editor Aspartame Advisory, 1997, Deep Times News Service, 1994-98. Founder Deep Politics Virtual Network, Internet, 1998; active Citizens for Truth in Kennedy Assasination, L.A., 1993—. Mem. Am. Assn. Family Practice (Calif. chpt.), Am. Assn. Physicians Surgeons, Am. Booksellers Assn., Am. Soc. Profl. Journalists, Union Am. Physicians Dentists. Mem. Zen Judaism Ch. Avocations: writing, photography, poetry, biking, motorcycling. Home: PO Box 4270 Torrance CA 90510-4270

STERN, SEYMOUR (SHOLOM), rabbi; b. N.Y.C., Oct. 29, 1920; s. Harry and Frances (James) S. BA, CCNY, 1939; MA, Hebrew Union Coll.-Jewish Inst. Religion, 1943; postgrad., U. of Judaism, L.A., 1952-57, U. So. Calif., 1955-57, Jewish Theol. Sem. Am., 1962; DD (hon.), Jewish Theol. Sem. Am., 1984, Hartman Inst., Jerusalem, 1987. Ordained rabbi, 1943. Rabbi congregations Bnai Abraham, Hagerstown, Md., 1942-43, East Liverpool, Ohio, 1943-44; rabbi Beth Israel Congregation, Waltham, Mass., 1944-47, Salinas, Ventura, Calif., 1948-56; chaplain Calif. State Dept. Mental Health, 1957-79; counselor Hillel Found. Brandeis U., 1944-45; chaplain Nat. Jewish Welfare Bd., San Francisco, 1947-48; officiated Pacific War Dead Repatriation Program. Chaplain surviving German Jews and Jewish Displaced Persons Occupied Germany, 1945-47; sec. Monterey County Jewish Community Coun., 1950-52; exec. dir. Ventura County Jewish Coun., 1953-56. Capt. U.S. Army, 1945-47, ETO. Recipient Presdl. Unit citation, 1949. Mem. The Rabbinical Assembly, Bd. Rabbis of So. Calif. Home: 360 S Burnside Ave Los Angeles CA 90036-5471

STERN, STANLEY, psychiatrist; b. N.Y.C., Apr. 5, 1933; s. Frank and Gussie S.; children: Marcus F., David S. BA cum laude, N.Y. U., 1953; MD, SUNY, 1957. Intern Ohio State U. Hosp., Columbus, 1957-58; resident in psychiatry Inst. Living, Hartford, Conn., 1958-60, Austen Riggs Ctr., Stockbridge, Mass., 1960-61; psychoanalytic tng. We. New Eng. Inst. for Psychoanalysis, New Haven, Conn., 1965-73; asst. clin. prof. psychiatry Yale U., New Haven, Conn., 1975-81; assoc. clin. prof. psychiatry U. Calif., San Diego, 1982-84; pvt. practice New Haven, 1965-82, La Jolla, Calif., 1982-84, Phoenix, 1984—; mem. faculty San Diego Psychoanalytic Inst., 1980-84; [illegible] Psychoanalytic Study Group, 1986-88, tng. and supervising analyst So. Calif. Psychoanalytic Inst., 1989; chmn. edn. com. Ariz. Pyschoanalytic New Tng. Facility, 1990-91; lectr., presenter, participant seminars and confs. in field. Contbr. article to profl. jours. Trustee Gesell Inst., New Haven, 1986-88, Ctr. for the Exceptional Patient, New Haven; bd. dirs. ACLU. Capt. USAF, 1961-63. Mem. Am. Coll. Psychoanalysts, Am. Psychoanalytic Assn. (cert.), Am. Psychiatric Assn., Am. Acad. Psychoanalysts, Irene Josselyn Group Advancement of Psychoanalysis, So. Calif. Psychoanalytic Inst. and Soc. (faculty), San Diego Psychoanalytic Inst., Council for the Advancement of Psychoanalysis (treas. 1972-73, pres.-elect 1973-74, pres. 1974-75, councillor 1975-80), Phi Beta Kappa, Beta Lambda Sigma, Psi Chi. Home and Office: PO Box 32685 Phoenix AZ 85064-2685 Address: 4438 E Arlington Rd Phoenix AZ 85018-1262

STERRETT, JAMES MELVILLE, accountant, business consultant; b. Chicago, Dec. 25, 1949; s. James McAnlis and Antoinette (Galligan) S.; m. Joyce Mieko Motoda, Sept. 1, 1989; 1 child, Victoria Hanako. BS in Acctg., Chaminade U., Honolulu, 1988; MBA, Chaminade U., 1991. CPA, Hawaii. Cons. Profitability Cons., Honolulu, 1985-87; pres. Sterrett Cons. Group, Honolulu, 1987-88; auditor Deloitte & Touche, Honolulu, 1988-90; acct., cons. pvt. practice, Honolulu, 1990—. Mem. Nat. Soc. Pub. Accts., Nat. Assn. Tax Practitioners, Hawaii Soc. CPA's, Delta Epsilon, Sigma. Office: 1314 S King St Ste 650 Honolulu HI 96814-1979

STEVENS, APRIL O'DELL, writer; b. Burbank, Calif., June 28, 1965; d. Robert George Stevens and Clois Freda Anton Roberts; m. Richard P. Chandler, Dec. 27, 1989 (div. Oct. 1998); children: Alex David, Zachary Allen. BA in Creative Writing, U. Calif., Santa Cruz, 1986. Printer The Sun, Bremerton, Wash., 1994-96; writer/corr. freelance, Port Orchard, Wash., 1994—; writer The Raymond Group, Poulsbo, Wash., 1998—. Chair pub. rels. South Kitsap Habitat for Humanity, Port Orchard, 1998, bd. dirs., exec. com.; pub. rels. cons. St. Vincent de Paul, Port Orchard, 1998—. Regents scholar, Calif., 1995. Home: 200 W Lippert F 128 Port Orchard WA 98366

STEVENS, CHARLES J., former prosecutor, lawyer. BA in English, Colgate U., 1979; JD, U. Calif., Berkeley, 1982. Assoc. Gibson, Dunn & Crutcher, L.A., 1982-84; ptnr. in charge Gibson, Dunn & Crutcher, Sacramento, 1987-93; asst. U.S. atty. Office U.S. Atty., L.A., 1984-87; U.S. atty. ea. dist. Calif. U.S. Dept. Justice, Sacramento, 1993-97; ptnr., lawyer Steven & O'Connell Law Office, Sacremento, 1997—; mem. Civil Justice Reform Act com. for ea. dist. Biden Com. of Ea. Dist., 1991—; panel spkr. and lectr. in field. Contbr. articles to profl. jours. Master Anthony M. Kennedy Am. Inn. of Ct.; mem. FBA (chair program com. Sacramento chpt. 1992-93), State Bar Calif. (bd. editors Criminal Law News 1991-93). Office: Stevens & O'Connell 400 Capitol Mall Ste 2100 Sacramento CA 95814-4412*

STEVENS, CLYDE BENJAMIN, JR., property manager, retired naval officer; b. Denver, Oct. 10, 1908; s. Clyde Benjamin and Maybelle Olive (Boot) S.; m. Lucile Lillian-Louise Kip, May 5, 1933; children: Jane Stevens White, Donald Kip, Patricia Louise Stevens Schley. BS, U.S. Naval Acad., 1930; postgrad., U.S. Naval Postgrad. Sch., Annapolis, Md., 1939, U.S. Naval War Coll., Newport, R.I., 1947. Registered profl. engr. Commd. ensign USN, advanced through grades to rear adm., 1959; comdg. officer USS R-20, S-33 Plaice and Platte, 1950-52; comdr. officer USS Platte 50-52 Destroyer Squad 6, 1954-55; with torpedo prodn. and undersea weapons div. Bur. Ordnance, Washington, 1947-59; with USS Platte, 1950-52, Destroyer squad., 1955-56; program dir. Bur. Ordnance, Washington, 1952-55, 56-59; ret., 1959; product mgr. TRW, Inc., Cleve., 1959-65; rsch. engr. Boeing Co., Seattle, 1965-74, torpedo cons., 1985; apt. owner and mgr. Seattle, 1965—; torpedo cons. Goodyear Aerospace Co., Akron, Ohio, 1965. Patentee automobile generator. Decorated Navy Cross, Silver Star with oak leaf cluster. Mem. Seattle Apt. Assn. (bd. dirs. 1967-91), Army and Navy Club, Rainier Club. Republican. Episcopalian. Home and Office: 2339 Franklin Ave E Seattle WA 98102-3331

STEVENS, ELEANOR SANDRA, domestic services executive; b. Oklahoma City, Nov. 1, 1932; d. Benjamin Franklin and Mary Lou (Smith) Williams; children: Fred W., Nathandra, Benjiman, Ola Enaid. AS in medicine, Fresno State U., 1954; student Fresno Adult Edn., Los Angeles Trade Tech., 1972-73. Radio disc jockey, Fresno, Calif., 1954-55; bookkeeper L.A. County Assessor, 1961-69; supervisor Holzman-Begue Real Estate Co., L.A., 1969-73; dist. mgr. United Systems, Inc., L.A., 1973-77; pub. relations cons. Harold G. Simon & Assoc., Vernon, Calif., 1977-81; pres. Stevens Personalized Svcs. (companion svcs. for sr. citizens), L.A., 1982—. Recipient cert. profl. devel. State of Calif., 1983. Mem. NAFE, Van Nuys Women's Referral Svc., D.B. & O. Charity and Social Club, Los Angeles Good Neighbor Council, Order Ea. Star. Methodist. Office: 3437 Edgehill Dr Los Angeles CA 90018-3639

STEVENS, HENRY AUGUST, insurance agent, educator; b. Frankfurt, Main, Germany, July 21, 1921; came to U.S., 1940; m. Rosemary O'Neil, Mar. 23, 1963; children: Michael, Patrick; children from previous marriage, H. Jack Fay, Sondra Fay. Student, U. Wis., 1943-44; grad., Dale Carnegie Sch., Richland, Wash., 1974. Theatre mgr. Sterling Theatres, Seattle, 1946-54, Alliance Amusement Co., Chgo., 1955-68; ins. agt. N.Y. Life Ins. Co., Richland, 1968—; regional v.p. Washington Assn. Life Underwriters, Richland, 1980; mem. adv. com. Wash. State Ins., Olympia, 1983-89. Chmn. bd. Richland YMCA, 1968; commr. Benton County Dyking Dist., Richland, 1970; chmn. Benton-Franklin Counties Bi-Centennial Commn., Tri-Cities, Wash., 1976; dist. chmn. Rep. Party, Benton County, 1980-96, 98—. Staff sgt. U.S. Army 1943-46. Recipient Nat. Quality award, Nat. Sales Achievement award. Mem. Tri-Cities Life Underwriters Assn. (pres. 1975, bd. dirs.), Tri-Cities Estate Planning Coun. (pres. 1984), Wash. State Assn. Life Underwriters (chmn. 1997), Kiwanis (pres. Chgo. club 1963, Richland club 1986-87, lt. gov. Pacific N.W. dist. 1983, chmn. dist. conv. 1971, 81, 91, sec. Pacific N.W. found. 1994—). Avocations: stamp collecting, preparing family tree. Home: 712 Riverside Dr Richland WA 99353-5216 Office: NY Life Ins Co 8203 W Quinault St Kennewick WA 99336-7117

STEVENS, JAN FREDERIK, phytochemist, researcher, pharmacist; b. Wildervank, The Netherlands, May 10, 1966; s. Carel Stevens and Marchiena (Groenwold) Stevens-Groenwold. MS cum laude, U. Groningen, The Netherlands, 1988, grad. in Pharmacy, 1990, PhD cum laude, 1995. Jr. rsch. assoc. Netherlands Orgn. for Sci. Rsch., Groningen, 1990-95; rschr. Oreg. State U., Corvallis, 1995—. Contbr. articles to profl. jours. Mem. Royal Netherlands Soc. Natural History, Royal Netherlands Soc. Advancement of Pharmacy, Netherlands Soc. Medicinal Plant Rsch. (F.H.L. van Os award 1989). Avocation: frisian horses. Home: J Kammingakade 17, 9648 KN Wildervank The Netherlands Office: Oreg State U Dept Chemistry Corvallis OR 97331

STEVENS, JANET, illustrator; b. Dallas, Jan. 17, 1953; d. Jack and Frances Stevens; m. Ted Habermann; children: Lindsey Habermann, Blake Habermann. BFA, U. Colo., 1975. Illustrator children's books, 1979—. Writer, illustrator: From Pictures to Words: A Book about Making a Book, 1995, My Big Dog, 1998, (with Susan Stevens Crummel) Cook-a-Doodle-Doo, 1999; reteller, illustrator: Animal Fair, 1981, The Princess and the Pea (Hans Christian Anderson), 1982, Old Bag of Bones, Tops and Bottoms; illustrator: Anansi and the Moss-Covered Rock, 1988, The Dog Who Had Kittens, 1991, Anansi Goes Fishing, 1992, To Market, To Market, 1997, others. Recipient Parents Choice award 1987, Notable Children's Trade Book in the Field of Social Studies citation Nat. Coun. for Social Studies-Children's Book Coun., 1987, Caldecott Honor citation Am. Libr. Assn., 1996, Notable Children's Book citation, 1996; recipient several state children's book awards. Avocations: mountain biking, camping, hiking, skiing. *

STEVENS, JOHN CLARKE, neurologist; b. Lloydminster, Sask., Can., Aug. 6, 1941; came to U.S., 1967; s. John Charles and Alice Ada (Clarke) S.; m. Patricia Marie Mosier, Jan. 4, 1991; children: David, Kimberly, Michael. MD, U. Alta. (Can.), Edmonton, 1965. Diplomate Am. Bd. Psychiatry and Neurology. Intern Royal Alexandra Hosp., Edmonton, Alberta, Can., 1965-66; resident in internal medicine Mayo Grad. Sch., [illegible] 1996; neurologist Mayo Clinic, Rochester, 1972-86; neurologist Mayo Clinic Scottsdale (Ariz.), 1987—, chair dept. neurology, 1995—. Fellow Am. Assn. Electrodiagnostic Medicine (bd. dirs. 1995-97), Am. Acad. Neuroology; mem. Am. Neurol. Assn. Office: Mayo Clinic Scottsdale 13400 E Shea Blvd Scottsdale AZ 85259-5499

STEVENS, NEAL, construction executive, financing executive; b. Trumann, Ark., May 1, 1941; s. Ester and Daisy Pauline (Estridge) S.; m. Jean Golden, June 4, 1960; children: Donna, Paul, Kimberly. Student, Kilgore (Tex.) Jr. Coll., 1959-60, Harbor Coll., Harbor City, Calif., 1961-62. Mfg. engr. Tridair Enterprises, Torrance, Calif., 1965-76; CEO, pres. E.O.S. Enterprises, Inc., Torrance, 1976—; pres., CEO E.O.S. Internat. Inc., Torrance, 1994—. Mem. NRA, Nat. Wild Life Fedn., N.Am. Wild Sheep, Soc. for Conservation of Big Horn Sheep, Safari Club Internat., Knights of Malta. Republican. Roman Catholic. Avocations: hunting, fishing, camping, hiking, rock hunting. Home: 40613 Via Diamonte Murrieta CA 92562-8504

STEVENS, RICK DARYL, entertainment industry executive; b. Los Angeles, Dec. 16, 1948; s. John and Lisa Mary (Sehl) S. B. in Bus., U. Miami, 1970. Product mgr. CBS Records, N.Y.C., 1970-73; asst. to pres. Polygram, N.Y.C., 1973-74, sr. v.p. artists repertoire, 1975-81; dir. mktg. Polydor/Metro-Goldwyn-Mayer Records, N.Y.C., 1974-75; personal mgr. Stevens-McGhee Entertainment, N.Y.C., 1982-84; pres. Summa Music Group, West Hollywood, Calif., 1984—; pres., co-founder Summa Artists, Inc., 1989—; pres. Summa Music Group and Record Plant, Inc.; cons. music pub. acquisitions Communications Tech. Group and Bear-Stearns, N.Y.C., 1983-85; chmn. EFX Systems; pres. Media Holdings Group. Author: About Music Publishing, 1984. Mem. Nat. Assn. Rec. Arts and Scis. Avocations: tennis, computers. Office: Summa Music Group 1032 N Sycamore Ave Los Angeles CA 90038-2308

STEVENS, ROBERT WILLIAM, church denomination administrator; b. Coquille, Oreg., Mar. 23, 1936; s. Stanton Frank and Eva R. (Mossholder) S.; m. Marilyn Ludlow, Sept. 10, 1957; children: Paul, Ruth. BA in Econs., Willamette U., 1958; postgrad., U. Wash., 1958-59. Treas. Pacific N.W. Ann. Conf., United Meth. Ch., Seattle, 1966—; del. Western Jurisdictional Conf., United Meth. Ch., 1968, 72, 76, 80, 84, 88, 92, 96, Gen. Conf., 1976, 80, 84, 88, 92, 96, mem. com. audit and rev. Gen. Coun. Fin. and Adminstrn., 1972-76, mem. Gen. Coun. Fin. and Adminstrn., 1976-84, mem. Gen. Bd. Pensions, 1984-92, v.p., 1988-92; chairperson Denominational Health Care Task Force, United Meth. Ch., 1989-91. Trustee Seabeck Christian Conf. Camp, Wash., 1973-84, 92-98, pres., 1982-84. Home: 13011 20th Ave NE Seattle WA 98125-4121 Office: United Meth Ch NW Ann Conf 2112 3rd Ave Ste 300 Seattle WA 98121-2310

STEVENS, STEPHEN EDWARD, psychiatrist; b. Phila.; s. Edward and Antonia S.; BA cum laude, LaSalle Coll., 1950; MD, Temple U., Phila., 1954; LLB, Blackstone Sch. Law, 1973; m. Isabelle Helen Gallacher, Dec. 27, 1953. Intern, Frankford Hosp., Phila., 1954-55; resident in psychiatry Phila. State Hosp., 1955-58; practice medicine specializing in psychiatry Woodland Hills, Calif., 1958-63, Santa Barbara, Calif., 1970-77; asst. supt. Camarillo (Calif.) State Hosp., 1963-70; cons. ct. psychiatrist Santa Barbara County, 1974-77; clin. dir. Kailua Mental Health Ctr., Oahu, Hawaii, 1977—. Author: Treating Mental Illness, 1961, Survival and the Fifth Dimension, 1997, Psychiatry, Survival and God, 1998. Served with M.C., USAAF. Diplomate Am. Bd. Psychiatry and Neurology. Decorated Purple Heart. Fellow Am. Geriatrics Soc. (founding); mem. Am. Acad. Psychiatry and Law, AMA, Am. Psychiat. Assn., Am. Legion, DAV (Oahu chpt. 1), Caledonia Soc., Am. Hypnosis Soc., Am. Soc. Adolescent Psychiatry, Hawaiian Canoe Club, Honolulu Club, Elks (BPOE 616), Aloha String Band (founder and pres.). Home: PO Box 26413 Honolulu HI 96825-6413

STEVENS, SUSAN MARIE, English educator, poet, editor; b. Austin, Tex., July 22, 1945; d. Walter MacDowell and Johnnye Joyce (Tyson) Cox; m. John David Fraivillig, Apr. 2, 1965 (div. June 1969); m. Gerald Lee Stevens, May 1, 1969 (div. Nov. 1971); 1 child, Brent Michael. BA in English, U. Redlands, Calif., 1974; MA in English, No. Arizona U., 1989. Cert. std. secondary tchg. Tchr., tutor lang. arts Many Farms H.S., Ariz., 1985-87, 89-90; editor, info. receptionist, collection officer USDA-Prescott (Ariz.) Nat. Forest, 1991-94; instr. English Ea. Ariz. Coll., Thatcher, 1996—; English tutor adj. English instr. Yavapai Coll., Prescott, 1994-96. Author fiction and poetry; editor: Queen of the Sun (E.J. Michael), 1995. Publicity dir. Zero Population Growth, Ridgecrest, Calif., 1969-71, Desert Cmty. Orch., Ridgecrest, 1969-71; book reviewer/feature writer, Parents Without Partners, Albany, Ga., 1982-83; bassoonist, Yavapai Cmty. Orchestra and Wind Quintet, Prescott, Ariz., 1987-88. Mem. Acad. of Am. Poets; Ea. Ariz. Coll. Faculty Assn. Democrat. Lutheran. Avocations: writing, vocal/instrumental music, hiking, reading. Fax: 520-428-8462. E-Mail: ssteven-s@eac.cc.az.us. Office: Eastern Arizona College US Hwy 70 Thatcher AZ 85558-0769

STEVENS, THEODORE FULTON, senator; b. Indpls., Nov. 18, 1923; s. George A. and Gertrude (Chancellor) S.; m. Ann Mary Cherrington, Mar. 29, 1952 (dec. 1978); children—Susan B., Elizabeth H., Walter C., Theodore Fulton, Ben A.; m. Catherine Chandler, 1980; 1 dau.; Lily Irene. B.A., U. Calif. at Los Angeles, 1947; LL.B., Harvard U., 1950. Bar: Calif., Alaska, D.C., U.S. Supreme Ct. bars. Pvt. practice Washington, 1950-52, Fairbanks, Alaska, 1953; U.S. atty. Dist. Alaska, 1953-56; legis. counsel, asst. to sec., solicitor Dept. Interior, 1956-60; pvt. practice law Anchorage, 1961-68; mem. Alaska Ho. of Reps., 1965-68, majority leader, speaker pro tem, 1967-68; U.S. senator for Alaska, 1968—, asst. Rep. leader, 1977-85; chmn. Sen. Appropriations Com. Served as 1st lt. USAAF, World War II. Mem. ABA, Alaska Bar Assn., Calif. Bar Assn., D.C. Bar Assn., Am. Legion, VFW. Lodges: Rotary, Pioneers of Alaska, Igloo #4. Home: PO Box 100879 Anchorage AK 99510-0879 Office: US Senate 522 Hart Senate Bldg Washington DC 20510

STEVENS, WILBUR HUNT, accountant; b. Spencer, Ind., June 20, 1918; s. John Vosburgh and Isabelle Jane (Strawser) S.; m. Maxine Dodge Stevens, Sept. 28, 1941; children: Linda Maxine Piffero, Deborah Anne Augello. BS, U. Calif., Berkeley, 1949, MBA, 1949. CPA, Calif.; cert. fraud examiner, fin. svcs. auditor; diplomate Am. Bd. Forensic Acctg. Staff acct. McLaren, Goode, West & Co., San Francisco, 1949-52; mng. ptnr. Wilbur H. Stevens & Co., Salinas, Calif., 1952-70; regional ptnr. Fox & Co., CPAs, Salinas, 1970-73; nat. dir. banking practice Fox & Co., CPAs, Denver, 1973-80; pres., chmn. Wilbur H. Stevens, CPA, PC, Salinas, 1980-94; chmn. Stevens, Sloan & Shah, CPAs, 1994—; adj. prof. acctg. U. Denver, 1975-78; faculty mem. Assemblies for Bank Dirs., So. Meth. U., Dallas, 1976-81, Nat. Banking Sch., U. Va., Charlottesville, 1979-87; chmn., dir. Valley Nat. Bank, 1963-71. Editor Issues in CPA Practice, 1975; contbr. articles to profl. jours. Capt. AUS, 1942-53. Decorated Bronze Star; Frank G. Drum fellow U. Calif., Berkeley, 1949. Mem. AICPA (v.p. 1971), Am. Acctg. Assn., Am. Assembly Collegiate Schs. Bus. (accreditation coun. 1975-78, 81-84), Nat. Assn. State Bds. Accountancy (pres. 1976-77, strategic initiatives com.), Calif. Soc. CPAs (pres. 1968-69, Disting. Svc. award 1988), Acctg. Rsch. Assn. (pres. 1973-75), Assn. Cert. Fraud Examiners, Am. Coll. Forensic Examiners, Nat. Assn. Fin. Svcs. Auditors, Burma Star Assn., CBI Vets. Assn., 14 AF Assn., Hump Pilots Assn., Acad. Acctg. Historians, Commonwealth Club Calif., Masons (master 1992, 97, Hiram award 1998, grand lodge com. taxation), Knight Templar, 32 degree Scottish Rite, Nat. Sojourners (pres. Monterey Bay chpt. 1996), Heroes of '76 (comdr John C. Fremont chpt. 1996-97), Salinas High Twelve Club (pres. 1995), QCCC, London, Rotary (dist. gov. 1983, chmn. internat. fellowship accounts 1994-96, Paul Harris fellow 1978), Phi Beta Kappa, Beta Gamma Sigma (v.p. 1949), Beta Alpha Psi. Republican. Methodist. Home: 38 Santa Ana Dr Salinas CA 93901-4136 Office: 975 W Alisal St Ste D Salinas CA 93901-1148

STEVENSON, GEORGE GUILFORD, information systems specialist; b. Glendale, Calif., Feb. 8, 1963; s. Haywood Thomas and Helen Marie (Moore) S.; m. Denise Lee Mascarenas, Feb. 21, 1981; 1 child, Katherine. Student, L.A. Trad-Tech., 1987-89, Glendale Cmty. Coll., 1991-93. Tel. operator Pacific Tel., Burbank, Calif., 1980-81; mail clk. Automobile Club Southern Calif., L.A., 1981-82, security, 1982-85, claims rep., 1985-86, facilities technician, 1986-89, constrn. technician, 1989-95; computer technician Tristar Computer Solutions, San Luis Obispo, Calif., 1995—. Republican. Protestant. Avocations: reading, writing, guitar, martial arts, prestidigitation. Home: 1674 Lima Dr San Luis Obispo CA 93405-6815 Office: Tristar Computer solutions 4401 El Camino Real G Atascadero CA 93422

STEVENSON, JAMES RALPH, school psychologist, author; b. Kemmerer, Wyo., June 29, 1949; s. Harold Ralph and Dora (Borino) S.; m. Alice M. Paolucci, June 17, 1972; children: Tiffany Jo, Brian Jeffrey. BA, U. No. Colo., 1971, MA, 1974, EdS, 1975. Diplomate Am. Psychotherapy Assn.; lic. elem. sch. counselor, sch. psychologist, Colo.; nationally cert. sch. psychologist. Sch. psychologist Jefferson County Pub. Schs., Golden, Colo., 1975-87, 89-91, Weld County Sch. Dist. 6, Greeley, Colo., 1987-89, Weld Bd. Coop. Edn. Svcs., LaSalle, Colo., 1991-95; spl. edn. coord. Weld Bd. Coop. Edn. Svcs., LaSalle, 1995; sch. psychologist Fort Lupton (Colo.) Schs., 1995-98; coord. of spec. edn. and gifted progs. Fort Lupton Sch. Dist., 1998—; ltd. pvt. practice sch. psychologist Pathways, Greeley, 1994—. Asst. coach Young Am. Baseball, Greeley, 1989, 90, head coach, 1992, 93; asst. basketball coach Recreation League for 6th-7th Grades, 1992, 93. U. No. Colo. scholar, 1974. Mem. NEA, NASP (alt. del. Colo. chpt. 1975-77, dir. Apple II users group Washington chpt. 1989-95), Assn. Play Therapy, Inc., Colo. Soc. Sch. Psychologists (chmn. task force on presch. assessment 1991-96), Colo. Edn. Assn., Ft. Lupton Edn. Assn., Jefferson County Psychologists Assn. (sec. 1986-87), Colo. Assn. for Play Therapy, Am. Orthopsychiat. Assn. Democrat. Roman Catholic. Avocations: travel, reading, sports events, plays, music. Home: 1937 24th Ave Greeley CO 80631-5027 Office: Fort Lupton Schs 301 Reynolds St Fort Lupton CO 80621-1329

STEVENSON, JAMES RICHARD, radiologist, lawyer; b. Ft. Dodge, Iowa, May 30, 1937; s. Lester Lawrence and Esther Irene (Johnson) S.; m. Sara Jean Hayman, Sept. 4, 1958; children: Bradford Allen, Tiffany Ann, Jill Renee, Trevor Ashley. BS, U. N.Mex., 1959; MD, U. Colo., 1963; JD, U. N.Mex. 1987. Diplomate Am. Bd. Radiology, Am. Bd. Nuclear Medicine, Am. Bd. Legal Medicine, 1989; Bar: N.Mex. 1987, U.S. Dist. Ct. N.Mex. 1988. Intern U.S. Gen. Hosp., Tripler, Honolulu, 1963-64; resident in radiology U.S. Gen. Hosp., Brook and San Antonio, Tex., 1964-67; radiologist, ptnr. Van Atta Labs., Albuquerque, 1970-88, Radiology Assocs. of Albuquerque, 1988—, pres., 1994-96; radiologist, ptnr. Civerolo, Hansen & Wolf, Albuquerque, 1988-89; adj. asst. prof. radiology U. N.Mex., 1970-71; pres. med. staff AT & SF Meml. Hosp., 1979-80, chief of staff, 1980-81, trustee, 1981-83. Author: District Attorney manual, 1987. Participant breast screening, Am. Cancer Soc., Albuquerque, 1987-88; dir. profl. divsn. United Way, Albuquerque, 1975. Maj. U.S. Army 1963-70, Vietnam; col. M.C. USAR, 1988—. Decorated Bronze Star. Allergy fellow, 1960. Med.-Legal Tort Scholar award, 1987. Fellow Am. Coll. Radiology (councilor 1980-86, mem. med. legal com. 1990-96), Am. Coll. Legal Medicine, Am. Coll. Nuclear Medicine, Radiology Assn. of Albuquerque; mem. AMA (Physicians' Recognition award 1969—), Am. Soc. Law & Medicine, Am. Arbitration Assn., Albbuquerque Bar Assn., Am. Coll. Nuclear Physicians (charter), Soc. Nuclear Medicine (v.p. Rocky Mountain chpt. 1975-76), Am. Inst. Ultrasound in Medicine, N.Am. Radiol. Soc. (chmn. med. legal com. 1992-95), N.Mex. Radiol. Soc. (pres. 1978-79), N.Mex. Med. Soc. (chmn. grievance com.), Albuquerque-Bernalillo County Med. Soc. (scholar 1959), Nat. Assn. Health Lawyers, ABA (antitrust sect. 1986—), N. Mex. State Bar, Albuquerque Bar Assn., Sigma Chi. Republican. Methodist. Club: Albuquerque Country. Lodges: Elks, Masons, Shriners. Home: 3333 Santa Clara Ave SE Albuquerque NM 87106-1530 Office: Medical Arts Imaging Ctr A-6 Med Arts Sq 801 Encino Pl NE Albuquerque NM 87102-2612

STEVENSON, PETER RENFREW, software engineer; b. Portland, Oreg., July 17, 1935; s. John Renfrew and Mary Louise (Hay) S.; m. Patricia Raemunda Peasley, Oct. 13, 1958; children: Greg, Mark, Sophia, Charles, Natasha, Joshua. BA in Math., U. Colo., 1964; MS in Computer Sci., U. Santa Clara, 1980. Solar observer High Altitude Observatory, Climax, Colo., 1961-64; jr. h.s. math tchr. Monte Vista (Colo.) Schs., 1965-66; mathematician U.S. Geol. Survey, Menlo Park, Calif., 1966-81; software engr. Lockheed Missiles and Space, Sunnyvale, Calif., 1981-85, Dalmo Victor/Singer, Tucson, 1985-88, Merdan Systems, Ft. Huahuaca, 1988, Lockheed Martin, Sunnyvale, 1988—. Contbr. articles to profl. jours. Area chair Christian Family Movement, 1972. With USNR, 1956-60. Mem. Assn. for Computing Machinery, SIGADA (local treas. 1981-88). Democrat. Roman Catholic. Avocations: photography, painting, fishing, outdoor exercise. Home: 5715 Makati Circle Dr #D San Jose CA 95123 Office: EA 40, B151 1111 Lockheed-Martin Way Sunnyvale CA 94089-1212

STEVENSON, ROBERT MURRELL, music educator; b. Melrose, N.Mex., July 3, 1916; s. Robert Emory and Ada (Ross) S. AB, U. Tex., El Paso, 1936; grad., Juilliard Grad. Sch. Music, 1938; MusM, Yale, 1939; PhD, U. Rochester, 1942; STB cum laude, Harvard U., 1943; BLitt, Oxford (Eng.) U.; Th.M., Princeton U.; DMus honoris causa, Cath. U. Am., 1991; LHD honoris causa, Ill. Wesleyan U., 1992; LittD honoris causa, Universidade Nova de Lisboa, 1993. Instr. music U. Tex., 1941-43, 46; faculty Westminster Choir Coll., Princeton, N.J., 1946-49; faculty research lectr. UCLA, 1981, mem. faculty to prof. music, 1949—; vis. asst. prof. Columbia, 1955-56; vis. prof. Ind. U., Bloomington, 1959-60, U. Chile, 1965-66, Northwestern U., Chgo., 1976, U. Granada, 1992; cons. UNESCO, 1977; Louis Charles Elson lectr. Libr. of Congress, Washington, 1969; inaugural prf. musicology Nat. U. Mex., 1996; spkr. Dumbarton Oaks Pre-Columbian Music Workshop, 1998. *He was the national winner of the Joseph M. Bearns Composition prize awarded by Columbia University in 1942. He headlined an entire program of his compositions at Town Hall, New York, in March, 1947. Leopold Stokowski conducted the Philadelphia Orchestra in premiere performances of two of his compositions in 1961. In Spain on May 8, 1997, he received in person the third gold medal awarded by the Real Conservatorio Superior. On July 17, 1997, he was Keynote Speaker at the 1997 Inter-American Conference on Black Music Research in Chicago. American achievements are as nothing unless they are written about and remembered. My mission has been to rescue the musical past of the Americas. Present-day composers are too busy making their own music to worry about their predecessors. As a result, every new generation of composers thinks that they are the first ones to descry Mount Olympus. Not so. The past is a succession of musical and artistic glories.* Author: Music in Mexico, 1952, Patterns of Protestant Church Music, 1953, La musica en la catedral de Sevilla, 1954, 85, Music Before the Classic Era, 1955, Shakespeare's Religious Frontier, 1958, The Music of Peru, 1959, Juan Bermudo, 1960, Spanish Music in the Age of Columbus, 1960, Spanish Cathedral Music in the Golden Age, 1961, La musica colonial en Colombia, 1964, Protestant Church Music in America, 1966, Music in Aztec and Inca Territory, 1968, Renaissance and Baroque Musical Sources in the Americas, 1970, Music in El Paso, 1970, Philosophies of American Music History, 1970, Written Sources for Indian Music Until 1882, 1972, Christmas Music From Baroque Mexico, 1974, Foundations of New World Opera, 1973, Seventeenth Century Villancicos, 1974, Latin American Colonial Music Anthology, 1975, Vilancicos Portugueses, 1976, Josquin in the Music of Spain and Portugal, 1977, American Musical Scholarship, Parker to Thayer, 1978, Liszt at Madrid and Lisbon, 1980, Wagner's Latin American Outreach, 1983, Spanish Musical Impact Beyond the Pyrenees, 1250-1500, 1985, La Música en las catedrales españolas del Siglo de Oro, 1993; contbg. editor: Handbook Latin Am. Studies, 1976—; editor Inter-Am. Music Rev., 1978—; contbr. to New Grove Dictionary of Music and Musicians, 17 other internat. encys. Served to capt. U.S. Army, 1943-46, 49. Decorated Army Commendation ribbon; fellow Ford Found., 1953-54, Gulbenkian Found., 1966, 81, Guggenheim Found., 1962, NEH, 1974, Comité Conjunto Hispano-Norteamericano (Madrid), 1989; recipient Fulbright rsch. awards, 1958-59, 64, 70-71, 88-89, Carnegie Found. tchg. award, 1955-56, Gabriela Mistral award OAS, 1985, Heitor Villa Lobos Jury award OAS, 1988, OAS medal, 1986, Cert. Merit Mexican Consulate San Bernardino, Calif., 1987, Silver medal Spanish Ministry Culture, 1989, Gold medal Real Conservatorio Superior, 1994, 97, 1st Lifetime Achievement award Sonneck Soc., 1999. Mem. Am. Musicol. Soc. (hon. life, Pacific SW chpt.), Real Academia de Bellas Artes, Hispanic Soc. Am., Am. Liszt Soc. (cons. editor), Heterofonia (cons. editor), Brazilian Musicol. Soc. (hon.), Portuguese Musicol. Soc. (hon.), Argentinian Musicol. Soc. (hon.), Orden Andrés Bello, Primera Clase, Venezuela, 1992. Avocation: playing piano. Office: UCLA Dept Music 405 Hilgard Ave Los Angeles CA 90095-9000

STEVENSON, SARAH SCHOALES, rancher, business owner; b. N.Y.C., Sept. 1, 1944; d. Dudley Nevison and Virginia Jocelyn (Vanderlip) Schoales; m. David Earl Hollatz, Jan. 27, 1968 (div. June 1985); children: Melissa Virginia, Peter David; m. Richard Stevenson, Sept. 1, 1995. BS, U. Wis., 1966; postgrad., U. So. Calif., L.A., 1966. Copywriter Max W. Becker Advt., Long Beach, Calif., 1966-67; advt. dir. officers news USN, Coronado, Calif., 1968-70; with syndicate dept. Morgan Stanley & Co., N.Y.C., 1970-72; lay-out asst. North Castle News, Armonk, N.Y., 1972-75; performer, writer Candy Band, Pound Ridge, N.Y., 1975-82; owner, mgr. Circle Bar Guest Ranch, Utica, Mont., 1983—; bd. dirs. Park Inn, Lewistown, Mont. Artist, composer: Play Me a Song, 1978, Going Home, 1980; composer: (mus. play) Elsie Piddock, 1979, Secret Garden, 1981, Windows, 1989. Soloist Hobson (Mont.) Meth. Ch., 1983—; founder What the Hay, Utica, 1990—. Mem. Mont. Emergency Med. Assn. (bd. dirs. 1990—), Dude Rancher's Assn. (bd. dirs. 1989—, pres. 1996, 97). Episcopalian. Avocations: horse breeding, literature, finance. Home and Office: Circle Bar Guest Ranch Utica MT 59452

STEWART, DAVID WAYNE, marketing educator, psychologist, consultant; b. Baton Rouge, Oct. 23, 1951; s. Wesley A. Stewart, Jr. and Edith L. (Richhart) Moore; m. Lenora Francois, June 6, 1975; children: Sarah Elizabeth, Rachel Dawn. BA, N.E. La. U., 1972; MA, Baylor U., 1973, PhD, 1974. Rsch. psychologist HHS, La., 1974-76; rsch. mgr. Needham, Harper & Steers Advt., Chgo., 1976-78; assoc. prof. Jacksonville (Ala.) State U., 1978-80; assoc. prof. Vanderbilt U., Nashville, 1980-86, sr. assoc. dean, 1984-86; prof. U. So. Calif., L.A., 1986-90, Ernest W. Hahn prof. mktg., 1990-91, Robert Brooker rsch. prof. mktg., 1991—, chmn. dept. mktg., 1995—; mgmt. cons., 1978—. Author, co-author: Secondary Research: Sources and Methods, Effective Television Advertising: A Study of 1000 Commericals, Consumer Behavior and the Practice of Marketing, Focus Group: Theory and Practice, Attention, Attitude, and Affect in Repsonse to Advertising, Nonverbal Communication and Advertising; editor: Jour. of Mktg., 1999—; contbr. articles to profl. jours.; editor: Jour. of Mktg., 1999—; mem. edtl. bd. Jour. Mktg. Rsch., Jour. Consumer Mktg., Jour. Pub. Policy & Mktg., Jour. Mktg., Jour. Advt., Jour. Promotion Mgmt., Current Issues and Rsch. in Advt., Jour. Internat. Consumer Mktg., Jour. Managerial Issues, Jour. Promotion Mgmt.; past pres. policy bd. Jour. Consumer Rsch., Acad. Mgmt. Fellow APA (coun. rep.), Am. Psychol. Soc. (charter); mem. Soc. for Consumer Psychology (past pres.), Inst. Mgmt. Scis., Decision Sci. Inst., Am. Mktg. Assn. (pres. acad. coun. 1997-98, v.p. fin. 1998-99), Assn. for Consumer Rsch., Am. Statis. Assn. (chair sect. on stats. in mktg. 1997), Acad. of Mgmt. Republican. Baptist. Office: U So Calif Sch Bus Adminstrn Dept Mktg Los Angeles CA 90089

STEWART, ISAAC DANIEL, JR., state supreme court justice; b. Salt Lake City, Nov. 21, 1932; s. Isaac Daniel and Orabelle (Iverson) S.; m. Elizabeth Bryan, Sept. 10, 1959; children: Elizabeth Ann, Shannon. BA with high honors, U. Utah, 1959, JD with high honors, 1962. Bar: Utah 1962, U.S. Dist. Ct. Utah 1962, U.S. Ct. Appeals (10th cir.) 1962, U.S. Ct. Appeals (4th cir.) 1963, U.S. Ct. Appeals (9th cir.) 1964, U.S. Ct. Appeals (8th cir.) 1965, U.S. Supreme Ct. 1965. Atty. antitrust divsn. Dept. Justice, Washington, 1962-65; asst. prof., then assoc. prof. U. Utah Coll. Law, 1965-70; ptnr. Jones, Waldo, Holbrook & McDonough, Salt Lake City, 1970-79; assoc. justice Utah Supreme Ct., 1979—, assoc. chief justice, 1986-88, 94-98, assoc. justice, 1999—; lectr. in field; mem. Utah Bd. Oil, Gas and Mining, 1976-78, chmn., 1977-78; Utah rep. Interstate Oil Compact Commn., 1977-78, exec. com. 1978-79; mem. adv. com. rules of procedure Utah Supreme Ct., 1983-87; chmn. com. on bar-press guidelines Utah Bar; mem. U. Utah search com., 1968-70; legal advisor, 1966-68. Editor-in-chief Utah Law Rev.; contbr. articles to legal jours. Chmn. subcom. on legal rights and responsibilities of youth Utah Gov's Com. on Youth, 1972; pres. Salt Lake chpt. Coun. Fgn. Rels., 1982; mem. Salt Lake City C. of C., 1974-79, mem. govtl. modernization com., 1976-78; missionary for Mormon Ch. in Fed. Republic Germany, 1953-56; bd. dirs. U. Utah Alumni Assn., 1986-89. Recipient Alumnus of Yr. award U. Utah Coll. Law, 1989. Mem. ABA, Utah Bar Assn. (com. on law and poverty 1967-69, com. on specialization 1977-78, pub. rels. com. 1968-69, chmn. com. on antitrust law 1977-78, com. on civil procedure reform 1968, mem. exec. com. bd. of appellate judges 1990—, liaison to supreme and adv. coms. evidence & profl. conduct 1986—, Appellate Judge of Yr. 1986), Salt Lake County Bar Assn., Am. Judicature Soc., Order of Coif, Phi Beta Kappa, Phi Kappa Phi, Sigma Chi (Significant Sig award 1987). Office: Utah Supreme Ct PO Box 140210 450 S State St Salt Lake City UT 84114-0210*

STEWART, JAMES WILLIAM, university administrator, minister; b. Springs, South Africa, Mar. 30, 1954; came to U.S., 1972, naturalized, 1978; s. James Henry and Beryl (Keevy) S.; m. Dawnella Darlene Annas; children: James, Joshua, Caleb, Whitney, Caitlyn. BA in Music, Bethany Coll., Scotts Valley, Calif., 1976; MA in Intercultural Studies, Assemblies of God Theol. Sem., Springfield, Mo., 1988; postgrad. in internat. comm., U. Wash. Pres. Assembly Bible Coll., Gaborone, Botswana, 1982-84, Swaziland Coll., Ezulwini, 1986-88; dir. relief and devel. Assemblies of God, Swaziland, Mozambique, 1985-88; sr. pastor Assemblies of God, No. Calif., 1989-96; adj. prof. Bethany Coll., 1992-96; dir. Ctr. for Adult Leadership Studies N.W. Coll., Kirkland, Wash., 1996—; regional dir. So. Africa Media Ministries, 1985-88. Contbr. articles to religious publs. Chmn. blood drive ARC, Bethany Coll., 1972-75; chaplain Rotary, Swaziland, 1987-88; tutor, counselor Siskiyou Schs., Happy Camp, Calif., 1976-78. Republican. Avocations: golf, wildlife photography. Office: NW Coll 5520 108th Ave NE Kirkland WA 98083

STEWART, JEFFREE ROBERT, environmental planner, artist; b. Concord, N.H., June 20, 1956; s. Robert Davison and Ruth Florence (Olney) S. BA, Evergreen State Coll., Olympia, Wash., 1983; postgrad., U. Wash., 1983-84, Inst. Creative Devel., 1989-91. River guide rafting Rio Bravo, Inc., Durango, Colo., 1981-82; forester, planner Wash. State Parks Commn., Olympia, 1983-84; fisheries biologist U. Wash., Seattle, Alaska and Aleutians, 1984-86; marine waste disposal project mgr. Washington Ecology Dept., Olympia, 1988-92, shorelands planner, 1992—; mem. art exhbns. com. Ecology Dept., Olympia, 1994, 95; mem. adv. bd. Washington Heritage Conf., Olympia, 1992; exhbns. team coord. Arts Olympia, 1993-94, chmn. steering group, 1995-96. One man shows include Batdorf & Bronson, Olympia, 1989, 91, 93, 94, Colophon Cafe, Bellingham, Wash., 1987, 96, Dancing Goats, Olympia, 1992, Thompson Gallery, 1995; exhibited in group shows at Janet Huston Gallery, LaConner, 1991, 92, 93, Wash. State Capitol Mus., Olympia, 1991, 92, 93, Childhoods End Gallery, 1995, 96, 97, Art-space Gallery, Bay City, Oreg., 1996, 97, Lucia Douglas Gallery, Bellingham, Wash., 1996, Evergreen State Coll., 1993, Wash. Ctr. Performing Arts, 1992, 93, 94, 95, 96, 97, Valley Mus. N.W. Art, 1994, 95, 96, 97, Tacoma Art Mus., 1995, also pvt. collections. Bd. trustees Evergreen State Coll., Olympia, 1981. Recipient Competent/Able Toastmaster awards Toastmasters Internat., 1989, 91, Oil Painting award of Merit Wash. State Capitol Mus., Olympia, 1993, Wash. Pub. Employees Assn. (bd. dirs. 1992-93), Meridian Toastmasters (pres., v.p. 1989-91). Mem. Artist Trust, Mus. N.W. Art, Tacoma Art Mus. Avocations: art collecting and curating, kayaking, freelance journalism, mountaineering. Home: PO Box 7397 Olympia WA 98507-7397 Office: Wash Ecology Dept PO Box 47775 Olympia WA 98504-7775

STEWART, JOHN L., architect; b. Detroit, June 7, 1948; s. Irvin Leroy and Virginia (Ashbolt) S.; m. Deborah E. Schreiber, Mar. 6, 1976;1 child, Jason Schreiber. BS in Interior Design, U. Wis., 1975; MArch, U. Wis., Milw., 1979. Registered architect, Calif. Prin. Stewart Assoc., San Carlos, Calif., 1983—. Mem. AIA, Nat. Coun. Architects. Avocation: sports. Home: 40 Oak Creek Ln San Carlos CA 94070 Office: Stewart Assoc. 1351 Laurel St San Carlos CA 94070

STEWART, LARRY RAY, engineer, financial director, quality consultant; b. Rock Springs, Wyo., Mar. 26, 1948; s. Raymond Melvin and Mary Jane (Fillin) S.; m. Della Jean Warren, Aug. 25, 1967; children: Stephanie M., Kara K., Gina R., Laura J. BS in Engring., U. Wyo., 1970, MS in Engring., 1972. Registered profl. engr., Ariz., Colo., Idaho, Mont., N.Mex., Oreg., Tex., Utah, Wyo. Mgr. apt. Willey Enterprises, Laramie, Wyo., 1966-70; grad. asst. U. Wyo., Laramie, 1970-72; systems analyst Dept. Def., Corona, Calif., 1972-73; engr. Mountain Bell, Cheyenne, Wyo., 1973-77; adminstr. Mountain Bell, Denver, 1977-79; mgr. Mountain Bell, Englewood, Colo., 1979-84; dist. mgr. Mountain Bell, Denver, 1985-87; dir. Bell TRICO Services, Englewood, 1984-85, U.S. West CGI, Denver, 1987-92; divsn. mgr. Hamlin Electric Services, Inc., Ft. Morgan, Colo., 1993-94; field engr. Colo. State U., Ft. Collins, 1994-95; state dir. MAMTC U. Wyo., Laramie, 1995—; mem. adv. bd. U. Wyoming Grad. Sch., Laramie, 1970-72; IOF co-chair AT&T/Bell System, Basking Ridge, N.J., 1980-83; curriculum advisor Network Tng., Englewood, 1980-83; fin. advisor Employee Suggestion Plan, Denver, 1984-86. Editor (coll. mag.) Enginews, 1970. Pres. Maplewood Homeowners, Arvada, Colo., 1986; key chair United Way, Denver, 1988.

Served with USAF, 1970-76. Mem. IEEE, Nat. Soc. Profl. Engrs. Republican. Lodge: Optimist (lt. gov. of Colo./Wyo. Dist.). Avocations: basketball, weight lifting, photography, traveling, hiking. Office: MAMTC U Wyo Wyo Hall Room 420 PO Box 3362 Laramie WY 82071-3362

STEWART, LUCILLE MARIE, special education coordinator; b. Pittsburgh, Feb. 24; d. William H. and Edna (Hoffman) S. BEd Duquesne U.; MEd, U. Pittsburgh; postgrad. courses Columbia U., U. Calif., Calif. State U. Cert. elem. and secondary tchr., spl. edn. tchr., supr., adminstr. Tchr. Lincoln (Ill). State Sch., 1953; group leader Retarded Education Alliance, N.Y.C., 1954-58; tchr. mentally retarded Ramapo Cen. Sch. Dist., Spring Valley, N.Y., 1958-60, seriously emotionally disturbed, 1960-64; program dir. Pomona (N.Y.) Camp for Retarded, summers 1960-63; tchr. Stockton Sch., San Diego, 1964-65, supr. presch. program for educationally disadvantaged Ramapo Ctrl. Sch. Dist., Spring Valley, N.Y., 1965-67; tchr. Cathdral City (Calif.) Sch., 1967-78; prog. specialist edn. Palm Springs Unified Sch. Dist., Calif., 1978-95; prin. elem. summer schs. Palm Springs (Calif.) Unified Sch. Dist., 1971-72; prin.-tchr. Summer Extended Sch. for Spl. Students, 1979—; mem. exec. com. U. Calif. Extension area adv. com. Mem. NEA, AAUW, Calif. Tchrs. Assn., Palm Springs Tchrs. Assn., Palm Springs Ednl. Leadership Assn., Calif. Assn. Program Specialists, Assn. for Supervision and Curriculum Devel., Am. Assn., Calif. Adminstrs. of Spl. Edn. (Desert community mental health childrens com.), Coun. Exceptional Children (admin., early childhood-learning handicap divsns.), Childhood Edn. Alpha Kappa Alpha, Phi Delta Kappa, Delta Kappa Gamma. Club: Toastmistress. Office: Palm Springs Unified Sch Dist 333 S Farrell Dr Palm Springs CA 92262-7905

STEWART, MARLENE METZGER, financial planning practitioner, insurance agent; b. Portland, Oreg., Nov. 1, 1937; d. Eddie Charles and Helen M. (Grant) Metzger; m. Robert W. Stewart, Aug. 1, 1964 (dec. Jan. 1967); m. Melvin N. McBurney, Feb. 14, 1985. BA, U. Oreg., 1959; MA, U. Tex., El Paso, 1971. Exec. dir. Summer 72 Youth Com. Office of Mayor, Portland, 1972; registered rep. Mut. Life Ins. Co. N.Y., Portland, 1973-76, Prudential Life Ins. Co., Portland, 1976-77; ptnr. N.W. Fin. Planning, Portland, 1977-79; pres. Horizons Unltd. Fin. Planning, Portland, 1979-86; prin. EMR Fin. Adv. Svcs., Inc., Portland, 1986-89; registered rep. KMS Fin. Svcs., Inc., Portland, 1979—; owner Stewart Fin. Group, 1991—. Mem.-at-large nat. bd. YMCA's, 1971-73; bd. dirs. Met. YMCA, Portland, 1971-75; bd. dirs. YWCA, Portland, 1989-92, treas., 1990-92, chmn. investment com.; chmn. planned giving com. Arthritis Found., 1984-86. Bill Bottler scholar Portland chpt. CLU and Chartered Fin. Cons., 1981. Mem. Inst. CFP's, Oreg. Soc. Inst. CFP's (treas. 1985-86), Internat. Assn. Fin. Planners (pres. Oreg. chpt. 1987-88), Nat. Assn. Life Underwriters, CLU's and ChFC's (treas. Portland chpt. 1985-86), Assocs. Good Samaritan (steering com., chmn. 1991-92), Rotary (chmn. World Cmty. com.). Republican. Presbyterian. Avocations: swimming, traveling, reading, knitting, sewing. Office: 4380 SW Macadam Ave Ste 525 Portland OR 97201-6408

STEWART, PATRICIA RHODES, retired clinical psychologist, researcher; b. Vallejo, Calif., Feb. 11, 1910; d. Butler Young Rhodes and Sarah Virginia (Ryan) Rhodes; m. John Kenneth Stewart (div.); children: John K., Nancy Rush. AB summa cum laude, Stanford U., 1930; MA, San Jose State U., 1959; PhD, U. London, 1963. Tchg. asst. San Jose State U., 1959-60; staff psychologist Napa State Hosp., 1964-77; pvt. practice in psychotherapy Berkeley, Calif., 1978-94; pvt. rsch. in adolescent deviance Berkeley, 1979-85; staff psychologist Westwood Mental Health Facility, Fremont, Calif., 1985-88. Author: Children in Distress: American and English Perspectives, 1976. Chair criminal justice com. No. Calif. region Am. Friends Svc. com., San Francisco, 1977-80, chair exec. com. 1970-74, 80-83, bd. dirs., 1980-83; bd. dirs. Friends Com. on Legis., Sacramento, 1985-88, No. Calif. Ecumenical Coun., Oakland, Calif., 1989-95. Mem. APA, AAAS, Phi Beta Kappa. Mem. Soc. of Friends. Home: 1225 Monterey Ave Berkeley CA 94707-2718

STEWART, PAUL ANTHONY, II, trade association executive, author; b. Oakland, Calif., Apr. 14, 1952; s. Paul Anthony Sr. and Hilda Hensley (Monger) S.; m. Stephanie Anne Pitts, July 8, 1972; children: Jana Lorraine, Robyn Lynne. BA, San Jose (Calif.) State U., 1974, MS, 1975. News editor various pubs., 1974-77; v.p. legis. svcs. Bldg. Industry Assn. of Superior Calif., Sacramento, 1977-82; exec. v.p. So. div. Bldg. Industry Assn. of No. Calif., San Jose, 1982-86; exec. v.p. Bldg. Industry Assn. of San Joaquin Valley, Fresno, Calif., 1986-90; CEO Bldg. Industry Assn. of Cen. Calif., Modesto, 1990-91, Rental Housing Assn. Contra Costa County, Walnut Creek, Calif., 1993-97; dir. pub. affairs Calif. Apt. Assn., 1997—. Host (TV show) Stewarts Sports Challenge, 1974 (Emmy nomination 1975); contbr. articles to profl. jours. Chmn. Transp. 2000 Steering LCom., San Jose, 1985-87; transp. commr. County of Santa Clara, Calif., 1986-87; pres. San Joaquin Valley Community Housing Leadership Bd., Fresno, 1988-90. Recipient Assn. Achievement award Calif. Apt. Assn., 1996, 97; named one of Outstanding Young Men of Am., U.S. Jaycees, 1984. Mem. Nat. Assn. Home Bldrs., Calif. Bldg. Industry Assn. (exec. officers coun., pres. 1990-91), Internat. Soc. Poets, Sigma Delta Chi. Baptist. Avocations: golf, softball, poetry, writing.

STEWART, PHILLIS, museum official. Pres. Nev. State Mus., Carson City. Office: Nev State Mus 600 N Carson St Carson City NV 89701-4004*

STEWART, ROBERT RAY, minister; b. Chandler, Ariz., Nov. 30, 1938; s. Eunice Alfred and Dona Belle (Weathers) S.; m. Violet Sue Ruth, May 27, 1957 (div. Feb. 1969); children: Terry Ray, Deborah Lynn; m. Gina Targosz, Feb. 12, 1990. Student, Bethany Coll., Santa Cruz, Calif., 1959-60. Ordained to ministry Assemblies of God, 1966. Evangelist Assemblies of God, Fremont, Calif., 1960-64; pastor 1st Assembly of God Ch., Coolidge, Ariz., 1964-65; founder, exec. dir. Teen Challenge Ariz., Inc., Phoenix, 1965-67; exec. dir. Teen Challenge, San Francisco, 1967-69; founder, exec. dir. City Harvest Ministry, Inc., Phoenix, 1990—; dist. mgr. Equitable Fin. Cos., Phoenix, 1970-90. Chmn. fund raiser ticket sales Palmer Drug Abuse Ctr., Phoenix, 1988-89; precinct committeeman Ariz. Rep. Com., Phoenix, 1989; bd. dirs. Teen Challenge Ariz., Inc., 1991—. With USN, 1956-59. Mem. Nat. Assn. Life Underwriters. Office: City Harvest Ministry Inc 6735 E Greenway Pkwy Apt 1121 Scottsdale AZ 85254-2110

STEWART, ROGER DEAN, university administrator; b. New Albany, Ind., July 27, 1950; s. Paul Daniel and Florence Elizabeth (Williams) S.; m. Laura Lan Stewart, Nov. 4, 1990; children: Christina, Jonathan. BA, Goddard Coll., Plainfield, Vt., 1974; MTS, Harvard U., 1976; PhD, Boston U., 1984. Assoc. dean of faculty U. So. Calif. Coll. Letters, Arts and Scis., L.A., 1980—. Office: U So Calif University Park Los Angeles CA 90089-4012

STEWART, SALLY, public relations practitioner; b. Phoenix, Mar. 1, 1955; d. Biven and Nancy Sue (Spurlock) S.; children: Padraic Haines, Colin Haines. BS in Broadcast Journalism, Ariz. State U., 1977, BA in Edn., 1980. Staff writer, media rep. Salt River Project, Phoenix, 1979-81; copy editor Mesa (Ariz.) Tribune, 1981-82; mktg. adminstrv. asst. Phoenix chpt. ARC, 1983; pub. info. asst. City of Scottsdale, Ariz., 1983-84; bus. editor, asst. city editor Scottsdale Progress Tribune, 1984-86; comms. mgr. Mesa Conv. and Visitors Bur., 1986-90; mgmt. asst. Neighborhood Improvement and Housing Dept., City of Phoenix, 1990-92, Pub. Info. Office, City of Phoenix, 1992-93; comm. cons. Ariz. Pub. Svc., Phoenix, 1993—. Mem. com. Fiesta Bowl, Phoenix, 1987-89; mem. pub. rels. com. Juvenile Diabetes Found., Phoenix, 1990; mem. pub. rels. com. Children's Garden Ground Breaking, Phoenix, 1993. Mem. Pub. Rels. Soc. Am. (accredited, bd. dirs. 1991-93, assembly del. 1993-95, pres. Valley of the Sun chpt. 1997). Avocations: travel, writing. Office: Ariz Pub Svc 2 Arizona Ctr 400 N 5th St Phoenix AZ 85004-3902

STEWART, SCOTT RICHARD, financial consultant; b. Salt Lake City, Mar. 10, 1966; s. John Richard and Bethany (Anderson) S.; m. Jami McCardell, Nov. 7, 1991. BFin, U. Phoenix, 1987. Cert. fin. planner. Tng. mgr. IDS Fin. Svcs., Salt Lake City, 1988-90; gen. ptnr. Stewart Enterprises, Salt Lake City, 1984—; pres. Alchemy Asset Mgmt. Group Ltd., Salt Lake City, 1990—; cons. The Money Mgmt. Group, Provo, Utah, 1990-92; advisor Hercules Credit Union, Salt Lake City, 1991—. Author: The Mortgage Reduction, 1989, Inevitable Wealth, 1991. Republican. Mormon. Avocation: motorcycling.

STEWART, STANFORD J., oncologist, immunologist; b. Big Spring, Tex., May 24, 1951; s. Merle J. and Elizabeth S. (Stanford) S.; m. Debra S. Echt, Nov. 5, 1978; children: Auston John, Allan Parker. BA, Rice U., 1973; MD, Baylor Coll. Medicine, 1977. Diplomate Am. Bd. Internal Medicine, Am. Bd. Med. Oncology. Resident Case Western Res. U., Cleve., 1977-80; fellow Stanford (Calif.) U., 1980-84; asst. prof. medicine Vanderbilt U., Nashville, 1984-92, assoc. prof. medicine, 1992-97; rsch. assoc. Nashville VA Med. Ctr., 1985-88, staff physician, 1988—; assoc. med. dir. Matrix Pharm., Inc., Fremont, Calif., 1997—; chmn. joint fellow com., program dir. divs. hematology and oncology Vanderbilt U., 1992-94. Contbr. articles to profl. jours. Mem. AAAS, Am. Fedn. Clin. Rsch., Am. Assn. Immunologists, So. Soc. for Clin. Investigation, Alpha Omega Alpha. Methodist.

STEWART, WALTER PRESTON, artist; b. San Francisco, July 14, 1931; s. Walter Preston and Frances Amelia (Blacklock) S. BA, U. of the Pacific, 1956; BPA, Art Ctr. Sch. Design, L.A., 1958. Co-host talk show Sta. WFAA-TV, Dallas, 1960-61; asst. art dir. Sta. WFAA-TV, 1961-66; artist Sta. KGO-TV, San Francisco, 1966, Sta. KRON-TV, San Francisco, 1967-74; courtroom artist Sta. KRON-TV and NBC, San Francisco, Burbank, 1974-96, CNN, San Francisco, Atlanta, 1996—. Courtroom artist for approximately 1,000 major trials including Oklahoma City bombing trials, Denver, 1996-98, Unabomber hearings, Sacramento, 1996-97; cartoonist/designer: (book) Broad Shoulders & Tight Ends, 1994, Dr. History's Sampler, 1995; spkr. at numerous functions. Named Alumnus of Yr. U. of the Pacific, 1998; recipient No. Calif. Emmy awards, 1981, 84, 88, AP award of excellence (for Angela Davis trial), 1971. Mem. San Francisco Soc. Illustrators, Air Force Art Program, Nat. Press Club, Broadcast Legends. Democrat. Avocations: watercolor painting, cartooning, fishing. Office: PO Box 621 Stinson Beach CA 94970-0621

STEWART-SCHLEGEL, SHARON DIANE, writer; b. Cleveland, Miss., June 16, 1951; d. Elton Stewart and Mary Ruth (Speights) Boyland; m. William E. Schlegel, Oct. 1998. BS in Mktg., San Diego State U., 1974; MBA, U. San Diego, 1977; AA in Tech. Writing, Mesa Coll., 1985. Sr. acctg. specialist Motorola Corp., San Diego, 1977-79; supr. acctg. Security Pacific Fin., San Diego, 1979-84; sr. acctg. specialist Sun Savs. and Loan, San Diego, 1984-85; publs. specialist Sundstrand Power Systems, San Diego, 1985-91; sr. analyst/editor MANTECH Advanced Tech., Pasadena, Calif., 1991-92; owner SDS Prodns., San Diego, 1981—; tech. editor Parsons Co., Pasadena, 1992-93; engring. writer Teledyne Laars, Moorpark, Calif., 1994-95; writer Harris Corp., Camarillo, CA, 1996—; instr. Mesa Coll., 1989-91. Contbr. articles to profl. jours. Vol. San Diego Police Dept., 1990-91, Glendale Police Dept., 1991—; vol. COMBO, 1982-83, Sta. KPBS Pub. Radio, 1984-87; chmn. Community Coll. Tech. Writing Coun., 1985-91; pres. Soc. for Technical COmms., 1993-95; mem. bd. dirs., chmn. Simi Valley Cultural Arts Ctr. Commn. & Found., 1994-97; mem. Simi Valley Neighbor D Coun., 1993-95. Lt. comdr. USNR, 1985—. Copley Assoc. scholar, 1983, Grocery Industry scholar, 1974; decorated Nat. Def. Svc. medal USNR, 1992. Mem. Naval Res. Assn. (v.p. 1987-90, Diamond in the Rough award 1990), Res. Officers Assn., Soc. Tech. Communicators, San Diego Writers Guild, Nat. Acad. TV Arts (acting chair 1984, cert. 1985), Toastmasters (Toastmaster of Yr. 1983). Republican. Baptist. Avocations: photography, jogging, gardening, cooking. Home: 78 E Bonita Dr Simi Valley CA 93065-2914 Office: Harris Corp 809 Calle Plano Camarillo CA 93012-8516

STICKEL, FREDERICK A., publisher; b. Weehawken, N.J., Nov. 18, 1921; s. Fred and Eva (Madigan) S.; m. Margaret A. Dunne, Dec. 4, 1943; children—Fred A., Patrick F., Daisy E., Geoffrey M., James E., Bridget A. Student, Georgetown U., 1939-42; BS, St. Peter's Coll., 1943. Advt. salesperson Jersey Observer daily, Hoboken, N.J., 1945-51; retail advt. salesperson Jersey Jour., Jersey City, 1951-55; advt. dir. Jersey Jour., 1955-66, publisher, 1966-67; gen. mgr. Oregonian Pub. Co., Portland, Oreg., 1967-72, pres., 1972-86, publisher, 1975—. Bd. regents U. Portland; mem. adv. bd. Portland State U.; bd. dirs. Portland Rose Festival Assn., United Way Oreg.; chmn. Portland Citizens Crime Commn.; mem. adv. bd. St. Vincent's Hosp. Capt. USMC, 1942-45. Mem. Assn. for Portland Progress (dir.), Portland C. of C. (dir.), Oreg. Newspaper Pubs. Assn. (past pres.), Pacific N.W. Newspaper Assn. (pres.), Am. Newspaper Pubs. Assn., University Club, Multnomah Athletic Waverley Country Club, Arlington Club, Rotary. Office: Oregonian Pub Co 1320 SW Broadway Portland OR 97201-3499

STICKLES, BONNIE JEAN, nurse; b. Waukesha, Wis., Nov. 24, 1944; d. Donald William and Betty Jane S.; B.S. in Nursing, U. Wis., 1967; M.S. in Nursing, Midwifery, Columbia U., 1974. Mem. nursing staff Grace Hosp., Detroit, 1970-73; mem. faculty and staff U. Minn. Sch. Nursing and Nurse-Midwifery Svc., Mpls., 1974-76; chief nurse-midwife, clin. instr. St. Paul-Ramsey Med. Ctr., 1976-84; midwifery supr. IHS/PHS Chinle Hosp., 1984-85; program mgr. maternal health sect. N.Mex. Dept. Health and Environ., 1985-90; Lovelace Med. Ctr., 1990-91; St. Vincent's Hosp., 1991-94; NMC Dialysis Divsn., 1994-95; blackjack dealer, 1995-97; with CNM Penitentiary N. Mex., 1997—. Mem. FDA Anesthetics, Life Support Adv. Com.; adv. bd. Childbirth Edn. Assn., 1980-85. Served with USNR, 1965-70. Decorated Letter of Commendation. Mem. Am. Coll. Nurse-Midwives (chmn. profl. affairs com. 1975-80), Nurses Assn. Am. Coll. Obstetricians and Gynecologists (charter), Aircraft Owners and Pilots Assn., Gt. Plains Perinatal Orgn., Alpha Tau Delta. Author articles in field; patentee teaching model.

STIEBER, TAMAR, journalist; b. Bklyn., Sept. 15, 1955; d. Alfred and Florence (Spector) S. Student, Rockland C.C., 1972-75, Rockland C.C., 1972-75, West London (Eng.) Coll., 1973-74; BA in Film cum laude, U. Calif., Berkeley, 1985, postgrad. in comparative lit., 1985-86; grad. police reserve academycum laude, Napa Valley Coll., 1988. Office mgr., confidential sec. AP, San Francisco, 1981-83; stringer Daily Californian, Berkeley, Calif., 1983-84; film rsch. teaching asst. U. California, Berkeley, 1984-86; libr. and rsch. asst. Pacific Film Archive, Berkeley, 1984-86; intern San Francisco Examiner, 1984; reporter Sonoma (Calif.) Index-Tribune, 1987-88, Vallejo (Calif.) Times-Herald, 1988-89, Albuquerque Journal, 1989-94. Recipient Pulitzer prize for specialized reporting, 1990, first place pub. svc. divsn. N.Mex. Press Assn., 1990, pub. svc. award Albuquerque Press Club, 1990; first place newswriting N.Mex. Press Assn., 1991; honorable mention Assn. Press Managing Editors, 1994. Mem. AAUW, Soc. Profl. Journalists, Investigative Reporters and Editors, Phi Beta Kappa. Home: PO Box 9835 Santa Fe NM 87504-9835

STIFEL, FREDERICK BENTON, pastor, biochemist, nutritionist; b. St. Louis, Jan. 30, 1940; s. Carl Gottfried and Alma J. (Clark) S.; m. Gail Joane Stewart, Aug. 10, 1963; children: Tim, Faith, Seth, Elizabeth. BS, Iowa State U., 1962, PhD, 1967; MDiv., Melodyland Sch. Theol., Anaheim, Calif., 1979. Ordained to ministry Evang. Presbyn. Ch., 1981. Lab. supr., research chemist U.S. Army Med. Research and Nutrition Lab., Denver, 1968-74, Letterman Army Inst. Research, San Francisco, 1974-76; intern pastor Melodyland Christian Ctr., Anaheim, 1979-80; assoc. pastor Faith Presbyn. Ch., Aurora, Colo., 1980—, moderator bd. deacons, 1997—; pastor Outreach and Missions, 1999—; chmn. care of candidates com. Presbytery of West, Denver, 1985-88, 91-94; mem. Denver Seminary Commn., 1995—, mem. world outreach com., 1998—; bd. dirs., v.p. Love Inc. of Metro Denver, 1987-90; regional coord. Nat. Assn. Single Adult Leaders, 1987-90, coord. Denver area, 1990-95; Colo. Pregnancy Ctrs., Inc., 1992-94, Rocky Mountain Prayer Network, 1994-96, Christian Family Svcs., 1990—; bd. dirs. St. James Bible Coll., 1995—, Profile Publs.; mem. faculty St. James Bible Coll., Kiev, Ukraine; bd. dirs. Internat. Project Adv. Bd., 1997—. Contbr. clin. med. and nutritional articles to profl. jours. Del. Iowa State Rep. Conv., Denver, 1984; mem. parent adv. coun. IMPACT drug intervention team Rangeview High Sch., Aurora, 1985-89, accountability com., 1989-96; mem. Friends of the Arts, 1992-96; young life leader Hinkley High Sch., Aurora, 1968-74; vice chmn. Young Life Com., Marin County, Calif., 1974-76. Capt. U.S. Army Med. Svc. Corps, 1967-70. Ralston Purina Rsch. fellow, 1962-63, Borden Agrl. scholar, 1962, recipient Sci. Achievement award U.S. Army Sci. Conf., West Point, N.Y., 1968, 70, Parents of the Yr. award Rangeview High Sch., 1992-93. Mem. Am. Inst. Nutrition, Am. Soc. Clin. Nutrition, Am. Sci. Affiliation, Evang. Theol. Soc., Phi Eta Sigma, Phi Kappa Phi, Alpha Zeta, Gamma Sigma Delta, Kappa Sigma, Sigma Xi. Avocations: reading, hiking, swimming, writing poetry, gardening. Home: 2102 S Blackhawk Way Aurora CO 80014-2900 Office: Faith Presbyn Ch [illegible]

STIGLICH, JACOB JOHN, JR., engineering consultant; b. Milw., Dec. 21, 1938; s. Jacob John Sr. and Augusta (Prezel) S. BSME, Marquette U., 1961; PhD, Northwestern U., 1970. Chief engr. Boride Products, Traverse City, Mich., 1971-74; mgr. ceramic materials Valeron Corp., Madison Heights, Mich., 1974-76; group leader, asst. dir. tech. Eagle Picher, Miami, Okla., 1976-78; program mgr. San Fernando Lab., Pacoima, Calif., 1978-84; tech. specialist Aerojet Ordnance Co., Tustin, Calif., 1984-85; cons. Colo., 1985-95; sr. scientist Materials Modification, Inc., Fairfax, Va., 1995—. Contbr. articles to profl. jours.; patentee in field. Col. USAR, 1961-92. Mem. AIME, Am. Soc. Metals, Am. Ceramic Soc., Mensa, Sigma Xi. Avocations: snow skiing, tennis.

STIGLITZ, JOSEPH EUGENE, economist; b. Gary, Ind., Feb. 9, 1943; s. Nathaniel David and Charlotte (Fishman) S.; m. Jane Hannaway, Dec. 23, 1978; children: Siobhan, Michael, Edward, Julia. B.A., Amherst Coll., Mass, 1964; DHL (hon.), Amherst Coll., 1974; Ph.D. in Econs., MIT, 1966; M.A. (hon.), Yale U., 1970; D in Econs. (hon.), U. Leuven, 1994. Prof. econs. Cowles Found., Yale U., New Haven, 1970-74; vis. fellow St. Catherine's Coll., Oxford, Eng., 1973-74; Joan Kenney professorship Stanford U., 1974-76, 88—; Oskar Morgenstern dist. fellow Inst. Advanced Studies Math., Princeton, N.J., 1978-79; Drummond prof. polit. economy Oxford U., Eng., 1976-79; prof. econs. Princeton U., 1979-88; sr. v.p., chief economist World Bank, Washington, 1995—; mem. Pres.'s Coun. Econ. Advisers, 1993-95, chmn. coun. econ. advisers, 1995-97, sr. v.p. devel. econs. and chief econs., exec. dir.; cons. World Bank, State of Alaska, Seneca Indian Nation, Bell Communications Rsch. Editor Jour. Econ. Perspectives, 1986-93; Am. editor Rev. of Econ. Studies, 1968-76; assoc. editor Am. Econ. Rev., 1968-76, Energy Econs., Managerial and Decision Econs.; mem. editl. bd. World Bank Econ. Rev. Recipient John Bates Clark award Am. Econ. Assn., 1979, Internat. prize Accademia Lincei, 1988, Union des Assurances de Paris prize, 1989; Guggenheim fellow, 1969-70. Fellow Inst. for Policy Rsch. (sr. 1991-93), Brit. Acad. (corr.); mem. Am. Econ. Assn. (exec. com. 1982-84, v.p. 1985), Am. Acad. Arts and Scis., Nat. Acad. Sci., Econometric Soc. Office: World Bank Group 1818 H St NW Rm Mc4-315 Washington DC 20433-0002

STILES, JOANNE MARY, secondary education educator; b. Columbus, Ohio, June 15, 1970; d. Joseph Mitchell and Mary Elizabeth (Worrall) Babcock; m. Jay Mitchell Stiles, July 8, 1994. AAS in Bus., Jefferson C.C., Watertown, N.Y., 1990; BA in English, SUNY, Oswego, 1992; MS in Tchg., SUNY, Potsdam, 1994. Cert. secondary English edn. English tchr. S.W. H.S., El Centro, Calif., 1995-98; English tchr., dept. chair Julian High Sch., Julian, Calif., 1998—. Mem. Nat. Coun. Tchrs. English, Calif. Tchrs. Assn. Home: 109 Alpine Village Dr Alpine CA 91901-2136

STILGENBAUER, ROBERT MELVIN, quality assurance professional; b. Coshocton, Ohio, Mar. 24, 1918; s. Jacob John and Clara Matilda (Hoffman) S.; m. Joan Marguerite Johnson, June 18, 1948; children: Gerald, Teresa, Emily, Ronald, Carolyn, John, Lorraine. Student, L.A. City Coll., 1959-60. Tester Hughes Aircraft Co., El Sugundo, Calif., 1951-62, facility engr., 1962-67, quality engr., 1967-86. Author: World's Largest Crossword Puzzle, 1949, Hypotenuse-Angle Table I, 1960, Composite and Prime Number Test, 1997, Johannes Hothem Families Book, 1998. Sgt. U.S. Army, 1942-45. Avocations: genealogy, mathematics, crossword puzzles. Home: 1660 Edgecliffe Dr Los Angeles CA 90026-1002

STILL, WILLIAM NORWOOD, JR., retired history educator, researcher; b. Columbus, Miss., Sept. 25, 1932; s. William Norwood and Helen (Morris) S.; m. Mildred Boling, June 4, 1953; children: Susan, Kathy, Norwood, Robert. BS, Miss. Coll., 1953; MA, U. Ala., 1958, PhD, 1964. From instr. to assoc. prof. Miss. Women's U., Columbus, 1959-68; from assoc. prof. to prof. East Carolina U., Greenville, N.C., 1968-94; dir. program in maritime history, underwater archaeology East Carolina U., Greenville, 1982-94; adj. researcher U. Hawaii, Honolulu, 1995—; rsch. chair Sec. of Navy USN, Washington, 1989-90; mem. adv. bd. Nat. Maritime Alliance, 1988; mem. US Commn. on Mil. History, 1990—. Author: Iron Afloat, 1970, American Sea Power in the Old World, 1980; co-author: Why the South Lost the Civil War, 1986; co-author, editor: The Confederate Navy, 1997; editor: Maritime History Series, 1986—; mem. editl. adv. bd. The American Neptune, 1984—, Civil War Times Illustrated, 1994—. Mem. Naval Hist. Found., 1980—. With USN, 1954-56. Recipient Jefferson Davis award The Confederate Mus., 1986, Pres. Harry Truman award Kansas City War Round Table, 1989, Christopher Crittenden Meml. award N.C. Lit. and History Assn., 1992. Mem. N.Am. Soc. Oceanic History (v.p. 1988-92, pres. 1992-94, Jack Bauer award for contributions to maritime history 1988), Soc. Civil War Historians (mem. adv. coun. 1987-97). Baptist. Avocation: tennis. Home: 75-234 Nani Kailua Dr Apt 67 Kailua Kona HI 96740-2077

STILLSON, ALAN, author; b. Bronx, N.Y., Dec. 16, 1945; s. Jacob and Rose Stillson; m. Sandra Rosenstein, June 17, 1967 (div. 1978); m. Gail Pechter, May 20, 1983; children: Jeffrey, Debi, Howard, Gary. BA in Math., Queens Coll., 1967, MS in Math., 1970; MBA, U. N. Mex., 1974. V.p. Beneficial Capital, L.A., 1981-83; pres./owner Calcomp Fin., Beverly Hills, Calif., 1983-95; mktg. coor. Best Buy, Calabasas, Calif., 1995—. Author: (book) The Mensa Genius ABC Quiz Book, 1998. Mem. Mensa, B'nai B'rith, Nat. Puzzlers League. Jewish. Avocations: writing, folksinging, puzzle solving, musician, family activities. Home: 5515 Keokuk Ave Woodland Hills CA 91367 Office: 5515 Keokuk Ave Woodland Hills CA 91367

STILLWELL, KATHLEEN ANN SWANGER, healthcare consultant; b. Glendale, Calif., Aug. 12, 1950; d. Robert Dowayne and Irene Margaret (Sawatzky) Swanger; m. Joseph Wayne Stillwell, Nov. 11, 1971; children: Shannon Kristine, Nathan Joseph. AA, Cypress Coll., 1971; AS & diploma, Golden West Coll., 1981; BA in English Lit., Long Beach State U., 1982; MPA, Health Svcs. Adminstrn., U. San Francisco, 1989. RN Calif. Staff nurse Long Beach (Calif.) Meml. Hosp., 1981-84; sr. claims analyst Caronia Corp., Tustin, Calif., 1984-87; dir. quality assurance & risk mgmt. St. Mary Med. Ctr., Long Beach, 1987-89; cons. quality assurance, risk mgmt. Am. Med. Internat., Costa Mesa, Calif., 1989-91; cons. healthcare, 1991—; adj. faculty U. San Francisco, Woodbury U., 1996, Woodbury U., 1995—; faculty Am. Soc. Healthcare Risk Mgrs. Cert. Program; v.p. Patient Care Assessment Coun., L.A., 1988-89, pres., 1989-90, bd. dirs.; pres. State Bd. Patient Care Coun., 1990-92, past pres., 1992-94; program dir. Ariz. Sch. Health Ins. Program, Inc., 1997—; mem. steering com. U.S.-China Quality Conf., Beijing, 1998; speaker in field. Vol. Calif. Health Decisions, Orange County, 1989—, PTA, Am. Cancer Soc., Patient Care Assessment Coun.; active Constnl. Rights Found.; mem. edn. com. Bus. in Soc., Bus. Leadership, 1995, World Future Soc., 1995. Mem. NLN, Am. Soc. Healthcare Risk Mgmt., Nat. Assn. Healthcare Quality (exec. fin. com. 1993-95), Am. Soc. for Quality (sec. healthcare divsn. 1995-96, chair membership 1994-95, chair-elect healthcare divsn. 1996-97, chair 1997-98, past chair 1998—, chair comms.), Am. Soc. Healthcare Risk Mgrs., So. Calif. Assn. Healthcare Risk Mgrs. (sec. 1989-90, mem. chmn. 1989-90, chair long-term care think tank 1997-98), Calif. League for Nurses (bd. dirs. 1993-95), Patient Care Assessment Coun. (v.p. So. Calif. 1988, pres. So. Calif. 1989-90, state bd. pres. 1990-92, state bd. dirs. 1992-94). Democrat. Lutheran. Avocations: reading, cooking, swimming, vol. activities. E-mail: kathleen-stillwell@prodigy.com. Home and Office: 825 Coastline Dr Seal Beach CA 90740-5810

STILLWELL, VALORIE CELESTE, secondary school mathematics educator; b. Merced, Calif., Nov. 26, 1960; d. Wallace Dee and Frances Estelle (Cagle) Sinclair; m. William Edward Stillwell, May 27, 1990. BS in Math. with highest honors, U. Calif., Davis, 1982, BS in Human Devel. with highest honors, 1982, track coaching credential with honors, 1983; MA in Edn., U.S. Internat., 1990. Cert. gifted and talented edn. and spl. edn. educator. Asst. track coach Woodland (Calif.) and Vacaville (Calif.) H.S., 1980-83; gifted and talented edn. math tchr., head track and field coach Irvington H.S., Fremont, Calif., 1983-87; gifted and talented edn. math tchr. Mission San Jose H.S., Fremont, 1987-90; math tchr., math dept. chairperson Edna Hill Mid. Sch., Brentwood, Calif., 1990-95, math mentor tchr., 1994-96; math. dept. chairperson Bristow Mid. Sch., Brentwood, 1995—; mem. liaison com. Irvington H.S., Fremont, 1983-87; mem. safety and facilities com. Mission San Jose H.S., Fremont, 1987-90; sch. site coun. chairperson Edna Hill Mid. Sch., 1990-92, reading com. chairperson; mem. [illegible]

1994-96. Ednl. Initiatives grantee, 1990. Mem. ASCD, Nat. Coun. Tchrs. of Math., Nat. Math. League, Calif. Math. Coun., Contra Costa County Math. (mem. adv. coun.), Diablo Math. Educators, Math Counts (peer tutor competition team). Avocations: reading, sports. Office: Bristow Sch 855 Minnesota Ave Brentwood CA 94513-1802

STILSON, WALTER LESLIE, radiologist, educator; b. Sioux Falls, S.D., Dec. 13, 1908; s. George Warren and Elizabeth Margaret (Zager) S.; m. Grace Beall Bramble, Aug. 15, 1933 (dec. June 1984); children: Carolyn G. Palmieri, Walter E., Judith A. Stirling; m. Lula Ann Birchell, June 30, 1985. BA, Columbia Union Coll., 1929; MD, Loma Linda U., 1934. Diplomate Am. Bd. Radiology, Nat. Bd. Med. Examiners. Intern White Meml. Hosp., Los Angeles, 1933-34; resident radiology Los Angeles County Gen. Hosp., 1934-36; instr. radiology Loma Linda (Calif.) U. Sch. Medicine, 1935-41, asst. prof., 1941-49, exec. sec. radiology, 1945-50, assoc. prof., 1949-55, head dept. radiology, 1950-55, prof. radiology, 1955-83, chmn. dept. radiology, 1955-69, emeritus prof., 1983—; chief radiology service White Meml. Hosp., Los Angeles, 1941-65, Loma Linda U. Med. Ctr., 1966-69; chmn. dept. radiologic tech. Sch. Allied Health Professions, 1966-75, med. dir. dept. radiologic tech., 1975-83. Contbr. articles to health jours. Fellow Am. Coll. Radiology; mem. AAAS, Los Angeles Radiol. Soc. (sec. 1960-61, treas. 1961-62, pres. 1963-64), Radiol. Soc. N.Am., Am. Roentgen Ray Soc., N.Y. Acad. Sci., Inland Radiol. Soc. (pres. 1971), Alpha Omega Alpha. Republican. Adventist. Avocations: photography, classical music, travel. Home: 25045 Crestview Dr Loma Linda CA 92354-3414 Office: Loma Linda Radiol Med Group 11234 Anderson St Loma Linda CA 92354-2804

STILWILL, BELLE JEAN, record company executive, printing company owner; b. Mackay, Idaho, Oct. 27, 1955; d. Allen LeRoy Stilwill and Galia Vee (Larter) Stilwill Dodd. Student, Ricks Coll., 1974-79, Def. Language Inst., 1980. Quality control Best Foods, Hermiston, Oreg., 1972-73; leader dance band Ricks Coll., Rexburg, Idaho, 1975-77; reporter Standard Jour., Rexburg, Idaho, 1976-77; news editor Chronicle-News, St. Anthony, Idaho, 1978; editor-in-chief The Scroll Ricks Coll., 1979-80; exec. asst. Rapid Printers, Monterey, Calif., 1981-82; corp. acct. Color-Ad Printers, Monterey, Calif., 1983-95; corp. acct. Bayshore Press, Scotts Valley, Calif., 1995—, v.p., 1995—; owner Stilwill & Hoover Group LLC. Author (record albums) 1st Step, 1988 (Sam Segal award 1988), Mixed Signals, 1989 (Sam Segal award 1990, Album of Month Sta. KOFE Radio Idaho), Lovin' Arms, 1990 (Sam Segal award 1991). Faculty scholar Ricks Coll., 1979-80. Mem. NAFE, NARAS, Nat. Assn. Ind. Record Distributors, Broadcast Music Industry. Home: 1199 Luxton St Seaside CA 93955-6008 Office: Bayshore Press 103 Whispering Pines Dr Ste E Santa Cruz CA 95066-4782

STIMSON, GRACE HEILMAN, editor; b. Wyndmoor, Pa., Dec. 25, 1907; d. Edgar James and Mary Alice (Bechtold) Heilman; m. Claude William Stimson, Feb. 7, 1953 (dec. June 1973). AB cum laude, Wilson Coll., Chambersburg, Pa., 1929; MA in History, U. Pa., Phila., 1937, PhD in History, 1949. Tchr. math. Linden Hall, Lititz, Pa., 1929-35; libr. Hist. Soc. Del., Wilmington, 1940-42; rsch. asst. Haynes Found., L.A., 1946-53; rsch. asst., free-lance editor Bur. Bus. and Econ. Rsch., UCLA, 1953-54; assoc. editor U. Calif. Press, UCLA Office, 1954-73; free-lance editor U. Calif. Press and U. Wash. Press, Seattle, 1973—. Editor: Calendar of Joel R. Poinsett Papers, 1941; co-author: Production Cost Trends in Selected Industrial Areas, 1948; author: Rise of Labor Movement in Los Angeles, 1955. Precinct worker Adlai Stevenson, Dem. party, 1952. Lt. USNR, 1942-46. Wilson Coll. Alumnae fellow, 1935-38, Moorefellow U. Pa., 1938-39; recipient scholarship U. Pa., 1936-37, prize Am. Hist. Assn., 1955. Mem. Phi Beta Kappa. Home and Office: 2661 Tallant Rd Apt 713 Santa Barbara CA 93105-4838

STINSON, AVIVA JOCHEBED, psychosocial nurse; b. Jerusalem, Palestine, Mar. 21, 1933; came to U.S., 1957; d. Solomon Isaac and Sarah (Dossik) Ostrovsky; m. Lawrence William Stinson, Jan. 19, 1956; children: Teresa Louise, Lawrence William Jr., John Durant. BS, U. Wash., 1981; MS, U. Alaska, 1987; postgrad., U. Minn., 1990-91. RN, Alaska, Wash., Minn., Ill.; cert. clin. specialist in adult psychiat. and mental health nursing; cert. advanced nurse practitioner. Staff nurse Paxton (Ill.) Gen. Hosp., 1957-58; staff nurse, head nurse Mercy Hosp., Urbana, Ill., 1966-72; staff nurse Guam (Micronesia) Meml. Hosp., 1973-74, Fairbanks (Alaska) Meml. Hosp., 1975-78, Swedish Hosp., Seattle, 1980-81; supr. nurse detox Fairbanks Native Assn., 1981-83; psychosocial nurse, therapist Fairbanks Psychiatric & Neurol. Clinic, Fairbanks, 1985-94; advanced nurse practitioner, psychotherapist Fairbanks, Alaska, 1994—. Bd. dirs. Child Abuse Task Force, Fairbanks, 1982-90, Fairbanks Cmty. Mental Health Ctr., 1985-90, 92-94. Mem. ANA (pres. Dist. IV 1986-89), Alaskan Nurses Assn. Avocations: aerobics, gourmet cooking, collecting native dolls. Home: PO Box 74958 Fairbanks AK 99707-4958 Office: 250 Cushman St Ste 5 Fairbanks AK 99701-4640

STITH, W(ILLIAM) MARK, real estate executive; b. Tucson, July 25, 1956; s. Sarah Josephine Lewis; m. Candace L. Starr, Mar. 18, 1991; children: Melissa Starr, Dawn Starr. BS in Pub. Adminstrn., U. Ariz., 1979, MEd in Counseling, 1981; student, Pima C.C., Tucson, 1990. Lic. profl. clin. counselor and marriage/family therapist, N.Mex.; lic. pvt. investigator, Ariz.; cert. emergency med. technician. Comml. realtor Breckenridge and eureka Realty, Tucson, 1982-88; dir. Childrens Protection Ctr. and Shelter, 7th Jud. Dist., Socorro, N.Mex., 1988-90; child protective svc. investigator State of Ariz., Pinal/Gila Counties, 1990; realty specialist, realtor Lauer & Assocs., Tucson, 1990-95; asst mgmt. realty specialist J.V. James & Assocs. Brokerage and Appraisals, Tucson, 1995—; lead investigator, chief rsch. Sierra Rsch., Tucson, 1991—; ind. contractor in asset mgmt. Dept. of Treasury/FDIC Resolution Trust Corp., Ariz. and N.Mex., 1991—. Author, developer: (book/manual) Operation Spiritfire, 1995. Bd. dirs. C.P.C. and S. Inc. Childrens Family Project, Tucson, 1994—. Mem. Nat. Assn. Realtors, Ariz. Assn. Realtors, Phi Alpha Alpha, Phi Theta Kappa. Address: PO Box 31754 Tucson AZ 85751-1754 also: 6657 E Victoria St Tucson AZ 85730-3226

STITT, MARI LEIPPER, writer; b. Salem, Ohio, May 1, 1923; d. Robert and Myrtle (Cost) Leipper; m. Rodney Dean Stitt, Apr. 22, 1944; children: Dana Lovelace, Rodney D. Jr. BA in Music, San Diego State U., 1946; MA in Human Rels., Calif. Western U., 1966. Dir. religious edn. Cen. Congl. Ch., 1941-50; tchr. sociology San Diego Evening Coll., 1966-84; writer poetry, 1984—. Home: 16686 Iron Springs Rd Julian CA 92036-9553

STITZINGER, JAMES FRANKLIN, religion educator, library director; b. Abington, Pa., July 27, 1950; s. James Franklin and Elizabeth (Kocher) S.; m. Deborah Lynn Benner, July 22, 1972; children: Rachael, James, David, Jonathan. BA, Northwestern Coll., Roseville, Minn., 1975; MDiv, Central Sem., 1975; ThM, Grace Theol. Sem., 1977; MLS, Drexel U., 1978; postgrad., Westminster Theol. Sem., 1991—. Acquisition libr. Grace Theol. Sem., Winona Lake, Ind., 1975-77; libr., prof. ch. history Calvary Bapt. Sem., Lansdale, Pa., 1977-87; dir. libr. svcs., assoc. prof. hist. theology The Master's Coll. and Sem., Sun Valley, Calif., 1987—; chief exec. officer Books for Libraries, Inc., North Hollywood, Calif., 1989—. Mem. Am. Theol. Libr. Assn., Am. Soc. Ch. History, Evang. Theol. Soc. Republican. Baptist. Office: The Masters Sem 13248 Roscoe Blvd Sun Valley CA 91352-3739

STOAKS, RALPH DUVAL, science administrator; b. Greenville, Miss., Apr. 8, 1935; s. Benjamin Duval and Joyce Fay (Neal) (div. 1968); 1 child, Kent Duval; m. Carolyn Jeanne Bush, Dec. 29, 1977. BA in Biology, McMurry Coll., Abilene, Tex., 1958; M of Natural Sci., U. Okla., 1967; PhD in Entomology, N.D. State U., 1975. Rsch. entomologist Bishop Mus. Natural History, Honolulu, 1978; urban entomologist, salesperson Orkin Pest Control, West Des Moines, Iowa, 1978-79; plant protection and quarantine officer USDA, Animal & Plant Health Inspection Svc., Plant Protection and Quarantine, San Diego, 1980-88; regional biotechnologist USDA, APHIS, PPQ, Sacramento, 1988-95, regional program mgr. biotech. and biol. control, 1996—. Contbr. numerous articles to profl. jours. and books. With U.S. Army N.G., 1959-64. Recipient Hammer award Vice Pres. Al Gore, 1997; NSF rsch. grantee U. Okla., 1960, 62, 66, N.D. State U., 1968; NIH rsch. fellow Bishop Mus., 1978. Mem. AAAS, Entomol. Soc. Am. (bd. cert. gen. entomologist), Am. Registry of Profl. Entomologists (bd. dirs. North Calif. br. 1989-91), Southwestern Assn. Naturalists, N.D. Natural Sci. Soc. (life), N.Am. Bethnological Soc. Home: 5888 Our Way Citrus Heights CA 95610-6746 Office: USDA APHIS PPQ Western Region 9580 Ste I Sacramento CA 95827

STOCKING, SHERL DEE, retail executive; b. Boise, Idaho, Aug. 20, 1945; s. Parley Dean and Iola Merrill (Linford) S.; m. Debra Lynn Hunt, Sept. 5, 1982. BS, Brigham Young U., 1968. Automotive specialist Bradshaw Auto Parts, Provo, Utah, 1964-68, J.C. Penney Co., Salt Lake City, 1969-70; store mgr. Uniroyal Tire Co., Salt Lake City, 1970-71; corp. tng. coordinator Uniroyal Tire Co., Houston, 1971, corp. advt. coordinator, 1972; store supr. Uniroyal Tire Co., Norfolk, Va., 1973-76; mgr. automotive dept. K-Mart Corp., Rapid City, S.D., 1976-79; dist. mgr. automotive dept. K-Mart Corp., N.Mex., 1979-80; mgr. Service Mdse. subs. K-Mart Corp., Denver, 1980-88; pres., owner S. & H. Svcs. Inc., Lynnwood, Wash., 1990—; antiques, petroliana, automobilia, Coca Cola, nostalgia dealer, Seattle. Pres. Quail Crossing Homeowner Assn., Denver, 1990—. Mem. Samuel Hall Soc., Coca Cola Collectors Club. Mormon. Home and Office: 115 146th St SE Lynnwood WA 98037-6711

STOCKTON, JOHN HOUSTON, professional basketball player; b. Spokane, Wash., Mar. 26, 1962; m. Nada Stepovich, Aug. 16, 1986; 1 child, John Houston. Grad., Gonzaga U., 1984. With Utah Jazz, Salt Lake City, 1984—; mem. U.S. Olympic Basketball Team, 1992. Named to NBA All-Star team, 1989-94; holder NBA single season rec. most assists, 1991; NBA Assists leader, 1987-1992; NBA Steals leader, 1989, 92; named NBA All-Star Co-MVP, 1993, All-NBA First Team, 1994. Led NBA in most assists per gaem, 1988-93; led NBA with highest steals per game avg., 1989,1992; shares single-game playoff record for most assists, 24, 1988. Office: Utah Jazz 301 W South Temple Salt Lake City UT 84101-1216*

STOCKTON, KEVIN W., insurance and investment professional; b. Ariz., Oct. 1, 1967; m. Suzanne M. (Tadra), June 13, 1992; children: Reilly G., Paige R. BS magna cum laude, U. Colo., 1992. CLU; ChFC; CFP; registered health underwriter. Sales rep. Merck Human Hlth. Div., Warren, Mich., 1992-94; agent, registered rep. Northwestern Mutual Life/Baird Sec., Troy, Mich., 1994, Denver, 1995-98; dir. mktg. The Madison Group, Inc., Denver, 1998—; fin. vice chmn., Boy Scouts of Am., Troy, Mich., 1992-94, U.S. Trnsplt. Games Steering Comm., Natl. Kidney Found., Ann Arbor, Mich, 1992-94, fin. comm., Denver, 1995, Distinguished Citizen Dinner Steering Comm., Boy Scouts of Am., Boulder, Colo., 1995-97, pres., chmn. bd. Gatsbys Cigar Merchants, Inc., Denver, 1996-97. Contrib. articles to profl. magazines, 1995. Cadet, Army, West Point, N.Y., 1985-87. Mem. Am. Soc. CLU's and ChFC, Internat. Assn. Fin. Planners, Nat. Assn. Life Underwriters, Inst. Cert. Fin. Planners, Million Dollar Round Table, Beta Gamma Sigma (life). Avocations: travel, fitness, family, music, reading. Office: The Madison Group Inc 4582 S Ulster St Ste 1300 Denver CO 80237-2639

STOCKTON, RODERICK ALAN, chemist; b. Lafayette, La., Jan. 18, 1951; s. Herbert Raymond and Olivet (Smith) S.; m. Pamela Sue Jones, Aug. 1, 1981 (div. 1992). BS, Stephen F. Austin State U., Nacogdoches, Tex., 1974; PhD, Tex. A&M U., College Station, 1985. Rsch. assoc. Tex. A&M U., College Station, 1975-85; sr. chemist Midwest Rsch. Inst., Kansas City, Mo., 1985-87, EG&G Idaho, Idaho Falls, 1987-89; prin. chemist Westinghouse Hanford Co., Richland, Wash., 1989-92; owner SLR Systems, Richland, 1992—; owner Stockton Consulting Svc., Richland, 1990-92. Contbr. articles to profl. jours. Welch Found. fellow. Mem. Am. Chem. Soc. Avocations: scuba diving, underwater photography, travel. Home: 3100 George Washington Way Richland WA 99352-1663 Office: SLR Systems 2600 NE Stapleton Rd Ste D Vancouver WA 98661-6581

STOEBUCK, WILLIAM BREES, law educator; b. Wichita, Kans., Mar. 18, 1929; s. William Douglas and Donice Beth (Brees) S.; m. Mary Virginia Fields, Dec. 24, 1951; children: Elizabeth, Catherine, Caroline. B.A., Wichita State U., 1951; M.A., Ind. U., 1953; J.D., U. Wash., 1959; S.J.D., Harvard U., 1973. Bar: Wash. 1959, U.S. Supreme Ct. 1967. Pvt. practice, Seattle, 1959-64; asst. prof. law U. Denver, 1964-67; assoc. prof. U. Wash., Seattle, 1967-70, prof., 1970-95; Judson Falknor prof., 1995—; of counsel Karr, Tuttle, Campbell, Seattle, 1988—. Author: Washington Real Estate: Property Law, 1995, Washington Real Estate: Transactions, 1995, Basic Property Law, 1989, Law of Property, 1984, 2d edit., 1993, Nontrespassory Takings, 1977, Contemporary Property, 1996; contbr. articles to legal jours. Bd. dirs. Cascade Symphony Orch., 1978-83, Forest Park Libr., 1975-80. Mem. Am. Coll. Real Estate Lawyers, Am. Coll. Mortgage Attys., Wash. State Bar Assn., Assn. Am. Law Schs., Order of Coif, Seattle Yacht Club. 1st lt. USAF, 1951-56. Home: 3515 NE 158th Pl Lk Forest Park WA 98155-6649 Office: U Wash Law Sch 1100 NE Campus Pkwy Seattle WA 98105-6605

STOERMER, DAPHNE CAROL, physical therapist, consultant; b. Vancouver, B.C., Feb. 6, 1939; came to the U.S., 1959; d. Douglas William Walker and Thelma Ray (Kelly) Whitelaw; m. Phillip Hilary Stoermer, Apr. 28, 1962; children: Hilary Anne, Mark Andrew, Claire Marie. Student, U. B.C., 1957-59; BSc, cert. in phys. therapy, U. So. Calif., L.A., 1961; lifetime teaching credential, UCLA, 1965. Registered phys. therapist. Staff phys. therapist U. So. Calif. Med. Ctr., L.A., 1962-64, San Gabriel (Calif.) Community Hosp., 1964-72; owner Lafayette (Calif.) Phys. Therapy, 1975—, Orinda (Calif.) Sports Fitness Ctr., 1981-91; cons. Consultation By Design, Lafayette, 1984—; bd. dirs. Phys. Therapy Provider Network Inc., Woodland Hills, Calif. Telephone help worker Contact Care, Lafayette, 1991-92. Mem. Am. Phys. Therapy Assn., N.Am. Back Sch., Internat. Dance Exercise Assn., Kappa Kappa Gamma (pub. rels. Psi chpt. 1988-90). Avocations: tennis, biking, running. Office: Lafayette Phys Therapy 978 2nd St # 240 Lafayette CA 94549-4512

STOKER, EUGENIA ELLEN EIDE, writer, former pediatrician; b. Ashland, Wis., Sept. 18, 1948; d. Onan and Sally Ella (Pieper) Eide; m. David Larry Stoker, June 19, 1972; children: Matthew Brian, Elizabeth Mary, Daniel James. BS in Chemistry, U. Ariz., 1970, MD, 1974. Intern in pediat. Ariz. Health Scis., Tucson, 1974; freelance writer Tucson, 1989—; leader parenting class Enrichment for Parents, Tucson, 1979-83. Author: (children's book) The King of Kindness, 1998; contbr. articles on child devel., parenting, tchg. to mags. Sunday sch. tchr. United Meth. Chs., Tucson, 1975-92; den leader Cub Scouts Pack 132, Tucson, 1983-91; sci. fair coord. Sewell Sch., Tucson, 1983, 84; Brownie and Jr. leader Girl Scouts, Tucson, 1985-87; chair family ministries Catalina United Meth. Ch., Tucson, 1991—; ch. news reporter Desert S.W. Conf., 1989-97. Mem. Soc. Children's Book Writers and Illustrators. Avocations: designing crafts, books and science projects for children, sewing crafts, gardening, designing teaching props. Home: 6002 E Wendrew Ln Tucson AZ 85711-2517

STOKES, ANDREA G., food service executive; b. Toronto, Ont., Can., May 30, 1966; d. Robert David and Kathleen Elizabeth (Wood) S. Diploma in hospitality & tourism, Centennial Coll. Applied Arts, 1988. Cert. meeting profl. Convention Liaison Coun. Sales & catering coord. Hotel Novotel, Toronto, 1988-89; food & beverage coord. The Royal Canadian, Toronto, 1989-93; catering sales mgr. Hotel Plaza II, Toronto, 1993-94, dir. catering, 1994-95; dir. catering & conf. svcs. Hilton Mesa (Ariz.) Pavilion, 1995—. Investment mgr. United Way, Mesa, 1997-98; exec. mem., bd. dirs. Boys & Girls Club East Valley, 1998—. Mem. Nat. Assn. Catering Execs. (sec. to bd. 1998), Meeting Profls. Internat. (mgr. of yr. 1997, 98). Avocations: hiking, travelling, rollerblading, shopping. Office: Hilton Mesa Pavilion 1011 W Holmes Ave Mesa AZ 85210-4986

STOKES, GORDON ARTHUR, educational company executive, author; b. Salt Lake City, Aug. 28, 1929; s. Lovell Arthur and Viola (Condie) S.; div.; 1 child, Michael Ross. Cert. in personology, Interstate Coll. Personology, Sacramento, 1965; cert., Inst. Counseling, San Dimas, Calif., 1977; cert. in psychodrama, Calif. Inst. Socioanalysis, Long Beach, 1978; cert. minister, The New Sem., N.Y.C., 1983. Mktg. mgr. parent effectiveness seminars Pace Seminars, Pasadena, Calif., 1970-72; internat. trainer Touch for Health, Pasadena, 1973-85; pres. Three in One Concepts, Burbank, Calif., 1976—. Co-author: Under the Code, 1980, Structural Neurology, 1984, Basic/Advanced One Brain, 1984, Body Circuits, Pain and Understanding, 1990, New Options for Decision Makers, 1992, Body Mind Integration, 1992, Without Stress Learning Can Be Easy, 1996 (Best Book North Am. Bookdealer Exchange, 1996). Pres. Internat. Assn. Specialized Kinesiology. Office: Three in One Concepts 2001 W Magnolia Blvd Bc Burbank CA 91506-1704

STOLROW, GREGORY, computer company executive; b. Burbank, Calif., Aug. 23, 1962; s. Walter Thomas and Margaret Ann (Fellows) S.; m. Elizabeth Ditmars, Sept. 5, 1992; 1 child, Hannah. BS in Acctg., U. So. Calif., 1984; MBA in Fin. and Policy, U. Chgo., 1992. CPA, Calif. Staff acct. Price Waterhouse, L.A., 1984-85; sr. tax staff Price Waterhouse, Newport Beach, Calif., 1985-88, tax mgr., 1989-90; mgr. litigation support Price Waterhouse, Balt., 1992-93; tax mgr. Price Waterhouse, Washington, 1993-94; exec. v.p., CFO, Computers for Tracts, Anaheim, Calif., 1994—. Treas. Young Execs. Am., 1987-89; pres. Trailwood HOA, Irvine, 1995—; co-chmn. Alumni Commn. Sigma Alpha Epsilon, Cal Gamma chpt., 1986-89. Scholar Price Waterhouse, U. Chgo., 1989. Republican. Presbyterian. Avocations: gardening, surfing, skiing, basketball, weight training. Home: 27 Runningbrook Irvine CA 92620-1214 Office: Computers For Tracts Inc 2910 E La Palma Ave Ste A Anaheim CA 92806-2618

STONE, CHARLES JOSEPH (JOE), columnist, law enforcement; b. Frizell, Kans., Jan. 21, 1913; s. Herbert Macklin and Laura (Belfield) S.; m. Catherine Lucille Bordner, Aug. 14, 1937; children: Milburn J., Norman Jene, Marilyn Jo, Herbert E., Sally Dee. Student, U. Wichita, 1937. Detective Wichita (Kans.) Police Dept., 1936-42, 45-46; chief petty officer, field investigator USCGR, 1942-45; reporter The Wichita (Kans.) Eagle, 1946-53, The San Diego (Calif.) Union Tribune, 1953-77; columnist Borrego Sun, Borrego Springs, Calif., 1997—. Writer (TV shows) Gunsmoke, 1950's, Restless Gun, 1950's; writer for Milburn Stone, 1950's. Honorary co-mayor Borrego Springs (Calif.) C. of C., 1998; vol. Anza-Borrego State Park, Borrego Springs, 1978-95. CPO, field investigator, USCGR, 1942-45. Recipient Bronze award AP, Calif., Nev., 1957, Ring of Truth award Copley Newspapers, San Diego, Calif., 1965, 66, 67, First Place award AP, Calif., Nev., 1986-87, Best Column-non daily award Soc. Profl. Journalists, San Diego, 1987; named hon. mem. Calif. State Park Rangers Assn. Mem. ASCAP, Writers Guild of Am. West. Democrat. Home: PO Box 103 Borrego Springs CA 92004-0103

STONE, DONALD D., investment and sales executive; b. Chgo., June 25, 1924; s. Frank J. and Mary N. (Miller) Diamondstone; student U. Ill., 1942-43; B.S., DePaul U., 1949; m. Catherine Mauro, Dec. 20, 1970; 1 child, Jeffrey. Pres., Poster Bros., Inc., Chgo., 1950-71, Revere Leather Goods, Inc., Chgo., 1953-71; owner Don Stone Enterprises, Chgo., 1954—; v.p. Horton & Hubbard Mfg. Co., Inc. div. Brown Group, Nashua, N.H., 1969-71, Neevel Mfg. Co., Kansas City, Mo., 1969-71. Mem. adv. bd. San Diego Opera; founder Don Diego Meml. Scholarship Fund; mem. bd. overseers U. Calif., San Diego, chancellor's assoc.; mem. exec. bd. Chgo. Area council Boy Scouts of Am. Served with U.S. Army, 1943-46. Clubs: Bryn Mawr Country (Lincolnwood, Ill.) (dir.), Carlton, La Jolla Beach and Tennis, La Jolla Country, Del Mar Thoroughbred. Home: 8240 Caminito Maritimo La Jolla CA 92037-2204

STONE, EDWARD CARROLL, physicist, educator; b. Knoxville, Iowa, Jan. 23, 1936; s. Edward Carroll and Ferne Elizabeth (Baber) S.; m. Alice Trabue Wickliffe, Aug. 4, 1962; children: Susan, Janet. AA, Burlington Jr. Coll., 1956; MS, U. Chgo., 1959, PhD, 1964; DSc (hon.), Washington U., Saint Louis, 1992, Harvard U., 1992, U. Chgo., 1992; BA (hon.), UCLA, 1998. Rsch. fellow in physics Calif. Inst. Tech., Pasadena, 1964-66, sr. rsch. fellow, 1967, mem. faculty, 1967—, prof. physics, 1976-94, David Morrisroe prof. physics, 1994—, v.p. for astron. facilities, 1988-90, v.p., dir. Jet Propulsion Lab., 1991—; Voyager project scientist, 1972—; cons. Office of Space Scis., NASA, 1969-85, mem. adv. com. outer planets, 1972-73; mem. NASA Solar System Exploration Com., 1983; mem. com. on space astronomy and astrophysics Space Sci. Bd., 1979-82; mem. NASA high energy astrophysics mgmt. operating working group, 1976-84, NASA Cosmic Ray Program Working Group, 1980-82, Outer Planets Working Group, NASA Solar System Exploration Com., 1981-82, Space Sci. Bd., NRC, 1982-85, NASA Univ. Relations Study Group, 1983, steering group Space Sci. Bd. Study on Major Directions for Space Sci., 1995-2015, 1984-85; mem. exec. com. Com. on Space Research Interdisciplinary Sci. Commn., 1982-86; mem. commn. on phys. scis., math. and resources NRC, 1986-89, mem. adv. com. NASA/Jet Propulsion Labs. vis. sr. scientist program, 1986-90; mem. com. on space policy NRC, 1988-89; chmn. adv. panel for The Astronomers, KCET, 1989—. Mem. editl. bd. Space Sci. Instrumentation, 1975-81, Space Sci. Rev., 1982-85, Astrophysics and Space Sci., 1982—, Sci. mag. Bd. dirs. W.M. Keck Found. Recipient medal for exceptional sci. achievement NASA, 1980, Disting. Svc. medal, 1981, 98, Disting. Pub. Svc. medal, 1985, Outstanding Leadership medal, 1986, 95, Am. Edn. award, 1981, Dryden award, 1983, Aviation Week and Space Tech. Aerospace Laureate, 1989, Sci. Man of Yr. award ARCS Found., 1991, Pres.'s Nat. medal of Sci., 1991, Am. Acad. Achievement Golden Plate award, 1992, COSPAR award for outstanding contbn. to space sci., 1992, LeRoy Randle Grumman medal, 1992, Disting Pub. Svc. award Aviation/Space Writers Assn., 1993, Internat. von Karman Wings award, 1996, Alumni award S.E. C.C., Burlington, Iowa, 1998, CEO of Yr. award ARC, 1998; Asteroid named for Edward C. Stone, 1996; Sloan Found. fellow, 1971-73; inducted to Hall of Fame Aviation Week and Space Tech., 1997. Fellow AIAA (assoc., Space Sci. award 1984, Von Karman lectureship in astronautics 1999), AAAS (award 1993), Am. Phys. Soc. (chmn. cosmic physics divsn. 1979-80, exec. com. 1974-76), Am. Geophys. Union, Internat. Astron. Union; mem. NAS, Internat. Acad. Astronautics, Am. Astron. Soc. (divsn. planetary scis. com. 1981-84, Space Flight award 1997), Am. Assn. Physics Tchrs., Am. Philos. Soc. (Magellanic award 1992), Calif. Assn. Rsch. in Astronomy (bd. dirs., vice chmn. 1987-88, 91-94, 97—, chmn. 1988-91, 94-97), Astron. Soc. Pacific (hon.), Nat. Space Club (bd. govs., Sci. award 1990), Calif. Coun. Sci. and Tech. Office: Jet Propulsion Lab 4800 Oak Grove Dr 180-904 Pasadena CA 91109-8001

STONE, GEORGE, artist, art educator. BA, Calif. State U., Long Beach, 1972; MFA, R.I. Sch. Design, 1974. Instr. R.I. Sch. Design, Providence, 1972-74; instr. sculpture Portsmouth (R.I.) Abbey Sch., 1973-74, Wayne State U., Detroit, 1974-75; vis. lectr., sculpture dept. Ohio U., Athens, 1976-77; instr., found. dept. Otis/Parsons Sch. Design, L.A., 1982-83; vis. lectr., sculpture dept. UCLA, 1986; assoc. prof. fine arts Art Inst. So. Calif., Laguna Beach, 1989-93; assoc. prof. visual art U. La Verne, Calif., 1994—; vis. artist Calif. State U. Long Beach, 1986, Crossroads H.S. for Arts and Sci., Santa Monica, 1987, Claremont (Calif.) Grad. Sch., 1987, 88, U. Calif. Santa Barbara, 1989, Art Ctr. Coll. Design, Pasadena, Calif., 1991, Yale U., New Haven, 1992, Chatham Coll., Pitts., 1992, Calif. State U. San Francisco, 1993; commd. artist City of West Hollywood, 1986, City of L.A. Cmty. Redevel. Agy., 1987, Metro Art L.A. County Met. Transp. Auth., 1990-97, City of L.A. Cultural Affairs Dept., 1995-97. Solo exhbns. include Forsythe Bldg., Detroit, 1975, Cline Bldg., Athens, Ohio, 1976, Lake Hope, Athens, 1977, Otis/Parsons Gallery, 1981, East Gallery Claremont Grad. Sch., 1985, Calif. State U. Long Beach Art Mus., 1986, Meyers/Bloom Gallery, Santa Monica, Calif., 1988, 91, Laguna Art Mus., Costa Mesa, Calif., 1990, Capp St. Project, 1991, New Langton Arts, San Francisco, 1991, Ruth Bloom Gallery, Santa Monica, 1993, Pitts. Ctr. Arts, 1994; 2-person exhbns. L.A. Contemporary Exhbns., 1985, Claremont Grad. Sch. Gallery, 1988; group exhbns. include Lehigh U. Art Gallery, Bethlemen, Pa., 1975, Wayne State U., 1975, U. Calif. Santa Cruz, 1978, Vanguard Gallery, L.A., 1979, L.A. Inst. Contemporary Art, 1979, NYU Art Gallery, N.Y.C., 1980, Charles Kobler and Assoc. Architects, L.A., 1983, Design Ctr. L.A., 1984, Univ. Art Mus. Calif. State U. Long Beach, 1985, IDM Corp. and Pub. Corp. Arts, Long Beach, 1985, CRA, L.A., 1987, Newport Harbor Art Mus., Newport Beach, Calif., 1988, Meyers/Bloom Gallery, 1989, Galerie Antoine Candeau, Paris, 1990, Sezon Mus. Art, Tokyo and Osaka, Japan, 1991, Muckenthaler Cultural Ctr., Fullerton, Calif., 1991, Contemporary Arts Ctr., New Orleans, 1993, Next Thread Waxing Space, N.Y.C., 1993, Contemporary Arts Forum, Santa Barbara, 1996, Armand Hammer Mus. Art and Cultural Ctr., UCLA, 1997, others; subject numerous catalogs, publs., and revs., 1984—. Home: 1815 Laurel Canyon Blvd Los Angeles CA 90046-2028*

STONE, HAZEL ANNE DECKER, artist; b. Salt Lake City, Oct. 30, 1934; d. Carl Marcellus and Hazel Sheets (Van Cott) Decker; m. William Samuel Stone, July 20, 1956; children: Cynthia Anne Stone Barkanic, Lisa Marie. BS, U. Utah, 1956, RN, 1956; postgrad. in arts and humanities, Ariz. State U., 1979-81; studied with various artists, Ariz., N.Mex., 1985—. Nurse out-patient dept. Salt Lake County Hosp., 1956-57; instr. med.-surg.

nursing U. Utah Coll. Nursing, 1957-59; watercolor fine artist. One-woman show Sun Cities Mus. of Art, Sun City, Ariz., 1997; exhibited in group show Chandler (Ariz.) Ctr. for the Arts, 1997; nat. juried exhbns. include Van Vechten-Lineberry Taos (N.Mex.) Art Mus., 1997, Wenatchee (Wash.) Valley Coll., 1997, Stables Gallery, Taos, 1996, Walton Arts Ctr., Fayetteville, Ark., 1995, Bareiss Gallery, Taos, 1995, Foothills Art Ctr., Golden, Colo., Tubac (Ariz.) Ctr. for Arts, 1999, Sangre de Cristo Arts Ctr., Pueblo, Colo., 1999, West Valley Art Mus., Surprise, Ariz., 1999, others. Docent Phoenix Art Mus., 1979-81, master docent, 1981-96. Mem. Ea. Washington Watercolor Soc., Ariz. Artists Guild (juried), Ariz. Watercolor Assn. (Award of Merit 1997, Merchant award 1994, bd. dirs. 1994—), Contemporary Watercolorists Ariz. (Merit award 1998, Award of Excellence 1997, chmn. spl. exhbns. 1998), Q Artists (chmn. exhbns. 1995—), Waterworks Artists, La. Watercolor Soc., N.W. Watercolor Soc., San Diego Watercolor Soc., Taos Soc. Watercolorists (signature), Watercolor Art Soc. Houston, Watercolor West (assoc.). Home and Studio: 3621 E Pasadena Ave Phoenix AZ 85018-1511

STONE, HERMAN HULL, internist; b. Noble, Ill., Dec. 12, 1915; s. Roy Edson and Carrie (Michels) S.; m. Marie Carlson Christensen; children, Patricia Marie Soln, Richard Allen. BS, U. Ill., 1937, MD, 1941. Resident in internal medicine U.S. VA Hosp., Hines, Ill., 1946-49; chief of medicine VA Hosp., Oklahoma City, 1949-50; with Riverside (Calif.) Med. Clinic, 1950-91; dir. Med. Libr., 1991—; clin. prof. medicine Loma Linda (Calif.) U., 1963—; founder, dir. Patients' Info. Libr., Riverside, 1991—; pres. citizens univ. com. U. Calif. Riverside, 1979-81; trustee Calif. Blue Shield. Served to maj. M.C., AUS, 1942-46. Recipient Outstanding award Nat. Soc. Fund Raising Execs., 1996. Fellow ACP (life); mem. L.A. Acad. Medicine (trustee), Rotary Club. Avocations: golf, books, travel. Office: Patients Info Libr 3660 Arlington Ave Riverside CA 92506-3912

STONE, JACK, screenwriter, musician, songwriter; b. Miami Beach, Fla., Oct. 14, 1958; s. Jack Stone and Elizabeth (Kuhn) Germann. AA in Liberal Arts, Miami Dade, 1976; BA in Comm. with honors, Loyola Marymount, 1996. Lic. realtor, Fla.; cert. audio/video engr. Realtor Divsn. Real Estate/Fla. Real Estate Commn., Fla., 1989—; audio/video engr. Soundmaster Rec., L.A., 1996—. Author poetry (1st prize Am. Poetry Contest 1991); author (screenplay) Vow of Silence, 1994; prodr., writer (musical) To Say Good-bye, 1995; author Objects in the Mirror, 1998 (pub. in Chicken Soup); film dir. Aint Whistlin Dixie, 1998. Mem. SAG. Avocations: fitness, health, webmaster, surfing, musician.

STONE, JAMES ROBERT, surgeon; b. Greeley, Colo., Jan. 8, 1948; s. Anthony Joseph and Dolores Concetta (Pietrafeso) S.; m. Kaye Janet Friedman, May 16, 1970; children: Jeffrey, Marisa. BA, U. Colo., 1970; MD, U. Guadalajara, Mex., 1976. Diplomate Am. Bd. Surgery, Am. Bd. Surg. Critical Care. Intern Md. Gen. Hosp., Balt., 1978-79; resident in surgery St. Joseph Hosp., Denver, 1979-83; pvt. practice Grand Junction, Colo., 1983-87; staff surgeon, dir. critical care Va. Med. Ctr., Grand Junction, 1987-88; dir. trauma surgery and critical care, chief surgery St. Francis Hosp., Colorado Springs, Colo., 1988-91; pvt. practice Kodiak, Alaska, 1991-92; with Summit Surg. Assocs., 1992-96; asst. dir. trauma Tristate Trauma System, Erie, Pa., 1996—; med. dir. LifeStar Aeromed, Erie, Pa., 1997—; asst. clin. prof. surgery U. Colo. Health Sci. Ctr., Denver, 1984-96; pres. Stone Aire Cons., Grand Junction, 1988—; owner, operator Jjnka Ranch, Flourissant, Colo.; spl. advisor CAP, wing med. officer, 1992-96; advisor med. com. unit, 1990-92; advisor Colo. Ground Team Search and Rescue, 1994-96. Contbr. articles to profl. jours.; inventor in field. Bd. djrs. Mesa County Cancer Soc., 1988-89, Colo. Trauma Inst., 1988-91. Colo. Speaks out on Health grantee, 1988; recipient Bronze medal of Valor Civil Air Patrol. Fellow Denver Acad. Surgery, Southwestern Surg. Congress, Am. Coll. Chest Physicians, Am. Coll. Surgeons (trauma com. Colo. chpt.), Am. Coll. Critical Care; mem. Am. Coll. Physician Execs., Soc. Critical Care (task force 1988—), Assn. Air Med. Physicians. Roman Catholic. Avocations: horse breeding, hunting, fishing.

STONE, JOHN HELMS, JR., admiralty advisor; b. Andalusia, Ala., Dec. 3, 1927; s. John Helms and Ruth May (Barker) S.;m. Mary Ham, July 24, 1950; children: Malcolm, Mary Ruth, Ronald, John T. Student Ga. Mil. Coll., U.S. Merchant Marine Sch., 1945; student, Tulane U., 1975. Master mariner, USCG. Master capt. Sea-Land Steamship, Port Newark, N.J., 1947-60; Lt. (jg) USNR, 1948-62; sr. pilot Panama Canal Co., Balboa Canal Zone, 1960-73; chief of transit op. Panama Canal Commn., Balboa Canal Zone, 1973-76; chmn. bd. local inspection Panama Canal Commn., Balboa, Republic of Panama, 1976-85; admiralty cons. John H. Stone & Assocs., Boulder, Colo., 1985—, Am. Registry Arbitrators, 1994—; admiralty advisor Phelps-Dunbar, New Orleans, 1958-79, Fowler White, Tampa, Fla., 1984, Terriberry & Assocs., New Orleans, 1992. County treas. Dem. Party, Boulder, 1989. Mem. NRA (v.p. 1970, master pistol and rifle shot), Master, Mates and Pilots Union (v.p. 1970-72). Presbyterian. Avocation: stock market. Home: 3795 Wild Plum Ct Boulder CO 80304-0460

STONE, MICHAEL DAVID, landscape architect; b. Moscow, Idaho, Apr. 11, 1953; s. Frank Seymour Stone and Barbara Lu (Wahl) Stone/Schonthaler; m. Luann Dobaran, Aug. 12, 1978; children: Stephanie Nicole, David Michael. B in Landscape Architecture, U. Idaho, 1976; postgrad., Oreg. State U., 1986, Harvard U., 1990; MA in Orgnl. Leadership, Gonzaga U., 1990. Registered landscape architect, Wash., cert. leisure profl.Nat. Recreation and Park Assn. Landscape designer Robert L. Woerner, ASLA, Spokane, Wash., 1976-77; pk. planner Spokane County Pks. and Recreation, 1977-82; landscape architect City of Spokane Pks. and Recreation, 1982-84, asst. pks. mgr., 1984-86, golf and cmty. devel. mgr., 1986-95, co-dir., 1995-96, spl. ops. mgr., 1996—; cons. Lake Chelan (Wash.) Golf Course, 1988. Pres. Sacred Heart Parish Coun., Spokane, 1987-89; v.p. Cataldo Sch. Bd. Dirs., Spokane, 1987-89; pres. South Spokane Jaycees, 1977-86; active Leadership Spokane, 1989, Nat. Exec. Devel Sch., 1993. Named Outstanding Young Man Am., 1980, 85, Outstanding Knight, Intercollegiate Knights, 1972-73, Jaycee of the Yr., South Spokane Jaycees, 1981, Vet. of the Yr., South Spokane Jaycees, 1984-85; recipient Holy Grail award Intercollegiate Knights, 1972-73. Mem. Nat. Recreation and Pk. Assn. (bd. dirs. golf mgmt. sect. 1995—), Am. Soc. Landscape Architects, Wash. Recreation and Pk. Assn., Nat. Inst. Golf Mgmt. (bd. dirs. 1995—), Beta Chi, Delta Tau Delta. Roman Catholic. Avocations: golf, basketball, photography, travel. Home: 2007 E 55th Ave Spokane WA 99223-8212 Office: City of Spokane 808 W Spokane Falls Blvd Spokane WA 99256-0001

STONE, NORMAN MICHAEL, psychologist; b. Balt., Mar. 23, 1949; s. Forrest Leon and Beverly Iola (Gendason) S.; m. Susan Foster Hoitt, May 18, 1981; children: Shannon, Caroline, Brittany Rain, Forrest. BA, UCLA, 1971; PhD, U. Iowa, 1976. Lic. psychologist, Tex., Calif. Chief youth and family svcs. Abilene (Tex.) Mental Health-Mental Retardation Regional Ctr., 1976-79; coord. family crisis team San Fernando Valley Guidance Clinic, Northridge, Calif., 1980-88, sr. clin. supr., 1989-95; sr. cmty. psychologist L.A. County Dept. Children's Mental Health, L.A., 1995—; mem. psychiat. panel of experts on dependency and family law Calif. Superior Ct., 1987-96; mem. adj. faculty Hardin-Simmons U., Abilene, 1977-79; vis. prof. UCLA, 1980-81; clin. prof. Fuller Theol. Sem., L.A., 1982-94. Contbr. numerous articles on psychology, psychiatry, law and social welfare to internat. profl. jours., books and film. USPHS fellow, 1972-76; Simon Found. rsch. grantee, 1982, 89. Mem. AAAPP, Am. Psychol. Soc., Sojourners. Avocations: poetry, theology. Office: LA County Dept Childrens Mental Health 550 S Vermont Ave Los Angeles CA 90020-1991

STONG, DAVID HENRY, artist, computer graphic artist; b. Milw., Dec. 2, 1950; s. Roland Oliver and Irene Marie (Gerrits) S. BBA, U Wis., Madison, 1980; MBA, U. Wis., 1985. Asst. mgr. Wis. Innovation Ctr., Whitewater, 1980-82; program assoc. Ctr. for Creative Leadership, Greensboro, N.C., 1982-85; owner Avatar Cons., Greensboro, N.C., 1985-87; owner Lightspeed GRAFX, Honolulu, 1987-92, 94-96, Glendale, Ariz., 1995—, art dir. Computer-Aided Tech., Inc., Honolulu, 1992-94; computer graphics adv. bd. Glendale C.C., 1998; spkr. Rocky Mt. Inventors Congress Colo., 1984. Graphic designer AmeriVox Collectible Phone Card, Hawaii, 1994, Logo for 50th Anniversary of the End of World War II, 1995. Creative dir. The Future Within Youth Group, Phoenix, 1998—; vol. child care Marcus House, Phoenix, 1995—. Recipient Emmy cert. Nat. Acad. TV Arts and Scis., 1992-93. Mem. Corel Hawaii User Group (pres. 1995-96). Avocations: music, fiction writing, [illegible] Home: [illegible] Dr Glendale AZ 85310-5686

STONG, JOHN ELLIOTT, retail electronics company executive; b. Elkater, Iowa, Sept. 20, 1921; s. Elliott Sheldon and Nora Elizabeth (Daly) S.; m. Olive Miriam Foley, Dec. 11, 1943; children: Mary Myers, Jon, Miriam. G-rad. U. Colo., 1943. Salesman, Purucker Music, Medford, Oreg., 1946-48, dept. mgr., 1949-56, store mgr., 1957, partner, 1958-61, owner, 1962-64; pres. Purucker Music Houses, Medford, 1965-67, Music West, Inc., Eugene, Oreg., 1968-70, Magnavox Centers, Medford, 1971—, exec. asst., Consultants Internat., 1972—. Served with USAF, 1943-45. Decorated Air medal. Mem. Nat. Assn. Music Mchts. (dir. 1969-72), Scull Mchts. Rsch. Group (dir., chmn.). Republican. Roman Catholic. Home: 2120 Woodlawn Dr Medford OR 97504-7678 Office: Cons Internat 111 N Central Ave Medford OR 97501-5925

STOORZA GILL, GAIL, corporate professional; b. Yoakum, Tex., Aug. 28, 1943; d. Roy Otto and Ruby Pauline (Ray) Blankenship; m. Larry Stoorza, Apr. 27, 1963 (div. 1968); m. Ian M. Gill, Apr. 24, 1981; 1 child, Alexandra Leigh. Student, N. Tex. State U., 1961-63, U. Tex., Arlington, 1963. Stewardess Cen. Airlines, Ft. Worth, 1963; advt. and acctg. exec. Phillips-Ramsey Advt., San Diego, 1963-68; dir. advt. Rancho Bernardo, San Diego, 1968-72; dir. corp. communications Avco Community Developers, San Diego, 1972-74; pres. Gail Stoorza Co., San Diego, 1974—, Stoorza, Ziegaus & Metzger, San Diego, 1974—; CEO Stoorza, Ziegaust, Metzger, Inc., 1993—; chmn. Stoorza/Smith, San Diego, 1984-85, Stoorza Internat., San Diego, 1984-85; CEO ADC Stoorza, San Diego, 1987—, Franklin Stoorza, San Diego, 1993—. Trustee San Diego Art Found.; bd. dirs. San Diego Found. for Performing Arts, San Diego Opera, Sunbelt Nursery Groups, Dallas. Names Small Bus. Person of Yr. Selest Com. on Small Bus., 1984, one of San Diego's Ten Outstanding Young Citizens San Diego Jaycees, 1979; recipient Woman of Achievement award Women in Communications Inc., 1985. Mem. Pubs. Soc. Am., Nat. Assn. Home Builders (residential mktg. com.), COMBO. Methodist. Clubs: Chancellors Assn. U. Calif. (San Diego), Pub. Relations, San Diego Press. Home: 3100 Front St Apt C San Diego CA 92103-5500 Office: Stoorza, Ziegaus & Metzger 225 Broadway 18th Flr San Diego CA 92101*

STOREY, ARTHUR WILLIAM, minister; b. Pitts., Dec. 4, 1945; s. Edmunt T. and Naomi Marie (Martin) S.; m. Carolyn Faye Witcher, June 21, 1966; children: Joye, Bill. Student, Sch. for Officer's Tng., San Francisco, 1974-76, Pasadena Nazarene Coll., 1964-67, Trevecca Nazarene Coll., Nashville, 1963-64. Ordained to ministry Salvation Army, 1975. Instr., staff mem. The Salvation Army, Rancho Palos Verdes, Calif., 1976-78; commanding officer The Salvation Army, Grand Junction, Colo., 1978-80, Denver, 1980-86, Cheyenne, Wyo., 1986—. Pres. Laramie County Sheriff's Dept., Cheyenne, Wyo., 1987—; pres. chaplain's corps Wyo. Vol. Orgn. Active in Disasters, 1987—; mem. Wyo. Critical Stress State Debriefing Team, 1990—. Named Masonic Citizen of Yr., 1990, Law Enforcement Officer of the Yr., Grand Junction Police Dept., 1982-83, Crimestopper Office of the Yr., Dallas, 1984. Mem. Kiwanis. Republican. Office: Salvation Army PO Box 1357 Riverside CA 92502-1357

STOREY, BRIT ALLAN, historian; b. Boulder, Colo., Dec. 10, 1941; s. Harold Albert and Gladys Roberta (Althouse) S.; m. Carol DeArman, Dec. 19, 1970; 1 child, Christine Roberta. AB, Adams State Coll., Alamosa, Colo., 1963; MA, U. Ky., 1965, PhD, 1968. Instr. history Auburn (Ala.) U., 1967-68, asst. prof., 1968-70; dep. state historian State Hist. Soc. Colo., Denver, 1970-71, acting state historian, 1971-72, rsch. historian, 1972-74; hist. preservation specialist Adv. Coun. on Hist. Preservation, Lakewood, Colo., 1974-88; sr. historian Bur. Reclamation, Lakewood, 1988—. Contbr. articles to profl. publs. Mem. Fed. Preservation Forum (pres. 1990-91), Nat. Coun. Pub. History (sec. 1987, pres.-elect 1990-91, pres. 1991-92), Orgn. Am. Historians (com. 1983-86, chmn. 1985-86), Victorian Soc. Am. (bd. dirs. 1977-79), Western History Assn. (chmn. com. 1982-86), Colo.-Wyo. Assn. Mus. (sec. 1974-76, pres. 1976-77), Cosmos Club (Washington). Avocation: birding. Home: 7264 W Otero Ave Littleton CO 80128-5639 Office: Bur Reclamation Denver Fed Ctr D 5300 Bldg 67 Denver CO 80225-0007

STOREY, FRANCIS HAROLD, business consultant, retired bank executive; b. Calgary, Alberta, Can., June 20, 1933; s. Bertwyn Morrell and Hilda Josephine (Masters) S.; m. Willomae Saiter, Apr. 25, 1954; children: Daryl, Elizabeth, Brian, Shelley. Student, Gonzaga U., 1953, Pacific Coast Bankers Sch., 1974-76. Designated Certified Profl. Cons. Bank trainee Wash. Trust Bank, Spokane, 1950-56; owner Storey & Storey, Spokane, 1956-64; agt. Bankers Life Nebr., Spokane, 1964-67; sr. v.p. Old Nat. Bank, Spokane, 1967-87, U.S. Bank of Wash., Spokane, 1987-90; pvt. practice cons. Spokane, 1990—; bd. dirs. Alloy Trailers Inc., 1990-98, Output Tech. Corp. bd. dirs. Coalition for Women on Streets (treas., finance chmn.). Bd. dirs. Spokane Bus. Incubator, 1985-96, United Way of Spokane, 1987-95; bd.dirs., treas., fin. chair, gen. conv. dep. Episc. Diocese Spokane Dep., 1969—; trustee Spokane Symphony Soc., 1986-93, Spokane Area Econ. Devel. Coun., 1982-89; mem. adv. bd. Intercollegiate Ctr. Nursing Edn., 1990-96, chair, 1996. Mem. Acad. Profl. Cons. and Advisors, Inland N.W. Soc. Cons. Profls., Spokane Rotary, Spokane Country Club, Spokane Club. Episcopalian. Avocations: golf, reading, travel. Home: 214 E 13th Ave Spokane WA 99202-1115

STOREY, NORMAN C., lawyer; b. Miami, Fla., Oct. 11, 1943. BA cum laude, Loyola U., L.A., 1965; JD, U. Ariz., 1968. Bar: Ariz. 1968. Law clk. to Hon. James A. Walsh U.S. Dist. Ct. Ariz.; ptnr. Squire, Sanders & Dempsey, Phoenix. Mem. State Bar Ariz., Am. Arbitration Assn. (panelist). Office: Squire Sanders & Dempsey 40 N Central Ave Ste 2700 Phoenix AZ 85004-4498

STORK, SUSAN DIANA, musician, composer; b. Bryn Mawr, Pa., May 31, 1951; d. George Frederick and Mary Ernestine (Weber) S.; m. William Teed Rockwell, Mar. 22, 1987. BA, Colby Coll., 1974. founder, dir. Festival of Harps concert series, 1990—, prodr., 1995—; dir. ednl. outreach program MultiCultural Music Fellowship and History of the Harp lectrs., 1995—; pvt. harp tchr. Harp performances include Grace Cathedral, San Francisco, Tlingit Tribal House, Haines, Alaska, Bremenale, Bremen, Germany Harp Fest, No. Italy, Morrison Planetarium, Acad. Scis., San Francisco, others; recs. include Harpestry, Herald of Spring, Harpdancing, others; co-prodr. Harpestry series, 1997; composer over 100 compositions for Celtic-style harp and ensembles; contbr. articles to profl. jours. Pres. Bay Area Folk Harp Soc. 2-Terms, 1994-96, bd. dirs., 1997—. Mem. Internat. Soc. Folk Harpers (Bay Area Folk Harp Soc. chpt., newsletter editor 1984-88, pres. 1987-90, bd. dirs. 1997—, founder, dir. Harp Day for Kids 1993—, founder, dir. Summer Harp Camp 1997), Am. Harp Soc., Hist. Harp Soc. Avocations: studying Buddhist thought, poetry, painting, hiking, dance. Home and Office: Multi-Cultural Music Fellowship 2419-A Tenth St Berkeley CA 94710

STORMES, JOHN MAX, instructional systems developer; b. Manila, Oct. 7, 1927; s. Max Clifford and Janet (Heldring) S.; m. Takako Sanae, July 29, 1955; children: Janet Kazuko Stormes-Pepper, Alan Osamu. BS, San Diego State U., 1950; BA, U. So. Calif., 1957, MA, 1967. Cert. secondary and community coll. tchr., sr. profl. human resources. Editing supr. Lockheed Propulsion Co., Redlands, Calif., 1957-61; proposals supr. Rockwell Internat., Downey, Calif., 1961-62; publs. dir. Arthur D. Little, Inc., Santa Monica, Calif., 1962-63; publs. coord. Rockwell Internat., Downey, 1963-68; project dir. Gen. Behavioral Systems, Inc., Torrance, Calif., 1969-73; tng. and comm. cons. Media Rsch. Assocs., Santa Cruz, Calif., 1973—; instrl. design supr. So. Calif. Gas Co., L.A., 1985—; lectr. Calif. State U., Northridge, 1991—; tng. cons. Nat. Ednl. Media, Chatsworth, Calif., 1966-81, communications cons. Opinion Rsch. Calif., Long Beach, 1974—. Co-author: TV Communications Systems For Business and Industry, 1970; contbg. author: ASTD's In Action series of casebooks, 1996-98. Curriculum adv. bd. communications dept. Calif. State U., Fullerton, 1964-78. Sgt. U.S. Army, 1952-55, Japan. Mem. Soc. Tech. Communication (... and ... Orange County chpt. 1962-63), Internat. Soc. Performance and Instruction (v.p. L.A. chpt. 1989, pres. 1990). Democrat. Episcopal. Avocations: photography, sailing. Home: 9140 Brookshire Ave Apt 207 Downey CA 90240-2963 Office: So Calif Gas Co ML 15H1 PO Box 3249 Los Angeles CA 90051-1249

STORMS, [illegible], retired veterinarian; b. [illegible], Wash., Oct. 13, 1920; s. Roy Lester and Helen Violet (Belshe) S.; m. Marjorie Louise Hudson, Apr. 10, 1943 (div.); children: Marjorie Maureen, Terry Jo, Sandra Diane. BS in Animal Husbandry, Wash. State U., 1951, DVM, 1952. Intern Portland, 1952; gen. practice vet. medicine Camas, 1952-54; dr.'s asst. pvt. practice vet. office, Hollywood, Calif., 1954, L.A., 1954, Whittier, Calif., 1954; vet. in charge pvt. practice vet. office, Artesia, Calif., 1955-56; owner, pvt. practice vet. medicine Buena Park, Calif., 1956-86; ret., 1986; mem. adv. bd. Guide Dogs for Blind, San Rafael, Calif., 1957-58; mem. steering com. Children's Hosp., Fullerton, Calif., 1960-61. With USN, 1940-51, PTO. Decorated Air medal with 3 gold stars, DFC.; recipient Pappy Pedigoe Meml. Trophy Calif. Sports Car Racing Assn., 1965. Mem. NRA, So. Calif. Vet. Medicine Assn. (life), Am. Vet. Medicine Assn., Orange County Vet. Medicine Assn. (pres. 1958), Olde '78 Fraser's Highlanders (chief-of-staff), Explorer's Club, Adventurer's Club L.A. (sec. 1984, bd. dirs., 1980-82, 95-97), Long Beach Yacht Club, Rotary (Paul Harris fellow, pres. Buena Park chpt. 1963), Masons, Shriners (capt., pres. 1999—, Legion of Honor). Avocations: race car driving, sailing, fishing, shooting. Home: 78th Frasers Highlanders 4316 Latona Ave Los Angeles CA 90031-1426

STOROZUM, STEVEN LEE, marketing professional; b. St. Louis, Jan. 14, 1954. AB, Washington U., St. Louis, 1975; MS, Carnegie Mellon U., 1976; postgrad., Va. Poly. U., 1979. Assoc. engr. IITRI-ECAC, Annapolis, Md., 1977; applications engr. ITT, Roanoke, Va., 1977-79; sr. engr. McDonnell Douglas Corp., St. Louis, 1979-82; mgr. LAN systems Am. Photonics, Inc., Brookfield, Conn., 1982-88; product mgr. PCO, Inc., Chatsworth, Calif., 1988-90, Fibermux Corp., Chatsworth, 1990-95; v.p. mktg. Video Products Group, Newbury Park, Calif., 1995—; cons. Wilton Industries, Ridgefield, Conn., 1988. Lighting designer theatrical prodns., 1978-79, 86-88; contbr. articles to profl. jours. Mem. Am. Phys. Soc., Optical Soc. of Am., Mensa. Avocations: theatre, music, travel.

STOSICH, DAVIDJOHN, company executive; b. Idaho Falls, Idaho, May 24, 1938; s. Vaughn T. and Esther (Smith) S.; m. Adeana Marshall, Aug. 28, 1962; children: Jennifer Lynne, Jacquelyn, Bryan, Jill, Jon, Anthony, Vaughndavid, Jelair, Hartman, Jeanne. BS, Brigham Young U., 1964; BPA in Profl. Illustrator, Art Ctr. Coll. Design, L.A., 1967. Graphic support Computer Scis. Corp., El Segundo, Calif., 1967-68; corp. communications staff Geotech, Salt Lake City, 1968-69; asst. to pres. Computer Update, Salt Lake City, 1969-70; corp. communications staff Omnico, Salt Lake City & Tacoma, 1970-71; support staff Big Sky of Mont., Big Sky, Mont., 1972-73; art dir. Artcraft, Bozeman, Mont., 1973-75; owner Stosich Advt., Idaho Falls, 1975-78; pres. Worldwide Achievements, Idaho Falls, 1980-81, Hive Systems, Idaho Falls, 1982-92; pres. Stosich Woodlock, Inc., Idaho Falls, 1986-94, CEO, 1994—. Graphic designer Tour Guide to Europe, 1988; sculptor woodlock wood sculptures. Graphic designer Crapo for U.S. Congress, Boise, 1992; active Idaho Falls Arts Coun., Exch. Club Am.; missionary to Switerland LDS Ch., 1958-61. Chosen one of Idaho's best QVC, 1995. Mem. Art Guild (Pocatello, Idaho). Republican. Avocations: drawing, woodwork, gardening, horses, hunting. Home: 2300 S Charlotte Dr Idaho Falls ID 83402-5675

STOTLER, ALICEMARIE HUBER, judge; b. Alhambra, Calif., May 29, 1942; d. James R. and Loretta M. Huber; m. James Allen Stotler, Sept. 11, 1971. BA, U. So. Calif., 1964, JD, 1967. Bar: Calif. 1967, U.S. Dist. Ct. (no. dist.) Calif. 1967, U.S. Dist. Ct. (cen. dist.) Calif. 1973, U.S. Supreme Ct., 1976; cert. criminal law specialist. Dep. Orange County Dist. Atty.'s Office, 1967-73; mem. Stotler & Stotler, Santa Ana, Calif., 1973-76, 83-84; judge Orange County Mcpl. Ct., 1976-78, Orange County Superior Ct., 1978-83, U.S. Dist. Ct. (cen. dist.) Calif., L.A., 1984—; assoc. dean Calif. Trial Judges Coll., 1982; lectr., panelist, numerous orgns.; standing com. on rules of practice and procedure U.S. Jud. Conf., 1991—, chair, 1993—; mem. exec. com. 9th Cir. Jud. Conf., 1989-93, Fed. State Jud. Coun., 1989-98, jury com., 1990-92, planning com. for Nat. Conf. on Fed.-State Judicial Relationships, Orlando, 1991-92, planning com for We. Regional Conf. on State-Fed. Judicial Relationships, Stevens, Wash., 1992-93; chair dist. ct. symposium and jury utilization Ctrl. Dist. Calif., 1985, chair atty. liason, 1989-90, chair U.S. Constitution Bicentennial com., 1986-91, chair magistrate judge com., 1992-93; mem. State Adv. Group. on Juvenile Justice and Delinquency Prevention, 1983-84, Bd. Legal Speciliazations Criminal Law Adv. Commn., 1983-84, victim/witness adv. com. Office Criminal Justice Planning, 1980-83, U. So. Calif. Bd. Councilors, 1993—; active team in tng. Leukemia Soc. Am., 1993, 95; legion lex bd. dir. U. So. Calif. Sch. Law Support Group, 1981-83. Winner Hale Moot Ct. Competition, State of Calif., 1967; named Judge of Yr., Orange County Trial Lawyers Assn., 1978, Most Outstanding Judge, Orange County Bus. Litigation Sect., 1990; recipient Franklin G. West award Orange County Bar Assn., 1985. Mem. ABA (jud. adminstrn. divsn.and litigation sect. 1984—, nat. conf. fed. trial judges com. on legis. affairs 1990-91), Am. Law Inst., Am. Judicature Soc., Fed. Judges Assn. (bd. dirs. 1989-92), Nat. Assn. Women Judges, U.S. Supreme Ct. Hist. Soc., Ninth Cir. Dist. Judges Assn., Calif. Supreme Ct. Hist. Soc., Orange County Bar Assn. (mem. numerous coms., Franklin G. West award 1984), Calif. Judges Assn. (mem. com. on judicial coll. 1978-80, com. on civil law and procedure 1980-82, Dean's coll. curriculum commn. 1981), Calif. Judges Found. Office: Ronald Reagan Fed Bldg and Courthouse 411 W 4th St Santa Ana CA 92701-4516

STOTT, DON EARL, family court mediator, educator; b. St. Helena, Calif., Oct. 25, 1945; s. Elwyn Guy and Cecile Verna (Brandon) S.; m. Clara A. Smith; children: Don Jr., Ron Dean. AA, Sacramento City Coll., Sacramento, Calif., 1973; BA, Calif. State Univ., 1975, MA, 1977. Family ct. mediator Amador County, Jackson, Calif., 1988—; psychology instr. San Jouguin Delta Coll., Stockton, Calif., 1994—; cons. 1994—. Contbr. articles to profl. jours.

STOTT, JAMES CHARLES, chemical company executive; b. Portland, Oreg., Sept. 5, 1945; s. Walter Joseph and Rellalee (Gray) S.; m. Caroline Loveriane Barnes, Dec. 7, 1973; children: William Joseph, Maryann Lee. BBA, Portland State U., 1969. Ops. mgr. Pacific States Express, Inc., Portland, 1970-73; bus. mgr. Mogul Corp., Portland, 1974-80; v.p. Market Transport, Ltd., Portland, 1980-85; pres., founder, chmn. bd. dirs. Chem. Corp. Am., Portland, 1985—, also bd. dirs.; chmn. bd. dirs. Carolina Industries, Portland. Mem. TAPPI. Republican. Roman Catholic. Club: University (Portland). Avocations: golf, outdoors.Fax: 503-885-9701. Home: 3842 Wellington Ct West Linn OR 97068-3600 Office: Chem Corp Am 19535 SW 129th Ave Tualatin OR 97062-8076

STOTT, PETER WALTER, forest products company executive; b. Spokane, Wash., May 26, 1944; s. Walter Joseph and Rellalee (Gray) S.; m. Julie L. Neupert, Oct. 12, 1996; 1 child, Preston. Student Portland State U., 1962-63, 65-68, U. Americas, Mexico City, 1964-65. Founder, chmn. bd. dirs. Market Transport Ltd., Portland, Oreg., 1969—; bd. dirpres., CEO, prin. Crown Pacific, Sunshine divsn. Portland Police Bur. (hon.), Liberty Northwest; assoc. mem. adv. bd. Pacific Crest Outward Bound Sch.; mem. pres.'s adv. bd. for athletics Portland State U.; trustee Lewis & Clark Coll. With USAR, 1966-72. Mem. Nat. Football Found. and Hall of Fame, Oreg. Sports Hall Fame (lifetime), SOLV (founders' circle), Arlington Club, Astoria Golf and Country, Mazamas Club, Multnomah Athletic Club, Portland Golf Club, Univ. Club, Waverley Country Club, Valley Club. Republican. Roman Catholic. Office: Crown Pacific 121 SW Morrison St Ste 1500 Portland OR 97204-3145

STOUFER, RUTH HENDRIX, community volunteer; b. Pitts., June 21, 1916; d. Walter Willits and Frances (Ponbeck) Hendrix; m. William Kimball Stoufer, Sept. 8, 1937 (dec.); children: Walter Hendrix, Frances Elizabeth Stoufer Waller (dec.). BS in Tech. Journalism, Iowa State U., 1937. Trustee Marcus J. Lawrence Meml. Hosp., 1989-96; devel. chairperson Sedona-Verde Valley Am. Heart Assn., 1988-91; mem. adv. bd. L.A. chpt. Freedom's Found., 1965-78; mem. coord. med. adv. bd. U. Ariz., 1986—; founding chairperson Muses of the Mus. No. Ariz., 1984-85, pres., 1986-87, mem. Sinagua Soc., 1983-96; bd. dirs. Nat. Charity League, L.A., 1962, Found. for Children, L.A., 1964, 65, 66; pres. Panhellenic adv. bd. U. So. Calif., 1964; key adv. U. So. Calif. chpt. Beta Alpha of Gamma Phi Beta, 1960-63. Named Woman of Yr., Intercity Coun., Gamma Phi Beta, 1965. Avocations: Southwestern U.S. history, bridge, piano, reading. Home: 87 Doodlebug Knl Sedona AZ 86336

STOUP, THOMAS R., bookstore owner, manager, retired educator; b. Sioux City, Iowa, June 8, 1932; s. Roy T. and Anne G. S.; m. Judith Mannen, Jan. 24, 1959 (div. Oct., 1980); m. Penny Patten, Dec. 10, 1992; children: Anne Rutzler Susan, John, Elizabeth Hardsley, Peter. BS, Nebr. U.; MA, San Diego (Calif.) State U.; DD (hon.), U. Life, Modesto. Tchr. San Diego City Schs., 1967-89; owner bookstore Bluedoor Bookstore, San Diego, 1988—. Bd. dirs. San Diego Jr. C. of C., 1963. Mem. San Diego Book Sellers Assn. (v.p.), Hillcrest Bus. Assn. (pres. 1993). Democrat. Avocation: reading. Home: 1083 Cypress Way San Diego CA 92103-4408

STOUT, ARTHUR PAUL, minister; b. Phoenix, Feb. 10, 1932; s. Floyd Hamilton and Lucille Catherine (Robinson) S.; m. Marilyn Sue Munsil, Aug. 15, 1953; children: Roger Paul, Kellie Joanne, Amanda Beth, Eric Revell. BA, Ariz. State U., 1953; STB, Boston U., 1956. Ordained to ministry, United Meth. Ch., 1956. Pastor Sunapee & Georges Mills (N.H.) Community Meth. Chs., 1958-60, Huachuca (Ariz.) Meth. Ch., 1960-65, St. Andrew Meth. Ch., Mesa, Ariz., 1972-76; assoc. pastor Christ United Meth. Ch., Tucson, 1976-82; pastor Ajo (Ariz.) Federated Ch., 1982-85, St. James United Meth. Ch., Tucson, 1985-91, White Mountain United Meth. Ch., Show Low, Ariz., 1991-92, Youngtown Meth. Ch., 1993-97; ret., 1997; pres. Cochise County Coun. Chs., Bisbee, Ariz., 1963, Tucson Ministerial Assn., 1989; chaplain Squadron 105, CAP, Tucson, 1996—. Contbr. editorials to newspapers. Mem. Optimist (pres. 1967), Toastmasters (pres. 1981, 84, 87), Gifted and Talented Edn. Home: 734 S Kenyon Dr Tucson AZ 85710-4607

STOUT, ELIZABETH WEST, foundation administrator; b. San Francisco, Mar. 4, 1917; d. Claudius Wilson and Sarah (Henderson) West; m. Bruce Churchill McDonald, Mar. 19 1944 (dec. 1952); children: Douglas, Anne; m. Charles Holt Stout, Oct. 27, 1958 (dec. 1992); stepchildren: Richard, George (dec.), Martha Stout Gilweit. Student, U. Nev., 1934-37; grad., Imperial Valley Coll., 1990. Cashier, acct. N.Y. Underwriters, San Francisco, 1937-42; sec. supply and accounts USN, San Francisco, 1942-44. Contbr. articles to profl. jours. Mem. adv. bd. Anza-Borrego Desert, Natural History Assn., 1974-84; founder Stout Paleontology Lab., Borrego Springs, Calif., 1982; found. trustee Desert Rsch. Inst., Reno, 1989—; active Black Rock Desert Project, 1989, Washoe Med. Ctr. League, 1953—, St. Mary's Hosp. Guild, 1953—. Named Disting. Nevadan U. Nev., 1993. Mem. Anza-Borrego Desert Natural History Assn. (dir. emeritus 1984), Soc. Vertebrate Paleontology, De Anza Desert Country Club, Kappa Alpha Theta. Republican. Episcopalian. Avocations: travel, writing, reading, golf.

STOUT, THOMAS MELVILLE, control systems engineer; b. Ann Arbor, Mich., Nov. 26, 1925; s. Melville B. and Laura C. (Meisel) S.; m. Marilyn J. Koebnick, Dec. 27, 1947; children: Martha, Sharon, Carol, James, William, Kathryn. BSEE, Iowa State Coll., 1946; MSE, U. Mich., 1947, PhD, 1954. Registered profl. engr., Calif. Jr. engr. Emerson Electric Co., St. Louis, 1947-48; instr., then asst. prof. U. Wash., Seattle, 1948-54; rsch. engr. Schlumberger Instrument Co., Ridgefield, Conn., 1954-56; dept. mgr. TRW/Bunker-Ramo Corp., Canoga Park, Calif., 1956-65; pres. Profimatics, Inc., Thousand Oaks, Calif., 1965-83; pvt. practice cons. Northridge, Calif., 1984—; active profl. engring. registration and certification; mem., bd. dirs. Accreditation Bd. for Engring. and Tech., 1995—. Contbr. articles, revs., papers to profl. publs., chpts. to books. Ens. USN, 1943-46. Fellow, hon. mem. Instrument Soc. Am.; mem. IEEE (sr. mem.), NSPE, AIChE, Am. Soc. for Engring. Edn., Calif. Soc. Profl. Engrs. Achievements include four patents in computer control of industrial processes; participant in early digital computer installations for industrial process control. Home and Office: 9927 Hallack Ave Northridge CA 91324-1120

STOWELL, KENT, ballet director; b. Rexburg, Idaho, Aug. 8, 1939; s. Harold Bowman and Maxine (Hudson) S.; m. Francia Marie Russell, Nov. 19, 1965; children: Christopher, Darren, Ethan. Student, San Francisco Ballet Sch., Sch. Am. Ballet; Lead dancer San Francisco Ballet, 1957-62, N.Y.C. Ballet, 1962-68; ballet dir., ballet master Frankfurt (Fed. Republic Germany) Opera Ballet, 1973-77; artistic dir. Pacific N.W. Ballet, Seattle, 1977—; prof. dance Ind. U., Bloomington, 1969-70; bd. dirs. Sch. of Am. Ballet, Dance/USA, Washington, 1986—. Choreographer: Silver Lining, Cinderella, Carmina Burana, Coppelia, Time & Ebb, Fauré Requiem, Hail to the Conquering Hero, Firebird, Over the Waves, Nutcracker, The Tragedy of Romeo and Juliet, Delicate Balance, Swan Lake, Time and Ebb, Through Interior Worlds, Quaternary, Orpheus. Bd. dirs. Sch. of Am. Ballet, N.Y.C., 1981—; mem. Goodwill Games Arts Com., Seattle, 1987—; chmn. dance panel NEA, 1981-85. Grantee NEA, 1980, 85; fellow NEA, 1979. Recipient Arts Service award King County Arts Commn., 1985, Outstanding Contbn. to Pacific N.W. Ballet State of Was., 1987, Best Dance Co. award The Weekly Newspaper, Seattle, 1987, Gov. Arts award, 1988, Dance Mag. award, 1996. Office: Pacific NW Ballet 301 Mercer St Seattle WA 98109-4600

STRACK, HAROLD ARTHUR, retired electronics company executive, retired air force officer, planner, analyst, author, musician; b. San Francisco, Mar. 29, 1923; s. Harold Arthur and Catheryn Jenny (Johnsen) S.; m. Margaret Madeline Decker, July 31, 1945; children: Carolyn, Curtis, Tamara. Student, San Francisco Coll., 1941, Sacramento Coll., 1947, Sacramento State Coll., 1948, U. Md., 1962, Indsl. Coll. Armed Forces, 1963. Commd. 2d lt. USAAF, 1943; advanced through grades to brig. gen. USAF, 1970; comdr. 1st Radar Bomb Scoring Group Carswell AFB, Ft. Worth, 1956-59; vice comdr. 90th Strategic Missile Wing SAC Warren AFB, Cheyenne, Wyo., 1964; chief, strategic nuclear br., spl. studies group Joint Chiefs of Staff, 1965-67, dep. asst. to chmn. JCS for strategic arms negotiations, 1968; comdr. 90th Strategic Missile Wing SAC Warren AFB, Cheyenne, 1969-71; chief Studies, Analysis and Gaming Agy. Joint Chiefs Staff, Washington, 1972-74, ret., 1974; v.p., mgr. MX Pacekeeper Program v.p. strategic planning Northrop Electronics Divsn., Hawthorne, Calif., 1974-88; ret., 1988. 1st clarinetist, Cheyenne Symphony Orch., 1969-71. Mem. Cheyenne Frontier Days Com., 1970-71. Decorated D.S.M., Legion of Merit, D.F.C., Air medal, Purple Heart; mem. Order Pour le Merite. Mem. Inst. Nav., Am. Def. Preparedness Assn., Air Force Assn., Aerospace Edn. Found., Am. Fedn. Musicians, Cheyenne Frontier Days "Heels". Home: 707 James Ln Incline Village NV 89451-9612

STRACK, STEPHEN NAYLOR, psychologist; b. Rome, N.Y., Nov. 13, 1955; s. Ralph and Grace (Naylor) S.; m. Leni Ferrero. BA, U. Calif., Berkeley, 1978; PhD, U. Miami, Fla., 1983. Psychologist L.A. County Dept. Mental Health, 1984-85; staff psychologist VA Outpatient Clinic, L.A., 1985—, dir. tng., 1992-97; clin. assoc. U. So. Calif., L.A., 1986-95; adj. prof. Calif. Sch. Profl. Psychology, L.A., 1989—; clin. prof. Fuller Grad. Sch. Psychology, Pasadena, Calif., 1986—. Author (test): Personality Adjective Check List, 1987; co-author (book): Differentiating Normal and Abnormal Personality, 1994, Death and the Quest for Meaning, 1997, Essentials of Million Inventories Assessment, 1999; cons. editor Jour. Personality Disorders, N.Y.C., 1992—, Omega, 1997—, Jour. Personality Assessment, 1999—. U.S. Dept. Vets Affairs grantee, 1986-93, 96—. Fellow APA, Soc. for Personality Assessment; mem. Internat. Soc. for the Study of Personality Disorders, Calif. Psychol. Assn., European Assn. Psychol. Assessment, Soc. for Rsch. in Psychopathology, Western Psychol. Assn., Sigma Xi. Office: VA Outpatient Clinic 351 E Temple St Los Angeles CA 90012-3328

STRAHAN, JULIA CELESTINE, electronics company executive; b. Indpls., Feb. 10, 1938; d. Edgar Paul Pauley and Pauline Barbara (Myers) Shawver; m. Norman Strahan, Oct. 2, 1962 (div. 1982); children: Daniel Keven, Natalie Kay. Grad. high sch., Indpls. With EG&G/Energy Measurements, Inc., Las Vegas, Nev., 1967—; sect. head EG&G Co., 1979-83, mgr. electronics dept., 1984—. Recipient award Am. Legion, 1952, Excellence award, 1986. Mem. NAFE, Am. Nuclear Soc. (models and mentors), Internat. Platform Assn. Home: 5222 Stacey Ave Las Vegas NV 89108-3078 Office: EG&G PO Box 1912 Las Vegas NV 89125-1912

STRAHLER, ARTHUR NEWELL, former geology educator, author; b. Kolhapur, India, Feb. 20, 1918; s. Milton W. and Harriet (Brittan) S.; m. Margaret E. Wanless, Aug. 10, 1940; children: Alan H., Marjorie E. A.B., Coll. Wooster, 1938; A.M., Columbia U., 1940, Ph.D. (Univ. fellow), 1944. Faculty Columbia U., 1941-71, prof. geomorphology, 1958-68, adj. prof. geology, 1968-71, chmn. dept. geology, 1959-62. Author: Physical Geography, rev. edit., 1975, The Earth Sciences, rev. edit., 1971, Introduction to Physical Geography, rev. edit., 1973, Planet Earth, 1971, Environmental Geoscience, 1973, Introduction to Environmental Science, 1974, Elements of Physical Geography, 2d edit., 1979, 3d edit., 1984, 4th edit., 1989, Principles of Earth Science, 1976, Principles of Physical Geology, 1977, Geography and Man's Environment, 1977, Modern Physical Geography, 1978, 4th edit., 1992, Physical Geology, 1981, Science and Earth History—The Evolution/Creation Controversy, 1987, Investigating Physical Geography, 1989, Understanding Science: An Introduction to Concepts and Issues, 1992, Physical Geography-Science and Systems of the Human Environment, 1996, Plate Tectonics, 1998. Fellow Geol. Soc. Am., Am. Geog. Soc.; mem. Am. Geophys. Union, Phi Beta Kappa, Sigma Xi. Home: 1039 Cima Linda Ln Santa Barbara CA 93108-1818

STRAIGHT, JAMES WESLEY, secondary education educator; b. Ely, Nev., Jan. 3, 1930; s. James Wesley Sr. and Mary Elizabeth (Hunter) S.; m. Gloria Frances Roysum, Aug. 22, 1954; children: James W. Jr., Elizabeth Straight Stevenson, Kathryn Straight Hernandez, Douglas Scott. BS in Geol. Engring., U. Nev., Reno, 1954. Cert. secondary tchr., Calif. Flotation operator Kennecott Copper Corp., McGill, Nev., 1954-57; soil engr. John F. Byerly, Bloomington, Calif., 1967-82; foreman Eagle-Picher, Lovelock, Nev., 1957-61; finish mill foreman Kaiser Steel, Fontana, Calif., 1962-67; tchr. indsl. arts Fontana Unified Schs., 1967-92; tchr. prospecting class Rialto (Calif) Unified Schs., 1969—; tchr. prospecting class U. Calif., Riverside, 1976. Author, pub.: Follow the Drywashers, 1988, vol. 2, 1990, vol. 3, 1993, Magnificent Quest, 1990, Advanced Prospecting and Detecting for Hardrock Gold, 1998, Successful Drywashing, 1996; contbg. editor mags. Popular Mining, Treas. Found., Western and Ea. Treas., Treas. Gold and Silver, Treas. Seekers, Internat. Calif. Mining Jour., Lost Treasure. Treas. San Bernadino (Calif.) Area Assn. for the Retarded, 1972; parent steering com. Inland Regional Ctr. 1st lt. U.S. Army C.E., 1955-57. Mem. Masons, San Bernardino Assn. for the Mentally Ill (bd. dirs.). Republican. Episcopalian. Avocation: amature radio. Home and Office: 19225 Mesa St Rialto CA 92377-4558

STRAIN, JOHN THOMAS, electronics engineer; b. Raymondville, Mo., Oct. 25, 1939; s. Thomas and Lillie (Merckling) S.; m. Bonnie J. Cline, 1967 (div. 1980); children: Robert Vidmar, Anthony Vidmar. BSEE, U. Mo., Rolla, 1964. Electronics technician Exec. Aircraft Co., Kansas City, Mo., 1960-61; electronic engring. technician Wilcox Electric Co., Kansas City, 1963, sr. electronics technician, 1964-67; sr. electronics technician Exec. Aircraft Co., 1964; electronic engring. tech. Gianni Voltex Co., San Diego, 1967-68; electronic fabricator Bendix Atomic Energy Commn., Kansas City, 1968; electronics engr. Electronic Research Corp., Overland Park, Kans., 1968-69, Monitor Products Co., South Pasadena, Calif., 1969-73, NBC, Burbank, Calif., 1973—. Designed and developed original TV stereo encoder; responsible (with Ron Estes) for first recorded stereo TV program (nominated for Emmy 1983); developer first DIP style crystal controled oscillator for use in computer and areospace industries. With USAF, 1964-65. Avocations: amateur radio, hiking, backpacking. Home: 6450 Clybourn Ave North Hollywood CA 91606-2728 Office: NBC 3000 W Alameda Ave Burbank CA 91523-0002

STRALING, PHILLIP FRANCIS, bishop; b. San Bernardino, Calif., Apr. 25, 1933; s. Sylvester J. and Florence E. (Robinson) S. BA, U. San Diego, 1963; MS in Child and Family Counseling, San Diego State U., 1971. Ordained priest Roman Catholic Ch., 1959, consecrated bishop, 1978. Mem. faculty St. John Acad., El Cajon, Calif., 1959-60, St. Therese Acad., San Diego, 1960-63; chaplain Newman Club, San Diego State U., 1960-72; mem. faculty St. Francis Sem., San Diego, 1972-76; pastor Holy Rosary Parish, San Bernardino, 1976-78; bishop Diocese of San Bernardino, 1978-95; pub. Inland Cath. newspaper, 1979-95; chmn. com. on lay ministry U.S. Cath. Conf./Nat. Cath. Conf. Bishops, 1993—; bishop of Reno, Nev., 1995—; bd. dirs. Calif. Assn. Cath. Campus Mins., 1960s; exec. sec. Diocesan Synod II, 1972-76; Episcopal vicar San Bernardino Deanery, 1976-78. Mem. Nat. Cath. Campus Ministries Assn. (bishop rep. 1992-98). Office: PO Box 1211 Reno NV 89504-1211

STRAND, ROGER GORDON, federal judge; b. Peekskill, N.Y., Apr. 28, 1934; s. Ernest Gordon Strand and Lisabeth Laurine (Phin) Steinmetz; m. Joan Williams, Nov. 25, 1961. AB, Hamilton Coll., 1955; LLB, Cornell U., 1961; grad., Nat. Coll. State Trial Judges, 1968. Bar: Ariz. 1961, U.S. Dist. Ct. Ariz. 1961, U.S. Supreme Ct. 1980. Assoc. Fennemore, Craig, Allen & McClennen, Phoenix, 1961-67; judge Ariz. Superior Ct., Phoenix, 1967-85, U.S. Dist. Ct. Ariz., Phoenix, 1985—; assoc. presiding judge Ariz. Superior Ct., 1971-85; lectr. Nat. Jud. Coll., Reno, 1978-87. Past pres. cen. Ariz. chpt. Arthritis Found. Lt. USN, 1955-61. Mem. ABA, Ariz. Bar Assn., Maricopa County Bar Assn., Nat. Conf. Fed. Trial Judges, Phi Delta Phi, Aircraft Owners and Pilots Assn. Lodge: Rotary. Avocations: computer applications, golf, fishing. Home: 5825 N 3rd Ave Phoenix AZ 85013-1537 Office: US Dist Ct Courthouse and Fed Bldg 230 N 1st Ave Ste 3013 Phoenix AZ 85025-0067

STRASBAUGH, WILLIAM EDWARD, writer, federal agency administrator, retired career officer; b. Vancouver, Wash., Mar. 14, 1945; s. Robert Ernest Strasbaugh and Edna Jean (Murrell) Hultberg; m. Marie K. Kruszewski, July 22, 1984; children: Jennifer Marie, Melissa Ann Angela May Joann, Erin Louise. Assoc. and assoc., Appy. Sci., High Line C.C., Des Moines, Wash., 1997, student, 1997-98. Aircraft crew chief USAF, 1963-67; test flight technician Boeing Aircraft Co., Seattle, 1967-72; indsl. engring. technician U.S. Govt., Ogden, Utah, 1972-82; shop supervisor Naval Reserve, 1976-82; mobility NCOIC Air Natl. Guard, 1982-93; project officer U.S. Govt., Ogden, Utah, 1982-86, contract adminstr., 1986-90, prodn. controller, 1990-93; writer Seattle, 1994—. Author: The Airlift, 1993, What Price Murder, 1996, A Price to Pay, 1998. With USAF, 1963-67, USNR, 1976-82, UT NAG, 1982-93. Decorated D.F.C., Purple Heart Air Medal. Mem. Wash. Lit. Assn., Libr. Technician Assn., Soc. Logistical Engrs., Method Time Mgmt. Assn. Roman Catholic. Home: 127 SW 154th St #348 Seattle WA 98166-2331

STRASBURG, LINDA ANN, transportation executive, college official, clinical hypnotherapist, radio talk show host; Price, Utah, Dec. 1, 1948; d. William Henry and Lillyan (O'Berto) Loomis; m. Nyle Taylor Strasburg, May 26, 1969; children—Sundee A., Sean T. Cert. in art Utah Tech. Coll., 1970. BS in Human Resource Mgmt. cum laude, 1987, M in Profl. Commn. Writing. Cert. clin. hypnotherapist, leadership trainer, Jump Start Entrepreneur Program. Telephone operator Mountain Bell Telephone Co., Salt Lake City, 1969-71; owner, operator Strasburg Machine, West Jordan, Utah, 1976-90; v.p. publs. Utah Tech. Coll., Salt Lake City, 1984—; payroll adminstr. Delta Air Lines, Salt Lake City, 1988—, owner Brauns & Co., owner Assolades Coaching & Cons.; tchr. workshops for motivation and developing creativity Lean Lifestyles, ins. coding instr., arbitrator Better Bus. Bureau. Group shows include West Jordan Women's Art Show, Granite Art Show, Utah Tech. Coll. Comml. Art Show. Pres. West Jordan Community Crime Watch, 1976-79; pub. speaker West Jordan Crime Prevention, Utah, 1976-78; commr. Utah Crime Prevention Assn., Salt Lake City, 1978; mem. masterplan com. West Jordan City, 1979, mem. assessment panel, 1980; mem. instl. council Salt Lake C.C., 1986—, alumni council, 1986-88; pres. Westland PTA, West Jordan, 1980-82, West Jordan Elem. PTA, 1982-83. Mem. Delta Epsilon Chi (3d place award in mktg. competition 1984), Delta Nu Alpha. Toastmasters. Home: 2303 Straw Cir West Jordan UT 84084-2106

STRATTON, GREGORY ALEXANDER, computer specialist, administrator, mayor; b. Glendale, Calif., July 31, 1946; s. William Jaspar and Rita Phyllis (Smith) S.; m. Yolanda Margot Soler, 1967 (div. 1974); 1 child, Tiffany Schwarzer; m. Edith Carter, Sept. 27, 1975; stepchildren: John Henkell, Paul Henkell, D'Lorah Henkell Wismar. Student, Harvey Mudd Coll., 1964-65; BS in Physics, UCLA, 1968; MBA, Calif. Luth. U., 1977. Elec. engr. Naval Ship Weapon System Engring. Sta., Port Hueneme, Calif., 1968-73; sr. staff mem. Univac, Valencia, Calif., 1973-74; v.p. Digital Applications, Camarillo, Calif., 1974-75; cons. Grumman Aerospace, Point Mugu, Calif., 1975-76; F-14 software mgr. Pacific Missile Test Ctr., Pt. Mugu, 1976-84; software mgr. Teledyne Systems, Northridge, Calif., 1984-92, dir. engring. software dept., 1992-93; dep. dir. software engring. Teledyne Electronic Systems, Northridge, Calif., 1993-94; software mgr. Litton Guidance and Controls, Northridge, Calif., 1995—. Mem. City Coun., City of Simi Valley, Calif., 1979-86, mayor, 1986-98; alt. Rep. County Cen. Com., Ventura County, 1986-88; mem. Rep. State Cen. Com., Calif., 1990—; bd. dirs. Simi Valley Hosp., 1987—. Mem. Assn. Ventura County Cities (chair 1990-91), Rotary (Paul Harris award Simi Sunrise chpt. 1989), Jaycees (pres. Simi Valley chpt. 1974-75, nat. bd. dirs. 1975-76, v.p. Calif. state 1976-77). Republican. Lutheran. Home: 254 Goldenwood Cir Simi Valley CA 93065-6771 Office: Litton Guidance and Controls 19601 Nordhoff Northridge CA 91324-2422*

STRATTON, WILLIAM ROBERT, physicist; b. River Falls, Wis., May 15, 1922; s. Charles Glen and Ada Viola (Ruby) S.; m. Beverly Mavis January, March 8, 1952; children: Nancy, Gail, Sheila. BA, U. Minn., 1948, PhD, 1952. Mem. staff Los Alamos (N. Mex.) Nat. Lab., 1952-82; prin., owner Stratton and Assocs., Los Alamos, N. Mex., 1982-87; pvt. practice Los Alamos, N. Mex., 1987—; adv. com. Pres. Comm. Accident at 3-mile Island, Washington. Fellow Am. Nuclear Soc. (special award 1981, 85); mem. Am. Physical Soc., Sigma Xi. Home: 2 Acoma Ln Los Alamos NM 87544-3801

STRAUSS, JON CALVERT, academic administrator; b. Chgo., Jan. 17, 1940; s. Charles E. and Alice C. (Woods) S.; m. Joan Helen Bailey, Sept. 19, 1959 (div. 1985); children: Susan, Stephanie; m. Jean Anne Sacconaghi, June 14, 1985; children: Kristoffer, Jonathon. BSEE, U. Wis., 1959; MS in Physics, U. Pitts., 1962; PhD in E.E., Carnegie Inst. Tech., 1965; LLD (hon.), U. Mass., 1996. Assoc. prof. computer sci., elec. engring. Carnegie Mellon U., Pitts., 1966-70; dir. computer ctr., prof. computer sci. Tech. U. Norway, Trondheim, Norway, 1970; vis. assoc. prof. elec. engring. U. Mich., Ann Arbor, 1971; assoc. prof. computer sci. Washington U., St. Louis, Mo., 1971-74, dir. computing facilities, 1971-73; dir. computing activities U. Pa., Phila., 1974-76, faculty master Stouffer Coll. House, 1978-80, prof. computer, info. scis., prof. decision sci. Wharton Sch., 1974-81, exec. dir. Univ. Budget, 1975-78, v.p. for budget, fin., 1978-81; prof. elec. engring. U. So. Calif., Los Angeles, 1981-85; sr. v.p. adminstrn. U. So. Calif., 1981-85; pres. Worcester Poly. Inst., Mass., 1985-94; v.p., chief fin. officer Howard Hughes Med. Inst., Chevy Chase, Md., 1994-97; pres. Harvey Mudd Coll., Claremont, Calif., 1997—; cons. Electronics Assocs., Inc., 1965, IBM Corp., 1960-64, Westinghouse Elec. Corp., 1959-60; bd. dirs. Transamerica Income Fund, Variable Ins. Fund, United Educators Ins. Contbr. articles on computer systems and university mgmt. to profl. jours.; co-holder patent. Bd. dirs. Presbyn.-U. Pa. Med. Ctr., Phila., 1980-81, U. So. Calif. Kenneth Norris Jr. Cancer Hosp., L.A., 1981-85, Med. Ctr. of Ctrl. Mass., 1986-94, Worcester Acad., 1986-91, Mass. Biotech. Rsch. Inst., 1985-94. Mem. New Eng. Assn. Schs. and Colls., Inc., Commn. on Instns. of Higher Edn., Nat. Collegiate Athletic Assn. (pres.'s commn. 1990-94). Avocations: rowing, running, sailing, swimming. Office: Harvey Mudd Coll 301 E 12th St Claremont CA 91711-5901

STRAWN, SUSAN HEATHCOTE, medical administrator; b. Pasadena, Calif., Feb. 10, 1940; d. Edward McNair and Ann Heathcote (Stevens) McNair; m. Harvey G. Holtz, June 24, 1960 (div. June. 1974); children: Christopher, Edward, David. AS, Butte Coll., 1973; lifetime tchg. credential, Calif. State U., Chico, 1987. Cert. respiratory therapist, 1974, cardiovascular tech., 1985. Respiratory therapist Feather River Hosp., Paradise, Calif., 1973-87; instr. respiratory therapy Butte Coll., Chico, 1982-87, instr. cardiovascular tech., 1987-95; cardiovasc. technologist Chico Cardiology, 1987-90; dir. cardiopulmonary dept. Oroville (Calif.) Hosp., 1990—; mem. adv. bd. Butte Coll., Chico, 1982—. Author 2-yr. cardiovasc. tech. program for Butte Coll., 1987. Mem. NOW, Am. Assn. Respiratory Care, Cardiovasc. Internat., Echo Soc., Calif. Soc. for Respiratory Care. Democrat. Episcopalian. Avocations: oil painting, traveling, reading, being a grandmother, raising black sheep. Home: 32 Humpyback Rd Oroville CA 95965-9104 Office: Oroville Hosp 2767 Olive Hwy Oroville CA 95966-6118

STREIFF, ARLYNE BASTUNAS, business owner, educator; b. Sacramento, Calif., Nov. 4; d. Peter James and Isabel (Gemnas) Bastunas; children: Peter Joshua, Joshua Gus. BS, U. Nev., 1965; postgrad., U. Calif., Davis, 1965-68, Calif. State U., Chico, 1968, 71. Cert. elem. tchr., Calif., Nev., cert. in English-specially designed lang. acad. instrn. devel. in English. Tchr. reading, lang. and kindergarten Enterprise Elem. Sch. Dist., Redding, Calif., 1965-98, tchr. kindergarten, 1988-98; owner, pres. Arlyne's Svcs., Redding, Calif., 1990—. Author: Niko and His Friends, 1989, Niko The Black Rottweiler, 1995, Color-Talk-Spell. Mem. Rep. Women, Five County Labor Coun., Redding, 1976-93, Calif. Labor Fedn., 1974-97, AFL-CIO, 1974-97. Named Tchr. of Yr., Enterprise Sch. Dist., 1969. Mem. AAUW, Am. Fedn. Tchrs., Calif. Tchrs. Assn. (bargaining spokesperson 1968-72, exec. bd. dirs.), United Tchrs. Enterprise (pres. 1979-80, chmn. lang. com.), Calif. Reading Assn., Enterprise Fedn. Tchrs. (pres. 1974, pres.-elect 1995-97), Calif. State Fedn. Tchrs. (v.p. 1974-75, exec. bd. 1995-97), Redding C. of C., Women of Moose, Elks. Avocations: home interior design, real estate, construction, creative writing, educational advancement. Office: Arlynes Svcs 1468 Benton Dr Redding CA 96003-3116

STRENA, ROBERT VICTOR, university research laboratory manager; b. Seattle, June 28, 1929; s. Robert Lafayette Peel and Mary Oliva (Holmes) S.; m. Rita Mae Brodovsky, Aug. 1957; children: Robert Victor, Adrienne Amelia. AB, Stanford U., 1952. Survey mathematician Hazen Engring., San Jose, Calif., 1952-53; field engr. Menlo Sanitary Dist., Menlo Park, Calif., 1954-55; ind. fin. reporter Los Altos, Calif., 1953-59; asst. dir. Hansen Labs. Stanford U., 1959-93, asst. dir. emeritus Ginzton Lab., 1993—; ind. fin. cons., Los Altos, 1965—; mem. restoration adv. bd., Moffett Fed. Airfield, 1994—. Active Edn. System Politics, Los Altos, 1965-80, local Boy Scouts Am., 1968-80, Maj. USAR, 1948-70. Mem. AAAS, Mus. Soc., Big X (Los Altos), Cherry Chase Golf Club. Republican. Avocations: golf, sailing. Home: 735 Raymundo Ave Los Altos CA 94024-3139 Office: Stanford U Ginzton Lab Stanford CA 94305

STRENGER, GEORGE, surgeon; b. N.Y., Sept. 5, 1906; s. Philip and Tillie (Strassman) S.; m. Florence Serxner, June 9, 1931; children: Philip J., Laurence N. BA, Columbia U., 1928, MD, 1931. Diplomate Am. Bd. Surg., 1942. surgeon Bklyn. Jew. Hosp., N.Y., 1934-72, Goldwater Meml. Hosp., N.Y., 1939-53; chief surg. svc. N.Y. regional office VA, 1948-72; surgeon Coney Island Hosp., N.Y., 1953-72; instr. Long Island Med. Coll., N.Y., 1934-36. Mem. Ditmas Pk. Assn. (pres. 1953-54). Comdr. field hosp. U.S. Army, 1942-46, ETO. Recipient commendation Gen. Eisenhower, 1945. Fellow Am. Coll. Surgeons. Avocations: music, languages, golf, tennis, swimming. Home: 31397 E Nine Dr Laguna Niguel CA 92677-2909

STRICHARTZ, JAMES LEONARD, lawyer; b. N.Y.C., Feb. 5, 1951; s. Morris Harvey and Estelle (Flatow) S. BA in Urban Studies, U. Mich., 1973, M in Pub. Policy, 1976, JD, 1977. Bar: Mich., 1977, D.C. 19878, Wash., 1980; diplomate Coll. of Comty. Assn. Lawyers. Law clk. Mich. Ct. Appeals, Detroit, 1977-78; assoc. atty. Weinrich, Gilmore & Adolph, Seattle, 1978-79; gen. counsel The 13th Regional Corp., Seattle, 1979-81; pvt. practice Seattle, 1981—; mem. Senate Jud. Com. Condo. Law Task Force, Seattle, 1986-87, Condo. Act Statutory Revision Com., 1987-91, Washington Common Interest Ownership Act Legis. Task Force, 1994-95; spkr. 22 and 23d nat. confs. Cmty. Assn. Inst., Alexandria, Va.; faculty Profl. Mgmt. Devel. Program, 1993. Pres., bd. dirs. Fremont Community Health Clinic, 1982-83, 45th St. Community Health Clinic, 1984-89; gen. counsel, trustee Wash. Trust for Hist. Preservation, 1982-87; mem. Corp. Coun. For The Arts, 1987-88, Coun. for Corp. Responsibility, 1984—; founding mem., founding dir. Shoreline Arts Coun., 1989-92. Mem. Comty. Assn. Inst., Nat. Conf. of Chpts. (vice chmn., N.W. region 1988-89, chmn. 1990-91), Comty. Assns. Inst. Wash. (bd. dirs. 1986-92, v.p. 1987, pres. 1988-90, faculty mem. ops. and mgmt. comty. assns. leadership tng. program 1987, 89, 90, 91, chmn. 1992, 93, faculty profl. mgmt. devel. program 1993-95), Comty. Assn. Inst. Rsch. Found. (chmn. symposium on comty. 1990, bd. dirs. 1991-96, speaker symposiums 1991, 93, v.p. 1994, treas. 1995). Democrat. Unitarian. Office: 200 W Mercer St # 511 Seattle WA 98119-3958

STRICKLAND, RONALD GIBSON, writer; b. Providence, R.I., Mar. 19, 1943; s. Edwin Theodore and Winifred (Gibson) S. BSFS, Georgetown, 1965, MA, 1968, PhD, 1976. Wildness activist Olympic Nat. Parks, Washington, D.C., 1968-76; founder The Pacific Northwest Trail, 1970; exec. dir. Pacific Northwest Trail Assn., Seattle, 1977-87; writer, 1978—. Contbr. articles to profl. jours. Avocation: long distance backpacking. Home: PO Box 10018 Seattle WA 98110-0018

STRICKLER, CAROLYN JEANETTE, writer, historian; b. Kansas City, Mo., Nov. 19, 1930; d. Clyde Cleveland and Eleanor Lowe; m. Peter Ness Strickler, June 9, 1951. Art editor L.A. Examiner, 1960-62; contbg. editor Ford's Travel Guides, L.A., 1964-77; West Coast editor Art Gallery Mag., L.A., 1971-72; co. historian L.A. Times, 1979-90; ind. writer, historian L.A. and Pasadena, Calif., 1990—. Contbr. articles to mags. Mem. Am. Soc. Journalists and Authors, Calif. Lawyers for the Arts, Hist. Soc. So. Calif., Pen Ctr. USA West. Democrat. Avocations: photography, travel. Home and Office: 960 San Pasqual St Apt 305 Pasadena CA 91106-3396

STRILER, RAY, distance education consultant; b. Crystal City, Mo., Dec. 21, 1938. BS in Edn., S.W. Mo. U., 1961; MS, Peabody Coll., Vanderbilt U., 1978; MA, Rider U., 1984; EdD, U.S. Internat. U., 1989. Prof., dept. chmn. Rider U., N.J.; tchr. coll. prep., Carlsbad, Calif.; dir. acad. programs and v.p. mil. programs Inst. for Profl. Devel., Phoenix; tech. cons. Voltek Inc., Belleville, Ill.; ptnr. Global Learning Techs., Oceanside, Calif.; pres. Edn. 2020 Inc. Alumni bd. dirs. U.S. Internat. U. Lt. col. U.S. Army, 1962-86.

STRINGER, NANETTE SCHULZE, lawyer; b. Stuttgart, Germany, May 29, 1952; came to U.S., 1952; d. Herbert Charles and Marie-Jeanne (Raphael) Schulze; m. James Cooper Stringer, Oct. 9, 1982; children: David, Sarah, Amy. BA, Harvard U., 1974; JD, Stanford U., 1978. Bar: Calif. 1978, U.S. Dist. Ct. (no. dist.) Calif. 1978. Atty. Keogh, Marer & Flicker, Palo Alto, Calif., 1979-81, Carr, McClellan, Burlingame, Calif., 1981-83, Lakin-Spears, Palo Alto, 1983-89, Law Ofc. of John Miller, Palo Alto, 1991-93; atty., owner Nanette S. Stringer, Atty. at Law, Palo Alto, 1993—. Sec., bd. mem. Palo Alto Little League, 1995—. Mem. Palo Alto Bar Assn. (lawyer referral svc. com.), Calif. State Bar (cert specialist family law bd. specialization, 1994—). Roman Catholic. Avocations: masters' swimming, running, gardening. Office: 375 Forest Ave Palo Alto CA 94301-2521

STRINGER, WILLIAM JEREMY, university official; b. Oakland, Calif., Nov. 8, 1944; s. William Duane and Mildred May (Andrus) S.; BA in English, So. Meth. U., 1966; MA in English, U. Wis., 1968, PhD in Ednl. Adminstrn., 1973; m. Susan Lee Hildebrand; children: Shannon Lee, Kelly Erin, Courtney Elizabeth. Dir. men's housing Southwestern U., Georgetown, Tex., 1968-69; asst. dir. housing U. Wis., Madison, 1969-73; dir. residential life, asso. dean student life, adj. prof. Pacific Luth., Tacoma, 1973-78; dir. residential life U. So. Calif., 1978-79, asst. v.p., 1979-84, asst. prof. higher and post-secondary edn., 1980-84; v.p. student life Seattle U., 1984-89, v.p. student devel., 1989-92, assoc. provost, 1989-95, assoc. prof. edn., 1990—, chair educational leadership, 1994—. Author: How to Survive as a Single Student, 1972, The Role of the Assistant in Higher Education, 1973. Bd. dirs. N.W. area Luth. Social Services of Wash. and Idaho, pres.-elect, 1989, pres., 1990-91; bd. dirs. Seattle Coalition Ednl. Equity. Danforth Found. grantee, 1976-77. Mem. AAUP, Am. Assn. Higher Edn., Nat. Assn. Student Pers. Adminstrs. (bd. dirs. region V 1985—, mem. editl. bd. Jour. 1995—), Am. Coll. Pers. Assn., Phi Eta Sigma, Sigma Tau Delta, Phi Alpha Theta. Lutheran. Home: 4553 169th Ave SE Bellevue WA 98006-6505 Office: Seattle U Dept Edn Seattle WA 98122

STROBER, MYRA HOFFENBERG, education educator, consultant; b. N.Y.C., Mar. 28, 1941; d. Julius William Hoffenberg and Regina Scharer; m. Samuel Strober, June 23, 1963 (div. Dec. 1983); children: Jason M., Elizabeth A.; m. Jay M. Jackman, Oct. 21, 1990. BS in Indsl. Rels., Cornell U., 1962; MA in Econs., Tufts U., 1965; PhD in Econs., MIT, 1969. Lectr., asst. prof. dept. econs. U. Md., College Park, 1967-70; lectr. U. Calif., Berkeley, 1970-72; asst. prof. grad. sch. bus. Stanford (Calif.) U., 1972-86, assoc. prof. sch. edn., 1979-90, prof., 1990—, assoc. dean acad. affairs, 1993-95, interim dean, 1994; program officer in higher edn. Atlantic Philanthropic Svcs., Ithaca, N.Y., 1998—; organizer Stanford Bus. Conf. Women Mgmt., 1974; founding dir. ctr. rsch. women Stanford U., 1974-76, 79-84, dir. edn. policy inst., 1984-86, dean alumni coll., 1992, mem. policy and planning bd., 1992-93, chair program edn. adminstrn. and policy analysis, 1991-93, chair provost's com. recruitment and retention women faculty, 1992-93, chair faculty senate com. on coms., 1992-93; mem. adv. bd. State of Calif. Office Econ. Policy Planning and Rsch., 1978-80; mem. Coll. Bd. Com. Develop Advanced Placement Exam. Econs., 1987-88; faculty advisor Rutgers Women's Leadership Program, 1991-93. Author: (with others) Industrial Relations, 1972, Sex, Discrimination and the Division of Labor, 1975, Changing Roles of Men and Women, 1976, Women in the Labor Market, 1979, Educational Policy and Management: Sex Differentials, 1981, Women in the Workplace, 1982, Sex Segregation in the Workplace: Trends, Explanations, Remedies, 1984, The New Palgrave: A Dictionary of Economic Theory and Doctrine, 1987, Computer Chips and Paper Clips: Technology and Women's Employment, Vol. II, 1987, Gender in the Workplace, 1987; editor: (with Francine E. Gordon) Bringing Women Into Management, 1975, (with others) Women and Poverty, 1986, (with Sanford M. Dornbusch) Feminism, Children and the New Families, 1988; mem. bd. editors Signs: Jour. Women Culture and Soc., 1975-89, assoc. editor, 1980-85; mem. bd. editors Sage Ann. Rev. Women and Work, 1984—; mem. editorial adv. bd. U.S.-Japan Women's Jour., 1991—; assoc. editor Jour. Econ. Edn., 1991—; contbr. chpt. to book, articles to profl. jours. Mem. rsch. adv. task force YWCA, 1989—; chair exec. bd. Stanford Hillel, 1990-92; bd. dirs. Resource Ctr. Women, Palo Alto, Calif., 1983-84; pres. bd. dirs. Kaider Found., Mountain View, Calif., 1990-96. Fellow Stanford U., 1975-77, Schiff House Resident fellow, 85-87. Mem. NOW (bd. dirs. legal def. and edn. fund 1993—), Am. Econ. Assn. (mem. com. status of women in the profession 1972-75), Am. Ednl. Rsch. Assn., Indsl. Rels. Rsch. Assn., Internat. Assn. for Feminist Econs. (pres. 1997—, assoc. editor Feminist Econs. 1994—). Office: Stanford U School of Education Stanford CA 94305 also: APS 120 E Buffalo St Ithaca NY 14850-4266

STROCK, DAVID RANDOLPH, brokerage house executive; b. Salt Lake City, Jan. 31, 1944; s. Clarence Randolph and Francis (Hornibrook) S.; m. Phyllis A. Tingley, Dec. 13, 1945 (div. June 15, 1982); children: Sarah, Heidi. AA, San Mateo Coll., 1967; BS, San Jose State U., 1970. Investment exec. Paine Webber, San Jose, Calif., 1970-78; corp. trainer Paine Webber, N.Y.C., 1978-79, rsch. coord., 1979-82; br. mgr. Paine Webber, Northbrook, Ill., 1982-84, Palos Verdes, Calif., 1984-89, Napa, Calif., 1989-90; investment exec. Paine Webber, Napa, 1990—. Contbr. articles to profl. jours. Mem. San Jose Jr. C. of C. (chmn. 1977, v.p. 1978), North Napa Rotary (past pres.), Moose. Republican. Avocations: racing, Indy car racing, formula one racing, biking, whitewater rafting. Home: 3324 Homestead Ct Napa CA 94558-4275 Office: Paine Webber 703 Trancas St Napa CA 94558-3014

STRODE, DEBORAH LYNN, English language educator; b. Ft. Dodge, Iowa, June 18, 1948; d. Franklin Max and Helen (Crook) S. BS in Speech and Theater, Parsons Coll., 1971; teaching cert., Boise State U., 1977; MS in Edn., So. Oreg. State U., 1985; adminstrv. cert., U. Alaska, Anchorage, 1986. Cert. tchr. Alaska, cert. adminstr., Nev. Tchr. U.S. Peace Corps., Liberia, West Africa, 1971-73; tchr., adminstr. North Slope Borough Sch. Dist., Barrow, Alaska, 1976-90; adminstr. fed. programs Iditarod Area Sch. Dist., McGrath, Alaska, 1990-91; vis. tchr. English Nishinomiya (Hyogo, Japan) Mcpl. Edn. Bd., 1993—; dir. childrens receiving home North Slope Borough Health Dept., Barrow, summer 1978. Supporting mem. Friends of Liberia, Washington; counselor McLaughlin Youth Detention Ctr., summer 1975; counselor Long and Short House Alaska Children's Svcs., 1974; treas. Barrow PTA; sponsor Internat. Thespian Soc.; active Fairfax County Pub. Access TV. Mem. NEA, Alaska Arts in Edn., Am. Theater Assn., Returned Peace Corps Vol. Assn., North Slope Adminstrn. Assn., North Slope Edn. Assn. (v.p.), Secondary Theater Assn., Childrens Theater Assn.

STRODE, GERALD MARVIN, physician assistant; b. Fargo, N.D., Sept. 25, 1946; s. Marvin Lloyd Strode and Ruth Elaine (Holt) Gabert; m. Cheryl Helen Ford, Sept. 25, 1982; children: Gerald John, Nicholas Daniel. Grad., U. Utah, 1976; DHL (hon.), U. Humanistic Studies, 1986. Cert. physician asst. With USNG, 1966-96; dir. rural outreach program Vets. Adminstrn., Salt Lake City, 1983-88; mem. staff physician assts. Valley Children's Hosp., [illegible] Medicine, Kirkland, Wash., 1994-95; owner Physician Asst. Surg. Svcs., Kirkland, 1995—; chmn. Wash. Gov. Com. on Employment of Handicapped, Olympia, 1976-78; advisor Wash. State Bd. Med. Examiners, Olympia, 1978-82. Decorated Navy Cross. Fellow Am. Acad. Physician Assts. (del.), Wash. Acad. Physician Assts. (pres. 1979, 81), Physician Assts. Orthop. Surgery (pres.-elect 1995); mem. Ducks Unltd. (area and zone chmn. 1988—, Disting. Svc. award 1993). Republican. Lutheran. Avocations: skiing, hunting, fishing, bicycle riding, sailing. Home: 15401 206th Ave NE Woodinville WA 98072-7764 Office: Physician Asst Surg Svcs Kirkland WA 98034

STROEMPLE, RUTH MARY THOMAS, social welfare administrator; b. Cleve., Jan. 31, 1923; d. Daniel William and Jeanette Alexandria (Webb) Thomas; m. Robert Theodore Stroemple, July 27, 1944 (dec. July 1991); children: Susan, George, Janet, Gayle. BA in Child Devel., Marylhurst Coll., 1981. Specialist infant care Oreg. Health Scis. U., Portland, 1976-85, Emanuel Hosp., Portland, 1986-87; mem. failure to thrive rsch. team Doernbecher Hosp., Portland, 1978-85; founder, dir. Newborn Connection, Portland, 1986-90; founder, dir. Med. Foster Parent Program Childrens' Svcs. Divsn., Portland, 1976-94; specialist infant assessment Foster Parent Program, Childrens' Svcs. Divsn., Portland, 1990-94, cons., trainer, 1991-94; team leader sensory stimulation program Infant Dystrophy Ctr., Romania; cons. in field. Author: (booklet) Infant Sensory Stimulation, 1986, (manual) Newborn Connection Hospital, 1986, (tng. manual) Medical Foster Parent Handbook, 1990. Ctr. Child Abuse & Neglect grantee, 1991; recipient Golden Rule award J.C. Penny, Portland, 1993. Mem. Infant Devel. Edn. Assn. (cert. instr.), Infant Massage Assn. (cert. instr.), Foster Parent Assn. Avocations: gardening, reading, hiking, family activities. Home: 12535 SW Tooze Rd Sherwood OR 97140-8442

STROHMEYER, JOHN, writer, former editor; b. Cascade, Wis., June 26, 1924; s. Louis A. and Anna Rose (Saladunas) S.; m. Nancy Jordan, Aug. 20, 1949; children: Mark, John, Sarah. Student, Moravian Coll., 1941-43; A.B., Muhlenberg Coll., 1947; M.A. in Journalism, Columbia, 1948; L.H.D. (hon.), Lehigh U., 1983. With Nazareth Item, 1940-41; night reporter Bethlehem (Pa.) Globe-Times, 1941-43, 45-47; investigative reporter Providence Jour.-Bull., 1949-56; editor Bethlehem Globe-Times, 1956-84, v.p., 1961-84, dir., 1963-84; African-Am. journalism tchr. in Nairobi, Freetown, 1964; Atwood prof. journalism U. Alaska Anchorage, 1987-88, writer-in-residence, 1989—. Author: Crisis in Bethlehem: Big Steel's Struggle to Survive, 1986, Extreme Conditions: Big Oil and The Transformation of Alaska, 1993. Lt. (j.g.) USNR, 1943-45. Pulitzer Traveling fellow, 1948; Nieman fellow, 1952-53; recipient Comenius award Moravian Coll., 1971; Pulitzer prize for editorial writing, 1972; Alicia Patterson Found. fellow, 1984, 85. Mem. Am. Soc. Newspaper Editors, Pa. Soc. Newspaper Editors (pres. 1964-66), Anchorage Racquet Club. Home: 6633 Lunar Dr Anchorage AK 99504-4550

STROLLE, JON MARTIN, language studies educator; b. Gaylord, Mich., Apr. 21, 1940; s. Edward Gustave and Nellie Dorothy (Yuill) S.; children: Carl, Thomas. BA, Oberlin Coll., 1962; MA, U. Wis., 1964, PhD, 1968. Asst. prof. Spanish Ind. U., Bloomington, 1967-74, SUNY Brockport, 1974-76; dean of the Spanish Sch. Middlebury (Vt.) Coll., 1976-80; edn. policy fellow U.S. Dept. Edn., Washington, 1980-81; dean of the coll. Jr. Coll. of Albany, N.Y., 1981-85; dean of lang. studies Monterey (Calif.) Inst. Internat. Studies, 1985-96, assoc. provost, 1996—; cons. NEH, Washington, 1980-85. Contbr. articles to profl. jours. Pres. bd. Monterey Bay Pub. Broadcasting, Monterey, 1989-92; mem. Monterey County Cultural Commn., 1997—. Woodrow Wilson fellow U. Wis., Madison, 1962, Mellon fellow Nat. Fgn. Lang. Ctr., 1994. Mem. Assn. Internat. Edn. Adminstrs. (exec. coun. 1994-96, bd. dirs. joint nat. com. for langs. 1996—), Rotary, Phi Beta Kappa. Office: Monterey Inst Internat Studies 425 Van Buren St Monterey CA 93940-2623

STROLLER, LOUIS A., film producer; b. Bklyn., Apr. 3, 1942; s. Mack and Shirley Stroller; m. Evelyne Bensimhon. BBA, Nichols Coll., 1963. Freelance asst. dir. N.Y.C., 1963-67, freelance prodn. mgr., 1967-77, exec. producer/producer, 1977-90; ind. producer, 1990—. Office: care Lucky L Prodns Inc 4860 Vanalden Ave Tarzana CA 91356-4717

STRONG, JAMES THOMPSON, management, security, human resources consultant; b. Boca Raton, Fla., Oct. 26, 1945; s. Earl William and Mary Joe (Thompson) S.; m. Lenore Jean Stager, Feb. 2, 1974; 1 child, Daria Nicole. BA in Polit. Sci., U. Calif., Riverside, 1973; MS in Strategic Intelligence, Def. Intelligence Coll., Washington, 1982. Factoring specialist. Commd. USAF, 1968, advanced through grades to maj., ret., 1990; faculty Def. Intelligence Coll., Washington, 1982-86; dir. translations USAF, 1986-88, dir. info. svcs., 1988-90; proprietary security mgr. McDonnell-Douglas Technologies, San Diego, 1990-92; owner Employment Svcs. for Bus., San Diego, 1995-97; adj. prof. internat. rels. U.S. Internat. U., 1996—, internat. bus. Palomar Coll., 1997—; factor broker. Author: The Basic Industrial Counter-Espionage Cookbook, 1993, The Government Contractor's OPSEC Cookbook, 1993; co-author: The Military Intelligence Community, 1985; mem. bd. editors Internat. Jour. Intelligence and Counterintelligence, 1986—; contbr. articles to profl. jours. Recipient Disting. EEO award USAF, 1987, Def. Meritorious Svc. medal 1986, Meritorious Svc. medal, 1981, 90, Joint Svc. Commendation medal Def. Intelligence Agy./NATO, 1982, 85. Mem. Nat. Mil. Intelligence Assn. (bd. dirs. 1984—, chpt. pres. 1989, 94), Ops. Security Profls. Soc. (chpt. chair 1993, 94-96), Nat. Cargo Security Coun., San Diego Roundtable (exec. coord. 1994, 95), Assn. Former Intelligence Officers (nat. scholarship adminstr. 1994—), Am. Soc. for Indsl. Security, Air Force Assn., San Diego Soc. for Human Resource Mgmt. Republican. Avocations: bridge, golf, reading. Home and Office: Applicant Background Checks 1142 Miramonte Gln Escondido CA 92026-1724

STRONG, JOHN OLIVER, plastic surgeon, educator; b. Montclair, N.J., Feb. 1, 1930; s. George Joseph and Olivia (LeBrun) S.; m. Helen Louise Vrooman, July 19, 1958 (dec. Mar. 1973); m. Deborah Sperberg, May 20, 1978; children: John Jr., Jean LeB., Andrew D. BS, Yale U., 1952; MD, U. Pa., 1957. Practice medicine specializing in plastic and reconstructive surgery Santa Ana, Calif., 1964-97; asst. clin. prof. plastic and reconstructive surgery U. Calif., Irvine, 1970—; chief of staff Western Med. Ctr., Santa Ana, 1996-97, interim chmn. bd., 1996-97, bd. dirs.; bd. dirs. United Western Med. Ctrs., Orange Health Found. Fellow ACS; mem. Calif. Med. Assn. (chmn. sci. adv. panel 1983-89), Calif. Soc. Plastic Surgeons (pres. 1991-92). Republican. Office: PO Box 94 Borrego Springs CA 92004-0094

STRONG, MAYDA NEL, psychologist, educator; b. Albuquerque, May 6, 1942; d. Floyd Samuel and Wanda Christmas (Martin) Strong; 1 child, Robert Allen Willingham. BA in Speech-Theatre cum laude, Tex. Western Coll., 1963; EdM, U. Tex., Austin, 1972, PhD in Counseling Psychology, 1978; lic. clin. psychologist, Colo., 1984; cert. alcohol counselor III, Colo., 1987, nat. master addiction counselor, 1996; Diplomate Am. Bd. Disability Analysts, Am. Bd. Psycholol. Specialties, Am. Bd. Forensic Examiners. Asst. instr. in ednl. psychology U. Tex., Austin, 1974-78; instr. psychology Austin C.C., 1974-78, Otero Jr. Coll., La Junta, Colo., 1979-89; dir. outpatient and emergency svcs. S.E. Colo. Family Guidance and Mental Health Ctr., Inc., La Junta, 1978-81; pvt. practice psychol. therapy, La Junta, 1981—; exec. dir. Pathfinders Chem. Dependency program, 1985-94, clin. cons., 1994—, chmn. adv. bd., 1995—; clin. psychologist Inst. Forensic Psychiatry, Colo. Mental Health Inst., Pueblo, 1989-94; adj. faculty Adams State Coll., 1992; dir. Revisions Behavior Mgmt. Program, 1996—; dir. Allstrong Enterprises, Inc., 1992-94; Del. to County Dem. Conv., 1988. Appeared in The Good Doctor, 1980, On Golden Pond, 1981, Chase Me Comrade, 1989, Plaza Suite, 1987, Moon Over Buffalo, 1997, OJC Players, 1997; co-dir. The Odd Couple, 1995. Bd. dirs. Picketwire Cmty. Theatre, 1995-98; dir. Brighton Beach Memoirs, Picketwire Cmty. Theatre, 1996. AAUW fellow, 1974-76. Mem. Am. Coll. Forensic Examiners, Bus. and Profl. People (legis. chairperson 1982-83, chmn. news election svc. 1982-88), Colo. Psychol. Assn. (legis. chmn. for dist.), Am. Contract Bridge League. Contbr. articles in field to profl. publs. Author poems in Chinook: Paths through the Puzzle, Decisions, Passion. Home: 24555 County Road 27 La Junta CO 81050-9609 Office: 315 W 3rd St Ste 204 La Junta CO 81050-1408

STRONSTAD, ROGER JONATHAN, college administrator; b. Turner [illegible] (Bendiksen) S.; m. Laurel Marion Smith, July 10, 1971. Diploma in theology, Western Pentecostal Bible Coll., 1971; M in Christian Studies, Regent Coll., 1975. Orained to ministry Pentecostal Assemblies Can., 1975. Minister Pentecostal Assemblies Can., Clinton, B.C., Can., 1971-73; instr. Western Pentecostal Bible Coll., Clayburn, B.C., 1974, assoc. prof., 1985, dean of edn., 1985—; lectr. various colls. Author: Models for Christian Living: A Commentary on First Peter, 1983, The Charismatic Theology of St. Luke, 1984; co-editor (with Lawrence M. Van Kleek): The Holy Spirit in the Scriptures and the Church, 1987; contbr. articles to profl. jours. Mem. Soc. Pentecostal Studies. Office: Western Pentecostal Bible Coll, PO Box 1700, Abbotsford, BC Canada V2S 7E7

STROPE, MICHAEL LEE, protective services official. BS cum laude, Drury Coll., 1975; MS, Cen. Mo. State U., 1978. From police officer to police lt. Mo. Police Dept., Springfield, 1970-84; chief of police City of Stillwater, Okla., 1984-87, City of College Station, Tex., 1987-92, Peoria (Ariz.) Police Dept., 1992—; instr. Ariz. State U., Phoenix, 1996—, Wayland U., Luke AFB, Ariz., 1993—; security-mgmt. cons. SSRS Properties, Inc., College Station, 1992; dept. chmn. criminal justice Blinn Coll., Brenham, Tex., 1992; project assessor Commn. on Accreditation for Law Enforcement Agencies, Inc., 1990; lectr. Okla. Mcpl. League, 1986; adj. faculty Columbia (Mo.) Coll., 1982-84, Drury Coll., Springfield, 1976-82; project dir. Mo. Police Dept., Springfield, 1979-81; adv. bd. chmn. Tex. A&M Engring. Ext. Svc. Police Acad., 1990-92. Contbr. articles to profl. jours. Criminal justice adv. com. Brazos Valley Cmty. Devel. Coun., 1987-92; exec. bd. dirs. Brazos Valley Coun. on Alcohol and Substance Abuse, 1987-91; dep. chmn. Brazos County Emergency Mgmt. Coun., 1987-92. Recipient Mayors award C. of C., 1996, Best of the West award Cmty. Svc., 1994, Cmty. Svc. award SAR, Tex., 1992, Spl. Recognition award Spl. Olympics, Okla., 1986, Outstanding Cmty. Svc. award Delta Tau Delta, 1985; named one of Outstanding Young Men of Am., 1983. Mem. Internat. Assn. Chiefs Police (tng. and edn. com. 1984-92, juvenile justice com. 1995—), FBI Nat. Acad. Assoc., Ariz. Police Chiefs Assn., Rotary. Office: Peoria Police Dept 8343 W Monroe St Peoria AZ 85345-6559

STROTE, JOEL RICHARD, lawyer; b. N.Y.C., Apr. 19, 1939; s. Jack and Fortuna (Benezra) S.; children: Jared, Noah, Sebastian; m. Elisa Ballestas, Dec. 14, 1991. BA, U. Mich., 1960; JD, Northwestern U., 1963. Bar: N.Y. 1964, D.C. 1965, Calif. 1967, U.S. Dist. Ct. (cen. dist.) Calif. 1967, U.S. Supreme Ct. 1971. Assoc. Damman, Blank, Hirsh & Heming, N.Y.C., 1964-65, ICC, Washington, 1965-66, Capitol Records, Hollywood, Calif., 1966-67; ptnr. Strote & Whitehouse, Beverly Hills, Calif., 1967-89; of counsel Selvin, Weiner & Ruben, Beverly Hills, Calif., 1989-94; ptnr. with Cohen, Strote & Young, 1992-94; sole practice law, 1994—; judge pro tem L.A. County Mcpl. Ct., 1973—; probation monitor Calif. State Bar Ct., L.A., 1985—; pres. Liberace Found., Las Vegas, Nev., 1987—; bd. chmn. Tuesday's Child, L.A., 1989-91. Mem. Thousand Oaks Arts Commn., 1997—. Cpl. USMC, 1963-64. Mem. Calif. State Bar Assn., L.A. County Bar Assn., L.A. Copyright Soc., Beverly Hills Bar Assn., Assn. Internat. Entertainment Lawyers, Internat. Fedn. of Festival Orgns. Democrat. Jewish. Avocations: swimming, bicycling, hiking, opera, travel. E-mail: Strote@IBM.net. Office: Joel R Strote Profl Corp 21700 Oxnard St Ste 340 Woodland Hills CA 91367-7560

STROUD, JOHN FRANKLIN, engineering educator, scientist; b. Dallas, June 29, 1922; s. Edward Frank and Ethel A. Stroud; m. Dorcas Elizabeth Stroud, Feb. 4, 1944; children: Kevin, Karen, Richard. BSME, Stanford (Calif.) U., 1949, postgrad., 1949-53; cert. in fin. mgmt. for sr. execs., U. Pa., 1984. Aero. rsch. scientist NASA Ames Rsch. Lab., Moffett Field, Calif., 1949-53; thermodynamics engr. Lockheed, Burbank, Calif., 1953-55, group engr. (mgr.) propulsion, 1955-63, dept. engr. (mgr.) propulsion, 1963-70, from dept. engr. to divsn. engr. (mgr.) propulsion, 1970-83, chief engr. (mgr.) flight scis., 1983-85, divsn. engr. (mgr.), 1985-90, ret., 1990; cons. spl. studies in econs. and engring. sci., 1990—; mem. ad hoc adv. congrl. subcom. on high tech wind tunnels, 1985. Contbr. articles to profl. jours.; author and speaker in field. Charity fund raiser United Way, 1970-80, others. Lt., naval aviator USN, 1942-45, ETO. Decorated Battle of Atlantic. Fellow AIAA (assoc., airbreathing propulsion com. 1966-68, 80-83, chmn. many sessions 1970—); mem. Soc. Automotive Engrs. (aviation div. air transport com., propulsion com., chmn. many sessions nat. confs. 1970—, co-chmn. AIAA/SAE nat. propulsion conf. 1978). Achievements include patent for low drag external compression supersonic inlet; design and development of integrated F-104A inlet and air inductions system, integrated inlet/air induction system into the total propulsion system and airframe; management of team that developed, designed, and integrated the aeropropulsion systems on the L1011 commercial transport; devised new theory for turbulent boundary layers in adverse pressure gradients; numerous other patents pending.

STROUP, ELIZABETH FAYE, librarian; b. Tulsa, Mar. 25, 1939; d. Milton Earl and Lois (Buhl) S. BA in Philosophy, U. Wash., 1962, MLS, 1964. Intern Libr. of Congress, Washington, 1964-65; asst. dir. North Cen. Regional Libr., Wenatchee, Wash., 1966-69; reference specialist Congl. Reference div. Libr. of Congress, Washington, 1970-71, head nat. collections Div. for the Blind and Physically Handicapped, 1971-73, chief Congl. Reference div., 1973-78, dir. gen. reference, 1978-88; city libr., chief exec. officer Seattle Pub. Libr., 1988-96; exec. dir. Wash. Literacy, Seattle, 1996—; cons. U.S. Info. Svc., Indonesia, Feb. 1987. Mem. adv. bd. KCTS 9 Pub. TV, Seattle, 1988—; bd. visitors Sch. Librarianship, U. Wash., 1988—; bd. dirs. Wash. Literacy, 1988—. Mem. ALA (pres. reference and adult svcs. div. 1986-87, div. bd. 1985-88), Wash. Libr. Assn., D.C. Libr. Assn. (bd. dirs. 1975-76), City Club, Ranier Club. Avocations: gardening, mountain climbing, reading. Office: Wash Literacy 220 Nickerson St Seattle WA 98109-1622

STROUP, RICHARD LYNDELL, economics educator, writer; b. Sunnyside, Wash., Jan. 3, 1943; s. Edgar Ivan and Inez Louise (Kellet) S.; m. Sandra Lee Price, Sept. 13, 1962 (div. Sept. 1981); children—Michael, Craig; m. Jane Bartlett Steidemann Shaw, Jan. 1, 1985; 1 child, David. Student, MIT, 1961-62; B.A., M.A., U. Wash., 1966, Ph.D. in Econs., 1970. Asst. prof. econs. Mont. State U., Bozeman, 1969-74; assoc. prof. econs. Mont. State U., 1974-78, prof. econs., 1978—; dir. Office Policy Analysis, Dept. Interior, Washington, 1982-84; vis. assoc. prof. Fla. State U., Tallahassee, 1977-78; sr. assoc. Polit. Economy Research Ctr., Bozeman, 1980—/lectr. summer univ., U. Aix (France), 1985—. Co-author: Natural Resources, 1983, Economics: Private and Public Choice, 8th edit., 1997, Basic Economics, 1993, What Everyone Should Know About Economics and Prosperity, 1993; also articles, 1972—; mem. editorial bd. Regulation, 1993—. Dir. Gallatin Valley Cmty. Sch. Adj. scholar Cato Inst., 1993—. Mem. Am. Econ. Assn., Western Econ. Assn., So. Econ. Assn., Mont Pelerin Soc., Phila. Soc., Pub. Choice Soc., Assn. of Pvt. Enterprise Edn. (dir.). Episcopalian. Home: 9 W Arnold St Bozeman MT 59715-6127 Office: PERC 502 N 19th Ave Ste 211 Bozeman MT 59718-3124

STRUBLE, DONALD EDWARD, mechanical engineer; b. Oakland, Calif., Oct. 10, 1942; s. Donald Edward and Marjorie E. (Griffin) S.; m. Allison Florence Dietrick, Dec. 20, 1964; children: Lisa Kathleen, Donald Lyman, John Dietrick. BS, Calif. Poly., 1964; MS, Stanford U., 1965; PhD, Ga. Inst. Tech., 1972. Asst. prof. Calif. Poly. State U., San Luis Obispo, Calif., 1970-74; sr. v.p. Minicars, Inc., Goleta, Calif., 1974-81; pres. Dynamic Sci., Inc., Phoenix, 1981-83; sr. engring. assoc. Cromack Engring. Assoc., Tempe, Ariz., 1983-85; cons. engr. Donald E. Struble, PhD, Phoenix, 1985-87; sr. engr. Collision Safety Engring., Phoenix, 1987—. Author: Fundamentals of Aerospace Structural Analysis, 1972; contbr. articles to profl. jours. Mem. Soc. Automotive Engrs., Assn. Advancement Automotive Medicine, Sigma Xi. Democrat. Episcopalian. Achievements include patent for Inflatable Restraint for Side Impactcs; research in experimental safety vehicles. Home: 842 Center St San Luis Obispo CA 93405-2314 Office: Collisions Safety Engring 2320 W Peoria Ave Ste B145 Phoenix AZ 85029-4766

STRUHL, STANLEY FREDERICK, real estate developer; b. Bklyn., Oct. 10, 1939; s. Isidore and Yvette (Miller) S.; BS with honors in Engring., UCLA, 1961, MBA in Data Processing, 1963; m. Patricia Joyce Wold, Feb. 26, 1966; children: Marc Howard, Lisa Lynn. Mem. tech. staff Hughes Aircraft Co., Fullerton, Calif., 1963-65; sr. asso. Planning Research Corp., [illegible] Calif., 1970-73; mgr. operations analysis System Devel. Corp., Santa Monica, Calif., 1973-77; gen. partner TST Developers, Canyon Country, Calif., 1977-81; pres. Struhl Enterprises, Inc., Northridge, Calif., 1977-85; owner Struhl Properties, Northridge, 1979—. Mem. planning sub. com. 12th council dist., L.A., 1986-98. Lic. real estate broker, Calif. Mem. San Fernando Valley Bd.

Realtors, Trail Dusters, Tau Beta Pi, Beta Gamma Sigma, Alpha Phi Omega. Home: 7309 Easthaven Ln West Hills CA 91307-1257

STRUTTON, LARRY D., newspaper executive; b. Colorado Springs, Colo., Sept. 12, 1940; s. Merril and Gladys (Sheldon) S.; m. Carolyn Ann Croak, Dec. 3, 1960; children—Gregory L., Kristen. A.A. in Electronics Engring., Emily Griffith Electronics Sch., 1968; B.S. in Bus. Mgmt. and Systems Mgmt., Met. State Coll., 1971; diploma in Advanced Mgmt. Program, Harvard U., 1988. Printer Gazette Telegraph, Colorado Springs, Colo., 1961-64; prodn. dir. Rocky Mountain News, Denver, 1964-80, pres., 1990, pres. and CEO, 1991—; exec. v.p. ops. and advt. Detroit Free Press, 1981-83; v.p. ops. Los Angeles Times, 1983-85, exec. v.p. ops., 1986-90; now pub. Rocky Mountain News, Denver. Mem. adv. com. Rochester Inst. Tech., 1984—. Mem. Am. Newspaper Pubs. Assn. (chmn. 1987, chmn. TEC com. 1985-86), R&E Council (research and engring. council of the Graphic Arts Industry Inc.). Club: Lakeside Golf (Los Angeles). Home: 182 Morgan Pl Castle Rock CO 80104-9061 also: Rocky Mountain News 400 W Colfax Ave Denver CO 80204-2607*

STRUTZEL, J(OD) C(HRISTOPHER), escrow company executive; b. L.A., Sept. 20, 1947; s. James Rudolph and Charlotte Elizabeth (Weiss) S.; m. Christine Melba Kemp, Dec. 28, 1969; children: Jason James, Jess Warren. BS in Bus. Mgmt., Calif. State U., Long Beach, 1970. Bellman Edgewater Hyatt House Hotel, Long Beach, 1970, night auditor, 1970-71; asst. mgr. Sands Resort Hotel, Palm Springs, Calif., 1971-72; gen. mgr. Sands Resort Hotel, Palm Springs, 1972-73; sales coordinator Bendix Home Systems, Santa Fe Springs, Calif., 1973-74; loan rep. J.E. Wells Fin. Co., L.A., 1974-75; v.p. Express Escrow Co., Huntington Beach, Calif., 1976-78; pres., chmn. bd., bd. dirs. Express Escrow Co., Westminster, Calif., 1978—; pres., chmn. bd., bd. dirs. Elsinore (Calif.) Escrow, Inc., 1977-79; bd. dirs. Sorrell Devel., Redondo Beach, Calif.; expert witness on escrow, litigation and cons., 1982—; chmn. liability reduction com. Escrow Agts. Fidelity Corp., 1983-84, legis. chmn., 1985-86, 87-90, 95-97, vice-chmn. bd., 1989-90, 94-95, treas., 1992-93; bd. dirs., sec. Discovery Escrow Co., 1989-94; drafted sections of Calif. Fin. Code, Health and Safety Code, Calif. Adminstrv. Code. Contbr. articles to trade publs. Campaign treas. Californians to Elect Ted Cook, 1982; bd. dirs. publicity chmn. Fountain Valley (Calif.) Youth Baseball, 1986-87; AD HOC com. on Escrow Regulations Dept. Housing and Cmty. Devel., 1980; escrow adv. com. Dept. Corps., 1990-93. Recipient J.E. Wells Meml. award, 1988, Chmn.'s award 1997. Mem. Escrow Agts. Fidelity Corp. (bd. dirs. 1983-90, 91-97), Escrow Inst. of Calif. (bd. dirs. 1991), Calif. Manufactured Housing Assn. (treas., bd. dirs. 1984-86), Calif. Manufactured Housing Inst. (bd. dirs. 1986—, treas. 1986-87, legis. chmn. 1993—, Polit. Action Com. Man of Yr. award 1988, Orange County chpt. Man of Yr. award 1988). Republican. Avocations: golf, war games, athletic coaching. Office: Express Escrow Co 7812 Edinger Ave Ste 300 Huntington Beach CA 92647-3727

STUART, DAVID EDWARD, anthropologist, author, educator; b. Calhoun County, Ala., Jan. 9, 1945; s. Edward George and Avis Elsie (Densmore) S.; B.A. (Wesleyan Merit scholar 1965-66), W.VA. Wesleyan Coll., 1967; M.A. in Anthropology, U. N.Mex., 1970, Ph.D., 1972, postdoctoral student, 1975-76; m. Cynthia K. Morgan, June 14, 1971. Research assoc. Andean Center, Quito, Ecuador, 1970; continuing edn. instr. anthropology U. N.Mex., 1971-72, research archeologist Office Contract Archeology, 1974, research coordinator, 1974-77, asst. prof. anthropology, 1975-77, assoc. prof. anthropology, 1984—, asst. v.p. acad. affairs, 1987-95, assoc. v.p. academic affairs, 1995—; asst. prof. Eckerd Coll., St. Petersburg, Fla., 1972-74; cons. archeologist right-of-way div. Pub. Service Co. N.Mex., Albuquerque, 1977-78; cons. anthropologist Bur. Indian Affairs, Albuquerque, 1978, Historic Preservation Bur. N.Mex., Santa Fe, 1978-81, Nat. Park Service, 1980, Albuquerque Mus., 1981; sr. research assoc. Human Systems Research, Inc., 1981-83, Quivira Research Center, Albuquerque, 1984-86; bd. dirs. Table Ind. Scholars, 1979-83, pres., bd. dirs. Rio Grande Heritage Found., Albuquerque and Las Cruces, 1985-87; advisor Human Systems Research, Inc., Tularosa, N.Mex., 1978-80, Albuquerque Commn. on Hist. Preservation, 1984-86. Grantee Eckerd Coll., 1973, Historic Preservation Bur., 1978-80. Essayist award N.Mex. Humanities Council, 1986. Mem. Am. Anthrop. Assn., Royal Anthrop. Inst. Gt. Britain, N.Mex. Archeol. Council, Albuquerque Archeol. Soc. (pres. 1986-88), Descs. Signers Declaration Independence, Sigma Xi, Phi Kappa Phi. Presbyterian. Co-author: Archeological Survey: 4 Corners to Ambrosia, N.Mex., 1976, A Proposed Project Design for the Timber Management Archeological Surveys, 1978, Ethnoarcheological Investigations of Shepherding in the Pueblo of Laguna, 1983; Author: Prehistoric New Mexico, 1981, 2d edit., 1984, 3d edit., 1988, Glimpses of the Ancient Southwest, 1985, The Magic of Bandelier National Monument, 1989, Power and Efficiency in Eastern Anasazi Architecture, 1994, others; columnist New Mexico's Heritage, 1983-87, Anasazi America, 2000, 1994, others. Editor: Archeological Reports, No. 1, 1975, No. 2, 1981. Office: U NMex Rm 200 Dane Smith Hall Albuquerque NM 87131

STUART, DAVID R., academic administrator. Asst. exec. dir. Faculty Assn. Calif. C.C.s, Sacramento, 1997—. Office: Faculty Assn Calif CC's 926 J St Ste 211 Sacramento CA 95814-2706*

STUART, DOROTHY MAE, artist; b. Fresno, Calif., Jan. 8, 1933; d. Robert Wesley Williams and Maria Theresa (Gad) Tressler; m. Reginald Ross Stuart, May 18, 1952; children: Doris Lynne Stuart Willis, Darlene Mae Stuart Cavalletto, Sue Anne Stuart Peters. Student, Calif. State U., Fresno, 1951-52, Fresno City Coll., 1962-64. Artist, art judge, presenter demonstrations at schs., fairs and art orgns. Calif., 1962—. Editor, art dir. Fresno High School Centennial 1889-1989, 1989; art advisor Portrait of Fresno, 1885-1985; contbg. artist Heritage Fresno, 1975; exhibited in group shows, including M.H. De Young Mus., San Francisco, 1971, Charles and Emma Frye Mus., Seattle, 1971, Calif. State U.-Fresno tour of China, 1974. Mem. adv. com. Calif. State Ken Maddy Ctrl. Calif. Conf. on Women, 1989—, Patrons for Cultural Arts, Fresno, 1987-92, bd. dirs., 1991-92. Recipient 53 art awards, 1966-84; nominated Woman of the Yr., Bus./Profl. of Fresno, 1990. Mem. Soc. Western Artists (bd. dirs. 1968-74, v.p. 1968-70), Fresno Womens Trade Club (bd. dirs. 1986-93, pres. 1988-90), Fresno Art Mus., Fresno Met. Mus., Native Daus. Golden West Fresno. Republican. Avocations: world travel, photography, collecting art and dolls of different cultures. Home and Office: 326 S Linda Ln Fresno CA 93727-5737

STUART, GERARD WILLIAM, JR., investment company executive, city official; b. Yuba City, Calif., July 28, 1939; s. Gerard William and Geneva Bernice (Stuke) S.; student Yuba Jr. Coll., 1957-59, Chico State Coll., 1959-60; A.B., U. Calif., Davis, 1962; M.L.S., U. Calif., Berkeley, 1963; m. Lenore Frances Loroña, 1981. Rare book librarian Cornell U., 1964-68; bibliographer of scholarly collections Huntington Library, San Marino, Calif., 1968-73, head acquisitions librarian, 1973-75; sec.-treas., dir. Ravenstree Corp., 1969-80, pres., chmn. bd., 1980—; pres., chmn. bd. William Penn Ltd., 1981—. Councilman City of Yuma, 1992-96, also dep. mayor, 1995; bd. dirs. Ariz. Humanities Coun., 1993—, Yuma Libr. Found., 1997—, chmn., 1997-98, 99—. Lilly fellow Ind. U., 1963-64. Mem. Bibliog. Soc. Am., Phi Beta Kappa, Alpha Gamma Sigma, Phi Kappa Phi. Clubs: Rolls-Royce Owners; Grolier (N.Y.C.); Zamorano (Los Angeles). Office: 204 S Madison Ave Yuma AZ 85364-1421

STUART, GREGORY M., nonprofit organization administrator; b. Amarillo, Tex., Nov. 18, 1958; s. Robert M. and Joyce E. (Miller) S.; m. Elaine Butcher, Dec. 31, 1988; children: Brooke, David. BS in Acctg., Ariz. State U., 1980; MPA, Calif. Luth. U., 1996. Program dir. Covenant House Calif., L.A., 1987-90; regional dir. Cath. Charities of L.a., 1991—; bd. dirs. Homeless No More, L.A., 1997-98. Recipient commendation County of Los Angeles, 1987, City of L.A., 1985, L.A. Olympic Com., 1984. Mem. L.A. Area C. of C. (bd. dirs. 1988-89), L.A. Jaycees (pres. 1986-88). Methodist. Avocations: leading Stephen Ministry, ultra marathon running, triathlon. Home: 418 Santa Barbara Cir Newbury Park CA 91320-2848

STUART, LAIRD JAMES, minister; b. Omaha, Nebr., Feb. 5, 1943; s. James Beecher and Virginia Simpson (Nevius) S.; m. Virginia Lee Kirkland, Jan 20, 1968; children: Carrie Rebekkah, Brodie Abigail, Rachel Alyssa. BA, Armherst Coll., 1965; MDiv, Princeton Theol. Sem., 1968, D in Ministry, 1981; DD, Waynesburg Coll., Westminster Coll., 1992. Ordained minister Presbyn. Ch. Min. 1st United Presbyn. Ch., Milford, Conn., 1968-72, South Presbyn. Ch., Bergenfield, N.J., 1972-76, First Presbyn. Ch., Grand Haven, Mich., 1976-80, Westminster Presbyn. Ch., Pitts., 1980-93, Calvary Presbyn. Ch., San Francisco, 1993—; moderator Palisades Presbytery, 1975, Pitts. Presbytery, 1986; adj. prof. Pitts. Theol. Seminary, Pa., 1985-93, bd. dirs., 1985-95, pres. bd. dirs., 1993. Bd. dirs. Allegheny Gen. Hosp., Pitts., 1985-93, Waynesburg (Pa.) Coll., 1983-85, A Christian Ministry in the Nat. Parks, 1982—. Charles Hiller Meml. fellow Princeton Theol. Seminary, 1968. Avocations: biking, hiking, sailing, golf, reading. Office: Calvary Presbyn Ch 2515 Fillmore St San Francisco CA 94115-1318

STUART, ROBERT D., electronics executive; b. Spokane, Wash., Dec. 1, 1957; s.John Calvin and Laura Belle (Mitchell) S.; m. Geri van Nus; children: Alasdair, Duncan. BSEE, Wash. State U., 1989. With USN, 1976-83; mfg. engr. Tektronix, Beaverton, Oreg., 1989-91, des. engr., 1991-92; appl. engr. Sharp Electr., Camas, Wash., 1992-95, prod. man., 1995—. Sr. chief USNR, 1984-97, ret. Mem. IEEE, co-chair Infrared Data Assoc. Office: Sharp Electronics 5700 NW Pacific Rim Blvd # Ms20 Camas WA 98607-9489

STUART, SIGNE MARGARET, artist; b. New London, Conn., Dec. 3, 1937; d. Carl Einar and Anna Louise (Gustafson) Nelson; m. Joseph Martin Stuart; 1 child, Lise Nelson Stuart. Student, Yale-Norfolk Art Sch., 1959; BA, U. Conn., 1959; MA, U. N.Mex., 1961. Prof. of art S.D. State U., Brookings, 1970-94; ind. artist Santa Fe, 1994—. One-woman shows included in Sheldon Meml. Art Gallery, Lincoln, 1972, Montgomery Mus. Art, Ala., 1977, Plains Art Mus., Fargo, N.D., 1998, Manitoba, Can., Arts Coun., 1992, 93, juror, S.D. Art Mus., 1995, WESTAF, Santa Fe, 1996; muralist: Landwave, 1977, Dakota Loft, 1985. NEA painting fellow, 1976; artist fellowship S.D. Arts Coun., 1986; artist residency U-Cross Found., 1990, Kans. State U., 1991. Mem. Friends of Contemporary Art.

STUBBLEFIELD, GARY L., retired career officer, consultant; b. Anaconda, Mont., Aug. 26, 1947; s. Glen Travic and Ellen Marie (Mayne) S.; m. Vickie E. Chapin Eld, June 21, 1971 (div. June 1981); m. Karen Suzie Weller, Feb. 21, 1994; children: Yong Hee, Michelle. BS in Botony, U. Idaho, 1969; MA in Internat. Affairs, Naval Postgraduate Sch., 1980. Commd. ensign USN, 1969, advanced through grades to comdr., 1986; stationed at Northern Arabian Gulf, 1988; commodore Special Boad Squadron ONE, San Diego, 1988-89; pres. Applied Marine Tech. Inc., San Diego, 1990-94, Vantage Systems Inc., Hamilton, Mont., 1994—. Author: Killing Zone, 1994, Inside U.S. Navy SEALs, 1995, Modern Day Piracy, 1998. Leader Boy Scouts, Republic of Korea, 1973-75. Decorated Bronze Star with combat V. Mem. Nat. Org. Underwater Instructors. Republican. Avocations: diving, hunting, camping, skiing, trekking. Home: 1027 Cherry Orchard Loop Hamilton MT 59840-9411

STUBBLEFIELD, JAMES IRVIN, emergency medicine physician, health facility administrator; b. Phila., Aug. 17, 1953; s. James Irvin Sr. and Geri (Harvey) S.; m. Linda Marie Simms, Aug. 12, 1978; children: Lindsay, Shannon. BSEE, MS in Bioengring., U. Pa., 1977; MD, Hahnemann U., Phila., 1982. Diplomate Am. Bd. Emergency Medicine, 1991. Mgr. energy engring. Norcross, Inc., Bryn Mawr, Pa., 1977-78; commd. 2d lt. U.S. Army, 1977, advanced through grades to lt. col., 1993; intern in gen. surgery Letterman Army Med. Ctr., San Francisco, 1982-83; flight surgeon, brigade surgeon 101st Airborne Div., Ft. Campbell, Ky., 1983-87; resident in emergency medicine Madigan Army Med. Ctr., Ft. Lewis, Wash., 1987-90; chief dep. emergency medicine and primary care Silas B. Hays Army Hosp., Ft. Ord, Calif., 1990-94; flight surgeon attack helicopter battalion Operation Desert Storm, Persian Gulf, 1991. Decorated Bronze Star, Air medal. Fellow Am. Coll. Emergency Physicians; mem. AMA, U.S. Army Flight Surgeon Soc., Assn. Mil. Surgeons U.S., Tau Beta Pi, Eta Kappa Nu, Alpha Epsilon Delta. Roman Catholic. Avocations: jogging, tennis, table tennis, martial arts, billiards. Home: 18506 Candace Ln Aromas CA 95004-9121

STUBBLEFIELD, JERRY MASON, religious educator, minister; b. Paducah, Ky., May 15, 1936; s. Bobbie and Lorene (Fleming) S.; m. Joanne McCaffrey, June 28, 1957; children: Robert, Mason, Alice. BA, Belmont U., 1957; MA, Vanderbilt U., 1958; BD, So. Bapt. Theol. Sem., 1961, MRE, 1962, PhD, 1967. Ordained to ministry So. Bapt. Conv., 1955. Pastor Victory Bapt. Ch., Shepherdsville, Ky., 1958-65; spl. instr. religious edn. Southeastern Bapt. Sem., Wake Forest, N.C., 1965-66; prof. religion Norman Coll., Norman Park, Ga., 1966-70; min. edn. First Bapt. Ch., Greenville, S.C., 1970-75; dir. ch. community ministry Greenville Bapt. Assn., 1975-77; assoc. prof. religious edn. Golden Gate Bapt. Theol. Sem., Mill Valley, Calif., 1977-83, prof., 1983-88, J.M. Frost Sunday sch. bd. chair Christian edn., 1988—; mem. various acad. coms. Golden Gate Bapt. Theol. Sem., Mill Valley; min. edn. Tiburion (Calif.) Bapt. Ch., 1978-81; trustee Calif. Bapt. Coll., 1984-88. Editor, contbg. author: A Church Ministering to Adults, 1986; contbg. author: Christian Education Handbook, 1981, 96; author: The Effective Minister of Education, 1993; contbr. articles to religious jours. Mem. Western Bapt. Religious Edn. Assn. (pres. 1983-84), So. Bapt. Religious Edn. Assn. (pres. 1988-89), North Am. Profs. Christian Edn. Avocations: golf, running, reading, travel, sports. Office: Golden Gate Bapt Theol Sem Strawberry Pt Mill Valley CA 94941

STUBBLEFIELD, THOMAS MASON, agricultural economist, educator; b. Taxhoma, Okla., Apr. 16, 1922; s. Temple Roscoe and Martha Lacy (Acree) S.; BS, N.Mex. State Coll., 1948; MS, A. and M. Coll. Tex., 1951, PhD, 1956; postgrad. U. Ariz., 1954; m. Martha Lee Miller, Mar. 7, 1943; children: Ellen (Mrs. Richard Damron), Paula (Mrs. James T. Culbertson), Thommye (Mrs. Gary D. Zingsheim). Specialist cotton mktg. N.Mex. State Coll., 1948; extension economist, then asst. agrl. economist U. Ariz., Tucson, 1951-58, from assoc. prof. to prof., 1958-64, prof. and agrl. economist, 1964-83, emeritus prof., 1983—, acting asst. dir. agrl. expt. sta., 1966-68, asst. to dir. sta., 1973-74, chief party Brazil contract, 1968-70. Mem. Pima Council Aging, 1974-77, 80-90; chmn. adv. com. Ret. Sr. Vol. Program, Pima County, 1974-77, 80-90, mem. 1974—. Chmn. bd. Saguaro Home Found., 1980-85. With AUS, 1942-45. Author bulls. in field. Adv. bd. Unified Cmty., 1994—. Home: 810 W Calle Milu Tucson AZ 85706-3925

STUBBS, DANIEL GAIE, labor relations consultant; b. Charleston, S.C., Nov. 13, 1940; s. Daniel Hamer and Esther Virginia (Garlow) S.; m. Sherrill Ann Sloan, July 8, 1984; children: Kimberly, Allison, Don; student U. Fla., 1959-60; BA, W.Va. U., 1965; postgrad. Temple U., 1965-67. Tchr., Sch. Dist. of Phila., 1965-67; rep. Am. Fedn. Tchrs., Washington, 1967; exec. sec. Calif. State Coll. Coun., Am. Fedn. Tchrs., AFL-CIO, L.A., 1967-68; rep. Am. Fedn. Tchrs., AFL-CIO, L.A., 1968-69, dir. orgn. Balt. Tchrs. Union, 1969-70; employee relations specialist Calif. Nurses Assn., L.A., 1971-72; exec. dir. United Nurses Assn. Calif., L.A., 1972-74; labor rels. cons. Social Svcs. Union, Svc. Employees Internat. Union, Local 535, AFL-CIO, L.A., 1974-76; exec. dir. Met. Riverside UniServ Unit, Calif. Tchrs. Assn., 1976-79, exec. dir. San Bernardino/Colton Uniserv Unit, 1979-80; gen. svcs. adminstr. Housing Authority, City of L.A., 1980-82; cons. Blanning & Baker Assocs., Tujunga, Calif., 1983-84; asst. exec. dir. adminstrv. svcs. L.A. Housing Authority, 1984-86; labor rels. cons., L.A., 1986—; lectr. in field. With U.S. Army, 1961-62. Recipient W.Va. U. Waitman Barbe Prize for creative writing, 1965. Mem. So. Calif. Indsl. Rels. Rsch. Assn., Orange County Indsl. Relations Research Assn., Indsl. Rels. Rsch. Assn., UCLA Inst. Indsl. Rels. Assn., Soc. of Profls. in Dispute Resolution, Town Hall Club of Calif. Presbyterian. Home: 3200 Fairesta St Apt 11 La Crescenta CA 91214-2681

STUBBS, STANFORD TODD, multimedia designer; b. Provo, Utah, July 10, 1955; s. W. Stanford and Marilynn (Scharman) S.; m. Joy E. Sargeant, June 23, 1978; children: Sarah, Matt, Amanda, Sam, Abby. BA, Brigham Young U., 1980; MEd, Utah State U., 1989. Tech. editor AIS, Inc., Orem, Utah, 1985-89; ednl. tech. Northeastern Utah Edn. Svcs., Heber City, Utah, 1989-94; project dir. Alpine Sch. Dist., Orem, 1993-94; multimedia designer Brigham Young U., Provo, 1994—. Named one of Top 100 Multimedia Prodrs., AV Video and Multimedia Prodr. Mag., 1998. Mem. Utah Coalition Edn. Tech. (editor 1992-95, pres. 1996-97). Mem. LDS Ch. Avocations: family, music, outdoors. Office: BYU Inst Tech Ctr Bldg B-34 Provo UT 84602

STUDEBAKER, IRVING GLEN, mining engineering consultant; b. Ellensburg, Wash., July 22, 1931; s. Clement Glen and Ruth (Krause) S.; (widowed); children: Ruth, Betty, Raymond, Karl, Donna. BS in Geol. Engring., U. Ariz., 1957, MS in Geology, 1959, PhD in Geol. Engring., 1977. Registered profl. engr., Wash., Nev., Ariz., Colo., Mont. Geophys. engr. Mobil, 1959-61; civil engr. City of Yakima, Wash., 1964-66; instr. Yakima Valley Coll., 1962-67; sr. rsch. geologist Roan Selection Trust, Kalulushi, Zambia, 1967-72; sr. mining engr. Occidental Oil Shale, Grand Junction, Colo., 1974-81; prof. Mont. Coll. Mining Sch., Butte, 1982-96; prof. emeritus, 1996—; cons. in field. Sgt. U.S. Army, 1951-54, Korea. Mem. N.W. Mining Assn., Geol. Soc. Am., Soc. for Mining and Metall. Engring., Soc. Econ. Geologists, Mont. Mining Assn., Sigma Xi (pres. Mont. tech. chpt. 1990-91). Avocations: golf, travel. Home and Office: 165 S 340th St Apt A Federal Way WA 98003-6629

STUDLEY, HELEN ORMSON, artist, poet, writer, designer; b. Elroy, Wis., Sept. 8, 1937; d. Clarence Ormson and Hilda (Johnson) O.; m. William Frank Studley, Aug. 1965 (div.); 1 son, William Harrison. Owner RJK Original Art, Sherman Oaks, Calif., 1979—; designer Aspen Series custom greeting cards and stationery notes, lithographs Love is All Colors, 1982, Flowers for Ruth (Best of Art Show award), Tex. Series original paintings and custom greeting cards. One woman show includes Sherman Oaks, Calif., 1991, Toluca Lake Art Festival, 1991, Art Show for Srs., 1992, Art Show for Youth, 1991; represented in numerous pub. and pvt. collections throughout U.S., Can., Norway, Sweden, Austria, Germany, Eng., France; group exhibits include Art Show for Homeless, L.A., 1990; author poetry Love is Care, Changes, 1988; contbr. poems to publs. Active Luth. Brotherhood, Emmanuel Luth. Ch. Honors include display of lithograph Snow Dreams, Snow Queens, Olympic Games, Lake Placid, N.Y., 1980, lithograph Summer Dreams, Summer Queens, Olympic Games, Los Angeles, 1984, lithograph Go for the Gold, Olympic Games, Atlanta, 1996; named finalist in competition for John Simon Guggenheim fellowship; recipient Golden Poet award World Poetry, 1987-92, Art Show for Youth, 1991, Art Show for Srs., 1992, Art Show at the Park, 1992, Diamond Pin award Carter Hawley Hale, 1991, 92, Outstanding Achievements in Poetry award, 1993, named Woman of the Year, 1993 Am. Biog. Inst., 1993. Mem. Internat. Soc. Poets (publ. in Disting. Poets Am. 1993), Soc. Illustrators, Am. Watercolor Soc., Internat. Soc. Artists, Internat. Platform Assn., Calif. Woman's Art Guild, Sons of Norway Club. Office: RJK Original Art 5020 Hazeltine Ave Sherman Oaks CA 91423-1174

STUFANO, THOMAS JOSEPH, criminologist; b. Newport, R.I., July 23, 1955; s. Thomas and Zoe Anne (Halsey) S.; 1 child, Christine Anne; m. Rene Ellen Goldfarb, Nov. 10, 1994. BSc in Criminal Justice, Pacific Western U., 1988, MBA, 1990; PhD in Criminal Justice, Clayton U., 1992; disting. grad., U.S. Air U., 1992; DSc in Mil. Scis., Eurotechnical Rsch. U., 1997. Legis. rschr. R.I. Ho. of Reps., Providence, R.I., 1978-79; sub com. investigator U.S. Ho. of Reps., Washington, 1979-81; law enforcement staff rschr. State of Fla., 1981-88; intelligence officer U.S. Govt., Washington, 1988—; CEO, dir. Diversified Intelligence Group, Inc., Colorado Springs, Colo., 1995—; exec. dir. Diversified Tech. Inc., Colorado Springs, Colo.; cons. crime commn. State of Fla., 1986-87, U.S. Govt., Washington, 1990-92, State of R.I., 1979-80; mem. Pres.' Commn. on Aviation Security and Terrorism. Author: Human Element in Business, 1992, Combating Terrorism, 1994, Investigators Pretext Investigation Manual, 1998, BEA Training Manual, 1998; Applied Impact Theory patentee, 1998; contbr. articles to profl. jours. Mem. Rep. Senatorial Inner Circle, Washington, 1992—; instr. ARC, Fla., 1994—; mem. adv. bd. Nat. Civil Def., Washington, 1988—; mem. Presdl. Round Table. Recipient Presdl. Commendation Pres. of U.S., 1988, 91, 94, Commendation U.S. Ho. of Reps. and Senate, 1982, 91, 94, commendation Prime Minister Lady Margaret Thatcher, 1991, Citation R.I. Ho. of Reps., 1980, Gov. of Mass., 1980, Tenn., Fla., Ky., 1990, Commendation U.S. Dept. of State, 1992, Min. Intelligence Security, Eng., 1996, Meritorious Achievement award for global antiterrorism, 1997, 20th Century Achievement award ABI, 1998, 500 Leaders of Influence award, 1998. Mem. Air Force Assn., Internat. Narcotic Enforcement Officers Assn., Res. Officers Assn., World Assn. of Investigators, Internat. Assn. Counter Terrorism and Security Profls., Civil Air Patrol (instr. search and recovery pilot), Aircraft Owners and Pilots Assn., Profl. Assn. of Diving Instrs. (instr., Platnuim Diving award 1989), Am. Kempo Karate Assn. (5th degree blackbelt), Order of Ky. Cols. Roman Catholic. Avocations: scuba diving, airplane pilot, parachuting, bicycling, karate.

STUMBLES, JAMES RUBIDGE WASHINGTON, multinational service company executive; b. Harare, Zimbabwe, Aug. 13, 1939; came to U.S., 1980; s. Albert R.W. and Mary Dallas (Atherstone) S.; m. Vyvienne Clare Shaw, Dec. 19, 1964; children: Christopher, Timothy, Jonathan. BA, U. Cape Town, Republic of South Africa, 1960, LLB, 1962. Adv. Supreme Ct. of S. Africa. Mng. dir. Rennies Confirming & Fin. Pty. Ltd., Johannesburg, 1971-72; group mng. dir., chmn. subsidiaries Pritchard Svcs. Group South Africa, Pty., Ltd., Johannesburg, 1972-80; dir. security, pres. subs. Pritchard Svcs. Group Am., Columbus, Ohio, 1980-83; exec. v.p., pres. subs. Mayne Nickless/ Loomis Corp., Seattle, 1984-87; v.p. N.W. Protective Svc. Inc., Seattle, 1987-91, pres., CEO, 1991—; pres., CEO Western Security Svc. Inc., Spokane, 1991—, Northwest Protective Svc. Inc.-Oreg., Portland, 1992—. Sec. Boy Scouts, Johannesburg, 1978-80. Mem. Rand Club, Rainier Club, Rotary, Kiwanis, Round Table (officer 1969-80). Avocations: tennis, boating, fishing. Office: NW Protective Svc Inc 2700 Elliott Ave Seattle WA 98121-1189

STUMP, BOB, congressman; b. Phoenix, Apr. 4, 1927; s. Jesse Patrick and Floy Bethany (Fields) S.; children: Karen, Bob, Bruce. B.S. in Agronomy, Ariz. State U., 1951. Mem. Ariz. Ho. of Reps., 1957-67; mem. Ariz. Senate, 1967-76, pres., 1975-76; mem. 95th-105th Congresses from 3rd Dist.Ariz., 1976—, mem. Nat. Security Com., chmn. vets. affairs com. With USN, 1943-46. Mem. Am. Legion, Ariz. Farm Bur. Republican. Seventh-day Adventist. Office: Ho of Reps 211 Canon Washington DC 20515-0303 also: 230 N 1st Ave Rm 5001 Phoenix AZ 85025-0230*

STUMP, D. MICHAEL, librarian; b. Santa Monica, Calif., Dec. 22, 1947; s. H. Walter and Margaret June (Stetler) S. B.A. in History, Pasadena Coll., 1971; M.L.S., U. So. Calif., 1977. Library asst. Calif. Inst. Tech., Pasadena, Calif., 1970-74; librarian First Baptist Ch. of Van Nuys, Calif., 1974-81, 1982-87, Laurence/2000, Van Nuys, 1981-82; Van Nuys Christian Coll., 1975-76, Hillcrest Christian Sch., Granada Hills, Calif., 1987—. Asst. scoutmaster San Fernando council Boy Scouts Am., 1970-73. Named to Outstanding Young Men Am. U.S. Jaycees, 1976. Mem. ALA, Am. Assn. Sch. Librs., Evang. Ch. Libr. Assn. (So. Calif. chpt.). Republican. Baptist. Office: Hillcrest Christian Sch 19700 Rinaldi St Porter Ranch CA 91326-4100

STUMPF, BERNHARD JOSEF, physicist; b. Neustadt der Weinstrasse, Rhineland, Germany, Sept. 21, 1948; came to U.S., 1981; s. Josef and Katharina (Cervinka) S. Diploma physics, Saarland U., Saarbrucken, West Germany, 1975, Dr.rer.nat., 1981. Rsch. asst. physics dept. Saarland U., Saarbrucken, 1976-81; rsch. assoc. Joint Inst. Lab. Astrophysics, U. Colo., Boulder, 1981-84; instr. physics, physics dept. NYU, N.Y.C., 1984-86, asst. rsch. scientist Atomic Beams Lab., 1984-85, assoc. rsch. scientist Atomic Beams Lab., 1985-86; vis. assoc. prof. physics dept. U. Windsor (Ont., Can.), 1986-88; assoc. prof. physics dept. U. Idaho, Moscow, 1988—; chmn. Conf. on Atomic and Molecular Collisions in Excited States, Moscow, 1990. Contbr. articles to profl. jours. German Sci. Found. postdoctoral fellow U. Colo., 1981-83. Mem. AAUP, German Phys. Soc., Am. Phys. Soc. Home: 825 W C St Moscow ID 83843-2108 Office: U Idaho Dept Physics Moscow ID 83844-0903

STUMPF, PAUL KARL, biochemistry educator emeritus; b. N.Y.C., N.Y., Feb. 23, 1919; s. Karl and Annette (Schreyer) S.; married, June 1947; children: Ann Carol, Kathryn Lee, Margaret Ruth, David Karl, Richard Frederic. AB, Harvard Coll., 1941; PhD, Columbia U., 1945. Instr. pub. health U. Mich., Ann Arbor, 1946-48; faculty U. Calif., Berkeley, 1948-58, prof., 1956-58; prof. U. Calif., Davis, 1958-84, prof. emeritus, 1984—; chief scientist Competitive Rsch. Grants Office USDA, Washington, 1988-91; cons. Palm Oil Rsch. Inst., Kuala Lumpur, Malaysia, 1982-92; mem. sci. adv. bd. Calgene, Inc., Davis, 1990-93; mem. sci. adv. panel Md. Biotech. Inst., 1990-92; Inaugural lectr. Tan Sri Dato'Seri B. Bek-Nielsen Found., Kuala Lumpur, 1996. Co-author: Outlines of Enzyme Chemistry, 1955, Outlines of Biochemistry, 5th edit., 1987; co-editor-in-chief Biochemistry of Plants, 1980; exec. editor Archives of Biochemistry/Biophysics, 1965-88;

contbr. over 250 articles to profl. jours. Mem. planning commn. City of Davis, 1966-68. Guggenheim fellow, 1962, 69, recipient Lipid Chemistry award Am. Oil Chemists Soc., 1974, Sr. Scientist award Alexander von Humboldt Found., 1976, Superior Svc. Group award USDA, 1992, Award of Excellence, Calif. Aggie Alumni Found., 1996. Fellow AAAS; mem. NAS, Royal Danish Acad. Scis., Am. Soc. Plant Physiologists (pres. 1979-80, chmn. bd. trustees 1986-90, Stephen Hales award 1974, Charles Reid Barnes Life Membership award 1992), Yolo Fliers Country Club (Woodland, Calif.). Avocation: golf. Home: 764 Elmwood Dr Davis CA 95616-3517 Office: Univ of Calif Molecular/Cellular Biology Davis CA 95616

STUNTZNER, GAY WURSTER, marketing professional; b. Denver, Colo., July 30, 1937; d. Charles Ivan and Pauline (Browning) Wurster; m. David Cranston Stuntzner, Dec. 24, 1960; children: Mark Cranston, Todd Browning, Brent David. BA, Northwestern U., 1960; postgrad., Queens Coll., 1964-65, U. Iowa, 1975-80, Iowa Wesleyan Coll., 1982-84. Dir. Henry county Arts Coun., Mt. Pleasant, Iowa, 1975-78; mgr. S.E. Iowa Symph. Orch., Mt. Pleasant, 1978-85; campaign asst. Jim Leach Congrl. Campaign, Burlington, Iowa, 1986; dir. devel. Young House Family Svcs., Burlington, 1986-92, Regis H.S., Stayton, Oreg., 1993—. Panel mem. Iowa Arts Coun., Des Moines, 1984-85; assoc. mem. Regis H.S. Found., Stayton, 1993—, Regis H.S. Bd., Stayton, 1993—. Avocations: hiking, canoeing, camping. Home: PO Box 686 1290 SW 1st Ave Mill City OR 97360-2519 Office: Regis HS PO Box 65 550 W Regis St Stayton OR 97383-1151

STUPPI, CRAIG, lawyer; b. San Francisco, Mar. 4, 1946. BA with honors, U. Calif., Santa Barbara, 1968; JD, Stanford U., 1971. Bar: Calif. 1972, U.S. Dist. Ct. (no., ctrl. and ea. dists.) Calif. 1972, U.S. Ct. Appeals (9th cir.) 1972, U.S. Supreme Ct. 1975. Ptnr. Bronson, Bronson & McKinnon LLP, San Francisco, 1992—. Mem. Am. Bankruptcy Inst., State Bar Calif., Bar Assn. San Francisco, Bar Area Bankruptcy Forum. Office: Bronson Bronson & McKinnon LLP 444 S Flower St 24th Fl Los Angeles CA 90071*

STURGEN, WINSTON, photographer, printmaker, artist; b. Harrisburg, Pa., Aug. 27, 1938; s. George Winston and Gladys Erma (Lenker) S.; m. Nancy Kathryn Otto, Jan. 23, 1959 (div. 1981); 1 child, Bruce Eugene Sturgen; m. Jessica Sheldon, Mar. 15, 1988. BS in Forestry, Pa. State U., 1960; postgrad., U. N.H., 1961-62; M of Forestry, Pa. State U., 1964; postgrad., U. Oreg., 1966-68. Cert. profl. photographer. Devel. engr. Weyerhaeuser Co., Longview, Wash., 1964-66; mgr. Wickes Lumber Co., Elkhorn, Wis., 1968-70; dir. ops. Wickes Wanderland, Inc., Delavan, Wis., 1970-72; owner, mgr. Sturgen's Cleaners, Delavan, 1972-80, Images by Sturgen, Delavan, 1980-84; instr. photography continuing edn. dept. Western N.Mex. U., 1988-90; juror numerous orgns., 1982—. One-man shows include Artesia (N.Mex.) Mus. and Art Ctr., 1992, Delavan Art Mus., 1984, Donnell Libr., N.Y.C., 1992; exhibited in group shows at Carlsbad (N.Mex.) Mus., 1992, Sister Kenny Inst., 1992, (3rd Pl.), 93 (1st Pl.), 94, Deming Ctr. for the Arts, N.Mex., 1991, Shellfish Collection, Silver City, N.Mex., 1989, 90, 91, 92, 93, Thompson Gallery, U. N.Mex., 1989, Profl. Photographers Assn. of N.Mex., 1985, 86, 87, 88 (awards), Union Gallery, U. N.Mex., 1987, Gallery Sigala, Taos, N.Mex., 1986, World Trade Ctr., N.Y.C., 1992, 93, 94, Internat. Exposition of Photography, 1983, 84, 85, 87, Beyond Photography Touring Exhibit, 1991-92, An Am. Collection Touring Exhibit, San Francisco, Washington, Brussels, Tokyo, 1993-95, Sapporo (Japan) Internat. Print Biennial, 1993, Very Spl. Arts/N.Mex. Touring Exhibit, 1993-94, Ctr. Contemporary Art, St. Louis, 1994 (purchase award), Internat. Photography Mus., Oklahoma City, 1999, numerous others; donation of all personal work Southwestern Regional Med. Ctr., N.Mex., 1996; pub. poetry, numerous articles in field; work reviewed in various publs. Founder, chmn. Winter Arts Festival, Silver City, N.Mex., 1988-90; com. mem. Taos Fall Arts Festival, 1985; com. chair Oktoberfest, Delavan, 1976-80; donated personal work to Southwestern Regional Med. Ctr., N.Mex., 1996; invitee Renaissance Weekend, Washington, 1997. Residency grant Wurlitzer Found., 1987, 89. Mem. Very Spl. Artists N.Mex., Very Spl. Artists Washington. Avocations: painting, printmaking, photography, disabled artists advocacy.

STURGES, JEFFERY ALAN, composer; b. Baton Rouge, Jan. 4, 1946; s. William Raymond Jr. and Margery Sturges; m. Sherry Lynn Fairbairn, Dec. 30, 1969; children: Allisun, Jeff Jr. (Jay). Student, La. State U., 1964-67, North Tex. State U., 1967-69, U. Nev., Las Vegas, 1969-70. Music dir. tours of Tom Jones, 1971-74, Connie Stevens, 1972-75, Engelbert Humperdinck, 1975-80, 91; composer TV series Legmen, Universal City, Calif., 1983-84, Hawaiian Heat, Universal City, 1984-85, T. J. Hooker, Burbank, Calif., 1984-86, Codename: Foxfire, Universal City, 1985, Simon & Simon, Universal City, 1986-89, Murder, She Wrote, Universal City, 1991-96, Walker, Texas Ranger, 1993. Condr., arranger (album) Barbara Streisand, 1984; co-writer song The Sharing of Love, Murder, She Wrote TV series, 1996. Mem. ASCAP, Am. Fedn. Musicians. Republican. Baptist. Avocation: fishing. Office: 2202 Indian Wells Ct Oxnard CA 93030-7703

STURGES, SHERRY LYNN, recording industry executive; b. Long Beach, Calif., Dec. 11, 1946; d. Howard George and Alice Myrtle Fairbairn; m. Jeffery Alan Sturges, Dec. 30, 1969; children: Allisun Malinda, Jay. Grad. high sch., Las Vegas, Nev. V.p. Soultime, Inc., Las Vegas, 1968-69, Universe, Inc., Las Vegas, 1971-76; co-developer, owner Fun Trax Music Video and Audio Recording Studios, Westwood, Calif., 1986—; creative cons. John Debella Show, 1990, M.T.V., L.A., 1990, KCET-TV, L.A., 1990, KTLA-TV, L.A., 1991. Co-writer song The Sharing of Love for TV series Murder, She Wrote, 1996, feature film The Ride, 1997; song writer (film) The Ride, 1997. Officer PTA, Woodland Hills, Calif., 1977-86, pres., 1984-86; vol. Connie Stevens Charity Orgn., Beverly Hills, Calif., 1980-84; vol. Crossroads Sch. for Arts and Sci., Westwood Meth. presch., West L.A. Bapt. Sch., Northridge United Meth. Ch., St. Vincent's Parents Coun., St. Joseph the Worker Sch., Chatsworth H.S., Sepulveda Nursery Sch., Nat. Neurofibromatosis Found., Life Steps Found., Westwood Village Assn. Recipient Outstanding Contribution award L.A. Unified Sch. Dist. Mem. Am. Soc. Composers, Authors and Pubs. Republican. Avocations: collecting dolls, plates and figurines.

STURGUL, JOHN ROMAN, mining engineering educator; b. Hurley, Wis., Jan. 3, 1940; s. Roman Harold and Isabelle Mary (Astor) S.; m. Alison Jean Miller, Jan. 23, 1965; children: Robert, Sarah. BS in Mining Engring., Mich. Tech. U., 1961; MS in Math., U. Ariz., 1963; PhD in Mining Engring., U. Ill., 1966. Assoc. prof. U. Ariz., Tucson, 1968-76; prof., head dept. N.Mex. Tech. Inst., Socorro, 1976-82; prof. U. South Australia, Adelaide, 1982-90; mng. dir. JRS Cons., Adelaide, 1990-92; prof. U. Idaho, Moscow, 1992—; vis. prof. U. N.S.W., U. Wollongong, Australia. Author: Fortran IV Programming; contbr. over 200 articles to profl. publs. Fulbright-Hays sr. scholar, U. Queensland, 1972; fellow U. Wollongong, 1990. Mem. Soc. Mining Engrs., Soc. for Computer Simulation, Am. Soc. Engring. Edn., Rotary. Avocation: bridge. E-mail: sturgul@uidaho.edu. Office: U Idaho Dept Met and Mining Moscow ID 83844-3024

STURGULEWSKI, ARLISS, state senator; b. Blaine, Wash., Sept. 27, 1927; B.A., U. Wash.; LLD (hon.) U. Alaska, Anchorage, 1993. Mem. Assembly Municipality of Anchorage, interim exec. dir. Alaska Sci. and Tech. Found., 1995; vice chmn. New Capital Site Planning Commn., mem. Capital Site Selection Com.; chmn. Greater Anchorage Area Planning and Zoning Commn.; mem. Alaska State Senate, 1978-93. Rep. nominee Office Gov. Alaska, 1986, 90. Home: 2957 Sheldon Jackson St Anchorage AK 99508-4469 Office: 3301 C St Ste 520 Anchorage AK 99503-3956

STUTT, MARILYN JEAN, publisher; b. St. Croix Falls, Wis., Aug. 25, 1927; d. Myron Lawrence and Margaret Julia (O'Neil) Heebink; student Stout Inst., Menomonie, Wis., 1945-46; divorced; children—Dena Margaret Heston, David Michael Stutt, Scott Patrick Anderson. Musician, arranger, vocalist with all girl orch. Sweethearts of Swing, 1947-53; music dir., disc jockey sta. KNIT, Abilene, Tex., 1958-59; writer sta. KRBC-TV, Abilene, also sta. KOAT-TV, Albuquerque, 1959-61; writer, editor U.S. Civil Service, Sandia Base, N.Mex., 1962-63; advt. dir. Roger Cox & Assocs. Enterprises, Albuquerque, 1974-77; owner Marilyn Stutt Advt. Agy., Albuquerque, also pres. Marilyn Stutt Enterprises, Inc., Albuquerque, 1977—; founder, pub. Albuquerque Singles Scene mag., 1979-84; pres. Singles Scene, Inc.; founder, pub. Sr. Scene Mag., 1987-89, nat. licensing network, 1981-85; founder, v.p. Unicorn Publs., Inc., 1984—; founder, pub. On the Scene Mag., 1985—. Mem. Mag. Pubs. Assn., N.Mex. Advt. Fedn., Albuquerque Women in Bus. Republican. Club: N.Mex. Press. Office: 3507 Wyoming Blvd NE Albuquerque NM 87111-4427

STYLES, BEVERLY, entertainer; b. Richmond, Va., June 6, 1923; d. John Harry Kenealy and Juanita Russell (Robins) Carpenter; m. Wilbur Cox, Mar. 14, 1942 (div.); m. Robert Marascia, Oct. 5, 1951 (div. Apr. 1964). Studies with Ike Carpenter, Hollywood, Calif., 1965—; student, Am. Nat. Theatre Acad., 1968-69; studies with Paula Raymond, Hollywood, 1969-70; diploma, Masterplan Inst., Anaheim, Calif., 1970. Freelance performer, musician, 1947-81; owner Beverly Styles Music, Joshua Tree, Calif., 1971—; v.p. spl. programs Lawrence Program of Calif., Yucca Valley, Calif.; talent coord., co-founder Quiet Place Studio, Yucca Valley, 1994; mem. exec. bd., awards dir. Am. chpt. Diogenes Process Group, 1996—. Composer, lyricist: (songs) Joshua Tree, 1975, Wow, Wow, Wow, 1986, World of Dreams, 1996, Thank You God, 1996, (music for songs) I'm Thankful, 1978, The Whispering, 1994; piano arrangements include Colour Chords and Moods, 1995, Desert Nocturne, 1996; records include The Perpetual Styles of Beverly, 1978; albums include The Primitive Styles of Beverly, 1977; author: A Special Plan to Think Upon, The Truth as Seen by a Composer, 1978, A Special Prayer to Think Upon, 1983. Mem. ASCAP (Gold Pin award), Profl. Musicians Local 47 (life), Internat. Platform Assn. Republican. Avocation: creating abstract art. Office: PO Box 615 Joshua Tree CA 92252-0615

SUBA, ERIC JOHN, physician; b. Columbia, Mo., Feb. 16, 1959; s. Antonio Ronquillo and Sylvia Marie (Karl) S. AB, Princeton U., 1980; MD, Washington U., 1984. Diplomate Am. Bd. Pathology. Resident U. Colo., Denver, 1984-88; fellow Washington U., St. Louis, 1988-90; physician The Permanente Med. Group, Redwood City, Calif., 1990—; dir. Friendship Bridge Pathology Tchg. Project, Evergreen, Colo., 1993-96; exec. dir. The Viet/Am. Cervical Cancer Prevention Project, San Francisco, 1996—. Fellow Internat. Acad. Pathology. Democrat. Roman Catholic. Office: Kaiser Permanente 1150 Veterans Blvd Redwood City CA 94063-2087

SUBACH, JAMES ALAN, information systems company executive, consultant; b. Lawrence, Mass., Mar. 24, 1948; s. Anthony John and Bernice Ruth (Pekarski) S. m. Marilyn Butler, Feb. 16, 1980. BS with distinction, U. Maine, 1970; MS, U. Ariz., 1975, PhD, 1979. Vis. scientist NASA Johnson Space Ctr., Houston, 1977-79; rsch. assoc. Baylor Coll. Medicine, Houston, 1977-79; pres. Subach Ventures, Inc., San Antonio, 1980-84, JAS & Assocs., Inc., Phoenix, 1984—, C.I.O. Inc., 1987-90; v.p. PTIMS, Inc., Phoenix, 1992-96; faculty assoc. Ariz. State U., Tempe, 1992-93; v.p. Multipoint Tax Systems, Scottsdale, Ariz., 1996-97; chief info. officer Multipoint Nat. Property Tax Info., Scottsdale, 1997—; co-founder Bridge Alliance LLC, Phoenix, 1998. Assoc. editor Jour. Applied Photog. Engring., 1973-78; author software Gen. Acctg. System, 1987; bus. computing columnist, 1987. Pres. Forest Trails Homeowners Assn., Phoenix, 1987-88. Mem. SPIE, Phoenix C. of C. (Pres.'s Roundtable, electronic comms. com.), Toastmasters (treas. Phoenix chpt. 1984), Ariz. Progress Users Group (pres. 1997), Tau Beta Pi, Sigma Pi Sigma. Republican. Avocations: publis speaking, cross-country skiing, photography, golf. Office: JAS & Assoc Inc 11326 N 7th St #4-276 Phoenix AZ 85022

SUBER, ROBIN HALL, former medical and surgical nurse; b. Bethlehem, Pa., Mar. 14, 1952; d. Arthur Albert and Sarah Virginia (Smith) Hall; m. David A. Suber, July 28, 1979; 1 child, Benjamin A. BSN, Ohio State U., 1974. RN, Ariz., Ohio. Formerly staff nurse Desert Samaritan Hosp., Mesa, Ariz. Lt. USN, 1974-80. Mem. ANA, Sigma Theta Tau.

SUBLETT, SCOTT W., screenwriting and film history educator, playwright; b. East Chicago, Ind., July 30, 1958; s. Albert Winfield and Rosetta M. Sublett. BS in Radio, TV, Film, Northwestern U., 1977; MFA in Screenwriting, UCLA, 1993. Film critic, feature writer The Washington Times, 1982-89; screenwriter L.A., 1989-96; tchr. screenwriting and film history San Jose (Calif.) State U., 1996—. Author, lyricist (musical comedy) Die, Die Diana, 1998.

SUBRAMANIAN, GOWRI, business executive, web technologies consultant; b. Kumbakonam, India, Aug. 20, 1969; came to U.S., 1991; s. Hariharan and Lakshmi Subramanian. B in Engring., Pondicherry Engring. Coll., India, 1991; MS, Tex. A&M U., 1993. Prodn. planning supr. Benchmark Electronics, Beaverton, Oreg., 1994-95; materials mgr. LMC West, Wilsonville, Oreg., 1995, ops. mgr., 1996-97; founder, CEO Aspire Systems, Wilsonville, 1997—, chmn., 1997—. Contbr. articles to profl. jours. Mem. Tau Beta Pi, Alpha Pi Mu. Avocations: flying, movies. Office: Aspire Systems 28550 SW Ashland Dr Apt 64 Wilsonville OR 97070-7764

SUBRAMANIAN, SUNDARAM, electronics engineer; b. Emaneswaram, Madras, India, July 9, 1934; came to U.S., 1968; s. Sundaram and Velammal (Subbiah) S.; m. Hemavathy Vadivelu, Feb. 18, 1968; children: Anand Kumar, Malathy. BE, Madras (India) U., 1959; PhD, Glasgow (Scotland) U., 1967; MBA, Roosevelt U., Chgo., 1977. Research engr. Zenith, Inc., Chgo., 1968-75; project engr. Motorola, Inc., Chgo., 1975-77; prof. Chapman Coll., Orange, Calif., 1977-78; cons. MCS, Orange, 1978-80; project engr. Endevco, San Juan Capistrano, Calif., 1980-84; project mgr. Unisys Corp., Mission Viejo, Calif., 1984—; bd. dirs. P.S.B. Inc., Torrance, Calif., 1984-93. Patentee in field. Bd. dirs. Tamil Nadu Found. Inc., Balt. and Washington, 1976-79; pres. S. India Cultural Assn., Villa Park, Calif., 1977-78. Mem. IEEE, Inst. Environ. Sci. (sr.). Avocations: internat. travelling, Vedantic research. Office: Unisys Corp 25725 Jeronimo Rd Mission Viejo CA 92691-2792

SUBRAMANYA, SHIVA, aerospace systems engineer; b. Hole-Narasipur, India, Apr. 8, 1933; s. S.T. Srikantaiah and S. Gundamma; m. Lee. S. Silva, Mar. 3, 1967; children: Paul Kailas, Kevin Shankar. BSc, Mysore U., Bangalore, India, 1956; MSc, Karnatak U., Dharwar, India, 1962; postgrad., Clark U., 1963; MBA, Calif. State U., Dominguez Hills, 1973; D in Bus. Adminstrn., PhD in Bus. Adminstrn., Nova Southeastern U., 1986. Sr. scientific officer AEC, Bombay, India, 1961-63; chief engr. TEI, Newport, R.I., 1964-67; prin. engr. Gen. Dynamics Corp., San Diego, 1967-73; asst. project mgr. def. and systems group TRW, Colorado Springs, Colo., 1973-87; asst. project mgr. space and def. group TRW, Redondo Beach, Calif., 1987-98; cons. aerospace industry Cerritos, Calif., 1998—; cons. Contbr. over 150 articles to profl. jours. V.p. VHP of Am., Berlin, Conn., 1984-88; pres. IPF of Am., Redondo Beach, 1981-88; appointed by Pres. of India to Atomic Energy Commn., India. Winner of dozens of awards and commendations from U.S. Dept. of Defense and the Aerospace Industry. Mem. Armed Forces Comm. and Electronics Assn. (v.p.-elect Rocky Mountain chpt. 1986—, Meritorious Svc. award 1985, Merit medal 1990), Am. Acad. Mgmt. Hindu. Avocation: social service. Home and Office: 12546 Inglenook Ln Cerritos CA 90703-7837

SUBRAMUNIYA, MASTER (SATGURU SIVAYA SUBRAMUNIYASWAMI), spiritual leader, publisher; b. Oakland, Calif., Jan. 5, 1927. Founder, head Saiva Siddhanta Ch., Kapaa, Hawaii, 1949—, Saiva Siddhanta Yoga Order, Kapaa, Hawaii, 1949—; head Kailasa Parampara, India, Sri Lanka; founder, pres. Himalayan Acad., Kapaa, Hawaii, 1957—; Hindu rep. Global Forum Spiritual Parliamentary Leaders Human Survival, Oxford, Moscow, Rio de Janiero, 1988, 90, 92; mem. Pres. assembly Parliament of World Religions, Chgo., 1993—. Author: Dancing with Siva, Hinduism's Contemporary Catechism, 1993, Loving Ganesha, 1996, Lemurian Scrolls, Angelic Prophecies Revealing Human Origins, 1998, Living with Siva Hinduisms Contemporary Culture; publisher Hinduism Today Mag., 1979—. Spiritual head Vision Kauai 2020, Hawaii, 1996-98. Recipient Jagadacharya award Parliament of World Religions, New Delhi, India, 1986. Hindu Heritage Endowment (founder, trustee 1995—). Fax: (808) 822-4351. Home and Office: Saiva Siddhanta Church 107 Kaholalele Rd Kapaa HI 96746-9304

SUCHENEK, MAREK ANDRZEJ, computer science educator; b. Warsaw, Poland, May 2, 1949; came to U.S., 1986; s. Tadeusz Aleksander and Barbara Krystyna (Zych) S.; m. Ewa Aleksandra Czerny, July 30, 1974 (div. 1991). MSc in Math. Engring., Warsaw Tech. U., 1973, PhD in Tech. Scis. with distinction, 1979. Instr. Warsaw Tech. U., 1973-79, asst. prof., 1979-88; assoc. Nat. Inst. for Aviation Rsch., Wichita, 1987-90; vis. asst. prof. Wichita (Kans.) State U., 1986 88, assoc. prof., 1988-89, assoc. prof., chair, 1989-90; prof. Calif. State U.-Dominguez Hills, Carson, 1990—, co-chair, 1996-97, chair, 1997-98; adj. prof. Pepperdine U., Malibu, Calif., 1999; mem. organizing com. Internat. Symposium on Methodologies for Intelligent Sys., 1989-90; program com. Ann. Ulam Math. Conf., 1990-91, Internat. Conf. on Computing and Info., 1992—; referee NSF, 1990-92, Annals of Math. and Artificial Intelligence, 1992-93, Jour. Logic Programming, 1992-94; presenter in field. Author: (with Jan Bielecki) ANS FORTRAN, 1980, (with Jan Bielecki) FORTRAN for Advanced Programmers, 1981, 2nd edit., 1983, 3rd edit., 1988 (Minister of Sci. Higher Edn. and Techs. prize 1982); reviewer Zentralblatt fur Mathematik, 1980-89, Math. Revs., 1989-91, Jour. Symbolic Logic, 1998—; mem. editl. bd. Ulam Quar., 1990—; contbr. articles to profl. jours. Rsch. grantee Polish Govt., 1974-76, 85-86, FAA, 1988-90, NASA, 1997. Mem. AAUP, The Assn. for Logic Programming, Computer Soc. IEEE, Assn. Symbolic Logic, Sigma Xi. Avocations: cats, collectibles, swimming, target shooting. Home: 830 N Juanita Ave Unit 4 Redondo Beach CA 90277-2270 Office: Calif State Univ Dominguez Hills 1000 E Victoria St Carson CA 90747-0001

SUDALNIK, JAMES EDWARD, educator, director, producer, writer; b. Chgo., Jan. 13, 1951. BS in Radio-TV Comm., U. Ill., 1972; MA in Pub. Visual Comm., So. Ill. U., 1977, PhD in Ednl. Media, 1986. Pres. Likeness Photographics, Chgo., 1968-71, Ravenswood Prodns., Chgo. and L.A., 1971—; cameraman Maj. Photo Co., Chgo., 1971-72; freelance photographer, designer Hinsdale, Ill., 1971-72; photographer Quality Photographics, Naperville, Ill., 1972; instr., producer, dir. Triton Coll., River Grove, Ill., 1972-76; freelance dir. Chgo. and L.A., 1976-78; supr. research Shawnee Nat. Forest Wilderness Evaluation Project/So. Ill. U., Carbondale, Ill., 1978-79; prof., coord. instnl. TV, Calif. State U. Dominguez Hills, Carson, 1980—, prof., 1990—; TV dir. Nat. Inst. on Alcoholism and Alcohol Abuse, Carbondale, 1977, producer U.S. Dept. Edn.-Compton (Calif.) Unified Sch. Dist., 1981; judge Internat. Exhbn. of Photography, L.A. County, 1983, Superfest Film and Video Festival, Los Angeles, 1986, Acad. Motion Picture Arts & Scis. Nicholl Fellowships in Screenwriting Competition, 1989; chmn. Comm. Dept. Calif. State U., Carson, 1998. Author: An Historical Survey of the Development of Cable TV, 1986, High-Definition Television: An Annotated Bibliography, 1994, Wilderness Preservation on the Shawnee National Forest, Wildeness: Preserving the American Heritage; contbg. author: A Resource Manual for Science Teachers in Southern Illinois; producer, dir. writer over 400 films, videos and commls.; contbr. articles to profl. jours. Recipient Excellence award Soc. for Tech. Communications, 1980, proudcer's finalist award Nat. Fedn. Local Cable Programmers, 1986, Telly award for promotional video, 1991, Golden Poet award World of Poetry Assn., 1987, Silver Poet award, 1990, Communicator award Distinction, 1995. Mem. Soc. Motion Picture and TV Engrs., Nat. Acad. TV Arts and Scis., Internat. Documentary Assn., Ind. Film Project West, Am. Film Inst., AAUP, Internat. Alliance Theatrical and Stage Employees, Sigma Chi Phi (v.p. local chpt. 1969). Avocations: music, travel, poetry, writing, reading. Office: Calif State U Dominguez Hills 1000 E Victoria St Carson CA 90747-0001

SUDDOCK, FRANCES SUTER THORSON, grief educator, writer; b. Estelline, S.D., Oct. 23, 1914; d. William Henry and Anna Mary (Oakland) Suter; m. Carl Edwin Thorson, July 6, 1941 (dec. Apr. 1976); children: Sarah Thorson Little, Mary Frances Thorson; m. Edwin Matthew Suddock, Aug. 7, 1982 (dec. Sept. 1986). BA, Iowa State Tchrs. Coll., 1936; postgrad., Syracuse U., 1940-41, U. Iowa, 1946; MA, Antioch U., San Francisco, 1981. Cert. tchr. Tchr. various high schs., Correctionville and Eagle Grove, Iowa, 1936-38, 38-40, 41-43, 45-47; chief clk. War Price and Rationing Bd., Eagle Grove, 1943-45; instr. (part time) Eagle Grove Jr. Coll., 1953-61; adminstr. Eagle Grove Pub. Library, 1961-77; facilitator Will Schutz Assocs., Muir Beach, Calif., 1987-88. Author: Whither the Widow, 1981. Vol. Nat. Trainer Widowed Persons Svc. Am. Assn. Retired Persons, 1989—, ret. sr. vol. program, Anchorage, 1988—; pres., bd. dirs. Anchorage Widowed Persons Svc., 1992-94; bd. dirs. North Iowa Mental Health Ctr., Mason City, 1959-76, Eagle Grove Cmty. Chest, 1960, Help Line, Inc., Ft. Dodge, Iowa, 1976-77; chmn. Cmty. Mental Health Fund, Eagle Grove, 1966-73; charter pres. Eagle Grove Concerned, Inc., 1973-77; active various civic orgns. Mem. AAUW (charter pres. Eagle Grove br. 1973-75), Am. Soc. on Aging, Alaska Assn. Gerontology (treas. 1992-94), Anchorage Woman's Club, P.E.O., Kappa Delta Pi. Home: 333 M St Apt 404 Anchorage AK 99501-1902

SUE, ALAN KWAI KEONG, dentist; b. Honolulu, Apr. 26, 1946; s. Henry Tin Yee and Chiyoko (Ohata) S.; m. Ginger Kazue Fukushima, Mar. 19, 1972; 1 child, Dawn Marie. BS in Chemistry with honors, U. Hawaii, 1968; BS, U. Calif., San Francisco, 1972, DDS, 1972. Film editor, photographer Sta. KHVH-TV ABC, Honolulu, 1964-71; staff dentist Strong-Carter Dental Clinic, Honolulu, 1972-73; dentist Waianae Dental Clinic, Honolulu, 1972-73; pvt. practice Pearl City, Hawaii, 1973—; chief exec. officer Dental Image Specialists, Pearl City, 1975—; dental dir. Hawaii Dental Health Plan, Honolulu, 1987—; dental cons. Calif. Dental Health Plan, Tustin, 1987—, Pacific Group Med. Assn., The Queen's Health Care Plan, Honolulu, 1993—; dental cons. Pacific Group Med. Assn., 1994—; cons. Hawaii Mgmt. Alliance Assn., 1996—; bd. dirs. Kula Bay Tropical Clothing Co., Hawaiian Ind. Dental Alliance; mem. exec. bd. St. Francis Hosp., Honolulu, 1976-78, chief dept. dentistry, 1976-78; mem. expert med. panel Am. Internat. Claim Svc., 1995—. Mem. adv. bd. Health Svcs. for Sr. Citizens, 1976—; mem. West Honolulu Sub-Area Health Planning Coun., 1981-84; mem. dental task force Hawaii Statewide Health Coordinating Coun., 1980, mem. plan devel. com., 1981-84; vol. oral cancer screening program Am. Cancer Soc.; v.p. Pearl City Shopping Ctr. Merchants Assn., 1975-84, 92-93, pres., 1994—. Regents' scholar U. Calif., San Francisco, 1968-72. Fellow Pierre Fauchard Acad., Acad. Gen. Dentistry; mem. ADA, Acad. Implants and Transplants, Am. Acad. Implant Dentistry, Hawaii Dental Assn. (trustee 1978-80), Honolulu County Dental Soc. (pres. 1982), Am. Acad. and Bd. Head, Facial, Neck Pain and TMJ Orthopedics, Intertel, Internat. Platform Assn., Mensa, Porsche Club, Pantera Owners Club, Mercedes Benz Club. Democrat. Avocations: cars, tennis, photography, gardening. Office: Dental Image Specialists 850 Kam Hwy Ste 116 Pearl City HI 96782-2691

SUE, MICHAEL ALVIN, physician; b. L.A., Apr. 15, 1956. MD, U. Chgo., 1980. Diplomate Am. Bd. Internal Medicine, Am. Bd. Allergy and Immunology. Intern, resident and fellow West Los Angeles VA Med. Ctr., L.A., 1980-86; allergist Kaiser Permanente, Panorama City, Calif., 1986—. Fellow Am. Coll. Allergy, Asthma, and Immunology; mem. Am. Acad. Allergy, Asthma, and Immunology. Office: Kaiser Permanente 13652 Cantara St Panorama City CA 91402-5497

SUGARMAN, KARLENE A, writer. MA, JFK U., 1993; BA, St. Mary's Coll., 1991; MA, JFK U., 1993. Intership supr. JFK U., San Francisco, 1995-98; pvt. practice Karlene Sugarman, MA, San Mateo, Calif., 1991—; sports psychology cons. U. San Francisco, 1994—; tchr. cons. Serra High School, San Mateo, Calif., 1996—, Mercy High School, Burlingame, Calif., 1996—; cons. Charles Schwab, San Francisco, 1997—. Author: Winning the Mental Way, 1998, contbr. articles to FastPitch World, 1996—, others. Mem. Assn. for the Advancement of Sports Psychology, U.S. Tennis Assn, No. Calif., (Sports Sci. Com.). Avocations: tennis, golf. Home: 490 Mariners Isl Blvd #319 San Mateo CA 94404

SUGIHARA, GEORGE, banker, oceanography educator; b. Tokyo; s. Shigeyoshi and Antonia (Vermeer) S.; m. Joan Dale Hall, Mar. 12, 1974; children: Emily, Peter, Nicholas. BS, U. Mich., 1972; MS, Princeton U., 1980, PhD, 1982. Wigner prize fellow Oak Ridge (Tenn.) Nat. Lab., 1982-85; prof. Scripps Inst. Oceanography, LaJolla, Calif., 1986—; John Dove Isaacs chair Scripps Inst. Oceanography, LaJolla, 1990; mng. dir. Deutsche Bank, San Diego, 1996—; vis. scholar Cornell U., Ithaca, N.Y., 1984, Imperial Coll. London/Wilwood Park, 1991-95, Japan Soc. Promotion of Sci., Tokyo, 1985-86; cons. Merrill Lynch, N.Y.C., 1989-90, Merrill Lynch Asia Pacific, Hong Kong, 1994-95, Deutsche Bank, Tokyo, 1995-96. Author: Fractals: A User's Guide, 1995. Organizer Pauma Creek Coalition, San Diego, 1995. Japan Soc. Promotion Sci. sr. rsch. fellow, Tokyo, 1986. Mem. Sierra Club, Nature Conservancy, Trout Unltd., Am. Rivers. Avocations: fly fishing, hunting, music. Home: 2505 Via Pisa Del Mar CA 92014-3815 Office: Deutsche Bank 402 W Broadway Ste 2050 San Diego CA 92101-8510

SUGIKI, SHIGEMI, ophthalmologist, educator; b. Wailuku, Hawaii, May 12, 1936; s. Sentaro and Kameno (Matoba) S.; m. Bernice T. Murakami, Dec. 28, 1958; children: Kevin S., Boyd R. *Shigemi Sugiki's son, Kevin, earned a D.D.S. and practices general dentistry in Honolulu and his other son, Boyd, earned a BFA and a MFA and is a glass artist in Seattle.* AB, Washington U., St. Louis, 1957; MD, Washington U., 1961. Intern St. Luke's Hosp., St. Louis, 1961-62; resident ophthalmology Washington U., St. Louis, 1962-65; chmn. dept. ophthalmology Straub Clinic, Honolulu, 1965-70, Queens Med. Ctr., Honolulu, 1970-73, 80-83, 88-90, 93—; clin. prof. ophthalmology Sch. Medicine U. Hawaii, 1997. Maj. M.C., AUS, 1968-70. Decorated Hawaiian NG Commendation medal, 1968. Fellow ACS; mem. Am., Hawaii med. assns., Honolulu County Med. Soc., Am. Acad. Ophthalmology, Contact Lens Assn. Opthalmologists, Pacific Coast Oto-Ophthal. Soc., Pan-Pacific Surg. Assn., Am. Soc. Cataract and Refractive Surgery, Am. Glaucoma Soc., Internat. Assn. Ocular Surgeons, Am. Soc. Contemporary Ophthalmology, Washington U. Eye Alumni Assn., Hawaii Ophthal. Soc., Rsch. To Prevent Blindness. Home: 2398 Aina Lani Pl Honolulu HI 96822-2024 Office: 1380 Lusitana St Ste 714 Honolulu HI 96813-2443

SUINN, RICHARD MICHAEL, psychologist; b. Honolulu, May 8, 1933; s. Maurice and Edith (Wong) S.; m. Grace D. Toy, July 26, 1958; children: Susan, Randall, Staci, Bradley. Student, U. Hawaii, 1951-53; B.A. summa cum laude, Ohio State U., 1955; MA in Clin. Psychology, Stanford U., 1957, PhD in Clin. Psychology, 1959. Lic. psychologist, Colo.; diplomate Am. Bd. Profl. Psychology (trustee 1996—). Counselor Stanford (Calif.) U., 1958-59, rsch. assoc. Med. Sch., 1964-66; asst. prof. psychology Whitman Coll., Walla Walla, Wash., 1959-64; assoc. prof. U. Hawaii, Honolulu, 1966-68; prof. Colo. State U., Ft. Collins, 1968—, head dept. psychology, 1972-93; cons. in field; psychologist U.S. Ski Teams, 1976, Olympic Games, U.S. Women's Track and Field, 1980 Olympic Games, U.S. Ski Jumping Team, 1988, U.S. Shooting Team, 1994; mem. sports psychology adv. com. U.S. Olympic Com., 1983-89; reviewer NIMH, 1977-80, 94-98. Author: The Predictive Validity of Projective Measures, 1969, Fundamentals of Behavior Pathology, 1970, The Innovative Psychological Therapies, 1975, The Innovative Medical-Psychiatric Therapies, 1976, Psychology in Sport: Methods and Applications, 1980, Fundamentals of Abnormal Psychology, 1984, 88, Seven Steps to Peak Performance, 1986, Anxiety Management Training, 1990; editorial bd.: Jour. Cons. and Clin. Psychology, 1973-86, Jour. Counseling Psychology, 1974-91, Behavior Therapy, 1977-80, Behavior Modification, 1977-78, Jour. Behavioral Medicine, 1978-83, Behavior Counseling Quar., 1979-83, Jour. Sports Psychology, 1980-91, Clin. Psychology: Science and Practice, 1994-97, Professional Psychology, 1994-97; author: tests Math. Anxiety Rating Scale, Suinn Test Anxiety Behavior Scale, Suinn-Lew Asian Self-identity Acculturation Scale. Mem. City Council, Ft. Collins, 1975-79, mayor, 1978-79; mem. Gov.'s Mental Health Adv. Council, 1983, Colo. Bd. Psychologist Examiners, 1983-86. Recipient cert. merit U.S. Ski Team, 1976, APA Career Contbn. to Edn. award, 1995; NIMH grantee, 1963-64; Office Edn. grantee, 1970-71. Fellow APA (chmn. bd. ethnic minority affairs 1982-83, chmn. edn. and tng. bd. 1986-87, policy and planning bd. 1987-89, publs. bd. 1993-97, bd. dirs. 1990-93, pres.-elect 1998), Behavior Therapy and Rsch. Soc. (charter); mem. Assn. for Advancement Psychology (trustee 1983-86), Assn. for Advancement Behavior Therapy (sec.-treas. 1986-89, pres. 1992-93), Asian Am. Psychol. Assn. (bd. dirs. 1983-88), Am. Bd. Behavior Therapy (bd. dirs. 1987—), Phi Beta Kappa, Sigma Xi. Home: 808 Cheyenne Dr Fort Collins CO 80525-1560 Office: Colo State U Dept Psychology Fort Collins CO 80523

SUISSA, DAVID, advertising executive. Exec. creative dir., chmn. bd. Suissa Miller Advt., L.A. Office: Suissa Miller Advt 11601 Wilshire Blvd Fl 16 Los Angeles CA 90025-1770*

SUITER, BROOKE JOHNSON, private school educator; b. Winston-Salem, N.C., July 22, 1946; d. John Griffith and Elizabeth Oliver (Clabaugh) Johnson; m. Harold Guthrie Suiter Jr., June 3, 1967; children: Katherine, Elizabeth, Tom. AB, Conn. Coll., 1968; MAT, Yale U., 1969. Tchr. Dept. Corrections, Montville, Conn., 1969-71, Bronx C.C., N.Y.C., 1971, Univ. City (Mo.) Schs., 1971-74, Forest Park C.C., St. Louis, 1973-76; chair bd. dirs. La Jolla (Calif.) United Meth. Ch. and Nursery Schs., 1981-85; dir. Christian edn. St. James Episcopal Ch., La Jolla, Calif., 1988-90; tchr. The Bishop's Sch., La Jolla, Calif., 1990—. Fellow Nat. Writing Project, 1994. Mem. Nat. Coun. Tchrs. English, Phi Beta Kappa. Democrat. Episcopalian. Avocations: reading, gardening. Home: 6315 Via Maria La Jolla CA 92037-6543 Office: The Bishops Sch 7607 La Jolla Blvd La Jolla CA 92037-4703

SUITER, THOMAS, advertising executive. Chief creative dir. CKS Partners, Cupertino, Calif. Office: 10443 Bandley Dr Cupertino CA 95014-1912*

SUKENICK, RONALD, author, English educator; b. Bklyn., July 14, 1932; m. Julia B. Frey. BA, Cornell U., 1955; PhD, Brandeis U., 1962. Prof. English U. Colo., Boulder, 1974—; dir. FC2/Black Ice Books, Normal, Ill., 1985—. Author: 98.6, 1996, Doggy Bag, 1995, Out, 1997, Mosaic Man, 1999; co-pub. Am. Book Rev., 1975—; pub. Black Ice mag., 1987. Office: U Colo Boulder Dept English, CB226 Boulder CO 80309

SUKO, LONNY RAY, judge; b. Spokane, Wash., Oct. 12, 1943; s. Ray R. and Leila B. (Snyder) S.; m. Marcia A. Michaelsen, Aug. 26, 1967; children: Jolynn R., David M. BA, Wash. State U., 1965; JD, U. Idaho, 1968. Bar: Wash. 1968, U.S. Dist. Ct. (ea. dist.) Wash. 1969, U.S. Dist. Ct. (we. dist.) Wash. 1978, U.S. Ct. Appeals (9th cir.) 1978. Law clk. U.S. Dist. Ct. Ea. Dist. Wash., 1968-69; assoc. Lyon, Beaulaurier & Aaron, Yakima, Wash., 1969-72; ptnr. Lyon, Beaulaurier, Weigand, Suko & Gustafson, Yakima, 1972-91, Lyon, Weigand, Suko & Gustafson, P.S., 1991-95; U.S. magistrate judge, Yakima, 1971-91, 95—. Mem. Phi Beta Kappa, Phi Kappa Phi. Office: PO Box 2726 Yakima WA 98907-2726

SUKOV, RICHARD JOEL, radiologist; b. Mpls., Nov. 13, 1944; s. Marvin and Annette Sukov; Susan Judith Grossman, Aug. 11, 1968; children: Stacy Faye, Jessica Erin. BA, BS, U. Minn., 1967, MD, 1970; student, U. Calif.-Berkeley, 1962-64. Diplomate Am. Bd. Radiology; lic. physician Minn., Calif. Intern pediatrics U. Minn., Mpls., 1970-71; resident radiology UCLA Ctr. for Health Sci., 1973-76; fellow in ultrasound and computed tomography UCLA, 1976-77; staff radiologist Centinela Hosp. Med. Ctr., Inglewood, Calif., 1977-85; staff radiologist Daniel Freeman Meml. Hosp., Inglewood, Calif., 1977—, dir. radiology, 1988-90; med. dir. dept. radiology Daniel Freeman Meml. Hosp., 1998—; asst. clin. prof. radiology UCLA Ctr. for Health Scis., 1977-83; adv. bd. Aerobics and Fitness Assn. Am., 1983—. Contbr. articles to profl. jours. Vol. Venice Family Clinic, 1985—. Lt. comdr. USPHS, 1970-72. U. Minn. fellow, 1964-65, 66, 70. Mem. Soc. Radiologists in Ultrasound (charter), Minn. Med. Alumni Assn., L.A. County Med. Assn., Calif. Med. Assn. Radiol. Soc. N.Am., L.A. Radiol. Soc. (continuing edn. com. 1990—, mgmt. com. 1996—, chmn., sec. 1997-98, treas. 1998—), L.A. Ultrasound Soc., Am. Coll. Radiology. Avocations: bicycling, skiing. Office: Inglewood Radiology 323 N Prairie Ave Ste 160 Inglewood CA 90301-4503

SULICH, VASSILI, artistic director; b. Island of Brac, Yugoslavia, Dec. 29, 1929; came to U.S., 1964; s. Thomas and Vjekoslava (Orlandini) Sulic. From co. mem. to Dancer Etoile various dancing cos., Paris, 1952-64; prin. dancer Broadway prodn. Follies Bergere, N.Y.C., 1964; prin. dancer, ballet master Las Vegas prodn. Follies Bergere, 1964-72; ind. choreographer Europe and U.S., 1964—; founder, artistic dir. Nev. Dance Theatre, Las Vegas, 1972-97, cons., advisor, 1997-98. Choreographer: Suite Lyrique, Oedipe roi, Idomeneo with Luciano Pavarotti; creator, choreographer numerous dance works including Mantodea, Walls in the Horizon, Cinderella; prin. dancer: La Dryade, L'Echelle, Combat, Cyrano de Bergerac, Lovers of Teruel; performer (TV show) Geraldine starring Geraldine Chaplin. Named Outstanding Individual Artist Gov. of Nev., 1981, Disting. Nevadan U. Nev. Bd. Regents, 1987. Office: Nev Theater Ballet 1555 E Flamingo Rd Las Vegas NV 89119-5258*

SULLIVAN, BARBARA JEAN, artist; b. Indpls., Jan. 7, 1935; d. Charles Arthur and Melida Mae Minnick; m. Charles Ray Poindexter, Dec. 31, 1990; children: Joseph Ruggless, Pamela Ruggless-Consoli, Diana Ruggless-Larsen, Milo Ballan.Z. Fine artist, 1978—. Author (paperback cover illustrations): The Horsemen, 1991, Winter Rage, 1992; one-woman show Artists' Gallery, Las Vegas, 1984; group shows: U.S. Federal Building Exhibition, Las Vegas, 1982, George Phippen Memorial Invitational Western Art Show, Prescott, Ariz., 1984, Burk Gallery, Boulder City, Nev., 1983, 7th Annual Western Art Show and Sale, Burk Gallery, 1983, 6th Annual Kalispell Art Show and Auction, Kalispell, Mont., 1983, 16th Annual C.M. Russell Auction of Original Western Art (silver medal), Great Falls, Mont., 1983, guest artist, Women Artists of American West, Pa-Jo's Gallery, Pinedale, WY, 1986, C.M. Russell Mus. Artist Invitational Exhibit, 1986, 8th Annual Western Art Show and Sale, Burk Gallery, 1987, Far Western Art Assn. Show, Caesars Palace, Las Vegas, 1987, Braithwaite Fine Arts Gallery, Cedar City, Utah, 1999; represented in permanent collections: Nevada National Bank, Virgin River Hotel and Casino., White House, Wash. D.C. Bd. dirs. Charles Arthur Minnick Sunset Meml. Park Found., Las Vegas, Nev., 1992-95; adv. bd. Las Vegas, 1992-95. Recipient First Place, Jaycee State Fair, 1976, 77, 5 awards Painting of Month Las Vegas Art Mus., 1978, Popular Award, San Gabriel Fine Arts Assn. Invitational, 1978, Reserve Grand Championship, Las Vegas State Fair, 1981, First Palce Oils Caliente Profl. Inivtational, 1982, Award of Excellence Am. Mothers State Competition, 1982, 83, honored by Mont. Gov. Ted Schwinden and C.M. Russell Auction of Original Western Art for Quick Draw, Best of Show award Las Vegas Art Mus., 1994, Judges Choice award, 1995. Mem. Las Vegas Art Mus., 1977—, juried mem. Am . Inst. Fine Art, 1984. Avocations: traveling, photography, horseback riding, subject research, visiting art galleries. Office: PO Box 81056 Las Vegas NV 89180-1056

SULLIVAN, CHARLES, university dean, educator, author; b. Boston, May 27, 1933; s. Charles Thomas and Marion Veronica (Donahue) S.; divorced; children: Charles Fulford, John Driscoll, Catherine Page; m. Shirley Ross Davis, Sept. 6, 1997. BA in English, Swarthmore Coll., 1955; MA, NYU, 1968, PhD in Social Psychology, 1973; MPA, Pa. State U., 1978. Predoctoral fellow NYU, 1964-68; postdoctoral fellow Ednl. Testing Svc., Princeton, N.J., 1973-74; asst. prof. psychology Ursinus Coll., Collegeville, Pa., 1973-78; mgmt. cons., 1978-86; adj. prof. Pa. State U., Radnor, Pa., 1978-80; prof., head dept. pub. adminstrn., dir. student svcs. Southeastern U., Washington, 1986-89; asst. dean Grad. Sch. Arts and Scis. Georgetown U., Washington, 1989-92, assoc. dean Grad. Sch. Arts and Scis., 1992-97, professorial lectr., dept. psychology, 1994-95; exec. dir. Doylestown Found., Doylestown, Pa., 1958-73; assoc. dean, prof. Coll. Profl. Studies U. San Francisco, 1997-98; adj. prof. social and behavioral scis. U. Md., 1984-96; lectr., spkr. on lit. and art Cooper-Hewitt Mus., N.Y.C., Nat. Soc. Arts and Letters, Washington, Martin Luther King Jr. Libr., Washington, Met. Mus. Art, N.Y.C., Smithsonian Instn., Washington, Children's Book Fair, N.Y.C., Nat. Mus. Women in Arts, Lombardi Cancer Rsch. Ctr., Georgetown U., Arts Club of Washington, Phillips Collection, Corcoran Gallery of Art, U. San Francisco Multicultural Lit. Program, Nat. Mus. Am. History, others. Author: Alphabet Animals, 1991, The Lover in Winter, 1991, Numbers at Play, 1992, Circus, 1992, Cowboys, 1993, A Woman of A Certain Age, 1994. Out of Love, 1996, American Folk, 1998; editor: America in Poetry, 1988, 2d edit., 1992, 3d edit., 1996, Imaginary Gardens, 1989, Ireland in Poetry, 1990, Children of Promise, 1991, Loving, 1992, American Beauties, 1993, Here Is My Kingdom, 1994, Fathers and Children, 1995, Imaginary Animals, 1996. Mem. bd. trustees Folger Poetry Bd., 1988-92; Nat. Soc. Arts and Letters, 1992-94, Am. Acad. Liberal Edn., 1995—; pres. Am. Found. Arts, 1995—. Mem. Am. Poetry Soc., Acad. Am. Poets, Cosmos Club, Commonwealth Club of Calif., The Family. Addres: 2121 Massachusets Ave NW Washington DC 20008

SULLIVAN, DANIEL MERCER, broadcast executive; b. Casa Grande, Ariz., June 13, 1940; s. Daniel Joseph and Margaret (Mercer) S.; m. Fredricka Schweizer, 1962 (div. 1967); 1 child, Daniel Mercer II; m. Delta M. Furse, Dec. 31, 1988. Student, Ariz. State U., 1958-62. Prodn. supr. UCLA TV Div., Los Angeles, 1965-69; nat. product mgr. Concord Electronics, Los Angeles, 1969-71; ops. mgr. Calif. Inst. of Arts, Valencia, 1971-75; lectr., media ctr. dir. U. Calif., San Diego, 1975-83; mgr. electronic news gathering Sta. KCBS-TV, Hollywood, Calif., 1983-87; mgr. video tape ops. CBS-TV City, Hollywood, 1987—. Dir. profl. automobile racing emergency services Formula One Grand Prix. Served as staff sgt. USAF, 1962-67. Recipient Award of Merit Internat. TV Assn., 1982. Mem. Acad. TV Arts & Scis., Soc. Motion Picture and TV Engrs. Republican. Roman Catholic. Clubs: Sportscar Club of Am., Calif. Sportscar (regional exec. 1983) (Los Angeles). Office: CBS-TV City 7800 Beverly Blvd Los Angeles CA 90036-2188

SULLIVAN, DEBRA KAE, elementary education educator; b. Iowa City, Iowa, Jan. 27, 1962; d. Raymond Francis and Jo Adele (Meyers) S. Cert. specialization in mgmt. devel., Am. Hotel & Motel Assn., 1985; BA, U. Iowa, 1989. Nev. tchg. lic. grades K-8. Reservations mgr. Holiday Inn, Iowa City, 1981-83; reservations clk. Holiday Inn Mart Plaza, Chgo., 1983-85; substitute tchr. grades K-12 Iowa City Sch. Dist., 1989-90; tchr. K-8 Clark County Sch. Dist., Las Vegas, Nev., 1990—; tchr. cons. Geog. Alliance in Nev., Las Vegas, 1994—; mem. geography curriculum task force Clark County Sch. Dist., Las Vegas, 1995; mem. geography task force State of Nev., Reno, 1996, mem. social studies task force, 1996; mem. Advanced Geography Inst., Geog. Alliance in Nev., Moscow, Russia, 1996, summer geography workshop Nat. Geographic Soc., Washington, 1998; chairperson 2d ann. GeoFest '96, Las Vegas. Host family Home Away From Home Program, U. Nev., Las Vegas, 1994-97. Mem. NEA, Nat. Coun. Social Studies, Nat. Coun. for Geog. Edn., People to People Internat., Social Studies Coun. Nev. (Elem. Sch. Social Studies Tchr. of the Yr. 1995-96). Avocations: reading, walking, collecting geography related objects, current events, cats. Home: 5709 Berwick Falls Ln Las Vegas NV 89129-5157 Office: Quannah McCall Elem Sch 800 E Carey Ave North Las Vegas NV 89030-5557

SULLIVAN, G. CRAIG, household products executive; b. 1940. BS, Boston Coll., 1964. With Procter & Gamble Co., 1964-69, Am. Express Co., 1969-70; regional sales mgr. Clorox Co., Oakland, Calif., 1971-76, v.p. mktg., 1976-78, mgr. food svc. sales devel., mgr. bus. devel., 1978-79, gen. mgr. food svc. products divsn., 1979-81, v.p. food svc. products divsn., 1981, v.p. household products, 1981-89, group v.p. household products, 1989-92, chmn. bd., pres., CEO, 1992—. Office: The Clorox Co PO Box 24305 Oakland CA 94623-1305

SULLIVAN, GEORGE ANERSON, orthodontist; b. Bon Aqua, Tenn.; s. Joe Marble and Ruby Christine (Luther) S.; m. Edie M. Timmons, May 11, 1957; children: Scott Patrick, Shawn Michael. AS, Henry Ford Community Coll., Dearborn, Mich., 1957; student, Eastern Mich. U., 1958-59; DDS, U. Mich., 1963, MS, 1966. Diplomate Am. Bd. Diplomates. Pvt. practice specializing in orthodontics Phoenix, 1966—; pres. Ammons Meml. Dental Clinic, Phoenix, 1979-80. Chmn. Phoenix Meml. Hosp., 1977-80. Served with USNR, 1955-63. Mem. Am. Assn. Orthodontics, Cen. Ariz. Dental Soc., Ariz. State Dental Assn., ADA, Ariz. Orthodontic Soc., Pacific Coast Soc. Orthodontics, Optimist Club (pres. Phoenix chpt. 1967-68), Lions (pres. 1972-73), Elks. Republican. Avocations: motorhome travel, fishing. Office: 4805 W Thomas Rd Ste D Phoenix AZ 85031-4005 also: 10752 N 89th Pl Ste 111 Scottsdale AZ 85260-6731

SULLIVAN, JAMES KIRK, retired forest products company executive; b. Greenwood, S.C., Aug. 25, 1935; s. Daniel Jones and Addie (Brown) S.; m. Elizabeth Miller, June 18, 1960; children: Hal N., Kim J. BS in Chemistry, Clemson U., 1957, MS, 1964, PhD, 1966; postgrad. program for sr. execs., MIT, 1975; DSc (hon.), U. Idaho, 1990. Prodn. supr. FMC Corp., South Charleston, W.Va., 1957-62; tech. supt. FMC Corp., Pocatello, Idaho, 1966-69; mktg. mgr. FMC Corp., N.Y.C., 1969-70; v.p. govtl. and environ. affairs Boise (Idaho) Cascade Corp., 1971-98; exec. com., chmn. trust and investment com., dist. bd. dirs. Key Bank of Idaho, 1983—; bd. dirs., chmn. audit com. Key Trust Co. of the West; chmn. adv. bd. U. Idaho Coll. Engring., 1966-70, 80-87, centennial campaign, 1987-89, rsch. found., 1980-82; mem. Accreditation Bd. Engring. and Tech., Inc., 1994—; bd. dirs. Pub. Employees Retirement Sys. of Idaho, St. Al's Hosp. Contbr. articles to profl. jours.; patentee in field. Mem. Coll. of Forest and Recreation Resources com. Clemson U., Idaho Found. for Pvt. Enterprise and Econ. Edn., Idaho Rsch. Found., Inc., Idaho Task Force on Higher Edn.; bd. dirs. Idaho Found. for Excellence in Higher Edn., Exptl. Program to Stimulate Competitive Rsch. NSF, N.W. Nazarene Coll., 1988-90, Boise Philharm., 1996—, mem. Len B. Jordan Pub Affairs Symposium; trustee Idaho Children's Emergency Fund, 1984—; trustee Bishop Kelly H.S., 1987-89, St. Als Reg. Med. Ctr.; chmn. Bishop Kelly Found., 1972-79, 85-89; chmn. adv. bd. U. Idaho Coll. Engring., Am. Forest and Paper Assn., Govtl. Affairs Com., Environ. Com., Options Adv. Group; bd. dirs. Boise Master Chorale, 1995—; bd. dirs. Silver Sage coun. Boy Scouts Am. 1st lt. U.S. Army, 1958-59. Recipient Presdl. Citation U. Idaho, 1990. Mem. AIChE, Am. Chem. Soc., Bus. Week Found. (chmn. Bus. Week 1980), Am. Forest and Paper Assn. (environ. and health coun., product and tech. com., solid waste task force), Bus. Roundtable (environ. com.), Idaho Assn. Commerce and Industry (past chmn. bd. dirs.), C. of C. of U.S. (pub. affairs com.). Republican. Home: 5206 Sorrento Cir Boise ID 83704-2347 Office: Boise Cascade Corp 1111 W Jefferson St PO Box 50 Boise ID 83728-0050

SULLIVAN, JAMES N., fuel company executive; b. San Francisco, 1937. Student, U. Notre Dame, 1959. Formerly v.p. Chevron Corp., until 1988, now vice chmn., dir., 1988—. Office: Chevron Corp 575 Market St San Francisco CA 94105-2856

SULLIVAN, MARTIN EDWARD, museum director; b. Troy, N.Y., Feb. 9, 1944; s. John Francis and Helen Edna (Lynch) S.; m. Katherine Mary Hostetter, May 9, 1981; children: Abigail, Bethany. BA in History, Siena Coll., 1965; MA in History, U. Notre Dame, 1970, PhD in History, 1974. Exec. dir. Ind. Commn. for Humanities, Indpls., 1972-75; dir. pub. programs NEH, Washington, 1976-81; pres. Inst. on Man and Sci., Rensselaerville, N.Y., 1981-83; dir. N.Y. State Mus., State Edn. Dept., Albany, N.Y., 1983-90, The Heard Mus., Phoenix, 1990—; trustee Am. Indian Ritual Object Repatriation Found., N.Y.C., 1992-98; chmn. U.S. Govt. Cultural Property Adv. Com., 1995—. Author: Museums, Adults and the Humanities, 1981, Inventing the Southwest: The Fred Harvey Company and Native American Art, 1996; contbr. articles to profl. jours. Trustee Phoenix Cmty. Alliance, 1991—, Am. Fedn. Arts, 1994-98; mem. Native Am. Repatriation Act Adv. Com., 1992—; chmn. Ariz. St. Libr. Adv. Coun., 1998—. With U.S. Army, 1966-68. Mem. Am. Assn. Mus. (v.p. 1990-93, mem. accreditation commn. 1997—). Democrat. Home: 4601 E Solano Dr Phoenix AZ 85018-1280 Office: The Heard Mus 22 E Monte Vista Rd Phoenix AZ 85004-1433

SULLIVAN, MICHAEL EVAN, investment and management company executive; b. Phila., Dec. 30, 1940; s. Albert and Ruth (Liebert) S.; BS, N.Mex. State U., 1966, MA (Ednl. Research Tng. Program fellow), 1967; BS, U. Tex., 1969; MBA, U. Houston, 1974; MS, U. So. Calif., 1976, MPA, 1977, PhD in Adminstrn., 1983; BS in Acctg., U. La Verne, 1981. Sr. adminstrv. and tech. analyst Houston Lighting & Power Co., 1969-74; electronics engr. U.S. Govt., Point Mugu, Calif., 1974-77; mem. tech. staff Hughes Aircraft Co., El Segundo, Calif., 1977-78; staff program adminstr. Ventura div. Northrop Corp., Newbury Park, Calif., 1978-79; div. head engring. div. Navastrogru, Point Mugu, 1979-82; br. head, div. head spl. programs head operational systems integraton office Pacific Missile Test Ctr., Calif., 1983-90, head tech. devel. office, head capability devel., 1993—; CNO, Dir. Rsch., Devel., and Acquisition in the Pentagon, Washington, 1987-88, dir. rsch. devel. test and evaluation and tech. in the Pentagon, 1990-93; pres., chmn. bd. Diversified Mgmt. Systems, Inc., Camarillo, Calif., 1978—. Author: The Management of Research, Development, Test and Evaluation Organizations; Organizational Behavior Characteristics of Supervisors-Public versus Private Sectors, Organizational Behavior Characteristics of Supervisors, Public versus Private Sectors; Self-Actualization in RDT & E Organizations; Self-Actualization in a Health Care Agency; others. V.p., bd. dirs. Ventura County Master Chorale and Opera Assn; bd. dirs. So. Calif. Assn. of Pub. Adminstrn. (also mem. fin. com., programs com., student aid com., exec. bd., exec. com. fed. lab. consortium). Served with U.S. Army, 1958-62. Ednl. Rsch. Info. Clearing House fellow, 1965-67. Mem. IEEE, Am. Math. Soc., Math. Assn. Am., Am. Statis. Assn., IEEE Engring. Mgmt. Soc., Am. Soc. Pub. Adminstrn., So. Calif. Assn. Pub. Adminstrn. (bd. dirs., various coms.), Assn. Fed. Tech. Transfer Execs., Fed. Mgrs. Assn., Am. Assn. Individual Investors, Mcpl. Mgmt. Assts. So. Calif., Fed. Lab. Consortium Exec. Coun. (head FLC far west region), Acad. Polit. Sci., Internat. Soc. for the Systems Scis., Assn. MBA Execs., Tech. Transfer Soc., Internat. Fedn. for Systems Rsch., Phi Kappa Phi, Pi Gamma Mu. Home: PO Box 273 Port Hueneme CA 93044-0273 Office: PO Box 447 Camarillo CA 93011-0447

SULLIVAN, ROBERT SCOTT, architect; b. Alexandria, La., Sept. 8, 1955; s. Robert Wallace and Harriette Henri (Fedric) S. BA cum laude, Tulane U., 1979, BArch, 1979. Registered architect, N.Y., Calif., La.; cert. Nat. Coun. of Archtl. Registrations Bds. Staff architect Cavitt, McKnight, Weymouth, Inc., Houston, 1979-81, Hardy, Holzman, Pfeiffer Assocs., N.Y.C., 1981-83; ptnr. Sullivan, Briggs Assocs., N.Y.C., 1983-86; cons. Butler, Rogers, Baskett, N.Y.C., 1985-86; prin. R. Scott Sullivan AIA, Berkeley, Calif., 1986-89; ptnr. Talbott Sullivan Archs., Albany, Calif., 1989-94, Scott Sullivan, Arch., Berkeley, 1994—; cons. Neometry Graphics, N.Y.C., 1983-86, dir, 1986—; bd. dirs. Middleton/Sullivan Inc., Alexandria, 1981—. Vestry St. Mark's Episc. Ch., Berkeley, 1988-89, 97—; bd. dirs. The Parsonage, Episcopal Diocese Calif., 1992-94; cons. Commn. Accessibility, Episcopal Diocese Calif., 1991-93, 95-96. Mem. AIA, Calif. Council Architects, Archtl. League N.Y.C., Nat. Trust for Hist. Preservation, Royal Archtl. Inst. of Can. (assoc.), Tau Sigma Delta. Democrat. Episcopalian.

SULLIVAN, STUART FRANCIS, anesthesiologist, educator; b. Buffalo, July 15, 1928; s. Charles S. and Kathryn (Duggan) S.; m. Dorothy Elizabeth Faytol, Apr. 18, 1959; children: John, Irene, Paul, Kathryn. BS, Canisius Coll., 1950; MD, SUNY, Syracuse, 1955. Diplomate Am. Bd. Anesthesiology. Intern Ohio State Univ. Hosp., Columbus, 1955-56; resident Columbia Presbyn. Med. Ctr., 1958-60; instr. anesthesiology Columbia U. Coll. Physicians and Surgeons, N.Y.C., 1961-62, assoc., 1962-64, asst. prof., 1964-69, assoc. prof., 1969-73; prof. dept. anesthesiology UCLA, 1973-91, vice chair anesthesiology, 1974-77, exec. vice chair, 1977-90, acting chmn., 1983-84, 87-88, 90-91, prof. emeritus, 1991—. Capt. M.C., USAR, 1956-58. Fellow NIH, 1960-61; recipient research career devel. award NIH, 1966-69. Mem. Assn. Univ. Anesthetists, Am. Physiol. Soc., Am. Soc. Anesthesiologists. Home: 101 Foxtail Dr Santa Monica CA 90402-2047 Office: UCLA Sch Medicine Dept Anesthesiology Los Angeles CA 90024

SULLIVAN, THOMAS JAMES, retired manufacturing company executive; b. Franklin, N.H., Mar. 26, 1923; s. James J. and Helen (Mullin) S.; m. Anne Clark, Aug. 31, 1963. A.B., Holy Cross Coll., 1947; J.D., Harvard U., 1949. With Gen. Dynamics Corp., 1949-61, asst. div. mgr., 1959-61; sr. assoc. Harbridge House, Cambridge, Mass., 1961-63; with Hydraulic Research & Mfg. Co., Valencia, Calif., 1963-71; v.p. Hydraulic Research & Mfg. Co., 1964-68, exec. v.p., 1968-69, pres., 1969-71; v.p. Textron, Inc., Providence, 1971-73; pres. Walker/Parkersburg (W. Va.) Co., 1973-81, Sprague Meter, Bridgeport, Conn., 1981-84, Dimetrics Inc., Diamond Springs, Calif., 1984-86. Served with USAAF, 1943-46. Fellow Nat. Contract Mgmt. Assn. Home: 2186 Augusta Ct San Luis Obispo CA 93401-4500

SULLIVAN, W. KIM, theatrical producer, actress; b. Balt.; d. William Edward and J. Fae Sullivan. AOS, Am. Acad. Dramatic Art; BA in English Lit., Susquehanna U. Former creative devel. specialist Dorothea G. Petrie Prodns., L.A. Theatre prodr. various prodns., including Faithful, Wallem and Tolan Do the Coast, Survival of the Heart. Mem. AFTRA, SAG, Women in Film, Actors Equity,. Avocation: music.

SULLIVAN-BOYLE, KATHLEEN MARIE, association executive; b. Tulsa, Feb. 9, 1958; d. Thomas Anthony and Jeanne Lee (Agnew) Sullivan; m. Thomas C. Boyle. BS in Polit. Sci., Ariz. State U., 1980; MA in Govt., Coll. William and Mary, 1982. Sec. Ariz. Rep. Party, Phoenix, 1980-81; rsch. asst. Pete Dunn for U.S. Senate Campaign, Phoenix, 1982; adminstrv. sec Ariz. Corp. Commn., Phoenix, 1983-84; pub. relations dir. Epoch Univs. Publ., Phoenix, 1984-86; membership dir. Tempe (Ariz.) C. of C., 1986-93; dir. legis. affairs, exec. dir. Ariz. Pharmacy Assn., 1994—. Sec., chmn. publicity Cactus Wren Rep. Women, Phoenix, 1983-89, Fiesta Bowl; bd. dirs. Tempe Leadership, Tempe YMCA; bd. govs. Tempe St. Luke's Hosp. Mem. Publ Rels. Soc. Am., Soroptimist (past pres.), Tempe C. of C. (bd. gos.),

Alpha Phi (chmn. conv.). Republican. Avocations: football, reading, needlepoint, music. Office: Ariz Pharmacy Assn 1845 E Southern Tempe AZ 85282-5831

SUMIDA, GREGORY ZIO, artist; b. L.A.. Grad., Alhambra H.S. One-man shows include Potlatch Art Gallery, 1976, Maxwell Galleries, San Francisco, 1977, Smith Gallery, N.Y.C., Zantman Galleries, Palm Desert, Calif., 1990, Legacy Gallery, 1991; group shows include Americana Gallery, Carmel, Calif., 1978, Fireside Gallery, Carmel, Calif., 1979, De Colores Gallery, Denver, 1979, Stremmel Galleries, Reno, 1980, Period Gallery West, Scottsdale, Ariz., 1981, Artist Union Gallery, 1982, 84, 85, Smith Gallery, N.Y.C., 1983, Artist Union Gallery, 1982, 84, 85, Hunter Art Gallery, San Francisco, 1984, For Art Lovers Only, Denver, 1984, Classic-Am. Show, 1988, 89, Legacy Gallery, Scottsdale, 1990, Zantman Galleries, Carmel, Calif., 1996, Urubamba Gallery, Paris, 1996; represented in numerous pub. and pvt. collections; included in numerous publications including Calif. Rev., 1989, Palm Springs Life, 1991, International Fine Art Collector, 1992, Art West, 1999. Office: PO Box 9210 Stockton CA 95208-1210

SUMME, KIMBERLY ANNE, lawyer; b. St. Louis, Oct. 6, 1969; d. Terry Hugh and Linda Kaye (Matthews) McC.; m. Philip N. Summe, Aug. 15, 1998. BA, Okla. State U., 1990; MSc, London Sco. Econs., 1991; BA in Law, MA in Law, Cambridge (Eng.) U., 1994; JD, U. Chgo., 1996. Bar: N.Y. 1997, Calif. 1998. Cons. Deloitte & Touche, Houston, 1991-92; assoc. atty. Sullivan & Cromwell, N.Y.C., 1996-97, Pillsbury Madison & Sutro, San Francisco, 1997-98. Contbr. articles to profl. jours. Methodist. Avocations: art, music, running.

SUMMERFIELD, NAN DRURY, gemologist, estate jewelry specialist; b. Waco, Tex., Dec. 22, 1957; d. Charles Edward and Nancy Lester (Summerfield) Uhrig. Student, U. Calif., Santa Barbara, 1976; grad., Gemological Inst. Am., Santa Monica, Calif., 1979. Staff gemologist Gemological Inst. Am. Gem Trade Lab., N.Y.C., 1979-80; instr. Gemological Inst. Am., N.Y.C., 1980-81; v.p., dept. head Sotheby's, N.Y.C., 1981-86, Beverly Hills, Calif., 1986-94; pres., owner Summerfield Jewels, Inc., Beverly Hills, 1994—; guest lectr. Am. Gem. Soc., 1990; auctioneer various charity orgns., 1986—. Bd. dirs. Los Angeles County Mus. Art, 1992—; bd. dirs., sec. Incline Beach Assn., Incline Village, Nev., 1996—. Mem. Am. Gem Trade Assn. (auctioneer, spectra judge 1991). Office: Summerfield Jewels Inc 433 N Camden Dr # 633 Beverly Hills CA 90210

SUMMERS, CAROL, artist; b. Kingston, N.Y., Dec. 26, 1925; s. Ivan Franklin and Theresa (Jones) S.; m. Elaine Smithers, Oct. 2, 1954 (div. Aug. 1967); 1 son, Kyle; m. Joan Ward, May 6, 1974. BA, Bard Coll., 1951, DFA (hon.), 1974. Tchr. Hunter Coll., Sch. Visual Arts, Haystack Mountain Sch. Crafts, Bklyn. Mus. Art Sch., Pratt Graphic Art Ctr., Cheltenham Twp. Art Ctr., Valley Stream Community Art Ctr., U. Pa., Columbia Coll., U. Calif., Santa Cruz, San Francisco Art Inst., U. Utah, Logan, Art Study Abroad, Paris, Casa de Espiritus Allegres Marfil, Mex., USIS workshop tour, India, 1974, 79. Represented in permanent collections at, Mus. Modern Art, Bklyn. Mus., N.Y. Pub. Libr., Libr. of Congress, Nat. Gallery, Victoria and Albert Mus., London, Bibliotheque Nationale, Paris, Kinstmuseum, Basil, Lugan (Switzerland) Art Mus. Grenchen (Switzerland) Art Mus., Malmo (Sweden) Mus., Los Angeles County Mus., Phila. Mus., Balt. Mus., Seattle Mus., Boston Mus., Art Inst. Chgo., Am. embassies in Russia, Can., India, Thailand, Fed. Republic Germany and Eng.; traveling exhibit, Mus. Modern Art, 1964-66; retrospective exhbn. Brooklyn Mus., 1977, Nassau County Mus. Art, 1990, Belles Artes, San Miquel de Allende, Mex., 1992, Miami U. Art Mus., Oxford, Ohio, 1995, Egon Schiele Centrum Česky Krumlov, Czech Republic, 1997-98, Mus. Art and History, Santa Cruz, 1999, Woodstock (N.Y.) Artists Assn., 1999. Served with USMCR, 1944-48, PTO. Italian govt. study grantee, 1954-55; Louis Comfort Tiffany Found. fellow, 1955, 60; John Simon Guggenheim Found. fellow, 1959; Fulbright fellow, Italy, 1961; Coun. for Internat. Exch. Scholars rsch. grantee, India, 1993-94. Mem. NAD, Calif. Soc. Printmakers. Address: 2817 Smith Grade Santa Cruz CA 95060-9764

SUMMERS, CATHLEEN ANN, film producer; b. Chgo.; d. Cecil Paul and Elizabeth Ann S.; m. Patrick Timothy Crowley. BA, U. So. Calif., 1973. Film editor, comml. producer, dir.'s asst. Roman Polanski, Rome, 1972; story editor Albert S. Ruddy Prodns. Paramount Pictures, L.A., 1973-74; exec. asst. Columbia Pictures, Burbank, Calif., 1974; story editor Columbia Pictures, 1974-76; devel. exec., v.p., producer Martin Ransohoff Prodns. Columbia Pictures, 1976; sr. v.p. Tri-Star Pictures, Century City, Calif., 1984-87; motion picture producer Cathleen Summers Prodns., L.A., 1989—; motion picture producer, ptnr. Summers-Kouf Prodns., Burbank, 1986-87; motion picture producer Cathleen Summers Prodns., L.A., 1987, Summers-Quaid Prodns., Century City, Culver City, Calif., 1988—. Producer: (motion picture) Stakeout, 1987, DOA, 1991, Vital Signs, 1990, Mystery Date, 1991, Dogfight, 1991, The Sandlot, 1993, Stakeout II, 1993. Co-founder Diane Thomas Scholarship-UCLA, 1988—; bd. dirs. L.A. chpt. Nat. Parkinson's Found. Mem. Am. Film Inst. (pres. 3d Decade Coun. 1995, 96, 97).

SUMMERS, WILLIAM KOOPMANS, neuropsychiatrist, researcher; b. Jefferson City, Mo., Apr. 14, 1944; s. Joseph S. and Amy Lydia (Koopmans) S.; m. Angela Forbes McGonigle, Oct. 2, 1972 (div. Apr. 1985); children: Elisabeth Stuart, Wilhelmina Derek. Student, Westminster Coll., Fulton, Mo., 1962-64; BS, U. Mo., 1966; MD, Washington U., St. Louis, 1971. Internal medicine intern Barnes Hosp-Washington U., St. Louis, 1971-72; resident in internal medicine Jewish Hosp., St. Louis, 1972-73; resident in psychiatry Rsch. Hosp., St. Louis, 1973-76; asst. prof. U. Pitts., 1976-78, U. So. Calif., L.A., 1978-82; asst. clin. prof. rsch. UCLA, 1982-88; rschr. Arcadia, Calif., 1988-92, Albuquerque, 1992—. Patentee in field. Mem. AMA, ACP, Am. Psychiat. Assn., Soc. Neurosci., N.Y. Acad. Scis., Am. Fedn. Clin. Rsch. Episcopalian. Avocation: gardening. Office: 4101 Indian Sch Rd Ste 360N Albuquerque NM 87110

SUN, GEORGE CHI, chemical engineering executive, consultant; b. Shanghai, Kiangsu, China, Feb. 14, 1930; m. Amy Cheng; 1 child, Leland. BSChemE, U. Calif., Berkeley, 1953; MSChemE, U. Mich., 1954. Rsch. engr. E.I. du Pont Co., Flint, Mich., 1954-60; plant mgr. Reichhold Chems., Inc., Hong Kong, 1961-65; new venture mgr. E.I. du Pont Co., Phila., 1966-70; pres. Amsun Industries, Inc., Irvine, Calif., 1970—. Patentee in field. Dir. Jr. C. of C., Flint, 1955,56; chmn. Am. Chem. Soc., Flint, 1959; active Peacful Uses Atomic Energy. Fellow Nash Kelvinator, Ann Arbor, Mich., 1954.

SUN, HAIYIN, optical engineer, educator; b. Kunming, Yunnan, China, July 27, 1958; came to the U.S., 1990; s. Qiyuan Sun and Shouzheng Wang; m. Nan Yang, Oct. 3, 1987; children: Tobias Y., Christina N. BS in Physics, Shanghai (China) Tchrs. U., 1982; MS in Photonics, Shanghai (China) Inst. Optics and Fine Mechanics, 1985; PhD in Photonics, U. Ark., 1994. Instr. Shanghai Tchr.'s U., 1982; asst. prof. Shanghai Inst. Optics and Fine Mechanics, 1986-88; vis. scientist Telecom. Network Rsch. Ctr. of Germany's Post, Darmstadt, 1988-90; optical engr. Power Tech., Inc., Little Rock, 1994-96; sr. optical engr. Coherent Inc., Auburn, Calif., 1996—; adj. prof. U. Ark., Little Rock, 1996—; prin. investigator various projects. Contbr. chpt. to book and numerous articles to profl. jours.; inventor several optical devices. Named Outstanding Rschr., The Justice Dept. USA Govt., 1995; rsch. grantee Ark. Sci. & Engring. Authority, 1993. Avocations: classical music, watching TV movies and sports, cooking. Home: 8328 Northvale Way Citrus Heights CA 95610-0803 Office: Coherent Inc 2303 Lindberg St Ste A90 Auburn CA 95602-9562

SUNDAR, VIJENDRA, lawyer educator; b. Nausori, Rewa, Fiji Islands, Oct. 27, 1940; came to U.S., 1966; s. Bisu R. and Pran Pati Sundar; m. Lynette Sue Schmid, June 13, 1987; children: Jesse Christopher Mikaele, Eric Lynn Kalani, Christina Elizabeth Ululani. BBA in Mktg., U. Hawaii, 1976; JD, Antioch U., 1979. Bar: U.S. Ct. Mil. Appeals 1983, Omaha Tribal Ct. 1983, U.S. Trust Ter. of Pacific 1983. Co-owner, mgr. Rewa Ice & Aerated Water Factory, Rewa Lodge & Cafe, Nausori, Fiji Islands, 1962-67; coord., instr. Pacific and Asia Linguistics Inst., Honolulu, 1968, Univ. Hawaii, Peace Corps Ctrs., 1968-98; paralegal Puget Sound Legal Asst. Found., Tacoma, Wash., 1975-76; atty. rschr. Inst. for Law and Rsch., Washington, 1980-81; atty. Legal Aid Soc., Inc., Omaha, 1982-84, Multnomah County Legal Aid Svcs., Inc., Portland, Oreg., 1984-85; instr. Platt Coll., Jefferson City, Mo., 1986-88; acting dir., vis. asst. prof. Columbia Coll., Columbia, Mo., 1989; acad. & legal cons., 1990-92; owner, operator, businessman Fairview Motel, Kemmerer, Wyo., 1996—. Town councillor Nausori (Fiji Islands) Town Coun., 1965-68; bd. dirs. Improvement Means People Allied for Change Together, Omaha, 1983-84; commn. mem. com. welfare of farm workers, 1985; parliamentarian, bd. dirs. Am. Indian Ctr., Omaha, 1983-84. Reginald Heber Smith Ctmty. Lawyer fellow Howard Univ., 1984-85. Mem. ABA. Avocations: swimming, fishing, traveling, cooking, acting. Address: PO Box 367 Kemmerer WY 83101-0367

SUNDARAM, SHANMUGAUELAYUTHAM KAMAKSHI, materials scientist, consultant; b. Vaigai, Tamilnadu, India, Apr. 30, 1958; came to U.S., 1990; s. S. and Saraswathy Velayutham; m. T.M. Nalini, Mar. 11, 1987; 1 child, Sudhandra. A.I.I. Ceramics, Indian Inst. Ceramics, Calcutta, 1983; M.Tech., Indian Inst. Tech., Kharagpur, 1986; PhD, Ga. Inst. Tech., 1994. Tradesman B Reactor Rsch. Ctr., Kalpakkam, India, 1977-79; tech. asst. Indian Inst. Tech., Kharagpur, 1979-87; rsch. engr. Tata Rsch. Devel. and Design Ctr., Pune, India, 1987-90; rsch. asst. Alfred (N.Y.) U., 1990-92; tchg./rsch. asst. Ga. Inst. Tech., Atlanta, 1992-94; postdoctoral fellow dept. energy Assoc. Western U., Richland, Wash., 1994-96; sr. rsch. scientist Pacific N.W. Nat. Lab., Richland, 1996—; vis. scientist MIT, 1998—; adj. faculty Wash. State U., 1997—; guest lectr. Ga. Inst. Tech., 1995—; literacy tutor Wash. State Literacy Program, 1995; vis. scientist Plasma Sci. and Fusion Ctr., MIT, 1998—; lectr. in field. Contbr. articles to profl. jours. Vol. elder care Benton-Franklin Counties, Wash., 1995—; spkr. Nat. Engrs. Week, 1995—. Recipient Ganpule award Indian Ceramic Soc., Calcutta, 1985, 86; AMIC Industries Ltd. award, Calcutta, 1983. Mem. AAAS, ASTM (com. mem. C.08.12 1995—), Am. Ceramic Soc. (phase diagrams editor 1992-94, abstractor 1992-94), Nat. Assn. Corrosion Engrs., Nat. Inst. Ceramic Engrs., Materials Rsch. Soc., Keramos. Avocations: writing, reading, museums, religions, international art film. Office: Pacific Northwest National Lab PO Box 999 MSIN: K6-24 Richland WA 99352-0999

SUNDEL, HARVEY H., marketing research analyst and consultant; b. Bronx, N.Y., July 24, 1944; s. Louis and Pauline (Brotman) S. BBA, St. Mary's U., San Antonio, 1969, MBA, 1970; PhD, St. Louis U., 1974. Asst. dir. research Lone Star Brewery, San Antonio, 1970-71; cons. Tri-Mark, Inc., San Antonio, 1972-73; asst. prof. mktg. Lewis and Clark Coll., Godfrey, Ill., 1973-74; asst. prof. mktg. Met. State Coll., Denver, 1974-77, chmn., prof. mktg., 1977-86; pres. Sundel Rsch., Inc., Denver, 1976—; cons. Frederick Ross Co., Denver, 1979-84, U.S. West Direct, Denver, 1986—, Monsanto Chems. Co., St. Louis, 1985—, Mountain Bell, Denver, 1979-88, U.S. West Comm., Denver, 1988—, AT&T, 1986-91, Melco Industries, 1987-90, Norwest Banks, 1990-94, PACE Membership Warehouse, 1992-93, U.S. Meat Export Fedn., 1992—, G.D. Searle, 1996—, Nextel Comms., 1996—; expert witness in legal cases. Contbr. papers and proceedings to profl. jours. Com. mem. Mile High United Way, Denver, 1975-80, Allied Jewish Fedn. Cmty. Rels. Action Com., 1995—, Hewlett Packard, 1998—. Jewish. Avocation: handball. Home: 1616 Glen Bar Dr Lakewood CO 80215-3014 Office: Sundel Rsch Inc 1150 Delaware St Denver CO 80204-3608

SUNDQUIST, LEAH RENATA, physical education specialist; b. El Paso, Tex., July 22, 1963; d. Dominic Joseph and Patricia Ann (Manley) Bernardi; m. David Curtis Sundquist, June 23, 1990. AA, N.Mex. Mil. Inst., 1983; BS, U. Tex., El Paso, 1986; MEd in Curriculum and Instrn., City U., Bellevue, Wash., 1996. Field exec. Rio Grande Girl Scout Coun., El Paso, 1983-84; customer teller M-Bank, El Paso, 1984-85; soccer coach St. Clements Sch., El Paso, 1985; substitute tchr. El Paso Sch. Dist., 1986; commd. 2nd lt. U.S. Army, 1983, advanced through grades to maj., 1997; plans/exercise officer U.S. Army, Ft. Lewis, Wash., 1990; ops. officer U.S. Army, Ft. Lewis, 1990-1991; comdr. hdqs. Hdqs. Co. 141st Support Bn. U.S. Army N.G., 1996-97; dir. Childrens World Learning Ctr., Federal Way, Wash., 1992-94; phys. edn. specialist, tchr. K-6 Kent (Wash.) Elem. Sch., 1994—. Coord. Nat. Conf. Christians and Jews, El Paso, 1979-81; v.p. Jr. Achievement, El Paso, 1980-81; adult tng. vol. Girl Scout Coun., bd. dirs. Pacific Peaks coun., 1993—, chair nominating com., 1996, jr. troop Girl Scout leader totem Girl Scout Coun., 1996, chair program policies rev. com., 1997, trainer instrn. of adults, 1997—; bd. dir. Jr. League Tacoma, 1993, 94. 3rd Res. Officer Tng. Corps scholar, 1981-83, H.P. Saunder scholar, 1982; recipient Humanitarian Svc. medal Great Fires of Yellowstone, U.S. Army, 1988, Gold award Girl Scouts U.S.A., 1981; decorated Nat. Def. Svc. medal Desert Storm; meritorius Svc. medal, 1991. Mem. NEA, Wash. Edn. Assn., Assn. U.S. Army, Air Def. Artillery Assn., Fellowship Christian Athletes, Soroptimist of Tacoma, Zeta Tau Alpha (sec. 1983-85, house mgr. 1984-86). Republican. Roman Catholic. Avocations: soccer, fishing, hunting, skydiving, rafting. Home: 31514 114th Pl SE Auburn WA 98092-3046

SUNDT, HARRY WILSON, construction company executive; b. Woodbury, N.J., July 5, 1932; s. Thoralf Mauritz and Elinor (Stout) S.; m. Dorothy Van Gilder, June 26, 1954; children: Thomas D., Perri Lee Sundt Touche, Gerald W. BS in Bus. Adminstrn., U. Ariz., 1954, postgrad., 1957-59. Salesman ins. VanGilder Agys., Denver, 1956-57; apprentice carpenter M.M. Sundt Constrn. Co., Tucson, 1957-58, estimator, 1958-59; adminstrv. asst. M.M. Sundt Constrn. Co., Vandenberg AFB, 1959-62; sr. estimator M.M. Sundt Constrn. Co., Tucson, 1962-64, div. mgr., 1964-65, exec. v.p., gen. mgr., 1965-75, pres., chmn., 1975-79; pres., chmn. Sundt Corp., Tucson, 1980-83, chmn., chief exec. officer, 1983-98; bd. dirs. Tucson Electric Power Co., Nations Energy Co. Pres. Tucson Airport Authority, 1982; bd. dirs. U. Ariz. Found. 1981. 1st lt. U.S. Army, 1954-56. Recipient Disting. Citizen award U. Ariz., 1982, Centennial Medallion award, 1989. Mem. Tucson Country Club. Republican. Episcopalian. Avocation: tennis. Home: 6002 E San Leandro Tucson AZ 85715-3014 Office: Sundt Corp PO Box 26685 4101 E Irvington Rd Tucson AZ 85714-2192

SUNIVILLE, HARRY FREDERICK, accountant; b. Ogden, Utah, Nov. 27, 1913; s. Herbert and Mary Adaline (Nantker) S.; m. Nadine Sullivent, Oct. 17, 1949; children: Harry F. Jr., Gerald Herbert, Thomas Gordon. AS, Weber State Univ., 1933; BS, Univ. Utah, 1935; M in commercial sci., Strayer Coll. Acct., 1937. CPA. Accounting, clerical U.S. Gov. Dept Agrl., Post Office & Internal Revenue, Washington, 1935-37; staff acct. Goddard Abbey Co., CPAs, Salt Lake City, Utah, 1938-40; chief fiscal auditor, asst. zone auditor U.S. Army Quartermaster Corps., Cheyenne, Wyo., Omaha, Nebr., 1940-41; chief project auditor Pine BLuff Arsenal U.S. Army Corps of Engrs., Pine Bluf, Ark., 1941-43; exec. acct. positions, 1943-45; sr. staff acct., sr. mng. ptnr. Suniville, Griffin & Smith, Salt Lake City, 1946—; cons., dir. M.H. Cook Pipeline Cons. Co., Salt Lake City, 1940-50. Scout com. Boy Scouts Am., Salt Lake City, 1953-63. Mem. Inst. of Mgmt. Accts.(pres. 1969-70), Weber & Wasatch Lodge, Utah Consistory No. 1 Scottish Rite, Shriners, Am. Inst. CPAs. Republican. Episcopalian. Avocations: fishing, camping, golfing, stamp collecting. Office: Smith Powell & Co LLC 68 S Main Ste 300 Salt Lake City UT 84101

SUNTREE, SUSAN FRANCES, English language educator, poet, playwright; b. L.A., May 19, 1946; d. Edward Francis and Beatrice Madaline (Hays) Stout; m. Philip James Daughtry, May 1, 1972 (div.); children: Sean Philip Daughtry, Califia Selene Suntree. BA in English, U. Ariz., 1968; MA, U. Kent, U.K., 1970. Instr. English La Familia Continuation H.S., Lancaster, Calif., 1970, Modesto (Calif.) C.C., 1970-75; instr. theatre arts Primitive Arts Inst., Grass Valley, Calif., 1976-83; vis. artist UCLA Arts Reach, Westwood, Calif., 1983-85; instr. English Santa Monica (Calif.) Coll., 1984-88, East L.A. Coll., Monterey Park, Calif., 1989—; instr., founder Writers Circle, Santa Monica, 1987—; vis. and resident artist Nev. County Cmty. Workshop, Grass Valley, 1981-82; dir. vis. poet Calif. Poets in Schs., Grass Valley, 1977-82; instr. English Tech. Univ., Helsinki, Finland, 1972; artistic dir. TheatreFlux, Santa Monica, 1985—; co-dir., cons. Simple Path-Arts for the Disabled, Santa Monica, 1982-89. Author: (poetry) Eye of the Womb, 1981, (book) Rita Moreno, 1992, numerous reviews, articles, essays, lectures; plays include: Seed to Snow: Plays for the Seasons, 1978-81, Origins of Praise, 1986, Symphony of Giordano Bruno, 1988, Sacred Sites/Los Angeles, 1992, many others; translator: Tulips (Ana Rossetti); numerous poetry pubs. and readings. Grantee Santa Monica Art Commn. and Santa Monica Art Found., 1986, Calif. Arts Coun., 1976, 78, 79, 80, 83, 84, 85, Ford Found. Cultural Enhancement at Calif. State U.-L.A. Mem. PEN, Dramatists Guild. Zen Buddhist. Avocations: mask making, gardening, singing. Home: 1223 11th St Santa Monica CA 90401-2002 Office: East LA Coll 1301 Avenida Cesar Chavez Monterey Park CA 91754-0001

SUPAN, RICHARD MATTHEW, finance company executive; b. Palo Alto, Calif., June 22, 1953; s. James Arthur and Nancy Ann (Rhein) S.; m. Bernadette Joan Bayer, Sept. 8, 1979; children: Raymond, Valerie, Joanna. AA, Foothill Coll., 1973; BSC, Santa Clara U., 1975, MBA, 1979. Cost acctg. supr. Electron Devices div. Litton Industries, San Carlos, Calif., 1975-78; cost acctg. mgr. Microwave Tube div. Varian Assocs., Palo Alto, Calif., 1978-81, ops. controller, 1981-84; dir. acctg. Varian Assocs., Palo Alto, Calif., 1984-85; controller Electron Device & Systems Group, Varian Assocs., Palo Alto, Calif., 1985-89, Oncology Systems, Varian Assocs., Palo Alto, Calif., 1989-95; v.p. ops. & fin. Intraop Med., Inc., Santa Clara, Calif., 1995-98; contr. Symantec Corp., Cupertino, Calif., 1998—. Mem. Beta Gamma Sigma (hon.). Avocation: coach, league official youth sports. Home: 5915 Amapola Dr San Jose CA 95129-3058 Office: 10201 Torre Ave Cupertino CA 95014-2131

SUPÉRNAW, WILLIAM MICHAEL (W. M. SUPÉRNAW), actor; b. Manhattan, N.Y., Oct. 1, 1938; s. Harold and Estelle (Rosen) S.; m. Shirley Zimmerman, Nov. 16, 1968 (div. June 1989); 1 child, Samantha; m. Phyllis Jean Savage, Mar. 16, 1990; stepchildren: Majeeda, Naimah, Ameerah, April-Dawn, Antar Nasser. Chief exec. officer Restaurant Cons., Inc., N.Y.C., 1960-68; pres. Actors League N.Y., Bronx, 1968-93; exec. dir. Playwrights, Actors and Dirs., Inc., Bklyn., 1980-93. Actor: (Broadway prodns.) The Third Best Sport, 1958, Becket (stand-by for Lord Laurence Olivier, Anthony Quinn, Arthur Kennedy), Critics' Choice (stand-by for Henry Fonda), (off-Broadway prodns.) Richard II, 1963, Richard III (played opposite Sir Alec Guinness), Macbeth (played opposite Sir John Gielgud), 1962, Twelfth Night, 1964, A Midsummer Night's Dream, 1945, Hamlet (479 consecutive performances), 1958-59, Crucible, Dracula, Death by Misadventure, Death is Called Sam, Year of Jubilee, Don Juan in Hell, The Littlest Tailor, Café Crown, H. Norman (by spl. request), (TV prodns.) H. Norman Schwarzkopf (by spl. request), Fireside Theatre, Studio One, Robert Montgomery Presents, US Steel Hour, Philco Playhouse, Playhouse 90, Play of the Week, Age of Kings, The Equalizer, As the World Turns, One Life To Live, Guiding Light, others, (films) Man is Man, 1961, Murphy's Law, 1977, Fort Apache-The Bronx, 1981, Beer, 1985, Heart, 1986; producer, dir. (play in Chgo.) No Exit; contbr. articles to Standby Publs., 1986. Active Civil Rights movement, 1960-69. Served with USCG, USCGR, 1958-66. Recipient Emmy award Nat. Acad. TV Arts and Scis., 1958, Elmer Rice award Theatre Guild, 1959, Spl. Antoinette Perry award Am. Theatre Wing, 1960, Joseph Jefferson commn. award, 1960, Silver award Cannes Film Festival, 1961. Mem. AFTRA (bd dirs nat. N.Y. local 1985-93, Stanley Greene award 1986), Actors Equity Assn., Actors Fund Am. Inc., SAG (Joseph C. Riley award 1979), Student Nat. Coordinating Com., SCLC, CORE, NAACP, Com. for Non-Violent Action. Democrat. Avocations: mountain climbing, fencing, horseback riding, writing, photography. Office: World Actors Network/PWD SPC #4 3315 W Adams Blvd Apt 7 Los Angeles CA 90018-1859

SUPOLA, SUSAN LENORA, secondary education educator, artist; b. Kalispell, Mont., Sept. 1, 1947; d. Kenneth R. and Beth J. (Cronemiller) Knapton; m. Sherman R. Supola, Mar. 14, 1967; children: Stephanie, Scott. BA in Edn. and Art, Whitworth Coll., 1989. Cert. secondary tchr., English and art, Mont. Tchr.'s aide/sec. Mead (Wash.) Jr. H.S., 1976-89; tchr. English Northwood Jr. H.S., Mead, 1990-91, Linderman Sch., Kalispell, 1992-93; tchr. art, English Flathead H.S., Kalispell, 1993—. Exhibited in group show Flathead Valley Art Show, 1996, 97. Mem. Nat. Coun. Tchrs. of English, Nat. Art Edn. Assn. Office: Flathead HS 644 4th Ave W Kalispell MT 59901-5206

SUPPA, RONALD ANTHONY, film producer, writer, entertainment lawyer; b. Phila., Oct. 21, 1948; s. Pasquale and Grace (Presto) S.; m. Lisa Moro, June 3, 1995; 1 child, Nicolas. BA in Lit., Pa. State U., 1970; JD, U. Wis., 1973. Bar: Wis. and Calif. 1973. Entertainment atty. Mitchell, Silberberg & Knupp, L.A., 1973-75; producer, ptnr. Force Ten Prodns. Ltd., L.A., 1975-80; ptnr. Krintzman & Suppa, L.A., 1980-82; pres. Ronald Suppa Prodns., Inc., Sherman Oaks, Calif., 1982-86, 87—; v.p. prodn. Kodiak Films, Inc., L.A., 1986-87; sr. instr. writing UCLA Ext., 1988—. Author: Reflections, 1975; screenwriter: Second Wind, 1985, Riding the Edge, 1987, Harry's War, 1990, Lord Byron's Daughter, 1991, The Shining Path, 1993, Hell's Angel, 1995; film producer: Paradise Alley with Sylvester Stallone, 1978, No Room to Run with Richard Benjamin, 1979, Barnaby and Me with Sid Caesar, 1980, Because He's My Friend with Karen Black, 1980, Defense Play with David Oliver, 1988, Maui Heat, 1996, others. Mem. Writers Guild Am. West, Calif. Bar Assn., Wis. Bar Assn., PEN Ctr. West. Democrat. Roman Catholic. Avocations: writing, skiing, traveling. Home and Office: 32063 Canterhill Place Westlake Village CA 91361-4817

SUPPES, PATRICK, statistics, education, philosophy and psychology educator; b. Tulsa, Mar. 17, 1922; s. George Biddle and Ann (Costello) S.; m. Joan Farmer, Apr. 16, 1946 (div. 1970); children: Patricia, Deborah, John Biddle; m. Joan Sieber, Mar. 29, 1970 (div. 1973); m. Christine Johnson, May 26, 1979; children: Alexandra Christine, Michael Patrick. BS, U. Chgo., 1943; PhD (Wendell T. Bush fellow), Columbia U., 1950; LLD, U. Nijmegen, Netherlands, 1979; Dr. honoris causa, Académie de Paris, U. Paris V, 1982. Instr., Stanford U., 1950-52, asst. prof., 1952-55, assoc. prof., 1955-59, prof. philosophy, statistics, edn. and psychology, 1959-92, prof. emeritus; founder, chief exec. officer Computer Curriculum Corp., 1967-90. Author: Introduction to Logic, 1957, Axiomatic Set Theory, 1960, Sets and Numbers, books 1-6, 1966, Studies in the Methodology and Foundations of Science, 1969, A Probabilistic Theory of Causality, 1970, Logique du Probable, 1981, Probabilistic Metaphysics, 1984, Estudios de Filosofía y Metodologí de la Ciencia, 1988, Language for Humans and Robots, 1991, Models and Methods in the Philosophy of Science, 1993; (with Davidson and Siegel) Decision Making, 1957, (with Richard C. Atkinson) Markov Learning Models for Multiperson Interactions, 1960, (with Shirley Hill) First Course in Mathematical Logic, 1964, (with Edward J. Crothers) Experiments on Second-Language Learning, 1967, (with Max Jerman and Dow Brian) Computer-assisted Instruction, 1965-66, Stanford Arithmetic Program, 1968, (with D. Krantz, R.D. Luce and A. Tversky) Foundations of Measurement, Vol. 1, 1971, (with M. Morningstar) Computer-Assisted Instruction at Stanford, 1966-68, 1972, (with B. Searle and J. Friend) The Radio Mathematics Project: Nicaragua, 1974-75, 1976 (with D. Krantz, R.D. Luce and A. Tversky) Foundations of Measurement, Vol. 2, 1989, Vol. 3, 1990, (with Colleen Crangle) Language and Learning for Robots, 1994, (with Mario Zanotti) Foundations of Probability with Applications, 1996. Served to capt. USAAF, 1942-46. Recipient Nicholas Murray Butler Silver medal Columbia, 1965, Disting. Sci. Contbr. award Am. Psychol. Assn., 1972, Tchrs. Coll. medal for disting. service, 1978, Nat. medal Sci. NSF, 1990; Center for Advanced Study Behavioral Scis. fellow, 1955-56; NSF fellow, 1957-58. Fellow AAAS, Am. Psychol. Assn., Am. Acad. Arts and Scis., Assn. Computing Machinery; mem. NAS, Math. Assn. Am., Psychometric Soc., Am. Philos. Assn., Am. Philos. Soc., Assn. Symbolic Logic, Am. Math Soc., Académie Internationale de Philosophie des Scis. (titular), Nat. Acad. Edn. (pres. 1973-77), Am. Psychol. Assn., Internat. Inst. Philosophy, Finnish Acad. Sci. and Letters, Internat. Union History and Philosophy of Sci. (div. logic, methodology and philosophy of sci., pres. 1975-79), Am. Ednl. Research Assn. (pres. 1973-74), Croatian Acad. Scis. (corr.), Russian Acad. Edn. (fgn.), Norwegian Acad. Sci. and Letters (fgn.), European Acad. Scis. and Arts, Chilean Acad. Scis., Sigma Xi.

SURFACE, STEPHEN WALTER, water treatment chemist, environmental protection specialist; b. Dayton, Ohio, Feb. 25, 1943; s. Lorin Wilfred and Virginia (Marsh) S.; m. Suzanne MacDonald, Aug. 29, 1964 (div.); 1 child, Jennifer Nalani; m. Sinfrosa Garay, Sept. 16, 1978; children: Maria Lourdes, Stephanie Alcantara. BS, Otterbein Coll., 1965; MA, U. So. Calif., 1970; postgrad., U. Hawaii, 1971. Cert. profl. chemist. Tchr. Hawaii State Dept. Edn., Honolulu, 1970-71; staff chemist Del Monte Corp., Honolulu, 1971; head chemist USNPearl Harbor, Honolulu, 1971-76; staff chemist USN Pearl Harbor, Honolulu, 1976-90; chief office installation svcs., environ. protection Def. Logistics Agy., Camp Smith, Hawaii, 1990—. Contbr. articles to profl. jours. Recipient DuPont Teaching award, U. So. Calif., 1966. Fellow Am. Inst. Chemists; mem. Am. Chem. Soc., Am. Def. Preparedness Assn., N.Y. Acad. Scis., Sigma Xeta, Phi Lambda Upsilon. Democrat. Methodist. Avocations: traveling, artifact collecting, landscaping. Home: 94-1139 Noheaiki St Waipahu HI 96797-4138 Office: Def Logistics Agy DPAC-W Camp H M Smith HI 96861

SUSSMAN, BRIAN JAY, meteorologist, weather broadcaster; b. L.A., Apr. 3, 1956; s. Alan E. and Beverly A. (Carlson) S.; m. Sue Ann Rittenhouse, June 18, 1978; chilren: Elisa, Samuel, Benjamin. BS, U. Mo., 1978. Reporter, anchor Sta. KCBJ-TV, Columbia, Mo., 1977-80; weather anchor Sta. KOLO-TV, Reno, 1980-83; on-air meteorologist Sta. KNTV-TV, San Jose, Calif., 1983-87, Sta. KDKA-TV, Pitts., 1987-89; substitute weatherman CBS This Morning, N.Y.C., 1988-93; on-air meteorologist Sta. KPIX-TV, San Francisco, 1989—. Co-author: (textbook) For Spacious Skies, 1987, rev. edit., 1989. Recipient Best Weathercast award Radio-TV News Dirs. Assn., 1987, 90-95, 97-98, AP, 1989, 90-98, Advancement of Learning Through Broadcasting award NEA, 1989. Mem. Am. Meteorol. Soc. (Seal of Approval cert.). Avocations: pub. speaking, adult ice-hockey. Office: Sta KPIX-TV 855 Battery St San Francisco CA 94111-1503

SUSTEK, RITAMARIE, fine arts appraiser; b. Chgo., Mar. 25, 1929; d. John Rehling and Elizabeth Garlin; m. John O. Sustek, March 1, 1952; children: Robert, Richard. BSc in Valuation Sci., Regis U., 1998. Accredited sr. appraiser. Mgr., cons. Bernard Galleries, Walnut Creek, Laguna Beac, Calif., 1984-93; prin., owner Ritamarie Sustek & Assocs., Walnut Creek, Calif., 1993—. Mem. Am. Soc. Appraisers (personal property chpt. dir. 1994, chpt. treas. 1995-96, personal property com. 1998, adv. com. 1998). Roman Catholic. Office: Sustek & Associates 712 Bancroft Rd # 197 Walnut Creek CA 94598-1531

SUSYNSKI, KENNETH, illustrator; b. Ft. Knox, Ky., May 10, 1965; s. Joseph F. and Barbara Jean (Jazwinski) S.; m. Catherine Angela Wilkins, Mar. 1, 1991; 1 child, Jack Wilkins. AA, U. Md., Munich, 1985; BA in Econs., U. Mass., 1987; postgrad., Sch. Visual Concepts, Seattle, 1997—. Sr. fin. dep. Fidelity Investments, Bethesda, Md., 1989-92; mgr. internat. trading Fidelity Brokerage Ltd., Tonbridge, U.K., 1992-94; v.p., br. mgr. Fidelity Investments, Seattle, 1994-97; freelance illustrator Seattle, 1997—; bd. dirs., trustee Neighborhood Children's Ctr., Seattle, 1998—. Mem. SPGA-Graphic Artists Guild, Soc. Children's Book Writers and Illustrators. Home and Office: 3938 Interlake Ave N Seattle WA 98103-8132

SUTCLIFFE, ERIC, lawyer; b. Calif., Jan. 10, 1909; s. Thomas and Annie (Beare) S.; m. Joan Basché, Aug. 7, 1937; children: Victoria, Marcia, Thomas; m. Marie C. Paige, Nov. 1, 1975. AB, U. Calif., Berkeley, 1929, LLB, 1932. Bar: Calif. 1932. Mem. firm Orrick, Herrington & Sutcliffe, San Francisco, 1943-85, mng. ptnr., 1947-78. Trustee, treas., v.p. San Francisco Law Libr., 1974-88; founding fellow The Oakland Mus. of Calif.; bd. dirs. Merritt Peralta Found., 1988; past bd. dirs. Hong Kong Bank of Calif., Friends of U. Calif. Bot. Garden, sec. Fellow Am. Bar Found (life); mem. ABA (chmn state regulation securities com. 1960-65), San Francisco Bar Assn. (chmn. corp. law com., 1964-65), San Francisco C. of C. (past treas., dir.), State Bar Calif., Pacific Union Club, Bohemian Club, Phi Gamma Delta, Phi Delta Phi, Order of Coif. Home: 260 King Ave Oakland CA 94610-1231 Office: Old Fed Reserve Bank Bldg 400 Sansome St San Francisco CA 94111-3304

SUTER, DAVID WINSTON, religion educator, minister; b. Staunton, Va., Mar. 1, 1942; s. Beverly Wills and Sarah Frances (Anderson) S.; m. Kristine Ann Pearson, July 8, 1978; 1 child, Jessica Eden. BA, Davidson Coll., 1964; BD, U. Chgo., 1967, MA, 1970, PhD, 1977. Ordained to ministry Presbyn. Ch. (U.S.A.), 1967. Pastor Longbranch (Wash.) Community Ch., 1986-90; prof. St. Martin's Coll., Lacey, Wash., 1983—, dean of humanities, 1991—. Author: Tradition and Composition in the Parables of Enoch, 1979; contbr. articles to profl. publs. Mem. Soc. Biblical Lit. Democrat. Office: St Martin's Coll 5300 Pacific Ave SE Lacey WA 98503-7500

SUTER, PEGGY JEAN, library director; b. Wilburton, Okla., July 18, 1937; d. Henry Paul and Violet Jessie Eads; m. James William Suter, May 15, 1954; children: Pauline Jeanette Owens, Jo Lavonne Ahlm. Grad., Hartshorne (Okla.) H.S., 1955. Cert. grade I libr., N.Mex. Piano tchr. Lovington, N.Mex., 1968-72, Eunice, N.Mex., 1973-88; kindergarten music tchr. First Meth. Ch., Lovington, 1970-73; substitute sch. tchr. Eunice Pub. Schs., 1978-81; libr. dir. Eunice Pub. Libr., 1981—. Organist First Meth. Ch., Eunice, 1982—. Mem. Am. Libr. Assn., N.Mex. Libr. Assn. (community Svc. award 1992), Lea County Libr. Assn. (v.p. 1982, pres. 1983, treas. 1984). Democrat. Methodist. Avocations: playing piano, singing, crochet. Office: Eunice Pub Libr Corner of 10th and Ave Eunice NM 88231

SUTHERLAND, BRUCE, composer, pianist; b. Daytona Beach, Fla.; s. Kenneth Francis and Norma (Williams) S.; Mus.B. cum laude, U. So. Calif., 1957, Mus.M., 1959; studies with Halsey Stevens, Ellis Kohs, Ethel Leginska, Amparo Iturbi. Harpsichord soloist with Telemann Trio in concert tour, 1969-70; tchr. master class for pianists U. Tex., Austin, 1971; dir. Bach festivals Music Tchrs. Assn. Calif., 1972-73, dir. Artists of Tomorrow Music Festivals Music Tchrs. Assn. Calif., 1984-88, compositions performed in numerous contemporary music festivals in U.S., 1957—; piano faculty Calif. State U. at Northridge, 1977—; tchr. master class for pianists UCLA, 1995—, adjudicator music competitions and auditions Nat. Guild Piano Tchrs. U. So. Calif., 1996, others; dir. Brentwood-Westwood Symphony ann. competition for young artists, 1981-88; composer: Allegro Fanfara for Orch., world premiere conducted by José Iturbi with Bridgeport Symphony Orch., 1970; Saxophone Quartet, 1971; Quintet for Flute, Strings, Piano, 1972; Notturno for Flute and Guitar, 1973; also string trio, piano and vocal works. Recipient grand prize Internat. Competition Louis Moreau Gottschalk, 1970; Stairway of Stars award Music Arts Soc., Santa Monica, 1973; named one of Los Angeles' Finest Piano Tchrs., New West Mag., 1977; honored as Dist. Tchr. of Anders Martinson, presdl. scholar in arts, 1991, Disting. Tchr. White House Commn. on Presidential Scholars, 1991; honored by Nat. Found. Advancement Arts 1989, 91, 93. Mem. Nat. Assn. Am. Composers and Condrs., Music Tchrs. Nat. Assn., Music Tchrs. Assn., Calif. Assn. Profl. Music Tchrs., Pi Kappa Lambda.

SUTHERLAND, DONALD WOOD, cardiologist; b. Kansas City, Mo., July 29, 1932; s. Donald Redeker and Mary Frances (Wood) S.; m. Margaret Sutherland, Sept. 11, 1954 (div. 1994); children: Kathleen Massar, Ellen Baltus, Richard, Ann, Julia McMurchie; m. Roslyn Ruggiero Elms, Mar. 31, 1995. BA, Amherst Coll., 1953; MD, Harvard U., 1957. Intern, resident Mass. Gen. Hosp., Boston, 1957-60; fellow in cardiology U. Oreg., Portland, 1961-63; pvt. practice Portland, 1963—; assoc. clin. prof. medicine Oreg. Health Sci. U., Portland, 1967—; chief of staff St. Vincent Hosp. and Med. Ctr., Portland, 1971-72. Contbr. articles to profl. jours. Fellow Am. Heart Assn., Am. Coll. Cardiology (pres. Oreg. chpt. 1972); mem. Multnomah Athletic Club, North Pacific Soc. Internal Medicine (pres. 1985), Pacific Interurban Clin. Club. Avocations: flying private planes, scuba diving. Home: 4405 SW Council Crest Dr Portland OR 97201-1534 Office: Columbia Cardiology Ltd 9155 SW Barnes Rd Ste 233 Portland OR 97225-6629

SUTHERLAND, DOUGLASS B., former mayor, tent and awning company executive; b. Helena, Mont., May 2, 1937; s. Chris and Marie Sutherland; m. Grace Sutherland, Sept. 5, 1986; children: Karen, Scott. B.A., Central Wash. U., 1959. Program specialist Boeing Co., Tacoma, Wash., 1960-71; owner, pres. Tacoma Tent & Awning, Inc., 1971-86; sec., pres., 1986-98. Bd. dirs. Tacoma-Pierce County Bd. Health, Tacoma-Pierce County Employment and Tng. Consortium; mayor City of Tacoma, 1982-89; pres. Puget Sound Regional Coun.; chair Urban County Caucus, Wash. Assn. of Counties. Mem. Assn. Wash. Cities, Tacoma-Pierce County C. of C. Republican. Lodge: Rotary. Avocation: sailing. E-mail: dsuther@co.pierce.wa.us. Office: Pierce County Executive 930 Tacoma Ave S Rm 737 Tacoma WA 98402-2100

SUTTER, DARRYL JOHN, former professional hockey coach. Player Chgo. Blackhawks, 1980-86, asst. coach, 1987-88, assoc. coach, 1991-92, head coach, 1992-95, cons., 1995-97; head coach San Jose Sharks, 1997—. Office: San Jose Sharks 525 W Santa Clara St San Jose CA 95113*

SUTTER, VIRGINIA JEAN, health administrator, mental health specialist; b. Ft. Washakie, Wyo.; d. Arlo and Gertrude (Ayers) Amos; m. D.A. Sutter (div. 1973); children: James E., Dennis D., Vicki M. Sutter Smolke. BS in Sociology, U. Colo., 1981; MSW, U. Okla., 1984, PhD in Pub. Adminstrn., 1995. Tchr. social work U. Okla. and Ctrl. Wyo. Coll., 1984-97; contract cons., mental health specialist, program developer Indian Health Svc., 1994-97; dir. social, health and edn. depts. Quinault Indian Nation, 1997—; dir., chairperson Wyo. Congl. Award Coun.; mem. protection and advocacy sys. Mental Health Adv. Coun., Wyo.; mem. project adv. panel, rschr. court cases in field of Indian Child Welfare Act, Washington, 1988. Contbr. articles to profl. jours. Bd. trustees Women of West Mus., Boulder, Colo.; dir. tribal rsch. and devel., chairperson No. Arapaho Bus. Coun. Wind River Reservation. Methodist. Avocations: writing, tribal activities. Home: PO Box 1485 3701 Auburn Ave F104 Auburn WA 98071 Office: We Indian Mgmt Svcs PO Box 1485 Auburn WA 98071

SUTTERBY, LARRY QUENTIN, internist; b. North Kansas City, Mo., Sept. 11, 1950; s. John Albert and Wilma Elizabeth (Henry) S.; m. Luciana Risos Magpuri, July 5, 1980; children: Leah Lourdes, Liza Bernadette. BA in Chemistry, William Jewell Coll., 1972; MD, U. Mo., Kans. City, 1976. Diplomate Am. Bd. Internal Medicine with qualifications in geriatric medicine, Am. Bd. Hospice & Palliative Care; cert. med. dir. Am. Med. Dirs. Assn., 1997. Resident in internal medicine Mt. Sinai Hosp., Chgo., 1976-79; physician Mojave Desert Health Svc., Barstow, Calif., 1979-86; pvt. practice Barstow, 1986—; med. dir. Rimrock Villa Convalescent Hosp., Barstow, 1995—, Mojave Valley Hospice, 1983—, VNA Hospice, Barstow, 1994—, Optioncare Home Health Svcs., 1995—. Recipient Loving Care award Vis. Nurse Assn. Inland Counties, 1988. Fellow ACP; mem. AMA, ACP, Am. Med. Dirs. Assn., Am. Diabetes Assn., Calif. Med. Assn., San Bernardino County Med. Soc., Am. Soc. Internal Medicine, Am. Geriatric Soc., Acad. Hospice Physicians, Nat. Hospice Orgn., Internat. Coll. Hospice and Palliative Care, Soc. Gen. Internal Medicine, Am. Numismatic Assn., Combined Orgns. Numismatic Error Collectors Am. Democrat. Roman Catholic. Avocations: astronomy. Office: 209 N 2nd Ave Barstow CA 92311-2222

SUTTERFIELD, KEVIN JAMES, lawyer, consultant; b. Long Beach, Calif., July 16, 1955; s. George Washington Sutterfield Jr. and Faun (Memmott) Hughes; m. Paula Sowards, May 20, 1987 (dec. Jan. 1998); children: Ashley, Hailey, Nathaniel, Taylor, Morgan. BA, Brigham Young U., 1979, JD, 1982. Bar: Utah 1982, U.S. Dist. Ct. Utah 1982, U.S. Ct. Appeals (10th cir.) 1984. Assoc. Dart & Stegall, Salt Lake City, 1982-83; assoc. Ray G. Martineau, Salt Lake City, 1983-86; mem. Howard, Lewis & Petersen, Provo, Utah, 1987-94; mem., founder Hickinger & Sutterfield, P.C., 1994—. Contbr. articles to profl. jours. Organizer, incorporator, gen. counsel, trustee Nat. Kidney Found. Utah, 1986-88. Mem. ATLA, Utah Trial Lawyers Assn. (bd. dirs. 1992—, editor in chief Utah Trial Jour. 1993—), Utah Bar Assn., Utah Cen. Bar Assn., Cougar Club, Riverside Country Club. Democrat. Mormon. Avocations: golf, tennis, snow and water skiing. E-mail: Kevin@Flickinger-Sutterfield.com. Office: Flickinger & Sutterfield 2750 N University Ave Provo UT 84604-3861

SUTTLES, VIRGINIA GRANT, advertising executive; b. Urbana, Ill., June 13, 1931; d. William Henry and Lenora (Fitzsimmons) Grant; m. John Henry Suttles, Sept. 24, 1977; step-children: Linda Suttles Daniels, Peg Suttles La Croix, Pamela Suttles Diaz, Randall. Grad. pub. schs., Mahomet, Ill. Media estimator and Procter & Gamble budget control Tatham-Laird, Inc., Chgo., 1955-60; media planner, supr. Tracy-Locke Co., Inc., Dallas and Denver, 1961-68; media dir., account exec. Lorie-Lotito, Inc., 1968-72; v.p., media dir. Sam Lusky Assos., Inc., Denver, 1972-86; ind. media buyer, 1984-89; mktg. asst. mktg. dept. Del E. Webb Communities, Inc., Sun City West, Ariz., 1985-88, with telemarketing dept., 1989-90, homeowner coord., 1993-97; mktg. coord. asst./media buyer, Del Webb Corp., Phoenix, 1990-93; lectr. sr. journalism class U. Colo., Boulder, 1975-80; condr. class in media seminars Denver Advt. Fedn., 1974, 77; Colo. State U. panelist Broadcast Day, 1978, High Sch. Inst., 1979, 80, 81, 82, 83. Founder, Del E. Webb Meml. Hosp. Found.; patron founder Tree of Life Nat. Kidney Found. of Colo.- Rockies Snow Mountain YMCA Ranch, Winter Park, Colo., Sun Health Found. Sun Cities, Ariz. State U. Found. Sundome Perfroming Arts Ctr. Mem. Denver Advt. Fedn. (bd. dir. 1973-75, program chmn. 1974-76, 80-82, exec. bd., v.p. ops. 1980-81, chmn. Alfie awards com. 1980-81, advt. profl. of Yr. 1981-82), Denver Advt. Golf Assn. (v.p. 1976-77, pres. 1977-78), Colo. Broadcasters Assn., Sun City West Bowling Assn. (bd. dirs. 1987-88), Am. Legion Aux. (Historian, pub. chmn. 1998—), VFW Aux., Air Force Sgt.'s Assn. Aux., Sun City Art Mus. Women's League. Republican. Congregationalist. Home: 20002 N Greenview Dr Sun City West AZ 85375-5579

SUTTON, DIANNA, foundation executive; b. Jacksonville, Fla., Sept. 11, 1952; d. Glenn Vernon, Sr. and Evelyn Louise (Barnes) S.; m. William Linhart Baumann, Nov. 21, 1993 (div. June 1997); 1 child, Jennifer Ryan Louise Selph. Student, U. Colo., 1986, U. No. Colo., 1997. Cert. fundraising exec. Nat. Soc. of Fund Raising Execs. Asst. to edn., opers. dir. Denver Mus. of Natural History, 1988-89; asst. dir. of devel. Opera Colo., Denver, 1989-91; sr. devel. assoc./major gifts program mgr. Denver Zool. Found., 1991-96; pres., CEO Yampa Valley Cmty. Found., Steamboat Springs, Colo., 1996—; editl. advisor Coun. on Founds., Washington, 1997-98; treas. Parker Cultural Commn., Colo., 1994-96; cons. non-profit orgns., 1994—; mentor Cmty. Resource Ctr., Denver, 1994—. County caucus rep. Dem. Party, Steamboat Springs, 1998. Mem. Rotary, nat. Soc. Fund Raising Execs. Presbyterian. Avocations: tennis, softball, jogging, chess. Home: PO Box 773914 Steamboat Springs CO 80477-3914 Office: Yampa Valley Cmty Found PO Box 774965 Steamboat Springs CO 80477-4965

SUTTON, L. PAUL, criminal justice educator; b. Munich, Aug. 16, 1948; s. William L. Sutton and Paulette Mikkelson. BS in Polit. Sci. and History, U. Kans., 1970; MA in Criminal Justice, SUNY, Albany, 1971, PhD in Criminal Justice, 1975. Asst. prof. sociology U. N.Mex., Albuquerque, 1976-78; rsch. assoc. Hindelang Criminal Justice Rsch. Ctr., Albany, N.Y., 1974-76; prof. criminal justice San Diego State U., 1981—; sr. rsch. assoc. Nat. Ctr. for State Cts., Williamsburg, Va., 1978-81; ind. filmmaker, N.Mex., Calif., 1982-92; cons. State of Calif. Dept. of Corrections, 1997-98; commr. cmty.-based punishment planning com., San Diego, 1996-97; bd. dirs. Nat. Forum on Criminal Justice, Springfield, Ill., 1980-81; expert witness on sentencing reform Nat. Acad. Scis., Washington, 1981. Producer documentary film Doing Time: Ten Years Later, 1991, Doing Time, 1979; co-author: The Search Warrant Process, 1984, Sentencing by Mathematics, 1982. Grantee Calif. State Dept. Corrections, 1997, NEH, 1979. Mem. AAUP, Am. Soc. Criminology,Acad. Criminal Justice Scis., Western Soc. Criminology, Phi Beta Kappa. Avocations: filmmaking, sailing, jogging. Office: San Diego State U Dept Criminal Justice San Diego CA 92182-4505

SUTTON, MARCELLA FRENCH, interior designer; b. Prague, Czechoslovakia, Sept. 4, 1946; came to U.S., 1952, naturalized, 1956; d. Eugen E. and Frances V. (Pruchovia) French; BS in Profl. Arts, Woodbury U., 1971; m. Michael D. Sutton, Feb. 11, 1978; 1 child, Kevin Christopher. Mgr. design dept. W. & J. Sloane, Beverly Hills, Calif., 1972-76; project dir. Milton I. Swimmer, Beverly Hills, 1977-78; owner, interior designer Marcella French Designs, Woodland Hills and La Crescenta, Calif., 1969-94; owner designer project mgr., constrn. and design Marcella French Designs, 1994—, prin. designer; property mgmt. coord., interior designer Home Savs. and Loan., State of Calif., L.A., 1979-82; regional premises officer, asst. v.p. regional hdqrs. Bank Am., L.A., 1981-86; v.p. M.D. Sutton Ins. Agy.; cons. pvt. residences, comml. bldgs., office and banks. Project mgr., 1st v.p. fundraising Shephard of the Valley Sch., 1989-90, enrichment chmn., 1990-91, mem. enrichment program pub. sch. calendar, 1991; active Young Reps., Vinyard Ch.; treas. West Hills Baseball Aux., 1989-93; arcades coord. Theatre Arts Festival for Youth, Agoura, 1992-94, co-chmn. ways and means RTRWF, 1992-94, 1st v.p., 1995-97, program chmn., 1996-97; judge Sci. Fair, 1993-95; treas. Taxpayers United for Fairness, 1994-99; co-organizer 9th and 10th Grade Parent Network Orgn. & Found., Chaminade, 1994-95; pres., area chmn. Paul Jhin, 1998—, del. C.R.A., alt. Los Angeles County ctrl. com., 1998—; Mamie Eisenhower chmn. for book donations LACFRW. Recipient various scholarships.

SUWINSKY, PAM POKORNEY, book publisher; b. Pittston, Pa., Aug. 28, 1954; d. Walter Francis and Sophia Marie (Matthews) Pokorney; m. Henry Frank Suwinsky, Jr., Apr. 7, 1990. BA in Classics, English, Pa. State U., 1976; MA in English, U. Chgo., 1977; postgrad., U. Ill., Chgo., 1983-85. Permissions asst. U. Chgo. Press., 1977-79, design and prodn. asst., 1979-81, prodn. coord., 1981-83, sr. prodn. coord., 1983-85; prodn. mgr. Beacon Press, Boston, 1985-88, design and prodn. mgr., 1988-90; prodn. editing mgr. Addison-Wesley, Menlo Park, Calif., 1991-98; dir. Thalia Pub. Svcs., Cupertino, Calif., 1998—. Prin. author: Chicago Guide to Electronic MSS, 1987. Mem. Bookbuilders of Boston (bd. dirs. 1989-91), Chgo. Book Clinic, Am. Inst. Graphic Art. Roman Catholic. Avocations: cooking, dance, theatre, reading, art.

SUYAMA, RUTH LEIKO, historian, educator; b. L.A., Apr. 15, 1937; d. Hajime and Kimi S.; m. Howard Kim. BA, San Jose (Calif.) State U., 1960; MA, Stanford U., 1962; EdD, Nova U., 1976. Prof. history Glendale (Calif.) Coll., 1965-75, L.A. City Coll., 1975-86, L.A. Mission Coll., Sylmar, Calif., 1986—; rev. Houghton Mifflin, 1994. Mem. Stanford Alumni Assn. (life). Office: LA Mission Coll 13356 Eldridge Ave Sylmar CA 91342-3200

SUZUKI, BOB H., university president. Formerly v.p. acad. affairs Calif. State Univ., Northridge; pres. Calif. State Poly. Univ., Pomona, 1991—. Office: Calif State Polytech Univ Office of Pres 3801 W Temple Ave Pomona CA 91768-2557

SUZUKI, DAVID TAKAYOSHI, geneticist, science broadcaster; b. Vancouver, B.C., Can., Mar. 24, 1936; s. Kaoru Carr and Setsu (Nakamura) S.; m. Joane Setsuko Sunahara, Aug. 20, 1958 (div. 1965); children—Tamiko Lynda, Troy Takashi, Laura Miya; m. Tara Elizabeth Cullis, Dec. 10, 1972; children—Severn Setsu, Sarika Freda. BA cum laude, Amherst Coll., Mass., 1958; PhD, U. Chgo., 1961; LLD (hon.), U. P.E.I., 1974, Queen's U., Ont., 1987; DSc (hon.), Acadia U., N.S., 1979, McMaster U., Ont., 1987, U. Windsor, Ont., 1979, Trent U., Ont., 1981, Lakehead U., Ont., 1986; DHL (hon.), Gov.'s State U., Ill., 1986. Research assoc. Oak Ridge Nat. Lab., 1961-62; asst. prof. U. Alta., Edmonton, Can., 1961-63; asst. prof. dept. zoology U. B.C., Vancouver, 1963-65, assoc. prof., 1965-69, prof., 1969—; vis. prof. UCLA, 1966, U. Calif.-Berkeley, 1969, 1976-77, U. Utah, Salt Lake City, 1971-72, U. P.R., 1972, U. Toronto, 1978. Host TV programs Suzuki on Sci., CBC, Vancouver, 1971-72, Sci. Mag., Toronto, 1974-79, Quirks & Quarks, Vancouver, 1974-79, Nature of Things, Toronto, 1979—; host series on sci. TV programs Interface, 1974-75, Just Ask, Inc., 1980, Night Video, 1984, Futurescan, 1984; radio program Discovery, 1983—; author: (textbook) Introduction to Genetic Analysis, 1976, David Suzuki Looks at Plants, 1985, David Suzuki Looks at Insects, 1986, David Suzuki Looks at Senses, 1986, Egg-Carton Zoo, 1986, Sciencescape: The Nature of Canada, 1986, British Columbia: Frontier for Ideas, 1986, From Pebbles to Computers, 1986; contbr. articles to profl. and popular publs. and mags. Bd. dirs. B.C. Civil Liberties Assn., 1973, Can. Civil Liberties Assn., 1982—. Decorated officer Order of Can.; recipient W.R. Steacie Meml. award Nat. Research Council Can., 1969-72; Sci. and Engring. medal Sci. Council B.C., 1981; UN Environ. Programme medal, 1985; grantee Can. Nat. Research Council, AEC, Nat. Cancer Inst. Can., NIH also others; recipient UNESCO Kalinga prize, 1986, Royal Bank award, 1986. Mem. Alliance of Can. TV and Radio Artists (award 1986), Genetic Soc. Am., Sci. Council Can. Mem. New Democratic Party. Avocations: scuba diving; fishing; skiing. Address: # 219, 2211 W 4th Ave, Vancouver, BC Canada V6K 4S4*

SVEE, GARY DUANE, newspaper editor, author, journalist; b. Billings, Mont., Nov. 11, 1943; s. Sigvart Oluf and Beatrice Evelyn (Lund) S.; m. C. Diane Schmidt, June 26, 1966; children—Darren Kirk, Nathan Jared. B.A., U. Mont., 1967. Unit mgr. Midland Bank, Billings, Mont., 1967-69; reporter Billings Gazette, 1969-76, opinion editor, 1982—; pub. Bridger (Mont.) Bonanza, 1976-77; feature editor Missoulian, Missoula, Mont., 1977-81. Author: Spirit Wolf, 1987, Incident at Pishkin Creek, 1989, Sanctuary, 1990 (Best Western novel Western Writers Am. 1990), Single Tree. vestryman St. Luke's Meml. Bd., Billings, 1989, Salvation Army, Missoula, 1980-82; vestryman Holy Spirit Parish, Missoula, 1980-82. Served to lt. USAR, 1966-72. Recipient Business Writing award U. Mo., 1974, Minority Affairs Reporting award N.W. region Sigma Delta Chi, 1980. Mem. Kiwanis (bd. dirs. Billings club 1988-89, 2d v.p. 1989, pres. 1990, 91-92), Theta Chi. Episcopalian. Avocations: fishing, golf, writing, sculpting, reading. Home: 474 Indian Trl Billings MT 59105-2706 Office: Billings Gazette PO Box 36300 Billings MT 59107-6300*

SVEEN, JAMES E., state official; b. Bremerton, Wash., June 11, 1953; s. Ernest J. and Laura Evelyn (Johnson) S.; m. Ann Lorraine Quinn, June 22, 1996; 1 child, Sarah Lorraine; children by previous marriage: James Christopher, Laurie Ann, Brita Denise. AAS, C.C. of Air Force, Tacoma, Wash., 1979; AS, St. Martin's Coll., Lacey, Wash., 1979, BA, 1982; MBA, U. S.D., 1985. Commd. lt. USAF, 1983-94, advanced through grades to capt.; chief policy devel. and compliance sect. 44th Strategic Missile Wing, Ellsworth AFB, S.D., 1983-87; dir. info. mgmt., human resource mgr., dir. edn., asst. prof U. Wash./Air Force Res. Officer Tng. Program, Seattle, 1987-91; contracts mgr. edn. with industry The Boeing Co. USAF, Seattle, 1991-92; contracts mgr. Milstar Satellite Comm. USAF, Hanscom AFB, Mass., 1992-94; contracts specialist Wash. State Mil. Dept., Fairchild AFB, 1995—; adj. faculty contract mgmt. cert. program Middlesex C.C., Bedford, Mass., 1994. Contbr. articles to profl. jours. Mem. ABA (govt. bus. assoc. pub. contract law sect.), Nat. Contract Mgmt. Assn. (cert., Boston chpt. awards chmn. 1993—, v.p. for edn. 1993-94, bd. dirs. 1993-94, pres.'s coun. 1993-94, contract mgmt. edn. and state and local govt. spl. topics com. 1993—, Puget Sound chpt. v.p. for ops. 1994-95), Nat. Assn. Purchasing Mgrs. (1st v.p. 1997—, Spokane affiliate, mem. MRO buyers group 1997—), Soc. of Fellows. Home: 3618 E 13th Ave Spokane WA 99202-5409 Office: 141 Civil Engring Squadron 2 S Olympia Ave Bldg 2001E Fairchild Air Force Base WA 99011-9650

SVIDOR, RHONA BEVERLY, real estate broker, elementary education educator; b. Boston, May 12, 1934; d. Sydney Z. and Bella (Shapiro) Zonis; m. Leonard Svidor, May 23, 1957; 1 child, Mark Allen. AA, UCLA, 1957; BA, Calif. State U., L.A., 1959, MA in Am. Studies, 1972. Lic. real estate broker; cert. elem. and secondary edn. tchr. Tchr. Rivera Sch. System, 1956-57, Hermosa Beach Sch. System, 1958-59, L.A. City Schs., 1959-88; real estate broker Rhona Realty, San Fernando Valley, Calif., 1977—. —, der art history group Valley U. Women, 1989-99, v.p. of programs, 1994; bd. dirs. SFV Bd. Brandeis U. Women's Com., 1993-94; leader Classical World Through Art and French, The Classical World Through Art, 1995—, co-leader Enjoying Poetry, 1997 Brandeis U. Women's Com., 1993—; program chmn. Pacific Asia Mus. Himalayan Arts Coun., 1993-94; bd. dirs. Natanya Na'amat USA, theatre chairperson. Mem. Toastmasters (v.p. membership 1993-94, 98, pres. 1994-95, chair 1993-94, v.p. programs 1995). Avocations: traveling, writing, reading, swimming.

SVIKHART, EDWIN GLADDIN, investment banker; b. Chgo., July 12, 1930; s. Edwin Gabriel and Mildred Charlotte (Slapnicka) S.; m. Joann Barbara Frisk, Aug. 22, 1954; children: David E., Robert E. BA, Beloit (Wis.) Coll., 1952; postgrad., Bradley U., 1957-59. With Caterpillar Tractor Co., Peoria, Ill., 1956-66; chief fin. officer Berglund Inc., Napa, Calif., 1966-71; chief fin. officer, treas. Galion (Ohio) Mfg. Co., 1971-77; chief operating officer constrn. equip. internat. div. Dresser Industries, Inc., Columbus, Ohio, 1977-81; chief operating officer Rocky Mountain Machinery Co., Salt Lake City, 1981-87; chief oper. officer Custom Equipment Corp., Salt Lake City, 1989-92; ptnr. Travis Capital Mkts., Salt Lake City, 1992—. Served to lt. (j.g.) USN, 1952-56.

SWAN, KENNETH CARL, surgeon; b. Kansas City, Mo., Jan. 1, 1912; s. Carl E. and Blanche (Peters) S.; m. Virginia Grone, Feb. 5, 1938; children: Steven Carl, Kenneth, Susan. A.B., U. Oreg., 1933, M.D., 1936. Diplomate: Am. Bd. Ophthalmology (chmn. 1960-61). Intern U. Wis., 1936-37; resident in ophthalmology State U. Iowa, 1937-40; practice medicine specializing in ophthalmology Portland, Oreg., 1945—; staff Good Samaritan Hosp.; asst. prof. ophthalmology State U. Iowa, Iowa City, 1941-44; asso. prof. U. Oreg. Med. Sch., Portland, 1944-45, prof. and head dept. ophthalmology, 1945-78; Chmn. sensory diseases study sect. NIH; mem. adv. council Nat. Eye Inst.; also adv. council Nat. Inst. Neurol. Diseases and Blindness. Contbr. articles on ophthalmic subjects to med. publs. Recipient Proctor Rsch. medal, 1953, Disting. Svc. award U. Oreg., 1963, Meritorious Achievement award U. Oreg. Med. Sch., 1968, Howe Ophthalmology medal, 1977, Aubrey Watzek Pioneer award Lewis and Clark Coll., 1979, Disting. Alumnus award Oreg. Health Scis. U. Alumni Assn., 1988, Disting. Svc. award, 1988, Mentor award Oreg. Health Scis. Found., 1996; named Oreg. Scientist of Yr. Oreg. Mus. Sci. and Industry, 1959. Mem. Assn. Research in Ophthalmology, Am. Acad. Ophthalmology (v.p. 1978, historian), Soc.

Exptl. Biology and Medicine, AAAS, AMA, Am. Ophthal. Soc. (Howe medal for distinguished service 1977), Oreg. Med. Soc., Sigma Xi, Sigma Chi (Significant Sig award 1977). Home: 4645 SW Fairview Blvd Portland OR 97221-2624 Office: Ophthalmology Dept Oreg Health Scis U Portland OR 97201

SWANK, ROY LAVER, physician, educator, inventor; b. Camas, Wash., Mar. 5, 1909; s. Wilmer and Hannah Jane (Laver) S.; m. Eulalia F. Shively, Sept. 14, 1936 (dec.); children: Robert L., Susan Jane (Mrs. Joel Keizer) Stephen (dec.); m. Betty Harris, May 23, 1987 (dec. June 1997); m. Luanna Kirksey, May 2, 1998. Student, U. Wash., 1926-30; MD, Northwestern U., 1935, PhD, 1935. House officer, resident Peter Bent Brigham Hosp., Boston, 1936-39; fellow pathology Harvard Med. Sch., 1938-39; mem. staff neurol. unit Boston City Hosp., 1945-48; asst. prof. neurology Montreal Neurol. Inst., McGill U., 1948-54; prof. medicine and neurology, head divsn. neurology Oreg. Med. Sch., 1954-75, prof. emeritus, 1975—; dir. Swank Multiple Sclerosis Clinic, Beaverton, Oreg., 1994—; pres. Pioneer Filters, 1970-78. Served to maj. M.C. AUS, 1942-46. Recipient Oreg. Gov.'s award for research in multiple sclerosis, 1966. Mem. Am. Physiol. Soc., Am. Neurol. Assn., European Microcirculation Soc., Sigma Xi. Achievements include invention of micro embolic filler; research of physical chemical changes in blood after fat meals and during surgical shock, platelet-leukocyte aggregation in stored blood in hypotensive shock; low-fat diet in multiple sclerosis; research of physical chemical changes in multiple sclerosis (plasma proteins); importance of plasma proteins in multiple sclerosis; investigation of breakdown of blood-brain barrier by infused micro emboli, and by in vitro produced micro emboli due to aggregated red blood cells. Home: 789 SW Summit View Dr Portland OR 97225-6185 Office: Swank Multiple Sclerosis Clin 13655 SW Jenkins Rd Beaverton OR 97005-1139

SWANSON, CHERYL ANN, small business owner, nurse; b. L.A., Feb. 17, 1967; d. Donald Herbert Cox and Mary Rosalie (Bowlds) Hook; m. Timothy Howard Swanson, Feb. 28, 1982 (div. Sept. 1987); 1 child, Christopher Michael. BSN magna cum laude, U. Ariz., 1995. RN, Ariz.; CCRN. Sales mgr. Double M Gem, Pocatello, Idaho, 1987-89, Desert Gem, Tucson, 1990-93; owner, mgr. AAA Loan & Jewelry, Tucson, 1993—; critical care nurse St. Joseph's Hosp., 1995. Scholar Idaho State U., 1988-89, M.B. and C.J. O'Connel scholar U. Ariz., 1995. Mem. ANA, Nat. League for Nursing, Golden Key, Sigma Theta Tau, Phi Kappa Phi. Democrat. Roman Catholic. Avocations: travel, writing, reading. Office: AAA Loan & Jewelry 1902 S Craycroft Rd Tucson AZ 85711-6621

SWANSON, DONALD ALAN, geologist; b. Tacoma, July 25, 1938; s. Leonard Walter and Edith Christine (Bowers) S.; m. Barbara Joan White, May 25, 1974. BS in Geology, Wash. State U., 1960; PhD in Geology, Johns Hopkins U., 1964. Geologist U.S. Geol. Survey, Menlo Park, Calif., 1965-68, 71-80, Hawaii National Park, 1968-71; sr. geologist Cascades Volcano Obs. U.S. Geol. Survey, Vancouver, Wash., 1980-90, rsch. scientist-in-charge, 1986-89; sr. geologist U.S. Geol. Survey, Seattle, 1990-96; assoc. dir. Volcano Systems Ctr. U. Wash., 1993-96; scientist-in-charge Hawaiian Volcano Obs., 1997—; affiliate prof. U. Wash., 1992—; cons. U.S. Dept. Energy, Richland, Wash., 1979-83; volcanologist New Zealand Geol. Survey, Taupo, 1984; advisor Colombian Volcano Obs., Manizales, 1986. Assoc. editor Jour. Volcanology and Geothermal Rsch., 1976—, Jour. Geophys. Rsch., 1992-94; editor Bull. of Volcanology, 1985-90, exec. editor, 1995—; contbr. numerous articles to profl. jours. Recipient Superior Service award U.S. Geol. Survey, 1980, Meritorious Service award U.S. Dept. Interior, 1985; postdoctoral fellow NATO, 1964-65. Fellow Geol. Soc. Am., Am. Geophys. Union; mem. AAAS, Sigma Xi. Avocation: hiking. Home: 417 Linaka St Hilo HI 96720-5927 Office: US Geol Survey Hawaiian Volcano Obs PO Box 51 Hawaii National Park HI 96718-0051

SWANSON, JANE BRADLEY, artist, realtor; b. Oak Park, Ill., Dec. 23; d. Willson Dorr Bradley and Lucille Mary Jane (Joyc) Tegen; m. Donald Glenn Earl Swanson, June 10, 1960; children: Lynne H. Suhling, Jon Glenn Bradley, Erik Donald Payson. BA, Rosary Coll., 1960. Lic. real estate agt., Ill., Hawaii; cert. master designer Florists Transworld Del. Assn., Ill. Substitute tchr. Brookfield, West Chester, Ill., 1960-70; lectr. Weight Watchers Chgo., Oak Brook, Ill., 1970-77; florist Darien, Ill., 1981-88, Aurora, Ill., 1986-89; realtor assoc. Murphy and Assoc., Naperville, Ill., 1988-89, ERA Maui Real Estate, Kihei, Hawaii, 1990—; artist Lahaina, Hawaii, 1990—. Mem. Plein Air Painters Maui (founder, treas. 1997—), Lahaina Arts Soc., Hui Noeau. Episcopalian. Avocations: photography, computer, reading. Home: 12 Alaiki Pl Makawao HI 96768-9310 Office: ERA Maui Real Estate 1847 Soikihei Rd # 103 Kihei HI 96753

SWANSON, JOHN AUGUST, artist; b. L.A., Jan. 11, 1938; s. John August and Mary Magdalene (Velasquez) S. LHD (hon.), Calif. Luth. U., 1996. lectr. in field. One-man shows include Mus. Art, Sci., & Industry, Bridgeport, Conn., 1987, Mus. History and Art, Ontario, Calif., 1987, L.A. Printmaking Soc., 1993 (Purchase award), Calif. Luth. U., Thousand Oaks, 1996, U. St. Thomas, St. Paul, 1996, Calvin Coll., Grand Rapids, Mich., 1998, Brauer Mus. Art, Valparaiso, Ind., 1998, Polis. Inst., Indpls., 1998; represented in permanent collections at Vatican Mus., Bibliotheque Nationale, Paris, Smithsonian Instn.-Nat. Mus. Am. Art, Nat. Mus. Am. History, Nat. Air and Space Mus.; collaborator: There is A Season, 1995 (Cath. Press award 1996); illustrator: Miidrashim, 1976. Fundraiser Nat. Assn. Hispanic Elderly, L.A., 1985-98. Mem. L.A. Printmaking Soc. Democrat. Roman Catholic. Avocations: violinist, music. Home: 2903 Waverly Dr Los Angeles CA 90039-2015

SWANSON, KENNETH J., museum administrator. Adminstr. Idaho State Hist. Mus., Boise. Office: Idaho State Hist Mus 610 Julia Davis Dr Boise ID 83702-7646*

SWANSON, PAUL RUBERT, minister; b. Bakersfield, Calif., May 13, 1943; s. Roland Hilding and Myrtle Isabelle (Magnuson) S.; m. Mary Elizabeth Greene, June 18, 1967; children: Kristen Ann, Karlynn Marie, Jonathan Paul. BA, Pacific Luth. U., 1966; MDiv, Luth. Sch. Theology, 1970. Ordained minister, Luth. Ch. Pastor 1st Luth. Ch., Anaconda, Mont., 1970-76, King of Kings Luth. Ch., Milwaukie, Oreg., 1976-84; asst. to bishop Pacific N.W. Synod-Luth. Ch. in Am., Portland, Oreg., 1984-87; bishop Oreg. Synod-Evang. Luth. Ch. Am., Portland, 1987—; bd. dirs. Legacy Health System, Portland. Regent Pacific Luth. U., Tacoma, 1987—; bd. dirs. Emanuel Hosp., Portland, 1987; chmn. bd. dirs. Hearthstone, Inc., Anaconda, 1973-76; bd. dirs. Ecumenical Ministries Oreg., Portland, 1984—. Recipient Disting. Svc. award Pacific Luth. U., 1993. Avocation: golf. *

SWANSON, RICHARD WILLIAM, retired statistician; b. Rockford, Ill., July 26, 1934; s. Richard and Erma Marie (Herman) S.; m. Laura Yoko Arai, Dec. 30, 1970. BS, Iowa State U., 1958, MS, 1964. Ops. analyst Stanford Rsch. Inst., Monterey, Calif., 1958-62; statistician ARINC Rsch. Corp., Washington, 1964-65; sr. scientist Booz-Allen Applied Rsch., Vietnam, 1965-67, L.A., 1967-68; sr. ops. analyst Control Data Corp., Honolulu, 1968-70; mgmt. cons., Honolulu, 1970-73; exec. v.p. SEQUEL Corp., Honolulu, 1973-75; bus. cons. Hawaii Dept. Planning and Econ. Devel., Honolulu, 1975-77, tax rsch. and planning officer Dept. Taxation, 1977-82; ops. rsch. analyst U.S. Govt., 1982-89; shipyard statisician U.S. Govt., 1989-97; ret., 1997. Served with AUS, 1954-56. Mem. Hawaiian Acad. Sci., Sigma Xi. Home: 583 Kamoku St Apt 3505 Honolulu HI 96826-5241

SWANSON, ROBERT KILLEN, management consultant; b. Deadwood, S.D., Aug. 11, 1932; s. Robert Claude and Marie Elizabeth (Kersten) S.; m. Nancy Anne Oyaas, July 19, 1958; children: Cathryn Lynn, Robert Stuart, Bart Killen. BA, U. S.D., 1954; postgrad., U. Melbourne, Australia, 1955. With Gen. Mills, Inc., Mpls., 1955-58, 71-79, v.p., 1971-73, group v.p., 1973-77, exec. v.p., 1977-79; with Marathon Oil Co., Findlay, Ohio, 1958-60; sr. v.p., dir. Needham, Harper & Steers, Inc., Chgo., 1961-69; joint mng. dir. S. H. Benson (Holdings) Ltd., Eng., 1969-71; pres., chief operating officer Greyhound Corp., Phoenix, 1980; chmn., chief exec. officer Del E. Webb Corp., Phoenix, 1981-87; chmn. RKS Inc., Phoenix, 1987—; bd. dirs. Am. [illegible] Ltd. 2d lt. U.S. Army, 1955. Fulbright scholar, 1954-55; Woodrow Wilson scholar. Mem. U.K. Dirs. Inst., U.S. Internat. Scholars Assn., English Speaking Union, Phoenix Country Club. Episcopalian. Office: RKS Inc 5600 N Palo Cristi Rd Scottsdale AZ 85253-7543

SWARD, JEFFREY EDWIN, information systems specialist; b. Milw., Jan. 16, 1953; m. Andrea J. Lankow, June 7, 1975. MusB, Calif. State U., Fullerton, 1975, BA in Math., 1976, postgrad. in photography, 1977, MusM, 1978; postgrad., Newport (Calif.) Sch. Photography, 1980, Orange Coast Coll., 1985-87. Computer programmer State of Calif., Fullerton, 1971-78; mem. tech. staff Computer Scis. Corp., Santa Ana, Calif., 1978-80; sr. programmer analyst Figgie Internat., Anaheim, Calif., 1980-81; applications systems specialist TRW, Orange, Calif., 1981-89; sr. programmer analyst Cox Comms., Irvine, Calif., 1989-96; sr. systems project specialist Automobile Club of So. Calif., Costa Mesa, 1996-98; sys. analyst CDB Infotek, Santa Ana, Calif., 1998—; freelance photographer, 1971—. Photographs exhibited at various local shows, 1987—. Choir dir. Garden Grove (Calif.) United Ch. of Christ, 1973-76; oboist Fullerton Civic Light Opera, 1974-87; oboist, English hornist Chapman Symphony, 1984-89; mem. Friends of Photography, 1986—, L.A. Ctr. for Photographic Studies, 1978—. Fine Arts scholar Bank of Am., 1971. Mem. Friends of Photography, Huntington Beach Art League, L.A. Ctr. for Photographic Studies, Phi Kappa Phi, Phi Kappa Lambda. Avocation: photography. Home: PO Box 7019 Huntington Beach CA 92615-7019

SWARD, ROBERT STUART, author; b. Chgo., June 23, 1933; s. Irving Michael and Gertrude (Huebsch) S.; life ptnr. Gloria K. Alford; children: Cheryl, Barbara, Michael, Hannah, Nicholas. *Grandparents Hyman David Swerdloff and wife, Bessie, left Poltava, Russia, in 1905 for New York where "Swerdloff" was Americanized to "Sward." Daughter Cheryl Cox Macpherson, is a Professor of Histology and Ethics at St. Georges University School Medicine, Grenada, West Indies. Her daughter, Maxine, was born in 1998. Daughter Barbara Kamala Joy owns Earth Matters, an environmental consulting firm in Novato, California. Married to David Webb. Two children: Aaron, born 1985; Robin born 1989. Son Michael is a master carpenter. Daughter, Hannah Davi Sward owns Patrick McCarthy Gallery in Los Angeles. She is author of Diary of a Non-Starlet. Son Nicholas Sward is a silkscreen artist.* BA with hons., U. Ill., 1956; MA, U. Iowa, 1958; postgrad., U. Bristol (Eng.), 1960-61, Middlebury (Vt.) Coll., 1956-60. Instr. English Conn. Coll., New London, 1958-59; writer-in-residence Cornell U., Ithaca, N.Y., 1962-64, U. Iowa, 1967-68; asst. prof. English/writer-in-residence U. Victoria (B.C.), 1969-73; editor/pubr. Soft Press, Victoria, 1970-79; radio broadcaster Can. Broadcasting Corp., Toronto, Ont., 1979-84; tech. writer Santa Cruz Op. (SCO), Santa Cruz, Calif., 1987-89; writer-in-residence extension program U. Calif., Santa Cruz, 1988—; writer-in-residence Cabrillo Coll., Aptos, Calif., 1988—; vis. poet creative writing program U. Calif., Santa Cruz, 1992—; writer in the schs. Ont. Arts Coun., Toronto, 1979-84, Cultural Coun., Santa Cruz, 1984—; cons. to pubs.; book reviewer Toronto Star, others. Author: Uncle Dog and Other Poems, 1962, Autobiography, CAAS, 1991, Poems: New and Selected, 1983, Four Incarnations: New and Selected Poems, 1957-91; (with Charles Atkinson, David Swanger and Tilly Shaw) Family, 1994, A Much-Married Man, A Novel, 1996, (poetry collection) Uncivilizing, 1997; editor eSCENE, 1996, Blue Penny Quar., summer 1996, Pares cum paribus, summer 1997. Tchr. Oak Bay Sr. Citizens, Victoria, 1973-74; editor, advisor Jazz Press, Poet Santa Cruz Pubs., 1985-87. With USN, 1951-54. Fulbright grantee, 1961, Guggenheim fellow, 1964-65, D.H. Lawrence fellow, U. N.Mex., 1966-67, Yaddo MacDowell Colony grantee, 1959-82; Djerassi Found. grantee, 1990—; recipient Villa Montalvo Lit. Arts award, 1989-90. Mem. League of Can. Poets, Writers Union of Can. (newsletter editor 1983-84), Nat. Writers Union. Democrat. Avocations: yoga, Macintosh computers, photography, swimming, book design. Home: PO Box 7062 Santa Cruz CA 95061-7062 Office: 435 Meder St Santa Cruz CA 95060-2307

SWART, BONNIE BLOUNT, artist; b. Shreveport, La., May 19, 1939; d. Jonathan Prescott and Alice Florence (Crawford) Blount; m. Carter Eaton Swart; children: Kathleen Anne, Nancy Laurie, Sherry Colleen. Student, U. Calif., Davis, Ventura Coll., 1984-88. Exhibited in group exhbns. at Am. Acad. Equine Art, 1989, 92, 93, 94, 96, 97, Nat. Mus. of the Horse, Lexington, Ky., Pastel Soc. of West Coast, Sacramento, 1995, 96, 97, Ann. Exhbn. on Animals in Art, La. State U., Baton Rouge, 1995, 96, Art at the Dog Show, Wichita, Kans., 1995, Harness Tracks of Am., Lexington, 1994, 96, Am. Acad. of Equine Art, Louisville, 1992, 93, 96, Arabian Jockey Club Art Auction, Delaware Park, Del., 1991, Equine Rsch. Benefit, Morvin Park, Leesburg, 1991, Arabian Horse Trust Art Auction, Scottsdale, 1990, 97-98, Women Artist's of the West, Biloxi, Miss., 1989, 97, 98, Internat. Arabian Horse Assn., Ky. Horse Park, Louisville, 1989, Arabian Horse Trust Mus. Exhibit, Westminster, Colo., 1987-89, Oil Painters of Am., Taos, N.Mex., 1997; represented in pvt. collections. Mem. Am. Acad. Equine Art (assoc.), Knickerbocker Artists (signature mem.), Pastel Soc. West Coast (signature mem.). Home: 2806 Gershwin Ct Lancaster CA 93536

SWARTZ, BETH AMES, artist; b. N.Y.C., Feb. 5, 1936. BS, Cornell U., 1957; MA, NYU, 1960. Co-founder Internat. Friends of Transformative Art, Phoenix, 1988; exec. dir. Culture Care, Phoenix, 1994; visual artist N.Y.C..Scottsdale/Phoenix, 1965—. Exhibited in solo shows at Ariz. State U, Phoenix, 1970, Rosenzweig Ctr. Gallery, Phoenix, 1970, Galleria Janna, Mexico City, 1971, Pavilion Gallery, Scottsdale, 1975, Springfield (Mo.) Art Mus., 1979, Frank Marino Gallery, N.Y.C., 1979, 81, Art Resources Gallery, Denver, 1983, U. Calif., Irvine, 1984, ACA Galleries, N.Y.C., 1985, Elaine Horwitch Galleries, Palm Springs, Calif., Scottsdale, Ariz., Salt Lake Art Ctr., Univ. Art Mus./U. Ariz., Tempe, Holtzman Art Gallery/Towson State U., 1990, Joy Tash Gallery, Scottsdale, Hermann Hesse Mus., Montqgnola, Switzerland; group shows in Scottsdale, Provincetown, Mass., Lake Forest, Ill., Gainesville, Fla., N.Y.C., Salt Lake City, Palm Springs, L.A., Spokane, St. Louis, Knoxville, Atlanta, Colorado Springs, Tucson, Reno, San Francisco, others; represented in collections at Albuquerque Mus. Art, Bklyn. Mus. ARt, Denver Art Mus., The Jewish Mus., N.Y.C., San Francisco Mus. Modern Art, skirball Mus./Hebrew Union Coll., U. Ariz. Mus. Art, Yuma Art Ctr., Ariz. Bank, Canyon Ranch, Home Petroleum, Nat. Bank Ariz., Phelps Dodge Corp., Subaru Corp., United Bank, numerous others; subject of numerous articles. Home: 5346 E Sapphire Ln Paradise Valley AZ 85253-2531

SWARTZ, CAROL I., academic administrator; b. Providence, Dec. 15, 1950; d. Leo L. and Lillian (Gordon) S. BA, U. R.I., 1973; MSW, Portland State U., 1977. Cert. social Worker, 1978. Social worker Children's Friend and Svcs., Providence, 1973-75; counselor S.E. Youth Svcs. Ctr., Portland, Oreg., 1975-77; dir. treatment Mt. Hood Treatment Ctr., Sandy, Oreg., 1977-79; coord. child devel. svcs. Corbett (Oreg.) Sch. Dist., 1978-80; clinician Homer (Alaska) Cmty. Mental Health Ctr., 1980-82; adj. instr. psychology and sociology U. Alaska, Kachemak Bay Campus, Homer, 1984-86; dir. U. Alaska, Kachemak Bay campus, Homer, 1986—; founding dir. So. Peninsula Women's Svcs., Homer, 1981-83; mgmt. cons. 1984-86; Alaska guardian ad litem, 1984-86. Trustee Homer Found., 1993—; mem. Homer Sister City Assn., 1992—; bd. dirs. Pratt Mus., Homer, 1992-94, Homer Coun. of Arts, 1993-95. Mem. Nat. Assn. of Higher Edn., Nat. Assn. Women in Edn., Nat. Assn. Women in C.C., Rotary Internat., Homer C. of C. (Citizen of Yr. nominee 1983, 86). Avocations: travel, reading, camping, sailing, hiking. Home: PO Box 2748 Homer AK 99603-2748

SWARTZ, ROSLYN HOLT, real estate investment executive; b. Los Angeles, Dec. 9, 1940; d. Abe Jack and Helen (Canter) Holt; m. Allan Joel Swartz, June 2, 1963. AA, Santa Monica (Calif.) Coll., 1970; BA summa cum laude, UCLA, 1975; MA, Pepperdine U., 1976. Cert. community coll. instr., student-personnel worker, Calif. Mgr. pub. relations Leader Holdings, Inc., L.A., 1968-75, pres., 1991—; sec., treas. Leader Holdings, Inc., North Hollywood, Calif., 1975-81, pres., 1981-91; chief exec. officer Beverly Stanley Investments, L.A., 1979—; pres. Leader Properties, Inc., The Leader Fairfax, Inc., Leader 358, Inc., Leader 359, Inc., Leader Ventura, Inc., 1996—. Condr. An Oral History of the Elderly Jewish Community of Venice, Calif. at Los Angeles County Planning Dept. Library, 1974. Founder L.A. County Mus. Art, Music Ctr. L.A. County, West Alumni Ctr., UCLA; mem. Club 100 of The Music Center of L.A. County; Hadassah (life), Friends of the Hollywood Bowl, Library Found of L.A. (sustaining mem.), bd. dirs. Am. Friends of Haifa Med. Ctr., West L.A. Symphony; capital patron Simon Wiesenthal Ctr. Fellow Phi Beta Kappa (bicentennial); mem. NAFE, [illegible] So. Calif. Coun. of The Nat. Museum of Women in the Arts, Natl. Mus. of Women in the Arts; Am. Pub. Health Assn., Am. Pharm. Assn., Comml. Real Estate Women, L.A. World Affairs Coun., Town Hall (life), Century City C. of C., Friends of Fox, UCLA Alumni Assn. (life), Women's Guild Cedars-Sinai Med. Ctr., L.A. County Mus. of Art Decorative Arts Coun.; Mus. Friends of the Graphis Arts, UCLA Prytanean Alumnae Assn., Santa Monica Coll. Alumni Assn. (life), ng mem.), Friends Fox, Phrateres Internat., Order of Eastern Star, Phi Alpha Theta. Alpha Gamma Sigma, Alpha Kappa Delta, Phi Delta Kappa, Pi Gamma Mu, Pi Lambda Theta. Avocation: horticulture. Office: PO Box 241784 Los Angeles CA 90024-9584

SWATT, STEPHEN BENTON, communications executive, consultant; b. L.A., June 26, 1944; s. Maurice I. and Lucille E. (Sternberger) S.; m. Susan Ruth Edelstein, Sept. 7, 1968; 1 child, Jeffrey Michael. BSBA, U. Calif., 1966, M in Journalism, 1967. Writer San Francisco Examiner, 1967; reporter United Press Internat., L.A., 1968-69; producer news Sta. KCRA-TV, Sacramento, Calif., 1969-70, reporter news, 1970-79, chief polit. and capitol corres., 1979-92; exec. v.p. Nelson Comm., Sacramento, 1992—; guest lectr. Calif. State U., Sacramento. Contbr. articles to profl. jours. With USCG, 1966. Recipient No. Calif. Emmy NATAS, 1976-77, Pub. Svc. award Calif. State Bar, 1977, Exceptional Achievement Coun. advancement and Support of Edn., 1976, Nat. Health Journalism award Am. Chiropractic Assn., 1978. Mem. Soc. Profl. Journalists (8 awards), Capitol Corres. Assn., U. Calif. Alumni Assn., Sacramento Press Club. Avocations: hiking, jogging, fishing. Office: Nelson Comms Group 1029 J St Ste 400 Sacramento CA 95814-2825

SWEENEY, CHRISTOPHER LEE, applied mathematics engineer; b. Denver, Oct. 14, 1959; s. Roger Lee Sweeney and Beverly Ann (Wagoner) Good; m. Susan Ann Merrell, May 24, 1986. Student, Community Coll. Denver; grad., U. Colo., 1988. Technician Ball Computer Products, Boulder, Colo., 1978-82, devel. engr., 1982-83; devel. engr. Ball Electronic Systems, Westminster, Colo., 1983-88; reliability engr. StorageTek, Louisville, Colo., 1989-94; mem. tech. staff Analysts Internat. Corp., Denver, 1994—. Inventor in field. Mem. Eta Kappa Nu, Tau Beta Pi. Home: 7974 W 108th Ave Broomfield CO 80021-2649 Office: Analysts Internat Corp 7800 E Union Ave Ste 600 Denver CO 80237-2755

SWEENEY, DOROTHY LOVE, minister, nurse; b. Worcester, Mass., May 22, 1922; d. Joseph Wilfred and Lillian Mary (Fagga) Fournier; children: Helen F. Hunter, Joseph Wayne Jodrey; m. John L. Sweeney, Mar. 15, 1986; stepchildren: Susan, Florence Moreno, Cathleen Bunn, John L., James, Thomas, Robert. Diploma in nursing, St. Mary's Hosp., 1963; ministerial diploma Religious Sci. Internat., 1973, DD, 1982, DD, United Ch. of Religious Sci., 1988. RN, Ga.; ordained to ministry Ch. of Religious Sci., 1980. Dir., Southeast States region VIII, United Ch. of Religious Sci., Beverly Hills, Calif., 1980 (internat. bd. trustees); staff min. World Ministry of Prayer, United Ch. of Religious Sci., Los Angeles, 1980-81, dir., v.p., Los Angeles, 1983-85 ; min., dir. Golden Circle Ch. of Religious Sci., Santa Ana, Calif., 1981-83; staff min. Redondo Beach Ch. Religious Sci.; ministerial staff cons. alcohol recovery services Tustin Community Hosp. (Calif.), Villa Recovery Home for Women, Santa Ana. Author: A Time for Healing, 1975; TV ministry: The Hour of New Thought, 1983. Mem. Southeast Clergy of Religious Sci. (sec., v.p., pres. 1974-77). Club: Toastmaster (treas., sec., v.p., pres. 1971-72). Home: 635 Paseo De La Playa Apt 303 Redondo Beach CA 90277-6547 Office: 907 Knob Hill Ave Redondo Beach CA 90277-4532

SWEENEY, MARVIN A., religious studies educator; b. Springfield, Ill., July 4, 1953; s. Jack H. and Leonore R. (Dorman) S. AB, U. Ill., 1975; MA, Claremont Grad. Sch., 1981, PhD, 1983. Head cataloguer Ancient Bibl. Manuscript Ctr., Claremont, Calif., 1979-83; asst. prof. U. Miami, Coral Gables, Fla., 1983-89; coord. pre-law advising U. Miami, Coral Gables, 1987-94, assoc. prof. religious studies, 1989-94; prof. Hebrew Bible Claremont Sch. Theology, 1994—; prof. religion Claremont Grad. U., 1994—. Author: Isaiah 1-4 and the Post-Exilic Understanding of the Isaianic Tradition, Isaiah 1-39; co-editor: New Visions of Isaiah. Bd. dirs. Hillel Jewish Student Orgn., Coral Gables, 1983—. Postdoctoral fellow Yad Hanadiv Barecha Found., Hebrew U. Jerusalem, 1989-90; Dorot Rsch. Prof. W.F. Albright Inst., Jerusalem, 1993-94; Lilly Theol. rsch. fellow, 1997-98. Mem. Soc. Bibl. Lit., Am. Acad. Religion, Assn. Jewish Studies, Am. Schs. Oriental Rsch., Nat. Assn. Profs. Hebrew, Am. Oriental Soc., Phi Kappa Phi. Jewish. Office: Claremont Sch Theology Dept Religious Studies 1325 N College Ave Claremont CA 91711

SWEENEY, ROBERT FRANK, foundation administrator; b. Craig, Colo., Feb. 13, 1938; s. Henry and June (O'Connell) S.; m. Gerri Keeling; children: Saundra Dorrance, Susan Good, Patrick, Sharon. BA in Social Sci., Colo. State U., 1959. Pres. colo. Press Assn., Denver; trustee U. No. Colo.; trustee, bd. Nat. Newspaper Assn., Wash.; bd. dirs. Sigma Chi Fraternity Found., Evanston, Ill.; exch. journalist, USSR, 1975. Dir. Rick's Sch., U. Denver, 1984-97. Capt. U.S. Army, 1959-60. Mem. Lions, Colo. Press Assn. Republican. Avocations: rollerblading, weight lifting, photography.

SWEENEY, VONNY HILTON, promotion company executive; b. Brownsville, Pa., Aug. 24, 1947; d. James and Ann Hilton; divorced; 1 child, Howard Hilton Sweeney. AA, Am. River Coll., 1971; BA, Calif. State U., Sacramento, 1974. Nat. promotion coord. Sussex Records, L.A., 1974; adminstr. asst. promotion and pub. rels. Playboy, L.A., 1974-76; mgr. Polydor rec. artists Alton McClain & Destiny, L.A., 1976-80; mgr. Polygram rec. artists Lace Wing, L.A., 1985-90; pres. James Brown West, Inc., Hollywood, Calif., 1990—; cons., publicist James Brown Prodns., Augusta, Ga., 1974—; founder, chair Annual Pre-Grammy Gala, L.A., 1980—. Asst. producer Ebony Music Awards, L.A., 1975. Fundraiser various politicians, L.A. and Sacramento, 1974—; mem. com. Miss Black L.A., 1990. Mem. Nat. Acad. Recording Arts and Scis., Am. Film Inst. Office: PO Box 691354 West Hollywood CA 90069-9354

SWEET, CYNTHIA KAY, business administrator; b. Highland, Kans., Feb. 21, 1949; d. Jack Wendull and Ruthanna (Dittemore) Hedrick; m. Roger Keith Alexander, 1968; children: Karen Joyce, Melinda Ruth Anne; m. Erich Christian Sweet, Oct. 31, 1990. Student, U. Kans., 1968, North Peralta Coll., 1973-74, U. Colo., 1976-79; BS in Bus. Tech., Empire State Coll., 1984. Computer operator Computer Ctr. U. Colo., Boulder, 1977-79; subscription coord. Inst. Arctic & Alpine Rsch., Boulder, 1979; computer operator Computer Ctr. Rensselaer Poly. Inst., Troy, N.Y., 1979-80, dir. devel. info. svcs., 1982-85; rsch. analyst N.Y. State Mus., Albany, 1979-80, project mgr., 1980-82; product mgr. Info. Assocs., Rochester, N.Y., 1985-89, sr. program mgr., 1990-92; applications mgr. Claris Corp., Santa Clara, Calif., 1989-90; custom programming mgr. Datatel, Fairfax, Va., 1992-94; exec. dir. advancement solutions TRG, Phoenix, 1994-96; dir. profl. svcs. USA Group Info. Solutions, Phoenix, 1996-97; v.p. InfoSolutions.edu, Phoenix, 1997-99; higher edn. practice lead Renaissance Worldwide, San Francisco, 1999—; freelance fundraising cons., Albany and Rochester, 1984-89. Contbr. articles to profl. jours. Activity coord. Info. Assocs./United Way, Rochester, 1985-89, 91-92; mem. festival staff meml. Art Gallery, Rochester, 1987-89; bd. dirs. Draper Dance Theatre, Rochester, 1988-92. Mem. NSFE, Coun. for Advancement and Support of Edn., Project Mgmt. Inst., Am. Mgmt. Assn. Avocations: camping, hiking, gardening, gourmet cooking, reading. Office: InfoSolutions.edu 4343 E Camelback Rd Ste 205 Phoenix AZ 85018-2756

SWEET, HARVEY, theatrical, scenic and lighting designer; b. Detroit, Oct. 27, 1943; s. Sam and Rose Sweet; m. Susan Perrett, Mar. 16, 1964 (div. Mar. 1975); children: Deborah Anne, Rebecca Lynn, Jason Aaron; m. Patricia Ravn, Sept. 9, 1978 (div. July 1987). BS, Ea. Mich. U., 1965; MS, U. Wis., 1967, PhD, 1974. Instr. U. N.D., Grand Forks, 1967-69; asst. prof. Boise (Idaho) State Coll., 1972-73; instr. U. Wis., Madison, 1973-74; prof. of theater arts U. No. Iowa, Cedar Falls, 1974-89; dir. lighting Landmark Entertainment Group, L.A. and Tokyo, 1989-91; cons. Advanced Tech., Tokyo, 1991; tech. writer Walt Disney Imagineering, Glendale, Calif., 1992; owner, operator Sweet Studios Theatrical Equipment, Cedar Falls, 1981-89; dir. theater tech. and design U. No. Iowa, 1974-87; project mgr., sr. designer, tech. writer Tru Roll, Inc., Glendale, Calif., 1993—. Author: Graphics for the Performing Arts, 1982, Handbook of Scenery, Properties and Lighting I and II, 1988, 2nd edit., 1995, The Complete Book of Drawing for the Theatre, 1995; scenic designer Summer Repretory Theatre, 1988, Timberlake Playhouse, 1988-89; lighting designer, scenic designer, tech. dir. various coll. theatrical prodns., 1964-89; themed lighting designer Sanrio Puroland, Tokyo, 1989, exec. dir. lighting, 1990. Mem. U.S. Inst. for Theatre Tech. (vice commn. 1979-81, commn. 1981-87, mem. graphic stds. bd. 1979-86; evaluation commn. 1983-88, mem. publs. com. 1986-89, bd. dirs. 1989).

Avocations: tennis, aerobics, cooking, photography. Office: Tru-Roll Inc 622 Sonora Ave Glendale CA 91201-2339

SWEITZER, MICHAEL COOK, healthcare product executive; b. Cin., July 29, 1961; s. Charles Samuel and Louise (Cook) S. BS in Biomedical Engring., Rensselaer Poly. Inst., 1983, M in Engring., 1985. Product specialist Siemens Med. Sys., Iselin, N.J., 1985-89, tech. mgr, 1989-90, nat. sales mgr., 1993-94, product mgr., 1994-96, cons., 1996-98; product specialist Siemens Med. Sys., San Francisco, 1990-92; product mgr. Toshiba Am. Med. Sys., S. San Francisco, 1992-93. Contbr. chpt. to MRI Guide for Technologists, 1994. Mem. Am. Healthcare Radiology Adminstrs., Inst. for Indsl. Engrs. Office: Varian Oncology Systems 3045 Hanover St # Msh-55 Palo Alto CA 94304-1129

SWENSON, DAVID AARON, computer scientist, educator; b. Fullerton, Calif., Mar. 22, 1965; s. Edwin Albert and Judith Lynn (Swanson) S. BS in Computer Sci., U. So. Calif., L.A., 1987; MS in Computer Sci., Rutgers U., 1990. Instr. N.Mex. State U., Carlsbad, 1990-92, asst. prof. computer sci., 1992—. Mem. Assn. Computing Machinery, Elks. Home: 1507 Monroe St Carlsbad NM 88220-4140 Office: New Mexico State Univ 1500 University Dr Carlsbad NM 88220-3509

SWENSON, ERICK LEE, fundraising administrator; b. San Jose, Calif., Oct. 16, 1964; s. Melvern LeRoy and Nancy Lee (Over) S. Degree in intercultural comm., U. Copenhagen, 1985; BA in Art History, San Jose State U., 1987, BS in Internat. Bus., 1987. Devel. and pub. rels. officer Eastfield Ming Quong, Campbell, Calif., 1987-90; pub. affairs officer Nat. ARC, Kansas City, Homestead, Fla., Burlingame, Calif., 1990-93; devel. mgr. Shanti Project, San Francisco, 1994-95; dir. devel. Episcopal Cmty. Svc., San Francisco, 1995—; instr. Ctr. for U.S./USSR Initiatives, Ukraine, 1989; del. Internat. Com. of Red Cross and Fedn. of Red Cross/Red Crescent Socs., 1991—. Editor Upside mag., 1990. Mem. rev. team Enterprise Cmty., San Francisco, 1996, 97, United Way of Bay Area, San Francisco, 1998. Mem. Pub. Rels. Soc. Am., Nat. Soc. Fundraising Execs., Delta Sigma Pi (Chancellor 1986-87), Alpha Lambda Delta. Congregationalist. Avocations: contemporary visual art, snake handling. Home: 1948 Alemany Blvd San Francisco CA 94112-3202

SWENSON, KATHLEEN SUSAN, music and art educator; b. Reno, Nev., Oct. 23, 1938; d. Harold Ruthaford McNeil and Hollyce Margaret (Scruggs) McNeil Biggs; m. James Michael Phalan, 1956 (div. 1974); children: David Michael, Jeanine Louise Phalan Lawrence, Gregory Shaun; m. Gerald Allen Swensen, Nov. 1976 (div. 1987); stepchildren: Craig Allen, Sarah Ann, Eric Sander. Student, U. Nev., Reno, 1956-58, Foothill Coll., 1966-68; AA, West Valley Coll.; BA, U. Calif., Santa Cruz, 1983. Concert pianist Nev.,Calif, 1950-64; pvt. piano instr. various locations, 1963—, pvt. art instr., 1970—, pvt. astrology instr., 1973—; founder, pres. AAM Triple Arts, Aptos, Calif., 1974—; founder, owner Aptos (Calif.) Acad. Music, 1991—. Producer, instr. art instrn. videos, music instrn. films, books. Mem. Soc Western Artists, Calif. Piano Tchrs. Assn., Los Gatos Art Assn. (pres. 1985-86), Saratoga Contemporary Artists (v.p. 1984-85), Nat. League Am. Pen Women (honorarian 1985), Soroptomists, Phi Beta Kappa. Republican. Episcopalian. Home and Office: Aptos Acad Music 3000 Wisteria Way Aptos CA 95003-3318

SWENSON, SUSAN ANN, engineering recruiting company executive; b. Lansing, Mich., July 30, 1948; d. Milton Cecil and Dorothy Frances (Manuel) Taylor; m. John William Deutschmann, Apr. 17, 1982 (div. Oct. 1995); 1 child, Danielle Cecile. BA in Sociology, U. Wis., 1971; MSW, Mich. State U., 1974. Cert. social worker. Vocat. rehab. counselor Portland, Oreg., 1982-88; recruiter rschr. Corp. Builders, Portland, 1989; engring. recruiter Fran Low, Ltd., Portland, 1989-91; owner Swenson & Assocs., Scottsdale, Ariz., 1991—; social and rehab. svcs. trainee U.S. Govt. Mich. State U., East Lansing, 1972-73, 73-74. Asst. coach Arcadia Scottsdale United Soccer Club, 1995; soccer player N.W. United Women's Soccer, 1980-93, DiHearts Soccer Team, 1996—; soccer player, mgr. Misfits Soccer Team, 1993-95. Mem. AAUW, Nationwide Interchange Svc., Inc., Ariz. Assn. Pers. Svcs. Democrat. Avocations: soccer, country line dancing, creative writing, reading. Home and Office: Swenson & Assocs 8502 E Cholla St Scottsdale AZ 85260-6612

SWETT, MARGARET CHRISTINE, finance executive; b. San Francisco, Sept. 14, 1959; d. Benson Payne Swett and Helen Irene (Frey) Iddings. BA in Econ., U. Calif., Santa Barbara, 1981; MBA, San Francisco State U., 1991. Acctg. supr. Geneva Group, Menlo Park, Calif., 1981-83; mgr. acctg. Pearl Cruises, San Francisco, 1983-87; mgr. acctg. and adminstrn. Seabourn Cruise Line, San Francisco, 1987-90, dir. fin. svcs., 1990-93, v.p. fin. and adminstrn., 1993—. Mem. NAFE, Nat. Honor Soc. (life), Beta Gamma Sigma. Avocations: photography, swimming, travel, humanities, literature. Home: 1400 Jones St Apt 201 San Francisco CA 94109-3292 Office: Seabourn Cruise Line 55 Francisco St Ste 710 San Francisco CA 94133-2128

SWICK, SEAN BOWMAN, software developer; b. Oceanside, Calif., Aug. 29, 1970; s. William Roy and Louella Austine (Goines) S.; 1 child, Daniel Bowman. AAS in Electronic Engring., ITT Tech. Inst., San Bernardino, Calif., 1990; BAS in Automated Mfg., ITT Tech. Inst., West Covina, Calif., 1992. Computer technician Banning (Calif.) Unified Sch. Dist., 1989-95; owner Swick Solutions Group, Banning, 1995-98; divsn. mgr. OCS Sys., Banning, 1998—; bd. dirs. Acad. Computer and Health Occupations, Banning. Author: (software) Academy Direct, 1995, Swick Solutions Group Web Site, 1996. Bd. dirs. Cabazon County Water Dist., 1997—. Mem. Downtown Banning Bus. Assn., Full Gospel Bus. Men Fellowship Internat., Banning Rotary Club. Republican. Avocations: hiking, camping, swimming, billiards. Home: PO Box 181 Banning CA 92220-0002 Office: 235 N Murray St # C Banning CA 92220-5511

SWIFT, SUSAN FREYA, writer, lawyer; b. St. Louis, Mar. 11, 1955; d. Sheldon Samuel and Sheila Louise (Lazarus) S.; m. Bruce Jeffrey Zweig, June 18, 1995. AB, U. Calif., Davis, 1976, MA, 1978; JD, U. Calif., San Francisco, 1981. Bar: Calif. Criminal def. atty. Sacramento, 1983—. Author short story; editor Comm/Ent Law Jour., 1981. Mem. Romance Writers Am. (events coord. 1998). Avocation: Karate. Office: 4880 San Juan Ave Fair Oaks CA 95628-4719

SWIFT, WILLIAM CHARLES, professional baseball player, Olympic athlete; b. Portland, Maine, Oct. 27, 1961. Student, Maine. Mem. U.S. Olympic Baseball Team, 1984; with Seattle Mariners, 1984-91; pitcher San Francisco Giants, 1991-94, Colo. Rockies, 1994-97; baseball player Balt. Orioles, Baltimore, MD, 1997; Baseball player Seattle Mariners, Seattle, WA, 1998. Nat. League Earned Run Average leader, 1992. Office: Seattle Mariners PO Box 4100 83 King Street Seattle WA 98104*

SWIG, ROSELYNE CHROMAN, community art consultant; b. Chgo., June 8, 1930; m. Richard Swig, Feb. 5, 1950 (dec.); children—Richard, Jr., Susan, Marjorie, Carol. Student, U. Calif.-Berkeley, UCLA; MFA (hon.), San Francisco Art Inst., 1988, DHL (hon.). Founder, pres. Roselyne C. Swig Artsource, San Francisco, 1977-94; apptd. by Pres. Clinton as dir. Art in Embassies Program U.S. Dept. of State, 1994-97. Trustee San Francisco Mus. Modern Art, U. Art Mus., Berkeley, Calif.; ex officio bd. mem. Jewish Mus. San Francisco; bd. dirs., treas. Am. Jewish Joint Distbn. Com.; vice chair fine art adv. panel FRS; past trustee Mills Coll., Oakland, Calif.; past past pres., bd. dirs. Jewish Cmty. Fedn. San Francisco, the Peninsula, Marin and Sonoma Counties; past commr. San Francisco Pub. Libr.; past bd. dirs. San Francisco Opera, Am. Coun. for Arts, KQED Broadcasting Sys.; past. pres. Calif. State Summer Sch. Arts, past chair bd. trustees San Francisco Art Inst.; past pres. San Francisco Arts Commn.; past nat. v.p. Am./Israel Pub. Affairs Com.; past trustee United Jewish Appeal; past chair bd. trustees Univ. Art Mus. Avocations: skiing; boating; tennis.

SWIGGER, NANCY DUNCAN, photographer; b. Albuquerque, May 18, 1942; m. Ronald T. Swigger, Aug. 24, 1963; children: Jocelyn, Elizabeth. BA, U. N.Mex., 1963; MA, Ind. U., 1965, PhD, 1969. Photographer Sound Portraits, Albuquerque, 1984—. Sculptor: Piano, 1998; newsletter editor: Am. Field Svc., 1997—. Former dir. Pan Am. Round Table, Albuquerque; past pres. LWV. Recipient 1st pl. in profl. divsn. Festival of the Cranes, 1995, 1st pl. wildlife Mus. of the Horse, 1996, Best of Show, 1st pl. in comml. Imagining Profl. of the S.W., 1997. Avocation: fluent in Spanish and Portuguese.

SWIHART, H. GREGG, real estate company executive; b. San Francisco, Sept. 25, 1938; s. Lawson Benjamin and Violet Mary (Watters) S.; B.A., U. Ariz., 1958; postgrad. U. Heidelberg (W.Ger.), 1958-59, Harvard U., 1959-60; M.A., Boston U., 1961; postgrad. U. Freiburg (West Germany), 1961-65; m. Ilse Paula Rambacher, Dec. 24, 1958; children—Tatjana Etta, Brett Marc, Natascha Theda. Stock broker Walston & Co., Tucson, 1966-71; with Solot Co., Tucson, 1971-74; pres. Cienega Properties, Inc., property mgmt. and investment, Tucson, 1975-77; pres. GT Realty Assocs., Ltd., Tucson, 1977—. Mem. Tucson Com. Fgn. Relations, 1973—; pres. Forum for Greater Outdoors, 1977-79; bd. dirs. Tucson Mus. Art, 1968-74, pres. 1969-70; pres. and trustee Canelo Hills Sch., 1977-79. Cert. property mgr. Mem. Tucson Bd. Realtors, Inst. Real Estate Mgmt. (pres. Tucson-So. Ariz. chpt. 1982, mem. nat. governing council 1985-87), Inst. Real Estate Mgmt. (governing council 1985-87, Property Mgr. of Yr. award So. Ariz. chpt. 1988), Realtors Nat. Mktg. Inst. Clubs: Harvard (pres. 1973-74), Active 20-30 (pres. 1969), Downtown Tucson. Home: Tunnel Springs Ranch PO Box 555 Sonoita AZ 85637-0555 Office: 4003 E Speedway Blvd Ste 110 Tucson AZ 85712-4555

SWIMM, THOMAS STEVEN, artist; b. Miami, Fla., May 14, 1950; s. Thomas Albert and Dorothy Marguerite (Royal) S.; m. Rosemary Patricia Ebenhoch, Mar. 10, 1976; 1 child, Jesse Thomas. Art dir. various advt. agys., Albany, 1970-82, Newport Beach, Calif., 1982-87. Recipient Bronze award, Art Calif., 1991, Gold award, 1994. Republican. Roman Catholic. Avocations: playwriting, piano. Address: 33936 La Serena Dr Dana Point CA 92629-2255

SWINDELLS, WILLIAM, JR., lumber and paper company executive; b. Oakland, CA, 1930; married. B.S., Stanford U., 1953. With Willamette Industries, Inc., Portland, Oreg., 1953—; sr. v.p. prodn., mktg. bldg. materials Willamette Industries, Inc., until 1978, exec. v.p., 1978-80, pres. forest products div., 1980-82, pres., chief exec. officer, 1982-96, also dir., chmn., 1984-97; chmn., CEO Willamette Industry, Portland, 1997—; dir. Oreg. Bank, Portland. Office: Willamette Industries 1300 SW 5th Ave Ste 3800 Portland OR 97201-5671

SWING, WILLIAM EDWIN, bishop; b. Huntington, W.Va., Aug. 26, 1936; s. William Lee and Elsie Bell (Holliday) S.; M. Mary Willis Taylor, Oct. 7, 1961; children—Alice Marshall, William Edwin. B.A., Kenyon Coll., Ohio, 1954-58; D.Div. (hon.), Kenyon Coll., 1980; M.A., Va. Theol. Sem., 1958-61, D.Div., 1980. Ordained priest Episcopal Ch. Asst. St. Matthews Ch., Wheeling, W.Va., 1961-63; vicar St. Matthews Ch., Chester, W.Va., 1963-69, St. Thomas Ch., Weirton, W.Va., 1963-69; rector St. Columba's Episcopal Ch., Washington, 1969-79; bishop Episcopal Ch. Calif., San Francisco, 1980—; chmn. bd. Ch. Div. Sch. of the Pacific, 1983-84; founder, chmn. Episcopal Found. for Drama, 1976—. Republican. Home: 2006 Lyon St San Francisco CA 94115-1610 Office: Episcopal Ch Diocesan Office 1055 Taylor St San Francisco CA 94108-2209*

SWITZER, TERI REYNOLDS, education educator, librarian; b. Tucson, Ariz., May 1, 1949; d. Ernest William and Lois Myrtle (Jensen) Reynolds; m. Ralph Vincent Switzer, Jr., June 30, 1973 (div. June 1989); children: Lois, R. Vincent III; m. Gene Joseph Luthman, July 17, 1993. BA, U. Ill., 1971, MS, 1973; MBA, Colo. State U., 1977. Instr. Colo. State U., Ft. Collins, 1973-77, asst. prof., 1988-95, assoc. prof., 1995—; media specialist St. Joseph Elem., Ft. Collins, 1985-88. Author: Telecommuters, 1997, Safe at Work?, 1999. Mem. ALA, Fedn. Info. and Documentation, Colo. Libr. Assn. Avocations: skiing, hiking. Home: 622 W Mountain Ave Fort Collins CO 80521-2609 Office: Colo State U 110 Morgan Libr Fort Collins CO 80523-1019

SWOFFORD, ROBERT LEE, newspaper editor, journalist; b. Berryville, Ark., Aug. 22, 1949; s. Andrew Madison and Verna Mae (England) S.; m. Karen King, Jan. 24, 1969 (div. 1977); children: Teri, Toby; m. Sandra Dunn, 1978 (div. 1979); m. B. Joanna Rongren, Feb. 14, 1981; 1 child, Tyler. AA, Coll. of the Sequoias, 1969; student, Calif. State U., 1969-71. Photographer, reporter, news editor The Advance-Register, Tulare, Calif., 1965-78; city editor The Record Searchlight, Redding, Calif., 1978-81; suburban editor, Neighbors editor The Sacramento Bee, 1981-86; assoc. metro. editor, cmty. editor The Orange County Register, Santa Ana, Calif., 1986-89; exec. news editor The Press Democrat, Santa Rosa, Calif., 1989-90, mng. editor, 1990—. Recipient Pulitzer prize for news photography Press Dem., 1997. Mem. Am. Soc. Newspaper Editors, Assoc. Press Mng. Editors, Calif. Soc. of Newspaper Editors (bd. dirs.). Office: The Press Democrat 427 Mendocino Ave Santa Rosa CA 95401-6385

SYKE, CAMERON JOHN, lawyer; b. Oak Park, Ill., Jan. 29, 1957; s. A. John and Rosemarie (Grasso) S.; m. Susan Royer, Jan. 2, 1982; children: Caroline, Jared. BSBA cum laude, U. Denver, 1977, LLM in Taxation, 1986; JD with honors, DePaul U., 1982. Bar: CPA, Colo. 1983, U.S. Tax Ct. 1985. Acct. Touche, Ross, Chgo., 1978-79, Denver, 1980-83; investment broker Boettcher & Co., Denver, 1983-84; CPA Laventhol & Horwath, Denver, 1984-85; assoc. Roath & Brega, Denver, 1985-87; dir. Hopper and Kanouff P.C., Denver, 1987-96; with Syke & Assocs., Englewood, colo., 1996—; adj. prof. U. Denver, 1985; instr. Colo. Soc. CPAs, 1986-87; lectr. Nat. Bus. Inst., 1986-87. Candidate councilman City of Denver, 1987. Mem. Colo. Bar Assn., Colo. Soc. CPAs. Republican. Presbyterian. Avocations: golf, tennis, weightlifting, travel, church ministry. Home: 6942 E Costilla Pl Englewood CO 80112-1110 Office: Syke & Assocs PC 9250 E Costilla Ave Ste 600 Englewood CO 80112-3649

SYKES, MICHAEL, publishing executive; b. N.Y.C., July 15, 1943; s. Richard Bishop Peter M'Cready and Barbara (Craig) S.; m. Pamela Collins, June 15, 1963 (div. June 1971); children: William Benjamin, Matthew Michael; m. Zoë Alexis Scott, Mar. 20, 1994. BA, San Francisco State U., 1966, MA, 1968. Writer/photographer Point Reyes/Cedarville, Calif., 1967-94; bookseller Punta de Los Reyes Bookstore, Point Reyes, 1969-74; editor/pub. Floating Island Publs., Point Reyes/Cedarville, 1976—; typographer Archetype West, Point Reyes, 1984-94; bookseller Gt. Basin Books, Cedarville, 1994—. Author: From an Island in Time, 1984. Recipient pub. fellowship Calif. Arts Coun., Sacramento, 1976, Coordinating Coun. of Literary Mags., N.Y.C., 1980, Nat. Endowment for the Arts, Washington, 1979, 80, 81. Avocations: outdoor activities, travel. Home: 540 Main St Cedarville CA 96104-0296 Office: Gt Basin Books & Floating Island Publs 540 D Main St Cedarville CA 96104-0296

SYLK, ROBERT F., casino marketing executive; s. Harry Sylk; 1 child, Kelly Jo. Pres. Sylk Corp., Marina del Rey, Calif.; prin. Travel Agts. Internat., Marina del Rey; del. Calif. Tourism and Trade Commn. Founder Marina del Rey Food and Wine Festival, Marina del Rey Music & Art Festival; pres., founder Marina/Venice chpt. City of Hope; chief precinct officer, sr. inspector County Registrar's dist. 4; former sr. v.p., mem. bd. dirs. Marina del Rey C. of C. Served with U.S. Army. 1997 City of Hope Man of Yr. Mem. Cornerstone Club of Marina del Rey (pres.). Office: 4143 Via Marina Ste 1118 Marina Del Rey CA 90292

SYLVESTER, EDWARD JOSEPH, science writer, journalism educator; b. Hackensack, N.J., Oct. 10, 1942; s. Edward Joseph Jr. and Ellen Marian (Hopkins) S.; m. Ginny Ross Gowanloch, Sept. 6, 1969; children: Daniel, Kathleen. AB, Princeton U., 1965; MA, CCNY, 1974. Reporter The Jersey Jour., Jersey City, 1962-63, The Morning Call, Paterson, N.J., 1968-69, Ariz. Star, Tucson, 1976-78, L.A. Times, 1978-80; rewriteman The Star Ledger, Newark, 1970-72; reporter, editor The Tucson Citizen, 1973-76; prof. Ariz. State U. Walter Cronkite Sch. Journalism, Tempe, 1980—; corr. Wall Street Jour., N.Y.C., 1975-78. Prin. author: The Gene Age, 1983, rev. edit., 1987; author: Target: Cancer, 1986, The Healing Blade: A Tale of Neurosurgery, 1993, rev. edit., 1997. With U.S. Army, 1965-67. Recipient teaching award Burlington Resources Found., 1991, Freedom Forum Pub. award, 1996; Wakonse Teaching fellow, 1994, Knight Inst. Jour. Excellence fellow, 1995. Mem. AAAS, Nat. Assn. Sci. Writers, Soc. Profl. Journalists, Investigative Reports and Editors, Assn. for Edn. in Journalism & Mass Communications. Office: Ariz State U Walter Cronkite Sch Journalism Tempe AZ 85287

SYMMES, DANIEL LESLIE, three-dimensional technology executive, producer, director; b. Los Angeles, June 26, 1949; s. Louis Leslie and Mary (Warkentine) S. Student, Columbia Coll., Hollywood, Calif., 1970-71. Co-founder Stereovision Internat., Inc., North Hollywood, Calif., 1971; cons. Dimension 3e, Beverly Hills, Calif., 1975-87; pres., chmn. Spatial Techs. Inc., 3D Video Corp., Hollywood, Calif., 1987-95; pres., CEO Dimension 3, Beverly Hills, 1995—; responsible for comml. 3D TV in U.S. and abroad; known worldwide as Mr. 3D. Author: Amazing 3-D; contbr. numerous articles to profl. jours.; dir. photography local 659 IATSE; patentee 3-D TV; inventor 1st reflex widescreen 3D filming system. Mem. SMPTE. Avocations: photography, expert scuba photography.

SYMMES, WILLIAM DANIEL, lawyer; b. Spokane, Wash., Sept. 10, 1938; s. William John and Sheila (Deacon) S.; m. Jayne Peters, June 20, 1959; children: Ashley, William. AB cum laude, Georgetown U., 1960; MBA, Columbia U., 1962; LLB, Stanford U., 1965. Bar: Calif. 1966, U.S. Ct. Appeals (9th cir.) 1966, Wash., 1968, U.S. Supreme Ct. 1982. Assoc. Burris & Lagerlof, L.A., 1965-68, Witherspoon, Kelley, Davenport & Toole, Spokane, 1968—; adj. prof. Gonzaga U., Spokane, 1971-77; part owner, officer, dir. Pacific Coast League AAA Spokane Indians, 1978-82, Las Vegas Stars, 1983-85. Bd. dirs. Greater Spokane Sports Assn., 1984—, Spokane Youth Sports Assn., 1985—, Focus 21, also others. Named Outstanding Young Man Yr. Spokane Jr. C. of C., 1969. Fellow Am. Coll. Trial Lawyers; mem. ABA, Am. Bd. Trial Advocates, Wash. State Bar Assn., Calif. Bar Assn., Spokane County Bar Assn. (chmn. jud. liaison com. 1982-84), Def. Rsch. Inst., Wash. Def. Lawyers Assn., Spokane C. of C., Focus 21, Empire Club, Spokane Club, Manito Golf and Country Club. Home: 3606 S Eastgate Ct Spokane WA 99203-1411 Office: Witherspoon Kelley Davenport & Toole 1100 Nat Bank Bldg Spokane WA 99201

SYMONDS, NORMAN LESLIE, computer programming specialist; b. Hawthorne, Calif., July 10, 1953; s. Malcolm F. and Nancy J. (Raab) S.; m. Catherine Anne Meades, Jan. 1, 1994. BA in Math., U. Calif., Berkeley, 1978; MBA in Mgmt. Sci., U. So. Calif., 1981. Programmer Burroughs Corp. (Unisys), Pasadena, Calif., 1978-81; sr. systems analyst Sungard Fin. Systems, Canoga Park, Calif., 1981-89; programming project leader Dames & Moore, L.A., 1989—. Avocations: chess, martial arts, tennis, hiking, fine dining. Home: 24120 Mariano St Woodland Hills CA 91367-5742 Office: Dames & Moore 911 Wilshire Blvd Ste 700 Los Angeles CA 90017-3499

SYMONS, JAMES MARTIN, theater and dance educator; b. Jacksonville, Ill., May 7, 1937; s. James and Pauline (Barton) S.; m. Judith White, Nov. 14, 1959; children: Tracy, Kelly, Carrie. BA, Ill. Coll., 1959; MA, So. Ill. U., 1964; PhD, Cornell U., 1970. Asst. prof. Yankton (S.D.) Coll., 1964-67; assoc. prof. Coll. St. Catherine, St. Paul, 1970-74, SUNY, Albany, 1974-77; prof., chair Trinity U., San Antonio, 1977-84; prof., chair theatre and dance dept. U. Colo., Boulder, 1984—; actor Off-Broadway, N.Y.C., 1959, Mo. Repertory Theatre, Kansas City, 1984; dir., actor Colo. Shakespeare Festival, Boulder, 1985—, producing artistic dir., 1994-95; leader People-to-People Del. of Theater Educators, USSR and Czechoslovakia, 1991. Author: Meyerhold's Theatre of the Grotesque, 1971 (Freedley Meml. award Theatre Libr. Assn. 1971); contbr. articles to scholarly jours. Lt. (j.g.) USN, 1960-63. Mem. Assn. for Theatre in Higher Edn. (pres. 1989-91), Assn. for Communication Adminstrn. (pres. 1990). Democrat. Methodist. Office: U of Colorado Dept Theatre And Dance Boulder CO 80309

SYMONS, ROBERT SPENCER, electronic engineer; b. San Francisco, July 3, 1925; s. Spencer W. and Avesia (Atkins) S.; m. Alice Faye Smith, Dec. 21, 1960; children: Julia Ann, Robert Spencer Jr. BS, Stanford U., 1946, MS, 1948. Engr. Eitel-McCullough, Inc., San Bruno, Calif., 1947, Heinz & Kaufman, South San Francisco, 1948, Pacific Electronics Co., Los Gatos, Calif., 1949; sr. engring. mgr. Varian Assocs., Palo Alto, Calif., 1950-83; tech. dir. Litton Industries, San Carlos, Calif., 1983—. Recipient Charles B. Thornton award for Advanced Technology Achievement, 1991. Patentee in field. Served to 1st lt. AUS, 1950-53. Fellow IEEE (assoc. editor Transactions on Electron Devices jour. 1980-83); mem. Phi Beta Kappa, Tau Beta Pi. Club: Commonwealth of Calif. Home: 290 Surrey Pl Los Altos CA 94022-2180 Office: Litton Industries 960 Industrial Rd San Carlos CA 94070-4194

SZABO, SANDOR, pathologist; b. Ada, Yugoslavia, Feb. 9, 1944; s. Gyorgy and Ilona (Komlos) S.; came to U.S., 1973, naturalized, 1981; M.D., U. Belgrade (Yugoslavia), 1968; M.Sc., U. Montreal (Que., Can.), 1971, Ph.D. (Med. Research Council Can. fellow), 1973; M.P.H., Harvard Sch. Pub. Health; m. Ildiko Mecs, Feb. 19, 1972; children—Peter, David. Intern, U. Belgrade Med. Sch. and Med. Center, Senta, Yugoslavia, 1968-69; vis. scientist Inst. Exptl. Medicine and Surgery, U. Montreal, 1969-70; resident in pathology Peter Bent Brigham Hosp. and Harvard U. Med. Sch., Boston, 1973-77, research fellow, 1975-77; asst. prof. pathology Harvard U., 1977-81, asso. prof., 1981—; cons. Recipient Physician's Recognition award AMA, 1976; Milton Fund award Harvard U., 1978; NIH grantee, 1978—. Mem. Am. Assn. Pathologists, Royal Coll. Pathologists, Am. Soc. Pharmacology and Exptl. Therapeutics, Soc. Exptl. Biology and Medicine, Am. Gastroenterol. Assn., Endocrine Soc., Internat. Acad. Pathology, N.Y. Acad. Scis. Roman Catholic. Contbr. articles to profl. publs. Office: VA Medical Ctr 113 5901 E 7th St Long Beach CA 90822-5201

SZABO, ZOLTAN, medical science educator, medical institute director; b. Szeged, Hungary, Oct. 5, 1943; came to U.S., 1967; s. Imre and Maria (Szikora) S.; m. Wanda Toy; children: Eva, Maria. Student, U. Med. Sch., Szeged, 1962-65; PhD, Columbia Pacific U., 1983. Tech. dir. microsurgery lab. R.K. Davies Med. Ctr., San Francisco, 1972-80; dir. Microsurgery and Operative Endoscopy Tng. (MOET) Inst., San Francisco, 1980—; assoc. dir. advanced laparoscopic surgery tng. ctr. Sch. Medicine U. Calif., San Francisco, 1992-96; rsch. assoc. oral and maxillofacial surgery U. of Pacific, San Francisco, 1980-83, adj. asst. prof., 1983—. Author: Microsurgery Techniques, vol. 1, 1974, vol. 2, 1984 (1st Place award for excellence in med. writing 1982); co-author: Tissue Approximation in Endoscopic Surgery, 1995; editor-in-chief Surgical Technology Internationa, Vol. 3, 1994, Vol. 4, 1995, Vol. 5, 1996, Vol. 6, 1997, Vol. 7, 1998; contbr. chpt. books, articles to profl. jours. With U.S. Army, 1969-71. Recipient cert. of Merit, AMA, 1978, commendation Accreditation Coun. for Continuing Med. Edn., 1982, 84, 90, 94, 98, Spl. Recognition award Sch. Medicine Cen. U. Venezuela, 1988, Sci. Poste Sessions Hon. Mention award Am. Urol. Assn., 1992, 1st prize Roundtable for New Techs. and Innovations we. sect., 1992, James Barrett Brown award Am. Assn. Plastic Surgeons, 1993. Fellow Internat. Coll. Surgeons (Disting. Svc. award 1994); mem. Hungarian Gynecol. Soc. (hon.), Medico-Dental Study Guild Calif., Internat. Microsurg. Soc., Soc. Am. Gastrointestinal Endoscopic Surgeons (hon., 1st prize Residents and Fellows Rsch. and Sci. Presentation 1992), Am. Fertility Soc., Am. Soc. Reconstructive Microsurgery (assoc.), Am. Soc. for Peripheral Nerve. Avocations: gardening, landscaping, oil painting, tennis, competitive air pistol target shooting. Office: Microsurgery Operative Endoscopy Tng Inst 153 States St San Francisco CA 94114-1403

SZAFRAN, ANITA G., research librarian; b. Exeter, Eng., Oct. 14, 1961; d. Jacek and Pamela (Zucker) S. BA, U. Calif., Berkeley, 1983; MLS, UCLA, 1991. Rsch. libr. Deloitte & Touche LLP, L.A., 1991—. Mem. Spl. Librs. Assn. Office: 1000 Wilshire Blvd Ste 1500 Los Angeles CA 90017-2457

SZCZERBA, VICTOR BOGDAN, electrical engineer, sales engineer; b. Chgo., Oct. 21, 1966; s. Bogdan and Zosia (Mika) S. BSEE, Marquette U., 1989; MBA, U. Calif., Berkeley, 1999. Sales engr. New Vision Computers, Milw., 1988-89; mktg. engr. Cypress Semicondr., San Jose, Calif., 1989-91; regional sales mgr. AMD/NEXGEN, Milpitas, Calif., 1991-96; sr. acct. mgr. Sun Micro Sys., Mountain View, Calif., 1996—; sales engr. Trinity Tech., Mountainview, Calif., 1991-92; cons. S3, Santa Clara, 1991-92; tutor Project Read. Mem. Knights of St. Patrick (pres. 1988-89), Sigma Phi Delta (v.p. 1987-88). Republican. Roman Catholic. Avocations: skiing, investing. Home: 235 Middlefield Rd Palo Alto CA 94301

SZEKELY, DEBORAH BEATRICE, entrepreneur; b. Bklyn., May 3, 1922; d. Harry and Rebecca (Seidman) Shainman; children: Sarah Livia Brightwood, Alex Szekely. Founder Rancho La Puerta, Tecate, Mexico, 1940—, Golden Door, San Marcos, Calif., 1958; pres. Inter-Am. Found., Arlington, Va., 1984-90; founder, chmn. Eureka Cmtys., Washington, 1990—. Author: Secrets of the Golden Door, 1978. Bd. mem. Claremont (Calif.) Grad. U., 1991—, Ptnrs. for Livable Cmtys., Washington, Nat. Coun. La Raza, Washington, Ford's Theatre, Washington. Recipient Living Legacy award Women's Internat. Ctr., San Diego, 1990, Disting. Sr. award United Srs. Health Coop, Washington, 1997, Cmty. Svc. award San Diego C. of C., 1998; named Small Businessperson of Yr., Small Bus. Adminstrn., San Diego, 1976. Mem. Internat. Women's Forum, Women's Forum Washington, Women Washington, Com. of 200. Avocations: gardening, reading, traveling. Office: Eureka Cmtys #802 1601 Connecticut Ave NW Washington DC 20009-1055

SZELENYI, IVAN, educator; b. Budapest, Apr. 17, 1938; came to the U.S., 1981; s. Gusztav and Julianna (Csapo) S.; m. Kataline Varady, Jan. 31, 1960; children: Szonja, Lilla, Balazs. PhD, Hungarian Acad. Scis., Budapest, 1973, DSc, 1990; hon. doctorate, Budapest U. Econs., 1992. Rsch. fellow Hungarian Acad. Scis., Budapest, 1963-75; found. prof. Flinders U., Adelaide, Australia, 1975-80; prof. U. Wis., Madison, 1981-86; disting. prof. CUNY Grad. Ctr., 1986-88; prof. UCLA, L.A., 1988—. Author: Urban Inequalities under State Socialism, 1983, Socialist Entrepreneurs, 1988 (C. Wright Mills award 1989); co-author: Intellectuals on the Road to Class Power, 1979. Mem. Hungarian Acad. Scis. *

SZERI, ANDREW JOHN, mechanical engineer, educator; b. Stafford, Eng., Jan. 9, 1964; s. Andras Zoltan and Mary Julie (Parkinson) S. BS, U. Pitts., 1984; MS, Cornell U., 1987, PhD, 1988. NSF grad. fellow Cornell U., Ithaca, N.Y., 1984-88; rsch. fellow Calif. Inst. Tech., Pasadena, 1988-89; lectr., postdoctoral researcher U. Calif., Santa Barbara, 1990-91; asst. prof. mech. engring. U. Calif., Irvine, 1991-95, assoc. prof., 1995-96; acting assoc. prof. mech. engring. U. Calif., Berkeley, 1997-98, assoc. prof., 1998—. Recipient young investigator award Office of Naval Rsch., 1993-97. Mem. Am. Physical Soc. (div. fluid dynamics), Acoustical Soc. Am., Soc. Rheology, Soc. Indsl. & Applied Math. Achievements include research in sonoluminescence, medical ultrasound, gas and surfactant transport at interfaces, nonlinear dynamics and pattern formation of orientable particles. Avocation: sailing. Office: U Calif Dept Mech Engring Berkeley CA 94720-1740

SZETO, ERIK K., family practice physician; b. Sept. 17, 1949; s. Yat and Siu-Fong (Ng) S.; m. Anita Y. Chan; children: Matthew, Eileen, Amanda, Jacob. BA in Chemistry, U. Ore., 1972; MS in Biochem. & Molecular Biophysics, Yale U., 1974; DO, Kirksville Coll. Osteopathic, 1978. Intern Botsford Hosp., Farmington Hills, 1978-79; pvt. family practice Portland, Ore., 1979—; chmn. quality assurance com. Family Care PCO of Oreg., 1991-94, Evergreen PCO of Oreg., 1991-94; chmn. gen. practice dept. Eastmoreland Hosp., Portland, 1985-87; health com. Gov. Roberts transitional team, 1990; com. for appt. diversion program med. dir. State of Oreg., 1992. Chmn., founder, bd. dirs. Chinese Svc. Ctr., Portland, 1983—; Chinese Cmty. Devel. Corp., 1991—; mem. leaders round table, Portland, 1992; chmn., exec. com. Asian Am. Coalition, 1992—. Mem. Am. Osteopathic Assn., Osteopathic Physicians and Surgeons of Ore., Ore. Med. Assn. Presbyn. Avocations: painting, sailing, tennis, music. Office: 4130 SE Division St Portland OR 97202-1647

SZETO, HUNG, publisher; b. Hoyping, Canton, People's Republic of China, Sept. 8, 1936; s. Cheong Yee and Sau King(Kwan) S.; m. Sau Hing Chow, Jan. 27, 1962; children: Roland, Lisa, Nancy. B in adminstrn., Tsing Hua Coll., Hong Kong, 1969. Mgr. Far East Trade Ctr., Seattle, 1975-81; editor Seattle Chinese Post, 1982; pres. APC Group, Seattle, 1986—; pub. Chinese Bus. Jour., 1989—. Mem. Asian Am. Journalists Assn., Chinese-Lang. Press Inst., Northwest Minority Pubs. Assn. Avocations: writing, consulting. Office: Chinese Bus Jour 659 S Weller St Seattle WA 98104-2944

SZIGETHY, NANCY SUE, accountant; b. Dallas, May 7, 1968; d. John William and Judy Ann (Jones) Smith; m. Stephen Michael Szigethy, May 18, 1991. AA, North Harris Coll., 1992; student, U. Houston, 1990-91, 92-93. Tax acct. Stewart & Stevenson, Houston, 1987-93; clk. cash receipts Reiss Media Enterprises, Englewood, Colo., 1994—. Mem. Inst. Mgmt. Accts. (dir. attendence 1988-93, award for 100% attendence 1988, 90, 92). Home: PO Box 280249 Lakewood CO 80228-0249

TAATGEN, HENDERIKUS ALBERT, university administrator, educator; b. Hellevoetsluis, The Netherlands, Oct. 21, 1951; came to U.S., 1979; s. Willem Taatgen and Ludwina Jantina Broens; m. Marga M. Kapka. BA in Geography, Nat. U., Groningen, The Netherlands, 1974, MA in Anthropology, 1979; PhD in Anthropology, SUNY, Stony Brook, 1988. Assoc. prof. Chapman U., Silverdale, Wash., 1995—, acad. program coord., 1997—; vis. asst. prof. Ind. U., Bloomington, 1989-93; chair COP Adv. Bd., Pt. Townsend, Wash., 1997—; planner Jefferson County Comty. Network, Bremerton, Wash, 1995; rschr. Roscrea (Ireland) Hist. Soc., 1985-86. Contbr. articles to profl. jours. Mem. Jefferson County Higher Edn. Access Com., Pt. Townsend, 1996—. Dissertation fellow Mildred and Herbert Weisinger Fund, 1987; Sigma Xi grantee, 1987. Mem. Soc. for Study of Social Problems (Erwin Smigel Fund award 1998, Activist and Fgn. Scholars Fund award 1998), Am. Coun. for Irish Students, Law and Justice Assn., Am. Conf. for Irish Studies, Jefferson County Law and Justice Assn. Home: 832 Hastings Ave Port Townsend WA 98368 Office: Chapman U PO Box 2120 Silverdale WA 98383-2120

TABASHNICK, SIMON MARK, multimedia producer, director, photographer; b. N.Y.C., Sept. 29, 1946; s. Herbert and Rose (Miller) T. AA, Miami (Fla.) Dade Jr. Coll., 1966; BS in Advt., U. Fla., 1968; DD (hon.), St. Mark's Coll., San Fernando, Calif., 1978. Lic. FCC. Disc jockey Sonny Mark Mobile Discotheques, Miami, 1974-76; sound mixer Jaguar Recording, Hollywood, Calif., 1978; rsch. cons. Soluk Films, L.A., 1983-87; prodr. sound effects MilchFilm Inc., Burbank, Calif., 1987-88; studio prodr. Limelite Studios, Miami, 1989-91; dir. devel. Rubber Dubbers Sound, Burbank, 1993; multimedia cons. AmeriKids USA, Marina del Rey, Calif., 1995—; prodr., dir. Mark Comm. Network, L.A., 1972—; real estate developer MCN Ltd., Tujunga, Calif., 1982-81; tech. cons. HI-X Tech., Miami, 1991-97. Dir. videotape More Yoga, 1995; prodr. sound effects Halloween 4, 1988; multimedia dir. CD-ROM Pony Express Rider, 1996 (Bessie award 1996). Social activist The Movement, San Francisco, 1968-72; civil libertarian ACLU, Miami, 1973-75. Innovations for Edn. grantee Oracle Group, 1996. Avocations: numismatics, philately, tennis, swimming, chess. Home: 14010 Captain Row Ste 337 Marina Del Rey CA 90292

TABOR, FRED, philosophy educator; b. Utica, N.Y., June 30, 1952; s. Matthew and Helen T.; m. Michelle Ester Abernathy, Aug. 17, 1985; 1 child, Drew Nikolai. BA, SUNY, Oswego, 1976; MS, U. Utah, 1983, MA, 1988. Instr. English/philosophy South Plains Coll., Levelland, Tex., 1988-90, Whatcom C.C., Bellingham, Wash., 1990—. Mem. Am. Fedn. Tchrs., Green Peace, Nature Conservancy, Union Concerned Scientists. Avocations: camping, hiking, parenting, gardening. Office: Whatcom CC 237 W Kellogg Rd Bellingham WA 98226-8033

TABRAH, RUTH MILANDER, minister, writer; b. Buffalo, N.Y., Feb. 28, 1921; d. Henry Milander and Ruth Harwood; m. Frank L. Tabrah, May 8, 1943 (div. Aug. 1970); children: Joseph, Thomas. BA, SUNY, Buffalo, 1941. Minister Honpa Hongwanji Mission of Hawaii, Honolulu, Hawaii, 1983—; lectr. in field. Author: Pulaski Place, 1949, Voices of Others, 1959, Emily's Hawaii, 1967, Hawaii Nel, 1967, The Red Shark, 1980, Buddhism, A Modern Way of Life and Thought, 1970, Lanai, Biography of an Island, 1976, Hawaii, a History, 1982, Niihau: The Last Hawaiian Island, 1987, Ajatasatu, The Story of Who We Are, 1988, Shin Sutras to Live By, 1991, The Monk Who Dared, 1995, The Natural Way of Shin Buddhism, 1994, Maui The Romantic Island, 1991-92, Kauai The Unconquerable Island, 1991-92, Golden Children of Hawaii, 1989; editor, text adaptor 9 titles Island Heritage Folktales and Legends, 1973-78; editor Buddhist Study Ctr. Press, 1979—; contbr. articles to jours. Founder Buddhist Study Ctr. Press, Honolulu, 1979; mem. Hawaii State Bd. Edn., Honolulu, 1966-78; chmn. [illegible] Buddhist Studies. E-mail: rutab@aloha.net. Fax: 808-593-9061. Home: 876 Curtis St Apt 3905 Honolulu HI 96813-5165

TABRISKY, JOSEPH, radiologist, educator; b. Boston, June 23, 1931; s. Henry and Gertrude Tabrisky; BA cum laude, Harvard U., 1952; MD cum laude, Tufts U., 1956; m. Phyllis Eleanor Page, Apr. 23, 1955; children: Joseph Page, Elizabeth Ann, William Page. Flexible intern U. Ill. Hosp., 1956-57; resident in radiology Fitzsimons Army Hosp., 1958-60; instr. radiology Tufts U. Med. Sch., 1964-65; cons. radiologist Swedish Med. Center, Denver, 1966-68; chief radiologist Kaiser Found. Hosp., Harbor City, Calif., 1968-72; mem. faculty UCLA Med. Sch., 1972—, prof. radiol. scis., 1975-92, prof emeritus, 1993—, vice chmn. dept., 1976-92 , exec. policy com. radiol. scis.; chmn. radiology dept. Harbor-UCLA Med. Ctr., 1975-92 , pres. faculty soc., 1979-80, exec. dir. MR/CT Imaging Ctr., bd. dirs. Rsch. Ednl. Inst., Harbor Collegium/UCLA Found.; chief exec. officer Vascular Biometrics Inc.; steering com. Harvard U., 1952; cons. L.A. County Dept. Pub. Health; chmn. L.A. County Radiol. Standards Com., 1979. Mem. Harvard-Radcliffe Schs. Com.; chmn., bd. dirs., treas., Harbor-UCLA Med. Found.; chmn. UCLA Coun. for Ednl. Devel. Maj. M.C., U.S. Army, 1957-63. Recipient Silver Knight award Nat. Mgmt. Assn., 1992. Diplomate Am. Bd. Radiology. Fellow Am. Coll. Radiology, Univ. Radcom Assn. (chief exec. officer 1987-89); mem. Radiol. Soc. N. Am., Calif. Med. Assn., Calif. Radiol. Soc., L.A. Med. Assn., L.A. Radiol. Soc., Alpha Omega Alpha. Contbr. articles to med. jours. Office: 1000 W Carson St Torrance CA 90502-2004

TACAL, JOSE VEGA, JR., public health official, veterinarian; b. Ilocos Sur, Philippines, Sept. 5, 1933; came to U.S., 1969; s. Jose Sr. and Cristina (Vega) T.; m. Lilia Caccam, 1959; children: Joyce, Jasmin, Jose III. DVM, U. Philippines, Quezon City, 1956; diploma, U. Toronto, 1964. Diplomate Am. Coll. Vet. Preventive Medicine; lic. vet., Calif. Provincial veterinarian Philippine Bur. Animal Industry, Manila, 1956-57; instr. vet. medicine U. Philippines, Quezon City, 1957-64, asst. prof., chmn. dept. vet. microbiology, pathology and pub. health, 1965-69; pub. health veterinarian San Bernardino (Calif.) County Dept. Pub. Health, 1970-83, sr. pub. health veterinarian, program mgr., sect. chief, 1984—; zoonotic diseases lectr. Calif. State U., San Bernardino, spring 1984; lectr. U. Calif. Extension, Riverside, spring, 1985; vis. prof. vet. pub. health U. Philippines at Los Banos, Laguna, 1988; participant 1st Internat. Conf. on Emerging Zoonoses, Jerusalem, 1996; program presenter 4th Internat. Symposium on Ectoparasites of Pets, U. Calif., Riverside, 1997; poster presenter 8th Annual Rabies in the Ams. Conf., Kingston, Ont., Can., 1997; mem. rabies and ferret adv. group Calif. Dept. Health Svcs., 1998. Columnist L.A. Free Press, 1991, Pilipinas Times, 1993, Mabuhay Times, 1994-95; contbr. more than 50 articles to profl. jours. Pres. Filipino Assn. of San Bernardino County, Highland, Calif., 1979; charter mem. Greater Inland Empire Filipino Assn., Highland, 1986—; del. First Filipino Media Conf. N.Am., L.A., 1993; mem. San Bernardino County Africanized Honey Bee Task Force, 1993—; participant 1st Internat. Conf. on Emerging Zoonoses, Jerusalem, 1996. Recipient Donald T. Fraser Meml. medal U. Toronto, 1964, Cert. of Merit, Philippine Vet. Med. Assn., 1965, Cert. of Appreciation Calif. State Bd. Examiners in Vet. Medicine, 1979, 84, Cert. of Recognition, Congressman George E. Brown Jr., 42d Congl. Dist. Calif., 1994, Assemblyman Joe Baca, 62d Assembly Dist., Calif. State Legis., 1994, Colombo Plan Study fellow Can./Philippine Govts., 1963-64. Mem. AAAS, AVMA, Orange Belt Vet. Med. Assn., Western Poultry Disease Conf., Soc. for Advancement of Rsch., Nat. Trust for Historic Preservation, N.Y. Acad. Scis., Phi Kappa Phi, Phi Sigma. Office: San Bernardino County Dept Pub Health 351 N Mountain View Ave San Bernardino CA 92401-1609

TADIAN, LUANNE F. B., financial analyst, consultant, researcher; b. Colorado Springs, Colo., Mar. 29, 1965; d. Carlos Solomon and Josie Dolores (Vigil) C'DeBaca; m. Nishan Thaddeus Tadian, Dec. 30, 1985; children: Joshua Abel, Zachary Solomon. BS in Psychology and Biology, U.N.Mex., 1988; MBA, Calif. State U., L.A., 199. Lic. in real estate law, series 6 and 63, Nat. Assn. Securities Dealers. Jr. v.p. prodn. Sentry Mortgage, Albuquerque, 1988-89; rsch. cons., L.A., 1991-93; account mgr. Beverly Hills Group Fin. Mgmt. Specialists, L.A., 1993-96; mgr. customer support Daylight Transport/DayWest Express, 1996—. Bd. dirs., chmn. vol. recognition, mem. pub. rels. and resource devel. coms. Calif. Litracy, San Gabriel, 1993—; del. Rep. Planning Com. Mem. NAFE, Nat. Assn. Women Bus. Owners, Nat. Assn. Life Underwriters, Beta Gamma Sigma. Republican. Roman Catholic. Home: House C 269 S Walnut Grove Ave San Gabriel CA 91776-1711

TAEKMAN, MICHAEL SEYMOUR, neurological surgeon; b. Chgo., June 30, 1937; s. Harry Joseph and Rose Anne (Sturner) T.; m. Ilene Roberta Erlich, Dec. 18, 1960; children—Jeffrey Marc, Jennifer Lynn, Jessica Beth. M.D., U. Ill.-Chgo., 1962. Diplomate Am. Bd. Neurol. Surgery. Intern, U. Ill., Chgo., 1962-63, resident, 1963-67; fellow U. Edinburgh, England, 1967; attending neurosurgeon Chgo. Mcpl. Contagious Disease Hosp., 1967; pres. East Bay Med. Group, Berkeley, Calif., 1969—; asst. clin. prof. U. Calif.-San Francisco, 1971—; instr. U. Ill.-Chgo., 1963-67, U. Calif.-San Francisco, 1968-71; lectr. U. Calif.-Berkeley, 1975—; chmn. dept. surgery Childrens Hosp. Med. Ctr., Oakland, Calif., 1980—; assoc. prof. U. Calif., San Francisco, 1990 . Author: Advances in Pituatary Disease, 1979. Contbr. articles to profl. jours. Adv. mem. San Rafael Sch. Bd., 1976-77; med. examiner State Calif., Berkeley, 1976—. Served to capt. USAF, 1964-71. Scholar Internat. Coll. Surgeons, 1967, Med. Research Council Great Britain, 1967. Fellow ACS, Am. Assn. Neurol. Surgeons, Am. Assn. Pediatric Neurol. Surgeons; mem. Calif. Acad. Medicine, Alameda Contra Costa Med. Assn., Phi Eta Sigma. Republican. Jewish. Club: Rafael Racket (San Rafael). Office: East Bay Med Group Inc 3000 Colby St Berkeley CA 94705-2058

TAFOYA, ARTHUR N., bishop; b. Alameda, N.Mex., Mar. 2, 1933; s. Nicholas and Rosita Tafoya. Ed., St. Thomas Sem., Denver, Conception (Mo.) Sem. Ordained priest Roman Cath. Ch., 1962. Asst. pastor Holy Rosary Parish, Albuquerque, 1962-65; pastor Northern N.Mex., from 1965, San Jose Parish, Albuquerque; rector Immaculate Heart of Mary Sem., Santa Fe; ordained bishop of Pueblo Colo., 1980—. Office: Diocese of Pueblo 1001 N Grand Ave Pueblo CO 81003-2915*

TAFT, DAVID ALLAN, surgeon; b. Madison, Wis., Dec. 26, 1933; s. Cyrus Alonso and Margaret Eleanor (Brubaker) T.; m. Sheila Blackwood, Apr. 20, 1968; children: Robert Matthew, Michael Cyrus. BS, Iowa State U., 1955; MD, U. Iowa, 1959; M in Med. Sci., Ohio State U., 1965. Diplomate Am. Bd. Surgery. Intern Ohio State U., Columbus, 1959-60, resident in surgery, 1960-64, chief resident, 1964-65; research fellow and jr. cons. Royal Infirmary U. Edinburgh, Scotland, 1965-66; surgeon The Mason Clinic, Seattle, 1969—; assoc. prof. surgery U. Wash., Seattle, 1979—. Contbr. articles to profl. jours. Served to comdr. USN, 1966-69, Vietnam. Decorated Navy Cross. Fellow ACS, Am. Bd. Surgery, Western Surgical Assn., North Pacific Surgical Assn.; mem. Pacific Coast Surgical Assn., Seattle Surgical Soc., Soc. Surgery Olinentary Tract, Sigma Xi. Republican. Presbyterian. Avocations: camping, hiking, outdoor activities. Home: 5757 64th Ave NE Seattle WA 98105-2041

TAGGART, SONDRA, financial planner, investment advisor; b. N.Y.C., July 22, 1934; d. Louis and Rose (Birnbaum) Hamov; children: Eric, Karen. BA, Hunter Coll., 1955. Cert. fin. planner; registered investment advisor; registered prin. Nat. Assn. Securities Dealers. Founder, dir., officer Copyright Svc. Bur., Ltd., N.Y.C., 1957-69; dir., officer Maclen Music, Inc., N.Y.C., 1964-69, The Beatles Ltd., 1964-69; pres. Westshore, Inc., Mill Valley, Calif., 1969-82; investment advisor, securities broker, chief exec. officer The Taggart Co. Ltd., 1982—. Editor: The Red Tapes: Commentaries on Doing Business With The Russians and East Europeans, 1978. Mem. Internat. Assn. Fin. Planners, Registry Fin. Planning Practitioners. Republican. Club: Bankers. Office: 9720 Wilshire Blvd Ste 205 Beverly Hills CA [illegible]

TAHMASSIAN, ARA ZARNEH, university director; b. Tehran, Iran, Apr. 15, 1953; came to U.S., 1981; s. Ohan Zarneh and Nashkoon (Asadourian) T.; m. Linda Khosrof Garabedian, Jan. 7, 1953; children: Levon Zarneh, Ani Verjeen. BSc in Nuclear Engring., London U., 1977; postgrad., Middlesex (Eng.) Poly. U., 1979; MSc in Radiol. Health, Salford (Eng.) U., 1980; PhD [illegible] Cons., Fremont, Calif., 1981-84, v.p. ops., 1987-88; dir. environ. health and safety Vets. Med. Ctr., San Francisco, 1984-87; mgr. radiation safety U. Calif., San Francisco, 1988-93, dir. environ. health and safety, 1993—; cons. various hosps., Calif., 1982—. Co-author papers in field, book chpt. Trustee St. Gregory's Ch., San Francisco, 1991-92; pres. Ararat Armenian Soc., San Francisco, 1991, Armenian Cultural Found., San Francisco, 1989; bd. dirs. Calif. Radioactive Forum, San Francisco, 1993. Mem. Soc. Nuclear Medicine, North Calif. Health Physics Soc. Republican. Armenian Orthodox. Avocations: soccer, cycling, boating. Home: 39537 Benavente Ave Fremont CA 94539-3002 Office: U Calif 50 Medical Center Way San Francisco CA 94143-8050

TAI, FRANK, aerospace engineering consultant; b. Omaha, Apr. 10, 1955; s. Shou Nan and May (Chuang) T.; m. Lorraine Mae Fesq, May 14, 1988. BSME, U. Calif., Berkeley, 1977; MS in Automatic Controls Engring., MIT, 1979. Design engr. satellite attitude control systems Ball Aerospace, Boulder, Colo., 1979-84; mgr. satellite attitude control systems TRW, Redondo Beach, Calif., 1984-88; mgr. engring. Microcosm, Inc., Torrance, Calif., 1988-89; pres., engring. cons., founder Tech. Advancements, Inc., Playa del Rey, Calif., 1989—. Contbr. articles to profl. jours. Mem. AIAA, Am. Astronautical Soc., Sigma Xi, Tau Beta Pi, Pi Tau Sigma. Office: Tech Advancements Inc 6738 Esplanade St # 300 Playa Del Rey CA 90293-7525

TAIFEL, ROMAN S., retired mortgage company executive; b. Freiburg, Germany, Oct. 11, 1936; came to U.S., 1949; s. Valentine and Valerie (Fisher) T.; m. Millee L. Buttery, July (, 1966. BS, Capitol Radio Engring., Washington, 1970. Lic. in real estate; comml. pilot. Engring. technician Western Union, Oakland, Calif., 1962-66; equipment inspector Western Union, Seattle, 1966-76, resident engr., 1977-89; real estate agt. Century 21, Seattle, 1992-93; owner RST Mortgage Svc., Seattle, 1994-99; sales mgr. U.S. Mortgage Reduction, Hilton Island, S.C., 1992-96; ind. distbr. Tex. Refinery Corp, Fort Worth, 1997-99. Mem. Rep. Nat. Com., Washington, 1980. Lt. comdr. USCGR, 1984—. Mem. Confederate Air Force (fin. officer 1980-84), VFW, Am. Legion. Avocations: flying, boating, dancing. Home: 4426 40th Ave SW Seattle WA 98116-4213

TAIMUTY, SAMUEL ISAAC, physicist; b. West Newton, Pa., Dec. 20, 1917; s. Elias and Samia (Hawatt) T.; BS, Carnegie Inst. Tech., 1940; PhD, U. So. Calif., 1951; m. Betty Jo Travis, Sept. 12, 1953 (dec.); children: Matthew, Martha; m. Rosalie Richards, Apr. 3, 1976; stepchildren: Charles Scott Holman, Martha Ruth Holman, Elizaeth Ann Holman. Physicist, U.S. Naval Shipyard, Phila. and Long Beach, Calif., 1942-46; rsch. asst. U. So. Calif., 1947-51; sr. physicist U.S. Naval Radiol. Def. Lab., 1950-52, SRI Internat., Menlo Park, Calif., 1952-72; sr. staff engr. Lockheed Missiles & Space Co., Sunnyvale, Calif., 1972-89; cons. physicist, 1971—. Mem. Am. Phys. Soc., Sigma Xi. Episcopalian. Contbr. articles to sci. publs. Patentee in field. Home: 3346 Kenneth Dr Palo Alto CA 94303-4217

TAINTER, JOSEPH ANTHONY, archaeologist; b. San Francisco, Dec. 8, 1949; s. George Washington and Elizabeth Anne (O'Reilly) T.; m. Bonnie Catherine Bagley, Nov. 4, 1977; 1 child, Emmet Bagley. BA, U. Calif., 1972; MA, Northwestern U., 1973, PhD, 1975. Asst. prof. U. N.Mex., Albuquerque, 1975-78; rsch. asst. prof. Eastern N.Mex. U., Portales, 1978-80; archaeologist USDA Forest Svc., Albuquerque, 1980-94; project leader Rocky Mountain Rsch. Sta., Albuquerque, 1994—; pres. N.Mex. Archaeol. Coun., Albuquerque, 1979-80; cons. U.S. Nat. Com. of Scientific Com. on Problems of the Environ., UN, 1995, Monts Mandingues Classified Forest, Bamako, Mali, 1992-93, Nat. Directorate of Arts and Culture, Mali, 1998; dirs. lectr. Getty Ctr. for the History of Art and the Humanities, 1994. Author: The Collapse of Complex Societies, 1988, 9th printing, 1996; co-editor: Evolving Complexity and Environmental Risk in the Prehistoric Southwest, 1996; co-author: Storia d'Europa II: Preistoria e Antichità, 1994. Grantee NSF, 1974-75. Mem. AAAS, Am. Anthropol. Assn., Soc. for Am. Archaeology. Achievements include developed and tested new theory explaining why societies and civilizations collapse; developed and tested new theory that relates economic sustainability to sociopolitical complexity; developed first archaeological research program in USDA Forest Service Research. Home: PO Box 145 Corrales NM 87048-0145 Office: Rocky Mountain Rsch Sta 2205 Columbia Dr SE Albuquerque NM 87106-3222

TAKAHASHI, EDWARD KATSUAKI, architect; b. L.A., Nov. 8, 1936; s. Seytsu Shodo and Suzue (Hasu) T.; m. Minnie Miyatake, Sept. 10 1961; children: Scott Hideyuki, Katherine Shoko, Mark Shoji. BArch, U. So. Calif., L.A., 1960. Registered arch., Calif.; registered disaster serv. worker, Calif.; cert. constrn. specifier; cert. third party insp. and moisture analyst. Draftsman O'Leary & Terasawa, L.A., 1959-66; arch., ptnr. O'Leary Terasawa Ptnrs., L.A., 1966-97; prin. Widom Wein Cohen O'Leary Terasawa, Santa Monica, Calif., 1998—; cons. archtl. arbitration; fallout shelter analyst; lectr. various arch. and law assns. Designed saftey nail gauge. Chmn. Ethics Comm., L.A. Chpt., 1993—; dir. Jap. Am. Optimist Club, 1967-74; pres. Calif. Basketball Assoc., 1989-91; commr. So. Calif. Women's athl. union, 1972-94; bd.dir. Little Tokyo Comm. Gym, 1996; active local Boy Scouts of Am. Recipient Silver Beaver award Boy Scouts Am., 1989; pres. award Constrn. Specification Inst., 1982. Mem. AIA, Contr. Specification Inst. (Pres. Award 1982), Roof Cons. Inst., Internat. Conf. Bldg. Ofcls. Republican. Buddhist. Avocations: ceramics, fishing, skiing, basketball. Office: Widom Wein et al Partners Ste 400 2020 Santa Monica Blvd Santa Monica CA 90404-2059

TAKAHASHI, GARY WAYNE, internist, hematologist, oncologist; b. Honolulu, Jan. 2, 1959; s. Kenneth Kiyoshi and Grace Setsuko (Ishigure) T. BS in Math. and Biology, Stanford U., 1980; MS in Anatomy/Reproductive Biology, U. Hawaii, 1983; MD, John A. Burns Sch. Medicine, Honolulu, 1984. Diplomate Nat. Bd. Med. Examiners, Am. Bd. Internal Medicine (Hematology, Med. Oncology). Intern, resident Oreg. Health Scis. U., Portland, 1984-87; chief resident St. Vincent Med. Ctr., Portland, 1987-88; fellow hematology/oncology U. Wash., Seattle, 1988-93; physician Hematology Clinic, Portland, Oreg., 1993-94, Oreg. Hematology Oncology Assocs., 1994—; clin. asst. prof. medicine Oreg. Health Scis. U., 1995—. Contbr. articles and abstracts to profl. publs. Recipient Achievement Rewards for Coll. Scientists scholarship, 1982, Merck, Sharp & Dohme Acad. award, 1982, Nat. Rsch. Svc. award fellowship NIH, 1990, March of Dimes Rsch. grant, 1993. Mem. Am. Coll. Physicians, Am. Soc. Hematology, Am. Soc. Clin. Oncology, Southwestern Oncology Group, Oreg. Med. Assn., Wash. Med. Assn., Oreg. Mycol. Soc. Avocations: music, computers, mycology. Office: Oreg Hematology Oncology Assocs 9155 SW Barnes Rd Ste 533 Portland OR 97225-6632

TAKAHASHI, MUNIO HOWARD See MAKUUCHI, MUNIO HOWARD

TAKARA, KEN T., software engineer, artist; b. Ann Arbor, Mich., May 12, 1955; s. Kenji and Florence Takara. BS in Computer Sci., U. Calif., Santa Barbara, 1982. Programmer Lockheed-Dialog Info. Systems, Mountain View, Calif., 1978-83; software engr. Tak Automation, Inc., Burlingame, Calif., 1983-85; project mgr. Power Up Software Corp., San Mateo, Calif., 1986-87; software engr. PE Biosystems, Foster City, Calif., 1989—. Office: PE Biosystems 850 Lincoln Center Dr Foster City CA 94404

TAKASUGI, ROBERT MITSUHIRO, federal judge; b. Tacoma, Sept. 12, 1930; s. Hidesaburo and Kayo (Otsuki) T.; m. Dorothy O. Takasugi; children: Jon Robert, Lesli Mari. BS, UCLA, 1953; LLB, JD, U. So. Calif., 1959. Bar: Calif. bar 1960. Practiced law Los Angeles, 1960-73; judge East Los Angeles Municipal Ct., 1973-75, adminstrv. judge, 1974, presiding judge, 1975; judge Superior Ct., County of Los Angeles, 1975-76; U.S. dist. judge U.S. Dist. Ct. (cen. dist.) Calif., 1976—; nat. legal counsel Japanese Am. Citizens League; guest lectr. law seminars Harvard U. Law Sch. Careers Symposium; commencement spkr.; mem. Legion Lex U. So. Calif. Law Ctr.; chmn. Pub. Defs. Indigent Def. & Psychiat. Panel Com., mem. Affirmative Action Com., Habeas Corpus-Death Penalty Com., Exec. Com., Jury Com., Settlement Rule Com., Adv. Com. on Codes of Conduct of the Jud. Conf. of the U.S., 1988-92, Code of Conduct of Judges. Mem. editorial bd. U. So. Calif. Law Rev., 1959; contbr. articles to profl. jours. Mem. Calif. adv. com. Western Regional Office, U.S. Commn. on Civil Rights; chmn. blue ribbon [illegible]

Theater U.S. Army, 1954, Jud. Excellence award Criminal Cts. Bar Assn., cert. of merit Japanese-Am. Bar Assn., Disting. Svc. award Asian Pacific Ctr. and Pacific Clinics, 1994, Freedom award Sertoma, 1995, Pub. Svc. award Asian Pacific Am. Legal Ctr. So. Calif., 1995, Trailblazer award So. Calif. region NAPABA, 1995, Spl. award Mex.-Am. Bar Assn., 1996, Spirit of Excellence award ABA, 1998; named Judge of Yr. Century City Bar Assn., 1995. Mem. U. So. Calif. Law Alumni Assn. (dir.). Office: US Dist Ct 312 N Spring St Los Angeles CA 90012-4701

TAKEI, TOSHIHISA, otolaryngologist; b. L.A., Apr. 19, 1931; s. Taketomi and Mitsue (Hagihara) T.; m. Emiko Kubota, Jan. 25, 1955; children: H. Thomas, T. Robert. BA, UCLA, 1954; MD, Boston U., 1962. Diplomate, Am. Bd. Otolaryngology. Intern L.A. County Harbor Gen. Hosp., 1962-63; resident in otolaryngology L.A. County/U. So. Calif. Med. Ctr., 1963-67; staff physician Covina (Calif.) Ear, Nose & Throat Med. Group, 1968—; asst. prof. Sch. Medicine, U. So. Calif., L.A., 1968—. 1st lt. U.S. Army, 1955-56, Korea. Fellow Am. Acad. Otolaryngology, Royal Soc. Medicine. Republican. Buddhist. Office: Covina ENT Med Group Inc 236 W College St Covina CA 91723-1902

TAKEUCHI, HAJIME JIM, airline executive, electrical engineer; b. Ishikawa, Japan, Nov. 4, 1941; came to U.S., 1961; s. Kazuo and Modori (Genmei) T.; m. Elaine Tsuha, Mar. 20, 1975; children: Mitsuko, Erica, Rodger. BSEE, U. Ill., 1966. Mgr. space shuttle United Svcs. Co., Cape Kennedy, Fla., 1982-83; contract mgr. Air Crew Tng. Co., Denver, 1983-84; engr. United Air Lines, San Francisco, 1967-76, staff engr., 1976-79; mgr. aircraft sales United Air Lines, Chgo., 1979-82; mgr. tech. svcs. United Air Lines, San Francisco, 1984-89, mgr. engring., 1989-91, dir. engring., 1991—. Home: 2436 Wright Ct South San Francisco CA 94080-5257 Office: United Airlines San Francisco Internat Airport San Francisco CA 94128

TALAMANTES, ROBERTO, developmental pediatrician; b. Juarez, Chihuahua, Mex., June 19, 1952; came to U.S., 1955; s. Cruz and Viviana (Monarez) T.; m. Blanca Yolanda Chavez, Aug. 19, 1972; children: Christian, Steven. BS in Biology, U. Colo., 1972; MD, U. Autonoma Ciudad Juarez, 1979. Rotating intern Baylor Coll. Medicine, Houston, 1980-81, pediat. resident, 1981-84, devel. pediat. fellow, 1984-86; pvt. practice Gen. Devel. Pediatrics, Las Cruces, N.Mex., 1986—; pres. IPA N.Mex., 1993-98; chmn. bd. dirs. Cimarron HMO, 1997—; pres. elect med. staff Meml. Med. Ctr., Las Cruces, 1993-94, pres., 1994-95, sec., 1992-94. With U.S. Army, 1972-74. Fellow Am. Acad. of Pediatrics, Soc. of Devel. Pediatrics; mem. N.Mex. Podiatric Soc., N.Mex. Med. Soc. Republican. Avocations: chess, guitar. Office: Hillside Circle Las Cruces NM 88011

TALBERT, MELVIN GEORGE, bishop; b. Clinton, La., June 14, 1934; s. Nettles and Florence (George) T.; m. Ethlelou Douglas, June 3, 1961; 1 child, Evangeline. BA, So. U., 1959; MDiv, Interdenominational Theol. Ctr., Gammon Theol. Sem., Atlanta, 1962; DD hon., Huston Tillotson Coll., Austin, 1972; LLD (hon.), U. Puget Sound, Tacoma, 1987. Ordained deacon, Meth. Ch., 1960 , elder, 1962, elected to episcopacy, United Meth. Ch., 1980. Pastor Boyd Chapel, Jefferson City, Tenn., 1960-61, Rising Sun, Sunrise, Tenn., 1960-61, St. John's Ch., L.A., 1961-62, Wesley Ch., L.A., 1962-64, Hamilton Ch., L.A., 1964-67; mem. staff So. Calif.-Ariz. Conf. United Meth. Ch., L.A., 1967-68; dist. supr. Long Beach dist. So. Calif.-Ariz. Conf. United Meth. Ch., 1968-73; gen. sec. Gen. Bd. Discipleship, Nashville, 1973-80; resident bishop Seattle area Pacific N.W. conf. United Meth. Ch., 1980-88, resident bishop San Francisco area Calif.-Nev. Conf., 1988—, sec. coun. bishops, 1988—; mem. exec. com. World Meth. Coun., 1976-81, 84—; mem. governing bd. Nat. Coun. Chs., 1980—; v.p., chmn. funding com. Gen. Commn. on Religion and Race, 1980-84, pres., 1984-88; chmn. Missional Priority Coordinating com. Gen. Coun. Ministries, 1980-84; mem. Gen. Commn. on Christian Unity and Interreligious Concerns, 1984—, African Ch. Growth and Devel. Com., 1981-84; pres. elect Nat. Coun. Ch. Christ in the U.S.A., pres. Mem. steering com. Student Non-Violent Coordinating com. Atlanta U. Ctr., 1960-61; trustee Gammon Theol. Sem., Atlanta, 1976—, U. Puget Sound, Tacoma, 1980-88 , Sch. Theology at Claremont, Calif., 1981-88, Pacific Sch. Religion, 1988—; bd. dirs. Glide Found., 1988—. Recipient award of merit for outstanding svc. in Christian edn. Gen. Bd. Edn., 1971; recipient Spl. achievement award Nat. Assn. Black Bus. Women, 1971; Nat. Meth. scholar, 1960; Crusade scholar, 1961. Mem. Theta Phi. Democrat. Home: 8735 W Camden Dr Elk Grove CA 95624-3037*

TALBOT, DAVID LYLE, editor; b. L.A., Sept. 22, 1951; s. Lyle and Margaret (Epple) T.; m. Camille Marie Peri, Dec. 9, 1989; children: Joseph, Nathaniel. Student, Univ. Calif., 1973. Environ. action staff writer Washington, D.C., 1979-81; sr. editor Mother Jones Mag., San Francisco, 1981-85; sr. editor San Francisco Examiner Image Mag., 1985-86, editor in chief, 1990-93, features editor, 1993-95; editor/CEO Salon Mag., San Francisco, 1995—. Co-author: Burning Desires: Sex in America, 1989, Creative Differences: Profiles of Hollywood Dissidents, 1978. Recipient Best Web Site award Time Mag., 1997, Best Web Mag. award Webby Awards, 1998. Office: Salon Mag 706 Mission St Fl 2 San Francisco CA 94103-3113

TALBOT, STEPHEN H., television producer, writer; b. Hollywood, Calif., Feb. 28, 1949; s. Lyle and Margaret (Epple) T.; m. Pippa Gordon; children: Dashiell, Caitlin. BA, Wesleyan U., 1970. Asst. to pres., lectr. Am. studies SUNY, Old Westbury, 1970-73; reporter Internews, Berkeley, Calif., 1973-79; producer, reporter KQED-TV, San Francisco, 1980-89; producer, writer Frontline (PBS), San Francisco, 1992—. Appeared in Leave It To Beaver as Gilbert, 1958-63, also Twilight Zone, Perry Mason, Lassie, others; producer, co-writer (documentary) The Long March of Newt Gingrich, 1996; producer: (documentary) The Best Campaign Money Can Buy, 1992 (Columbia Univ. Dupont award), (PBS-TV) Beryl Markham, 1986, Ken Kesey, 1987, Carlos Fuentes, 1989, Maxine Hong Kingston, 1990, John Dos Passos, 1994; producer, writer: (documentary) The Case of Dashiell Hammett, 1982 (Peabody award, Edgar Allan Poe award), 1968: The Year That Shaped a Generation, 1998; co-producer, reporter: (documentary) Broken Arrow, 1980 (George Peabody & George Polk award), others. Recipient Thomas Storke Internat. Journalism award World Affairs Coun. No. Calif., San Francisco, 1983, 86, Golden Gate award San Francisco Film Festival, 1986, 89, Emmy award, NATAS, 1980-81, 82-83, 87-88, 90-91. Mem. Writer's Guild Am. West, Am. Fedn. TV and Radio Artists. Office: Ctr Investigative Reporting 500 Howard St Ste 206 San Francisco CA 94105-3000

TALBOTT, GEORGE ROBERT, physicist, mathematician, educator; b. San Diego, Oct. 1, 1925; s. George Fletcher and Mary (Lanz) T.; BA with honors, UCLA, 1960; DSc, Ind. No. U., 1973. Physicist, mem. tech. staff Rockwell Internat. Co., Anaheim, Calif., 1960-85; mem. faculty thermodynamics Pacific States U., 1971-77, prof., 1972-80, chmn. dept. math. studies, 1973-80; lectr. computer sci. Calif. State U., Fullerton, 1979—; cons. physics, computer sci.; disting. guest lectr. Brunel U., London, 1974, 76; spl. guest Forschungsbibliothek, Hannover, W. Ger., 1979; assoc. editor KRONOS jour., Glassboro (N.J.) U., 1978—; chief computer scientist and ednl. videotape dir. Specialized Software, Wilmot, Wis., 1982—; phys. scientist and rsch. assoc. San Diego Mus. Man, 1993—. With M.C., U.S. Army, 1956. Recipient Vis. Scholar's award Western Mich. U., 1979; elected to Herbert Hoover H.S. Hall Fame, San Diego, 1998. Mem. Am. Soc. Med. Technologists, Am. Math. Soc., Math. Assn. Am., Am. Soc. Clin. Pathologists (lic. med. lab. technologist), Sigma Xi. Buddhist. Author: Electronic Thermodynamics, 1973; Philosophy and Unified Science, 1977, Computer Applications, 1989, Sir Arthur and Gravity, 1990, Fermat's Last Theorem, 1991, The Signal Processing Library, 1995; co-inventor burner. Home: 4031 E Charter Oak Dr Orange CA 92869-2611

TALBOTT, JOHN, mayor; m. Claudia Field; 2 children. BA in Soc. Sci., Coll. Great Falls, 1976; MA in Polit. Sci., Cen. Mich. U., 1978. Enlisted USAF, advanced through grades to col., ret., 1982, served in various assignments including Joint Svc. Commands; past comdr. commn. squadron USAF, Malstrom AFB, Mont.; with Jet Propulsion Lab, to 1989; mayor City of Spokane, Washington. Active cmty. devel. and politics, Spokane, 1989—. Office: Office of Mayor City Hall 5th Fl 808 W Spokane Falls Blvd Spokane WA 99201-3335*

TALIAFERRO, ROBERT See BROOKE, TAL

TALKE, FRANK EBERHARD, education educator; b. Dresden, Germany, Sept. 10, 1939; came to U.S., 1965; s. Artur and Louise T.; m. Kathryn Ann Talke; children: Stefan, Kristen, Kurt. Diploma Engring., U. Stuttgart, Germany, 1965; MS, U. Calif., Berkeley, 1966, PhD, 1968. Mgr. IBM, San Jose, Calif., 1969-86; prof. U. Calif. San Diego, 1986—, chair AMES dept., 1993-95; vis. prof. U. Calif. Berkeley, 1984. Author numerous tech. papers; patentee in field. Mem. ASME, IEEE (chair local sect. 1990-92). Office: U Calif San Diego 9500 Gilman Dr La Jolla CA 92093-5003

TALLERICO, PAUL JOSEPH, electrical engineer; b. N.Y.C., Nov. 30, 1938; s. Joseph Anthony and Marie Antonette (Dideo) T.; m. Mary Ellen Healy, Aug. 23, 1962; children: Catherine Ann, Elen Barbara. BSEE, MIT, MSEE; PhDEE, U. Mich., 1968. Staff mem. Internat. Baumess Machine Rsch. Lab., Yorktown Heights, N.Y., 1962-63; staff mem. Los Alamos (N.Mex.) Nat. Lab., 1968-96, team leader, 1996—; vis. prof. U. Paris, Orsay, 1985-86. Co-patentee in field. Patroller, Los Alamos Ski Patrol, 1992—. Mem. IEEE (sr., vice chair, then chair Los Alamos sect. 1995-97). Home: 238 Loma Del Escolar St Los Alamos NM 87544-2526 Office: Los Alamos Nat Lab PO Box 1663 M/S H827 Los Alamos NM 87545

TALLMAN, RICHARD C., lawyer; b. Oakland, Calif., Mar. 3, 1953; s. Kenneth A. and Jean M. (Kemppe) T.; m. Cynthia Ostolaza, Nov. 14, 1981. BSC, U. Santa Clara, 1975; JD, Northwestern U., 1978. Bar: Calif. 1978, Wash. 1979, U.S. Dist. Ct. (no. dist.) Calif. 1979, U.S. Dist. Ct. (we. dist.) Wash. 1979, U.S. Ct. Appeals (9th cir.) 1979, U.S. Dist. Ct. Hawaii 1986, U.S. Supreme Ct. 1997, U.S. Dist. Ct. (ea. dist.) Wash. 1998. Law clk to Hon. Morrell E. Sharp U.S. Dist. Ct. (we. dist.) Wash., Seattle, 1978-79; trial atty. U.S. Dept. Justice, Washington, 1979-80; asst. U.S. atty. U.S. Dist. Ct. (we. dist.) Wash., Seattle, 1980-83; ptnr. Schweppe, Krug & Tausend, PS, Seattle, 1983-89; mem. Bogle & Gates, PLLC, Seattle, 1990—; chmn. western dist. Wash. Lawyer Reps. to Ninth Cir. Jud. Conf., 1996-97. Instr. Nat. Park Svc. Seasonal Ranger Acad., Everett and Mt. Vernon, Wash., 1983-93; chmn. Edmonds C.C. Found., Lynnwood, Wash., 1990-92; gen. counsel Seattle-King County Crime Stoppers, 1987—; mem. exec. bd. Chief Seattle coun. Boy Scouts Am., 1997—. Mem. ABA, FBA (trustee 1992-93, v.p. 1994, pres. 1995), Seattle-King County Bar Assn., Rainier Club, Wash. Athletic Club. Avocations: hunting, hiking, fishing. Office: Bogle & Gates Two Union Sq # 4700 601 Union St Ste 4700 Seattle WA 98101-2346

TALMADGE, PHILIP ALBERT, state supreme court justice, former state senator; b. Seattle, Apr. 23, 1952; s. Judson H., Jr., and Jeanne C. T.; m. Darlene L. Nelson, Sept. 6, 1970; children: Adam, Matthew, Jessica, Jonathan, Annemarie. BA magna cum laude with high honors in Polit. Sci., Yale U., 1973; JD, U. Wash., 1976. Bar: Wash. 1976. Assoc. Karr Tuttle Campbell, 1976-89; pres. Talmadge & Cutler, P.S., 1989-95; senator State of Wash., 1979-95; justice Supreme Ct. Wash., 1995—; chair Senate Judiciary Com., 1981, 83-87, Senate Health and Human Svcs. Com., 1992-95, Wash. Senate, 1978-94, ways and means com., children and family svc. com., edn. com. Fellow Am. Assn. Appellate Lawyers; mem. King County Bar Assn., Wash. State Bar Assn., Seattle-King County Bar Assn. Author: The Nixon Doctrine and the Reaction of Three Asian Nations, 1973; editor Law Rev., U. Wash., 1975-76; contbr. articles to profl. jours.

TALMAGE, KENNETH KELLOGG, business executive; b. Morristown, N.J., Jan. 16, 1946; s. Edward Taylor Hunt Jr. and Dorothy Rogers Talmage. BA, Claremont Men's Coll., 1968; MBA, Boston U., Brussels, 1976. Asst. to chmn. Fin. Com. to Re-elect President Nixon, 1972-73; assoc., Hon. Leonard K. Firestone, L.A., 1973-74; attaché Am. Embassy, Brussels, 1974-77; mgmt. cons. strategic planning and fin. Arthur D. Little, Inc., Cambridge, Mass., 1977-80; sr. v.p. Boston Safe Deposit & Trust Co., 1980-87; pres. Lloyd's Furs, Inc., Denver, Colo., 1987-92; bd. dirs. Monterey Water Co., 1992—, pres., 1995-97, chmn., CEO, 1997—; bd. dirs. Pure West Industries, Inc., vice-chmn., 1993-95. Trustee Colo. Outward Bound Sch., 1990-96, vice chmn., 1995-96, bd. govs., 1996—. Vols. for Outdoor Colo., 1988-94, Breckenridge Outdoor Edn. Ctr., 1989-92; advisor Hurricane Island Outward Bound Sch., Maine, 1987—, trustee, 1979-87, chmn. bd. trustees, 1980-83; mem. exec. com. Outward Bound, U.S.A., 1980-85. With USNR, 1968-69. Mem. The Country Club (Mass.), Denver Country Club. Home: PO Box 1526 Carmel CA 93921-1526 Office: Monterey Water Co 1158 S Main St Manteca CA 95337-9505

TALT, ALAN R., lawyer; b. Stockton, Calif., June 17, 1929; s. Daniel Henry and Josephine (LeSaffre) T.; m. Marjorie Schutte, Sept. 12, 1953; children: Bradley Alan, Stephen Scott, Mark Kevin, Karen Talt Beardsley. BA, U. Calif., Berkeley, 1951, JD, 1954. Bar: Calif. 1955, U.S. Dist. Ct. (no. and so. dists.) Calif. 1955, U.S. Ct. Appeal (9th cir.) 1955. Law clk. to the chief judge U.S. Ct. Appeal (9th cir.), San Francisco, 1954-55; pvt. practice L.A. and Pasadena, Calif., 1955—; gen. counsel, sec., bd. dirs. Kirkhill Rubber Co., Brea, Calif., 1988—; gen. counsel, bd. dirs. KAPCO, Brea, 1985—; gen. counsel Caine, Farber & Gordon, Pasadena, 1986—. Asst. editor: Williston Casebook Contract Law, 1953. Pres. San Gabriel Valley Learning Soc., Pasadena, 1976-77; nat. v.p. Newman Clubs Am., 1949-50. Samuel Bell-McKee fellow, 1948; U. Calif. Berkeley Alumni scholar, 1947. Mem. Calif. State Bar, Jonathan Club, Valley Club (pres.), Ironwood Country Club. Avocations: fly fishing, philately. Home: 1375 Saint Albans Rd San Marino CA 91108-1860 Office: Law Offices Alan R Talt 790 E Colorado Blvd Ste 710 Pasadena CA 91101-2113

TALUS, DONNA J., educator; b. Salem, Oreg., Sept. 13, 1931; d. Ralph V. and Estella R. (Barber) Sebern; m. Hank M. Talus, June 5, 1955 (dec.); children: Dottie Hofford, Steve, Stacy. BA in PE, Williamette U., 1953. Cert. ARC First Aid instr., travel agent. Secondary tchr. Langlois (Oreg.) H.S., Oreg., 1953-54, Heppner H.S., 1954-55; tchr. Stanfield (Oreg.) H.S., Oreg., 1955-57, Riverside (Oreg.) H.S., 1960; also bd. mem. Oreg.; secondary tchr. Myrtle Creek (Oreg.) H.S., 1960-67; caseworker Grant County Ctrl. Sch. Dist., John Day, Oreg., 1967-68; tchr. Prairie City (Oreg.) H.S., 1968-69; secondary tchr. Grant Union H.S., John Day, Oreg., 1969-75, Mt. Vernon (Oreg.) H.S., 1975-86, North Marion H.S., Aurora, Oreg., 1992-94; water fitness instr. Salem (Oreg.) Family YMCA, 1990—. Pres. PTA, Myrtle Creek, Oreg., 1966-67; Camp Fire guardian, Roseburg-John Day, Oreg., 1966-79; den mother Boy Scouts Am.; tchr. Meth. Ch. Sch. Camp, Oreg. Mem. NEA, AAUW (del. UN seminar 1982, pres. Oreg. State 1983-85). Republican. Methodist. Avocations: music, water fitness, bowling, line dancing. Home: 29650 SW Courtside Dr # 22 Wilsonville OR 97070-7482

TALVI, SILJA JOANNA ALLER, freelance journalist, writer; b. Helsinki, Finland, Apr. 25, 1970; d. Ilkka Ilari Talvi and Judith F. Aller; m. Brian Kei Tanaka, Mar. 26, 1995. BA in Ethnic Studies with honors, Mills Coll., 1991; MA in Women Studies, San Francisco State U., 1993. Cert. to work with battered women, HIV pre and post-test counselor. Freelance writer San Francisco and Seattle, 1992—; program coord. The Women's Bldg., San Francisco, 1993-94; non-profit cons. San Francisco, 1994-97; outreach coord., rschr. Health Initiatives for Women, San Francisco, 1995-96. Contbr. articles to mags. and profl. jours. Recipient Palladium award Mills Coll., 1990, Scholarship award Nat. Coun. Jewish Studies, 1991-92, Grad. award Marjorie Hefter Stern, 1992, Davis-Putter award for scholarly excellence and grassroots activism, 1992. Mem. Nat. Writers Union, Cassell Network Writers. Avocations: bicycling, snowboarding, poetry.

TAMEZ, LORRAINE DIANE, writer, nurse; b. Pueblo, Colo., Nov. 26, 1950; d. Daniel and Mary Ann (Abeyta) Tamez; children: David, Christopher, Lauren. Cert. in nursing, Trinidad State Jr. Coll., Colo., student. poetry editor Purgatoire Mag. Author: Prairie Woman, 1989; contbr. poetry (as L.D. Thames) various mags. With U.S. Army, 1969-71. Mem. PEN, Poets and Writers. Democrat. Roman Catholic. Avocations: photography, photojournalism, writing poetry. Home and Office: PO Box 181 Trinidad CO 81082-0181

TAMKIN, CURTIS SLOANE, real estate development company executive; b. Boston, Sept. 21, 1936; s. Hayward and Etta (Goldfarb) T.; m. Priscilla Martin, Oct. 18, 1975; 1 child, Curtis Sloane. BA in Econs., Stanford U., 1958. V.p., treas., dir. Hayward Tamkin & Co., Inc., mortgage bankers, L.A., 1963-70; mng. ptnr. Property Devel. Co., L.A., 1970-82; pres. The Tamkin Co., 1982—. Mem. bd. govs. Music Ctr. L.A., 1974-98; pres. L.A. Master Chorale Assn., 1974-78; mem. vis. com. Stanford U. Librs., 1982-86; bd. dirs. L.A. Philharm. Assn., 1985—. Lt. (j.g.) USNR, 1960-63. Mem. Founders League L.A. Music Ctr. (pres. 1988-98, chmn. emeritus 1998), L.a. Jr. C. of c.. (dir. 1968-69), Pacific Coun. Internat. Policy, Burlingame Country. Home: 1230 Stone Canyon Rd Los Angeles CA 90077-2920 Office: 9460 Wilshire Blvd Beverly Hills CA 90212-2732

TAMMANY, ALBERT SQUIRE, III, trust and bank executive; b. Paget, Bermuda, Aug. 21, 1946; s. Albert Squire Jr. and Marion Genevieve (Galloway) T.; m. Teresa Reznor, Sept. 8, 1973. BA, Stanford U., 1968; MBA, U. Pa., 1973. Budget and planning officer Tuskegee Univ., Ala., 1973-74; budget analyst contrs. dept. Chase Manhattan Bank, N.Y.C., 1974-75; v.p., div. contr. Wells Fargo Bank, San Francisco, 1975-78, v.p., retail group contr., 1978-79; v.p., contr. Imperial Bank, L.A., 1979-81, sr. v.p. fin., 1981-83; exec. v.p., First Network Savs. Bank, L.A., 1983-87, chief oper. officer, 1987-89, North Am. Trust Co., San Diego, 1990-93, Trustguard, San Diego, 1993-93; sr. trust officer, Exchange Bank, Santa Rosa, Calif., 1993—. cons. Inst. for Svcs. to Edn., Inc., 1973-74. Woodrow Wilson fellow U. Pa. Served with USMC, 1968-71. Wharton Pub. Policy fellow, 1972. Mem. Am. Bankers Assn. (trust ops. com.), Wharton Club, Stanford Club.

TAMURA, CARY KAORU, fundraiser, consultant; b. Honolulu, Jan. 9, 1944; s. Akira and Harue T.; m. Denise Jeanne Mitts, Oct. 17, 1987; children: Jennifer Joy, Matthew D. Student, U. Hawaii, 1961-63; BA in Philosophy, Nyack Coll., 1966; MA in Theology, Fuller Sem., 1986. Cert. fund-raising exec. Dir. svc. tng. ops. Fin. Adv. Clinic of Hawaii, Honolulu, 1972-76; dir. planned giving The Salvation Army, Honolulu, 1976-78; planned giving cons. InterVarsity Christian Fellowship, Portland, Oreg., 1978-80; account exec. Am. Income Life, Portland, Oreg., 1980-81; dir. planned giving The Salvation Army, Portland, Oreg., 1981-84, L.A., 1984-85; dir. devel., planned giving U. So. Calif., 1985-90; dir. gift planning UniHealth America, Burbank, Calif., 1990-94; charitable gift planning cons. Brea, Calif., 1995—; bd. dirs. Nat. Com. on Planned Giving, Indpls., 1991-93, sec. exec. com., 1993; mem. adv. com., adj. faculty UCLA Extension; lectr. in field. Bd. dirs. Japanese Evang. Missionary Soc., 1990-95, v.p., 1993, bd. deacons Evang. Free Ch., 1992-95. With U.S. Army, 1969-72. Mem. Planned Giving Round Table So. Calif. (pres. 1989-91, Pres.'s award 1992), Nat. Soc. Fund Raising Execs., (bd. dirs. Greater L.A. chpt. 1990-97, v.p. 1993, 95, chmn. Fund Raising Day 1994, treas. 1996-97, Profl. Fund Raiser of Yr. award 1995), So. Calif. Assn. Hosp. Developers. Republican. Avocations: photography, golf, travel. Home and Office: 1413 Robert Ct Brea CA 92821-2165

TAMURA, DANIEL MASANORI, tax specialist; b. Honolulu, June 2, 1923; s. Jitsudo and Kaneyo (Ishida) T.; m. Toshiko Tamura; children: Sharon Sato, Gail Nishihara, Irwin, Marian Genovia. Student, LaSalle Ext. U. Office and pers. supt. Libby, McNeill & Libby, Honolulu, 1941-70; employment supr. Dole, Honolulu, 1970-71; office mgr., treas. Cen. Pacific Boiler, Honolulu, 1971-84; tax preparer, office supr. H & R Block, Honolulu, 1968-72, 84—. Pres., treas. Seicho No Ie, 1957—. Sgt. maj. U.S. Army, 1944-47. Mem. Disabled Am. Vets. (comdr. 1950—), Lions Club (lion tamer 1950-57). Avocations: golf, gardening. Home: 1704 Ala Amoamo St Honolulu HI 96819-1713 Office: H & R Block 98-019 Kam Hwy Aiea HI 96701-4909

TAMURA, KEITH AICHI, architect, consultant; b. Waimea, Hawaii, Jan. 6, 1951; s. Yoichi and Hilda Aiko (Shimomura) T. BS, U. Calif., Berkeley, 1972; BArch, U. Hawaii, 1982. Draftsman, designer Wimberly Whisenand Allison Tong and Goo, Honolulu, 1984-86; office mgr., architect Riecke, Sunnland, Kono Architects Ltd., Honolulu, 1986-91; architect AM Ptnrs., Honolulu, 1991-92; v.p. John Bowen Designer, Inc., Honolulu, 1992-98; sr. architect Leo A. Daly, Honolulu, 1998—. Bd. dirs. Honolulu Japanese Jr. C. of C., 1982-85. Named Chmn. of Yr., Honolulu Japanese Jaycees, 1978. Mem. AIA, U. Hawaii Archtl. Sch. Alumni Assn., (chmn. publs. com. 1991-93, bd. dirs. 1992-94). Office: Leo A Daly Ste 1000 1357 Kapiolani Blvd Honolulu HI 96814

TAN, COLLEEN WOO, communications educator; b. San Francisco, May 6, 1923; d. Mr. and Mrs. S.H. Nq Quinn; m. Lawrence K.J. Tan; children: Lawrence L., Lance C. BA in English/Am. Lit., Ind. U., 1950, MA in English, 1952; MA in Speech Arts, Whittier Coll., 1972; postgrad., U. Calif. Berkeley, 1952-53. Cert. secondary edn. tchr., K-12, community coll., Calif. Tchng. aide English U. Calif., Berkeley, 1952-53; tchr. English and Social Studies Whittier (Calif.) High Sch., 1957-60; prof. speech comms. Mt. San Antonio Coll., Walnut, Calif., 1960-94; dir. forensics, 1969-80; sen. acad. senate Mt. San Antonio Coll., Walnut, Calif., 1982-90, faculty rep., 1990—; mem. numerous collegiate coms., campus advisor to Chinese Club and Asian Students Assn. Recipient Woman of Achievement Edn. award San Gabriel Valley, Calif. YWCA, 1995; named Outstanding Prof. Emeritus, Mt. San Antonio Coll. Found., 1994. Mem. AAUW (pres. Whittier Br. 1982, cultural interests chair Calif. state divsn. 1985-87, Fellowship award 1973-74, Las Distinguidas award 1992), Calif. Asian-Am. Faculty Assn., Delta Kappa Gamma, Phi Beta Kappa (Outstanding Educator of Am. award 1972). Roman Catholic. Avocations: creative writing, reading fiction, attending theater, music, dance. Home: 13724 Sunrise Dr Whittier CA 90602-2547 Office: Mt San Antonio 1100 N Grand Ave Walnut CA 91789-1341

TAN, F. DONG, electronic engineer; b. Nanchang, China, Oct. 15, 1955; came to U.S., 1989; s. Yifei Tan and Yunzhang Fang; m. Fang Liu, 1984; 1 child, Taige Tan. BES, Jiangxi Poly. U., Nanchang, 1979; PhD, Calif. Inst. Tech., 1993. Profl. engr., Calif. Lectr. Jiangxi Poly. U., 1980-85; vis. asst. prof. U. Waterloo, Ont., Can., 1986-88; lab. mgr. Calif. Inst. Tech., Pasadena, 1989-93; sr. technologist, tech. mgr. avionics electronics dept. TRW Space and Electronics Group, Redondo Beach, Calif., 1995—. Contbr. articles to profl. pubs. including IEEE jours. Recipient award for Excellence in Tchg., Jiangxi Poly., 1980, TEC award Mix Found., 1995, award as nationally recognized technologist TRW, 1995, 2 Patent awards TRW, 1996. Mem. Power Electronics Soc. of IEEE (sr., chmn. L.A. coun. chpt., chmn. various programs and confs., assoc. editor jour.). Achievements include 1 patent in field, patents pending; being first to employ bifurcation theory to investigate nonlinear instability problem of switching converters, first to measure analog current loopgain in switching converters; design of 1st series of high-density, high-efficiency high-voltage-bus DC/DC converters for space and military applications. Office: TRW R9 2873 One Space Park Redondo Beach CA 90278

TAN, MARIANO BUENDIA, physician; b. Quezon City, Philippines, Sept. 25, 1930; came to U.S., 1958; m. Bella Lim, July 14, 1961; children: Maribelle, Marvin, Mariano Jr., Michael. MD, U. Santo Thomas, Manila, Philippines, 1957. Resident pediat. Cook County Hosp., Chgo., 1958-61, chief resident, 1962; asst. clin. prof. U. Maniboba, Winnipeg, 1970-76; commd. ensign USN, 1977, advanced through grades comdr., 1985; pediat. officer USN, Long Beach, Calif., 1977-85; pediatrician Kaiser Permanente, Bellflower, Calif., 1985-96. Fellow Am. Acad. Pediat. Home: 9732 Avenida Monterey Cypress CA 90630-3446

TAN, WILLIAM LEW, lawyer; b. West Hollywood, Calif., July 25, 1949; s. James Tan Lew and Choon Guey Louie; m. Shelly Mieko Ushio. BA, U. Pa., 1971; JD, U. Calif. Hastings Coll. Law, San Francisco, 1974. Bar: Calif. 1975, U.S. Dist. Ct. (cen. dist.) Calif. 1975, U.S. Ct. Appeals (9th cir.) 1975, U.S. Supreme Ct. 1979. Assoc. Hiram W. Kwan, Los Angeles, 1974-79; ptnr. Mock & Tan, Los Angeles, 1979-80; sole practice Los Angeles, 1980-81; ptnr. Tan & Sakiyama, L.A., 1981-86, 88—, Tan & Sakiyama, P.C., L.A., 1986-88; bd. dirs. Am. Bus. Network, L.A.; pres., bd. dirs. Asian Rsch. Cons., L.A., 1983-85; mem. adv. bd. Cathay Bank, 1990-91; bd. dirs. Asian Pacific Am. Legal Ctr. Co-founder Asian Pacific Am. Roundtable, L.A., 1981; chmn. bd. dirs. Leadership Edn. for Asian-Pacifics, L.A., 1984-87; alt. del. Dem. Nat. Conv., San Francisco, 1984; mem. Calif. State Bd. Pharmacy, Sacramento, 1984-92, v.p., 1988-91, pres., 1991-92; mem. L.A. City and County Crime Crisis Task Force, 1981, L.A. Asian Pacific Heritage Week Com., 1980-85, Asian Pacific Women's Network, L.A., 1981, L.A. City Atty.'s Blue Ribbon Com. of Advisors, 1981, cmty. adv. bd. to Mayor of L.A., 1984, allocations vol. liaison team health and therapy divsn. United Way, L.A., 1986, mem. nominating com. bd. dirs. 1994—; bd. dirs. Chinatown Svc. Ctr., L.A., 1983; conf. advisor U.S.-Asia, L.A., 1981-83; mem. L.A. city atty. Housing Adv. Com.; mem. Pacific Bell Consumer Product Adv. Panel, 1986-90; vice chair cmty. adv. bd. Sta. KCET-TV, PBA, 1993-94; mem. adv. commn. State of Calif. Com. on State Procurement

Practices, 1989-90; mem. L.A. City Attys. Citizens' Task Force on Pvt. Club Discrimination, 1989-90; mem. Calif. Med. Summit, 1993; mem. Mayor's Commn. Children, Youth and Families, 1993-96; mem. pub. access subcom. Mayor's Spl. adv. Com. on Tech. Implementation, 1994-96. Named one of Outstanding Young Men of Am., 1979. Mem. Calif. State Bar Assn. (vice chmn. com. ethnic minority rels. 1983-85, chmn. pub. affairs com. 1981-82, mem. others), L.A. County Bar Assn. (trustee 1984-86, vice chair human rights com. 1980-82, mem. numerous coms.), So. Calif. Chinese Lawyers Assn. (pres. 1980-81, chmn. 1987-88, mem. various coms.), Minority Bar Assn. (chmn. 1981-82, sec. 1980-81, chmn. adv. bd. 1982-83), Asian Pacific Bar of Calif., Nat. Asian Pacific Am. Bar, Japanese Am. Bar Assn., Bench and Bar Media Coun., Consumer Attys. of Calif., Soc. Intercultural Edn. (conf. coord., advisor panelist tng. and rsch. com. 1983). Avocations: gourmet cooking, bicycling, swimming, tennis, water color painting. Office: Ste 390 201 S Figueroa St Los Angeles CA 90012

TAN, ZHIQUN, biomedical scientist; b. Lichuan, China, July 23, 1964; came to U.S., 1996; s. Yuankun and Shiming (Sun) T.; m. Tu Wenli, Mar. 27, 1993. MD, Tongji Med. U., Wuhan, China, 1985; PhD, Wuhan U., 1993. Lectr. Wuhan U., China, 1989-93, assoc. prof., 1993-96; postdoctoral fellow U. So. Calif. Med. Sch., L.A., 1997—; adj. scientist Wuhan Inst. Hydrobiology, 1990-96. Author: Eutrophication of Lakes in China, 1990. Fellow N.Y. Acad. Scis.; mem. AAAS, Soc. Neurosci. Am., Soc. Environ. Toxicology and Chemistry U.S.A. Achievements include research on molecular events in neurodegeneration, the surface/interface interations in water and their ecological significance, removal of toxic contaminants (heavy metals, phenols) in waters using decaying leaves of plants, and gene expression in neuro-disorders and aging.

TANAKA, JANICE, artist, educator; b. L.A., Sept. 9, 1940; d. Koto Jack and Lily Yuviko (Yamate) T.; children: Rebecca Eiko Gallardo, David Eitaro Gallardo. Studied with B. Stone and R. Cameron, Stone-Cameron Ballet, 1954-56; studied with R. Lunnon and D. Tempest, Allegro Am. Ballet, 1956-57; student, Conserv. de Musica, Mex., 1962-64; BFA, Sch. of Art Inst. of Chgo., 1978, MFA, 1980. Studio/field prodr. UCLA, 1981-82; lectr. Columbia Coll., Chgo., 1982-83; assoc. prof. U. Colo., Boulder, 1985-89; vis. assoc. prof. visual comm. design UCLA, 1990—; vis. artist Northwestern U., Evanston, Ill., 1983, U. Calif., San Diego, 1982, 85, U. Ill., Chgo., 1983, U. Wis., Madison, 1983, U. Md., Balt., 1984, U. Mich., Mt. Pleasant, 1984, U. Mo., Kansas City, 1984, U. Wis., Stevens Point, 1985, UCLA, 1988, U. Ariz., Tucson, 1989, U. Hawaii, Monoa, 1990, U. Minn., Mpls., 1991, Calif. Inst. Arts, Valencia, 1991, U. Calif., Riverside, 1991, Otis Parsons Sch. Design, L.A., 1992, U. Calif., Irvine, 1992, U. So. Calif., L.A., 1992, Sch. Art Inst. Chgo., 1993. Freelance prodr./dir.; one-woman shows include Mus. Modern Art, N.Y.C., 1991, 93, Wight Art Gallery, L.A., 1992, Biennale, Whitney Mus. Am. Art, N.Y.C., 1991, 93; exhibited in group shows at L.A. Mcpl. Art Theater, 1994, Vancouver Art Gallery, B.C., Can., 1994, Walter Phillips Gallery, Banff, Alta., Can., 1994, Nat. Mus. Contemporary Art, Korea; represented in permanent collections at Carnegie Mus. Art, Pitts., Japanese Am. Nat. Mus., L.A., Long Beach (Calif.) Mus. Art. Bd. dirs. Ctr. New TV, 1983-85, Film Forum, 1993. NEA Western Regional Media Arts fellow, 1994; Nat. Endowment Art media grantee, 1993; recipient Best Exptl. award Atlanta Film/Video Festival, 1992, James D. Phelan award, 1992, Bronze Appleaward Nat. Edn. Film & Video Festival, 1993, Bronze award WorldFest Houston Internat. Film Festival, 1993, Jorors award Atlanta Film/Video Festival, 1993, Gold Jurors Choice award Charlotte Film and Video Festival, 1993, Bronze Plaque award Film Coun. Greater Columbus, 1993. Office: CAL ARTS 24700 Mcbean Pkwy Valencia CA 91355-2340

TANAKA, JEANNIE E., lawyer; b. L.A., Jan. 21, 1942; d. Togo William and Jean M. Tanaka. BA, Internat. Christian U., Tokyo, 1966; MSW, UCLA, 1968; JD, Washington Coll., 1984. Bar: Calif. 1984, U.S. Dist. Ct. (cen., no. dists.) Calif. 1985, U.S. Ct. Appeals (9th cir.) 1985, D.C. 1987. Instr. Aoyama Gakuin, Meiji Gakuin, Sophia U., Tokyo, 1968-75; with program devel. Encyclopedia Britannica Inst., Tokyo, 1976-78; instr. Honda, Mitsubishi, Ricoh Corps., Tokyo, 1975-80; with editorial dept. Simul Internat., Tokyo; assoc. Seki and Jarvis, L.A., 1984-86, Jones, Day, Reavis & Pogue, L.A., 1986-87, Fulbright, Jaworsky and Reavis, McGrath, L.A., 1987-89; asst. counsel Unocal, L.A., 1989-91; pvt. practice L.A., 1991—; counsel Calif. Dept. Corps., L.A., 1993—. Active Japan-Am. Soc., L.A., 1984-95, Japanese-Am. Citizens League, L.A., 1981, 92—, Japanese Am. Cultural and Cmty. Ctr., 1986-89; vol. Asian Pacific Am. Legal Ctr. So. Calif., 1985-86. Mem. Japanese-Am. Bar Assn., Mensa. Democrat. Mem. Foursquare Meth. Ch. Avocations: Japanese language, Chinese language, U.S.-Far East relations, martial arts.

TANAKA, RICHARD KOICHI, JR., architect, planner; b. San Jose, Calif., Oct. 16, 1931; s. Richard Inoru and Mae Yoshiko (Koga) T.; m. Barbara Hisako Kumagai, Oct. 7, 1961; children: Craig, Todd, Sandra, Trent. BArch, U. Mich., 1954; M in Urban Planning, Calif. State U., San Jose, 1978. Exec. v.p. Steinberg Group, San Jose, L.A., 1954—; chair, bd. dirs. Happi House Restaurants, Inc., 1972—. Author: American on Trial, 1988. Dir. Human Rels. Com., San Jose, 1969-73; dir., pres. Bicentennial Com., San Jose, 1974-77; bd. dirs. Santa Clara County Sch. Bd. Assn., 1980—; pres. Internment of Local Japanese Ams., San Jose, 1984—; past pres., trustee East Side H.S. Dist., San Jose, 1971-92, Japanese Am. Citizens League, San Jose; mem. bd. govs. Boy Scouts Am., San Jose, 1978—, NCCJ, San Jose, 1976—; past pres. Tapestry and Talent, 1976-80; trustee San Jose/ Evergreen C.C., 1992—, pres., 1993-94, 97-98; bd. dirs., pres. Calif. C.C. Trustees, 1997-98. Mem. AIA, Am. Planning Inst., Constrn. Specification Inst., Rotary. Avocations: golf, painting. Home: 14811 Whipple Ct San Jose CA 95127-2570 Office: 60 Pierce Ave San Jose CA 95110-2819

TANAKA, STANLEY KATSUKI, optometrist, consultant; b. Honolulu, Sept. 19, 1932; s. Tomikichi and Hatsue T.; m. Esther K. Kokubun, Oct. 31, 1959; children: Glen A., Fay M. Student U. Hawaii, 1950-52; BS, U. Okla., 1952; OD magna cum laude (Jackson award), Ill. Coll. Optometry, 1956. Enlisted U.S. Army, 1957, advanced through grades to col. Res., 1981; optometrist Hawaii Permanente Med. Group, Honolulu, 1968—; cons. opthalmic firms. Named Hawaii Optometrist of Yr., 1984. Mem. Am. Optometric Assn., Hawaii Optometric Assn., Armed Forces Optometric Soc., Contact Lens Soc., Am. Optometric Found., Optometric Extension Program, Beta Sigma Kappa. Democrat. Club: Toastmasters. Home: 2645 Oahu Ave Honolulu HI 96822-1722 Office: 1831 S King St Honolulu HI 96826-2137

TANAKA, TOGO W(ILLIAM), retired real estate and financial executive; b. Portland, Oreg., Jan. 7, 1916; s. Masaharu and Katsu (Iwatate) T.; m. Jean Miho Wada, Nov. 14, 1940; children: Jeannie, Christine, Wesley. AB cum laude, UCLA, 1936. Editor Calif. Daily News, 1935-36, L.A. Japanese Daily News, 1936-42; documentary historian War Relocation Authority, Manzanar, Calif., 1942; staff mem. Am. Friends Service Com., Chgo., 1943-45; editor to head publs. div. Am. Tech. Soc., 1945-52; pub. Chgo. Pub. Corp., 1952-56; pub. School-Indsl. Press, Inc., L.A., 1956-60; chmn. Gramercy Enterprises, L.A.; dir. T.W. Tanaka Co., Inc.; city commr. Community Redevel. Agy., L.A., 1973-74; dir. L.A. Wholesale Produce Market Devel. Corp., 1979-89, Fed. Res. Bank, San Francisco, 1979-89; mem. adv. bd. Calif. First Bank, L.A., 1976-78, bd. dirs. Meth. Hosp., So. Calif., 1978-93. Author: (with Frank K. Levin) English Composition and Rhetoric, 1948; (with Dr. Jean Bordeaux) How to Talk More Effectively, 1948; (with Alma Meland) Easy Pathways in English, 1949. Mem. citizens mgmt. rev. com. L.A. Unified Sch. Dist., 1976-77; adv. coun. to assessor L.A. County, 1981-84; bd. dirs. Goodwill Industries of So. Calif.; trustee Wilshire United Meth. Ch., 1976-78, Calif. Acad. Decathlon, 1978-81; adv. bd. Visitors and Conv. Bur., 1984-88, Am. Heart Assn., 1984-88, New Bus. Achievement, Inc., YMCA Met. L.A., 1977-91, Boy Scouts Am. Coun., 1980-86; mem. adv. council Calif. World Trade Commn., 1986-87; active Nat. Strategy Info. Ctr. N.Y., Nat. Wellness Community, Western Justice Ctr. Found.; trustee Whittier Coll.; chmn. L.A. chpt. Nat. Safety Coun.; [illegible] award Internat. Council Indsl. Editors, 1955, UNESCO Literacy award, 1974, L.A. Archbishop's Ecumenical award, 1986, Frances Larkin award ARC, 1993, Spirit of Wellness award, 1995. Mem. [illegible] Japan-Am. Soc. So. Calif. (coun. [illegible]), [illegible] Rotary (dir., pres. L.A.

club 1983-84, Svc. award 1995), Phi Beta Kappa, Pi Sigma Alpha, Pi Gamma Mu. Home: 949 Malcolm Ave Los Angeles CA 90024-3113 Office: 626 Wilshire Blvd Los Angeles CA 90017-3209

TANCREDO, THOMAS G., congressman; b. North Denver, Colo., Dec. 20, 1945; m. Jackie Tancredo; 2 children. BA, U. Colo., 1968. Mem. Colo. Ho. Reps., 1977-81; regional rep. U.S. Dept. Edn., 1981-93; mem. 106th Congress from 6th Colo. dist., 1999—; mem. edn. and workforce, internat. rels., and resources coms. Office: 1123 Longworth House Office Bldg Washington DC 20515 also: 5601 S Broadway Ste 370 Littleton CO 80120*

TANG, JUMING, food engineering educator; b. Changsha, Hunan, China, May 8, 1959; arrived in Can., 1985; s. Shenxuo Tang and Dajen Tan; m. Yanyin Zeng, June 15, 1984; children, Zhao, Mitchell. BS, Ctrl.-S. U. Tech., Shangsha, China, 1981; MS, U. Guelph, Ont., Can., 1987; PhD, U. Saskatoon, Can., 1991. Fellow U. Saskkatoon, 1991; asst. prof. Acadia U., Wolfville, N.S., Can., 1991-94, S.D. State U., Brookings, 1994-95, Wash. State U., Pullman, 1995-97; cons. Scotian Gold Coop. Ltd., Kentiville, N.S., 1993-94, Indsl. Rsch. Asst. Program of Can., Halifax, N.S., 1993-94. Contbr. articles to Jour. Food Sci., Food Engring., Drying Tech. Mem. Am. Soc. Agrl. Engrs., Assn. Profl. Engrs. N.S., Inst. Food Technologists (George F. Steward Internat. Rsch. Paper Competition award 1993-94), Internat. Microwave Power Inst. Achievements include devel. of gen. saturation criteria for high moisture biol. mass during compression, gen. predictive equation for gelling temperature of gellan solution as function of composition, procedure to accurately measure specific heat capacity of seeds using differential scanning calorimetry; research in microwave and radio frequency heating in food processing, drying technology and food gel rheology. Home: 880 SE Edge Knoll Dr Pullman WA 99163-2408 Office: Wash State Univ Dept Biol Systems Engring Pullman WA 99164-6120

TANG, PAUL CHI LUNG, philosophy educator; b. Vancouver, B.C., Can., Jan. 23, 1944; came to U.S., 1971; s. Pei-Sung and Violet (Wong) T. *Dr. Paul Tang's father, Dr. Pei-Sung Tang, is one of China's most distinguished scientists. Educated at the University of Minnesota, Johns Hopkins University and Harvard University, Pei-Sung Tang is now Director Emeritus of the Institute of Botany, Academia Sinica, Beijing, China and Professor of General Physiology at Beijing University. Pei-Sung Tang is son of Tang Hua-lung, one of the small group of men associated with Sun Yat-Sen, who led the overthrow of the Manchus and the establishment of the Chinese Republic. Tang Hua-lung became the Minister of Education for China before he was assassinated in 1918.* BSc with high distinction, U. B.C., 1966; MA in Edn., Simon Fraser U., Vancouver, 1971; MA, Washington U., St. Louis, 1975, PhD, 1982; cert. in ethics, Kennedy Inst. Ethics, 1983; diploma in piano, U. Toronto, 1962. Teaching asst. philosophy of edn. Simon Fraser U., 1969-71; instr. philosophy St. Louis C.C. at Meramec, Kirkwood, Mo., 1975-82; instr., lectr. philosophy Washington U., 1972-76; adj. asst. prof. Harris-Stowe State Coll., St. Louis, 1980-82; asst. prof. philosophy Grinnell (Iowa) Coll., 1982-85; asst. prof. to assoc. prof. to prof. dept. philosophy Calif. State U., Long Beach, 1985—, chmn. dept. philosophy, 1988-94; vis. lectr. philosophy So. Ill. U., Edwardsville, 1978-79. *Dr. Paul Tang has won the California State University system-wide Trustee's Outstanding Professor Award; the California State University, Long Beach Outstanding Professor Award; the California State University, Long Beach Distinguished Faculty Teaching Award; the College of Liberal Arts Most Valuable Professor Award; the Associated Students Faculty Advisor of the Year Award (four times); and the Student Philosophy Association Outstanding Graduate Professor Award. He was also awarded a Certificate of Recognition for continued commitment to education from the California State Senate. He has also won several University research grants.* Contbr. numerous articles and revs. to profl. publs.; editor Philosophy of Sci. Assn. Newsletter, 1985-90; asst. editor Philosophy of Sci. acad. jour., 1972-75. Senator Internat. Parliament for Safety and Peace, Palermo, Italy. Decorated knight Templar Order of Jerusalem, knight Order Holy Cross of Jerusalem, knight comdr. Lofsenic Ursinius Orer, chevalier Grand Crois de Milice du St. Sepulcre; recipient cert. of merit Student Philosophy Assn., 1988-90, 93-94, spl. award, 1992; named faculty advisor of yr. Assoc. Students, 1987, 90, 91, 95, Highland Lord of Camster, Scotland, 1995; Paul Tang prize in philosophy named in his honor, 1996—; fellow Washington U., 1971, summer rsch. fellow Calif. State U., 1988, NEH fellow Harvard U., 1988, NEH Summer Seminar fellow, 1968; internat. scholar Phi Beta Delta, interdisciplinary scholar Phi Kappa Phi, 1993; grantee vis. philosophers program Coun. for Philos. Studies, 1987, 91, 92; Disting. Vis. Scholars and Artists Fund, Calif. State U., 1988, 89, rsch. grantee, summer 1996. Fellow World Lit. Acad.; mem. Am. Philos. Assn. (Excellence in Tchg. award 1995, 97), Philosophy of Sci. Assn., History of Sci. Soc., Kennedy Inst. Ethics, Hastings Ctr., Iowa Philos. Soc. (pres. 1985-86), Internat. Platform Assn., Brit. Soc. Philosophy of Sci., Soc. Philosophy and Psychology, Maison Internat. des Intellectuels de l'Acad. Francaise, Internat. Order Merit (Eng.), Golden Key (hon., Internat. Man of Yr. 1995-96), Order Internat. Fellowship (Eng.), numerous others. Avocations: hiking, tennis, chess, music, travel. Home: 5050 E Garford St Apt 228 Long Beach CA 90815-2859 Office: Calif State U Dept Philosophy 1250 N Bellflower Blvd Long Beach CA 90840-0006

TANG, TOM, banking executive; b. Tiensuei, Peoples Republic of China, Nov. 24, 1946; came to the U.S., 1974; s. Hsun Hui and Hui Hsing (Fan) T.; m. Gloria Tang, Aug. 13, 1974; children: Jonathan, Kevin. BA, Nat. Chung Hsing U., Taipei, Taiwan, 1974; MBA, Okla. State U., 1977; postgrad., UCLA Ext., 1978-79, Inst. Fin. Edn., L.A., 1979-82. Loan officer Topa T&L, Lakewood, Calif., 1977-78; acct. Gibraltar Savs., Beverly Hills, Calif., 1978-80; asst. v.p., br. mgr. 1st Pub. Savs. Bank, L.A., 1980-84; v.p. Gateway Savs. Bank, L.A., 1984-85; v.p., regional mgr. East-West Fed. Bank, San Marino, Calif., 1985-90; sr. v.p. Far-East Nat. Bank, L.A., 1990—. Fellow Optimists (Outstanding Svc. award 1984); mem. Chinese Coll. Alumni Basketball Assn. So. Calif. (chairperson 1990-91), Nat. Chung-Hsing U. Alumni Assn. So. Calif. (bd. dirs. 1987-94, pres. 1989-90, v.p. 1988-89, 90-91), Joint Chinese Coll. Alumni Assn. So. Calif. (bd. dirs. 1988-93), Monterey Park C. of C. (bd. dirs. 1983-84, chairperson Chinese-Am. com. 1984). Avocations: cooking, gourmet food, sports, classical music. Home: PO Box 80558 San Marino CA 91118-8558 Office: Far East Nat Bank 105 E Valley Blvd Alhambra CA 91801-5131

TANIGUCHI, TOKUSO, surgeon; b. Eleele, Kauai, Hawaii, June 26, 1915; s. Tokuichi and Sana (Omaye) T.; BA, U. Hawaii, 1941; MD, Tulane U., 1946; 1 son, Jan Tokuichi. Intern Knoxville (Tenn.) Gen. Hosp., 1946-47; resident in surgery St. Joseph Hosp., also Marquette Med. Sch., Milw., 1947-52; practice medicine, specializing in surgery, Hilo, Hawaii, 1955—; chief surgery Hilo Hosp.; teaching fellow Marquette Med. Sch., 1947-49; v.p., dir. Hawaii Hardware Co., Ltd. Capt. M.C., AUS, 1952-55. Diplomate Am. Bd. Surgery. Fellow Internat., Am. colls. surgeons; mem. Am., Hawaii med. assns., Hawaii County Med. Soc., Pan-Pacific Surg. Assn., Phi Kappa Phi. Contbr. articles in field to profl. jours. Patentee automated catheter. Home: 277 Kaiulani St Hilo HI 96720-2530

TANIMOTO, GEORGE, agricultural executive, farmer; b. Gridley, Calif., Feb. 10, 1926; s. Hikoichi and Rewa Tanimoto; m. Hanami Yamasaki, Dec. 19, 1946; 1 child, Patricia. Grad., Coyne Electric Sch., Chgo., 1950. Elec. technician, 1951, owner peach and prune orchards, 1952; founder Kiwifruit Nursery, Calif., 1965; pres. Tanimoto Bros., Gridley, Calif., 1977—, Tanimoto Enterprises, Inc., Gridley, 1979—; bd. dirs. Blue Anchor, Inc., Sacramento; chmn. Calif. Fruit Exchange, Inc.; U.S. rep. Internat. Kiwifruit Orgn., Lake Tahoe, Calif., 1985, Rome, 1986, Biarritz, France, 1987, Hong Kong, 1988, chmn. Orgn.,Rome, 1986; dir. Butte County Agrl. Adv. Commn., Oroville, Calif.; founder, chmn. Calif. Kiwifruit Commn., 1980-84, 1988-89, vice chmn. 1985-87. Pres. South Shore Assn., Bucks Lake, Calif., 1989. Mem. Kiwifruit Growers Calif. (founder, bd. dirs., pres. 1973-80), Kiwifruit Mktg. Assn. Calif. (founder, chmn. 1989-97), Gridley Sportsman Club (founder, pres. 1975-78). Republican. Buddhist. Avocations: fishing, boating, photography. Pioneered the first comml. planting and devel. of cultural practice for kiwifruit in Calif. Home: 948 River Ave Gridley CA 95948-9774

TANNER, DEE BOSHARD, retired lawyer; b. Provo, Utah, Jan. 16, 1913; s. Myron Clark and Marie (Boshard) T.; m. Jane Barwick, Dec. 26, 1936 (div. Aug. [illegible]); children: Barry, Diane McDowell; m. [illegible] 6, 1981. BA, U. Utah, 1935; LLB, Pacific Coast U., 1940; postgrad., Harvard U., 1936, Loyola U., L.A., 1937. Bar: Calif. 1943, U.S. Dist. Ct. (so. dist.) Calif. 1944, U.S. Ct. Appeals (9th cir.) 1947, ICC 1964, U.S. Dist. Ct. (ea. dist.) Calif. 1969, U.S. Supreme Ct. 1971. Assoc. Spray, Davis & Gould, L.A., 1943-44; pvt. practice L.A., 1944; assoc. Tanner and Sievers, L.A., 1944-47, Tanner and Thornton, L.A., 1947-54, Tanner, Hanson, Meyers, L.A., 1954-64; ptnr. Tanner and Van Dyke, L.A., 1964-65, Gallagher and Tanner, L.A., 1965-70; pvt. practice Pasadena, Calif., 1970-95; retired, 1995. Mem. L.A. Bar Assn., World Affairs Assn., Harvard Law Sch. Assn., Lawyers' Club L.A. Home and Office: 1720 Lombardy Rd Pasadena CA 91106-4127

TANNER, JOHN DOUGLAS, JR., history educator, writer; b. Quantico, Va., Oct. 2, 1943; s. John Douglas and Dorothy Lucille (Walker) T.; m. Jo Ann Boyd, Jan. 1964 (div. Aug. 1966); 1 child, Lorena Desiree; m. Laurel Jean Selfridge, Dec. 19, 1967 (div. Oct. 1987); children: John DouglasIII, Stephen Douglas, Elizabeth Jane; m. Karen H. Olson, Apr. 16, 1988. BA, Pomona Coll., 1966; MA, Claremont Grad. U., 1968; postgrad., U. Calif., Riverside, 1976, 84-86, U. Calif., San Diego, 1984-87, U. Pacific, 1993. Cert. tchr., Calif. Asst. swimming, water polo coach Pomona Coll., 1966-69; rsch. asst. history dept. Claremont Grad. U., 1967-69; assoc. prof. history Palomar Coll., San Marcos, Calif., 1969—, pres. faculty, 1970-71, v.p. faculty senate, 1971-72. Author: Olaf Swenson and his Siberian Imports jour., 1978 (Dog Writers Assn. Am. Best Series award 1979), Campaign for Los Angeles, 1846-47, 69; co-editor: Don Juan Forster, 1970, Alaskan Trails, Siberian Dogs, 1998; contbr. articles to profl. jours. Mem. citizens com. Fallbrook (Calif.) San. Dist., 1980; merit badge counselor Boy Scouts Am., 1975-85; Martin County Hist. Soc., Morgan County Hist. Soc., Fallbrook Hist. Soc., San Diego Opera Guild, San Diego Classical Music Soc., Opera Pacific Guild. Chautauqua fellow NSF, 1979. Mem. Nat. Assn. for Outlaw and Lawman History, Inc., Western Outlaw-Lawman History Assn. (adv. bd.), Custer Battlefield Hist. and Mus. Assn. (life), Western Writers Am., Old Trail Drivers Assn. Tex., The Westerners, Siberian Husky Assn. Am. (bd. dirs. 1974-78, 1st v.p. 1978-79), So. Calif. Siberian Husky Assn. (pres. 1972-79), U.S. Shooting Team (Inner Circle), Sons of the Rep. of Tex., Western History Assn. Republican. Episcopalian. Avocations: collecting S.W. Indian art, backpacking, wine making, writing, opera. Home: 2308 Willow Glen Rd Fallbrook CA 92028-8605 Office: Palomar Coll 1140 W Mission Rd San Marcos CA 92069-1415

TANNER, JORDAN, state legislator; b. Provo, Utah, July 26, 1931; s. Vasco Myron and Annie (Atkin) T.; m. Patricia Nowell, Sept. 16, 1960; children: Eric, Jeffrey, Timothy. BS, U. Utah, 1954; MBA, U. Calif., Berkeley, 1961. Fgn. svc. officer USIA, Washington, 1960-87; state rep. Utah Ho. of Reps., Salt Lake City, 1990—. Commr. Utah Centennial Commn., Salt Lake City, 1993—. Lt. USN, 1954-56. Republican. Mem. LDS Ch. Home and Office: 677 W Lakeview Dr Alpine UT 84004

TANNO, RONALD LOUIS, dentist; b. San Jose, Calif., Dec. 17, 1937; s. George Anthony and Rose Marie (Manghisi) T. BS magna cum laude, Santa Clara U., 1959; DDS, U. of Pacific, 1963. Dentist Santa Clara County Health Dept., San Martin, Calif., 1965-67, Alameda County Health Dept., Oakland, Calif., 1965-67; pvt. practice San Jose, 1966—; dental cons. Found. Med. Care, San Jose, 1977-81, Dental Ins. Cons., Saratoga, Calif., 1980-88, Santa Clara County Sch. Dists. Dental Plan, San Jose, 1983—; cons. quality rev. Delta Dental Plan Calif., San Francisco, 1983—; mem. dental staff Los Gatos (Calif.) Community Hosp., 1978-94, chief dental dept., 1983, 84. Capt. USAF, 1963-65. Mem. ADA, Calif. Dental Assn., Santa Clara County Dental Soc., Elks, Lions, Xi Psi Phi, Omicron Kappa Upsilon. Avocations: snow skiing, dancing, Corvette sports cars. Office: 1610 Westwood Dr Ste 3 San Jose CA 95125-5110

TANSEY, ROGER KENT, lawyer; b. Waterloo, Iowa, Aug. 23, 1955; s. Roger Kent Tansey Sr. and Judith Lea Hertz; m. Tucker. AB in English, Case Western Res. U., 1977; JD, Boston Coll., 1983. Bar: Calif. 1983. Rsch. asst. Winston Churchill III, MP, House of Commons, London, 1977-80; fed. law clk. Hon. Volney Brown, U.S. judge, ctrl. dist. Calif., L.A., 1983-85; assoc. Tuttle & Taylor, L.A., 1985-87; v.p. and counsel Home Savs. of Am., L.A., 1987-91; dir. legal svcs. AIDS Project Los Angeles, L.A., 1991-93, AIDS Svc. Ctr., Pasadena, Calif., 1993-95; exec. dir. OneDay-Family AIDS Project, Denver, 1995-97, AID for AIDS, West Hollywood, Calif., 1997—. Chmn. State Bar of Calif. com. on human rights, 1989-91; mem. Gay and Lesbian Task Force of the City of West Hollywood, 1987-88. Office: AID for AIDS 8235 Santa Monica Blvd Ste 200 West Hollywood CA 90046-5981

TANZI, CAROL ANNE, interior designer; b. San Francisco, Apr. 9, 1942; d. Raymond Edward and Anne Marie Giorgi. BA, U. San Jose, Calif., 1966. Teaching credential, Calif.; cert. interior designer, Calif. Home furnishings coord. R.H. Macy's, San Francisco, 1966-72; owner, pres. Carol A. Tanzi & Assocs., Burlingame, Calif., 1972—; instr. interior design Recreational Ctrs., Burlingame/Foster City, Calif., 1972-85; design cons. Am. Cancer Soc., San Mateo, Calif., 1994-95; mem. adv. com. for interior design students Coll. San Mateo, 1984-87; head designer San Mateo Battered Women's Shelter Pro Bono, 1993. Interior designer mags. Sunset, 1982, House Beautiful, 1992, 1001 Home Ideas, 1983; monthly cable TV program Interior Design by Tanzi, 1994—. Pres. Aux. to Mission Hospice, Burlingame, 1988-89, Hist. Soc. Burlingame, 1992-93; pres. Cmty. for Edn., Burlingame, 1996; mem. adv. com. Breast Ctr./Mills Peninsula Hosp., 1994—; mem. Oaks Hist. Adv. Bd., 1993-94; commr., pres. San Mateo County Commn. on Status of Women, 1990-95; chair San Mateo County Pvt. Industry Coun., 1997. Recipient Recogniton of Outstanding Performance Rotary Club of Burlingame, 1988-93, Congl. Recognition U.S.A., Burlingame, 1994, Commendation Bd. Suprs., County of San Mateo, 1994, Recognition Calif. Legis. Assembly, Burlingame, 1994, Hon. Svc. award for Outstanding Svc. to children and youth Calif. State PTA, 1997; named Superior Interior Designer Bay Area San Francisco Examiner, 1991, Woman of Distinction Soroptimist Internat., Burlingame/San Mateo, 1994. Mem. Am. Soc. Interior Designers (v.p. 1988, Presdl. Citation for disting. svc. 1986, 87, 88, Calif. Peninsula Chpt. Design award 1995), Burlingame C. of C. Women's Forum (chair 1986-95), Rotary Club of Burlingame (sec. 1994-97). Avocations: miniatures, reading, exercising, basketball. Home: 1528 Columbus Ave Burlingame CA 94010-5512 Office: Carol A Tanzi & Assocs PO Box 117281 Burlingame CA 94011-7281

TAO, CHIA-LIN PAO, humanities educator; b. Soochow, Kiangsu, China, July 7, 1939; came to U.S., 1961; d. Tsung-han and Hoi-chin Pao; m. Jingshen Tao, Aug. 22, 1964; children: Rosalind, Jeanne, Sandy. BA, Nat. Taiwan U., Taipei, 1961; MA, Ind. U., 1963, PhD, 1971. Assoc. prof. Nat. Taiwan U., Taipei, 1969-76, 78-79; vis. assoc. prof. U. Ariz., Tucson, 1976-78, 79-85, assoc. prof., 1989—; v.p. Hist. Soc. for 20th Century China in N.Am., 1992-93, pres., 1993-94. Editor, author: Studies in Chinese Women's History 4 vols., 1979-95. Mem. Tucson-Taichung Sister-City Com., Tucson, 1984—; sec. Ariz. Asian Am. Assn., 1989, dir., 1989-93. Rsch. grantee Nat. Sci. Coun., Taipei, 1971-72, 73-74, Harvard-Yenching Inst., Cambridge, Mass., 1972-74, Pacific Cultural Found., Taipei, 1984-85. Mem. Assn. for Asian Studies (pres. Western conf. 1994), Tucson Chinese Am. Profl. Soc. (pres. 1996), Tucson Chinese Assn. (bd. dirs. 1996-98). Democrat. Office: U Ariz Dept E Asian Studies Tucson AZ 85721

TAPPAN, JANICE RUTH VOGEL, animal behavior researcher; b. Pasadena, Mar. 13, 1948; d. Robert Samuel and Etta (Berry) Vogel; m. David Stanton Tappan IV, Dec. 20, 1970; children: Stacey, Christina, Danny. BA in Anthropology, U. Calif., Berkeley, 1970. Rsch. asst. L.A. Zoo, 1982—; owner Fiddlers Crossing, Pasadena, 1989—. Calif. Arts Coun. folklore grantee, 1989-90. Mem. Scottish Fiddling Revival (v.p. 1986—, judge fiddling 1989—), Scottish Fiddlers of Calif. (v.p. 1986—), Calif. Traditional Music Soc. (devel. dir. 1990-94, v.p. 1994—), Scottish Fiddlers of L.A. (music dir. 1990—). Phi Beta Kappa. Democrat. Soc. of Friends. Avocations: music. Home: 1938 Rose Villa St Pasadena CA 91107-5046

[illegible] India, June 11, 1921; came to U.S., 1966; naturalized, 1972; s. Nand and Isar (Kaur) Singh; m. Rani Surinder, Dec. 29, 1954; children: Nina, Roopinder, Sylvia, Sonya. BS with honors, Punjab U., 1944, MS with 1st class honors, [illegible] R.B. Woodward Harvard U., 1950-51; Post doctorate fellow NRC, Can.,

1953-54; prof. chemistry govt. colls., Punjab, India, 1954-58; prin. govt. colls., India, 1958-64; rsch. and devel. chemist PEBOC Ltd., Northolt, Eng., 1964-65, Unilever Rsch. Lab., Isleworth, Eng., 1965-66; prin. investigator rsch. projects Aldrich Chem.Co., Milw., 1966-76; rsch. and devel. chemist Polyscis., Inc., Warrington, Pa., 1976-88, Calbiochem, La Jolla, Calif., 1989-94; pres. One World Publ. Co., San Diego, 1996—; prin. investigator rsch. projects. Author: The Educational Problem of India, 1955, An Outline of the Philosophy of Creative Education, 1959, Evolution of the Soul, 1970, Universal Creative Religion for Peace, Love and Light, 1978, 2d edit., 1994, Human Sacrifice and Cannibalism in the Holy Bible, 1996, Sex Stories of the Holy Bible, 1996; contbr. numerous articles to profl. jours. Mem. Am. Chem. Soc. Avocations: studies in comparative religions, meditation. Home: 4202 Appleton St San Diego CA 92117-1901 Office: One World Publ Co PO Box 178206 San Diego CA 92177-8206

TARAKJI, GHASSAN, engineering educator; b. Aleppo, Syria; m. Rasha Tarakji, July 9, 1994. B in Civil Engring., Am. U., Beirut, Labanon, 1978; MCE, U. Fla., Gainesville, 1980; PhD in Civil Engring., Clemson U., S.C., 1983. Lic. profl. engr.,Fla., Calif. Site engr. OTAC Contracting, Dubai, 1978-79; asst. prof. Fla. State U., Tallahassee, 1983-86; prof. San Francisco State U., 1986—; pres. Sigma Engrs., Hayward, Calif., 1989—; interm chmn. FSU-FAMU C.E. Dept., Tallahassee, Fla., 1983-84; cons. 1984—; expert witness Judicial Sys., Oakland, Calif., 1994; chair Promotions and Tenure Com. Sch. Engring., San Francisco, 1994—. Author: (monogram) Birariate Normal Tables, 1989; contbr. papers and articles to profl. jours. Recipient Meritorious Performance award San Francisco State U., 1990. Mem. ASCE, Transp. Rsch. Bd. Avocations: tennis, photography, travel, reading. Home: Sigma Engr PO Box 27141 San Francisco CA 94127 Office: San Francisco State U Sch Engring 1600 Holloway Ave San Francisco CA 94132-1722

TARANIK, JAMES VLADIMIR, geologist, educator; b. Los Angeles, Apr. 23, 1940; s. Vladimir James and Jeanette Downing (Smith) T.; m. Colleen Sue Glessner, Dec. 4, 1971; children: Debra Lynn, Danny Lee. B.Sc. in Geology, Stanford U., 1964; Ph.D., Colo. Sch. Mines, 1974. Chief remote sensing Iowa Geol. Survey, Iowa City, 1971-74; prin. remote sensing scientist Earth Resources Observation Systems Data Ctr., U.S. Geol. Survey, Sioux Falls, S.D., 1975-79; chief non-renewable resources br., resource observation div. Office of Space and Terrestrial Applications, NASA Hdqrs., Washington, 1979-82; dean mines Mackay Sch. Mines U. Nev., Reno, 1982-87, prof. of geology and geophysics, 1982—, Arthur Brant chair of geology and geophysics, 1996—; pres. Desert Research Inst., Univ. and C.C. Sys. Nev., 1987-98, Regents's prof. and pres. emeritus, 1998—; adj. prof. geology U. Iowa, 1971-79; vis. prof. civil engring. Iowa State U., 1972-74; adj. prof. earth sci. U. S.D., 1976-79; program scientist for space shuttle large format camera expt. for heat capacity mapping mission, liaison Geol. Scis. Bd., Nat. Acad. Scis., 1981-82; dir. NOAA Coop. Inst. Aerospace Sci. & Terrestrial Applications, 1986-94; program dir. NASA Space Grant consortium Univ. and Community Coll. System Nev., Reno, 1991—; team mem. Shuttle Imaging Radar-B Sci. Team NASA, 1983-88, mem. space applications adv. com., 1986-88; chmn. remote sensing subcom. SAAC, 1986-88; chmn. working group on civil space commercialization Dept. Commerce, 1982-84, mem. civil operational remote sensing satellite com., 1983-84; bd. dirs. Earth Satellite Corp.; mem. adv. com. NASA Space Sci. and Applications Com., 1988-90, Nat. Def. Exec. Res., 1986—, AF studies bd., com. on strategic relocatable targets, 1989-91; mem. pre-launch rev. bd., NASA, Space Radar Lab., 1993-94; mem. fed. lab. rev. task force, NASA, 1994—; prin. investigator Japanese Earth Resources Satellite, 1991-94; mem. environ. task force MEDEA, Mitre Corp., McLean, Va., 1993—; cons. Jet Propulsion Lab., Calif., Hughes Aircraft Corp., Lockheed-Marietta Corp., Mitre Corp., TRW; developer remote sensing program and remote sensing lab. for State of Iowa, ednl. program in remote sensing for Iowa univs. and U. Nev., Reno; program scientist for 2d space shuttle flight Office Space and Terrestrial Applications Program; mem. terrestrial geol. applications program NASA, 1981—; co-investigator Can. Radarsat Program, 1995—; program dir. NASA EPSCOR, Nev., 1998—. Contbr. to profl. jours. Served with C.E. U.S. Army, 1965-67; mil. intellegence officer Res. Decorated Bronze Star medal; recipient Spl. Achievement award U.S. Geol. Survey, 1978, Exceptional Sci. Achievement medal NASA, 1982, NASA Group Achievement award Shuttle imaging radar, 1990, NASA Johnson Space Ctr. Group Achievement award for large format camera, 1985; NASA prin. investigator, 1973, 83-88, prin. investigator French Spot-1 Program to Evaluate Spot 1986-88; NDEA fellow, 1968-71. Fellow AAAS, Geol. Soc. Am., Explorers Club, Am. Soc. Photogrammetry Remote Sensing; mem. IEEE (sr.), AIAA (sr.), Am. Astron. Soc. (sr.), Internat. Acad. Astronautics, Soc. Exploration Geophysicists, Am. Geophys. Union, Am. Assn. Petroleum Geologists, Soc. Mining Engrs. Am., Inst. Metallurgical Engrs., Soc. Econ. Geologists, Bohemian Club San Francisco. Home: PO Box 7175 Reno NV 89510-7175

TARBI, WILLIAM RHEINLANDER, secondary education educator, curriculum consultant, educational technology researcher; b. San Bernardino, Calif., Feb. 23, 1949; s. William Metro and Sue (Rheinlander) T.; m. Jenny Workman, Apr. 10, 1980 (div. 1985); m. Michele Hastings, July 4, 1990; children: Amy, Melissa. AA, Santa Barbara City Coll., 1969; BA in History, U. Calif., Santa Barbara, 1976; MA, U. Redlands, 1992. Cert. secondary edn. social studies tchr., Calif. Reporter AP, Santa Barbara, Calif., 1976-80, UPI, Seattle, 1980-85, Golden West Radio Network, Seattle, 1980-85; tchr. Redlands (Calif.) Unified Sch. Dist., 1988—; cons. IMCOM, Redlands, 1985—. Mrm. E Clampus Vitus, Phi Delta Kappa. Avocations: painting, photography, writing, gardening, fencing.

TARIO, TERRY C(HARLES), broadcasting executive; b. L.A., Aug. 28, 1950; s. Clifford Alexander and Marion Charlene (Olive) T.; 1 child; Brian Paul. Grad. high sch., Hermosa Beach, Calif., 1968. Gen. mgr. South Bay Power Tools, Hermosa Beach, 1973-76; v.p., gen. mgr. Sta. KEZJ-FM, Twin Falls, Idaho, 1976—; pres. Money Music, music and record pub. co., Twin Falls, 1995—; dir. mktg. Pet Complex, Boise and Salt Lake City, 1985-90; v.p. Admagination. Creator commls. John Lennon Meml. (Best of Yr. award 1982), Pets Unltd., 1983 (Best of Yr. award 1983), Depot Grill, 1984 (Best of Yr. award 1984), Eyecenter (Best of Yr. award 1986). Served with USN, 1968-72. Recipient Best of Yr. Pub. Svc. award, 1990. Mem. BMI, Idaho Broadcasters Assn. (Best Pub. Svc. award 1990), Advt. and Mktg.Cons. (pres.). Avocations: skiing, running, writing. Office: Stas KEZJ FM and KLIX-AM-FM 415 Park Ave Twin Falls ID 83301-7752

TARKOWSKI, LARRY MICHAEL, municipal official; b. Flint, Mich., May 15, 1952; s. Lavern Joseph and Barbara Ann (Wade) T.; children: Jonathon, Logan. B in Gen. Studies, U. Mich., Ann Arbor, 1974. Supt. Warren Smith Contracting, Flagstaff, Ariz., 1979-89; dir. pub. works Town of Prescott Valley, Ariz., 1989—. Chmn. No. Ariz. Coun. Govt. Transp. Bd., Flagstaff, 1990-97; mem. Ariz. Town Hall, 1997; gov. appointee State Groundwater Users Adv. Coun. Named Profl. Man of Yr., Prescott Valley Rotary Club, 1993. Mem. Am. Water Works Assn., Am. Pub. Works Assn. (pres. No. Ariz. br. 1995), Solid Waste Assn. N.Am., Ctrl. Yavapai Transp. Planning Orgn., Prescott Valley Hist. Soc., Prescott Valley C. of C., Lions (pres. 1994), Yavapai Soccer Club (coord. 1992—, bd. dirs. 1997—), Prescott Valley C. of C. (roastee). Avocations: soccer, softball, skiing, hiking.

TARN, NATHANIEL, poet, translator, educator; b. Paris, June 30, 1928; s. Marcel and Yvonne (Suchar) T.; children : Andrea, Marc. BA with honors, Cambridge (Eng.) U., 1948, MA, 1952; postgrad., U. Sorbonne, U. Paris, 1949-51; MA, U. Chgo., 1952, PhD, 1957; postgrad., London Sch. Econs., 1953-58. Anthropologist Guatemala, Burma, Alaska, and other locations, 1952—; prof. comparative lit. Rutgers U., 1970-85, prof. emeritus modern poetry, comparative lit, anthropology, 1985; vis. prof. SUNY, Buffalo and Princeton, 1969-70. Author: Old Savage/Young City, 1964, Where Babylon Ends, 1968, The Beautiful Contradictions, 1969, October, 1969, A Nowhere for Vallejo, 1971, Lyrics for the Bride of God: Section: The Artemision, 1972, The Persephones, 1974, Lyrics for the Bride of God, 1975, The House of Leaves, 1976, Birdscapes, with Seaside, 1978, The Desert Mothers, 1985, At the Western Gates, 1985, Palenque, 1986, Seeing America First, 1989, Flying the Body, 1993, Multitude of One, 1995, Views from the Weaving Mountain: Selected Essays in Poetics and Anthropology, 1991, Scandals in the House of Birds: Shamans & Priests on Lake Atitlan, 1997; co-author: (with Janet Rodney) The Forest, 1978, Atitlan/Alashka, 1979, The Ground of Our Great Admiration of Nature, 1978; contbg. author: Penguin Modern Poets No. Seven: Richard Murphy, Jon Silkin, Nathaniel Tarn, 1965, A.P.E.N. Anthology of Contemporary Poetry, 1966, The Penguin Book of Modern Verse Translation, 1966, Poems Addressed to Hugh MacDiarmid, 1967, Music and Sweet Poetry: A Verse Anthology, 1968, Frontier of Going: Anthology of Space Poetry, 1969, Shaking the Pumpkin, 1972, America: A Prophecy, 1973, Open Poetry, 1973, Active Anthology, 1974, Symposium of the Whole, 1983, Random House Book of Twentieth Century French Poetry, 1983, Beneath a Single Moon: Buddhism in American Poetry, 1991, American Poetry since 1950: Innovators and Outsiders, 1993; translator: The Heights of Macchu Picchu (Pablo Neruda), 1966, Stelae (Victor Segalen), 1969, Zapotec Struggles, 1993; editor, co-translator: Con Cuba: An Anthology of Cuban Poetry of the Last Sixty Years, 1969, Selected Poems (Pablo Neruda), 1970; editor Cape Edits. and founder-dir. Cape Goliard Press, J. Cape Ltd., 1967-69. Recipient Guinness prize for poetry, 1963. Office: PO Box 8187 Santa Fe NM 87504-8187

TARSON, HERBERT HARVEY, university administrator emeritus; b. N.Y.C., Aug. 28, 1910; s. Harry and Elizabeth (Miller) T.; m. Lynne Barnett, June 27, 1941; 1 son, Stephen. Grad., Army Command Gen. Staff Coll., 1942, Armed Forces Staff Coll., 1951, Adavnced Mgmt. Sch. Sr. Air Force Comdrs., George Washington U., 1954; B.A., U. Calif., Los Angeles, 1949; Ph.D., U.S. Internat. U., 1972. Entered U.S. Army as pvt., 1933, advanced through grades to maj., 1942; transfered to U.S. Air Force, 1947, advanced through grades to lt. col., 1949; adj. exec. officer Ft. Snelling, Minn., 1940-42; asst. adj. gen. 91st Inf. Div., 1942-43; chief of personnel, advance sec. Comd. Zone, ETO, 1944-45; dir. personnel services 8th Air Force, 1946-47; dep. dir. dept. info. and edn. Armed Forces Info. Sch., 1949-51; dir. personnel services Japan Air Def. Force, 1951-53, Continental Air Command, 1953-62; dir. adminstrv. services, spl. asst. to Comdr. 6th Air Force Res. Region, 1962-64; ret., 1964; asst. to chancellor L.I. U., Brookville, 1964-69; dean admissions Tex. State Tech. Inst., San Diego Indsl. Center, 1970-72; v.p. acad. affairs Nat. U., San Diego, 1972-75, sr. v.p., 1975-88, founding sr. v.p. emeritus, 1988—. Decorated Bronze Star medal with oak leaf cluster, Air Force Commendation medal with 2 oak leaf clusters. Fellow Bio-Med Research Inst.; mem. Doctoral Soc. U.S. Internat. U., Am. Soc. Tng., Devel., World Affairs Council, Air Force Assn., Navy League U.S., Pres.'s Assos. of Nat. U. (presidential life). Home: 4611 Denwood Rd La Mesa CA 91941-4803

TARTAKOVSKY, DANIEL MIRON, hydrologist, applied mathematician; b. Kazan, Russia, Sept. 1, 1969; came to U.S., 1993; s. Miron D. and Nina Z. (Edelstein) T. MS, Kazan State U., 1991; PhD, U. Ariz., 1996. Rschr. Inst. Math. and Mechanics, Kazan, 1990-93; grad. rsch. assoc. U. Ariz., Tucson, 1993-96; rsch. assoc. Los Alamos (N.Mex.) Nat. Lab., 1996—. Contbr. articles to profl. jours. Recipient scholarship Kazan State U., 1987-91, award Russian Academia Sci., 1993, grant Soros Found., 1995. Mem. European Geophys. Soc., Am. Geophys. Union.

TARTER, CURTIS BRUCE, physicist, science administrator; b. Louisville, Sept. 26, 1939; s. Curtis B. and Marian Turner (Cundiff) T.; m. Jill Cornell, June 6, 1964 (div. 1975); 1 child, Shana Lee; m. Marcia Cyrog Linn, Sept. 6, 1987. BS, MIT, 1961; PhD, Cornell U., 1967. Tchg. asst. Cornell U., Ithaca, N.Y., 1961-63, rsch. asst., 1964-67; physicist Lawrence Radiation Lab., Livermore, Calif., summers 1962, 63; staff mem. theoretical physics divsn. U. Calif., Lawrence Livermore Nat. Lab., 1967-69, group leader macroscopic properties of matter, 1969-71, assoc. divsn. leader, 1971-74, group leader opacities, 1972-78, divsn. leader, 1974-84; dep. assoc. dir. for physics Lawrence Livermore Nat. Lab., 1984-88, assoc. dir. for physics, 1988-94, dep. dir., 1994; dir., 1994—; sr. scientist Applied Rsch. Labs. Aeronutronic divsn. Philco-Ford Corp., 1967; lectr., grad. student advisor dept. applied sci., U. Calif., Davis/Livermore, 1970—; cons. Hertz Found., 1970—, field com. study on astronomy in the 80's, NRC, 1980; mem. Army Sci. Bd., Washington, 1989-96; mem. Calif. Coun. on Sci. and Tech., 1996—; mem. Pacific Coun. on Internat. Policy, 1998. Contbr. numerous articles to profl. jours. Recipient Roosevelts Gold Medal award for sci. Fellow Am. Phys. Soc.; mem. AAAS, Am. Astron. Soc., Internat. Astron. Union. Republican. Avocations: golf, squash, bridge. Home: 676 Old Jonas Hill Rd Lafayette CA 94549-5214 Office: Lawrence Livermore Nat Lab PO Box 808 Livermore CA 94551-0808

TASH, GRAHAM ANDREW, JR., automobile retail company executive; b. Seattle, Dec. 18, 1956; s. Graham Andrew and Charlotte Eleanor (Hawes) Tash; m. Julie Thompson Titus, Aug. 8, 1981; children: Jacqueline E., Katherine J., Graham A. III. BA, U. Puget Sound, 1979. Dist. mgr. Kenworth Truck Co., Atlanta, 1984-86; ops. mgr. Titus-Will Ford/Toyota, Tacoma, Wash., 1987-90, gen. mgr., 1991-94; pres. Titus-Will Ford/Toyota, Tacoma, 1994—, bd. dirs.; bd. dirs. Titus-Will Ent. Bd. dirs. Christian Brotherhood Acad., Tacoma, 1996—; mem. activities coun. Tacoma Art Mus., 1993, 94, 95. Recipient Chairman's award Ford Motor Co., 1986, 87, 92, Pres.'s award Toyota Motor Sales USA, 1991, 92, 94, 95, 96. Mem. Tacoma C. of C. (bd. dirs. 1996—), Tacoma Country and Golf Club, Wash. Athletic Club, Tacoma Lawn Tennis Club. Republican. Episcopalian. Avocations: snow skiing, boating, hunting, golf. Office: Titus-Will Ford/Toyota Sales Inc 3606 S Sprague Ave Tacoma WA 98409-7444

TASHIMA, ATSUSHI WALLACE, federal judge; b. Santa Maria, Calif., June 24, 1934; s. Yasutaro and Aya (Sasaki) T.; m. Nora Kiyo Inadomi, Jan. 27, 1957; children: Catherine Y., Christopher I., Jonathan I. AB in Polit. Sci., UCLA, 1958; LLB, Harvard U., 1961. Bar: Calif. 1962. Dep. atty. gen. State of Calif., 1962-67; atty. Spreckels Sugar divsn. Amstar Corp., 1968-72, v.p., gen. atty., 1972-77; ptnr. Morrison & Foerster, L.A., 1977-80; judge U.S. Dist. Ct. (ctrl. dist.) Calif., L.A., 1980-96, U.S. Ct. Appeals (9th cir.), Pasadena, Calif., 1996—; mem. Calif. Com. Bar Examiners, 1978-80. With USMC, 1953-55. Mem. ABA, State Bar Calif., Los Angeles County Bar Assn. Democrat. Office: US Ct Appeals PO Box 91510 125 S Grand Ave Pasadena CA 91105-1652*

TATA, GIOVANNI, publishing executive; b. Taranto, Italy, Apr. 26, 1954; came to U.S., 1974, naturalized, 1982; s. Vito and Angela (Colucci) T.; m. Brenda Susan Smith, Feb. 14, 1978; children: Elizabeth Ariana, Katherine Allison, Margaret Anne, Michael Anthony. BS cum laude (scholar), Brigham Young U., 1977, MA, 1980; grad. cert. area studies U. Utah, 1980; PhD, 1986; postgrad. U. Turin (Italy), 1980-81. Archaeologist, Utah State Hist. Soc., Salt Lake City, 1979; instr. dept. langs. U. Utah, Salt Lake City, 1983-85; Mediterranean specialist Soc. Early Hist. Archaeology, Provo, Utah, 1978-91; mus. curator Pioneer Trail State Park, Salt Lake City, 1982-83; instr. dept. art Brigham Young U., Provo, 1982-84; research fellow Direzione Generale per la Cooperazione Scientifica Culturale e Technica, Rome, 1980-81; research curator Utah Mus. Fine Arts, Salt Lake City, 1985-87; chmn. 35th Ann. Symposium on the Archaeology of the Scriptures, 1986; pres. Transoft Internat., Inc., 1988—, Mus. Info. Systems, 1987-93; chmn. Taras Devel. Corp., 1994-97; dir. creative works Brigham Young U., 1996—. Chmn. MuseuMedia, Inc., 1995—. Republican. Mem. Ch. Jesus Christ of Latter-day Saints. Mem. Am. Assn. Museums, Internat. Coun. Museums, Utah State Hist. Soc. Home: PO Box 2194 Provo UT 84603-2194 Office: Transoft Internat 3325 N University Ave Ste 300 Provo UT 84604-7412

TATARSKII, VALERIAN IL'ICH, physics researcher; b. Kharkov, USSR, Oct. 13, 1929; s. Il'ya A. and Elizabeth A. (Lapis) T.; m. Maia S. Granovskaia, Dec. 22, 1955; 1 child, Viatcheslav V. MS, Moscow State U., 1952; PhD, Acoustical Inst. Acad. Scis., 1957; DSc, Gorky State U., 1962. Scientific rschr. Geophys. Inst. Acad. Sci. USSR, Moscow, 1953-56; scientific rschr. Inst. Atmospheric Physics, Acad. Sci. USSR, Moscow, 1956-59, sr. scientific rschr., 1959-78, head lab., 1978-90; head dept. Lebedev. Phys. Inst. Acad. Sci., Moscow, 1990-91; sr. rsch. assoc. U. Colo. Coop. Inst. for Rsch. in Environ. Sci., Boulder, 1991—, NOAA/ERL. Environ. Tech. Lab., Boulder. Author: Wave Propagation in a Turbulent Medium, 1961, 67, The Effect of the Turbulent Atmosphere on Wave Propagation, 1971, Principles of Statistical Radiophysics, 1989; contbr. articles to profl. jours. Recipient of Max Born award, 1994, Optical Soc. of Am., USSR State prize, 1990. Fellow Optical Soc. Am. (Max Born award 1994); mem. Russian Acad. Sci., U.S.A. Nat. Acad. Engring. (fgn. assoc.), N.Y. Acad. Sci. Avocations: classical music, kayaking. Office: NOAA ERL ETL 325 Broadway St Boulder CO 80303-3337

TATE, CARL ROY, management consultant, real estate broker; b. Inglewood, Calif., Sept. 19, 1935; s. Roy Kenneth and Elizabeth Marion (Campbell) T.; m. Dalene Ellen Holland, June 17, 1962; children: Tiffany Ellen Leppelman, Tracy Elizabeth, Tammy Erin Alenis, Brian Roy. AA in Bus. Adminstrn., El Camino Coll., Torrance, Calif., 1958; BA in Bus. Adminstrn., Calif. State U., Long Beach, 1960, BS in Bus. Edn., 1961; MBA in Bus. Adminstrn., Columbia State U., Metairie, La., 1976. C.C. tchg. credential, Calif.; cert. adminstr., Calif.; lic. real estate broker, Calif. Exec. dir. F.H.P., Inc., Long Beach, Calif., 1960-62; dir. employee health Rockwell Internat., El Segundo, Calif., 1962-68; regional adminstr. Health Care Corp. Inc., Newport Beach, Calif., 1968-70, Cmty. Psychol. Ctrs., Alhambra, Calif., 1970-72; assoc. adminstr. Torrance Meml. Hosp., 1972-74; regional ops. analyst, hosp. adminstr. Am. Medicorp, Inc., Venice, Calif., 1974-76; dist. mgr. provider svcs. Blue Cross So. Calif., L.A., 1976-77; pres., CEO C. Tate & Assocs., Victorville, Calif., 1977—. Bd. dirs. Tri-City Mental Health Authority, Pomona, Calif., 1970-72; chmn. health planning task force Inland Counties Health Systems Agy., Grand Terrace, Calif., 1978-83; v.p. governing bd. Spring Valley Lake Assn., Victorville, Calif., 1980-89; pres. bd. trustess Victor Valley C.C. Dist., Victorville, 1987—. Sgt. USMC, 1953-56. Named Outstanding Healthcare Exec. in Victor Valley, Inland Counteis Health Systems Agy., Grand Terrace, 1980; recipient Cmty. Svc. award City of Pomona, 1972. Mem. C.C. League Calif. (state legislation fin. com. 1995—), Apple Valley C. of C. (membership chmn. 1987-97), Spring Valley Lake Country Club (governing bd. 1978-96). Republican. Avocations: handcrafted cars, travel, reading professional journals, attending sports activities. Home: 8087 Svl Box Victorville CA 92392-5121 Office: C Tate & Assocs 8087 Svl Box Victorville CA 92392-5121

TATUM, RONALD WINSTON, physician, endocrinologist; b. Joplin, Mo., Apr. 29, 1935; s. Dorothy Elizabeth (Messick) T.; m. Phyllis Wainman, June 25 (div. May 1974); children: Jeffrey, Stacey; m. Yvonne Marie Laug, Oct. 8, 1994; children: Christina, Candice. AB, Harvard U., 1957; MD, U. Rochester, 1961. Intern Strong Meml. Hosp., Rochester, N.Y., 1961-62; resident U. Rochester, 1962-64, fellow, 1964-66; clin. endocrinologist in pvt. practice Albuquerque, 1966—; active staff Presbyn. Hosp. and St. Joseph Hosp., Albuquerque, 1966—; med. dir. Cottonwood Treatment Ctr., Albuquerque, 1985-90, N.Mex. Monitored Treatment Program, Albuquerque, 1990—; clin. endocrine cons. Charter Hosp. and Heights Psychiat. Hosp., Albuquerque, 1985—. Contbr. articles to profl. jours. Mem. med. adv. com. Hospice Home Health Care, Albuquerque, 1991—. Mem. Am. Assn. Clin. Endocrinologists (charter), Am. Assn. Internal Medicine, Am. Diabetes Assn. (pres. N.Mex. chpt. 1970, 74), Am. Soc. Addiction Medicine, Assn. for Med. Rsch. in Substance Abuse. Avocations: photography, computer investing. Home: 408 Poinsettia Pl SE Albuquerque NM 87123-3916 Office: 7520 Montgomery Blvd NE Albuquerque NM 87109-1521

TATUM, THOMAS DESKINS, film and television producer, director; b. Pineville, Ky., Feb. 16, 1946; s. Clinton Turner and Gaynelle (Deskins) T.; m. Laura Ann Smith, Aug. 15, 1968 (div. 1974); m. Suzanne Pettit, Sept. 29, 1983 (dec. 1998); children: Rhett Cowden, Walker Edwin; m. Kathryn Vinson, Nov. 28, 1998. BA, Vanderbilt U., 1968; JD, Emory U., 1974. Bar: Ga. 1974, D.C. 1980. Spl. asst. City of Atlanta, 1974-76; dep. dir. fed. relations Fed. Relations Nat. League of Cities, Washington, 1977-78; dir. communications Office of Conservation and Solar Energy, Washington, 1979-80; chmn. exec. producer Tatum Communications., Inc., Telluride, and Burbank, Calif., 1981—; chmn., pres. Western Film & Video, Inc., Telluride, Colo., 1987—; pres., COO Planet Central TV, 1995-96. Prodr. feature film Winners Take All, 1987; prodr., dir. documentaries Double High, 1982 (award), Maui Windsurf, 1983, home videos Greenpeace in Action, Girls of Winter/Skiing mag., US Pro Ski tour, 1983-90, Action Sports of the 80's ESPN, 1984-88, Am. Ultra Sports with Prime Network, 1989-94, various TV, cable and home video sports and health programs, 1982—, series Eco Sports, 1995—, Body, Mind, and Spirit, 1996-97. Dep. campaign mgr. Maynard Jackson, 1973, Jimmy Carter campaign, 1976, staff conf. Dem. Mayors, 1974-75, media cons. Greepeace, 1988; bd. dirs. Atlanta Ballet, v.p., 1975; nat. urban affairs coord. Carter Mondale campaign 1976, mem. Carter Mondale transition team 1976-77; mem. adv. bd. Solar Electric Light Fund, Washington, 1990-98, Green Peace. Mem. Ga. Bar Assn., Hollywood Film and TV Soc., L.A. Tennis Club. Presbyterian. Avocations: skiing, sailing, Yoga, tennis, travel. Home: PO Box 944 Telluride CO 81435-0944 Office: Tatum Comm Inc 2219 W Olive Ave Ste 173 Burbank CA 91506-2625

TAUBE, DANIEL ORIN, psychology and law educator; b. Stamford, Conn., July 7, 1953; s. George S. and Marsha Y.; m. Debra A. Warshaw, July 26, 1981; 1 child, Gabriel Michael. BA in Psychology, Sonoma State U., Rohnert Park, Calif., 1975; JD, Villanova U., 1985; PhD in Clin. Psychology, Hahnemann U., 1987. Lic. psychologist, Calif. Psychology intern Friens Hosp., Phila., 1985-86; rsch. assoc. Ctr. Excellence, Addiction Treatment Rsch. U Medicine & Dentistry N.J. Sch. Medicine, Camden, 1986-89; eval. coord. Alameda County Mental Health, Oakland, Calif., 1989-90; asst. prof. psychology Calif. Sch. Profl. Psychology, Alameda, Calif., 1990-96, assoc. prof., 1996—. Contbr. articles to profl. jours. Mem. APA (mem. ethics appeals hearing panel 1993—), Am. Profl. Soc. on Abuse of Children, Am. Psychology-Law Soc., Calif. Psychol. Assn. Office: Calif School Profl Psychology 1005 Atlantic Ave Alameda CA 94501-1148

TAUBE, HENRY, chemistry educator; b. Sask., Can., Nov. 30, 1915; came to U.S., 1937, naturalized, 1942; s. Samuel and Albertina (Tiledetski) T.; m. Mary Alice Wesche, Nov. 27, 1952; children: Linda, Marianna, Heinrich, Karl. BS, U. Sask., 1935, MS, 1937, LLD, 1973; PhD, U. Calif., 1940; PhD (hon.), Hebrew U. of Jerusalem, 1979; DSc (hon.), U. Chgo., 1983, Poly. Inst., N.Y., 1984, SUNY, 1985, U. Guelph, 1987; DSc honoris causa, Seton Hall U., 1988; Lajos Kossuth U. of Debrecen, Hungary, 1988; DSc, Northwestern U., 1990; hon. degree, U. Athens, 1993. Instr. U. Calif., 1940-41; instr., asst. prof. Cornell U., 1941-46; faculty U. Chgo., 1946-62, prof., 1952-62, chmn. dept. chemistry, 1955-59; prof. chemistry Stanford U., 1962-90; prof. emeritus chemistry Stanford U, 1990—; Marguerite Blake Wilbur prof. Stanford U., 1976, chmn. dept., 1971-74; Baker lectr. Cornell U., 1965. Hon. mem. Hungarian Acad., Scis., 1988. Guggenheim fellow, 1949, 55; recipient Harrison Howe award, 1961, Chandler medal Columbia U., 1964, F. P. Dwyer medal U. NSW, Australia, 1973, Nat. medal of Sci., 1976, 77, Allied Chem. award for Excellence in Grad. Tchg. and Innovative Sci., 1979, Nobel prize in Chemistry, 1983, Bailar medal U. Ill., 1983, Robert A. Welch Found. award in Chemistry, 1983, Disting. Achievement award Internat. Precious Metals Inst., 1986, Brazilian Order of Sci. Merit award, 1994, Hon. fellowship Royal Soc. Can., 1997. Fellow Royal Soc. Chemistry (hon.), Indian Chem. Soc. (hon.); mem. NAS (award in chem. scis. 1983), Am. Acad. Arts and Scis., Am. Chem. Soc. (Kirkwood award New Haven sect. 1965, award for nuclear applications in chemistry 1955, Nichols medal N.Y. sect. 1971, Willard Gibbs medal Chgo. sect. 1971, Disting. Svc. in Advancement Inorganic Chemistry award 1967, T.W. Richards medal NE sect. 1980, Monsanto Co. award in inorganic chemistry 1981, Linus Pauling award Puget Sound sect. 1981, Priestley medal 1985, Oesper award Cin. sect. 1986, G.M. Kosolapoff award Auburn sect. 1990), Royal Physiographical Soc. of Lund (fgn. mem.), Am. Philos. Soc., Finnish Acad. Sci. and Letters, Royal Danish Acad. Scis. and Letters, Coll. Chemists of Catalonia and Beleares (hon.), Can. Soc. Chemistry (hon.), Hungarian Acad. Scis. (hon. mem.), Royal Soc. (fgn. mem.), Brazilian Acad. Scis. (corr.), Engring. Acad. Japan (fgn. assoc.), Australian Acad. Scis. (corr.), Chem. Soc. Japan (hon. mem. 1993), Phi Beta Kappa, Sigma Xi, Phi Lambda Upsilon (hon.). Office: Stanford U Dept Chemistry Stanford CA 94305-5080

TAUER, PAUL E., mayor, educator; b. 1935; m. Katherine Eldredge, Sept. 1, 1956; children: Paul E. Jr., Edward, Roch, Eugene, Kathryn, Tammie, Andrew, Timothy. BA in Historyand Edn., Regis Coll., 1961; MA in Edn. Adminstrn., U. No. Colo., 1964. Tchr. Denver Pub. Schs., 1961-92; ret., 1992. Mayor City of Aurora, Colo., 1987—, mem. Aurora City Coun., 1979-1987; mem. Adams County Coordinating Com., Gov.'s Met. Transp. Roundtable; active Aurora airport coms. Mem. Noise. Office: Office of Mayor 1470 S Havana St Aurora CO 80012-4014

TAVEGGIA, THOMAS CHARLES, management consultant; b. Oak Lawn, Ill., June 15, 1943; s. Thomas Angelo and Eunice Louise (Harriss) T.; m. Brigitte I. Adams, Jan. 23, 1965; children: Michaela, Francesca. BS, Ill. Inst. Tech., 1965; MA, U. Oreg., 1968, PhD, 1971. Prof., U. Oreg., Eugene, 1970, U. B.C. (Can.), Vancouver, 1970-73, U. Calif.-Irvine, 1973-74, Ill. Inst.

Tech., Chgo., 1974-77; mgmt. cons. Towers, Perrin, Forster & Crosby, Chgo., 1977-80; ptnr. Manplan Cons., Chgo., 1980-81; ptnr. Coopers & Lybrand, San Francisco, 1981-86; ptnr. Touche Ross, San Francisco, 1986-88; prof. Calif. Sch. Profl. Psychology, Berkeley, 1988-98. NDEA Title IV fellow, 1967-71; U. B.C. faculty rsch. grantee, 1970, 71, 73. Faculty Rsch. grantee Calif. Sch. Profl. Psychology, 1993-98. Mem. Acad. Mgmt. Soc., Nat. Bur. Profl. Mgmt. Cons. Presbyterian. Author: (with R. Dubin and R. Arends) From Family and School To Work, 1967; (with Dubin) The Teaching-Learning Paradox: A Comparative Analysis of College Teaching Methods, 1968; (with Dubin and R.A. Hedley) The Medium May Be Related to the Message: College Instruction by TV, 1969; contbr. numerous articles to books and profl. jours. Home: 1506 W Canada Hills Dr Tucson AZ 85737

TAVERNA, RODNEY ELWARD, financial services company executive; b. Springfield, Ill., Aug. 8, 1947; s. Jerome Thomas and Virginia (Holcomb) T.; m. Cheryl Ann Walters, Sept. 4, 1968 (div. 1983); children: Lara Lyn, Melinda Marie, Ryan Thomas; m. Caroline Whiffen, Apr. 1985. BA, U. Mo., 1969; MBA in Fin., Nat. U., 1988. Commd. 2d lt., supply officer USMC, 1969, advanced through grades to maj.; 1979; supply officer Central Svcs. Agy., Danang, Vietnam, 1970-71, Marine Air Control Squadron, Futenma, Okinawa, 1977-78; logistics officer Hdqrs. Marine Corps Recruit Depot, Paris Island, S.C., 1972-75; support officer Marine Barracks, Treasure Island, San Francisco, 1975-77; regimental supply officer 1st Marine Divsn., Camp Pendleton, Calif., 1978-79; asst divsn. supply officer 1st Marine Divsn., 1985-88; brigade supply officer 1st Marine Brigade, Kaneohe Bay, Hawaii, 1980-82; exec. officer 1st Maintenance Bn., Camp Pendleton, 1982-85; asst div. supply officer 1st Marine Div., 1985-88; pres. Freedom Fin. Group, 1991—; br. mgr. WMA Securities, Inc., 1994-97; sr. field dir. Premier Fin. Am., 1997—; owner, mgr. Opportunities Unltd., Oceanside, Calif. 1985-91; cons. Incentive Leasing Corp., San Diego, 1985-86, The Profit Ctr., Santa Ana, Calif., 1991; founding mgr. Meditrend Internat., San Diego, 1987-88; founding dir. Am. 3-D Corp., Henderson, Nev., 1990-91. Republican. Avocations: computers, snow skiing, racquetball, scuba diving. E-mail: FreedomFinancial@home.com. Home and Office: 1632 Avenida Andante Oceanside CA 92056-6905

TAVERNETTI, SUSAN PISONI, film studies educator, film critic; b. Salinas, Calif., Dec. 16, 1950; d. Edward John and Jane Pisoni; m. Russell Eugene Tavernetti, July 27, 1974; children: Tessa Jane, Rhett Eugene. BA in Psychology and English summa cum laude, U. of the Pacific, 1973; MA in Cinema, U. So. Calif., 1978. Film studies instr. De Anza Coll., Cupertino, Calif., 1975—; film critic Palo Alto (Calif.) Weekly, 1986—; dir. Palo Alto Film & Video Festival, 1985-89; lectr. cinema dept. San Francisco State U., 1989, 94-95; film studies instr. Foothill Coll., Los Altos Hills, Calif., 1988; film festival juror; cons. in field. Co-author: The Critical Eye: An Introduction to Looking at Movies, 1998; prodr.: The Palo Alto Film Festival, 1985-86. Mem. Foothill-De Anza Faculty Assn. Office: De Anza Coll Film-TV Dept 21250 Stevens Creek Blvd Cupertino CA 95014-5702

TAYLOR, ALAN SHAW, history educator; b. Portland, Maine, June 17, 1955; s. Ruel Edward Jr. and Virginia (Craig) T. BA, Colby Coll. Waterville, Maine, 1977; PhD, Brandeis U., 1986. Instr. Colby Coll., 1984-85; fellow, asst. prof. Inst. Am. History and Culture, Williamsburg, Va., 1985-87; asst. prof. history Boston U., 1987-92, assoc. prof., 1992—. Author: Liberty Men and Great Proprietors, 1990; author articles and revs. NEH fellow Am. Antiquarian Soc., Worcester, Mass., 1990; Ctr. for History of Freedom fellow, St. Louis, 1991; Nat. Humanities Ctr. fellow, Research Triangle Park, N.C., 1993; Huntington Libr. fellow, San Marino, Calif., 1994. Mem. Am. Hist. Assn., We. Hist. Assn., Orgn. Am. Historians, Soc. for Historians of the Am. Republic, Peripheral Studies Assn. Avocations: tennis, town ball, following the Boston Red Sox,pool. Office: U Calif Dept History 1 Shields Ave Davis CA 95616

TAYLOR, ALEX, painter, sculptor, exhibit designer; b. Wichita, Kans., Aug. 13, 1952; s. Lewis W. and Jane (Barclay) T.; m. Vickie Halverson, July 1, 1978; 1 child: Charles Ethan. BFA in Painting, Ariz. State U., 1976. Exhibit and graphic designer Phoenix Zoo, 1972-76; exhibit designer Minn. Zoo, Apple Valley, 1976-78; imagineer Walt Disney Co., Glendale, Calif., 1979-83; owner Emerge Design, Alhambra, Calif., 1983-90; painter, sculptor La Cañada, Calif., 1990—. Patentee press fit sign framing sys. Mem. L.A. Art Assn., Huntington Westerners. Democrat. Mem. Soc. of Friends. Avocations: collecting books, studying American history.

TAYLOR, ANTHONY TODD, career officer, pilot; b. Graysville, Ala., July 5, 1968; s. Ted Levon and Lawanda Faye (Baker) T.; m. Shelaine Faith Davis, Sept. 2, 1995. BA, U. Ala., Birmingham, 1990; MS, Troy (Ala.) State U., 1998. Commd. 2d lt. USAF, 1990, advanced through grades to capt., 1994; asst. dir. ops. Combat Camera, Charleston, S.C., 1992-94; student pilot, 1994-95; chief of flight safety, instr. pilot 40th Rescue Flight, Great Falls, Mont., 1995—. Decorated Air Force Commendation medal. Mem. Co. Grade Officers Assn. Mem. Ch. of God. Avocations: history, working with dogs, fly fishing, upland game hunting, international relations. Home: 4946A Locust St Great Falls MT 59405-6616

TAYLOR, BARRY E., lawyer; b. Mineola, N.Y., Mar. 14, 1948. BA magna cum laude, U. Va., 1970, JD, 1975. Bar: Calif. 1975. With Wilson, Sonsini, Goodrich & Rosati P.C., Palo Alto, Calif. Mem. ABA, State Bar Calif., Order Coif, Phi Beta Kappa. Office: Wilson Sonsini Goodrich & Rosati PC 650 Page Mill Rd Palo Alto CA 94304-1050

TAYLOR, CHERYAL A., artist, educator; b. Mather AFB, Calif., Sept. 7, 1947; d. Gerard Elbert Baranowski and Doris Mae (Huie) Williford; children from previous marriage: Christian Nimsky, Erich Nimsky; m. Robert James Taylor, Mar. 22, 1989. BA, Ariz. State U., 1986, MEd in Counselor Edn., 1991. Cert. cmty. coll. tchr. Pvt. practice graphic designer, 1979-93, pvt. practice artist, 1980—; instr. Scottsdale (Ariz.) C.C., 1987—, graphic design 1990-97; instr. U. St. Francis, Joliet, Ill., 1995, 97; instr.-on-call Ea. Ariz. Coll., Globe, 1987—; cons. graphic design, Column Graphics, Seattle, 1993-95, Intellimed Internat. Inc., Phoenix, 1992, Blue Circle West, Phoenix, London, 1989; co-owner Art Directory, 1978-79. Exhibited in group shows at Kerr Cultural Ctr. Gallery, Scottsdale, 1983, Scottsdale C.C., various 1984-93, Ariz. State U., Tempe, 1987; represented in pub. and pvt. collections; editor Copper Canyon Ranch News, Globe, 1994-98. Recipient 2d place award Fountain Hills (Ariz.) Art Show, 1985, Juror's Choice award Scottsdale C.C., 1985, 1st place award, 1984. A. Avocations: bow hunting, back packing, camping, pistol shooting. Home: 8508 E Highland Ave Scottsdale AZ 85251-1823 Office: Scottsdale CC 9000 E Chaparral Rd Scottsdale AZ 85250-2614

TAYLOR, CLIFFORD PAUL, architect; b. Los Angeles, Apr. 5, 1947; s. William Paul and Doree Jane (Williams) T.; m. Bianca Gabrielle Flake, Feb. 8, 1986. BA, R.I. Sch. of Design, 1977, BArch, 1978. Registered architect, R.I., Colo. Instr. design Brigham Young U., Provo, Utah, 1971; intern architect Donald J. Prout, AIA, Cranston, R.I., 1979-81; project architect Fred M. Briggs, AIA, Laguna Beach, Calif., 1981—. Prin. works include office bldg. for Elixir Industries, 1983 (Grand award 1986), Kwon residence, 1983, Pikes Peak Summit House. Mem. AIA (lobbyist R.I. chpt. 1980). Office: 219 W Colorado Ave Ste 304 Colorado Springs CO 80903-3338

TAYLOR, DONALD STEWART, English literature educator; b. Portland, Oreg., Aug. 8, 1924; s. Donald Munro and Eva Jane (Tucker) T.; m. Joanne Seidler, Dec. 6, 1952; children: Leon, Benjamin, Matthew. BA, U. Calif., Berkeley, 1947; MA, U. Calif., 1948, PhD, 1950. Instr. English lit. Northwestern U., Evanston, Ill., 1950-54; from instr. to assoc. prof. U. Wash., Seattle, 1954-68; prof. U. Oreg., Eugene, 1968-89, English lit. historian, 1989—. Author: Thomas Chatterton's Art, 1978. R.G. Collingwood: A Bibliography, 1988; editor: Complete Works of Thomas Chatterton, 1971; contbr. articles and short stories to lit. publs. With U.S. Army, 1944-46. [illegible] reading music cooking. Home: [illegible] Eugene OR 97403-1630

[illegible line]
21, 1959; d. Louet Maxwelton and Inez Rita (Dupré) T.; m. Ernie Robert

---

Silva, July 20, 1991; 1 child, Robert Taylor Silva. BA cum laude, Claremont-McKenna Coll., 1981; JD with honors, George Washington U., 1984. Bar: Calif. 1985. Intern U.S. Ho. of Reps., Washington, 1979; staff mem. Jim Lloyd for Congress Com., Calif., 1980; staff asst. Senate Dem. Policy Com., Washington, 1982-84; program instr. Close Up Found., Arlington, Va., 1984-85; tchr. Providence High Sch., Burbank, Calif., 1985-87; dir. law and govt. programs Constnl. Rights Found., L.A., 1987-97; dir. alumni rels. Claremont (Calif.) McKenna Coll., 1997—. Mem. ABA. Democrat. Roman Catholic. Avocations: music, crafts. Office: Claremont McKenna Coll Office Alumni Rels Heggblade Ctr Claremont CA 91711

TAYLOR, GARY L., federal judge; b. 1938. AB, UCLA, 1960, JD, 1963. Assoc. Wenke, Taylor, Evans & Ikola, 1965-86; judge Orange County Superior Ct., 1986-90, U.S. Dist. Ct. (ctrl. dist.) Calif., Santa Ana, 1990—. With U.S. Army, 1964-66. Mem. Am. Coll. Trial Lawyers, State Bar Calif., Orange County Bar Assn. (bd. dirs. 1980-82, founder, chmn. bus. litigation com., Disting. Svc. award 1983). Office: US Dist Cts 751 W Santa Ana Blvd Rm 801 Santa Ana CA 92701-2085*

TAYLOR, GEORGE FREDERICK, newspaper publisher, editor; b. Portland, Oreg., Feb. 28, 1928; s. George Noble and Ida Louise (Dixon) T.; m. Georga Bray, Oct. 6, 1951; children—Amelia Ruth, Ross Noble. BS, U. Oreg., 1950. Reporter Astoria (Oreg.) Budget, 1950-52, Portland Oregonian, 1952-54; copy reader Wall St. Jour., 1955-57, reporter, 1957-59, Detroit Bur. chief, 1959-64, Washington corr., 1964-68; asst. mng. editor Wall St. Jour., San Francisco, 1968-69; mng. editor Wall St. Jour., N.Y.C., 1970-77, exec. editor, 1977-86; pub. North Bend (Oreg.) News, 1986—, Prime Time, 1987—, Coquille Valley Sentinel, 1989—. Lt. USAF, 1955-57. Mem. Oregon Newspaper Publishers Assn. (bd. dirs. 1997—). Office: 1 Bartons Aly Coquille OR 97423-1270

TAYLOR, GUY WATSON, symphonic conductor; b. Anniston, Ala., Dec. 25, 1919; s. Stokely Brackston and Ola Mae (Shaw) T.; m. Renee Lifton, Oct. 19, 1947; children: Eric Anthony, Ellen Jane. Diploma, Birmingham Conservatory of Music, 1941, Juilliard Sch. Music, 1948; pvt. studies and workshops with, Dimitri Mitropoulos, 1941-42, L'Ecole Monteux, 1949, Eugene Ormandy, 1953, George Szell, 1956. Conductor Springfield (Ohio) Symphony Orch., 1948-51, Nashville Symphony Orch., 1951-59, Phoenix Symphony Orch., 1959-69, Fresno Philharmonic Orch., 1969-84; guest conductor, U.S., Gt. Britain, Philippines, P.R., Can. and Mexico City; musical commentator Springfield News & Sun, 1948-51, Ariz. Republic, 1959-61, Fresno Bee, 1970-76. Has appeared on, BBC Radio, CBS-TV. Served with AUS, 1942-45. Recipient Conductor Recognition award Am. Symphony Orch. League, 1960, Alice M. Ditson Orch. award, 1961, citation for adventuresome programming of contemporary music ASCAP, 1977. Mem. Am. Symphony Orch. League, Phi Mu Alpha Sinfonia.

TAYLOR, HELEN SHIELDS, civic worker; b. Bloomington, Ind., Nov. 27, 1922; d. Lester Howard Shields and Mary Margaret (Galyan) Shields-Fleener; m. Richard R. Hurst, July 29, 1945 (div. Feb. 1959); children: Pamela Hurst Hayes, Richard S.; m. Clyde Leon Taylor, Dec. 2, 1961; 1 child, John P. AA, Coll. Sequoias, 1975; BA, Calif. State U., Fresno, 1979. bd. dirs. Taylor Machinery, Inc., Visalia, Calif. Author: Japanese Invasion of the Philippines, 1977, Russia Today, 1979. Bd. dirs. Town Hall, Inc., Fresno, 1990-96; past pres. Tulare County Symphony, Visalia, Meth. Women, Visalia, 1952-96; mem. Ice House Theatre, Visalia, Meth. Mem. AAUW (grantee 1979), U.S. Fgn. Policy Assn. (co-chair 1986-96), Alpha Gamma Sigma. Democrat. Avocations: investing, travel, book reviewing, public speaking. Home: 1545 S Chinowth St Visalia CA 93277-3909 Office: Taylor Machinery Inc 5736 W Lisendra Dr Visalia CA 93277-9270

TAYLOR, IRVING, mechanical engineer, consultant; b. Schenectady, N.Y., Oct. 25, 1912; s. John Bellamy and Marcia Estabrook (Jones) T.; m. Shirley Ann Milker, Dec. 22, 1943; children: Bronwen D., Marcia L., John I., Jerome E. BME, Cornell U., 1934. Registered profl. engr., N.Y., Mass., Calif. Test engr. Gen. Electric Co., Lynn, Mass., 1934-37; asst. mech. engr. M.W. Kellogg Co., N.Y.C., 1937-39; sect. head engring. dept. The Lummus Co., N.Y.C., 1939-57; research engr. Gilbert and Barker, West Springfield, Mass., 1957-58, Marquardt Corp., Ogden, Utah, 1958-60, Bechtel, Inc., San Francisco, 1960-77; cons. engr. Berkeley, Calif., 1977-91; adj. prof. Columbia U., 1950-60, NYU, 1950-60. Contbr. articles to profl. jours. Fellow ASME (life, Henry R. worthington medal 1990); mem. Pacific Energy Assn. Soaring Soc. Am. (life), Sigma Xi (assoc.). Unitarian. Avocations: sailplane soaring, skiing, lawn bowling. Home: 300 Deer Valley Rd Apt 2P San Rafael CA 94903-5514

TAYLOR, JAMES JARED, III, artist, sculptor; b. Cin., May 14, 1958; s. James Jared Jr. and Anne (Mitchell) T.; m. J. Shelby Stone, Nov. 30, 1991; 1 child, Samara. BFA, Kansas City Art Inst., 1981; MFA, Rutgers U., 1986. Assoc. dir. Calif. Sculpture Ctr., Palm Desert, 1988-90; head art dept. Mt. San Jacinto H.S., Palm Springs, Calif., 1994—; adj. faculty Coll. of the Desert, Palm Desert, 1989—, Calif. State U., San Bernardino, 1993—. One-man shows include Princeton Day Sch., N.J., 1982, Johnson Atelier, Princeton, 1983, Mason Gross Sch. of Arts, Rutgers U., 1986, Extension Gallery, 1987, Henry Chauncey Ctr., Princeton, 1988, Riverside Arts Found., Palm Springs, 1992, Rose Watkins Gallery, Palm Desert, 1996; group shows include U. Mo. Kansas City, 1979, The Kemper Gallery, Kansas City, 1981, Anne Reid Gallery, Princeton, 1982, Robeson Ctr. Gallery, Newark, 1983, Warner Commn., N.Y.C., 1984, Mercer County Cultural Heritage Commn., N.J., 1985, Voorhees-Zimmerli Art Mus., 1986, The Morris Mus., Morristown, N.J., 1987, Carnegia Ctr., Princeton, 1988, The Calif. Sculpture Ctr., Palm Desert, 1989, Aerie Sculpture Garden, Palm Desert, 1990, Valeriue Miller Fine Art, Palm Desert, 1992, Edward Dean Mus., Cherry Valley, Calif., 1993, La Quinta Arts Festival, 1993, 94, Left Bank Gallery, Palm Desert, 1996, Malton Gallery, Cin., 1996, Gallery Blu, Palm DEsert, 1997, others; represented in permanent collectionsElectronic Data Systems, L.A., Wright-Reiman Labs., N.J., Am. Acad. Family Physicians, Kansas City, Children's Mercy Hosp. Kansas City, Mr. and Mrs. Harry Gordon, Lambertville, N.J., Mr. and Mrs. Dana Stewart, Lambertville, Mr. and Mrs. Wayne Gittinger, Indian Wells, Calif., Ms. Marcia Broderick, Palm Desert, Mr. and Mrs. Vincent Neary, Berkeley, Calif., Imago Galleries, Palm DEsert, Mr. Steve Sobcyck, Cathedral City, Calif., numerous others. N.J. State Coun. on Arts fellow, 1985. Mem. Nat. Art Edn. Assn., Coll. Art Assn. Democrat. Episcopalian. Avocations: hiking, surfing, reading. Home: 1866 N Jacques Rd Palm Springs CA 92262-3113

TAYLOR, JAMES WALTER, marketing consultant; b. St. Cloud, Minn., Feb. 15, 1933; s. James T. and Nina C. Taylor; m. Joanne Syktte, Feb. 3, 1956; children: Theodore James, Samuel Bennett, Christopher John. BBA, U. Minn., 1957; MBA, NYU, 1960; DBA, U. So. Calif., 1975. Mgr. research div. Atlantic Refining, Phila., 1960-65; dir. new product devel. Hunt-Wesson Foods, Fullerton, Calif., 1965-72; prof. mktg. Calif. State U., Fullerton, 1972-95; mng. dir. Innovative Mgmt. Devel. Co., Laguna Beach, Calif., 1995—; cons. Smithkline Beecham Corp., Tokyo, Govt. of Portugal, Lisbon, Austrade, Govt. of Australia, Hagenfeldt-Affarerna AB, Stockholm. Author: Profitable New Product Strategies, 1984, How to Create a Winning Business Plan, 1986, Competitive Marketing Strategies, 1986, The 101 Best Performing Companies in America, 1987, The Complete Manual for Developing Winning Strategic Plans, 1988, Every Manager's Survival Guide, 1989, Developing Winning Strategic Plans, 1990, How to Develop Successful Advertising Plans, 1993, Marketing Planning: A Step by Step Guide, 1997. Fulbright scholar Ministry of Industry, Lisbon, Portugal, 1986-87, U. We. Sydney, Australia, 1989-90; recipient Merit award Calif. State U., 1986-90. Mem. The Planning Forum, Am. Mktg. Assn., Strategic Mgmt. Assn., Assn. for Consumer Rsch., Acad. Mktg. Sci. Home: 3190 Mountain View Dr Laguna Beach CA 92651-2056

TAYLOR, JUDITH ANN, marketing and sales executive; b. Sheridan, Wyo., July 3, 1944; d. Milo G. and Eleanor M. (Wood) Rinker; m. George [illegible] Montgomery Ward, Sheridan, 1968-73; pers. mgr., asst. mgr. Dan's Ranchwear, Sheridan, 1973-80; sales/prodn. coord. KWYO Radio, Sheridan, 1981-83; sales mgr., promotions coord. KROE Radio, Sheridan, 1984-96; [illegible] & [illegible] Food [illegible] 1990 [illegible] for dir. sales and marketing best western Sheridan Ctr., 1996—; notary pub. State of Wyo., 1985—; lectr. instr. BSA

Merit U.; lectr. acad. achievement LVA Adv. Bd., 1993—, instr. Tongue River Middle Sch. Academic Enrichmen t Program, 1994-95; S.C. Ambs., 1980—, pres., 1995-96. Mng. editor BOUNTY Publ., 1993-96. Sec.-treas. Sheridan County Centennial Com., 1986-89; local sec.-treas. Wyo. Centennial Com., Sheridan, 1986-90; exec. dir. Sheridan-Wyo. Rodeo bd., 1983—; bd. dirs. Sheridan County Fair Bd., 1991-96, treas., 1995—; bd. dirs. "Christmas in April" Sheridan County, 1992—, Cowboy Mus. of the West, 1998—; mem. WJTP Coun., Cheyenne, 1990-92; mem. adv. coun. Tutor-Literacy Vols. of Am., 1993—; Sheridan High Sch. Key Club sponsor, 1994—; Sheridan Jr. High Sch. Builders Club sponsor, 1996—; City of Sheridan CVB bd., 1996—; Mrs. Santa Claus for local groups; vol. coord. AIDS Quilt; local chmn. March of Dimes Walkamerica, 1997—; mem. steering com. Ronald McDonald House. Named Person of Week, Sheridan County Cmty., 1998. Mem. Wyo. Assn. Broadcasters, S.C.C. of C. (bd. 1988—, pres. 1989-91, 97-98), UMWA Aux. (pres. 1982-89), Kiwanis (v.p. 1992—, pres.-elect 1993, pres. 1994), S.C. Ambassadors (pres. 1995-96), Ft. Phil Kearney/Bozeman Trail (bd. dirs. 1995—). Republican. Christian Ch. Office: Best We Sheridan Ctr PO Box 4008 Sheridan WY 82801-1208

TAYLOR, KENDRICK JAY, microbiologist; b. Manhattan, Mont., Mar. 17, 1914; s. William Henry and Rose (Carney) T.; BS, Mont. State U., 1938; postgrad. (fellow) U. Wash., 1938-41, U. Calif. at Berkeley, 1952, Drama Studio of London, 1985; m. Hazel Marguerite Griffith, July 28, 1945; children: Stanley, Paul, Richard. Rsch. microbiologist Cutter Labs., Berkeley, Calif., 1945-74; microbiologist Berkeley Biologicals, 1975-86. Committeeman Mount Diablo coun. Boy Scouts Am., 1955, dist. vice-chmn., 1960-61, dist. chmn., 1962-65, cubmaster, 1957, scoutmaster, 1966; active Contact Ministries, 1977-80; bd. dirs. Santa Clara Community Players, 1980-84; vol. instr. English as a Second Lang., 1979-80; vol. ARC Blood Ctr., VA Hosp., San Jose; life mem. PTA; census taker, 1980; mem. Berkly Jr. C. of C., 1946-49. Served with AUS, 1941-46, lt. col. Res., ret. Recipient Scout's Wood badge Boy Scouts Am., 1962; recipient Golden Diploma Mont. State U., 1988, Silver Diploma, 1998. Mem. Am. Soc. Microbiology (chmn. local com. 1953, v.p. No. Calif. br. 1963-65, pres. 1965-67), Sons and Daus. Mont. Pioneers, Mont. State Univ. Alumni Assn., Mont. Hist. Soc., Gallatin County Hist. Soc., Headwaters-Heritage Hist. Soc., Am. Legion Post 89, Parent-Tchrs. Assn. Calif. (life) Presbyterian (trustee 1951-53, elder 1954—). Home: 550 S 13th St San Jose CA 95112-2361

TAYLOR, LEIGH HERBERT, college dean; b. Chgo., Oct. 23, 1941; s. Herbert and Leona Taylor; m. Nancy E. Young; children: Jennifer, Jeremiah. BA, U. Tulsa, 1964, JD, 1966; LLM, NYU, 1969. Bar: Okla. 1966, Ill. 1976. Trial atty. Civil Rights div. Dept. Justice, Washington, 1966-68; prof. DePaul U. Coll. Law, Chgo., 1969-77; asst. dean DePaul U. Coll. Law, 1972-73; assoc. dean, 1973-77; dean Coll. Law, Ohio No. U., Ada, 1977-78, Sch. Law Southwestern U., L.A., 1978—; mem. adv. bd. 1st Woman's Bank of Calif. U. L.A. 1981-85; dir. Law Sch. Admissions Svcs., Inc., 1982-86; chmn. audit com. Law Sch. Admissions Coun., 1989-91, trustee, 1991-98, chair-elect, 1994-95, chair, 1995-97; mem. bd. trustees Coun. on Legal Edn. Opportunity, 1993-96. Editor-in-chief Tulsa Law Jour., 1966; author: Strategies for Law-Focused Education, 1977; (with others) Law in a New Land, 1972; mem. editorial bd. Family Law Quarterly, 1977-78. Bd. dirs. Criminal Def. Consortium Cook County (Ill.), Inc., 1975-77, L.A. Press Club Found. With AUS, 1959. Fellow Am. Bar Found.; mem. ABA (accreditation com. 1991-95), Law in Am. Soc. Found., Ill. Bar Assn., Chgo. Bar Assn. (rec. sec.), L.A. County Bar Assn., Okla. Bar Assn. Office: Southwestern U Sch Law Office of Dean 675 S Westmoreland Ave Los Angeles CA 90005-3905

TAYLOR, LESLIE GEORGE, mining and financial company executive; b. London, Oct. 8, 1922; came to U.S., 1925; s. Charles Henry and Florence Louisa (Renouf) T.; m. Monique S. Schuster, May, 1964 (div. 1974); children: Leslie G. Anthony II, Sandra J. Mira, Linda S. Marshall; m. Wendy Ann Ward, July 4, 1979. BBA, U. Buffalo, 1952. Asst. to pres. Kelsey Co., 1952-60; pres. Aluminum Industries and Glen Alden Co., Cin. and N.Y.C., 1960-63; pres., chmn. bd. dirs. DC Internat. (and European subs.), Denver, 1963-68; prin. Taylor Energy Enterprises, Denver, 1968—, Taylor Mining Enterprises, Denver, 1968—; Leslie G. Taylor and Co., Denver, 1968—; dir., pres. Internat. Global Health, Inc., Boulder, Colo., Can., 1998—; del. Internat. Astronautical Soc., Stockholm, 1968, London, 1969, Speditur Conv., 1976; bd. dirs. AlFresh Foods, Merendon Mining Internat., Calgary, Alta. Mem. USCG Aux. Mem. Soc. Automotive Engrs., Denver Country Club, Shriners, Masons, Scottish Rites. Republican. Episcopalian. Office: Global Health Inc 5031 S Ulster Pkwy Ste 200 Denver CO 80237-2810

TAYLOR, LISA C., marketing professional; b. Montreal, Quebec, Can., June 17, 1966; came to U.S., 1994; d. Michael Christie and Clare Patricia (Cavanagh) T.; m. Jeffrey Mead Drummond, Aug. 4, 1990 (div. 1996). B in Journalism with hons., Carleton U., 1989. Prodr., acct. exec. Stonehaven Comm., Montreal, 1989-94; owner Infowest Travel, Moab, Utah, 1994-96; dir. devel. Canyonlands Field Inst., Moab, 1996—. Trustee KZMU Pub. Radio, Moab, 1995-96; trainer Superhost, Moab, 1995—; mem. adv. bd. Grand Co. Travel Coun., Moab, 1997—, Canyonlands Travel Region, Utah, 1997—. Recipient Silver Video Prodn. award Mercomm, 1991, Gold Video Prodn. award, 1992, Bronze Video Prodn. award Internat. Fest. Film and Video, 1993. Mem. Moab C. of C. (liaison 1997—), Nature Conservancy, Canyonlands Natural History Assn., Western Folklife Ctr. Avocations: hiking, tennis, writing, rafting, traveling. Office: Canyonlands Field Inst PO Box 68 Moab UT 84532-0068

TAYLOR, MINNA, lawyer; b. Washington, Jan. 25, 1947; d. Morris P. and Anne (Williams) Glushien; m. Charles Ellett Taylor, June 22, 1969; 1 child, Amy Caroline. BA, SUNY, Stony Brook, 1969; MA, SUNY, 1973; JD, U. So. Calif., 1977. Bar: Calif. 1977, U.S. Dist. Ct. (cen. dist.) Calif. 1978. Extern to presiding justice Calif. Supreme Ct., 1977; field atty. NLRB, L.A., 1977-82; dir. employee rels., legal svcs. Paramount Pictures Corp., L.A., 1982-85, v.p. employee rels. legal svcs., 1985-89; dir. bus. and legal affairs Wilshire Ct. Prodns., L.A., 1989-91; sr. counsel Fox Broadcasting Co., L.A., 1991-92, v.p. legal affairs, 1992-97, sr. v.p. legal affairs, 1997—. Editor notes and articles: U. So. Calif. Law Rev., 1976-77. Mentor MOSTE, L.A., 1986-87, 88-89; pres. Beverly Hills chpt. ACLU, L.A., 1985. Fellow ABA, Calif. State Bar (mem. copyright subcom. 1994-95), L.A. County Bar Assn.; mem. Beverly Hills Bar Assn., L.A. Bead Soc. (membership sec. 1992-94, mem. bd. dirs. 1994-95), Order of Coif. Office: Fox Broadcasting Co 10201 W Pico Blvd Los Angeles CA 90064-2606

TAYLOR, NIGEL BRIAN, financial planner; b. Winchester, June 17, 1953. Grad., Coll. Fin. Planning, Denver, 1993. Cert. Fin. Planner; lic. NASD Series 6, 7, 24; registered prin.; lic. to practice in European Cmty. Owner Family Trust Planners, domestic and internat. retirement, estate planning, asset protection, L.A. and Santa Monica, Calif., 1988—; mgr. Fin. Planning Expo '96, L.A. Author: Domestic and International Estate and Asset Protection for the Resident Alien, 1996, Ethical Considerations in Financial Planning the Practice Standards Debate, 1997; mem. editl. rev. bd. Jour. Fin. Planning. Mem. Santa Monica Bar (assoc.), Inst. CFPs (registered practitioner, bd. dirs., pres. L.A. Soc.). Office: 1011 4th St Apt 209 Santa Monica CA 90403-3843

TAYLOR, PETER VAN VOORHEES, advertising and public relations consultant; b. Montclair, N.J., Aug. 25, 1934; s. John Coard and Mildred (McLaughlin) T.; m. Janet Kristine Kirkebo, Nov. 4, 1978; 1 son, John Coard III. BA in English, Duke U., 1956. Announcer Sta. WQAM, Miami, 1956; announcer, music dir. Sta. KHVH, Honolulu, 1959-61; promotion mgr. Sta. KPEN, San Francisco, 1962; with Kaiser Broadcasting, 1962-74, GE Broadcasting Co., 1974-78; program/ops. mgr. Sta. KFOG, San Francisco, 1962-66; mgr. Sta. WXHR AM/FM, Cambridge, Mass., 1966-67; gen. mgr. Sta. WJIB, Boston, 1967-70; v.p., mgr. FM divsn. Kaiser Broadcasting, 1969-72; v.p., ag. mgr. Sta. KFOG, San Francisco, 1970-78; pres. Taylor Comms., 1978-90, 97—, Baggott & Taylor, Inc., 1990-91, Taylor Advt. & Pub. Rels., 1991-96, Nov. 1998. Broadcasters Assn., 1974-76, [illegible] Broadcasters Assn., 1982-84, KCRH Chabot Coll., 1982-93, San Francisco Boys & Girls Club, 1991-93, Coast Guard Found., 1991—, Leukemia Soc., San Francisco, [illegible]. [illegible] and Long Wave Radio Clubs, Worldwide TV/FM Dx Assn., Rotary

(San Francisco - bd. dirs. 1988-93, 94-95, 1st v.p. 1990-91, pres. 1991-92, dist. 5150 - pub. rels. chmn. 1986-89, conf. chmn. 1990, area rep. 1992-93, dist. gov. nom., 1995-96), Golden Gate Breakfast Club (bd. dirs. 1995-96, v.p. 1995-96). Lt. USCGR, 1957-63. Home and Office: 6002 Bayview Dr NE Tacoma WA 98422-1227

TAYLOR, PHILIP CRAIG, physics educator; b. Paterson, N.J., Mar. 17, 1942; s. Philip D. and Elizabeth (Erdman) T.; m. Muriel Allison Taylor, Dec. 20, 1969; children: Allison L., Heather M. AB, Carleton Coll., 1964; PhD, Brown U., 1969. Research physicist Naval Research Lab., Washington, 1971-80, supervisory research physicist, 1980-82; prof. physics U. Utah, Salt Lake City, 1982—, chmn. dept. physics, 1989-98, assoc. dir. laser inst., 1987-98, dir. laser inst., 1998—. Fellow Am. Phys. Soc.; mem. AAAS, Materials Rsch. Soc., Am. Assn. Physics Tchrs. Office: U Utah Dept Physics Salt Lake City UT 84112

TAYLOR, REESE HALE, JR., lawyer, former government administrator; b. Los Angeles, May 6, 1928; s. Reese Hale and Kathryn (Emery) T.; m. Lucille Langdon, Dec. 29, 1948 (div. 1959); children: Reese Hale (dec.), Stuart Langdon, Anne Kathryn, Lucille Emery; m. Jolene Yerby, June 30, 1972. B.A. with distinction, Stanford U., 1949; LL.B., Cornell U., 1952. Bar: Calif. 1954, Nev. 1966. Assoc. Gibson, Dunn & Crutcher, Los Angeles, 1952-58; pvt. practice Los Angeles, 1958-65; assoc. Wiener, Goldwater & Galatz, Las Vegas, Nev., 1966-67; chmn. Nev. Pub. Service Commn., Carson City, 1967-71; ptnr. Laxalt, Berry & Allison, Carson City, 1971-78, Allison, Brunetti, MacKenzie & Taylor, Carson City, 1978-81; chmn. ICC, Washington, 1981-85; ptnr. Heron, Burchette, Ruckert & Rothwell, Washington, 1986-90, Taylor & Morell, Washington and Long Beach, Calif., 1990-91, Taylor, Morell & Gitomer, Washington and Long Beach, 1992-94; of counsel Keesal, Young & Logan, Long Beach, 1994—; vice chmn. Nev. Tax Commn., Carson City, 1967-69; mem. Nev. Gov.'s Cabinet, Carson City, 1967-70, Carson City Bd. Equalization, 1979-81, chmn., 1979-80; bd. dirs. U.S. Rail Assn., Washington, 1981-85. Del. Republican Nat. Conv., Kansas City, Mo., 1976, mem. platform com., 1976, alt. del., Detroit, 1980; mem. Rep. Nat. Com., 1980-81. Mem. ABA, Am. Judicature Soc., Cornell Club (N.Y.), Order of Coif, Phi Gamma Delta, Phi Delta Phi. Episcopalian. Office: Keesal Young & Logan Union Bank Bldg PO Box 1730 Long Beach CA 90801-1730

TAYLOR, RICHARD EDWARD, physicist, educator; b. Medicine Hat, Alta., Can., Nov. 2, 1929; came to U.S., 1952; s. Clarence Richard and Delia Alena (Brunsdale) T.; m. Rita Jean Bonneau, Aug. 25, 1951; 1 child, Norman Edward. B.S., U. Alta., 1950, M.S., 1952; Ph.D., Stanford U., 1962; Docteur honoris causa, U. Paris-Sud, 1980; DSc, U. Alta., 1991; LLD (hon.), U. Calgary, Alta., 1993; DSc (hon.), U. Lethbridge, Alta., 1993, U. Victoria, B.C., Can., 1994; Dr. honoris causa, U. Blaise Pascal, 1997. Boursier Lab. de l'Accelerateur Lineaire, Orsay, France, 1958-61; physicist Lawrence Berkeley Lab., Berkeley, Calif., 1961-62; staff mem. Stanford (Calif.) Linear Accelerator Ctr., 1962-68, assoc. dir., 1982-86, prof., 1968—. Fellow Guggenheim Found., 1971-72, von Humboldt Found., 1982; recipient Nobel prize in physics, 1990. Fellow AAAS, Am. Acad. Arts and Scis., Am. Phys. Soc. (W.K.H. Panofsky prize div. particles and fields 1989), Royal Soc. Can., Royal Soc. London; mem. Can. Assn. Physicists, Nat. Acad. Scis. (fgn. assoc.). Office: Stanford Linear Accelerator Ctr PO Box 4349 Stanford CA 94309-4349

TAYLOR, RUTH ANNE, lawyer; b. Honolulu, Feb. 18, 1961; d. Gerald Lou and Charlotte Anne (Nelson) Allison; m. Thomas Scott Taylor, Dec. 28, 1985; children: Kyle Thomas, Kelly Gerald, Kory Scott. BA in Journalism, U. So. Calif., 1984; JD, N.Y. Law Sch., 1987. Bar: Calif. 1987, U.S. Dist. Ct. (so. dist.) Calif., U.S. Ct. Appeals (9th cir.). Assoc. Carlsmith, Wichman, Case Mukai & Ichiki, L.A., L.A., 1987-89, Christensen, White, Miller, Fink & Jacobs, L.A., 1989-93; assoc. gen. counsel Warner Bros. Records, Inc., 1993-98, v.p. legal and bus. affairs, 1998—. Mem. Los Angeles County Bar Assn., Beverly Hills Bar Assn. Republican. Avocations: scuba diving, skiing, photography, cooking.

TAYLOR, STEVEN BRUCE, agriculture company executive; b. Salinas, Calif., Dec. 29, 1954; s. Edward Horton and Joanne (Church) T.; m. Kathryn Hagler, Dec. 17, 1978; children: Meghan Jean, Kyle Hagler, Christian Steven. BA, U. Calif., Berkeley, 1978; MBA, Harvard U., 1985. Pres. Fresh Concepts, San Marino, Calif., 1985-87; mktg. staff Bruce Church, Inc., Salinas, Calif., 1987-91; pres. Fresh Express Retail Mktg., Salinas, 1991-93; pres. Fresh Internat., Salinas, 1991-93, CEO, chmn., 1993—; v.p. Salinas Valley Lettuce Co-op, Salinas, 1990—; bd. dirs. Produce for Better Health, Del., 1991—. Bd. Elders First Presbyn. Ch., Salinas, 1989-92, personnel com. 1989-94, bldg. com. 1990—; founding mem. Lincoln Club of Monterey County, Salinas, 1990. Avocations: basketball, skiing, soccer coach, bible study, board games. Home: 515 Santa Paula Dr Salinas CA 93901-1517 Office: Fresh Internat 1020 Merrill St Salinas CA 93901-4409

TAYLOR, TIMOTHY TYRONE, artist; b. Kernersville, N.C., Aug. 15, 1960; s. Arwisters and Marline Deloris (Archie) T. BA, U. N.C., 1982; MDiv, Duke U., 1986. Gallery dir. African-Am. Hist. and Cultural Soc., San Francisco, 1991-92; curator Richmond (Calif.) Art Ctr., 1991-92; mus. technician San Francisco Internat. Airport Mus., 1996—; lectr. in field. Author numerous poems; one-man shows include Paul Gallery, Tokyo, Kato Gallery, Tokyo, Mary Lou William's Ctr. Gallery, Duke U.; group shows include St. Louis U. Mus. Cont. Religious Art and Bomani Gallery, San Francisco. Com. mem. San Francisco Sunshine Task Force, 1997; active San Francisco Art Commn. Artists Adv. Com., 1996—. Recipient 2d pl. Books, Inc. Poetry Contest, San Francisco, 1998. Home: 1005 Market St Ste 311 San Francisco CA 94103-1625

TAYLOR, WALTER WALLACE, lawyer; b. Newton, Iowa, Sept. 18, 1925; s. Carrol W. and Eva (Greenly) T.; A.A., Yuba Coll., 1948, A.B., 1950; M.A., U. Calif., 1955, J.D., McGeorge Coll. Law, 1962; m. Mavis A. Harvey, Oct. 9, 1948; children—Joshua Michael (dec. 1980), Kevin Eileen, Kristin Lisa, Jeremy Walter, Margaret Jane, Melissa E., Amy M. Adminstrv. analyst USAF, Sacramento, 1951-53; personnel, research analyst Calif. Personnel Bd., Sacramento, 1954-56; civil service, personnel analyst, chief counsel, gen. mgr. Calif. Employees Assn., Sacramento, 1956-75; staff counsel, chief profl. standards Calif. Commn. Tchr. Credentialing, 1975-88, ret. 1988; staff counsel State Office Real Estate appraiser Licensing and Certification, 1992-94, ret.; tchr. discipline civil service, personnel cons. Served USCGR, 1943-46. Mem. Calif. State Bar, Am., Sacramento County bar assns. Democrat. Author: Know Your Rights, 1963-64. Home: 4572 Fair Oaks Blvd Sacramento CA 95864-5336

TAYLOR, WILLIAM AL, state supreme court justice; b. Lusk, Wyo., Nov. 2, 1928; m. Jane Y.; 3 children. BA, U. Wyo., 1951, LLD, 1959. Bar: Wyo. 1959. Teacher Lusk, 1950-51,54-55, pvt. practice, 1959-78; city atty. Town of Lusk, 1962-74; atty. Niobrara County, Wyo., 1964-77; judge Wyo. Dist. Ct. (8th dist.), Cheyenne, 1980-93; justice Wyoming Supreme Ct., 1993—, chief justice, 1996-98; Exec. dir. Wyo. State Bar, 1977-80. Staff sgt. U.S. Army, 1951-53. Mem. Wyo. State Bar (Civil Rules com.), Wyo. Judicial Conf. (chmn. 1984-85),Tenth Cir. Bar Assn., Nat. Trial Judges, Am. Legion, Sigma Alpha Epsilon. Office: Wyo Supreme Ct Supreme Court Bldg 2301 Capitol Ave Cheyenne WY 82001-3644

TAYLOR, WILLIAM MALCOLM, environmentalist, educator, executive recruiter; b. South Hiram, Maine, June 18, 1933; s. William Myers and Gladys Marie (Weldy) T.; stepmother Edna (Tyson) Taylor; m. Carrie Mae Fiedler, Aug. 31, 1957 (div. Sept. 1980); children: William Stephan, Alyson Marie, Eric Fiedler; m. Elizabeth Van Horn, June 18, 1983. Student, George Sch., 1948-50; BA in Liberal Arts, Pa. State U., 1956; MEd, U. N.C., 1962. Instr. ESL Anatolia Coll., Am. Lang. Ctr., Salonica, Greece, 1956-58; tchr. biology-chemistry Coral Shores H.S., Tavernier, Fla., 1961-62; pk. naturalist Everglades Nat. Pk., Fla., 1962-65; tech. editor Nat. Pk. Svc., Washington, 1965-67; chief interpretation Canyonlands Nat. Pk., Utah, 1967-71; environ. edn. specialist western regional office Nat. Pk. Svc., Calif., 1971-77; dir. program devel. Living History Ctr., Novato, Calif., 1981-83; exec. recruiter, ptnr. Van Horn, Taylor & Assocs, Biotech-Biomed. Rsch., Santa Cruz, Calif., 1983-95, 98—; mem. 2d World Conf. on Nat. Parks and Equivalent Reserves, 10th Internat. Seminar on Nat. Parks, U.S., Can., Mex. Author: The Strands Walk, Exercises in Guided Inquiry for Children; founder, developer (with Sally Berlant) ednl. program Environ. Living Program, 1973 (Calif. Bicentennial Commn. award 1974, Don Perryman award Calif. Social Studies Coun., 1975, Nat. Bicentennial Adminstrn. sponsorship 1976). Bd. dirs. Novato Environ. Quality Com., 1973-76; mem. Calif. Conservation Com., 1973-76; mem. Utah Environ. Com., 1968-71, Internat. Sonoran Desert Alliance; vol. Ariz. Symphony Orch. Assn. Mem. Civil Air Patrol. Mem. Am. Bonanza Soc., Lighthawk, Flying Samaritans, Tucson Soaring Club, Wright Flight, Mensa, Phi Delta Kappa. Avocations: flying, birding, natural history. Home: 2321 S Circle X Pl Tucson AZ 85713-6703

TAYLOR BARDWELL, MARY-BETH ANNE, artist, sculptor; b. Glen Cove, N.Y., July 21, 1962; d. John Joseph and Anne Ruth (Robinson) Taylor; m. Tennyson Bardwell, Oct. 21, 1989; 1 child, Tennyson Taylor Bardwell. BA, Fashion Inst. Tech., SUNY, 1986. One-woman shows include Rose Café, Venice, Calif., 1996, 97, inkfish, Santa Monica, Calif., 1996, 97, Abbot's Habit, Venice, 1996, 97, The Palm, East Hampton, N.Y., 1997, 98, Coach Gallery, East Hampton, 1997, 98, Apple Bank, Sag Harbor, N.Y., 1998, Bank of N.Y., Montauk, N.Y., 1998, Caswell's, Montauk, 1998, Bridgehampton (N.Y.) Café, 1998; group exhibits include Guild Hall, East Hampton, 1998, Apple Bank, Sag Harbor, 1998, Gallery East, East Hampton, 1998, Chrysalis Gallery, Southampton, N.Y., 1998, 99; represented in numerous pvt. collections; various commd. pieces. Recipient Excellence award First St. Gallery, N.Y., 1995, Critics Pick award Manhattan Arts Internat., N.Y., 1995, Cover Art award Montauk Pioneer, N.Y., 1997. Mem. Montauk Art Assn. Home: PO Box 1901 Montauk NY 11954 also: 536 1/2 Altair Pl Venice CA 90291

TAYLOR-BROWN, CAMERON ANN, artist, educator, consultant; b. L.A., Oct. 2, 1953; d. James Hutton and Ann Rossner (Hinsdale) Taylor; m. Charles Albert Brown, July 8, 1978; children: Julia, Peter. Student, Vassar Coll., 1970-71; BA, U. Calif., Berkeley, 1975; BS, Phila. Coll. Textiles, 1977. Fabric stylist Cheney Bros., N.Y.C., 1977-79; design instr. Phila. Coll. Textiles, 1979-83; rsch. assoc., curator Goldie Paley Design Ctr., Phila., 1980-83; arist, educator Phila. and L.A., 1979—; regional rep. fibers L.A., 1983—; ednl. cons. ACCESS Cultural Liaison Svcs., L.A., 1997—; mem. com. Getty Edn. Inst./Fairfax Family Sch., L.A., 1997; lectr., workshop presenter Bobbinwinders, Creative Weavers Guild, the Shepherdess, South Coast Spinners and Weavers, So. Calif. Guild Handweavers. Artist, contbr. Fiberarts mag., 1985, 87, Fiberarts Design Book 4, 1991, Design Book 5, 1995, Shuttle, Spindle & Dyepot, 1997; exhbns. include Artspace Gallery, Woodland Hills, Calif., 1992, Del Mano Gallery, 1994, Downey Mus. Arts, 1995, Riverside Mus. Art, 1997. Mem. program devel. com., fundraiser, cmty. outreach com., grant writer Friends of Third St. Sch., L.A., 1989—, co-pres., 1997—. Recipient Woman of Larchmont Cmty. Svc. award Larchmont Chronicle, 1997. Mem. Textile Group L.A. (bd. dirs. 1984-90), Designing Weavers (Bd. dirs. 1992-95, 97-98), Calif. Fibers (regional liaison 1993—). Avocations: reading, gardening, travel, skiing.

TAZZA, DAVID ROBERT, editor; b. Pitts., Nov. 14, 1956; s. Albert Francis and Doris Mae (Huss) T. Grad. h.s., Pitts. Authorization for svc. cert. for vt. postsecondary schs., Calif. Instr. Computer Learning Ctr., Anaheim, Calif., 1982-84, Inst. Computer Tech., L.A., 1984-85; metal smith Anvil Arts, Anaheim, 1986-88; loan officer DP Fin., Orange, Calif., 1989-94; freelance writer Riverside (Calif.) Bus. Jour., 1996-98; editor Darnell Group, Norco, Calif., 1994-95, project coord., 1998—; editor multi-title news Darnell Group, 1994-96; advisor Riverside C.C., 1996-97; cons. editing various cos., Mira Loma, Calif., 1995-98. Contbr. articles to newspapers. Vol. Jurupa Alive, Riverside, 1997-98; vol. Jurupa Valley H.S., Mira Loma, 1995-96, band vol., 1996-98. Recipient Golden Poet award World of Poetry, 1991. Avocations: collecting pre-depression era textbooks, designing and building electric guitars.

TCHAICOVSKY, BENY, artist, musician; b. Rio de Janeiro, Brazil, Nov. 3, 1954; came to U.S., 1976; s. Jacob and Fany T. Owner, pres. Zoe Prodns., Fairfax, Calif., 1993-98; cons. Artnetwork Comms., Sausalito, Calif., 1994—. Composer record album Explorer, 1983; executed poster at Cannes Film Festival (first place award), 1996, 3D animation home video program, 1997. Recipient Gold Medal award Internat. Exhibition ABD, Rio, Brazil, 1982, Best of Show award Natsoulas Novelozo Gallery, Davis, Calif., 1988, Comendator of the Brazilian Assn. Fine Arts title, Rio, 1990, Hon. Mention award Eurographic's, 1998. Avocations: travel. E-mail: zoe@3dzoe.com. Fax: (415) 454-4925. Home and Office: 92 Piper Ln Fairfax CA 94930-1022

TEAGUE, DON, telecommunications company executive; b. Myrtle Springs, Tex., Aug. 20, 1942; s. Harold Davis and Laverne Syble (Griggers) T.; m. Janet Carol Leech, Aug. 11, 1962 (div. May 1972); m. Ginger Carroll Bernard, Jan. 8, 1977; children: Austin, Jonathan, Ginger. AA, Lon Morris Coll, Jacksonville, Tenn., 1962; BBA, U. Tex., 1964, LLB, 1966; LLB, Harvard U., 1967. Bar: Tex. 1966, N.Y. 1969, Colo. 1993. Asst. prof. law Rutgers U., Newark, N.J., 1967-69; assoc. Debevoise & Plimpton, New York, NY, 1969-70, Vinson & Elkins, Houston, 1970-94; sr. v.p. legal Falcon Seaboard Cos., Houston, 1994-97; exec. v.p. legal ICG Comm. Inc., Denver, 1997—. Mem. Denver C. of C. Home: 140 Downing St Denver CO 80218-3917 Office: ICG Comm Inc 161 Inverness Dr W Englewood CO 80112-5003

TEAGUE, JANE LORENE, lay worker; b. Brainerd, Minn., May 27, 1918; d. Willis Ernest and Ellenora Christine (Yde) Lively; m. Jasper Uriah Teague, Nov. 26, 1939; children: Jack, James, Janet. Grad., high sch. Pres. Women's Aux., L.A. Bapt. City Mission Soc., 1968-69; leadership devel. chairperson Am. Bapt. Women, 1969-70, conf. chairperson, 1971-75, v.p., program chmn., 1975-77, pres. Pacific S.W. region, 1980-83, pres. local ch., 1983-85; pres. Am. Bapt. Chs. of Pacific S.W., 1973, bd. mgrs., exec. com., chmn. bd. edn., 1975-76, also mem. nominating and camping coms., reps. from L.A. Bapt. Assn.; mem. gen. bd. Am. Bapt. Chs. in U.S.A., 1974—; moderator L.A. Assn., 1974—, mem. bd. nat. housing ministries, 1985—; mem. com. local arrangements, women's dept. Bapt. World Alliance, 1983-85; chairperson bd. edn. 1st Bapt. Ch., North Hollywood, Calif., 1985-95; mem. Prayer Task Force Am. Bapt. Chs. of Pacific S.W., 1990—, bd. mgrs., 1990—; program chairperson Children's Bapt. Home Aux., 1968-69; bd. dirs. Atherton Bapt. Homes, exec. search com., 1994; bd. dirs. Am. Bapt. Homes of West, Children's Bapt. Home, Inglewood, Calif.; White Cross chairperson L.A. Valley Assn., 1989-92. Pres. Am. Bapt. Women's Ministries 1st Bapt. Ch. Pasadena, 1997—, local chmn. Tng. Day, 1998—. Address: 1030 E Valencia Ave Burbank CA 91501-1551

TEAGUE, LAVETTE COX, JR., systems educator, consultant; b. Birmingham, Ala., Oct. 8, 1934; s. Lavette Cox and Caroline Green (Stokes) T.; student Auburn U., 1951-54; B.Arch., MIT, 1957, M.S.C.E., 1965, Ph.D., 1968; MDiv with distinction Ch. Div. Sch. Pacific, 1979. Cert. computer profl. Inst. Cert. of Computer Profls. Archtl. designer Carroll C. Harmon, Birmingham, 1957, Fred Renneker, Jr., Birmingham, 1958-59; architect Rust Engrng. Co., Birmingham, 1959-62, Synergetics, Inc., Raleigh, N.C., 1962-64, Rust Engrng. Co., Birmingham, 1964-68; research asst., inst., research assoc. MIT, Cambridge, 1964-68; dir. computer services Skidmore, Owings & Merrill, San Francisco, Chgo., 1968-74; postdoctoral fellow UCLA, 1972; adj. assoc. prof. architecture and civil engrng. Carnegie-Mellon U., Pitts., 1973-74; archtl. systems cons., Chgo., 1974-75, Berkeley, Calif., 1975-80, Pasadena, Calif., 1980-82, Altadena, Calif., 1982—; lectr. info. systems Calif. State Poly. U., Pomona, 1980-81, prof., 1981—, asst. chair, 1990-91, chair, 1991-93, 96-98. Fulbright lectr., Uruguay, 1985. Co-author: Structured Analysis Methods for Computer Information Systems, 1985. Recipient Tucker-Voss award M.I.T., 1967; Fulbright scholar, 1985. Mem. AIA (Arnold W. Brunner scholar 1966), Assn. Computing Machinery, Sigma Xi, Phi Eta Sigma, Scarab, Scabbard and Blade, Tau Beta Pi, Chi Epsilon, Beta Gamma Sigma. Episcopalian. Home: 1696 N Altadena Dr Altadena CA 91001-3623 Office: 3801 W Temple Ave Pomona CA 91768-2557

TECSON, HERMINIGILDO LISARONDO, sculptor, painter; b. Manila, Philippines, Apr. 6, 1950; came to U.S., 1979; s. Marcelino Ermita and Generosa T.; m. Lorna Abdon, July 27, 1994. BFA, U. East Sch. Fine Arts, Manila, 1972; student, Calif. State U., Long Beach, 1980-82, Otis Parson Sch. Art, 1983-85. Pvt. practice Calif. Paintings published in Am. References Calif. Art Review, 1988, Encyclopedia of the Living Artist in Am., 1993; one-man shows include Hermila Art Gallery, Long Beach, Calif., 1987, the Brix Gallery, Makati, Philippines, 1992; group shows include Silangan Art Gallery, Manila, 1975, 76, Mus. Philippine Art, 1977, Rear Room Gallery, Manila, 1979, C.F. Pablo & Sons Gallery, Manila, 1980, Hermila Art Gallery, Long Beach, 1986, 87, 88, Philippine Art Guild, Glendale, Calif., 1992, Glendale Galleria, 1993, others. Recipient First prize Long Beach (Calif.) Art Assn., 1984, First prize Art from the Heart of Cmty., Lakewood, Calif., 1984. Mem. Internat. Sculpture Ctr. Roman Cath. Office: Willow Art Gallery 1418 W Willow St Long Beach CA 90810-3119

TEDARDS, DOUGLAS MANNING, English language educator; b. Greenville, S.C., Feb. 12, 1944; s. Connor and Adair (Manning) T.; m. Judy Lynn Tillotson, June 5, 1976; children: Morgan, Mandy, Colin, Ryan. BA, Vanderbilt U., 1966; MA, U. Fla., 1968; D of Arts, U. Pacific, 1976. Instr. Paine Coll., Augusta, Ga., 1970-72; lectr. U. Calif., Santa Barbara, 1978-81; assoc. prof. U. of the Pacific, Stockton, Calif., 1982—; mem. adv. bd. Calif. Writing Project, Berkeley, 1994—. Contbr. poetry to mags., revs. Fellow NEH, 1985. Democrat. Avocations: golf, poetry readings. Office: U of the Pacific 3601 Pacific Ave Stockton CA 95211-0110

TEDFORD, CHARLES FRANKLIN, biophysicist; b. Lawton, Okla., June 26, 1928; s. Charles E. and Loula B. (Waters) T.; m. Julie Reme Sauret, Sept. 15, 1951; children: Gary Franklin, Mark Charles, Philip John. BS with distinction in Chemistry, S.W. Tex. State U., 1950, MS, 1954; postgrad. in radiobiology Reed Coll., 1957, in biophysics U. Calif., Berkeley, 1961-63. Enlisted USN, 1945-47, commd. ensign, 1950, advanced through grades to capt., 1968; biochemist U.S. Naval Hosp., San Diego, 1953-54, U.S. Naval Biol. Lab., Oakland, Calif., 1954-56; sr. instr., radiation safety officer Nuclear, Biol. and Chem. Warfare Def. Sch., Treasure Island, Calif., 1956-61; asst. chief nuclear medicine div. Navy Med. Sch., Bethesda, Md., 1963-66; adminstrv. program mgr. radiation safety br. Bur. Medicine and Surgery, Washington, 1966-72; dir. radiation safety and health physics program Navy Regional Med. Center, San Diego, 1972-74; mgr. Navy Regional Med. Clinic, Seattle, 1974-78, ret., 1978; dir. radiation health unit Ga. Dept. Human Resources, Atlanta, 1978-79; dir. Ariz. Radiation Regulatory Agy., Tempe, 1979-91; chief, Radiological Health Prog., Juneau, Alaska, 1991-93, ret. 1993; cons. 1993—. elected chmn. Conf. Radiation Program Dirs., 1987; named Ariz. Southwestern Low Level Radioactive Waste Compact Commr., 1990. Recipient Ariz. Adminstr. of Yr. award Ariz. Adminstrs. Assn., 1988; decorated Legion of Merit, Meritorious Service medal. Mem. Health Physics Soc., Am. Nuclear Soc. Contbr. articles on radiation safety to profl. publs.

TEDFORD, JACK NOWLAN, III, construction executive, small business owner; b. Reno, Jan. 1, 1943; s. Jack Nowlan Jr. and Elizabeth (Kolhoss) T.; m. Nancy Joanne Stiles, Feb. 27, 1971; children: Jack Nowlan IV, James Nathan. BS, U. Nev., 1966, MBA, 1969. Bus. mgr. Los Angeles Bapt. Coll., Newhall, Calif., 1969-71; v.p. Jack N. Tedford, Inc., Fallon, Nev., 1971-98; owner/broker Tedford Realty, Fallon, 1974-94; owner/mgr. Tedford Bus. Systems, Fallon, 1978-94; pres. JNT, Inc., Fallon, 1994—; pres., Jack N. Tedford, Inc., 1998—. Author numerous computer programs. Mem. Selective Svc. Local Bd., Fallon, 1971-76; chmn. City of Fallon Bd. Adjustment, 1975-95, chmn. Churchill Co. Reps., Fallon, 1976-80; mem. ctrl. com. Nev. Reps., 1976—; del. Nat. Conv., Detroit, 1980, Dallas, 1984; former coun. ofcls. Western Nev. Devel. Dist.; former treas. Lahontan Valley Environ. Alliance. Mem. Assn. Gen. Contractors (pres., former v.p., treas. Nev. chpt., nat. dir.), Nat. Bd. Realtors, State Bd. Realtors, Fallon Bd. Realtors, CEDA Bus. Coun. (formerly mem. bd. dirs.), Nev. Motor Transport Assn., Nat. Asphalt Pavement Assn. (quality improvement com.), Rotary (bd. dirs. 1969-71), Master's Coll. (bd. dirs. 1971-95), Slavic Gospel Assn. (bd. dirs. 1995—), Nat. Assn. Gen. Contractors (open shop com., closely held bus. com.), Fellowship of Cos. for Christ Internat. Republican. Baptist. Avocations: skiing, computers, family activities, golf. Home: 115 N Bailey St Fallon NV 89406-2720 Office: 235 E Williams Ave Fallon NV 89406-3027

TEEL, JOYCE, supermarket and drugstore retail executive; b. 1930. Dir. Raley's, West Sacramento, 1950—; co-chmn., 1991—. Office: Raleys & Belaire 500 W Capitol Ave West Sacramento CA 95605*

TEERLINK, J(OSEPH) LELAND, real estate developer; b. Salt Lake City, July 16, 1935; s. Nicholas John and Mary Luella (Love) T.; student U. Utah, 1953-55; m. Leslie Dowdle, Nov. 5, 1975; children: Steven, David, Andrew, Suzanne, Benjamin. Sales rep. Eastman Kodak Co., Salt Lake City, 1960-69; founder Graphic Systems, Inc., Salt Lake City, 1969-82, pres., 1969-79, chmn. bd., 1979-82; founder Graphic Ink Co., Salt Lake City, 1973, pres., 1975-79, chmn. bd., 1979-82; founder G.S.I. Leasing Co., Salt Lake City, 1975, pres., 1975-82; chmn. bd. Graphic Systems Holding Co., Inc., Salt Lake City, 1978-82; dir. leasing and acquisitions Terra Industries, Inc., real estate developers, 1982-86, ptnr., 1986—; bd. dirs. ARC, Salt Lake City, 1979-82; co-founder, dir. Hope Living Ctr. Found. for Mothers and Children, 1993—; vice consulate of the Netherlands for Utah, 1977-92; mem. active corps of execs., SBA, 1979-83; mem. adv. bd. House of Hope Mothers and Children Utah Alcoholism Found., 1992-94. Recipient Masters award Salt Lake Bd. Realtors, 1993; named Small Businessman of the Yr. for Utah, SBA, 1978. Mem. Graphic Arts Equipment and Supply Dealers of Am. (dir. 1978-82), Printing Industry of Am., Nat. Assn. Indsl. and Office Parks (pres. Utah chpt., 1986-87), Nat. Fedn. Ind. Businessmen, Million Dollar Club (life). Republican. Mormon. Home: 2984 Thackeray Pl Salt Lake City UT 84108-2517 Office: 6925 Union Park Ctr Midvale UT 84047-4142

TEETERS, DOROTHY IRENE, book store administrator; b. San Francisco, Mar. 2, 1962; d. John LeRoy Dunlap and Carole Ann (Murphy) Bratton; m. Vaughn A. Teeters, Oct. 1 1994. BS in Mktg., U. Nev., 1986. Media buyer Dunn Draper-Glenn Marz, Reno, 1986-88; store mgr. Walden Books, Silverdale, Wash., 1988-92; asst. mgr. T. J. Maxx, Federal Way, Wash., 1992-96; employment cons. Bus. Careers, Tacoma, Wash., 1996-97; store mgr. Armchair Books, Port Orchard, Wash., 1997—. Campaign worker Barbara Vucanovich for Congress, Reno, 1986-88. Mem. Am. Mktg. Assn., Literacy Coun. Kitsap (bd. dirs., fundraising com. 1997—). Reno Women in Advt. (bd. dirs. 1987-88), Pacific N.W. Booksellers Assn., Internat. Soc. Folk Harpers and Craftsmen (Orca chpt. pres. 1997—). Avocations: harpist, choir member, historical recreationist. Home: PO Box 488 Wauna WA 98395-0488 Office: Armchair Books 1700 SE Mile Hill Dr Ste 202 Port Orchard WA 98366-3553

TEETS, JOHN WILLIAM, retired diversified company executive; b. Elgin, Ill., Sept. 15, 1933; s. John William and Maudie Teets; m. Nancy Kerchenfaut, June 25, 1965; children: Jerri, Valerie Sue, Heidi Jayne, Suzanne. Student, U. Ill.; LLD (hon.), Trinity Coll., 1982; DBA in Foodsvc. Mgmt. (hon.), Johnson and Wales U., 1991; D in Comml. Sci. (hon.), Western Internat. U., 1992. Pres., ptnr. Winter Garden Restaurant, Inc., Carpenterville, Ill., 1957-63; v.p. Greyhound Food Mgmt. Co.; pres. Post Houses, Inc., and Horne's Enterprises, Chgo., 1964-68; pres., chief operating officer John R. Thompson Co., Chgo., 1968-71; pres., corp. v.p. pub. restaurant divsn. Canteen Corp., Chgo., 1971-75; divsn. pres. Jacques Restaurant Group, 1975; exec. v.p., CEO Bonanza Internat. Co., Dallas, 1975; group v.p. food svcs., pres. Greyhound Food Mgmt., Inc. (now named Restaura), Phoenix, 1975; vice chmn. The Greyhound Corp., Phoenix, 1980; chmn., CEO Greyhound Corp. (now The Dial Corp), Phoenix, 1981-96; chmn., pres., CEO The Dial Corp, Phoenix, 1996-97; vice chmn. Pres.' Conf. on Foodservice Industry. Recipient Silver Plate award, Golden Plate award Internat. Foodsvc. Mgrs. Assn., 1980, Bus. Leadership award Harvard Bus. Sch. Club Ariz., 1985, Order of the Crown, Kingdom of Belgium, 1990, Ellis Island medal of honor Nat. Ethnic Coalition of Orgns. Found., 1995; named Top Bus. Spkr. of Yr., Forbes Mag., 1990, Capt. of Achievement, Acad. of Achievement, 1992, CEO of Yr., Leaders Mag., 1986. Mem. Nat. Inst. Foodsvc. Industry (trustee), Am. Mgmt. Assn., Christian Businessmen's Assn. (chmn. steering com. 1977). Office: JW Teets Enterprises LLC 1850 N Central Ave Phoenix AZ 85004-4527

TEETS, WALTER RALPH, accounting educator; b. Boulder, Colo., Oct. 1, 1950; s. Otis E. and Elsie (Purchase) T.; m. Mary Anne Clougherty. B in Music Edn., U. Colo., 1973; MMus, U. Wis., Madison, 1976; MS in Edn., U. Wis., Whitewater, 1981, MS in Acctg., 1985; PhD, U. Chgo., 1989. CPA. Asst. prof. Wash. U., St. Louis, 1986-89, U. Ill., Urbana-Champaign, Ill., 1989-94, Gonzaga U., Spokane, Wash., 1994—; continuing profl. edn. spkr. Gonzaga U., 1996-99. Contbr. articles to profl. jours. Acad. acctg. fellow Office of Chief Acct., U.S. SEC, 1997-98. Mem. Am. Acctg. Assn., K.C.

(fin. sec. 1990-93). Avocations: music, cross-country skiing, four-wheeling. Office: Gonzaga Univ 502 E Boone Ave Spokane WA 99258

TEGUH, COLLIN, osteopathic physician, educator; b. Medan, Indonesia, Aug. 25, 1957; s. Tonga and Tsit Wati (Salim) T.; m. Lisa Hom; children: Justen W., Branden C., Brittany Lisa. BA, U. Calif. San Diego, 1983; DO, U. Osteo. Medicine Des Moines, 1991. Rsch. asst. Scripp Meml. and Whittier Inst. for Endocrinology & Diabetes, LaJolla, Calif., 1983-87, U. Osteo. Medicine and Health Scis., Des Moines, 1988-90; intern, resident San Bernardino (Calif.) County Med. Ctr., 1991-93; pvt. practice San Diego, 1999—; asst. clin. prof. U. Calif. San Diego, LaJolla, 1995—, Coll. Osteo. Medicine, Pomona, Calif., 1995—. Contbr. articles to profl. jours. Mem. Am. Osteo. Assn., Am. Acad. Family Physician, San Diego Osteo. Med. Assn. (exec. bd.), San Diego Acad. Family Physicians, U. Calif. San Diego Alumni Assn., U. Osteo. Medicine and Health Scis. Alumni Assn. Avocations: snorkeling, hiking, reading, horticulture, travel. Office: North Park Med Ctr 3780 El Cajon Blvd San Diego CA 92105-1033

TEHRANI, FLEUR TAHER, electrical engineer, educator, researcher; b. Tehran, Iran, Feb. 16, 1956; came to U.S., 1984; d. Hassan and Pourandokht (Monfared) T.; m. Akbar E. Torbat, June 16, 1997. BS in Elec. Engring., Arya-Mehr U. of Tech., Tehran, 1975; DIC in Comm. Engring., Imperial Coll. Sci. and Tech., London, 1977; MSc in Comm. Engring., U. London, 1977, PhD in Elec. Engring., 1981. Registered profl. engr., Calif. Comm. engr. Planning Orgn. of Iran, Tehran, 1977-78; lectr. A elec. engring. Robert Gordon's Inst. Tech., Aberdeen, U.K., 1982-83; lectr. II elec. engring. South Bank U., London, 1984; asst. prof. elec. engring. Calif. State U., Fullerton, 1985-91, assoc. prof. elec. engring., 1991-94, prof. elec. engring., 1994—; vis. assoc. prof. elec. engring. Drexel U., Phila., 1987-88; sys. cons. Telebit Corp., Cupertino. Calif., 1985; engring. cons. PRD, Inc., Dresher, Pa., 1989-92; mem. NASA/Am. Soc. Engring. Edn. summer faculty Jet Propulsion Lab., Calif. Inst. Tech., Pasadena, 1995, 96. Contbr. articles to profl. jours.; patentee in field. Recipient Best Ann. Rsch. Manuscript award Assn. for the Advancement of Med. Instrumentation, 1993, NASA/Am. Soc. Engring. Edn. Recognition award for rsch. contbns., 1995, 96, Outstanding Recognition award for creative and scholarly activities Calif. State U., Fullerton, 1998. Mem. IEEE, Women in Sci. and Engring. (chair Calif. State U. chpt. 1990-91), Assn. Profs. and Scholars of Iranian Heritage (pres. 1991-92), Sigma Delta Epsilon. Avocations: music, literature, poetry, stamp collecting. Office: Calif State U Dept Elec Engring 800 N State College Blvd Fullerton CA 92831-3547

TEHRANIAN, MAJID, political economy and communications educator; b. Iran, Mar. 22, 1937; m. Katharine Kia; children: Terrence, Yalda, John, Maryam. BA in Govt., Dartmouth Coll., 1959; MA in Middle Eastern Studies, Harvard U., 1961, PhD in Polit. Economy and Govt., 1969. Asst. prof. econs. Lesley Coll., 1964-69; assoc. prof. polit. sci. New Coll. U. South Fla., 1969-71; dir. social planning Plan Orgn. of Iran, 1971-72; sr. analyst, dir. rsch. Indsl. Mgmt. Inst., 1972-74; dir. prospective planning project Nat. Iranian Radio & TV, 1974-75; prof., founding dir. Iran Communications & Devel. Inst., 1976-78; program specialist communication planning and studies Div. Devel. of Communication Systems UNESCO, Paris, 1979-80; fellow Communication Inst., East West Ctr., 1981-82; chair dept. communication U. Hawaii, Manoa, 1986-88, prof. dept. communication, 1981—, dir. Matsunaga Inst. Peace, 1990-92, dir. Toda Inst. Global Peace Policy Rsch., 1996—; vis. scholar Inst. for Communication Rsch., Stanford U., 1977; vis. fellow St. Anthony's Coll., Oxford U., 1978-79; vis. scholar Ctr. for Internat. Affairs MIT, 1980-81, Can., U.S. and USSR universities, 1988; rsch. affiliate Ctr. for Middle Eastern Studies, Harvard U., 1980-81; vis. prof. dept. govt. Harvard Summer Sch., 1989-90; dir.-elect and dir. Inst. for Peace, U. Hawaii, coun. and exec. com., 1986—; rsch. fellow Social Sci. Rsch. Inst., U. Hawaii, Manoa, 1982-83, 84-86; lectr. in field. Author: Towards a Systematic Theory of National Development, 1974, Socio-Economic and Communications Indicators in Development Planning, 1981, Technologies of Power, 1990; co-author: The Middle East: Its Government and Politics, 1972, The Global Context of the Formation of Domestic Communications Policies, 1975, Policy Towards Social Sciences in Asia and Oceania, 1978, Worlds Apart: Human Securityand Global Goverance, 1999, Asia Peace: Security and Goverance in the Asia Pacific Region, 1999, Global Communication and World Politics, 1999, Choose Dialogue, 1999; editor: Communications Policy for Development, 1977, Letters from Jerusalem, 1990, Deconstructing Paradise: Dependency, Development and Discourse in Hawaii, 1990, Peace and Policy; co-editor: Restructuring for World Peace: On the Threshold of the 21st Century, 1992, World Apart: Human Security and Global Governance, 1999, Asian Peace: Security and Governance in the Asia-Pacific Region, 1999, Choose Dialogue, 1999; contbr. articles to profl. jours.; reviewer in field. Scholar Dartmouth Coll., 1955-59, Fujio Matsuda scholar, 1990-91; Jane Addams Peace Found. fellow, 1961, Ford Found. fellow Harvard U., 1959-61, fellow St. Anthony's Coll., Oxford, 1978-79, fellow East West Ctr. Communication Isnt., 1977, 81, 82; rsch. grantee Social Sci. Rsch. Inst., U. Hawaii, Manoa, 1982-85, UNESCO rsch. grantee, 1983-84, Can. Studies Faculty Enrichment grantee, 1988, Hawaii Interactive TV System Curriculum Devel. grantee, 1989; recipient Dartmouth Colby & Grimez Prizes, 1959, Excellence in Teaching award 1989, Soka U. award of highest honor, Disting. Svc. award Assn. Edn. in Journalism and Mass Communication, 1998. Fellow World Acad. Art & Sci.; mem. Internat. Inst. Communications (bd. trustees 1979-81), Internat. Communication Assn. (conf. theme chair for Asia 1989), Pacific Telecommunication Coun., Middle East Studies Assn. N.Am., Middle East Econs. Assn. (nat. adv. bd.), Soc. for Iranian Studies (founding exec. sec. 1967-71), Worldview Internat. Found. Avocations: swimming, tennis, chess, poetry. Home: 2627 Manoa Rd Honolulu HI 96822-1767 Office: U Hawaii Dept Communication Honolulu HI 96822 also: Toda Inst 1600 Kapiolani Blvd Ste 1111 Honolulu HI 96814-3806

TEIRSTEIN, PAUL SHEPHERD, physician, health facility administrator; b. N.Y.C., July 5, 1955; s. Alvin Stanley and Alice Teirstein. BA in Biology, Vassar Coll., 1976; MD, CUNY, 1980. Diplomate Am. Bd. Internal Medicine and Cardiovascular Diseases. With Lab. of Vision Rsch. NIH, Bethesda, Md., 1977-79; intern and resident Brigham & Women's Hosp., Boston, 1980-83; fellow in cardiology Stanford (Calif.) U., 1983-86; fellow in advanced coronary angioplasty Mid-Am. Heart Inst., Kansas City, Mo., 1986-87; fellow in stents, artherectomy and lasers NIH, Bethesda, 1987; dir. interventional cardiology Scripps Clinic and Rsch. Found., La Jolla, Calif., 1987—; presenter at Am. Coll. Cardiology, 1987-94, Am. Heart Assn., 1990-93, The French Hosp., San Luis Obispo, Calif., 1989, St. Luke's Med. Ctr., Phoenix, 1989, Cardiology for the Cons., Rancho Santa Fe, 1989, U. Calif., Irvine, 1989, ACP, Scottsdale, Ariz., 1989, Presbyn. Hosp., Whittier, Calif, 1989, St. Jude Med. Ctr., Fullerton, Calif., 1990, Oscala Med. Ctr., Osaka, Japan, 1992, Cedars-Sinai Med. Ctr., L.A., 1993, European Congress of Cardiology, Nice, France, 1993, Tokyo U., 1993, Lenox Hill Hosp., N.Y., 1993, Japanese Soc. Internat. Cardiology, 1994, Nat. Hindu Hosp., Bombay, 1994, G.B. Pant Hosp., Delhi, India, 1994, Escort's Hosp., 1994, B.M. Birla Hosp., Calcutta, 1994, Shaare Zedek Med. Ctr., Jerusalem, 1994, XV Gongresso da Sociedad de Cardiology de Sao Paulo, Ribeirao Preto, Brazil, 1994, and others. Grantee NSF, 1975. Fellow Am. Coll. Cardiology, Assn. for Rsch. in Vision and Ophthalmology, Beta Beta Beta, Alpha Omega Alpha. Office: Scripps Clinic & Rsch Found 10666 N Torrey Pines Rd La Jolla CA 92037-1092

TEITELBAUM, LEE E., dean; b. New Orleans, La., Nov. 4, 1941. BA magna cum laude, Harvard Coll., 1963; LLB, Harvard U., 1966; LLM, Northwestern U., 1968. Bar: Ill. Staff atty. Chgo. Lawyer Project, 1966-68; asst. prof. law U. N.D., 1968-70; assoc. prof. law SUNY, Buffalo, 1970-73; vis. assoc. prof. law U. N.Mex. Law Sch., 1972, assoc. prof. law, 1973-74, prof. law, 1974-87; prof. law, dir. Ctr. for the Study of Legal Policy Relating to Children Ind. U. Law Sch., 1980-81, vis. prof., 1987; vis. prof. U. Utah Coll. Law, 1985, prof. law, 1986—, assoc. dean acad. affairs, 1987-90, acting dean, 1988, dean, 1990-98, Alfred C. Emery prof. law, 1994—; fellow legal history program U. Wis., Madison, 1984; mem. test audit subcom. Law Sch. Admissions Coun. Author: (with A. Gough) Beyond Control: Status Offenders in the Juvenile Court, 1977 (with W.V. Stapleton) In Defense of [illegible] articles to profl. jours.; bd. editors Law & Soc. Rev., 1982-87, Law & Policy, Jour. Legal Edn., 1990-92. Fellow ABA (reporter ABA-IJA project on standards for juvenile justice, standards relating to the role of counsel for pvt. parties 1979); mem. Law & Soc. Assn. (bd. trustees 1977-80), Utah Minority Bar Assn. (award), Assn. Am. Law Schs. Office: Univ of Utah College of Law Salt Lake City UT 84112-8909*

TELLER, PAULINE IVANCOVICH, artist; b. Ross, Calif., May 3, 1914; d. Baldo Aloysius and Marien Barron Ivancovich; m. Frederic de Peyster Teller II, Aug. 29, 1941; children: Joan Teller Coda, Peter Ivancovich, Anne Teller Wallace, Frederic de Peyster III. BFA, Dominican Coll., 1936. One-woman shows include San Francisco Mus. Modern Art, 1940, Dominican Coll. Libr., 1975, Ross Valley Clinic, 1976, Marin Civic Ctr. Adminstrn. Bldg Gallery, 1981, Mus. Mission San Juan Capistrano, 1987, Hobar Gallery, Santa Barbara, Calif., 1989; exhibites include San Francisco Art Assn., 1939, Fine Arts Bldg GGIE, 1940, San Francisco Women Artists, 1945, Marin Soc. Artists, 1936-85, Terra Linda Art Assn., 1936-85, Soc. Western Artists, 1936-85, Marin Art Guild, 1970-85, Calif. State Fair, Sacramento, 1970-85, Gilbert Gallery, San Francisco, 1970-85, Shorebirds Gallery, Tiburon, 1970-85, L.A. Design Ctr., 1987, Village Artistry, Carmel, Calif., 1988-89, Linda Vida Gallery, Ruidoso, N.Mex., 1988-89, Hobar Gallery, Santa Barbara, Calif., 1989-90, Vigil Gallery, Sonoma, Calif., 1990, Nevada City, Calif., 1990, Linda Lundeen Gallery, Las Cruces, N.Mex., 1991, Projects Gallery, San Rafael, Calif., 1991, Arlene Siegel Gallery, N.Mex.; represented in permanent collections at Mrs. J.H. Dollar, Hr., Kentfield, Dr. Gary Boero, San Rafael, Dominican Coll., Leafy Mayhew, Sacramento, Stanford (Calif.) U., San Domenico Sch. San Anselmo, Calif., Stanford U. Hosp., Saiter Packard Children's Hosp., Stanford, Calif., others. Mem. Nat. Mus. Women in Arts (charter). Home: 290 Harvard Dr Larkspur CA 94939-1112

TELLINGTON, WENTWORTH JORDAN, engineer; b. Gorham, N.H., Oct. 11, 1916; s. Jesse James and Myrtle Meneleh (Jordan) T.; m. Elizabeth Haman-Ashley, Apr. 29, 1939 (div. 1956); children: Wentworth J. Jr., Joan Elizabeth Gabert. Grad., Phillips Andover Acad., 1935; student, Norwich U., 1939; AB, Columbia U., 1940, postgrad., 1946-47; postgrad., U. So. Calif., 1957-59, UCLA, 1959. Instr. U.S. Mil. Acad., West Point, N.Y., 1941-45; field supr. Century Geophys. Corp., Tulsa, 1946-48; chief geophysicist Pacific Petroleums Ltd., Calgary, Alberta, Can., 1949-51; exec. v.p. Overland Inds. Ltd., Edmonton, Alberta, Can., 1952-55; head math. dept. Chadwick Sch., Rolling Hills, Calif., 1956-60; proprietor Pacific Coast Equestrian Rsch. Farm, Badger, Calif., 1961-70, Whitehurst Products Co., San Francisco, 1970-75, Deep Moon Gold Mine, Downieville, 1982-92; CEO Seadeck Corp., Tucson, 1995—, 1995—; adj. prof. Prescott (Ariz.) Coll., 1972-75. Author: (books) Military Maps and Air Photos, 1979, Endurance and Competitive Trail Riding, 1979, Gold and a Hideaway of Your Own, 1993, Crazy in America, 1994; inventor: vehicle tracker, device for tracking and recording locations, 1944, floating airport, 1995, floating platform, 1996. Engr. ethics com. Soc. Profl. Engrs., Can., 1953-54; bd. govs. Western States Trail Assn., Auburn, Calif., 1962-80. Recipient Creative Citizenship in Calif. award Gov. Ronald Reagan, 1968. Mem. Am. Assn. Petroleum Geologists. Republican. Congregationalist. Achievements include patents for Vehicle Tracker, device for tracking and recording locations, 1944, Floating Airport, 1995, Floating Platform, 1996. Avocations: tennis, riding, aerobatic flying.

TEMKO, ALLAN BERNARD, writer; b. N.Y.C., Feb. 4, 1924; s. Emanuel and Betty (Alderman) T.; m. Elizabeth Ostroff, July 1, 1950 (dec. Aug. 1996); children: Susannah, Alexander. AB, Columbia U., 1947; postgrad, U. Calif., Berkeley, 1949-51, Sorbonne, 1948-49, 51-52. Lectr. Sorbonne, 1953-54, Ecole des Arts et Metiers, Paris, 1954-55; asst. prof. journalism U. Calif., Berkeley, 1956-62, lectr. in city planning and social scis., 1966-70, lectr. Grad. Sch. Journalism, 1991; prof. art Calif. State U., Hayward, 1971-80; lectr. art Stanford U., 1981, 82; architecture critic San Francisco Chronicle, 1961-93, art editor, 1979-82; archtl. planning cons.; chmn. Yosemite Falls Design Workshop, 1992; Pulitzer Prize juror, 1991-92. Author: Notre Dame of Paris, 1955, Eero Saarinen, 1962, No Way To Build a Ballpark and Other Irreverent Essays on Architecture, 1993; contbr. articles to U.S. and fgn. mags. and newspapers; West Coast editor, Archtl. Forum, 1959-62. Served with USNR, 1943-46. Recipient Gold medal Commonwealth Club Calif., 1956, Silver medal, 1994, Journalism award AIA, 1961, Silver Spur award San Francisco Planning and Urban Renewal Assn., 1985, AIA Inst. Honor award, 1991, Nathaniel A. Owings award AIA Calif. Coun., 1995, 1st prize in archtl. criticism Mfrs. Hanover/Art World, 1986, Critic's award Mfrs. Hanover/Art World, 1987, Profl. Achievement award Soc. Profl. Journalists, 1988, Pulitzer Prize for criticism, 1990; grantee Rockefeller Found., 1962-63, 20th Century Fund, 1963-66, NEA, 1988, Graham Found., 1990; Guggenheim fellow, 1956-57. Home: 1015 Fresno Ave Berkeley CA 94707-2517

TEMKO, FLORENCE, author. Student, London U. cons. Mingei Internat. Mus. Author: Traditional Crafts From the Caribbean: Japan; China, 1998-99, From Africa; From Mexico and Central America; From Native North America, 1996, Funny Money, 1998, One Thousand Cranes, 1998, Money Folding 2, 1997, Wedding Origami, 1994, Bible Origami-New Testament, 1994, Paper Jewelry, 1989, For Your Eyes Only-13 Ways to Fold Secret Notes 1994, Papier Pleins D'Idees, 1994, 96, Made with Paper, 1991, 2d edit., 1993, Scary Things, 1991, Paper TricksII, 1990, Paper Tricks, 1988, New Knitting, 1984, Elementary Art Games and Puzzles, 1982, Chinese Papercuts; Their Story, How to Use Them and Make Them, 1982, Let's Take a Trip; Come to My House, Guess Who!, 1982, many others. Mem. Authors Guild, Am. Soc. of Journalists and Authors, San Diego Press Club, Origami USA (founding bd. dirs.). Home and Office: 5050 La Jolla Blvd Apt Pc San Diego CA 92109-1707

TEMPLE, PATRICIA COLLINS, medical director; b. Oregon City, Oreg., Feb. 10, 1942; d. John F. and Sherla (Stewart) Collins; m. Gary F. Temple, Mar. 14, 1965 (div. Jan. 1979); m. Steven G. Gabbe, July 26, 1981; children: Adam, Erica, Amanda, Daniel. BA, Mills Coll., 1964; MD, MS, Oreg. Health Scis. U., 1969; MPH, Harvard U., 1975. Dir. quality assurance San Francisco Gen. Hosp., 1977-81; pediatrician in pvt. practice, dir. Bryn Mawr (Pa.) Hosp., 1981-86; med. dir. Health Pass, Phila., 1986-87, Ohio State U. Health Plan, Columbus, 1987-96, U. Wash., Seattle, 1996—. Contbr. articles to profl. jours. Bd. dirs. Family Support Svcs., 1984-87, Child Guidance Svcs., Columbus, Ohio, 1989-96. Mem. Am. Acad. Pediatrics, Am. Coll. Physician Execs., Ambulatory Pediatrics. Avocation: cooking. Office: U Wash 1910 Fairview Ave E Ste 304 Seattle WA 98102-3620

TEMPLE, PETER JOHN MASKELL, producer, communication consultant; b. London, Feb. 3, 1950; came to Can., 1952; s. George Edward Maskell and Diana Pirie (Watson) T. B of Applied Arts, Ryerson Poly., Toronto, 1974. Comml. producer CFAC TV, Calgary, Alta., Can., 1975-78; creative dir. CFCN TV, Calgary, 1979; pres. Palmer Jarvis & Assocs., Calgary, 1980-85; mgr. comms. Imperial Oil Ltd., Edmonton, Alta., 1985; pres. Media One Comms., Calgary, 1986—. Producer, dir., writer TV series Investing in Art, 1992, 93, 94. Mem. Can. Pub. Rels. Soc., Internat. Assn. Bus. Communicators, Mktg. Profls. Internat. (bd. dirs.), Can. Film and TV Prodn. Assn., Alta. Motion Picture Industries Assn., Calgary C. of C. Avocation: sailing. Home: 2034 21 Ave SW, Calgary, AB Canada T2T 0N7 Office: Media One Comms Ltd, 700 6th Ave SW Ste 300, Calgary, AB Canada T2P 0T8

TEMPO, HOLLY JANE, artist, educator; b. Mpls., Feb. 3, 1964; d. Mary Jane (Riley) Jacobs; m. John Charles Eichinger, June 27, 1987 (div. 1993). BA, Pitzer Coll., 1986; MFA, Claremont Grad. U., 1991. Lectr. Scripps Coll., Claremont, Calif., 1993-94; adminstrv. asst. D'Agnenica Angels Project, L.A., 1994; dir. Lucky Nun Gallery, L.A., 1994-95; instr. art Riverside (Calif.) C.C., 1995—, Mt. San Antonio Coll., Walnut, Calif., 1995—; lectr. Artsreach program UCLA, 1995; dir. Seeking It Through Exhbns. SITE, L.A., 1995-97; guest artist, lectr. Pomona Coll., Claremont, Calif., 1994, Calif. State U., Fullerton, 1994; guest curator Aria Noir Gallery, Pomona, 1995, Da Gallery, Pomona, 1990; grants panelist L.A. Cultural Affairs Dept., 1997, Los Angeles County Arts Commn., 1997; solo exhibn. San Jose City Coll., 1998; loan fund panelist Arts Inc., 1998—. Exhibited in group shows, including Kohn Turner Gallery, 1994, William Turner Gallery Annex, 1995, Calif. State U., L.A., 1996, Ruth Bacholfner Gallery, 1997, [illegible] Kitchen Studios, 1997. Organizer of exhibition for Coun. of Chs., Homeless Pomona-Inland Valley, 1994. Recipient Honorarium L.A. Contemporary Exhibitions, 1991; Elsie DeWolf Found. scholar, 1986; Change Inc. grantee, 1998. Mem. Support Assocs. Grad. Art (v.p. 1994-96). Avocations: reading women's literature, antiques, gardening, interior decorating. Home: 642 Moulton Ave Apt E32 Los Angeles CA 90031-3717

TENG, MIN, research scientist; b. Jilin, China, Nov. 9, 1963; came to U.S., 1986; d. Yunsheng and Fengchun (Liu) T.; m. Yazhong Pei, July 7, 1988; 1 child, Bradley Minxing. BS, Jilin U., Changchun, 1985; PhD, SUNY, Stonybrook, 1991. Postdoctoral fellow U. Notre Dame, Ind., 1991-93; rsch. scientist Allergan Pharmacy, Irvine, Calif., 1993-95, sr. rsch. scientist, 1995-97; sr. scientist I Alanex Corp., San Diego, 1997—. Mem. Am. Chem. Soc. Avocations: oil painting, piano, tennis. Office: Alanex Corp 3550 General Atomics Ct San Diego CA 92121-1122

TENGBOM, LUVERNE CHARLES, religion educator; b. Poskin, Wis., May 30, 1919; s. Carl John and Ida Carolina (Carlson) T.; m. Mildred Helena Hasselquist, May 23, 1953; children: Daniel, Judith, Janet, David. BA, Gustavus Adolphus Coll., 1943; MDiv, Augustana Sem., 1946; ThM, Luther Sem., St. Paul, 1962; PhD, Hartford Sem. Found., 1977. Ordained to ministry Luth. Ch. in Am., 1946. Pastor 1st Luth. Ch., Calgary, Alta., Can., 1946-56; missionary, mem. bd. world missions Augustana Luth. Ch., Tanzania, 1956-67; prof. Luth. Bible Inst., Anaheim, Calif., 1967-85, acad. dean, 1976-85, prof., 1987-91; sec. Can. Conf., Augustana Luth. Ch., 1950-56; mem. commn. on world mission Pacific S.W. Synod, Luth. Ch. in Am., 1981—, bd. world missions, 1985-87; prof. Trinity Theol. Coll., Singapore, Singapore Bible Coll., 1985-87. Author: Fill My Cup, Lord, 1978, Bible Readings for Families, 1981. sec. Luth. Bible Inst., Camrose, Alta, 1946-56; dean Luth. Bible Sch., Moshi, Tanzania, 1960-61. Home: 789 N Cambridge Ave Claremont CA 91711-4258

TENNENBAUM, MICHAEL ERNEST, private investor; b. St. Petersburg, Fla., Sept. 17, 1935; s. Reubin and Frieda (Miller) T.; m. Suzanne Stockfisch; children by previous marriage—Mark Stephen, Andrew Richard. BS, Ga. Inst. Tech., 1958; MBA with honors, Harvard U., 1962. Assoc. Burnham & Co., N.Y.C., 1962-64; assoc. Bear, Stearns & Co., N.Y.C., 1964-69, sr. mng. dir., 1969-96, vice chmn. investment banking div., 1988-93; chmn. bd. dirs. Tech. Park, Atlanta, 1978-81; mng. mem. Tennenbaum & Co., LLC, L.A., 1996—; bd. dirs. ICF Kaiser Internat., Inc., 1998—; chmn. fin. com., mem. exec. com. ICF Kaiser Internat., Inc., 1998—; bd. dirs. TelePacific Corp. Bd. govs., nat. bd. trustees Boys and Girls Clubs Am.; mem. nat. adv. bd. Ga. Inst. Tech., 1971-77; mem. vis. com. Harvard U. Sch. Bus., Cambridge, Mass., 1986-92, bd. assocs., 1992—; bd. trustees Ga. Inst. Tech. Found., Inc., Atlanta, 1988-96; bd. dirs. Joffrey Ballet, 1990-92, chmn. exec. com., 1991-92; bd. dirs. Music Ctr. L.A. County Unified Fund Cabinet, 1990-91; chmn. L.A. Mayor's Spl. Adv. Com. on Fiscal Adminstrn., 1993-94; commr. Calif. Intercity HighSpeed Ground Transp. Commn.; chmn. Calif. High Speed Rail Authority, 1998—. Mem. Malibu Racquet Club. Home: 118 Malibu Colony Rd Malibu CA 90265-4642 Office: Tennenbaum & Co LLC Ste 1010 1999 Avenue Of The Stars Los Angeles CA 90067-4611

TENNENT, VALENTINE LESLIE, accountant; b. Apia, Western Samoa, Apr. 5, 1919; came to U.S., 1922; s. Hugh Cowper and Madge Grace (Cook) T.; m. Jeanne Marie Elder, Dec. 10, 1941; children: Madeline Jeanne Walls, Hugh Cowper II, Michael Waller, Val Leslie, Paul Anthony. Student, U. Calif., Berkeley, 1938-40. CPA, Hawaii, La. Mgr. Tennent & Greaney, CPAs, Hilo, Hawaii, 1945-50; ptnr. Cameron, Tennent & Dunn, CPAs, Honolulu, 1950-56; ptnr. KPMG Peat Marwick LLP, Honolulu, 1956-79, cons., 1979-84; ind. rschr. pub. fin. and banking, polit. economy, moral philosophy, San Diego, 1984—. Founding trustee, pres., treas. Tennent Art Found., Honolulu, 1955-77; trustee, treas. Watumull Found., Honolulu, 1963-90; bd. dirs. Iolani Sch., Inst. for Human Svcs., Honolulu, Lyman Mus., Hilo. Capt. USAF, 1941-45. Recipient Bishop's Cross for disting. svc. Protestant Episcopal Ch., Dist. Hawaii, 1965, G.J. Watumull award for disting. achievement Watumull Found., Honolulu, 1982. Mem. AICPA (governing coun. 1961-64), Hawaii Soc. CPAs (pres. 1960). Episcopalian. Avocations: swimming, fine arts, music, literature. Home and Office: 700 Front St Unit# 1607 San Diego CA 92101-6063

TENNISON, WILLIAM RAY, JR., financial planner, stockbroker, resort owner; b. Deming, N.Mex., July 22, 1941; s. William Ray and Mildred Rose (Frei) T.; m. Mary Kay Reid, Jan. 27, 1963; children: William Ervin, Bradley Joseph, Stephanie Kay (dec.). BS in Indsl. Mgmt., Ariz. State U., 1963; MBA in Econs., U. Ariz., 1966. Indsl. engr. USAF, 1963-71; from account exec. to br. office mgr., stockbroker E. F. Hutton & Co., Mesa, Ariz., 1971-88, first v.p., also mem. Dirs. Adv. Coun.; sr. v.p., stockbroker Kemper Security Group, Mesa, Ariz., 1988-91, sr. v.p. Boettcher divsn., also Kemper Exec. Coun.; bd. dirs. D.E. Frey, Denver, 1991—; pres. Tennison and Assocs., Inc., Paonia, Carbondale and Somerset, Colo., 1991—, Mesa and Sedona, Ariz., 1991—; owner Crystal Meadows Ranch Resort, Inc., Somerset, Colo.; speaker in field at sales confs. and conventions. Author: (book/tng. program) Bill Tennison Master Class, 1990.; featured in Registered Representative Mag., 1989, 92, 95, Rsch. Mag., 1992, 93, 95, Broker Hall of Fame, 1995, Arizona Business Mag., 1993; contbr. articles to profl. jours; presenter weekly radio show Pub. Radio, Western Colo. Mem. East Valley Sr. Found., 1986-96; pres. Paonia (Colo.) C. of C., 1994-95, Stephanie Kay Tennison Meml. Scholarship Found. Mem. Paonia (Colo. Club, pres.) Rotary Club (dir.). Republican. Methodist. Avocations: hunting, fishing. E-mail: Wtennisonj@aol.com. Home: Crystal Meadows Ranch Resort 30682 County Rd # 12 Somerset CO 81434 Office: Tennison & Assocs Inc DE Frey & Co Inc 40 N Center Ste 106 Mesa AZ 85201-7300

TENNYSON, PETER JOSEPH, lawyer; b. Winona, Minn., Mar. 18, 1946; s. Richard Harvey and Sylvia Josephine (Jadrich) T.; m. Mary Eileen Fay, Jan. 3, 1970; children: Mark Christian, Rachel Christine, Matthew Patrick, Erica Ruth/. BA, Purdue U., 1968; JD, U. Va., 1975. Bar: Calif. Assoc. atty. O'Melveny & Myers, L.A., 1975-82; v.p., gen. counsel Cannon Mills Co., Kannapolis, N.C., 1982-84; ptnr. Stradling, Yocca, Newport Beach, Calif., 1984-89, Jones, Day, Reavis & Pogue, Irvine, Calif., 1990-95, Paul, Hastings, Janofsky & Walker, Costa Mesa, Calif., 1995—; mem. Calif. Commn. on Future of Legal Profession and State Bar, 1994; lectr. in field. Mem. adv. com. St. Joseph Hosp., Orange, Calif., 1987-93; bd. dirs. Lincoln Club Orange County, 1991-93, South Coast Symphony, 1989-92. Capt. U.S. Army, 1968-72. Mem. Orange County Bar Assn., Performing Arts Bus. Alliance South Coast Repertory Silver Circle. Roman Catholic. Avocations: down hill skiing, swimming. Home: 2621 Circle Dr Newport Beach CA 92663-5616 Office: Paul Hastings Janofsky & Walker LLP 695 Town Center Dr Fl 17 Costa Mesa CA 92626-1924

TEODORO, LAWRENCE BELANDRES, export documentation company executive, consultant; b. Quezon City, The Philippines, Oct. 23, 1965; came to U.S., 1984; s. Efren and Lynn (Belandres) T. BSBA, Menlo Coll., Atherton, Calif., 1988. Gen. mgr. Dakin, Inc., Brisbane, Calif., 1988-90, mgr. prodn. ops., 1988-90; traffic mgr. Rarewoods, Inc., Burlingame, Calif., 1990-92; 0dir. ops. Great Explorations, San Francisco, 1992-94; pres., CEO Teodoro Group Cos., Menlo Park, Calif., 1994—. Roman Catholic. Avocation: collecting wine. Office: Teodoro Group 1259 El Camino Real Ste 142 Menlo Park CA 94025-4227

TERADA, ALICE MASAE, retired elementary school teacher, writer; b. Hilo, Hawaii, Nov. 13, 1928; d. David Matsuo and Mitsuko (Sekido) Marutani; m. Harry T. Terada, Aug. 25, 1951; children: Suzanne T. Henderson, Keith Y., Lance S. Diploma, Queen's Hosp. Sch. Nursing, 1950; BS, We. Res. U., 1953; MEd, U. Hawaii, 1971. Cert. tchr., Hawaii. Registered nurse County Meml. Hosp., Hilo, Hawaii, 1950-51, U. Hosps., Cleve., 1952-53; lang. arts tchr. Dept. Edn., Honolulu, 1967-68; reading tchr. Reading Ctr., Honolulu, Hawaii, 1968-82; ret. Author: Under the Starfruit Tree, 1989, The Magic Crocodile, 1994. Mem. AAUW, Internat. Reading Assn., Zonta Club Internat., Zonta Club Honolulu (bd. dirs. 1996-97). Avocations: art, art history, porcelain antiques, yoga, swimming.

TERESI, JOSEPH, publishing executive; b. Mpls., Mar. 13, 1941; s. Cliff I.A. and Helen Ione (Leslie) T.; divorced; 1 child, Nicholas. Chief exec. officer Jammer Cycle Products Inc., Burbank, Calif., 1968-80, Paisano Pubs. [illegible] riders Video Mag. Pub. (mags.) Easyriders, 1971—, In the Wind, 1974—, Biker Lifestyle, 1986—, Tattoo, 1986—, Am. Rodder, 1987, Womens Enterprise, 1987-89, Eagles Eye, 1989—, Tattoo Flash, 1993—, Tattoo Savage, 1993—, VQ, 1994—, Early-Riders, 1994-96, Quick Throttle, 1995—,

Roadware, 1995—. Holds world speed record for motorcycles set at 322 miles per hour, 1990. Avocations: motorcycles, race cars, boats, marlin fishing, skiing. Office: Paisano Pubs Inc PO Box 3000 Agoura Hills CA 91376-3000

TERMINELLA, LUIGI, critical care physician, educator; b. Catania, Italy, Nov. 15, 1960; came to U.S., 1961; s. Roberto and Josephine (Bartolotta) T. MD summa cum laude, U. Catania, 1986. Pathology asst. Brotman Med. Ctr., Culver City, Calif., 1987-89; transitional resident Miriam Hosp./Brown U., Providence, 1989-90; resident in internal medicine U. Hawaii, Honolulu, 1990-92; tng. in critical care/internal medicine U. Hawaii/Queen's Med. Ctr., Honolulu, 1992-93; transfusion svc. physician Blood Bank of Hawaii, Honolulu, 1992-93; internal medicine physician Hawaii Physician Svcs., Honolulu, 1993—; critical care physician Queen's Med. Ctr., Honolulu, 1993—; mem. clin. faculty John H. Burns Sch. Medicine, U. Hawaii, Honolulu, 1994—; pres. Pualani Family Health, SRL, Corp., Honolulu. Recipient Clementi award U. Catania, 1986, others. Mem. ACP, AMA, Am. Soc. Internal Medicine, Hawaiian Soc. Critical Care, Soc. Critical Care Medicine. Avocations: photography, law, architecture. Office: Queen's Med Ctr 1301 Punchbowl St # 4B Honolulu HI 96813-2413

TERRELL, A. JOHN, university telecommunications director; b. Pasadena, Calif., Dec. 27, 1927; s. Harry Evans and Elizabeth (Eaton) T.; m. Elizabeth Schalk, June 6, 1949; children—Patricia Elyse, Marilee Diane, John Scott. Student, Chaffey Coll., 1947-48; BBA, U. N. Mex., 1952. Communications cons. Mountain States Tel. & Tel., Albuquerque, 1951-56; mgr. office and communications services A.C.F. Industries, Inc., Albuquerque, 1956-62; mgr. communications and services Norton Simon Industries, Inc., Fullerton, Ca., 1962-68; v.p. gen. mgr. Wells Fargo Security Guard Service Div. Baker Industries, Fullerton, Ca., 1968-71; adminstrv. mgr., budget adminstr. Hyland div. Baxter-Trevenol Labs. Inc., Costa Mesa, CA, 1971-77; exec. v.p. Am. Tel. Mgmt. Inst Inc., Newport Beach, Calif., 1977-78; telecommunications dir. UCLA, 1978-89, retired, 1989. Contbr. articles to profl. jours. Republican. candidate for state rep., Albuquerque, 1960; precinct chmn. and mem. Bernalillo County Rep. Central Com., 1961-62; Rep. candidate for N. Mex. State Bd. Edn., 2nd Jud. Dist., 1962; colonial aide-de-camp Gov. N. Mex., Santa Fe, 1968. Served with U.S. Mcht. Marine, 1944-45, U.S. Army, 1946-47, USAR, 1947-50. Mem. Nat. Assn. Accts. (dir. 1967-77) (Most Valuable mem. 1974-75), Telecommunications Assn., Am. Legion, VFW. Episcopalian. Lodges: Greater Irvine Lions (charter pres. 1975-76), Albuquerque Jaycees (v.p., treas. 1956-62). Home: 2727 Island View Ln Corona Del Mar CA 92625-1309

TERRELL, HOWARD BRUCE, psychiatrist; b. Feb. 19, 1952. BS magna cum laude, Calif. State U., Hayward, 1974; MD, U. Calif., San Diego, 1980. Diplomate in psychiatry and in forensic psychiatry Am. Bd. Psychiatry and Neurology. Intern. Kaiser Found. Hosp., Oakland, Calif., 1980-81; resident in psychiatry U. Calif., San Francisco/Fresno, 1982-85; staff psychiatrist Kings View Corp., Reedley, Calif., 1985-87, sr. staff psychiatrist, 1987-88, dir. outpatient psychiatry, 1988-89; dir. dual diagnosis and affective disorders programs Sierra Gateway Hosp., Clovis, Calif., 1989-91; asst. clin. prof. psychiatry U. Calif. Sch. Medicine, San Francisco; lectr. in field. Contbr. articles to profl. jours. Fellow Am. Coll. Forensic Psychiatry; mem. Am. Acad. Psychiatry and the Law, Am. Psychiat. Assn., Ctrl. Calif. Psychiat. Soc. (pres. Sierra chpt. 1996-98). Avocations: golf, computers, photography, enology, music. Office: 3100 Willow Ave Ste 102 Clovis CA 93612-4741

TERRILL, KAREN STAPLETON, retired medical planning consultant; b. Milw., Mar. 21, 1939; d. Thomas John and Olive Patrea (Thorbjornsen) Stapleton; m. Max Kurt Winkler, Dec. 18, 1965 (dec. June 1976); m. Richard Terrill, Jan. 23, 1991 (dec. May 1991). BS in Nursing, U. Mich., 1961; MBA, U. Nev., 1974. RN, Calif. Project nurse Langley Porter N.P.I., San Francisco, 1962-64; asst. dir. nursing Milw. County Mental Health Ctr., 1964-66; instr. Fond du Lac (Wis.) Sch. Dist., 1966-67; sch. nurse Inglewood (Calif.) Sch. Dist., 1968-69; instr. nursing U. Nev., Reno, 1969-74; health planner manpower State of Nev. Comp B. Agy., Carson City, 1974-75; planning analyst St. Mary's Hosp., Reno, 1974-76; sr. system analyst U. Calif., San Francisco, 1976-79; med. planning cons. Stone Marraccini & Patterson, San Francisco, 1979-93. Mem. citizen's adv. group City of Richmond, Calif., 1987-88; founding dir. of B.O.A.T. non-profit corp. to promote ferry transit on San Francisco Bay. Mountain State Regional Planning Commn. grantee, 1973-74. Home: 1308 Mallard Dr Richmond CA 94801-4113

TERRILL, W(ALLACE) ANDREW, international security analyst, educator; b. Pasadena, Calif., Aug. 15, 1954; s. Wallace and Gloria (Acheson) T. BA in Polit. Sci., Calif. State Poly. U., 1975; MA in Polit. Sci., U. Calif., Riverside, 1976; PhD in Internat. Rels., The Claremont Grad. Sch., 1983. Rsch. asst. Analytical Assessments Corp., L.A., 1978-80, rsch. assoc., 1980-87; part-time instr. Calif. State Poly. U., Pomona, 1987-89; asst. prof. polit. sci. Old Dominion U., Norfolk, Va., 1989-93; sr. internat. security analyst Lawrence Livermore Nat. Lab., Livermore, Calif., 1993—; vis. prof. U.S. Air War Coll., Maxwell AFB, Ala., 1998—; cons. Sys. Rsch. and Devel. Corp., L.A., 1987-89; adj. asst. prof. Occidental Coll., L.A., 1988-89; workshop leader; interviewed on TV, radio and in print media on Mid. Eastern and nonproliferation issues. Contbr. numerous book revs. and articles to acad. jours. Served with USAR, 1976—, lt. col., 1997. Decorated Meritorious Svc. medal; recipient Haynes Found. dissertation fellowship, 2 Claremont Grad. Sch. full-tuition fellowships.

TERRY, CHRISTOPHER THOMAS, artist; b. Stamford, Conn., Jan. 8, 1956; s. William W. and Jane (McCartan) T.; m. Diane Graham, June 9, 1979; children: Graham Christopher, Christine McCartan. BA, R.I. Coll., 1978; MFA, U. Wis., 1981. Vis. artist Calif. State U., Long Beach, 1985-88; assoc. prof. Utah State U., Logan, 1988—. Recipient regional painting fellowship WESTAF/NEA, 1994-95, Fulbright scholarship CIES, Essen, Germany, 1995, Visual Artist fellowship Utah Arts Coun., 1990, residency Millay Colony for the Arts, Austerlitz, N.Y., 1990. Office: Utah State U Art Dept UMC 4000 Logan UT 84322-0001

TERRY, FRANK JEFFREY, bishop. Bishop Diocese of Spokane, Wash., 1991—. Office: Episcopal Diocese of Spokane 245 E 13th Ave Spokane WA 99202-1114*

TERRY, MICHAEL JOSEPH, courtroom clerk; b. Mount Ayr, Iowa, Aug. 26, 1957; s. John Stanley and Kathryn Marie (Williams) T. BS in Psychology, Santa Clara U., 1979, paralegal cert., 1987. Dep. ct. clk. Santa Clara County Mcpl. Ct., San Jose, Calif., 1980-86; ct. attendent Santa Clara County Superior Ct., San Jose, 1986-87; courtroom clk. Santa Clara County Superior Ct., San Jose, Calif., 1987—. Editor: Crimson Warrior Pub., 1992—. Mem. ACLU, Courtroom Clks. Assn., World Affairs Coun., Phi Delta Phi (life). Democrat. Avocations: literature, travel, theatre. Office: Superior Ct 170 Park Center Plz San Jose CA 95113-2219

TERRY, RICHARD FRANK, data transcriber; b. Ogden, Utah, July 19, 1949; s. Frank Nebeker and Gertrude Angeline (Berghout) T. BA, Weber State Coll., 1979. Data transcriber IRS, Marriott, Utah, 1976—. Mem. Ch. of Jesus Christ of Latter Day Saints. Avocation: reading the Spanish Bible.

TERRY, STEVEN SPENCER, mathematics educator, consultant; b. Hoodriver, Oreg., July 9, 1942; s. Steven Bliss and Kathryn (Spencer) T.; m. Vivian Hickman, Aug. 20, 1964; children: Yvette, Kathryn, S. Matthew, Spencer, Stuart, Heather. BS, Utah State U., 1964, MS, 1967. Tchr. math Clayton Jr. High, Salt Lake City, 1964-67, 29 Palms (Calif.) High Sch., 1967-68; tchr. math, coach Yucca Valley (Calif.) High Sch., 1968-76; prof. math. Ricks Coll., Rexburg, Idaho, 1976—; chmn. dept. Author: (textbook) Elementary Teachers' Math, 1985. Pres. Yucca Valley City Coun., 1972-76, mem. water bd., fire and streets bd., lighting bd., recreation bd.; judge Young Woman of Yr. contests, Idaho; officer Madison County (Idaho) Baseball Assn.; mem. Rexburg Airport Bd. Recipient Outstanding Tchrs. award San Bernardino and Riverside Counties, Calif., 1976, Outstanding Secondary Educator, 1974, 75. Mem. Am. Math. Assn. Two-Yr. Colls. (v.p. 1980-86, dir. Summer Inst., Outstanding Contbn. award 1982, 94, 96, co-chair Summer Inst. at Ricks Coll., co-chair 1988 internat. conv.), Nat. Coun. Tchrs. Math., NEA (life), Phi Delta Kappa (life, sec. 1974-76, Outstanding Contbn. award 1984). Republican. Mormon. Avocations: racquetball, basketball, outdoor activities, skiing, horseback riding. Home: 221 S 2nd E # D Rexburg ID 83440-2202 Office: Ricks Coll Rexburg ID 83460-0515

TERWILLIGER, ROBERT ALAN, auditor; b. Middletown, N.Y., Sept. 11, 1947; s. Clarence Lawrence and Grace Mae (Fuller) T.; m. Marilyn E. Walsh, July 29, 1972; children: Catherine, Matthew. BA, SUNY, Stony Brook, 1969; MPA, SUNY, Albany, 1970; JD, U. Puget Sound/Seattle U., 1977. Bar: Wash. 1977. Adminstrv. asst. SUNY, Albany, 1972-74; dep. prosecuting atty. Snohomish County, Everett, Wash., 1978-80; atty. Breskin Robbins Bastian, Seattle, 1980-83; chief dep. auditor Snohomish County, Everett, 1983-93, county auditor, 1993—. Mem. 44th legis. dist. Snohomish County, Bothell, Wash., 1984-91, mem. 1st legis. dist., 1992—; bd. dirs. Snohomish County United Way, Everett, Wash., 1990-96, 97—, Snohomish King Youth Club, Edmonds, Wash., 1991-98; precinct com. officer Snohomish County Dems., Everett, 1984—. Mem. Everett Rotary Club. Democrat. Presbyterian. Avocations: gardening, season ticket holder Seattle Seahawks football. Home: 21603 Oak Way Brier WA 98036-8176 Office: Snohomish County Auditor 3000 Rockefeller Ave Everett WA 98201-4046

TESH, JOHN, television talk show host, musician; b. Garden City, N.Y., 1953; s. John and Mildred Tesh; m. Connie Sellecca, Apr. 4, 1992; children: Gib, Prima. Co-host Entertainment Tonight, 1986—; host One-On-One with John Tesh, 1991; co-host John and Leeza from Hollywood, 1993. Television appearances include: The U.S. Open Tennis Championship, 1985, Macy's Thanksgiving Day Parade, 1987, Wimbledon, 1991, TV film Holyrock-a-Bye Baby, 1993; film appearances include Shocker, 1989, Soapdish, 1991, Love Affair, 1996; albums include Tour de France, 1988, The Early Years, 1990, Ironman, 1992, The Games, 1992, Monterey Nights, 1993, A Romantic Christmas, 1993, Wintersong, Sax by the Fire, Sax on the Beach, John Tesh Live at Red Rocks, Discovery, Avalon, A Family Christmas, 1995, Music in the Key of Love, 1995, Choirs of Christmas, 1996, Holiday Collection, 1996, Victory: The Sports Collection, 1997, Sax All Night, 1997, Grand Passion, 1998; composers theme music Bobby's World, 1990, The Knife and Gun Club, 1990, One on One, 1991, NFL Live. Recipient 4 Emmy awards for composing, 2 Emmy awards for reporting. Office: care GTSP Records John Tesh Prodns 13749 Riverside Dr Sherman Oaks CA 91423*

TESHIMA, RONALD S., landscpae architect. AA, Merritt Coll., 1966; BS in Ornamental Hort., Calif. State Poly Coll., 1968, B of Landscape Architecture, 1971. Prin., dir. design Wimmer Tamada Assocs., San Deigo, 1971-88; prin.-in-charge Teshima Design Group, San Deigo, 1988—. Bd. dirs. YMCA, San Diego, 1985; mem. Orchids & Onions Cmty. Awareness, San Deigo, 1984. Mem. ASLA (pres. San Diego chpt. 1978, v.p. San Diego chpt. 1977), Rotary. Office: Teshima Design Group 9903 Businesspark Ave Ste C San Diego CA 92131-1120

TESLER, LAWRENCE GORDON, software company executive; b. N.Y.C., Apr. 24, 1945; s. Isidore and Muriel (Krechmer) T.; m. Shelagh Elisabeth Leuterio, Oct 4, 1964 (div. 1970); 1 child, Lisa Traci; m. Colleen Ann Barton, Feb. 17, 1987. BS in Math., Stanford U., 1965. Pres. Info. Processing Corp., Palo Alto, Calif., 1963-68; rsch. asst. Stanford U. Artificial Intelligence Lab., 1968-73; mem. rsch. staff Xerox Corp., Palo Alto, 1973-80; sect. mgr. Lisa div. Apple Computer, Inc., Cupertino, Calif., 1980-82, cons. engr., 1983-86, v.p. advanced tech., 1986-90, v.p. advanced products, 1990-92, v.p. engring., 1992-93, chief scientist, 1993-97, v.p. AppleNet divsn., 1996-97; pres. Stagecast Software, Inc., Palo Alto, Calif., 1997—; bd. dirs. ARM Holdings, PLC; mem. Computer Sci. and Telecom. Bd., 1991-94. Contbr. articles to profl. jours., various computer software. Bd. dirs. Peninsula Sch., Menlo Park, Calif., 1974-78. Mem. Assn. Computing Machinery (conf. co-chmn. 1987-88). Office: Stagecast Software Inc 580 College Ave Palo Alto CA 94306-1434

TESS, ROY WILLIAM HENRY, chemist; b. Chgo., Apr. 25, 1915; s. Reinhold W. and Augusta (Detl) T.; m. Marjorie Kohler, Feb. 19, 1944; children: Roxanne, Steven. BS in Chemistry, U. Ill., 1939; PhD, U. Minn., 1944. Rsch. chemist, group leader Shell Devel. Co., Emeryville, Calif., 1944—, rsch. supr., 1959-61, 63-66; rsch. supr. Royal Dutch/Shell Plastics Lab., Delft, The Netherlands, 1962-63; tech. planning supr. Shell Chem. Co., N.Y.C., 1967-70; tech. mgr. solvents Shell Chem. Co., Houston, 1970-77, cons., 1977-79; ind. cons. Fallbrook, Calif., 1979—; pres. Paint Rsch. Inst., Phila., 1973-76; lectr. air pollution tech., Shell Kagaku, Tokyo. Editor, organizer: Solvents Theory and Practice, 1973; (with others) Applied Polymer Science, 1975, Applied Polymer Science, 2d edit., 1985. Pres. Assn. Indsl. Scientists, Berkeley, Calif., 1948-50, Minerinda Property Owners Assn., Orinda, Calif., 1965-67, Houston Camellia Soc., 1973-74. Fellow Am. Inst. Chemists; mem. Nat. Paint and Coatings Assn. (air quality com. 1967-79), Fedn. Socs. Coatings Tech. (bd. dirs. 1973-76, Roon award 1957, Heckel award 1978), Am. Chem. Soc. (divsn. polymeric materials chmn. 1978, established Roy W. Tess award in Coatings 1985, exec. com. 1977—, Disting. Svc. award 1993), Sigma Xi, Alpha Chi Sigma, Phi Kappa Phi, Phi Lambda Upsilon. Achievements include discovery, development and recommendation of uses for existing and potential petrochemical raw materials in coatings, resins and polymer industries; research in Epon resins, in high polymer latices based on acrylates, styrene, ethylene and vinyl esters, in drying oils and alkyds, and in solvent blends based on solution theory. Expertise in air pollution technology including lecture tours in Japan sponsored by Shell Kagaku of Tokyo. Home and Office: 1615 Chandelle Ln Fallbrook CA 92028-1707

TESSIER, DENNIS MEDWARD, paralegal, lecturer, legal advisor, consultant; b. Royal Oak, Mich., Sept. 20, 1956; s. Medward James and Marilyn (Pitsos) T.; m. Michelle Terri Zeichick, July 28, 1990; 1 child, Brian Jae. Cert. paralegal, U. West L.A., 1987, cert. atty. practice, 1990; cert. in epidemiology, U.S. CDC, 1991. Reprodn. analyst Burroughs Corp., Detroit, 1975-76; mixologist Holiday Inn, Inc., Belair, Calif., 1977-83; spl. asst. office of the gen. counsel U.S. Jud. Intelligence Agy., Pacific Sta., L.A., 1981—; mixologist R.W. Grace Inc., Marina Del Rey, Calif., 1984-86; paralegal O'Melveny & Myers, L.A., 1986, Haight, Brown & Bonesteel, Santa Monica, Calif., 1987-93, Helsell & Fetterman, Seattle, 1993-94, Nintendo of Am. Inc., Redmond, Wash., 1994-96, Tousley Brain PLLC, Seattle, 1996-99, Preston, Gates and Ellis, Seattle, 1999—; family law cons. Helping Svcs., L.A., 1990-93, L.A. Clinic, 1990; researcher Tessier & Assocs. Rsch., Topanga Canyon, Calif., 1983—; with Starlight Found., Redmond, Wash., 1993—. Author: Beauty in Motion, 1983, Champerty and Barratry, 1998. Creek Rat Esquire, 1999; contbr. articles to profl. jours. Mem. ABA (sci. and tech. law, jud. adminstrn. sects.), ATLA, Soc. Epidemiology Rsch., Assn. Investigative Scis., U.S. Nat. Acad. Scis. Academe Industry Program (spkr. CLE). Democrat. Lutheran. Avocations: music, arts. Home: 21100 Pioneer Way Edmonds WA 98026-6947 Office: Preston Gates and Ellis Columbia Ctr Ste 5000 701 Fifth Ave Seattle WA 98104-7078

TESTA, GABRIEL, real estate broker; b. N.Y.C., Dec. 17, 1928; s. Morris and Sophie (Cohen) T.; m. Nadine Sylvia Gross, June 17, 1954; children: Pamela Marsha, Simone Lena, Harry, Robert Maurice. Student, Conservatory of Music, 1954, Lumbleau U. Lic. real estate broker, Calif. Asst. mgr. May Co., L.A., 1949-51; with Railway Express, L.A., 1954-60; chief rte. clk., chief router, surveillance guard R.E.A. Air Express, L.A., 1960-75; real estate agt., assoc. broker Active Realty, Hawthorne, Calif., 1976—. Campaigner Dem. Party, Hawthorne, 1980—. Sgt. U.S. Army, 1951-53, Korea. Mem. Am. Legion. Avocations: golf, baseball, swimming, chorus singing, gambling.

TESTA, STEPHEN MICHAEL, geologist, consultant; b. Fitchburg, Mass., July 17, 1951; s. Guiseppe Alfredo and Angelina Mary (Pettito) T.; m. Lydia Mae Payne, July 26, 1986; 1 child, Brant Ethan Gage. AA, Los Angeles Valley Jr. Coll., Van Nuys, 1971; BS in Geology, Calif. State U., Northridge, 1976, MS in Geology, 1978. Registered geologist, Calif., Oreg.; cert. profl. geol. scientist., Idaho, Alaska; cert. engring. geologist, Calif.; registered environ. assessor, Calif. Engring. geologist R.T. Frankian & Assocs., Burbank, Calif., 1976-78, Bechtel, Norwalk, Calif., 1978-80, Converse Cons., Seattle, 1980-82; sr. hydrogeologist Ecology Environment, Seattle, 1982-83; sr. geologist Dames & Moore, Seattle, 1983-86; v.p. Engring. Enterprises, Long Beach, Calif., 1986-89; CEO Applied Environ. Svcs., San Juan Capistrano, Calif., 1990-94; pres. Testa Environ. Corp., Foothill Ranch, Calif., 1994—. Author: Restoration of Petroleum Contaminated Aquifers, 1990, Principles of Technical Consulting and Project Management, 1991, Geological Aspects of Hazardous Waste Management, 1994, The Reuse and Recycling of Contaminated Soil, 1997, Petroleum in the Environment, 1999; editor: Geologic Field Guide to the Salton Basin, 1988, Environmental Concerns in the Petroleum Industry, 1989, Environmental Geology, 1999, Petroleum Geology, 1999, Mining Geology, 1999, Engineering Geology, 1999, Hydrogeology, 1999; contbr. more than 60 articles to profl. jours., a preface and chpts. to books. Mem. AAAS, Am. Inst. Profl. Geologists (mem. profl. devel. com. 1986, mem. continuing edn. com. program chmn., 1988—, mem. nat. screening bd. 1992-94, chmn. 1995—, exec. bd. del. 1993, nat. v.p. 1994, found. trustee 1995—, honors and awards com. 1996-97, found. trustee 1997—, internat. affairs com. 1998, nat. pres. 1998, presdl. Cert. of Merit 1987, 94), L.A. Basin Geol. Soc. (pres. 1991-92), Geol. Soc. Am. (Roy J. Shlemon mentor program honorarium 1998, found. trustee 1998—), Am. Geol. Inst. (found. trustee), Geol. Soc. Am. (found. trustee), Am. Assn. Petroleum Geologists (Pacific sect. environ. com., co-chmn. 1993—, chmn. liaison com. divsn. environ. geoscis. 1997, geoenviron. forum 1998, cert. of merit 1997, editor-in-chief Jour. Environ. Geoscis. 1998—), Am. Mineral. Soc., Am. Geol. Inst. (found. trustee 1998—), South Coast Geol. Soc., Nat. Assn. State Bds. Geology (coun. examiners 1998—), Assn. Ground Water Scientists and Engrs., Assn. Engring. Geologists, Assn. Mil. Engrs., Environ. Assessment Assn., Mineral Soc. Can., Hazardous Materials Rsch. Inst., Calif. Water Pollution Control Assn., Sigma Xi. Roman Catholic. Achievements include research igneous and metamorphic petrology, asphalt chemistry; development of methods for subsurface hydrogeologic characterization and remediation, proprietary processes for incorporation of contaminated soil and other materials considered toxic and hazardous via recycling into a variety of cold-mix asphaltic products. Home: 19814 Jesus Maria Rd Mokelumne Hill CA 95245-9559 Office: Testa Environ Corp Ste 1E-446 27641 Portola Pky Foothill Ranch CA 92610-1743

TETHER, ANTHONY JOHN, aerospace executive; b. Middletown, N.Y., Nov. 28, 1941; s. John Arthur and Antoinette Rose (Gesualdo) T.; m. Nancy Engle Pierson, Dec. 27, 1963 (div. July 1971); 1 child, Jennifer; m. Carol Suzanne Dunbar, Mar. 3, 1973; 1 child, Michael. AAS, Orange County C.C., N.Y., 1961; BS, Rensselaer Poly Inst., 1963; MSEE, Stanford (Calif.) U., 1965, PhD, 1969. V.p., gen. mgr. Sys. Control Inc., Palo Alto, Calif., 1968-78; dir. nat. intelligence Office Sec. of Def., Washington, 1978-82; dir. strategic tech. DARPA, Washington, 1982-86; corp. v.p. Ford Aerospace, Newport Beach, Calif., 1986-90, LORAL, Newport Beach, 1990-92; corp. v.p., gen. mgr. Sci. Application Internat., Inc., San Diego, 1992-94; CEO Dynamics Tech. Inc., Torrance, Calif., 1994-96; CEO, pres. Sequoia Group, Newport Beach, Calif., 1996—; chmn., bd. dirs. Condyne Tech., Inc., Orlando, Fla., 1990-92; dir. Orincon, La Jolla, Calif. Contbr. articles to profl. jours. Recipient Nat. Intelligence medal DCI, 1986, Civilian Meritorious medal U.S. Sec. Def., 1986. Mem. IEEE, Cosmos Club, Sigma Xi, Eta Kappa Nu, Tau Beta Pi. Avocations: ham radio, skiing. Home: 4518 Roxbury Rd Corona Del Mar CA 92625-3125

TETLOW, WILLIAM LLOYD, infotech consultant; b. Phila., July 2, 1938; s. William Lloyd and Mary Eleanor (Ferris) T.; m. Amber Jane Riederer, June 13, 1964; children: Jennifer Kay, Rebecca Dawn, Derek William. Student, Cornell U., 1956-60; B in Gen. Edn., U. Omaha, 1961; MA, Cornell U., 1965, PhD, 1973. Dir. instl. research Cornell U., Ithaca, N.Y., 1965-70; dir. planning U. B.C., Vancouver, Can., 1970-82; dir. NCHEMS Mgmt. Products, Boulder, Colo., 1982-85; pres., dir. Vantage Info. Products, Inc., Boulder, 1985-87; pres., propr. Vantage Computer Svcs., Boulder, 1986-96; infotech cons. U. Colo., 1986—; cons. various univs. U.S., Can. and Australia, 1970—. Editor/author: Using Microcomputers for Planning and Decision Support, 1984; contbr. numerous articles to profl. jours. Mem. Mt. Calvary Luth. Ch. Coun., 1985-86, 89-92, pres., 1991-92, U.S. Mex. C. of C. (webmaster Rocky Mountain chpt.). Served to 1st lt. AUS, 1961-63. Recipient U. Colo. medal, 1987; Kiwanis Hixon fellow, 1996, Kiwanis Lusche fellow, 1996. Mem. Assn. Inst. Rsch. (sec. 1973-75, v.p. 1980-81, pres. 1981-82), Concordia, Kiwanis (pres. 1996-97). Avocations: outdoor sports, woodworking. Home: 312 Diamond Cir Louisville CO 80027-3202

TETTEGAH, SHARON YVONNE, education educator; b. Wichita Falls, Tex., Jan. 14, 1956; d. Lawrence Guice and Doris Jean (Leak) Oliver; 1 child, Tandra Ainsworth; m. Joseph Miller Zangai, Dec. 22, 1978 (div. 1983); 1 child, Tonia Monjay Zangai; m. George Tettegah, Apr. 28, 1989; children: Nicole Jennifer, Michael Scott. AA, Coll. Alameda, 1985; BA, U. Calif., Davis, 1988, teaching cert., 1989, MA, 1991; PhD in Ednl. Psychology, U. Calif., Santa Barbara, 1997. Cert. elem. tchr., Calif. Clk. II Alameda County Mcpl. Ct., Oakland, Calif., 1976-77; acct. clk. Alameda County Social Svcs., Oakland, 1977-78, eligibility technician, 1978-82; supervising clk. Alameda County Health Care Svcs., Oakland, 1982-84; tchr. Davis (Calif.) Joint Unified Sch. Dist., 1988-89, L.A. Unified Schs., L.A., 1990-92; tchr. Oakland Unified Sch. Dist., Oakland, 1992—, tchr. sci. mentor, 1993—; teaching asst. U. Calif., Santa Barbara, 1993-94; adminstrv. intern Oxnard Unified Sch. Dist., 1994, U. Calif. Cultural Awareness Program, Santa Barbara, 1994—; rsch. cons. to vice chancellor students affairs, cons. tchr. edn. program, facilitor registrar's office U. Calif., Santa Barbara, 1995-96, rsch. asst. Grad. Sch. Edn., 1996—; asst. prof. tchr. edn. Calif. State U., Hayward, 1998—; cons. U. Calif. , Davis, 1988-89, Montessori Ctr. Sch., Santa Barbara, Calif., 1996, Oakland-Hayward Sch. Partnership, Oakland, 1998-99; multicultural cons. Davis Unified Sch. Dist., 1988-89; edn. cons. Ednl. Testing Svc., Emeryville, Calif., 1994; chair diversity com. of Santa Barbara Village Charter Sch.; mem. academic senate com. undergrad enrollment and admissions U. Calif. Santa Barbara, 1995, tchr. cross-cultural interactions course, summer, 1995; mem. academic affairs affirmative action com. U. Calif. Santa Barbara, 1995-96, grad. sch. of edn., grad. affairs and affirmative action comms. U. Calif. Santa Barbara, 1995-96; rsch. cons. Oakland Unified Sch. Dist., 1998-99, African Am. Literacy and Culture Project, Oakland Pub. Schs., Oakland, 1998—; gubernatorial appointee to State Interagy. Coord. Coun., 1999—. Contbr. articles to profl. jours. Mem. U. Calif. Santa Barbara Acad. Senate Bd. Undergraduate Admissions and Records; co-chair Diversity Com. Montecito-Santa Barbara Charter Sch.; pres. African-Am. Grad. and Profl. Students Orgn., Davis, 1988-89; gubernatorial appointee State Interagy. Coordinating Coun., Calif., 1999. Recipient Charlene Richardson Acad. Honors award Coll. Alameda, 1985; Calif. State Acad. fellow, 1989-91, Grad. Opportunity Acad. Excellence fellow, 1994-95, Vice Chancellors Acad. Achievement fellowship U. Calif. Santa Barbara, 1995-96, Vice Chancellors Acad. Fellowship Grad. Divsn., 1995-96, 96-97. Mem. Am. Ednl. Researchers Assn., Calif. Sci. Tchrs. Assn., Calif. Advocacy for Math and Sci., Calif. Tchrs. Assn., Calif. Media Libr. Educators Assn., PTA, Multicultural Curriculum Assn., Supervision and Curriculum Leadership Assn., Bay Area Sci. and Tech. Educators Corsortium, Pan-African Students Assn., Kappa Delta Pi. Avocations: travelling, reading, preparing gourmet foods, tennis. Home: PO Box 56715 Hayward CA 94542 Office: U Calif Santa Barbara Sch Edn/Ednl Psychology Santa Barbara CA 93106

TETZLAFF, KAREN MARIE, state official; b. Florence, Oreg., Mar. 9, 1950; d. Chester Arthur and Martha Jane (Howell) Mitchell; m. Sterling Franklin Tetzlaff, July 16, 1988; children: Michelle René Davis, André Scott Matney, Derrick Anthony Matney, Anissa Barret. Diploma, Chemeketa C.C., Salem, Oreg., 1981. Notary pub., Oreg. Sec. Oreg. Corrections div., Madras, 1977-78; intake-release data clk. community corrections Oreg. Corrections div., Salem, 1979-80, correctional officer, 1980-83, records mgr., 1983—, instr., 1990—; master facilitator trainer breaking barriers Oreg. Corrections div., 1995—; facilitator, trainer breaking barriers Gordon Graham & Co., Salem, 1992—, developing capable people, Salem, 1993—; instr., law enforcement data system rep. Oreg. Women's Correctional Ctr., Salem, 1984—, facilitator, 1993—. Head usher John Jacobs Evangelistic Assn., Salem, Medford, Redmond, Oreg., 1990-92; youth worship leader South Salem Foursquare Ch., Salem, 1990-92; vol. Driving Under Influence Tng. Task Force, Salem, 1992—; v.p. Salem Gospel Cente Womens Ministry, 1993-95, Marion County chpt. Mothers Against Drunk Driving, 1994-95; dir. Pentecostal Holiness N.W. Dist. Women's Ministry, 1996—; worship and music dir., youth leader Salem Gospel Ctr., 1996—. Recipient 5-yr. outstanding svc. award Law Enforcement Data System, 1990, Investing in People, Svc. to State Tng. award Exec. Dept., 1992, traffic safety award Oreg. Dept. Transp., 1993, Employee of Quarter award Oreg. Women's Correctionala Ctr., 1993. Mem. Am. Correctional Assn., Oreg. Corrections Assn., Nat. Notary Assn., Cognitive Restructuring Network (letter of ap-

preciation 1993). Republican. Avocations: paralegal studies, reading, singing. Office: Oreg Women's Correctional Ctr 2809 State St Salem OR 97310-1307

TEUTSCH, CHAMPION KURT, psycho-geneticist; b. Leipzig, Germany, Feb. 10, 1921; came to U.S., 1939; s. Friedrich Wilhelm and Elizabeth (Babette) T.; m. Joel Marie Noel, Apr. 24, 1954 (dec. Mar. 1992); 1 child, Lee Brooks. BCE with high honors, U. Fla., 1942; degree, U. So. Calif., L.A., 1948-49, 57; postgrad., Harvard U., 1947-48; MS in Psychology, Calif. Coast U., Santa Ana, 1975, PhD in Psychology, 1976. Sr. engr., tech. writer, editor various aerospace firms, Columbus, San Francisco, L.A., 1946-60; cons., gene-physicist, psycho-geneticist L.A., 1960—; pres. Acad. Teutsch Ideal Method, L.A., 1981—; chmn. bd. dirs. Internat. Human Rsch. Ctr. Sunray, Moscow State U., 1993—; cons. med. clinics, law firms, real estate, computer, electronics ins. firms, automobile agys., entertainment orgns., various locations, 1964—; guest nat. and local TV programs, 1968—; cons. Bush Presdl. campaign, L.A., 1988; lectr. Moscow State U., 1993, U. St. Petersburg, 1993, Zaparoche, Ukraine, 1994, Med. Coll. U. Fla., 1994; vis. prof. medicine U. Fla., 1996—. Co-author: Understand and Raise Your Consciousness--From Here to Happiness!, 1959, 75, Victimology: An Effect of Consciousness, Interpersonal Dynamics and Human Physics, 1973, Stress, Genetics and Interpersonal Relationships--The Type D Complex, 1979, From Human Bondage to Liberty: An Introduction to Genephysics, 1993, A Nonmedical Andwer to Cancer and Other Diseases, 1994, Ideal Israel, Tel Aviv, 1996; developer (with J.M. Noe! Teutsch) genogram and basic inner drive, direction or desire. Served to 1st lt. USAF, 1942-52. Mem. Friar's Club, Vikings Club, Optimist Internat. (pres. 1982). Avocation: tennis, skiing. Home: Unit 401 10418 Ilona Ave Los Angeles CA 90064-2304 Office: Acad Teutsch Ideal Method 2049 Century Park E Ste 2730 Los Angeles CA 90067-3272

TEVIOTDALE, ELIZABETH COVER, museum curator; b. N.Y.C., Nov. 15, 1955; d. David Ramsay Wilson and Anne Cover (Barton) T. BA in Music, SUNY, Buffalo, 1979; MA, U. N.C., 1981, PhD, 1991; MA, Tulane U., 1985; BA in History, SUNY, Buffalo, 1979. Predoctoral fellow Samuel H. Kress Found., Warburg Inst., 1988-90; guest scholar Swedish Inst., Stockholm, 1989; vis. instr. U. Iowa, Iowa City, 1991; vis. asst. prof. Davidson (N.C.) Coll., 1991-92; asst. curator J. Paul Getty Mus., L.A., 1992-97, assoc. curator, 1997—; assoc. Ctr. for Medeival and Renaissance Studies, UCLA, 1995—. Contbr. articles to profl. publs. Travel grantee Fulbright Commn., Free U., Berlin, 1983-84. Mem. Am. Musicological Soc., Coll. Art Assn., Internat. Ctr. Medieval Art, Medieval Acad. Am. Avocation: slow pitch softball. Home: 9814 Regent St Apt 2 Los Angeles CA 90034-5126 Office: J Paul Getty Mus 1200 Getty Center Dr Ste 1000 Los Angeles CA 90049-1687

TEVIS, BARRY LEE, television producer, marketing executive; b. Pasadena, Calif., Feb. 5, 1956; s. John Larry Tevis and Renee Lydia Clement; m. Julie Marie Knauss, Mar. 31, 1990; children: Ben, Ann Marie, Hilary, Andrew. Student, Bates Vocat. Tech. Inst., Tacoma, 1973-75. Master control operator KTBN-TV, Santa Ana, Calif., 1975-76; producer, dir. KOTI-TV, Klamath Falls, Oreg., 1976-77, KPAZ-TV, Phoenix, Ariz., 1977-78; prodn. mgr., dir. advt. and promotion KTVL-TV, Medford, Oreg., 1978—. Sound dir. Rogue Valley Fellowship Ch., Medford. Recipient various broadcast awards. Mem. Promax Internat. (award of merit 1990). Republican. Avocations: photography, travel. Office: KTVL-TV 1440 Rossanley Dr Medford OR 97501-1751

TEVRIZIAN, DICKRAN M., JR., federal judge; b. Los Angeles, Aug. 4, 1940; s. Dickran and Rose Tevrizian; m. Geraldine Tevrizian, Aug. 22, 1964; children: Allyson Tracy, Leslie Sara. BS, U. So. Calif., 1962, JD, 1965. Tax acct. Arthur Andersen and Co., Los Angeles, 1965-66; atty., ptnr. Kirtland and Packard, Los Angeles, 1966-72; judge Los Angeles Mcpl. Ct., Los Angeles, 1972-78, State of Calif. Superior Ct., Los Angeles, 1978-82; ptnr. Manatt, Phelps, Rothenberg & Tunney, Los Angeles, 1982-85, Lewis, D'Amato, Brisbois & Bisgaard, Los Angeles, 1985-86; judge U.S. Dist. Ct., Los Angeles, 1986—. Named Trial Judge of the Yr., Calif. Trial Lawyers Assn., 1987, L.A. County Bar Assn., 1994-95. Mem. Calif. Trial Lawyer's Assn. (trial judge of yr. 1987), L.A. County Bar Assn. (trial judge of yr. 1994-95), Malibu Bar Assn. (fed. ct. trial judge of yr. 1998). Office: US Dist Ct Royal Federal Bldg 255 E Temple St Los Angeles CA 90012-3334

THALL, RICHARD VINCENT, school system administrator; b. San Francisco, Sept. 12, 1940; s. Albert Vincent and Alice Stella (O'Brien) T.; m. Ellyn Marie Wisherop, June 15, 1963; children: Kristen Ellyn, Richard Vincent Jr. AA, City Coll. San Francisco, 1961; BA, San Francisco State Coll., 1964; MA, San Francisco State U., 1971. Cert. elem. tchr., Calif.; cert. secondary tchr., Calif.; cert. community coll. tchr., Calif. Tchr. biology San Francisco Unified Sch. Dist., 1965-66; tchr. biology Mt. Diablo Unified Sch. Dist., Concord, Calif., 1966-79, program dir. water environ. studies program, 1979—; ranger/naturalist State of Calif., Brannan Island, 1973-78; naturalist Adventure Internat., Oakland, Calif., 1979-81; lectr. Princess Cruise Lines, 1982—, Sea Goddess, 1986—, Sun Lines, 1987, Sitmar Lines, 1989, Royal Caribbean Internat., 1991-98; lectr. naturalist Posh Talks, Inc., 1982—; spkr. commencements U. Calif., Berkeley, 1989. Author: Ecological Sampling of the Sacramento-San Joaquin Delta, 1976; Water Environment Studies Program, 1986; co-author: Project MER Laboratory Manual, 1982. Mem. Contra Costa County (Calif.) Natural Resources Commn., 1975-78, vice-chmn., 1977-78; active Save Mt. Diablo, Concord, 1969-76, v.p., 1974-75; mem. citizens com. Assn. Bay Area Govt. Water Quality, 1979-82, vice-chmn., 1980-82; active John Marsh Home Restoration Com., Martinez, Calif., 1977-78; troop com. chmn. Boy Scouts Am., Concord, 1984-86, asst. scoutmaster, 1985-87. Recipient Recognition and Excellence cert. Assn. Calif. Sch. Adminstrs., 1984, Wood Badge award Boy Scouts Am., 1986; grantee State Calif., 1982, 84, San Francisco Estuary Project, 1992, EPA, 1992, Shell Oil Co., 1993. Mem. AAAS, Nat. Assn. Biology Tchrs., Nat. Audubon Soc., Am. Mus. Natural Hist., Nat. Geog. Soc., Smithsonian Instn. (assoc.). Republican. Roman Catholic. Avocations: skiing, jogging, reading, hiking, photography. Home: 1712 Lindenwood Dr Concord CA 94521-1109 Office: Mt Diablo Unified Sch Dist 1936 Carlotta Dr Concord CA 94519-1358

THAMES, CARROLL THOMAS, financial consultant; b. Webbers Falls, Okla., Sept. 26, 1938; s. Carroll Hilton and Opal (Gillespie) T.; m. Ramona Pepin, Dec. 16, 1961 (div. July 1980); children: Kimberly Ann, Gavin Thomas. BA, Coll. of Notre Dame, Belmont, Calif., 1972; MBA, U. Santa Clara, 1974. CLU, chartered fin. cons.; cert. fin. planner. Chief industr. engr. Kaiser Aluminum Chem. Corp., Oakland, Calif., 1966-83; registered prin. SunAmerica Securities, Inc., Phoenix, 1980—; pres. Capital Mgmt. Network, Inc., Woodbridge, Calif., 1985—; lectr. U. Calif., Santa Cruz, 1986, Golden Gate U., Monterey, Calif., 1984-85, Hartnell Coll., Salinas, Calif., 1986-87. Contbr. fin. planning articles to profl. jours. Bd. dirs. YMCA, Salinas, 1986-87. Mem. Internat. Assn. for Fin. Planning Inc. (pres.-chmn. Monterey Bay chpt. 1985-88), Am. Soc. CLU & Chartered Fin. Consultants (pres. Monterey Bay chpt. 1984-85), Calif. Assn. for Fin. Planning (sec. 1986-87), Inst. Cert. Fin. Planners, Internat. Bd. Cert. Fin. Planners, Alpha Gamma Sigma. Republican. Avocations: golf, tennis, bridge, trap, skiing. Office: PO Box 1024 Woodbridge CA 95258-1024

THANHOUSER, EDWIN WAY, marketing manager; b. N.Y.C., Jan. 18, 1949; s. Lloyd Frank and Alice (Way) T.; m. Diane Kopecky, July 15, 1968 (div. Feb. 1977); 1 child, Lisa Anne; m. Anne Attebury, Dec. 18, 1980; children—Edwin Way, Spencer Kallin, William Lloyd, Michael Severn. B.S. in Computer Sci., Trinity U., San Antonio, 1973. With Tektronix, Inc., 1977-82; marketing mgr. Intel Co., Hillsboro, Oreg., 1982—. Inventor Intermixing refresh and DVST graphics, 1977. Mem. Assn. Computing Machinery, Spl. Interest Group Graphics, Computer Graphics Pioneer (charter), Mazamas Club (climbing com. 1983-86), Multnomah Athletic Club, Portland Golf Club. Home: 703 NW Albemarle Ter Portland OR 97210-3114 Office: Intel Co 5200 NE Elam Young Pkwy Hillsboro OR 97124-6497

THAYER, MARTHA ANN, small business owner; b. Santa Fe, N.Mex., May 8, 1936; d. Duren Howard and Lena Odessa (Fox) Shields; m. Norman S. Thayer Jr., Jan. 30, 1960; children: Murray Norman, Tanya Noelle. BS, U. N.Mex., 1960. Child welfare worker State of N.Mex., Farmington and Santa Fe, 1961-64; owner Baskets by Thayer, Albuquerque, 1975-85, Noelle's, Albuquerque, 1985-89; ptnr., co-owner Indian Originals, Albuquerque, 1989-94, Native Design, 1995-96; owner Martha A. Thayer, 1996-98; treas. DHS Properties, Inc., 1994—; agt. for Elizabeth Abeyta, Adrian Quintana, Alexandria Rohrscheib, Albuquerque, 1995—; owner Martha A. Thayer Enterprises L.L.P., 1998—; co-owner Shields Investments Enterprises L.L.P., 1998—; crafts instr. Village Wool, Continuing Edn., Albuquerque, 1975-78; trustee Shields Trust, 1994—. Contbr. articles, revs. to craft publs.; juried show, Mus. of Internat. Folk Arts, 1975; baskets exhibited in group shows at N.Mex. State Fair, 1980 (1st place award), Women's Show, 1983 (1st place award). Campaign mgr. Dem. Candidate for State Supreme Ct., Bernalillo County, N.Mex., 1970; founding mem. Women's Polit. Caucus, Bernalillo County; chmn. Mother's March of Dimes, Bernalillo County, 1974. Mem. Hist. Preservation Soc., Petroleum Club, Genealogy Club of Albuquerque Pub. Libr., Mus. Albuquerque (assoc.). Avocations: genealogy, gardening, anthropology, politics, antiques, Native American art collector.

THAYER, MICHAEL J., secondary education educator. Tchr. Las Cruces (N.Mex.) Mid. Sch., 1972-94, Las Cruces H.S., 1994—. Named N.Mex. Tchr. of Yr., 1992. Office: Las Cruces HS 1755 El Paseo St Las Cruces NM 88001-6011*

THEE, THOMAS WILLIAM, management consultant; b. Aurora, Ill., Nov. 18, 1937; s. John William and Della Mae (Chrystal) T.; m. Marcia Lee Olauson, Feb. 15, 1982; 1 child, Jonathan William. BS, No. Ill. U., 1964. Dir. child guidance Loyal Order of Moose, Mooseheart, Ill., 1964-65; mgr. of mgmt. employment United Air Lines, Inc., Elk Grove Village, Ill., 1965-67; dir. mgmt. devel. Cone Mills Corp., Greensboro, N.C., 1967-70; v.p. Hodge Cronin Assocs., Chgo., 1970-71; v.p. indsl. and pub. rels. Am. Hosp. Supply Corp, Two Rivers, Wis., 1971-73, v.p. mktg. and sales, 1973-76, v.p., gen. mgr., 1976-82; exec. v.p., gen. mgr. The Am. Consulting Group, Los Gatos, Calif., 1982—. Dir. Manpower Devel. Program, Greensboro N.C. C. of C., 1968; bd. dirs. United Fun, Two Rivers, Wis., 1975-80. With USAF, 1957-60, Japan. Avocations: golf, reading, sports activities. Office: The Am Consulting Group 170 Knowles Dr Ste 210 Los Gatos CA 95030

THEURER, BYRON W., aerospace engineer, business owner; b. Glendale, Calif., July 1, 1939; s. William Louis and Roberta Cecelia (Sturgiss) T.; m. Sue Ann McKay, Sept. 15, 1962 (div. 1980); children: Karen Marie, William Thomas, Alison Lee. BS in Engring. Sci., USAF Acad., 1961; MS in Aero. Sci., U. Calif., Berkeley, 1965; MBA, U. Redlands, 1991. Commd. USAF, 1961, advanced through grades to lt. col., ret. 1978; project officer Space Shuttle Devel. Prog., Houston, 1971-76; chief of test F-15 Systems Prog. Office Wright Patterson AFB, Ohio, 1976-78; sr. engr. Veda, Inc., Dayton, 1979-81, Logicon Inc., Dayton, 1981-83; project mgr. Support Systems Assocs., Inc., Dayton, 1983-84, CTA Inc., Ridgecrest, Calif., 1985-89; owner, operator The Princeton Rev. of Ctrl. Calif., Ridgecrest, 1989-92, San Luis Obispo, 1993—; cons. in field. Decorated Silver Star, D.F.C., Air Medals (16); named Officer of the Yr., Air Force Flight Test Ctr., Edwards AFB, 1970. Mem. Air Force Assn., Assn. Old Crows, USAF Acad. Assn. Grads. (nat. bd. dirs. 1972-75, chpt. pres. 1981-83). Republican. Episcopalian. Avocations: long distance running. Home: PO Box 697 Cayucos CA 93430-0697

THIELE, GLORIA DAY, retired librarian, small business owner; b. Los Angeles, Sept. 4, 1931; d. Russell Day Plummer and Dorothy Ruby (Day) Plummer Thi.; m. Donald Edward Cools, June 13, 1953 (div.); children: Michael, Ramona, Naomi, Lawrence, Nancy, Rebecca, Eugene, Maria, Charles. MusB, Mt. St. Mary's Coll., L.A., 1953. Libr. asst. Anaheim (Calif.) Pub. Libr., 1970-73, head Biblioteca de la Comunidad, 1973-74, children's libr. asst., 1974-76, children's br. specialist, 1976-78, children's libr., 1978-81; head children's svcs. Santa Maria (Calif.) Pub. Libr., 1981-85; cons. Literature Continuum, Santa Maria Sch. Dist., 1981-85; cons. Organizational Ch.-Sch. Libr., L.A., 1980; guest lectr. children's lit. Allan Hancock Coll., Santa Maria, 1981-85; owner, founder Discovery Garden, Grass Valley, Calif., 1989-93. Libr. liaison Casa Amistad Community Svc. Group, Anaheim, 1973-74; mem. outreach com. Santiago Libr. System, Orange County, 1973-74, mem. children's svcs. com., 1971-81; mem. Community Svcs. Coordinating Council, Santa Maria, 1982-85; chairperson children's svcs. com. Black Gold Libr. System, 1983-84; cons. children's libr. programs, 1986—; profl. storyteller, 1989—; Allegro Alliance vol. for music in the mountains, 1994-98. Contbr. poems to Amherst Soc.'s Am. Poetry Ann., 1988. Mem. So. Calif. Council Lit. for Children and Young People, Kiwanis (sec., publicity chair 1996—), Delta Epsilon Sigma. Republican. Roman Catholic.

THIGPEN, MARY CECELIA, city official, consultant; b. L.A., Jan. 27, 1949; d. Tom Allen and Inell Theresa (Evans) Johnson; m. Willie Edward Thigpen, Apr. 30, 1971; children: Sonna Aminata, Monifa Ayodele. BA, Xavier U., New Orleans, 1971; MS in Urban Planning, U. New Orleans, 1979. Planner Urban Systems, Inc., New Orleans, 1977-79, Grimball/Garrandon/Savoy Engrs. and Architects, New Orleans, 1979-80; planner, cons. Mayor's Office, City of New Orleans, 1979; grants program evaluator Pinellas County Manpower Council, Clearwater, Fla., 1980-81; personnel mgmt. specialist Pinellas County Personnel Dept., Clearwater, 1981-83; adminstrv. analyst U. Calif., San Diego, 1983-85; sr. and personnel analyst City of Chula Vista, Calif., 1985—; planning cons. Mayor's office, New Orleans, 1979; b.p. bd. dirs. Cajon Valley Ednl. Found., El Cajon, Calif., 1988—. Writer poetry. Named Woman of Distinction, San Diego County Women, Inc., 1990; named Mother of Yr., Delta Sigma Theta of San Diego County, 1996. Mem. Nat. Med. Assn. Aux. (v.p. 1986—), Jack and Jill Am, Calif. Women in Govt., Internat. Pers. Mgmt. Assn., Am. Planning Assn. Roman Catholic. Avocations: fashion design, arts promotion, handcrafts, writing poetry and plays. Home: 1551 Heron Ave El Cajon CA 92020-8810

THILL, JOHN VAL, communications professional, writer, consultant; b. Milw., Dec. 27, 1953; s. Lewis Dominic and Carol Jean (Werner) T. BS, San Diego State U., 1977; MBA, U. San Diego, 1982. Mgr. Pacific Bell, San Diego, 1979-82; CEO Comm. Specialists of Am., San Diego, 1982—; pres. Bovee & Thill LLC; bd. dirs. Comm. Rsch. Inst., L.A. Author: Excellence in Business Communication, 1997, Business Today, 1998, Business Communication Today, 1999. Named Outstanding Bus. Communicator Am. Soc. Journalists, 1982, Nat. Cmty. Leadership award, 1997. Mem. Assn. Bus. Communication, 1985, Text and Acad. Authors Assn. Avocations: swimming, racquetball. Office: Bovee & Thill LLC 2950 E Flamingo Rd Ste B Las Vegas NV 89121

THOLLANDER, EARL GUSTAVE, artist, author; b. Kingsburg, Calif., Apr. 13, 1922; s. Gus Alfred and Helen Marie (Peterson) T.; m. Janet Marie Behr; May 31, 1947; children: Kristie, Wesley. BA, U. Calif., Berkeley, 1944. Staff artist Patterson and Hall, San Francisco, 1946-47, San Francisco Examiner, 1947-57, Landphere and Assocs., 1957-60; free-lance artist, writer, 1960—. Author: Back Roads of California, 1971, revised 1988; Back Roads of New England, 1974, Barns of California, 1974, Back Roads of Arizona, 1978 (now called Arizona's Scenic Byways), revised 1992, Back Roads of Oregon, 1979, revised 1993, Back Roads of Texas, 1980, Back Roads of Washington, 1981, revised 1993, Earl Thollander's Back Roads of California, 1983, revised 1994, Back Roads of the Carolinas, 1985, Earl Thollander's San Francisco, 1994. Served to lt. (j.g.) USN, 1942-45, PTO. Democrat. Unitarian. Home and Studio: 19210 Hwy 128 Calistoga CA 94515-9502

THOMAS, ALTA PARKER, secondary school educator; b. Butte, Mont., Sept. 18, 1940; d. Charles Clayton and Sarah Elizabeth (Bennett) Parker Hopkins; m. Vivian William Thomas Jr., Aug. 19, 1962; children: Christine Michelle Thomas Walters, Tracyy Ann Thomas, Lisa Janine Thomas Julson. BS, Mont. State U., 1962; MEd, Walla Walla Coll., 1991. Cert. tchr., Wash. Rsch. chemist Dow Chem. Co., Midland, Mich., 1962-64; tchr. Granite Sch. Dist., Salt Lake City, 1964-65; home and hosp. tchr. Richland (Wash.) Schs., 1975-77; sci. tchr. Kennewick (Wash.) Sch. Dist., 1977-84, high sch. biology tchr., 1984—, sci. dept. chair, 1992-94; coord. Internat. Baccalaureate Kennewick Sch. Dist., 1994—, chmn. sci. curriculum com., 1987-89, rep. dist. circle com., 1991-93; coach sci. olympiad team Kennewick H.S., 1988-94, mem. staff devel. com., 1986-91, site coun., 1996. Patented oven cleaner formula; editor: Curnutt Family Cookbook, 1986. Founder acad. booster club Kennewick High Sch., 1985. REST fellow Battelle Pacific N.W. Lab., 1988. Mem. Nat. Assn. Biology Tchrs., NEA, Wash. Edn. Assn., Kennewick Edn. Assn. (rep., negotiator 1977—), Wash. Sci. Tchr. Assn., Delta Kappa Gamma (membership chair, polit. affairs chair 1984—). Presbyterian. Avocations: birding, hiking, cross stitch, quilting, reading. Home: 4029 S Cascade St Kennewick WA 99337-5185 Office: Kennewick High Sch 500 S Dayton St Kennewick WA 99336-5674

THOMAS, BRIAN CHESTER, state legislator, engineer; b. Tacoma, Wash., May 19, 1939; s. Ralph R. and Katheryne (Chester) T.; m. Judith Lynn Adams, Feb. 20, 1965; children: Jeffrey, Kyle, Cheryl. BS in Engring., Oreg. State U., 1961; postgrad., U. Wash., 1968-70; MBA, Pacific Luth. U., 1979. Civil engr. U.S. Coast Guard, Seattle, 1962-63; ops. officer U.S. Coast Guard, Astoria, Oreg., 1964-65; sr. sales engr. Puget Sound Power & Light Co., Bellevue, Wash., 1965-70, mgr. market rsch., 1971-80, rsch. adminstr., 1981-89, prin. engr., 1989-97; mem. Wash. Ho. of Reps., Olympia, 1993—, mem. forecast coun., 1996—, mem. joint select com. on edn. restructuring, 1995—, chmn. fin. com., 1995—, energy, utilities coms., 1997—, chmn. Sch. Constrn. Task Force, 1998—; chair EEI Rsch. Mgmt. Com., Washington, 1988-89, EPRI Renewable Com., Palo Alto, Calif., 1989-90; adv. bd. Nat. Renewable Energy Lab., Golden, Colo., 1990-92; mem. adv. bd. sch. elec. engring. Oreg. State U., Corvallis, 1991-97; dep. dir. region 10 U.S. Dept. Transp. Emergency Orgn., Seattle, 1989-93. Bd. dirs. Issaquah (Wash.), Sch. Dist., 1989-93. Capt. USCGR, 1961-84. Mem. Issaquah Rotary (pres. 1982-83). Republican. Avocation: restoring Studebakers. Home: 14715 182nd Pl SE Renton WA 98059-8028 Office: Wash Ho Reps PO Box 40610 Olympia WA 98504-0610

THOMAS, CLAUDEWELL SIDNEY, psychiatry educator; b. N.Y.C., Oct. 5, 1932; s. Humphrey Sidney and Frances Elizabeth (Collins) T.; m. Carolyn Pauline Rozansky, Sept. 6, 1958; children: Jeffrey Evan, Julie-Anne Elizabeth, Jessica Edith. BA, Columbia U., 1952; MD, SUNY, Downstate Med. Ctr., 1956; MPH, Yale U., 1964. Diplomate Nat. Bd. Med. Examiners, Am. Bd. Psychiatry, Am. Bd. Forensic Medicine, Am. Bd. Psychological Splties. From instr. to assoc. prof. Yale U., New Haven, 1963-68, dir. Yale tng. program in social community psychiatry, 1967-70; dir. div. mental health service programs NIMH, Washington, 1970-73; chmn. dept. psychiatry U.M.D.N.J., Newark, 1973-83; prof. dept. psychiatry Drew Med. Sch., 1983—, chmn. dept. psychiatry, 1983-93; prof. dept. psychiatry UCLA, 1983-94, vice chmn. dept. psychiatry, 1983-93, prof. emeritus dept. psychiatry, 1994—; med. dir. Tokanui Hosp., TeAwamutu, N.Z., 1996; cons. A.K. Rice Inst., Washington, 1978-80, SAMSA/PHS Cons., 1991—; mem. L.A. County Superior Ct. Psych. Panel, 1991-97. Author: (with B. Bergen) Issues and Problems in Social Psychiatry, 1966; editor (with R. Bryce LaPorte) Alienation in Contemporary Society, 1976, (with J. Lindenthal) Psychiatry and Mental Health Science Handbook; mem. editorial bd. Internat. Jour. Mental Health, Adminstrn. In Mental Health. Bd. dirs. Bay Area Found., 1987—. Served to capt. USAF, 1959-61. Fellow APHA, Am. Psychoanalytic Assn. (hon.), Am. Psychiat. Assn. (life), Royal Soc. Health, N.Y. Acad. Sci., N.Y. Acad. Medicine; mem. Am. Sociol. Assn., Am. Coll. Mental Health Adminstrs., Am. Coll. Forensic Examiners, L.A. Acad. Med. Avocations: tennis, racquetball, violin, piano. Home and Office: 30676 Palos Verdes Dr W Palos Verdes Peninsula CA 90274

THOMAS, CRAIG, senator; b. Cody, Wyo., Feb. 17, 1933; s. Craig E. and Marge Oweta (Lynn) T.; m. Susan Roberts; children: Peter, Paul, Patrick, Alexis. BS, U. Wyo., 1955. V.p. Wyo. Farm Bur., Laramie, 1959-66; with Am. Farm Bur., 1966-75; gen. mgr. Wyo. Rural Elec. Assn., 1975-89; mem. Wyo. Ho. of Reps., 1984-89; rep. from Wyo. U.S. Ho. of Reps., Washington, 1989-94; U.S. senator from Wyo. Washington, 1995—; mem. energy and natural resources com., environment and pub. works com., fgn. rels. com., Indian affairs com. Former chmn. Natrona County (Wyo.) Rep. Com.; state rep. Natrona County Dist.; del. Rep. Nat. Conv., 1980. Capt. USMC. Mem. Am. Soc. Trade Execs., Masons. Methodist. Office: US Senate 109 Hart Senate Office Bldg Washington DC 20510-5001*

THOMAS, DAVID G., advertising executive; b. Ogden, Utah, Oct. 15, 1950; s. Glenn and Norma (Beard) T.; m. Kathleen Lynn Alford, Aug. 27, 1969; children: Troy, Matthew, Brett. BS, Weber State Coll., 1977; MS, Brigham Young U., 1980. Musician Utah, 1968-77; tchr., counselor Sandridge Jr. High Sch., Roy, Utah, 1977-81; writer, producer Salt Lake City, 1981-82; chmn. Thomas/Phillips/Clawson Advt., Salt Lake City, 1982-86; exec. v.p., mng. dir. Cole & Weber Advt., Inc., Salt Lake City, 1986—; pres. Publicis, Salt Lake City. Councilman, asst. mayor, Plain City, Utah, 1972-78; scout master Boy Scouts Am., Farmington, Utah, 1977-85. Recipient Clio finalist award, 198-86, IBA awards (7) Hollywood Broadcasters, N.Y. Film and Video Gold awards N.Y. Film Soc., 1987. Mem. Utah Advt. Fedn. (43 Gold awards 1981-87), AAAA. Democrat. Mormon. Avocations: skiing, water skiing, camping. Home: 2073 Kingston Rd Farmington UT 84025-4107 Office: Publicis 110 Social Mall Ave Salt Lake City UT 84111*

THOMAS, DAVID SNOW, plastic surgeon; b. Chgo., Feb. 7, 1951; s. Allan Perry and Verna Bea (Snow) T.; m. Becky Williams Thomas, Aug. 25, 1973; children: Nathan David, Abigail, Elizabeth. BA, U. Utah, 1974, MD, 1978. Diplomate Am. Bd. Plastic Surgery, Am. Bd. Surgery. Resident surgery UCLA, 1978-83, resident plastic surgery, 1983-85, fellow craniofacial surgery, 1985; pvt. practice Salt Lake City, 1986—; chief plastic surgery Primary Childrens Med. Ctr., Salt Lake City, 1988-90, LDS Hosp., 1993—; clin. asst. prof. U. Utah Plastic Surgeons, Salt Lake City, 1986-89, assoc. prof. surgery, 1990-93, clin. assoc. prof., 1993—. Bd. Dirs. AMICUS, Salt Lake City, Utah, 1990-92. Fellow Am Coll. Surgeons; mem. Am. Soc. Plastic & Reconstructive Surgery, Am. Soc. Maxillofacial Surgery, Am. Cleft Palate Craniofacial Assn., Am. Soc. Aesthetic Plastic Surgery, Interplast (pres. Salt Lake City, 1992—, bd. dirs. Palo Alto, Calif., 1992—), The Country Club (Salt Lake City). Office: 370 9th Ave Ste 200 Salt Lake City UT 84103-2877*

THOMAS, EDWARD DONNALL, physician, researcher; b. Mart, Tex., Mar. 15, 1920; married; 3 children. BA, U. Tex., 1941, MA, 1943; MD, Harvard U., 1946; MD (hon.), U. Cagliari, Sardinia, 1981, U. Verona, Italy, 1991, U. Parma, Italy, 1992, U. Barcelona, Spain, 1994, U. Warsaw, Poland, 1996, U. Jagiellonski, Cracow, Poland, 1996. Lic. physician Mass., N.Y., Wash.; diplomate Am. Bd. Internal Medicine. Intern in medicine Peter Bent Brigham Hosp., Boston, 1946-47, rsch. fellow hematology, 1947-48; NRC postdoctoral fellow in medicine dept. biology MIT, Cambridge, 1950-51; chief med. resident, sr. asst. resident Peter Bent Brigham Hosp., 1951-53, hematologist, 1953-55; instr. medicine Harvard Med. Sch., Boston, 1953-55; rsch. assoc. Cancer Rsch. Found. Children's Med. Ctr., Boston, 1953-55; physician-in-chief Mary Imogene Bassett Hosp., Cooperstown, N.Y., 1955-63; assoc. clin. prof. medicine Coll. Physicians and Surgeons Columbia U., N.Y.C., 1955-63; attending physician U. Wash. Hosp., Seattle, 1963-90; prof. medicine Sch. Medicine U. Wash., Seattle, 1963-90, head divsn. oncology Sch. Medicine, 1963-85, prof. emeritus medicine Sch. Medicine, 1990—; dir. med. oncology Fred Hutchinson Cancer Rsch. Ctr., Seattle, 1974-89, assoc. dir. clin. rsch. programs, 1982-89, mem., 1974—; mem. hematology study sect. NIH, 1965-69; mem. bd. trustees and med. sci. adv. com. Leukemia Soc. Am., Inc., 1969-73; mem. clin. cancer investigation review com. Nat. Cancer Inst., 1970-74; 1st ann. Eugene C. Eppinger lectr. Peter Bent Brigham Hosp. and Harvard Med. Sch., 1974; Lilly lectr. Royal Coll. Physicians, London, 1977; Stratton lectr. Internation Soc. Hematology, 1982; Paul Aggeler lectr. U. Calif., San Francisco, 1982; 65th Mellon lectr. U. Pitts. Sch. Medicine, 1984; Stanley Wright Meml. lectr. Western Soc. Pediatric Rsch., 1985; Adolfo Ferrata lectr. Italian Soc. Hematology, Verona, Italy, 1991. Mem. editl. bd. Blood, 1962-75, 77-82, Transplantation, 1970-76, Proc. of Soc. for Exptl. Biology and Medicine, 1974-81, Leukemia Rsch., 1977-87, Hematological Oncology, 1982-87, Jour. Clin. Immunology, 1982-87, Am. Jour. Hematology, 1985—, Bone Marrow Transplantation, 1986—. With U.S. Army, 1948-50. Recipient A. Ross McIntyre award U. Nebr. Med. Ctr., 1975, Philip Levine award Am. Soc. Clin. Pathologists, 1979, Disting. Svc. in Basic Rsch. award Am. Cancer Soc., 1980, Kettering prize Gen. Motors Cancer Rsch. Found., 1981, Spl. Keynote Address award Am. Soc. Therapeutic Radiologists, 1981, Robert Roesler de Villiers award Leukemia Soc. Am., 1983, Karl Landsteiner Meml. award Am. Assn. Blood Banks, 1987, Terry Fox award Can., 1990, Internat. award Gairdner Found., 1990, N.Am. Med. Assn. Hong Kong prize, 1990, Nobel prize in medicine 1990, Presdl. medal of sci. NSF, 1990,. Mem. NAS, Am. Assn. Cancer Rsch., Am. Assn. Physicians (Kober medal 1992), Am. Fedn. Clin. Rsch., Am. Soc. Clin. Oncology (David A. Karnoksky Meml. lectr. 1983), Am. Soc. Clin. Investigation, Am. Soc. Hematology (pres. 1987-88, Henry M. Stratton lectr. 1975), Internat. Soc. Exptl. Hematology, Internat. Soc. Hematology,

Academie Royale de Medicine de Belgique (corresponding mem.), Swedish Soc. Hematology (hon.), Swiss Soc. Hematology, Royal Coll. Physicians and Surgeons Can. (hon.), Western Assn. Physicians, Soc. Exptl. Biology and Medicine, Transplantation Soc., Nat. Acad. Medicine (hon.). Office: Fred Hutchinson Cancer Ctr 1100 Fairview Ave N D5-100 PO Box 19024 Seattle WA 98109-1024

THOMAS, ESTHER MERLENE, elementary education educator; b. San Diego, Oct. 16, 1945; d. Merton Alfred and Nellie Lida (Von Pilz) T. *The Thomas family came from Wales. Esther's great-grandfather James Thomas was born in 1807, married Jane Walker, and died at age 106 in Missouri. Great-grandfather Calvin Thomas married Mellissa Mattingly who was Cherokee. Great-great-grandfather John Dabbs from Tennessee married Margaret Jones. Great-great-grandfather Dr. Logan Wallace was born in North Carolina in 1803. His family made musical instruments in England. He married Anna Chiles. Great-grandfather Bernhart Von Pilz was born in Germany. He married Minna Handle,daughter of Godeif Handel. Great-grandparents Friedrick Ziegler and Henrietta Yunge came to America from Germany in 1887.* AA with honors, Grossmont Coll., 1966; BA with honors, San Diego State U., 1969; MA, U. Redlands, 1977. Cert. elem. and adult edn. tchr. Tchr. Cajon Valley Union Sch. Dist., El Cajon, 1969—; sci. fair coord. Flying Hills Sch.; tchr. Hopi and Navajo Native Americans, Ariz., Utah, 1964-74, Goose and Gander Nursery Sch., Lakeside, Calif., 1964-66; dir., supt. Bible and Sunday schs. various chs., Lakeside, 1961-87; mem. sci. com., math. coun. Cajon Valley Union Sch. Dist., 1990-91, libr. com., 1997-98. Author: Individualized Curriculum in the Affective Domain; contbg. author: Campbell County, The Treasured Years, 1990, Legends of the Lakeside; songwriter for Hilltop Records, Hollywood, Calif.; songs released Never Trouble Trouble, Old Glory, Jesus Is Our Lord, Daniel's Prayer, There Lay Jesus, God's Hands, 1996-97, Washing Machine Charlie, Playmates, 1998; songwriter for Amerecord Records, Hollywood; songs released Born to Win, 1996; songwriter for Hollywood Artists Records, Hollywood; songs released Clear the Path Lord, Aqua Forte, In the Volume of the Book, 1996, Home is Where the Heart Is, You Don't Even Know Who I Am, No Place to Cry, To Walk With God., Ixnay, If You Never Loved Me, 1997; songwriter for Columbine Records Corp., Hollywood; song released Life of a Single Woman, 1997, Take This Pain Away, 1998; contbr. articles to profl. jours. and newspapers. Tem. U.S. Senatorial Club, Washington, 1984—, Conservative Caucus, Inc., Washington, 1988—, Ronald Reagan Presdl. Found., Ronald Reagan Rep. Ctr., 1988, Rep. Presdl. Citizen's Adv. Commn., 1989—, Rep. Platform Planning Com., Calif., 1992, at-large del. representing dist. #45, Lakeside, Calif., 1992, 1995—, Am. Security Coun., Washington, 1994, Congressman Hunter's Off Road Adv. Coun., El Cajon, Calif., 1994, Century Club, San Diego Rep. Century Club, 1995; mem. health articulation com. project AIDS, Cajon Valley Union Sch. Dist., 1988—, Concerned Women Am., Washington, Recruit Depot Hist. Mus., San Diego, 1989, Citizen's Drug Free Am., Calif., 1989—, The Heritage Found., 1988—; charter mem. Marine Corps Mus.; mem. Lakeside Centennial Com., 1985-86; hon. mem. Rep. Presdl. Task Force, Washington, 1986; del. Calif. Rep. Senatorial Mid-Term Conv., Washington, 1994; mus. curator Lakeside Hist. Soc., 1992-93. Recipient Outstanding Svc. award PTA, 1972-74; recognized for various contbns. Commdg. Post Gen., San Diego Bd. Edn., 1989. Mem. Tchrs. Assn., Calif. Tchrs. Assn., Cajon Valley Educators Assn. (faculty advisor, rep. 1980-82, 84-86, 87-88), Nat. Trust for Hist. Preservation, Christian Bus. and Profl. Women, Trust for Hist. Preservation, Ridgecrest Golden Terrace Park Assn. (pres. 1998), Nashville Songwriters Assn., Capitol Hill Women's Club, Am. Ctr. for Law and Justice, Internat. Christian Women's Club (Christian amb. to Taiwan, Korea, 1974). Republican. Avocations: world traveling, Christian teaching, vocal music, piano, guitar. Home: 13594 Hwy 8 # 3 Lakeside CA 92040-5235 Office: Flying Hills Elem Sch 1251 Finch St El Cajon CA 92020-1433

THOMAS, FRANK JOSEPH, retired nuclear engineer; b. Pocatello, Idaho, Apr. 15, 1930; s. Emil C. and Jean (Jones) T.; m. Carol Jones, Feb. 4, 1949; children: Dale, Wayne, Keith. BSEE, U. Idaho, 1952; MS, U. Calif., Berkeley, 1957. Registered profl. mech. engr., Calif. Engr. Sandia Corp., Albuquerque, 1952-56; mgr. engring. div. Aerojet Gen., San Ramon, Calif., 1957-64; dir. nuclear program Office Sec. Defense, Washington, 1964-67; sr. scientist Rand Corp., Santa Monica, Calif., 1967-71; chmn. Pacific-Sierra Rsch. Corp., L.A., 1971-98, ret., 1998; lectr. U. Calif., Berkeley, 1956-58; chmn. treaty evaluation panel Def. Advanced Rsch. Projects Agy., Washington, 1969-71; clear sky panel USAF, Washington, 1967-73. Author: Evasive Foreign Nuclear Testing, 1971, Blackjack Strategy, 1961; contbr. articles to profl. jours. including Nature, Physics Letters. Recipient Master Design award Product Engring. Mag., 1963. Mem. AAAS, Am. Inst. Aeronautics and Astro. Achievements include development and operation of the first closed-cycle gas turbine power plant in the U.S. Office: Pacific Sierra Rsch Corp 2901 28th St Santa Monica CA 90405-2938

THOMAS, FRANKLIN ROSBOROUGH, retired animator; b. Santa Monica, Calif., Sept. 5, 1912; s. Frank Waters and Ina Marcella (Gregg) T.; m. Jeanette Armentrout, Feb. 16, 1946; children: Ann Winfield, Gregg Franklin, Theodore William, Douglas Craig. Student, Fresno State Coll., 1929-31; AB magna cum laude, Stanford U., 1933; postgrad., Choinard Art Sch., 1933-34, Walt Disney Studio, 1934. Directing animator Walt Disney Co., Burbank, Calif., 1934-78; ret., 1978; lectr., spkr. in field; chmn. jury N.Y. Internat. Animated Film Festival, 1975. Animator for numerous films, including Show White and the Seven Dwarfs, 1937, Pinocchio, 1940, Bambi, 1942, The Three Caballeros, 1945, The Many Adventures of Winnie the Pooh, 1977; directing animator The Adventures of Ichabod and Mr. Toad, 1949, Cinderella, 1950, Alice in Wonderland, 1951, Peter Pan, 1953, Lady and the Tramp, 1955, Sleeping Beauty, 1959, 101 Dalmatians, 1961, Sword in the Stone, 1963, Mary Poppins, 1964, The Jungle Book, 1967, The Aristocats, 1970, Robin Hood, 1973, The Rescuers, 1977; supervising animator: The Fox and the Hound, 1981; also animator for numerous shorts; co-author: Disney Animation -- The Illusion of Life, 1981, Too Funny for Words, 1987, Bambi-The Story and the Film, 1990, Jungle Book Portfolio, 1993, Disney Villains, English edit., 1993, French edit., 1995; contbr. editor to sketch book series; Dixieland jazz pianist Firehouse Five Plus 2, 1949-68, appearing on radio and TV programs The Bing Crosby Show, The Milton Berle Show, Ed Wynn TV Shows, others; subject of documentary Frank and Ollie; exhibited drawings in Whitney Mus., N.Y.C., 1981. Guest spkr. Russian Govt. and Soyuzmultifilm and other East European countries, 1976, U.S. Info. Agy. Cultural Exch. Program, 1986. With USAF, 1942-45. Recipient numerous award, including Annie award Internat. Animated Film Soc., 9 Old Men award Hon. Cinema Soc. Mem. Phi Beta Kappa. Address: 758 Flintridge Ave Flintridge CA 91011-4027

THOMAS, GEORGE THORP, editor, publisher; b. Dayton, Ohio, Oct. 20, 1937; s. George Thorp Thomas and Christina (McCall) Field; children: Sean, Patrick, Eva. BA in English, U. Dayton, 1964; MA in English, Ea. Wash. U., 1979, MFA in Creative Writing, 1981. Founder, editor Willow Springs Mag., Cheney, Wash., 1977-80; pub., editor, writer George & Mertie's Place, Spokane, Wash., 1994—; pub., editor Heliotrope mag., Spokane, 1997—. Contbr. poetry and short stories to periodicals and anthologies. Mem. Peace and Justice Action League, Spokane. Mem. Am. Acad. poets. Democrat. Deist. Avocations: conversation, reading. Office: Dick Diver Enterprises PO Box 10335 Spokane WA 99209-1335

THOMAS, HAYWARD, manufacturing company executive; b. Los Angeles, Aug. 9, 1921; s. Charles Sparks and Julia (Hayward) T.; m. Phyllis Mary Wilson, July 1, 1943; children: H. David, Steven T. BS, U. Calif., Berkeley, 1943. Registered profl. engr. Staff engr. Joshua Hendy Corp., Los Angeles, 1946-50; prodn. mgr. Byron Jackson Co., Los Angeles, 1950-55; mgr. mfg. Frigidaire div. Gen. Motors Corp., Dayton, Ohio, 1955-70; group v.p. White Motor Corp., Cleve., 1971-73; sr. v.p. Broan Mfg. Co., Hartford, Wis., 1973-85; pres. Jensen Industries, Los Angeles, 1985-87; retired, 1987. Served to lt. USNR, 1943-46. Mem. Soc. Mfg. Engrs. (chmn. mfg. mgmt. council 1984-86). Republican. Episcopalian. Avocations: tennis, fishing. Home: 1320 Granvia Altamira Palos Verdes Peninsula CA 90274-2006

THOMAS, HOWARD PAUL, civil engineer, consultant; b. Cambridge, Mass., Aug. 20, 1942; s. Charles Calvin and Helen Elizabeth (Hook) T.; m. Ingrid Nybo, Jan. 4, 1969; children: Kent Michael, Lisa Karen, Karina Michelle. BS in Engring., U. Mich., 1965, MS in Engring., 1966. Registered profl. engr., Alaska, Calif. Engr. Ove Arup & Ptnrs., London, 1966-67; project engr. Woodward-Clyde Cons., San Francisco, 1967-73; assoc. Woodward-Clyde Cons., Anchorage, 1975-89; spl. cons. Cowiconsult Cons., Copenhagen, 1973-75; prin. engr. Harding-Lawson Assocs., Anchorage, 1989-90; v.p., chief engr. EMCON Alaska, Inc., Anchorage, 1991-94; gen. mgr. Internat. Tech. Corp., Anchorage, 1994-96; assoc. GeoEngrs., Inc., Anchorage, 1996—; mem. Anchorage Mayor's Geotech. Adv. Commn., 1997—; chmn. Nat. Tech. Coun. Cold Regions Engring., 1988-89, chmn. com. program and publs., 1982-84; chmn. 4th Internat. Conf. Cold Regions Engring., Anchorage, 1986; liaison NAS/Nat. Rsch. Coun. Polar Rsch. Bd., 1989—. Contbr. articles to profl. jours. Named Alaskan Engr. Yr., 1986. Fellow ASCE (pres. Anchorage chpt. 1985-86, chair mgmt. group A. 1996-97, pres. Alaska sect. 1998—); mem. Soc. Am. Mil. Engrs., Cons. Engrs. Coun. Alaska (pres. 1989-90), Am. Cons. Engrs. Coun. (nat. dir. 1990-91), Project Mgmt. Inst. (v.p. Alaska chpt. 1991-95), Toastmasters (pres. Anchorage club 1984), Sons of Norway (v.p. Anchorage lodge 1997—). Lutheran. Avocations: playing French Horn in Anchorage Civic Orchestra, travel, skiing, sailing. Home: 2611 Brittany Dr Anchorage AK 99504-3332

THOMAS, JEANETTE MAE, public accountant; b. Minn., Dec. 19, 1946; d. Herbert and Arline Harmon; m. Gerald F. Thomas, Aug. 9, 1969; children: Bradley, Christopher. BS, Winona State U., 1968; postgrad., Colo. State U.; CFP, Coll. for Fin. Planning, Denver, 1985. Enrolled agt.; cert. fin. planner; registered rep. NASD; registered investment advisor; accredited tax advisor. Tchr. pub. schs. systems Colo., N.Mex., Mich., 1968-72; adminstrv. asst. Bus. Men's Svcs., Ft. Collins, Colo., 1974-75; tax cons. Tax Corp. Am., Ft. Collins, Colo., 1972-80; chief acct. Jayland Enterprises, La Porte, Colo., 1981—; pres., CEO Thomas Fin. Svcs. Inc., Ft. Collins, 1980—. Contbr. articles to newspapers and profl. newsletters. Bd. dirs. local PTO, 1984-85; treas. Boy Scouts Am., 1985-88; master food safety advisor coop. ext. Colo. State U., 1988—; spkr., steering com. AARP Women's Fin. Info. Program, 1988—; past chair adv. bd. Larimer County Coop. Ext., Colo. State U.; quality rev. com., sch. to career adv. bd. Poudre R-1 Schs. Mem. Internat. Assn. Fin. Planning (past officer), Am. Soc. Women Accts. (bd. dirs. 1984-86, 96-98), Pvt. Industry Coun. (chair 1994-95), Nat. Soc. Accts., Colo. Soc. Pub. Accts., Inst. CFPs, Am. Notary Assn., Ft. Collins C. of C. (red carpet com. bus. assistance coun. 1989-96). Avocations: sewing, bread baking, food preservation, bicycling, fly fishing, golf. Home: PO Box 370 Laporte CO 80535-0370 Office: 400 S Howes St Ste 2 Fort Collins CO 80521-2802

THOMAS, JIM, professional basketball team executive. Mng. gen. ptnr. Sacramento Kings. Office: Sacramento Kings 1 Sports Pkwy Sacramento CA 95834-2301*

THOMAS, JOHN GILBERT, producer; b. Miami, Fla., Jan. 19, 1948; s. John G. and Caroline W. Thomas; m. Vegie Anderson, Jan. 3, 1969 (div. 1982); m. Galina K., Sept. 17, 1995; children: Melissa Ann, Masha. BA in Cinema, U. So. Calif., 1971. developer Easy Budget Software, L.A., 1990—; cons. DirecTV, El Segunda, Calif., 1996-97, IBM Global Svcs., 1997-99. prodr., dir. Tin Man, 1983, Banzai Runner, 1985, Arizona Heat, 1989, Healer, 1995; prodr. Hurricane Hugo Disaster Relief Show, ARC, 1990, Fred, 1999—; freelance writer L.A. Times, 1999—. Mem. Writers' Guild Am., Screen Actor's Guild. Republican. Methodist. Avocations: flying.

THOMAS, JOSEPH FLESHMAN, architect; b. Oak Hill, W.Va., Mar. 23, 1915; s. Robert Russel and Effie (Fleshman) T.; m. Margaret Ruth Lively, Feb. 28, 1939 (dec.); children: Anita Carol, Joseph Stephen; m. Dorothy Francene Root, Apr. 29, 1967 (div.); m. Bonnie Abbott Buckley, June 15, 1991. Student, Duke, 1931-32; B.Arch., Carnegie-Mellon U., 1938. Practice architecture various firms W. Va., Va., Tenn., Calif., 1938-49; staff architect Calif. Div. Architecture, Los Angeles, 1949-52; prin. Joseph F. Thomas, architect, Pasadena, Calif., 1952-53; pres. Neptune & Thomas (architects-engrs.), Pasadena and San Diego, 1953-78; Mem. Pasadena Planning Commn., 1956-64, chmn., 1963-64; pres. Citizens Coun. for Planning, Pasadena, 1966-67; mem. steering com. Pasadena NOW, 1970-74; mem. Pasadena Design Com., 1979-86; mem. adv. bd. Calif. Office Architecture and Constrn., 1970-72; mem. archtl. adv. com. Calif. State U. System, 1981-84; mem. adv. coun. Sch. Environ. Design Calif. Poly. Inst., 1983—; mem. outreach for architecture com. Carnegie Mellon U., 1989—, pres.'s devel. com., 1991—. Prin. works include Meth. Hosp., Arcadia, Calif., Foothill Presbyn. Hosp., Glendora, Calif., master plans and bldgs., Citrus Coll., Azusa, Calif., Riverside (Calif.) Coll., Westmont Coll., Monticeto, Calif., Northrop Inst. Tech., Inglewood, Calif, Indian Valley Coll., Marin County, Calif., Pepperdine U., Malibu, Calif., UCLA, U. Calif., San Diego, Long Beach (Calif.) State U., Calif. Inst. Tech., Pasadena, Calif., other coll. bldgs. Pacific Telephone Co., Pasadena, L.A. County Superior Ct. Bldg., U.S. Naval Hosp., San Diego. Trustee Almansor Edn. Ctr., 1986-92; bd. dirs., co-founder Syncor Internat., 1973-83; founding dir. Bank of Pasadena, 1962-65. Lt. (j.g.) USNR, 1943-46. Recipient Service award City of Pasadena, 1964; Disting. Service award Calif. Dept. Gen. Services, 1972; Gold Crown award Pasadena Arts Council, 1981. Fellow AIA (4 awards honor, 13 awards merit 1957-78, dir. Calif. coun. 1966-68, exec. com. 1974-77, pres. Pasadena chpt. 1967, chmn. Calif. sch. facilities com. 1970-72, mem. nat. jud. bd. 1973-74, nat. dir. 1974-77, treas. 1977-79, exec. com., planning com., chmn. finance com.); mem. Breakfast Forum (chmn. 1983), Annandale Golf Club, Pi Kappa Alpha. Republican. Methodist. Home: 330 San Miguel Rd Pasadena CA 91105-1446

THOMAS, KEITH VERN, bank executive; b. Provo, Utah, Oct. 21, 1946; s. Vern R. and Lois (Doran) T.; m. Sherrie Hunter, Oct. 7, 1969; children: Genevieve, Joshua, Rachel, William, Rebecca. AA, Dixie Coll., 1969; BS, Brigham Young U., 1971; MBA, St. Mary's Coll., 1980. From examiner to asst. dir. Fed. Home Loan Bank Bd., San Francisco, 1971-85; sr. v.p., dir. exams. and supervision Fed. Home Loan Bank, Seattle, 1985-88; exec. v.p., COO Frontier Savings Assn., Las Vegas, Nev., 1988-89, pres., CEO, dir., 1989-90; sr. v.p. Am. Fed. Savs. Bank, Las Vegas, 1991-96; pres., CEO Frontier Fin. Corp., Las Vegas, 1996-97; chmn. of the bd., pres., CEO U.S. Savings Bank, Las Vegas, 1997—; bd. dirs., chmn. Nev. Cmty. Reinvestment Corp.; bd. dirs. So. Nev. Housing Corp., U.S. Savs. Bank. Editor: Real Estate Textbook, 1983-84. Trustee Nev. Sch. Arts; mem. fin. com. North Las Vegas Neighborhood Housing Svcs.; mem. cmty. reinvestment and housing com. Western League Savs. Instns.; bd. dirs., dist. vice chmn., coun. tng. dir. Boulder Dam Area coun. Boy Scouts Am.; active Leadership Las Vegas; bd. dirs. Nev. Cmty. Found., Local Initiatives Support Corp.; mem. Clark County Cmty. Housing Adv. Com.; mem. contract com. United Way; mem. Leadership Las Vegas Alumni Assn. Recipient Silver Beaver award Boy Scouts Am., 1997; named Outstanding Instr., Inst. Fin. Edn. 1984. Mem. Nev. Clearing House Assn. (v.p., bd. dirs.), Nat. Assn. Rev. Appraisers and Mortgage Underwriters, Brigham Young Mgmt. Soc., So. Nev. Exec. Coun. (bd. dirs., past pres.), Las Vegas C. of C. (Cmty. Achievement award 1996), Nev. Devel. Authority, So. Nev. Home Builders Assn., Las Vegas S.W. Rotary (bd. dirs.). Republican. Mem. Ch. Jesus Christ LDS. Avocations: sports, reading, music, family, computers. Office: US Savings Bank PO Box 81796 Las Vegas NV 89180-1796

THOMAS, LAURA MARLENE, artist, private antique dealer; b. Chico, Calif., Apr. 29, 1936; d. Boyd Stanley Beck and Lois Velma (Behnke) Lyons; m. Charles Rex Thomas; children: Tracy Loraine, Jeffory Norris. AA in Fine Arts, Sacramento City Coll., 1978; BA in Fine Arts, Calif. State U., 1981. Tchrs. asst. Hanford Elem. Sch., Hanford, Calif., 1963-68; asst. dir. RSVP: Retired Sr. Vol. Program, Hanford, 1971-74; dir. of Art Bank Sacramento City Coll., Sacramento, 1976-78; pub. asst. Student Activities Calif. State Univ., Sacramento, 1978-81; antique dealer pvt. practice, Sacramento, 1981—, arts and crafts bus., 1976—; social worker Cath. Social Svcs., Sacramento, 1985-93. Artist: weaving, Double Image, 1977, 2nd Place 1977; ceramic sculptor, Bird. Charter mem. YWCA, Sacramento, 1972, Folsum Hist. Soc., 1988. Cert. of appreciation, Carmellia City Ctr. Adv. Council, Sacramento, 1986. Mem. Statue of Liberty-Ellis Island Found., 1985, North Shore Animal League (Benefactors award 1985), Calif. State U. Alumni Assn., Hanford Sportsman Club (v.p. 1963-68). Republican. Protestant. Avocations: tennis, needlepoint, gourmet cooking. Home: 2719 I St Apt 4 Sacramento CA 95816-4354

THOMAS, LOWELL, JR., author, lecturer, former lieutenant governor, former state senator; b. London, Oct. 6, 1923; s. Lowell Jackson and Frances (Ryan) T.; m. Mary Taylor Pryor, May 20, 1950; children: Anne Frazier, David Lowell. Student, Taft Sch., 1942; BA, Dartmouth Coll., 1948; postgrad., Princeton Sch. Pub. and Internat. Affairs, 1952. Asst. cameraman Fox Movietone News, S.Am., 1939, Bradford Washburn Alaskan mountaineering expdn., 1940; illustrated lecturer, 1946—; asst. economist, photographer with Max Weston Thornburg, Turkey, 1947, Iran, 1948; film prodn. Iran, 1949; Tibet expdn. with Lowell Thomas, Sr., 1949; field work Cinerama, S.Am., Africa, Asia, 1951-52; travels by small airplane with wife, writing and filming Europe, Africa, Middle East, 1954-55; mem. Rockwell Polar Flight, first flight around the world over both poles, Nov., 1965; mem. Alaska State Senate, 1967-74; lt. gov. State of Alaska, 1974-79; owner Talkeetna Air Taxi, Inc., air contract carrier, Anchorage, Alaska, 1980-94. Producer series of films Flight to Adventure, NBC-TV, 1956; producer, writer TV series High Adventure, 1957-59; producer documentary film Adaq, King of Alaskan Seas, 1960; producer two films on Alaska, 1962, 63, film on U. Alaska, 1964, South Pacific travel documentary, 1965, film on Arctic oil exploration, Atlantic-Richfield Co., 1969. Author: Out of this World, A Journey to Tibet, 1950, (with Mrs. Lowell Thomas, Jr.) Our Flight to Adventure, 1956, The Silent War in Tibet, 1959, The Dalai Lama, 1961, The Trail of Ninety-Eight, 1962, (with Lowell Thomas Sr.) More Great True Adventures, 1963, Famous First Flights that Changed History, 1968. past pres. Western Alaska coun. Boys Scouts Am.; bd. dirs. Anchorage unit Salvation Army, Alaska Conservation Found. 1st lt. USAAF, 1943-45. Mem. Nat. Parks and Conservation Assn. (bd. dirs.), Alaska C. of C., Aircraft Owners and Pilots Assn. Clubs: Explorers, Marco Polo, Dutch Treat (N.Y.C.); Rotary, (Anchorage), Press (Anchorage); Dartmouth Outing; American Alpine. Address: 10800 Hideaway Lake Dr Anchorage AK 99516-1145

THOMAS, LYNN MARIE, artist, retired dude ranch owner, operator; b. L.A., Nov. 20, 1939; d. Eugene Leonard and Genevie Juanita (Hupp) Pfeifer; m. Joe Glen Thomas, Dec. 2, 1969 (div.); children from previous marriage: Beverly Linda Hahn, Deborah Jean Hahn, Michelle Marie Hahn (dec.). Grad h.s., Henderson, Nev. One-woman shows include Burk Gallery, Boulder City, Nev., 1976, 78, Pa-Jo's Western Art Gallery, Pinedale, Wyo., 1976, 80, 89, Bank of Nev., Las Vegas, 1976, 78, Energy Rsch. & Devel. Adminstrn., Las Vegas, 1977, U. Nev., Las Vegas, 1979, Rock Springs (Wyo.) Fine Arts Ctr., 1988, 89, White Mountain Libr., Rock Springs, 1990, 92, Green River (Wyo.) Libr., 1990, 93; group exhbns. include Wyo. Artists Assn. (Best of Show, Artist's Choice, People's Choice, Pres.'s Choice, 4 1st pl., 14 misc. awards), Sweetwater County Art Guild Nat. (Best of Show, People's Choice, 2 1st pl. in profl. divsn., misc. other awards), Seven State Regional (3 awards for 3 pieces), Black Canyon Show (2 1st pl., 3 misc. awards), Cody Western & Wildlife Classic (Purple ribbon), Audubon Nat. Wildlife Art Show (2 1st in oil prizes), Women Artists of West (Artist's Artist, 1987, 1st pl. in oils, 10 misc. awards), Cheyenne Frontier Days Old West Mus. (Beanie Herzog award 1985), Am. Mothers (Sweepstakes award 1979, 83, several misc. awards), Las Vegas Elks Helldorado Show (1st pl. oils 1975, 84, 3 misc. awards), Sublett County Fair (36 1st pl. awards, 10 Best of Show awards, 6 Overall Champion awards, 23 Champion awards, 13 misc. awards), Daisy Patch Gallery, Casper, Wyo., 1996, Savage Gallery, Sioux Falls, S.D., 1996, High Desert Gallery, Rock Springs, Wyo., 1996, ; represented in permanent collections including Las Vegas Rev. Jour., 1st Wyo. Bank, Big Piney, Sublett County Wyo. Libr., Las Vegas Elks Western Art Collection, Rock Springs Fine Arts Ctr., Ft. Huachuca Post Cavalry Mus., Green River Valley Mus., Big Piney; contbr. art to numerous pubs. and profl. jours. Mem. Nat. Cowgirl Hall of Fame, Hereford, Tex., Cowboy Artists of Am. Mus., Kerrville, Tex., Mus. of the Mountain Man, Pinedale, Wyo., Wyo. Coun. on Arts, Flaming Gorge Natural History Assn., Sublette County Hist. Soc., Green River Valley Mus.; charter mem. Nat. Mus. for Women in the Arts, Washington, Nat. Mus. of the Am. Indian, Washington. Mem. Women Artists of the West (emeritus), Pinedale Fine Arts Coun., Sublette County Artists Guild, Mixed Media, Wyo. Artists Registry, Nev. Artists Register, Wyo. Artists Assn. Avocations: photography, outdoors, horses, music, poetry. Home and Studio: House on Muddy 105 Richie Rd Boulder WY 82923

THOMAS, MICHAEL STEVEN, software company executive; b. Denver, June 1, 1954; s. Robert A. and Marilyn Jo (Malloy) T., m. Mary Shiela Conway, Dec. 29, 1958; children: Kelly Louise, Edward Joseph. BS in Bus. and Fin., U. Colo., 1976; MBA, Regis U., Denver, 1995. Cert. purchasing mgr. Subcontract adminstr. Martin Marietta Corp., Denver, 1985-93; sr. subcontract adminstr. Union Pacific Corp., Boulder, Colo., 1993-94; contract adminstrv. mgr. Environ. Sci. and Engring., Englewood, Colo., 1994-95; purchasing mgr. Space Imaging, Inc., Thornton, Colo., 1995-96; mgr. corp. purchasing and contracts J.D. Edwards & Co., Denver, 1996—. Contbr. articles to profl. jours. Leader Boy Scouts Am., Lakewood, Colo. Fellow Nat. Contract Mgmt. Assn.; mem. Am. Mgmt. Assn., Nat. Assn. Purchasing Mgmt. Republican. Roman Catholic. Avocations: skiing, backpacking, hiking, mountain climbing, phesant hunting. Home: 2407 S Holman Cir Lakewood CO 80228-4893 Office: JD Edwards & Co 8055 E Tufts Ave Ste 1200 Denver CO 80237-2886

THOMAS, PATRICIA STATON, dollhouse designer, educator, writer; b. Manhattan, N.Y., Feb. 25, 1946; d. Harry Parker and Patricia (Hall) Staton; m. Noel Russell Thomas, Mar. 4, 1975; 1 child, Robin Birkland. BS in drama, Skidmore Coll., 1968. Copywriter Needham, Harper & Steers Adv., L.A., 1971-73; radio announcer Sta. KSWB, Seaside, Ore., 1975-76; columnist Dollhouse Miniatures, Waukesha, Wis., 1981-98, Miniature Collector Mag., Mich., 1998—; freelance poet, playwright, essayist Seaview, Wash., 1991—, freelance dollhouse maker, tchr., 1974—. Author: (play) Life with the Deadman, or How I Fell for Entropy, 1998, numerous poems. Founding pres. Water Music Festival, Seaview, 1984-86 (bd. mem. 1987-89); coord. vis. writers workshops for area residents, Seaview, 1991—; mem. steering com. Colombia Pacific Arts Forum, Astoria, Ore., 1994-97. Named to Nat. Assn. Miniature Enthusiasts Acad. Honor, Carmel, Ind., 1986; recipient Lit. fellow in poetry Artist Trust, NEA, Seattle, 1995. Fellow Internat. Guild Miniature Artisans (Crystal award for excellence, 1978, Lifetime Achievment award). Protestant. Avocations: gardening, reading.

THOMAS, RICHARD MCKENNON, II, college administrator; b. Ft. Morgan, Colo., Nov. 5, 1961; s. Richard McKennon and Ann Rae (Douglass) T.; m. Shannon Lisa Wells, Jan. 10, 1987; children: Jamison Scott, Christopher Patrick, Madilynn Samantha. BS, Colo. State U., 1993, MS, 1995. Asst. mgr. Walsh Auto Parts, Englewood, Colo., 1979-83; mgr. D & S Auto Parts, Littleton, Colo., 1983-85; salesman Continental VW, Littleton, 1985-86; mgr. Auto Parts Profls., Denver, 1986-90; athletic parking coord. Colo. State U., Ft. Collins, 1990-95, asst. informal recreation coord., 1993-95; assoc. dir. housing and residence life Mesa State Coll., Grand Junction, 1996—; informal recreation rep. Colo. State U., Ft. Collins, 1993-94, chair recreation adv. bd., 1994-95; new residence hall com. mem. Mesa State Coll., Grand Junction, Colo., 1996—. Reader bd. mem. Jour. Student Affairs, 1994-95. Asst. coach Ft. Collins Soccer Club, 1993-95; league coord. Littleton Soccer Assn., 1995; coach T-ball Grand Mesa Little League, Grand Junction, 1996, Grand Mesa Youth Soccer Assn. U9-Boys, 1996—. Mem. Nat. Intramural Recreational Sports Assn., Nat. Assn. Student Pers. Adminstrs., Assn. Coll. and Univ. Housing Officers. Avocations: running, windsurfing. Office: Mesa State Coll PO Box 2647 Grand Junction CO 81502-2647

THOMAS, RICHARD VAN, state supreme court justice; b. Superior, Wyo., Oct. 11, 1932; s. John W. and Gertrude (McCloskey) T.; m. Lesley Arlene Ekman, June 23, 1956; children: Tara Lynn, Richard Ross, Laura Lee, Sidney Marie. B.S. in Bus. Adminstrn. with honors, U. Wyo., 1954, LL.B. with honors, 1956; LL.M., NYU, 1961. Bar: Wyo. 1956, U.S. Ct. Appeals (10th cir.) 1960, U.S. Ct. Mil. Appeals 1960, U.S. Supreme Ct. 1960. Law clk. to judge U.S. Ct. Appeals (10th Circuit), Cheyenne, 1960-63; asso. firm Hirst & Applegate, Cheyenne, 1963-64; partner firm Hirst, Applegate & Thomas, Cheyenne, 1964-69; U.S. atty. Dist. Wyo., Cheyenne, 1969-74; justice Wyo. Supreme Ct., Cheyenne, 1974—, chief justice, 1985-86. Pres. Laramie County United Way, 1972, trustee, 1973-74, chmn. admissions and allocations com., 1968-69, chmn. exec. com., 1973, chmn. combined fed. campaign, 1974; bd. dirs. Goodwill Industries Wyo., Inc., 1974-77; exec. com. Cheyenne Crusade for Christ, 1974; v.p., exec. com. Wyo. Billy Graham Crusade, 1987; bd. dirs. Cheyenne Youth for Christ, 1978-81; chancellor Episcopal Diocese of Wyo., 1972—, lay dep. gen. conv., 1973—, chmn. search evaluation nomination com., 1976-77, lay reader, 1969—; bd. dirs. Community Action of Laramie County, 1977-82; chmn. Cheyenne dist. Boy Scouts Am., 1977-78, mem. nat. council, 1982-84, mem. Longs Peak council, 1977—, v.p. dist. ops., v.p. membership relationships, 1979-81, pres.,

1981-83; mem. North Cen. Region Exec. Bd., 1986—, pres. Old West Trails Area, 1988—; chmn. Laramie County Health Planning Com., 1980-84. Served with JAGC USAF, 1957-60. Named Boss of Year, Indian Paintbrush chpt. Nat. Secs. Assn., 1974; Civil Servant of Year, Cheyenne Assn. Govt. Employees, 1973; Vol. of Yr., Cheyenne Office, Youth Alternatives, 1979; recipient St. George Episcopal award, 1982, Silver Beaver award Boy Scouts Am., 1985. Mem. Am., Laramie County bar assns., Wyo. State Bar, Phi Kappa Phi, Phi Alpha Delta, Omicron Delta Kappa, Sigma Nu. Clubs: Kiwanis (Cheyenne) (program com. 1969-70, dir. 1970-72, chmn. key club com. 1973-76, disting. pres. 1980-81), Masons (Cheyenne) (33 deg., past master); Shriners; Nat. Sojourners (Cheyenne). Office: Wyo Supreme Ct Supreme Ct Bldg 2301 Capitol Ave Cheyenne WY 82002*

THOMAS, ROGER PARRY, interior designer, art consultant; b. Salt Lake City, Nov. 4, 1951; s. E. Parry and Peggy Chatterton T.; m. Marilyn Harris Hite, Nov. 21, 1976 (div. Apr. 1979); m. H. Andrea Wahn, Nov. 20, 1982 (div. Dec. 1996); 1 child, Andrew Chatterton. BFA, Tufts U., 1973. Pres. Miller-Thomas, Inc., Las Vegas, Nev., 1973-76; v.p. Yates-Silverman, Inc., Las Vegas, 1976-81; v.p. design Atlandia Design a Mirage Resorts Inc. Co., Las Vegas, 1981—. Mem. Nev. Arts Cou. Office: Atlandia Design 3260 Industrial Rd Las Vegas NV 89109-1132

THOMAS, SHIRLEY, author, educator, business executive; b. Glendale, Calif.; d. Oscar Miller and Ruby (Thomas) Annis; m. W. White, Feb. 22, 1949 (div. June 1952); m. William C. Perkins, Oct. 24, 1969. BA in Modern Lit., U. Sussex, Eng., 1960, PhD in Comm., 1967; diploma, Russian Fedn. Cosmonautics, 1995. Actress, writer, producer, dir. numerous radio and TV stas., 1942-46; v.p. Commodore Prodns., Hollywood, Calif., 1946-52; pres. Annis & Thomas, Inc., Hollywood, 1952—; prof. technical writing U. So. Calif., L.A., 1975—; Hollywood corr. NBC, 1952-56; editor motion pictures CBS, Hollywood, 1956-58; corr. Voice of Am., 1958-59; now free lance writer; cons. biol. scis. communication project George Washington U., 1965-66; cons. Stanford Rsch. Inst., 1967-68, Jet Propulsion Lab., 1969-70. Author: Men of Space vols. 1-8, 1960-68, Spanish trans., 1961, Italian, 1962; Space Tracking Facilities, 1963, Computers: Their History, Present Applications and Future, 1965; The Book of Diets, 1974. Organizer, chmn. City of L.A. Space Adv. Com., 1964-73, Women's Space Symposia, 1962-73; founder, chmn. Aerospace Hist. Soc. Inc.; chmn. Theodore von Karman Postage Stamp Com., 1965—, stamp issued 1992; bd. dirs. World Children's Transplant Fund, 1993—, Achievement Rewards for Coll. Scients. Recipient Aerospace Excellence award Calif. Mus. Found. 1991, Nat. Medal Honor DAR, 1992, Yuri Gagarin Medal Honor, 1995. Fellow Brit. Interplanetary Soc.; mem. AIAA, AAAS, Internat. Acad. Astronautics, Internat. Soc. Aviation Writers, Air Force Assn. (Airpower Arts and Letters award 1961), Internat. Acad. Astronautics, Nat. Aero. Assn., Nat. Asn. Sci. Writers, Soc. for Tech. Communications, Am. Astronautical Soc., Nat. Geog. Soc., Am. Soc. Pub. Adminstrn. (sci. and tech. in govt. com. 1972—), Achievement Awards for Coll. Scientists, Muses of Calif., Theta Sigma Phi, Phi Beta. Home: 8027 Hollywood Blvd Los Angeles CA 90046-2510 Office: U So Calif Profl Writing Program University Park Waite-Phillips Hall 404 Los Angeles CA 90089-4034

THOMAS, STEVE D., infosystem specialist; b. Butte, Mont., Aug. 8, 1951; s. William James and Catherine (Murphy) T.; m. Kathy Ann McCarthy, Aug. 22, 1971; children: Shawn, Heather. Programmer analyst Anaconda Co., Butte, 1973-81, systems analyst, 1981-82; systems programmer ARCO Metals, Columbia Falls, Mont., 1982-83, supr. ops. and tech. support, 1983-85; supt. of mgmt. info. systems Columbia Falls Aluminum Co., 1985-96, info. sys. mgr., 1996—. Home: 1872 Riverwood Rd PO Box 731 The Dalles OR 97058-0731 Office: CFAC 2000 Aluminum Dr Columbia Falls MT 59912-9424

THOMAS, SUSAN DUNCAN, fundraising consultant; b. New Britain, Conn., Feb. 14, 1937; d. Philip Duncan and Jean French T.; m. Loyall F. Sewall, Sept. 12, 1958 (div. Jul. 1975); children: Sarah, Rebecca, Loyall F. BA, Harvard Univ., 1983, Tufts Univ., 1985, Syracuse Univ., 1987; MA, Mt. Holydu Coll. Dir. of devel. Trustees of Reservations, Mitton, Mass., 1980-82; dir. of corp. and found. rels. Brandesi Univ., Waltham, Mass., 1982-84; dir. corp. and found. rels. Harvard Medical Sch., Boston, 1984-88; v.p. institutional res. Pine Manor Coll., Chestnut Hill, Mass., 1988-91; prin. Thomas B. Weinstein, 1991—; vol. Porttaro Mus. of Art, 1965-70, bd. dirs. Rau Island Dance Co., 1965-70. Contbr. articles to profl. jours. Active in historic preservation in Maine Greater Portland Landmarks, 1971, 72. Mem. Nat. Soc. Fundraising Execs. (bd. dirs. 1986-88), Coun. in Advancement and Supple of Edn., Estate Planning COun. of Santa Fe, Small Point Club. Avocations: art, hiking, travel.

THOMAS, TERESA ANN, microbiologist, educator; b. Wilkes-Barre, Pa., Oct. 17, 1939; d. Sam Charles and Edna Grace T. BS cum laude, Coll. Misericordia, 1961; MS in Biology, Am. U. Beirut, 1965; MS in Microbiology, U. So. Calif., 1973; cert. in ednl. tech. U. Calif., San Diego, 1998. Tchr., sci. supr., curriculum coord. Meyers High Sch., Wilkes-Barre, 1962-64, Wilkes-Barre Area Public Schs., 1961-66; rsch. assoc. Proctor Found. for Rsch. in Ophthalmology U. Calif. Med. Ctr., San Francisco, 1966-68; instr. Robert Coll. of Istanbul (Turkey), 1968-71, Am. Edn. in Luxembourg, 1971-72, Bosco Tech. Inst., Rosemead, Calif., 1973-74, San Diego Community Coll. Dist., 1974-80; prof. math. Sch. Math Scis. and Engring. Southwestern Coll., Chula Vista, Calif., 1980—, pres. acad. senate, 1984-85, del., 1986-89; chmn., coord., steering com. project Cultural Rsch. Educational and Trade Exchange, 1991—, Southwestern Coll.-Shanghai Inst. Fgn. Trade; coord. Southwestern Coll. Great Teaching Seminar, 1987, 88, 89, coord. scholars program, 1988-90; mem. exec. com. Acad. Senate for Calif. C.Cs., 1985-86, Chancellor of Calif. C.Cs. Adv. and Rev. Council Fund for Instrnl. Improvement, 1984-86; co-project dir. statewide, coord. So. Calif. Biotech Edn. Consortium, 1993-95, steering com., 1993—; adj. asst. prof. Chapman Coll., San Diego, 1974-83, San Diego State U., 1977-79; chmn. Am. Colls. Istanbul Sci. Week, 1969-71; mem. adv. bd. Chapman Coll. Community Center, 1979-80; cons. sci. curriculum Calif. Dept. Edn., 1986-89; pres. Internat. Relations Club 1959-61; mem. San Francisco World Affairs Coun., 1966-68, San Diego World Affairs Coun., 1992—; v.p. Palomar Palace Estates Home Owners Assn., 1983-85, pres. 1994—. mem. editorial rev. bd. Jour. of Coll. Sci. Teaching, NSTA, 1988-92; ; bd. dirs. San Diego-Leon Sister Cities Soc., 1991-94. Mem. Chula Vista Nature Interpretive Ctr. (life), Internat. Friendship Commn., Chula Vista, 1985-95, vice chmn. 1989-90, chmn. 1990-92, Chula Vista, Calif., 1987-95; mem. U.S.-Mex. Sister Cities Assn., nat. bd. dirs., 1992-94, gen. chair 30th nat. conv., 1993; mem. City of Chula Vista Resource Conservation Commn., 1996—. NSF fellow, 1965; USPHS fellow, 1972-73; recipient Nat. Teaching Excellence award Nat. Inst. Staff and Orgnl. Devel., 1989; recognized at Internat. Conf. Teaching Excellence, Austin, 1989; Pa. Heart Assn. research grantee, 1962; named Southwestern Coll. Woman of Distinction, 1987. Mem. NIH (mem. steering com., mentor bridge to future program Southwestern Coll. and San Diego State U. 1993-98), Am. Soc. Microbiology (So. Calif. Microbe Discovery Team 1995—), Nat. Sci. Tchrs. Assn. (life, internat. com., coord. internat. honors exchange lectr. competition sponsored with Assn. Sci Educators Great Britain, 1986), Nat. Assn. Biology Tchrs. (life), Soc. Coll. Sci. Tchrs., S.D. Zool. Soc., Calif. Tchrs. Assn., NEA, Am. Assn. Community and Jr. Colls., Giraffes, Am.-Lebanese Assn. San Diego (chmn. scholarship com., pres. 1988-93), Am. U. of Beirut Alumni and Friends of San Diego (1st v.p. 1984-91), Lions Internat. (bull. editor 1991-93, best bull. award 1992, 93, 2nd v.p. 1992-93, 1st v.p. 1993-94, editor Roaring Times Newsletter 1993-94, chmn. dist. internat. rels. and cooperations com. 1993-95, with pub. rels., 1997-98, pres. SW San Diego County chpt. 1994-95, Sweetwater Zone chmn. dist. 4-L6 1996-97, pub. rels. 1997-98), Japan Soc. San Diego and Tijuana, Chula Vista-Odawara (Japan) Sister Cities Assn. (founding pres. 1995—), Kappa Gamma Pi (pres. Wilkes-Barre chpt. 1963-64, San Francisco chpt. 1967-68), Sigma Phi Sigma, Phi Theta Kappa, Alpha Pi Epsilon (hon. life mem., founder, advisor Southwestern Coll. chpt. 1989-90, Am. Lebanese Syrian Ladies Club (pres. 1982-83).

THOMAS, TOM EDWARD, call center consultant; b. Findlay, Ohio, July 12, 1954; s. John L. and Madge L. (L[illegible]) T.; m. Mary Beth [illegible], July 1, 1997. BS, Ohio State U., 1977; MBA, Case Western Res. U., 1980. Mgr. MCI, Denver, 1982-87; dir. Whirlpool Corp., Denver, 1988-89; mgr. DHL, Phoenix, 1989-92, pres. Thomas & Assocs., Phoenix, 1992—; mem. telecom. and tech. adv. coun. Maricopa C.C., 1996-98, curriculum developer in call ctr. mgmt. U. Phoenix; coord. Call Ctr. Network Group. Author coll. course Call Ctr. Mgmt., 1997. Mem. Call Ctr. Network Group (regional coord., co-chair). Avocations: mountain bicycle racing, running.

THOMAS, VERNEDA ESTELLA, retired perfusionist; b. Chgo., June 21, 1936; d. Russel Huston and Verneda (Williams) T. BS, Graceland Coll., Lamoni, Iowa, 1973. Cardiovascualr technician Michael Reese Hosp., Chgo., 1962; cardiopulmonary technician Chgo. State Tuberculosis Sanitorium, Chgo., 1962-66, Loyola U. Sch. Medicine, Maywood, Ill., 1966-68; physiology technician Loyola U. Sch. Medicine, 1968-69; med. technologist Cook County Hosp., Chgo., 1969-71; rsch. assoc. Queen's Med. Ctr., Honolulu, 1973-78; intra aortic balloon pump technician Queen's Med. Ctr., 1973-95; perfusionist for pvt. med. practice Honolulu, 1978-82; perfusionist Mid Pacific Perfusion, Honolulu, 1982-88, Psicor, Inc., Honolulu, 1988-96; ret., 1996; referee, U.S. Volleyball Assn., 1978. Contbr. articles to med. publs. Mem. U.S. Pan-Am. high jump team, Mex., 1955; mem. U.S. Olympic volleyball team, Tokyo, 1964. Mem. Am. Soc. Cardiopulmonary Technology, Am. Bd. Cardiovascular Perfusion. Baptist. Avocations: bodyboarding, camping, board games. Home: 217 Prospect St Apt D7 Honolulu HI 96813-1755

THOMAS, WILLIAM GORDON, writer, educator; b. Los Angeles, June 5, 1931; s. Ernest Leslie and Marian (Bowers) T.; m. Diane R. McCulloch, Sept. 8, 1951; children—Gregory, Mark, Scott, Christopher. Student, Occidental Coll., 1949-50, U. Calif. at Berkeley, 1952-54; B.A., U. Calif. at Los Angeles, 1956, M.A., 1957, Ed.D., 1965. Instr. speech and drama Immaculate Heart and Mt. St. Marys Colls., 1956-57; dir. cultural programs U.S. Forces in Europe, 1957-59; dir. pub. relations Immaculate Heart Coll., Los Angeles, 1959-61; coll. and univ. placement adviser U. Calif., Los Angeles, 1961-62; assoc. dean students, mgr. U. Calif. (Student and Alumni Placement Center), 1962-67; also instr. U. Calif. (U. Calif. Extension); dean students Calif. State U., Northridge, 1967-69; dean ednl. career services U. Calif., Los Angeles, 1969-75; also dean exptl. ednl. programs; chancellor Johnston Coll. U. Redlands, 1975-76; dean Los Angeles Community Colls., 1976-82; prof. Calif. State U., Dominguez Hills and L.A., 1982-90; prof. English Los Angeles Trade Tech. Coll., 1982—; cons. mgmt., 1982-95. Co-author, editor books; contbr. articles to profl. jours. Pres. Northridge Western Boys Baseball Assn.; bd. mgrs. YMCA. Served with USN, 1950-54; commr. San Clemente Pks. and Recreation Dept., 1998—. Mem. Am. Assn. Higher Edn., Westlake Village C. of C. (pres., chief exec. officer 1985-87), Phi Delta Kappa, Alpha Tau Omega. Club: Rotary. Home: 2506 Calle Jade San Clemente CA 92673-3905

THOMAS, WILLIAM MARSHALL, congressman; b. Wallace, Idaho, Dec. 6, 1941; s. Virgil and Gertrude Thomas; m. Sharon Lynn Hamilton, Jan. 1968; children: Christopher, Amelia. B.A., San Francisco State U., 1963, M.A., 1965. Mem. faculty dept. Am. govt. Bakersfield (Calif.) Coll., 1965-74, prof., 1965-74; mem. Calif. State Assembly, 1974-78, 96th-105th Congress from 18th, now 21st Calif. Dist., 1979—; vice chmn. of House Task Force on Campaign Fin. Reform; mem. Ho. of Reps. Ways and Means Com.; chmn. Com. on House Oversight, Ways & Means Health Subcom.; mem. Ways & Means subcom on Trade; mem. del. to Soviet Union, by Am. Council Young Polit. Leaders, 1977; chmn. Kern County Republican Central Com., 1972-74; mem. Calif. Rep. Com., 1972-80; del. Republican Party Nat. Conv., 1980, 84, 88; mem. Rep. Leader's Task Force on Health Care Reform. Office: Ho of Reps 2208 Rayburn Ho Office Bldg Washington DC 20515-0521*

THOMAS, YVONNE LINDER, psychologist; b. L.A.; d. G. and L. Linder; m. M. Thomas. BA in Psychology cum laude, Calif. State U., Northridge, 1986; MA in Psychology, Calif. State U., L.A., 1987; PhD in Psychology, Calif. Grad. Inst., L.A., 1992. Licensed psychologist. Psychol. intern The Counseling Ctr. West Los Angeles, Calif., 1988-92; registered psychol. asst. The Beverly Hills (Calif.) Counseling Ctr., 1992-96, psychologist, 1996—; guest radio therapist KIEV-870 AM Radio, Glendale, Calif., summer 1993; guest TV psychologist Century Cable Pub. Access, Santa Monica, Calif., 1996. Mem. APA, Calif. Psychol. Assn., L.A. County Psychol. Assn. (mem. media com., multi-cultural diversity com.), Golden Key, Psi Chi. Office: The Beverly Hills Counseling Ctr 9570 W Pico Blvd Ste 200 Los Angeles CA 90035-1216

THOMAS-COTE, NANCY DENECE, office products manufacturing company executive; b. Long Beach, Calif., Feb. 20, 1959; d. Alan Thomas and Barbara Jean (Rush) Tuthill; m. Gary Cote. V.p. BTE, Inc., Long Beach, 1978-88; gen. mgr. BTE, Inc., Huntington Beach, Calif., 1982-88, pres., 1988-95, CEO, 1995—; pres. Omni Label, Inc., Huntington Beach, 1985-90; co-owner LeMac Leasing, La Canada, Calif., 1985-90; owner Dayspring Wedding Cons., Long Beach, 1991-93. V.p. Long Beach Spl. Charities, Inc., 1987; pres. Long Beach Spl. Charities, Inc., 1988; mem. Long Beach Sch.-to-Career Coalition, 1997; bd. dirs. Greater Long Beach Area Girl Scouts Coun., 1999. Mem. Am. Health Info. Mgmt. Assn., Calif. Health Info. Assn., Bus. Products Industry Assn., Nat. Assn. Women Bus. Owners (bd. dirs. L.A. chpt. 1995-96), An Income of Her Own. Office: BTE Inc 5672 Bolsa Ave Huntington Beach CA 92649-1113

THOMPSON, ADRIAN, communications executive; b. Breckenridge, Tex., May 7, 1953; s. Demetris Sanders and Effie J. Thompson. Owner, operator Baisha Comms., Las Cruces, N.Mex. Comms. officer NAACP, Las Cruces, N.Mex., 1981-98. Served with USN, 1972-81. Republican. Home: 1540 E Idaho Ave Apt G Las Cruces NM 88001-4369 Office: Baisha Comms 1540 E Idaho Ave Apt G Las Cruces NM 88001-4369

THOMPSON, ALAN MCFADDEN, institute administrator; b. Richmond, Va., Jan. 14, 1964; s. James Disney and Arluvene Bernice (Grossman) T.; m. Christine Neff, Mar. 19, 1993; 1 child, Vincent Orion Thompson Neff. BA in Internat. Devel., Bethel Coll., North Newton, Kans., 1990, BA in Peace Studies, 1990. English tchr. AEON Corp., Kashiwa, Japan, 1991-92; sr. sec. U. Wash. Law Sch., Seattle, 1992-94; devel. dir. Rural Devel. Inst., Seattle, 1994—. Organizer, Alliance for Survival, L.A., 1983-84; vol. Missionaries of Charity, Kathmandu, Nepal, 1987; reporter World Neighbors, Kathmandu, 1988. Mem. Wallingford Toastmasters (v.p. edn. 1998). Avocations: writing children's literature, public speaking, travel. Office: Rural Devel Inst 4746 11th Ave NE Apt 504 Seattle WA 98105-4671

THOMPSON, ARLENE RITA, nursing educator; b. Yakima, Wash., May 17, 1933; d. Paul James and Esther Margaret (Danroth) T. BS in Nursing, U. Wash., 1966, Masters in Nursing, 1970, postgrad., 1982—. Staff nurse Univ. Teaching Hosp., Seattle, 1966-69; mem. nursing faculty U. Wash. Sch. Nurses, Seattle, 1971-73; critical care nurse Virginia Mason Hosp., Seattle, 1973—; educator Seattle Pacific U. Sch. Nursing, 1981—; nurse legal cons. nursing edn., critical care nurse. Contbr. articles to profl. jours. USPHS grantee, 1969; nursing scholar Virginia Mason Hosp., 1965. Mem. Am. Assn. Critical Care Nurses (cert.), Am. Nurses Assn., Am. Heart Assn., Nat. League Nursing, Sigma Theta Tau, Alpha Tau Omega. Republican. Presbyterian. Avocations: sewing, swimming, jogging, bicycle riding, hiking. Home: 2320 W Newton St Seattle WA 98199-4115 Office: Seattle Pacific U 3307 3rd Ave W Seattle WA 98119-1997

THOMPSON, BETTY JANE, small business owner; b. Ladysmith, Wis., Nov. 18, 1923; d. Edward Thomas and Mayme Selma (Kratwell) Potter; m. Frederick Sturdee Thompson, Apr. 19, 1945 (div. Apr. 1973); children: Denise Alana, Kent Marshall; m. J.R. Critchfield, Feb. 14, 1977 (div. 1989). Student, Jamestown (N.D.) Coll., 1946-47, U. Calif., Long Beach, 1964-69; AA, Orange Coast Coll., 1976; postgrad., Monterey Peninsula Coll., 1979-80; SBA Cert., Hartnell Coll., 1982. Cert. fashion cons. Owner, mgr., buyer Goodview (Minn.) Food Mart, 1947-50; dist. mgr. Beauty Counselor of Minn., Winona County, 1951-61; Boy Scout liaison J.C. Penney Co., Newport Beach, Calif., 1969-72; dept. mgr. and buyer boyswear At Ease, Newport Beach, 1972-77, mgr. Top Notch Boys Wear, Carmel, Calif., 1977-83, buyer, 1984-88; owner, mgr. Top Notch Watch, Sun City, Ariz., 1989-95; editor H&R Block, 1995-98; v.p., chmn. Don Loper Fashion Show, [illegible] employment program, 1998—. Co-editor Aux. Antics mag., 1965. Vol. fundraising leadership Family Svc. Assn., Orange County, Calif., 1962-68, other [illegible] publicity, study group, Sunday sch. tchr., Congl. Ch., Winona, [illegible] Civic Club, 1948; active Norwest Bank Silver Bullets, Sr. Citizens of the Sun Cities, Phoenix, 1998—. Recipient Athena award Panhellenic Assn. Orange City, Calif., 1968, El Camino Real Dist. Svc. award Orange Empire coun. Boy Scouts Am., Baden-Powell award, Outstanding Leadership award, El Camino Real Dist., Calif., 1972J. Ringling North award, 1949; named Outstanding Svc. Vol. Family Svc. Assn., 1969. Mem. Carmel Bus. Assn. Avocations: travel, photography, ballroom dance, bicycling, skiing. Home and Office: 10048 W Hawthorn Dr Sun City AZ 85351-2829

THOMPSON, BEVERLY PIFFORD, vice-principal; b. Mebane, N.C., Aug. 22, 1946; d. William Davis and Bessie Mae (Palmer) Pittard; m. Lawrence J. Thompson, Oct. 28, 1972; children: Kelsey, Kory. BS in English, East Carolina U., Greenville, N.C., 1968; MA in Religious Edn., Loyola Marymount U., L.A., 1988; M in Ednl. Adminstrn. with distinction, Calif. State U., Northridge, 1996. Calif. adminstrv. credential, Tier I, Calif. clear single subject English. Tchr. English New Bern (N.C.) Sr. H.S., 1968-73; adminstrv. sec. R.K. Summy, Inc., Bakersfield, Calif., 1977-81; tchr. religious studies Garces Meml. H.S., Bakersfield, 1981-92; vice prin., dean curriculum Bishop Garcia Diego H.S., Santa Barbara, Calif., 1992-98; asst. prin. Dos Pueblos H.S., Galeta, Calif., 1998—; guest lectr. Young Adult Conf., Santa Barbara, 1996-97. Mem. Nat. Assn. Supervision and Curriculum Devel., Nat. Assn. Secondary Sch. Prins., Assn. Calif. Sch. Adminstrs., Calif. Assn. Supervision and Curriculum Devel., Nat. Cath. Edn. Assn., Phi Kappa Phi. Roman Catholic. Avocations: horseback riding, gardening, reading, walking. Home: 67 Deerhurst Dr Goleta CA 93117-1936 Office: Dos Pueblos HS 7266 Alameda Ave Galeta CA 93117

THOMPSON, C. MICHAEL, congressman; b. St. Helena, Calif., Jan. 24, 1951; s. Charles Thompson and Beverly (Forni) Powell; m. Janet Thompson, Mar. 8, 1982; children: Christopher, Jon. MA, Chico State U. Owner, maintenance supr. Beringer Winery; mem. Calif. State Senate, 1990-99, 106th Congress from 1st Calif. dist., 1999—; chair select com. on Calif.'s Wine Industry; chair Senate budget com.; vice chair Senate natural resources com. Staff sgt. U.S. Army, Vietnam. Decorated Purple Heart. Named Freshman Legislator of the Yr. Calif. Sch. Bds. Assn., 1990, Legislatorof the Yr. Calif. Abortion Rights Action League, Legislator of the Yr. Calif. Assn. Persons with Handicaps, Legislator of the Yr. Police Officers Rsch. Assn. Calif., Legislator of the Yr. Disabled in State Svc., 1994, Senator of the Yr. Calif. Assn. Homes and Svcs. for Aging, 1995; Recipient Disting. Svc. award Calif. State Assn. Counties, Disting. Svc. award Calif. Assn. Hosps., Legis. Leadership award Calif. Assn. Health Svcs. Home, 1994, Disting. Svc. award Aids Project L.A., 1995, Outstanding Senator award Planned Parenthood Affiliates Calif., 1996, Outstanding Senator of the Yr. award Calif. Sch. Bds. Assn., 1996, Outstanding Senator of the Yr. award Calif. Profl. Firefighters, 1996. Democrat. Roman Catholic. Office: 415 Cannon House Office Bldg Washington DC 20515*

THOMPSON, CHARLOTTE ELLIS, pediatrician, educator, author; b. Sept. 5, 1928; d. Robert and Ann Ellis; divorced; children: Jennifer Ann, Geoffrey Graeme. BA, Stanford U., 1950, MD, 1954. Diplomate Am. Bd. Pediat. Intern Children's Hosp., San Francisco, 1953-54; resident UCLA, 1960-61, L.A. Children's Hosp., 1962-63; pvt. practice La Jolla, Calif., 1963-75; dir. Muscle Disease Clinic, Univ. Hosp.-U. Calif. Sch. Medicine, San Diego, 1969-80, asst. clin. prof. pediat., 1969—; dir. Ctr. for Handicapped Children and Teenagers, San Francisco, 1981—; cons. U.S. Naval Hosp., San Diego, 1970-91; dep. dir. Santa Clara County Child Health and Disability, Santa Clara, Calif., 1974-75; dir. Ctr. for Multiple Handicaps, Oakland, Calif., 1976-81; co-dir. Muscle Clinic Children's Hosp., San Diego, 1963-69. Author: Raising a Handicapped Child: A Helpful Guide for Parents of the Physically Disabled, 1986, 4th edit., 1991, Allein leben: Ein umfassendes Handbuch für Frauen, 1993, Making Wise Choices: A Guide for Women, 1993, Raising a Child with a Neuromuscular Disorder, 1999, Raising A Handicapped Child, 1999; contbr. articles to med. jours., including Clin. Pediat., New Eng. Jour. Medicine, Neurology, Jour. Family Practice, Mothering, Jour. Pediatric Orthopedics, Pediatrician, Am. Baby, Pediatric News, also chpts. to books. Mem. Calif. Children's Svc. Com., 1977—. Fellow Am. Acad. Pediatrics; mem. Am. Women's Med. Assn., Internat. Music Box Soc. Avocations: tennis, ice skating, opera. Office: Ctr for Handicapped Children and Teenagers 2000 Van Ness Ave Ste 307 San Francisco CA 94109-3020

THOMPSON, CRAIG SNOVER, corporate communications executive; b. Bklyn., May 24, 1932; s. Craig F. and Edith (Williams) T.; m. Masae Sugizaki, Feb. 21, 1957; children: Lee Anne, Jane Laura. Grad., Valley Forge Mil. Acad., 1951; B.A., Johns Hopkins U., 1954. Newspaper and radio reporter Easton (Pa.) Express, 1954-55, 57-59, Wall St. Jour., 1959-60; account exec. Moore, Meldrum & Assocs., 1960; mgr. pub. relations Cen. Nat. Bank of Cleve., 1961-62; account exec. Edward Howard & Co., Cleve., 1962-67; v.p. Edward Howard & Co., 1967-69, sr. v.p., 1969-71; dir. pub. relations White Motor Corp., Cleve., 1971-76; v.p. pub. relations No. Telecom Inc., Nashville, 1976-77, White Motor Corp., Farmington Hills, Mich., 1977-80; v.p. corp. communications White Motor Corp., 1980-81; dir. exec. communications Rockwell Internat. Corp., Pitts., 1981-86, El Segundo, Calif., 1986-91; dir. exec. communications Rockwell Internat. Corp., Seal Beach, Calif., 1992-97, sr. communications exec., 1997; pres. Craig S. Thompson. Inc., 1997—. Bd. dirs. Shaker Lakes Regional Nature Center, 1970-73. Served to 1st lt., inf. U.S. Army, 1955-57. Mem. Pub. Rels. Soc. Am. (accredited), Alumni Assn. Valley Forge Mil. Acad. (bd. dirs. 1988-94).

THOMPSON, DAVID RENWICK, federal judge; b. 1930. BS in Bus., U. So. Calif., 1952, LLB, 1955. Pvt. practice law with Thompson & Thompson (and predecessor firms), 1957-85; judge U.S. Ct. Appeals (9th cir.), 1985—. Served with USN, 1955-57. Mem. ABA, San Diego County Bar Assn., Am. Bd. Trial Lawyers (sec. San Diego chpt. 1983, v.p. 1984, pres. 1985). Office: US Ct Appeals 940 Front St San Diego CA 92101-8994*

THOMPSON, DENNIS PETERS, plastic surgeon; b. Chgo., Mar. 18, 1937; s. David John and Ruth Dorothy (Peters) T.; m. Virginia Louise Williams, June 17, 1961; children: Laura Faye, Victoria Ruth, Elizabeth Jan. BS, U. Ill., 1957, BS in Medicine, 1959, MS in Physiology, MD, 1961. Diplomate Am. Bd. Surgery, Am. Bd. Plastic Surgery. Intern Presbyn.-St. Lukes Hosp., Chgo., 1961-62; resident in gen. surgery Mayo Clinic, Rochester, Minn., 1964-66, fellow in gen. surgery, 1964-66; resident in gen. surgery Harbor Gen. Hosp., Los Angeles, 1968-70; resident in plastic surgery UCLA, 1971-73, clin. instr. plastic surgery, 1975-82, asst. clin. prof. surgery, 1982-97, assoc. clin. prof. surgery, 1998—; private medicine specializing in plastic and reconstructive surgery, Los Angeles, 1974-78, Santa Monica, Calif., 1978—; chmn. plastic surgery sect. St. John's Hosp., 1986-91; mem. staff Santa Monica Hosp., UCLA Ctr. Health Scis.; chmn. dept. surgery Beverly Glen Hosp., 1978-79; pres. Coop. of Am. Physicians Credit Union, 1978-80, bd. dirs., 1980-97, chmn. membership devel. com., 1983-97, treas., 1985-97. Contbr. articles to med. jours. Moderator Congl. Ch. of Northridge (Calif.), 1975-76, chmn. bd. trustees, 1973-74, 80-82; bd. dirs. L.A. Bus. Coun., 1987-90. Am. Tobacco Inst. research grantee, 1959-60. Fellow ACS; mem. AMA (Physicians Recognition award 1971, 74, 77, 81, 84, 87, 90, 93, 96), Calif. Med. Assn., L.A. County Med. Assn. (chmn. bylaws com. 1979-80, chmn. ethics com. 1980-81, sec.-treas. dist. 5 1982-83, program chmn. 1983-84, pres. 1985-86, councilor 1988-96), Pan-Pacific Surgical Assn., Am. Soc. Plastic and Reconstructive Surgeons, Calif. Soc. Plastic Surgeons (chmn. bylaws com. 1982-83, chmn. liability com. 1983-85, councilor 1988-91, sec. 1993-95, v.p. 1995-96, pres.-elect 1996-97, pres. 1997-98), L.A. Soc. Plastic Surgeons (sec. 1980-82, pres. 1982-97), Lipoplasty Soc. N.Am., UCLA Plastic Surgery Soc. (treas. 1983-84, v.p. 1996-98, pres. 1998—), Am. Soc. Aesthetic Plastic Surgery, Am. Assn. Accreditation of Ambulatory Surg. Facilities (bd. dirs. 1995-97), Western Los Angeles Regional C. of C. (bd. dirs. 1981-84, 86-89, chmn. legis. action com. 1978-80), Phi Beta Kappa, Alpha Omega Alpha, Nu Sigma Nu, Phi Kappa Phi, Delta Sigma Delta, Omega Beta Pi, Phi Eta Sigma. Republican. Office: 2001 Santa Monica Blvd Santa Monica CA 90404-2102

THOMPSON, DWIGHT ALAN, vocational rehabilitation expert; b. [illegible] m. Irene Anita Arden, June 18, 1977; children: Dwight Christopher, Meredith Irene, Hilda Arden. *Wife Irene Arden is a licensed psychologist for University of Washington-Bothel. She received a BA in History from the University of Washington in 1977, an MA in Education from Seattle*

University in 1982 and a Edd in Counseling Psychology from Northern Arizona University in 1995. An avid Girl Scout leader she is also a member of the Husky Sports Hall of Fame at the University of Washington. BA in Social Welfare, U. Wash., 1978, MSW, 1980. Registered vocat. rehab. counselor, Wash., Oreg.; cert. social worker, Wash.; cert. case mgr.; diplomate Am. Bd. Clin. Examiners in Social Work; cert. disability mgmt. Specialist Commn. Houseparent Parkview Home for Exceptional Children, Seattle, 1976-77; rsch. analyst Wash. State Ho. Reps., Olympia, 1979-81; v.p. The James L. Groves Co., Everett, Wash., 1982-86; exec. dir. Evaluation & Tng. Assocs., Seattle, 1984-86; CEO, owner Rehab. & Evaluation Svcs. Inc., Seattle, 1986—; v.p., founder Next Generation Technologies, Inc., Seattle, 1994—; social work officer 50th Gen. Army Res. Hosp., Seattle, 1982-87, 91-93; med. adminstrv., social worker officer Operation Desert Storm, Riyadh, Saudi Arabia, 1990-91; aide-de-camp 2d Hosp. Ctr., San Francisco, 1987-88, pub. affairs officer, 1988-90; acting commdr. 1972d MED DET-Combat Stress Control, 1993, exec. officer, 1994-97, comdr., 1998—. Co-author Correction Study Report, 1981. Registered lobbyist Wash. State, 1983-87; conf. pres. St. Vincent de Paul Soc., 1975-78; lt. Thurston County Fire Dist #6, East Olympia, Wash., 1980-83; alumni rep. COS Track Com. U. Wash., 1984-87; primary candidate Dem. Primary for State Rep., Renton, Wash., 1984; mem. Wash. Vocat. Rehab. adv. com. Dept. Labor Industries, 1992-96; tech. advisor Com. on Vocat. Rehab., 1997—; pres. Sheridan Beach Cmty. Club, Inc., 1994-95; chair human svcs. commn. City Lake Forest Park, Wash, 1995; mem. city coun., 1996—; mem. Girl Scouts of Am.; trustee First Ave Svc. Ctr., 1998—; scoutmaster World Jamboree Western Region Boy Scouts Am., 1999. Fellow Am. Acad. Pain Mgmt. (cert.); Mem. NASW (cert.), Nat. Assn. Rehab. Profls. (pvt. sector, Wash. legis. chair), Acad. Cert. Social Workers, Wash. Self-Insurers Assn., Assn. Mil. Surgeons U.S., Res. Officers Assn., Nat. Eagle Scout Assn., Am. Bd. Forensic Examiners, Case Mgmt. Soc. Am., Boy Scouts Am., Nat. Assn. Rehab. Profls. (Kevin Karr award for Most Innovative Rehab. Program 1995), Theta Xi (pres. 1975-77). Roman Catholic. Home: 16270 Beach Dr NE Lk Forest Park WA 98155-6704 Office: Rehab and Evaluation Svcs 226 Summit Ave E Seattle WA 98102-5619

THOMPSON, ELBERT ORSON, retired dentist, consultant; b. Salt Lake City, Aug. 31, 1910; s. Orson David and Lillian (Greenwood) T.; m. Gayle Larsen, Sept. 12, 1935; children: Ronald Elbert, Karen Thompson Toone, Edward David, Gay Lynne. Student, U. Utah, 1928-30, 33-35; DDS, Northwestern U., 1939; hon. degree, Am. Coll. Dentistry, Miami, Fla., 1958, Internat. Coll. Dentistry, San Francisco, 1962. Pvt. practice dentistry Salt Lake City, 1939-78; ret., 1978; inventor, developer and internat. lectr. postgrad./undergrad. courses various dental schs. and study groups, 1953-83; developer, tchr. Euthenics Dentistry Concept; also, sit-down dentistry, four handed dentistry, lounge-type dental chair, washed field dentistry, euthenics dental operating chair; cons. in field. Contbr. numerous dental articles to profl. jours. Life mem. Rep. Presdl. Task Force, Washington, 1985—. Recipient Merit Honor award U. Utah, 1985; named Dentist of the Yr. Utah Acad. Gen. Dentistry, 1991, Father of Modern Dentistry, 1991. Mem. ADA (life), Utah Dental Assn. (life, sec. 1948-49, Disting. Svc. award 1980, E.O. Thompson Recognition award 1995), Salt Lake City Dental Soc. (life, pres. 1945-46), Utah Dental Hygiene Soc. (hon.), Am. Acad. Dental Practice Adminstrn. (life, pres. 1965-66), Internat. Coll. Dentists, Am. Coll. Dentists, Sons of Utah Pioneers (life), Dinorators Club (charter), Northwestern U. Alumni Assn. (Merit award 1961), Omicron Kappa Upsilon. Mormons. Avocations: temple service, golf, photography, computer, writing. Home: 112 Gamble Ave Preston ID 83263-1055

THOMPSON, GEORGE LEWIS, lawyer; b. N.Y.C., June 12, 1944; s. Thomas Vincent and Belle (Sherman) T.; m. Daphne J. Mackey, Aug. 14, 1982. BA, Bard Coll., 1966; JD, Duke U., 1970. Bar: N.Y. 1971. Atty. advisor Gen. Counsel U.S. Dept. Transp., Washington, 1970-71; gen. atty. Rocky Mountain region FAA, Denver, 1971-74; assoc. regional counsel New Eng. region FAA, Boston, 1974-85; regional counsel N.W. Mountain region FAA, Seattle, 1985-89, asst. chief counsel, 1989—. Avocations: sailing, gardening, tennis, reading. Office: FAA NW Mountain Region 1601 Lind Ave SW Renton WA 98055-4099

THOMPSON, GORDON, JR., federal judge; b. San Diego, Dec. 28, 1929; s. Gordon and Garnet (Meese) T.; m. Jean Peters, Mar. 17, 1951; children—John M., Peter Renwick, Gordon III. Grad., U. So. Calif., 1951, Southwestern U. Sch. Law, Los Angeles, 1956. Bar: Calif. 1956. With Dist. Atty.'s Office, County of San Diego, 1957-60; partner firm Thompson & Thompson, San Diego, 1960-70; U.S. dist. judge So. Dist. Calif., San Diego, 1970—, chief judge, 1984-91, sr. judge, 1994—. Mem. ABA, Am. Bd. Trial Advocates, San Diego County Bar Assn. (v.p. 1970), San Diego Yacht Club, Delta Chi. Office: US Dist Ct 940 Front St San Diego CA 92101-8994

THOMPSON, HERBERT ERNEST, tool and die company executive; b. Jamaica, N.Y., Sept. 8, 1923; s. Walter and Louise (Joly) T.; student Stevens Inst. Tech., 1949-51; m. Patricia Elaine Osborn, Aug. 2, 1968; children: Robert Steven, Debra Lynn. Foreman, Conner Tool Co., 1961-62, Eason & Waller Grinding Corp., 1962-63; owner Endco Machined Products, 1966-67, Thompson Enterprises, 1974—; pres. Method Machined Products, Phoenix, 1967; pres., owner Quality Tool, Inc., 1967-96. Served to capt. USAAF, 1942-46. Decorated D.F.C., Air medal with cluster. Home: 14009 N 42nd Ave Phoenix AZ 85053-5306 Office: 4223 W Clarendon Ave Phoenix AZ 85019-3618

THOMPSON, JACK ERNEST, state official; b. Cleve., Jan. 17, 1943; s. Ernest Wilfred and Veneta Lena (Miller) T.; m. Donna Jeanne Campbell, Oct. 22, 1966; children: Darci, Chad. BS, USAF Acad., Colorado Springs, Colo., 1965; MBA, U. Colo., 1976. Program mgr. Mission Rsch. Corp., Albuquerque, 1985-87, group leader, 1987-91; cons. U. N.Mex., Albuquerque, 1991-93; dir. mfg. Bio-Recovery Systems, Las Cruces, N.Mex., 1993-94; dir. State Transp. Authority, Albuquerque, 1995-96; dep. sec. N.Mex. Corrections Dept., Santa Fe, 1996—. With USAF, 1965-85. Mem. AIAA. Republican. Home: 14353 Marquette Dr NE Albuquerque NM 87123-1966 Office: Corrections Dept PO Box 27116 Santa Fe NM 87502-0116

THOMPSON, JAMES AVERY, JR., bankruptcy specialist, consumer credit consultant; b. Whiteville, N.C., Oct. 3, 1947; s. James Avery and Mary Elizabeth (Davis) T.; m. Julia Lee Stephens Thompson, June 7, 1969 (div. July 1979); 1 child, Marlee Amanda Elizabeth Thompson; m. Susannah Elizabeth Rupp Thompson, May 16, 1987; 1 child, Sarah Mary Elizabeth Thompson. AA (hon.), Marion (Ala.) Mil. Inst., 1967; BA, U. Ala., Tuscaloosa, 1969; MLS, 1973; MBA, So. Calif. Inst., Claremont, 1988; JD, Am. Coll. of Law, 1988. Mus. curator U. Ala., Birmingham, 1972-73, med. libr., 1973-82; asst. law libr. U. Laverne (Calif.) Law Sch., 1985-86; ref. libr. Western State U. Sch. Law, Fullerton, Calif., 1986-88; prof., instr. Am. Coll. Law, Brea, Calif., 1988-89; dir., instr. U. West L.A. Law Libr., 1988-90; legal intern Law Office Frank Phillips, Yorba Linda, Calif., 1990-91, Law Office Susannah Thompson, Temecula, Calif., 1991-98, Law Office Chris Mullen, Temecula, Calif., 1998—. Author numerous periodicals in field. Campaign chmn. Med. Libr. United Way, Birmingham, Ala., 1979-80; mem. Lions Club, Tarrant, Ala., 1975-77; dir., spon. Tennis Assn. Pleasant Grove, Ala., 1980-82. Recipient Eagle Scout award, Order of Arrow Boy Scouts Am., 1963; named pres. Student Bar Assn., Am. Coll. Law, Brea, Calif., 1987-88, editor Law Review Am. Coll. Law, Brea, Calif., 1988. Mem. Royal Numismatic Soc. Can., Royal Philatelic Soc. Can., U.S. Tennis Assn., Am. Numismatic Assn., Delta Theta Phi, Alpha Sigma Phi. Democrat. Methodist. Avocations: numismatics, philately, tennis, anthropology, ice skating. Office: Law Office Chris Mullen Ste 206 41743 Enterprise Circle N Temecula CA 92590-4858

THOMPSON, JAMES WILLIAM, lawyer; b. Dallas, Oct. 22, 1936; s. John Charles and Frances (Van Slyke) T.; BS, U. Mont., 1958, JD, 1962; m. Marie Hertz, June 26, 1965 (dec. 1995); children: Elizabeth, Margaret, John; m. Linda Dozier, May 2, 1998. Acct., Arthur Young & Co., N.Y.C., summer 1959; instr. bus. adminstrn. Eastern Mont. Coll., Billings, 1959-60, U. Mont., Missoula, 1960-61; admitted to Mont. bar, 1962; assoc. Cooke, Moulton, Bellingham & Longo, Billings, 1962-64, James R. Felt, Billings, 1964-65; asst. atty. City of Billings, 1963-64, atty., 1964-66; ptnr. Felt, Speare & Thompson, Billings, 1966-72, McNamer, Thompson & Cashmore, 1973-86, McNamer & Thompson Law Firm PC, 1986-89, McNamer, Thompson, Werner & Stanley, P.C., 1990-93, McNamer Thompson Law Firm PC, 1993-98, Wright Tolliver Guthals Law Firm PC, 1999—; bd. dirs. Associated Employers of Mont., Inc., 1989-98; mem. adv. coun. Sch. Fine Arts U. Mont., 1997—. Mem. Billings Zoning Commn., 1966-69; v.p. Billings Community Action Program (now Dist. 7 Human Resources Devel. Council), 1968-70, pres., 1970-75, trustee, 1975—; mem. Yellowstone County Legal Services Bd., 1969-70; City-County Air Pollution Control Bd., 1969-70; pres. Billings Symphony Soc., 1970-71; bd. dirs. Billings Studio Theatre, 1967-73, United Way Billings, 1973-81, Mont. Inst. of Arts Found., 1986-89, Downtown Billings Assn., 1986-90, Billings Area Bus. Incubator, Inc., 1991-94, Found. of Mont. State U., Billings, 1992-98, Mont. Parks Assn., 1997—, Rimrock Opera Co., 1998—; mem. Diocesan exec. council, 1972-75; mem. Billings Transit Commn., 1971-73; mem. City Devel. Agy., 1972-73. CPA, Mont. Mem. ABA, Am. Acad. Estate Planning Attys., Nat. Acad. Elder Law Attys., State Bar Mont., Yellowstone County Bar Assn. (bd. dirs. 1983-87, pres. 1985-86), C. of C., Elks, Kiwanis (pres. Yellowstone chpt. 1974-75), Sigma Chi (pres. Billings alumni assn. 1963-65). Episcopalian. Home: 123 Lewis Ave Billings MT 59101-6034 Office: 300 US Bank Bldg Billings MT 59101

THOMPSON, JEREMIAH BEISEKER, international medical business executive; b. Harvey, N.D., July 20, 1927; s. Linden Brown and Ferne Althea (Beiseker) T.; m. Paula Maria Ketchum, Feb. 5, 1960; children: Cole, Per, Gover, Susannah. BS, U. Minn., 1949, MD, 1966. Rsch. assoc. U. Colo. Med. Sch., Denver, 1955-56, U. Calif. Med. Sch., San Francisco, 1956-57, Stanford U., 1957-59; applications rsch. scientist Beckman/Spinco Co., Palo Alto, Calif., 1959-61; mgr. Asia and Africa Hewlett Packard Co., Palo Alto, 1966-72; med. cons. Alyeska Pipeline Co., Anchorage, 1973-76; mgr. Asia, Africa, Australasia Corometrics Med. Systems, Wallingford, Conn., 1976-82; dir. internat. ops. Oximetrix (Abbott), Mountain View, Calif., 1982-84, Novametrix Med. Systems, Wallingford, 1984-88; ptnr. TMC Internat., Tokyo and Concord, Calif., 1988—; advisor, cons. Yokogawa-Hewlett Packard, Tokyo, 1966-70; cons. Kupat Holim, Tel Aviv, Israel, 1967-92, Itochu, Tokyo, 1984-99, Nat. Heart-Lung Inst., Beijing, China, 1984-99. Project dir. Comparative Study of Western and Japanese Medicine in Taisho and Showa Eras, 1991—. With USN, 1945-46; PTO. Founding fellow Brit. Interplanetary Soc.; assoc. Japan Found., Assn. Asian Studies; mem. Kokusai Bunka Kaikan, Tokyo, World Affairs Coun., Mechanics Inst. Achievements include cancer research, joint Japan/U.S. project screening and evaluation for anti-cancer activity of halogenated methane derivatives, augmentation of irradiation effects by chemotherapy. Home and Office: TMC Internat 3718 Barrington Dr Concord CA 94518-1614

THOMPSON, JOEL ERIK, lawyer; b. Summit, N.J., Sept. 15, 1940; s. Maurice Eugene and Charlotte Ruth (Harrington) T.; m. Deborah Ann Korp, Dec. 24, 1980 (div. Jan. 1987); children: Janice Santiesteban, Amber. Student, Va. Poly. Inst., 1958, Carnegie Inst. Tech., 1960-61; BSME cum laude, Newark Coll. Engring., 1966; JD, Seton Hall, 1970. Bar: N.J. 1970, Ariz. 1975, U.S. Tax Ct. 1972, U.S. Ct. Claims 1972, U.S. Customs Ct., 1972, U.S. Ct. Mil. Appeals, 1972, U.S. Ct. Customs and Patent Appeals 1972, U.S. Dist. Ct. N.J. 1970, Ariz. 1975, U.S. Ct. Appeals (9th cir.) 1975, U.S. Supreme Ct. 1975; cert. specialist criminal law Ariz. Bd. Legal Specialization; lic. profl. engr., N.J. Sr. technician Bell Tel. Labs., Inc., Murray Hill, N.J., 1965-67; patent agent Bell Tel. Labs., Inc., Murray Hill, 1967-70, staff atty., 1970-73; sr. trial atty. N.J. Pub. Defender's Office, Elizabeth, N.J., 1973-74; assoc. Cahill, Sutton and Thomas, Phoenix, 1974-76; trial lawyer Maricopa County Pub. Defender's Office, Phoenix, 1976-80; trial lawyer, criminal law specialist Henry J. Florence, Ltd., Phoenix, 1980-86; pvt. practice Phoenix, 1987—; judge Superior Ct. Ariz., Phoenix, 1987-95; instr. Phoenix Regional Police Acad., 1976-80, Glendale C.C., 1977, Ariz. State U. Sch. of Law, 1978, Am. Inst., 1990; pres., CEO Eagle Master Corp., Phoenix, 1995—; presenter in field. Contbr. articles to profl. jours. Mem. planning com., Phoenix, 1992-98, mayor's select com., Phoenix, 1997, blue ribbon com. Maricopa Assn. Govs., 1996-97; chmn. planning com. Camelback East Village, Phoenix, 1993-96. Mem. Ariz. Bar Assn., Nat. Assn. Criminal Def. Lawyers, Ariz. Attys. Criminal Justice (charter), Maricopa Bar Assn. (CLE com. 1990-94, bench and bar com. 1992-96, Cert. Appreciation), Ariz. Assn. Pvt. Investigators (hon.), Internat. Assn. Identification (hon.), Tau Beta Pi, Pi Tau Sigma. Office: 3104 E Camelback Rd # 521 Phoenix AZ 85016-4502

THOMPSON, JOHN, museum director. Gen. mgr. Copper King Mus., Butte, Mont., 1990—. Office: Copper King Mansion 219 W Granite St Butte MT 59701-9235*

THOMPSON, JOHN WILLIAM, international management consultant; b. Hurricane, Utah, Oct. 14, 1945; s. Thomas Thurman and Lula (Brinkerhoff) T.; m. Pamela Ruth Williams, Sept. 14, 1991. BSEE, Utah State U., 1969, MBA, 1972; PhD, U. Oreg., 1978. Rsch. asst. Utah State U., Logan, Utah, 1967-69, tching. asst., 1971-72; elec. engr. Collins Radio, Newport Beach, Calif., 1969-72; tching. fellow U. Oreg., Eugene, 1972-78; tng. dir. Lifespring Inc., San Rafael, Calif., 1978-80; pres., CEO Human Factors Inc., San Rafael, Calif., 1980—; chmn. bd. Acumen Internat., San Rafael, Calif., 1985—. Author: The Human Factor: An Inquiry into Communication and Consciousness, 1983, Leadership in the 21st Century in New Traditions in Business, 1992, The Renaissance of Learning in Learning Organizations: Developing Cultures for Tomorrow's Workplace, 1994, The Human Factor, 1996; author of software based management assessment programs, system theory based management development courses, 1980-92. Rockefeller Found. grantee, 1971. Avocations: sailing, breeding Koi, gardening, bicycling, scuba diving. Office: Human Factors Inc 4000 Civic Center Dr Ste 500 San Rafael CA 94903-4152

THOMPSON, JOSIE, nurse; b. Ark., Apr. 16, 1949; d. James Andrew and Oneda Fay (Watson) Rhoads; m. Mark O. Thompson, Feb. 14, 1980. Diploma, Lake View Sch. Nursing, 1970; student, Danville C.C., 1974-75, St. Petersburg Jr. Coll., 1979. RN, Ill., Wyo. Staff nurse St. Elizabeth Hosp., Danville, Ill., 1970-78, Osteopathetic Hosp., St. Petersburg, Fla., 1980-81, Wyo. State Hosp., Evanston, 1981-83; staff nurse Wyo. Home Health Care, Rock Springs, 1984—, adminstr., 1986-95; pres. Home Health Care Alliance Wyo., 1991-92; staff nurse home health Interim Health Care, Cheyenne, Wyo., 1996-97; staff nurse Rocky Mountain Home Health Care, Green River, Wyo., 1997—. Mem. nursing program adv. bd. Western Wyo. Community Coll.; mem. Coalition for the Elderly, Spl. Needs Com. Sweetwater County, 1992-93. Home: PO Box 1154 Rock Springs WY 82902-1154 Office: Rocky Mountain Home Health Care 535 Uinta Dr Green River WY 82935-4818

THOMPSON, JUDITH ANN, editor, educator, writer; b. Long Beach, Calif., Feb. 28, 1938; d. William Pollhill and Jean Louise (Wilson) Blackmore; children: Terri Anne, David Ross, Rebecca Jean, Michael Jai. BAE with honors, U. Fla., 1959; MA in English Lit., U. Hawaii, 1971. Cert. tchr., Hawaii, Oreg. Tchr. Le Jardin d'Enfants, Kailua, Hawaii, 1968-69; tchr. Yoga Coll. of India, Honolulu, San Francisco, 1971-73, Gateway Montessori Sch., San Francisco, 1972-73, Hawaii Dept. Edn., 1975-80; exec. editor Inst. for Polynesian Studies Brigham Young U. Hawaii campus, Laie, 1980-84; illustrator Health Skills for Life, Eugene, Oreg., 1985-87; dir. Ramedica Internat. Corp., Eugene, 1988-92; editor, pub. rels. cons. Nissim Koen, Portland, 1995-97; founder Blackmore & Blackmore Pub., Portland, 1996—; editor Portland br. Yoga Coll. of India newsletter. Author: Healthy Pregnancy the Yoga Way, 1977; co-author: Polynesian Canoes and Navigation, 1981; illustrator: (children's book) Honolulu Zoo Riddles, 1974; editor/designer: The Cry of the Humble by Paul Lavender, 1998; contbr. articles to profl. jours. Avocations: yoga, swimming, painting. Office: 117 NW Trinity Pl Ste C Portland OR 97209-1925

THOMPSON, JUDITH KASTRUP, nursing researcher; b. Marstal, Denmark, Oct. 1, 1933; came to the U.S., 1951; d. Edward Kastrup and Anna Hansa (Knudsen) Pedersen; m. Richard Frederick Thompson, May 22, 1960; children: Kathryn Marr, Elizabeth Kastrup, Virginia St. Claire. BS, RN, U. Oreg., 1958, MSN, 1963. RN, Calif., Oreg. Staff nurse U. Oreg. Med. Sch., Eugene, 1957-58; staff nurse U. Oreg. Med. Sch., Portland, 1958-61, head staff nurse, 1960-61; instr. psychiat. nursing U. Oreg. Sch. Nursing, Portland, 1963-64; rsch. asst. U. Oreg. Med. Sch., Portland, 1964-65, U. Calif., Irvine, 1971-72; rsch. assoc. Stanford (Calif.) U., 1982-87; rsch. asst. Harvard U., Cambridge, Mass., 1973-74; rsch. assoc. U. So. Calif., L.A., 1987—. Contbg. author: Behavioral Control and Role of Sensory Biofeedback, 1976; contbr. articles to profl. jours. Treas. LWV, Newport Beach, Calif., 1970-74; scout leader Girl Scouts Am., Newport Beach, 1970-78. Named Citizen of Yr. State of Oreg., 1966. Mem. Soc. for Neurosci., Am. Psychol. Soc. (charter), ANA, Oreg. Nurses Assn. Republican. Lutheran. Avocations: art collecting, travel, tennis. Home: 28 Sky Sail Dr Corona Del Mar CA 92625-1436 Office: U So Calif University Park Los Angeles CA 90089-2520

THOMPSON, LOIS JEAN HEIDKE ORE, psychologist; b. Chgo., Feb. 22, 1933; d. Harold William and Ethel Rose (Neumann) Heidke; m. Henry Thomas Ore, Aug. 28, 1954 (div. May 1972); children: Christopher, Douglas; m. Joseph Lippard Thompson, Aug. 3, 1972; children: Scott, Les, Melanie. BA, Cornell Coll., Mt. Vernon, Iowa, 1955; MA, Idaho State U., 1964, EdD, 1981. Lic. psychologist, N.Mex. Tchr. pub. schs. various locations, 1956-67; tchr., instr. Idaho State U., Pocatello, 1967-72; employee/orgn. devel. specialist Los Alamos (N.Mex.) Nat. Lab., 1981-84, tng. specialist, 1984-89, sect. leader, 1989-93; pvt. practice indsl. psychology and healthcare, Los Alamos, 1988—; sec. Cornell Coll. Alumni Office, 1954-55, also other orgns.; bd. dirs. Parent Edn. Ctr., Idaho State U., 1980; counselor, Los Alamos, 1981-88. Editor newsletter LWV, Laramie, Wyo., 1957; contbr. articles to profl. jours. Pres. Newcomers Club, Pocatello, 1967, Faculty Womens Club, Pocatello, 1968; chmn. edn. com. AAUW, Pocatello, 1969. Mem. APA, N.Mex. Psychol. Assn. (bd. dirs. divsn. II 1990, sec. 1988-90, chmn. 1990), N.Mex. Soc. Adlerian Psychology (pres. 1990, treas. 1991-97, bd. dirs. 1996—), Soc. Indsl. and Orgn. Psychology. Mem. LDS Ch. Avocations: racewalking, backpacking, skiing, tennis, biking. Home and Office: 340 Aragon Ave Los Alamos NM 87544-3505

THOMPSON, LYLE EUGENE, electrical engineer; b. Pocatello, Idaho, May 16, 1956; s. Clyde Eugene and Doris (Pratt) T.; m. Barbara Mae Dickerson, Dec. 31, 1986. Grad. high sch. Sr. diagnostic engr. Calma/GE, Santa Clara, Calif., 1978-83; mem. tech. staff Telecommunications Tech., Inc., Milpitas, Calif., 1983-84; proprietor/cons. Lyle Thompson Cons., Fremont, Calif., 1984-87; sys. analyst Raynet Corp., Menlo Park, Calif., 1987-88; proprietor/cons. Lyle Thompson Cons., Hayward, Calif., 1988-89; mgr. sys. design Raylan Corp., Menlo Park, Calif., 1989-90; dir. system design Raylan Corp., Menlo Park, 1990-91; pvt. practice cons. San Lorenzo, Calif., 1991-96; pres., CEO HelioSoft, Inc., San Lorenzo, Calif., 1996—; cons. in field. Patentee in field. Mem. ACM, IEEE. Avocations: skiing, music, role playing, golf. Home: 664 Paseo Grande San Lorenzo CA 94580-2364

THOMPSON, LYNN KATHRYN SINGER, educational director; b. Ames, Iowa, Nov. 30, 1947; d. William Andrew and Virginia Preston (Russell) Singer. BA, Cornell Coll., Mt. Vernon, Iowa, 1970; MA in Edn., Ariz. State U., 1980; EdD, No. Ariz. U., 1990. Cert. tchr. and adminstr., Ariz. Tchr. Crane Elem. Dist., Yuma, Ariz., 1970-81, 86-90; coord. fed. programs Crane Elem Dist., Yuma, Azri., 1981-83, asst. prin., 1983-85; dir. lang. acquisition and fed. programs, 1990—. Bd. dirs. Yuma Fine Arts Assn., 1982-84; mem. Ariz. State Com. Practitioners, Phoenix, 1994—. Recipient Golden Bell award Ariz. Sch. Bds. Assn., 1992; Delta Kappa Gamma scholar, 1987, 89. Mem. PEO Internat., Delta Kappa Gamma (pres. 1988-90), Phi Delta Kappa (bd. dirs., rsch. chair 1991-95), ZONTA Internat. (bd. dirs. Yuma 1991, pres. 1996-97, 98). Avocations: home restoration, camping, antiques, reading. Office: Crane Elem Dist 4250 W 16th St Yuma AZ 85364-4031

THOMPSON, PAUL HAROLD, university president; b. Ogden, Utah, Nov. 28, 1938; s. Harold Merwin and Elda (Skeen) T.; m. Carolyn Lee Nelson, Mar. 9, 1961; children: Loralyn, Kristyn, Shannyn, Robbyn, Daylyn, Nathan. BS, U. Utah, 1964; MBA, Harvard U., 1966, D Bus. Adminstrn., 1969. Rsch. assoc. Harvard U., Cambridge, Mass., 1966-69; asst. prof. Harvard U., Cambridge, 1969-73; assoc. prof. bus. Brigham Young U., Provo, Utah, 1973-78, prof., 1978-84, asst. dean, 1978-81, dean, 1984-89, v.p., 1989-90; pres. Weber State U., Ogden, Utah, 1990—; cons. Goodyear, Hughes Aircraft, Portland GE, Esso Resources Ltd., GE. Co-author: Organization and People: Readings, Cases, and Exercises in Organizational Behavior, 1976, Novations: Strategies for Career Management, 1986; also articles. Named Outstanding Prof. of Yr., Brigham Young U., 1981; Baker scholar Harvard U., 1966. Mem. Am. Assn. State Colls. and Univs. (com. 1991—), Ogden C. of C. (exec. com. 1990—), Rotary (prograam com. Ogden 1991—, Harris fellow 1992—), Phi Beta Kappa. Office: Weber State U Presidents Office 3750 Harrison Blvd Ogden UT 84408*

THOMPSON, PETER LAYARD HAILEY, SR., golf course architect; b. Modesto, Calif., Apr. 26, 1939. BS in East Asian Studies, U. Oreg., 1962, B in Landscape Architecture, 1971, M in Urban Planning, 1971; postgrad., U. Calif., Berkeley, 1975, Nat. U. Registered landscape arch., Calif., Oreg., Wash., Nev. With Oreg. Planning Commn., Lane County, 1965-70; commr. Oreg. Planning Commn., Eugene, 1981-83; sr. assoc. Ruff, Cameron, Lacoss, Eugene, 1971-75; prin. Peter L. H. Thompson & Assocs., Eugene, 1975-83, John H. Midby & Assocs., Las Vegas, Nev., 1983-86, Thompson-Wihlborg, Ltd., Corte Madera, Calif., 1982-89, Thompson Planning Group (now Thompson Golf Planning), Ltd., San Rafael, Calif., 1989—; with Oreg. Planning Commn., commr., 1981-83, Novato, Calif. Planning Commn., commr. 1989-93, pres. 1989-93; spkr. Oreg. Home Builders Conf., 1980, Pacific Coast Builders Conf., 1984, Tacoma Country Club Pro-Pres. Tournament, 1991, Madrona Links Men's Golf Club, 1991, Twin Lakes Country Club Pro-Pres. Tournament, 1992, Golf Expo, Palm Springs, Calif., 1993, 95, Golf Expo, Nashville, 1993, Golf Expo, Monterey, Calif., 1994, others. Contbr. articles to mags. Mem. citizen's adv. bd. City of Eugene, Oreg., City of Las Vegas. Mem. USGA, Am. Soc. Landscape Archs., Am. Assn. Planners, Nat. Golf Found., Urban Land Inst., Rotary Internat. Office: Thompson Golf Planning Ltd 2175 Francisco Blvd E Ste A San Rafael CA 94901-5524

THOMPSON, RENA LOUISE, elementary education educator; b. Long Beach, Calif., Aug. 1, 1961; d. Cloyd Roy Bower and Melody Mae (Montgomery) Smith; m. Floyd Fewel Thompson, Nov. 15, 1986; children: Kyle Fewel, Collin Odell. AA, Cypress Jr. Coll., 1982; BA, Calif. State U., Long Beach, 1985; MA, Calif. State U., L.A., 1991. Preliminary adminstrv. credential, spl. edn.-learning handicapped credential, resource spl. program cert. of competence, multi-subject credential, Calif. 6-8 Special Day Class tchr. East Middle Sch. Downey (Calif.) Unified Sch. Dist., 1987-91, 4th grade tchr. Williams Sch., 1991-95, summer prin. Williams Sch., 1995, K-5 math mentor, 1995-97, K-5 RSP tchr. Imperial Sch., 1995-97; summer prin. Downey (Calif.) Unified Sch. Dist.-Lewis Sch., summer 1996; PQR cons. Freeway Consortium, Lakewood, Calif., 1995—. Mem. Delta Kappa Gamma (sec. 1995-97, pres. 1997—), Alpha Omicron Pi Alumnae (v.p. 1985—). Democrat. Avocations: cooking, reading, crafts, family, outdoors. Home: 2121 W Crone Ave Anaheim CA 92804-3524 Office: Imperial Sch 8133 Imperial Hwy Downey CA 90242-3794

THOMPSON, RICHARD DICKSON, lawyer; b. Lexington, Ky., Aug. 14, 1955; s. Lawrence Sidney and Algernon Smith (Dickson) T.; m. Bobbi Dale Magidoff, Aug. 3, 1980; children: Anne Katherine, Harrison Asher. AB, Harvard U., 1977; JD, Stanford U., 1980. Bar: Calif. 1980, U.S. Dist. Ct. (so. dist.) Calif. 1980. Assoc. Rosenfeld Meyer & Susman, Beverly Hills, Calif., 1980-83, Silverberg Rosen Leon & Behr, L.A., 1983-86; ptnr. Silverberg Rosen Leon & Behr, 1986-89; assoc., then ptnr. Silverberg Katz Thompson & Braun, L.A., 1989-95. Bd. trustees L.A. Copyright Soc. Mem. Order of the Coif, Phi beta Kappa. Office: Bloom, Hergott, Cook Diemer & Klein 150 S Rodeo Dr Fl 3 Beverly Hills CA 90212-2410*

THOMPSON, RICHARD FREDERICK, psychologist, neuroscientist, educator; b. Portland, Oreg., 1930; s. Frederick Albert and Margaret St. Clair (Marr) T.; m. Judith K. Pedersen, May 22, 1960; children: Kathryn M., Elizabeth K., Virginia St. C. B.A., Reed Coll., 1952; M.S., U. Wis., 1953, Ph.D., 1956. Asst. prof. med. psychology Med. Sch. U. Oreg., Portland, 1959-63, assoc. prof., 1963-65, prof., 1965-67; prof. psychobiology U. Calif. Irvine, 1967-73, 75-80; prof. psychology Harvard U., Cambridge, Mass., 1973-74; Lashley chair prof. Harvard U., Cambridge, 1973; prof. psychology, Bing prof. human biology Stanford U., Palo Alto, Calif., 1980-87; Keck prof. psychology and biol. scis. U. So. Calif., L.A., 1987—, dir. neuroscience program, 1989—. Author: Foundations of Physiological Psychology, 1967,

(with others) Psychology, 1971, Introduction to Physiological Psychology, 1975; Psychology editor (with others), W.H. Freeman & Co. publs., chief editor, Behavioral Neurosci., 1983—; editor: Jour. Comparative and Physiol. Psychology, 1981-83; regional editor: (with others) Physiology and Behavior; contbr. (with others) articles to profl. jours. Fellow AAAS, APA (Disting. Sci. Contbn. award 1974, governing coun. 1974—), Soc. Neurosci. (councilor 1972-76); mem. NAS, Am. Acad. Arts and Scis., Internat. Brain Rsch. Orgn., Psychonomic Soc. (gov. 1972-77, chmn. 1976), Am. Psychol. Soc. (pres. 1994-96), Western Psychol. Assn. (pres. 1994-95), Soc. Exptl. Psychology (Warren medal). Office: Univ of So Calif Neuroscis Program HNB 122 Univ Park Los Angeles CA 90007

THOMPSON, ROBERT CHARLES, lawyer; b. Council, Idaho, Apr. 20, 1942; s. Ernest Lavelle and Evangeline Montgomery (Carlson) T.; m. Marilyn Anne Wilcox, Jan. 17, 1960 (dec. Mar. 1962); m. Patricia Joan Price, June 1, 1963 (div. 1969); m. Jan Nesbitt, June 29, 1973 (dec. May 1998); m. Shari Lewis, Feb. 7, 1999; children: Tanya, Christopher, Eric. AB, Harvard U., 1963, LLB, 1967. Bar: Mass. 1967, Calif. 1983, U.S. Dist. Ct. (ea. dist.) Mass. 1975, U.S. Ct. Appeals (1st cir.) 1976, U.S. Ct. Appeals (9th cir.) 1984, U.S. Dist. Ct. (no. dist.) Calif. 1983, U.S. Dist. Ct. (ea. dist.) Calif., 1996. Assoc. Choate, Hall & Stewart, Boston, 1967-73; asst. regional counsel EPA, Boston, 1973-75, regional counsel, 1975-82, assoc. gen. counsel, 1979-82; regional counsel EPA, San Francisco, 1982-84; ptnr. Graham & James, San Francisco, 1984-91, LeBoeuf, Lamb, Greene & MacRae, San Francisco, 1992—. Contbr. articles to profl. jours. Bd. dirs. Peninsula Indsl. and Bus. Assn., Palo Alto, Calif., 1986-98, chmn. Cambridge (Mass.) Conservation Commn., 1972-74; co-chmn. The Clift Confs. on Environ. Law, 1983-98; assoc. mem. Ban Conservation and Development Commission, 1998-. John Russell Shaw traveling fellow Harvard Coll., 1963-64; recipient Regional Administrs. Bronze medal EPA, 1976, 84. Mem. ABA (natural resources sect., com. on native Am. natural resources law, spl. com. on mktg.), Natural Resources Def. Coun., Sierra Club, Commonwealth Club, Phi Beta Kappa. Democrat. Episcopalian. Avocations: personal computers, yoga, antiques, wines, cooking. Office: LeBoeuf Lamb Greene & MacRae One Embarcadero Ctr San Francisco CA 94111

THOMPSON, ROBERT SAMUEL, lawyer; b. Cleve., Nov. 2, 1930; s. Wayne Charles Thompson and Cornelia Irene (Anderson) Thompson Baker; m. Dorothy "JoAnne" Courtney; children: Robert Dale, Richard Wayne. BA, Hamilton Coll., 1953; JD, U. Mich., 1956; postgrad., Air Command and Staff Coll., Montgomery, Ala., 1967-68. Bar: Mich. 1956, Ohio 1962, U.S. Supreme Ct. 1962, Oreg. 1973. Judge advocate USAF, 1956-77; pvt. practice McMinnville, Oreg., 1977-98. Judge mcpl. ct., 1977—. Maj. USAF, 1977. Maj. USAF, 1997. Mem. Oreg. Soc. SAR (pres. 1989-90), Oreg. Mcpl. Judges Assn. (pres. 1992-93), Rotary (bd. dirs. McMinnville chpt. 1989), Am. Legion, Masons. Home and Office: 127 NW 19th St Mcminnville OR 97128

THOMPSON, RONALD EDWARD, lawyer; b. Bremerton, Wash., May 24, 1931; s. Melville Herbert and Clara Mildred (Griggs) T.; m. Marilyn Christine Woods, Dec. 15, 1956; children—Donald Jeffery, Karen, Susan, Nancy, Sally, Claire. B.A., U. Wash., 1953, J.D., 1958. Bar: Wash. 1959. Asst. city atty. City of Tacoma, 1960-61; pres. firm Thompson, Krilich, LaPorte, West & Lockner, P.S., Tacoma, 1961—; judge pro tem Mcpl. Ct., City of Tacoma, Pierce County Dist., 1972—, Pierce County Superior Ct., 1972—. Chmn. housing and social welfare com. City of Tacoma, 1965-69; mem. Tacoma Bd. Adjustment, 1967-71, chmn., 1968; mem. Tacoma Com. Future Devel., 1961-64, Tacoma Planning Commn., 1971-72; bd. dirs., pres. Mcpl. League Tacoma; bd. dirs. Pres. Tacoma Rescue Mission, Tacoma Pierce County Cancer Soc., Tacoma-Pierce County Heart Assn., Tacoma-Pierce County Council for Arts, Econ. Devel. Council Puget Sound, Tacoma Youth Symphony, Kleiner Group Home, Tacoma Community Coll. Found., Pierce County Econ. Devel. Corp., Wash. Transp. Policy Inst.; Coalition to Keep Wash. Moving, precinct committeeman Republican party, 1969-73. Served with AUS, 1953-55; col. Res. Recipient Internat. Community Service award Optimist Club, 1970, Patriotism award Am. Fedn. Police, 1974, citation for community service HUD, 1974, Disting. Citizen award Mcpl. League Tacoma-Pierce County, 1985; named Lawyer of the Yr. Pierce County Legal Secs. Assn., 1992. Mem. Am. Arbitration Assn. (panel of arbitrators), ABA, Wash. State Bar Assn., Tacoma-Pierce County Bar Assn. (sec. 1964, pres. 1979, mem. cts. and judiciary com. 1981-82), Assn. Trial Lawyers Am., Wash. State Trial Lawyers Assn., Tacoma-Pierce County C. of C. (bd. dirs. exec. com., v.p., chmn.), Downtown Tacoma Assn. (com. chmn., bd. dirs. exec. com., chmn.), Phi Delta Phi, Sigma Nu. Roman Catholic. Clubs: Variety (Seattle); Lawn Tennis, Tacoma, Optimist (Tacoma, Internat. Pres. 1973-74). Home: 3101 E Bay Dr NW Gig Harbor WA 98335-7610 Office: 524 Tacoma Ave S Tacoma WA 98402-5416

THOMPSON, RONALD MACKINNON, family physician, artist, writer; b. N.Y.C., Oct. 19, 1916; s. George Harold and Pearl Anita (Hatfield) T.; m. Ethel Joyce Chastant, June 30, 1950; children: Phyllis Anita, Walter MacKinnon, Charles Chastant, Richard Douglas. BS, U. Chgo., 1947, MS, 1948, MD, 1949. Diplomate Am. Bd. Family Practice. Intern U. Mich., Ann Arbor, 1950-51; resident in psychiatry U. Tex., Galveston, 1951-52; pvt. practice, family and internal medicine South Dixie Med. Ctr., West Palm Beach, Fla., 1952-85; instr. Anatomy, U. Chgo., 1946-47, Pharmacology, 1948-49. Contbr. more than 125 poems and short stories to lit. mags., also articles to med. jours.; 7 one-man shows (over 30 awards for painting in regional and nat. shows); represented in permanent collections at 5 mus. Former mem. bd. dirs. Norton Mus. of Art, West Palm Beach. With Fla. N.G., 1936-40; cadet USAAF, Force, 1943-44. Over thirty awards for painting in juried regional and nat. shows. Fellow Am. Acad. Family Physicians; mem. AMA, Fla. Med. Assn., Fla. Acad. of Family Physicians, Palm Beach County Med. Soc., Nat. Watercolor Soc., Ariz. Watercolor Soc. Republican. Episcopalian. Avocations: chess, tennis, writing, square and round dancing. Home: 308 Leisure World Mesa AZ 85206-3142

THOMPSON, TERENCE WILLIAM, lawyer; b. Moberly, Mo., July 3, 1952; s. Donald Gene and Carolyn (Stringer) T.; m. Caryn Elizabeth Hildebrand, Aug. 30, 1975; children: Cory Elizabeth, Christopher William, Tyler Madison. BA in Govt. with honors and high distinction, U. Ariz., 1974; JD, Harvard U., 1977. Bar: Ariz. 1977, U.S. Dist. Ct. Ariz. 1977, U.S. Tax Ct. 1979. Assoc. Brown & Bain P.A., Phoenix, 1977-83, ptnr., 1983-92; ptnr. Gallagher and Kennedy, P.A., Phoenix, 1992—; legis. aide Rep. Richard Burgess, Ariz. Ho. of Reps., 1974; mem. bus. adv. bd. Citibank Ariz. (formerly Great Western Bank & Trust, Phoenix), 1985-86. Mem. staff Harvard Law Record, 1974-75; rsch. editor Harvard Internat. Law Jour. , 1976; lead author, editor-in-chief: Arizona Corporate Practice, 1996; contbr. articles to profl. jours. Mem. Phoenix Mayor's Youth Adv. Bd. 1968-70, Phoenix Internat.; active 20-30 Club, 1978-81, sec. 1978-80, Valley Leadership, Phoenix, 1983-84, citizens task force future financing needs City of Phoenix, 1985-86; exec. coun. Boys and Girls Clubs of Met. Phoenix, 1990—; bd. dirs. Phoenix Bach Choir, 1992-94; deacon Shepherd of Hills Congl. Ch., Phoenix, 1984-85; pres. Maricopa County Young Dems., 1982-83, Ariz. Young Dems., 1983-84, sec. 1981-82, v.p. 1982-83; exec. dir. Young Dems. Am., 1985, exec. com. 1983-85; others. Fellow Ariz. Bar Found.; mem. State Bar Ariz. (vice chmn. internt. law sect. 1978, sec. securities law sect. 1990-91, vice chmn. sect. 1991-92, chmn.-elect 1992-93, chmn. 1993-94, exec. coun. 1988—, sec. bus. law sect. 1992-93, vice chmn. 1993-94, chmn. 1994-95), Nat. Assn. Bond Lawyers, Am. Acad. Healthcare Attys., Nat. Health Lawyers, Blue Key, Phi Beta Kappa, Phi Kappa Phi, Phi Eta Sigma. Home: 202 W Lawrence Rd Phoenix AZ 85013-1226 Office: Gallagher & Kennedy PA 2600 N Central Ave Ste 1800 Phoenix AZ 85004-3099

THOMPSON, WILLIAM BENBOW, JR., obstetrician, gynecologist, educator; b. Detroit, July 26, 1923; s. William Benbow and Ruth Wood (Locke) T.; m. Constance Carter, July 30, 1947 (div. Feb. 1958); 1 child, William Benbow IV; m. Jane Gilliland, Mar. 12, 1958; children: Reese Ellison, Belinda Day. AB, U. So. Calif., 1947, MD, 1951. Diplomate Am. Bd. Ob-Gyn. Resident Gallinger Mun. Hosp., Washington, 1952-53, George Washington U. Hosp., Washington, 1953-55; asst. ob-gyn. La. State U., 1955-56; asst. clin. prof. UCLA, 1957-64; assoc. prof. U. Calif.-Irvine Sch. Med., Orange, 1964-92, dir. gynecology, 1977-92, prof. emeritus, 1993—, vice chmn. ob-gyn., 1978-89; assoc. dean U. Calif.-Irvine Coll. Med., Irvine, 1969-73. Inventor: Thompson Retractor, 1976; Thompson Manipulator, 1977. Bd. dirs. Monarch Bay Assn. Laguna Niguel, Calif. 1969-77, Monarch Summitt II A ssn. 1981-83. With U.S. Army, 1942-44, PTO. Fellow ACS, Am. Coll. Ob Gyn. (life), L.A. Ob-Gyn. Soc. (life); mem. Orange County Gynecology and Obstetrics Soc. (hon.), Capistrano Bay Yacht Club (commodore 1975), Internat. Order Blue Gavel, Dana West Yacht Club. Avocation: boating. Office: UCI Med Ctr OB/GYN 101 The City Dr S Orange CA 92868-3201

THOMPSON, WILLIAM JOSEPH, secondary school educator, coach; b. Sedalia, Mo., Jan. 4, 1953; s. Robert Clark and Maxine Flavia (Pettyjohn) T.; m. Deborah Ann St. Germaine, Dec. 21, 1992; children: Bleys Kueck, Jordan Kueck, Seth Thompson. BA in History, Okla. State U., 1975; MA in History, U. Mo., 1981. Cert. tchr.Colo., Mo. Grad. tchg. asst. history U. Mo., Columbia, 1975-79; social studies tchr. Rampart H.S., Colorado Springs, Colo., 1983—, sch. writing assessment com., 1991-93, mem. sch. accountability com., 1993-94. Named Coach of Yr., Gazette Telegraph, 1986. Mem. Nat. Coun. for the Social Studies, Colo. H.S. Activities Assn., Nat. Soccer Coaches Assn. Am., Phi Delta Kappa. Office: Rampart HS 8250 Lexington Dr Colorado Springs CO 80920-4301

THOMSON, GRACE MARIE, nurse, minister; b. Pecos, Tex., Mar. 30, 1932; d. William McKinley and Elzora (Wilson) Olliff; m. Radford Chaplin, Nov. 3, 1952; children: Deborah C., William Earnest. Assoc. Applied Sci., Odessa Coll., 1965; extension student U. Pa. Sch. Nursing, U. Calif., Irvine, Golden West Coll. RN, Calif., Okla., Ariz., Md., Tex. Dir. nursing Grays Nursing Home, Odessa, Tex., 1965; supr. nursing Med. Hill, Oakland, Calif.; charge nurse pediatrics Med. Ctr., Odessa; dir. nursing Elmwood Extended Care, Berkeley, Calif.; surg. nurse Childrens Hosp., Berkeley; med./surg. charge nurse Merritt Hosp., Oakland, Calif.; adminstr. Grace and Assocs.; advocate for emotionally abused children; active Watchtower and Bible Tract Soc.; evangelist for Jehovah's Witnesses, 1954—.

THOMSON, JANYCE K., quality assurance administrator. MSN, U. Oreg., 1982. Nursing care cons. State of Wash., Spokane, 1974-80; discharge coord. VA Hosp., Portland, Oreg., 1981-83; assoc. dir. nursing King Khalid U. Hosp., Kingdom of Saudi Arabia, 1983-84; nursing care cons. supr. State of Wash., Olympia, 1985-88, nursing home survey mgr., 1988-89, quality assurance chief nursing home svcs., 1990-95; cmty. svcs. quality assurance adminstr. Aging and Adult Svcs., State of Wash., Olympia, 1995-99; cons., 1999—. E-mail: LEEJAN@Olywa.net.

THOR, PAUL VIETS, computer science educator, software engineer, consultant; b. Schenectady, N.Y., Mar. 10, 1946; s. Donald D. and Eleanor B. (Viets) T.; m. Barbara K. Nelson, Mar. 27, 1982 (div. Dec. 1993). BSME, U. Denver, 1968; MS in Engrng. Mgmt., UCLA, 1976; MS in Computer Sci., George Mason U., 1993; postgrad., Colo. Tech. U., 1996—. Engr. Martin Marietta Corp., Denver, 1968-69; commd. 2d lt. USAF, 1969, advanced through grades to maj., 1982; pilot trainee USAF-Williams AFB, Phoenix, Ariz., 1970-71; pilot C141A 15 MAS-Norton AFB, San Bernardino, Calif., 1971-75, pilot C141B, 1981-84; communications and computer officer 2044 CG-Pentagon, Washington, 1977-81; air field mgr. 18TFW-Kadena AB, Okinawa, Japan, 1984-86; pilot C12 1402 MAS-Andrews AFB, Washington, 1986-87; comm. and computer officer 7 Comm. Group-Pentagon, Washington, 1987-89; cons. George Mason U., Fairfax, Va., 1990-93; pvt. practice cons. Colorado Springs, Colo., 1993—; wing flight examiner 63 MAW-Norton AFB, San Bernardino, 1981-84; acquisitions officer 7th Comms. Group-Pentagon, 1987-89; assoc. prof. computer sci. Colo. Tech. U., Colorado Springs, 1993—. Mem. Computer Soc. of IEEE, Assn. Computer Machinery, Air Force Assn. (life), Ret. Officers Assn. Avocations: personal computers, woodworking, crafts, photography, book collector. E-mail: pthor@iex.net. Home: 3262 Muirfield Dr Colorado Springs CO 80907-7805 Office: Colo Tech U 4435 N Chestnut St Colorado Springs CO 80907-3812

THORNBURG, RON, newspaper editor. BA in Polit. Sci., Purdue U., 1971. Reporter Jour. and Courier, Lafayette, Ind., 1972-73; mng. editor The Evening Times, Melbourne, Fla., 1973-75; met. editor, asst. news editor, copy editor, bur. chief Today, Melbourne, 1975-78, mng. editor, 1978-80; exec. editor News Press, Fort Myers, Fla., 1980-86; news exec. Comty. Newspapers, Gannet Co., Inc., 1986-88; editor Burlington (Vt.) Free Press, 1988-94; mng. editor Standard Examiner, Ogden, Utah, 1994—. Office: Standard-Examiner 455 23rd St Ogden UT 84401-1596*

THORNBURY, JOHN ROUSSEAU, radiologist, physician; b. Cleve., Mar. 16, 1929; s. Purla Lee and Gertrude (Glidden) T.; m. Julia Lee McGregor, Mar. 20, 1955; children: Lee Allison, John McGregor. A.B. cum laude, Miami U., Oxford, Ohio, 1950; M.D., Ohio State U., 1955. Diplomate: Am. Bd. Radiology. Intern Hurley Hosp., Flint, Mich., 1955-56; resident U. Iowa Hosps., Iowa City, 1958-61; instr., asst. prof. radiology U. Colo. Med. Center, Denver, 1962-63; practice medicine specializing in radiology Denver, 1962-63, Iowa City, 1963-66, Seattle, 1966-68, Ann Arbor, Mich., 1968-79, Albuquerque, 1979-84, Rochester, N.Y., 1984-89, Madison, Wis., 1989-94; mem. staff U. Wisconsin Hosp., Madison; prof. radiology, chief sect. of body imaging, U. Wis. Med. Sch., 1989-94, prof. emeritus, 1994—; asst. prof. radiology U. Iowa Hosps., 1963-66, U. Wash. Hosp., Seattle, 1966-68; assoc. prof. radiology U. Mich. Med. Ctr., 1968-71; prof. radiology, chief divsn. diagnostic radiology Sch. Medicine, U. N.Mex., 1979-84; prof. radiology U. Rochester Sch. Medicine, 1984-89, acting chmn., 1985-87; chmn. sci. com. on efficacy studies Nat. Coun. on Radiation Protection, 1980-95; rapporteur/mem. sci. group on indications/limitations of x-ray diagnostic procedures WHO, 1983; cons. com. on efficacy of magnetic resonance nat. health tech. adv. panel Australian Inst. Health, 1986; invited U.S. cons. MRI program, Nijmegen, The Netherlands, 1992; mem. planning group Low Back Pain Collaboratives and Nat. Congress, Inst. for Health Care Improvement, 1997-98; mem. adv. com. to bd. dirs. Soc. Health Svcs. Rsch. in Radiology, 1998—; mem. methodologic rsch. issues working group NIH and Pub. Health Svc.-Office of Women's Health, 1998; cons., spkr. Royal Australasian Coll. Radiologists, Melbourne, Australia, 1997; cons. tech. assessment and outcomes rsch., 1994—; cons. to Am. Soc. Neuroradiology, 1995—; lectr. in field. Co-author/cons. Clin. Efficacy Assessment Project, Am. Coll. Physicians, 1986-89; assoc. editor: Yearbook of Radiology, 1971-82; mem. editl. bd.: Contemporary Diagnostic Radiology, 1977-84, Urologic Radiology, 1977-84. Bd. dirs. Sally Jobe Found., Denver, 1996—. Capt., M.C. USAF, 1956-58. Grantee Agy. Health Care Policy and Rsch., 1986-91, U. Rochester, 1986-89, U. Wis., Madison, 1989-91, NIH, 1999—. Fellow Am. Coll. Radiology (imaging network, outcomes and quality of life subcom.); mem. Soc. Uroradiology (pres. 1976-77, dir. 1977-79), Assn. Univ. Radiologists (pres. 1980-81), Radiol. Soc. N.Am., Am. Roentgen Ray Soc. (Caldwell medal 1993), Soc. for Health Svcs. Rsch. in Radiology (adv. com. to bd. dirs. 1998—), Colo. Radiol. Soc., Phi Beta Kappa, Delta Tau Delta, Omicron Delta Kappa, Phi Chi. Republican. Lutheran. Home: 185 Morgan Pl Castle Rock CO 80104-9061

THORNE, DAVID W., lawyer; b. Walla Walla, Wash., Aug. 9, 1945. BA, Wash. State U., 1967; MBA, U. Wash., 1969, JD, 1974. Bar: Wash. 1974. Mem. Davis Wright Tremaine LLP, Seattle. Mem. ABA, Am. Coll. Real Estate Lawyers, Am. Coll. Mortgage Attys., Am. Land Title Assn. Lender Counsel Group, Wash. State Bar Assn. (past mem. exec. com. real property, probate and trust sect., past chmn. 1991-92), Pacific Real Estate Inst. (past pres. 1994, founding trustee 1989-96), Phi Delta Phi. Office: Davis Wright Tremaine LLP 2600 Century Sq 1501 4th Ave Ste 2600 Seattle WA 98101-1688

THORNE, KATE RULAND, writer, publisher, editor; b. Del Norte, Colo., Dec. 15, 1937; d. Joseph Lydian Norman and Avis Frances Kiemsteadt; m. Edwin G. Ruland, Aug. 20, 1960 (div. 1984); children: Gregory, Jeanie, Rebecca. BA, So. Meth. U., 1976. Speech pathologist Shady Brook Sch., Dallas, 1960-61, Hillside Rehab., Grand Junction, Colo., 1962-72; pub. Thorne Enterprises Pub. Inc., Sedona, Ariz., 1989—; editor, pub. Thorne/Swiftwind Pub., Sedona, 1993—; owner Sedona Books and Music, Ariz., 1998—; hostess TV show Celebrity Spotlight, Geronimo Cable, 1998—; lectr. in field. Author: Lion of Redstone, 1980, Experience Sedona: Legends and Legacies, 1990; (screenplay) Blood Oath; author, editor: Experience Jerome and the Verde Valley: Legends and Legacies, 1992, The Yavapai: People of the Red Rocks, 1993, The Legacy of Sedona Schnebly, 1994, Upon This Rock, 1995, The Hitchenbirds, 1996; editor, columnist Sedona Mag., 1986-87; columnist Art Talk, Directions Mag.; contbr. numerous articles to mags. and newspapers; 1st woman editor Sedona Red Rock News, 1987-88. Founder, pres. Ariz. Indian Living Treasures, 1990-91; founding mem., sec. Western Am. Week, 1990-94. Mem. Ariz. Small Pub. Assn. (founding mem.), Sedona Hist. Soc. (pres.). Avocations: reading, hiking, swimming, travel. Home and Office: 149 Gambel Ln Sedona AZ 86336-7119

THORNHILL, FRANKLIN, lawyer; b. Irvington, N.J., May 1, 1939; s. Travis and Vashti (Compton) T.; m. Eileen Coral, Sept. 7, 1960 (div. 1979); children: Robert, Clayton, Sharon; m. Christine Weavers, Oct. 12, 1980 (div. 1983); m. Felicia Trumble, May 14, 1984 (dec. 1986); 1 child, Candice. BA, Bklyn. Coll., 1961; JD, Yale U., 1964. Bar: D.C. 1965, N.Y. 1965, Calif. 1980, U.S. Supreme Ct. 1971. Law clk. to Hon. H. Barringer U.S. Ct. Appeals, 1965-66; assoc. Flounders, Treffinger & Campbell, Washington, 1966-70; ptnr. Brown & Thornhill, N.Y.C., 1971-81, Thornhill, Richards & Werik, Palo Alto, Calif., 1982—; lectr. and cons. in field. Author: Marriage: The Perfect Contract, 1988, The Enlightened Consumer, 1990; contbr. articles to profl. jours. Chmn. consumers right com. Bolten Sr. Citizen Coun., Palo Alto, 1989—; bd. dirs. Windhill Symphony, 1991-95, Can Do Found., 1993-97, Today's Child Tomorrows Future, 1997—. Fulbright scholar, 1960; recipient numerous grants. Mem. ABA, Am. Assn. Trial Lawyers, Pala Alto Bar Assn., Phi Beta Kappa. Lutheran. Democrat. Avocations: swimming, reading, music, chess. Office: Thornhill Richards & Werik 260 Sheridan Ave Ste 216 Palo Alto CA 94306-2009

THORNTON, CAMERON MITCHELL, financial planner; b. L.A., Sept. 30, 1954; s. H. Walter and Naomi L. (Brown) T.; m. Jane Kubasak, June 18, 1978; children: Mitchell, Kathryn, Andrew. BA, U. So. Calif., L.A., 1976; MBA, U. La Verne, 1983. CFP. Planner Lockheed Calif. Co., Burbank, 1980-84; adv. assoc. Fin. Network Investment Corp., Burbank, 1983—, fin. cons., 1983—, prin., br. mgr., 1997—; prin. Cameron Thornton Assocs., Burbank, 1982—; prin. lic. charitable gift planner Renaissance Inc., 1992—; lic. charitable gift planner Renaissance Inc., 1992—. Author: (manual) Computer Aided Planning System, 1982-83. Mem., vice chair St. Joseph Med. Ctr. Found., 1988-92, chmn. planned giving dept., 1991-92; mem., chair Burbank Police Commn., 1981-85, Burbank Planning Commn., 1989-93; with ARC, Burbank, 1984-88, chmn. 1985-87; scoutmaster troop 209 Boy Scouts of Am., Burbank, 1997—. Named Friend of Campfire, Camp Fire Coun., Pasadena, Calif., 1989, 92. Mem. Nat. Assn. Renaissance Advisors, Inst. CFP's, Internat. Assn. for Fin. Planning, Cert. Fin. Planner Bd. Standards, Burbank C. of C. Republican. Roman Catholic. Avocations: fishing, reading, snow skiing, water skiing. Office: Cameron Thornton Assocs 290 E Verdugo Ave Ste 205 Burbank CA 91502-1342

THORNTON, CHARLES VICTOR, lawyer; b. Takoma Park, Md., July 18, 1942; s. Charles Victor and Margaret Louise (Wiggins) T.; m. Suzanne Thorne, May 16, 1970; children: Christopher, Matthew, Joshua, Jeremy. AB, Cornell U., 1964; JD, U. Mich., 1967. Bar: Calif. 1969, U.S. Dist. Ct. (cen. dist.) Calif. 1969. Instr. U. Pa. Law Sch., Phila., 1967-68; assoc. Paul, Hastings, Janofsky & Walker, L.A., 1968-74; ptnr. Paul, Hastings, Janofsky & Walker, 1975—, mng. ptnr. L.A. office, 1992-96, mng. partner San Francisco office, 1997—. Contbr. articles to publs. Pres. Info. and Referral Fedn. Los Angeles County, 1988-95; mem. exec. com. Los Angeles County United Way, 1988-92. Named Bd. Vol. of Yr. United Way, 1986. Mem. Calif. Club, Los Angeles Country Club, San Francisco YMCA (bd. dirs. 1998—). Avocations: running, golf. Office: Paul Hastings Janofsky & Walker 345 California St San Francisco CA 94104

THORNTON, J. DUKE, lawyer; b. Murray, Ky., July 11, 1944; s. Arthur Lee and Ruth Maxine (Billings) T.; m. Carol Caceres, Dec. 26, 1966 (dec.); children: Jennifer, Carey. BBA, U. N.Mex., Albuquerque, 1966, JD, 1969. Bar: N.Mex. 1969, U.S. Ct. Appeals (10th cir.) 1969, N.Y. 1985, U.S. Supreme Ct. 1992. With Butt, Thornton & Baehr, P.C., Albuquerque, 1971—, now chmn. bd.; legal counsel N.Mex. Jaycees, 1972; clk. N.Mex. Supreme Ct., Santa Fe, 1969; mem. com. N.Mex. Uniform Jury Instructions, 1987-88. Author: Trial Handbook for New Mexico Lawyers, 1992. Bd. dirs. N.Mex. Bd. of Dentistry, Santa Fe, 1987-88; commr. N.Mex. Racing Commn., Albuquerque, 1988-95. Mem. ABA, Assn. Coll. and Univ. Counsel, Internat. Assn. Ins. Counsel, Am. Bd. Trial Advs., Albuquerque Bar Assn. (bd. dirs. 1978-79), Nat. Collegiate Athletic Assn. (agt.). Avocation: pilot. Office: Butt Thornton & Baehr PC PO Box 3170 Albuquerque NM 87190-3170*

THORNTON, JOHN S., IV, bishop. Bishop Diocese of Idaho, Boise, 1990—. Office: Episcopal Diocese of Idaho Box 936 510 W Washington St Boise ID 83702-5953

THORP, EDWARD OAKLEY, investment management company executive; b. Chgo., Aug. 14, 1932; s. Oakley Glenn and Josephine (Gebert) T.; B.A. in Physics, UCLA, 1953, M.A., 1955, Ph.D. in Math., 1958; m. Vivian Sinetar, Jan. 28, 1956; children: Raun, Karen, Jeffrey. Instr., UCLA, 1956-59, C.L.E. Moore instr. MIT, Cambridge, Mass., 1959-61; asst. prof. N.Mex. State U., 1961-63, assoc. prof. math., 1963-65, U. Calif., Irvine, 1965-67, prof. math., 1967-82, adj. prof. fin., 1982-87; regents lectr. U. Calif., Irvine, 1992-93; vis. prof. UCLA, 1991; chmn. Oakley Sutton Mgmt. Corp., Newport Beach, Calif., 1972-91; mng. gen. ptnr. Princeton/Newport Ptnrs., Newport Beach, 1969-91, OSM Ptnrs., MIDAS Advisors, Newport Beach, 1986-89; gen. ptnr. Edward O. Thorp & Assocs., L.P., Newport Beach, 1989—; portfolio mgr., cons. Glenwood Investment Corp., Chgo., 1992-94; prin., cons. Grosvenor Capital Mgmt., Chgo., 1992-93; pres. Noesis Corp., 1994—. Grantee NSF, 1954-55, 62-64, Air Force Office Sci. Research, 1964-73. Fellow NSF, Inst. Math. Stats.; mem. Phi Beta Kappa, Sigma Xi. Author: Beat The Dealer: A Winning Strategy for the Game of Twenty-One, 1962, rev. edit., 1966, Elementary Probability, 1966, The Mathematics of Gambling 1984; co-author: Beat The Market, 1967; The Gambling Times Guide to Blackjack, 1984; columnist Gambling Times, 1979-84. Avocations: astronomy, distance running. Office: Edward O Thorp & Assocs LP 620 Newport Center Dr Ste 880 Newport Beach CA 92660-8008

THORPE, DOUGLAS L., lawyer; b. Wahoo, Nebr., Jan. 25, 1937. BSCE, U. Nebr., 1959; JD cum laude, So. Meth. U., 1968. Bar: Calif. 1969. Mem. Perkins Coie, L.A., 1988—; bd. dirs. Pub. Counsel, 1980-83. Mem. ABA (antitrust law sect., corp., banking and bus. law sect., litigation sect., econs. of law practice sect.), State Bar Calif., L.A. County Bar Assn. (del. to State Bar Conf. of Dels. 1981, 1983-84, exec. com. antitrust law sect. 1981-83), Century City Bar Assn. (bd. govs. 1982-85), Order of the Coif, Barristers, Phi Delta Phi, Sigma Tau, Tau Beta Pi, Chi Epsilon. Office: Perkins Coie 1999 Ave Of Stars Fl 9 Los Angeles CA 90067-6022*

THORPE, GARY STEPHEN, chemistry educator; b. Los Angeles, Mar. 9, 1951; s. David Winston and Jeanette M. (Harris) T.; m. Patricia Marion Eison, Apr. 13, 1949; children: Kristin Anne, Erin Michelle. BS, U. Redlands, 1973; MS, Calif. State U., Northridge, 1975. Tchr. L.A. Schs., 1975-80, L.A. Community Colls., 1976-81, Beverly Hills (Calif.) High Sch., 1980—; instr. chemistry Coll of the Canyons, Santa Clarita, Calif., 1998—. Author: AP Chemistry Study Guide, 1993. Res. police officer L.A. Police Dept., 1991; CEO For Our Kids Found., L.A., 1999—. Recipient Commendation L.A. County Bd. Suprs., 1983, 84, Beverly Hills City Coun., 1983, 84, City of L.A., 1995, REsolution of Commendation State of Calif. Senate and Assembly, 1983, 84, Cert. of Appreciation L.A. County Bd. Edn., 1984-85, Gov. George Deukmejian, Sacrament, 1984-85. Mem. Am. Chem. Soc. (exec. dir. So. Calif. divsn. 1995—, bd. dirs. 1998—, selected as Outstanding Chemistry Tchr. of So. Calif. 1989, 92), NEA, Calif. Tchrs. Assn., Phi Delta Kappa. Republican. Lutheran. Lodge: Masons. Avocations: ham radio, computer application. Home: 6127 Balcom Ave Encino CA 91316-7207

THORSEN, JAMES HUGH, aviation director, airport manager, retired; b. Evanston, Ill., Feb. 5, 1943; s. Chester A. and Mary Jane (Currie) T.; m. Nancy Dain, May 30, 1980. BA, Ripon Coll., 1965. FAA cert. comml. pilot, flight instr. airplanes and instruments. Bd. dirs. Internat. Northwest Aviation Coun.; pres. Thorsen Aviation Cons. Recipient Region Safey award PAA N.W. Mountain. Mem. Am. Assn. Airport Execs. (past pres. N.W. chpt., Disting. Svc. award 1999), Mensa, Quiet Birdmen, Sigma Alpha Epsilon. Home: 334 Westmorland Dr Idaho Falls ID 83402-4607

THORSEN, NANCY DAIN, real estate broker; b. Edwardsville, Ill., June 23, 1944; d. Clifford Earl and Suzanne Eleanor (Kribs) Dain; m. David Massie, 1968 (div. 1975); 1 child, Suzanne Dain Massie; m. James Hugh Thorsen, May 30, 1980. BSc in Mktg., So. Ill. U., 1968, MSc in Bus. Edn., 1975; grad. Realtor Inst., Idaho, 1983. Cert. resdl. and investment specialist, fin. instr.; Designated Real Estate Instr. State of Idaho; accredited buyer rep. Personnel officer J.H. Little & Co. Ltd., London, 1969-72; instr. in bus. edn. Spl. Sch. Dist. St. Louis, 1974-77; mgr. mktg./ops. Isis Foods, Inc., St. Louis, 1978-80; asst. mgr. store Stix, Baer & Fuller, St. Louis, 1980; assoc. broker Century 21 Sayer Realty, Inc., Idaho Falls, Idaho, 1981-88, RE/MAX Homestead Realty, 1989—; speaker RE/MAX Internat. Conv., 1990, 94, RE/MAX Stars Cruise, 1993, RE/MAX Pacific N.W. Conv., 1994, Century 21 Austral-Asia, 1995, women's seminar Clemson U., 1996, 98; real estate fin. instr. State of Idaho Real Estate Commn., 1994; founder Nancy Thorsen Seminars, 1995. Bd. dirs. Idaho Vol., Boise, 1981-84, Idaho Falls Symphony, 1982; pres. Friends of Idaho Falls Libr., 1981-83; chmn. Idaho Falls Mayor's Com. for Vol. Coordination, 1981-84; power leader Power Program, 1995; ; mem. Mtn. River Valley Red Cross (chair capital campaign), cmty. gifts chair ARC. Recipient Idaho Gov.'s award, 1982, cert. appreciation City of Idaho Falls/Mayor Campbell, 1982, 87, Civitan Disting. Pres. award, 1990, Bus. Woman of the Yr. award C. of C., 1998; named to Two Million Dollar Club, Three Million Dollar Club, 1987, 88, Four Million Dollar Club, 1989, 90, Top Investment Sales Person for Eastern Idaho, 1985, Realtor of Yr. Idaho Falls Bd. Realtors, 1990, Outstanding Realtors Active in Politics, Mem. of Yr. Idaho Assn. Realtors, 1991, Women of Yr. Am. Biog. Inst., 1991, Profiles of Top Prodrs. award Real Estate Edn. Assn., Above the Crowd award 1997; named Western Region Power Leader, Darryl Davis Seminars. Mem. Nat. Spkrs. Assn., Idaho Falls Bd. Realtors (chmn. orientation 1982-83, chmn. edn. 1983, chmn. legis. com. 1989, 95—, chmn. program com. 1990, 91), Idaho Assn. Realtors (pres. Million Dollar Club 1988—, edn. com. 1990-93), So. Ill. U. Alumni Assn., Idaho Falls C. of C. (Bus. Woman of the Year - Professions, 1997), Newcomers Club, Civitan (pres. Idaho Falls chpt. 1988-89, Civitan of Yr. 1986, 87, outstanding pres. award 1990), Hall of Fame, 1998, Real Estate Educators Assn. Office: RE/MAX Homestead Inc 1301 E 17th St Ste 1 Idaho Falls ID 83404-6273

THRELKELD, STEVEN WAYNE, civil engineer; b. La Jolla, Calif., Feb. 22, 1956; s. Willard Wayne and Sylvia Eileen (Daugherety) T.; m. Sheree Leslie Chabot, Nov. 17, 1984; children: Tristan David, Kayla Lee. BS in Geol. Scis., San Diego State U., 1985. Geophys. trainee Western Geophys., Bakersfield, Calif., 1985; civil engr. Dee Jaspar & Assocs., Bakersfield, 1986, Bement, Dainwood & Sturgeon, Lemon Grove, Calif., 1987, Calif. Dept. Transp., San Diego, 1988—; comml. scuba diver, San Diego, 1987-88. Photo editor Montezuma Life Mag., San Diego, 1981; portrait photographer Coast Prodns., San Diego, 1975. Mem. Profl. Engrs. in Calif. Govt. (San Diego chpt.), Planetary Soc., Union Concerned Scientists, Common Cause, Nat. Parks and Conservation Assn., World Wildlife Fund, Planning and Conservation League. Avocations: traveling, writing, music, art, photography. Home: 4262 Bancroft Dr La Mesa CA 91941-6744

THRONDSON, EDWARD WARNER, residential association administrator; b. Woodland, Calif., May 22, 1938; s. Edward J. and Arden Warner (Law) T.; m. Marjorie Jean Waite, June 25, 1960 (div. 1993); children: Mark Edward, Kimberly Anne, Sulin Marget; m. Mary Jo Riddell Law, Jan. 13, 1994. BS, Stanford U., 1960; MBA, Harvard U., 1962. Profl. Community Assn. Mgr., Community Assn. Inst. Asst. br. mgr. Pacific Delta Gas, Santa Rosa, Calif., 1962-65; corp. staff asst. Pacific Delta Gas, San Jose, Calif., 1965-72; regional mgr. Pargas, San Jose, 1972-86; gen. mgr., COO The Villages Golf and Country Club, San Jose, 1986-93; sr. v.p. West Coast Community Assocs., Campbell, Calif., 1994-95; assn. mgr. Cmty. Assns. Consulting, Napa, Calif., 1996-97, Oakmont Village Assn., Santa Rosa, Calif., 1997—. Mem. Cmty. Assns. Inst. (com. chair 1991—, Pres.'s Appreciation award 1991), Calif. Assn. Cmty. Mgrs. (cert., founding mem., com. chair 1992—, author course 1992, 94, 96). Avocations: golf, stamp collecting, geneology.

THUMS, CHARLES WILLIAM, designer, consultant; b. Manitowoc, Wis., Sept. 5, 1945; s. Earl Oscar and Helen Margaret (Rusch) T. B. in Arch., Ariz. State U., 1972. Ptnr., Grafic, Tempe, Ariz., 1967-70; founder, prin. I-Squared Environ. Cons., Tempe, Ariz., 1970-78; designer and cons. design morphology, procedural programming and algorithms, 1978—. Author: (with Jonathan Craig Thums) Tempe's Grand Hotel, 1973, The Rossen House, 1975; (with Daniel Peter Aiello) Shelter and Culture, 1976; contbg. author: Tombstone Planning Guide, 5 vols., 1974. Office: PO Box 3126 Tempe AZ 85280-3126

THUNDER, SPENCER K., retired elementary school principal; b. Longview, Wash., Dec. 5, 1939; s. Maynard King and Aarah Avona (Hearn) T.; m. Joyce Marie Sjogren, June 22, 1959 (div. June 1972); children: Scott, Mark, Karen; m. Jeanine Louise Pratt. BA, Cen. Wash. U., 1962; MEd, U. Wash., 1975. Cert. elem. educator, prin., reality therapist. Tchr. jr. and sr. high Yakima (Wash.) Sch. Dist., 1962-66; tchr. elem. Olympia (Wash.) Sch. Dist., 1966-67; tchr. high sch. Edmonds (Wash.) Sch. Dist., 1967-71, program mgr., high sch. spl. edn., 1971-76; prin. Maplewood Handicapped Children's Ctr., Edmonds, 1976-87, Mountlake Terrace (Wash.) Elem. Sch., 1987-94; adj. prof. Seattle Pacific U., 1991—; supr. tchg. interns City U., Renton, Wash., 1994—, Western Wash. U., 1996; instr. Edmonds C.C., 1978—; vis. faculty Ctrl. Wash. U., Ellensberg, 1976; instr. Olympia Vocat. Tech., 1966-67, Yakima Valley Coll., 1964-66. Author: (pamphlet) Work Eval in Schools, 1975; contbr. articles to profl. jours. Bd. dirs. Smithwright Estates Group Home, Edmonds, 1980-96. Sgt. Wash. N.G., 1955-63. Avocations: collecting political memorabilia, world stamps. Home: 708 Hoyt Ave Everett WA 98201-1320

THURSTON, WILLIAM RICHARDSON, oil and gas industry executive, geologist; b. New Haven, Sept. 20, 1920; s. Edward S. and Florence (Holbrooke) T.; m. Ruth A. Nelson, Apr. 30, 1944 (div. 1966); children: Karin R., Amy R., Ruth A.; m. Beatrice Furnas, Sept. 11, 1971; children: Mark P., Stephen P., Douglas P., Jennifer P. AB in Geol. Sci. with honors, Harvard U., 1942. Field geologist Sun Oil Co., Corpus Christi, Tex., 1946-47; asst. to div. geologist Sun Oil Co., Dallas, 1947-50; chief geologist The Kimbark Co., Denver, 1952-59; head exploration dept. Kimbark Exploration Co., Denver, 1959-66; co-owner Kimbark Exploration Ltd., Denver, 1966-67, Kimbark Assocs., Denver, 1967-76, Hardscrabble Assocs., Denver, 1976-80; pres. Weaselskin Corp., Durango, Colo., 1980—. Bd. dirs. Denver Bot. Gardens, 1972-90, Crow Canyon Ctr. for Archaeology, Cortez, Colo., 1980-92. Comdr. USNR, World War II, Korea. Decorated D.F.C. with 2 stars. Mem. Am. Assn. Petroleum Geologists, Denver Assn. Petroleum Landmen, Rocky Mountain Assn. Petroleum Geologists, Four Corners Geol. Soc. Republican. Avocations: photography, gardening, reading. Office: Weaselskin Corp 12995 Highway 550 Durango CO 81301-6674

THYDEN, JAMES ESKEL, diplomat, educator, lecturer; b. L.A., Apr. 10, 1939; s. Eskel A. and Mildred Aileene (Rock) T.; m. Patricia Irene Kelsey, Dec. 15, 1959; children: Teresa Lynn, Janice Kay, James Blaine. BA in Biology, Pepperdine U., 1961; MA in Scandinavian Area Studies, U. Wash., 1992. Cert. secondary tchr., Calif., Wash. Tchr. Gompers Jr. High Sch., L.A., 1962-64; fgn. svc. officer U.S. Dept. State, Washington, 1964-90; rschr. U. Wash., Seattle, 1992-93; exec. dir. Seattle chpt. UN Assn., 1993-96; travel lectr. Cunard Lines' Royal Viking Sun, 1995, and Royal Caribbean's Splendour of the Seas, 1997. Editor govt. report, ann. human rights reports, 1983-86; author, editor in-house govt. reports, documents. Dir. Office of Human Rights, 1983-86; counselor Embassy for Polit. Affairs, Am. Embassy, Oslo, Norway, 1986-90. Named Outstanding Young Man Am., 1969, Alumnus of Yr., Pepperdine U., 1984. Mem. Am. Fgn. Svc. Assn., World Affairs Coun. Seattle. Avocations: travel, reading, gardening. Home: 5631 153rd Pl SW Edmonds WA 98026-4239

TIBBITTS, JOHN CODDING, publisher; b. Geneva, Ohio, Oct. 15, 1911; s. Francis Embury and Neva Grace (Codding) T.; m. Edith Ellen Boomershine, Jul. 7, 1934 (dec. June 1995); children: Loren Jay, James Embury. Student, Jr. Coll., Riverside, Calif., 1930-32. Labor C.C.C., Camp Radford, Calif., 1933; asst. area acct. Sera Transcient Svc., San Bernardino, Calif., 1933-35; timekeep clerk, cashier V.S.F.S. Forestry Svc. Dept. Motor Vehicles, Riverside, Calif., 1936-37; statistical clerk Dept. Employment Divsn. Hwys., San Diego, 1938-46; shop chief clerk Dept. Employment Divsn. Hwys., Sacramento, Calif., 1946-52, state chief clerk, 1952-66; author, publ. Sacramento, Calif., 1967—. Contbr. articles to profl. jours. Inducted in Hall of Fame Fed. of Historics Bottle Assn., 1985. mem. Calif. State Employees Assn. Retired Mems. (state del., chpt. pres.), Quarter Century. Republican. Methodist. Avocations: fishing, antiques, desert camping. Home: 3161 56th St Sacramento CA 95820-1732

TICE, BRADLEY SCOTT, humanities educator; b. Palo Alto, Calif., Oct. 6, 1959; s. Lilburn Trent and Paula Nanette (Osborne) T. AA, De Anza Coll., Cupertino, Calif., 1983; BA in History, San Jose State U., 1987; PhD in Chemistry, Fairfax U., Baton Rouge, 1996; Diploma in Ayurvedic Medicine, The Ayurvedic Inst.; Diploma in Stress therapy, Internat. Yoga Sch.; LittD in Tchg., St. Clements Univ., The Carribean, 1998. Prof. Pacific Lang. Inst., Cupertino, Calif., 1992—; dir. rsch. Advanced Human Design, Cupertino, 1992—; CEO Tice Pharms., San Jose; intern. NASA Ames Rsch. Ctr., Moffett Field, Calif., 1997-98. Editor Jour. Pacific Lang. Inst., 1995-96; mem. editl. bd. The Story of Life. Recipient Pres.'s award Nat. Author's Registry, 1996, editor's choice award (3), The Nat. Libr. of Poetry, 1995, (2), 1996, Cert. Merit for essay, Pharmacia Biotech and Sci. prize for young scientists, 1997. Mem. ACS, IEEE, AIAA, COSPAR, Am. Physical Soc., N.Y. Acad. Scis., Assn. Computing Machinery, Am. Soc. Microbiology, Tchrs. English to Spkrs. of Other Langs., Calif. Assn. Bilingual Edn., Internat. Assn. Tchrs. English as a Fgn. Lang., Internat. Soc. Poets, Mars Soc. (found. mem.). Avocations: weight training, fencing, bicycling, swimming, archery. Office: Pacific Language Inst PO Box 2214 Cupertino CA 95015-2214

TICE, CAROLYN KAY, magazine editor; b. Kansas City, Mo., June 20, 1945; d. Clyde Prather and Hazel Adelyn (Best) Coleman; m. Arthur Raymond Tice, June 1, 1968. AA, Kansas City C.C., 1965. Office mgr. Litho-Comp Art Assocs., Kansas City, 1965-67; layout editor Spencer Printing Co., Kansas City, 1967-68; prodn. mgr. InterTec Pub. Co., Lenexa, Kans., 1968-70; assoc. editor Farm and Power Equipment Mag., St. Louis, 1970-79; exec. sec. Custodis Constrn. Co., Salt Lake City, 1979; mng. editor Fin. Freedom Report Mag., Salt Lake City, 1980—; exec. editor Home Bus. News Mag., Am. Home Bus. Assn., 1994—. Active Nat. Humane Soc., Washington, 1988—, Humane Soc. Salt Lake City, 1988—. Mem. Nat. Assn. Real Estate Editors, Phi Theta Kappa. Republican. Lutheran. Avocations: snow skiing, reading, swimming, golf, travel. Office: Am Home Bus Assn 4505 Wasatch Blvd Salt Lake City UT 84124-4709

TIDBALL, LEE FALK, elementary education educator; b. Waukon, Iowa, Feb. 26, 1955; s. John Harlow and Katherine Jane (Falk) T.; m. Catherine Susan Cooper, June 14, 1975 (div. Aug. 1982); children:: Aaron Matthew, Jonathan Michael. BS, Le Tourneau U., Longview, Tex., 1979. Cert. elem. tchr., Calif. Youth dir. Centenary Meth. Ch., Modesto, Calif., 1979-80; recreation dir. Crestwood Manor Hosp., Modesto, Calif., 1980; substitute tchr. Modesto City Schs., 1981-83; 7th grade tchr. Orangeburg Christian Sch., Modesto, 1983-84; 5th & 6th tchr. Bret Harte Elem., Modesto, 1984-91, gifted edn. tchr., 1991-97; tchr. 6th grade Beard Elem. Sch., Modesto, 1997—. *A gifted and talented teacher at a culturally and economically diverse school, Mr. Tidball pioneered a site-based, multi-age, full-day program for teacher-selected 4th-6th grade gifted students featuring major differentiations designed specifically to meet their special needs. These included a reading program emphasizing higher-level thinking skills, numerous cross-age projects, running and exercise, and intergration of performing arts. Particularly unique was his Social Studies program, a course in both history and leadership based on the lives of key historical figures. In 1998, Lee also published his first novel, Windfork Secrets, a work of juvenile fiction.* Head coach, pres. Silverwings Track Club, Modesto, 1982—; actor Modesto Performing Arts, 1994-96. Named Outstanding Young Religious Leader, Mason City (Iowa) Jaycees, 1976. Mem. NEA, Calif. Assn. for the Gifted, Modesto Tchrs. Assn., Pacific Assn., U.S.A. Track and Field, Soc. Children's Book Writers and Illustrators. Avocations: singing, writing, running. Home: 1228 W Roseburg Ave Apt D Modesto CA 95350-4982 Office: Beard Elem Sch 915 Bowen Ave Modesto CA 95350-3096

TIDWELL, GEOFFREY MORGAN, medical company executive; b. San Diego, Aug. 16, 1958; s. Morgan Alfred and Dorothy (Doolittle) T. BA in Psychology, U.S. Internat. U., 1991; MBA in Health Care Adminstrn., Nat. U., 1996. Rsch. asst. San Marcos (Calif.) Clinic, 1988-91; area svc. mgr. Nat. Med. Sys., Frederick, Md., 1993-94, Life Med. Svcs., San Diego, 1994-95; intern San Diego County Med. Soc., 1995-96; adminstrn. resident dept. interventional radiology U. Calif., San Diego, 1995-96; v.p., dir. clin. svcs. M&G Med. Svc., San Diego, 1995—; vis. scholar U. Calif. Sch. Medicine, San Diego, 1996, 97, 98; radio personality Sta. KOWF, Escondido, Calif., 1989-90, Sta. KKYY, San Diego, 1990-91, Sta. KRMX, San Diego, 1990-91, Sta. KGB, San Diego, 1991-97.r. clin. svcs., v.p. sales and mktg. M&G Med. Svc., San Diego, 1995— Co-author chpts. Podiatry Today, vol. 10 # 7, 1997. Vol. telethon Muscular Dystrophy Assn., San Diego, 1991, Easter Seals, San Diego, 1991. Mem. Am. Coll. Healthcare Execs. (assoc.), Med. Group Mgmt. Assn. (assoc.), Emergency Med. Assembly (assoc.), Healthcare Coalition San Diego County (assoc.), Psi Chi. Republican. Methodist. Avocations: fitness training, horseback riding, target shooting, reading, guitar. Office: M&G Med Svcs 4198 Convoy St San Diego CA 92111-3702

TIEN, CHANG-LIN, engineer, educator; b. Wuhan, China, July 24, 1935; came to U.S., 1956, naturalized, 1969; s. Yun Chien and Yun Di (Lee) T.; m. Di-Hwa Liu, July 25, 1959; children: Norman Chihnan, Phyllis Chihping, Christine Chihyih. BS, Nat. Taiwan U., 1955; MME, U. Louisville, 1957; MA, PhD, Princeton U., 1959; PhD (hon.), U. Louisville, 1991, U. Notre Dame, 1992, Hong Kong U. Sci. and Tech., 1993, U. Conn., 1994, U. Waterloo, Can., 1995, U. Ill., 1995, Ohio State U., 1996, Hong Kong Bapt. U., 1996, Ariz. State U., 1996, Mills Coll., 1997, SUNY, Stony Brook, 1998. Acting asst. prof. dept. mech. engring. U. Calif., Berkeley, 1959-60, asst. prof., 1960-64, assoc. prof., 1964-68, prof., 1968-88, 90—, A. Martin Berlin chair prof., 1987-88, 90-97; Disting. prof. U. Calif., Irvine, 1988-90, NEC Disting. prof. engring, 1997—; chmn. divsn. thermal sys. U. Calif., Berkeley, 1969-71, also vice chancellor for research, 1983-85, chair dept. mech. engring., 1974-81; exec. vice chancellor U. Calif., Irvine, 1988-90; chancellor U. Calif., Berkeley, 1990-97; councillor Nat. Acad. Engring., 1998—; chair exec. com. Internat. Ctr. for Heat and Mass Transfer, 1980-82; hon. prof., dir. Xi'an Jiaotong U. Engring. Thermodynamics Rsch. Inst., 1987—; mem. adv. bd. Hong Kong U. Sci. and Tech., 1991—; chair internat. adv. panel Nat. U. Singapore, 1993—, U. Tokyo Inst. Indsl. Sci., 1995; tech. cons. Lockheed Missiles and Space Co., GE; gov. bd. dirs. Com. of 100, 1991—; bd. dirs. Wells Fargo Bank, Raychem Corp., 1996, Kaiser Permanente, AirTouch Comm., Chevron Corp., 1997; mem. coun. Fgn. Rels., 1996; active Aspen Inst. Domestic Strategy Group, 1992-97; chmn. Bay Area Econ. Forum, 1997—, Chief Exec.'s Commn. Innovation and Tech., Hong Kong, 1998-99, Asia Found. Bd. Trustees, 1999—; cons. in field. Author one book; editor Internat. Commn. Heat and Mass Transfer, 1981—, Internat. Jour. of Heat and Mass Transfer, 1981—; editor-in-chief Exptl. Heat Transfer, 1987—, Microscale Thermophysical Engineering, 1997—, ; editor twelve vols.; contbr. articles to profl. jours. Bd. dirs. Com. 100, 1991—; trustee Chiang Indsl. Charity Found., Ltd., Hong Kong, 1991—, Princeton U., 1991-95, U.S. Com. Econ. Devel., 1994—, Carnegie Found. Advancement Tchg., 1994-97; trustee Asia Found., 1993—, chmn., 1998—. John Simon Guggenheim fellow, 1965, Sr. U.S. Sci. fellow Japan Soc. for Promotion of Sci., 1980; recipient Sr. U.S. Sci. award Alexander von Humboldt Found., 1979, Pi Tau Sigma award for Excellence in Tchg., 1972 ; named Most Disting. Chinese scholar, Soc. Hong Kong Scholars, 1989, Li Ka Shing Disting. Lectr., U. Hong Kong, 1994, Gordon Wu Disting. Lectr., Princeton U., 1995, Martin Martel Lectr., Brown U., 1996. Fellow AAAS (bd. dirs. 1992—), ASME (hon., chair exec. com. heat transfer divsn. 1980-81, v.p. basic engring. 1988-90, Heat Transfer Meml. award 1974, Gustus L. Larson Meml. award 1975, AIChE/ASME Max Jakob Meml. award 1981, Disting. Lectr. award 1987-91), AIAA (Thermophysics award 1977), Am. Acad. Arts and Scis. (hon. 1991), Academia Sinica (hon., Taiwan 1988); mem. NAE (mem. internat. affairs adv. com. 1987-90, chair mech. engring. peer com. 1989-90, councillor 1998—), Am. Soc. Engring. Edn. (mem. nat. adv. coun. 1993—), Heat Transfer Soc. Japan (hon. 1995), Chinese Acad. Scis. (fgn. mem., Hon. Prof., Inst. Thermophysics 1981—). Office: Dept Mech Engring U Calif 6101 Etcheverry Hall # 1740 Berkeley CA 94720-1741

TIERNEY, MICHAEL, filmmaker; b. Pasadena, Calif., Jan. 24, 1965; s. Edward Michael and Anne (Winterburn) T. lead singer, songwriter The Weird, L.A., 1993—; writer, prodr., dir. Evicted Prodns., L.A., 1999. Writer, dir.: Evicted, 1998. Office: Evicted Prodns PO Box 2832 Los Angeles CA 90078-2832

TIFFANY, SANDRA L., state legislator; b. Spokane, Wash., June 30, 1949; m. Ross M. Tonkens; 1 child, Courtney. Student, U. Calif. Mem. Nev. Assembly, 1993—. Mem. Nev. Rep. Women's Club, Green Valley Cmty. Assn. Home: 2156 Sun Swept Way Henderson NV 89014-4273 Office: Nev Assembly State Capitol Carson City NV 89710

TIGER, PETER ERROL, controller; b. Bloemfontein, South Africa, Aug. 23, 1962; s. Siegfried Esau and Judy Shirley T.; m. Lynn Karen Seehoff Tiger, July 9, 1987; children, Nicole Lee, Jason Warren. BS, San Diego State U., 1981-85. CPA. Staff auditor Gunnarson, Broomfield CPAs, San Diego, 1985-86; sr. auditor Laventhol and Horwath CPAs, L.A., 1986-90; controller Superba, Inc., L.A., 1990—. Editor National Association of CPAs Magazine, 1984-85, Community Type Magazine, 1991—. Chmn., treas. Fathers Day Coun. West Coast, L.A., 1992—. Recipient Outstanding Client Svc. award Laventhol & Horwath CPAs, L.A., 1990. Mem. Am. Inst. CPAs, Calif. Soc. CPAs. Avocations: tennis coaching, tennis, skiing, cycling, reading. Office: Superba Inc 1735 S Santa Fe Ave Los Angeles CA 90021-2940

TIGUE, WILLIAM BERNARD, adult education educator; b. Wilkes-Barre, Pa., Aug. 20, 1945; s. Joseph Francis and Susanna Agatha (Opet) T.; m. Faye Gage Cox, Dec. 10, 1977 (div. 1980); m. Dolores Cruz Arriaga, Apr. 17, 1993. BA, Kings Coll., 1967; MA, East Tenn. State U., 1969; TESOL cert., UCLA, 1997. Acct. exec. Carl Byoir & Assocs., San Francisco; editor internal publs. Crocker Nat. Bank, San Francisco; copywriter acct. exec. Doremus & Co., San Francisco; assoc. publ., sales mgr. Calif. Bicyclist Yellow Jersey Enterprises, San Francisco; English tchr. LACCD, L.A.; tchr. adult edn. L.A. Unified Sch. Dist. Mem. Women Educators of So. Calif. Democrat. Roman Catholic. Avocations: reading, cooking, AAA profl. baseball. Home: 329 California Ave Apt 8 Santa Monica CA 90403-5014

TILDEN, WESLEY RODERICK, author, retired computer programmer; b. Saint Joseph, Mo., Jan. 19, 1922; s. Harry William and Grace Alida (Kinnaman) T.; m. Lorraine Henrietta Frederick, June 20, 1948. Grad., Navy Supply Corps Sch., 1945; BS, UCLA, 1948; BA, Park Coll., Mo., 1990. Purchasing agent Vortox Co., Claremont, Calif., 1951-61; lang. lab. dir. Mount San Antonio Coll., Walnut, Calif., 1962-65; computer programmer, operator General Dynamics, Pomona, Calif., 1967-70; ret., 1970. Author: (book) Scota, The Egyptian Princess, 1994, Merit-Sekhet: Foster Mother of Moses?, 1996; photographer, textbooks, mags., newspaper, catalogs. Historian Claremont Sister City Assn., 1963-66. Lt. USNR, 1942-46 PTO. Recipient with Lorraine Tilden People to People award Reader's Digest Found., 1963-64, 1964-65; named Hon. Citizen Guanajuato, Mexico, 1963. Mem. Soc. Mayflower Descendants, Scottish Clans, UCLA Alumni Assn., Park Coll. Alumni Assn., Univ. Club of Claremont. Republician. Avocations: history, genealogy, photography, gardening. Home: 351 Oakdale Dr Claremont CA 91711-5039

TILLER, WILLIAM ARTHUR, retired science educator, scientific researcher; b. Toronto, Ont., Can., Sept. 18, 1929; came to the U.S., 1955; s. Arthur and Vere Eden Emma (Pash) T.; m. Jean Elizabeth Ackroyd, June 28, 1952; children: Andrea, Jeff. BASc, U. Toronto, 1952, MASc, 1953, PhD, 1955. Sr. physicist Westinghouse Rsch. Lab., Churchill Borough, Pa., 1955-64; full prof. dept. materials sci. and engring. Stanford (Calif.) U., 1964-66, dept. chmn., 1966-71, full prof., 1971-92, emeritus prof., 1992—; cons. Dupont de Nemours & Co., Wilmington, Del., 1965-90, Memc Materials Co., St. Peters, Mo., 1990-96, Durance & Ditron LLC, Excelsior, Minn., 1995—; bd. dirs. Astron Antennaco, Washington. Author: Science of Crystallization I, 1991, Science of Crystallization II, 1992, Science and Human Transformation, 1997; co-author: Computer Simulation, 1982; contbr. articles to profl. jours. Avocations: psychoenergetics research, walking. Home: 909 S Pinecone St Payson AZ 85541 Office: Stanford U Dept MSE Stanford CA 94305-2205

TILLMAN, BETTY BANKS (TALIBAH TILLMAN), secondary school educator; b. New Orleans, Sept. 8, 1944; d. Buster and Elsie (Stallworth) Banks; children: Sherman W. III, Kamau B. Abayomi. BA in English Edn. and Drama, Dillard U., New Orleans, 1966; MA in Theatre and Comm., U. New Orleans, 1974; AA in Theology, E.C. Reems Bible Inst., Oakland, Calif., 1990. Tchr. lang. arts and drama Orleans Parish Schs., New Orleans, 1966-74; tchr. English and drama Oakland Unified Sch. Dist., 1974-82; artist in schs. Calif. Arts Fund Found., Sacramento, 1982-83; mentor tchr. English San Francisco Unified Sch. Dist., 1984-90, English coord. Access program, 1990-91, tchr. English, 1992—; founding mem., actress Dashiki Theatre, New Orleans, 1968-74, chair English dept. San Francisco Unified Sch. Dist., 1998—, participant extended literacy collaborative, 1997-98; mem. Wallenberg Site Coun., pres., 1997-98, chair English dept. Wallenberg H.S., 1997—; mem. San Francisco Lit. Recommendation Com. Editor, pub. newsletter Talibah Speaks, 1985-87. Sponsor Black Student Union, Wallenberg Traditional H.S., San Francisco, 1986—, sponsor, counselor student travel, 1987—; big sister Big Bros. and Sisters, San Francisco, 1990-91; youth advisor YWCA, San Francisco, 1992-93; youth counselor, tchr. Acts Full Gospel Ch., Oakland, 1996—, San Francisco Literature Recommendation com. Recipient Outstanding Educator award San Francisco Alliance Black Educators, 1992. Mem. Nat. Coun. Tchrs. of English, Calif. Tchrs. Assn., Women Writers Assn., San Francisco Alliance Black Educators. Avocations: reading fiction, travel, photography, writing. Office: Wallenberg Traditional HS 40 Vega St San Francisco CA 94115-3826

TILLMAN, JOHN LEE, principal; b. Mesa, Ariz., Jan. 31, 1947; s. W.L. and Juanita (Johnson) T.; m. Judith Ann Tuxhorn, May 31, 1980; children Matthew Lee, Andrew Lee. BA, Adams State Coll., 1969, MA, 1975. Cert. tchr., Colo., Va.; cert. adminstr., Colo. Music tchr. Mountain Valley Sch., Saquache, Colo., 1969-70; dir. music Hargrave Mil. Acad., Chatham, Va., 1970-76; music tchr. Sargent Sch. Dist., Monte Vista, Colo., 1976-82; secondary prin. Sargent Sch. Dist., Monte Vista, 1982-95, dir. devel., 1995—; bd. control Colo. H.S. Activities Assn., Denver, 1990-93; alumni bd. dirs. Adams State Coll., Alamosa, Colo., 1990-93. Music dir. Calvary Bapt. Ch., Monte Vista, 1976—. Mem. Am. Assn. Sch. Adminstrs., Colo. Assn. Sch. Execs., Colo. Music Educators Nat. Conf., Phi Delta Kappa. Baptist. Avocations: computers, music, electronics, woodworking. Office: Sargent Sch Dist 7090 N County Road 2 E Monte Vista CO 81144-9756

TILLMAN, JOSEPH NATHANIEL, engineering executive; b. Augusta, Ga., Aug. 1, 1926; s. Leroy and Canarie (Kelly) T.; m. Alice Lavonia Walton, Sept. 5, 1950 (dec. 1983); children: Alice Lavonia, Robert Bertram; m. Areerat Usahaviriyakit, Nov. 24, 1986. BA magna cum laude, Paine Coll., 1948; MS, Northrop U., 1975, MBA, 1976; DBA, Nova U., 1989. Dir. Rockwell Internat., Anaheim, Calif., 1958-84; pres. Tillman Enterprises, Corona, Calif., 1985—; guest lectr. UCLA, 1980-85. Contbr. articles to profl. jours. Capt. USAF, 1948-57, Korea. Recipient Presdl. Citation Nat. Assn. for Equal Opportunity in Higher Edn., 1986. Mem. Acad. Mgmt. (chmn. 1985-86), Soc. Logistics Engrs. (pres. 1985-86), Paine Coll. Alumni Assn. (v.p. 1976—), NAACP (pres. 1984-88). Avocations: duplicate bridge, travel, swimming, skiing, hiking. Office: Tillman Enterprises 1550 Rimpau Ave Trlr 45 Corona CA 91719-3206

TILLOTSON, HAYDEE VELAZQUEZ, real estate developer, property manager; b. New Orleans, Dec. 19, 1938; d. Manuel Velazquez Blanco and Haydee (Lopez) Grefe; m. John Henry Tillotson Jr., Sept. 5, 1959; children: John Henry III, Erik Michael. Grad. in Interior Design, Interior Designers Guild, Newport Beach, Calif., 1979. Bookkeeper Union Bank, L.A., 1958-60; pvt. practice Creative Decor Concepts Group, Hungtington Beach, Calif., 1979-97; real estate developer Tillotson Enterprises, Hungtington Beach, Calif., 1985—. Mem. Rep. Women Federate, Washington, 1970—; commr. Orange County Commn. on Status of Women, 1982-85; mem. Anti Crime Coalition, Huntington Beach, 1990—; planning commr. Orange County, 1993-94, Huntington Beach, 1995-98; founding chmn. Project Self Sufficiency Found., Huntington Beach, 1993-95; bd. dirs. Huntington Beach Hosp. and Med. Ctr., 1994—, chmn. bd., 1997, 98, 99; bd. dirs. Lincoln Club Orange

County, 1996-98, Orange County Coun. Boy Scouts Am., 1997—, Vets. Charities, Orange County, 1996, 97—; mem. citizens adv. bd. Automobile Club So. Calif., L.A., 1995—; pres. Pacific Harbours Rep. Women Federated, Huntington Beach, 1996-97, 98-99; vice chmn. Pacific Liberty Information Bank, Huntington Beach, 1997. Recipient Huntington Beach 2000 Devel. award, 1988, Woman of Yr. award State of Calif. Legis., 58th Assembly Dist., 1992, Citizen of Yr. award City of Huntington Beach, Calif. Police Assn., 1994, Woman of Yr. award State of Calif. Legis.-Sen. Ross Johnson, 1996, Outstanding Citizen of Yr. award Huntington Beach, 1997. Mem. Orange County Bus. Coun. (bd. dirs. 1995-97), Huntington Beach C. of C. (chmn. 1991-92, Bus. of Yr. award 1990), Soroptimist Internat. (Woman of Distinction award 1991). Republican. Roman Catholic. Avocations: traveling, reading, walking. Office: Tillotson Enterprises 15272 Bolsa Chica St Huntington Beach CA 92649-1243

TILSON, DANIEL, elementary education educator. Tchr. Eastwood Elem. Sch., Roseburg, Oreg., 1985—. Recipient Excellence in Sci. Tchg. award, 1990, Milken Nat. Edn. award, 1992, State Tchr. of Yr. elem. award Oreg., 1992; Christa McAuliffe fellow, 1988. Office: Eastwood Elem Sch 2550 SE Waldon Ave Roseburg OR 97470-3805

TILSON THOMAS, MICHAEL, symphony conductor; b. L.A., 1944; s. Ted and Roberta T. Studies with, Ingolf Dahl, U. So. Calif., others; student conducting, Berkshire Music Festival, Tanglewood, Mass.; student conducting (Koussevitsky prize 1968); LL.D., Hamilton Coll.; L.H.D. (hon.), D'Youville Coll., 1976. Asst. condr. Boston Symphony Orch., 1969, assoc. condr., 1970-72, prin. guest condr., 1972-74; also Berkshire Music Festival, summer 1970, 74; music dir., condr. Buffalo Philharmonic Orch., 1971-79; music dir., prin. condr. Great Woods Ctr. for Performing Arts, 1985-88; prin. condr. London Symphony Orch., 1988-95; artistic dir. New World Symphony, Fla., 1988—; prin. guest condr. London Symphony Orch., 1995—; music dir. San Francisco Symphony, 1995—. Condr., dir., N.Y. Philharmonic Young People's Concerts, CBS-TV, 1971-77; vis. condr. numerous orchs., U.S., Europe, Japan; chief condr. Ojai Festival, 1967, dir., 1972-77; opera debut, Cin., 1975; condr.: Am. premiere Lulu (Alban Berg), Santa Fe Opera, summer 1979; prin. guest condr., L.A. Philharm., 1981-85, Am. premiere Desert Music (Steve Reich), 1984; prin. condr. Gershwin festival London Symphony Orch., Barbcan Ctr., 1987; composer: Grace (A Song for Leonard Bernstein), 1988, Street Song (for Empire Brass Quintet), 1988, From the Diary of Anne Frank (for orchestra and narrator Audrey Hepburn and New World Symphony), 1990; commd. by UNICEF for Concerts for Life's European premiere, 1991; recording artist Sony Classical/CBS Masterworks, 1973—; co-artistic dir. Pacific Music Festival, 1990—, with Leonard Bernstein 1st ann. Pacific Music Festival, Sapporo, Japan, 1990; co-artistic dir. 2d ann. Pacific Music festival, 1991, Salzburg Festival, 1991; conducted Mozart Requiem. Named Musician of Year, Musical Am. 1970; recipient Koussevitsky prize, 1968, Grammy award for Carmina Burana with Cleve. Orch., 1976, for Gershwin Live with Los Angeles Philharm., 1983, Grammy nomination, Best Classical Album - Debussy: Le Martyre de Saint Sebastien (with the London Symphony Orchestra), 1994. Office: 888 7th Ave Fl 37 New York NY 10106-3799 also: San Francisco Symphony Davies Symphony Hall 201 Van Ness Ave San Francisco CA 94102*

TIMM, ROBERT MERLE, wildlife specialist, administrator; b. Pomona, Calif., Oct. 7, 1949; s. Herbert Merle and Mary Elsie (Beasley) T.; m. Janice Howard Hawthorne, May 31, 1986; children: Anna Elizabeth Howard, Sarah Beatrice Howard, Jesse Robert Howard. BS, U. of Redlands, 1971; MS, U. Calif., Davis, 1973, PhD, 1977. Extension wildlife specialist, assoc. prof. U. Nebr., Lincoln, 1978-87; supt., extension wildlife specialist Hopland Rsch. and Ext. Ctr., U. Calif., Hopland, 1987—; cons. rodent control USAID/Denver Wildlife Rsch. Ctr.-USDA, Bangladesh, 1989. Editor: Prevention and Control of Wildlife Damage, 1993, co-editor, 1994; contbr. articles to profl. publs. Chmn. coun. 1st Evang. Covenant Ch., Lincoln, 1983-85; group study exch. mem. Rotary Internat. to Natal province, Republic South Africa, 1982. Named Outstanding New Specialist, NE Coop. Extension Assn., Lincoln, 1982. Mem. Soc. for Range Mgmt., Am. Soc. Mammalogists, Nat. Animal Damage Control Assn. (editor newsletter 1990—), The Wildlife Soc. (wildlife damage mgmt. working group, profl. devel. com., cert. wildlife biologist), Sigma Xi, Gamma Sigma Delta. Fin. sec. United Ch. Christ-Congl., Cloverdale, Calif. Achievements include statewide Integrated Pest Management project focused on rodent damage control; Predator Damage Control project to reduce coyote predation on sheep, funded by California Department of Pesticide Regulation. Home: 968 Riverside Dr Ukiah CA 95482-9666 Office: U Calif Hopland Rsch and Ext Ctr 4070 University Rd Hopland CA 95449-9717

TIMMINS, JAMES DONALD, venture capitalist; b. Hamilton, Ont., Can., Oct. 3, 1955; came to U.S., 1979; s. Donald G. and Myrna L. (Seymour) T. BA, U. Toronto, 1977; law degree, Queen's U., 1979; MBA, Stanford U., 1981. Investment banker Wood Gundy, Toronto, 1980, Salomon Bros., San Francisco, 1981-84; mng. dir. and chief exec. officer McKewon & Timmins, San Diego, 1984-87; ptnr. Hambrecht & Quist, San Francisco, 1987-90, Redwood Ptnrs., Menlo Park, 1991-98; ptnr. NIF Ventures, San Francisco, 1998—; bd. dirs. Artios Corp., Irvine, Micronics Computers, Inc., Fremont, Calif.; with Harmony Software, Inc., Los Gatos, Calif., Sierra Vista Rsch. Corp., Spectra Switch Inc., Santa Rosa, Calif. Mem. Olympic Club of San Francisco. Home: 735 Laurelwood Dr San Mateo CA 94403-4058 Office: NIF Ventures USA Inc 525 Market St Ste 3420 San Francisco CA 94105

TIMMONS, EVELYN DEERING, pharmacist; b. Durango, Colo., Sept. 29, 1926; d. Claude Elliot and Evelyn Allen (Gooch) Deering; m. Richard Palmer Timmons, Oct. 4, 1952 (div. 1968); children: Roderick Deering, Steven Palmer. BS in Chemistry and Pharmacy cum laude, U. Colo., 1948. Chief pharmacist Meml. Hosp., Phoenix, 1950-54; med. lit. rsch. librarian Hoffman-LaRoche, Inc., Nutley, N.J., 1956-57; staff pharmacist St. Joseph's Hosp., Phoenix, 1958-60; relief mgr. various ind. apothecaries, Phoenix, 1960-68; asst. then mgr. Profl. Pharmacies, Inc., Phoenix, 1968-72; mgr. then owner Mt. View Pharmacy, Phoenix and Paradise Valley, Ariz., 1972—; pres. Ariz. Apothecaries, Ltd., Phoenix, 1976—, dir. compounding 1976—; mem. profl. adv. bd., bereavement counselor Hospice of Valley, 1983-96; mem. profl. adv. bd. Upjohn Health Care and Svcs., Phoenix, 1984-86; bd. dirs. Am. Council on Pharm. Edn., Chgo., 1986-92, v.p. 1988, 89, treas., 1990-91; mem. expert adv. con. compounding pharms. U.S. Pharmacoepial Conv., 1992—; preceptor U. Ariz., 1997—, Midwestern Coll. Pharmacy, Ariz. Campus, 1998—. Author poetry; contbr. articles to profl. jours. Mem. Scottsdale (Ariz.) Fedn. Rep. Women, 1963; various other offices Rep. Fedn.; mem. platform com. State of Ariz., Nat. Rep. Conv., 1964; asst. sec. Young Rep. Nat. Fedn., 1963-65; active county and state Rep. coms.; mem. Internat. Jour. of Pharm. Compounding (adv. bd. 1996—), fin. chmn. Internat. Leadership Symposium: Women in Pharmacy, London, 1987; treas. Leadership Internat. Women Pharmacy, 1991—; mem. founders circle Gladys Taylor McNarey Med. Found., 1996—. Named Outstanding Young Rep. of Yr., Nat. Fedn. Young Reps., 1965, Preceptor of Yr., U. Ariz./Syntex, 1984; recipient Disting. Public Svc. award Maricopa County Med. Soc., 1962, Disting. Alumni award Wasatch Acad., 1982, Career Achievement award Kappa Epsilon, 1983, Leadership and Achievement award Upjohn Labs., 1985-86, Outstanding Achievement in Profession award Merck, Sharp & Dohme, 1986, award of Merit Kappa Epsilon, 1988, Disting. Coloradoan award U. Colo., 1989, Vanguard award Kappa Epsilon, 1991, Unicorn award Kappa Epsilon, 1993, Compounding Pharmacist of the Yr. award Profl. Compounding Corp. of Am., 1995, 96, Healing Heart Award Gladyl Taylor McGally Found., 1998. Fellow Am. Coll. of Apothecaries (v.p. 1982-83, pres. 1984-85; chmn. bd. dirs. 1985-86, adv. coun. 1986-92, Chmn. of Yr. 1980-81 Victor H. Morganroth award 1985, J. Leon Lascoff award 1990) Internat. Acad. of Compounding Pharmacists (bd. dirs. 1993—); mem. Ariz. Soc. of Hosp. Pharmacists, Am. Pharm. Assn. (Daniel B. Smith award 1990), Ariz. Pharmacy Assn. (Svc. to Pharmacy award 1976, Pharmacist of Yr. 1981, Bowl of Hygeia 1989, 1st Innovative Pharmacy award 1994), Maricopa County Pharmacy Assn. (pres. 1977, Svc. to Pharmacy award 1977), Am. Soc. of Hosp. Pharmacists, Am. Aircraft Owners and Pilots Assn., Air Safety Found., Nat. Assn. of Registered Par- [illegible] Vanguard award 1991, Unicorn award 1993). Lodge: Civinettes (pres. Scottsdale chpt. 1960-61). Avocations: flying, skiing, swimming, backpacking, hiking, writing. Office: Mt View Pharmacy 10565 N Tatum Blvd Ste D118 Scottsdale AZ 85253-1035

TIMMONS, WILLIAM MILTON, producer, freelance writer, retired cinema arts educator, publisher, film maker; b. Houston, Apr. 21, 1933; s. Carter Charles and Gertrude Monte (Lee) T.; m. Pamela Cadorette, Dec. 24, 1975 (div. 1977). BS, U. Houston, 1958; MA, UCLA, 1961; PhD, U. So. Calif., 1975. Child actor Houston Jr. Theater, 1945-46; staff announcer Sta. KMCO, Conroe, Tex., 1951-52; prodn. asst. Sta. KUHT-TV, Houston, 1953-54, 56-57; teaching fellow UCLA, 1960-61; ops. asst. CBS-TV, Hollywood, Calif., 1961-62; prof. speech and drama Sam Houston State U., Huntsville, Tex., 1963-67; chmn. dept. cinema Los Angeles Valley Coll., Van Nuys, Calif., 1970-91, ret., 1992; prodr. Sta. KPFK, L.A., 1959-60, 83-95; pub. Acad. Assocs., L.A., 1976; proofreader, cons. Focal Press Pub. Co., N.Y.C., 1983-92. Author: Orientation to Cinema, 1986; contbr. articles to mags.; prodr., dir.: (radio programs) Campus Comments, 1963-67, numerous ednl. films, 1963—; prodr. ednl. series for cable TV, 1993—. With USNR, 1954-56. Named Hon. Tex. Ranger, State of Tex., Austin, 1946; U. Houston scholar, 1957. Mem. Mensa, U. So. Calif. Cinema-TV Alumni Assn., Red Masque Players, Secular Humanists L.A., Alpha Epsilon Rho, Delta Kappa Alpha. Democrat. Avocations: reading, writing, viewing movies.

TIMMRECK, THOMAS C., health sciences and health administration educator; b. Montpelier, Idaho, June 15, 1946; s. Archie Carl and Janone (Jensen) T.; m. Ellen Prusse, Jan. 27, 1971; children: Chad Thomas, Benjamin Brian, Julie Anne. AA, Ricks Coll., 1968; BS, Brigham Young U., 1971; MEd, Oreg. State U., 1972; MA, No. Ariz. U., 1981; PhD, U. Utah, 1976. Program dir. Cache County Aging Program, Logan, Utah, 1972-73; asst. prof. div. health edn. Tex. Tech U., Lubbock, 1976-77; asst. prof. dept. health care adminstrn. Idaho State U., Pocatello, 1977-78; dept. chair, asst. prof. health services program No. Ariz. U., Flagstaff, 1978-84; cons., dir. grants Beth Israel Hosp., Denver, 1985; prof. dept. health scis. and human ecology, coordinator grad. studies, coordinator health adminstrn. and planning Calif. State U., San Bernardino, 1985—; pres. Health Care Mgmt. Assocs., 1985—; presenter at nat. confs.; dept. chair health and wellness dept., faculty Loretto Heights Coll., Denver; adj. faculty Dept. Mgmt. U. Denver, Dept. Mgmt. and Health Adminstrn. U. Colo., Denver, dept. bus. adminstrn. U. Redlands (Calif.), U. So. Calif., L.A., Chapman U. Author: Dictionary of Health Services Management, rev. 2d edit., 1987, Health Services Cyclopedic Dictionary, 3d edit., An Introduction to Epidemiology, 1994, 2d edit., 1998, Planning and Program Development and Evaluation: A Handbook for Health Promotion, Aging, and Health Services, 1995; mem. editl. bd. Jour. Health Values, 1986—, Basic Epidemiological Methods and Biostats., Dictionary of Epidemiology and Public Health, 1996; contbr. numerous articles on health care adminstrn., behavioral health, gerontology and health edn. to profl. jours. Chmn., bd. dirs. Inland Counties Health System Agy.; mem. strategic planning com. chmn. Vis. Nurses Assn. of Inland Counties; bd. dirs. health svc. orgns. With U.S. Army, 1966-72, Vietnam. Mem. Assn. Advancement of Health Edn., Am. Acad. Mgmt., Assn. Univ. Programs in Health Care Adminstrn., Healthcare Forum. Republican. Mormon. Office: Calif State U Dept Health Scis and Human Ecology San Bernardino CA 92407

TIMSARI, BIJAN, engineering educator; b. Tehran, Sept. 11, 1967; s. Rostam and Parvin (Bondarian) T. BS, Sharif U. of Tech., Tehran, 1990; MS in Telecomms., Isfehan U. Tech., Iran, 1993; MSEE, U. So. Calif., L.A., 1997, postgrad., 1998—. Rschr. Iran Telecomms. Rsch. Ctr., Tehran, 1988-94, Electronic Rsch. Ctr., Tehran, 1990-94; software analyst, cons. Genesis 2000, Inc., Calabasas, Calif., 1996—; rsch. asst. U. So. Calif., L.A., 1997—, 1994—; adj. prof. Sharif U. Technology, Tehran, 1993-94. Mem. IEEE, Internat. Soc. for Optical Engring., Assn. for Computing Machinery. Office: Signal & Image Processing Inst Univ So Calif EE424 3740 Mcclintock Ave Los Angeles CA 90007-4012

TINDLE, CHARLES DWIGHT WOOD, broadcasting company executive; b. Bryn Mawr, Pa., Jan. 13, 1950; s. Charles Wood and Nancy (Sapp) T. Student, Kenyon Coll., 1968-71. Pres. Dwight Karma Broadcasting, Mesa, Ariz., 1971-76, Natural Broadcasting System, Mesa, 1976-79; producer, fellow Am. Film Inst. Ctr. for Advanced Film Studies, 1979-81; pres. Network 30, Scottsdale, Ariz., 1985—; owner Sta. KDKB-AM-FM, Mesa, Sta. KSML-FM, Lake Tahoe, Calif., Sta. KNOT-AM-FM, Prescott, Ariz., Sta. KBWA, Williams, Ariz. Recipient Peabody award U. Ga., 1976. Republican. Seventh Day Adventist. Home: 4445 E Flower St Phoenix AZ 85018-6452 Office: 644 N Country Club Dr Mesa AZ 85201-4948

TINGAY, STEVEN JOHN, astronomer; b. Bendigo, Victoria, Australia, Feb. 19, 1970; s. Stanley Joseph and Elaine Margret (Cook) T.; m. Sonia Mary Erle, June 7, 1992. BS with honors, U. Melbourne, Victoria, Australia, 1992; PhD, Australian Nat. U., Canberra, Australian Capital Terr., 1997. Rsch. assoc. Jet Propulsion Lab., Pasadena, Calif., 1996—. Contbr. articles to profl. jours. Mem. N.Y. Acad. Scis. Avocations: fishing, athletics. Fax: (818) 393-6890. E-mail: stingay@earthlink.net, tingay@hyaa.jpl.nasa.gov. Home: 11360 Ovada Pl Apt 11 Los Angeles CA 90049-2131 Office: Jet Propulsion Lab (MS 238-332) 4800 Oak Grove Dr Pasadena CA 91109-8001

TINGLEY, WALTER WATSON, computer systems manager; b. Portland, Maine, July 24, 1946; s. Edward Allen Tingley and Ruth Annie (Howard) Tuttle; m. Elizabeth A. Fletcher, May 1970 (div. 1975); m. Carol S. Gadoury, Dec. 1998. BS, U. Md., 1974. Programmer analyst U.S. Ry. Assn., Washington, 1974-80, Digital Equipment Corp., Maynard, Mass., 1980-81, Interactive Mgmt. Sys., Belmont, Mass., 1981; sys. designer Martin Marietta Data Sys., Greenbelt, Md., 1982-84; mgr. computer ops. Genex, Rockville, Md., 1984; sys. mgr. Applied Rsch. Corp., Landover, Md., 1985; programmer analyst Input/Output Computer Svcs., Washington, 1986-87, Lockheed Engring. and Scis., Las Vegas, Nev., 1987-91, Los Alamos (N.Mex.) Nat. Lab., 1992-96, Miller Internat., Denver, 1997—. Author tech. book revs., software revs. With USAF, 1964-68. Mem. Computer Soc. of IEEE, Assn. Computing Machinery. Avocations: skiing, hiking, swimming. Home: 8271 Johnson Ct Arvada CO 80005-2155

TINNIN, THOMAS PECK, real estate professional; b. Albuquerque, May 15, 1948; s. Robert Priest and Frances (Ferree) T.; m. Jamie Tinnin Garrett, Dec. 12, 1986; children: Megan Ashley, Courtney Nicole, Robert Garrett. Student, U. Md., 1969-72; BA, U. N.Mex., 1973. Ins. agt. Occidental Life of Calif., Albuquerque, 1972—; gen. agt. Transamerica-Occidental Life, Albuquerque, 1978-93; pres. Tinnin Investments, Albuquerque, 1978—, Tinnin Enterprises, Albuquerque, 1978—, Tinnin Real Estate & Devel., Albuquerque, 1989—; mem. N.Mex. State Bd. Fin., Santa Fe., 1985-87, 90—, sec. 1990-96; del. White House Conf. on Small Bus., Washington, 1986; bd. dirs. Albuquerque Econ. Devel., 1987-88. Bd. dirs. Albuquerque Conv. and Visitor's Bureau, 1982-84, St. Joseph's Hosp. Better Bus. Bur., 1983, Albuquerque, 1984-86, N.Mex. Jr. Livestock Found., pres. 1988, Presbyn. Heart Inst., 1989-91, N.Mex. First Confs., 1992, chair-elect; chmn. Manzano Dist. Boy Scouts Am., 1981-82; chmn. Manzano Dist. Finance, 1983; del. White House Conf. Small Bus., 1986; trustee N.Mex. Performing Arts Coun., 1989-90; chmn. N.Mex. State Fair, 1997—; bd. mem. Mus. Natural History, 1997—. Mem. NALU, N.Mex. Life Leaders Assn., Nat. Assn. Real Estate Appraisers, Albuquerqye Armed Forces Adv. Assn., Albuquerque C. of C. (bd. dirs. 1978-84, chmn. ambassador's com. 1983), N.Mex. Life Underwriters Assn., Albuquerque Country Club. Republican. Presbyterian. Avocations: hunting, fishing, skiing, water skiing. Home: 2303 Candelaria Rd NW Albuquerque NM 87107-3055 Office: Tinnin Enterprises 2303 Candelaria Rd NW Albuquerque NM 87107-3055

TIPTON, GARY LEE, retired services company executive; b. Salem, Oreg., July 3, 1941; s. James Rains and Dorothy Velma (Dierks) T. BS, Oreg. Coll. Edn., 1964. Credit rep. Standard Oil Co. Calif., Portland, Oreg., 1964-67; credit mgr. Uniroyal Inc., Dallas, 1967-68; ptnr., mgr. bus. Tipton Barbers, Portland, 1968-94; ret., 1994. Mem. Rep. Nat. Com., 1980—, Sen. Howard Baker's Presdl. Steering Com., 1980; dep. dir. gen. Internat. Biog. Ctr., Cambridge, Eng., 1987—, mem. U.S. Congl. adv. bd. Am. Security Coun., 1984-93; mem. steering com. Coun. on Fgn. Rels. Portland Com., 1983-84, chmn. 1984-86, mem. exec. com., 1988-90, bd. dirs., 1990-91. Recipient [illegible] 1982, cert. Disting. Contbn. Sunset High Sch. Dad's Club, 1972, 73, Cert. of Perfection award Tualatin Valley Fire and Rescue Dist., 1994. Fellow Internat. Biog. Assn. (life, Kay award 1993, U.K.); mem. Sunset Mchts. Assn. (co-founder, treas. [illegible]), [illegible]

sonian Assocs., UN Assn. (steering com. UN day 1985), World Affairs Coun. of Oreg., City Club of Portland.

TIPTON, KAREN, middle school educator; b. Junction City, Kans., Aug. 29, 1935; d. Clarence Calvert and Olive Ann (Bennett) T.; m. Merle Francis Channel, July 5, 1951 (div. Mar. 1983); children: Gloria Jeane Channel McKim, Steven Blair, Michael Curtis, Patrick Rock Channel. BS in Math., U. So. Colo., 1972; MA in Edn., Lesley Coll., 1990. Cert. tchr., Colo. Tchr. Pueblo (Colo.) Sch. Dist. 70, 1973—. Mem. NEA, AAUW, Pueblo County Tchrs. Assn., Colo. State Hist. Soc., Elks, Eagles. Home: 316 W 21st St Pueblo CO 81003-2516

TIRABASSI, LINDA SUE, secondary education educator; b. Niagara Falls, N.Y., Aug. 31, 1950; d. Alfred Angelo and Carmela Dolores T. AA, Niagara County Cmty. Coll., Niagara Falls, 1970; BS, SUNY (Brockport), 1972; MS, Calif. State U. (Fullerton), 1992. Tchr. St. Edward's Sch., Corona, Calif., 1977-81; tchr., pub. rels. Notre Dame H.S., Riverside, Calif., 1981-88; tchr. Ramona H.S., Riverside, Calif., 1988—; conflict resolution coord. Ramona H.S., 1994—. Mem. Calif. Assn. Peer Programs. Office: Ramona HS 7675 Magnolia Ave Riverside CA 92504-3627

TISDALE, DOUGLAS MICHAEL, lawyer; b. Detroit, May 3, 1949; s. Charles Walker and Violet Lucille (Battani) T.; m. Patricia Claire Brennan, Dec. 29, 1972; children: Douglas Michael, Jr., Sara Elizabeth, Margaret Patricia, Victoria Claire. BA in Psychology with honors, U. Mich., 1971, JD, 1975. Bar: Colo. 1975, U.S. Dist. Ct. Colo. 1975, U.S. Ct. Appeals (10th cir.) 1976, U.S. Supreme Ct. 1979. Law clk. to chief judge U.S. Dist. Ct. Colo., Denver, 1975-76; assoc. Brownstein Hyatt Farber & Madden, P.C. ; ptnr., dir. Brownstein Hyatt Farber & Strickland, P.C., 1976-92; shareholder Popham, Haik, Schnobrich & Kaufman, Ltd., 1992-97, dir. 1995-97; ptnr. Baker & Hostetler LLP, Denver, 1997—; Home: 4662 S Elizabeth Ct Cherry Hl Vlg CO 80110-7106 Office: Baker & Hostetler LLP 303 E 17th Ave Denver CO 80203-1235

TISHNER, KERI LYNN, secondary education educator; b. Santa Ana, Calif., June 1, 1964; d. Albert John, Jr. and Barbara Ann (Milner) Geverink; m. David Jackson Tishner, Apr. 27, 1985. BA in Art with distinction, Calif. State U., Long Beach, 1988, tchg. credentials, 1991; postgrad., Calif. State U., San Bernardino, 1994—. State D coaching license Calif. Youth Soccer Assn. Art tchr. Apple Valley (Calif.) H.S., 1991-99; art tchr. Granite Hills H.S., Apple Valley, 1999—, dept. chair performing arts, 1999—; mentor teacher, 1998—. Presenter in field of art. Participant Calif. Arts Project, San Bernardino, 1995. Mem. NEA, Nat. Art Edn. Assn., Calif. Tchrs. Assn., Calif. Art Edn. Assn., Los Angeles County Mus. Art, Norton Simon Mus. Art, Apple Valley Unified Tchrs. Assn., Kappa Delta Pi. Avocations: roller blading, weaving, computers, playing soccer, painting. Office: Granite Hills HS 22900 Esaws Rd Apple Valley CA 92307

TITUS, EDWARD DEPUE, psychiatrist, administrator; b. N.Y.C., May 24, 1931; s. Edward Kleinhans and Mary (Brown) Chadbourne; m. Virginia Van Den Steenhoven, Mar. 24, 1963 (div.); m. Catherine Brown, Apr. 22, 1990. BA, Occidental Coll., 1953; MS, U. Wis., 1955; MD, Stanford U., 1962; PhD, So. Calif. Psychoanalytic Inst., 1977. Mng. ptnr. Hacker Clinic Assn., Lynwood, Calif., 1968-90; chief psychiatrist parole outpatient clinic region III Calif. Dept. Corrections, L.A., 1991—; asst. clin. prof. psychiatry U. So. Calif., 1993—; chmn. dept. psychiatry St. Francis Hosp., Lynwood, 1979-80. Fellow Am. Psychiat. Assn.; mem. Calif. Med. Assn. (ho. of dels. 1981-95), So. Calif. Psychiat. Soc. (sec. 1984-85, 98—), Los Angeles County Med. Assn. (dist. pres. 1980-81, pres. sect. psychiatry 1990-92). Avocations: photography, backpacking. Office: Parole Outpatient Clinic 600 St Paul Ave Los Angeles CA 90017-2014

TITUS, VICTOR ALLEN, lawyer; b. Nevada, Mo., Sept. 2, 1956; s. Charles Allen and Viola Mae (Cliffman) T.; m. Laraine Carol Cook, Oct. 13, 1974 (div. Feb. 1982); 1 child, Matthew; m. Deborah Diane Carpenter, Apr. 10, 1984; 1 child, Jacquelynn. BS, Ctrl. Mo. State U., 1978, BA, 1978; JD, U. Mo., 1981. Bar: N.Mex. 1981, U.S. Dist. Ct. N.Mex. 1981, Mo. 1982, U.S. Ct. Appeals (10th cir. 1983), U.S. Supreme Ct. 1986, Colo. 1989, Ariz. 1995. Lawyer Jay L. Faurot, P.C., Farmington, N.Mex., 1981-83; ptnr. Faurot & Titus, P.C., Farmington, N.Mex., 1983-85; lawyer, sole proprietor Victor A. Titus, P.C., Farmington, N.Mex., 1985—; arbitrator in civil disputes Alternative Dispute Resolution-Arbitration; liquor lic. hearing officer City of Farmington, 1989-94. Contbr. articles to profl. jours. Adult Behind Youth, Boys & Girls Club, Farmington, 1987—; mem. hosp. adv. bd. San Juan Regional Med. Ctr., Farmington, 1988-93. Recipient San Juan County Disting. Svc. award N.Mex. Bar Assn., 1984; named one of Best Lawyers in Am., 1995-96, 97—. Mem. Assn. Trial Lawyers of Am., N.Mex. Trial Lawyers (bd. pres. 1983—, pres. 1993-94), State Bar of N.Mex. (disciplinary bd. 1997—, specialization com. 1992—, legal advt. com. 1990), San Juan County Bar Assn. (pres. 1984), Nat. Assn. Criminal Def. Lawyers, Colo. Trial Lawyers. Democrat. Avocation: sports. Home: 5760 Pinehurst Farmington NM 87402-5078 Office: Victor A Titus PC 2021 E 20th St Farmington NM 87401-2516

TKACHUK, KEITH, professional hockey player; b. Melrose, Mass., Mar. 28, 1972. With Phoenix Coyotes formerly Winnipeg (Canada) Jets, 1992—. Named to Hockey East All-Rookie team, 1990-91, NHL All-Star second team, 1994-95, Sporting News All-Star team, 1996. Office: Phoenix Coyotes 2 N Central Ste 1930 1 Renaissance Sq Phoenix AZ 85004

TOBER, MARK ROBERT, investment representative, stockbroker; b. Arcadia, Calif., Sept. 15, 1959; s. Robert and Joanne Marie (Leuschner) T.; m. Carol Lynne Weeshoff, Apr. 4, 1987; children: William Robert, Christian Michael. BA, U. So. Calif., 1981; JD, Western State U., Fullerton, Calif., 1992. CFP. Ins. broker Rossmore Property & Casualty, L.A., 1981-84, Aetna Life & Casualty, Orange, Calif., 1984-86, Elmco Ins., Inc., Santa Ana, Calif., 1986-91; investment rep. Edward D. Jones & Co., San Clemente, Calif., 1991-94; fin. advisor Linsco/Private Ledger, San Clemente, 1994—. Recipient Am. Jurisprudence award for legal writing & criminal law Am. Jurisprudence, 1988, 89. Fellow Internat. Bd. CFPs, San Clemente C. of C., Kiwanis, Sigma Alpha Epsilon (pres. 1980-81). Republican. Avocations: golf, weight tng. Office: LINSCO/Private Ledger De Los Mares #105 San Clemente CA 92673

TOBIAS, MARILYN, historian, educator, writer; b. Bronx, N.Y., Oct. 13, 1942; d. Henry and Elsie A. (Roskin) T. BA, Hunter Coll., 1963, MA, 1966; PhD, NYU, 1977. Tchr. Wagner Jr. H.S., N.Y.C., 1963-66, Flushing H.S., Queens, N.Y., 1966-73; adj. lectr., asst. dir. Rsch. Inst. Bklyn. Coll., 1973-75; pub. historian, rschr., cons. Washington, 1977-79; pres., bd. scholars Potomac Ednl. Resources, Inc., Washington, 1979-85; pub. historian N.Y.C., 1984-93; pub. historian, ind. scholar Thousand Oaks, Calif., 1993—; adj. asst. prof. NYU, N.Y.C., 1983-84, adj. assoc. prof., 1990; adj. asst. prof. Hunter Coll., N.Y.C., 1984-85, Pace U., N.Y.C., 1984-87, adj. assoc. prof., 1987-92, adj. prof., 1992-93; alt. Am. Fellowships Panel, 1997—; cons. numerous ednl., profl., govt. and cmty. entities; lectr. in field. Author: Old Dartmouth on Trial: The Transformation of the Academic Community in Nineteenth Century America, 1982; co-author: History of Education Quarterly, idex. vols. 11-20, 1984; contbr. articles to profl. jours. including Jour. Policy History, and to reference books including Enclyopedia of New York City, Am. Nat. Biography. Mem. N.Y. County Dem. Com., N.Y.C., 1973-77, 87-93, Calif. Dem. State. Com., 1996—; elected mem. Ventura County Dem. Ctrl. Com., Calif., 1996—. Mem. AAUW (N.Y.C. and Thousand Oaks chpts., proposal reviewer, panel mem. commn. internat. fellowships and awards Ednl. Found. 1982-84, svc. award middle Atlantic region 1985, svc. award Ednl. Found. 1985, disting. svc. award N.Y.C. chpt. 1986, chair centennial 1986, ednl. com. 1992-93, chair, moderator edn. and equity roundtable 1992-93, name honored Ednl. Found. N.Y.C. br. 1993), Nat. Women's Polit. Caucus, Nat. Coun. Pub. History, Western Assn. Women Historians, History Edn. Soc., Organ. Am. Historians. Democrat. Jewish. Avocation: volunteer work. Home: 555 Laurie Ln Apt G8 [illegible]

TOBIN, RONALD WILLIAM, French language educator; b. N.Y.C., June 19, 1936; s. William R. and Mary (Jadoff) T.; m. Ann L. Pollmann, Feb. 20, [illegible]

fellow), Princeton U., 1959, Ph.D., 1962; Fulbright fellow, U. Lille, France, 1959-60. Instr. French Williams Coll., Williamstown, Mass., 1961-63; asst. prof. U. Kans., 1963-65, asso. prof., chmn. dept. French and Italian, 1965-69; prof. French U. Calif. at Santa Barbara, 1969—, chmn. dept. French and Italian, 1969-71, 75-80, assoc. vice chancellor for acad. programs, 1989—; Vis. prof. Claremont (Calif.) Coll. Grad. Div., 1972, U. Ariz., 1972, UCLA, 1973, 80, 81; mem. univ. adv. council to Inst. Life Ins., 1969-80. Author: Racine and Seneca, 1971, Tarte à la crème: Comedy and Gastronomy in Molière's Theater, 1990, 98; editor: L'Esprit Créateur: Seventeenth-Century Studies in Honor of E.B.O. Borgerhoff, 1971, L'Esprit Createur: Myth and Mythology in the Seventeenth Century, 1976, Papers on French Seventeenth Century Literature: Esthétique et Société au XVIIe Siècle, 1977, Littérature et gastronomie, 1985; editor in chief: French Rev., 1986—. Am. Philos. Soc. grantee, 1963, 67; Am. Council Learned Socs. grantee, 1978, 81; fellow Nat. Endowment for Humanities, 1967; decorated Chevalier, Acad. Palms, 1972, Officier, 1987; Chevalier Order of Merit, 1984. Mem. Chevalier Order of Arts & Letters, Modern Humanities Research Assn., Société d'Etude du 17e siècle, Alliance Française. Democrat. Roman Catholic. Home: 26 La Cumbre Cir Santa Barbara CA 93105-4442

TOBIN, VINCENT MICHAEL, professional sports team executive; b. Burlington Junction, Mo., Sept. 29, 1943. BE, U. Mo., 1965, M in Guidance and Counseling, 1966. Def. ends coach Missouri, 1967-70, def. coord., 1971-76; def. coord. Brit. Columbia Lions CFL, 1977-82, Phila./Balt. Stars USFL, 1983-85, Chgo. Bears NFL, 1986-92, Indpls. Colts NFL, 1994-95; head coach Ariz. Cardinals, 1996—. Office: Arizona Cardinals PO Box 888 Phoenix AZ 85001-0888*

TOBIN, WILLIAM JOSEPH, newspaper editor; b. Joplin, Mo., July 28, 1927; s. John J. and Lucy T. (Shoppach) T.; m. Marjorie Stuhldreher, Apr. 26, 1952; children—Michael Gerard, David Joseph, James Patrick. BJ, Butler U., 1948. Staff writer AP, Indpls., 1947-52, news feature writer, N.Y.C., 1952-54, regional membership exec., Louisville, 1954-56, corr., Juneau, Alaska, 1956-60, asst. chief of bur., Balt., 1960-61, chief of bur., Helena, Mont., 1961-63; mng. editor Anchorage Times, 1963-73, assoc. editor, 1973-85, gen. mgr., 1974-85, v.p., editor-in-chief, 1985-89, editor editorial page, 1990, asst. pub., 1991, senior editor Voice of the Times, 1991—; bd. dirs. Enstar Corp., 1982-84. Mem. devel. com. Anchorage Winter Olympics, 1984-91, bd. dirs. Anchorage organizing com., 1985-91; bd. dirs. Alaska Coun. on Econ. Edn., 1978-84, Boys Clubs Alaska, 1979-83, Anchorage Symphony Orch., 1986-87, Blue Cross Wash. and Alaska, 1987—, chmn. 1990-91; chmn. Premera Corp., 1994—; mem. adv. bd. Providence Hosp., Anchorage, 1974-91, chmn., 1980-85. Served to sgt. AUS, 1950-52. Mem. Alaska AP Mems. Assn. (pres. 1964), Anchorage C. of C. (bd. dirs. 1969-74, pres. 1972-73), Alaska World Affairs Council (pres. 1967-68), Phi Delta Theta. Clubs: Alaska Press (pres. 1968-69), Commonwealth North (Anchorage). Home: 2130 Lord Baranof Dr Anchorage AK 99517-1257 Office: Anchorage Times PO Box 100040 Anchorage AK 99510-0040

TOCHO, LEE FRANK, mechanical engineer; b. New Orleans, Sept. 21, 1955; s. John Reaves Jr. and Grace Felice (Weekley) T.; m. Linda Varela, May 13, 1989; 1 child, Alexander Varela. BSME, Auburn U., 1977. Mech. engr. NOPSI, New Orleans, 1978-91, HC&S, Puunene, Hawaii, 1991—; gov. Hawaii Sugar Technologists, Aiea, 1994-98, pres., 1998. Dir. Riverland Credit Union, New Orleans, 1987-91. Mem. ASME, NFPA, Maui Engring. Soc. Libertarian. Mem. LDS Ch. Achievements include invention of shrouded condenser entrance, direct contact de-superheater and power plant condenser automatic cleaner. Home: PO Box 814 Makawao HI 96768-0814 Office: Hawaiian Comm & Sugar Co PO Box 266 Puunene HI 96784-0266

TODARO, PATRICIA ANNE, painter, singer; b. Rockville Centre, N.Y., Feb. 24, 1933; d. Russell Norman and Grace Ruth (Eyerman) Sheidow; m. Raymond Ashman, Feb. 6, 1958 (div.); children: Robert Ashman, Richard Ashman, Kathryn Ashman. Student, Sullins Coll., 1950-51, Art Students League, 1954, Susquehanna U., 1952-54, Coll. of William and Mary, 1982-84. With programming dept. ABC, 1954-55; with travel dept. Rand, Santa Monica, Calif., 1955-56; pres. Seltzer Gallery, N.Y.C., 1986, 87. One-woman shows include Seltzer Coll., 1985-87, Seltzer Gallery, Phoenix Visual Arts Ctr., 1988, Kerr Cultural Ctr., Scottsdale, Ariz., 1989, Williamsburg Duke of Glouster Show, 1984, Albert Einstein Med. Ctr., N.Y.C., 1987, Seltzer Gallery, represented in pvt. collections Albi-France, 1986, Leo House, N.Y.C., 1986-87, Shanti-AIDS Home, Phoenix, Ariz., 1988, Unipas Gallery, N.Y.C., 1991. Recipient Silver medal Salon D'Automne, Albi, France, 1986; scholar Am. Theatre Wing, 1954-58. Mem. Am. Fedn. Musicians. Avocations: cantor and organist with church, sailing, biking.

TODD, ALDEN, writer, editor; b. Washington, Jan. 12, 1918; s. Laurence and Constance Davis (Leupp) T.; m. Jean Goldman, Apr. 20, 1941 (dec. Mar. 1988); children: Paul, Philip. Diploma, Phillips Exeter Acad., 1935; BA, Swarthmore Coll., 1939. Tchr. Friends Sch., Wilmington, Del., 1940-42; outside machinist Sun Shipbuilding Co., Chester, Pa., 1942-43; news reporter Federated Press, Washington, 1946-50, 55-56; freelance writer Washington and N.Y.C., 1956-67; editor, publs. dir. Deloitte Haskins & Sells, N.Y.C., 1968-83; adj. prof. NYU, N.Y.C., 1966-86; lectr., N.Y.C. and L.A., 1970-82. Author: (books) Abandoned, 1961, Justice on Trial, 1964 (Gavel award ABA 1965), A Spark Lighted in Portland, 1966, Richard Montgomery, Rebel of 1775, 1967, Finding Facts Fast, 1972, 79: co-author: (book) Favorite Subjects in Western Art, 1968; contbr. articles to popular mags., also book revs. Bd. dirs. Friends of the Libr., Anchorage, 1996—; active Anchorage Libr. Adv. Bd., 1998—. Cpl. U.S. Army, 1943-46. Mem. Am. Soc. Journalists & Authors, 101st Airborne Divsn. Assn., Alaska Soc. Mayflower Desc. (treas. 1997-98), Phi Beta Kappa. Avocations: research and research methods, correspondence. Home: 1303 H St Anchorage AK 99501

TODD, CATHERINE JACKSON, writer; b. L.A., Jan. 31, 1947; d. Hubert Edward and Carolyn Arden (Laws) Jackson; m. Timothy Gordon Todd, Aug. 24, 1968. AB cum laude, Occidental Coll., 1968; MA, Stanford U., 1969. Cert. tchr., Calif. Tchr. English, French Sequoia Union H.S., Redwood City, Calif., 1968-73, Country Day Sch., San José, Costa Rica, 1970-72; tchr. English Grossmont Union H.S., La Mesa, Calif., 1991-93; bus. svcs. writer San Diego, 1993—. Author: Bond of Honor, 1981, Marian, 1991, (as Elizabeth Jackson) A Brilliant Alliance, 1993, (as Elizabeth Jackson) Galatea's Revenge, 1993, (as Elizabeth Jackson) Rogue's Delight, 1995, Making Waves, 1997, Staying Cool, 1997; contbr. articles to profl. jours. Mem. Authors Guild, Romance Writers Am., Phi Beta Kappa. E-mail: CathETodd@aol.com. Home: 6027 Adobe Falls Rd San Diego CA 92120-4626

TODD, FRANCES EILEEN, pediatrics nurse; b. Hawthorne, Calif., Aug. 20, 1950; d. James Clark and Jean Eleanor (McGinty) Nailen; m. Steven Charles Todd, Oct. 25, 1975; 1 child, Amanda Kathryn. ASN, El Camino Jr. Coll., 1974; BSN, Calif. State Coll., Long Beach, 1982, postgrad. RN, Calif.; cert. pub. health nurse, Calif.; cert. PNP; cert. provider pediat. advanced life support, Am. Heart Assn. Nursing attendant St. Earne's Nursing Home, Inglewood, Calif., 1973; clinic nurse I Harbor-UCLA Med. Ctr., Torrance, Calif., 1974-77, evening shift relief charge nurse, clinic nurse II, 1977-85, pediatric liaison nurse, 1984-90, pediatric nurse practitioner, 1985—; steward Local Union 660, 1995—; tutor Compton (Calif.) C.C., 1988, clin. instr., 1987-88; lectr. faculty dept. pediatrics UCLA Sch. Medicine, 1980—; lectr. in field. Co-author: Judges and Stewards Handbook, 1992; contbr. articles to profl. jours. Past co-chairperson parent support group Sherrie's Schs., Lomita, Calif. Mem. Nat. Assn. Pediat. Nurse Assocs. and Practitioners, L.A. Pediat. Soc., Emergency Nurses Assn., Local 660 (shop steward), Svc. Employees Int. Union, local 660 (union steward), Peruvian Paso Horse Registry N.Am. (co-chair judge's accreditation com. 1989-98, judge's Andalusian horses). Avocations: Peruvian Paso horses, orchids, jewelery design. Office: Harbor UCLA Med Ctr 1000 W Carson St Torrance CA 90502-2004

TODD, HAROLD WADE, association executive, retired air force officer; b. Chgo., Jan. 17, 1938; s. Harold Wade and Jeanne (Fayal) T.; m. Wendy Yvonne Kendrick, July 12, 1981; children by previous marriage: Hellen J. Wilson, Kenneth J., Stephen D., Joseph M., Michelle M. Adams, Mark A.; stepchildren: Jamie Y. White, James K. Mills, Timothy S. Emerson. BS, U.S. Air Force Acad., 1959; grad., Nat. War Coll., 1975. Commd. 2d lt. U.S. Air Force, 1959, advanced through grades to maj. gen., 1982; aide to comdr. (2d Air Force (SAC)), Barksdale AFB, La., 1970-71; exec. aide to comdr.-in-chief U.S. Air Forces Europe, Germany, 1971-74; spl. asst. chief of staff USAF, 1975-76; chief Concept Devel. Div., 1976-77, chief Readiness and NATO Staff Group, Hdqrs. USAF, 1977-78; exec. asst. to chmn. Joint Chiefs Staff Washington, 1978-80; comdr. 25th region N. Am. Aerospace Def. Command McChord AFB, Wash., 1980-82; chief staff 4th Allied Tactical Air Force Heidelberg, 1982-85; commandant Air War Coll., 1985-89; vice comdr. Air U., 1985-89, ret., 1989; ind. cons. Colorado Springs, Colo., 1989-95; pres., CEO, Nat. Stroke Assn., Englewood, Colo., 1995—. Founder, pres. Bossier City (La.) chpt. Nat. Assn. for Children with Learning Disabilities, 1970-71. Decorated Def. D.S.M., Air Force D.S.M. (2), Legion of Merit (2), D.F.C., Air medal (8), Air Force Commendation medal. Mem. Air Force Assn., USAF Acad. Assn. Grads., Nat. War Coll. Alumni Assn. Home: 1250 Big Valley Dr Colorado Springs CO 80919-1015*

TODD, MICHAEL CULLEN, sculptor, painter; b. Omaha, June 20, 1935; s. Patrick Cullen and Helen Lorraine (Round) T.; m. Kathryn Asako Doi, June 16, 1974 (div. 1986); 1 child, Mia Doi; m. Patricia Ann Alexakis, Nov. 29, 1986. B.F.A. magna cum laude, U. Notre Dame, 1957; M.A., UCLA, 1959. Exhbns., in Paris, London, N.Y.C., Boston, Detroit, Los Angeles, Washington and San Diego, 1960—; represented in permanent collections, Whitney Mus., Los Angeles County Mus. Art, La Jolla Mus., San Diego, Oakland (Calif.) Mus., Norton Simon Mus., Pasadena, Calif., Met. Mus. Art, N.Y., Hirshhorn Mus., Washington. (Woodrow Wilson fellow 1957-59, Fulbright fellow 1961-63, recipient award Nat. Endowment Arts 1974-75). Address: 2817 Clearwater St Los Angeles CA 90039-2807

TODD, RICHARD EMERSON, administrator; b. Owosso, Mich., Jan. 21, 1942; s. George Evans and Hazel Elaine (Harris) T. AA, Mott C.C., 1963; BS, Western Mich. U., 1965, MA, 1971. Tchr. visual arts Kalamazoo (Mich.) Pub. Schs., 1966-87; prof. visual arts San Diego Mesa Coll., 1987-91, San Diego City Coll., 1991-95; coord. pub./cultural arts City of Chula Vista (Calif.), 1996—; architecture design Fashion Inst. Design & Mdse., San Diego, 1988-92; art cons. San Diego Unified Schs., 1987-91; chair person Calif. Assembly Local Art Agys./So. Calif.; bd. dirs. San Diego Black Film Festival, Gold Coast Classic for Black Colls. and Univs.; bd. cons. Calif. Ballet Co. Coro Found. fellow, San Diego, 1996. Mem. African Am. Mus. Fine Arts (bd. dirs., pres. 1994-97, co-chair 1997—). Office: City of Chula Vista 276 4th Ave Chula Vista CA 91910-2699

TODD, WILLIAM MICHAEL, counselor, educator; b. Dayton, Ohio, Jan. 4, 1957; s. J.T. and Bessie Kate (Lowe) T.; 1 child, Katie Janeese. BA in Psychology, Ottawa U., 1993, MA in Profl. Counseling, 1994. Cert. cmty. coll. tchr., 1995. Counselor Arrowstar Counseling, Phoenix, 1992—; prof. psychology Glendale (Ariz.) C.C., 1994; bus. owner Antique Market, MT Constrn., Arrowstar Cons., Phoenix, 1983—. Assoc. pastor Nazarene Ch., Phoenix, 1991-93, youth min., 1993; counselor Boys and Girls Club, Phoenix, 1993-94. Mem. Am. Counselors Assn., Am. Clin. Mental Health Assn., Marriage and Family Counseling Assn., Phi Theta Kappa. Home: 3507 E Windsor Ave Phoenix AZ 85008-1231 Office: Arrowstar Counseling 3520 E Indian School Rd Phoenix AZ 85018-5115

TODUS, GINA MARIE, filmmaker, media artist; b. L.A., Aug. 15, 1966; d. Harold Dean and Sheri Lynn (Krtek) T. BA, U. Calif., San Diego, 1989; MFA, Rutgers U., 1995. Prodn. technician Harvard U., Cambridge, Mass., 1989-92; tchg. asst. Rutgers U., New Brunswick, N.J., 1993-95; traffic coord. NYU, N.Y.C., 1995-96, programming coord., 1996-97. Dir., writer: (exptl. film) The Travelogue and Souvenirs, 1994; co-prodr.: (documentary) The Fat of the Land, 1995; co-prodr., dir. Truck Stop, 1999. Dodge fellow Internat. Film Seminar, 1997, N.J. Coun. on the Arts fellow, 1998; grantee Phila. Coun. on Arts, 1995, Ben & Jerry's Found., 1995. Mem. AIVF, IDA. Mem. Green Party. Avocations: travel, Asian studies and cinema, conversational Chinese.

TOEPPE, WILLIAM JOSEPH, JR., retired aerospace engineer; b. Buffton, Ohio, Feb. 27, 1931; s. William Joseph Sr. and Ruth May (Hipple) T. BSEE, Rose-Hulman Inst. Tech., Terre Haute, Ind., 1953. Engr. Electronics divsn. Ralph M. Parsons Co., Pasadena, Calif., 1953-55; pvt. practice cons. Orange, Calif., 1961-62; engring. supr. Lockheed Electronics Co., City of Commerce, Calif., 1962-64; staff engr. Interstate Electronics Corp., Anaheim, Calif., 1957-61; engring. supr. Interstate Electronics Corp., Anaheim, 1964-89, ret., 1989. Author: Finding Your German Village, 1990, Gazetteers and Maps of France for Genealogical Research, 1990, GGSA Library User's Guide, 1995, Sandusky County, Ohio, Births, Infant-Name Soundex Index, 1997. Pres. Golden Cir. Home Owners' Assn., Orange, 1989-95. With U. S. Army, 1955-57. Mem. Ohio Geneal. Soc. (life), So. Calif. Geneal. Soc., German Geneal. Soc. Am. (bd. dirs. 1993-97). Avocations: genealogy, music. Home: 700 E Taft Ave Apt 19 Orange CA 92865-4400

TOFTNESS, CECIL GILLMAN, lawyer, consultant; b. Glasgow, Mont., Sept. 13, 1920; s. Anton Bernt and Nettie (Pedersen) T.; m. Chloe Catherine Vincent, Sept. 8, 1951. AA, San Diego Jr. Coll., 1943; student, Purdue U., Northwestern U.; BS, UCLA, 1947; JD cum laude, Southwestern U., 1953. Bar: Calif. 1954, U.S. Dist. Ct. (so. dist.) Calif. 1954, U.S. Tax Ct. 1974, U.S. Supreme Ct. 1979. Pvt. rpactice palos Verdes Estates, Calif., 1954—; chmn. bd., pres., bd. dirs. Fishermen & Mchts. Bank, San Pedro, Calif., 1963-67; v.p., bd. dirs. Palos Verdes Estates Bd. Realtors, 1964-65; participant Soc. Expdn. through the Northwest Passaage. Chmn. cpaital campaign fund Richstone Charity, Hawthorne, Calif., 1983; commencement spkr. Glasgow H.S., 1981. Served to lt. (j.g.) USN, 1938-46, ETO, PTO, commdg. officer USS Ptormigon, 1941-45. Decorated Bronze Star; mem. Physicians for Prevention of Nuclear War which received Nobel Peace prize, 1987; named Man of Yr., Glasgow, 1984. Mem. South Bay Bar Assn., Southwestern Law Sch. Alumni Assn. (class rep. 1980—), Themis Soc.-Southwestern Law Sch., Schumacher Founders Cir.-Southwestern Law Sch. (charter), Kiwanis (sec.-treas. 1955-83, v.p., pres., bd. dirs.), Masons, KT. Democrat. Lutheran. Home: 2229 Via Acalones Palos Verdes Pen CA 90274 Office: 2516 Via Tejon Palos Verdes Estates CA 90274-6802

TOGNAZZINI, BRUCE, software designer, engineer; b. San Francisco, Mar. 26, 1945; s. Roland Erwin Tognazzini and Page Pashel (Pressley) Solomon; m. Julia Frances Moran, June 26, 1986; children: Joshua, Rebecca. CEO Carr Electronics Corp., San Francisco, 1967-78; software engr. Apple Computer Inc., Cupertino, Calif., 1978-92; disting. engr. Sun Microsys., Menlo Park, Calif., 1992-96; lead designer Heatheon Corp., Santa Clara, Calif., 1996—; mem. steering com. every-citizen interface com. NRC, Washington, 1995-97. Author: Tog on Interface, 1992, Tog on Software Design, 1996; patentee in field. Avocations: flying, scuba diving.

TOHILL, BRUCE OWEN, geologist; b. Chgo., Oct. 21, 1941; s. Kenneth Fay and Jane Fayette (Dickinson) T.; Mary Alice (Wieber) Tohill; children—Damon, Kevin, Brian. B.S., U. Nebr., 1964, M.S., 1965. Geologist, Humble Oil & Refining Co., Kingsville, Tex., 1965-67, Amoco Prodn. Co., Denver, 1967-72, Pubco Petroleum Corp., Denver, 1972-73; ptnr. Peppard & Assocs., Denver, 1973-83, Basin Analysis Cons., Denver, 1983-92, Tohill & Assocs., Inc., 1992—; mem. adv. bd. dept. geology U. Nebr., 1981-85. Contbr. articles to profl. jours. Recipient Disting. Svc. award dept. geology U. Nebr. Rocky Mountain Assn. Geologists. Mem. Calif. Explorationists Group (founder), Rocky Mountain Assn. Geologists, Am. Assn. Petroleum Geologists (chmn. ho. of dels. 1983-84), Soc. Econ. Paleontologists and Mineralogists (pres. sect. 1975), Am. Inst. Profl. Geologists (bd. dirs. 1977, v.p. 1979), U. Nebr. Alumni Club (pres. 1976), Masons, Shriners. Republican. Methodist. Home: 3327 W 114th Cir Unit B Westminster CO 80030-7113

TOKOFSKY, JERRY HERBERT, film producer; b. N.Y.C., Apr. 14, 1936; s. Julius H. and Rose (Trager) T.; m. Myrna Weinstein, Feb. 21, 1968 (div.); children: David, Peter; m. Fiammetta Bettuzzi, 1970 (div.); 1 child, Tatianna; m. Karen Oliver, Oct. 4, 1981. BS in Journalism, NYU, 1956, LLD, 1959. Talent agt. William Morris Agy., N.Y.C., 1953-59; v.p. William Morris Agy., L.A., 1959-64; exec. v.p. Columbia Pictures, L.A., 1964-69; v.p. Paramount Pictures, London, 1970; exec. v.p. MGM, London, 1971; pres. Jerry Tokofsky Prodns., L.A., 1972-82; exec. v.p. Zupnik Enterprises, L.A., 1982-92; pres. Jerry Tokofsky Entertainment, Encino, Calif., 1992—; prof. Sch. TV and Film U. So. Calif. Sch. Bus. Prodr. films: Where's Poppa, 1971, Born to Win, 1972, Dreamscape, 1985, Fear City, 1986, Wildfire, 1988, Glengarry Glen Ross, 1992, The Grass Harp, 1995, American Buffalo, 1995, Double Down, 1997, Life on Mars, 1997, God's Anvil and Out on My Feet, 1997, Alibi Store, 1998, Virgin, 1998. With U.S. Army, 1959, res. 1959-63. Named Man of Yr. B'nai B'rith, 1981; recipient L.A. Resolution City of L.A., 1981. Mem. Variety Club Internat. Avocations: skiing, tennis, golf, chess.

TOLAND, FLORENCE WINIFRED, printing company executive, retired business educator; b. Paola, Kans., Aug. 6, 1906; d. Frederick W. and Bertha G. (Cartwright) Arzberger; BA, U. Ariz., 1935, MS in Bus. Adminstrn., 1946; m. Jess William Toland, Dec. 23, 1934 (dec. 1954); 1 child, Ronald William. Tchr. grade sch., Dos Cabezos, Willcox and Mascot, Ariz., 1925-32, jr. high and high sch., 1934-36, 38-42, amphitheater sch., Tucson; asst. prof. U. Ariz., Tucson, 1942-71, asst. prof. emeritus, 1971—; cons., semi-ret.. Mem. Ariz. Bus. Educators Assn. (life), Nat. Bus. Educators Assn., Western Bus. Educators Assn., Order Ea. Star, Pi Omega Pi, Pi Lambda Theta. Democrat. Co-author: Transcription Method Shorthand, 1946. Home: 5461 N Paseo Espejo Tucson AZ 85718-5229 Office: 110 S Park Ave Tucson AZ 85719-5746

TOLANEY, MURLI, environmental engineering executive; b. 1941. BS in Civil Engring., U. Kans., MS in Environ. Engring. Jr. engr. Coun. Sci. and Indsl. Resources, New Delhi, 1963-66; project engr. L.A. County Sanitary Dist., 1966-70; with Montgomery Watson Assn., Pasadena, Calif., 1970—, now pres., CEO. Office: Montgomery Watson Ams 300 N Lake Ave Fl 12 Pasadena CA 91101-4109*

TOLBERT, BETH WILLDEN, real estate company owner, broker; b. Delta, Utah, Apr. 7, 1935; d. Delbert B. and Mildred (Twitchell) Willden; m. Stanley Tolbert, May 12, 1955; children: Keven, Tracy, Troy. Student, Brigham Young U., 1953-54. Cert. residential specialist. Realtor Harding Realty, Am. Fork, Utah, 1976-82; associate broker Pine Valley Realty, Alpine, Utah, 1982-97; prin., owner Beth Tolbert Realty Group, St. George, Utah, 1997—. Apptd. Utah Real Estate Commn., Salt Lake City, 1993—, chair 1993-94; bd. trustees Utah Valley State Coll., Orem, 1991—, chair 1996-97; pres. Nat. Womens Coun. Realtors, 1994. Recipient Realtor of Yr. award Utah Assoc. Realtors, 1984, Distinguished Svc. award 1994, Realtor of Yr. award Utah County Bd. Realtors, 1984. Home: 1825 W Mathis Park Pl 45 Saint George UT 84770

TOLDANES, RONI DE JESUS, journalist; b. Manila, Philippines, Sept. 29, 1963; s. Vicente and Lourdes (De Jesus) T. BSBA, Tarlac State U., 1982; LLB, Ateneo de Manila U., 1985. Polit. reporter Malaya, Manila, 1983-84; mng. editor Asahi Shimbun, Tokyo, 1984-89; chief editor Agencia EFE, Madrid, Spain, 1989-94; editor-in-chief Philippine Times, L.A., 1995-96, Herald, L.A., 1995-96; editor GunGames Mag., Moreno Valley, Calif., 1996—; editl. cons. Diario Veritas, San Diego, 1998—; contbg. editor The Press Enterprise, San Diego, 1998—. Named journalist of yr. Pamana Awards, L.A., 1997, Hollywood Celebrity Shoot, Burbank, Calif., 1998, writer of yr. World Fast Draw Assn., 1998. Mem. Fgn. Corr. Assn., Nat. Press Club, Assn. Filipino Journalists. Roman Catholic.

TOLENTINO, CASIMIRO URBANO, lawyer; b. Manila, May 18, 1949; came to U.S., 1959; s. Lucio Rubio and Florence (Jose) T.; m. Jennifer Masculino, June 5, 1982; 2 children: Casimiro Masculino, Cristina Cecelia Masculino. BA in Zoology, UCLA, 1972, JD, 1975. Bar: Calif. 1976. Gen. counsel civil rights div. HEW, Washington, 1975-76; regional atty. Agrl. Labor Relations Bd., Fresno, Calif., 1976-78; regional dir. Sacramento and San Diego, 1978-81; regional atty. Pub. Employment Relations Bd., Los Angeles, 1981; counsel, west div. Writers Guild Am., Los Angeles, 1982-84; dir. legal affairs Embassy TV, Los Angeles, 1984-86; sole practice Los Angeles, 1986-87; mediator Ctr. Dispute Resolution, Santa Monica, Calif., 1986-87; asst. chief counsel Dept. of Fair Employment and Housing, State of Calif., 1986-92, adminstrv. law judge dept. social svcs., 1992—. Editor: Letters in Exile, 1976; contbr. articles and revs. to Amerasia Jour. Chmn. adv. bd. UCLA Asian Am. Studies Ctr., 1983-90; chmn. bd. Asian Pacific Legal Ctr., L.A., 1983-93 (Decade award); pres. bd. civil svc. commrs. City of L.A., 1984-85, 90-93; bd. dirs. met. region United Way, 1987-95; bd. dirs. Rebuild L.A., 1992-97; mem. Asian-Pacific Am. adv. coun. L.A. Police Commn., 1995-97; mem. adv. coun. L.A. Children's Scholarship Fund, 1998—. Mem. Nat. Asian-Am. Legal Consortium (bd. dirs. 1991—), State Bar Calif. (exec. com. labor law sect. 1985-88), Los Angeles County Bar Assn., Minority Bar Assn. (sec. 1984-85), Philippine Lawyers of So. Calif. (pres. 1984-87, Award of Merit 1982). Democrat. Roman Catholic. Avocations: history, photography, travel.

TOLES, GEORGE EDWARD, JR., marketing communications executive; b. Memphis, Jan. 9, 1939; s. George Edward and Annie Jane (Arnold) T.; m. Elizabeth Claire Wyngarden, Aug. 25, 1961; children: Anne Elizabeth Stanczak, Laura Jane Hinkley, Andrew John. BA in Speech, Wheaton (Ill.) Coll., 1961; M of T.V., U. Ill., 1962. Announcer, newscaster, program dir. various radio stas., Mich. and Wash., 1964-70; creative dir., acct. exec. Sta. KJR-AM, Seattle, 1970-73; gen. mgr. Kaye-Smith Prodns., Seattle, 1974; acct. exec. Sta. KISW-FM, Seattle, 1974-75; owner The Toles Co., Edmonds, Wash., 1975—; cleints include Seattle Internat. Auto Show, Olympic Boat Ctrs., John L. Scott Real Estate, others; pub. address announcer Detroit Pistons, 1965-67, Seattle Sonics, 1967-86. Chmn. exec. com. Pro Athletes Outreach, Issaquah, Wash., 1986—, bd. dirs., 1986—; mem. steering com. Sch. Bus. and Econ., Seattle Pacific U., 1988—, mem. Exec. Adv. Coun., 1988—; emcee city-wide mayor's and leadership prayer breakfasts, Seattle and Bellevue, 1977-93. 1st lt. Signal Corps, U.S. Army, 1962-64. Avocations: reading, public speaking.

TOLIVER, LEE, mechanical engineer; b. Wildhorse, Okla., Oct. 3, 1921; s. Clinton Leslie and Mary (O'Neall) T.; m. Barbara Anne O'Reilly, Jan. 24, 1942; children: Margaret Anne, Michael Edward. BSME, U. Okla., 1942. Registered profl. engr., Ohio. Engr. Douglas Aircraft Co., Santa Monica, Calif., 1942, Oklahoma City, 1942-44; engr. Los Alamos (N.Mex.) Sci. Lab., 1946; instr. mech. engring. Ohio State U., Columbus, 1946-47; engr. Sandia Nat. Labs., Albuquerque, 1947-82; instr. computer sci. and math. U. N.Mex., Valencia County, 1982-84; number theory researcher Belen, N.Mex., 1982—. Author: (computer manuals with G. Carli, AF. Schkade) Experience with an Intelligent Remote Batch Terminal, 1972; (with C.R. Borgman, T.I. Ristine) Transmitting Data from PDP-10 to Precision Graphics, 1973, Data Transmission-PDP-10/Sykes/Precision Graphics, 1975; Relations Between Prime and Relatively Prime Integers, 1998. With Manhattan Project (Atomic Bomb) U.S. Army, 1944-46. Mem. Math. Assn. Am., Am. Math. Soc. Achievements include devel. of 44 computer programs with manuals. Home: 206 Howell St Belen NM 87002-6225

TOLLETT, GLENNA BELLE, accountant, mobile home park operator; b. Graham, Ariz., Dec. 17, 1913; d. Charles Harry and Myrtle (Stapley) Spafford; m. John W. Tollett, Nov. 28, 1928; 1 child, Jackie J., 1 adopted child, Beverly Mae Malgren. Bus. cert., Lamson Coll. Office mgr. Hurley Meat Packing Co., Phoenix, 1938-42; co-owner, sec., treas. A.B.C. Enterprises, Inc., Seattle, 1942—; ptnr. Bella Investment Co., Seattle, 1962—, Four Square Investment Co., Seattle, 1969—, Warehouses Ltd., Seattle, 1970—, Tri State Partnership, Wash., Idaho, Tex., 1972—; pres. Halycon Mobile Home Park, Inc., Seattle, 1979—; co-owner, operator Martha Lake Mobile Home Park, Lynwood, Wash., 1962-73. Mem. com. Wash. Planning and Community Affairs Agy., Olympia, 1981-82, Wash. Mfg. Housing Assn. Relations Com., Olympia, 1980-84; appointed by Gov. Wash. to Mobile Home and RV Adv. Bd., 1973-79. Named to RV/Mobile Home Hall of Fame, 1980. Mem. Wash. Mobile Park Owners Assn. (legisl. chmn., lobbyist 1976-85, cons. 1984, pres. 1978-79, exec. dir. 1976-84, This is Your Life award 1979), Wash. Soc. of Assn. Execs. (Exec. Dir. Service award 1983), Mobile Home Old Timers Assn., Mobile Home Owners of Am. (sec. 1972-76, Appreciation award 1976), Nat Fire Protection Assn. (com. 1979-86), Aurora Pkwy. North C. of C.)sec. 1976-80), Fremont C. of C. Republican. Mormon. Avocations: needlework, gardening, fishing, swimming, trailering. Home: 18261 Springdale Ct NW Seattle WA 98177-3228 Office: ABC Enterprises Inc 3524 Stone Way N Seattle WA 98103-8924

TOLMAN, MARVIN NELSON, education educator; b. Salt Lake City, Mar. 3, 1939; s. Olester and Anna Urilla (Nelson) T.; m. Judy Harmon, June 8, 1963; children: Todd, Gregory, Valorie, Regina, Randy, Aaron. MEd, U. Utah, 1969; EdD, Utah State U., 1975. Tchg. prin. La Sal (Utah) Sch., 1964-66; tchr. grade 5 Peteetneet Sch., Payson, Utah, 1966-68; intern coord. Grant Sch., Springville, Utah, 1969-71; tchr. grade 3-5 Grant Sch., Springville, 1971-75; prof. elem. edn. Brigham Young U., Provo, Utah, 1975—; sci. insvc. provider Utah State Office of Edn., 1980—. Author: Hands on Earth Science Activities, 1995, Hands on Physical Science Activities, 1995, Discovering Elementary Science, 1995, Hands on Life Science Activities, 1996. Mem. Nat. Coun. Tchrs. Maths., Nat. Assn. Rsch. in Sci. Tchg., Nat. Sci. Tchrs. Assn., Internat. Assn. Sci. Educators, Utah Soc. Environ. Edn., Utah Sci. Tchrs. Assn. (bd. dirs. 1991-95, Outstanding Sci. Educator 1996), Utah Coun. Tchrs. of Maths., Utah Coun. Computers in Edn. (bd. dirs. 1990-92), Coun. Elem. Sci. Internat. Mem. LDS Ch. Office: Brigham Young U 210-F MCKB Provo UT 84602

TOM, CREIGHTON HARVEY, aerospace engineer, consultant; b. Oakland, Calif., Mar. 29, 1944; s. Harvey and Katherine (Lew) T. BS in Forestry, U. Calif., Berkeley, 1966; MS in Stats., Colo. State U., 1972, PhD in Computer Sci., 1978. Sr. environ. analyst HRB-Singer, Inc., Ft. Collins, Colo., 1977-78; staff scientist Sci. Applications, Golden, Colo., 1979-80; cons. Golden, 1981; scientist, specialist ConTel Info. Systems, Littleton, Colo., 1981-84; sr. staff engr. Hughes Aircraft Co., Aurora, Colo., 1984-91; shuttle astronaut cand. NASA, Houston, 1980; cons. to companies and schs. Contbr. articles to profl. jours. Adviser CAP, Golden, 1981—; mem. YMCA. Served to maj. U.S. Army, 1966-67, with Res. 1967—. Decorated Bronze Star and Air medals, U.S. Army, 1967. Mem. Am. Soc. Photogrammetry, AAAS, NRA, Mensa, Intertel, Sigma Xi, Xi Sigma Pi, Phi Kappa Phi. Republican. Methodist. Avocations: astronomy, popular and fiction writing, photography, sci. fiction, survivalism. Home: 4057 S Bannock St Englewood CO 80110-4603 Office: C&H Enterprises Littleton CO 80120-4432

TOM, LAWRENCE, engineering executive; b. L.A., Jan. 21, 1950; BS Harvey Mudd Coll., 1972; JD Western State U., San Diego, 1978; spl. diploma U. Calif., San Diego, 1991. Design engr. Rockwell Internat., L.A., 1972-73; design engr. BFGoodrich Aerospace (formerly Rohr, Inc.), Chula Vista, Calif., 1973-76, sr. design engr., 1980, computer graphics engring. specialist, 1980-83, chief engring. svs., 1989-91, chief engring. quality, 1991-93, project mgr., 1993-98, info. tech. specialist, 1998—; sr. engr. Rohr Marine, Inc., Chula Vista, 1977-79; chief exec. officer Computer Aided Tech. Svcs., San Diego, 1983-87; software cons. Small Systems Software, San Diego, 1984-85; computer graphics engring. specialist TOM & ROMAN, San Diego, 1986-88; dir. Computervision Users Group, 1986-88, vice chmn. 1988-91, pres., 1991-93, exec. chmn., 1992-94, regional chmn., 1996—; bd. dirs. Exec. Program for Scientists and Engrs.-Alumni Assn. U. Calif., San Diego, 1991—; pres. Art to Art, San Diego, 1994—; cons. in field. George H. Mayr Found. scholar, 1971, Bates Found. Aero. Edn. scholar, 1970-72. Mem. Nat. Mgmt. Assn. (chpt. v.p.), Aircraft Owners and Pilots Assn., Infiniti Club. Office: 7770 Regents Rd Ste 113-190 San Diego CA 92122-1937

TOMAN, JIŘÍ, educator, institute director; b. Prague, Czechoslovakia, Nov. 5, 1938; s. Jaroslav and Eugenie (Pithard) T.; m. Jaroslava Bartoš-Wišata, Sept. 19, 1969; 1 child, Jaroslava. Diploma, Faculty Comparative Law, Luxembourg, 1964; JUDR, Charles U., Prague, 1966; PhD, U. Geneva, 1980, Grad. Inst. Internat. Studies, Geneva. Asst. prof. Sch. Econs., Prague, 1962-70; reader African Inst. Geneva, 1968-69, U. Geneva, 1973-98; rsch. dir. Henry Dunanat Inst., Geneva, 1969-92, dir., 1986-87, 92-98; prof. law Santa Clara (Calif.) U., 1998—; cons., assoc. econ. affairs officer UN Conf. on Trade and Devel., Geneva, 1968-69; cons. UN Disaster Relief Coord., Geneva, 1985-86, UN Human Rights Ctr., Geneva, 1986-88, UNESCO, Paris, 1983-88; founding mem. Internat. Ctr. Sociol., Penal and Penitentiary Studies, Messina; adminstr. Tory Ltd., Lepero Ltd., 1991—. Editor: The Laws of Armed Conflicts, 1973, 83, 88 (in English), 96 (in French), The Spirit of Uppsala, 1984, Protection of Cultural Property in the Event of Armed Conflicts, 1994 (in French), 1996 (in English). Named Academician Acad. Natural Scis. Fedn. Russia, Moscow, 1994. Mem. Am. Soc. Internat. Law, Inter-Am. Bar Assn. (co-chmn. internat. law com. 1985-87), Intercenter Intl. Ctr. for Sociological and Penitentiary Studies (bd. dirs.). Avocations: classical music, golf, protection of cultural property. Fax: 408-554-4426. E-mail: jtoman@scu.edu. Home: Rue des Pervenches 5, 1227 Geneva Switzerland Office: Santa Clara U Sch Law 500 El Camino Real Santa Clara CA 95050-4345

TOMASI, DONALD CHARLES, architect; b. Sacramento, Calif., Oct. 24, 1956; s. Thomas M. and Anita (Migliavacca) T.; m. Loretta Elaine Goveia, Feb. 1, 1986; children: Jeffrey, Genna, Michael. AB in Architecture with honors, U. Calif., Berkeley, 1979; MArch, U. Wash., 1982. Registered architect, Calif. Project mgr. Robert Wells and Assocs., Seattle, 1982-84, Milbrandt Architects, Seattle, 1984, T.M. Tomasi Architects, Santa Rosa, Calif., 1984-86; prin. Tomasi Architects, Santa Rosa, 1986-93, TLCD Architecture, Santa Rosa, 1993—. Grad. Leadership Santa Rosa, 1992; mem. design rev. com. Sonoma County, 1988-90; chmn. Santa Rosa Design Rev. Bd., 1990-97. Recipient Honor award Coalition for Adequate Sch. Housing, 1991, 93, 96, Merit award, 1991. Mem. AIA (chpt. bd. dirs. 1990-91, 98, v.p. 1999, Merit award 1986). Avocations: snow skiing, wine, travel.

TOMASSON, HELGI, dancer, choreographer, dance company executive; b. Reykjavik, Iceland, 1942; m. Marlene Rizzo, 1965; children: Kristinn, Erik. Student, Sigridur Arman, Erik Bidsted, Vera Volkova, Sch. Am. Ballet, Tivoli Pantomime Theatre, Copenhagen. With Joffrey Ballet, 1961-64; prin. dancer Harkness Ballet, 1964-70, N.Y.C. Ballet, 1970-85; artistic dir. San Francisco Ballet, 1985—, also dir. Debut with Tivoli Pantomime Theatre, 1958; created roles in A Season of Hell, 1967, Stages and Reflections, 1968, La Favorita, 1969, The Goldberg Variations, 1971, Symphony in Three Movements, 1972, Coppélia, 1974, Dybbuk Variations, 1974, Chansons Madecasses, 1975, Introduction and Allegro, 1975, Union Jack, 1976, Vienna Waltzes, 1977; choreographer Theme and Variations, Polonaise, Op. 65, 1982, Ballet d'Isoline, 1983, Menuetto (for N.Y.C. Ballet) 1984, Beads of Memory, 1985, Swan Lake, 1988, Handel-a Celebration, 1989, Sleeping Beauty, 1990, Romeo and Juliet, 1994, others. Decorated Knight Order of Falcon (Iceland), 1974, Comdr. Order of Falcon, 1990; recipient Silver medal Internat. Moscow Ballet Competition, 1969, Golden Plate award Am. Acad. Achievement, 1992, Dance Mag. award, 1992. Office: care San Francisco Ballet 455 Franklin St San Francisco CA 94102-4438*

TOMBRELLO, THOMAS ANTHONY, JR., physics educator, consultant; b. Austin, Tex., Sept. 20, 1936; s. Thomas Anthony and Jeanette Lilian (Marcuse) T.; m. Esther Ann Hall, May 30, 1957 (div. Jan. 1976); children: Christopher Thomas, Susan Elaine, Karen Elizabeth; m. Stephanie Carhart Merton, Jan. 15, 1977; 1 stepchild, Kerstin Arusha. BA in Physics, Rice U., 1958, MA, 1960, PhD, 1961; doctoral degree (hon.), Uppsala U., 1997. Rsch. fellow in physics Calif. Inst. Tech., Pasadena, 1961-62, 64-65, asst. prof. physics, 1965-67, assoc. prof., 1967-71, prof., 1971—, tech. assessment officer, 1996—, William R. Kenan Jr. prof., 1997—, chair divsn. physics, math. and astronomy, 1998—; asst. prof. Yale U., New Haven, 1963; cons. in field; disting. vis. prof. U. Calif.-Davis, 1984; v.p., dir. rsch. Schlumberger-Doll Rsch., Ridgefield, Conn., 1987-89; mem. U.S. V.P.'s Space Policy Adv. Bd., 1992; mem. sci. adv. bd. Ctr. of Nanoscale Sci. and Technology, Rice U., 1995—; mem. tech. adv. bd. Internat. Isotopes, Inc.; bd. dirs. Schlumberger Tech. Corp., Schlumberger Found. Assoc. editor Nuc. Physics, 1971-91, Applications of Nuc. Physics, 1980—, Radiation Effects, 1985-88, Nuc. Instruments and Methods B, 1993—. Recipient Alexander von Humboldt award von Humboldt Stiftung, U. Frankfurt, Germany, 1984-85; named Disting. Alumnus, Rice U., 1998; NSF fellow Calif. Inst. Tech. 1961-62; A.P. Sloan fellow, 1971-73. Fellow Am. Phys. Soc.; mem. AAAS, Materials Rsch. Soc., Phi Beta Kappa, Sigma Xi, Delta Phi Alpha. Avocations: reading, jogging. Democrat. Office: Calif Inst Tech Dept Physics Mail Code 91125 Pasadena CA 91125

TOMICH-BOLOGNESI, VERA, educator; b. L.A.; d. Peter S. and Yovanka (Ivanovich) T.; m. Gino Bolognesi, July 12, 1969. AA, John Muir Jr. Coll., Pasadena, Calif., 1951; BA in Polit. Sci., UCLA, 1953, MEd, 1955, EdD, 1960. Cert. secondary tchr., Calif., cert. secondary sch. adminstrn., Calif.; cert. jr. coll. tchr., Calif. Tchg. asst. dept. edn. UCLA, 1956; tchr., dept. chmn. Culver City (Calif.) Unified Sch. Dist., 1956-91; rschr., writer U.S. Dept. Edn., Washington, 1961, del. to Yugoslavia, 1965; co-owner, exec. Metrocolor Engring., San Gabriel, Calif., 1973—; cons., Continental Culture Specialists, Inc., Glendale, Calif., 1985-92; rsch. asst. Law Firm of Driscoll & Tomich, San Marino, Calif., 1989—. Author: Education in Yugoslavia and the New Reform, 1963, Higher Education and Teacher Training in Yugoslavia, 1967; screenplay editor 1996—. Bd. trustees St. Sava Serbian Orthodox Ch., San Gabriel, 1975-95, mem., 1960—. Recipient Episcopal Gramata, Serbian Orthodox Ch. of Western Am., 1996; named in Outstanding Young Women of Am., 1966. Mem. NEA (life), Calif. Tchrs. Assn., UCLA Alumni Assn., Alpha Gamma Sigma, Pi Lambda Theta. Home: 100 E Roses Rd San Gabriel CA 91775 Office: Metrocolor Engring 5110 Walnut Grove Ave San Gabriel CA 91776

TOMKIEL, JUDITH IRENE, small business owner; b. St. Louis, Nov. 4, 1949; d. Melvin Charles William and Mildred Neva (Kayhart) Linders; m. William George Tomkiel, Dec. 15, 1972; children: Soteara, William, Kimberli, Jennifer, Christopher. Order filler Baker & Taylor Co., Sommerville, N.J., 1972-74; owner, founder The Idea Shoppe, Garden Grove, 1983-90; seamstress, crafts person Cloth World, Anaheim, Calif., 1987-89; mgr. S.M.T. Dental Lab., San Clemente, Calif., 1990-94, pres., 1994—; Vol. Reading Is Fundamental Program, Garden Grove, 1988-89; freedom writer Amnesty Internat., Garden Grove, 1988-91. Author numerous poems; pub., editor (newsletter) Shoppe Talk, 1987-90; pub. Fakatale, 1988. Fellow World Literary Acad.; mem. NAFE, Nat. Writer's Club, Soc. Scholarly Pub., Dental Lab Owners Assn. (pres. S.M.T. Dental Lab., Inc. 1994). Avocations: sewing, writing, music, printing, gardening.

TOMLINSON, WILLIAM M., lawyer; b. Paris, France, Sept. 2, 1948. BA, Princeton U., 1970; JD, U. Oreg., 1974. Bar: Oreg. 1974, Wash. 1986. Atty. Lindsay, Hart, Neil & Weigler, Portland, Oreg. Mem. ABA (mem. torts and ins. practice sect.), Oreg. State Bar, Oreg. Assn. Def. Counsel, Wash. State Bar Assn., Multnomah County Bar Assn. Office: Lindsay Hart Neil & Weigler 1300 SW 5th Ave Ste 3400 Portland OR 97201-5640

TOMOMATSU, HIDEO, chemist; b. Tokyo, June 8, 1929; came to U.S., 1959; s. Shinsai Nasu and Suma T.; m. Yuko Ito, Nov. 12, 1967; 1 child, Tadao. *Hideo's father, the 16th superior of Saigan-ji Buddhist Temple in Tokyo is the second son of Shin-ei Nasu, the 25th Superior of Jigan-ji Temple in Tochigi Prefecture which was founded in 1223 AD by his ancestor, Priest Shingan, one of the twenty four disciples of Holy Priest Shinran. Priest Shingan was, before his conversion, a warrior named Sukemura Nasu, a second cousin of Yoichi Nasu, the mostfamous archer in Japanese history who established his fame in 1185 AD in the Yashima Naval Battle of the Gen-Pei War. Hideo's mother is a daughter of a superior of Gon-nen-ji Temple in Tokyo. Hideo is a rare non-priest professional among his relatives.* BSChemE., Waseda U., 1952; MS in Chemistry, U. of the Pacific, 1960; PhD in Chemistry, Ohio State U., 1964. Registered profl. engr., Tex., U.S. patent agt. Chem. Hodogaya Chem. Co., Tokyo, 1952-59, Texaco Chems. Co., Austin, Tex., 1964-72; Quaker fellow Quaker Oats Co., Barrington, Ill., 1972-96; cons. Functional Food Resources, Inc., Escondido, Calif., 1996—. *Hideo is an executive research scientist with recognized expertise in the field of nutraceutical foods, especially physiologically functional oligosaccharides. His prior achievements include discoveries of a natural sweetener fifty times sweeter than sucrose, methods to synthesize brilliantly colored new food pigments, a method to calculate final water activity of a food mixture, a method to produce a slab of synthetic adipose, a new method producing flavored rice or pasta, catalytic systems yielding high polymers from cyclic ethers, and a process yielding furan dialdehyde, and structure determination of heparin in part.* Contbr. articles to profl. jours.; patentee in field. Mem. Am. Chem. Soc., Am. Assn. Cereal Chemists, Inst. Food Technologists. Home: 2555 Seascape Gln Escondido CA 92026-3862

TOMPKINS, ROBERT WALTER, retired civil engineer; b. Phila., June 21, 1924; s. Walter Clair and Loraine Alberta (Hoffman) T.; m. Hedwig Berta Reiss Kafer, May 9, 1953 (wid. Nov. 1987); children: Helmut Kafer, Herta Kafer Cooper, Waltraud Kafer Glaab, Lily Tompkins Payton, Heidi Tompkins Ruby Orley; m. Shirley Diane Harrison Statham, Oct. 6, 1992. Supervisory civil engr. Corps of Engrs., Phila., 1954-60; supervisory gen. engr. Base Civil Engr. AF, Elmendorf AFB, Alaska, 1960-67, 67-74; draftsman Dowl Engrs., Anchorage, 1976. Author: (booklet) Bridge for Six, 1989; author various board games. With U.S. Army, 1943-46, ETO. Mem. Am. Legion. Conservative Ind. Avocations: game designing, golf, softball, collecting coins, stamps, flags and other items, dancing. Home: 2440 Nancy Cir Anchorage AK 99516

TOMS, MICHAEL ANTHONY, broadcast journalist, editor, writer, producer; b. Washington, June 7, 1940; s. Austin Herman Toms and Margaret Dorothy (Pitcher) Slavinsky; m. Justine Willis, Dec. 16, 1972; children: Michael Anthony, Robert Welch. Student, U. Miami, 1959-60, U. Va. Extension, 1961-63; postgrad., Calif. Inst. Integral Studies, San Francisco, 1973-75; DrTheology, Sem. St. Basil the Great, Sydney, Australia, 1981; DHL (hon.), U. Humanistic Studies, San Diego, 1983. Field govt. rep. VariTyper Corp., Washington, 1960-64; sales mgr. VariTyper Corp., San Francisco, 1964-67; regional sales mgr. VariTyper Corp., San Bernardino, 1967-68; pres. Creative Mktg. Assocs., San Francisco, 1968-73; chmn. bd. The Response Mktg. Group, San Francisco, 1971-73; CEO Michael A. Toms & Assocs., San Francisco, 1973-76; pres. New Dimensions Found., San Francisco, 1973—; sr. acquisitions editor Harper Collins, San Francisco, 1989-95; exec. prodr., host nat. pub. radio interview series New Dimensions, 1980—; chmn. bd. emeritus Calif. Inst. Integral Studies, San Francisco, 1979-83; exec. dir. Audio Inds., Inc., San Francisco, 1981-83; adj. prof. Marylhurst Coll. Grad. Sch. of Bus., 1993—, Union Grad. Sch., 1994—; founder, CEO New Dimensions Broadcasting Network, 1994—; exec. editor New Dimensions Book Series, 1993—; mem. bd. dirs. KQED, Inc., San Francisco, 1980-83, Green Earth Found., 1989—, KZYX-FM, Mendocino County, Calif., 1989-91; mem. bd. adv. The Great Round, 1989—. Author: Worlds Beyond, 1978, The New Healers, 1980, An Open Life, 1988, At The Leading Edge, 1991. Mem. Task Force to Promote Self Esteem and Personal and Social Responsibility, Mendocino County, Calif., 1988-89; mem. internat. adv. bd. Radio for Peace Internat.; bd. dirs. Human Potential Audio Found., 1994-97; mem. adv. bd. New Road Map Found., 1991—. Mem. Internat. Assn. for Socially Responsible Radio (founding dir. 1991—). Avocations: travel, writing, reading. Home: PO Box 1029 Ukiah CA 95482-1029 Office: New Dimensions Found PO Box 569 Ukiah CA 95482-0569

TONELLO-STUART, ENRICA MARIA, political economist; b. Monza, Italy; d. Alessandro P. and Maddalena M. (Marangoni) Tonello; m. Albert E. Smith; m. Charles L. Stuart. BA in Internat. Affairs, Econs., U. Colo., 1961; MA, Claremont Grad. Sch., 1966, PhD, 1971. Sales mgr. Met. Life Ins. Co., 1974-79; pres., CEO, ETS R&D, Inc., Palos Verdes Peninsula, Calif., 1977—; dean internat. studies program Union U., L.A. and Tokyo; lectr. internat. affairs and mktg. UCLA Ext., Union U. Pub., editor Tomorrow Outline Jour., 1963—, The Monitor, 1988; pub. World Regionalism-An Ecological Analysis, 1971, A Proposal for the Reorganization of the United Nations, 1966, The Persuasion Technocracy, Its Forms, Techniques and Potentials, 1966, The Role of the Multinationals in the Emerging Globalism, 1978; developed the theory of social ecology and econsociometry. Organizer 1st family assistance program Langley FB Tactical Air Command, 1956-58. Recipient vol. svc. award VA, 1956-58, ARC svc. award, 1950-58. Mem. Corp. Planners Assn. (treas. 1974-79), Investigative Reporters and Editors, World Future Soc. (pres. 1974-75), Asian Bus. League, Soc. Environ. Journalists, Chinese Am. Assn. (life), Japan Am. Assn., L.A. World Trade Ctr., Palos Verdes C. of C. (legis. com.), L.A. Press Club (bd. dirs.), Zonta (chmn. internat. com. South Bay), Pi Sigma Alpha. Avocations: writing, collecting old books and maps, community service, travel.

TONG, CHILING, trade and commerce administrator; b. Taipei, Taiwan, Mar. 19, 1958; d. Ping Tong and Shin-Mei Shui; m. Joel Szabat. BA in English Lit., Chinese Cultural U., Taipei, 1981; MBA, Calif. State U., Long Beach, 1985-87. Dir. pub. affairs Am. Chinese Bus., L.A., 1988-89; employer rep. Employment Devel. Dept., Sacramento, 1989-92, comt. rels. profl., 1992-94; dir. Calif. Office in Taipei, 1994—; asst. sec. Trade & Commerce, Sacramento, 1998. Pub., (newsletter) CA Connection, 1994—, transl., Crown Book, 1988. Commr. Sacramento Arts Commn., 1994; chairperson L.A. County Comty. Action Bd., 1992; v.p. Comty. Rels. Commn., Monterey Park, Calif., 1991; bd. dirs. El Sereno (Calif.) Luther Day Care Ctr., 1988. Named Hon. Treas., Miss. State, 1995; recipient Outstanding Women award YWCA, 1993, Outstanding Svcs. award, 1992, Outstanding Achievement award Monte Jade Sci., 1997; fellow CORO Found., 1984—. Mem. Global Fedn. of Chinese Bus. Women, Am. State Office Assn. (v.p. 1995—), Friends of Calif. Assn. (hon. chmn. 1995—), Am. C. of C. in Taipei, Rotary Club Taiwan, Taiwan's Srs. Jaycee Club. Lutheran. Office: Calif Office Trade/Investment, 5 Hsin Yi Rd Sect 5, Taipei 110, Taiwan

TONG, RICHARD DARE, anesthesiologist; b. Chgo., Oct. 20, 1930; s. George Dare and June (Jung) T.; student U. Calif., Berkeley, 1949-52; MD, U. Calif., Irvine, 1956. m. Diane Helene Davies, Apr. 12, 1970; children: Erin, Jason; m. Deanna Johnson, Jan. 5, 1993; stepchildren: Jeffery Johnson, Ryan Johnson. Intern, Phoenix Gen. Hosp., 1956-57; resident in anesthesiology UCLA, 1965-67; pvt. practice, Lakewood, Calif., 1967—; clin. instr. UCLA Sch. Medicine, 1968—. Dep. sheriff reserve med. emergency team, L.A. County. With USNR, 1947-53. Diplomate Am. Bd. Anesthesiology. Fellow Am. Coll. Anesthesiology; mem. Am. Soc. Anesthesiologists, AMA, Calif. Med. Assn., L.A. County Med. Assns. Office: PO Box 1131 Lakewood CA 90714-1131

TONG, SIU WING, computer programmer; b. Hong Kong, May 20, 1950; came to U.S., 1968; BA, U. Calif., Berkeley, 1972; PhD, Harvard U., 1979; MS, U. Lowell, 1984. Research assoc. Brookhaven Nat. Lab., Upton, N.Y., 1979-83; software engr. Honeywell Info. Systems, Billerica, Mass., 1984-85; sr. programmer, analyst Hui Computer Cons., Berkeley, Calif., 1985-88; sr. v.p. devel., chief fin. officer Surgicenter Info. Systems, Inc., Orinda, Calif., 1989-94; sr. sys. specialist Info. Sys. Divsn. Contra Costa County Health Svcs., Martinez, Calif., 1995-97; info. tech. supr. Info. Sys. Divsn. Contra Costa County Health Svcs., Martinez, 1997—. Vol. tchr. Boston Chinatown Saturday Adult Edn. Program of Tufts Med. Sch., 1977-79. Muscular Dystrophy Assn. fellow, 1980-82. Mem. AAAS, IEEE, Assn. Computing Machinery, N.Y. Acad. Scis. Home: 17 Beaconsfield Ct Orinda CA 94563-4203 Office: Contra Costa County Health Svcs 595 Center Ave Ste 210 Martinez CA 94553-4634

TONG, THEODORE G., pharmacy educator, dean; b. La Jolla, Calif., Oct. 8, 1942; s. Raymond and Guey Kay (Dear) T.; m. Esther D. Lee, June 29, 1968. BS, U. So. Calif., 1964, Oreg. State U., 1965; DPharm, U. Calif., 1969; postgrad., Harvard Inst., 1990. Diplomate Am. Bd. Applied Toxicology; lic. pharmacist, Ariz., Calif. From clin. instr. to assoc. clin. prof. U. Calif. Sch. Pharmacy, San Francisco, 1969-82, prof., 1982—; assoc. dean Coll. Pharmacy U. Ariz., Tucson, 1987—; exec. dir. Ariz. Poison Control Sys., Tucson, 1984—; mem. non prescription durgs adv. com. FDA/DHHS, Rockville, Md., 1994—, adv. panel substance abuse and clin. toxicology U.S. Pharmacopeia, Rockville, 1990—. Contbr. 29 chpts. to books, 52 articles to profl. jours. Recipient Disting. Leadership Dr. Martin Luther King Jr. Ctr. U. Ariz., 1992, Outstanding Faculty Asian Am. Faculty Staff Alumni Assn. U. Ariz., 1994. Fellow Am. Acad. Clin. Toxicology (trustee 1997—); mem. Am. Pharm. Assn. (chair-elect clin. sci. sect. acad. pharm. rsch. and sci. 1996—), Am. Coll. Clin. Pharmacy, Am. Assn. Poison Control Ctrs., Am. Assn. Colls. Pharmacy. Office: U Ariz Coll Pharmacy 1703 E Mabel St Tucson AZ 85719

TONINI, LEON RICHARD, sales professional; b. Pittsfield, Mass., May 16, 1931; s. John Richard and Mabel Grayce (Rushbrook) T.; B.A. in Mgmt., U. Md., 1951; m. Helen Jo, Aug. 15, 1966; 1 son, John Richard, II. Enlisted in U.S. Army, 1947, advanced through grades to master sgt., 1968; service in W.Ger., Korea and Vietnam; ret., 1974; dir. vets. employment and assistance Non-Commd. Officers Assn., San Antonio, 1974-75; supr. security Pinkerton's Inc., Dallas, 1975-78; gen. mgr. civic center Travelodge Motor Hotel and Restaurant, San Francisco, 1978-85; sales representative Vernon Co., 1985—. Chmn. San Francisco Vets. Employment Com., 1981. Served as sgt. maj. Calif. N.G., res. Decorated Bronze Star; Republic Vietnam Honor medal 2d class. Mem. San Francisco Hotel Assn. (dir.), Non-Commd. Officers Assn. (dir. Calif. chpt.), Am. Legion, Regular Vets. Assn. (nat. sr. vice comdr.), Amvets, Patrons of Husbandry. Republican. Baptist. Club: Masons. Home and Office: 205 Collins St Apt 9 San Francisco CA 94118-3429

TONJES, MARIAN JEANNETTE BENTON, education educator; b. Rockville Center, N.Y., Feb. 16, 1929; d. Millard Warren and Felicia E. (Tyler) Benton; m. Charles F. Tonjes (div. 1965); children: Jeffrey Charles, Kenneth Warren. BA, U. N.Mex., 1951, cert., 1966, MA, 1969; EdD, U. Miami, 1975. Dir. recreation Stuyvesant Town Housing Project, N.Y.C., 1951-53; tchr. music., phys. edn. Sunset Mesa Day Sch., Albuquerque, 1953-54; tchr. remedial reading Zia Elem. Sch., Albuquerque, 1965-67; tchr. secondary devel. reading Rio Grande High Sch., Albuquerque, 1967-69; rsch. asst. reading Southwestern Coop. Ednl. Lab., Albuquerque, 1969-71; assoc. dir., vis. instr. Fla. Ctr. Tchr. Tng. Materials U. Miami, 1971-72; asst. prof. U.S. Internat. U., San Diego, 1972-75; prof. edn. Western Wash. U., Bellingham, 1975-94, prof. emerita, 1994—; dir. summer study at Oriel Coll. Oxford (Eng.) U., 1979-94; adj. prof. U. N.Mex., Albuquerque, 1995—, reading supr. Manzanita Ctr., 1968; vis. prof. adult edn. Palomar (Calif.) Jr. Coll., 1974; vis. prof. U. Guam, Mangilao, 1989-90; spkr., cons. in field; invited guest Russian Reading Assn., Moscow, 1992. Author: (with Miles V. Zintz) Teaching Reading/Thinking Study Skills in Content Classroom, 3rd edit., Secondary Reading, Writing and Learning, 1991, (with Ray Wolpow and Miles Zintz) Integrated Content Literacy, 1999, Secondary Reading, Writing and Learning, 1991; contbr. articles to profl. jours. Tng. Tchr. Trainers grantee, 1975; NDEA fellow Okla. State U., 1969. Mem. Am. Reading Forum (chmn. bd. dirs. 1983-85), Adult and Adolescent Literacy Confs. (spkr. 1991-94), Internat. Reading Assn. (mem. travel, interchange and study tours com. 1984-86, mem. non-print media and reading com. 1980-83, workshop dir. S.W. regional confs. 1982, mem. com. internat. devel. N.Am. 1991-96, Outstanding Tchr. Educator 1988-90), U.K. Reading Assn. (spkr. 1977-93), European Conf. in Reading (spkr. Berlin 1989, Edinburgh 1991, Malmo 1993, Budapest 1995), European Coun. Internat. Schs. (The Hague, spkr. 1993), World Congress in Reading Buenos Aires (spkr. 1994), PEO (past chpt. pres.), Nat. Coun. Tchrs. English, Internat. Reading Assn., Am. Reading Forum, Delta Delta Delta. Avocations: miniatures, tennis, bridge, art, travel.

TONJES, ROBERT ERNST, artist; b. Port Arthur, Tex., Apr. 13, 1937; s. Ernst and Rowena (Booraem) T.; m. Donna Jean, June 1963 (div. Sept. 1971); 1 child, Susan Lynn; m. Theresa, Aug. 25, 1987; 1 child, Robin Jean. AA, El Camino Coll., 1961; BFA, U. So. Calif., 1963. Advt. sales/layout The Richmond (Calif.) Ind., 1964-67; printing sales Jeffries Lithograph Co., L.A., 1967-70, Continental Graphics, L.A., 1970-75, Ealzer-Shopes Engraving, San Francisco, 1975-80; creative dir. Recreation Pubs., Alameda, Calif., 1980-82; printing sales mgr. Signature Press, Sacramento, Calif., 1982-92; picture framer Bob Tonjes Franes, Sacramento, Calif., 1992—; co-owner New Artworks Gallery, Fair Oaks, Calif., 1997. Represented in over 100 pvt. collections. With USNR, 1955-60. Mem. Calif. Art League (pres. 1996-97), Watercolor Artists (v.p. 1995). Avocations: sailing, swimming. Home and office: 2314 Knight Way Sacramento CA 95822-2828

TONN, ELVERNE MERYL, pediatric dentist, dental benefits consultant; b. Stockton, Calif., Dec. 10, 1929; s. Emanuel M. and Lorna Darlene (Bryant) T.; m. Ann G. Richardson, Oct. 28, 1951; children: James Edward, Susan Elaine Tonn Yee. AA, La Sierra U., Riverside, Calif., 1949; DDS, U. So. Calif., 1955; BS, Regents Coll., U. State N.Y., 1984. Lic. dentist; cert. tchr., Calif. Pediatric dentist, assoc. Walker Dental Group, Long Beach, Calif., 1957-59, Children's Dental Clinic, Sunnyvale, Calif., 1959-61; pediatric dentist in pvt. practice Mountain View, Calif., 1961-72; pediatric dentist, ptrn. Pediatric Dentistry Assocs., Los Altos, Calif., 1972-83; pediatric dentist, ptnr. Valley Oak Dental Group, Manteca, Calif., 1987—; from clin. instr. to assoc. prof. U. Pacific, San Francisco, 1964-84; assoc. prof. U. Calif., San Francisco, Calif., 1984-86; ; pediatric dental cons. Delta Dental Plan, San Francisco, 1985—; chief dental staff El Camino Hosp., Mountain View, 1964-65, 84-85; lectr. in field. Weekly columnist Manteca Bull., 1987-92; producer 2 teaching videos, 1986; contbr. articles to profl. jours. Lectr. to elem. students on dental health Manteca Unified Sch. Dist., 1982—; dental health screener Elem. Schs., San Joaquin County Pub. Health, 1989-90; dental cons. Interplast program Stanford U. Sch. Medicine. Capt. U.S.

Army, 1955-57. Fellow Internat. Coll. Dentists, Am. Acad. Pediatric Dentistry, Am. Coll. Dentists, Royal Soc. Health (Eng.), Acad. of Dentistry for Handicapped, Pierre Fauchard Acad., Acad. Dental Materials, Am. Soc. Dentistry for Children; mem. ADA, Internat. Assn. Pediatric Dentistry, Internat. Assn. Dental Rsch., Fedn. Dentaire Internationale, Am. Assn. Dental Cons., Calif. Dental Assn., Calif. Soc. Dentistry for Children (pres. 1968), Calif. Soc. Pediatric Dentists, N.Y. Acad. Scis., Calif. Acad. Sci., Rotary Internat., Am. Bd. Quality Assurance and Utilization Rev. Physicians (diplomate, cert. dental benefits cons.), Nat. Assn. for Healthcare Quality, Am. Coll. Med. Quality. Republican. Avocations: photography, travel, medieval history. Home: 374 Laurelwood Cir Manteca CA 95336-7122 Office: Valley Oak Dental Group Inc 1507 W Yosemite Ave Manteca CA 95337-5182

TONSING, CECILIA ANN DEGNAN, lay worker, foundation administrator; b. Washington, Apr. 20, 1943; d. Peter David and Elizabeth (Corcoran) Degnan; m. Michael John Tonsing, Jan. 29, 1966; children: Catherine Michele, Michael John Jr. BA, Holy Names Coll., Oakland, Calif., 1965; MPA, Calif. State U., Hayward, 1976. Tchr. Our Lady of Angels Cath. Ch., Claremont, Calif., 1966; instr. confirmation St. Perpetua's Cath. Ch., Lafayette, Calif., 1970-72; educator youth and family liturgy Corpus Christi Cath. Ch., Piedmont, Calif., 1981-83, eucharistic min., 1983—, reader, lector, 1985—; pres., chief exec. officer Providence Hosp. Found., Oakland, 1984-87, St. Luke's Hosp. Found., San Francisco, 1987—; mem. devel. com. Corpus Christi Sch., Piedmont, 1981-90; mem. fund raising com. Episc. Charities Appeal, San Francisco, 1989-91. Chmn. Calif. Heritage Preservation Commn., Sacramento, 1984—; trustee Calif. State Archives Found., Sacramento, 1986—; vol., trainer Girl Scouts U.S., N.Y.C., 1989—. Fellow Nat. Assn. Hosp. Devel.; mem. Nat. Soc. Fund Raising Execs. (cert.), Nat. Com. on Planned Giving, No. Calif. Planned Giving Coun., Claremont Country Club, Women's Athletic Club, Lakeview Club. Republican. Roman Catholic. Home: 911 Longridge Rd Oakland CA 94610-2444 Office: St Lukes Hosp Found 3555 Army St San Francisco CA 94110-4403

TOOKEY, ROBERT CLARENCE, consulting actuary; b. Santa Monica, Calif., Mar. 21, 1925; s. Clarence Hall and Minerva Maconachie (Anderson) T.; BS, Calif. Inst. Tech., 1945; MS, U. Mich., 1947; m. Marcia Louise Hickman, Sept. 15, 1956; children: John Hall, Jennifer Louise, Thomas Anderson. With Prudential Ins. Co. Am., Newark, 1947-49; assoc. actuary in group Pacific Mut. Life Ins. Co., Los Angeles, 1949-55; asst. v.p. in charge reins. sales and service for 17 western states Lincoln Nat. Life Ins. Co., Ft. Wayne, Ind., 1955-61; dir. actuarial services Peat, Marwick, Mitchell & Co., Chgo., 1961-63; mng. prin. So. Calif. office Milliman & Robertson, cons. actuaries, Pasadena, 1963-76; pres. Robert Tookey Assos., Inc., 1977—. Committeeman troop 501 Boy Scouts Am., 1969-72. Served to lt. (j.g.) USNR, 1943-45, 51-52. Fellow Soc. Actuaries, Conf. Consulting Actuaries; mem. Am. Acad. Actuaries, Pacific Ins. Conf., Rotary Club (Pasadena), Union League Club (Chgo.). Home and Office: PO Box 646 La Canada CA 91012-0646

TOOLEY, CHARLES FREDERICK, communications executive, consultant; b. Seattle, Sept. 29, 1947; s. Creath Athol and Catherine Ella (Wainman) T.; m. Valerie Adele Gose, Mar. 7, 1981 (dec. Feb. 1991); children: Paige Arlene Chytka, Marni Higdon Tooley; m. Joan Marie Stapleton, Feb. 21, 1998. BA, Lynchburg Coll., 1968. Producer, stage mgr., tech. dir. various theatre cos. and performing arts orgns., 1965-74; field underwriter N.Y. Life Ins. Co., Billings, Mont., 1974-77; market administr. Mountain Bell Telephone Co., Butte and Billings, Mont., 1978-83; pres. BCC Inc., Billings, Mont., 1983—. Active Mont. Arts Coun., 1982-92, Billings/Yellowstone County Centennial, 1981-82, Mont. Cultural Advocacy, 1982-92; bd. dirs. Yellowstone 89ers, 1987-89, Christian Chs. in Mont., 1983—, divsn. of overseas ministries Christian Ch. Disciples of Christ, 1997 ; elder Ctrl. Christian Ch., Billings, 1983—, chmn. trustees, 1983-85; mem. Mont. Dem. Exec. Bd., 1982-87; mem. adv. bd. Salvation Army, Billings, 1984—; del. Dem. Nat. Conv., 1980; Dem. candidate Mont. Ho. of Reps., 1986; mem. Billings City Coun., 1988-94, mayor pro tem, 1992-94; mayor City of Billings, 1996—; mem. Common Global Missions Bd., 1997—. Sgt. U.S. Army, 1969-72, Vietnam. Mem. Billings Coun. Fgn. Rels., Toastmasters (Div. Gov.'s Cup 1978), Kiwanis (bd. dirs. 1981-88), Masons, Shriners, Elks. Mem. Disciples of Christ. Avocations: theatre productions.

TOPE, DWIGHT HAROLD, retired management consultant; b. Grand Junction, Colo., Aug. 29, 1918; s. Richard E. and Elizabeth (Jones) T.; m. Carolyn Stagg, Apr. 29, 1949; children: Stephen R., Chris L. AS, Mesa Coll., 1940; student, George Washington U. With Fgn. Funds Control, a Div. of U.S. Treasury Dept.; staff adjuster Fire Cos. Adjustment Bur., Denver, Albuquerque, 1946-48; br. mgr. Gen. Adjustment Bur., Deming, N.Mex., 1948-50; spl. agt. Cliff Kealey State Agy., Albuquerque, 1950-56; pres. Dwight Tope State Agy., Inc., Albuquerque, 1956-84; with Fgn. Funds Control divsn. U.S. Dept. Treasury, Albuquerque; sr. cons. Dwight Tope State Agy., Inc., Albuquerque, 1985 87. Life mem. adv. bd. Salvation Army, Albuquerque, 1974—, Meals on Wheels, 1987-97; life mem. bd. dirs., past chmn. bd., pres. Presbyn. Heart Inst., Albuquerque, 1977-94. Maj. Coast Arty. Anti-Aircraft, 1941-45. Mem. N.Mex. Ins. Assn. (past chmn.), Ins. Info. Inst. (past chmn.), N.Mex. Surplus Lines Assn. (past pres.), Air Force Assn., Assn. of U.S. Army, Am. Legion, Albuquerque C. of C. (mil. rels. com.), Rotary, Masons, Shriners, Albuquerque Country Club, Petroleum Club. Republican. Avocations: boating, fishing, hunting. Home: 1812 Stanford Dr NE Albuquerque NM 87106-2538 Office: 8100 Mountain Rd NE Ste 204E Albuquerque NM 87110-7833

TOPILOW, CARL S., symphony conductor; b. Jersey City, N.J., Mar. 14, 1947; s. Jacob Topilow and Pearl (Roth) Topilow Josephs; m. Shirley; 1 child, Jenny Michelle. B.Mus., Manhattan Sch. of Mus., 1968, M.Mus., 1969. Exxon/Arts Endowment Condr. Denver Symphony Orch., 1976-79, asst. condr., 1979-80; mus. dir. Denver Chamber Orch., 1976-81, Denver Youth Orch., 1977-80, Grand Junction Symphony, Colo., 1977-80, Nat. Repertory Orch., Breckenridge, Colo., 1978—; dir. orchs. Cleve. Inst. Mus., 1981—, condr. Summit Brass 1986—, Cleve. Pops Orch., 1995—. Recipient Conducting fellowship Nat. Orch. Assn., N.Y.C., 1972-75, Aspen Mus. Festival, Colo., 1976; winner 1st place Balt. Symphony Conducting Competition, Md., 1976. Office: Cleve Inst of Music 11021 East Blvd Cleveland OH 44106*

TOPJON, ANN JOHNSON, librarian; b. Los Angeles, Dec. 2, 1940; d. Carl Burdett and Margaret Elizabeth (Tildesley) Johnson; m. Gary M. Topjon, 1963; children: Gregory Eric and Cynthia Elizabeth (twins); m. Philip M. O'Brien, 1990. BA, Occidental Coll., 1962; MLS, UCLA, 1963. Reference asst. Whittier (Calif.) Pub. Libr., 1973-78; pub. svc. and reference libr. Whittier Coll., 1981—. Author (bibliography) Carl Larsson, 1992 (portions also published in catalogs). Faculty rsch. grantee Whittier Coll., 1987-88, 91-92, 95-96; grantee The Am.-Scandinavian Found., N.Y., 1991. Mem. Calif. Acad. and Rsch. Librs. (liaison at Whittier Coll. 1990—), AAUW (Whittier br. 1968-77, Brea-La Habra br., Calif. 1977—, chmn. lit. group, 1977—, chmn. scholarship fund raising 1988-89). Office: Whittier Coll Wardman Libr 7031 Founders Rd Whittier CA 90608

TOPP, ALPHONSO AXEL, JR., environmental scientist, consultant; b. Indpls., Oct. 15, 1920; s. Alphonso Axel and Emilia (Karlsson) T.; m. Mary Catherine Virtue, July 7, 1942; children: Karen, Susan, Linda, Sylvia, Peter, Astrid, Heidi, Eric, Megan, Katrina. BS in Chem. Engring., Purdue U., 1942; MS, UCLA, 1948. Commd. 2d lt. U.S. Army, 1942, advanced through grades to col., 1966, ret., 1970; environ. scientist Radiation Protection Sect., State of N.Mex., Santa Fe, 1970, program mgr., licensing and registration sect., 1978, chief radiation protection bur., 1981-83; cons., 1984—. Decorated Legion of Merit, Bronze Star with 2 oak leaf clusters. Mem. Rotary, Sigma Xi. Republican. Presbyterian. Home and Office: 872 Highland Dr Los Osos CA 93402-3902

TOPSY-ELVORD, DORIS LOUISE, municipal official; b. Vicksburg, Miss., June 17, 1931; d. Clyde Julius Walker and Mary Lee Rose; m. Urlee Topsy, Apr. 5, 1953; children: Gerald, Stanley, Stephen; m. Ralph Elvord, Dec. 29, 1984. BA in Social Welfare, Calif. State U., 1969; MA in Criminal Justice, Chapman Coll., 1981. Group supr. Calif. Youth Authority, 1956-59; procurement officer L.A. County Sheriff's Dept., 1961-66, recreation leader, 1966-69, dep. probation officer, 1969-88, civil svc. commr., 1988-92; mem. City Coun., Long Beach, Calif., 1992—; vice Mayor City of Long Beach, 1996—; v.p. Long Beach Unified Sch. Dist. Pers. Commn., 1991-92. Bd. dirs. Pacific Hosp., Long Beach, 1991—, NCCJ, 1993—, NAACP; active Nat. Black Caucas, 1992—. Recipient Outstanding award McCobb Boys Home, 1984, Spl. award Dorothy Brown Sch., 1986. Mem. Nat. Coun. Negro Women, Eta Phi Beta (v.p. Kappa chpt. 1984-86, pres. 1986-88, Soror of Yr. 1982). Avocations: travel, reading. Home: 2373 Olive Ave Long Beach CA 90806-3236 Office: 333 W Ocean Blvd Fl 14 Long Beach CA 90802-4604

TORBET, LAURA, author, artist, photographer, graphic designer; b. Paterson, N.J., Aug. 23, 1942; d. Earl Buchanan and Ruth Claire (Ehlers) Robbins; BA, BFA, Ohio Wesleyan U., 1964; m. Bruce J. Torbet, Sept. 9, 1967 (div. 1971); m. Peter H. Morrison, June 19, 1983 (dec. Nov. 1988); m. Salam Habibi, Aug. 23, 1995. Mng. editor Suburban Life mag., East Orange, N.J., 1964-65; asst. public relations dir. United Funds N.J., Newark, 1965-67; art dir. Alitalia Airlines, N.Y.C., 1967-69; propr. Laura Torbet Studio, N.Y.C., 1969-84; author: Macrame You Can Wear, 1972, Clothing Liberation, 1973, Leathercraft You Can Wear, 1975, The T-Shirt Book, 1976, The Complete Book of Skateboarding, 1976, How To Do Everything With Markers, 1977; (with Doug McLaggan) Squash: How to Play, How to Win, 1977; The Complete Book of Mopeds, 1978; (with Luree Nicholson) How to Fight Fair With Your Kids...and Win!, 1980; editor: Helena Rubenstein's Book of the Sun, 1979, The Encyclopedia of Crafts, 1980; (with George Bach) A Time for Caring, 1983, The Innter Enemy, 1983; (with Hap Hatton) Helpful Hints for Hard Times, 1982, The Virgin Homeowners Handbook, 1984, Helpful Hints for Better Living, 1984; (with James Braly) Dr. Braly's Optimum Health Program, 1985; (with Bernard Gittelson) Intangible Evidence, 1987; (as writer for Harville Hendrix) Keeping the Love You Find, 1992, The Couples Companion, 1994, The Personal Companion, 1996; editor, ghost writer, co-author books. Pres., bd. dirs. The Living/Dying Project. Mem. Boss Ladies. Home and Office: 1111 Butterfield Rd San Anselmo CA 94960-1181

TORMEY, CARLOTTA ANN, artist; b. Oakland, Calif., Sept. 12, 1947; d. Arthur Joseph Tormey and Sheila Theresa (Doyle) Weems; m. Mark Walter Greenfeldt, Jan. 10, 1969 (div. June 1983); 1 child, Michael Donovan. Student, Laney Jr. Coll., Calif. State U., Hayward. Illustrator, layout artist, art dir. Liberty House Dept. Store, Oakland, 1972-83; illustrator, designer Compendium, San Francisco, 1983-87; illustrator, designer, art dir. Mühlhaüser & Young, San Francisco, 1987-91; fashion illustrator, instr. Acad. Art, San Francisco, 1984-85; illustrator, designer, art dir. Carlotta Tormey/Illustration Sta., Oakland, 1992—. Author, illustrator fairy tale calendar, 1988, 93, 94. Recipient 4 ANDY awards, 1985. Mem. Graphic Artist Guild, San Francisco Soc. Illustrators. Avocations: art history, photography, theatrical performance, fencing, biking.

TORRES, ART, state senator; b. L.A.; children: Joaquin, Danielle. AA, East L.A. C.C.; BA, U. Calif., Santa Cruz; JD, U. Calif. John F. Kennedy teaching fellow Harvard U.; senator State of Calif., L.A.; chmn. Senate Com. Ins., Claims and Corps., Assembly Health Com., Senate Toxics and Pub. Safety Mgmt. Com., Select Com. Pacific Rim, Senate Spl. Rask Force on New L.A.; founder Calif. EPA; sr. mem. Senate Edn. Com.; author 1992 Immigrant Workforce Preparation Act; mem. Nat. Conf. State Legislatures Coalition on Immigration, Senate Appropriations Com., Senate Energy and Pub. Utilities Com., Senate Govtl. Orgn. Com., Senate Judiciary Com., Senate Natural Resources Com., Senate Transp. Com., chmn. California Dem. Party. Mem. Coun. Fgn. Rels., N.Y., Nat. Commn. Internat. Migration and Econ. Devel.; participant IVth Nobel Prizewinners Meeting Nova Spes Internat. Found., Vatican, Rome, 1989—. Recipient Legislator of Yr. award Calif. Orgn. Policy and Sheriffs, 1990, Outstanding Legislator of Yr. award Calif. Sch. Bd. Assn., 1990, Outstanding Alumnus award U. Calif. Santa Cruz, Dreamer award Boys and Girls Club Am., 1990, Achievement award Latin Am. Law Enforcement Assn., 1992. Office: 911 20th St Sacramento CA 95814-3115*

TORRES, BARBARA WOOD, technical services professional; b. Coudersport, Pa., Sept. 18, 1945; d. Ken and Myrna (Nelson) Wood; m. James Torres, July 3, 1965; children: James C. II, William D. BS in Physics, U. N.Mex., 1969, MS in Physics, 1972. Mem. staff EG&G, Albuquerque, 1972-76, Mission Rsch. Corp., Albuquerque, 1977-78; from staff mem. to v.p. test engring. TRW (formerly BDM Internat.), Albuquerque, 1978—; dir. test engring. TWR (formerly BDM Internat.), Albuquerque, 1998—; mem. N.Mex. State Sci. and Tech. Commn., 1983-86; mem. com. NEWTEC Joint Venture, N.Mex., 1998—. Mem. adv. bd. N.Mex. Comprehensive Regional Ctr. for Minorities, 1993-96; judge N.Me. Regional and State Sci. Fair, 1986-96; bd. dirs. M.Mex. Network for Women in Sci., Albuquerque, 1988-92. Recipient Gov. award for Outstanding N.Mex. Women, 1988; named Outstanding Grad., Rio Grande H.S., 1995. Mem. Am. Phys. Soc., Am. Bus. Women's Assn. (nat. sec. 1996-97, dist. v.p. 1995-96, One of Top 10 Bus. Women, 1982), Internat. Test and Evaluation Assn., Internat. Electronic and Elec. Engrs. Avocations: travel, mystery and spy novels, walking. Home: PO Box 478 Tijeras NM 87059 Office: TRW 6001 Indian Sch NE Albuquerque NM 87110

TORRES, ESTEBAN EDWARD, congressman, business executive; b. Miami, Ariz., Jan. 27, 1930; s. Esteban Torres and Rena Baron (Gomez) T.; m. Arcy Sanchez, Jan. 22, 1955; children: Carmen D'Arcy, Rena Denise, Camille Bianca, Selina Andre, Esteban Adrian. Student, East Los Angeles Coll., 1960, Calif. State U., Los Angeles, 1963, U. Md., 1965, Am. U., 1966; PhD (hon.), Nat. U., 1987. Chief steward United Auto Workers, local 230, 1954-63, dir. polit. com., 1963; organizer, internat. rep. United Auto Workers (local 230), Washington, 1964; asst. dir. Internat. Affairs Dept., 1975-77; dir. Inter-Am. Bureau for Latin Am., Caribbean, 1965-67; exec. dir. E. Los Angeles Community Union (TELACU), 1967-74; U.S. ambassador to UNESCO, Paris, 1977-79; chmn. Geneva Grp., 1977-78; chmn. U.S. del. Gen. Conf., 1978; spl. asst. to pres. U.S., dir. White House Office Hispanic Affairs, 1979-81; mem. 98th-103rd Congresses from 34th Dist. Calif., 1983—, mem. appropriations com., subcom. fgn. ops., subcom. transp.; campaign coordinator Jerry Brown for Gov., 1974; Hispanic coordinator Los Angeles County campaign Jimmy Carter for Pres., 1976; mem. Sec. of State Adv. Group, 1979-81; v.p. Nat. Congress Community Econ. Devel., 1973-74; pres. Congress Mex.-Am. Unity, 1970-71, Los Angeles Plaza de la Raza Cultural Center, 1974; dir. Nat. Com. on Citizens Broadcasting, 1977; cons. U.S. Congress office of tech. assessment, 1976-77; del to U.S. Congress European Parliament meetings, 1984—; ofcl. congl. observer Geneva Arms Control Talks; chmn. Congl. Hispanic Caucus, 1987; speaker Wrights Del. to USSR, 1987; Dem. dep. Whip, 1990. Contbr. numerous articles to profl. jours. Co-chmn. Nat. Hispanic Dems., 1988—; chmn. Japan-Hispanic Inst. Inc.; bd. visitors Sch. Architecture U. Calif. at Los Angeles, 1971-73; bd. dirs. Los Angeles County Econ. Devel. Com., 1972-75, Internat. Devel. Conf., 1976-78; chmn. Congrl. Hispanic Caucus, 1985-86; pres. Plaza de la Raza Cultural Ctr., 1972-73; trustee Am. Coll. Paris, 1977-79. Served in AUS, 1949-53, ETO. Recipient Congrl. award Nat. Leadership award 1997. Mem. Americans for Dem. Action (exec. bd. 1975-77), VFW Post 6315, Pico Rivera, Calif., Am. Legion, Smithsonian Inst. (regent 1997—), S.W. Voter Inst. Office: Ho of Reps 2269 Rayburn HOB Washington DC 20515-0005

TORRES, RALPH CHON, minister; b. San José, Calif., Oct. 18, 1948; s. Chon Poncé and Dora (Grijalva) T.; m. Pamela Ellen Hansen, Mar. 6, 1971; children: Chon, Brita, Samuel, Sarah. BTh, L.I.F.E. Bible Coll., L.A., 1970. Ordained to ministry Internat. Ch. of the Foursquare Gospel, 1981. Missionary asst. Internat. Ch. of Foursquare Gospel, Mexicali, Mex., 1970; youth pastor Internat. Ch. of Foursquare Gospel, Redondo Beach, Calif., 1971-72, Pueblo, Colo., 1972-74; sr. pastor Internat. Ch. of Foursquare Gospel., Pasadena, Calif., 1984—; youth pastor Ch. on the Way, Van Nuys, Calif., 1975-84; asst., dir. children's camps, Jr. and Sr. High camps for So. Calif. Dist. Foursquare Chs., 1978—; tchr. L.I.F.E. Bible Coll., L.A., 1979-86; bd. dirs. Holy Ghost Repair Svc., Hollywood, Calif., Centrum of Hollywood, Christians in Govt., L.A., Camp Cedar Crest, Running Springs, Calif.; bd. dirs., speaker Mainstream Inc., Tacoma, 1978-83. Composer: Kids of the Kingdom, 1976. Mem. Prop. 98 Sch. Report Card Com., Pasadena, 1989-90; adv. com. Marshall Fundamental Sch., Pasadena, 1989-90, Pasadena Unified Sch. Dist., 1990—. Recipient commendation for svc. Mayor of Pasadena, 1990. Office: Pasadena Foursquare Ch 174 Harkness Ave Pasadena CA 91106-2007*

TORREZ, NAOMI ELIZABETH, editor, librarian; b. Scranton, Pa., July 3, 1939; d. Sterling E. and Naomi (Reynolds) Hess; m. Lupe F. Torrez, Dec. 23, 1961; children: Sterling Edward, Stanley Marshall. BA, U. Ariz., 1961; MA, U. Calif., Berkeley, 1964, MLS, 1970; DRE, Golden State Sch. Theology, Oakland, Calif., 1988; cert. in travel industry, Vista C.C., 1993. Libr. asst. Oakland Pub. Libr., 1966-67, U. Calif. Libr., Berkeley, 1967-70; tutor-couns. Sonoma State Hosp., Eldridge, Calif., 1973-77, libr. tech. asst., 1977-79; health scis. libr. Kaiser Hosp., Vallejo, Calif., 1979-87; copyright rev. editor, med. libr. Kaiser Dept. Med. Editing, Oakland, 1987—; past instr. Bay Cities Bible Inst., Oakland; mem. faculty Golden State Sch. Theology, Oakland, 1984—; participant Statewide Latino Congress, 1994. Author: Not in My Pew, 1990, GSST Research Manual, 1990; contbr. to Co-op Low Cost Cookbook, 1965. Active Albany 75th Anniversary Com., 1983, Women's Health Initiative, 1995—; officer Ariz. Fedn. of the Blind, Calif. Coun. of the Blind, 1959-66; bd. dirs. Castilleja del Arroyo Home Owners Assn. Woodrow Wilson fellow, 1961; Nat. Merit scholar, 1957-61. Mem. Kaiser Permanente Latino Assn., Kaiser Affirmative Action Com., Kaiser Health Edn. Com., K.P. Regional Librs. Group (chair 1988), Phi Beta Kappa, Phi Kappa Phi. Baptist. Home: 1009 Murrieta Blvd Apt 15 Livermore CA 94550-4134 Office: Kaiser Dept Med Editing 1800 Harrison St Fl 16 Oakland CA 94612-3429

TORRISI, RALPH JOSEPH, labor union executive; b. Lawrence, Mass., Feb. 29, 1932; s. Sebastiano Edward and Nellie Marie (Laudani) T.; m. Mary Esperanza Guillen, June 26, 1954; children: Debra Ann Marie Torrisi Negrete, Denise Marie Bernadette Torrisi Nuno. Pres. Teamsters #296, San Jose, Calif., 1965-80, sec., treas., CEO, 1980—; sec., treas. Teamster Joint Coun. # 7, San Francisco, 1974—; mem. policy com. Western Conf. Teamsters, 1983-94. Mem. adv. bd. Santa Clara County Sheriff's Dept., San Jose, 1981—, reserve dep., 1994—; bd. dirs. State Compensation Ins. Fund, San Francisco, 1985—; trustee numerous pension and health trusts, 1972—. Sgt. USAF, 1951-55. Named Labor Man of Yr., Bay Area Union Labor Party, 1995. Mem. Calif. State Sheriffs' Assn. (charter), KC (various offices, award 1974), Capitol Club of Silicon Valley (charter). Democrat. Roman Catholic. Avocations: antique firearms, golf, western art, watches, pool. Office: Teamsters Local Union # 296 1165 Park Ave Ste 201 San Jose CA 95126-2922

TOSO, NORMAN EREC, English language educator; b. Sierra Vista, Ariz., Aug. 20, 1956; s. Norman Conrad and Phyllis Marlene (Peterson) T.; m. Margaret Lynn Schrag, July 10, 1987; children: Aaron Kyle, Sean Conrad. BA, U. Wis., 1980; MA, U. Ariz., 1987, PhD, 1996. ESL tchr. Colegio Americano, Quito, Ecuador, 1985-86; rsch. assoc. U. Ariz., Tucson, 1986-87; tchg. assoc. U. Ariz., 1988-95; English tchr. Tucson H.S., 1987-88, Tucson Unified-U. H.S., 1990; English instr. Ariz. State U., Tempe, 1995-98, English lectr., 1998; sr. lectr. U. Ariz., Tucson, 1998—. Author essays, poems. Bd. dirs. El Presidio Hist. Dist. adv. bd., Tucson, 1989-93. Mem. NCTE, Ariz. English Tchrs. Assn. Avocations: cycling, running, cmty. bldg.

TOSTI, DONALD THOMAS, psychologist, consultant; b. Kansas City, Mo., Dec. 6, 1935; s. Joseph T. Tosti and Elizabeth M. (Parsons) Tosti Addison; m. Carol J. Curless, Jan. 31, 1957 (dec. 1980); children: Rene, Alicia, Roxanna, Brett, Tabitha, Todd Marcus; m. Annette Brewer, Dec. 29, 1989. BS in Elec. Engring., U. N. Mex., 1957, MS in Psychology, 1962, PhD in Psychology, 1967. Chief editor Teaching Machines Inc., Albuquerque, 1960-64; div. mgr. Westinghouse Learning Corp., Albuquerque, 1964-70; founder, sr. v.p. Ind. Learning Systems, San Raphael, Calif., 1970-74, pres., 1974-76; chmn. bd. Omega Performance, San Francisco, 1976-77; pres. Operants Inc., San Rafael, 1978-81; v.p. Forum corp., San Rafael, 1981-83; mng ptnr. Vanguard Cons. Group, San Francisco, 1983—. Author: Basic Electricity, Advanced Algebra, Fundamentals of Calculus, TMI Programmed Series, 1960-63; Behavior Technology, 1970; A Guide to Child Development; Tactics of Communication; co-author: Learning Is Getting Easier, 1973; Introductory Psychology, 1981, Usibility Factors in Hardware and Software Design, 1982, Comparative Usibility, 1983, Performance Based Management, Positive Leadership, 1986, Strategic Alliances, 1990, The Professional Manager, 1995, Power and Governance, 1996, Global Fluency, 1999. Mem. APA, Internat. Soc. for Performance Improvement (v.p. rsch. 1983-85, treas. 1997—, Outstanding Mem. award 1984, Life Membership award 1984, Outstanding Product award 1974). Home: 41 Marinita Ave San Rafael CA 94901-3443

TOTH, J., engineering executive, consultant; b. Honolulu, Apr. 11, 1971; s. Andrew and Shirley (Yoshimura) T. BSEE, U. Hawaii, 1994. Dir. FCCC, Honolulu, 1986-89; cons. Strategic Info. Solutions, Inc., Honolulu, 1990-94, prin., 1994-96; v.p. engring. JMCS, Inc., Honolulu, 1996—; bd. dirs. Daedalus Corp., Honolulu, IDIC, Inc., Honolulu, JMCS, Inc., Net Enterprise, Inc. Mem. supervisory com. ARC, Honolulu, 1992—, chair, 1994-97, chair quality assurance com., 1999—, mem. health and safety svcs. bd., 1994-97, 99—; mem. Instr. Trainer edn. cadre, 1993—. Mem. IEEE, Internet Soc. Office: JMCS Inc 1088 Bishop St Ste 609 Honolulu HI 96813-3116

TOUCH, JOSEPH DEAN, computer scientist, educator; b. Bristol, Pa., Apr. 20, 1963; s. Ralph Benjamin and Filomena (Cianfrani) T. BS in Biophysics and Computer Sci., U. Scranton, 1985; MS in Computer Sci., Cornell U., 1987; PhD in Computer Sci., U. Pa., 1992. Cons., indsl. undergrad. rsch. participation program student GTE Labs., Inc., Waltham, Mass., 1983-85; cons. The Software Engring. Inst., Pitts., 1986; rsch. asst. Cornell U., Ithaca, N.Y., 1985-87; cons. Bell Comm. Rsch., Morristown, N.J., 1987-88; grad. rsch. fellow, AT&T Bell Labs. Rsch. assistantship U. Pa., Phila., 1988-92; cons. NASA Goddard Space Flight Ctr., Greenbelt, Md., 1992; computer scientist, project leader U. So. Calif. Info. Scis. Inst., Marina del Rey, Calif., 1992—; rsch. asst. prof. U. So. Calif., L.A., 1994—; mem. U. Scranton Acad. Computing Adv. Coun., 1983-85; univ. coun. com. on comm. U. Pa., 1989-90, com. on rsch. policy, 1990-91, acad. planning and budget com., 1990-91; reviewer various jours.; lectr. in field. Contbr. articles to profl. jours.; patentee in field. Mem. IEEE, Assn. for Computing Machinery (chpt. pres. 1984-85), IEEE Comm. Soc. (tech. program com. 1993), U. Scranton Phila. Alumni Soc. (v.p. 1990-91), Sigma Xi, Alpha Sigma Nu, Sigma Pi Sigma, Upsilon Pi Epsilon. Democrat. Roman Catholic. Avocations: rollerblading, volleyball, guitar, bicycling, sketching. Home: 14005 Palawan Way Ph 23 Marina Del Rey CA 90292 Office: USC Info Scis Inst 4676 Admiralty Way Marina Del Rey CA 90292

TOURTELLOTTE, WALLACE WILLIAM, neurologist, educator; b. Great Falls, Mont., Sept. 13, 1924; s. Nathaniel Mills and Frances Victoria (Charlton) T.; m. Jean Esther Toncray, Feb. 14, 1953; children: Wallace William, George Mills, James Millard, Warren Gerard. PhB, BS, U. Chgo., 1945, PhD, 1948, MD, 1951. Intern Strong Meml. Hosp. U. Rochester (N.Y.) Sch. Medicine and Dentistry, 1951-52; resident in neurology U. Mich. Med. Ctr., Ann Arbor, 1952-55, asst. prof. neurology, 1955-59, assoc. prof., 1959-66, prof., 1966-71; prof. UCLA, 1971—; prof. dept. neurology, 1996—; vis. assoc. prof. Washington U., St. Louis, 1963-64; mem. med. adv. bd. Nat. Multiple Sclerosis Soc., 1968—, So. Calif. Multiple Sclerosis Socs., 1972—; dir. Multiple Sclerosis Rsch. and Treatment Ctr., Nat. Neurol. Rsch. Specimen Bank, 1971—; vice chmn. dept. neurology UCLA, 1971-96; chief neurology svc. West L.A. VA Med. Ctr., 1971—, dir. tng. program, 1991—. Co-editor (with Cedric Raines, Henry McFarland): Multiple Sclerosis, Clinical and Pathogenetic Basis, 1997; mem. editorial bd. Jour. Neurol. Sci., Revue Neurologica, Italian Jour. Neurol. Sci., Multiple Sclerosis Jour. Lt. (j.g.) M.C., USNR, 1952-54. Recipient Disting. Alumni Service award U. Chgo., 1982. Fellow Am. Acad. Neurology (S. Weir Mitchell Neurology Reseach award 1959); mem. Am. Assn. Univ. Neurol. Prof., Am. Neurol. Assn. (counselor 1982—, v.p. 1992), World Fedn. Neurology (founding mem.), Am. Assn. Neuropathologists, Internat. Soc. Neurochemsitry (founding mem.), Am. Soc. Pharmacology and Exptl. Therapeutics, Am. Soc. Neurochemistry (founding mem.), Soc. Neurosci., Confrerie de la Chaine des Rotisseur, Argentier du Baillage de Los Angeles, Ordre Mondial des Gourmets Degustateurs Etats-Unis, Pasadena Wine and Food Soc., Physician Wine & Food Soc., Soc. Med. Friends of Wine, Sigma Xi. Republican. Presbyterian. Home: 1140 Tellem Dr Pacific Palisades CA 90272-2244 Office: West Los Angeles VA Med Ctr 11301 Wilshire Blvd Los Angeles CA 90073-1003

TOVAR, CAROLE L., real estate management administrator; b. Toppenish, Wash., May 19, 1940; d. Harold Max and Gertrude Louisa (Spicer) Smith;

m. Duane E. Clark, Aug. 1959 (div. 1963); 1 child, David Allen; m. Vance William Gribble, May 19, 1966 (div. 1989), m. Conrad T. Tovar, June 25, 1992. Student, Seattle Pacific Coll. Cert. profl. exec.; cert. profl. of occupancy. With B.F. Shearer, Seattle, 1950-60, Standard Oil, Seattle, 1960-62, Seattle Platen Co., 1962-70; ptnr. West Coast Platen, Los Angeles, 1970-87, Waldorf Towers Apts., Seattle, 1970—, Cascade Golf Course, North Bend, Wash., 1970-88; co-owner Pacific Wholesale Office Equipment, Seattle and L.A., 1972-87; owner Pacific Wholesale Office Equip., Seattle, L.A. and San Pablo, Calif., 1988-92, Pac Electronic Service Ctr., Commerce and San Pablo, Calif., 1988-90, Waldorf Mgmt. Co. dba Tovar Mgmt. Co., 1988—; Tovar Properties, 1993—. Mem. Nat. Ctr. Housing Mgmt. (cert. occupancy specialist), Assisted Housing Mgmt. Assn. (nat. cert., Wash. bd. dirs. 1995-96). Methodist. Avocations: genealogy, music, low income housing for seniors. Office: PO Box 13675 Mill Creek WA 98082-1675

TOVAR, NICHOLAS MARIO, mechanical engineer; b. Ogden, Utah, Jan. 18, 1960; s. Gerdo and Alice (Martinez) T.; m. Suzanne Oxborrow, Sept. 17, 1982; children: Ashley, Nicholas Brock, Clinton Gregory, Lance Edward, Marshall Prescott, Jarrett Stanley. BSME in Logistics Engring., Weber State U., 1986; BSME in Mech. Engring. and Mfg., Nat. U., 1990. Logistics contr. Utah-Idaho Supply Co., Salt Lake City, 1985-86; sr. manufacturing engr. Aerojet Propulsion div. GenCorp., Sacramento, 1986-93; sr. quality engr. BP Chems. Adv. Materials Divsn., Stockton, 1993-94; dir. quality engring. Indsl. Testing Internat., Lincoln, 1994-95; quality assurance mgr. Siemens Transp. Systems, Sacramento, 1996-98; dir. quality assurance Rocklin (Calif.) Precision Machining, Inc., 1998—. Republican. Mormon. Avocations: athletics, wargames, history, music. Home: 11428 Sabalo Way Gold River CA 95670-6207 Office: Rocklin Precision Machining Inc divsn Kleinfelder Corp 4180 Duluth Ave Rocklin CA 95765-1400

TOWE, A. RUTH, museum director; b. Circle, Mont., Mar. 4, 1938; d. David and Anna Marie (Pedersen) James; m. Thomas E. Towe, Aug. 21, 1960; children: James Thomas, Kristofer Edward. BA, U. Mont., 1960, MA, 1970; postgrad., Am. U., 1964. Bookkeeper, copywriter Sta. KGVO, Missoula, Mont., 1960-61; grad. asst. Sch. of Journalism U. Mont., Missoula, 1961-62; editorial asst. Phi Gamma Delta mag., Washington, 1964; reporter The Chelsea (Mich.) Standard, 1965-66; dir. Mont. Nat. Bank, Plentywood, 1966-73; bookkeeper, legal sec. Thomas E. Towe, Atty. of Law, Billings, Mont., 1967-68; dir. Mont. Nat. Bank, Browning, 1972-73; mus. exec. dir. The Moss Mansion Mus., Billings, 1988—. Mem. Mont. Coun. of Family Rels. & Devel., 1970; pres. Mont. Assn. of Symphony Orchs., 1987-88; sheriff Yellowstone Corral of Westerners, Billings, 1993; pres. Yellowstone Hist. Soc., 1998—; vice-chmn. Yellowstone Dem. Ctrl. Com., Billings, 1983-84; judge flower show Nat. Coun. State Garden Clubs; mem. Billings Friends Mtg., 1986—. Mem. AAUW, PEO, Mus. Assn. Mont. (pres. 1990-92, bd. dirs. 1989—), Jr. League, Theta Sigma Phi (hon.). Avocation: gardening. Office: The Moss Mus 914 Division St Billings MT 59101-1921

TOWER, SUE WARNCKE, artist; b. Seattle, Mar. 25, 1940; d. Edgar Dean and Ione Althea (Smith) T.; m. Donald Frank Speyer, Dec. 31, 1958 (div. June 1968); children: Stacy, Monte. BFA, Pacific N.W. Coll. Art, 1982. vis. artist So. Oreg. State Coll., 1996; performing artist (slide presentation) Oreg. Arts Commn. Arts-in-Edn. Program, Salem region, 1996-98; featured artist Oreg. Symphony's Composer Program Cover Art Project, 1997. One woman exhibits include Jacobs Gallery Hult Ctr. Performing Arts, Eugene, Oreg., 1993, Littman Gallery, Portland (Oreg.) State U., 1994, BICC Libr., Oreg. Health Scis. U., 1994, City of Las Vegas Reed Whipple Cultural Ctr., 1996; group exhibits inlcude Bellvue Art Mus., 1992, Galerie Bratri Capku and The Okresni Mus., Prague and Jicin, Czech Republic, 1995, State Capital, Salem, Oreg., 1995, Maryhill Mus. of Art, Goldendale, Wash., 1998, Blackfish Gallery, 1998, Orange County Art Ctr., 1998, Beaverton Arts Commn., 1998. Fundraiser, donor Blackfish Gallery, Pacific N.W. Coll. Art, 1994; donor Cascade AIDS Project Benefit Art Auction, 1996. Avocations: ballet. Office: Sue Tower Studio 930 SW Gibbs St Apt 14 Portland OR 97201-7321

TOWERS, BERNARD LEONARD, medical educator; b. Preston, Eng., Aug. 20, 1922; s. Thomas Francis and Isabella Ellen (Dobson) T.; m. Carole Ilene Lieberman (div. 1992); 1 child, Tiffany Sabrina; children from previous marriage: Helena Marianne, Celia Marguerite, Julie Carole. M.B., Ch.B., U. Liverpool, 1947; M.A., U. Cambridge, 1954. House surgeon Royal Infirmary, Liverpool, 1947; lectr. U. Bristol, 1949-50, U. Wales, 1950-54, Cambridge U., 1954-70; fellow Jesus Coll., 1957-70, steward, 1961-64, tutor, 1964-69; dir. med. studies, 1964-70; prof. pediatrics UCLA, 1971-84, prof. anatomy, 1971-91, prof. psychiatry, 1983-91, prof. emeritus anatomy and psychiatry, 1991—, convenor, moderator medicine and soc. forum, 1974-89; pvt. practice integrative medicine, 1991-98, ret., 1998; co-dir. Program in Medicine, Law and Human Values, 1977-84; cons. Inst. Human Values in Medicine, 1971-84; adv. bd. Am. Teilhard Assn. for Future of Man, 1971-98; v.p. Teilhard Centre for Future Man, London, 1974-98. Author: Teilhard de Chardin, 1966, Naked Ape or Homo Sapiens?, 1969, Concerning Teilhard, 1969; also articles, chpts. on sci. and philosophy.; Editor anat. asst.: Brit. Abstracts Med. Scis, 1954-56, Teilhard Study Library, 1966-70; adv. bd.: Jour. Medicine and Philosophy, 1974-84. Served to capt. RAMC, 1947-49. NIH grantee, 1974-78; NEH grantee, 1977-83. Fellow Cambridge Philos. Soc., Royal Soc. Medicine; mem. Brit. Soc. History of Medicine, Soc. Health and Human Values (pres. 1977-78), Anat. Soc. G.B., Worshipful Soc. Apothecaries London, Am. Assn. for Study Mental Imagery, Western Assn. Physicians, Societe Europeene de Culture Venise.

TOWLER, SUREVA, publisher, writer; b. Washington, Sept. 22, 1932; d. Martin and Ella (April) Codel; m. David Allen Towler, 1973 (dec. 1991); 1 child, Judith Keller. BA, N.Y.U. Dir. rsch. Nat. Endowment for the Arts, Washington, 1965-67; dir. publs. U.S. Dept. of Housing and Urban Devel., Washington, 1970-72; county adminstr. Routt County, Steamboat Springs, Colo., 1976-81; pub. The Meeker (Colo.) Herald, 1992-93; cons. Steamboat Springs, 1994—. Author: Federal Funds and Services for the Arts, 1966, Washington and the Arts, 1970, Economic Aspects of the Performing Arts, 1972, The Historical Guide to Routt County, 1978, The History of Skiing at Steamboat Springs, 1987, Recipes from the Farm, 1989, The Cream of Tartar Story, 1996, Faster Horses, Younger Women, Older Whiskey, 1996; contbr. articles to mags. Bd. dirs. East Routt Libr., 1977-81, Tread of Pioneers Mus., 1975-88, Routt County EMS, 1980-86, Routt County Archives, 1980-88, United Way, 1979. Recipient Best Friend award Bud Werner Meml. Libr., 1990, Financial Devel. award Gale Rsch. Co., 1991, Hazie Werner award for excellence Steamboat Ski & Resort Corp., 1996. Mem. Western Writers of Am., Women Writing the West, Colo. Author's League (Top Hand award 1997). Office: White River Publishing Co Box 768 Steamboat Springs CO 80477

TOWNER, LARRY EDWIN, consulting company executive; b. Gallup, N.Mex., Sept. 27, 1937; s. Edwin Robert and Esther Kathryn (Kern) T.; m. D. Yvonne Turner, Mar. 12, 1966; children: Kristina Kay, Jennifer Kate. BS in Tech. Mgmt., Am. U., Washington, 1976. Project mgr. Wolf Research, Houston, 1965-66, Gulton SRG, Arlington, Va., 1966-67; dep. for database devel. USN, Washington, 1967-79; mgr., BTP teleprocessing RCA, Cherry Hill, N.J., 1979-80; mgr., data base adminstrn., solid state div. RCA, Somerville, N.J., 1980-82; mgr., systems devel. Hughes Aircraft, El Segundo, Calif., 1982-89; pres. TCSI, Richland, Wash.—. Author: Ads/Online Cookbook, 1986, A Professionals Guide, 1989, Case: Concepts and Implementation, 1989, Oracle: The Professionals Reference, 1991; contbr. articles to profl. jours. Treas. Va. Hills Recreation Assn., Alexandria, 1970-72, pres. 1975-77; active Civil Air Patrol, Alexandria, 1968-79; bd. dirs. Northwest Citizens Radio Emergency Service, Spokane, Wash., 1960-63. Recipient Meritorious Service award Civil Air Patrol, 1976. Mem. IDMS User Assn. (bd. dirs. Outstanding Svc award 1984 Hall of Fame award 1992), Amateur Radio Relay League, Assn. for Sys. Mgmt. (v.p. Columbia chpt. 1993, pres. 1994), Richland Rotary Club, Hughes Mgmt. Club. Methodist. Avocations: flying, computers, amateur radio. Home and Office: TCSI 266 Adair Dr Richland WA 99352-0453

TOWNES CHARLES HARD physics educator; b. Greenville, S.C., July May 4, 1941; children: Linda Lewis, Ellen Screven, Carla Keith, Holly Robinson. B.A., B.S., Furman U., 1935; M.A., Duke U., 1937; Ph.D., Calif. Inst. Techn. 1939. Mem. tech. staff Bell Telephone Lab. 1939-47; assoc. prof. physical Columbia Univ. 1948-50 prof. physics 1950 61;

Columbia Radiation Lab., 1950-52, chmn. physics dept., 1952-55; provost and prof. physics MIT, 1961-66, Inst. prof., 1966-67; v.p., dir. research Inst. Def. Analyses, Washington, 1959-61; prof. physics U. Calif, Berkeley, 1967-86, 94, prof. physics emeritus, 1986-94, prof. grad. sch., 1994—; Guggenheim fellow, 1955-56; Fulbright lectr. U. Paris, 1955-56, U. Tokyo, 1956; lectr., 1955, 60; dir. Enrico Fermi Internat. Sch. Physics, 1963; Richtmeyer lectr. Am. Phys. Soc., 1959; Scott lectr. U. Cambridge, 1963; Centennial lectr. U. Toronto, 1967; Lincoln lectr., 1972-73, Halley lectr., 1976, Krishnan lectr., 1992, Nishina lectr., 1992; Rajiv Gandhi lectr., New Delhi, India, 1997, Weinberg lectr. Oak Ridge (Tenn.) Nat. Lab., 1997, Rajiv Gandhi lectr., 1997, Weinberg lectr., 1997, Henry Norris Russell lectr. Am. Astron. Soc., 1998; dir. Gen. Motors Corp., 1973-86, Perkin-Elmer Corp., 1966-85; mem. Pres.'s Sci. Adv. Com., 1966-69, vice chmn., 1967-69; chmn. sci. and tech. adv. com. for manned space flight NASA, 1964-70; mem. Pres.'s Com. on Sci. and Tech., 1976; researcher on nuclear and molecular structure, quantum electronics, interstellar molecules, radio and infrared astrophysics. Author: Making Waves, 1996, (with A.L. Schawlow) Microwave Spectroscopy, 1955; author, co-editor: Quantum Electronics, 1960, Quantum Electronics and Coherent Light, 1964; editorial bd. Rev. Sci. Instruments, 1950-52, Phys. Rev., 1951-53, Jour. Molecular Spectroscopy, 1957-60, Procs. Nat. Acad. Scis., 1978-84, Can. Jour. Physics, 1995—; contbr. articles to sci. publs.; patentee masers and lasers. Trustee Calif. Inst. Tech., Carnegie Instn. of Washington, Grad. Theol. Union, Calif. Acad. Scis.; mem. corp Woods Hole Oceanographic Instn. Decorated officier Légion d'Honneur (France); recipient numerous hon. degrees and awards including Nobel prize for physics, 1964; Stuart Ballantine medal Franklin Inst., 1959, 62; Thomas Young medal and prize Inst. Physics and Phys. Soc., Eng., 1963; Disting. Public Service medal NASA, 1969; Wilhelm Exner award Austria, 1970; Niels Bohr Internat. Gold medal, 1979; Nat. Sci. medal, 1982, Berkeley citation U. Calif., 1986; named to Nat. Inventors Hall of Fame, 1976, Engring. and Sci. Hall of Fame, 1983; recipient Common Wealth award, 1993, ADION medal Observatory Nice, 1995; Henry Norris Russell Lectureship Am. Astron. Soc., 1998. Fellow IEEE (life, Medal of Honor 1967), Am. Phys. Soc. (pres. 1967, Plyler prize 1977), Optical Soc. Am. (hon., Mees medal 1968, Frederick Ives medal 1996), Indian Nat. Sci. Acad., Calif. Acad. Scis.; mem. NAS (coun. 1968-72, 78-81, chmn. space sci. bd. 1970-73, Comstock award 1959, Carty medal 1962), Am. Philos. Soc., Am. Astron. Soc., Am. Acad. Arts and Scis., Royal Soc. (fgn. mem.), Russian Acad. Scis. (fgn. mem.), Pontifical Acad. Scis., Max-Planck Inst. for Physics and Astrophysics (fgn. mem.), N.Y. Acad. Scis. (hon. life); elected to NAE 1998. Office: U Calif Dept Physics 366 LeConte #7200 Berkeley CA 94720-7300

TOWNSEND, ALVIN NEAL, artist; b. Rock Island, Tex., Oct. 26, 1934; s. Archie Lee and Synthia Ellen (Westbook) T.; m. Phyllis Virginia Keyes (div.); 1 child, Phyllis Lynn; m. Bestsy Rose Brown; children: Brita, Lissi, Shana, Kristinn. BFA, U. N.Mex., 1961, MFA, 1962. Base crafts dir. U.S. Civil Svc., Ft. Belvoir, Va., 1962-69, post crafts dir., 1969-70; prof. art edn. U. N.Mex., 1970-91, prof. emeritus, 1991—; artist-in-residence Otago Polytech., Dunedin, New Zealand, 1988; vis. prof. art No. Ariz. U., Flagstaff, 1984; vis. artist New Zealand Soc. of Potters, New Zealand, 1988. More than 200 exhbns., including Mus. of Internat. Folk Art, 1959, 60, 62, 66, Mus. of Fine Arts, U. N.Mex., 1968, Tweed Mus., Duluth, Minn., 1975, Salzbrand, Galerie Handwerkskammgr, Kublenz, Germany, 1983, 86, 89, 93, IX Bienne de Ceramique d'Art, Vallautas, France, 1984, Fletcher Brownbuilt Exhbn., Auckland, New Zealand, 1982, Clay Az Art, Rotorua, New Zealand, 1987, As 220 Exchange, Providence, R.I., 1997, Free Spirits Mus. of the Horse, Ruidoso, N.Mex., 1998, Durango Art Ctr., Durango, Colo., 1999, Hardwood Art Ctr., Albuquerque, N.Mex., 1999. Named Artist of Month Binney & Smith, Inc., 1997; faculty rsch. grant U. N.Mex., 1986-87, 82-83, 79-80. Democrat. Avocations: camping, fishing. Home: 2583 Ramirez Rd SW Albuquerque NM 87105 Office: Townsend Studios 2583 Ramirez Rd SW Albuquerque NM 87105 also: Studio B-2/Harwood Art Ctr 1114 7th St NW Albuquerque NM 87102

TOWNSEND, RUSSELL HENRY, lawyer; b. Ft. Lewis, Wash., Dec. 27, 1949; s. Peter Lee and Irma Matilda (Greisberger) T.; children: Alexander Peter, Jennifer Sabrina. BS, Calif. Maritime Acad., 1971; JD, Lincoln U., San Francisco, 1979. Bar: Calif., U.S. Dist. Ct. (no. and ea. dists.) Calif. Title examiner Western Title Ins. Co., Oakland, Calif., 1971-74; clk. Garrison, Townsend, Hall and predecessor, San Francisco, 1974-79; ptnr. Amberg & Townsend, San Francisco, 1980-83, Townsend and Bardellini, San Francisco, 1983-87, Townsend, Bardellini, Townsend and Wechsler, San Francisco, 1988-92. Lt.j.g. USNR, 1971-75. Mem. ABA, State Bar Calif., Marin County Bar Assn. Republican. Fax: 415-899-9666. Home: 18018 Comstock Ave Sonoma CA 95476-4215 Office: Townsend Law Offices 1620 Grant Ave Ste 3 Novato CA 94945

TOY, PEARL TAK-CHU YAU, transfusion medicine physician; b. Hong Kong, July 31, 1947; came to U.S., 1965; d. Tse-Wah Yau and Grace Liang; m. Larry Toy, Dec. 12, 1970; 1 child, Jennifer. BA, Smith Coll., 1969; MD, Stanford U., 1973. From asst. prof. to assoc. prof. dept. lab. medicine U. Calif. Sch. Medicine, San Francisco, 1980-91, prof. dept. lab. medicine, 1991—; chief blood bank and donor ctr. Moffitt-Long Hosp., U. Calif., San Francisco, 1991—; chair expert panel on autologous transfusion NIH, Bethesda, Md., 1988-94, chair rsch. tng. rev. com., 1992. Contbr. articles to profl. jours., chpts. to books. Recipient numerous grants NIH, 1983—. Mem. Phi Beta Kappa, Sigma Xi, Alpha Omega Alpha. Achievements include research in autologous blood transfusion; blood transfusions.

TOYOMURA, AKIKO CHARLOTTE, health administrator, nurse; b. Kahuku, Hawaii, Sept. 14, 1923; d. Torajiro and Mika Nakamura; m. Dennis T. Toyomura, May 29, 1949; children: Wayne J., Gerald F., Amy J., Lyle D. Diploma, St. Francis Hosp., Honolulu, 1945; postgrad. certs., Cook County Med. Hosp., Chgo., 1949; Assoc. degree, Kapiolani C.C., U. Hawaii, 1981, cert. of achievement, 1980, 81. RN HI, Ill.; sch. health aide; cert. first aid ARC, CPR, Hawaii. Head nurse Women's & Children's Hosp., Chgo., 1949-51; nurse civil svc. U.S. Army, Honolulu, 1952-53; school nurse Luth. Evang. School, Chgo., 1953-58; nurse Rehab. Hosp., Honolulu, HI, 1962-63, Kaiser Med. Ctr., 1963-66; sr. health aide State of Hawaii, Honolulu, 1983—; developer basic health and nursing program Luth. Evang. Sch., Chgo., 1953-58. Home: 2602 Manoa Rd Honolulu HI 96822-1703 Office: State of Hawaii 1240 7th Ave Honolulu HI 96816-2644

TRABITZ, EUGENE LEONARD, aerospace company executive; b. Cleve., Aug. 13, 1937; s. Emanuel and Anna (Berman) T.; m. Caryl Lee Rine, Dec. 22, 1963 (div. Aug. 1981); children: Claire Marie, Honey Caryl; m. Kathryn Lynn Bates, Sept. 24, 1983; 1 stepchild, Paul Francis Rager. BA, Ohio State U., 1965. Enlisted USAF, 1954, advanced through grades to maj.; served as crew commdr. 91st Strategic Missile Div., Minot, S.D., 1968-70; intelligence officer Fgn. Tech. Div., Dayton, Ohio, 1970-73; dir. external affairs Aero Systems Div., Dayton, 1973-75; program mgr. Air Force Armament Div., Valparaiso, Fla., 1975-80; dir. ship ops. Air Force Ea. Test Range, Satellite Beach, Fla., 1980-83; dep. program mgr. Air Force Satellite Text Ctr., Sunnyvale, Calif., 1983-84; ret., 1984; sr. staff engr. Ultrasystems Inc., 1984-86; pres. TAWD Systems Inc., Palo Alto, Calif., 1986-92, Am. Telenetics Co., San Mateo, Calif., 1992—; cons. Space Applications Corp., Sunnyvale, 1986-87, Litton Computer Svcs., Mountain View, Calif., 1987-91, Battelle Meml. Inst. Columbus, 1993—. V.p. Bd. County Mental Health Clinic, Ft. Walton Beach, Fla., 1973-75. Decorated Bronze Star. Mem. DAV (life), World Affairs Coun., U.S. Space Found. (charter), Air Force Assn. (life), Assn. Old Crows, Nat. Sojourners, Commonwealth Club Calif., Masons (32 degree). Avocations: golf, tennis, racketball, sailing, bridge. Home: 425 Anchor Rd Apt 317 San Mateo CA 94404-1058

TRACHT, DAVID ADAMS petroleum products consultant; b. Ft. Worth, Oct. 2, 1916; s. Sherwood Alonzo and Virginia Bell (Evans) T.; m. Margie Evelyn Johnson, July 25, 1941 (div. Oct. 1973); m. Margie Virginia Estonson, June 29, 1979; 1 child, Delene Spencer. BA, U. Redlands, 1939; postgrad. in chem. engring., U. Houston, Baytown, 1967. Inspector ship tanks Esso Std. Oil Co., Baytown, Tex., 1942-61; marine chemist Homble co., Baytown, 1942-61; sr. staff coord. Exxon, Benicia, Calif., 1969-78; v.p. jet fuel Sevedz Oil Co., 1983-94; adv. bd. Contra Costa County St. Calif. Martinez, Calif., 1974-78; cons. pet products blending, 1984-89. Vice pres. Boy Scouts Am., U. gov. Kiwanis, pres., 1974. Fellow Inst. for Advance-

Automotive Engrs. (chmn. So. Calif.), Nat. Pet Refining Assn., Internat. Std. Orgn. Republican. Methodist. Avocations: football, basketball officiating. Home: 1500 NE 15th Ave Apt 428 Portland OR 97232-4418

TRACY, GEORGE S., healthcare service company executive; b. Buffalo, Mar. 6, 1963; s. Daniel A. Jr. and Mary J. (Tronolone) T.; m. Amy E. Wildblood, Sept. 5, 1987; children: Daniel E., Steven J. Student, Syracuse U., 1985. Various positions Spectrum Healthcare Resources, St. Louis, 1985-90, bus. mgr., 1990-94, dir. ops., 1994-96, v.p., 1996—. Mem. Country Club of Colo., Syracuse U. Alumni of Colo., Canisius H.S. of Buffalo Alumni, Zeta Psi (Rocky Mountain Assn. pres. 1989-91), Syracuse Assn. Zeta Psi. Roman Catholic. Avocations: golfing, hiking, bicycle riding. Office: Spectrum Healthcare Resources 6760 Corporate Dr Ste 200 Colorado Springs CO 80919

TRACY, JAMES JARED, JR., accountant, law firm administrator; b. Cleve., Jan. 17, 1929; s. James Jared and Florence (Comey) T.; m. Elizabeth Jane Bourne, June 30, 1953 (div. 1988); children: Jane Mackintosh, Elizabeth Boyd, James Jared IV, Margaret Gardiner; m. Judith Anne Cooper, Feb. 18, 1989. AB, Harvard U., 1950, MBA, 1953. CPA, Ohio. Acct., mgr. Price Waterhouse & Co., Cleve., 1953-65; treas., CFO Clevite Corp., Cleve., 1965-69; asst. treas. Republic Steel Corp., Cleve., 1969-70, treas., 1970-75; v.p., treas. Johns-Manville Corp., Denver, 1976-81; v.p., treas., CFO I. T. Corp., L.A., 1981-82; exec. dir. Hufstedler, Miller, Carlson & Beardsley, L.A., 1983-84, Shank, Irwin & Conant, Dallas, 1984-85, Pachter, Gold & Schaffer, L.A., 1985-86; v.p., sr. cons. Right Assocs., L.A., 1987-91; dir. adminstrn. Larson & Burnham, Oakland, Calif., 1991-95; ret., 1995; adminstrv. dir. Law Offices of Thomas E. Miller, Newport Beach, Calif., 1996-97; human resources adminstr. Baker & McKenzie, San Francisco, 1997-98; dir. adminstrn. Wartnick, Chaber, Harowitz, Smith & Tigerman, San Francisco, 1998—; trustee and v.p. Miss Hall's Sch., Pittsfield, Mass., 1970-78; dir. Union Commerce Bank, Cleve., 1971-76; adv. bd. mem. Arkwright-Boston Ins. Co., Boston, 1976-81. Trustee and v.p. Cleve. Soc. for Blind, 1965-76; trustee Western Res. Hist. Soc., Cleve., 1972-76; treas. St. Peters by the Sea Presbyn. Ch., Palos Verdes, Calif. 1981-91. Recipient Alumni award Harvard U., Denver, 1981. Mem. AICPA, Ohio Soc. CPAs, Assn. Legal Adminstrs., Piedmont Montclair Rotary Club (pres. 1995-96), Harvard Club San Francisco, Harvard Bus. Sch. Club No. Calif. Avocations: sailing, golf, gardening. Home: 126 Lombardy Ln Orinda CA 94563-1111

TRACY, JAMES MICHAEL, building manufacturing executive; b. Watertown, S.D., May 11, 1959; s. Gerald Eugene and Virginia Mary (Brown) T.; m. Sarah Jane Alderink, Apr. 19, 1980; children: Ryan James, Jamie Alderink. BSBA, U. S.D., 1983. Sales engr. Lundell Mfg., Plymouth, Minn., 1983-85; product mgr. Advance Foam Plastics, Denver, 1985-91; pres. Legacy Builders Ltd., Thornton, Colo., 1991-93; divsn. gen. mgr. Premier Bldg. Sys., Fife, Wash., 1993-98; dir. internat. bus. Premier Industries, Tacoma, 1998—; chmn. product adv. bd. AFM Corp., Excelsior, Minn., 1988-90. Patentee Insul-Beam. Mem. zoning bd. appeals City of Thornton, 1990-93; del. Colo. Rep. party, Adams County, 1992. Named Colo. Chmn. of Yr., Ducks Unltd., Memphis, 1990; recipient Disting. Svc. award Colo. Power Coun., Denver, 1989. Mem. Structural Insulated Panel Assn. (pres. 1998, bd. dirs. 1996-98). Evangelical. Office: Premier Bldg Sys 4609 70th Ave E Fife WA 98424-3711

TRACY, JAMES WAYNE, pastor, educator; b. Tulsa, Nov. 17, 1945; s. James Kenneth and Margaret Eunice (Pickett) T.; m. Carolyn Marie Haugan, Aug. 7, 1976; children: Keith Scott, Tonya Raylene; m. Judith Ann Cornwall, Sept. 12, 1967 (div. 1972); 1 child, James Robert. BA, So. Calif. Coll., Costa Mesa, 1970; MA, Calif. Grad. Sch. of Theol., Glendale, 1985. Cert. sch. adminstr. Assn. Christian Schs. Internat. Assoc. pastor 1st Assembly of God, Grants Pass, Oreg., 1967-68; christian sch. tchr. Wilmington (Calif.) Christian Sch., 1968-70, 72-75; assoc. pastor 1st Assembly of God, Salem, Oreg., 1970-72, New Life Christian Ctr., Fresno, Calif., 1976-81, Assembly of God, Hawthorne, Calif., 1981; pastor Calvary Chapel, Los Alamos, N.Mex., 1982—. Author: Divorce Re Marriage: The Letter of the Law vs. The Spirit if the Law, 1985. Active mem. United Way Funding Com., Los Alamos, N.Mex., 1987. Mem. Assn. Christian Schs., Internat., Assn. Christian Schs. Internat. Adminstrs. Fellowship. Republican. Office: Calvary Chapel 580 N Mesa Rd Los Alamos NM 87544-2775

TRAFTON, STEPHEN J., bank executive; b. Mt. Vernon, Wash., Sept. 17, 1946; m. Diane Trafton; children: John, Roland. BS in Zoology, Wash. State U., 1968. V.p., mgr. dept. money market Seattle-First Nat. Bank, 1968-79; v.p., mgr. bank consulting group Donaldson Lufkin Jennrette, N.Y.C., 1980; exec. v.p., treas. Gibraltar Savings Bank, L.A., 1980-84; banking cons., 1984-86; v.p., treas. Hibernia Bank, San Francisco, 1986-88; sr. v.p., treas. Goldome Bank, Buffalo, N.Y., 1988-90; sr. exec. v.p., CFO Glenfed Inc., 1990-91, vice chmn., CFO, 1991—, pres., 1992—; sr. exec. v.p., CFO Glendale Fed. Bank, 1990-91, vice chmn., CFO, 1991, pres., COO, 1991-92, chmn. bd., pres., CEO, 1992—, COO, also bd. dirs. Mem. Phi Eta Sigma. Office: Golden State Bancorp Inc. 401 N Central Ave Glendale CA 91203-2001

TRAGER, RUSSELL HARLAN, advertising consultant; b. Cambridge, Mass., Sept. 26, 1945; s. Nathan Allan and Shirley (Gibbs) T.; m. V. Jan Adams, Aug. 19, 1968 (div. July 1975); 1 child, Eric Todd; m. Edna Marie Sanchez, Feb. 16, 1980; children: Felice Rosanne, Justin Tomas. AA, Newton Jr. Coll., 1965; BS, U. Miami, 1968; postgrad., Harvard U., 1968-69. Account rep. Hervic Corp., Sherman Oaks, Calif., 1972-75; Canon USA, Lake Success, N.Y., 1975-78; key account sales rep. Yashica Inc., Glendale, Calif., 1978-79; sales rep. Region I United Pubs. Corp., Beverly Hills, Calif., 1979-81, sales mgr., 1981-83; regional pres. United Pubs. Corp., Carson, Calif., 1983-86, region v.p., 1986-88; v.p. sales United Pubs. Corp. divsn. of Nynex Co., El Segundo, Calif., 1988-91; dir. sales Yelex Corp., L.A., 1991-92; sales mgr. Trader Pub. Co., L.A., 1992-93; cons. Russ Trager & Assocs., Manhattan Beach, Calif., 1994—. Avocations: salt-water fishing, photography, collecting art. Home and Office: Russ Trager & Assocs 3308 Pacific Ave Manhattan Beach CA 90266-3518

TRAM, KENNETH KHAI KT, internist; b. Saigon, Vietnam, Oct. 29, 1961; came to U.S., 1978; s. Felix Ngan and Lisa Hong (Pham) T.; m. Christine Tram-Hong Tran, June 19, 1993. BS summa cum laude, U. Calif., Irvine, 1984; MD, UCLA, 1988. Diplomate Am. Bd. Internal Medicine, Am. Bd. Geriatric Medicine. Resident in internal medicine UCLA-San Fernandny Valley, 1988-91; geriatric medicine fellow UCLA Sch. Medicine, 1992-94; clin. instr./assoc. investigator Sepulveda (Calif.) VA Med. Ctr., 1991-94, acting med. dir., 1994; internist Facey Med. Group, Sepulveda, 1994—. Contbr. articles to profl. jours. Mem. CPAG/CHOMS, Calif., 1991—. Recipient Solomon Scholars Resident award UCLA Sch. Medicine, 1991, Nat. Kidney Found. Fellowship award, 1991-92, VA Rsch. and Devel. Career Devel. award, 1992-94. Mem. ACP, AAAS, AMA, Am. Soc. for Bone and Mineral Rsch., U.S. Table Tennis Assn., Nat. Geog. Soc., Mus. Heritage Soc. Home: 28309 Azurite Pl Valencia CA 91354-1504 Office: Facey Medical Group Inc 11211 Sepulveda Blvd Mission Hills CA 91345-1196

TRAN, JACK NHUAN NGOC, gas and oil reservoir engineer; b. Quang Binh, Vietnam, Sept. 21, 1933; came to U.S., 1975; s. Dieu Ngoc and Ly Thi (Nguyen) T.; m. Qhang Thi Huynh; Children: Quoc Dung, Ann Nga Huyen, Ephram Anh Dung, John Hung Dung. BS, U. San Francisco, 1977, MBA, 1978. With Republic of Vietnam Mil., 1952-67; cadet Rep. Vietnam Mil. Acad., Dalat, 1952-53; 1st lt., co. comdr. 1st Republic of Vietnam Bn., South Vietnam, 1953-54; editor-in-chief Republic of Vietnam Revs., Saigon, 1955-57; commandant Republic of Vietnam Aerial Photo Ctr., Saigon, 1958-61; Republic of Vietnam Mil. Intelligence Sch., Cajmal and Bulgon, 1968-69; mem. Republic of Vietnam Senate, 1967-73; v.p. The Meteco Corp., Saigon, Vietnam, 1971-72; pres., chmn. bd. Metevco-Vinaseco Co., Saigon, 1972-75; air photo analyst Std. Oil Co., San Francisco, 1975-79; gas and oil engr. Chevron Oil Co., San Francisco, 1980—; col. U.S. Intelligence, Calif., 1980-90. Author: Flower in the Battle Field, 1956, Geological Survey of the 19th and 20th centuries Mekong River Oil Development, 1984, The Military Life, City, City of Omaha, Nebr., 1989, Hon. Citizen City of Fayetteville, N.C., 1969; Resolution of Recognition, Senate of State of Hawaii, 1969, Senate of State of Texas, 1989, mem. The U. of San Francisco Alumni Assn., Rotary

Internat. Roman Catholic. Avocations: swimming, music, reading, traveling. Home: 1418 Lundy Ave San Jose CA 95131-3310

TRAPP, GERALD BERNARD, retired journalist; b. St. Paul, May 7, 1932; s. Bernard Edward and Lauretta (Mueller) T.; m. Bente Joan Moe, Jan. 29, 1954; children—Eric Gerald, Lise Joan, Alex Harold. B.A., Macalester Coll., St. Paul, 1954. Editor Mankato (Minn.) Free Press, 1954-57; with AP, 1957-80; nat. broadcast exec. charge sales AP, East of Miss., 1966-68; gen. broadcast news editor AP, N.Y.C., 1968-79; dep. dir. broadcast services AP, 1979-80, liaison broadcast networks, 1968-80; v.p., gen. mgr. Intermountain Network, Salt Lake City, 1980-87; v.p., dir. mktg. Travel Motivation, Inc., Salt Lake City, 1987-88; ops./program mgr. Mountain Cable Network, Inc., Salt Lake City, 1988-89; sr. v.p. Travel Motivation, Inc., Salt Lake City, 1990-92; mktg. specialist Morris Travel, 1992-95, pricing analyst, 1995-97. Bd. dirs. Westminster Coll. Found. Mem. Radio TV News Dirs. Assn., Oratorio Soc. Utah (bd. dirs.), Pro Musica, Sigma Delta Chi. Mem. United Ch. Christ. Home: 785 Three Fountains Cir Apt 17 Salt Lake City UT 84107-5063 Office: 240 Morris Ave Salt Lake City UT 84115-3223*

TRASK, KAREN DALE, publisher, artist; b. Dearborn, Mich., May 27, 1955; d. Benjamin Zygmund and Florence Lottie (Wozniak) S.; m. William Stephens Trask, Apr. 21, 1989. BFA, Kendall Coll. Art and Design, Grand Rapids, Mich., 1986. Tech. illustrator Med. & Aerospace, Tempe, Ariz., 1978-82; artist Mesa, Ariz., 1983-84; art instr. various pub. sch. sys., 1985-88; prodn. artist PCS, Inc., Scottsdale, 1988-89, PCS Health Sys., Scottsdale, 1994-95; mktg. and prodn. artist Margie Gail, Inc., Scottsdale, 1990-94; pub. Cornerstone Artists Publishing Group, Fountain Hills, Ariz., 1995—; also bd. dirs. Author: For The Sake of Appearances, 1997. Bd. dirs. Fountain Hills Arts Coun., 1996-97; pres. Fountain Hills Art League, 1996-97. Mem. Nat. Oil and Acrylic Painters Soc., Colored Pencil Soc. Am., Ariz. Book Publishing Assn., Cornerstone Artists (founding). Avocations: photography, camping. Office: Cornerstone Artists Pub Grp PO Box 19036 Fountain Hills AZ 85269-9036

TRASK, ROBERT CHAUNCEY RILEY, author, lecturer, foundation executive; b. Albuquerque, Jan. 2, 1939; s. Edward Almon Trask and Florence Jane (White) Jones; m. Katie Lucille Bitters (div. 1981); m. Mary Jo Chiarottino, Dec. 1, 1984; 1 child, Chauncey Anne. Student pub. schs., San Diego. Lic. master sea capt. Entertainer, singer, comedian, 1964—; founder, pres. Nat. Health & Safety Svcs., San Francisco, 1968-71, ARAS Found., Issaquah, Wash., 1978—; capt., dive master San Diego Dive Charters, 1972-75; sr. capt., dive master Pacific Sport Diving Corp., Long Beach, Calif., 1975-77; lectr., bus. cons., 1978—; cons., tng. developer Nissan, Gen. Dynamics, AT&T, religious orgns., also other corps., 1978—. Author: (manual) Tulip, 1971, Living Free, 1982, God's Phone Number, 1987, (video program for adolescents) Breaking Free, also seminar manuals. Mem. SAG. Avocations: fishing, boating, diving, exploring, gardening. Office: ARAS Found Ste 93 3020 Issaquah Pine Lake Rd SE Issaquah WA 98029-7255

TRASK-TYRELL, NANCY, management company executive; b. Deer Lodge, Mont., June 1, 1936; arrived in Eng., 1969; d. Frank S. and Cora Isabelle (Nichols) Trask; m. William James Paul, Sept. 17, 1960 (div. 1982); children: William James, Elisa Anne, Michael Justin; m. David Alan Tyrell, Apr. 11, 1992. BA, U. Mont., 1958, MA, 1962. Assoc. Mgmt. Facilitation Inst., London, 1977-80; owner Paul Mgmt. Assn., London, 1980-87; mng. ptnr. Excel Internat., London, 1987—. Author: Right To Be You, 1985; co-author: Principles of Project Management, 1989; author (video) Making Meeting Work, 1989; contbr. articles to profl. jours. Mem. Internat. Inst. Transactional Analysis, Inst. Transactional Analysis (founder, v.p. 1982-85), Renaissance Group (founder). Episcopalian. Avocations: antique porcelain, mountain climbing, gardening, skiing, people. Office: Excel Internat 2810 Contour Rd Missoula MT 59802-3376

TRAUD, DONALD ROBERT, public relations, marketing executive; b. McKeesport, Pa.. BS in Journalism and Pub. Rels., U. Fla., 1979; MA in Pub. Adminstrn., Troy State U., 1985. Commd. 2d lt. USAF, 1979, advanced through grades to capt., 1983, resigned, 1992; internal info. officer USAF, Chanute AFB, Ill., 1979-81; media rels. officer USAF, Maxwell AFB, Ala., 1981-83; dep. commdr. USAF, Yong San, Korea, 1983-84; chief of pub. affairs USAF, Hellenikon, Greece, 1984-87; chief cmty. rels. sec. of Air Force USAF, L.A., 1987-92; owner MJ Pub. Rels., L.A., 1992-93; mktg. mgr. Triple Check, Montrose, Calif., 1993—; pub. rels. cons. Am. Youth Symphony, L.A. Contbr. numerous articles to mags. and newspapers. Mem. Am. Mktg. Assn. Office: Triple Check 2441 Honolulu Ave Montrose CA 91020-1864

TRAUNTER, JOHN JAMES, real estate executive; b. Simpson, Minn., Dec. 4, 1935; s. John Slyvester and Oridena Francis (Baker) T.; m. Carol Lee Rowberry, July 12, 1974 (div. May 1981); 1 child, Lindsey D.; m. Kathy N. Bucy, July 19, 1992; children: Theresa, Carrie, John; 1 stepchild, Victor. AA, Anchorage C.C., 1968; BBA, U. Alaska, 1970, MbA, 1971. Lic. comml. pilot. Adminstr. pub. affairs RCA Svc. Co., Anchorage, 1965-70; dir. adminstrn. and pub. rels. Alyeska Resort Inc., Girdwood, Alaska, 1970-71; mgmt. cons. State Alaska, Juneau, 1972-73; exec. dir. City of Lost River, Alaska, 1973-74; v.p., gen. mgr. C. Bruce Ficke Investments, Girdwood, 1974-76; pres., gen. mgr. Gateway Inc., Girdwood, 1975-85; CEO Alyeska Mgmt. Svc., Girdwood, 1985—; mem. MD49 Coun. Govs., Fairbanks, Alaska, 1996-97. Patentee in field. Chmn. Jr.-Inter-Fraternity Coun., Seattle, 1957-58, Girdwood Cmty. Coun., 1976-78; fire chief City of Girdwood, 1972-75; chmn., mem. Girdwood Bd. Suprs., 1992-95. With U.S. Army, 1953-54, Korea. Recipient cert. ARC, 1966, Melvin Jones fellowship Internat. Assn. Lions, Chgo., 1993-94. Mem. Am. Legion, Disabled Vets. Fgn. Wars, Internat. Assn. Lions Clubs (dist gov. 1996-97), Girdwood, Turnagain Arm Lions Club (pres. 1992). Republican. Roman Catholic. Avocations: photography, music, fine arts, dog training, humanitarianism. Home: NHN Cortina Rd Girdwood AK 99587 Office: Alyeska Mgmt Svcs PO Box 909 Girdwood AK 99587-0909

TRAUTH, PATRICIA MARY, landscape architect; b. Cin., Nov. 8, 1955; s. Albert Edward and Martha Beatrice (Donelan) T.; m. John Gregory Rollinson, Aug. 5, 1995; children: Stephanie, Jack, Nicole. BFA, Bowling Green State U., 1979, BS in Art Edn., 1979; M of Landscape Architecture, U. Ariz., 1987. Registered profl. landscape architect, Calif. Assoc. Gillespie Delorenzo & Assocs., San Diego, 1987-89; landscape architect JP Engring., San Diego, 1989-92; project mgr. WYA, San Diego, 1992-93; prin. Circa 9, San Diego, 1992-93; instr. Mesa C.C., San Diego, 1990-94, New Sch. Architecture, San Diego, 1995; staff San Diego Univ., 1998—; assoc. Kawasaki Theilacker Ueno & Assocs., San Diego, 1993—; spkr. in field. Active curriculum devel. Built Environment Edn. Program, San Diego, 1993-95; dir. devel. lesson plans edn. program. Mem. Am. Soc. Landscape Architects (v.p. local chpt. 1995-96, newsletter editor 1990-93), Calif. Women Environ. Design (state pres. 1994-95, dir. So. Calif. 1992-95). Home: 1638 Edilee Dr Cardiff By The Sea CA 92007-1104

TRAVAGLINI, JOSEPH, educational consultant; b. Phila., Sept. 17, 1932; m. Marilyn Irene Gordon, Dec. 26, 1956; children: Mark D., David H. BSBA, Drexel U., 1955; M of Govtl. Adminstrn., U. Pa., 1960; PhD, U. Md., 1974. Dir. personnel svcs. Antioch Coll., Yellow Springs, Ohio, 1960-65; mgr. adminstrv. svcs. U. Chgo., 1965-66; asst. bur. chief Pa. State Dept. Edn., Harrisburg, 1966-67; asst. to pres. Essex C.C., Baltimore County, Md., 1967-75; program mgr. individualized degree programs Ctrl. Mich. U., Mt. Pleasant, 1975-88; dean grad. and external programs Coll. Santa Fe, 1988-89; assoc. dean, dir. The Union Inst., San Diego Ctr., Cin., 1989-92; ednl. cons. San Diego, 1993—; co-chair accreditation study Essex C.C., 1969-70; team leader program learning seminar U. Mich., Ann Arbor, 1982; reviewer Calif. Postsecondary Edn. Commn., Sacramento, 1990-91; cons. to pres. La Jolla U., San Diego, 1993. Author: (chpt.) Personalized Instruction in Education Today, 1970; co-author: (chpt.) The University and the Inner City, 1980. Pres. Joppatowne (Md.) Civic Assoc., 1969-74; county coun. candidate Harford County, Bel Air, Md., 1974; alumni amb. Drexel U., Phila., 1997—; vol. auditor Balboa Pk. Japanese Friendship Garden, San Diego, 1995—. With U.S. Army, 1955-57. Recipient Samuel S. Fels scholarship U. Pa., 1958-60, fellowship U. Colo., 1968. Mem. Wharton Alumni Club So. Calif., Sierra Club, World Wildlife Fund, Nature Conservancy, Phi Delta Kappa (emeritus). Democrat. Avocations: environment, international travel, jogging, music, politics. Home: 3375 Date St San Diego CA 92102

TRAVERS, DAVID OWENS, chaplain; b. Lynn, Mass., June 27, 1934; s. Daniel Otis and Helena (Owens) T. BA, Boston Coll., 1961, MDiv, 1969; MEd, Tufts U., 1969. Ordained priest Roman Cath. Ch., 1968. Retreat dir. Jesuit Ctr., Boston, 1969-74; chaplain Boston City Hosp., 1974-76; commd. 2d lt. USN, 1970, advanced through grades to commdr., 1982, chaplain, 1976—. Mem. Jesuits of New England. Home: 800 Kaheka St Honolulu HI 96814-3728 Office: Chaplains Office Marine Corps Air Station M C B H Kaneohe Bay HI 96863

TRAVERS, JUDITH LYNNETTE, human resources executive; b. Buffalo, Feb. 25, 1950; d. Harold Elwin and Dorothy (Helsel) Howes; m. David Jon Travers, Oct. 21, 1972; 1 child, Heather Lynne. BA in Psychology, Barrington Coll., 1972; cert. in paralegal course, St. Mary's Coll., Moraga, Calif., 1983; postgrad., Southland U., 1982-84. Exec. sec. Sherman C. Weeks, P.A., Derry, N.H., 1973-75; legal asst. Mason-McDuffie Co., Berkeley, Calif., 1975-82; paralegal asst. Blum, Kay, Merkle & Kauftheil, Oakland, Calif., 1982-83; CEO, bd. dirs. Dela Pers. Svcs. Inc., Concord, Calif., 1983—; pres. All Ages Sitters Agy., Concord, 1986-95; CEO, bd. dirs. Guardian Security Agy., Concord, Calif., 1992—; sec., bd. dirs. Per Diem Staffing Systems, Inc.; bd. dir. Securicorp. Vocalist record album The Loved Ones, 1978. vol. local Congl. campaign, 1980, Circle of Friends, Children's Hosp. No. Calif., Oakland, 1987—; mem. Alameda County Sheriff's Mounted Posse, 1989, Contra Costa Child Abuse Prevention Coun., 1989; employer adv. coun. Ctrl. Contra Costa County, 1993—. Mem. NAFE, Am. Assn. Respiratory Therapy, Soc. for Human Resource Mgmt., Am. Mgmt. Assn., Gospel Music Assn., Palomino Horse Breeders Am., DAR, Barrington Oratorio Soc., Commonwealth Club Calif., Nat. Trust Hist. Preservation, Alpha Theta Sigma. Republican. Baptist. Avocations: boating, horses. Home: 3900 Brown Rd Oakley CA 94561-2664 Office: Delta Pers Svcs Inc 1820 Galindo St Ste 3 Concord CA 94520-2447

TRAVOUS, KENNETH E., state agency administrator. Exec. dir. Ariz. State Parks Bd., Phoenix. Office: Ariz State Parks Bd 1300 W Washington St Phoenix AZ 85007-2929*

TRAXLER, BUCK, newspaper editor; b. Missoula, Mont., Jan. 9, 1948; s. Jack Eugene and Dorothy (Shepherd) T.; m. Elizabeth Marie Traxler, Apr. 15, 1972 (div. 1984). Degree in photography, San Diego City Coll., 1974. Editor Phillips County News, Malta, Mont., 1985-86, Independent Observer, Conrad, Mont., 1986—. Mem. Conrad City Coun., 1998—; ctrl. committeeman Rep. Party, Conrad, 1988—. With USN, 1968-72. Decorated Meritorious Unit commendation, Nat. Def. Svc. medal, Combat Action ribbon. Mem. Conrad C. of C. (pres. 1991, 93), Conrad Crimestoppers (sec. 1988-91), Pondera Golf Club (v.p., dir. 1990-93, sec. 1998—), Lions (sec. 1995—), Moose, VFW. Avocations: golf, hunting. Home: 616 S Delaware St Conrad MT 59425-2511 Office: Independent Observer PO Box 966 Conrad MT 59425-0966

TRAYLOR, WILLIAM ROBERT, publisher; b. Texarkana, Ark., May 21, 1921; s. Clarence Edington and Seba Ann (Talley) T.; m. Elvirez Sigler, Oct. 9, 1945; children: Kenneth Warren, Gary Robert, Mark Daniel, Timothy Ryan. Student, U. Houston, 1945-46, U. Omaha, 1947-48. Div. mgr. Lily-Tulip Cup Corp., N.Y.C., 1948-61; asst. to pres. Johnson & Johnson, New Brunswick, N.J., 1961-63; mgr. western region Rexall Drug & Chem. subs. Dart Industries, L.A., 1963-67; pres. Prudential Pub. Co., Diamonds Springs, Calif., 1967—; cons. to printing industry, 1976-98; syndicated writer (under pseudonym)s. Bill Friday's Bus. Bull., 1989—. Author: Instant Printing, 1976 (transl. into Japanese), Successful Management, 1979, Quick Printing Encyclopedia, 1982, 8th edit., 1998, How to Sell Your Product Through (Not to) Wholesalers, 1980; pubr. Professional Estimator and Management Software for Printing Industry, 1997, Small Press Printing Encyclopedia, 1994. With USCG, 1942-45. Named Man of Yr. Quick Printing Mag., 1987. Mem. Nat. Assn. Quick Printers (hon. lifetime), C. of C., Kiwanis, Toastmasters. Democrat. Avocations: snow skiing, boating.

TREACY, STEPHEN DELOS, marine mammalogist, actor, playwright; b. Huntington, W.Va., Oct. 31, 1943; s. James Joseph and Laura Ellen (Moore) T.; m. Ann Hundley Collins, Sept. 29, 1968; children: Michael Starbuck, David Galway. BA in Biol. Sci., Marshall U., 1971; postgrad., U. Calif., Berkeley, 1978, U. Wash., 1980. Wildlife biologist Wash. Game Dept., Astoria, Oreg., 1980-84; wildlife biologist U.S. Minerals Mgmt. Svc., Anchorage, 1984-96, sr. wildlife biologist, 1996—; rsch. mgr. Bowhead Whale Aerial Survey Project, U.S. Minerals Mgmt. Svc., Anchorage, 1987—. Actor: Aerial Surveys of Endangered Whales in the Beaufort Sea, 1987-98, (movie) Magnum Force, 1974; playwright Winter Bird, 1995; actor profl. theaters. Vol. U.S. Peace Corps, Panamá, 1966-68; baseball coach Little League, Anchorage, 1993; judge H.S. drama tournaments, Anchorage, 1993—. Mem. SAG (chair Conservatory Film Workshop 1975-78, San Francisco Exec. Coun. 1977-78), Soc. for Marine Mammalogy (charter), Actors' Equity Assn., The Dramatists Guild, Inc., Cook Inlet Hist. Soc. Avocations: biking, canoeing, genealogy, mycology, zymurgy. Home: 3020 Redwood St Anchorage AK 99508 Office: US Minerals Mgmt Svc 949 E 36th Ave Anchorage AK 99508

TREADWAY-DILLMON, LINDA LEE, athletic trainer, actress, stuntwoman; b. Woodbury, N.J., June 4, 1950; d. Leo Elmer and Ona Lee (Wyckoff) Treadway; m. Randall Kenneth Dillmon, June 19, 1982. BS in Health, Phys. Edn. & Recreation, West Chester State Coll., 1972, MS in Health and Phys. Edn., 1975; postgrad., Ctrl. Mich. U., 1978; Police Officer Stds. Tng. cert. complaint dispatcher, Goldenwest Coll., 1982. Cert. in safety edn. West Chester State Coll.; cert. EMT, Am. Acad. Orthopaedic Surgeons. Grad. asst., instr., asst. athletic trainer West Chester (Pa.) State Coll., 1972-76; asst. prof., program dir., asst. athletic trainer Ctrl. Mich. U., Mt. Pleasant, 1976-80; police dispatcher City of Westminster, Calif., 1980-89; oncology unit sec. Children's Hosp. Orange County, Orange, Calif., 1989-96; control clk. food & beverage Marriott Hotel, Anaheim, Calif., 1996—. Stuntwoman, actress United Stunt Artists, SAG, L.A., 1982—; dancer Disneyland, Anaheim, Calif., 1988—; contbr. articles to profl. jours. Athletic trainer U.S. Olympic Women's Track and Field Trials, Frederick, Md., 1972, AAU Jr. World Wrestling Championships, Mt. Pleasant, Mich., 1977, Mich. Spl. Olympics, Mt. Pleasant, 1977, 78, 79. Recipient bronze and gold Spirit of Disneyland Resort awards, 1997; named Outstanding Phys. Educator, Delta Psi Kappa, Ctrl. Mich. U., 1980, Outstanding Young Woman of Am., 1984; named to Disneyland Entertainment Hall of Fame, 1995. Mem. SAG, Nat. Athletic Trainers Assn. (cert., women and athletic tng. ad hoc com. 1974-75, placement com. 1974-79, program dirs. coun. 1976-80, ethics com. 1977-80, visitation team 1978-80, 25 Yr. award 1997), U.S. Field Hockey Assn. (player), Pacific S.W. Field Hockey Assn. (player, Nat. Champion 1980, 81, 82), L.A. Field Hockey Assn. (player), Swing Shift Dance Team (dancer). Presbyterian. Avocations: flying, piano, athletics, stitchery, travel. Home: 18073 Scanlan Ct Fountain Valley CA 92708-5865

TREECE, JAMES LYLE, lawyer; b. Colorado Springs, Colo., Feb. 6, 1925; s. Lee Oren and Ruth Ida (Smith) T.; m. Ruth Julie Treece, Aug. 7, 1949 (div. 1984); children—James (dec.), Karen Treece, Teryl Wait, Jamilyn Smyser, Carol Crowder. Student Colo. State U., 1943, Colo. U., 1943, U.S. Naval Acad., 1944-46; B.S., Mesa Coll., 1946; J.D., U. Colo., 1950; postgrad. U. N.C., 1976-77. Bar: Colo. 1952, U.S. Dist. Ct. Colo. 1952, U.S. Ct. Appeals (10th cir.) 1952, U.S. Supreme Ct. 1967. Assoc., Yegge, Hall, Treece & Evans and predecessors, 1951-59, ptnr., 1959-69; U.S. atty., Colo., 1969-77; pres. Treece & Bahr and predecessor firms, Littleton, Colo., 1977-91; mcpl. judge, 1967-68; mem. faculty Nat. Trial Advocacy Inst., 1973-76, Law-Sci. Acad., 1964. Chmn. Colo. Dept. Pub. Welfare, 1963-68; chmn. Colo. Dept. Social Services, 1968-69; mem. Littleton Bd. Edn., 1977-81. Served with USNR, 1944-46. Recipient awards Colo. Assn. Sch. Bds., 1981, IRS, 1977, FBI, 1977, DEA, 1977, Fed. Exec. Bd., 1977. Mem. Fed. Bar Assn. (pres. Colo. 1975, award 1975), Colo. Bar Assn. (bd. govs.), Denver Bar Assn. (v.p., trustee). Republican. Episcopalian. Home: 12651 N Pebble Beach Dr Sun City AZ 85351-3327

TREFNY, JOHN ULRIC, academic administrator, dean; b. Greenwich, Conn., Jan. 28, 1942; s. Ulric John and Mary Elizabeth (Leech) T.; m. Sharon Livingston, 1992; 1 child from previous marriage, Benjamin Robin. BS, Fordham U., 1963; PhD, Rutgers U., 1968. Rsch. assoc. Cornell U., Ithaca, N.Y., 1967-69; asst. prof. physics Wesleyan U., Middletown, Conn., 1969-77; asst. prof. physics Colo. Sch. Mines, Golden, 1977-79, assoc. prof., 1979-85, prof. 1985—, dir. Amorphous Materials Ctr., 1986-90, assoc. dean rsch., 1988-90, head physics dept., 1990-95, v.p. for acad. affairs, dean faculty, 1995—; cons. Solar Energy Rsch. Inst., Golden, Energy Conversion Devices, Troy, Mich., others. Contbr. articles to profl. jours. Recipient Teaching award AMOCO Found., 1984, Friend of Sci. Edn. award, 1990. Mem. Colo. Assn. Sci. Tchrs. (bd. dirs. 1986-88), Sigma Xi (N.W. region co-dir. 1994—), Sigma Pi Sigma. Avocations: golfing, traveling, whiskey. Home: 14268 W 1st Ave Golden CO 80401-5354

TREGLE, LINDA MARIE, dance educator; b. Fort Sill, Okla., Sept. 8, 1947; d. Franklin and Helen Marie (Diggs) T. BA, Mills Coll., Stockton, Calif., 1970, MA, 1974; life credential, U. Calif., 1974. founder, dir., choreographer Internat. Studios, Inc., Stockton, 1970—; dance instr. San Joaquin Delta Coll., Stockton, 1970—; program cons., choreographer Alpha Kappa Alpha, Stockton, 1984—, choreographer SDW Motion Pictures, Stockton, 1983—; advisor Internat. Dance Club San Joaquin, 1970—; founder, dir. Tregles Internat. Dance Co., 1970—; mem. Ruth Beckford's Dance Studio. Directed and choreographed numerous dance prodn. videos. Mem. NAACP, Black Employment Trends (community rep. 1988—), Calif. Tchrs. Assn., Alpha Kappa Alpha. Avocations: creative writing, table sports, drama, arts, dance. Home: 2411 Arden Ln Stockton CA 95210-3256 Office: San Joaquin Delta Coll 5151 Pacific Ave Stockton CA 95207-6304

TREICH, RICHARD D., communication executive; b. Morristown, N.J., Oct. 9, 1953; s. Robert F. and Jeannette Treich; m. Nancy S. Dimatteo, Aug. 9, 1981; children:Cameron, Branden. BS in Bus. Adminstrn., Susquehanna U., 1975. Mgr. Ebasco, Dallas, 1975-82; dir. Coopers & Lybrand, Dallas, 1982-84; prin. KPMG Peat Marwick, Denver, 1984-95; v.p. regulation TCI Comm., Englewood, Colo., 1995—. Office: TCI Comm 5619 Dtc Pkwy Englewood CO 80111-3017

TREJOS, CHARLOTTE MARIE, humanities educator, consultant; b. Trout Lake, Mich., July 5, 1920; d. Charles Floyd and Lula May (Force) Draper; m. J. Mario Trejos, Jan. 8, 1961; 1 child, J. Mario Jr. Tchg. credentials, State of Calif., 1989; MA (hon.), Hawthorne Coll., 1975; DD (hon.), Min. Salvation Ch., 1986. Tchr. English El Colegio Anglo-Am., Cochabamba, Bolivia, 1965-66; tchr. Hawthorne (Calif.) Christian Sch., 1966-75; owner Trejos Literary Cons., Carson, Calif., 1976—. Author: My Carson, Your Carson, 1987, Variegated Verse, 1973, Yesterday Was Sunday, 1994; contbg. editor Health Care Horizons, 1979-89; contbr. articles to profl. jours. Voter registerer Democrats, Carson, 1975—. With U.S. Army, 1942-43. Named Poet of Yr. Nat. Poetry Pub. Assn., 1974; recipient Cert. of Merit Dictionary of Internat. Biography, 1974, Medal of Honor Am. Biog. Inst., 1987, Golden Poet award World of Poetry, 1993. Mem. Soc. Ibero-Am. Escritores de Los Estados Unidos Am. (pres. 1985—, Cert. Recognition 1986), Profl. Writers L.A. Chpt. Avocations: music, tap dancing, art, gardening. Home and Office: 22325 S Vermont Ave # 13 Torrance CA 90502-2427

TREMBLY, CRISTY, television executive; b. Oakland, Md., July 11, 1958; d. Charles Dee and Mary Louise (Cassidy) T. BA in Russian, German and Linguistics cum laude, W.Va. U., 1978, BS in Journalism, 1978, MS in Broadcast Journalism, 1979; advanced cert. travel, West L.A. Coll., 1982; advanced cert. recording engring., Soundmaster Schs., North Hollywood, Calif., 1985. Videotape engr. Sta. WWVU-TV, Morgantown, W.Va., 1976-80; announcer, engr. Sta. WVVW Radio, Grafton, W.Va., 1979; tech. dir., videotape supr. Sta. KMEX-TV, L.A., 1980-85; broadcast supr. Sta. KADY-TV, Oxnard, Calif., 1988-89; news tech. dir. Sta. KVEA-TV, Glendale, Calif., 1985-89; asst. editor, videotape technician CBS TV Network, Hollywood, Calif., 1989-90; videotape supr. Sta. KCBS-TV, Hollywood, 1990-91, mgr. electronic news gathering ops., 1991-92; studio mgr., engr.-in-charge CBS TV Network, Hollywood, 1992—; radio operator KJ6BX Malibu Disaster Comm., 1987—. Prodr. (TV show) The Mountain Scene, 1976-78. Sr. orgn. pres. Children of the Am. Revolution, Malibu, Calif., 1992—; chmn. adminstrv. coun. Malibu United Meth. Ch., 1993—, choir 1995—; sec., mem. adv. com. Tamassee (S.C.) Sch., 1992—; vol. Ch. Coun., L.A. Riot Rebldg., Homeless shelter work, VA Hosps., Mus. docent; sponsor 3 overseas foster children. Named one of Outstanding Young Women of Am., 1988; recipient Asst. editor Emmy award Young and the Restless, 1989-90, Golden Mike award Radio/TV News Assn., 1991, 92. Mem. ATAS (mem. exec. com. on electronic prodn. 1992—, mem. awards com. 1994-96, 97-98, engring. awards com. 1997-98, judge local and nat. Emmys 1991—, mem. membership com. 1994-96), DAR (state chair jr. membership 1987-88, state chair scholarships 1992-94, state chmn. jr. contest 1994-96, others, Malibu organizing regent 1991, state chair motion pictures radio and TV Calif. 1988-90, Mex. 1990—, Nat. Outstanding Jr. 1993, nat. vice-chair broadcast media 1995-98, state chair pub. rels. 1996—, nat. vice-chair units overseas Mex. 1998—), Am. Women in Radio and TV (So. Calif. bd. 1984-85, 93—, pres.-elect 1995-96, pres. 1996-97, dist. dir. 1997-98), Soc. Profl. Journalists, Women in Comms., Travelers Century Club (program chair 1987—), Soc. Broadcast Engrs. (1995—), Mensa (life), Soc. Motion Picture/TV Engrs. (pres. 1995-97), Beta Sigma Phi. Democrat. Methodist. Avocations: singing, cooking, travel, genealogy, languages. Home: 2901 Searidge St Malibu CA 90265-2969 Office: CBS TV City 7800 Beverly Blvd Los Angeles CA 90036-2188

TREMBOUR, FRED WILLIAM, foreign service officer, metallurgist; b. Watervliet, N.Y., Sept. 19, 1912; s. Max Rudolf and Margaret Rose (Ellinger) T.; m. Margaret Culbertson (div. June 1951); children: Richard, William; m. Mary Leone Egerman, Dec. 1, 1951; children: Alice, Karla Trembour Irvin. BS in Metall. Engring., Carnegie Inst. Tech., 1940; postgrad., U. Colo., 1971-73. Rsch. engr. Westinghouse Electric & Mfg. Co., East Pittsburgh, Pa., 1938-42; prodn. engr. Ferrotherm Co., Cleve., 1942-46; fgn. svc. officer Dept. Commerce, Dept. War, USIA, Dept. Def., Dept. State, various locations, 1946-69; rsch. assoc. U.S. Geol. Survey Dating Lab., Denver, 1974—; rsch. affiliate U. Colo. Inst. Arctic and Alpine Rsch., Boulder, 1988—. Contbr. articles to profl. jours. Carnegie Inst. Tech. scholar. Mem. AAAS, Archaeol. Inst. Am. Democrat. Avocations: numismatics, lithics in archaeology, non-fiction reading in social sciences. Home: 365 S 43rd St Boulder CO 80303-6005

TRENBERTH, KEVIN EDWARD, atmospheric scientist; b. Christchurch, New Zealand, Nov. 8, 1944; came to U.S., 1977; s. Edward Maurice and Ngaira Ivy (Eyre) T.; m. Gail Neville Thompson, Mar. 21, 1970; children: Annika Gail, Angela Dawn. BSc with honors, U. Canterbury, Christchurch, 1966; ScD, MIT, 1972. Meteorologist New Zealand Meteorol. Service, Wellington, 1966-76, supt. dynamic meteorology, 1976-77; assoc. prof. meteorology U. Ill., Urbana, 1977-82, prof., 1982-84; scientist Nat. Ctr. Atmospheric Research, Boulder, Colo., 1984-86, sr. scientist, 1986—, leader empirical studies group, 1987, head sect. climate analysis, 1987—; dep. dir. climate and global dynamics divsn. Nat. Ctr. Atmospheric Rsch., Boulder, Colo., 1991-95; mem. joint sci. com. for world climate programme, com. climate changes and the ocean Tropical Oceans Global Atmosphere Program Sci. Steering Group, 1990-94; mem. Climate Variability and Predictability Sci. Steering Group, 1995—, co-chair, 1996—; mem. joint sci. com. World Climate Rsch. Program, 1999—. Editor: Climate System Modeling, 1992, Earth Interactions, 1996-98; contbr. articles to profl. jours. Grantee NSF, NOAA, NASA. Fellow Am. Meteorol. Soc. (editor sci. jour. 1981-86, com. chmn. 1985-87, Editor's award 1989), AAAS (coun. del. sect. atmosphere and hydrosphere sci. 1993-97), Royal Soc. New Zealand (hon.); mem. NAS (earth scis. com. 1982-85, tropical oceans global atmosphere adv. panel 1984-87, polar rsch. bd. 1986-90, climate rsch. com. 1987-90, global oceans atmosphere land sys. panel 1994-98), Atmosphere Obs. Panel of Globe Climate Observing Sys., Meterol. Soc. New Zealand. Home: 1445 Landis Ct Boulder CO 80303-1122 Office: Nat Ctr Atmospheric Research PO Box 3000 Boulder CO 80307-3000

TRESSLAR, NOLA V., artist, retired foundation administrator, marketing professional; b. Tacoma, Wash., Mar. 10, 1942; d. Arthur and Viola Mafalda (Sirianni) De Caro; m. Lloyd E. Montgomery, Dec. 8, 1961 (div. 1971); children: Gina N. Montgomery, Melissa R. Montgomery; m. Walter B. Swain, Mar. 11, 1977 (div. 1994); m. Guy E. Tresslar, May 16, 1997. Student, U. Puget Sound, 1959-62. First woman cert. real estate appraiser, Wash. Appraiser/assesor Pierce County Assessors Office, Tacoma, 1971-77; chief appraiser Otero Savs. & Loan, Colorado Springs, 1977-78; pvt. fee appraiser, co-owner N.W.S. & Assocs., Colorado Springs, 1978—; pres., designer N.V.S. Enterprises, Colorado Springs, 1980-89; dir. mktg. U S

WEST Edn. Found., Seattle, 1990-92, exec. dir. Northwest Baby Talk, 1993-95, fund devel., pub. rels. mgr. Child Abuse Prevention Resources, 1995—. Designer numerous gift items. Recipient Women at Work award Council on Working Women, 1985, Pub. Service award Colorado Springs Assn. Life Underwriters, 1985, Salesman With A Purpose Club Booster of Yr. award, 1986. Mem. NAFE, NOW, Urban League, Tacoma Jr. League (cmty. adv. bd.), Soc. Real Estate Appraisers (candidate, treas. 1978, bd. dirs. 1982-84), Chi Omega Alumnae. Democrat. Avocations: traveling, sumi painting, crafts, photography, volunteering.

TRETIKOFF, ELENA HELEN, writer; b. Newhalen, Alaska, Apr. 14, 1954; d. Evon and Okalena Tretikoff; m. Peter Joseph; m. John Kruscke Sr.; children: Norman, Curtis, Ricco, Viola, Hylda, John, Naidene, Sophia. Postal clk. Iliamna, Alaska, 1974-75; health rep Bristol Bay Area Health, Alaska, 1975-81; store owner Newhalen, Alaska, 1975-81; job corp employee Palmer, Alaska, 1994-95; writer Iliamna, 1995—. village rep. Newhalen City, Alaska, 1975-81, mayor, 1983. Recipient award Libr. Congress, 1996. Russian Orthodox. Home: Box 54 Iliamna AK 99606

TREVITHICK, RONALD JAMES, underwriter; b. Portland, Oreg., Sept. 13, 1944; s. Clifford Vincent and Amy Lois (Turner) T.; m. Delberta Russell, Sept. 11, 1965; children: Pamela, Carmen, Marla, Sheryl. BBA U. Wash., 1966. CLU, CPA, ChFC, accredited estate planner. Mem. audit staff Ernst & Ernst, Anchorage, 1966, 68-70; pvt. practice acctg., Fairbanks, Alaska, 1970-73; with Touche Ross & Co., Anchorage, 1973-78, audit ptnr., 1976-78; exec. v.p., treas., bd. dirs. Veco Internat., Inc., 1978-82; pres., bd. dirs. Petroleum Contractors Ltd., 1980-82; bd. dirs. P.S. Contractors A/S, Norcon, Inc., OFC of Alaska, Inc., V.E. Systems Svcs., Inc., Veco Turbo Services, Inc., Veco Drilling, Inc., Vemar, Inc., 1978-82; with Coopers & Lybrand, Anchorage, 1982-85; field underwriter, registered rep. New York Life Ins., 1985—; instr. acctg. U. Alaska, 1971-72; lectr. acctg. and taxation The Am. Coll., 1972, 97, instr. adv. sales Life Underwriters Tng. Coun., 1988-89; bd. dirs. Ahtna Devel. Corp., 1985-86. Div. chmn. United Way, 1975-76, YMCA, 1979; bd. dirs., fin. chmn. Anchorage Arts Coun., 1975-78, Am. Diabetes Assn., Alaska affiliate, 1985-91, chmn. bd. 1988-89, chmn. hon. bd. 1992-96, Am. Heart Assn., Alaska affiliate, 1986-87, Anchorage dist. com., 1994-96, treas. 1996-98, Alaska State Youth Soccer Assn.; mem. Anchorage Estate Planning Coun., 1996—, treas., 1998—. With U.S. Army, 1967-68. Mem. Fin. Execs. Inst. (pres. Alaska chpt. 1981-83), Soc. Fin. Svcs. Profs. (v.p. Alaska chpt. 1993-94, pres. 1994-96), Alaska Assn. Life Underwriters (sec., treas. 1987-90), Alaska Planned Giving Counc., Beta Alpha Psi. Clubs: Alaska Goldstrikers Soccer (pres. 1992-93, youth coach 1985-95), Petroleum (treas. 1996—). Home: 4421 Huffman Rd Anchorage AK 99516-2211 Office: 1600 A St Ste 110 Anchorage AK 99501-5146

TREWHELLA, JILL, biophysicist; b. Sydney, Australia, Jan. 24, 1953; d. Leonard John and Ivy Joy (Kingsley) T.; m. David Louis Ollis, July 1974 (div. 1982); 1 child, Graham Andrew; m. Don Merrill Parkin, June 1991. BSc, U. NSW, 1975, MSc, 1978; PhD, U. Sydney, 1981. Postdoctoral assoc. Yale U., New Haven, Conn., 1980-84; staff mem. Los Alamos (N.Mex.) Nat. Lab., 1984-88, sect. leader, 1988-90, dep. group leader, 1990-91, scientific advisor, staff mem. 1991-92, group leader, 1992-95, lab. fellow, 1995—; study sect. mem. NIH divsn. rsch. grants, molecular and cellular biophysics, 1996—; chairperson Nat. Inst. of Stds. Tech. Col. Neutron Rsch. Facility Program adv. com. 1991-98; mem. biophysics rev. panel NSF, 1989-91. Editor: Stable Isotope Applications in Biomolecular Structure and Mechanisms, 1995; mem. adv. editl. bd. European Physics Jour., 1996—; contbr. articles to profl. jours. including Jour. Molecular Biology, Biochemistry, Jour. Biol. Chemistry, Nature, Protein Sci., Biophys. Jour., others. Recipient Commonwealth Postgrad. award Australian Govt., 1975-79, Los Alamos Nat. Lab. Fellows prize, 1995. Mem. Biophys. Soc. (coun. 1993-96, exec. bd. 1994-96, chair publs. com. 1996—, sec. elect 1998), Neutron Scattering Soc. of Am. (exec. com. 1993-96), Am. Crystallographic Soc. (chair small angle scattering spl. interest group 1997-98). Achievements include research in advances in understanding the structural basis for regulation of biochemical processes. Home: 1417 Big Rock Loop Los Alamos NM 87544-2875 Office: Biosci and Biotech Group Chem Sci and Tech Divsn Mail Stop G758 Los Alamos NM 87545

TRIBBLE, RICHARD WALTER, brokerage executive; b. San Diego, Oct. 19, 1948; s. Walter Perrin and Catherine Janet (Miller) T.; m. Joan Catherine Sliter, June 26, 1980. BS, U. Ala., Tuscaloosa, 1968; grad. Gulf Coast Sch. Drilling Practices, U. Southwestern La., 1976. Stockbroker Shearson, Am. Express, Washington, 1971-76; ind. oil and gas investment sales, Falls Church, Va., 1976-77; pres. Monroe & Keusink, Inc., Falls Church and Columbus, Ohio, 1977-87; instnl. investment officer FCA Asset Mgmt., 1983-85; fin. cons. Merrill Lynch Pierce, Fenner & Smith, Inc., Phoenix, 1987—, cert. fin. mgr., 1989—, sr. fin. cons., 1992—, asst. v.p., 1993—. Served with USMC, 1969-70. Republican. Methodist. Office: 2525 E Camelback Rd Phoenix AZ 85016-4219

TRICOLES, GUS PETER, electromagnetic engineer, physicist, consultant; b. San Francisco, Oct. 18, 1931; s. Constantine Peter and Eugenia (Elias) T.; m. Beverly Mildred Ralsky, Dec. 20, 1953 (dec. Dec. 1974); children: Rosanne, Robin; m. Aileen Irma Aronson, Apr. 1, 1980 (div. June 1980). BA in Physics, UCLA, 1955; MS in Applied Math., San Diego State U., 1958; MS in Applied Physics, U. Calif., San Diego, 1962, PhD in Applied Physics, 1971. Engr. Convair div. Gen. Dynamics, San Diego, 1955-59, engr. Electronics div., 1962-75, engring. mgr. Electronics div., 1975-89, sr. engring. staff specialist, 1989-92; engr. Smyth Rsch. Assn., San Diego, 1959-61; rsch. asst. Scripps Instn. Oceanography, La Jolla, Calif., 1961-62; sr. engring. staff specialist G.D.E. Systems, Inc., San Diego, 1992—; cons. Ga. Inst. Tech., Atlanta, 1972, 79-80, Transco Industries, L.A., 1973, Aero Geo Industries, San Antonio, 1980-82, Vantage Assocs., San Diego, 1988; rsch. reviewer NRC, NAS, Boulder, Colo., 1986-88. Author: (with others) Radome Engineering Handbook, 1970, Antenna Handbook, 1988; contbr. articles to profl. jours.; holder 19 patents. With USN, 1952-53. Fellow IEEE (antenna standards com. 1980—, advancement com. 1988), Optical Soc. Am. (local sect. v.p. 1966); mem. N.Y. Acad. Scis., Am. Geophys. Union. Avocations: woodworking, photography. Home: 4633 Euclid Ave San Diego CA 92115-3226 Office: GDE Sys Inc PO Box 92150 San Diego CA 92150-9009

TRIEWEILER, TERRY NICHOLAS, state supreme court justice; b. Dubuque, Iowa, Mar. 21, 1948; s. George Nicholas and Anne Marie (Oastern) T.; m. Carol M. Jacobson, Aug. 11, 1972; children: Kathryn Marie, Christina Marie, Anna Theresa. BA, Drake U., 1970, JD, 1972. Bar: Iowa 1973, Wash. 1973, U.S. Dist. Ct. (so. dist.) Iowa 1973, U.S. Dist. Ct. (we. dist.) Wash. 1973, Mont. 1975, U.S. Dist. Ct. Mont. 1977. Staff atty. Polk County Legal Services, Des Moines, 1973; assoc. Hullin, Roberts, Mines, Fite & Rowland, Seattle, 1973-75, Morrison & Hedman, Whitefish, Mont., 1975-77; sole practice, Whitefish; justice Mont. Supreme Ct., Helena, 1991—; lectr. U. Mont. Law Sch., 1981—; mem. com. to amend civil proc. rules Mont. Supreme Ct., Helena, 1984, commn. to draft pattern jury instrns., 1985; mem. Gov.'s Adv. Com. on Amendment to Work Compensation Act, adv. com. Mont. Work Compensation Ct. Mem. ABA, Mont. Bar Assn. (pres. 1986-87), Wash. Bar Assn., Iowa Bar Assn., Assn. Trial Lawyers Am., Mont. Trial Lawyers Assn. (dir., pres.). Democrat. Roman Catholic. Home: 1615 Virginia Dale St Helena MT 59601-5823 Office: Mont Supreme Ct Justice Bldg Rm 410 215 N Sanders St Helena MT 59620-4522*

TRIGIANO, LUCIEN LEWIS, physician; b. Easton, Pa., Feb. 9, 1926; s. Nicholas and Angeline (Lewis) T.; children: Lynn Anita, Glenn Larry, Robert Nicholas. Student Tex. Christian U., 1944-45, Ohio U., 1943-44, 46-47, Milligan Coll., 1944, Northwestern U., 1945, Temple U., 1948-52. Intern, Meml. Hosp., Johnstown, Pa., 1952-53; resident Lee Hosp., Johnstown, 1953-54; gen. practice, Johnstown 1953-59; med. dir. Pa. Rehab. Center, Johnstown, 1959-62, chief phys. medicine and rehab., 1964-70; physics medicine and rehab. N.Y. Inst. Phys. Medicine and Rehab., 1962-64; dir. rehab. medicine Lee Hosp., 1964-71, Ralph K. Davies Med. Center, San Francisco, 1978-83, Rehab. Ctr. of Nev., Las Vegas, 1998—; asst. prof. phys. medicine and rehab. Temple U. Sch. Medicine; founder Disability Alert. Served with USNR, 1944-46. Diplomate Am. Bd. Phys. Medicine and Rehab. Mem. AMA, A.C.P., Pa. San Francisco County Med. socs., Am. Acad. Phys. Medicine and Rehab., Am. Congress Phys.

TRIMBLE, STEPHEN, writer, photographer; b. Denver, Oct. 30, 1950; s. Donald Eldon and Isabelle Virginia (Brinig) T.; m. Joanne Carol Slotnik, Oct. 11, 1987; children: Dory Elizabeth, Jacob Douglas. BA magna cum laude, Colo. Coll., 1972; MS, U. Ariz., 1979. Park ranger/naturalist Utah, Wash., Colo., 1972-75; dir. Mus. No. Ariz. Press, 1980-81. Author: The Bright Edge: A Guide to the National Parks of the Colorado Plateau, 1979, Longs Peak: A Rocky Mountain Chronicle, 1984, Canyon Country, 1986, Our Voices, Our Land, 1986, Talking With the Clay: the Art of Pueblo Pottery, 1987, The Sagebrush Ocean: A Natural History of the Great Basin, 1989, The People: Indians of the American Southwest, 1993; co-author: The Geography of Childhood: Why Children Need Wild Places, 1994, Testimony: Writers of the West Speak on Behalf of Utah Wilderness, 1996; editor: Blessed By Light: Visions of the Colorado Plateau, 1986, Words from the Land: Encounters with Natural History Writing, 1988; photographer: Earth Fire: A Hopi Legend of the Sunset Crater Eruption, 1987, Navajo Pottery: Traditions and Innovations, 1987, The Nepal Trekker's Handbook, 1989, Earthtones: A Nevada Album, 1995, Mud Matters: Stories From a Mud Lover, 1998; author (children's book) The Village of Blue Stone, 1990. Mem. Authors Guild, Am. Soc. Media Photographers, PEN West, Gentlemen's Book Group. Avocations: camping, photography, books, natural history, education of children. Home and Office: PO Box 1078 Salt Lake City UT 84110-1078

TRIPOLI, MASUMI HIROYASU, financial consultant and diplomat; b. Fukuyama, Japan, Apr. 23, 1956; d. Yoshimi and Suzuko Hiroyasu; 1 child, Mona Lisa Tripoli. BA cum laude, U. Wash., 1978; MA, Sophia U., Tokyo, 1981; MBA, Ecole des Hautes Etudes Comml, Jouy-en-Josas, France, 1983. CFP; chartered fin. cons. Corp. planning mgr. Kowa Corp., Osaka, Japan, 1983-85; internat. bond trader Banque Baribas, Tokyo, 1985-86, Westpac Bank, Tokyo, 1987-88; fin. cons. Sagemark Consulting/Lincoln Fin. Advisors, Glendale, Calif., 1989—; Tripoli & Assocs., Glendale, Calif., 1989—; anchor newscaster United TV, L.A., 1989-92; condr. seminars in field. Contbr. articles to profl. jours. Grantee Sophia U., 1979, H.E.C., 1983. Mem. Internat. Bd. Cert. Fin. Planners. Avocations: child education, horseback riding. Office: Tripoli and Assocs 330 N Brand Blvd Ste 400 Glendale CA 91203-2308

TRIPP, KEVIN FRANCIS, priest; b. New Bedford, Mass., May 17, 1942; s. Philip Francis and Helen Catherine (FitzGerald) T. BA, St. John's Sem., Brighton, Mass., 1964, MDiv., 1968; postgrad., Notre Dame U., 1965-68. Ordained priest Roman Cath. Ch., 1968. Parish priest Diocese of Fall River (Mass.), 1968-74; dir. religious ministries St. Luke's Hosp., New Bedford, Mass., 1974-83; dir. clin. pastoral edn. Our Lady of the Lake Regional Med. Ctr., Baton Rouge, La., 1983-87; dir. chaplain svcs. St. Mary's Hosp. and Med. Ctr., San Francisco, 1987-93; pres. SpiritHealth, 1994—; exec. dir. Marin Interfaith Coun., 1997—. Contbr. articles to profl. jours. Recipient Disting. Svc. award Mass. Jaycees, Fall River, 1970. Mem. Nat. Assn. Cath. Chaplains (Disting. Svc. award 1987, 95, pres. elect 1991, pres. 1993-95). Avocations: sailing, reading, playing piano, listening to classical music. Home: 14551 Redwood Ln Guerneville CA 95446-9662 Office: Marin Interfaith Coun 650 Las Gallinas Ave San Rafael CA 94903-3620

TRIPP, SUSAN LYNN, small business owner; b. Long Beach, Calif., May 1, 1953; d. Fred Robert and Marion Mary (Swales) Mulker; m. Gary Elliot Wolf, July 3, 1977 (div. Aug. 1986); 1 child, Daniel Gary; m. Robert Rolan Tripp, Mar.22, 1987. BA in Liberal Arts, San Jose State U., 1976. Cert. tchr., Calif. Dir.- San Jose (Calif.) State Housing, 1975-77; dir. Wonderland Presch., San Jose, 1978; tchr. Hillbrook Sch., Los Gatos, Calif., 1979-87; owner, mgr. TeleVet, San Jose, 1987-90; mgr. La Mirada Animal Hosp., Santa Fe Springs, Calif., 1989-90, owner, mgr., 1990—; spkr. Vet. Mgmt. Co., Ft. Collins, Colo., 1992, Ebell Club, La Mirada, 1993; cons., 1993; TV appearances include La Mirada Cable, 1993. Author: Sex is Good, Abuse is Wrong, 1986-93. Pub. safety commr. La Mirada, Calif., 1993—; campaign chair Sch. Bd. candidate, 1993; coord. Neighborhood Watch Program, La Mirada, 1993; chair Com. to Elect Pat Ruiz, La Mirada, 1993; mem. La Mirada Gang Task Force, 1993-94, La Mirada Disaster Steering Com., 1993-94; elder Cmty. Presbyn. Ch., La Mirada, 1994. Mem. La Mirada C. of C. Avocation: pets, hiking, travel, computer, advertising. Office: La Mirada Animal Hosp 13914 Rosecrans Ave Santa Fe Springs CA 90670-5210

TRIPPEL, STUART ANDREW THOMAS, economist, consultant; b. Auburn, Wash., Jan. 19, 1964; s. Richard Lee and Lola Myrth (Simmons) T. BA, U. Wash., 1988. Economist CH2M HILL, Bellevue, Wash., 1987-89; mgmt. cons. McKinley Group, Seattle, 1989-90; economist Econ. Engring. Svcs., Inc., Bellevue, 1990-96; v.p. EES Cons., Inc., Bellevue, 1996-97; pvt. practice Seattle, 1997—. Bd. trustees Municipal League King County, Seattle, 1990-92; adv. com. Catherine of Siena Inst., Seattle, 1997—. Mem. Am. Economic Assn., Orgn. Am. Historians. Republican. Roman Catholic. E-mail: stuart.trippel@worldnet.att.net. Fax: 206-652-8487. Office: 506 2nd Ave Ste 1718 Seattle WA 98104-2348

TROISPOUX, CHRISTIANNE VALERIE ANN, psychologist; b. Pasadena, Calif., June 10, 1968; d. Claude and Georgette (Guestault) T. BA in Psychology, Mt. St. Mary's Coll., 1990; MA in Psychology, Calif. State U., Northridge, 1993. Cert. sch. psychologist. Ednl. therapist Hillside Devel. Learning Ctr., La Canada, Calif., 1990-93; sch. psychologist L.A. Unified Sch. Dist., 1993—. Mem. Calif. Assn. Sch. Psychologists, NOW. Democrat. Roman Catholic. Avocations: arts and crafts, biking, hiking, reading. Office: LAUSD Spl Edn 450 N Grand Ave Los Angeles CA 90012-2123

TROMMER, ROSEMERRY WAHTOLA, writer, poet, editor; b. Grand Forks, N.D., Nov. 2, 1969; d. Charles Henry and Julianne (Stoll) Wahtola; m. Eric William Trommer, Oct. 21, 1995; 1 stepchild, Shawnee Adelson. BA in English, Colo. Coll., 1992; grad., Denver Pub. Inst., 1992; MA in English Lang. and Linguistics, U. Wis., 1994. Tchr. writing, ESL U. Wis., Madison, 1993-94; arts writer Telluride (Colo.) Times-Jour., 1994-85, arts editor, 1995-97; editor Telluride Pub., 1997—; freelance writer, 1995—; poetry specialist Telluride Acad., 1998—; cons. McGinley & Assoc., Telluride, 1998—; editor Buildingzone.com, Ridgway, Colo., 1998—; bd. dirs. Anhaa Sch. of the Arts. Contbr. poetry and feature stories to lit. publs. Bd. dirs. Telluride Edn. Found., 1997—; soprano Heartbeat, 1994—; Telluride Chamber Choir, 1995—. Recipient Poets in Person award NEH, Telluride, 1997-98, Native Am. Poetry award Amelia, 1998; Homegrown grantee Colo. Commn. for Arts, 1997-98, 98-99. Mem. Colo. Press Assn. (Best Feature Story award 1996, Best Column, Humor award 1997), Telluride Writers Guild (bd. dirs. 1998—, Mark Fischer Poetry prize 1997), Phi Beta Kappa. Avocations: hiking, rafting, singing, cooking, yoga. Office: Telluride Pub PO Box 964 Telluride CO 81435

TROST, BARRY MARTIN, chemist, educator; b. Phila., June 13, 1941; s. Joseph and Esther T.; m. Susan Paula Shapiro, Nov. 25, 1967; children: Aaron David, Carey Daniel. BA cum laude, U. Pa., 1962; PhD, MIT, 1965; D (hon.), U. Claude Bernard, Lyons, France, 1994, Technion, Israel, 1997. Mem. faculty U. Wis., Madison, 1965—, prof. chemistry, rsch. prof. chemistry U. Wis., prof. chemistry Stanford U., 1987—; Tamaki prof. humanities and scis., 1990, chmn. dept., 1996—; cons. Merck, Sharp & Dohme, E.I. duPont de Nemours; Chem. Soc. centenary lectr., 1982. Author: Problems in Spectroscopy, 1967, Sulfur Ylides, 1975; editor-in-chief Comprehensive Organic Synthesis, 1991—, ChemTracts/Organic Chemistry, 1993—; editor: Structure and Reactivity Concepts in Organic Chemistry series, 1972—; assoc. editor Jour. Am. Chem. Soc., 1974-80; mem. editl. bd. Organic Reactions series 1971—, Chemistry A European Jour., 1995—, Sci. of Synthesis, Houben-Weyl Methods of Molecular Transformations, 1995—; contbr. numerous articles to profl. jours. Recipient Dreyfus Found. Tech.-Scholar award, 1970, 77, Creative Work in Synthetic Organic Chemistry award, 1981, Baekeland award 1990, Janssen prize, 1990, Roger Adams award Am. Chem. Soc. 1995, Presdl. Green Univ. Challenge award, 1998; named Chem. Pioneer, Am. Inst. Chemists, 1983; NSF fellow, 1963-65, Sloan Found. fellow, 1967-69, Am. Swiss Found. fellow 1975, Zinpora fellow 1997, Guggenheim 1989. Mem. AAAS, Am. Chem. Soc. (award in pure chemistry 1977, Roger Adams

award 1995, Herbert C. Brown award for creative rsch. in synthetic methods 1999), Nat. Acad. Scis., Am. Acad. Arts and Scis., Chem. Soc. London. Office: Stanford U Dept Chemistry Stanford CA 94305

TROTT, STEPHEN SPANGLER, federal judge, musician; b. Glen Ridge, N.J., Dec. 12, 1939; s. David Herman and Virginia (Spangler) T.; divorced; children: Christina, Shelley. BA, Wesleyan U., 1962; LLB, Harvard U., 1965; LLD (hon.), Santa Clara U., 1992. Bar: Calif. 1966, U.S. Dist. Ct. (cen. dist.) Calif. 1966, U.S. Ct. Appeals (9th cir.) 1983, U.S. Supreme Ct. 1984. Guitarist, mem. The Highwaymen, 1958—; dep. dist. atty. Los Angeles County Dist. Atty.'s Office, Los Angeles, 1966-75; chief dep. dist. atty. Los Angeles County Dist. Atty.'s Office, 1975-79; U.S. dist. atty. Central Dist. Calif., Los Angeles, 1981-83; asst. atty. gen. criminal div. Dept. Justice, Washington, 1983-86; mem. faculty Nat. Coll. Dist. Attys., Houston, 1981-83; central dist. Calif. Law Enforcement Coordinating Com.; Houston, 1981-83; coordinator Los Angeles-Nev. Drug Enforcement Task Force, 1982-83; assoc. atty. gen. Justice Dept., Washington, 1986-88; chmn. U.S. Interpol, 1986-88; judge U.S. Ct. of Appeals 9th Cir., Boise, Idaho, 1988—. Trustee Wesleyan U., 1984-87; bd. dirs., pres. Children's Home Soc., Idaho, 1990—; bd. dirs. Boise Philharm. Assn., 1995—, v.p., 1997—. Recipient Gold record as singer-guitarist for Michael Row the Boat Ashore, 1961, Disting. Faculty award Nat. Coll. Dist. Attys., 1977. Mem. Am. Coll. Trial Lawyers, Wilderness Fly Fishers Club (pres. 1975-77), Brentwood Racing Pigeon Club (pres. 1977-82), Magic Castle, Internat. Brotherhood Magicians, Idaho Classic Guitar Soc. (founder, pres. 1980—). Republican. Office: US Ct Appeals 9th Cir 666 US Courthouse 550 W Fort St Boise ID 83724-0101*

TROTTER, F(REDERICK) THOMAS, retired academic administrator; b. L.A., Apr. 17, 1926; s. Fred B. and Hazel (Thomas) T.; m. Gania Demaree, June 27, 1953; children—Ruth Elizabeth, Paula Anne (dec.), Tania, Mary. AB, Occidental Coll., 1950, DD, 1968; STB, Boston U., 1953, PhD, 1958; LHD, Ill. Wesleyan U., 1974, Cornell Coll., 1985, Westmar Coll., 1987; LLD, U. Pacific, 1978, Wesleyan Coll., 1981; EdD, Columbia Coll., 1984; LittD, Alaska Pacific U., 1987. Exec. sec. Boston U. Student Christian Assn., 1951-54; ordained elder Calif.-Pacific, Methodist Ch., 1953; pastor Montclair (Calif.) Meth. Ch., 1956-59; lectr. So. Calif. Sch. Theology at Claremont, 1957-59, instr., 1959-60, asst. prof., 1960-63, assoc. prof., 1963-66, prof., 1966, dean, 1961; prof. religion and arts, dean Sch. Theology Claremont, 1961-73; mem. Bd. Higher Edn. and Ministry, United Meth. Ch., 1972-73, gen. sec., 1973-87; pres. Alaska Pacific U., Anchorage, 1988-95; ret., 1995; dir. Inst. for Antiquity and Christianity at Claremont. Author: Jesus and the Historian, 1968, Loving God with One's Mind, 1987, God Is with Us, 1997, Politics, Morality, and Higher Education, 1997, weekly column local newspapers; editor-at-large: Christian Century, 1969-84. Trustee Dillard U. Served with USAAF, 1944-46. Kent fellow Soc. for Values in Higher Edn., 1954; Dempster fellow Meth. Ch., 1954. Mem. Rotary Internat. (Anchorage Downtown), Commonwealth North. Home: 75-136 Kiowa Dr Indian Wells CA 92210

TROUNSTINE, PHILIP JOHN, editor, journalist; b. Cin., July 30, 1949; s. Henry P. and Amy May (Joseph) Trounstine; children: Jessica, David; m. Deborah Williams, May 1, 1993; children: amy, Ryan, Patrick Wilkes. Student, U. Vt., 1967-68, Stanford U., 1968-70; BA in Journalism, San Jose State U., 1975. Graphic artist Eric Printing, San Jose, Calif., 1972-75; reporter Indpls. Star, Ind., 1975-78; reporter San Jose Mercury News, Calif., 1978-83, editl. writer, 1983-86, polit. editor, 1986—; ednl. cons. Teen Recovery Strategies, 1995—. Co-author: Movers & Shakers: The Study of Community Power, 1981. Creator, writer SPJ Gridiron Show, San Jose, 1981-91. Pulliam fellow, 1975, Duke U., 1991, J.S. Knight Stanford U., 1993-94. Mem. Soc. Profl. Journalists (mem. nat. ethics com. 1993-96). Jewish. Avocations: golf, fishing. Home: 912 46th St Sacramento CA 95819-3431 Office: San Jose Mercury News 750 Ridder Park Dr San Jose CA 95190-0001

TROUPE, MICHAEL EUGENE, career officer; b. Lake City, Fla., Jan. 28, 1962; s. Etheridge Estelle and Marie Melrose (Pafford) T. AA, U. Md., 1991. From student to tech. support U.S. Navy, Pearl Harbor, Hawaii, 1982—. Avocations: reading, internet, music.

TROUT, LINDA COPPLE, state supreme court justice; b. Tokyo, Sept. 1, 1951. BA, U. Idaho, 1973, JD, 1977. Bar: Idaho 1977. Judge magistrate divsn. Idaho Dist. Ct. (2d jud. divsn.), 1990-91; dist. judge Idaho Dist. Ct. (2d jud. divsn.), Lewiston, 1991-92; acting trial ct. adminstr. Idaho Dist. Ct. (2d jud. divsn.), 1987-91; justice Idaho Supreme Ct., 1992—, chief justice, 1997—; instr. collection law U. Idaho, 1983, 88. Mem. Idaho State Bar Assn., Clearwater Bar Assn. (pres. 1980-81).

TROUT, MONROE EUGENE, hospital systems executive; b. Harrisburg, Pa., Apr. 5, 1931; s. David Michael and Florence Margaret (Kashner) T.; m. Sandra Louise Lemke, June 11, 1960; children: Monroe Eugene, Timothy William. AB, U. Pa., 1953, MD, 1957; LLB, Dickinson Sch. of Law, 1964, JD, 1969; LLD (hon.), Dickinson Sch. Law, 1996, Bloomfield Coll., 1994. Intern Great Lakes (Ill.) Naval Hosp., 1957-58; resident in internal medicine Portsmouth (Va.) Naval Hosp., 1959-61; chief med. dept. Harrisburg State Hosp., 1961-64; dir. drug regulatory affairs Pfizer, Inc., N.Y.C., 1964-68; v.p., med. dir. Winthrop Labs., N.Y.C., 1968-70; med. dir. Sterling Drug, Inc., N.Y.C., 1970-74, v.p., dir. med. affairs, 1974-78, sr. v.p., dir. med. affairs, bd. dirs., mem. exec. com. 1978-86; pres., CEO Am. Healthcare Sys., Inc., 1986-95, chmn., 1987-95; also bd. dirs. Am. Healthcare Systems, Inc.; chmn. emeritus Am. Healthcare Sys., Inc., 1995—; interim CEO Cytran Inc., 1996; bd. dirs. Baxter Internat., SAIC, West Co., Inc.; chmn. bd. dirs. Cytyc Inc., Am. Excess Ins. ltd., 1990-95; adj. assoc. prof. Bklyn. Coll. Pharmacy; spl. lectr. legal medicine, trustee Dickinson Sch. Law, 1970-93; trustee Ariz. State U. Sch. Health Adminstrn., 1988-91; mem. Sterling Winthrop Rsch. Bd., 1977-86, Joint Commn. Prescription Drug Use, 1976-80; sec. Commn. on Med. Malpractice, HEW, 1971-73, cons., 1974; co-chmn. San Diego County Health Commn., 1992-94; past dir. Biotransplantation, Inc., Gensia, Inc., Cytran, Inc., Criticare Inc., 1991-95. Mem. editl. bd. Hosp. Formulary Mgmt., 1969-79, Forensic Sci., 1971—, Jour. Legal Medicine, 1973-79, Reg. Tox. and Pharmac, 1981-87, Med. Malpractice Prevention, 1985—; editl. reviewer Annals of Internal Medicine; contbr. articles to profl. jours. Exec. com. White House Mini Conf. on Aging, 1980; Rep. dist. leader, New Canaan, Conn., 1966-68; mem. Nat. Health Adv. AAA, N.Y. State Commn. Substance Abuse, 1978-80, Town Coun., New Canaan, 1978-86, vice chmn., 1985-86; bd. dirs. New Canaan Interchurch Svc. Com., 1965-69, Athletes Kidney Found., Circle in Sq. Theatre Inc., 1984-86; trustee Cleve. Clinic, 1971-87, Albany Med. Coll., 1977-86, St. Vincent DePaul Ctr. for the Homeless, 1987-90, U. Calif.-San Diego Thornton Hosp. and Med. Ctr., 1990-97, San Diego Mus. Art, 1996-98; trustee, vice chmn. Morehouse Med. Sch., 1980-89; assoc. trustee U. Pa., bd. visitors U. Pa. Sch. Nursing, 1988-92; pres. bd. trustees U. Calif. San Diego Found., 1994-97; vice chmn. Med. Commn. for Food and Shelter, Inc.; chmn. bd. Am. Coll. Legal Medicine Found., 1983-87; chmn. Internat. B'nai B'rith Dinner, 1989, 94. Recipient Alumni award of merit U. Pa., 1953, Disting. Alumni award Dickinson Sch. Law, 1989, Nat. Healthcare award Internat. B'nai B'rith, 1991, Entrepreneur of Yr. award San Diego, 1994, Horatio Alger award, 1995, Salvation Army Tradition of Caring award, 1996, Civis Universitatus award U. Calif. San Diego, 1997, Gold Medal award, 1998. Mem. Am. Coll. Legal Medicine, Fellow Am. Coll. Legal Medicine (v.p., pres., bd. govs.); mem. AMA (Physician's Recognition awards 1969, 72, 76, 82, 85, 88, 92), Med. Execs. (pres. 1975-76), Delta Tau Delta (Alumni Achievement award 1996). Lutheran. Office: PO Box 8052 Rancho Santa Fe CA 92067-8052

TROVER, ELLEN LLOYD, lawyer; b. Richmond, Va., Nov. 23, 1947; d. Robert Van Buren and Hazel (Urban) Lloyd; m. Denis William Trover, June 12, 1971; 1 dau., Florence Emma. AB, Vassar Coll., 1969; JD, Coll. William and Mary, 1972. Asst. editor Bancroft-Whitney, San Francisco, 1973-74; owner Ellen Lloyd Trover Atty.-at-Law, Thousand Oaks, Calif., 1974-82; ptnr. Trover & Fisher, Thousand Oaks, 1982-89; pvt. practice law, Thousand Oaks, 1990—. Author, editor: Chronology and Documentary Handbooks of State Chronologies, 1972. Trustee, Conejo Future Found., Thousand Oaks, 1978-91, trustee emeritus, 1992—, vice chmn., 1982-84, chmn., 1984-88; pres. Zonta Club Conejo Valley Area, 1978-79; trustee Hydro Help for the Handicapped, 1980-85, Atlantis Found., 1994—. Mem. State Bar Calif., Va. State Bar, Phi Alpha Delta. Democrat. Presbyterian.

Home: 11355 Presilla Rd Camarillo CA 93012-9230 Office: 1107E E Thousand Oaks Blvd Thousand Oaks CA 91362-2816

TROWBRIDGE, THOMAS, JR., mortgage banking company executive; b. Troy, N.Y., June 28, 1938; s. of Thomas and Elberta (Wood) T.; m. Delinda Bryan, July 3, 1965; children: Elisabeth Tacy, Wendy Bryan. BA, Yale U., 1960; MBA, Harvard U., 1965. V.p. James W. Rouse & Co., Balt., 1965-66, Washington, 1966-68, San Francisco, 1968-73, 76-78; pres. Rouse Investing Co., Columbia, Md., 1973-76; pres. Trowbridge, Kieselhorst & Co., San Francisco, 1978-97, CEO, chmn., 1997—. Bd. dirs. Columbia Assn., 1975-76; trustee, treas. The Head-Royce Sch., Oakland, Calif., 1980-84; trustee, pres. Gen. Alumni Assn. Phillips Exeter Acad., 1984-90. Lt. USNR, 1960-63. Mem. Urban Land Inst., Calif. Mortgage Bankers Assn. (bd. dirs. 1991-98, pres. 1996-97), Mortgage Bankers Assn. Am. (bd. govs. 1993—), Olympic Club, Pacific Union Club, Lambda Alpha Internat. Republican. Presbyterian. Avocations: running, golf. Home: 4 Ridge Ln Orinda CA 94563-1318 Office: Trowbridge Kieselhorst & Co 555 California St Ste 2850 San Francisco CA 94104-1604

TROWE, PAUL BIAGIO, computer scientist; b. Bklyn., Apr. 6, 1971; s. Samuel Henry and Lucia Adeline (Cernese) T. BS, Fla. State U., 1994. Asia regional sales mgr. Internat. Hi-Tech Mktg., Miami, Fla., 1994-95; assoc. prodr. Sierra-On-Line, Oakhurst, La., 1995-96; prodr./dir. Activision, Santa Monica, Calif., 1997-98; v.p. OEM sales Gremlin Interactive, Sheffield, Eng., 1998—; sr. cons. CompuFox, Miami, 1994—. Mem. adv. bd. Lesbian & Gay Cmty. Svcs. Ctr., Orlando, 1992-94; tutor/tchr. Edgewood Children's Ranch, Orlando, Fla., 1992-94. Mem. Computer Game Developer Assn., Am. Mktg. Assn., Students Party (charter, chmn. bd. dirs.), Gama Sutra. Avocations: exotic travel, tchg. Home: 230 The Strand Hermosa Beach CA 90254-5048

TROXELL, MARY THERESA (TERRY TROXELL), geriatrics services professional; b. Syracuse, N.Y., Aug. 29, 1950; d. Henry and Mary (McDermott) Flynn; 1 child, Melissa Lee. BSN, U. Pa., 1971. Cert. quality improvement specialsit; cert. gerontol. nurse specialist; cert. case mgr. Supr. neonatal ICU St. Joe's, Syracuse, 1976-79; dir. nursing Hillhaven, Phoenix, 1979-81; quality assurance nurse long term care Maricopa County, Phoenix, 1981-83; dir. nursing Desert Haven Nursing Home, Phoenix, 1983-84; team leader, surveyor health care licensure State of Ariz., Phoenix, 1985-87, program mgr. long term care licensure and certification, 1987-89, program mgr. enforcement and compliance licensure and cert., 1989-91; dir. profl. svcs. SunQuest Healthcare, Phoenix, 1991-94, v.p. clin. ops., 1994-96; sr. v.p. clin. and ancillary ops. Unison Healthcare, 1996—. Author: (manuals) Licensure Procedures, 1990, Quality Improvement, Restorative Nursing: A Key to Quality, 1992, Director of Nursing Manual, 1996, Clinical Operations Series, 1997. Developer legislation for adult care homes, health care licensure laws State of Ariz., 1990. Mem. Ariz. Health Care Assn. (chair legis. com. 1992-94, chair devel./revision nursing facility laws 1992-94), Am. Health Care Assn. (nat. facility stds. com. 1992-96, nat. multifacility com. 1993-96, LTC nurses coun. 1995, nat. quality com. 1996-97, regional v.p. region XI, adv. com.), Quality Improvement Nurses Assn., Gerontol. Nurses Assn., Am. Health Care (v.p. region XI). Home: 10791 N 101st Way Scottsdale AZ 85260-6331 Office: Unison Health Care Ste 245 8800 N Garney Center Dr Scottsdale AZ 85258

TRUCKER, ALBERT, plastic surgeon; b. St. Joseph, Mich., Aug. 5, 1924; s. Albert and Louise (Goebel) T. BA, Johns Hopkins U., 1951; MD, U. Md., 1956. Diplomate Am. Bd. Plastic Surgery. Intern in gen. surgery U. Calif., San Francisco, 1956-59; resident in plastic surgery Mayo Clinic, Rochester, Minn., 1959-62; pvt. practice Santa Rosa, Calif., 1962—. Mem. Am. Soc. Plastic Surgery, Calif. Soc. Plastic Surgery. Office: 200 Montgomery Dr Santa Rosa CA 95404-6633

TRUETT, HAROLD JOSEPH, III (TIM TRUETT), lawyer; b. Alameda, Calif., Feb. 13, 1946; s. Harold Joseph and Lois Lucille (Mellin) T.; 1 child, Harold Joseph IV; m. Anna V. Billante, Oct. 1, 1983; 1 child, James S. Carstensen. BA, U. San Francisco, 1968, JD, 1975. Bar: Calif. 1975, Hawaii 1987, U.S. Dist. Ct. (ea., so., no., and cen. dists.) Calif. 1976, Hawaii 1987, U.S. Ct. Appeals (9th cir.) 1980, U.S. Supreme Ct. 1988, U.S. Ct. Fed. Claims, 1995. Assoc. Hoberg, Finger et al, San Francisco, 1975-78, Bledsoe, Smith et al, San Francisco, 1979-80, Abramson & Bianco, San Francisco, 1980-83; mem. Ingram & Truett, San Rafael, 1983-90; prin. Law Office of H.J. Tim Truett, San Francisco, 1991-93, Winchell & Truett, San Francisco, 1994—; lectr. trial practice Am. Coll. Legal Medicine, 1989, 90, Calif. Continuing Edn. of the Bar. Bd. dirs. Shining Star Found. 1991—, Marin County, Calif.; mem. Marin Dem. Coun., San Rafael, 1983-90. Lt., aviator USN, 1967-74. Mem. ABA, Hawaii Bar Assn., Assn. Trial Lawyers Am., Calif. Bar Assn. (com. for adminstrn. of justice, conf. of dels.), San Francisco Bar Assn., Calif. Trial Lawyers Assn., Lawyers Pilots Assn. Roman Catholic. Home: 2622 Leavenworth St San Francisco CA 94133-1614

TRUJILLO, AUGUSTINE, university administrator; b. Swink, Colo., May 5, 1940; s. Roque and Manclovia (Chavez) T.; m. Martha cordelia Velasquez, June 19, 1969; children: Augustine Christopher, Melissa Ann, Brian Anthony, Clarissa Frances. AA, Otero Jr. Coll., La Junta, Colo., 1968; BA, Adams State Coll., 1971; PhD, U. Colo., 1983. Tchg. cert., Colo. Social studies tchr. Swink H.S., 1971-72; southwest regional fellow Leadership Devel. Program/Ford Found., Albuquerque, 1972-73; athletic dir. Naco (Ariz.) Elem./Jr. H.S., 1973-74; asst. dir. spl. svcs. program U. So. Colo., Pueblo, 1975-76; coord. STW program L.Am. Rsch. and Svc. Agy., Denver, 1980-81; asst. dir. high sch. equivalency U. So. Colo., Pueblo, 1981-84; dir. Ctr. for Ethnic Student Affairs U. Utah, Salt Lake City, 1984—. Mem. Bd. of State History, Utah, Salt Lake City, 1995; chmn. Hispanic adv. bd. Utah State Office Edn., Salt Lake City, 1987-92, chmn. coalition of minority coun., 1991; bd. dirs. math, engring, sci. achievement bd. U. Utah, 1988-94. With USAF, 1961-64. Ford Found. fellow, 1972-73, Title III Bilingual fellow Dept. HEW, 1976-80; Adams State U. grad. assistantship, 1975. Democrat. Roman Catholic. Avocations: fishing, volunteering to assist at-risk youths. Home: 647 E 800 S Salt Lake City UT 84102-3533 Office: University of Utah Ad16 14 318 Union Building Salt Lake City UT 84112-1192

TRUJILLO, LORENZO A., lawyer, educator; b. Denver, Aug. 10, 1951; s. Filbert G. and Marie O. Trujillo; m. Ellen Alires; children: Javier Antonio, Lorenzo Feliciano, Kristina Alires. BA, U. Colo., 1972, MA, 1974, postgrad.; EdD, U. San Francisco, 1979; JD, U. Colo., 1993. Bar: Colo. 1994, U.S. Dist. Ct. Colo. 1994, U.S. Ct. Appeals (10th cir.) 1994, U.S. Supreme Ct. 1999; cert. edn. tchr., prin., supt., Colo., Calif. Exec. assoc. Inter-Am. Rsch. Assocs., Rosslyn, Va., 1980-82; exec. dir. humanities Jefferson County Pub. Schs., Golden, Colo., 1982-89; pvt. practice edn. cons. Lakewood, Colo., 1989-93; gen. corp. counsel Am. Achievement Schs., Inc., Lakewood, Colo., 1994-96; atty. Frie, Arndt & Trujillo Law Firm, Arvada, Colo., 1994-96, ptnr., 1995-97; dist. hearing officer, dir. of instrn. Adams County Sch. Dist. 14, 1997—, dir. human resources, 1998—; co-chair Mellon fellowships The Coll. Bd., N.Y.C., 1987-93; cons. U.S.I.A. Fulbright Tchr. Exch. Program, Washington, 1987-93; editorial advisor Harcourt, Brace, Jovanovich Pub., Orlando, Fla., 1988-93. Contbr. numerous articles to profl. jours. Mem. panel of arbitrators Am. Arbitration Assn., 1994. Recipient Legal Aid Clinic Acad. award Colo. Bar Assn., 1993, Pro Bono award, 1993, Loyola U. Acad. award, 1993, Gov.'s award for excellence in the arts State of Colo., 1996. Mem. Colo. chpt. Am. Assn. Tchrs. of Spanish and Portuguese (pres. 1985-88), Am. Immigration Lawyers Assn., Nat. Sch. Bds. Coun. Sch. Attys., Nat. Assn. Judiciary Interpreters and Translators, Colo. Bar Assn. (probate and trust sect., grievance policy com. 1995-97, ethics com. 1995-96), U. San Francisco Alumni Assn. (founder, pres. 1987-90), Phi Delta Kappa (chair internat. edn. com. 1988-89), Phi Alpha Delta. Avocation: violinist. Office: Adams County Sch Dist 14 Divsn Human Resources 4720 E 69th Ave Commerce City CO 80022-2380

TRUJILLO-CUTHRELL, LORETTA MARIE, chemical engineer; b. Santa Fe, N.Mex., May 22, 1959; d. Jose E.F. and Irene D. (Fernandez) Trujillo; m. Robert Blair Cuthrell, May 16, 1987. BSChemE, U. N.Mex., 1988. Process engr. Kerr McGee Chem., Trona, Calif., 1989-91; chem. engr. N.Am. Chem. Co., Trona, 1991—, quality coord., 1992-98; quality coord. IMC Chem., Trona, Calif., 1998—. Mem. AICE (vice-chair 1995—), Women in Mining. Office: Argus Facility IMC Chem Inc Trona CA 93592

TRULY, DIANE ELIZABETH, tax board administrator; b. Omaha, Aug. 15, 1943; d. Joseph and Elizabeth Ann (Lyle) Robbie; m. Reginald Wesley Vinson, Sept. 14, 1963 (div. Dec. 1971); 1 child, Laura Elizabeth; m. William Arthur Truly, Oct. 20, 1972 (div. June 1982); 1 child, Mara Yvonne. BA, Calif. State U., L.A., 1968; postgrad., Calif. State U., Sacramento, 1978-81. Planning cons. Franchise Tax Bd., Sacramento, 1982-83, mgr./legis. analysis and devel., 1983-84; dist. mgr. Franchise Tax Bd., San Jose, Calif., 1984-87, San Francisco, 1987-89; area adminstr. Franchise Tax Bd., L.A., 1989-92; dist. office bur. dir. Franchise Tax Bd., Sacramento, 1992-95; v.p., bd. dirs. Nelson Labs., Sioux Falls, S.D. Bd. dirs. Women Escaping a Violent Environ., Sacramento, 1993—, Nat. Coun. on Alcoholism and Drug Dependence, Sacramento chpt., 1994—. Democrat. Home: 925 Piedmont Dr Sacramento CA 95822-1701

TRULY, RICHARD H., academic administrator, former federal agency administrator, former astronaut; b. Fayette, Miss., Nov. 12, 1937; s. James B. Truly; m. Colleen Hanner; children: Richard Michael, Daniel Bennett, Lee Margaret. B.Aero. Engring., Ga. Inst. Tech., 1959. Commd. ensign U.S. Navy, 1959; advanced through grades to vice adm., assigned Fighter Squadron 33, served in U.S.S. Intrepid, served in U.S.S. Enterprise; astronaut Manned Orbiting Lab. Program USAF, 1965-69; astronaut NASA, from 1969, comdr. Columbia Flight 2, 1981; comdr. Columbia Flight 2 Challenger Flight 3, 1983; dir. Space Shuttle program, 1986-89; adminstr. NASA, 1989-92; v.p., dir. Georgia Tech Rsch. Inst., Atlanta, Ga.; dir. Nat. Renewable Energy Lab., Golden, Colo. Recipient Robert H. Goddard Astronautics award AIAA, 1990. Office: Nat Renewable Energy Lab 1617 Cole Blvd Golden CO 80401-3393*

TRUMAN, JAMES, editor. Newspaper reporter London; Am. editor, columnist The Face, N.Y.C.; featured editor Vogue Mag., 1988-90; editor-in-chief Details Mag., 1990-94; editl. dir. Archtl. Digest (Conde Nast Pubs.), 1994—. Contbr. articles to The Village Voice, The London Sunday Times, HG, others. Office: 6300 Wilshire Blvd Los Angeles CA 90048-5204

TRUMBLE, BEVERLY JANE, artist; b. Milw., Oct. 31, 1934; d. Harvey George and Rachel Rebecca (Wagner) Bowers; m. Henry Esser; children: Gail Lorraine, Deann Loreen; m. Morris M. Trumble, July 28, 1968. Student, Colo. U., 1958, Arts Students League, 1976-83, Daniel Green Workshop, 1984. Sec. bd. dirs. West Side Arts Coalition, N.Y.C., 1985-87, co-chair visuals, 1987-88, speaker, moderator, 1988-89, dir. gallery, 1988-90; co-chair pastel sect. Pen & Brush, Inc., N.Y.C., 1989-91; bd. dirs. com. Summit County Arts Coun., Breckenridge, Colo., 1993. One-woman shows include The Pen and Brush, 1987, Internat. House, 1989, Pleiades Gallery, N.Y.C., 1993, U. Denver, 1993, Duncan Galleries, Koelbel Libr., 1994; exhibited in numerous group art exhbns. Dir. studio tours various civic orgns., N.Y.C., 1988-90; speaker Littleton Pub. Sch., Littleton, Colo., 1992. Recipient merit scholarship Art Students, N.Y.C., 1982, Solo Exhibit award The Pen and Brush, 1985, Artists Guild award Mamaroneck (N.Y.) Artists Guild, 1988, Salmagundi Pen and Brush award Salmagundi Club, 1989, 1st place award Colo. Mountain Coll., 1992. Mem. Pastel Soc. Am., Soc. Layerists in Multi-Media, Art Students League N.Y. (Life), New York Artists Equity Assn. Inc. (nominating com. 1987), Taos Art Assn. (visual arts com. 1995-96). Home: 6946 Ndcbu Taos NM 87571-6243

TRUNDLE, W(INFIELD) SCOTT, publishing executive newspaper; b. Maryville, Tenn., Mar. 24, 1939; s. Winfield Scott and Alice (Smith) T.; m. Elizabeth Latshaw, Oct. 14, 1989; children: Stephen, Allison. BA, Vanderbilt U., 1961, JD, 1967. Bar: Tenn. 1967. Spl. agt. U.S. Secret Service, 1963-66; asso. to partner firm Hunter, Smith, Davis & Norris, Kingsport, Tenn., 1967-72; pub. Kingsport (Tenn.) Times-News, 1972-78; pres. Greensboro (N.C.) Daily News, 1978-80; exec. v.p. Jefferson Pilot Publs., Inc., Greensboro and Clearwater, Fla., 1980-82; v.p., bus. mgr. Tampa Tribune (Fla.), 1982-91; sr. v.p. Hillsborough C.C., 1991-93; publisher Ogden (Utah) Standard Examiner, 1993—; assoc. prof. East Tenn. State U., 1973-77; sec., bd. dirs. Ogden Indsl. Devel. Corp.; bd. dirs. Weber Econ. Devel. Corp. Bd. dirs. Downtown Ogden, Inc. Mem. Tenn. Bar Assn., Utah Press Assn. (bd. dirs.), Weber Ogden C. of C. (bd. dirs.). Methodist. Home: 1580 Maule Dr Ogden UT 84403-0413 Office: Ogden Publ Corp PO Box 951 Ogden UT 84402-0951

TRUSIAK, JEFFREY J., electronics executive; b. Cleve., Feb. 2, 1965; s. Kenneth Stanley Trusiak and Diana Marie (Chunzinsky) O'Loughlin; m. Marlène Jean Trusiak, Mar. 23, 1996; children: Sam, Bud, Brian, Josef. BS in Finance, Ariz. State U. Account exec. Ecliptek, Costa Mesa, Calif., 1988-91; regional sales dir. Inductor Supply, Orange, Calif., 1991-92; owner, v.p. ops. Abracon Corp., Aliso Viejo, Calif., 1992—, also bd. dirs., 1992—. Avocations: skiing, bicycling, basketball. Home: 24972 Wilkes Pl Laguna Hills CA 92653-4925

TRUTA, MARIANNE PATRICIA, retired oral and maxillofacial surgeon, educator, author; b. N.Y.C., Apr. 28, 1951; d. John J. and Helen Patricia (Donnelly) T.; m. William Christopher Donlon, May 28, 1983; 1 child Sean Liam Riobard Donlon. BS, St. John's U., 1974; DMD, SUNY, Stonybrook, 1977. Intern The Mt. Sinai Med. Ctr., N.Y.C., 1977-78, resident, 1978-80, chief resident, 1980-81; asst. prof. U. of the Pacific, San Francisco, 1983-85, clin. asst. prof., 1985-94; asst. dir. Facial Pain Rsch. Ctr., San Francisco, 1986-92; pvt. practice oral and maxillofacial surgery Peninsula Maxillofacial Surgery, South San Francisco, Calif., 1985-97, Burlingame, Calif., 1988-97, Redwood City, Calif., 1990-95, San Carlos, Calif., 1995-96. Contbr. articles to profl. jours., chpts. to textbooks. Mem. Am. Assn. Oral Maxillofacial Surgeons, Am. Dental Soc. Anesthesiology, Am. Soc. Cosmetic Surgery, Am. Assn. Women Dentists, Western Soc. Oral Maxillofacial Surgeons, No. Calif. Soc. Oral Maxillofacial Surgeons, San Mateo County Dental Soc. (bd. dirs. 1995-96). Office: Peninsula Maxillofacial Surgery 1860 El Camino Real Ste 300 Burlingame CA 94010-3114

TRZYNA, THADDEUS CHARLES, academic institution administrator; b. Chgo., Oct. 26, 1939; s. Thaddeus Stephen and Irene Mary (Giese) T.; divorced; 1 child, Jennifer. BA in Internat. Rels., U. So. Calif., 1961; PhD in Govt., Claremont Grad. U., 1975. Vice consul U.S. Govt., Elisabethville, Katanga, Zaire, 1962-63; consul U.S. Govt., Leopoldville, Republic of Congo, 1963-64; sec. Nat. Mil. Info. Disclosure Policy Com. U.S. Govt., Washington, 1964-67; pres. Calif. Inst. Pub. Affairs, Claremont, 1969-89, Sacramento, 1989—; sr. assoc. Sch. of Politics and Econs., Claremont Grad. U., 1989—; dir. Interant. Ctr. for Environment and Pub. Policy, 1990—; mem. coun. Internat. Union for Conservation of Nature and Natural Resources, 1990-96, chmn. commn. on environ. strategy and planning, 1990-96; chmn. Calif. Forum on Hazardous Materials, 1985-88, Calif. Farmlands Project Task Force, 1981-84; cons. U.S. and Calif. State Agys. on Environ. Policy; cons. on devel. of natural resources Univ. for Peace, Costa Rica; lectr. internat. rels. Pomona Coll. Author: The California Handbook, rev. 8th edit. 1999, The Power of Convening, 1990, A Sustainable World, 1995. Mem. Am. Fgn. Service Assn., Sierra Club (v.p. 1975-77, chmn. internat. com. 1977-79). Democrat. Office: Calif Inst Pub Affairs PO Box 189040 Sacramento CA 95818-9040

TSAI, PETER YING-SHIH, minister; b. TaiChung, Taiwan, Taiwanese, Jan. 7, 1923; s. James Yu and Chien-Ju (Lee) T.; m. Mary Su-Chin Chiang, July 22, 1949; children: Geoge Hsin-Tao, Hsin-Cheng, Hsin-Sheng, Hsin-Mei. Grad., Tokyo Theol. Sem., 1987; M of Missions, Kyoritsu Christian Inst., 1988. Elec. engr. Taiwan Power Co., 1949-79; com. mem. Gen. Assembly Presbyn. Ch., Taiwan, 1977-80; chief fin. dept. Presbyn. Ch., Taiwan, 1978-80; minister, 1983—; dir. Fund of Taiwanese Religious Edn. in Am., L.A., 1991—. Home and Office: Ste 185 9557 Laurel Canyon Blvd Apt 208 Pacoima CA 91331-4238

TSANG, DAVID D., computer company executive. Chmn., CEO, pres. Oak Tech, Sunnyvale, Calif. Office: Oak Tech 139 Kifer Ct Sunnyvale CA 94086-5120*

T'SANI, NOLAN, ballet company director; b. Coral Gables, Fla, Feb. 4, 1948; s. Gilbert Onderdonk and Evelyn Marion (Nolan) Jacobs. Student N.C. Sch. Arts, 1967-69, Sch. Am. Ballet, N.Y.C., 1969-70. Dancer, N.Y.C. Ballet, 1970-78; guest artist/choreographer Oakland Ballet, Calif., 1978-79, Milw. Ballet, 1979-80; artistic dir. Capitol City Ballet, Sacramento, 1979-90, guest choreographer, ballet master, master tchr; ballet master Ballet Du Nord, Roubaix, France, 1991, Hong Kong Ballet, 1992-94; master tchr. Sacramento Ballet, 1994—, Calif. State U. Sacramento, 1995—. Office: Sacramento Ballet 1631 K St Sacramento CA 95814

TSCHACHER, DARELL RAY, mortgage banking executive; b. Wendell, Idaho, Oct. 17, 1945; s. Lewis Edward and Erma Irene (Parmely) T.; m. Judith Allyn Evers, Dec. 30, 1966; children: Kendall Ray, Kristin Allyn. Grad. high sch. Cert. bus. counselor; lic. real estate broker, Calif., Idaho. Ptnr. KD Air Svc., Apple Valley, Calif., 1967-68; real estate broker Calif., 1968-73; v.p., dir. mktg. Chism Homes, Inc., Las Vegas, Nev., 1973-78; self-employed real estate, fin., bus. cons., 1978-87; regional v.p. br. ops. Nat. First Mortgage Co., 1987-88; sr. v.p., western reg. mgr. Nat. 1st Mortgage Co., Rancho Cordova, Calif., 1988-91; v.p., div. mgr. Ryland Mortgage Co., Rancho Cordova, 1991-94; v.p., regional mgr. Ryland Mortgage Co., Woodland Hills, Calif., 1995; v.p., project mgr., prodn. redesign Ryland Mortgage Co., Columbia, Md., 1996—; pres. Premier Escrow Co., Woodland Hills, Calif., 1996; self employed business cons., 1997—; pres. Home Acquisition Systems, Inc., Affinity Mortgage Corp., Boise, Idaho, 1997—. Bd. dirs. Tomorrow's Hope, Boise, 1985; exec. com. MDA of No. Calif., Sacramento, 1991. With USAF, 1963-67. Mem. Homebuilders of S.W. Idaho (bd. dirs. 1976-78), Idaho Home Owners Warranty Coun. (bd. dirs. 1977), Treasure Valley Exchangors (bd. dirs. 1980-84, Exchangor of the Yr. 1982), Soc. Exchange Counselors. Republican. Avocations: flying, golf. Home: 792 Nicklaus Ln Eagle ID 83616-5358

TSCHERNISCH, SERGEI P., academic administrator. BA, San Francisco State U.; MFA in Theatre, Stanford U.; student, San Francisco Actors' Workshop, Stanford Repertory Theatre. Founding mem. Calif. Inst. of Arts, 1969, mem. faculty, assoc. dean Sch. Theatre, dir., 1969-80; prof. dept. theatre U. Md., College Park, 1980-82; dir. divsn. performing and visual arts Northeastern U., Boston, 1982-92; dean Coll. of Comm. and Fine Arts Loyola Marymount U., L.A., 1992-94; pres. Cornish Coll. of Arts, Seattle, 1994—; advisor NEA; mem. com. USIA; cons. to many festivals. Office: Cornish Coll of Arts 710 E Roy St Seattle WA 98102-4604*

TSE, DANY YUI, dentist, dental administrator; b. Swatow, China, Mar. 23, 1950; came to U.S., 1971; s. Bik Ka and Chor Chun (Chan) T.; m. Debbie S. Cham, Feb. 14, 1972; children: May H., Key M., Yen H., Win M. BS, Portland State U., 1978; DMD, OREG. Health Scis. U., 1979; Cert., Harvard U., 1994. Founder, co-chmn. Gentle Dental, Vancouver, Wash., 1979—; gen. ptnr. LTL Devel., Vancouver, Wash., 1985—; dir. HOSTS Corp., Vancouver, 1989-95, Am. Acad. Dental Group Practice, Phoenis, 1993—. Dir. World Relief Corp., Wheaton, Ill., 1993—, United Way, Portlant, Alumni Assn., Sch. Dentistry, Portland, 1995—; trustee Gordon Conwell Sem., Boston, 1995—. Mem. Am. Assn. Dental Consultants (cert.). Avocations: sports enthusiast. Office: Gentle Dental 900 Washington St Ste 1100 Vancouver WA 98660-3409

TSE, MAN-CHUN MARINA, special education educator; b. Kai-Ping, China, Dec. 14, 1948; came to U.S., 1972; d. Sun-Poo and Su-ling Cheung; m. Richard Anderson, Aug. 17, 1997. BA in English, U. Chinese Culture, Taipei, Taiwan, 1970; MS in Spl. Edn., U. So. Calif., 1974. Cert. tchr., spl. edn. tchr., Calif. Rsch. asst. lit. U. Chinese Culture, 1970-72; English tchr. Tang-Suede Mid. Sch., Taiwan, 1970-72; instr. Willing Workers, Adult Handicapped Program L.A. Sch. Dist., 1976-77; instr. ESL Evans Adult Sch., L.A., 1977-82; instr. ESL, polit. sci. Lincoln Adult Sch., L.A., 1986-94; spl. edn. tchr. Duarte (Calif.) Unified Sch. Dist., 1977—; commr., program co-chair Calif. Spl. Edn. Adv. Commn., Sacramento, 1994-96; mem. Calif. State Bd. Edn., 1996—; mem. Calif. State Summer Sch. for the Arts, 1998—; coun. mem. L.A. County Children Planning Coun., 1995—; com. mem. L.A. County Sci. & Engring. Fair Com., 1993—; bd. dirs. Asian Youth Ctr., San Gabriel City, Calif., 1992—; mem. exec. bd. Pres. Com. on Employment of People with Disabilities (U.S.), 1997—; com. mem. tchr. devel. project Nat. Assn. State Bd. Edn., 1977—; mem. Calif. State Supts. Art Task Force, 1997—, Calif. Supt. Pre-Sch. Task Force, 1997—; advisor Calif. Coun. Tech., 1996—. Appeared on numerous TV and radio programs. Bd. trustee Bruggemeyer Libr., Monterey Park, Calif., 1993—; pres. L.A. County Coun. Reps., 1994—; mem. Calif. Statewide Focus Group Diversity, Sacramento, 1995-97; chair Chinese Am. Edn. Assn., 1993—, co-chair, co-founder Multi-Cultural Cmty. Assn., 1992—; bd. dirs. Rosemead-Taipei Sister City, 1993—, San Gabriel Valley Charity Night Com., 1992—; chair L.A. County/Taipei County Friendship Com., 1996—. Recipient Recognition cert. Duarte Edn. Found., 1990, cert. Valley View Sch., 1991, award State Calif., 1991, Appreciation award City Rosemead, 1992, Commendation cert. Alhambra Sch. Dist., 1992-93, Edn. award Asian Youth Ctr., 1992, 1992, Commendation cert. City L.A., 1992, commendation County L.A., 1992, award U.S. Congress, 1993, Recognition cert. Calif. Legis. Assembly, 1993, Proclamation City Alhambra, 1993, Chinese Am. PTA award, 1993, John Anson Ford award L.A. County Human Rels. Com., 1993, Appreciation cert. Chinese Consolidated Benevolent Assn., 1994, Recognition cert. Calif. State Senate, 1994, Appreciation cert. City Monterey Park, 1995, Spl. Achievement award Calif. Spl. Edn. Adv. Commn., 1997, Outstanding Comm. Svc. award City of Duarte, Calif., 1997, Spl. Achievement award Duarte United Edn. Ctr., 1997, Disting. Woman of Yr. award Calif. 24th Dist. Sen.'s Office, 1997, Svc. award Calif. Fedn. Exceptional Children Coun., 1998. Mem. Calif. Tchr. Assn., Chinese Edn. Assn., Internat. Platform Assn., Nat. Assn. State Bds. Edn. Office: Duarte Unified Sch Dist 1620 Huntington Dr Duarte CA 91010-2534

TSENG, FELIX HING-FAI, accountant; b. Kowloon, Hong Kong, May 11, 1964; s. Hin-Pei and Selena Suk-Ching Tseng; m. Rachel Wai-Chu, Feb. 16, 1992; children: Walter Fan-Kong, Riley Fan-Wei. BS, Pepperdine U., 1985, MBA, 1989. CPA; cert. mgmt. acct., cert. fin. mgr. Acct. Ronald A. Stein CPA, Woodland Hills, Calif., 1989-93; contr. Benebase Investment Inc., Monterey Park, Calif., 1991-98; exec. dir. Benebase Ltd. Partnership, 1998—; prin. Lilly Property Mgmt., L.A., 1995—. Editor (newsletter) El Toro, 1993-96. Mem. AICPA, Inst. Mgmt. Accts. (v.p. comm. 1994-95, pres. 1995-96, regional dir. 1998—), Calif. Soc. CPA, So. Calif. Soc. CMAs, Assn. MBA Execs. Avocations: sports, fishing, bridge, good foods. Office: Benebase Ltd Partnership 108 N Ynez Ave Ste 211 Monterey Park CA 91754-1680

TSENG, WILLIAM HING-WAY, architect; b. Hong Kong, Hong Kong, Jan. 30, 1959; came to U.S., 1977; s. Cheng and Han S.; m. Camellia, Feb. 25, 1984; 1 child: Alex. BArch, Ill. Inst. Tech., 1982. Registered architect, Calif. Asst. arch., dept. pub. works City of L.A., 1984-86, assoc. arch., dept. recreation and parks, 1986-88; project mgr. Port of L.A., 1988—. Mem. AIA. Avocation: military models. Office: Port of LA 425 S Palos Verdes St Fl 3 San Pedro CA 90731-3309

TSINIGINE, ALLEN, educator; b. Tuba City, Ariz., Feb. 25, 1952; s. Claw and Desbah (Martin) T.; 1 child, Ryan Allen. BS in Elem. Edn., No. Ariz. U., 1974. Cert. tchr., Ariz. Tchr. Page (Ariz.) Unified Sch. Dist. # 8, 1974-85; asst. dir., instr. LeChee Vocat. Tech. Ctr., Page, 1987-93; instr. pre-algebra, algebra Coconino County C.C., Page, 1992—; instr. math. Coconino C.C., Page, 1992—; presdl. appointee, exec. staff asst. Navajo Dept. Edn., 1993-95; mem. Nat. Indian Policy Ctr., George Washington U., 1995-96; edn. com. co-chair Nat. Congress Am. Indians, 1995-96. Mem. gov. bd. dirs. Page Unified Sch. Dist. #8, 1987-93, pres., 1988-90, 91-92, clk., 1990-91, 92-93; sec.-treas. LeChee chpt. Navajo Nation, 1979-87; mem. Navajo Way, Inc., Window Rock, Ariz., 1987-92. Mem. Nat. Sch. Bds. Assn., Native Am. Caucus, Nat. Ind. Edn. Assn. (pres.). Avocations: ranching, livestock. Home: PO Box 292 Page AZ 86040-0292 Office: LeChee Vocat Tech Ctr Coppermine Rd-LeChee Page AZ 86040

TSO, TOM, law educator; b. Teecnospos, Ariz., Mar. 7, 1945; s. Horace Hosteen and Lena (Saltwater) T.; m. Louise Anne Chee, Jan. 8, 1970; children: Travis, Dempsey, Delsey Renee, Dorothy Mae, Wanda L. BS in Polit. Sci., City U. L.A., 1988; JD (hon.), CUNY. Plant operator Air Reduction Co., Teecnospos, 1968-69; tribal park ranger Navajo Nation, Window Rock, Ariz., 1969; interpreter, investigator, ct. advocate Legal Aid & Defender Svc., Window Rock, 1970-73; ct. advocate, equal opportunity asst. Navajo Housing Authority, Window Rock, 1973-74; interpreter, investigator, ct. advocate Legal Aid & Defender Svc., Window Rock, 1974; tribal ct. advocate Law Firm of Louis Denetsosie, Window Rock, 1976-77; dir. tribal law

devel. and litigation unit DNA-People's Legal Svcs., Window Rock, 1977-81; dist. ct. judge Window Rock Dist. Ct., Window Rock, 1981-85; chief justice Navajo Nation Supreme Ct., Window Rock, 1985-91; with Bur. Indian Affairs Agy., 1991; cmty. rels. advisor Mobil Exploration and Producing U.S. Inc., Cortez, Colo., 1994-96; tchr. law advocacy Crownpoint (N.Mex.) Inst. Tech., 1996—; cons. ENRON Corp., Houston, 1998—; chmn. adv. tng. com. Legal Svcs. Corp., Washington, 1977-78; mem. advocate tng. com. Ariz. Statewide Legal Svcs., 1978-79; chmn. Navajo Nation Bar Admissions Com., Window Rock, 1979-81; bd. dirs. Nat. Indian Justice Ctr., San Francisco, 1985-92; mem. Ariz. State Gov.'s Adv. Coun. Juvenile Justice, 1988-93; mem. labor mgmt. com. Gallup-McKinley County Pub. Schs., 1994—; mem., vp. Navajo Engrng. and Constrn. Authority, Shiprock, N.Mex., 1995—; mem. adv. bd. Tribal Law and Policy Inst., San Francisco, 1997—. assisting cons. Navajo Legal Glossary, Fed. Dist. Ct., 1983; contbr. articles to profl. jours. Bd. dirs. Gallup Friendship House, Gallup, N.Mex., 1979-80; pres. Day Care Ctr., Ft. Defiance, Ariz., 1978-79; mem. Window Rock Christian Reformed Ch., 1978-85; mem. adv. bd. to the Gov.'s Office on Women/Children in Poverty, Phoenix, 1986-87. Sgt. USMC, 1965-67, Vietnam. Decorated Purple Heart; recipient Petra Found. award, 1991, award of appreciation Indian Bar Assn., 1991, State Bar Ariz., 1992, Disting. Jud. Svc. award State Bar N.Mex., 1992. Mem. Navajo Nation Bar Assn. (v.p. 1979-81, chmn. bar admission com. 1979-81, cert. appreciation 1985), Fleet Marine Assn., Disabled Ams. Assn. Mem. Christian Reformed Ch.

TSOHANTARIDIS, TIMOTHEOS, minister, religion educator; b. Katerini, Greece, Feb. 7, 1954; came to U.S., 1967; s. Ioannis and Parthena (Karipidis) T.; m. Valerie Ann Hoffman, July 11, 1977; children: Demetrius, Thaddeus. BA, Barrington Coll., 1977; MDiv, Gordon-Conwell, 1980; MA, Ashland Theol. Sem., 1985. Ordained to ministry Evang. Friends Ch., 1986. Ch. planter Ea. region Evang. Friends Ch., North Ridgeville, Ohio, 1980-85; prof. religion, Greek, dir. Christian life, soccer coach George Fox Coll., Newberg, Oreg., 1985—; bd. didrs. Greek Evang. Camps, 1989—. Author: (in Greek) Greek Evangelicals: Pontus to Katerini, 1985. Mem. Am. Acad. Religion, Soc. Bibl. Lit., Nat. Soccer Coaches Athletic Assn. (soccer coach, Nat. Coach of Yr. 1989). Home: 414 N Meridian St Newberg OR 97132-2625 Office: George Fox Coll 414 N Meridian St Newberg OR 97132-2625

TSUJIO, HIROKAZU, computer consultant; b. Tokyo, Oct. 7, 1955; came to U.S., 1995; s. Hiroshi and Kazuko (Kimoto) T.; m. Marjolaine Gagnon, Oct. 4, 1980 (div. Sept. 1994); children: Jonathan, Stephanie. Student, Prince Hotel Sch., Tokyo, 1976. Maitre'd Restaurant Katsura, Montreal, 1977-83; MIS dir. Scotpage, Montreal, 1983-92; cons. Techsyscom Inc., Montreal, 1992—; ind. Oracle database cons. Beaverton, Oreg., 1995—. Avocations: travel, skiing, net surfing, jazz. Home and Office: 9511 NW Engleman St Portland OR 97229-9131

TSUMURA, YUMIKO, Japanese language and culture educator, consultant; b. Gobo City, Wakayama, Japan, Mar. 8, 1939; came to the U.S., 1972; s. Yoshio and Masako (Moriguchi) T.; m. Motoi Umano, Apr. 13, 1961 (dec. Apr. 1962); 1 child, Junko; m. Samuel B. Grolmes, Mar. 2, 1969. BA, Kwansei Gakuin U., Nishinomiya, Japan, 1961, MA, 1965, postgrad., 1965-66; MFA, U. Iowa, 1968. Lectr. Baika Women's Coll., Osaka, Japan, 1970-72, Calif. State U., San Jose, 1973-74, U. Santa Clara, Calif., 1975-77, West Valley Coll., Saratoga, Calif., 1974-79; assoc. prof. Foothill Coll., Los Altos Hills, Calif., 1974—; asst. prof. Coll. San Mateo, Calif., 1975—; asst. prof. Japanese lang. and culture, shodo Cañada Coll., Redwood City, Calif., 1974—; U.S.-Japan intercultural cons. Apple Computer, Inc., Cupertino, Calif., 1984—, NASA Ames Rsch. Ctr., Mountain View, Calif., 1987-93, Hewlett Packard Co., Santa Clara, 1992—, Kobe Steel U.S.A., Inc., San Jose, 1992—. Co-translator: (with Sam Grolmes) (Japanese poetry and fiction) New Directions Annual, 1970-74; contbr. poetry to lit. jours., 1967—. Artist rep. Junko Tsumura, Igor Scedrov piano cello duo Cultural Comm. and Cons., Palo Alto, 1988—; lectr. and demonstrator on Shodo Galerija Foruma Mladih, Varazdin, Croatia, 1993; bd. dirs. Japanese Cultural Ctr., Foothill Coll., 1994. Honor scholar Kwansei Gakuin U., Nishinomiya, 1958-59; Travel grantee Fulbright-Hayes Commn., Tokyo, 1966, Internat. Peace Scholarship grantee P.E.O. Internat. Peace Fund, Des Moines, 1967-68. Mem. No. Calif. Tchrs. Assn. Avocations: poetry, Shodo ink brush art, classical music, dance, cooking. Home: 723 Torreya Ct Palo Alto CA 94303-4160 Office: Foothill Coll 4000 Middlefield Rd Palo Alto CA 94303-4739

TSUO, ANNE LI, database specialist; b. Taipei, Taiwan, Republic of China, June 5, 1950; d. Bing-Ching Benn and Chong-Jye (Liang) Lee; m. Yuan-Huai Simon Tsuo, Apr. 7, 1974; children: Lee Kirjohn, Leo Kirtie. M in Computer Info. Sci., U. Denver, 1989; postgrad., NYU. Therapeutic dietitian Coney Island Hosp., Bklyn., 1974-75; dietitian Carlton Nursing Home, Bklyn., 1975-76; therapeutic dietitian Flatbush Gen. Hosp., Bklyn., 1976-78; clin. dietitian Johnston-Willis Hosp., Richmond, Va., 1978, Mercy Med. Ctr., Denver, 1982-87; cons. nutritionist Nutrition Cons. Svc., Golden, Colo., 1982—; data analyst Colo. Found. for Med. Care, Denver, 1989-90, tech. program coord., 1990-92; database specialist Nat. Renewable Energy Lab., Golden, 1992-96; mem. tech. staff application software engr., technical lead info. tech. U.S. West Com., Denver, 1996—; speaker for health and nutrition subjects The Rocky Mountain Engring. and Sci. Coun., Denver, 1989-92. Contbr. articles to profl. jours. Bd. dirs. The Colo. Chinese Club, Denver, 1991-93; record custodian The Boy Scout of Am., Troop 166, Lakewood, Colo., 1992—. Fellow The Am. Dietetic Assn.; mem. The Colo. Dietetic Assn., The Denver Dietetic Assn., The Data Processing Mgmt. Assn., Rocky Mountain Oracle User Group, Oracle Devel. Tools User Group. Democrat. Roman Catholic. Avocations: reading, music, tennis, swimming, photography. Home: 2850 Joyce St Golden CO 80401-1323

TSUTAKAWA, EDWARD MASAO, management consultant; b. Seattle, May 15, 1921; s. Jin and Michiko (Oka) T.; student U. Wash., 1941, Wash. State U., 1949; m. Hide Kunugi, Aug. 11, 1949; children: Nancy Joyce, Margaret Ann Langston, Mark Edward. Free-lance comml. artist, Spokane, 1943-47; artist Maag & Porter Comml. Printers, Spokane, 1947-54; organizer Litho Art Printers, Inc., Spokane, 1954—, gen. mgr., pres., 1965-80; charter organizer, dir. Am. Comml. Bank, 1965-80; prin. E.M. Tsutakawa Co., bus. cons. U.S., Japan Trade Negotiator, 1980-89; v.p., operation officer, dir. Mukogawa Ft. Wright Inst. Pres. emeritus Spokane-Nishinomiya Sister City Soc., Sister Cities Assn. of Spokane; mem Eastern Wash. State Hist. Soc.; bd. dirs. Spokane Regional Internat. Trade Alliance, Leadership Spokane. Recipient Disting. Svc. medal Boy Scouts of Japan, 1967, Cultural medal in Edn., Japan, 1985, Disting. Svc. award City of Nishinomiya, 1971, Disting. Svc. to Expo '74 State of Wash., 1974, Book of Golden Deeds award Exchange Club, 1978, Disting. Community Scv. award UN Assn., 1979, Whitworth Coll., 1987, Svc. to Youth award Spokane YMCA, 1988, Silver Hawk medal Boys Scouts Japan, 1997; decorated Order of Sacred Treasure medal Govt. of Japan, 1984. Mem. Japanese Am. Citizens League, Japan Am. Soc. Wash. State (pres.'s award 1991). Methodist. Clubs: Kiwanis (Spokane). Home: 4116 S Madelia St Spokane WA 99203-4229

TU, JOHN, engineering executive; b. 1941. With Motorola Co., Wiesbaden, Germany, 1966-74; pres. Tu Devel., L.A., 1975-82, Camintonn Corp., Santa Ana, Calif., 1982-85; v.p., gen. mgr. AST Rsch., Irvine, Calif., 1985-87; pres. Newgen Systems Corp., Fountain Valley, Calif., 1987—; CEO Kingston Tech., Fountain Valley, 1988—. Office: Kingston Tech Co 17600 Newhope St Fountain Valley CA 92708-4220*

TU, TRANG DANG, urban planner, fitness professional; b. Saigon, Vietnam, Aug. 3, 1972; came to U.s., 1975; d. Cam Bo Tu and Nguyet Minh Dang. BA in Econs., Harvard U., 1994, M in Urban Planning, 1997. Rschr. Lincoln Inst. of Land Policy, Cambridge, Mass., 1995-97; cons. Codman Sq. Neighborhood Devel. Corp., Boston, 1996; rschr. World Bank, Washington, 1997; urban planner Interim Cmty. Devel. Orgn., Seattle, 1997—. Pub. svc. fellow Pforzheimer Found., 1994-95; recipient Buttenweiser award, 1992. Office: City of Seattle 600 4th Ave Fl 3D Seattle WA 98104-1850

TUAZON, JESUS OCAMPO, electrical engineer, educator, consultant; b. Manila, Jan. 2, 1940; came to U.S., 1963; s. Filomeno and Patrocino (Ocampo) T.; m. Norma Mamangun, Oct. 12, 1963; children: Maria, Noel, Norman, Mary, Michelle. BSEE, Mapua Inst., Manila, 1960; MSEE, Iowa State U., 1966, PhD, 1969. Elec. prof. Calif. State U., Fullerton, Calif.

1969—; scientist Jet Propulsion Lab., Pasadena, Calif., 1984—; computer cons. Hughes Aircraft, Fullerton, 1977, Gen. Dynamic, Pomona, Calif., 1983, U.S. Naval Weapon Sta., Seal Beach, Calif., 1978-83. Author of papers for profl. confs. Mem. IEEE, Am. Assn. Engring Educators. Democrat. Roman Catholic. Avocations: jogging, swimming, chess. Home: 816 S Verona St Anaheim CA 92804-4035 Office: Calif State Univ 800 N State College Blvd Fullerton CA 92831-3547 also: Jet Propulsion Lab 4800 Oak Grove Dr Pasadena CA 91109-8001

TUCK, EDWARD FENTON, business consultant, venture capitalist; b. Memphis, July 5, 1931; s. Edward Fenton and Jane Florence (Lewis) T.; m. Janet Allene Barber, July 6, 1957; children: Jean, Ann. BSEE, Mo. Sch. Mines, 1953; elec. engr. (hon.), U. Mo., 1980, D Engring. (hon.), 1997. Registered profl. engr., Calif. Various engring. and mfg. mgmt. positions Lenkurt Elec. Co. div. GTE, San Carlos, Calif., 1957-62; v.p., co-founder Kebby Microwave Corp., San Carlos, 1962-64; v.p., tech. dir. ITT Telecommunications, N.Y.C., 1965-72; gen. mgr., pres. Tel-Tone Corp., Kirkland, Wash., 1972-74; v.p. mktg. and engring. Am. Telecommunications Corp., El Monte, Calif., 1975-79; pres. Edward Tuck & Co., Inc., West Covina, Calif., 1979-86; gen. ptnr. The Boundary Fund, West Covina, 1986-95; with Kinship Ptnrs. II, 1990—; prin. Falcon Fund, 1982—; TriQuint Semiconductors, Beaverton, Oreg.; chmn. Endgate Corp., Sunnyvale, Calif.; with Teledesic Corp., Kirkland, Wash. Contbr. articles to profl. jours. Trustee U. Mo., Rolla, mem. jet propulsion lab. comml. adv. com. Served with U.S. Army, 1954-56. Named mem. Acad. Elec. Engring. U. Mo. Fellow Instn. Radio, Elec. and Electronic Engrs. Australia; mem. IEEE (sr., 1st prize for article 1962), Assn. Profl. Cons. (pres., bd. dirs. 1979-86), AAAS. Democrat. Office: Kinship Partners II 1900 W Garvey Ave S Ste 200 West Covina CA 91790-2653

TUCK, MICHAEL RAY, technical services executive; b. Pocatello, Idaho, Aug. 9, 1941; s. Amos R. and Phyllis (Day) T.; m. Heather K. Fowler, Oct. 22, 1962; children: Lisa M., Jennifer A., M. Mark. BS in Math., Idaho State U., 1964; MS in Math., U. Idaho, 1971. Programmer analyst Argonne Nat. Labs., Idaho Falls, 1964-69; computer scientist Argonne Nat. Labs., Idaho Falls, 1969-76; engr., mgr. computer div. Montana Energy Inst., Butte, Mont., 1976-81; v.p. MultiTech Inc. div. MSE Inc., Butte, 1981-82, pres., 1982-83, v.p., 1983-87; sr. v.p., COO MSE Tech. Applications, Inc., Butte, 1987-94; pres. MSE Tech. Applications Inc., Butte, 1994—, also bd. dirs.; cons. TMA Assocs., Butte, 1982-83. Mem. Exchange Club. Methodist. Office: MSE Tech Applications Inc PO Box 4078 Butte MT 59702-4078

TUCKER, JANET PIKE, employment agency owner; b. Mercedes, Tex., Aug. 21, 1944; d. Herbert McDowell and Marjorie Evelyn (Hale) Pike; m. Edwin Hal Tucker, Sept. 28, 1966; children: Stephanie Anne, Gregory McDowell. BA, Trinity U., San Antonio, 1966. Cert. tchr., Tex., N.Mex. Tchr. San Antonio Ind. Sch. Dist., 1966, Weslaco (Tex.) Ind. Sch. Dist., 1968-69, Farmington (N.Mex.) Ind. Sch. Dist., 1978-82; exec. dir. San Juan United Way, Farmington, 1982-83; co-owner Horizons Travel, Farmington, 1983-84; owner, pres. Temporarily Yours, Inc., Farmington, 1984—. Bd. dirs., v.p. Four Corners Opera Assn., Farmington, 1978-82; bd. dirs., div. head San Juan United Way, Farmington, 1984-85; bd. dirs. San Juan Coll. Found., Farmington, 1985—; pres. Anasazi Pageant Found., Farmington, 1988—; bd. dirs. FIDS/San Juan Econ. Devel. Svcs., 1986—; mem. N.Mex. Pvt. Industry Coun., 1987-92; bd. dirs. Assn. of Commerce and Industry. Named Citizen of Yr. C. of C., 1990. Mem. N.Mex. Assn. Pers. Cons., Nat. Assn. Pers. Cons., Nat. Assn. Temp. Svcs., Assn. Commerce and Industry, Nat. Fedn. Ind. Bus., Rotary (bd. dirs. Farmington chpt. 1989—). Republican. Methodist. Avocations: golf, skiing, reading, volunteer work. Office: Temporarily Yours Inc 111 N Behrend Ave Farmington NM 87401-8413

TUCKER, JONATHAN BRIN, political scientist; b. Boston, Aug. 2, 1954; s. Leonard Walter and Deborah Alice (Brin) T.; m. Karen Fern Fifer, Aug. 27, 1980 (div.). BS in Biology, Yale U., 1975; MA in Internat. Rels., U. Pa., 1982; PhD in Polit. Sci., MIT, 1990. Mem. bd. editors Scientific Am. mag., N.Y.C., 1976-79; freelance sci. writer Phila., 1979-83; sr. editor High Tech. mag., Boston, 1983-85; arms control fellow U.S. Dept. of State, Washington, 1989-90; def. policy analyst U.S. Congress Office of Tech. Assessment, Washington, 1990-93; fgn. affairs splst. U.S. Arms Control and Disarmament Agy., Washington, 1993-95; sr. policy analyst Presdl. Adv. Com. on Gulf War Vets. Ilnesses, Washington, 1995; dir. chem., biol weapons nonproliferation project Ctr. for Nonproliferation Studies Monterey Inst. Internat. Studies, Calif., 1996—. Author: Ellie: A Child's Fight Against Leukemia, 1982; govt. reports; contbr. articles to profl. jours.; mem. editl. adv. bd. Politics and the Life Scis., 1996—. Recipient Spl. Recognition award Leukemia Soc. Am., 1984. Mem. Assn. for Politics and the Life Scis., Arms Control Assn., Robert Bosch Found. Fellowship Alumni Assn., Sierra Club, Monterey Aquarium. Democrat. Avocations: ballroom dancing, hiking. Office: Ctr for Nonproliferation Studies/MIIS 425 Van Buren St Monterey CA 93940-2623

TUCKER, MARCUS OTHELLO, judge; b. Santa Monica, Calif., Nov. 12, 1934; s. Marcus Othello Sr. and Essie Louvonia (McLendon) T.; m. Indira Hale, May 29, 1965; 1 child, Angelique. BA, U. So. Calif., 1956; JD, Howard U., 1960. Bar: Calif. 1962, U.S. Dist. Ct. (cen. dist.) Calif. 1962, U.S. Ct. Appeals (9th cir.) 1965, U.S. Ct. Internat. Trade 1970, U.S. Supreme Ct. 1971. Pvt. practice, Santa Monica, 1962-63, 67-74; dep. atty. City of Santa Monica, 1963-65; asst. atty. U.S. Dist. Ct. (Cen. Dist.) Calif., 1965-67; commr. L.A. Superior Ct., 1974-76; judge mcpl. ct. Long Beach (Calif.) Jud. Dist., 1976-85; judge superior ct. L.A. Jud. Dist., 1985—; supervising judge L.A. County Dependency Ct. L.A. Superior Ct., 1991-92, presiding judge Juvenile divsn., 1993-94; asst. prof. law Pacific U., Long Beach, 1984, 86; justice pro tem U.S. Ct. Appeals (2nd cir.), 1981; mem. exec. com. Superior Ct. of L.A. County, 1995-96. Mem. editl. staff Howard U. Law Sch. Jour., 1959-60. Pres. Community Rehab. Industries Found., Long Beach, 1983-86, Legal Aid Found., L.A., 1976-77; bd. dirs. Long Beach coun. Boy Scouts Am., 1978-92. With U.S. Army, 1960-66. Named Judge of Yr. Juvenile Cts. Bar Assn., 1986, Disting. Jurist Long Beach Trial Trauma Coun., 1987, Honoree in Law Handy Community Ctr., L.A., 1987, Bernard S. Jefferson Jurist of Yr. John M. Langston Bar Assn. Black Lawyers, 1990, Judge of Yr. Long Beach Bar Assn., 1993; recipient award for Law-Related Edn. Constl. Rights Found./L.A. County Bar Assn., 1992, commendation L.A. County Bd. Suprs., 1994. Fellow Internat. Acad. Trial Judges; mem. ABA, Calif. Judges Assn. (chmn. juvenile law com. 1986-87), Langston Bar Assn. (pres. bd. dirs. 1972, 73), Calif. Assn. Black Lawyers, Santa Monica Bay Dist. Bar Assn. (treas. 1969-71), Am. Inns of Ct., Selden Soc. Avocations: comparative law, traveling. Office: 415 W Ocean Blvd Dept 245 Long Beach CA 90802-4512

TUCKER, STEVEN J., oncologist; b. St. Louis, July 24, 1967; s. R. Thomas and Elaine A. (Susman) T.; m. Asa Humg, Dec. 27, 1997. BA, Ind. U., 1989; MD, U. Mo., 1994. Resident UCLA, 1994-96, fellowship, 1996—. Office: UCLA Med Ctr 200 Medical Plaza #120 Los Angeles CA 90024

TUELL, JACK MARVIN, retired bishop; b. Tacoma, Nov. 14, 1923; s. Frank Harry and Anne Helen (Bertelson) T.; m. Marjorie Ida Beadles, June 17, 1946; children—Jacqueline, Cynthia, James. B.S., U. Wash., 1947, LL.B., 1948; S.T.B., Boston U., 1955; M.A., U. Puget Sound, 1961, DHS, 1990; D.D., Pacific Sch. Religion, 1966; LLD, Alaska Pacific U., 1980. Bar: Wash. 1948; ordained to ministry Meth. Ch., 1955. Practice law with firm Holte & Tuell, Edmonds, Wash., 1948-50; pastor Grace Meth. Ch., Everett, Wash., 1950-52, South Tewksbury Meth. Ch., Tewksbury, Mass., 1952-55, Lakewood Meth. Ch., Tacoma, 1955-61; dist. supt. Puget Sound dist. Meth. Ch., Everett, 1961-67; pastor 1st United Meth. Ch., Vancouver, Wash., 1967-72; bishop United Meth. Ch., Portland, Oreg., 1972-80, Calif.-Pacific Conf., United Meth. Ch., L.A., 1980-92; interim sr. pastor First United Meth. Ch., Boise, Idaho, 1995; Mem. gen. conf. United Meth. Ch., 1964, 66, 68, 70, 72; pres. coun. of Bishops United Meth. Ch., 1989-90. Author: The Organization of the United Methodist Church, 1970, 8th edit. 1997. Pres. Tacoma U.S.O., 1959-61, Vancouver YMCA, 1968; v.p. Ft. Vancouver Seamens Cnt., 1964-72, vice chmn. Vancouver Human Rels. Commn., 1970-72; pres. Oreg. Coun. Alcohol Problems, 1972-76; trustee U. Puget Sound, 1961-73, Vancouver Meml. Hosp., 1967-72, Alaska Meth. U., Anchorage, 1972-80, Willamette U., Salem, Oreg., 1972-80, Willamette View Manor, Portland, 1972-80, Rogue Valley Manor, Medford, Oreg., 1972-76, Sch. Theology at Claremont, Calif., 1980-92, Methodist Hosp., Arcadia, Calif., 1983-92; pres. nat. div. bd. global ministries United Meth. Ch., 1972-76, pres. ecumenical and interreligious concerns div., 1976-80, Commn. on Christian Unity and intereligious concerns, 1980-84, Gen. Bd. of Pensions,1984-92, Calif. Coun. Alcohol Problems, 1985-88. Jacob Sleeper fellow, 1955. Mem. Lions. Home and Office: 816 SE 16th St # 637 Des Moines WA 98198

TUFTE, CAROL SUE, artist, international publishing executive. BFA, U. Iowa, 1978; Cert. in Music Recording, San Francisco State U., 1991. Asst. dir. internat. sales Music West Records, San Rafael, Calif., 1988-92; v.p. bus. affairs Triloka, Inc., Venice, Calif., 1993-94; dir. internat. pub. Megatrax Prodn. Music, Inc., Studio City, Calif., 1995—. Christian. Office: Megatrax Prodn Music 11648 Ventura Blvd # 978 Studio City CA 91604-2613

TUGEND, THOMAS JOSEPH, communications executive; b. Berlin, June 30, 1925; came to U.S., 1939; s. Gustav and Irene Frederika (Fontheim) Tugendreich; m. Rachel Spitzer, Oct. 7, 1956; children: Orlee, Alina, Ronit. BA, U. Calif., Berkeley, 1950; Bachelor's Cert., U. Madrid, 1954; MA, UCLA, 1957. Reporter San Francisco Chronicle, 1951-54; pub. info. officer UCLA, 1957-84, dir. communications Sch. Engring. and Architecture, 1984-89; west coast corr. Jerusalem Post, Israel, 1974—; west coast corr. Jewish Chronicle, U.K., Jewish Telegraphic Agy., N.Y.; pub. relations cons. Weizmann Inst. Sci., Rehovot, Israel, 1963-91. Contbg. editor Jewish Jour., L.A. Bd. dirs. So. Calif. Jewish Hist. Soc., Los Angeles; Machal West (Am. Vet. of Israel), L.A. Served as sgt. U.S. Army, 1944-46, ETO, 1950-51; Israel Def. Forces, 1948-49. Recipient Journalism award for Excellence, Greater Los Angeles Press Club, 1984, 86, Simon Rockower award, 1987. Mem. Nat. Assn. Sci. Writers, Am. Jewish Press Assn. Jewish. Avocations: tennis, swimming, motion picture history.

TULLIS, RICHARD BARCLAY, artist, photographer; b. Phila., Jan. 26, 1962; s. Garner Handy and Holly (Gano) T.; m. Karen McKissick, Sept. 9, 1990. BA, U. Calif., Davis, 1984. Studio asst. Exptl. Printmaking, San Francisco, 1978-82; printmaker Garner Tullis Workshop, Emeryville, Calif., 1982-85; master printer, papermaker Tullis Workshop, Santa Barbara, Calif., 1985-90; owner, collaborator Atelier Richard Tullis, Santa Barbara, Calif., 1990—. Photographer: (book) Sean Scully, Monotypes of Sam Francis, 1994, Per Kirkeby Arken Museum, 1996, Garner Tullis "Art of Collaboration", 1998. Mem. chancellor's coun. U. Calif., Santa Barbara, 1994-97. Home: PO Box 2370 Santa Barbara CA 93120-2370 Office: Atelier Richard Tullis 1 N Calle Cesar Chavez Ste 9 Santa Barbara CA 93103-5613

TUMA, SUZANNE TULLOSS, artist; b. Pocatello, Idaho, July 24, 1946; d. Harold Edward and JoAnne (Tulloss) T. AA, Casper Coll., 1966; BFA, Univ. Wyo., 1970, MFA, 1972. Teaching asst. Univ. Wyo., Laramie, 1971-72; interior designer Shade-Rite Inc., Casper, Wyo., 1973-92, Design Crafter, Casper, Wyo., 1992—. Exhibited in group shows including West Wind Gallery, 1982, 84, Missoula Mus. of The Arts, 1986, Black Hills State Coll., 1979, Gallery 323, 1973, Gallery 234, 1986, Wenatchee Valley Coll., 1990. Bd. dirs. Wyo. Coun. on the Arts, 1975-78; founder bd. dirs. Artcore Arts Coord. Rep., 1992—. Mem. Am. Soc. Interior Designers Allied. Avocations: dance, crafts, gardening, remodeling houses. Office: Artcore PO Box 874 Casper WY 82602-0874

TUNG, PRABHAS, plastic surgeon; b. Ubol, Thailand, Apr. 3, 1944; s. Sathee and Seng (Ngium) T.; m. Patarin C. Sinjin; children: Tony, Tommy. MD, Mahidol U., Bangkok, 1968. Diplomate Am. Bd. Plastic Surgery. Plastic surgeon pvt. practice, Flint, Mich., 1980-82, Sacramento, Calif., 1982—. Office: 2801 K St Ste 200 Sacramento CA 95816-5118

TUNG, YEISHIN, research scientist; b. Taipei, Taiwan, Aug. 27, 1962; came to U.S., 1987; s. Wei and Kuoing (Wu) T. BSChemE, Chung Yuan U., Chun Li, Taiwan, 1984; MS in Materials Sci., Rutgers U., 1989, PhD in Materials Sci., 1993. Rsch. asst. Rutgers U., New Brunswick, N.J., 1989-93; rsch. assoc. Fisk U., Nashville, 1994-97, rsch. asst. prof., 1997-98; staff analyst accelerator techiques group Charles Evans & Assocs., Redwood City, Calif., 1998—. Author: (book chpt.) Hyphenated Techniques in Polymer Characterization, 1994. 2d lt. Taiwan infantry, 1984-86. Recipient Coblentz Soc. award Coblentz Soc., 1993. Mem. Am. Phys. Soc., Am. Vacuum Soc., Materials Rsch. Soc., Am. Chem. Soc. Achievements include observation of surface phonon mode of semiconductor quantum dots; measurement of sublimation rates of high explosives.

TUNISON, ELIZABETH LAMB, education educator; b. Portadown, Northern Ireland, Jan. 7, 1922; came to U.S., 1923; d. Richard Ernest and Ruby (Hill) Lamb; m. Ralph W. Tunison, Jan. 24, 1947 (dec. Apr. 1984); children: Eric Arthur, Christine Wait, Dana Paul. BA, Whittier Coll., 1943, MEd, 1963. Tchr. East Whittier (Calif.) Schs., 1943-59; tchr. T.V. TV Channels 13 and 28, So. Calif. Counties, 1960-75; dir. curriculum Bassett (Calif.) Schs., 1962-65; elem. sch. prin. Rowland Unified Schs., Rowland Heights, Calif., 1965-68; assoc. prof. edn. Calif. State Poly. U., Pomona, 1968-71; prof. Whittier Coll., 1968-88, prof. emerita, 1988—; bd. dirs. Restless Legs Syndrome Found., facilitator for So. Calif. Orgn. Bd. dirs. Presbyn. Intercmty. Hosp. Found.; founder Restless Legs Support Group (chmn. 1995—). Recipient Whittier Coll. Alumni Achievement award 1975; Helen Hefernan scholar 1963. Mem. AAUP, Assn. Calif. Sch. Adminstrs. (state bd., chmn. higher edn. com. 1983-86, region pres. 1981-83, Wilson Grace award 1983), PEO (pres. 1990-92), Assistance League of Whittier (v.p. 1994-96), Delta Kappa Gamma (v.p. 1996-97). Home: 5636 Ben Alder Ave Whittier CA 90601-2111

TUNNELL, MICHAEL O'GRADY, education educator; b. Nocona, Tex., June 14, 1950; s. Grady Tolan and Trudy (Müller) Chupp; m. Glenna Maurine Henry, June 12, 1972; children: Heather Anne Wall, Holly Lyne Argyle, Nikki Leigh, Quincy Michael. BA, U. Utah, 1973; MEd, Utah State U., 1978; EdD, Brigham Young U., 1986. Cert. tchr., Utah. Tchr. Uintah Sch. Dist., Vernal, Utah, 1973-75; tchr., libr. media specialist Wasatch Sch. Dist., Heber City, Utah, 1976-85; asst. prof. Ark. State U., Jonesboro, 1985-87, No. Ill. U., DeKalb, 1987-92; assoc. prof., prof. Brigham Young U., Provo, Utah, 1992—. Author: Chinook! (Am. Booksellers Pick of the Lists), The Joke's on George (Assn. Mormon Letters award in Children's Lit., 1993), Beauty and the Beastly Children (Am. Booksellers Pick of the Lists), The Children of Topaz (Carter G. Woodson Honor Book, Parents' Choice award, 1997 Notable Children's Book in the Field of Social Studies), Mailing May (ALA Notable Book, Parent's Choice award, 1998 Tchr.'s Choices Book), School Spirits (Parent's Choice Recommended Story Book), Children's Literature, Briefly, The Story of Ourselves: Teaching History Through Children's Literature, The Prydain Companion, Lloyd Alexander: A Biobibliography; contbr. to children's mags., profl. jours. Mem. ALA, Nat. Coun. Tchrs. of English (bd. dirs. 1995-97), Internat. Reading Assn., Soc. of Children's Book Writers and Illustrators. Democrat. Mem. LDS Ch. Avocations: reading, photography. Office: Brigham Young U Dept Tchr Edn 210 A McKay Bldg Provo UT 84602

TURNAGE, JEAN A., state supreme court justice; b. St. Ignatius, Mont., Mar. 10, 1926. JD, Mont. State U., 1951; D Laws and Letters (non.), U. Mont., 1995. Bar: Mont. 1951, U.S. Supreme Ct. 1963. Formerly ptnr. Turnage, McNeil & Mercer, Polson, Mont.; formerly Mont. State senator from 13th Dist.; pres. Mont. State Senate, 1981-83; chief justice Supreme Ct. Mont., 1985—. Mem. Mont. State Bar Assn., Nat. Conf. Chief Justices (past pres.), Nat. Ctr. State Courts (past chair). Office: Mont Supreme Ct 215 N Sanders St Helena MT 59601-4522

TURNER, BONESE COLLINS, artist, educator; b. Abilene, Kans.; d. Paul Edwin and Ruby (Seybold) Collins; m. Glenn E. Turner; 1 child, Craig Collins. BS in Edn., U. Idaho, MEd; MA, Calif. State U., Northridge, 1974. Instr. art L.A. Pierce Coll., Woodland Hills, Calif., 1964—; prof. art Calif. State U., Northridge, 1986-87; art instr. L.A. Valley Coll., Van Nuys, 1987-89, Moorpark (Calif.) Coll., 1988—, Arrowmont Coll. Arts & Crafts, Gatlinburg, Tenn., 1995-96; advisor Coll. Art and Arch. U. Idaho, 1988—; juror [illegible] Watercolor Soc., 1980, 91, San Diego Art Inst., Brand Nat. Watermedia Exhbn., 1980, 96-97, prin. gallery Orlando Gallery, Sherman Oaks, Calif. Represented in permenant collections The White House, Smithsonian Inst., Olympic Arts Festival, L.A., Royal Birmingham Soc. of Artists Gallery, Birmingham, Eng., Westminster Gal-

leries, London; one-woman shows include Angel's Gate Gallery, San Pedro, Calif., 1989, Art Store Gallery, Studio City, Calif., 1988, L.A. Pierce Coll. Gallery, 1988, Brand Art Gallery, Glendale, Calif., 1988, 93, Coos (Oreg.) Art Mus., 1988, U. Nev., 1987, 98, Orlando Gallery, Sherman Oaks, Calif., 1993, 98, Brand Libr., Glendale, Calif., 1998; prin. works in pub. collections Hartung Performing Arts Ctr., Moscow, Idaho, Home Savs. and Loan, San Bernardino Sun Telegram Newspapers, Oreg. Coun. for the Arts, Newport, Nebr. Pub. Librs., Brand Libr., Glendale, Lincoln (Nebr.) Indsl. Tile Corp. Recipient Springfield (Mo.) Art Mus. award, 1989, Butler Art Inst. award, 1989, Nat. award Acrylic Painters Assn. Eng. and U.S.A., 1996. Mem. Nat. Acrylic Painters Assn. of Eng. (award 1996), Nat. Mortar Bd. Soc., Nat. Watercolor Soc. (life, past pres., Purchase prize 1979), Watercolor U.S.A. Honor Soc. (award), Watercolor West. Avocations: tennis, bicycling, music, singing.

TURNER, FLORENCE FRANCES, ceramist; b. Detroit, Mar. 9, 1926; d. Paul Pokrywka and Catherine Gagal; m. Dwight Robert Turner, Oct. 23, 1948; children: Thomas Michael, Nancy Louise, Richard Scott, Garry Robert. Student, Oakland C.C., Royal Oak, Mich., 1975-85, U. Ariz., Yuma, 1985, U. Las Vegas, 1989—. Pres., founder Nev. Clay Guild, Henderson, 1990-94, mem. adv. bd., 1994—; workshop leader Greenfield Village, Dearborn, Mich., 1977-78, Plymouth (Mich.) Hist. Soc., 1979, Las Vegas Sch. System, 1989-90, Detroit Met. area, 1977-85. Bd. dirs. Las Vegas Art Mus., 1987-91; corr. sec. So. Nev. Creative Art Ctr., Las Vegas, 1990-94. Mem. So. Nev. Rock Art Enthusiasts, Las Vegas Gem Club, Nev. Camera Club, Golden Key, Phi Kappa Phi. Avocations: photography, collecting gems, travel. Office: Nev Clay Guild PO Box 50004 Henderson NV 89016-0004

TURNER, GEORGE MASON, lawyer; b. Butte, Mont., Sept. 2, 1935; s. William Dale and Bernice (Ownby) T.; m. Angela Gloria Aparicio, Oct. 14, 1995; children: Esther, Lesley, Allyson, Aarin, Alexander. BS in Polit. Sci., Brigham Young U., 1959, MS in Polit. Sci., 1960; JD, UCLA, 1968. Bar: Calif. 1969, U.S. Dist. Ct. Calif. 1969, U.S. Supreme Ct. 1976, U.S. Ct. Claims 1981, U.S. Tax Ct. 1981. Assoc. Munns & Kofford, Pasadena, Calif., 1969-72; ptnr. Turner & Smart, Pasadena, 1972-85, Turner & Schofield, Pasadena, 1985—; instr. estate tax law Am. Coll. Bryn Maur, Pa., 1976; monitor Continuingdn. of Bar, Calif., 1985. Author: Revocable Trusts, 1983, 4th edit., 1998, Irrevocable Trusts, 1985, 3d edit., 1997, Trust Administration and Fiduciary Responsibility, 1993, Revocable Trusts: The Centerpiece of Estate Planning, 1998. V.p. San Gabriel Valley Boy Scouts Am., Pasadena, 1976-78; pres. San Gabriel Valley Estate Planning Co., Pasadena, 1979-80; bd. dirs., chmn. bd. Calif. Family Study Ctr., Burbank, 1975-92, Ettie Lee Homes, Los Angeles, 1984-90. Recipient Silver Beaver award Boy Scout Am., 1979. Mem. ABA, Calif. Bar Assn., Los Angeles Bar Assn., Pi Sigma Alpha. Republican. Mormon. Avocation: photography.

TURNER, HAL WESLEY, state agency administrator; b. Winchester, Mass., Nov. 18, 1932; s. Wesley Francis and Anna Louise (Hodgkins) T.; m. Jean Marie Turner; children: Julie, Karen. BA, U. Sioux Falls, S.D., 1955. Cert. Govtl. Fin. Mgr. Mem. tech. and mgmt. staff Boeing Computer Svcs., Seattle, 1958-69; mgr. prodn. systems Kennecott Copper Corp., Salt Lake City, 1970-71; dir. MIS State of Idaho, Boise, 1971-74, adminstr. of budget, 1974-77; sales assoc. White Riedel Realtors, Boise, 1978-81; chief dep. Idaho State Controller's Office, Boise, 1981—; pres., Student Loan Fund Idaho, Inc., Fruitland, 1978—. Mem. Boise Samaritan Village Health Facility Adv. Bd.; region 4 chmn. Idaho Com. for Employer Support of Guard and Res. With U.S. Army, 1955-57. Mem. Nat. Assn. State Auditor's Comptr. and Treas., Nat. Assn. Govtl. Accts., Elks, Broadmore Country Club. Democrat. Methodist. Avocations: golf, racquetball. Home: 554 E Riverchase Way Eagle ID 83616-6338 Office: State Contrs Office PO Box 83720 Boise ID 83720-3720

TURNER, LILLIAN ERNA, nurse; b. Coalmont, Colo., Apr. 22, 1918; d. Harvey Oliver and Erna Lena (Wackwitz) T. BS, Colo. State U., 1940, Columbia U., 1945; cert. physician asst., U. Utah, 1978. Commd. 2d lt. Nurse Corps, U.S. Army, 1945; advanced through grades to lt. comdr. USPHS, 1964; 1st lt. U.S. Army, 1945-46; U.S. Pub. Health Svc., 1964-69; dean of women U. Alaska, Fairbanks, 1948-50; head nurse Group Health Hosp., Seattle, 1950-53; adviser to chief nurse Hosp. Am. Samoa, Pago Pago, 1954-60; head nurse Meml. Hosp., Twin Falls, Idaho, 1960-61; shift supr. Hosp. Lago Oil and Transport, Siero Colorado, Aruba, 1961-63; nurse adv. Province Hosp., Danang, South Vietnam, 1964-69, Cho Quan Hosp., South Vietnam, 1970-72; chief nurse, advisor Truk Hosp., Moen, Ea. Caroline Islands, 1972-74; nurse advisor Children's Med. Relief Internat., South Vietnam, 1975; physician's asst. U. Utah, 1976-78, Wagon Circle Med. Clinic, Rawlins, Wyo., 1978-89, Energy Basin Clinic Carbon County Meml. Hosp., Hanna, Wyo., 1989-96; ret., 1996. Named Nat. Humanitarian Physician Asst. of Yr., 1993, Wyo. Physician Asst. of Yr., 1992, Disting. Alumnus of Yr., Columbia U.-Presbyn. Hosp., N.Y.C., 1997. Mem. Wyo. Acad. Physician Assts. (bd. dirs. 1982-83), Am. Acad. Physician Assts., Nat. Assn. Physician Assts. Avocations: reading, wood carving, sewing, hiking, beach combing, watching Denver Bronco football. Home: PO Box 337 Hanna WY 82327-0337

TURNER, MICHAEL SETH, public relations and marketing executive; b. San Diego, July 28, 1948; s. Charles Irwin and Lee (Yomin) T., m. Marlene Carol Meyer, Sept. 7, 1981. BS, San Diego State U., 1970; MS, Iowa State U., 1971. Instr. U. Nebr., Omaha, 1971-72; news dir. Sta. KFJM-AM-FM, Grand Forks, N.D., 1972-78; sta. mgr. Sta. KUOP-FM, Stockton, Calif., 1978-79; dir. pub. relations Sta. KCSN-FM, Northridge, Calif., 1980-92; prin. Turner-Meyer Communications, Chatsworth, Calif., 1989—; dir. pub. rels. L.A. Jewish Home for Aging, Reseda, Calif., 1992—; cons. Calif. State U., Northridge, 1987. Host, producer radio shows Morning Jour., 1972-78, L.A. Connection, 1980-87; freelance restaurant critic, 1989-92. Bd. dirs. Pine-to-Prairie coun. Girl Scouts U.S., 1972-78; bd. dirs. N. Hills Jaycees, 1980-84, Northridge Recreation and Parks Festival, 1982-84; mem. communication coms. Greater L.A. affiliate Am. Heart Assn., 1989-944, N. Angeles region United Way, 1989-96. Participant Rotary Internat. Group Study Exchange, Philippines, 1978; named one of Outstanding Young Men of Am., U.S. Jaycees, 1982-84. Mem. So. Calif. Broadcasters, Pub. Interest Radio and TV Ednl. Soc. (pres. 1984-87), Publicity Club L.A. (pres. 1988-89), Healthcare Pub. Rels. and Mktg. Assn. So. Calif. (v.p. 1996—). Avocation: gourmet cooking. Home: 10341 Canoga Ave Apt 29 Chatsworth CA 91311-2213

TURNER, PAUL REGINALD, biologist; b. Oxford, England, Mar. 26, 1958; s. Herbert John George and Laura Pamela Ellen (Messer) T.; m. Pamela Foley, Sept. 28, 1990; 1 child, Natasha D. B, Univ. London, 1979; PhD, Univ. Conn., 1987. Rsch. asst. King's Coll. Hosp., London, 1979-81; fellow Univ. Calif., Berkeley, 1987-91; charge de mission Assn. Francaise Contre les Myopathies, Gif-sur-Yvette, France, 1991-93; fellow Univ. Calif., San Francisco, 1993-97, asst. rsch. endocrinologist, 1997—. Author: The Cell Biology of Fertilization, 1989; contbr. articles to profl. jours.; mural exhibited at M.B.L., Mass. Active British Labor Party, 1996—. Mem. Am. Soc. Bone and Mineral Rsch. Avocations: painting, drawing, chess, reading, music, French. Office: Univ Calif Endocrine Unit 4150 Clement St San Francisco CA 94121-1545

TURNER, ROBERT ELWOOD, physicist; b. Covington, Ky., Dec. 8, 1937; s. Elwood Fletcher and Margaret Belle (Gunn) T. BS in Physics, U. Cin., 1959, MS in Physics, 1960; MA in Physics, Columbia U., 1963; PhD in Physics, Washington U., St. Louis, 1970. Research physicist U. Mich., Ann Arbor, 1970-73, Environ. Research Inst. Mich., Ann Arbor, 1973-77; sr. scientist Sci. Applications Internat. Corp., Monterey, Calif., 1977—; rsch. assoc. Inst. for Space Studies, NASA, N.Y.C., 1962, Washington U., 1964-69; astronomer McDonnell Planetarium, St. Louis, 1965-68; lectr. U. Mich., 1971-77; Gordon Conf. lectr., 1980. Contbr. articles to profl. jours. and books. Rep. precinct leader, Ann Arbor, 1972. Laws fellow, 1959; recipient Group Achievement award NASA, 1976. Mem. AAAS, Am. Assn. Physics Tchrs., Monterey Inst. Rsch. in Astronomy, N.Y. Acad. Scis., Toastmasters (ednl. v.p. Dayton 1986, pres. 1987, sec. 1989, treas. 1991), Sigma Xi (programs co-chair Air Force chpt. 1988-89). Methodist. Club: Toastmasters (ednl. v.p. Dayton 1986, pres. 1987, sec. 1989). Avocations: swimming, tennis, ice skating, hiking. Home: 930 Casanova Ave Apt 40 Monterey CA 93940-6821 Office: Sci Applications Internat 550 Camino El Estero Ste 205 Monterey CA 93940-3231

TURNER, WALLACE L., reporter; b. Titusville, Fla., Mar. 15, 1921; s. Clyde H. and Ina B. (Wallace) T.; m. Pearl Burk, June 12, 1943; chldren: Kathleen Turner, Elizabeth Turner Everett. B.J., U. Mo., 1943; postgrad. (Nieman fellow), Harvard U., 1958-59. Reporter Springfield (Mo.) Daily News, 1943, Portland Oregonian, 1943-59; news dir. Sta. KPTV, Portland, 1959-61; asst. sec. HEW, Washington, 1961-62; reporter N.Y. Times, San Francisco, 1962—; bur. chief N.Y. Times, 1970-85, Seattle bur. chief, 1985-88. Author: Gamblers Money, 1965, The Morman Establishment, 1967. Recipient Heywood Broun award for reporting, 1952, 56; Pulitzer Prize for reporting, 1957. Office: Box 99269 Magnolia Sta Seattle WA 98199-4260

TURNER, WILLIAM COCHRANE, international management consultant; b. Red Oak, Iowa, May 27, 1929; s. James Lyman and Josephine (Cochrane) T.; m. Cynthia Dunbar, July 16, 1955; children: Scott Christopher, Craig Dunbar, Douglas Gordon. BS, Northwestern U., 1952, LLD (hon.), Am. Grad. Sch. Internat. Mgmt., 1993. Pres., chmn. bd. dirs. Western Mgmt. Cons., Inc., Phoenix, 1955-74, Western Mgmt. Cons. Europe, S.A., Brussels, 1968-74; U.S. amb., permanent rep. OECD, Paris, 1974-77, vice chmn. exec. com., 1976-77, U.S. rep. Energy Policy Com., 1976-77, mem. U.S. dels. internat. meetings, 1974-77; U.S. Rep. Consultative Group parent org. Coord. Com. (COCOM) Multilateral Export Controls Communist Nations, Paris, 1974-77; mem. western internat. trade group U.S. Dept. Commerce, 1972-74; chmn., CEO Argyle Atlantic Corp., Phoenix, 1977—; chmn. European adv. coun., 1981-88, Asia Pacific adv. coun. AT&T Internat., 1981-88; founding mem. Pacific Coun. Internat. Policy, L.A., 1995—; mem. U.S.-Japan Bus. Coun., Washington, 1987-93, European adv. coun. IBM World Trade Europe/Mid. East/Africa Corp., 1977-80; mem. Asia Pacific adv. coun. Am. Can Co., Greenwich, Conn., 1981-85, GE of Brazil adv. coun. GE Co., Coral Gables, Fla., 1979-81, Caterpillar of Brazil adv. coun. Caterpillar Tractor Co., Peoria, Ill., 1979-84, Caterpillar Asia Pacific Adv. Coun., 1984-90, U.S. adv. com. Trade Negotiations, 1982-84; bd. dirs. Goodyear Tire & Rubber Co., Akron, Ohio, Rural/Metro Corp., Microtest, Inc., Phoenix; chmn. bd. dirs. GO Wireless Internat. Ltd., Melbourne, Fla., 1995-97; chmn. internat. adv. coun. Avon Products, Inc., N.Y.C., 1985-98; mem. Spencer Stuart adv. coun. Spencer Stuart and Assocs., N.Y.C., 1984-90; chmn., mem. internat. adv. coun. Advanced Semiconductor Materials Internat. NV., Bilthoven, The Netherlands, 1985-88; bd. dirs. The Atlantic Coun. of U.S., Washington, 1977-92; co-chmn. internat. adv. bd. Univ. of Nations, Kona, Hawaii, 1985—; bd. dirs. World Wildlife Fund/U.S., 1983-85, World Wildlife Fund/The Conservation Found., 1985-89, Nat. Coun., 1989-95, 1996—; bd. govs. Joseph H. Lauder Inst. Mgmt. and Internat. Studies, U. Pa., 1983—; trustee Heard Mus., Phoenix, 1983-86, mem. nat. adv. bd., 1986-93; trustee Am. Grad. Sch. Internat. Mgmt., 1972—, chmn. bd. trustees, 1987-89; bd. govs. Atlantic Inst. Internat. Affairs, Paris, 1977-88; adv. bd. Ctr. Strategic and Internat. Studies, Georgetown U., 1977-81; dir. Pullman, Inc., Chgo., 1977-80, Nabisco Brands, Inc., Parsippany, N.J., 1977-85, Salomon Inc., N.Y.C., 1980-93, AT&T Internat., Inc., Basking Ridge, N.J., 1980-84, Atlantic Inst. Found., Inc., N.Y.C., 1984-90; mem. European Cmty.-U.S. Businessmen's Coun., 1978-79; bd. govs. Am. Hosp. of Paris, 1974-77; trustee Nat. Symphony Orch. Assn., Washington, 1973-83, Am. Sch., Paris, 1976-77, Orme Sch., Mayer, Ariz., 1970-74, Phoenix Country Day Sch., 1971-74; mem. nat. coun. Salk Inst., 1978-82; mem. U.S. Adv. Com. Internat. Edn. and Cultural Affairs, 1969-74; nat. rev. bd. Ctr. Cultural and Tech. Interchange between East and West, 1970-74; mem. vestry Am. Cathedral, Paris, 1976-77; pres., bd. dirs. Phoenix Symphony Assn., 1969-70; chmn. Ariz. Joint Econ. Devel. Com., 1967-68; exec. com., bd. dirs. Ariz. Dept. Econ. Planning and Devel., 1968-70; chmn. bd. Ariz. Crippled Children's Services, 1964-65; treas. Ariz. Rep. Com., 1956-57; chmn. Ariz. Young Rep. League, 1955-56; chmn. bd. Mercy Ships Internat., Inc., A Ministry of Youth With A Mission, Lindale, Tex., 1985—; mem. trade and environment com. Nat. Adv. Coun. for Environ. Policy and Tech.-U.S. EPA, Washington, 1991-95; dir. exec. com., chmn. internat. com. Ariz. Econ. Coun., Phoenix, 1989-93; dir. exec. com. Orgn. for Free Trade and Devel., Phoenix, 1991-93; chmn. Internat. Adv. Coun. Plasma Tech., Inc., Sante Fe, 1992-97. Recipient East-West Ctr. Disting. Svc. award, 1977. Mem. U.S. Coun. Internat. Bus. (trustee, exec. com.), Coun. Fgn. Rels., Coun. of Am. Ambs. (vice chmn. bd.), Nat. Adv. Coun. on Bus. Edn., Coun. Internat. Edn. Exchange (greater Phoenix leadership 1979-97), Govs. Strategic Partnership Econ. Devel., Phoenix, 1992-95, Met. Club, Links Club (N.Y.C.), Paradise Valley (Ariz.) Country Club, Bohemian Club. Episcopalian. Office: 4350 E Camelback Rd Ste 240B Phoenix AZ 85018-8338

TURNER, WILLIAM WEYAND, author; b. Buffalo, N.Y., Apr. 14, 1927; s. William Peter and Magdalen (Weyand) T.; m. Margaret Peiffer, Sept. 12, 1964; children: Mark Peter, Lori Ann. BS, Canisius Coll., 1949. Spl. agt. in various field offices FBI, 1951-61; free-lance writer Calif., 1963—; sr. editor Ramparts Mag., San Francisco, 1967—; investigator and cons. Nat. Wiretap Commn., 1975; U.S. del. J.F.K. Internat. Seminar, Rio de Janeiro, 1995. Author: The Police Establishment, 1968, Invisible Witness: The Use and Abuse of the New Technology of Crime Investigation, 1968, Hoover's F.B.I.: The Men and the Myth, 1970, Power on the Right, 1971, (with Warren Hinckle and Eliot Asinof) The Ten Second Jailbreak, 1973, (with John Christian) The Assassination of Robert F. Kennedy, 1978, (with Warren Hinckle) The Fish is Red: The Story of the Secret War Against Castro, 1981, updated, expanded, retitled as Deadly Secrets: The CIA-Mafia War Against Castro and the Assassination of JFK, 1992; contbg. author: Investigating the FBI, 1973; contbr. articles to popular mags. Dem. candidate for U.S. Congress, 1968. Served with USN, 1945-46. Mem. Authors Guild, Internat. Platform Assn., Press Club of San Francisco. Roman Catholic. Avocation: tennis. Home and Office: 163 Mark Twain Ave San Rafael CA 94903-2820

TURNEY, STEVEN CRAIG, architect; b. Lima, Ohio, Sept. 18, 1958; s. Paul Raymond and Barbra Jean (Metzger) T.; m. Mary Hollis Von Dach, July 24, 1991. AS, Boise State U., 1982; BArch, U. Idaho, 1990. Iron worker, welder Hartman Mfg., Boise, Idaho, 1976-80; crew chief T.W. Blasingame & Assocs., Boise, 1982-86; intern architect Walter H. Miller AIA, Clarkston, Wash., 1989-90; project mgr. Hosford & Larson AIA, Boise, 1990-91; project architect ZGA Archs. Planners, Boise, 1991—. Mem. Local Govt. Com., Boise, 1992. Mem. AIA, NCARB, Constrn. Specifications Inst. (v.p. Idaho chpt. 1995, pres.-elect 1996, pres. 1997), Boise C. of C., Golden Key, Tau Sigma Delta. Home: 4096 E Driftwood Dr Meridian ID 83642-6026 Office: 815 Park Blvd Ste 350 Boise ID 83712-7762

TURPEN, LOUIS A., airport terminal executive. Pres., CEO Greater Toronto Airports Authority (formerly Lester B. Pearson Internat. Airport), Ont., Can., 1996—; dir., San Francisco Airports Commn. Office: Grtr Toronto Airports Auth, PO Box 6031, Toronto, ON Canada L5P 1B2

TURRENTINE, DANIEL BRUCE, appraiser; b. Hereford, Tex., Mar. 3, 1923; s. Daniel Eugene and Bess Price (Ridgway) T.; m. Shirley Gay LaPorte, July 13, 1947 (dec. May 1997); children: Sheryl Ann, William Bruce. BA in Bus. Adminstrn., San Jose State U., 1949. Auctioneer LaPorte's Inc., Monterey, Calif., 1949-88; appraiser LaPorte's Appraisal Svc., Pacific Grove, Calif., 1988—. City councilman Pacific Grove, Calif., 1964-68. Lt. (j.g.) USN, 1943-46. Mem. Rotary (pres. 1979-80), Masons (master 1961-62). Republican. Presbyterian. Avocation: photography. Address: PO Box 20 Pacific Grove CA 93950-0020

TURRENTINE, LYNDA GAYLE, interior designer; b. Carrizozo, N.Mex., Apr. 12, 1941; d. Edward Franklyn and Lora Olive (Allen) Adams; m. Frank George Turrentine, Sept. 5, 1961 (div. 1974); 1 child, Teri Lynn. BA, U. North Tex., 1964. Interior Designer Marsh and Assoc., Denton, Tex., 1964-65, Stewart Office Supply, Dallas, 1965-66, The Paper Mill, Las Cruces, N.Mex., 1966-74; gen. mgr. and interior designer Design Plaza, Las Cruces, 1974-79; acct. rep. Cholla Bus. Interiors, Tucson, 1979-80; owner Interior Concepts, Tucson, 1980—; affiliated with Friedman, Keim, McFerror Architects, Tucson, 1987-92; speaker at several univs.; judge portfolio U. Ariz., 1983-85; com. chmn. Designer Showhouse, Tucson, 1983, 84, 86, 88, 90, 93, co-chair design com., 1988, 90, participant, 1983, 84, 86, 88, 90, 93, 95. Mem. Arts Coun. Las Cruces, 1977-79, PTA, Las Cruces, 1977-84; cookie chmn. Girl Scouts, La. Cruces, 1978; mem. ch. choir; donor Tucson Mus. Art; com. Casa de los Ninos Angel Nursery Interiors; donor Brewster House for Abused Women; supporter Desert S.W. Soroptimist; chair Ronald McDonald House, libr. com.; bd. mem. Lester St. Ronald McDonald House remodeling com.; co-chair bldg. com. St. Paul's United Meth. Ch. Mem. Am. Soc. Interior Designers (pres. 1981-83, nat. bd. dirs. 1981-83, 87-89, Presdl. citation, treas. Ariz. south chpt. 1983-85, bd. dirs. 1981-88, 94-95, Medalist award 1985), Las Cruces C. of C., Tucson C. of C., Sahuraro Bus. (bd. dirs. Tucson, 1981-88), Chi Omega Sorority Assn., U. North Tex. Alumni Assn. Republican. Avocations: church work, swimming, furniture design, theater, jewelry design. Office: Interior Concepts 812 N Crescent Ln Tucson AZ 85710-2646

TUSHINSKY, FRED CHARLES, manufacturing executive; b. St. Louis, Apr. 15, 1938; s. Jacques and Fanny (Landman) T.; m. Elaine Tushinsky; 1 child, Jesse Eric. Sr. v.p. Superscope, Inc., Chatsworth, Calif., 1957-62; pres., CEO Marantz Co. Inc., Chatsworth, 1962-89, CD Labs., Inc., North Hollywood, Calif., 1992—. Recipient commendation for consumer protection and consumer/bus. rels. White Ho., Washington, 1975. Avocations: aviation, photography. Office: CD Labs Inc 10643 Riverside Dr North Hollywood CA 91602

TUTASHINDA, A.K. KWELI (BRIAN P. ALTHEIMER), chiropractic physician, educator; b. Wynne, Ark., May 14, 1956; s. Joe Porché and Lura Ella (Darden) Altheimer; divorced; 1 child, Chinyere R.; m. Leonor Quiñonez, June 13, 1987; children Xihuanel, Rukiya, Jomoké. BA in Philosophy summa cum laude, U. Ark., 1978; D of Chiropractic cum laude, Life Chiropractic Coll. West, San Lorenzo, Calif., 1989. Tchr. English Oakland (Calif.) Pub. Schs., 1984-86; tchr. spl. programs U. Calif., Berkeley, 1984-92, 94-95, 98; instr. phys. diagnosis and chiropractic tech. Life Chiropractic Coll. West, San Lorenzo, Calif., 1989—; pvt. practice chiropractic physician Oakland, Berkeley, 1990—; owner Imhotep Chiropractic & Wellness Clinic; dir. Imhotep Wellness Workshops & Seminars. Editor, pub. Foresight Mag., 1982-84; author, pub. Toward a Holistic Worldview, 1985; contbr. articles to Chiropractic History. Recipient 1st degree Black Belt Tae Kwon Do, 1976. Mem. Assn. Chiropractic History, Somatics Soc. Mem. Sufi Order of the West, Naqshbandi Sufi Order. Islam. Avocations: yoga, martial arts, writing, reading, jogging. Office: 3358 Adeline St Berkeley CA 94703-2737

TUTT, MARGARET HONNEN, retail store owner; b. Garden City, Kans., Oct. 11, 1951; d. Russell Thayer and Louise (Honnen) T.; m. Frank John Steinegger, Sept. 7, 1974 (div. Aug. 1981); children: John F. Steinegger, Elisabeth Sophia Tutt Steinegger. BA, U. Denver, 1974. Owner Foster & Son-The Gift Collection, Denver, 1992—. Docent Denver Zoo Assocs., 1976-81, chair, 1979-80; bd. dirs. Hist. Denver, Inc., 1986-92; chmn. fundraising Newborn Hope, Inc., Denver, 1990, treas., 1996—; fundraiser Kent Denver Sch., 1993—; spl. events chair Colo. Preservation, Inc., 1995—; pres. Historic Denver Guild, 1996—. Mem. Jr. League of Denver (lectr. on volunteering for cmty. orgns. 1991, 92), Glenmoor Country Club (golf com.), Centennial Club (chair 1989-90). Republican. Episcopalian. Avocations: golf, skiing, walking. Office: Foster & Son-The Gift Collection 5925 E Princeton Cir Englewood CO 80111-1038

TUUL, JOHANNES, physics educator, researcher; b. in Valuste Elementary School where both parents taught; Tarvastu, Viljandi, Estonia, May 23, 1922; came to U.S., 1956, naturalized, 1962; s. Johan and Emilie (Tulf) T.; m. Marjatta Murtoniemi, July 14, 1957 (div. Aug. 1971); children: Melinda, Melissa; m. Sonia Esmeralda Manosalva, Sept. 15, 1976; 1 son, Johannes. Elementary Teaching Credential, Tartu Normal School (Estonia), 1941; teacher, Valuste Elementary School, 1941-43; escaped to Finland, December, 1943; after Finland surrendered to Russia in 1944, escaped to Sweden; diploma in Electrical Engineering, Stockholm Tech. Inst., 1947; Instructor, Stockholm Tech. Inst., 1947-49; Lab. Eng., Elec. Prospecting Co., Stockholm, 1949-53; Elec. Eng., LM Ericsson Telephone Co., Stockholm, 1954-55: studied Astronomy, Mathematics and Physics, Univ. of Stockholm, 1951-56; B.S. U. of Stockholm, 1955, M.A., 1956; Sc.M., Brown U., 1957, Ph.D., 1960. Research physicist Am. Cyanamid Co., Stamford, Conn., 1960-62; sr. research physicist Bell & Howell Research Center, Pasadena, Calif., 1962-65; asst. prof., assoc. prof. Calif. State Poly. U., Pomona, 1965-68; vis. prof. Pahlavi U., Shiraz, Iran, 1968-70; chmn. phys. earth sci. Calif. State Poly. U., Pomona, 1971-75, prof. physics, 1975-91, prof. emeritus, 1992—; cons. Bell & Howell Research Center, Pasadena, Calif., 1965, Teledyne Co., Pasadena, 1968; guest researcher Naval Weapons Center, China Lake, Calif., 1967, 72; resident dir., Calif. State U. Internat. Programs in Sweden and Denmark, 1977-78. Author: Physics Made Easy, 1974; contbr. articles in field to profl. jours. Pres. Group Against Smoking Pollution, Pomona Valley, Calif., 1976; foster parent Foster Parents Plan, Inc., Warwick, R.I., 1964—; block capt. Neighborhood Watch, West Covina, Calif., 1982-84. Citizen Ambassador of People to People Internat., 1990—; Physics Edu. Delegation to Peoples Republic of China, 1990; Baltic Assist Delegation, 1992. Special Award, Travelers' Century Club, 1998.; Brown U. fellow, 1957-58; U. Namur (Belgium) research grantee, 1978; Centre Nat. de la Recherche Scientifique research grantee, France, 1979; recipient Humanitarian Fellowship award Save the Children Fedn., 1968. Mem. AAAS (life), N.Y. Acad. Scis., Am. Phys. Soc., Republican. Roman Catholic. Avocations: research in energy conservation and new energy technologies.

TUXON, LINDA LOUISE, banking officer; b. Everett, Wash., May 4, 1943; d. James Gilbert Novotney and Dolores Marie (LaCombe) Hahn; m. Michael Roy Tuxon, May 27, 1967; children: Darrin Dean, James Michael. Diploma, Northwestern U., Evanston, Ill., 1991; Cert. Fin. Svcs. Counselor, Am. Bankers Assn., Evanston, Ill., 1991. Cert. trust and fin. advisor, 1992. Accounts receivable Continental Ill. Bank and Trust, Salt Lake city, 1962-63; sec., payroll sec. Nespelem (Wash.) Rural Elec. Coop., 1963; sec. Dept. of Hwys./State of Utah, 1964; utility clk. First Interstate Bank of Nev., Reno, 1964-71; bookkeeper, asst. cashier and ops. officer to asst. v.p. Pioneer Citizens Bank, Reno, 1975—; mem. Estate Planning Coun., 1986—. Tchr. Jr. Achievement of Reno, 1992. Mem. Am. Inst. Banking, Am. Field Trial Corp. of Am., Fin. Women Internat., Nat. Assn. Women in Constrn. Avocations: reading fiction, needlepoint, field trials with pointing dogs, gardening. Home: 2250 W Holcomb Ln Reno NV 89511-6551 Office: Pioneer Citizens Bank Trust Dept PO Box 2351 Reno NV 89505-2351

TWEEDT, ANNE ELIZABETH, lawyer, legislative policy analyst; b. Hartford, Conn., May 29, 1966; d. William Patrick and Irene Fallon (Kelley) Murray; m. Darin Edward Tweedt, Sept. 11, 1993; children: Madeleine Clare, Samuel Edward. BA, Conn. State U., 1988; JD, Willamette U. Coll. Law, 1993. Bar: Oreg. 1993. Legis. asst. to Spkr. of Ho. Conn. Gen. Assembly, Hartford, 1987-89, fin. com. clk., 1989-90; atty. pvt. practice, Salem, Oreg., 1993-95; health and human svcs. policy analyst Legis. Policy and Rsch., Salem, Oreg., 1995—. Roman Catholic. Office: Policy and Rsch Office State Capitol Salem OR 97310

TWIFORD, JIM, state legislator; b. Wheaton, Wy., Nov. 17, 1942; m. Jenne Lee Twiford. Pres. senate Wy. Ho. of Reps. Roman Catholic. Fax: 307-358-3515. E-mail: jimjenne@aol.com. Office: 43 Fairway Estates Douglas WY 82633*

TWINE, BRUCE DAVID, information services administrator; b. Cleve., May 25, 1942; s. James Henry and Gertrude Mary (Neway) T.; m. Diane Mary Murray, Sept. ;9, 1967; children: Leah Christine, Kyler Elizabeth. BA in Psychology, Kenyon Coll., 1964; MBA, U. Okla., 1977. Commd. 2d lt. USAF, 1964, advanced through grades to col., ret., 1991; adminstr. Dept. Family Svcs., Cheyenne, Wyo., 1992—. Lector Holy Trinity Cath. Ch., Cheyenne, 1991. Mem. APHA (bd. dirs. Info. Sys. Mgmt. sect. 1997—), Nat. Assn. for Welfare Rsch. and Stats. (bd. dirs. 1995—), Laramie County Master Gardeners. Avocations: fishing, reading, golf, skiing. E-mail: btwine@missc.state.wy.us. Home: 2843 Olive Dr Cheyenne WY 82001-5736 Office: Dept Family Svcs 2300 Capitol Ave Cheyenne WY 82001-3644

TWISS, ROBERT MANNING, prosecutor; b. Worcester, Mass., Aug. 2, 1948; s. Robert Sullivan Jr. and Marion (Manning) T.; m. Joan Marie Callahan, Aug. 4, 1979. BA, U. Mass., 1970; JD, U. San Francisco, 1975; MA in Criminal Justice, Wichita State U., 1979; LLM, Georgetown U., 1981. Bar: Mass. 1976, Calif., 1988, U.S. Ct. Mil. Appeals 1976, U.S. Dist. Ct. Mass. 1976, U.S. Ct. Appeals (1st cir.) 1976, U.S. Ct. Appeals (5th cir.) 1986, U.S. Ct. Appeals (9th cir.) 1988, U.S. Dist. Ct. (ea. and cen. dist.) Calif. 1989. Atty. office chief counsel IRS, Washington, 1980-86; trial atty.

criminal div. U.S. Dept. Justice, Washington, 1986-87; asst. U.S. atty. U.S. Dept. Justice, Sacramento, 1987-93, 94- , chief organized crime and narcotics, 1991-92, 1st asst. U.S. atty., 1992-93, U.S. atty., 1993, exec. assst. U.S. atty., 1994. Contbr. articles to profl. jours. Capt. JAGC, U.S. Army, 1976-80. Named to McAuliffe Honor Soc. U. San Francisco, 1975; recipient Markham award Office Chief Counsel IRS, Washington, 1985. Avocation: athletics. Office: Office US Atty 501 I St 10th Fl Sacramento CA 95814-2400

TWIST, ROBERT LANPHIER, farmer, rancher, cattle feeder; b. Memphis, Dec. 27, 1926; s. Clarence C. and Edith G. Twist; student Springfield (Ill.) Jr. Coll., 1943; B.S. in Agr., U. Ill., 1950; postgrad. U. Edinburgh (Scotland); m. Joy Twist; 1 child Marilyn Edith Ten Hope. Owner, operator farm lands, Twist, Ark., 1949—, Bow Fiddle Ranch, Laramie, Wyo., 1961—, Lost Creek Ranch, Masters, Colo., 1963, Rolling T Ranch, Ft. Morgan, Colo., 1965—, R.L. Twist Ranches Cattle Feeding Enterprises, Greeley, Colo. and Ft. Morgan, 1974—; prin. R.L. Twist Land & Investments, Paradise Valley, Ariz., 1974—; Rocker M Ranch, Douglas, Ariz., 1981—, Circle J Ranch, Gunnison, Colo., 1993; cons. agrl. mgmt. Justice of Peace, Twist, Ark., 1954. Served with USAAF, 1944-46. Mem. Colo. Farm Bur., Wyo. Farm Bur., Nat. Cattlemen's Assn. (charter). Republican. Presbyterian. Home: 4612 E Sparkling Ln Paradise Valley AZ 85253

TWITCHELL, KENT, mural artist; b. Lansing, Mich., Aug. 17, 1942; s. Robert E. and Wilma Doris (Berry) T.; m. Susan Catherine Fessler, Dec. 27, 1975 (div. 1986); m. Pandora Seaton, Feb. 23, 1990; children: Rory, Artie. AA, East L.A. Coll., 1969; BA, Calif. State U., 1972; MFA, Otis Art Inst., 1977; DA (hon.), Biola U., 1989; DFA (hon.), Otis Coll. Art and Design, 1996. Illustrator USAF, 1960-65; display artist J.C. Penney Co., Atlanta, 1965-66; abstract artist, painter L.A., 1968-70, mural artist, 1971—; instr. L.A. County High Sch. for the Arts, L.A., 1987-90, Otis/Parsons Art Inst., L.A., 1980-83; cons. Olympic Murals Program, L.A., 1983-84. Executed exterior murals at Union at 12th St. (Steve McQueen monument), L.A., 1971, Hollywood Fwy. (The Freeway Lady), L.A., 1974, Hill St. at Olympic (Edward Ruscha monument), 1987, 405 Fwy. (La Marathon mural), Inglewood, Calif., 1987, 1420 Locust St. (Dr J monument), Phila., 1989, Harbor Fwy. (La Chamber Orch.), L.A., 1991-93, (Will Rogers Monument), Calif. Theater, San Bernardino, Calif., 1998; one-man shows include: L.A. Mcpl. Art Gallery, 1980, Loyola Marymount U., L.A., 1985, Thinking Eye Gallery, L.A., 1986, Valparaiso (Ind.) U. Art Mus., 1987, Westmont Coll. Art Gallery, Santa Barbara, Calif., 1987, Biola U. Art Gallery, La Mirada, Calif., 1987, Vincent Price Gallery-East L.A. Coll., 1990, Lizardi-Harp Gallery, Pasadena, Calif., 1991, U. Redlands Art Gallery, 1997, Koplin Gallery, L.A., 1998; exhibited in group shows at L.A. Mcpl. Art Gallery, 1977, 81, 94, 96, Calif. Polytech. U., Pomona, 1978, Santa Monica Coll., 1978, L.A.C.E. Gallery, L.A., 1981, Otis/Parsons Art Inst., L.A., 1987, Mayer Schwarz Gallery, Beverly Hills, 1988, 90, Principia Coll., Elsah, Ill., 1989, Koplin Gallery, Santa Monica, 1992, 95, 98, L.A. County Mus. Art, 1992, Robert Berman Gallery, Santa Monica, 1995, Art Ctr./Coll. Design, Pasadena, 1996, Riverside (Calif.) Art Mus., 1996. Mem. adv. bd. Artists Equity Assn., 1980-88, Mural Conservancy of L.A., 1988—. Grantee Calif. Arts Coun., 1978, Nat. Endowment for Arts, 1986. Avocation: theology. E-mail address: artkent@saber.net. Home and Studio: 9505 Main St PO Box 145 Upper Lake CA 95485-0145

TWITCHELL, THEODORE GRANT, music educator and composer; b. Melrose, Kans., Jan. 26, 1928; s. Curtis and Sarah Frances (Lane) T.; m. Rebecca Janis Goldsmith, Nov. 18, 1989; stepchildren: Ralph Norman, Russell Norman, Dawn Jiricek. AA in Music, L.A. City Coll., 1949; BA in Social Studies, Calif. State U., L.A., 1951, MA in Secondary Edn., 1955; EdD in Secondary and Higher Edn., U. So. Calif., L.A., 1964. Tchr. Barstow (Calif.) Union High Sch., 1952, Burbank (Calif.) Unified Sch. Dist., 1954-66; dean instrn., dir. evening divsn., dir. summer sessions, 1966-69; pres. Palo Verde Coll., Blythe, Calif., 1969-70; adult tchr. L.A. Unified Sch. Dist., 1977-78; faculty Columbia West U., L.A., 1993—; pvt. English tutor, 1979—. Composer: The Gettysburg Address, Tidewater, The Pride of Monticello, Labor Day March, Valley Forge, Normandy Prayer, Christmas in L.A., L.A., Overture to Tidewater, The Joy of Snow, Walt Whitman and Friends, over 90 others; contbr. articles to profl. jours.; author: Dear Mr. President, 1982, Courage, Conflict and Love, 1988, The Magnificent Odyssey of Michael Young, 1992. With U.S. Army, 1952-53. Recipient Coll. Faculty Senate Award for Achievements for the coll., Palo Verde Coll., Student Body award. Mem. Internat. Poetry Hall Fame, Cmty. Coll. Pres.'s Assn., Am. Assn. Composers, Authors and Pubs., Calif. PTA (hon. life mem.), Rho Delta Chi. Republican. Methodist. Avocations: music, writing, travel, hiking, photography. Home: 2737 Montrose Ave Apt 10 Montrose CA 91020-1318

TWOMLEY, BRUCE CLARKE, commissioner, lawyer; b. Selma, Ala., Jan. 23, 1945; s. Robert Clarke and Eleanor Jane (Wood) Anderson T.; m. Sara Jane Minton, June 13, 1979; children: Christopher Mario, Jonathan Marion. BA in Philosophy, Northwestern U., 1967; LLM, U. Calif., San Francisco, 1970; postgrad. Nat. Jud. Coll., Reno, Nev., 1983, 88. Bar: Calif. 1972, Alaska 1973, U.S. Dist. Ct. Alaska, 1973, U.S. Ct. Appeals (9th cir.) 1982. VISTA vol., Anchorage, 1972-73; lawyer Alaska Legal Services Corp., Anchorage, 1973-82; commr. Alaska Comml. Fisheries Entry Commn., Juneau, 1982-83, chmn., 1983—; mem. Gov.'s Fisheries Cabinet, 1983—, Child Support Enforcement Divsn. Rural Task Force, 1985—, Alaska Fedn. of Natives Task Force on IRS and Alaska Native Fishermen, 1994; cons. IRS, Sta. WNED-TV, Buffalo, 1988; mem. Bristol Bay Native Assn. Blue Ribbon Commn. on Ltd. Entry, 1994—; Contbr.: Limited Access Management: A Guidebook to Conservation, 1993. Recipient Alaska Legal Services Disting. Service award, 1983, 92. Mem. Juneau Racquet Club (adv. bd. 1989—), Kappa Sigma (pres. interfraternity council 1966-67). Home: PO Box 20972 Juneau AK 99802-0972 Office: Alaska Comml Fisheries Entry Commn 8800 Glacier Hwy Ste 109 Juneau AK 99801-8079

TYCHOWSKI, CHRISTOPHER ROMAN, engineer; b. Chorzow, Poland, Sept. 20, 1937; came to U.S., 1973; s. Feliks and Maria Jadwiga (Napierala) T.; m. Slavomira Maria Zbierska, Sept. 16, 1975 (div. Mar. 1979). Bachelors Degree, Poznan (Poland) Tech. Coll., 1958; Masters Degree, Poznan Politechnik, 1965; PhD, Warsaw (Poland) Inst. Tech., 1972. Sr. project engr. Warsaw Inst. Tech., 1969-73; project engr. Arthur G. McKee, San Mateo, Calif., 1974-76; pvt. practice cons. Phoenix, 1976-78; civil engr. W.B.C. Cons., Phoenix, 1978-79; project engr. Peter A. Lendrum Architects, Phoenix, 1979-80; sr. structural engr. Sullivan-Mason, Inc. Architects-Engrs., Phoenix, 1981-83; plans rev. engr. City of Phoenix Bldg. Safety Dept., 1981-83; sr. project engr. Magadini Alagia Assoc., Phoenix, 1983-84; pres. C.R.T. Corp., Tempe, Ariz., 1984—; realtor Realty Experts, Inc., Phoenix, 1987—; pres. Alliance Bldg. Corp., Phoenix, 1988—, Acorn Bldg. Corp.; exec. v.p. Gemcraft Constrn. Co., Inc., Phoenix, 1988—. Patentee in field. Recipient Recognition awards, Polish Assn. of Architects, 1968, 70, Tech. Excellence award Polish Normalization Com., 1971, Best Sports Pub. of Yr. award Polish Nat. Olympic Com., 1972. Mem. Am. Inst. Steel Constrn., Structural Engrs. Assn., Phoenix Bd. Realtors. Republican. Roman Catholic. Avocations: stamp collecting, tennis, classical music. Office: CRT Corp 1370 E 8th St Ste 2 Tempe AZ 85281-4383

TYKESON, DONALD ERWIN, broadcasting executive; b. Portland, Oreg., Apr. 11, 1927; s. O. Ansel and Hillie Martha (Haveman) T.; m. Rilda Margaret Steigleder, July 1, 1950; children: Ellen, Amy, Eric. BS, U. Oreg., 1951. V.p., dir. Liberty Comm., Inc., Eugene, Oreg., 1963-67, pres., CEO, dir., 1967-83; mng. ptnr. Tykeson/Assocs. Enterprises, 1983—; chmn. bd. Bend Cable Comm., Inc., 1983—, Telecomm Svcs. Inc., 1988—, Ctrl. Oreg. Cable Advt., Inc., 1992—, Bend Cable Data Svcs. LLC, 1998—. Bd. dirs. Nat. Multiple Sclerosis Soc., 1987—, Nat. Coalition Rsch. in Neurol. and Communicative Disorders, 1984-89, Sacred Heart Med. Ctr. Found., 1995—; chmn. Nat. Coalition in Rsch. pub. and govt. info. com., 1986-89, C-SPAN 1980-89; mem. bus. adv. coun. U. Oreg. Coll. Bus. Adminstrn., 1973—, steering com. 1997—, dean search com., 1998-99; trustee U. Oreg. Found., [illegible] rsch. and med. programs com., 1986—; trustee Eugene Art Found., 1980-85, Oreg. Health Scis. U. Found., 1988-91, investment com., 1992-95; mem. Oreg. Investment Coun. State of Oreg., vice-chmn., 1988-92. Mem. Nat. Assn. Broadcasters, Nat. Cable TV Assn. (dir. 1976-83), Chief Execs. Orgn., Vintage Club (bd. dirs. 1996—, chmn. fin. com., treas. 1996—, pres. Custom Lot Assn. 1992-97), Country Club Eugene (dir. 1975-77, sec. 1976, v.p. 1977), Multnomah Athletic Club, Arlington Club, Rotary, Elks. Home: 447 Spyglass Dr Eugene OR 97401-2091 Office: Tykeson/Assocs Enterprises PO Box 70006 Eugene OR 97401-0101*

TYL, NOEL JAN, baritone, astrologer, writer; b. West Chester, Pa., Dec. 31, 1936. BA, Harvard U., 1958. Bus. mgr. Houston Grand Opera Assn., 1958-60; account exec. Ruder and Finn Pub. Rels., N.Y.C., 1960-62; profl. astrologer, 1970—; editor Astrology Now mag., 1974-79; pres. Tyl Assocs., Inc. pub. rels. and advt., 1980-89; media spokesman; internat. lectr., locations including U.S., Moscow, London, Oslo, Copenhagen, Berlin, Amsterdam, The Netherlands, Toronto, Ont., Tel Aviv, Bologna. Winner Am. Opera Auditions, 1964; opera singer U.S. and Europe, 1964-80; Wagner specialist; appearances include Vienna State Opera, Düsseldorf, Rome, Milan, Barcelona, N.Y.C. Opera, also throughout U.S.; author: Principles and Practice of Astrology, 12 vols., 1973-75, Teaching and Study Guide, 1976, The Horoscope as Identity, 1974, Holistic Astrology, 1980, Prediction in Astrology, 1991, Synthesis and Counseling in Astrology, 1994, Astrology of the Famed, 1995, Predictions for a New Millennium, 1996, Astrological Timing of Critical Illness, 1998. Mem. Astrology's World Orgn./AFAN (presiding officer). Home: 17005 E Player Ct Fountain Hills AZ 85268-5721

TYLER, DARLENE JASMER, dietitian; b. Watford City, N.D., Jan. 26, 1939; d. Edwin Arthur and Leola Irene (Walker) Jasmer; BS, Oreg. State U., 1961; m. Richard G. Tyler, Aug. 26, 1977 (dec.); children: Ronald, Eric, Scott. Clin. dietitian Salem (Oreg.) Hosp., 1965-73; sales supr. Sysco Northwest, Tigard, Oreg., 1975-77; clin. dietitian Physicians & Surgeons Hosp., Portland, Oreg., 1977-79; food svc. dir. Meridian Park Hosp., Tualatin, Oreg., 1979—. Registered dietitian. Mem. Am. Dietetic Assn., Oreg. Dietetic Assn., Portland Dietetic Assn., Am. Soc. Hosp. Food Svc. Adminstrs. Episcopalian. Home: 9472 SW Hume Ct Tualatin OR 97062-9039 Office: 19300 SW 65th Ave Tualatin OR 97062-7706

TYLER, GAIL MADELEINE, nurse; b. Dhahran, Saudi Arabia, Nov. 21, 1953 (parents Am. citizens); d. Louis Rogers and Nona Jean (Henderson) Tyler; m. Alan J. Moore, Sept. 29, 1990; 1 child, Sean James. AS, Front Range C.C., Westminster, Colo., 1979; BS in Nursing, U. Wyo., 1989. RN. Ward sec. Valley View Hosp., Thornton, Colo., 1975-79; nurse Scott and White Hosp., Temple, Tex., 1979-83, Meml. Hosp. Laramie County, Cheyenne, Wyo., 1983-89; dir. DePaul Home Health, 1989-91; field staff nurse Poudre Valley Hosp. Home Care/Poudre Care Connection, 1991-98, RVNA, 1999—. Avocations: collecting internat. dolls, sewing, reading, travel.

TYLLIA, FRANK MICHAEL, university official, educator; b. Rossland, B.C., Can., Dec. 1, 1942; came to U.S., 1942; s. Alex J. and Lenora M. (Janni) T.; m. Kathryn A. McWalter, Mar. 21, 1970. BBA, Gonzaga U., 1965, BA in Edn., 1967; MA in Edn., Seattle U., 1972. Tchr. pub. schs., Seattle, 1967-72, prin., 1972-78; prin. Edmonds Sch. Dist., Lynnwood, Wash., 1978-97; field supr. M Tchg. City U., Bellevue, Wash., 1997—; adj. prof. Seattle Pacific U., 1990—. Active alumni mentoring program Gonzaga U., Seattle, 1993—; active Kirkland conf. com. King County Juvenile Justice, 1997—, mem. diversion adv. bd., 1998—. Mem. ASCD, Assn. Wash. Sch. Prins. (various coms.), Washington Athletic Club, Phi Delta Kappa. Home and Office: 4527 103d Ln NE Kirkland WA 98033-7639

TYRRELL, ELEANORE DAY, health program evaluation specialist; b. Phila., Aug. 9, 1938; d. Peter Aloysius Tyrrell and Elsie Amelia Day. BA in Psychology, U. Richmond, 1960; MA in Psychology, Pepperdine U., 1980. Rsch. assoc. U. Pa. Med. Sch., Phila., 1961-62; with UCLA, 1962-91; rsch. assoc. to lab. supr. to co-adminstr. Marijuana Rsch. Program, coord. Program in Psychiatry, Law & Human Sexuality; program and policy analyst Alzheimer's Disease Program, Ctr. for Gerontology, Calif. Dept. Health Svc.-Inst. for Health and Aging, U. Calif., San Francisco, 1991—; exec. dir. Ctr. for Drug Edn. and Brain Rsch., L.A., 1987-88; cons. rschr. Beverly Hills Headache & Pain Med. Group, L.A., Los Alamos (N.Mex.) Nat. Labs., SUNY, Stony Brook, So. Calif. Neuropsychiat. Inst., La Jolla, others. Contbr. articles and rsch. papers to profl. jours. Pres. The Opera Assocs., L.A.; dir. publicity and pub. rels. L.A. and western regions Met. Opera Nat. Coun. Auditions. Recipient Adminstrv. and Profl. Staff award U. Calif. San Francisco, 1994, Outstanding Performance award U. Calif. San Francisco, 1996. Mem. Sacramento Area Pepperdine U. Alumni (v.p.), Psi Chi. Home: 3421 Toledo Way Sacramento CA 95821-2437

UBEROI, MAHINDER SINGH, aerospace engineering educator; b. Delhi, India, Mar. 13, 1924; came to U.S., 1945, naturalized, 1960; s. Kirpal Singh and Sulaksha (Kochar) U. B.S., Punjab U., Lahore, India, 1944; M.S., Calif. Inst. Tech., 1946; D.Eng., Johns Hopkins U., 1952. Registered profl. engr. Mem. faculty U. Mich., Ann Arbor, 1953-63, prof. aeros., 1959-63, vis. prof., 1963-64; prof. aerospace engring. U. Colo., Boulder, 1963—, chmn. dept. aerospace engring., 1963-75; fellow Joint Inst. for Lab. Astrophysics, Boulder, 1963-74; hon. rsch. fellow Harvard U., 1975-76; invited prof. U. Que., Can., 1972-74; vis. scientist Max Planck Inst. for Astrophysics, Munich, 1974. Author numerous rsch. publs. on dynamics of ionized and neutral gases and liquids with and without chem. reactions, gravity and electromagnetic fields; editor Cosmic Gas Dynamics, 1974. Council mem. Ednl. TV Channel 6, Inc., Denver, 1963-66. Guggenheim fellow Royal Inst. Tech., Stockholm, Sweden, 1958; exchange scientist U.S. Nat. Acad. Scis.; exchange scientist Soviet Acad. Scis., 1966. Mem. Am. Phys. Soc., Tau Beta Pi. Home: 819 6th St Boulder CO 80302-7418

UBERSTINE, MITCHELL NEIL, bank executive; b. N.Y.C., Apr. 27, 1956; s. Elliott and Barbara Marilyn (Wernick) U.; m. Janice Diane Wemple, Dec. 26, 1987; children: Jeffrey Aaron, Andrew Louis. AA, Pierce Coll., Woodland Hills, Calif., 1975. Purchasing agt. Workshop West, Inc., Beverly Hills, Calif., 1975-78, Allianz Ins., L.A., 1978-79, Allstate Savs., Glendale, Calif., 1979-80; gen. svc. supr. First Fed. Bank Calif., Santa Monica, 1980-83, asst. v.p., 1983-86, v.p., 1986-93, sr. v.p., 1994—. Contbr. articles to profl. jours. Bd. dirs., v.p. Jewish Family Svc., Santa Monica, 1991—; bd. dirs. Santa Monica region NCCJ. Mem. Purchasing Mgmt. Assn. L.A. Republican. Jewish. Avocations: camping, fishing, paintball, photography. Office: First Fed Bank Calif 401 Wilshire Blvd Ste 220 Santa Monica CA 90401-1416

UDALL, CALVIN HUNT, lawyer; b. St. Johns, Ariz., Oct. 23, 1923; s. Grover C. and Dora (Sherwood) U.; m. Doris Fuss, Dec. 11, 1943; children: Fredric, Margaret Udall Moses, Julie (Mrs. Blair M. Nash), Lucinda Johnson, Tina Udall Rodriguez. LL.B., U. Ariz., 1948. Bar: Ariz. 1948. Ptnr. Fennemore Craig, 1953—; Ariz. spl. counsel Arizona v. California, 1954-62; mem. Coun. on Legal Edn. Opportunity, 1983-93. Mem. cast, Phoenix Mus. Theatre, 1959-65. Fellow Am. Bar Found. (bd. dirs. 1986-89, fellows chmn. 1988-89), Ariz. Bar Found. (Disting. Svc. award 1993), Am. Coll. Trial Lawyers; mem. ABA (ho. dels. 1962-92, bd. govs. 1981-84, exec. com. 1983-84, chmn. task force on minorities 1984-86), Maricopa County Bar Assn. (pres. 1957, Disting. Pub. Svc. award 1986), State Bar Ariz. (bd. govs. 1960-65), Ariz. Law Coll. Assn. (bd. dirs. 1967-80, pres. 1978-79, U. Ariz. Disting. Citizen award 1984, bd. visitors 1991—). Office: Fennemore Craig 3003 N Central Ave Ste 2600 Phoenix AZ 85012-2913

UDLAND, DUANE S., protective services official; m. Judi Udland; 1 child, Eric. Grad., Spokane Police Acad., 1973; BA in Sociology, Ea. Washington State Coll., 1973; grad., FBI Nat. Acad., 1987. From law enforcement officer to detective Spokane (Wash.) County Sheriffs Office, 1972-78; from patrol officer to sgt. Soldotna Police Dept., 1978-82; from patrol officer to dep. chief Anchorage Police Dept., 1988-97, apptd. chief, 1997—; bd. dirs. Alaska Native Justice Ctr.; past chmn. Cen. Peninsula 911 Bd.; mem. Govs. Juvenile Justice Conf. on Youth and Justice; criminal justice adv. bd. State of [illegible] Police Minority Rels. Task Force. Mem. FBI Nat. Acad. Assn., Internat. Assn. Chiefs of Police, Alaska Assn. Chiefs of Police, Alaska Peace Officers Assn., Anchorage C. of C. (crime com.). Home: 1743 W 15th Ave Anchorage AK 99501-4911 Office: Anchorage Police Dept 4501 S Bragaw St Anchorage AK 99508*

UDOD, HRYHORY, priest, church official; b. Kharkiw, Ukraine, Jan. 30, 1925; s. Ivan and Vera (Pisarewsky) U.; m. Alice Levchenko, July 20, 1957; children: Taras, Greg. BD, St. Andrews Coll., Winnipeg, Man., Can., 1958, BA with honors, BE, 1972; MA, U. Sask., 1974; PhD, Ukrainian Free U., Munich, 1975. Ordained priest Ukrainian Greek Orthodox Ch. Can., 1958. Parish priest various parishes New Westminster, B.C., Westlock, Alta., Ft. Frances, Ont., Sheho, Sask., Kamsack, Sask.; parish priest Ukrainian Orthodox Cathedral, Saskatoon, Sask., Can., 1966-80; chmn. presidium Ukrainian Orthodox Ch. Can., Winnipeg, Man., 1980-85; parish priest Canora, Sask., 1991—. Author books; contbr. articles to profl.jours.; radio broadcaster. Office: Box 425, Canora, SK Canada S0A 0L0

UDVAR-HAZY, STEVEN F., leasing company financial executive; b. Budapest, Hungary, Feb. 23, 1946; came to U.S., 1958.; m. Christine L. Henneman, June 7, 1980; 3 children. BA, UCLA, 1968; HHD (hon.), U. Utah (Dixie Coll.), 1990. Cert. airline transp. jet pilot. Pres. Internat. Lease Fin. Corp., Beverly Hills, Calif., 1973—; bd. dirs. Sky West Inc., St. George, Utah. Mem. Wings Club (Achievement to Aviation award 1989). Office: Internat Lease Fin Corp Ste 3900 1999 Avenue Of The Stars Los Angeles CA 90067*

UDWADIA, FIRDAUS ERACH, engineering educator, consultant; b. Bombay, Aug. 28, 1947; came to U.S., 1968.; s. Erach Rustam and Perin P. (Lentin) U.; m. Farida Gagrat, Jan. 6, 1977; children: Shanaira, Zubin. BS, Indian Inst. Tech., Bombay, 1968; MS, Calif. Inst. Tech., 1969, PhD, 1972; MBA, U. So. Calif., 1985. Mem. faculty Calif. Inst. Tech., Pasadena, 1972-74; asst. prof. engring. U. So. Calif., Los Angeles, 1974-77, assoc. prof. aerospace and mech. engring., 1977-83, prof. mech. engring., civil engring. and bus. adminstrn., 1983-86; prof. engring. bus. adminstrn. U. So. Calif., 1986—; also bd. dirs. Structural Identification Computing Facility U. So. Calif.; cons. Jet Propulsion Lab., Pasadena, 1978—, Argonne Nat. Lab., 1982-83, Air Force Rocket Lab., Edwards AFB. Calif., 1984—; vis. prof. applied mechanics and mech. engring. Calif. Inst. Tech., Pasadena, 1993. Assoc. editor: Applied Mathematics and Computation, Jour. Optimization Theory and Applications, Jour. Franklin Inst., Jour. Differential Equations and Dynamical Sys., Nonlinear Studies, Jour. Mathematical Analysis and Applications, Jour. Mathematical Problems in Engring.; author: Analytical Dynamics, A New Approach, 1996; mem. adv. bd. Internat. Jour. Tech. Forecasting and Social Change; mem. publs. com. Jour. Aerospace Engring.; contbr. articles to profl. jours. Bd. dirs. Crisis Mgmt. Ctr., U. So. Calif. NSF grantee, 1976—; recipient Golden Poet award, 1990. Mem. AIAA, ASCE, Am. Acad. Mechanics, Soc. Indsl. and Applied Math., Seismological Soc. Am., Sigma Xi (Earthquake Engring. Research Inst., 1971, 74, 84). Avocations: writing poetry, piano, chess. Home: 2100 S Santa Anita Ave Arcadia CA 91006-4611 Office: U So Calif 430K Olin Hall University Park Los Angeles CA 90007

UEHLING, BARBARA STANER, educational administrator; b. Wichita, Kans., June 12, 1932; d. Roy W. and Mary Elizabeth (Hilt) Staner; children: Jeffrey Steven, David Edward. B.A., U. Wichita, 1954; M.A., Northwestern U., 1956, Ph.D., 1958; hon. degree, Drury Coll., 1978; LLD (hon.), Ohio State U., 1980. Mem. psychology faculty Oglethorpe U., Atlanta, 1959-64, Emory U., Atlanta, 1966-69; adj. prof. U. R.I., Kingston, 1970-72; dean Roger Williams Coll., Bristol, R.I., 1972-74; dean arts scis. Ill. State U., Normal, 1974-76; provost U. Okla., Norman, 1976-78; chancellor U. Mo.-Columbia, 1978-86, U. Calif., Santa Barbara, 1987-94; sr. vis. fellow Am. Council Edn., 1987; mem. Pacific Rim Pub. U. Pres. Conf., 1990-92; exec. dir. Bus. and Higher Edn. Forum, Washington, 1995-97; cons. North Ctr. Accreditation Assn., 1974-86; mem. nat. educator adv. com. to Compt. Gen. of U.S., 1978-79; mem. Commn. on Mil.-Higher Edn. Rels., 1978-79, Am.Coun. on Edn., bd. dirs. 1979-83, treas., 1982-83, mem. Bus.-Higher Edn. Forum, 1980-94, exec. com. 1991-94; Commn. on Internat. Edn., 1992-94, vice chair 1993; bd. dirs. Coun. of Postsecondary Edn., 1986-87, 90-93, Meredith Corp., 1980—; mem. Transatlantic Dialogue, PEW Found., 1991-93. Author: Women in Academe: Steps to Greater Equality, 1979; editorial bd. Jour. Higher Edn. Mgmt., 1986—; contbr. articles to profl. jours. Bd. dirs., chmn. Nat. Ctr. Higher Edn. Mgmt. Sys., 1977-80; trustee Carnegie Found. for Advancement of Teaching, 1980-86, Santa Barbara Med. Found. Clinic, 1989-94; bd. dirs. Resources for the Future, 1985-94; mem. select com. on athletics NCAA, 1983-84, also mem. presdl. commn.; mem. Nat. Coun. on Edn. Rsch., 1980-82. Social Sci. Research Council fellow, 1954-55; NSF fellow, 1956-57; NIMH postdoctoral research fellow, 1964-67; named one of 100 Young Leaders of Acad. Change Mag. and ACE, 1978; recipient Alumni Achievement award Wichita State U., 1978, Alumnae award Northwestern U., 1985, Excellence in Edn. award Pi Lambda Theta, 1989. Mem. Am. Assn. Higher Edn. (bd. dirs. 1974-77, pres. 1977-78), Western Coll. Assn. (pres.-elect 1988-89,k pres. 1990-92), Golden Key, Sigma Xi.

UHDE, LARRY JACKSON, joint apprentice administrator; b. Marshalltown, Iowa, June 2, 1939; s. Harold Clarence and Rexine Elizabeth (Clemens) U.; m. Linda-Lee Betty Best, Nov. 19, 1960; children: Mark Harold, Brian Raymon. Student, Sacramento City Coll., 1966, Am. River Coll., Sacramento, 1975. Equipment supr. Granite Constrn., Sacramento, 1962-69; truck driver Iowa Wholesale, Marshalltown, Iowa, 1969-70; mgr. Reedy & Essex, Inc., Sacramento, 1970-71; dispatcher Operating Engrs. Local Union 3, Sacramento, 1971-73; tng. coord. Operating Engrs. Joint Apprenticeship Com., Sacramento, 1973-83, apprenticeship div. mgr., 1983-87, adminstr., 1987-95; ret., 1995; chmn. First Women in Apprenticeship Seminar, 1972, Calif. Apprentice Coun., 1992, chair Blue Ribbon com.; com. mem. Sacramento Gen. Joint Apprenticeship Com., 1973-74; rep. Sacramento Sierra's Bldg. and Constrn. Trades Coun., 1973-75; com. mem. Valley Area Constrn. Opportunity Program, 1974-77; commr. State of Calif. Dept. Indsl. Rels., Calif. Apprenticeship Coun., chmn. 1992; mem. Apprenticeship Adv. Com. Internat. Union Oper. Engrs. Contbr. articles to trade papers. Mgr., v.p. Little League, 1971-75; co-chmn. Fall Festival St. Roberts Ch., 1973-75; v.p. Navy League Youth Program, 1978-81; instr. ARC, 1978-87; counselor United Way 1980—; bd. mem. County CETA Bd., 1981-82; coun. mem. Calif. Balance of State Pvt. Industry Coun., 1982-83, Sacramento Pvt. Industry Coun., 1982-83; coord. Acholic Recovery Program, 1984—. With USN, 1956-60. Inducted into Calif. Apprenticeship Hall of Fame, 1996. Mem. Western Apprenticeship Coords. Assn. (statewide dir. 1987—), U.S. Apprenticeship Assn., Sacramento Valley Apprenticeship Tng. Coords. Assn. (rep.), Rancho Murieta County, U.S. Golf Assn., Bing Maloney Golf Club. Democrat. Roman Catholic. Avocations: golf, archery, bowling, hunting, camping, dancing.

UHL, PHILIP EDWARD, marine artist; b. Toledo, Aug. 19, 1949; s. Philip Edward and Betty Jean (Mayes) U. Student, Dayton Art Inst., 1967-68, Art Students League, 1974. Creative dir. Ctr. for Civic Initiative, Milw., 1969-71; VISTA vol. Office Econ. Opportunity, 1969-71; artist, photographer Assn. Honolulu Artists, 1974-77; pres. Uhl Enterprises div. Makai Photography, Honolulu, 1977—, Videoscapes div. Channel Sea TV, Honolulu, 1977—; cons. Pan Am. Airways, N.Y.C., Honolulu, 1979-84, ITTC Travel Ctr., Honolulu, 1982-83, Royal Hawaiian Ocean Racing Club, Honolulu, 1984—, Sail Am.-Am's Cup Challenge, Honolulu, 1985-86, Am. 3 Found., Am. Cup Def., San Diego, 1991-92, Am. 3 Found. Womens Team, 1994-95. Co-prodr. video documentary White on Water, 1984 (Emmy 1984), Racing the Winds of Paradise (Golden Monitor award Internat. TV Assn. 1989); prodr.: Joy of Life (Golden Monitor award Internat. TV Assn. 1988), Sailors on the Sea, 1990, Teamwork, Talent, Technology (Tele award 1993); cameraman, prodr.: Pan Am. Clipper Cup 1980, 82, 84, Kenwood Cup, 1986, 88, 90, 92, 94, 96, 98 (2 Tele awards 1994), ESPN Kenwood Cup, 1990, 92, 94, ESPN Am.'s Cup, 1991-92, 94-95, Transpac, 1991, 93, 95, 97 (video documentary) Rocking the Boat, 1994-95, Datelinbe NBC Setting Sail 1994-95, numerous spls., reports on ABC-TV, NBC-TV, CBS-TV, PBS, NHK, BBC, TFI, F1, TVNZ and numerous other major worldwide broadcast networks; photographer: (book) Nautical Quar. (Soc. Pub. Designer award 1984); contbr. numerous articles, photos to yachting publs. Mem. Am. Film Inst., Internat. Platform Assn., Soc. Internat. Nautical Scribes, Am. Soc. Media Photographers, Honolulu Printmakers, Hawaii Computer Art Soc., U.S. Sailing Assn., Royal Hawaiian Ocean Racing Club, Tutukaka S. Pacific Yacht Club, Waikiki Yacht Club. Office: UHL Enterprises 1750 Kalakaua Ave Honolulu HI 96826-3766

ULIN, DAVID LAWRENCE, writer, editor, educator; b. N.Y.C., Aug. 21, 1961; s. Richard Irwin and Susan Dana (Borkow) U.; m. Rae Dubow, Aug.

27, 1988; children: Noah Dubow, Sophie Dubow. BA, U. Pa., 1984. Contbr. L.A. Times, 1991—; book editor L.A. Reader, 1993-96; instr. UCLA Extension, 1993—; contbr. Newsday, Melville, N.Y., 1994—, L.A. Weekly, 1996—, Chgo. Tribune, 1997—. Author: Cape Cod Blues, 1992. Trustee Beyond Baroque Literary Arts Ctr., Venice, Calif., 1995. Mem. PEN West (treas. 1995—), Nat. Book Critics Cir. (bd. dirs. 1994—).

ULIN, SAMUEL ALEXANDER, computer systems developer; b. Nov. 8, 1955; s. Webster Beattie Ulin and Ann (Fletcher) Rainier; m. Lida Ohan, May 30, 1992. Student, U. Del., 1973-78. Systems design cons. Alpha Ro Inc., Wilmington, Del., 1982-83, Command Computer Svcs., N.Y.C., 1983-84; systems designer DBS Films, Inc., Malvern, Pa., 1984-86; dir. engring. Flight Safety Inc., ISD, Malvern, 1986-87, Irving, Tex., 1987-89; sr. system designer Litigation Scis., Culver City, Calif., 1989-96; v.p. engring. IDEA, Inc., Seattle, 1996—. Designer software for interactive tng. on aircraft sys., 1983, one of first interactive ct. evidence presentation systems used in fed. ct., 1987. Avocations: electronics, stamp and coin collecting, winter sports. Home: 449 E Providencia Ave Apt K Burbank CA 91501-2916 Office: IDEA Inc 11351 Blue Heron Ln NE Bainbridge Island WA 98110-1212

ULLERY, PATRICIA ANNE, marketing professional; b. Casper, Wyo., July 13, 1949; d. Warren James and Nella Marie (Hammack) U.; m. Royce Edward Gilpatric, Apr. 1, 1968 (div. 1992); children: Royce Edward Gilpatric II, Eric Wynn Gilpatric. AA, Oakland C.C., Auburn Hills, Mich., 1978; student, Oakland U., 1979; BS in Internat. Bus. and Econs., Regis U., 1992; postgrad., U. Colo., 1994—. Divsn. editor Richardson Vick, Inc., Phila., 1979-81; dir. mktg. Rocky Mountain region Flack & Kurtz, Denver, 1982-86; dir. mktg. western region M.A. Mortenson Co., Denver, 1986-88; dir. mktg. Associated Gen. Contractors Colo., Denver, 1990-91; mgr. comml. devel. Cybercon Corp., Denver, 1992—; mem. real estate coun. U. Colo.; bd. dirs. Lower Downtown Dist., Inc., mktg. com., 1993-94. Mem. steering com. Great City Symposium '84, Urban Design Forum, Met. Denver's Great Neighborhoods, 1985, Parks and Pub. Spaces, 1986, bd. dirs. 1986-89; chair New Denver Airport design conf., 1987; mem. mktg. and mgmt. com. lower downtown task force Downtown Plan, 1986; mem. comprehensive plan land use/urban design task force City of Denver, 1987-88; bd. dirs. Community Housing Svcs., 1994; mem. Downtown Denver, Inc., 1982—. Recipient Outstanding Bus. Comm. Merit award Internat. Assn. Bus. Communicators, 1982, Fifty for Colo. award Colo. Assn. for Commerce and Industry, 1988, Ace Constrn. Excellence award Associated Gen. Contractors Colo., 1988, 91, Bus. in Arts award COlo. Bus. Com. for Arts, 1991. Mem. Soc. for Mktg. Profl. Svcs. (publicity chair Colo. chpt. 1984, v.p. 1985, pres. 1986, chair editorial com. Marketer, 1986-87, nat. bd. dirs. 1987-90, Leonardo award 1986), Ctrl. City Opera House Assn. (bd. dirs., pres. OperaPros 1993-94). Republican. Methodist. Avocations: skiing, golf, hiking, gardening, piano/. Home: 7880 W Woodard Dr Denver CO 80227-2438 Office: Cybercon Corp 1050 17th St Ste 1800 Denver CO 80265-1801

ULLMAN, MYRON EDWARD, III, retail executive; b. Youngstown, Ohio, Nov. 26, 1946; s. Myron Edward Jr. and June (Cunningham) U.; m. Cathy Emmons, June 20, 1969; children: Myron Cayce, Denver Tryan, Peter Brynt, Benjamin Kyrk, Kathryn Kwynn, Madylin Ming Yan. BS in Indsl. Mgmt., U. Cin., 1969; postgrad. Inst. Ednl. Mgmt., Harvard U., 1977. Internat. account mgr. IBM Corp., Cin., 1969-76; v.p. bus. affairs U. Cin., 1976-81; White House fellow The White House, Washington, 1981-82; exec. v.p. Sanger Harris div. Federated Stores, Dallas, 1982-86; mgr. dir., chief oper. officer Wharf Holdings Ltd., Hong Kong, 1986-88; chmn., CEO, dir. R.H. Macy & Co. Inc., N.Y.C., 1986-95; dir. Federated Dept. Stores, Inc.; group chmn., dir. DFS Group Ltd., San Francisco, 1995-98, group chmn., 1999—; pres. Selective Distbn. Group LVMGT, Louis Vitton Moet Hennesy, Paris, 1999—; mng. dir. Lane Crawford Ltd., Hong Kong, 1986-88; bd. advisors Gt. Traditions Corp., Cin.; dep. chmn. Omni Hotels, Hampton, N.H., 1988; vice chmn. bd. dirs. Mercy Ships Internat. Internat. v.p. U. Cin. Alumni Assn., 1980—; bd. dirs. Nat. Multiple Sclerosis Soc., N.Y.C.; bd. dirs. Brunswick Sch., Greenwich, Conn., U. Cin. Found., Lincoln Ctr. Devel., Deafness Rsch. Found., 1997—, U. Calif. Med. Ctr. Found., San Francisco, 1998—. Mem. White House Fellow Alumni Assn., Econ. Club N.Y.C. (bd. dirs., exec. com.), Nat. Retail Fedn. (vice chmn., bd. dirs., exec. com. 1993—), Delta Tau Delta (treas. 1967-68). Republican. Office: DFS Group Ltd 575 Market St San Francisco CA 94105-2823 Other: LVMH, 30 Ave Hoche, 75008 Paris France

ULMER, FRANCES ANN, state official; b. Madison, Wis., Feb. 1, 1947; m. Bill Council; children: Amy, Louis. BA in Econs. and Polit. Sci., U. Wis.; JD with honors, Wis. Sch. Law. Polit. advisor Gov. Jay Hammond, Alaska, 1975-81; former mayor City of Juneau, Alaska; mem. Alaska Ho. of Reps., 1986-94, minority leader, 1992-94; lt. gov. State of Alaska, 1995—. Home: 1700 Angus Way Juneau AK 99801-1411 Office: Office of the Lt Gov PO Box 110015 Juneau AK 99811-0015*

ULRICH, JOHN AUGUST, microbiology educator; b. St. Paul, May 15, 1915; s. Robert Ernst and Mary Agnes (Farrell) U.; m. Mary Margaret Nash, June 6, 1940 (dec. May 1985); children: Jean Anne, John Joseph, Robert Charles, Karl James, Mary Ellen, Lenore Alice; m. Mary Matkovich, July 19, 1986. BS, St. Thomas Coll., 1938; PhD, U. Minn., 1947. Instr. De La Salle High Sch., Mpls., 1938-41; rsch. asst. U. Minn., Mpls., 1941-45, 49, Hormel Inst., U. Minn., Austin, 1945-49; instr. Mayo Clinic, U. Minn., Rochester, 1949-55; asst. prof. Mayo Found., U. Minn., Rochester, 1955-66; assoc. prof. U. Minn., Mpls., 1966-69; prof. U. N.Mex., Albuquerque, 1969-82, prof. emeritus, 1982—; chmn. Bacteriology & Mycology Study Sect., NIH, Washington, 1961-64, Communicable Diseases Study Sect., Atlanta, 1968-69; cons. VA Hosp., Albuquerque, 1970—, Sandia Labs., Albuquerque, 1971—, U.S. Hosp. Supply, 1978, Internat. Chem. Industries, U.S., 1979—, Minn. Mining and Mfg. Co., 1980—, Johnson and Johnson, 1981; mem. com. on surface sampling APHA, 1974; mem. FDA-Over the Counter Drugs Panel, 1975-77, FDA-Hosp. and Personal Use Device Panel, 1978-80; mem. internat. working group on air handling in hosps. and energy conservation U. Minn., 1978-79; rsch. chmn. in field; others. Chmn. Zumbro Valley exec. bd. Boy Scouts Am., Rochester, 1953-55; mem. Gamehaven exec. bd. Boy Scouts Am., Rochester, 1952-62, Dem. Com., Olmsted County, Minn., 1964-69. Recipient Silver Beaver award Boy Scouts Am., 1962, Bishop's award Winona Diocese, 1962, Katahli award U. N.Mex., 1980. Mem. Am. Soc. Microbiology (coun. mem. 1978-80), Am. Chem. Soc., Am. Bd. Med. Mycology, Am. Acad. Microbiology, Am. Acad. Dermatology (affiliate) Elks. Democrat. Roman Catholic. Achievements include discoveries in food preservation; survival of microorganisms at low temperatures; urinary amino acid excretions in variety of disease states; post-operative wound infections; bacterial skin populations; hospital epidemiology. Home: 3807 Columbia Dr Longmont CO 80503-2122

ULRICH, PAUL GRAHAM, lawyer, author, publisher, editor; b. Spokane, Wash., Nov. 29, 1938; s. Donald Gunn and Kathryn (Vandercook) U.; m. Kathleen Nelson Smith, July 30, 1982; children—Kathleen Elizabeth, Marilee Rae, Michael Graham. BA with high honors, U. Mont., 1961; JD, Stanford U., 1964. Bar: Calif. 1965, Ariz. 1966, U.S. Supreme Ct. 1969, U.S. Ct. Appeals (9th cir.) 1965, U.S. Ct. Appeals (5th cir.) 1981. Law clk. judge U.S. Ct. Appeals, 9th Circuit, San Francisco, 1964-65; assoc. Lewis and Roca, Phoenix, 1965-70, ptnr., 1970-85; pres. Paul G. Ulrich P.C., Phoenix, 1985-92, Ulrich, Thompson & Kessler, P.C., Phoenix, 1992-94, Ulrich & Kessler, P.C., Phoenix, 1994-95, Ulrich, Kessler & Anger, P.C., Phoenix, 1995—; owner Pathway Enterprises, 1985-91; judge pro tem divsn. 1, Ariz. Ct. Appeals, Phoenix, 1986; instr. Thunderbird Grad. Sch. Internat. Mgmt., 1968-69, Ariz. State U. Coll. Law, 1970-73, 78, Scottsdale C.C., 1975-77, also continuing legal edn. seminars. Author and pub.: Applying Management and Motivation Concepts to Law Offices, 1985; editor, contbr.: Arizona Appellate Handbook, 1978—, Working With Legal Assistants, 1980, 81, Future Directions for Law Office Management, 1982, People in the Law Office, 1985-86; co-author, pub.: Arizona Healthcare Professional Liability Handbook, 1992, supplement, 1994, Arizona Healthcare Professional Liability Defense Manual, 1995, Arizona Healthcare Professional Liability Update Newsletter, 1992—; co-author: Federal Appellate Practice Guide: Ninth Circuit, 1994, 2d edit., 1999; contbg. editor Law Office Econs. and Mgmt., 1984-97, Life, Law and the Pursuit of Balance, 1996, 2d edit., 1997. Mem. Ariz. Supreme Ct. Task Force on Ct. Orgn. and Adminstrn., 1988-89; mem. com. on appellate cts. Ariz. Supreme Ct., 1990-91; bd. visitors Stanford U. Law Sch., 1974-77; adv. com. legal assisting program Phoenix Coll., 1985-95; atty. rep. 9th Cir. Jud. Conf., 1997—. With U.S. Army, 1956. Recipient continuing legal edn. award State Bar Ariz., 1978, 86, 90, Harrison Tweed spl. merit award Am. Law Inst./ABA, 1987. Fellow Ariz. Bar Found. (founding 1985—); mem. ABA (chmn. selection and utilization of staff pers. com., econs. of law sect. 1979-81, mem. standing com. legal assts. 1982-86, co-chmn. joint project on appellate handbooks 1983-85, co-chmn. fed. appellate handbook project 1985-88, chmn. com. on liaison with non-lawyers orgns. Econs. of Law Practice sect. 1985-86), Am. Acad. Appellate Lawyers, Am. Law Inst., Am. Judicature Soc. (Spl. Merit citation 1987), Ariz. Bar Assn. (chmn. econs. of law practice com. 1980-81, co-chmn. lower ct. improvement com. 1982-85, co-chmn. Ariz. appellate handbook project 1976—), Coll. Law Practice Mgmt., Maricopa County Bar Assn. (bd. dirs. 1994-96), Calif. Bar Assn., Phi Kappa Phi, Phi Alpha Delta, Sigma Phi Epsilon. Democrat. Home: 2529 E Lupine Ave Phoenix AZ 85028-1823 Office: Ste 250 3707 N Seventh St Phoenix AZ 85014-5059

ULRICH, ROBERT GUSTAV, film editor; b. Winnipeg, Man., Can., Jan. 12, 1958; came to U.S., 1965; s. Robert G. Sr. and Eleanor Anne (Kershaw) U.; m. Lisa Langlois, Oct. 8, 1994. BFA, Art Acad. of Cin., 1982; directing fellow, Am. Film Inst., L.A., 1983. Projectionist Cin., 1975-77; dir./producer commls., ind. short films, 1977-78; laser projection operator Laserworks, Inc., 1978-79; comml. freelance photographer N.Y.C., 1979-80; asst. propmaster/spl. effects Hellnight, 1980-81; prodn. mgr. Bluebird, Coast Prodns. N. Lee Lacy & Co., 1981; spl. effects design Jennie & Co., N.Y.C., 1981, Perkins/Sinclair, Kinsman/Taylor, London, 1982; asst. dir./prodn. mgr. Joseph Pipher & Co., 1982; editor Filmcore, 1984-85; editl. animation specialist Def. Audio Visual Assn., Norton AFB, 1985-86; 2d unit dir. Out of the Dark Cinetel Films, 1987; supr./ops. Film Completion Svcs., 1988-89; dir. various prodns. various, 1989—, art dir. various prodns., 1990—. Automated Dialogue Replacement supr., editor, dialogue editor on numerous films. Recipient Telly award, 1992, Emmy nomination, 1996. Mem. Motion Picture Sound Editors (bd. govs.), Motion Picture Editors Guild. Office: Maplewood 1223 Wilshire Blvd Ste 242 Santa Monica CA 90403-5400

ULRICH, WALLACE, political organization administrator. Chmn. Wyo. Rep State Com., Casper. Fax: (307) 473-8640. Office: Wyo Rep State Com Ste 314 400 E 1st St Casper WY 82601*

UMLANDT, MICHAEL WAYNE, public relations executive; b. Muscatine, Iowa, June 21, 1952; s. Peter W. and Evelyn L. (Fowler) U.; m. Carol S. Buttgen, Aug. 16, 1974; children: Christopher, Jared, Jonathan, April. BA, U. Iowa, 1975. Mng. editor Moody Mag., Chgo., 1982-88; sr. editor, pub. rels. coord. Luis Palau Evangelistic Assn., Portland, 1989—. Editor: The Only Hope for America, 1996; editor (newsletter Proclaim!, 1996. Office: Luis Palau Evangelistic Assn 1500 NW 167th Pl Beaverton OR 97006-7342

UNDERHILL, LOUISE FLYNN, retired educator, poet; b. DuQuoin, Ill., May 17, 1908; d. Edward and Celeste Flynn; m. Charles Underhill, 1972 (dec.). AB in Edn., Georgetown Coll., 1930. Tchr. Ill., Colo.; with State Dept. Edn., Cheyenne, Wyo., 1948; tchr. English Carey Jr. H.S., Cheyenne, 1954-72, ret., 1972; with Tuberculosis and Health Assn., Cheyenne, 1948. Author 12 books poetry. Laramie County libr. publicist, 1972-75; past mem. Friendship Force; mem. 1st Presbyn. Ch., Gen. Fedn. Women's Clubs, Gen. Fedn. Rep. Women. Recipient Disting. Alumna award Georgetown Coll., 1980; named Cheyenne's 1st poet laureate; one of her poems was placed in cornerstone of Capitol during state's centennial celebration. Mem. Wyo. Media Profls.

UNDERWOOD, ANTHONY PAUL, lawyer; b. Atlanta, June 25, 1955; s. Paul L and Charlene B. (Snider) U.; m. Joan Carol Butler, May 27, 1978; children: Andrew Ryan, Elizabeth Kaitlin, Caroline MacKenzie. BA, U. North Ala., 1977; MA, Samford U., 1980, JD, 1980; MS, Johns Hopkins U., 1983; LLM, Judge Adv. Gen.'s Sch., 1994. Bar: Ala. 1980, U.S. Claims Ct. 1982, U.S. Ct. Mil. Appeals 1982. Trial atty. U.S. Army, various locations, 1980-87; sr. assoc. Doke & Riley, Dallas, 1987-89; legal counsel, dir. contracts Hughes Aircraft Co., Torrence, Calif., 1989-93; mgr., contracts Hughes Missile Systems Co., Tucson, Ariz., 1993-95; dir., contracts & licensing Lockheed Martin Internat. Launch Svcs., San Diego, 1995—. Author: A Progressive History of the Young Men's Business Club of Birmingham, Ala.: 1946-70, 1980. Lt. col. USAR, 1980—. Mem. ABA (vice chair various coms., pub. contract law sect). Republican. Avocations: travel, running, reading, attending sports events. Office: Lockhead Martin Internat Launch Svcs Inc 101 W Broadway Ste 2000 San Diego CA 92101-8221

UNDERWOOD, MAX, architect, educator; b. Loma Linda, Calif., Dec. 24, 1954; s. Joseph Douglas and Flora Belle (Black) U. BS in Architecture, U. So. Calif., 1977; MArch, Princeton U., 1979. Registered architect, Ill., Tex., Ariz. Grad. teaching asst. Princeton (N.J.) U., 1977-79; assoc. prof. Ariz. State U., Tempe, 1985—; vis. asst. prof. U. Ill., Chgo., 1980-83, U. Miami, Coral Gables, Fla., 1981, U. Tex., Arlington, 1983-85; vis. prof. Cath. U., Washington, 1983-86; designer Office of Charles & Ray Eames, Venice, Calif., 1976; architect pvt. practice, Chgo., Dallas, Phoenix, 1982-95, Max Underwood & Barbara Crisp, Tempe, 1995—. Chair Heritage Sq. & Sci. Park, Phoenix, 1989—; cmty. resource spkr. Ariz. Humanities Coun., Phoenix, 1990—. Mem. AIA, Phoenix Arts Commn., Ariz. State U. Art Mus. Office: Ariz State U Sch Arch Tempe AZ 85287-1608

UNDERWOOD, RALPH EDWARD, computer systems engineer; b. Houston, Sept. 26, 1947; s. Harry Anson and Ethel Jackson Underwood; m. Linda Sue Merkel, Apr. 10, 1976. BS in Biology, Baker U., 1969; JD, Washburn U., 1973; MS in Computer Sci., Kans. U., 1984. Bar: Kans. 1973. Free-lance stock and options trader Prairie Village, Kans., 1974-79; mem. staff BDM Corp., Leavenworth, Kans., 1982-84; sr. research and devel. engr. Ford Aerospace and Communications Corp., Colorado Springs, Colo., 1984-87, subcontract adminstr., 1987-89; sr. engr., program mgr. CTA Inc., Colorado Springs, 1989-93; sr. staff system engring. MCI Telecomms. Corp., Englewood, Colo., 1993-95; cons. in computer security and risk mgmt. Englewood, Colo., 1995—. Patentee in field. Mem. Kans. Bar Assn., Upsilon Pi Epsilon, Sigma Phi Epsilon (social chmn. 1968, asst. house mgr. 1968, sec./treas. sr. coun. 1969), Phi Alpha Delta. Avocations: hunting, fishing, tennis, skiing.

UNDERWOOD, ROBERT ANACLETUS, congressional delegate, university official; b. Tamuning, Guam, July 13, 1948; m. Lorraine Aguilar; 5 children. BA with honors in History, Calif. State U., 1969, MA in History, 1971; cert. edn. adminstrn., U. Guam, 1976; DEd, U. So. Calif., 1987. Loader, sorter United Parcel Svc., L.A., 1966-72; tchr. George Washington High Sch., 1972-74, asst. prin. for bus. and student pers., 1974-76; asst. and acting prin. Inarajan Jr. High Sch., 1976; instr., dir. bilingual bicultural tng. program U. Guam, 1976-81, asst. prof., 1981-83, dir. bilingual edn. assistance for Micronesia project, 1983-88, dean Coll. Edn., 1988-90, acad. v.p., 1990—; del. 103d-105th Congress from Guam, 1993—; mem. House resources com., nat. security com.; vice chair Asian Pacific Caucus; part-time curriculum writer Guam Bilingual Edn. Project, 1973-76; chair Chamorro Lang. Commn., 1979-90. Named citizen of yr. Nat. Assn. Bilingual Edn., 1996. Roman Catholic. E-mail: guantodc@mail.house.gov. Office: US Ho Reps 424 Cannon Ho Office Bldg Washington DC 20515-5301*

UNDERWOOD, THOMAS WOODBROOK, communications company executive; b. Royal Oak, Mich., Nov. 29, 1930; s. Elmer and Della Marie (Zimmer) U.; m. Louise Virginia, May 24, 1953 (dec. Feb. 1979); children: Ann Marie Underwood Shuman, Dan and Dave (twins). BAS in Elec. Engring., Milw. Sch. Engring., 1957. Service analyst, writer ITT Gillfillan, Los Angeles, 1958-60; sr. tech. editor, writer Smithkline Beckman, Fullerton, Calif., 1960-78; tech. com. mgr. Smithkline Beckman, Brea, Calif., 1978-85; pres. Tranwood Communications, Santa Ana, Calif., 1985—. Tech. editor, writer manuals for manned space flights to Mars and the moon. Served to staff sgt. USAF, 1950-54, Korea. Fellow Soc. Tech. Comms. (Orange County chpt., assoc., pres. 1992, 93, treas. 1966, 88), Am. Med. Writers Assn, U.S. C. of C., Santa Ana C. of C. Democrat. Office: Tranwood Communications PO Box 5578 Buena Park CA 90622-5578

UNDERWOOD, VERNON O., JR., grocery stores executive; b. 1940. With Young's Market Co., L.A., pres., 1976-97, chmn. bd., 1989—, also CEO, 1997—. Office: Young's Market Co 2164 N Batavia St Orange CA 92865-3109

UNGER, STEPHEN ALAN, executive recruiter; b. N.Y.C., May 31, 1946; s. Oliver Archibald and Virginia Vera (Speed) U.; m. Kathleen Sloto Meisel, June 16, 1979. Student, NYU, 1967-68; BA, Syracuse U., 1967. V.p. internat. sales Marwi Capital Development, Paris, 1970-78; v.p. internat. sales and acquisitions Universal Pictures, Universal City, Calif., 1978-80; v.p. internat. sales and distbn. CBS Theatrical Films, Studio City, Calif., 1980-82; pres. Unger Internat. Film Distbg., Studio City, 1982-88; ptnr. Korn/Ferry Internat., Century City, Calif., 1988-91; ptnr., mng. dir. worldwide entertainment and comm. practice Spencer Stuart, L.A., 1991—; instr. UCLA, 1991. Bd. dirs., mem. pres. coun. Starbright Found., 1990—.

UNGERLEIDER, DOROTHY FINK, educational therapist; b. Chgo., Apr. 22, 1934; d. Theodore I. and Florence R. (Jacobson) Fink; m. J. Thomas Ungerleider, Dec. 19, 1954; children: John, Margot Ellen. BSEd in Spl. Edn. with honors, U. Mich., 1955; MA in Spl. Edn. with honors, Calif. State U., Northridge, 1975. Cert. ednl. therapist; cert. elem. and spl. edn. tchr., Calif. Edn. therapist in pvt. practice, Encino, Calif., 1968—; lectr. in field. Author: Reading, Writing and Rage, 1985, 2d edit., 1996; contbr. articles to profl. jours. Pro bono cons., ednl. therapist Juvenile Justice Connection Project, New Directions for Youth, Van Nuys H.S. Tech. Program. Fellow Assn. Ednl. Therapists (founding pres. 1979-82, chair adv. bd. 1983—, honoree Ann. Conf. 1994). Avocations: hiking, speed walking, adventure travel, skiing. E-mail: dotrwr@earthlink.net. Office: Assn Ednl Therapists 1804 W Burbank Blvd Burbank CA 91506-1315

UNIS, RICHARD L., judge; b. Portland, Oreg., June 11, 1928. Grad., U. Va., U. Oreg. Bar: Oreg. 1954, U.S. Dist. Ct. Oreg. 1957, U.S. Ct. Appeals (9th cir.) 1960, U.S. Supreme Ct. 1965. Judge Portland Mcpl. Ct., 1968-71; judge Multnomah County Dist. Ct., 1972-76, presiding judge, 1972-74; former judge Oreg. Cir. Ct. 4th Judicial Dist., 1977; former sr. dep. city atty. City of Portland; spl. master U.S. Dist. Ct. House, Portland; adj. prof. of local govt. law and evidence Lewis & Clark Coll. Northwestern Sch. Law, 1969-76, 77-96; spl. master supr. La.-Pacific Inner-Seal Siding nationwide class action litig.; faculty mem. The Nat. Judicial Coll., 1971-96; former faculty mem. Am. Acad. Judicial Edn. Author: Procedure and Instructions in Traffic Court Cases, 1970, 101 Questions and Answers on Preliminary Hearings, 1974. Bd. dirs. Oreg. Free from Drug Abuse; mem. Oreg. Adv. Com. on Evidence Law Revision, chmn. subcom., 1974-79. Maj. USAFR, JAGC, ret. Recipient Meritorius Svc. award U. Oregon sch. Law, 1988; named Legal Citizen of Yr. Oreg. Law Related Edn., 1987; inducted into The Nat. Judicial Coll. Hall of Honor, 1988. Mem. Am. Judicature Soc. (bd. dirs. 1975), Am. Judges Assn., Multnomah Bar Found., Oregon Judicial Conf. (chmn. Oreg. Judicial Coll. 1973-80, legis. com. 1976—, exec. com. of judicial edn. com., judicial conduct com.), N.Am. Judges Assn. (tenure, selection and compensation judges com.), Dist. Ct. Judges of Oreg. (v.p., chmn. edn. com.), Nat. Conf. Spl. Ct. Judges (exec. com.), Oreg. State Bar (judicial adminstrn. com., sec. local govt. com., com. on continuing certification, uniform jury instrn. com., exec. com. criminal law sect., trial practice sect. standards and certification com., past chmn., among others), Oreg. Trial Lawyers Assn. (named Judge of Yr. 1984). Office: US Dist Ct House 1000 SW Third Ave Portland OR 97204*

UNSER, AL, professional auto racer; b. Albuquerque, May 29, 1939; s. Jerry H. and Mary C. (Craven) U.; m. Wanda Jesperson, Apr. 22, 1958 (div.); children: Mary Linda, Debra Ann, Alfred; m. Karen Barnes, Nov. 22, 1977 (div.). Auto racer U.S. Auto Club, Speedway, Ind., 1964-94. Placed 3d in nat. standings, 1968, 2d in 1969, 77, 78, 1st in 1970, 4th in 1976; winner Indpls. 500, 1970, 71, 78, 87, Pocono 500, 1976, 78, Ont. 500, 1977, 78; placed 3d in U.S. Auto Club Sports Car Club Am. Formula 5000, 1975, 2d place, 1976; Internat. Race of Champions champion, 1978; 2d pl. Indpls. Motor Speedway, 1983; CART/PPG Indy Car champion, 1983, 85. Home: 7625 Central Ave NW Albuquerque NM 87121-2115*

UPHOFF, JOSEPH ANTHONY, JR., artist; b. Mar. 15, 1950. AA in Fine Arts, El Paso Community Coll., 1975; BA in Fine Arts, U. Colo., 1977. Mem. music, fine arts commn. First United Meth. Ch., Colorado Springs, Colo., 1979-81; asst. karate instr. The Judo and Karate Acad. Colo. Inc., Colorado Springs, 1986-87; karate instr. The Inst. Martial Arts, Colorado Springs, 1990-91. One-man shows include Weidman Realty, Colorado Springs, 1980, The Commonwheel Gallery, Manitou Springs, Colo., 1981, U.S. Space Command Hdqrs., Colorado Springs, 1985; contbr. articles to profl. jours; author numerous poems. Performer Nat. Libr. Week, 1990. With U.S. Army, 1970-73. Recipient 1st Pl. Profl. award Pikes Peak Artists Assn., 1981, 84; named Man of Achievement Internat. Biog. Ctr., 1990-91. Mem. Am. Ju-Jitsu Assn. Avocations: karate (black belt). Office: Inst Martial Arts Inc 2374 Academy Pl Colorado Springs CO 80909-1604

URENA-ALEXIADES, JOSE LUIS, electrical engineer; b. Madrid, Spain, Sept. 5, 1949; s. Jose L. and Maria (Alexiades Christodulakis) Urena y Pon. MSEE, U. Madrid, Spain, 1976; MS in Computer Science, UCLA, 1978. Rsch. asst. UCLA, 1978; systems analyst Honeywell Info. Systems, L.A., 1978-80; mem. tech. staff Jet Propulsion Lab., Pasadena, Calif., 1980-91; exec. dir. Empresa Nacional de Innovacion S.A., L.A., 1991-96; sr. technologist Hughes Space & Comm., L.A., 1996—. Contbr. various articles to profl. jours. Two times recipient NASA Group Achievement award. Mem. IEEE, IEEE Computer Soc., IEEE Communications Soc., Assn. for Computer Machinery, World Federalist Assn., Spanish Profl. Am. Inc. Roman Catholic. Avocations: amateur photographer, Master's swimming. Home: 904 Dickson St Marina Dl Rey CA 90292-5513 Office: Hughes Space & Comm Mail Stop: S50-x366 1700 E Imperial Hwy Los Angeles CA 90059-2559

URETZ, MICHAEL ALBERT, health and fitness executive; b. Chgo., Oct. 19, 1942; s. George and Frances (King) U. JD, DePaul U., 1966. Asst. states atty. Ill. States Atty., Chgo., 1967-70; atty. pvt. practice, L.A., 1972-88; pres. World Gym Lic. Ltd., Santa Monica, Calif., 1983—. Mem. Eldorado Polo Club, Empire Polo Club, Sigma Chi (life). Independent. Avocation: polo. Office: World Gym Lic Ltd 2210 Main St Santa Monica CA 90405-2275

URI, GEORGE WOLFSOHN, accountant; b. San Francisco, Dec. 8, 1920; s. George Washington and Ruby Uri; m. Pamela O'Keefe, May 15, 1961. AB, Stanford U., 1941, IA, 1943, MBA, 1946; postgrad., U. Leeds, Eng., 1945. CPA, Calif.; CFP. CMA, ChFC; Accredited Estate Planner. Mem. acctg., econs. and stats. depts. Shell Oil Co., Inc., San Francisco, 1946-48; ptnr. Irelan, Uri, Mayer & Sheppie, San Francisco; pres. F. Uri & Co., Inc.; instr. acctg. and econs. Golden Gate Univ., 1949-50. Contbr. articles to profl. jours. Chmn. San Rafael Redevel. Adv. Com., 1977-78, mem., 1978-91, mem. emeritus, 1991— ; bd. dirs. San Francisco Planning and Urban Renewal Assn., 1958-60. Served with AUS, 1942-46, to col. Res. (ret.). Recipient Key Man award San Francisco Jr. C. of C.; Meritorious Service medal Sec. of Army, 1978. Mem. AICPA (hon., cert. personal fin. specialist), INFORMS (treas. No. Calif. chpt. 1961-62), Calif. Soc. CPAs (hon.; sec.-treas. San Francisco chpt. 1956-57, dir. 1961-63, state dir. 1964-66, mem. Forbes medal com. 1968-69, chmn. 1969-71), Am. Econs. Assn., Inst. Mgmt. Accts., San Francisco Estate Planning Coun. (dir. 1965-68, Am. Soc. Mil. Comptrollers, Execs. Assn. San Francisco (pres. 1965-66), Inst. Cert. Mgmt. Accts. (Disting. Performance cert. 1978), Inst. Cert. Fin. Planners, Am. Soc. CLUs and ChFC, World Trade Club (San Francisco), Commonwealth Club (quar. chmn. 1971), Stanford (San Francisco; dir. 1990—), Army and Navy (Washington). Office: 100 Pine St Ste 2300 San Francisco CA 94111-5209

URMER, DIANE HEDDA, management firm executive, financial officer; b. Bklyn., Dec. 15, 1934; d. Leo and Helen Sarah (Perlman) Leverant; m. Albert Heinz Urmer, Sept. 2, 1952; children: Michelle, Cynthia, Carl. Student U. Tex., 1951-52, Washington U., St. Louis, 1962-63; BA in Psychology, Calif. State U.-Northridge, 1969. Asst. auditor Tex. State Bank, Austin, 1952-55; v.p., contr. Enki Corp., Sepulveda, Calif., 1966-70, also dir., 1987—; v.p., fin. Cambia Way Hosp., Walnut Creek, Calif., 1973-78; v.p., contr. Enki Health & Rsch. Sys., Inc., Reseda, Calif., 1978—, sr. v.p., 1993—; also dir. Contbr. articles to profl. jours. Pres. Northridge PTA, 1971; chmn. Northridge Citizens Adv. Council, 1972-73. Mem. Women in

Mgmt. Club: Tex. Execs. Avocations: bowling, sailing, handcrafts, golf. Office: Enki Health and Rsch Systems Inc 21601 Devonshire St Chatsworth CA 91311-2946

USSERY, ALBERT TRAVIS, lawyer, investment company executive; b. Gulfport, Miss., Mar. 12, 1928; s. Walter Travis and Rosamond (Sears) U.; m. Margaret Grosvenor Paine, Nov. 22, 1950; children: Margaret Rosamond, John Travis, Marilyn Ann, Meredith Lee. AB, Washington U., St. Louis, 1950; LLB, U. N.Mex., 1951, JD, 1968; LLM, Georgetown U., 1955. Bar: N.Mex. 1951. Ptnr. Gallagher and Ussery, Albuquerque, 1951-53, Threet, Ussery & Threet, Albuquerque, 1957-60; assoc. with Alfred H. McRae, Albuquerque, 1961-63; ptnr. McRae, Ussery, Mims, Ortega & Kitts, Albuquerque, 1964-65; chmn. Am. Bank Commerce, 1966-70, pres., 1967-70; ptnr. Ussery, Burciaga & Parrish, Albuquerque, 1969-79; pres. Ussery & Parrish, P.A., Albuquerque, 1980—; spl. counsel to Albuquerque on water law, 1956-66; chmn. Rio Grande Valley Bank, Albuquerque, 1972-83, Bank of S.W., 1980-83; lectr. mil. law U. N.Mex., 1956, instr. corp. fin., 1956-57, lectr. bus. law, 1960-61; bd. dirs. 1st City Investment Brokers, Inc., 1983-85, Lovelace Med. Systems and Techs., Inc., 1983-84. Chmn. water adv. com. Albuquerque Indsl. Devel. Svc., 1960-66; vice chmn. N.Mex. Coun. on Econ. Edn., 1969-74; mem. N.Mex. Regional Export Expansion Council, 1969-74, mem. Albuquerque Armed Forces Adv. Assn., 1977—. Trustee Village Los Ranchos de Albuquerque, 1970-72; chmn. adv. bd. Lovelace-Bataan Med. Ctr., 1976-78; trustee Lovelace Med. Found., 1978-96, vice chmn., 1988-96; trustee Lovelace Respiratory Rsch. Inst., 1996—, chmn., 1966—; bd. dirs. Goodwill Industries N.Mex., 1957-65, Albuquerque Travelers Assistance, 1956-66, Family Consultation Svc., 1961-64, Albuquerque Symphony Assn., 1964-68, Hispanic Culture Found., 1983-92, Lovelace Health Plan Inc., 1985-89; bd. dirs. N.Mex. Arthritis Found., 1969-74, pres., 1971. Mem. Am., Fed., Albuquerque (treas. 1957-60) bar assns., State Bar N.Mex., Estate Planning Coun. Albuquerque (pres. 1962), N.Mex. Zool. Soc. (dir., pres. 1977-78), Am. Legion (comdr. 1962-63), Lawyers Club. (pres. 1983-84). Lodge: Kiwanis (dir. 1957-60). Home: 37 Chaco Loop Sandia Park NM 87047-8505 Office: Ussery and Parrish PA 200 Rio Grande Valley Bldg 501 Tijeras Ave NW Albuquerque NM 87102-3174

USUI, LESLIE RAYMOND, retired clothing executive; b. Wahiawa, Hawaii, Feb. 2, 1946; s. Raymond Isao and Joyce Mitsuyo (Muramoto) U.; m. Annie On Nor Hom, Oct. 23, 1980; 1 child, Atisha. BA in Zool., U. Hawaii, 1969, MA in Edn., 1972. Cert. tchr., Hawaii. Flight steward United Airlines, Honolulu, 1970; spl. tutor Dept. Edn., 1971-73; v.p. Satyuga, Inc., Honolulu, 1974-80; pres. Satyuga, Inc., 1980—; also bd. dirs., now ret.; cons. Hawaii Fashion Guild, 1978-79. Composer: Song to Chenrayzee, Song to Karmapa. Co-founder, bd. dirs. Kagyu Thegchen Ling Meditation Ctr., 1974—, pres., 1997-99; bd. dirs. Maitreya Inst., 1983-86, Palpung Found., 1984—; mem. U.S. Senatorial Bus. Adv. Bd., Washington, 1988; charter mem. Citizens Against Govt. Waste, 1988—, Citizens for Sound Economy, 1987-91, Nat. Tax Limitation Com., 1988-89. Mem. Am. Biog. Inst. (life, bd. govs. 1990), Internat. Biog. Centre (life), World Inst. Achievement (life), Cousteau Soc., Nature Conservancy, Waikiki Aquarium. Republican. Buddhist. Avocations: oriental gardening, music. Home: 1417 Laamia Pl Honolulu HI 96821-1403 Office: Satyuga Inc PO Box 161257 Honolulu HI 96816-0926

UTHEZA, HERVE JEAN LOUIS, communications executive; b. Toulouse, France, Mar. 26, 1967; s. Guy and Jacqueline (Couget) U. BA, Lycee Pierre de Fermat, Toulouse, France, 1989; MBA, Hautes Etudes Commerciales, Paris. Pres., CEO HEC Jr. Conseil, Paris, 1989-90; U.S. rep. Thomson CSF Ventures, Palo Alto, Calif., 1991-93; fin. analyst Thomson Multimedia, Palo Alto, Calif., 1993-94; contracts and licensing mgr. Thomson Sun Interactive, Mountainview, Calif., 1994-96; bus. devel. mgr. Navio Comm., Sunnyvale, Calif., 1997-98; bus. devel. mgr. Europe Network Computer, Redwood Shores, Calif., 1998—. Author: Valeur Ajoutée et Taxe Professionelle, 1989, (poetry) Silences Murmurés, 1993; author mkt. studies Investing in Florida, 1990, Venture Capital in Silicon Valley, 1992; dir. Pay TV Europe. Mem. French-Am. C. of C. Avocations: philosophy, writing, painting, photography, cooking. Home: 27 Levant St San Francisco CA 94114-1409 Office: Network Computer 1000 Bridge Pkwy Redwood City CA 94065-1157

UTHOFF, MICHAEL, dancer, choreographer, artistic director; b. Santiago, Chile, Nov. 5, 1943; came to U.S., 1962; s. Ernst and Lola (Botka) U.; m. dau., Michelle. Grad. biology, high sch., Chile; dance tng. with Juilliard Sch., 1962-65, Martha Graham, 1962-63, Joffrey Ballet, 1965-68, Sch. Am. Ballet, 1962-64; Laureate in Humanities, St. Joseph Coll., Hartford, Conn. Leading dancer Jose Limon Dance Co., 1964-65, City Center Joffrey Ballet, 1965-68, N.Y.C. Opera, 1968-69; leading dancer, asst. dir. First Chamber Dance Co. N.Y., from 1969; artistic dir. Hartford Ballet Co., 1972-92, Ballet Ariz., 1992—; mem. faculty Juilliard Sch. Music, N.Y.C., from 1969; guest artist, tchr. Princeton Ballet Soc.; prof. dance SUNY, Purchase, 1972-74; instr. dance and drama movement, Yale U.; works premiered by Compania Nacional de Danzas, Mexico City, 1989; guest choreographer Shanghai Ballet, Republic of China, 1986; led Hartford Ballet on 3-week 11-city tour of Peoples Republic of China by invitation of Shanghai Internat. Culture Assn., 1988, 5-week 9-country tour Latin Am., 1991. Choreographer, dancer-actor film Seafall, 1968; opera prodns. Aida and La Cenerentola, Honolulu, 1972, Conn. Opera Romeo et Juliette, 1989, Pitts. Opera Aida, 1988; choreographer Quartet, City Center Joffrey Ballet, 1968, The Pleasure of Merely Circulating, Juilliard Sch. Music, 1969, Windsong, Reflections, Dusk, Promenade, First Chamber Dance Co., 1969-70, Mozart's Idomeneo for Caramoor Music Festival, 1970, Concerto Grosso for Ballet Clasico 70 of Mexico, also restaged Dusk, 1972, Aves Mirabiles, 1973, Danza a Quattro, 1973, Marosszek Dances, 1973, Duo, 1974, Pastorale, 1974, Brahms Variations, 1974, Autumalal, 1975, Mir Ken Geharget Veren, 1976, Tom Dula, 1976, Unstill Life, 1977, Songs of a Wayfarer, 1977, Ask Not..., 1977, White Mountains Suite, 1978, Bach Cantata, 1978, The Nutcracker, 1979, Romeo and Juliet, 1981, Cachivaches, 1981, Reflections on the Water, 1981, Weeping Willow, 1982, Carmencita Variations, 1982, Hansel and Gretel, 1983, Coppelia, 1986, Speak Easy, 1986, New England Triptych, 1986, Los Copihues, 1988, Petrouchka, 1988, RFD #1, 1989, Classical Symphoniette, 1990, Alice in Wonderland, 1991, Nocturnes, 1991, Sinfonia Danzante, 1991; Nat. Endowment Arts commns. for choreography: Primavera, Minn. Dance Theatre, 1975, Panvezitos, Greater Houston Civic Ballet, 1976, Sonata, The Prodigal Son, Hartford Ballet, 1977, 79. Recipient award for best choreography for Murmurs of the Stream, Chilean Nat. Press, 1983, Critic's Circle Best of Yr. in Arts award, Chile, 1984, Milagno en la Alameda award for Chilean Nat. Women, 1995; grantee various founds. Office: Ballet Ariz 3645 E Indian School Rd Phoenix AZ 85018-5126*

UTTAL, WILLIAM R(EICHENSTEIN), psychology and engineering educator, research scientist; b. Mineola, N.Y., Mar. 24, 1931; s. Joseph and Claire (Reichenstein) U.; m. Michiye Nishimura, Dec. 20, 1954; children: Taneil, Lynet, Lisa. Student, Miami U. Oxford, Ohio, 1947-48; B.S. in Physics, U. Cin., 1951; Ph.D. in Exptl. Psychology and Biophysics, Ohio State U., 1957. Staff Psychologist, mgr. behavioral sci. group IBM Research Center, Yorktown Heights, N.Y., 1957-63; assoc. prof. U. Mich., Ann Arbor, 1963-68, prof. psychology, 1968-86, research scientist, 1963-86, prof. emeritus, 1986—; grad. affiliate faculty dept. psychology U. Hawaii, 1986-88; research scientist Naval Ocean Systems Ctr.-Hawaii Lab., Kailua, 1985-88; prof., chmn. dept. psychology Ariz. State U., Tempe, 1988-92, prof. dept. indsl. engring., 1992—, affiliated prof., Dept. of Computer Sci. and Engring., 1993-98, prof. emeritus, 1999—; vis. prof. Kyoto (Japan) Prefectural Med. U., 1965-66, Sensory Sci. Lab., U. Hawaii, 1968, 73, U. Western Australia, 1970-71, U. Hawaii, 1978-79, 80-81, U. Auckland, 1996, U. Freiburg, Sydney, 1997; pres. Nat. Conf. on On-Line Uses Computers in Psychology, 1974. Author: Real Time Computers: Techniques and Applications in the Psychological Sciences, 1968, Generative Computer Assisted Instruction in Analytic Geometry, 1972, The Psychobiology of Sensory Coding, 1973, Cellular Neurophysiology and Integration: An Interpretive Introductin, 1975, An Autocorrelation Theory of Visual Form Detection, 1975, The Psychobiology of Mind, 1978, A Taxonomy of Visual Processes, 1981, Visual Form Detection in Three Dimensional Space, 1983, Principles of Psychobiology, [illegible] Perception of Dotted Forms, 1987, On Seeing Forms, 1988, The Swimmer: A Computational Model of a Perceptual Motor System, 1992, Toward a New Behaviorism: The Case Against Perceptual Reductionism, 1998, A Computational Model of Vision: The Role of Combination, 1999; also numerous articles; editor: Readings in Sensory Coding, 1972; assoc. editor Behavioral Research Method and Instrn., 1968-90, Computing: Archives for Electronic Computing, 1963-75, Jour. Exptl. Psychology: Perception and Performance, 1974-79; cons. editor Jour. Exptl. Psychology: Applied, 1994—. Served to 2d lt. USAF, 1951-53. USPHS spl. postdoctoral fellow, 1965-66; NIMH research scientist award, 1971-76. Fellow AAAS, Am. Psychol. Soc. (charter), Soc. Exptl. Psychologists (chmn. 1994-95); mem. Psychonomics Soc. Patentee in field. Office: Ariz State U Dept Indsl and Mgmt Systems Engring Tempe AZ 85287-1104

UTTER, ROBERT FRENCH, retired state supreme court justice; b. Seattle, June 19, 1930; s. John and Besse (French) U.; m. Elizabeth J. Stevenson, Dec. 28, 1953; children: Kimberly, Kirk, John. BS, U. Wash., 1952; LLB, 1954. Bar: Wash. 1954. Pros. atty. King County, Wash., 1955-57; individual practice law Seattle, 1957-59; ct. commr. King County Superior Ct., 1959-64, judge, 1964-69; judge Wash. State Ct. Appeals, 1969-71; judge Wash. State Supreme Ct., 1971-95, chief justice, 1979-81; ret., 1995; lectr. in field, leader comparative law tour People's Republic of China, 1986, 87, 88, 91, USSR, 1989, Republic of South Africa, 1997, Ukraine, Hungarian and Czech Republic, 1998; adj. prof. constl. law U. Puget Sound, 1987, 88, 89, 90, 91, 92, 93, 94; cons. CEELI, 1991, 93—, USIA, 1992; visitor to Kazakhstan, Kyrgystan Judiciary, 1993, 94, 95, 96, Outer Mangolia, 1997; lectr. to Albanian Judiciary, 1994, 95. Editor books on real property and appellate practice. Pres., founder Big Brother Assn., Seattle, 1955-67; pres., founder Job Therapy Inc., 1963-71; mem. exec. com. Conf. of Chief Justices, 1979-80, 81-86; pres. Thurston County Big Bros./Big Sisters, 1984; lectr. Soviet Acad. Moscow, 1991; USIA visitor to comment on jud. system, Latvia, 1992, Kazakstan, 1993-94; trustee Linfield Coll. Named Alumnus of Yr., Linfield Coll., 1973, Disting. Jud. Scholar, U. Ind., 1987, Judge of Yr., Wash. State Trial Lawyers, 1989, Outstanding Judge, Wash. State Bar Assn., 1990, Outstanding Judge, Seattle-King County Bar Assn., 1992, Conder-Faulkner lectr. U. Wash. Sch. Law, 1995, Disting. Alumnus Sch. Law U. Wash., 1995. Fellow Chartered Inst. Arbitrators; mem. ABA (commentator on proposed constns. of Albania, Bulgaria, Romania, Russia, Lithuania, Azerbaijan, Uzbekistan, Byelarus, Kazakhstan & Ukraine), Am. Judicature Soc. (Herbert Harley award 1983, Justice award 1998, sec. 1987—, chmn. bd. dirs., mem. exec. com.), Order of Coif. Baptist.

UTZ, SARAH WINIFRED, nursing educator; b. San Diego; d. Frederick R. and Margaret M. (Gibbons) U.; BS, U. Portland, 1943, EdM, 1958; MS, UCLA, 1970; PhD, U. So. Calif., 1979. Clin. instr. Providence Sch. Nursing, Portland, Oreg., 1946-50, edn. dir., 1950-62; edn. dir. Sacred Heart Sch. Nursing, Eugene, Oreg., 1963-67; asst. prof. nursing Calif. State U., L.A., 1969-74, assoc. prof., 1974-81, prof., 1981—, assoc. chmn. dept. nursing, 1982—; cons. in nursing curriculum, 1978—; healthcare cons., 1991—; past chmn. ednl. adminstrs., cons., tchrs. sect. Oreg. Nurses Assn., past pres. Oreg. State Bd. Nursing; mem. rsch. program Western Interstate Commn. on Higher Edn. in Nursing; chmn. liaison com. nursing edn. Articulation Coun. Calif. Author articles and lab manuals. Served with Nurse Corps, USN, 1944-46. HEW grantee, 1970-74, Kellogg Found. grantee, 1974-76, USDHHS grantee, 1987—; R.N., Calif., Oreg. Mem. Am. Nurses Assn., Calif. Nurses Assn (edn. commr. region 6 1987—, chair edn. interest group region 6, 1987—), Am. Ednl. Rsch. Assn., AAUP, Phi Delta Kappa, Sigma Theta Tau. Formerly editor Oreg. Nurse; reviewer Western Jour. Nursing Rsch. Home: 1409 Midvale Ave Los Angeles CA 90024-5454 Office: 5151 State University Dr Los Angeles CA 90032-4226

UVEZ, KURSAT, software engineer; b. Ankara, Turkey, Oct. 21, 1965; s. Sakir and Gulser (Caner) U. BS in Math., Bogazici U., Istanbul, Turkey, 1989; MS in Computer Sci., N.J. Inst. of Tech., 1996. Dir. of PC dept. Turkish Commerce Bank, Istanbul, 1991-93; product devel. mgr. Ulukom, Ltd., Istanbul, 1993-94; software engr. Traveling Software, San Mateo, Calif., 1996-97; lead software engr. Brio Tech., Palo Alto, Calif., 1997—. Mem. Assn. Computing Machinery, IEEE. Home: 2295 Francisco St Apt 303 San Francisco CA 94123-1962

UYEHARA, CATHERINE FAY TAKAKO (YAMAUCHI), physiologist, educator, pharmacologist; b. Honolulu, Dec. 20, 1959; d. Thomas Takashi and Eiko (Haraguchi) Uyehara; m. Alan Hisao Yamauchi, Feb. 17, 1990. BS, Yale U., 1981; PhD in Physiology, U. Hawaii, Honolulu, 1987. Postdoctoral fellow SmithKline Beecham Pharms., King of Prussia, Pa., 1987-89; asst. prof. in pediatrics U. Hawaii John Burns Sch. Medicine, Honolulu, 1991—; rsch. pharmacologist Kapiolani Med. Ctr. for Women and Children, Honolulu, 1990-91; statis. cons. Tripler Army Med. Ctr., Honolulu, 1984-87, 89—, chief rsch. pharmacology, 1991—, dir. collaborative rsch. program, 1995—; asst. prof. pharmacology U. Hawaii John A. Burns Sch. Medicine, 1993—; grad. faculty Interdisciplinary Biomed. Sci. program, 1995—. Contbr. articles to profl. jours. Mem. Am. Fedn. for Med. Rsch., Am. Physiol. Soc., Soc. Uniformed Endocrinologists, Endocrine Soc., We. Soc. Pediatric Rsch., N.Y. Acad. Scis., Sigma Xi. Democrat. Mem. Christian Ch. Avocations: swimming, diving, crafts, horticulture, music. Office: Tripler Army Med Ctr 1 Jarrett White Rd Bldg 40 Tripler Army Medical Center HI 96859

VAGNINI, LIVIO LEE, chemist, forensic consultant; b. North Bergen, N.J., Apr. 26, 1917; s. Frank S. and Margaret (Avondo) V.; m. Daniele Hogge, Sept. 29, 1949; children: Frank, Stephen, Eric. BS in Chemistry, Fordham U., 1938; postgrad., U. Md. Med. Sch., 1938-39. Diplomate Am. Bd. Forensic Examiners. Chemist H.A. Wilson Co. div. Englehard Industries, Inc., 1940-42; chief chemist U.S. Army Graves Registration, Liege, Belgium, 1946-48; chief forensic chemist U.S. Army Criminal Investigation Lab., Frankfurt, Fed. Republic Germany, 1948-60; sr. chemist FDA, Washington, 1960-62, CIA, Washington, 1963-73; project engr. Mitre Corp., McLean, Va., 1973-75; staff scientist Planning Research Corp., McLean, 1975-77; program dir. L. Miranda Assocs., Washington, 1978-81; forensic cons. Carmel, Calif., 1981—. Contbr. articles to profl. publs. Mem. Ft. Ord (Calif.) Retireee Coun., 1988, 89—; treas. Alliance Francaise Monterey Peninsula; adv. commn. Monterey County Commn. Vets. Svcs., 1990, 91, 92; Assn. Former Intelligence Officers, 1973—. Served with U.S. Army, 1942-46, lt. col. ret., 1975. Decorated Bronze Star. Fellow Am. Inst. Chemists, Am. Acad. Forensic Scis.; mem. Nat. Assn. for Uniformd Svcs. (Monterey chpt.)Internat. Soc. Blood Transfusion, Internat. Soc. Forensic Scientists, Ret. Officers Assn. (pres. Monterey County chpt. 1985), Sons in Retirement (pres. Pebble Beach br. 1986), Am.-Scandinavian Soc. (1st v.p., program dir. Monterey County 1989). Roman Catholic. Home: 26069 Mesa Dr Carmel CA 93923-8952

VAHUR, MARTIN, systems analyst; b. San Francisco, Jan. 30, 1964; s. Peeter and Maimu (Joosep) V.; m. Brenda Tom, July 19, 1997. BS, San Francisco State U., 1987; postgrad., U. San Francisco. Sys. analyst Hewlett-Packard Co., Palo Alto, Calif., 1987-92, tng. mgr., 1992-95, edn. mgr., 1995-98, IT project mgr., 1998—. Mem. Golden Key, Beta Gamma Sigma. Home: 15905 Soda Springs Rd Los Gatos CA 95033-8642

VAIL, MICHAEL EDWARD, viticulturist, agronomist; b. Beech Grove, Ind., June 28, 1963; s. Charles and Kitty Belle (Soukup) V. BS, Purdue U., 1986; MS, U. Calif., Davis, 1990. Cert. profl. agronomist Am. Registry of Cert. Profls. in Agronomy Crops and Soils. Soils technician Purdue U., West Lafayette, Ind., 1981-83; botany technician Purdue U., West Lafayette, 1983, rsch. assoc., 1983-86, tchg. asst., 1986; rsch. asst. U. Calif., Davis, 1986-89; viticulture prodn. specialist Crop Care Assocs., Inc., St. Helena, Calif., 1989-92; viticulturist Vino Farms Inc., Healdsburg, Calif., 1992—; herbicide rsch. intern Monsanto Ag Products Co., St. Louis, summer 1985; rsch. intern PPG Industries, Inc., Indpls., summer 1986; invited spkr. U. Calif., Davis, 1989, cooperator, 1991-97; radiation safety officer Vino Farms, Inc., Lodi, Calif., 1992-97; mem. rsch. com. Lodi-Woodbridge Wine Grape Commn. Contbr. articles to profl. jours. Mem. Am. Phytopathol. Soc., Am. Soc. Agronomy, Am. Soc. for Enology and Viticulture (pesticide subcom. 1992-95), Sonoma County Vineyard Tech. Group, Lodi-Woodbridge Winegrape Commn. (rsch. com.), Sigma Xi, Alpha Zeta. Achievements include developed a new technique to quantify grape cluster tightness. Avocations: winemaking, international travel, gardening. Home: 9417 Lazy Creek Dr Windsor CA 95492-8825 Office: Vino Farms Inc 16651 Eastside Rd Healdsburg CA 95448-9490

VALDEZ, ARNULFO, dentist, lawyer; b. Mojave, Calif., June 27, 1954; s. Stephen Monarez Jr. and Mary Lou (Esparza) V.; m. Brandy Radovich, Dec. 31, 1994; children: Bayleigh, Briton, Barrington. BS in Biol. Sci., Calif. State U., Hayward, 1976; BS in Dental Sci. and DDS, U. Calif., San Francisco, 1982; MBA, Calif. State Poly. U., 1985; BS and JD cum laude, Pacific West Coll. Law, 1995. Bar: Mex., 1996; diplomate Am. Bd. Forensic Medicine, Am. Bd. Forensic Dentistry; cert. ind. med. examiner, qualified med. examiner, Calif. Pvt. practice specializing in temporomandibular joint and Myofascial Pain Dysfunction Disorders Pomona, Calif., 1982, Claremont, Calif., 1982—; CEO Valcom, 1994—; assoc. Marin, O'Connell & Meché, 1996; CEO Valcom-A Telecom. Corp.; mem. adv. com. dental assisting program Chaffey Coll., Rancho Cucamonga, Calif., 1982—; mem. staff Pomona Valley Hosp. Med. Ctr.; ptnr. Marin, O'Connell & Meché. Vol. dentist San Antonio Hosp. Dental Clinic, Rancho Cucamonga, 1984—, Pomona Valley Assistance League Dental Clinic, 1986—; bd. dirs. Pacific West Coll. Law, 1993—, v.p. fgn. devel., 1996—. Fellow Am. Coll. Forensic Examiners, Acad. Gen. Dentistry (mastership 1994); mem. ADA, Am. Equilibration Soc., The Cranial Acad., Newport Harbor Acad. Dentistry, Calif. Dental Assn., Tri-County Dental Soc. (co-chmn. mktg. 1986, chmn. sch. screening 1987, Golden Grin award), Acad. Gen. Dentistry, U. Calif.-San Francisco Alumni Assn., U. So. Calif. Sch. Dentistry Golden Century Club, Toastmasters, Psi Omega, Delta Theta Phi. Democrat. Roman Catholic. Avocations: skiing, gymnastics, kenpo karate (black belt), racquet sports, dancing. Home: 515 Seaward Rd Corona Del Mar CA 92625-2600 Office: 410 W Baseline Rd Claremont CA 91711-1607

VALDEZ, JAMES GERALD, automotive aftermarket executive; b. Vallejo, Calif., Jan. 26, 1945; s. Charles Arthur and Margaret Ellen (Chavez) V.; m. Cathy Evelyn Gudiewski, Oct. 9, 1970; children: Mitchell Charles, Jason Garrett. BS in Engring. Tech., Calif. Poly. U., 1967; MBA in Mktg., Pepperdine U., 1975. Sales engr. Shell Oil Co., L.A., 1969-70; regional mgr. Ethyl Corp., L.A., 1970-76; dir. product engring. Pennzoil Co., Houston, 1976-84; owner, operator Valco Enterprises, L.A., 1984-86; sr. v.p. mktg. Analysis, Inc., L.A., 1986-88; dir. sales and mktg. Castrol Inc., L.A., 1988-93; v.p., gen. mgr. CSF, Inc., L.A., 1993—, also dir.; cons. in field, 1984-86. Major USAR, 1967-80. Decorated Commendation medal. Mem. SAE (chmn. various coms., gen. materials coun. 1980), Am. Petroleum Inst. (chmn. lubricants com. 1980-84), Havenhill Homeowners Assn. (pres.). Republican. Home: 5850 E Trapper Trl Anaheim CA 92807-4734

VALDEZ, JOANNE MARINDA, critical care, medical and surgical nurse; b. Moundsville, W.Va., Nov. 12, 1935; d. Byron L. and Marinda Gould (Thompson) Dunn; m. Joseph V. Valdez, Dec. 24, 1953; children: Joseph V. II, M. Louise, Alice, Robert, Richard, Michael, Elizabeth. Lic. practical nurse, St. Vincent's Sch., Santa Fe, 1974; ADN, No. N.Mex. Community Coll., 1985; BSN, U. N.M., 1992. Lic. practical nurse, N.Mex.; RN, N.Mex.; cert. in BLS, ACLS, Pediatric Life Support. Practical nurse post cardiac unit St. Vincent's Hosp., Santa Fe, 1974-77, practical nurse ICU, 1977-80, practical nurse CCU, practical nurse renal and med.-surg. floor, 1983-86, nurse oncology floor and med.-surg. unit, 1986-87, nurse post anesthesia care unit, 1987-96; ret., 1996; participant N.Mex. Gov.'s Conf. on Nursing, 1989. Recipient 20-yr. Svc. award St. Vincent's Hosp., 1989. Mem. ANA, NAFE, Nat. League Nursing, Post Anesthesia Nurse Assn. N.Mex. Home: 1013 Calle La Resolana Santa Fe NM 87505-5112

VALENTINE, GENE C., securities dealer; b. Washington, Pa., June 19, 1950; s. John N. and Jane S. Valentine. BS in Psychology, Bethany Coll., 1972; student, U. Vienna, Austria, 1971-72. Commd. ensign USN, 1972, advanced through grades to lt., 1987, hon. discharged, 1978; owner Horizon Realty, San Francisco, 1978-82; dir. land acquisitions Windfarms Ltd. subs. Chevron, U.S.A., San Francisco, 1980-82; v.p. mktg. Christopher Weil & Co., Sherman Oaks, Calif., 1982-85; chmn., CEO Pacific Asset Group Inc. (name now Fin. West Group, Inc.), Westlake Village, Calif., 1985—; bd. dirs. Fin. West Group, Inc., Paradox Holdings, Kennsington Holdings; founder, chmn., dir. Second Byte Found. Bd. trustees Bethany Coll., W.Va., 1998—; mem. Rep. Party, L.A. Mem. NASD, Internat. Assn. Fin. Planning (bd. dirs. L.A. chpt. 1982-87). Episcopalian. Avocations: equestrian, sailing, tennis, golf, running. Fax: 805-495-9935. E-mail: fw6inc@aol.com. Office: Fin West Group Inc Branch # 200 2663 Townsgate Rd Westlake Village CA 91361-2702

VALENTINE, JOHN LESTER, state legislator, lawyer; b. Fullerton, Calif., Apr. 26, 1949; s. Robert Lester and Pauline C. (Glood) V.; m. Karen Marie Thorpe, June 1, 1972; children: John Robert, Jeremy Reid, Staci Marie, Jeffrey Mark., David Emerson, Patricia Ann. BS in Acctg. and Econs., Brigham Young U., 1973, JD, 1976. Bar: Utah 1976, U.S. Dist. Ct. Utah, U.S. Ct. Appeals (10th cir.), U.S. Tax Ct.; CPA. Atty. Howard, Lewis & Petersen, Provo, Utah, 1976—; mem. Utah Ho. Reps., 1988-98, Utah Senate, 1999—; instr. probate and estates Utah Valley State Coll.; instr. fin. planning., adj. prof. law Brigham Young U.; chmn. revenue and taxation com. Utah Senate, 1999—, vice chmn. exec. appropriations com., judiciary com., pub. edn. subcom.; mem. exec offices, cts., corrections and legis. appropriations subcom., Utah Ho. of Reps., 1988-90, capital facilities subcom., 1988-90, retirement com., 1988-90, judiciary com., 1988-92, strategic planning steering com., 1988-90, interim appropriations com., 1988-94, tax. review commn., 1989-98, ethics com., 1990-92, human svcs. and health appropriations subcom., 1990-92, revenue and taxation com., 1988-98, vice chmn. 1990-92; vice chmn. exec. appropriations., 1990-92; chmn. exec. appropriations com., 1992-94, chmn. rules com., 1994-96, higher edn. appropriations com. 1994-96, asst. majority whip, 1996-98; bd. dirs. Utah Corrections Industries; chmn. Utah State Sen., 1998, chmn. revenue and taxation, vice chmn. exec. appropriations; mem. Pub. Educator Appropriations sub com. Mem. adv. bd. Internat. Sr. Games, 1988—; active Blue Ribbon Task Force on Local Govt. Funding, Utah League Cities and Towns, 1990-94, Criminal Sentencing Guidelines Task Force, Utah Judicial Coun., 1990-92, Access to Health Care Task Force, 1990-92, Utah County Sheriff Search and Rescue, Orem Met. Water Bd., Alpine Sch. Dist. Boundary Line Com., Boy Scouts Am.; bd. regents Legis. Adv. Com. UVCC; mem. exec. bd. Utah Nat. Parks Coun.; mem. adv. coun. Orchard Elem. Sch., Mountainlands Com. on Aging; bd. trustees Utah Opera Co.; judge nat. and local competitions Moot Ct.; voting dist. chmn.; state, county del.; lt. incident command sys. Utah County Sheriff. Recipient Silver Beaver award Boy Scouts Am., Taxpayer Advocate award Utah Taxpayer Assn. Mem. ABA (tax sect.), Utah State Bar, CPA Com., Tax Sect. Specialization Com., Bicentennial Com. Republican. Mormon. Avocation: mountain climbing. Office: Howard Lewis & Petersen 120 E 300 N Provo UT 84606-2907

VALENTINO, STEPHEN ERIC (IL CONTÉ VALENTINO), production and entertainment company executive, actor, singer; b. N.Y.C., Apr. 2, 1954; s. Joseph and Ina Mae (Diamond) V. Student, Hofstra U., N.Y.C., 1972-74, San Francisco Conservatory Music, 1974-78, Am. Inst. Mus. Studies, Graz, Austria, 1982. Gen. dir., chmn. bd. Mastic Community Theatre, Mastic Beach, N.Y., 1971-74; dir. advt. Marin Opera Co., San Rafael, Calif., 1979-80, Marin Ctr., San Rafael, 1983-85; pres., chief exec. officer Valentino & Assocs., Novato, Calif., 1978—; pres., CEO, co-founder Celebrity Events Internat., 1992—. Food and wine critic, contbg. editor San Francisco Mag., 1995—; contbg. author: Come Barefoot Eating Sensuous Things, 1979; prodr. Miss Julie, San Francisco; appeared in Firestorm, 1992, La Boheme, Daughter of the Regiment, (world premier) Calisto and Melibea, U. Calif., Davis, La Cenerentola, La Nozze de Figaro, The Merry Widow, La Traviata, The Bartered Bride, The Twelfth Night, Barber of Seville, Carmen, Die Fledermaus, Gianni Schicchi, I Pagliacci, Hansel and Gretel, The Magic Flute, Old Maid and the Thief, The Mikado, The Merry Wives of Windsor, (comml.) Ind. Live Ins. Corp. Am., (play) Feuerbach, Mary Stewart as Earl of Leister, 1996. Celebrity coord. Kids Say No To Drugs, 1987, MADD, 1987, ARC, San Jose, Calif., 1989; entertainment coord. Earthquake Relief Fund, San Francisco, 1989, Christmas Tree Program for the Needy, San Francisco, 1986, San Francisco Grand Prix BMW Polo Classic, Marin Suicide Prevention Ctr., 1987, Calif. Health Rsch. Found., 1988, UNICEF San Francisco, 1985, Little Sisters of The Poor, 1985, San Francisco Child Abuse Coun., 1988, 92; fundraiser Easter Seals, Marin County, Calif., 1988, Toys for Tots, Bay Area, Calif., 1987—, Global Youth Resource Orgn., Sunnyvale, Calif., 1989-90; mem. Dem. Nat. Com., 1988-90; commr. Bus. [illegible] 1992, celebrity basketball game Easter Seals Soc., 1993, entertainer Shelters for the Homeless of L.A. Earthquake, 1994. Recipient Cert. of Honor, Bd. Suprs., City and County San Francisco, 1986, Awards of Appreciation [illegible] H.R.H. Prince Leonard of the Hutt River Principality, Queensland, Aus-

tralia, 1995. Mem. AFTRA, SAG. Home and Office: Valentino and Assocs 73 Corte Roble Novato CA 94949-5925

VALESKIE-HAMNER, GAIL YVONNE, information systems specialist; b. San Francisco, May 16, 1953; d. John Benjamin and Vera Caroline (Granstrand) Valeskie; m. David Bryan Hamner, May 21, 1983. Student, Music Conservatory, Valencia, Spain, 1973, U. Valencia, 1973; BA magna cum laude, Lone Mountain Coll., 1973, MA, 1976. Fgn. exchange broker trainee Fgn. Exchange Ltd., San Francisco, 1978-79; fgn. exchange remittance supr. Security Pacific Nat. Bank, San Francisco, 1979-81; exec. sec. Bank of Am., San Francisco, 1981-83, fgn. exchange ops. supr, 1983-84; word processing specialist Wolborg-Michelson, San Francisco, 1984-86; office mgr. U.S. Leasing Corp., San Francisco, 1986-88; cons. Valeskie Data/Word Processing, San Francisco, 1987-89, pres., 1989—. Soc. chmn., mem. mission edn. com. Luth. Women's Missionary League, Vallejo, Calif., 1986-94; vol. Luth. Braille Workers, Vallejo, 1987; organist Shepherd of Hills Luth. Ch., San Francisco, 1988—. Mem. NAFE, Profl. Assn. Secretarial Svcs. (pres. 1993—), Am. Guild Organists, Am. Choral Dirs. Assn. Avocations: singing, ceramics, piano, needlework, writing.

VALFRE, MICHELLE WILLIAMS, nursing educator, administrator, author; b. Reno, Feb. 12, 1947; d. Robert James and Dolores Jane (Barnard) Williams; m. Adolph A. Valfre, Jr., Nov. 1998. BSN, U. Nev., Reno, 1973; M Health Svc., U. Calif., Davis, 1977. RN, Oreg. Staff nurse VA Hosp., Reno, 1973-77; family nurse practitioner Tri-County Indian Health Svc., Bishop, Calif., 1977-78; instr. nursing Roque C.C., Grants Pass, Oreg., 1978-82; psychiat. nurse VA Hosp., Roseburg, Oreg., 1982; dir. edn. Josephine Meml. Hosp., Grants Pass, 1983-84; geriat. nurse practitioner Hearthstone Manor, Medford, Oreg., 1984-86; chmn. nursing dept. Roque C.C., Grants Pass, Oreg., 1986-89, instr. social scis., 1997-98; prin. Health and Ednl. Cons. Inc., Tucson, 1989—; DON Highland House Nursing Ctr., Grants Pass, 1990; bd. dirs. Tri-County Indian Health Svc.; cons. for nursing svcs. in long-term care facilities. Author: Professional Skills for Leadership, Foundations of Mental Health Nursing, 1997; contbr.; Fundamental Nursing: Concepts and Skills. Mem. Josephine County Coalition for AIDS, Grants Pass, 1990. With USN, 1965-69. Mem. NAFE, Nat. League Nursing, Oreg. Ednl. Assn., Oreg. State Bd. Nursing (mem. re-entry nursing com. 1992-93).

VALLBONA, MARISA, public relations counselor; b. Houston, Jan. 2, 1964; d. Carlos and Rima (Rothe) Vallbona; m. Don R. Rayner Jr., July 12, 1986 (div.); children: Donald R. Rayner III, Timothy Carlos Rayner. Student, U. Colo., U. de Dijon, France; BS in Journalism, U. Tex. Account exec. Jae Stefan & Assocs., Austin, Tex., 1987-88; media rels. asst. America's Cup XXVII, 1988; sr. account exec. pub. rels. Berkman & Daniels, 1988-90; prin. Rayner & Vallbona Inc. Advt. & Pub. Rels., San Diego, 1990-97; pres. CIM, Inc., San Diego, 1997—. Editor: Flowering Inferno, 1994, Soldiers Cry By Night, 1994, Assumed Name, 1994, People on the Prowl, 1995; contbr. articles to profl. jours. Pub. rels. chair, bd. dirs. Women of St. James Episc. Ch., 1994, 1st v.p., 1995; mem. pub. affairs disaster task force ARC, 1993—; pub. rels. chair Sunkist Am. Cancer Soc. Cup Regatta, 1989; mem. elections mktg. task force City of San Diego, 1989. Mem. Pub. Rels Soc. Am. (accredited, San Diego chpt. chair accreditation com. 1994, dir.-at-large 1995, bd. dirs. 1996—, sec. 1997, dir. 1998, assembly del. 1999), Am. Soc. Health Care Mktg. and Pub. Rels., Health Care Communicators San Diego (v.p., bd. dirs. 1994, sec. 1993, numerous awards), United Cerebral Palsy Assn., Pub. Rels. Club San Diego (exec. bd. dirs. 1991-92, various awards), Jr. League San Diego. Avocations: snow skiing, tennis, sailing, golfing. Office: CIM Inc 6961 Petit St San Diego CA 92111-3303

VALLERAND, PHILIPPE GEORGES, sales executive; b. Montreal, Que., Can., June 12, 1954; came to U.S., 1982; s. Louis Philippe and Beatrice (Goupil) V.; m. Laura Jean Frombach, Sept. 25, 1979; children: Harmonie May, Jeremy Thomas, Emilie Rose. Student, U. Montreal, 1974, U. Sherbrooke, 1975, U. Que., 1976, White Mgmt. Sch., London, 1981. Cert. mktg. and sales ISO 9000. Dir. resort Club Mediterranee Inc., Bahamas, Switzerland,, Africa,, Guadelupe, West Indies, 1978-80; v.p. Franglo/Sunsaver Inc., London and Hyeres, France, 1980-82; v.p. sales Source Northwest, Inc., Woodinville, Wash., 1982-93; pres., CEO Prime Resource Group. Sr. comdr. Royal Rangers Boys Club, Monroe, Wash., 1988-96; bd. mem. Christian Faith Ctr., Monroe, 1988-94; mem. Rep. Nat. Com. Named to 500 Inc. Mag., 1983, 89; recipient Disting. Sales & Mktg. Exec. award Internat. Orgn. Sales & Mktg. Execs., 1993, 96. Mem. Am. Mktg. Assn. (adv. bd.), Sales and Mktg. Execs. Internat. Avocations: skiing, archery.

VALLES, JUDITH, mayor, former academic administrator; b. San Bernardino, Calif., Dec. 14, 1933; d. Gonzalo and Jovita (Lopez-Torices) V.; m. Chad Bradbury, Sept. 30, 1956 (dec. Sept. 1969); children: Edith Renella, Nohemi Renella, Chad; m. Harry Carl Smith, Oct. 13, 1985. BA in English, Redlands (Calif.) U., 1956; MA in Spanish Lit., U. Calif., Riverside, 1966. Instr. Spanish San Bernardino (Calif.) Valley Coll., 1963-64, head dept. fgn. lang., 1971-76, chair div. humanities, 1976-81, dean extended day, 1981-83, adminstrv. dean acad. affairs, 1983-87, exec. v.p. acad. and student affairs, 1987-88; pres. Golden West Coll., Huntington Beach, Calif., 1988—; mayor San Bernardino, 1998—; mem. adv. com. Police Officers Standards and Trng. Commn., Scaramento, 1991—. Author fgn. lang. annals and sociol. abstracts. Speaker statewide edn. and community orgns., 1988—; bd. dirs. exec. coun. and chief exec. officers Calif. Community Colls., 1990—. Named One of Outstanding Women Orange County YWCA, 1990, Citizen of Achievement LWV, 1989; inducted into Hall of Fame, San Bernardino Valley Coll. Mem. Women's Roundtable Orange County, Conf. and Visitors Bur., C. of C. (Vanguard), Kiwanis, Charter 100. Avocations: opera, theater, reading. Office: Office of Mayor 300 North D St San Bernardino CA 92418*

VALLIANT, JAMES STEVENS, lawyer; b. Glendale, Calif., Sept. 29, 1963; s. William Warren and Carol Dee (Heath) V.; m. Holly Lynne White. BA, NYU, 1984; JD, U. San Diego, 1989. Bar: Calif. 1989. Law instr. U. San Diego, 1988-89; dep. dist. atty. Dist. Atty.'s Office, San Diego, 1989—; host talk show WJM Prodns., Hollywood, Calif., 1996. Recipient Citation of Appreciation MADD, 1993. Republican. Office: Dist Attys Office 330 W Broadway San Diego CA 92101-3825

VALONE, KEITH EMERSON, clinical psychologist; b. Austin, Tex., Aug. 3, 1953; s. James Floyd and Elizabeth Niles (Emerson) V.; m. Leona Marie Lagace, July 22, 1978; children: Kyle Stephen James, Christienne Marie. BA, U. So. Calif., 1975; MA, U. Ill., 1979, PhD, 1981; PsyD, Inst. Contemporary Psychoanaly, L.A., 1995. Lic. psychologist, Calif. Pvt. practice Pasadena, Calif., 1983—; dir. psychology Ingleside Hosp., Rosemead, Calif., 1990-92; candidate Inst. of Contemporary Psychoanalysis, L.A., 1991-95; clin. asst. prof. dept. psychology Fuller Theol. Sem., Pasadena, Calif., 1984-85; asst. clin. prof. dept. psychology UCLA, 1984-87; chief psychology svc. Las Encinas Hosp., Pasadena, 1988. Contbr. articles to profl. jours. Mem. APA, Calif. State Psychol. Assn., Phi Beta Kappa. Episcopalian. Office: 301 S Fair Oaks Ave # 401 Pasadena CA 91105-2536

VAN ALLEN, KATRINA FRANCES, painter; b. Phoenix, Feb. 18, 1933; d. Benjamin Cecile Sherrill and Magdalen Mary (Thomas) Adams; m. Ray C. Bennett II, Dec. 31, 1950 (div. 1955); m. William Allen Van Allen, Mar. 15, 1963 (dec. Mar. 1971); m. Donovan Wyatt Jacobs, Apr. 22, 1972; children: Ray Crawford Bennett III, Sherri Lou Bennett Maraney. Student, Stanford U., 1950, 51, 52, Torrance C.C., 1962, 63; MA, U. Tabriz, Iran, 1978; studied with Martin Lubner, Jerold, Burchman, John Leeper, L.A.; student, Otis Art Inst., Immaculate Heart Coll.; studied with the late Russa Graeme, 1968, 69, 70. Office mgr. H.P. Adams Constrn. Co., Yuma, Ariz., 1952-59; nurse Moss-Hathaway Med. Clin., Torrance, Calif., 1962-63; interviewer for various assns. N.Y.C., 1964-70. Solo shows include: Zella 9 Gallery, London, 1972, Hambleton Gallery, Maiden Newton, Eng., 1974, Intercontinental Gallery, Teheran, Iran, 1976, USIA Gallery, Teheran, 1977, 78, Coos Art Mus., Coos Bay, Oreg., 1993; exhibited in group shows at La Cienega Gallery, L.A., 1970, 80, 81, 82, Design Ctr. Gallery, Tucson, 1985, Coos Art Mus., 1992-97, 98; represented in permanent collections at Bankers Trust Bd. Room, London, Mfrs. Hanover Bank, London, U. Iowa Med. Sch., Iowa City, Bank of Am., Leonard E. Blakesley Internat. Law Offices, Marina del Rey, Calif., and numerous pvt. collections. Bd. dirs. Inst. for Cancer and Leukemia Rsch., 1966-67, 68. Recipient Five City Tour and Honorarium, Iran Am. Soc., 1977. Mem. Nat. Women in the Arts, L.A. Art Assn., Coos Bay Art Assn., Coos Bay Power Squadron, Lower Umpqu Flycasters, Coos Country Club. Avocations: fly-fishing, hiking, bridge, golf, the arts. Home and Studio: 3693 Cape Arago Hwy Coos Bay OR 97420-9604

VANARSDEL, ROSEMARY THORSTENSON, English studies educator; b. Seattle, Sept. 1, 1926; d. Odin and Helen Catherine (McGregor) Thorstenson; m. Paul P. VanArsdel Jr., July 7, 1950 (dec. Jan. 1994); children: Mary M., Andrew P. BA, U. Wash., 1947, MA, 1948; PhD, Columbia U., 1961. Grad. tchg. asst. Columbia U., N.Y.C., 1948-50; acting instr. U. Wash., Seattle, 1961-63; asst. prof. U. Puget Sound, Tacoma, Wash., 1967-69; assoc. prof. U. Puget Sound, Tacoma, 1970-77, prof. English, 1977-87, disting. prof. emeritus, 1987—, dir. Writing Inst., 1976-86, dir. semester abroad, 1977, dir. Legal English program Sch. Law, 1973-77; vis. prof. Gonzaga U., Pacific Luth. U., Whitman Coll., Willamette U., 1977. Author: Victorian Periodicals: A Guide to Research, Vol. I, 1978, Vol. II, 1989, George Eliot: A Centenary Tribune, 1982, Victorian Periodicals and Victorian Society, 1994, Periodicals of Queen Victoria's Empire, An Exploration, 1996; mem. editl. bd. Wellesley Index for Victorian Periodicals, 1968-89; contbr. articles to profl. jours. Recipient Doris Bronson Morrill award Kappa Kappa Gamma, 1982, Disting. Alumnae award Broadway H.S., Seattle, 1991. Mem. MLA, Royal Soc. Lit., Oxford Bibliog. Soc., Nat. Coun. Tchrs. English (Achievement awards, dir. 1974-77), Rsch. Soc. for Victorian Periodicals (pres. 1981-83). Home: 4702 NE 39th St Seattle WA 98105-5205

VAN ASPEREN, MORRIS EARL, banker; b. Wessington, S.D., Oct. 5, 1943; s. Andrew and Alyce May (Flagg) Van A.; m. Anne Virginia Merritt, July 2, 1966; 1 child, David Eric. BS in Math., U. Okla., 1966; MBA, Pepperdine U., 1979. Mgr. western dist. Svc. Rev. Inc., Northbrook, Ill., 1970-77; v.p. Hooper Info. Systems Inc., Tustin, Calif., 1977-78; v.p., chief fin. officer ATE Assocs. Inc., Westlake Village, Calif., 1978-84; mgmt. cons. Thousand Oaks, Calif., 1984-94; sr. v.p. Nat. Bank Calif., L.A., 1986—; chmn. liaison com. region IX SBA, 1990-94; adj. faculty U. Phoenix, 1997—; bd. dirs. Logical Imaging Solutions, Inc., Santa Ana, Calif., 1997—. Nat. advocate fin. svcs. SBA, 1989. Lt. USN, 1966-70. Mem. Nat. Assn. Govt. Guaranteed Lenders (bd. dirs. 1990-93), Robert Morris Assocs., Nat. Assn. Credit Mgmt., Am. Legion (bd. dirs. Post 339 1995). Avocations: art, music. Office: Nat Bank Calif 145 S Fairfax Ave Los Angeles CA 90036-2171

VANASSE, DEB LYNN, secondary education educator, writer; b. St. Paul, Sept. 12, 1957; d. Louis Lehmann and Laura Mae (Koerner) Jones; m. Timothy Vanasse, July 27, 1980; children: Lynx, Jessica. BS, Bemidji (Minn.) State U., 1978; MA, Calif. State U., Dominguez Hills, 1991. Tchr. high sch. Lower Kuskakwim Schs., Bethel, Alaska, 1979-82; instr. devel. studies U. Alaska, Fairbanks, 1982-88; chair dept. lang. arts North Pole (Alaska) H.S., 1988—. Author: A Distant Enemy, 1997; contbr. chpt to book: United in Diversity, 1998; assoc. editor: The Camai Book, 1981. Mem. Nat. Coun. Tchrs. of English, Greater Fairbanks Bd. Realtors. Mem. Assembly of God Ch. Home: 322 Rambling Rd Fairbanks AK 99712 Office: North Pole HS 601 NPHS Blvd North Pole AK 99705

VAN BEBBER, ANNIE, business developer; b. Chgo., Aug. 12, 1948; d. Louis and Raye (Yablonky) Friedman; m. Terry Reed, 1971; children: Coreen Van Bebber, Taylor Van Bebber. Student, Valley Coll., Van Nuys, Calif., 1968, Pasadena City Coll., 1972, Northridge U. With Drake-Chenault, Canoga Park, Calif., 1968-71; assoc. editor Radio & Records, Century City, Calif., 1972-75; gen. mgr. Inside 12X12/Retail Record Report, Woodland Hills, Calif., 1975-76, Computer Park West, Long Island City, N.Y., 1978-81; ind. agt., cons. Internat. Computer Group, Can., 1992-95, v.p. bus. devel. Attitude Network, Naples, Fla., 1995-96; CEO, owner Digital Maven, Glendale, Calif., 1996—; founder Holiday Videos; new bus. developer Internet Developer's Assn.; new media chmn., Internet specialist Rec. Artist Against Drunk Drivers; pres. Traffic Mgr.'s Conf. of Calif.; event planner Glendale C. of C. Mem. Edn. Tech. Planning Team; coord. nat. radiothon Nat. Leukemia Broadcast Coun.; vol. Children's Cancer Study Group, Nat. Childhood Cancer Found., T.J. Martell Found.; founders bd., chmn. events and dinners Neil Bogart Meml. Fund; corp. sponsor March of Dimes 10 yrs. invitational ski race; cruise event cons. AMFAR; mem. adv. bd., Internet specialist SafeHaven. Mem. Internat. Interactive Comms. Soc., Acad. Interactive Arts and Scis., Delta Nu Alpha. Avocations: skiing, sailing, cruising, traveling. Home: 1421 El Miradero Ave Glendale CA 91201-1201

VAN BRUNT, EDMUND EWING, physician; b. Oakland, Calif., Apr. 28, 1926; s. Adrian W. and Kathryn Anne (Shattuck) Van B.; m. Claire Monod, Feb. 28, 1949; children: Karin, Deryk, Jahn. BA in Biophysics, U. Calif., Berkeley, 1952; MD, U. Calif., San Francisco, 1959; ScD (hon.), U. Toulouse, France, 1978. Postdoctoral fellow NIH, 1961-63; rsch. assoc. U. Calif., San Francisco, 1963-67; staff physician Kaiser Permanente Med. Ctr., San Francisco, 1964-91; dir. div. rsch. Kaiser Permanente Med. Program, Oakland, Calif., 1979-91; assoc. dir. Kaiser Found. Rsch. Inst., Oakland, 1985-91, sr. cons., 1991—; Kaiser Permanente Med. Program No. Calif. region; adj. prof. U. Calif., San Francisco, 1975-92; chmn. instnl. rev. bd. Kaiser Permanente No. Calif. region, 1986—; pres. bd. trustees French Found. Med. Rsch. and Edn., San Francisco, 1992-98. Contbr. articles to profl. books and jours. With U.S. Army, 1944-46. Fellow ACP, Am. Coll. Med. Informatics; mem. AAAS, Calif. Med. Assn., U. Calif. Emeritus Faculty Assn., Sigma Xi. Avocations: flying, photography, swimming.

VAN DE KAMP, ANDREA LOUISE, academic administrator; b. Detroit, July 28, 1943; m. John K. Van De Kamp; 1 child, Diana. BA, Mich. State U., 1966; MA, Columbia U., 1972. Dir. recruitment Columbia U., N.Y.C., 1968-71; asst. dean admissions Dartmouth Coll., Hanover, N.H., 1971-74; assoc. dean admissions Occidental Coll., L.A., 1974-77; exec. dir. Internat. Acad. Estate Trust Law, L.A., 1976-79, Coro Found., L.A., 1977-80; dir. devel. Mus. Contemporary Art, L.A., 1980-81; dir. pub. affairs Carter Hawley Hale Stores, Inc., L.A., 1981-87; pres. Ind. Colls. So. Calif., L.A., 1987-89; chmn. West Coast ops. Sotheby's N.Am., Beverly Hills, Calif., 1989—; bd. dirs. City Nat. Bank, Jenny Craig Corp., Walt Disney Co. Bd. dirs., officer, Music Ctr. Operating Co., L.A.; chmn. Music Ctr., L.A. County; trustee Pomona Coll.; sec. Calif. Cmty. Found. Mem. Women in Pub. Affairs. Avocations: sports. Office: 9665 Wilshire Blvd Beverly Hills CA 90212-2340

VAN DE KAMP, JOHN KALAR, lawyer; b. Pasadena, Calif., Feb. 7, 1936; s. Harry and Georgie (Kalar) Van de K.; m. Andrea Fisher, Mar. 11, 1978; 1 child, Diana. BA, Dartmouth Coll., 1956; JD, Stanford U., 1959. Bar: Calif. 1960. Asst. U.S. atty. L.A., 1960-66, U.S. atty., 1966-67; dep. dir. Exec. Office for U.S. Attys., Washington, 1967-68, dir., 1968-69; spl. asst. Pres.'s Commn. on Campus Unrest, 1970; fed. pub. defender L.A., 1971-75; dist. atty. Los Angeles County, 1975-83; atty. gen. State of Calif., 1983-91; with Dewey Ballantine, L.A., 1991-96, of counsel, 1996—; pres. Thoroughbred Owners, Calif., 1996—; bd. dirs. United Airlines. Mem. Calif. Dist. Attys. Assn. (pres. 1975-83), Nat. Dist. Attys. Assn. (v.p. 1975-83), Peace Officers Assn. L.A. County (past pres.), Nat. Assn. Attys. Gen. (exec. com. 1983-91), Conf. Western Attys. Gen. (pres. 1986). Office: Dewey Ballantine 333 S Hope St Ste 3000 Los Angeles CA 90071-3039

VANDENBERG, PETER RAY, magazine publisher; b. Geneva, Ill., Sept. 8, 1939; s. Don George and Isabel (Frank) V.; m. Kathryn Stock, June 1973 (div. Apr. 1977). BBA, Miami U., 1962. Creative adminstr. E.F. McDonald Incentive Co., Dayton, Ohio, 1966-73; mfrs.' rep. Denver, 1974-75; mgr. Homestake Condominiums, Vail, Colo., 1975-76; desk clk. Vail Run Resort, 1976-77; sales rep. Colo. West Advt., Vail, 1977-79, pres., 1980-83; pres. Colo. West Publ., Vail, 1983—. With U.S. Army, 1963-66. Mem. Sigma Chi. Avocations: sports, music, reading.

VANDENBERGHE, RONALD GUSTAVE, accountant, real estate developer; b. Oakland, Calif., July 1, 1937; s. Anselm Henri and Margaret B. (Bygum) V.; B.A. with honors, San Jose State Coll., 1959; postgrad. U. Calif. at Berkeley Extension, 1959-60, Golden Gate Coll., 1961-63; CPA, Calif.; m. Patricia W. Dufour, Aug. 18, 1957; children: Camille, Mark, Matthew. Real estate investor, pres. VandenBerghe Fin. Corp., Pleasanton, Calif., 1964—. Instr. accounting U. Cal., Berkeley, 1963-70; CPA, Pleasanton, 1963—. Served with USAF. Mem. Calif. Soc. CPAs. Republican. Presbyterian. Mason (Shriner). Home: PO Box 803 Danville CA 94526-0803 Office: 20 Happy Valley Rd Pleasanton CA 94566-9792

VANDER ARK, GARY DUANE, neurosurgeon; b. Ellsworth, Mich., Aug. 3, 1937; s. Harry G. and Dorothy W. (Horrenga) Vander A.; m. Phyllis J. Quist, May 31, 1958; children: Tom, Jillane. BS, Calvin Coll., 1958; MD, U. Mich., 1962. Diplomate Am. Bd. Neurosurgery. Intern, then resident U. Hosp., Ann Arbor, Mich., 1962-68; pvt. practice, Englewood, Colo.; chief neurosurgery Denver Gen. Hosp., 1971-76; pres. Colo. Neurol. Inst., Denver, 1988—. Author: A Primer of EEG, 1970; contbr. over 50 articles to med. jours., chpts. to books. Pres. Doctors Care, Denver, 1988—. Maj. MC, U.S. Army, 1968-71. Recipient Robbins cmty. svc. award Colo. Med. Soc., 1990, svc. to manking award local, dist. and regional Sertoma, 1992, Disting. Alumni award Calvin Coll., 1993. Fellow ACS; mem. Am. Assn. Neurol. Surgeons, Western Neurosurg. Soc., Colo. Nerosurg. Soc. (pres. 1995-96), Colo. Med. Soc. (pres.-elect 1996-97, pres. 1997-98), Arapahoe Med. Soc. (pres. 1985-86). Republican. Mem. Christian Reformed Ch. Avocations: mountain climbing, biking. Home: 79 Glenmoor Dr Englewood CO 80110-7116 Office: Rocky Mountain NA Alliance 701 E Hampden Ave Englewood CO 80110-2736

VANDERFORD, THOMAS NEIL, JR., lawyer; b. Fresno, Calif., Oct. 24, 1960; s. Thomas Neil Sr. and Janet (Rosewall) V.; m. Madelene Pink, Sept. 28, 1985; children: Ryan Joseph, Ty Winston, Jack Thomas Calvin. BA, UCLA, 1982; JD cum laude, Loyola U., L.A., 1985. Bar: Calif. 1985. Assoc. Lawler, Felix & Hall, L.A., 1985-86, Pillsbury, Madison & Sutro, L.A., 1986-92; sr. counsel Hyundai Motor Am., Fountain Valley, Calif., 1992—. Mem. ABA, Orange County Bar Assn., Loyola Law Sch. Alumni Assn., Tau Kappa Epsilon (bd. dirs. L.A. chpt. 1986-90). Democrat. Roman Catholic. Office: Hyundai Motor Am 10555 Talbert Ave Fountain Valley CA 92708

VANDERGRIFF, JERRY DODSON, retired computer store executive; b. Ft. Leonard Wood, Mo., Nov. 6, 1943; s. Oliver Wyatt Vandergriff and Mary Ella (Perkins) Myers; m. Donna Jean Niehof, Aug. 14, 1976 (div. Nov. 1987); children: Robert Lee II, William Oliver; m. Lisa Ann Marrett, Aug. 10, 1996. BS in Bus., Emporia State U., 1974. Customer svc. mgr. Pictures, Inc., Anchorage, 1975-83, v.p., gen. mgr., 1983-87; gen. mgr. Pictures-The Computer Store, Anchorage, 1987-96; ret., 1996. Bd. dirs. Community Schs. Coun., Anchorage, 1986-87; mem. Gov.'s Coun. on Edn., 1989-90; bd. dirs. Romig Jr. High Sch., 1989-90, pres. PTSA, 1990-92; mem. exec. bd. Alaska's Youth Ready for Work, 1989-92. Mem. VFW. Republican. Avocations: movies, reading, pool, fishing, scuba diving. Home: 3831 Balchen Dr Anchorage AK 99517-2446

VANDERHEIDEN, RICHARD THOMAS, government official, lawyer; b. Omaha, Nov. 10, 1947; s. Frederick Joseph and Margaret (Burke) V.; m. Mary Margaret Schuster, June 1, 1969; children: Brian, Paul. BS, U. Nebr., 1970, JD, 1973. Bar: Nebr. 1974. Dep. county atty. Merrick County, Central City, Nebr., 1974-75; ptnr. Phares Torpin Vanderheiden & Mesner, Central City, 1976-87; v.p. Founders Bank of Ariz., Scottsdale, 1987-88, Chase Trust Co. of Ariz., Scottsdale, 1988-91; pub. fiduciary Maricopa County, Phoenix, 1991—; jud. nominating commn. 21st Jud. Dist., Nebr., 1984-86; bd. dirs. Merrick County Mental Health Ctr., 1975-82, Mericopa County Justice Com., 1991—, exec. team, 1991; chmn. Maricopa County Deferred Compensation Bd., 1994—, NaCo Deferred Compensation Adminstrv. Com., 1995—. Pres. Bd. Edn., Central City, 1975-82; chpt. chmn. ARC, Central City, 1976-80; co-chair United Way Campaign, Maricopa County; chmn. cert. com. Nat. Guardianship Assn. Mem. ABA, Nat. Guardianship Assn. (bd. dirs. 1992-97, v.p. 1995), Nat. Guardianship Found. (bd. trustees 1997—, vice chair 1997-98), Scottsdale Bar Assn., Valley Estate Planners (pres. 1990-91), Ariz. Bankers Assn. (trust com. 1989-91), Sertoma Internat. (pres. 1979), Central City C. of C. (bd. dirs. 1980-84). Roman Catholic. Avocations: tennis, hiking, running, reading. Office: First Am Title Bldg 111 W Monroe St Fl 5 Phoenix AZ 85003-1716

VANDERHOEF, LARRY NEIL, academic administrator; b. Perham, Minn., Mar. 20, 1941; s. Wilmar James and Ida Lucille (Wothe) V.; m. Rosalie Suzanne Slifka, Aug. 31, 1963; children: Susan Marie, Jonathan Lee. B.S., U. Wis., Milw., 1964, M.S., 1965; Ph.D., Purdue U., 1969. Postdoctorate U. Wis., Madison, 1969-70; research assoc. U. Wis., summers 1970-72; asst. prof. biology U. Ill., Urbana, 1970-74; assoc. prof. U. Ill., 1974-77, prof., 1977—, head dept. plant biology, 1977-80; provost Agrl. and Life Scis., U. Md., College Park, 1980-84; exec. vice chancellor U. Calif., Davis, 1984-91, exec. vice chancellor, provost, 1991-94; chancellor, 1994—; vis. investigator Carnegie Inst., 1976-77, Edinburgh (Scotland) U., 1978; cons. in field. NRC postdoctoral fellow, 1969-70, Eisenhower fellow, 1987; Dimond travel grantee, 1975, NSF grantee, 1972, 74, 76, 77, 78, 79, NATO grantee, 1980. Mem. AAAS, Am. Soc. Plant Physiology (bd. editors Plant Physiology 1977-82, trustee, mem. exec. com., treas. 1982-88, chmn. bd. trustees 1994—), Nat. Assn. State Univ. and Land Grant Colls. Home: 16 College Park Davis CA 95616-3607 Office: U Calif Davis Office Chancellor Davis CA 95616

VANDER HOOF, JILL, stone sculptor, educator; b. Concord, Calif., Feb. 2, 1945; d. Vertress Lawrence Vander Hoof. BA in Biology, San Francisco State U., 1968; postgrad., Studio Silverio Paoli, Pietrasanta, Italy, 1983-86. Asst. prof. Westmont Coll., Santa Barbara, Calif., 1993—; docent Santa Barbara Mus. Art, 1979-83. Mem. Santa Barbara Sculptors' Guild (pres. 1996-98). Avocation: international travel. Home: PO Box 50214 Santa Barbara CA 93150 Office: Westmont Coll 955 La Paz Rd Santa Barbara CA 93108

VANDERHOOFT, JAN ERIC, orthopedic surgeon, educator; b. Salt Lake City, May 16, 1962; s. Gerard F. and Else-Marie Vanderhooft; m. Sheryll Jo Vanderhooft, Mar. 25, 1984; children: Peter, Lauren. BS, Stanford (Calif.) U., 1984; MD, U. Utah, 1988. Cert. Am. Bd. Orthopaedic Surgeons, added qualification in hand surgery. Resident, fellow U. Wash., Seattle, 1988-94; attending physician Salt Lake Orthopedic Clinic, 1994—; clin. dir. orthop. rotation St. Mark's Hosp. U. Utah, 1998—; clin. dir. family medicine residency orthop. rotation Columbia St. Mark's, 1998—; clin. instr. U. Wash., 1993-94; asst. clin. prof. dept. orthopedics U. Utah. Contbr. articles to profl. jours. and chpts. to textbooks. Bd. dirs. Turn Cmty. Svcs., Salt Lake City, 1996—. Recipient: Family Medicine Res. award for excellence in tchg., 1995, 96, 98. Fellow Am. Acad. Orthopaedic Surgeons; mem. Western Musculoskeletal Assn. (bd. dirs. 1995-96), Am. Soc. for Surgery of the Hand, Utah Med. Assn., Western Orthop. Assn., Alpha Omega Alpha. Office: Salt Lake Orthopedic Clinic 1160 E 3900 S Ste 5000 Salt Lake City UT 84124-1247

VANDERLINDEN, CAMILLA DENICE DUNN, telecommunications industry manager; b. Dayton, July 21, 1950; d. Joseph Stanley and Virginia Danley (Martin) Dunn; m. David Henry VanderLinden; Oct. 10, 1980; 1 child, Michael Christopher. Student, U. de Valencia, Spain, 1969; BA in Spanish and Secondary Edn. cum laude, U. Utah, 1972, MS in Human Resource Econs., 1985. Asst. dir. Davis County Community Action Program, Farmington, Utah, 1973-76; dir. South County Community Action, Midvale, Utah, 1976-79; supr. customer service Ideal Nat. Life Ins. Co., Salt Lake City, 1979-80; mgr. customer service Utah Farm Bur. Mutual Ins., Salt Lake City, 1980-82; quality assurance analyst Am. Express Co., Salt Lake City, 1983-86, quality assurance and human resource specialist, 1986-88; mgr. quality assurance and engring. Am. Express Co., Denver, 1988-91; mgr. customer svc. Tel. Express Co., Colorado Springs, Colo., 1991-97; dir. Call Ctr. United Membership Mktg. Group, Lakewood, Colo., 1997-98; telesvcs. industry mgr. Piton Found., Denver, 1998—; mem. adj. faculty Westminster Coll., Salt Lake City, 1987-88. mem. adj. faculty, mem. quality adv. bd. Red Rocks Community Coll., 1990-91. Vol. translator Latin Am. community; vol. naturalist Roxborough State Park; internat. exch. coord. EF Fgn. Exch. Program. Mem. Internat. Customer Svc. Orgn. (officer call ctr. chpt.), Colo. Springs Customer Svc. Assn. (officer). Christian. Avocations: swimming, hosting fgn. exchange students. Home: 10857 Snow Cloud Trail Littleton CO 80125-9211

VAN DER MEULEN, JOSEPH PIERRE, neurologist; b. Boston, Aug. 22, 1929; s. Edward Lawrence and Sarah Jane (Robertson) VanDer M.; m. Ann

Irene Yadeno, June 18, 1960; children—Elisabeth, Suzanne, Janet. A.B., Boston Coll., 1950; M.D., Boston U., 1954. Diplomate: Am. Bd. Psychiatry and Neurology. Intern Cornell Med. div. Bellevue Hosp., N.Y.C., 1954-55; resident Cornell Med. div. Bellevue Hosp., 1955-56; resident Harvard U., Boston City Hosp., 1958-60, instr., fellow, 1962-66; assoc. Case Western Res. U., Cleve., 1966-67; asst. prof. Case Western Res. U., 1967-69, assoc. prof. neurology and biomed. engring., 1969-71; prof. neurology U. So. Calif., L.A., 1971—; also dir. dept. neurology Los Angeles County/U. So. Calif. Med. Center; chmn. dept. U. So. Calif., 1971-78, v.p. for health affairs, 1977—, dean Sch. Medicine, 1985-86, 95-97; vice dean med. affairs, 1995-97; dir. Ind. Health Professions, L.A., 1991—; vis. prof. Autonomous U. Guadalajara, Mex., 1974; pres. Norris Cancer Hosp. and Research Inst., 1983-98. Contbr. articles to profl. jours. Mem. med. adv. bd. Calif. chpt. Myasthenia Gravis Found., 1971-75, chmn., 1974-75, 77-78; med. adv. bd. Amyotrophic Lateral Sclerosis Found., Calif., 1973-75, chmn., 1974-75; mem. Com. to Combat Huntington's Disease, 1973—; bd. dirs. Calif. Hosp. Med. Ctr., Good Hope Med. Found., Doheny Eye Hosp., House Ear Inst., L.A. Hosp. Good Samaritan, Children's Hosp. of L.A., Phila. Health Edn. Corp., Barlow Respiratory Hosp., USC U. Hosp., chmn., 1991—; bd. govs. Thomas Aquinas Coll.; bd. dirs. Assn. Acad. Health Ctrs., chmn., 1991-92; pres. Scott Newman Ctr., 1987-89; pres., bd. dirs. Kenneth Norris Cancer Hosp & Rsch. Inst. Served to lt. M.C. USNR, 1956-58. Nobel Inst. fellow Karolinska Inst., Stockholm, 1960-62; NIH grantee, 1968-71. Mem. AMA, Am. Neurol. Assn., Am. Acad. Neurology, L.A. Soc. Neurology and Psychiatry (pres. 1977-78), L.A. Med. Assn., Mass. Med. Soc., Ohio Med. Soc., Calif. Med. Soc., L.A. Acad. Medicine, Alpha Omega Alpha (councillor 1992—), Phi Kappa Phi. Home: 39 Club View Ln Palos Verdes Peninsula CA 90274-4208 Office: U So Calif 1540 Alcazar St Los Angeles CA 90033-4500

VANDERMEY, HERMAN RONALD, dean, religion educator; b. Buffalo, Sept. 28, 1952; s. Robert Benjamin and Marion Isabel (Reed) V.; m. Denise Bonta Tart, June 5, 1982. BA, Masters Coll., 1974; MDiv, Biola U., 1977, ThM, 1980; EdD, Faith Sem., 1988; LittD (hon.), Faith-Los Angeles Sch. of Theology, 1989. Cert. secondary edn. tchr., Calif. Youth min. Bethany Bible Presbyn. Ch., Glendale, Calif., 1973—; dir. Verdugo Christian Day Camps, Glendale, 1973—; dean, prof. ch. history Cohen Theol Sem, L.A., 1988—; tchr. Glendale Unified Schs., 1985—; vice chmn. India Nat. Inland Mission, Glendale, 1985—; moderator S.W. Presbyn., L.A., 1985—; vice moderator Bible Presbyn. Synod, 1998—. Author: Hosea/Amos, 1981. Republican. Office: Bethany Bible Presbyn Ch 3229 N Verdugo Rd Glendale CA 91208-1633

VANDERMOLEN, SUSAN ANN, library media specialist; b. Monticello, N.Y., Mar. 22, 1960; d. Irwin Charles and Sharon Joyce (Goldfin) Price; m. Garry Van Der Molen Jr., Apr. 20, 1980; children: Elizabeth Ann, Melissa May, George Garry. AA, West Hills C.C., 1997; postgrad., Chapman U., 1997—. Plant dept. mgr., cashier, non-foods worker Shop Rite, Middletown, N.Y., 1978-82; tchr. aide Admiral Akers Elem. Sch., 1991-93, classified libr. media specialist, 1993—. Staff writer: (newspaper) The Golden Eagle, 1993. Red Cross vol. Naval Hosp., Lemoore Naval Air Sta., 1985-88; parent vol. Akers Sch., 1988-91; pres. PTA, Lemoore, Calif., 1993-94; book chairperson Women's Aglow, Lemoore, 1996—, corr. sec. Mem. Calif. Schs. Libr. Assn., Computer Using Educators. Republican. Avocations: gardening, crocheting, bowling, golf. Home: 1413 San Simeon Dr Lemoore CA 93245 Office: Cen Union Sch Dist PO Box 1339 Lemoore CA 93245

VANDERSPEK, PETER GEORGE, management consultant, writer; b. The Hague, Netherlands, Dec. 15, 1925; came to U.S., 1945; s. Pieter and Catherine Johanna (Rolf) V.; m. Charlotte Louise Branch, Aug. 18, 1957. Student, Tilburg (Netherlands) U., 1944; MA in Econs., Fordham U., 1950, PhD in Econs., 1954; postgrad., George Washington U., 1967-68. Internat. economist Mobil Oil Corp., N.Y.C., 1956-59; mgr. internat. market rsch. Celanese Corp., N.Y.C., 1959-63; internat. economist Bethlehem (Pa.) Steel Corp., 1964-65; sr. tech. adviser Battelle Meml. Inst., Washington, 1965-66; indsl. adviser Inter-Am. Devel. Bank, Washington, 1967-69; economist Fed. Res. Bank, N.Y.C., 1970-72; mgr. internat. market rsch. Brunswick Corp., Skokie, Ill., 1973-76; mgr. advanced planning Sverdrup Corp., St. Louis, 1979-87; cons. Sverdrup Corp., 1988-90; pres. OBEX, Inc., San Luis Obispo, Calif., 1988—. Author: Planning for Factory Automation, 1993; contbr. to profl. jours. Thomas J. Watson fellow, IBM-Fordham U., 1945-49. Mem. Nat. Assn. Bus. Economists, Mensa. Avocations: travel, writing, dog training. Home and Office: 1314 Vega Way San Luis Obispo CA 93405-4815

VAN DERVEER, TARA, university athletic coach; b. Niagara Falls, N.Y., June 26, 1953. Grad., Indiana U., 1975. Coach women's basketball Stanford U. Cardinals, 1985—, U.S. Nat. Women's Team, 1995—; coach gold medalist Women's Olympic Team, 1996. Champions NCAA Divsn. 1 A, 1990, 92. Office: Stanford U Womens Basketball Dept of Athletics Palo Alto CA 94305

VAN DER VEUR, PAUL ROSCOE, communication educator, researcher; b. Honolulu, Dec. 17, 1958; s. Paul W.J. van der Veur and Karol Ann (Kaiser) Niemi; m. Shirley L. Morrow, July 23, 1983; 1 child, Luke Marius. BA, MTS Vakschool, 1982; MFA, Ohio U., 1985, PhD, 1996. Ednl. advisor U.S. Peace Corps, Mokhotlong, Lesotho, 1985-87; comms. specialist Govt. of Lesotho, Maseru, 1987-89; collections cons. Athens, Ohio, 1989-91; faculty advisor Ohio U., Athens, 1992, tchg. assoc., 1990-93; asst. prof. Mont. Tech. of the U. of Mont., Butte, 1993-96; assoc. prof. Mont. Tech., Butte, 1996—; advisor KMSM Radio Sta., Butte, 1993—, Technocrat Newspaper, Butte, 1993—. Author: Colonial Legacies in Mass Education and Mass Communications in Southern Africa with Special Reference to Radio Broadcasting in Botswana: 1920-1995. Founder Citizens for Preservation and Revitalization; vol. My Sister's Place, Athens, 1995; big brother Big Bros. and Sisters, Butte, 1993—. John Houk rsch. grant Ohio U., 1993, instrnl. grant Mont. Tech., 1994. Mem. African Studies Assn., Assn. for Edn. in Journalism and Mass Comms. (James W. Markham award 1993), Returned Peace Corps Vol. Avocations: reading, writing, skiing, hiking, swimming. Office: Mont Tech of the U of Mont 1300 W Park St Butte MT 59701-8932

VAN DER WERFF, TERRY JAY, management consultant, professional speaker, futurist; b. Hammond, Ind., May 16, 1944; s. Sidney and Johanna (Oostman) van der W.; m. Renee Marie Leet, Mar. 2, 1968; children: Anne Cathleen, Valerie Kay, David Edward, Michele Renée, Julia Leigh. SB and SM, MIT, 1968; DPhil, Oxford (Eng.) U., 1972. Registered profl. engr., Colo., South Africa; prof. biomed. engr., South Africa. Staff engr. ARO, Inc., Tullahoma, Tenn., 1968; asst. prof. mech. engring., physiology and biophysics Colo. State U., Ft. Collins, 1970-73; vis. asst. prof. medicine U. Colo., Denver, 1973-74; head biomed. engring. U. Cape Town/Groote Schuur Hosp., Cape Town, South Africa, 1974-80; dean of sci. and engring. Seattle U., 1981-90; exec. v.p. for acad. affairs St. Joseph's U., Phila., 1990-91; pres. van der Werff Global Ltd., Seattle, 1991—. Co-author: Mathematical Models of the Dynamics of the Human Eye; author 175 book revs., monthly newspaper and mag. columns; contbr. over 40 articles to profl. jours. Recipient Ralph R. Teetor award Soc. Automotive Engrs., Detroit, 1972. Fellow Royal Soc. South Africa, Biomed. Engring. Soc. South Africa; mem. AAAS, Nat. Spkrs. Assn., Soc. Competitive Intelligence Profls., World Affairs Coun., Inst. Mgmt. Cons., Strategic Leadership Forum, Sigma Xi. Republican. Roman Catholic. Home: 2410 NE 123rd St Seattle WA 98125-5241

VAN DEUSEN, LARRY MILTON, artist; b. Sydney, N.Y., Jan. 31, 1952; s. C.D. and Ruth I. (Westin) Van D. BA in Sculpture, Calif. State U., Hayward, 1975. One-man shows include Calif. State U., Hayward, 1976, Olive Hyde Gallery, Fremont, Calif., 1978, Calif. State U. Art Gallery, Hayward, 1984, So. Exposure Gallery, San Francisco, 1985, San Francisco Women Artist Gallery, 1988, Davis Art Ctr., Calif., 1989, Hayward Main Libr., 1993, San Francisco State U. Art Gallery, 1995, A.R.C. Gallery, Chgo., 1996, Hayward Theater Gallery, 1997, Triobol Gallery, Castro Valley, 1998, Stanford U. Gallery, Palo Alto, 1998; group shows include Capricorn/Asunder Gallery, San Francisco, 1979, Nanny Goat Hill Gallery, San Francisco, 1983, Works Gallery, San Jose, Calif., 1987, Arts Coun. Annex Gallery, Hayward, 1993, Lower Columbia Coll. Gallery, Longview, Wash., 1994, Downtown Gallery, Hayward, 1993, 94, 95, 96, Phantom Gallery, Hayward, 1994, Sun Gallery, Hayward, 1996, Art Gallery, McNeese State U., Lake Charles, La., 1996, Gallery 303, Statesboro, Ga., 1996, others. Home: 25376 Morse Ct Hayward CA 94542-1134

VANDEVER, JUDITH ANN, county official; b. Hemstead, N.Y., Aug. 6, 1941; d. John Anthony Klym and Kathryn M. (Lane) Trexler; children: Garret, Kimberlee Vandever Johnson. Student, U. Nev. Dep. recorder Clark County Recorder, Las Vegas, Nev., 1979-91, chief dep. recorder, 1991-93, asst. recorder, 1993-94, county recorder, 1995—. State chair. Nev. Young Woman of the Yr., 1991; mem. S.M.A.R.T. Team Clark County Sch. Dist., 1994-95, ctrl. com. State/County Dem. Ctrl. Com., 1988—; state dir. Women Officials Nat. Assn. Counties, 1997. Recipient Leadership Dedication award Amigos De HIP, 1996, Women Elected Ofcls. Spotlight award Women's Dem. Club, 1996. Mem. ASPA, Nat. Assn. County Recorders and Clks., Assn. of Profl. Mortage Women,Assn. of Recorders Mgrs. and Adminstrs., U. Nev.-Las Vegas Jean Nidetch Women's Ctr. (original founder), Leadership Las Vegas Alumni Assoc., Las Vegas C. of C. (bd. of trustees, cmty. coun. 1995-98). Office: Clark County Recorder 500 S Grand Central Pkwy Las Vegas NV 89106-4506

VAN DUSEN, DONNA BAYNE, communication consultant, educator, researcher; b. Phila., Apr. 21, 1949; d. John Culbertson and Evelyn Gertrude (Godfrey) Bayne; m. David William Van Dusen, Nov. 30, 1968 (div. Dec. 1989); children: Heather, James; m. L. John Maki, Dec. 27, 1996. BA, Temple U., 1984, MA, 1986, PhD, 1993. Instr. Kutztown (Pa.) U., 1986-87, Ursinus Coll., Collegeville, Pa., 1987-96; cons., rschr. Comm. Rsch. Assoc., Valley Forge, Pa., 1993-96; rschr. Fox Chase Cancer Ctr., Phila., 1985-86; adj. faculty Temple U. Law Sch., 1994—, LaSalle U., 1994-96, Wharton Sch., U. Pa., 1994-95; asst. prof. Beaver Coll., Glenside, Pa., 1995-96; faculty Internat. U., 1996—, Metro State U., Denver, 1997—; cons. Human Comm. Resources and Solutions, 1997—. Writer Mountain Connection, 1998—. Vol. Friends in Transition. Mem. AAUP, Nat. Comm. Assn. Avocations: oil painting, creative writing, sailing, gardening, reading. Home: 1631 Crow Valley Rd Bailey CO 80421-2304

VANE, SYLVIA BRAKKE, anthropologist, publisher, cultural resource management company executive; b. Fillmore County, Minn., Feb. 28, 1918; d. John T. and Hulda Christina (Marburger) Brakke; m. Arthur Bayard Vane, May 17, 1942; children: Ronald Arthur, Linda, Laura Vane Ames. AA, Rochester Jr. Coll., 1937; BS with distinction, U. Minn., 1939; postgrad., Radcliffe U., 1944; MA, Calif. State U., Hayward, 1975. Med. technologist Dr. Frost and Hodapp, Willmar, Minn., 1939-41; head labs. Corvallis Gen. Hosp., Oreg., 1941-42; dir. lab. Cambridge Gen. Hosp., Mass., 1942-43, Peninsula Clinic, Redwood City, Calif., 1947-49; v.p. Cultural Systems Rsch., Inc., Menlo Park, Calif., 1978—; pres. Ballena Press, Menlo Park, 1981—; cons. cultural resource mgmt. So. Calif. Edison Co., Rosemead, 1978-81, San Diego Gas and Elec. Co., 1980-83, Pacific Gas and Elec. Co., San Francisco, 1982-83, Wender, Murase & White, Washington, 1983-87, Yosemite Indians, Mariposa, Calif., 1982-91, San Luis Rey Band of Mission Indians, Escondido, Calif., 1986-89, U.S. Ecology, Newport Beach, Calif., 1986-89, Riverside County Flood Control and Water Conservation Dist., 1985-95, Infotec, Inc., 1989-91, Alexander & Karshmer, Berkeley, Calif., 1989-92, Desert Water Agy., Palm Springs, Calif., 1989-90, Metropolitan Water Dist., Nat. Park Svc., 1992—, Applied Earthworks, Inc., 1997—. Author: (with L.J. Bean), California Indians, Primary Resources, 1977, rev. edit., 1990, The Cahuilla and the Santa Rosa Mountains, 1981, The Cahuilla Landscape, 1991, Ethnology of the Alta California Indians, vol. I Pre Contact, vol. II Post Contact, 1992, Spanish Borderlands Sourcebooks, vols. 3, 4; contbr. chpts. to several books. Bd. dirs. Sequoia Area coun. Girl Scouts U.S., 1954-61; bd. dirs., v.p., pres. LWV, S. San Mateo County, Calif., 1960-65. Fellow Soc. Applied Anthropology, Am. Anthropology Assn.; mem. Southwestern Anthrop. Assn. (program chmn. 1976-78, newsletter editor 1976-79), Soc. for Am. Archaeology, Soc. Calif. Archaeology (Martin A. Baumhoff Spl. Achievement award 1998). Mem. United Ch. of Christ. Office: Ballena Press 823 Valparaiso Ave Menlo Park CA 94025-4206

VAN EMBURGH, JOANNE, lawyer; b. Palmyra, N.J., Nov. 18, 1953; d. Earl Henry and Clare (Kemmerle) Van E.; m. Samuel Michael Surloff, July 6, 1993. BA summa cum laude, Catholic U., 1975; JD cum laude, Harvard Law Sch., 1978. Bar: Calif. 1978. Assoc. atty. Agnew Miller & Carlson, L.A., 1978-82; ptnr. Sachs & Phelps, L.A., 1982-91, Heller, Ehrman, White & McAuliffe, L.A., 1991-93; mng. counsel Toyota Motor Sales, USA, Inc., Torrance, 1993—. Mem. ABA. Avocations: reading, cooking, sports. Office: Toyota Motor Sales USA Inc 19001 S Western Ave Torrance CA 90509*

VAN ETTEN, PETER WALBRIDGE, hospital administrator; b. Boston, May 10, 1946; s. Royal Cornelius Van Etten and Peggy June (Walbridge) Hutchins; m. Mary Peters French, Sept. 5, 1968; children: Molly, Clarissa, Ellen. BA, Columbia U., 1968; MBA, Harvard U., 1973. Br. mgr. BayBanks, Brookline, Mass., 1968-71; loan officer Bank of Boston, 1973-76; CFO Univ. Hosp., Boston, 1976-79; exec. v.p., CFO New Eng. Med. Ctr., Boston, 1979-89; pres., CEO Transitions Systems, Boston, 1986-89; dep. chancellor U. Mass. Med. Ctr., Worcester, 1989-91; CFO Stanford (Calif.) U., 1991-94; pres., CEO Stanford Univ. Hosp., 1994-97; CEO UCSF Stanford Health Care, 1997—; exec. com. U. Healthsystem Consortium, 1997—, vice chmn., 1998—; dir. Calif. Healthcare Assn., 1998—; dir. Transition Sys., Inc., 1996-98. Chair campaign United Way San Francisco, 1998—. Office: UCSF Stanford Health Care San Francisco CA 94134

VAN EXEL, NICKEY MAXWELL, professional basketball player; b. Kenosha, Wis., Nov. 27, 1971; s. Nickey Maxwell and Joyce Van Exel; 1 child, Nickey Maxwell III. Attended, Trinity Valley C.C., 1989-91, U. Cin., 1993. Profl. basketball player L.A. Lakers, 1993-98; guard Denver Nuggets, 1998-. Named to NBA All-Rookie 2d team, 1994. Office: Denver Nuggets 1635 Clay St Denver CO 80204-1743*

VAN GELDER, NANEENE SUE, English language educator; b. Glendale, Calif., Sept. 3, 1946; d. Jack Phelps and Bernett (Clarke) Van G.; m. Stephen H. Ellis, June 15, 1968 (Feb. 1979); children: Blake Ellis, Jacquelyn Ellis. BA, Occidental Coll., 1968; MA, San Diego State U., 1973. Cert. tchr., Calif. V.p. Ellis Corp., San Diego, 1974-78; freelance writer, editor San Diego, 1978-88; instr. English Santa Rosa (Calif.) Jr. Coll., 1988—; chair learning cmty. steering com. Santa Rosa Jr. Coll., 1994-98. Editor: A Clinical Hypnosis Primer, 1985, Aerobic Instructor Manual, 1987; editor (mag.) Dance-Exercise Today, 1985-87; editor (newsletter) Fit Cop, 1988-89. Mem. Assn. for Study of Lit. and Environ., Faculty Assn. Calif. C.C.s. Avocations: hiking, dancing. Home: 2120 Northwwod Dr Santa Rosa CA 95404

VAN GELDEREN, ELLY, English linguistics educator; b. Geertruidenberg, The Netherlands, Sept. 20, 1958; d. Antonij Johannes and Elsje (Schuttevaar) van G.; m. Harry McFarland Bracken, June 19, 1985. Kandidaats, U. Utrecht, The Netherlands, 1979, doctoraal, 1981; PhD, McGill U., Montreal, Que., Can., 1986. Instr. humanities John Abbott Coll., Montreal, 1986-89; lectr. linguistics McGill U., 1989; vis. asst. prof. Queen's U., Kingston, Ont., Can., 1989-90; asst. prof. English linguistics U. Groningen, The Netherlands, 1990-95; asst. prof. Ariz. State U., Tempe, 1995-98, assoc. prof., 1998—. Author: The Rise of Functional Categories, 1993, Verbal Agreement and the Grammar Behind its Breakdown: Minimalist Feature Checking, 1997; co-editor: German: Syntactic Problems - Problematic Syntax, 1997; contbr. articles to profl. jours. Chmn. Can. sect. Amnesty Internat., Ottawa, Ont., 1985-86; del. Internat. Coun. Mtg., Helsinki. Mem. Linguistic Soc. Am., Linguistic Assn. Can. and U.S., Internat. Soc. for Hist. Linguistics, Linguistic Soc. The Netherlands, Internat. Linguistic Assn., Soc. Linguistica Europaea, also others. Home: 9107 E Avenida Las Noches Apache Junction AZ 85219-4676 Office: Ariz State U English Dept Tempe AZ 85287-0302

VAN HENGEL, DRUSILLA RUTH, social ecologist; b. North Tarrytown, N.Y., Sept. 9, 1963; d. Maarten and Drusilla Ruth (Riley) van H.; m. Joshua Conrad Patlak, Nov. 10, 1996. BA, Dartmouth Coll., 1985; MA, U. Calif., Irvine, 1993, PhD, 1996. Rsch. asst. Inst. Transp. Studies, Irvine, 1992-96, postdoctoral rschr., 1996-97; author bicycle master plan City of Santa Barbara, Calif., 1997-98, mobility coord. City of Santa Barbara, 1999—. Bd. dirs. Newport Aquatic Ctr., Newport Beach, Calif., 1996-98; sec. sprint racing com. of U.S. Canoe and Kayak Team, Indpls., 1996-98. Mem. 1996 Olympic team U.S. Canoe and Kayak Team, Atlanta, 1996; mem. world kayak team U.S. Canoe and Kayak Team, 1997, 98; del. to Internat. Olympic Acad., U.S. Olympic Com., Olympica, Greece, 1997. Mem. Offshore Canoe Club. Avocations: watercolor painting, swimming, creative writing.

VAN HOOMISSEN, GEORGE ALBERT, state supreme court justice; b. Portland, Oreg., Mar. 7, 1930; s. Fred J. and Helen F. (Flanagan) Van H.; m. Ruth Madeleine Niedermeyer, June 4, 1960; children: Geroge T., Ruth Anne, Madeleine, Matthew. BBA, U. Portland, 1951; JD, Georgetown U., 1955, LLM in Labor Law, 1957; LLM in Jud. Adminstrn., U. Va., 1986. Bar: D.C. 1955, Oreg. 1956, Tex. 1971, U.S. Dist. Ct. Oreg. 1956, U.S. Ct. Mil. Appeals 1955, U.S. Ct. Customs and Patent Appeals 1955, U.S. Ct. Claims 1955, U.S. Ct. Appeals (9th cir.) 1956, U.S. Ct. Appeals (D.C. cir.) 1955, U.S. Supreme Ct. 1960. Law clk. for Chief Justice Harold J. Warner Oreg. Supreme Ct., 1955-56; Keigwin teaching fellow Georgetown Law Sch., 1956-57; dep. dist. atty. Multnomah County, Portland, 1957-59; pvt. practice Portland, 1959-62; dist. atty. Multnomah County, 1962-71; dean nat. coll. dist. attys., prof. law U. Houston, 1971-73; judge Cir. Ct., Portland, 1973-81, Oreg. Ct. Appeals, Salem, 1981-88; assoc. justice Oreg. Supreme Ct., Salem, 1988—; adj. prof. Northwestern Sch. Law, Portland, Willamette U. Sch. Law, Portland State U.; mem. faculty Am. Acad. Judicial Edn., Nat. Judicial Coll.; Keigwin Teaching fellow Georgetown U. Law Sch. Mem. Oreg. Ho. of Reps., Salem, 1959-62, chmn. house jud. com. With USMC, 1951-53; col. USMCR (ret.). Recipient Disting. Alumnus award U. Portland, 1972. Master Owen M. Panner Am. Inn of Ct.; mem. ABA, Oreg. State Bar, Tex. Bar Assn., Oreg. Law Inst. (bd. dirs.), Arlington Club, Multnomah Athletic Club, Univ. Club. Roman Catholic. Office: Oreg Supreme Ct 1163 State St Salem OR 97310-1331

VAN HORN, O. FRANK, retired counselor, consultant; b. Grand Junction, Colo., Apr. 16, 1926; s. Oertel F. and Alta Maude (Lynch) Van H.; m. Dixie Jeanne MacGregor, Feb. 1, 1947 (dec. Nov. 1994); m. Evelyn Anne Carroll, Mar. 22,1998; children: Evelyn, Dorothy. AA, Mesa Coll., 1961; BA, Western State Colo., 1963; MEd, Oreg. State U., 1969. Counselor, mgr. State of Oreg.-Employment, Portland and St. Helens, 1964-88; pvt. practice counselor and cons. St. Helens, 1988-96; chair Task Force on Aging, Columbia County, 1977-79; advisor Western Interstate Commn. on Higher Edn., Portland, 1971, Concentrated Employment and Tng., St. Helens, 1977, County Planning Bd., Columbia County, Oreg., 1977-80, City Planning Bd., St. Helens, 1978, Youth Employment Coun., St. Helens, 1978, Task Force on Disadvantaged Youth, St. Helens, 1980; counselor Career Mgmt. Specialists Internat.; instr. Portland C.C. Mem. ACA, Oreg. Counseling Assn., Internat. Assn. Pers. in Employment Svc. (Outstanding Achievement award 1975), Nat. Employment Counselors Assn. Democrat. Home: 220 MacArthur St Saint Helens OR 97051-1118

VAN HORSSEN, CHARLES ARDEN, manufacturing executive; b. Mpls., June 28, 1944; s. Arden Darrel and Margaret E. (Ellingsen) V H.; m. Mary Katherine Van Kempen, Sept. 11, 1967 (div. 1975); children: Lisa, Jackie; m. Mary Ann Pashuta, Aug. 11, 1983; children: Vanessa, Garrett. BSEE, U. Minn., 1966. Design engr. Sperry Univac, Mpls., 1966-68; sr. project engr. Sperry Univac, Salt Lake City, 1975-80; systems engr. EMR Computer, Mpls., 1968-75; pres. A&B Industries Inc., Phoenix, 1980—, Axis Tech Inc., Phoenix. Patentee in field. Mem. Ariz. Tooling and Machining Assn. (bd. dirs., v.p. 1987-89, pres. 1989-91). Republican. Episcopalian. Office: Axis Tech Inc 21622 N 14th Ave Phoenix AZ 85027-2841

VAN HUDSON, MARK VALENTINES, religion educator; b. Pitts., Aug. 26, 1949; s. Paul Franklin van Hudson. BS in Engring., U. N.Mex., 1971; MS, Cogate Rochester Sem., 1985; PhD, Georgetown U., 1990. Asst. prof. Georgetown U., Washington, 1989—; chmn. Asian Theol. Congress, Singapore, 1983-84; chmn. Hist. Lit. Symposium, 1988; del. Congress Bibl. Archeologists, 1990; chmn. S.W. Spiritual and Theol. Conf, 1991. Author: Ballal and Christ, 1982, Urban Christianity in the 1st Century, 1989, Berashith and Minor Prophets, 1990; editor: the Mimetic Jesus, 1985; editor Agama-Apoliti, Jakarta, Indonesia, 1978-82, Asian Religious Lit. Jour. Singapore, 1982-84, Am. Theologian, 1986-89; contbg. editor S.W. Spirituality, 1991—. Del. U.S. Bicentennial Commn., Washington, 1987-90. Mem. Am. Congress Bibl. Lit. (sec. gen. 1991), Soc. Bib. Lit., Am. Acad. Religion (assoc.), Assn. Am. Hebrew Scholars (pres. 1990-91), Md. Hist. Restoration Soc. (pres. 1987). Home: PO Box 80314 Albuquerque NM 87198-0314

VANIER, JERRE LYNN, art director; b. Phoenix, June 11, 1957; i. Jerry Dale Barber and Betty Jane (Brady) Barber Hughes; m. Kent Douglas Wick, May 4, 1979 (div. June 1994); 1 child, Jared Kent Wick; m. Jay David Vanier, June 6, 1994; 1 child, Jolie Jacqueline. BA in Art History magna cum laude, Ariz. State U., 1978, MA in Humanities. Chmn., vice chmn. Internat. Friends of Art, Scottsdale, Ariz., 1990-96; dir. 19th and 20th century art Joy Tash Gallery, Scottsdale, 1996-97; dir. estate art Vanier Fine Art, Ltd., Scottsdale, 1997-98, dir., 1998—. Mem. pub. art collection adv. bd. Scottsdale Cultural Coun., 1990—. Mem. DAR (Ariz. page continental congress 1993, Ariz. vice chmn. Jr. Am. Citizen com. 1998, 3d vice regent Camelback chpt. 1993), Colonial Dames Am., Daus. Republic of Tex. (nonresident), Nat. Soc. Arts and Letters (Valley of Sun chpt. bd. dirs. 1988-92, art chmn. 1988-90, membership chmn. 1990-92), Jr. League Phoenix, Alpha Delta Pi, Phi Kappa Phi. Republican. Avocations: genealogy, collecting contemporary art. Office: Vanier Art Ltd 7106 E Main St Scottsdale AZ 85251-4316

VAN KARNES, KATHLEEN WALKER, realtor; b. Providence, June 17, 1944; d. Robert Edward Walker and Mary Antoinette (Brouillard) Holl; m. Eugene Sergei Tolegian, Dec. 3, 1966 (div. 1987); children: Elisabeth Ani, Aram Eugene; m. Karl Robert Van Karnes, Mar. 31, 1990. Student, East L.A. Coll., 1970-71, Pan Am. Coll., 1962-63. Sec. 3M Co., L.A., 1963-68; office adminstr. Imperial Clin. Lab., Inc., Lynwood, Calif., 1978-80, v.p., chief fin. officer, 1980-87; realtor Bliss Keeler, Inc., San Marino, Calif., 1986-90; realtor Fred Sands Realtors, San Marino, 1990—, Pasadena, 1997; co-owner VK Enterprises, 1991. Co-chmn. program L.A. chpt. founding mem. Foothill affiliate Am. Diabetes Assn., 1987. Mem. White Ho. Confederacy Mus. (founding), Nat. Assn. Realtors, Calif. Assn. Realtors, Braille Aux. Pasadena (pres. 1991-93). Republican. Presbyterian. Avocations: tennis, folk dancing, creative writing. Office: Fred Sands Realtors 751 Cordova St Pasadena CA 91101-2617

VAN KILSDONK, CECELIA ANN, retired nursing administrator, volunteer; b. Beaver Dam, Wis., Sept. 28, 1930; d. Walter and Pauline (Yagodzinski) Klapinski; (div.); children: Dan, James, Paula, Steve. Diploma, Mercy Hosp. Sch. Nursing, 1951; BS, Coll. of St. Frances, Peoria, Ill., 1983. Clin. nurse Divsn. of Ambulatory Care, Phoenix, 1965-70, clin. charge nurse, 1970-82, regional nursing supr., 1982-87, nurse adminstr., 1987-92; mgr. nursing svc. Maricopa County Health Dept. Svcs., Phoenix. Mem. Continuing Edn. review Com., 1989—; vol. Primary Care Ctr.; disaster nurse ARC. Mem. ANA, Ariz. Nurse's Assn., Nat. League for Nursing, Phi Theta Kappa. Home: 11041 N 18th Ave Phoenix AZ 85029-3712

VAN KIRK, JOHN ELLSWORTH, cardiologist; b. Dayton, Ohio, Jan. 13, 1942; s. Herman Corwin and Dorothy Louise (Shafer) Van K.; m. Patricia L. Davis, June 19, 1966 (div. Dec. 1982); 1 child, Linnea Gray. BA cum laude, DePauw U., Greencastle, Ind., 1963; BS, Northwestern U., Chgo., 1964, MD with distinction, 1967. Diplomate Am. Bd. Internal Medicine, Am. Bd. Internal Medicine subspecialty in cardiovasc. disease; cert. Nat. Bd. Med. Examiners. Intern Evanston (Ill.) Hosp., 1967-68; staff assoc. Nat. Inst. of Allergy & Infectious Diseases., Bethesda, Md., 1968-70; resident internal medicine U. Mich. Med. Ctr., Ann Arbor, 1970-72, fellow in cardiology, 1972-74, instr. internal medicine, 1973-74; staff cardiologist Mills Meml. Hosp., San Mateo, Calif., 1974—, vice-chief medicine, 1977-78, dir. critical care, 1978-96, critical care utilizaton rev., 1988—, dir. pacemaker clinic, 1976—; staff cardiologist Mills Peninsula Hosp., Burlingame, Calif., 1996—; dir. transitional care, 1996—; mem. courtesy staff Sequoia Hosp., 1984—. Contbr. rsch. articles to profl. jours. Recipient 1st prize in landscaping Residential Estates, State of Calif., 1977. Fellow Am. Coll. Cardiology; mem. AMA (Physician's Recognition award 1968, 72, 75, 77, 80, 82, 85, 87, 89, 93, 97), Calif. Med. Assn., San Mateo County Med. Soc., Am. Heart

Assn., San Mateo County Heart Assn. (bd. dirs. 1975-78, mem. Bay area rsch. com. 1975-76, mem. edn. com. 1975-77, pres.-elect 1976-77, pres. 1977-79), Alpha Omegaa Alpha. Republican. Mem. United Brethren Ch. Avocations: gardening, computer science, tennis, woodworking, electronics, ham radio. Office: Unified Med Clinics of Peninsula 50 S San Mateo Dr Ste 270 San Mateo CA 94401-3859

VAN KIRK, RICHARD LEE, management consultant; b. Omaha, Sept. 23, 1936; s. Reo P. and Rose R. (Turco) Van Kirk; B.S.M.E., (Hinrichs Meml. award), Calif. Inst. Tech., 1958; postgrad. Los Angeles State Coll., 1963-64, Long Beach State Coll., 1960-62; M.B.E., Claremont Grad. Sch., 1971; m. Janet Carol Labory, July 12, 1959; children—Richard Lee, Karen Evelyn, Douglas Harley. Indsl. engr., prodn. mgr. Procter & Gamble Co., Long Beach, Calif., 1958-63; assoc. dir. devel. Calif. Inst. Tech., 1963-65; prodn. supt. Riverside Cement Co. (Calif.), 1965-67; cons. Arthur Young & Co., Los Angeles, 1967-76, dir. mgmt. services, 1976-78, West region dir. mgmt. services, 1978-85, dir. Mgmt. Cons. Group, West Region, 1985-89, nat. dir. Mfg. Cons. Group, 1985-89; dir. Mfg. and Aerospace Consulting, West Region, Ernst and Young, 1989-94; pres., CEO Spl. Olympics So. Calif., 1995—; tech. advisor Gov.'s Coun. on Phys. Fitness, 1995—. Co-author: The Complete Guide to Special Event Management, 1992. Trustee Woodbury U., 1979-85, chmn., 1982-84; mem. Los Angeles County Citizens Productivity Adv. Com., 1981-85, vice chmn., 1982-85; v.p. tech. Los Angeles Olympic Organizing Com., 1984. Registered profl. engr., Calif. Mem. Inst. Mgmt. Cons. (cert.), Am. Inst. Indsl. Engrs. Republican. Methodist. Office: 6071 Bristol Pkwy Culver City CA 90230-6601

VAN KLEEK, LAURENCE MCKEE (LAURIE VAN KLEEK), minister, librarian, educator; b. Vancouver, B.C., Can., Dec. 14, 1944; m. Darlene H. Van Kleek, May 11, 1974; children: Lineke E., Kyle L., Benjamin C. ThB diploma, Western Pentecostal Bible Coll., 1969; BA, Wilfrid Laurier U., 1971; MDiv, Waterloo Luth. Sem., 1972; MA, Assemblies of God Theol. Sem., 1977; libr. technician diploma, U. Coll. of Fraser Valley, 1984; MLS, U. B.C., 1988. Ordained to ministry Pentecostal Assemblies Can., 1975. Lectr. Western Pentecostal Assemblies Can., 1975; lectr. Western Pentecostal Bible Coll., Abbotsford, B.C., 1972-76, libr., asst. prof., 1978—; supply chaplain Regional Psychiat. Centre, Abbotsford, B.C., 1978-85. Vol. in prison ministry Regional Psychiat. Centre, 1975-77. Gale-Beitel Meml. scholar, 1965. Mem. Assn. Christian Librs., Northwest Assn. Christian Librs. (pres. 1994-96). Home: 32216 Mouat Dr, Abbotsford (Clearbrook), BC Canada V2T 4H9 Office: Western Pentecostal Bible Coll, 35235 Straiton Rd, Clayburn, BC Canada also: PO Box 1700, Abbotsford, BC Canada V2S 7E7

VAN LOUCKS, MARK LOUIS, venture capitalist, business advisor; b. Tampa, Fla., June 19, 1946; s. Charles Perry and Lenn (Bragg) Van L.; m. Eva Marianne Forsell, June 10, 1986; children: Brandon, Charlie. BA in Comm. and Pub. Policy, U. Calif., Berkeley, 1969. Sr. v.p. mktg., programming and corp. devel. United Cable TV Corp., Denver, Colo., 1970-81, advisor, 1983-89; sr. v.p., office of chmn. Rockefeller Ctr. TV Corp., N.Y.C., 1981-83; advisor United Artists Commun. Corp., Englewood, 1989-91; investor, business advisor in pvt. practice Englewood, 1983—; founder, prin. owner Glory Hole Saloon & Gaming Hall, Central City, Colo., 1990—, Harrah's Casino, Black Hawk, Colo., 1990—; chmn., CEO Bask Internat., Englewood, 1990—; bd. dirs. Wild West Devel. Corp., Denver; sr. v.p. bd. dirs. GSI Cable TV Assocs., Inc., San Francisco, 1984-90; guest lectr. on cable TV bus., 1985-91; cons. Telecommunications, Inc., Denver, 1989-93. Producer HBO spl. Green Chili Showdown, 1985; producer TV spl. 3 Days for Earth, 1987; producer, commd. artist nuclear war armament pieces; contbr. articles to profl. jours. Chmn. Cops in Crisis, Denver, 1990—; bd. dirs. The NOAH Found., Denver, 1976—; founding dir. Project for Responsible Advt., Denver, 1991-92; chmn. mayor's mktg. adv. bd., Central City, Colo. Named hon. capt. Denver Police Dept., 1991—, fin. advisor L. Rose Co., 1995—. Mem. Casino Owners Assn. (founding dir. 1989—), Colo. Gaming Assn. (dir. 1990—), recipient S'nnaeel Evol award, 1995), Glenmoor Country Club, The Village Club. Republican. Jewish. Avocations: music, woodworking, philanthropy, vintage autos. Office: MLVL Inc 333 W Hampden Ave Ste 1005 Englewood CO 80110-2340

VAN MAERSSEN, OTTO L., aerospace engineer, consulting firm executive; b. Amsterdam, The Netherlands, Mar. 2, 1919; came to U.S., 1946; s. Adolph L. and Maria Wilhelmina (Edelmann) Van M.; m. Hortensia Maria Velasquez, Jan. 7, 1956; children: Maria, Patricia, Veronica, Otto, Robert. BS in Chem. Engring., U. Mo., Rolla, 1949. Registered profl. engr., Tex., Mo. Petroleum engr. Mobil Oil, Caracas, Venezuela, 1949-51; sr. reservoir engr. Gulf Oil, Ft. Worth and San Tome, Venezuela, 1952-59; acting dept. mgr. Sedco of Argentina, Comodoro Rivadavia, 1960-61; export planning engr. LTV Aerospace and Def., Dallas, 1962-69, R & D adminstr. ground transp. div., 1970-74, engr. specialist new bus. programs, 1975-80; mgr. cost and estimating San Franciso and Alaska, 1981-84; owner OLVM Cons. Engrs., Walnut Creek, Calif., 1984—; cons. LTV Aerospace and Def., Dallas, 1984—. Served with Brit. Army. Intelligence, 1945, Germany. Mem. Soc. Petroleum Engrs. (sr.), Toastmasters (sec.-treas. Dallas chpt. 1963-64), Pennywise Club (treas. Dallas chpt. 1964-67). Democrat. Roman Catholic. Avocations: travel, photography. Home and Office: OLVM Cons Engrs 1649 Arbutus Dr Walnut Creek CA 94595-1705

VAN MOLS, BRIAN, publishing executive; b. L.A., July 1, 1931; s. Pierre Matthias and Frieda Carthyll (MacArthur) M.; m. Barbara Jane Rose, Oct. 1, 1953 (dec. 1968); children—Cynthia Lee, Matthew Howard, Brian; m. Nancy Joan Martell, June 11, 1977; children—Thomas Bentley, Cynthia Bentley, Kristi. A.B. in English, Miami U., Oxford, Ohio, 1953. Media supr. McCann-Erickson Inc., 1955-58; salesman Kelly Smith Co., 1959; with sales Million Market Newspaper Inc., 1959-63; sales mgr. Autoproducts Mag., 1964; sr. salesman True Mag., 1965-68, Look Mag., 1969-70; regional advt. dir. Petersen Pub. Co., Los Angeles, 1971-74; pub. Motor Trend, 1982-84; nat. automotive mktg. mgr. Playboy Enterprises, Inc., N.Y.C., 1984-85, nat. sales mgr., 1985—; western advt. dir. Playboy mag., 1985-86; assoc. pub., advt. dir. Cycle World CBS, Inc., Newport Beach, Calif., 1974-81, pub., 1981; v.p., advt. dir. Four Wheeler Mag., Canoga Pk., Calif., 1986-88; v.p., dir. advt. western div. Gen. Media, Inc., 1988-91; v.p., dir. new bus. devel. Paisano Pub., Inc., Agoura Hills, Calif., 1991-92; dir. mktg. Crown Publs., 1993-94; exec. v.p. Voice Mktg. Inc., Thousand Oaks, Calif., 1994, DMR The Reis Co., Tustin, Calif., 1995-96; COO Mesa Exhaust Products, Inc., Costa Mesa, Calif., 1996-97; mktg. dir. McMullen Argus Pub., Inc., Placentia, Calif., 1998—. Served with U.S. Army, 1953-55. Mem. Los Angeles Advt. Club, Adcraft Club Detroit, Advt. Sportsmen of N.Y. Republican. Episcopalian. Home: 5 Odyssey Ct Newport Beach CA 92663-2349

VANNIX, C(ECIL) ROBERT, programmer, systems analyst; b. Glendale, Calif., June 14, 1953; s. Cecil H. Jr. and Gloria Jenny (Zappia) V.; married, 1980; children: Robert Jeremy, Leslie Ann. AS in Plant Mgmt., BS in Indsl. Arts, Loma Linda U., 1977; AS in Info. Systems, Ventura City Coll., 1985. Instr. indsl. arts Duarte (Calif.) High Sch., 1977-79, Oxnard (Calif.) High Sch., 1979-81; computer cons. Litton Data Comand Systems, Agoura, Calif., 1976-81, sr. engr. instr., 1981-85; computer cons. McLaughlin Research Corp., Camarillo, Calif., 1976-77, sr. program analyst, 1985-88; sr. program analyst Computer Software Analysts, Camarillo, Calif., 1988-90; sr. systems analyst, mgr. S/W systems devel. V.C. Systems, 1990—. Recipient Spl. Achievement award One Way Singers, Glendale, 1975. Mem. Apple PI Computer Club, Litton Computer Club (pres. 1975-76), West Valley Xbase Users Group. Republican. Adventist. Avocations: woodworking, automotives, photography, skiing. Home and Office: 407 Appletree Ave Camarillo CA 93012-5125

VAN NOY, TERRY WILLARD, health care executive; b. Alhambra, Calif., Aug. 31, 1947; s. Barney Willard and Cora Ellen (Simms) V.; m. Betsy Helen Pothen, Dec. 27, 1968; children: Bryan, Mark. BS in Bus. Mgmt., Calif. State Poly. U., 1970; MBA, Pepperdine U., 1991. CLU. Group sales rep. Mutual of Omaha, Atlanta, 1970-74, dist. mgr., 1974-77; regional mgr. Mutual of Omaha, Dallas, 1977-82; nat. sales mgr. Mutual of Omaha, Omaha, Neb., 1982-83; v.p. group mktg. Mutual of Omaha, Omaha, 1983-87; div. dir. Mutual of Omaha, Orange, Calif., 1987-95; pres., CEO, Amil Internat., Las Vegas, 1995—; bd. dirs. State Nev. Reinsurance Program. Presenter in field. Vice chmn. Morning Star Luth. Ch., Omaha, 1987; mem. adv. bd. Chapman U. Sch. Bus.; mem. exc. com. ABL Orgn.; trustee Desert Rsch. Inst.; mem. State of Nev. Reins. Bd. Mem. Am. Soc. CLU, Orange County Employee Benefit Coun., We. Pension and Benefits Conf. Republican. Avocations: skiing, scuba diving. Home: 2312 Prometheus Ct Henderson NV 89014-5324 Office: Amil Internat 1050 E Flamingo Rd Ste E120 Las Vegas NV 89119-7427

VANNOZZI, THOMAS, cameraman; b. Apr. 3, 1951; s. Isidor and Mary V. Student, U. Nev., Las Vegas, 1969-71; student, UCLA, 1973. Freelance video camera operator Las Vegas and Los Angeles, 1971—; video camera operator ABC, HBO, NBC, Fox,, Hollywood, Calif.; Handheld, pedestal, lighting cameraman, videography. *Created boxing camera shots walk-in and rope drop with early hand held cameras in early 1970's. Created and produced a music variety special for American troops in the Persian Gulf War. Produced founding video/teleconference convention for a statewide organization. Authoring member Committee to draft First Nevada State Democratic Party Charter 1973/74, Committee to Re-write Nevada State Democratic Party Charter and By-Laws 1997/98. Treasurer for Nevada Carter Presidential Campaign, 1975. State coordinator Nevadans for Brown Presidential Campaign, 1992. Delegate and Floor coordinator for Nevada at Democratic National Convention.* Recipient Emmy award for Outstanding Camera on a Spl., 1993, L.A. Emmy award for Camera on Live Sports Event, 1995; nominated for L.A. Sports Emmy, 1994. Democrat. Roman Catholic. Avocations: running.

VAN ORDEN, AMANDA KAY MITCHELL, insurance consultant; b. McAlester, Okla., Feb. 11, 1953; d. Fane LeRoy and Norma Evelyn (Magruder) Mitchell. BA magna cum laude, U. Utah, 1975. Registered health underwriter. V.p. Nirvana, Inc., Phoenix, 1978—. Vol. PHX Open, 1980—; vol. reader Sun Sounds, Phoenix, 1987-95; pledge dr. vol. PBS, Tempe, Ariz., 1988—; vol. Spl. Olympics, Phoenix, 1988—, Make a Wish Foundation, 1992—; co-leader Daisy coun. Girl Scouts U.S.A., 1993. Mem. Health Care Choice Coalition (membership dir. 1993, comm. chmn. 1993—), Women Life Underwriters, Greater Phoenix Assn. Health Underwriters, Greater Phoenix Assn. Life Underwriters, Jr. League of Phoenix, Christian Bus. Women's Assn., Phoenix Art Mus., U. Utah Alumnae (founding mem.), Chi Omega (treas. 1985-92). Republican. Mem. ChristianCh. Avocations: tennis, golf, reading, travel, collecting teddy bears. Home: 10624 N 7th Pl Phoenix AZ 85020-5816 Office: Nirvana Inc 1240 E Missouri Ave Phoenix AZ 85014-2912

VAN RELLIM, TIM, film producer; b. New Forest, Eng., May 6, 1944; came to the U.S., 1994; s. Thomas Wilfred and Dolores Anthea (Cromie) Wellesley; m. Barbara Jane Coleridge, Mar. 29, 1978; children: Christina Joanna, Natasha Louise, Andrew Daniel. Student, Lódź (Poland) Film Sch., 1968. external examiner Royal Coll. Art, London. Prodr. (feature films) Viking Sayas, 1993, K2, 1994, Snow White, 1996, Ravenous, 1998. Knight fellow The Ancient and Noble Order of the Knights Templar, 1996. Avocations: sailing, skiing.

VAN REMMEN, ROGER, management consultant; b. Los Angeles, Sept. 30, 1950; s. Thomas J. and Elizabeth (Vincent) V.; B.S. in Bus., U. So. Calif., 1972. Account mgr. BBDO, Los Angeles, 1972-78; account mgr. Dailey & Assocs. Advt., L.A., 1978—, v.p., mgmt. supr., 1980-84, sr. v.p., 1985-90; dir. mktg. communications, Teradata, 1990-91, ptnr. Brown, Bernardy, Van Remmen Exec. Search, L.A., 1991—. Bd. dirs. Advt. Emergency Relief Fund., Richstone Family Ctr. Mem. Univ. So. Calif. Alumni Assn., Advt. Club of Los Angeles. Roman Catholic. Home: 509 3rd St Manhattan Beach CA 90266-6414 Office: Brown Bernardy Van Remmen 12100 Wilshire Blvd Ste M40 Los Angeles CA 90025-7117

VAN RY, GINGER LEE, school psychologist; b. Alexandria, Va., June 26, 1953; d. Ray Ellsworth Hensley and Bernice Anne (Weidel) Wolter; m. Willem Hendrik Van Ry, Aug 23, 1986; 1 child, Anika Claire. AA, U. Nev., Las Vegas, 1973; BA, U. Wash., 1983, MEd, 1985. Cert. sch. psychologist (nationally). Psychometrist The Mason Clinic, Seattle, 1980-84, supr., psychology lab., 1984-86; sch. psychologist Everett (Wash.) Sch. Dist., 1986—; mem. profl. ednl. adv. bd. U. Wash. Sch. Psychology, Seattle, 1995—. Author: (with others) Wash. State Assn. of Sch. Psychologists Best Practice Handbook, 1993. Co-pres. Lake Cavanaugh Hghts. Assn., Seattle, 1994-95, chmn. long-range planning com., 1995—. Mem. AAUW, NEA, Nat. Assn. Sch. Psychologists (cert. sch. psychologist), Wash. State Assn. Sch. Psychologists (chair profl. devel. com. 1995—), Wash. State Edn. Assn., U. Wash. Alumni Assn. Democrat. Avocations: reading, travel, fgn. cultures, woodworking, horticulture. Office: The Everett Sch Dist PO Box 2098 Everett WA 98203-0098

VAN SCHOONENBERG, ROBERT G., corporate lawyer; b. Madison, Wis., Aug. 18, 1946; s. John W. and Ione (Henning) Schoonenberg. BA, Marquette U., 1968; MBA, U. Wis., 1972; JD, U. Mich., 1974. Bar: Calif. 1975, Fla. 1976. Atty. Gulf Oil Corp., Pitts., 1974-81; sr. v.p., gen. counsel, sec. Avery Dennison Corp., Pasadena, Calif., 1981—; judge pro tem Pasadena Mcpl. Ct., 1987-89. Dir., v.p. fin. adminstrn. Am. Cancer Soc., San Gabriel Vally Unit, 1987—; v.p., treas., dir., v.p. investments Pasadena Symphony Assn.; bd. dirs. Pasadena Recreation and Parks Found., 1983-84; mem. Pasadena Citizens Task Force on Crime Control, 1983-84; dir. Boy Scouts, San Gabriel Valley Coun., dir. public coun.; bd. dirs. Verugo Hills Hosp. Found. Mem. ABA, Am. Corp. Counsel Assn. (bd. dirs.), Am. Soc. Corp. Secs. (bd. dirs., pres. Southern Calif. chpt.), L.A. County Bar Assn. (past chair, corp. law dept. sect.), Corp. Counsel Inst. (bd. govs.), Jonathon Club, Flint Canyon Tennis Club, Pasadena Athletic Club, Wis. Union. Clubs: Athletic (Pasadena); Wis. Union. Office: Avery-Dennison Corp 150 N Orange Grove Blvd Pasadena CA 91103-3534*

VAN SCOTTER, RICHARD DALE, education policy executive; b. Elkhorn, Wis., Sept. 2, 1939; s. Henry Irving and Helen Evelyn (MaGill) Van S.; m. Suzanne Starmer, Feb. 29, 1964 (div.); children: Shannon, Philip; m. Pamela Gale Burnett, Aug. 15, 1987; 1 child, Caitlin. BA, Beloit (Wis.) Coll., 1961; MA, U. Wis., 1966; PhD, U. Colo., 1971. Tchr. Homewood Flossmoor H.S., Flossmoor, Ill., 1966-68; adj. prof. U. Colo., Boulder, 1971-77; asst. prof. Grinnell (Iowa) Coll., 1973-77; curriculum dir. Social Issues Resources, Inc., Boca Raton, Fla., 1977-83; project dir., writer IBM Corp., Boca Raton, 1983-86; v.p. edn. Jr. Achievement, Inc., Colorado Springs, Colo., 1986—; adj. prof. U. Colo., Colorado Springs, 1993—; mem. editl. bd. Citizens' Goals, Colorado Springs, 1992—. Author: Public Schooling in America, 1991, Social Foundations of Education. Mem. advocacy com. Citizens' Goals, 1993; bd. dirs. Citizen's Project, 1995. Lt. USN, 1961-65. Mem. ASCD, Nat. Coun. Social Studies. Avocations: running, bicycling. Office: Jr Achievement Inc One Education Way Colorado Springs CO 80906

VANSELOW, CARL ROBERT, JR., physician assistant; b. Sewickley, Pa., Aug. 18, 1949; s. Carl Robert and Audrey May (DeShong) V.; m. Kathleen Lee Bouvier, Apr. 17, 1971 (div. Mar. 1976); 1 child, Christopher Robert; m. Susan Mikulski, Dec. 31, 1994. AA in Engring., Glendale (Ariz.) C.C., 1969; MB in Primary Care Medicine, U. Utah, 1982, Physician Asst. Cert., 1980; postgrad., U. Nev., 1992. Lic. physician asst., Nev.; registered cardiovascular technologist. Indsl. designer U-Haul Internat., Phoenix, 1969-72; cardiovascular technologist St. Joseph's Hosp., Phoenix, 1971-74; instr. animal rsch. techniques Ariz. State U., Tempe, 1974-76; assoc. fellow in cardiovascular rsch. R.S. Flinn Found./Ariz. Heart Inst./St. Joseph's Hosp., Phoenix, 1974-76; chief cardiovascular technologist, head cardiology dept. Maricopa County Hosp., Phoenix, 1975-76; cardiovascular technologist Presbyn. Hosp. and Med. Ctr., Albuquerque, 1976-77, Lovekin Cardiology Assocs., Albuquerque, 1977-78; physician asst., tech. dir. Cardiovascular Cons., Las Vegas, 1978-95; physician asst. cardiology sect. Sunrise Hosp., Las Vegas, 1978—, Desert Springs Hosp., Las Vegas, 1990—, Valley Hosp., Las Vegas, 1995—; physician asst./clin. co-investigator Cardiovascular Ctr., Las Vegas, 1995—; physician asst. cardiology sect. Mountain View Hosp., 1996—; physician asst. advisor Nev. State Bd. Med. Examiners, Reno, 1987—; mem. Nev. Medicare Reform Task Force, U.S. Ho. of Reps., 1995. Contbr. articles to profl. jours. Active 200 Men's Club/Boys and Girls Club, Las Vegas, 1994-96. Fellow Soc. Nuclear Medicine (mem. sect. for cardiovascular imaging), Am. Acad. Physician Assts. (ho. of dels.), Nev. Acad. Physician Assts. (chief del., legis. coord., past pres., bd. dirs.); mem. Nev. Soc. Nuclear Medicine, Am. Heart Assn. (so. Nev. affiliate, mem. coun. on basic sci., coun. on clin. cardiology Laennec Soc.). Avocations: sailing, scuba diving/dive medicine, veterinary medicine. Home: 5680 Edna Ave Las Vegas NV 89146-6840 Office: Cardiovascular Ctr So Nev 7200 Cathedral Rock Dr Ste 220 Las Vegas NV 89128-0441

VAN SICKLE, FREDERICK L., federal judge; b. 1943; m. Jane Bloomquist. BS, U. Wis., 1965; JD, U. Wash., 1968. Ptnr. Clark & Van Sickle, 1970-75; prosecuting atty. Douglas County, Waterville, Wash., 1971-75; judge State of Wash. Superior Ct., Grant and Douglas counties, 1975-79, Chelan and Douglas Counties, 1979-91; judge U.S. Dist. Ct. (ea. dist.) Wash., Spokane, 1991—; co-chair rural ct. com. Nat. Conf. State Trial Judges, 1987-91. 1st lt. U.S. Army, 1968-70. Mem. ABA (nat. conf. fed. judges jud. adminstrn.), Am. Adjudicature Soc., Wash. State Bar Assn., Masons (pres. Badger mountain lodge 1982-83), Scottish Rite, Spokane Rotary, Shriners. Office: US Dist Cts US Courthouse PO Box 2209 920 W Riverside Ave Rm 914 Spokane WA 99201-1010

VANSICKLE, SHARON DEE, public relations executive; b. Portland, Oreg., Nov. 10, 1955. BA in Mktg. and Journalism, U. Portland, 1976, postgrad., 1977-79. Reporter Willamette Week, Portland, 1976-77; dir. pub. rels. Tektronix, Portland, 1977-83; prin. pub. rels. Karakas VanSickle Ouellette Advt. and Pub. Rels., Portland, 1983—; chmn. Pinnacle Worldwide, bd. dirs. pub. rels. coun. Mem. Am. Electronics Assn., Pub. Rels. Soc. Am. (pres. Portland chpt. 1994-95, chair-elect N. Pac. dist.). Office: Karakas VanSickle Ouellette Advt and Pub Rels 200 SW Market St Ste 1400 Portland OR 97201-5741

VAN TAMELEN, JANE ELIZABETH, artist, filmmaker; b. Madison, Wis., Aug. 14, 1953; d. Eugene Earl and Mary Ruth (Houtman) Van T.; m. Eric Neville Luke, Sept. 11, 1982 (div. Mar. 1993); children: Kristin Johanna, Alexandra Carlen. BA with honors, Art Ctr. Coll. Design, 1995. Freelance artist Santa Monica, Calif., 1983-91; artist, multimedia art dir., filmmaker Studio City, Calif., 1995-96.

VAN TUYLE, GREGORY JAY, nuclear engineer; b. Chgo., Feb. 19, 1953; s. Willard D. and Mary E. (Kershner) Van T.; m. Frances A. Weinstein, Aug. 16, 1994; 1 child, William Steven. BSE magna cum laude, U. Mich., 1975, MSE, 1976, PhD of Nuclear Engring., 1978. From dep. divsn. head to program mgr. Brookhaven Nat. Lab., Upton, N.Y., 1978-97; sr. sci. & strategic planning adv. nat. project dir. Los Alamos (N.Mex.) Nat. Lab., 1997-99, lead project leader accelerator transmutation waste project, 1999—, project leader, Accelerator Transmutation of Waste Project, 1999—. Contbr. articles to profl. jours. Mem. Am. Nuc. Soc. (Reactor Safety divsn. program com. sec. to vice-chmn. 1991-96, chmn. 1996-97, past pres., v.p., treas. L.I. chpt. 1979-97, founder and chair Accelerator Applications Tech. Group 1996-98), Am. Phys. Soc., Brookhaven Nat. Lab. Toastmasters (pres., v.p. 1990-95, awards 91, 92, 94). Achievements include performing computer simulation of Chernobyl-4 accident based on Soviet explanation prior to release of Soviet analyses, subsequently cross-comparing analyses, confirming similarities and evaluating differences. Office: Los Alamos Nat Lab Mail Stop H813 PO Box 1663 Los Alamos NM 87544-0600 :

VAN TUYLE, JEAN CLAIRE, playwright, producer; b. Cin., Dec. 31, 1933; d. Emmett Anthony and Hildagarde (Obermeyer) McGuff; m. Robert VanTuyle (div. Dec. 1988); children: Edith, Robert, Andrew. Pres., prodr. MGR Prodns., Pasadena, Calif., 1989-98; pres. Footlighters, L.A., 1995-96; gov. Theatre L.A., 1992-98. Writer play Ida, 1993. Pres., bd. dirs. Christ Child Soc., Pasadena, 1989—, Footlighters; commencement spkr. Mayfield Sr. Sch., Pasadena, 1996. Mem. Women in Theatre (award for Outstanding Contbn. to Theatre in L.A. 1994), Dramatists Guild. Roman Catholic. Home: 3560 Grayburn Rd Pasadena CA 91107-4627

VAN VALKENBURGH, HOLLY VIOLA, librarian, consultant; b. N.Y.C., Nov. 22, 1936; d. Horace Bulle III and Viola Frieda (Gerfe) Van V.; children: Leland V. Lammert, Jeni L. Moradi, Gary F. Ohm. BA, U. Colo., 1957; MA, U. Denver, 1965; MEd, Lesley Coll., Cambridge, Mass., 1988. Elem. sch. tchr. Tenn., 1958-60; elem. sch. tchr. Colo., 1961-62, sch. librarian, 1962-66; sch. librarian Wyo., 1984-88; coll. librarian Sheridan (Wyo.) Coll., 1966-74, Morrison Coll., Reno, Nev., 1989-92; owner, operator Nanny Placement Agy., Reno, 1991-96, Word Pro, Carson City, Nev., 1996—; cons. Nev. State Libr., Carson City, 1993—; adminstr. weatherization assistance project Dept. of Energy, Sheridan, 1975-84. Bd. dirs. Grassroots Lobby, Carson City, 1995—; vice chair Nev. Women's History Project, Reno, 1996—; treas., mem. Sheridan County Recreation Bd., 1972-78. Josephine Halverson Morris scholar U. Denver, 1965. Mem. AAUW (newsletter editor, pres. local chpts. 1972, 73, 96-97, 97-98), Nat. Assn. Van Valkenburgh Family (newsletter editor, 1991—, bd. dirs. 1998—), Nev. Libr. Assn. (newsletter editor 1996—). Avocations: white water rafting, reading. Home: 184 Lake Glen Dr Carson City NV 89703-5215 Office: Nev State Libr and Archives 100 N Stewart St Carson City NV 89701-4285

VAN VELZER, VERNA JEAN, retired research librarian; b. State College, Pa., Jan. 22, 1929; d. Harry Leland and Golda Lillian (Cline) Van V. BS in Library Sci., U. Ill., 1950; MLS, Syracuse U., 1957. Head librarian Orton Library, Ohio State U., Columbus, 1952-54; serials assoc. Syracuse (N.Y.) U. Library, 1954-57; head cataolger SRI Internat., Menlo Park, Calif., 1957-58; head librarian GE Microwave Lab., Palo Alto, Calif., 1958-64, Fairchild Rsch. and Devel. Lab., Palo Alto, 1964-65, Sylvania Intelligence Library, Mountain View, Calif., 1965-66; rsch. librarian ESL Inc. subs. TRW, Sunnyvale, Calif., 1966-92; cons. in field. Vol. Lantos Re-election Campaign, San Mateo, Calif., 1972—, Wildlife Rescue, Palo Alto, 1980—; mem. Barron Park Assn., Palo Alto, 1975—; mem. Calif. Polit. Action Com. for Animals, San Francisco, 1986—. Recipient Commemorative medal of Honor, Am. Biographical Inst., 1946, Paul Revere Cup, Santa Clara Camellia Soc., 1968, Internat. Cultural Diploma of Honor, Am. Biographical Inst., 1988. Mem. Spl. Librs. Assn., IEEE, AIAA, Calif. Holistic Vet. Assn., Internat. Primate Protection League, People for Ethical Treatment of Animals, Assn. Old Crows, In Def. of Animals, Primarily Primates, Sierra Club, World Wildlife Club, Greenpeace. Avocations: horticulture, ecology, koi, music, literature. Home: 4048 Laguna Way Palo Alto CA 94306-3122

VAN WAGENEN, STERLING, film producer, director; b. Provo, Utah, July 2, 1947; s. Clifton Gray and Donna Anna (Johnson) Van W.; m. Marilee Jeppson; children: Sarah, Kristina, Arthur, William, Hugh, Andrew. BA, Brigham Young U., 1972. Exec. dir. U.S. Film Festival, Park City, Utah, 1978-80; exec. dir. Sundance Inst., Salt Lake City, 1980-84, v.p., 1984-86; adj. prof. film Brigham Young U., 1992—. Dir. plays King Lear, 1974, Othello, 1984, Hamlet, 1972, The Flies, 1970, Blind Dates, 1995, (film) Christmas Snows, Christmas Winds (2 regional Emmy awards), Alan and Naomi, 1990, Great American West, 1995; prodr. films Faith of an Observer, 1984, The Trip to Bountiful, 1986 (Acad. award Best Actress), Yosemite: The Fate of Heaven, 1988, The Witching of Ben Wagner, 1989, Convicts, 1989, Secrets of the Pharaohs, 1994, Ancestors, 1996, Yellowstone: America's Eden, 1997, The Dead Sea Scrolls: The Final Mystery, 1998, The Dead Sea Scrolls and the End of Days, 1998. Office: 2230 E 6014 S Salt Lake City UT 84121

VAN WHY, REBECCA RIVERA, retired guidance counselor; b. Casa Blanca, N.Mex., Sept. 14, 1932; d. Charles and Doris (Thompson) Rivera; m. Raymond Richard Van Why, Aug. 27, 1955; children: Raymond R., Ronald R., Randall R. BS, U. N.Mex., 1959. Tchr. Bur. of Indian Affairs, Albuquerque, 1960-62, guidance counselor, 1969-94, tchr., supr., 1973-74, acting dir. student life, 1987, ret., 1994; head tchr. Laguna (N.Mex.) Headstart OEO, 1967-69, acting dir., 1969. Appt. N.Mex. Youth Conservation Corps Commn., 1992-98. Recipient Cert. of Recognition, Sec. of Interior, 1975, Cert. of Appreciation, State of N.Mex., 1986, N.Mex. Commn. on the Status of Women, 1993; named honoree Internat. Women's Day, U. N.Mex., 1987. Republican. Avocations: sewing, traveling, boating, fishing, dancing. Home: 14417 Central Ave NW Albuquerque NM 87121-7756

VARELA, MANUEL FRANCISCO, microbiologist; b. Santa Fe, Dec. 3, 1962; s. Phil and Josephine (Flores) V.; m. Ann Frances Higgins, Apr. 6, 1990. BA in Biochemistry, U. N.Mex., 1987, MS in Biochemistry, 1989, PhD in Biomed. Scis., 1994. Rsch. analyst U. N.Mex. Sch. Medicine, Albuquerque, 1983-89; postdoctoral fellow Harvard U. Med. Sch., Boston, 1994-97; asst. prof. biology Eastern N.Mex. U., Portales, 1997—. NSF grantee,

1999—; rsch. fellow Am. Soc. for Cell Biology, 1991, NIH postdoctoral fellow, 1994-97. Mem. AAAS, Am. Soc. for Microbiology, Phi Kappa Phi, Sigma Xi. Avocations: photography, golf. Email: Manuel.Varela@enmu.edu. Office: Eastern NMex U Dept Biology Sta #33 Portales NM 88130

VARGA, STEVEN CARL, reinsurance company executive, consultant; b. Columbus, Ohio, Jan. 19, 1952; s. Stephen Thomas and Eva Jeney V.; BA in Psychology and Philosophy magna cum laude, Carthage Coll., 1977, MSA with honors Cen. Mich. U., 1986; m. Michelle L. Auld, Nov. 17, 1973; children: Zachary Steven, Joshua Lewis. Svc. mgr. Chem-Lawn Corp., Columbus, 1972-75; respiratory therapist St. Catherine's Hosp., Kenosha, Wis., 1975-77; policy analyst Nationwide Ins. Cos., Columbus, 1978-79, asst. mgr. Corp. Tng. Ctr., 1979-86; dir. ednl. tng. Sullivan Payne Co., Seattle, 1986-88, asst. v.p. human resource devel., 1989-93; v.p. Reinsurance Solutions, Inc., Seattle, 1994-95; sr. v.p. Unltd. Potential, Inc., 1995—. Mem. civic action program com., 1979-86, Nat. Mental Health Assn., 1972-79; mem. occupational adv. coun. Bellevue C.C., 1989—; v.p. Kenosha County chpt., 1975-77; mem. Franklin County (Ohio) Mental Health Assn., 1978-86. Rhodes scholar, 1976-77. Mem. Am. Soc. Tng. and Devel., Soc. Broadcast Engrs., Ins. Inst. Am. (contbg. author Principles of Reinsurance, vol. I and II, nat. advisory com. assoc. in reinsurance program), Brokers and Reinsurers Markets Assn. (edn. and tng. co-chair), Am. Psychol. Assn., Am. Mgmt. Assn., Soc. of Ins. Trainers and Educators (chmn. regional area planning com.), Carthage Coll. Alumni Assn., Phi Beta Kappa, Psi Chi. Home: 15586 Sandy Hook Rd NE Poulsbo WA 98370-7869 Office: Unltd Potential Inc 400 Warren Ave Ste 410 Bremerton WA 98337-1487

VARGAS, HERNAN ISAAC, surgeon; b. Lima, Peru, June 3, 1961; came to U.S., 1987; MD, Cayetano Heredia U., Peruana, 1986. Cert. in surgery. Intern Cayetano Heredia U. Hosp., Lima, 1985-86; resident in gen. surgery Harbor-UCLA Med. Ctr., Torrance, Calif., 1987-93; fellow in surg. oncology NIH/NCI/Surgery Br., Bethesda, Md., 1994-96; chief surg. oncology Harbor-UCLA Med. Ctr., Torrance, 1996—. Office: Surg Oncology Box 25 1000 W Carson St Torrance CA 90502-2004

VARGAS, MARSHA LYNN, art dealer, appraiser; b. New Orleans, Oct. 26, 1943; d. Edward Wesley Jr. and Johnnie Fay (Rogers) Austermuehle; m. Robert Louis Vargas, Nov. 23, 1970. Cert. in classified splty. of Asian art. Wholesaler antique oriental ceramics, 1970-73; pres. Oriental Corner, Los Altos, Calif., 1973—; appraiser, lectr. in field. Mem. connoisseur's coun. Asian Art Mus. San Francisco. Mem. Am. Soc. Appraisers (sr.; pres. San Jose chpt. 1982-83), Netsuke Dealers Assn., Inc. (v.p. 1980—). Fax: 650-941-3297. Office: Oriental Corner 280 Main St Los Altos CA 94022-2908

VARIO, JOYCE, graphic designer; b. Warwick, R.I., July 28, 1959; d. Ralph Peter and Irene Louise (Beauregard) V. Grad., Art Inst. Boston, 1981. Prodn. artist Fin. Publ. Co., Boston, 1982-84; art dir., prodn. mgr. Kasmar Publs., Inc., Torrance, Calif., 1986-89; asst. mgr. desktop Copy Spot Printing, Santa Monica, Calif., 1989-90; graphic designer Crestec L.A., Inc., Gardena, Calif., 1990-92, Canter & Assocs., Inc., Santa Monica, Calif., 1992-97; owner Joyce Vario Illustration/Graphic Design, Inglewood, Calif., 1992—. Recipient Maggie Cert. Excellence in Design Kitchens by Profl. Designers, 1989. Mem. Nat. Corvette Owners Assn., Nat. Coun. Corvette Clubs, Southwest Corvettes, Nat. Corvette Restorers Soc. (bd. dirs. So. Calif. chpt., chmn.), L. A. Macintosh Users Group. Avocations: Corvettes, collecting record albums. Office: Illustration/Graphic Design 1324 Welton Way Inglewood CA 90302-1309

VARO, MARTON-GEZA, sculptor; b. Szekelyudvarhely, Hungary, Mar. 15, 1943; came to U.S., 1989; s. Gyorgy and Viola (Tomori) V.; 1 child, Kata; m. Ilona Magdolna Kalmar, Sept. 25, 1979; children: Marton, Ilona. Diploma in Fine Arts, Ion Andreescu U., Cluj, Romania, 1966. Sculptor in limestone and marble. Works include sculptures at Conv. Ctr. Budapest, 1984, Breaking Free, Brea, Calif., 1990, Peace Meml., Palm Desert, Calif., 1992, Dallas Plaza of the Americas, 1992, marble sculpture at Volos, Greece, 1988, Tustin Ranch Market Place, Calif., Art Inst. of So. Calif., Laguna Beach, Calif., Bass Hall, Ft. Worth, 1998. Recipient award Studio of Young Artists, Hungary, 1976, Munkacsy prize Ministry of Culture, Hungary, 1984; Derkovits grantee Ministry of Culture, 1972-75; Fulbright scholar, 1989-91. Avocation: fishing. Home: 2 Charity Irvine CA 92612-3255

VARONA, LUCIA TAROT, Spanish language educator, researcher; b. Coban, Guatemala, Sept. 15, 1952; came to U.S., 1986; d. Paul Tarot and Carlota Sierra Barrientos; m. Joaquin Lainfiesta, Nov. 24, 1971 (div. Sept. 1982); children: Ana Lainfiesta, Mario Lainfiesta; m. Federico Varona, June 30, 1984. Grad., u. Rafael Landivar, Guatemala, 1986; MS in Edn., U. Kans., 1989; EdD, U. San Francisco, 1996. Tchr. Parroquia de Esquipulas, Guatemala City, Guatemala, 1979-82; edn. coord. Proyecto Nueva Vida, Guatemala City, 1982-85; Spanish instr. U. Kans., Lawrence, 1987-89; asst. to pres. Christian found. for Children and Aging, Kansas City, Kans., 1989-91; adj. lectr. San Jose (Calif.) State U., 1992-96; adj. lectr. Santa Clara (Calif.) U., 1992-96, Spanish lectr., 1992—; ednl. cons. Parroquia de Esquipulas, Guatemala City, 1982-86; mem. adv. bd. Centro Audiovisual Semilla, Guatemala City, 1982-86. Editor: Service Learning in Spanish, 1998; author audivisual tchg. material and artices. Avocations: hiking, gardening, creative writing. Home: 2774 White Acres Dr San Jose CA 95148-3691 Office: Santa Clara U 500 El Camino Real Santa Clara CA 95053

VASCHE, MARK, editor. Exec. editor Modesto (Calif.) Bee, 1997—. Office: Modesto Bee 1325 H St PO Box 5256 Modesto CA 95352*

VASILEIADIS, SAVVAS, chemical, environmental engineering educator; b. Thessaloniki, Greece, Apr. 18, 1963; came to U.S., 1988; s. Prodromos and Eugenia Vasileiadis; m. Zoe Dimitrios Ziaka, Feb. 17, 1985; children: Eugenia-Melina, Artemis-Dimitria. Diploma in Chem. Engring., Aristotle U., Thessaloniki, Greece, 1987; MS in Chem. and Materials Engring., Syracuse U., 1990; PhD in Chem. Engring., U. So. Calif., 1994. Registered prof. engr., European cmty. countries. Prodn. engr. Chem. Industries of No. Greece, Thessaloniki, 1985-86; rsch. assoc. Syracuse U., N.Y., 1988-90; rsch. assoc. U. So. Calif., L.A., 1990-94, rsch. fellow, 1994-96, faculty, 1997—; engring. cons. ZIVATECH, L.A., 1994—; activities coord. grad. student orgn., U. So. Calif., 1993. Author papers in field; contbr. articles to profl. jours.; patents pending. Recipient paper award R.J. Kokes, 1993, 95, AIChE, 1993, 95, 96, Materials Rsch. Soc., 1994, U. So. Calif. Pres.' award, 1996; fellow Norwegian Ednl. Coun., 1987. Mem. AIChE, Materials Rsch. Soc., N.Am. Catalysis Soc. Ea. Orthodox. Achievements include novel reactor-membrane permeator process design for methane-steam reforming, methane-CO2 reforming, and the water gas shift, with applications in methanol and synthetic gasoline synthesis, in power generation cycles and fuel cells; original research on membrane reactor and membrane separation chem. processes, chem. kinetics and mechanics, materials and polymers sci. and engring. Avocations: hiking, traveling, soccer. Home: 15549 Dearborn St North Hills CA 91343-3267 Office: Univ So Calif Sch Engring KAP 230C Los Angeles CA 90089-2531

VASQUEZ, EDMUNDO EUSEBIO, religious organization administrator; b. Chacon, N.Mex., May 14, 1932; s. Eusebio and Dora (Ortiz) V.; B.A., N.Mex. Highlands U., 1953; postgrad. U. Colo., 1958, Brigham Young U., 1959; M.A., Stanford U., 1961; postgrad. U. Costa Rica, 1966; m. Carol Vallendar, June 16, 1957 (div. Aug. 1978); children—Amarante, Daniel, Amalio; m. Jane Atkins, Nov. 1983. With Sta. KFUN, 1949-53; dean Wasatch Acad., Mt. Pleasant, Utah, 1955-65; dean Colegio Americano, Ibagué, Colombia, 1966-71; pres. Menaul Sch., (Albuquerque, 1971-78; agt. Nat. Life of Vt. and Northwestern Mut. Life, Albuquerque, 1978-81; dir. So. Calif. Found., 1981—; rep. United Presbyn. Found., 1981—; cons. in field; lectr., cons. Hispanic affairs; cons. multicultural edn. Bd. dirs. United [illegible] 75, ARC, 1979-82, trustee San Francisco Theol. Sem., San Anselmo, Calif., 1982—; fundraiser charitable and polit. orgns. Served with USAF, 1953-55. Mem. Assn. Supervision and Curriculum Devel., Nat. Assn. Life Underwriters, [illegible] Rotary, Lions, Masons. Office: So Calif Found 1501 Wilshire Blvd Los Angeles CA 90017-2205

VASSALLI, SHORTY See **COLLINGS, CELESTE LOUISE**

VASUDEVAN, RAMASWAMI, engineering consultant; b. Trichi, Tamil Nad, India, Nov. 28, 1947; came to U.S., 1970; s. Rajagopal and Jembakalakshmi; m. Padmini Vasudevan, mar. 20, 1980 (div. 1992). BE, Madras U., India, 1970; MS, UCLA, 1972. Registered profl. engr., Calif.; cert. plant engr., Calif. Project engr. Anco Engrs., Culver City, Calif., 1971-77; mgr. Wyle Labs., Norco, Calif., 1977-78, EDAC, Palo Alto, Calif., 1978-82; project mgr. Los Alamos (N.Mex.) Tech. Assocs., 1982-85; assoc. EQE Inc., Irvine, Calif., 1985-87; pres. Sidhi Cons., Inc., Santa Ana, Calif., 1987—. Contbr. articles to profl. jours. Mem. ASME, IEEE (stds. com. 1982-84), EERI, NFPA, EPRI-EQAG, Am. Inst. Plant Engrs., Am. Facilities Engrs., Nat. Elec. Testing Assn. Republican. Avocations: photography, sailing, bicycling. Office: Sidhi Cons Inc 4642 E Chapman Ave # 210 Orange CA 92869-4111

VAUGHAN, ALAN, parapsychologist; b. Akron, Ohio, Dec. 28, 1936; s. Robert L. and Millie M. (Denny) V.; m. Diane Dudley, June 20, 1975; children: Lauren, Thomas, Jonathan. AB in Greek and Latin, U. Akron, 1958; PhD in Parapsychology (hon.), El Inst. de Ciencias Parapsicologicas, Granada, Spain, 1977; PhD in Therapeutic Counseling, Open Internat. U., 1993. Editor Psychic mag., San Francisco, 1970-77; parapsychology editor New Realities, San Francisco, 1977; editor Reincarnation Report, Malibu, Calif., 1982-83; intuitive cons. Los Angeles, 1981—; founder Mind Tech. Systems, 1988. Author: Patterns of Prophecy, 1973, Incredible Coincidence, 1979, The Edge of Tomorrow, 1982, The Power of Positive Prophecy, 1991, Doorways to Higher Consciousness, 1998; co-author: Dream Telepathy, 1973. Research grantee Parapsychology Found., N.Y.C., 1967. Mem. Parapsychol. Assn. (assoc.), Assn. for the Study of Dreams, Intuition Network. Home: 1446 Yale St # C Santa Monica CA 90404-3108

VAUGHAN, AUDREY JUDD, paralegal, musician; b. Washington, May 8, 1936; d. Deane Brewster and Elizabeth (Melamed) Judd; m. Arthur Harris Vaughan Jr., Feb. 7, 1959 (div. June 1976); 1 child, Erik Brewster. BA, Cornell U., 1958; postgrad., Eastman Sch. Music, 1959-62; cert. in paralegal studies, UCLA, 1977. Tchr. music Rochester (N.Y.) Sch. Sys., 1961-64, Gooden Sch., Sierra Madre, Calif., 1975-78; paralegal Nossaman, Kruger & Marsh, L.A., 1978-80, Latham Watkins, L.A., 1980-84, Ammirato Palumbo, Pasadena, Calif., 1984—; dir. Los Grillos, medieval and renaissance music performing group, Pasadena, 1965—. Organizer studies and presentations, bd. dirs., spkr. LWV, Pasadena, 1965-73. Mem. L.A. Paralegal Assn. (com. for paralegal edn., spkr. 1985—), Baroquen Consort and Baroque Instrumental Ensemble, Silverlake Baroque Ensemble. Avocations: singing, playing renaissance instruments, playing harpsichord, hiking. Home: 2034 Glenview Ter Altadena CA 91001-2808

VAUGHAN, PAUL IRVINE, minister; b. Toronto, Ont., Can., Sept. 11, 1937; came to U.S., 1987; s. Irvine John and Doris Bernice (Price) V.; married Nov. 8, 1958; children: Steven, Bryan, Grayden. BA, Can. Christian Coll., 1982, BTh, 1982, MA, 1983, D of Ministry, 1984. Ordained to ministry Christian Ch., 1975. Pastoral counselor Toronto, 1975—; chaplain, maj. CAP, Calif., 1975—; missionary to East Africa Kenya, 1985; pastor Yours for Life Ministries Inc., Santa Ana, Calif. Past leader Boy Scouts of Can., Toronto; active St. John Ambulance/Red Cross, Dominon of Can. Office: Yours For Life Ministries PO Box 27023 Santa Ana CA 92799-7023

VAUGHAN, RALPH EUGENE, municipal administrator; b. Laurium Village, Mich., Sept. 16, 1954; s. Ralph Eugene and Barbara Jean (Fowler) V.; m. Patricia Ellen Windham, June 28, 1974; children: Christopher, Marissa. AS in Criminology, Southwestern Coll., Chula Vista, Calif., 1974, AA in History, 1982. Battalion clk., photojournalist U.S. Army, Ft. Campbell, Ky., Augsburg, Germany, 1975-81; prodn. editor Lemon Grove (Calif.)/Spring Valley News, 1982; mng. editor Greenleaf Classics, Inc., San Diego, 1982-87; quality assurance editor Rosenblatt & Son Naval Architects, San Diego, 1987-88; payroll specialist City of San Diego, 1988—; recording sec. Auditor's/Risk Mgmt. joint com. City of San Diego, 1995—. Author: Adventure of the Ancient Gods, 1991, The Secrets of Dreamland, 1997, Holmes: The Dreaming Detective, 1993; editor: Mars! Planet of Dreams, 1995. Avocations: archaeology, stamp collecting, ancient coins, jewelry design, cartography. Home: 265 5th Ave Chula Vista CA 91910-2442

VAUGHAN, RUSSELL FREDRIC, internet executive; b. Mount Vernon, Wash., Jan. 13, 1941; s. James Henry and Nellie Sena (Marihugh) V.; m. Carroll Agnes Leen, Sept. 22, 1962; children: Nola Kay Vaughan-Rassmussen, Sean Jeffrey Vaughan. BS in Physics, U. Wash., 1963. Engr. North Am. Aviation, L.A., 1963-64, The Boeing Co., Kent, Wash., 1965-83, 87-98; v.p. Kay Vaughan Racing Stables, Inc., Enumclaw, Wash., 1983-87; pres. World Wide Web Hosting, Federal Way, Wash., 1998—. Editor Gift of Fire, 1996—; contbr. articles to profl. jours.; patentee in field. Named Leading Race Horse Owner, Wash. Horse Breeding Assn., Renton, 1982, 83, 84; recipient Outstanding Paper award IEEE, 1979. Mem. Prometheus High IQ Soc. (editor 1996, pres. 1998). Avocations: writing essays, computer graphics, reading, travel, koi ponds. Home: 35813 3rd Ave SW Federal Way WA 98023-7362 Office: World Wide Web Hosting PO Box 24513 Federal Way WA 98093-1513

VAUGHN, KATHY, municipal official. Pres. bd. commrs. Pub. Utility Dist., Everett, Wash. also: PO Box 1107 Everett WA 98206 Office: Office Bd Commrs Pub Utility Dist 2320 California St Everett WA 98201-3750*

VAUGHT, LOY, basketball player; b. Feb. 24, 1968. Forward L.A. Clippers. Office: c/o LA Clippers 3939 S Figueroa St Los Angeles CA 90037-1200

VAWTER, DONALD, retired personnel management consultant; b. Spokane, Wash., May 19, 1920; s. Edgar F. and Lina M. Vawter; m. Margaret Schroeder, May 5, 1950; children: Charlotte, Sara. Student in Polit. Sci., Wash. State U., 1946-49. Supr. employer svcs. Wash. State Employment Svc., Seattle, 1950-58; employment mgr. Sundstrand Data Control, Redmond, Wash., 1958-72; profl. recruiter DBA Bellevue Employment Agy., Bellevue, Wash., 1972-73; pers. mgr., workers compensation adminstr. Crown Zellerbach, Omak, Wash., 1973-82; bd. dirs. Pacific N.W. Pers. Mgmt. Assn. 1974-78; apptd. Gov's. Svcs. Coun., 1977-83. Served with USCGR, 1942-46, 50-53, comdr. Res. ret., 1968. Mem. Am. Soc. Pers. Adminstrn. (accredited pers. mgr.). Home: PO Box 296 Tonasket WA 98855-0296

VAYSMAN, SEMEN, writer, mechanic; b. Kiev, Ukraine, Sept. 16, 1940; came to U.S., 1993; s. Phishel and Veyla (Krupnick) V.; m. Valentina Firshteyn, Jan. 29, 1971; children: Marina, Emiliya. Grad. H.S., Kiev, 1964. Mechanic Ukraine Hotel Goloseevsky, Kiev, 1984-90. Author: The Miracle of Dream, 1996. With USSR Army, 1958-61. Avocations: swimming, running, collecting stamps, reading. Home: 921 E Broadway Apt 401 Long Beach CA 90802-5342

VAZ, KATHERINE ANNE, English language educator, writer; b. Castro Valley, Calif., Aug. 26, 1955; d. August Mark and Elizabeth (Sullivan) Vaz; m. Michael Trudeau, May 1, 1994. BA, U. Calif., Santa Barbara, 1977; MFA, U. Calif., Irvine, 1991. Assoc. prof. English U. Calif., Davis, 1995—; keynote or featured spkr. at Libr. of Congress (1997), literary confs. at U. of the Azores, U. Calif. Berkeley, U. Mass., Dartmouth U., Rutgers U. *Vaz is the first Portuguese-American to have her work recorded for the archives of the Library of Congress (Hispanic Division) alongside recordings by Gabriel Garcia Marquez, Octavio Paz, Pablo Neruda, and others. She was on the six-person U.S. Presidential Delegation sent to represent the U.S. at the Expo 98/World's Fair in Lisbon, 1998 and was selected by Luso-Americano as one of the Top 50 influential Luso-Americans of the 20th Century. The Library of Congress picked MARIANA as one of the top 30 international books of 1998.* Author: (novel) Saudade, 1994, Mariana (6 langs.), 1997, (short [illegible]). Recipient grant fellowship Nat. Endowment for the Arts, 1993, Davis Humanities Inst., U. Calif. Davis, 1998-99; recording of interview and reading at the Libr. of Congress was the 1st for a Portuguese-Am., 1997. Mem. Authors Guild, Pen/Am., Portuguese-Am. Leadership Coun. of the U.S., U.S. Presidential Delegation to Expo 98/World's Fair, Lisbon, Portugal. Democrat. Roman Catholic. Office: U Calif 1 Shields Ave Davis CA 95616-5270

VEBLEN, JOHN ELVIDGE, lawyer; b. Seattle, Feb. 14, 1944. AB magna cum laude, Harvard U., 1965; BA, MA with first class honors, Oxford U., Eng., 1967; JD, Yale U., 1971. Bar: Wash. 1971, N.Y. 1973. Law clerk U.S. Ct. Appeals (9th cir.), 1971-72; ptnr. Stoel Rives LLP, Seattle, 1972—. Mem. ABA, Wash. State Bar Assn., Seattle-King County Bar Assn., Phi Beta Kappa. Office: Stoel Rives LLP One Union Sq 600 University St Ste 3600 Seattle WA 98101-4109*

VECCHIO, THOMAS JAMES, medical researcher, consultant; b. N.Y.C., June 14, 1924; s. James and Mildred (Lepre) V.; m. Helaine Bjorndahl, June 23, 1951 (div. 1970); children: Karen, Claudia, Theodore; m. Lisa Wasleski, July 17, 1977. BS, Manhattan Coll., 1944; MD, Harvard U., 1948. Diplomate Am. Bd. Internal Medicine. Intern, resident; pvt. practice Grand Rapids, Mich., 1954-56; assoc. chief, internal medicine Miners Meml. Hosp., Williamson, W.Va., 1956-57, Middlesboro, Ky., 1958-59; worldwide mgr., cardiology and gastroenterology The Upjohn Co., Kalamazoo, Mich., 1960-83; med. dir. Syntex, Palo Alto, Calif., 1984-90; pharm. cons. Bodega Bay, Calif., 1990—. Author: Birth Control by Injection; The Story of Depo-Provera, 1992; contbr. 16 articles to profl. jours. 1st lt. U.S. Army Med. Corps, 1951-53. Fellow ACS. Avocations: music, reading, travel. Home: PO Box 1014 Bodega Bay CA 94923-1014

VEGA, BENJAMIN URBIZO, retired judge, television producer; b. La Ceiba, Honduras, Jan. 18, 1916; m. Janie Lou Smith, Oct. 12, 1989; AB, U. So. Calif., 1938, postgrad., 1939-40; LLB, Pacific Coast U. Law, 1941. Bar: Calif. 1947, U.S. Dist. Ct. (so. dist.) Calif. 1947, U.S. Supreme Ct. 1958. Assoc. Anderson, McPharlin & Connors, L.A., 1947-48, Newman & Newman, L.A., 1948-51; dep. dist. atty. County of L.A., 1951-66; judge L.A., County Mcpl. Ct., East L.A. Jud. Dist., 1966-86, retired, 1986; leader faculty seminar Calif. Jud. Coll. at Earl Warren Legal Inst., U. Calif-Berkeley, 1978. Mem. Calif. Gov.'s Adv. Com. on Children and Youth, 1968; del. Commn. of the Califs., 1978; bd. dirs. Los Angeles-Mexico City Sister City Com.; pres. Argentine Cultural Found., 1983. Recipient award for outstanding services from Mayor of L.A., 1973, City of Commerce, City of Montebello, Calif. Assembly, Southwestern Sch. Law, Disting. Pub. Service award Dist. Atty. L.A. Mem. Conf. Calif. Judges, Mcpl. Ct. Judges' Assn. (award for Outstanding Services), Beverly Hills Bar Assn., Navy League, L.A. County, Am. Judicature Soc., World Affairs Council, Rotary (hon.), Pi Sigma Alpha. Home: 101 California Ave Apt 1207 Santa Monica CA 90403-3525

VEGA, JOSE GUADALUPE, psychologist, clinical director; b. San Benito, Tex., June 4, 1953; s. Jose Guadalupe and Bertha (Saenz) V.; children: Lilian Anna, Jose Guadalupe III; m. Alberta L. Valdez, Oct. 5, 1990. BA, Pan. Am. U., Edinburg, Tex., 1975; MA, U. Denver, 1976, PhD, 1979. Lic. psychologist, Colo., 1983, profl. counselor, Tex., 1982; diplomate Am. Bd. Med. Psychotherapists, Am. Bd. Vocat. Neuropsychology, Am. Bd. Profl. Disability Cons., Am Bd. Forensic Examiners, Am. Bd. Psychol. Specialties (forensic neuropsychology); cert. adminstrn. Halste ad-Reitan Neuropsychology test batteries. With Oasis of Chandala, Denver, 1978-79, Maytag-Emrick Clinic, Aurora, Colo., 1979; psychologist Spanish Peaks Mental Health Ctr., Pueblo, Colo., 1980-85; pvt. practice Assocs. for Psychotherapy and Edn., Inc., 1985-86; co-owner Affiliates in Counseling, Psychol. Assessment and Consultation, Inc., Pueblo, 1986-87; psychologist Parkview Psychol. Testing Clinic, Pueblo, 1987-93, Colo. Dept. Corrections, 1994-96; pvt. practice, Pueblo, 1993—; mem. state grievance bd. Psychology Augment Panel, 1988-95. Active Colo. Inst. Chicano Mental Health, Community Youth Orgn., Boys Club Pueblo; mem. health and human svcs. com. City of Pueblo. Mem. APA, ACA, Nat. Acad. Neuropsychology, Internat. Neuropsychol. Soc., Colo. Neuropsychol. Soc. (charter), Reitan Soc. (charter), Colo. Psychol. Assn. (bd. dirs. non-metro rep. 1995—), Nat. Hispanic Psychol. Assn., Hispanic Neuropsychol. Soc., Phi Delta Kappa, Kappa Delta Pi. Democrat. Roman Catholic. Office: 222 W B St Pueblo CO 81003-3404

VEITCH, PATRICK LEE, performing arts entrepreneur; b. Beaumont, Tex., Mar. 26, 1944; s. Melvin Wood and Sarah Irene Turner (Barton) V.; BA, North Tex. State U., 1967; cert. Not for Profit Mgmt. Columbia U., 1978; m. Kathleen Norris, Dec. 27, 1979; 1 dau., Alexandra Norris. Acct. exec. Ketchum, MacLeod & Grove, N.Y.C., 1967-70; dir. publications Manhattan Coll., N.Y.C., 1970-73; dir. mktg. Met. Opera, N.Y.C., 1973-81; gen. mgr. The Australian Opera, Sydney, 1981-86; producer stage musicals and arts festivals, 1986—; lectr. arts mgmt. Columbia U., 1978-80, N.Y. U., 1979-80; cons. in field. Mem. Theatrical Proprietors and Entrepreneurs Assn. Australia (dir. 1981—). Home: 148 S Reeves Dr Beverly Hills CA 90212-3005 Office: Ctr Theatre Group 135 N Grand Ave Los Angeles CA 90012-3013

VELA, STEVEN RENE, portfolio manager; b. Las Vegas, N.Mex., Sept. 13, 1964; s. Jose A and Julia C. (Bowers) V.; m. Linda M. Billings, Jan. 18, 1997; 1 child Alexander J. BA, Colo. Coll., 1986; MBA, So. Meth. U., 1989. CFA. Acct. The Schuck Corp., Colorado Springs, Colo., 1985-88; portfolio mgr. Ramsay Investment Counsel, Inc., Colorado Springs, Colo., 1989-97, Ramsay, Stattman, Vela & Price, Inc., Colorado Springs, Colo., 1997—. Asst. treas. The Joseph Henry Edmondson Found., Colorado Springs, 1992—; bd. dirs. Pikes Peak Found. for Mental Health, Colorado Springs, 1993-98, Arthritis Found., Colorado Springs, 1997-98. Mem. El Paso Club. Fax: (719) 473-8379. E-mail: raminvest@aol.com. Office: Ramsay Stattman Vela & Price Inc 2 N Cascade Ave Ste 810 Colorado Springs CO 80903-1627

VELASQUEZ, GLORIA LOUISE, language educator, writer; b. Loveland, Colo., Dec. 21, 1949; d. John E. and Frances (Molinar) V.; children: Robert John Velasquez Trevino, Brandi Lynn Trevino. BA, U. No. Colo., 1978; MA, Stanford U., 1982, PhD, 1985. Prof. Calif. Polytech. State U., San Luis Obispo, 1985—. Author: (books) Juanita Fights the School Board, 1994, Maya's Divided World, 1995, Tommy Stands Alone, 1995, Rina's Family Secret, 1998; (poetry) I Used to be a Superwoman, 1997. Recipient Premier et Dieuxieme Prix Poetry, Stanford U., 1979, 11th Chicano Literary Prize (book) U. Calif., Irvine, 1985; named Honored Alumni, U. No. Colo., 1985, Hall of Fame, 1989. Democrat. Avocation: guitar. Office: Calif Polytech State U Dept Modern Langs & Lit San Luis Obispo CA 93407

VELLUTATO, JAMES LEE, music publisher; b. Phoenix, June 12, 1958; s. Joseph Dominic and Donna Lee (Roth) V.; m. Lorraine Marie Provost, Feb. 6, 1987; 1 child, Dominique Marie. BA, UCLA, 1981. Mail rm. worker Chappell Intersong Music, L.A., 1982-83, profl. mgr., 1983-85; creative dir. Famous Music/Paramount Pictures, L.A., 1986-88, sr. creative dir., 1988—; musical dir. plays UCLA, 1982-83, 83-84. Avocations: golf, tennis, volleyball, producing. Office: Sony ATU Music Pub 2100 Colorado Ave Santa Monica CA 90404-3512

VEMULA, NARASIMHARAO, physician; b. Repalle, India, May 12, 1948; s. Kodanda Ramaiah and Rajeswari (Bysani) V.; married; children: Gauthami, Radhika, Raaga. MD, Guntur Med. Coll., 1974. Diplomate Am. Bd. Internal Medicine and Gastroenterology. Pvt. practice of gastroenterology Hobbs, N.Mex., 1981. Fellow Am. Coll. Physicians, Am. Coll. Gastroenterology; mem. Am. Gastroenterology Assn., N.Mex. Med. Soc. Avocation: golf. Home: 109 W Coal Ave Hobbs NM 88240-1944 Office: 5419 N Lovington Hwy Ste 5 Hobbs NM 88240-9135

VENABLE, GIOVAN HARBOUR, lawyer; b. Winston-Salem, N.C., Dec. 10, 1956; d. Joel William and Jo Ann (Harbour) V. AB in Music magna cum laude, Dartmouth Coll., 1979; MDiv, Harvard U., 1983; JD, Stanford U., 1988. Bar: Calif. 1989, D.C. 1990, U.S. Supreme Ct. 1994; ordained minister Congregational Ch. 1984. Assoc. Wyman Bautzer Kuchel & Sibert, [illegible] pvt. practice L.A., 1992—. Contbr. articles to profl. jours.; editor Cal West Congregationalist, 1990—. Active 1st Congl. Ch., L.A., 1983—; mem. Intermission, L.a., 1989—. Mem. Ebell Club (v.p. membership 1988—). Phi Beta Kappa. [illegible] Office: 110 N Larchmont Blvd Los Angeles CA 90004-3013

VENDITTI, PHILLIP NORRIS, institute president; b. Pueblo, Colo., Aug. 7, 1951; s. Frederick Phillip and Jesse Anne (Caldwell) V.; m. Yuna Min, Aug. 17, 1978; children: Amelia Anne, Claire Elien. BA, U. Colo., 1971; MS in English Edn., U. Tenn., 1975; M Internat. Adminstrn., Sch. Internat. Tng., Brattleboro, Vt., 1981; PhD in Ednl. Adminstrn., U. Tex., 1987. Student affairs officer Wash. State U., Pullman, 1981-85; English instr. Austin (Tex.) C.C., 1985-87; asst. to pres. Moraine Valley C.C., Palos Hills, Ill., 1987-89; assoc. dean acad. affairs Genesee C.C., Batavia, N.Y., 1989-92; v.p. acad. affairs W.Va. No. C.C., Wheeling, 1992-94; exec. v.p. Pacific Internat. Inst., Lewiston, Idaho, 1994-96; pres. Am. Culture & Lang. Inst., Lewiston, 1996—. Editor: Let's Look at America, 1979, Profiles in Success, 1990. Bd. dirs. Wash. Idaho Symphony, Lewiston, 1996—. Nat. merit scholar U. Tenn., 1968; named Master Tchr., Nat. Inst. Staff Orgnl. Devel., Austin, 1992.. Mem. Clarkston Rotary Club (bd. dirs., chair Youth Exch. 1994-96), Leadership Lewiston (chmn. 1995), Lewiston C. of C. Unitarian. Avocations: unpopular music, jogging. Home and Office: Am Culture and Lang Inst 511 Crestline Circle Dr Lewiston ID 83501-6704

VENEMA, JON ROGER, educator, pastor; b. Modesto, Calif., Apr. 11, 1953; s. Roger Edwin and Marilyn Ailene (Johnson) V.; m. Shelley Elizabeth, Mar. 29, 1974; children: Jordan Christopher Wilder, Susanna Lee. AA, Modesto (Calif.) Jr. Coll., 1974; BA magna cum laude, Simpson Coll., 1976; MDiv, Mennonite Brethren Bibl. Sem., 1980; PhD, Golden Gate Bapt. Theol. Sem., 1995. Instr. bibl. and religious studies Fresno Pacific Coll., Modesto, 1980-84; sr. pastor 1st Bapt. Ch., So. San Francisco, 1984-94; acad. dean Western Seminary No. Calif., San Jose, Sacramento, 1997—; adj. faculty Fresno Pacific Coll., 1984-87, Simpson Coll., San Francisco, 1987-88; instr. St. James Coll., Pacifica, Calif., 1987-90; adj. prof. Golden Gate Bapt. Theol. Sem., Marin, Calif., 1992, Highland Christian Coll., San Bruno, Calif., 1992-93, Western Conservative Bapt. Theol. Sem., 1994—; acad. dean, devel. coord. Western Sem., Sacramento, 1995-96; acad. dean Western Sem. No. Calif., Sacramento, 1995-96, Sacramento and San Jose, 1997—, asst. prof. N.T. lang. and lit., 1996—. Mem. Soc. Bibl. Lit., Evang. Theol. Assn., Delta Epsilon Chi. Republican. Avocations: sports, art and illustration, backpacking. Home: 2228 Canadian Cir Modesto CA 95356-2700 Office: Western Conserv Baptist Sem 2924 Becerra Way Sacramento CA 95821-3939 also: 16330 Los Gatos Blvd Ste 100 Los Gatos CA 95032-4520

VENGER, BENJAMIN HERSCHEL, neurosurgeon, medical consultant; b. Dearborn, Mich., Dec. 27, 1957; s. Norman and Sally Rita (Friedman) V. BA in Zoology, Pomona Coll., 1979; MD, U. Tex., Houston, 1983. Diplomate Am. Bd. Neurol. Surgery. Surg. intern Baylor Coll. Medicine, Houston, 1983-84; neurosurg. resident Baylor Coll. Medicine, Houston, 1984-89; pvt. practice Las Vegas, 1989—. Co-author: Guide to Human Anatomy, 1985; contbr. articles to profl. jours., chpts. to books. Fellow ACS; mem. AMA, Am. Assn. Neurol. Surgeons, Congress of Neurol. Surgeons, Nev. State Mental Assn., Clark County Med. Soc., Phi Beta Kappa, Sigma Xi, Alpha Omega Alpha. Avocation: flying. Office: 3006 S Maryland Pkwy Ste 265 Las Vegas NV 89109-6206

VENIS, LINDA DIANE, academic administrator, educator; b. Pasadena, Calif., Nov. 15, 1948; d. Ashton Harwood Venis and Grace (Bullock) Miller; m. Gary Arther Berg, Mar. 9, 1991; 1 child, Laura Grace Berg. BA magna cum laude, UCLA, 1970, PhD, 1978. Lectr. English UCLA, 1982-85, adj. asst. prof. Dept. English, 1987-90; lectr. Sch. Fine Arts U. So. Calif., L.A., 1985—; assoc. dir. studies UCLA/London & Cambridge Programs UCLA Extension, 1986-91, head writers program, 1985—, dir. dept. arts, 1992—. Contbr. articles to profl. jours. Recipient Profl. Contbrns. to Continuing Edn. award Continuing Edn. Assn., UCLA Disting. Tchg. award, 1985. Mem. PEN USA/West (bd. dirs. 1993—, adv. bd. 1992-93), Women in Film, Assn. Acad. Women. Office: UCLA Extension The Arts 10995 Le Conte Ave Los Angeles CA 90024-2883

VENKATESHWARAN, RAGHU, engineer; b. Bangalore, Karnataka, India, May 6, 1966; Came to U.S. May 4, 1990; s. Venkateshwaran Venkat and Nagamani (Joshi) Venkateshwaran; m. Lakshmi Srinivasan, June 16, 1966, . BS, U. Mysore, India, 1987. Engr. Taligent, Sunnyvale, Calif., 1995-97; sr. engr. IBM, San Jose, Calif., 1998—. Democrat. Hindu. Avocations: tennis, skating, books, travel. Home: 201 W California Ave Sunnyvale CA 94086-5063

VENNE, GEORGIA PACHECO, artist; b. Alamosa, Colo., Aug. 10, 1957; d. Joe Manuel and Cleo Maria (Espinoza) Pacheco; m. Robert J. Venne, July 29, 1952; 1 child, Leigh April. BA in Art cum laude, Adams State Coll., 1998. Bus. owner Alamosa, 1985—; with interlibr. loan office Adams State Libr., Alamosa, 1996-98; artist Chamber Gallery, Alamosa, 1997-98; photographer Great Sand Dunes, Alamosa, 1998. Exhibited in group shows at Hatfield Gallery, 1998, Alamosa, 1998, Installation 214, 1998. Mem. Am. Youth Soccer Orgn. (coach 1992-94). Avocations: theater, concerts, photography, gardening, cooking. Home: 7991 S 103d Alamosa CO 81101

VENTRIGLIA, PHILLIP J., lawyer; b. Somerville, NJ, July 17, 1944; s. Salvatore and Carmella (DeMaio) V.; m. Lynn R. Moreno, Sept. 28, 1967; 1 child, James Phillip. BA, Rutgers U., 1966, JD, 1969. Bar: N.J. 1969, Nev. 1973. Assoc. Pearl, Kline, Jadach & Assocs., Piscataway, NJ, 1970-73; ptnr. Ventriglia, Werick, Possien & Romano, Las Vegas, 1973—; vis. prof. U. Nev. Las Vegas, 1980—. Contbr. articles to profl. jours. Bd. dirs. Carson City United Way, 1991-95, Profl. Resume Svc., Inc., Las Vegas. Mem. ABA, Nev. Bar Assn., Order of the Coif, Elks. Democrat. Roman Catholic. Avocations: silk screening, traveling, cooking. Office: Ventriglia Werick Possien & Romano 3305 Spring Mtn Rd Ste 60 Las Vegas NV 89102

VENZKE, RAY FRANK, psychotherapist; b. Wood County, Wis., Sept. 7, 1933; s. Herman A. and Christina (Sojka) V.; m. Dawn Woltman, June 14, 1953 (div. Feb. 1972); 1 child, Diane W. Doersch; m. Joy Leadbetter, June 21, 1972 (div. Nov. 1985); m. DeMaris Hafner Unruh, May 31, 1986. BA in Ednl. Psychology, Wartburg Coll., 1955; MDiv, Trinity Sem., Columbus, Ohio, 1959; MA in Psychology, U. N.D., 1974. Lic. clin. profl. counselor, Mont. Pastor Bearlake Luth. Parish, Twin Lakes, Minn., 1959-63; missionary Thailand Luth. Mission, 1963-64; pastor First Luth. Parish, Washburn, N.D., 1965-67; addiction counselor Heartview Found., Mandan, N.D., 1971-74; therapist, program evaluator Badlands Human Svc. Ctr., Dickinson, N.D., 1975-85; psychotherapist Dickinson, N.D., 1985-87, Chrysalis Counseling Svcs., Helena, Mont., 1988—; cons. New Beginnings in Wellness, 1997—, Lewis and Clark County Law Enforcement Chaplains, Helena, 1988-95. Narrator Mont. Talking Book Librs., Helena, 1990—; chair task force CISM Mont. Dept. Disaster, 1994-97; mem. Mont. Gov.'s Task Force on Mental Health Medicaid, Helena, 1993-97, State Manage Care Oversight Com., 1997—. Mem. Am. Counselors Assn., Am. Mental Health Counselors, Mont. Clin. Mental Health Counselors (treas. 1992-94, counselor of yr. award 1996), Mont. Counselors Assn., Lions (Dist. Gov. 5NW award 1983), Am. Philatelic Soc. Avocations: stamp collecting, reading, photography. Office: Chrysalis Counseling Svc 2019 Missoula Ave Helena MT 59601-3245

VERANT, WILLIAM J., state agency administrator; b. Washington, Dec. 19, 1941; m. Donna M. Verant; children: Bill Jr., Sharon. BSBA, Am. U. Various sr. mgmt. positions various comml. banks, savs. and loan and mortgage banks, Washington, Calif., N.Mex.; dir. fin. instns. divsn., regulation and licensing dept. State of N.Mex., Santa Fe, 1995—, acting dir. securities divsn.; acting dir. securities divsn. State of N.Mex. Avocation: restoring old cars. Office: State of New Mexico PO Box 25101 725 Saint Michaels Dr Santa Fe NM 87504-7605

VERDIELL, JEAN-MARC, communications company executive; b. Tournai, Belgium, Feb. 7, 1964; s. Jean-Baptiste and Frida (Raszewski) V.; m. Hoang-Oanh Vo, Dec. 24, 1996. Diploma in engring., Ecole Poly., Palaiseau, France, 1986; PhD, U. Paris, 1990. Rsch. asst. Thomson-CSF Ctrl. Rsch. Labs., Orsay, France, 1987-90; rsch. assoc. U. Md., College Park, 1990-91; mem. tech. staff AT&T Bell Labs., Holmdel, N.J., 1991-94; staff scientist SDL Inc., San Jose, Calif., 1994-97; founder, CEO LightLogic Inc., Palo Alto, Calif., 1998—; reviewer Electronics Letters, 1991—; cons. optoelectronics tech. NASA Jet Propulsion Lab., Pasadena, 1997—. Contbr. over 50 articles to profl. jours.; patentee in field. Mem. IEEE, Laser and Electro Optics Soc., Optical Soc. Am. (selection com. 1996-97). Avocation: classical piano.

VERGAMINI, JUDITH SHARON ENGEL, counselor, educator; b. Milw., May 21, 1941; d. Max E. and Rose (Ladish) Engel; m. Jerome Carl Vergamini, May 1, 1965; children: Michael David, Beth Allison, Daniel Carl. BS, U. Wis., 1963, postgrad., 1964, 66-76; MS, U. Oreg., 1978, postgrad., 1980—. Nat. cert. counselor; lic. profl. counsellor, tchr., sch. counselor, marriage and family therapist. Elem. tchr. Crestwood Elem. Sch., Northbrook, Ill., 1963-64, Odana Elem. Sch., Madison, Wis., 1964-65, Fitzmorris Elem. Sch., Arvada, Colo., 1965-66; tchr. Headstart, Madison, Wis., 1966; coord., founder parent vols. program Alternate Sch., Eugene, Oreg., 1976-77; pvt. practice counselor Eugene, 1978—; instr. Lane C.C., Eugene, Oreg., 1978—; lectr. Addictions Treatment Hosp. Program, 1989-92; mental health specialist Headstart of Lane County, Oreg., 1993-94; resource counselor Newman Ctr. U. Oreg., Eugene, 1979—, adj. prof., 1994—; presenter in field. Recipient Appreciation award Eugene Edn. Assn., 1980, Svc. to Edn. award, Oreg. Edn. Assn., 1980, Dedication and Performance award Nat. Disting. Svc. Registry, 1990, Outstanding Merit award Nat. Bd. Cert. Counselors, 1991. Fellow Am. Orthopsychiatric Assn.; mem. AACD, Am. Assn. for Marriage and Family Therapy (clin.), Am. Mental Health Counselors Assn., Oreg. Counseling Assn. Avocations: art, theatre. Home: 1047 Brookside Dr Eugene OR 97405-4913 Office: 1508 Oak St Eugene OR 97401-4042

VERHEY, JOSEPH WILLIAM, psychiatrist, educator; b. Oakland, Calif., Sept. 28, 1928; s. Joseph Bernard and Anne (Hanken) V.; BS summa cum laude, Seattle U., 1954; MD, U. Wash., 1958; m. Darlene Helen Seiler, July 21, 1956. Intern, King County Hosp., Seattle, 1958-59; resident Payne Whitney Psychiatric Clinic, N.Y. Hosp., Cornell Med. Center, N.Y.C., 1959-62, U. Wash. Hosp., Seattle, 1962-63; pvt. practice, Seattle, 1963-78; mem. staff U. Providence Hosp., 1963-78, Fairfax Hosp., 1963-78, VA Med. Center, Tacoma, 1978-83, chief inpatient psychiatry sect., 1983—; clin. instr. psychiatry U. Wash. Med. Sch., 1963-68, clin. asst. prof. psychiatry, 1968-82, clin. assoc. prof., 1982—; cons. psychiatry U.S. Dept. Def., Wash. State Bur. Juvenile Rehab.; examiner Am. Bd. Psychiatry and Neurology. Diplomate Am. Bd. Psychiatry and Neurology. Fellow N. Pacific Soc. Psychiatry and Neurology, Am. Psychiat. Assn.; mem. AMA, Am. Fedn. Clin. Rsch., World Fedn. Mental Health, Soc. Mil. Surgeons of U.S., Wash. Athletic Club, Swedish Club (life). Home: 1100 University St Seattle WA 98101-2848 Office: VA Med Ctr Tacoma WA 98493

VERMEER, WANDA BETH, healthcare consultant; b. Orange City, Iowa, Dec. 9, 1954; d. Bernard E. and Wilminia (Vander Schaaf) V. BSN, Augustana Coll., 1977; MBA, Ariz. State U., 1985. Head nurse Good Samaritan Med. Ctr., Phoenix, 1980-86; spl. projects dir. Good Samaritan Regional Med. Ctr., Phoenix, 1987-88; physician hosp. orgn. project mgr. Iowa Meth. Health System, Des Moines, 1989-92; v.p. Tokos Med. Corp./Matryx Health Ptnrs., Phoenix, 1992-96; pres. Vermeer & Assocs., 1997—. Office: Vermeer & Assoc 2406 E Mountain Vista Dr Phoenix AZ 85048-4216

VERNIERO, JOAN EVANS, special education educator; b. Wilkes-Barre, Pa., Nov. 30, 1937; d. Raymond Roth and Cary Hazel (Casano) Evans; m. Daniel Eugene Verniero Jr., Jan. 7, 1956; children: Daniel Eugene III, Raymond Evans. BA, Kean Coll., 1971; MS in Edn. Adminstrn., Monmouth U., West Long Branch, N.J., 1974; postgrad., Calif. Coast U., 1986-92. Cert. elem. sch. tchr., spl. edn. tchr., sch. adminstr., N.J., N.Mex., Colo.; nat. registered emergency med. technician. Tchr. Children's Psychiat. Ctr., Eatontown, N.J., 1965-69; tchr. Arthur Brisbane Child Treatment Ctr., Farmingdale, N.J., 1969-71, prin., 1971-75; prin. S.A. Wilson Ctr., Colorado Springs, Colo., 1976-82; tchr. pub. schs. Aurora, Colo., 1982-93; retired, 1993; edn. rep. Aurora Pub. Schs. Crew leader Black Forest (Colo.) Rescue Squad 1979-85, treas., bd. dirs. Fire Protection Dist., 1980-85; evaluator Arson divsn. Aurora (Colo.) Fire Dept., 1993—. Mem. Phi Delta Kappa. Republican. Presbyterian. Avocations: nature photography, travel. Home: 671 S Paris St Aurora CO 80012-2315

VERNON, BRIAN THOMAS, dancer, choreographer, dance educator; b. Milw., Jan. 22, 1967; s. Kenneth Leo and Pauline Ann (Oliviér) V. BFA, U. of the Arts, 1992; MFA, U. Calif., Irvine, 1994. Dance instr. U. of the Arts, Phila., 1988-92, U. Calif., Irvine, 1992-94; asst. prof. dance Mesa State Coll., Grand Junction, Colo., 1995—; Asst. artistic dir. Mesa State Coll. Repertory Dance Co., Grand Junction, 1995—; dir., choreographer, performer music theatre, concert dance, TV, comml. and films, 1985—; annual guest artist and master dance tchr. South Am.; guest artist, workshop presenter, lectr. in field. Featured performer Black and Blue, 1996-97. Mem. vis. scholars program Mesa State Coll., Grand Junction, 1997—; cons., guest spkr. Grand Junction Art Ctr., 1997—. Recipient Outstanding Grad. Student Achievement award Nat. Dance Assn., 1994; Chancellor's fellow U. Calif., Irvine, 1992-94. Mem. Internat. Tap Assn., Am. Coll. Dance Festival Assn. (guest artist), Rocky Mountain Theatre Assn. (guest artist). Avocations: music, traveling, swimming, theme parks, reading. Office: Mesa State Coll Fine Arts PO Box 2647 Grand Junction CO 81502-2647

VERNON, TIMOTHY, artistic director. Artistic director Pacific Opera, Victoria, Can. Office: 1316B Govt St, Victoria, BC Canada V8W 1Y8*

VERPLOEGEN, LORRAINE JEAN, elementary school educator; b. Havre, Mont., Mar. 15, 1950; d. Edwin Edgar and Donna Lee (Perry) Larson; m. Frank Edward Verploegen, Nov. 17, 1973; children: Eric James, Erin Jean. BS in Edn., Mont. State U., Billings, 1972; MEd, Mont. State U., Havre, 1991. Remedial reading tchr. Huntley Project, Worden, Mont., 1972; primary resource tchr. Havre Pub. Schs., 1972-75, 78-79, 1991-92, intermediate resource tchr., 1989-91, tchr. grades 1, 2 and 3, 1976-79, 79-80, reading recovery tchr. leader, 1992—; itinerant resource tchr. Bear Paw Coop, Chinook, Mont., 1988; primary resource tchr. Rocky Boy Elem. Sch., Box Elder, Mont., 1988; tchr. K-6 Cottonwood Country Sch., Havre, 1982-86. 4-H leader Hill County 4-H, Havre, 1984-94. Mont. State Reading Coun. Tchr. Project grantee, 1993-94. Mem. NEA, Tri-County Reading Coun. (pres., v.p.), Mont. State Reading Coun. (state chair 1982-92, Leadership award 1991), Havre Edn. Assn. (pres.), Internat. Reading Assn. Avocations: reading, cross-stitch, crocheting, music. Home: HC 30 Box 79B Havre MT 59501-9706

VERRONE, PATRIC MILLER, lawyer, writer; b. Glendale, N.Y.C., Sept. 29, 1959; s. Pat and Edna (Miller) V.; m. Margaret Maiya Williams, 1989; children: Patric Carroll Williams, Marianne Emma Williams. BA, Harvard U., 1981; JD, Boston Coll., 1984. Bar: Fla. 1984, Calif. 1988, U.S. Dist. Ct. (mid. dist.) Fla. 1984, U.S. Dist. Ct. (ctrl. dist.) Calif. 1995, U.S. Ct. Appeals (9th cir.) 1995. Assoc. Allen, Knudsen, Swartz, DeBoest, Rhoads & Edwards, Ft. Myers, Fla., 1984-86; writer The Tonight Show, Burbank, Calif., 1987-90; temp. judge Santa Monica Mcpl. Ct., 1999—; adj. prof. Loyola Law Sch., L.A., 1998-99. Dir., producer, writer The Civil War--The Lost Episode, 1991; writer The Larry Sanders Show, 1992-94, The Critic, 1993-95; producer, writer The Simpsons, 1994-95, Muppets Tonight!, 1995-97 (Emmy award Best Children's Program 1998), Pinky and the Brain, 1998, Futurama, 1998—; editor Harvard Lampoon, 1978-84, Boston Coll. Law Rev., 1983-84, Fla. Bar Jour., 1987-88, L.A. Lawyer, 1994—; issue editor: Ann. Entertainment Law Issue, 1995-99; contbr. articles to profl. jours. including Elysian Fields Quar., Baseball and the American Legal Mind, White's Guide to Collecting Figures. Bd. dirs. Calif. Confedn. of Arts, 1994-98, Mus. Contemporary Art, 1994-95. Mem. ABA (vice chair arts, entertainment and sports law com. 1995-96), Calif. Bar, Calif. Lawyers for Arts, L.A. County Bar Assn. (sec. barristers exec. com., chair artists and the law com., steering com. homeless shelter project, intellectual property and entertainment law sect., state appelate jud. evaluation com., legis. activity com.), Fla. Bar Assn., Writers Guild Am. West (exec. com. animation writers caucus), Harvard Club Lee County (v.p. 1985-86), Harvard Club So. Calif. Republican. Roman Catholic. Avocation: baseball. Home and Office: PO Box 1428 Pacific Palisades CA 90272-1428

VERSCH, ESTHER MARIE, artist; b. Santa Monica, Calif., May 27, 1927; d. Claro Contreras Santellanes and Juana Hernandez; m. Chester Ray Fraelich, Nov. 14, 1943 (div. Nov. 1964); children: Joe Fraelich, Diane Fraelich Preston; m. Terry Lee Versch, June 21, 1969; stepchildren: Fred, Roman, Joseph, Terry Jr., Michael. Student, East L.A. Coll., Pasadena City Coll. Lic. vocat. nurse. Nurse pvt. dr.'s office L.A., 1968-69, U. So. Calif. Med. Ctr., L.A., 1963-68; artist Altadena, Calif., 1972—. Artist: (front cover) Library Services L.A., 1983, Christmas card for Western Greeting Inc.; group exhibitions: Women Artists of the West Internat. Exhibition and Sale, George Ohr Cultural Arts and Cultural Ctr., Biloxi, Miss., 1998; collections: Johnson Humrick House Mus., Coshocton, Ohio, and other private collections. Vol. Arroyo Rep., Pasadena, Calif., St. Luke Hosp., Pasadena, 1990-94. Recipient Gold medal for watercolor San Gabriel Fine Arts, 1979, Best of Show award for watercolor Am. Indian and Western, 1990, Hon. mention San Gabriel Fine Arts, 1990. Mem. Women Artists of the West (emeritus mem., treas., asst. sec., editor West Wind, 1st pl. award for watercolor 1979). Republican. Roman Catholic. Avocations: walking, gardening, sewing.

VER STEEG, DONNA LORRAINE FRANK, nurse, sociologist, educator; b. Minot, N.D., Sept. 23, 1929; d. John Jonas and Pearl H. (Denlinger) Frank; m. Richard W. Ver Steeg, Nov. 22, 1950; children: Juliana, Anne, Richard B. BSN, Stanford, 1951; MSN, U. Calif., San Francisco, 1967; MA in Sociology, UCLA, 1969, PhD in Sociology, 1973. Clin. instr. U. N.D. Sch. Nursing, 1962-63; USPHS nurse rsch. fellow UCLA, 1969-72; spl. cons., adv. com. on physicians' assts. and nurse practitioner programs Calif. State Bd. Med. Examiners, 1972-73; asst. prof. UCLA Sch. Nursing, 1973-79, assoc. prof., 1979-94, asst. dean, 1981-83, chmn. primary ambulatory care, 1976-87, assoc. dean, 1983-86, prof. emeritus (recalled 1994-96), chair primary care, 1994-96, emeritus, 1996—; co-prin. investigator PRIMEX Project, Family Nurse Practitioners, UCLA Extension, 1974-76; assoc. cons. Calif. Postsecondary Edn. Commn., 1975-76; spl. cons. Calif. Dept. Consumer Affairs, 1978; accredited visitor Western Assn. Schs. and Colls., 1985; mem. Calif. State Legis. Health Policy Forum, 1980-81; mem. nurse practitioner adv. com. Calif. Bd. RNs, 1995-97; mem. Edn. Industry Interface, Info. Devel. Mktg. Sub Coms., Calif. Strategic Planning Com. Nursing/Colleagues in Caring Project, 1995—. Contbr. chpts. to profl. books. Recipient Leadership award Calif. Area Health Edn. Ctr. System, 1989, Commendation award Calif. State Assembly, 1994; named Outstanding Faculty Mem. UCLA Sch. Nursing, 1982. Fellow Am. Acad. Nursing; mem. AAAS, AAUW, ANA (pres. elect Calif. 1977-79, pres. Calif. 1979-81), ANA C interim chair Calif. 1995-96, Nat. League Nursing, Calif. League Nursing, N.Am. Nursing Diagnosis Assn., Am. Assn. History Nursing, Stanford Nurses Club, Sigma Theta Tau (Alpha Eta chpt. Leadership award Gamma Tau chpt. 1994), Sigma Xi. Home: 708 Swarthmore Ave Pacific Palisades CA 90272-4353 Office: UCLA Sch Nursing Box 956917 Los Angeles CA 90095-6917

VERTS, LITA JEANNE, university administrator; b. Jonesboro, Ark., Apr. 13, 1935; d. William Gus and Lolita Josephine (Peeler) Nash; m. B. J. Verts, Aug. 29, 1954 (div. 1975); 1 child, William Trigg. BA, Oreg. State U., 1973; MA in Lingustics, U. Oreg., 1974; postgrad., U. Hawaii, 1977. Librarian Forest Research Lab., Corvallis, Oreg., 1966-69; instr. English Lang. Inst., Corvallis, 1974-80; dir. spl. svcs. Oreg. State U., Corvallis, 1980—, faculty senator, 1988-96; ret., 1996. Editor ann. book: Trio Achievers, 1986, 87, 88; contbr. articles to profl. jours. Precinct com. Rep. Party, Corvallis, 1977-80; adminstrv. bd. 1st United Meth. Ch., Corvallis, 1987-89, mem. fin. com., 1987-93, tchr. Bible, 1978—; bd. dirs. Westminster Ho., United Campus Ministries, 1994-95; adv. coun. Disabilities Svc., Linn, Benton, Lincoln Counties, 1990—, vice-chmn., 1992-93, chmn. 1993-94; citizen adv. bd. on Transit, 1998—, intercity steering com., 1999—, Cowalis Downtown Parking Commn., 1999—. Mem. N.W. Assn. Spl. Programs (pres. 1985-86), Nat. Coun. Ednl. Opportunities Assn. (bd. dirs. 1984-87), Nat. Gardening Assn., Alpha Phi (mem. corp. bd. Beta Upsilon chpt. 1990-96). Republican. Methodist. Avocations: gardening, photography, golf. Home: 530 SE Mayberry Ave Corvallis OR 97333-1866 Office: Spl Svcs Project Waldo 337 OSU Corvallis OR 97331

VEST, HYRUM GRANT, JR., horticultural sciences educator; b. Salt Lake City, Sept. 23, 1935; s. Hyrum and Josephine Gwendolyn (Lund) V.; m. Gayle Pixton, Sept. 18, 1958; children: Kelly, Lani, Kari, Kamille, Kyle. B.S., Utah State U., 1960, M.S., 1964; Ph.D., U. Minn., 1967. Pathologist, agronomist U.S. Dept. Agr., Beltsville, Md., 1967-70; vegetable breeder Mich. State U., East Lansing, 1970-76; dept. head dept. hort. and landscape architecture Okla. State U., Stillwater, 1976-83; head dept. hort. scis. Tex A & M U., College Station, 1983-89; head dept. plants, soils and biometeorology Utah State U., Logan, 1989-95, assoc. dir. Utah Agrl. Experiment Sta., 1995—; mem. Nat. Plant Genetics Resource Bd., Washington, 1982-88. Served to 1st lt. U.S. Army, 1960-63. Univ. research fellow Utah State U., 1963-64. Fellow Am. Soc. Hort. Sci. Republican. Mem. LDS Ch. Home: 368 Spring Creek Rd Providence UT 84332-9432 Office: Utah State U Utah Agrl Experiment Sta Logan UT 84322-4810

VEST, ROSEMARIE LYNN TORRES, secondary school educator; b. Pueblo, Colo., Jan. 16, 1958; d. Onesimo Bernabe and Maria Bersabe (Lucero) Torres; m. Donald R. Vest, May 1, 1982. BA, U. So. Colo., 1979, BS, 1991; cert. travel agt., Travel Trade Sch., Pueblo, 1986. Cert. secondary tchr., Colo. Tutor U. So. Colo., Pueblo, 1977-79; sales rep. Intermountain Prodns., Colorado Springs, Colo., 1979-80; tutor, Pueblo, 1980-82, 84-85; travel agt. So. Colo. Travel, Pueblo, 1986-88; children's program facilitator El Mesias Family Support Program, Pueblo, 1987-88; substitute tchr. social studies Sch. Dist. 60, Pueblo, 1990—, Freed Mid. Sch., Pueblo, 1991, 92; Chpt. 1 Summer Reading Program, 1992, 93, 94, 95; instr. Travel and Tourism Dept. Pueblo C.C., 1994-95, Dept Social Studies, 1996-97. Tchr. Sunday sch., chairperson adminstrv. bd. cert. lay spkr., lay rep. to ann. conf. Ch. Evangelism, co-chmn. Trinity United Meth. Ch., Pueblo, 1989-94, parish coun. rep. to Trinity/Bethel Coop. Parish; sponsor United Meth. Youth United Meth. Ch.; tchr. Sunday Sch., co-coord. vacation Bible sch., edn. chairperson, 1994—, cert. lay spkr., ministerial program asst., lay leader Bethel United Meth. Ch., 1994—; craft facilitator Integrated Health Svcs., Pueblo, 1991—; spiritual devotions/worship leader Pueblo Manor Nursing Home, 1993—; vol. resident svcs. Pueblo County Bd. for Developmental Disabilities, 1989—; mem. conf. leadership team, parliamentarian Rocky Mountain Conf. United Meth. Ch., 1995, dist. rep., 1997—; ministerial candidate United Meth. Ch.; conf. rep. Rocky Mountain Conf. Coun. on Fin. and Adminstrn., 1996—. Recipient Excellence in Tchg. award Freed Mid. Sch., 1992, Vol. of Yr. award IHS of Pueblo, 1995. Mem. Assn. Am. Geographers, Nat. Oceanog. Soc., Nat. Geog. Soc. Democrat. Avocations: crafts, photography, reading, cross-stitch, listening to music. Home: 125 W Grant Apt C Pueblo CO 81004-2000

VESTAL, JOSEPHINE BURNET, lawyer; b. Iowa City, June 13, 1949; d. Allan Delker and Dorothy (Walker) V. Student Williams Coll., 1970; B.A., Mount Holyoke Coll., 1971; J.D., U. Wash., 1974. Bar: Wash. 1974, U.S. Dist. Ct. (we. dist.) Wash. 1974, U.S. Ct. Appeals (9th cir.) 1984, U.S. Ct. Appeals (D.C. cir.) 1984, U.S. Dist. Ct. (ea. dist.) Wash. 1993. Ptnr. Selinker, Vestal, Klockars & Andersen, Seattle, 1974-80; assoc. Williams, Kastner & Gibbs, Seattle, 1981-87; mem. Williams, Kastner & Gibbs PLLC, 1988—. Mem. ABA (mem. labor and employment sect., mem. labor and employment sect. Def. Rsch. Inst.), Wash. State Bar Assn., King County Bar Assn. Office: Williams Kastner & Gibbs 4100 Two Union Square 601 Union St Ste 4100 Seattle WA 98101-2380

VIANELLO, FRANCO, sculptor, gallery owner; b. Venice, Italy, May 29, 1937; came to U.S., 1960; s. Primo and Giovanna (Conedo) V.; m. Jane Nourse, Feb. 17, 1964; 1 child, Elizabeth. MA, Inst. Arts, Venice, 1959. Asst., master, dept. head Inst. of Arts and Technique, Venice, Italy, 1956-59; pres. Cera Persa, Berkeley, Calif., 1960-62, Art Bronzes, Richmond, Calif., 1964-79; prin., owner Vianello Studios, Napa, Calif., 1979—; cons. Ohio State U. Art Dept., Columbus, 1959-60, U. Calif., Berkeley, 1960-62. Prin. works include bronze sculptures titled Pony Express, 1978, Bucking Horse, 1980, Coming Through the Rye, 1981, Leif Ericson, 1962, Tunaman Memorial, 1987. With U.S. Army, 1962-64. Recipient Best of Show, Fifth Army, 1964, Gold Medal award Western Heritage Ctr. Cowboy Hall of Fame, Okla. City, 1981, Purchase award San Francisco Arts Commn., 1985. Avocations: fishing, boating, woodworking, glassworking. Home and Office: Vianello Studios 2040 Oak Knoll Ave West Napa CA 94558-1340

VIBBER, JAMES CHARLES, software engineer; b. Culver City, Calif., Sept. 15, 1951; s. Jack Gordon and Ruth Marie (Seabold) B.; m. Lee Weigle, Sept. 18, 1971; children: Kelson, Brion. BS in Math., Calif. Inst. of Tech., 1973, BS in Biology, 1974; MS in Bio-Electronics, U. Calif., Berkeley. Cert.

systems engr., Microsoft. R&D engr. Edwards Pacemaker Systems, Irvine, Calif., 1977-80; project scientist Med. Specialties Bus., Irvine, 1980-83; sr. R&D engr. Am. Edwards Labs., Irvine, 1983-86; project mgr., expert systems Tokos Med. Corp., Santa Ana, Calif., 1986-95; sr. software engr. Wonderware, Irvine, 1995—. Mem. IEEE. Avocations: sci. fiction, bodybuilding, drawing, music. Home: 14121 Woodlawn Ave Tustin CA 92780-5145 Office: Wonderware 100 Technology Dr Irvine CA 92618-2401

VICE, LISA, writer, educator; b. Tipton, Ind., July 25, 1951; d. Eddie Franklin V.; life partner: Martha Clark Cummings, 1989; 1 child, Zoe. BA, Hunter Coll., N.Y.C., 1985, MA, 1987. Adj. prof. Hunter Coll., 1987-92; lectr. U. Calif., Santa Cruz, 1992—; Tumblewords lectr. Wyo. Arts. Coun., Cheyenne, 1998-2000. Author: Reckless Driver, 1995 (silver medal Commonwealth Club 1996), Preacher's Lake, 1998. Wyo. Arts Coun. Lit. fellow, 1999. Mem. Nat. Writers Union. Avocations: gardening, hiking.

VICK, AUSTIN LAFAYETTE, civil engineer; b. Cedervale, N.Mex., Jan. 28, 1929; s. Louis Lafayette and Mota Imon (Austin) V.; BSCE, N.Mex. State U., 1950, MSCE, 1961; m. Norine E. Melton, July 18, 1948; children: Larry A., Margaret J., David A. Commd. 2d lt. USAF, 1950, advanced through grades to capt., 1959, ret., 1970; ordnance engr. Ballistics Rsch. Lab., White Sands Proving Ground, Las Cruces, N.Mex., 1950-51, civil engr., 1951-55, gen. engr. White Sands Missile Range, 1957-73, phys. scientist adminstr., 1955-57, supr. gen. engr., 73-84; owner A.V. Constrn., Las Cruces, 1979-93; realtor Campbell Agy., Las Cruces, 1979-84; cons. test and evaluation, instrumentation systems, ops. maintenance and mgmt. to Dept. of Def., major comml. firms, 1984—; pres., treas. Survey Tech., Inc., 1985—; cons. in field, Las Cruces, 1984—. Mem. outstanding alumni awards com. N.Mex. State U., 1980. Recipient Outstanding Performance award Dept. Army, White Sands Missile Range, 1972, Spl. Act awards, 1967, 71, 75, Disting. Alumni award N.Mex. State U. Coll. Engring., 1996. Mem. Mil. Ops. Research Soc. (chmn. logistics group 1968-69), Am. Def. Preparedness Assn. (pres. 1970-72), Assn. U.S. Army (v.p. 1970-71), Am. Soc. Photogrametry, Am. Astronautical Soc. (sr. mem.), N.Mex. State U. Acad. Civil Engring. Contbr. articles to profl. jours. Home and Office: 4568 Spanish Dagger Las Cruces NM 88011-9635

VICKER, RAY, writer; b. Wis., Aug. 27, 1917; s. Joseph John and Mary (Young) V.; m. Margaret Ella Leach, Feb. 23, 1944. Student, Wis. State U., Stevens Point, 1934, Los Angeles City Coll., 1940-41, U.S. Mcht. Marine Officers' Sch., 1944, Northwestern U., 1947-49. With Chgo. Jour. Commerce, 1946-50, automobile editor, 1947-50; mem. staff Wall St. Jour., 1950-83; European editor Wall St. Jour., London, Eng., 1960-75. Author: How an Election Was Won, 1962, Those Swiss Money Men, 1973, Kingdom of Oil, 1974, Realms of Gold, 1975, This Hungry World, 1976, Dow Jones Guide to Retirement Planning, 1985, The Informed Investor, 1990; also numerous articles. Served with U.S. Merchant Marine, 1942-46. Recipient Outstanding Reporting Abroad award Chgo. Newspaper Guild, 1959; Best Bus. Reporting Abroad award E. W. Fairchild, 1963, 67; hon. mention, 1965; Bob Considine award, 1979; ICMA Journalism award, 1983. Mem. Soc. Profl. Journalists, Authors Guild. Roman Catholic. Clubs: Overseas Press (Reporting award 1963, 67) (N.Y.C.); Press (Chgo.). Home and Office: Apt 15201 7500 N Calle Sin Envidia Tucson AZ 85718-7375

VICKERS, DEBORAH JANICE, electrical engineer, researcher; b. Blandford, Dorset, Eng., Jan. 30, 1961; came to U.S., 1986; d. William Hedley and Kathryn Rosemary (Purvis) V. BS in Physics, Queen Mary Coll., London, 1982; MSEE, U. Coll. London, 1985; PhD in Elec. Engring., U. Calif., L.A., 1996. Rsch. scientist Gen. Motors Rsch. Labs., Warren, Mich., 1986-94; staff rsch. scientist Hughes Rsch. Labs., Malibu, Calif., 1994-99, sr. staff rsch. scientist, 1999—; rsch. asst. U. Coll. London, 1982-85. Mem. IEEE, Inst. Physics (assoc.), Tau Beta Pi. Achievements include patent for Fibre Optic Pressure Sensor. Office: Hughes Rsch Labs 3011 Malibu Canyon Rd Malibu CA 90265-4797

VICKERY, BYRDEAN EYVONNE HUGHES (MRS. CHARLES EVERETT VICKERY, JR.), retired library services administrator; b. Belleview, Mo., Apr. 18, 1928; d. Roy Franklin and Margaret Cordelia (Wood) Hughes; m. Charles Everett Vickery, Jr., Nov. 5, 1948; 1 child, Camille. Student, Flat River (Mo.) Jr. Coll., 1946-48; BS in Edn., S.E. Mo. State Coll., 1954; MLS, U. Wash., 1964; postgrad. Wash. State U., 1969-70. Tchr. Ironton (Mo.) Pub. Schs., 1948-56; elem. tchr. Pasco (Wash.) Sch. Dist. 1, 1956-61, jr. high sch. libr., 1961-68, coord. librs., 1968-69; asst. libr. Columbia Basin Community Coll., Pasco, 1969-70, head libr., dir. Instructional Resources Ctr., 1970-78, dir. libr. svcs., 1979-87, assoc. dean libr. svcs., 1987-90, ret., 1990; owner Vickery Search & Research, 1990—; chmn. S.E. Wash. Libr. Svc. Area, 1977-78, 88-90. Bd. dirs. Pasco-Kennewick Community Concerts, 1977-88, pres., 1980-81, 87-88, Pasco-Kennewick Community Concerts, treas., 1991—; bd. dirs. Mid-Columbia Symphony Orch., 1983-89; trustee Wash. Commn. Humanities, 1982-85; bd. mem. Arts Coun. Mid-Columbia Region, 1991-93. Author, editor: Library and Research Skills Curriculum Guides for the Pasco School District, 1967; author (with Jean Thompson), also editor Learning Resources Handbook for Teachers, 1969. Recipient Woman of Achievement award Pasco Bus. and Profl. Women's Club, 1976. Mem. ALA, AAUW (2d v.p. 1966-68, corr. sec. 1969), Wash. Dept. Audio-Visual Instrn., Wash. Libr. Assn., Am. Assn. Higher Edn., Wash. Assn. Higher Edn., Wash. State Assn. Sch. Librs. (state conf. chmn. 1971-72), Tri-Cities Librs. Assn., Wash. Libr. Media Assn. (community coll. levels chmn. 1986-87), Am. Assn. Rsch. Libr., Soroptimist Internat. Assn. (rec. sec. Pasco-Kennewick chpt. 1971-72, treas. 1973-74, pres. 1978-80, v.p. 1989-90, treas. 1991, found. & awards chmn. 1995-96), Columbia Basin Coll. Adminstrs. Assn. (sec.-treas. 1973-74), Pacific N.W. Assn. Ch. Libr., Women in Communications, Pasco Bus. and Profl. Women's Club, PEO, Beta Sigma Phi, Delta Kappa Gamma, Phi Delta Kappa (sec. 1981-82, Outstanding Educator award 1983). Home: 3521 S Fisher Ct Kennewick WA 99337-2559

VIDAL, ALEJANDRO LEGASPI, architect; b. Kawit, Cavite, The Philippines, May 3, 1934; came to U.S. 1954; s. Antonio and Patrocinia Santonil (Legaspi) V.; m. Fe Del Rosario, Aug. 16, 1962; 1 child, Alex Anthony. BS in Architecture, Mapua Inst. Tech., 1962. Registered arch., The Philippines. Prin. A.L. Vidal Arch., Manila, The Philippines, 1962-63; staff arch. Vinnell Wall & Green, Agana, Guam, 1963-64; project engr. Dillingham Corp. of Nevada, Hawaii and Guam, 1964-74; sr. project mgr., preconstrn. svc. mgr. Fletcher-Pacific Constrn. Co. Ltd., Honolulu, 1974-96; prin. A.L. Vidal Constrn. Cons., Honolulu, 1996—, A.L. Vidal Arch., Cavite, The Philippines, 1996—. Designer, builder first application of integrated aluminum forming sys. for high rise concrete construction. Active Rep. Presdl. Task Force, Washington, 1980-88, Rep. Senatorial Com., Washington, 1980-88. With USN, 1954-58, Korea. Mem. Am. Concrete Inst., Am. Mgmt. Assn., Soc. Am. Mil. Engrs., Am. Legion, U. Hawaii Found., Chancellor's Club, Disabled Am. Vets., Comdrs. Club, Oxford Club. Roman Catholic. Avocations: golf, swimming, volunteer work. Home: 1051 Kaluanui Rd Honolulu HI 96825-1321

VIEIRA, LINDA MARIE, administrative and technical coordinator, endoscopy technician; b. San Jose, Calif., July 8, 1961; d. Albert Sequeira and Catherine Marie (Souza) Vieira; m. John Bettencourt Ramos, June 12, 1982 (div. July 1993). AA, De Anza Coll., 1986; BA, St. Mary's Coll. Calif., Moraga, 1988; student, De Anza Coll., Cupertino, Calif., 1997—. Cert. gastrointestinal clinician, aerobic instr. Endoscopy technician O'Connor Hosp., San Jose, 1979-94, Good Samaritan Health Sys., Los Gatos, Calif., 1994—, Alexian Bros. Hosp., San Jose, Calif., 1995—; adminstrv. and tech. coord. South Bay Endoscopy Ctr., San Jose, Calif., 1997—; aerobic instr. Mountain View (Calif.) Athletic Club, 1984-95, Decathlon Club, Santa Clara, 1991—, Golds Gym, Mountain View, 1994—, Silicon Valley Athletic Club, Santa Clara, 1995—. Contbr. articles to profl. jours. Vol. O'Connor Hosp., 1975-79; active campaign Santa Clara City Council, 1980-81. Fellow Irmandade Da Festa Do Espirito Santo (sec. 1974-82, queen 1975-76), Soc. Gastrointestinal Assts., No. Soc. Gastrointestinal Assts., Soc. Espirito Santo of Santa Clara, Luso Am. Fraternal Fedn. (state youth pres. 1979-80, youth leader local coun. Santa Clara Mountain View 1979-87, scholar 1979 founder, organizer Mountain View-Santa Clara chpt. 1980, pres. local region 1980-84, state 20-30 pres. 1984-85, state dir. youth programs 1988-94, state dir. 1991—), mem. Aerobics and Fitness Assn. Am., Am. Coun. on Exercise (cert. aerobics instr. 1991—). Republican. Roman Catholic. Avocations: aerobic dance, weight lifting, reading, piano, sewing, wine tasting. Home: 1618 Roll St Santa Clara CA 95050-4024 Office: South Bay Endoscopy Ctr 455 Oconnor Dr Ste 340 San Jose CA 95128-1644

VIERHELLER, TODD, software engineering consultant; b. Winter Park, Fla., June 22, 1958; s. Irvin Theodore and Jeanne Marie (Zeller) V.; m. Susan Lindhe Watts, Dec. 22, 1984; children: Renate Jeanne, Clark, Lindhe Marie, Kent. BS in Computer Sci., U. Mo., Rolla, 1980; MA in Bibl. Studies, Multnomah Sch. Bible, Portland, Oreg., 1986. Tech. writer, software engr. Tektronix, Beaverton, Oreg., 1981-86, software engring. mgr., 1988-89; software engr., supr. Intel Corp., Hillsboro, Oreg., 1986-88; software engring. mgr. Summation, 1989-90; sr. software cons. Quality First, Lynnwood, Wash., 1990—; software engring. cons. Digital Equipment Corp., Bellevue, Wash., 1990-91, GTE, Bothell, Wash., 1990-91, Frank Russell Co., Tacoma, Wash., 1992-93, InterConnections, Inc., Bellevue, 1993, Novell, San Jose, Calif., 1993, Heartstream, Inc., 1996, N.Am. Morpho Sys., Inc., 1996, Air Touch Cellular, 1996-97; software engring. mgmt. cons. Weyerhauser, Federal Way, Wash., 1991-92, Frank Russell, Tacoma, Wash., 1994, ConnectSoft, Inc., Bellevue, 1994, Microsoft, Redmond, Wash., 1995-96, Nordstrom, Seattle, 1997-98, Ernst & Young, LLP, Seattle, 1998—; tech. writer, cons. Air Touch Cellular, Bellevue, Wash., 1996-97. Mem. IEEE, NRA, Upsilon Pi Epsilon, Kappa Mu Epsilon. Republican. Mem. Evang. Christian Ch. Avocations: camping, bicycling, shooting sports, kung fu. Home: 23617 36th Pl W Brier WA 98036-8411 Office: Quality First PO Box 6212 Lynnwood WA 98036-0212

VIGGAYAN, ROBERTO ALMAZAN, architect; b. Manila; s. Wilfredo Palingayan Viggayan and Honorata Domingo Almazan. BS in Arch., Far Ea. U., Manila, 1968. Registered profl. arch., Philippines, Calif., Hawaii. Prof. Far Ea. U. Inst. Arch. and Fine Arts, Manila, 1971; sr. assoc. dir. design WWAT & G, Inc., Honolulu, 1973-87; dir. design Hemmeter Design Group, Honolulu, 1989-90; dir. comml. design CYP, Inc., Costa Mesa, Calif., 1991-92; pres. Roberto Viggayan & Assocs., Newport Beach, Calif., 1987—; Treas. Constrn. Specification Inst. Project designer The Ritz Carlton Hotel, Laguna Niguel, The Four Seasons Hotel, Newport Beach, The Hilton Tapa Tower Hotel, Waikiki, Hawaii, Hyatt Regency Hotel, Maui, The Keppel Ctr., Philippines. Mem. AIA (corp., mem. com. on hist. preservation, mem. com. on interiors), United Archs. of the Philippines (corp.), Philippine Inst. Archs. (corp.), Oahu Filipino Jaycees, Porsche Club Am., Sports Car Club Am., Sigma Kappa Chi (pres. 1964-68), Sigma Phi Omega. Avocations: sports cars, painting cards, gardening, traveling, animals. Office: Roberto Viggayan & Assocs 2207 Golden Cir Newport Beach CA 92660-3307

VIGIL, DANIEL AGUSTIN, academic administrator; b. Denver, Feb. 13, 1947; s. Agustin and Rachel (Naranjo) V.; m. Claudia Cartier. BA in History, U. Colo., Denver, 1978, JD, 1982. Bar: Colo. 1982, U.S. Dist. Ct. Colo. 1983. Project mgr. Mathematics Policy Rsch., Denver, 1978; law clk. Denver Dist. Ct., 1982-83; ptnr. Vigil and Bley, Denver, 1983-85; asst. dean sch. law U. Colo., Boulder, 1983-89; assoc. dean sch. law U. Colo., 1989—; apptd. by chief justice of Colo. Supreme Ct. to serve on Colo. Supreme Ct. Ad Hoc Com. on miniority participation in legal profession; adj. prof. U. Colo. Sch. Law; bd. dirs. Continuing Legal Edn. in Colo., Inc.; mem. Gov. Colo. Lottery Commn., 1990-97. Editor (newsletter) Class Action, 1987-88; co-editor (ethics com. column) Colo. Lawyer, 1995-97. Bd. dirs. Legal Aid Soc. Met. Denver, 1986—, chmn. bd. dirs., 1998—; past v.p. Colo. Minority Scholarhip Consortium, pres. 1990-91; mem. Task Force on Community Race Rels., Boulder, 1989-94; past mem. jud. nomination rev. com. U.S. Senator Tim Wirth. Mem. Colo. Bar Assn. (mem. legal edn. and admissions com. 1989-94, chmn. 1989-91, bd. govs. 1991, 97—), Hispanic Nat. Bar Assn. (chmn. scholarship com. 1990-95), Colo Hispanic Bar Assn. (bd. dirs. 1985-89, pres. 1990), Denver Bar Assn. (joint com. on minorities in the legal profession), Boulder County Bar Assn. (ex-officio mem., trustee), Phi Delta Phi (faculty sponsor). Roman Catholic. Avocations: skiing, cosmology. Home: 828 3d Ave PO Box 518 Lyons CO 80540-0518 Office: U Colo Sch Law PO Box 401 Boulder CO 80303

VIGIL, M(ARIA) DOLORES, secondary education educator; b. Pecos, N.Mex., Aug. 21, 1941; d. Jose Simon and Valentina (Bowles) V.; m. Robert D. White, Feb. 1, 1969 (div. 1986); children: Robert J., Melissa A., Melanie K.; m. R. Orlando Vigil, June 3, 1995. BA, N.Mex. Highlands U., 1965; MS, Ea. Mich. U., 1977. Cert. tchr., N.Mex. Tchr. Monterey (Calif.) Penninsula Sch. Dist., 1965-69; adult edn. techr. Plymouth (Mich.) Canton Sch. Dist., Mich., 1970-85; tchr. home econs. Archdiocese, Santa Fe, 1985-86; tchr. English Pecos (N.Mex.) Ind. Schs., 1986—; cmty. edn. educator Schoolcraft C.C., Livonia, Mich., 1982-85; ESL instr. Santa Fe C.C., 1996—. Vol. Women's Resource Ctr., Livonia, 1980-85; pres. St. Anthony's Cath. Ch., Pecos, 1990-98, fin. coun., 1990-98, pastoral coun., 1995-98; vol. naming streets and numbering houses for easier UPS delivery and making 911 possible, East Pecos, summer 1997. Mem. Nat. Coun. Tchrs. English, Pecos Am. Fedn. Tchrs. Democrat. Office: Pecos Ind Schs PO Box 368 Pecos NM 87552

VIGIL-GIRON, REBECCA, state official; b. Taos, N.Mex., Sept. 4, 1954; d. Felix W. and Cecilia (Santistevan) Vigil; m. Rick Giron; 1 child, Andrew R. AA in Elem. Edn., N.Mex. Highlands U., 1978, BA in French, 1991. Sec., project monitor, customer svc. rep. Pub. Svc. Co. N.Mex., 1978-86; sec. of state N.Mex., 1987-90, 98—; exec. dir. N.Mex. Commn. Status of Women, 1991; electoral observer UN, Angola, Africa, 1992; electoral observer Internat. Found. Electoral Sys., Dominican Republic, 1994, Equatorial Guinea, Africa, 1996, Washington, 1996; participant AMPART, Mex., 1991. Dem. nominee U.S. Ho. Reps., 1990. Named among 100 MOst Influential Hispanics in Nation, Hispanic Bus. Mag., 1990; recipient Trio Achievers award S.W. Assn. Student Assistance Programs, 1993, Gov.'s award Outstanding N.Mex. Women, 1994. Mem. Albuquerque Hispano C. of C. (membership rep., sr. sales mktg. rep., corp. rels. coord.). Office: Sec State State Capitol Rm 420 Santa Fe NM 87503*

VIGLIONE, EUGENE LAWRENCE, automotive executive; b. Paterson, N.J., Nov. 23, 1931; s. Fred and Caroline (Cantilina) V.; m. Vera Yonkens, June 12, 1954 (div. June 1976), m. Evila (Billie) Larez Viglione, Sept. 19, 1976; children: Victoria, David, Valerie, Vanessa, Francine, Margaret, Robert. Student, Cooper Union, N.Y., 1950-51. Pres. Lahaina News, Ridgewood, N.J., 1995—; sales mgr. Carlton Motors, Frankfurt, Germany, 1966-67, Jones Minto Ford, Burlingame, Calif., 1967-72, Terry Ford, Pompano Beach, Fla., 1974-75; gen. mgr. Kohlenberg Ford, Burlingame, 1975-76; v.p. Morris Landy Ford, Alameda, Calif., 1976-80, Burlingame Ford, 1980-85; emeritus chmn. bd. Valley Isle Motors, Wailuku, Hawaii, 1985—; pres. Marriott Luau, Lahaina, Hawaii, 1989—; gen. mgr., v.p. Jim Falk Lexus of Beverly Hills, 1996—; pres. Maui Auto Dealers Assn., Wailuku, 1986-87, pres. VIG Music C., 1996. Del. Rep. State Conv., Honolulu, 1988, State House of Reps.; 1992; v.p. Rep. Party Precinct, Lahaina, 1988, trustee Rep. Presdl. Task Force, Washington, 1983-88; pres. Maui County Rep. Party, 1983; treas. Beverly Hills Rep. Club, 1998; pres. Big Bros./Big Sisters, 1993; pres. Light Bringers; bd. dirs. Following Maui Symphony, Lahaina Action Com., Maui United Way, Homeless Resource Ctr., Maple Counseling Ctr. Named Top 250 Exec. Hawaii Bus. Mag., 1986-92. Mem. Nat. Auto Dealers Assn., Internat. Auto Dealers Assn., Nat. Fed. of Ind. Bus., Maui Rotary, Lahaina Yacht Club, Maui Country Club, Frairs Club of Calif., Gideons, Maui C. of C., Beverly Hills Rotary Club, Mountain Gate Country Club, Vista Del Mar (bd. mem.). Avocations: sailing, fishing, golf, tennis, flying. Home: 2481 Kaanapali Pky Lahaina HI 96761-1910 Office: Valley Isle Motors 221 S Puunene Ave Kahului HI 96732-2426 also: 9230 Wilshire Blvd Beverly Hills CA 90212-3329

VILARDI, AGNES FRANCINE, real estate broker; b. Monson, Mass., Sept. 29, 1918; d. Paul and Adelina (Mastrioanni) Vetti; m. Frank S. Vilardi, Dec. 2, 1939; children: Valerie, Paul. Cert. of dental assisting Pasadena Jr. Coll., 1934. Lic. real estate broker. Real estate broker, owner Vilardi Realty, Yorba Linda, Calif.; cons. in property mgmt. Mem. Am. Dental Asst. Assn., North Orange County Bd. Realtors (sec./treas. 1972), Yorba Linda Country Club, Desert Princess Country Club. Home and Office: 18982 Villa Ter Yorba Linda CA 92886-2610

VILLARAIGOSA, ANTONIO R., state official; m. Corina; children: Marisela, Prisila, Antonio Jr., Natilia Fe. Mem. assembly State of Calif., 1995, Dem. whip and mem. appropriations and budget coms., majority leader, 1997; speaker Calif. State Assembly, 1998. Mem. Greater Eastside Voter Registration and Edn. Project, Jobs with Peace, LAUSD Mex. Am. Edn. Commn., L.A. Ctr. for Law and Justice. Office: Calif Assembly PO Box 942849 Rm 219 Sacramento CA 94249-0001 also: 1910 W Sunset Blvd Ste 500 Los Angeles CA 90026*

VILLARREAL, SHARON MARIE, elementary education educator; b. Ventura, Calif., Mar. 26, 1961; d. José G. and Sharon N. (Kay) V.; 1 child, Elizabeth Maribel. BA in Spanish, U. Calif., Davis, 1985; bilingual cert. competence in Spanish, Calif. State U., Dominguez Hills, 1988, multiple subject tchg. credential, 1993. Cert. multiple subject tchr. with bilingual emphasis, Calif. Tchr. Nevin Avenue Elem. Sch., L.A. Unified Sch. Dist., 1985—, bilingual coord., 1989-93, mem. sch. leadership coun., 1991. Mem. Booster Club, St. Andrew Sch., Pasadena, Calif., 1993—; tchr. religious edn. St. Andrew Parish, 1994—. Mem. NEA, Am. Fedn. Tchrs., Union Tchrs. L.A., Calif. Aggie Alumni Assn. Democrat. Avocations: camping, basketball, Spanish literature, volleyball, poetry. Office: Nevin Avenue Elem Sch 1569 E 32nd St Los Angeles CA 90011-2213

VILNROTTER, VICTOR ALPÁR, research engineer; b. Kunhegyes, Hungary, Nov. 8, 1944; came to U.S., 1957; s. Nicholas and Aranka (Vidovits) V.; m. Felicia D'Auria, Jan. 20, 1974; children: Katherine, Brian. BSEE, NYU, 1971; MS, MIT, 1974; PhD in EE, U. So. Calif., L.A., 1978. Teaching asst. MIT, Cambridge, Mass., 1972-74; rsch. engr. Jet Propulsion Lab., Pasadena, Calif., 1979—. Contbr. articles to profl. jours.; patentee in field. Mem. IEEE (referee in communications soc. 1980—), N.Y. Acad. Scis., Sigma Xi, Eta Kappa Nu. Achievements include development and demonstration of real-time array-feed antenna compensation system for future deep-space missions; development of robust receiver structures for autonomous monitoring of spacecraft beacon signals; development of optimum frequency estimators for use during high-dynamic spacecraft maneuvers such as orbit-insertion, and development of optimum receivers for tracking and detecting very weak signals from deep space. Avocations: astronomy, chess, hiking, backpacking, music. Home: 1334 Greenbriar Rd Glendale CA 91207-1254

VINCENT, DAVID RIDGELY, management consulting executive; b. Detroit, Aug. 9, 1941; s. Charles Ridgely and Charlotte Jane (McCarroll) V.; m. Margaret Helen Anderson, Aug. 25, 1962 (div. 1973); children: Sandra Lee, Cheryl Ann; m. Judith Ann Gomez, July 2, 1978; 1 child, Amber; stepchildren: Michael Jr., Jesse Joseph Flores (dec.). BS, BA, Calif. State U.-Sacramento, 1964; MBA, Calif. State U.-Hayward, 1971; PhD Somerset U, 1991. Cert. profl. cons. to mgmt., 1994. Sr. ops. analyst Aerojet Gen. Corp., Sacramento, 1960-66; contr. Hexcel Corp., Dublin, Calif., 1966-70; mng. dir. Memorex, Austria, 1970-74; sales mgr. Ampex World Ops., Switzerland, 1974-76; dir. product mgmt. NCR, Sunnyvale, Calif., 1976-79; v.p. Boole & Babbage Inc., gen. mgr. Inst. Info. Mgmt., Sunnyvale, Calif., 1979-85; pres., CEO The Info. Group, Inc., Santa Clara, Calif., 1985—. USSF soccer referee emeritus. Author: Perspectives in Information Management, Information Economics, 1983, Handbook of Information Resource Management, 1987, The Information-Based Corporation: stakeholder economics and the technology investment, 1990, Reengineering Fundamentals: Business Processes and the Global Economy, 1994-96; contbr. monographs and papers to profl. jours. Mem. Nat. Alliance Bus. Economists, Am. Electronics Assn., Soc. Competitive Intelligence Profls., World Future Soc., Inst. Mgmt. Cons. Home: 2803 Kalliam Dr Santa Clara CA 95051-6838 Office: PO Box Q Santa Clara CA 95055-3756

VINCENT, STEVE, environmental engineer; b. 1951. BS in Oceanography, U. Wash., 1974. With Weyerhaeuser, Tacoma, 1974-85; with Columbia Analytical Svc., Kelso, Wash., 1986—, now pres. Office: Columbia Analytical Svc 1317 S 13th Ave Kelso WA 98626-2845*

VINCENT, VERNE SAINT, protective services official. Chief police Aurora (Colo.) Police Dept., 1995—. Office: Aurora Police Dept 15001 E Alameda Dr Aurora CO 80012-1546*

VINES, CONNIE, writer; b. Panama City, Fla.; d. Charles Evan and Virginia Lee (Wolford) Misso; m. Jimmie M. Vines, July 27, 1975; children: Aaron Michael, Corey Mathew. contest judge nat. br. Romance Writers of Am., 1990-98. Author: (novels) Rachel and the Texan, 1998, Whisper Upon the Water. Contest judge Outreach Internat., 1996-97; bd. sec. Title IX Indian Edn., San Bernardino, Calif., 1995, 98; pres. PTA, Ontario, Calif., 1986-88, sec., 1984-86. Recipient 1st place award of excellence, Outreach Internat., 1997, 2nd place Tara Romance Writers, 1998, Rocky Mountain Fiction Writers, 1993, Va. Romance Writers Assn., 1991, others. Mem. Young Adult Writer's Network (bd. sec. 1996—), Romance Writers of Am., Pomona Valley Writers Assn. (sec. 1986-89), Mystery and Suspense Writers, Fantasy, Futuristic, Paranormal Writers Assn. Republican. Home: PO Box 1035 Guasti CA 91743-1035

VINES, HIGH, JR., minister, educator; b. Texarkana, Tex., Jan. 12, 1930; s. High Sr. and Pinkie (Keeling) V.; m. Greta Myra Thomptson, July 7, 1969; children: Richard, Michelle, Reginald, Deirdre, Greta, Marla. AA, Ventura Coll., 1951; BA in Bible, Talist Theol. Sem., 1958, BD, 1961, ThM, 1978; DLitt, Caleb Sch. Theology, 1998. Pastor Bapt. Ch., L.A., 1956-62; pres., Bible instr. Bible Tng. Sch., L.A., 1963-65; owner hardware and paint retail store, Compton, Calif., 1970-74; pres., instr. Caleb Sch. Theology, Compton, 1982—. Author: Two Kinds of Pastors, 1990, My Enemy is My Best Friend, 1992, The Gambling Preachers, 1995; prodr. Look and Live cable broadcast, 1990—. Pres. Citizens Against Corruption on Govt., Compton, 1996—. With USN, 1951-55. Recipient Prodr. of Yr. award Cable Access, 1992, Access CATV award, 1996, 50 Yrs. in Ministry award Evangelistic Brotherhood, Inc., 1998. Mem. NAACP. Democrat. Avocations: chess, reading, camping, travel. Home and Office: 12628 S Halo Dr Compton CA 90221-1829

VINTON, ALICE HELEN, real estate company executive; b. McMinnville, Oreg., Jan. 10, 1942; d. Gale B. and Saima Helen (Pekkola) V. Student, Portland State Coll., Northwestern Sch. Commerce. Lic. real estate broker, Hawaii. In real estate, 1976—; owner, prin. broker Vinton Realty, Honolulu, 1976—. Founder, bd. dirs. Kekuaanaui, Hawaii Big Sisters, 1972-76; former vol. Child and Family Svc., women's divsn. Halawa Prison; bd. dirs. Kindergarten and Children's Aid Assn., 1977-88, advisor, mem. long-range planning com. 1988-90; former mem. tuition aid com., chmn. nominating com. and capital improvements com. Laura Morgan Pre-Sch.; bd. dirs. Hawaii Theatre Ctr., 1985-86; mem. Lyon Arboretum Assn. Recipient proclamation Hawaii Ho. of Reps., cert. of merit for disting. svc. to community, Dictionary of Internat. Biography, Vol. XXI, 1990. Mem. Nat. Assn. Realtors, Hawaii Assn. Realtors, Honolulu Bd. Realtors, Honolulu C. of C., Acad. Arts, Bishop Mus. Assn., Wildlife Fedn., Honolulu, Friends of Iolani Palace, Smithsonian Inst., Honolulu Press Club (membership chmn. 1988-90), Rainbow Girls Club (life), Hawaii Humane Soc., Sierra Club, Hist. Hawaii, Cen. Bus. Club Honolulu, Nature Conservancy Hawaii, YWCA, Coustea Soc., Wolf Haven, Honolulu Polo Club, Orchid Soc. Manoa, North Shore Animal League, Nat. Pks. and Conservation Assn., Wilderness Soc. Republican. Episcopalian. Avocations: music, art, animals, crafts, history. Office: Vinton Realty 49 S Hotel St Ste 306 Honolulu HI 96813-3143

VIOLET, WOODROW WILSON, JR., retired chiropractor; b. Columbus, Ohio, Sept. 19, 1937; s. Woodrow Wilson and Alice Katherine (Woods) V.; student Ventura Coll., 1961-62; grad. L.A. Coll. Chiropractic, 1966; m. Judith Jane Thatcher, June 15, 1963; children: Woodina Lonize, Leslie Alice. Pvt. practice chiropractic medicine, Santa Barbara, Calif., 1966-73, London, 1973-74, Carpinteria, Calif., 1974-84; past mem. coun. roentgenology Am. Chiropractic Assn. Former mem. Parker Chiropractic Rsch. Found., Ft. Worth. With USAF, 1955-63. Recipient award merit Calif. Chiropractic Colls., Inc., 1975, cert. of appreciation Nat. Chiropractic Antitrust Com. 1977. Mem. Nat. [illegible] Soc., Delta Sigma. Patentee surg. instrument. Home: 210 N Mall Dr Unit 140 Saint George UT 84790-1477

VIOLETTE, GLENN PHILLIP, construction engineer; b. Hartford, Conn., Nov. 15, 1950; s. Reginald Joseph and Marielle Theresa (Bernier) B.; m.

Susan Linda Begam, May 15, 1988. BSCE, Colo. State U., 1982. Registered profl. engr., Colo. Engring. aide Colo. State Hwy. Dept., Glenwood Springs, Colo., 1974-79, hwy. engr., 1980-82; hwy. engr. Colo. State Hwy. Dept., Loveland, Colo., 1979-80; project engr. Colo. State Hwy. Dept., Glenwood Canyon, Colo., 1983-97; resident engr. Colo. State Dept. Transp., Craig, 1998—; guest speaker in field. Contbg. editor, author, photographer publs. in field. Recipient scholarship Fed. Hwy Adminstrn., 1978. Mem. ASCE, Amnesty Internat., Nat. Rifle Assn., Siera Club, Audubon Soc., Nature Conservancy, World Wildlife Fund, Cousteau Soc., Chi Epsilon. Office: Colo Dept Transp 270 Ranney St Craig CO 81625-2840

VISCO, FRANK JOSEPH, biology educator, consultant; b. Burbank, Calif., Nov. 23, 1944; s. Louie Visco and Phyllis Rosemarie (Borgia) Grimes; m. Jaqueline Marie (Weiand) Gray, May 27, 1967 (div.); children: Lisa Marie, Michelle Marie; m. Kim Kelly, Sept. 10, 1988. BA, Calif. State U., L.A., 1967, MA, 1968; std. tchg. credential, Calif. Bd. Edn., 1968. Prof. biology Orange Coast Coll., Costa Mesa, Calif., 1968—, chair dept. biology, 1977-97; environ. cons. The Benz Group, Pasadena, Calif., 1972—; v.p. FLD, Inc., Pasadena, 1991—; tech. sci. cons. Soil Wash Technologies, Inc., San Diego, 1992—; fin. advisor Geminia Plastic Enterprises, Inc., Maywood, Calif., 1996—; CFO, Customized Box Co., San Fernando, Calif., 1997—. Contbr. articles to sci. publs. Founder Orange Coast Coll. Recyling Ctr., 1969. Grantee NSF, 1979. Roman Catholic. Avocations: volleyball, music, theater. Office: Orange Coast Coll 2701 Fairview Rd Costa Mesa CA 92626-5563

VISCO, KIM KELLY, biologist, educator, financial consultant; b. L.I., N.Y., Feb. 15, 1965; d. Francis John and Elizabeth Veronica (Gambino) Kelly; m. Frank Joseph Visco, Sept. 10, 1988; stepchildren: Lisa Marie, Michelle Marie. AA, Orange Coast Coll., 1983; BA, Calif. State U., 1988. Cert. Calif. C.C. life. Sec.-treas. ALWS, Inc., Stanton, Calif., 1987-93; instr. biology Orange Coast Coll., Costa Mesa, Calif., 1988—; lab. dir. Benz/Gabbita Cons., Westminster, Calif., 1989-91; environ. cons. Benz Group, Pasadena, Calif., 1991—; fin. cons. FLD Corp., Pasadena, 1995—; fin. advisor Gemini Plastics Enterprises, Inc., Maywood, Calif., 1996—; bd. dirs. The Customized Box Co., San Fernando, Calif. Editor, contbr.: Biology 100 Lab Manual, 1995, Biology 181 Lab Manual, 1996; cons., contbr. (video) Soil Wash Technologies, 1996; patentee in field. Republican. Roman Catholic. Avocations: theatre, music, volleyball, skiing, physical fitness. Home: 21171 Amberwick Ln Huntington Beach CA 92646-7309 Office: Orange Coast Coll 2701 Fairview Rd Costa Mesa CA 92626-5563

VISCONTI-TILLEY, VICKI LORRAINE, illustrator; b. Gallup, N.Mex., Apr. 17, 1956; d. Ronald G. and Charlene (Slaughter) W.; m. William W. Gilland, May 17, 1975 (div. Mar. 1985); 1 child, Shannon Michelle; m. Russell Ray Tilley, Aug. 31, 1985. Cert., Al Collins Graphic Sch. Design, 1987; student, Western N.Mex. U., 1988-96. Illustrator Maiden Silver Art Studio, Silver City, N.Mex., 1988—; tchr. art Silver Consol. Schs., Silver City, 1994-99; founding mem., artist Yankie Creek Coop. Gallery, Silver City, 1994-95; graphic designer TotalGraphix, Silver City, 1987-92; designer, juror Winter Arts Festival, Silver City, 1991; designer Mimbres Region Arts Coun., Silver City, 1990-92; owner Maiden Silver Art Gallery, 1992—; cons., tchr. art Re-Learning N.Mex., 1996; art workshop dir. Silver Consolidated Schs. grant program, Silver City, 1998. Illustrator: Creative Colored Pencil-Rockport, 1995, Fractures In Rhyme, 1997, (CD ROM) Atlantis to the Stars and Dragons and Dinosaurs, 1996-97, Urth (CD-ROM RPG) Dragon Multimedia, 1997, In Oceans of Color (semifinalist L. Ron Hubbard's Illustrator of Future, 1998), A Child's Garden, 1999, From the Gilded Quill, 1999; included in American Artist's, An Illustrated Survey, 1990. Mem. Pandora's Mgmt. Sys., Houston, 1997—, agent 1997—; founding mem. Art Against AIDS, 1998—. Avocations: travel, renaissance fairs. Home: PO Box 1475 Silver City NM 88062-1475 Office: c/o PMS Prodns PO Box 800212 Houston TX 77280-0212

VISGATIS, CHARLES ANTHONY, artist, gallery director; b. Chgo., June 14, 1930; s. Anton and Pauline Visgatis; m. Geraldine Visgatis, Mar. 27, 1954; 1 child, Brad Lee. BA, Art Inst. Chgo., 1957; MA, Northwestern U., 1963; EdD, U. Oreg., 1977. Dist. art supr., tchr. Sch. Dist. 110, Deerfield, Ill., 1956-64; art instr. h.s. Sch. Dist. 113, Highland Park, Ill., 1964-68; coord. art edn., asst prof. art Oreg. State U., Corvallis, 1969-76; art educator Calif. State U., Long Beach, 1977-81; dir., artist Tambra Gallery, Salem, Oreg., 1994—. Recipient 1st pl. award for mixed media All Oreg. Art Ann., 1991, Corvallis Art Ctr., 1975. Office: Tambra Gallery 222 Commercial St NE Salem OR 97301-3410

VISSCHER, BARBARA RUTH, epidemiologist, researcher; b. Memphis, Jan. 23, 1927; d. Maurice B. and Gertrude (Pieters) V.; m. Fredrick H. Kahn, Feb. 14, 1952; children: Susan, Kathryn, William. BA, U. Minn., 1947, MD, 1951; MPH, UCLA, 1968, PhD, 1973. Intern San Francisco Hosp., 1951-52; asst. prof. UCLA Sch. Pub. Health, 1974-80, assoc. prof., 1980-86, prof., 1986-94, prof. emeritus, 1994—; mem. rsch. review com. NIH, 1986-90; mem. sci. adv. bd. Am. Found. AIDS Rsch., 1990—. Reviewer sci. jours.; contbr. over 90 articles to profl. jours. Fellow Am. Coll. Epidemiology; mem. APHA, Soc. Epidemiologic Rsch., Am. Epidemiol. Soc., Internat. Epidemiol. Assn., Phi Beta Kappa, Alpha Omega Alpha, Delta Omega. Democrat. Unitarian. Office: UCLA Sch Pub Health Los Angeles CA 90095

VITRAC, JEAN-JACQUES CHARLES, international business consultant; b. Paris, May 31, 1942; came to U.S., 1972; s. Jean Bernard Vitrac and Paulette Aimée (Buisson) Mannerheim; m. Roswitha Kahling, Sept. 11, 1965; children: Emmanuel, François, Catherine. *Vitrac's mother, a widow, was married in 1964 to Carl Eric Mannerheim, the nephew of Carl Gustav Mannerheim, President of Finland (1944-46), also known as "The Liberator of Finland" for successfully resisting the Soviet aggression against his country. Vitrac's family is deeply rooted in eight countries, including the United States.* Diploma, Faculty of Law, Aix, France, 1963; post grad. in mktg., Institut National Du Marketing, Paris, 1972; post grad. in econ. scis., Institut Superieur Sciences Economiques, Paris, 1979. Devel. officer Europe-Africa Internat. Jaycees, Geneva, 1968-70; dir. econ. affairs Internat. Jaycees, Coral Gables, Fla., 1970-72; mktg. cons. Bernard Krief Internat., Paris, 1973-79; strategy cons. Euro-PacRim Internat., Walnut Creek, Calif., 1980—; chair task force on multinat. strategies Ctrl. Bank of France, Paris, 1974-78; mktg. cons. Aérospatiale, Paris, 1978; bd. dirs. Capsule Française Inc., Napa, Calif.; asst. prof. mktg. Inst. Français de Gestion, Paris, 1973-79; U.S. chmn. L'Entreprise Demain, Brussels, 1982-98; no. Calif. chmn. World Tech. Execs. Network, 1987-90. *Since 1972, Mr. Vitrac has worked with government and business leaders, to improve economic development and job creations in Africa, Latin America, California and France. As a strategic consultant for a number of politicians and regions worldwide, his effort resulted in major economic improvements. In 1989, he organized a tele-video conference on global economy between California, Belgium, and France, which resulted in new business ventures. He also led a number of trade missions for new technologies between California and France. More recently, he formed with a select group of leading California economic experts, a permanent task force to promote economic development, competitiveness and business incubators worldwide.* Author: Discover Export, 1974; co-author: Doing Business in California, 1989; editor World Tech. Execs. Network Review, 1989-90. Mem. E. Bay Internat. Trade Coun., 1996-97; chair parish coun. St. Patrick's Ch., 1998. Named knight Equestrian Order of Holy Sepulchre of Jerusalem. Mem. KC (dep. grand knight 1998), Am. Assn. Polit. Cons., Art Ranaissance Found. (hon., chair Calif. chpt. 1994—), Classical Philharmonic (v.p. 1995-96), Cal-France Coun. (v.p. 1996-97), Kiwanis Internat (gov.'s cabinet, dir. com. svc. 1996-97), French War Vets. (No. Calif. chpt. pres. 1996-97), Napa Kiwanis Club (disting. pres. 1993). Republican. Roman Catholic. Home: Becket's Ranch PO Box 467 Valley Springs CA 95252 Office: Euro PacRim Int Corp 2173 Hwy 12 East PO Box 1418 Valley Springs CA 95252

VITTI, GARY JOHN, athletic trainer, business owner; b. Stamford, Conn., Apr. 17, 1954; s. Mario Olindo and Sylvia Blanch (Conetta) V.; m. Christine Jane Mohrlock, Sept. 19, 1981; children: Rachel, Emelia. BA, So. Conn. State U., 1976; MS, U. Utah, 1982. Cert. athletic trainer. Sales & customer rels. rep. H.R.M., N.Y.C., 1976-77; sales & mktg. rep. Calderon, N.Y.C., 1977-78, Johnson and Johnson, Milltown, N.J., 1978-79; athletic trainer U. Utah, Salt Lake City, 1980-82, instr. dept. phys. edn., 1981-82; athletic trainer, cons. Snowbird (Utah) Ski Resort, 1981-82; asst. athletic trainer Utah Jazz, NBA, Salt Lake City, 1981-82; head athletic trainer athletic dept. U. Portland, Oreg., 1982-84; head athletic trainer L.A. Lakers, NBA, 1984—; owner R.E. Techs.; adj. asst. instr. edn. dept. U. Portland, 1982-84; cons. Pro Health, Phoenix, 1990—; bd. advisors Pro Heat, Phoenix, 1990—; invited speaker, lectr. Contbr. over 30 articles to profl. jours.; author video on tng. techniques for profl. basketball players. Consiglieri Onorario Orgn. Italian Trainers, Forli, Italy, 1992—. Mem. Am. Coll. Sports Medicine, Nat. Athletic Trainers' Assn., Nat. Basketball Trainers' Assn. (Trainer of Yr. award 1991-92), Calif. Athletic Trainers' Assn. Avocations: collecting jazz & classical music, jogging, strength training, studying Italian. Office: LA Lakers PO Box 10 Inglewood CA 90306-0010

VIVIAN, LINDA BRADT, sales and public relations executive; b. Elmira, N.Y., Nov. 22, 1945; d. Lorenz Claude and Muriel (Dolan) Bradt; m. Robert W. Vivian, Apr. 5, 1968 (div. Sept. 1977). Student, Andrews U., 1963-66. Adminstrv. asst. Star-Gazette, Elmira, 1966-68; editor Guide, staff writer Palm Springs (Calif.) Life mag., 1970-75; dir. sales and mktg. Palm Springs Aerial Tramway, 1975-97; domestic tourism mgr. Palm Springs Desert Resorts, Rancho Mirage, Calif., 1998—; sec. Hospitality and Bus. Industry Coun. Palm Springs Desert Resorts, 1989-91, 1997, vice-chmn. 1991-94, chmn., 1994-95. Mem. Hotel Sales and Mktg. Assn. (allied nominating chmn. Palm Springs chpt. 1986-88), Am. Soc. Assn. Execs., Travel Industry Assn., Hospitality Industry and Bus. Coun. of Palm Springs Resorts (sec. 1989-91, vice-chmn. 1991-94, chmn. 1994-95), Nat. Tour Assn. (co-chair Team Calif. promotions com. 1993-97), Calif. Travel Industry Assn., Hospitality Bus. Industry Coun., Palm Springs C. of C. (bd. dirs. 1984-85). Republican. Avocations: golf, reading. Office: Palm Springs Deserts Resorts CVB 69-930 Hwy 111 # 201 Rancho Mirage CA 92270

VLASAK, WALTER RAYMOND, state official, management development consultant; b. Hartsgrove, Ohio, Aug. 31, 1938; s. Raymond Frank and Ethel (Chilan) V.; m. Julia Andrews, Feb. 25, 1966; children: Marc Andrew, Tanya Ethel. BSBA, Kent State U., 1963; MA, U. Akron, 1975. Commd. 2d lt. U.S. Army, 1963; platoon leader, anti-tank platoon leader and battalion adjutant 82d Airborne Div., 1963-65; combat duty Viet Nam, 1965-66, 68-69; exec. officer, co. comdr. and hdqrs. commandant of the cadre and troops U.S. Army Sch. Europe, Oberammergau, Fed. Republic Germany, 1966-68; asst. prof. Mil. Sci. Kent (Ohio) State U., 1970-74; infantry battalion exec. officer 9th Infantry Div., Ft. Lewis, Wash., 1976-77, orgnl. effectiveness cons. to commanding gen., 1977-79, brigade exec. officer, 1980-82; orgnl. effectiveness cons. to commanding gen. 8th U.S. Army, U.S. Forces, Korea, 1979-80; advanced through ranks to lt. col. U.S. Army, 1980, ret., 1984; pres. Comsult, Inc., Tacoma, 1984—; mgr. employee devel. tng. dept. social and health svcs. State of Wash., Tacoma, 1985—. Decorated Legion of Merit, Bronze Star with V device and two oak leaf clusters, Air medal, Purple Heart, Vietnamese Cross of Gallantry with Silver Star. Mem. Am. Soc. for Tng. and Devel., Assn. U.S. Army (bd. dirs. Tacoma 1984—). Avocations: hiking, camping, fishing. Home: 10602 Hill Terrace Rd SW Tacoma WA 98498-4337 Office: State of Wash Dept Social and Health Svcs 8425 27th St W Tacoma WA 98466-2722

VO, HUU DINH, pediatrician, educator; b. Hue, Vietnam, Apr. 29, 1950; came to U.S., 1975; s. Chanh Dinh and Dong Thi (Pham) V.; m. Que Phuong Tonnu, Mar. 22, 1984; children: Katherine Hoa-An, Karyn Bao-An. MD, U. Saigon, 1975. Diplomate Am. Bd. Pediat. Adminstr. bilingual vocat. tng. Cmty. Care and Devel. Svc., L.A., 1976-77; resident in pediat. Univ. Hosp., Jacksonville, Fla., 1977-80; physician, surgeon, chief med. officer Lanterman Devel. Ctr., Pomona, Calif., 1980-92, chief med. staff, 1984-88, coord. med. ancillary svc., 1984-88, 91—; physician Pomona Valley Cmty. Hosp., 1988-90; asst. clin. prof. Loma Linda (Calif.) Med. Sch., 1985-92; chief med. officer So. Reception Ctr. and Clinic., Norwalk, Calif., 1992—; bd. dirs. Pomona Med. Clinic Inc. Radio talk show host (weekly), 1997—. Pres. Vietnamese Cmty. Ponoma Valley, 1983-85, 87-95, chmn., 1993-95; nat. co-chair mem. Vietnamese Am. Cmty. in U.S.A., 1993-95, chmn., bd. comptrollers, 1998—; bd. dirs. YMCA, Pomona, 1988-92, Sch.-Cmty. Partnership, Ponoma, 1988-92, ARC. Mem. AMA (Physician recognition award 1989, 1992, 98), L.A. Pediat. Soc., Vietnamese-Am. Physicians Assn. La. and Orange County (founding mem., sec. 1982-84, bd. dirs. 1987-90). Republican. Buddhist. Avocations: tennis, soccer, reading, singing, music. Home: 1074 S Rexford Ln Anaheim CA 92808 Home: 13200 Bloomfield Ave Norwalk CA 90650-3253 Office: Pomona Med Clinic 1182 E 40th Ave Pomona CA 91767

VOBEJDA, WILLIAM FRANK, aerospace engineer; b. Lodgepole, S.D., Dec. 5, 1918; s. Robert and Lydia (Stefek) V.; m. Virginia Parker, Oct. 24, 1942; children—William N., Margaret, Mary Joan, Barbara, Lori. B.C.E., S.D. Sch. Mines and Tech., 1942. Registered profl. engr., Colo. Stress analyst Curtiss Wright Corp., Columbus, Ohio, 1942-45; civil/hydraulic engr. Bur. Reclamation, Denver, 1945-54; mech. supr. Stearns Roger Corp., Denver, 1954-62; mgr. Martin Marietta Corp., Denver, 1962-86, mgr. engring. M-X Program, 1978-86; pres. BV Engring., Inc., Englewood, Colo., 1986-89. Active Boy Scouts Am. Recipient Silver Beaver award. Mem. Englewood City Council 1984-87, Englewood Water and Sewer Bd., 1990—. Mem. AIAA. Democrat. Roman Catholic. Clubs: St. Louis Men's, K.C., Martin Marietta Chess, Lions Internat. (sec.).

VODOPEST, EDWARD L., mechanical engineer; b. Kansas City, Kans., Aug. 29, 1949; s. Edward Frank and Peggy Joyce (Nuzum) V.; m. Judith Kay Ross, June 24, 1972; children: Mark Edward, Sarah Diane. BSME, Kans. State U., 1972; MBA, Wash. State U., 1997. Control sys. engr. Black & Veatch, Kansas City, Mo., 1972-81; instrument/control engr. Brown & Root, San Ramon, Calif., 1981-83; sr. prin. control sys. engr. ICF Kaiser Hanford/Kaiser Engrs. Hanford, Richland, Wash., 1983-96; sr. design engr. Fluor Daniel N.W., Richland, 1996—. Mem. ASME, IEEE, ISA, Internat. Soc. for Measurement and Control (exec. bd. 1996—). Avocations: snow skiing, soccer refereeing and coaching. Home: 8929 Millstone Dr Lenexa KS 66220-2553 Office: Fluor Daniel Northwest PO Box 1050 Richland WA 99352-1050

VOELKER, MARGARET IRENE (MEG VOELKER), gerontology, medical, surgical nurse; b. Bitburg, Germany, Dec. 31, 1955; d. Lewis R. and Patricia Irene (Schaffner) Miller; 1 child, Christopher Douglas. Diploma, Clover Park Vocat.-Tech., Tacoma, Wash., 1975, diploma in practical nursing, 1984; ASN, Tacoma C.C., 1988; postgrad., U. Wash., Tacoma, 1992-95. Cert. ACLS. Nursing asst. Jackson County Hosp., Altus, Okla., 1976-77; receptionist Western Clinic, Tacoma, 1983; LPN, Tacoma Gen. Hosp., 1984-88, clin. geriatric nurse, 1988-90, clin. nurse post anesthesia care unit perioperative svcs., 1990—; pre-admit clinic nurse, 1995-97; mem. staff nurse coun. Tacoma Gen. Hosp., 1990-91, procedural sedation nurse, 1996—. Editor NPANA newsletter, 1998—. Recipient G. Corydon Wagner endowment fund scholarship. Mem. Am. Soc. PostAnesthesia Nurses, N.W. PostAnesthesia Nurses Assn., Phi Theta Kappa, Sigma Theta Tau.

VOGEL, NADINE ORSOFF, foundation executive; b. Bronx, N.Y., Oct. 21, 1963; d. Eli H. and Phyllis S. (Landskroner) Orsoff; m. Douglas Albert Vogel, June 15, 1985; 1 child, Gretchen Ashley. Student, U. South Fla., 1981-83; BS, Coll. of Charleston, 1985; MBA, Golden Gate U., 1987. Account rep., asst. mgr. Met Life, L.A., 1987-89, br. agy. mgr., 1989-93, account exec., 1993—; pres., founder, exec. dir. Spl. Needs Advocate for Parents, L.A., mem3—; instr. Life Underwriter Tng. Coun., Monterey, Calif., 1988-89; spkr. on spl. needs to numerous orgns., 1993—. Author: Special Needs Planning, The Process, 1996. Fin. Liason Lea Baeck Temple FYC Com., Belair, Calif., 1994-96; creator, bd. dirs. Spl. Needs Awareness Day, Beverly Hills, Calif., 1994; v.p. Good Beginnings neonatal ICU Cedars Sinai Med. Ctr., 1993-96; mem. adv. bd. Computer Access Ctr., 1994-95; mem. region C planning bd. L.A. Unified Sch. Dist., 1994; bd. dirs. Westside Coastal Early Start Joung Coun., 1993-95, Profl. Women's Network, Monterey, 1987-90. Recipient Vol. award Cedars Sinai Med. Ctr., 1994. Mem. Nat. Assn. Life Underwriters (v.p. 1988-93, 93-96, Achievement award 1988, 89, 94, 95, Agt. of Yr. award 1988, 89), Nat. Orgn. Rare Disorders, Calif. Perinatal Assn. (mem. coun., bd. dirs. 1994-96), Nat. Assn. Security Dealers, Million Dollar Round Table (mem. conf. com. 1989, 96, 97, 98), Parent Care, Bus. and Profl. Women's Assn. (bd. dirs. 1987-90, Outstanding Young Profl. Woman of Yr. award 1988, 89). Avocations: piano, guitar, swimming, working out.

VOGEL, RICHARD WIEDEMANN, business owner, ichthyodynamicist, educator; b. N.Y.C., Apr. 12, 1950; s. Jack and Edna Jeanne (Wiedemann) V.; m. Pamela Jane Gordon, Aug. 7, 1974; children: Amy Jane, Katy Lynn, Gina Marie, Krista Jeanne. Postgrad. Owner, operator ichthyol. rsch. and comml. fishing vessel Santa Barbara, Calif., 1973-88; designer advanced hydrodynamic curvature Clark Foam Factory, Laguna Beach, Calif., 1994—; lectr. Surfrider Found. Conf., U. Calif., San Diego, 1994. Inventor in field. Episcopalian. Avocations: music, athletic tng. and fitness. Office: Ichthyodynamics PO Box 1167 Hanalei HI 96714-1167

VOGET, JANE J., city official, lawyer; b. Montréal, Que., Can., Jan. 2, 1949; d. Frederick Wilhelm and Mary Kay (Mee) V. BA in German and Anthropology, So. Ill. U., 1971, MS in Planning and Cmty. Devel., 1977; JD, Lewis and Clark Coll., 1990. Bar: Wash. 1991. Program mgr. Ill. Dept. Local Govt. Affairs, Springfield, 1975-78, U.S. Dept. Housing and Urban Devel., Washington, 1978; mem. staff The White House, Office Asst. to Pres. for Intergovtl. Affairs, Washington, 1979-80; housing project mgr. Multnomah County, Portland, Oreg., 1985-88; sr. project mgr. City of Seattle, 1989—; pvt. practice, Seattle, 1991—. Author, co-author govtl. publs. Vol. lawyer West Seattle Legal Clinic, 1994—, Na Hanu 'O ku'ulei Aloha, 1996—. Mem. ABA (mem. affordable housing fin. com. 1991-96), Wash. State Bar Assn. (real property probate and trust sect.), King County Bar Assn. (Housing Justice Project atty.), Orca Alliance (bd. dirs.). Avocations: swimming, Hawaiian music and dance, animal rights advocate. Office: 500 Union # 450 Seattle WA 98101 Office: City of Seattle 618 2nd Ave Seattle WA 98104-2222 also: 500 Union Ste 450 Seattle WA 98101

VOGT, EVON ZARTMAN, III (TERRY VOGT), merchant banker; b. Chgo., Aug. 29, 1946; s. Evon Zartman Jr. and Catherine C. (Hiller) V.; m. Mary Hewit Anschuetz, Sept. 26, 1970; 1 child, Elizabeth Christine. AB, Harvard U., 1968; MBA, U. Colo., 1976. Vol., then staff mem. U.S. Peace Corps., Brazil, 1968-72; v.p. Wells Fargo Bank, Sao Paulo, Brazil, 1977-81; mng. dir. Wells Fargo Internat. Ltd., Grand Cayman, 1982-84; mgr. global funding Wells Fargo Bank, San Francisco, 1984-86; pres. ARBI Transnational, Inc., San Francisco, 1986—; also bd. dirs. Arbi Transnational, Inc., San Francisco; bd. dirs. Magtech Ammunition Co., Inc., Las Vegas, 1990—. Bd. dirs. Internat. Diplomacy Coun., San Francisco, 1990-98, pres. 1995-97; active No. Calif. C.A.R.E. Found., 1993-95, The Mex. Mus., 1994-96; bd. dirs. World Affairs Coun. of No. Calif., 1996—. Recipient Order of Rio Branco, Brazilian Govt., 1996. Mem. Brazil Soc. No. Calif. (pres. 1989-94), Pan Am. Soc. Calif. (bd. dirs., pres. 1991-94), World Affairs Coun. No. Calif. (bd. dirs.). Office: ARBI Transnational Inc 601 California St San Francisco CA 94108-2805

VOGT, HUGH FREDERICK, minister, college administrator; b. Aberdeen, Sask., Can., Mar. 30, 1916; came to U.S., 1938; s. Harry F. and Queena Elva (Morrison) V.; divorced; children: Heather, Keren, Barbara; m. Kathleen Josephine D'Angelo, Oct. 21, 1983; children: Gregg, Steven, Scott, Michael. BA, Pasadena Coll., 1944; MA, U. Calif., L.A., 1958; DD (hon.), Ernest Holmes Coll., L.A., 1980; D of Religious Sci. (hon.), Ernest Holmes Coll., 1985. Ordained to ministry Ch. of the Nazarene, 1945. Min. Ch. of the Nazarene, Oroville, Calif., 1944-45, Pomeroy, Wash., 1945-48, Richland, Wash., 1948-51, Vancouver, Wash., 1951-56; min. Mile Hi Ch. of Religious Sci., Denver, 1966—; tchr. homiletics and ch. adminstrn. Ernest Holmes Coll., Denver, 1988—; mem. United Ch. Religious Sci., L.A. (trustee 1975-80, pres. 1982-88; Min. of Yr. 1978, Pres. award 1982); dir. Ernest Holmes Coll., Denver, 1988—. Author: Up Your Bracket, 1980, Keys to Life, Ride the Wild Horses, 1986; host TV program New Design For Living (Angel award, 1989). Mem. United Clergy Religious Sci., Assn. Counselors and Therapists, Lakewood C. of C. (trail boss 1982-84), Rolling Hills Country Club. Republican. Office: Mile Hi Ch 9277 W Alameda Ave Lakewood CO 80226-2858

VOLAN, WENDY TYSON, marketing professional; b. Phila., July 21, 1953; d. James Robert and Caroline Helen (Macintyre) Tyson; m. Gregory D. Volan, Jan. 21, 1978. Student, U. Colo., 1971-75. Customer svc. mgr. Pallas Photo Labs, Inc., Denver, 1976-79; prin., dir. grafic design Volan Design Assocs., Boulder, Colo., 1979—. Mem. mktg. com. Boulder County United Way. Mem. Am. Ctr. Design, Inst. Packaging Profls., Rock Mountain Writers Guild. Avocations: sports cars, photography, bicycling. Office: Volan Design Assocs 1800 38th St Boulder CO 80301-2622

VOLBORTH, ALEXIS VON, geochemistry and geological engineering educator; b. Viipuri, Finland, July 11, 1924; came to U.S. 1955, naturalized; m. Nadia Hasso, 1947; children: Tatyana, Swetlana, Maria, Gregory, Anna, Nicholaus H.W., Elisabeth. *First church records on the Volborth family appear with Herman Volbordt (dec. 1622) in Barby, a Swedish settlement on River Elbe, Saxony. His son Herman (b. 1609) moved to Nordhausen, Harz. His son was Johann Christian Volborth (b. 1738, Nordhausen). His son, Johann Friedrich August von Volborth (b. 1768), emigrated to St. Petersburg, Russia around 1790. He was pastor general in St. Petersburg and vice president, General Consortium, Evangelical Lutheran Church of Russia. He was granted hereditary nobility by Czar Nicholas I in 1824. His son was Alexis von Volborth's great grandfather, Carl Alexander (b. 1800), who was a doctor of medicine, paleontologist, mineralogist, founder of the Mineralogical Society of Russia, state counselor, and chief physician at the Royal Marine Hedaquaters, St. Petersburg. The mineral Volborthite and a fossil Volborthella were named in his honor. Alexis von Volborth's grandfather, Woldemar (b. 1838), served as Chancellor, Royal Chancellory, St. Petersburg. His father, Alexis (b. 1889) has a PhD in Chemistry from Universtiy of Bonn. He was a colonel in the Semyonovsky regiment in WWI, and emigrated to Finland in 1920. The origin of the Volborth clan may be traced to Sweden as indicated by the original spelling of Herman Volbordt, endings later germanized to nn and th. The word probably stems from the Old Swedish fullborda, meaning to fulfill. In the family survives a tale about an early ancestor who served a Danish king in the Middle Ages as advisor and court jester when Denmark controlled Southern Sweden.* PhC, U. Helsinki, 1950, PhLic and PhD in Geology-Mineralogy, 1954. Mineralogist, rsch. assoc., assoc. prof., prof. U. Nev., Reno, 1956-68; Killam vis. prof. geology, Killam rsch. prof. Dalhousie U., Can., 1968-72; vis. prof. NASA Lunar Sci. Inst., U. Houston, 1972-73; vis. rsch. chemist U. Calif., Irvine, 1973-76; prof. geology and chemistry N.D. State U., 1975-78; prof. geology, scientist Nucleaar Radiation Ctr., Wash. State U., Pullman, 1978-79; prof. geochemistry and chemistry Mont. Coll. Mineral Sci. and Tech., Butte, 1979-94, prof. geol. engring., 1987-92, dir. accelerator lab., 1983-86, sr. radiation safety officer, 1983-86; prof. emeritus Mont. Tech./U. Mont., Butte, 1995—; prin. investigator Stoichiometry Study Lunar Rocks, NASA, 1972-73; cons. AEC, 1961-63, NASA, 1965-73, Anaconda Co., 1968, Atomic Energy Orgn. Iran, 1975, King Abdul Aziz U., Jeddah, Saudi Arabia, 1975-76, Johns Manville Corp., Chevron, 1980-83, Pegasus Gold Inc., 1987, Placer Dome Inc., Echo Bay, Inc., 1990; U.S. rep., del. 2d Conf. on Natural Reactors, IAEC, Paris, 1977; U.S. rep. Internat. Geol. Correlation Program, 1990-96; interpreter, Russian translator in Soviet Siberia for U.S. and Can. mining cos., 1990-96. Contbr. articles to profl. jours. Traveling rsch. fellow Outokumpu Found., U. Vienna, U. Heidelberg, 1954-55, Hoover fellow Calif. Inst. Tech., 1955-56, sr. fellow Australian Acad. Sci., 1965, fellow Guggenheim Found., 1965-66; fossil Elkoceras Volborthi named in his honor. Fellow Mineral. Soc. Am., Am. Inst. Chemists; mem. Am. Chem. Soc., Am. Nuclear Soc., Soc. Econ. Geologists, Internat. Precious Metals Inst. Home and Office: PO Box 80 Dayton MT 59914-0080

VOLCKMANN, RUSSELL WILLIAM, III, artist; b. Charlottesville, Va., Dec. 28, 1958; s. Russell William and Mary Jane (Green) V.; m. Ayumi Akasaka (Feb. 12, 1993 (div. Aug. 1997). Student, Santa Rosa Jr. Coll., Santa Rosa, Calif., 1984, San Francisco State Univ., 1992. Elec. tech. Hewlett Packard, Santa Rosa, 1984-90; pres., exec. prodr. Volksmedia, San Francisco, 1992—; creative dir. Internat. Interactive Communications Soc., San Francisco, 1995-97; adv. Multimedia Devel. Group, 1993; affirmative action communications com. Hewlett Packard Corp., Santa Rosa, 1989. Animator Printz Showreel, 1994. Recipient Japan Soc. award Japan Soc. Northern Calif., 1991. Mem. Best Internet Developers. Avocations: swimming, scuba, Muay Thai kickboxing, Didgeridoo. Office: Volksmedia 2343 3rd St Ste 295 San Francisco CA 94107-3132

VOLK, ROBERT HARKINS, aviation company executive; b. East Orange, N.J., Nov. 27, 1932; s. Harry Joseph and Marion (Waters) V.; m. Barbara

June Klint, Sept. 10, 1954; children: Christopher G., William W., Laura L., Elisabeth M. BA, Stanford U., 1954, LLB, 1958. Bar: Calif. 1959. Assoc. Adams Duque & Hazeltine, L.A., 1959-62; ptnr. Adams Duque & Hazelyine, L.A., 1962-67; commr. of corps. State of Calif., Sacramento, 1967-69; pres. Union Bancorp, L.A., 1969-73; pres., chmn. Union Am., L.A., 1973-79; owner, chief exec. officer Martin Aviation Inc., Santa Ana, Calif., 1980-90, Media Aviation L.P. Burbank, 1984——. Sgt. USAF, 1955-57. Mem. Calif. Bar Assn. Republican. Avocations: skiing, golf, tennis. Home: 332 Conway Ave Los Angeles CA 90024-2604 Office: Media Aviation LP 2800 N Clybourn Ave Burbank CA 91505-1010

VOLKERSZ, WILLEM ALDERT, artist, educator; b. Amsterdam, The Netherlands, Aug. 3, 1939; s. E. Gerald and Elly (Merens) V.; m. Diane Power, Dec. 20, 1965; 1 child, Jason Alexander. BA, U. Wash., 1965; MFA, Mills Coll., 1967. Instr. Ohio State U., Columbus, 1967-68; prof. Kansas City (Mo.) Art Inst., 1968-86, Mont. State U., Bozeman, 1986-; vis. lectr. Jacob Kramer Coll., Leeds, Eng., 1972-73; mem. nat. faculty Union of Ind. Colls. of Art, Kansas City, 1979-80; dir. admissions Kansas City Art Inst., 1981-83. One man shows include Western Wash. U., Bellingham, WA, 1994, Plains Art Mus., Fargo, ND, 1994, Salt Lake Art Ctr., Salt Lake City, 1995, Nicolaysen Art Mus., Casper, WY, 1998, Mont. State U., Bozeman, Mont., 1999, Mus. N.W. Art, La Conner, Wash., 1999. Mem. folk art adv. bd. Plains Art Mus., Fargo, N.D., 1998—; trustee Beall Park Art Ctr., Bozeman, 1993-95. Recipient Fulbright Sr. Scholar award Coun. for Internat. Exch. of Scholars, 1990-91; individual artist fellow Mont. Arts Coun., 1997-98; grantee Exceptional Opportunities, Mont. State U., 1999, Mont. Com. for Humanities, 1999. Mem. Coll. Art Assn., Folk Art Soc. Am. (mem. nat. adv. bd. 1990-97), Phi Kappa Phi. Home: 12299 Portnell Rd Bozeman MT 59718-9552 Office: Mont State U Sch of Art 241 Haynes Bozeman MT 59717

VOLLACK, ANTHONY F., former state supreme court justice; b. Cheyenne, Wyo., Aug. 7, 1929; s. Luke and Opal Vollack; m. D. Imojean; children: Leah, Kirk. Bar: Colo. 1956. Pvt. practice law Colo., from 1956; former state senator; judge Colo. Dist. Ct. (1st jud. dist.), 1977-85; justice Colo. Supreme Ct., 1986—, chief justice, 1995-98; ret., 1998. Office: Colo Supreme Ct Colorado State Judicial Bldg 2 E 14th Ave Denver CO 80203-2115*

VOLPE, RICHARD GERARD, insurance accounts executive, consultant; b. Sewickley, Pa., Apr. 10, 1950; s. Ralph Carl and Louise P. (Cosentino) V.; m. Janet Lynn Henne, May 10, 1986; 1 child, John Ralph. BA, Vanderbilt U., 1972. CPCU. Trainee, asst. mgr. Hartford (Conn.) Ins. Group, 1973-74; v.p. sales Roy E. Barker Co., Franklin, Tenn., 1975-80; asst. v.p., product mgr. comml. ins. Nat. Farmers Union Ins., Denver, 1980-82; prin. R.G. Volpe & Assocs, Denver, 1982-85; account exec. Millers Mut. Ins., Aurora, Colo., 1985-89; pres, CEO AccuSure, Inc., Arvada, Colo., 1989—; account exec. J.R. Misken, Inc., Denver, 1990-92, The Prudential, Colorado Springs, 1992—; edn. chmn. Insurors Tenn., Nashville, 1978-79; new candidate chmn. Mid-Tenn. chpt. CPCU, Nashville, 1979-80; cons. Bennett Nat. Bank Colo., mktg. mgr., 1989-90; cons. Plains Ins., Inc., 1987-90. Contbr. articles to profl. jours. Dem. chmn. Williamson County, Tenn., 1979; campaign mgr. legis., Franklin, 1979-98; legis. chmn. Centennial Life Underwriters, 1998; del. Rep. State Caucus, 1998. Named Hon. Col. Gov. Tenn., 1979. Mem. Soc. Property and Casualty Underwriters, Centennial Life Underwriters, South Metro Denver C. of C. Roman Catholic. Avocations: skiing, camping, hiking, biking, sailing. Home: 10908 Snow Cloud Trl Littleton CO 80125-9210 Office: The Prudential 3151 S Vaughn Way Ste 500 Aurora CO 80014-3514

VONDERHEID, ARDA ELIZABETH, nursing administrator; b. Pitts., June 19, 1925; d. Louis Adolf and Hilda Barbara (Gerstacker) V.; diploma Allegheny Gen. Hosp. Sch. Nursing, 1946; B.S. in Nursing Edn., Coll. Holy Names, Oakland, Calif., 1956; M.S. in Nursing Adminstrn., UCLA, 1960. Head nurse Allegheny Gen. Hosp., Pitts., 1946-48; staff nurse Highland-Alameda County Hosp., Oakland, Calif., 1948-51, staff nurse poliomyelitis units, 1953-55; pvt. duty nurse Directory Registered Nurses Alameda County, Oakland, 1951-53; adminstrv. supervising nurse Poliomyelitis Respiratory and Rehab. Center, Fairmont, Alameda County Hosp., Oakland, 1955-58; night supr., relief asst. dir. nursing Peninsula Hosp., Burlingame, Calif., 1960, adminstrv. supr., 1961-62, inservice educator, 1963-69; staff nurse San Francisco Gen. Hosp., 1969, asst. dir. nurses, 1969-72; mem. faculty continuing edn. U. Calif., San Francisco, 1969-71; dir. nursing services Kaiser Permanente Med. Center, South San Francisco, 1973-1982, asst. adminstr. Med. Center Nursing Services, 1982-85; asst. adminstr. Kaiser Hosp., San Francisco, 1985-87; ret. 1987. Chmn. edn. com. San Mateo County (Calif.) Cancer Soc., 1962-69; bd. dirs. San Mateo County Heart Assn., 1968-71; mem., foreman pro tem San Mateo County Civil Grand Jury, 1982-83; mem. San Mateo County Health Council, 1982-85, vice chmn., 1984; mem. all ch. coms. Cert. advanced nursing adminstrn. Mem. AAAW (bd. dirs.), San Mateo County (dir. 1964-69, pres. elect 1967-68, pres. 1968-70), Golden Gate (1st v.p. 1974-78, dir. 1974-78), Calif., Am. nurses assns., Nat. League Nursing, Soc. for Nursing Service Adminstrs., State Practice and Edn. Council, Maui Hospice Assn. (vol.), San Mateo County Grand Jury Assn., Calif. Grand Jury Assn., AARP (chpt. 3184 Lahaina, Hawaii 1995-98, pres. 1998—), Maui Christian Women's Club (bd. dirs. 1995-98, chmn. 1996-98), Sigma Theta Tau. Republican. Club: Kai-Perm. Contbr. articles in field to profl. jours. Home: 150 Puukolii Rd Apt 47 Lahaina HI 96761-1961

VON DOEPP, CHRISTIAN ERNEST, psychiatrist; came to U.S., 1949; s. Philip and Elizabeth von Doepp; m. Janet Carol Brown, Jan. 2, 1994; children: Heidi Louise von Doepp Lemon, Peter Anders, Niels Christian. Student, U. Heidelberg, Germany, 1955; BA, DePauw U., 1957; MD, Stanford U., 1961; intern, Boston City Hosp., Tufts U., 1962. Diplomate Am. Bd. Psychiatry and Neurology, Nat. Bd. Med. Examiners. Resident psychiatry Langley Porter Psychiat. Inst. U. Calif., San Francisco, 1968; house call physician Permaennte Med. Group, San Francisco, 1966-68; consulting psychiatrist Somerville (Mass.) Child Guidance Ctr., 1969; brig psychiatrist and cons. to correctional program Boston Naval Sta., 1968-69; lectr. and preceptor Calif. Dept. Health, Health Tng. Resource Ctr., Berkeley, Calif., 1970-77; dir. day hosp. and aftercare programs San Mateo (Calif.) Ctrl. County Psychiat. Svcs., 1970-87; sr. psychiatrist San Mateo County Mental Health Divsn., 1987—; cons. psychiatrist Calif. Med. Facility,CDC, Vacaville, 1995—; fellow Inst. Pathology, U. Freiberg, Germany, 1960, Lab. Cmty. Psychiatry, Harvard Med. Sch., Boston, 1969; supr., coord. cmty. psychiatry rotation for residents U.S. Naval Hosp., Oakland, Calif., 1970-81; med. examiner State of Calif., 1971-78; cons. Counseling and Assistance Ctr., U.S. Naval Sta., Treasure Island, Calif., 1974-76; asst. clin. prof. dept. psychiatry U. Calif. San Francisco, 1971—; chmn. or mem. numerous coms. San Mateo County Mental Health Div., 1970—. Bd. dirs. Tahoma Meadows Homeowners Assn., 1986-92, pres., 1980-81; pres. Tahoma Mut. Water Co., 1978-80. With M.C., USN, 1962-65; capt. USNR, 1965—. Mem. Am. Psychiat. Assn., No. Calif. Psychiat. Soc., San Mateo County Psychiat. Soc. (sec.-treas. 1987-89, bd. dirs. 1987-93), Calif. Med. Assn., San Mateo County Med. Assn., Faculty-Alumni Assn. Dept. Psychiatry U. Calif. San Francisco (bd. dirs. 1985-90). Office: 19 W 39th Ave Ste 4 San Mateo CA 94403-4549

VON DRACHENFELS, SUZANNE HAMILTON, writer; b. L.A., May 26, 1928; d. Augustus Adolphus and Floribel Hargett (Kelly) Hamilton; m. James True Luscombe, July 14, 1950 (div. 1969); children: James Hamilton Luscombe, Kelly Ann Luscombe, Elizabeth Scott Buckingham, Patricia Jane Pecoulas; m. Louis Wood Robinson, Aug. 1972 (div. 1988); m. Alec Verner, Baron von Drachenfels, Aug. 14, 1990. BS, U. So. Calif., 1950. Tabletop cons., spkr. Fitz & Floyd, Dallas, 1983-90; contbg. editor Giftware News, Chgo., 1987-91. Vol., mem. bd. Jr. League Pasadena, 1958-83; docent Huntington Libr. & Art Gallery, San Marino, 1962-68, L.A. County Mus. of Art, 1969-74; pres. Jr. League Sustainers, Pasadena, 1977. Republican. Episcopalian. Avocations: study of and collecting Oriental porcelain, reading history of tableware and tablemanners, travel. Home: 149 Littlefield Rd [illegible]

VON KALINOWSKI, JULIAN ONESIME, lawyer; b. St. Louis, May 19, 1916; s. Walter E. and Maybelle (Michaud) von K.; m. Penelope Jayne Dyer, June 29, 1980; children by previous marriage: Julian Onesime, Wendy Jean

von Kalinowski. BA, Miss. Coll., 1937; JD with honors, U. Va., 1940. Bar: Va. 1940, Calif. 1946. Assoc. Gibson, Dunn and Crutcher, L.A., 1946-52, ptnr., 1953-85, mem. exec. com., 1962-82, adv. ptnr., 1985—; CEO, chmn. Litigation Scis., Inc., Culver City, Calif., 1991-94; chmn. emeritus Litigation Scis., Inc., Torrance, Calif., 1994-96, Dispute Dyamics, Inc., Torrance, Calif., 1996—; instr. Columbia Law Sch., Parker Sch. Fgn. and Cooperative Law, summer 1981; instr. antitrust law and litigation So. Meth. Sch. of Law, 1982-84, bd. visitors, 1982-85; v.p., bd. dirs., mem. exec. com. W.M. Keck Found.; mem. faculty Practising Law Inst., 1971, 76, 78, 79, 80; instr. in spl. course on antitrust litigation Columbia U. Law Sch., N.Y.C., 1981; mem. lawyers dels. com. to 9th Cir. Jud. Conf., 1953-67; UN expert Mission to People's Republic China, 1982. Contbr. articles to legal jours.; author: Antitrust Laws and Trade Regulation, 1969, desk edit., 1981; gen. editor: World Law of Competition, 1978, Antitrust Counseling and Litigation Techniques, 1984; gen. editor emeritus Antitrust Report. With USN, 1941-46, capt. Res. ret. Fellow Am. Bar Found., Am. Coll. Trial Lawyers (chmn. complex litigation com. 1984-87); mem. ABA (ho. of dels. 1970, chmn. antitrust law sect. 1972-73), State Bar Calif., L.A. Bar Assn., U. Va. Law Sch. Alumni Assn., Calif. Club, L.A. Country Club, La Jolla Beach and Tennis Club, The Sky Club (N.Y.C.), Phi Kappa Psi, Phi Alpha Delta. Republican. Episcopalian. Home: 12320 Ridge Cir Los Angeles CA 90049-1151

VON KAMINSKY, ELAINE ISABELLE, financier, congresswoman; b. Geneva, Switzerland, Nov. 26, 1963; came to U.S., 1964; d. Peter Johannes and Juliette Isabelle (Bourbon et Bourbon) Von K.; m. Laurenz DiMedici, June 11, 1974; 1 child, Alfonso Sebastian Von Kaminski DiMedici deBourbon. Student, Oberlin Coll., 1984, Fullerton (Calif.) Coll., 1983-86, U. So. Calif. 1986-88, U. Geneva, 1988-90; JD, Harvard U., 1988, BA, MM, BS. Pres. Sapho & Co., L.A., 1991—; CEO Sapho Bank Corp., San Francisco, 1991—; researcher Presdl. Adv. Com., Washington, 1992—; mem. Ho. of Reps., Washington, 1991—; CEO Sapho Bank Corp, S.F., Royal Bank of Russa, NBR., N.A.; del.-at-large Rep. Platform Com., 1991—; mem. nat. Rep. senatorial com., 1992—. Columnist for Washington Post/ ABC-TV. Republican. Roman Catholic. Avocation: farming. Address: 9951 Platanal Dr Villa Park CA 92861-4225

VON KRENNER, WALTHER G., artist, writer, art consultant and appraiser; b. W. Ger., June 26, 1940; s. Frederick and Anna-Marie (von Wolfrath) von K.; m. Hana Renate Geue, 1960; children—Michael P., Karen P. Student of Southeast Asia studies, Buddhist U., Bankok,Thailand; postgrad. and field work, Cambodia. Curator, v.p. Gallery Lahaina, Maui, Hawaii; pres. Internat. Valuation Honolulu, 1973-80; owner Al Hilal Arabians, Mont.; instr. aikido, 1962—; founder, dir. Sandokan Aikido Schs., 1995. Mem. A.I m. Soc. Appraisers: sr. mem.; pres., dir.). Home: PO Box 1338 Kalispell MT 59903-1338

VON LINSOWE, MARINA DOROTHY, information systems consultant; b. Indpls., July 21, 1952; d. Carl Victor and Dorothy Mae (Quinn) von Linsowe; m. Clayton Albert Wilson IV, Aug. 11, 1990; children: Kira von Linsowe Parker, Lara Carla von Linsowe-Wilson, Tami Cheri von Linsowe-Wilson. Student Am. River Coll., Portland State U. Verbal operator Credit Bur. Metro, San Jose, Calif. and Portland, Oreg., 1970-72; computer clk. Security Pacific Bank, San Jose, Calif. and Portland, Oreg., 1972-73; proof clk. Crocker Bank, Seaside, Calif., 1973-74; proof supr. Great Western Bank, Portland, 1974-75; bookkeeper The Clothes Horse, Portland, 1976-78; computer operator Harsh Investment Co., Portland, 1978-79; data processing mgr. Portland Fish Co., 1979-81; data processing mgr. J & W Sci. Inc., Rancho Cordova, Calif., 1981-83; search and recruit specialist, data processing mgr. Re:Search Exec. Recruiters, Sacramento, Calif., 1983; sr. systems analyst Unisys Corp. (formerly Burroughs), 1983-91; sr. systems cons. FileNet Corp., Portland, Oreg., 1991-92; owner Optimal System Svcs., Portland, Oreg., 1992—; mfg. specialist, computer conversion cons., bus. sys. analyst Portland. First violinist Am. River Orch. Recipient Bank of Am. Music award, 1970. Mem. NAFE, Am. Prodn. and Inventory Control Soc. (cert.), Am. Mgrs. Assn., MENSA, Data Processing Mgmt. Assn. Republican. Lutheran.

VON PASSENHEIM, JOHN B., lawyer; b. Calif., Nov. 25, 1964; s. Burr Charles and Kathryn E. (Kirkland) Passenheim. BA in English with honors, U. Calif.-Santa Barbara, 1986; JD, U. Calif., Hastings, 1989. Bar: Calif. 1989, U.S. Dist. Ct. (so. dist.) Calif. 1991. Pvt. practice San Diego, 1990—; organizer Rock The Vote, San Diego, 1992; primary atty. Calif. Lawyers for the Arts, San Diego; panelist Ind. Music Seminar, 1992, 93, 94; mem. Surfrider Found. Nat. Adv. Bd., 1995—; gen. counsel Greyboy Records, Post Boy Records, Alchemical, Inc. Contbg. staff DICTA mag., 1990-94; editor (legal column) It's the Law, 1990-93. Exec. counsel San Diego chpt. Surfrider Found., 1991-95; vol. atty. San Diego Vol. Lawyer Program, 1990-93. Office: 4425 Bayard St Ste 240 San Diego CA 92109-4089

VON SAUERS, JOSEPH F., lawyer; b. N.Y.C.; s. Joseph F. and Margaret von Sauers; m. June A. von Sauers. BEE, Manhattan Coll., 1980; MBA, Pepperdine U., 1987; JD, Southwestern U., 1991; LLM, Columbia U., 1995. Bar: Calif. 1992, D.C. 1993, Minn. 1993, Tex. 1993, Colo. 1994, U.S. Patent and Trademark Office. Contracts negotiator Hughes Aircraft Co., El Segundo, Calif., 1985-92; atty. Jones, Day, Reavis & Pogue, Dallas, 1992-94, Loeb & Loeb, LLP, L.A., 1995-97, Gray, Cary, Ware & Freidenrich, Palo Alto, Calif., 1997-98; dep. gen. coun. Roland Corp. U.S., L.A., 1998—; active Calif. Lawyers for Arts, L.A., 1996; guest spkr. Loyola U., L.A., 1996. Contbr. articles to profl. jours. Mem. Am. Legion. Comdr. USNR. Recipient Kuwait Liberation medal Saudi Arabian/Kuwaiti Govts., 1992, 96; Wildman scholar Southwestern U., 1987-91. Mem. Naval Res. Assn., L.A. County Bar Assn. Avocations: sailing, golf, tennis.

VON STUDNITZ, GILBERT ALFRED, state official; b. Hamburg, Germany, Nov. 24, 1950; came to U.S., 1954.; s. Helfrid and Rosemarie Sofie (Kreiten) von S.; m. Erica Lynn Hoot, May 26, 1990. BA, Calif. State U., L.A., 1972. Adminstrv. hearing officer State of Calif., Montebello, 1987-91; mgr. III driver control policy unit Dept. Motor Vehicles State of Calif., Sacramento, 1991-93; ops. mgr. Driver Safety Review, 1993-95; contract mgr. State Dept. Health Svcs., 1995-97; staff mgr. licensing ops. policy Dept. Motor Vehicles, Sacramento, 1997—. Author: Aristocracy in America, 1989; editor publs. on German nobility in U.S., 1986—. Active L.A. Conservancy, West Adams Heritage Assn., dir., 1989-91. Mem. Calif. State Mgrs. Assn., Assn. German Nobility in N.Am. (pres. 1985—), Driver Improvement Assn. Calif. (v.p. 1992-96, dir. media rels. 1996—), Benicia Hist. Soc., Sierra Club, Intertel, Mensa, Orders and Medals Soc. Am., Nat. Assn. Managed Care Regulators, Phi Sigma Kappa (v.p. chpt. 1978). Roman Catholic. Avocations: genealogical research, collecting. Home: 1101 W 2nd St Benicia CA 94510-3125

VON TILSIT, HEIDEMARIE, information management specialist; b. Heinrichswalde, Germany, Sept. 26, 1944; came to U.S., 1967; d. Heinz and Kaethe Krink; m. Leonard Wierzba, May 14, 1969 (div. 1990). Buchhandel, Dt. Buchh. Schule, Kiel, Germany, 1965; profl. cert., Coll. of Further Edn., Oxford, Eng., 1966; BA, Calif. State U., Fullerton, 1979. Library asst. Allergan, Inc., Irvine, Calif., 1975-76; info. analyst Allergan Pharms., Irvine, Calif., 1976-79, library supr., 1979-81, mgr. corp. info. ctr., 1982—; cons. in field, Irvine, 1980—; owner, pres. Unitran, Corona, Calif., 1980—; mem. adv. bd. Coil & Assocs. Career Cons., Orange, Calif., 1987—; mem. adv. bd. for univ.-industry rsch. and tech. U. Calif., Irvine, 1992—; mem. adv. bd. Info. Libr./Info. Sci. Continuing Edn., Calif. State U. Fullerton. Editor/writer articles sci. and information mgmt. Vol. AIDS Svcs. Found., 1994—; bd. mem. Elections Com. of the County of Orange, 1998; mem. Eleanor Roosevelt Dem. Club, 1996—; co-chair Inland Empire Lesbian & Gay Dem. Club, 1997—. Mem. Am. Soc. Info. Sci., Spl. Librs. Assn., Pharm. Edn. & Rsch. Inst. (com. info. mgmt. sect. 1985—). Democrat. Avocations: dramatic arts, horseback riding, sporting clays. Home: 1543 San Rafael Dr Corona CA 91720-3709 Office: Allergan Inc 2525 Dupont Dr Irvine CA 92612-1599

[illegible line] **TU[illegible] JOHN LEAVY,** [illegible] 16, 1941; s. Lloyd William and Elsie Irene (Bousselot) V. BA in History, U. Iowa, 1951; BA in Journalism, U. Wash., 1953. Tchr. Oelwein (Iowa) High Sch., 1951-52; columnist Seattle Post-Intelligencer, 1953-71; critic Seattle Times, 1971-98. With U.S. Army, 1946-48. Democrat.

VOORHIES, JANICE LEAVITT, secondary education educator; b. Las Vegas, Nev., Oct. 10, 1946; d. Max V. and Marba Rose (Wilcox) Leavitt; m. Bruce James Voorhies, June 6, 1969; children: Leah, Mark, James, Ben, David, Michael, Rachel, Nathan. BA, Brigham Young U., 1968; MEd, Westminster Coll., 1996. Tchr. Alpine Dist., Orem, Utah, 1968-69, Jordan Dist., Sandy, Utah, 1988—. Contbr. numerous articles to mags. and newspapers. Regional chmn. fundraising, exec. com. Primary Children's Hosp., Salt Lake City, 1991-95. Recipient White House Disting. Tchr. award, Washington, 1996. Mem. Nat. Coun. Tchrs. English. Republican. Ch. Jesus Christ LDS. Avocations: gardening, counted cross stitching, traveling. Office: Bingham HS 2160 W 10400 S South Jordan UT 84095-8353

VORIS, WILLIAM, academic administrator emeritus; b. Neoga, Ill., Mar. 20, 1924; s. Louis K. and Faye (Hancock) V.; m. Mavis Marie Myre, Mar. 20, 1949; children: Charles William II, Michael K. BS, U. So. Calif., 1947, MBA, 1948; PhD, Ohio State U., 1951; LLD, Sung Kyun Kwan U. (Korea), 1972, Eastern Ill. U., 1976. Teaching asst. Ohio State U., Columbus, 1948-50; prof. mgmt. Wash. State U., Pullman, 1950-52; prof., head dept. mgmt. Los Angeles State Coll., 1952-58, 60-63; dean Coll. Bus. and Pub. Adminstrn., U. Ariz., Tucson, 1963-71; pres. Am. Grad. Sch. Internat. Mgmt., Glendale, Ariz., 1971-89, pres. emeritus, 1989—, adj. prof., 1994—. Ford Found. research grantee Los Angeles State Coll., 1956; prof. U. Tehran (Iran), 1958-59; Ford Found. fellow Carnegie Inst. Tech., Pitts., 1961; prof. Am. U., Beirut, Lebanon, 1961, 62; cons. Hughes Aircraft Co., Los Angeles, Rheem Mfg. Co., Los Angeles, Northrop Aircraft Co., Palmdale, Calif., Harwood Co., Alhambra, Calif., ICA, Govt. Iran. Served with USNR, 1942-45. Fellow Acad. Mgmt.; mem. Ariz. Acad., Beta Gamma Sigma, Alpha Kappa Psi, Phi Delta Theta. Author: Production Control, Text and Cases, 1956, 3d edit., 1966; Management of Production, 1960. Research in indsl. future of Iran, mgmt. devel. in Middle East. Home: Thunderbird Campus Glendale AZ 85306

VORPAGEL, WILBUR CHARLES, historical consultant; b. Milw., Feb. 26, 1926; s. Arthur Fred and Emma (Hintz) V.; Betty J. Hoch, June 19, 1952; stepchildren: Jerry L., Sharon Belveal Sullenberger. Student Army specialized tng. program, U. Ill., 1943-44; BBA, U. Wis., 1949; MBA, U. Denver, 1953. Cert. tchr., Colo. Instr. Montezuma County High Sch., Cortez, Colo., 1950-51; coord. bus. edn. Pueblo (Colo.) Pub. Schs., 1951-56; pvt. practice bus. cons. Pueblo and Denver, 1956—; tchr. bus. edn. Emily Griffith Opportunity Sch., Denver, 1959-69; various positions with Denver & Rio Grande Western R.R. Co., Denver, 1959-88; cons. in field. Bd. dirs. Colo. Ret. Sch. Employees Assn., Denver, 1988—; rep. Custer Battlefield Hist. & Mus. Assn. Sgt. U.S. Army, 1944-46, ETO. Mem. Augustan Soc., St. John Vol. Corp., S.E. Colo. Geneal. Soc., Rio Grande Vets. Club (bd. dirs. Pueblo chpt.), Biblical Archaeol. Soc. (contbg. writer), Nat. Huguenot Soc., Colo. Huguenot Soc. (organizing pres. 1979-95), 70th Inf. Divsn. Assn., Shriners, Masons. Republican. Mem. Christian Ch. Avocations: archeo-astronomy, militaria, numismatics, autographs, incunabula. Home and Office: 335 Davis Ave Pueblo CO 81004-1019

VOSBECK, ROBERT RANDALL, architect; b. Mankato, Minn., May 18, 1930; s. William Frederick and Gladys (Anderson) V.; m. Phoebe Macklin, June 21, 1953; children: Gretchen, Randy, Heidi, Macklin. BArch, U. Minn., 1954. Various archtl. positions, 1956-62; ptnr. Vosbeck-Vosbeck & Assocs., Alexandria, Va., 1962-66, VVKR Partnership, Alexandria, 1966-79; exec. v.p. VVKR Inc., 1979-82, pres., 1982-88; prin. Vosbeck/DMJM, Washington and Alexandria, Va., 1989-94; v.p. DMJM Arch. and Enginerg., 1990-94; pvt. practice archtl. cons., 1994—; mem. Nat. Capital Planning Commn., 1976-81, U.S./USSR Joint Group on Bldg. Design and Constrn., 1974-79; mem. Nat. Park System Adv. Bd., 1984-88. Archtl. works include Pub. Safety Ctr., Alexandria, Va., 1987, Yorktown (Va.) Visitors Ctr, 1976, Frank Reeves Mcpl. Office Bldg., Washington, 1986, Fed. Bldg., NOrfolk, Va., 1979, Jeff Davis Assocs. Office Complex, Arlington, Va., 1991, Westminster Continued Care Retirement Community, Lake Ridge, Va., 1993. Pres. Alexandria Jaycees, 1960-61; v.p. Va. Jaycees, 1962-63; pres. Alexandria Ch. of Com., 1974-75. Engring. officer USMC, 1954-56. Recipient Plaque of Honor Fedn. Colegios Architects (Republic of Mexico); named to Outstanding Young Men of Am., Jaycees, 1963, Acadamecian. Internt. Acad. Architecture, hon. fellow Royal Archtl. Inst. Can., Soc. Architects of Mexico; recipient hon. fellowship Colegios Architects Spain, Union Bulgarian Architects. Fellow AIA (bd. dirs. 1976-78, v.p. 1979-80, pres. 1981), Internat. Union Architects (coun. 1981-87), Nat. Trust Hist. Preservation, Alexandria C. of C. (pres. 1974-75). Presbyterian. Home and Office: 770 Potato Patch Dr Unit A Vail CO 81657-4462

VOSEVICH, KATHI ANN, writer, editor, scholar; b. St. Louis, Oct. 12, 1957; d. William and Catherine Mildred (Kalinowski) V.; m. James Hughes Meredith, Sept. 6, 1986. AB with honors, St. Louis U., 1980, MA, 1983; PhD, U. Denver, 1988. Tchg. fellow St. Louis U., 1980-83, acad. advising fellow, 1983-84; tchg. fellow U. Denver, 1985-87; prof. ESL, BNM Talensch., Uden, The Netherlands, 1988-91; instr. English, mentor U. Ga., Athens, 1992-94; vis. asst. prof. Colo. Coll., Colorado Springs, 1994; sr. tech. writer and editor Titan Client/Server Techs., Colorado Springs, 1994-96, head documentation, libr., 1996-97; documentation mgr. Beechwood, Colorado Springs, 1997—; forensic judge USAF Acad., Colo., 1987-88; edn. officer Volkel (The Netherlands) Air Base, 1988-91; instr. English European divsn. U. Md., The Netherlands and Belgium, 1989-91. Author: Customer Care User's Guide, 1996, Interview with Joseph Heller, 1998, Conversations with Joseph Heller in Understanding the Literature of World War II, 1999; editor: Subscription Services System Documentation, 1996, Titan Process Documentation, 1994-96; copy editor: Language, Ideas, and American Culture; War, Literature and the Arts; contbr. over 100 electronic texts and articles to profl. jours. Colo. scholar U. Denver, 1985-86, grad. dean scholar, 1988; NEH fellow U. Md., 1994. Mem. MLA, Phi Beta Kappa, Alpha Sigma Nu. Roman Catholic. Avocations: writing, drawing, raising Bernese mountain dogs. Office: Beechwood 7150 Campus Dr Ste 200 Colorado Springs CO 80920-3178

VOTH, ALDEN H., political science educator; b. Goessel, Kans., May 4, 1926; s. John F. and Helena (Hildebrandt) V.; m. Norma E. Jost, Aug. 18, 1956; children: Susan, Thomas. BA, Bethel Coll., 1950; MS in Econs., Iowa State U., Ames, 1953; PhD in Internat. Rels., U. Chgo., 1959. Assoc. prof. polit. sci. Upland (Calif.) Coll., 1960-63; prof. polit. sci. San Jose (Calif.) State U., 1963-65, 67-91, prof. emeritus, 1991—; vis. prof. polit. sci. Am. U. in Cairo, 1965-67. Author: Moscow Abandons Israel, 1980, (with others) The Kissinger Legacy, 1984. Trustee Pomona (Calif.) Valley Am. Assn. UN, 1963; participant China Ednl. Exch., 1966. Am. U. in Cairo Rsch. grantee, 1966; Nat. Coun. on US-Arab Rels. fellow, 1990—. Home: 1385 Kimberly Dr San Jose CA 95118-1426 Office: San Jose State U One Washington Sq San Jose CA 95192

VREELAND, PATRICIA ANNE MARTIN, secondary education educator, teacher educator; b. Milw., Aug. 25, 1948; d. Philip Patrick and Mary Kathleen (Howe) Martin; m. John E. Vreeland, Jr., July 5, 1969; children: Erica Anne, Sara Elizabeth. BA in English cum laude, U. San Diego, 1970; MA in English, San Diego State U., 1994; postgrad., U. Calif., San Diego. Cert. secondary tchr. English, social sci., crosscultural lang., acad. devel. and gifted/talented edn. Tchr. Sweetwater H.S. Dist., Chula Vista, Calif., 1970-76; instr. San Diego Cmty. Colls., 1977-91; tchr., chair dept. San Diego City Schs., 1991-95; tchr. educator, supr. U. Calif., San Diego, La Jolla, 1995—; assessor Nat. Bd. for Profl. Tchg. Standards, Princeton, N.J., 1994-96; mem. planning conf. Internat. Conf. on Tchr. Rsch., San Diego, 1998; presenter at confs. Contbr. revs. and articles to Voices from the Middle, Applause, Family Press, others. Vol. Mission Bay Girls Softball, San Diego, 1985-89; mem. San Diego Mus. Art, YMCA, Dimensions; subscriber Old Globe Theater, 1994—. Grantee Edna McConnell Clark Found., Calif. Coun. on Tchr. Credentialing, others. Mem. NEA, San Diego Area Writing Project, Nat. Writing Project, Nat. Coun. Tchrs. English, Calif. Assn. Tchrs. English, Calif. Tchrs. English to Speakers of Other Langs. Avocations: tennis, skiing, cookbook collecting. Office: USCD Intern Support Program 4606 Ingraham St San Diego CA 92109

VREELAND, ROBERT WILDER, electronics engineer; b. Glen Ridge, N.J., Mar. 4, 1923; s. Frederick King and Elizabeth Lenora (Wilder) V.; m. Jean Gay Fullerton, Jan. 11, 1947; 1 son Robert Wilder. BS, U. Calif. Berkeley, 1947. Electronics engr. Litton Industries, San Carlos, Calif., 1948-

55; sr. devel. electronics engr. U. Calif. Med. Ctr., San Francisco, 1955-89; ret.; cons. electrical engring; speaker 8th Internat. Symposium Biotelemetry, Dubrovnik, Yugoslavia, 1984, RF Expo, Anaheim, Calif., 1985, 86, 87. Contbr. articles to profl. jours., also to internat. meetings and symposiums; patentee in field. Recipient Chancellor's award U. Calif., San Francisco, 1979; cert. appreciation for 25 years' service U. Calif., San Francisco, 1980. Mem. Nat. Bd. Examiners Clin. Engring. (cert. clin. engr.), IEEE, Assn. Advancement Med. Instrumentation (bd. examiner), Am. Radio Relay League (pub. service award 1962). Home: 45 Maywood Dr San Francisco CA 94127-2007 Office: U Calif Med Ctr 4th and Parnassus Sts San Francisco CA 94143

VREUGDENHIL, RALPH LYLE, minister; b. Venus, Nebr., Feb. 21, 1940; s. Harmen and Eunice Rachel (Bennett) V.; m. Velera Faye Downer, Apr. 3, 1964; children: John Alan, Timothy James. BA in Religion, Miltonvale (Kans.) Wesleyan Coll., 1961; MEd, U. Portland, 1975. Ordained to ministry Wesleyan Ch., 1970. Tchr. Dakota Mission to the Philippines, Luzon, The Philippines, 1961-62; pastor Guymon (Okla.) Wesleyan Ch., 1967-69; counselor Youth Outreach Inc., Vancouver, Wash., 1968-77; dir. men's div. Tacoma Rescue Mission, 1982-89; administrv. pastor Puyallup (Wash.) Ch. of the Nazarene, 1989—; elder Wash./Pacific Dist. Nazarene Ch., 1981-91. Developed New Life Program, 1982. Mem. Christian Mgmt. Assn., Wash. Ch. Adminstrs., Kiwanis, Rotary.

VROMAN, CHARLES ALVIN, technical writer, programmer; b. Key West, Fla., Dec. 30, 1953; s. Henry Alvin and Georgene Mae (Austin) V.; m. Susan Denise Church, Oct. 25, 1975; 1 child, Charles. BS, Chapman U., 1997. Served in USN, 1972-93; tech. writer, programmer Applied Tech. Sys., Bremerton, Wash., 1995—. Home: 2756 NE Athens Way Bremerton WA 98311-8408

VROOM, STEVEN MICHAEL, director university gallery; b. Dearborn, Mich., Feb. 26, 1961; s. Edmond Montcrief Montbatten-Bain and Gisela Mathilda (Ansbach) Vroom. BPh, Cornell Coll., Mt. Vernon, Iowa, 1986, B in Spl. Studies, 1986; MA, U. Iowa, 1989. Gallery technician Armstrong Gallery, Mt. Vernon, Iowa, 1981-85; mgr. Lazy T Motor Lodge, Estes Park, Colo., 1983-87; asst to th curator Office of Visual Materials, Iowa City, Iowa, 1987-88; tchg. asst. U. Iowa, Iowa City, 1988-89; vis. asst. prof. St. Ambrose U., Davenport, Iowa, 1989; dir. exhibits Iowa City, Johnson County Arts, 1991-93; instr. U. Iowa, Iowa City, 1990-93; vis. assoc. prof. Knox Coll., Galesburg, Ill., 1993; dir. Univ. Gallery, Sewanee, Tenn., 1993—; chmn. Strike for the Arts Com., Iowa City, 1990. Author: (book) Form and Meaning: The Taj Mahal, 1989; (art catalogs), 6 Americans, 1993, The Romantic Vision of J.A. Oertel, 1995, New Sculpture: Geoff Bowie, 1996. Bd. dirs. Iowa City Childrens Theatre, 1989-91, Iowa City Arts Ctr., 1991-93. Recipient Shaw scholarship Cornell Coll., Mt. Vernon, Iowa, 1982-86, Grad. Coll. scholarship U. Iowa, Iowa City, 1990. Mem. Coll. Art Assn., Am. Assn. Mus., Tenn. Assn. Mus. (recording sec. Nashville, 1996, Hon. Mention 1994, Award of Excellence, 1996), Am. Fedn. of Art, Am. Coll. and Univ. Galleries, People for the Am. Way. Democrat.

VU, QUAT THUONG, electrical engineer; b. Vietnam, Aug. 5, 1944; came to U.S., 1988; s. Mao Quy and Phung Thi Vu; m. Lethuy Thi, Dec. 22, 1973; children: Hien T., Duc T. BSEE, U. Ky., 1965; MSEE, Calif. Inst. of Tech., 1967, PhDEE, 1970. Dean MINH-DUC U. Coll. Engring., Saigon, Vietnam, 1971-75; rschr. Hochiminh City, Vietnam, 1977-87, CNRS-CRN, Strasbourg, France, 1987-88, Calif. Inst. of Tech., Pasadena, 1989-90; components rschr. Intel Corp., Santa Clara, Calif., 1990—. Achievements include several patents in field. Office: Intel Corp M/S SC1-03 3065 Bowers Ave Santa Clara CA 95054-3293

VUCANOVICH, BARBARA FARRELL, former congresswoman; b. Fort Dix, N.J., June 22, 1921; d. Thomas F. and Ynez (White) Farrell; m. Ken Dillon, Mar. 8, 1950 (div. 1964); children: Patty Dillon Cafferata, Mike, Ken, Tom, Susan Dillon Stoddard; m. George Vucanovich, June 19, 1965. Student, Manhattanville Coll. of Sacred Heart, 1938-39. Owner, operator Welcome Aboard Travel, Reno, 1968-74; Nev. rep. for Senator Paul Laxalt, 1974-82; mem. 98th-104th Congresses from 2d Nev. dist., 1983-96; chmn. appropriations subcom. on military construction; Rep. natl. woman Nev. Rep. Party, 1996—. Pres. Nev. Fedn. Republican Women, Reno, 1955-56; former pres. St. Mary's Hosp. Guild, Lawyer's Wives. Roman Catholic. Club: Hidden Valley Country (Reno). Office: Rep State Cen Comm Nevada 6114 W Charleston Blvd Las Vegas NV 89146-1127

VUK, MELVIN MARVIN, college director, educator; b. Carlsbad, N.Mex., Dec. 12, 1941; s. Melvin M. and Florence Grace (Oshell) V.; m. Cynthia S. Johnson, Sept. 17, 1968; children: Melissa, Alisa. BA, U. Ill., 1964, MA, 1966; PhD, Oreg. State U., 1975. Commd. lt. col. USAF, 1966, advanced through grades to lt. col., 1987; staff officer U.S. Intel, Allied Air Forces Ctrl. Europe, Germany, 1988-91; chief Intel edn. and tng. USAF Air Staff, Pentagon, Washington, 1991-92; assoc. dean Joint Mil. Intel Coll., Washington, 1992-94; ret. USAF, 1994; assoc. prof. geography N.Mex. State U., Carlsbad, 1994-97; campus dir. Coll. of S.W., Carlsbad, 1997—; mgr. environ. planning Union Pacific RR, Omaha, 1976-80; program mgr. Environ. Rsch. and Tech., Ft. Collins, 1980-84; mem. adv. bd. Assn. Small Aerospace Cos., Colorado Springs, Colo., 1983-85. Bd. dirs. Parking Commn., Ft. Collins, 1984-85, Carlsbad Mus. Arts, 1995—, Carlsbad Dept. Econ. Devel., 1994—; pres. Shephardson Sch. PTO, Ft. Collins, 1983-85, Ramstein (Germany) H.S. PTO, 1989-91. Decorated Bronze star USAF, 1968; recipient Svc. award VFW, Carlsbad, 1995, Outstanding Volunteerism award United Way Carlsbad and Eddy Co., 1997. Mem. Am. Assn. Geographers, Air Force Assn., Carlsbad C. of C. Avocations: auto repair, hiking, bicycling, softball, travel. Home: 1001 N Ural Dr Carlsbad NM 88220-4052 Office: 500 W Church St Carlsbad NM 88220-5135

VUONG, FRANK PHENG, insurance company executive; b. Phnom-penh, Cambodia, Apr. 16, 1953; s. Dac-Tran and Hoa (Huynh) V.; m. Michelle Lau Vuong; children: Genevieve, Gelene. AA, St. John Coll., Macau, 1974, City Coll. San Francisco, 1977; BA, San Francisco State Univ., 1979. CPA. With M.S.P. Agy., San Francisco, 1978-81; agt N.Y. Life Ins. Co., San Francisco, 1981-86, sales mgr., 1987-89, assoc. gen. mgr., 1989-95, ptnr., 1995-97, mng. ptnr., 1998—. Author: Mission Possible, 1997. Bd. dirs. Tio Chew Cmty. Ctr., San Francisco, 1991-93; prin. Tio-Chem Chinese Sch., San Francisco, 1991-93. Recipient Nat. Mgr. award Gold level award Gen. Agts. & Mgrs. Assn., 1991-98, Silver Level award, 1990, Bronze level award, 1989, Career Devel. award, 1988-98, Master Agy. award, 1993, 97, 98. Mem. San Francisco Life Underwriters Assn., Gen. Agents & Mgrs. Assn. Avocations: travel, jogging. Office: N Y Life Ins Co 100 Pine St Ste 3000 San Francisco CA 94111-5216

WACHBRIT, JILL BARRETT, accountant, tax specialist; b. Ventura, Calif., May 27, 1955; d. Preston Everett Barrett and Lois JoAnne (Fondersmith) Batchelder; m. Michael Ian Wachbrit, June 21, 1981; children: Michelle, Tracy. AA, Santa Monica City Coll., 1975; BS, Calif. State U., Northridge, 1979; M in Bus. Taxation, U. So. Calif., 1985. CPA. Supervising sr. tax acct. Peat, Marwick, Mitchell & Co., Century City, Calif., 1979-82; sr. tax analyst Avery Internat., Pasadena, Calif., 1982-83; tax mgr., asst. v.p. First Interstate Leasing, Pasadena, 1983-88, Gibraltar Savs., 1988, Security Pacific Corp., L.A., 1988-92; tax mgr., acct. El Camino Resources Ltd., Woodland Hills, Calif., 1992-95; tax mgr. Herbalife Internat. of Am., Century City, Calif., 1995-97; with PMC, Inc., Sun Valley, Calif., 1997—. Republican. Jewish. Avocations: reading, travel, collecting.

WACHTEL, ALBERT, writer, educator; b. N.Y.C., Dec. 20, 1939; s. Jacob and Sarah Rose (Kaplansky) W.; m. Sydelle Farber, Mar. 9, 1958; children: Sally Rose, Seth Laurence, Stephanie Allyson, Synthia Laura, Jonathan Benjamin, Jessica Eden, Jacob Ethan. BA, CUNY, 1960; PhD, SUNY, Buffalo, 1968. Instr. SUNY, Buffalo, 1963-66, asst. to dean, 1966-68; asst. prof. U. Calif., Santa Barbara, 1968-74; prof. English, creative writing Pitzer Coll., The Claremont (Calif.) Colls., 1974—. Playwright: Paying the Piper, 1968, Prince Hal, 1995; co-editor Modernism: Challenges and Perspectives, 1986; author: The Cracked Looking Glass: James Joyce and the Nightmare of History, 1992; contbr. stories, creative essays to lit. jours., newspapers, and mags. NDEA fellow, 1960-63, fellow Creative Arts Inst., U. Calif., Berkeley, 1970, NEH Summer Inst., Dartmouth Coll., 1987; Danforth Found. assoc., 1978, NEH Seminar, Cornell U., 1998. Jewish. Office: Pitzer Coll Claremont Colls Claremont CA 91711-6101

WACHTEL, THOMAS LEE, surgeon; b. Mansfield, Ohio, July 25, 1938; s. Earl J. and Lorena Fredona (Lehman) W.; m. Carolyn Coleman, May 15, 1965; children: John Matthew, David Earl-Martin, Julianne Maria. AB, Western Res. U., Cleve., 1960; MD, St. Louis U., 1964; cert. naval flight surgeon, Naval Flight Sch., Pensacola, Fla., 1970. Diplomate Am. Bd. Surgery; cert. added qualification in surg. critical care. Intern in surgery U. Ky., Lexington, 1964-65, resident in surgery, 1965-66; resident in surgery St. John's Mercy Hosp., St. Louis, 1966-69; pvt. practice Hamilton & Wachtel, Corbin, Ky., 1973-74; mem. surg. faculty U. N.Mex., Albuquerque, 1974-77; mem. surg. faculty U. Calif., San Diego, 1978-84, 91-96, burn dir., 1980-84, head trauma divsn., 1982-84; med. dir. trauma Samaritan Regional Med. Ctr., Phoenix, 1984-90; program dir. Phoenix Integrated Surg. Residency, 1986-90; med. dir. trauma Sharp Meml. Hosp., San Diego, 1990-96; chmn. bioengring. faculty Ariz. State U., 1984-90; dir. trauma Centura Health St. Anthony Hosp. Ctrl., Denver, 1996—; mem. surg. faculty F. Edward Hebert Sch. Medicine USPHS, Bethesda, 1988—; mem. surg. faculty U. Ariz., Tucson, 1993—; mem. nat. faculty Advanced Burn Life Support, Omaha, 1988—; mem. surg. faculty U. Colo., Denver, 1996—. Author: Medical Exploring, 2 edits., 1973, 76, Current Topics in Burn Care, 1983, Burns of the Head and Neck, 1984; editor: A Symposium on Burns, 1985. Mem. Nat. Commn. on Exploring Boy Scouts Am., Arlington, Tex., 1972-85; mem. Flynn Found. on Commn. on Med. Manpower, Phoenix, 1987-88. With USNR, 1969-97, capt. Res. Recipient Family Practice Teaching award Am. Acad. Family Practice, Phoenix, 1985; rsch. grantee U.S. Army, NIH, HSA-HEW. Fellow ACS (gov. 1995—), Am. Assn. Surgery of Trauma, Am. Coll. Critical Care Medicine; mem. Am. Burn Assn. (pres. 1989-90), Phi Gamma Delta, Phi Chi (pres. Phi Rho chpt. 1963-64), Omicron Delta Kappa, Sigma Delta Psi. Roman Catholic. Avocations: travel, hiking, woodworking, fishing, skiing. Office: Centura Health St Anthony Hosp Ctrl Trauma Dept 4231 W 16th Ave Denver CO 80204-1335

WADAS, JOHN W., fundraiser, marketing executive; b. Rahway, N.J., Nov. 17, 1944; s. Charles J. and Gertrude Sue (Gregerson) W.; m. Glenda G. Varnum, May 24, 1966 (div. June 1993); m. Louise Ann Stanger, June 18, 1994; children: James J., Rober M.; stepchildren: Sydney Stanger, Felicia Stanger, Shelby Stanger. BS, Long Beach State U., 1970; MS, Ariz. Sate U., 1972. Nat. cert. fund raising exec. Head wrestling coach Long Beach (Calif.) State U., 1970-71; head wrestling coach Ariz. State U., Tempe, 1971-74, assoc. athletic dir., 1974-82; athletic dir. U. South Fla., Tampa, 1982-86; exec. dir. found. San Diego State U., 1986-93; fund raising cons. self employed, La Jolla, Calif., 1993—; exec. dir. Sun Devil Club, Tempe, 1972-82; dir. devel. San Diego Hall of champions, 1993-95, San Diego Aerospace Mus., 1995—. Bd. dirs. YMCA, La Jolla, 1998—. With USN, 1963-67, Vietnam. Named Coll. Rookie Coach of Yr., NCAA, 1970. Mem. Nat. Fund Raising Execs. Avocations: sports, golf, running, tennis, racquetball. Home: 5558 Taft Ave La Jolla CA 92037-7642

WADDELL, THEODORE, painter; b. Billings, Mont., Oct. 6, 1941. Student, Bklyn. Mus. Art Sch., 1962; BS, Ea. Mont. Coll., 1966; MFA, Wayne State U., 1968. One-man shows include U. Calif., San Diego, 1984, Cheney Cowles Meml. Mus., Spokane, Wash., 1985, The New West, Colorado Springs, 1986, Bernice Stein Baum Gallery, N.Y., 1992; exhibited in group shows 38th Corcoran Biennial, Corcoran Gallery, Washington, 1983; represented in permanent collections Ea. Mont. Coll., Yellowstone Art Ctr., Billings, Sheldon Meml. Art Gallery, U. Nebr., Lincoln, City of Great Falls, Mont., Dallas Mus. Art, San Jose (Calif.) Mus. Office: care Stremmel Gallery 1400 S Virginia St Reno NV 89502-2806*

WADDINGHAM, JOHN ALFRED, artist, journalist; b. London, Eng., July 9, 1915; came to U.S., 1927, naturalized, 1943; s. Charles Alfred and Mary Elizabeth (Coles) W.; m. Joan Lee Larson, May 3, 1952; children: Mary Kathryn, Thomas Richard. Student, Coronado (Calif.) Sch. Fine Arts, 1953-54, Portland Art Mus., 1940-65, U. Portland, 1946-47; pupil, Rex Brandt, Eliot Ohara, George Post. Promotion art dir. Oreg. Jour., Portland, 1946-59; with The Oregonian, Portland, 1959-81; editl. art dir. The Oregonian, 1959-81; tchr. watercolor Oreg. Soc. Artists, 1954-56; tchr. art Oreg. Sch. Arts and Crafts, 1981—, Portland C.C., Multnomah Athletic Club, Mittleman Jewish Cmty. Ctr.; represented by several galleries, Oreg. and Wash. One man shows include Art in the Gov.'s Office, Oreg. State Capitol, 1991 and more than 30 shows in the Northwest; rep. mus. rental collections, Portland Art Mus., Bush House, Salem, Ore., U. Oreg. Mus., Vincent Price collection, Ford Times collection, also Am. Watercolor Soc. Travelling Show; paintings included in Salmagundi Club, N.Y.C., UN Bldg., Watercolor, U.S.A. of Springfield, Mo., others; judge art events, 1946—, over 50 one-man shows; ofcl. artist, Kiwanis Internat. Conv., 1966; designed, dir. constrn. cast: concrete mural Genesis, St. Barnabas Episcopal Ch., Portland, 1960; spl. work drawings old Portland landmarks and houses; propr. John Waddingham Hand Prints, fine arts serigraphs and silk screen drawings, 1965—; featured artist: Am. Artist mag., Watercolor mag., among others. Artist mem. Portland Art Mus. With USAAF, 1942-46. Recipient gold medal Salone Internazionale dell' Umorismo, Italy, 1974, 76, 80; honored with a 45 yr. retrospective Assignment: The Artist as Journalist Oreg. Hist. Soc., 1991; winner Palme do Oro in three exhbns., Bordighera, Italy. Mem. Portland Art Dirs. Club (past pres.), N.W. Watercolor Soc., Am. Watercolor Soc. (hon. sustaining), Watercolor Soc. Oreg., Oreg. Soc. Artists (watercolor tchr.), Multnomah Athletic Club, Jewish Community Ctr., Univ. Oreg. Med. Sch., Art in the Mounts., Oreg. Old Time Fiddlers, Clan Macleay Bagpipe Band. Home and Studio: 955 SW Westwood Dr Portland OR 97201-2744

WADE, ANDREW E., engineer; b. Sioux City, Iowa; s. Irvin E. and Selma Theresa (Corchine) W.; m. Gail Ann Greenstein Wade, Aug. 12, 1973; children: Nathalie Sarah, Ariel Erica. BS in Physics, MIT, 1973; PhD in Math. Physics, U. Calif., Berkeley, 1980. Tchr. edn. dept. U. Calif., Berkeley, 1975-80; engr. H.P., Cupertino, Calif., 1980-81; group v.p. Daisy Systems, Mountain View, Calif., 1981-86; v.p. engring. Digital, Santa Clara, Calif., 1986-87; cons. Wade & Assocs., Los Altos, Calif., 1987-88; founder, v.p. Objectivity, Inc., Mountain View, Calif., 1988-98; v.p. engring. Molecular Applications Group, Palo Alto, Calif., 1998—; spkrs. confs. in field. Contbr. articles to profl. jours. Mem. Assn. Computing Machinery, Phi Beta Kappa, Sigma Xi. Democrat. Jewish. Avocations: running, hiking, dancing. Home: 1528 Gilmore St Mountain View CA 94040-2917 Office: Molecular Application Grp PO Box 51110 Palo Alto CA 94303-0687 Address: 1528 Gilmore St Mountain View CA 94040-2917

WADE, JUDY LEE, journalist; b. St. Cloud, Minn., Mar. 12, 1939; d. Howard Walter and Mildred Mary (Jung) Wittmayer; m. Gerald H. Wade, Mar. 3, 1969 (div. Apr. 1988); m. William S. Baker Jr., June 22, 1991. BA, U. Minn., 1960. Freelance travel writer, 1960—. Author: Disneyland and Beyond: The Ultimate Guide, 1992, California Travel Bug, 1994, Seasonal Guide to the Natural Year, 1997, Arizona Guide, 1998. Mem. Am. Soc. Journalists and Authors, Soc. Am. Travel Writers. Avocations: scuba diving, sailing, bicycling. Home and Office: 11640 S 44th St Phoenix AZ 85044-2447

WADE, RODGER GRANT, financial systems analyst; b. Littlefield, Tex., June 25, 1945; s. George and Jimmie Frank (Grant) W.; m. Karla Kay Morrison, Dec. 18, 1966 (div. 1974); children: Eric Shawn, Shannon Annelle, Shelby Elaine; m. Carol Ruth Manning, Mar. 28, 1981. BA in Sociology, Tex. Tech. U., 1971. Programmer First Nat. Bank, Lubbock, Tex., 1971-73, Nat. Sharedata Corp., Odessa, Tex., 1973; asst. dir. computing ctr. Odessa Community Coll., 1973-74; programmer/analyst Med. Sci. Ctr., Tex. Tech U., Lubbock, 1974-76; sys. mgr. Hosp. Info. Sys., Addison, Tex., 1976-78; programmer, analyst Harris Corp., Grapevine, Tex., 1978-80, Joy Petroleum, Waxahachie, Tex., 1980-82; owner R&C Bus. Sys./Requerdos de Santa Fe, N.Mex., 1982-84; fin. sys. analyst Los Alamos (N.Mex.) Tech. Assocs., 1984-95; cons. mngr. Unidata Corp., Denver, 1995-98; cons. Interlink Group, Denver, 1998—; owner El Rancho Herbs, Santa Fe, 1988-91, Wade Gallery, Santa Fe, 1990-91, Wade Systems, Santa Fe, 1992—. Vol. programmer Los Alamos Arts Coun., 1987-88; mem. regulations task force N.Mex. Gov.'s Health Policy Adv. Com.; vol. systems support Amigos Unidos of Taos, 1990-95. Republican. Avocation: photography. Home: 7160 Berthoud St Westminster CO 80030-5633 Office: Interlink Group Inc 857 Grant St Denver CO 80203-2904

WADLEY, STEPHEN ALEXANDER, foreign language educator; b. Provo, Utah, Feb. 5, 1954; s. Alexander and Nelda (Beckstrand) W.; m. Malinda Larie Bastian, Aug. 17, 1991. BA, Brigham Young U., 1978; MA, U. Wash., 1980, PhD, 1987. Asst. prof. Brigham Young U., Provo, 1985-89; asst. prof. Portland (Oreg.) State U., 1991-96, assoc. prof., 1996—; bd. dirs. Oreg. State Sys. Higher Edn. China Bd., Portland. Editor: (periodical) Saksaha: A Review of Manchu Studies, 1995—; author: (monograph) The Mixed-Language Verses from the Manchu Dynasty in China, 1991; co-author: (book) Instructional Materials for the Teaching of Chinese, 1989. Fellow Inter-Univ. Program, Taipei, Taiwan, 1990-91; Outstanding Jr. Faculty Devel. grantee Portland State U., 1992. Mem. Am. Oriental Soc. (sec.-treas. Western br. 1995—, exec. com. 1992-95), Assn. for Asian Studies, N.W. China Coun. Democrat. Mormon. Home: 9941 SW 59th Ave Portland OR 97219-5603 Office: Portland State U Dept Fgn Lang & Lit Portland OR 97207

WADLOW, JOAN KRUEGER, academic administrator; b. LeMars, Iowa, Aug. 21, 1932; d. R. John and Norma I. (IhLe) Krueger; m. Richard R. Wadlow, July 27, 1958; children: Dawn, Kit. B.A., U. Nebr., Lincoln, 1953; M.A. (Seacrest Journalism fellow 1953-54), Fletcher Sch. Law and Diplomacy, 1956; Ph.D. (Rotary fellow 1956-57), U. Nebr., Lincoln, 1963; cert., Grad. Inst. Internat. Studies, Geneva, 1957. Mem. faculty U. Nebr., Lincoln, 1966-79; prof. polit. scis. U. Nebr., 1964-79, assoc. dean Coll. Arts and Scis., 1972-79; prof. polit. scis., dean Coll. Arts and Scis., U. Wyo., Laramie, 1979-84, v.p. acad. affairs, 1984-86; prof. polit. sci., provost U. Okla., Norman, 1986-91; chancellor U. Alaska, Fairbanks, 1991—; cons. on fed. grants; bd. dirs. Alaska Sea Life Center, Key Bank Alaska; mem. Commn. Colls. N.W. Assn. Author articles in field. Bd. dirs. Nat. Merit Scholarship Corp., 1988-97, Lincoln United Way, 1976-77, Bryan Hosp., Lincoln, 1978-79, Washington Ctr., 1986—, Key Bank of Alaska, Alaska SeaLife Ctr.; v.p., exec. commr. North Cen. Assn., pres., 1991; univ. pres. mission to Isreal, 1998; pres. adv. bd. Lincoln YWCA, 1970-71; mem. def. adv. com. Women in the Svcs., 1987-89; mem. community adv. bd. Alaska Airlines; mem. Univ. Pres.'s Mission to Israel, 1998. Recipient Mortar Board Teaching award, 1976, Disting. Teaching award U. Nebr., Lincoln, 1979, Rotary Internat. Alumni Scholar Achievement award, 1998; fellow Conf. Coop. Man, Lund, Sweden, 1956. Mem. NCAA (divsn. II pres. coun. 1997—), Internat. Studies Assn. (co-editor Internat. Studies Notes 1978-91), Nat. Assn. State Univs. and Land-Grant Colls. (exec. com. coun. acad. affairs 1989-91, chair internat. affairs counsel 1996-97), Western Assn. Africanists (pres. 1980-82), Assn. Western Univs. (pres. 1993), Coun. Colls. Arts and Scis. (pres. 1983-84), Greater Fairbanks C. of C., Gamma Phi Beta. Republican. Congregationalist. Office: U Alaska Fairbanks Singers Hall Ste 320 Fairbanks AK 99775

WADMAN, WILLIAM WOOD, III, educational director, technical research executive, consulting company executive; b. Oakland, Calif., Nov. 13, 1936; s. William Wood, Jr., and Lula Fay (Raisner) W.; children: Roxanne Alyce Wadman Hubbling, Raymond Alan (dec.), Theresa Hope Wadman Boudreaux; m. Barbara Jean Wadman; stepchildren: Denise Ellen Varine Skrypkar, Brian Ronald Varine. M.A., U. Calif., Irvine, 1978. Cert. program mgr. tng. Radiation safety specialist, accelerator health physicist U. Calif. Lawrence Berkeley Lab., 1957-68; campus radiation safety officer U. Calif., Irvine, 1968-79; dir. ops., radiation safety officer Radiation Sterilizers, Inc., Tustin, Calif., 1979-80; prin., pres. Wm. Wadman & Assocs. Inc., 1980—; mem. operational review team Princeton U. Rsch. Campus TOKOMAK Fusion Test Facility, 1993-94; technical project mgr. for upgrades projects Los Alamos Nat. Lab. 1994-96, tech. project mgr. for 3 projects, 1995—; mem. team No. 1, health physics appraisal program NRC, 1980—, operational readiness review team to Princeton U. Rsch. Campus TOKOMAK Fusion Test Facility, 1993-94; cons. health physicist to industry; lectr. sch. social ecology, 1974-79, dept. community and environ. medicine U. Calif., Irvine, 1979-80, instr. in environ. health and safety, 1968-79, Orange Coast Coll., in radiation exposure reduction design engring. Iowa Electric Light & Power; trainer Mason & Hanger-Silas Mason Co., Los Alamos Nat. Lab.; instr. in medium energy cyclotron radiation safety UCLBL, lectr. in accelerator health physics, 1966, 67; curriculum developer in field; subject matter expert Los Alamos Nat. Lab., Earth and Environ. Scis., Tech. Support Office. Active Cub Scouts; chief umpire Mission Viejo Little League, 1973. Served with USNR, 1955-63. Recipient award for profl. achievement U. Calif. Alumni Assn., 1972, Outstanding Performance award U. Calif., Irvine, 1973. Mem. Health Physics Soc. (treas. 1979-81, editor proc. 11th symposium, pres. So. Calif. chpt. 1977, Professionalism award 1975), Internat. Radiation Protection Assn. (U.S. del. 4th Congress 1977, 8th Congress 1992), Am. Nuclear Soc., Am. Public Health Assn. (chmn. program 1978, chmn. radiol. health sect. 1979-80), Campus Radiation Safety Officers (chmn. 1975, editor proc. 5th conf. 1975), ASTM, Project Mgmt. Inst. Club: UCI Univ. (dir. 1976, sec. 1977, treas. 1978). Contbr. articles to tech. jours. Achievements include research in radiation protection and environmental sciences; Avocations: sailing, Tae Kwon Do, wood working, numesmantics. Home: 3687 Red Cedar Way Lake Oswego OR 97035-3525 Office: 675 Fairview Dr Ste 246 Carson City NV 89701-5428

WAFER, THOMAS J., JR., newspaper publisher. Pub. The Daily Breeze, Torrance, Calif., 1993—. Office: 5215 Torrance Blvd Torrance CA 90503*

WAGENER, ROBERT JOHN, bioethicist, mediator; b. Buffalo, N.Y., Mar. 6, 1946; s. Philip John and June Augusta (Bartels) W. BA, Houghton Coll. and SUNY, Buffalo; MDiv, McCormick Theol. Sem., Chgo.; MA, Canisius Coll. Founder, pres. Ctr. for Med. Ethics and Mediation, San Diego, 1992—; mediation coord. Am. Arbitration Assn., 1993—; cons. U. Calif. San Diego Ethics Consultation Svc., 1985—; lectr., mediator, mentor, trainer in field. Contbr. articles to profl. jours. Bd. dirs. Hospice Buffalo, Victim Offender Reconciliation Program, San Diego, U. Calif. San Diego Med. Ctr. Ethics Com.; cons. San Diego Hospice Chaplaincy Project; mem. adv. bd. Dignita Hospice, San Diego; vice chair Hotel Dieu Hosp. Hospice, New Orleans; v.p. Sudden Infant Death Found. Western N.Y. Mem. ABA (dispute resolution sect.), Am. Soc. Law, Medicine and Ethics, Soc. Profls. in Dispute Resolution, So. Calif. Mediation Assn., Internat. Bioethics Inst., Hastings Ctr. for Bioethics. Avocations: racquetball, skiing, antiques. Office: Ctr for Med Ethics & Mediation Ste 111 1081 Camino Del Rio S San Diego CA 92108-3543

WAGGENER, THERYN LEE, law enforcement professional; b. Cedar Rapids, Iowa, Sept. 7, 1941; s. Hollis Angisa (Fowler) W.; m. Zoetta Jean Hamilton, May 30, 1967; 1 child, Drugh Kincade. BBA, Nat. U., 1977, MBA, 1979; JD, Western State Coll. Law, 1980. Traffic officer Calif. Hwy. Patrol, San Diego, 1966-72; owner, operator Am. Nat. Chem., San Diego, 1972-82; chief investigator N.Mex. Real Estate Commn., Albuquerque, 1983-86, Nev. Real Estate Div., Carson City, 1986-89; lt., shift comdr. Nev. Dept. Prisons, Ely, 1989—; prof., Sierra Nev. Coll., Incline Village, 1988-89, Western Nev. Community Coll., Carson City, 1987-89; No. Nev. C.C., 1992—. Mem. Washoe County (Nev.) Rep. Cen. Com., 1989. With USN, 1960-65. Mem. Nat. Assn. Real Estate Lic. Law Ofcls. (enforcement and investigative com. 1987-89), Toastmasters, Rotary, Lions, Masons, Shriners, Nu Beta Epsilon. Avocations: skiing, golf, horses, flying.

WAGNER, ARTHUR, actor, director, educator; b. N.Y.C., May 11, 1923; s. Moses and Fanny (Spiro) W.; m. Molli Joan Mercer, June 16, 1956; children: Wayne Louis, Michelle Patrice. BA, Earlham Coll., Richmond, Ind., 1946; MA, Smith Coll., 1948; PhD, Stanford U., 1962. Chmn. dept. theater Rollins Coll., Winter Park, Fla., 1956-65; prof. theater Tulane U., New Orleans, 1965-67; prof. Ohio U., Athens, 1967-69, Temple U., Phila., 1969-72; chmn. dept. theater U. Calif., San Diego, 1972-77, prof., head actor tng. program, 1974-91; treas. League Profl. Theatre Tng. Programs, 1971-72; v.p. Am. Theatre Assn., 1976-78; pres. Nat. Theatre Conf., 1978-81. Actor, dir. numerous prodns. Served with U.S. Army, 1943-46. Danforth Found. grantee, 1961. Mem. Nat. Theatre Found. (pres. 1978-81), Horton Plaza Theatre Found. (pres. 1987—), Actors Equity Assn. Avocations: tennis, squash, skiing, bicycling. Home: 7 Burnett Ave N # 1 San Francisco CA 94131-3322 Office: U Calif Dept Theatre La Jolla CA 92093

WAGNER, DANA ERIC, roofing company executive; b. Sacramento, Sept. 20, 1958; s. Gary Don and Marjorie (Melvold) W.; children: Chelsea Rae, Dane Douglas. Grad., Encino H.S., Sacramento, 1976. Owner Wagner Roofing, Sacramento, Calif. Avocations: fishing, hunting.

WAGNER, DAVID JAMES, lawyer; b. Cleve., Feb. 7, 1946; m. Martha Wilson, June 22, 1979; 1 child, Diana Jane. BS, USAF Acad., 1969; JD, Georgetown U., 1973. Bar: Colo. 1973, U.S. Supreme Ct. 1975, U.S. Dist. Ct. of Colo. 1973, U.S. Tax Ct. 1974. Asst. assoc. gen. counsel Presdl. Clemency Bd., Washington, 1974-75; sec., gen. counsel Cablecomm-Gen. Inc., Denver, 1975-77; adj. prof. law Metro. State Coll., Denver, 1975-80; atty., mng. prin. Wagner & Waller, P.C., Denver, 1977-84; chmn. bd. GILA Comm., Inc., Denver, 1987; pvt. practice David Wagner & Assocs., P.C., Englewood, Colo., 1984—. Editor Am. Criminal Law Rev., Georgetown U. Law Sch., 1972-73. Trustee Kent Denver Sch., Cherry Hills Village, Colo., 1990-96, treas., 1992, pres., 1992-96; treas., dir. Denver Chamber Orch., 1979-81; dir. Leadership Denver Assn., 1978-80. Capt. USAF, 1973-75. Republican. Episcopalian. Office: David Wagner & Assocs PC Penthouse 8400 E Prentice Ave Ph Englewood CO 80111-2927

WAGNER, JOHN LEE, food products executive; b. Mt. Vernon, Wash., Aug. 24, 1943; s. John Orville and Gladys Annina (Hansen) W.; m. Judith Ann Murray, June 17, 1965 (div. Oct. 1991); 1 child, Trevor John; m. Claudia Ruth Littleton, Feb. 27, 1996. BA, U. Wash., 1965. Bank official Seattle First Nat. Bank, 1970-78; pres. Bank of Wash., Bellingham, 1978-83, Talbot Investment Co., Seattle, 1982-83; pres., owner Resource Pacific, Inc., Seattle, 1982—. Pres. Bellingham C. of C., 1980, Whatcom County Devel. Coun., 1981; bd. dirs. Western Wash. U. Found., 1984-88. Capt. USMC, 1965-70. Recipient Paul Harris Fellowship award Rotary Internat., 1989. Mem. Columbia Tower Club, Seattle Club, Rotary (pres. local dist. 1984). Republican. Avocations: gardening, golf, fishing.

WAGNER, JUDITH BUCK, investment firm executive; b. Altoona, Pa. Sept. 25, 1943; d. Harry Bud and Mary Elizabeth (Rhodes) B.; m. Joseph E. Wagner, Mar. 15, 1980; 1 child, Elizabeth. BA in History, U. Wash., 1965; grad. N.Y. Inst. Fin., 1968. Registered Am. Stock Exch., N.Y. Stock Exch., investment advisor. Security analyst Morgan, Olmstead, Kennedy & Gardner, L.A., 1968-71; security analyst Boettcher & Co., Denver, 1972-75; pres. Wagner Investment Mgmt., Denver, 1975—; chmn., bd. dirs. The Women's Bank, N.A., Denver, 1977-94, organizational group pres., 1975-77; chmn. Equitable Bankshares Colo., Inc., Denver, 1980-94; bd. dirs. Equitable Bank of Littleton, 1983-88, pres., 1985; bd. dirs. Colo. Growth Capital, 1979-82; lectr. Denver U., Metro State, 1975-80. Author: Woman and Money series Colo. Woman Mag., 1976; moderator 'Catch 2' Sta. KWGN-TV, 1978-79. Pres. Big Sisters Colo., Denver, 1977-82, bd. dirs., 1973-83; bd. fellows U. Denver, 1985-90; bd. dirs. Red Cross, 1980, Assn. Children's Hosp., 1985, Colo. Health Facilities Authority, 1978-84, Jr. League Community Adv. Com., 1979-82, Brother's Redevel., Inc., 1979-80; mem. agy. rels. com. Mile High United Way, 1978-81, chmn. United Way Venture Grant com., 1980-81; bd. dirs. Downtown Denver Inc., 1988-95; bd. dirs., v.p., treas. The Women's Found. Colo., 1987-91; treas., trustee, v.p., Graland Country Day Sch., 1990—, pres. 1994—; trustee Denver Rotary Found., 1990-95; trustee Hunt Alternatives Fund, 1992-97, The Colo. Trust, 1998—. Recipient Making It award Cosmopolitan Mag., 1977, Women on the Go award, Savvy mag., 1983, Minouri Yasoui award, 1986, Salute Spl. Honoree award, Big Sisters, 1987; named one of the Outstanding Young Women in Am., 1979; recipient Woman Who Makes A Difference award Internat. Women's Forum, 1987. Fellow Assn. Investment Mgmt. and Rsch.; mem. Women's Forum of Colo. (pres. 1979), Women's Found. Colo., Inc. (bd. dirs. 1986-91), Denver Soc. Security Analysts (bd. dirs. 1976-83, v.p. 1980-81, pres. 1981-82), Colo. Investment Advisors Assn., Rotary (treas. Denver chpt. found., pres. 1993-94), Leadership Denver (Outstanding Alumna award 1987), Pi Beta Phi (pres. U. Wash. chpt. 1964-65). Office: Wagner Investment Mgmt Inc Ste 240 3200 Cherry Creek South Dr Denver CO 80209-3245

WAGNER, PATRICIA HAMM, lawyer; b. Gastonia, N.C., Feb. 1, 1936; d. Luther Boyd and Mildred Ruth (Wheeler) Hamm; married; children: David Marion, Michael Marion, Laura Marion. AB summa cum laude, Wittenberg U., 1958; JD with distinction, Duke U., 1974. Bar: N.C. 1974, Wash. 1984. Asst. univ. counsel Duke U., Durham, N.C., 1974-75, assoc. univ. counsel health affairs, 1977-80; atty. N.C. Meml. Hosp., 1975-77; assoc. N.C. Atty. Gen. Office, 1975-77; assoc. Powe, Porter & Alphin, Durham, 1980-81, prin., 1981-83; assoc. Williams, Kastner & Gibbs, 1984-86, Wickwire, Goldmark & Schorr, 1986-88; spl. counsel Heller, Ehrman, White & McAuliffe, 1988-90, ptnr., 1990—; arbitrator Am. Arbitration Assn., 1978—; arbitrator, pro tem judge King County Superior Ct., 1986—; tchr. in field. Mem. bd. vis. Law Sch. Duke U., 1992-98; bd. dirs. Seattle Edn. Ctr., 1990-91, Metroctr. YMCA, 1991-94, Cmty. Psychiat. Clinic, Seattle, 1984-86; bd. dirs., sec.-treas. N.C. Found. Alternative Health Programs, Inc., 1982-84; bd. dirs., sec.-treas. N.C. Ctr. Pub. Policy Rsch., 1976-83, vice-chmn., 1977-80; mem. task force on commitment law N.C. Dept. Human Resources, 1978; active Def. Rsch. Inst. 1982-84; bd. dirs. Law Fund, 1992—, v.p., 1993-97; mem. ADR Roundtable, 1996—. Fellow Am. Bar Found.; mem. ABA (mem. ho. dels. Seattle-King County Bar Assn. 1991-94, mem. litigation sect.), Am. Soc. Hosp. Attys., Wash. State Bar Assn. (mem. domestic rels. task force 1991-93), Seattle-King Bar Assn. (mem. bd. trustees 1990-93, sec. bd. 1989-90, chair judiciary and cts. com. 1987-89, mem. King County Superior Ct. delay reduction task force 1987-89, mem. gender bias com. 1990-94, chair 1990-91), Wash. Def. Trial Lawyers (chmn. ct. rules and procedures com. 1987, co-editor newsletter 1985-86), Wash. State Soc. Hosp. Attys., Wash. Women Lawyers (treas. 1986, 87). Office: Heller Ehrman White & McAuliffe 6100 Columbia Ctr 701 5th Ave Ste 6100 Seattle WA 98104-7098

WAGNER, RACHEL ANNETTE, systems analyst, consultant; b. Santa Ana, Calif., July 5, 1958; d. Roger Wilfred and Rita Janette (Plante) Remillard; m. Richard Henry Wagner, July 28, 1979 (div. May 1985); 1 child, Nicole Elaine. BA in Sociology, Calif. State U., Fullerton, 1981; M of MIS, West Coast U., 1997. Customer liaison Dustin Assocs., Santa Ana, 1984-87; pub. supr. Eaton Corp., Westlake Village, Calif., 1987-90; sr. sys. analyst Amgen, Inc., Thousand Oaks, Calif., 1990-98; sr. cons. pub. svcs. KPMG Peat Marwick, Woodland Hills, Calif., 1998—; conf. spkr. Drug Info. Assn., various locations, 1995—, Internat. Inst. Rsch., various locations, 1996—. Pres. mother/child program YMCA, Camarillo, Calif., 1992-93. Office: KPMG 21700 Oxnard St Ste 1200 Woodland Hills CA 91367-7303

WAGNER, RICHARD, athletics consultant, former baseball team executive; b. Central City, Nebr., Oct. 19, 1927; s. John Howard and Esther Marie (Wolken) W.; m. Gloria Jean Larsen, May 10, 1950; children—Randolph G., Cynthia Kaye. Student, pub. schs., Central City. Gen. mgr. Lincoln (Nebr.) Baseball Club, 1955-58; mgr. Pershing Mcpl. Auditorium, Lincoln, 1958-61; exec. staff Ice Capades, Inc., Hollywood, Calif., 1961-63; gen. mgr. Sta. KSAL, Salina, Kans., 1963-65; dir. promotion and sales St. Louis Nat. Baseball Club, 1965-66; gen. mgr. Forum, Inglewood, Calif., 1966-67; asst. to exec. v.p. Cin. Reds, 1967-70, asst. to pres., 1970-74, v.p. adminstrn., 1975, exec. v.p., 1975-78, gen. mgr., 1977-83, pres., 1978-83; pres. Houston Astros Baseball Club, 1985-87; spl. asst. Office of Baseball Commr., 1988-93; asst. to chmn. Major League Exec. Coun., 1993-94; pres. RGW Enterprises, Inc., Phoenix, 1978-97. Served with USNR, 1945-47, 50-52. Named Exec. of Yr., Minor League Baseball, Sporting News, 1958. Republican. Methodist.

WAGNER, ROB LEICESTER, newspaper editor, writer; b. Pasadena, Calif., Nov. 17, 1954; s. Howard Leicester and Jill (Hisey) W.; m. Deniece Heredia, July 8, 1978; children: Nicholas, Selena, Danielle. AA in Journalism, Pasadena City Coll., 1975. Reporter Meredith Newspapers, L.A., 1978-80, Corona (Calif.) Daily Ind., 1980-83, Daily Report, Ontario, Calif., 1983-85, San Gabriel Valley Tribune, Covina, Calif., 1985-86; reporter, city editor Inland Valley Daily Bull., Ontario, 1986-95, mng. editor, 1995—; sr. writer, Inland Bus. Mag., Ontario, 1987-89; writer L.A. Daily Jour., 1986-89. Author: Classic Cars, 1996, Fire Engines, 1996, Toy Tractors, 1996, Kings of the Road, 1997, Fabulous Fins of the Fifties, 1997, John Wayne, 1997, Volkswagens, 1998, Pickup Trucks, 1998, Style and Speed, 1998, Hot Rods, 1999, American Chrome, 1999, Fire Rescue, 1999; contbr. articles to mags. Recipient Best Series award Calif. Newspaper Pubs. Assn., San Diego, 1982, Outstanding Svcs. award League United L.Am. Citizens, 1982, Best Investigative Story award Soc. Profl. Journalists, 1989. Mem. Grosse Il Hist. Soc., United Empire Loyalists Assn. Can. Avocations: genealogy, travel. Home: 10711 Katrina Ct Riverside CA 92505-2838 Office: Inland Valley Daily Bull 2041 E 4th St Ontario CA 91764-2605

WAGNER, RONALD DEAN, petroleum engineer; b. Findlay, Ohio, Apr. 6, 1958; s. Richard Dean and Betty Lou (Jones) W.; m. Vicki Marie James, Aug. 16, 1980; children: Ronald Dean Jr., Lara Marie. AS, Casper (Wyo.) Coll., 1978; BS in Petroleum Engring., U. Wyo., 1981. Registered profl. engr., Wyo. Petroleum engr. I Oxy USA, Inc., Gillette, Wyo., 1981-82, petroleum engr. II, 1982-85, staff petroleum engr., 1985-86; sr. petroleum engr. Oxy USA, Inc., Gillette and Midland, Tex., 1986-91; profl. petroleum engr. Amerada Hess Corp., Williston, N.D., 1991-93; v.p. prodn. Pathfinder Energy, Inc., Gillette, Wyo., 1993—. Mem. Soc. Petroleum Engrs. (profl. regulatory com. 1994—), Masons. Republican. Methodist. Achievements include research in reduced paraffin treating of 15,000 bopd from $1,000,000 per year to $250,000 by use of chemical treating versus hot oil treating. Office: Pathfinder Energy Inc PO Box 187 Gillette WY 82717-0187

WAGNESS, LORRAINE MELVA, gifted education educator; b. Bellingham, Wash., June 11, 1933; d. William Barkley and Laura Iola (Starr) Nattrass; m. Lee Wagness, Aug. 24, 1969; 1 child, Kathryn Lorraine. BA, Western Wash. State U., 1955; MA, City U., Seattle, Wash., 1993. Cert. tchr. grades kindergarten through 12, Wash. Tchr. Bellingham Sch. Dist., 1955-57, Eugene (Oreg.) Sch. Dist., 1957-59; tchr. talented and gifted, libr., arts specialist Seattle Pub. Schs., 1959—; chmn. Science Fair, 1995, 96, Art Show, 1995, 96. Photographer various publs., 1984-90; exhibited batik/paintings area shows (1st pl. Wash. Arts Contest 1990). Vol., demonstrator weaving and spinning Woodland Pk. Zoo Guild, Seattle, 1984—; pres. Sigma Kappa Mothers' Club, U. Wash., 1982-84. Sci. scholar Wash. State Garden Clubs, Seattle, 1960; partnership grantee Lafayette Sch. PTA, Seattle, 1994, 95. Mem. NEA (bldg. rep. 1980-90), Wash. Edn. Assn. (bldg. rep. 1980-90), Seattle Tchrs. Assn. (bldg. rep. 1980-90), AAUW (Outstanding Sr. award 1955), Internat. Reading Assn. (mem. coms. 1990-96), Associated Women Students (pres. 1955), Gen. Fedn. Women's Clubs (sec., treas. 1988-92, Club Woman of Yr. 1986, 90), Evergreen Garden Club (treas., sec. 1985—), Delta Kappa Gamma (v.p. Beta Beta chpt. 1991-96), Pi Lambda Theta (mem. coms. Seattle area chpt. 1988—). Presbyterian. Avocations: international travel, arts and crafts, gardening, reading, photography. Home: 17040 Sylvester Rd SW Seattle WA 98166-3434

WAGONER, DAVID EVERETT, lawyer; b. Pottstown, Pa., May 16, 1928; s. Claude Brower and Mary Kathryn (Groff) W.; children: Paul R., Colin H., Elon D., Peter B., Dana F.; m. Jean Morton Saunders; children: Constance A., Jennifer L., Melissa J. BA, Yale U., 1950; LLB, U. Pa., 1953. Bar: D.C. 1953, Pa. 1953, Wash. 1953. Law clk. U.S. Ct. Appeals (3d cir.), Pa., 1955-56; law clk. U.S. Supreme Ct., Washington, 1956-57; ptnr. Perkins & Coie, Seattle, 1957-96; panel mem. of arbitration forum worldwide including People's Republic of China, B.C. Internat. Comml. Arbitration Ctr., Hong Kong Internat. Arbitration Centre, Asian/Pacific Ctr. for Resolution of Internat. Bus. Disputes and the Ctr. for Internat. Dispute Resolution for Asian/Pacific Region. Mem. sch. com. Mcpl. League Seattle and King County, 1958—, chmn., 1962-65; mem. Seattle schs. citizens coms. on equal ednl. opportunity and adult vocat. edn., 1963-64; mem. Nat. Com. Support Pub. Schs.; mem. adv. com. on community colls., to 1965, legislature interim com. on edn., 1964-65; mem. community coll. adv. com. to state supt. pub. instrn., 1965; chmn. edn. com. Forward Thrust, 1968; mem. Univ. Congl. Ch. Council Seattle, 1968-70; bd. dirs. Met. YMCA Seattle, 1968; bd. dirs. Seattle Pub. Schs., 1965-73, v.p., 1966-67, 72-73, pres., 1968, 73; trustee Evergreen State Coll. Found., chmn. 1986-87, capitol campaign planning chmn.; trustee Pacific NW Ballet, v.p. 1986. Served to 1st lt. M.C., AUS, 1953-55. Fellow Am. Coll. Trial Lawyers (mem. ethics com., legal ethics com.), Chartered Inst. Arbitrators, Singapore Inst. Arbitrators; mem. ABA (chmn. standing com. fed. jud. imprisonment, chmn. appellate advocacy com., mem. commn. on separation of powers and jud. independence), Wash. State Bar Assn., Seattle-King County Bar Assn., Acad. Experts, Swiss Arbitration Assn., Comml. Bar Assn. London, Nat. Sch. Bds. Assn. (bd. dirs., chmn. coun. Big City bds. edn. 1971-72), English-Speaking Union (v.p. Seattle chpt. 1961-62), Chi Phi. Home: 4215 E Blaine St Seattle WA 98112-3229 Office: Internat Arbitration Chambers US BankCtr 1420 5th Ave Fl 22 Seattle WA 98101-4087

WAGONER, NANCY ANN, university admissions executive, writer; b. Roswell, N. Mex., June 7, 1954; d. Frank Lafayette and Corine Marie (Davis) W.; 1 child, Joshua. AA in Social Sci., Eastern N. Mex. U., 1978; BS in Psychology, N. Mex. Inst. Mining & Tech., 1990. Process control operator Intel Corp., Rio Rancho, N. Mex., 1984-85; indsl. engring. tech. II Intel Corp., Rio Rancho, 1985-86; inspector Eagle Pitcher, Inc., Socorro, N. Mex., 1987-88; printers asst. N. Mex. Inst. Mining & Tech., Socorro, N. Mex., 1988; project asst. N. Mex. Inst. Mining & Tech., Socorro, 1988-90, asst. dir. admissions, 1990-93, assoc. dir. admissions, 1993—; chairperson and judge N. Mex. State Sci. and Engring. Fair, Socorro, N. Mex., 1992-98; spl. awards judge Intel Internat. Sci. and Engring. Fair, Fort Worth, Tex., 1998,. Editor: (book) New Mexico's Environment: Dance of the Interests, 1990. Grantee: Coalition to Increase Minority Degrees, Tucson, 1993-97, N. Mex. State U., Las Cruces, N. Mex., 1993—, Western Assn. to Expand Student Opportunities, Tucson, 1997—. Mem. Nat. Assn. for Coll. Admission Counseling, Rocky Mt. Assn. for Coll. Admission Counseling, N. Mex. Assn. Collegiate Registrars and Admission Officers (sec.-treas. 1994-95, pres. 1995-98, Svc. award 1997). Democrat. Baptist. Avocations: reading, writing short stories and essays, jazz, walking, aerobics. Office: N Mex Inst Mining & Tech 801 Leroy Pl Socorro NM 87801-4681

WAHL, BERNT RAINER, mathematician, writer, software engineer; b. Santa Monica, Calif., June 24, 1960; s. Bruno W. and Ursula (Nunn) W. BA in Math., U. Calif., Santa Cruz, 1984, BS in Physics, 1986; MBA, U. Calif., Davis, 1998. Founding mem. BMUG Inc., Berkeley, Calif., 1984—; CEO Dynamic Software, Berkeley, Calif., 1986—; mem. Bootstrap Inst., Fremont, Calif., 1996—; CEO R.Q. Labs Inc., Berkeley, Calif.; tech. advisor Reliacom, Reston, Va., Quantal, Berkeley, Calif., Jhane Barnes, Inc., N.Y., 1995—; lectr. U. Calif., Berkeley, U. Calif., Davis, 1995-96. Author: Exploring Fractals, 1995; host (video series) Fractals, 1995, Info. Tech., 1996; film dir./prodr.: Swing City. Avocations: Olympic photography, America Cup Heart of Am. E-mail: bernt@wahl.org. Office: Dynamic Software PO Box 13991 Berkeley CA 94712-4991 also: RQ Labs Inc 1936 University Ave Ste 355 Berkeley CA 94704-1000

WAHLBERG, MAX, safety director; b. Payson, Utah, Dec. 30, 1951; s. Joseph Leonard and Joan (Sorenson) W.; m. Georgina Wahlberg, Apr. 30, 1986 (div. Aug. 1991); m. Mary Michelle McConnell, Aug. 11, 1950; children: April Lynn, Max Joseph. Mine-shift foreman Anaconda Copper, Tooele, Utah; mine supt. Crested Corp., Austin, Nev.; safety tng. coord. Echo Bay Minerals, Battle Mt., Nev., Coeur Rochester, Lovelock, Nev.; v.p. Occu-Family Care, Spark, Nev.; safety dir. Pegasus Gold, Jorlay, Nev., Kilborn Internat., Denver. EMT, West Juab Ambulance, Eureka, Utah, 1975-82; fireman Eureka City, 1975-82, mem. Search and Rescue, Eureka, 1975-82; advisor 6 County Emergency Med. Svcs. Avocations: flying, golf. Home: 605 Oak Ct Battle Mountain NV 89820-2706

WAHLKE, JOHN CHARLES, political science educator; b. Cin., Oct. 29, 1917; s. Albert B.C. and Clara J. (Ernst) W.; m. Virginia Joan Higgins, Dec. 1, 1943; children: Janet Parmely, Dale. A.B., Harvard U., 1939, M.A., 1947, Ph.D., 1952. Instr., asst. prof. polit. sci. Amherst (Mass.) Coll., 1949-53; assoc. prof. polit. sci. Vanderbilt U., Nashville, Tenn., 1953-63; prof. polit. sci. SUNY, Buffalo, 1963-66, U. Iowa, 1966-71, SUNY, Stony Brook, 1971-72, U. Iowa, Iowa City, 1972-79; prof. polit. sci. U. Ariz., Tucson, 1979-87, prof. emeritus, 1988—, retired. Author: (with others) The Legislative System, 1962, Government and Politics, 1966, The Politics of Representation, 1978; co-author: Introduction to Political Science—Reason, Reflection, and Analysis, 1997;. Served to capt., F.A. AUS, 1942-46. Decorated Air medal with 2 oak leaf clusters. Mem. AAAS, Am. Polit. Sci. Assn. (past pres.), Internat. Polit. Sci. Assn., So. Polit. Sci. Assn., Midwest Polit. Sci. Assn. (past pres.), Western Polit. Sci. Assn., Southwestern Polit. Sci. Assn., Assn. Politics and the Life Scis., Internat. Soc. of Polit. Psychology. Home: 3462 N Entrada Catorce Tucson AZ 85718-4851 Office: U Ariz Social Science Bldg Rm 515 Dept Political Science Tucson AZ 85721*

WAINESS, MARCIA WATSON, legal management consultant; b. Bklyn., Dec. 17, 1949; d. Stanley and Seena (Klein) Watson; m. Steven Richard Wainess, Aug. 7, 1975. Student, UCLA, 1967-71, 80-81, UCLA Grad. Sch., 1987-88. Office mgr., paralegal Lewis, Marenstein & Kadar, L.A., 1977-81; office mgr. Rosenfeld, Meyer & Susman, Beverly Hills, Calif., 1981-83; adminstr. Rudin, Richman & Appel, Beverly Hills, 1983; dir. adminstrn. Kadison, Pfaelzer, L.A., 1983-87; exec. dir. Richards, Watson and Gershon, L.A., 1987-93; legal mgmt. cons. Wainess & Co., L.A., 1993—; faculty UCLA Legal Mgmt. & Adminstrn. Program, 1983, U. So. Calif. Paralegal Program, L.A., 1985; adv. bd. atty. asst. tng. program UCLA, 1984-88; adj. faculty U. West L.A. Sch. Paralegal Studies, 1997-98. Mem. ABA (chair Displaywrite Users Group 1986, legal tech. adv. coun. litig. support working group 1986-87), Inst. Mgmt. Consultants, L.A. County Bar Assn. (exec. com. law office mgmt. sect.), San Fernando Valley Bar Assn., Assn. Legal Adminstrs. (mem. editl. adv. bd. 1998—, bd. dirs. 1990-92, asst. regional v.p. Calif. 1987-88, regional v.p. 1988-89, pres. Beverly Hills chpt. 1985-86, membership chair 1984-85, chair new adminstrn. sect. 1982-84, mktg. mgmt. sect. com. 1989-90, internat. conf. com.), Beverly Hills Bar Assn. (chair law practice mgmt. sect. 1998—). Avocations: historic preservation, antiques, interior design. Office: 23d Fl 11601 Wilshire Blvd Fl 23D Los Angeles CA 90025-1770

WAINIO, MARK ERNEST, insurance company consultant; b. Virginia, Minn., Apr. 18, 1953. BA, Gustavus Adolphus Coll., 1975. Cert. safety profl., assoc. loss control mgmt., assoc. risk mgmt., assoc. claims, CPCU. Carpenter ABI Contracting Inc., Virginia, 1975-77; co-owner Mesabi Builders, Albuquerque and Eveleth, Minn., 1977-79; sr. engring. rep. Aetna Life & Casualty, Albuquerque, 1979-86; loss control specialist CNA Ins. Cos., Albuquerque, 1986-91, loss control cons., 1991-94, mgr. loss control svcs., 1994-95, dir. loss control svcs., 1995-97, asst. v.p. loss control svcs., 1997—; owner MEW Safety and Risk Mgmt., 1989—; pres. MW Enterprises, 1990—. Mem. Am. Soc. Safety Engrs., CPCU. Avocations: golf, fishing, hunting, swimming, Karate. Office: CNA Ins Cos 8500 Menaul Blvd NE Albuquerque NM 87112-2298

WAINIONPAA, JOHN WILLIAM, computer equipment company executive; b. Quincy, Mass., July 13, 1946; s. Frank Jacob and Jennie Sofia (Kaukola) W.; m. S. Linda Rapo, Oct. 18, 1969; children: Heidi Liisa, Erik David, Sinikka Lin. BSEE, U. N.Mex., 1972; MS in Aero. Engring., Naval Postgrad. Sch., 1981. Engr.-in-tng., Colo. Enlisted USN, 1968, commd. ens., 1972, advanced through grades to lt. comdr., 1982; flight instr. Tng. Squadron 27, Corpus Christi, Tex., 1973-75; aircraft, mission comdr. Patrol Squadron 49, Jacksonville, Fla., 1976-79; ops. officer Anti-Submarine Warfare Ops. Ctr., Kadena, Okinawa, Japan, 1982-84; launch and control systems officer Naval Space Command, Dahlgren, Va., 1984-86; naval space systems ops. officer U.S. Space Command, Colorado Springs, 1986-88; ret. USN, 1988; sys. engr. CTA Inc., Colorado Springs, 1988-95, tng. coord., 1993-94, profl. devel. orgn. mgr., 1994-95; product mgr. Digital Equipment Corp., Colorado Springs, 1995—. Merit badge counselor Boy Scouts Am., Colorado Springs, 1986—; classroom instr. Jr. Achievement, Colorado Springs, 1995—. Mem. AIAA (sr.), IEEE, U.S. Naval Inst., Sigma Tau, Eta Kappa Nu. Avocations: music, skiing, drama, volunteer church activities. Office: Digital Equipment Corp CX01-2/P22 301 S Rockrimmon Blvd Colorado Springs CO 80919-2398

WAKATSUKI, LYNN Y., commissioner. Commr. fin. instns. Honolulu. Office: 1010 Richards St Rm 602A Honolulu HI 96813-2920

WAKE, DAVID BURTON, biology educator; b. Webster, S.D., June 8, 1936; s. Thomas B. and Ina H. (Solem) W.; m. Marvalee Hendricks, June 23, 1962; 1 child, Thomas Andrew. BA, Pacific Luth. U., 1958; MS, U. So. Calif., 1960, PhD, 1964. Instr. anatomy and biology U. Chgo., 1964-66, asst. prof. anatomy and biology, 1966-69; assoc. prof. zoology U. Calif., Berkeley, 1969-72, prof., 1972-89, prof. integrative biology, 1989—, John and Margaret Gompertz prof., 1991-97; dir. Mus. Vertebrate Zoology U. Calif., Berkeley, 1971-98; curator Herpetology Mus. Vertebrate Zoology, U. Calif., 1971—. Author: Biology, 1979; co-editor: Functional Vertebrate Morphology, 1985, Complex Organismal Functions: Integration and Evolution in the Vertebrates, 1989. Recipient Quantrell Teaching award U. Chgo., 1967, Outstanding Alumnus award Pacific Luth. U., 1979, Joseph Grinnell medal Mus. Vertebrate Zoology, 1998; grantee NSF, 1965—; Guggenheim fellow, 1982. Fellow AAAS, NAS, NRC (bd. biology 1986-92), Am. Philos. Soc., Am. Acad. Arts and Scis.; mem. Internat. Union for Conservation of Nature and Natural Resources (chair task force on declining amphibian populations 1990-92), Am. Soc. Zoologists (pres. 1992), Am. Soc. Naturalists (pres. 1989), Am. Soc. Ichthyologists and Herpetologists (bd. govs.), Soc. Study Evolution (pres. 1983, editor 1979-81), Soc. Systematic Biology (coun. 1980-84), Herpetologist's League (Disting. Herpetologist 1984). Home: 999 Middlefield Rd Berkeley CA 94708-1509

WAKS, DENNIS STANFORD, lawyer; b. Decatur, Ill., Apr. 2, 1949; s. Paul and Regina W.; m. Jaclyn Hoyle; 1 child, Kelly. BA, U. Wis., 1971; JD, U. Miss., 1973; LLM, U. Mo., Kansas City, 1975. Bar: Miss. 1973, Ill. 1975, U.S. Dist. Ct. (no. dist.) Miss. 1973, U.S. Dist. Ct. (so. dist.) Ill. 1975, U.S. Dist. Ct. (ea. dist.) Calif. 1988, U.S. Ct. Apeals (9th cir.) 1989, Calif. 1989. Dir. prison legal svcs. project So. Ill. U. Sch. Law, Carbondale, Ill., 1976-77; asst. pub. defender Jackson County Pub. Defenders Office, Murphysboro, Ill., 1977-80, chief pub. defender, 1980-85; spl. prosecutor Perry County States Atty. Office, Pinckneyville, Ill., 1985; prof. dept. law enforcement So. Ill. U., Carbondale, 1978-87; pvt. practice Murphysboro, 1985-87; asst. atty. Fed. Pub. Defenders Office Ea. Dist. Calif., Sacramento, 1988—, supervising sr. atty., 1990-96; chief asst. Fed. Pub. Defender, 1996—; faculty Ill. Defender Program, Chgo., 1982-86, bd. dirs.; faculty masters thesis and doctoral com. So. Ill. U., Carbondale, 1978-87; mem. planning com. U.S. Dist. Ct. (ea. dist.) Calif.; mem. Unibomb def. team. Editor Miss. Law Rev., 1973. Organizer Paul Simon for Senator, Carbondale, 1984; bd. dirs. Hill Ho. Resdl. Ctr. for Substance Abuse, Carbondale, 1981-87, v.p. 1984-87. Named Outstanding Young Man of Am., 1985. Mem. ABA, Nat. Assn. Criminal Def. Attys., Ill. Pub. Defender Project, Ill. Pub. Defenders Assn., Calif. Attys. for Criminal Justice, Calif. Pub. Defenders Assn. Democrat. Avocations: reading, weightlifting, politics. Office: Fed Defenders Office 801 K St 10th Fl Sacramento CA 95814-3518

WALASEK, OTTO FRANK, chemical engineer, biochemist, photographer; b. Park Falls, Wis., Mar. 11, 1919; s. Frank Otto and Mary (Swoboda) W.; m. Annie May Stockton (div. Nov. 1959); 1 child, Richard A.; m. Joan Constance Ashton, Sept. 18, 1965; children: Arthur, Carl. BS in Chem. Engring., U. Wis., 1946; MS in Biochemistry, U. Ill., 1968; postgrad., Loyola U., 1968-72. Penicillin processing product engr. I Abbott Labs., North Chgo., Ill., 1946-49; antibiotic process rsch. and devel. Abbott Labs., North Chgo., 1950-55, biochemical rsch., 1956-68, sr. biochemist, 1968-77, staff Leukemia project, 1978-80; pvt. photographer Sonora, Calif., 1981—. Patentee in field; contbr. articles to profl. jours. Recipient Excellence award Fedn. Internat. of Art Photographic, Switzerland, 1972; named Hon. Master of Profl. Photography, Profl. Photographic Assns., Taiwan, 1990. Mem. Photographic Soc. Am. (associateship), Royal Photographic Soc., Nat. Stereoscopic Soc., Internat. Stereoscopic Union. Democrat. Avocations: nature, wilderness, canoeing adventures, travel.

WALCHER, ALAN ERNEST, lawyer; b. Chgo., Oct. 2, 1949; s. Chester R. and Dorothy E. (Kullgren) W.; m. Penny Marie Walcher; children: Dustin Alan, Michael Alan, Christopher Ray; 1 stepchild, Ronald Edwin Culver. BS, U. Utah, 1971, cert. in internat. rels., 1971, JD, 1974. Bar: Utah 1974, U.S. Dist. Ct. Utah 1974, U.S. Ct. Appeals (10th cir.) 1977, Calif. 1979, U.S. Dist. Ct. (cen. dist.) Calif. 1979, U.S. Ct. Appeals (9th cir.) 1983, U.S. Dist. Ct. (ea., no., and so. dists.) Calif. 1994. Sole practice, Salt Lake City, 1974-79; ptnr. Costello & Walcher, L.A., 1979-85, Walcher & Scheuer, 1985-88, Ford & Harrison, 1988-91, Epstein Becker & Green, 1991—; judge pro tem Los Angeles Mcpl. Ct., 1986-91; dir. Citronia, Inc., Los Angeles, 1979-81. Trial counsel Utah chpt. Common Cause, Salt Lake City, 1978-79. Robert Mukai scholar U. Utah, 1971. Mem. Soc. Bar and Gavel (v.p. 1975-77), ABA, Fed. Bar Assn., Los Angeles County Bar Assn., Century City Bar Assn., Assn. Bus. Trial Lawyers, Phi Delta Phi, Owl and Key. Club: Woodland Hills Country (Los Angeles). Home: 17933 Sunburst St Northridge CA 91325-2848 Office: Epstein Becker & Green 1875 Century Park E Ste 500 Los Angeles CA 90067-2506

WALCHER, JENNIFER LYNNE, city official; b. Denver, Feb. 8, 1956; d. Donald Robert and Winifred Edmunde (O'Dell) W. AS in Adminstrn. of Justice, Arapahoe C.C., Littleton, Colo., 1984; BS in Criminal Justice, Columbia Coll., Aurora, Colo. and Columbia, Mo., 1986; AS in Occupl. Safety, Trinidad State Jr. Coll., 1994. Cert. water distbn. sys. technician, Colo. Security patrolman Mission Viejo, Highlands Ranch, Colo., 1983-84; security officer Denver Water Dept., 1985-87, water serviceman I, 1987-88, safety and loss control specialist, 1988—. Contbr. articles to profl. publs. Instr. CPR and first aid Colo. Safety Assn., Denver, 1988—; instr. defensive driving Nat. Safety Coun., 1988—. With USN, 1974-81. Mem. Am. Soc. Safety Engrs., Phi Theta Kappa. Lutheran. Avocations: golf, camping, fishing, ceramics, writing poetry. Home: 2720 S Newland St Denver CO 80227-3519 Office: Denver Water Dept 1600 W 12th Ave Denver CO 80204-3412

WALD, MALVIN DANIEL, screenwriter, producer; b. N.Y.C., Aug. 8, 1917; s. Rudolph and Bella (Danglo) W.; m. Sylvia Blanche Fish, June 22, 1946; children: Alan Russell, Jenifer Diane. BA, Bklyn. Coll., 1936; JD, Woodland U., 1976. Screenwriter various film studios, Hollywood, Calif., 1939-42; screenwriter, producer various film and TV studios, worldwide, 1946—; adj. prof. writing U. So. Calif., L.A., 1949—; playwright, actor ANTA, West Burbank, Calif., 1985-93; guest appearances Hollywood Commandos, AMC Channel, 1997, Rogues Gallery, Discovery Channel, 1997, Visiting With Huell Howser, PBS, 1996. Author: (book and screenplay) The Naked City, 1949 (Acad. award nomination for best story 1949); editor: (textbook) Three Major Screenplays, 1972; contbr. (reference book) American Screenwriters, 1984, 86, Scribner's Encyclopedia of American Lives, 1998, The Search For Reality, 1999; contbr. articles to profl. publs. Dir. info. Am. Vets. Com., L.A., 1945-46; bd. dirs. Housing for Entertainment Profls., Hollywood, 1986-93. Tech. sgt. USAAF, 1942-46. Recipient Gold medal Venice Film Festival, 1956, Critics award Locarno (Switzerland) Film Festival, 1960, Spl. Film award Cairo Film Festival, 1965; inducted into Producers Guild Hall of Fame, 1993. Mem. Writers Guild Am. West (bd. dirs. 1983-85), Writers Guild Found. (trustee 1986-97), Univ. Film and Video Found. (adv. bd. 1987-91), Acad. Motion Picture Arts and Scis. (documentary awards com. 1950-80, Acad. award nomination 1958, editl. bd. creative screenwriting, editl. bd.). Home: 4525 Greenbush Ave Sherman Oaks CA 91423-3111

WALDEN, JOSEPH LAWRENCE, career officer; b. Paducah, Ky., Oct. 2, 1956; s. Thomas Lorenzo and Betty Jo (Miller) W.; m. Julia Kay Johnson, Oct. 9, 1982; children: Amber Marie, Bobbi Michelle. BS in Rural Sociology, N.C. State U., 1978; MBA, Fla. Inst. Tech., Melbourne, 1988; MS in Sys. Mgmt., Fla. Inst. Tech., 1989; grad., USAF Air War Coll., 1997. Commd. U.S. Army, 1978, advanced through grades to lt. col., to date; supply platoon leader 25th Inf. divsn. U.S. Army, Schofield Barracks, Hawaii, 1979-81; supply control officer U.S. Army, 1981-82; installation supply officer Signal Sch. U.S. Army, Ft. Gordon, Ga., 1983; brigade logistics officer 2d Signal Brigade U.S. Army, Ft. Gordon, 1983-84; co. comdr. Co. B, 3rd Batallion, 2d Signal Brigade, Ft. Gordon, 1984-86; logistics plans officer Combat Devel., Quartermaster Sch., Ft. Lee, Va., 1988-89; chief gen. support U.S. Army Quartermaster Sch., Ft. Lee, 1989-91; assigned to U.S. Army Command and Gen. Staff Coll., Ft. Leavenworth, Kans., 1991-92; exec. officer 19th Corps Materiel Mgmt. Ctr., Wiesbaden, Germany, 1992-94; chief supply mgmt. 3D Corps Support Command, Wiesbaden, 1994-95; comdr. Materiel Mgmt. Ctr., Ft. Irwin, Calif., 1995-97; program mgr. Logistics Reengring., Ft. Lee, Va., 1997—; mem. adj. faculty St. Leo Coll., Ft. Lee, 1988-91; mem. faculty City Coll. of Chgo., 1994-95; pres. Walden Fitness Systems, Ft. Leavenworth, 1984-92. Contbr. articles to profl. jours. Mem. Bldg. Code Appeals Bd., City of Hopewell, 1988-91. Mem. APICS, Internat. Soc. of Logistics, The Warehousing Edn. and Rsch. Coun., Nat. Strength Conditioning Assn., Va. Assn. of U.S. Powerlifting Fedn. (pres. 1989-91), Am. Sunbathing Assn., Fellowship Christian Athletes, Fla. Sheriffs Assn., San Diego Zool. Soc., Assn. Quartermasters, Mus. Tolerance, Las Vegas Sun Club, Save the Manatee Club. Republican. Methodist. Avocations: powerlifting (1992 Nat. Champion), naturist.

WALDRON, JILL GENEVIEVE, English language educator; b. Evanston, Ill., Dec. 17, 1936; d. Frank Wesley Rorabach and Helen Montgomery (Davenport) Davee; m. Benny Lee Bohlander, June 10, 1958 (div. 1966); m. Raymond Wilson Keller, June 1, 1971 (div. 1983); 1 child, Eric Douglas Bohlander. BA, Ill. Wesleyan U., 1958; MA, U. Ill., 1959; postgrad., UCLA, 1965-68. English tchr. Danvers (Ill.) H.S., 1958-59; English instr. Ill. State U., Normal, 1959-63, UCLA, 1965-68, Santa Monica City Coll., 1968; English prof. Pierce Coll., Woodland Hills, Calif., 1968—; mem. instrnl. TV com. L.A.C.C. Dist.-ITV, 1969—. Author: The Scope of Recognition, 1971; contbr. poetry to profl. publs. Talk show host Sta. KCRW, Santa Monica, 1981-82; bd. dirs. Welsh Pony Found., Pacific Saddlebred Assn. Named San Fernando Valley Tchr./Poet of Yr., 1995. Mem. Pacific Saddlebred Assn. (bd. dirs., writer). Democrat. Avocations: driving ponies and riding. Home: PO Box 723 Topanga CA 90290

WALEN, JOANNE MICHELE, secondary education educator, consultant; b. Reno, Nev., July 8, 1942; d. John Baptista and Helen Hattie (Laakonen) Pollastro; m. Wallace Donald Walen, Feb. 20, 1961; children: Lisa M. Mays, Kevin M. Walen. BA, U. Nev., Reno, 1965, MA, 1974. Cert. secondary sch. tchr., curriculum supr., Nev. Tchr. Washoe County Sch. Dist., Reno, Nev., 1965-85; English program coord. Washoe County Sch. Dist., Reno, 1985-95; dir. WCSD Shakespeare in the Schs., Reno, 1985-95; cons. Shakespeare Express, Reno, 1995—, McDougal Littell, 1998—; head reader, trainer Nev. State Dept. Edn., Carson City, 1980—; co-dir. Lit. Inst. U. Nev., Reno, 1986-90; essay reader ETS, Princeton, N.J., 1990-94; cons. IBEU, Rio de Janiero, Brazil, 1996, 98; cons. in field. Sr. editor (book) Secondary Writing Guide, 1995; author: (booklet) Handbook for Writing Traits, 1993; contbr. articles to profl. jours. Founder, dir. Shakespeare Performance Festival, Reno, 1986-95; co-dir. Washoe K-16 Coun. Lang. Consortium, Reno, 1995-96. Recipient Humanities award Nev. Humanities Com. State of Nev., 1991; grantee Summer Seminar NEH, Stratford Upon Avon, UK, 1994. Mem. NEA, Nat. Coun. Tchrs. of English (liaison officer 1994—, chair CEE commn 1996-98), Internat. Reading Assn., No. Nev. Writing Project, Alpha Delta Kappa (pres. 1982-84). Lutheran. Avocations: reading, theater, travel. Home: 11500 Pickens Dr Reno NV 89511-9445

WALENDOWSKI, GEORGE JERRY, accounting educator; b. Han-Minden, Germany, Mar. 25, 1947; came to U.S., 1949; s. Stefan (dec.) and Eugenia (Lewandowska) W. AA, L.A. City Coll., 1968; BS, Calif. State U., L.A., 1970, MBA, 1972. Cert. community coll. instr. acctg. and mgmt., Calif. Acct. Unocal (formerly Union Oil Co. Calif.), L.A., 1972-76, data control supr., 1976-78, acctg. analyst, 1978-79; sr. fin. analyst Hughes Aircraft Co., El Segundo, Calif., 1979-83, fin. planning specialist, 1983-84, program controls specialist, 1984-86, bus. mgmt. specialist, 1986-92, bus. analyst, 1993-95; adj. instr. bus. math. L.A. City Coll., 1976-80, adj. instr. acctg., 1980-97, substitute instr. acctg., 1997—, mem. acctg. adv. com., 1984, 87, 89; adj. instr. acctg. Pasadena City Coll., 1996—; reviewer conf. papers Western Acad. Mgmt., 1996, 97. Contbr. articles to profl. jours.; reviewer conf. papers Inst. Behavior and Applied Mgmt., 1997. Mem. commn. Rep. Pres. Task Force, 1986. Recipient Medal of Merit, Rep. Presdl. Task Force, 1984, cert. of merit, named registered life mem. commn., 1986, named Honor Roll life mem., 1989; recipient Vice-Presdl. Cert. of Commendation, Rep. Nat. Hall of Honor, 1992, Rep. Congl. cert. of Appreciation, 1993, Rep. Congl. Order of Freedom award Nat. Rep. Congl. Com., 1995, Recognition award L.A. chpt. Strategic Leadership Forum, 1983. Mem. Acad. Mgmt. (reviewer social issues in mgmt. divsn. 1991, mgmt. edn. and devel. divsn. program rev. com. 1998), Am. Fin. Assn., Inst. Mgmt. Accts. (author's cir. L.A. chpt. 1980, Robert Half author's trophy 1980, cert. of appreciation 1980, 83), Am. Acctg. Assn. (competitive manuscript com. 1997-98, reviewer tchg. curr. sect. 1998-99), Nat. Bus. Edn. Assn., Nat. Mgmt. Assn., Fin. Mgmt. Assn., Soc. Advancement Mgmt., U.S. Chess Fedn., Beta Gamma Sigma. Republican. Roman Catholic. Home: 426 N Citrus Ave Los Angeles CA 90036-2632 Office: Pasadena City Coll Bus Edn 1570 E Colorado Blvd Pasadena CA 91106-2003

WALI, DEBRA ANN, human resources administrator; b. St. Petersburg, Fla., Mar. 29, 1967; d. Larry Dombrowski and Jana Lou Wolff Dombrowski-Swete; m. Chip Wali, Sept. 2, 1995. BS in Hotel and Restaurant Mgmt., Calif. Poly. U., Pomona, 1990. Human resources adminstr. All-New Stamping, El Monte, Calif., 1990-93; corp. human resources mgr. Stanton Industries, Tualatin, Oreg., 1993-95; human resources mgr. Bullseye Glass, Portland, Oreg., 1995—. Mem. Soc. for Human Resource Mgmt. Avocations: reading, gardening, travel. Office: Bullseye Glass Co 3722 SE 21st Ave Portland OR 97202-2994

WALKER, BARBARA MONIKA ANN, trade association executive, lawyer; b. Denver, May 26, 1953; d. John S. Jr. Walker; m. Philip A. Feigin, June 6, 1987. BS in Journalism, U. Colo., 1976; JD in Law, U. Denver, 1978. Atty. Isaacson, Rosenbaum, et al, Denver, 1984, Brenman, Raskin, Friedlob, et al, Denver, 1985; sr. asst. atty. gen. Colo. Att. Gen.'s Office, Denver, 1990; adminstrv. law judge Colo. Pub. Utilities Commn., Denver, 1991; Colo. state banking commr. Colo. Divsn. Banking, Denver, 1996; spl. counsel McKenna & Cuneo, LLP, Denver, 1996-98; exec. officer Ind. Bankers Colo., Denver; staff atty. U.S. Securities and Exch. Commn., Denver, 1978-83. Registered lobbyist Ind. Bankers Colo., 1997—; mem. customer adv. coun. Fed. Res. Bank Kansas City, Denver br., 1997—. Democrat. Avocations: gardening, cross country skiing, bicycling, reading, furniture refinishing. Office: Ind Bankers Colo 1580 Logan St Ste 510 Denver CO 80203-1941

WALKER, BURTON LEITH, engineering writer, psychotherapist; b. Mt. Morris Twp., Mich., Oct. 23, 1927; s. Dalton Hugh and Muriel Joyce (Black) W.; m. Norva Jean Trochman, June 28, 1949; children: Paul, Cynthia Halverson, Mark; m. Carol Jean D'Andrea, July 31, 1981. Cert. psychology. tchr., lic. psychotherapist, hypnotherapist, Calif. A.A., Allan Hancock Coll., 1971; B.A., Chapman Coll., 1974, M.A., 1975. Contract estimator Ryan Aeronaut., San Diego, 1949-59; logistics rep. GD/A, San Diego, 1960-62; systems engr., cons. fgn. svc. Ralph M. Parsons, L.A., 1962-68; lead engring. writer, sr. analyst Fed. Electric, Vandenberg AFB, Calif., 1969-86; psychotherapist Access, Vandenberg Village, Family Guidance Svc., Santa Ynez, Calif., 1974—; part time prof. Allan Hancock Coll., Santa Maria, Calif., 1974-93, ret.; small bus. owner 1974-86. Active Santa Ynez Valley Presbyn. Ch. Mem. Am. Assn. Christian Counselors, Nat. Mgmt. Assn. (Outstanding Svc. award 1982), Calif. Assn. Marriage and Family Therapists, Assn. Advancement Ret. People. Republican. Home: 3149 E Hwy 246 Santa Ynez CA 93460-9634

WALKER, CAROLYN PEYTON, English language educator; b. Charlottesville, Va., Sept. 15, 1942; d. Clay M. and Ruth Peyton. BA with distinction in Am. History and Lit., Sweet Briar Coll., 1965; cert. in French, Alliance Francaise, Paris, 1966; EdM, Tufts U., 1970; MA in English and Am. Lit., Stanford U., 1974, PhD in English Edn., Stanford U., 1977. Tchr. Elem. and jr. high schs. in Switzerland, 1967-69; tchr. elem. grades Boston Sch. System, 1966-67, 69-70; Newark (Calif.) Unified Sch. System, 1970-72; instr. div. humanities Canada Coll., Redwood City, Calif., 1973, 76-78; instr. Sch. Bus., U. San Francisco, 1973-74; evaluation cons. Inst. Profl. Devel., San Jose, Calif., 1975-76; asst. dir. Learning Assistance Ctr., Stanford U., Calif., 1972-77, dir., 1977-84, lectr. Sch. Edn., 1975-84, dept. English, 1977-84, supr. counselors, tutors and tchrs., 1972-84; assoc. prof. dept. English, San Jose State U., Calif., 1984-93; dir. English dept. Writing Ctr., 1986-93, Steinbeck Rsch. Ctr., 1986-87; mem. faculty U. Calif., Berkeley and Santa Cruz, 1995—; corp. trainer, 1993—; pres. Waverley Edn., Inc., Ednl. Cons., 1983-91, tchr. writing and Am. culture for fgn. profls., U. Calif. at Berkeley, 1995—, pvt. prac. corp. trng., 1983—; head cons. to pres. to evaluate coll.'s writing program, San Jose City Coll., 1985-87; cons. U. Tex., Dallas, 1984, Stanford U., 1984, 1977-78, CCNY, 1979, U. Wis., 1980, numerous testing programs; cons. to pres. San Diego State U., 1982, Ednl. Testing Svc., 1985-88, also to numerous univs. and colls.; condr. reading and writing workshops, 1972—; reviewer Random House Books, 1978—, Rsch. in the Teaching of English, 1983—, Course Tech., Inc., 1990—; cons. Basic Skills Task Force, U.S. Office Edn., 1977-79, Right to Read, Calif. State Dept. Edn., 1977-82, Program for Gifted and Talented, Fremont (Calif.) Unified Sch. Dist., 1981-82; bd. dirs. high tech. sci. ctr., San Jose, 1983-84; speaker numerous profl. confs. Author: (with Patricia Killen) Handbook for Teaching Assistants at Stanford University, 1977, Learning Center Courses for Faculty and Staff: Reading, Writing, and Time Management, 1981, How to Succeed as a New Teacher: A Handbook for Teaching Assistants, 1978, ESL Courses for Faculty & Staff: An Additional Opportunity to Serve the Campus Community, 1983, (with Karen Wilson) Tutor Handbook for the Writing Center at San Jose State University, 1989, (with others) Academic Tutoring at the Learning Assistance Center, 1980, Writing Conference Talk: Factors Associated with High and Low Rated Writing Conferences, 1987, Lifeline Mac: A Handbook for Instructors in the Macintosh Computer Classrooms, 1989, Communications with the Faculty: Vital Links for the Success of Writing Centers, 1991, Coming to America, 1993, Teacher Dominance in the Writing Conference, 1992, Instant Curriculum: Just Add Tutors and Students, 1993; contbr. chpts. to Black American Literature Forum, 1991; contbr. articles to profl. jours. Vol. fundraiser Peninsula Ctr. for the Blind, Palo Alto, Calif., 1982—, The Resource Ctr. for Women, Palo Alto, 1975-76. Recipient Award for Outstanding Contbns., U.S. HEW, 1979, award ASPIRE (federally funded program), 1985, two awards Student Affirmative Action, 1986, award Western Coll. Reading & Learning Assn., 1984; numerous other awards and grants. Mem. MLA, Coll. Reading & Learning Assn. (treas. 1982-84, bd. dirs. 1982-84), Nat. Coun. Tchrs. English, No. Calif. Coll. Reading Assn. (sec.-treas. 1976-78), Am. Assn. U. Profs., Jr. League Palo Alto (bd. dirs. 1977-78, 83-84). Home: 2350 Waverley St Palo Alto CA 94301-4143

WALKER, DAPHINE BROADHEAD, construction executive; b. Nephi, Utah, Oct. 29, 1903; d. Hyrum and Polly Victoria (Jennings) Broadhead; widowed Oct. 1930; children: Raymond Walker, Darrell Walker, Jacqueline Nadel. LittD (hon.), Willamette U., 1992. Aircraft mechanic Fla. Aircraft Corp., Orlando, 1941-46; sec. Air Force Operational Test Ctr., Elgin AFB, Fla., 1947; manuscript reproduction and layout specialist supr. Air Rsch. and Devel. Ctr., Elgin AFB, Fla., 1948; sec. Bonneville Power, Eugene, Oreg., 1948-50; dist. clk. Forest Svc., Eugene, 1950-55; mgr. various apt. houses, Eugene; owner and mgr. constrn. bus. Eugene. Author and editor: Through the Years, 1970, My Last Chapter, 1994. Named Woman of the Yr. and one of Top Ten Women Am. Bus. Women's Assn., 1968. Avocations: stamp collecting, sewing. Home: 16057 NW Claremont Dr Portland OR 97229-7841

WALKER, DEWARD EDGAR, JR., anthropologist, educator; b. Johnson City, Tenn., Aug. 3, 1935; s. Deward Edgar and Matilda Jane (Clark) W.; m. Candace J. Arroyo; children: Alice, Deward Edgar III, Mary Jane, Sarah, Daniel, Joseph Benjamin. Student, Ea. Oreg. Coll., 1953-54, 56-58, Mexico City Coll., 1958; BA in Anthropology with honors, U. Oreg., 1960-61, PhD in Anthropology, 1964; postgrad., Wash. State U., 1962. Asst. prof. anthropology George Washington U., Washington, 1964-65; asst. prof. anthropology Wash. State U., Pullman, 1965-67, research collaborator, 1967-69; assoc. prof., chmn. dept. Sociology/Anthropology, lab. dir. U. Idaho, Moscow, 1967-69; prof. U. Colo., Boulder, 1969—, research assoc. in population processes program of inst. behavioral sci., 1969-73, assoc. dean Grad. Sch., 1973-76; founder, v.p. Walker Rsch. Group, Ltd., Boulder, Colo. Founder, co-editor Northwest Anthropol. Rsch. Notes, 1966—; editor, Plateau Vol.: Handbook of North American Indians, 1971-98; author, co-author 150 books, reports, articles and papers. Mem. tech. steering panel Hanford Environ. Dose Reconstrn. Project, 1988-95, Basalt Waste Isolation Project, Hanford, 1986-88; advisor on Native Am. affairs. With U.S. Army, 1954-62. Fellow NSF, 1961, NDEA, 1961-64. Fellow Am. Anthropol. Assn. (assoc. editor Am. Anthropologist 1973-74), Soc. Applied Anthropology (hon. life, exec. com. 1970-79, treas. 1976-79, chmn. 1980-95, cons., expert witness tribes of N.W., editor Human Orgn. 1970-76, rschr. over 65 projects with 150 monographs, articles, reports, and papers, editor High Plains Applied Anthropologist); mem. AAAS, Am. Acad. Polit. and Social Scis., N.W. Anthropol. Conf. Avocations: geology, mining. Home: PO Box 4147 Boulder CO 80306-4147 Office: U Colo PO Box 233 Boulder CO 80309-0233

WALKER, DORIS I., author, historian, educator; b. Cleve.; d. Alphonse Charles and Rose Emma (Gibbons) Isaak; divorced; children: Brent Evan Walker, Blair Dana Walker. AB, Case Western Reserve U.; postgrad., Northwestern U., U. Calif., Irvine. Pub. rels. mgr., publs. editor Dana Point (Calif.) Harbor Assn., 1970-84; field rsch. writer Kessler Exch., L.A., Calif., 1984-89; instr. Calif. history Saddleback Coll., Mission Viejo; lectr. Chapman Coll., Calif. State U., Fullerton, tchr. seminars Orange County Marine Inst., Capistrano Unified Sch. Dist.; lectr. in field. Author: Sections of Orange, Home Port for Romance, Adventurer's Guide to Dana Point, Mission Viejo: The Ageless Land, Orange County Adventures With Children, The Whales of Capistrano Bay, A Guide Book of Numismatic-Philatelic Covers; contbr., editor, photographer newspapers, mags. Commr. Orange County Hist. Commn., 1994—; coord. Dana Point Festival of Whales, 1975-84. Recipient numerous awards including Am. History award DAR, Clarion award, Unique Coverage award Women in Comm., Woman of Distinction award Capistrano Bay Area, Soroptimist Internat., Crisis Comm. Award Internat. Coun. Indsl. Editors, cert. of recognition Calif. State Senate; named Orange County Woman of Achievement in Comm., YWCA. Mem. AAUW (pres. San Clemente-Capistrano Bay br.), Nat. Fedn. Press Women (Nat. first place book award history), Calif. Media Profls., Calif. Press Women (pres. Orange County dist., state sec.), Dana Point Hist. Soc. (hon. life, founder, dir.), San Juan Capistrano Hist. Soc. (dir.), Orange County Hist. Soc. (dir.). Avocations: travel, photography, granddaughter. Office: Box 546 Dana Point CA 92629-0546

WALKER, DUNCAN EDWARD, retired career officer; b. Washington, Aug. 2, 1942; s. Edward John and Katherine Edith (Duncan) W. BA in Indsl. Psychology, N.Mex. State U., 1965; MS in Systems Mgmt., U. So. Calif., 1978; MPA, Golden Gate U., 1980. Commd. 2d lt. USAF, 1965, advanced through grades to lt. col., 1981; weapons contr. 21st air divsn. USAF, McGuire AFB, 1965-68; weapons contr. 620 tactical control squadron USAF, Dan Nang, Vietnam, 1968-69; instr., crew comdr. Minuteman II ICBM 351st strategic millile wing USAF, Whiteman AFB, Mo., 1969-74; divsn. weapons contr. tng. officer 314th air divsn. USAF, Osan AB, Korea, 1974-75; grad. Squadron Officers Sch., 1973, Air Command and Staff Coll., 1974, Indsl. Coll. Armed Forces, 1977; chief Minuteman flight test mgmt. 1st strategic aerospace divsn. Indsl. Coll. Armed Forces, Vanderbilt AFB, Calif., 1975-81; dep. for ICBM ops. and evaluation Air Force Operational Test and Evaluation Ctr., Vandenberg AFB, Calif., 1984-88; chief devel. and deployment br. ICBM requirements SAC, Offutt AFB, Nebr., 1981-84; program engr. Fed. Svcs. Corp., Western Space and Missile Ctr., Vandenberg AFB, Calif., 1988-92; ret., 1992, pvt. cons., 1992—. Mission coun. exec. Boy Scouts of Am., 1993-95. Decorated Bronze Star, Meritorious Service medal with two oak leaf cluster, Air Force Commendation medal with three oak leaf clusters. Mem. VFW, Order Pour Le Merite, Air Force Assn., Am. Legion, Elks (past exalted ruler), Order Moose, Vietnam Vets. of Am. Republican. Methodist. Home: 113 N Y St Lompoc CA 93436-5514

WALKER, ELJANA M. DU VALL, civic worker; b. France, Jan. 18, 1924; came to U.S., 1948; naturalized, 1954; m. John S. Walker, Jr., Dec. 31, 1947; children: John, Peter, Barbara. *Daughter Barbara is executive director of the Independent Bankers of Colorado organization. The former state banking commissioner was appointed by Colorado governor Roy Romer to be the first woman to serve in that position in the state. She also serves as special counsel with McKenna & Cuneo, a Denver law firm. She was staff attorney for the U.S. Securities and Exchange Commission for four years. She holds a journalism degree from the University of Colorado and a law degree from the University of Denver. She is married to Philip Feigin, the state's securities commissioner.* Pres. Loyola Sch. PTA, 1959-59; bd. dirs. Santa Claus Shop, 1959-73; treas. Archdiocese Denver Catholic Women, 1962-64; rep. Cath. Parent-Tchr. League, 1962-65; pres. Aux. Denver Gen. Hosp., 1966-69; precinct committeewoman Arapahoe County Women's Com., 1973-74; mem. re-election com. Arapahoe County Rep. Party, 1973-78, Reagan election com., 1980; block worker Arapahoe County March of Dimes, Heart Assn., Hemophilia Drive, Muscular Dystrophy and Multiple Sclerosis Drive, 1979-81, cen. city asst. Guild Debutante Charities, Inc. Recipient Dist. Svc. award Am.-by-choice, 1966; nmaed to Honor Roll, ARC, 1971. Mem. Cherry Hills Symphony, Lyric Opera Guild, Alliance Francaise (life mem.), ARC, Civic Ballet Guild (life mem.), Needlework Guild Am. (v.p. 1980-82), Kidney Found. (life), Denver Art Mus., U. Denver Art and Conservation Assns. (chmn. 1980-82), U. Denver Women's Lib. Assn., Chancellors Soc., Passage Inc., Friends of the Fine Arts Found. (life), Children's Diabetes Found. (life), Littleton Pub. Sch. Pioneers, Union (Chgo.), Denver Athletic, 26 (Denver), Welcome to Colo. Internat. Roman Catholic. Address: 2301 Green Oaks Dr Greenwood Village CO 80121-1562

WALKER, ETHEL PITTS, theatre arts educator; b. Tulsa, Feb. 4, 1943; d. Opie Donnell Pitts and Wilhelmina Teresa Miller; m. Phillip Eugene Walker, Aug. 6, 1977; 1 child, Travis Donnell. BS in Edn., Lincoln U., 1964; MA, U. Colo., 1965; PhD in Theatre, U. Mo., 1975. Instr. speech and theatre dept. Southern U., Baton Rouge, 1965-68; asst. prof. speech and drama dept. Lincoln U., Jefferson City, Mo., 1968-77; asst. prof. Afro-Am. studies dept. U. Ill., Urbana, 1977-79; sec. BankAm. Corp., San Francisco, 1980-88; vis. lectr. Afro-Am. studies U. Calif., Berkeley, 1988; vis. lectr. theatre dept. Wayne State U., Detroit, 1988-89; prof. theatre arts dept. San Jose (Calif.) State U., 1989—; exec. dir. African-Am. Drama Co., San Francisco, 1978—; pres. Black Theatre Network, Gainesville, Fla., 1986-88, Calif. Ednl. Theatre Assn., San Francisco, 1996-98, Calif. Legis. Action Coalition for Arts Edn., Concord, Calif., 1998—. Editor: New/Lost Plays by Ed Bullins, 1995; contbr. articles to profl. jours. Active 3rd Bapt. Ch., San Francisco, 1979—. Recipient Life Membership award Black Theatre Network, 1992, Pres.'s award Calif. Ednl. Theatre Assn., 1998; named to Consortium of Drs., Savannah, Ga., 1993, one of honored alumni women Lincoln U., 1994. Mem. Nat. Coun. Negro Women, Nat. Conf. African-Am. Theatre. Avocations: reading, swimming. Home: 195 Ney St San Francisco CA 94112-1642 Office: San Jose State U Theatre Arts Dept 1 Washington Sq San Jose CA 95192-0001

WALKER, ETTA L., lawyer; b. Tribune, Kans., Oct. 27, 1959; d. Ralph D. and Cathryn A. (Woodman) W.; 1 child, Catherine Missouri Walker Jenkinson. BA, U. Kans., 1981; JD, U. Colo., 1991. Bar: Colo., Nev. Operator, family grain elevator business, Sharon Springs, Kans., 1983-85; rd. mgr. Great Plains Chautauqua, Bismark, N.D., 1986-88; law clk. Land and Water Fund, Boulder, Colo., 1989-91; rsch. asst. U. Colo., Boulder, 1989-91, Am. Indian Resources Inst., Boulder, 1990-91; law clk. Hon. Procter R. Hug Jr.-U.S. Ct. Appeals 9th cir., Reno, Nev., 1991-94; atty. Lionel Sawyer & Collins, Reno, 1994—. Mem. ABA, Am. Inns. of Ct. (barrister Bruce Thompson chpt. 1997-98), Nev. Bar Assn., Colo. Bar Assn., No. Nev. Women Lawyers Assn. Office: Lionel Sawyer & Collins 50 W Liberty St Ste 1100 Reno NV 89501-1951

WALKER, FRANCIS JOSEPH, lawyer; b. Tacoma, Aug. 5, 1922; s. John McSweeney and Sarah Veronica (Meechan) W.; m. Julia Corinne O'Brien, Jan. 27, 1951; children: Vincent Paul, Monica Irene Hylton, Jill Marie Nudell, John Michael, Michael Joseph, Thomas More. BA, St. Martin's Coll., 1947; JD, U. Wash., 1950. Bar: Wash. Asst. atty. gen. State of Wash., 1950-51; pvt. practice law, Olympia, Wash., 1951—; gen. counsel Wash. Cath. Conf., 1967-76. Lt. (j.g.) USNR, 1943-46; PTO. Home and Office: 2723 Hillside Dr SE Olympia WA 98501-3460

WALKER, FRANKLIN CURTIS, national park administrator; b. Sept. 10, 1945; s. Howard and Edna Walker; m. Judy Provins, May 29, 1967; children: Mark, Kathy, Phillip. BS in Biology, N.Mex. State U., 1967. Park ranger White Sands Nat. Monument Nat. Park Svc., 1970-72, park ranger Jefferson Nat. Expansion Meml., 1972-73, park ranger Gulf Islands Nat. Seashore, 1973-77, naturalist south dist. Yellowstone Nat. Park, 1977-80, chief of interpretation Carlsbad Caverns Nat. Park, 1980-85, park supt. Ft. Clatsop Nat. Meml., 1985-90; supt. Nez Perce Nat. Hist. Park Nat. Park Svc., Idaho, Oreg., Wash., Mont., 1990-98; supt. Saguaro Nat. Park Nat. Park Svc., Tucson, 1998—. 1st lt. U.S. Army, 1967-69. Home: 3510 7th St E Lewiston ID 83501-5110 Office: Saguaro Nat Park 3693 S Old Spanish Trail Tucson AZ 85730-5601*

WALKER, GAIL JUANICE, electrologist; b. Bosque County, Tex., Sept. 3, 1937; d. Hiram Otis and Hazel Ruth (Carmichael) Gunter; cert. Shults Inst. Electrolysis, 1971; children—Lillian Ruth, Deborah Lynn. In quality control Johnson & Johnson, San Angelo, Tex., 1962-70; owner, pres., electrologist Ariz. Inst. Electrolysis, Scottsdale, 1979—; ednl. cons. Gail Walker's Internat. Sch. Electrolysis, Tokyo, 1980; area corr. Hair Route mag., 1981; co-founder Gailshay Worldwide Bio-Tonique and Epluche Skin Care Products; CEO, J. Ransom Network Mktg. Travel and Telecomm. Products; participant continuing edn. program in electrology Shelby State Coll., 1981. Editor

Electrolysis World. Cert., Pvt. Bus. and Tech. Schs., State of Ariz. Mem. Ariz. Assn. Electrologists (pres. 1980—), Am. Electrolysis Assn., Internat. Guild Profl. Electrologists, Nat. Fedn. Ind. Businessmen, Ariz. Assn. Electrologists (organizer 1980). Republican. Baptist. Club: Order of Eastern Star. Co-developed Bio-Tonique Skin Care product line, 1990, pvt. label Epluche Skin Care product line, 1994.

WALKER, GEORGE ALPHONSO, artist, minister, skin care consultant; b. Kingston, Jamaica, Feb. 19, 1962; s. George Alfonso Walker and Myrtle Joni Hurst. AS in Fashion Design, Fashion Inst. of Tech., N.Y.C., 1985; minister, Univ. Life Minisry, 1997. Fashion designer Sheila's Designs, Bklyn., N.Y., 1979-83; staff Plaza Temps, N.Y.C., 1983-85; fashion designer Fed. Allied Stores, N.Y.C., 1986-87, Brawn of Calif., San Diego, 1990-96, pvt. practice, San Diego, 1996—. Artist: work exhibited at Manhattan Art Internat. Artist in the 90's, 1994, 95, 96 (Excellent Merit award), published in Encyclopedia of Living Artists, 1996, exhibited at Kunst & Moon Gallery, Switzerland, 1998. Mem. San Diego Regional Artists (bd. dirs. 1997). Avocations: reading, teaching, swimming, exotic cooking. Home: 2149 Front St San Diego CA 92101-1958

WALKER, JOHN SUMPTER, JR., lawyer; b. Richmond, Ark., Oct. 13, 1921; s. John Sumpter, Martha (Wilson) W.; m. Eljana M. duVall, Dec. 31, 1947; children: John Stephen, Barbara Monika Ann, Peter Mark Gregory. *Daughter Barbara is executive director of the Independent Bankers of Colorado organization. The former state banking commissioner was appointed by Colorado governor Roy Romer to be the first woman to serve in that position in the state. She also serves as special counsel with McKenna & Cuneo, a Denver law firm. She was staff attorney for the U.S. Securities and Exchange Commission for four years. She holds a journalism degree from the University of Colorado and a law degree from the University of Denver. She is married to Philip Feigin, executive director, North American Securities Administrators Association, Inc., Washington D.C.* BA, Tulane U., 1942; MS, U. Denver, 1952, JD, 1960; diploma Nat. Def. U., 1981. Bar: Colo. 1960, U.S. Dist. Ct. Colo. 1960, U.S. Supreme Ct., 1968, U.S. Ct. Appeals (10th cir.) 1960, U.S. Tax. Ct., 1981. With Denver & Rio Grande Western R.R. Co., 1951-61, gen. solicitor, 1961-89; pres. Denver Union Terminal Ry. Co. Apptd. gen. counsel Moffat Tunnel Commn., 1991; life mem. Children's Diabetes Fund. With U.S. Army, 1942-46. Decorated Bronze Star. Mem. Colo. Bar Assn., Arapahoe County Bar Assn., Alliance Francaise (life), Order of St. Ives, U. Denver Chancellors' Soc., Cath. Lawyers Guild, Denver Athletic Club. Republican. Roman Catholic.

WALKER, JOYCE MARIE, secondary school educator; b. Kansas City, Kans., Jan. 24, 1948; d. Frank Cornelius and Inez (Pennington) W.; divorced; 1 child, Kevin Cornelius. BS, U. Ark., Pine Bluff, 1972. Cert. ch. adminstr. Bus. tchr. U.S. Trade Sch., Kansas City, 1972-74; exec. sec. Kansas City Mo. Sch. Dist., 1974-77; tchr. vocat. bus. Aurora (Colo.) Pub. Sch., 1977—; vocat. bus. tchr. Pioneer Community Coll., 1975-77. Mem. Aurora Human Rels. Martin Luther King Jr. Com., 1986—; asst. sec. Sunday sch. Macedonia Bapt. Ch., 1985—, evangelism counselor, 1992—; 2d v.p. E.L. Witchfield Missionary Soc., 1989; chmn. We. States Fgn. Mission, 1990. Mem. Nat. Coun. Negro Women, Nat. Assn. Bus. Educators, NAACP (Aurora br. 1990—), Delta Sigma Theta (v.p. Denver chpt. 1998—). Avocations: tennis, bowling, sewing. Home: 12948 E 48th Ave Denver CO 80239-4408 Office: Aurora Pub Schs 11700 E 11th Ave Aurora CO 80010-3758

WALKER, JUANIE NATALIE, communication educator; b. Lubbock, Tex., Dec. 30, 1963; d. Woodrow Raymond and Hideko (Kabetani) Lane; m. Michael George Walker, Aug. 3 1, 1986; 1 child, Jacob Oliver Lane. BA, Pepperdine U., 1984, MA, 1987; PhD, U. So. Calif., L.A., 1994. Comm. coord. Bateman, Eichler, Hill, Richards Fin. Svcs., L.A., 1987; asst. dir., grant writer founds. and grants Pepperdine U., Malibu, Calif., 1987-90, adj. prof., 1989-90, 93, asst. prof. comm. divsn., 1994—; asst. lectr. U. So. Calif., L.A., 1991-94. Deacon Malibu Presbyn. Ch., 1997—; mem. Christians for Bibl. Equality, 1996—. Mem. Nat. Comm. Assn., Internat. Comm. Assn., Western States Comm. Assn. Avocations: jogging, vegetarian cooking, hiking. Office: Pepperdine U Comm Divsn Malibu CA 90263

WALKER, KEITH LEE, writer, publisher; b. Palo Alto, Calif., June 24, 1923; s. Willard Porter and Elizabeth (Tallmon) W.; m. Mary Roberta Sheehan, July 27, 1946 (div. Jan. 1974); children: Linda Lee Walker Kelly, Mary Roberta Walker Duggan, Marcella Kathryn Walker McCleary, Daniel Keith; m. Anne Therese Schlaadt, Mar. 9, 1974; 1 child, Laurie Anne Walker Brenner. Student, San Jose State Coll., 1941-42, U. Calif., Davis, 1942-43, Calif. Poly. Coll., 1943-44; BS in Agrl. Journalism, Iowa State Coll., 1946. Reporter Palo Alto Times, 1946-47; asst. editor Menlo Park (Calif.) Recorder, 1947-48; expediter Stanford (Calif.) U. Press, 1949-50; reporter Burlingame (Calif.) Advance, 1950-55; courthouse reporter Peninsula Newspapers, Inc., Redwood City, Calif., 1955-79; writer Sonora and Santa Rosa, Calif., 1979-94; author, pub. Golden Door Press, Santa Rosa, 1994—. Author: The Escape, 1970, How to Survive Financially, 1991, A Trail of Corn, 1995, (children's book) The Dilapidated Dragon, 1994. Republican. Evangelical. Avocations: home crafts, wood splitting, auto maintenance. Home: 4969 Hoen Ave Santa Rosa CA 95405-7457 Office: Golden Door Press 4969 Hoen Ave Santa Rosa CA 95405-7457

WALKER, LARRY KENNETH ROBERT, professional baseball player; b. Maple Ridge, B.C., Dec. 1, 1966. Grad. high sch., B.C., Can. With Montreal Expos, 1989-94; outfielder Colo. Rockies, 1995—. Named "The Sporting News" Nat. League All-Star Team, 1992, "The Sporting News" NAt. League Silver Slugger Team, 1992; recipient Gold Glove as outfielder, 1992-93. Office: Colo Rockies Coors Field 2001 Blake St Denver CO 80205-2008*

WALKER, LYNN CHERYL, code compliance officer, consultant; b. Dearborn, Mich., 1944; d. Leonard and Margaret W.; m. James W. Welch, Aug. 22, 1972 (div. July 1977). BA, Calif. State U., Northridge, 1966. Certified code enforcement officer, Calif. Bus. lic. inspector City of La Mesa, Calif., 1977-80; prin., owner retail store, La Mesa, Calif., 1980-83; mktg. adv. Peace Corps., Nairobi, Kenya, 1983-85; code conformance office City of Nat. City, Calif., 1986-92; bus. adv. United Nations, Gizo, Soloman Islands, 1992-93; recruiter Occupl. Training Svcs. Inc., San Diego, 1994; code compliance officer City of Poway, Calif., 1994—. Vol. Returned Peace Corps Vols., U.S., 1998. Mem. Soroptimists Internat. (treas. 1981-82), Assn. Bus. Lic. Inspectors (dir. 1978-79), So. Calif. Assn. Code Enforcement Officials, Inc. (dir. 1995-97), San Diego Mus. Art. Avocations: running, swimming, hiking, gardening, reading. Home: 4675 Vista St San Diego CA 92116-4848

WALKER, MARGARET SMITH, real estate company executive; b. Lancashire, Eng., Oct. 14, 1943; came to U.S., 1964; d. Arthur Edward and Doris Audrey (Dawson) Smith; m. James E. Walker, Feb. 6, 1992. Lic. real estate agt., Hawaii. Broker Lawson-Worrall Inc. (now Mary Worrall/Sotheby), Honolulu, 1974-81; pres. Maggie Parkes & Assocs., Inc., Honolulu, 1981—. Bd. dirs. Hawaii Combined Tng. Assn., Honolulu, 1985-97; com. chmn. Hawaii Opera Theatre, 1997, chmn. Opera Ball, 1997. Mem. Am. Horse Shows Assn., Hawaii Horse Shows Assn., Outrigger Canoe Club. Episcopalian. Avocations: dressage riding, horse show management. Office: PO Box 25083 Honolulu HI 96825-0083

WALKER, MOIRA KAYE, sales executive; b. Riverside, Calif., Aug. 2, 1940; d. Frank Leroy and Arline Rufina (Roach) Porter; m. Timothy P. Walker, Aug. 30, 1958 (div. 1964); children: Brian A., Benjamin D., Blair K., Beth E. Student, Riverside City Coll., 1973. With Bank of Am., Riverside, 1965-68, Abitibi Corp., Cucamonga, Calif., 1968-70; with Lily div. Owens-Illinois, Riverside, 1970-73; salesperson Lily div. Owens-Illinois, Houston, 1973-77; salesperson Kent H. Landsberg div. Sunclipse, Montebello, Calif., 1977-83, sales mgr., 1983-85; v.p., sales mgr. Kent H. Landsberg div. Sunclipse, Riverside, 1985—. Mem. NAFE, Women in Paper (treas. 1978-84), Kent H. Landsberg President's Club (1st female to make club, 1994, 95, 96). Lutheran. Office: Kent H Landsberg Div Sunclipse 1180 W Spring St Riverside CA 92507-1327

WALKER, OLENE S., lieutenant governor; b. Ogden, Utah, Nov. 15, 1930; d. Thomas Ole and Nina Hadley (Smith) W.; m. J. Myron Walker, 1957; children: Stephen Brett, David Walden, Bryan Jesse, Lori, Mylene, Nina, Thomas Myron. BA, Brigham Young U., 1954; MA, Stanford U., 1954; PhD, U. Utah, 1986; HHD (hon.), Weber State U., 1997. V.p. Country Crisp Foods, 1969-92; mem. Utah Ho. of Reps. Dist. 24; lt. gov. State of Utah, 1993—. Mem. Salt Lake Edn. Found. bd. dirs. 1983-90; dir. community econ. devel.; mem. Ballet West, Sch. Vol., United Way, Commn. on Youth, Girls Village, Salt Lake Conv. and Tourism Bd.; mem. adv. coun. Weber State U. Mem. Nat. Assn. Secs. of State (Western chmn., nat. lt. gov.'s conf., pres. 1997-98). Mormon. Office: Lt Gov 203 State Capitol Bldg Salt Lake City UT 84114-1202

WALKER, PHILIP EUGENE, producer, educator; b. Chgo., Jan. 9, 1950; s. Welmon and Mary Ann (Brefford) W.; m. Ethel Louise (Pitts) Walker, Aug. 6, 1977; 1 child: Travis Donnell. BA in Theater, Loyola Univ., Chgo., 1972; MA in Theater, Univ. of Ill., 1973; MFA in Acting, U. Calif., Davis, 1979. Cert. Calif. C.C. Instr. Theater instr. Lincoln Univ., Jefferson City, Mo., 1973-75; artistic dir. African Am. Drama Co., San Francisco, 1977—; theater instr. U. Ill., 1977-78; touring coord. Calif. Arts Coun., Sacramento, 1981-83; speech and drama chmn. Fisk Univ., Nashville, 1986-87; multicultural instr. Am. Conservatory Theater-Summer Congress, San Francisco, 1997; head master African Am. Acting Acad., San Francisco, 1997—; advisor Western Alliance of Arts Adminstr., San Francisco, 1994; creator Calif. African Am. Student Programming Summit, Santa Clara, Calif., 1997; adj. lectr. Santa Clara U., Calif., 1997; creator Nat. Black Talent/Presenter Tour Mrtg. Summit, New Orleans, 1998; pres. Oakland Ensemble Theatre, 1998—. Appeared in movies Howard the Duck, Peggy Sue Got Married; dir. (play) Can I Sing For You Brother?, 1992; author/actor Can I Speak For You Brother?, 1983, 90. Co-found., adminstrv. Children's Performance Ctr., 1987—; assoc. rep. Nat. Assn. for Campus Activities-Pacific N.W., 1998—; Program prodr. 3d Bapt. ch., San Francisco, 1998—. Recipient Outstanding Young Men of Am., 1983, Key to the City, Tuskegee, Ala., 1985; nominee NACA Campus Entertainment awards, Columbia, S.C., 1992, 93. Mem. Nat. Assn. of Dramatic and Speech Arts, Black Talent Showcasing Assn., v.p. Avocation: match collector. Office: African Am Drama Co 195 Ney St San Francisco CA 94112-1642

WALKER, RAYMOND FRANCIS, business and financial consulting company executive; b. Medicine Lake, Mont., Nov. 9, 1914; s. Dennis Owen and Rose (Long) W.; m. Patricia K. Blakey, May 15, 1951; children: Richard A., Mark D., Maxie R. Forest, Victoria L. Le Huray, Suzanne J. Buhl, Tracy Walker Stampanoni. Grad. pub. schs.; student, Edison Vocat. Sch., 1935-39. Truck mgr. Pacific Food Products, Seattle, 1939-42; machinist Todd Shipyard, Seattle, 1943-45; owner Delbridge Auto Sales, Seattle, 1945-48; pres. Pacific Coast Acceptance Corp., 1949-60; v.p. West Coast Mortgage, Seattle, 1960-67, United Equities Corp., Seattle, 1965-69; pres. Income Mgmt. Corp., Seattle, 1970-90; v.p. Internat. Mint and Foundry, Redmond, Wash., 1983-87; pvt. practice bus. and fin. cons. Sequim, Wash., 1987—; cons. Life Ins. Co. Am., Bellevue, Wash., 1982-87, Consumer Loan Svc., Lynwood Wash., 1980-92; dir., cons., v.p. fin. Am. Campgrounds, Bellevue, 1971-79; cons., bd. dirs. Straits Forest Products, Inc. , Port Angeles, Wash.; dir., cons. Synergy Techs., Inc., Sequim, 1990-97, co-founder, dir. Sequim Tech., Inc., 1994-97. Mem. Nat. Assn. Security Dealers. Methodist. Lodge: Elks. Home: 3347 W Sequim Bay Rd Sequim WA 98382-8430

WALKER, RICHARD HUGH, orthopaedic surgeon; b. Elgin, Ill., Jan. 29, 1951; m. Wendy Allen; children: Ashley Elizabeth, Blake Allen, Emily Paige. AB cum laude, Occidental Coll., 1973; MD, U. Chgo., 1977. Diplomate Nat. Bd. Med. Examiners, Am. Bd. Orthopaedic Surgery. Jr. resident in surgery UCLA, 1977-79; jr. resident in orthopaedic surgery Stanford (Calif.) U., 1979-81, sr. resident, 1981-82, chief resident, 1982-83; clin. mem. divsn. orthopaedic surgery, sect. lower extremity reconstructive surgery Scripps Clinic and Rsch. Found., La Jolla, Calif., 1983—, co-dir. lower extremity reconstructive surgery fellowship, divsn. orthopaedic surgery, 1989—, assoc. head. divsn. orthopaedic surgery, 1990-97, chmn. dept. surgery, 1998—; staff physician dept. surgery Green Hosp. of Scripps Clinic, La Jolla, 1983—, mem. exec. com. 1994—, chief of staff, 1995-97, chmn. dept. surgery, 1998—; team physician San Diego Padres, 1983-86, 95—; clin. instr. dept. orthopaedics and rehab. U. Calif., San Diego, 1983-92, asst. clin. prof., 1992—; mem. bd. dirs. Scripps Clinic Med. Group, La Jolla, 1992—, mem. exec. com. 1998—; mem. bd. govs. Scripps Clin., 1992—, mem. joint exec. bd., 1992-93, mem. joint coun. Scripps Health, 1995-97; mem. physicians coun. Scripps Insts. of Medicine and Sci., 1995-97; presenter, lectr. in field. Cons. reviewer Clin. Orthopaedics and Related Rsch., 1989—, Jour. Bone and Joint Surgery, 1994—; contbr. articles to profl. jours. Mem. AMA, Am. Acad. Orthopaedic Surgeons, We. Orthopaedic Assn. (program chmn. San Diego chpt. 1994-95, treas. 1995-96, v.p. 1996-97, pres. 1997-98, Resident Paper award 1983), Calif. Orthopaedic Assn., Assn. Arthritic Hip and Knee Surgery (charter mem. 1991), Am. Assn. Hip and Knee Surgeons, Assn. Bone and Joint Surgeons (Nicholas Andry Rsch. award 1997). Office: Scripps Clinic Divsn Orthopaedic Surgery 10666 N Torrey Pines Rd La Jolla CA 92037-1092 also: 15025 Innovation Dr San Diego CA 92128-3409

WALKER, RICHARD K., lawyer; b. Knoxville, Tenn., Oct. 21, 1948. BA with honors, U. Kans., 1970, JD, 1975; student, U. Bonn, Germany; grad. student, U Tübingen, Germany. Bar: Ariz. 1975, D.C. 1977, U.S. Supreme Ct. 1977. Asst. prof. law U. S.C., 1977-81, assoc. prof. law, 1981-82; ptnr. Bishop, Cook, Purcell & Reynolds, Washington, 1981-90, Winston & Strawn, Washington, 1990-93; dir. Streich Lang, Phoenix, 1993—. Bd. trustees Ariz. Theatre Co., 1995—. Fulbright Direct Exchange scholar. Mem. ABA, Labor and Employment Law Sec. (mem. equal employment opportunity law com. devel. of the law under the NLRA com., 1979—), Litigation Sec. (mem. class actions and derivitive suits com. and trial pratice com., 1998—, mem. employment rels. and labor law com., 1979—), Ariz. Assn. Def. Counsel (bd. dirs. 1997—). Office: Streich Lang Renaissance One 2 N Central Ave Fl 2 Phoenix AZ 85004-2391

WALKER, ROBERTA SMYTH, school system administrator; b. Tacoma, June 18, 1943; d. Robert Middleton and Maxine (Hartl) Smyth; m. Ronald E. Walker, Apr. 1962 (div. Mar. 1965); 1 child, David M.; m. James R. Hawkins, July 19, 1985 (dec. Sept. 1991). BA, Evergreen State Coll., Olympia, Wash., 1982; MS, Seattle Pacific U., 1989. Pers. analyst Seattle Sch. Dist., 1977-83, dir. staff rels., 1983-86; exec. dir. employee rels. Renton (Wash.) Sch. Dist., 1986—; adj. faculty Seattle Pacific U., 1989—, Western Wash. U., 1995—. Vol. Crisis Clinic, Seattle, 1993—. Recipient Angel in Seattle award AT&T Wireless and Intiman Theatre, 1995. Mem. Wash. Assn. Sch. Adminstrs., Employee Rels. and Negotiations Network (pres. 1991-92), Sno-King Negotiators. Office: Renton Sch Dist 435 Main Ave S Renton WA 98055-2700

WALKER, T. MIKE, creative writing and literature educator; b. Aurora, Ill., Nov. 2, 1937; s. Hugh Fairbanks and Irene Walker; m. Kay Leona Karpus, Aug. 1956 (div. 1962); children: Pamela, Connie, Griffon, Arianna; m. Sandra Vines, Dec. 21, 1995; stepchildren: Stefani, John, Ian. MA in Lang. Arts, San Francisco State U., 1962. Cert. tchr., Calif. Police officer San Francisco Police Dept., 1960-62; creative writing instr. dept. Engish San Francisto State U., 1962-65; English tchr. Poly. H.S., San Francisco, 1966-68; creative writing and lit. instr. Cabrillo C.C., San Francisco, 1968-98, faculty emeriti, 1998—; freelance writer, traveling min. Santa Cruz, Calif., 1998—. Author: Voices From the Bottom of the World: A Policeman's Journal, 1970 (Yale Younger Poets Hon. Mention award); assoc. editor Etc. Mag. of Gen. Semantics, 1963-68. Pres., newsletter editor, negotiator Cabrillo Fedn. Tchrs., 1988-97; v.p. No. Calif. chpt. Am. Fedn. Tchrs., 1995-97. Recipient Cert. of Recognition Calif. State Senate, 1998, Calif. State Assembly, 1998. Mem. Nat. Writer's Union (former newsletter editor, del.). Buddhist. Avocations: music, keyboard, drums, Middle East, jazz, photography. Office: Town Scribe Agy & Traveling Min 1516 Delaware Ave Santa Cruz CA 95060-6434

WALKER, VAUGHN R., federal judge; b. Watseka, Ill., Feb. 27, 1944; s. Vaughn Rosenworth and Catharine (Miles) W. AB, U. Mich., 1966; JD, Stanford U., 1970. Intern economist SEC, Washington, 1966, 68; law clk. to the Hon. Robert J. Kelleher U.S. Dist. Ct. Calif., L.A., 1971-72; assoc. atty. Pillsbury Madison & Sutro, San Francisco, 1972-77, ptnr., 1978-90; judge U.S. Dist. Ct. (no. dist.) Calif., San Francisco, 1990—; mem. Calif. Law Revision Commn., Palo Alto, 1986-89. Cert. of Achievement in Bay Area, San Francisco, 1979-83, St. Francis Found., San Francisco, 1991-97.

Woodrow Wilson Found. fellow U. Calif., Berkeley, 1966-67. Fellow Am. Bar Found.; mem. ABA (jud. rep., antitrust sect. 1991-95), Lawyers' Club of San Francisco (pres. 1985-86), Assn. Bus. Trial Lawyers (dir. 1996-98), Am. Law Inst., Am. Saddlebred Horse Assn., San Francisco Mus. Modern Art, Bohemian Club, Olympic Club. Office: US Dist Ct 450 Golden Gate Ave Ste 36052 San Francisco CA 94102-3482

WALKER, WALTER FREDERICK, professional basketball team executive; b. Bradford, Pa., July 18, 1954; m. Linda Walker. Diploma, U. Va.; MBA, Stanford U., 1987; BA, U. Va., 1976. Chartered Fin. Analyst. Player Portland (Oreg.) Trail Blazers, 1976-77; player Seattle SuperSonics, 1977-82, pres., gen. mgr., 1994—; player Houston Rockets, 1982-84; with Goldman Sachs and Co., San Francisco, 1987-94; prin. Walker Capital, Inc., San Francisco, 1994; mem. USA gold medal World Univ. Games basketball team, 1973; broadcaster basketball Raycom Network, 1989-94; cons. Seattle SuperSonics, 1994. Vice chmn. Capital Campaign; bd. dirs. Red Hook Ale Brewery; bd. dirs. Interpoint Corp., Gargoyles Performance Eyeware. Named 1st team Acad. All-Am. U. Va.; named to Pa. State Sports Hall of Fame. Office: Seattle SuperSonics 190 Queen Anne Ave N Ste 200 Seattle WA 98109-4926

WALKER, WANDA MEDORA, retired elementary school educator, consultant; b. San Diego, Aug. 28, 1923; d. Bryant Hereford and Anna Genevieve (Barnes) Howard; m. Elmer Manfred Walker, Nov. 23, 1949 (dec. Aug. 1978); children: Kathleen May Stewart (dec.), Mary Ellen Quessenberry, Sydney Edward, Jessie Ann Meacham. BA, San Diego State U., 1947; MA, U. Wash., 1948; PhD, Calif. Western U., 1967. Cert. (life) spl. secondary music tchr., elem. tchr., sch. adminstr. Elem. tchr. Lakeside (Calif.) Elem. Dist., 1948-50, La Mesa (Calif.) Sch. Dist., 1951-53; elem. tchr. San Diego Schs. Dist., 1953-57, cons. gifted, 1957-59, vice prin., 1959-62, prin., 1962-88; rep. San Diego Schs. War Against Litter, 1971-76; pres. Assn. Calif. Sch. Adminstrs. Ret., 1992-94. Poet, composer. Recipient Am. Educators medal Freedoms Found. Valley Forge, 1973, Woman of Yr. award Pres. Coun. Women's Svc., Bus. & Profl. Clubs San Diego, 1980, Woman of Action award Soroptomists Internat. El Cajon, 1992. Mem. Am. Assn. Women (parliamentarian 1989—, Appreciation award 1992), Calif. Retired Tchrs., Assn. Calif. Sch. Adminstrs. (pres. 1978-79), Singing Hills Women's Golf, Sr. Resource Ctr. (adv. bd., chmn. 1991—). Avocations: photography, painting, gardening, golf, music. Home: 13208 Julian Ave Lakeside CA 92040-4312

WALKER, WELMON, JR. (RUSTY WALKER), publisher, consultant; b. Chgo., Dec. 28, 1947; s. Welmon Sr. and Mary Ann (Befford) W.; m. Nedra Kay Carlson, Dec. 30, 1972; children: Welmon III, Whitney O. Student, U. Alaska, 1970-74; AA, Tanana Valley Community Coll., 1984; BS, U. of the State of N.Y., 1985; MBA, U. Phoenix, 1996; student, The Grad. Sch. Am. Gen. mgr. Sta. KMPS (name now Sta. KSUA-FM), Fairbanks, Alaska, 1971-74; duty dir. Sta. KUAC-TV, Fairbanks, 1973-74; staff photographer Sta. KFAR-TV, Fairbanks, 1974-75; bus. mgr. Nat. Painting Corp., Fairbanks, 1975-76; instr. Fairbanks Native Assn., 1975-76; asst. mgr. Wometco-Lathrop Co., Fairbanks, 1978-79; pres. That New Pub. Co., Fairbanks, 1977-93, Honolulu, 1993—; instr. U. Alaska, Fairbanks, 1979-80, Commonwealth Internat. U. Author: Alaska Corp Manual, 1977, Publishing Manual, 1987, Finding The Lowest Quality Print Bid For Your Short Run Book Project, 1997, Hawaii Corp Manual, 1997; contbr. articles to profl. jours. Dir. Lost Lake Camp, Midnight Sun Coun. Boys Scouts Am., 1986-87, bd. dirs., 1978—; pres., bd. dirs. Fairbanks Youth Svcs., Inc., 1979—; dir. Bapt. Tng. Union, St. John Bapt. Ch., Fairbanks, 1969; pres., 1994-95, bd. dirs., 1993— Luth. Ch. of Honolulu; student affairs chmn. univ. assembly U. Alaska, 1971-74. With U.S. Army, 1968-70. Mem. Small Pubs. Assn. N.Am. (charter), Pubs. Mktg. Assn., Star Fleet Club (lt. comdr. 1983-86), Rotary. Avocations: computer programming, chess. Office: That New Pub Co PO Box 621 Aiea HI 96701-0621

WALKER-HILL, HELEN SIEMENS, musicologist, piano instructor; b. Winnipeg, Manitoba, Can., May 26, 1936; d. George and Margaret (Toews) Siemens; m. George Walker, July 23, 1960 (div. Feb. 1975); children: Gregory, Ian; m. Robert Hadley Hill, Nov. 27, 1981 (div. June 1991). BA, U. Toledo, 1957; diplome, Ecole Normale de Musique, Paris, 1958; MA, Smith Coll., 1965; DMA, U. Colo., 1981. Cert. secondary tchr., Ohio. Asst. prof. adj. U. Colo., Boulder, 1983-90; ind. scholar, 1990—; vis. asst. prof. U. Wyo., Laramie, 1993-98; mem. internat. dictionary black composers adv. bd. Ctr. Black Music Rsch., Chgo., 1995—. Author: Piano Music by Black Women Composers, 1992, Music by Black Women Composers, 1995; compiler, editor (music anthology) Black Women Composers, 1992; project dir., pianist (CD recording) Kaleidoscope: Music by African-Am. Women, 1995. Fulbright fellow, 1957-58, Rockefeller fellow Ctr. Black Music Rsch., Columbia Coll., 1998; scholar-in-residence Schomburg Ctr. Rsch. in Black Culture, N.Y.C., 1995-96; grantee Nat. Endowment for Arts, 1993.

WALKLET, JUDITH KULA, printing company executive; b. Boston, May 18, 1958; d. Eric Bertil and Gulli Ingegerd (Ahs) K. BA, Middlebury Coll., 1980; postgrad., Radcliffe U., 1980, Harvard U., 1991. Sales rep. R.R. Donnelley & Sons Co., N.Y.C., 1980-87; sales rep. Maxwell Communication Corp., N.Y.C., 1987-88, v.p. sales, 1988, sr. v.p. sales, 1988-90; sr. v.p. sales Quebecor Printing (USA) Corp., N.Y.C., 1990-93, sr. v.p. strategic planning, 1994-97, v.p. strategic mktg., 1997—. Recipient Luminaire award Women In Prodn., N.Y.C., 1990, Good Scout award Graphic Arts divsns. Boy Scouts Am., 1996. Mem. Mag. Publishers Assn., Graphic Communications Assn., Gravure Assn. Am. Avocations: running, skiing, photography, travel, languages. Office: Quebecor Printing USA Corp 696 E Trimble Rd San Jose CA 95131-1222

WALL, BRIAN RAYMOND, forest economist, business consultant, researcher, author, policy analyst, telemarketing sales executive; b. Tacoma, Wash., Jan. 26, 1940; s. Raymond Perry and Mildred Beryl (Pickert) W.; m. Joan Marie Nero, Sept. 1, 1962 (div. Aug. 1990) children: Torden Erik, Kirsten Noel. BS, U. Wash., 1962; MF, Yale U., 1964. Forestry asst. Weyerhaeuser Timber Co., Klamath Falls, Oreg., 1960; inventory forester West Tacoma Newsprint, 1961-62; timber sale compliance forester Dept. Nat. Resources, Kelso, Wash., 1963; rsch. forest economist Pacific N.W. Rsch. Sta., USDA Forest Svc., Portland, Oreg., 1964-88, cons. 1989—; co-founder, bd. dirs. Cordero Youth Care Ctr., 1970-81; owner Brian R. Wall Images and Communications; owner, Nikken ind. distbr. Sage Mentor Lifestyles; owner Sage Mentors Bus. Consultancy; ind. distbr. NIKKEN; cons. to govt. agys., Congress univs., industry, small bus.; freelance photographer. Co-author: An Analysis of the Timber Situation in the United States, 1982; contbr. articles, reports to profl. publs., newspapers. Interviewed and cited by nat. and regional news media. Recipient Cert. of Merit U.S. Dept. Agr. Forest Service, 1982. Mem. ACLU, Soc. Am. Foresters (chmn. Portland chpt. 1973, Forester of Yr. 1975), Conf. of Western Forest Economists Inc. (founder, bd. dirs. 1988-91, treas. 1982-87), Portland Photographic Forum, Common Cause, Oregon Economists Assn., Nat. Audubon Soc., Amnesty Internat., Zeta Psi. Home: 989 Netzel St Oregon City OR 97045-3405 Home and Office: Sage Mentors Consultancy F-1162 10117 SE Sunnyside Rd # F-1162 Clackamas OR 97015-9765

WALL, LLOYD L., geological engineer; b. Jerome, Idaho, Feb. 2, 1936; s. Lloyd and Ola (Buck) W.; m. Myrna Bradshaw, Aug. 25, 1954; children: Jeffrey B., Julie, Neil S., Charlene, Gail, Matthew W., Suzzane, Michael L., Connie. AS in Chemistry, Coll. Eastern Utah, 1956; BS in Geology, Brigham Young U., 1958. Pres., owner Cons. Geologist, Salt Lake City and Brigham City, 1958—; plant mgr. Thiokol, Brigham City, Utah, 1958-66; mgr. ops. Sealcraft, Salt Lake City, 1966-68; mgr. programs Eaton-Kenway, Bountiful, Utah, 1968-76; pres., owner HydraPak, Inc., Salt Lake City, 1976-86; pres. Kolt Mining Co., Salt Lake City, 1979—; owner Lloyd L. Wall & Assocs., Salt Lake City, 1986—. Author: Seal Technology, 1993; developer largest rocket motor vacuum casting system in free world, only high pressure water reclaimation system for solid propellant rocket motors in free world, only acceptable seal mfg. process for NASA Space Shuttle rocket motor. Vol. tchr. Alta Acad., Salt Lake City, 1983—. Served as sgt. N.G., 1954-62. Mem. Geol. Soc. Am., Utah Geol. Assn. Republican. Mormon. Avocations: hunting, fishing, mountain climbing, photography, flying. Home: 8100 Claybourne Ave Salt Lake City UT 84109-1727

WALL, SONJA ELOISE, nurse administrator; b. Santa Cruz, Calif., Mar. 28, 1938; d. Ray Theothornton and Reva Mattie (Wingo) W.; m. Edward Gleason Holmes, Aug. 1959 (div. Jan. 1968); children: Deborah Lynn, Lance Edward; m. John Aspesi, Sept. 1969 (div. 1977); children: Sabrina Jean, Daniel John; m. Kenneth Talbot LaBoube, Nov. 1, 1978 (div. 1989); 1 child, Tiffany Amber. BA, San Jose Jr. Coll., 1959; BS, Madonna Coll., 1967; student, U. Mich., 1968-70; postgrad., Wayne State U., 1967-68. RN, Calif., Mich., Colo. Staff nurse Santa Clara Valley Med. Ctr., San Jose, Calif., 1959-67, U. Mich. Hosp., Ann Arbor, 1967-73, Porter and Swedish Med. Hosp., Denver, 1973-77, Laurel Grove Hosp., Castro Valley, Calif., 1977-79, Advent Hosp., Ukiah, Calif., 1984-86; motel owner LaBoube Enterprises, Fairfield, Point Arena, Willits, Calif., 1979—; staff nurse Northridge Hosp., L.A., 1986-87, Folsom State Prison, Calif., 1987; co-owner, mgr. nursing registry Around the Clock Nursing Svc., Ukiah, 1985—; critical care staff nurse Kaiser Permanente Hosp., Sacramento, 1986-89; nurse Snowline Hospice, Sacramento, 1989-92; carepoint home care and travel nurse Hosp. Staffing Svcs. Inc., Placerville, Calif., 1992-94, interim home health nurse, 1994-95; nurse Finders Home Health Care, 1996; owner Sunshine Manor Resdl. Care Home, Placerville, Calif., 1995—; owner Royal Plantation Petites Miniature Horse Farm. Contbr. articles to profl. jours. Leader Coloma 4-H, 1987-91; mem. mounted divsn. El Dorado County Search and Rescue, 1991-93; docent Calif. Marshall Gold Discovery State Hist. Park, Coloma, Calif. Mem. AACN, NAFE, Oncology Nurses Assn., Soc. Critical Care Medicine, Am. Heart Assn. (CPR trainer, recipient awards), Calif. Bd. RNs, Calif. Nursing Rev., Calif. Critical Care Nurses, Soc. Critical Care Nurses, Am. Motel Assn. (beautification and remodeling award 1985), Nat. Hospice Nurses Assn., Cmty. Residential Care Assn. Calif., Soroptimist Internat. Calif., Am. Miniature Horse Assn. (winner nat. grand championship 1981-83, 85, 89), DAR (Jobs Daus. hon. mem.), Kiwanis, Cameron Park Country Club. Republican. Episcopalian. Avocations: pinto, paint, Thoroughbred and miniature horses, real estate devel., swimming. Home and Office: Sunshine Manor Residental Care Home & Around Clock Nursing 3112 Washington St Placerville CA 95667-5825

WALL, TERESA LAURINE, nursing and healthcare administrator; b. Redmond, Oreg., May 22, 1951; d. Monroe James and Arlene (Manuel) W.; 1 child, Richard James. BSN, Ariz. State U., 1981; MPH in Health Adminstrn., U. Okla. Health Scis. Ctr., 1990. Pub. health nurse trainee Gila River Indian Community, Sacaton, Ariz., 1982, pub. health nurse, 1985-88; clin. nurse USPHS Indian Health Svc., Sacaton, 1982-85; pub. health nurse USPHS Indian Health Svc., Watonga, Okla., 1988-90; exec. dir. Gila River Indian Community Dept. Health Svcs., 1990—; bd. dirs. Gila River Care Ctr., treas., 1992—; alt. mem. Indian Health Svc., Phoenix Indian Med. Ctr. Instnl. Rev. Bd., 1993—; commn. mem. Ariz. Area Health Edn. Ctr., 1993—. Lt. USPHS, 1983-86. Mem. APHA, Am. Coll. Healthcare Execs. (assoc.), Okla. Coll. Pub. Health Alumni Assn., Arizonans for Prevention. Democrat. Avocations: reading, beauty consultant. Home: 1762 W Mariposa Ct Chandler AZ 85224-6605

WALLACE, J. CLIFFORD, federal judge; b. San Diego, Dec. 11, 1928; s. John Franklin and Lillie Isabel (Overing) W.; m. Elaine J. Barnes, Apr. 8, 1996; 9 children. B.A., San Diego State U., 1952; LL.B., U. Calif., Berkeley, 1955. Bar: Calif. 1955. With firm Gray, Cary, Ames & Frye, San Diego, 1955-70; judge U.S. Dist. Ct. for So. Dist. Calif., 1970-72; judge U.S. Ct. Appeals for 9th Circuit, San Diego, 1972-96, sr. circuit judge, 1996—. Contrbr. articles to profl. jours. Served with USN, 1946-49. Mem. Am. Bd. Trial Advocates, Inst. Jud. Adminstrn. Mem. LDS Ch. (stake pres. San Diego East 1962-67, regional rep. 1967-74, 77-79). Office: US Ct Appeals 9th Cir 940 Front St Ste 4192 San Diego CA 92101-8941

WALLACE, JULIA DIANE, newspaper editor; b. Davenport, Iowa, Dec. 3, 1956; d. Franklin Sherwood and Eleanor Ruth (Pope) W.; m. Doniver Dean Campbell, Aug. 23, 1986; children: Emmaline Livingston Campbell, Eden Jennifer Campbell. BS in Journalism, Northwestern U., 1978. Reporter Norfolk (Va.) Ledger-Star, 1978-80, Dallas Times Herald, 1980-82; reporter, editor News sect. USA Today, Arlington, Va., 1982-89, mng. editor spl. projects, 1989-92; mng. editor Chgo. Sun-Times, 1992-1996; exec. editor Statesman Jour., 1996—. Mem. Am. Soc. Newspaper Editors. Office: Statesman Journal 280 Church St NE Salem OR 97301-3762

WALLACE, KENNETH ALAN, investor; b. Gallup, N.Mex., Feb. 23, 1938; s. Charles Garrett and Elizabeth Eleanor (Jones) W. A.B. in Philosophy, Cornell U., 1960; postgrad. U. N.Mex., 1960-61; m. Rebecca Marie Odell, July 11, 1980; children: Andrew McMillan, Aaron Blue, Susanna Garrett, Megan Elizabeth, Glen Eric. Comml. loan officer Bank of N.Mex., Albuquerque, 1961-64; asst. cashier Ariz. Bank, Phoenix, 1964-67; comml. loan officer Valley Nat. Bank, Phoenix, 1967-70; pres. WWW, Inc., Houston, 1970-72; v.p. fin. Hometels of Am., Phoenix, 1972-77, Precision Mech. Co., Inc., 1972-77; ptnr. Schroeder-Wallace, 1977-93; dir. Marlin Mech.; chmn. Shalako Corp., Phoenix; mng. ptnr., pres. Blackhawk, Inc., Phoenix, 1977—, also, bd. dirs.; pres., chmn. bd. AlphaSat Corp., Phoenix, 1990—; pres. chmn. bd. dirs. Black Diamond Cable Co., LLC, Park City, Utah; gen. ptnr. Wallco Enterprises, Ltd., Mobile, Ala., Am. Entertainment Network, LLC, Phoenix; mng. gen. ptnr. The Village at University Heights, Flagstaff; mem. AEN Cable Ventures, LLC; bd. dirs. Complete, Inc., Nashville, Telecomm., Inc., Phoenix. Loaned exec. Phoenix United Way, 1966, Tucson United Way, 1967; mem. Valley Big Bros., 1970—; bd. dirs. Phoenix Big Sisters, 1985-87; mem. Alhambra Village Planning Com.; fin. dir. Ret. Sr. Vol. Program, 1973-76; mem. Phoenix Men's Arts Coun., 1968—, dir., 1974-75; mem. Phoenix Symphony Coun., Packards Internat. Campaign committeeman Rep. gubernatorial race, N.Mex., 1964; mem. AEN CableVentures, LLC; treas. Phoenix Young Reps., 1966; mem. Cornell U. Adv. Coun., 1996—, Coll. Arts and Scis. Coun. Cornell U., 1996—; bd. dirs. Devel. Authority for Tucson, 1967. Mem. Soaring Soc. Am. (Silver badge), Am. Rifle Assn. (life), Nat. Mktg. Assn. (Mktg. Performance of Year award 1966), Nat. Assn. Skin Diving Schs., Pima County Jr. C. of C. (bd. dir. 1967), Phoenix Little Theatre, Phoenix Musical Theatre, S.W. Ensemble Theatre (bd. dir.), Wheelmen of Am., Cornell Univ. Coun., Cornell Univ. Arts & Scis., Packards Internat., Masons, Shriners, Kona Kai Club (San Diego), Paradise Valley Country Club, Alpha Tau Omega. Office: The Wallace Group of Cos PO Box 7703 Phoenix AZ 85011-7703

WALLACE, LORRAINE D., secondary school educator; b. Rexburg, Idaho, Nov. 3, 1943; d. Walter J. and Myrle (Chantrill) Davis; m. Olani D. Wallace, July 21, 1962 (dec. July, 1997); children: Jeff, Nalani, David, Brent, Lorriann, Jennifer, Scott. AA, Coll. So. Idaho, 1984; BA in English, Secondary Edn., Idaho State U., 1986; MEd in Edn. Leadership, Brigham Young U., 1997. Cert. tchr. secondary schs., Utah, Idaho. Tchr. Raft River H.S., Malta, Idaho, 1986-87, Juab H.S., Nephi, Utah, 1987—; adj. faculty Utah Valley state Coll., Orem, 1998—. Named Lang. Arts Tchr. of Yr. Utah Coun. Tchrs. English, 1998. Office: Juab HS 802 N 650 E Nephi UT 84648

WALLACE, MATTHEW WALKER, retired entrepreneur; b. Salt Lake City, Jan. 7, 1924; s. John McChrystal and Glenn (Walker) W.; m. Constance Cone, June 22, 1954 (dec. May 1980); children—Matthew, Anne; m. Susan Struggles, July 11, 1981. BA, Stanford U., 1947; MCP, MIT, 1950. Prin. planner Boston City Planning Bd., 1950-53; v.p. Nat. Planning and Research, Inc., Boston, 1953-55; pres. Wallace-McConaughy Corp., Salt Lake City, 1955-69; pres. Ariz. Ranch & Metals Co., Scottsdale, Ariz., 1969-84; pres. Idaho TV Corp., Channel 6, ABC, Boise, 1976-78; chmn. Wallace Assocs., Inc., Salt Lake City, 1969-98 ; dir. 1st Interstate Bank, Salt Lake City, 1956-90, dir. Arnold Machinery Co., 1988—, dir. Roosevelt Hot Springs Corp., 1978—; mem. adv. bd. Mountain Bell Telephone Co., Salt Lake City, 1975-85. Pres., Downtown Planning Assn., Salt Lake City, 1970; chmn. Utah State Arts Coun., Salt Lake City, 1977; mem. Humanities and Scis. Coun., Stanford U., also mem. athletic bd., bd. vis. sch. law; mem. nat. adv. bd. Coll. Bus., U. Utah; lifetime dir. Utah Symphony Orch.; chmn. arts adv. coun. Westminster Coll. Lt. (j.g.) USN, 1944-46; PTO. Recipient Contbn. award Downtown Planning Assn., 1977, Govs. Award in the Arts, 1991, Utah Nat. Guard Minuteman award, 1994. Mem. Am. Inst. Cert. Planners (charter), Am. Arts Alliance (bd. dirs. 1991), Alta Club (dir.), Cottonwood Club (pres. 1959-63), Salt Lake Country Club (dir.), Desert Island Golf and Country Club (Rancho Mirage, Calif.), Flat Rock Club (Island Pk., Idaho pres. 1994-95), Phi Kappa Phi (hon., life). Home: 2510 Walker Ln Salt Lake City UT 84117-7729

WALLACE, ROBERT JOSEPH, systems engineer; b. Las Cruces, N.Mex., June 12, 1956; s. Duane Robert and Millicent Ann (Eastly) W.; m. Kathryn Louise Macmurray, Aug. 13, 1981; children: Jessica, Heather, Scott, Daniel, Morgan, Matthew. BSME, Brigham Young U., 1984; postgrad., Ariz. State U., 1988-92, San Diego State U., 1994—. Aero-thermo engr. Garrett Turbine Engine Co., Phoenix, 1985-86, computer methods engr., 1986-92; computer methods engr. Solar Turbines Inc., San Diego, 1992-94, controls design engr., 1996-97, group leader controls devel., 1997—. Lay leader LDS Ch., Phoenix, 1985—; troop leader Boy Scouts Am., Ramona, Calif., 1994—. Mem. ASME. Avocations: backpacking, canoeing, computers. Office: Solar Turbines Inc 9250 Sky Park Ct San Diego CA 92123-5398

WALLACE, WILLIAM ARTHUR, JR., environmental engineering executive; b. N.Y.C., Dec. 6, 1942; s. William Arthur and Helene Marie (Hoene) W.; m. Diane Marie Guillot, July 11, 1964; children: Kathleen Marie, Jane Coventry. BSChemE, Clarkson U., 1964; MS in Mgmt., Rensselaer Poly. Inst., 1971; advanced mgmt. program course, Harvard U., 1989. Chief plans and programs U.S. Naval Ammunition Depot, Hawthorne, Nev., 1973-75; chief hazardous waste enforcement EPA, Washington, 1975-78; chief enforcement br. U.S. Dept. Interior, Washington, 1978-79; v.p. Fred C. Hart Assocs., N.Y.C., 1979-81; engring. exec. mktg. and strategic planning CH2M Hill, Bellevue, Wash., 1981—; testified Overview of Superfund Cleanup Techs. U.S. Ho. Reps., Washington, 1985, Overview of Superfund, 1988, 91, Soil Contaminants: PCB, 1988, U.S. Senate inquirey into environ. tech., 1993. Bd. dirs. Hazardous Waste Action Coalition, 1986—, treas., 1990-91, pres., 1996—; invited panel mem. Office of Tech. Assesment Nuclear Waste Remediation Workshop, Washington, 1990; mem. sci. adv. com. Western Regional Hazardous Substance Rsch. Ctr. Stanford U., 1989-95; mem. panel ad hoc criteria group environ. tech., We. Govs.' Assn., 1993-95; mem. Enterprise for the Environment, 1996—. Recipient George A. Hogaboom award Am. Electroplaters Soc., 1968, Bronze Medal award EPA, 1978, Outstanding Citizenship award Met. Law Enforcement Assn., Denver, 1980. Mem. Met. Club, Greenwood Athletic Club. Avocations: sailing, skiing, reading, cycling. Office: CH2M Hill 6060 S Willow Dr Greenwood Village CO 80111-5142

WALLACH, LESLIE ROTHAUS, architect; b. Pitts., Feb. 4, 1944; s. Albert and Sara F. (Rothaus) W.; m. Susan Rose Berger, June 15, 1969; 1 child, Aaron. BS in Mining Engring., U. Ariz., 1967, BArch, 1974. Registered architect, Ariz.; registered contractor, Ariz. Prin. Line and Space LLC, Tucson, 1978—; mem. awards jury Sunset mag., 1997, Ariz. Homes of Yr., 1997, L.A. AIA; keynote spkr. various confs.; chair Coll. of Arch. Design Coun., U. Ariz., 1998. Representative projects include Ariz. Sonora Desert Mus. Restaurant Complex, Tucson, Elgin Elem. Sch., Ariz., Hillel Student Ctr. U. Ariz., Tucson, Boyce Thompson Southwestern Arborteum Vis. Ctr., Superior, Ariz., San Pedro Riparian Ctr., Sierra Vista, Ariz., Nat. Hist. Trails Ctr., Casper, Wyo., 1996; contbr. Sunset Mag., Architecture Mag. and Fine Homebuilding; exhibited at U. Ariz., AIA Nat. Conv., Washington; spkr. in field. Bd. dirs Tucson Regional Plan, Inc. Recipient Roy P. Drachman Design award, 1982, 85, 93, Electric League Ariz. Design award, 1987, 88, Gov. Solar Energy award, 1989, Desert Living awards citation, 1991, Ariz. Architect's medal, 1989, Disting. Alumni award U. Ariz., 1998, also 25 additional design awards, including 4 received in 1995. Fellow AIA (Ariz. Honor award 1989, 92, 96, AIA/ACSA Nat. Design award 1991, Western Mountain region Design award 1992, 96, CA AIA/Phoenix Homes and Gardens Home of the Yr. Honor award 1992, 96, Western Region Silver medal 1996); mem. SAC AIA (past pres., Design award 1985, 88, 90). Office: Line and Space 627 E Speedway Blvd Tucson AZ 85705-7433

WALLACH, PATRICIA, mayor; b. Chgo.; m. Ed Wallach; 3 children. Grad., Pasadena City Coll. Mem. city coun. City of El Monte, Calif., 1990-92, mayor, 1992—; ret. tchr.'s aide Mountain View Sch. Dist. Past trustee El Monte Union High Sch. Dist., L.A. County High Sch. for the Arts; chief amb. of goodwill Zamora, Michoacan, Mex., Marcq-en-Baroeul, France, Yung Kang, Hsiang, Republic of China, Minhang, Peoples Republic of China; mem. L.A. County Libr. Commn.; chairperson of bd. Cmty. Redevel. Agy.; mem. bd. El Monte Cmty. Access TV Corp.; mem. PTA, Little League Assns.; v.p. exec. bd., treas. Foothill Transit. Mem. League of Calif. Cities, San Gabriel Valley Coun. of Govts., Independent Cities Assn., U.S./Mex. Sister Cities Assn., Sister Cities Internat., Women of the Moose, El Monte Women's Club. Office: 11333 Valley Blvd El Monte CA 91731-3210

WALLER, LARRY GENE, mortgage banking executive; b. Corpus Christi, Tex., Nov. 18, 1948; s. Paul Hobson and Marie (Armellini) W.; m. Mary Sandra Cupp, Dec. 27, 1969 (div. 1987); children: Stacey Ann, Jaime Lynn; m. Sharon Elizabeth Falls, Jan. 28, 1988; 1 child, Lisa Suzanne Cantello. AA, Bakersfield Jr. Coll., 1970. Lic. real estate broker, Calif., Nev. Asst. v.p. Bank of Am., Stockton, Calif., 1970-78, Wells Fargo Mortgage Co., Sacramento, 1978-81; regional v.p. Weyerhaeuser Mortgage Co., Sacramento, 1981-89; sr. v.p. Koll Realty Advisors, Sacramento, 1989-91; pres. L. G. Waller Co., 1991-93; pres., CFO Waller, Kaufman & Sutter, Sacramento, 1991—, Waller, Kaufman & Sutter of Nev., Reno, 1995—. Mem. Nat. Assn. Indsl. and Office Parks (bd. dirs. Sacramento chpt.), Mortgage Bankers Assn. (income property com.), Calif. Mortgage Bankers Assn., North Tahoe Bus. Assn. Home: PO Box 2810 Kings Beach CA 96143-2810 Office: 2277 Fair Oaks Blvd Ste 400 Sacramento CA 95825-5598 also: PO Box 6670 Incline Village NV 89450-6670

WALLER, PETER WILLIAM, public affairs executive; b. Kewanee, Ill., Oct. 1, 1926; s. Ellis Julian and Barodel (Gould) W.; m. Anne-Marie Appelius van Hoboken, Nov. 10, 1950; children: Catherine, Hans. BA with hons., Princeton U., 1949; MA with hons., San Jose State U., 1978. Bur. chief Fairchild Publs., San Francisco, 1953-55; freelance writer Mountain View, Calif., 1956-57; pub. relations coord. Lockheed Missiles and Space, Sunnyvale, Calif., 1957-64; info. mgr. for 1st missions to Jupiter, Saturn, Venus NASA Ames Rsch. Ctr., Mountain View, 1964-83, mgr. pub. info., 1983-95; cons. NASA-Ames Galileo, Lunar Prospector, 1996-97; prodr. space films PacPAW Assoc., 1998—; speechwriter for pres. Lockheed Missiles and Space, 1960-64. Producer (documentary) Jupiter Odyssey, 1974 (Golden Eagle, 1974); producer, writer NASA Aero. program, 1984; contbr. articles to profl. jours, encyclopedias. Cons. on preservation of Lake Tahoe, Calif. Resources Agy., Sacramento, 1984. Mem. No. Calif. Sci. Writers Assn., Sierra Club. Democrat. Congregationalist. Avocations: rock climbing, skiing, travel, architecture, construction. Home: 3655 La Calle Ct Palo Alto CA 94306-2619

WALLER, STEPHEN, air transportation executive; b. 1949. Student, New Zealand U., 1970-74. Courier, country mgr., european mktg. mgr. DHL Airways, Inc., London, 1975-80, Tehran, Iran, 1975-80; sr. v.p. Network Trans divsn. DHL Airways, Inc., Redwood City, Calif., 1981—. Office: DHL Airways Inc 333 Twin Dolphin Dr Ste 100 Redwood City CA 94065-1496

WALLERSTEDT, JAMES DOUGLAS, information technology consultant; b. Kansas City, Mo.; s. John Irving Wallerstedt. B Mgmt. Sci., Tulane U., 1979; M Internat. Affairs, U. Calif., San Diego, 1998. Programmer analyst Pool Offshore, New Orleans, 1980-82; asst. mgr. cust. svc. Entre Computer, San Diego, 1982-83; cons. Prin. Automated Sys., San Diego, 1983-90; dir. info. ctr. Shell Nigeria, Port Harcourt, 1990-92; prin., founder Productivity Sys., San Diego, 1993-95; sys. architect T.E.C. Inc., San Diego, 1996-97. Author: White Paper, 1998, (software) Telemagic, 1987. Bd. dirs. San Diego chpt. Nat. Acctg. Assn., 1985-87. Mem. Computer Exec. Mktg. Assn. (founding mem.). E-mail: jwaller@earthlink.net. Home: PO Box 948625 La Jolla CA 92037-9406

WALLERSTEIN, JUDITH SARETSKY, marriage and divorce researcher; b. N.Y.C., Dec. 27, 1921; d. Samuel Saretsky and Augusta (Tucker) Weinberger; m. Robert S. Wallerstein, Jan. 27, 1949; children—Michael, Nina, Amy. B.A., Hunter Coll., N.Y.C., 1943; M.S., Columbia U., 1946; Ph.D. in Psychology, Lund U. (Sweden) 1978. Sr. lectr. U. Calif.-Berkeley, 1966-91, sr. lectr. emeritus, 1991—; dir. Calif. Children of Divorce Project, Marin County, Calif., 1971—; founder, former exec. dir. Judith Wallerstein Ctr. Family in Transition, Corte Madera, Calif., 1980-93. Prin. investigator follow-up study effects of divorce on children and their parents, study of good marriages. Mem. adv. com. on family law Calif. Senate Subcom. on Adminstrn. of Justice, 1977-79; mem. task force on Family equity Calif. State Senate, 1986. Author 3 books; contbr. 90 articles to profl. jours. Recipient Koshland award in Social Welfare San Francisco Found., 1975, René Spitz award Denver Psychoanalytic Soc., 1991, Geri Taylor Meml. award No. Calif. Psychiat. Soc., 1993, Presdl. Citation Am. Psychol. Assn. Divsn. of Family Psychol., 1995, Dale Richmond award Am. Acad. Pediat., 1996; others. Fellow Ctr. Advanced Study in the Behavioral Scis., Stanford, Calif., 1979-80, Rockefeller Found. Study Ctr., Bellagio, Italy, 1992. Mem. NASW, Am. Psychoanalytic Assn. (hon.), N.Y. Freudian Soc. (hon.), San Francisco Psychoanalytic Soc. (interdisciplinary mem.), Am. Orthopsychiatric Assn., Assn. Child Psychoanalysis (mem. exec. council 1977-80), Assn. Family Conciliation Courts, Phi Beta Kappa.

WALLERSTEIN, ROBERT SOLOMON, psychiatrist; b. Berlin, Jan. 28, 1921; s. Lazar and Sarah (Guensberg) W.; m. Judith Hannah Saretsky, Jan. 26, 1947; children—Michael Jonathan, Nina Beth, Amy Lisa. B.A., Columbia, 1941, M.D., 1944; postgrad., Topeka Inst. Psychoanalysis, 1951-58. Assoc. dir., then dir. rsch. Menninger Found., Topeka, 1954-66; chief psychiatry Mt. Zion Hosp., San Francisco, 1966-78; tng. and supervising analyst San Francisco Psychoanalytic Inst., 1966—; clin. prof. U. Calif. Sch. Medicine, Langley-Porter Neuropsychiat. Inst., 1967-75, prof., chmn. dept. psychiatry, also dir. inst., 1975-85, prof. dept. psychiatry, 1985-91, prof. emeritus, 1991—; vis. prof. psychiatry La. State U. Sch. Medicine, also New Orleans Psychoanalytic Inst., 1972-73, Pahlavi U., Shiraz, Iran, 1977, Fed. U. Rio Grande do Sul, Porto Alegre, Brasil, 1980; mem., chmn. rsch. scientist career devel. com. NIMH, 1966-70; fellow Ctr. Advanced Study Behavioral Scis., Stanford, Calif., 1964-65, 81-82, Rockefeller Found. Study Ctr., Bellagio, Italy, 1992. Author 18 books and monographs; mem. editl. bd. 19 profl. jours.; contbr. over 250 articles to profl. jours. Served with AUS, 1946-48. Recipient Heinz Hartmann award N.Y. Psychoanalytic Inst., 1968, Disting. Alumnus award Menninger Sch. Psychiatry, 1972, J. Elliott Royer award U. Calif., San Francisco, 1973, Outstanding Achievement award No. Calif. Psychiat. Soc., 1987, Mt. Airy gold medal, 1990, Mary Singleton Sigourney award, 1991. Fellow ACP, Am. Coll. Psychoanalysts, Am. Psychiat. Assn., Am. Orthopsychiat. Assn.; mem. Am. Psychoanalytic Assn. (pres. 1971-72), Internat. Psychoanalytic Assn. (v.p. 1977-85, pres. 1985-89), Group for Advancement Psychiatry, Brit. Psycho-Analytical Soc. (hon.), Phi Beta Kappa, Alpha Omega Alpha. Home: 290 Beach Rd Belvedere CA 94920-2472 Office: 655 Redwood Hwy Ste 261 Mill Valley CA 94941-3011

WALLIS, ERIC G., lawyer; b. Astoria, N.Y., Jan. 8, 1950. AB magna cum laude, U. Pacific, 1972; JD, U. Calif., Hasting Coll. of Law, 1975. Bar: Calif. 1975. Mem. Crosby, Heafey, Roach & May P.C., Oakland, Calif., 1982—. Editorial assoc. Hastings Law Jour., 1974-75. Mem. ABA (sect. litigation), State Bar Calif., Alameda County Bar Assn. Office: Crosby Heafey Roach & May PC PO Box 2084 Oakland CA 94604-2084

WALLIS, WENDY S., sales and management consultant; b. Beacon, N.Y., Apr. 22, 1948; d. Kenneth Brooks and Dorothy Marie (Albrecht) G.; m. Michael Wallis, Dec. 14, 1973 (div. 1981); 1 child, Brooke Allison. BS, S.W. Mo. State U., 1971. Mktg. mgr. Bell Atlantic, Phila., 1974-82, RCA, Inc., Cherry Hill, N.J., 1982-84; dir. strategic planning ONYX & IMI, Inc., San Jose, Calif., 1984-85; pres., CEO Intelligent Peripheral Devices, Los Gatos, Calif., 1985-87; founder Evergreen Mgmt. Co., Oakland, Calif., 1987-90, The Wallis Group, 1990-94, Exec. Skills Dynamics, 1994-98; prin. Gair Labs, Inc, Alamo, Calif., 1998—. Treas. Jon Sims Ctr. Performing Arts, San Francisco, 1991—. mem. NAFE, NASD, Inst. Cert. Fin. Planners (assoc.), Nat. Assn. Women Bus. Owners (treas. 1992-93), Natl. Assn. Seminar Leaders. Democrat. Lutheran. Avocations: swimming, hiking, horseback riding, biking. Office: Gair Labs Inc 170F Alamo Pla Ste 120 Alamo CA 94507

WALLISCH, CAROLYN E., principal; b. Denver, Aug. 23, 1939; d. Morgan Franklin and Margaret C. (Kopf) White; m. Darrell Dean Wallisch, June 9, 1963; children: Michael Dean, Kerri Elise. BA in Elem. Edn., U. No. Colo., 1961, MA in Elem. Edn., 1965; postgrad., Denver U., 1989. Cert. tchr. grades K-8, adminstrn. grades K-12. Tchr. grade 1 San Jose Unified Sch. Dist., 1961-62, Greeley (Colo.) Pub. Schs., 1962-69; tchr. grades 2-8, dean of students Jefferson County Schs., Lakewood, Colo., 1984-94; prin. grades K-5 Littleton (Colo.) Pub. Schs., 1994—. Contbr. articles to profl. jours. Leader 4-H Clubs of Am., Littleton, 1982-84, Girl Scouts U.S.A., Littleton, 1979-82; den leader Boy Scouts Am., Littleton, 1976-78; precinct committeewoman Littleton, 1984-90. Named one of Outstanding Young Women of Am., 1965, Model Tchr., ABC News Peter Jennings Who's Happening in Edn., 1993, Instr. Mag., 1993. Mem. ASCD, Internat. Reading Assn. (Colo. coun. 1989—), Colo. Coun. Tchrs. Math. (conf. presenter), Colo. Assn. Sch. Execs. (conf. presenter), PTO (v.p. 1994—), Kiwanis, Kappa Delta Pi (bd. dirs.), Sigma Sigma Sigma (bd. dirs.), Alpha Delta Kappa (bd. dirs.), Phi Delta Kappa (bd. dirs., rsch. chmn. 1987—). Republican. Avocations: tennis, golf. Home: 5549 W Hinsdale Ave Littleton CO 80128-7021 Office: Highland Elem Sch 711 E Euclid Ave Littleton CO 80121-2312

WALLS, HERBERT LEROY, school system administrator; b. Springfield, Ohio, July 12, 1944; s. James Edward and Hattie Beatrice (Jackson) W.; m. Vonzile Green, Feb. 4, 1967 (div. 1975); children: Herbert Le Roy Jr., Jomica Yvette. BA in English, Calif. State U., L.A., 1972; MA in Spl. Edn., Calif. State U., Dominguez Hills, 1982; MEd, U. LaVerne, 1992, EdD, 1998; HHD (hon.), Mt. Zion Bible Sem., 1991. Cert. English tchr., spl. edn. tchr., adminstr., Calif. Tchr. Golden Day Schs., L.A., 1971-72; English tchr. M.L. King Jr. Middle Sch., Boston, 1972-74; spl. edn. tchr. Arnold RE-ED West, Carmichael, Calif., 1974-75; adminstr., tchr. Golden Day/Univ. Alternative Sch., L.A., 1975-79; dir. spl. edn. Dorothy Brown Sch., L.A., 1979-84; prin., tchr. Westside Acad., L.A., 1984-86; tchr. spl. edn. Sacramento City (Calif.) Unified Sch. Dist., 1987-93, prin., 1993—; dean Christ Temple Bible Inst., Sacramento, 1991-93; ednl. cons. Little Citizen Schs., L.A., 1994. Contbr. poetry to anthologies. Sgt. USMC, 1962-66, Vietnam. Mem. ASCD, Calif. State U. Alumni Assn. (L.A.), Alumni U. La Verne Assn., Mt. Zion Sem. Alumni Fellowship, Phi Delta Kappa. Mem. Apostolic Ch. Avocations: watercolor impressionist painting, piano, drama, singing gospel and classical music. Home: 2600 Cadjew Ave Sacramento CA 95832-1424

WALLSTRÖM, WESLEY DONALD, bank executive; b. Turlock, Calif., Oct. 4, 1929; s. Emil Reinhold and Edith Katherine (Lindberg) W.; student Modesto Jr. Coll., 1955-64; certificate Pacific Coast Banking Sch., U. Wash., 1974; m. Marilyn Irene Hallmark, May 12, 1951; children: Marc Gordon, Wendy Diane. Bookkeeper, teller First Nat. Bank, Turlock, 1947-50; v.p. Gordon Hallmark, Inc., Turlock, 1950-53; asst. cashier United Calif. Bank, Turlock, 1953-68, regional v.p., Fresno, 1968-72, v.p., mgr., Turlock, 1972-76; founding pres., dir. Golden Valley Bank, Turlock, 1976-84; pres. Wallström & Co., 1985—. Campaign chmn. United Crusade, Turlock, 1971; chmn., founding dir. Covenant Village, retirement home, Turlock, 1973-94, treas. Covenant Retirement Communities West; founding pres. Turlock Regional Arts Coun., 1974, dir., 1975-76. Served with U.S. N.G., 1948-56. Mem. Nat. Soc. Accts. for Coops., Ind. Bankers No. Calif., Am. Bankers Assn., U.S. Sailing, No. Calif. Golf Assn., Turlock C. of C. (dir. 1973-75), Stanislaus Sailing Soc. (commodore 1980-81), Pacific Inter-Club Yacht Assn. (bd. dirs. 1994—, vice commodore), Turlock Golf and Country Club (pres. 1975-76, v.p., 1977, dir. 1977, 83), Stockton Sailing Club, Grindstone Joe Assn., Recreational Boaters Calif. (dir. 1998), Masons, Rotary. Republican. Mem. Covenant Ch. Home: 1720 Hammond Dr Turlock CA 95382-2850 Office: Wallstrom & Co 2925 Niagra St Turlock CA 95382-1056

WALRATH, HARRY RIENZI, minister; b. Alameda, Calif., Mar. 7, 1926; s. Frank Rienzi and Cathren (Michlar) W.; AA, City Coll. San Francisco, 1950; BA, U. Calif. at Berkeley, 1952; MDiv, Ch. Div. Sch. of Pacific, 1959; m. Dorothy M. Baxter, June 24, 1961; 1 son, Gregory Rienzi. Dist. exec. San Mateo area council Boy Scouts Am., 1952-55; ordained deacon Episcopal Ch., 1959, priest, 1960; curate All Souls Parish, Berkeley, Calif., 1959-61; vicar St. Luke's, Atascadero, Calif., 1961-63, St. Andrew's, Garberville, Calif., 1963-64; asso. rector St. Luke's Ch., Los Gatos, 1964-65, Holy Spirit Parish, Missoula, Mont., 1965-67; vicar St. Peter's Ch., also headmaster St. Peter's Schs., Litchfield Park, Ariz., 1967-69; chaplain U. Mont., 1965-67; asst. rector Trinity Parish, Reno, 1969-72; coordinator counciling svcs. Washoe County Council Alcoholism, Reno, 1972-74; adminstr. Cons. Assistance Svcs., Inc., Reno, 1974-76; pastoral counselor, contract chaplain Nev. Mental Health Inst., 1976-78; contract mental health chaplain VA Hosp.,

Reno, 1976-78; mental health chaplain VA Med. Ctr., 1978-83, staff chaplain, 1983-85, chief, chaplain service, 1985-91, also triage coord. for mental health, ret., 1991; per diem chaplain Washoe Med. Ctr., Reno, 1993; assoc. priest Trinity Episcopal Ch., Reno, 1995; assoc. Mountain Ministries, Susanville, Calif., 1995—; dir. youth Paso Robles Presbytery; chmn. Diocesan Commn. on Alcoholism; cons. teen-age problems Berkeley Presbytery; mem. clergy team Episcopal Marriage Encounter, 1979-85, also Episc. Engaged Encounter, chaplian Make A Wish Found., 1998—. Author: God Rides the Rails-Chapel Cars on American Railroads at the Turn of the Century, 1994. Mem. at large Washoe dist. Nev. area council Boy Scouts Am., scoutmaster troop 73, 1976, troop 585, 1979-82, asst. scoutmaster troop 35, 1982-92, assoc. adviser area 3 Western region, 1987-89, regional com. Western Region, 1989-90; lodge adviser Tannu Lodge 346, Order of Arrow, 1982-87; docent coun. Nev. Hist. Soc., 1992; South Humboldt County chmn. Am. Cancer Soc. Trustee Community Youth Ctr., Reno. Served with USNR, 1944-46. Decorated Pacific Theater medal with star, Am. Theater medal, Victory medal, Fleet Unit Commendation medal; recipient dist. award of merit Boy Scouts Am., St. George award Episc. Ch.-Boy Scouts Am., Silver Beaver award Boy Scouts Am., 1986, Founders' award Order of the Arrow, Boy Scouts Am., 1985; performance awards VA-VA Med. Ctr., 1983, 84; named Arrowman of Yr., Order of Arrow, Boy Scouts Am. Cert. substance abuse counselor, Nev. Mem. Ch. Hist. Soc., U. Calif. Alumni Assn., Nat. Model R.R. Assn. (life), Sierra Club Calif., Missoula Council Chs. (pres.), Alpha Phi Omega. Democrat. Club: Rotary. Home: 4822 Ramcreek Trl Reno NV 89509-8029

WALSH, DANIEL FRANCIS, bishop; b. San Francisco, Oct. 2, 1937. Grad., St. Joseph Sem., St. Patrick Sem., Catholic U. Am. Ordained priest, Roman Catholic Ch., 1963. Ordained titular bishop of Tigia, 1981; aux. bishop of San Francisco, 1981-87, bishop of Reno-Las Vegas, 1987—. Home: 2809 Cameo Cir Las Vegas NV 89107-3213 Office: Diocese of Reno-Las Vegas Office of Bishop PO Box 18316 Las Vegas NV 89114-8316*

WALSH, FRANCIS RICHARD, law educator, lawyer, arbitrator; b. Newark, Jan. 1, 1924; s. Loretta Anne (Norton) W.; m. Ethel Anne Walsh, Mar. 12, 1944; 1 child, Jeffrey R. BSBA, Seton Hall U., 1943; JD, Georgetown U., 1948. Prof. Law Sch. Georgetown U., Washington, 1949-51; law clk. to presiding justice U.S. Ct. Appeals (9th cir.), San Francisco, 1948-49; chief broadcast bur. FCC, Washington, 1970-71; pvt. practice San Francisco, 1954-70; prof. law U. San Francisco, 1951-54, 71-74, dean, prof. law, 1957-70; prof. law Hastings Coll. of Law, U. Calif., San Francisco, 1974—. Lt. USNR, 1934-46, PTO. Avocations: golf, travel. Home: 28 Spring Rd San Rafael CA 94904-2625 Office: Hastings Coll Law 200 Mcallister St San Francisco CA 94102-4707

WALSH, JOHN, museum director; b. Mason City, Wash., Dec. 9, 1937; s. John J. and Eleanor (Wilson) W.; m. Virginia Alys Galston, Feb. 17, 1962; children: Peter Wilson, Anne Galston, Frederick Matthiessen. B.A., Yale U., 1961; postgrad., U. Leyden, Netherlands, 1965-66; MA, Columbia U., 1965, PhD, 1971. Lectr., rsch. asst. Frick Collection, N.Y.C., 1966-68; assoc. higher edn. Met. Mus. Art, N.Y.C., 1968-71; assoc. curator European paintings Met. Mus. Art, 1970-72, curator dept. European paintings, 1972-74, vice-chmn., 1974-75; adj. asso. prof. art history Columbia U., N.Y.C., 1969-72; adj. prof. Columbia U., 1972-75; prof. art history Barnard Coll., Columbia U., N.Y.C., 1975-77; Mrs. Russell W. Baker curator paintings Mus. Fine Arts, Boston, 1977-83; dir. J. Paul Getty Mus., Malibu, Calif., 1983—; vis. prof. fine arts Harvard U., 1979; mem. governing bd. Yale U. Art Gallery, 1975—, Smithsonian Coun., 1990—. Contbr. articles to profl. jours. Mem. Dem. County Com., N.Y.C., 1968-71; mem. vis. com. Fogg Mus., Harvard U., 1982-87; bd. fellows Claremont U. Ctr. and Grad. Sch., 1988—. With USNR, 1957-63. Fulbright grad. fellow The Netherlands, 1965-66. Mem. Coll. Art Assn., Am. Assn. Mus., Archaeol. Inst. Am., Am. Antiquarian Soc., Assn. Art Mus. Dirs. (trustee 1986—, pres. 1989-90), Century Assn. N.Y.C. Office: J Paul Getty Mus Ste 1000 1200 Getty Center Dr Los Angeles CA 90049-1687*

WALSH, KENNETH ANDREW, biochemist; b. Sherbrooke, Que., Can., Aug. 7, 1931; s. George Stanley and Dorothy Maud (Sangster) W.; m. Deirdre Anne Clarke, Aug. 22, 1953; children: Andrew, Michael, Erin. BSc in Agr., McGill U., 1951; MS, Purdue U., 1953; PhD, U. Toronto, 1959. Postdoctoral fellow U. Wash., Seattle, 1959-62, from asst. prof. to assoc. prof. Biochemistry, 1962-69, prof. Biochemistry, 1969—, chair, 1990—. Author (book) Methods in Protein Sequence Analysis, 1986. Mem. The Protein Soc. (sec.-treas. 1987-90), Am. So. Biochemistry/Molecular Biology. Office: U Wash PO Box 357350 Seattle WA 98195-7350

WALSH, MADGE RICHARDSON, editor, writer; b. Berkeley, Calif., Mar. 1, 1931; d. Russell David and Jessie Dewey (Cutting) Richardson; m. Bert Thompson Walsh, Dec. 20, 1958; children: David, Caitilin. BA in Dramatic Lit. cum laude, U. Calif., Berkeley, 1952, MA in Anthropology, 1959. Cons. Redding (Calif.) Mus. Art & History, 1986—, Dogtown Territorial Quarterly, Paradise, Calif., 1993—; Shasta Hist. Soc. rep., Assn. Redding Museums, 1987-88. Author: A Century of Saints, 1878-1978, 1978, Carpenter With a Camera, 1993; compiler: Shasta County Voters, 1866-1884, 1993; contbr. articles to hist. jours.; editor Shasta Hist. Soc., 1987-96; script writer, dir. Shasta Hist. Soc. Presents video programs, 1996. Cataloger, v.p. Shasta Hist. Soc., Redding, Calif., 1974-75, bd. dirs., 1975-76, 88-90; sec., bd. dirs. Anderson Hist. Soc., 1997—. Named Woman of Yr. St. Andrews Presbyn. Ch., Portland, 1983. Mem. Calif. Hist. Soc., Calif. Native Plant Soc., Conf. Calif. Hist. Socs., Turtle Bay Museums, Assn. for No. Calif. Records and Rsch., Shasta Hist. Soc., Anderson Hist. Soc. (sec., bd. dirs. 1997—), Horsetown-Clear Creek Preserve. First Christian Disciple. Avocations: historic costume and design, gardening, genealogy, needlework. Office: Shasta Hist Soc 1449 Market St Redding CA 96001-1026

WALSH, MASON, retired newspaperman; b. Dallas, Nov. 27, 1912; s. Herbert C. and Margaret (Hayes) W.; m. Margaret Anne Calhoun, Mar. 7, 1947; children: Margaret Anne (Mrs. James G. Dunn), Timothy Mason, Kevin Calhoun. B.A. in Polit. Sci., So. Meth. U., 1934. Staff Dallas Evening Jour., 1929-37; staff Dallas Dispatch-Jour. (later Dallas Jour.), 1938-42; editor Austin (Tex.) Tribune, 1942; dir. employee relations N.Am. Aviation, Dallas, 1942-45; with Dallas Times-Herald, 1945-60, mng. editor, 1952-60; mng. editor Phoenix Gazette, 1960-66; gen. mgr. Phoenix Newspapers, Inc., 1966-75, asst. pub., 1975-78; pub. Ariz. Republic and Phoenix Gazette, 1978-80, pub. emeritus, 1980—. Profl. musician, 1929-35. Chmn. Ariz. Dept. Econ. Planning and Devel. Bd., 1968-71; bd. dirs., v.p. Goodwill Industries Central Ariz., 1978-84, v.p., 1982-83; bd. dirs. Western Newspaper Found., 1974-81; trustee Desert Found., Scottsdale, 1982-85; mem. Nat. Def. Exec. Res., 1964-80. Mem. A.P. Mng. Editors Assn. (dir. 1956-63, pres. 1963), A.P. Assn. Calif., Ariz., Hawaii and Nev. (pres. 1976-77), Ariz. Acad. (dir. 1973-81, v.p. 1980-81), Valley Forward Assn. (dir. 1970-87), Newcomen Soc., Phoenix 40, Sigma Delta Chi. Episcopalian. Club: Arizona. Home: 4102 N 64th Pl Scottsdale AZ 85251-3110

WALSH, SARAH ELIZABETH (ELIZABETH WALSH), English language educator; b. Cumberland, Md., May 30, 1933; d. William Concannon and Sarah Elizabeth (Nee) W. BA, Manhattanville Coll., Purchase, N.Y., 1955; MA, Manhattanville Coll., Albany, N.Y., 1963; PhD, Harvard U., 1973. Joined Soc. Sacred Heart, Roman Cath. Ch., 1955. Secondary tchr. Acad. Sacred Heart, Greenwich, Conn., 1959-63, Albany, 1964-67; dean freshman class Manhattanville Coll., Purchase, 1967-68; teaching fellow Harvard U., Cambridge, Mass., 1969-73, instr. English, 1973-74; asst. prof. La. State U., Baton Rouge, 1974-75; asst. prof., assoc. prof. English, U. San Diego, 1975-83, prof., 1983—, chmn. dept., 1985, 90-91, dir. grad. program in English, 1985-91, chmn. dept., 1991-92; participant NEH summer seminar Columbia U., N.Y.C., 1989, 96, NEH summer inst. Yale U., New Haven, 1991. Editor: The Tale of Ralph the Collier, 1989, Light of Learning: Selected Essays of Morton W. Bloomfield, 1993; contbr. articles to profl. jours. N.Y. Regents fellow, 1965-69, Rsch. grantee Harvard U., 1973, Harvard travel grantee, 1969, Dexter travelling fellow, Eng., Italy, 1973, USD Rsch. grantee 1979, 80, 88, 89, 90, 92, 93, 94, 95, 96. Mem. MLA, Dante Soc., Medieval Acad., Medieval Assn. of the Pacific, New Chaucer Soc., Kappa Gamma Pi. Democrat. Avocations: drama, music, politics. Home and Office: U San Diego 5998 Alcala Park San Diego CA 92110-2492

WALSH, WILLIAM, former football coach; b. Los Angeles, Nov. 30, 1931. Student, San Mateo Jr. Coll.; BA, San Jose State U., 1954, MA in Edn., 1959. Asst. coach Monterey Peninsula Coll., 1955, San Jose State U., 1956; head coach Washington Union High Sch., Fremont, Calif., 1957-59; asst. coach U. Calif., Berkeley, 1960-62, Stanford U., 1963-65, Oakland Raiders, Am. Football League, 1966-67, Cin. Bengals, 1968-75, San Diego Chargers, Nat. Football League, 1976; head coach Stanford U., 1977-78; head coach, gen. mgr. San Francisco 49ers, NFL, 1979-89, exec. v.p., 1989; broadcaster NBC Sports, 1989-91; head coach Stanford U., 1992-95; cons. San Francisco Forty Niners, 1996—. Named NFL Coach of Yr., Sporting News, 1981; coached Stanford U. winning team Sun Bowl, 1977, Bluebonnet Bowl, 1978, Blockbuster Bowl, 1993, San Francisco 49ers to Super Bowl championships, 1981, 84, 88; elected to Pro Football Hall of Fame, 1993. Office: Bill Walsh Enterprises 3000 Sand Hill Rd Ste 200 Menlo Park CA 94025-7113

WALSH, WILLIAM DESMOND, investor; b. N.Y.C., Aug. 4, 1930; s. William J. and Catherine Grace (Desmond) W.; m. Mary Jane Gordon, Apr. 5, 1951; children: Deborah, Caroline, Michael, Suzanne, Tara Jane, Peter. BA, Fordham U., 1951; JD, Harvard U., 1955. Bar: N.Y. State bar 1955. Asst. U.S. atty. So. dist. N.Y., N.Y.C., 1955-58; counsel N.Y. Commn. Investigation, N.Y.C., 1958-61; mgmt. cons. McKinsey & Co., N.Y.C., 1961-67; sr. v.p. Arcata Corp., Menlo Park, Calif., 1967-82; gen. ptnr. Sequoia Assocs., 1982—; pres., chief exec. officer Atacra Liquidating Trust, 1982-88; chmn. bd. dirs. Consol. Freightways Corp., Menlo Park, Calif., Clayton Group, Inc., Tampa, Fla., Newell Mfg. Corp., Lowell, Mich., Newell Indsl. Corp., Roanoke, Va., Neuroscis. Inst./Scripps; bd. dirs. URS Corp., San Francisco, Basic Vegetable Products, San Francisco, UNOVA, Beverly Hills, Calif., Newcourt Credit Corp., Toronto, Ont., Can., Crown Vantage, Oakland, Calif., Bemiss Jason Corp., Newark, Calif., Am. Ireland Fund. Mem. bd. visitors Harvard Law Sch., co-chair dean's adv. bd.; trustee Fordham U.; mem. bd. overseers Hoover Inst. Mem. N.Y. State Bar Assn., Harvard Club (N.Y.C. and San Francisco), Fordham Club No. Calif., Knights of Malta. Home: 279 Park Ln Atherton CA 94027-5448 Office: 3000 Sand Hill Rd Ste 140 Menlo Park CA 94025-7113

WALSHAW, L. SCOTT, commissioner. BA in Art History, Calif. State U., BA in Econ.; MBA, U. Nev. Sr. examiner Nev. Fin. Instns., Carson City, Nev.; asst. nat. bank examiner Office the Comptr. the Currency, Carson City, Nev.; commr. Fin. Instns., Carson City, Nev., 1983—; past chmn. Am. Coun. State Savs. Supr.; past. chmn., trustee Inst. Supr. Edn.; past mem. state liaison com. Fed. Fin. Instns. Examination Coun. Office: State of Nev Fin Instns Divsn 406 E 2nd St Ste 3 Carson City NV 89701-4758

WALSTON, RODERICK EUGENE, state government official; b. Gooding, Idaho, Dec. 15, 1935; s. Loren R. and Iva M. (Boyer) W.; m. Margaret D. Grandey; children: Gregory Scott W., Valerie Lynne W. A.A., Boise Jr. Coll., 1956; B.A. cum laude, Columbia Coll., 1958; LL.B. scholar, Stanford U., 1961. Bar: Calif. 1961, U.S. Supreme Ct. 1973. Law clk to judge U.S. Ct. Appeals 9th Cir., 1961-62; dep. atty. gen State of Calif., San Francisco, 1963-91, head natural resources sect, 1969-91, chief asst. atty. gen. pub. rights div., 1991—; spl. dep counsel Kings County, Calif., 1975-76; mem. environ. and natural resources adv. coun. Stanford (Calif.) Law Sch. Contbr. articles to profl. jours.; bd. editors: Stanford Law Rev., 1959-61, Western Natural Resources Litigation Digest, Calif. Water Law and Policy Reporter; spl. editor Jour. of the West. Co-chmn. Idaho campaign against Right-to-Work initiative, 1958; Calif. rep. Western States Water Coun., 1986—; environ. and natural resources adv. coun., Stanford Law Sch. Nat. Essay Contest winner Nat. Assn. Internat. Rels. Clubs, 1956, Stanford Law Rev. prize, 1961; recipient Best Brief award Nat. Assn. Attys. Gen., 1997; Astor Found. scholar, 1956-58. Mem. ABA (chmn. water resources com. 1988-90, vice chmn. and conf. chmn. 1985-88, 90—), Contra Costa County Bar Assn., U.S. Supreme Ct., Hist. Soc., Federalist Soc., World Affairs Coun. No. Calif. Office: Calif Atty Gen's Office 1300 I St Ste 1720 Sacramento CA 95814-2919

WALTER, GEORGE PAUL, insurance agency executive; b. Cedar Rapids, Iowa, May 31, 1942; s. Paul George and Velda (Smart) W.; m. Kathleen Ann Wolf, Nov. 27, 1965 (div. 1984); children: Adam, Aaron, Andrew, Susan; m. Roberta Ray Krueger Lorenz, Nov. 26, 1994. AD, Everett C.C. Car salesman Wood Motors, Everett, Wash., 1965-68, 72-74; car lot owner Little Auto City, Denver, 1968-72; ins. salesman Mid Assn. Luth., Everett, 1974-88; car sales Lincoln Liberty, Weratchee, Wash., 1988-91; ins. agy. owner A Ins. Svcs., Denver, 1991—. With USAF, 1961-65. Mem. Nat. Assn. Life Underwriters. Republican. Lutheran. Avocations: flying, golf. Home: 3130 W 63d Ave Denver CO 80221 Office: A Ins Svcs PO Box 12100 4999 W 47th Ave Denver CO 80212

WALTER, MICHAEL CHARLES, lawyer; b. Oklahoma City, Nov. 25, 1956; s. Donald Wayne and Viola Helen (Heffelfinger) W. BA in Polit. Sci., BJ, U. Wash., 1980; JD, Univ. Puget Sound, 1983. Bar: Wash. 1985, U.S. Dist. Ct. (9th cir. 1985). Ptnr. Keating, Bucklin & McCormack, Seattle, 1985—; instr. Bellevue (Wash.) C.C., 1983—. FAX: 206-223-9423. Mem. ABA, Wash. State Bar Assn., Reporters Com. for Freedom of Press, Seattle-King County Bar Assn., Wash. Assn. Def. Counsel, Seattle Claims Adjustors Assn., Wash. Assn. Mcpl. Attys., Def. Rsch. Inst., Am. Planning Assn., Def. Rsch. Inst. Avocations: running, swimming, hiking, coin collecting, photography. Fax: (206) 223-9423. Home: 11920 27th Pl SW Burien WA 98146-2438 Office: Keating Bucklin & McCormack 4141 SeaFirst 5th Ave Pla Seattle WA 98104

WALTERS, ANNA LEE, writer, educational administrator, educator; b. Pawnee, Okla., Sept. 9, 1946; d. Luther and Juanita Mae (Taylor) McGlaslin; children: Anthony, Daniel. BA Goddard Coll. Dir. Navajo Community Coll. Press, Tsaile (Navajo Nation), Ariz., 1982—; contbg. author: The Man to Send Rainclouds, 1974, Warriors of the Rainbow, 1975, Shantih, 1976, The Third Woman, 1979, The Remembered Earth, 1979, American Indians Today, Thought, Literature, Art, 1981, Spider Woman's Granddaughters, Traditional Tales and Contemporary Writing by Native American Women, 1989, Tapestries of Life, Women's Work Women's Consciousness and the Meaning of Daily Experience, Talking Leaves, Contemporary Native American Short Stories, Growing Up Native American-An Anthology, Native Heritage-Personal Accounts by American Indians 1790 to Present, Walking the Twilight-Women Writers of the Southwest, Reinventing the Enemy's Languages, Contemporary Native Women Writings of Native America; coauthor textbook: The Sacred Ways of Knowledge, Sources of Life, 1977; author: The Otoe-Missiouria Tribe, Centennial Memoirs, 1881-1981, 1981; Earth Power Coming, 1983; The Sun is Not Merciful, 1985, Ghost Singer, 1988, The Spirit of Native America, 1989, Talking Indian, 1993, Neon Pow Wow, Reflections on Survival and Writing, the Two-Legged Creature-An Otoe Story (retold by Anna Lee Walters); contbr. articles to jours.; guest editor Frauen Offensive, 1978; also poet, feature writer; editor: Neon Pow-Wow, 1994, The Two Legged Creature, 1994. Recipient Am. Book award The Before Columbus Found., 1986, Virginia Scully McCormick Lit. award, 1986. Office: Dine Coll Humanities Dept Tsaile AZ 86556

WALTERS, DAVID WAYNE, history and government educator, tennis coach; b. Corona, Calif., Aug. 7, 1956; s. Kenneth Richard Walters and Ellen Louise (Masters) Deitrick; m. Shelia Faye Young, June 25, 1977; children: Jeremy Andrew, Joshua Allen. BA, Calif. Poly. U., 1990; MEd, Azusa Pacific U., 1997. Cert. social sci. tchr., Calif. Salesmen United Van Lines, Monrovia, Calif., 1980-84; mktg. dir. Chino (Calif.) Valley Chamber, 1986-89; tchr. Bloomington (Calif.) H.S., 1991-96; asst. prin. Ruth O. Harris Mid. Sch., Bloomington, 1996—. Mem. Calif. Coun. Social Scis. (Student Tchr. of Yr. 1990), Calif. Tchr.'s Assn.

WALTERS, JESSE RAYMOND, JR., judge; b. Rexburg, Idaho, Dec. 26, 1938; s. Jesse Raymond and Thelma Rachael (Hodgson) W.; m. Harriet Payne, May 11, 1959; children—Craig T., Robyn, J. Scott. Student Ricks Coll., 1957-58; B.A. in Polit. Sci., U. Idaho, 1961, J.D., 1963; postgrad. U. Washington, 1962; LL.M. U. Va., 1990. Bar: Idaho 1963, U.S. Dist. Ct. Idaho 1964, U.S. Ct. Appeals (9th cir.) 1970. Law clk to chief justice Idaho Supreme Ct., 1963-64; sole practice, Boise, Idaho, 1964-77; atty. Idaho senate, Boise, 1965; dist. judge 4th Jud. Dist., Idaho, Boise, 1977-82, adminstrv. dist. judge, 1981-82; chief judge Idaho Ct. Appeals, Boise, 1982—. [illegible] services; chmn. Criminal Pattern Jury Instrn. Com.; mem. Civil Pattern Jury Instrn. Com; Republican committeeman, Boise, 1975-77; mem. Ada County Rep. Central Com., 1975-77. Mem. Idaho Bar Assn. (bankruptcy com.), Idaho Adminstrv. Judges Assn., ABA, Am. Judicature Soc., Assn. Trial Lawyers Am. Idaho Trial Lawyers Assn., Council Chief Judges Ct. Appeals (pres. 1994-95), Boise Estate Planning Council, Jaycees (nat. dir. 1969-70, pres. Boise chpt. 1966-67). Mormon. Lodges: Lions, Elks, Eagles. Office: Supreme Ct of Idaho PO Box 83720 Boise ID 83720-3720

WALTERS, KATHLEEN JANE, office manager; b. Grand Island, Nebr., Apr. 19, 1947; d. Francis J. and Mary Jane (Thrasher) Albrecht; m. Richard Lee Walters, July 25, 1968; children: Sara Jane, Joshua Lee. BS in Edn., Ea. Mont. Coll., 1969. Lic. realtor Mont. State Bd. Realty Regulation. Aquatics/health club dir. Rocky Mountain Coll., Billings, 1977-93; owner Indsl. Lubricants Co., Billings, Mont., 1993-96; office mgr. Jan Barry Ct. Reporting, Billings, 1993—; realtor Century 21, Billings, 1993-96; emergency telecomm. operator City of Billings, 1996-97; vol. coord. Cmty. Crime Prevention Coun., Billings, 1997-98; tutor, Billings, 1992—. Guest columnist: (newspaper) Billings Gazette, 1984. Vice-chairperson Pks., Recreation, Pub. Lands Bd., Billings, 1984-90; water safety chairperson ARC, Billings, 1980-88; com. mem. Habitat for Humanity, 1992-98; commr. Local Govt. Rev. Com., Billings, 1994-96; membership com. ACLU, Billings, 1993; vestry mem. St. Stephen's Episcopal Ch., Billings, 1984-88; mem. Mont. Women's Lobby, Helena, 1990—. Mem. Mont. Arabian Horse Assn. (sec. 1992-93, editor periodical 1986, Dir.'s award 1990). Democrat. Avocations: showing and training Arabian horses, fishing, biking, auto racing. Home: 3104 Radcliff Dr Billings MT 59102-0731 Office: Cmty Crime Prevention Coun 201 S 30th St Billings MT 59101-4044

WALTERS, KENNETH C., retired educator; b. Constantine, Mich., Apr. 2, 1913; s. Roy Irvin and Pearl Valentine (Ashbaugh) W. Student, Western Mich. U., 1931-35; MA in Math., MA in Edn., U. Mich., 1948; PhD in Math., U. Fla., 1952. Tchr. coll. level, 1936-52. One man shows, Thousand Oaks, Calif.; author: (novels) Gone with the Winter, 1980, I, the President, 1980, (comedy, play) Irene, The Nurse's Aide, 1980, (instrnl.) Beginners Play Piano in 60 Minutes, 1996, over 100 poems; copyright 6,200 songs; standup comedian. Advisor to Bill Clinton. 4-yr. scholar Western Mich. U., 1931-35. Mem. Burbank Catalina Art Assn. (pres.), San Fernando Art Club. Avocation: composing songs. Home: 2233 N Catalina St Burbank CA 91504-3246

WALTERS, KIM G., librarian; b. Torrington, Conn., July 1, 1955; d. Robert Bruce Walters and Gladys V. (Porter) Loughlin; m. Chris D. Coleman; 1 child, Nathaniel M.W. BA, Western Conn. State U., 1973; MA, So. Meth. U., 1982; MLIS, San Jose State U., 1988. Libr. Unisys, Santa Clara, Calif., 1984-89, Marin Inst. for Prevention of Alcohol & Other Drug Problems, San Rafael, Calif., 1989-90; libr. dir. S.W. Mus., L.A., 1990—. Editor numerous books. Mem. Spl. Libr. Assn., Soc. Calif. Archivists. E-mail: library@southwestmuseum.org. Office: SW Mus 234 Museum Dr Los Angeles CA 90065-5000

WALTERS, PAUL, protective services official; b. Reading, Eng., 1945; (parents Am. citizens); m. Linda Koskewich; children: Gary, Michael. AA, Orange Coast Coll., 1972; BA in Criminal Justice, Calif. State U., Fullerton, 1986; MPA, U. So. Calif., 1992; JD, Am. Coll. of law; grad., Calif. Command Coll., 1986, Police Exec. Rsch. Forum, Sr. Mgmt. Inst., Harvard U. From patrol officer to capt. City of Santa Ana (Calif.) Police Dept., 1971-88, chief of police, 1988—. Sgt. USAF. Recipient Appreciation cert. Orange County Bar Assn., 1990, Commendation cert. Orange County Human Rels. Commn., 1990, Orange County Cmty. Policing award, 1994. Mem. Orange County Chiefs of Police and Sheriff's Assn. (mem. exec. com., past pres.). Office: Santa Ana Police Dept M-97 PO Box 1981 Santa Ana CA 92702-1981

WALTERS, THOMAS BYRON, metrology analyst; b. Gresham, Oreg., Feb. 23, 1964; s. Wesley James and Carol Ann (Guthu) W.; m. Erin Holden Gilreath Cooper, Aug. 16, 1997. BS in Mech. Engring. Tech., Oreg. Inst. Tech., 1986. Cert. locksmith, Oreg. Layout inspector Precision Castparts Corp., Portland, Oreg., 1986-92; metrology analyst Precision Castparts Corp., Portland, 1992-98, Clackamas, Oreg., 1994—. Donor Paralyzed Vets. Am., 1992—, Disabled Am. Vets., 1992—. Cpl. USMC, 1988-91, Persian Gulf. Oreg. scholar Oreg. Dept. Edn., 1982. Mem. VFW, Am. Legion. Republican. Evangelical. Avocations: personal fitness, competitive softball, locksmithing. E-mail: twalters@pccsmtp.precast.com, twalters@inetarena.com. Home: 15122 SE Pinegrove Loop Clackamas OR 97015 Office: Precision Castparts Corp 13340 SE 84th St Clackamas OR 97015

WALTON, NEPHI A., multimedia producer, consultant; b. Woods Cross, Utah, Sept. 3, 1974. Student, U. Utah, 1990-95. Dir. multimedia Am. Digital, Salt Lake City, 1994—. Author: (multimedia project) Virtual Anatomy, 1996. Recipient Best Interface Design award N.Y. Festivals, 1997, Best Healthcare Application award, 1997. Avocations: art, hiking, fishing, hunting, web development. Office: Am Digital 624 N 300 W Salt Lake City UT 84103-1308

WALTON, ROGER ALAN, public relations executive, mediator, writer; b. Denver, June 25, 1941; s. Lyle R. and Velda V. (Nicholson) W.; m. Helen Anderson. Attended, U. Colo., 1960-63. Govt. rep. Continental Airlines, Denver, 1964-72; dir. pub. affairs Regional Transp. Dist., Denver, 1972-77; pub. affairs cons. Denver, 1977—; res. pub. info. officer Fed. Emergency Mgmt. Agy., 1995-96; pres. Colo. Times Pub. Co. Author: Colorado-A Practical Guide to its Government and Politics, 1973, 6th rev. edit., 1990, Colorado Gambling - A Guide, 1991; columnist The Denver Post newspaper, 1983—, The Rocky Mountain Jour., 1977-81. Mem. U.S. Presdl. Electoral Coll., Washington, 1968; commr. U.S. Bicentennial Revolution Commn., Colo., 1972-76, U.S. Commn. on the Bicentennial of U.S. Constn., Denver, 1985-90, pres.; trustee Arapahoe County (Colo.) Libr. Bd., 1982-86; chmn. lobbyist ethics com. Colo. Gen. Assembly, 1990-91. Republican. Avocations: reading, fishing, photography. Home and Office: 12550 W 2d Dr Lakewood CO 80228-5012

WALTZ, MARCUS ERNEST, retired prosthodontist; b. Brownsville, Oreg., July 29, 1921; s. Roswell Starr and Eva Ione (Cherrington) W.; m. Constance Jean Elwood, May 31, 1952 (div. Nov. 1973); children: Melody Ann, Martha Louise, Kathryn Jean, Holly Jay, Joy Evalyn, Ross Elwood; m. Shelby Annette Schwab, June 10, 1975. AB, Willamette U., 1942; DMD, U. Oreg., 1945. Cert. Nev. State Bd. Dental Examiners. Practice dentistry Forest Grove, Oreg., 1946-52; practice dentistry specializing in prosthodontics Reno, 1954-95, ret., 1995; councillor Pacific Coast Dental Conf.; pres. Pacific Coast Soc. of Prosthodontics, 1983; mem. Nev. State Bd. Dental Examiners, 1960-66, pres., 1964. Mem. State of Nev. Selective Svc. Appeals Bd., 1970-76, pres., 1974-76. Lt. USN, 1945-46, 52-54, Korea. Decorated Combat Medics award, Battle Stars (oak leaf cluster),. Fellow Internat. Coll. Dentistry, Acad. Dentistry Internat.; mem. ADA, Northern Nev. Dental Soc. (pres. 1959), Nev. Dental Assn., Nev. Acad. Gen. Dentistry (pres. 1974), Sigma Chi, Omicron Kappa Upsilon. Democrat. Methodist. Club: Reno Exec. (dir. 1960-66, pres. 1964-65). Lodges: Sigma Tau (pres. 1941-42), Masons (32 degree), Shriners. Avocation: outdoor activities. Home: 715 Manor Dr Reno NV 89509-1944

WALUNGA, ALLEN R., writer, researcher; b. Gambell, Alaska, Oct. 21, 1951; s. Willis and Nancy (Ugloowuk) W. AA in Social Scis. cum laude, Boise State U., 1980; BA in acctg. Bookkeeper Industries, Boise, Idaho, 1980-83; adminstrv. asst. Stillwater Sys., Lino Lakes, Minn., 1987-89; computer typesetter OMR, Stillwater, Minn., 1989-90; rsch., mktg. rep. Insight, Inc., Lino Lakes, 1992-95; freelance writer, 1979—; founder, chmn. Lit. Devel., Boise, 1979-82, founder, editor Stillwater Quarterly, 1988-90. Author: Loving in the Truth, 1982, Changes in Native Alaska, 1997, Addiction/Deliverance, 1998; patentee sportswear. Supporting mem. Jay Cees Juneau, Alaska, Minn., 1978, 87-90, pres. Full Gospel Bus., Boise, 1980-80, treas. Native Culture Coun. Juneau, 1995—. Brother Heritage Found., mem. Native Culture Coun. Republican. Presbyterian. Avocations: classical music, art, scrabble, chess, jogging. Home: PO Box 103 Gambell AK 99742-[illegible]

WAMBOLT, THOMAS EUGENE, financial consultant; b. Scottsbluff, Nebr., Aug. 9, 1938; s. Andrew, Jr. and Anne (Altergott) W.; B.S., Met. State Coll., Denver, 1976; cert. Total Quality Mgmt. m. Linda E. Shifflett, Oct. 31, 1967; 1 son, Richard Duane King. Pres. Universal Imports Co., Westminster, Colo., 1967-71; printer Rocky Mountain News, Denver, 1967-78; propr., accountant Thomas E. Wambolt Co., Arvada, Colo., 1974-77, fin. cons., 1977—. Baptist. Address: 6035 Garrison St Arvada CO 80004-5345

WAN, FREDERIC YUI-MING, mathematician, educator; b. Shanghai, Jan. 7, 1936; arrived in U.S., 1947; s. Wai-Nam and Olga Pearl (Jung) W.; m. Julia Y.S. Chang, Sept. 10, 1960. SB, MIT, 1959, SM, 1963, PhD, 1965. Mem. staff MIT Lincoln Lab., Lexington, 1959-65; instr. math. MIT, Cambridge, 1965-67, asst. prof., 1967-69, assoc. prof., 1969-74; prof. math., dir. Inst. Applied Math. and Stats. U. B.C., Vancouver, 1974-83; prof. applied math. and math. U. Wash., Seattle, 1983-95, chmn. Dept. Applied Math., 1984-88, assoc. dean scis. coll. arts and scis., 1988-92; prof. math., prof. mech. and aero. engring. U. Calif., Irvine, 1995—, vice chancellor rsch., dean grad. studies, 1995—; program dir. Divsn. Math. Sci. NSF, 1986-87, divsn. dir., 1993-94; cons. indsl. firms and govt. agys.; mem. MIT Ednl. Coun. for B.C. Area of Can., 1974-83. Assoc. editor Jour. Applied Mechancs, 1991-95, Can. Applied Math. Quar., Studies in Applied Math., Jour. Dyn. Discrete, Continuous and Impulsive Sys., 1994-97, Internat. Jour. Solids & Structures; contbr. articles to profl. jours. Sloan Found. award, 1973, Killam sr. fellow, 1979. Fellow AAAS, ASME, Am. Acad. Mechanics (sec. fellows 1984-90, pres.-elect 1992-93, pres. 1993-94), Soc. Indsl. and Applied Math., Can. Applied Math. Soc. (coun. 1980-83, pres. 1983-85, Arthur Beaumont Disting. Svc. award 1991), Am. Math. Soc., Math. Assn. Am., Sigma Xi. Home: 22 Urey Ct Irvine CA 92612-4077 Office: U Calif Irvine Office Rsch & Grad Studies 155 Administration Irvine CA 92697-3175

WANG, CHARLES PING, scientist; b. Shanghai, Republic of China, Apr. 25, 1937; came to U.S., 1962; s. Kuan-Ying and Ping-Lu (Ming) W.; m. Lily L. Lee, June 29, 1963. BS, Taiwan U., Republic of China, 1959; MS, Tsinghua U., Singchu, Republic of China, 1961; PhD, Calif. Inst. Tech., 1967. Mem. tech. staff Bellcomm, Washington, 1967-69; research engr. U. San Diego, 1969-74; sr. scientist Aerspace Corp., Los Angeles, 1976-86; pres. Optodyne, Inc., Compton, Calif., 1986—; adj. prof. U. Calif., San Diego, 1979-90; pres. Chinese-Am. Engr. and Scientists Assn. So. Calif., Los Angeles, 1979-81; program chmn. Internation Conf. of Lasers, Shanghai, 1979-80; organizer and session chmn. Lasers Conf., Los Angeles, 1981-84, program chmn., Las Vegas, 1985. Editor in chief Series in Laser Tech., 1983-91; contbr. articles to profl. jours.; inventor discharge excimer laser. Calif. Inst. Tech. scholar, 1965. Fellow Am. Optical Soc., AIAA (assoc., jour. editor 1981-83). Office: Optodyne Inc 1180 W Mahalo Pl Compton CA 90220-5443

WANG, CHEN CHI, electronics company, real estate, finance company, investment services, and international trade executive; b. Taipei, Taiwan, Aug. 10, 1932; came to U.S., 1959, naturalized, 1970; s. Chin-Ting and Chen-Kim Wang; m. Victoria Rebisoff, Mar. 5, 1965; children: Katherine Kim, Gregory Chen, John Christopher, Michael Edward. B.A. in Econs., Nat. Taiwan U., 1955; B.S.E.E., San Jose State U., 1965; M.B.A., U. Calif., Berkeley, 1961. With IBM Corp., San Jose, Calif., 1965-72; founder, chief exec. officer Electronics Internat. Co., Santa Clara, Calif., 1968-72, owner, gen. mgr., 1972-81, reorganized as EIC Group, 1982, now chmn. bd., chief exec. officer; dir. Systek Electronics Corp., Santa Clara, 1970-73; founder, sr. ptnr. Wang Enterprises (name changed to Chen Kim Entrprises 1982), Santa Clara, 1974—; founder, sr. ptnr. Hanson & Wang Devel. Co., Woodside, Calif., 1977-85; chmn. bd. Golden Alpha Enterprises, San Mateo, Calif., 1979—; mng. ptnr. Woodside Acres-Las Pulgas Estate, Woodside, 1980-85; founder, sr. ptnr. DeVinc & Wang, Oakland, Calif., 1977-83; Van Heal & Wang, West Village, Calif., 1981-82; founder, chmn. bd. EIC Fin. Corp., Redwood City, Calif., 1985—; chmn. bd. Maritek Corp., Corpus Christi, Tex., 1988-89; chmn. EIC Internat. Trade Corp., Lancaster, Calif., 1989—, EIC Capital Corp., Redwood City, 1990—. Served to 2d lt., Nationalist Chinese Army, 1955-56. Mem. Internat. Platform Assn., Tau Beta Pi. Mem. Christian Ch. Author: Monetary and Banking System of Taiwan, 1955, The Small Car Market in the U.S., 1961. Home: 195 Brookwood Rd Woodside CA 94062-2302 Office: EIC Group Head Office Bldg 2055 Woodside Rd # 2075 Redwood City CA 94061-3355

WANG, COLLEEN IONA, medical association administrator, writer; b. Mpls., Oct. 23, 1953; d. Dillard Wayne and Nova Bardeen (Vaught) Greenwood; m. Hansen Stephen Wang, Aug. 22, 1976; children: Hansen Jeremiah, Nathaniel Stephen. AS in Nursing, Loma Linda U., 1994. Registered nurse, Calif. Staff nurse cardio-thoracic ICU Loma Linda (Calif.) U. Med. Ctr., 1975-77, staff nurse pediats. ICU, 1978-80; staff nurse med.-surg. cardiothoracic ICU St. Bernardine's Hosp., San Bernardino, Calif., 1977-78; nurse medically fragile, high risk infants, foster care San Bernardino County, Alta Loma, Calif., 1980-87; coord. support group So. Calif. chpt. San Bernardino-Riverside County Tourette Syndrome Assn., Loma Linda, 1987-97; med. liaison So. Calif. chpt. Tourette Syndrome Assn., Redlands, 1991—, nursing educator, 1993—; bd. dirs. med. liaison Tourette Syndrome Assn., Encino, 1993-96; chmn. western regional med. conf. Tourette Syndrome Assn., Pasadena, 1994; bd. dirs., pres. Tourette Syndrome Assn., Encino, 1996-98; host chmn. with Tourette Syndrome Assn. N.Y. Tourette Syndrome Assn., Burbank, 1996; chmn. educators conf. Tourette Syndrome Assn., San Diego, 1998. Co-author, editor: Tourette Syndrome: A Continuing Education Program for Nurses, 1993, updated, 1996 (Outstanding Chpt. Achievement award Nat. Tourette Syndrome Assn. Inc. 1994); contbr. articles to profl. jours. Vol. instr. gifted and talented math Mariposa Elem. Redlands (Calif.) Sch. Dist., 1990-91; mem. PTA Mariposa Elem., Redlands, Calif., 1992-95, vol. instr. first aid Flash Class, 1990-92; presenter-in-svc. edn. Multiple Schs. San Bernardino County, Riverside County, L.A. County, 1992—; mem. PTA Moore Middle Sch., Redlands, 1995-97, Redlands H.S., 1994—. Mem. Ams. for Nonsmoker's Rights, Tourette Syndrome Assn. (nat. membership Bayside, N.Y. emm. com. underserved area conf. 1986-97). Avocations: computers, snorkeling, travel. Office: Tourette Syndrome Assn So Calif 30733 E Sunset Dr S Redlands CA 92373-7350

WANG, FU-QUAN, electrical engineer, researcher; b. Dazhu, Sichuan, China, Apr. 14, 1963; came to U.S., 1989; s. Shao Rong Wang and Baoying Zhang; m. Yu Yang, Aug. 9, 1991; children: Angela M., Anton Y. BS in Post and Telecomms., Beijing U., 1982, MS in Post and Telecomms., 1985; PhD, U. Notre Dame, 1993. Lectr. Beijing U., 1985-88; rsch. assoc. U. Notre Dame, Ind., 1993-94; cons. Microunity Sys., Sunnyvale, Calif., 1994; sr. engr. Vocal Techs., Ltd., Buffalo, 1994-95; staff engr. ESS Tech., Inc., Fremont, Calif., 1995-96; project mgr. ESS Tech., Inc., Fremont, 1996—. Contbr. articles to IEEE Trans. Mem. IEEE, N.Y. Acad. Sci. Achievements include application of sequential decoding algorithms to trellis coding; construction of optimum and good trellis codes for sequential decoding; development of host based modem products. Office: ESS Tech Inc 48401 Fremont Blvd Fremont CA 94538-6581

WANG, HUAI-LIANG WILLIAM, mechanical engineer; b. Hsinchu, Taiwan, Republic of China, Apr. 4, 1959; came to U.S., 1984; s. Feng-Chi and Hu-Mei (Chou) W.; m. Wen-Pei Chen, June 28, 1986; children: James, Edward. BSME, Tatung Inst. of Tech., Taipei, Taiwan, 1981; MSME, Okla. State U., 1985. Asst. engr. Teco Electric and Machinery Corp., Taipei, Taiwan, 1984; electro-mech. engr. Microsci. Internat. Corp., Sunnyvale, Calif., 1987-89; engr. Lockheed Engring. and Scis. Co., Houston, 1989-91, sr. engr., 1991-92; mgr. mech. engring. Orbiter Tech. Co., Fremont, Calif., 1992; sr. engr. Avatar Sys. Corp., Milpitas, Calif., 1993, Quantum Corp., Milpitas, 1994—. Mem. IEEE, ASME. Office: Quantum Corp 500 Mccarthy Blvd Milpitas CA 95035-7909

WANG, I-TUNG, atmospheric scientist; b. Peking, People's Republic of China, Feb. 16, 1933; came to U.S., 1958; s. Shen and Wei-Yun (Wen) W.; m. Amy Hung Kong; children: Cynthia P., Clifford T. BS in Physics, Nat. Taiwan U., 1955; MA in Physics, U. Toronto, 1957; PhD in Physics, Columbia U., 1965. Rsch. physicist Carnegie-Mellon U., Pitts., 1965-67, asst. prof., 1967-70; environ. systems engr. Argonne (Ill.) Nat. Lab., 1970-76; mem. tech. staff Environ. Monitoring and Svcs. Ctr. Rockwell Internat., Creve Coeur, Mo., 1976-80, Newbury Park, Calif., 1980-84; sr. scientist, combustion engr. Environ. Monitoring and Svcs. Inc., Newbury Park, Camarillo, 1984-88; sr. scientist ENSR Corp (formerly ERT), 1988; pres. EMA Co., Thosand Oaks, Calif., 1989—; tech. advisor Bur. of Environ. Protection, Republic of China, 1985; environ. cons. ABB Environ, 1989-92, ARCO, 1990-91, Du Pont (SAFER Sys. Divsn.), 1992-93, So. Calif. Edison, 1993-95, So. Coast Air Quality Mgmt. Dist., 1995-96, Tetra Tech., 1996—. Contbr. papers to profl jours. Grantee Bureau of Environ. Protection, Taiwan, 1985. Mem. N.Y. Acad. of Scis., Air and Waste Mgmt. Assn., Sigma Xi. Avocations: violin and chamber music. Office: EMA Co Ste 435 2219 E Thousand Oaks Blvd Thousand Oaks CA 91362-2930

WANG, QUN, English language educator; b. Shanghai, Apr. 28, 1956; came to U.S., 1983; s. Yi Wang and Huiying Jian; m. Lori A. Lee, Sept. 12, 1986; children: Sophia, Eugenia. BA, East China Normal U., Shanghai, 1979, MA, 1982; PhD, U. Oreg., 1990. Asst. prof. U. Wis., River Falls, 1990-95; assoc. prof. Calif. State U. Monterey Bay, Seaside, 1995—. Author: The Illusory World of Contemporary American Drama, 1990; editor jour. Race, Gender and Class, Asian American Voices, 1997. Mem. MLA, Assn. Asian Am. Studies, Multicultural and Ethnic Lits. of U.S. Home: 1027 Funston Ave Pacific Grove CA 93950-5429 Office: Calif State U Monterey Bay 100 Campus Ctr Seaside CA 93955-8000

WANG, SUWEN, physicist, consultant; b. Yangzhou, China, May 14, 1959; came to U.S., 1982; s. Changrong Wang and Yun Zhang; m. Xiao Shuang Fu, Apr. 3, 1994; children: Oliver Shizi Wang, Alice Fuzi Wang. BS, Nanjing (China) U., 1982; MS, La. State U., 1983; PhD, Duke U., 1988. Postdoctoral fellow Duke U., Durham, N.C., 1988-89; postdoctoral rsch. assoc. Manchester (Eng.) U., 1989-90; rsch. assoc. U. Mass., Amherst, 1990-92; sr. rsch. scientist Stanford (Calif.) U., 1992—; cons. Simplex Solutions, Inc., Sunnyvale, Calif., 1996—. Contbr. articles to sci. jours.; inventor in field. Mem. Am. Phys. Soc., Sigma Xi. Achievements include being one of the first to discover non wetting of superfluid helium on cesium substrate with the third sound technique; contributions to the field of crit. phenomena by studying properties of liquid helium; contributions to developing a milli-arc-sec cryogenic star tracker for Relativity Mission-an experiment for testing general relativity. Office: Stanford Univ GP-B HEPL Stanford CA 94305

WANG, XIAODONG, corporate executive, consultant; b. Yunhe, Zhejiang, China, Sept. 10, 1957; s. Wendou and Huizhong (Yang) W.; m. Hong Xue, Oct. 1, 1982; children: Cindy, Lawrence. Med. practitioner cert., Yunhe Med. Sch., China, 1977; BS, Zhejiang U., Hangzhou, China, 1983; MBA, Boise State U., 1993. Practitioner Shaxi Hosp., Yunhe, China, 1977-78; sect. chief Lishui Hosp., China, 1983-84; project engr. Fujian Investment & Enterprise Co., Fuzhou, China, 1984-86; dep. dir. SHP Corp., Fuzhou, 1986-90; project coord. Simplot Co., Boise, Idaho, 1992-93, gen. mgr. China ops., 1994—; cons. Chendou Hydro Design Inst., Chendou, China, 1988-90, Hunan (China) Electric Power Bur., 1989-90. Author: Poems, Essays and Short Stories, 1972-82 (Best Works 1982). Mem. Mgmt. Assn. China, Collegiate Entrepreneur Assn., MBA Assn. (advisor 1991-92). Home: PO Box 15033 Boise ID 83715-5033 Office: Simplot Co 6360 Federal Way Boise ID 83716-9617

WANGER, OLIVER WINSTON, federal judge; b. L.A., Nov. 27, 1940; m. Lorrie A. Reinhart; children: Guy A., Christopher L., Andrew G., W. Derek, Oliver Winston II. Student, Colo. Sch. Mines, 1958-60; BS, U. So. Calif., 1963; LLB, U. Calif., Berkeley, 1966. Bar: Calif. 1967, U.S. Dist. Ct. (ea. dist.) Calif. 1969, U.S. Tax Ct. 1969, U.S. Dist. Ct. (cen. dist.) Calif. 1975, U.S. Dist. Ct. (so. dist.) Calif. 1977, U.S. Dist. Ct. (no. dist.) Calif. 1989, U.S. Ct. Appeals (9th cir.) 1989. Dep. dist. atty. Fresno (Calif.) County Dist. Atty., 1967-69; ptnr. Gallagher, Baker & Manock, Fresno, 1969-74; sr. ptnr. McCormick, Barstow, Sheppard, Wayte & Carruth, Fresno, 1974-91; judge U.S. Dist. Ct. (ea. dist.) Calif., Fresno, 1991—; adj. prof. law Humphreys Coll. Law, Fresno, 1968-70. Fellow Am. Coll. Trial Lawyers, Internat. Acad. Trial Lawyers; mem. Am. Bd. Trial Advs. (pres. San Joaquin Valley chpt. 1987-89, nat. bd. dirs. 1989-91), Am. Bd. Profl. Liability Attys. (founder, diplomate), Calif. State Bar (mem. exec. com. litigation sect. 1989-92, mem. com. on fed. cts. 1989-90), San Joaquin Valley Am. Inn of Ct. (pres. 1992-93), Beta Gamma Sigma. Office: US Dist Ct 5104 US Courthouse 1130 O St Fresno CA 93721-2201

WANGSGARD, CHRIS PRINCE, lawyer; b. Ogden, Utah, July 16, 1941; s. Scott Maughn and Elizabeth (Prince) W.; m. Erica Gwilliam, June 25, 1979; children: Kirk, Sten, Dane. BS, U.S. Military Acad., 1963; JD, U. Utah, 1972. Bar: Utah 1972, U.S. Dist. Ct. (Utah) 1972, U.S. Ct. Appeals (10th cir.) 1972. Commd. 2d lt. U.S. Army, 1963, advanced through grades to capt., resigned, 1969; atty. Van Cott, Bagley, Cornwall & McCarthy, Salt Lake City, 1972-91, ptnr., 1977-91; ptnr. Parsons Behle & Latimer, Salt Lake City, 1991—; adj. prof. Coll. of Law U. of Utah, 1983-87. Mem. Am. Inns of Ct. (Master of the Bench). Office: Parsons Behle & Latimer 201 S Main St Ste 1800 Salt Lake City UT 84111-2218

WANNEBO, ODE, religious organization executive, opera-concert singer, educator; b. Namsos, Trondelag, Norway, Mar. 11, 1932, came to U.S., 1963; s. Odin Mayer and Johanne (Alvhilde) W. Pres., min. music, concert singer, coord.-condr. vocal master class seminar tng. Odewind Prodns., North Hollywood, Calif., 1972—; founder, pres., counselor drugs addiction and alcoholics Victor's Circle, Van Nuys, Calif., 1982—; comml. artist Art & Handcraft Sch., Oslo, 1957-58; opera-concert singer, composer, songwriter Acad. Music and Performing Arts, Vienna, Austria, 1958-63. Composer music and lyrics for numerous sacred-secular songs; composer, producer Classical-Folk Cantata, 1974; appeared in movie A Day at Dandelions Sea, 1981; also several recs. including one with London Symphony. Founder support group Iron sharp ends Iron. Recipient Hon. Westerner award Can. Govt., 1967, Gold medal Norwegian Swimming Assn., 1973; Norwegian Govt. scholar, 1959-63. Mem. ASCAP, Sons of Norway. E-Mail: Odew@aol.com. Office: Odewind Prodns PO Box 5316 North Hollywood CA 91616-5316

WANSTREET, BRENT LEE, company executive; b. Clarksburg, W.Va., Apr. 13, 1954; s. Paul and Mary (Hurley) M.; m. Juli (Vargo), Apr. 20, 1974; children: Matthew, Amanda, Jessica. Student, Vol. State C.C., Gallatin, Tenn., 1979-81, County Coll. Morris, Flanders, N.J., 1988-91. Gen. mgr. Rickel Home Ctr., N.J., 1981-87; ops. mgr. Hoboken Wood Floors, Hoboken, NJ, 1987-89; area dir. of stores Toys R Us, Paramus, N.J., 1989-94; dist. mgr. Michaels Stores, Dallas, 1994-96, metro mgr., 1996; v.p. ops. Aaron Bros. (Divsn. Michaels Stores), Commerce, Calif., 1996—. With USAF, 1972-73. Named one of Outstanding Young Men of Am., 1976. Republican. Roman Catholic. Home: 26 Laurelwood Irvine CA 92620-1299 Office: Aaron Bros 1270 Goodrich Blvd Los Angeles CA 90022-5107

WARADY, PHYLIS ANN, novelist; b. Sault Ste. Marie, Mich., Sept. 18, 1930; d. Desirs Gabriel and Henrietta Christina (Curry) Rastrom; m. Gordon Zane Warady; children: Anne Christine, April Carolyn, Stephen MacDougal. AA, Compton Jr. Coll., Compton, Calif., 1950. Author: Scandal's Daughter, 1990, The Earl's Comeuppance, 1991, The Golden Swan, 1994, The Peristent Suitor, 1995. Mem. Novelists, Inc., Romance Writers of Am. (pres. 1989-90), Sierra Writers (pres. 1990, v.p. 1999), Authors Guild. Avocations: reading, bridge.

WARD, ALBERT EUGENE, research center executive, archaeologist, ethnohistorian; b. Carlinville, Ill., Aug. 20, 1940; s. Albert Alan and Eileen (Boston) W.; m. Gladys Anena Lea, Apr. 26, 1961 (div. Apr. 4, 1974); children—Scott Bradley, Brian Todd; m. Stefanie Helen Tschaikowsky, Apr. 24, 1982. AA, Bethany Luth. Jr. Coll., Mankato, Minn., 1961; BS, No. Ariz. U., 1968; MA, U. Ariz., 1972. Lab. asst., asst. archeologist Mus. No. Ariz., Flagstaff, 1965-67; research archeologist Desert Research Inst., U. Nev., Las Vegas, 1968; research archeologist Archeol. Survey, Prescott Coll., Ariz., 1969-71, research assoc., 1971-73; research archeologist Ariz. Archeol. Ctr., Nat. Park Service, Tucson, 1972-73, research collaborator Chaco Ctr., Albuquerque, 1975; founder, dir. archaeol. research program Mus. Albuquerque, 1975-76; founder, dir., 1976-79 pres. bd. dirs. Ctr. Anthrop. Studies, Albuquerque, 1976—; lectr. U. N.Mex. C.C., 1974-77, others; contract archaeol. salvage and research projects in N.Mex. and Ariz. Editorial adv. bd. Hist. Archeology, 1978-80; editor publs. Ctr. Anthrop. Studies, 1978—. Contbr. articles to scholarly jours. Grantee Mus. No. Ariz., 1972, S.W. Monuments Assn., 1973, CETA, 1975-79, Nat. Park Service, 1978-79. Mem. Soc. Am. Archeology, Soc. Hist. Archeology, No. Ariz. Soc. Sci. and Art, Ariz. Archeol. and Hist. Soc., Archeol. Soc. N.Mex., Albuquerque Archeol. Soc., Am. Anthrop. Assn., S.W. Mission Research Ctr., Am. Soc. Conservation Archeology, Soc. Archeol. Scis., Southwestern Anthrop. Assn., N.Mex. Archeol. Council, Living Hist. Farms and Agrl. Mus. Assn. Republican. Lutheran.

WARD, ANTHONY JOHN, lawyer; b. L.A., Sept. 25, 1931; s. John P. and Helen C. (Harris) W.; A.B., U. So. Calif., 1953; LL.B., U. Calif. at Berkeley, 1956; m. Marianne Edle von Graeve, Feb. 20, 1960 (div. 1977); 1 son, Mark Joachim; m. 2d, Julia Norby Credell, Nov. 4, 1978. Admitted to Calif. bar, 1957; asso. firm Ives, Kirwan & Dibble, Los Angeles, 1958-61; partner firm Marapese and Ward, Hawthorne, Calif., 1961-69; individual practice law, Torrance, Calif., 1969-76; partner firm Ward, Gaunt & Raskin, 1976—. Served to 1st lt. USAF, 1956-58. Mem. ABA, Blue Key, Calif. Trial Lawyers Assn., Lambda Chi Alpha. Democrat. Home: 24962 Paseo Cipres Lake Forest CA 92630-2247 Office: Pavilion A 21525 Hawthorne Blvd Torrance CA 90503-6600

WARD, CARL EDWARD, research chemist; b. Albuquerque, Oct. 16, 1948; s. Joe E. and Loris E. (Wenk) W.; m. Bertha R. Schloer, June 9, 1970. BS in Chemistry, N.Mex. Inst. Mining and Tech., 1970; MS in Chemistry, Oreg. Grad. Ctr., 1972; PhD in Chemistry, Stanford U., 1977. Research chemist Union Carbide Corp., Charleston, W.Va., 1977-79, Dynapol Corp., Palo Alto, Calif., 1979-80; research chemist Chevron Chem. Co., Richmond, Calif., 1980-85, sr. research chemist, 1986-88; apptd. supr. chemical synthesis Chevron Chem. Co., Richmond, 1988-90; sr. rsch. assoc. Chevron Rsch. & Tech. Co., Richmond, 1990-91, staff scientist, 1991—; staff scientist Chevron Products Co.-Global Lubricants, Richmond, 1997—. Referee Jour. Organic Chemistry, 1983—; patentee in field; contbr. articles to profl. jours. Recipient NSF traineeship, Stanford U., 1972-73; Upjohn fellow, Stanford U., 1976-77, NLGI fellow, 1998; recipient Clarence E. Earle Meml. award, 1995. Mem. Soc. Tribologists and Lubrication Engrs., Nat. Lubricating Grease Inst. (Clarence E. Earle Meml. award 1995), Am. Chem. Soc., Calif. Acad. Sci., N.Mex. Inst. Mining and Tech. Pres. Club, Stanford U. Alumni Assn. Democrat. Avocations: gardening, camping, fishing. Home: 1355 Nisich Dr San Jose CA 95122-3061 Office: Chevron Rsch & Tech Co PO Box 1627 Richmond CA 94802-1796

WARD, HERBERT ARTHUR, JR., priest, child care executive; b. Jackson, Miss., Mar. 30, 1937; s. Herbert Arthur Sr. and Frances Florence Ivy (Slaymaker) W.; m. Nancy Ruth Miles, Mar. 28, 1978; children: Timothy David, Kathleen Megan. BA with honors, Millsaps Coll., 1958; Sacrosancta Theologia Magister, Gen. Theol. Sem., N.Y.C., 1961; DD, Nashotah House Sem., 1990. Vicar St. Mark's Ch., Mississippi City, Miss., 1961-65; curate, headmaster nat. hdqs. St. George's Ch. and Sch., New Orleans, 1965-70; pres., CEO St. Judge's Ranch for Children, Boulder City, Nev., 1970—. Episcopalian. Office: St Jude's Ranch for Children 100 Saint Judes St Boulder City NV 89005-1614

WARD, JOHN J., bishop; b. Los Angeles, 1920. Student, St. John's Sem., Camarillo, Calif., Catholic U. Am. Ordained priest, Roman Catholic Ch., 1946. Apptd. titular bishop of Bria, aux. bishop Diocese of Los Angels Roman Cath. Ch., 1963—; vicar gen. Roman Cath. Ch., Los Angeles., 1963—. *

WARD, JULIE MCDUFF, real estate marketing specialist; b. Birmingham, Ala., Mar. 26, 1946; d. Oliver Tabor and Julia Frances (Cooper) McDuff; m. David William Ward, Jan. 19, 1968; 1 child, Brian William. BS in Edn., U. Ala., 1968. Mgmt. trainee Bell Telephone Co., Birmingham, 1964-68; tchr. elem. edn. Huntsville (Ala.) City Schs., 1969-73; real estate agt. Frontier Better Homes and Gardens, Littleton, Colo., 1988—. Mem. pers. com. Ken Caryl Bapt. Ch., Littleton, 1992-95. Mem. Colo. Assn. Realtors (grad. realtor inst. designation), Jefferson County Assn. Realtors. Avocations: reading, physical fitness, cross-country skiing. Office: Frontier Better Homes 5944 S Kipling St Ste 100 Littleton CO 80127-2590

WARD, MICHAEL ALAN, public information consultant; b. L.A., Oct. 10, 1936; s. Carl Franklin and Verna Grace (Somerton) W.; m. Barbara Lee Maziarz, July 22, 1972; 1 child, Jennifer Lorraine. BA, Calif. State U., L.A., 1959; MS in Journalism, UCLA, 1962. Asst. city editor San Gabriel Valley Tribune, West Covina, Calif., 1965-72; reporter L.A. Times, 1972-93; co-owner Ward Pub. Rels., Upland, Calif., 1993—; lectr. Calif. State U., Fullerton, 1993, Calif. State U., San Bernardino, 1993-94. Mem. Soc. Profl. Journalists. Home: 1582 Maywood Ave Upland CA 91786-2135

WARD, MILTON HAWKINS, mining company executive; b. Bessemer, Ala., Aug. 1, 1932; s. William Howard and Mae Ivy (Smith) W.; m. Sylvia Adele Randle, June 30, 1951; children: Jeffrey Randle, Lisa Adele. BS in Mining Engring., U. Ala., 1955, MS in Engring., 1981; MBA, U. N.Mex., 1974; DEng (hon.), Colo. Sch. of Mines, 1994; PhD, U. London. Registered profl. engr., Tex., Ala. Supr., engr. San Manuel (Ariz.) Copper Corp., 1955-60; gen. supt. of mines Kerr-McGee Corp., Oklahoma City, N.Mex., 1960-66; gen. mgr. Homestake Mining Co., Grants, 1966-70; v.p. ops. Ranchers Exploration & Devel. Corp., Albuquerque, 1970-74; pres., COO Freeport-McMoRan, Inc., New Orleans, 1974-92, also bd. dirs.; chmn., pres. CEO Cyprus Amax Minerals Co., Englewood, Colo., 1992—; dir. Kinross Gold (formerly Amax Gold Inc.), 1993—; bd. dirs. Mineral Info. Inst., Inc., Internat. Copper Assn.; mem. Geoscience and Environment Ctr's. adv. bd. Sandia Nat. Labs., 1998—. Bd. trustees Western Regional Coun.; bd. dirs. Smithsonian Nat. Mus. Natural History, Nat. Mining Hall of Fame and Mus.; disting. engring. fellow U. Ala., mem. Pres.'s cabinet. Recipient Daniel C. Jackling award and Saunders gold medal Soc. Mining, Metallurgy and Exploration, 1992; inductee Am. Mining Hall of Fame, State of Ala. Engring. Hall of Fame, 1996; Honoree of Yr. Achievement Rewards Coll. Scientists, 1998-99. Fellow Inst. Mining and Metallurgy (London); mem. Nat. Acad. Engring., AIME (former sect. chmn., Disting. Mem. award), Am. Mining Congress, Nat. Mining Assn. (dir.), Am. Australian Assn., Mining and Metall. Soc. Am. (pres., exec. com.), Can. Inst. Mining and Metall., Nat. Rsch. Coun. (com. on earth and scis.), NAM (natural resources com.), Internat. Copper Assn. (bd. dirs.), Copper Club, Met. Club (Washington), Met. Club (Englewood), Las Campanas Country Club (Santa Fe, N.M.), Ventana Canyon Country Club (Tucson, Ariz.). Republican. Presbyterian. Office: Cyprus Amax Minerals Co 9100 E Mineral Cir Englewood CO 80112-3401

WARD, ROBERT RICHARD, lawyer; b. Spencer, Iowa, Nov. 7, 1948. BA, U. Calif., Berkeley, 1971; MBA, Calif. State U., Hayward, 1974; JD, Pepperdine U., 1978. Bar: Calif. 1978; U.S. Dist. Ct. (cen. dist.) 1979; U.S. Supreme Ct. 1978. Sr. ptnr. Mainstreet Law Offices, Inc., Yorba Linda, Calif., 1981—; real estate broker Award Properties, Yorba Linda, Calif., 1990—; bd. dirs. Colorbrite, Inc., Huntington Beach, Calif., 1990-96, Nat. Recreational Corp., San Jose, 1983-96, Ednl. Found., Yorba Linda, 1992-94, Sino Am., Dalian, China, 1992-96. Co-author: Alaska Pipeline Legislation, 1977. Pres. Placentia (Calif.) C. of C.; chmn. Planning Commn., Placentia; bd. dirs. Yorba Linda C. of C. Mem. Orange County Bar Assn., ATLA, Rotary Club, Exchange Club. Avocations: hunting, fly fishing, scuba diving. Office: Main St Law Offices Inc 4895 Main St Yorba Linda CA 92886-3413

WARD, SETH, history and Judaic studies educator; b. N.Y.C., Dec. 15, 1952; s. Aba and Bernice (Hamerman) W.; m. Carol Evelyn Kozak, July 4, 1978; children: Gila M., Shoshana E., Simcha Z., Raphael M. BA, Yale U., 1974, MA, 1978, PhD, 1984. Instr. Yale U., New Haven, Conn., 1984-85; lectr. U. Haifa, Israel, 1985-88, Ben Gurion U. of the Negev, Beersheva, Israel, 1988, Technion, Haifa, 1989-91; asst. prof. history and Judaic studies U. Denver, 1991—; dir. Inst. Islamic Judaic Studies, U. Denver, 1991—; dir., pres. Hispano Crypto Judaic Resource Ctr., Denver, 1997—; coord. religious svcs. Allied Jewish Apts., Denver, 1994—. Author: Synagogues and Churches in Islamic Law, 1984; contbr. articles to profl. jours. Pres. Colo. Hebrew Chorale, 1993—; mem. Family Support Svcs. Coun., Denver, 1995—, spl. needs edn. com. Ctrl. Agy. for Jewish Edn., Denver, 1991—. Jewish. Office: U Denver Dept Judaic Studies Denver CO 80208

WARDER, WILLIAM, artist; b. Guadalupita, N.Mex., July 23, 1920; s. Julian and Benita (Cordova) W.; m. Sylvia Ann Shipley, May 1, 1942 (div. June 1947); children: Alice O., Benita A., Thomas S.; m. Betty Lorena Caldwell, Oct. 2, 1947; children: Susan J., Rebecca J., Margaret E., Emily

A. BFA, U. N.Mex., 1946; postgrad., UCLA, Art Students League, N.Y.C., Taos (N.Mex.) Sch. Fine Arts. Tchr. APS, Albuquerque, 1948-50; artist-in-residence Las Vegas, Espanola & Albuquerque Pub. Schs., 1971-84. Author: Art as an Alternative Approach to Education, Answering an Inner Voice, 1993; writer, prodr., host tv art series How to be an Artist. Chmns. grantee Nat. Endowment for the Arts. Home: 400 Sandstone Dr NE Rio Rancho NM 87124-4456

WARDLAW, KIM A.M., judge; b. San Francisco, July 2, 1954; m. William M. Wardlaw, Sept. 8, 1984. Student, Santa Clara U., 1972-73, Foothill C.C., Los Altos Hills, Calif., 1973-74; AB in Comm. summa cum laude, UCLA, 1976, JD with honors, 1979. Bar: Calif., U.S. Dist. Ct. (cen. dist.) Calif. 1979, U.S. Dist. Ct. (so. dist.) Calif. 1982, U.S. Dist. Ct. Nev. 1985, U.S. Dist. Ct. (no. dist.) Calif. 1992, U.S. Dist. Ct Mont. 1993, U.S. Dist. Ct. Minn. 1994, U.S. Dist. Ct. (no. dist.) Ala. 1994, U.S. Dist. Ct. (so. dist.) Miss. 1995, U.S. Supreme Ct. Law clk. U.S. Dist. Ct. Cen. Dist. Calif. 1979-80; assoc. O'Melveny and Myers, 1980-87, ptnr., 1987-95; circ. judge U.S. Dist. Ct. Calif., L.A., 1995—; presdl. transition team Dept. Justice, Washington, 1993; mayoral transition Team City of L.A., 1995—; bd. govs., vice-chair UCLA Ctr. for Comm. Policy, 1994—; cons. in field. Co-author: The Encyclopedia of the American Constitution, 1986; contbr. articles to profl. jours. Pres. Women Lawyers Pub. Action Grant Found., 1986-87; del. Dem. Nat. Conv., 1992; founding mem. L.A. Chamber Orchestra, 1992—; active Legal Def. and Edn. Fund, Calif. Leadership Coun., 1993—, Blue Ribbon of L.A. Music Ctr., 1993—. Named one of Most Prominent Bus. Attys. in L.A. County, L.A. Bus. Jour., 1995; recipient Buddy award NOW, 1995. Mem. ABA, NOW, Mex.-Am. Bar Assn. L.A. County, Calif. Women Lawyers, Women Lawyers Assn. L.A., L.A. County Bar Assn. (trustee 1993-94), Assn. Bus. Trial Lawyers (gov. 1988—), Orgn. Women Execs., Downtown Women Ptnrs, Chancery Club, Breakfast Club, Hollywood Womens Polit. Com., City Club Bunker Hill, Phi Beta Kappa. Office: US Dist Ct 9th Cir 125 S Grand Ave Pasadena CA 91105*

WARD-SHAW, SHEILA THERESA, nurse; b. N.Y.C., June 20, 1951; d. Arthur and Cynthia Melba (Mapp) Jenkins; m. Howard J. Ward, Nov. 1977 (div. 1981); m. Thomas N. Shaw, Sept. 1988; children: Tanyatta, Barbara, Thomas. Student, Rockland Community Coll., 1973, U. Nev., Las Vegas, 1984, San Jose State U., 1994-95; BSN, San Jose State U., 1995. Charge nurse Hillcrest (N.Y.) Nursing Home, 1973-74; infirmary nurse St. Agatha's Home for Children, Nanuet, N.Y., 1974-75; temp. bldg. charge nurse Letchworth Village, Thiells, N.Y., 1976; charge nurse New Paltz (N.Y.) Nursing Home, 1977; non secure detention, foster bdg. parent St. Agatha's Home for Children, Nanuet, 1977-79; asst. nursing supr., inservice coord., infection control nurse So Nev. Mental Retardation, Las Vegas, 1979-84; psychiat. nurse II evening duty officer Harbor View Devel. Ctr., Valdez, Alaska, 1987-89; infection control, employee health nurse, unit coord. North Star Hosp., Anchorage, 1989-92; psychiat. nurse, infection control Oak Creek Hosp., San Jose, Calif., 1992-93, writer, producer OSHA precaution tng. staff video, 1993; psychiat. nurse Menlo Park divsn. VA Hosp., Palo Alto, 1992-95, psychiat. nurse Palo Alto divsn., 1995-96, nursing supr. Livermore divsn., 1996—; nursing supr. Kaiser Permanente Hayward Med. Ctr., 1997—. Campaign worker Nev. Gov. Bryan Dem. Candidate, Las Vegas, 1983-84, Pearson for County Commn. Race, Las Vegas, 1984; pres. Clark County Health Educators, 1983; mem. APIC., 1980-85. Mem. Nat. Assn. Black Nurses, South Bay Black Nurses Assn. (corr. sec. 1996-98), San Jose State U. Students of African Descent Assn. (chmn. pub. affairs, newsletter editor 1995), San Jose State U. Coll. Applied Sci. and Art Friends and Alumni Sch. Nursing (editor newsletter 1995-96), San Jose State U. Alumni Assn., Assn. for Practioners of Infection Control, Nat. Assn. Black Nurses., San Jose State U. Alumni Assn., San Jose State U. Sch. Nursing Alumni and Friends. Roman Catholic. Avocation: traveling. Office: VA Hosp Palo Alto MPD 3801 Miranda Ave Palo Alto CA 94304-1207

WARE, JAMES W., federal judge; b. 1946. BA, Calif. Luth. U., 1969; JD, Stanford U., 1972. Assoc. Blase, Valentine & Klein, Palo Alto, Calif., 1972-77, ptnr., 1977; judge Santa Clara County Superior Ct., U.S. Dist. Ct. (no. dist.) Calif., 1990—; pro bono East Palo Alto Law Project. Active Am. Leadership Forum; mem. bd. visitors Stanford Law Sch.; active Martin Luther King Papers Project. 2nd lt. USAR, 1969-86. Office: US Dist Cts 280 S 1st St Rm 4150 San Jose CA 95113-3095*

WARENSKI, MARILYN, writer; b. Salt Lake City, May 9, 1931; d. Charles Russell and Vaughn (Tuttle) Liston; m. James Carl Warenski, Sept. 9, 1953; children: Lisa, Jane, James, Paul. BA, U. Utah, 1952; design degree, N.Y. Sch. Interior Design, 1962; MFA in Writing, Vt. Coll., 1988. Tchr. pub. sch. sys. Salt Lake City, 1952-53; tchr. pub. sch. Teaneck, N.J., 1953-55; tchr. U. Utah, Salt Lake City, 1969-72; freelance interior designer, Salt Lake City, 1962-75; pub. spkr. in field, we. U.S., 1978-84. Author: (book) Patriarchs and Politics: The Plight of the Mormon Woman, 1978 (ERA Alice Paul award 1984). Spkr. Utah Women's Polit. Caucus, Salt Lake City, 1978-84; vol. Jr. League Salt Lake City, 1963-71; bd. dirs. Chamber Music Soc., Salt Lake City, 1986-90. Recipient Nat. Best Dressed Table Design award Gorham Co., 1971, Utah Women's Polit. Caucus award 1983. Democrat. Avocations: traveling, tennis, cooking, reading. Home: 4135 Mathews Way Salt Lake City UT 84124

WARK, ROBERT RODGER, art curator; b. Edmonton, Can., Oct. 7, 1924; žame to U.S., 1948, naturalized, 1970; s. Joseph Henry and Louise (Rodger) W. B.A., U. Alta., 1944, M.A., 1946, LLD (hon.), 1986; A.M., Harvard, 1949, Ph.D., 1952. Instr. art Harvard U., 1952-54; instr. history art Yale U. 1954-56; curator art Henry E. Huntington Library and Art Gallery, San Marino, Calif., 1956-90; lectr. art Calif. Inst. Tech., 1960-91, UCLA, 1966-80. Author: Sculpture in the Huntington Collection, 1959, French Decorative Art in the Huntington Collection, 1961, Rowlandson's Drawings for a Tour in a Post Chaise, 1963, Rowlandson's Drawings for the English Dance of Death, 1966, Isaac Cruikshank's Drawings for Drolls, 1968, Early British Drawings in the Huntington Collection 1600-1750, 1969, Drawings by John Flaxman, 1970, Ten British Pictures 1740-1840, 1971, Meet the Ladies: Personalities in Huntington Portraits, 1972, Drawings from the Turner Shakespeare, 1973, Drawings by Thomas Rowlandson in the Huntington Collection, 1975, British Silver in the Huntington Collection, 1978; editor: Sir Joshua Reynolds: Discourses on Art, 1959. Served with RCAF, 1944-45; Served with RCNVR, 1945. Mem. Coll. Art Assn. Home: 1330 Lombardy Rd Pasadena CA 91106-4120 Office: Huntington Libr 1151 Oxford Rd San Marino CA 91108-1299

WARKENTIN, LARRY RAY, music educator, composer; b. Reedley, Calif., Aug. 14, 1940; s. Pete D. and Marie G. (Janzen) W.; m. Paula B. Berg, Aug. 17, 1962; children: Richard, Rhonda. AB, Tabor Coll., 1962; MA, Calif. State U., Fresno, 1964; DMA, U. So. Calif., 1967. Chmn. music dept. Fresno Pacific U., 1967—. Composer: Invitation to Joy, 1981, This is a Holy Day, 1978, Koinonia, 1978 (commd. by Mennonite World Conf.), Academic Variations, 1984, Crazy Quilt, 1987, Concerto in G for Piano and Orchestra, 1988, Music Critic for the Fresho Bee, 1993, Ostinati for Orchestra, 1993, Symphony No. 1 "Doxology." Recipient 1st prize for composition Calif. Music Tchrs. Assn., 1984, Spl. award for classical music ASCAP, 1996. Mem. Music Tchrs. Assn. Calif. (chmn. composition competition, 1982-86), Fresno Nat. Soc. Arts and Letters (pres. 1984-86), ASCAP. Mem. Mennonite Brethren Ch. Avocations: travel, gardening. Office: Fresno Pacific Univ 1717 S Chestnut Ave Fresno CA 93702-4709

WARNAS, JOSEPH JOHN, municipal official; b. Boston, Aug. 31, 1933; s. Augustas and Nellie (Pipiras) W.; m. Bernice Gearlene Sarver (dec. July 1983); children: Robert John, Kimberly Joanne; m. Ruth Ellen Haaker, Jan. 12, 1985. BS in Mgmt., Boston Coll., 1955; MBA in Mgmt., Ariz. State U. 1971. Administr. subcontract Gen. Motors, Oak Creek, Wis., 1958-65; mgr. purchasing Sperry Rand Corp., Phoenix, 1965-70; dir. material mgmt. dept. Maricopa County, Phoenix, 1971-93; founder, pres. Apex Constrn. Mgmt. Co., Inc., 1996; Mem. Joint Fed., State and local Govt. Adv. Bd USA, Washington, 1974; mem. exptl. tech. adv. com. Nat. Inst. Govt. Purchasing & GSA, Washington, 1975; mem. lectr Ariz. State U. Tempe, Glendale Community Coll.; instr. seminars Nat. Inst. Govt. Purchasing, Washington. Assoc. editor Aljian's Purchasers Handbook, 4th rev. edit., 1982; contbr. articles to profl. jours. Mem. State Ariz. Purchasing Rev. Bd., Phoenix, 1980, Men's Bus Aux., Phoenix 1978; Served as 1st lt. U.S. Army, 1951-58. Mem. Nat. Inst. Govt. Purchasing (pres. 1971-72, dir. 1971-74) nat.

to Internat. Fedn. Purchasing and Mgmt. 1983), Ariz. State Capitol Chpt. Nat. Inst. Govtl. Purchasing Inc. (founder, pres. 1977), Purchasing Mgmt. Assn. Ariz. (pres. 1973), Sigma Iota Epsilon. Republican. Roman Catholic. Avocations: hunting, fishing, camping, hiking, literature. Home: 12511 N 76th Pl Scottsdale AZ 85260-4839

WARNER, FRANK SHRAKE, lawyer; b. Ogden, Utah, Dec. 14, 1940; s. Frank D. and Emma (Sorensen) W.; m. Sherry Lynn Clary. JD, U. Utah 1964. Bar: Utah 1964. Assoc. Young, Thatcher, Glasmann & Warner, and predecessor, Ogden, 1964-67, ptnr., 1967-72; chmn. Pub. Svc. Commn. Utah, Salt Lake City, 1972-76; ptnr. Warner & Wikstrom, Ogden, 1976-79, Warner, Marquardt & Hasenyager, Ogden, 1979-82; pvt. practice, Ogden, 1982-89, Warner & Phillips, 1989-96, Warner Law Firm, 1996—. Mem. Utah Gov.'s Com. on Exec. Reorgn., 1978-80. Mem. Utah Bar Assn. (ethics and discipline com. 1981-90), Ogden Gun Club (past pres.). Office: 868 25th St Ogden UT 84401-2611

WARNER, MICHAEL D., museum director; b. Salt Lake City, Nov. 1, 1949; s. Reed H. and Alma (Henline) W.; m. Ilene G. Reflow, Nov. 9, 1973; children: Ryan D., Joshua T. Student, Met. State Coll., 1969-71. Dist. mktg. mgr. Frontier Airlines, Inc., Denver, 1970-80; gen. mgr. Frontier Airlines, Inc., Colorado Springs, Colo., 1980-85; exec. dir. ProRodeo Hall of Fame, Colorado Springs, 1985-94. Editor: (mag.) Roundup. Dir. Pikes Peak Sertoma, Colorado Springs, 1990, Tax Adv. Com., Colorado Springs, 1985-89; pres. Conv. and Vis. Bur., Colorado Springs, 1984. Republican. Avocations: golf, fishing, western art. Office: PRO Rodeo Hall Fame & Mus Am Cowboy 101 Pro Rodeo Dr Colorado Springs CO 80919-2396*

WARNER, ROLLIN MILES, JR., economics educator, real estate broker; b. Evanston, Ill., Dec. 25, 1930; s. Rollin Miles Warner Sr. and Julia Herndon (Polk) Clarkson. BA, Yale U., 1953; cert. in law, Harvard U., 1956; MBA, Stanford U., 1960; cert. in edn. adminstrn., U. San Francisco, 1974. Lic. real estate broker, Calif. Asst. to v.p. fin. Stanford U., 1960-63; instr. history Town Sch., San Francisco, 1963-70; instr. econs. and history, dean Town Sch., 1975—; prin. Mt. Tamalpais, Ross, Calif., 1972-74; dir. devel. Katharine Branson Sch., Ross, 1974-75, instr. econs., history, mathematics, outdoor edn., math, computer-aided design; sponsor Nat. Ctr. for Fin. Edn., San Diego, 1986—. Author: America, 1986, Europe, 1986, Africa, Asia, Russia, 1986, Greece, Rome, 1981, Free Enterprise at Work, 1986. Scoutmaster to dist. commr. Boy Scouts Am., San Francisco, 1956—. Served to lt. USNR, 1953-55, Korea, Pacific, Vietnam. Recipient Silver Beaver award Boy Scouts Am., 1986, Town Sch. medal Town Sch. for Boys Alumni Coun., 1995. Mem. Assn. for Asian Studies, Groliей Club N.Y., Univ. Club San Francisco, San Francisco Yacht Club (Belvedere, Calif.), Am. Econs. Assn., Math. Assn. Am., Marines Meml. Assn., Calif. Real Estate Edn. Assn., IEEE Computer Soc., Am. Hist. Assn., Am. Camping Assn., Central Valley Assn. Realtors. Office: Town Sch 2750 Jackson St San Francisco CA 94115-1195

WARNER, VINCENT W., bishop. Bishop Diocese of Olympia, Seattle, 1990—. Office: Diocese of Olympia PO Box 12126 1551 10th Ave E Seattle WA 98102-4298*

WARNER, WALTER DUKE, corporate executive; b. Davenport, Iowa, Feb. 26, 1952; s. Robert Martin and Opal Louise (Gibbons) W.; m. Susan Dee Hafferkamp, Nov. 15, 1975 (div. 1982); 1 child, Natalie. BS, Drake U., 1975. Ops. officer Iowa-Des Moines Nat. Bank, 1975-78; from v.p. ops. to v.p. mktg. and pub. rels. Cen. Savs. and Loan Assn., San Diego, Calif., 1978-84; pres. The Lomas Santa Fe Cos., Solana Beach, Calif., 1985-91; pres., cofounder Ebert Composites Corp., San Diego, 1991—, also bd. dirs.; pres., CEO Strongwell Ebert LLC, San Diego, 1998—, also bd. dirs.; bd. dirs. Torrey Pines Bank, Solana Beach, Lomas Group Inc. Del Mar, Calif., Madison Valley Properties, Inc., La Jolla, Calif., Nature Preserved of Am. Inc., San Clemente, Calif.; pres., bd. dirs. Regents Park Comml. Assn., La Jolla, Strongwell Ebert. Bd. dirs. Inst. of the Ams., La Jolla, 1986—, mem. internat. council, 1986—; chmn. bd. dirs.; pres. San Diego chpt. Arthritis Found., 1985-87; dir., pres. Gildred Found., Solana Beach, 1986—; founding dir., treas. Golden Triangle Arts Found. Mem. Calif. League of Savs. and Loans (mktg. and ops. com. 1982-84), Internat. Forum for Corp. Dirs., Iowa Club San Diego (founding dir. 1984-85). Republican. Protestant. Avocations: tennis, piano.

WARNOCK, LARRY EDWARD, software engineer; b. Davenport, Iowa, Apr. 22, 1953; s. Clarence and Gwen (McClure) W. BA, Trinity U., 1975. Sr. programmer May Dept. Stores, L.A., 1984-87, 92-94, First Interstate Bank, L.A., 1987-92, VISA Internat., Foster City, Calif., 1994—; bd. dirs. Achenbach Graphic Arts Council, San Francisco; organizer mus. travel tours. Contbr. articles to newsletter. Peer counselor Shanti, L.A., 1984-87. Grantee Nat. Presby. Scholarship Found., 1971, San Antonio (Tex.) Adv. Found., 1973. Democrat. Avocations: collecting 1st edition rare books, collecting art, woodworking. Office: VISA Internat PO Box 8999 San Francisco CA 94128

WARPINSKI, TERRI L., academic administrator, artist; b. Green Bay, Wis., June 2, 1955; d. Robert J. and Lucille J. (Kehoe) W.; m. David J. Schroeder, July 5, 1986. BA, U. Wis., 1979; MA, U. Iowa, 1982, MFA, 1983. Vis. instr. Sch. Art, U. Fla., Gainesville, 1983-84; asst. prof. art dept. fine arts U. Oreg., Eugene, 1984-90, dir. Malheur Photography Workshop, 1984—, assoc. prof. art, 1990—, assoc. dean Sch. Architecture and Allied Arts, 1997—; mem. vis. faculty Arrowmont Sch. Arts and Crafts, Gatlinburg, Tenn., 1990, 92, 94, 96, 98; vis. artist North Harris Coll., Linfield Coll., Coll. St. Catherine, U. Arts, Phila. One person show at Internat. PhotoFest, Houston, 1996; exhibited in group show at Murray State U., 1998 (Juror's award 1998). Active Oreg. Natural Desert Assn., 1991—. Summer Rsch. grantee U. Oreg., 1989; Rsch. grantee Ctr. for the Study of Women in Soc., 1996. Mem. Internat. Coun. Fine Arts Deans, Coll. Art Assn., Soc. Photographic Edn. (regional dir. 1987-92). Avocations: backpacking, cross-country skiing, gardening. Fax: (541) 346-3626. E-mail: warpinsk@darkwing.uoregon.edu. Office: Sch Architecture & Allied Arts 5249 U Oreg Eugene OR 97403-5249

WARREN, CHRISTOPHER CHARLES, electronics executive; b. Helena, Mont., July 27, 1949; s. William Louis and Myrtle Estelle (Moren) W.; m. Danette Marie Geordge, Apr. 21, 1972; 1 child, Jeffrey Scott. Grad. high sch., Helena, 1967. Electrician Supreme Electronics, Helena, 1972-81; v.p., svc. technician Capital Music Inc., Helena, 1981—; state exec. Amusement & Music Operators Assn. Coun. of Affiliated States, Chgo., 1990-92. Sgt. USAF, 1968-72, Vietnam. Mem. Internat. Flipper Pinball Assn. (sec./treas. 1991-92, pres. 1993-94), Mont. Coin Machine Operators Assn. (pres. 1989-91 v.p.), Mont. Coin Machine Operators State 8-Ball (chmn.), Valley Nat. 8 Ball Assn. (charter), Amusement and Music Operators Assn. (bd. dirs. 1992-95, v.p. 1995—), Ducks Unltd., Eagles, Moose, Rocky Mountain Elk Found. Avocations: photography, restoring old cars and trucks, hunting, fishing. Home: 8473 Green Meadow Dr Helena MT 59602-8312 Office: Capital Music Inc 3108 Broadwater Ave Helena MT 59602-9222

WARREN, DAVID HARDY, psychology educator; b. Chelsea, Mass., July 28, 1943; s. Roland Leslie and Margaret (Hodges) W.; m. Katherine V. Warren; children: Michael Jonathan Warren, Gabriel Kristopher Coy. A.B. in Psychology, Yale U., 1965; Ph.D. in Child Devel. U. Minn., 1969. Prof. psychology U. Calif., Riverside, 1969—, dean Coll. Humanities and Social Scis., 1977-85, dir. Univ. honors program, 1989-92, chair dept. psychology, 1992-94, exec. vice chancellor, 1994—. Author: Blindness and Early Childhood Development, 1977, 84, Blindness and Children: An Individual Differences Approach, 1994; contbr. articles to profl. jours. Mem. Psychonomic Soc., AAAS. Office: U Calif Office of Exec Vice Chancellor Riverside CA 92521

WARREN, FAN LEE, artist, educator; b. Birmingham, Ala., Dec. 31, 1957; d. Hattie May W. BFA, Ill. State U., 1982; MFA, Sch. of Art Inst., Chgo., 1983. Dir. Woman Made Gallery, Chgo., 1992-94, exhbn. com. mem. Urban Gateways, Chgo., 1990-93, Mexican Mus., San Francisco, 1994-98, Chabot C.C., Hayward, Calif., 1995—, Las Positas Coll., Livermore, Calif., 1997—. Artist-in-residence Emeryville Gallery, 1998, Berkeley Arts Ctr., 1997—, Pro Arts Gallery, 1998—, Oakland, Calif. Commns. Lawrence Hall of Science, Berkeley, Calif., 1998—; Asian-Am. Dance

tive Artist fellow Cultural Arts divsn., City of Oakland, Calif., 1998; Cmty. Arts grantee Dept. Cultural Affairs, Chgo., 1989, 91, Artist in Residence grantee Calif. Arts Coun., 1995. Mem. Coll. Art Assn. Home: 3607 Maple Ave Oakland CA 94602-3338

WARREN, JAMES RONALD, retired museum director, author, columnist; b. Goldendale, Wash., May 25, 1925; stepson H.S. W.; m. Gwen Davis, June 25, 1949; children: Gail, Jeffrey. B.A., Wash. State U., 1949; M.A., U. Wash., 1953, Ph.D., 1963. Adminstrv. v.p. Seattle Community Coll., 1965-69; pres. Edmonds Community Coll., Lynnwood, Wash., 1969-79; dir. Mus. of History and Industry, Seattle, 1979-89; lectr. in field. Author history books; columnist Seattle Post Intelligencer, 1979-92, Seattle Times, 1992-96. Served with U.S. Army, 1943-45, ETO, prisoner-of-war, Germany. Mem. VFW, Am. Ex-POW Assn., 42d (Rainbow) Div. Vets., Rotary, also others. Home and Office: 3235 99th Ave NE Bellevue WA 98004-1803

WARREN, JUDI DELL, minister; b. L.A., Feb. 25, 1940; d. Raymond Oliver Perry and Maria Luz (Wistler) Tumilty; m. Charles Robert Deemer (div.); 1 child, Christine Nel Deemer-Fonseca; m. Paul Blaisdell Warren, Aug. 22, 1981. Student, San Jose State U. 1959-62; BA in Edn., Calif. State U., L.A., 1964. Ordained to ministry Ch. of Inner Light, 1977, Ch. of Truth, 1985. Sr. pastor Ch. of Truth, Pasadena, Calif., 1978-89; founder, dean Albert Grier Sch. Religious Studies, Pasadena, 1982-84, instr., 1982—; founder, pres. Internat. Alliance of Chs. of Truth, Pasadena, 1987—; min. emeritus Ch. of Truth, Pasadena, 1989—; dir. Soc. for the Study of Metaphysical Religion, Santa Barbara, Calif., 1988—. Life mem. Internat. New Thought Alliance. Office: Internat Alliance Chs Truth 690 E Orange Grove Blvd Pasadena CA 91104-4452

WARREN, KATHERINE VIRGINIA, art gallery director; b. Balt., Aug. 10, 1948; d. Joseph Melvin and Hilda Virginia (Thiele) Heim; m. David Hardy Warren; 1 child, Gabriel Kristopher Coy; 1 stepchild, Michael Jonathan Warren. BA, U. Calif., Riverside, 1976, MA, 1980. Asst. curator Calif. Mus. Photography, Riverside, 1979-80, acting dir., 1980-81, asst. dir., curator of edn., 1981-84; dir. univ. art gallery U. Calif., Riverside, 1980—. Bd. dirs. Riverside Arts Found., 1980-89, chmn. bd., 1986-88. Marius De Brabant fellow U. Calif., 1977-79. Mem. Am. Assn. Mus., Western Mus. Conf. Office: Sweeney Art Gallery U Calif Riverside Riverside CA 92521

WARREN, LARRY MICHAEL, clergyman; b. Bonne Terre, Mo., Nov. 25, 1946; s. Orson Wesley and Ruth Margaret (Stine) W.; m. Bonnie Jean Monk Chandler, Apr. 9, 1983; children: Samantha Chandler, John, Abigail Chandler, Anne, Meredith. BA cum laude, Lincoln U., 1969; MDiv with honors, St. Paul Sch. Theology, Kansas City, Mo., 1976; D of Ministry, San Francisco Theol. Sem., 1987. Ordained elder United Meth. Ch., 1978. Pastor Cainsville (Mo.) United Meth. Ch., 1975-76, Lakelands Parish, Rathdrum, Idaho, 1976-78; assoc. pastor Audubon Park United Meth. Ch., Spokane, Wash., 1978-83; pastor Faith United Meth. Ch., Everett, Wash., 1983-90, Tacoma First United Meth. Ch., 1990-95; co-pastor Renton First United Meth. Ch., 1995—; adviser Kairos Prison Ministry Wash., Monroe, 1984-92; conf. rep. grad. bd. St. Paul Sch. Theology, Kansas City, 1984, 94-96. Contbr. to col. Dialogue Everett Herald, 1984-88. Adviser DeMolay, Spokane, 1979-81; team mem. Night-Walk, inner-city ministry, Spokane and Everett, 1981, 85; vol. chaplain Gen. Hosp. Everett, 1983-90; trustee Deaconess Children's Svcs., Everett, 1983-88. Recipient Legion of Honor DeMolay Internat., 1982. Mem. Fellowship of Reconciliation, North Snohomish County Assn. Chs. (v.p. 1985-89), Pacific N.W. Ann. Conf. Bd. Global Ministries (sec. 1988-92, pres. 1993-97), Renton Ecumenical Assn. Chs. (pres. 1996-98). Democrat. Avocations: reading, traveling, stamps and coins, woodworking. Home: 121 Monterey Pl NE Renton WA 98056-4032 Office: Renton First United Meth Ch 2201 NE 4th St Renton WA 98056-4073

WARREN, RICHARD WAYNE, obstetrician and gynecologist; b. Puxico, Mo., Nov. 26, 1935; s. Martin R. and Sarah E. (Crump) W.; m. Rosalie J. Franzoia, Aug. 16, 1959; children: Lani Marie, Richard W., Paul D. *Daughter Lani Marie, MD 1988, University of Minnesota, was a resident in OB-GYN at Valley Medical Center, San Jose, California. She specializes in ob-gyn and is a partner in the Warren Medical Corp. Son Paul Douglas, MD 1991, Harvard University, was a resident in orthopedic surgery at Texas Tech University. A fellow in foot and ankle surgery at Galveston, Texas. His Practice is in orthopedic surgery at Tuscon, Arizona. Wife Rosalie L. and Son Richard W. manage the Warren Medical Corp* BA, U. Calif., Berkeley, 1957; MD, Stanford U., 1961. Intern, Oakland (Calif.) Naval Hosp., 1961-62; resident in ob-gyn Stanford (Calif.) Med. Ctr., 1964-67; practice medicine specializing in ob-gyn, Mountain View, Calif., 1967—; mem. staff Stanford and El Camino hosps.; pres. Warren Mexical Corp.; assoc. clin. prof. ob-gyn Stanford Sch. Medicine. Served with USN, 1961-64. Diplomate Am. Bd. Ob-Gyn. Fellow Am. Coll. Ob-Gyn; mem. AMA, Am. Fertility Soc., Am. Assn. Gynecologic Laparoscopists, Calif. Med. Assn., San Francisco Gynecol. Soc., Peninsula Gynecol. Soc., Assn. Profs. Gynecology and Obstetrics, Royal Soc. Medicine, Shufelt Gynecol. Soc. Santa Clara Valley. Contbr. articles to profl. jours. Home: 102 Atherton Ave Menlo Park CA 94027-4021 Office: 2500 Hospital Dr Mountain View CA 94040-4106

WARREN, STEPHAN J. (STEVE), transportation executive; b. Badwiessee, Germany, Sept. 21, 1944; came to U.S., 1946; s. Arthur L. and Tatjiana (Muller) W.; m. Peggy L., May 5, 1965. AA, Ventura Coll., 1965; BA, U. Calif., Long Beach, 1972. Mgr. internat. sales Am. Airlines, L.A., 1966-76; regional sales mgr. Korean Airlines, L.A., 1976-79; mgr. internat. sales Am. Airlines, 1980-85; v.p. cargo Mercury Svcs., Inc., 1985-88; pres. Pelican Cargo, Inc., 1988-93, Nighthawk Svcs., Inc., 1993—. Office: Nighthawk Svcs Inc 5430 Rosecrans Ave Lawndale CA 90260-1119

WARRICK, BROOKE, marketing executive. MS in Psychology, San Francisco State U. Past mktg. dir. VALS program Stanford Rsch. Inst.; pres. Am. Lives, San Francisco; internat. spkr. in field; condr. tng. sessions various orgns. Author: The Builder's Guide to Moveup Buyers; prodr. (video) An American Portrait. Office: Am LIVES Inc 6114 Lasalle Ave Ste 590 Oakland CA 94611-1825*

WARRIN, DONALD OGDEN, retired foreign language educator; b. Montclair, N.J., Apr. 17, 1933; s. Donald Preater and Elizabeth Ogden (Brouwer) W.; m. Anne Marie Doherty, Apr. 29, 1961 (div.); children: Paul Ogden, Jeffrey Preater, John Michael, David Francis; m. Diane Ruth Beeson, Aug. 17, 1986. BA in English, U. So. Calif., 1960; MA in Portuguese, N.Y.U., 1967, PhD in Portuguese, 1973. Prof. Calif. State U. Hayward, 1969-97; emeritus, 1997—; chair Dept. of Modern Langs. and Lits., Calif. State U. Hayward, 1983-93; dir. Coop. Edn. Program, 1986-88. Editor: (book) Aguarelas Florentinas, 1986, Cem Anos de Poesia Portuguesa na California, 1986; creator photo exhbns. The Portuguese in Nevada, Portuguese Men and Women on the Western Frontier; contbr. articles to profl. jours. Recipient Causa Portuguesa award Portuguese Union of Calif., 1987. Mem. Western Hist. Assn., Calif. Hist. Soc., Nev. Hist. Soc., Hist. Inst. of Terceira, Azores, Portugal. Avocations: sports, photography. Office: Calif State U Dept Modern Langs & Lits 25800 Carlos Bee Blvd Hayward CA 94542-3001

WARRIS, ANNA CUMMINGS, religious organization executive; b. Phila., Aug. 8, 1912; d. James Emlen and Anna May (Mock) Cummings; widow; 1 child, Joseph Emlen. Student, Wheaton Coll., 1931-32, Albany Bible Inst., 1933-34, Pa. State U., 1934-35, U. Calif., 1955-56, Temple U., 1958-59. Cert. SEC, Nat. Ass. Security Dealers. Soil conservationist USDA, 1941-42; acctg. clk. Lansdale (Pa.) Tube Co., 1943-48; office mgr. Clark and Co. Tucson, 1952-54; head acctg. dept. Philco (formerly Lansdale Tube Co.), Spring City, Pa., 1956-61; comptr., then exec. asst. to pres. De Moss Assocs., King of Prussia, Pa., 1961-66; field underwriter, pension trust work and estate planning N.Y. Life Ins. Co, Phila. 1966-91; pres. Bible Women Internat., 1974—; spkr. in field. Author: Foretaste of Glory, 1979, 2nd edit., 1982, Braille edit., 1994, Come Travel with Me, 1984, Seed of David...Son of God, 1991, 2nd edit., 1993. Mem. ad hoc fin. com. Ariz. State Opera, 1975-76, active Montgomery County War Bd., 1941-42, So. Ariz. Estate Planning Com., 1975, 76. Recipient Kemper Merriam award U. Ariz., 1972; named Hon. Citizen of South Korea. Mem. Nat. Assn. Arts Immorial. M. als

Tuscon chpt.), Nat. Women's Leaders Round Table (nat. pension leader). Republican. Mem. Brethren Ch. Avocations: reading, writing books. Home: 6245 E Broadway Blvd Ste 510 Tucson AZ 85711-4019 Office: Bible Women Internat 3941 E Desmond Ln Tucson AZ 85712-3304

WASDON, DOROTHY, secondary educator; b. Bossier City, La.; d. Lawrence Clifford and Ella Mae (Wheeler) York; m. Ernest Lee Wasdon, July 29, 1972 (div. Feb. 1976). AA, Ctrl. Jr. Coll., McPherson, Kans., 1965; BS, Lincoln U., Jefferson City, Mo., 1968; MS, San Francisco U., 1982. Life secondary credentials. Project mgr. City of Richmond, Calif., 1968-72; tchr. Willard Jr. H.S., Berkeley, Calif., 1972-76, Berkeley (Calif.) H.S., 1976—; mem. adv. bd. Computer Acad., Berkeley, 1987—. Pres., usher St. John Missionary Bapt. Ch., Richmond, 1990-97. Named Outstanding Tchr., Ford Found., Union City, Calif., 1996, Sponsor of Yr. Future Leaders World, Sacramento, Calif., 1974. Mem. NAACP, Calif. Tchr. Assn., Berkeley Fedn. Tchrs., Order Eastern Star (sec. Star of Love 1986-96, grand sec. Golden Poppy Grand chpt. 1985—), 22's Social Club (pres. 1988-90), Elks (escort 1992-94, award 1994), Chi Beta Sigma. Democrat. Baptist. Avocations: bowling, camping, horseback, tennis, softball. Home: 6047 Bernhard Ave Richmond CA 94805-1209

WASHBURN, HARRIET CAROLINE, secondary education educator; b. Hallock, Minn., Mar. 15, 1920; d. John W. and Anna Melinda (Younggren) Swanson; m. Edward James Washburn, Jan. 22, 1971 (dec. 1993); children: Jacqueline Ann Batt, stepchild, Margaret; m. Ohls Batt. BA cum laude, Macalester Coll., 1941; MA in Pupil Personnel Svcs., San Jose State U., 1969. Tchr. Latin, English, phys. edn. Renville (Minn.) Pub. Sch., 1941-43; tchr. phys. edn. St. Cloud (Minn.) Jr. H. S., 1943-44, Fremont (Calif.) Unified Sch. Dist., 1958-69; recreation specialist City Recreation Dept., Lincoln, Nebr., 1946-50; dir. youth activities Trinity Meth. Ch., Lincoln, 1950-53; counselor Milpitas (Calif.) Unified Sch. Dist., 1969-75, head counselor, 1975-80; cons., trainer, speaker Stockton, Calif., 1980—; coord. bank acct. Bank of Stockton, 1989—; mem., presenter Internat. Tng., Anaheim, 1978—; cons. personal, profl. devel. Personal Dynamics, Inc., Mpls., 1980-87. Guest speaker Kiwanis, Lions, Candy Stripers, Ctrl. Meth. Ch., MCClellan AFB, and numerous others, 1980—, presenter Asian Am. Found., Stockton, 1995—. With USN, 1944-46. Recipient Sch. Counselor Svc. award Calif. Sch. Counselor Assn., Milpitas, 1980. Mem. AAUW, Beginners Luck Investment Club, Alliance for the Mentally Ill of S.J. County, Rep. Women's Club. Presbyterian. Avocations: bridge, Bible study, reading, writing. Office: Bank of Stockton 301 E Miner Ave Stockton CA 95202-2585

WASHBURN, JON, artistic director. Founder, condr., artistic dir. Vancouver (B.C., Can.) Chamber Choir, 1971—; condr., artistic dir., exec. dir. Phoenix (Ariz.) Bach Choir, 1992-98; guest condr. CBC Vancouver Orch., Masterpiece Ensemble, Phoenix Chamber Orch., Calgary, Edmonton, Nova Scotia, Phoenix and Vancouver Symphony Orchs.; guest condr. Santa Fe Desert Chorale, Estonian Philharmonic Chamber Choir, L.A. Master Chorale; assoc. composer Can. Music Ctr.; mem. artistic juries Can. Coun.; mem. adv. coun. Internat. Music Festivals in U.S.; tchr. in field. Composer, arranger Rossetti Songs, The Star, A Stephen Foster Medley, Chinese Melodies, Rise!Shine!, Noel Sing We; co-author God's Lamb; gen. choral editor Jaymar Music Ltd. Co-recipient Music award Vancouver Awards; recipient Govt. of Can. Celebration 88 cert. of merit, Queen Elizabeth's Silver Jubilee medal, Disting. Svc. award Assn. Can. Choral Condrs., Margaret Hillis award for choral excellence, 1998. Mem. Chorus Am. (bd. dirs.). Office: Vancouver Chamber Choir, 1254 W Seventh Ave, Vancouver, BC Canada V6H 1B6

WASHINGTON, JAMES WINSTON, JR., artist, sculptor; b. Gloster, Miss., Nov. 10, 1909; s. James and Lizie (Howard) W.; m. Janic R. Miller, Mar. 29, 1943. Student, Nat. Landscape Inst., 1944-47; D.F.A., Center Urban-Black Studies, 1975. tchr. summer class N.W. Theol. Union Seattle U., 1988. One man shows U.S.O. Gallery, Little Rock, 1943, Foster-White Gallery, Seattle, 1974, 78, 80, 83, 89 (also at Bellevue Art Mus., 89), Charles and Emma Frye Art Mus., Seattle, 1980, 95, Mus. History and Industry, Seattle, 1981; exhibited in group shows Willard Gallery, N.Y.C., 1960-64, Feingarten Galleries, San Francisco, 1958-59, Grosvenor Gallery, London, Eng., 1964, Lee Nordness Gallery, N.Y.C. 1962 Woodside Gallery, Seattle, 1962-65, Foster-White Gallery, Seattle, 1974, 76, 89, 92, Smithsonian Instn., 1974, San Diego, 1977, others; retrospective exhbn. Bellevue Art Mus., Washington, 1989; represented in permanent collections Seattle, San Francisco, Oakland art museums, Seattle First Nat. Bank, Seattle Pub. Libr. YWCA, Seattle, Meany Jr. H.S., Seattle World's Fair, Expo 70 Osaka, Japan, Whitney Mus. Am. Art, N.Y.C.; commd. sculpture: Bird With Covey, Wash. State Capitol Mus., Olympia, 1983, Obelisk with Phoenix and Esoteric Symbols of Nature in granite, Sheraton Hotel Seattle, 1982, Life Surrounding the Astral Alter, In Matrix, owner T.M. Rosenblume, Charles Z. Smith & Assocs., Seattle, 1986, The Oracle of Truth (6 1/2 ton sculpture) Mt. Zion Bapt. Ch., Seattle, 1987, commd. sculptures King County Arts Commn., 1989, Bailey Gatzert Elem. Sch., Seattle, 1991, Twin Eaglets of the Cosmic Cycle (Quincy Jones), 1993, Fountain of Triumph (Bangasser Assocs. Inc.), 1992-93, Seattle, 1993-94, 94-95, Child in Matrix, 1995, Blunt Tail Owl, 1996, Bunny Rabbit and Robbin, 1996; author book of poetry Poems of Life, 1997 (Internat. Hall of Fame Nat. Soc. Poets). Passover leader Mt. Zion Baptist Ch., Seattle, 1974-87; founder James W. Washington, Jr. and Mrs. Janie Rogella Washington Found. Recipient Spl. Commendation award for many contbns. to artistic heritage of state Gov., 1973, plaque City of Seattle, 1973, plaque Benefit Guild, Inc., 1973, arts service award King County Arts Commn., 1984, cert. of recognition Gov. of Wash., 1984, Editor's Choice award Outstanding Achievement in Poetry Nat. Libr. Poetry, 1993; named to Wash. State Centennial Hall of Honor, Wash. State Hist. Soc., 1984; home and studio designated historic landmark (city and state), 1991; Dr. James W. Washington Jr. and Mrs. Janie Rosella Washington Found. established, 1997. Mem. Internat. Platform Assn., Internat. Soc. Poets (life, awards 1993), Profl. Artists Phila., Masons (33d degree). Home: 1816 26th Ave Seattle WA 98122-3110

WASHINGTON, REGINALD LOUIS, pediatric cardiologist; b. Colorado Springs, Colo., Dec. 31, 1949; s. Lucius Louis and Brenette Y. (Wheeler) W.; m. Billye Faye Ned, Aug. 18, 1973; children: Danielle Larae, Reginald Quinn. BS in Zoology, Colo. State U., 1971; MD, U. Colo., 1975. Diplomate Nat. Bd. Med. Examiners, Am. Bd. Pediatrics, Pediatric Cardiology. Intern in pediatrics U. Colo. Med. Ctr., Denver, 1975-76, resident in pediatrics, 1976-78, chief resident, instr., 1978-79, fellow in pediatric cardiology, 1979-81, asst. prof. pediatrics, 1982-1988, assoc. prof. pediatrics, 1988-90, assoc. clin. prof. pediatrics, 1990—; staff cardiologist Children's Hosp., Denver, 1981-90; v.p. Rocky Mountain Pediatric Cardiology, Denver, 1990—; mem. admissions com. U. Colo. Sch. Medicine, Denver, 1985-89; chmn., bd. dirs. Coop. Health Care Agreements, 1994-98; chmn. dept. pediatrics Presbyn./St. Lukes Med. Ctr, Denver, 1996-99, pres.-elect med. staff, 1997-99; adv. coun. Nat. Heart Lung Blood Inst., NIH, 1996-98. Cons. editor Your Patient and Fitness, 1989-92. Chmn. Coop. Health Care Agreements Bd., State of Colo., 1994-98; adv. bd. dirs. Equitable Bank of Littleton, Colo., 1984-86; bd. dirs. Ctrl. City Opera, 1989-95, Cleo Parker Robinson Dance Co., 1992-94, Rocky Mountain Heart Fund for Children, 1984-89, Rainbo Ironkids, 1989-95; nat. bd. dirs. Am. Heart Assn., 1992-96; bd. dirs. Nat. Coun. Patient Info. and Edn., 1992-98, Children's Heart Alliance, 1993-94, Colo. State U. Devel. Coun., 1994—, Caring for Colo. Found., 1999—; trustee Denver Ctr. Performing Arts, 1994—, Regis U., 1994—; mem. Gov.'s Coun. Phys. Fitness, 1990-91; mem. Colo. State Bd. Agr., 1996—, adv. coun. of NMCBI of the NCM, 1995-98. Named Salute Vol. of Yr. Big Sisters of Colo., 1990; honoree NCCJ, 1994, Physician of Yr., Nat. Am. Heart Assn., 1995. Fellow Am. Acad. Pediatrics (cardiology subsect.), Am. Coll. Cardiology, Am. Heart Assn. (coun. on cardiovascular disease in the young, exec. com. 1988-91, nat. devel. program com. 1990-94, vol. of yr. 1989, pres. Colo. chpt. 1989-90, Torch of Hope 1987, Gold Heart award Colo. chpt. 1990, bd. dirs. Colo. chpt., exec. com. Colo. chpt. 1987—, grantee Colo. chpt. 1983-84, mem. editorial bd. Pediatric Exercise Scis. 1988—), Soc. Critical Care Medicine; mem. Am. Acad. Pediatrics/Perinatology, , Am. Acad. Pediatrics/Pediatric Cardiology (exec. com. 1996—), N.Am. Soc. Pediatric Exercise Medicine (pres. 1986-87), Colo. Med. Soc. (chmn. sports medicine coun. 1993-94), Leadership Denver 1990, Denver Athletic Club, Met. Club, Glenmoor Golf Club. Democrat. Roman Catholic. Avocations: golf, fishing. Office: Rocky Mountain Pediat Cardiology 1601 E 19th Ave Ste 5600 Denver CO 80218-1255

WASHINGTON-KNIGHT, BARBARA J., career officer, nurse; b. Chgo., July 13, 1948; d. Lewis and Carrie Mae (Randolph) Washington; m. William S. Knight, Aug. 23, 1986; children: Carlton, Carrie. Diploma, St. Elizabeth's Hosp., Chgo., 1971; B in Health Scis., Chapman Coll., 1979, postgrad. CCRN. Commd. lt. USAF, 1972, advanced through grades to lt. col.; asst. head nurse med. unit USAF, Fairfield, Calif., 1976-78, asst. head nurse orthopedic unit, 1978-79; asst. head nurse spl. care unit USAF, Montgomery, Ala., 1979-80, head nurse spl. care unit, 1980-82; head nurse spl. care unit USAF, Riverside, Calif., 1982-85; head nurse surg. ICU USAF, San Antonio, 1985-87, clin. supr. dept. of critical care, 1987-88; head nurse spl. care unit USAF, Sacramento, Calif., 1988-91, coord. quality improvement, 1990-92; asst. chief nurse, clin. nurse specialist inpatient svcs. USAF, Tinker AFB, Oklahoma City, 1992-93; clin. nurse post critical care unit Moreno Valley (Calif.) Cmty. Hosp., 1993—. Mem. Soc. Ret. Air Force Nurses, Am. Assn. Critical Care Nurses, Am. Assn. Legal Nurse Cons. (cert.), Air Force Assn., Air War Coll. Assn., Women's Meml. Found., Nat. Coun. Negro Women, Ret. Officers Assn., Citizen Amb.

WASNIEWSKI, JOHN, computer company executive; b. Waukegan, Ill., Sept. 21, 1946; m. Sharon Smith, 1990; 1 child, Sarah. BA, St. Louis (Mo.) U., 1969; MBA, Northwestern, 1975. Mgr. mfg. Gen. Instrument, 1981-91; mgr. strategic initiatives Applied Materials, 1991-98; mgr. process innovations Fujitsu, Milpitas, Calif., 1998—. Mem. Am. Soc. Quality. Avocations: military history.

WASSERMAN, BARRY L(EE), architect; b. Cambridge, Mass., May 25, 1935; s. Theodore and Adelaide (Levin) W.; m. Wilma Louise Greenfield, June 21, 1957 (div. 1971); children: Tim Andrew, Andrew Glenn; m. Judith Ella Michalowski, Apr. 22, 1979. B.A., Harvard U., 1957, M. Arch., 1960. Registered architect, Calif. Assoc. John S. Bolles Assocs., San Francisco, 1960-69; prin. Wasserman-Herman Assocs., San Francisco, 1969-72; prin., dir. Office Lawrence Halprin U Assocs., San Francisco, 1972-76; dep. state architect State of Calif., Sacramento, 1976-78, state architect, 1978-83; prof. dept. architecture, dir. Inst. Environ. Design, Sch. Environ. Design Calif. State Poly. U., Pomona, 1983-87, chair dept. architecture, Coll. Environ. Design, 1988-96; cons. architecture, Sacramento, 1983—; program advisor Fla. A&M U., Tallahassee, 1981-83. Architect Wasserman House, San Rafael, Calif., 1963 ((AIA-Sunset Mag. award of Merit) 1965-66), Anna Waden Library, San Francisco, 1969 ((AIA award of Merit 1970)), Capitol Area Plan, Sacramento, 1977 (Central Valley chpt. AIA Honor award 1979). Recipient Awards citation Progressive Architecture 26th awards Program, 1979. Fellow AIA chmn. architecture in govt. com. (1979). Democrat. Jewish. Home: 6456 Fordham Way Sacramento CA 95831-2218

WASSERMAN, BRUCE ARLEN, dentist, mail order company executive; b. San Mateo, Calif., June 7, 1954; s. Albert and Dunia (Frydman) W.; children: Rachael, Rebecca, Meir, Keren; m. Debra Elizabeth Wright, Apr. 14, 1996. BA in Mass Communications, Winona State U., 1981; DDS, U. Pacific, 1985. Apprentice blacksmith Reuben Syhre Blacksmith Shop, Pine River, Minn., 1973-74; blacksmith Walden Forge, Pine River, 1974-79; founding dir. Team Redeemed, San Mateo, 1984-92; pvt. practice dentistry San Mateo, 1985—; pres. Manx USA, San Mateo, 1987-92. Editor: (quar. jour.) Cycle Lines, 1983-85, Good News, 1984-92, No. Calif. Reporter, 1987-90; assoc. editor: Internat. Communicator, 1988-89, editor, 1990; editor: (mo. jour.) The Mouthpiece, 1986-89; author: A Manual of Uniforming. Cubmaster Boy Scouts Am., San Mateo, 1986 87; fund raiser Am. Lung Assn., San Mateo County, 1986-90, bd. dirs., 1989-94, chmn. Bike Trek, 1989, fund devel. com., 1989-90, membership com., 1991; chmn. Sofitel Bastille Tour, 1992-93. Recipient Disting. Young Alumni award Winona State U., 1988; Mosby scholar Tau Kappa Omega, 1985. Fellow Am. Acad. Dentistry Internat. (editor 1990, mem. bylaws com. 1990), Am. Coll. Dentists, Royal Soc. Health, Pierre Fauchard Acad. (chmn. No. Calif. sect. 1992-95); mem. ADA (cert. recognition 1987, 89, 90), Calif. Dental Assn. (Disting. Svc. award 1987), San Mateo County Dental Soc. (exec. bd. 1986-89, editor 1986-89, Pres. award 1989, Bd. Dirs. award 1987, bd. dirs. 1991-92), Christian Classic Bikers Assn. (Calif. rep. 1983-94), Order Ky. Cols., 78th Fraser's Highlanders Regiment (lt./capt., recruiting officer 1993-94, maj. O.C. 77th Montgomery Highlanders Regiment Headquarters Garrison), Pacific Road Riders (pres., editor 1983-85). Avocations: bicycling, motorcycling, writing, metalworking, hiking. Office: 410 N San Mateo Dr San Mateo CA 94401-2418

WASSERMAN, LEW R., film, recording and publishing company executive; b. Cleve., Mar. 15, 1913; m. Edith T. Beckerman, July 5, 1936; 1 dau., Lynne Kay. D (hon.), Brandeis U., NYU. Nat. dir. advt. and publicity Music Corp. Am., 1936-38, v.p., 1938-39, became v.p. charge motion picture div., 1940; now chmn., chief exec. officer, dir., mem. exec. com. MCA, Inc., also chmn. bd., chief exec. officer, dir. subsidiary corps.; now chmn. emeritus; chmn. emeritus Assn. Motion Picture and TV Producers. Trustee John F. Kennedy Libr., John F. Kennedy Ctr. Performing Arts, Jules Stein Eye Inst., Carter Presdl. Ctr., Lyndon Baines Johnson Found.; pres. Hollywood Canteen Found.; chmn. Rsch. to Prevent Blindness Found.; hon. chmn. bd. Ctr. Theatre Group L.A. Music Ctr.; bd. dirs. Amateur Athletic Found. of L.A. (chmn. fin. com.), L.A. Music Ctr. Found.; bd. gov.'s Ronald Reagan Presdl. Found. Recipient Jean Hersholt Humanitarian award Acad. Motion Picture Arts and Scis., 1973. Democrat. Office: Universal City Studios Inc 100 Universal City Plz Universal City CA 91608-1085*

WASSERMAN, STEPHEN IRA, physician, educator; b. Los Angeles, Dec. 17, 1942; m. Linda Morgan; children: Matthew, Zachary. BA, Stanford U., 1964; MD, UCLA, 1968. Diplomate Am. Bd. Internal Medicine, Am. Bd. Allergy and Immunology. Intern, resident Peter B. Brigham Hosp., Boston, 1968-70; fellow in allergy, immunology Robert B. Brigham Hosp., Boston, 1972-75; asst. prof. medicine Harvard U., Boston, 1975-79, assoc. prof., 1979; assoc. prof. U. Calif.-San Diego, La Jolla, 1979-85, prof., 1985—, chief allergy tng. program Sch. Medicine, 1979-85, chief allergy div. Sch. Medicine, 1985-93, acting chmn. dept. medicine, 1986-88, chmn. dept. medicine, 1988—, Helen M. Ranney prof., 1992—; co-dir. allergy sect. Robert B. and Peter B. Brigham Hosps., 1977-79; dir. Am. Bd. Allergy and Immunology, Am. Bd. Internal Medicine. Contbr. articles to profl. jours. Served to lt. comdr. USPHS, 1970-72, San Francisco. Fellow Am. Acad. Allergy and Immunology (pres.-elect 1996-97); mem. Am. Soc. Clin. Investigation, Assn. Am. Physicians, Am. Assn. Immunologists, Collegium INternationale Allergologicum, Phi Beta Kappa, Alpha Omega Alpha. Office: U Calif San Diego Med Ctr 402 Dickinson St Ste 380 San Diego CA 92103-6902

WASSERMAN, WILLIAM JACK, chemistry educator; b. N.Y.C., Apr. 27, 1925; s. Leon and Dora (Dyer) W.; m. Harriet Jo Marsh, July 19, 1959; children: Wayland, Wyeth. BS in Chemistry, UCLA, 1947; MS in Organic Chemistry, U. So. Calif., 1950; PhD in Organic Chemistry, U. Wash., 1954. Asst. prof. Humboldt State U., Arcata, Calif., 1954-57; sr. research chemist Martin-Marietta Corp., Seattle, 1957-62, Truesdail Labs., Los Angeles, 1962-63; asst. prof. chemistry San Jose (Calif.) State U., 1963-67; instr. Seattle Cen. Community Coll., 1967-96; cons. Counselors in Chemistry, Seattle, 1958—. Contbr. articles to profl. jours. Served with USN, 1944-46, PTO. Mem. Am. Chem. Soc. (chmn. Puget Sound sect. 1981, chmn. nat. meeting 1983), Sigma Xi, Phi Lambda Upsilon. Democrat. Avocations: collections, theater and concert events. Home: 1247 20th Ave E Seattle WA 98112-3530

WASSMAN, ROSE MARIE MADELINE, English language educator; b. Bklyn., Oct. 28, 1931; d. Dominick and Theresa (Signore) Abbruzzese; m. Robert Ray Wassman, May 7, 1967. Student, Hunter Coll., N.Y.C., 1949-56; BA in English, Wayne State U., 1959, MA in English, 1963; cert. in reading, Calif. State U., Hayward, 1970; cert. ESL, San Francisco State U., 1992. Cert. secondary edn. educator., Calif. Sec. various orgns., 1951-55; adminstrv. asst. Ford Internat., Dearborn, Mich., 1956-59; tchr. English, Cooley H.S., Detroit, 1959-64; instr. English, lit. Schoolcraft Coll., Livonia, Mich., 1964-67; tchr. English, reading Ravenswood H.S., East Palo Alto, Calif., 1967-69; instr. English, reading Ohlone Coll., Fremont, Calif., 1969-70; semi-ret. prof. reading DeAnza Coll., Cupertino, Calif., 1971—; cons. various colls., 1976-79. Co-author: (textbook) A Reader's Handbook, 1985, Vocabulary Strategies, 1996, Effective Reading Change of Word, 2d edit., 1997, also software. Recipient award for innovative devel. U. Tex. League for Innovation, Austin, 1977; Apple Found. grantee, 1982, Rsch. and Innovation grantee DeAnza Coll., 1975. Mem. Coll. Reading and Learning Assn. (conf. mgr. 1980), Nat. Assn. Devel. Edn., No. Coll. Reading Assn. (pres. 1976-79). Roman Catholic. Avocations: travel, gardening, cooking. Home: 9 Russell Ave Portola Vally CA 94028-7246 Office: DeAnza Coll 21250 Stevens Creek Blvd Cupertino CA 95014-5702

WASSMER, THEODORE MILTON, artist; b. Salt Lake City, Feb. 23, 1910; s. Theodore James and Hester Sadie (Hall) W.; m. Julia Farnsworth Lund, Dec. 8, 1945 (dec. May 1996). Student, Art Students League, N.Y.C., 1947-51; student under Raphael Soyer, Am. Art Sch., N.Y.C., 1949-51. Employed by engraving and wholesale hardware cos. Salt Lake City, 1925-42; artist N.Y.C., 1946-52, Woodstock, N.Y., 1952-85, Salt Lake City, 1985—; apprentice to Florence E. Ware painting murals for the WPA, 1934-39. More than 2,000 works are in museums, colls., schs. and pvt. collections in U.S., Europe and Japan; with wife donated more than 900 works to Springville Mus. of Art, Snow Coll., Brigham City Mus.-Gallery, Fairview Mus. of History and Art and Nora Eccles Harrison Mus. Art, Utah; solo show at Albany (N.Y.) Inst. History and Art, 1974; other solo shows in Alaska, Ariz., Tex., Utah, Fla., N.Y. and Calif.; in Art Access Gallery traveling show (Utah), exhibited with 4 other artists over 80, 1994; solo show of 50 recent works at Myra Powell Gallery, Ogden, Utah, 1997; works reproduced in various publs. Sgt. U.S. Army Air Force, 1942-45. Springville Mus. Art honored his 80th yr. with reception and 60-yr. retrospective show, 1930-90, showing 100 of his works and issuing a 24-page catalog. Avocation: collecting art. Home: 130 S 1300 E Apt 501 Salt Lake City UT 84102-1761

WATANABE, CORINNE KAORU AMEMIYA, lawyer, judge, state official; b. Wahiawa, Hawaii, Aug. 1, 1950; d. Keiji and Setsuko (Matsumiya) Amemiya; m. Edwin Tsugio Watanabe, Mar. 8, 1975; children: Traciann Keiko, Brad Natsuo, Lance Yoneo. BA, U. Hawaii, 1971; JD, Baylor U., 1974. Bar: Hawaii 1974. Dep. atty. gen. State of Hawaii, Honolulu, 1974-84, 1st dep. atty. gen., 1984-85, 87-92, atty. gen., 1985-87; assoc. judge Hawaii Intermediate Ct. Appeals, Honolulu, 1992—. Mem. ABA, Hawaii Bar Assn. Democrat. Office: Hawaii Intermediate Ct Appeals PO Box 2560 Honolulu HI 96804-2560

WATARU, WESTON YASUO, civil engineer; b. Honolulu, Mar. 30, 1957; s. Ralph Mitsuo and Anna Setsuko (Ogami) W.; m. Celine Jacqueline Teasdale, Nov. 1, 1986; children: Maile, Hope, Amber, Adam. BS, U. Hawaii, 1980. Registered profl. engr., Hawaii. Asst. engr. Dames and Moore, Honolulu, 1980-82; civil engr. I City and County of Honolulu Dept. Pub. Works, 1982-84, civil engr. IV, 1985-87, civil engr. V, 1987-89, svc. engr., civil engr. VI, 1989-98; civil engr. VI City and County of Honolulu Dept. Planning and Permitting, 1998—; mem. utilities coord. com. City and County of Honolulu, 1989—, mem. permit streamlining task force, 1995—. Mem. ASCE, NSPE, Am. Pub. Works Assn., Hawaii Govt. Employees Assn. Avocations: family, sporting events, basketball, reading. Office: City and County of Honolulu Dept Planning and Permitting 650 S King St Dept And Honolulu HI 96813-3078

WATERBURY, DAVID A., music producer, composer; b. Chgo., Feb. 29, 1956; s. Fredrick C. and Dorothy (Schlag) W. Wrote 18 songs used in films, TV and movies, 1985-98, wrote 22 songs on CD and albums, 1985-98; played with several groups including Mariah, Encounter, Vision; toured with Boxtops, 1982-83 and others. Organized charities events for Last Orphanage in L.A., 1996, 97. Recipient Good Hands award Hillary Clinton, Washington, 1996. Home: 12116 Hartsook St Studio City CA 91607

WATERMAN, DAVID MOORE, lawyer; b. San Francisco, July 23, 1947; s. Joseph and Muriel Yvette (Moore) W.; divorced; children: Kymberley Anne, Kevin David. BA, U. Ariz., 1970, JD, 1973; postgrad., U. Wash., 1978-80. Bar: Ariz. 1973, U.S. Dist. Ct. Ariz. 1973, U.S. Ct. Appeals (9th cir.) 1973. Assoc. Law Offices of William Berlat, Tucson, 1973-74, Law Offices of David K. Wolfe, Tucson, 1976-78, Rabinovitz, Dix & Rehling, Tucson, 1981-84; ptnr. Dix, Rehling & Waterman, Tucson, 1984-86, Dix & Waterman, Tucson, 1986-91; propr. Law Offices of David M. Waterman, 1991-95; ptnr. Taylor & Assocs., Tucson, 1996-98; pvt. practice Tucson, 1998—; adj. prof. bus. law U. Puget Sound, Tacoma, Wash., 1978-80; instr. Highline C.C., Midway, Wash., 1978-79, U. Phoenix, 1992-93; staff assoc. Office of Atty. Gen., Seattle, 1978. Mem. ABA, ATLA, Ariz. Assn. Lawyers for Injured Workers, So. Ariz. Workers' Compensation Applicant's Assn. (pres. 1986-88), State Bar Ariz. Worker's Compensation (co-chair sect. 1985), Am. Soc. Law and Medicine. Office: 900 E River Rd Ste 204 Tucson AZ 85718-5697

WATERMAN, MIGNON REDFIELD, public relations executive, state legislator; b. Billings, Mont., Oct. 13, 1944; d. Zell Ashley and Mable Erma (Young) Redfield; m. Ronald Fredrick Waterman, Sept. 11, 1965; children: Briar, Kyle. Student, U. Mont., 1963-66. Lobbyist Mont. Assn. Chs., Helena, 1986-90; senator State of Mont., Helena, 1990—; with pub. rels. dept. Mont. Coun. Tchrs. Math., Helena, 1991-96; mem. edn., pub. welfare and instns. sub-com. fin. and claims commn. Mont. Senate, rev. oversight com., 1995—, post-secondary policy & budget com., 1995—. Sch. trustee Helena (Mont.) Sch. Dist. 1, 1978-90; bd. dirs. Mont. Hunger Coalition, 1985—; pres. Mont. Sch. Bds. Assn., 1989-90; active Mont. Alliance for Mentally Ill (Mon Ami award 1991). Recipient Marvin Heintz award Mont. Sch. Bds. Assn., 1987, Friends of Edn. award Mont. Assn. Elem. and Middle Sch. Prins., 1989, Child Advocacy award Mont. PTA, 1991, award Mont. Alliance for Mentally Ill, 1991, Outstanding Adv. award Nat. Easter Seals Soc., 1997, Pres.'s award Mont. Assn. Rehab., 1997. Mem. Mont. Sch. Bds. Assn. (Marvin Heintz award 1988, pres.1989-90), Mont. Elem. Sch. Prins., Mont. Parent, Teacher, Student Assn. (child advocacy award 1991). Democrat. Methodist. Home and Office: 530 Hazelgreen Ct Helena MT 59601-5410 Office: Mt State Senate State Capitol Helena MT 59620

WATERS, ANTHONY EDWARD, adult education educator, volunteer; b. Torrance, Calif., Dec. 17, 1957; s. James E. Waters and Virginia Benson; m. Dagmar H. Kaletsch, July 17, 1987; children: Christopher, Kirsten. BS in Internat.Agrl. Devel., U. Calif. (Davis), 1978, PhD in Sociology, 1995; MS in Biology, Calif. Poly., 1986. Peace Corps vol. Malaria (Thailand) Zone Office, 1980-82; sanitarian Internat. Rescue Com., Thailand, 1982-83; spl. projects officer Luth. World Fedn., Tanzania, 1984-87, program officer, 1994-96; various tchg. positions U. Calif. (Davis), 1989-94; asst. prof., lectr. Calif. State U., Chico, 1996—. Author: Crime and Immigrant Youth, 1999; contbg. author: (with others) Essential Outsiders: Chinese and Jews in the Modern Transformation of Southeast Asian and Eastern Europe, 1997, Corporate Links and Direct Foreign Investment in Asia and the Pacific, 1995, Origins and Destinations: 41 Essays on Chinese America; also author of articles on crime in the immigrant cmty. youth, urban life, devel. aid in E. Africa, and refugees. Adminstr. Luth. World Fedn., UN High Commn. for Refugees funded Rwandan and Burundian refugees in Tanzania; evaluator Calif. Youth Authority Positive Parenting Parolees program, 1997-98. Recipient Rotary Club Study Exch. award, Phillipines, 1989. Mem. Africa Studies Assn., Am. Sociol. Assn. Lutheran. Home: 23236 Baker Ct Auburn CA 95602-8546 Office: California State Univ Dept Sociology and Social Work Dept Sociology and Social Work Chico CA 95929-0445

WATERS, KEITH JOHN, music educator, pianist; b. Locust Valley, N.Y., Nov. 29, 1958; s. Robert Frances and Evelyn (McGowan) W. B in Music, U. N.C., 1982; M in Music, New Eng. Conservatory of Music, 1985; PhD, U. Rochester, 1997. Jazz pianist Greensboro, N.C., Boston, 1983-85, Washington, 1985-90; tchr. Eastman Sch. of Music, Rochester, 1990-95; prof. U. Colo., Boulder, 1995—. Rsch. grant Paul Sacher Stiftung, 1994. Mem. Soc. for Music Theory, Rocky Mountain Soc. for Music Theory. Avocations: hiking, reading. Office: U Colo at Boulder Coll of Music PO Box 301 Boulder CO 80309-0301

WATERS, M. BRUCE, engineering technician; b. Houston, Apr. 17, 1950; s. Wayland O. and Snellah G. (Holt) W.; m. Jean H. Sudduth, June 26, 1971; 1 child, Tegan Joy. Student, La. State U., 1968-69, 70-74, U. Houston, 1969, San Jacinto Jr. Coll., Deer Park, Tex., 1969. Engring. aide I La. Dept. Highways, Baton Rouge, 1971-73, engring. aide II, 1973-74; sta. mgr. Cliff Brice Gas Stas., Boulder, Colo., 1975; mill worker Red Dale Coach, Longmont, Colo., 1975; engring. aide B Colo. Dept. Highways, Boulder, 1975-76, engring. aide C, 1976-91, engring tech. I, 1991—. Blood donor Belle Bonfils, Boulder, Colo., 1975—; mem. Vols. for Outdoor Colo.; sec.

Libertarian Party of Boulder County, 1991-93, 95-96; appointed to 20th Judicial Dist. Domestic Violence Treament Providers Cert. Bd., 1998—. Eagle Scout, 1967. Mem. Nat. Inst. Cert. Engring. Techs., Chpt. C Freewheelers (sec. 1993-95, 98-99, Rider of Yr. 1998), Am. Motorcyclist Assn., Soc. for Preservation and Encouragement of Barbershop Quartet Singing in Am. Avocations: collecting antique motorcycles, skiing, reading, music. Office: Colo Dept Transp 1050 Lee Hill Dr Boulder CO 80302-9404

WATERS, MAXINE, congresswoman; b. St. Louis, Aug. 15, 1938; d. Remus and Velma (Moore) Carr; m. Sidney Williams, July 23, 1977; children: Edward, Karen. Grad. in sociology Calif. State U., L.A.; hon. doctorates, Spelman Coll., N.C. Agrl. & Tech. State U., Morgan State U. Former tchr. Head Start; mem. Calif. Assembly from dist. 48, 1976-91, Dem. caucus chair, 1984; mem. 102nd-105th Congresses from Dist. 35, Calif., 1991—; mem. Banking, Fin., Urban Affairs com., Ho. subcom. on banking, capitol subcom. on banking, employment and tng. subcom. on vets., veterans affairs com., banking and fin. svcs. com., ranking house subcom. on gen. oversight and investigations; chair Congl. Black Caucus. Mem. Dem. Nat. Com., Dem. Congrl. Campaign com.; del. Dem. Nat. Conv., 1972, 76, 80, 84, 88, 92, mem. rules com. 1984; mem. Nat. Adv. Com. for Women, 1978—; bd. dirs. TransAfrica Found., Nat. Women's Polit. Caucus, Ctr. Nat. Policy, Clara Elizabeth Jackson Carter Found. Spellman Coll., Nat. Minority AIDS Project, Women for a Meaningful Summit, Nat. Coun. Negro Women, Black Women's Agenda; founder Black Women's Forum. Office: US Ho of Reps 2344 Rayburn Washington DC 20515-0535*

WATKIN, VIRGINIA RUTH, banker; b. Pomona, Calif., Sept. 25, 1955; d. Charles Robertson Williams and Effie Ruth (Jones) Kettmann; m. Thomas Peter Watkin, Sept. 10, 1977. AA Mt. San Antonio Coll., 1975; postgrad. Calif. State U.-Fullerton, U. Guadalajara, Riverside City Coll. Mgmt. trainee Local Loan Co., La Puente, Calif., 1977, Morris Plan of Calif., Corona, 1977-78; cons. loan processor Glendale Fed. Riverside, Calif., 1978-81, cons. loan officer, Riverside and Downey, Calif., 1981-84, sr. cons. loan officer, Glendale, Calif., 1984-86; asst. v.p./consumer loan mgr. Hemet (Calif.) Fed. Savs. and Loan, 1986—; instr. Inst. Fin. Edn. Hemet/San Jacinto (Calif.) chpt. Consumer Fin. Rep. Calif. Community and Jr. Coll. Assn., Walnut, 1975. Mem. Nat. Assn. Female Execs., Calif. Savs. and Loan League (consumer loan com.), Hemet C. of C. Republican. Roman Catholic. Lodge: Soroptimists (v.p. Riverside 1982, pres. Riverside 1983). Avocations: reading, water skiing, fishing, camping, gourmet cooking. Home: 17754 Siskiyou Rd Apple Valley CA 92307-1224 Office: Hemet Fed Savs and Loan 3600 Tyler St Riverside CA 92503-4180

WATKINS, CHARLES REYNOLDS, medical equipment company executive; b. San Diego, Oct. 28, 1951; s. Charles R. and Edith A. (Muff) W.; children: Charles Devin, Gregory Michael. BS, Lewis and Clark Coll., 1974; postgrad., U. Portland, 1976. Internat. salesman Hyster Co., Portland, Oreg., 1975-80, Hinds Internat. Corp., Portland, 1980-83; mgr. internat. sales Wade Mfg. Co., Tualatin, Oreg., 1983-84; regional sales mgr. U.S. Surg., Inc., Norwalk, Conn., 1984-86; nat. sales mgr. NeuroCom Internat., Inc., Clackamas, Oreg., 1986-87; pres. Wave Form Systems, Inc., Portland, 1987-98; pres., dir. Wave Form Mfg., Inc., Portland, 1998—; prin. Wave Form Lithotripsy LLC, Portland, 1998—; pres. Wave Form Mfg., Inc., 1998—. Bd. dirs. Portland World Affairs Coun., 1980. Mem. Am. Soc. Laser Medicine and Surgery, Am. Assn. Gynecol. Laparoscopists, Ind. Med. Distbrs. Assn., Portland City Club. Republican. Avocations: flying, photography, travel. Office: Wave Form Sys Inc PO Box 3195 Portland OR 97208-3195

WATKINS, EUGENE LEONARD, surgeon, educator; b. Worcester, Mass., Jan. 4, 1918; s. George Joseph and Marcella Katherine (Akels) W.; A.B. with honors in biology, Clark U., 1940; M.D. (Hood scholar), Harvard U., 1943; m. Victoria Peake, Sept. 23, 1944; children: Roswell Peake, Priscilla Avery. Intern, Roosevelt Hosp., N.Y.C., 1944; resident in surgery, 1944-46, 49-50, asst. resident in surgery, 1948-49; fellow in surgery, clin. rsch. fellow Mass. Gen. Hosp., Boston, 1947-48; practice medicine specializing in surgery, N.Y.C., 1950-56, Morristown, N.J., 1950-90, Denville, N.J., 1956-85, Boonton, N.J., 1961-85; mem. staff Morristown Meml. Hosp., 1950, vice chmn. dept. surgery, 1974-77, chmn., 1959-61, mem. corp.; cons. surgeon St. Clare's Hosp., Denville, N.J., Riverside Hosp., Boonton, N.J., Community Med. Center, Morristown; courtesy surg. staff St. Luke's-Roosevelt Hosp. Center, N.Y.C.; asst. clin. prof. surgery Rutgers U. Coll. Medicine and Dentistry, New Brunswick, N.J., 1972-85; asst. clin. prof. surgery Columbia U. Coll. Phys. and Surg., 1985-90; v.p. chmn. fin. com. Morristown Bd. Health, 1954-56. Served to 1st lt., AUS, 1946. Diplomate Am. Bd. Surgery. Fellow ACS (chmn. N.J. Adv. Com. 1965-77, chmn. N.J. State com. Trauma, 1960); mem. N.J., Morris County med. socs., AMA, Soc. Surgeons N.J. (1st v.p. 1982, pres. 1983), Am. Thoracic Soc., AAAS, Harvard Med. Soc. N.Y. (pres. 1960-61), West Side Med. Soc., Roosevelt Hosp. Alumni Assn. Republican. Presbyterian. Clubs: Harvard (N.Y.C.), Morristown, Morristown Field. Achievements include development of spring-loop surgical suture holder. Home: PO Box 1037 Buffalo WY 82834-1037

WATKINS, GLORIA THOMAS, health care worker; b. Memphis, May 25, 1937; d. James Victor and Louise (Bowers) Thomas; m. William Edward Carnes, Dec. 2, 1953 (div. May 1972); children: Denzil Carnes (dec.), Vincent Carnes, Francesca Brande, Trent Carnes; m. Calvin Floyd Watkins, June 17, 1972. BS, Calif. State U., 1978. Wirer, solderer Douglas Aircraft, Ocean Park, Calif., 1962; teller Bank Am., Westwood, Calif., 1962-63, City Nat. Bank, Beverly Hills, Calif., 1963-64; tchr. Project Headstart Delta Sigma Theta, L.A., 1964-73; instr. Southwest Industries, Gardena, Calif., 1974-76; care provider Los Angeles County Sys., L.A., 1979—. Author: Definitions of Common Words and Phrases in The King James Bible, 1994; inventor Back Zipper Opener, 1995. Avocations: crossword puzzles, reading, music. Home: 1918 W 81st St Los Angeles CA 90047-2639

WATKINS, JOHN GOODRICH, psychologist, educator; b. Salmon, Idaho, Mar. 17, 1913; s. John Thomas and Ethel (Goodrich) W.; m. Evelyn Elizabeth Browne, Aug. 21, 1932; m. Doris Wade Tomlinson, June 8, 1946; m. Helen Verner Huth, Dec. 28, 1971; children: John Dean, Jonette Alison, Richard Douglas, Gregory Keith, Rodney Philip, Karen Stroobants, Marvin R. Huth. Student, Coll. Idaho, 1929-30, 31-32; BS, U. Idaho, 1933, MS, 1936; PhD, Columbia U., 1941. Instr. high sch. Idaho, 1933-39; faculty Ithaca Coll., 1940-41, Auburn U., 1941-43; assoc. prof. Wash. State U., 1946-49; chief clin. psychologist U.S. Army Welch Hosp., 1945-46; clin. psychologist VA Hosp., American Lake, Wash., 1949-50; chief clin. psychologist VA Mental Hygiene Clinic, Chgo., 1950-53, VA Hosp., Portland, Oreg., 1953-64; prof. psychology U. Mont., Missoula, 1964-84; prof. emeritus U. Mont., 1984—, dir. clin. tng., 1964-80; lectr. numerous univs.; clin. asso. U. Oreg. Med. Sch., 1957; pres. Am. Bd. Examiners in Psychol. Hypnosis, 1960-62. Author: Objective Measurement of Instrumental Performance, 1942, Hypnotherapy of War Neuroses, 1949, General Psychotherapy, 1960, The Therapeutic Self, 1978, (with others) We, The Divided Self, 1982, Hypnotherapeutic Techniques, 1987, Hypnoanalytic Techniques, 1992, Ego States: Theory and Therapy, 1997; contbr. articles to profl. jours. Mem. Internat. Soc. Clin. and Exptl. Hypnosis (co-founder, pres. 1965-67, recipient awards 1960-65), Soc. Clin. and Exptl. Hypnosis (pres. 1969-71, Morton Prince award), Am. Psychol. Assn. (pres. divsn. 30 1975-76, recipient award 1993), Sigma Xi, Phi Delta Kappa. Home and Office: 413 Evans Ave Missoula MT 59801-5827

WATKINS, JUDITH ANN, nurse administrator; b. Chgo., Mar. 11, 1942; d. Russell and Louise Bernadine (Aloy) Keim; m. Thomas H. Watkins III, Dec. 24, 1961; children: Tamara Sue, Randall Scott. Grad. in nursing, Knapp Coll. Nursing, Santa Barbara, Calif., 1963; BSN, Pacific Union Coll., 1991, PHN cert., 1991; MHA, U. LaVerne, 1995. Cert. CPR instr., vocat. edn. instr. Obstetrics supr. Bowling Green (Ky.) Warren County Hosp., 1963-67; clin. staff nurse Chula Vista (Calif.) Med. Clinic, 1967-69; nurse aide instr. Sawyers Coll., Ventura, Calif., 1972; ob-gyn. supr. Westlake (Calif.) Community Hosp., 1972-77; RN acute patient care Medical Personnel Pool, Bakersfield, Calif., 1984; med. asst. instr., dir. of allied health [illegible] Med. Ctr., 1988-91, dir. client svcs., 1991-94, asst. adminstr. clin. svcs., 1994-98; asst. prof. UCLA, 1998—; v.p. clin. svcs. Regal Med. Group, [illegible] Mother of the Yr., Frazier Pk. (Calif.) Community Ch., 1979, Instr. of the Yr., 1986. Mem. Kern County RN Soc., Kern County Trade Club, Pine Mt. Golf Club (founder Lilac Festival 1982, Lady of the Yr. 1983) Sundale Country Club, Seven Oaks Country Club, Toastmasters Internat. Avocations: swimming, golf. Home: 8004 Nairn Ct Bakersfield CA 93309-4276 Office: Bakersfield Family Med Ctr 4580 California Ave Bakersfield CA 93309-7013

WATKINS, LOIS IRENE, English educator; b. Sterling, Nebr., Mar. 12, 1926; d. August Ralph and Magdalena Anna (Foss) Bargman; m. Morris Grant Watkins, Dec. 28, 1947 (dec. May 1996); children: Sharon Thomas, Stephen, Mark, Paul, Debra Walters, Joanna Hutchinson, David. Student, Concordia Tchrs. Coll., 1945-47; BA in Applied Linguistics, Calif. State U., Fullerton, 1976, MA in Applied Linguistics, 1978. 2d grade tchr. Canoga Park (Calif.) Luth. Sch., 1961-62; asst. prof. William Carey U., Pasadena, Calif., 1978-80; asst. to pres. All Nations Lit., Calif., Ind., Wash., 1972-92; dir. literature and literacy All Nations Lit., Colorado Springs, Colo., 1992-94, pres., bd. dirs., 1994-96; ESL curriculum specialist Internat. Bible Soc., Colorado Springs, Colo., 1996—; missionary wife Luth. Ch.-Mo. Synod, Uyo, Nigeria, 1950-52, Ogojo, Nigeria, 1959-63. Author, sr. instr. manual and video series Bridge of Love, 1994; co-editor: All Nations English Dictionary, 1990. Mem. Rep. Nat. Com., Washington. Mem. Luth. Soc. for Missiology (bd. dirs. 1994—). Avocations: reading, writing, gardening, computer graphics. Home: 5475 Jennifer Ln Colorado Springs CO 80917-1420

WATKINS, THOMAS HENRY, writer, educator; b. Loma Linda, Calif., Mar. 29, 1936; s. Thomas Francis and Orel Rhea (Roller) W.; m. Elaine Otakie, Jan. 13, 1957 (div. Nov. 1970); children: Lisa Lynn, Kevin Blair; m. Ellen Joan Parker, June 12, 1976. AA, San Bernardino Valley Coll., 1956; BA, U. Redlands, 1958. Mng. editor The Am. West, Palo Alto, Calif., 1966-68, editor, 1969-70; v.p. Am. West Pub. Co., Palo Alto, 1967-70; sr. editor Am. Heritage, N.Y.C., 1976-82; editor Wilderness, Washington, 1982-97; Wallace Stegner prof. western Am. studies Mont. State U., Bozeman, 1997—. Author: San Francisco in Color, 1968, California in Color, 1970, Gold and Silver in the West, 1971, California, 1973, 83, On the Shore of the Sundown Sea, 1973, Vanishing Arctic, 1987, Time's Island, 1989, Righteous Pilgrim, 1990, 92 (L.A. Times Book award for biography 1991), The Great Depression, 1993,94, Natural America, 1998, The Hungry Years, 1999, others; author, photographer: Stone Time, 1994; co-author: Here Today, 1968, The Water Hustlers, 1971, The Lands No One Knows, 1974, Mirror of the Dream, 1976, These American Lands, 1994, Western Art Masterpieces, 1996, others; co-editor: The West, 1994, 1995; contbr. articles and revs. to Nat. Geographic, Am. Heritage, S.D. Rev., Smithsonian, Audubon, Calif. History, Constn., N.Y. Times, Condé Nast's Traveler, Sierra, others. Chmn. non-fiction judges panel for Nat. Book awards Nat. Book Found., N.Y.C., 1996; chmn. PenCtr/USA West rsch. non-fiction book award panel, L.A. Recipient John Collier Meml. award Forest History Soc., 1992. Mem. PEN Am. Ctr., Wilderness Soc. (v.p. 1986-97, Robert Marshall award 1988), Phi Beta Kappa. Democrat. Avocations: hiking, photography.

WATKISS, ERIC JOHN, career officer; b. East Point, Ga., May 17, 1964; s. George Philip Watkiss and Barbara Anne Seaman; m. Lynne Lee Novak, Nov. 25, 1989. B of Aerospace Engring., Ga. Inst. Tech., 1986; MS in Aero. Engring., Naval Postgrad. Sch., 1994; grad., U.S. Naval Test Pilot Sch., 1995. Lic. pvt. pilot FAA. Airport mgr. Aerocountry Airport, McKinney, Tex., 1981-86; advanced through grades to lt. comdr. USN, 1996, naval flight officer, 1986—, EA-6B Prowler electronic countermeasures officer, 1989—, naval flight test officer, 1995-96, naval test pilot sch. instr., 1996-98, EA-6B Prowler weapon sys. support activity mil. lead, 1998—. Decorated two Navy Achievement medals, 1990, 91, one Navy Commendation medal. Mem. AIAA (winner 1st pl. aircraft design competition 1993. 94), MENSA, Aircraft Owners and Pilots Assn. Republican. Episcopalian. Avocations: flying, mountain biking, skiing. Home: 1200 Rigel Dr Point Mugu Nawc CA 93041 Office: Naval Weapons Test Squadron Point Mugu Nawc CA 93042

WATNE, DONALD ARTHUR, accountant, educator; b. Gt. Falls, Mont., Jan. 18, 1939; s. Arthur Leonard and Anne (Salo) W.; m. Patricia Elaine Schick, Aug. 12, 1961; children—Elizabeth Anne, Michael Arthur. BA with high honors, U. Mont., 1960, MA, 1961; PhD, U. Calif.-Berkeley, 1977. CPA, Oreg. Acct., Piquet & Minihan, Eugene, Oreg., 1961-65; mgr. capital investment analysis Weyerhaeuser Co., Tacoma, 1965-68; mktg. rep. IBM Corp., Portland, Oreg., 1968-70; dir. EDP Ctr. in Concejo Mcpl., Barquisimeto, Venezuela, 1971-72; prof. acctg. Portland State U., 1976—; vis. prof. Xiamen (Fujian, People's Rep. China), 1985-86, U. Otago, Dunedin, New Zealand, 1985-86, U. Newcastle, Australia, 1985-86; cons. in field; mem. acctg. qualifications com. Oregon State Bd. of Acctg., 1989-98, mem. CPE com., 1998—. Del. to Soviet Union citizen amb. program People to People Internat., 1990; mem. Tng. the Trainers Program, Vilnius, Lithuania, 1993. Mem. AICPA, Am. Acctg. Assn., Oreg. Soc. CPAs, Mazamas Mountain Climbing Club, Mensa. Author: (with Peter B.B. Turney) Auditing EDP Systems, 2d. edit. 1990; contbr. articles in field, chpts. in handbooks. Home: 2826 NE 26th Ave Portland OR 97212-3503 Office: Portland State U Sch Bus Adminstrn PO Box 751 Portland OR 97207-0751

WATRING, WATSON GLENN, gynecologic oncologist, educator; b. St. Albans, W.Va., June 2, 1936; m. Roberta Tawell. BS, Washington & Lee U., 1958; MD, W.Va. U., 1962. Diplomate Am. Bd. Ob-Gyn, Am. Bd. Gynecol. Oncology. Intern The Toledo Hosp., 1963; resident in ob-gyn Ind. U., Indpls., 1964-66, Tripler Gen. Hosp., Honolulu, 1968-70; resident in gen. and oncologic surgery City of Hope Nat. Med. Ctr., Duarte, Calif., 1970-71, assoc. dir. gynecol. oncology, sr. surgeon, 1973-77; fellow in gynecol. oncology City of Hope Nat. Med. Ctr. and UCLA Med. Ctr., 1972-74; asst. prof. ob-gyn UCLA Med. Ctr., 1972-77; assoc. prof., sr. gynecologist, sr. surgeon Tufts New Eng. Med. Ctr. Hosp., Boston, 1977-80, asst. prof. radiation therapy, 1978-80; practice medicine specializing in ob-gyn Boston, 1980-82; assoc. prof. ob-gyn U. Mass., Worcester, 1982; regional dir. gynecol. oncology So. Calif. Permanente Med. Group, Los Angeles, 1982—, asst. dir. residency tng., 1985—; dir. gynecol. oncology St. Margarets Hosp. for Women, Dorchester, Mass., 1977-80; clin. prof. ob-gyn U. Calif., Irvine, 1982—. Contbr. articles to profl. jours. Mem. ch. council Luth. Ch. of the Foothills, 1973-75. Served to lt. col. M.C., U.S. Army, 1965-71. Fellow Am. Coll. Ob-Gyn, Los Angeles Obstet. and Gynecol. Soc.; mem. AAAS, ACS (Calif. and Mass. chpts.), Boston Surg. Soc., AMA, Mass. Med. Soc., Mass. Suffolk Dist. Med. Soc., Internat. Soc. Gynecol. Pathologists, Western Soc. Gynecologists and Obstetricians, Am. Soc. Clin. Oncology, Soc. Gynecol. Oncologists, Western Assn. Gynecol. Oncologists (sec.-treas. 1976-81, program chmn. 1984, pres. 1985—), New Eng. Assn. Gynecol. Oncologists (chmn. charter com.), New Eng. Obstet. and Gynecol. Soc., Obstet. Soc. Boston, Am. Radium Soc., Soc. Study Breast Disease, New Eng. Cancer Soc., Internat. Gynecol. Cancer Soc., Daniel Morton Soc., Sigma Xi. Republican. Avocations: golf, skiing, horticulture.

WATSON, DAVID COLQUITT, electrical engineer, educator b. Linden, Tex., Feb. 9, 1936; s. Colvin Colquitt and Nelena Gertrude (Keasler) W.; m. Flora Janet Thayn, Nov. 10, 1959; children: Flora Janeen, Melanie Beth, Lorrie Gaylene, Cheralyn Gail, Nathan David, Amy Melissa, Brian Colvin. BSEE, U. Utah, 1964, PhD in Elec. Engring. (NASA fellow), 1968. Electronic technician Hercules Powder Co., Magna, Utah, 1961-62; rsch. fellow U. Utah, 1964-65, rsch. asst. microwave devices and phys. electronics lab., 1964-68; sr. mem. tech. staff ESL, Inc., Sunnyvale, Calif., 1968-78, head dept. Communications, 1969-70; sr. engring. specialist Probe Systems, Inc., Sunnyvale, 1978-79; sr. mem. tech. staff ARGO Systems, Inc., Sunnyvale, 1979-90; sr. mem. tech. staff GTE Govt. Systems Corp., Mountain View, Calif., 1990-91; sr. cons. Watson Cons. Svcs., 1991-92; sr. staff engr. ESL, Inc., 1992— ; mem. faculty U. Santa Clara, 1978-81, 1992—, San Jose State U., 1981—, Coll. Notre Dame, 1992—, Chapman U., 1993—. Contbr. articles to IEEE Transactions, 1965-79; co-inventor cyclotron-wave rectifier; inventor gradient descrambler. Served with USAF, 1956-60. Mem. IEEE, Phi Kappa Phi, Tau Beta Pi, Eta Kappa Nu. Mem. LDS Ch. Office: Space Sys Loral 3825 Fabian Way Palo Alto CA 94303-4604

WATSON, HAROLD GEORGE, ordnance company executive, mechanical engineer; b. Phoenix, Oct. 19, 1931; s. Clarence Elmer and Eunice A. [illegible] Ruth, Linda Darlene, Harold George; m. Katherina Anna Kish, Sept. 22, 1990. B.S., U. Ariz., 1954. Engr. Shell Oil Co., L.A., 1954; project engr. Talco Engring. Co., Hamden Conn., 1956, area mgr., Mesa, Ariz., 1956-57, chief engr. Rocket Power, 1958-61, dir. engring., 1961-64; dir. engring. Space Ordnance Systems, El Segundo, Calif., 1964-68; dir. engring. Universal Propulsion Co., Riverside, Calif., 1968-70, gen. mgr., v.p. engring., Tempe, Ariz., 1970-76, v.p., mgr., 1976-77, pres., gen. mgr., Phoenix, 1977—. Patentee in field. 1st lt. USAR, 1954-56. Mem. Am. Mgmt. Assn., SAFE Assn. (past pres.), AIAA, Air Force Assn., Internat. Pyronetics Soc., Am. Def. Preparedness Assn. Office: Universal Propulsion Co Inc 25401 N Central Ave Phoenix AZ 85027-7899

WATSON, LARRY SULLIVAN, editor, educator; b. Oklahoma City, May 3, 1941; s. Levi Sullivan and Betty Wilma (Galyean) W. BA, Okla. State Univ., 1963; MA, Ctrl. Mo., 1964; student, Northwestern Univ., 1964-65. Asst. prof. Carson-Newman Coll., Jefferson City, Tenn., 1965-66; prof., rschr., writer U. Mo., Columbia, 1969-79; editor, owner HISTREE, Yuma, Ariz., 1979—; instr. Cen. Mo., Warresnburg, 1964, Northwestern Univ., Evanston, Ill., 1965; assoc. faculty Western Ariz. Coll., Yuma, 1995—. Author over 200 books; contbg. editor Heritag Quest, Orting, Wash., 1995; contbr. articles to profl. publs. Dir. Key Club, 4-H, Okla., 1959-64; sec. Ariz. Geneal. Adv. Bd., 1995-96, comms. chmn., 1997. With U.S. Army, 1966-68. Fellow Ark.-La.-Tex. Genealogy Soc.; mem. Nat. Genealogy Soc., New Eng. Hist. Soc., Genealogy Soc. Yuma (v.p. 1996, pres. 1997), Ariz. Genealogy Soc. (adv. bd.). Republican. Avocations: bridge. Office: HISTREE PO Box 5982 Yuma AZ 85366-5982

WATSON, MARILYN FERN, writer, artist; b. Oklahoma City, July 30, 1934; d. Charles Haddon and Mary Perle (Knotts) Rounds; m. Donald Wayne Watson, Aug. 14, 1954; 1 child, Lyndon Lee. BS in Psychology magna cum laude, Ea. N.Mex. U., 1973, postgrad., 1980-81. Apprentice technician, Sante Fe Opera, 1982. Geol. draftsman Lion Oil Co., Roswell, N.Mex., 1956-57; freelance writer, artist Roswell, N.Mex., 1960—; pvt. tutor learning disabled, gifted children, 1976-77; founder, owner Creativity Unltd., Roswell, N.Mex., 1994—. Contbr. articles to mags. and profl. jours. Ofcl. centennial historian, artist United N.Mex. Bank, Roswell, 1990; chairperson/sponsor Heritage awards Hist. Ctr. S.E. N.Mex., Roswell, 1995, found. bd., 1996-97. Recipient Writer's Digest Mag. award, 1959, Guideposts Fedn. award, 1978. Mem. Psi Chi, Phi Kappa Phi. Methodist. Avocations: gardening, hiking, reading/collecting classic literature, designing stained glass, sculpture. Home: 100 S Pennsylvania Roswell NM 88201 Office: Creativity Unltd 100-1/2 S Penn Roswell NM 88201

WATSON, MATHEW D., optical scientist; b. L.A., Feb. 9, 1958. BS in Physics, San Jose State U., 1984; MS in Optical Scis., U. Ariz., 1989, PhD in Optical Scis., 1991. Mem. tech. staff Uniphase, Inc., San Jose, Calif., 1984-86; rsch. assoc. Optical Scis. Ctr., Tucson, Ariz., 1986-91; electro optical engr. ILX Lightwave, Inc., Bozeman, Mont., 1991-93; sr. optical engr. Quest Integrated, Inc., Kent, Wash., 1994-96; pres. Eclipse Optical Rsch., Bellevue, Wash., 1997—. Contbr. articles to profl. jours.; patentee in field. Grad. rsch. scholar Optical Scis. Ctr., 1989; recipient ARCS scholarship ARCS Found., 1983. Mem. Optical Soc. Am., IEEE/Laser and Electro-optic Soc., Soc. Photometric and Instrumentation Engrs. Home: 10439 NE 28th Pl Bellevue WA 98004-2043 Office: Eclipse Optical Rsch 10439 NE 28th Pl Bellevue WA 98004-2043

WATSON, OLIVER LEE, III, aerospace engineering manager; b. Lubbock, Tex., Sept. 18, 1938; m. Judith Valeria Horvath, June 13, 1964; 1 child, Clarke Stanford. BSEE, U. Tex., 1961; MSEE, Stanford U., 1963; MBA, Calif. State U., Fullerton, 1972; cert., U. So. Calif., 1980. Mgr. ballistic analysis Rockwell Internat. Autonetics Div., Anaheim, Calif., 1973-78, mgr. minuteman systems, 1978-83, mgr. preliminary engring., 1983-84; mgr. analysis group autonetics divsn. Rockwell Internat., Anaheim, Calif., 1984-85, mgr. aircraft sys. autonetics dept., 1985-93, dep. dir. integrated product devel. N.Am. aircraft modification divsn., 1993-94, dep. dir. engring. N.Am. aircraft modification divsn., 1994-96; dep. dir. engring. comm. and combat sys. divsn. Boeing N.Am., Anaheim, 1996-98; skills, process and metrics mgr. Comm. and Battle Mgmt., Anaheim, 1998—; lectr. engring. Calif. State U., Fullerton, 1981-90, mem. indsl. adv. bd., 1994—, vice chmn., 1995-97; spkr. welcome address Engring. & Computer Sci. Commencement, 1997. Co-author Digital Computing Using Fortran IV, 1982; Fortran 77, A Complete Primer, 1986. Bd. dirs. Olive Little League, Orange, 1980; vol. Stanford U. Engring. Fund, Orange County, Calif., 1983, regional chmn. 1984-86, So. Calif. chmn. 1986-91; mem. Stanford Assocs., 1988—. Recipient Stanford Assocs. Centennial Medallion award, 1991; fellow N.Am. Aviation Sci.-Engring., L.A., 1962, 63, Inst. Advancement Engring., L.A., 1976. Mem. IEEE (sr., sec. v.p. 1974-75, sect. chmn. 1975-76), Jaycees (v.p. Orange chpt. 1973-74), Rockwell-Calif. State Univ. Alumni Club (v.p. 1993, pres. 1993-94), Lido Sailing Club. Republican. Avocations: sailing, swimming, humor writing, scriptwriting, reading. Office: Boeing NAm 031-DA62 3370 E Miraloma Ave Anaheim CA 92806-1911

WATSON, SHARON GITIN, psychologist, executive; b. N.Y.C., Oct. 21, 1943; d. Louis Leonard and Miriam (Myers) Gitin; m. Eric Watson, Oct. 31, 1969; 1 child, Carrie Dunbar. B.A. cum laude, Cornell U., 1965; M.A., U. Ill., 1968, Ph.D., 1971. Psychologist City N.Y. Prison Mental Health, Riker's Island, 1973-74; psychologist Youth Services Ctr., Los Angeles County Dept. Pub. Social Services, Los Angeles, 1975-77, dir. clin. services, 1978, dir. Youth Services Ctr., 1978-80; exec. dir. Crittenton Ctr. for Young Women and Infants, Los Angeles, 1980-89, Assn. Children's Svcs. Agys. of So. Calif., L.A., 1989-92, L.A. County Children's Planning Coun., 1992—; mem. L.A. delegation Pres.'s Summit for Am.'s Future, 1997. Mem. Commn. for Children's Svcs. Family Preservation and Family Support Policy Com., Mayor's Com. on Children, Youth and Families, 1993-95, L.A. County Welfare Reform Network, United Way of Greater L.A. Cmty. Devel. Cabinet, Interagy. Coun. Child Abuse and Neglect Policy Com., L.A. Unified Sch. Dist. Bd. Edn.'s Com. on Student Health and Human Svcs., LISC Health Sector Partnership, L.A. Roundtable for Children, 1988-94, Adolescent Pregnancy Childwatch, 1985-89; trustee L.A. Ednl. Alliance for Restructuring Now; co-chmn. Los Angeles County Drug and Alcohol Abuse Task Force, 1990. Mem. APA, Calif. Assn. Svcs. for Children (sec.-treas. 1983-84, pres. elect 1985-86, pres. 1986-87), Assn. Children's Svcs. Agys. So. Calif. (sec. 1981-83, pres. elect 1983-84, pres. 1984-85), Town Hall L.A., mem. Jr. Olympics Com. U.S. Olympics Com., bd. dirs. U.S. Figure Skating Assn. (chair, membership com. 1996—, sanctions and eligibility 1993-96), So. Calif. Inter-Club Assn. of Figure Skating Clubs (vice chair 1989-91, chair 1991-93), Pasadena Figure Skating Club (pres. 1985-87, 89-90). Home: 4056 Camino Real Los Angeles CA 90065-3928 Office: LA County Children's Planning Coun 500 W Temple St Ste B26 Los Angeles CA 90012-2722

WATTERS, RICHARD JAMES, professional football player; b. Harrisburg, Pa., Apr. 7, 1969. Degree in design, U. Notre Dame. With San Francisco 49'ers, 1991-94; running back Phila. Eagles, 1995-98, Seattle Seahawks, 1998—. Selected to Pro Bowl, 1992-94. Achievements include member San Francisco 49'ers Super Bowl XXIX Champions, 1994, holds NFL postseason single game for most points (30), most touchdowns (5), Jan. 15, 1994 vs N.Y. Giants. Office: Seattle Seahawks 11220 NE 53d St Kirkland WA 98033*

WATTS, MARVIN LEE, minerals company executive, chemist, educator; b. Portales, N.Mex., Apr. 6, 1932; s. William Ellis and Jewel Reata (Holder) W.; m. Mary Myrtle Kiker, July 25, 1952; children: Marvin Lee, Mark Dwight, Wesley Lyle. BS in Chemistry and Math., Ea. N.Mex. U., 1959, MS in Chemistry, 1960; postgrad. U. Okla., 1966, U. Kans., 1967. Analytical chemist Dow Chem. Co., Midland, Mich., 1960-62; instr. chemistry N.Mex. Mil. Inst., Roswell, 1962-65, asst. prof., 1965-67; chief chemist AMAX Chem. Corp., Carlsbad, N.Mex., 1967-78, gen. surface supt., 1978-84; pres. N.Mex. Salt and Minerals Corp., 1984—; chem. cons. Western Soils Lab., Roswell, 1962-67; instr. chemistry N.Mex. State U., Carlsbad, 1967—; owner, operator cattle ranch, Carlsbad and Loving, N.Mex., 1969—; bd. dirs. Mountain States Mutual Casualty Co., 1991; gen. mgr. Eddy Potash, Inc., 1987—, v.p. and gen. mgr., 1987-95; cons. Potash Industry, [illegible] Coun., 1994; chmn. Eddy County Land USF Commn., Eddy County Labor Rels. Bd.; dir. Soil Conservation Svc.; mem. Roswell dist. adv. bd. Bur. Land [illegible] bd. Roswell dist. Bur. Land Mgmt., mem. Eddy County Fair Bd., 1970—,

chmn., 1978, 82; mem. pub. sch. reform com.; chmn. higher edn. reform com.; mem. sponsor of N.Mex. Pub. Sch. Reform Act; bd. dirs. Carlsbad Regional Med. Ctr., 1976-78; pres. bd. Carlsbad Found., 1979-82; adv. bd. N.Mex. State U. at Carlsbad, 1976-80; vice chmn. bd. Guadalupe Med. Ctr.; bd. dirs. N.Mex. State U. Found.; state senator N.Mex. Legis., 1984-89. Mem. Rep. State Exec. com., 1972—; Rep. chmn. Eddy County (N.Mex.), 1970-74, 78-82. dirs. Conquistador coun. Boy Scouts Am., Regional Environ. Ednl. Rsch. and Improvement Orgn. Served with Mil. Police Corps, AUS, 1953-55; Germany. Recipient Albert K. Mitchell award as outstanding Rep. in N.Mex., 1976; hon. state farmer N.Mex. Future Farmers Am.; hon. mem. 4-H. Fellow N.Mex. Acad. Sci.; mem. Am. Chem. Soc. (chmn. subsect.), Western States Pub. Lands Coalition, Carlsbad C. of C. (dir. 1979-83), N.Mex. Mining Assn. (dir.), AIME (chmn. Carlsbad potash sect. 1975), Carlsbad Mental Health Assn., N.Mex. Inst. Mining and Tech. (adv. bd. mining dept.), Am. Angus Assn., Am. Quarter Horse Assn., N.Mex. Cattle Growers Assn. (bd. dirs. 1989—), Carlsbad Farm and Ranch Assn., Nat. Cattleman's Assn. Baptist. Kiwanis (Disting. lt. gov.), Carlsbad Mental Health Assn. (pres. 1994—), Elks. Home: PO Box 56 Carlsbad NM 88221-0056 Office: PO Box 31 Carlsbad NM 88221-5601

WATZ, MARTIN CHARLES, brewery consultant; b. St. Louis, Oct. 31, 1938; s. George Michael and Caroline Theresa (Doggendorf) W.; m. Deborah Perkowski; children: Pamela, Kathlene, Karen. BS in Chemistry and Microbiology, SE Mo. State U., 1961; MBA, Washington U., 1966-67. Safety engr. McDonnell-Douglas, 1962-64; sr. brewing chemist Anheuser-Busch, Inc., St. Louis, 1965-68, asst. brewmaster, Columbus, Ohio, 1968-79, sr. asst. brewmaster, St. Louis, 1979-82, resident brewmaster, Baldwinsville, N.Y., 1982-84, Williamsburg, Va., 1984-87; v.p. bakers yeast divsn. Anheuser-Busch Indsl. Products Corp., St. Louis, 1987-88, dir. brewing ops., 1988-89; sr. brewmaster Anheuser-Busch, Ft. Collins, Colo., 1989-99; brewing cons., 1999—. Patentee in field. With USAF, 1962-65. Mem. Master Brewers Assn. Am. (pres., nat. bd. govs.), Am. Soc. Brewing Chemists, Internat. Food Tech. Assocs., Aircraft Owners and Pilots Assn., U.S. Pilots Assn. Avocation: flying. Home and Office: 1417 N County Rd # 3 Fort Collins CO 80524-9312

WAX, ARNOLD, physician; b. Bklyn., Mar. 11, 1949; s. Emanuel and Eleanor (Greenfield) W.; m. Francine Wax; children: Erin, Rachael, Adam, Benjamin. BS in Pharm. Scis., Columbia U., 1971; MD, SUNY, Buffalo, 1976. Diplomate Nat. Bd. Med. Examiners, Am. Bd. Internal Medicine, Am. Bd. Quality Assurance and Utilization Rev. Physicians, Am. Acad. Pain Mgmt.; lic. physician, Fla., Calif., N.D., Minn., N.Y., Nev., Ariz. Intern, resident Millard Fillmore Hosp., Buffalo, 1976-79; clin. asst. instr. SUNY, 1977-79; instr. medicine U. Rochester, N.Y., 1979-81; dir. internal medicine U. N.D., Grand Forks, 1982-83, clin. asst. prof., 1982-85; pvt. practice Las Vegas, Nev., 1987—; mem. staff Sunrise Hosp., Las Vegas, Desert Springs Hosp., Las Vegas, Nathan Adelson Hospice, Las Vegas. Contbr. articles to profl. jours. Grantee So. Nev. Cancer Rsch. Found., Ea. Coop. Oncology Group, Gynecol. Oncology Group, North Ctrl. Cancer Treatment Group, S.W. Oncology Group. Fellow Am. Coll. Physicians; mem. AMA, Am. Cancer Soc. (fellow 1979), Am. Soc. Clin. Oncology, Am. Coun. Physicians (gov. State of Nev.), Nev. Oncology So. (v.p.), Nev. Med. Soc., Clark County Med. Soc. (trustee, peer rev. com., treas.), Nev. Peer Rev. Orgn., U. Nev. Las Vegas Found., Nev. Dance Theater, Nev. Opera Theater, Las Vegas Symphony, Nev. Inst. Contemporary Art, Lied Mus., Allied Arts Coun., James Platt White Soc., U. Buffalo Found., Rho Chi (Bronze medal 1971). Home: 2224 Chatsworth Ct Henderson NV 89014-5309 Office: 3920 S Eastern Ave Ste 202 Las Vegas NV 89119-5171

WAX, STEPHEN MARTIN, personal manager; b. Queens, N.Y., Jan. 31, 1943; s. Walter and Theresa (Bonnet) W.; m. Roberta Stepel, Mar. 27, 1965 (div. Jan. 1985); children: Lisa, Jody. BBA, Pace Coll., 1964. Dir. nat. promotions Bell Records, N.Y.C., 1968-73; pres. Elektra Asylum Records, L.A., 1973-79; music cons. Warner Bros. Pictures, Burbank, Calif., 1979-83; cons. to Jose Menedez RCA, Hollywood, Calif., 1983-85; personal mgr. Stiletto Mgmt., L.A., 1985—. Mem. NARAS, ASCAP, BMI.

WAXMAN, HENRY ARNOLD, congressman; b. Los Angeles, Sept. 12, 1939; s. Louis and Esther (Silverman) W.; m. Janet Kessler, Oct. 17, 1971; children: Carol Lynn, Michael David. B.A. in Polit. Sci. UCLA, 1961, J.D., 1964. Bar: Calif. 1965. Mem. Calif. State Assembly, 1969-74, chmn. com. on health, until 1994; mem. 94th-104th Congresses from 24th (now 29th) Calif. dist., 1975—, ranking minority mem. house subcom. on health and environment, 1979—, mem. govt. reform & oversight com., mem. commerce com. Pres. Calif. Fedn. Young Democrats, 1965-67. Mem. Calif. Bar Assn., Guardians Jewish Home for Aged, Am. Jewish Congress, Sierra Club, B'nai B'rith, Phi Sigma Alpha. Office: US Ho of Reps 2204 Rayburn HOB Washington DC 20515-0529*

WAYBURN, EDGAR, internist, environmentalist; b. Macon, Ga., Sept. 17, 1906; s. Emanuel and Marian (Voorsanger) W.; m. Cornelia Elliott, Sept. 12, 1947; children: Cynthia, William, Diana, Laurie. AB magna cum laude, U. Ga., 1926; MD cum laude, Harvard U., 1930. Hosp. tng. Columbia-Presbyn. Hosp., N.Y.C., 1931-33; assoc. clin. prof. Stanford (Calif.) U., 1933-65, U. Calif., San Francisco, 1960-76; practice medicine specializing in internal medicine San Francisco, 1933-1985; mem. staff Pacific Presbyn. Med. Ctr., San Francisco, 1959-86, chief endocrine clinic, 1959-72, vice chief staff, 1961-63, hon. staff, 1986—. Editor: Man Medicine and Ecology, 1970; contbr. articles to profl. and environ. jours. Mem. Sec. of Interior's Adv. Bd. on Nat. Park System, 1979-83, commn. on nat. parks and protected areas Internat. Union for Conservation Nature and Natural Resources; leader nat. campaigns Alaska Nat. Interest Lands Conservation Act; trustee Pacific Presbyn. Med. Ctr., 1978-86; chmn. People For a Golden Gate Nat. Recreation Area, 1971—; mem. citizens' adv. commn. Golden Gate Nat. Recreation Area, San Francisco, 1974—, leader nat. campaigns, 1978-86; prin. citizen advocate Redwood Nat. Park, 1968, 78; dir. The Antarctica Project; mem. adv. bd. Pacific Forest Trust; hon. chmn. Tuolomne River Preservation Trust; bd. dirs. Garden Sullivan Hosp., 1965-78; prin. adv. Enlargement of Mt. Tamal Pais State Pk.; leader campaign to establish Golden Gate Nat. Recreation Area, 1972. Maj. USAF, 1942-46. Recipient Douglas award Nat. Pks. and Conservation Assn., 1987, Leopold award Calif. Nature Conservancy, 1988, Fred Packard award Internat. Union Conservation Nature, 1994, Laureate of Global 500 Roll of Honour award U.N. Environment Programme, 1994, 1st Conservation award Ecotrust, 1994, Albert Schweitzer prize, 1995. Fellow ACP; mem. AMA, Am. Soc. Internal Medicine, Calif. Med. Assn. (del. 1958-83, Recognition award 1986, Leadership and Quality awards 1986), San Francisco Med. Soc. (pres. 1965, Resolution of Congratulations 1986), Sierra Club (pres. 1961-64, 67-69, John Muir award 1972, hon. pres. 1993), Sierra Club Found. (dir. 1960-87, pres. 1971-78, hon. pres. 1998—), Fedn. Western Outdoor Clubs (pres. 1953-55). Avocations: exploration, hiking. Home: 314 30th Ave San Francisco CA 94121-1705

WAYBURN, PEGGY (CORNELIA ELLIOTT WAYBURN), author, editor; b. N.Y.C., Sept. 2, 1917; d. Thomas Ketchin and Cornelia (Ligon) E.; m. Edgar Wayburn Sept. 12, 1947; children: Cynthia, William, Diana, Laurie. BA cum laude, Barnard, 1942. Copywriter Vogue Mag., N.Y.C., 1943-45, J. Walter Thompson, San Francisco, 1945-47; self employed freelance writer, San Francisco, 1948—; Author: Adventuring in the San Francisco Bay Area, Adventuring in Alaska; (prize-winning audio visual series) Circle of Life; contbr. articles to mags. and profl. jours. Mem. bd. advisors Am. Youth Hostels; trustee Sierra Club Found. Recipient annual award Calif. Conservation Assn., 1966. Mem. Sierra Club (spl. svc. award 1967, women's award 1995), Phi Beta Kappa. Avocations: traveling, hiking, river-running. Home: 314 30th Ave San Francisco CA 94121-1705

WAYLAND, NEWTON HART, conductor; b. Santa Barbara, Calif., Nov. 5, 1940; s. L.C. Newton and Helen Bertha (Hart) W.; m. Judith Anne Curtis, July 3, 1969 (div. 1986). MusB, New Eng. Conservatory Music, 1964, MusM, 1966. Host, composer, performer Sta. WGBH-TV, Boston, 1963-82; pianist, harpsichordist Boston Symphony Orch., 1964-71; music dir. Charles Playhouse, 1965-67; pianist, guest condr., arranger Boston Pops Orch., 1971-74; resident Pops condr. Midwest Pops Orch., South Bend, Ind., 1979-91, Oakland Symphony Orch., Calif., 1980-85, Houston Symphony Orch., 1986-93; prin. Pops condr. Denver Symphony Orch., 1987-89, Vancouver (B.C.) Symphony Orch., 1993—; guest condr. numerous orchs. U.S. and Canada, 1977—. Recs. include: Music for Zoom (PBS Emmy-winning TV show), 1971-78, Music for Nova (award-winning PBS-TV show), 1972-78, America Swings, 1987, Gershwin Plays Gershwin, 1987, Pop Go the Beatles, 1987, Classical Jukebox, 1988, Stompin' at the Savoy, 1988, Sophisticated Ladies, 1988, A Touch of Fiedler, 1989, Prime Time, 1989; arranger, performer: Jazz Loves Bach, 1968, Fiedler in Rags, 1974; arranger, condr.: Berlin to Broadway with Kurt Weill, 1972; condr. Oedipus Tex (Grammy award 1991); arranger, composer, performer (songs A&M Records) Come On and Zoom, Zoom Tunes. Recipient highest honors New Eng. Conservatory Music, 1974, Chadwick Disting. Achievement medal New Eng. Conservatory Music, 1966. Avocations: hiking, history, theatre. Home and Office: 2970 Hidden Valley Ln Santa Barbara CA 93108-1619

WAYMAN, COOPER HARRY, environmental legal counsel; b. Trenton, N.J., Jan. 29, 1927; s. Cooper Ott and Helen Viola (Unverzagt) W.; m. Ruth Treier, June 16, 1951; children: Carol Beth Withers, Andrea Lee Daschbach. BS, Rutgers U., 1951; MS, U. Pitts., 1954; PhD, Mich. State U., 1959; JD, U. Denver, 1967. Bar: Colo. 1969, Tex. 1972; registered profl. engr., Colo.; cert. real estate broker, Colo.; cert. and registered environ. mgr. Rsch. chemist U.S. Geol. Survey, Lakewood, Colo., 1960-65; assoc. prof. chemistry Colo. Sch. Mines, Golden, 1965-70; regional counsel EPA, Dallas, 1971-74; asst. to regional adminstr. EPA, Denver, 1974-83; exec. asst. to mayor City of Denver, 1981-85; dir. environment compliance Cord Labs., Inc., Broomfield, Colo., 1986-88; environ. and permits mgr. Chem. Waste Mgmt. Inc., Port Arthur, Tex., 1988-92; regional regulatory mgr. Chem. Waste Mgmt., Inc., Houston, 1992-94; compliance branch mgr. Adv. Scis., Inc., Carlsbad, N.Mex., 1994-95; area office legal counsel Waste Isolation Project, Dept. Energy, Carlsbad, N.Mex., 1995—, lead counsel WIPP litigation team; dir. energy office EPA, Denver, 1974-78; adj. prof. law U. Denver, 1981-84; mem. State of Colo. Air Pollution Commn., Denver, 1969-70. Author: Detergents and Environment, 1965, Permits Handbook for Coal Development, 1981; contbr. 60 articles to profl. jours. With USNR, 1945-46. Grantee U.S. Fish and Wildlife Svc., 1967; fellow, rsch. assoc. MIT, 1956-58. Fellow Am. Inst. Chemists, 1993. Avocations: skiing, golf, photography, art. Home: 901 Fountain Dr Carlsbad NM 88220-3073 Office: US Dept Energy Carlsbad Area Office PO Box 3090 Carlsbad NM 88221-3090

WAYMAN, MORRIS, chemical engineering educator, consultant; b. Toronto, Can., Mar. 19, 1915; s. Harry and Martha (Alt) W.; m. Sara Gertrude Zadkin; children: Michael Lash, Thomas Ethan; m. Mary Chabot. B.A., U. Toronto, 1936, M.A., 1937, Ph.D., 1941. Registered profl. engr., Ont. Researcher Can. Internat. Paper Co., Hawkesbury, Ont., 1942-52; tech. dir. Columbia Cellulose Co., Prince Rupert, B.C., 1958-63; prof. chem. engring. U. Toronto, 1963-93, prof. forestry, 1973-93; pres. Morris Wayman, Ltd., Toronto, 1966—; adj. prof. chem. engring. U. Alberta, 1993—; cons., Can., U.S., Brazil, Sweden, UN. Author: Guide for Planning Pulp and Paper Enterprises, 1973, Wealth and Welfare, 1978, Biotechnology of Biomass Conversion: fuels and chemicals from renewable resources, 1990; contbr. numerous articles to sci. jours.; patentee in field. Mem. Ont. Waste Mgmt. Adv. Bd., 1975-80, Edmonton Philharm Orch. Hon. fellow Innis Coll., Toronto, 1977. Fellow AAAS, Royal Soc. Can., Chem. Inst. Can.; mem. Can. Wood Chemistry Symposium (chmn. 1979-82), Sigma Xi.

WAYNE, KYRA PETROVSKAYA, writer; b. Crimea, USSR, Dec. 31, 1918; came to U.S., 1948, naturalized, 1951; d. Prince Vasily Sergeyevich and Baroness Zinaida Fedorovna (Fon-Haffenberg) Obolensky; m. George J. Wayne, Apr. 21, 1961; 1 child, Ronald George. BA, Leningrad Inst. Theatre Arts, 1939, MA, 1940. Actress, concert singer, USSR, 1939-46, actress, U.S., 1948-59; enrichment lectr. Royal Viking Line cruises, Alaska-Can., Greek Islands-Black Sea, Russia/Europe, 1978-79, 81-82, 83-84, 86-87, 88. Author: Kyra, 1959, Kyra's Secrets of Russian Cooking, 1960, 93, The Quest for the Golden Fleece, 1962, Shurik, 1971, 92, The Awakening, 1972, The Witches of Barguzin, 1975, Max, The Dog That Refused to Die, 1979 (Best Fiction award Dog Writers Assn. Am. 1980); Rekindle the Dreams, 1979, Quest for Empire, 1986, Li'l Ol' Charlie, 1989, Quest for Bigfoot, 1996. Founder, pres. Clean Air Program, Los Angeles County, 1971-72; mem. women's coun. KCET-Ednl. TV; mem. Monterey County Symphony Guild, 1989-91, Monterey Bay Aquarium, Monterey Peninsula Mus. Art, Friends of La Mirada, Fresno Art Mus., Fresno Met. Mus., Valley Children's Hosp. Served to lt. Russian Army, 1941-43. Decorated Red Star, numerous other decorations USSR; recipient award Crusade for Freedom, 1955-56; award Los Angeles County, 1972, Merit award Am. Lung Assn. L.A. County, 1988. Mem. Soc. Children's Book Writers, Authors Guild, P.E.N., UCLA Med. Faculty Wives (pres. 1970-71, dir. 1971-75) UCLA Affiliates (life), L.A. Lung Assn. (life), Friends of the Lung Assn. (pres. 1988), Carmel Music Soc. (bd. dirs. 1992-94), Idyllwild Sch. Music, Art and Theatre Assn. (trustee 1987), Los Angelenos Club (life), Fresno Philharmonic Condr.'s Cir., Fresno Philharmonic Women's League. Home: 561 E Mariners Cir Fresno CA 93720-0848

WAYNE, PHILIP LOUIS, costume designer; b. Burbank, Calif., Feb. 3, 1952; s. Philip J. and Ellen Margaret (O'Connor) W. AA, Los Angeles Valley Coll., Van Nuys, Calif., 1973. Freelance designer and costumer various studios, L.A., 1971-79; staff costumer ABC-TV, L.A., 1979-92; costume supr. ABC-TV Gen. Hosp., L.A., 1992—. Costume designer A Touch of the Poet, 1974; costume supr. Early AM, 1989 (Emmy Nomination), AM L.A., 1988-91. Recipient Outstanding Contbn. award Permanent Charities, L.A., 1992, awards for costume design and supervision. Mem. Acad. TV Arts and Scis. (peer group exec. 1994—). Republican. Roman Catholic. Avocations: genealogical research, photography. Home: 6843 Teesdale Ave North Hollywood CA 91605-5313 Offie: Sta ABC-TV 4151 Prospect Ave Los Angeles CA 90027-4524

WEAGRAFF, PATRICK JAMES, psychology educator, writer; b. Buffalo, May 27, 1940; s. Harry Edward and Donnabelle (O'Brien) W.; children from a previous marriage: Michael, Patrick Jr., Kim Marie, Susan Lynn; m. Sandra Weagraff; 1 stepchild, Nicholas Turner. BS, SUNY, Buffalo, 1963; MEd, U. Md., 1965; EdD, UCLA, 1970, PhD, 1971. Cert. psychology, post secondary edn., secondary edn., ednl. adminstrn., drug and alcohol counseling. Assoc. dir. U.S. Peace Corps, Lagos, Nigeria, 1965-68; ednl. adminstr. Calif. Dept. Edn., Sacramento, 1971-75; assoc. commr. edn. Mass. Dept. Edn., Boston, 1975-76; psychologist Sierra View Mental Health, Auburn, Calif., 1978-81; chief clin. svcs. Calif. Dept. Mental Health, Sacramento, 1981-93; clin. dir. St. Joseph's Hosp., Stockton, Calif., 1993-95; prof. psychology Profl. Sch. Psychology, Sacramento, 1993-98; assoc. prof. Nat. U., Stockton, Calif., 1983—. Author 9 books including Careers in Focus, 1993, Communications, 1993, Public Service Occupations, 1993, Construction Occupations, 1993, Decision Making, 1995, Making Decisions Work, 1997. Trustee Crossroads Inc., Sacramento, 1982-90; bd. dirs. Golden Empire Scouts, Sacramento, 1985-91; trustee Western Inst. Therapeutic Studies, 1996—. Edn. Profession Devel. Act fellow UCLA, 1970. Mem. Phi Delta Kappa, Epsilon Pi Tau. Jewish. Avocation: classic cars. Home: 9229 Cambra Ct Elk Grove CA 95758-4013

WEAKLAND, ANNA WU, artist, art educator; b. Shanghai, China, May 1, 1924; came to the U.S., 1947; d. Tse-Chien and Kwei-Ying (Sze) Wu; m. John H. Weakland, Feb. 11, 1950; children: Alan Wade, Lewis Francis, Joan. BA, U. Shanghai, China, 1943; MA, Columbia U., 1948; postgrad., Stanford U., 1953-55. art instr. U. Calif., 1968, 72, 78, 82, 84, Stanford (Calif.) U., 1990; vis. art prof. Zhejiang Acad. Arts, Hangzhou, China, 1991. One-woman shows include De Young Mus., San Francisco, 1959, San Francisco Mus. Modern Art, 1961, Chathan Gallery, Hong Kong, 1963, Seattle Art Mus., 1964, Ashmolian Mus., Oxford, Eng., 1964, Sale Internat./Palacio De Bellas, Mexico City, 1966, Downtown Gallery, N.Y., 1967, Victoria (Can.) Art Mus., 1967, Heritage Gallery, L.A., 1971, Wells Fargo Bank Hdqs., San Francisco, 1973, Macy's, Palo Alto, 1976, I. Magnin, Palo Alto, 1981, Tresidor Union Gallery, Stanfor U., 1982, Palo Alto (Calif.) Med. Found., 1984, Stanford (Calif.) Mus. Art, 1988, Hewlett-Packard Co. Art Gallery, Palo Alto, 1989, Gump's Art Gallery, San Francisco, 1990, Marin County Civic Ctr., San Rafael, Calif., 1994; represented in permanent collections including Ashmolean Mus., Oxford, Eng., U. B.C., Vancouver, Fukuoka (Japan) U., Stanford U., Seattle (Wash.) Art Mus., IBM Corp., others. Named Artist of the Yr., Friends of The Libr. award, Palo Alto, Calif., 1979, Artist of the Month, No. Calif. Home and Garden Mag., Redwood City, Calif., 1992. Mem. Am. Women Caucas for Art, Asian Am. Women Artists Assn. Avocations: music, tennis, aerobic dancing, cooking, photography. Home: 4245 Manuela Ct Palo Alto CA 94306-3731

WEART, WENDELL D., nuclear waste management scientist; b. Brandon, Iowa, Sept. 24, 1932; s. J. Everett and Mary E. W.; m. Nancy Ruth Andress, June 31, 1954; children: Brian, Kathleen, Craig; m. Leanne L. Jercinovic, Aug. 8, 1981; children: Randy, Scott, Heather. BA, Cornell Coll., 1953; PhD, U. Wis., 1961. From mem. staff to sr. fellow Sandia Nat. Lab., Albuquerque, 1959-98, sr. scientist, 1995-97, sr. fellow, 1997—. Mem. Am. Geophysical Union. Avocations: photography. E-mail: wdullweart@msn.com. Home: 5500 Edwards Dr NE Albuquerque NM 87111-1985 Office: Sandia Nat Lab Albuquerque NM 87185-0771

WEATHERHEAD, LESLIE R., lawyer; b. Tacoma, Sept. 28, 1956; s. A. Kingsley and Ingrid A. (Lien) W.; m. Anali C. Torrado, June 24, 1985; children: Spencer, Madeleine, Audrey. BA, U. Oreg., 1977; JD, U. Wash., 1980. Bar: Wash. 1980, Oreg. 1996, U.S. Ct. Appeals (9th cir.) 1981, U.S. Dist. Ct. (ea. dist.) Wash. 1984, U.S. Ct. Internat. Trade 1984, Hawaii 1987, U.S. Dist. Ct. (we. dist.) Wash. 1989, Idaho 1989, U.S. Dist. Ct. Idaho 1989, U.S. Supreme Ct. 1994, Colville Tribal Ct. 1993, U.S. Ct. Apeals (10th cir.) 1995, U.S. Ct. Fed. Claims 1995. Asst. terr. prosecutor Territory of Guam, Agana, 1980-83; spl. asst. U.S. Atty. Dist. of Guam and No. Marianas, Agana, 1982-83; atty. Witherspoon, Kelley, Davenport & Toole, Spokane, 1984—; lawyer-rep. 9th cir. jud. conf., 1989-95, lawyer-rep. chmn., 1995; adj. faculty Gonzaga U. Sch. of Law, 1994-95. Contbr. articles on Indian law and administrv. investigations to profl. jours. Bd. dirs. Spokane Uptown Opera, 1989-96, pres., 1992-94. Mem. ABA, Fed. Bar Assn. (pres. ea. dist. 1996-97), Hawaii Bar Assn., Idaho Bar Assn., Wash. State Bar Assn., Oreg. State Bar Assn. Avocations: sailing, scuba, skiing. Office: Witherspoon Kelley Davenport & Toole 428 W Riverside Ave Spokane WA 99201-0301

WEATHERLEY-WHITE, ROY CHRISTOPHER ANTHONY, surgeon, consultant; b. Peshawar, India, Dec. 1, 1931; S. Roy and Elfreda (Milward) Boehm, m. Dorian Jeanne Freeman Weatherley-White, Dec. 27, 1961; children: Carl Christopher, Matthew Richard, Larissa Chantal. MA, Cambridge U., 1953; MD, Harvard U., 1958. Surgeon Biomedical Cons., Denver, 1970—; pres. Plastic Surgery Group, Denver, 1992-97; chmn. Plastic Surgery Rsch. Coun., 1975-76; pres. Rocky Mountain Assn. Plastic Surgeons, 1973-74; v.p. Am. Cleft Palate Assn. Author: Plastic Surgeru of the Female Breast, 1982; contbr. over 45 articles to profl. jours. Cons. Colo. Biomedical Venture Ctr., Denver, 1993—. Recipient Rsch. award Am. Soc. Plastic Surgery, 1962, 64. Mem. Harvard Club of N.Y., Oxford-Cambridge Club, Denver Country Club, Denver Athletic Club. Episcopalian. Avocations: flying, skiing, scuba diving, archaeology. Home: 100 S Humboldt St Denver CO 80209-2516 Office: Plastic Surgery Group 4500 E 9th Ave Ste 470 Denver CO 80220-3923*

WEATHERUP, ROY GARFIELD, lawyer; b. Annapolis, Md., Apr. 20, 1947; s. Robert Alexander and Kathryn Crites (Hesser) W.; m. Wendy Gaines, Sept. 10, 1977; children: Jennifer, Christine. AB in Polit. Sci., Stanford U., 1968, JD, 1972. Bar: Calif. 1972, U.S. Dist. Ct. 1973, U.S. Ct. Appeals (9th cir.) 1975, U.S. Supreme Ct. 1980. Assoc. Haight, Brown & Bonesteel, L.A., Santa Monica and Santa Ana, Calif., 1972-78, ptnr., 1979—; judge Moot Ct. UCLA, Loyola U., Pepperdine U.; arbitrator Am. Arbitration Assn.; mem. com. Book Approved Jury Instructions L.A. Superior Ct. Mem. ABA, Calif. Acad. Appellate Lawyers, Town Hall Calif., L.A. County Bar Assn. Republican. Methodist. Home: 17260 Rayen St Northridge CA 91325-2919 Office: Haight Brown & Bonesteel PO Box 680 1620 26th St Ste 4000 Santa Monica CA 90404-4060

WEAVER, BETH ANN, sales manager; b. Danville, Ill., Feb. 27, 1958; d. John Francis and Margaret Ann (Orr) Bjorback; m. Mark M. Weaver, Feb. 2, 1980; 1 child, Bailey Alexandra. BS, U. Mo., 1989. Paralegal Gray Plant Mooty Mooty, Mpls., 1986-87, Bryan Cave, St. Louis, 1987-90; sales mgr. Weekender Casual Wear, Chgo., 1993—. Com. chair Danville-Alamo Newcomers, Danville, 1994, chair programs and luncheons, 1995. Mem. AAUW, Women's Network Contra Costa County. Avocations: gourmet cooking, tennis, reading.

WEAVER, ERIC GORDON, fitness trainer, nutrition consultant; b. San Gabriel, Calif., Apr. 24, 1971; s. Thomas Gordon Weaver and Melody Ann Martyn; 1 child, Austinn Pierce Weaver. Student, Citrus Coll., Glendora, Calif., 1990, 92. Cert. personal trainer. Owner Get-Fit Personal Tng., Torrance, Calif., 1989—; trainer L.A. Fitness, Pomona, Calif., 1989-90; with sales dept. Bulldog Gym, Irwindale, Calif., 1990-91; mgr. Family Fitness Ctr., Industry, Calif., 1991-94, Powerhouse Gym, Rancho Palos Verdes, Calif., 1994-95. Republican. Avocations: roller blading, snow skiing, video games, golf, body building. Office: Get-Fit PO Box 783 Redondo Beach CA 90277-0783

WEAVER, HOWARD C., newspaper executive; b. Anchorage, Oct. 15, 1950; s. Howard Gilbert and Lurlene Eloise (Gamble) W.; m. Alice Laprele Gauchay, July 16, 1970 (div. 1974); m. Barbara Lynn Hodgin, Sept. 16, 1978. BA, Johns Hopkins U., 1972; MPhil, Cambridge U., 1993. Reporter, staff writer Anchorage Daily News, 1972-76, columnist, 1979-80, mng. editor, 1980-83, editor, 1983-95; editor, owner Alaska Advocate, Anchorage, 1976-79; asst. to pres., McClatchy Newspapers, 1995-97, editor of editl. pages, 1997—; internat. co-chair Northern News Svc., 1989-94; disting. lectr. journalism U. Alaska, Fairbanks, 1991. Pulitzer Prize juror, 1988, 89, 94, 95. Recipient Pulitzer prize, 1976, 89, Pub. Svc. award AP Mng. Editor's Assn., 1976, 89, Headliner award Press Club of Atlantic City, 1976, 89, Gold medal Investigative Reporters and Editors, 1989. Mem. Am. Soc. Newspaper Editors, Investigative Reporters and Editors, Sigma Delta Chi (Nat. award 1989), Alaska Press Club (bd. dirs. 1972-84), Upper Yukon River Press Club (pres. 1972). Avocations: ice hockey, foreign travel, opera.

WEAVER, JUDITH A., museum director. Acting dir. Mus. of the Rockies, Bozeman, Mont. Office: Mus of the Rockies care Mont State U Bozeman MT 59717-0272*

WEAVER, MAX KIMBALL, social worker, consultant; b. Price, Utah, Apr. 4, 1941; s. Max Dickson and Ruth (Kimball) W.; m. Janet Hofheins, Sept. 13, 1963; children: Kim, Cleve, Chris, Wendy, Michael, Amyanne, Heather. Student, So. Utah State Coll., 1959-60; BS, Brigham Young U., 1965; MSW, U. Utah, 1967. Lic. clin. social worker and marriage counselor, Utah. Cons. Utah State Tng. Sch. (now Devel. Ctr.), American Fork, 1966; dir. Dept. Pub. Welfare, Cedar City, Utah, 1967-70; social worker Latter Day St. Social Services, Cedar City, 1970-75; with Mental Retardation Devel. Disabled Adult Services Dept. Social Services, Cedar City, 1975—; cons. nursing homes, Utah, 1974-95; tchr. So. Utah State Coll., Cedar City, 1972, 77; home health social worker, 1993—. Contbr. articles to mags. Pres. Am. Little League Baseball, 1977-84, 86, Cedar High Booster Club, 1984-95; chmn. Rep. Precinct #1, 1984; v.p. Big League Baseball, 1986-95. Recipient Silver Beaver award, 1996. Mem. Nat. Assn. Social Work (nominating com., licensing com.), Am. Pub. Welfare Assn., Utah Pub. Employees Assn. Mormon. Lodge: Rotary. Avocations: reading, sports, scouting, gardening. Home: 157 Rountree Dr Cedar City UT 84720-3532 Office: Dept Social Svcs 106 N 100 E Cedar City UT 84720-2608

WEAVER, MICHAEL JAMES, lawyer; b. Bakersfield, Calif., Feb. 11, 1946; s. Kenneth James and Elsa Hope (Rogers) W.; m. Valerie Scott, Sept. 2, 1966; children: Christopher James, Brett Michael, Karen Ashley. AB, Calif. State U., Long Beach, 1968; JD magna cum laude, U. San Diego, 1973. Bar: Calif., 1973, U.S. Dist. Ct. (so. dist.) Calif. 1973, U.S. Ct. Appeals (9th cir.) 1975, U.S. Supreme Ct. 1977. Law clk. to chief judge U.S. Dist. Ct. (so. dist.) Calif., San Diego, 1973-75; assoc. Luce, Forward, Hamilton & Scripps, San Diego, 1975-80, ptnr., 1980-86; ptnr. Sheppard, Mullin, Richter & Hampton, San Diego, 1986-99, Latham & Watkins, San Diego, 1999—; judge pro tem San Diego Superior Ct.; master of the Bench of the Inn, Am. Inns of Ct., Louis M. Welch chpt.; lectr. Inn of Ct., San Diego, 1981—, Continuing Edn. of Bar, Calif., 1983—, Workshop for Judges U.S. Ct. Appeals (9th cir.), 1990; mem. task force on establishment of bus. cts. sys. Jud. Coun. Calif., 1996-97. Editor-in-chief: San Diego Law Rev., 1973; contbr. articles to profl. jours. Bd. dirs., pres. San Diego Kidney

Found., 1985-90; bd. dirs. San Diego Aerospace Mus., 1985-97; trustee La Jolla (Calif.) Playhouse, 1990-91. Served to lt. USNR, 1968-74. Fellow Am. Coll. Trial Lawyers; mem. San Diego Assn. Bus. Trial Lawyers (founding mem., bd. govs.), San Diego Def. Lawyers Assn. (dir.), Am. Arbitration Assn., 9th Cir. Jud. Conf. (del. 1987-90), Safari Club Internat. (San Diego chpt.), San Diego Sportsmen's Club. Republican. Presbyterian. Avocations: reading, family activities, flying, skiing. Office: Latham & Watkins 701 B St Ste 2100 San Diego CA 92101

WEAVER, ROGER KEYS, retired English language educator; b. Portland, Oreg., Feb. 2, 1935; s. Glen Leon and Effie Winbern (Keys) W.; m. Sharron Louise Beckett, June 23, 1962 (div. Jan. 1974); children: Eric Beckett, Roger Kevin. BA, U. Oreg., 1957, MFA, 1967; MA, U. Wash., 1962. Mem. faculty Oreg. State U., Corvallis, 1962-96, prof. English emeritus, 1996—. Author: (books of poetry) The Orange and Other Poems, 1967, 21 Waking Dreams, 1976, Traveling on The Great Wheel, 1991. Founder non-profit orgn. Poetry Enterprises, Corvallis, 1996. Mem. Lions. Mem. Soc. of Friends. Avocation: gardening. Home: 712 NW 13th St Corvallis OR 97330-5953

WEAVER, ROY A., national monument officer. Supt. Bandelier Nat. Monument, Los Alamos, N.Mex. Office: Bandelier Nat Monument HCR1 Box 1 Ste #15 Los Alamos NM 87544-9701*

WEAVER, SARA LEE, sales executive; b. Jefferson City, Mo., Apr. 4, 1962; d. Thomas Henry and Majorie Gwendolyn (Jones) W. BJ, BA, U. Mo., 1984; student, U. London, 1980, Université Laval, 1983. Sales asst. Katz Communications, Dallas, 1985-87, Chgo., 1987-88; media systems trainer Katz Communications, N.Y.C., 1988-90; sales exec. Katz Communications, Chgo., 1990-94, Sta. KGO-TV, San Francisco, 1994-97, ABC Nat. TV Sales, San Francisco, 1998—. Bd. dirs. Art Span, San Francisco, Scottish Games, Oakland, Calif.; pres. ArtSpan, San Francisco; mem. Scottish Dance Performance Team. Mem. AAUW (v.p. membership San Francisco br.), Omicron Delta Kappa, Sigma Rho Sigma, Kappa Epsilon Alpha, Pi Beta Phi. Democrat. Presbyterian. Avocations: bicycling, snow skiing, reading, golf, Scottish country dancing. Office: ABC Nat TV Sales 900 Front St San Francisco CA 94111-1427

WEAVER, VELATHER EDWARDS, small business owner; d. Willie and Ethel Edwards; m. Ellerson Weaver; children: Frank Mattox Jr., Terence Mattox, Christopher Williams, Sharon, Shelley, Stephanie. Student, Sonoma State Coll., 1972, U. Calif., Berkeley, 1972; BA, Calif. State U., Hayward, 1973; MBA, St. Mary's Coll., Moraga, Calif., 1989. Coach, counselor Opportunities Industrialization Ctr., Oakland, Calif., 1967-69; tchr. Berkeley Headstart, 1969-70; instr., cons. external degree program Antioch Coll.-West, San Francisco, 1971-74; market analyst World Airways, Inc., Oakland, 1972-75, affirmative action adminstr., 1975-78; cons. A.C. Transit, Oakland, 1982; owner, mgr. Val's Designs and Profl. Svcs., Lafayette, Calif., 1980—; mgr. adminstrn., tng. supr. North Oakland Pharmacy, Inc., 1970—, also bd. dirs.; adv. bd. The Tribune, Oakland, 1982-88. Author RAPRO Self Mgmt. Program, 1985. Program coord., mem. publicity com. Lafayette Arts and Sci. Found., 1982-83; mem. admission bd. St. Mary's Coll. Grad. Sch. Bus., 1990; bd. dirs. Acalanes H.S., Lafayette, 1980-82, Lafayette Elem. Sch., 1975-80; mem. Lafayette Econ. Devel. Task Force, 1994-95; vice chmn. Lafayette Econ. Devel. Commn., 1995—. Mem. Calif. State Pharmacists Assn. Aux. (pres. Contra Costa Aux. 1980, pres. state aux. 1986-88, recognition award 1987), Calif. Pharmacists Polit. Action Com. (appreciation award 1988), Diablo Valley Bus. and Profl. Women (pub. rels. com. 1986-87, best local orgn. award 1987, author yearbook 1987), No. Calif. Med., Dental and Pharm. Assn. Aux. (bd. dirs., com. chair 1975—, pres. elect 1991, pres. 1991-93), Internat. Platform Assn., Links, Inc. Avocations: reading, researching family businesses, travel, attending auctions. Office: North Oakland Pharmacy Inc 5705 Market St Emeryville CA 94608-2811

WEAVER, WILLIAM BRUCE, astronomer, operations analyst; b. Catskill, N.Y., Sept. 1, 1946; s. William Ray and Bette (Martino) W.; m. Sandra Dale Wilford, Feb. 1967; children: Cristina Dawn, Robert Bruce Glen. BS, U. Ariz., 1968; MS, Case Inst. Tech., 1971; PhD, Case Western Res. U., 1972. Astronomer Montery (Calif.) Inst. for Rsch. in Astronomy, 1972—, dir., 1985—; sr. prin. staff BDM, Monterey, 1973—. Contbr. articles to books and profl. jours. NSF fellow, 1968-72. Fellow Royal Astron. Soc.; mem. Am. Astron. Soc., Internat. Astron. Soc., Astron. Soc. of Pacific. Avocations: orchids, wine, cooking. Office: Montery Inst Rsch Astronomy 200 8th St Marina CA 93933-6002

WEAVER, WILLIAM SCHILDECKER, electric power industry executive; b. Pitts., Jan. 15, 1944; s. Charles Henry and Louise (Schildecker) W.; m. Janet Kae Jones, Mar. 7, 1981. BA, Hamilton Coll., 1965; JD, U. Mich., 1968. Bar: Wash. 1968. Assoc. Perkins Coie, Seattle, 1968-74; ptnr. Perkins COIE, Seattle, 1975-91; exec. v.p., CFO Puget Sound Power & Light Co., Bellevue, Wash., 1991-97; vice chmn., chmn. unregulated subsidiaries Puget Sound Energy, 1997—, pres., COO, 1997, pres., CEO, 1998—, also bd. dirs.; bd. dirs. Hydro Electric Devel. Co., Bellevue, Connex T, Inc., Seattle. Bd. dirs. Wash. Rsch. Coun., Seattle, 1991-97, chmn., 1995-97; trustee Seattle Repertory Theatre, 1992-95, Corp. Coun. Arts, 1995-98, Pacific Sci. Ctr., 1997—. Mem. ABA, Wash. State Bar Assn., Seattle Yacht Club, Rainier Club. Office: Puget Sound Energy PO Box 97034-obc- Bellevue WA 98009

WEBB, ANDREW HOWARD, minister; b. Monterey Park, Calif., Dec. 28, 1945; s. Samuel Gorden and Jeannie (Stewart) W.; m. Marjorie Jean Pattison, June 20, 1970; children: Karen Jean, James Patrick. AB, San Diego State U., 1968, MA, 1975; postgrad., Mennonite Brethren Bibl. Sem., 1982—. Ordained deacon, 1983, ordained to ministry Free Meth. Ch., 1983. Min. Christian edn. and outreach Modesto (Calif.) Free Meth. Ch., 1981-85; pastor Oak Ave Free Meth. Ch., Orangevale, Calif., 1985—; dir. children's ministry Calif. Conf., 1978-83, bd. adminstrn., 1983—, chair bd. Christian edn., 1983—. V.p. Inter-Faith Ministries, Modesto, 1985; pres. Lemon Grove (Calif.) Tchrs. Assn., 1972-74, Imperial Valley coun. Internat. Reading Assn., El Centro, Calif., 1969; bd. dirs. Empire Union Sch. Dist., Calif., 1979-83; pres. Twin Lakes Food Bank, 1988—. Mem. Nat. Assn. Evangelists (pres. Sacramento County chpt. 1989-92), Twin Lake Ministerial Assn. (pres. 1986-88), Wesleyan Theol. Soc., Kiwanis Internat. (life; past pres., past lt. gov.), Alpha Phi Omega, Alpha Delta. Home: 6218 Calgary Ave Sacramento CA 95841-2002 Office: 8790 Oak Ave Orangevale CA 95662-2449

WEBB, LEWIS M., retail executive; b. 1934. Owner Webb's Texaco Svc., Los Alamitos, Calif., 1960-72; pres. Bargain Rent-A-Car Inc., Cerritos, Calif., 1960—, L.M. Webb & Sons, Inc., Mission Viejo, Calif., 1988—; pres., CFO Webb Automotive Group, Inc., Cerritos, Calif., 1989—; pres. Buick Mart Inc., Cerritos, Cerritos Body Works, Inc., Irvine, Calif., Kit Fit Inc., Buena Park, Calif., Lew Webb's Irvine Toyota, Mr. Wheels Inc., Cerritos. Office: Webb Automotive Group Inc 44 Auto Center Dr Irvine CA 92618-2802

WEBB, WELLINGTON E., mayor; BA in Edn. Colo. State Coll., 1964, MA in Edn. Univ. No. Colo., 1970; teacher, 1964-76; elected Colo. House of Reps., 1972, 74, 76; regional dir. HEW, 1977-81, governor's cabinet, 1981-87; elected auditor City of Denver, 1987-91, mayor, 1991—. Chmn. U.S. Conf. of Mayor's Task Forces on Violence, 1993—. Office: Office of Mayor City & County Bldg Rm 350 1437 Bannock St Denver CO 80202-5337*

WEBBER, CHRIS, III (MAYCE EDWARD CHRISTOPHER WEBBER), professional basketball player; b. Detroit, Mar. 1, 1973; s. Mayce and Doris Webber. Student, U. Mich., 1991-93. Drafted Orlando (Fla.) Magic, 1993; forward Golden State Warriors, San Francisco, 1993-94, Washington Bullets, 1994-98, Sacramento Kings, 1998-. Founder Timeout Found. Drafted 1st round Orlando Magic, 1993, named Nat. H.S. Player of Yr., 1990-91, Mr. Basketball State of Mich., 1991, Coca-Cola Classic NBA Player of Yr., 1994, Brut Bullets Player of Yr., 1994-95, NBA All-Rookie 1st Team, 1994. Avocations: collecting signed historical documents of prominent African-Americans. Office: Sacremento Kings One Sports Parkway Sacremento CA 95834*

WEBBER, MARILYN ASPEN KAY, writer; b. Abilene, Tex., Nov. 22, 1961; d. [illegible] Journalism, U. Okla., 1984; MFA in Screen Writing, Am. Film Inst., 1991. Tchrs. asst. Tarleton State U., Stephenville, Tex., 1988-89; writer, assoc. producer AFI, L.A., 1989-91; TV animation writer Gunther-Wahl Prodns.-ABC, L.A., 1992, Ruby/Spears-ABC, L.A., 1993-94; TV writer children's programs ABC-Greengrass Prodns., L.A., 1993-94, CBS-Allegra Films, L.A., 1994; children's programs animation writer ABC, L.A., 1994; Saturday morning animation writer DIC Entertainment-ABC, L.A., 1994; cons., Tex., 1993. Writer: (screenplays) How to Kill Howie?, 1987 (best screenplay), Mouth of the Cat, 1993 (semi-finalist Am.'s best), Captain Zoom: Zoom On Trial; writer/dir. ind. film A Place Called Harmony. Mem. World Wildlife Fund, 1991; supporter Union Rescue Mission, L.A., 1991, Feed the Children, Oklahoma City, 1994, Habitat for Humanity Internat., Americus, Ga., 1994. Recipient Acad. award nomination Motion Picture Acad., 1992, Most Notable Children's Video award Am. Libr. Assn., 1993, nomination Humanitas, 1994, award for advancement of learning in broadcasting NEA, 1994. Episcopalian. Avocations: travel, portrait drawing, ice skating, sports, reading classic literature.

WEBBER, NANCY WILDERMUTH, artist, educator; b. St. Louis, Mo., May 14, 1937; d. Frederick A. and Myra (Leach) Wildermuth; 1 child, Sophia C. BA, Dominican Univ., 1959; MA, Pius XII Inst., Florence, Italy, 1961; MFA, Mills Coll., 1962. Prof. art L.A. Harbor Coll., Wilmington, Calif., 1965—; film instr. Orange Coast Coll., Costa Mesa, Calif., 1997—. Exhibited in solo exhibitions including Martin Schweig Gallery, St. Louis, 1989, Nat. Ctr. for Performing Arts, Bombay, India, 1990, The Palos Verdes Art Ctr Norris Gallery, 1994, Jr. Chamber of Commerce, L.A., 1995, SAFECO Ins. Fountain Calley, Calif., 1996, Exit Gallery, 1997, Agnes Gallery, 1998, Islip Art Mus., Long Island, N.Y., 1998, Irvine Fine Arts Ctr., Irvine, Calif., 1997, Jan Kesner Gallery, L.A., 1996, Univ. San Antonio Art Gallery, 1996, Houston Ctr. for Photography, 1995, Riverside Art Mus., 1995, The Armand Hammer Mus., 1995, and numerous others. Bd. dirs. Angels Gate Cultural Ctr., 1998; artist coun. mem. Long Beach Mus. of Art, 1998—. Recipient Visual Art award Metro Blue LIne Photo Mual, 1991, The J. Paul Getty Trust fund, 1992; Fulbright Hayes seminar, 1994. Mem. Mus. of Contemporary Art, L.A. County Mus. Art, Mus. of Latin Am. Art. Avocations: film history, film appreciation. Fax: 310-833-5831. Office: L A Harbor Coll 1111 Figueroa Pl Wilmington CA 90744-2311

WEBBER, PEGGY, actress, producer, director, writer; b. Laredo, Tex., Sept. 15, 1925; d. Mathew Edward and Margaret Ann (Pierce) Weber; m. Robert Sinskey, Aug. 8, 1951 (div. 1968); children: Teresa Dickinson, Patricia Wynn, Robert Marshall Jr.; m. Sean McClory, Mar. 17, 1983. Student, U. So. Calif., L.A., 1942-44; AA, CUESTA, 1973; student, Calif. Poly. U. Founder Calif. Artists Repertory and Radio Theater, 1972. Actress, writer, dir., prodr.: (TV drama) Treasures of Literature (Outstanding Prodn. award Acad. TV Arts and Scis., 1948-49); writer, dir., prodr. C.A.R.T., Mysteries in the Air; actress network radio, network and radio shows; actress: (films) Orson Welles' Macbeth, Hitchcock's The Wrong Man, Farrow's Submarine Command, others; exec. dir. 7 theatres. Recipient Ray Bradbury Creativity award Woodbury U., L.A., 1998, 24 nat. and internat. awards. Mem. AFTRA, SAG, Actors Equity Assn., PPB (bd. dirs.). Avocations: walking, history, genealogy, archaeology. Office: Calif Artists Repretory and Radio Theater 6612 Whitley Ter Los Angeles CA 90068-3221

WEBBER, WILLIAM DIDERICHSEN, clergyman; b. St. Charles, Ill., July 1, 1930; s. Leroy Dewey and Freda Franklina (Diderichsen) W.; m. Marilynn Joyce Carlson, June 15, 1952; children: Sharon Linnea Webber Scott, Stephen William. BA with honors, Wheaton (Ill.) Coll., 1952; MDiv, No. Bapt. Theol. Sem., 1955; D Ministry, Midwestern Theol. Sem., 1975. Ordained to ministry Am. Bapt. Chs., 1955. Sr. pastor First Bapt. Ch., Park Forest, Ill., 1960-66, University Heights Bapt. Ch., Springfield, Mo., 1966-77, Seattle First Bapt. Ch., 1977-79, First Bapt. Ch., Stockton, Calif., 1979-86; adminstr. Mt. Rubidoux Manor Retirement Community, Riverside, Calif., 1986—; pres. Am. Bapt. Chs. Ill. and Mo., 1974-75; exec. com. Am. Bapt. Chs. U.S.A., Valley Forge, Pa., 1980-86, Bapt. Internat. Ministries, Valley Forge, 1980-86; bd. dirs. Am. Bapt. Chs. of Pacific S.W. Calif., Hawaii, Ariz., 1989-90. Author plays: Is It I, Lord, 1987, Robrt Rackes, Isaac Bachus. Mem. Downtown Adv. Com., Riverside, 1990—. Named Pastor of Yr., Coun. Am. Bapt. Men, Chgo., 1960. Mem. Am. Assn. Homes for the Aging, Am. Bapt. Homes and Hosps., Calif. Assn. Homes for the Aging. Home: 275 Celeste Dr Riverside CA 92507-3118 Office: Mt Rubidoux Manor 3993 10th St Riverside CA 92501-3574

WEBER, ALOIS HUGHES, principal; b. Clay County, Mo., Dec. 19, 1910; d. William Swan and Nora Mildred (Elam) Hughes; m. Frank Thomas Ewing Weber, May 28, 1934 (dec. 1980); children: Patricia Katherine Weber Brusuelas, Susan Weber Mills. BA, William Jewell Coll., Liberty, Mo., 1932; MA, U. Mo., Kansas City, 1971. Elem. prin. Linden (Mo.) Sch. Dist. #72, 1931-34; elem. tchr. Eugene (Mo.) Sch. Dist., 1935-38, Sycamore Sch., Boone County, Mo., 1938-41; reserve tchr. Kansas City (Mo.) Schs., 1941-55, contract tchr., 1955-63; head tchr. Allen Sch., Kansas City, 1963-67; remedial reading tchr. Benjamin Franklin Sch., Kansas City, 1967-69; reading cons. Div. Urban Edn., Kansas City, 1969-73; coord. Title I Elem. Reading and Compensatory Edn., Kansas City, 1974-79; ret.; instr., trainer ARC, Am. Assn. Ret. Persons, Staying Healthy After Fifty, State of N.Mex., 1987-89, Growing Old with Health and Wisdom, 1989-95; tutor Literacy Vols. of Am., Inc., Rio Rancho, N.Mex., 1990-93; spkr. AARP Health Care Reform, Health Care Am., 1992—, Lovelace Sr. Adv. Group, 1993-98. Vol. Corrales Libr., 1980-88; bd. dirs. Read West, Literacy Vols. Am., Rio Rancho, 1989-92; bd. dirs. Adobe Comty. Theatre, Corrales, 1989-90; lectr. in field; mem. State of N.Mex. steering com. Growing Old with Health and Wisdom, 1989-95; asst. state coord. Am. Assn. Ret. Persons, Health Advocacy Svcs., N.Mex., 1995-98. Recipient Area Comty. Svc. award AARP, State of N.Mex., 1988, Cert. of Appreciation, ARC, 1988, Cert. of Appreciation for outstanding comty. svc. N.Mex. Legislature, State Senate, 1997, Cert. of Appreciation Rio Rancho, N.Mex. Dept. Pub. Safety Srs. and Law Enforcement Together, 1997; NSF grantee, 1973. Mem. AAUW, N.Mex. Assn. Edn. Retirees (exec. com. 1987-89), Albuquerque Assn. Edn. Retirees (exec. sec., bd. dirs. 1990-95), PEO (chpt. BD chaplain, 1990—), West Mesa Assn. Ednl. Retirees (membership chmn. 1991, v.p. 1993, pres. 1994), Grad. Club Albuquerque. Democrat. Baptist. Avocations: bridge, reading, travel. Home: 3321 Esplanade Cir SE Rio Rancho NM 87124-2198

WEBER, ARNOLD I., lawyer; b. Little Cedar, Iowa, Oct. 4, 1926; divorced; children: Katherine Weber Hickle, Thomas, Margaret Weber Robertson. PhB magna cum laude, Marquette U., 1949; MA, Harvard U., 1950; JD, George Washington U., 1954, LLM, 1956. Bar: D.C. 1954, Md. 1961, Calif. 1962, U.S. Dist Ct. D.C. 1954, (no. dist.) Calif. 1962, (cen. dist.) Calif. 1992, U.S. Ct. Claims 1960, U.S. Tax Ct. 1965, U.S. Ct. Appeals (D.C. cir.) 1954, (9th cir.) 1962, (fed. cir.) 1991, U.S. Supreme Ct. 1959. Lawyer Housing and Home Fin., Washington, 1954; pvt. practice Washington, 1954-55; lawyer Tariff Commn., Washington, 1954-55, FCC, Washington, 1955-56, IRS, Washington, 1956-61; assoc. Brobeck, Phleger & Harrison, San Francisco, 1961-64; sr. gen. atty. So. Pacific Transp., San Francisco, 1964-84; western tax counsel Santa Fe Pacific Corp., San Francisco, 1985-88; pvt. practice San Francisco, 1988—. With USNR, 1944-54, PTO. Mem. ABA, Olympic Club, Bar Assn. San Francisco, State Bar of Calif. Office: 57 Post St Ste 502 San Francisco CA 94104-5020

WEBER, DENNIS MILLARD, music educator; b. Scottsbluff, Nebr., May 20, 1944; s. Millard F. and Beth V. (Davis) W.; m. Linda M. Parks, Aug. 21, 1965; children: Sara, Joel, Jeremy, Anna Lynne. Diploma in sacred music, Moody Bible Inst., 1965; MusB, Jacksonville U., 1967; MA in Music, Kent State U., 1972; D in Musicology, U. Paris, 1993. Min. of music and youth Glendale Cmty. Ch., Jacksonville, Ohio, 1965-69; music tchr. Cuyahoga Valley Christian Acad., Stow, Ohio, 1969-71; prof. European Bible Inst., Lamorlaye, France, 1973-93; assoc. prof. Simpson Coll. and Grad. Sch., Redding, Calif., 1995—; acad. dean European Bible Inst., Lamorlaye, 1976-81. Translator: Music of the Bible Revealed, 1992; author: Manuel d'accompagner les cantiques au piano, 1994; editor: (hymnal) Celebration, 1982, 3d edit., 1994. Choirmaster All Saints Episcopal Ch., Redding, 1997—; v.p. Found. Roi David, Paris, 1978—; choral conductor Simpson Coll., Redding, 1995—; active Redding Symphony Orch. Choral Soc., 1995—. Recipient [illegible] 1997. Episcopalian. Avocation: archaeology. Office: Simpson Coll & Grad Sch 2211 College View Dr Redding CA 96003-8601

WEBER, EICKE RICHARD, physicist; b. Muennerstadt, Germany, Oct. 28, 1949; s. Martin and Irene (Kistner) W. BS, U. Koeln, Fed. Republic of Germany, 1970, MS, 1973, PhD, 1976, Dr.Habil., 1983. Sci. asst. U. Koeln, 1976-82; rsch. asst. U. Lund, Sweden, 1982-83; asst. prof. Dept. Material Sci. U. Calif., Berkeley, 1983-87, assoc. prof., 1987-91, prof. materials sci., 1991—; prin. investigator Lawrence Berkeley Lab., 1984—; vis. prof. Tohoku U., Sendai, Japan, 1990; cons. in field; internat. fellow Inst. for Study of Defects in Solids, SUNY, Albany, 1978-79; chmn. numerous confs.; mem. founding com. CAESAR Found., Bonn, 1995-97, mem. scientific coun. 1999—; lectr. in field. Editor: Defect Recognition and Image Processing in III-V Compounds, 1987, Imperfections in III-V Compounds, 1993; co-editor: Chemistry and Defects in Semiconductor Structures, 1989, others; series co-editor: Semiconductors and Semimetals, 1991—; contbr. over 370 articles to profl. jours. Recipient IBM Faculty award, 1984, Humboldt U.S. Sr. Scientist award, 1994; rsch. grantee Dept. of Energy, 1984—, Office Naval Rsch., 1985—, Air Force Office Sci. Rsch., 1988—, NASA, 1988-90, Nat. Renewable Energy Lab., 1992—. Mem. IEEE (sr.), Am. Phys. Soc., Materials Rsch. Soc. Achievements include first identification of point defects formed by dislocation motion in silicon; determination of the energy levels of antisite defects in GaAs, of 3d transition metal solubility and lattice site in silicon, of mechanism of internal gettering in silicon; research in defects formed in III/V thin films and interfaces; on lattice mismatched heteroepitaxial growth; in structure and electronic properties of metal GaAs heterostructures; in nature and electronic properties of defects in GaAs, GaN, and related compounds; in MBE growth of GaN and related compounds; in low-temperature MBE growth of As-rich GaAs; in transition metal gettering in silicon; polysilicon for photovoltaic applications; scanning tunneling microscopy of semiconductor thin films and interfaces; on electron paramagnetic resonance of defects in semiconductors. E-mail: weber@socrates.berkeley.edu. Office: 587 Evans Hall U Calif Dept Materials Sci 587 Evans Hall Berkeley CA 94720-1775

WEBER, FRANCIS JOSEPH, archivist, museum director; b. Jan. 22, 1933; s. Frank J. and Katherine E. (Thompson) W. Student, L.A. Coll., 1953, St. Johns Coll., 1955, St. Johns Seminary, 1959, Cath. U. Am., 1962, Am. U., Washington. Ordained priest Roman Cath. Ch., 1959. Archivist Archdiocese L.A., 1962—; prof. history Queen Angels Sem., 1962-72; chaplain St. Catherine Mil. Sch., 1972-75; pastor San Buenaventura Mission, 1975-81; dir. Borromeo Guild, 1984-87; dir. San Fernando Mission, 1981—. Editor The Tidings, 1990, Hoja Volante, 1984-95, Miniature Book Soc. Newsletter, 1995-97; contbr. articles to profl. jours. Pres. Zamorano Club, 1991-93; sheriff L.A. Corral Westerners, 1995; hist. rev. commn. Diocese of Monterey. Decorated Grand Cross Isabel la Catolica, 1993, Knighthood of The Holy Sepulchre; recipient Commendation award El Pueblo do L.A. State Historic Park, 1970, L.A. County Bd. Supr., 1972, L.A. City Coun., 1981, L.A. County Bd. Supr., 1992, Merit award Rounce and Coffin Club, 1969, 71, 75, 77, 79-80, 84-86, 88, 92-95, Archivist Excellence award Calif. Heritage Preservation Commn., 1995. Fellow Calif. Hist. Soc. (Merit award 1972, 83), Hist. Soc. So. Calif. (bd. dirs.); mem. Assn. Cath. Diocesan Archivists (pres. 1996-97), Santa Barbara Mission Archves (bd. dirs.), Assn. Cath. Diocesan Archives (bd. dirs.). Democrat. Roman Catholic. Office: Hist Mus Archival Ctr 15151 San Fernando Mission Blv Mission Hills CA 91345-1109

WEBER, FRED J., retired state supreme court justice; b. Deer Lodge, Mont., Oct. 6, 1919; s. Victor N. and Dorothy A. (Roberts) W.; m. Phyllis M. Schell, June 2, 1951; children: Anna Marie, Donald J., Mark W., Paul V. B.A., U. Mont., 1943, J.D., 1947. Bar: Mont. 1947. Atty. Kuhr & Weber, Havre, Mont., 1947-55, Weber, Bosch & Kuhr, and successors, 1956-80; justice Supreme Ct. Mont., Helena, 1981-95. Served to capt. inf. U.S. Army, 1943-46. Fellow Am. Bar Found., Am. Coll. Probate Counsel; mem. ABA, Am. Judicature Soc.

WEBER, GEORGE RICHARD, financial consultant, writer; b. The Dalles, Oreg., Feb. 7, 1929; s. Richard Merle and Maud (Winchell) W.; m. Nadine Hanson, Oct. 12, 1957; children: Elizabeth Ann Weber Katooli, Karen Louise Weber Zaro, Linda Marie. BS, Oreg. State U., 1950; MBA, U. Oreg., 1962. CPA, Oreg. Sr. trainee U.S. Nat. Bank of Portland (Oreg.), 1950-51; jr. acct. Ben Musa, CPA, The Dalles, 1954; tax and audit asst. Price Waterhouse, Portland, 1955-59; sr. acct. Burton M. Smith, CPA, Portland, 1959-62; pvt. practice, Portland, 1962—, assoc. World Mktg. Alliance, 1996—; lectr. acctg. Portland State Coll.; expert witness fin. and tax matters. Sec.-treas. Mt. Hood Kiwanis Camp, Inc., 1965. Exec. counselor SBA; mem. fin. com., powerlifting team U.S. Powerlifting Fedn., 1984, amb. People to People, China, 1987. Arty. officer AUS, 1951-53. Decorated Bronze Star. Mem. AICPA, Internat. Platform Assn., Oreg. Hist. Soc.,Oreg. City Traditional Jazz Soc., Order of the Holy Cross Jerusalem, Order St. Stephen the Martyr, Order St. Gregory the Illuminator, Knightly Assn. St. George the Martyr., World Literary Acad., Portland C.S. Lewis Soc., Beta Alpha Psi, Pi Kappa Alpha. Republican. Lutheran. Clubs: Kiwanis, Portland Track, City (Portland); Multnomah Athletic; Sunrise Toastmasters. Author: Small Business Long-term Finance, 1962, A History of the Coroner and Medical Examiner Offices, 1963, CPA Litigation Service References, 1991, Letters to a Friend, 1995; contbr. to profl. publs. and poetry jours. Home: 2603 NE 32d Ave Portland OR 97212-3611 Office: 4380 SW Macadam Ave Ste 210 Portland OR 97201-6404

WEBER, LAVERN JOHN, marine science administrator, educator; b. Isabel, S.D., June 7, 1933; s. Jacob and Irene Rose (Bock) W.; m. Shirley Jean Carlson, June 19, 1959 (div. 1992); children: Timothy L., Peter J., Pamela C., Elizabeth T.; m. Patricia Rae Lewis, Oct. 17, 1992. AAS, Everett Jr. Coll., 1956; BA, Pacific Luth. U., 1958; MS, U. Wash., 1962, PhD, 1964. Instr. U. Wash., Seattle, 1964-67, asst. prof., 1967-69, acting state toxicologist, 1968-69; assoc. prof. Oreg. State U., Corvallis, 1969-75, prof., 1976—, asst. dean grad. sch., 1974-77; dir. Hatfield Marine Sci. Ctr. Oregon State U., Newport, 1977—, supt. Coastal Oreg. Marine Exptl. Sta., 1989-98, assoc. dean Coll. Agrl. Sci., 1998—. Pres., trustee Newport Pub. Libr., 1991-92, Yaquina Bay Econ. Found., Newport, 1991-92; chmn. Oreg. Coast Aquarium, 1983-95. Recipient Pres. award Newport Rotary, 1984-85. Mem. South Slough Mgmt. Commn., Am. Soc. Pharm. and Exptl. Therapy, West Pharm. Soc., Soc. Toxicology, Soc. Exptl. Biol. Med. (n.w. divsn., pres. 1978, 82, 87) , Pacific N.W. Assn. Toxicologists (chair 1985-86, coun. 1991-93), Western Assn. Marine Lab. (pres. 1993). Avocations: woodworking, reading, walking, scuba, gardening. Office: Oregon State Univ Hatfield Marine Sci Ctr 2030 SE Marine Science Dr Newport OR 97365-5229

WEBER, RICHARD DEAN, physician, primary care practitioner, researcher; b. Downey, Calif., Aug. 26, 1938; s. Leslie Ward and Ethel Lucille (Kalangvin) W.; m. Fratie Gevedia Jackson, Aug. 30, 1958; children: Debra Lynn Weber Riley, Shelley Annette. D Naturapathic Medicine magna cum laude, Am. U. Natural Therapeutics, Mesa, Ariz., 1980; MD Homeopathic, Western U., Phoenix, 1982; PhD in Psychol. Counseling, Golden State U., L.A., 1984; D of Oriental Medicine and Acupuncture, Calif. Acupuncture Coll., San Diego, 1986. Diplomate in preventive medicine. Engr. Kern County Fire Dept., 1966-71, capt., 1971-76; chief paramedic, CEO Flynn Ambulance Co., Bakersfield, Calif., 1974-76; primary care assoc. physician in medicine North Kern Hosp., Wasco, Calif., 1976-78; naturopathic physician, dir. rsch. Southwestern U.S. Rsch. Ctr., Monett, Mo., 1978-80; homeopathic physician Bakers Holistic Health Ctr., Lake Geneva, Fla., 1980-81, Hollywood (Fla.) Treatment Ctr., 1981-83; naturopathic physician, dir. rsch. Sooutwestern U.S. Rsch. Ctr., Prescott, Ariz., 1983-87; Oriental medicine physician, acupuncturist, dir. rsch. Bio-Systems and Pain Ctr., Escondido, Calif., 1987—; qualified med. evaluator, acupuncturist State of Calif. Workmen's Compensation, Sacramento, 1992—; rsch. physician Rsch. Ctr., Prescott, 1978-87; v.p. bd. dirs. Calif. Acupuncture Coll., San Diego, 1985-86. Author (paper) Silver Amalgam, 1981. Sec. Nevada Naturopathic Med. Assn., Las Vegas, 1982-95. Grantee primary care assoc. Stanford U., 1978. Mem. Calif. Soc. Indsl. Medicine and Surgery, Calif. Soc. Oriental Medicine and Acupuncture, Am. Assn. Acupuncture and Oriental Medicine. Republican. Mormon. Avocations: golf, astronomy, amateur radio, computer technology. Office: Bio-Systems and Pain Ctr 301 E Washington Ave Ste B Escondido CA 92025-2855

WEBER, SAMUEL, editor, retired; b. N.Y.C., July 31, 1926; s. Bernard and Gertrude (Ellenberg) W.; m. Eileen Gloria Hornstein, Mar. 5, 1950; children—Bruce Jay, Robert Matthew. B.S. in Elec. Engring, Va. Poly. Inst., 1947. Engr. N.Y. Bd. Transp., 1948-50, U.S. Naval Shipyard, Bklyn., 1950-52, Barlow Engring. Co., N.Y.C., 1952-54; engring. supr. Curtiss Wright Corp., Woodridge, N.J., 1954-56; electronics engr. Loral Electronics Corp., N.Y.C., 1957-58; with Electronics mag., N.Y.C., 1958-67, assoc. mng. editor, 1968-70, exec. editor, 1970-79, editor in chief, 1979-84, exec. tech. editor, 1984-88, editor-at-large, 1988-92; editor in chief Electrotechnology mag., N.Y.C., 1968—; pres. Samuel Weber & Assocs., 1988-91, Samuel Weber & Assocs., Inc., 1991-96; contbg. editor Asic & Eda Magazine, 1991-94; spl. projects editor Electronic Engring. Times, 1992-96, ret., 1997. Author: Modern Digital Circuits, 1964, Optoelectronic Devices and Circuits, 1968, Large and Medium Scale Integration, 1974, Circuits for Electronics Engineers, 1977, Electronic Circuits Notebook, 1981. Served with AUS, 1944-46. Mem. IEEE (life). Home and Office: 4242 E Allison Rd Tucson AZ 85712-1039

WEBER, STEPHEN LEWIS, university president; b. Boston, Mar. 17, 1942; s. Lewis F. and Catherine (Warns) W.; m. Susan M. Keim, June 27, 1965; children: Richard, Matthew. BA, Bowling Green State U., 1964; postgrad., U. Colo., 1964-66; PhD, U. Notre Dame, 1969; EdD (hon.), Capital Normal U., China, 1993. Asst. prof. philosophy U. Maine, Orono, 1969-75, assoc. prof., 1975-79, asst. to pres., 1976-79; dean arts and scis. Fairfield (Conn.) U., 1979-84; v.p. acad. affairs St. Cloud (Minn.) State U., 1984-88; pres. SUNY Oswego, 1988-95; interim provost SUNY, Oswego, 1995-96; pres. San Diego State U., 1996—; participant Harvard Inst. Ednl. Mgmt., Cambridge, Mass., 1985. Contbr. numerous articles on philosophy and acad. adminstrn. to profl. jours. Mentor Am. Coun. Edn. Fellowship Program, Am. Coun. on Edn., Commn. on Internat. Edn. and Commn. on Govtl. Rels.; bd. govs. The Peres Ctr. for Peace, San Diego Found.; bd. dirs. San Diego Regional Econ. Devel. Corp.; mem. internat. adv. bd. Found. for the Children of the Californias. Named Outstanding Humanities Tchr., U. Maine, 1975; Rsch. fellow U. Notre Dame, 1968-69. Mem. Am. Philos. Assn., Am. Assn. Higher Edn. Democrat. Avocations: art, woodworking, swimming, boating. Office: Office of the Pres San Diego State U San Diego CA 92182-8000

WEBER, STEPHEN ROSS, broadcast technician; b. Fresno, Calif., Dec. 12, 1922; s. Andrew Edward and Florence Lucretia (Ross) W.; m. Deane Laverne Davis, Feb. 16, 1942 (dec. Jan. 1997); children: June Marie Ward, Anita Ann Dodson, Stephen Ross Jr.; m. Charlene Sue Bartholomew, Dec. 12, 1997. Grad. H.S., Fresno, 1940; mgmt. tng. course, Purdue U., 1978, 79; Dale Carnegie, 1970, 78. Lic. radio telephone operator. Aircraft electronics technician U.S. Civil Svc., Sacramento, Fresno, 1942-45; chief engr. Radio Sta. KERO, Bakersfield, Calif., 1945-48; radio engr. Radio Sta. KFRE, Fresno, 1948-53; engring. supr. KFRE Radio & TV, Fresno, 1953-65; chief engr. KFRE/KFSN Radio & TV, Fresno, 1965-85; ret., 1985; TV consulting engr. various, 1985-88. Mem. Soc. Broadcast Engrs. (local pres. 1970—), Fresno Amateur Radio Club (pres. 1952). Republican. Avocations: fly, skiing, ham radio (W6QON), exercising. Home: 170 Twin Peaks Dr PO Box 297 Toledo WA 98591-0297

WEBSTER, KENNETH FEWINGS, painter, consultant; b. Buffalo, Dec. 27, 1923; s. Gilbert Arthur and Llorene Jeannette (Fewings) W.; m. E. Janis Kenline Christenson, Sept. 1951 (div. Apr. 1974); children: Ford, Michael, Kim; m. Cheryl Ivy Burnett, June 1975. Student, U. Buffalo, 1946-48; cert., Pratt Inst., 1952. Creative dir., founder Design Directions, Reno, 1965-73; mem. design team audio-visual USN F-14 Top Gun Program, Miramar, Calif., 1976-77; exec. dir. art N.W. Ayer, Inc., San Francisco, 1978-80; creative cons. Shaklee Corp., San Francisco, 1981-86; instr. dept. art Coll. of Redwoods, Eureka, Calif., 1987-89; represented by Christopher Bell Collection, Alvarado Mall, Monterey, Calif., 1986—; illustrator USAF Art Program, 1970-84. Author, artist: Southeast Asia Sketchbook, 1982; exhibited at Bolling Air Base, Washington, 1970, 82, N.Y. Soc. Illustrators, 1985, USAF Collection, Wright-Patterson Air Base. Recipient San Francisco Soc. Communicating Art award, 1980, Best Work award San Francisco Art Dirs. Show, 1983, Cert. of Excellence, Calif. Design, 1985. Home and Studio: 556 Redwood Rd Shelter Cove Whitethorn CA 95589-9090

WECHSLER, MARY HEYRMAN, lawyer; b. Green Bay, Wis., Jan. 8, 1948; d. Donald Hubert and Helen (Polcyn) Heyrman; m. Roger Wechsler, Aug. 1971 (div. 1977); 1 child, Risa Heyrman; m. David Jay Sellinger, Aug. 15, 1981; 1 stepchild, Kirk Benjamin; 1 child, Michael Paul. Student, U. Chgo., 1966-67, 68-69; BA, U. Wash., 1971; JD cum laude, U. Puget Sound, 1979. Bar: Wash. 1979. Assoc. Law Offices Ann Johnson, Seattle, 1979-81; ptnr. Johnson, Wechsler, Thompson, Seattle, 1981-83; pvt. practice Seattle, 1984-87; ptnr. Mussehl, Rosenberg et al, Seattle, 1987-88, Wechsler, Becker, Erickson, Ross, Roubik & Hunter, Seattle, 1988—; mem. Bd. of Ct. Edn., 1998; bd. dirs. U. Wash. Law Sch. Child Advocacy Clinic, 1996—; mem. Walsh Commn. on Jud. Selection, 1995-96; mem. commn. on domestic rels. Wash. State Supreme Ct., 1996-97; mem. law-related edn. com., 1997; chair edn. com. Access to Justice Bd., 1996-98; presenter in field. Author: Family Law in Washington, 1987, rev. edit., 1988, Marriage and Separation, Divorce and Your Rights, 1994; contbr. articles to legal publs. Mem. Wash. State Ethics Adv. Com., 1992-95; bd. dirs. Seattle LWV, 1991-92. Fellow Am. Acad. Matrimonial Lawyers (sec.-treas. Wash. state chpt. 1996, profl. com. nat. 1996-97, v.p. 1997, 98, pres. 1999); mem. ABA (chmn. Wash. state 1987-88), Wash. State Bar Assn. (exec. com. family law sect. 1985-91, chair 1988-89, ct. improvement com. 1998—, legis. com. 1991-96, Outstanding Atty. of Yr. family law sect. 1988, comms. com. 1997-98), Wash. Women Lawyers, King County Bar Assn. (legis. com. 1985—, vice-chair 1990-91, chair family law sect. 1986-87, chair domestic violence com. 1986-87, trustee 1988-90, policy planning com. 1991-92, 2d v.p. 1992-93, 1st v.p. 1993-94, pres. 1994-95, long-range planning com. 1998—), Nat. Conf. of Bar Pres. (commn. com. 1994-95, long range planning com. 1998-99), King County Bar Found. (trustee 1997—). Office: Wechsler Becker Erickson Ross Roubik & Hunter 701 5th Ave Seattle WA 98104-7016

WEED, RONALD DE VERN, engineering consulting company executive; b. Indian Valley, Idaho, Sept. 1, 1931; s. David Clinton and Grace Elizabeth (Lavendar) W.; m. Doris Jean Hohener, Nov. 15, 1953; children: Geraldine Gayle, Thomas De Vern, Cheryl Ann. BSChemE, U. So. Calif., 1957; MS in Chem. Engring., U. Wash., 1962; LLB, La Salle U., Chgo., 1975; postgrad., Century U., Beverly Hills, Calif., 1979—. Registered profl. engr., Washington, Calif. Devel. engr. GE Co., Richland, Washington, 1957-65, Battelle N.W. Labs., Richland, 1965-68; oper. plant engr. NIPAK, Inc., Kerens, Tex., 1968-72; aux. systems task engr. Babcock & Wilcox Co., Lynchburg, Va., 1972-74; materials and welding engr. Bechtel Group Cos., San Francisco, 1974-85; cons. engr. Cygna Energy Svcs., Walnut Creek, Calif., 1985-91; with inter city fund Cygna Energy Svcs., Oakland, Calif., 1991-94; corrosion engr. Gen. Physics Corp., Oakland, 1994—; sr. environ. engr. Jacobs Engring. Group. Contbr. rsch. reports, papers and chpts. in books; patentee in field. With U.S. Army, 1951-53. Mem. Am. Inst. Chem. Engrs., Am. Welding Soc., Nat. Assn. Corrosion Engrs. (cert., sect. vice chmn. and chmn. 1962-68). Avocations: reading, photography, gardening. Home and Office: 74 Sharon St Bay Point CA 94565-1527 *Deceased.*

WEEKS, DENNIS LEROY, English language educator; b. Manhattan, Kans., Aug. 18, 1948; s. Harlan L. and Winifred O. (Kraemer) W. BA, Western Ill. U., 1970, MA, 1980; PhD, St. Louis U., 1990. Tchg. fellow St. Louis U., 1981-83; instr. N.W. Mo. State U., Maryville, 1985-87; asst. prof. English S.W. Mo. State U., Springfield, 1987-91; assoc. prof. English Ky. State U., Frankfort, 1991-96; prof. English U. Great Falls (Mont.), 1996-99; chair humanities and social scis. Schenectady County C.C., Schenectady, N.Y., 1999—. Editor: Time, Memory & the Verbal Arts: Essays on Walter Ong, 1998, To Love the World So Well: Essays on Robert Penn Warren, 1996, Classical Rhetorical Thought, 1995; author: Steps Toward Salvation, 1993. With U.S. Army, 1970-72. Mem. MLA, Ky. Philological Assn., Robert Penn Warren Cir. Democrat. Presbyterian. Home: 4216 Central Ave Great Falls MT 59405-1621 Office: U Great Falls 1301 20th St S Great Falls MT 59405-4934

WEEKS, ROBERT LEE, electronic engineer, program manager; b. Woonsocket, R.I., Mar. 8, 1957; s. Joseph Bernard and Claire Lorraine (Jolicoeur) W.; m. Christine Ann Bentley; children: Barbara Ann, Christopher Lee. BSEE, U. Ariz., 1985, postgrad., 1987; MBA, U. Phoenix, 1996. Laborer ASARCO Mine Inc., Sahuarita, Ariz., 1979-82; test engr. EMI and TEMPEST br. U.S. Army Electronic Proving Ground, Ft. Huachuca, Ariz., 1985-88, chief EMI and TEMPEST br., 1988-95; chief electromagnetics br. U.S. Army Electronic Proving Ground, Ft. Huachuca, 1995-96, mgr. R&D program, 1996—; mem. MIL-STD-461 Joint Working Group, 1989-94; mem. DOD and industry E3 standards com. Dept. Def., 1994—. Bd. dirs. Bristol Park Neighborhood Assn., Tucson, 1994—; vol. YMCA, 1994—. With USMC, 1975-79. Mem. IEEE (named Engr. of Yr. local chpt. 1994), Electromagnetic Compatibility Soc. of IEEE, Nat. Assn. Radio and Telecomms. Engrs. (cert. electromagnetic compatibility engr.). Democrat. Roman Catholic. Avocations: basketball, bowling, hiking. Office: US Army Electronic Proving Ground STEWS-EPG-TE Fort Huachuca AZ 85613

WEEKS, WILLIAM RAWLE, JR., oil company executive; b. Denver, Oct. 23, 1920; s. William Rawle Sr. and Besse Elizabeth (Griffith) W.; m. June Suzanne Stephens, Jan. 22, 1944 (div. 1980); children: Stephen R., Tacy A. Weeks Hahn. BA, Stanford U., 1943. With book prodn. divsn. Stanford U. Press, 1948-49; advt. exec. Palo Alto, Calif., 1949-50; with CIA, 1951—; gen. ptnr. Weeks, Brewer & Assocs., 1971; CEO Fort Collins Consol. Royalties, Inc., Cheyenne, Wyo., 1983—. Author: Knock and Wait Awhile, 1957 (Edgar Allan Poe award 1958, Commonwealth award 1958). Nat. press and media advance man Muskie Vice Presdl. Campaign, 1968. 2nd lt. U.S. Army, 1943-46. Mem. Nat. Press Club, Denver Petroleum Club, Heather Ridge Country Club. Avocations: flying, skiing, golfing, hiking. Home: 1201 Williams St Apt 11C Denver CO 80218-2678 Office: Fort Collins Consol Royalties Inc 1508 Stillwater Ave Cheyenne WY 82009-7349

WEEMS, MARY ANN, business owner; b. Carlsbad, N.Mex., June 12, 1948; d. Myer and Nadine Lolita (Miller) Rosenberg; div. 1993; children: Elizabeth Nadine, Brian Eli. BS in Art cum laude, William Woods Coll., 1970. Cert. tchr., Mo., Tex. Tchr. art Lubbock (Tex.) Pub. Sch., 1970-71; profl. artist Albuquerque, 1972-77; owner Weems Galleries & Framing, Albuquerque, 1981—, Weems Artfest, Albuquerque, 1982—, Weems Gallery - Old Town, Albuquerque, 1994—; bd. dirs. N.Mex. Arts and Crafts Fair, Albuquerque, 1972-76, Rio Grande Arts and Crafts Fair, 1974-77. Mem. Albuquerque Conv. and Visitors Bur., 1981—, bd. dirs., 1990-92; loan fund mem. West Corp., Albuquerque, 1992-95; bd. dirs. Albuquerque Mus., 1986-88; mem. N.Mex. Arts Commn., 1998—. Named one of Women on the Move YWCA, 1996, 10 Top Smart, Savvy, Successful Albuquerque Women's Mag., 1997; named #1 Fine Arts and Crafts Fair in N.Mex. Harris List, 1996. Mem. Internat. Festivals and Events Assn. (Pinnacle award 1996), S.W. Festivals and Events Assn., Albuquerque C. of C., Albuquerque Gallery Assn. (pres. 1984-86). Jewish. Avocations: tennis, performing arts. Office: Weems Galleries and Framing 2801 Eubank Blvd NE Ste M Albuquerque NM 87112-1300

WEESE, BRUCE ERIC, pharmaceutical sales executive; b. Chewelah, Wash., Mar. 22, 1942; s. Harry M. and Roberta B. (Carman) W.; m. Elaine M. Smith, June 18, 1962 (div. July 1972); children: Sandra G., Michael D.; m. Vera B. Reed, Mar. 22, 1975; stepchildren: Kevin E. Bayron, Kelly M. Bayron. BA in Edn., Ea. Wash. State U., Cheney, 1964; MBA, Pepperdine U., 1981. Tchr. Grant Joint Union High Sch. Dist., Sacramento, 1964-70; pharm. sales McNeil Labs., San Jose, Calif., 1970-77, Adria Labs., San Francisco, 1977-83, Serono Labs., San Francisco, 1983-84; pharm. sales Boehringer Ingelheim, Santa Rosa, Calif., 1984-91, mgr. govt. affairs (lobbyist) for western states, 1991-97, area mgr. managed care, 1997-98; pharm. sales rep. Guerneville, Calif., 1998—. Bd. dirs. Russian River Health Ctr., Guerneville, Calif., 1994-95, 98—, Redwood Empire br. Am. Lung Assn., 1998—. Mem. United Anglers, Sequoia Paddlers, Santa Rosa Sailing Club, Sierra Club. Democrat. Avocations: kayaking, sailing, fishing. Home and Office: 16149 Fern Way Guerneville CA 95446-9611

WEGGE, LEON LOUIS FRANÇOIS, retired economics educator; b. Breendonk, Antwerp, Belgium, June 9, 1933; came to U.S., 1959; s. Petrus Maria and Alberta (De Maeyer) W.; m. Beate Maria Teipel, Nov. 22, 1962; children: Simone, Robert, Elizabeth. B in Thomistical Philosophy, Cath. U. Louvain, Belgium, 1957, Licentiate in Econ. Sci., 1958; PhD in Indsl. Econs., MIT, 1963. Assoc. lectr. U. New S. Wales, Kensington, Australia, 1963-66; prof. econs. U. Calif., Davis, 1966-94, retired, 1994—; vis. prof. U. Bonn, Fed. Republic Germany, 1980-81. Assoc. editor Jour. Internat. Econs., 1971-84; contbr. articles to profl. jours. Rsch. fellow Ctr. for Ops. Rsch. and Econometrics, 1972-73, fellow The Netherlands Inst. for Advanced Study, 1987-88. Mem. Econometric Soc., Am. Statistical Assn. Roman Catholic. Home: 26320 County Rd # 98 Davis CA 95616

WEGNER, LUCY SIEFERT, information specialist; b. Santa Monica, Calif., Dec. 11, 1953. MLS, MBA, UCLA, 1987; MA, Calif. State U., Northridge, 1980. Dir. Ctr. for Scholarly Tech. U. So. Calif., 1993-97, head strategic planning coord., 1998—. Mem. ALA, Am. Soc. for Info. Sci., Assn. for Computing Machinery. Democrat. Avocations: travel, music. Office: Univ So Calif LVL 130 MC 0182 Los Angeles CA 90089

WEH, ALLEN EDWARD, airline executive; b. Salem, Oreg., Nov. 17, 1942; s. Edward and Harriet Ann (Hicklin) W.; m. Rebecca Ann Roberton, July 5, 1968; children: Deborah Susan, Ashley Elizabeth, Brian Roberton. BS, U. N.Mex., 1966, MA, 1973. Asst. to chief adminstrv. officer Bank N.Mex., Albuquerque, 1973; pres. N.Mex. Airways, Inc., Albuquerque, 1974; dep. dir. N.Mex. Indochina Refugee Program, Santa Fe, 1975-76; dir. pub. affairs UNC Mining & Milling Co., Albuquerque, 1977-79; pres., CEO, CSI Aviation Svcs., Inc., Albuquerque, 1979—. Mem. steering com. Colin McMillan for lt. gov., Albuquerque, 1982; bd. dirs. N.Mex. Symphony Orgh., Albuquerque Conv. and Visitors Bur., 1982; mem. Albuquerque Police Adv. Bd., 1977-78; mem. fin. com. Heather Wilson for Congress, 1998. Capt. USMC, 1966-71, Vietnam; col. USMCR, 1971-97, Col. USMC, 1990-91, Persan Gulf, 1992-93, Somalia. Decorated Legion of Merit, Bronze Star with V device, Purple Heart with two gold stars, Meritorious Svc. medal with gold star, Air medal. Mem. Marine Corps Res. Officers Assn. (life, bd. dirs. 1973, 86), Res. Officers Assn. U.S. (life), SCV (life), Mil. Order Stars and Bars (life), SAR, Soc. of the Descendants of Washington's Army at Valley Forge. Republican. Episcopalian. Home: 6722 Rio Grande Blvd NW Albuquerque NM 87107-6330 Office: CSI Aviation Svcs Inc 3700 Rio Grande Blvd NW Albuquerque NM 87107-3042

WEHINGER, PETER AUGUSTUS, astronomer, educator; b. Goshen, N.Y., Feb. 18, 1938; s. George Edward and Elizabeth Marie (Goode) W.; m. Susan Wyckoff, July 29, 1967. BS in Physics, Union Coll., Schenectady, N.Y., 1960; MA in Astronomy, Ind. U., 1962; PhD, Case Western Reserve U., 1966. NASA predoctoral fellow Case Western Reserve U., Cleve., 1963-65; instr. U. Mich., Ann Arbor, 1965-67, asst. prof., 1967-70; assoc. prof. U. Kans., Lawrence, 1970-72; vis. assoc. prof. Tel Aviv U., Ramat-Aviv, Israel, 1972-75; prin. rsch. fellow Royal Greenwich Observatory, Herstmonceux, Sussex, Eng., 1975-78; vis. sr. scientist Max Planck Inst. for Astronomy, Heidelberg, Germany, 1978-80; vis. prof. Ariz. State U., Tempe, 1981-84, rsch. prof., 1984—; staff astronomer Steward Obs., U. Ariz., 1997—; project mgr. 1.3 meter telescope Astronomy Dept. U. Mich., 1966-70; tech. cons. Boller & Chivens Divsn., Perkin Elmer Corp., S. Pasadena, Calif., 1974-75, Photek Ltd., St. Leonard's-on-the-Sea, Sussex, Eng., 1992-94, Torus Precision Optics, Iowa City, 1997—; vis. prof. Astronomy Ctr. U. Sussex, Brighton, Eng., 1975-78, sr. rsch. fellow Astronomy dept. Ohio state U., Columbus, 1978-79; vis. prof. Physics-Astronomy dept. No. Ariz. U., Flagstaff, 1981-82; discipline specialist in spectroscopy Internat. Halley Watch, NASA/JPL, 1982-89; vis. rsch. fellow Mt. Stromlo Observatory and Siding Spring, Australian Nat. Univ., Canberra, 1986—; assoc. dir. Ariz./NASA Space Grant Consortium, Ariz. State U., 1990-94; adj. staff astronomer Steward Observatory U. Ariz., 1991-97; mem. Ariz. Sci. Ctr. Adv. Bd., 1995—; vis. prof. physics and astronomy Mesa C.C., 1996-98; faculty assoc. plant biology Ariz. State U., 1998—. Contbr. 105 articles to profl. jours.; editor: (conf. proceedings) Observations of Recent Comets, 1990; editor electronic newsletter On Periodic Comets, 1985-90; co-editor (CDROM Archives) Spectroscopic Observations of Comets, 1990. Grantee: NASA 1982-90, 1983-93, 1989-94, 1995-99, GTE-Sprint, 1985-87, NSF, 1985-87, 1994-97, Ariz. Pub. Svc. Corp., 1998-99. Fellow Royal Astron. Soc.; mem. Am. Astron. Soc. (divsn. planetry scis.), Astron. Soc. of the Pacific, Internat. Astron. Union, Sigma Xi. Achievements include measurement of carbon isotope abundances in comets; titanium isotope abundances in red giant stars, identification of H_2O in comets; digital imaging and spectroscopy of quasar host galaxies detected at their cosmological distances; spectroscopy of sodium torus associated with Jupiter and Io. E-Mail: pwehinger@as.arizona.edu. Home: 2135 E Loma Vista Dr Tempe AZ 85282-2927 Office: Ariz State Univ Physics-Astronomy Dept Tempe AZ 85287-1504

WEHRLI, JOHN ERICH, biotechnology executive; b. Bogota, Colombia, Dec. 1, 1963; came to U.S., 1969; s. Werner Freiderich and Graciela Wehrli; m. Vicki Lee Burnett, Aug. 18, 1991; children: Sophia Cristina, Sarina Darlene. BS summa cum laude in Mgmt. and Econs., Golden Gate U., 1993; Tax cert., Foothill Coll., 1994; JD, U. Calif., San Francisco, 1998; MBA, U. Calif., Berkeley, 1998. Analytical chemist dept. Chem. Analysis Syva Diagnostics Co., 1985-87; robotics specialist dept. Automation Tech. Syntex Rsch. Inc., 1987-89, rsch. chemist Inst. Pharm. Scis., dept. Pharm. Chemistry, 1987-91, sr. sci. analyst programmer, sys. mgr. Rsch. Info. Sys., 1991-93, sys. analyst, sr. sys. mgr., 1993-94; part-time fin. cons. assoc. Shearson Lehman Bros., San Francisco, 1989; v.p. Precision Instrument Design Inc., Tahoe City, Calif., 1989-96; legal intern patent and tech. licensing Lawrence Berkeley Nat. Lab., 1995-96; dir. Raptographics, LLC, Mountain View, Calif., 1995-97; pres. Wehrli Tech. Cons., Mountain View, Calif., 1995-96; atty. Cooley Godward LLP, 1996-99; v.p. bus. devel. and intellectual property NaviCyte Inc., Sparks, 1996-98; sr. dir. legal affairs and corp. sec. Trega Biosciss., Inc., 1998—. Contbr. articles to profl. jours. Enterprise scholar Golden Gate U., 1992, Kanze scholar, 1993, Univ. Honors scholar, 1993, Pres.'s scholar Foothill Coll., 1993. Mem. AAAS, ABA (sci. and tech. sect.), Am. Chem. Soc. (chem. info. and computer scis. sect.), Assn. Univ. Tech. Mgrs., Licensing Execs. Soc., Am. Intellectual Property Law Assn., N.Y. Acad. Scis., Phi Alpha Delta. Avocations: wildlife preservation, animal cruelty prevention, fractal mathematics, non-linear systems, Graeco Roman history. Home: 1879 Springer Rd Apt B Mountain View CA 94040-4052 Office: NaviCyte Inc Reno NV 89501

WEIDEMAN, WARREN MILO, producer; b. Houston, Mar. 4, 1944; s. George and Marion (Rand) W. BA, U. Ark., 1970. Creative dir. Weidman & Whitney Advt., Hartford, Conn., 1972-77; mktg. dir. CMR-Playboy Enterprise Coll. Divsn., 1977-79; mktg. cons. 20th Century Fox, Universal, 1979-84; co-founder Krown, Inc., Beverly Hills, Calif., 1984-88; mng. dir. Krown/Y&R, Culver City, Calif., 1988-91; pres. 1st Look Prodns., L.A., 1991-95; pres., CEO Harmony Entertainment, L.A., 1995—; spkr. in field. V.p. Free Arts Clinic for Abused Children, Malibu, Calif., 1985-95. with USAF, 1962-66. Office: Harmony Entertainment 420 S Beverly Dr Ste 100 Beverly Hills CA 90212-4410

WEIDNER, MARK, environmental research executive; b. 1952. MS in Analytical Chemistry, Purdue U., 1976. With Mich. State U., East Lansing, 1976-78; instr. Finnigan Corp., San Jose, Calif., 1978-80; sr. chemist Metro Lab., Seattle, 1980-85; now pres., treas. Analytical Resources, Inc., Seattle, 1985—. Office: Analytical Resources Inc 333 9th Ave N Seattle WA 98109-5187*

WEIGAND, WILLIAM KEITH, bishop; b. Bend, Oreg., May 23, 1937. Ed., Mt. Angel Sem., St. Benedict, Oreg., St. Edward's Sem. and St. Thomas Sem., Kenmore, Wash. Bishop Diocese Salt Lake City, 1980-93, Diocese Sacramento, 1993—; Ordained priest Roman Cath. Ch., 1963. Office: Diocese of Sacramento 2110 Broadway Sacramento CA 95818-2518*

WEIGEND, GUIDO GUSTAV, geographer, educator; b. Zeltweg, Austria, Jan. 2, 1920; came to U.S., 1939, naturalized, 1943; s. Gustav F. and Paula (Sorgo) W.; m. Areta Kelble, June 26, 1947 (dec. 1993); children: Nina, Cynthia, Kenneth. B.S., U. Chgo., 1942, M.S., 1946, Ph.D., 1949. With OSS, 1943-45; with mil. intelligence U.S. War Dept., 1946; instr. geography U. Ill., Chgo., 1946-47; instr. then asst. prof. geography Beloit Coll., 1947-49; asst. prof. geography Rutgers U., 1949-51, assoc. prof., 1951-57, prof., 1957-76, acting dept. chmn., 1951-52, chmn. dept., 1953-67, assoc. dean, 1972-76; dean Coll. Liberal Arts, Prof. geography Ariz. State U., Tempe, 1976-84, prof. geography, 1976-89; ret., 1989; Fulbright lectr. U. Barcelona, 1960-61; vis. prof. geography Columbia U., 1963-67, NYU, 1967, U. Colo., summer 1968, U. Hawaii, summer 1969; liaison rep. Rutgers U. to UN, 1950-52; invited by Chinese Acad. Scis. to visit minority areas in Chinese Cent. Asia, 1988; mem. U.S. nat. com. Internat. Geog. Union, 1951-58, 61-65; chmn. Conf. on Polit. and Social Geography, 1968-69. Author articles, monographs, bulls. for profl. jours.; contbr.: (4th edit.) A Geography of Europe, 1977; geog. editor-in-chief: Odyssey World Atlas, 1966. Bd. adjustment Franklin Twp., N.J., 1959; mem. Highland Park (N.J.) Bd. Edn., 1973-75, v.p., 1975; mem. Ariz. Coun. on Humanities and Pub. Policy, 1976-80; vice chmn. Phoenix Com. on Fgn. Rels., 1976-79, chmn., 1979-81; mem. exec. com. Fedn. Pub. Programs in Humanities, 1977-82; bd. dirs. Coun. Colls. Arts and Scis., 1980-83, Phoenix Chamber Music Soc., 1995—; commr. N. Cen. Assn. Colls. and Schs., 1976-80, bd. dirs. commn. on instns. of higher edn., 1980-83. Research fellow Office Naval Research, 1952-55, Rutgers Research Council, 1970-71; grantee Social Sci. Research Council, 1956, Ford Found., 1966, Am. Philos. Soc., 1970-71, German Acad. Exchange Service, 1984; Fulbright travel grantee Netherlands, 1970-71. Mem. Assn. Am. Geographers (chmn. N.Y. Met. divsn. 1955-56, editl. bd. 1955-59, mem. coun. 1965-66, chmn. N.Y.-N.J. divsn. 1965-66), Am. Geog. Soc., Phoenix Chamber Mus. Soc. (bd. dirs. 1995—), Sigma Xi (pres. Ariz. State U. chpt. 1989-91). Home: 2094 E Golf Ave Tempe AZ 85282-4046 Office: Ariz State U Dept Geography Tempe AZ 85287

WEIGLE, WILLIAM OLIVER, immunologist, educator; b. Monaca, Pa., Apr. 28, 1927; s. Oliver James and Caroline Ellen (Alsing) W.; m. Kathryn May Lotz, Sept. 4, 1948 (div. 1980); children—William James, Cynthia Kay; m. Carole G. Romball, Sept. 24, 1983. B.S., U. Pitts., 1950, M.S., 1951, Ph.D., 1956. Research assoc. pathology U. Pitts., 1955-58, asst. prof. immunochemistry, 1959-61; assoc. div. exptl. pathology Scripps Rsch. Inst., La Jolla, Calif., 1961-62, assoc. mem. div., 1962-63; mem. dept. exptl. pathology Scripps Rsch. Inst., La Jolla, 1963-74, mem. dept. immunopathology, 1974-82, chmn. dept. immunopathology, 1980-82, mem., vice chmn. dept. immunology, 1982-85, mem. dept. immunology, 1982-97, chmn. dept. immunology, 1985-87, prof. dept. immunology, 1997-98, prof. emeritus, 1998—; adj. prof. biology U. Calif., San Diego; McLaughlin vis. prof. U. Tex., 1977; mem. adv. bd. Immunetech Pharms., San Diego, 1988-93; cons. in field. Author: Natural and Acquired Immunologic Unresponsiveness, 1967; assoc. editor: Clin. and Exptl. Immunology, 1972-79; Jour. Exptl. Medicine, 1974-84; Immunochemistry 1964-71; Procs. Soc. Exptl. Biology and Medicine, 1967-72; Jour. Immunology, 1967-71; Infection and Immunity, 1969-86, Aging: Immunology and Infectious Disease, 1987-96; sect. editor: Jour. Immunology, 1971-75; editorial bd.: Contemporary Topics in Immunobiology, 1971-93; Cellular Immunology, 1984-96; contbr. articles to profl. jours. Emeritus Coun. of the Trustees, Lovelace Inst., Albuquerque, 1996—. Pub. Health Research fellow, Nat. Inst. Neurol. Diseases and Blindness, 1956-59; NIH sr. research fellow, 1959-61, Research Career award, 1962. Mem. Am. Assn. Immunologists, Am. Soc. Exptl. Pathology (Parke Davis award 1967), Am. Soc. Microbiology, N.Y. Acad. Scis., Am. Assn. Pathologists, Soc. Exptl. Biology and Medicine. Home: 688 Via De La Valle Solana Beach CA 92075-2461 Office: Scripps Rsch Inst Dept Immunology IMM9 10550 N Torrey Pines Rd La Jolla CA 92037-1000

WEIGNER, BRENT JAMES, secondary education educator; b. Pratt, Kans., Aug. 19, 1949; s. Doyle Dean and Elizabeth (Hanger) W.; m. Sue Ellen Weber Hume, Mar. 30, 1985; children: Russell John Hume, Scott William Hume. BA, U. No. Colo., 1972; MEd, U. Wyo., 1977, PhD, 1984. Counselor, coach Olympia Sport Village, Upson, Wyo., summer 1968; dir. youth sports F.E. Warren AFB, Cheyenne, summers 1973, 74; instr. geography Laramie County Community Coll., Cheyenne, 1974-75; tchr. social sci. McCormick Jr. High Sch., Cheyenne, 1975—, Laramie County Sch. Dist. 1, Cheyenne, 1975—; head social studies dept. McCormick Jr. High Sch., 1987—; curriculum adv. coun. chmn. Laramie County Sch. Dist. No. 1, 1988-89; lectr. ednl. methods U. Wyo., 1989, mem. clin. faculty, 1992-94; nat. chmn. Jr. Olympic cross-country com. AAU, Indpls., 1980-81; pres. Wyo. Athletic Congress, 1981-87; tchr. cons. Nat. Geog. Soc. Geography Inst., summer 1991; bd. dirs. Shadow Mountain Lodge, Aspen, Colo., 1992-93, United Med. Ctr. of Wyo. Found., 1995—. Fgn. exch. student U. Munich, 1971-72; head coach Cheyenne Track Club, 1976—, pres., 1980; deacon 1st Christian Ch., Cheyenne, 1987-90, elder, 1991-93; rep. candidate gen. election Wyo. Legis., 1991. Named Wyoming State bd. edn. Disting.

Educator, Wyo. U.S. West Outstanding Tchr., 1989, Wyo. Coun. for the Social Studies K-8 Tchr. of Yr., 1994-95, Jr. High Coach of Yr., Wyo. Coaches Assn., 1996; fellow Taft Found., 1976, Earthwatch-Hearst fellow, Punta Allen, Mex., summer 1987, Christa McAuliffe fellow, 1991-92, Wyo. Christa Mcauliffe Selection Com., 1994, 95; Fulbright grantee, Jerusalem, summer 1984; Fulbright scholar Ghana and Senegal, 1990; People-to-People Internat. Ambassador to Vietnam, 1993; recipient Masons of Wyo. Disting. Tchr. award 1994. Mem. ASCD, NEA, Nat. Network for Ednl. Renewal, Nat. Coun. Social Studies, Nat. Coun. Geog. Edn., Dominican Rep. Nat. Coun. for Geog. Edn. (Cram scholarship 1992), Wyo. Geog. Alliance (steering com., Amazon Workshop Fellowship 1998), Cheyenne Tchrs. Edn. Assn. (govtl. rels. com., instrn. and profl. devel. com.), U. No. Colo. Alumni Assn., Cheyenne C. of C., Wyo. Heritage Soc., Wyo. Edn. Assn. (World Book Ency. classroom rsch. project cons. 1976—, accountability task force 1989-90), Fulbright Alumni Assn. (life), U. Wyo. Alumni Assn. (life), Cheyenne Sunrise, Lions (bd. dirs. Cheyenne 1987, pres. 1995-96, 1st v.p. 1993-94, Melvin Jones Fellowship, 1995), Phi Delta Kappa (life, bd. dirs. Cheyenne 1989—, v.p., edn. award for rsch. 1990, pres. 1992-93, ednl. found. rep. 1993-94, area 4-D coord. 1994-95, Gerald Read Internat. Seminar scholar 1994; mem. outstanding doctoral dissertation com. 1994, 96). Home: 402 W 31st St Cheyenne WY 82001-2527 Office: McCormick Jr HS 6000 Education Dr Cheyenne WY 82009-3991

WEIL, LOUIS ARTHUR, III, newspaper publishing executive; b. Grand Rapids, Mich., Mar. 14, 1941; s. Louis Arthur, Jr. and Kathryn (Halligan) W.; m. Mary Elizabeth Buckingham, Sept. 7, 1963 (div. June 1977); children: Scott Arthur, Christopher Davison, Timothy Buckingham; m. Daryl Hopkins Goss, Jan. 26, 1980. B.A. in English, Ind. U., 1963; DHL (hon.), Mercy Coll., Grand Valley State U. Various positions Times Herald, Port Huron, Mich., 1966-68; personnel dir., pub. Journal and Courier, Lafayette, Ind., 1968-73; gen. mgr., pub. Gannett Westchester Rockland Newspapers, White Plains, N.Y., 1973-74, pres., gen. mgr., 1974-77, pres., pub., 1977-79; v.p. devel. Gannett Co., Inc., N.Y.C., 1979-83, sr. v.p. planning and devel., 1982-86; chmn., pub. Gannett Westchester Rockland Newspapers, White Plains, 1984-86; pres. The Detroit News, 1986-89, pub., 1987-89; U.S. pub. Time Mag., 1989-91; pub., chief exec. officer, exec. v.p. Ariz. Republic, Phoenix Gazette, Ariz. Bus. Gazette, 1991-96; pres., CEO Central Newspapers, Inc., Phoenix, 1996—; bd. dirs. Ctrl. Newspapers, Inc., Prudential. Bd. trustees, adv. bd. Ariz. Cancer Ctr. at U. Ariz., Eugene C. Pulliam Trust, Am. Grad. Sch. Internat. Mgmt.; chmn. adv. bd. Kids Voting USA; bd. dirs. Ariz. Cmty. Found., Ind. U. Found.; campaign chmn. Valley of the Sun United Way, 1992; past chmn. Greater Phoenix Leadership; past pres. bd. trustees Phoenix Art Mus. With USN. Office: Ctrl Newspapers Inc 200 E Van Buren St Phoenix AZ 85004-2238

WEILAND, DAVE ALLEN, broadcast engineer; b. Oct. 12, 1960; s. Norbert and Amy Weiland; m. Meegan Agee, Sept. 4, 1993. AS, Pierce Coll., 1980; BA, Calif. State U., Northridge, 1987. Mem. staff entertainment divsn. Universal Studios, Universal City, Calif., 1980-83; owner Dawco, Northridge, Calif., 1983—; chief engr. Time Warner/West Valley Studios, Chatsworth, Calif., 1988—. Mem. Internat. TV Assn., Soc. Motion Picture and TV Engrs., Soc. Broadcast Engrs., Audio Engring. Soc.

WEILER, DOROTHY ESSER, librarian; b. Hartford, Wis., Feb. 21, 1914; d. Henry Hugo and Agatha Christina (Dopp) Esser; A.B. in Fgn. Langs., Wash. State U., 1935; B.A.L., Grad. Library Sch., U. Wash., 1936; postgrad. U. Ariz., 1956-57, Ariz. State U., 1957-58, Grad. Sch. Librarianship, U. Denver, 1971; m. Henry C. Weiler, Aug. 30, 1937; children—Robert William, Kurt Walter. Tchr.-librarian Roosevelt Elem. Schs., Dist. #66, Phoenix, 1956-59; extension librarian Ariz. Dept. Library and Archives, Phoenix, 1959-67; library dir. City of Tempe (Ariz.), 1967-79; assoc. prof., dept. library sci. Ariz. State U., 1968; vis. faculty Mesa Community Coll., 1980-84. Mem. public relations com. United Fund; treas. Desert Samaritan Med. Ctr. Aux., 1981, v.p. community relations Hosp., 1982, vol. asst. chaplain, 1988—, pastoral care vol. Named Ariz. Librarian of Yr., 1971; recipient Silver Book award Library Binding Inst., 1963. Mem. Tempe Hist. Soc., Ariz. Pioneers Hist. Soc., Am. Radio Relay League, Am. Bus. Women's Assn., ALA, Southwestern Library Assn., Ariz. State Libr. Assn. (pres. 1973-74), Ariz. Libr. Pioneer. Roman Catholic. Clubs: Our Lady of Mt. Carmel Ladies' Sodality, Soroptimist Internat. Founder, editor Roadrunner, Tumbling Tumbleweed; contbr. articles to mags. Home: 1605 E Southern Ave Tempe AZ 85282-5610

WEILER, MARY PAULINE, lawyer, nurse; b. Portland, Oreg., Nov. 11, 1957; d. Alfred John Weiler and Pauline Marguerite Roberts. BSN, BA in Psychology, U. Wash., 1980; JD cum laude, Lewis & Clark Coll., 1989. Bar: Ariz. 1989, Wash. 1990, Oreg. 1990, U.S. Dist. Ct. Ariz. 1989. Adminstr./dir. Kimberly Svcs., Inc., Portland, Oreg., 1984-86; med. cons. Spears, Lubersky et al, Portland, Oreg., 1986-88; atty. Gallagher & Kennedy, Phoenix, 1989-90; sr. health plan counsel, dir. contract adminstrn. Kaiser Found. Health Plan of the Northwest, Portland, 1990—. Advisor Animal Aid, Portland, 1988—. Mem. Oreg. State Bar Assn. (mem.-at-large exec. com. health law sect. 1995-97, mem. corp. counsel sect. 1995—), Wash. State Bar Assn. (health law sect. 1990—, corp. counsel sect. 1995—). Democrat. Avocations: sailing, reading. Office: Kaiser Found Health Plan NW 500 NE Multnomah St Ste 100 Portland OR 97232-2031

WEILL, LOUIS ARTHUR, III (CHIP), publishing executive; b. Grand Rapids, Mich., Mar. 15, 1941; m. Daryl Goss; children: Scott, Chris, Tim. BA in English, Ind. U.; LLD, Mercy Coll., Grand Valley State U. Several circulation and advt. positions Times Herald, Port Huron, Mich., 1966-68; personnel dir., then pub. Lafayette (Ind.) Jour. & Courier, 1968-1979; v.p. devel. Gannett Westchester Rockland Newspapers, 1979-82, sr. v.p. planning & devel., 1982-86; pres., then pres. & pub. Detroit News, 1986-89; pub., CEO Phoenix Newspapers, Inc., 1991-96; chmn., pres., CEO Ctrl. Newspapers, Inc., Paradise Valley, Ariz., 1996—; bd. trustees Am. Grad. Sch. Internat. Mgmt. Bd. trustees, mem. adv. bd. Ariz. Cancer Ctr., U. Ariz.; campaign chmn. Valley of Sun United Way, 1982; chmn. Greater Phoenix Leadership, past pres. bd. trustees Phoenix Art Mus. Mem. Newspaper Assn. Am. (bd. dirs.), Ariz. Cmty. Found. (bd. dirs.), Ind. U. Found. (bd. dirs.). Office: PO Box 2245 Phoenix AZ 85002-2245

WEILL, SAMUEL, JR., automobile company executive; b. Rochester, N.Y., Dec. 22, 1916; s. Samuel and Bertha (Stein) W.; student U. Buffalo, 1934-35; m. Mercedes Weil, May 20, 1939 (div. Aug. 1943); children: Rita and Eric (twins); m. Cléanthe Kimball Carr, Aug. 12, 1960 (div. 1982); m. Jacqueline Natalie Bateman, Jan. 5, 1983. Co-owner, Brayton Air Coll., St. Louis, 1937-42; assoc. editor, advt. mgr., bus. mgr. Road and Track Mag., Los Angeles, 1951-53; pres. Volkswagen Pacific, Inc., Culver City, Calif., 1953-73, Porsche Audi Pacific, Culver City, 1953-73; chmn. bd. Minto Internat., Inc., London; v.p. fin. Chieftain Oil Co., Ojai, Calif. Recipient Tom May award Jewish Hosp. and Research Center, 1971. Served with USAAF, 1943-45. Home: 305 Palomar Rd Ojai CA 93023-2432 Office: Chieftain Oil Co 214 W Aliso St Ojai CA 93023-2502

WEIMER, DAWN, sculptor; b. Denver, June 11, 1943; d. Morton Weil and Elsie Ione (Gudgel) Griswold; m. Thomas Eugene Weimer, June 14, 1964; 1 child, Heath. Executed bronzes for City of Westminister, Colo., 1996, City of Fort Collins, Colo., 1996-97, City of Loveland, Colo., 1996-97, City of Greeley, Colo., 1996-97; represented in permanent collections Lockheed-Martin Corp., Bethesda, Md., Express Pers. Internat. Hdqs., Oklahoma City, Okla., Bliss Industries Inc. Internat. Hdqs., Ponca City, Okla., Am. Quarter Horse Mus., Amarillo, Tex.; one-person shows include Bank One, Loveland, 1997. Recipient Best of Show, First Place award Draft Horse Classic, 1996, Philip Isenberg award Pen and Brush Sculpture Exhibit, 1994, Anna Hyatt Huntington award Am. Artists Pro League, 1993. Mem. Nat. Sculpture Soc., Catharine Lorillard Wolfe Art Club (Leila Gardin Sawyer award 1992), We. Art Assn., We. Heritage Artists. Office: Western Dawn Studio 1125 Centennial Rd Fort Collins CO 80525-2573

WEINBERG, HEDY LEAH, journalist; b. Utica, N.Y., Oct. 15, 1939; d. S. [illegible] 1960; children: Benjamin Thomas, Shira Beth, Adam Jerome. BA, NYU, 1961; student, Brandeis U., 1957-60; M in Spl. Studies, U. Denver, 1985. Substitute tchr. N.Y. Bd. Edn., Bklyn., 1961-64; staff writer, contbg. editor St. Edition USA, Denver, 1987-91, instr. writing divsn. extended studies U. Colo., Denver, 1992-94; v.p. Weinberg Group, Inc., Denver, 1996—. Co-author: Living with Hepatitis C: A Survivor's Guide, 1997 (1st Place Non-Fiction, Colo. Press Women 1998). Recipient Journalism award Leukemia Soc. Am., 1987, Third Place Personality Profile, Nat. Fedn. Press Women, 1989, First Place Articles/Essays, Nat. Writers Assn., 1995. Mem. Authors Guild, Soc. Profl. Journalists, Colo. Press Women/Nat. Fedn. Press Women, Colo. Authors League. Office: 4025 S Oneida St Denver CO 80237

WEINBERGER, FRANK, information management consultant; b. Chgo., Sept. 18, 1926; s. Rudolph and Elaine (Kellner) W.; m. Beatrice Natalie Fixler, June 27, 1953; children: Alan J., Bruce I. BSEE, Ill. Inst. Tech., Chgo., 1951; MBA, Northwestern U., 1959; DBA, U.S. Internat. U., San Diego, 1996. Registered profl. engr., Ill, Calif. Engr. Admiral Corp., Chgo., 1951-53; sr. engr. Cook Rsch., Chgo., 1953-59; mem. tech. staff Rockwell Internat., Downey, Calif., 1959-80, info. systems advisor, 1980-95; info. mgmt. cons., 1995—. Pres. Temple Israel, Long Beach, Calif., 1985-87, bd. dirs. 1973-85. With USN, 1944-46. Mem. Assn. for Computer Machinery. Democrat. Jewish. Avocation: microcomputers. Home and Office: 3231 Yellowtail Dr Los Alamitos CA 90720-5253

WEINER, FERNE, psychologist; b. N.Y.C., June 14, 1928; d. Irving Kapp and Peggy (Finkelstein) Hessberg; m. Howard Weiner, July 20, 1948; children: Irving Kenneth, Laurie. BA, Skidmore Coll., 1965; MA, Sarah Lawrence Coll., 1971; PhD, U. Hawaii, 1975. Lic. psychologist, Conn., Hawaii. Asst. prof. West Oahu Coll. U. Hawaii, Honolulu, 1975-77; staff psychologist Cmty. Guidance Clinic, Manchester, Conn., 1978-83; chief cons. psychologist Consultation and Evaluation Ctr., Meriden, Conn., 1984-85; psychologist cons. Disability Determination Svcs., Hartford, Conn., 1986-87, Honolulu, 1988—; police psychologist Honolulu Police Dept., 1988; pvt. practice, Greenwich, Conn., 1983-87, Honolulu, 1988—; cons. Adopt-A-Sch. Project, Honolulu, 1991-94; interviewer, therapist Sexual Abuse Treatment Team, Manchester, 1979-83; cons., trainer Conn. schs., day care, ch. groups, 1979-87. Contbr. articles to profl. jours. Active Disaster Assistance Mgmt. Team, Hawaii, 1994-95; v.p., sec. Queens Court at Kapiolani Bd., Honolulu, 1992-95; admissions rep. Hawaii Sarah Lawrence Coll., Honolulu, 1970-80; cons. to adoptees search Orphan Voyage, Conn., 1980-87; mentor Girl Scout Coun. Am., Oahu, 1993-94. Mem. Am. Psychol. Assn. (clin. psychotherapy and neuropsychology divsn.), Hawaii Psychol. Assn., Nat. Registry Health Svcs. Providers, Outrigger Canoe Club, Honolulu Club. Democrat. Jewish. Avocations: aerobics, interior design, property renovation, gourmet cooking, travel. Home: 3004 Hibiscus Dr Honolulu HI 96815-4725 Office: Behavior Therapy Clinic Kahala Office Ctr 4211 Waialae Ave Honolulu HI 96816-5319 also: Disability Determination Br 1580 Makaloa St Honolulu HI 96814-3237

WEINER, NORMAN, pharmacology educator; b. Rochester, N.Y., July 13, 1928; m. Diana Elaine Weiner, 1955; children: Steven, David, Jeffrey, Gareth, Eric. BS, U. Mich., 1949; MD, Harvard U., 1953. Diplomate Am. Bd. Med. Examiners. Intern 2d and 4th Harvard Med. Svc., Boston City Hosp., 1953-54; rsch. med. officer USAF, 1954-56; instr. dept. pharmacology-biochemistry Sch. of Aviation Medicine, San Antonio, 1954-56; from instr. to asst. prof. Harvard Med. Sch., Boston, 1956-67; prof. pharmacology U. Colo. Health Sci. Ctr., Denver, 1967—, disting. prof., 1989, chmn. dept. pharmacology, 1967-87; vis. prof. U. Calif., Berkeley, 1973-76; interim dean U. Colo. Sch. Medicine, 1983-84; Allan D. Bass lectr. sch. medicine Vanderbilt U., Nashville, 1983, divsn. v.p. Abbott Labs., Abbott Park, Ill., 1985-87; Pfizer lectr. Tex. Coll. Osteo. Medicine, Ft. Worth, 1985; disting. prof. UCHSC, 1989. Editor: Drugs and the Developing Brain, 1974, Structure and Function of Monoamine Enzymes, 1977, Regulation and Function of Monoamine Enzymes, 1981, Neuronal and Extraneuronal Events in Autonomic Pharmacology, 1984. Recipient Rsch. Career Devel. award USP HS, 1963, Kaiser Permanente award, 1974, 81, Otto Krayer award Am. Soc. Pharmacology and Exptl. Therapeutics, 1985; Spl. fellow USPHS, London, 1961-62; Disting. Volwiler Rsch. fellow Abbott Labs., 1988; Norman Weiner Festschrift, 1993; Julius Axelrod medal for outstadning scholarship in catecholamine rsch., 1993. Mem. AAAS, Am. Soc. for Pharmacology and Exptl. Therapeutics (Otto Krayer award 1985), N.Y. Acad. Scis., Assn. Med. Sch. Pharmacology, Am. Soc. Neurochemistry, Western Pharmacology Soc., Am. Coll. Neuropsychopharmacology, Soc. Neurosci., Biochem. Soc., Internat. Brain Rsch. Orgn., Internat. Soc. Neurochemistry, Rsch. Soc. on Alcoholism, Phi Beta Kappa, Sigma Xi, Alpha Omega Alpha, Phi Eta Sigma, Phi Lambda Upsilon, Phi Kappa Phi. Office: U Colo Health Sci Ctr Pharmacology Dept 4200 E 9th Ave Denver CO 80220-3706

WEINER, PETER H., lawyer; b. N.Y.C., July 10, 1944. BA, Harvard U., 1966; MSc, London Sch. Econs., 1967; LLB, Yale U., 1970. Bar: Calif. 1971. Ptnr. Paul, Hastings, Janofsky & Walker LLP, San Francisco, 1997—. Mem. Phi Beta Kappa. Office: Paul Hastings Janofsky & Walker LLP 345 California St Fl 29 San Francisco CA 94104-2606*

WEINER, SANDRA SAMUEL, critical care nurse, nursing consultant; b. N.Y.C., Jan. 12, 1947; d. Herbert A. and Ruth (Wallerstein) Samuel; m. Neil D. Weiner, June 15, 1969 (div. June 1980); 1 child, Jaime Michelle. BS in Nursing, SUNY, Buffalo, 1968; cert. in critical care, Golden West Coll., 1982; postgrad. UCLA, U. West L.A. Sch. of Law, 1992. RN, Pa., Calif. Staff nurse N.Y. Hosp.-Cornell Med. Ctr., 1968-69; head nurse med.-surg. nursing Abington (Pa.) Hosp., 1969; assoc. prof. Sch. Nursing, U. Pa., Phila., 1970; instr. nursing Coll. of Med. Assts., Long Beach, Calif., 1971-72; surg. staff nurse Med. Ctr. of Tarzana, Calif., 1978-79, Cedar-Sinai Med. Ctr., L.A., 1979-81; supr. recovery room Beverly Hills Med. Ctr., L.A., 1981-92; Post Anesthesia Care Unit nurse Westside Hosp., 1992-96, Midway Hosp., Beverly Hills, Calif., 1996—; med. cons. RJA & Assocs., Beverly Hills, Calif., 1984-92; instr. CPR, L.A., 1986-95. Mem. women's aux. Ctr. Theater Group Vols., L.A., 1986—, Maple Ctr., Beverly Hills, 1987-96. Mem. Am. Nursing Assn., Am. Soc. Post-Anesthesia Nursing, Am. Assn. Critical Care Nurses, Heart and Lung Assn., Post Anesthesia Nurses Assn., U.S. Ski Assn. Democrat. Jewish. Avocations: skiing, aerobics, travel, theater, ballet. Fax: (818) 509-8975. Home: 12633 Moorpark St Studio City CA 91604-4537

WEINER, STEWART GEORGE, magazine editor, writer, book publisher; b. Cin., Sept. 11, 1945; s. Dr. Alfred Lawrence and Janet Katherine (Lackner) W.; m. Ellen Faye Lustbader, Feb. 14, 1987; 1 child, Maxwell Spencer. Bachelor of Journalism, U. Mo., 1967. Founder bailey/erskine/roberts, Cin., 1968-73; editor-in-chief Writer's Digest, Cin., 1973-75; editor Provincetown mag., Cape Cod, Mass., 1976-77; sr. editor Playboy Enterprises, L.A., 1977-80; pub., owner The Galliard Press, L.A., 1983-84; editor-in-chief Caesars World's SEVEN mag., L.A., 1988-90; sr. editor Calif. mag., L.A., 1989—; dep. bur. chief TV Guide, L.A., 1992—; editor-in-chief Palm Springs (Calif.) Life, 1994—. Pub.: Radio Eyes, 1984; author: GERI, 1984. Avocations: music, film. Home: 73450 Calliandra St Palm Desert CA 92260-6067 Office: 303 N Indian Canyon Dr Palm Springs CA 92262-6015 Address: 73450 Calliandra St Palm Desert CA 92260-6067

WEINGARTEN, SAUL MYER, lawyer; b. Los Angeles, Dec. 19, 1921; s. Louis and Lillian Dorothy (Alter) W.; m. Miriam Ellen Moore, Jan. 21, 1949; children: David, Steven, Lawrence, Bruce. AA, Antelope Valley Coll., 1940; AB, UCLA, 1942; cert., Cornell U., 1943; JD, U. Southern Calif., 1949. Prin. Saul M. Weingarten Assocs., Seaside, Calif., 1954—; atty. City of Gonzales, Calif., 1954-74, City of Seaside, 1955-70; gen. counsel Redevel. Agy., Seaside, 1955-76, Security Nat. Bank, Monterey, Calif., 1968-74; bd. dirs., exec. com. Frontier Bank, Cheyenne, Wyo., 1984—, Mariposa Hall Inc., 1989—. Author: Practice Compendium, 1950; contbr. articles to profl. jours. Del. Internat. Union of Local Authorities, Brussels, Belgium, 1963, 73; candidate state legislature Dem. Com., Monterey County, 1958; counsel Monterey Peninsula Mus. of Art, Inc., 1972-80; gen. counsel Monterey County Symphony Assn., Carmel, Calif., 1974-98, Mountain Plains Edn. Project, Glasgow, Mont., 1975-81; chmn. fund raising ARC, Monterey, 1964; chmn., bd. dirs. fund raising United Way, Monterey, 1962-63; pres., bd. dirs. Alliance on Aging, Monterey, 1968-82; bd. dirs. Family Svc. Agy., [illegible] Found., 1982—; dir., mem. exec. com. Monterey Bay Performing Arts Ctr., 1990. Served to commdr. USN, 1942-46, 50-54, Korea. Grad. fellow Coro Found., 1949-50. Mem. Calif. Bar Assn., Monterey County Bar Assn., Monterey County Trial Lawyers Assn., Rotary (pres. 1970-71, 82-83), Commonwealth Club, Meadowbrook Club. Jewish. Avocations: tennis, travel. Home: 4135 Crest Rd Pebble Beach CA 93953-3008 Office: 1123 Fremont Blvd Seaside CA 93955-5759

WEINHARDT, J. W., computer company executive. Chmn. bd. dirs., CEO SJW Corp., San Jose, Calif. Office: SJW Corp 374 W Santa Clara St San Jose CA 95113-1502*

WEINMANN, ROBERT LEWIS, neurologist; b. Newark, Aug. 21, 1935; s. Isadore and Etta (Silverman) W.; m. Diana Weinmann, Dec. 13, 1980 (dec. Dec. 1989); children: Paul, Chris, Dana, Paige. BA, Yale U., 1957; MD, Stanford U., 1962. Diplomate Am. Bd. of EEG and Neurophysiology, v.p.; diplomate Am. Acad. Pain Mgmt., Am. Bd. Forensic Medicine. Intern Pacific Presbyn. Med. Ctr., San Francisco, 1962-63; resident in neurology Stanford U. Hosp., 1963-66, chief resident, 1965-66; pvt. practice San Jose, Calif., 1969—; former clin. instr. neurology, Stanford (Calif.) U. Chmn. editl. bd. Clin. EEG Jour.; mem. editl. bd. Jour. Am. Acad. Pain Mgmt.; formerly mem. editl. bd. Clin. Evoked Potentials Jour.; contbr. articles to various publs. Capt. M.C., U.S. Army, 1966-68, Japan. Recipient award State of R.I., Santa Clara County Med. Soc., Epilepsy Soc., Calif. State Assembly, other orgns.; fellow Univ. Paris, 1957-58. Fellow Am. Coll. Forensic Medicine; mem. Union of Am. Physicians and Dentists (pres. 1990—, bd. dirs. 1972—, pres. Calif. fedn. 1990—). Avocations: softball, tennis, music, theater, martial arts. Office: Union Am Physicians & Dentists 1330 Broadway Ste 730 Oakland CA 94612-2589

WEINRICH, JAMES DONALD, psychobiologist, educator; b. Cleve., July 2, 1950; s. Albert James and Helen (Lautz) W. AB, Princeton U., 1972; PhD, Harvard U., 1976. Postdoctoral fellow, then instr. Johns Hopkins U., Balt., 1980-82; rsch. assoc., then asst. rsch. prof. psychiatry Boston U., 1983-87; asst. rsch. psychobiologist, project mgr. U. Calif., San Diego, 1987-89, asst. rsch. psychobiologist, ctr. mgr., 1989-91, sr. investigator sexology, 1991-93, prin. investigator sexology project, 1994—; bd. dirs. Found. Sci. Study of Sexuality, Mt. Vernon, Iowa. Author: Sexual Landscapes, 1987; co-editor: Homosexuality: Social, Psychological and Biological Issues, 1982, Homosexuality: Research Implications for Public Policy, 1991; cons. editor Jour. of Sex Rsch., 1997—. Mem. Internat. Acad. Sex Rsch., Soc. for Sci. Study of Sex (Hugo Beigel award 1987), Am. Coll. Sexologists (cert.), Phi Beta Kappa. Avocations: computers, photography. Office: Univ Calif San Diego 2760 5th Ave Ste 200 San Diego CA 92103-6325

WEINSHIENK, ZITA LEESON, federal judge; b. St. Paul, Apr. 3, 1933; d. Louis and Ada (Dubov) Leeson; m. Hubert Troy Weinshienk, July 8, 1956 (dec. 1983); children: Edith Blair, Kay Anne, Darcy Jill; m. James N. Schaffner, Nov. 15, 1986. Student, U. Colo., 1952-53; BA magna cum laude, U. Ariz., 1955; JD cum laude, Harvard U., 1958; Fulbright grantee, U. Copenhagen, Denmark, 1959; LHD (hon.), Loretto Heights Coll., 1985; LLD (hon.), U. Denver, 1990. Bar: Colo. 1959. Probation counselor, legal adviser, referee Denver Juvenile Ct., 1959-64; judge Denver Mcpl. Ct., 1964-65, Denver County Ct., 1965-71, Denver Dist. Ct., 1972-79; judge, then sr. judge U.S. Dist. Ct. Colo., Denver, 1979—. Precinct committeewoman Denver Democratic Com., 1963-64; bd. dirs. Crime Stoppers. Named one of 100 Women in Touch with Our Time Harper's Bazaar Mag., 1971, Woman of Yr., Denver Bus. and Profl. Women, 1969; recipient Women Helping Women award Soroptimist Internat. of Denver, 1983, Hanna G. Solomon award Nat. Coun. Jewish Women, Denver, 1986. Fellow Colo. Bar Found., Am. Bar Found.; mem. ABA, Denver Bar Assn., Colo. Bar Assn., Nat. Conf. Fed. Trial Judges (exec. com., past chair), Dist. Judges' Assn. of 10th Cir. (past pres.), Colo. Women's Bar Assn., Fed. Judges Assn., Denver Crime Stoppers Inc. (bd.dirs.), Devner LWV, Women's Forum Colo., Harvard Law Sch. Assn., Phi Beta Kappa, Phi Kappa Phi, Order of Coif (hon. Colo. chpt.). Office: US Dist Ct US Courthouse Rm C-418 1929 Stout St Denver CO 80294-0001*

WEINSTEIN, RACHEL, clown; b. Edmonton, Alta., Can., Jan. 30, 1912; came to U.S., 1952; d. Samuel and Rebecca (Rabinovich) Caplan; m. Sam Weinstein, June 1952 (div. 1962); 1 child, Lee Gray. Cert. Completion, Prince Albert Bus. Coll., Sask., 1941; Master Clown Cert., Lane C.C., Eugene, Oreg., 1992; studied with clown Frosty Little, 1997. Founder, mgr. Strand Shoe Store, Prince Albert, 1932-41; chief window display decorator Hudson's Bay Co., Victoria, B.C., Can., 1942-45; founder Dominion Paint Co., Victoria, B.C., Can., 1945-52; owner, mgr. Rachel Weinstein Bus. and Tax Cons. Svc., Eugene, 1962-85, Rachel Weinstein Vita and Resume Svc., Eugene, 1962-85; entertainer Tango the Clown, Eugene, 1985—. Editor/pub.: Cow Creek Valley Memories, 1971, Genealogy of Mrs. Chatt, 1975. Recipient Gov. Gen.'s medal Province of Sask., 1926, Outstanding Achievement Commendation, Prince Albert Bus. Coll., 1941. Mem. AAI Investors, World Clown Assn., Rental Owner's Assn. Avocations: piano playing, music theory. Office: PO Box 1722 Eugene OR 97440-1722

WEINSTOCK, HAROLD, lawyer; b. Stamford, Conn., Nov. 30, 1925; s. Elias and Sarah (Singer) W.; m. Barbara Lans, Aug. 27, 1950; children—Nathaniel, Michael, Philip. B.S. magna cum laude, N.Y. U., 1947; J.D., Harvard, 1950. Bar: Conn. bar 1950, Ill. bar 1950, Calif. bar 1958. Atty. SEC, Washington, 1950-52, IRS, 1952-56; tax atty. Hunt Foods & Industries, Inc., Los Angeles, 1956-58; pvt. practice Beverly Hills, Calif., 1958-71, Los Angeles, 1971—; mem. Weinstock, Manion, Reisman, Shore & Neumann (and predecessor firms), 1958—; Lectr. extension div., estate planning courses U. Calif. at Los Angeles, 1959—; estate planning and taxation courses Calif. Continuing Edn. of the Bar, 1960—. Author: Planning An Estate, 4th edit., 1995; contbr. articles to profl. publs. Nat. trustee Union Am. Hebrew Congregations, 1976-79; bd. trustees Jewish Cmty. Found., L.A.; adv. bd. Estate Planning Inst. UCLA Law Sch., 1979-92, NYU Inst. on Fed. Taxation, 1986-95. Mem. ABA, Calif. Bar Assn., Beverly Hills Bar Assn. (chmn. probate and trusts com. 1967-68), Los Angeles Bar Assn., Beverly Hills Estate Planning Council (pres. 1968-69), Estate Counselors Forum of Los Angeles (pres. 1963-64). Jewish (pres. temple 1974-76). Office: Weinstock Manion 1875 Century Park E 15th Fl Los Angeles CA 90067-1702

WEINSTOCK, RONALD JAY, research and development company executive; b. L.A., Mar. 14, 1960; s. Howard Frank and Anne Carol (Schneider) W.; m. Sigrid Lipsett, June 11, 1988; children: Rachel, Brent. Student, U. Calif., San Diego, 1978-80, U. Calif., Santa Barbara, 1980-81. CEO Magnetic Resonance Diagnostics Corp., Thousand Oaks, Calif., 1989—; vice chmn. Magnetic Resonance Rsch. Soc., Tokyo, 1991—; lectr. in field. Co-developer Magnetic Resonance Analyzer; contbr. articles to profl. jours. CPR instr. Am. Heart Assn., Beverly Hills, 1981; EMT, UCLA, 1980; chmn. police dept. disaster response team City of Thousand Oaks, 1995—.

WEIR, ALEXANDER, JR., utility consultant, inventor; b. Crossett, Ark., Dec. 19, 1922; s. Alexander and Mary Eloise (Field) W.; m. Florence Forschner, Dec. 28, 1946; children: Alexander III, Carol Jean, Bruce Richard. BSChemE, U. Ark., 1943; MChemE, Poly Inst. Bklyn., 1946; PhD, U. Mich., 1954; cert., U. So. Calif. Grad. Sch. Bus. Adminstrn., 1968. Chem. engr. Am. Cyanamid Co., Stamford Rsch. Labs., 1943-47; with U. Mich., 1948-58; rsch. assoc., project supr. Engring. Rsch. Inst., U. Mich., 1948-57; lectr. chem. and metall. engring. dept. U. Mich., 1954-56, asst. prof., 1956-58; cons. Ramo-Woolridge Corp., L.A., 1956-57; mem. tech. staff, sect. head, asst. mgr. Ramo-Wooldridge Corp., L.A., 1957-60, incharge Atlas Missile Captive test program, 1956-60; tech. adv. to pres. Northrop Corp., Beverly Hills, Calif., 1960-70; prin. scientist for air quality So. Calif. Edison Co., L.A., 1970-76, mgr. chem. sys. R & D, 1976-86, chief rsch. scientist, 1986-88; utility cons. Playa Del Rey, Calif., 1988—; rep. Am. Rocket Soc. to Detroit Nuc. Coun., 1954-57; chmn. session on chem. reactions Nuc. Sci. and Engring. Congress, Cleve., 1955; U.S. del. AGARD (NATO) Combustion Colloquium, Liege, Belgium, 1955; Western U.S. rep. task force on environ. R & D goals Electric Rsch. Coun., 1971; electric utility advisor Electric Power Rsch. Inst., 1974-78, 84-87, industry advisor dept. chemistry and biochemistry Calif. State U., L.A., 1981-88. Author: Two and Three Dimensional Flow of Air through Square-Edged Sonic Orifices, 1954; (with D.D. Morrison and T.C. Anderson) Notes on Combustion, 1955, also tech. papers; inventor acid rain prevention device used in 5 states. Sea scout leader, Greenwich, Conn., 1944-48, Marina del Rey, Calif., 1965-70; bd. govs., past pres. Civic Union Playa del Rey, chmn. sch., police and fire, nominating; civil def.; army liaison [illegible] Westchester

YMCA, chmn. Dads sponsoring com., active fundraising; chmn. nominating com. Paseo del Rey Sch. PTA, 1961; mem. L.A. Mayors Cmty. Adv. Com.; asst. chmn. advancement com., merit badge dean Cantinella dist. L.A. Area coun. Boy Scouts Am. Recipient Nat. Rsch. Coun. Flue Gas Desulfurization Industrials Scale Reliability award NAS, 1975, Power Environ. Achievement award EPA, 1980, Excellence in Sulfur Dioxide Control award EPA, 1985. Mem. AIChE, Am. Geophys. Union, Navy League U.S. (v.p. Palos Verdes Peninsula coun. 1961-62), N.Y. Acad. Scis., Sci. Rsch. Soc. Am., Am. Chem. Soc., U.S. Power Squadron (hon. capt. of fleet 1997), St. Andrew Soc. So. Calif., Clan Macnachtan Assn., Clan Buchanan Soc. Am., Clan Farquharson Assn., Betty Washington Lewis Soc. of Children of Am. Revolution (past pres.), Ark. Soc. of Children of Am. Revolution (past pres.), Santa Monica Yacht Club (lifetime hon. cannoneer), Sigma Xi, Phi Kappa Phi, Phi Lambda Upsilon, Alpha Chi Sigma, Lambda Chi Alpha. Office: 8229 Billowvista Dr Playa Del Rey CA 90293-7807

WEIR, CHARLENE MARTHA, writer; b. Atheson, Kans., Nov. 10, 1937; d. George Julius and Clara Ernestine (Wissman) Kettner; children: Jon Christopher, Leslie Alane. RN, Kans. Writer El Cerrito, Calif. Author: Winter Widow, 1991, Consider the Crows, 1993, Family Practice, 1995, Murder Take Two, 1998. Mem. Mystery Writers Am., Sisters in Crime, Am. Crime Writers League.

WEIR, JIM DALE, small business owner; b. Phoenix, Feb. 2, 1956; s. Jim Earl and Laverne Alice (Mahan) W.; m. Myra Yvonne Anglin, July 19, 1980; children: Justin, Kevin, Amanda, Jordan. Student, Phoenix Coll., 1978; BS, Grand Canyon Coll., 1980. Owner Quality S Mfg., Phoenix, 1980—. Vol. Tempe (Ariz.) Ch. of the Nazarene, 1987-89, Latin Am. Ch. of the Nazarene, Phoenix, 1988-89. Recipient Key of City award Phoenix, 1987, Fast Growth award Inc. mag., 1988. Republican. Avocations: sports, outdoors, family. Home: PO Box 23910 Phoenix AZ 85063-3910

WEIS, ANDREW (ANDY) JEROME, musician, educator; b. St. Marys, Pa., July 28, 1954; s. Leo Benten and Audrey Mary (Wendel) W.; m. Virginia Lee Wortman, June 15, 1984 (div.); 1 child, Audrey Anna. Profl. diploma, Berklee Coll. Music, 1975; student, Navy Sch. Music, 1980. drum tchr. jazz camps Monterey Jazz Festival and Youth Music Monterey. With U.S. Army, 1980-83. Mem. Am. Fedn. Musicians. Roman Catholic. Avocations: drum restoration, drum consulting. Home and Office: 625 Major Sherman Ln Monterey CA 93940-4620

WEISBERG, MAGGIE, public relations executive; b. Arad, Hungary, Feb. 22, 1917; came to U.S., 1922; d. Matyas and Roszika (Kobol) Kiss; widowed. Student, UCLA. Pvt. practice pub. rels. Tarzana, Calif., 1960-71; ptnr. M & M Assocs., Ft. Jones, Calif., 1971—. Author children's stories. Home and Office: PO Box 1020 12424 Main St Fort Jones CA 96032

WEISENBURGER, THEODORE MAURICE, judge, poet, educator, writer; b. Tuttle, N.D., May 12, 1930; s. John and Emily (Rosenau) W.; children: Sam, Jennifer, Emily, Todd, Daniel, Dwight, Holly, Michael, Paul, Peter; m. Maylyne Chu, Sept. 19, 1985; 1 child, Irene. BA, U. N.D., 1952, LLB, 1956, JD, 1969; BFT, Am. Grad. Sch. Internat. Mgmt., Phoenix, 1957. Bar: N.D. 1963, U.S. Dist. Ct. N.D. 1963. County judge, tchr. Benson County, Minnewaukan, N.D., 1968-75, Walsh County, Grafton, N.D., 1975-87; tribal judge Devils Lake Sioux, Ft. Totten, N.D., 1968-84, Turtle Mountain Chippewa, Belcourt, N.D., 1974-87; U.S. magistrate U.S. Dist. Ct., Minnewaukan, 1972-75; Justice of the Peace pro tem Maricopa County, Ariz., 1988-92; instr. Rio Salado C.C., 1992—; tchr. in Ethiopia, 1958-59. 1st lt. U.S. Army, 1952-54. Author: Poetry and Other Poems, 1991. Recipient Humanitarian award U.S. Cath. Conf., 1978, 82, Right to Know award Sigma Delta Chi, 1980, Spirit of Am. award U.S. Conf. Bishops, 1982. Home: 4353 E Libby St Phoenix AZ 85032-1732

WEISER, FRANK ALAN, lawyer; b. L.A., Dec. 12, 1953; s. Carl and Rose (Klein) W.; m. Susan Koenig, Aug. 12, 1983. BA, UCLA, 1976; JD, Southwestern U., L.A., 1979; LLM in Taxation, U. San Diego, 1986. Bar: Calif. 1979, U.S. Dist. Ct. (cen. dist.) Calif. 1981, U.S. Tax Ct. 1982, U.S. Ct. Appeals (9th cir.) 1982, U.S. Supreme Ct. 1987, U.S. Ct. Claims 1987, U.S. Ct. Mil. Appeals 1988, U.S. Ct. Appeals (fed. cir.) 1989, U.S. Ct. Internat. Trade 1989, U.S. Ct. Appeals Temporary Emergency Ct., 1989, U.S. Ct. Vets. Appeals 1990, U.S. Dist. Ct. (no. and so. dists.) Calif. 1993. Tax cons., advanced underwriter Transam. Occidental Life Ins. Co., L.A., 1979-80; assoc. Law Offices Herman English, 1980-81; atty., owner Frank A. Weiser-A Law Corp., L.A., 1981—; judge pro tem L.A. County Mcpl. Ct., 1987—. Editor So. Calif. mag., 1987—; contbr. articles to profl. jours. Bd. suprs. Michael Antonovich Election Com., 1988; mem. World Affairs Coun., L.A.; mem. U.S. Ct. of Vets. Appeals, 1990; assoc. mem. Calif. Rep. Cen. Com. Recipient official resolutions from Calif. State Legislature, 1989, joint rules com. resolution for state assembly and sate senate, 1990, Calif. State Assembly and Senate, 1989, L.A. County Bd. of Suprs., 1989, City Coun. of L.A., 1987, Congressional Cert. of Appreciation; tribute to him placed into official Congl. record, 1989; Nat. Merit scholar, 1971. Mem. ABA (internat. labor com., arts control and disarmament com., internat. employment practices com., editorial advisor internat. law and practive sect. publs. com., internat. property, estate and trust com., fgn. investment in U.S. com.), Fed. Bar Assn. (internat. law com.), Inter-Am. Bar Assn., Am. Judicature Soc., Assn. Trial Lawyers Am., Calif. Trial Lawyers Assn., L.A. Trial Lawyers Assn., Internat. Bar Assn., World Affairs Coun. L.A., World Inst. Achievement, L.A. Athletic Club. Office: 3460 Wilshire Blvd Ste 903 Los Angeles CA 90010-2230

WEISER, JANET KAYE, computer company executive; b. Rushville, Nebr., Sept. 12, 1951; d. John Ulrich and Mary Eilhelmina (Janssen) Lehman; m. Alan Warren Weiser, Jan. 1, 1985; children: Carla Marie, Dana Lauren. BA summa cum laude, Met. State Coll., 1973; MPH, U. N.C., 1979. Chief statistical analyst Colo. Dept. Health, Denver, 1971-93; pres. JK, Inc., Denver, 1983—; cons. Colo. State U., Boulder, 1984-94. Mem. Am. Pub. Health Assn., Nat. Assn. Pub. Health Statistics and Info. Systems. Home: 4925 Highway 34 Wheatland WY 82201-8626 Office: JK Inc 8333 Greenwood Blvd Denver CO 80221-4481

WEISKOPF, KIM ROBERT, television producer, writer; b. N.Y.C., Apr. 10, 1947; s. Robert Jerome and Eileen May (Ito) W.; m. Jo Ellen Erwin Legendre, May 17, 1980; 1 child, Kathleen. BA in English Lit., San Francisco State U., 1969. Story editor, writer TV show Good Times, Hollywood, Calif., 1977; exec. script cons., writer TV show Three's Company, L.A., 1979-80; prodr., writer TV show 9 to 5, L.A., 1981; exec. prodr., writer TV show What's Happening Now, Burbank, Calif., 1985-87; prodr., writer TV show Full House, Culver City, Calif., 1988-91; supervising prodr., writer TV show Rachel Gunn, R.N., Hollywood, 1992-93; supervising/co-exec. prodr., writer TV show Married...With Children, Columbia TV, Culver City and Hollywood, 1994-96; exec. prodr., writer TV show Malcolm & Eddie, Tri-Star TV, Culver City, 1996—; co-exec. prodr., writer TV show Sister, Sister Paramount, Hollywood, Calif., 1997.

WEISKOPF, WILLIAM HARVARD, accountant; b. Chgo., Feb. 18, 1938; s. William Herman and Josephine (Marron) W.; m. Carol Ruth Soderstrom, June 14, 1958; children: Cheryl Ruth, William Helge, Richard Harvard. BSBA, Northwestern U., 1960, MBA, 1967. CPA, Colo., Ill. Controller Clare Ceramics, Cary, Ill., 1960-63; chief fin. officer S.C. Lawlor Co., Melrose Park, Ill., 1964-65; staff acct. Ernst & Young, Chgo., 1967-69; staff acct. Ernst & Young, Denver, 1970-71, mgr., 1972-75, sr. mgr., 1976-78, ptnr., 1979-91; exec. dir. Colo. Sch. Mines Found., Inc., Golden, Colo., 1992—. Mem. exec. bd. Denver Coun. Boy Scouts Am., 1981—. Mem. AICPA (coun. mem. 1989-92), Colo. Soc. CPAs (pres. 1988-89), Leadership Denver Assn., Colo. Alliance of Bus. (dir., treas. 1986-91). Republican. Avocations: skiing, tennis. Office: Colo Sch Mines Found Inc PO Box 4005 Golden CO 80401-0005

WEISMAN, MARTIN JEROME, manufacturing company executive; b. N.Y.C., Aug. 22, 1930; s. Lewis E. and Estelle (Scherer) W.; m. Sherrie Cohen, Jan. 27, 1952; children: Jane Dory, Andrea Sue, Amy Ellen. B in Chem. Engring., N.Y.U., 1951. Sr. chem. engr. Ideal Toy Corp., Hollis, N.Y., 1951-57; research chemist Chesebrough-Ponds, Stamford, Conn., 1957-62; mgr. nail products lab. Max Factor and Co., Hollywood, Calif., 1962-81; v.p., tech. dir. Sher-Mar Cosmetics div. Weisman Industries, Inc., Canoga Park, Calif., 1981-97; owner Weisman Industries, Inc., Westlake Vlg., CA, 1997—. Patentee in field. Mem. Soc. Cosmetic Chemists, Los Angeles Soc. Coatings Tech., Am. Chem. Soc. Home and Office: Weisman Industries 32132 Canyon Crest Ct Westlake Village CA 91361-4800

WEISS, HERBERT KLEMM, retired aeronautical engineer; b. Lawrence, Mass., June 22, 1917; s. Herbert Julius and Louise (Klemm) W.; m. Ethel Celesta Giltner, May 14, 1945 (dec.); children: Janet Elaine, Jack Klemm (dec.). BS, MIT, 1937, MS, 1938. Engr. U.S. Army Arty. Bds., Ft. Monroe, Va, 1938-42, Camp Davis, N.C., 1942-44, Ft. Bliss, Tex., 1944-46; chief WPN Systems Lab., Ballistic Research Labs., Aberdeen Proving Grounds, Md, 1946-53; chief WPN systems analysis dept. Northrop Aircraft Corp., 1953-58; mgr. advanced systems devel. mil. systems planning aeronutronic div. Ford Motor Co., Newport Beach, Calif., 1958-61; group dir., plans devel. and analysis Aerospace Corp., El Segundo, Calif., 1961-65; sr. scientist Litton Industries, Van Nuys, Calif., 1965-82; cons. mil. systems analysis, 1982-90; Mem. Sci. Adv. Bd. USAF, 1959-63, sci. adv. panel U.S. Army, 1965-74, sci. adv. commn. Army Ball Research Labs., 1973-77; advisor Pres.'s Commn. Law Enforcement and Adminstrn. Justice, 1966; cons. Office Dir. Def., Research and Engring., 1954-64. Contbr. articles to profl. jours. Patentee in field. Recipient Commendation for meritorious civilian service USAF, 1964, cert. appreciation U.S. Army, 1976. Fellow AAAS, AIAA (assoc.); mem. IEEE, Ops. Rsch. Soc. Am., Cosmos Club. Republican. Home: PO Box 2668 Palos Verdes Peninsula CA 90274-8668

WEISS, LOREN ELLIOT, lawyer, law educator; b. Cleve., Sept. 28, 1947; s. Harry and Gertrude (Rapport) W.; m. Gina Dalton. BA with honors, UCLA, 1969; JD cum laude, U. San Diego, 1972. Bar: Calif. 1972, U.S. Dist. Ct. (so. dist.) Calif. 1972, Utah 1983, U.S. Dist. Ct. (cen. dist.) Calif. 1983, U.S. Dist. Ct. Utah 1983, U.S. Ct. Appeals (9th cir.) 1972, U.S. Ct. Appeals (10th cir.) 1986. With various law firms, San Diego, 1972-80; owner, gen. mgr. Mid-Mountain Lodge, Park City, Utah, 1980-83; pvt. practice, Salt Lake City, 1983-89, 93—; of counsel Purser, Okazaki & Berrett, Salt Lake City, 1989-93; prin. Weiss Berrett Petty, Salt Lake City, 1996—; mem. Utah Com. Bar Examiners, Salt Lake City, 1989-93; mem. ann. meeting com. Utah State Bar, 1985-91, chmn., 1994-95; liaison, panel atty. rep. U.S. Jud. Conf.Com. on Defender Svc., 1992-95; mem. mandatory cont. legal edn. bd. Utah Judicial Conf., 1995—; adj. prof. J. Reuben Clark Law Sch., Brigham Young U., 1990-98. Contbr. articles to legal jours. Trustee Utah Trout Found., Salt Lake City, 1988—. Mem. FBA, Calif. Bar Assn., Utah Bar Assn., Nat. Assn. Criminal Def. Lawyers (co-chmn. continuing legal edn. com. 1992-93, co-chair indigent svcs. com. 1994-95), Am. Bd. Trial Advocates. Avocations: fly fishing, reading. Fax: (801) 531-7711. Office: # 530 50 S Main St Salt Lake City UT 84101

WEISS, MARTIN HARVEY, neurosurgeon, educator; b. Newark, Feb. 2, 1939; s. Max and Rae W.; m. R. Debora Rosenthal, Aug. 20, 1961; children: Brad, Jessica, Elisabeth. AB magna cum laude, Dartmouth Coll., 1960, BMS, 1961; MD, Cornell U., 1963. Diplomate Am. Bd. Neurol. Surgery (bd. dirs. 1983-89, vice chmn. 1987-88, chmn. 1988-89). Intern Univ. Hosps., Cleve., 1963-64; resident in neurosurgery Univ. Hosps., 1966-70; sr. instr. to asst. prof. neurosurgery Case Western Res. U., 1970-73; asso. prof. neurosurgery U. So. Calif., 1973-76, prof., 1976-78, prof., chmn. dept., 1978—, Martin H. Weiss chair in neurol. surgery, 1997—; chmn. neurology B study sect. NIH; mem. residency rev. com. for neurosurgery Accreditation Commn. for Grad. Med. Edn., 1989—, vice chmn., 1991-93, chmn., 1993-95, mem. appeals coun. in neurosurgery, 1995—; Courville lectr. Loma Linda U. Sch. Medicine, 1989; Edgar Kahn vis. prof. U. Mich., 1987; W. James Gardner lectr. Cleve. Clinic, 1993; Edwin Boldrey vis. prof. U. Calif., San Francisco, 1994; hon. guest San Francisco Neurol. Soc., 1994, Australian Neurosurg. Soc., 1996; Aurthur Ward vis. prof. U. Wash., 1988; John Raff vis. prof. U. Oreg., 1995; Afrox traveling prof. South African Congress Neurol. Surgeons, 1989; Loyal Davis lectr. Northwestern U., 1990; vis. prof. U. Melbourne, 1996, U. Sydney, 1996; Wagner lectr. U. Medicine and Dentistry N.J., 1997. Author: Pituitary Diseases, 1980; editor-in-chief Clin. Neurosurgery, 1980-83; assoc. editor Bull. L.A. Neurol. Socs., 1976-81, Jour. Clin. Neurosci., 1981—; mem. editl. bd. Neurosurgery, 1979-84, Neurol. Rsch., 1980—, Jour. Neurosurgery, 1987—, chmn., 1995—, assoc. editor, 1996. Served to capt. USAR, 1964-66. Spl. fellow in neurosurgery NIH, 1969-70; recipient Jamieson medal Australasian Neurosurg. Soc., 1996. Mem. ACS (adv. coun. neurosurgery 1985-88), Soc. Neurol. Surgeons (v.p. 1999—), Neurosurg. Soc. Am., Am. Acad. Neurol. Surgery (exec. com. 1988-89, v.p. 1992-93), Rsch. Soc. Neurol. Surgeons, Am. Assn. Neurol. Surgeons (bd. dirs. 1988-91, sec. 1994-97, pres.-elect 1998—, pres. 1999—), Congress Neurol. Surgeons (v.p. 1982-83), Western Neurosurg. Soc., Neurosurg. Forum, So. Calif. Neurosurg. Soc. (pres. 1983-84), Phi Beta Kappa, Alpha Omega Alpha. Home: 357 Georgian Rd La Canada-Flintridge CA 91011-3520 Office: 1200 N State St Los Angeles CA 90033-1029

WEISS, ROBERT MARK, education administrator; b. L.A., Apr. 5, 1953; s. Murray John and Twyla Bernice (Yorkshire) W.; m. Karen Sue Basin, Mar. 24, 1985 (div. Feb. 1994). AB, U. So. Calif., 1975, MA, 1978; PhD, UCLA, 1985. Cert. instr., Calif. Cmty. Colls. Instr. Mt. San Antonio Jr. Coll., Walnut, Calif., 1989-90, So. Oreg. U., Ashland, 1991-92; dir. Medford (Oreg.) Edn. Internat., 1993—; cons. U. Calif., San Diego, 1985-86. Author: Prospect: Portrait of an Uper Rogue Community, 1989, Laurelhurst: Lost Community of the Upper Rogue, 1991; translator: I Give My Heart to Children, 1997. Mem. Bear Creek Greenway Com., Medford, Oreg., 1991, Rogue Valley Civic League, Medford, 1998. Recipient Writing grant So. Oreg. Hist. Soc., 1990, Sukhomlinskij medallion Tchrs. Tng. Inst. Kiev, Ukraine, 1996. Mem. MLA, Am. Assn. Tchrs. Slavic and East European Langs., Phi Beta Kappa. Avocations: musical theater, mineral collecting, book collecting, rafting. Home: 1776 Rogue River Dr Eagle Point OR 97524 Office: Medford Edn Internat 214 Stark St Medford OR 97504

WEISSENBUEHLER, WAYNE, former bishop, pastor. Bishop of Rocky Mountain Evang. Luth. Ch. in Am., Denver, 1993; pastor Bethany Luth. Ch., Englewood, Colo., 1993—. Office: Bethany Luth Ch 4500 E Hampton Englewood CO 80110*

WEISSFELD, AMY M., sales executive; b. Buffalo, Dec. 17, 1968; d. Richard Alan and Carol Joan (Loewensberg) W.; m. Kenneth L. Levy, Aug. 1, 1993. BA in English, U. Mich., 1991; student, Ariz. State U. Asst. account exec. Sheila Sloan Pub. Rels., Inc., Southfield, Mich., 1989-90; Japanese ski host Park City (Utah) Ski Corp., 1991-92; asst. account exec. C&S Creative Svcs., Inc., Park City, 1992-93; promotion mgr. Continental Promotion Group, Inc., Tempe, Ariz., 1993-95, nat. sales mgr., 1995—. Office: Continental Promotion Group, Inc 422 S Madison Dr Tempe AZ 85281-7221

WEISSMAN, SHANE ANDREW, automobile accessories company owner; b. Artesia, Calif., Sept. 30, 1956; s. George Elliott and Claire Belle Weissman; m. Carla Jean Peters, July 3, 1976. Student, Poly. U., San Fernando/Van Nuys, Calif., 1974. Dispatcher Doug Scott & Co. subs. L.A. Coroners Office, L.A., 1976-78; pin striper Trim Line No. Calif., Redding, 1979-85; owner Shane's Auto Accessories, Shasta Lake, Calif., 1986—. Author: Nifty Nursery Rhymes, 1997; songwriter: (lyrics) If You Really Loved Me You'd Have Never Said "I Do," 1996, If She Hadn't Been So Pretty, I Would Have Seen the Train, 1996. Avocations: unicycle riding, motivational public speaking. Office: Shane's Auto Accessories PO Box 5273 Shasta Lake CA 96089-5273

WEITZEL, JOHN QUINN, bishop; b. Chgo., May 10, 1928; s. Carl Joseph and Patricia (Quinn) W. BA, Maryknoll (N.Y.) Sem., 1951, M of Religious Edn., 1953; PMD, Harvard U. Ordained priest Roman Cath. Ch., 1955. With ednl. devel. Cath. Fgn. Mission Soc. of Am., Maryknoll, 1955-63, nat. dir. vocations for Maryknoll, dir. devel. dept. and info. services, 1963-72, mem. gen. council, 1972-78; asst. parish priest Cath. Ch., Western Samoa, 1979-81, pastor, vicar gen., 1981-86; consecrated bishop, 1986; bishop Cath. Ch., Am. Samoa, 1986—. Office: Diocese Samoa-Pago Pago Fatuoaiga PO Box 596 Pago Pago AS 96799-0596

WELCH, DOMINIC, publishing executive. Pres., pub. The Salt Lake Tribune, Salt Lake City, Utah. Office: 400 Tribune Bldg Salt Lake City UT 84111*

WELCH, MATTHEW LEE, journalist; b. Bellflower, Calif., July 31, 1968; s. Peter William Welch and Mary Bobbitt Townsend; m. Emmanuelle Marie Richard, July 26, 1997. Night prodn. mgr. Daily Nexus, Santa Barbara, Calif., 1988-90; founder, owner, editor Prognosis, Prague, Czechoslovakia, 1990-95; corr. UPI, Bratislava, Slovakia, 1992-94; musician Van Diamond, The Royal Supremems, 1995; mng. editor Budapest Bus. Jour., 1995-97; project mgr. New World Pub., Budapest, 1997; contbg. writer Online Journalism Rev., L.A., 1998—; news editor Tabloid, San Francisco, 1998—; cons., contbg. editor Velvet Mag., Prague, 1995-96; cons. Viper Radio, Skopje, Macedonia, 1996. Writer, performer mus. cassettes. Home: 4627 Pepperwood Ave Long Beach CA 90808

WELCH, RICHARD LEROY, personal improvement company executive; b. Lincoln, Nebr., Oct. 15, 1939; s. Raymond Nathanial and Helen Lila (Ludwig) W.; m. Donna Lee Gysegem, Nov. 3, 1991; children: Terri L. Flowerday, Julie A. Kuhl; 1 stepchild, Shannon Panzo. Student, U. Nebr., 1958-59. Agt. Gurantee Mut. Life, Lincoln, Nebr., 1960-61; agt., mgr. Mut. of Omaha, 1962-68; gen. agt. Loyal Protective Life, Omaha, 1969-70; mgr. Mut. Benefit Life, Dallas, 1971-73; br. mgr. Great West Life, San Jose, Calif., 1973-74; pres. Internat. Speedreading Inst., Phoenix, 1975-80; founder, pres. Educom, Inc./Subliminal Dynamics, Aurora, Colo., 1980—; mem. adv. bd. Great West Life, San Jose, 1973; pres. bd. dirs. Internat. Speedreading Inst., Phoenix, 1975-80, Subliminal Dynamics, Inc., San Jose, 1980-93, Educom, Inc., Aurora, 1993—; scientist, spkr., author, educator in field. Author: Brain Management, 1996. Mem. Shriners, Masons (32d degree). Democrat. Avocations: sports, music, travel. Office: Educom Inc DBA Subliminal Dynamics 19744 E Union Dr Aurora CO 80015-3486

WELCHERT, STEVEN JOSEPH, public affairs consultant; b. Davenport, Iowa, June 16, 1956; s. Richard Marshall and Norma Jean (Waters) W.; m. Kathleen Ann Agnitsch, June 13, 1981; children: Sarah Elizabeth, Matthew Joseph. BGS, U. Iowa, 1979. Nat. field staff Ted Kennedy for President, 1979-80; polit. dir. Lucero for U.S. Senate, Denver, 1984; legis. dir. for Gov. Richard Lamm, Denver, 1984-87, sr. edn. advisor for, 1985-87; issues dir. for Mayor Federico Peña, Denver, 1987; v.p. Bonham/Shlenker & Assocs., Denver, 1988-90; pres. The Welchert Co., Denver, 1990—; staff chmn. Nat. Govs. Assn., Washington and Denver, 1986; on-air analyst Sta. KMGH-TV, Denver, 1987-94; Wis. dir. Gore for Pres., Milw., 1988; floor whip Dem. Nat. Platform Com., 1988; dir. Western Hemisphere Trade and Commerce Forum Hosting Trade Mins. and Bus. Leaders, 1995. Writer radio series Ind. Thinking, 1987-88. Advisor Cultural Facilities Dist., Denver, 1988; bd. dirs. Citizens for Denver's Future, 1989-90; mem. Denver Baseball Commn., 1986-89, also chmn. govt. com., Rocky Mt. chpt. Am. Ireland Fund. Named Rising Leader for 90's Colo. Bus. Mag., 1990. Mem. Am. Assn. Polit. Cons. (Pollie awards 1st pl. Best Free Media, 2d pl. Print Graphics and Collateral Material 1995). Democrat. Roman Catholic. Avocations: hiking, mountain biking, youth coaching. Office: The Welchert Co 1525 Market St # 200 Denver CO 80202-1607

WELCHMAN, JOHN, art educator. BA, Clare Coll. Cambridge U., 1981; MPhil, Courtauld Inst. Art London U., 1984; MA, Cambridge U., 1990; PhD, Courtauld Inst. Art London U., 1991. Dir. studies English lang. & lit. The Oxford Study Ctr., Oxford, 1979; course coord. Internat. Cmty. Sch., London, 1982-84; lectr. The Open U., Oxford, England, 1984-85; vis. asst. prof. UCLA, 1988, Arts Ctr., Pasadena, Calif., 1988; acting asst. prof. U. Calif., San Diego, 1988-90; from lectr. to sr. lectr. visual arts Monash U., Melbourne, 1990-93; vis. asst. prof. Harvard U., Cambridge, Mass., 1995; assoc. prof. visual arts U. Calif., San Diego, 1996—. Fulbright found. fellow, 1984-85, NEH fellow, 1989, others. Author: Modernism Relocated: Towards a Cultural Studies of Visual Modernity, 1995, Invisible Colors: A Visual History of Titles, 1997; co-author: The Dada and Surrealist Word-Image, 1989, Techniques of Modern Art, 1983, editor: Rethinking Borders, 1996, Please to the Table, 1990, Terrific Pacific, 1995; contbr. articles to profl. jours. Office: U Calif Dept Visual Arts 0327 9500 Gilman Dr La Jolla CA 92093-5003

WELDEN, LARRY TRUMAN, artist; b. Berkeley, Calif., Sept. 30, 1922; s. Raymond David W. and Frances Christine (Welch) W. Russell; m. Jean Louise Ellickson, Nov. 24, 1953; children: Jay David, Kim Jennifer Welden Ganoung, Sidney Lynn Welden Futrell, Drew Ethen, Bryan Lee. BA in Edn., Calif. Coll. Arts & Crafts, 1951; MA in Art, Calif. State U., 1959. Instr. art Kit Carson Jr. H.S., Sacramento, 1951-54, Peter Lassen Jr. H.S., Sacramento, 1954-58, Airan Johnson H.S., Sacramento, 1958-60; prof. art Sacramento City Coll., 1960-85; retired, 1985. One-man shows include Sacramento State Coll., 1957, Calif. Palace of Legion of Honor, San Francisco, 1960, Artist Contemporary Gallery, Sacramento, 1962, 65, 68, 70, 76, 86, 88, 90, 92, 95, Little Gallery, Sacramento, 1968, 77, Crocker Art Mus., Sacramento, 1981, Calif. State Capital, Sacramento, 1986, Jennifer Pauls Gallery, Sacramento, 1986, Solemon Dupnick Gallery, Sacramento, 1997; group shows include Crocker Art Mus., 1960, 65, 67, 73, 76, Calif. Palace of Legion of Honor, 1961, Shasta Coll. Art Exhbn., Redding, Calif., 1964, San Francisco Mus. Modern Art, 1965, San Francisco Art Inst., 1970, Calif. State U., Sacramento, 1977, 88, U. Calif., Davis, 1979, Dana Reich Art Gallery, San Francisco, 1980, Gumps, San Francisco, 1982, Artist Contemporary Gallery, 1982, 83, 85, 91, 92, 96, Himovitz Art Gallery, Sacramento, 1989, Yosemite Renaissance VII, 1993, 96, Wells Fargo Ctr., Sacramento, 1996, Solemon Dupnick Gallery, 1996; represented in permanent collections Crocker Art Mus., Sacramento City Coll., Shasta Coll., Calif. Coll. Arts & Crafts, U. Calif. Davis Med. Ctr., Kaiser Permanente Hosp., Sacramento & Oakland, Calif., Farror and William, Sacramento, Donald Joseph Co., Sacramento, DeLa Vergue and McMurty Law Office, Sacramento, Dr. & Mrs. David Warren, Mr. Gregory Favre, Mr. & Mrs. William Parker, Sacramento, Dulury Acctg. Corp., Sacramento, Burnett Miller & Son, Sacramento, Mr. & Mrs. Malcolm Shyte, Mill Valley, Calif., Shirley Soleman Dupnick, Sacramento, Serrano County Club, El Dorado Hills, Calif., others. Democrat. Avocations: sailing, classical music, art history, travel. Home: 7107 West Ln Granite Bay CA 95746

WELK, RICHARD ANDREW, plastic surgeon; b. Aug. 9, 1956. BS, U. Mich., 1977, MD, 1981. Diplomate Am. Bd. Surgery, Am. Bd. Plastic Surgery. Resident gen. surgery Grand Rapids, Mich., 1981-86; resident plastic surgery U. Calif., Irvine, 1986-88; plastic surgeon pvt. practice, Kirkland, Wash., 1988-91, Polyclinic, Seattle, 1991—. Mem. Am. Soc. Plastic & Reconstructive Surgery, Am. Soc. Aesthetic Plastic Surgery, Wash. State Med. Assn., Wash. Soc. Plastic Surgeons (pres. 1995-96). Office: Polyclinic 1145 Broadway Seattle WA 98122-4299*

WELKE, ELTON GRINNELL, JR., publisher, writer; b. Berkeley, Calif., June 15, 1941; s. Elton Grinnell and Elsie Maud (Shattuck) W.; m. Anna Lange, July 28, 1963 (div. 1980); children: Allison Espy, Erik Grinnell; m. Bonnie Jean Lum, Jan. 24, 1981; 1 child, Erin Irene. BA in Zoology, U. Calif., Berkeley, 1962. Staff writer Sunset mag., Menlo Pk., Calif., 1962-65, assoc. editor, 1965-69, sr. editor, 1978-80; travel editor Better Homes & Gardens, Des Moines, 1969-71; mng. editor Apt. Life mag., Des Moines, 1971-72; exec. editor Sunset Spl. Interest mags., Menlo Pk., 1972-78; freelance editorial cons. San Francisco and Seattle, 1981-84; v.p., dir. Livingston & Co., Seattle, 1984-89; publisher Microsoft Press, 1989-98; chmn. North Wave Comms., Inc., Alaska, 1996—; bd. dirs. Advance Online, Inc., Seattle; cons. Holland Am. Line, Seattle, 1983-84, Livingston & Co. Advt., Seattle, 1983-84. Author: How to Survive Being Alive, 1977, Place's to go With Children Around Puget Sound, 1987. Bd. dirs. Olympic Nat. Pk. Assocs., Washington, 1965-69, March of Dimes, Western Washington, 1987-92, chmn. campaign com., 1989-92. Recipient 1st Pl. award Washington Press Assn., 1985, 86, 88, WPA award, 1987. Mem. Soc. A. Travel Writers, PRSA, Internat. Assn. Bus. Communicators (Golden Quill award 1985), Washington Athletic Club, Safari Club, Sierra Club, Alpha Delta Phi. Republican. Avocations: gardening, plant collecting, fly fishing, cattle ranching, Asian art. Home: 11329 NE 103d St Kirkland WA 98033-5178 Office: 11329 NE 103d St Kirkland WA 98033-5178

WELLER, DEBORAH SUE, investment company executive; b. L.A., Sept. 9, 1950; d. Paul Earl and Irene (Doctorow) W.; m. Barry Avaron White, June 17, 1978; children: Alyssa, Devin. BA, Calif. State U., Northridge, 1973. Lic. tax. cons., Oreg. Legal adminstr. White, Getgey & Meyer, Cin., 1976-78; owner Elk Creek Toy Co., Gresham, Oreg., 1981-83; legal adminstr. O'Connell et al, Portland, Oreg., 1983-84; investment advisor Weller Fin.

Adv. Svcs., Portland, Oreg., 1984—. Active Clackamas H.S. Site Coun., Milwaukie, Oreg., 1998—. Avocations: golf, swimming, reading, art. Fax: (503) 255-9804. E-mail: debsw@teleport.com. Office: Weller Fin Adv Svcs 10735 SE Stark St Ste 206 Portland OR 97216-2765

WELLER, DEBRA ANNE, elementary educator; b. New Orleans, Feb. 4, 1954; d. James Garretson and Elizabeth Gene (Blakely) Hyatt; m. Bruce Weller, June 15, 1974; children: Jenny, Todd. AA in Art, St. Petersburg Jr. Coll., 1974; BA in Art Edn., Glassboro State Coll., 1983; MS in Curriculum and Instrn., Nat. U., 1991. Cert. tchr. Profl. storyteller Mission Viejo, Calif., 1980—; tchr. Capistrano Unified Sch. Dist., San Juan Capistrano, Calif., 1989—; elem. tchg. asst. prin. Bathgate Elem., 1998—; edn. dir. South Coast Storytellers Guild, Costa Mesa, Calif., 1990—; workshop presenter Orange County Dept. Edn., Costa Mesa, 1991—, Imagination Celebration, Irvine, Calif., 1993—; bd. mem. Calif. Kindergarten Assn. Author: (pamphlet) Image-U-Telling Clubs, 1995. Sec. Mission Viejo Cultural Com., 1995—. Cultural Arts grantee Dana Point (Calif.) Cultural Commn., 1993. Mem. NEA, Nat. Storytelling Assn. (Pacific region liaison), Calif. Tchrs. Assn., Calif. Kindergarten Assn. (bd. dirs.). Mormon. Avocations: calligraphy, composing, playing banjo, dulcimer and guitar.

WELLES, JOHN GALT, retired museum director; b. Orange, N.J., Aug. 24, 1925; s. Paul and Elizabeth Ash (Galt) W.; m. Barbara Lee Chrisman, Sept. 15, 1951; children: Virginia Chrisman, Deborah Galt, Barton Jeffery, Holly Page. BE, Yale U., 1946; MBA, U. Pa., 1949; LHD (hon.) U. Denver, 1994. Test engr. Gen. Electric Co., Lynn, Mass., 1947; labor relations staff New Departure div. Gen Motors Corp., Bristol, Conn., 1949-51; mem. staff Mountain States Employers Coun., Denver, 1952-55; head indsl. econs. div. U. Denver Research Inst., Denver, 1956-74; v.p. planning and devel. Colo. Sch. Mines, Golden, 1974-83; regional adminstr. EPA, Denver, 1983-87; exec. dir. Denver Mus. Natural History, 1987-94, exec. dir. emeritus, 1994—. Sr. cons. Secretariat, UN Conf. Human Environment, Geneva, 1971-72; cons. Bus. Internat., S.A., Geneva, 1972; trustee Tax Free Fund of Colo., N.Y., 1987—, Denver Pub. Libr. Friends Found., 1996—; mem. Rocky Mountain regional adv. bd. Inst. Internat. Edn., 1996—; exec. com. Denver Com. on Fgn. Rels., 1987—; bd. dirs Gulf of Maine Found., 1995—; chmn. Colo. Front Range Project, Denver, 1979-80. Contbr. articles to profl. jours., newspapers. Recipient Disting. Svc. award Denver Regional Coun. Govts., 1980, Barnes award EPA, 1987. Mem. AAAS, Am. Assn. Museums (ethics commn. 1991-94, v.p. 1992-95), Sustainable Futures Soc. (nat. adv. bd. 1994—), Met. Denver Exec. Club (pres. 1967-68), World Future Soc., Univ. Club (Denver) Denver Athletic Club, Tau Beta Pi, Blue Key. Republican. Episcopalian.

WELLES, MELINDA FASSETT, artist, educational psychologist; b. Palo Alto, Calif., Jan. 4, 1943; d. George Edward and Barbara Helena (Todd) W. Student, San Francisco Inst. Art, 1959-60, U. Oreg., 1960-62; BA in Fine Arts, UCLA, 1964, MA in Spl. Edn., 1971, PhD in Ednl. Psychology, 1976; student fine arts and illustration Art Ctr. Coll. Design, 1977-80. Cert. ednl. psychologist, Calif. Asst. prof. Calif. State U., Northridge, 1979-82, Pepperdine U., L.A., 1979-82; assoc. prof. curriculum, teaching and spl. edn. U. So. Calif., L.A., 1980-89; prof. liberal studies Art Ctr. Coll. Design, 1978—; mem. acad. faculty Pasadena City Coll., 1973-79, Otis Coll. Art and Design, L.A., 1986—, UCLA Extension, 1980-84, Coll. Devel. Studies, L.A., 1978-87, El Camino C.C., Redondo Beach, Calif., 1982-86; cons. spl. edn.; pub. adminstrn. analyst UCLA Spl. Edn. Rsch. Program, 1973-76; exec. dir. Atwater Park Ctr. Disabled Children, L.A., 1976-78; coord. Pacific Oaks Coll. in svc. programs for L.A. Unified Schs., Pasadena, 1978-81; mem. Southwest Blue Book, The Blue Ribbon, Friends of Robinson Gardens, Freedom's Found. at Valley Forge, The Mannequins, Costume Coun. L.A. County Mus. of Art., Assistance League of So. Calif. Author: Calif. Dept. Edn. Tech. Reports, 1972-76; editor: Teaching Special Students in the Mainstream, 1981, Educating Special Learners, 1986, 88, Teaching Students with Learning Problems, 1988, Exceptional Children and Youth, 1989, Left Brain Right Brain, 1997; group shows include: San Francisco Inst. Art, 1960, U. Hawaii, 1978, Barnsdall Gallery, L.A., 1979, 80; represented in various pvt. collections. HEW fellow, 1971-72; grantee Calif. Dept. Edn., 1975-76, Calif. Dept. Health, 1978. Mem. Am. Psych. Assn., Calif. Learning Disabilities Assn., Am. Council Learning Disabilities, Calif. Scholarship Fedn. (life), Alpha Chi Omega. Office: 700 Levering Ave Apt 1 Los Angeles CA 90024-2795

WELLISCH, WILLIAM JEREMIAH, social psychology educator; b. Vienna, Austria, July 3, 1938; came to U.S., 1940; s. Max and Zelda (Schanser) W.; m. Geraldine Eve Miller (dec. Feb. 1970); children: Garth Kevin, Miriam Rhoda; m. Claudine Abbey Truman, Sept. 5, 1971; children: Rebecca Colleen, Marcus Joshua, Gabriel Jason. MA in Sociology, U. Mo., 1965, PhD in Sociology, 1968. Researcher urbanization Hemispheric Consultants, Columbia, Mo., 1968-69; cons. to local govt. ofcl. on L.Am. Bi-cultural Consultants, Inc., Denver, 1969-70; prof. Red Rocks Coll., Lakewood, Colo., 1970-76, 77—. Author: Bi-Cultural Development, 1971, Honduras: A Study in Sub-Development, 1978. Mem. citizen's adv. bd. Sta. KCFR Pub. Radio, Denver, 1989—. Republican. Mem. Unification Ch. Avocations: still-life photography, landscape gardening. Home: 2325 Clay St Denver CO 80211-5123 Office: Red Rocks CC 13300 W 6th Ave Golden CO 80401-5357

WELLIVER, CHARLES HAROLD, hospital administrator; b. Wichita, Kans., Feb. 14, 1945; married. BA, Wichita State U., 1972; MHA, U. Mo., 1974. Asst. dir. St. Luke's Hosp., Kansas City, 1974-79, assoc. dir., 1979-80; adminstr. Spelman Meml. Hosp., Smithville, Mo., 1980-82; sr. adminstr., COO Good Samaritan Med. Ctr., Phoenix, 1982-86, v.p., CEO, 1989—; v.p., CEO Thunderbird Samaritan Hosp., Glendale, Ariz., 1986-89; COO Good Samaritan Med. Ctr., Glendale. Office: Good Samaritan Regional Med Ctr 1441 N 12th St Phoenix AZ 85006-2837

WELLS, GEORGE HENRY, minister; b. Durant, Okla., May 14, 1940; s. Philip Yancy and Delta Iona (Harlin) W.; m. Deborah Lynn Lehman, Mar. 21, 1984. BAEd, U. Okla., 1961; BD, St. Andrews U., Scotland, 1964; MDiv, San Francisco Theol. Sem., 1980, DMin, 1984. Ordained to ministry So. Bapt. Conv., 1962, United Presbyn. Ch. USA, 1980. Pastor Francis (Okla.) Bapt. Ch., 1960-61; min. evangelism and youth First Bapt. Ch., Ada, Okla., 1961-63; dir. crusades Haggai Evang. Assn. Atlanta, 1965-69; pastor adminstrn. First Presbyn. Ch., Bakersfield, Calif., 1969-76; assoc. pastor Fair Oaks (Calif.) Presbyn. Ch., 1976-83, co-pastor, 1983-84, pastor, 1985—; Bd. dirs. HIS Farm, Inc., Sacramento. Author: Electronic Church Awareness Guide, 1983. Chmn. Greater Sacramento Concert of Prayer, 1989-90; bd. dirs. Law Enforcement Chaplaincy, 1988-90; chaplain NBA Sacramento Kings, 1985—. Named one of Outstanding Young Men in Am. U.S. Jaycees, 1974; Rotary Found. fellow St. Andrews U., 1964. Mem. Nat. Assn. Christian Bus. Adminstrs., Nat. Assn. Evangs., Alpha Chi. Republican. Home: 4941 Susan Hollow Ct Fair Oaks CA 95628-8159 Office: Fair Okas Presbyn Ch 3127 Eastern Ave Sacramento CA 95821-4006

WELLS, MERLE WILLIAM, historian, state archivist; b. Lethbridge, Alta., Can., Dec. 1, 1918; s. Norman Danby and Minnie Muir (Huckett) W.; student Boise Jr. Coll., 1937-39; A.B., Coll. Idaho, 1941, L.H.D. (hon.), 1981; M.A., U. Calif., 1947, Ph.D., 1950; L.H.D., U. Idaho, 1990. Instr. history Coll. Idaho, Caldwell, 1942-46; assoc. prof. history Alliance Coll., Cambridge Springs, Pa., 1950-56, 58, dean students, 1955-56; cons. historian Idaho Hist. Soc., Boise, 1956-58, historian and archivist, 1959—; hist. preservation officer, archivist State of Idaho, Boise, 1968-86. Treas., So. Idaho Migrant Ministry, 1960-64, chmn., 1964-67; nat. migrant adv. com. Nat. Council Chs., 1964-67, gen. bd. Idaho council, 1967-75; bd. dirs. Idaho State Employees Credit Union, 1964-67, treas., 1966-67; mem. Idaho Commn. Arts and Humanities, 1966-67; mem. Idaho Lewis and Clark Trail Commn., 1968-70, 84-88; mem. Idaho Bicentennial Commn., 1971-76; bd. dirs. Sawtooth Interpretive Assn., 1972—, dept. history United Presbyn. Ch., 1978-84; v.p. Idaho Zool. Soc., 1982-84, bd. dirs., 1984-94, treas., 1988-90, historian, 1990—. Named Disting. Alumnus Boise State U., 1997. Mem. [illegible] State Hist. Preservation Officers (dir. 1976-81, chmn. Western states council on geog. names 1982-83), Am. Hist. Assn., Western History Assn. (council 1973-76), AAUP, Am. Assn. State and Local History (council 1973-77), Soc. Am. Archivists, Assn. Idaho Historians (pres. 1991), others. Author: Anti-Mormonism in Idaho, 1978, Boise: An Illustrated History, 1982, Gold

Camps and Silver Cities, 1984, Idaho: Gem of the Mountains, 1985. Office: Idaho State Hist Soc 210 Main St Boise ID 83702-7264

WELLS, ROGER STANLEY, software engineer; b. Seattle, Apr. 13, 1949; s. Stanley A. and Margaret W. BA, Whitman Coll., 1971; postgrad., U. Tex., Austin, 1973-74; BS, Oreg. State U., 1977. Software evaluation engr. Tektronix, Beaverton, Oreg., 1979-83; computer engr. Aramco, Dhahran, Saudi Arabia, 1983-84; software engr. Conrac Corp., Clackamas, Oreg., 1984-85, Duarte, Calif., 1985; software analyst Lundy Fin. Systems, San Dimas, Calif., 1986-89; contract software analyst for various orgns. Seattle, 1989-92; sr. project engr. Illuminet (formerly U.S. Intelco. Networks), Olympia, Wash., 1993—, mem. Exec. Yr. 2000 com., 1998-99. Bd. dirs. The Sci. Fiction Mus., Salem, Oreg., 1993—; co-founder, bd. dirs., pres. Oreg. Sci. Fiction Conv., 1979-81; mem. Illuminet exec. year 2000 com., 1998-99. Mem. IEEE, Nat. Speakers Assn., Am. Philatelic Soc., Nat. Assn. Parliamentarians, Am. Inst. Parliamentarians (chpt. v.p. 1996-97, pres. 1997-98), Fantasy Amateur Press Assn., Portland Sci. Fiction Soc., N.W. Sci. Fiction Soc., Internat. Platform Assn. (2d place Monologue contest 1997, mem. conv. com. 1998-99), Mensa, Assn. Computing Machinery, L.A. Sci. Fantasy Soc., Melbourne (Australia) Sci. Fiction Club, Toastmasters Internat. (pres. 1980, v.p. edn. 1994-95, area gov. 1994-95, dist. 32 parliamentarian 1996—). Designer of software program to transfer billing records for regional telephone companies. Avocations: travel, public speaking, science fiction, stamp collecting. Home: 4820 Yelm Hwy SE Apt B-102 Lacey WA 98503-4903

WELLS, SALLY ANN, elementary education educator; b. Milw., July 15, 1953; d. John Dorr and Martha (McGonagle) Wakefield; m. James Donald Wells, Oct. 24, 1987; children: Todd, Brendan. Student, Ohio Wesleyan U., 1971-73; BA, U. Oreg., 1976; MA in Tchg., Lewis and Clark Coll., Portland, Oreg., 1989. Coord. data processing Sierra Designs, Oakland, Calif., 1976-78; tchr. Washington County Sch. Dist., Portland, 1978-79, Jarrow Montessori Sch., Boulder, Colo., 1979-86; wilderness coord. U.S. Forest Svc., Trout Lake, Wash., 1987-89; tchr. mid. sch. White Salmon Valley Sch. Dist., White Salmon, Wash., 1989—; presenter Northwest Coun. Computer Educators, 1997, 99, Nat. Sch. Bd. Assn., 1998. Contbr. chpt. to book. Washington State Competitive grantee, 1996—. Mem. N.W. Coun. Computer Educators. Avocations: skiing, biking, hiking, weaving, gardening. Home: PO Box 93 Trout Lake WA 98650 Office: Henkle Mid Sch 480 NW Loop Rd White Salmon WA 98672

WELLS, THELMA M., educator, educational administrator; b. St. Louis, Apr. 21, 1939; d. Berry and Isabel M. (Griffin) Williams; m. Harold Wells, July 2, 1960 (div. July 1963); children: Berri Ann, O. Wiley Warren. B of Liberal Studies, Pepperdine U., 1975, MPA, 1977. RN, Calif. Nursing instr. King/Drew Med. Ctr. L.A. County, L.A., 1981-88, Compton C.C., L.A., 1995-97; mem. faculty, dir. Charles R. Drew U., L.A., 1990—; internat. fellow to East Africa, Internat. Found. for Edn. and Self Help, Phoenix, 1995-96; instr. emergency medicine technician 1 L.A. Trade Tech., 1981-88. Mem. ASTD, Nat. Soc. Allied Health, Am. Assn. Higher Edn., Homer G. Phillips Sch. of Nursing Alumni Assn., Pepperdine U. Alumni Assn., Beta Pi Sigma. Democrat. Church of God in Christ. Avocations: traveling, handicrafts, reading, movies, walking. Home: 1140 E Ocean Blvd Unit 105 Long Beach CA 90802-5662 Office: Charles R Drew U 1831 E 118th St Los Angeles CA 90059-2531

WELSH, JOHN RICHARD, state official; b. Neillsville, Wis., May 27, 1938; s. Francis Richard and Bernice Margaret (Schneider) W.; m. Carol Kay Ableidinger, Sept. 30, 1961; children: Tony, Becky, Cathy, Michael, Chelley. BBA, Loyola U., Chgo., 1977; MEd, No. Ariz. State U., 1996. Benefit mgr. George F. Brown & Sons, Chgo., 1968-69, Marsh & McLennon, Chgo., 1969-71; adminstrv. mgr. Kemper Ins. Group, Long Grove, Ill., 1971-73; benefits mgr. 1st Nat. Bank of Chgo., 1973-79, The Arizona Bank, Phoenix, 1979-81; cons. Phoenix, 1981-84; benefits mgr., arbitrator Frontier Airlines, Inc., Denver, 1984-85; benefits mgr. Dept. Adminstrn., State of Ariz., Phoenix, 1985-91; retirement officer, seminar facilitator Ariz. State Retirement Sys., Phoenix, 1991—; team leader, benefits adv. Total Quality Mgmt. Ariz. State Retirement System, Phoenix, 1995. High sch. football ofcl. Ariz. Interscholastic Assn., Phoenix, 1980-93; football coach Portage Park Sports, Chgo., 1969-79, baseball coach, 1969-79; basketball coach K.C., Durand, Wis., 1966-68. With USN, 1956-59. Mem. Nat. Assn. for Pre-Retirement Edn., Loyola U. Alumni Assn. (Phoenix chpt.), Notre Dame Club of Phoenix, Bellaire Men's Golf Assn. Roman Catholic. Avocations: golf, snow skiing, reading, walking, swimming. Home: 4141 W Hayward Ave Phoenix AZ 85051-5751 Office: Ariz State Retirement Sys 3300 N Central Ave Phoenix AZ 85012-2501

WELSH, MARY MCANAW, educator, family mediator; b. Cameron, Mo., Dec. 7, 1920; d. Francis Louis and Mary Matilda (Moore) McA.; m. Alvin F. Welsh, Feb. 10, 1944 (dec.); children: Mary Celia, Clinton F., M. Ann. AB, U. Kans., 1942; MA, Seton Hall U., 1960; EdD, Columbia U., 1971. Reporter, Hutchinson (Kans.) News Herald, 1942-43; house editor Worthington Pump & Machine Corp., Harrison, N.J., 1943-44; tchr., housemaster, coordinator Summit (N.J.) Pub. Schs., 1960-68; prof. family studies N.Mex. State U., Las Cruces, 1972-85; adj. faculty dept. family practice Tex. Tech. Regional Acad. Health Ctr., El Paso, 1978-82, Family Mediation Practice, Las Cruces, 1986—. Mem. AAUW (pres. N.Mex. 1981-83), N.Mex. Council Women's Orgn. (founder, chmn. 1982-83), Delta Kappa Gamma, Kappa Alpha Theta. Democrat. Roman Catholic. Author: A Good Family is Hard to Found, 1972; Parent, Child and Sex, 1970; contbr. articles to profl. jours.; writer, presenter home econs. and family study series KRWG-TV, 1974; moderator TV series The Changing Family in N.Mex./LWV, 1976. Home and Office: University Park 4150 Tesota Dr Las Cruces NM 88011-7647

WELSH, STACEY LAU, investment banker; b. Honolulu, Nov. 30, 1960; d. Timothy Shao Yu and Violet Yuk Kung (Lee) Lau; m. John Anthony Welsh, May 15, 1993. BS, San Francisco State U., 1984; MBA, U. Chgo., 1989. CPA, Calif. Office mgr. Markle, Stuckey, Clark & Co., San Francisco, 1982-84, acct., 1984-87; v.p. Citicorp Real Estate, Inc., San Francisco, 1989—; pres. Capajava, Stamford, Conn., 1992-94. Sponsor, Student/Sponsor Partnership, N.Y.C., 1990-94. Avocations: entrepreneurial ventures, golf, skiing. Home: 40 Sea Cliff Ave San Francisco CA 94121-1132 Office: Citicorp Real Estate Inc Global Real Estate Equity 1 Sansome St San Francisco CA 94104-4448

WELSOME, EILEEN, journalist; b. N.Y.C., Mar. 12, 1951; d. Richard H. and Jane M. (Garity) W.; m. James R. Martin, Aug. 3, 1983. BJ with honors, U. Tex., 1980. Reporter Beaumont (Tex.) Enterprise, 1980-82, San Antonio Light, 1982-83, San Antonio Express-News, 1983-86, Albuquerque Tribune, 1987-94. Recipient Clarion award, 1989, News Reporting award Nat. Headliners, 1989, John Hancock award, 1991, Mng. Editors Pub. Svc. award AP, 1991, 94, Roy Howard award 1994, James Aronson award, 1994, Gold Medal award Investigative Reporters and Editors, 1994, Sigma Delta Chi award, 1994, Investigative Reporting award Nat. Headliners, 1994, Selden Ring award, 1994, Heywood Broun award, 1994, George Polk award, 1994, Sidney Hillman Found. award, 1994, Pulitzer Prize for nat. reporting, 1994; John S. Knight fellow Stanford U., 1991-92.

WELTER, LINDA ALLAIRE, development executive; b. Bayonne, N.J., Aug. 11, 1949; d. Godfrey Adolf and Grace Elizabeth (Buss) W. BA in Philosophy and Polit. Sci., Drew U., 1971, postgrad., 1972-73; postgrad., Harvard U., 1985; MBA, Boston Coll., 1987. Development asst. Harvard U., Cambridge, Mass., 1980-83, development assoc., 1983-85, dir. class and area programs, 1985-86, sr. development officer, 1986-87; from capital campaign dir. to asst. v.p. for resources Wellesley (Mass.) Coll., 1987-93; v.p., gen. mgr. for development ops. ARC, Washington, 1993-94; dir. major gifts U. Calif., Berkeley, 1994—; instr. Stonehill Coll., Easton, Mass.; lectr. Northeastern U., Boston; cons. Vassar Coll.; fundraising cons. Dimock Cmty. Health Ctr., Boston, 1992. Vol. co-chair fundraising Ruah, mem. capital campaign com. Fenway Cmty. Health Ctr.; vol. Nat. Network on Women as Philanthropists. Mem. Women in Development (bd. dirs., chair city svc. project), Coun. for Advancement and Support of Edn. (teaching faculty 1985—), Women in Philanthropy. Avocations: Alpine and Nordic skiing, sailing, mountain climbing, writing, photography. Address: 116 W Willow Grove Ave Philadelphia PA 19118-3961 Office: U Calif Univ Rels 2440 Bancroft Way Berkeley CA 94704-1603

WELTON, CHARLES EPHRAIM, lawyer; b. Cloquet, Minn., June 23, 1947; s. Eugene Frances and Evelyn Esther (Koski) W.; m. Nancy Jean Sanda, July 19, 1969 (div.); children: Spencer Sanda, Marshall Eugene. BA, Macalester Coll., 1969; postgrad., U. Minn., 1969-70; JD, U. Denver, 1974. Bar: Colo. 1974, U.S. Dist. Ct. Colo. 1974, U.S. Supreme Ct. 1979, U.S. Ct. Appeals (10th cir.) 1980. Assoc. Davidovich & Wanifuchi, Denver, 1974-77, Charles Welton and Assocs. and successor firms, Denver, 1978-86; ptnr. OSM Properties, Denver, 1982-97, Brock House, LLC, Denver, 1997—; prin. Charles Welton, P.C., 1986—; grievance com., panelist, arbitrator Colo. Supreme Ct., 1996—; adj. prof. Inst. Advanced Legal Studies U. Denver, 1991—; polit. and social commentator; lectr. in field; instr. Nat. Inst. Trial Advocacy, 1998—. Author instrnl. materials; editor profl. publications; contbr. articles to profl. jours. Sch. pres. PTSA, Denver, 1983-84; coach Colo. Jr. Soccer League, 1980-85; coach Odessey of Mind (formerly Olympics of Mind), 1986-88; bd. dirs. Virginia Vale Swim Club, officer, 1989-91, Pioneer Jr. Hockey Assn., 1990-92. Served alt. mil. duty Denver Gen. Hosp., 1970-72. Mem. ATLA, Denver Bar Assn. (facilitator bench/bar retreat 1995, 96, legal fee arbitration com.), Colo. Bar Assn. (legal fee arbitration com.), Colo. Trial Lawyers Assn. (bd. dirs. 1985-90, chmn. seminar com. 1986-88, exec. com. 1987-88, legis. com. 1988-94, case assistance com. 1995—, keyperson 1997—), Am. Bldg. a Lasting Earth (founder), Exec. Ventures Group of Am. Leadership Forum (founding adv. bd. 1987-90). Democrat. Lutheran. Home: 680 Vista Ln Lakewood CO 80215-6037 Office: The Brock House 1800 Gaylord St Denver CO 80206-1211

WELTON, MICHAEL PETER, dentist; b. Milw., Apr. 19, 1957; s. Lloyd Peter and Allegra (Nimmer) W.; m. Etsuko Suehiro, Nov. 21, 1986 (div. Nov. 1993); m. Lucia Aldon, Jan. 29, 1994. BS in Biology, Carroll Coll., 1979; DDS, U. Minn., 1983. Commd. lt. USN, 1983; resident Naval Hosp. Camp Pendleton, Oceanside, Calif., 1983-84; with periodontics dept. Naval Dental Clinic, Yokosuka, Japan, 1984-85; clinic dir. Negishi Dental Annex, Yokohama, Japan, 1985-87; gen. dentistry Br. Dental Clinic Mare Island Naval Sta., Vallejo, Calif., 1987-90; pvt. practice gen. dentistry Vacaville, Calif., 1990—; legis. extern Am. Student Dental Assn., Washington, 1982; student rep. Minn. Dental Assn., Mpls., 1980. Fellow Acad. Dentistry Internat.; mem. ADA, Calif. Dental Assn. (ho. of dels. 1996-98, com. rules and order 1998), Napa-Solano Dental Soc. (exec. com. 1995-98, bd. dirs. 1990-95, pres. 1997), Art Deco Soc. Calif., No. Calif. Golf Assn., Vacaville C. of C., Tilden Park Golf Club, Delta Sigma Delta (treas. Mpls. chpt. 1982-83, Outstanding Mem. award 1982-83), Vacaville Sunrise Rotary Club (dir. 1997—), Ducks Unlimited (dinner com. 1997—). Avocations: golf, skiing, tennis, reading, gardening, hunting. Home: 480 Evelyn Cir Vallejo CA 94589-3259 Office: 3000 Alamo Dr Ste 103 Vacaville CA 95687-6345

WELTY, JOHN DONALD, academic administrator; b. Amboy, Ill., Aug. 24, 1944; s. John Donald and Doris (Donnelly) W.; m. Sharon Welty; children: Anne, Elisabeth, Bryan, Darren, Heather. B.S., Western Ill. U., 1965; M.A., Mich. State U., 1967; Ed.D., Ind. U., 1974. Asst. v.p. for student affairs SW State U., Marshall, Minn., 1973-74; dir. residences SUNY-Albany, 1974-77, assoc. dean for student affairs, 1977-80; v.p. for student and univ. affairs Indiana U. of Pa., 1980-84, pres., 1984-91; pres. Calif. State U., Fresno, 1991—; lectr. in field. Contbr. articles to profl. jours. Chmn. Small Bus. Incubator of Indiana, 1985-91; bd. dirs. Open Door Crises and Counseling Ctr., Indiana, Big Bros./Big Sisters, Indiana, 1980-84. Recipient Chancellor's award SUNY, 1977. Mem. Fresno Bus. Coun., Fresno Econ. Devel. Commn., Sunnyside Country Club. Roman Catholic. Lodge: Rotary. Office: Calif State U 5241 S Maple Ave Fresno CA 93725-9739

WEMPLE, JAMES ROBERT, psychotherapist; b. Hardin, Mont., May 31, 1943; s. Charles Clifford and Lillian Louise (Smith) W.; m. Sarah Ann House, May 7, 1983; children: Brian Matthew, Laura Ashley, Kerri Ann, Jaime Marie, Kevin James. BA, U. Mont., 1966, MA, 1970, postgrad., 1970-71; PhD, Wash. State U., 1979. Diplomate Am. Acad. Pain Mgmt. Tchr., coach Custer County High Sch., Miles City, Mont., 1966-67; sch. psychologist Missoula, Mont., 1970-71; grad. asst. U. Mont., Missoula, 1970-71; dir. counseling Medicine Hat (Alberta) Coll., Canada, 1971-73; counselor Lethbridge (Alberta) C.C., 1973-76; head resident Wash. State U., Pullman, 1976-79; mental health specialist Missoula Rehab., 1979-82; clin. mental health counselor Missoula, 1982—. With U.S. Army, 1960-69, Korea. Fellow Am. Bd. Med. Psychotherapists; mem. Am. Psychol. Assn., Soc. for Clin. and Exptl. Hypnosis, Am. Soc. for Clin. Hypnosis, Internat. Soc. for Hypnosis, Nat. Acad. Cert. Clin. Mental Health Counselors, Soc. for Personality Assessment, AACD, Phi Kappa Phi. Avocations: fishing, hunting. Home: 2410 Clydesdale Ln Missoula MT 59804-9297 Office: 255 W Front St # B Missoula MT 59802-4301

WENDLE, KEVIN, computer company executive. News producer WABC-TV, N.Y.C.; founding pres., COO Quincy Jones Entertainment; exec. v.p. Fox Entertainment Group; exec. prodr. CNET: The Computer Network; developed, supervised Married...With Children, The Simpsons, Beverly Hills 90210; exec. produced Fresh Prince of Bel-Air. Office: CNET 150 Chestnut St San Francisco CA 94111-1004*

WENDLINGER, ROBERT MATTHEW, communications and memory consultant; b. N.Y.C.; s. Harry and Rose (Pollock) W.; m. Dalis Peralta, 1955 (div. 1973); children: David, Marcella, Marta; m. Joan Hays Cole, June 23, 1984. Student U. Calif., Berkeley, 1942-43, Columbia U., 1947-52. Script editor Radio Free Europe, N.Y.C., 1950-52; assoc. editor Ind. Film Jour., N.Y.C., 1953-57; gen. mgr. Kermit Rolland and Assos., Princeton, N.J., 1957-59; exec. asst. in charge editorial services United Hosp. Fund of N.Y., N.Y.C., 1959-60; mgr. info. sect. Com. for Air and Water Conservation, Am. Petroleum Inst., N.Y.C., 1966-67; with Bank of Am. NT & SA, San Francisco, 1967-78, asst. v.p. communications, 1977-78; pres. Communications Cons. and Services, Berkeley, Calif., 1978-82; pres. Proust Press, Oakland, Calif., 1994—; mem. grad. faculty St. Mary's Coll., Moraga, Calif., 1975-78; mem. Astron Corp. Fellow Am. Bus. Communication Assn.; mem. Indsl. Communication Council (past pres.). Author: (with James M. Reid, Jr.) Effective Letters: A Program in Self-Instruction, 1964, 3d edit., 1978, Japanese edit., 1996, The Memory Triggering Book: Using Your Memories to Enhance Your Life and Your Relationships, 1995; contbr.: Everybody Wins; TA Applied to Organizations, 1973; Affirmative Action for Women, 1973; McGraw-Hill Ency. Professional Management, 1978. Office: 20 Treasure Hill Oakland CA 94618-2331

WENDT, STEVEN WILLIAM, business educator; b. Rockford, Ill., Sept. 18, 1948; s. Roy W. Wendt and Betty Lou (Phillips) Wendt Oser. AAS, Clark County Community Coll., North Las Vegas, Nev., 1982; BS, U. Nev., 1985, MBA, 1987. Cert. vocat. adult educator, Nev. Electronics tech. engr. Rockford Automation, Inc., 1972-74; owner, operator S.W. Ltd., Rockford, 1972-76, S.W. Enterprises, Henderson, Nev., 1977—; instr. electronics Nev. Gaming Sch., Las Vegas, 1977-83; gen. mgr., corp. sec. treas. Customs by Peter Schell, Las Vegas, 1977-83; field engr. Bell & Howell Mailmobile Ops. div., Zeeland, Mich., 1982-90; instr. bus. U. Nev., Las Vegas, 1985—; dir. Wing Fong & Family Microcomputer Labs. Coll. Bus. and Econs. U. Nev., 1990-97; sr. arbitrator Better Bus. Bur., Las Vegas, 1982—; bus. cons. Small Bus. Devel. Ctr., Las Vegas, 1985—; incorporator, v.p. Info. Sys., Warren, Mich., 1990-91; fin. officer, gen. ptnr. Obsidian Pub. Press, Henderson, Nev., 1991-96; mem. faculty senate U. Nev., 1993-96; bd. dirs. Gem Crafters Inc., Warren. Author: Intro to Microcomputers, For Future PC Experts, 1992. Treas. U. Nev. Grad. Student Assn, 1986-87. Served with USN, 1967-71. Recipient Cert. Appreciation UNICEF, 1984. Mem. IEEE, Computer Soc., Assn. Info. Systems, Fin. Mgmt. Assn. (Nat. Honor Soc. 1985), Strategic Gaming Soc., U. Nev. Computer User Group (exec. com., chair stds. com.), U. Nev. Alumni Assn., Am. Legion, VFW (life), Phi Lambda Alpha. Avocations: geology, numismatics, philatelitics. Home: 1325 Chestnut St Henderson NV 89015-4208 Office: U Nev 4505 S Maryland Pkwy Las Vegas NV 89154-9900

WENTWORTH, THEODORE SUMNER, lawyer; b. Bklyn., July 18, 1938, s. Theodore Sumner and Alice Ruth (Wortmann) W.; AA, Am. River Coll., 1958; JD, U. Calif., Hastings, 1962; m. Sharon Linelle Arkush, 1965 (dec. 1987); children: Christina Linn, Kathryn Allison; m. Diana Webb von Welanetz, 1989; 1 stepchild, Lexi von Welanetz. Bar: Calif. 1963, U.S. Dist. Ct. (no., ctrl. dists.) Calif., U.S. Ct. Appeals (9th cir.), U.S. Supreme Ct.; cert. trial specialist; diplomate Nat. Bd. Trial Advocacy; assoc. Am. Bd. Trial Advocates. [illegible] Hunt & Martin, Santa Ana, Calif., 1963-66; ptnr.

Hunt, Liljestrom & Wentworth, Santa Ana, 1967-77; pres. Solabs Corp.; chmn. bd., exec. v.p. Plant Warehouse, Inc., Hawaii, 1974-82; prin. Law Offices of Wentworth & Paoli, specializing in personal injury, product liability, profl. malpractice, bus. fraud, fire loss litigation, human rights issues, Newport Beach and Temecula, Calif.; judge pro tem Superior Ct. Attys. Panel, Harbor Mcpl. Ct.; owner Eagles Ridge Ranch, Temecula, 1977—. Pres., bd. dirs. Santa Ana-Tustin Community Chest, 1972; v.p., trustee South Orange County United Way, 1973-75; pres. Orange County Fedn. Funds, 1972-73; bd. dirs. Orange County Mental Health Assn. Mem. ABA, Am. Bd. Trial Advocates (assoc.), State Bar Calif., Orange County Bar Assn. (dir. 1972-76), Am. Trial Lawyers Assn., Calif. Trial Lawyers Assn. (bd. govs. 1968-70), Orange County Trial Lawyers Assn. (pres. 1967-68), Lawyer-Pilots Bar Assn., Aircraft Owners and Pilots Assn., Bahia Corinthian Yacht Club, Balboa Bay Club, The Center Club, Pacific Club, Newport. Research in vedic prins., natural law, quantum physics and mechanics. Office: 4631 Teller Ave Ste 100 Newport Beach CA 92660-8105 also: Wells Fargo Bank Bldg 41530 Enterprise Cir S Temecula CA 92590-4816

WENTZ, JEFFREY LEE, information systems consultant; b. Philippi, W.Va., Nov. 29, 1956; s. William Henry and Edith Marie (McBee) W. AS in Data Processing, BS in Acctg., Fairmont (W.Va.) State Coll., 1978. Programmer/analyst U.S. Dept. Energy, Morgantown, W.Va., 1978-79; analyst Middle South Svcs., New Orleans, 1979-81; sr. analyst Bank of Am., San Francisco, 1981-83; pres., cons. Wentz Cons. Inc., San Francisco, 1983—. Office: Wentz Consulting Inc 1378 34th Ave San Francisco CA 94122-1309

WERBACH, MELVYN ROY, physician, writer; b. N.Y.C., Nov. 11, 1940; s. Samuel and Martha (Robbins) W.; m. Gail Beth Leibsohn, June 20, 1967; children: Kevin, Adam. BA, Columbia Coll., N.Y.C., 1962; MD, Tufts U., Boston, 1966. Diplomate Am. Bd. Psychiatry and Neurology. Intern VA Hosp., Bklyn., 1966-67; resident in psychiatry Cedars-Sinai Med. Ctr., L.A., 1969-71; dir. psychol. svcs., clin. biofeedback UCLA Hosp. and Clinics, 1976-80; pres. Third Line Press, 1986—; asst. clin. prof. Sch. Medicine, UCLA, 1978—; mem. nutritional adv. bd. Cancer Treatment Ctrs. Am., 1989-93; mem. adv. com. The Dead Sea Confs., Israel, 1990—; mem. adv. bd. Longevity Rsch. Ctr., 1996—. Author: Third Line Medicine, 1986, Nutritional Influences on Illness, 1987, 2d edit., 1993, Nutritional Influences on Mental Illness, 1991, Healing Through Nutrition, 1993, Foundations of Nutritional Medicine, 1997; co-author: Botanical Influences on Illness, 1994; mem. editl. bd. Jour. of Nutritional Medicine, 1993—, Health News and Rev., 1991—, Jour. Optimal Nutrition, 1993—, Alt. Medicine Digest, 1994—; mem. internat. adv. bd. Jour. Bodywork and Movement Therapies, 1996—; mem. adv. bd. HealthWorld Online, 1996—; mem. med. adv. bd. Let's Live Mag., 1989-93; columnist Internat. Jour. Alt. and Complementary Medicine, 1992—, Townsend Letter for Doctors, 1993—, Australasian Jour. Nutrition and Environ. Medicine, 1994—, Jour. Orthomolekulare Medizin, 1997—, Nutrition Sci. News, 1997—; mem. panel What Doctors Don't Tell You, 1993—; contbr. articles to med. jours. Mem. Am. Coll. Nutrition, Biofeedback Soc. Calif. (hon. life mem., pres. 1977, Cert. Honor 1985), Australian Coll. Nutritional and Environ. Medicine (hon.).

WERDEGAR, KATHRYN MICKLE, state supreme court justice; b. San Francisco, CA; d. Benjamin Christie and Kathryn Marie (Clark) Mickle; m. David Werdegar; children: Maurice Clark, Matthew Mickle. Student, Wellesley Coll., 1954-55; AB with honors, U. Calif., Berkeley, 1957; JD with distinction, George Washington U., 1962; JD, U. Calif., Berkeley, 1990. Bar: Calif. 1964, U.S. Dist. Ct. (no. dist.) Calif. 1964, U.S. Ct. Appeals (9th cir.) 1964, Calif. Supreme Ct. 1964. Legal asst. civil rights divsn. U.S. Dept. Justice, Washington, 1962-63; cons. Calif. Study Commn. on Mental Retardation, 1963-64; assoc. U. Calif. Ctr. for Study of Law and Soc., Berkeley, 1965-67; spl. cons. State Dept. Mental Hygiene, 1967-68; cons. Calif. Coll. Trial Judges, 1968-71; atty., head criminal divsn. Calif. Continuing Edn. of Bar, 1971-78; assoc. dean acad. and student affairs, assoc. prof. Sch. Law, U. San Francisco, 1978-81; sr. staff atty. Calif. 1st Dist. Ct. Appeal, 1981-85, Calif. Supreme Ct., 1985-91; assoc. justice Calif. 1st Dist. Ct. Appeal, 1991-94, Calif. Supreme Ct., San Francisco, 1994—. Author: Benchbook: Misdemeanor Procedure, 1971, Misdemeanor Procedure Benchbook, 1975, 83; contbr. California Continuing Education of the Bar books; editor: California Criminal Law Practice series, 1972, California Uninsured Motorist Practice, 1973, I California Civil Procedure Before Trial, 1977. Recipient Charles Glover award George Washington U., J. William Fulbright award for disting. pub. svc. George Washington U. Law Sch. Alumni Assn., award of excellence Calif. Alumni Assn., also 5 Am. Jurisprudence awards. Mem. Nat. Assn. Women Judges, Calif. Judges Assn., Nev./Calif. Women Judges Assn., Order of the Coif. Office: Calif Supreme Court 350 McAllister St San Francisco CA 94102-3600

WERNER, DAVID ROBERT, English language educator; b. Madison, Wis., Oct. 22, 1946; s. George McKinley and Vivian Elida (Saline) W.; m. Mara Eleanor Fagin, Sept. 10, 1971 (div. May 1981); 1 child, Anna Teresa. BA, San Francisco State Univ., 1971, MA, 1974. Assoc. prof. Eng. Univ. La Verne, La Verne, Calif., 1976—, dir. epic program, 1976—. Author: In The Shadow/Hunter, 1997, Correctional Education, 1990; editor: From the Inside Out, 1991. Co-chair San Gabriel Valley Men's Coun., 1990-96; mem. retreat orgn. coun. L.A. Men's Coun., 1996. Mem. Correctional Edn. Assn. (editorial bd. 1986—, post. sec. SIG chair, 1988—, book rev. editor 1987—), Nat. Coun. Tchrs. of Eng. Democrat. Episcopalian. Avocations: woodworking, sailing, hiking. Home: 539 Wayland Ct Claremont CA 91711-5001 Office: Univ La Verne 1950 3d St La Verne CA 91750-4443

WERNER, MARLIN SPIKE, speech pathologist and audiologist; b. Portland, Maine, Aug. 15, 1927; s. Leonard Matthews and Margaret (Steele) W.; m. Caroline Emma Paul, Dec. 23, 1985; children: Leo Hart, Joseph Hart. BA in Sociology and Social Work, U. Mo., 1950; ScM in Audiology and Speech Pathology, Johns Hopkins U., 1957; PhD in Speech and Hearing Sci., Ohio State U., 1966. Lic. in audiology, hearing aid dispensing, speech pathology, Hawaii; lic. in audiology and speech pathology, Calif. Audiologist/speech pathologist, dir. Speech and Hearing Ctr. Asheville (N.C.) Orthopedic Hosp., 1960-64; assoc. prof. speech pathology and audiology We. Carolina U., Cullowhee, N.C., 1965-69; assoc. prof. speech pathology, audiology and speech sci. Fed. City Coll. (now U. D.C.), Washington, 1969-73; pres. Friends of Nepal's Hearing Handicapped, Oakland, Calif., 1979-84; audiologist, speech pathologist pvt. practice, Oakland and Lafayette, Calif., 1973-85; pvt. practice Lafayette, 1985-87; pvt. practice speech pathology and audiology Hilo, Hawaii, 1987—; speech and hearing cons. VA Hosp., Oteen, N.C., 1960-64; clin. cons. Speech and Hearing Clinic, Asheville Orthopedic Hosp., 1966-67; lectr., presenter in field. Contbr. articles to profl. jours.; contbr. to Ency. Brit., Am. Heritage Book of Natural Wonders, others. Hearing impaired svcs. task force State of Hawaii Dept. Health, 1987-88; mem. Hawaii County Mayor's Com. for Persons with Disabilities, 1988-94; adv. bd. Salvation Army, 1992; bd. dirs. Hawaii chpt. Am. Arthritis Found.; past pres. Big Island Safety Assn.; mem. Hawaii Gov.'s Bd. Hearing Aid Dealers and Fitters; mem. adv. com., pres. Older Adult Resource Ctr., Laney Coll., Oakland, Calif.; v.p. Hawaii Speleol. Survey; chmn. Hawaii Grotto of Nat. Speleol. Soc., others; mem. adv. bd. Hilo Bay Clinics. MCH fellow Johns Hopkins U., 1954, Pub. Health fellow Ohio State U., 1964. Fellow Nat. Speleological Soc.; mem. AAAS, Am. Speech and Hearing Assn., Acoustical Soc. Am., Calif. Speech and Hearing Assn., Calif. Writers Club (bd. dirs., past pres.), Hawaii Speech, Lang. and Hearing Assn., Fellowship Interest Learning Motivation (F.I.L.M. Club). Avocations: collecting and making musical instruments, graphic arts, photography, cave exploring, writing. Home: 27-683 Kalaoa Mauka Papaikou HI 96781 Office: 400 Hualani St Ste 191-a Hilo HI 96720-4383

WERNER, ROGER HARRY, archaeologist; b. N.Y.C., Nov. 11, 1950; s. Harry Emile and Rena (Roode) W.; m. Kathleen Diane Engdahl, Feb. 20, 1982; children: Meryl Lauren, Sarah Melise, Jeremy Marshall; 1 stepchild, Amber Fawn. BA, Belknap Coll., 1973; MA, Sonoma State U., Rohnert Park, Calif., 1982. Curatorial aide Anthro. Lab. Sonoma State Coll., 1975-76, curatorial asst., 1976-77, staff archaeologist, 1977-80; staff archaeologist Planning Dept., Lake County, Calif., 1977; cir. riding archaeologist western region Nat. Park Service, Tucson, Ariz., 1978; prin. investigator ASI Cartography and Geog. Info. Sys., Stockton, Calif., 1979—; pres. Cmty. Wide Web of Stockton, 1995-97; cons. Calif. Indian Legal Svcs., Ukiah, 1977, Geothermal Rsch. Impact Projection Study, Lakeport, Calif., 1977—, Delta Net Comms., Stockton, Calif., 1995—; instr. Ya-Ka-Ana Indian Ednl. Ctr., Santa Rosa, Calif., 1978-79; lead archaeologist No. Calif., WESTEC Svcs., Inc., San Diego, 1979-81; adj. prof. U. Puget Sound, summer 1995. Sec. Colonial Hts. PTA, 1983-84, 2d v.p., 1985-86, historian, 1986-87, v.p., 1987-88; cons., instr. Clovis Adult Sch., 1984-85; instr. U. Pacific Lifelong Learning Ctr., 1987—, San Joaquin Delta Coll., 1990—, Calif. State U., Fresno, 1992—; bd. dirs. Valley Mountain Regional Ctr., 1987-88, treas., 1988-89, v.p., 1989-90, pres.-elect, 1990-91, pres., 1991-92; bd. trustees Stockton Chorale, treas., 1992-93, youth chorale rep., 1993-94; active Spl. Olympics, Stockton, Calif.; adminstr. Minor A divsn. Sundown Little League of Stockton, Inc., 1998. Anthropology dept. research grantee, Sonoma State U., 1980. Mem. Geol. Soc. Am., Soc. for Am. Archaeologists, Great Basin Anthropol. Conf., Soc. for Calif. Archaeology, Assn. for Retarded Citizens. Democrat. Avocations: reading, community activities, computers. Home: 1117 Aberdeen Ave Stockton CA 95209-2625 Office: ASI Cartography & GIS 8026 Lorraine Ave Ste 218 Stockton CA 95210-4224

WERNER, WILLIAM ARNO, architect; b. San Francisco, Dec. 11, 1937; s. William Arno and Sophie (Menutis) W.; m. Wendy Rolston Wilson, Feb. 3, 1963 (div. Jan. 1983); 1 child, Christa Nichol. BA with honors, Yale U., 1959, BArch, 1962, MArch, 1963. Drafter Serge Chermayeff, Paul Rudolph and Charles Brewer, New Haven, 1961-63; project designer Johnson, Poole & Storm, San Francisco, 1963-64; project designer Leo S. Wou & Assocs., Honolulu, 1965-66, v.p. of design, 1971-72; project architect John Tatom Assocs., Honolulu, 1965-66; sr. designer Skidmore, Owings & Merrill, San Francisco, 1968-71, assoc./project architect, 1972-76; prin. W.A. Werner Assocs., San Francisco, 1976-80; ptnr. Werner & Sullivan, San Francisco, 1980—; mem. planning commn. City of Sausalito, Calif.; bd. govs. Yale U., New Haven; visitorship in architecture U. Auckland Found., New Zealand, 1994. Prin. works include Alameda Mcpl. Credit Union, Lane Pub. Co., Menlo Park, Calif., Pacific Data Images, Mountain View, Calif., Saga Corp., Menlo Park, Tiffany & Co., Union Square, San Francisco, Somerset Collection, Troy, Mich., Touche Ross & Co., Oakland, U.S. Post Office, San Francisco, (renovations) Fed. Express Co., San Francisco, KD's Grog N' Grocery, San Francisco, Jessie Street. Substation, San Francisco, Lakeside Tower Health Ctr./Mt. Zion Hosp., Qantas Bldg, San Francisco, Women's Care, San Francisco, Moon Residence, Dillon Beach, Calif., Shenkar Residence, San Francisco, Tacker Residence, Denver, Lasky Residence, San Francisco, Starring Residence, San Francisco, Whitehead Residence, Monte Rio, Calif., various laboratories, theatres and rsch. facilities, urban design. Recipient Progressive Architecture Design award Jessie St. Substation, 1980, DuPont Co. Design award Touche Ross & Co., 1983, award of Excellence Woodwork Inst. of Calif., 1989, USPS/NEA Nat. Honor award for Design Excellence, 1990, Tucker Design Excellence award Bldg. Stone Inst., Tiffany & Co., 1992. Mem. AIA (San Francisco chpt.), Found. for San Francisco's Architectural Heritage (hon.). Home: 213 Richardson St Sausalito CA 94965-2422 Office: Werner & Sullivan 207 Powell St Ste 800 San Francisco CA 94102-2209

WERNING, JOSEPH ROBERT, computer company executive; b. Kansas City, Mo., Nov. 9, 1928; s. Joe and Hester Clair (Casebeer) W.; m. Martha Kollas, Aug. 24, 1952 (div. 1960); m. Lucia Diller, Oct. 10, 1960 (deceased); children: Catherine, Gryf, Dirk, Cort. BS in Math., Oregon State U., 1952, BS in Chem. Engring., 1953; PhD in Phys. Chemistry, U. Calif., Berkeley, 1958. Chem. engr. Dupont, Wilmington, 1953-55; engring. mgr. IBM Corp., San Jose, Calif., 1958-69, Memorex Corp., Santa Clara, Calif., 1969-75, System Industries, San Jose, 1975-80, Anderson-Jacobson, San Jose, 1980-82; founder, exec. v.p. On Target Tech., Santa Clara, 1982—. Contbr. articles to profl. jours.; patentee in field. With USMC, 1946-48. Avocations: ornithology, philately, horticulture. Home: 215 Vineyard Dr San Jose CA 95119-1863 Office: On Target Tech 3350 Scott Blvd Santa Clara CA 95054-3104

WERSTIUK, LINDA, hairstylist, photographic artist; b. Bronx, N.Y., Apr. 23, 1959; d. Louis and Lenora (Masciandaro) Mariano; m. Kenneth Werstiuk, Feb. 20, 1983; children: Eric Jon, Alexa Taylor. Grad., Cosmetology Sch., Middletown, N.Y., 1977; grad. in Photography, West Valley Occupl., 1993. Photographic artist Northridge, Calif., 1990—; hairstylist, haircolorist Hugh O'Brien Salon, North Hollywood, Calif., 1991—; photo illustrator, Northridge; photo hand colorist, Northridge; instr. photo hand coloring Encino (Calif.) Media Ctr.; instr. hand coloring B&W photos The Learning Annes, L.A. Published works include photo illustration, Children's Def. Fund, 1996, CASA Assn., 1996, Parent Press, 1997, Whole Person Calendar, 1998, Our Children Mag., 1998. Chair health and safety com. Lorne Street Sch. PTA, Northridge, 1994—; absolute chalk-artist The Light Bringer Project, Pasadena, Calif., 1996, 97, 98; chairperson Nat. PTA Reflections Art Program; art docent making friends with gt. works Lorne Sch. Republican. Avocations: fine art chalk art on pavement, Mendhi-henna body painting.

WERTHEIMER, ROBERT E., paper company executive; b. 1928; married. BSME, U. Wash., 1950; MBA, Harvard U., 1952. With Longview (Wash.) Fibre Co., 1952—, package engr., 1955-59, asst. mgr. container ops., 1959-60, asst. mgr. container sales, 1960-63, v.p. container sales West, 1963-75, v.p. prodn., 1975, group v.p. containers, now exec. v.p., dir. Office: Longview Fibre Co 120 Montgomery St Ste 2200 San Francisco CA 94104-4325

WESKAMP, KELLEY S., account manager, real estate liquidation; b. Boulder City, Nev., Jan. 9, 1964; d. Dale P. and Phyllis J. (Cooper) W. BA in English Lang. Lit. with distinctio, Loretto Heights Coll., 1985. Cons. Ely Leadership Mgmt., Lakewood, Colo., 1985-88; budget asst. Bureau Reclamation, Denver, 1988-90; real estate owned technician FDIC, Denver, 1990-93; real estate specialist Westfall and Co., Westminster, 1993-95; account mgr. Westfall and Co., 1995-97, Castle Advisors subs. Chgo. Title, 1998—; participant Bench Mark Study, Pete Marwick Assocs., 1997. Contbr. article to mag. Democrat. Catholic. Avocations: weaving, reading, travel, cooking. Home: 12080 W Mexico Ave Lakewood CO 80228

WESSLER, CHARLES B., film producer; b. Spencer, Mich.; s. Richard and Ruth W. Film producer Wessler Entertainment, West Hollywood, Calif. Producer: (feature films) It's Pat, Cold Feet, Dumb and Dumber, There's Something About Mary, 1998, Bushwacked, The Locusts. With IDF, 1972-74. Office: Wessler Entertainment # 300 9056 Santa Monica Blvd West Hollywood CA 90069-5545

WESSLER, MARY HRAHA, marketing and management executive; b. Des Moines, Nov. 4, 1961; d. Francis M. and Shirley A. (Malone) Hraha; 1 child, Nick. BA in Mass Communications, Iowa State U., 1984; postgrad., U. Denver, 1990. Asst. mktg. dir. Des Moines Ballet Co.; asst. press sec. Governor State of Iowa, Des Moines; dir. mktg. Real Estate Mgmt. Corp., Scottsdale, Ariz., 1984-87; v.p. Great West Mgmt. and Realty, Ltd., Denver, 1987-97; reg. v.p. AIMCO, Denver, 1997—; instr., spkr. for apt. assns., Multi-Housing World and IREM. Mem. Nat. Apt. Assn., Colo. Apt. Assn. (bd. dirs. 1995-97), Apt. Assn. of Metro Denver (sec., bd. dirs., treas., pres.-elect, pres. 1997-98, Owner of Yr. 1992-93, 95, 97, Woman of Yr. 1989-90), Met. Club. Home: 9400 E Iliff Ave #134 Denver CO 80231-3974

WESSLER, MELVIN DEAN, farmer, rancher; b. Dodge City, Kan., Feb. 11, 1932; s. Oscar Lewis and Clara (Reiss) W.; grad. high sch.; m. Laura Ethel Arbuthnot, Aug. 23, 1951; children: Monty Dean, Charla Cay, Virgil Lewis. Farmer-rancher, Springfield, Colo., 1950—; dir., sec. bd. Springfield Co-op. Sales Co., 1964-80, pres. bd., 1980—. Pres., Arkansas Valley Co-op. Council, SE Colo. Area, 1965-87, Colo. Co-op. Council, 1969-72, v.p. 1974, sec. 1980-86; community com. chmn. Baca County, Agr. Stablzn. and Conservation Svc., Springfield, 1961-73, 79—, vice chmn. Baca County Com., 1980-90; mem. spl. com. on grain mktg. Far-Mar-Co.; mem. adv. bd. Denver Bapt. Bible Coll., 1984-89; chmn., bd. dirs. Springfield Cemetery Bd., 1985—; apptd. spl. com. Farmland Industries spl. project Tomorrow, 1987—. Recipient The Colo. Cooperator award The Colo. Coop Coun., 1990. Mem. Colo. Cattlemen's Assn., Colo. Wheat Growers Assn., Southeast Farm Bus. Assn. (bd. dirs. 1991-95), Big Rock Grange (treas. 1964-76, master 1976-82), Southwest Kans. Farm Bus. Assn. (dir. 1996—). Address: 18363 County Road Pp Springfield CO 81073

WEST, BILLY GENE, public relations executive; b. Richmond, Ind., Nov. 22, 1946; s. Billy D. and Jean C. (Cox) W. AA, Cerritos Coll., 1966; BA, U. So. Calif., 1969; MA, U. Minn., 1971. Salesman, Marina Art Products, L.A., 1967-73; v.p. Am. Telecon Network, Dallas, 1974-77; gen. mgr. Phoenix Publs., Houston, 1977-78; pres. San Dark, Inc., San Francisco, 1978-82; gen. ptnr. Billy West & Assocs., 1982—; pres. V.G. Prodns., 1983—; chief exec. officer Westmarking, San Francisco, 1989— ; exec. dir. Young Ams. for Freedom, Minn. and Wis., 1970-72; pres. S.F.P.A., San Francisco, 1982-83. Mem. Assn. MBA Execs. Mem. Am. Ref. Ch.

WEST, EDWARD ALAN, graphics communications executive; b. L.A., Dec. 25, 1928; s. Albert Reginald and Gladys Delia (White) W.; m. Sonya Lea Smith, Jan. 2, 1983; children: Troy A., Tamara L.; stepchildren: Debra, Chris, Donna. AA, Fullerton Coll., 1966; student, Cerritos Coll., 1957, UCLA, 1966-67. Circulation mgr. Huntington Park (Calif.) Signal Newspaper, 1946-52; newspaper web pressman Long Beach (Calif.) Press Telegram, 1955-62; gravure web pressman Gravure West, Los Angeles, 1966-67; sales engr. Halm Jet Press, Glen Head, N.Y., 1968-70; salesman Polychrome Corp., Glen Head, 1970-74; supr. reprographics Fluor Engring & Construction, Irvine, Calif., 1974-81; dir. reprographics Fluor Arabia, Dhahran, Saudi Arabia, 1981-85, Press Telegram, Long Beach, 1986-97; with Suburban LA Newspaper Group, 1998—; printing advisor Saddleback C.C., Mission Viejo, Calif., 1979, 80. Author: How to Paste up For Graphic Reproduction, 1967. Sgt. USMC, 1952-55, Korea. Mem. In-Plant Printing Assn. (cert. graphics comm. mgr. 1977, editor newsletter 1977, pres. Orange County chpt. 1979-80, Internat. Man of Yr. award 1980), 1st Marine Divsn. Assn. (life), VFW (life), Am. Legion, Internat. Assn. Legions of Honor (emeritus), Western Shrine Assn. (comdr. 1996-97), Shriners (pres. South Coast club 1991, editor blue and gold unit Legion of Honor El Bekal Temple 1989-92, comdr. Legion of Honor 1992 (life), Shriner of Yr. award 1994), Masons, KT, Internat. High Twelve 500 (Capistrano pres. 1995, 96). Presbyterian. Home: 198 Monarch Bay Dr Dana Point CA 92629-3437 Office: Suburban LA Newspaper Group 1210 N Azusa Canyon Rd West Covina CA 91790-1003

WEST, HUGH STERLING, aircraft leasing company executive; b. Kansas City, Kans., Apr. 5, 1930; s. Gilbert Eugene and Dorothy (Johnson) W.; BS, U. Va., 1952; BS in Aero., U. Md., 1959; grad. U.S. Naval Test Pilot Sch., 1959; m. Willa Alden Reed, Jan. 16, 1954; children: Karen, Phillip, Susan. Commd. 2d lt. U.S. Marine Corps., 1948, advanced through grades to maj., 1961; exptl. flight test pilot, U.S. Naval Air Test Center, Patuxent River, Md.; resigned, 1961; program mgr. Boeing Aircraft Co., Seattle and Phila., 1961-66, dir. airworthiness, comml. airplane divsn., 1969-71; dir. aircraft sales Am. Airlines, Tulsa, 1971-76; v.p. equipment mgmt. GATX Leasing Corp., San Francisco, 1976-80; v.p. tech., partner Polaris Aircraft Leasing Corp., San Francisco, 1980-85; v.p., co-founder U.S. Airlease, Inc. divsn. Ford Motor Co., 1986-96, ret., 1996; pres. Hugh S. West & Assocs., Comml. Aircraft Cons. Mem. Soc. Exptl. Test Pilots, Army Navy Country Club. Republican. Episcopalian. Home and Office: 387 Darrell Rd Hillsborough CA 94010-6763

WEST, JACK HENRY, petroleum geologist; b. Washington, Apr. 7, 1934; s. John Henry and Zola Faye (West) Pigg; m. Bonnie Lou Ruger, Apr. 1, 1961; children: Trent John, Todd Kenneth. BS in Geology, U. Oreg., 1957, MS, 1961. Cert. petroleum geologist. Geologist Texaco Inc., L.A and Bakersfield, Calif., 1961-72; asst. dist. devel. geologist Texaco Inc., L.A., 1972-78; geologist Oxy Petroleum Inc., Bakersfield, 1978-80, div. geologist, 1980-83; exploitation mgr. Oxy U.S.A. Inc./Cities Svc. Oil and Gas, Bakersfield, 1983-89; sr. petroleum advisor WZI Inc., Bakersfield, 1990-92, petroleum cons., 1993—. Active Beyond War, Bakersfield, 1983-90. Mem. Am. Assn. Petroleum Geologists (pres. Pacific sect. 1988-89, adv. coun. 1992-94, sec. divsn. profl. affairs 1995—), San Joaquin Geol. Soc. (pres. 1984-85), Alfa Romeo Owners Club. Republican. Methodist. Avocations: music, sports cars.

WEST, JERRY ALAN, professional basketball team executive; b. Chelyan, W.Va., May 28, 1938; s. Howard Stewart and Cecil Sue (Creasey) W.; m. Martha Jane Kane, May, 1960 (div. 1977); children: David, Michael, Mark; m. Karen Christine Bua, May 28, 1978; 1 son, Ryan. BS, W.Va. Coll.; LHD (hon.), W.Va. Wesleyan Coll. Mem. Los Angeles Lakers, Nat. Basketball Assn., 1960-74, coach, 1976-79, spl. cons., 1979-82, gen. mgr., 1982-94; exec. v.p. basketball operations L. A. Lakers, 1994—; mem. first team Nat. Basketball Assn. All-Star Team, 1962-67, 70-73, mem. second team, 1968, 69; mem. NBA champion L.A. Lakers, 1972. Author: (with William Libby) Mr. Clutch: The Jerry West Story, 1969. Capt. U.S. Olympic Basketball Team, 1960; named Most Valuable Player NBA Playoff, 1969, All-Star Game Most Valuable Player, 1972; named to Naismith Meml. Basketball Hall of Fame, 1979, NBA Hall of Fame, 1980; mem. NBA 35th Anniversary All-Time Team, 1980; named NBA Exec. of Yr. Sporting News, 1994-95. Office: LA Lakers PO Box 10 Inglewood CA 90306-0010*

WEST, NATALIE ELSA, lawyer; b. Greenwich, Conn., Mar. 11, 1947. AB, Smith Coll., 1968; JD, U. Calif., Berkeley, 1973. Bar: Calif. 1974. Counsel Calif. Fair Polit. Practices Commn., Sacramento, 1975-79; city atty. City of Berkeley, Calif., 1980-85, City of Novato, Calif., 1985-92, City of Brentwood, Calif., 1994-99; gen. counsel Livermore-Amador Valley Water Mgmt. Agy., 1996—; shareholder McDonough, Holland & Allen, Oakland, Calif., 1991—. Pres. city attys. dept. League of Calif. Cities, 1986-87, bd. dirs., 1995-97. Mem. State Bar Calif., Alameda County Bar Assn. Office: McDonough Holland & Allen 1999 Harrison St Ste 1300 Oakland CA 94612-3582

WEST, ROBERT L., JR., marketing professional; b. Wilmington, N.C., Oct. 5, 1958; s. Robert L. Sr. and Elsie S. (Skipper) W.; m. Elena F., Nov. 21, 1992. BSBA, Pembroke State U., 1981; postgrad., U. Pa., 1988-90. Divsn. controller Royster Co., Norfolk, Va., 1982-84; regional fin. mgr. Rohm & Haas Co., Memphis, 1984-86; head Asian ops. Franklin Mint, Hone Kong, 1986-88; head corp. cost improvement Franklin Mint, Phila., 1988-89; head European ops. Franklin Mint, London, 1989-90; v.p. fin. & ops. Paradise Galleries, Inc., San Diego, 1990-91; v.p., chief fin. officer Georgetown Collection, Inc., Portland, Maine, 1992-95; v.p. worldwide ops. Nat. Media Corp., Phoenix, 1995-96; pres., founder DCA Internat., Phoenix, 1990—; cons. to CEO J Cres, N.Y.C., 1990-91. V.p Maxton (N.C.) Conservative Response, 1980-82. Mem. Am. Mgmt. Assn., Am. Fin. Assn., Inst. Mgmt. Accts., World Affairs Coun. Republican. Avocations: biking, flying, model railroading, tennis, long distance running. Home: 800 Roundwood Dr Scarborough ME 04074-8219 Office: DCA Dynamic Cons Assocs 3646 E Ray Rd Ste B16-60 Phoenix AZ 85044-7116

WEST, ROBERT SUMNER, surgeon; b. Bowman, N.D., Nov. 20, 1935; s. Elmer and Minnie (DeBode) W.; m. Martha W. Hopkins, Mar. 23, 1957; children: Stephen, Christopher, Anna Marie, Catherine, Sarah. BA, U. N.D., 1957, BS in Medicine, 1959; MD, Harvard U., 1961. Diplomate Am. Bd. Surgery. Intern U.S. Naval Hosp., Chelsea, Mass., 1961-62; resident in surgery U. Vt. Med. Ctr. Hosp., 1965-69; pvt. practice Coeur d'Alene, Idaho, 1969—; coroner Kootenai County, Coeur d'Alene, 1984—. Trustee, pres. Coeur d'Alene Sch. Dist. 271 Bd. Edn., 1973-77; bd. dirs. PRO-WEST, 1989—. Lt. M.C., USN, 1960-65. Fellow ACS (pres. Idaho chpt. 1985, gov. at large); mem. Idaho Med. Assn. (pres. 1989-90, trustee), Kiwanis. Republican. Methodist. Avocation: sailing. Office: 920 W Ironwood Dr Coeur D Alene ID 83814-2643

WEST, TONY, state official; b. Phoenix, Ariz., Oct. 29, 1937; m. Margaret O'Malley, 1962; 3 children: William A., III, John Patrick, Stephen Michael. BS, Ariz. State Univ., 1961. Formerly pres., chief exec. officer Shenendoah Ranches; Ariz. state rep., 1973-82, former Ariz. state senator, dist. 18, Ariz. state treas., 1998; corp. commr. Ariz. Corp. Commn., Phoenix, 1999—. Mem. Ariz. Club (formerly pres.), Ariz. Found. for Handicapped (pres.), John C. Lincoln Hosp. Found. Republican. Office: Ariz Corp Commn 1200 W Washington St Phoenix AZ 85007-2812*

WESTBO, LEONARD ARCHIBALD, JR., electronics engineer; b. Tacoma, Wash., Dec. 4, 1931; s. Leonard Archibald and Agnes (Martinson) W.; B.A. in Gen. Studies, U. Wash., 1958. Electronics engr. FAA, Seattle Air Route Traffic Control Center, Auburn, Wash., 1961-72; asst. br. chief electronics engring. br. 13th Coast Guard Dist., Seattle, 1972-87. Served with

USCG, 1951-54, 1958-61. Registered profl. engr., Wash. Mem. Aircraft Owners and Pilots Assn., IEEE, Am. Radio Relay League. Home and Office: 10528 SE 323d St Auburn WA 98092-4734

WESTCOTT, BRIAN JOHN, manufacturing executive; b. Rexford, N.Y., June 19, 1957; s. John Campbell and Norma (Cornell) W.; m. Andrea Belrose, Apr. 23, 1988; children: Sarah Katharine, Paul Brian. BS, Lehigh U., 1979; MS, Stanford U., 1980, PhD, 1987. Engr. Combustion Engring., Windsor, Conn., 1980-81; rsch. engr. Gen. Electric Corp. Rsch., Niskayuna, N.Y., 1981-83; rsch. fellow Stanford (Calif.) Grad. Sch. Bus., 1987-88; mgr. Gen. Electric Corp. Mgmt., Bridgeport, Conn., 1988-89; prin. A.T. Kearney Tech. Inc., Redwood City, Calif., 1989—; chief exec. officer Westt, Inc., Menlo Park, Calif., 1990—. Author: (with others) Paradox and Transformation, 1988; contbr. articles to profl. jours.; inventor, patentee in field. Mem. Menlo Park Vitality Task Force, 1993-94. Recipient Tech 500 award Westt, Inc., 1996, 97, 98, Inc. 500 award, 1997, Silicon Valley Tech fast 50 award, 1997, 98; postdoctoral rsch. fellow Stanford U. Grad. Sch. Bus., 1987, 88; rsch. fellow Electric Power Rsch., Stanford, 1983-87. Mem. ASME. Avocations: sports, politics. Office: Westt Inc 1090 Obrien Dr Menlo Park CA 94025-1409

WESTER, KEITH ALBERT, film and television recording engineer, television executive; b. Seattle, Feb. 21, 1940; s. Albert John and Evelyn Grayce (Nettell) W.; m. Judith Elizabeth Jones, 1968 (div. Mar. 1974); 1 child, Wendy Elizabeth. AA, Am. River Coll., Sacramento, 1959; BA, Calif. State U., L.A., 1962; MA, UCLA, 1965. Lic. multi-engine rated pilot. Prodn. asst. Sta. KCRA-TV, Sacramento, 1956; announcer Sta. KSFM, Sacramento, 1960; film editor, sound rec. technician Urie & Assocs., Hollywood, Calif., 1963-66; co-owner Steckler-Wester Film Prodns., Hollywood, 1966-70; owner Profl. Sound Recorders, Studio City, Calif., 1970—, Aerocharter, Studio City, 1974—; owner Wester Devel., Sun Valley, Coeur d'Alene, Idaho, 1989—, also Studio City, 1989—; majority stockholder Channel 58 TV, Coeur d'Alene/Spokane, Idaho, 1993—. Prodn. sound mixer: (films) Never Been Kissed, 1999, Runaway Bride, 1999, Armageddon, 1998, Mouse Hunt, 1997, Air Force One, 1997 (Acad. award co-nominee for best sound 1998), Shadow Conspiracy, 1996, G.I. Jane, 1997, The Rock, 1996 (Acad. award co-nominee for best sound, 1997), Waterworld, 1995 (Acad. award co-nominee for best sound 1996), The Shadow, 1994, Wayne's World II, 1993, Coneheads, 1993, Body of Evidence, 1992, Indecent Proposal, 1992, School Ties, 1991, Frankie and Johnny, 1991, Another You, 1991, Thelma and Louise, 1990, Shattered, 1990, Desperate Hours, 1989, Joe vs. the Volcano, 1989, Black Rain, 1989, Sea of Love, 1988, Real Men, 1985, Mask, 1984, Thief of Hearts, 1983, Young Doctors in Love, 1982, First Monday in October, 1981. Mem. NATAS (Emmy award An Early Frost 1986, Emmy nominations in 1982, 84, 85, 87), SAG, Acad. Motion Picture Arts and Scis. (Acad. award nomination for best sound Black Rain 1990, Waterworld 1996, The Rock 1997, Air Force One 1998), Brit. Acad. Film and TV Arts (award nomination for The Rock 1997), Cinema Audio Soc. (sec. 1985-91, Sound award 1987), Soc. Motion Picture and TV Engrs., Internat. Sound Technicians, Local 695, Assn. Film Craftsmen (sec. 1967-73, treas. 1973-76), Aircraft Owners and Pilots Assn. (Confederate Air Force col.), Am. Radio Relay League (K6DGN). Home: 4146 Bellingham Ave Studio City CA 91604-1601 Office: Profl Sound Recorders 22440 Clarendon St Woodland Hills CA 91367-4467

WESTERDAHL, JOHN BRIAN, nutritionist, health educator; b. Tucson, Dec. 3, 1954; s. Jay E. and Margaret (Meyer) W.; m. Doris Mui Lian Tan, Nov. 18, 1989; 1 child, Jasmine Leilani. AA, Orange Coast Coll., 1977; BS, Pacific Union Coll., 1979; MPH, Loma Linda U., 1981. Registered dietitian, mastered herbalist; cert. nutrition specialist. Nutritionist, health educator Castle Med. Ctr., Kailua, Hawaii, 1981-84, health promotion coord., 1984-87, asst. dir. health promotion, 1987-88, dir. health promotion, 1988-89, dir. health promotion and nutritional svcs., 1998—; dir. nutrition and health rsch. Health Sci., Santa Barbara, Calif., 1989-90; sr. nutritionist, project mgr. Shaklee Corp., San Francisco, 1990-96; dir. nutrition Dr. McDougall's Right Foods, Inc., South San Francisco, 1996—; mem. faculty staff, dir. continuing edn. Am. Acad. Nutrition, 1996—; talk show host Nutrition and You, Sta. KGU Radio, Honolulu, 1983-89; nutrition com. mem. Hawaii div. Am. Heart Assn., Honolulu, 1984-87; mem. nutrition study group Govs. Conf. Health Promotion and Disease Prevention for Hawaii, 1985. Author: Medicinal Herbs: A Vital Reference Guide, 1998, The Millennium Cookbook, 1998; editor: Nourish Mag., 1995-96; nutrition editor: Veggie Life Mag., 1995—. Mem. AAAS, Am. Coll. Sports Medicine, Am. Dietetic Assn. (Calif. coord. vegetarian nutrition dietetic practice group), Am. Nutritionists Assn., Am. Coll. Nutrition, Soc. for Nutrition Edn., Nat. Wellness Assn., Nutrition Today Soc., Am. Soc. Pharmacognosy, Inst. Food Technologists, Hawaii Nutrition Coun. (v.p. 1983-86,m pres.-elect 1988-89, pres. 1989), Hawaii Dietetic Assn., Calif. Dietetic Assn., N.Y. Acad. Scis., Seventh-day Adventist Dietetic Assn., several other profl. assns. Republican. Seventh-Day Adventist. Avocations: swimming, scuba diving. Office: Castle Ctr Health Promotion 46-001 Kamehameha Hwy Ste 104 Kaneohe HI 96744-3720

WESTERMAN, DONNA DAY, artist; b. Detroit, June 22, 1940; d. James McAdam and Mary Elizabeth (McGibbon) Day; m. Jan Hendrik Westerman, Sept. 28, 1967; 1 child, Johanna Louise. Student, U. Mich., 1958-60, Boston Mus. Sch., 1962; BFA, MFA, Otis Art Inst., L.A., 1966. Tchr. art various mus. and schs., Mass. and Calif., 1960-76; prof., chmn. art dept. Orange Coast Coll., Costa Mesa, Calif., 1976—, founder and dir. computer graphics program, 1979-90; owner Saltlick Studios, Costa Mesa, Calif., 1987—; curator confs. and symposiums; spkr. in field. Author: One-Of-A-Kind Artists Books; author, reviewer mag. Bookways, 1993; artist, creator cast glass, cast bronze and carved wood, archtl. commns.; exhibited in various shows, 1954—. Dir., vol. art program Santiago Sch., Santa Ana, 1976-78; mem. support group Big Bros./Big Sisters, Orange County, Calif., 1987—; mem. edn. com. Bowers Mus., Santa Ana, 1975-80. Recipient Outstanding Calender Design award Printing Inst. Am., 1975; State of Calif. grantee, 1983-84. Mem. L.A. Printmaking Soc. (bd. dirs., pres.), L.A. Women of Letters, Alliance for Contemporary Book Arts, Guild of Book Workers, Western Assn. Art Conservators, Orange County Arts Alliance (officer, bd. dirs.), Am. Craft Coun. Avocations: photography, book binding, sailing, gardening, walking. Office: Orange Coast Coll 2701 Fairview Rd Costa Mesa CA 92626-5563

WESTERN, CAROLE ANN, literary agent; b. Nuneaton, Warwickshire, England, Jan. 17, 1945; d. Ernest and Agnes Nancy (Webster) Gummery; m. Daniel Ray Western, May 4, 1938; children: Rick Matthew, Jeff Lawrence, Jason Scott, Tracie Rae, Kellie Lee. RSA, London Univ., 1965. Tchr. East H.S., Salt Lake City, Utah, 1993-95, Salt Lake City Sch., Salt Lake City, Utah, 1993-95, Pioneer Craftshouse, Salt Lake City, Utah, 1990—; v.p. Nebula Books, 1998—. Author: Ancient Circle, Fire Goddess, Winds of the Karazan, Crystal Pyramid, Swamp Spirits, Nightmare Cafe. Cub scout leader, 1988-92; com. Utah League of Writers. Mem. Montgomery West Agy. (pres. 1988—). Avocations: writing screenplays and books, editing, publishing, teaching. Home: 7450 Butler Hills Dr Salt Lake City UT 84121-5008

WESTFALL, STEPHEN DONALD, accountant, small business owner; b. Moscow, Idaho, Sept. 20, 1953; s. Donald Eugene and Elizabeth Ann (Morgan) W.; m. Joyce Beck, Aug. 29, 1976; children: Erin Kay, Corey Stephen. BS, U. Idaho, 1975. CPA, Idaho. Ptnr. Westfall & Westfall, C.P.A's, Burley, Idaho, 1975—; bd. dirs. Cassia Meml. Hosp. and Med. Ctr., Burley, 1983—, vice-chmn. 1994-96, chmn., 1996—; bd. dirs. First Fed. Savings Bank, Twin Fall, Idaho, 1992—; bd. dirs., pres. Burle Racquet and Health Corp., 1982—; bd. dirs., treas. Burley Regatta, Inc., Craters of the Moon Devel.; bd. dirs. ARC Mini Cossia chpt. 1994-96. Mem. AICPA, Idaho Soc. CPAs, Burley Area C. of C. (bd. dirs. 1986-91, pres. 1989), Elks Club. Republican. Presbyterian. Avocations: golf, racquetball, biking, travel. Home: 17 Granada Pl Burley ID 83318-1705 Office: Westfall & Westfall CPAs 1329 Albion Ave Burley ID 83318-1898

WESTON, IDANTHEA BEYETTE, school director; b. Paris, July 12, 1930; came to U.S., 1932; d. Hubert Ward and Jessica Idanthea (Moffat) Beyette; m. William Bunker Weston Jr., June 10, 1951; children: William Bunker III, Perrin Idanthea, Bonnie Emerson. BA, Scripps Coll., 1951. Tchr. Challenger Sch., San Jose, Calif., 1963-73; dir., founder Old Orchard Sch., Campbell, Calif., 1973—. Vol. Jr. League, San Jose, 1954—. Republican. Episcopalian. Avocations: reading, travel, needlepoint design. Home: 620 Twin Ln Soquel CA 95073-9543

WESTON, JANE SARA, plastic surgeon, educator; b. Oceanside, N.Y., May 21, 1952; m. Jan K. Horn; 1 child, Jonathan Spencer Horn. MD, Stanford U., 1975-79. Diplomate Am. Bd. Plastic Surgery. Resident gen. surgery Sch. Medicine Stanford (Calif.) U., 1979-82, resident plastic surgery Sch. Medicine, 1982-83; fellow craniofacial surgery Hopital des Enfants Malades, Paris, 1983-84; plastic surgeon Kaiser Permanente Med. Group, San Jose, Calif., 1985-90; pvt. practice Palo Alto, Calif., 1990—; mem. faculty Stanford U. Med. Sch., 1994-95. Active Leadership Palo Alto, 1993. Fellow ACS; mem. Am. Soc. Plastic and Reconstructive Surgeons (chair women plastic surgeons com. 1993-96). Avocation: harp. Office: 750 Welch Rd Ste 321 Palo Alto CA 94304-1510*

WETCH, LYLE JEFFREY, electrical engineer; b. Billings, Mont., Aug. 17, 1962; s. Leroy Delbert and Rita Annette (Lorsen) W.; m. Regina Marie Kroneberger, Oct. 9, 1993; 1 child, Derek Hunter. BSEE, Mont. State U., 1990. Product test engr. Tex. Instruments, Midland, Tex., 1990-91; asic design engr. Tex. Instruments, Sherman, Tex., 1991-93; product engr. Toko Am., Colo. Springs, Colo., 1993-94; asic design engr. NCR Microelectronics, Ft. Collins, Colo., 1994-95; field application engr. Actel Corp., Arvada, Colo., 1995—; cons., Arvada, Colo., 1997—. Mem. Internat. Elec. Electronic Engrs. Republican. Roman Catholic. Avocations: fishing, hunting, biking. Home and Office: 7275 Nile Ct Arvada CO 80007-7078

WETSCH, PEGGY A., information systems specialist, publisher, educator, nurse; b. San Diego; d. Harvey William Henry and Helen Catherine (Thorpe) Brink; m. Gearald M. Wetsch, June 26, 1971; children: Brian Gearald, Lynette Kirstiann Nicole. Diploma, Calif. Hosp. Sch. Nursing, 1971; BSN cum laude, Pepperdine U., 1980; MS in Nursing, Calif. State U., L.A., 1985. Cert. in nursing adminstrn., human resource devel. Clin. nurse Orange County Med. Ctr./U. Calif. Irvine Med. Ctr., Orange, Calif., 1971-75; pediatric head nurse U. Calif. Irvine Med. Ctr., 1975-79; clin. nurse educator Palm Harbor Gen./Med. Ctr. Garden Grove, Calif., 1980-81; dir. ednl. svcs. Med. Ctr. of Garden Grove, 1981-85; dir. edn. Mission Hosp. Regional Med. Ctr., Mission Viejo, Calif., 1986-92; coord. computer and learning resources L.A. Med. Ctr. Sch. Nursing, 1992-95; assoc. part time faculty Saddleback Coll., 1990-94; cons. ptnr. nur.SYS-Edn. systems Cons., 1995-97; sys. adminstr. Info. Resources Group, Pasadena, Calif., 1997-98, chief info. officer, 1998—; pres., pub. Info. Resources Group, L.A., 1998—; lectr. statewide nursing program Calif. State U., Dominguez Hills, 1986-92; ednl. cons. Author: (with others) Nursing Diagnosis: Guidelines to Planning Care, 1993, 2d edit., 1994, 4th edit., 1999; contbr. articles to profl. jours. Treas. Orange County Nursing Edn. Coun., 1986-87, 88-90, pres., 1987-88. Mem. ANA, NLN, Am. Nursing Informatics Assn. (pres. 1997-98, elections com. So. Calif. chpt. 1994, coord. continuing edn., conf. planning com.), N.Am. Nursing Diagnosis Assn. (secondary reviewer Diagnostic Rev. 1989-90, expert adv. panel 1990-92, mem. diagnosis rev. com. 1992-96, chair diagnostic rev. com. 1996-98, program com. 1998—), Soc. Calif. Nursing Diagnosis Assn. (membership chmn. 1984-92, pres. 1992-94), Nat. Am. Mgmt. Assn. (charter L.A. County, U. So. Calif. Med. Ctr. chpt.), Spina Bifida Assn. Am., Phi Kappa Phi, Sigma Theta Tau (pres. Iota Eta chpt. 1990-92). Home: 1520 San Clemente Ln Corona CA 91720-7949

WETZBARGER, DONNA KAY, secondary education educator; b. Madison, S.D.; d. D.H. and E.M. (Gray) Krug; m. Dale G. Wetzbarger; children: Taylor, Erin. BA, Ottawa (Kans.) U., 1973; MA, U. No. Colo., 1979. Cert. secondary edn. tchr., Colo. Tchr. Ft. Morgan, Colo., 1973-84; instr. Midland (Tex.) Coll., 1984-86; tchr. Sheridan Coll., Gillette, Wyo., 1986-87, Niwot (Colo.) H.S., 1987—; reading specialist Improvement Plus, Longmont, Colo., 1990—. Incentive grantee St. Vrain, 1996; Sch. to Career grantee, 1997-98. Mem. NEA, Colo. Edn. Assn., Nat. Coun. Tchrs. of English. E-mail: jake2343@cris.com. Home: 2343 Smith Ct Longmont CO 80501-1149 Office: Niwot HS 8989 E Niwot Rd Longmont CO 80503

WETZEL, JODI (JOY LYNN WETZEL), history and women's studies educator; b. Salt Lake City, Apr. 5, 1943; d. Richard Coulam and Margaret Elaine (Openshaw) Wood; m. David Nevin Wetzel, June 12, 1967; children: Meredith (dec.), Richard Rawlins. BA in English, U. Utah, 1965, MA in English, 1967; PhD in Am. Studies, U. Minn., 1977. Instr. Am. studies and family social sci. U. Minn., 1973-77, asst. prof. Am. studies and women's studies, 1977-79, asst. to dir. Minn. Women's Ctr., 1973-75, asst. dir., 1975-79; dir. Women's Resource Ctrs. U. Denver, 1980-84, mem. adj. faculty history, 1981-84, dir. Am. studies program, dir. Women's Inst., 1983-84; dir. Women in Curriculum U. Maine, 1985-86, mem. coop. faculty sociology, social work and human devel., 1986; dir. Inst. Women's Studies and Svcs. Met. State Coll. Denver, 1986—, assoc. prof. history, 1986-89, prof. history, 1990—; speaker, presenter, cons. in field; vis. prof. Am. studies U. Colo., 1985. Co-author: Women's Studies: Thinking Women, 1993; co-editor: Readings Toward Composition, 2d edit., 1969; contbr. articles to profl. publs. Del. at-large Nat. Women's Meeting, Houston, 1977; bd. dirs. Rocky Mountain Women's Inst., 1981-84; treas. Colo. Women's Agenda, 1987-91. U. Utah Dept. English fellow, 1967; U. Minn. fellow, 1978-79; grantee NEH, 1973, NSF, 1981-83, Carnegie Corp., 1988; named to Outstanding Young Women of Am., 1979. Mem. Am. Hist. Assn., Nat. Assn. Women in Edn. (Hilda A. Davis Ednl. Leadership award 1996, Sr. Scholar 1996), Am. Assn. for Higher Edn., Am. Studies Assn., Nat. Women's Studies Assn., Golden Key Nat. Honor Soc. (hon.), Alpha Lambda Delta, Phi Kappa Phi. Office: Met State Coll Denver Campus Box 36 PO Box 173362 Denver CO 80217-3362

WEWER, WILLIAM PAUL, lawyer; b. San Diego, May 27, 1947; s. William P. and Helen E. (Helm) Wewer; m. Katheleen Marquardt, Dec. 6, 1987. BA with honors, Pomona Coll., 1970; JD with high honors, George Washington U., 1977. Bar: D.C. 1977, U.S. Ct. Appeals (D.C. cir.) 1977, Calif. 1980, U.S. Ct. Appeals (9th cir.) 1980, U.S. Dist. Ct. D.C. 1981, U.S. Dist. Ct. (no. dist.) Calif. 1982, U.S. Supreme Ct. 1982, Colo. 1989, Mont., 1994, U.S. Dist. Ct. (ctrl. dist.) Calif. 1996. Legisl. asst. U.S. Senator Howard W. Cannon, Washington, 1970-74; profl. staff mem. Rules Com. U.S. Senate, Washington, 1974-77; assoc. Sutherland, Asbill & Brennan, Washington, 1977-79; ptnr. Wewer & Mahn, P.C., Washington, 1979-83, Wewer Law Firm, Washington, San Francisco, Denver, Helena, 1983-97, Wewer & Kalera, Washington, San Francisco, Helena, 1998—, Bleak House Publishing Co., Bethesda, Md., 1988-89; cons. various candidates nationwide, 1966—; mem. faculty CLE courses Nat. Bus. Inst. Contbr. articles to profl. jours. and nationally syndicated newspaper column. Bd. dirs. Am. Tax Reduction Movement, Washington, 1980-89, pres., 1989-91; bd. dirs. Howard Jarvis Taxpayers Assn., L.A., 1980-89, Am. Tax Reduction Found., Washington, 1983-90, Nat. Com. to Preserve Social Security and Medicare, Washington, 982-87, Montanans for Better Govt. Found., Helena, 1995-97; sec. Beer Drinkers Am., Sacramento, 1994—; treas. Dr. Lynch Found., L.A., 1995— ; treas. various non-profit groups nationwide; mem. legal adv. bd. and exec. com. Defenders of Property Rights, Washington, 1992—; sec. Subscription TV Assn., Wasington, 1979-83, Calif. Apt. Law Info. Found., L.A., 1989—. Mem. ABA (mem. exempt orgns. com. sect. taxation). Republican. Home: 2636 Van Ness Ave Apt 401 San Francisco CA 94109-1611 Office: PO Box 555 21 N Last Chance Gulch #207 Helena MT 59624-0555 also: 1592 Union St San Francisco CA 94123-4531 also: Internat Sq 1825 I St NW Ste 185 Washington DC 20006-5403

WEXLER, HOWARD ADAM, director of photography; b. L.A., Sept. 20, 1949; s. Sy and Helen (Nager) W; 1 child, Aaron Rene. Student, U. S.C., 1970-71. Dir. photography (feature films) Hot Under the Collar, Guns, Virgin High, Savage Beach, The Favorite, Jigsaw Murders, Angel III, Reform School Girls, Picasso Trigger, Arizona Heat, Hard Ticket to Hawaii, Banzai Runner; producer, dir. (theatre) Loving Lulu, 1991; also numerous edn. med. and documentary films. Avocations: camping, bicycling, yoga, cooking. Home: 961 Vernon Ave Venice CA 90291-2838

WEYAND, FREDERICK CARLTON, retired military officer; b. Arbuckle, Calif., Sept. 15, 1916; s. Frederick C. W. and Velma Semans (Weyand); m. Lora Arline Langhart, Sept. 20, 1940; children: Carolyn Ann, Robert Carlton, Nancy Diane. A.B., U. Calif.-Berkeley, 1939, LL.D. (hon), U. Akron, 1975. Officer U.S. Army, advanced to gen. chief of staff, 1940-76; sr. v.p. First Hawaiian Bank, Honolulu, 1976-82; trustee Estate of S.M. Damon, Honolulu, 1982—; bd. dirs. First Hawaiian, Inc., Ltd., First Hawaiian Bank, First Hawaiian Credit Corp. Chmn. ARC, Honolulu, 1982, Hawaiian Open golf Tourney, 1981-82. Decorated D.S.C. U.S. Army, 1967, D.S.M. Army (3), Dept. Def. (1), 1966-76, other U.S. and fgn. mil. decorations. Mem. Am. Def. Preparedness Assn., Assn. U.S. Army, U.S. Strategic Inst. (v.p. 1976—), USAF Assn. Lutheran. Clubs: Waialae Country. Lodge: Masons. Home: 2121 Ala Wai Blvd Ph 1 Honolulu HI 96815-2211 Office: SM Damon Estate 999 Bishop St Fl 28 Honolulu HI 96813-4423*

WEYERHAEUSER, GEORGE HUNT, forest products company executive; b. Seattle, July 8, 1926; s. John Philip and Helen (Walker) W.; m. Wendy Wagner, July 10, 1948; children: Virginia Lee, George Hunt, Susan W., Phyllis A., David M., Merrill W. BS with honors in Indsl. Engring., Yale U., 1949. With Weyerhaeuser Co., Tacoma, 1949—, successively mill foreman, br. mgr., 1949-56, v.p., 1957-66, exec. v.p., 1966-88, pres., chief exec. officer, 1988, chmn. bd., chief exec. officer, 1988-91, chmn. bd., past CEO, also bd. dirs.; bd. dirs. Boeing Co., SAFECO Corp., Chevron Corp.; mem. Bus. Coun., Bus. Roundtable, Wash. State Bus. Roundtable. Office: Weyerhaeuser Fin Svcs CH 5B Tacoma WA 98477-0001

WEYGAND, LEROY CHARLES, service executive; b. Webster Park, Ill., May 17, 1926; s. Xaver William and Marie Caroline (Hoffert) W.; BA in Sociology cum laude, U. Md., 1964; m. Helen V. Bishop, Aug. 28, 1977; children: Linda M. Weygand Vance (dec.), Leroy Charles, Cynthia R., Janine P. Enlisted in U.S. Army, 1944, commd. 2d lt., 1950, advanced through grades to lt. col., 1966; service in Korea, 1950; chief phys. security U.S. Army, 1965-70; ret., 1970; pres. Weygand Security Cons. Srvcs., Anaheim, Calif., 1970—, W & W Devel. Corp., 1979—; security dir. Jefferies Banknote Co., 1972-78; pres. Kern County Taxpayers Assn., 1986—; dir. Mind Psi-Biotics, Inc. Bd. dirs. Nat. Assn. Control Narcotics and Dangerous Drugs. Decorated Legion of Merit. Mem. Am. Soc. Indsl. Security. Contbr. articles profl. jours. Patentee office equipment locking device. Home: 12110 Backdrop Ct Bakersfield CA 93306-9707 Office: Kern County Taxpayers Assn 1415 18th St Ste 407 Bakersfield CA 93301-4442

WHALEN, MARGARET CAVANAGH, retired secondary school educator; b. Des Moines, Iowa, Mar. 9, 1913; d. Thomas J. and Ann Lenore (Paul) Cavanagh; m. George Hubert Whalen, Aug. 3, 1946; children: Michael T., Ann Whalen Carrillo, George Patrick (dec.), Cheryl Joan. BS in Commerce, St. Teresa Coll., Winona, Minn., 1935. Head bus. dept. St. Augustine H.S., Austin, Minn., 1935-36, Parochial H.S., Caledonia, Minn., 1936-37; clk., typist U.S. Govt., Dept. Social Security, Des Moines, 1937-38; county investigator for old age asst., aid to blind Marion County, Knoxville, Iowa, 1938; hydro dept. U.S. Weather Bur. Regional Office, Iowa City, Kansas City, Mo., 1939-42; head bills/warrants dept. Regioinal office IRS, Des Moines, 1942-46; substitute tchr. Los Gatos (Calif.) H.S., 1961-65, Saratoga (Calif.) H.S., 1961-65. Vol. Girl Scouts U.S.A., Boy Scouts Am., Saratoga, Calif., 1957-62; poll insp. Santa Clara County Regional Voters, Saratoga, Calif.; precinct insp. Saratoga for Santa Clara County Registrar of Voters; organizer, vol. Saratoga Area Sr. Coord. Coun., 1979—; Eucharistic minister, lector, commentator Sacred Heart Ch., Saratoga, 1986—; charter pres. Oz chpt. Children's Home Soc. Calif., Saratoga; mem. Sacred Heart Women's Club, Our Lady of Los Gatos (Calif.) # 197 Young Ladies Inst. Recipient Papal Bronze medal for Pub. Rels. Nat. Coun. Cath. Women, Saratoga, 1958, Merit award Friends of Saratoga Librs., 1975—, Merit award Saratoga Area Sr. Coord. Coun., 1981. Mem. AAUW (corr. sec. Los Gatos-Saratoga br., chmn. social arts, bridge, hospitality, Friday Matinee sect., book rev. sect.), Saratoga Hist. Found., Alumnae Assn. St. Teresa Coll., Montalvo Assn., Saratoga Foothill Club. Democrat. Roman Catholic. Avocations: bridge, reading, crocheting, family dinner parties, travel. Home: 14140 Victor Pl Saratoga CA 95070-5425

WHALEY, ROBERT HAMILTON, judge; m. Lucinda schilling; 1 child. BA, Princeton U., 1965; JD, Emory U., 1968. Litigator land and natural resources divsn. Dept. Justice, 1969-71; asst. U.S. atty. U.S. Dist. Wash. (ea. dist.), 1971-72; assoc. Winston & Cashatt, Spokane, Wash., 1972-76; ptnr. Winston & Cashatt, 1976—; judge Spokane County Superior Ct., 1992-95, U.S. Dist. Ct., Spokane, 1995—. Office: US Dist Ct Wash PO Box 283 920 Riverside Ave W Spokane WA 99210*

WHAN, NORMAN WENDELL, minister; b. Aurora, Ill., Jan. 13, 1943; s. Lawrence Donald and Evelyn Irene (Nash) W.; m. Judith Ann Williams, Feb. 23, 1963; children: Jeffrey, Victoria, Tamara, Scott. Grad., Peoria, Ill., 1961. Dir. ch. planning Friends S.W. Yearly Meeting, Whittier, Calif., 1985-88; pres., founder Ch. Growth Devel. Internat., Brea, Calif., 1988—, Canning Hunger, Inc., Orange, Calif.; bd. dirs. Missions Internat., Nashville, 1987—, Internat. Light & Life Network, Pasadena, Calif., 1988—, Ch. Growth Devel. Internat., Brea, 1988—; bd. advisors Ch. Planting Ctr., Orlando, Fla., 1990—. Author: (book kit) The Phone's for You, 1985; co-author: Keeping in Touch, 1989; editor newsletter Hook, Line, & Sinker, 1988. Mem. N.Am. Soc. Ch. Growth. Republican. Fax: 714-279-6575. Office: Ch Growth Devel Internat 131 E Grove Ave Orange CA 92865-3301

WHARTON, THOMAS WILLIAM, mining executive; b. St. Louis, Nov. 20, 1943; s. Thomas William and Elaine Margaret (Bassett) w.; divorced; children: Thomas William, Christopher John. BSc in Econs., U. Mo., 1967; M in Health Adminstrn., U. Ottawa, Ont., Can., 1978. Asst. to exec. dir. Ottawa Civic Hosp., 1978-80; exec. dir. Caribou Meml. Hosp., Williams Lake, B.C., Can., 1980-83; dir. clinic and rehab. services Workers' Compensation Bd., Vancouver, B.C., 1983-89; dir. Conquistador Gold Mines, Vancouver, 1989-98; pres. Diagnostic and Health Cons., Vancouver, 1989—; dir. Citrine Holdings, Ltd., Vancouver, B.C., Can., 1994-98; bd. dirs. USV Telemanagement, Inc., Vancouver, Leopardus Resources, Inc., Vancouver, Can. Med. Placement Svc., Vancouver, 1998. Recipient Founder award Cariboo Musical Soc., 1983; named Lord of the Manors of Wharton and Kirkby Stephen (Eng.), 1991. Avocations: music, art.

WHEADON, KATHLEEN ROSE, university development director; b. Seattle, Apr. 29, 1966; d. William Joseph III and Penny (Millar) Thayer; m. Kenneth E. Wheadon, May 16, 1998. BA in Architecture, U. Wash., 1988. Intern arch. Gustavson Assoc. Archs., Salt Lake City, 1989-90, Enninger Fetzer Tholen Archs., Salt Lake City, 1990-95; devel. dir. Grad. Sch. Architecture, U. Utah, Salt Lake City, 1995—; bd. dirs. pub. affairs com. U. Utah, 1995-98. Chair staff adv. com. Lowell Bennion Cmty. Svc. Ctr., Salt Lake City, 1995—; big sister Big Bros./Big. Sisters, Salt Lake City, 1994-97. Mem. Coun. for Advancement and Support of Edn., Utal Archtl. League (bd. dirs., v.p.), Contemporary Arts Group (pres. 1996-98). Avocations: bicycling, backpacking, cooking, gardening, reading. Office: Univ Utah Grad Sch Architecture 375 S 1530 E # 235 Salt Lake City UT 84112-8945

WHEATLEY, BARNARESE P. (BONNIE WHEATLEY), health services consultant; b. New Iberia, La., Nov. 6, 1942; d. Ervin and Elizabeth (Pierce) Politte; m. Horace Wheatley, Oct. 9, 1967; children: Adrienne K., Alanna M. BS, Calif. State U., Hayward, 1989; MPH, San Jose State U., 1994. Project dir. breast cancer early detection program Alameda County Med. Ctr., Oakland, Calif., 1989-93; health svc. cons. Alameda County, Oakland, 1993—. Co-author: Wellness Perspective, 1993. Treas. Leadership Am., 1992-93; coord. Nat. Black Leadership No. Calif., 1992—; bd. dirs. Susan B. Komen Found., 1994—, Breast Cancer Action, 1994-96, Nat. Breast Cancer Coalition, 1993-96 ; adv. com. Cancer Info. Svc., 1993—; active Calif. Breast Cancer Rsch. Coun., Healthy City Fund Bd. Recipient Community Svcs. Outreach award Calif. Legislature, 1989, Outstanding Svc. award Nat. Assn. Bench and Bar Spouses, 1992, Reaching People Through Partnerships award, 1996. Mem. Women and Girls Against Tobacco (bd. dirs.). Democrat. Avocation: gardening. Home: 42 La Salle Ave Piedmont CA 94611-3549 Office: Alameda County Med Ctr 1411 E 31st St Oakland CA 94602-1018

WHEATLEY, MELVIN ERNEST, JR., retired bishop; b. Lewisville, Pa., May 7, 1915; s. Melvin Ernest and Gertrude Elizabeth (Mitchell) W.; m. Lucile Elizabeth Maris, June 15, 1939; children: Paul Melvin, James Maris, John Sherwood (dec.). AB magna cum laude, Am. U., 1936, DD, 1958; BD summa cum laude, Drew U., 1939; DD, U. of Pacific, 1948. Ordained to ministry Meth. Ch., 1939. Pastor area Meth. ch., Lincoln, Del., 1939-41; assoc. pastor First Meth. Ch., Fresno, Calif., 1941-43, pastor Centenary Meth. Ch., Modesto, Calif., 1943-46, Cen. Meth. Ch., Stockton, Calif., 1946-

54, Westwood Meth. Ch., L.A., 1954-72; bishop Denver Area, 1972-84, ret., 1984; instr. philosophy Modesto Jr. Coll., 1944; summer session instr. Hebrew-Christian heritage U. of Pacific; instr. Homiletics U. So. Calif., So. Calif. Sch. Theology, Claremont; lectr. St. Luke's Lectures, Houston, 1966; mem. Bd. of Ch. and Soc., Commn. on Status and Role of Women, United Meth. Ch., 1976-84; condr. European Christian Heritage tour, 1961, Alaska and Hawaii Missions, 1952, 54. Author: Going His Way, 1957, Our Man and the Church, 1968, The Power of Worship, 1970, Family Ministries Manual, 1970, Christmas Is for Celebrating, 1977; contbr. articles to profl. jours. Chmn. Community Rels. Conf. So. Calif., 1966-69; pres. So. Calif.-Ariz. Conf. Bd. Edn., 1960-68; hon. trustee Iliff Sch. Theology; hon. dir., active mem. Parents and Friends of Lesbians and Gays, 1980—. Recipient Disting. Alumnus award Am. U., 1979, Ball award Meth. Fedn. Social Action, 1984, Prophetic Leadership award The Consultation on Homosexuality, Tolerance and Roman Cath. Theology, 1985, Human Rights award Universal Fellowship of Met. Community Congregations, 1985. Home: 859 Ronda Mendoza Unit A Laguna Hills CA 92653-5940

WHEATON, ALICE ALSHULER, administrative assistant; b. Burbank, Calif., Mar. 20, 1920; d. Elmore and Anzy Jeanette (Richards) Wheaton; m. Robert Edward Alshuler, Sept. 19, 1942 (div. 1972); children: John Robert, Katherine Alshuler Voss. BA in Edn., UCLA, 1942. CPS (Certified Profl. Sec.); cert. tchr. Owner, dir. The Fitness Studio, Washington, 1974-85; staff asst. Pres. Coun. Phys. Fitness and Sports, Washington, 1980-89; coord. Fed. Inter Agy. Health Fitness Coun., Washington, 1986-89; expert cons. U.S. Office Pers. Mgmt., Washington, 1986-89; adminstrv. asst. North County Bank, Escondido, Calif., 1990-95; sec. Pala Mesa Village Homes Assn., 1994-96, bookkeeper, 1997—; cons. Pres. Coun. Phys. Fitness and Sports. Editor: The Federal FitKit-Guidelines for Federal Agencies, 1988. Recipient Gold Key award L.A. Area United Way, 1966. Mem. (IAAP) Internatl. Assn. of Admin. Profls. (pres. Palomar chpt. 1993-95), UCLA Gold Shield Hon. (pres.), UCLA Alumni Assn. (v.p., Disting. Com. Svc. award 1968), San Diego Hist. Soc., North County Kappa Kappa Gamma Alumnae Assn. (pres. 1995-97). Republican. Episcopalian. Avocations: historical research, gardening.

WHEELER, CHARLES MERVYN, retired chemistry educator; b. Moundsville, W.Va., Oct. 29, 1921; s. Charles Mervyn, Sr. and Olive Ila (Powell) W.; m. May Kathleen Wickers, Dec. 18, 1943; children: Charles M. III, W. Randolph, Jennifer L., N. Kathleen, Timothy A., Anne O. BS, W. Va. U., 1947, MS, 1948, PhD, 1950. Asst. prof. chemistry U. N.H., Durham, 1950-55, assoc. prof. chemistry, 1955-75, prof., 1975-83, prof. emeritus, 1983—, dean of students, 1960-61; cons. U. de San Marcos, Lima, Peru, 1957, 59, 60, NSF, India, 1965, 67, 68, 69; chmn. grad. chem. dept. Madurai U., India, 1968-69; panelist UNESCO Internat. Workshop Evaluation Chem., U. Ceylon, 1968. Mem. Zoning Bd. of Adjustment, Durham, 1961-78; mem. Durham Sch. Bd., 1962-66; vol. U.S. Fish and Wildlife Svc., 1965-98. Maj. U.S. Army, 1942-46, PTO. Recipient John Barton Payne scholarship W. Va. U., Morgantown, 1942; grantee Rsch. Corp., Durham, 1954, Atomic Energy Commn., Durham, 1955. Mem. Am. Chem. Soc., AAUP, Sigma Xi, Phi Lambda Upsilon, Phi Kappa Phi. Republican. Methodist. Avocations: bird watching, reading, hiking, travel. Home: 250 E Alameda Apt 204 Santa Fe NM 87501

WHEELER, DENICE MCINTIRE, real estate and investments professional, lecturer; b. Springville, Utah, July 24, 1929; d. Glenn L. and Elizabeth Marie (Jolley) Dallin; widowed; children: Shelley Marie McIntire Lee, Mark Douglas, Gregory Wayne. BA, Brigham Young U., 1966; postgrad., U. Utah, 1970. profl. lectr. on women's issues. Author: (book) The Feminine Frontier: Wyoming Women 1850-1900; co-author: First Ladies of Wyoming; contbr. articles to profl. jours. and publs. Apptd. by Pres. Clinton to chair Bear River Commn., 1995—; apptd. by Gov. Herschler to Wyo. Commn. for Women, chair; apptd. by Gov. to Dept. Health Adv. Bd., 1998 ; active in securing Safe Houses for abused women and children, others. Recipient numerous awards in field and from civic orgns., including Wyo. State hist. Soc. awards for Hist. Preservation, recognition for contbns. to AARP, 1986—, J.C. Penney Golden Rule award for Volunteerism, 1998, Nat. Press Women Writing award, 1988, Gov.'s Vol. award for Wyo., 1989, others. Avocations: white water rafting, travel, camping, sports. Home: PO Box 106 Evanston WY 82931-0106

WHEELER, FRANK KNOWLES BLASDELL, retired military officer, business consultant; b. Mpls., Oct. 29, 1912; s. Walter Hall and Eva Maude (Blasdell) W.; widowed, Oct. 1991; children: Mary Ann Wheeler Masker, Frances Blasdell Wheeler Kindle, Charles Knowles. BS in Mech. Electrics, U.S. Naval Acad., 1935, PhD (Equivalent) Electronics, 1944. Registered profl. engr., Calif. Commd. ensign USN, 1935, advanced through grades to capt., 1954; commdg. officer U.S.S. Kearney, 1944-46; mem. various fleets/electronics staffs USN, 1946-60, ret., 1960; mfg. mgr. Hewlett Packard Co., Palo Alto, Calif., 1960-70; pres., bus. cons. Wheeler & Assocs., Los Altos Hills, Calif., 1970—. Mem. IEEE. Republican. Presbyterian. Avocations: electronics, preparing historical video productions. Home and Office: 27174 Elena Rd Los Altos CA 94022-3343

WHEELER, GERALDINE HARTSHORN, historian; b. Pomona, Calif., Feb. 5, 1919; d. Albion True and Beatrice Osa (Barnes) Hartshorn; m. Lloyd Franklyn Wheeler, Dec. 2, 1938 (dec. Mar. 1996); children: Russell Lloyd, Robert Gerald. *Her intense interest in history led Geraldine Hartshorn Wheeler into researching her family roots and the social life of earlier times. Her love of the flow of words has led to writing essays for local newspapers, giving lectures, and now into transcribing old family diaries. She also has a special interest in the historical side of earthquakes, where and when they happened, and how people reacted under the stress of the events. She also enjoys doing volunteer activities which started at the age of seven and still involved in.* AA, Santa Barbara (Calif.) C.C., 1950's. Co-owner Atheling's, Santa Barbara, Calif., 1971-76, Pomona, 1976-90; chmn. bd. trustees Atheling Heritage Trust, Claremont, Calif., 1994—. Pub., editor (mag.) Atheling's, 1974-75; pub. editor (newsletter) Grand Priory of America Order of St. Lazarus, 1974-86; editor, founder St. Margaret's Jour., 1975—. Vol. PTA, Fontana and Santa Barbara, 1945-60; active Hist. Soc. Pomona Valley, 1950—; mem. various coms. and choir First Congl. Ch., Santa Barbara, 1952-72; leader Cub Scouts Am., Santa Barbara, 1953-56; grey lady unit chmn. Santa Barbara chpt.-ARC, 1958-62; women's project bd. v.p., activities chmn., active various coms. Santa Barbara Hist. Soc., 1960-74; exec. sec. 1960 Nixon for Pres. Campaign, Santa Barbara, 1960; mem. spkrs. bur. Nixon for Gov. Campaign, Santa Barbara, 1962; mem. Rep. state ctrl. com. State of Calif., 1962-64; blitz chmn. Rockefeller for Pres. Campaign, Santa Barbara, 1964; coord. vol. svcs. Office of Civil Def., City of Santa Barbara, 1965-76; coord. tv series on earthquakes Sta. KEYT, Office of Civil Def., Santa Barbara, 1968; bd. dirs. Calif. Ctrl. Coast Area, U.S.O., 1968-76, treas. bd., 1970-76; supporter Vis. Nurses and Hospice Assn., 1994—; others. Decorated Dame of Grace, Mil. and Hospitaller Order of St. Lazarus of Jerusalem, Cert. of Merit, 1973, The Alan Weaver Hazelton award; recipient Cert. of Merit, Santa Barbara Jr. Coll., 1954-55, Medal of Appreciation SAR, 1972, Cert. of Award Nat. Soc. Daus. of Founders and Patriots of Am., 1997. Mem. Calif. Hist. Soc., New Eng. Hist. and Geneal. Soc., The Pomona Ebell (pres. 1998—). Republican. Avocations: book collecting, reading, genealogy, classical music, needlework. Home: 1047 E Baseline Rd Claremont CA 91711-1577

WHEELER, LARRY RICHARD, accountant; b. Greybull, Wyo., Nov. 30, 1940; s. Richard F. and Olive B. (Fredrickson) W.; m. Patricia C. Marturano, Dec. 3, 1977; children: Anthony, Richard, Teresa, Kara. BS, U. Wyo., 1965. CPA, Colo. Staff acct. H. Greger CPA, Ft. Collins, Colo., 1965-66, sr. acct. Lester Draney & Wickham, Colorado Springs, Colo., 1966-67; acct., controller/treas., J.D. Adams Co., Colorado Springs, 1967-74; ptnr. Wheeler Pierce & Hurd, Inc., Colorado Springs, 1974-80; gen. mgr., v.p. Schneebeck's, Inc., Colorado Springs, 1980-81; prin. L.R. Wheeler & Co., P.C., Colorado Springs, 1981-94; pres. Wheeler & Gilmartin Assocs., P.C., Colorado Springs, 1994—, L.R. Wheeler & Co., P.C., 1995; dir. Schneebeck's Industries, Williams Printing, Inc., Inc. Mem. U.S. Taekwondo Union; bd. dirs. Domestic Violence Prevention Ctr. Paul Stock Found. grantee, 1962. Mem. Nat. Assn. Cert. Valuation Analysts, AICPA, Colo. Litigation Support Group. Office: 317 E San Rafael St Colorado Springs CO 80903-2405

WHEELER, MALCOLM EDWARD, lawyer, law educator; b. Berkeley, Calif., Nov. 29, 1944; s. Malcolm Ross and Frances Dolores (Kane) W.; m. Donna Marie Stambaugh, July 21, 1981; children: Jessica Ross, M. Connor. SB, MIT, 1966; JD, Stanford U., 1969. Bar: Calif. 1970, Colo. 1992, U.S. Dist. Ct (cen. dist.) Calif. 1970, U.S. Ct. Appeals (9th cir.) 1970, U.S. Ct. Appeals (10th cir.) 1973, U.S. Dist. Ct. (no., so., ea. and cen. dists.) Calif. 1975, U.S. Ct. Appeals (11th cir.) 1987, U.S. Ct. Appeals (D.C. cir.) 1987, U.S. Supreme Ct. 1976, U.S. Ct. Appeals (3d cir.) 1989, (4th cir.) 1992, (8th cir.) 1993, (5th cir.) 1995, (Fed. cir.) 1998. Assoc. Howard, Prim, Smith, Rice & Downs, San Francisco, 1969-71; assoc. prof. law U. Kans., Lawrence, 1971-74; assoc. Hughes Hubbard & Reed, Los Angeles, 1974-77, ptnr., 1977-81, 83-85, cons., 1981-83; ptnr. Skadden, Arps, Slate, Meagher & Flom, Los Angeles, 1985-91; dir. Parcel, Mauro, Hultin & Spaanstra P.C., Denver, 1991-98, Wheeler Trigg & Kennedy, P.C., Denver, 1998—; vis. prof. U. Iowa, 1978, prof., 1979; prof. U. Kans., Lawrence, 1981-83; chief counsel U.S. Senate Select Com. to Study Law Enforcement Undercover Activities, Washington, 1982-83. Mem. editorial bd. Jour. Products Liability, 1984—; bd. editors Fed. Litigation Guide Reporter, 1986—; contbr. articles to profl. jours. Mem. ABA, Calif. Bar Assn., Colo. Bar Assn., Am. Law Inst. Home: 100 Humboldt St Denver CO 80218-3932

WHEELER, MICHAEL DAVID, career officer, aviator, instructor; b. Oakland, Calif., Apr. 15, 1968; s. Anthony Allen and Shirley Patricia (Nielsen) W.; m. Tracy Dawn Falconer, Dec. 16, 1995. BS in Astrophysics, UCLA, 1991. Fleet svc. clk. Am. Airlines, Burbank, Calif., 1988-91; commd. ensign USN, 1991, advanced through grades to lt., naval aviator, 1991—; instr. pilot USN, Nas Barbers Pt, Hawaii, 1997—; mission commdr. USN, 1997—; mem. flight adv. bd. Dept. Exec. Transport-USN, Nas Barbers Pt., 1997—, check pilot, 1997—. Mem. Nat. Space Soc. Republican. Avocations: skiing, surfing, roller hockey, hiking. Home: 88 Aikahi LP Kailua HI 96734 Office: USN Dept Exec Transp Barbers Point N A S HI 96862

WHEELER, STEVEN M., lawyer; b. Evanston, Ill., Jan. 5, 1949. AB, Pricneton U., 1971; JD with distinction, Cornell U., 1974. Bar: Ariz. 1974. Mem. Snell & Wilmer, Phoenix, ptnr., 1980—. Mng. editor Cornell Law Review, 1973-74; contbr. articles to profl. jours. Mem. ABA, Order Coif, Phi Kappa Phi. Office: Snell & Wilmer 1 Arizona Ctr Phoenix AZ 85004-0001*

WHEELER, WILLIAM EARLING (BILL WHEELER), artist, gallery owner; b. Pomona, Calif., Sept. 1, 1948; s. William Adelbert and Hazel Esther (Wolfe) W. AA, Chaffey Coll., Rancho Cucamonga, Calif., 1968; BFA, Otis Art Inst., L.A., 1971; MFA, Otis Art Inst., 1973. Master printer The Printmakers, Studio City, Calif., 1972-77; owner, dir. Studio 1617, L.A., 1976—. Represented in permanent collections AMOCO Learning Ctr., Downer's Grove, Ill., Epicentre Restaurant, L.A., Escondido (Calif.) City Hall, Gen. Am. Life Ins. Co., St. Louis, Pacific Bell, San Francisco, Princess Cruise Lines, Saks, Boca Raton, Fla., Chevy Chase, Md., Kansas City, Mo., San Diego State U., Scottsdale (Ariz.) Meml. Hosp., U.S. Air Terminal, Phoenix Internat. Airport, ANA Sheraton Hotel, Osaka, Japan, Apple Computer, Avery Label, Bank of Am., Columbia Pictures, CitiCorp, Detroit Edison, Dow Chem., Emerson Electric, St. Louis, Ency. Britannica, FDIC, Fireman's Fund Ins., Ford Motor Co., GM, Getty Oil, Holiday Inns, Home Savs. and Loan Assn., Hyatt Hotels, IBM, K-Mart/Kresge Corp. Hdqs., Kaiser-Permanente, Calvin Klein Cosmetics, Litton Industries, MCI Telecomm., Mitsui Mfr.'s Bank, Mobil Oil, Nordstrom's, Pa. Life, Price Waterhouse, Prudential Savs., Samaritan Health Svcs., So. Calif. Edison, So. Calif. Gas Co., Toyota Motor Co., TRW, Warner Records, Xerox. Elsie de Wolfe scholar, 1973-74. E-mail: wheelerb@studio1617.com. Office: Studio 1617 1617 Silver Lake Blvd Los Angeles CA 90026-1310

WHEELON, ALBERT DEWELL, physicist; b. Moline, Ill., Jan. 18, 1929; s. Orville Albert and Alice Geltz (Dewell) W.; m. Nancy Helen Hermanson, Feb. 28, 1953 (dec. May 1980); children—Elizabeth Anne, Cynthia Helen; m. Cicely J. Evans, Feb. 4, 1984. B.Sc., Stanford U., 1949, Ph.D., Mass. Inst. Tech., 1952. Teaching fellow, then rsch. assoc. physics MIT, Boston, 1949-52; with Douglas Aircraft Co., 1952-53, Ramo-Wooldridge Corp., 1953-62; dep. dir. sci. and tech. CIA, Washington, 1962-66; with Hughes Aircraft Co., L.A., 1966-88, chmn., chief exec. officer, 1987-88; vis. prof. MIT, 1989; mem. Def. Sci. Bd., 1968-76; mem. Pres.'s Fgn. Intelligence, 1983-88; mem. Presdl. Commn. on Space Shuttle Challenger Accident, 1986; trustee Aerospace Corp., 1990-93, Calif. Inst. Tech., Rand Corp. Author 30 papers on radiowave propagation and guidance systems. Recipient R.V. Jones Intelligence award, 1994. Fellow IEEE, AIAA (Von Karman medal 1986, Goddard Astronautics award 1997); mem. NAE, Am. Phys. Soc., Sigma Chi. Republican. Episcopalian. Address: 181 Sheffield Dr Montecito CA 93108-2242

WHELCHEL, SANDRA JANE, writer; b. Denver, May 31, 1944; d. Ralph Earl and Janette Isabelle (March) Everitt; m. Andrew Jackson Whelchel, June 27, 1965; children: Andrew Jackson, Anita Earlyn. BA in Elem. Edn., U. No. Colo., 1966; postgrad. Pepperdine Coll., 1971, UCLA, 1971. Elem. tchr. Douglas County Schs., Castle Rock, Colo., 1966-68, El Monte (Calif.) schs., 1968-72; br. librarian Douglas County Libraries, Parker, Colo., 1973-78; zone writer Denver Post, 1979-81; reporter The Express newspapers, Castle Rock, 1979-81; history columnist Parker Trail newspapers, 1985-93; columnist Gothic Jour. 1994; writing tchr. Aurora Parks and Recreation, 1985-91; writing instr. Arapahoe C.C., 1991—; exec. dir. Nat. Writers Assn., 1991—; editor Authorship mag., 1992-98; lit. agent NWLA 1996—; contbr. short stories and articles to various publs. including: Genre Sampler, Writer's World, Writer's Open Forum, Writer's Jour., Reunions, Fresno Bee, Ancestry Newsletter, Empire mag., Calif. Horse Rev., Host mag., Jack and Jill, Child Life, Children's Digest, Peak to Peak mag.; author (non-fiction books): Your Air Force Academy, 1982, A Guide to the U.S. Air Force Acad., 1990, Parker, Colorado: A Folk History, 1990, The Beginning Writer's Writing Book, 1996, A Folk History of Parker and Hilltop, 1996; co-author: The Writer's Office, 1998; (coloring books): A Day at the Cave, 1985, A Day in Blue, 1984, Pro Rodeo Hall of Champions and Museum of the American Cowboy, 1985, Pikes Peak Country, 1986, Mile High Denver, 1987; co-author: The Register, 1989; lectr. on writing and history. Mem. Colo. Author's League, Nat. Writers Club (treas. Denver Metro chpt. 1985-86,, v.p. membership 1987, sec. 1990, bd. dirs. 1990-91, pres. 1990-91, v.p. programs 1992), Parker Area Hist. Soc. (pres. 1987, 88, 89).

WHIDDON, CAROL PRICE, writer, editor, consultant; b. Gadsden, Ala., Nov. 18, 1947; d. Curtis Ray and Vivian (Dooly) Price; m. John Earl Caulking, Jan. 18, 1969 (div. July 1987); m. Ronald Alton Whiddon, Apr. 13, 1988. Student, McNeese State U., 1966-68; BA in English, George Mason U., 1984. Flute instr. Lake Charles, La., 1966-68; flutist Lake Charles Civic Symphony, 1966-69, Beaumont (Tex.) Symphony, 1967-68; freelance editor The Washington Lit. Rev., 1983-84, ARC Hdqrs., Washington, 1984; writer, editor Jaycor, Vienna, Va., 1985-87; writer, editor Jaycor, Albuquerque, 1987-90, publs. mgr., 1990-91; writer, editor Proteus Corp., Albuquerque, 1991-92; owner Whiddon Editorial Svcs., Albuquerque, 1989—; mem. S.W. Writer's Workshop, 1991—. Co-author: The Spirit That Wants Me: A New Mexico Anthology, 1991; contbr. various articles to Albuquerque Woman and mil. dependent pubs. in Fed. Rpublic Germany. Bd. dirs. Channel 27-Pub. Access TV, 1991-93, exec. bd. sec., 1992, v.p., 1993; dep. mgr. Fed. Women's Program, Ansbach, Fed. Republic Germany, 1980-81; pres. Ansbach German-Am. Club, 1980-82; sec. Am. Women's Activities, Fed. Republic Germany, 1980-81, chairwoman, 1981-82. Recipient cert. of appreciation from Am. amb. to Germany Arthur T. Burns, 1982, medal of appreciation from comdr. 1st Armored Div., Ansbach, Germany, 1982. Mem. NAFE, Women in Comm. (newsletter editor 1989-90, 91-92, 94-95, v.p. 1990-91, pres.-elect 1992-93, pres. 1993-94, chair programs com. Nat. Profl. Conf. 1994), Soc. Tech. Comm. (sr., membership dir. 1993-94), Nat. Assn. Desktop Pubs., Am. Mktg. Assn., Greater Albuquerque C. of C., N.Mex. Cactus Soc. (historian 1989-94, sec. 1991, newsletter editor 1992—, various show ribbons 1989-91). Republican. Avocations: reading, writing, gardening, camping, music. Home: 1129 Turner Dr NE Albuquerque NM 87123-1917

WHIPPLE, DANIEL SAWYER, JR., writer; s. Daniel Sawyer and Sara Johanna (Brown) W.; m. Kathleen Anne Bogan, Sept. 4, 1983; children: Jacob, Carl. Student, Georgetown U., 1970. Corr. Bus. Week, Houston, 1979-80; editor High Country News, Lander, Wyo., 1980-83; editor/writer No. Lights, Missoula, Mont., 1984-88, Casper (Wyo.) Star Tribune, 1988-95; freelance writer Eugene, Oreg., 1983-84, Broomfield, Colo., 1995—. Author: National Geographic Driving Guide to the Heartland, 1998, numerous articles. Ted Scripps fellow in environ. journalism, Boulder, Colo., 1997-98. Mem. Soc. Environ. Journalists. Avocations: classical guitar, fantasy baseball. Home: 3295 W 11th Avenue Ct Broomfield CO 80020-6754

WHISNAND, REX JAMES, housing association executive; b. Van Nuys, Calif., Jan. 2, 1948; s. Harold Theodore Whisnand and Laura Fay Brigham Whisnand Brown; m. Cathy Ladeane Bennett, Apr. 1, 1978; 1 child, Bryce James. BS in Agrl. Bus. Mgmt., Calif. Poly State U., San Luis Obispo, 1970; BSBA, Calif. State U., Sacramento, 1976; MPA in Housing Adminstrn., U. San Francisco, 1985; grad., U.S. Naval Submarine Sch., New London, Conn., 1972, Stanford U., 1992; postgrad. Inst. Orgn. Mgmt., C. of C. of U.S. Generalist W & W Hardware Store, Orcutt, Calif., 1964-70; state park ranger Calif. Dept. Parks and Recreation, Lompoc and Sacramento, 1969-75; exec. asst. Constrn. Industry Legis. Coun., Sacramento, 1974-75; dir. assn. svcs. Bldg. Industry Assn. Superior Calif., Sacramento, 1976-79; exec. v.p. West Bay divsn. Bldg. Industry Assn. No. Calif., Redwood City, 1980-84; exec. v.p. Bldg. Industry Assn., Tacoma/Pierce County, 1984-86; supr. Lumberjack Store, Lodi, Calif., 1988-90; exec. v.p. Rental Housing Owners Assn. of So. Alameda County, Hayward, Calif., 1990-96; field rep. Am. Housing Survey, 1997-98, crew leader Census 2000, 1999—; mem. com. Calif. Bldg. Industry Assn., Sacramento, 1976-84; mem. exec. officers coun., local govt. com. Calif. Apt. Assn., 1991-96; mem. Alameda County Housing Rsch. Adv. Bd., Hayward, Calif., 1990-93; bd. dirs. Pacific Bay Fed. Credit Union, Credit Union Execs. Soc., Internat. Credit Assn., Pronet; adj. faculty U. San Francisco; customer svc. rep. Oakland Athletics, Oakland Raiders, Golden State Warriors, 1997-99; bus. sales rep. CompUSA. Editor Pierce County Builder, 1984-86 (Assn. Achievement awards Nat. Assn. Home Builders 1984, 85), Superior California Builder Mag., 1978-80. Active 20-30 Club Internat. #1, Sacramento, 1976-80, officer, 1981-82; mem. South Sacramento Area Cmty. Planning Adv. Bd., 1978-79; grad. Pleasanton Leadership, 1995; chmn. Coastside Coalition for Safe Hwys., Half Moon Bay, 1983-84; bd. congregations Family Emergency Shelter Coalition Alameda County, 1995—; mem. Pleasanton Gen. Plan Econ./Fiscal Growth Com., 1994-96, Bay Area Indsl. Edn. Coun., 1995-96, Hayward Coalition for Youth, 1995-96; officer Half Moon Bay C. of C., 1982-84; cert. basketball coach Nat. Youth Sports Assn., 1994—. With USNR, 1970-76, U.S. Army, N.G., 1990-92. Named Outstanding Young Man. in Am., Jr. C. of C., Foster City, Calif., 1983. Mem. Internat. Assn. Bus. Communicators (pres. Sacramento chpt. 1979, pres. Peninsula chpt. 1981), Am. Soc. Assn. Execs. (cert.), No. Calif. Soc. Assn. Execs. (bd. dirs. 1994-97, com. chmn. 1993-95), Pleasanton C. of C. (econ. devel. com. 1990-96), Wash. State Home Builders Assn. (pres. exec. officers coun. 1985), Western Conf. Assn. Execs. (mem. com. 1995-96), So. Alameda County Assn. Realtors, Hayward C. of C. (govt. rels. coun. 1990-95), Calif. Vocat. Indsl. Clubs Am. (bd. dirs. 1977-80), Nat. Apt. Assn., Calif. Polytech. Alumni Assn., World Future Soc., Alpha Gamma Rho (charter, com. chair 1969-96). Episcopalian. Avocations: Boy Scouts, coach and bd. dirs. Pony League baseball and youth basketball, dog training, genealogy. Home: 5435 Black Ave Ste 3 Pleasanton CA 94566-5966

WHISNER, PEGGY JANELLE, accountant; b. Lovington, N.Mex., Aug. 28, 1966; d. Floyd Pleasant and Imogene (Gage) Green; m. Gregory David Hoskins, Aug. 13, 1988 (div. Apr. 1992); m. Charles Whisner, Jan. 27, 1995. Student, Wayland Bapt. U., 1984-86; BBA, Eastern N.Mex. U., 1988. Bookkeeper Gen. Welding Supply, Inc., Lovington, N.Mex., 1985; bookkeeper Manpower, Hobbs, N.Mex., 1987; cashier, bookkeeper Alco, Portales, N.Mex., 1989; bookkeeper Parson's Inc., Tatum, N.Mex., 1989-90; sales rep. Dunlaps, Hobbs, 1990-93; acct. Lea County Treas., Lovington, 1993—. Mem. Nat. Trust Hist. Preservation, 1993—. Mem. NAFE, Delta Mu Delta. Republican. Baptist. Avocations: piano, crosstitch, collecting coins, travel.

WHITACRE, JOHN, apparel executive; b. 1953. Student, U. Wash. With Nordstrom Inc., 1976—; co-chmn. Nordstrom Inc., Seattle, 1995-97, chmn., 1997—. Office: Nordstrom Inc 1501 5th Ave Seattle WA 98101-1603

WHITAKER, CYNTHIA ELLEN, nurse; b. Dearborn, Mich., June 15, 1948; d. John Harold and Marion Violet (Malmsten) Fields; m. Elbert Charles Whitaker, Sept. 7, 1968; children: Shannon Kaye, Kaycee Susan. ADN, Oakland C.C., Union Lake, Mich., 1982; BSN, U. Mich., 1985. RN, Calif.; cert. case mgr. Nurse Wheelock Meml. Hosp., Goodrich, Mich., 1982-86; clin. nursing instr. Oakland C.C., Union Lake, Mich., 1985-86; rehab. nurse Continental Ins.-UAC, Southfield, Mich., 1987-88; med. mgmt. cons. Continental Rehab. Resources, Sacramento, 1988-89; pres. RNS Healthcare Cons., Inc., Sacramento, 1989—; spkr. in field; mem. core task force Ctr. for Case Mgmt. Accountability; vice chair case mgmt. adv. bd. Am. Accreditation Healthcare Commn./Utilization Rev. Accreditation Commn., Washington, 1998—. Co-author: (book) Infectious Disease Handbook, 1981, (booklet) Standards of Practice for Case Management, 1995; contbr. articles to profl. jours. Mem. adv. bd. grad. sch. nursing San Francisco State U., 1994—; mem. cmty. adv. bd. Mercy Healthcare Sacramento, 1993-95, Kentfield (Calif.) Rehab. Hosp., 1993—, North Valley Rehab. Hosp., Chico, Calif., 1991-93. Dean's Fellow Scholarship awardee U. Mich., 1986. Mem. Am. Assn. Legal Nurse Cons., Case Mgmt. Soc. Am. (co-founder No. Calif. chpt., affiliate dir. 1993-95, affiliate pres. 1992-93, nat. sec. 1995-96, nat. pres. 1997-98), Case Mgmt. Soc. Internat. (bd. dirs.). Republican. Avocations: international travel, swimming, snow skiing, reading, hiking. Home: 800 Elmhurst Cir Sacramento CA 95825-6605 Office: 1010 Hurley Way Ste 525 Sacramento CA 95825-3218

WHITAKER, VICTORIA MARIE, English educator; b. Glendale, Calif., Nov. 26, 1947; d. Jack Bowles and Margie Marie (Hutson) W.; 1 child, Jacqueline Rae Huggins. BA, Calif. State U., Northridge, 1970; MA, U. No. Colo., 1978. Cert. tchr., Colo., Calif., N.Mex. Ski instr. Winter Park (Colo.) Ski Sch., 1976-88; sub. tchr. Modesto (Calif.) City Schs., 1988-91; interim instr. Calif. State U., Turlock, 1989-91; tchr. Farmington (N.Mex.) Mcpl. Schs., 1991—; steering com. English Expo, Albuquerque, 1997—. Contbg. author: (coll. text) Understanding Film, 1998. Mem. Dem. Party, N.W. N.Mex., 1998. Mem. NEA, Nat. Coun. Tchrs. English. Avocations: reading, playing Mah Jong on computer, gardening, organizing and enjoying my home, taking long walks with my dog. E-mail: msvic@cyberport.com. Home: 45 Rd 3141 Aztec NM 87410

WHITCHURCH, CHARLES AUGUSTUS, art gallery owner, humanities educator; b. Long Beach, Calif., Sept. 29, 1940; s. Charles Augustus and Frances Elizabeth (White) W.; m. Michèle Elizabeth Cartier, Aug. 17, 1968 (div. 1977); 1 child, Gialisa Elizabeth; m. Mary Susan Ornelas, Jan. 28, 1984; 1 child, Marisa Tatiana. BA in History, Santa Clara U., Irvine, 1962; MA in Comparative Lit., U. Calif., Irvine, 1970. Cert. grad. secondary teaching credential. Asst. ops. officer United Calif. Bank, Inglewood, 1965-66; tchr. English Laguna Beach (Calif.) High Sch., 1966-68; teaching assoc., fellow U. Calif., Irvine, 1968-70; prof. lit. and humanities Golden West Coll., Huntington Beach, Calif., 1971—; owner, dir. Charles Whitchurch Fine Arts, Huntington Beach, Calif., 1978—; cons. Pyo Gallery, Seoul, Dem. Peoples Rep. Korea, 1989-90, Gordon Gallery, Santa Monica, Calif., 1989-96; judge, spkr. in field. Author mus. catalogues; contbr. articles to profl. jours. Founding mem., mem. adv. coun. Modern Mus. Art, Santa Ana, Calif., 1987-92. NEA grantee; named One of Outstanding Young Men Am., 1977. Mem. Nat. Coun. Tchrs. English, Art Dealers Assn. of Calif. (bd. dirs. 1988—, sec. 1988-90, pres. 1990-92), Huntington Beach Art Assn. (founding mem. 1990), Robert Gumbiner Found. for the Arts (bd. dirs. 1994-95), Found. Creative Arts (bd. dirs. 1996—), The Libra Group (pres. 1994—), Santa Clara Alumni Assn., Alpha Sigma Nu, Phi Sigma Tau. Avocations: swimming, weight tng., writing, baseball coaching, reading.

WHITE, BETTY, actress, comedienne; b. Oak Park, Ill., Jan. 17, 1922; m. Allen Ludden, 1963 (dec.). Student pub. schs., Beverly Hills, Calif. Appearances on radio shows This Is Your FBI, Blondie, The Great Gildersleeve; actress: (TV series) including Hollywood on Television, The Betty White Show, 1954-58, Life With Elizabeth, 1953-55, A Date With The Angels, 1957-58, The Pet Set, 1971, Mary Tyler Moore Show, 1974-77, The Betty White Show, 1977, The Golden Girls, 1985-92 (Emmy award for best actress 1986), The Golden Palace, 1992-93, Maybe This Time, 1995—, The Story of Santa Claus, 1996, A Weekend in the Country, 1996; (TV

miniseries) The Best Place to be, 1979, The Gossip Columnist, 1980, (films) Advise and Consent, 1962, Dennis the Menace 2, 1998, Hard Rain, 1998 ; guest appearances on other programs; summer stock appearances Guys and Dolls, Take Me Along, The King and I, Who Was That Lady?, Critic's Choice, Bells are Ringing. Recipient Emmy award NATAS, 1975, 76, 86; L.A. Area Emmy award, 1952. Mem. AFTRA, Am. Humane Assn., Greater L.A. Zoo Assn. (dir.). Office: care William Morris Agy/Betty Fanning 151 S El Camino Dr Beverly Hills CA 90212-2704*

WHITE, BEVERLY JANE, cytogeneticist; b. Seattle, Oct. 9, 1938. Grad., U. Wash., 1959, MD, 1963. Diplomate Nat. Bd. Med. Examiners, Am. Bd. Pediatrics, Am. Bd. Med. Genetics; lic physician and surgeon, Wash., Va., N.J., Calif. Rsch. trainee dept. anatomy Sch. Medicine U. Wash., Seattle, 1960-62, pediatric resident dept. pediatrics, 1967-69; rotating intern Phila. Gen. Hosp., 1963-64; rsch. fellow med. ob-gyn. unit Cardiovascular Rsch. Inst. U. Calif. Med. Ctr., San Francisco, 1964-65; staff fellow lab. biomed. scis. Nat. Inst. Child Health and Human Devel. NIH, Bethesda, Md., 1965-67, sr. staff fellow, attending physician lab. exptl. pathology Nat. Inst. Arthritis, Metabolism and Digestive Diseases, 1969-74, acting chief sect. cytogenetics, 1975-76, rsch. med. officer, attending physician sect. cytogenetics lab. cellular biology and genetics, 1974-86, dir. cytogenetics unit, interinstitute med. genetics program clin. ctr., 1987-95; dir. cytogenetics Corning Clin. Labs., Teterboro, N.J., 1995-96; assoc. med. dir. cytogenetics Nichols Inst.-Quest Diagnostics, San Juan Capistrano, Calif., 1996-97, med. dir. cytogenetics, 1998—; vis. scientist dept. pediat. divsn. genetics U. Wash. Sch. Medicine, 1983-84; intramural cons. NIH, 1975-95; cons. to assoc. editor Jour. Nat. Cancer Inst., 1976; cons. dept. ob-gyn. Naval Hosp., Bethesda, 1988-89; lectr., presenter in field. Recipient Mosby Book award, 1963, Women of Excellence award U. Wash. and Seattle Profl. chpt. Women in Comm., 1959, Reuben award Am. Soc. for Study Sterility, 1963. Fellow Am. Coll. Med. Genetics (founding), Am. Acad. Pediatrics; mem. AMA. Am. Soc. Human Genetics, Assn. Genetic Technologists (program com. 1989). Home: One St Maxime Laguna Niguel CA 92677 Office: Nichols Inst/Quest Diagnostics Inc Dept Cytogenetics San Juan Capistrano CA 92690-6130

WHITE, BONNIE YVONNE, management consultant, retired educator; b. Long Beach, Calif., Sept. 4, 1940; d. William Albert and Helen Iris (Harbaugh) W. BS, Brigham Young U., 1962, MS, 1965, EdD in Ednl. Adminstrn., 1976, postgrad. Harvard U., 1987. Tchr., Wilson High Sch., Long Beach, Calif., 1962-63; grad. asst. Brigham Young U., Provo, Utah, 1963-65; instr., dir. West Valley Coll., Saratoga, Calif., 1965-76; instr., evening adminstr. Mission Coll., Santa Clara, Calif., 1976-80; dean gen. edn. Mendocino Coll., Ukiah, Calif., 1980-85; dean instrn. Porterville (Calif.) Coll., 1985-89, dean adminstrv. svc., 1989-93; rsch. assoc. SAGE Rsch. Internat., Orem, Utah, 1975-99. Del. Tulare County Ctrl. Com. Rep. Party, 1993-94; pres. community adv. bd. Calif. Conservation Corps, 1989-93; v.p. Porterville Community Concerts, 1990-94; bd. dirs. United Way North Bay, Santa Rosa, Calif., 1980-85, St. Vincent de Paul, 1993-97; mem. Calif. Commn. on Basic Skills, 1987-89, Calif. Commn. on Athletics, 1987-90. Mem. AAUW, Faculty Assn. Calif. C.C.'s, Calif., Coun. Fine Arts Deans, Assn. Calif. C.C. Adminstrs. Assn. Calif. Community Coll. Adminstrs. Liberal Arts, Zonta (intern), Soroptimists (intern). Republican. Mem. LDS Ch.

WHITE, BRITTAN ROMEO, manufacturing company executive; b. N.Y.C., Feb. 13, 1936; s. Brittan R. and Matilda H. (Baumann) W.; m. Esther D. Friederich, Aug. 25, 1958 (dec. May 1981); children: Cynthia E., Brittan R. VII; m. Peggy A. Lee, Aug. 30, 1990. BSChemE, Drexel U., 1958; MBA, Lehigh U., 1967; JD, Loyola U., Los Angeles, 1974; MA, Pepperdine U., 1985. Bar: Calif., U.S. Dist. Ct. Calif.; registered profl. engr., Calif. Process engr. Air Reduction Co., Bound Brook, N.J., 1958-64; area supr. J.T. Baker Chem. Co., Phillipsburg, N.J., 1964-66; asst. plant mgr. Gamma Chem. Co., Great Meadows, N.J., 1966-69; plant mgr. Maquite Corp., Elizabeth, N.J., 1969-70; purchasing mgr. Atlantic Richfield Co., Los Angeles, 1970-79; dir. mfg. Imperial Oil, Los Angeles, 1979-82; mgr. chem. mgmt. program Hughes Aircraft Co., Los Angeles, 1982-94; pres. The Crawford Group, 1994—; bd. dirs. Diversified Resource Devel. Inc., Los Angeles, 1979—; seminar moderator and speaker Energy Conservation Seminars, 1979-83. Editor Rottweiler Rev., 1979-81; chief award judge Chem. Processing mag., 1976, 78, 80; contbr. articles to profl. jours. Vice chmn. Bd. Zoning and Adjustment, Flemington, N.J., 1970-72; pres. bd. dirs. Homeowners' Assn., Palm Springs, Calif., 1983-90, Prescott, Ariz., 1997—; vice chmn. State Legis. Com., 1998—; mem. indsl. adv. com. sci., tech. and globalization program Embry-Riddle Aeronaut. U., 1998—. Capt. C.E., U.S. Army, 1958-60, res., 1960-68. Mem. ABA, Am. Inst. Chem. Engrs., Am. Chem. Soc., Mensa, Psi Chi. Republican. Lodge: Elks. Avocations: antiques, show dogs, psychology. Home: 1091 Pine Country Ct Prescott AZ 86303-6403 Office: The Crawford Group PO Box 3020 Prescott AZ 86302-3020

WHITE, CECIL RAY, librarian, consultant; b. Hammond, Ind., Oct. 15, 1937; s. Cecil Valentine and Vesta Ivern (Bradley) W.; m. Frances Ann Gee, Dec. 23, 1960 (div. 1987); children—Timothy Wayne, Stephen Patrick. B.S. in Edn., So. Ill. U., 1959; cert. in Czech., Syracuse, U., 1961; M. Div., Southwestern Bapt. Sem., 1969; M.L.S., N. Tex. State U., 1970, Ph.D., 1984. Librarian, Herrin High Sch. (Ill.), 1964-66; acting reference librarian Southwestern Sem., Ft. Worth, 1968-70, asst. librarian, 1970-80; head librarian Golden Gate Bapt. Sem., Mill Valley, Calif., 1980-88; head librarian West Oahu Coll., Pearl City, Hawaii, 1988-89; dir. spl. projects North State Coop. Library System, Yreka, Calif., 1989-90; dir. library St. Patrick's Sem., Menlo Park, Calif., 1990—; library cons. Hist. Commn., So. Bapt. Conv., Nashville, 1983-84, Internat. Bapt. Sem., Prague, Czech Republic, 1996; mem. Thesaurus Com., 1974-84; mem. adv. bd. Cath. Periodical and Lit. Index, 1995—. Bd. dirs. Hope and Help Ctr., 1986-88, vice chmn. 1987-88. With USAF, 1960-64. Lilly Found. grantee Am. Theol. Library Assn., 1969. Mem. Am. Theol. Library Assn. (coord. consultation svc. 1973-78, program planning com. 1985-88, chmn., 1986-88), Nat. Assn. Profs. Hebrew (archivist 1985—), ALA, Assn. Coll. and Rsch. Librarians, Cath. Libr. Assn. (mem. exec. bd. 1999—), Phi Kappa Phi, Beta Phi Mu. Democrat. Baptist. Home: 40509 Ambar Pl Fremont CA 94539-3630 Office: St Patricks Sem 320 Middlefield Rd Menlo Park CA 94025-3563

WHITE, CELESTE (EMILY), writer, publisher; b. Kans. City, Mo., Dec. 15, 1952; d. Halbert Lynn and Emily (Roach) W.; m. Richard Bladworth Hardie III, June 15, 1974. BA, Wellesley Coll., 1974; MS, U. Mass., 1982. Freelance writer, editor Calif., 1977—; cover copy writer Bantam and Avon Books, N.Y.C., 1986-89; asst. to v.p. Davis Pubs., N.Y.C., 1987; project mgr. Assn. Health & Spiritual Devel., Redding, Calif., 1993-95; prin., owner Keswick House Pub., Redding, Calif., 1996—. Author: Legend of the Flying Hotdog, 1989 (best kids books Parent's Mag. 1989), Natural Remedies for Common Ailments, 1996, Nat. Asthma and Allergy Manual, 1997, Planet Dreams, 1998. Scholar Wellesley (Mass.) Coll., 1974; fellow U. Mass., Amherst, 1976-77. Avocations: classical piano, found object art, roller-blading, mountain biking, molecular biology.

WHITE, CHARLES OLDS, aeronautical engineer; b. Beirut, Apr. 2, 1931; s. Frank Laurence and Dorothy Alice (Olds) W.; m. Mary Carolyn Liechty, Sept. 3, 1955; children—Charles Cameron, Bruce Blair. B.S. in Aero. Engring., MIT, 1953, M.S., 1954. Aero. engr. Douglas Aircraft Long Beach, 1954-60, aero. engr. Ford Aerospace & Communication Corp., Calif., 1960-79, sr. engr. specialist, 1979-80, staff office of gen. mgr. DIVAD div., 1980-81, tech. mgr. DIVAD Fuzes, 1981-82, supr. design and analysis DIVAD div., 1982-85; tech. mgr. Advanced Ordnance Programs, 1985-87, PREDATOR Missile, 1987-90, cons. 1990-93; engring. tech. prin. Aerojet Corp., 1993-94; tech. prin. OCSW Ammunition Olin Ordinance, 1994-97, cons., 1997—. Mem. AIAA, AAAS, Nat. Mgmt. Assn., Am. Aviation Hist. Soc., Sigma Gamma Tau. Republican. Presbyterian. Clubs: Masters Swimming, Newport Beach Tennis. Contbr. articles to profl. jours.

WHITE, DANNY LEVIUS, counselor, consultant, educator; b. Temple, Tenn., Oct. 9, 1956; s. Chester Allen and Elizabeth (Jimmerson) W.; m. Phemonia Lyvette Miller, July 23, 1988; 1 child, Amadi Najuma. AA, Mesa (Ariz.) Community Coll., 1976; BA, Ottawa (Kans.) U., 1982; postgrad., [illegible] No. Ariz. U., 1993. Clinician I Phoenix South Mental Health, 1982-85, therapist I Ariz. Dept. of Correction, Tucson, 1985-87; cons. Tucson Urban League, 1987-88; counselor, assessment specialist Pima County Atty.'s Office, Tucson, 1988-96; pres., CEO Family Matters Counseling and Cons. Svcs., Tucson, 1996—; adj. faculty Pima C.C., 1993-95; mem. com. So. Ariz. Task Force Against Domestic Violence, Tucson, 1989—, outreach coord., Day of Unity chmn., 1993, 94, 95; psychology assoc. II minor's unit Ariz. Dept Corrections, 1996. Dem. precinct committeeman, Tucson, 1988-92; del. 1988 Nat. Dem. Conv.; dep. registrar Pima & Maricopa County Recorders Office, Phoenix and Tucson, 1983-90; mem. citizens adv. coun. Phoenix Elem. Sch. Dist. 1, 1983-85; chair radiothon membership drive com. Tucson chpt. NAACP, 1990-93, chair health fair drive, 1992-93; pres. bd. dirs. P.A.S.A.R., Tucson, 1989-91; booster Spl. Olympics, 1980-90; spl. friend Ariz. Children's Home Foster Care, 1990; implemented Will to Win and Stay In Sch. drive programs, 1987-91; vol., blooddrive coord. United Blood Svcs., Phoenix, 1983-87. Named Outstanding West Campus Adj. Faculty Mem., Pima C.C., 1994-95; recipient Robert L. Horn Outstanding Cmty. Svc. award NAACP, 1996, Tucson NAACP Presidents award, 1998, No. Az. U. Alumme Citizen of Yr., 1998. Mem. United Parent and Youth League Inc. (pres. bd. dirs. 1984-85), Gov.'s Alliance Against Drugs (bd. dirs. 1989-91), Omega Psi Phi (named Man of Yr. Ariz. chpts. 1983, 85, 92, pres. Tucson grad. chpt. 1991-95), Delta Alpha Alpha. Avocations: photography, music, plants, people. Home: PO Box 1135 Tucson AZ 85702-1135

WHITE, DAVID OLDS, researcher, former educator; b. Fenton, Mich., Dec. 18, 1921; s. Harold Bancroft and Doris Caroline (Olds) W.; m. Janice Ethel Russell, Sept. 17, 1923; children: John Russell, David Olds Jr., Benjamin Hill. BA, Amherst Coll., 1943; MS, U. Mass., 1950; PhD, U. Oreg., 1970. Tchr. human physiology Defiance (Ohio) Coll., summer 1950; sci. tchr. Roosevelt Jr. High Sch., Eugene, Oreg., 1951-52; prin. Glide (Oreg.) High Sch., 1952-56; tchr. Munich Am. Elem. Sch., 1957-69; prin. Wurzburg (Fed. Republic Germany) Am. High Sch., 1959-60, Wertheim (Fed. Republic Germany) Am. Elem. Sch., 1960-61; tchr. Dash Point Elem. Sch., Tacoma, 1961-63, Eugene (Oreg.) Pub. Schs., 1963-81; internat. rschr. in field. Contbr. articles to profl. publs.; patentee electronic model airplane. Staff sgt. U.S. Army, 1942-45, PTO. Fulbright grantee, 1956-57, 72-73. Mem. NEA, Fulbright Alumni Assn., Phi Delta Kappa. Avocations: skiing, camping, tennis, hunting, piano. Home: 4544 Fox Hollow Rd Eugene OR 97405-3904

WHITE, DEVON MARKES, professional baseball player; b. Kingston, Jamaica, Dec. 29, 1962. With Calif. Angels, 1981-90, Toronto Blue Jays, 1990-95, Florida Marlins, Miami, 1996—; outfielder Los Angeles Dodgers, 1998-; player Am. League All Star Team, 1989, 93. Recipient Gold Glove award, 1988-89, 91-94; named Am. League leader put outs by outfielder, 1987, 91-92. Office: Los Angeles Dodgers 1000 Elysian Park Ave Los Angeles CA 90012*

WHITE, DON WILLIAM, rancher, minister; b. Santa Rita, N.Mex., June 27, 1942; s. Thomas Melvin and Barbara (Smith) W.; m. Jacqueline Diane Bufkin, June 12, 1965; children: Don William Jr., David Wayne. BBA, Western N.Mex. U., 1974, MBA, 1977. Field acct. Stearns Roger Corp., Denver, 1967-70; controller, adminstrv. mgr. USNR Mining and Minerals Inc., Silver City, N.Mex., 1970-72; devel. specialist County of Grant, Silver City, 1973-77; divisional controller Molycorp. Inc., Taos, N.Mex., 1977-78; mgr. project adminstrn. Kennecott Minerals Co., Hurley, N.Mex., 1978-83; sr. v.p. Sunwest Bank Grant County, Silver City, N.Mex., 1983-84, exec. v.p., 1984-85, pres., chief exec. officer, 1985-97; rancher Deming, N.Mex., 1997—; bd. dirs. Bank of Grant County. Bd. dirs. Sunwest Bank of Grant County, Silver City/Grant County Econ. Devel., 1983—; councilman Town of Silver City, 1977; chmn. Dems. for Senator Pete Domenici, 1986; pres. Gila Regional Med. Found., 1989-92; pres. SWNM Econ. Devel. Corp., 1984—; trustee Indian Hills Bapt. Ch., 1988-89; chmn. State of N.Mex. Small Bus. Adv. Coun.; vice chmn. vocat. edn. adv. com. Western N.Mex. U., 1989; mem. Silver Schs.-Sch./Bus. Partnership Coun. Named Outstanding Vol., Silver City/Grant County Econ. Devel., 1987, 94, FFA, 1985, Western N.Mex. U. Outstanding Alumni, 1998. Mem. Am. Bankers Assn., N.Mex. Bankers Assn., Bank Adminstrn. Inst., Assn. Commerce and Industry (bd. dirs. 1988-91), N.Mex. Mining Assn. (assoc.), Rotary (past pres., dist. gov. rep.). Avocations: snow skiing, water skiing, hunting, fishing, golf. Office: Sunwest Bank of Grant County 1203 N Hudson St Silver City NM 88061-5519

WHITE, DONALD HARVEY, physics educator emeritus; b. Berkeley, Calif., Apr. 30, 1931; s. Harvey Elliott and Adeline White; m. Beverly Evalina Jones, Aug. 8, 1953; children: Jeri, Brett, Holly, Scott, Erin. AB, U. Calif., Berkeley, 1953; PhD, Cornell U., 1960. Rsch. physicist Lawrence Livermore (Calif.) Nat. Lab., 1960-71, cons., 1971-90; prof. physics Western Oreg. U., Monmouth, 1971-95; ret.; vis. rsch. scientist Inst. Laue-Langevin, Grenoble, France, 1977-78, 84-85, 91-92. Author: (with others) Physics, an Experimental Science, 1968, Physics and Music, 1980. Pres. Monmouth-Independence Cmty. Arts, 1983. DuPont scholar, 1958; Minna-Heineman Found. fellow, Hannover, Fed. Republic Germany, 1977. Mem. Am. Phys. Soc., Oreg. Acad. Sci. (pres. 1979-80), Phi Kappa Phi (pres. West Oreg. chpt. 1989-90). Democrat. Presbyterian. Home: 411 S Walnut Dr Monmouth OR 97361-1948

WHITE, GARY RICHARD, electrical engineer; b. Detroit, Nov. 15, 1962; s. Thomas Richard and Davene (Reynolds) W. BSEE, Wayne State U., 1986. Electronics engr. U.S. Army Info. Sys. Engring. Command, Ft. Belvoir, Va., 1987-88, Ft. Shafter, Hawaii, 1988-92; elec. worker U.S. Navy Pub. Works Ctr., Pearl Harbor, Hawaii, 1992-96; plant operator helper U.S. Navy Pub. Works Ctr., Pearl Harbor, 1996—. Mem. IEEE, NRA, NSPE, Assn. Computing Machinery, Am. Assn. Individual Investors, Am. Mgmt. Assn. Avocations: weightlifting, cooking, hardware and software, rock concerts, movies. Office: PO Box 19055 Honolulu HI 96817-9055

WHITE, GAYLE CLAY, aerospace company executive; b. Wyandotte, Mich., Sept. 28, 1944; s. John Leonard and Irene Frances (Clay) W.; m. Sharon Wong, June 8, 1968; children: Lai Jean, Quinn Yee. BBA, Ea. Mich. U., 1967; MBA, Utah State U., 1971; MPA, Auburn U., 1976; postgrad., Nova U., 1985—. Computer system analyst USAF Logistics Command, Odgen, Utah, 1967-71, U.S.-Can. Mil. Officer Exec., Ottawa, Ont., 1971-73; mgr. software devel. USAF Data System Design Ctr., Montgomery, Ala., 1973-77; data base adminstr. Supreme Hdqrs. Allied Powers Europe, Casteau, Belgium, 1977-81; mgr. software configuration System Integration Office, Colorado Springs, Colo., 1981-83; mgr. computer ops. N.Am. Aerospace Def. Command, Colorado Springs, 1983-84; dir. ops. 6 Missile Warning Squadron, Space Command, Cape Cod, Mass., 1984-86, comdr., 1986-87; mgr. program devel. Rockwell Internat., Colorado Springs, 1987-96; mgr. bus. devel. The Boeing Co., Colorado Springs, 1996—; mem. faculty computer sci. and bus. Regis U., Colorado Springs, 1981-97. Treas. Christian Ctr. Ch., Colorado Springs, 1989-95; v.p. European Parents, Tchrs. and Students Assn., 1979-81. Recipient Mil.-Civilian Rels. award Otis Civilian Adv. Coun., 1987, awarded cert. Data Processing Mgmt. Assn., 1973. Mem. Armed Forces Comm. Electronics Assn., Inst. Nav. (treas. Rocky Mountain sect. 1996-97), Global Positioning Sys. Internat. Assn., Air Force Assn., SHAPE Officers Assn., Nat. Security Indsl. Assn. (bd. dirs. Rocky Mountain chpt. 1990-97, vice chmn. space com. ctrl. region 1996-97, space com. bd. dirs. 1997—, pres. Rocky Mountain chpt. 1997—), Christian Businessmen's Assn., Lynmar Racquet Club, Alpha Kappa Psi, C. of C. mil. affairs steering com. Republican. Avocations: racquetball, camping, coin collecting. Office: Boeing 1250 Academy Park Loop Ste 134 Colorado Springs CO 80910-3790

WHITE, IAN PHILLIP, personal care facilitator; b. Cheltenham, Eng., Sept. 3, 1966; came to U.S., 1993; s. Frank William and Janice Grace (Webb) W.; m. Carol Allison Lynn, Sept. 1, 1994 (dec. Oct. 1996). BSc with honors, U. Bradford, Yorkshire, Eng., 1989; mktg. cert., Luton (Eng.) Inst. Higher Edn., 1990. Personal asst. N&P Bldg. Soc., Bradford, Yorkshire, Eng., 1986-87; mktg. mgr. Brit. Telecom., Bedford, Eng., 1990-91; cons. IFF Rsch., London, 1991-92; founder The Effective Consultancy, Findhorn, Scotland, 1992-94, Body Works, Findhorn, 1992-94, Energy Empowerment, Orem, Utah, 1994—; co-founder L.E.T.S., Findhorn, 1991-93; practitioner Findhorn Health Ctr., 1991-93. Author (cassette series) Energy Work, 1994, [illegible] Empowerment Series, 1995. Avocations: mountain biking, hiking, cross-country skiing, yoga, Edgu. Home and Office: Advanced Realisation Ctr 51 W Center St # 101 Orem UT 84057-4605

WHITE, J(OB) BENTON, retired religion educator; b. Birmingham, Ala., Sept. 3, 1931; s. Edith Branch (Benton) White; m. Mary Lou White, July 19, 1958; children: Thomas Raymond, Matthew Louis. BS, U. Ala., 1953; BD, Emory U., 1956; MTh, Pacific Luth. Theol. Sem., 1969. Ordained to ministry United Meth. Ch., as deacon, 1954, as elder, 1956. Assoc. dir. Wesley Found., U. Nebr., Lincoln, 1959-61; dir. Wesley Found. San Jose (Calif.) State U., 1961-67, ombudsman, 1967-69, asst. to pres., 1969-70, prof. religious studies, coord. religious studies program, 1970-92; vis. prof. Santa Clara U., 1992—. Author: From Adam to Armageddon: A Survey of the Bible, 1986, 3d edit., 1994, Taking the Bible Seriously: Honest Differences About Biblical Interpretation, 1993; contbr. articles to profl. jours., mags. Capt. USAF, 1956-59. Mem. Am. Acad. Religion (v.p., pres. western region). Democrat. Home: 2503 Briarwood Dr San Jose CA 95125-4902

WHITE, JON MCCLENDON, engineering educator, geologist; b. Hamilton, Ohio, Sept. 20, 1946; s. Frank William and Hattie Lee (McClendon) W.; m. Sandy Frances DuRant, June 2, 1972; children: Travis DuRant McClendon, Clinton McClendon. Grad. geology engr., Colo. Sch. Mines, 1968; MS, S.D. Sch. Mines & Tech., 1973, PhD, 1975; MA in Ethics & Policy Studies, U. Nev., 1996. Mining engr. U.S. Geol. Survey, Billings, Mont., 1975-78; regulatory affairs coordinator Carter Mining Co., Gillette, Wyo., 1978-80; asst. prof. U. Wyo., Laramie, 1980-82, U. Petroleum & Minerals, Dhahran, Saudi Arabia, 1982-84; dir. Rock Mechanics and Explosives Rsch. Ctr., Sch. Mines & Metallurgy, U. Mo., Rolla, Mo., 1985-89; site mgr. U.S. Dept. Energy, Las Vegas, 1989—; chmn. rsch. policy com., U. Mo.; cons. Delphic Assocs., Inc., Falls Church, Va., 1987-88. Editor: Proc. 3d Internat. Conf. Innovative Mining Systems, 1988; contbr. articles to profl. jours. Mem. St. Louis Com. on Fgn. Relations, 1986—. 1st lt. C.E., U.S. Army, 1969-71, Vietnam. Mem. Soc. Mining Engrs., Inc.., Internat. Pyrotechnic Soc., U.S. Strategic Inst. Republican. Baptist. Avocations: karate, competition marksmanship. Office: US Dept of Energy PO Box 30307 North Las Vegas NV 89036-0307

WHITE, KATHLEEN MERRITT, geologist; b. Long Beach, Calif., Nov. 19, 1921; d. Edward Clendenning and Gladys Alice (Merritt) White; m. Alexander Kennedy Baird IV, Oct. 1, 1965 (dec. 1985); children: Pamela Roberts, Peter Madlem, Stephen Madlem, Mari Afify. Attended, Sch. Boston Mus. Fine Arts, 1939-40, Art Students League, 1940-42; BS in Geology, Pomona Coll., 1962; MS in Geochemistry, Claremont Grad. Sch., 1964. Rsch. asst. geology Pomona Coll., Claremont, Calif., 1962-66, rsch. assoc. geology, 1966-75; cons. geology Claremont, Calif., 1975-77; sr. scientist Jet Propulsion Lab./NASA, Pasadena, 1977-79, mem. tech. staff, 1979-86; ind. rschr. Claremont, 1986—; owner Kittie Tales, Claremont, 1992—. Contbr. Geosat Report, 1986; contbr. articles to profl. jours.; author, illustrator children's books. Grantee NASA, 1984, 85; Pomona Coll. scholar, 1963. Fellow Am. Geophys. Union; mem. Geol. Soc. Am. (invited paper 1994), Pomona Coll. Alumni Assn. Republican. Avocations: painting, piano playing, weaving, hiking, swimming. Home: 265 W 11th St Claremont CA 91711-3804

WHITE, LERRILL JAMES, clinical pastoral educator; b. Lafayette, Ind., Mar. 13, 1948; s. Joe Lloyd and Wanita Irene (Robertson) W.; m. Deborah June Brown, Dec. 27, 1969; children: Krister Colin Brant, Kourtney Cassidy Benay. BA, Abilene Christian U., 1970, MS, 1973; MDiv, Princeton Theol. Sem., 1975; postgrad., Pa. State U., 1980-89. Ordained to ministry Ch. of Christ, 1975. Clin. chaplain Ft. Logan Mental Health Ctr., Denver, 1975-76, Meml. Med. Ctr., Corpus Christi, Tex., 1976-78; sr. pastor Centre Community Ch. of Christ, State Coll., Pa., 1978-87; assoc. dir. pastoral care Geisinger Med. Ctr., Danville, Pa., 1983-87; dir. pastoral care Yuma (Ariz.) Regional Med. Ctr., 1987-95; pres. well i b enterprises inc., 1995—; author, presenter tng. courses, 1987—. Contbr. articles to profl. jours.; creator interview instrument P.C. Ranking Instrument, 1981. Bd. dirs. Behavioral Health Svcs., Yuma, 1991-96; mem., coach Yuma Youth Soccer Assn., 1987-93. Fellow Coll. Chaplains (state rep.- Ariz.); m. Assn. Clin. Pastoral Edn. (supr. 1983—, regional cert. com. Pacific region 1990—), Ariz. Chaplain's Assn. (exec. com. 1988-93, pres. 1989-90), Greater Yuma Ministerium.

WHITE, LORAY BETTY, public relations executive, writer, actress, producer; b. Houston, Nov. 27, 1934; d. Harold White and Joyce Mae (Jenkins) Mills; m. Sammy Davis Jr., 1957 (div. 1958); 1 child, Deborah R. DeHart. Student, UCLA, 1948-50, 90-91, Nichiren Shoshu Acad., 1988-92; AA in Bus., Sayer Bus. Sch., 1970; study div. mem. dept. L.A., Soka U., Japan, 1970-86. Editor, entertainment writer L.A. Community New, 1970-81; exec. sec. guest rels. KNBC Prodns., Burbank, Calif., 1969-75; security specialist Xerox X10 Think Tank, L.A., 1975-80; exec. asst. Ralph Powell & Assocs., L.A., 1980-82; pres., owner, producer LBW & Assocs. Pub. Rels., L.A., 1980—; owner, producer, writer, host TV prodn. co. Pub. Pub. Rels., L.A., 1987—; dir., producer L.B.W. Prodn. "Yesterday, Today, Tomorrow, L.A., 1981—. Actress (film) Ten Commandments, 1956, (Broadway) Joy Ride; appeared in the following endorsements including Budweiser Beer, Old Gold Cigarettes, Salem Cigarettes, TV commls. including Cheer, Puffs Tissue, Coca Cola, Buffern, others; entertainment editor L.A. Community News, 1970-73; writer (column) Balance News, 1980-82. Vol. ARC, 1995; mem. Habitat for Humanity Internat, Nat. Com. Preserve Soc. Sec. and Medicare, 1998-99, Nat. Black Network Assn., AARP, So. Calif. Com. Sr. Citizens, re-elect Scott Wildmen Rep. campaign. Recipient Cert. of Honor, ARC, 1984, Internat. Orgn. Soka Gakkai Internat. of Japan, Cmty. Vols. of Am. award, 1994; named Performer of Yr. Cardella Demillo, 1976-77. Mem. ARC (planning, mktg., prodn. event com. 1995), UCLA Alumni Assn., Lupus Found. Am. (So. Calif. chpt.), Nat. Fedn. Blind, Myohoji-Hokkeko Internat., Libr. of Congress Assocs. (charter). Buddhist. Avocations: singing, acting, TV writing and producing.

WHITE, ONEIDA ELIZABETH, Daycare provider; b. Waco, Tex., Feb. 3, 1922; d. Oscar Eulali and Jim Lovey (Warner) W. BS, Bradley U., 1963; MA, Nova U., 1980; MA in Bibl. Studies, Bay Cities Sem., 1984. Libr. Peoria (Ill.) Jour. Star, 1965-67, tchr. primary sch., 1961-75, 67-71; asst. prin. Peoria Dist. 150, 1965-66; tchr. Oakland (Calif.) Unified Sch. Dist., 1971-86, substitute tchr., 1986—; pianist Sunday sch. Cuomosris Mission Union, 1983—; pres. pastor aid soc. Foothill Missionary Bapt. Ch., 1986—. Active Dem. Party, 1990. Baptist. Avocations: reading, missionary worker. Home: 540 21st St Apt 905 Oakland CA 94612-1638

WHITE, RAYMOND, health facility administrator. BS in Microbiology, U. Oreg., 1965; PhD in Microbiology, MIT, 1971; postdoctoral study, Stanford U. Assoc. prof. Microbiology Dept. U. Mass. Sch. Medicine, Worcester, 1978-80; assoc. prof. Cellular, Viral & Molecular Biology U. Utah Sch. Medicine, Salt Lake City, 1980-84; investigator Howard Hughes Med. Inst. U. Utah, 1980-94; co-chair Human Genetics Dept. U. Utah Sch. Medicine, 1984-94, dir. Huntsman Cancer Inst., 1994—, chmn. Dept. Oncological Scis., 1994—. Recipient Rosenthal Found. award Am. Assn. Cancer Rsch., Charles S. Mott prize for Cancer Rsch. Gen. Motors Found., Nat. Med. Rsch. award Nat. Health Coun., Allan award for Cancer Rsch. Am. Soc. Human Genetics, Friedrich von Recklinghausen award Nat. Neurofibromatosis Found., Lewis S. Rosenstiel award for Disting. Work in Med. Scis. Brandeis U. Mem. NAS. Achievements include developing the molecular tools for construction of a map of genetic markers for the human genome, discovery of genes for neurofibromatosis and familial polyposis; research interests include identifying and characterizing genes associated with inherited cancer syndromes. Office: U Utah EIHG #533 Rm 7410 Salt Lake City UT 84112*

WHITE, RICK, congressman; b. Nov. 6, 1953. BA in Govt. and French, Dartmouth Coll., 1975; postgrad., Pantheon-Sorbonne; JD, Georgetown U., 1980. Mem. 104th to 105th Congresses from 1st Wash. dist., 1995—; mem. house commerce com.; founder Congl. Internet Caucus. Founder Books for Kids. Republican. Office: 116 Cannon Ho Office Bldg Washington DC 20515*

WHITE, ROBERT C., air transportation executive; b. 1943. Student, Wake Forest U., 1961-65. With Procter & Gamble, Columbus, Ohio, 1971-73; asst. [illegible] (Fla.) Regional Airport, 1975-78; dep. dir. aviation Jacksonville (Fla.) Port

Authority, 1978-80; exec. dir. Peninsula Airport Commn., Newport News, Va., 1980-82; dir./cons. Lockheed Air Terminal, Burbank, Calif., 1982—; exec. dir. Reno Tahoe Internat. Airport, 1988—. With USN, 1966-71. Office: Reno Tahoe Internat Airport PO Box 12490 Reno NV 89510-2490

WHITE, ROBERT GORDON, research director, biology educator; b. Lithgow, NSW, Australia, Jan. 17, 1938; s. Richard Robert and Francis Elsie (Schubert) W.; m. Sandra Elizabeth Ferrier, Dec. 9, 1961 (dec. May 1995); children: Robert Ian, Andrew Douglas; m. Lura Peck Elverson, Aug. 2, 1997. B. in Agrl. Sci., Melbourne U., Australia, 1962; M in Rural Sci./Physiology, U. New Eng., Australia, 1968, PhD, 1974. Rsch. asst. Melbourne U., 1962-63; demonstrator U. New Eng., Armidale, Australia, 1963-66, tchr. fellow, 1966-69; asst. prof. zoophysiology and nutrition U. Alaska, Inst. Arctic Biology, Fairbanks, 1970-75, assoc. prof., 1975-81, prof., 1981-98, prof. emeritus, 1998—, acting dir., 1985, 92, dir., 1993-98, dir. Large Animal Rsch. Sta., 1979-98. Co-editor: (with Hudson) Bioenergetics of Wild Herbivores, 1985; editor: (proceedings, with Klein, Keller) First International Muskox Symposium, 1984 (proceedings, with Luick, Lent, Klein) First International Reindeer and Caribou Symposium, 1975; editorial bd.: Rangifer/Biol. Papers U. Alaska; contbr. over 100 papers to profl. jours. Pipe major Fairbanks Red Hackle Pipe Band, 1975-90; pres. Fairbanks Nordic Ski Club, 1973-75. NATO Rsch. fellow, Trondheim, Norway, 1975-76. Fellow AAAS (Alaska chmn. 1985, 94), Arctic Inst. N.Am.; mem. Am. Physiol. Soc., Wildlife Soc., Am. Soc. Mammologists, Australasian Soc. Willdlife Mgmt., Australian Soc. Animal Prodn., Australian Soc. Biochemistry and Molecular Biology, Sigma Xi. Avocations: cross country skiing, river boating, hunting, playing bagpipes. Office: U Alaska Inst Arctic Biology Fairbanks AK 99775

WHITE, ROBERT RANKIN, writer and historian, hydrologist; b. Houston, Feb. 8, 1942; s. Rankin Jones and Eleanor Margaret (White) W. BA in Geology, U. Tex., 1964; MS in Hydrology, U. Ariz., 1971; PhD in Am. studies, U. N.Mex., 1993. Hydrologist Tex. Water Devel. Bd., Austin, 1972-74; hydrologist U.S. Geol. Survey, Las Cruces, N.Mex., 1974-78, Santa Fe, 1978-80, Albuquerque, 1980-89; writer, historian Albuquerque, 1989—; mem. planning bd. N.Mex. Art History Conf., Taos, N.Mex., 1987—. Author: The Lithographs and Etchings of E. Martin Hennings, 1978, The Taos Soc. of Artists, 1983 (rev. edit. 1998); co-author: Pioneer Artists of Taos, 1983, Bert Geer Phillips and The Taos Art Colony, 1994; contbr. articles to profl. jours. Bd. dirs. Friends of U. N.Mex. Librs., Albuquerque, 1984-90. With U.S. Army, 1965-68. Mem. NRA (life), Hist. Soc. N.Mex. (pres. 1991-93), N.Mex. Book League (pres. 1994, exec. dir. 1996—), Taos County Hist. Soc. Episcopalian. Home and Office: 1409 Las Lomas Rd NE Albuquerque NM 87106-4529

WHITE, ROBERT STEPHEN, physics educator; b. Ellsworth, Kans., Dec. 28, 1920; s. Byron F. and Sebina (Leighty) W.; m. Freda Marie Bridgewater, Aug. 30, 1942; children: Nancy Lynn, Margaret Diane, John Stephen, David Bruce. AB, Southwestern Coll., 1942, DSc hon., 1971; MS, U. Ill., 1943; PhD, U. Calif., Berkeley, 1951. Physicist Lawrence Radiation Lab., Berkeley, Livermore, Calif., 1948-61; head dept. particles and fields Space Physics Lab. Aerospace Corp., El Segundo, Calif., 1962-67; physics prof. U. Calif., Riverside, 1967-92, dir. Inst. Geophysics and Planetary Physics, 1967-92, chmn. dept. physics, 1970-73, prof. emeritus physics dept., rsch. physicist, 1992—; lectr. U. Calif., Berkeley, 1953-54, 57-59. Author: Space Physics, 1970, Why Science?, 1998; contbr. articles to profl. jours. Officer USNR, 1944-46. Sr. Postdoctoral fellow NSF, 1961-62; grantee NASA, NSF, USAF, numerous others. Fellow AAAS, Am. Phys. Soc. (exec. com. 1972-74); mem. AAUP, Am. Geophys. Union, Am. Astron. Soc. Home: 5225 Austin Rd Santa Barbara CA 93111-2905 Office: U Calif Inst Geophysics & Planetary Physics Riverside CA 92521

WHITE, RODNEY CURTIS, paralegal, legal assistant; b. Pueblo, Colo., Aug. 20, 1958; s. Richard Robert and Mary Alice (Valdez) W. Student, Pueblo C.C., 1987-89; Diploma Paralegal/Legal Asst., So. Career Inst., Boca Raton, Fla., 1990, student, 1996—. Freelance paralegal Pueblo, 1991-95; UA technician/security Crossroads Managed Care Sys., Pueblo, 1995—, billing clerk/client intake, 1998—; investigator/legal rschr. various law firms, 1989-90; notary public, 1989—. Campaign coord. Elect George Bush for Pres. campaign, So. Colo., 1988 89, Rau for County Clerk and Recorder; pres. Viva Bush com. Rep. Nat. Hispanic Assembly, Washington, 1985-89; mem. Rep. Nat. Com., Washington, 1988-89; Colo. state hosp. employee rep. Am. Fed. State County Mcpl. Employees, Pueblo, 1985-88; fund raiser Crime Stopper, Pueblo. Mem. Colo. Trial Lawyers Assn. Republican. Home: 2581 Lynwood Ln Pueblo CO 81005-2719

WHITE, RUTH BRYANT, media consultant, analyst, counselor, minister; b. Denver, May 6, 1955; d. Volleny Bryant Sr. and Ruth Ada (Washington) Smith; m. Steven Alan White, Nov. 21, 1980; children: Pershaun R., LeJeune B., LaVonda M. Ed. high sch., Denver. Ordained to ministry Christian Ch., 1988. With acctg. sect. U.S. Govt., Denver and L.A., 1972-81; remittance processor Auto Club So. Calif., L.A., 1981-84; with acctg. dept. various agys. L.A., 1984-91; sr. adminstrv. support specialist Infonet, L.A., 1991—; media cons. on interracial relationships. Author: Free Indeed: The Autobiography of an Interracial Couple, 1989; coordinating prodr. Hollywood Post Oscar Showcase, 1996; appeared on talk shows. V.p. A Place for Us, Gardena, Calif., 1984—. Mem. Assn. Multiethnic Ams. (charter, regional v.p. western U.S. 1991-93). Avocation: research on prejudice, racism, and interracial issues, public speaking. Office: A Place for Us Nat PO Box 357 Gardena CA 90248-0357

WHITE, W. ROBIN, author; b. Kodaikanal, Madras, India, July 12, 1928; came to U.S., 1944; s. Emmons Eaton and Ruth Esther (Parker) W.; m. Marian Lucille Biesterfield, Feb. 3, 1948 (dec. Mar. 1983); children: Christopher, Parker, Shelley. BA, Yale U., 1950; MA, Calif. State Poly. U., 1991. Instr. writers program UCLA, 1985-93; lectr. Calif. State Poly. U., Pomona, 1985-93; exec. officer Calif. State Regional Ctrs., Ukiah, Calif., 1973-79. Author: Elephant Hill, 1959 (Harper prize), House of Many Rooms, 1958, Men and Angels, 1961, Foreign Soil, 1962, All in Favor Say No, 1964, His Own Kind, 1967, Be Not Afraid, 1972, The Special Child, 1978, The Troll of Crazy Mule Camp, 1979, Moses the Man, 1981, The Winning Writer: Studies in the Art of Self-Expression, 1997; anthologies include: Best American Stories, O. Henry Prize Stories, Best Modern Short Stories, Seventeen's Stories, others; contbr. numerous mags. including Harper's, The New Yorker, New York Times, L.A. Times, Harper's Bazaar, Saturday Evening Post, Ladies' Home Jour., Seventeen, Nat. Wildlife, Mademoiselle, The Reporter; author poetry (Poetry award 1993, 94, 95); editor-in-chief Per/Se Internat. Quar., 1965-69; fiction editor UCLA West/Word, 1989-90. Class rep. Kodai-Woodstock Found., 1986—; elder Presbyn. Session, Claremont, Calif., 1988-91; mem. libr. commn. Pasadena Presbyn. Ch., 1996—. Recipient Disting. Achievement award Ednl. Press Assn., 1974, North Coast Regional Ctr., Ukiah, 1978; Bread Loaf fellow Middlebury Coll., 1956, Stegner fellow Stanford U., 1956-57. Mem. Calif. State Poetry Soc., Authors Guild. Democrat. Presbyterian. Avocations: backpacking, gardening, photography, birds. Home: 1940 Fletcher Ave South Pasadena CA 91030-4625

WHITEAKER, LINDA JOYCE, minister, educational administrator; b. Cookeville, Tenn., May 4, 1942; d. Beecher and Thelma Lee (Roberson) W. Student U. Hawaii, 1965, Hancock Jr. Coll., 1970—; Th.B., Clarksville Sch. Theology, 1980, M.Th., 1983; grad. Calif. Assn. Realtors, 1968. Lic. to ministry Ch. of God, 1960. Pastor, Ch. of God, Lahaina, Hawaii, 1962-64; dir. youth and Christian edn. Ch. of God, Hawaii, 1964-65; pastor Santa Maria Ch. of God, Calif., 1965—; owner/broker Lin*Etta Realty, Santa Maria, 1972—; builder. Founder, pastor, adminstr. Accelerated Christian Sch., 1976—; founder, pres. Lady Ministers Fellowship Internat., 1981—; mem. Santa Maria/Orcutt Gen. Plan Adv. Com., 1979-84; mem. Santa Maria Planning Commn., 1984-89, chmn., 1988-89; mem. congl. task force com. U.S. Ho. of Reps., 1983. Mem. Santa Maria Bd. Realtors (pres. 1978-79, legis. chmn. 1980), Calif. Assn. Realtors (bd. dirs. 1977-81), Nat. Assn. Realtors (bd. dirs. 1978-81), Santa Maria C. of C. (speakers club). Republican. Avocations: walking; collecting Bibles; travel; photography. Home and Office: PO Box 1342 Santa Maria CA 93456-1342

WHITEHEAD, GRAHAM GRANT ROBIN, theater director; b. Cairo, July 30, 1941; came to U.S., 1992; s. John Hallworth and Eunice Ivy (Willis) W.; m. Ruth Holmes Everett, July 24, 1972; 1 child, Sarah Robin Holmes; m. Margaret Louise Latzer, Dec 28, 1991. BA, Cambridge (Eng.) U., 1962; MA, U. New Brunswick, Can., 1964; PhD, U. Toronto, Can., 1972. Asst. prof. Dalhousie U., Halifax, NS, Can., 1972-76; assoc. prof. Ariz. State U., Tempe, AZ, 1992-94; artistic assoc. Childs Play Inc., Tempe, 1998—.

WHITEHOUSE, N. VIRGINIA, communications studies educator; b. France, Oct. 28, 1964. BA, Samford U., 1986; MA, U. Mo., 1992, PhD, 1997. Reporter Franklin (Tenn.) Review Appeal, 1986-88; tchr. English, Korea Bapt. Sem., Taejon, Rep. of Korea, 1989-90; corr. Bapt. Press, Taejon, Rep. of Korea, 1989-90; reporter Montgomery (Ala.) Advertiser, 1991; asst. prof. dept. comm. studies Whitworth Coll., Spokane, Wash., 1996—. Contbr. articles to profl. jours. Guardian Ad Litem, CASA, Spokane County, 1997—. Study/travel grantee U.S. Dept. Edn., Rep. of Korea, 1997-98. Mem. Assn. Edn. in Journalism and Mass Comm., Inland N.W. Soc. Profl. Journalists (advisor student chpt. 1997—). Lutheran. Office: Whitworth Coll Comm Studies Spokane WA 99251

WHITEHOUSE, PHYLLIS JEANNE, public relations executive; b. Chgo., Apr. 10, 1923; d. Philip Bernard II and Emily (Soravia) Stockhausen; m. Walter L. Forward Jr., Feb. 19, 1958 (div. 1963); m. Jack Pendleton Whitehouse, Mar. 6, 1964 (div. Nov. 1984); 1 child, Mark Philip. BS in Chemistry, U. Ill., 1944. Chemist Lucent Labs., Murray Hill, N.J., 1944-46; flight attendant, then with sales dept. Am. Airlines, 1946-62; mem. sales staff, 1980—; pres. Whitehouse Enterprises, L.A. Mem. Internat. Visitors' Program. Mem. Who's Who Internat., Lahaina Yacht Club. Avocations: tennis, bridge, travel, symphony, opera. Home: 424 Kelton Ave Apt 310 Los Angeles CA 90024-2095

WHITENER, PHILIP CHARLES, aeronautical engineer, consultant; b. Keokuk, Iowa, July 9, 1920; s. Henry Carroll and Katherine Ethel (Graham) W.; m. Joy Carrie Page, Oct. 9, 1943; children: David A., Barbara C., Wendy R., Dixie K. BSME, U. N.Mex., 1941. Ordained to elder Presbyn. Ch., 1956. Engr. Boeing Airplane Co., Seattle, 1941-47, supr. wind tunnel model design, 1947-57, project engr. B-52 flight test, 1957-62, engrng. mgr. Fresh I hydrofoil, 1962-65, configurator supersonic transport, 1965-70, with preliminary design advanced concepts, 1970-83, ret., 1983; pres., chief engr. Alpha-Dyne Corp., Bainbridge Island, Wash., 1983-98; mgr. Advanced Marine Concepts, LLC, 1998—. Inventee in field. Organizer Trinity Ch., Burien, Wash., 1962, Highline Reformed Presbyn., Burien, 1970, Liberty Bay Presbyn., Poulsbo, Wash., 1978; pres. Whitener Family Found., Bainbridge Island, 1979; bd. dirs. Mcpl. League of Bainbridge, 1993—, v.p., 1994, pres., 1996—; pres. Mcpl. League Found., 1994-98, bd. dirs., 1998—. Republican. Avocations: designing, computers, boating. Home: 5955 NE Battle Point Dr Bainbridge Island WA 98110

WHITESIDE, LOWELL STANLEY, seismologist; b. Trinidad, Colo., Jan. 7, 1946; s. Paul Edward and Carrie Belle (Burgess) W. BS, Hamline U., 1968; postgrad., Oswego State U. of N.Y., 1970-72; MS, U. Nebr., 1985; postgrad., Ga. Inst. of Tech., 1986-88, U. Colo., 1990-94. Instr. U.S. Peace Corps, Mhlume, Swaziland, 1968-71; rsch. assoc. CIRES, U. Colo., Boulder, 1988-90; geophysicist in charge of internat. earthquake data base NOAA, Nat. Geophys. Data Ctr., Boulder, 1990—; vis. rschr. Nuclear and Geol. Scis. Inst., Wellington, New Zealand, 1997; gen. ssec. UN Workshop on Forecasting Nat. Disasters by Geomagnetic Methods, Beijing, 1998, on Geomagnetic Methods, Beijing, 1998; co-chair Internat. Workshop on Statis. Earthquake Predicition, Hangzhou, China, 1998. Scoutmaster Boy Scouts Am., St. Paul, Lincoln, Nebr., 1968-80, camp counselor, 1968-76. Recipient Eagle Scout award Boy Scouts Am., 1968, NGDC/NOAA Customer Svc. award, 1995. Mem. AAAS (chmn. 1986-87, vice chmn. 1985-86, Geology-Geography, Rocky Mountain sect., Outstanding Articles Referee 1992, Best Student Paper award 1984, 85), Seismol. Soc. of Am., Am. Geophys. Union, Sierra Club, Planetary Soc. Presbyterian. Avocations: hiking, camping, music, biking, running. Home: PO Box 3141 Eldorado Springs CO 80025-3141 Office: NOAA/NGDC/NESOIS 325 Broadway St Boulder CO 80303-3337

WHITE-VONDRAN, MARY-ELLEN, retired stockbroker; b. East Cleveland, Ohio, Aug. 21, 1938; d. Thomas Patrick and Rita Ellen (Langdon) White; m. Gary L. Vondran, Sr., Nov. 25, 1961; children: Patrick Michael, Gary Lee Jr. BA, Notre Dame Coll., South Euclid, Ohio, 1960; postgrad., John Carroll U., 1960, U. Mass., 1961, U. S.C., 1969, San Jose State U., 1971-75, U. Santa Clara, Calif., 1972, Stanford U., 1989; MSL, Peninsula U., Mountain View, Calif., 1994; intern program para-legal dept., DeAnza Coll., Calif., 1996-97; postgrad., Newport U., 1998—. Cert. life secondary tchr., Calif.; lic. NASD series 7, 18 & 63 broker. Tchr. Cleve. Sch. Dist., 1960-61, East Hartford (Conn.) Sch. Dist., 1961-62, San Francisco Bay Area Sch. Dist., 1970-75; life and disability agt. Travelers Ins. Co. and BMA Ins. Co., San Jose, Calif., 1975-77; stockbroker Reynolds, Bache, Shearson, Palo Alto, Calif., 1977-78, Schwab & Co., San Francisco, 1980; adminstr. pension and profit Crocker Nat. Bank, San Francisco, 1980-82; stockbroker Calif. Fed./Invest Co., San Francisco, 1982-83; head trader, br. mgr. Rose & Co., San Francisco, 1983-84; ret., 1984; tchr. citizenship for fgn. born adult community edn. Fremont Union High Sch. Dist., Sunnyvale, Calif., 1988—. Author: Jo Mora-Renaissance Man, 1973, Visit of Imperial Russian Navy to San Francisco, 1974, John Franklin Miller, 1974, 1905 Quail Meadow Road. Sec. Quota Internat., Los Altos, Calif., 1987; constn. chairperson LWV, Los Altos, 1985—, lectr. speakers bur. 1987, moderator, co-producer TV/Cable programs; precinct capt. 1988 & 90 Elections, Los Altos; appointee ad hoc com. for transp. of mobility impaired Santa Clara County, 1988; vol. tchr. English in Action; usher lively arts Stanford U.; mem. tele com. Peninsula Dem. Coalition; active Internat. Vis. Com., Palo Alto, People for Accessible Health Care, Women in History Mus., Calif. History Ctr., Cupertino, Palo Alto Neighbors Abroad; legal intern Slenkovich & Flanagan, Mountain View Mediations Svcs., Sr. Adult Legal Assistance; intern Support Network for Battered Women. Recipient Valley Cable Recognition award, 1988. Mem. AAUW, ACLU, NOW (speakers bur. coord.), ABA (student), ATLA (student), World Affairs Forum, Women in History Assn., The Great War Soc., Am. Assn. Retired Persons, Older Women's League, Los Altos Women in Bus., Women's Internat. League for Peace & Freedom, Irish Cultural Soc., South Bay Scottish Soc., Commonwealth Club (steering com., program com. Palo Alto/Midpeninsula chpt.), Kenna Club. Democrat. Roman Catholic. Avocations; reading, community activities, Dem. politics, swimming, Irish dancing, music, and lit.

WHITFORD, JOSEPH P., lawyer; b. N.Y.C., Apr. 30, 1950. BA, Union Coll., 1972; JD, Syracuse U., 1975; LLM in Taxation, George Washington U., 1978. Bar: N.Y. 1976, D.C. 1977, Wash. 1979. Staff atty. divsn. corp. fin. SEC, Washington, 1975-78; assoc. Foster Pepper & Shefelman, Seattle, 1978-83, mem., 1983—; chmn. bd. dirs. MIT Forum on the Northwest, 1992-93. Office: Foster Pepper & Shefelman PLLC 1111 3rd Ave Ste 3400 Seattle WA 98101-3207*

WHITING, JUDITH A., education educator; b. Coos Bay, Oreg., Sept. 8, 1941; d. Allen Luther and Lorraine Beatrice 9Pollock) Rogers; m. Floyd Ira Whiting, Aug. 18, 1963; children: Michael A., Marcia E. Whiting Yamagata. BA, Willamette U., 1963; MS, Portland State U., 1969. Tchr. David Douglas H.S., Portland, Oreg., 1963-68; instr. U. Nev., Reno, 1985-93; instr., cons. Truckee Meados C.C., Reno, Nev., 1986—, 94—; coor. Writing Ctr., Truckee Meadows C.C./OTM Br. Campus, Reno, 1997-98. Mem. Nat. Coun. Tchrs. of English, Alpha Phi Internat. (collegiate pres. 1962, alumni pres. 1979). Avocations: crossword puzzles, walking, cross-country skiing, travel. Office: Truckee Meadows Comm Coll Mail 056 7000 Dandini Blvd Reno NV 89512-3999

WHITING, VAN ROBERT, JR., political science educator; b. Balt., Jan. 26, 1950; s. Van Robert Sr. and Sara Frances (Hollister) W.; m. Christine Mary Lux, June 5, 1971; children: Van Michael, Stephen Hollister. BA magna cum laude, Yale U., 1973; MA, Harvard U., 1978, PhD in Polit. Sci., 1981. Mellon fellow/vis. lectr. U. Calif., Berkeley, 1981-82; asst. prof. Brown U., Providence, R.I., 1982-89; sr. rsch. fellow U. Calif., San Diego, 1990—; dir. N.Am. Competitiveness Project, 1993-97; vis. scholar Ctr. for Internat. Affairs, Harvard U., Cambridge, Mass., 1984; bd. dirs. Brown/Mexico program, Providence, 1986-89; cons. Internat. Inst. R.I., 1983, 89; project dir. Liberalization and Competitiveness; cons. Telescan, Inc.; prin. Internat. Polit. Advisory; founder Global Convergence, Inc.; dir. Congl. Briefings, 1993, 94; spkr. World Affairs Coun., World Pres. Orgn., others. Author: The Political Economy of Foreign Investment in Mexico, 1992; author: (with others) The Dynamics of Regional Integration; editor, author: Liberalization and Competitiveness, 1995, Regionalization in Asia-Pacific, NAFTA and the Americas, 1995; contbr. articles to profl. jours. and books. Recipient Distinction in Polit. Sci. award, Charles Washburn Clark prize Yale U., 1973, grad. fellowship NSF, 1974-79, Fulbright, Social Sci. Rsch. Coun. fellowships to Mexico, 1978-79, Wriston fellowship Brown U., 1984, Indo-Am. Fulbright fellowship to India, 1990. Mem. Am. Polit. Sci. Assn., Latin Am. Studies Assn., Internat. Studies Assn., Internat. Platform Assn., Yale Club. Home: 4240 Porte De Palmas Unit 52 San Diego CA 92122-5157 Office: U Calif San Diego 0510 9500 Gilman Dr Dept 510 La Jolla CA 92093-0510

WHITING, WALLACE BURTON, II, chemical engineer, educator; b. Hartford, Conn., Sept. 6, 1952; s. Harold Alan and Lillian Anne (Jones) W.; m. Patricia Rose Headington Moore, June 17, 1978; children: Sharon E. Moore, Cynthia L. Moore Restivo. BS, Rensselaer Polytechnic Inst., 1974; MSChemE, Polytechnic Inst. N.Y., 1976; PhD, U. Calif., Berkeley, 1982. Registered profl. engr., Calif., W.Va., Nev. Asst. mech. engr. Pratt & Whitney Aircraft Co., East Hartford, Conn., 1973; chem. process engr. Dorr-Oliver Inc., Stamford, Conn., 1974-76; rsch. assoc. Lawrence Berkeley Lab., Berkeley, Calif., 1976-82; prof. W.Va. U., Morgantown, 1982—; program dir. NSF, 1991, 94; vis. prof. UCLA, 1992; prof., chair U. Nev., Reno, 1996—. Co-author: Analysis, Synthesis and Design of Chemical Processes, 1997; editor Fluid Phase Equilibria Jour.; contbr. articles to profl. jours. Grantee NSF, U.S. Dept. Energy. Mem. AIChE (nat. program chair for edn. 1988—), Am. Soc. Engrng. Edn. (bd. dirs. nat. projects 1990—, chair programming chem. engrng. and edn. divsn. 1986-90, Dow Outstanding Faculty award 1986, Centennial Svc. award 1993), Am. Chem. Soc., Internat. Gesellschaft Fuer Ingenieurpaedagogik, Assn. Environ. Engrng. Profs., Sigma Xi, Tau Beta Pi. Achievements include development of a new approach to mixing rules for equations of state for asymmetric mixtures, and a new approach to quantifying uncertainties in process design caused by thermodynamic uncertainties. Office: U Nev Chem and Metallurg Engring 170 Reno NV 89557

WHITLEY, DAVID SCOTT, archaeologist; b. Williams AFB, Ariz., Mar. 5, 1953; s. Edgar Duer and Yvonne Roca (Wightman) W.; m. Tamara Katherine Koteles, Feb. 13, 1987; 1 child, Carmen. AB in Anthrop. & Geog. (magna cum laude), U. Calif., 1976, MA in Geography, 1979, PhD in Anthropology, 1982. Soc. Profl. Archeology. Chief archeologist Inst. Archeology UCLA, L.A., 1983-87; rsch. fellow Archeology Dept. U. Witwatersrand, Johannesburg, S. Africa, 1987-89; pres. W&S Cons., Simi Valley, Calif., 1989—; U.S. rep. internat. com. rock art Internat. Coun. Monuments and Sites, 1992—, exec. com., 1997-99, mem. coun. dirs., 1997—. Author: A Guide to Rock Art Sites: Southern California and Southern Nevada, 1996, L'Art des chamanes: art rupestre en Californie, 1997; editor: archeological monographs; contbr. articles to profl. jours. Prehistoric Archeologist, State of Calif. Hist. Resources Commn., 1986-87; mem. rsch. adv. com. Chauvet Cave, France, 1996—. Recipient post doctoral fellowship, Assn. for Field Archeology, 1983, tech. specialist grant, U.S. Aid, 1986. Fellow Am. Anthrop. Assn.; mem. Soc. Am. Archeology, SAR, Sons of the Indian Wars, Mayflower Soc. Home: 447 3d St Fillmore CA 93015-1413 Office: W&S Consultants 2422 Stinson St Simi Valley CA 93065

WHITLOW, WILLIAM LA FOND, minister, theology school planter; b. Mpls., Oct. 20, 1932; s. George Lester and Wanona Nadine (Ridgeway) W.; m. Donna Mae Magnuson, June 13, 1953; children: Debra, Cathleen, Lisa Mae. Ministerial diploma, Eugene (Oreg.) Bible Coll., 1953; postgrad., Seattle Pacific U., 1961, BTh, ThM, Internat. Sem., Orlando, Fla., 1981, ThD summa cum laude, 1986, DD (hon.), 1984; LittD, Evangel Christian U. Am., 1992. Ordained to ministry Open Bible Standard Chs., 1954, Biltmore Bible Ch., 1988. Asst. and pastor Oreg. chs., 1949-55; dean pers. Calif. Open Bible Inst., Pasadena, 1957-58; pres., island supt. Bible Inst., Montego Bay, Jamaica, 1958-59, San Fernando, Trinidad, 1960-65; sr. pastor Biltmore Bible Ch., Phoenix, 1967—; pres. Biltmore Bible Sch. Theology, Phoenix, 1982-86; extension sch. rep. Internat. Sem., Orlando, 1984-91; adj. faculty mem. Evang Theol. Sem., Dixon, Mo., 1989-91; affiliate prof. Vision Christian U., Ramona, Calif., 1991. Author, compiler: Basic Bible School Builder, 1986-91; also numerous Bible tng. courses. Recipient Outstanding Acad. Achievement award Internat. Sem., 1987. Office: Biltmore Bible Christian Ctr 3330 E Camelback Rd Phoenix AZ 85018-2310

WHITMORE, DONALD CLARK, retired engineer; b. Seattle, Sept. 15, 1932; s. Floyd Robinson and Lois Mildred (Clark) W.; m. Alice Elinor Winter, Jan. 8, 1955; children: Catherine Ruth, William Owen, Matthew Clark, Nancy Lynn, Peggy Ann, Stuart John. BS, U. Wash., 1955. Prin. engr. The Boeing Co., Seattle, 1955-87, ret., 1987; developer, owner mobile home pk., Auburn, Wash., 1979—. Author: Towards Security, 1983, (monograph) SDI Software Feasibility, 1990, Characterization of the Nuclear Proliferation Threat, 1993, Rationale for Nuclear Disarmament, 1995. Activist for arms control, Auburn, Wash., 1962—; chmn. Seattle Coun. Orgns. for Internat. Affairs, 1973, Auburn Citizens for Schs., 1975; v.p. Boeing Employees Good Neighbor Fund, Seattle, 1977, Spl. Svc. award, 1977; pres. Abe Keller Peace Edn. Fund, 1998—; pres., founder Third Millennium Found., 1994 . Avocations: hiking, travel, collecting. Home and Office: 16202 SE Lake Moneysmith Rd Auburn WA 98092-5274

WHITNEY, DAVID, prosecutor; b. Alamosa, Colo., Apr. 25, 1942; s. Robert F. and Clarissa I. (Wilson) W.; m. Martha Green, Sept. 26, 1980; children from previous marriage: LeAnn Gonzalez, Christopher. AB in Philosophy, UCLA, 1968, JD, 1971, postgrad., 1971-72. Bar: Calif. 1972, U.S. Dist. Ct. (cen. dist.) Calif. 1973, U.S. Ct. Appeals (9th cir.) 1981, U.S. Supreme Ct. 1985. Dep. pub. defender L.A., 1972-74, pvt. practice, 1974-78; pvt. practice San Bernardino, Calif., 1978-86; dep. dist. atty. Dist. Atty.'s Office, San Bernardino, 1986—, death penalty coord., psychiat. issues coord., 1988—, lead atty. major crimes unit, 1996—; expert witness, lectr. in field. Chmn. Fire Commn., Forest Falls, Calif., 1988—. Mem. Calif. Dist. Attys. Assn. (mem. state death penalty com. 1995—), Forensic Mental Health Assn. Calif. (pub. policy com. 1996—), Criminal Cts. Bar Assn. (bd. dirs. 1982-84), County Bar Assn. (jud. evaluation com. 1987-89, co-chmn. 1988, bench/bar com. 1989, chmn. office mgmt. adv. com. 1995, domestic violence prosecutions com. 1995). Democrat. Office: Office of Dist Atty 316 Mountain View San Bernardino CA 92415

WHITNEY, JANE, foreign service officer; b. Champaign, Ill., July 15, 1941; d. Robert F. and Mussette (Cary) W. BA, Beloit Coll., 1963; CD, U. Aix, Marseille, France, 1962. Joined Fgn. Service, U.S. Dept. State, 1965, vice consul, Saigon, Vietnam, 1966-68, career counselor, 1968-70, spl. asst. Office of Dir. Gen., 1970-72, consul, Stuttgart, Fed. Republic Germany, 1972-74, Ankara, Turkey, 1974-76, spl. asst. Office of Asst. Sec. for Consular Affairs, 1976-77, mem. Bd. Examiners Fgn. Service, 1977-78, 79-81, consul, Munich, Germany, 1978-79, Buenos Aires, Argentina, 1981-82, ethics officer Office of Legal Adviser, 1982-85, advisor Office of Asst. Sec. for Diplomatic Security, 1985-86, dep. prin. officer, consul, Stuttgart, 1986-90, prin. officer, consul gen., Perth, Australia, 1990-91. Recipient awards U.S. Dept. State, 1968, 70, 81, 85, 87, 90. Mem. Presbyterian Ch.

WHITNEY, NATALIE WHITE, primary school educator; b. Pasadena, Calif., Mar. 26, 1917; d. Walter Patton and Natalie May (Brokaw) White; m. John Parker Whitney, Mar. 17, 1943 (dec. July 1969); children: John Parker, Jr., Sarah Carpenter. Student, Univ. Ariz., 1936-38, Claremont Coll., 1940-43; BA, Whittier Coll., 1940. Kindergarten primary tchr. credential, Calif. Asst. dir. M.B. Eyer Nursery Sch., Scripps Coll., Claremont, 1940-43; dir. kindergarten Westridge Sch. Girls, Pasadena, 1943-45; tchr. kindergarten Oak Grove Sch. Dist., San Jose, Calif., 1971-73, 73-86, primary tchr., 1973—. Author: Pumpkins, 1996 (also Spanish edit. Calabazas 1996), The Tiny Dot, 1996 (also Spanish edit. El puntito 1996). Gray Lady, ARC, Pasadena, 1943; sponsor Ford Country Day Sch., Los Altos, Calif., 1955-58, Children's Country Sch. (name now Hillbrook Sch.), Los Gatos, Calif., 1958-64, Youth Sci. Mus., San Jose, 1971-86; den mother Boy Scouts Am., Los Altos, 1956-58; mem. women's aux. San Jose Symphony, 1963; asst. gift shop Alexian Bros. Hosp. League, 1965. Recipient Merit award ARC, 1951. Mem. Mayflower Soc. (life), Valle Monte League (sustaining), Los Altos

Hunt Club (resident), Kappa Kappa Gamma. Republican. Episcopalian. Avocations: reading, interior decorating, gourmet cuisine, gardening, hostessing. Home: 15785 Alta Vista Way San Jose CA 95127-1702

WHITNEY, RALPH ROYAL, JR., financial executive; b. Phila., Dec. 10, 1934; s. Ralph Royal and Florence Elizabeth (Whitney) W.; m. Fay Wadsworth, Apr. 4, 1959; children: Lynn Marie, Paula Sue, Brian Ralph. BA, U. Rochester, 1957, MBA, 1972. Spl. agt. Prudential Ins. Co., Rochester, N.Y., 1958-59, divsn. mgr., 1959-63; gen. agt. Nat. Life Vt., Syracuse, 1963-64; contr. Wadsworth Mfg. Assocs. Inc., Syracuse, 1964-65, v.p., 1965-68, pres., 1968-71; pres. Warren (Pa.) Components Corp., 1968-72; pres., mng. prin. ptnr. Hammond Kennedy Whitney & Co., N.Y.C., 1972—; chmn. IFR Sys., Inc., Seneca Printing Inc., Control Devices Inc.; chmn., CEO Grobet File Co., Am. Maine Rubber Co.; bd. dirs. Excel Industries, Inc., Baldwin Tech. Corp., Selas Corp. Am., M. Mossberg & Son, Inc., MedTek Inc., Wyo. Bus. Coun., Relm Wireless Comms. Inc., Ind. Internet Bank, Horton Emergency Vehicles, Morehouse Group. Bd. trustees U. Rochester. Mem. N.Y. Yacht Club, Lotus Club (N.Y.C.), Century Club (Syracuse), Merion Cricket Club, Princeton Club. Episcopalian. Home: 3441 Highway 34 Wheatland WY 82201-8714

WHITSEL, RICHARD HARRY, biologist, entomologist; b. Denver, Feb. 23, 1931; s. Richard Elstun and Edith Muriel (Harry) W.; m. Laurie Pearson, May 25, 1997; children by previous marriages: Russell David, Robert Alan, Michael Dale, Steven Deane. BA, U. Calif., Berkeley, 1954; MA, San Jose State Coll., 1962. Sr. rsch. biologist San Mateo County Mosquito Abatement Dist., Burlingame, Calif., 1959-72; environ. program mgr., chief of watershed mgmt., chief of planning, chief of wetlands planning office Calif. Regional Water Quality Control Bd., Oakland, 1972—; mem. grad. faculty water resource mgmt. U. San Francisco, 1987-89. Served with Med. Service Corps, U.S. Army, 1954-56. Mem. Entomol. Soc. Am., Entomol. Soc. Wash., Am. Mosquito Control Assn., Calif. Alumni Assn., The Benjamin Ide Wheeler Soc., Nat. Parks and Conservation Assn. (life), Sierra Club. Democrat. Episcopalian. Contbr. articles to profl. jours. Home: 5218 Muirwood Dr Pleasanton CA 94588-3636 Office: Calif Regional Water Quality Control Bd 1515 Clay St Oakland CA 94612-1499

WHITSITT, ROBERT JAMES, professional basketball team executive; b. Madison, Wis., Jan. 10, 1956; s. Raymond Earl and Dolores June (Smith) W.; m. Jan Leslie Sundberg; children: Lillian Ashley, Sean James. BS, U. Wis., Stevens Point, 1977; MA, Ohio State U., 1978. Intern Indiana Pacers, Inpls., 1978, bus. tickets mgr., 1979, dir. bus. affairs and promotions, 1980, asst. gen. mgr., 1981-82; v.p. mktg. Kansas City (Mo.) Kings, 1982-84, v.p., asst. gen. mgr., 1984-85; v.p., asst. gen. mgr. Sacramento Kings, 1985-86; pres. Seattle Supersonics, 1986-97, Portland Trail Blazers, 1997—. Mem. Nat. Basketball Assn. (alternate gov., mem. competition and rules com.). Republican. Lutheran. Lodge: Rotary. Avocations: skiing, jogging, reading, music. Office: Portland Trailblazers 1 Center Ct Ste 200 Portland OR 97227-2103*

WHITTAKER, PAUL EMERSON, physician, army officer; b. Miami, Fla., Dec. 25, 1954; s. Denis Alfred and Della Ann Whittaker; m. Ann Elizabeth Edwards, June 24, 1978; children: Lisa, Tracy, David. BSE, Duke U., 1976; MD, U. Md., 1980; grad., Army War coll., 1996. Diplomate Am. Bd. Family Practice. Commd. capt. U.S. Army, 1976, advanced through grades to col.; div. surgeon 3d Inf. Divsn., Wuerzburg, Germany, 1991-93; staff family physician Madigan Army Med. Ctr., Tacoma, 1993-94, chief family care svc., 1994-95, chief soldier care svc., 1995-96, chief Family Practice Residency Clinic, 1996-98; command surgeon I Corps, Ft. Lewis, Wash., 1998—; clin. instr. U. Wash., Seattle, 1994—; clin. asst. prof. Uniformed Svcs. U., Bethesda, Md., 1994—. Contbr. articles to profl. jours. Active Cub Scouts, Boy Scouts Am., Gig Harbor, Wash., 1997-98. Decorated Bronze Star, Meritorious Svc. medal. Fellow Am. Acd. Family Physicians; mem. AMA, Uniformed Svcs. Acad. Family Physicians (health svcs. com. 1996-97), Phi Kappa Psi. Republican. Unitarian. Avocations: tennis, bridge, skiing, basketball. Home: 4108 4th St NW Gig Harbor WA 98335-7703 Office: Hdqrs I Corps 4th and Pendleton Sts Fort Lewis WA 98433

WHITTAKER, SUE MCGHEE, music educator, pianist; b. Chgo., Feb. 17, 1942; d. Chester O. and Bevie Faye (Smith) McGhee; m. Jerry Roy Whittaker, Aug. 9, 1968; children: Judd, Eric, Holly. BME, Roosevelt U., Chgo., 1965, MM, 1966; DMA, U. Ariz., 1996. Faculty Lee Coll., Cleveland, Tenn., 1965-68; gen. music tchr. Madison Sch. Dist., Phoenix, 1969-72; faculty Ariz. Coll. of the Bible, Phoenix, 1983-92; founding dir. North Valley Sch. of the Arts, Scottsdale, Ariz., 1995—. Guest soloist (as part of 2-piano team Whittaker and Ross) Mesa Symphony, Scottsdale Symphony, Phoenix Symphony, others; accompanist Phoenix Little Theatre, Masterworks Chorale, Met. Opera auditions, Scottsdale Symphony Chorale. Named to Outstanding Young Women of Am., 1967. Mem. Music Educators Nat. Conf., Music Tchrs. Nat. Assn., Nat. Conf. Piano Pedagogy (mem. rsch. com. 1988—), Ariz. State Music Tchrs. Assn. (adjudicator 1980—). Republican. Avocations: antiques, reading, travel. Home: 15009 N 93d Way Scottsdale AZ 85260-2860

WHITTEN, PHILLIP, writer, editor in chief; b. Phila., Aug. 19, 1943; s. Clifton L. and Sylvia (Klaufer) W.; m. Cynthia Lee Waring, Mar. 31, 1967 (div. June 1971); 1 child, Russell; m. Donna Lee Tunnell, May 22, 1993. BA, San Jose State U., 1965, MA, 1967; EdM, Harvard U., 1968, EdD, 1976. Assoc. pub., prodr. CRM, Del Mar, Calif., 1970-71; pub. Dushkin Publ. Group/CBS Group Pubs., Guilford, Conn., 1971-74; assoc. prof. Bentley Coll., Waltham, Mass., 1980-89; rsch. assoc. Harvard U., Cambridge, 1989-93; editor-in-chief Sports Publs., L.A., 1993—; pres. intergrad. sch. coun., Harvard U., 1969-70. Author of 17 books including The Complete Book of Swimming, 1994, Anthropology: Contermorary Perspectives, The Encyclopedia of Anthropology, 1976, The Study of Antropology, 1976, Race and Politics in S. Africa, 1979, Criminology, 1980; prodr. three films; contbr. articles to profl. jours. Mem. Fin. Com., Marblehead, Mass., 1991-93; chmn. Sch. Bd., Marblehead, 1993-94, pres. exec. dir. Internat. Com. for Nigeria/Biafra Relief, 1969-71. Recipient Media award Am. Swim Coaches Assn., Ft. Lauderdale, Fla., 1998. Avocations: swimming, bicycling, traveling. Office: Sports Publs Inc Ste 200 90 Bell Rock Plaza Sedona AZ 86351

WHITTINGHAM, CHARLES EDWARD, thoroughbred race horse owner and trainer; b. San Diego, Apr. 13, 1913; s. Edward and Ellen (Taylor) W.; m. Peggy Boone, Oct. 12, 1944; children: Michael Charles, Charlene. T-rainer thoroughbred horses, Calif., 1930-42; asst. trainer Luro Pub. Stable, N.Y., 1945-49; owner, trainer Whittingham Pub. Stable, Sierra Madre, Calif., 1949—; winner Ky. Derby with Ferdinand, 1986, with Sunday Silence, 1989. Mem. Rep. Senatorial Inner-Circle, Washington, 1983—, nat. advisor bd. Am. Security Council, Washington, 1976—; campaigner mem. Rep. Nat. Com., Washington, 1976—. Served to master sgt. USMC, 1942-45, PTO. Recipient Eclipse awards Thoroughbred Race Track Assn./Daily Racing Form/Nat. Turf Writers Assn., 1971, 82, 89; named to Nat. Racing Hall of Fame, 1974, Brietbard Hall of Fame/Hall of Champions, San Diego, 1993. Mem. Horsemens Benevolent & Protective Assn. (v.p 1976—). Republican. Roman Catholic. Avocation: anything related to thoroughbred race horses. Home and Office: 444 Mariposa Ave Sierra Madre CA 91024-2308

WHYBROW, PETER CHARLES, psychiatrist, educator, author; b. Hertforshire, Eng., June 13, 1939; U.S. citizenship, 1975; s. Charles Ernest and Doris Beatrice (Abbott) W.; children: Katherine, Helen. Student, Univ. Coll., London, 1956-59; MB BS, Univ. Coll., 1962; diploma psychol. medicine, Conjoint Bd., London, 1968; MA (hon.), Dartmouth Coll., 1974, U. Pa., 1984. House officer endocrinology Univ. Coll. Hosp., 1962, sr. house physician psychiatry, 1963-64; house surgeon St. Helier Hosp., Surrey, Eng., 1963; house officer pediatrics Prince of Wales Hosp., London, 1964; resident psychiatry U. N.C. Hosp., 1965-67, instr., research fellow, 1967-68; mem. sci. staff neuropsychiat. research unit Charshalton, Surrey, 1968-69; dir. residency tng. psychiatry Dartmouth Med. Sch., Hanover, N.H., 1969-71; prof. psychiatry Dartmouth Med. Sch., 1970-84, chmn. dept., 1970-78, exec. dean, 1980-84; prof., chmn. dept. psychiatry U. Pa., Phila., 1984-96, Ruth Meltzer prof. psychiatry, 1992; psychiatrist-in-chief Hosp. U. Pa., 1984-96; prof. psychiatry and biobehavioral scis., chmn. dept. psychiatry Sch. Medicine UCLA, 1996—; dir. Neuropsychiatric Inst., 1996—; physician-in-chief Neuropsychiatric Hosp., 1996—; dir. psychiatry Dartmouth Hitchock Affiliated Hosp., 1970-78; vis. scientist NIMH, 1978-79; cons. VA, 1970—, NIMH, 1972— ; chmn. test com. Nat. Bd. Med. Examiners, 1977-84; researcher psychoendrocrinology. Author: Mood Disorders: Toward a New Psychobiology, 1984, The Hibernation Response, 1988, A Mood Apart, 1997; editor: Psychosomatic Medicine, 1977; mem. editl. bd. Cmty. Psychiatry, Psychiat. Times, Directions in Psychiatry, Neuropsychopharmacology, Depression; contbr. articles to profl. jours. Recipient Anclote Manor award psychiat. rsch. U. N.C., 1967, Sr. Investigator award nat. Alliance for Rsch. into Schizophrenia and Depression, 1989; Josiah Macy Jr. Found. scholar, 1978-79; fellow Cen. for Advanced Studies in Behavioral Sci., Stanford, 1993-94; recipient Lifetime Investigator award NDMDA, 1996; decorated Knight of Merit, Sovereign Order of St. John of Jerusalem, 1993. Fellow AAAS, Am. Psychiat. Assn., Royal Coll. Psychiatrist (founding mem.), Am. Coll. Psychiatrists, Ctr. Advanced Study of Behavioral Scis. (hon.), Soc. Psychosomatic Rsch. London (hon.); mem. Am. Assn. Chmn. Depts. Psychiatry (pres. 1977-78), Royal Soc. Medicine, Am. Psychopath Assn., Am. Coll. Neuropsychopharmacology, Soc. Biol. Psychiatry, N.Y. Acad. Scis., Soc. Neurosci., Sigma Xi, Alpha Omega Alpha. Office: UCLA Sch Medicine Neuropsychiat Rsch Inst 760 Westwood Plz Los Angeles CA 90095-8353

WHYTE, NANCY MARIE, performing arts educator; b. Myrtlepoint, Oreg., Mar. 12, 1948; d. Lawrence Edward and Carol Elizabeth (Johnson) Guderian; m. Anthony John Whyte, Aug. 7, 1967 (div. Sept. 1968); 1 child, Charles Lawrence; m. Douglas Brian Graff, June 27, 1971 (div. Oct. 1974); m. Lawrence Hanson, Mar. 12, 1976 (div. Aug. 1984); m. Joseph Paul Deacon, Aug. 10, 1985; 1 child, Nina Alexandra. Student, U. Wash., 1969-72, Am. Sch. Dance, 1972; BA, Evergreen State Coll., 1987. Owner, dir. Nancy Whyte Sch. Ballet, Bellingham, Wash., 1969—; artistic dir. Garden St. Dance Players, Bellingham, Wash., 1969-72; co-dir. Exptl. Performance Workshop, Bellingham, 1975-77; instr. creative dance St. Paul's Primary Sch., Bellingham, 1993-97; facilitator dance workshop Allied Arts/Whatcom Co., Bellingham, 1995—; guest lectr. Western Wash. U., Bellingham, 1976-83, 96—; guest faculty Dance Theatre Northwest, Tacoma, Wash., 1995—. Author: Memoirs of a Child of Theatre Street, 1993; soloist Raduga Folk Ballet/N.Y. Character Ballet, N.Y.C., 1978-79; choreographer numerous ballets, 1972—. Mem. Nat. Dance Assn., Regional Dance Am. (assoc.). Democrat. Avocations: voice, writing. Office: MT Baker Ballet 1412 Cornwall Ave PO Box 2393 Bellingham WA 98227-2393

WHYTE, RONALD M., federal judge; b. 1942. BA in Math., Wesleyan U., 1964; JD, U. So. Calif., 1967. Bar: Calif. 1967, U.S. Dist. Ct. (no. dist.) Calif. 1967, U.S. Dist. Ct. (cen. dist.) Calif. 1968, U.S. Ct. Appeals (9th cir.) 1986. Assoc. Hoge, Fenton Jones & Appel, Inc., San Jose, Calif., 1971-77, mem., 1977-89; judge Superior Ct. State of Calif., 1989-92, U.S. Dist. Ct. (no. dist.) Calif., San Jose, 1992—; judge pro-tempore Superior Ct. Calif., 1977-89; lectr. Calif. Continuing Edn. of Bar, Rutter Group, Santa Clara Bar Assn., State Bar Calif.; legal counsel Santa CLara County Bar Assn., 1986-89; mem. county select com. Criminal Conflicts Program, 1988. Bd. trustees Santa Clara County Bar Assn., 1978-79, 84-85. Lt. Judge Advocate Gen.'s Corps, USNR, 1968-71. Recipient Judge of Yr. award Santa Clara County Trial Lawyers Assn., 1992, Am. Jurisprudence award. Mem. Calif. Judges Assn., Assn. Bus. Trial Lawyers (bd. govs. 1991-93), Santa Clara Inn of Ct. (exec. com. 1993—), San Francisco Bay area Intellectual Property Inn of Ct. (exec. com. 1994—). Office: US Courthouse 280 S 1st St Rm 2112 San Jose CA 95113-3002

WIATROWSKI, CLAUDE ALLAN, computer executive; b. Chgo., Dec. 27, 1946; s. Alex F. and Emilie N. (Macias) W.; m. Margaret A. Ammeson, Nov. 23, 1967; children: Kevin Douglas, Karen Elaine. BS in Physics, Ill. Inst. Tech., 1968; MSEE, U. Ariz., 1970, PhDEE, 1973. Design engr. Burr Brown Research Corp., Tucson, 1973-75; asst. prof. engring. U. Colo., Colorado Springs, 1975-81; pres. Mountain Automation Corp., Woodland Park, Colo., 1976—; chief scientist Scott Sci. and Tech., Colorado Springs, 1981-84; v.p. Parkcon, Inc., Woodland Park, 1986—. Author: Logic Ckts and Microcomputer, 1980, Cog Wheel Route, 1982, From C To Modula-2 And Back, 1987, Teller County, 1987, Visual Object Oriented Programming Using Delphi, 1997; VLSI editor Simulation mag., 1986—, producer, Pikes Peak Route, 1999. Recipient Outstanding Teaching award U. Colo., 1978. Mem. Nat. Ry. Hist. Soc. (bd. dirs. 1977-80). Avocations: RRs, music, photography. Home: PO Box 4590 Woodland Park CO 80866-4590 Office: Mountain Automation Corp PO Box 6020 Woodland Park CO 80866-6020

WICK, DANIEL LEWIS, educator, writer; b. Logan, Utah, Sept. 3, 1944; s. Earl Joseph and Helen Edith (Mack) W.; m. Jeanne Lorraine Hébert, Aug. 22, 1970. AB, San Francisco State U., 1970, MA, 1972; PhD, U. Calif., Davis, 1977. Coord. undergrad. instructional improvement, acad. asst. to vice chancellor acad. affairs U. Calif., 1979—, lectr. integrated studies program, 1980—, dir. summer sessions, 1984—. Author: A Conspiracy of Well-Intentioned Men: The Society of Thirty and the French Revolution, 1987; author several revs.; contbr. more than 70 articles to profl. jours. Recipient William Koerner award Soc. For French Hist. Studies, 1980. Mem. Western Assn. Summer Sessions Adminstrs. (dir. 1990—, pres. 1992-93, Outstanding Adminstr. Achievement award 1987, Best Summer Catalog award 1987). Office: Univ Calif-Davis Office Summer Sessions Davis CA 95616

WICKER, MARJORIE ARLENE, elementary education educator; b. Long Beach, Calif., July 1, 1935; d. Philip Bowen and Ave Marie (Boyer) Kimball; m. Duane Roland Wicker, May 16, 1954 (div. Apr. 1980); children: Randy Stephen, Carole Lyn Wicker Gerchy. AA, Santa Ana Coll., 1973; BA, Calif. State U., Fullerton, 1976, MA, 1983. 4th grade tchr. Castle Rock Sch.-Walnut Sch. Dist., Diamond Bar, Calif., 1976-98; 3rd, 4th and 5th grade tchr. Maple Hill-Walnut (Calif.) Sch. Dist., 1980-90; 3rd grade tchr. Vejar Sch.-Walnut (Calif.) Sch. Dist., 1990—. Mem. Calif. Tchrs. Assn., Calif. State Fullerton Reading Assn., San Gabriel Valley Reading Assn. Republican. Episcopalian. Avocations: boating, hiking, traveling, theater, reading. Home: 1662 S Heritage Cir Anaheim CA 92804-6561 Office: Vejar Sch 20222 Vejar Sch Walnut CA 91789

WICKIZER, CINDY LOUISE, elementary school educator; b. Pitts., Dec. 12, 1946; d. Charles Sr. and Gloria Geraldine (Cassidy) Zimmerman; m. Leon Leonard Wickizer, Mar. 21, 1971; 1 child, Charlyn Michelle. BS, Oreg. State U., 1968. Tchr. Enumclaw (Wash.) Sch. Dist., 1968—. Mem. NEA, Wash. Edn. Assn., Enumclaw Edn. Assn., Am. Rabbit Breeders Assn. (judge, chmn. scholarship found. 1986-87, pres. 1988-94, 96-98, dist. dir. 1994-96, Disting. Svc. award 1987, Hall of Fame 1998), Wash. State Rabbit Breeders Assn. (life, Pres.'s award 1983, 94, sec., dir., v.p. 1995-97), Vancouver Island Rabbit Breeders Assn., Wash. State Rabbit and Cavy Shows Inc. (sec. 1994—), Evergreen Rabbit Assn. (sec., v.p., pres.), Alpha Gamma Delta. Home: 26513 112th St E Buckley WA 98321-9258

WICKWIRE, PATRICIA JOANNE NELLOR, psychologist, educator; b. Sioux City, Iowa; d. William McKinley and Clara Rose (Pautsch) Nellor; m. Robert James Wickwire, Sept. 7, 1957; 1 child, William James. BA cum laude, U. No. Iowa, 1951; MA, U. Iowa, 1959; PhD, U. Tex., Austin, 1971; postgrad. U. So. Calif., UCLA, Calif. State U., Long Beach, 1951-66. Tchr., Ricketts Ind. Schs., Iowa, 1946-48; tchr., counselor Waverly-Shell Rock Ind. Schs., Iowa, 1951-55; reading cons., head dormitory counselor U. Iowa, Iowa City, 1955-57; tchr., sch. psychologist, adminstr. S. Bay Union High Sch. Dist., Redondo Beach, Calif., 1962-82, dir. student svcs. and spl. edn.; cons. mgmt. and edn.; pres. Nellor Wickwire Group, 1981—; mem. exec. bd. Calif. Interagency Mental Health Coun., 1968-72, Beach Cities Symphony Assn., 1970-82; chmn. Friends of Dominguez Hills (Calif.), 1981-85. Lic. ednl. psychologist, marriage, family and child counselor, Calif.; pres. Calif. Women's Caucus, 1993-95. Mem. APA, AAUW (exec. bd., chpt. pres. 1962-72), Nat. Career Devel. Assn. (media chair 1992-98), Am. Assn. Career Edn. (pres. 1991—), L.A. County Dirs. Pupil Svcs. (chmn. 1974-79), L.A. County Personnel and Guidance Assn. (pres. 1977-78), Assn. Calif. Sch. Adminstrs. (dir. 1977-81), L.A. County SW Bd. Dist. Adminstrs. for Spl. Edn. (chmn. 1976-81), Calif. Assn. Sch. Psychologists (bd. dirs. 1981-83), Am. Assn. Sch. Adminstrs., Calif. Assn. for Measurement and Evaluation in Guidance (dir. 1981, pres. 1984-85, 98—), ACA (chmn. Coun. Newsletter Editors 1989-91, mem. com. on women 1989-92, mem. com. on rsch. and knowledge, 1994—, chmn. 1995—, chmn. 1996—, mem. and chmn. bylaws com. 1990—), Assn. Measurement and Eval. in Guidance (Western regional editor 1985-87, conv. chair 1986, editor 1987-90, exec. bd. dirs. 1987-91), Calif. Assn. Counseling and Devel. (exec. bd. 1984—, pres. 1988-89, jour. editor 1990—), Internat. Career Assn. Network (chair 1985—), Pi Lambda Theta, Alpha Phi Gamma, Psi Chi, Kappa Delta Pi, Sigma Alpha Iota. Contbr. articles in field to profl. jours. Office: The Nellor Wickwire Group 2900 Amby Pl Hermosa Beach CA 90254-2216

WIDAMAN, GREGORY ALAN, financial executive, accountant; b. St. Louis, Oct. 4, 1955; s. Raymond Paul Sr. and Louise Agnes (Urschler) W. BS in Bus. Econs. cum laude, Trinity U., 1978. CPA, Tex. Sr. auditor Arthur Andersen & Co., Houston, 1978-82; sr. cons. Price Waterhouse, Houston, 1983-85; fin. advisor to segment pres. Teledyne, Inc., Century City, Calif., 1985-95; sr. mgr. ops. planning for consumer products ABC Broadcasting/TV The Walt Disney Co., Burbank, Calif., 1995-97; dir. internal audit & spl. projects Hilton Hotels Corp., Beverly Hills, Calif., 1997—; cons. Arthur Andersen & Co., Price Waterhouse, Teledyne, Walt Disney Co., Hilton Hotels Corp. Mem. AICPAs, Calif. Soc. CPAs, Christian Bus. Mens com. of U.S.A., World Affairs Coun., MIT/Calif. Tech. Enterprise Forum. Republican. Avocations: white water rafting, water and snow skiing, camping, business. Home: 1416 S Barrington Ave # 4 Los Angeles CA 90025-2363 Office: Hilton Hotels Corp 9336 Civic Center Dr Beverly Hills CA 90210-3604

WIDENER, MARY LEE, non-profit financial executive; b. Schaal, AK, July 6, 1938; d. Mert and Johnnie (Newton) Thomas; m. Warren Widener Sr., Apr. 4, 1959; children: Warren Jr., Michael, Stephen. Diploma, Heald Bus. Coll., 1956; Pub. Adminstrn. Program, U. San Francisco Sch. Profl. Studies, 1978; Hon. Doctor of Laws, John F. Kennedy U., 1979. Adminstrv. asst. to exec. v.p. U. Calif., Berkeley, 1959-69, office mgr. gifts and endowments, 1959-69; urban programming coord. Fed. Home Loan Bank Bd., Washington, 1972-73; housing cons. Ford Found., N.Y.C., 1973-74; exec. dir. Oakland Neighborhood Housing Svcs., Oakland, 1973-76; program cons. Urban Reinvestment Task Force, Washington, 1974-76; pres., CEO Neighborhood Housing Svcs. of Am., Inc., Oakland, 1974—; chmn. bd. dirs. Fed. Home Loan Bank, San Francisco, 1994—; bd. dirs. Pvt. Mortgage Ins. Group , San Francisco, 1995—. Author: (with others) Housing America, 1993. Trustee emeritus San Francisco Found; adv. bd. PEW Charitable Trusts Partnership for Civic Change, Phila.; former dir. KQED, San Francisco; former state chair Calif. Dem. Ctrl. Com., San Francisco; former mem. U.S. Senate Housing Task Force, Washington, Commn. on Homelessness, Oakland. Recipient award Nat. Coalition of 100 Black Women, N.Y., 1989, San Francisco LWV Women who could be Pres. award, 1996. Democratic. Methodist. Avocations: tennis, traveling, golf. Office: Neighborhood Housing Svc Am Inc 1970 Broadway 4th Flr Oakland CA 94612-2216

WIEBE, J. E. N., province official. Lt. gov. Govt. Saskatchewan, Regina, Can. Fax: 306-787-7716. Office: Office of the Lt Gov, Govt House 4607 Dewdney Ave, Regina, SK Canada S4P 3V7

WIEBELHAUS, PAMELA SUE, school administrator, educator; b. Stanley, Wis., May 28, 1952; d. Wilbur Leroy and Marjorie Jean (Bernse) Thorne; m. Mark Robert Wiebelhaus, Apr. 27, 1985; 1 child, Sarah Jean. AS in Nursing, No. Ariz. U., 1973, BS in Gen. Home Econs., 1974. R.N. Ariz., Colo; cert. post secondary vocat. tchr., Colo. Nurse Flagstaff (Ariz.) Community Hosp., 1973-75, Children's Hosp., Denver, 1975, St. Joseph's Hosp., Denver, 1980; office nurse, surg. asst. OB-Gyn Assocs., P.C., Aurora, Colo., 1975-78; nursing coordinator perinatal services Community Hosp. Smaritan Health, Phoenix, 1978-79; nurse, mem. personnel pool Good Samaritan Hosp., Phoenix, 1979-80, J. Bains, MD, Phoenix, 1979-80; file clk. Pharm. Card Systems, Inc., Phoenix, 1979-80; office nurse S. Eisenbaum, MD, Aurora, Colo., 1980; instr., coordinator med. office program T.H. Pickens Tech. Ctr., Aurora (Colo.) Pub. Schs., 1980—; med. supr. healthfair sites, Denver, 1982-85; mem. adv. com. Emily Griffith Opportunity Sch., Denver, 1984-90; mem. survey team North Ctrl. Bd. Edn., 1985, Colo. Bd. Edn., Denver, 1987; book reviewer proposal and new edit. ins. text-reference book W.B. Saunders, 1992—; chair adv. com. Media Ctr., Pickens Tech., 1995—. Acad. scholar No. Ariz. U., 1970, nat. def. grantee, 1970-74; PTA and Elks Club scholar, 1970. Mem. Am. Assn. Med. Assts. (cert.; membership chmn. Capitol chpt. Colo. Soc. 1981). Lutheran.

WIEDEN, DAN G., advertising executive; b. 1945. With Georgia-Pacific Corp., Portland, Oreg., 1967-72; free-lance writer, 1972-78; with McCann-Erickson, Portland, 1978-80, William Cain, Portland, 1980-82; pres. Wieden & Kennedy, Portland, 1982—. Office: Wieden & Kennedy Inc 320 SW Washington St Portland OR 97204-2640*

WIEDER, JUDY SARA, editor-in-chief; b. N.Y.C., Mar. 22, 1944; d. Jack E and Paula (Rosenberg) W. BA, Univ. Calif., Berkeley, 1966. Editor, creater Right On! Mag., Hollywood, Calif., 1969-72; songwriter L.A., 1976—; editor BLAST, Encino, Calif., 1987-88; contbr. editor RIP Mag., L.A., 1988-89; assoc. editor Creem Mag., L.A., 1989-90; editor Genre Mag., L.A., 1991-93; art and entertainment editor The Advocate, L.A., 1993-94, sr. arts & entertainment editor, 1995, exec. editor, 1996, editor-in-chief, 1996—. Author: 100 Soul Stars, 1971, How To Make A Record Deal, 1970. Recipient 3 Gold Albums, 1977, 78, Grammy award, 1978, Platinum Album award, 1990; named #1 dance hit song Billboard Mag., 1997. Mem. Nat. Acad. of Recording Arts & Scis., Human Rights Campaign. Avocation: tiling. Office: The Advocate 6922 Hollywood Blvd Los Angeles CA 90028-6117

WIEDERRICK, ROBERT, museum director. Pres. Lemhi County Hist. Mus., Salmon, Idaho. Office: Lemhi County Hist Mus 210 Main St Salmon ID 83467-0645*

WIEDLE, GARY EUGENE, real estate management company executive; b. San Antonio, July 28, 1944; s. Eugene Wiley and Melba Frances (Keeney) W.; m. Regena Zokosky, July 7, 1977 (div. June 1983); children: Ana Lauren, Aric Brandt. AA, Coll. of the Desert, Palm Desert, Calif., 1975; BA, Calif. State U., Long Beach, 1967; MA, U. So. Calif., 1973. Lic. real estate broker, Calif.; cert. profl. community assn. mgr. Adminstrv. asst. City of Inglewood, Calif., 1967-68, asst. city mgr., 1970-74; exec. dir. Coachella Valley Assn. of Govts., Palm Desert, 1974-84; mgr. The Springs Country Club, Rancho Mirage, Calif., 1984-87; prof. polit. sci. Coll of the Desert, Palm Desert, 1987-90; owner Fortune West Mgmt., Palm Desert, 1990—; cons. polit. orgns., bus. and community groups, Riverside County, Calif., 1984—. State comdr. DAV, Dept. Calif., 1982. 1st lt. U.S. Army, 1968-70, Vietnam. Decorated Bronze Star for valor, Purple Heart, Commendation of valor. Mem. Am. Inst. Cert. Planners (cert. planner), Cmty. Assns. Inst. (pres. 1986-89), Calif. Assn. Cmty. Mgrs., Real Estate Educators Cert. Inst., Bd. Realtors Palm Desert, Am. Planning Assn., Western Govtl. Rsch. Assn., Gideons Internat. Republican. Lutheran. Avocation: reading history. Home: 82-362 Gable Dr Indio CA 92201-7439 Office: Fortune West Mgmt GE Wiedle Co 73-900 El Paseo Rear Palm Desert CA 92260-4336

WIEFELS, PAUL HAROLD, management consultant; b. Los Angeles, Jan. 20, 1954; s. Frank Leonard and Nancy Jean (Allen) W.; B.S., U. So. Calif., 1975, M.B.A., 1977. Assoc. product mgr. Nissan Motor Corp., Gardena, Calif., 1977-79; account exec., Foote, Cone and Belding, Los Angeles, 1979-80; account supr. SSC & B:Lintas, Los Angeles, 1980-81; account supr. Ketchum Communications, San Francisco, 1981-82; advt. mgr. Apple Computer, Inc., Cupertino, Calif., 1982-85, group mgr. internat. mktg., 1985-88; dir. product mktg. Ingres Corp., Alameda, Calif., 1988-90, dir. mktg. consulting, Landor Assocs., 1990-91, sr. ptnr. The Chasm Group, 1991—. Mem. Am. Mktg. Assn., Commerce Assocs. U. So. Calif. Office: 411 Borel Ave Ste 550 San Mateo CA 94402-3520

WIELGUS, RONALD STANLEY, retired architect, entomologist, author; b. Chgo., Aug. 22, 1933; s. Roman and Josephine (Gorski) W.; m. Alyn Joy Hurd, Dec. 26, 1956; children: Dale, Jeanne, Roger. BArch, Ill. Inst. Tech., 1956. Registered architect, Calif., Ariz., Nev., Ill. Archtl. draftsman various archtl. firms, Chgo., 1958-59; project architect various archtl. firms, Phoenix, 1959-65, Wilsey & Ham, San Mateo, Calif., 1965-67; pres., owner Ronald S. Wielgus Architect, Phoenix, 1967-82, Sierra Vista, Ariz., 1982-89, Tucson, 1989-94. Author: Arizona's Golden Secret, 1992, Yours For the Taking,

1993, Grow Your Own Crystals, 1994, Arizona's Little-Known Gold Placers, 1996; contbr. articles to Jour. Rsch on the Lepidoptera, Bull. of the Allyn Mus. Served with U.S. Army, 1956-58. New species of moth named Argyotaenia Wielgusi, Smithsonian Instn., 1990, Gazoryctra Wielgusi, U. Conn., 1991, Carmenta Wielgusi, State of Calif., 1989. Avocations: geology, gold prospecting, electronics. Home: 1230 E Placita Del Cervato Tucson AZ 85718-2946

WIEMER, ROBERT ERNEST, film and television producer, writer, director; b. Highland Park, Mich., Jan. 30, 1938; s. Carl Ernest and Marion (Israelian) W.; m. Rhea Dale McGeath, June 14, 1958; children: Robert Marshall, Rhea Whitney. BA, Ohio Wesleyan U., 1959. Ind. producer, 1956-60; dir. documentary ops. WCBS-TV, N.Y.C., 1964-67; ind. producer of television, theatrical and bus. films N.Y.C., 1967-72; exec. producer motion pictures and TV, ITT, N.Y.C., 1973-84; pres. subs. Blue Marble Co., Inc., Telemontage, Inc., Alphaventure Music, Inc., Betaventure Music, Inc. ITT, 1973-84; founder, chmn., chief exec. officer Tigerfilm, Inc., 1984—; chmn., bd. dirs. Golden Tiger Pictures, Hollywood, Calif., 1988—; pres, CEO Tuxedo Pictures Corp., Hollywood, Calif., 1993—; bd. dirs., v.p. prodn. Las Vegas Internat. Film Festival; v.p. prodn. Cinevegas. Writer, prodr., dir.: (feature films) My Seventeenth Summer, Witch's Sister, Do Me a Favor, Anna to the Infinite Power, Somewhere, Tomorrow, Night Train to Kathmandu; exec. prodr.: (children's TV series) Big Blue Marble (Emmy and Peabody awards); dir. (TV episodes) New York Undercover, seaQuest DSV, Star Trek: The Next Generation, Deep Space Nine, The Adventures of Superboy; composer (country-western ballad) Tell Me What To Do. Recipient CINE award, 1974, 76, 77, 79, 81, Emmy award, 1978. Mem. NATAS, ASCAP, Info. Film Producers Assn. (Outstanding Producer award), Nat. Assn. TV Programming Execs., Am. Women in Radio and TV, N.J. Broadcasters Assn., Dirs. Guild Am., v.p., bd. mem. CineVegas The Las Vegas Internat. Film Festival. Office: Golden Tiger Pictures 3896 Ruskin St Las Vegas NV 89147-1097

WIENER, VALERIE, senator, communications consultant, positioning strategist, writer; b. Las Vegas, Nev., Oct. 30, 1948; d. Louis Isaac Wiener and Tui Ava Knight. BJ, U. Mo., 1971, MA, 1972; MA, U. Ill., Springfield, 1974; postgrad., McGeorge Sch. Law, 1976-79. Producer Checkpoint Sta. KOMU-TV, Columbia, Mo., 1972-73; v.p., owner Broadcast Assocs., Inc., Las Vegas, 1972-86; pub. affairs dir. First Ill. Cable TV, Springfield, 1973-74; editor Ill. State Register, Springfield, 1973-74; prodr. and talent Nevada Realities Sta. KLVX-TV, Las Vegas, 1974-75; account exec. Sta. KBMI (now KFMS), Las Vegas, 1975-79; nat. traffic dir. six radio stas., Las Vegas, Albuquerque and El Paso, Tex., 1979-80; exec. v.p., gen. mgr. Stas. KXKS and KKJY, Albuquerque, 1980-81; exec. adminstr. Stas. KSET AM/FM, KVEG, KFMS and KKJY, 1981-83; press sec. U.S. Congressman Harry Reid, Washington, 1983-87; adminstrv. asst Friends for Harry Reid, Nev., 1986; press sec. U.S. Senator Harry Reid, Washington, 1987-88; owner Wiener Comm. Group, Las Vegas, 1988—; senator State of Nev., 1996—. Author: Power Communications: Positioning Yourself for High Visibility (Fortune Book Club main selection 1994, Money Book Club selection 1995), Gang Free: Friendship Choices for Today's Youth, 1995, 2d edit., 1996, The Nesting Syndrome: Grown Children Living at Home, 1997; contbg. writer The Pacesetter, ASAE's Comm. News. Sponsor Futures for Children, Las Vegas, Albuquerque, El Paso, 1979-83; mem. El Paso Exec. Women's Coun., 1981-83; mem. VIP bd. Easter Seals, El Paso, 1982; media chmn. Gov.'s Coun. Small Bus., 1989-93; mem. Gov.'s Commn. on Aging, 1997—, Clark Coun. Sch. Dist. and Bus. Cmty. PAYBAC Spkrs. and Partnership Programs, 1989—; med. dir. 1990 Conf. on Women, Gov. of Nev.; media chmn. Congl. Awards Coun., 1989-93; vice-chmn. Gov.'s Commn. on Post-secondary Edn., 1992-96; bd. dirs. BBB So. Nev. Named Outstanding Vol., United Way, El Paso, 1983, SBA Nev. Small Bus. Media Adv. of Yr., 1992; recipient Woman of Achievement in Media award, 1992, Outstanding Achievement award Nat. Fedn. Press Women, 1991, Disting. Leader award Nat. Assn. for Cmty. Leadership, 1993, over 120 other comm. awards. Mem. Nev. Press Women (numerous 1st place media awards 1990—), Nat. Spkrs. Assn., Small Pubs. Assn. N.Am. (media chmn., nat. rep. So. Nev. 1990-91, Nev. Adv. of Yr. award 1992), Dem. Press Secs. Assn., El Paso Assn. Radio Stas., U.S. Senate Staff Club, Las Vegas C. of C. (Circle of Excellence award 1993), Soc. Profl. Journalists. Democrat. Avocations: reading, writing, fitness training, pub. speaking, community involvement. Office: 1500 Foremaster Ln Ste 2 Las Vegas NV 89101-1103

WIENS, BEVERLY JO, educator; b. Oildale, Calif., Oct. 2, 1947; d. Ernest and Irene Josephine (Klassen) Bartel; m. Gary D. Wiens, Aug. 19, 1967; children: Nicole Marie Wiens Cook, Katie Lyn Wiens. BA, San Jose State U., 1969, MA, 1971; MA, Santa Clara U., 1992. Lic. counselor, Calif. Tchr. West Valley Coll., Saratoga, Calif., 1971-76, San Jose (Calif.) City Coll., 1974-75, San Jose State U., 1978; marriage, family therapist Coalition of Counseling Centers, Los Gatos, Calif., 1982-86; assoc. prof. San Jose Bible Coll., 1982-87; prof., dept. chair San Jose Christian Coll., 1988—; lectr. in field. Mem. Am. Assn. Christian Counselors, Am. Counseling Assn., Assn. Religious Value in Counseling, Assn. Counselor Training, Supervision, Calif. Assn. Marital Family Therapists. Republican. Mem. Mennonite Brethren. Office: San Jose Christian Coll 790 S 12th St San Jose CA 95112-2304

WIESE, KEVIN GLEN, entrepreneur; b. Ogden, Utah, Mar. 19, 1960; s. Glen James and Kay Jon (Mildon) W. BS in Fin. and Mktg., U. Utah, 1982; MBA, Golden State U., 1987; PhD in Internat. Bus., Columbia Pacific U., 1987. Fin. advisor Silverstein Fin., L.A., 1983-85; fin. cons. Christopher Weil & Co., Inc., L.A., 1985-87; chief exec. officer, pres. Internat. Venture Enterprises, L.A., 1988—, Internat. Venture Rsch., L.A., 1988—, Internat. Leadership Performance Advisors, L.A., 1988—, Internat. Wealth Group, Ltd., L.A., 1988—; chief oper. officer Albatross Sportcoaer, Inc., Huntington Beach, Calif., 1990—; adj. prof. Loyola Marymount U., Los Angeles, 1986-87, Coll. for Fin. Planning Denver, 1986-87; cons. United Industries, L.A., 1987-88, Rouse Fin. Network, Phoenix, 1989—; researcher Harvard U., Boston, 1987—, Oxford U., Eng., 1987—, Stanford U., Palo Alto, Calif., 1987—, Cambridge U., Eng., 1987—; cons. Concierge Mgmt. Group, 1990, Heuristics Search, Inc., 1990; resident bus. expert on Fin. News Network cable program The Am. Entrepreneur; pub. speaker in field. Pub. Trend Newsletter for Small Bus. Entrepreneurs, 1990—. Bus. liaison Mega-Cities Project L.A. Sect., 1988—; vol. Hugh O'Brian Youth Found., L.A., 1986-88, assoc. mem. community leadership, 1989—; mem. HOBY Assocs. Mem. Internat. Assn., for Fin. Planning (bd. dirs. L.A. chpt. 1985-86, sec., treas. 1984-85), Inst. Cert. Fin. Planning. Republican. Avocations: fencing, karate, skiing, romance langs., mus. instruments. Office: Internat Wealth Group Ltd 7101 La Tijera Blvd Apt 207 Los Angeles CA 90045-2177

WIESE, NEVA, critical care nurse; b. Hunter, Kans., July 23, 1940; d. Amil H. and Minnie (Zemke) W. Diploma, Grace Hosp. Sch. Nursing, Hutchinson, Kans., 1962; BA in Social Sci., U. Denver, 1971; BSN, Met. State Coll., 1975; MS in Nursing, U. Colo., Denvr, 1978; postgrad., U. N.Mex., 1986; PhD, Kennedy Western U., 1999. RN, N.Mex.; CCRN. Cardiac ICU nurse U. N.Mex. Hosp., Albuquerque; coord. critical care edn. St. Vincent Hosp., Santa Fe, charge nurse CCU, clin. nurse III intensive and cardiac care. Recipient Mary Atherton Meml. award for clin. excellence St. Vincent Hosp., 1986. Mem. ANA (cert. med. surg. nurse), AACN (past pres., sec. N.Mex. chpt., Clin. Excellence award 1991, Lifetime Achievement award 1997), N.Mex. League Nursing (past v.p., bd. dirs., sec., membership com. 1992-97).

WIETING, GARY LEE, federal agency executive; b. Huron, S.D., Apr. 24, 1937; s. LeRoy Charles and Edna Lorraine (Crawley) W.; m. Nancy Lou Clark, July 9, 1961 (div. 1991); children: Kevin Clark, Brian David; m. Julia Gladys Eli, Dec. 31, 1998. *Gary Wieting's father and mother were highly successful farmers near Blackstone, Illinois for 40 years, retiring in 1977. His maternal grandparents, Clifton Crawley and Rose Hendershot Crawley, homesteaded in Montana in the 1930's. His paternal great-grandparents immigrated from Northern Germany to South Dakota in the 1870's. His paternal grandparents, Willie George Wieting and Mary Helen Puffer, were married in Hitchcock, South Dakota, on January 1, 1898.* BA, U. Ill., 1961; MBA, Lake Forest Sch. Mgmt., 1983; travel and tourism diploma, Heritage Coll., Las Vegas, Nev., 1997. Logistics mgr. U.S. Army, Vietnam, 1967-68, NATO/Shape Support Group, Belgium, 1968-72, 8th U.S. Army, Korea, 1972-73, U.S. Army Readiness Region, Ft. Sheridan, Ill., 1973-77, U.S. Army Recruiting Command, Ft. Sheridan, Ill., 1977-83; rsch. and devel. logistics mgr. Belvoir Rsch. and Devel. Ctr., Ft. Belvoir, Va., 1983-85, 88-90; personal svcs. logistics mgr. Hdqrs. Dept. of Army, Washington, 1985-88; logistics mgr., assoc. program mgr. for adv. automation FAA, Washington, 1990-94; ret., 1994. *Gary Wieting has thirty-five years of progressively responsible experience with the United States Army and the Federal Aviation Administration. While at Headquarters, Department of the Army in Washington, DC, he chaired the committee revising and implementing the Department of Defense policy on evacuation of human remains from military operations, a policy that was in effect during Operation Desert Storm in 1990-91. He finished his government career as a senior logistician developing supply, maintenance and training support for the $7 billion Air Traffic Automation System, the next generation of the Federal Aviation Administration's air traffic control system.* Travel counselor, 1997; mem. So. Nev. Area Mil. Retiree Coun., 1998. Capt. U.S. Army, 1957-77, ret. lt. col., 1986. Decorated Army Commendation medal, Bronze Star medal; recipient Comdr. Award for Civilian Svc., U.S. Army, 1988. Avocations: collecting art, U.S. and internat. travel, playing bridge. Home: 2421 Flower Spring St Las Vegas NV 89134-1822

WIGFIED-PHILLIP, RUTH GENIVEA, genealogist, author, researcher; b. Couer d' Alene, Idaho, Dec. 1, 1918; d. Arthur and Jenivea Caroline (Crisp) Wigfield; m. Milton Fred Phillip, May 14, 1942 (dec. Nov., 1984); children: Rochelle Ruth, Gloria Genivea, Nancy Lenore, Douglas Fred, Andrea Arleen. BA, U. Montana, Missoula, 1939; registered genealogist, Augustine Genealogy Sch., Torrance, Calif., 1985, Desc. of William the Conquerer, 1997, Desc. of Companion of William Conquerer, 1997. Med. technician Deaconess Hosp., Great Falls, Mont., 1939-42; social worker Mont. State Welfare Dept., Helena, 1944-46; musical instr. Mont. Music Tchrs. Assn., Great Falls, 1947-62, Missoula, 1962-72; genealogy rschr. Phillip Heritage House, Missoula, 1962-66, writer, author, 1972—. Author, editor: (5 newsletters on genealogy) Wigfield Genealogy, 1972—, Crisp Genealogy, 1981—, Lipscomb Genealogy, 1981, Martin Genealogy, 1981, New Race, 1985—. Mem. Immanuel Luth. Ch., Sunday sch. supt., 1965-72; sec. Mont. State Music Tchrs. Union, 1969-71. Recipient music scholarship Harlowtown Music Dept., Harlowtown, Mont., 1932-35. Mem. DAR (regent Bitterroot chpt. 1973-75, state Indian chmn. 1976-90, 25 yr. h on. award Bitterroot chpt. 1997), Guild of St. Margaret of Scotland (grand dame Mont., 1986—), Eastern Star (organist), Rebecca Lodge (organist). Avocations: bridge, garden club, travel, fishing, golf. Home and Office: Phillip Genealogy Heritage House 605 Benton Ave Missoula MT 59801-8633

WIGGINS, CHARLES EDWARD, judge; b. El Monte, Calif., Dec. 3, 1927; s. Louis J. and Margaret E. (Fanning) W.; m. Yvonne L. Boots, Dec. 30, 1946 (dec. Sept. 1971); children: Steven L., Scott D.; m. Betty J. Koontz, July 12, 1972. B.S., U. So. Calif., 1953, LL.B., 1956; LL.B. (hon.) Ohio Wesleyan, 1975, Han Yang. U., Seoul, Korea, 1976. Bar: Calif. 1957, D.C. 1978. Lawyer, Wood & Wiggins, El Monte, Calif., 1956-66, Musick, Peeler & Garrett, Los Angeles, 1979-81, Pierson, Ball & Dowd, Washington, 1982-84, Pillsbury, Madison & Sutro, San Francisco, 1984; mem. 90-95th congresses from 25th and 39th Calif. Dists.; judge U.S. Ct. Appeals (9th cir.), 1984-96, sr. judge, 1996—. Mayor City of El Monte, Calif., 1964-66; mem. Planning Commn. City of El Monte, 1956-60; mem. Commn. on Bicentennial of U.S. Constitution, 1985—, mem. standing com. on rules of practice and procedure, 1987—. Served to 1st lt. U.S. Army, 1945-48, 50-52, Korea. Mem. ABA, State Bar Calif., D.C. Bar Assn. Republican. Lodge: Lions.*

WIGGINS, KIM DOUGLAS, artist, art dealer; b. Roswell, N.Mex., Apr. 8, 1959; s. Walton Wray Wiggins and Barbara Jo (Chesser) Ortega; m. Mary Allison Raney, Sept. 4, 1977 (div. May 1984); children: Rebekah, Mona; m. Maria C. Trujillo, June 17, 1995; children: Gianna Josiah, Elisha Douglas. Student, Ea. N.Mex. U., Roswell, 1977, 83-84, San Antonio Coll., 1978-79, Ind. Bapt. Coll., Dallas, 1982-83, Santa Fe Inst. Fine Art, 1989, Rhema C.B.S., Tulsa, 1997. Dir. Clarke-Wiggins Fine Art, Palm Springs, Calif., 1986-89; owner, mgr. Wiggins Fine Art, Santa Fe, 1989-93, Wiggins Studio, Roswell, 1991—; owner Print & Promise, Roswell, 1996—; cons. Mus. N.Mex., Santa Fe, 1992—. Cline Fine Art, Santa Fe, 1993—. One man shows at Altermann Morris Galleries, Houston, Dallas, 1992-99, Studio Gallery, Laguna Beach, San Diego, 1998; exhibited in group shows Pa. Acad. Fine Art, Phila., 1992-96, M.H. DeYoung Mus., San Francisco, 1993-96, Autry Mus. Western Heritage, L.A., 1999; represented in permanent collections Mus. of N.Mex., Anschutz Collection, Denver; editor: K. Douglas Wiggins: Sense of Spirit, 1993; pub., contbr.: Art of the American West, 1999. Mem. NRA, HOG, CMA, Internat. Platform Assn., Soc. Am. Impressionists, Coun. for Art of West, Gladney Ctr., Assurance Home. Republican. Avocations: printmaking, poetry, pottery, motorcycles, scuba diving. Home: 6 El Arco Iris Dr Roswell NM 88201-7711 Studio: Altermann & Morris Galleries 225 Canyon Rd Santa Fe NM 87501-2755

WIGHTMAN, THOMAS VALENTINE, rancher, researcher; b. Sacramento, Oct. 7, 1921; s. Thomas Valentine and Pearl Mae (Cutbirth) W.; m. Lan Do Wightman. Student, U. Calif., Berkeley, 1945-46, B of Animal Husbandry, U. Calif., Davis, 1949; student, Cal. Poly. Inst., 1949-50. Jr. aircraft mechanic SAD (War Dept.), Sacramento, Calif., 1940-42; rancher Wightman Ranch, Elk Grove, Calif., 1950-59; machinest Craig Ship-Bldg. Co., Long Beach, Calif., 1959-70; rancher Wightman Ranch, Austin, Nev., 1970-88; dir. Wightman Found., Sacramento, 1988—. Dir. med. rsch. Staff sgt. U.S. Army, 1942-45. Recipient scholarship U.S. Fed. Govt., 1945-50. Fellow NRA, VFW, U. Calif. Alumni Assn., U. Calif. Davis Alumni Assn., Bowles Hall Assn.; mem. Confederate Air Force, The Oxford Club. Republican. Avocations: antique automobiles and aircraft. Home and Office: Wightman Found 2130 51st St Apt 129 Sacramento CA 95817-1507

WIGINTON, MORRIS S., III, data processing executive; b. Austin, Tex., June 13, 1950; s. Morris S. Wiginton Jr. and Bernice (Moreland) Lilley; m. Deborah Joyce, Aug. 8, 1978 (dec. Aug. 1984); m. Gerry, Feb. 7, 1987. U. Houston, 1972. Mgr. transit dept. 1st City Bank, Houston, 1973-76; br. mgr. Univ. Computer Svcs., San Antonio, 1976-80; gen. mgr. Universal Computer Forms, Inc., Houston, 1980-87; regional mgr., Western U.S. Universal Computer Systems, Houston, 1983-87, v.p. tng. and installations, 1982-87, v.p. mktg., 1984-87. Pres. Netcom Bus. Technologies, 1988-93; pres., CEO Summit Consulting, 1996—. Mem. Mensa, Rocky Mt. Elk Found. Republican. Avocations: flying (pvt. pilot), hunting, skiing, billiards, writing. Home: 2989 S Olympia Cir Evergreen CO 80439-8833

WIGTON, CHESTER MAHLON, family physician; b. Pueblo, Colo., Jan. 12, 1928; s. Washington Irving and Bessie Marie (Ramsey) W.; m. Marjorie Chanak, Aug. 29, 1953 (dec. Jan. 1981); children: Robin, Renee, Kent, Lance, Bruce, Scott; m. Anita Kay Nelson, July 4, 1993; children: Sallie Michelle Short, Sadie Kay Short. BS cum laude, Colo. Coll., 1950; MD, U. Colo., Denver, 1954. Diplomate Am. Bd. Family Practice. Intern Swedish Hosp., Seattle, 1954-55; pvt. practice family medicine, Durango, Colo., 1957—; emeritus active Med. Mercy Hosp., Durango, 1990—, v.p. staff, 1970-73; med. dir. Hacienda Nursing Home, Bloomfield, N.Mex., 1992-95. Pres. CAMP Inc., Durango, 1970, CEOW Inc., Durango, 1964; treas. Tamarron Owners Assn. Bd., Durango, 1986-95; sec. Durango Sch. Bd., 1969-73; dir. San Juan Devel., Durango, 1971. Lt. (j.g.) USPHS, 1955-57; sec. Cmty. Hosp. Bd., Durango, 1986-92. Fellow Am. Acad. Family Practice; mem. Durango C. of C. (pres. 1965-66), Durango Rotary Club (pres. 1968), Electra Lake Sporting Club (pres. 1982-85), Delta Epsilon, Sigma Nu, Nu Sigma Nu. Republican. Presbyterian. Avocations: skiing, tennis, golf, fishing, hunting. Home: 151 Riverview Dr Durango CO 81301-4349 Office: 3575 Main Ave Durango CO 81301-4028

WIKSTROM, FRANCIS M., lawyer; b. Missoula, Mont., Aug. 20, 1949. BS, Weber State Univ., 1971; JD, Yale U., 1974. Bar: Utah 1974, U.S. Supreme Ct. 1980. Asst. U.S. atty. U.S. Dist. Ct. Utah, 1979-80, U.S. atty., 1981; mem., chmn. litigation dept. Parsons Behle & Latimer, Salt Lake City; mem. Utah State Bar Commn.; chmn. Utah Judicial Conduct Commn.; mem. adv. com. on rules civil procedure Utah Supreme Ct.; mem. 10th Cir. Adv. Com. Fellow Am. Bar Found., Am. Coll. Trial Lawyers; mem. ABA, Salt Lake County Bar Assn. (pres. 1993-94), Am. Inns Ct. II (master bench). Office: Parsons Behle & Latimer PO Box 45898 One Utah Ctr 201 S Main St Ste 1800 Salt Lake City UT 84111-2218

WIKTOROWICZ, ANDREW CHARLES, consultant technology-based business development; b. Valevade, India, Nov. 25, 1945; came to U.S., 1951; s. Janusz Stanislaus and Kristina (Dziedzic) W.; m. Karen Wolff, Aug. 15, 1993; children by previous marriage: Tanya, Daniel, Dustin. BS in Physics, Ill. Inst. Tech., 1967. Instrument physicist CPC Internat., Argo, Ill., 1967-70; project engr. Fluor Corp., Irvine, Calif., 1970-73; engring. group leader Bechtel Power Corp., Norwalk, Calif., 1973-74; engr. chief controls Ameron Process Systems Div., Santa Ana, Calif., 1974-76; v.p. J.P.W. Industries, Orange, Calif., 1976-78; pres. Automated Dynamics Corp., Laguna Hills, Calif., 1978-85; v.p. Nova Power, Inc., Santa Ana, 1985-89; pres. Unigen Corp., Thousand Oaks, Calif., 1990—; exec. dir. Western Coun. of Constrn. Consumers, Torrance, Calif., 1995—; bd. dirs. Unigen, Mission Viejo, Calif., 1987—; prof. engring. Calif. Dept. Consumer Affairs, Sacramento, 1975, 78. Co-author: Instrument Engineers' Handbook-Programmable Controllers, 1985; contbr. articles to profl. jours. Expert examiner control systems Calif. Dept. Consumer Affairs-Bd. Profl. Engring., Sacramento, 1976—; trustee welfare fund Internat. Brotherhood of Electrical Workers, Orange, 1976-80. Undergrad. research grantee NSF, Washington, 1966. Mem. Instrument Soc. Am. Internat. (v.p. 1981-83, bd. dirs. 1981-83, fin. com. 1983—, dir. publs., 1983—, long-range planning com. 1988—), Orange County Instrument Soc. Am., Western Coun. Constrn. Consumers (program com. 1987, exec. dir. 1995—). Republican. Roman Catholic. Avocations: racquetball, horseback riding, golfing, tennis, chess. Home and Office: Unigen 1941 Coventry Ct Thousand Oaks CA 91362-1810

WILCOX, BRENT KEITH, information systems specialist; b. Seattle, Wash., Sept. 2, 1952; s. Archie Elmer Wilcox and Lillian Eileen Miller; m. Valerie Jean Munn (div.); m. Susan Maria Dixon, Nov. 9, 1981; 1 child, Benjamin Virgil. BA, U. Wash., 1974; MS, Troy State U., 1978; MA, Webster U., 1991. Advanced through ranks to maj. USAF, 1974-94; chief ops. 6947 ESG, Homestead AFB, Fla., 1980-82; chief C3CM ops. 690.3 ESG, OSan Air Base, Korea, 1982; jr. officer career cryptologic program Nat. Security Agy., Ft. Meade, Md., 1983-85; chief flight ops. 6920 ESG, Misawa Air Base, Japan, 1985-88; program mgr. CONSTANT WEB HQ Electronic Security Commd., San Antonio, 1988-91; chief current analysis and reporting ctr. Europe 6950 ESG, RAF Chicksands, Eng., 1991-94; info. tech. mgr. Johnson Matthey Electronics, Spokane, Wash., 1994—; Cert. software mgr., 1994, radio engr. Soc. Broadcast Engrs. Author: Wilcox History, 1988. Asst. precinct committeeman 32d Dist., King County, Wash., 1973; v.p. sch. bd. Misawa Christian Acad., Misawa Air Base, 1987, pres., 1988. Decorated Joint Svc. Commendation medal (2), Air Force Commendation medal (2), Air Force Achievement medal. Mem. Assn. Profl. Inventory Control Sys., Friends of Seven, Guthrie County Geneal. Soc. Republican. Methodist. Avocations: genealogy, photography, woodworking, fitness, wine. Home: 727 E Glencrest Dr Spokane WA 99208-9723 Office: Johnson Matthey Electronics 15128 E Euclid Ave Spokane WA 99216-1895

WILCOX, EDWARD R., engineering executive; b. Youngstown, Ohio, Apr. 11, 1953; s. Edward R. And Dolores (Vanca) W. Enlisted USAF, 1976; maintenance technician USAF, Hickham AFB, Hawaii, 1977-81; maintenance instr. USAF, Norton AFB, Calif., 1982-84, technician, 1984-93, prodr. tng. films, 1987-91, quality assurance inspector, 1991-92, electro-optics rschr., 1990-93, non-destructive inspection technician, 1992-93; owner Wilcox Engring. & Rsch., Vacaville, Calif., 1993—; mem. mil. S.W.A.T. team 63 Security Police Squadron, San Bernardino, Calif., 1984-93. Night vision repair technician San Bernardino Sheriff's Dept., 1992-93, San Bernardino Police Dept., 1992-93. Roman Catholic. Achievements include patents in field; finding of repairability of MX-10160/UV. Avocation: helping people. Office: Wilcox Engring & Rsch PO Box 6503 Vacaville CA 95696-6503

WILCOX, MARY MARKS, Christian education consultant, educator; b. Madison, Wis., Apr. 23, 1921; d. Roy and Mary Celia (Leary) Marks; m. Ray Everett Wilcox, Nov. 28, 1942; children: Peter, Anne, Susan, Steven. BA, U. Wis., 1942; MRE, Iliff Sch. Theology, Denver, 1968. Cert. Christian educator. Cons. local chs., Lakewood, Littleton, Wheat Ridge, Colo., 1963-74; instr., leader numerous seminars throughout U.S. and Can., 1963—; interim parish cons. 1st Presbyn. Ch., Lakewood, 1988-90; profl. assoc. for faith devel. 1st Presbyn. Ch., Lakewood, Colo., 1993-97; mem. adj. faculty Iliff Sch. Theology, 1970—. Author: Developmental Journey, 1979; co-author: Viewpoints, 1998; contbr. articles to various publs., chpts. to books. Trustee, mem. exec. bd. Nat. Ghost Ranch Found., Abiquiu, N. Mex., 1983-93. Recipient award Iliff Alumni Assn., 1989. Mem. Assn. Profs. and Researchers in Religious Edn. (presenter), Religious Edn. Assn., Assn. Presbyn. Christian Educators (past mem. exec. bd.), Moral Edn. Assn. Democrat. Presbyterian. Home: 3590 Estes St Wheat Ridge CO 80033-5933

WILCOX, RHODA DAVIS, elementary education educator; b. Boyero, Colo., Nov. 4, 1918; d. Harold Francis and Louise Wilhelmina (Wilfert) Davis; m. Kenneth Edward Wilcox, Nov. 1945 (div. 1952); 1 child, Michele Ann. BA in Elem. Edn., U. No. Colo., 1941; postgrad., Colo. Coll., 1955-65. Life cert. tchr., Colo. Elem. tchr. Fruita (Colo.) Pub. Sch., 1938-40, Boise, Idaho, 1940-42; sec. civil service USAF, Ogden, Utah, 1942-43, Colorado Springs, Colo., 1943-44; sec. civil service hdqtrs. command USAF, Panama Canal Zone; sec. Tech. Libr., Eglin Field, Fla., 1945-46; elem. tchr. Colorado Springs Sch. Dist. 11, 1952-82, mem. curriculum devel. com., 1968-69; lectr. civic, profl. and edn. groups, Colo.; judge for Excellence in Literacy Coldwell Bankers Sch. Dist. 11, Colo. Coun. Internat. Reading. Assn. Author: Man on the Iron Horse, 1959, Colorado Slim and His Spectacklers, 1964, (with Jean Pierpoint) Changing Colorado (Social Studies), 1968-69, The Founding Fathers and Their Friends in Denver Posse of the Westerners Brand Bank, 1971, The Bells of Manitou, 1973, (with Len Froisland) In the Footsteps of the Founder, 1993. Mem. hist. adv. bd. State Colo., Denver, 1976; mem. Garden of the Gods master plan rev. com. City of Colorado Springs, 1987—; mem. cemetery adv. bd. City of Colorado Springs, 1988-91; mem. adv. bd. centennial com., 1971; mem. steering com. Spirit of Palmer Festival, 1986; judge Nat. Hist. Day, U. Colo., Colorado Springs, and Colo. Coll., Colorado Springs; hon. trustee Palmer Found., 1986—; mem. Am. the Beautiful Centennial Celebrations, Inc., 1992-93; active Friends of the Garden of the Gods, Friends of Winfield Scott Stratton, Friends of the Libr. Named Tchr. of the Yr., Colorado Springs Sch. Dist. 11, 1968. Mem. AAUW (Woman of Yr. 1987), Colo. Ret. Educators Assn., Colorado Springs Ret. Educators Assn., Helen Hunt Jackson Commemorative Coun., Women's Ednl. Soc. Colo. Coll. Avocations: lecturing, conducting tours and writing tour scripts, volunteering in Pioneers Mus. Archives, Ecumenical Social Ministries, Garden of the Gods, Rock Ledge Ranch. Home: 1620 E Cache La Poudre St Colorado Springs CO 80909-4612

WILD, BONITA MARIE, healthcare company executive; b. Chgo., Jan. 14, 1949; d. Edward and Veronica (Hlad) Orzechowski; m. Forrest Wild; 1 child, Monica. Student, U. Chgo., 1973-75; BS, Roosevelt U., 1977; MA, U. Ariz., 1984. Sales rep. and dist. trainer Ortho Pharm. Corp., Raritan, N.J., 1978-82; v.p. and mktg. dir. Golden Era, Phoenix, 1982-84; sales rep. Surgikos, Arlington, Tex., 1984-88, Johnson & Johnson Med., Inc., Arlington, 1988-90; profl. products mgr. Johnson & Johnson Internat., Johnson & Johnson Poland, Warsaw, 1991-92; account bus. mgr. Johnson & Johnson Hosp. Svcs., New Brunwick, N.J., 1990-91, corp. bus. mgr., 1993—; corp. dir. Johnson & Johnson Health Care Sys., 1995—; counsellor Mariposa Women's Ctr., Orange, Calif., 1984-89. Mem. Franklin Honor Soc. at Roosevelt U. Republican. Roman Catholic. Avocations: skiing, travel, hiking, golf. Home: 506 Nyes Pl Laguna Beach CA 92651-4145

WILDE, DAVID, publisher, writer, biographer; b. Hereford, Nov. 12, 1944; s. Elizabeth Lillian (Price-Slawson) W. Diploma, Kneller Hall, London, 1965; pvt. mus. studies with Carmello Pace, Malta, 1964-68; student, Cardiff (Wales) Coll. Music, 1970-71; diploma in art, Open U., Leicester, Eng., 1980; student, Lancaster (Eng.) U., 1980-81, U. N.Mex., 1984. With BBC Radio, Eng., 1975-79; resident mem. wind ensemble Loughborough (Eng.) U., 1976-79; oil field worker Western Oceanic Inc. and Bawden Drilling, North Sea, Scotland, 1983-84; tutor U. N.Mex., Albuquerque, 1986-88, tchr. dept. continuing edn., 1989-90; musician/composer Civic Orch., Albuquerque, 1988-89; legal rschr. Wilde & Sprague, Albuquerque, 1988-90; pub., author Wilde Pub., Albuquerque, 1989—; clerical officer Severn-Trent Water, Eng., 1972-74, Social Security, Eng., 1983; rschr. Ctr. Southwest Rsch. U. N.Mex., 1994-97; spkr. in field. Author: The Spirit That Wants Me, 1989, In the South: The Five Year Diary of a Journey Across America, 1991, Route 66: The Five Year Diary of a Journey Across America, 1991, Wildeland: Prose,

1992, North Sea Saga, 1960s: Opera of Oil, 1993, Desert Meditations: A Fairy Tale of New Mexico, 1993, Black Innocence: The Immigrant, 1993, Poems, People, Places: Travels on My Own, 1994, Basic Horn Technique: Studies for the French Horn, 1994, The Life and Times of Cdr. E.C. Zeke Cortez, USNR, 1996, Snow Bow: A Children's Story, 1999, Pinis: (novel), 1998, (with others) La Puerta: A Doorway Into the Academy, 1997, Collected Short Stories, 1999; contbr. to National Library of Poetry, 1996; editor 6 books; actor Geronimo prodn. Turner Network TV, 1993; extra various prodns., 1969-84. Rschr. SRIC, Albuquerque, 1989-96; cons. N.Mex. Bd. Appraisers, Albuquerque, 1989-90. Roman Catholic. Avocations: travel, classical music, spirituality, history, mathematics. Office: 105 Stanford Dr SE Albuquerque NM 87106-3537 also: Wilde Pub PO Box 4581 Albuquerque NM 87196-4581

WILDE, TERUKO, artist; b. Nagoya, Mie, Japan, Apr. 20, 1945; d. Sadao and Moto (Minami) Takeuchi; m. Davis S. Wilde, June 27, 1970 (div. Feb. 26, 1987); 1 child, Emily. Student, U. Cin., 1962-64, Columbus Coll. Arts & Design, 1967-69. Graphic artsit Nationwide Ins. Co., Columbus, Ohio, 1968-70; owner Teruko's Studio Gallery, Willard, Ohio, 1971-80; co-pub., mktg. dir. Prisum Mag., Willard, 1980-82, Willard Junction, Willard, 1982-85; artist self-employed, Taos, N.Mex., 1986—. Founder Prism, 1980-82, Willard Junction, 1982-85; exhibited in one-person and group shows. Bd. dirs. Willard Fine Arts, Inc., 1981-85, City Mgrs. Adv. Com., Willard, 1984-86; tchr. First United Meth. Ch., Willard, 1976-80; art tchr. Sandusky (Ohio) Cultural Ctr., 1973-74. Named Best in Painting Mansfield Art Ctr., 1979, Best of Show Columbia Art Show, 1976. Mem. Taos Art Assn. Avocations: reading, music, tennis. Home: PO Box 2060 Taos NM 87571-2060

WILDER, JAMES D., geology and mining administrator; b. Wheelersburg, Ohio, June 25, 1935; s. Theodore Roosevelt and Gladys (Crabtree) W.; children: Jaymie Deanna, Julie Lynne. Graduated high sch., Wheelersburg. Lic. real estate agt., Ohio. Real estate agt. Portsmouth, Ohio; mgr. comml. pilots, fixed base operator Scioto County Airport, Ohio; mgr. and part owner sporting goods store, Portsmouth; cons. geologist Paradise, Calif., 1973-81; pres. Mining Cons., Inc., Paradise, 1981-84; dir. geology and devel. Para-Butte Mining, Inc., Paradise, 1984-88, pres., 1988-90, pres., chief exec. officer, 1990—. Served with U.S. Army, 1956-57. Avocations: hunting, fishing, camping. Home and Office: Para-Butte Mining Inc PO Box 564 Paradise CA 95967-0564

WILDER, JENNIFER ROSE, interior designer; b. Washington, Nov. 23, 1944; d. Winfield Scott and Blanche Irene (Taylor) Wilder; m. Scott Harris Smith, 1973 (div. 1987); children: Jason W., Adam S., Molly L., Whitney W. AA, Colo. Woman's Coll., Denver, 1965, BA, 1967. Interior designer Jamaica St. Interiors, Aurora, Colo., 1969-71; mgr./interior designer Interior Systems, Denver, 1971-73; owner/interior designer Jennifer Smith Designs, Denver, 1973-85, Inside Image Ltd., Castle Rock, Colo., 1985-86; interior designer Greenbaum Home Furnishings, Bellevue, Wash., 1986-94; mgr., interior designer Westbay Interiors, Gig Harbor, Wash., 1994—; instr. Tacoma C.C., Gig Harbor, Wash., 1995—. Recipient Design for Better Living award Am. Wood Coun., Seattle, 1987, Silver Mame awards Master Bldrs. Assn., 1992, 1st place Internat. Design Competition, Shintaku Daiwa, Hokaido, Japan,1 992. Mem. Am. Soc. Interior Design (allied mem.). Avocations: foreign languages, classical piano. Office: Westbay Interiors 408 Buena Vista Ave Fircrest WA 98466-7037

WILDER, KING, film director, computer consultant; b. L.A.; s. Kawika Kahanu and Rae Wilder; m. Julie Avola. Editor Empire Prodns., Hollywood, Calif., 1986-90; dir., prodr. SteppinStone Entertainment, Universal City, Calif., 1990—, website designer/creator, 1995—. Co-prodr. (films) including Puppet Master II, 1990; dir., co-prodr. (TV) including series Ultraman, 1992-93; screenwriter Across the Border, 1994. Mem. AFTRA, Aloha Golf Club (bd. dirs. 1994—). Office: Gizmo Beach Web Design PO Box 8417 Universal City CA 91618

WILDERMUTH, RONALD E., public relations professional; married; two children. BA in Internat. Rels. and Sociology, St. Ambrose Coll.; MS in Pub. Rels. with honors, Am. U.; MS in Naval Sci., Naval War Coll.; honor. grad., U. Okla. Commd. ensign USN, 1968, advanced through grades to capt., 1992; line officer USS Catamount, Comphibron 5, 1968-71; pub. rels. for Navy recruiting USN, 1971-75, pub. rels. staff Office of Info. dept., 1975-78; pub. rels. officer U.S. European Command, 1978-81; student Naval War Coll., Newport, R.I., 1981-82; dep. dir. pub. rels. U.S. Atlantic Command, Norfolk, Va., 1982-84; pub. rels. advisor Joint Chiefs of Staff, 1984-86; pub. rels. dir. Naval Air Forces, Pacific Fleet, 1986-88; pub. rels. advisor Gen. Schwarzkopf, 1989-92; dir. corp. rels. The Parsons Corp., Pasadena, Calif., 1992—; spokesman, pub. rels. counselor, speech writer in field, 1984-91. Active Feline Conservation Ctr., Greater Pasadena Bus. Ptnrs., Pasadena NOW; bd. dirs., mem. exec. com. Pasadena-Foothill br. L.A. Urban League. Decorated two Meritorious Svc. medals Dept. Def., two Meritorious Svc. medals USN, Personal Achievement medal USN, Legion of Merit medal Gen. H. Norman Schwarzkopf; recipient Accolades award for cmty. svc., Easter Seals Appreciation award for cmty. svc., Navy League Appreciation award for cmty. svc., Armed Forces YMCA Appreciation award for cmty. svc., others. Mem. Pub. Rels. Soc. Am., Am. Mktg. Assn., L.A. C. of C., Pasadena C. of C. (bd. dirs., mem. exec. com.), U.S. C. of C. Avocations: golf, study of African animals and art, jogging, painting and sculpture. Office: The Parsons Corp 100 W Walnut St Pasadena CA 91124-0001

WILEY, BONNIE JEAN, journalism educator; b. Portland, Oreg.; d. Myron Eugene and Bonnie Jean (Galliher) W. BA, U. Wash., 1948; MS, Columbia U., 1957; PhD, So. Ill. U., 1965. Mng. editor Yakima (Wash.) Morning Herald; reporter, photographer Portland Oregonian; feature writer Seattle Times; war correspondent PTO AP; western feature editor AP, San Francisco; reporter Yakima Daily Republic; journalism tchr. U. Wash., Seattle, Cen. Wash. U., Ellensburg, U. Hawaii, Honolulu; mem. grad. faculty Bangkok U., Thailand, 1991; mem. faculty journalism program U. Hawaii, Honolulu, 1992—; Adminstr. Am. Samoa Coll., Pago Pago; news features advisor Xinhua News Agy., Beijing, Yunnan Normal U., Kumming, China, 1995. Mem. Women in Communications (Hawaii Headliner award 1985, Nat. Headliner award 1990), Theta Sigma Phi. Home: 1434 Puanakau St # 1212 Honolulu HI 96818-1933

WILEY, DAVID COLE, producer; b. Long Beach, Calif., Sept. 12, 1948; s. Norman Cole and Bettigene Rosamond W. Ind. prodr., 1987—. Prodr. Abduction - the UFO Soap, 1987, Speak-Out, 1988-89, Coal Canyon BMX, 1989, PC 101 - Computer Repair, 1989, Young Lives, 1990, A Slice of Life, 1990, 91, Hidden Talents, 1992, Rock Talk, 1992—, History of the Santa Ana Canyon, 1994—, Buena Park Journal, 1994—; (documentaries) In Search of the Butterfield Trail, 1990, George Key Ranch - Centennial Celebration, 1993, Visitors from Catalan, 1996, History of the Santa Ana River, 1997, The Steam Kalliope, 1998. Recipient Western Access Video Excellence award Nat. Fedn. Local Cable Programmers, 1992, CABY Comcast Cablevision, 1996. Mem. Santa Ana Canyon Hist. Coun. (v.p., 1995—), Alliance Cmty. Media. Address: PO Box 6481 Fullerton CA 92834-6481

WILHELM, ROBERT OSCAR, lawyer, civil engineer, developer; b. Balt., July 7, 1918; s. Clarence Oscar and Agnes Virginia (Grimm) W.; m. Grace Sanborn Luckie, Apr. 4, 1959. BSCE, Ga. Tech. Inst., 1947, MSIM, 1948; JD, Stanford U., 1951. Bar: Calif. 1952, U.S. Supreme Ct. Mem. Wilhelm, Thompson, Wentholt and Gibbs, Redwood City, Calif., 1952—; gen. counsel Bay Counties Gen. Contractors; pvt. practice civil engring., Redwood City, 1952—; pres. Bay Counties Builders Escrow, Inc., 1972-88. With C.E., AUS, 1942-46. Mem. Bay Counties Civil Engrs. (pres. 1957), Peninsula Builders Exchange (pres. 1958-71, dir.), Calif. State Builders Exchange (treas. 1971), Del Mesa Carmel Cmty. Assn. (bd. dirs. 1997-99), Mason, Odd Fellows, Eagle, Elks. Author: The Manual of Procedures for the Construction Industry, 1971, Manual of Procedures and Form Book for Construction Industry, 9th edit., 1995; columnist Law and You in Daily Pacific Builder, 1955—; author: Construction Law for Contractors, Architects and Engineers. Home: 134 Del Mesa Carmel Carmel CA 93923-7950 Office: 702 Marshall St Ste 310 Redwood City CA 94063-1820

WILK, DIANE LILLIAN, architect, educator; b. L.A., July 14, 1955; d. Stefan Piotr and Wanda Helen (Harasimowicz) W. BS in Architecture, U. So. Calif., 1977; MArch, Yale U., 1981; postgrad., Stanford U., 1981-82. Registered architect, Calif., Colo.; cert. Nat. Coun. Archtl. Registration Bds. Project designer Daniel, Mann, Johnson & Mendenhall, L.A., 1981, Boyd Jenks Architect, Palo Alto, Calif., 1982-84; project arch. HED Architects, Redwood City, Calif., 1984-86; assoc. prof. architecture U. Colo., Denver, 1986—, assoc. dir. architecture program, 1991-92; dir. arch. grad. program, dept. U. Colo., 1997—. Author: Historic Denver Guides, 1995, 2nd edit., 1997; contbg. author: The Avant Garde and The Landscape, 1991; editor: Avant Garde; contbr. articles to profl. jours.; cellist Redwood Symphony, Redwood City, 1982-85, Centennial Orch., 1997. Assoc. dir. Polish Music Reference Ctr. U. So. Calif.; co-chair, mem. adv. bd. Polish Inst. Arts and Scis. Am. Recipient faculty rsch. award U. Colo. Sch. Architecture, 1988, 92; grantee Graham Found., 1989. Mem. AIA, Soc. Archtl. Historians, Tau Sigma Delta (award student chpt. 1990), Alpha Rho Chi, Alpha Lambda Delta. Avocations: music, sailing, skiing, golf, cycling. Office: U Colo Campus Box 126 PO Box 173364 Denver CO 80217-3364

WILKENING, LAUREL LYNN, academic administrator, planetary scientist; b. Richland, Wash., Nov. 23, 1944; d. Marvin Hubert and Ruby Alma (Barks) W.; m. Godfrey Theodore Sill, May 18, 1974. BA, Reed Coll., Portland, Oreg., 1966; PhD, U. Calif., San Diego, 1970; DSc (hon.), U. Ariz., 1996. From asst. prof. to assoc. prof. U. Ariz., Tucson, 1973-80, dir. Lunar and Planetary Lab., head planetary scis., 1981-83, vice provost, prof. planetary scis., 1983-85, v.p. rsch., dean Grad. Coll., 1985-88; divsn. scientist NASA Hdqrs., Washington, 1980; prof. geol scis., adj. prof. astronomy, provost U. Washington, Seattle, 1988-93; prof. earth system sci., chancellor U. Calif., Irvine, 1993-98; dir. Seagate Tech., Inc., 1993—, Rsch. Corp., 1991—, Empire Ranch Found., 1998—; vice chmn. Nat. Commn. on Space, Washington, 1984-86, Adv. Com. on the Future of U.S. Space Program, 1990-91; chair Space Policy Adv. Bd., Nat. Space Coun., 1991-92; co-chmn. primitive bodies mission study team NASA/European Space Agy., 1984-85; chmn. com. rendezvous sci. working group NASA, 1983-85; mem. panel on internat. cooperation and competition in space Congl. Office Tech. Assessment, 1982-83; trustee NASULGC, 1994-97, UCAR, 1988-89, 97-98, Reed Coll., 1992—. Editor: Comets, 1982. Bd. dirs. Empire Ranch Found., 1998—. U. Calif. Regents fellow, 1966-67; NASA trainee, 1967-70. Fellow Meteoritical Soc. (councilor 1976-80), Am. Assn. Advanced Sci.; mem. Am. Astron. Soc. (chmn. div. planetary scis. 1984-85), Am. Geophys. Union, AAAS, Planetary Soc. (dir. 1994—, v.p. 1987—), Phi Beta Kappa. Democrat. Avocations: gardening, camping, swimming.

WILKENS, STEVE, software marketing and sales executive; b. Burbank, Calif., Nov. 14, 1962; s. Martin Allen and Eileen Elizabeth (Jacobson) W.; m. Georgia Jean Lalonde, Dec. 31, 1987; children: Andrea, Stefani. BA in Mgmt., St. Mary's Coll. of Calif., Moraga. Account exec. Dean Witter, San Francisco; sales mgr. WPS/IBM, Houston; regional sales mgr. The McCosker Corp., San Ramon, Calif.; terr. mgr. Aldon Computer Corp., Oakland, Calif.; regional sales mgr. Smith Dennis & Gaylord, Santa Clara, Calif.; prin. Texsys Rd, San Francisco. Sgt. U.S. Army, 1981-85. Decorated Army Commendation medal, Achievement medal, Good Conduct medal, French Commando, Italian Airborne Wings. Mem. 82d Airborne Assn. Methodist.

WILKIE, JAMES W., history educator; s. Waldo Wallace and Lucile (Likins) W. BA, Mexico City Coll., 1958; PhD, U. Calif., Berkeley, 1965. Instr. Ohio State U., 1965-68; prof. UCLA, 1968—; chair program on Mex., co-chair Latin Am. Grad. Studies UCLA; pres. Globalization Strategies; founding dir. UCMEXUS U. Calif. Consortium on Mex. and U.S.; founder PROFMEX, 1984—; dir. Latin Am. Oral History Project. Author: The Mexican Revolution (1910-1976): Federal Expenditure and Social Change, Frente a la Revolución Mexicana: 17 Entrevistas de Historia Oral, 4 vols., others; contbr. articles to profl. jours.; founder PROFMEXIS Info. Sys.; co-editor: (web jour.) Mex. and the World; editor: SALA-Statis. Abstract of Latin am. and Analytical Publs. Fax: (310) 454-3109. E-mail: Wilkie@UCLA.EDU. Home: 1242 Lachman Ln Pacific Palisades CA 90272-2257 Office: UCLA Program on Mex 11361 Bunche Hall Los Angeles CA 90095-1487

WILKINS, AMY P., publishing executive. Pres. Teen mag., L.A. Office: care Teen mag Petersen Pub Co LLC 6420 Wilshire Blvd Los Angeles CA 90048-5502

WILKINSON, JOAN KRISTINE, nurse, pediatric clinical specialist; b. Rochester, Minn., June 15, 1953; d. A. Ray and Ruth Audrey (Wegwart) Kubly; m. Robert Morris Wilkinson, June 14, 1975; children: Michael Robert, Kathryn Ann. BS in Nursing, U. Wis., 1975; MS, U. Colo., 1986. RN, clin. nurse specialist. Team leader Mendota Mental Health Inst., Madison, Wis., 1975-76; care leader Boulder (Colo.) Psychiat. Inst., 1976-78; pub. health nurse, head nurse Rocky Mountain Poison Ctr., Denver, 1978-83; research teaching asst. U. Colo. Health Scis. Ctr., Denver, 1986-87. Disaster nurse ARC, Boulder, 1976—; participant community service United Way, Denver, 1981-84; vol. nurse Channel 9 Health Fair, Boulder, 1983. Fellow U. Colo. Health Scis. Ctr., 1986; recipient Recognition cert. ARC, Madison, 1978, Gold award United Way, Denver, 1981, Outstanding Citizen award Boulder, 1990, Torch award for outstanding leader Girl Scouts, 1995. Mem. Colo. Nurses Assn. (dist. 12 scholar 1983-86), Am. Nurses Assn., World Health Assn., Sigma Tau Theta. Lutheran. Home: 1195 Hancock Dr Boulder CO 80303-1101 Office: Denver Vis Nurse Assn 390 Grant St Denver CO 80203-4022

WILKINSON, RICHARD FRANCIS, JR., marketing executive; b. L.A., Jan. 25, 1944; s. Richard Francis and Doris Louise (Courtion) W.; m. Judith Anne Polodna, Sept. 13, 1966; children: Michael Francis, Mark William, Misty Anne, Michelle Louise. AA in Sci., Pasadena (Calif.) City Coll., 1965; BS in Microbiology, Calif. State Polytech. U., 1968; MS in Biology, Utah State U., 1972, PhD in Genetics, 1974. Microbiologist Space Gen. Corp., El Monte, Calif., 1967-68; rsch. fellow U. Wash. Marine Labs., Friday Harbor, 1972; post doctoral fellow, instr. Harvard Med. Sch., Boston, 1974-76; asst. prof. U. So. Calif., L.A., 1976-77; tech. mgr. N. Am. Sci. Assocs., Irvine, Calif., 1977-79; mgr., biol. scis. Am. Pharmaseal Corp., Irwindale, Calif., 1979-81; self employed - agr., 1981-84; rsch. assoc. U. Tex. Med. Sch., Houston, 1984-85; tech. dir. LifeCell Corp., Woodlands, Tex., 1986-87; sales mgr. Hyclone Labs., Inc., Logan, Utah, 1987-89, dir. mktg., 1989-92, sr. tech. dir., 1992-. Contbr. articles to profl. jours. Asst. scoutmaster Boy Scouts Am., El Toro, Calif., 1980, scoutmaster, Rupert, Idaho, 1984, dist. chmn., Houston, 1985, cubmaster, Hyde Park, Utah, 1991. Mem. World Trade Assn. Utah, Acad. Model Aeros., Utah Pilots Assn., Aircraft Owners Pilots Assn., Cache Anglers. Republican. Mem. LDS Ch. Avocations: private pilot, fly fishing, photography, hiking, model aviation. Office: HyClone Labs Inc 1725 Hyclone Rd Logan UT 84321-6299

WILKS-OWENS, DIXIE RAE, conference/meeting planner, workforce preparation specialist; b. Oakland, Calif., Nov. 1, 1943; d. James D. Wilks and Pauline Ruth (Peoples) Biddulph; m. August Edward Slagle (div. 1974); children: Tonya Davina Slagle, Victor Scott Slagle; m. Howard Laverne Owens, Dec. 15, 1984. AA, Ohlone Coll., 1973; attended, U. Calif., Davis, 1993-94; cert. mgmt. effectiveness, U. So. Calif. Unemployment ins. specialist, employment and tng. generalist. Employment supr. Calif. Employment Devel. Dept., Sacramento, 1969-86, employment specialist, 1986-88, legis. analyst, 1988-90, legis. re-employment ctr. mgr., 1990-91, mktg. mgr., 1991-94, mgr. workforce preparation conf., 1994-98; pres. Meeting Masters, Sacramento, 1996—; state mgr. Dept. Labor's Nationwide One-Stop Career Ctr. Conf., 1997, 98. Bd. dirs., membership chair Sacramento Women's Campaign Fund, 1993-97. Mem. Internat. Assn. Pers. in Employment Security (mem. internat. rels. com. 1991, Calif. chpt. pres. 1992-94, bd. dirs. conf. planning bd. 1993-94, legis. chair 1995-98), Soc. Govt. Meeting Profls. Democrat. Unitarian Universalist. Avocation: conference planner. Office: Meeting Masters 1151 Oak Hall Way Sacramento CA 95822-3209 also: State Job Tng Coord Coun 800 Capitol Mall # C67 Sacramento CA 95814-4807

WILLANS, JEAN STONE, religious organization executive; b. Hillsboro, Ohio, Oct. 3, 1924; d. Homer and Ella (Keys) Hammond; student San Diego Jr. Coll.; D.D. (hon.) Am. Coll. Sems., 1996; m. Richard James Willans, Mar. 28, 1966; 1 dau., Suzanne Jeanne. Asst. to v.p. Family Loan Co., Miami, Fla., 1946-49; civilian supr. USAF, Washington, 1953-55, Ordained archdeacon, 1996, ordained priest, 1997, consecrated bishop, 1998, Ch. of the East; founder, dir. Blessed Trinity Soc., editor Trinity mag., Los Angeles, 1960-66; co-founder, exec. v.p., dir. Soc. of Stephen, Altadena, Calif., 1967—, exec. dir., Hong Kong, 1975-81; lectr. in field. Republican. Author: The Acts of the Green Apples, 1974, rev. edit 1995; co-editor: Charisma in Hong Kong, 1970; Spiritual Songs, 1970; The People Who Walked in Darkness, 1977; The People Who Walked in Darkness II, 1992. Recipient Achievement award Nat. Assn. Pentecostal Women, 1964; monument erected in her honor Kowloon Walled City Park, Hong Kong Govt., 1996. Office: Soc of Stephen PO Box 6225 Altadena CA 91003-6225

WILLARD, GARCIA LOU, artist; b. Huntington, W.Va., Apr. 15, 1943; d. Harry Lee and Laura Lillian (Riley) Hall; m. Victor Percy Young, Sept. 2, 1972 (dec. Mar. 1980); m. Roger Lee Willard, Aug. 22, 1988. Student, Marshall U., 1978-83, W.Va. U., 1993, U. N.D., 1994-95. Owner, pres. Young's Fine Art, Huntington, 1975-85, Dyna Line, Wheeling, W.Va., 1980-85; instr. pastel and drawing Oglebay Mus.'s Stifel Fine Art Ctr., Wheeling, 1984-87; instr. pastel and portraiture Ohio U., Athens, 1987; owner, operator Outlines, Phoenix, Ariz., 1988-91; contbg. artist Sonoran Gallery, Phoenix, 1993—; mem. adv. bd. Profl. Art League, St. Clairsville, Ohio, 1984-85; lectr. and exhbn. juror various art orgns., Ohio, W.Va., Pa., 1987-88; art cons. Journey's End Designs, Wheeling, 1987. One woman shows include: Delf-Norona Mus., Moundsville, W. Va., Ariel Gallery, N.Y.C., Sonoran Gallery, Phoenix; Group shows include: Pen & Brush Club, N.Y.C., 1988, Hermitage Found. Mus., Va., 1988; contbr., illustrator: (book) Dr. Horton on African Art, 1985. Advisor Ariz. Fine Arts Commn., Phoenix, 1989-92. Recipient Best of Show award Delf-Norona Mus., 1985, Molly Guion award for graphics Catharine Lorillard Wolfe Art Club, 1988, Douglas Pickering Carnegie Mellon award, 1986. Fellow Am. Artists Profl. League (Pastel award 1988); mem. Pastel Soc. Am. (artist mem., A & M design award, 1988), Acad. Artists Assn. (artist mem., award for pastel portrait 1989), Degas Pastel Soc. (artist mem., M. Grumbacher award for pastel excellence 1988), Nat. Drawing Assn., Art Assn. Harrisburg (artist mem.). Republican. Avocations: archeology, astronomy, paper-making, attending symphonies, traveling. Home: 16215C N 37th Dr Phoenix AZ 85053-2806 Office: Sonoran Gallery 8819 W Corrine Dr Peoria AZ 85381-8166

WILLARD, H(ARRISON) ROBERT, electrical engineer; b. Seattle, May 31, 1933; s. Harrison Eugene and Florence Linea (Chelquist) W.; BSEE, U. Wash., 1955, MSEE, 1957, PhD, 1971. Staff assoc. Boeing Sci. Research Labs., Seattle, 1959-64; rsch. assoc. U. Wash., 1968-72, sr. engr. and rsch. prof. applied physics lab., 1972-81; sr. engr. Boeing Aerospace Co., Seattle, 1981-84; dir. instrumentation and engring. MetriCor Inc. (previously Tech. Dynamics, Inc.), 1984—. Served with AUS, 1957-59. Lic. profl. engr., Wash. Mem. IEEE, Am. Geophys. Union, Phi Beta Kappa, Sigma Xi, Tau Beta Pi. Contbr. articles to tech. jours. Patentee in field. Office: 17525 NE 67th Ct Redmond WA 98052-4939

WILLARD, HELEN W., newswriter, photographer; b. Onoto, W.Va., June 7, 1913; d. John Roland and Daisy Mary (Hill) Campbell; m. Leon J. Willard, Dec. 13, 1941 (dec. 1985); children: James L., Mary Jane. BA, Ellensburg Normal, 1940. Tchr. Newaukum Hill, Chehalis, Wash., 1932-34; tchr. Ilwaco, Wash., 1934-37, Tacoma, 1939-41; writer, photographer Prosser (Wash.) Record Bulletin, 1959-94; ruralite Benton Rea, Prosser, 1970-95. Author: Pow Wow-Indian, 1950, The Way It Was, Vol. 1, 1996, Vol. 2, 1997. Vice chmn. Rep. Com., Wash., 1979-80. Mem. Rotary, Prosser C. of C. Republican. Methodist. Avocaitons: camping, hiking, traveling. Home and Office: Roza Run Pub 57301 N Mcdonald Rd Prosser WA 99350-8657

WILLARD, THOMAS KIRT, artist; b. Topeka, Kans., Oct. 14, 1928; s. Gordon Herman and Lucy Ellen (Greathouse) W.; m. Bonnie Jean King, Sept. 8, 1959 (dec. Aug. 1982); 1 child, Pamela. AA, Univ. Alaska, 1991. Serviceman U.S. Army, Japan, 1949-53; field rep. Equifax, Inc., Emporia, Kans., 1953-84; artist, writer, 1988—. Author: Demons of Stony River, 1996; contbr. articles to profl. jours. Recipient Outstanding Svc. award Kenai Peninsula Botanical Soc., 1995. Mem. N.Am. Hunting Club, Nat. Rifle Assn., Kenai Peninsula Botanical Soc. (pres. 1994, v.p., 1995, sec., treas. 1996—), Kenai River Sport Fishing Inc. Republican. Quaker. Avocations: flying, hunting, fishing, botany, naturalist. Home: 1618 Tanaga Cir Kenai AK 99611-7909

WILLBANKS, ROGER PAUL, publishing and book distributing company executive; b. Denver, Nov. 25, 1934; s. Edward James and Ada Gladys (Keller) W.; m. Beverly Rae Masters, June 16, 1957; children: Wendy Lee, Roger Craig. B.S., U. Denver, 1957, M.B.A., 1965. Economist, bus. writer, bus. forecaster Mountain States Tel. Co., Denver, 1959-66; dir. pub. relations Denver Bd. Water Commrs., 1967-70; pres. Royal Publs. Inc., Denver, 1971—, Nutri-Books Corp., Denver, 1971—, Inter-Sports Book and Video, 1986—. Editor Denver Water News, 1967-70, Mountain States Bus., 1962-66. Mem. Gov. of Colo.'s Revenue Forecasting Com., 1963-66. Served with U.S. Army, 1957-58. Recipient Pub. Rels. award Am. Water Works Assn., 1970, Leadership award Nat. Inst. of Nutritional Edn., 1989, Medal of Freedom, U.S. Senate, 1994. Mem. Am. Booksellers Assn., Nat. Nutritional Foods Assn., Pub. Rels. Soc. Am. (charter mem. health sect.), Denver C. of C., SAR. Republican. Lutheran. Clubs: Aspen Glen Club, Denver Press, Auburn Cord Duesenberg, Rolls Royce Owners, Classic Car of Am., Denver U. Chancellor's Soc., Ferrari. Address: Royal Publs Inc PO Box 5793 Denver CO 80217-5793

WILLEMS, WALLY, health facility administrator; b. Fresno, Calif., Oct. 25, 1932; s. Henry Neufield and Alice Dortheia (Buhler) W.; m. Norma Jean White, Dec. 31, 1974; children: Rhonda, Rick. Race horse trainer Calif., 1951-58, Elobe Farms/Burns Steamship Line, 1958-62; truck driver Squoia Forest Products, Dinuba, Calif., 1962-68, McCarthy Farms, Lemorre, Calif., 1968-85; cert. nurse asst. Kings Convalescent, Hanford, Calif., 1985-88; lic. vocat. nurse Pacific Gardens, Fresno, Calif., 1988-94; pres. Valley Quality Home Care, Fresno, Calif., 1994—, also bd. dirs. Mem. Christian Bus. Mens Club. Republican. Baptist. Avocations: photography, camcorder, family history, writing short stories. Home: 860 E Grangeville Blvd Spc 173 Hanford CA 93230-2296 Office: Valley Quality Home Care 1900 N Gateway Blvd Ste 152 Fresno CA 93727-1630

WILLENBORG, JONATHAN EDWARD, computer specialist; b. Fountain Valley, Calif., May 26, 1975; s. Edward Eugene Willenborg and Diana Danielle (Willis) Trace. AA, Orange Coast Coll., 1996; student, Calvary Chapel Bible Coll., 1998—. Data entry asst. Marriott Corp., Newport Beach, Calif., 1993-95; prodn. engr. JVC Info. Sys., Irvine, Calif., 1994-95; asst. MIS DA Ins. Brokers, Huntington Beach, Calif., 1996-97; computer technician All Purpose Computers, Huntington Beach, 1997-98; network technician Accurate Computer Tech., Irvine, Calif., 1997-98; cons. All Purpose Computers, 1997—. Mem. Calvary Chapel, Costa Mesa, Calif. Republican. Avocations: flying, tchg., speaking, learning, thinking. Home: 14312 Riviera Dr Huntington Beach CA 92647-2002

WILLES, MARK HINCKLEY, media industry executive; b. Salt Lake City, July 16, 1941; s. Joseph Simmons and Ruth (Hinckley) W.; m. Laura Fayone, June 7, 1961; children: Wendy Anne, Susan Kay, Keith Mark, Stephen Joseph, Matthew Bryant. AB, Columbia Coll., 1963, PhD, 1967. Mem. staff banking and currency com. Ho. of Reps., Washington, 1966-67; asst. prof. fin. Wharton Sch. U. Pa., Phila., 1967-69; economist Fed. Res. Bank, Phila., 1967, sr. economist, 1969-70, dir. research, 1970-71, v.p., dir. research, 1971, 1st v.p., 1971-77; pres. Fed. Res. Bank of Mpls., 1977-80; exec. v.p., chief fin. officer Gen. Mills, Inc., Mpls., 1980-85, pres., chief oper. officer, 1985-92, vice chmn., 1992-95; chmn., pres., CEO Times Mirror Co., L.A., 1995—; pub. Los Angeles Times, 1997—. Office: Times Mirror Co Times Mirror Sq Los Angeles CA 90053

WILLEY, CHARLES WAYNE, lawyer; b. Dillon, Mont., Oct. 7, 1932; s. Asa Charles and Elizabeth Ellen Willey; m. Helene D., July 21, 1962 (div.); children: Stephen Charles, Heather Helene, Brent David, Scott D.; m. Alexis W. Grant, Jan. 26, 1986. BS with honors, Mont. State U., 1954; JD with high honors, U. Mont., 1959. Bar: Mont. 1959, Calif. 1960, U.S. Ct. Claims 1973, U.S. Tax Ct. 1973, U.S. Ct. Appeals (9th cir.) 1959, U.S. Ct. Appeals (Fed. cir.) 1983, U.S. Supreme Ct. 1972. Law clk. to presiding judge U.S. Ct. Appeals (9th cir.), 1959-60; ptnr. Price, Postel & Parma, Santa Barbara, Calif., 1960-77; pvt. practice Santa Barbara, 1977—; prof. law corp.; instr. Santa Barbara City Coll., 1961-63, U. Calif., Santa Barbara, 1963-64; lectr.

Mont. Tax Inst., 1990, 92, Am. Agr. Law Assn., 1993, 96. Chief editor Mont. Law Rev., 1958-59. Pres. Legal Aid Found. Santa Barbara, 1970; mem. Laguna Blanca Sch. Bd., pres. 1980-81; v.p. Phoenix of Santa Barbara. Served to capt. USAF, 1954-56. Mem. Santa Barbara County Bar Assn. (pres. 1972-73), Phi Kappa Phi, Phi Eta Sigma, Phi Delta Phi. Republican. Episcopalian. Lodge: Kiwanis. Avocations: reading, writing, traveling. Office: 1114 State St Ste 315 Santa Barbara CA 93101-2735

WILLIAMS, ARTHUR COZAD, broadcasting executive; b. Forty Fort, Pa., Feb. 12, 1926; s. John Bedford and Emily Irene (Poyck) W.; m. Ann Cale Bragan, Oct. 1, 1955; children: Emily Williams Van Hoorickx, Douglas, Craig. Student, Wilkes U., 1943-44; B.A. cum laude, U. So. Calif., 1949. With Kaiser Aluminum, 1949, Sta. KPMC, 1950-51; v.p., mgr. KFBK and KFBK-FM Radio Stas., Sacramento, 1951-80; with public relations dept. Sacramento Bee, McClatchy Newspapers, 1981-86; dir.-treas. Norkal Opportunities, Inc.; pres. Sacramento Bee Credit Union. Served with AUS, 1944-46. Mem. Sigma Delta Chi. Clubs: Rotary, Sutter, Valley Hi Country, Masons, Shriners. Home: 1209 Nevis Ct Sacramento CA 95822-2532 Office: 1125 Brownwyk Dr Sacramento CA 95822-1028

WILLIAMS, BEAU WILSON, health services administrator; b. Lynwood, Calif., Sept. 13, 1957; s. William Gene and Martha Maria (Hernandez) Bobo; m. Heysert Amparo Moreno, Dec. 1, 1984; children: Ryan, Kevin. AA in Anthropology, Calif. State U., Carson, 1997. Sr. issue clk. Prudential Ins. Co., L.A., 1978-80; contract analyst William M. Mercer, Inc., L.A., 1980-85, United Ins., Chatsworth, Calif., 1985-88; mgr. contracts Health Net, Woodland Hills, Calif., 1988—. Mem. Am. Health Lawyers Assn. Democrat. Roman Catholic. Avocations: fiction writing, reading, bowling, bicycling. Office: Health Net 21600 Oxnard St Ste 600 Woodland Hills CA 91367-4975

WILLIAMS, CHARLES (CHAD) MADISON, III, music company executive; b. San Francisco, Oct. 1, 1963; s. Charles Madison Williams II and Lorraine (Murphy) Shook; m. Teresa Anne Valadez, Aug. 22, 1960. Computer technician Record Factory, San Francisco, 1982-83, photo artist, 1983-84; typographer Display Lettering, San Francisco, 1984-86; graphic designer Arrow Graphics, San Francisco, 1986-88, Gardner Comm., San Francisco, 1988-90, Mattel Inc., L.A., 1991-95; label owner Resist Label Group, L.A., 1995—; cons. for Indie start-ups, L.A., 1996—. Author: Quease, 1998; composer: (contemporary) Wait for Nothing--Blink, 1996; prodr.: (jazz) Jack Kervorkian--A Very Still Life, 1997, Subjazz Proxy (with Gerald Wiggins), 1997. Mem. Am. Fedn. Musicians. Avocations: mountain biking, hiking, tennis, motorcycle racing, travel. Office: Resist Label Group 2408 Penmar Ave Venice CA 90291-5049

WILLIAMS, CHARLES PRESTON, sound effects storyteller, author; b. St. Petersburg, Fla., Nov. 14, 1967; s. Larry and Cyntia (Wright) W.; m. Melody Ann Williams, Apr. 20; children: Kylie Lynn, C.J. Grad., Principia Upper Sch., St. Louis, 1986. Tchr. M-Care-McDonnel Douglas Early Childhood Ctr., St. Louis, 1987-90; disc jockey KRAL-KIQZ Radio, Rawlins, Wyo., 1996-97; libr. Carbon County Libr., Rawlins, 1996-98, Natrona County Libr., Casper, Wyo., 1996-98; cartoonist Rawlins Daily Times, 1996—, Casper (Wyo.) Star Tribune, 1996—; storyteller, 1998—; standup comic St. Louis Funnybone, 1987-91; presenter Wyo. Arts Coun., Cheyenne, 1996—. Author: (cartoon books) No Services, 1996, Don't Feed the Vultures, 1999; (children's books) Sounds Around You, 1995, Bathtime, 1998. Mem. Nat. Storytelling Assn. Home: 1112 E 2d St Casper WY 82601-2904

WILLIAMS, CLARENCE, protective services official; b. Shreveport, La., Oct. 1, 1945; s. Leonard and Hearlean (Willis) W.; m. Mary K. Mannings, Nov. 30, 1974 (div. 1982); 1 child, Makala Deloris; m. Paulette Maria Guyton, Nov. 9, 1991; children: Kevin Michael, Maleah Requal. Student, So. U., 1963-64, Seattle C.C., 1968. Aerospace mechanic Boeing Aircraft Co., Seattle, 1965-68; fire fighter Seattle Fire Dept., 1968-76, engr., driver, 1976-82, emergency med. tech., 1976—, lt., 1982—; accreditation inspector Nat. Fire Protection Assn., Quincy, Mass., 1990—; cons. Pryor McClendon Counts Investment Bankers, 1993. Chmn. bd. trustees Mt. Zion Bapt. Ch., Seattle, 1992—; active Leadership Tomorrow, Seattle, 1986—, N.W. Conf. Black Pub. Ofcls., Wash., 1980—. With Wash. NG, 1965-71. Named one of Outstanding Young Men Am., 1978, 81, Most Outstanding Fire Fighter in State of Wash. Wash. State Jaycees, 1979; recognized for furthering cause of human rights UN Assn. U.S.A., 1979. Mem. Internat. Assn. Black Profl. Fire Fighters (pres. 1984-88), NAACP (membership com. 1976), Seattle Urban League (scholarship com. 1978), Seattle Black Fire Fighters Assn. (pres. 1968), So. U. Alumni Assn. Democrat. Office: Internat Assn Black Profl Fire Fighters PO Box 22005 Seattle WA 98122-0005

WILLIAMS, DAVID ALEXANDER, pilot; b. Helena, Mont., May 29, 1939; s. Daniel samuel and Dorothy (Alexander) W.; m. Jacquoline anders, Feb. 14, 1964 (div. Mar. 1988); children: Daniel Alexander, Darryl Jackson. BA, U. So. Calif., L.A., 1962. Lic. airline transport pilot, FAA. Commd. ensign USNR, 1963, advanced through grades to capt., 1985; tng. and test pilot McDonnel Douglas, Long Beach, Calif., 1980-87, chief pilot flight stds. and safety, 1987-97; chief pilot flight stds. and safety Douglas Products divsn. Boeing, Long Beach, 1997—; mem. internat. adv. com. Flight Safety Found., Washington, 1987—; mem. windshear tng. aid task force FAA/industry, Washington, 1985-87; mem. CFIT tng. com. Flight Safety Found./FAA, 1992-96, joint safety analysis team FAA Industry, 1997—. Author: Turbulence Education and Training Aid FAA/Industry, 1996-97. Mem. Naval Res. Assn., catalina Conservancy. Republican. Avocations: scuba diving, sailing. Home: 436 N Bellflower Blvd Unit 311 Long Beach CA 90814-4302 Office: Boeing IMC DO94-0012 3855 N Lakewood Blvd # Imc94-12 Long Beach CA 90846-0003

WILLIAMS, DAVID KEITH, technical trainer; b. Exeter, N.H., Mar. 4, 1965; s. Horace Robert and Arlene Emily (Locke) W. BS, U. N.H., 1987. Software engr. Micro-Integration, Newmarket, N.H., 1988-89, Alloy Computer Products, Marlboro, Mass., 1989-90; sr. software engr. Cabletron Systems, Inc., Rochester, N.H., 1990-95, tech. trainer, 1995-97; sr. tech. trainer Infinity-A SunGard Co., Mountain View, Calif., 1997—; cons. in computer software. Asst. scoutmaster Boy Scouts Am., Newton Junction, N.H., 1986-91; bd. dirs. Newton Junction Fireman's Assn., 1983-95. Mem. Amnesty Internat. Ptnrs. of Conscience. Baptist. Avocations: foreign languages, musical instruments, hiking, skiing, karate.

WILLIAMS, DAVID MICHAEL, manufacturing executive; b. Bklyn., Feb. 25, 1936; s. Robert Irving and Patricia Margaret (Flanagan) W.; m. Carol Bultmann, Nov. 13, 1965; children: Mark, Jennifer. Cert., NYU, Ctr. for Safety Engring., Manhattan, N.Y., 1960. Mgr. various mfrs., 1956-79; pres. D.M. Williams, Inc., Livermore, Calif., 1979—; cons. various mfrs., 1979—. Candidate for Gov., Calif., 1990; candidate for Congress, Calif., 1986, 88, 89, 92, 94, 96, 98; active Rep. Ctrl. Com., Calif., 1987-88. Cole grantee NYU, 1960. Mem. Inst. Packaging Profls. (bd. dirs. no. Calif. chpt., 1982-85, chmn. 1985-86), ASTM, Mensa (founder interest group 1983-86). Roman Catholic. Avocation: politics. Office: 1560 Kingsport Ave Livermore CA 94550-6149

WILLIAMS, DAVID WELFORD, federal judge; b. Atlanta, Mar. 20, 1910; s. William W. and Maude (Lee) W.; m. Ouida Maie White, June 11, 1939; children: David Welford, Vaughn Charles. A.A., Los Angeles Jr. Coll., 1932; A.B., UCLA, 1934; LL.B., U. So. Calif., 1937. Bar: Calif. 1937. Practiced in Los Angeles, 1937-55; judge Mcpl. Ct., Los Angeles, 1956-62, Superior Ct., Los Angeles, 1962-69, U.S. Dist. Ct. (cen. dist.) Calif., Los Angeles, 1969—; now sr. judge U.S. Dist. Ct. (cen. dist.) Calif.; judge Los Angeles County Grand Jury, 1965. Recipient Russwurm award Nat. Assn. Newspapers, 1958; Profl. Achievement award UCLA Alumni Assn., 1966. Office: US Dist Ct US Courthouse 312 N Spring St Ste 1621 Los Angeles CA 90012-4718

WILLIAMS, DEREK, JR., pharmaceutical professional; b. Ft. Rucker, Ala., June 25, 1958; s. Derek W. Sr. and Carol E. (Kaufman) W.; m. Penny L. Bradly, Apr. 22, 1991; children: Jason Brian, Courtney Elizabeth. AS, U. Nev., 1981; BA, U. Colo., 1984; MA, U. Nev., 1986; postgrad., Pepperdine U. Cert. Inst. Regulatory Affairs, 1997. Rsch. asst. U. Nev., Reno, 1984-86; surgical counselor St. Lukes Hosp., Denver, 1987-89; pub. health advisor Ctrs. for Disease Control, Atlanta, 1989-91; clin. rsch. assoc. Amgen, Inc., Thousand Oaks, Calif., 1991-92, regulatory affairs specialist, 1992-97; mgr. regulatory affairs SangStat Med. Corp., Menlo Park, Calif., 1997-98; assoc. dir. regulator affairs Nexell Therapeutics, Inc., Irvine, Calif., 1998—. Named Outstanding Young Men of Am., 1989-90. Mem. Regulatory Affairs Profls. Soc., Brit. Inst. Regulatory Affairs., Commonwealth Club of Calif., European Soc. for Regulatory Affairs, Am. Assn. Pharm. Scientists. Avocations: sports, history, literature. Office: Nexell Therapeutics Inc 9 Parker Irvine CA 92618

WILLIAMS, DEWAYNE ARTHUR, JR., artist, environmental resource specialist; b. San Diego, Aug. 20, 1943; s. DeWayne Arthur Sr. and Mary Elizabeth (Cardell) W.; m. Suelynn D. Davison, Jan. 18, 1964; children: Regan Lane, Rani Chellane Garcia, DeWayne Arthur III. BA in Biol. Sci., Fla. State U., 1966; MA in Interdisciplinary Studies, Oreg. State U., 1974; postgrad., U. Idaho, 1997—. Aquatic biologist Oreg. Game Commn., Corvallis, 1966-72; biol. technician EPA, Corvallis, 1974-75; crafts shop dir., instr. U.S.Army, Ft. Gulick, Canal Zone, 1975-79; artist/mus. curator U. Mont., Missoula, 1980-88; artist, author, editor, photographer Artistwork, Missoula, 1988-93; biol. technician (fish) Nat. Marine Fisheries Svc., Honolulu, 1994; exhibit specialist Nat. Pk. Svc., Homestead, Fla., 1994-96; environ. protection asst. U.S. Army Corps of Engrs., Boise, Idaho, 1996—; fine arts dir. student union Oreg. State U., Corvallis. Author, editor, photographer, pub.: Montana Tribute, 1990 (Mont. Best Seller 1991); photograph Black into White, 1984 (Purchase award Danadell Gallery 1986), Erotic Art by Living Artists, 1988. Scoutmaster, cubmaster, advancement chmn. Boy Scouts Am., various locations, 1967-93. Democrat. Episcopalian. Avocations: hunting, fishing, camping. Fax: 208-343-9914. Home: 11130 Highlander Rd Boise ID 83709-5247 Office: US Army Corps Engrs HC 33 Box Hc-33 Box Boise ID 83716-9804

WILLIAMS, DONNA REILLY, counselor, writer, personnel consultant; b. Dauphin, Man., Can., Mar. 18, 1945; came to U.S., 1986; d. Allen Leslie and Mary Mabel (McNicol) Reilly; m. Clifford Neil Williams, May 31, 1966; children: Mary, Kevin, David, Laura. Diploma in Theol. Studies (distinction), Newman Theol. Coll., Edmonton, Alta., Can., 1985; MA in Pastoral Studies, Loyola Marymount U., L.A., 1990; postgrad. marriage and family therapy program, Presbyn. Counseling Svcs., Seattle, 1996; postgrad. mediator tng. program, Pacific Family Mediation Inst., Bellevue, Wash., 1997. Staff chaplain Edmonton Gen. Hosp., 1985-86; sr. theology tchr. Sacred Heart of Jesus H.S., L.A., 1987-88; pastoral min. Archdiocese of L.A., 1988-89; dir. support svcs. AIDS Healthcare Found., L.A., 1989-90; counselor, cons. Woodinville, Wash., 1991—; advanced hypnotherapy and release therapy intern Wellness Inst., Issaquah, Wash., 1996; employee assistance program coord. Assoc. Cath. Cemeteries, Seattle, 1994—. Author: Grief Ministry: Helping Others Mourn, 1990, (children's) Morgan's Baby Sister, 1992, Our Family is Divorcing, 1996, When Dreams Don't Work: Professional Caregivers and Burnout, 1997; contbr. articles to profl. jours. Mem. sr. citizen's action com. Beverly Hosp., Montebello, Calif., 1986-89. Fellow Am. Assn. Grief Counselors; mem. ACA, Assn. for Death Edn. and Counseling (cert.), Internat. Assn. Marriage & Family Counselors, Heart-Centered Hypnotherapy Assn. Avocations: ceramics, public speaking and teaching, retreat direction. E-mail: donna@healplace.com. Office: 18327 147th Ct NE Woodinville WA 98072-9294

WILLIAMS, DOUGLAS ARRON, courier; b. San Lorenzo, Calif., Feb. 6, 1968; s. Arthur Grant and Elizabeth Ann (Whittaker) W.; m. Lori Jacqualine Williams, Mar. 8, 1997. Student, San Diego State Univ., 1996—. Alterations Elegant Penguin, San Jose, Calif., 1986-88; sales Nordstrom, San Jose, Calif., 1986-88, 1988-89; truck driver M.A.T. Express, San Jose, Calif., 1989, Nippon Express, San Jose, Calif., 1989-90; courier DHL Worldwide Express, San Jose, Calif., 1990—; editor: SDFWA, San Diego, 1998. Media rels. RNC Conv., 1996. Mem. Soc. Profl. Journalists. Republican. Avocations: woodworking, writing. Home: 3936 Clairemont Dr San Diego CA 92117-5511

WILLIAMS, ELISA ANN, journalist; b. Springfield, Mass., Dec. 30, 1961; m. William Wesley Carter. BA, Miami U., Oxford, Ohio, 1984. Intern Cin. Mag., 1984; editl. asst. Palm Beach Life, West Palm Beach, Fla., 1984-86; journalist Palm Beach Post, West Palm Beach, 1986-90, Washington Times, 1990-92, Orange County Register, Santa Ana, Calif., 1993-97, The Oregonian, Portland, 1997—; Treas., pres.-elect Orange County Press Club, 1995-96. Recipient Davenport Fellowship in Bus. and Economic Reporting U. Mo., 1989; winner 1st pl. for Best Reporting Washington Press Club, 1990-91.

WILLIAMS, ELIZABETH YAHN, author, lecturer, lawyer; b. Columbus, Ohio, July 20, 1942; d. Wilbert Henry and Elizabeth Dulson (Brophy) Yahn. BA cum laude, Loyola Marymount U., 1964; secondary tchg. credential, UCLA, 1965; JD, Loyola U., 1971. Cert. tchr. h.s. and jr. coll. law, English and history. Writer West Covina, Calif., 1964—; designer West Covina, 1966-68; tchr. jr./sr. h.s. L.A. City Schs., Santa Monica, Calif., 1964-65, La Puente (Calif.) H.S. Dist., 1965-67; legal intern, lawyer Garvey, Ingram, Baker & Uhler, Covina, Calif., 1969-72; lawyer, corp. counsel Avco Fin. Svcs., Inc., Newport Beach, Calif., 1972-74; sole practitioner and arbitrator Santa Ana, Calif., 1974-80, Newport Beach, 1980-87; mem. faculty continuing edn. State Bar of Calif., 1979; adj. prof. Western State U. Sch. Law, Fullerton, Calif., 1980; mem. fed. cts. com. Calif. State Bar, San Francisco, 1977-80. Author: (1-act plays) Acting-Out Acts, 1990, Grading Graciela, 1992, Boundaries in the Dirt, 1993; author, lyricist: (1-act children's musical) Peter and the Worry Wrens, 1995; editor: The Music of Poetry, 1997; contbr. articles to profl. jours.; panelist TV show Action Now, 1971; interviewee TV show Women, 1987; scriptwriter, dir. TV show Four/Four, 1994, (3-act adaptation) Saved in Sedona, 1995; scriptwriter, prodr., host TV show Guidelights to Success, 1996. Mem. alumni bd. Loyola-Marymount Coll., L.A., 1980-84; mem. adv. bd. Rancho Santiago Coll., Santa Ana, 1983-84; spkr. Commn. on Status on Women, Santa Ana, 1979. Recipient Editor's Choice award Nat. Libr. of Poetry, 1995-96, Telly award finalist, 1996; grantee Ford Found., 1964-65; French scholar Ohio State U., 1959, acad. scholar Loyola-Marymount U., 1960-64. Mem. Calif. Women Lawyers (co-founder, life, bd. dirs. 1975-76), Orange County Bar Assn. (faculty Orange County Coll. Trial Advocacy 1982, chmn. human and individual rights com. 1974-75, comml. law and bankruptcy com. 1978-79, corp. and bus. law sect. 1980-81), Soc. of Children's Book Writers and Illustrators, Magee Park Poets, Nat. League Am. Penwomen (La Jolla br.), Pub. Mktg. Assn., San Diego Pub. Alliance, Phi Theta Kappa (most disting. hon. life mem.). Avocation: directing and producing ensemble and liturgical dramas and musicals. Address: PO Box 233 San Luis Rey CA 92068

WILLIAMS, ENID JO, writer; b. Laverne, Okla., Feb. 6, 1920; d. Oliver John and Esther (Root) Bourgois; m. Edward L. Williams, Aug. 8, 1936; children: Loretta June Smith, Gary L. *Ms. Williams is one of eight children. She's married, 63 years, to Edward L. Williams, her high school sweetheart. She has two children, Lt. Col. Gary L. Williams, Fort Knox, Kentucky, Loretta June Smith, Lakewood, California. Paternal grandfather was grade school teacher in Louisiana. Her father left school at 16 to work the oil fields of Laverne, Oklahoma to support the family after his father died. Maternal grandmother was widowed and raised three children, Benjamin, Esther, and Ruby, by turning her home into a Catholic Convent School. Ms. Williams and her husband retired to Deming, New Mexico where she's still a prolific writer.* Grad., Excelsior H.S., Norwalk, Calif., 1936. Tchr. Sunday sch. Full Gospel, Bellflower, Calif., 1950-55; with Shady Acres, Redding and Ctrl. City, Calif., 1968-74; office mgr. Little Moe Zarellas, Long Beach, Calif., 1980—. Songwriter; contbg. poet: Best Poems of 1997, Best Poems of the 90's, Poetry in New Libr. of Congress. Named in top 2% of poets Nat. Libr. Poetry, 1997, recipient Golden Poet award, 1990, 91; named Top Song Writer, Chapel Recording Co., 1995. Mem. ASCAP, Am. Nat. Libr., Nat. Libr. Congress, Internat. Libr. Poets, Internat. Soc. Poets (life, Copper medallion 1997), Rebekah Lodge. Republican. Methodist. Avocations: reading, writing, flowers. Home: 2075 Camino Dos SW Deming NM 88030-1023

WILLIAMS, EVAN THOMAS, college dean, chemistry educator; b. N.Y.C., May 17, 1936; s. Clarke and Margaret (Button) W.; m. Lise Reinholdt Jacobsen, Sept. 19, 1959; children: Elisabeth Clarke, John Reinholdt. AB, Williams Coll., 1958; PhD, MIT, 1963. Rsch. assoc. Rsch. Establishment Risø, Roskilde, Denmark, 1963-65; asst. prof. dept. chemistry Bklyn. Coll., CUNY, 1965-71, assoc. prof., 1971-75, prof., 1976-92, chmn. dept., 1981-84, dean undergrad. studies, 1989-92; dean, v.p. acad. affairs Lewis & Clark Coll., Portland, Oreg., 1992-95, prof. chemistry, 1992—, asst. to pres., 1995-97, chmn. environ. studies program, 1997—; cons. Geos Corp., Mt. Vernon, N.Y. Contbr. over 40 rsch. articles to sci. jours. Pres. Cobble Hill Assn., Bklyn., 1972-73; mem. Bklyn. Solid-Waste Adv. Bd., 1981-92; trustee Packer Collegiate Inst., Bklyn., 1978-87. Mem. AAAS, Am. Chem. Soc., Am. Phys. Soc., Phi Beta Kappa, Sigma Xi. Office: Lewis & Clark Coll Chemistry Dept 0615 SW Palatine Hill Rd Portland OR 97219-7879

WILLIAMS, FRANCIS LEON, engineering executive; b. McGill, Nev., Sept. 19, 1918; s. Leon Alfred and Mazie Arabella (Blanchard) W.; m. Ailsa Bailey, Oct. 1944 (div.); children: Rhonda, Grapham, Alison; m. Marita I. Furry, Feb. 23, 1974. Student, Calif. Inst. Tech., 1940-41, UCLA, 1946-47, Am. TV Labs., 1948; BME, Sydney U., Australia, 1952; postgrad., San Jose State Coll., 1958-60, Foothill Coll., 1961, Regional Vocat. Ctr., San Jose, Calif., 1962, Alexander Hamilton Inst., 1971-72, Lane Community Coll., 1978-85. Project engr., prodn. supr. Crompton, Parkinson, Australia Pty., Ltd., Sydney, 1949-50; field and sales engr. Perkins Australia Pty., Ltd., Sydney, 1951-54; chief mech. engr. Vicon Corp., San Carlos, Calif., 1955-60; design engr., group leader Lockheed Missiles and Space Co., Sunnyvale, Calif., 1960-70; prin. Astro-Tech Cons. Co., Los Altos, Calif., 1971-72; mech. designer Morvue and Morden Machines, Portland, Oreg., 1973-74; sr. mech. design engr. Chip-N-Saw div. Can-Car of Can., Eugene, Oreg., 1974-75; sales mgr. Indsl. Constrn. Co., Eugene, 1975-76, gen. mgr., 1977-78; ops. mgr. Steel Structures, Eugene, 1976-77; mech. design and project engr. Carothers Co., Eugene, 1978-80; chief engr. Bio Solar and Woodex Corps., Eugene and Brownsville, Oreg., 1980-83; cons. and design engr. Am. Fabricators, Woodburn, Oreg., 1983-84; design engr., draftsman Peterson Pacific Corp., Pleasant Hill, Oreg., 1984-85, Jensen Drilling Co., Glenwood, Oreg., 1985; design engr. Judco & Ball Flight Dryers, Inc., Harbor City, Calif., 1985-86; sr. v.p. The Richelsen Co., also cons.; chief engr. Peterson Pacific Corp., Eugene, 1984-93, mgr. new product devel. R&D, 1993—; owner, designer Williams Machine Design, Eugene, 1995—; also cons.; advisor solid waste recovery County Bd. Commr.'s Office, Eugene, 1984-85. Contbr. articles to profl. jours.; patentee in field. Chmn. bldg. and grounds Westminster Presbyn. Ch., Eugene, 1984-86. Served with USAF, 1941-45. Democrat. Lodge: Elks. Avocation: writing. Home: 2324 Lillian St Eugene OR 97401-4916

WILLIAMS, HAROLD MARVIN, foundation official, former government official, former university dean, former corporate executive; b. Phila., Jan. 5, 1928; s. Louis W. and Sophie (Fox) W.; m. Nancy Englander; children: Ralph A., Susan J., Derek M. AB, UCLA, 1946; JD, Harvard U., 1949; postgrad. U. So. Calif. Grad. Sch. Law, 1955-56; DHL (hon.), Johns Hopkins U., 1987, Occidental Coll., 1997, Calif. State U., 1998. Bar: Calif. 1950; practiced in Los Angeles, 1950, 53-55; with Hunt Foods and Industries, Inc., Los Angeles, 1955-68, v.p. 1958-60, exec. v.p., 1960-68, pres., 1968; gen., mgr. Hunt-Wesson Foods, 1964-66, pres., 1966-68; chmn. finance com. Norton Simon, Inc., 1968-70, chmn. bd., 1969-70, dir., 1959-77; dir. Times-Mirror Corp., SunAmerica, Calif. Endowment, Pub. Policy Inst.; prof. mgmt., dean Grad. Sch. Mgmt., UCLA, 1970-77; pres., dir. Special Investments & Securities Inc., 1961-66; chmn. SEC, Washington, 1977-81; pres., CEO J. Paul Getty Trust, 1981-98, pres. emeritus; of counsel Skadden Arps et al., 1998—; regent U. Calif., 1983-94. Mem. Commn. for Econ. Devel. State of Calif., 1973-77; energy coordinator City of Los Angeles, 1973-74; public mem. Nat. Advt. Review Bd., 1971-75; co-chmn. Public Commn. on Los Angeles County Govt.; mem. Coun. on Fgn. Rels., Com. for Econ. Devel.; commn. to rev. Master Plan for Higher Edn., State of Calif., 1985-87; co-chair Calif. Citizens Commn. Higher Edn.; trustee Nat. Humanities Ctr., 1987-93; dir. Ethics Resource Ctr.; mem. Pres.' Com. on Arts and Humanities; mem. Commn. on the Acad. Presidency. Served as 1st lt. AUS, 1950-53. Mem. State Bar Calif. Office: J Paul Getty Trust 1200 Getty Center Dr Ste 400 Los Angeles CA 90049-1681

WILLIAMS, HARRY EDWARD, management consultant; b. Oak Park, Ill., July 20, 1925; s. Harry E. and Mary E.; m. Jean Horner; 1 child, Jeanne. Student, West Coast U., Los Angeles, 1958-60; BS in Engring., Calif. Coast Coll., Santa Ana, 1975; MA, Calif. Coast Coll., 1975; PhD, Golden State U., Los Angeles, 1981. Registered profl. engr., Calif. Mgr. Parker Aircraft Co., Los Angeles, 1958-60, Leach Corp., Los Angeles, 1968-69, Litton, Data Systems, Van Nuys, Calif., 1969-72; dir. Electronic Memories, Hawthorne, Calif., 1972-78, Magnavox Co., Torrance, Calif., 1978-80; v.p. Stacoswitch Inc., Costa Mesa, Calif., 1981-87; mgmt. cons., Westminster, Calif., 1987—; cons. in field. Contbr. articles to profl. jours. With USAF, 1943-46. Recipient Mgr. of the Yr. award Soc. for Advancement of Mgmt., 1984, Phil Carroll award for outstanding contbns. in field of ops. mgmt., 1985, Profl. Mgr. citation, 1984. Fellow Internat. Acad. Edn. Republican. Methodist. Avocation: target shooting.

WILLIAMS, HOWARD WALTER, aerospace engineer, executive; b. Evansville, Ind., Oct. 18, 1937; s. Walter Charles and Marie Louise (Bollinger) W.; m. Phyllis Ann Scofield, May 4, 1956 (div. Sept. 1970); m. Marilee Sharon Mulvane, Oct. 30, 1970; children: Deborah, Steven, Kevin, Glenn, Lori, Michele. AA, Pasadena City Coll., 1956; BSME, Calif. State U., Los Angeles, 1967; BSBA, U. San Francisco, 1978; PhD in Comml. Sci. (hon.), London Inst. Applied Rsch., 1992. Turbojet, rocket engr. Aerojet-Gen. Corp., Azusa, Calif., 1956-59, infrared sensor engr., 1959-60, rocket, torpedo engr., 1960-66; power, propulsion mgr. propulsion divsn. Aerojet-Gen. Corp., Sacramento, 1967-73, high speed ship systems mgr., 1974-78, combustion, power mgr., rocket engine and energy mktg. mgr., 1979-89, dir. strategic planning, 1989-94; strategic analyst, program mgr. Pratt & Whitney Space Propulsion, San Jose, Calif., 1995—. Author: (with others) Heat Exchangers, 1980, Industrial Heat Exchangers, 1985, History of Liquid Rocket Engine Development in the U.S., 1992, Aerojet: The Creative Company, 1997; co-inventor Closed Cycle Power System, 1969. Recipient Energy Innovation award U.S. Dept. Energy, 1985. Mem. AIAA (sr., Best Paper 1966), Am. Soc. Metals (organizing dir. indsl. heat exch. confs. 1985). Avocations: bicycling, grandchildren.

WILLIAMS, ISABEL MAFNAS, computer systems engineer, computer consultant; b. Austin, Tex., Sept. 21, 1965; d. Juan Crisostomo and Isabel (Iglesias) Mafnas; m. Dereck S. Williams, June 10, 1995. BA in Statistics, U. Calif., Berkeley, 1987; postgrad., Chabot Coll., 1989-91, Merritt Coll., 1991-92. Stats. tutor, stats. reader U. Calif., Berkeley, 1986-87; stats. reader U. Calif. Extension, Berkeley, 1987-89; instrnl. asst. II Chabot Coll., Hayward, 1988-92, computer lab. specialist, 1992-96; systems engr. III MDL Info. Systems, Inc., San Leandro, Calif., 1996—; tchr. computers Eureka!-Girls Inc., San Leandro, 1993-96. Author: (Software user's guide) Academic Session Time Keeper, 1990, 91, 92, 94, 96. Recipient Newspaper Carrier scholarship Gannett Found., Inc., Guam, 1983, Gannett Spl. scholarship Gannett Found., Inc., Guam, 1983. Office: MDL Info Systems Inc 14600 Catalina St San Leandro CA 94577-6608

WILLIAMS, J. D., state controller; b. Malad, Idaho; m. Rosemary Zaugg; 4 daus. MPA, Brigham Young U.; JD, Am. Univ. Bar: Idaho, D.C., several fed. cts.; cert. govt. fin. mgr. Apptd. law clk. D.C. Ct. Appeals; dep. Idaho Atty. Gen. Boise; lawyer Preston, Idaho; mayor City of Preston; appt. auditor State of Idaho, Boise, 1989-94, elected controller, 1994—; mem. Info. Tech. Res. Coun., Idaho. Past mem. Idaho Law Enforcement Planning Commn., past chmn. Idaho Youth Commn.; past chmn. Preston Sch. Dist. Excellence in Edn. com.; past mem. Idaho Water Resource Bd. Named. Fin. Mgr. of Yr., Idaho. Nat. Assn. State Comptrollers (past pres.), Nat. Assn. State Auditors, Comptrollers and Treasurers (former mem. exec. com., Pres.'s award for outstanding svc. in fin. mgmt. to U.S.). Office: Office of State Controller State Capital Boise ID 83720-0001

WILLIAMS, JACK JEFF, realtor, retired executive administrator; b. Cushing, Okla., July 28, 1936; s. Jeff Davis and Pauline Vera (Meyers) W.; m. Mary Ann Hill, June 1, 1957; children: Janet Lee Williams Charlin, Jeff Brian. BA in Econs., U. Calif., Dominguez Hills, 1974. Lic. real estate sales, Calif. Exec. adminstr. TRW Space & Electronics, Redondo Beach, Calif.; realtor Moore & Assocs. Hermosa Bch. (Top ten agent); cons. Delta Airlines, Atlanta, Aerospace Corp., El Segundo, Calif., Amdahl Corp., Santa Clara, Calif., Continental Airlines, L.A. Author, editor: Meyers from Moyers, 1996. Mem. TRW Retirees Assn. (v.p. 1997, pres. 1998), Torrance

Rose Float Assn. (bd. dirs. 1996—, v.p., 1997—), South Bay Genealogy Soc., Snow Valley Ski Club (coord.), Masons (sr. deacon 1993). Republican. Baptist. Avocation: genealogy research. Home: 5216 Emerald St Torrance CA 90503-2724 Office: Moore & Assocs Realtors 2615 Pacific Coast Hwy Ste 100 Hermosa Beach CA 90254-2278

WILLIAMS, JAMES DAVID, lawyer; b. New Orleans, Nov. 21, 1962; s. David Lufe and Alice (Beckworth) W. BA, Am. U., 1985; JD, Northwestern Sch. Law, Portland, 1994. Bar: Oreg. Agrl. ext. vol. U.S. Peace Corps, Mauritania, 1987-89; in-house counsel Confederated Tribes of the Umatilla Indian Reservation, Pendleton, Oreg., 1995—. Avocations: artist, outdoor sports enthusiast. Office: Confederated Tribes of Umatilla India Reservation PO Box 638 Pendleton OR 97801-0638

WILLIAMS, JOAN ELAINE, podiatric surgeon, educator; b. La Mesa, Calif.; d. William E. and Dottie B. Williams; m. Edward Homewood Miller, 1987; children: Carol Martins, William Baerg, Michael Baerg. BS, Calif. Coll. Podiatric Med., 1978, D of Podiatric Medicine, 1981; MS, Pepperdine U., 1979. Diplomate Am. Bd. Podiatric Surgery, Am. Bd. Podiatric Orthopedics and Primary Podiatric Medicine. Chief podiatric medicine and surgery dept. vets. affairs Puget Sound Health Care System, Seattle, 1982—; clin. asst. prof. podiatric medicine Calif. Coll. Podiatric Medicine, San Francisco, 1982—, U. Osteo. Medicine and Health Sci., Des Moines, Iowa, 1982-90; clin. assoc. prof. U. Osteo. Medicine and Health Scis., Des Moines, Iowa, 1990—; oral bd. examiner Am. Bd. Podiatric Orthopedics, Chgo., 1988; reviewer merit rev. grant Vets. Affairs Ctrl. Office, Washington, 1989; lic. exam reviewer Nat. Bd. Podiatric Med. Examiners, State College, Pa., 1993—. Editor: Preferred Practice Guidelines, 1992-94; contbr. articles to profl. jours. County del. Wash. State Rep. Party, Seattle, 1994. Recipient Acad. scholarship Pepperdine U., 1979. Fellow Am. Coll. Foot and Ankle Surgeons, Am. Coll. Foot and Ankle Orthopedics. Presbyterian. Avocations: classical music, playing cello. Office: Puget Sound Health Care Sys Dept Vets Affairs 1660 S Columbian Way Seattle WA 98108-1532

WILLIAMS, JOHN CHARLES, II, data processing executive; b. Dayton, Ohio, Jan. 29, 1955; s. John Charles and Frances Jerline (McKean) W.; m. Diane Catherine Busch, Feb. 11, 1978; 1 child, Tabitha Anne. Programmer Kino Starr, Tucson, 1977-78, City of Boise (Idaho), 1978; data processing mgr. Nat. Assn. Ind. Businesses, Inc., Boise, 1978-79; chief exec. officer Williams Rsch. Assoc., Boise, 1979-80, MRW Data Systems, Inc., Tucson, 1981-82, Computer Security, Tucson, 1983-86, Modern Magic, Tucson, 1986-88; tech. support dir. Program Sources, Inc., Tucson, 1988-89; chief exec. officer Cactus Explosives Corp., 1989-90, Systems Cons. Assocs., Tucson, 1990-94; sr. systems analyst Desert Diamond Casino, 1994-97; program analyst Muscular Dystrophy Assn., Tuscon, 1997—. Area coord. Kolbe For Congress Campaign, Tucson, 1984; Ariz. Rep. State Committeeman, 1986—; mem. Ariz. Sonora Desert Mus., Tucson, 1983—. Republican. Avocations: leather crafting, horsemanship, numismatics. Address: PO Box 64203 Tucson AZ 85728-4203

WILLIAMS, JOHN CHRISTOPHER RICHARD, bishop; b. Sale, Cheshire, Eng., May 22, 1936; arrived in Can., 1960; s. Frank Harold and Ceridwen Roberts (Hughes) W.; m. Rona Macrae Aitken, Mar. 18, 1964; children: Andrew David, Judith Ann. BA in Commerce, Manchester U., Eng., 1958; diploma in theology, Cranmer Hall, Durham, Eng., 1960; DD, Emmanuel St. Chad Coll., Saskatoon, Can., 1997. Ordained deacon Anglican Ch. of Can., 1960, priest, 1962. Missionary in charge Anglican Ch. Can., Sugluk, Que., Can., 1961-72, Cape Dorset, N.W.T., Can., 1972-75, Baker Lake, N.W.T., 1975-78; archdeacon of the Keewatim Anglican Ch. Can., 1975-87; rector Holy Trinity Anglican Ch. Can., Yellowknife, N.W.T., 1978-87; bishop suffagan Diocese of the Arctic, Can., 1987-90, diocesan bishop, 1990—; trustee Can. Churchman, Anglican Ch. Can., 1976-82, mem. nat. exec. com., 1976-79, 92-95. Coord., trans. into Eskimo Inukkitut New Testament, 1992. Avocations: reading, skiing, swimming. *

WILLIAMS, JOHN JAMES, JR., architect; b. Denver, July 13, 1949; s. John James and Virginia Lee (Thompson) W.; m. Mary Serene Morck, July 29, 1972. BArch, U. Colo., 1974. Registered architect, Colo., Calif., Idaho, Va., Utah, Nev., N.Mex., Wyo., Ohio. Project architect Gensler Assoc. Architects, Denver, 1976, Heinzman Assoc. Architects, Boulder, Colo., 1977, EZTH Architects, Boulder, 1978-79; prin. Knudson/Williams PC, Boulder, 1980-82, Faber, Williams & Brown, Boulder, 1982-86, John Williams & Assocs., Denver, 1986-97; John Williams Architecture P.C., 1997-98; panel chmn. U. Colo. World Affairs Conf.; vis. faculty U. Colo. Sch. Architecture and Planning, Coll. Environ. Design, 1986-91. Author (with others) State of Colorado architect licensing law, 1986. Commr. Downtown Boulder Mall Commn., 1985-88; bd. dirs. U. Colo. Fairway Club, 1986-88; mem. Gov's. Natural Hazard Mitigation Coun., State of Colo., 1990. Recipient Teaching Honorarium, U. Colo. Coll. Architecture and Planning, 1977, 78, 79, 80, 88, Excellence in Design and Planning award City of Boulder, 1981, 82, Citation for Excellenc, WOOD Inc., 1982, 93, Disting. Profl. Svc. award Coll. Environ. Design U. Colo., 1988, James Sudler Svc. award AIA, Denver, 1998. Mem. AIA (sec. 1988, bd. dirs. Colo. North chpt. 1985-86, chair Colo. govtl. affairs com. 1995-98, Design award 1993, pres. 1990, sec. Colo. chpt. 1988, ednl. fund Fisher I traveling scholar 1988, state design conf. chair 1991, North chpt. Design award 1993, treas. Denver chpt. 1998, v.p. 1999), Architects and Planners of Boulder (v.p. 1982), Nat. Coun. Architect Registration Bd., Nat. Golf Found. (sponsor), Kappa Sigma (chpt. pres. 1970). Avocations: golf, polit. history, fitness and health. Home: 1031 Turnberry Cir Louisville CO 80027-9594 Office: John Williams Architecture PC 821 17th St Ste 502 Denver CO 80202-3018

WILLIAMS, JOHN PHILIP, osteopathic physician; b. Waco, Tex., Nov. 1, 1957; s. Frank and Ginette (Gazell) W.; m. Laurel Karen Stagnitto, Sept. 30, 1984; children: Lauren Katherine, Nathan Micheal. BS, U. New Eng., Biddeford, Maine, 1981; MS, Calif. State U., San Bernardino, 1985; DO, U. New Eng. Coll. Osteo. Med., 1989; internship, Osteo. Hosp. of Maine, Portland, 1990-91. Intern Osteo. Hosp. Maine, Portland, 1990-91; resident in internal medicine Loma Linda (Calif.) U. Med. Ctr., 1991-95; staff physician in internal medicine North Calif. Med. Assns., Willits, 1995—, North Calif. Med. Assnns., Willits, 1994—, Calif. Med. Found. of Adventist Health Sys., 1997-98; med. dir. Mendocino Calif. Med. Found., 1997-98; chmn. ICU Howard Meml. Hosp. Mem. AMA, ACP, Am. Osteo. Assn., Am. Coll. Osteo. Internal Medicine, Am. Coll. Laser Medicine, Alpha Omega Alpha. Republican. Seventh-day Adventist. Avocations: bicycling, camping. Office: 82 Madrone St Willits CA 95490-4249

WILLIAMS, JOHN RAYMOND, JR., real estate regional director; b. Pitts., May 14, 1958; s. John Raymond Sr. and Patricia (Sollick) W. BS in Fin., Duquesne U., 1980. Banking officer Mellon Bank, Pitts., 1980-82; asst. v.p. Dollar Bank, Pitts., 1982-85; real estate mgr. Westinghouse Credit Corp., Pitts., 1985-87; real estate sr. mgr. Westinghouse Credit Corp., Irvine, Calif., 1987-89; regional dir. comml. real estate Westinghouse Credit Corp., San Francisco, 1989—; dir. First Hotel Investment Corp., dir., v.p. WES-K/W, dir. WES-W&H. Mem. Urban Land Inst., Bay Area Mortgage Assn. Roman Catholic. Avocations: running, skiing, music. Office: Westinghouse Credit Corp 1800 Broadway Apt 205 San Francisco CA 94109-2232

WILLIAMS, JOYCE MARILYN, artist, business owner; b. Waterbury, Conn., Sept. 12, 1933; d. Carl Vosburgh and Arline Dorothy (Cummings) Miller; m. Ralph Gray, Apr. 8, 1949 (div. 1955); children: Diane Leslie, Jerri Joyce-Gray; m. Charles Edward Williams, July 24, 1958; 1 child, Carol Lea. Grad. h.s., San Mateo, Calif., 1950. Pres., owner JC Enterprises, Phoenix, Ariz., 1993—; art instr. Sta. KHIZ-TV, Victorville, Calif., 1995; judge fine art San Bernardino County Fair, Victorville, 1995. Author: (instrn. books) Painting Portraits, 1994, Painting Horses, 1995; author, artist: (videos) Painting Portraits, 1993, Painting Horses, Wildlife, 1995; numerous portrait commns., U.S. and Can.; commd. cover art for world's largest Arabian horse show. Recipient numerous 1st pl. awards various art shows, 1985-95. Mem. High Desert Art League, High Desert GD (editor newsletter 1992-95). Avocations: teaching art, giving demonstrations, painting for galleries, writing. Office: JC Enterprises PO Box 82815 Phoenix AZ 85071-2815

WILLIAMS, KENNETH, secondary education educator, consultant; b. El Centro, Calif., Nov. 18, 1937; s. Roy Evance and Lily Mae (Sprenger) W.; m. Muriel Pauline Blake, Nov. 19, 1955; children: Marcelle, Melissa, Michelle. AA in English, Modesto Jr. Coll., 1957; student, U. Calif., Berkeley, 1958-59; BA in Liberal Arts, Calif. State U., Stanislaus, Turlock, 1961. Cert. secondary tchr., Calif. Tchr. English and reading Walter White Jr. H.S., Ceres, Calif., 1961-63; tchr. English and journalism Modesto (Calif.) H.S., 1963-98; dist. resource tchr. lang. arts Modesto City Schs., 1976-87, dist. lang. arts chair, 1987-97; founding dir. Great Valley Writing Project, Turlock, 1983-94; tchr. cons. Bay Area Writing Project, Berkeley, 1976—; ednl. cons., Modesto, 1976—; publs. advisor Citizens for Excellence in Edn., Modesto, 1980—. Co-author: (textbook series) Voices in Literature, Language and Composition, 1969, New Voices in Literature, Language and Composition, 1984; editor newspapers Advance, BEST, 1980—. Recipient Vasche award Calif. State U., Stanislaus, 1961, Outstanding Educator in Am. award, 1974. Mem. NEA, Calif. Tchrs. Assn. (Jose Calmanares award 1995), Modesto Tchrs. Assn., Ctrl. Calif. Coun. Tchrs. of English (chair curriculum study commn. 1994-99), Nat. Coun. Tchrs. English. Avocations: photography, collecting folklore, videography. Home: 3600 Jeffrey Dr Modesto CA 95357-0704

WILLIAMS, KENNETH JAMES, retired county official; b. Eureka, Calif., Apr. 28, 1924; s. E. J. and Thelma (Hall) W.; student Humboldt State Coll., 1942-43; B.S., U. Oreg., 1949, M.Ed., 1952; m. Mary Patricia Warring, Sept. 3, 1949; children—James Clayton, Susan May, Christopher Kenneth. Engaged as mountain triangulation observer with U.S. Coast and Geodetic Survey, 1942; instr. bus. and geography Boise (Idaho) Jr. Coll., 1949-51; tchr. Prospect High Sch., 1952-54; prin. Oakland (Oreg.) High Sch., 1954-58; supt. prin. Coburg Public Schs., 1958-64; supt. Yoncalla (Oreg.) Public Schs., 1964-66, Amity (Oreg.) Public Schs., 1966-72; adminstr. Yamhill County, McMinnville, Oreg., 1974-85; cons., 1985—; county liaison officer Land and Water Conservation Fund, 1977-85. Dist. lay leader Oreg.-Idaho ann. conf. United Methodist Ch., 1968-80, bd. dirs. western dist. Ch. Extension Soc., 1976-97; mem. Mid-Willamette Manpower Council, 1974-85; bd. dirs. Lafayette Noble Homes, 1970-72; mem. adv. com. local budget law sect. State of Oreg. Served with AUS, 1943-46. Decorated Purple Heart. Mem. NEA, Oreg. Edn. Assn., Oreg. Assn. Secondary Prins., Nat. Assn. Secondary Prins., AAUP, Oreg., Am. Assn. Sch. Adminstrs., Assn. Supervision and Curriculum Devel., Nat. Sch. Pub. Relations Assn., Phi Delta Kappa. Mason (Shriner), Lion. Home: 21801 SE Webfoot Rd Dayton OR 97114-8832

WILLIAMS, LEONA RAE, lingerie shop owner, consultant; b. Fairfield, Nebr., July 1, 1928; d. Melton M. and Helga D. (Sorensen) Brown; m. Eugene F. Williams, June 6, 1946; 1 child, Dennis D. Grad. high sch., Fairfield. Owner Alice Rae Apparel Shop, Tucson, 1953-96, second location, 1967-96, Green Valley, Ariz., 1976-93, Sun City, Ariz., 1979-96; ret., 1996; cons. in field. Sponsor Distributive Edn. Program, 1978-82; coord. fashion shows Am. Cancer Soc., Tucson, 1987, 88, 89. Mem. Exec. Women's Internat. Assn. (chpt. pres. 1994), Mchts. Assn. (pres. 1987-89), Soroptomists, C. of C. Better Bus. Bur. Republican. Baptist.

WILLIAMS, LOUISE RAE, artist, educator; b. Phoenix, Mar. 7, 1947; d. Walter Landon and Lillian Grace (Snowdon) Lyons; m. Robert Alan Williams, Apr. 1, 1967 (div. Apr. 1982); children: Michael Scott, Lisa Beth; m. Thomas James Lineham, Aug. 4, 1990. BA with honors, San Jose State U., 1969; BA, The Evergreen Coll., 1979; MFA, Ctrl. Wash. U., 1985. Asst. to dir. Indochinese refugee program Centralia Coll., Olympia, Wash., 1980-81, adj. instr., 1992; grad. asst. Ctrl. Wash. U., Ellensburg, 1982-85; instr. Yakima (Wash.) Valley C.C., 1984; vis. faculty The Evergreen State Coll., Olympia, 1988, 91, 93-97, 97—; asst. prof. Webster U., St. Louis, 1989-90; adj. instr. South Puget Sound C.C., Olympia, 1988-89, Centralia Coll., winter 1992. Solo exhibit King Art Gallery, 1994; represented in pub. collections Wash. State Art In, Pub. Places Collection, Tacoma Housing Authority. Sec. Alliance for the Mentally Ill, Thurston/Mason County, Washington, 1998. Artist in Residence, Ucross Found., 1987, Centrum Found., 1995. Mem. Coll. Art Assn.

WILLIAMS, MARION LESTER, government official; b. Abilene, Tex., Dec. 1, 1933; s. Martin Lester and Eddie Faye (Wilson) W.; m. Johnnie Dell Ellinger, Dec. 14, 1957; children: Tammy Dawn Cole, Pamela DeAnn Ritterbush. BS, Tex. A&M U., 1956; MS, U. N.Mex., 1967; PhD, Okla. State U., 1971. Test engr. Sandia Nat. Labs., Albuquerque, 1959-61; weapons sys. engr. Naval Weapons Evaluation Facility, Albuquerque, 1961-66; ops. rsch. analyst Joint Chiefs of Staff/Joint Task Force II, Albuquerque, 1966-68; chief reliability div. Field Command DNA, Albuquerque, 1969-71; prin. scientist SHAPE Tech. Ctr., The Hague, Netherlands, 1971-74; chief tech. advisor HQ AF Test & Evaluation Ctr., Albuquerque, 1974-81; chief scientist HQ AF Operational Test & Evaluation Ctr., Albuquerque, 1981-89; tech. dir. HQ AF Operational Test & Evaluation Ctr., 1989—; vis. adv. com. Okla. State U., Stillwater, 1988—; adv. com. U. N.Mex., Albuquerque, 1985—. Editor T&E Tech. Jour., 1987—; contbr. articles to profl. jours. Sci. advisor N.Mex. Sci. & Tech. Oversigh Com., Albuquerque, 1988; bd. advisors U. N.Mex. Cancer Ctr., 1987—; bd. dirs. Contact Albuquerque, 1986-87. 1st lt. USAF 1956-59. Recipient Presdl. Rank award, 1987, 92. Fellow Mil. Ops. Rsch. Soc. (pres. 1982-83, bd. dirs. 1976-81, Wanner award 1991), Internat. Test & Evaluation Ctr. (bd. dirs. 1984-86, 88-90, v.p. 1990, pres. 1992-93), Ops. Rsch. Soc. Am., Tau Beta Pi, Phi Eta Sigma, Alpha Pi Mu, Sigma Tau, Kappa Mu Epsilon. Democrat. Baptist. Avocations: skiing, computers. Home: 1416 Stagecoach Ln SE Albuquerque NM 87123-4429 Office: HQ AF Operational Test Ctr Kirtland AFB Albuquerque NM 87117-7001

WILLIAMS, MICHAEL ANTHONY, lawyer; b. Mandan, N.D., Sept. 14, 1932; s. Melvin Douglas and Lucille Ann (Gavin) W.; m. Marjorie Ann Harrer, Aug. 25, 1962 (div. 1989); children: Ann Margaret, Douglas Raymond, David Michael; m. Dorothy Ruth Hand, 1989. B.A., Coll. of St. Thomas, 1954; LL.B., Harvard U., 1959. Bar: Colo. 1959, N.D. 1959, U.S. Dist. Ct. Colo. 1959, U.S. Ct. Appeals (10th cir.) 1959, U.S. Supreme Ct. 1967. Assoc. Sherman & Howard and predecessor Dawson, Nagel, Sherman & Howard, Denver, 1959-65, ptnr., 1965-91; pres. Williams, Youle & Koenigs, P.C., Denver, 1991—. Served as 1st lt. USAF, 1955-57. Mem. Am. Coll. Trial Lawyers, Am. Bd. Trial Advs., Colo. Bar Found., Am. Law Inst., ABA, Colo. Bar Assn., Denver Bar Assn., Arapahoe County Bar Assn. Office: Williams Youle & Koenigs PC 950 17th St Ste 2450 Denver CO 80202-2828

WILLIAMS, MICHAEL JAMES, health care services consultant; b. Royal Oak, Mich., Sept. 23, 1951; s. Robert Burgett and Elizabeth (McGuire) W.; m. Juliana Caitlin. BA in Police Adminstrn., Wayne State U., 1974, BS in Psychology, 1974; MPA, Calif. State U., Fullerton, 1978. Asst. mgr. Suburban Ambulance Co., Royal Oak, 1970-74; dir. Emergency Med. Services Imperial County, El Centro, Calif., 1974-76, Orange County, Santa Ana, Calif., 1976-80; pres. EMS Systems Design, Irvine, Calif., 1980-89, The Abaris Group, Tustin, 1989—; instr., trainer ACLS, Am. Heart Assn., 1978-80, CPr, 1989—; spl. cons. Hosp. Coun. So. Calif., Calif. Assn. Hosps. and Health Systems; EMS med. coord. trauma emergencies Pyramid Films, Santa Monica, Calif., 1989 (Am. Film Inst. Blue Ribbon award). Contbr. numerous articles to profl. jours. Recipient Recognition award Orange County Emergency Care Commn., 1980, Appreciation award UCI Med. Ctr., Orange, Calif., 1980, Orange County Fire Chiefs Assn., 1980. Mem. Healthcare Fin. Mgmt. Assn., Am. Trauma Soc., Am. Heart Assn. (bd. dirs. Orange County chpt., 1976-82), No. Calif. Healthcare Execs., Orange County Trauma Soc. (bd. dirs. 1981-89, program achievement award, 1987), Internat. Assn. Fire Chiefs (EMS sect.), EMS Adminstrs. Assn. Calif. (founding). Democrat. Avocations: jogging, racquetball, fishing. Office: 700 Ygnacio Valley Rd Ste 250 Walnut Creek CA 94596-3871

WILLIAMS, MIKEL H., magistrate judge; b. 1946. Chief magistrate judge Boise. Office: US Dist Ct Idaho Fed Bldg US Courthouse 550 W Fort St MSC 039 Boise ID 83724-0101*

WILLIAMS, PAT, former congressman; b. Helena, Mont., Oct. 30, 1937; m. Carol Griffith, 1965; children: Griff, Erin, Whitney. Student, U. Mont., 1956-57, William Jewell U.; BA, U. Denver, 1961; postgrad., Western Mont. Coll.; LLD (hon.), Carroll Coll., Montana Coll. of Mineral Sci. and Tech. Mem. Mont. Ho. of Reps., 1967, 69; exec. dir. Hubert Humphrey Presdl. campaign, Mont., 1968; exec. asst. to U.S. Rep. John Melcher, 1969-71; mem. Gov.'s Employment and Tng. Council, 1972-78, Mont. Legis. Reapportionment Commn., 1973; co-chmn. Jimmy Carter Presdl. campaign, Mont., 1976; mem. 96th-102nd Congresses from 1st Mont. dist., 1979-96; sr. fellow Ctr. Rocky Mountain W. U. Mont., Missoula, 1996—; ranking mem. postsecondary edn. subcom. Coordinator Mont. Family Edn. Program, 1971-78. Served with U.S. Army, 1960-61; Served with Army N.G., 1962-69. Mem. Mont. Fedn. Tchrs. Democrat. Lodge: Elks. Home: 210 High Park Way Missoula MT 59803-2246 Office: U Montana Ctr for Rocky Mountain West Millwaki Station Fl 12 Missoula MT 59812*

WILLIAMS, PHILIP ANTHONY, engineering executive. Student, Long Beach City Coll., 1978-91. Advanced tng. cert. Comm. Workers Am., 1979; Digital Network Automatic Switch cert. LARSE Corp., Sunnyvale, Calif., 1983; cert. income tax preparer Am. Schs., 1992; cert. comty. alcohol and drug abuse tng. City of Long Beach, 1995. Electrician Naval Post Grad. Sch., Monterey, Calif., 1972-73; electrician helper Long Beach (Calif.) Naval Shipyard, 1977; equipment maintainer GTE, Thousand Oaks, Calif., 1978-81; engr. III GTE, Thousand Oaks, 1981-83, sr. engr., 1983-86, staff engr., 1986—. Contbr. articles to profl. jours.; inventor Bupger Dog. Founder, CEO Mentor 2000; participant Long Beach Leadership Program; bd. mem. Long Beach Midnight Basketball League; vol. United Way-Greater L.A./Harbor Area, Calif. Police Summer Games, Long Beach, Sr. Olympics, Long Beach. With U.S. Army, 1969-76. Mem. VFW, Am. Legion, Vietnam Vets. Am. Home and Office: PO Box 5017 Long Beach CA 90805-0017

WILLIAMS, RAY RALPH, advisory engineer; b. Blackfoot, Idaho, Aug. 6, 1935; s. Millard William Roberts and Ardell Lydia Evans; m. Beverly Boyce, June 17, 1957; children: Serena Ardell, Steven Ray, David Tim, Travis Ralph, Brannon Dean. BA in Econs. and Bus., Chapman U., 1975; MS in Sys. Mgmt., U. So. Calif., 1979; B in Indsl. Tech., U. Idaho, 1987. Cert. quality engr.; cert. quality auditor. Master chief petty officer USN, 1974-77; tech. asst. to corp. quality mgr. San Diego Gas and Electric, 1977-79; sr. project engr. Exxon Nuc. Idaho, Idaho Falls, Ind., 1979-82; start up mgr. Union Electric-Callaway Nuclear Power Plant, Fulton, Mo., 1982-84; start up engr. Ill. Power, Clinton, 1984-85; sr. engr. Rockwell Corp., Idaho Falls, 1985-89; staff engr. EG&G Idaho Corp., Idaho Falls, 1989-94, chmn. quality assn., 1992-93; advisory engr. Lockheed Martin Idaho Tech., Idaho Falls, 1994—. With USN, 1974-77. Decorated Submarine Patrol pin USN; recipent Navy Achievment medals. Mem. VFW, Am. Soc. Quality (chmn. sect. 1992-93, scholarship chair 1994-96), Am. Nuc. Soc., Navy Res. Assn., Am. Legion. Republican. Mem. LDS Ch. Home: 4190 E 460 N Rigby ID 83442-5529 Office: Lockheed Martin Idaho Technologies Dept Packaging and Transp PO Box 1625 Idaho Falls ID 83415-0001

WILLIAMS, RICHARD KENT, electrical engineer; b. Quincy, Ill., July 10, 1958; s. Robert Gene and Mary Adele (Wheelan) W.; m. Dorothy LLising Aquino, July 4, 1985; children: Laura, Alyssa. BSEE, U. Ill., 1980; MSEE, Santa Clara U., 1987. lectr. in field. Over 40 patents in field; contbr. articles to profl. jours., chpts. to books. Mem. AAAS, IEEE (tech. reviewer), Electrochem. Soc., Internat. Symposium on Power Semiconductor Devices and ICs. Office: Siliconix Inc 2201 Laurelwood Rd Santa Clara CA 95054-1593

WILLIAMS, ROBERT STONE, protective services official; b. Mathews, Va., Jan. 22, 1952; s. Charles H. and Anne (Stone) W.; m. Danielle Williams, July 1987. AAS, Rowan Tech. Inst., 1972; BS in Fire Protection and Safety Engring., Okla. State U., 1975, MBA, 1976. Adminstrv. specialist Oklahoma City Fire Dept., 1977-79; dep. fire chief Clovis Fire Dept., N.Mex., 1979-82; fire chief Billings Fire Dept., Mont., 1982-88; fire chief City of Spokane, Wash., 1988—. Mem. Wash. State Bldg. Code Coun., 1989-94; bd. dirs. Salvation Army, Billings, 1984-85, Am. Heart Assn., Clovis, N.Mex., 1980-82; chmn. Internat. Fire Code Inst., 1993-94, 94-95, mem., 1990—. Named Fireperson Yr. Billings Downtown Exchange Club, 1988. Mem. Western Fire Chiefs Assn. (1st v.p. 1984-85, pres. 1985-86), Internat. Assn. Fire Chiefs, Nat. Fire Protection Assn., Curry County Jaycees (v.p. 1981-82, Jaycee of Yr. 1982), Billings Jaycees (bd. dirs. 1983-87, v.p. community devel. 1985, Outstanding Jaycee 1983, Disting. Service award 1985), Mont. Jaycees (treas. 1986-87, speak-up program mgr. 1986-87, Outstanding Young Montanan award 1985-86). Roman Catholic. Office: Spokane Fire Dept W 44 Riverside Ave Spokane WA 99201-0114*

WILLIAMS, ROGER, musician; b. Omaha, Oct. 1, 1924; s. Frederick Jacob and Dorothea Wertz; m. Louise Decarlo Williams; children: Laura, Alice, James. Bachelors, Idaho State U., 1950; Masters, Drake U., 1952; postgrad., Juilliard, 1953. Home: 16150 Clear Valley Pl Encino CA 91436-3312

WILLIAMS, RONALD DEAN, minister, religious organization executive; b. Decatur, Ill., Oct. 23, 1940; s. Henry Lawrence and Ella Loudica Williams; m. Carole Jeanette Lane, June 16, 1962; children: Scott Allan, Mark Lawrence, Derek James. BTh, LIFE Bible Coll., L.A., 1965; DD, Internat. Ch. Foursquare Gospel, L.A., 1992. Ordained to ministry Internat. Ch. Foursquare Gospel, 1966. Pastor Foursquare Gospel Ch., Surrey, B.C., Can., 1965-69; missionary Foursquare Gospel Ch., Hong Kong, 1969-85; prof. LIFE Bible Coll., 1985-95; mng. editor Foursquare World ADVANCE, 1993—; comm. officer Internat. Ch. of Foursquare Gospel, 1988—; bd. dirs. Foursquare Gospel Ch.; pres. exec. bd. Internat. Pentecostal Press Assn., Oklahoma City, 1990-98; comm. officer Pentecostal/Charismatic Chs. North Am., Memphis, 1994—; coord. E. Coun. Foursquare Miss., 1979-82. Editor: The Vine and The Branches, 1992; mng. editor Foursquare World ADVANCE mag., 1985. With USAF, 1958-61. Avocations: writing, golf, reading, music. Office: Internat Ch Foursquare Gospel 1910 W Sunset Blvd Ste 200 Los Angeles CA 90026-3295

WILLIAMS, RONALD LEE, pharmacologist; b. Koleen, Ind., June 26, 1936; s. Marion Raymond and Doris May (Lynch) W.; m. Sondra Sue Cobb, June 7, 1957; children: Robin Lee, Christopher P., David R., Jonathan V. BS, Butler U., 1959, MS, 1961; PhD, Tulane U., 1964. Registered pharmacist, Colo. From instr. to assoc. prof. pharmacology La. State U., New Orleans, 1964-84, assoc. prof. medicine, 1978-84, ret., 1984; asst. dir. Dept. of Corrections Hosp. Pharmacy, Canon City, Colo., 1986-93; with Canon Pharmacy, Canon City, Colo., 1994-95; clin. pharmacist VA Med. Ctr., Ft. Lyon, Colo., 1996—; expert adv. panel renal drugs U.S. Pharmacopeia Drug Info., 1981-85; cons. in field. Mem. editl. bd. Pharmacology, 1979; reviewer jour. Pharmaceutical Sci., 1976; contbr. articles to profl. jours. La. Heart Assn. grantee, 1964, 66. Mem. Am. Soc. Pharmacology, N.Y. Acad. Sci., Fedn. Am. Soc. Exptl. Biology, So. Colo. Soc. Hosp. Pharm. Assn., Sigma Xi, Rho Chi. Republican. Baptist. Avocations: hiking, camping, back-packing, hunting, book collector.

WILLIAMS, RONALD OSCAR, systems engineer; b. Denver, May 10, 1940; s. Oscar H. and Evelyn (Johnson) W. BS in Applied Math., U. Colo. Coll. Engring., 1964, postgrad. U. Colo., U. Denver, George Washington U. Computer programmer Apollo Systems dept., missile and space divsn. Gen. Electric Co., Kennedy Space Ctr., Fla., 1965-67, Manned Spacecraft Ctr., Houston, 1967-68; computer programmer U. Colo., Boulder, 1968-73; computer programmer analyst def. systems divsn. System Devel. Corp. for NORAD, Colorado Springs, 1974-75; engr. def. systems and command-and-info. systems Martin Marietta Aerospace, Denver, 1976-80; systems engr. space and comm. group, def. info. systems divsn. Hughes Aircraft Co., Aurora, Colo., 1980-89; rsch. analyst Math Rsch. Ctr., 1990—, sr. rsch. mathematician, 1996—. Vol. fireman Clear Lake City (Tex.) Fire Dept., 1968; officer Boulder Emergency Squad, 1969-76, rescue squadman, 1969-76, liaison to cadets, 1971, pers. officer, 1971-76, exec. bd., 1971-76, award of merit, 1971, 72, emergency med. technician 1973—; spl. police officer Boulder Police Dept., 1970-75; spl. dep. sheriff Boulder County Sheriff's Dept., 1970-71; nat. adv. bd. Am. Security Coun., 1979-91, Coalition of Peace through Strength, 1979-91. Served with USMCR, 1958-66. Decorated Organized Res. medal; recipient Cost Improvement Program award Hughes Aircraft Co., 1982, Systems Improvement award, 1982, Top Cost Improvement Program award, 1983. Mem. AAAS, AIAA (sr.), Math. Assn. Am., Am. Math. Soc., Soc. Indsl. and Applied Math., Math. Study Unit of the Am. Topical Assn., Armed Forces Comm. and Electronics Assn., Assn. Old Crows, Nat. Def. Industrial Assn., Marine Corps Assn., Air Force Assn., U.S. Naval Inst., Nat. Geog. Soc., Smithsonian Instn., Soc. Amateur Radio Astronomers, Met. Opera Guild, Colo. Hist. Soc., Hist. Denver, Inc., Historic Boulder, Inc., Mountain Hist. Soc., Denver Botanic Gardens, Denver Mus. Natural History, Denver Zool. Found., Inc., Mensa. Lutheran.

WILLIAMS, ROSS EVANS, planner, landscape architect; b. Newark, Feb. 26, 1955; s. Gwynne Pierce and Francis Louise (Smith) W.; m. Janet Kay Hartshorn, Apr. 10, 1983; children: Jonathan Ross, Pamela Kay. BS, Colo. State U., 1977. Park planner City of Longmont, Colo., 1977-82, City of Lakewood, Colo., 1982—; mem. Colo. Profl. Certification Bd. Leisure Profls., Denver, 1990-96. Mem. Am. Planning Assn., Am. Soc. Landscape Archs., Nat. Recreation and Parks Assn. (cert. leisure profl.), Colo. Parks and Recreation Assn. Republican. Presbyterian. Office: City of Lakewood 445 S Allison Pkwy Lakewood CO 80226-3105

WILLIAMS, RUTH LEE, clinical social worker; b. Dallas, June 24, 1944; d. Carl Woodley and Nancy Ruth (Gardner) W. BA, So. Meth. U., 1966; M Sci.in Social Work, U. Tex., Austin, 1969. Milieu coordinator Starr Commonwealth, Albion, Mich., 1969-73; clin. social worker Katherine Hamilton Mental Health Care, Terre Haute, Ind., 1973-74; clin. social worker, supr. Pikes Peak Mental Health Ctr., Colorado Springs, Colo., 1974-78; pvt. practice social work Colorado Springs, 1978—; pres. Hearthstone Inn, Inc., Colorado Springs, 1978—; practitioner Jin Shin Jyutsu, Colorado Springs, 1978—; pres., v.p. bd. dirs. Premier Care (formerly Colorado Springs Mental Health Care Providers Inc.), 1986-87, chmn. quality assurance com., 1987-89, v.p. bd. dirs., 1992-93; bd. dirs. Beth Haven, Inc., JAC Svcs. Author, editor: From the Kitchen of The Hearthstone Inn, 1981, 2d rev. edit., 1986, 3d rev. edit., 1992. Mem. Am. Bd. Examiners in Clin. Social Work (charter mem., cert.), Colo. Soc. Clin. Social Work (editor 1976), Nat. Assn. Soc. Workers (diplomate), Nat. Bd. Social Work Examiners (cert.), Nat. Assn. Ind. Innkeepers, So. Meth. U. Alumni Assn. (life). Avocations: gardening, hiking, sailing. Home: 11555 Howells Rd Colorado Springs CO 80908-3735 Office: 536 E Uintah St Colorado Springs CO 80903-2515

WILLIAMS, SALLY, landscape designer; b. Kansas City, Mo., June 30, 1955; d. Douglas John and Margaret Ann (Paul) Williams; m. Siegfried Peter Duray-Bito, June 16, 1984; children: Cassie, Alana. BA, Metro State Coll., Denver, 1979. Bus. mgr. Muse, Denver, 1985-87; exec. dir. Colo. Fedn. of the Arts, Denver, 1987-88; owner Perennial Garden Planning, Littleton, Colo., 1992—. Advanced master gardener Arapahoe County Ext. Svc., Littleton, 1985-96. Avocations: watercolor painting, sketching, reading. Home and Office: Perennial Garden Planning 5000 Aspen Dr Littleton CO 80123-1502

WILLIAMS, SPICE, actress; b. Burbank, Calif., Apr. 26, 1952; d. Robert Lee Williams and Gladys Marie (Elherman) Williams-Mulligan; m. Charles Fassert, May 12, 1982 (div. June 1989); m. Gregory Crosby, Aug. 26, 1989; 1 child, Luke Gregory. Student, L.A. Valley Coll.; med. transcriber, Sawyers Occupl. Treatment nurse Convalescent Homes, L.A., 1967-70; musician, singer, entertainer Sugar N Spice AF of M, 1970-78; songwriter 20th Century Records, L.A., 1978-79; actress and stuntwoman Hollywood, Calif., 1978—; food mfr. Spice of Life Meatless Meats and Jerky, Sherman Oaks, Calif., 1993—; nutritional advisor MS Fitness Mag., Corona, Calif., 1980—; founder, prodr. Power Source Day annual benefit, 1986—. Appeared in films Shattered Illusions, Cherokee Kid, Terminal Force, Star Trek V, Naked Truth, The Guyver, Stranded, The Killing Touch, Educating Crystal; appeared in TV movies Dangerous Affection, Getting Physical, Murder in High Places; appeared on TV in Buffy the Vampire Slayer, The Smart Guy, Roseanne, Step By Step, Young and The Restless, Bold & Beautiful, Melrose Place, Brisco County Jr., Acapulco Heat, Hat Squad, My Two Dads, Women in Prison, Out of This World, Mama's Family, others; stunt woman for films Spawn, Batman & Robin, Batman II, Natural Born Killers, Ghostbusters II, Twins, A Simple Plan, Acts of Betrayal, From Dusk Til Dawn, High School High, Backstreet Justice, CIA #2, Sleepwalker, For the Love of the Game, many others; stuntwoman for TV shows The Smart Guy, Roseanne, Lois & Clark, Melrose Place, Deep Space Nine, My Two Dads, Day's Of Our Lives, 7th Heaven, Murder She Wrote, Reasonable Doubts, Fall Guy, Stir Crazy, Knots Landing, Falcon Crest, many others. Mem. AFTRA (nat. bd. 1994-97, local bd. 1998—), SAG (stunt and safety com. 1994-95), Stuntwomen's Assn. Motion Pictures (bd. mem., treas.), Acad. TV Arts and Scis. Avocations: body building, kickboxing, horseback riding, skiing, precision driving. Office: Spice of Life Co Ste 115 15445 Ventura Blvd Sherman Oaks CA 91403

WILLIAMS, SUSAN ELAINE, stockbroker, financial planner; b. Hartford, Conn., Aug. 14, 1965; d. Werner Sigmund Schild and Elllinor Kay (Whitehead) Davidson; m. Mark Shelton F. Williams, Sept. 5, 1993; 1 child, Eric Shelton Schild. BA, Lafayette Coll., Easton, Pa., 1987. Asst. v.p. Chem. Bank, N.Y.C., 1987-92; asst. portfolio mgr. Thornburg Mgmt. Co., Santa Fe, N. Mex., 1992-93; registered rep. S G Long & Co., Missoula, Mont., 1993—. Treas. Missoula Downtown Assn., 1995—. Mem. Rotary Internat. Avocations: skiing, hiking, backpacking, biking, outdoor activities. Office: S G Long & Co 283 W Front St Ste 302 Missoula MT 59802-4328

WILLIAMS, VIVIAN LEWIE, college counselor; b. Columbia, S.C., Jan. 23, 1923; d. Lemuel Arthur Sr. and Ophelia V. (McDaniel) Lewie; m. Charles Warren Williams, Apr. 4, 1947 (div. 1967); children: Pamela Ann Williams-Coote, Charles Warren Jr. (dec.). *Lemuel Arthur Lewis's (father) paternal ancestors date back to 1790, when George (Lewey) Lewie came to America. Father Lemuel A. Lewie, D.D.S., was one of the early black dentists in South Carolina beginning his practice in 1907. He had attended New York City College and received his D.D.S. from Howard University in 1907. Husband, C. W. Williams, M. D. was a leading surgeon in Charlotte, North Carolina. Together, they developed Hyde Park Estates (89.9 acres upper middle class division) in 1961. Many family members entered the medical field: sister, R. Marguerite Lewie, M. D., son, Charles Warren, Jr., M.D., and niece, R. Maria Lewie, M.D.* BA, Allen U., 1942; MA, U. Mich., 1946, postgrad., 1946, 48; MS, U. So. Calif., 1971, postgrad., 1971-72. Cert. marriage, family and child counselor, Calif.; cert. Calif. C.C. counselor. Asst. prof. psychology Tenn. State Agrl. and Indsl. U., Nashville, 1946-47; asst. prof. edn. Winston-Salem (N.C.) State U., 1947-50; asst. prof. edn., dir. tchr. edn. Allen U., Columbia, S.C., 1951-53; specialist reading, coord. lang. arts Charlotte (N.C.) Mecklenburg Schs., 1963-67, cons. comprehensive sch. improvement project, 1967-69; asst. prof. edn., psychology Johnson C. Smith U., Charlotte, 1967-69; counselor, team leader Centennial, U. So. Calif. Tchr. Corps, L.A., 1970-73; counselor Compton (Calif.) C.C., 1973—, adv. fgn. student, 1975-85; co-developer Hyde Park Estates and The Moors, Charlotte, N.C., 1960-63. Pres. bd. dirs. Charlotte Day Nursery, 1956-59; bd. dirs. Taylor St. USO, Columbia, S.C., 1951-53; sec. southwest region Nat. Alliance Family Life, 1973-74; sec. bd. dirs. NCCJ, Charlotte, 1959-62. Recipient Faculty Audit Program award Ford/Carnegie Found., Harvard U., Cambridge, Mass., 1968, Pub. Svc. Achievement award WSOC Broadcasting Co.; fellow U. Mich., 1946. Mem. NAACP (life, Golden Heritage mem. 1992), AAUW (life), NEA (life), Am. Fedn. Tchrs., Faculty Assn. Calif. C.C., Nat. Acad. Counselors and Family Therapists (life, clin. mem., pres. S.W. region 1989), C.C. Counselors Assn., The Links, Inc. (Harbor area chpt. historian 1985-87, chaplain 1990-94, 96-98), Jack and Jill Am. (charter mem., organizer Charlotte chpt., pres. 1954-56), Women on Target, Calif. Tchrs. Assn., Delta Sigma Theta, Alpha Gamma Sigma (Golden Apple award 1981). Democrat. Methodist. Avocations: sewing, crafts, photography. Home: 6621 Caro St Paramount CA 90723-4755 Office: Compton Community Coll 1111 E Artesia Blvd Compton CA 90221-5314

WILLIAMS, WALTER BAKER, mortgage banker; b. Seattle, May 12, 1921; s. William Walter and Anna Leland (Baker) W.; m. Marie Davis Wilson, July 6, 1945; children: Kathryn Williams-Mullins, Marcia Frances Williams Swanson, Bruce Wilson, Wendy Susan. BA, U. Wash., 1943; JD, Harvard U., 1948. With Bogle & Gates, Seattle, 1948-63, ptnr., 1960-63; pres. Continental Inc., Seattle, 1963-91, chmn., 1991-97, chmn. emeritus, 1997—; bd. dirs. United Graphics Inc., Seattle, 1973-86, Fed. Nat. Mortgage Assn., 1976-77; chmn. Continental Savings Bank, 1991—. Rep. Wash. State Ho. of Reps., Olympia, 1961-63; sen. Wash. State Senate, Olympia, 1963-71; chmn. Econ. Devel. Council of Puget Sound, Seattle, 1981-82; pres. Japan-Am. Soc. of Seattle, 1971-72; chmn. Woodland Park Zoo Commn., Seattle, 1984-85. Served to capt. USMC, 1942-46, PTO. Recipient Brotherhood Citation, NCCJ, Seattle, 1980, First Citizen award Seattle-King County Asn. Realtors, 1997. Mem. Mortgage Bankers Assn. Am. (pres. 1973-74), Wash. Mortgage Bankers Assn. (pres. 1971), Fed. Home Loan Mortgage Corp. (adv. com.), Wash. Savs. League (bd. dirs., chmn. 1991-92), Rotary (pres. local club 1984-85), Rainier Club Seattle (pres. 1987-88). Republican. Congregationalist. Office: Continental Inc 601 Union St Ste 2000 Seattle WA 98101-2326

WILLIAMS, WALTER DAVID, aerospace executive, consultant; b. Chgo., July 22, 1931; s. Walter William and Theresa Barbara (Gilman) W.; m. Joan Haven Armstrong, Oct. 22, 1960; children: Latham Lloyd, Clayton Chapell, William Haven. BS, Ohio U., 1951; MBA, Harvard U., 1955; MS, MIT, 1972. Supr. fin. policy and systems Hughes Aircraft Co., Culver City, Calif., 1955-57; staff mem. Rand Corp. and SDC, Santa Monica, Calif., 1957-60; mgr. adminstrn. and fin. Microwave Div. TRW Inc., Canoga Park, Calif., 1960-63; exec. asst. Space Labs. Northrop Corp., Hawthorne, Calif., 1963-66; fin. mgr. comml. group Aircraft Div. Northrop Corp., Hawthorne, Calif., 1966-72; dir. internat. plans Northrop Corp., L.A., 1972-74, dir. internat. mkt. devel., 1974-77, exec. dir. internat., 1977-93; pres. Williams Internat. Assocs., L.A., 1994—; export advisor U.S. Sec. Commerce, Washington, 1986-98. Author (study/lect. series) Internat. Def. Mktg., 1982. Dir. KCET Men's Coun., L.A., 1970; pres. Westwood Rep. Club, L.A., 1970; assoc. mem. Rep. State Ctrl. Com., Calif., 1968; div. chmn. Rep. Ctrl. Com., L.A. County, 1968. Served to capt. U.S. Army, 1951-53. Recipient fellowship Alfred P. Sloan Found., 1971-72. Mem. AIAA, Soc. Sloan Fellows, MIT Club, Harvard Bus. Sch. Assn., Newcomen Soc., Chaine des Rotisseurs, L.A. Country Club, Harvard Club, Soc. Bacchus Am., Order of Malta, Delta Sigma Pi, Pi Kappa Alpha. Avocations: golf, tennis, paddle tennis. Office: Williams Internat Assocs PO Box 491178 Los Angeles CA 90049-9178

WILLIAMS, WILLIAM COREY, theology educator, consultant; b. Wilkes-Barre, Pa., July 12, 1937; s. Edward Douglas and Elizabeth Irene (Schooley) W.; m. Alma Simmenroth Williams, June 27, 1959; 1 child, Linda. Diploma in Ministerial Studies, NE Bible Inst., 1962; BA in Bibl. Studies, Cen. Bible Coll., 1963, MA in Religion, 1964; MA in Hebrew and Near Ea. Studies, NYU, 1966, PhD in Hebrew Lang. and Lit., 1975; postgrad., Hebrew U., 1977-78, Inst. Holyland Studies, 1986. Ref. libr. Hebraic section Libr. of Congress, Washington, 1967-69; prof. Old Testament So. Calif. Coll., Costa Mesa, 1969—; adj. prof. Old Testament Melodyland Sch. Theology, Anaheim, Calif., 1975-77; vis. prof. Old Testament Fuller Theol. Sem., Pasadena, Calif., 1978-81, 84, Asian Theol. Ctr. for Evangelism and Missions, Singapore and Sabah, E. Malaysia, 1985, Continental Bible Coll., Saint Pieters-Leeuw, Belgium, 1985, Mattersey Bible Coll., Eng., 1985, Inst. Holy Land Studies, Jerusalem, 1986, Regent U., 1994; transl. cons. and reviser New Am. Std. Bible, 1969-94; transl. cons. The New Internat. Version, 1975-76, New Century Version, 1991, The New Living Translation, 1992-95, New Internat. Version, Reader's Version, 1993-94; transl. cons. and editor Internat. Children's Version, 1985-86. Author: (books, tapes) Hebrew I: A Study Guide, 1986, Hebrew II: A Study Guide, 1986; contbr. articles to International Standard Bible Encyclopedia, New International Dictionary of Old Testment Theology and Evangelical Dictionary of Biblical Theology; contbr. articles to profl. jours.; contbr. notes to Spirit Filled Life Study Bible. Nat. Def. Fgn. Lang. fellow NYU, 1964-67; Alumni scholar N.E. Bible Inst., 1960-61; NEH fellow, summer 1992; recipient Disting. Educator's award Assemblies of God, 1997. Mem. Soc. Bibl. Lit., Evang. Theol. Soc. (exec. office 1974-77), Am. Acad. Religion, Nat. Assn. Profs. of Hebrew, Inst. Bibl. Rsch., The Lockman Found. (hon. mem. bd. dirs. 1992-94, mem. editorial bd. 1974-94). Home: 1817 Peninsula Pl Costa Mesa CA 92627-4591 Office: So Calif Coll 55 Fair Dr Costa Mesa CA 92626-6520

WILLIAMS JONES, ELIZABETH, financial planner, business consultant; b. San Francisco, Jan. 16, 1948; d. John and Myrtle Mary (Thierry) W.; children: Brian, Jonathan; m. Archie W. Jones Jr. Cert. in bus., U. Calif., 1979. Cert. computers loan processing. Manpower coord., fed. programs U.S. Govt., San Francisco; patient svc. rep. Health Care Svc., Oakland, Calif.; ins. and real estate cons.; pres. Investments Unlimited, Oakland, EWJ & Assocs. Mktg. Firm; leisure svcs. commr. City of Pitts.; CEO Ultimate Vacations Inc. Mem. NAACP. Recipient Pub. Speaking award; European Investment fellow. Mem. AAUW, NAFE, Nat. Real Estate Owners Assn., Nat. Notary Assn., Order Ea. Star, Heroines Jericho, Daus. Isis, Toastmistress Club. Home: PO Box 523 Pittsburg CA 94565-0052

WILLIAMS-LOHMAR, JUDITH ANN, technical and engineering services company executive; b. Lancaster, Calif., Aug. 10, 1954; d. Robert Melvin Williams and Cora Lee (Clemow) Williams Campbell. AA, Ventura Coll., 1979; BA in Communications, U. Wash., 1982. Editor NOAA, Seattle, 1982; liaison asst. Naval Ship Weapon Systems Engring. Sta., Washington, 1983; mgmt. analyst Triton Assocs., Inc., 1983-84; program mgr. Tech. Applications, Inc., Alexandria, Va., 1984-86; logistics analyst Value Systems Engring. Corp., Alexandria, 1986-87; tng. analyst Designers & Planners, Inc., Arlington, Va., 1987; prin. Ind. Profl. Writers & Assoc., Alexandria, 1987-88; sr. logistician Support Mgmt. Svcs., Inc., Oxnard, Calif., 1989-91; sys. engr. GE Govt. Svcs., Oxnard, 1991-92, Martin Marietta Svcs., Inc., Oxnard, 1993-94, Lockheed Martin Svcs., Oxnard, Calif., 1995—. Author newsletter articles, 1986-88. Mem. Soc. Naval Architects and Marine Engrs. (assoc. dir. 1987-88), Navy League U.S. (dir. pub. affairs 1986-87, mng. editor newsletter 1986), Soc. Logistics Engrs., Ventura County Writers' Club. Christian. Avocations: creative writing, reading, quilting, cooking, walking.

WILLIAMSON, CHILTON, JR., magazine editor; b. N.Y.C., Apr. 25, 1947; s. Chilton and Frances (Philpotts) W.; m. Norma Boles, Mar. 12, 1981 (div. Apr. 1992). BA, Columbia Coll., 1969. History editor St. Martin's Press, N.Y.C., 1973-75; literary editor Nat. Rev., N.Y.C., 1976-89, sr. editor, 1986-89; sr. editor Chronicles: A Magazine of American Culture, Rockford, Ill., 1989—. Author: Saltbound: A Block Island Winter, 1980, Roughnecking It, 1982, Desert Light, 1987, The Homestead, 1990, The Immigration Mystique, 1996, (monthly column) The Hundredth Meridian for Chronicles. Roman Catholic. Avocations: hunting, horses, music, bullfighting. Home: 5021 Redland Dr Las Cruces NM 88011-7915

WILLIAMSON, CORLISS, basketball player; b. Dec. 4, 1973. Forward Sacramento Kings. Office: care Sacramento Kings 1 Sports Pkwy Sacramento CA 95834-2300

WILLIAMSON, EDWARD HENRY, chaplain, army officer; b. Jackson, Miss., Dec. 9, 1957; s. Oliver Frank and Edith Elise (Berch) W.; m. Jeanne Marie Lazio, May 28, 1988. B History, Miss. Coll., 1983; MDiv, Golden Gate Sem., 1988. Ordained to ministry So. Bapt. Ch., 1988. Chaplain Letterman Army Med. Ctr. USAR, San Francisco, 1988-90; post chaplain U.S. Army, Camp Parks, Calif., 1990; chaplain 1-14th AV U.S. Army, Ft. Rucker, Ala., 1991, chaplain 46th engr., 1992; chaplain 1-503rd rgt. U.S. Army, Camp Casey, South Korea, 1993-94; chaplain 5-29th Field arty. U.S. Army, Ft. Carson, Colo., 1994-96, chaplain 1-72 Armor, 1996-97, chaplain 68th corps support, 1997-99; retired from active duty, 1999. Mem. Army Aviator Assn. Am., VFW (jr. v.p. post 4061), Pi Gamma Mu, Phi Alpha Theta. Republican. Avocations: chess, model aircraft, computer programming, hiking, swimming. Home: 305 Rudd Ave Canon City CO 81212-3255

WILLIAMSON, EDWIN LEE, wardrobe and costume consultant; b. Downey, Calif., Dec. 2, 1947; s. Cecil Earnest and Edwina Louise (Tedie) W. AA, L.A. City Coll., 1967-70; BA in Theater and Music Edn., 1971, MA in Theater and Music Edn., 1973; student, U. So. Calif., 1971-73. Wardrobe master Ice Capades, 1973-76; mem. wardrobe dept. Paramount Studios, 1976-78, Disney Studios, 1978-81; freelance wardrobe and costume cons., L.A., 1981—; editor spl. events & theatre presentations Nightlife Mag. Appeared as Michael in original mus. Peter Pan. Mem. adv. bd. Halfway House and AIDS Hospsice, Valley Presbyn. Hosp.; founder West Coast Singers L.A., Inner City Athletic Union L.A.; founding mem. Gay Mens Chorus, Gt. Am. Yankee Freedom Band L.A., L.A. Gay and Lesbian Community Ctr.; hon. mem. bd. dirs. U. So. Calif. Idylwild Sch. Music and Arts.; bd. dirs. One Christopher St. West; founding vol. Gay Community Svc. Ctr.; emperor Imperial Ct. of San Fernando Valley. Scholar U. So. Calif., 1971-73; nominee Tony award Best Supporting Actor in musical Happy Time. Mem. SAG, AFTRA, Wardrobe Union, Masons. Lutheran. Home and Office: 4741 Elmwood Ave Apt 4 Los Angeles CA 90004-3135 Also: Nightlife Pubs 1800 N Highland Ave Ste 604 Hollywood CA 90028-4525

WILLIS, ANDRÉ MAURICE, electrical engineer, computing service executive; b. Fairfield, Ala., Oct. 16, 1957; s. Lamar and Marie (Davis) W.; m. Selene Yvette Lowe, Mar. 4, 1958. BSEE, Tuskegee U., 1981; postgrad., Focus Automation, 1993-94. Cert. in elec. sys. FAA, network engr. Novell. Project engr. Arco, Port Arthur, Tex., 1980; sys. engr. Dictaphone Corp., Milford, Conn., 1982-86, project engr., 1986; mgr. avionic flight test McDonnell Douglas Corp., Long Beach, Calif., 1987-93; info. sys. cons. EDP, L.A., 1994, So. Calif. Presbyn. Homes, Glendale, Calif., 1994; network sys. analyst Weyerhauser Mortgage, Woodland Hills, Calif., 1995; sr. network engr. CB Comml. Real Estate, Torrance, Calif., 1995—, project mgr., 1997—; tech. customer adv. bd. Cheyenne divsn. Intel & Computer Assocs., 1998; corp. mgr. tng. McDonnell Douglas, 1990; info. sys. cons. EDP/Contract Svcs., L.A., 1994-95; pres., owner Datronics, L.A., 1996—. Vol. Going to Coll. program UCLA, 1997-98. Tuskegee U. Sch. Engring. scholar, 1976-80; recipient CB Comml Real Estate Project award IT, 1997. Mem. IEEE, ASME. Avocations: tennis, swimming, reading, chess, camping.

WILLIS, BARRY, education educator, writer; b. Utica, N.Y., Nov. 15, 1952; s. William and Virginia (Valenti) W. BS in Journalism, Utah State U., 1974, MEd in Instrnl. Tech., 1976; EdD in Instrnl. Tech., Ind. U., 1981. Dir. instrnl. devel. U. Alaska, Anchorage, 1981-86, assoc. vice chancellor, 1986-88, statewide dir. distance edn., 1988-93; prof. edn., dir. outreach Coll. Engring. U. Idaho, Moscow, 1993—. Author: Distance Education: A Practical Guide, 1993; editor: Distance Education: Strategies and Tools, 1994; contbg. editor Jour. Ednl. Tech., 1992—; contbr. Alaska Mag., 1992-93. Avocations: flying, flyfishing. Home: 1075 Idlers Rest Rd Moscow ID 83843-9163 Office: U Idaho Dept Engring Outreach Moscow ID 83844-0001

WILLIS, CLIFFORD LEON, geologist; b. Chanute, Kans., Feb. 20, 1913; s. Arthur Edward and Flossie Duckworth (Fouts) W.; m. Serreta Margaret Thiel, Aug. 21, 1947 (dec.); 1 child, David Gerard. BS in Mining Engring., U. Kans., 1939; PhD, U. Wash., 1950. Geophysicist The Carter Oil Co. (Exxon), Tulsa, 1939-42; instr. U. Wash., Seattle, 1946-50, asst. prof., 1950-54; cons. geologist Harza Engring. Co., Chgo., 1952-54, 80-82, chief geologist, 1954-57, assoc. and chief geologist, 1957-67, v.p., chief geologist, 1967-80; pvt. practice cons. geologist Tucson, Ariz., 1982—; cons. on major dam projects in Iran, Iraq, Pakistan, Greece, Turkey, Ethiopia, Argentina, Venezuela, Colombia, Honduras, El Salvador, Iceland, U.S. Lt. USCG, 1942-46. Recipient Haworth Disting. Alumnus award U. Kans., 1963. Fellow Geol. Soc. Am., Geol. Soc. London; mem. Am. Assn. Petroleum Geologists, Soc. Mining, Metallurgy and Exploration Inc., Assn. Engring. Geologists, Sigma Xi, Tau Beta Pi, Sigma Tau, Theta Tau. Republican. Roman Catholic. Avocations: travel, reading. Home: 4795 E Quail Creek Dr Tucson AZ 85718-2630

WILLIS, EDWARD OLIVER, management consultant, state official; b. St. Louis, Apr. 6, 1948; s. George Washington and Mary (Fantroy) W.; m. Jennifer Linnea Johnson, June 17, 1972 (div. Dec. 1991); children: Linnea, Eric; m. Linda Diane Clark, Aug. 8, 1992. AA, Am. River Coll., Sacramento, 1972; BS in BA, Calif. State U., Sacramento, 1974; MBA in Mgmt., Golden Gate U., San Francisco, 1978. Divsn. ops. supr., casualty claims investigator Allstate Ins. Co., Menlo Park, Sacramento, 1974-75; budget analyst Dept. Fin., State of Calif., Sacramento, 1975-77; assoc. govtl. program analyst Dept. Health, Medi-Cal Procurement Project, State of Calif., Sacramento, 1977-78; chief fiscal br. solid waste mgmt. bd. State of Calif., Sacramento, 1978-79, mgr. adminstrv. svcs. state lands commn., 1979-80, asst. to assoc. supt. pub. instrn. dept. edn., 1980-82, dep. dir. adminstrn. dept. fish and game, 1982-90, acting adminstr. office of oil spill prevention and response, 1990-92, dep. dir. adminstrn. dept. developmental svcs., 1992-93, dep. dir. adminstrv. svcs. program dept. toxic substances, 1993-94, asst. sec. policy devel. Calif. Environ. Protection Agy., 1994-95, chief dep. dir. Calif. Conservation Corps, 1995—; owner, prin. cons. WW Assocs., 1994—; part-time instr. Cosumnes River Coll., Sacramento, 1980-83. Author: Business Employment Equity Plan, 1994. Vol. United Way Campaign, United Negro Coll. Fund, Sacramento Children's Home, YMCA; 1st v.p. Nat. Black Child Devel. Inst., Sacramento, 1981-82; chmn. Black Adv. Com. to State Pers. Bd., 1984-85; mem. St. Francis of Assisi Sch. Bd., Sacramento, 1996—, pres., 1991-93; bd. trustees Black Advocates in State Svc., 1992; bd. dirs. Nat. Forum for Black Pub. Adminstrs., Washington, 1993—, pres., 1991-93, 1st v.p. 1990-91); Little League coach, 1996—. With USAF, 1966-70. Decorated Air medals (4). Mem. Nat. Forum for Black Pub. Adminstrs. (Sacramento chpt. bd. dirs. 1993—, 1st v.p. 1990-91, pres. 1991-93), Am. Soc. Pub. Adminstrn. (Pub. Adminstr. of the Yr.). Avocations: golf, softball. Home: 1065 Almaden Village Ln San Jose CA 95120-3361 Office: Conservation Corps State of California 1719 24th St Sacramento CA 95816-7114

WILLIS, HAROLD WENDT, SR., real estate developer; b. Marion, Ala., Oct. 7, 1927; s. Robert James and Della (Wendt) W.; student Loma Linda U., 1950, various courses San Bernardino Valley Coll.; m. Patsy Gay Bacon, Aug. 2, 1947 (div. Jan. 1975); children: Harold Wendt II, Timothy Gay, April Ann, Brian Tad, Suzanne Gail; m. Vernette Jacobson Osborne, Mar. 30, 1980 (div. 1984); m. Ofelia Alvarez, Sept. 23, 1984; children: Ryan Robert, Samantha Ofelia. Ptnr., Victoria Guernsey, San Bernardino, Calif., 1950-63, co-pres., 1963-74, pres., 1974—; owner Quik-Save, 9th & Waterman shopping ctr., 1966—, Ninth and Waterman Shopping Ctr., San Bernardino, 1969—; pres. Energy Delivery Systems, Food and Fuel, Inc. San Bernardino City water commr., 1965—, pres. bd. water commrs., 1994—. Bd. councillors Loma Linda (Calif.) U., 1968-85, pres., 1971-74; mem. So. Calif. Strider's Relay Team (set indoor Am. record in 4x800 1992, set distance medley relay U.S. and World record for 60 yr. old 1992). Served as officer U.S. Mcht. Marine, 1945-46. Mem. Calif. Dairy Industries Assn. (pres. 1963, 64), Liga Internat. (2d v.p. 1978, pres. 1982, 83). Seventh-day Adventist (deacon 1950-67). Lic. pvt. pilot; rated multi engr. in 601 P aerostar. Office: PO Box 5607 San Bernardino CA 92412-5607

WILLIS, SELENE LOWE, electrical engineer, software consultant; b. Birmingham, Ala., Mar. 4, 1958; d. Lewis Russell and Bernice (Wilson) Lowe; m. André Maurice Willis, June 12, 1987. BSEE, Tuskegee U., 1980; postgrad., UCLA, 1993-94, U. So. Calif., 1996. Component engr. Hughes Aircraft Corp., El Segundo, Calif., 1980-82; reliability and lead engr. Aero Jet Electro Sys. Corp., Azusa, Calif., 1982-84; sr. component engr. Rockwell Internat. Corp., Anaheim, Calif., 1984, Gen. Data Comm. Corp., Danbury, Conn., 1984-85; design engr. Lockheed Missile & Space Co., Sunnyvale, Calif., 1985-86; property mgr. Penmar Mgmt. Co., L.A., 1987-88; aircraft mechanic McDonnell Douglas Corp., Long Beach, 1989-93; Unix sys. adminstrn. Santa Cruz Ops., 1994; tech. staff Space Applications Corp., El Segundo, Calif., 1995-96; bus. ops. mgr., cons. New Start, Santa Monica, Calif., 1995; software developer Nat. Advancement Corp., 1996; entrepreneur Datatronics, 1996—; exec. v.p., owner L.A. Network Engr. Jet Propulsion Lab., L.A., 1996—; software engr., network engr., application engr. Jet Propulsion Lab, Pasadena, Calif., 1996—, lead engr., 1997—; lead UNIX engr. Jet Propulsion Lab, L.A., 1998—; mgr. Tech. Jet Propulsion Lab., Pasadena, 1998—; cons., software designer Kern & Wooley, attys., Westwood, Calif., 1995; software developer Nat. Advancement Corp., Santa Ana, Calif., 1995—. Vol. Mercy Hosp. and Children's Hosp., Birmingham, 1972-74; mrm. L.A. Gospel Messengers, 1982-84, West Angeles Ch. of God and Christ, L.A., 1990; cons., mgr. bus. ops. New Start/Santa Monica (Calif.) Bay Area Drug Abuse Coun., 1995; vol. Pres. Clinton's Going-To-Coll. Program through UCLA, 1997—; chair UCLA Transfer Coll. Scholarship Program, 1998. Scholar Bell Labs., 1976-80, UCLA, 1994. Mem. IEEE, ASME, Aerospace and Aircraft Engrs., So. Calif. Profl. Engring. Assn., Tuskegee U. Alumni Assn., UCLA Alumni Assn. (scholarship and adv. com.), Eta Kappa Nu. Mem. Christian Ch. Avocations: piano, computers, softball, real estate.

WILLIS, STEPHEN C., contractor; b. Colorado Springs, Colo., Feb. 6, 1952; s. Robert K. and Isabelle (Craft) W.; m. Suzanne Sprenger, Mar. 12, 1976; children: Michael, Kevin. BBA, U. Colo., 1974. Constrn. mgr. Terrawest Co., Colorado Springs, 1975-82; pres. Terrawest Co., 1983-88, Willis Constrn., 1988-91; v.p. Master Bilt Homes, 1991-94; pres. Willis Homes, 1995—. Bd. dirs. Cheyenne Creek Water Dept., Colorado Springs, 1990—, Regional Bldg. Dept., Colorado Springs, 1995—. Mem. Home Builders Assn. of Colorado Springs (Bldr. of Yr. 1997). Avocations: bicycling, flower gardening. Home: 411 W Cheyenne Rd Colorado Springs CO 80906-2445 Office: Willis Homes Inc PO Box 38101 Colorado Springs CO 80937-8101

WILLOUGHBY, JAMES RUSSELL, artist; b. Toronto, Ohio, Apr. 22, 1928; s. Russell Lee and Edna Gertrude (McKeown) W.; m. Dorothy M. Ponder, Sept. 12, 1952 (div. 1958); children: Jim Jr., David; m. Susan N. Boettjer, Nov. 28, 1980. AA, Pasadena City Coll., 1951; postgrad., Art Ctr. Sch. Mem. staff Chrysler Corp., Maywood, Calif., 1951-57; adminstrv. asst., tech. artist Ramo-Wooldridge, El Segundo, Calif., 1957-59; adminstr. asst. Space Tech. Labs., El Segundo, 1959-61; intelligence analyst Aerospace Corp., El Segundo, 1961-65; freelancer Calif., 1965-72, Filmation Studios, Reseda, Calif., 1972-82, various orgns., 1982—; storyboard designer Hanna-Barbera, Disney Studios, 1987-90. Author, illustrator: Cowboy Country Cartoons, 1988, Birds of the Southwest, 1997, Do YOu Pray, Duke?, 1999; co-author, illustrator: Cowboy Cartoon Cookbook, 1990, Cactus County, 1992, Sharlot Hall Coloring Book, 1994, Cowboy Cartoons: Quick on the Draw, 1996, A Dude's Guide to the West, 1996; illustrator: Cowpies Ain't No Dish You Take To The County Fair, 1997; contbr. editorial cartoons to journs. Mem. Nat. Cartoonist Soc., Westerners Internat., Prescott Corral. Avocations: hiking. Home: 1407 Sierra Vista Dr Prescott AZ 86303-4545

WILLOUGHBY, JIMMY RAY, minister; b. San Antonio, Sept. 27, 1953; s. Jack Henry and Mildred Lucille (Moree) W.; m. Ireta June Owen, Aug. 28, 1976; children: Vielka Renee, Jamie Rae Ann. Student, Berean Sch. Bible, Springfield, Mo., 1980. Ordained to ministry Echos of Faith Revivals Inc., 1974, Assemblies of God, 1980. Assoc. pastor Echos of Faith Ch., Ontario, Calif., 1974-79; evangelist Jim Willoughby Ministries, Montclair, Calif., 1979-81; sr. pastor Echos of Faith Christian Ctr., Ontario, 1981—; del. Traditional Values Coalition, Anaheim, Calif., 1985—; dir. Agape Outreach, Ontario, 1986—; area dir. Internat. Conv. Faith Ministries, Little Rock, 1990—; mem. adv. bd. Athletics Internat. Ministries, Phoenix, 1991—. Author: Trick or Treat, Satan's Game, 1991; editor Faith Tabloid mag., 1986-89; host radio show The Uncompromising Word, 1984—. Organizer July 4th Freedom Celebration, Chino, Calif., 1984—; mem. Police Task Force on Satanic Crimes, Chino, 1990. Republican. Office: Echos of Faith PO Box 3100 Ontario CA 91761-0910

WILLOUGHBY, STUART CARROLL, contractor; b. Tucson, Mar. 19, 1951; s. Stuart Carroll and Margeret Ann (Thornton) W.; m. Beth Anne Willoughby; children: Julie Ann, Aimee Sue, Scott Tyler, John Christopher, Jeremy Luke. Student, U. Ariz., 1970-74, U. Ariz., 1973. Owner Willcox (Ariz.) Realty and Constrn. Co., 1974-75, Willoughby Constrn. and Devel. Corp., Tucson, 1975—; owner, broker Red Baron Realtors, Inc., Tucson, 1978—; owner Willoughby Plumbing Corp., Tucson, 1985—, Sunshine Solar Co., Tucson, 1980—. Leader 4H Club. Mem. So. Ariz. Home Builders Assn. (bd. dirs. 1978—, life dir., Bd. Mem. of Yr. award 1981, honored PAC com. 1985, 86, 87), Tucson Bd. Realtors, Nat. Assn. of Home Builders (Life Spike award 1980). Republican. Avocations: water and snow skiing, beekeeping, flying, remote controlled airplanes, sailing and racing catamarans and monohulls. Home: 9781 E Burnett St Tucson AZ 85730-4427

WILLS, JOHN ELLIOT, JR., history educator, writer; b. Urbana, Ill., Aug. 8, 1936; s. John Elliot and George Anne (Hicks) W.; m. Carolin Connell, July 19, 1958; children: Catherine, Christopher John, Jeffrey David, Joanne, Lucinda. BA in Philosophy, U. Ill., 1956; MA in East Asian Studies, Harvard U., 1960, PhD in History and Far Ea. Langs., 1967. History instr. Stanford (Calif.) U., 1964-65; history instr. U. So. Calif., L.A., 1965-67, asst. prof., 1967-72, assoc. prof., 1972-84, prof., 1984—, acting chair East Asian Langs. and Cultures, 1987-89; dir. East Asian Studies Ctr. USC-UCLA Joint East Asian Studies Ctr., L.A., 1990-94; rsch. abroad in The Netherlands, Taiwan, China, Japan, Macao, Philippines, Indonesia, India, Italy, Spain, Portugal, Eng. Author: Pepper, Guns, and Parleys: The Dutch East India Company and China, 1662-1681, 1974, Embassies and Illusions: Dutch and Portuguese Envoys to K'ang-hsi, 1666-1687, 1984, Mountain of Fame: Portraits in Chinese History, 1994; co-editor: (with Jonathan D. Spence) From Ming to Ch'ing: Conquest, Region, and Continuity in Seventeenth-Century China, 1979; contbr. articles to profl. jours. Grantee Nat. Acad. Scis., 1985, Am. Coun. Learned Soc., 1979-80; Younger Humanist fellow NEH, 1972-73. Mem. Assn. for Asian Studies, Am. Hist. Assn., Phi Beta Kappa, Phi Kappa Phi (Recognition award 1986, 95). Avocation: travel. Office: U So Calif Dept History Los Angeles CA 90089-0034

WILLSON, HARRY, writer; b. Montoursville, Pa., July 23, 1932; s. Harry Gilbert and Jessie Gibb (Walker) W.; m. Christine Kuhn, Aug. 24, 1952 (div. Jul. 1970); children: Mary Christine Harrigan, Thomas Andrew, John Mark. AB, Lafayette Coll., 1953; MDv, Princeton Theological Sem., 1958; student, Univ. de Madrid, Madrid, Spain, 1957, Univ. New Mexico, Albuquerque, N.Mex., 1983. Pastor Alameda & Placitas Presby. Ch., Alameda, N.Mex., 1958-66; tchr. Albuquerque Acad., Albuquerque, 1966-73; tchr., dept. head Sandia Preparatory, Albuquerque, 1973-76; owner Draperies by Adela, Albuquerque, 1976—; writer Amador Publ., Albuquerque, 1986—. Author: Duke City Tales, 1986, A World for the Meek, 1987, Souls & Cells Remember, 1988, This'll Kill Ya, 1990, Little Brown Roadrunner, 1992, Vermin, 1996; editor: Caesar of Sante Fe, 1990, Eva's War, 1990, Twelve Gifts, 1991, Hunger in the First Person Singular, 1992, Ancestral Notes, 1994, Christmas Blues, 1995, Amerika? America!, 1997, The Pianist Who Loved AYN Rand, 1998. Pres. U.N. Orgn., 1976; host Servas, Albuquerque, 1986-94; activist CItizens for Alternatives to Radioactive Dumping, 1980—; active ABQ Center for Peace and Justice, 1984—. Democrat. Avocations: gardening, chair caning, photography, Spanish language, travel. Home: 607 Isleta Blvd SW Albuquerque NM 87105-3827 Office: Amador Publ PO Box 12335 Albuquerque NM 87195-0335

WILMOT, MARLENE JUNE, writer; b. McCook, Neb., Nov. 10, 1933; d. Lloyd J. and Freda (Voigt) Harvey; m. William A. Wilmot, Aug. 5, 1952; children: Janell Renea Wilmot Ambrosier, David Harvey Wilmot. Grad. H.S., Norton, Kans. Writer Greeley, Colo., 1995—; v.p. Longview Crop Ins., Greeley, 1984-94; mktg. specialist, USDA, Kansas City, Mo.; dist. dir., USDA, Norton, Kans., 1964-81. Author Bluff-to-Bluff, 1994, Bluff-to-Bluff, too!, 1995, Hardship Trail, 1996. 1st woman to be chosen dist. dir. by Fed. Crop Ins. Corp.-USDA, 1981. Methodist. Avocations: travel, history, reading, speaking. Home and Office: 2625 58th Ave Greeley CO 80634-4529

WILNER, PAUL ANDREW, journalist; b. N.Y.C., Feb. 12, 1950; s. Norman and Sylvia (Rubenstein) W.; m. Alyson Paula Bromberg, June 3, 1980; children: Anne Charlotte, Daniel Joseph. Student, U. Calif., Berkeley, 1968; BA, CUNY, 1976. Copy clk. N.Y. Times, 1976-80; reporter L.A. Herald Examiner, 1980-85; mng. editor Hollywood Reporter, L.A., 1985-87; asst. mng. editor features San Francisco Examiner, 1987—; sr. instr. U. So. Calif., L.A., 1983-85. Author: (poetry) Serious Business, The Paris Rev., 1977. Office: SF Examiner Mag 110 5th St San Francisco CA 94103-2972

WILSON, ALMON CHAPMAN, surgeon, physician, retired naval officer; b. Hudson Falls, N.Y., July 13, 1924; s. Almon Chapman and Edith May (Truesdale) W.; m. Sofia M. Bogdons, Jan. 24, 1945; 1 child, Geoffrey Peter. B.A., Union Coll., Schenectady, 1946; M.D., Albany Med. Coll., 1952; M.S., George Washington U., 1969; student, Naval War Coll., Newport, R.I., 1968-69. Diplomate: Am. Bd. Surgery. Served as enlisted man and officer U.S. Navy, 1943-46, lt. j.g., M.C., 1952, advanced through grades to rear adm., 1976; intern U.S. Naval Hosp., Bremerton, Wash., 1952-53; resident VA Hosp., Salt Lake City, 1954-58; chief of surgery Sta. Hosp. Naval Sta., Subic Bay, Philippines, 1959-61; staff surgeon Naval Hosp., San Diego, 1961-64; asst. chief surgery Naval Hosp., Chelsea, Mass., 1964-65; comdg. officer 3d Med. Bn., 3d Marine Div. Fleet Marine Force, Pacific, Vietnam, 1965-66; chief surgery Naval Hosp., Yososuka, Japan, 1966-68; assigned Naval War Coll., 1968-69; fleet med. officer, comdr. in chief U.S. Naval Forces, Europe; sr. med. officer Naval Activities London, 1969-71; dep. dir. planning div. Bur. Medicine and Surgery Navy Dept., Washington, 1971-72; dir. planning div. Navy Dept., 1972-74; with additional duty as med. adv. to dep. chief naval ops. (logistics) and personal physician to chmn. Joint Chiefs of Staff, 1972-74; comdg. officer Naval Hosp., Great Lakes, Ill., 1974-76; asst. chief for material resources Bur. Medicine and Surgery Navy Dept., Washington, 1976-79; comdg. officer (Navy Health Scis. Edn. and Tng. Command), 1979-80; the med. officer U.S. Marine Corps., 1980-81, project mgr. Fleet Hosp. Programs, 1981-82, dir. Resources Div., 1982-83, dep. dir. naval medicine, dep. surgeon gen. Dept. Navy, 1983-84; ret., 1984; mem. grad. med. edn. adv. com. Dept. Def. Decorated Legion of Merit with gold V (2 stars), Meritorious Service medal, Joint Service Commendation medal. Fellow ACS (gov.); mem. Assn. Mil. Surgeons U.S.

WILSON, BART ALLEN, media director, marketing consultant, educator; b. North Miami Beach, Fla., Aug. 28, 1962; s. John Trevette and Elaine Ann (Rafalowski) W.; m. Tanya Katherine Worthington, Oct. 3, 1984. AAS, Coll. of the Air Force, 1983, Coll. of the Air Force, 1985. Cert. Netscape solutions expert. Art dir. Pro-Print, Dallas, 1987-89; digital applications mgr.-MIS Levenson & Hill, Dallas, 1989-91; photo CD platform mgr. Eastman Kodak, Raleigh, N.C., 1991-93; product mktg. mgr. DayStar Digital, Flowery Branch, Ga., 1993-94; dir. new media Hayduk-King Advt., Santa Fe, 1994—. Author (software) PhotoFolio Pro, 1994; author: Not of This Fold, 1997. Sgt. USAF, 1981-87. Recipient Presdl. award Pres. George Bush, 1989. Mem. Electronic Times Photojournalism Workshops (bd. dirs. 1991-92), Nat. Press Photographers Assn., Apple Developers. Republican. Jewish. Avocations: public speaking, racquetball, digital video. Home: 11 Lauro Rd Santa Fe NM 87505-9169 Office: Hayduk King Advt Worldwide 1219 Luisa St Ste 3 Santa Fe NM 87505-4176

WILSON, BLENDA JACQUELINE, academic administrator; b. Woodbridge, N.J., Jan. 28, 1941; d. Horace and Margaret (Brogsdale) Wilson; m. Louis Fair Jr. AB, Cedar Crest Coll., 1962; AM, Seton Hall U., 1965; PhD, Boston Coll., 1979; DHL (hon.), Cedar Crest Coll., 1987, Loretto Heights Coll., 1988, Colo. Tech. Coll., 1988, U. Detroit, 1989; LLD (hon.), Rutgers U., 1989, Ea. Mich. U., 1990, Cambridge Coll., 1991, Schoolcraft Coll., 1992. Tchr. Woodbridge Twp. Pub. Schs., 1962-66; exec. dir. Middlesex County Econ. Opportunity Corp., New Brunswick, N.J., 1966-69; exec. asst. to pres. Rutgers U., New Brunswick, N.J., 1969-72; sr. assoc. dean Grad. Sch. Edn. Harvard U., Cambridge, Mass., 1972-82; v.p. effective sector mgmt. Ind. Sector, Washington, 1982-84; exec. dir. Colo. Commn. Higher Edn., Denver, 1984-88; chancellor and prof. pub. adminstrn. & edn. U. Mich., Dearborn, 1988-92; pres. Calif. State U., Northridge, 1992—; Am. del. U.S./U.K. Dialogue About Quality Judgments in Higher Edn.; adv. bd. Mich. Consolidated Gas Co., Stanford Inst. Higher Edn. Rsch., U. So. Col. Dist. 60 Nat. Alliance, Nat. Ctr. for Rsch. to Improve Postsecondary Teaching and Learning, 1988-90; bd. dirs. Alpha Capital Mgmt.; mem. higher edn. colloquium Am. Coun. Edn., vis. com. Divsn. Continuing Edn. in Faculty of Arts & Scis., Harvard Coll., Pew Forum on K-12 Edn. Reform in U.S. Dir. U. Detroit Jesuit High Sch., Northridge Hosp. Med. Ctr., Arab Cmty. Ctr. for Econ. and Social Svcs., Union Bank, J. Paul Getty Trust, James Irvine Found., Internat. Found. Edn. and Self-Help, Achievement Coun., L.A.; dir., vice chair Met. Affairs Corp.; exec. bd. Detroit area coun. Boy Scouts Am.; bd. dirs. Commonwealth Fund, Henry Ford Hosp.-Fairlane Ctr., Henry Ford Health System, Met. Ctr. for High Tech., United Way Southeastern Mich.; mem. Nat. Coalition 100 Black Women, Detroit, Race Rels. Coun. Met. Detroit, Women & Founds., Greater Detroit Interfaith Round Table NCCJ, Adv. Bd. Valley Cultural Ctr., Woodland Hills; trustee assoc. Boston Coll.; trustee emeritus Cambridge Coll.; trustee emeritus, bd. dirs. Found. Ctr.; trustee Henry Ford Mus. & Greenfield Village, Sammy Davis Jr. Nat. Liver Inst. Mem. AAUW, Assn. Governing Bds. (adv. coun. of pres.'s), Edn. Commn. of the States (student minority task force), Am. Assn. Higher Edn. (chair-elect), Am. Assn. State Colls. & Univs. (com. on policies & purposes, acad. leadership fellows selection com.), Assn. Black Profls. and Adminstrs., Assn. Black Women in Higher Edn., Women Execs. State Govt., Internat. Women's Forum, Mich. Women's Forum, Women's Econ. Club Detroit, Econ. Club, Rotary. Office: Calif State Univ Office of President 18111 Nordhoff St Northridge CA 91330-0001*

WILSON, CARL ARTHUR, real estate broker; b. Manhasset, N.Y., Sept. 29, 1947; s. Archie and Florence (Hefner) W.; children: Melissa Starr, Clay Alan; m. Jacquie Elcox; 1 stepchild: Christie Cash. Student, UCLA, 1966-68, 70-71. Tournament bridge dir. North Hollywood (Calif.) Bridge Club, 1967-68, 70-71; computer operator IBM, L.A., 1967-68, 70-71; bus. devel. mgr. Walker & Lee Real Estate, Anaheim, Calif., 1972-76; v.p. sales and mktg. The Estes Co., Phoenix, 1976-82, Continental Homes Inc., 1982-84; pres. Roadrunner Homes Corp., Phoenix, 1984-86, Lexington Homes, Inc., 1986, Barrington Homes, 1986-90; gen. mgr. Starr Homes, 1991—, pres., 1996—; pres. Offsite Utilities, Inc., 1992-98; adv. dir. Liberty Bank; sec., treas. Treasure Valley Hearing Aid Ctr. Mem. Glendale (Ariz.) Citizens Bond Coun., 1986-87, Ariz. Housing Study Commn. 1988-89, Valley Leadership, 1988-98; pres.'s coun. Am. Grad. Sch. Internat. Mgmt., 1985-89; vice-chmn. Glendale Planning and Zoning Commn., 1986-87, chmn. 1987-91; mem. bd. trustees Valley of Sun United Way, 1987-92; chmn. com. Cmty. Problem Solving and Fund Distbn., 1988-89; mem. City of Glendale RTC Task Force, 1990, Maricopa County Citizens Jud. Reform Com., 1990-92, Maricopa County Citizens Jud. Adv. Coun., 1990-91; co-founder, bd. dirs. Leadership West, Inc., 1993-94; mem. Maricopa County Trial Ct. Appointment Commn., 1993-98; mem. bd. adjustments City of Glendale, 1976-81, chmn. 1980-81, mem. bond coun., 1981-82; mem. real estate edn. adv. coun. State Bd. C.C., 1981-82; precinct committeeman, dep. registrar, 1980-81. With U.S. Army, 1968-70. Mem. Nat. Assn. Homebuilders (bd. dirs. 1985-93, nat. rep. Ariz. 1990-92), Cen. Ariz. Homebuilders Assn. (adv. com. 1979-82, treas. 1986, sec. 1987, v.p. 1987-89, chmn. 1989-90, bd. dirs. 1985-98, life dir. 1994—), Glendale C. of C. (dir. 1980-83, 89-91), Sales and Mktg. Coun. (chmn. edn. com. 1980, chmn. coun. 1981-82, Mame grand award 1981). Home: PO Box 4565 Boise ID 83711-4565 Office: Treasure Valley Hearing Aid Ctr 10390 Fairview Ave Boise ID 83704-8013

WILSON, CATHERINE PHILLIPS, elementary education educator; b. Calif., July 19, 1935; d. Harry Leland and Catherine (Waterbury) Phillips; m. Henry S. Wilson Jr., Apr. 12, 1958 (dec. Jan. 1979); children: Lee, Janell, Carey, Kimberly, Blake. Student, U. of the Pacific, 1953-54; BA in Edn. and Psychology, Calif. State Coll., San Jose, 1957; postgrad., Portland State U., 1981-89, Chapman U., Danville, Calif., 1990-93. Cert. tchr., Oreg. Sales coord. The Donatello Hotel, San Francisco, 1981-82; ind. mgmt. cons. A. Cal Rossi, Inc., San Francisco, 1983-84; tchr. 5th grade Portland (Oreg.) Pub. Schs., 1985, tchr. Glencoe Sch., 1987-89; tchr. 1st grade Oakland (Calif.) Unified Dist., 1989-90; tchr. 2d grade Martin Luther King Elem. Sch. Portland Pub. Schs., 1990-93, tchr. 2d grade Lent Elem. Sch., 1993—. Author: Soaring to Success, 1986, Escape to Freedom, 1987, Journey Through the Galazies, 1988. Named Oreg. Tchr. of Yr., U.S. West, 1991, Spirit of the N.W., KATU Channel 2, Portland, 1992; recipient Tchrs. Making a Difference award Nationwide Ins., 1994, Impact II award Reading in a Castle of Dreams, 1994, KEX-Fred Meyer Tchr. award, 1994. Mem. Oreg. Edn. Assn., Kiwanis Early Risers, Kappa Alpha Theta, Alpha Delta Kappa. Republican. Roman Catholic. Avocations: reading, writing, collecting, speaking to groups. Office: Lent Elem Sch 5105 SE 97th Ave Portland OR 97266-3747

WILSON, CHARLES LEE, neuroscientist, epilepsy researcher, educator; b. Phoenix, June 6, 1941; s. Francis Lee and Leila Frances (Harris) W.; m. Brenda Cox, Jan. 14, 1967; children: Jennine, Nicole. AB, U. Calif., Berkeley, 1964; MA, San Francisco State U., 1967; PhD, SUNY, Stony Brook, 1972. Postdoctoral fellow UCLA, 1972-74, asst. rschr., 1974-78; asst. rsch. neurologist Med. Sch., 1978-84, asst. prof. neurology, 1984-92, assoc. prof., 1992-97, prof., 1997—. Contbr. articles to profl. jours. and books. Rsch. grantee in epilepsy NIH, UCLA Med. Sch., 1984—. Mem. AAAS, Soc. Neurosci., Am. Epilepsy Soc., Am. Clin. Neurophysiology Soc., Internat. Brain Rsch. Orgn. Democrat. Avocations: backpacking, mountain climbing. Office: UCLA Med Sch Dept Neurology Los Angeles CA 90095

WILSON, CHARLES ZACHARY, JR., newspaper publisher; b. Greenwood, Miss., Apr. 21, 1929; s. Charles Zachary and Ora Lee (Means) W.; m. Doris J. Wilson, Aug. 18, 1951 (dec. Nov. 1974); children: Charles III, Joyce Lynne, Joanne Catherine, Gary Thomas, Jonathan Keith; m. Kelly Freeman, Apr. 21, 1986; children: Amanda Fox, Walter Bremond. BS in Econs., U. Ill., 1952, PhD in Econs. and Stats., 1956. Asst. to v.p. Commonwealth Edison Co., Chgo., 1956-59; asst. prof. econs. De Paul U., Chgo., 1959-61; assoc. prof. bus. SUNY, Binghamton, 1961-67, prof. econs. and bus., 1967-68; prof. mgmt. and edn. UCLA, 1968-84, vice chancellor acad. programs, 1985-87; CEO, pub., pres. Cen. News-Wave Publs., L.A., 1987-93; pres. Czand Assocs., Pacific Palisades, Calif., 1994—; CEO Wave Cmty. Newspapers, L.A., 1997—; mem. adv. council Fed. Res. Bank, San Francisco, 1986-88, 2001 com. Office of Mayor of Los Angeles, 1986-89. Author: Organizational Decision-Making, 1967; contbr. articles on bus. to jours. Bd. dirs. Los Angeles County Mus. Art, 1978-81; mem. Com. on L.A. City Revenue, 1975-76, UN Assn. Panel for Advancement of U.S. and Japan Rels., N.Y.C. 1972-74; chmn. L.A. Mayor's task force on Africa, 1979-82; mem. L.A. Charter Reform Commn. Fellow John Hay Whitney, U. Ill., 1955-56, Ford Found., 1960-61, 81-82, 84, Am. Council of Edn., UCLA, 1967-68, Aspen Inst. for Human Studies; named one of Young Men of Yr., Jaycees, 1965. Mem. AAAS, Am. Econ. Assn., Nat. Newspaper Pub. Assn., Am. Mgmt. Assn., Alpha Phi Alpha (pres., pledgemaster 1952-54), Phi Kappa Phi, Order of Artus (pres.). Avocations: tennis, jogging, collecting old bus. texts. Home: 1053 Tellem Dr Pacific Palisades CA 90272-2243 Office: Cen Newspaper Publs 2621 W 54th St Los Angeles CA 90043-2614

WILSON, DARRYL B(ABE), teacher, writer; b. Fall River Mills, Calif., Nov. 21, 1939; s. Herman Ira Wilson and Laura (Larillard) Carmony; m. Donna Lee Griffith (div.); children: Sonny, Lance, Erik, Cory; life ptnr. Danell Rene Garcia (dec.); children: Theodoro, Seterro (twins). BA, U. Calif., Davis, 1992; MA, U. Ariz., 1994, postgrad., 1995—. With Am. Indian Lang. Devel. Inst. U. Ariz., Tucson, 1994—; tchr. Lawrence Intermediate Sch., Yaqui Reservation, Ariz., 1995. Author: Wellen Auf Dem Meer Der Zeit, 1974, The Sound of Rattles and Clappers, 1993, Wilma Mankiller, Principal Chief of the Cherokee Nation, 1995; co-author: (with Lois Hogle) Voices from the Earth, 1997; contbg. author: (short story anthologies) Earth Song, Sky Spirits, 1993, Coming to Light, 1994, Native American Oral Traditions, Collaboration and Interpretation, The California Reader; contbr. articles to profl. jours.; co-editor: Dear Christopher, 1993. With USMC, 1957-61. Grantee Fund for Folk Cuolture, 1993, SEVA, 1993; fellow Ford Found., 1994. Home and Office: 5405 Prospect Rd Apt 4 San Jose CA 95129-4846

WILSON, DIERDRE LYNN, theater and dance educator, director, choreographer, psychotherapist, drama therapist; b. La Mesa, Calif., Feb. 21, 1945; d. Joseph Herbert Wilson and Audrie Ilene (Branin) W.; m. Douglas John Hammel, Aug. 18, 1978; children: Devon, Galen. AA, Grossmont Coll., 1977; BA in Clin. Psychology, Antioch U., 1979; MEd in Counseling Psychology, Wash. State U., 1983, MA in Theatre, 1985, EdD in Counseling Psychology, 1994; student Agnes Moorehead Actor's Workshop, Los Angeles, 1967, Lee Strasberg Inst., Los Angeles, 1969, Odyssey Improvisation Theatre, Los Angeles, 1969, Theatre East Actor's Workshop, Los Angeles, 1969, Am. Conservatory Theatre, San Francisco, 1970-71; City Coll. San Francisco, 1975; dance tng. San Francisco Ballet, San Francisco Dance Spectrum, San Francisco Dance Theatre, Marguerite Ellicot Sch. Ballet, Pacific Ballet Acad., Gene Maranaccio Sch. Ballet, Roland Dupree Dance Acad., Wash. State U. Registered drama therapist, mental health counselor. Ballet instr. Ed Mock Studios, San Francisco, 1974-75, San Francisco Dance Theatre, 1974-75; tchr. creative dramatics Ballet Folk, Moscow, Idaho, 1980; instr., curriculum designer creative arts for handicapped Wash. State U., Pullman, 1980, instr. ballet, 1980, instr. acting, 1982-83, mem. senate, 1981; founding dir., adminstr. Acad. Performing Arts, Pullman, 1986—; dir. Ctr. for Counseling and Devel., Pullman; dir. Wash. Jr. Concert Ballet; dance cons., choreographer; mem. San Francisco Ballet; soloist San Francisco Opera Co.; appeared in numerous musicals, with various ballet cos., in several films; cons. Wash. Commn. for Humanities, 1984. Author: Introduction to Theatre for the Aged Disabled, 1977. Chmn. disabled services adv. council San Diego Parks and Recreation Dept., 1978; dir. Safe Harbor Children's Bereavement Program. San Diego Theatre for Disabled grantee, 1978; Wash. State U. grantee, 1982; Wash. Commn. for Humanities grantee, 1983, 84. Mem. Actor's Equity Assn., Am. Guild Musical Artists, Nat. Assn. Drama Therapists, Am. Assn. for Counseling Devel., Am. Counseling Assn., Phi Delta Kappa. Office: Ctr for Counseling and Devel Fiddlehead Marina Bldg 611 Columbia St NW Olympia WA 98501-1000

WILSON, DONALD KENNETH, JR., lawyer, publisher; b. Lancaster, Pa., Mar. 5, 1954; s. Donald Kenneth and Gloria (Payne) W.; m. Lauren Elaine O'Connor, Sept. 3, 1977; children: Donald, Tameka, Veronica, Matthew. BA, U. So. Calif., 1976; JD, N.Y. Law Sch., 1979. Bar: Calif. 1979, U.S. Ct. Appeals (9th cir.) 1979, U.S. Ct. Appeals (ea. dist.) Mich., 1996, U.S. Ct. Appeals, Colo. 1997. Ptnr. Law Office, L.A., 1987-92; pres., chief operating officer Quincy Jones Productions, L.A., 1983-86; assoc. Garey, Mason & Sloane, L.A., 1979-82; pres., CEO 4 Kids Music, L.A., 1989—, Dotevema Music, L.A., 1989—; of counsel Law Offices Johnnie L. Cochran Jr., L.A., 1992—. Producer: (video documentary) Frank Sinatra, 1984 (Vira award 1985, Grammy nomination 1985); contb. articles to newspapers. Trustee First African Meth. Episc. Ch., 1989-97; mem. NAACP, L.A., 1990. Recipient Citizenship award, Am. Legion, 1972; named Outstanding Young Men of Am., 1982, 83, Outstanding Contbr. to Community, Entertainment Civic Orgn., 1986. Avocations: tennis, reading, walking, fishing. Office: Law Offices Johnnie L Cochran Jr 4929 Wilshire Blvd Ste 1010 Los Angeles CA 90010-3825

WILSON, ELEANOR MCELROY, county official; b. Lancaster, Pa., Sept. 10, 1938; d. Hartford Ford and Jane Ann (Bowker) McElroy; m. Frank Eugene Wilson, July 17, 1976 (dec. Jan. 1980). AA, Monterey Peninsula Jr. Coll., Monterey, Calif., 1959; BA in Edn., San Jose State U., 1963; MA in Bus. Adminstrn./Mgmt., Webster U., St. Louis, 1981; MA in Internat. Rels., Salve Regina Coll., Newport, R.I., 1990; MA in Nat. Security/Strategic Studies, Naval War Coll., Newport, 1991. Sec. Geo. Dovolis Real Estate, Monterey, 1957-59; legal sec. Thompson & Thompson Attys., Monterey, 1959-61; legal asst., supr. Thomson J. Hudson, Atty., Monterey, 1963-68, legal asst., 1972-74. Mem. Orange County Grand Jury, Superior Ct., Santa Ana, Calif., 1982-83; citizen mem. Orange County Parole Bd., Santa ana, 1993-96; mem. Orange County Juvenile Justice Commn., Orange, 1992—. Col. USMCR, 1968-98. Decorated Meritorious Svc. medal, Navy Commendation medal, others. Mem. Marine Corps Hist. Found. (bd. dirs.), Marine Corps Aviation Assn. (bd. dirs.), Linda Sloan Mundy Found. (bd. dirs.). Republican. Episcopalian. Avocations: reading, golf, tennis, travel. Home: 22476 Alcudia Mission Viejo CA 92692-1157

WILSON, EMILY MARIE, sales executive; b. Aberdeen, Wash., Mar. 24, 1951; d. Charles Robert and Alice Adele (Robinson) W.; m. Michael A. Rich, July 1, 1976. Student, U. Puget Sound, 1969-71, Austro-Am. Inst., Vienna, 1971; BA in Polit. Sci., U. Wash., 1973. U.S. sales mgr. Clairol, Inc., Seattle, 1975-81, sales rep. N.W. Wash., drug-mass mdse. div., 1975-77, sales rep. Met. Seattle, 1977-78, dist. mgr. sales western Wash., 1978-81; trainer territorial sales reps., mgr. dist. dollar sales, and dist. sales mgr. of Wash., Oreg., Idaho and Mont., Clorox, Inc., Seattle, 1981-82, assoc. regional mgr. Western div. spl. markets, 1982-83; regional mgr. Olympic Stain Co., Bellevue, Wash., 1983-86; dir. sales Inscape Products The Weyerhauser Co., Tacoma, 1986-88; dir. ops. Wildland Journeys, Seattle, 1988-89; Traveller World Wide Explorations, 1989—; sales mgr. Adventures Abroad, Seattle, 1990-92; owner Emily Unltd. Organizational Svcs. and Mgmt., 1992—. Mem. Nat. Assn. Profl. Organizers, Transcendental Meditation Soc., Oreg. Hist. Soc., Sons and Daus. of Oreg. Pioneers, Pioneer Assn. Wash., Seattle Hist. Soc., Sidha of the Age of Enlightenment World Govt. Assn., Grad. Sci. of Creative Intelligence, Women's Profl. Managerial Network. Office: 4417 54th Ave NE Seattle WA 98105-4942

WILSON, GARY THOMAS, engineering executive; b. Pitts., Sept. 26, 1961; s. Charles Zachary and Doris Jean (Thomas) W.; m. Georgiann E. Wilson, Dec. 31, 1994. AB, Dartmouth Coll., 1983, BEEE, 1984; MSEE, Calif. State U., Long Beach, 1992; postgrad., UCLA, 1992—. Elec. engr. AiResearch, Man., Garrett, Torrance, Calif., 1983; sr. mem. tech. staff TRW Space & Electronics Group, Redondo Beach, Calif., 1984-93; v.p. of R&D CZAND Assocs., L.A., 1993—; rsch. asst. UCLA Flight System Rsch. Ctr., Westwood, Calif., 1994-96; scientist payload sys. Hughes Space & Comms., 1996—; cons. CZAND Assocs., L.A., 1985-93; instr. electronics UCLA Smarts Program. Tutor math. and sci. TRW Bootstrap, Redondo Beach, 1991-93. Recipient Meritorious Svc. award United Negro Coll. Fund, 1989; TRW master's fellow, doctoral incentive fellow Calif. State U., 1993. Mem. IEEE, Nat. Soc. Black Engrs. (pres. Dartmouth chpt. 1982-83), Dartmouth Soc. Engrs. Avocations: tennis, golf, chess, basketball, cycling.

WILSON, GORDON RUSSEL, art educator; b. Portland, Oreg., Jan. 6, 1947; s. Leo Barney Wilson and Evelyn Elizabeth (Craig) Wilson Ramus; children: Anthony, Christine. BS, Portland State U., 1970; MFA, Ft. Wright Coll., 1972. Art instr. Spokane (Wash.) Studio Sch., 1972-74, artist in residence, 1971-76; assoc. prof. in art Whitworth Coll., Spokane, 1976—; art program coord. Whitworth Coll., 1982-86; juror paper selection for Intercollegiate Ctr. for Nursing, Spokane, 1981, 5th Congl. Dist. Art, Spokane, 1990, 2d Ann. Wash. Art Instrs. of Higher Learning Invitational, Polack Gallery, Seattle; dir. Koehler Gallery, Whitworth Coll., 1991—; instr.

art, Paris and Nice, France, 1980, 86, 92; artist-in-resident Nature Art Life and Liberty Assn., Vence, France, 1993. One man shows include Cheney Cowles Mus. Spotlight Series, 1979, Spokane Art Sch., 1987, Whitworth Coll., Spokane, 1987, 92, Eclectic Electric Gallery, 1998; artist whose paintings, drawings, mixed media have been exhibited in a wide range of exhibits including Spokane Painters '75 Invitational, Carnegie Art Ctr. Ann. Regional Juried Art, 1979, 84 (1st pl. drawing 1983), Berkeley Nat. 1983, 84, N.W. Juried Art 1983, 88, A Spokane Sampler 1981, 82, 84, 85, 87, 89, 90, 92, 93, 94, Hockaday Ctr. for the Arts, Kalispell Montana, 1984, NIC Coll., Coeur d'Alene, Idaho, 1988, 89; art at work program Cheney Cowles Mus., Spokane, 1987-94. Invited participant in Goodwill Games Exhibit, Spokane, 1990. Mem. Nat. Art Educators Assn., Wash. Art Educators Assn., Christians in the Visual Arts, Cheney Cowles Mus. Home: 11814 N Anna J Dr Spokane WA 99218-2708 Office: Whitworth Coll Hawthorne Rd Spokane WA 99251

WILSON, HEATHER ANN, congresswoman; b. Keene, N.H., Dec. 30, 1960; d. George Douglas Wilson and Martha Lou Wilson-Kernozicky. BS, USAF Acad., 1982; M. Philosophy, Oxford U., 1984, PhD, 1985. U.S. mission NATO, Brussels, 1987-89, Nat. Security Coun., Washington, 1989-91; pres. Keystone Internat., Inc., Albuquerque, 1991-95; cabinet sec. N.Mex. Dept. Children, Youth and Families, Santa Fe, 1995-98; mem. 105th-106th Congresses from 1st N.Mex. Dist., Washington, 1998—; adj. prof. U. N.Mex.; mem. Def. Adv. Com. on Women in the Svcs. Contbr. articles to profl. jours. Capt. USAF, 1982-89. Decorated Def. Meritorious Svc. medal, USAF Meritorious Svc. medal; Rhodes scholar, 1982. Republican. Avocations: rowing, hiking, skiing. Office: 2404 Rayburn House Office Bldg Washington DC 20515-3101*

WILSON, IAN HOLROYDE, management consultant, futurist; b. Harrow, England, June 16, 1925; came to U.S., 1954; s. William Brash and Dorothy (Holroyde) W.; m. Page Tuttle Hedden, Mar. 17, 1951 (div. Dec. 1983); children: Rebecca, Dorothy, Ellen, Holly, Alexandra; m. Adrianne Marcus, July 12, 1992. MA, Oxford U., 1948. Orgn. cons. Imperial Chem. Industries, London, 1948-54; various staff exec. positions in strategic planning, mgmt. devel. Gen. Electric Co., Fairfield, Conn., 1954-80; sr. cons. to maj. U.S. and internat. cos. SRI Internat., Menlo Park, Calif., 1980-93; prin. Wolf Enterprises, San Rafael, Calif., 1993—; exec. in residence Va. Commonwealth U., Richmond, 1976; fellow Va. Ctr. for Creative Arts, 1998. Author: Planning for Major Change, 1976, The Power of Strategic Vision, 1991, Rewriting the Corporate Social Charter, 1992, Managing Strategically in the 1990s, 1993, Executive Leadership, 1995; contbg. editor Learning from the Future, 1998; mem. editl. bd. Planning Rev., 1973-81; Am. editor Long Range Planning Jour., London, 1981-89; sr. editor Strategy and Leadership, 1993—. Mem. adv. bd. Technol. Forecasting and Social Change, 1989—; chmn. Citizen's Long Range Ednl. Goals Com., Westport, Conn., 1967-70; mem. strategic process com. United Way of Am., Alexandria, Va., 1985-94. Capt. Brit. Army, 1943-45, ETO. Va. Ctr. Creative Arts fellow, 1998. Mem. AAAS, Strategic Leadership Forum, World Future Soc. Unitarian. Avocations: travel, writing, photography. Home and Office: 79 Twin Oaks Ave San Rafael CA 94901-1915

WILSON, IRA LEE, middle school educator; b. Taylor, La., Dec. 20, 1927; d. Henry and Sadie Mae (Milbon) Parker; m. Odie D. Wilson, Jr., May 11, 1946; children: Ervin Charles, Annie Jo, Carrido Michelle. BS, Grambling State U., 1954; postgrad., Pepperdine U., 1974, Pepperdine U., 1976; MEd, La Verne Coll., 1976. Tchr. Willowbrook Sch. Dist., Los Angeles, 1955-67, Compton (Calif.) Unified Sch. Dist., 1968—; grade level chairperson Roosevelt Middle Sch. P.T.A., Compton, 1988—; corr. sec., 1988—, sch. site leadership resource team; mem. associated student body coun. advisor Roosevelt Middle Sch., 1993-95, mem. discipline com., 1994-95. Asst. sec. Los Angeles Police Dept. Sweethearts Area Club, Los Angeles, 1988-95; mem. planning activities com. L.A. Football Classic Found., 1989; chairperson higher edn. Travelers Rest Bapt. Ch., 1992—. Recipient Perfect Attendance award Compton Unified Sch. Dist., 1987-88, S.W. Area Sweethearts for Outstanding Svcs. Los Angeles Police Dept., 1988, Disting. Svc. award Compton Edn. Assn., 1987-88, 83, Cert. of Achievement Roosevelt Jr. High Sch., 1984-85, Perfect Attendance award Roosevelt Middle Sch., 1984, Cert. of Achievement Mayo Elem. Sch., 1973-74, Roosevelt Mid. Sch., 1989, Disting. Svc. award Compton Edn. Assn., 1987-88, Key of Success award Am. Biog. Inst., Inc., 1990. Mem. NEA, Calif. Tchr. Assn., Grambling State U. Alumni Assn. (life, asst. activity chairperson 1987—), Black Women's Forum, Block Club. Democrat. Baptist. Avocations: reading, horticulture, attending sports events. Home: 828 W 126th St Los Angeles CA 90044-3818

WILSON, JAMES BRIAN, English as a second language educator; b. Ventura, Calif., Aug. 14, 1961; s. Arthur James and Patricia (Fottrell) W. BA in French, U. Calif., Irvine, 1983, tchr. ESL cert., 1994; MA in Comparative Lit., Calif. State U., Fullerton, 1992. Tchr. ESL, Claremont H.S., Huntington Beach, Calif., 1994; instr. adult basic edn.-ESL, Pasadena (Calif.) City Coll. Cmty. Edn. Ctr., 1994-96; instr. ESL, Mt. San Antonio Coll., Walnut, Calif., 1994—; lectr. ESL, Pasadena City Coll., 1996—. Tutor South Coast Literacy Coun., Irvine, 1993-94. Mem. TESOL, Calif. Tchrs. English to Spkrs. Other Langs., Orange County Guitar Circle. Avocation: playing classical and Celtic music guitar.

WILSON, JAMES RICKER, physicist, consultant; b. Berkeley, Calif., Oct. 21, 1922; s. Leslie Ramsey and Ethel Frances (Banker) W.; m. Demetra George Corombos, Feb. 25, 1949; children: Leslie, Marika, George, Tasia, Peter. BS in Chemistry, U. Calif., Berkeley, 1943, PhD in Physics, 1952. Physicist Sandia Corp., Berkeley, 1952-53; physicist Lawrence Livermore (Calif.) Nat. Lab., 1953-88, lab. assoc., 1991—; cons. Lawrence Livermore Nat. Lab., 1988-90. Author: Numerical Modeling in Physics, 1991. With U.S. Army, 1944-46. Fellow Am. Phys. Soc., Murdock Found.; mem. Am. Astron. Soc., Internat. Astronomy Union. Democrat. Achievements include establishment of neutrino heating mechanism for supernova explosions and a mechanism for explaining gamma ray bursts. Home: 2993 Chateau Way Livermore CA 94550-6845 Office: Lawrence Livermore Nat Lab PO Box L-35 Livermore CA 94551-0808

WILSON, JAMES ROSS, communications educator, broadcasting executive; b. Petaluma, Calif., Nov. 25, 1939; s. Stanley Thomas and Billie (Ross) W.; m. Elizabeth Ann Buckleman, Dec. 29, 1964 (div. 1982); children: Greg, Tom. BA, Fresno State Coll., 1961; MA, Calif State U., Fresno, 1976. Radio and TV instr. Dept. Def. Info. Sch., Ft. Slocum, N.Y., 1962-65; news dir. Sta. KVON, Napa, Calif., 1965, Sta. KTIM, San Rafael, Calif., 1966; news reporter Sta. KMJ, Fresno, 1966-67, news dir., 1967-71; program dir. Sta. KMJ/KNAX-FM, Fresno, 1971-78, v.p., gen. mgr., 1978-82; news assignment editor Sta. KFSN-TV, Fresno, 1982-83; prof. mass comm., gen. mgr., faculty advisor KFSR-FM Calif. State U., Fresno, 1983—; jazz disk jockey Sta. KVPR, Valley Pub. Radio, Fresno, 1984-90; weekend news anchor KMPH-FM News Radio, 1994-96. Co-author: Mass Media/Mass Culture, 4th edit., 1997. Recipient Best Newscast award Calif. AP-TV-Radio Assn., 1971, Best News Documentary award Calif. AP-TV-Radio Assn., 1973-74, Broadcast Excellence award Billboard mag., 1976; Calif. State U. grantee, 1987. Mem. Broadcast Edn. Assn., Cen. Calif. Broadcasters Assn. (treas., bd. dirs. 1980-83), Assn. for Edn. in Journalism and Mass Communication, Sigma Delta Chi, Alpha Epsilon Rho, Phi Kappa Phi. Home: 4747 E Holland Ave Fresno CA 93726-2914 Office: Calif State U Dept Mass Comm/Journalism Fresno CA 93740

WILSON, JAN ELIZABETH, art dealer; b. Lexington, N.C., May 6, 1955; d. Richard Baxter and Frances Fay (Thomason) W. BA in Sociology, U. N.C., Greensboro, 1979; AOS in Culinary Arts, Calif. Culinary Acad., 1996. Social worker Forsyth County DSS, Winston-Salem, N.C., 1980-85; supr. values divsn. Jefferson-Pilot Life Ins. Co., Greensboro, 1985-89; exec. dir. U.S. Amputee Athletic Assn., Charlotte, N.C., 1989-90; mgr. summer competition Nat. Handicapped Sports, Colorado Springs, Colo., 1990-92; mgr. disabled sports svcs. U.S. Olympic Com., Colorado Springs, 1992-94; owner Jan Wilson Gallery, Sun Valley, Idaho, 1996—; mem. Mayor's Com. for Handicapped, Winston-Salem, N.C., 1982-85, chairperson, 1984-85; U.S. del. XIII gen. assembly Internat. Sprots Orgn. for disabled, Ottawa, Can., 1989, IX gen. assembly, Cairo, 1992alt. mem. com. on sports for disabled U.S. Olympic Com., Colorado Springs, 1981-84, 90-92; faculty guest spkr., athlete panel Am. Acad. Orthotists & Prosthetists Continued Edn. Cours, Raleigh, N.C., Syracuse, N.Y., 1990, 92; co-founder Amputee Support Group Colorado Springs, 1991-92; U.S. del. leader Winter Paralympic Games, Lillehammer, Norway, 1992. Bd. dirs. Sagebrush Equine Tng. Ctr., 1998—. Recipient Bronze medal U.S. Disabled Sports Team/Olympics for Disabled, 1980, Gold medal (five), Silver medal U.S. Amputee Team/Can. Nat. Championships, 1983, Gold medal, Silver medal (three), Bronze medal U.S. Disabled Sports Team/Internat. Games for Disabled, 1984, Gold medal (two) U.S. Amputee Team/Australian Nat. Amputee Championships, 1988, Silver medal (three), Bronze medal U.S. Disabled Sports Team/VII Paralympic Games, 1988; Named Handicapped Citizen of Yr. Mayor's Com. for Handicapped Banquet, 1982, Outstanding Female Athlete of Yr., U.S. Amputee Athletic Assn. Nat. Championships, 1983, 88, Outstanding Female Athlete of Yr. Amputee Sports, Colo. Amateur Sports Corp., 1988; named to U.S. Amputee Athletic Assn. Hall of Fame, 1987. Mem. Amputee Coalition Am. (bd. dirs. 1991), Sun Valley/Ketchum C. of C. (bd. dirs.). Avocations: skiing, swimming, cycling, equestrian, kayaking. Office: Jan Wilson Gallery 320 First Ave N Ketchum ID 83340

WILSON, JIM HAROLD, musician; b. Greenville, S.C., Aug. 18, 1955; s. James Wilson and Lillian (Cotnoir) Doyle; 1 child, Jason Ihbe. Owner L.A. Piano Svcs., Sherman Oaks, Calif., 1978—; recording artist Angel/EMI Classics, N.Y.C., 1998—; owner VelvetVista Music, Sherman Oaks, 1997—; recording artist Angel/EMI Classics, N.Y.C., 1998—; devel. cons. midi-adaptor for acoustic piano Forte Midi-Mod, 1984. Composer, artist (CD) Northern Seascape, 1998. Founder Our Children's World Found., Hollywood, 1990. Mem. NARAS (chpt. bd. govs. 1997—). Avocations: freestyle skiing, scuba diving, hiking, travelling. Office: VelvetVista Music 5152 Sepulveda Ste 123 Sherman Oaks CA 91403

WILSON, JOHN FRANCIS, religion educator, archaeologist; b. Springfield, Mo., Nov. 4, 1937; s. Frederick Marion and Jessie Ferrell (Latimer) W.; m. L. Claudette Faulk, June 9, 1961; children: Laura, Amy, Emily. BA, Harding U., Searcy, Ark., 1959; MA, Harding U., Memphis, 1961; PhD, U. Iowa, 1967. Dir. Christian Student Ctr., Springfield, 1959-73; prof. religious studies S.W. Mo. State U., Springfield, 1961-83; prof. of religion, dean Seaver Coll. Arts, Letters and Scis. Pepperdine U., Malibu, Calif., 1983-98; dir. Inst. for the Study of Religion and Archaeology, 1998—. Author: Religion: A Preface, 1982, 2d edit., 1989; co-author: Discovering the Bible, 1986, Excavations at Capernaum, 1989; contbr. articles, revs. to profl. publs. Mem. Archaeol. Inst. Am., Am. Schs. of Oriental Rsch., Soc. Bib. Lit., Am. Numismatic Soc., Palestine Exploration Soc. Mem. Ch. of Christ. Office: Pepperdine U Seaver Coll 24255 Pacific Coast Hwy Malibu CA 90263-0002

WILSON, JOHN PASLEY, law educator; b. Newark, Apr. 7, 1933; s. Richard Henry and Susan Agnes (Pasley) W.; m. Elizabeth Ann Reed, Sept 10, 1955 (div.); children: David Cables, John, Jr., Cicely Reed. AB, Princeton U., 1955; LLB, Harvard U., 1962. Bar: N.J. 1962, U.S. Dist. Ct. N.J. 1962, Mass. 1963, U.S. Dist. Ct. Mass. 1963. Budget examiner Exec. Office of Pres., Bur. of Budget, Washington, 1955-56; assoc. Riker, Danzig, Scherer & Brown, Newark, 1962-63; asst. dean Harvard U. Law Sch., Cambridge, Mass., 1963-67; assoc. dean Boston U. Law Sch., 1968-82; dean Golden Gate U. Sch. Law, San Francisco, 1982-88, prof., 1988—; vis. prof. dept. health policy and mgmt. Harvard U., 1988; cons. Nat. Commn. for the Protection of Human Subjects of Biomed. and Behavioral Rsch.; mem. Mass. Gov's. Commn. on Civil and Legal Rights of Developmentally Disabled; former chmn. adv. com. Ctr for Community Legal Edn., San Francisco. Author: The Rights of Adolescents in the Mental Health System. Contbr. chpts. to books, articles to profl. jours. Bd. dirs. Greater Boston Legal Svcs., Chewonki Found.; mem. Health Facilities Appeals Bd., Commonwealth of Mass.; assoc. mem. Democratic Town Com., Concord; chmn. Bd. Assessors, Concord; bd. overseers Boston Hosp. for Women, past chmn. med. affairs com.; past mem. instl. rev. bd. Calif. Pacific Hosp., San Francisco. Served to lt. (j.g.) USNR, 1956-59. NIMH grantee, 1973. Mem. Nat. Assn. Securities Dealers (arbitrator). Office: Golden Gate U Sch Law 536 Mission St San Francisco CA 94105-2967

WILSON, JOHNNY LEE, editor-in-chief; b. Santa Maria, Calif., Oct. 20, 1950; s. John Henry and Bobbie Lou (Henson) W.; m. Susan Lynne Leavelle, Aug. 28, 1970 (div. 1998); children: Jennifer Lynne, Jonathan Lee. BA, Calif. Bapt. Coll., Riverside, 1972; MDiv, Golden Gate Bapt. Seminary, Mill Valley, Calif., 1975; ThM, So. Bapt. Theol. Seminary, Louisville, 1978, PhD, 1981. Pastor Rollingwood Bapt. Ch., San Pablo, Calif., 1974-75, Temple Bapt. Ch., Sacramento, Calif., 1975-77, Hermosa-Redondo Beach (Calif.) Ministries, 1981-82, Immanuel. Bapt. Ch., La Puente, Calif., 1982-86; asst. editor Computer Gaming World, Anaheim, Calif., 1986-89, editor, 1989-94; editor-in-chief Computer Gaming World, San Francisco, 1993—; pres. and prof. of Old Testament Calif. Korean Bapt. Seminary, Walnut, 1990-93; adj. prof. O.T. studies So. Calif. Ctr., Garden Grove, Calif., 1981-86; mem. com. Software Pub. Assn. Ratings Group, Washington, 1994; mem. adv. coun. Recreation Software Adv. Coun., 1995; bd. govs. Acd. Interactive Arts and Scis., 1995. Author: The Sim City Planning Commission Handbook, 1990, The Sim Earth Bible, 1991; co-author: The Mercer Dictionary of Bible, 1990, Sid Meier's Civilization: Rome on 640K A Day, 1992. Named to Outstanding Young Men of Am., Jaycees, Ala., 1977, Best Software Reviewer, Software Pubs. Assn., Washington, 1990. Avocations: drama, miniatures gaming, writing. Home: 2051 Shoreline Dr Apt 303 Alameda CA 94501-6114 Office: Ziff-Davis Pub 135 Main St Fl 14 San Francisco CA 94105-1812

WILSON, JUDITH FALTYSEK, development executive; b. Oak Park, Ill., Jan. 22, 1945; d. Paul Holmes and Mary Jane (Ward) Faltysek; m. Anthony Parks Wilson, Aug. 20, 1966; children: Catherine Holmes, Christopher Ward. BS, Northwestern U., 1967. Tchr. Ewing Twp. Schs., Trenton, N.J., 1967-70; cons. Bensinger, DuPont & Assoc., Chgo., 1981-90; assoc. dir. devel. Lawrenceville (N.J.) Sch., 1990-94; dir. of devel. Out-of-Door Acad., Sarasota, Calif., 1995. Bd. dirs., chmn. Jr. League of Chgo., 1976-81; bd. dirs., benefit chmn. Infant Welfare Soc. Chgo., 1978-86; mem. founders group Women in Devel., Princeton, N.J., 1992-95. Named Vol. of Yr. for drug edn. of parents Chgo. Mag., 1983. Mem. Nat. Soc. Fundraising Execs., Jr. League of San Francisco. Episcopalian. Home: 2900 Pacific Ave Apt 101 San Francisco CA 94115-1065

WILSON, KAREN LOUISE, artist, educator; b. Ford Ord, Calif., Mar. 22, 1962; d. Donald and Elaine (Jones) W. BFA, U. Wash., 1986; MFA, U. Chgo., 1995. Tchg. asst. U. Chgo., 1994-95; instr. Tacoma (Wash.) Cmty. Coll., 1996-97, South Seattle Cmty. Coll., 1996-98; lectr. Pacific Luth. U., Tacoma, Wash., 1998—. One-woman shows include Smith Tower Art Gallery, Seattle, 1993, Tacoma (Wash.) Ctr. Art Gallery, 1998; exhibited in group shows at Sch. Fine Art Gallery, Seattle, 1986, Rainier Square Atrium, Seattle, 1987, Exec. Offices King County Courthouse, Seattle, 1988, Chgo. Humanities Inst., 1995, Artemisia Gallery, Chgo., 1996, Commencement Art Gallery, Tacoma, Wash., 1998, Tacoma (Wash.) Art Mus. at the Tacoma Convention Ctr., 1998, others. Nat. delegate Dem. Party, N.Y.C., 1992; precinct capt. Dem. Party, Seattle, 1992-93; com. mem. Cath. Cmty. Svcs. Art, Tacoma, 1998. Recipient Honorarium, King County Arts Commn., Seattle, 1988, 93; Merit award Sch. Fine Art Gallery, U. Wash., Seattle, 1986, fellow U. Chgo., 1993-95. Mem. Women's Caucus Art, Coll. Art Assn. Avocations: reading, walking. Office: 5437 S Tacoma Way Studio C Tacoma WA 98409

WILSON, LERRY, public relations executive. Prin. Wilson McHenry Co, San Mateo, Calif. Office: Wilson McHenry Co 393 Vintage Park Dr Ste 140 Foster City CA 94404-1172*

WILSON, MARGIE (MARJORIE) JEAN, elementary education educator, writer; b. San Francisco, Nov. 2, 1950; d. Robert Barry and Priscilla Jean (Small) Clarfield; m. Michael E. Wilson, July 3, 1976; children: Christopher Michael, Robert Alexander. BA, U. Calif., Santa Barbara, 1972; postgrad., Calif. State U., Hayward; postgrad. Contra Costa Adult Edn., U. Calif. Berkeley ext. Cert. elem. tchr., Calif. Adminstrv. asst. Spreckels Sugar, San Francisco, 1974-76; sales exec. Cromwell & Co., Nashville, Tenn., 1976-77; legal sec., paralegal Latham & Watkins, L.A., 1977-79; legal sec. James C. Monroe, Santa Rosa, Calif., 1979-81; adminstrv. asst. Benefit Plan Securities, Santa Rosa, 1982-84, Bruce Kassel, MSW, Santa Rosa, 1984-85, Curriculum Assoc., Santa Rosa, 1985-86; editor Events Mag., Santa Rosa, 1987-95; contract editor/proofreader Kodansha Internat. Pubs., Tokyo, 1996—; substitute tchr. West Sonoma County (Calif.) Schs., 1995—; ptnr. WORDSWORTH, Santa Rosa, 1983—; publicity coord., dir. Jack London Found., Glen Ellen, Calif., 1990—. Author: Jack London Coloring and Activity Book, 1993, 500 Ways to Say Said, 1985, The Wit & Wisdom of Jack London, 1995; editor: Animal Origami, 1997, True Love Poems from the Heart, 1996, As I Recall, 1993, Beauty and the Feast, 1995, Young Jack London, 1996, Jack London's Klondike Adventure, 1997, Ozark Hillbilly CEO, 1999; contbr. articles to various publs. Vol. USA-USSR Inst., San Francisco, 1974-76, Oak Grove & Forestville Unified Sch. Dist., Sonoma County, 1986—, Russian River Rodeo, Guerneville, 1996—; Market Day coord. U. Calif. Santa Barbara, Hot Breakfast program, Goleta, Calif., 1973, 74, Dem. party Sonoma and Santa Barbara counties, 1970—, Redwood Empire Lyric Theater, Santa Rosa, 1990—, Save the Redwoods, 1990—, SuperPlayground, Sebastopol, Calif., 1992. Mem. Calif. Scholarship Found. (life), Delta Kappa Gamma (life), Internat. Assn. Machinists & Aerospace Workers, Eastern Star. Home: 2524 S Edison St Graton CA 95444-9352 Office: WORDSWORTH PO Box 7132 Santa Rosa CA 95407-0132

WILSON, MARK, library media specialist; b. Richmond, Va., Oct. 30, 1949; s. Earl Everett and Dorothy (Chamlee) W. BA, U. Houston, 1972; MEd, U. Va., 1976. Tchr. Houston Ind. Sch. Dist., 1978-80, Temple (Tex.) Ind. Sch. Dist., 1980-94, Puyallup (Wash.) Ind. Sch. Dist., 1994-97; libr. media specialist University Place (Wash.) Sch. Dist., 1997—. Recipient Golden Apple Temple Daily Telegram, 1987. Mem. NEA. Avocations: swimming, racquetball, hiking, biking.

WILSON, MARY SUSAN, writer, publisher; b. Danville, Ill., Aug. 1, 1957; d. Anthony Joseph and Katie (Shahadey) Lattood; m. Bruce Raymond Wilson, Jan. 17, 1987. BA, So. Ill. U., 1981. Author, publisher (book) No Ordinary Day, 1995. Avocations: crafts, antiques, internet development.

WILSON, MATTHEW FREDERICK, newspaper editor; b. San Francisco, May 10, 1956; s. Kenneth E. and Verna Lee (Hunter) W. BA in Philosophy, U. Calif., Berkeley, 1978. Copy person San Francisco Chronicle, summers 1975, 76, 77, copy editor, 1978-82, editorial systems coord., 1982-84; budget analyst San Francisco Newspaper Agy., 1984085; asst. news editor San Francisco Chronicle, 1985-87, asst. to exec. editor, 1987-88, mng. editor, 1988-95, exec. editor, 1995—. Mem. Am. Soc. Newspaper Editors, AP Mng. Editors, Calif. Soc. Newspaper Editors. Office: San Francisco Chronicle 901 Mission St San Francisco CA 94103*

WILSON, MELVIN EDMOND, civil engineer; b. Bremerton, Wash., Aug. 3, 1935; s. Edmond Curt and Madeline Rose (Deal) W.; m. Deanna May Stevens, Nov. 22, 1957 (div. Mar. 1971); children: Kathleen, Debra Wilson Frank. BSCE, U. Wash., 1957, MSCE, 1958. Registered profl. engr., Wash. Asst. civil engr. City of Seattle, 1958-60, assoc. civil engr., 1960-64, sr. civil engr., 1964-66, supervising civil engr., 1966-75, sr. civil engr., 1975-77, mgr. X, 1977-88; owner Wilson Cons. Svcs., Seattle, 1988-89; transp. sys. dir. City of Renton, Wash., 1989-96, ret., 1996; owner Mel Wilson Photographer, Seattle, 1975-84. Contbr. reports to profl. jours. Rep. Renton transp. work group King County (Wash.) Growth Mgmt. Policy Com.; rep. Renton tech. adv. com. South County Area Transp. Bd., King County, 1992-96, developer svc. policy (adopted by Puget Sound Govtl. Conf.) to encourage travel by transit. successfuly led effort to make Renton first suburban city to receive direct transit svc. under Met. King County Plan, 1994. Mem. ASCE, Am. Pub. Works Assn., Inst. Transp. Engrs., Tau Beta Pi, Sigma Xi. Avocations: photography, weight lifting, hiking.

WILSON, MICHAEL GREGG, film producer, writer; b. N.Y.C., Jan. 21, 1942; s. Lewis Gilbert Wilson and Dana (Natol) Broccoli; m. Coila Jane Hurley; children: David, Gregg. BS, Harvey Mudd Coll., 1963; JD, Stanford U., 1966. Bar: D.C., Calif., N.Y. Legal advisor FAA-DOT, Washington, 1966-67; assoc. Surrey, Karasik, Gould, Green, Washington, 1967-71; ptnr. Surrey and Morse, Washington and N.Y.C., 1971-74; legal advisor Eon Prodns., London, 1974-78, producer, mng. dir., 1978—. Writer/prodr.: For Your Eyes Only, 1981, Octopussy, 1983, View to a Kill, 1985, The Living Daylights, 1987, Licence to Kill, 1989; prodr.: Goldeneye, 1995; author: Pictorialism in California, Getty Museum, 1994. Avocation: 19th and 20th century photograph collecting.

WILSON, MIRIAM GEISENDORFER, retired physician, educator; b. Yakima, Wash., Dec. 3, 1922; d. Emil and Frances Geisendorfer; m. Howard G. Wilson, June 21, 1947; children—Claire, Paula, Geoffrey, Nicola, Marla. B.S., U. Wash., Seattle, 1944, M.S., 1945; M.D., U. Calif., San Francisco, 1950. Mem. faculty U. So. Calif. Sch. Medicine, L.A., 1965—, prof. pediatrics, 1969—. Office: U So Calif Med Ctr 1129 N State St Rm 1g24 Los Angeles CA 90033-1044

WILSON, MYRON ROBERT, JR., retired psychiatrist; b. Helena, Mont., Sept. 21, 1932; s. Myron Robert Sr. and Constance Ernestine (Bultman) W. BA, Stanford U., 1954, MD, 1957. Diplomate Am. Bd. Psychiatry and Neurology. Dir. adolescent psychiatry Mayo Clinc, Rochester, Minn., 1965-71; pres. and psychiatrist in chief Wilson Ctr., Faribault, Minn., 1971-86; ret., 1986; chmn. Wilson Ctr., 1986-90; ret., 1990; assoc. clin. prof. psychiatry UCLA, 1985—. Contbr. articles to profl. jours. Chmn., CEO C.B. Wilson Found., L.A., 1986—; mem. bd. dirs. Pasadena Symphony Orchestra Assn., Calif., 1987; vestryman, treas. St. Thomas' Parish, L.A., 1993-96. Lt. comdr., 1958-60. Fellow Mayo Grad. Sch. Medicine, Rochester, 1960-65. Fellow Am. Psychiat. Assn., Am. Soc. for Adolescent Psychiatry, Internat. Soc. for Adolescent Psychiatry (founder, treas. 1985-88, sec. 1985-88, treas. 1988-92); mem. Soc. Sigma Xi (Mayo Found. chpt.). Episcopalian. Office: Wilson Found 8033 W Sunset Blvd # 4019 West Hollywood CA 90046-2427

WILSON, PETE, former governor; b. Lake Forest, Ill., Aug. 23, 1933; s. James Boone and Margaret (Callaghan) W.; m. Betty Robertson (div.); m. Gayle Edlund, May 29, 1983. B.A. in English Lit., Yale U., 1955; J.D., U. Calif., Berkeley, 1962; LL.D., Grove City Coll., 1983, U. Calif., San Diego, 1983, U. San Diego, 1984. Bar: Calif. 1962. Mem. Calif. Legislature, Sacramento, 1966-71; mayor City of San Diego, 1971-83; U.S. Senator from Calif., 1983-91; gov. State of Calif., 1991-98. Trustee Conservation Found.; mem. exec. bd. San Diego County council Boy Scouts Am.; hon. trustee So. Calif. Council Soviet Jews; adv. mem. Urban Land Inst., 1985-86; founding dir. Retinitis Pigmentosa Internat.; hon. dir. Alzheimer's Family Ctr., Inc., 1985; hon. bd. dirs. Shakespeare-San Francisco, 1985. Recipient Golden Bulldog award, 1984, 85, 86, Guardian of Small Bus. award, 1984, Cuauhtemoc plaque for disting. svc. to farm workers in Calif., 1991, Julius award for outstanding pub. leadership U. So. Calif., 1992, award of appreciation Nat. Head Start, 1992; named Legislator of Yr., League Calif. Cities, 1985, Man of Yr. N.G. Assn. Calif., 1986, Man of Yr. citation U. Calif. Boalt Hall, 1986; ROTC scholar Yale U., 1951-55. Mem. Nat. Mil. Family Assn. (adv. bd.), Phi Delta Phi, Zeta Psi. Republican. Episcopalian. Office: 2121 Ave of Stars 34th Fl Century City CA 90067*

WILSON, RICHARD RANDOLPH, lawyer; b. Pasadena, Calif., Apr. 14, 1950; s. Robert James and Phyllis Jean (Blackman) W.; m. Catherine Goodhugh Stevens, Oct. 11, 1980; children: Thomas Randolph, Charles Stevens. BA cum laude, Yale U., 1971; JD, U. Wash., 1976. Bar: Wash. 1976, U.S. Dist. Ct. (we. dist.) Wash. 1976, U.S. Ct. Appeals (9th cir.) 1977. Assoc. Hillis, Phillips, Cairncross, Clark & Martin, Seattle, 1976-81, ptnr., 1981-84; ptnr. Hillis, Cairncross, Clark & Martin, Seattle, 1984-87; ptnr. Hillis Clark Martin & Peterson, Seattle, 1987—, chmn. land use and environ. group; bd. dirs. Quality Child Care Svcs., Inc., Seattle; pres. Plymouth Housing Group, Seattle, 1998—, trustee, 1998—; lectr. various bar assns., 1980—. Contbr. articles to profl. jours. Chmn. class agts. Yale U. Alumni Fund, New Haven, 1985-87, class agt., 1971—, mem. class coun., 1991-96, mem. Western Wash. exec. com. Yale capital campaign, 1992-97, vice chmn. leadership gifts com. Yale 25th reunion, 1995-96; mem., vice chmn. Medina (Wash.) Planning Commn., 1990-92; chmn. capital campaign Plymouth Congrl. Ch., Seattle, 1995, moderator, pres. ch. coun., 1998—. Mem. ABA, Wash. State Bar Assn. (dir. environ. and land use law sect. 1985-88), Seattle-King County Bar Assn., Kingsley Trust Assn. (pres. 1996-98), Yale Assn. of Western Wash. Congregationalist. Avocations: acting, singing, rare book collecting. Home: 2305 86th Ave NE Bellevue WA 98004-2416 Office: Hillis Clark Martin & Peterson 1221 2nd Ave Ste 500 Seattle WA 98101-2925

WILSON, ROBERT LLEWELLYN, clinical psychologist, educator; b. Cleveland, Tenn., Oct. 11, 1954; s. Robert Anderson and Louise Bell (Bible) W.; m. Belen Aurita, June 22, 1996. BA, U. Tenn., 1976; MS, Auburn U., 1980, PhD, 1988; grad. (hon.), Fed. Law Enforcement Tng. Ctr., 1988. Lic. psychologist, Calif.; cert. profl. healthcare quality. Dir. child and family svcs. Wiregrass Mental Health Sys., Sothan, Ala., 1982-83; clin. dir. Family Violence Program, Montgomery, Ala., 1983-84; psychologist Correctional Med. Sys., 1985-88; dir. child and family svcs. Wiregrass Mental Health System, Dothan, Ala., 1982-83; clin. dir. Family Violence Program, Montgomery, Ala., 1983-84; psychologist Correctional Med. Systems, Martinez, 1985-88; staff psychologist Fed. Bur Prisons, Pleasanton, Calif., 1988-89; chief of psychology Fed. Bur Prisons, Pleasanton, 1989-90; assoc. chief mental health VA Med. Clinic, Martinez, Calif., 1990—; adj. faculty Auburn U., Montgomery, Ala., 1977-78, Los Positas Coll., Calif., 1990—, Diablo Valley Coll., Calif., 1998; clin. instr. psychiatry U. Calif.-Sch. Medicine, Davis, 1990—; external cons. Readjustment Counseling Ctr., Concord, Calif., 1993—; trainer quality improvement VA, No. Calif., 1994—, mem. nat. facilitation com., Cleve., 1995—, VA Nat. Nonclin. Comm. Tng. Com., Salt Lake City, 1997—, bioethics steering com.-Sierra Pacific Health Care Network, San Francisco, 1997—; chmn. bioethics com. No. Calif. Health Care System, 1997—; faculty mem. Bayer Inst. Comm., New Haven, 1996—; mem. Diablo Coll. Faculty Senate, 1998—. Mem. social com. Gateview Homeowners, Albany, Calif., 1996—. Recipient Estes Kefauver Meml. Endowment Fund scholarship 1976, Sustained Superior Svc. award Fed Bur. Prisons, 1990, Spl. Contbn. award No. Calif. Health Care System 1996. Mem. Mensa Internat., Calif. Psychol. Assn., Psi Chi. Democrat. Avocations: Karate, weightlifting, theater performance. Home: 555 Pierce St Apt 1009 Albany CA 94706-1003 Office: VA NCHCS 150 Muir Rd Martinez CA 94553-4668

WILSON, ROBERT MCCLAIN, plastic surgeon, educator; b. Cornwall, N.Y., Dec. 6, 1942; s. James Van Gorder and Isabel Mae (Steele) W.; m. Dorothea Louise Figge; children: Michael McClain, Sara Malia. MD, U. Colo., Denver, 1968. Diplomate Am. Bd. Surgery, Am. Bd. Plastic Surgery. Commd. U.S. Army, 1967, advanced through ranks to Col., 1993; intern Tripler Army Med. Ctr., Honolulu, 1968-69, resident gen. surgery, 1970-74; resident orthopaedic surgery Martin Army Hosp., Ft. Benning, Ga., 1969-70; resident plastic surgery Walter Reed Army Med. Ctr., Washington, 1974-76, asst. chief plastic surgery svcs., 1976-78; chief plastic surgery svcs. Landstuhl Army Regional Med. Ctr., Germany, 1978-81, 90-93, 1996—; chief plastic surgery svcs. Fitzsimons Army Med. Ctr., Aurora, Colo., 1993-96; plastic surgeon Wenatchee (Wash.) Valley Clinic, 1981-90. Fellow ACS; mem. AMA, Am. Soc. Plastic Surgeons, Assn. Mil. Surgeons of U.S. Luth. Avocations: skiing, bicycling, kayaking, hiking, camping. Home: Adam Müller Strasse #9, 66894 Gerhardsbrunn Germany Office: Landstuhl Regional Med Ctr Cmr 402 Box 734 APO AE 09180-0734

WILSON, ROBERT MICHAEL ALAN, writer; b. Jamestown, N.Y., June 19, 1944; s. Harry Garfield and Hazel Virginia (Groscost) W.; m. Ursula Lieselotte Frank, May 14, 1987; 1 child, Jeffrey Aryan. BS, Calif. State U., 1974; MPA, U. So. Calif., 1976; JD, Western State U., 1983. Deputy sheriff L.A. County Sheriff's Dept., 1968-92; traffic safety advocate San Bernardino (Calif.) Police Dept., 1992-94; free-lance writer, Moreno Valley, Calif., 1992—. Author: Bad Wimpfen, 1994, Nolocaust, 1995, The Only Good Indian..., 1996, Drenched in Blood, Rigid in Death, The True Story of the Wickenburg Massacre, 1997. Creator, mgr. 999 Run for Abused Kids, Industry, Calif., 1988-91; creator, chmn. Masonic Essay Contest Against Drugs, Moreno Valley, 1991—. Sgt. USAF, 1964-67. Recipient award of merit Calif. Peace Officers Assn., 1991, Disting. Svc. award Nat. Commn. Against Drunk Drivers, Washington, 1991. Mem. Masons (Hiram award 1992), Shriners. Republican. Avocations: boating, fishing. Home: 10837 Cloud Haven Dr Moreno Valley CA 92557-4211

WILSON, ROBERT SIDNEY, banker; b. Philipsburg, Pa., May 2, 1947; s. Sidney Milford and Dorothy Hazel (Edelblute) W.; m. Ann Marie Mills, Dec. 19, 1969; children: Matthew, Amanda, Courtney. BBA in Mktg., U. Akron, 1974. Mgmt. trainee Cen. Trust Co. Northeastern Ohio, Canton, 1974-76; mng. officer Cen. Trust Co., Canton, 1976-79; asst. cashier 1st Nat. Bank Cin., 1979-81, asst. v.p., 1981-82, regional v.p., 1982-85; corp. v.p. Citibank Ariz. (formerly United Bank Ariz.), Phoenix, 1985-93; v.p. Norwest Bank Ariz. (formerly Citibank), Phoenix, 1993—; chmn. 1994 Ariz./NASA Regional Aerospace Conf., 1993-94. Fin. chmn., bd. dirs. Tempe (Ariz.) YMCA, 1986-88; bd. dirs. Tempe chpt. Am. Cancer Soc., 1986-87; mem. East Valley Ptnrship., Tempe, 1986-92; vice chmn. Tempe campaign United Way, 1988—; bd. dirs. Valley of Sun United Way, 1989-92; bd. dirs., treas. St. Luke's Health System Found., 1990—, vice chmn., 1992-93, chmn., 1993-94, chmn. joint investment com., 1991-92; bd. dirs. Tempe Impact Edn. Found., 1992—; mem. Stonier Grad. Sch. Banking Ruters U., 1984-85; mem. task force Vision Tempe, 1990—, pres., 1991—; mem. adv. com. Tempe Elem. Sch. Dist. Community-Bus.-Edn. Partnership, 1990; mem. fin. com. Symington for Gov., 1990; mem. campaign support com. Gary Richardson for State Rep., 1990, 92; campaign fin. chmn. Bev Hermon for Congress, 1994; mem. Joint Legis. Com. Sch. Consol., 1991-92; bd. dirs. Tempe Conv. and Visitors Bur., 1990-91; charter mem. City of Tempe Bus. Roundtable, 1991—; hon. bd. dirs. Tempe Ctr. for Habilitation, 1993—; active Tempe Community Found., 1991-93, Tempe Elem. Sch. Dist. Task Force, 1992; bd. dirs. Chicano Museo, 1994—. Recipient City of Tempe Community Svc. award, 1989, 90, 91, 92. Mem. Robert A. Morris & Assocs. (regional assoc.), Am. Inst. Banking, Tempe C. of C. (bd. dirs., vice chmn. Svcs. award 1987, pres. 1990), Am. Electronics Assn. (bd. dirs. Ariz. coun. 1990-91). Republican. Office: Norwest Bank Ariz 3300 N Central Ave # 9028 Phoenix AZ 85012-2501

WILSON, ROBIN SCOTT, university president, writer; b. Columbus, Ohio, Sept. 19, 1928; s. John Harold and Helen Louise (Walker) W.; m. Patricia Ann Van Kirk, Jan. 20, 1951; children: Kelpie, Leslie, Kari, Andrew. B.A., Ohio State U., 1950; M.A., U. Ill., 1951, Ph.D., 1959. Fgn. intelligence officer CIA, Washington, 1959-67; prof. English Clarion State Coll., (Pa.), 1967-70; assoc. dir. Com. Instnl. Cooperation, Evanston, Ill., 1970-77; assoc. provost instrn. Ohio State U., Columbus, 1977-80; univ. pres. Calif. State U., Chico, 1980-93, pres. emeritus, 1993—. Author: Those Who Can, 1973, Death By Degrees, 1995, Paragons, 1996; short stories, criticism, articles on edn. Lt. USN, 1953-57. Mem. AAAS, Phi Kappa Phi.

WILSON, STEPHEN VICTOR, federal judge; b. N.Y.C., Mar. 26, 1942; s. Harry and Rae (Ross) W. B.A. in Econs., Lehigh U., 1963; J.D., Bklyn. Law Sch., 1967; LL.M., George Washington U., 1973. Bars: N.Y. 1967, D.C. 1971, Calif. 1972, U.S. Ct. Appeals (9th cir.) U.S. Dist. Ct. (so., cen. and no. dists.) Calif. Trial atty. Tax div. U.S. Dept. Justice, 1968-71; asst. U.S. atty., L.A., 1971-77, chief spl. prosecutions, 1973-77; ptnr. Hochman, Salkin & Deroy, Beverly Hills, Calif., from 1977; judge U.S. Dist. Ct. (cen. dist.) Calif., L.A., 1985—; adj. prof. law Loyola U. Law Sch., 1976-79; U.S. Dept. State rep. to govt. W.Ger. on 20th anniversary of Marshall Plan, 1967; del. jud. conf. U.S. Ct. Appeals (9th cir.), 1982-86. Co-editor Tax Crimes--Corporate Liability, BNA Tax Management Series, 1983; contbr. articles to profl. jours. Recipient Spl. Commendation award U.S. Dept. Justice, 1977. Mem. ABA, L.A. County Bar Assn., Beverly Hills Bar Assn. (chmn. criminal law com.), Fed. Bar Assn. Jewish. Contbr. articles to profl. jours. Home: 9100 Wilshire Blvd Beverly Hills CA 90212-3415 Office: US Courthouse Rm 217 J 312 N Spring St Los Angeles CA 90012*

WILSON, THEODORE HENRY, retired electronics company executive, aerospace engineer; b. Eufaula, Okla., Apr. 23, 1940; s. Theodore V. and Maggie E. (Buie) W.; m. Barbara Ann Tassara, May 16, 1958 (div. 1982); children: Debbie Marie, Nita Leigh, Wilson Axten, Pamela Ann, Brenda Louise, Theodore Henry II, Thomas John, Margaret Mariana; m. Colleen Fagan, Jan. 1, 1983 (div. 1987); m. Karen L. Lerohl, Sept. 26, 1987 (div. 1997); m. Sandra Rivadeneira, Mar. 27, 1997. BSME, U. Calif., Berkeley, 1962; MSME, U. So. Calif., 1964, MBA, 1970, MSBA, 1971. Sr. rsch. engr. N.Am. Aviation Co. div. Rockwell Internat., Downey, Calif., 1962-65; propulsion analyst, supr. div. applied tech. TRW, Redondo Beach, Calif., 1965-67, mem. devel. staff systems group, 1967-71; sr. fin. analyst worldwide automotive dept. TRW, Cleve., 1971-72; contr. systems and energy group TRW, Redondo Beach, 1972-79; dir. fin. control equipment group TRW, Cleve., 1979-82; v.p. fin. control indsl. and energy group, 1982-85; mem. space and def. group TRW, Redondo Beach, 1985-95, ret., 1995; [illegible], mem.

com. acctg. curriculum UCLA Extension, 1974-79. Mem. Fin. Execs. Inst. (com. govt. bus.), Machinery and Allied Products Inst. (govt. contracts coun.), Nat. Contract Mgmt. Assn. (bd. advisors), Aerospace Industries Assn. (procurement and fin. coun.), UCLA Chancellors Assocs., Tau Beta Pi, Beta Gamma Sigma, Pi Tau Sigma. Republican. Avocations: golf, bridge. Home: 3617 Via La Selva Palos Verdes Peninsula CA 90274-1115

WILSON, THOMAS WOODROW, III, research scientist, consultant; b. Greensboro, N.C., Mar. 29, 1956; s. Thomas Woodrow Jr. and Ruth Hanes (Friddle) W. BS in Textile Chemistry with honors, N.C. State U., 1978, MS in Textile Chemistry, 1981, PhD in Fiber and Polymer Sci., 1986. Registered patent agent. Polymer scientist Rsch. Triangle Inst., Research Triangle Park, N.C., 1989-91; rsch. scientist Family Health Internat., Research Triangle Park, N.C., 1991-93, sr. rsch. scientist, 1993-94, assoc. dir., 1994-95; mgr. intellectual property and regulatory affairs Mayer Labs., Oakland, Calif., 1996-97; materials rschr. Nike, Beaverton, Oreg., 1997—; cons. IPAS, Carrboro, N.C., 1991-94. Patentee med. devices; contbr. articles to profl. jours. Grantee USDA, NASA, NIH/Nat. Inst. Dental Rsch., 1986. Mem. AAAS, Am. Chem. Soc. (polymeric materials sci. and engring. divsn., polymer divsn., rubber divsn., chemistry and law divsn.), ASTM, Sigma Xi. Avocations: leatherworking, woodworking, writing fiction. Office: Nike IHM 15705 SW 72nd Ave Portland OR 97224-7937

WILSON, TISH, children's services administrator; b. San Diego, Feb. 27, 1950; d. Kelley Frank and Evelyn Jewel (Parr) Scott; m. David Alexander Stephenson, Apr. 17, 1983; children: Wes, Dwight. BS, San Diego State U., 1973; MS, Utah State U., 1976. Tchr. Neighborhood Assoc./Head Start, San Diego, 1970-72, San Diego Unified Schs., 1972-73; instr. Utah State U., Logan, 1973-78; edn. coord. Ute Indian Tribe, Ft. Duchesne, Utah, 1975-78; edn. specialist Community Devel. Inst., Kansas City, Mo., 1978-79; exec. dir. Community Devel. Inst., Albuquerque, 1979-88; divsn. head early childhood multicultural edn. program Santa Fe C.C., 1988-95; dirs. opers. devel. children's svcs. Presbyn. Med. Svcs., Santa Fe, 1995—; bd. dirs. Community Devel. Inst., Albuquerque, Work Systems by Design, Kansas City, Twisted Pine Nursery, Inc., Santa Fe; validator Acad. of Early Childhood Programs, Washington, 1984—; rep. Cun. for Early Childhood Profl. Recognition, Washington, 1978—. Mem. City of Santa Fe Children & Youth Commn., 1990-92; task force mem. State of N.M., House Meml., Santa Fe, 1989-95, Senate Joint Meml., 1996—. Recipient Gov.'s Outstanding N.Mex. Women award, 1995. Mem. Nat. Assn. for the Edn. of Young Children, N.Mex. Head Start Assn. Democrat. Avocations: hiking, swimming, camping. Office: Presbyn Med Svcs PO Box 2267 1422 Paseo De Peralta Santa Fe NM 87504

WILSON-CANNON, MARGARET ELIZABETH, artist, educator; b. Marquette, Mich., May 26, 1923; d. Carl Arthur and Elizabeth Justina Erickson; m. John Pershing Cannon, Sept. 4, 1947 (dec. Aug. 6, 1983); children: Michael, Jennifer, Colleen Cannon Nicholson, Ericka Cannon Kramer; m. Robert Carlton Wilson, Aug. 16, 1992. BA in Art Edn., U. Americas, Mexico D.F. (now Puebla); MA in Drawing and Painting, U. Calif., Fullerton. Tchr. art appreciation, art history U. Americas, Puebla, Mexico; tchr. art appreciation, art history, drawing and painting Cypress and Fullerton Colls., Calif.; art history, art appreciation, life drawing Calif. U., Fullerton; tchr. drawing and painting Cerritos, Escuela de Artes Activo, Ensenada, Mex.; lectr., art critic, editor, illustrator; adj. prof. Chapman U. Artist: one woman shows include Paideia Gallery, La Cienega, Hollywood, Calif., others; group exhibitions: Laguna Mus. of Art, Cerritos Coll. Gallery, Calif. U. at Fullerton, U. Americas, Mex., La Mirada Festival of the Arts, Orange County Art Assn., L.A. Art Assn.; invited to exhibit Fine Arts Assn., Warsaw, Poland. Home and Studio: 1640 Maple Dr Chula Vista CA 91911-5942

WILT, ADAM JAY, engineering consultant, filmmaker, videographer; b. Austin, Tex., May 4, 1959; s. Edward J. and Mary Anne (Smith) W. BS, Princeton U., 1982; M of Engring., Carnegie-Mellon U., 1986. Software engr. Circuit Studios, Washington, 1986-88; sr. software engr. Abekas Video Sys., Redwood City, Calif., 1988-91, Borland Internat., Scotts Valley, Calif., 1991-92, Louth Automation, Menlo Park, Calif., 1993-94, Pinnacle Sys., Mt. View, Calif., 1994-97; self-employed cons. engr. Menlo Park, 1997—; Dir. photography (film) The Beautiful Thing, 1998; dir. photography, editor, co-dir. (film) For Reasons Unknown, 1980. Mem. Soc. Motion Picture and T.V. Engrs. (San Francisco sect. mgr. 1996—). Avocations: flying, cycling. E-mail: adam@adamwilt.com. Office: PO Box 4153 Menlo Park CA 94026-4153

WILTON, PETER CAMPBELL, marketing educator; b. Adelaide, S.A., Australia, Jan. 28, 1951; came to U.S., 1975; s. Murray and Kathleen (Ratcliffe) W. B in Commerce with hons., U. New South Wales, Sydney, 1972; PhD in Mgmt., Purdue U., 1979. Product mgr. Colgate Palmolive, Sydney, 1973-75; mktg. prof. U. Calif., Berkeley, 1979-87, 92—; COO Myer Pacific Corp., Melbourne, Australia, 1987-90; sr. assoc. Melbourne U., 1990, Sir Donald Hibberd lectr., 1991; vis. fellow Griffith U., Brisbane, Australia, 1982; vis. assoc. prof. Duke U., Durham, N.C., 1985-86; pres., dir. Applied Mktg. Analysis, Inc., Wilmington, Del., 1987—, Orbis Assocs., San Francisco, 1992—. Contbr. articles to profl. jours. Recipient Mktg. Rsch. Soc. Australia prize, 1973; Australian Govt. fellow, 1975-79; grantee NSF, 1981, 84. Mem. Assn. Pub. Opinion Rsch. (officer 1985), Am. Mktg. Assn. (officer 1982-84), Australian-Am. C. of C. (dir. 1993-95). Avocations: flying, sailing, music, travel.

WINCHELL, ROBERT ALLEN, government agency administrator, accountant, auditor; b. Ft. Monmouth, N.J., Oct. 28, 1945; s. Robert Winslow Winchell; B.A., U. Calif., Santa Barbara, 1967; M.B.A., U. Pa., 1969. CPA, Calif. Air Force Audit Agy., El Segundo, Calif., 1972-73; accountant Scholefield, Bellanca & Co., W. Los Angeles, 1974-75, So. Calif. Gas Co., Los Angeles, 1975-76; auditor Def. Contract Audit Agy., Dept. Def., Los Angeles, 1976-86, supervisory auditor, 1986-96; ret., 1996; internal auditor UCLA, 1998—. Served with AUS, 1969-71; Vietnam. Decorated Bronze Star. Mem. Assn. Govt. Accountants, Am. Inst. C.P.A.'s, Alpha Kappa Psi. Republican. Presbyterian. Club: Los Angeles Country. Home: 2008 California Ave Santa Monica CA 90403-4506

WINCHESTER, ED, protective services official. Chief of police Fresno, Calif. Office: 2323 Mariposa St Fresno CA 93721-1824*

WINDER, DAVID KENT, federal judge; b. Salt Lake City, June 8, 1932; s. Edwin Kent and Alma Eliza (Cannon) W.; m. Pamela Martin, June 24, 1955; children: Ann, Kay, James. BA, U. Utah, 1955; LLB, Stanford U., 1958. Bar: Utah 1958, Calif. 1958. Assoc. firm Clyde, Mecham & Pratt Salt Lake City, 1958-66; law clk. to chief justice Utah Supreme Ct., 1958-59; dep. county atty. Salt Lake County, 1959-63; chief dep. dist. atty., 1965-66; asst. U.S. atty. Salt Lake City, 1963-65; partner firm Strong & Hanni, Salt Lake City, 1966-77; judge State of Utah Dist. Ct., Salt Lake City, 1977-79; U.S. Dist. judge Utah, 1979-93, chief U.S. Dist. judge, 1993-97; sr. judge US. Dist. Utah, 1997—; examiner Utah Bar Examiners, 1975-79, chmn., 1977-79; mem. jud. resources com. Served with USAF, 1951-52. Mem. Am. Bd. Trial Advocates, Utah State Bar (Judge of Yr. award 1978), Salt Lake County Bar Assn., Calif. State Bar. Democrat. Office: US Dist Ct 110 US Courthouse 350 S Main St Salt Lake City UT 84101-2180*

WINDING, EZSHWAN KRAUS, artist; b. North Chicago, Ill., Aug. 13, 1934; d. Joseph and Hermina Lang Kraus; m. Kai C. Winding (dec. May 1983); children: Valarie, Renee, Cynthia Hamilton. BFA, U. Ill., 1956; student, Art Inst. Chgo., 1962, Barat Coll., 1968-69, UCLA, 1977. Pres. Artisimo Art Gallery, Scottsdale, Ariz., 1991-97; yoga tchr. N.Y.C., Chgo., Spain, 1971-87. Author: Yoga for Musicians, 1982; exhibited in invitational and juried shows including U. Oreg., 1998, Rouge C.C., Bennington (Vt.) Ctr. for the Arts, 1997, represented in collections at Casa Grande Mus., Ariz., Pendelton Corp., Whittman-Hart, Inc., Chgo., Cleve., Indpls., Dallas, others. Home and Office: 210 Suncrest Rd Unit 3 Talent OR 97540-8620

WINDSOR, WILLIAM EARL, consulting engineer, sales representative; b. Evansville, Ind., Jan. 24, 1927; s. Charles H. and Lora E. (Archey) W.; divorced; children: Kim, William, Robert. Student, Purdue U., 1946-50. Field engr. Philco Corp., Phila., 1950-53, Europe, Africa, Arabia, studio ops.

engr. Sta. WFBM, Indpls., 1953-55; field engr. RCA Svc. Co., Cherry Hill, N.J., 1955-56; audio facilities engr. ABC, N.Y.C., 1956-62; rsch. engr. Fine Recording, Inc., N.Y.C., 1962-66; chief engr. A & R Recording, Inc., N.Y.C., 1966-68; chief engr., corp. sec. DB Audio Corp., N.Y.C., 1968-70; pres. Studio Cons., Inc., N.Y.C., 1970-72; sr. v.p., v.p., gen. mgr. Quad Eight Electronics-Quad Eight/Westrex, San Fernando, Calif., 1972-85; sr. mktg. exec. Mitsubishi Pro Audio Group, San Fernando, Calif., 1985-89; pres., CEO Quad Eight Electronics, Inc., Valencia, Calif., 1989-90; ind. cons., Valencia, 1991—. Inventor monitor mixer for multitrack audio consoles, 1967, update function for audio console automation, 1973; designer of new architecture for film scoring and film re-recording sound mixing consoles, 1974 (Acad. award 1974). Served with USNR, 1945-50. Fellow Audio Engring. Soc. (chmn. N.Y. sect. 1970); mem. Soc. Motion Picture & TV Engrs. Avocations: photography, foreign travel, art collecting. Home and Office: 23112 Yvette Ln Valencia CA 91355-3060

WINFIELD, ROY A., pharmaceutical company executive. CEO Incyte Pharms., Palo Alto, Calif. Office: Incyte Pharms 3174 Porter Dr Palo Alto CA 94304-1212*

WINFREY, SUSAN CAROL, small business owner; b. San Luis Obispo, Calif., July 19, 1949; d. Alfred and Marguerette (Beck) Ricioli; m. John L. Biddle, 1966 (div. 1977); children: John Glenn, Sherry Lee; m. Jerry Andrew Winfrey, Aug. 26, 1979 (div. 1997). In-home support counselor AmTech, Anchorage, Alaska, 1984-86; officer mgr. House of Harley-Davidson, Anchorage, 1987-89; co-owner Wind-Free Trucking Co., Kasilof, Alaska, 1988-97; officer mgr. Westminster (Calif.) Harley-Davidson, 1993-94; gen. mgr. Kenai Peninsula Harley-Davidson, Soldotna, Alaska, 1997—. Author: Misadventure on the Sea of Gold, 1997. Mem. NRA, A.B.A.T.E., Soldotna C. of C., Kenai C. of C., Ladies of Harley. Republican. Avocations: hiking, fishing, hunting, motorcycle riding, boating.

WING, ROGER, management consultant; b. N.Y.C., May 26, 1945; s. John A. and Norma M. (LeBlanc) W.; m. Judith A. King, June 7, 1963 (div. 1980); m. Peggy J. McFall, Aug. 27, 1983; children: Roger, Karin, Nicole, Sean, Nathan, Alexandra. BBA, Cleve. State U., 1972, MBA, 1975. Supr. Am. Greetings Co., Brooklyn, Ohio, 1969-74; dir. Revco D.S. Inc., Twinsburg, Ohio, 1974-78; mgr. Hughes Aircraft Co., Los Angeles, 1978-79; sr. dir., v.p. Continental Airlines, Los Angeles, 1979-81; dir., practice leader Coopers & LyBrand, Los Angeles, 1981-83; pres. Huntington Cons. Group, Huntington Beach, Calif., 1983—; prof. Cleve. State U., 1977-78. Named Systems Man of Yr., Assn. Systems Mgmt., 1978. Avocations: tennis, skiing, photography, travel, Christian ministry. Office: The Huntington Cons Group 8531 Topside Cir Huntington Beach CA 92646-2117

WINGER, WALTER ORVAL, minister; b. Kindersley, Saskat., Can., July 14, 1929; came to U.S., 1967; s. Marshal A. and Mary Ethel (Bitner) W.; m. Lois Pauline, Aug. 21, 1951; children: Larry Aldon, Marshal Lee, Wayne Scott. BTh, Ont. Bible Coll., 1960; MS, Temple U., 1972; D of Ministry, Eastern Bapt. Theol. Seminary, Phila., 1976. Ordained to ministry Brethren in Christ Ch., 1960. Sr. pastor Port Colborne (Ont.) Brethren in Christ Ch., 1955-67, Carlisle (Pa.) Brethren in Christ Ch., 1967-79; pres. Niagra Christian Coll., Fort Erie, Ont., Can., 1979-83; sr. pastor Browncroft Community Ch., Rochester, N.Y., 1983-89, Upland (Calif.) Brethren in Christ Ch., 1989—; adj. lectr. Messiah Coll., Grantham, Pa., 1973-79, Roberts Wesleyan Coll., Rochester, 1983-84, Azusa (Calif.) Pacific U., 1990—. Fellow Profl. Soc. Doctors of Ministry; mem. Kiwanis (bd. dirs. Carlisle chpt. 1970-79, com. chmn. Upland chpt. 1990—). Home: 845 W Arrow Hwy Upland CA 91786-4517 Office: Upland Brethren Christ Ch 845 W Arrow Hwy Upland CA 91786-4517

WINMILL, B. LYNN, judge; m. Judy Winmill; 3 children. BA, Idaho State U.; JD, Harvard U. Atty. Holland and Hart, Denver; trial lawyer Hawley, Troxell, Ennis and Hawley, Pocatello, Idaho; judge Idaho Sixth Jud. Dist. Ct., Boise, Idaho, 1987—. Office: US Dist Ct Idaho 6th Fl 550 W Fort St # 040 Ste 039 Boise ID 83724*

WINN, H. RICHARD, surgeon; b. Chester, Pa., 1947. MD, U. Pa., 1968; BA, Princeton U., 1964. Diplomate Am Bd. Neurological Surgeons. Intern U. Hosp., Cleve., 1968-69, resident surgery, 1969-70; resident neurolog. surgery U. Hosp. Va., Charlottesville, 1970-74; neurol. surgeon U. Wash. Hosp., Seattle, 1983—; prof., chmn. neurol. surgery U. Wash., Seattle, 1983—; dir. Am. Bd. Neurol. Surgery. Founding editor Neurosurgical Clinics of North Amercia; mem. editl. bd. Jour. Neurosurgery, Am. Jour. Physiology, Am. Jour. Surgery. Fellow AAAS, ACS (gov.), Soc. Brit. Neurol. Surgeons (hon.); mem. AMA, Am. Assn. Neurol. Surgeons. Office: U Wash Dept Neurosurg 325 9th Ave # 359766 Seattle WA 98104-2420*

WINNER, KARIN, newspaper editor. Editor San Diego Union-Tribune, 1995—. Office: Copley Press Inc 350 Camino De La Reina San Diego CA 92108-3003*

WINNER, RAMONA, writer; b. San Manuel, Ariz., Aug. 24, 1957; d. Pablo L. and Mary (Dominguez) Moreno; m. Robert L. Winner, July 8, 1978; children: Robert G., Lucas. Pub. rels. and awards sec. Santa Barbara (Calif.) Bd. Realtors, 1980-81; with Calif. Preferred Providers, 1983-84; exec. sec. Vantage PPO, 1984-87; recruiter Network Mgmt., Inc., 1987-88; patient adv. Systemetrics, Santa Barbara, 1988-93; freelance writer, 1993—; project coord. Breast Care Ctr., 1995-96; with Goleta Valley Cmty. Hosp. Found., 1997-98; cons. grant writing LaBelle Found., Santa Barbara, Calif., 1997-98, Unity Shoppe, Inc., Santa Barbara, 1998. Author: It's Okay To Be Different! i Esta Bien Ser Diferente!, 1996. Cpl. USMC, 1975-79. Mem. Small Pubs., Artists and Writers Network. Avocations: walking, reading, crafts. Office: Brainstorm 3000 PO Box 42246 Santa Barbara CA 93140-2246

WINSKILL, ROBERT WALLACE, manufacturing executive; b. Tacoma, Oct. 30, 1925; s. Edward Francis William and Margaret Eyre (Myers) W. BA, Coll. Puget Sound, Tacoma, 1947. Field rep. Ray Burner Co., San Francisco, 1954-57, nat. sales mgr., 1960-69; v.p. sales Western Boiler Co., L.A., 1957-60; gen. sales mgr. Ray Burner Co., San Francisco, 1973-82; v.p., chief exec. officer Orr & Sembower, Inc., Middletown, Pa., 1969-73; pres. Combustion Systems Assocs., Inc., Mill Valley, Calif., 1982—; bd. dirs. Sino-Am. Boiler Engring. Co., Shanghai, China, S. T. Johnson Co., Oakland, Calif. Contbr. articles to profl. jours.; columnist Marin Scope, Mill Valley Harold, 1991—. With U.S. Army, 1943-44. Mem. ASME, Olympic Club (San Francisco), Rotary. Avocation: vineyard. Office: Combustion Systems Assocs Inc PO Box 749 Mill Valley CA 94942-0749

WINSLOW, BETTE KILLINGSWORTH, dance studio owner; b. Springfield, Mo., Dec. 10, 1919; d. Troy Kenwood andWinifred Elizabeth (Reed) Killingsworth; m. Kenelm Crawford Winslow, Sept. 5, 1947; children: Katherine, Jeanette, Kenelm, Elizabeth, Priscilla. Student, Christian Coll., 1937-39, Perry Mansfield Theater Arts Camp, summer 1938; studied with, George Balanchine, 1939-41, Pierre Vladimiroff, Anatole O'Boukhoff, Anatole Vilzak, Ludmila Shollar, Muriel Stuart, Jack Stanley, Jose Fernandez, Doris Humphrey, Jose Limon, Martha Graham, Nimura. Dancer Vogue Ballet, Rodeo, Vincent Youman Concert Revue, Met. Opera Ballet, N.Y.C., Boston and Can., 1939-44; program dir. overseas clubs ARC, New Guinea, Philippines and Korea, 1944-47; owner dance studios, pvt. tchr. dance Hermon, N.Y., Ishpeming, Mich., and Taos, N.Mex., 1947—; dir. Dance Taos summer workshops, 1986-92. Choreographer numerous dance prodns., original ballets. Recipient Disting. Alumni award Columbia Coll., 1996, Taos Living Treasure award, 1998. Avocation: sewing. Home: PO Box 927 El Prado NM 87529-0927 Office: PO Box 425 Taos NM 87571-0425

WINSLOW, DAVID ALLEN, chaplain, retired naval officer; b. Dexter, Iowa, July 12, 1944; s. Franklin E. and Inez Maude (McPherson) W.; m. Frances Lavinia Edwards, June 6, 1970; children: Frances, David. BA, Bethany Nazarene Coll., 1968; MDiv, Drew U., 1971, STM, 1973; cert. of achievement Emergency Mgmt Inst. FEMA, 1997. Ordained to ministry United Meth. Ch., 1969; cert. FEMA instr. Clergyman, 1969—; assoc. minister All Sts. Episcopal. Ch., Millington, N.J., 1969-70; asst. minister Marble Collegiate Ch., N.Y.C., 1970-71; min. No. N.J. Conf., 1971-75; joined chaplain corps USN, 1971, advanced through grades to lt. comdr., [illegible]

disaster cons. Ch. World Svc., Cupertino, Calif., 1997—; NDMS/DMAT, CA-6, Contra/Costa County, Calif., 1997—. Author: The Utmost for the Highest, 1993, Epiphany: God Still Speaks, 1994, Be Thou My Vision, 1994, Evening Prayers At Sea, 1995, Wiseman Still Adore Him, 1995, God's Power At Work, 1996; (with Walsh) A Year of Promise: Meditations, 1995, editor: The Road to Bethlehem: Advent, 1993, Preparation for Resurrecton: Lent, 1994, God's Promise: Advent, 1994, The Way of the Cross: Lent, 1995; contbr. articles to profl. jours. Bd. dirs. disaster svcs. and family svcs. ARC, Santa Ana, Calif., 1988-91, Child Abuse Prevention Ctr., Orange, Calif., 1990-91; bd. dirs. Santa Clara County Coun. Chs., 1993-94, del., 1995-98; bd. dirs. Salvation Army Adult Rehab. Ctr. Adv. Coun., San Jose, Calif; bd. dirs. emergency svcs. Santa Clara Valley chpt. ARC, San Jose, 1995-98; bd. dirs. disaster svcs. Interfaith Svc., Inc., San Jose Internat. Airport. Fellow Am. Acad. Experts in Traumatic Stress (cert. expert); mem. ACA, USN League (hon.), Sunrise Exch. Club (chaplain 1989-91), Dick Richards Breakfast Club (chaplain 1988-91), Kiwanis, Masons (charter), Shriners, Scottish Rite. Avocations: golf, skiing, sailing. Home: 20405 Via Volante Cupertino CA 95014-6318

WINSLOW, FRANCES EDWARDS, city official; b. Phila., Sept. 12, 1948; d. Harry Donaldson and Anna Louise (McColgan) E.; m. David Allen Winslow, June 6, 1970; children: Frances Lavinia, David Allen Jr. BA, Drew U., 1969, MA, 1971; M Urban Planning, NYU, 1974, PhD, 1978. Cert. in hazardous material mgmt.; cert. emergency mgmt. mgr. Adminstrv. asst. Borough of Florham Park, N.J., 1970-73; instr. Kean Coll., Union, N.J., 1973-75; adminstrv. analyst Irvine (Calif.) Police Dept., 1984-86; coord. emergency svcs. City of Irvine, 1986-91; dir. emergency svcs. City of San Jose, Calif., 1991—; instr. U. Calif., Irvine ext., 1990-91, Berkeley ext., 1996—, Santa Cruz ext., 1997—; adj. prof. San Jose State U., 1999; mem. Calif. Seismic Safety Commn., 1991-95, Calif. Hosp. Bldg. Safety Bd., 1994-95. Editor NCEER Workshop Procs., 1990, 92; contbr. chpts. in books and articles to profl. jours. Vice pres. San Diego Chaplain's Wives, 1976-79; treas. Girl Scouts U.S.A., Yokohama, Japan, 1980-81; treas. Camp Pendleton Officer's Wives Club, 1982-83, pres., 1983-84; vice chmn. curriculum ARC Disaster Acad., 1989-90, chmn., 1991; mem. community disaster preparedness com. ARC, 1992-97; del. Nat. Coordinating Com. on Emergency Mgmt., 1990—; bd. dirs. Calif. Earthquake Safety Found., 1997—. Recipient Vol. Svc. award Navy Relief Soc., 1984; Lasker Found. fellow, 1972; named one of Women of Distinction, Soroptimists Internat., 1991. Mem. ASPA (program chmn. Orange County 1984-85, chmn. criminal justice sect. award com. 1988-92, Santa Clara County bd. dirs., co-chmn. mini-conf. 1993, sec. 1994-95, pres. 1995-98, bd. mem., chair sect. emergency mgmt., nat. policy com., nat. membership chair 1996-97, nat. coun. 1998—), Am. Planning Assn. (regional conf. planning com. 1989-90), Internat. City Mgrs. Assn., Assn. Environ. Profls., Assn. Police Planning and Res. Officers (past sec., v.p. Orange County 1984-90), Creekers Club (pres. 1985-88), San Jose Mgmt. Assn. (bd. dirs. 1992-98), Calif. Emergency Svcs. Assn. (conf. program com. 1992, 95, 98, legis. chair 1997-98, Platinum award 1998, Gold award 1998), Santa Clara County Emergency Mgrs. Assn. (sec. 1995, v.p. 1996, pres. 1997), Yokohama Internat. Women's Club (v.p. for social svcs. 1979-81). Republican. Methodist. Avocations: amateur radio, music, reading, biking, swimming. Home: 20405 Via Volante Cupertino CA 95014-6318 Office: City of San Jose 855 N San Pedro St # 404 San Jose CA 95110-1718

WINSLOW, NORMAN ELDON, business executive; b. Oakland, Calif., Apr. 4, 1938; s. Merton Conrad and Roberta Eilene (Drennen) W.; m. Betty June Cady, Jan. 14, 1962 (div. Aug. 1971); 1 child, Todd Kenelm; m. Ilene Ruth Jackson, Feb. 3, 1979. BS, Fresno (Calif.) State U., 1959. Asst. mgr. Proctors Jewelers, Fresno, 1959-62; from agt. to dist. mgr. Allstate Ins. Co., Fresno, 1962-69; ins. agt. Fidelity Union Life Ins., Dallas, 1969-71; dist. and zone mgr. The Southland Corp., Dallas, 1971-78; owner Ser-Vis-Etc., Goleta, Calif., 1978—. Pub./editor FranchiserviceNews; author: Hands in Your Pockets, 1992; contbr. numerous articles to profl. jours. With USAFNG, 1961-67. Mem. Nat. Coalition of Assn. of 7-11 Franchises (affiliate, mem. adv. bd. Glendale, Calif. chpt. 1984-90), Am. Arbitration Assn. (expert witness/cons. Calif. superior cts.). Republican. Methodist. Avocations: gardening, photography, traveling. Home: 1179 N Patterson Ave Santa Barbara CA 93117-1813 Office: Ser-Vis-Etc PO Box 8276 Goleta CA 93118-8276

WINSLOW, PHILIP CHARLES, agriculturist, marketing consultant; b. Carthage, Ind., Jan. 13, 1924; s. William Howard and Ione (Morris) W.; m. Arlis Brown, Oct. 6, 1951; children: Mark, Jay, Julie. BS, Purdue U., 1948. Successively dist. mgr., regional product mgr., asst. div. sales mgr., div. sales mgr., nat. product mgr., nat. mktg. mgr. Ralston Purina Co., 1950-1970; v.p. mktg. Namolco, Inc., Willow Grove, Pa., 1971-84; dir. mktg. Liquid Products Divsn. Cargill, Inc., Willow Grove, 1984-85; nat. mktg. cons. Cargill, Inc., Mpls., 1986-88; v.p. The Montgomery Group, Huntingdon, Tenn., 1989—; pres., dir. Winslow Farms, Inc., Carthage, 1982—. Sgt. U.S. Army, 1948-50. Mem. Am. Feed Industry Assn. (com. chmn. 1975-76, com. sec. 1982-83), Big 10 Club Phila. (pres. 1981), Shadowridge Golf Club (sec.-treas. 1992, pres. 1993, bd. govs. 1993-94), Purdue Club Phila. (v.p. 1982-83, pres. 1983-86), Purdue Club San Diego. Republican. Lutheran. Avocation: golf. Home and Office: 1305 La Salle Ct Vista CA 92083-8945

WINSLOW, THOMAS SCUDDER, III, naval architect, marine consultant; b. N.Y.C., Oct. 1, 1939; s. Thomas Scudder Jr. and Elizabeth (Russell) W.; m. Nancy Lester, Feb. 8, 1964 (div. Jan. 1975); 1 child: Alexandra; m. Sheila Pearson, May 24, 1980; 1 child: Jonathan Scudder. B Engring. Sci., Johns Hopkins U., 1963; MS, U. Calif., Berkeley, 1970. Registered profl. engr., Calif. Naval arch. David J. Seymour, Ltd., San Francisco, 1970-72, Thomas T. Lunde, Inc., San Francisco, 1973-75; chief naval arch. Am. Pres. Lines, Oakland, Calif., 1975-84; engring. dir. Am. Pres. Lines, Oakland, 1984-98; pvt. practice naval arch.-marine cons. Oakland, 1998—; cons. Marine Bd., Nat. Rsch. Coun. and Nat. Acad. of Scis., Washington, 1990—. Contr. articles to profl. jours. Lt. USN, 1963-68, Pacific. Mem. Soc. of Naval Archs. and Marine Engrs. (chmn. No. Calif. sect. 1985-86, David W. Taylor medal 1998), Intergov. Maritime Orgn. (U.S. del. 1990-93), Am. Bureau of Shipping (naval arch. com. 1986-91, tech. com. 1991—). Republican. Episcopalian. Achievements include design of largest containership in world; design for most power put on ships propeller for single-screw propulsion. Home and Office: 7210 Woodrow Dr Oakland CA 94611-1435

WINSOR, DAVID JOHN, cost consultant; b. Duluth, Minn., May 27, 1947; s. Alphonse Joseph and Sylvia Mae (Petrich) W.; m. Linda Kay Sanders, Dec. 22, 1968 (div. Mar. 1974). BA in Bus., U. Puget Sound, 1978; M of Mech. Engring., Pacific Western U., 1979. Jr. engr. J.P. Head Mech., Inc., Richland, Wash., 1965-67; estimator, project engr. Subs. of Howard S. Wright Co., Seattle, 1972-75; sr. estimator Massart Co., Seattle, 1975-76; project mgr. Univ. Mechanical, Portland, Oreg., 1976; cons. Kent, Wash., 1976-79; owner Leasair, Federal Way, Wash., 1978-83; pres., owner Expertise Engring. & Cons., Inc., Bellevue, Wash., 1979-82, 90-95; cons. Winsor & Co., Walnut Creek, Calif., 1983—; estimator IDC, Portland, Oreg., 1996—; cons. NASA, Mountain View, Calif., 1986, Lockheed Missile & Space, Sunnyvale, Calif., 1984-87, The Boeing Co., Seattle, 1979-82. Author: (with others) Current Construction Costs, 1987, 88, 89, Construction Materials Inventory Systems, 1973, 74, Construction Inflation Trends, 1975, 76, 77, 78, 79, 80, 81, Construction Claims and Prevention, 1981, 82. Served to sgt. USAF, 1967-71. Mem. Jaycees (state dir. 1972-73, state chmn. 1973-74). Republican. Roman Catholic. Avocations: flying, golf, car and gun collecting.

WINTER, RICHARD SAMUEL, JR., computer training company owner, writer; b. Denver, Mar. 17, 1958; s. Richard Samuel and Jerryl Dene (Gano) W.; m. Karen Annette Hansen, May 27, 1989. Student, Griffith U., Brisbane, Australia, 1979; BA in Internat. Environment, Colo. Coll., 1981; MA in Pub. Adminstrn., U. Colo., Denver, 1989. Range aide U.S. Forest Svc., Desert Exptl. Station, Utah, 1976-77; pub. health investigator, lab. technician Denver Health Dept., 1982-84; projects mgr. Colo. Statesman, Denver, 1984-85; editor Mile Hi Prep, Denver, 1985; fin. analyst Pan Am. World Airways, N.Y.C., 1985-88; sr. ptnr., owner PRW, Denver, 1988—; pres. info. systems Trainers, Denver, 1994. Co-author, revisor: MicroRef Quick Reference Bd. Lotus 1-2-3 Rel. 3.0, 1990, MicroRef Quick Reference Gd. Lotus 1-2-3 Rel. 2.2, 1990, Que Q&A QueCards, 1991, Que 123 Release 2.3 QuickStart, 1991, Que 123 Release 2.4 QuickStart, 1992, Que Look Your Best with Excel, 1992, Que Excel for Windows Sure Steps, 1993, Que Using Lotus 123 Release 4, 1994, Que Using Excel 5, 1994, Que Using Microsoft Office, 1994, Que Using Microsoft Office 95, 1995, Que Special Edition Using Microsoft Office Professional for Windows 95, 1996, Que Special Edition Using Microsoft Office 97 Professional, 1997, Que Microsoft Access 97 Quick Reference Guide, 1997, Que Using Microsoft Office 95, 1998, Que Microsoft Office 97 User Manual, 1998. Chmn. N.Y. Victims for Victims, N.Y.C., 1986-87; bd. dirs. Colo. Common Cause, Denver, 1984-85; steering com. Voter Registration "Motor Voter" Amendment, Denver, 1983-84; pres. Broadway Commons Homeowners Assn., Denver, 1982-84; pres. Info. Systems Trainers, 1994, bd. dirs. 1990-96; Dist. Accountability Adv. Com. budget chair Clear Creek Sch. Dist., 1996-98; chair Clear Creek Imagine Ednl. Excellence, 1997-99. Recipient Vigil Honor, Order of the Arrow, 1976, Disting. Svc. award Info. Sys. Trainers, 1996. Mem. Phi Beta Kappa, Alpha Lambda Delta.

WINTERER, AUDREY LYN, writer, public relations consultant; b. Manchester, N.H., Mar. 24, 1963; d. Allen George Winterer and Barbara Jean (Grace) Winterer-Schulz. AA, Mesa (Ariz.) C.C., 1985; BA in Lit./Writing, U. Calif., San Diego, 1991. Writing cons. Oasis Writing Ctr., San diego, 1989-90; sci. and tech. translator Landry & Locke, Goettingen, Germany, 1990-93; lang. and sci. tutor DeAnza Coll., Cupertino, Calif., 1993-95; rsch. asst. Human Performance Rsch. Lab., NASA/Ames Rsch. Ctr., Moffett Field, Calif., 1994-95; pub. rels. coord. Threshold Enterprises, Inc., Scotts Valley, Calif., 1995-96; pub. rels. account mgr. MCA, Inc., Mountain View, Calif., 1996-97; freelance writer Scotts Valley, 1997—. Vol., sanctuary steward Save Our Shores, Santa Cruz, Calif., 1996—. Mem. Pub. Rels. Soc. Am. Avocations: geology, aviation. Home: 245M Mount Hermon Rd # 133 Scotts Valley CA 95066-4007

WINTERER-SCHULZ, BARBARA JEAN, art designer, author; b. Manchester, N.H., Apr. 1, 1938; d. John Edward and Elizabeth Virginia Grace; m. Allen George Winterer, Mar. 30, 1959 (div. 1977); children: Audrey Lyn Winterer, Amy Jo Winterer DeNoble; m. James Robert Schulz, May 28, 1983. AA, Mesa (Ariz.) C.C., 1980; BS summa cum laude, U. Md., Heidelberg, Germany, 1996. Art designer Morningstar Art Design Studio, Cortez, Colo., 1988—. Contbr. articles to newspapers and jours. Ofcl. U.S. reporter at World Eskimo Indian Olympics, Faribanks, Alaska, 1994; asst. dir. Ariz. Myasthenia Gravis Found., 1977-80. Recipient Humanitarian award Phila. Inst. Human Potential, 1972, Chancellor of Germany award for acad. achievement, 1986, Citation of Meritorious Achievement award in the arts and humanitarianism Internat. Biograph. Ctr., 1997. Mem. AAUW, Libr. of Congress (assoc.), Alpha Sigma Lambda, Phi Theta Kappa. Avocations: gardening, gourmet cooking. Office: Morningstar Art Design Studio 201 W Downey Ave Cortez CO 81321-2727

WINTERMAN, CRAIG L., lawyer; b. Denver, Oct. 29, 1950. BS, U. Oreg., 1973; JD, Southwestern U., 1976. Bar: Calif. 1977, U.S. Dist. Ct. (cen. dist.) Calif. 1977, U.S. Dist. Ct. (so. and no. dists.) Calif. 1980, U.S. Ct. Appeals (9th cir.) 1980, U.S. Supreme Ct. 1980. Ptnr. Herzfeld & Rubin, L.A., 1986—. Mem. State Bar Calif., Assn. So. Calif. Def. Counsel, Assn. Advancement Auto. Medicine. Office: Herzfeld & Rubin 1925 Century Park E Ste 600 Los Angeles CA 90067-2783*

WINTERS, RICHARD ALLEN, mineral economist; b. Butte, Mont., Feb. 19, 1963; s. Allen S. and Doris Ellen (Taylor) W. BS in Fin. and Econs., U. Mont., 1986; MS in Mineral Econs., Colo. Sch. Mines, 1990, postgrad., 1991-93. Office engr. Morrison Knudsen Engrs., Richland, Wash., 1986-88; project acct. Morrison Knudsen Engrs., Richland, 1987-88; ops. analyst Echo Bay Mines, Denver, 1989; instr. Colo. Sch. Mines, Golden, Colo., 1991-92; cons. Coors Brewing Co., Golden, 1991-92; sr. rsch. engr. Phelps Dodge Mining Co., Morenci, Ariz., 1992-94; gold analyst Robertson, Stephens and Co., San Francisco, 1994-95; v.p. corp. devel. Golden Star Resources Ltd., Denver, 1995—. Pres. Mineral Econ. Grad. Student Assn., 1989-90. Mem. Soc. Mining, Metallurgy and Exploration, Assn. Environ. Resource Economists, Mineral, Econs. and Mgmt. Soc. Avocations: outdoors, jewelry craft. Office: Golden Star Resources Ltd Denver CO 80203

WINTER-SWITZ, CHERYL DONNA, travel company executive; b. Jacksonville, Fla., Dec. 6, 1947; d. Jacqueline Marie (Carroll) Winter; m. Frank C. Snedaker, June 24, 1974 (div. May 1976); m. Robert William Switz, July 1, 1981. AA, City Coll. of San Francisco, 1986; BS, Golden Gate U., 1990, MBA, 1992. Bookkeeper, agt. McQuade Tours, Ft. Lauderdale, Fla., 1967-69; mgr. Boca Raton (Fla.) Travel, 1969-76; owner, mgr. Ocean Travel, Boca Raton, 1976-79; ind. contractor Far Horizons Travel, Boca Raton, 1979-80; mgr. Tara/BPF Travel, San Francisco, 1981-84; mgr. travel. dept. Ernst & Whinney/Lifeco Travel, San Francisco, 1984-86; travel cons. Siemer & Hand Travel, San Francisco, 1989—; instr. Golden Gate U., 1986—, U. San Francisco. Mem. Amateur Trapshooting Assn., Hotel and Restaurant Mgmt. Club. Republican. Episcopalian. Avocations: trap shooting, gardening, cooking, travelling, reading. Home: 642 Brussels St San Francisco CA 94134-1902 Office: Siemer & Hand Travel 750 Battery St Ste 300 San Francisco CA 94111-1525

WINTHROP, JOHN, wines and spirits company executive; b. Salt Lake City, Apr. 20, 1947; m. Marilyn MacDonald, May 17, 1975; children: Grant Gordon, Clayton Hanford. AB cum laude, Yale U., 1969; JD magna cum laude, U. Tex., 1972. Bar: Calif. 1972. Law clk. 9th cir. U.S. Ct. Appeals, L.A., 1972-73; conseil juridique Coudert Freres, Paris, 1973-75; v.p. gen. counsel MacDonald Group, Ltd., L.A., 1976-82; pres., CEO MacDonald Mgmt. Corp. and MacDonald Group Ltd., L.A., 1982-86; pres., chief exec. officer MacDonald Corp. (gen. contractors), L.A., 1982-86; chmn., CEO Comstock Mgmt. Co., L.A., 1986—; pres., CEO Winthrop Investment Properties, Los Angeles, 1986—; CEO Veritas Imports, L.A., 1995—; bd. dirs. Plus Prods., Tiger's Milk Prods., Inc., Irvine, Calif., 1977-80. Contbr. articles to profl. jours. Bd. dirs., sec. L.A. Sheriff's Dept. Found.; bd. dirs. L.A. Opera. Mem. Nat. Eagle Scout Assn. (life), French-Am. C. of C. (bd. dirs. 1982-87), Urban Land Inst., Yale Club N.Y., Calif. Club, The Beach Club, Elizabethan Club, Order of the Coif, Beta Theta Pi. Republican. Office: Veritas Imports Penthouse 9460 Wilshire Blvd Beverly Hills CA 90212-2720

WINTHROP, KENNETH RAY, insurance executive; b. N.Y.C., Dec. 29, 1950; s. Ralph and Lore (Bruck) W.; m. Sharon Swinnich, 1976 (div. 1978); m. Diane Louise Denney, June 27, 1981; children: Alyssa Louise, Matthew Lawrence, Andrew Lee. BA in English, SUNY, Buffalo, 1972. Chartered life underwriter. Agt. Northwestern Mut. Life Ins., Woodland Hills, Calif., 1975-78, Nat. Life of Vermont, L.A., 1978-93; mgr. Mass Mut., L.A., 1993-97, agt., 1997—. Referee Am. Youth Soccer Orgn., L.A., 1996. Mem. Million Dollar Round Table (life). Avocations: racquetball, snow skiing, trout fishing, gardening. E-mail: kwinthrop@massmutual.com. Home: 7609 W 83rd St Playa Del Rey CA 90293-7979 Office: 4601 Wilshire Blvd Fl 3 Los Angeles CA 90010-3880

WINTLE, ROSEMARIE, bio-medical electronic engineer; b. Brigham City, Utah, Sept. 13, 1951; d. DeVere and Kathleen (Layton) W. Student, Weber State U., 1972-76, Brigham Young U., 1978-79, U. Utah, 1980-87, ITT Electronic Tech. Inst., 1986-88, Utah State U., 1991-92. Engr. Morton Internat., Brigham City, Utah; computer technician Salt Lake City; engr. Nuclear Med., Mesa, Ariz., 1976-77, U. Utah Hosp. Lab., Salt Lake City, 1980-87; electronic engr. Varian Assocs., Inc., Salt Lake City, 1987-88; electronic bio-med. experiment and rsch. engr. Clin. Rsch. Assocs., Provo, Utah, 1988-89. Contbr. articles to profl. jours. Designer, builder Honeyville (Utah) town playground equipment; designer, mgr. Honeyville town water system. Recipient grant Brigham City. Mem. IEEE (pres.), NSPE, Inst. for Sci. Info., Am. Statis. Assn., Sci. Am. Libr., Computer Club, Amnesty Internat., Libr. of Science, Newbridge Book Club. Mem. LDS Ch. Avocations: chess, sports, computers.

WINZELER, JUDITH KAY, foundation administrator; b. Canton, Ohio, Dec. 17, 1942; d. Charles and Pauline Doris (Werstler) Wenzlawski; m. Robert Lee Winzeler, Nov. 4, 1961; children: Elizabeth Ann, Alice Louise Winzeler Smith. BA, U. Nev., 1971, MA, 1981. Instr. anthropology Western Nev. C.C., Reno, 1976-77; program developer Nev. Humanities Com., Reno, 1977-78, asst. dir., 1978-80, assoc. dir., 1980-84, exec. dir., 1984—; panelist NEH, 1991; mem. Hilliard Found. Com., Reno, 1984—; mem. program com. Fedn. of State Humanities Couns., Washington, 1989; mem. selections com. Grace A. Griffen Chair in History, Reno, 1992. Mem. Nev. Commn. on Bicentennial of U.S. Constn., 1985-91; pres. Luth. Ch. of Good Shepherd, Reno, 1987-89; mem. nominating com. Evang. Luth. Ch. Am., Sierra Synod, Oakland, Calif., 1991-94; bd. dirs., officer Reno/Sparks Metro Min., Reno, 1987—; adv. bd. Nev. Ctr. for the Book, 1998—; ad hoc mem. Adv. Com. Participatory Democracy, 1997—; active Nev. Hist. Soc., Nev. State Mus., Nev. Mus. Art, Western Folklife Ctr., Friends of Washoe County Libr. Mem. Reno Rotary Club (Paul Harris fellow). Avocation: traveling. Home: 1579 Belford Rd Reno NV 89509-3907 Office: Nev Humanities Com 1034 N Sierra St Reno NV 89503-3721

WIRKKALA, JOHN LESTER, cable company executive; b. Wadena, Minn., Sept. 25, 1947; s. Rueben Richard and Virginia Grace (Plank) W.; m. Connie Lee Cardarelle (div.); children: Scott, Todd; m. Lynn Diane Braund, Feb. 14, 1984; children: Scott, Seth, Shawn. AS in Electronic Tech., Brown Inst., 1982. Acct. La Maur Inc., Mpls., 1969-72, regional sales mgr., 1976-78; controller Nat. Beauty Supply, Mpls., 1972-76; store mgr. Schaak Electronics, Mpls., 1980-82; divsn. mgr. Mktg. Link, Denver, 1982-85; owner, operator Computer Systems Cons., Aurora, Colo., 1985-87; v.p. sales and mktg. Mgmt. Info. Support, Lakewood, Colo., 1987-89; sales mgr. Foothills Software Inc., Littleton, Colo., 1989-93; ops. mgr. Data Packaging Corp., Denver, 1993-96; pres. Practical Bus. Concepts, Aurora, Colo., 1996; dir. corp. devel. Across Media Network, Golden, Colo., 1996—. Contbr. articles to profl. jours. and mags.; speaker at seimnars and industry trade shows. With U.S. Army, 1966-69, Vietnam. Mem. VFW (quartermaster post # 6331 1993-94). Home and Office: 11211 Winona Ct Westminster CO 80030-7811

WIRT, SHERWOOD ELIOT, writer, minister; b. Oakland, Calif., Mar. 12, 1911; s. Loyal Lincoln and Harriet Eliot (Benton) W.; m. Helen Winola Wells, July 2, 1940 (dec. Sept. 1986); 1 child, Alexander Wells; m. Ruth Evelyn Love, Aug. 29, 1987. BA, U. Calif., Berkeley, 1932; BD, Pacific Sch. Religion, Berkeley, 1943; PhD, Edinburgh (Scotland) U., 1951. Ordained to ministry, 1943. Pastor 1st Congl. Ch., Collinsville, Conn., 1943-44, Knox Presbyn Ch., Berkeley, 1951-55, Hillside Presbyn. Ch., Oakland, Calif., 1955-59; editor Decision mag. Billy Graham Evangelistic Assn., 1959-76; min. to students U. Wash., 1946-49. Author 27 books including Crusade at the Golden Gate, 1959, Not Me, God, 1966, Social Conscience of the Evangelical, 1968, Translation, Confessions of Augustine, 1971, Jesus Power, 1972, Topical Encyclopedia of Living Quotations, 1974, Afterglow, 1975, A Thirst for God, 1980, The Doomsday Connection, 1986, The Making of a Writer, 1987, The Book of Joy, 1994, Billy, 1997, Spiritual Awakening, 1987 (Gold Medallion Book award Evang. Christian Pub. Assn.), Jesus, Man of Joy, 1999; editor 7 books. Pres. San Diego Gilbert and Sullivan Soc., 1980-81; scoutmaster Boy Scouts Am., 1936. Capt. USAAF, 1944-46. Recipient Freedom of Valley Forge Found. award, 1968; named Hon. Col., State of Tenn. Mem. Associated Ch. Press (life), Evang. Press Assn. (life, pres. 1969-71), San Diego County Christian Writers Guild (founder/convener 1977-96), Theta Chi, Sigma Delta Chi. Republican. Avocations: hiking, swimming, tennis, golf. Home: 14140 Mazatlan Ct Poway CA 92064-3964

WISBAR, TANIA, company executive; b. Berlin, Jan. 9, 1936; came to U.S., 1938; d. Frank and Eva (Kroy) W.; m. John Mahoney, July 11, 1980. BA, Mills Coll., 1957; MA, Calif. State U., Northridge, 1971; PhD, Walden U., 1978. Pres. B.E.L.I. Inc., Alhambra, Calif., 1976—; cons. in field. Co-author: (novel) Last Cemetery in Berlin, 1996, (film) In a World Alone, 1975. Home: PO Box 5429 Playa Del Rey CA 90293

WISCHMANN, LESLEY BROOK, writer, researcher; b. Mineola, N.Y., Oct. 20, 1952; d. William John and Rita D. (Wallace) W.; m. Lawrence Alan Jansen, Dec. 9, 1972. BA, Western Coll., Oxford, Ohio, 1973; postgrad., U. Wyo., Laramie, 1977-79. Social worker HHWP Cmty. Action Com., Findlay, Ohio, 1975-77; paralegal advocate Wyo. Protection and Advocacy, Cheyenne, 1978-81; dir. Disability Rsch., Laramie, 1981-84, website designer Oreg.-Calif. Trails Assocs., Independence, Mo., 1996—; writer, rschr., photographer self employed, Laramie, 1985—; cons. Wyo. Protection and Advocacy, 1990-91; co-moderator Overland Trails Mailing List,1995—; workshop and symposium presenter. Contbg. author: American Passages, 1997; contbr. articles to Am. History Illus., Am. Heritage. Election judge Albany County, Wyo., 1996-98,. Recipient various awards for website design. Mem. Wyo. State Hist. Soc., Wyo. Assn. Profl. Historians, Oreg.-Calif. Trails Assn. (pubs. rels. dir. 1992—, dir. 1997—). Democrat. Avocations: genealogy, travel. Home: 712 S 2d St Laramie WY 82070-3620

WISE, JANET ANN, college official; b. Detroit, Aug. 8, 1953; d. Donald Price and Phyllis (Licht) W.; m. Peter Anthony Eisenklam, Oct. 16, 1976 (div. Aug. 1982); m. Edward Henry Moreno, Mar. 31, 1984; 1 child, Talia. Student, U. N.Mex., 1971-73; BA in English, Coll. of Santa Fe, 1989. Editl. asst., writer The New Mexican, Santa Fe, 1975-77; press asst., press sec. Office of Gov. N.Mex., Santa Fe, 1979-82; dir. pub. rels. City of Santa Fe, 1983-84, Coll. of Santa Fe, 1984—. Bd. dirs. Santa Fe Bus. Bur., 1984-87, Santa Fe Girl's Club, 1986-89. Recipient Exemplary Performance award Office Gov. of N.Mex., Santa Fe., 1981, 3 Grand awards for publs. Coun. for Advancement and Support of Edn., 1993-95. Mem. Pub. Rels. Soc. Am., N.Mex. Press Women, Santa Fe Media Assn. (pres. 1989-91). Democrat. Unitarian. Avocation: piano. Home: 7 Conchas Ct Santa Fe NM 87505-8803 Office: Coll of Santa Fe 1600 Saint Michaels Dr Santa Fe NM 87505-7615

WISE, KITTY, writer, composer; b. Plaindealing, La., June 26, 1947; d. Warren G. Wise. BA in English, U. Wyo., 1992. Cert. educator, Wyo. CEO, sec., v.p. Precision Well Svc., Inc., Gillette, Wyo., 1982-89; founder, CEO, sec.-treas. Wisewords Pub., Inc., Gillette, 1997—. Author: A Lost Soul, 1990, Somewhere Beyond Tomorrow, 1997, (trilogy) The Wind In My Hair, 1992, Listen To The Wind, 1996, Anywhere The Wind Blows, 1997; co-author, editor, artist (work book) The Empowered Exec's Handbook for Life THE LABYRINTH A Journey Into Your Personal Power, 1997; author of short stories; composer various songs. Recipient Svc. award Gillette Jaycees, 1976-77, Am. Legion, Gillette, 1997. Office: Wisewords Pub PO Box 2878 Gillette WY 82717-2878

WISE, WOODROW WILSON, JR., small business owner; b. Alexandria, Va., Mar. 9, 1938; s. Woodrow Wilson Sr. and Helen (Peverill) W.; m. Barbara Jean Hatton, Oct. 6, 1956 (div. 1975); m. Sandra Kay Habitz, Dec. 17, 1983; children: Anthony P., Laura J. Gen. mgr. Alexandria (Va.) Amusement Corp., 1956-73; curator Harold Lloyd Estate, Beverly Hills, Calif., 1973-75; pres. Discount Video Tapes, Inc., Burbank, Calif., 1975—. Office: Discount Video Tapes Inc PO Box 7122 833A N Hollywood Way Burbank CA 91505-2814

WISECHILD, LOUISE MARIE, writer, researcher; b. Centralia, Wash., July 26, 1954. BA, U. Wash., 1976; postgrad., Stanford U., 1977-78, Union Inst., 1995—. Freelance writer, 1983—, freelance lectr., 1988—; pvt. practice in counseling Vashon Island, Wash., 1988—; importer, shop owner Beautiful Magic, Vashon Island, Wash., 1996—. Author: The Obsidian Mirror, 1988, The Mother I Carry, 1993; editor: She Who Was Lost Is Remembered, 1991. Recipient scholarship Union Inst., 1997. Mem. Green Party. Avocations: jewelry making, yoga, song writing. Home: PO Box 1803 Vashon WA 98070-1803

WISEMAN, JAY DONALD, photographer, mechanical designer and contractor; b. Salt Lake City, Dec. 23, 1952; s. Donald Thomas and Reva (Stewart) W.; m. Barbara Helen Taylor, June 25, 1977; children: Jill Reva, Steve Jay. Ed. Utah State U., Logan, U. Utah. Cert. profl. photographer. Pvt. practice photography; owner, pres. JB&W Corp.; judge Utah State Fair, 1991, 93, 95, 96, 97. Recipient Grand prize Utah State Fair, 1986, Kodak Crystal for Photographic Excellence, 1986, 87, Master of Photography degree, 1989, Best of Show award, 1991-92; Profl. Photographer Mag. cover photo, 1988; numerous photos inducted for permanent collection Internat. Photographic Hall of Fame, 1989; photo named one of World's Greatest, Kodak, 1987-88; 2 photos named among World's Best, Walt Disney World and Profl. Photographers Assn., 1988, 2 prints tied for Masters Best of Show award RMPPA Regional contest, 1991-92; recipient Gold Medallion award Best in Show (world wide). Mem. Profl. Photographers Assn. Am. (one of top 10 scores internat. photo contest), Rocky Mountain Profl.

Photographers (Best of Show, highest score ever 1987, Master Photographer of Yr. 1991, Ct. of Honour 1981-91), Inter-Mountain Profl. Photographers Assn. (Master's Trophy Best of Show 1982, 86, 88, Photographer of Yr. award 1986, Ct. of Honour 1981-91), Photographers Soc. Am (Best of Show award Utah chpt. 1986). Latter Day Saints. Represented in Salt Lake City Internat. Airport permanent photo exhibit, various traveling loan collections, U.S. and Europe, 1988, loan collection Epcot Ctr., 1988-91; photographs published numerous profl. jours.

WISNIEVITZ, DAVID, film producer; b. Mexico City, May 16, 1950; came to U.S., 1972; s. Rafael and Yoja (Rosenberg) W.; m. Lourdes Martin, June 10, 1985 (div. 1994); children: Maya, Elishaya. MFA, San Francisco Art Inst., 1976. Prodn. mgr., sound and camera: (film documentary) Raiders of the Lost Ark, 1980 (Emmy nomination 1981); assoc. producer, prodn. mgr.: (film) The Ballad of Gregorio Cortez, 1981, Ghostdad, 1989, White Sands, 1991; L.A. line producer: (film) Flight of the Spruce Goose, 1985; producer: (film) Valentino Returns, 1985; prodn. mgr.: (film) The Milagro Beanfield War, 1986; exec. producer: (film) Old Gringo, 1987, 88, A Civil Action, 1998; co-exec. prodr.: Selena, 1996; exec. producer, prodn. mgr.: (film) Talent For The Game, 1989, 90; co-prodr.: Searching for Bobby Fisher, 1992-93, Fallen Angels, 1993, Chasers, 1993, Bushwacked, 1994, Marvin's Room, 1995, Sliding Doors, 1997; producer many commls. Office: Sunnyside Films Inc 656 W Knoll Dr # 301 West Hollywood CA 90069

WISNIEWSKI, STEPHEN ADAM, professional football player; b. Rutland, Vt., Apr. 7, 1967. Student, Pa. State U. Offensive guard L.A. Raiders, 1989–. Named All-Pro Team Guard by Sporting News, 1990-93, Coll. All-Am. Team, 1987, 88. Played in Pro Bowl, 1990-91, 93. Office: L A Raiders 1220 Harbor Bay Pkwy Alameda CA 94502-6501

WITHERINGTON, JENNIFER LEE, sales and marketing executive, meeting planner; b. Albuquerque, Sept. 8, 1960; d. Terrence Lee and Pamela Ann (Hoerter) W. BA in Polit. Sci., James Madison U., 1982. Cert. meeting profl. Asst. press sec. U.S. Senate, Washington, 1983-85; nat. sales mgr. Madison Hotels, Washington, 1986-88; dir. sales Madison Air Charter Svcs., Washington, 1987-88; nat. sales mgr. Ritz-Carlton Hotels, Palm Springs, Calif., 1988-90; dir. sales and mktg. Cappa and Graham, Inc., San Francisco, 1990-95; gen. mgr. USA Hosts, San Francisco, 1995-98; v.p. sales and mktg. Key Events, Inc., San Francisco, 1998—; spkr. in field. Contbr. articles to profl. jours. Vol. San Francisco Emergency Rescue Team, Yerba Buena Ctr. for Arts. Mem. Am. Soc. Assn. Execs., Soc. Incentive Travel Execs., Profl. Conv. Mgmt. Assn. (pres. San Francisco chpt. 1994-97), Meeting Profls. Internat. (bd. dirs. 1997-99). Republican. Roman Catholic. Avocations: golf, wine. Home: 1565 Green St Apt 304 San Francisco CA 94123-5129 Office: Key Events Inc 888 Brannan St San Francisco CA 94103-4928

WITHERS, RICHARD ALLEN, JR., security firm executive, consultant; b. Kansas City, Mo., Oct. 8, 1957; s. Richard Allen and Edith Ethel (McLaughlan) W. BS criminal sci., criminology, Univ. Md., 1994; MA in security mgmt., Webster Univ., 1996. MA computer resources, 1997. Pvt. to gunnery sergeant U.S. Marine Corps, 1976-84, chief warrant officer, 1985-89, limited duty officer, 1990-97; owner/pres. Tech. Security & Countermeasures Cons., Carlsbad, Calif., 1997—; cons. U.S. Govt., 1997—. Capt. U.S. Marine Corp, 1976-97. Mem. Am. Soc. Industrial Security, Internat. Computer Security Assn., Nat. Tech. Investigators Assn., Marine Corps Counterintelligence Assn., Marine Mustang Assn. Office: TSCC Inc PO Box 666 Carlsbad CA 92018-0666

WITKIN, JOEL-PETER, photographer; b. Bklyn., Sept. 13, 1939; s. Max and Mary (Pellegrino) W.; m. Cynthia Jean Bency, June 30, 1978; one child, Kersen Ahanu. B.F.A., Cooper Union, 1974; M.F.A., U. N.Mex., 1986; student (fellow), Columbia U., 1973-74. Artist in residence Zerybthia Rome, Italy, summer 1996; represented by Pace/McGill (now named Pace Wilden-Stein MacGill), N.Y.C., Fraenkel Gallery, San Francisco, Baudion Lebon Gallery, Paris; artist in residence Berlin, fall 1998, Paris, winter 1998; lectr. Am. Acad. Rome, 1996, Camera Work, Berlin, El Escorial, Spain, 1998. Exhibited in Projects Studio One, N.Y.C., 1980, Galerie Texbraun, Paris, 1982, Kansas Ctiy Art Inst., 1983, Stedelijk Mus., Amsterdam, 1983, Fraenkel Gallery, 1983-84, 87, 91, 93, 95, 97, Pace Wilden-Stein MacGill Gallery, N.Y.C., 1983, 84, 87, 89, 91, 93, 95, 97, San Francisco Mus. Modern Art, 1985, Bklyn. Mus., 1986, Galerie Baudoin Lebon, Paris, 1987, 89, 91, 95, Centro de Arte Reina Sofia Mus., Madrid, 1988, Palais de Tokyo, Paris, 1989, Fahey/Klein Gallery, L.A., 1987, 89, 91, 97, Mus. Modern Art, Haifa, Israel, 1991, Photo Picture Space Gallery, Osaka, Japan, 1993, Guggenheim Mus., N.Y.C., 1995, Interkamera, Prague, 1995, Il Castello de Rivoli Mus., Turin, 1995, Encontros de Fotografia, Colombia, Portugal, 1996, Rencontres de la Photographie, Arles, France, 1996, Taipei Photo Gallery, Taiwan, 1994, 96, 98, Museum of Fine Arts, Santa Fe, 1998, Wildenstein Gallery, Tokyo, 1998; group shows: Mus. Modern Art, N.Y.C., 1959, San Francisco Mus. Moder Art, 1981, Whitney Biennial, 1985, Palais de Tokyo, Paris, 1986, La Phorographie Contemporaine en France, 1996, Foto Masson, Goteberg, Sweden, 1997, Hanlin Museum, So. Korea, 1997, Bogardenkapel, Bruges, 1998, Hayward Gallery, London, 1997; represented in permanent collections, Mus. Modern Art, N.Y.C., San Francisco Mus. Modern Art, 1980, Nat. Gallery Art, Washington, Victoria and Albert Mus., London, George Eastman House, N.Y., The Getty Collection, Moder Museet, Stockholm, Sweden, Whitney Mus., N.Y.C., The Guggenheim Mus., N.Y.C., Tokyo Met. Mus. Photography; subject of monographs: Joel-Peter Witkin, 1985, 88-89, 91, 93, 95-96, 98; editor: Masterpieces of Medical Photography, 1987, Harms Way, 1994; artist residency, Rome, 1996, Berlin, 1998, Paris, 1998. Served with U.S. Army, 1961-64. Decorated Chevalier Des Arts et de Lettres (France), 1990, The Augustus Saint Gaudens medal The Cooper Union, 1996; recipient Disting. Alumni award The Cooper Union, 1986, Internat. Ctr. Photography award, 1988; Ford Found. grantee, 1977, 78, Nat. Endowment in Photography grantee, 1980, 81, 86, 92. Address: 1707 Five Points Rd SW Albuquerque NM 87105-3017

WITMAN-GLENN, LAURA KATHLEEN, writer, security guard, silent alarm monitor; b. Pottstown, Pa., Mar. 4, 1957; d. William Tedford and Kathleen (Nieman) Witman; m. David Dale Roripaugh, Oct. 11, 1985 (div.); life ptnr. Marjorie Lorraine Witman-Glenn, May 17, 1989; 1 child, Scotty Levengood Witman-Glenn. Student, San Bernardino Valley Coll., 1976-79; Degree in Actg. magna cum laude, Adelphi Bus. Coll., San Bernardino, Calif., 1985. Cert. acctg. bookkeeper. Silent alarm monitor, payroll acct. Comml. Security Alliance, San Bernardino, Calif., 1985—. Author: The Sun, 1994; (poetry) World of Poetry, 1990, National Library of Poetry, 1992, 94, 95, 96, 98, Sparrowgrass, 1993; (short story) Antivivesection Soc., 1993, Animal Voice, 1994, Paws Newsletter, 1993, 94, 96, A Dogs Day Newsletter, 1994, House Rabbit Soc., 1994, 95. Mem. Bette Midler Fan Club, San Bernardino's Gay/Lesbian Cmty. Ctr., Bark Animal Rights Orgn., Dog Fancy's Pet Owners Club, House Rabbit Soc. Mem. Obsessive Compulsive Disorder Found., People for Ethical Treatment of Animals, House Rabbit Soc., Gay and Lesbian Cmty. Ctr., Bette Midler Fan Club. Democrat. Home: 2001 N Rancho Ave Apt 27A Colton CA 92324-1211

WITMER, DIANE F., communications educator; b. Pasadena, Calif., Jan. 20, 1945; d. Stanley Lamar and Mary Evelyn Witmer; 1 child, David William Penkoff. AA, Golden West Coll., Huntington Beach, Calif., 1977; BS in BA, U. LaVerne (Calif.), 1980; MS in Sys. Mgmt., U. So. Calif., L.A., 1989; MA in Communication Arts, U. So. Calif., 1993, PhD in Orgnl. Comm., 1994. Dir. pub. rels. Weight Watchers, Santa Ana, Calif., 1980-84; dir. comm. March of Dimes, Costa Mesa, Calif., 1986-90; prin. Penkoff Comm. Resources, L.A., 1990-92; instr. Calif. State U., Fullerton, 1994-96; asst. lectr. comm. arts and scis. U. So. Calif., University Park, 1991-94; asst. prof. Purdue U., West Lafayette, Ind., 1994-97; assoc. prof. Calif. State U., Fullerton, 1997—. Editor, The Paper Weight, 1981-84. Chmn. award com. March of Dimes, Costa Mesa, nat. vol., 1990—; also chair speakers bur. Sagemore divsn., mem. exec. com. Mem. Pub. Rels. Soc. Am. (accredited mem.), U. So. Calif. Alumni Assn., Pacific Chorale. Avocations: singing.

WITT, JOHN WILLIAM, municipal lawyer; b. Los Angeles, Aug. 30, 1932; s. John Udo and Alice (Westervelt) W.; m. Lenora Jane Ticknor, Sept. 1, 1961; children: John David, Stephanie Anne Witt Mills, William Westervelt. AB, Stanford U., 1954; LLB, 1956. Bar: Calif. 1957, U.S. Dist. Ct. (ctrl. dist.) Calif. 1961, U.S. Dist. Ct. (so.) Calif. 1967, U.S.

Supreme Ct. 1969. Dep. city atty. City of San Diego, 1961-64, chief criminal dep. city atty., 1964-67, chief dep. city atty., 1967-69, city atty., 1969-96; spl. counsel Lounsbery Ferguson Altona & Peak, LLP, San Diego, 1996—. Contbr. articles to profl. jours. Pres. Boys' Clubs San Diego, 1985-87; bd. dirs. St. Paul's Episcopal Home, Inc., San Diego, 1982-88, 97—; exec. bd. San Diego County Council Boy Scouts Am, 1970-81, chmn. leadership tng. com., 1970-73, Bicentennial chmn., 1974-76, chmn. Jamboree com., 1977. Served with USMC, 1954-57, col. res. ret. Named Pub. Lawyer of Yr. San Diego County Bar Assn., 1986, Disting. Eagle Scout Boy Scouts Am., 1975. Mem. ABA (state and local govt. law sec., coun. mem. 1980-84, 85-89, 96-98, chair 1992-93, mem. ho. dels. 1993-96, Nelson award 1996), Internat. Mcpl. Law Officers Assn. (pres. 1985-86, bd. trustees 1976-87, Outstanding Nat. Pub. Svc. award 1986), League Calif. Cities (bd. dirs. 1985-96), League Calif. Cities City Atty.'s Dept. (pres. 1976-77), Calif. Dist. Attys. Assn. (bd. dirs. 1980-82), Southwestern Legal Found. (adv. bd. mem. mcpl. legal studies ctr. 1981—), State Bar Calif. (exec. com. pub. law sect. 1980-83), San Diego County Bar Assn. (chair pub. lawyers com. 1997-98), San Diego Lions Club (bd. trustees welfare found. 1983-87, 90-97, chair 1992-93, pres. 1990-91, Diocesan standing com. 1974-78, 82-86, Diocesan bd. dirs. 1998—, dep. to gen. convention 1985-97), Phi Alpha Delta. Republican. Episcopalian. Avocations: writing, travel, sports. Office: Lounsbery Ferguson Altona & Peak LLP 1010 2d Ave Ste 1902 San Diego CA 92101-4910

WITT, MELVIN SYLVAN, editor, publisher; b. Stockton, Calif., Dec. 25, 1925; s. Arnold and Sarah (Peletz) W.; m. Dorothy Halling, June 17, 1949; children: Ann, Mallory. BS, U. Calif., Berkeley, 1948; LLB, U. Calif., San Francisco, 1951. Bar: Calif. 1952. Trial atty. State Compensation Ins. Fund, L.A., 1954-57; appellate atty. Calif. Indsl. Accident Commn., San Francisco, 1957-60, trial referee, 1961-64; pvt. practice Berkeley, 1966-68; rsch. atty. Calif. Continuing Edn. of Bar, Berkeley, 1969-75; sec. dep. commr. Calif. Workers' Compensation Appeals Bd., San Francisco, 1964-66, chmn., 1975-80; chmn. Calif. Workers' Compensation Adv. Commn. to Calif. State Bar, 1974-75; founder, editor, pub. Calif. Workers' Compensation Reporter, Berkeley, 1973—; adj. prof. law Golden Gate U., San Francisco, 1971-75, 81, McGeorge Law Sch., U. of Pacific, Sacramento, 1973-75. Editor, co-author: California Workers' Compensation Practice, 2nd edit., 1973. With inf., U.S. Army, 1944-46, ETO. Named Pub. Ofcl. of Yr., Calif. Applicants' Attys. Assn., Sacramento, 1980; recipient commendation by resolution Calif. State Legislature, Sacramento, 1981. Mem. 78th Inf. Divsn. Vets. Assn. Democrat. Avocations: WWII history, travel. Office: Calif Workers Compensation Reporter PO Box 975 Berkeley CA 94701

WITTEN, MARK LEE, lung injury research scientist, educator; b. Amarillo, Tex., June 23, 1953; s. Donald Lee and Polly Ann (Warren) W.; m. Christine Ann McKee, June 10, 1988; 1 child, Brandon Lee. BS in Phys. Sci., Emporia State U., 1975; PhD, Ind. U., 1983. Postdoctoral fellow U. Ariz., Tucson, 1983-88; instr. in medicine Harvard Med. Sch., Boston, Mass., 1988-90; rsch. prof. U. Ariz., Tucson, 1990—, head Airborne Particulates Rsch. Ctr., 1998—, head Lung Injury Lab., 1998; cons. Ames Life Scis. Space Sta. program NASA; grant cons. USAF, Washington, 1991—, NSF, 1995, U.S. Army, 1995. Contbr. articles to profl. jours.; patentee in field. Grantee USAF, 1991—, Tng. grant Dept. of Def., 1992—, NIH, 1991—, Upjohn Pharm., 1992, Dept. of Army, 1993. Mem. AIAA, Am. Physiol. Soc., N.Y. Acad. Scis., Soc. Toxicology. Methodist. Achievements include first animal model of cigarette smoke exposure to show cigarette smoke increases lung permeability, animal model of passive cigarette smoke, to demonstrate pulmonary edema in a microgravity model, studies of fluid regulation in space biology models; patent for immunostimulatory properties of substance P. Office: U Ariz Dept Pediatrics AHSC 1501 N Campbell Ave Tucson AZ 85724

WITTER, WENDELL WINSHIP, financial executive, retired; b. Berkeley, Calif., Oct. 16, 1910; s. George Franklin Jr. and Mary Ann (Carter) W.; m. Florence Corder, Oct. 18, 1935 (div. Oct. 1973); 1 child, Wendelyn; m. Janet Hutchinson Alexander, Dec. 12, 1973 (dec. 1977); m. Evelyn Grinter Harkins Gooding, Mar. 26, 1978. BA, U. Calif., Berkeley, 1932; Diploma, Investment Bankers Inst., Wharton Bus. Sch., 1955. Salesman Dean Witter & Co., San Francisco, 1933-50, ptnr., 1950-68, exec. v.p., 1968-76; cons. Dean Witter, Reynolds, Inc., San Francisco, 1976-82, retired cons., 1982—. Past Regent U. Calif., 1969-70; mem. Coordinating Coun. Higher Edn., Calif., 1970-71; trustee State Univs., Long Beach, Calif., 1971-79; past bd. dirs. San Francisco Symphony, ARC Golden Gate Chpt., Met. YMCA, Grace Cathedral, Better Bus. Bur. Lt. col. Army Air Force, 1941-46. Mem. San Francisco Bond Club (pres. 1955), Assn. of Stock Exch. Firms (pres. 1962), Investment Bankers Assn. Am. (pres. 1965), U. Calif. Alumni Assn. (pres. 1969-70), Berkeley Fellows, Pacific Union Club, San Francisco Golf Club, Bohemian Club, Zeta Psi. Republican. Episcopalian. Avocations: golf, fishing. Home: 1400 Geary Blvd Apt 2109 San Francisco CA 94109-6572

WITTROCK, MERLIN CARL, educational psychologist; b. Twin Falls, Idaho, Jan. 3, 1931; s. Herman C. and Mary Ellen (Baumann) W.; m. Nancy McNulty, Apr. 3, 1953; children: Steven, Catherine, Rebecca. BS in Biology, U. Mo., Columbia, 1953, MS in Ednl. Psychology, 1956; PhD in Ednl. Psychology, U. Ill., Urbana, 1960. Prof. grad. sch. edn. UCLA, 1960—, founder Ctr. Study Evaluation, chmn. divsn. ednl. psychology, chmn. faculty, exec. com.; univ. com. on outstanding teaching; dir. math. and humanities program, 1997; co-founder Urban Tchr. Edn. Program, 1996; co-dir. Imagination Project, 1998; fellow Ctr. for Advanced Study in Behavioral Scis., 1967-68; vis. prof. U. Wis., U. Ill., Ind. U., Monash U., Australia; bd. dirs. Far West Labs., San Francisco; chmn. com. on evaluation and assessment L.A. Unified Sch. Dist.; mem. nat. adv. panel for math. scis. NRC of NAS, 1988-89; chmn. nat. bd. Nat. Ctr. for Rsch. in Math. Scis. Edn., chmn. charges com. UCLA; adv. bd. Kauffman Found., Kansas City, Mo., 1995—; bd. dirs. Western Edn. Lab. for Edn. Rsch., Far West Lab. Author, editor: The Evaluation of Instruction, 1970, Changing Education, 1973, Learning and Instruction, 1977, The Human Brain, 1977, Danish transl., 1980, Spanish transl., 1982, The Brain and Psychology, 1980, Instructional Psychology: Education and Cognitive Processes of the Brain, Neuropsychological and Cognitive Processes of Reading, 1981, Handbook of Research on Teaching, 3d edit., 1986, The Future of Educational Psychology, 1989, Research in Learning and Teaching, 1990, Testing and Cognition, 1991, Generative Science Teaching, 1994, Metacognitiion 1995. Mentor Edn. Leadership Program. Capt. USAF, 1953-55. Recipient Thorndike award for outstanding psychol. rsch., 1987, Disting. Tchr. of Univ. award UCLA, 1990; Ford Found. grantee. Fellow AAAS, APA (pres. divsn. ednl. psychology 1984-85, assn. coun. 1988-91, award for Outstanding Svc. to Ednl. Psychology 1991, 93, Disting. Svc. award for svc. to sci. adv. coun.), Am. Psychol. Soc., (charter fellow), Am. Ednl. Rsch. Assn. (chmn. ann. conv., chmn. publs. 1980-83, assn. coun. 1986-89, bd. dirs. 1987-89, chmn. com. on ednl. TV 1989—, Outstanding Contbns. award 1986, Outstanding Svc. award 1989), Phi Delta Kappa. Office: UCLA 3339 Moore Hall Los Angeles CA 90095

WITZLER, SUZANNE ILIFF, publishing executive; b. Washington, Sept. 9, 1943; d. William Seward and Dorothy (Keller) I.; m J.L. Witzler, Oct. 29, 1966. BA, Denison U., 1965; MA, U. Chgo., 1966. Asst. editor Cahners Publ., Denver, 1970-71; editorial dir. Industry Media, Inc., Denver, 1972-84; group editor Advanstar Communications, Denver, 1984-93; v.p., editor, Injection Molding Mag. Abby Communications, Denver, 1993—. Editor: Pocket Specs for Injection Molding, 1994. Trustee Iliff Sch. Theology, 1992—; vol. lectr. Colo. State Univ., 1985-91. Ford Found. fellow, 1965-66, Top Women in Plastics award Plastics Mag., 1978. Mem. Soc. Plastics Engrs. (sr.), Jr. League of Denver. Home: 5401 E Dakota Ave Apt 11 Denver CO 80246-1456 Office: Abby Communications 55 Madison St Ste 770 Denver CO 80206-5432

WIZARD, BRIAN, publisher, author; b. Newburyport, Mass., June 24, 1949, s. Russell and Ruth (Hidden) Willard. BA, Sonoma (Calif.) State U., 1976; D of Metaphysics, Universal Life Ch., 1997. Ordained to ministry Universal Life Ch., 1997. Pvt. practice as jeweler, sculptor and craftsman Calif., 1974-79; Wallowa, Oreg., 1991—; prin. The Starquill Pub. Port Douglas, Queensland, Australia, 1981-86; owner Starquill Internat., Wallowa, Oreg. Author: (trilogy) The Will He Make it Saga (nominee Pulitzer prize), Permission to Kill 1988, Permission to Live 1992, Back in the World 1992, (co-author) The Enchanted Coming True 1988. Coming of

Age, 1990, Pollution IV, 1993; (short stories) Tropical Pair, 1986, Metempsychosis, 1988 (In Search of) The Silver Lining, 1994, The Moon Whistling By on a Cloud, 1994, (The Princess of the) Wildflowers, 1995, Mushroom Magic, 1996; contbr. to Smithsonian Inst.'s The Vietnam War Generation; contbr. to SpaceArc; prodr. (video documentary) Thunderhawks, 1987, Swift Action Newsteam, Tope Creek Lookout, 1995; songwriter, prodr. (cassette) Brian Wizard Sings for His Supper, 1989 (cert. of achievement Billboard 1993); songwriter, singer, prodr. (I Don't Want) Permission to Kill, 1989, Busker's Theme Song, Living in North Queensland, Circus Act, Hitch Hiking Man, Self-Portrait, The Love We Share Will Never End, 1994, Never Met a Girl Like You, Folk-Rock Opera: A Cover Story: After That Ugly Saloon Incident; contbr. to America's Finest Songwriter and Lyricists CD, 1997, (novels, video and music) Brian Wizard's 20th Century Anthology, 1998. Renovator hist. landmark The Tope Creek Lookout (Skyship); mem. Nat. Hist. Lookout Register; sponsor Adopt A Hwy., 1995; min. Universal Life Ch. With U.S. Army, 1967-70. Decorated Air medals (26), Aviator Flight Wings; recipient Cert. of Appreciation, Pres. Richard M. Nixon. Mem. Vietnam Helicopter Crewmember Assn., 145th Combat Aviation Bn. Assn., Vietnam Combat Vets. Assn., Vietnam Vets. Am., Vietnam Vets. Australia Assn. Office: PO Box 42 Wallowa OR 97885-0042

WOESSNER, FREDERICK T., composer, pianist; b. Teaneck, N.J., July 23, 1935; s. Fred and Bertha W.; m. Lise, Feb. 14, 1960 (div. 1973); children: Betty, Allison. Student, Peabody Conservatory of Music, Balt., 1960-61; MBA, NYU, 1968; MA, Calif. State U., Los Angeles, 1975; pvt. study with, David Diamond, Charles Haubiel, Albert Harris. Owner Al-Fre-Bett Music, Los Angeles, 1980—. Composer (for orch.) Nursery Song, Variations on an Irish Air, Reflections for Strings, Fanfare for Winds, String Quartet, Concerto No. 1 and Concerto No. 2 for Piano Improvisations and Orch., Secret Gospels (Cantata), Sonic studies for Piano I Elegy for Trumpet and Winds, Victorian Atmosphere Overture, Far Far Away for Chorus and Orchestra, (for chorus) Fantasia in Ragtime, (for chorus and orchestra) May the Olympic Spirit Guide Us and Fanfare (Millennium 2000), (music for films) Sky Bandits, Gunbus, Pale Horse, Pale Rider, The Curb Your Appetite Diet, Centerfold, (title music for TV) Actors Forum, (for stage) From Berlin to Broadway, Oh Atlantis, Kurt, Lil Nell, Another Town, Victorian Atmospheres; composer and pianist, album-film/video, Vincent Moreaux, His Finest Hour In My Forest Cathedral, Songs from the Sea; rec. artist Sonic Arts and Repertoire Records. Pres. bd. dirs. Inst. for Recording and Multimedia Arts; mem. bd. govs.Music and the Arts Found. of Am., Inc.; dir. West Coast Musical Theatre Lab. Mem. ASCAP, NARAS, Dramatists Guild, Soc. Composers and Lyricists, Am. Fedn. Musicians, Am. Soc. Music Arrangers and Composers (treas. 1978—), Composers and Arrangers Found. Am. (sec.). Democrat. Office: Al-Fre-Bett Music PO Box 45 Los Angeles CA 90078-0045

WOGSLAND, JAMES WILLARD, retired heavy machinery manufacturing executive; b. Devils Lake, N.D., Apr. 17, 1931; s. Melvin LeRoy and Mable Bertina (Paulson) W.; m. Marlene Claudia Clark, June 1957; children: Karen Lynn, Steven James. BA in Econs., U. Minn., 1957. Various positions fin. dept. Caterpillar Tractor Co., Peoria, Ill., 1957-64, treas., 1976-81; mgr. fin. Caterpillar Overseas S.A., Geneva, 1965-70, sec.-treas., 1970-76; dir.-pres. Caterpillar Brasil S.A., São Paulo, 1981-87; exec. v.p. Caterpillar, Inc., Peoria, 1987-90, also bd. dirs., vice-chmn., 1990-95; bd. dirs. Ameren Corp., St. Louis. Mem. adv. bd. St. Francis Hosp., Peoria, 1987-95; bd. dirs. Peoria Area Cmty. Found., 1986-92; trustee Eureka Coll., 1987-95; commr. Kootenai County Planning and Zoning Commn., 1997—. Sgt. USAF, 1951-55. Mem. Hayden Lake Golf and Country Club. Republican. Presbyterian. Home: 9675 Easy St Hayden Lake ID 83835-9526

WOHL, ARMAND JEFFREY, cardiologist; b. Phila., Dec. 11, 1946; s. Herman Lewis and Selma (Paul) W.; m. Marylouise Katherine Giangrossi, Sept. 4, 1977; children: Michael Adam, Todd David. Student, Temple U., 1967; MD, Hahnemann U., 1971. Intern Bexar County Hosp., San Antonio, 1971-72; resident in internal medicine Parkland Hosp., Dallas, 1972-74; fellow in cardiology U. Tex. Southwestern Med. Ctr., Dallas, 1974-76; chief of cardiology USAF Hosp. Elmendorf, Anchorage, 1976-78; chief cardiologist Riverside (Calif.) Med. Clin., 1978-79; cardiologist Grossmont Cardiology Med. Group, La Mesa, Calif., 1980-84; pvt. practice, La Mesa, 1985—; chief of cardiology Grossmont Hosp., La Mesa, 1988-90; assoc. clin. prof. Sch. Medicine. U. Calif., San Diego, 1990—. Contbr. articles to profl. jours. Bd. dirs. Grossmont Healthcare Dist., 1995-98, San Diego County chpt. Am. Heart Assn., 1981-87. Maj. USAF, 1976-78. Fellow Am. Coll. Cardiology (councilor Calif. chpt. 1991-99), ACP, Coun. on Clin. Cardiology. Avocations: tennis, travel. Office: 5565 Grossmont Center Dr La Mesa CA 91942-3020

WOHLETZ, LEONARD RALPH, soil scientist, consultant; b. Nekoma, N.D., Oct. 22, 1909; s. Frank and Anna (Keifer) W.; m. Jane Geisendorfer, Sept. 1, 1935; children: Mary Jane, Leonard Ralph Jr., Elizabeth Ann, Catherine Ellen, Margaret Lee. BS, U. Calif., Berkeley, 1931, MS, 1933. Jr. soil expert USDA Soil Erosion Svc., Santa Paula, Calif., 1934; asst. regional chief soil surveys USDA Soil Conservation Svc., Santa Paula, 1935; asst. regional chief soil surveys USDA Soil Conservation Svc., Berkeley, 1939-42, soil survey supr., 1942-45, state soil scientist, 1945-68, asst. to state conservationist, 1969-71; cons. soil scientist Berkeley, 1973—. Author: Survey Guide, 1948; contbr. articles to profl. publs. including Know Calif. Land, Soils and Land Use Planning, Planning by Foresight and Hindsight. Mem. Waste Mgmt. Commn., Berkeley, 1981; chmn. com. Rep. for Congress, 8th Dist. Calif., 1980; pres. State and Berkeley Rep. Assembly, 1985—. Recipient Soil Conservationist of Yr., Calif. Wildlife Fedn., 1967. Mem. Soil and Water Conservation Soc. (chmn. organic waste mgmt. com. 1973—, sect. pres., Dist. Svc. award, charter and life mem., Disting. Svc. award 1971, Outstanding Svc. award 1983), Soil Sci. Soc. Am. (emeritus), Internat. Soc. Soil Sci., Profl. Soil Sci. Assn. Calif., Commonwealth Club Calif., San Francisco Farmers Club. Roman Catholic. Achievements include expedition of soil surveys, interpretations, funding and publications in California, improvement of methods of conveying technical soils interpretations, land use, waste management information. Home: 510 Vincente Ave Berkeley CA 94707-1522

WOIKE, LYNNE ANN, computer scientist; b. Torrance, Calif., Oct. 20, 1960; d. Stephen J. and Virginia (Ursich) Shane; m. Thomas W. Woike, Feb. 13, 1988; 1 child, Karla. BSc in Computer Sci. cum laude, Calif. State U., Dominguez Hills, 1994. Computer cons. Unocal Oil Co., Wilmington, Calif., 1992-94; x-window/motif software developer Logican Inc., San Pedro, Calif., 1994-95; reticle engr. TRW, Inc., Redondo Beach, Calif., 1982-88, sr. mem. tech. staff product data mgmt. database adminstr., 1995-98, chmn. product data mgmt. change control bd., 1995-98; sr. IT programmer/analyst DirecTV, Inc., El Segundo, Calif., 1998—. Mem. IEEE, IEEE Computer Sci., Assn. for Computing Machinery (chmn. student chpt. 1993-94), Calif. State U. Sci. Soc. (computer sci. rep. 1993-95). Office: DirecTV Inc 200 N Sepulveda Blvd El Segundo CA 90245-4340

WOJNICKI, TADEUSZ ISRAEL, writer, educator; b. Wolica, Poland, Sept. 13, 1944; came to U.S., 1971; s. Stefan and Zofia (Dobrowolski) W.; m. Maria Sujkowska, Mar. 15, 1969 (div. 1982); 1 child, Iwona Barbara. MA, Cath. U. Lublin, Poland, 1970, PhD, 1977; MA, San Francisco State U., 1996. Instr. Def. Lang. Inst., Monterey, Calif., 1982-89, Am. Online Campus, 1996-99, Hartnell Coll., 1999—. Author: Lie Under the Fig Trees, 1996, Scrowls on a Crate of Oranges, 1987. Officer Steinbeck Festival, Salinas, Calif., 1997—; cmty. leader Jewish Cmty. Online AOL, 1996—. Recipient Excellence in Leadership award Angels by the Sea, 1995-96, Nobel Comm. award The Heartlight Jour., 1993. Mem. Nat. Writers' Union. Jewish. Avocations: international travel, wilderness hiking, Torah study. Office: PO Box 3198 Carmel CA 93921

WOJNO, BRADLEY NELSON, financial sales executive; b. Akron, Ohio, Feb. 14, 1964; s. George Alexander and Mary Elizabeth (Hoover) W. Student, Muskingum Coll., 1986. Sales mgr. The Auto Lease, Akron, Ohio, 1989-90; reg. sales leader GE Capital Fleet Svcs., Balt., 1990-96; area mgr. Ford Motor Co., Balt. 1996-97; dist. mgr. ARI San Mateo, Calif., 1997—. Asst. scout master Boy Scouts Am., Akron, 1986-90; pres. Coll. Reps. 1984-86. Mem. Akron Rotary Club (bd. dirs. 1987-90). Avocations: swimming, water and snow skiing. Home: 700 Beauty Dr Apt 000 Foster

City CA 94404-2610 Office: ARI 1825 S Grant St Ste 305 San Mateo CA 94402-2660

WOLANDE, GENE JAMES, writer, actor, director; b. Chgo., Sept. 3, 1956; s. Sam Charles and Marie J. (Riccio) W. BA, U. Dallas, 1978; MFA, Trinity U., 1981. Writer Wonder Years, Star Trek, Deep Space 9, Cost of Living, Silvers Oakley, Time Frame, Two-Way Street; appeared in L.A. Confidential, The Negotiator, A Civil Action, Robo Cop. Office: Canvas Entertainment 7095 Hollywood Blvd Ste 104-399 Los Angeles CA 90028-8903

WOLANER, ROBIN PEGGY, internet and magazine publisher; b. Queens, N.Y., May 6, 1954; d. David H. and Harriet (Radlow) W.; m. Steven J. Castleman, 1992; children: Terry David, Bonnie Lee. BS in Indsl. and Labor Rels., Cornell U., 1975. Sr. editor Viva Mag., N.Y.C., 1975-76; editor Impact Mag., N.Y.C., 1976-77; circulation mgr. Runner's World Mag., Mountain View, Calif., 1977-79; cons. Ladd Assocs., San Francisco, 1979-80; gen. mgr. Mother Jones Mag., San Francisco, 1980-81, pub., 1981-85; founder, pub. Parenting Mag., San Francisco, 1985-91, pres., 1991-92; v.p. Time Pub. Ventures, 1990-96; pres., CEO Sunset Pub. Corp., 1992-95; exec. v.p. CNET, 1997—; bd. dirs. Burnham Pacific Properties, Health Ctrl. Com., OnLine Ptnrs. Com. Jewish. Office: 2240 Hyde St San Francisco CA 94109-1509

WOLD, DAVID C., bishop. Bishop of Southwestern Wash. Evang. Luth. Ch. in Am., Tacoma, 1988—. Office: Synod of Southwestern Washington 420 121st St S Tacoma WA 98444-5218*

WOLD, MARGARET BARTH, religion educator; b. Chgo., Mar. 6, 1919; d. Frank Philip and Esther Sophie (Pedersen) Barth; m. Erling Henry Wold, Oct. 4, 1942; children: John, Michael, Kristi Wold de Merlier, Stephen Ganzkow-Wold, Erling Jr. BA, Luther Coll., 1941; MA, Luther Sch. Theology, Chgo., 1950; DD (hon.), Luther Coll., 1986; LittD (hon.), Calif. Luth. U., 1973; DD (hon.), Wartburg Sem., 1985. Exec. bd. Am. Luth. Ch. Women, Mpls., 1966-73, exec. dir., 1973-74; dir. for ministry in changing communities So. Pacific dist., Am. Luth. Ch., 1977-84; assoc. prof. N.T. Calif. Luth. U., Thousand Oaks, 1985-89, coord. sr. mentor program, 1986—; cons. Pub. Welfare Bd., Bismarck, N.D., 1967-68; v.p. So. Calif. West Synod, Evang. Luth. Ch. in Am., 1987-90; keynote speaker Luth. World Fedn. Assembly, Budapest, Hungary, 1984; C.C. Hein Meml. lectr., 1985. Author: The Shalom Woman, 1975, The Critical Moment, 1978, Women of Faith and Spirit, 1987, The Power of Ordinary Christians, 1988; also 5 books co-authored with Erling H. Wold. Bd. dirs. Grand Forks (N.D.) Unified Sch. Dist., 1968-70; bd. dirs. Pacific Luth. Theol. Sem., Berkeley, Calif., 1974-86, pres. bd. dirs., 1978-84. Recipient Martin Luther 450th Anniversary award Luth. Brotherhood, 1967, Disting. Svc. award Luther Coll., 1968, 125th Anniversary award Augustana Coll., S.D., 1968. Mem. Am. Acad. Religion, Soc. for Bibl. Lit. Democrat. Office: Calif Luth U 60 W Olsen Rd Thousand Oaks CA 91360-2787

WOLF, ALAN STEVEN, lawyer; b. Jersey City, Jan. 5, 1955; s. Lester Joel and Beatrice (Spiegel) W.; m. Donna Snow Wolf, Aug. 31, 1980; children: Lauren, Bradley. BA, Dartmouth Coll., 1977; JD, Southwestern U., L.A., 1980. Bar: Calif. 1980, U.S. Dist. Ct. (no., so., ea. and cen. dists.) Calif. 1980. With Alvarado, Rus & McClellen, Orange, Calif., 1981-84; ptnr. Cameron Dreyfuss & Wolf, Orange, 1984-89; pres. Gordon & Wolf, Newport Beach, Calif., 1989-91, Wolf & Pfeifer, Newport Beach, Calif., 1991-97, Wolf & Richards, Newport Beach, 1997—. Pres., founding dir. Laguna Beach (Calif.) Pop Warner Football, 1995-96, sec., 1996; chief Indian Princess Tribe, Laguna Beach, 1993. Mem. U.S. Foreclosure Network (bd. dirs. 1990-95, Com. Mem. of Yr. 1994), Calif. Mortgage Bankers Assn. (chmn. legal issues com. 1994-95), Dartmouth Club (pres. Orange County club 1991); fellow Am. Coll. Mortgage Attys. Avocations: computers, Internet. Office: Wolf & Richards 18 Corporate Plaza Dr Newport Beach CA 92660-7901

WOLF, ALFRED, rabbi; b. Eberbach, Germany, Oct. 7, 1915; came to U.S., 1935, naturalized, 1941; s. Hermann and Regina (Levy) W.; m. Miriam Jean Office, June 16, 1940; children: David B., Judith C. (dec.), Dan L. BA, U. Cin., 1937; MHL, Hebrew Union Coll., 1941; DD, 1966; PhD, U. So. Calif., 1961; DHL, U. Judaism, 1987, Loyola Marymount U., 1990. Ordained rabbi, 1941. Rabbi Temple Emanuel, Dothan, Ala., 1941-46; S.E. regional dir. Union Am. Hebrew Congregations, 1944-46; Western regional dir. Union Am. Hebrew Congregations, Los Angeles, 1946-49; rabbi Wilshire Blvd. Temple Los Angeles, 1949-85, rabbi emeritus, 1985—; dir. Skirball Inst. on Am. Values of Am. Jewish Com., 1985-95; founding dir., 1996—; lectr. U. So. Calif., 1955-69, Hebrew Union Coll., Jewish Inst. Religion, Calif., 1963-65, 74; lectr. religion Seven Seas div. Chapman Coll., 1967; adj. prof. theology Loyola U. Los Angeles, 1967-74; lectr. sociology Calif. State U., Los Angeles, 1977; co-chair First Nationwide Conf. for Cath. Jewish and Protestant seminaries, Chgo., 1993. Author: (with Joseph Gaer) Our Jewish Heritage, 1957, (with Monsignor Royale M. Vadakin) Journey Of Discovery - A Resource Manual for Catholic-Jewish Dialogue, 1989; editor Teaching About World Religions: A Teacher's Supplement, 1991. Mem. camp commn. adminstrv. com. Camp Hess Kramer, 1951—; mem. L.A. Com. on Human Rels., 1956-72, mem. exec. bd., 1960—, chmn., 1964-66, hon. mem., 1972—; pres. Anytown U.S.A., 1964-66; mem. United Way Planning Coun. Bd., chmn., 1974-78; mem. youth adv. com. NCCJ, 1968-72, exec. bd., 1972-93; founding pres. Interreligious Coun. So. Calif., 1970-72; chmn. clergy adv. com. L.A. Sch. Dist., 1971-81; chmn. Nat. Workshop on Christian-Jewish Rels., 1978; bd. govs. Hebrew Union Coll., bd. alumni overseers, 1972—; mem. L.A. 2000 Com., 1986-89, The 2000 Partnership, 1989-95, Berlin Sister City Com., L.A., 1987-89; bd. dirs. Jewish Fedn. Coun., 1978-85, bd. govs., 1985—; bd. dirs. Jewish Family Svc. L.A., sec., 1978-80. Recipient Samuel Kaminker award as Jewish educator of year Western Assn. Temple Educators, 1965, John Anson Ford Human Relations award County Commn. on Human Relations, 1972, 90, Harry Hollzer Meml. award Los Angeles Jewish Fedn. Council, 1978, Volpert Community Service award, 1986, Community Service award United Way of Los Angeles, 1980, Leadership award Los Angeles Bd. Edn., 1981, Service to Edn. award Associated Adminstrs. Los Angeles, 1983, Pub. Service award Jewish Chautauqua Soc., 1986, N.Am. Interfaith Leadership award Nat. Workshop for Christian-Jewish Rels., 1990, Lifetime Achievement award U. So. Calif., 1998. Mem. Bd. Rabbis So. Calif. (pres.), Am. Jewish Com. (exec. com. Los Angeles chpt., Max Bay Meml. award 1986), Central Conf. Am. Rabbis (exec. bd., mem. commn. on Jewish edn. 1970-72, treas. 1975-79, chmn. interreligious activities com. 1975-79, hon. mem. 1991—), Pacific Assn. Reform Rabbis (pres.), So. Calif. Assn. Liberal Rabbis (pres.), Synagogue Council Am. (mem. com. interreligious affairs), Alumni Assn. Hebrew Union Coll.-Jewish Inst. Religion, Town Hall, Los Angeles World Affairs Council, U. So. Calif. Alumni Assn. Home: 3389 Ley Dr Los Angeles CA 90027-1315 Office: Skirball Inst on Am Values 635 S Harvard Blvd Ste 214 Los Angeles CA 90005-2501

WOLF, ARTHUR HENRY, museum administrator; b. New Rockford, N.D., June 18, 1953; s. Louis Irwin and Vivian Joyce (Grinde) W.; m. Holly M. Chaffee, Oct. 18, 1984. BA in Anthropology, U. Nebr., 1975; MA, U. Ariz., 1977. Lab. asst., acting curator anthropology U. Nebr. State Mus., Lincoln, 1973-75; rsch. asst. Ariz. State Mus., Tucson, 1975-77; curator of collections Sch. Am. Rsch., Santa Fe, N.Mex., 1977-79; dir. Millcent Rogers Mus., Taos, N.Mex., 1979-87, Nev. State Mus. and Hist. Soc., Las Vegas, 1988-92, Mus. of Rockies, Bozeman, Mont., 1992-96; pres. High Desert Mus., Bend, Oreg., 1996—; speaker in field; cons. Pueblos of Zuni, Picuris, San Ildefonso and Taos. Contbr. articles and revs. to profl. jours. Trustee Kokopelli Archeol. Rsch. Fund, Bozeman, 1992-96; active Mont. Ambs. Recipient Young Alumnus award U. Nebr. Lincoln, 1990. Mem. Am. Assn. Mus. (bd. dirs. 1994—, vis. com. roster 1989—, vice chair 1996-97), Rotary, Assn. Sci. Mus. Dirs. Avocations: travel, reading, music. Home: 110 NW Wau St Bend OR 97701 Office: The High Desert Museum 59800 South Hwy 97 Bend OR 97702*

WOLF, CHARLES, JR., economist, educator; b. N.Y.C., Aug. 1, 1924; s. Charles and Rosalie W.; m. Theresa van de Wint, Mar. 1, 1947; children: Charles Theodore, Timothy van de Wint. B.S., Harvard U., 1943, M.P.A., 1948, Ph.D. in Econs., 1949. Economist, fgn. service officer U.S. Dept. State, 1945-47, 49-53; mem. faculty Cornell U., 1953-54, U. Calif., Berkeley, 1954-55; sr. economist The Rand Corp., Santa Monica, Calif., 1955-67, head econs. dept., 1967-81; dean The Rand Grad. Sch., 1970-97, sr. econ. advisor, 1981—, corp. fellow in internat. econs., 1996—; sr. fellow Hoover Inst., 1988—; bd. dirs. Capital Income Builder Fund, Capital World Growth Fund; mem. adv. com. UCLA Clin. Scholars Program; lectr. econs. UCLA, 1960-72; mem. adv. bd. grad. sch. pub. policy Carnegie-Mellon U., 1992—. Author: The Costs and Benefits of the Soviet Empire, 1986, Markets or Governments: Choosing Between Imperfect Alternatives, 1988, 93, Linking Economic Policy and Foreign Policy, 1991, Defense Conversion and Economic Reform in Russia and Ukraine, 1994, Long-Term Economic and Military Trends: The United States and Asia, 1994-2015, 1995, The Economic Pivot in a Political Context, 1997; bd. editors Korean Jour. of Def. Econs., 1995—; editl. adv. bd. Society, 1997—; contbr. articles to profl. jours. Mem. Assn. for Public Policy Analysis and Mgmt. (pres. 1980-81), Am. Econs. Assn., Econometric Soc., Coun. on Fgn. Rels., Internat. Inst. Strategic Studies London. Clubs: Cosmos (Washington); Riviera Tennis (Los Angeles); Harvard (N.Y.). Office: The Rand Grad Sch 1700 Main St Santa Monica CA 90401-3297

WOLF, CYNTHIA TRIBELHORN, librarian, library educator; b. Denver, Dec. 12, 1945; adopted d. John Baltazar and Margaret (Kern) Tribelhorn; m. H.Y. Rassam, Mar. 21, 1969 (div. Jan. 1988); children: Najma C., Yousuf J.; adopted children: Leonard Joseph Lucero, Lakota E. Rassam-Lucero, Macinley William Osborn, Kevin Trey. BA, Colo. State U., 1970; MLS, U. Denver, 1985. Cert. permanent profl. librarian, N.Mex. Elem. tchr. Sacred Heart Sch., Farmington, N.Mex., 1973-78; asst. prof. library sci. edn. U. N.Mex., Albuquerque, 1985-90, dir. libr. sci. edn. divsn., 1989-90; pres. Info. Acquisitions, Albuquerque, 1990—; libr. dir. Southwestern Coll., Santa Fe, 1992-94; mem. youth resources Rio Grande Valley Libr. Sys., Albuquerque, 1994-95, adult reference svc., 1995-98; with Albuquerque Pub. Schs., 1998—; instr. U. N.Mex., 1998-99; fine arts resource person for gifted edn. Farmington Pub. Schs., 1979-83; speaker Unofficial Mentorships and Market Rsch., 1992-98. Mem. Farmington Planning and Zoning Commn., 1980-81; bd. dirs. Farmington Mus. Assn., 1983-84; pres. Farmington Symphony League, 1978. Mem. ALA, N.Mex. Library Assn., LWV (bd. dirs. Farmington, 1972-74, 75, pres.). Avocations: mixed media graphics design, market research, creative approaches to personal journals, board game design.

WOLF, FREDERICK GEORGE, environmentalist; b. Paterson, N.J., Aug. 30, 1952; s. Frederick George and Doris (Miller) W. BS, U. S.C., 1974; postgrad., Clemson U., 1976-77; MS in Environ. Health, East Tenn. State U., 1978; MS in Sys. Mgmt., U. Denver, 1990; DBA in Mgmt., Nova Southeastern U., 1998. Cert. profl. geologist, Alaska. Phys. scientist U.S. Army Environ. Hygiene Agy., Edgewood, Md., 1974-75, S.C. Dept. Health and Environ. Control, Columbia, 1977-78; hydrogeologist EPA, Atlanta, 1978-79; hydrologist Boston, 1979-81; regional hydrogeologist Seattle, 1981-86; mgr. hazardous waste sect. Parametrix Inc., Bellevue, Wash., 1986-88; regional mgr. environ. affairs Elf Atochem N.Am., Tacoma, 1988—. Lt. USNR, 1974-87. Recipient Spl. Svc. award EPA, 1982; decorated Bronze medal, 1983. Mem. Am. Inst. Profl. Geologists (cert. profl. geol. scientist), Acad. of Hazardous Materials Mgmt. (cert. hazardous materials mgr. master level), Soaring Soc. Am. (Bronze badge number 338), Sigma Xi, Epsilon Nu Eta. Office: Elf Atochem NAm 2901 Taylor Way Tacoma WA 98421-4330

WOLF, HANS, opera company director; b. Hamburg, Germany. Grad., U. Vienna, New Vienna Cons. of Music; PhD, New Vienna Cons. of Music. Conductor Innsbruck (Austria) Symphony Orch., orchs. in Germany and Austria; music dir. Remington Records, Vienna, 1950-52, Livingston (N.J.) Audio Products, 1952-60; conductor Riverside (Calif.) Opera Co., 1961-69; assoc. conductor, chorus master Seattle Opera Assn., 1969-83; co-founder Tacoma Opera, 1981, artistic dir., conductor, 1981-95; with Cmty. Outreach Prodns., Seattle, 1974—. Office: Seattle Opera PO Box 9248 Seattle WA 98109-0248

WOLF, HANS ABRAHAM, retired pharmaceutical company executive; b. Frankfurt, Fed. Republic Germany, June 27, 1928; came to U.S., 1936, naturalized, 1944; s. Franz Benjamin and Ilse (Nathan) W.; m. Elizabeth J. Bassett, Aug. 2, 1958; children: Heidi Elizabeth, Rebecca Anne, Deborah Wolf Streeter, Andrew Robert. AB magna cum laude, Harvard U., 1949, MBA, 1955; PhB, Oxford U., 1951. Math instr. Tutoring Sch., 1946-47; statis. research Nat. Bur. Econ. Research, N.Y.C., 1948-49; researcher Georgetown U., 1951-52; confidential aide Office Dir. Mut. Security, Washington, 1952; analyst Ford Motor div. Ford Motor Co., Dearborn, Mich., summer 1954; foreman prodn. M&C Nuclear Inc., Attleboro, Mass., 1955-57; asst. supt. prodn. Metals & Controls Corp., Attleboro, 1957-59, mgr. product dept., 1959-62, controller, 1962-67; asst. v.p., controller materials and services group Tex. Instruments Inc., Dallas, 1967-69, treas., v.p., 1969-75; v.p. fin., chief fin. officer Syntex Corp., Palo Alto, Calif., 1975-78, exec. v.p., 1978-86, vice chmn., chief adminstrv. officer, 1986-92, vice chmn., 1992-93, also bd. dirs., 1986-93; bd. dirs. Clean Sites, Inc., Alexandria, Va., Tab Products Co., Palo Alto, Calif., chmn., 1995—; bd. dirs. Network Equipment Techs., Redwood City, Calif., chmn., 1996—; bd. dirs. Satellite Dialysis Ctrs., Inc., Redwood City, Hyal Pharms., Mississauga, Ont. Author: Motivation Research—A New Aid to Understanding Your Markets, 1955. Mem. Norton (Mass.) Sch. Bd., 1959-62, chmn., 1961-62; pres., bd. dirs. Urban League Greater Dallas, 1971-74; bd. dirs. Dallas Health Planning Coun., mem. community adv. com., 1973-75; bd. dirs., pres. Children's Health Coun. of the Mid Peninsula; cubmaster Boy Scouts Am., 1976-78; elder United Ch. Christ, 1970-73, vice chmn. gen. bd., 1970-71, moderator, 1978-80; trustee Pacific Sch. Religion, 1986-94, chmn., 1990-94; trustee World Affairs Coun. San Francisco, 1986-92, 94-97; dir. Tech Mus. San Jose, 1992-98. With USAF, 1952-53. Mem. Am. Mgmt. Assn. (planning council fin. div. 1970-76), Phi Beta Kappa.

WOLF, PATRICIA B., museum director. Dir., exec. dir. Anchorage Mus. History and Art, 1989—. Office: Anchorage Mus History and Art 121 W 7th Ave Anchorage AK 99501-3611*

WOLFCHIEF-GHIDOSSI, MARIE ANTONETTE VICARIO, artist; b. Sacramento, Nov. 27, 1948; d. Edward Francis Edwards and Antonette Nathalie (Vicario) Hallmark; m. David Allen Clark, Aug. 1967 (div.); m. Stanley Everett Ghidossi, Mar. 25, 1989; 1 child, Amber Carol Marie Antonette Catherine Cheryl. BA in Environ. Apology and Illustration, Calif. State U., Sacramento, 1986. Cert. emerg. tchr. credential. Substitute tchr. Stockton (Calif.) Unified Sch., 1988-92, Native Am. Indian tchr., 1992-94; lectr. Stockton Unified Sch., 1989-94. Sculptor and textile artist. Underground writer Welfare Reform Now, Placerville, Calif., 1983. Avocations: gardening, wool felting, basketry, ethnobotany.

WOLFE, BRIAN AUGUSTUS, retired sales executive, small business owner; b. Mexico City, Nov. 23, 1946; came to U.S., 1947; s. Steward Augustus and Vivia Idalene (Fouts) W.; m. Holly Joyce Gilhart, Dec. 29, 1981; 1 child, Derek Augustus. BSME, Tex. A&M U., 1968. Project engr. Tex. Power & Light Co., Dallas, 1968-72; service engr. Babcock & Wilcox, Chgo., 1972-74; sales engr., New Eng. dist. Babcock & Wilcox, Boston, 1974-79; area mgr., Far East, internat. bus. Babcock & Wilcox, Barberton, Ohio, 1979-81; dist. sales mgr. Babcock & Wilcox, Sheridan, Colo., 1981-97; owner Wolfe Environ. Svcs., Lakewood, Colo., 1996—. Mem. Water Environment Assn., Rocky Mountain Elec. League (bd. dirs. 1988-96, v.p. 1990-91, pres.-elect 1991-92, pres. 1992-93). Avocations: auto racing, basketball, caving. Home and Office: 7285 W Vassar Ave Lakewood CO 80227-3303

WOLFE, CAMERON WITHGOT, JR., lawyer; b. Oakland, Calif., July 7, 1939; s. Cameron W. and Jean (Brown) W.; m. Frances Evelyn Bishopric, Sept. 2, 1964; children: Brent Everett, Julie Frances, Karen Jean. AB, U. Calif.-Berkeley, 1961, JD, 1964. Bar: Calif. 1965, U.S. Dist. Ct. (no. dist.) Calif. 1965, U.S. Ct. Appeals (9th cir.) 1965, U.S. Tax Ct. 1966, U.S. Ct. Claims 1977, U.S. Ct. Appeals (3d cir.) 1980, U.S. Ct. Appeals (fed. cir.) 1983, U.S. Supreme Ct. 1986 . Assoc., then ptnr. Orrick, Herrington & Sutcliffe, San Francisco, 1964—; bd. dirs. Crowley Maritime Corp.; mem. steering com. Western Pension Conf. Pres. League to Save Lake Tahoe, 1979, 80; chmn. League to Save Lake Tahoe Charitable Trust, 1966-91, Piedmont Edn. Fund Campaign, 1982-83; pres. Piedmont Edn. Found., 1986-90; bd. dirs. Yosemite Fund., 1993—. Served with U.S. Army, 1957, with USAR, 1957-65. Mem. ABA (mem. taxation com.), Calif. State Bar, San Francisco Bar Assn., Order of Coif, Phi Beta Kappa. Clubs: Pacific Union (San Francisco); Claremont Country (Oakland, Calif.). Home: 59 Lakeview Ave Piedmont CA 94611-3514 Office: Orrick Herrington & Sutcliffe 400 Sansome St San Francisco CA 94111-3143

WOLFE, CLIFFORD EUGENE, architect, writer; b. Harrington, Wash., Mar. 26, 1906; s. Delwin Lindsley and Luella Grace (Cox) W.; m. Frances Lillian Parkes, Sept. 12, 1936 (dec.); children: Gretchen Yvonne Wolfe Mason, Eric Von; m. Mary Theye Worthen. A.B. in Architecture, U. Calif.-Berkeley, 1933. Registered architect, Calif. Assoc. architect John Knox Ballantine, Architect, San Francisco, 1933-42; supervising architect, prodn. engr. G.W. Williams Co. Contractors, Burlingame, Calif., 1942-44; state-wide coord. med. schs. and health ctrs. office archs. and engrs. U. Calif.-Berkeley, San Francisco and Los Angeles, 1944-52; sec. council on hosp. planning Am. Hosp. Assn., Chgo., 1952-59; dir. planning dept. Office of York & Sawyer, Architects, N.Y.C., 1959-74; prin. Clifford E. Wolfe, AIA-E, Oakland, Calif., 1974-88; ret.; assoc. designer State of Calif. Commn. for Golden Gate Internat. Exposition, San Francisco, 1938-39; cons. Fed. Hosp. Council, Washington, 1954-60; mem. Pres.'s Conf. on Occupational Safety, Washington, 1955; rsch. architect Hosp Rsch. and Ednl. Trust, Chgo., 1957-59; instr. hosp. planning Columbia U., N.Y.C., 1961-73. Author, editor manuals on hosp. planning, engring. and safety, 1954-58. Author: Ballad of Humphrey The Humpback Whale, 1985; contbr. poetry to Tecolote Anthology, 1983, The Ina Coolbrith Circle, 1985, 87, 89, 91, 93, 95, 97 (Grand prize Ina Coolbrith award 1986, Cleone Montgomery award 1990), Islandia, 1986, Tidings, 1989, Calif. Fedn. Chaparral Poets (pres. Tecolote chpt. 1982-86, 91-95). Hosp. planning research grantee USPHS, 1956. Mem. AIA (chmn. honor awards com. Chgo. chpt. 1958-59, chmn. activities com. N.Y. chpt. 1972-74, mem. emeritus East Bay chpt. 1974—). Address: 3900 Harrison St Apt 306 Oakland CA 94611-4525

WOLFE, EDWARD WILLIAM, II, music educator, composer; b. Albuquerque, Sept. 24, 1946; s. Edward William and Mary Ellen (Gabriele) W.; m. Nancy Jean Brown, Aug. 16, 1980. B in Music Edn., U. N.Mex., 1968, MA, 1973. Cert. tchr., N.Mex., Calif. Tchr. Grant Jr. High Sch., Albuquerque, 1970-75, Manzano High Sch., Albuquerque, 1974-75, Hoover Mid. Sch., Albuquerque, 1975-77, San Dimas (Calif.) High Sch., 1977-85; instr. music Calif. Poly. State U., Pomona, Calif., 1984; tchr. Bonita High Sch., LaVerne, Calif., 1985-89, Lone Hill Mid. Sch. and Feeders, San Dimas, Calif., 1989—; tchr. Hummingbird Music Camp, Jemez, N.Mex., 1970-76; cons. BUSD, San Dimas, 1980—; presenter jazz edn. SCSBOA fall conf., 1995. Author: The Language of Music, 1974, rev. 1993; composer Quartet for Horns, 1967, Oboe Sonata, 1967, Trio for Flute, Violin and Horn, 1968, Caverna, 1972, Quintet for Brass, 1993, numerous compositions and jazz arrangements, 1972—. Mem. Task Force on Mid. Sch. Reform, 1990. Recipient award Juvenile Justice Commn. City of San Dimas, 1984, 93; named to BUSD Hall of Fame, 1991. Mem. Music Educators Nat. Conf. (adjudicator 1969-77, 80—, v.p. dist. 7 1972, pres. 1975-76), Calif. Music Educators Assn. (task force on mid. sch. reform 1990, Outstanding Music Edn. cert. 1991), Nat. Assn. Jazz Educators (adjudicator 1980—, treas. N.Mex. chpt. 1972), Calif. Tchrs. Assn., So. Calif. Sch. Band and Orch. Assn., Bonita United Teaching Assn., Phi Mu Alpha. Avocation: model railroader. Home: 817 S Dumaine Ave San Dimas CA 91773-3808

WOLFE, WILLIAM DOWNING, public utility administrator; b. Zanesville, Ohio, Nov. 14, 1947; s. William Jr. and Wava Benetta (Downing) W.; m. Laura Olivia Soza, July 29, 1972; children: Lisa Anne, Erin Nicole. BBA, U. Ariz., 1969. Instr. RTV Internat., N.Y.C., 1969-70; mgr. prodn. Sta. KUAT-TV/AM/FM, Tucson, 1969-76; lectr. U. Ariz., Tucson, 1970-78; mgr. prodn. Sta. KGUN-TV, Tucson, 1976-79; exec. producer Sta. KTVK-TV, Phoenix, 1979-82; writer, producer Ariz. Pub. Svc. Co., Phoenix, 1982-83, supr. pub. info., 1983-86; coord. emergency planning Palo Verde Nuclear Generating Sta., Phoenix, 1986—; cons. Nat. Student Films, Hollywood, Calif., 1975, Warner for Gov., Phoenix, 1986, various advt. agys., Tucson, Phoenix, various U.S. locations, 1974-83. writer, producer, dir. over 800 TV and multi-media programming and comml. advertisements for PM Mag., Wide World Sports, Good Morning Am., local, others, 1969—. Advisor Jr. Achievement, Tucson, 1976; chmn. com. Ariz. Citizens for Edn., Phoenix, 1988—; mem. budget adv. com., long-range planning com., supt. search profile com., supt. search com., bond election com., curriculum exit outcomes planning com., campus improvement team, strategic planning team Deer Valley Sch. Dist., bd. dirs. So. Ariz. chpt. Muscular Dystrophy Assn., 1976-79. Grantee Ford Found., 1969; recipient Golden Sch. Bell award Ariz. Dept. Edn., 1974-79, Emmy nomination Nat. Acad. TV Arts and Scis., 1979, Bronze Anvil nat. award Pub. Rels. Soc. Am., 1983, award Excellence Internat. Assn. Bus. Communicators. Mem. Nat. Emergency Mgmt. Assn., Nat. Radiol. Emergency Preparedness Conf. (Intercom 190, presdl. adv. com. on EBS system 1992—). Democrat. Roman Catholic. Avocations: music. Office: Palo Verde Nuclear Generating Sta PO Box 52034 Phoenix AZ 85072-2034

WOLFE, WILLIAM JEROME, librarian, English language educator; b. Chgo., Feb. 24, 1927; s. Fred Wiley and Helen Dorothea (Lovaas) W.; m. ViviAnn Lundin O'Connell, June 25, 1960 (div. 1962); 1 child, Lund. *Son Lund, Navy veteran and graduate of the University of Arizona, is a computer programmer. Father Fred Wolfe, World War I U.S. Army veteran, worked in the Railway Mail Service 1920-61 and practiced law in Chicago 1928-63. Grandparents Ludvig Lovaas (cabinetmaker) and Anna Anderson immigrated from Norway in 1888. Grandfather Alfred Wolfe, graduate of Tri-State Normal College, taught school in Kosciusko County, Indiana, 1897-1930. Great-grandfather James Knox Polk Wiley, from Ohio, served in the Union Army at the Battle of Shiloh. Great-great-great-grandfather Garret Wolfe served in the Pennsylvania militia during the American Revolution.* AB, U. Chgo., 1948; BA, Roosevelt U., Chgo., 1953; MEd, Chgo. State U., 1963; AA with high honors, Pima C.C., 1992; BA in Art magna cum laude, U. Ariz., 1994. Tchr. English John Marshall High Sch., Chgo., 1956-60; libr. Safford Jr. High Sch., Tucson, Ariz., 1961-71, Santa Rita High Sch., Tucson, 1971-75, Tucson High Sch., 1975-87; tutor Eastside Ctr., Tucson Adult Lit. Vols., 1988—, supr., 1993—. Co-founder Tucson Classic Guitar Soc., 1969-72; docent U. Ariz. Mus. Art, Tucson, 1989—; mem. adv. bd. U. Ariz. Sch. Music, 1995—; singer U. Ariz. Collegium Musicum, 1981-96, Lane Justus Chorale, 1996—. With U.S. Army, 1945-46, ETO. Mem. U. Ariz. Pres. Club, U. Ariz. Old Main Club, Am. Legion, Norsemen's Fedn., Phi Kappa Phi, Phi Theta Kappa. Mem. Ch. of Christ Scientist. Avocations: poetry writing, drawing, singing, piano, classical guitar. Home: 8460 E Rosewood St Tucson AZ 85710-1702

WOLFF, BRIAN RICHARD, metal manufacturing company executive; b. L.A., Dec. 11, 1955; s. Arthur Richard and Dorothy Virginia (Johnson) W.; divorced; children: Ashley Rachael, Taryn Nicole. BSBA, Calif. State U., Chico, 1980; postgrad., U. Phoenix, 1990—. Registered counseling practitioner, Calif., 1996, guidance practitioner, Calif., 1996; ordained min. Progressive Universal Life Ch., 1996. Sales rep. Federated Metals Corp./ASARCO, Long Beach, Calif., 1980-82, dist. sales mgr., 1983-84; sales mgr. Copper Alloys Corp., Beverly Hills, Calif., 1982-83; dir. mktg. Federated-Fry Metals/Cookson, Long Beach, Industry and Paramount, Calif., 1984-87; regional sales mgr. Colonial Metals Co., L.A., 1987-91; nat. sales mgr. Calif. Metal X/Metal Briquetting Co., L.A., 1991-93; sales engr. Ervin Industries, Inc., Ann Arbor, Mich., 1993-95; sales mgr. Southbay Bronze, San Jose, Calif., 1996—; tech. sales mgr. GSP Metals & Chems. Co., 1987-91; cons. sales Calif. Metal Exch., L.A., 1987-91, Atlas Pacific Inc., Bloomington, Calif., 1993—; sales mgr. Southbay Bronze, San Jose, Calif., 1996—; dealer Mason Shoe Co., 1996—; co-owner Sober Creatures, Huntington Beach, Calif., 1998—. Mem. citizens adv. com. on bus. Calif. Legis., 1983; ordained min. Universal Life, 1996. Mem. Non Ferrous Founders Soc., Am. Foundrymen Soc., Calif. Cast Metals Assn., Steel Structures Painting Coun., Am. Electroplaters Soc., Soc. Die Cast Engrs., NRA. Republican. Presbyterian. Avocations: scuba diving, tennis, freshwater fishing, trap shooting, hunting.

WOLFF, JOEL HENRY, human factors engineer, lawyer; b. New Rochelle, N.Y., Oct. 29, 1966; s. s. Richard Eugene and Elise Leonora (Wolff) A. BA, U. Nev. at Las Vegas, 1991; JD, Gonzaga U., 1995. Computer operator Sun Teleguide, Henderson, Nev., 1987-90; engring. aide Wojcik Engring., Las Vegas, 1989-90; computer cons. Ax Med. Interfaces, Las Vegas, 1990-91; programmer Biosoft, Las Vegas, 1991-92; rule 9 legal intern, 1994-95, univ. legal assistance, 1994; computer cons., sys. analyst Wolff Legal Engines,

1995—; mem. corp. legal dept. Graham and James LLP/Riddell-Williams P.S., Seattle, Wash., 1997-98; contractor for litigation dept. Preston, Gates and Ellis LLP, Seattle, 1998; legal database programmer and designer King County Prosecutor's Ofc.-Civil Divsn.-Employment Law, Seattle, 1998—; legal database designer and cons., King County Prosecuting Atty.'s Office, civil divsn., employment law sect., Seattle, 1998-99. Named Eagle Scout Boy Scouts Am., 1984. Mem. ASCE (sec. student chpt. 1986-87), ABA (law student divsn. 1992-95), Internat. Law Soc. of Gonazaga Univ., Nat. Eagle Scout Assn., Wash. State Bar Assn., Phi Alpha Delta, Sigma Nu. Achievements include rsch. on systems engring. with emphasis of man/machine interface; stats. analysis of social power structures and how they interface with sci. and tech. Home: 11309 NE 128th St Apt F-301 Kirkland WA 98034-6365

WOLFGANG, BONNIE ARLENE, musician, bassoonist; b. Caribou, Maine, Sept. 29, 1944; d. Ralph Edison and Arlene Alta (Obetz) W.; m. Eugene Alexander Pridonoff, July 3, 1965 (div. Sept. 1977); children: George Randall, Anton Alexander, Stephan Eugene. MusB, Curtis Inst. Music, Phila., 1967. Soloist Phila. Orch., 1966; soloist with various orchs. U.S., Cen. Am., 1966-75; prin. bassoonist Phoenix Symphony, 1976—, with Woodwind Quintet, 1986—. Home: 9448 N 106th St Scottsdale AZ 85258-6056*

WOLFSCHMIDT, WILLI See FLINT, WILLIS WOLFSCHMIDT

WOLINSKY, LEO C., newspaper editor. BA in Journalism, U. So. Calif., 1972. Journalist, 1972—; staff writer L.A. Times, 1977-86, dep. chief Sacramento bur., 1987-89, city editor, 1990, Calif. polit. editor, 1991, metro editor, asst. mng. editor, 1994-97, mng. editor, 1997—. Office: Los Angeles Times Times Mirror Sq Los Angeles CA 90053

WOLK, BRUCE ALAN, dean; b. Bklyn., Mar. 2, 1946; s. Morton and Gertrude W.; m. Lois Gloria Krepliak, June 22, 1968; children: Adam, Daniel. BS, Antioch Coll., 1968; MS, Stanford U., 1972; JD, Harvard U., 1975. Bar: D.C. 1975. Assoc. Hogan & Hartson, Washington, 1975-78; prof. U. Calif. Sch. Law, Davis, 1978—, acting dean, 1990-91, dean, 1993-98. Danforth Found. fellow, 1970-74, NSF fellow, 1970-72, Fulbright sr. research fellow, 1985-86. Mem. ABA, Am. Law Inst. Office: Univ Cal-Davis Sch Law King Hall 400 Mrak Hall Dr Davis CA 95616-5201*

WOLK, MARTIN, physicist, electronics engineer; b. Long Branch, N.J., Jan. 13, 1930; s. Michael and Tillie (Barron) W.; 1 child, Brett Martin. BS, George Washington U., 1957, MS, 1968; PhD, U. N.Mex., 1973. Physicist Naval Ordnance Lab., White Oak, Md., 1957-59, Nat. Oceanic and Atmospheric Adminstrn., Suitland, Md., 1959-66; solid state physicist Night Vision Lab., Fort Belvoir, Va., 1967-69; rsch. asst. U. N.Mex., Albuquerque, 1969-73; electronics engr. Washington Navy Yard, 1976-83, TRW, Inc., Redondo Beach, Calif., 1983-84; physicist Metrology Engring. Ctr., Pomona, Calif., 1984-85; electronics engr. Naval Aviation Depot North Island, San Diego, 1985—; cons. Marine Corps Logistics Base, Barstow, Calif., 1985—, Naval Weapons Station, Fallbrook, Calif., 1987-89, Naval Weapons Support Ctr., Crane, Ind., 1989—. Contbr. articles to Jour. Quantitative Spectroscopy and Radiative Transfer, Monthly Weather Rev., Proceedings of SPIE, Procs. of EUROPTO. Cpl. 11th Airborne Div., 511 Parachute Infantry Reg., U.S. Army, 1946-49, Japan. Mem. IEEE, Soc. Photo-Optical Instrumentation Engring., European Optical Soc., Sigma Pi Sigma, Sigma Tau. Achievements include development of first Tiros meteorological satellites; research on electron-beam for micro-circuit device fabrication; development of electro-optical calibration systems for the TOW missile system optical and night vision sights for the Marine Corps; development of visible and infrared spectral radiometric system utilizing a Fourier Transform Interferometer spectrometer and dual conjugate Cassegrainian optical telescopes for primary standards calibration of thermal radiation sources for the Navy. Home: 740 Eastshore Ter Unit 91 Chula Vista CA 91913-2421

WOLKOV, HARVEY BRIAN, radiation oncologist, researcher; b. Cleve., Feb. 8, 1953; s. Sidney and Norma (Levin) W.; m. Lauren Cronin, Jan. 9, 1993. BSc, Purdue U., 1975, MSc, 1977; MD, Medical Coll. Ohio, 1979. Diplomate Am. Bd. Radiology. Intern U. Calif., San Francisco, 1979-80; res. Stanford Med. Ctr., Stanford, Calif., 1980-83; rsch. asst. Stanford (Calif.) U., 1982; from asst. clin. prof. to assoc. clin. prof. U. Calif., Davis, 1983-97, assoc. clin. prof., 1997—; medical dir. Mercy Hosps., Sacramento, Calif., 1987-90; med. dir. Sutter Cancer Ctr. Dept. Radiation Oncology, Sacramento, Calif., 1990—; co-prin. investigator Pediat. Oncology Group, Chgo., 1989—; adv. bd. Nat. Graves Disease Found., Jacksonville, Fla., 1993—; bd. dirs. Sutter Hosps. Found., Sacramento. Author: (with others) Intraoperative Radiation, 1989, Frontiers in Radiation, 1991, Textbook Radiation Oncology, 1998; contbr. 25 articles to profl. jours. Fellow Am. Cancer Soc., 1978, 1983, Am. Coll. Radiology, 1997; recipient Travel award Am. Soc. Therapeutic Radiology Oncology, Reston, Va., 1987. Mem. Am. Coll. Radiolgy (chmn. standards accreditation com. 1997—), Am. Cancer Soc. (reviewer 1990—), Assn. Residents Radiation Oncology (exec. com. 1997—), Council Affiliated Radiation Oncology Soc. (pres. elect, 1998), Northern Calif. Radiation Oncology Soc. (pres elect 1996—), Radiaion Therapy Oncology Group (com. chair 1986—). Jewish. Avocations: oil painting, sculpture, travel. Office: Sutter Cancer Center 2800 L St Ste 10 Sacramento CA 95816-5616

WOLLEGA, RAS M., small business owner, artist; b. Cin., June 7, 1956; s. Frank and Juanita (Vinegar) Welbon. Grad. h.s., Cin. One-man shows include Contemporary Arts Gallery, Berkeley, Calif., 1984, 86; group exhibits include Kottler Gallery, N.Y.C., 1976, Wolfe Gallery, Burlingame, Calif., 1985, Art Rise Gallery, San Bruno, Calif., 1986, Art Exposure, Stockton, Calif., 1989, Bloomington Art Gallery, Sacramento, 1996. Avocations: walking, biking, yoga. Home: 691 Rollins Rd Apt 9 Burlingame CA 94010-2770

WOLLENBERG, RICHARD PETER, paper manufacturing company executive; b. Juneau, Alaska, Aug. 1, 1915; s. Harry L. and Gertrude (Arnstein) W.; m. Leone Bonney, Dec. 22, 1940; children: Kenneth Roger, David Arthur, Keith Kermit, Richard Harry, Carol Lynne. BSME, U. Calif., Berkeley, 1936; MBA, Harvard U., 1938; grad., Army Indsl. Coll., 1941; D in Pub. Affairs (hon.), U. Puget Sound, 1977. Prodn. control Bethlehem Ship, Quincy, Mass., 1938-39; with Longview (Wash.) Fibre Co., 1939—, safety engr., asst. chief engr., chief engr., mgr. container operations, 1951-57, v.p., 1953-57, v.p. ops., 1957-60, exec. v.p., 1960-69, pres., 1969-78, pres., chief exec. officer, 1978-85, pres., chief exec. officer, chmn. bd., 1985—, also bd. dirs.; mem. Wash. State Council for Postsecondary Edn., 1969-79, chmn., 1970-73; mem. western adv. bd. Allendale Ins. Bassoonist SW Washington Symphony. Trustee Reed Coll., Portland, 1962—, chmn. bd. 1982-90. Served to lt. col. USAAF, 1941-45. Recipient Alumni Achievement award Harvard U., 1994. Mem. NAM (bd. dirs. 1981-86), Pacific Coast Assn. Pulp and Paper Mfrs. (pres. 1981-92), Inst. Paper Sci. and Tech. (trustee), Wash. State Roundtable. Home: 1632 Kessler Blvd Longview WA 98632-3633 Office: Longview Fibre Co PO Box 606 Longview WA 98632-7391

WOLLMER, RICHARD DIETRICH, statistics and operations research educator; b. L.A., July 27, 1938; s. Herman Dietrich and Alice Myrtle (Roberts) W. BA in Math., Pomona Coll., 1960; MA in Applied Math., Columbia U., 1962; MS in Engring. Sci., U. Calif., Berkeley, 1963, PhD Engring. Sci., 1965. Scientist Rand Corp., Santa Monica, Calif., 1965-70; prof. info. systems Calif. State U., Long Beach, 1970—; vis. prof. Calif. State U., Northridge, 1981-82; cons. McDonnell Douglas, Long Beach, Calif., 1978-80, 82, 85-91, Logicon, San Pedro, Calif., 1979-81, Behavioral Tech. Labs., U. So. Calif., 1973-75; vis. assoc. prof. Stanford U., 1976; rsch. scientist Electric Power Rsch. Inst., Palo Alto, Calif., 1977; rsch. engr. Jet Propulsion Lab., Pasadena, Calif., 1971. Contbr. articles to profl. jours. Deacon Bel Air Presbyn. Ch., L.A., 1982-84, treas. 1983. Mem. So. Calif. Inst. Mgmt. Sci.-Ops. Rsch. Soc. (chmn. 1981, 89, vice chmn., 1980, 88, treas. 1979), Ops. Rsch. Soc. Am., Inst. Mgmt. Sci., Internat. Fedn. Ops. Rsch. Mgmt. Sci., Internat. Fedn. Ops. Rsch. and Mgmt. Sci., So. Calif. INFORMS (treas. 1999). Republican. Avocations: classical music, sports, reading, antique cars. Home: 6132 Fernwood Dr Huntington Beach CA 92648-3524 Office: Calif State U 1250 N Bellflower Blvd Long Beach CA 90840-0001

WOLTERS, CHRISTIAN HEINRICH, systems engineer; b. Kalkar, Germany, July 19, 1965; came to U.S., 1994; s. Heinrich and Hedwig (Terhorst) W. MS in Physics, RWTH-Aachen, 1990, PhD in Physics, 1994. Rsch. asst. ACCESS, Aachen, 1988-90, project leader, 1990-94; postdoctoral rsch. assoc. Nat. High Magnetic Field Lab.-Fla. State U., Tallahassee, 1994-96; instrumentation physicist NHMFL-Fla. State U., Tallahassee, 1996-97; sr. sys. engr. KLA-TENCOR, Milpitas, Calif., 1997—. Achievements include patents in field. Avocations: private pilot, rowing, piano. Office: KLA-Tencor 5 Technology Dr Milpitas CA 95035-7916

WOMACK, THOMAS HOUSTON, manufacturing company executive; b. Gallatin, Tenn., June 22, 1940; s. Thomas Houston and Jessie (Eckel) W.; Linda Walker Womack, July 20, 1963 (div. Dec. 1989); children: Britton Ryan, Kelley Elizabeth; m. Pamela Ann Reed, Apr. 20, 1991. BSME, Tenn. Tech. U., Cookeville, 1963. Project engr. U.S. Gypsum Co., Jacksonville, Fla., 1963-65; project mgr. Maxwell House Div. Gen. Foods Corp., Jacksonville, 1965-68; mfg. mgr. Maxwell House Div. Gen. Foods Corp., Hoboken, N.J., 1968-71, div. ops. planning mgr., 1971-73; industry sales mgr. J.R. Schneider Co., Tiburon, Calif., 1973-79; pres., CEO Womack Internat., Inc., Mare Island, Calif., 1979—; chmn., CEO Ceramic Microlight Technologies, Inc., Mare Island, Calif., 1995—; pres., CEO WestAmerica Engring. and Mfg. Co., 1997—. Holder 5 U.S. patents. Mem. Soc. Tribologists and Lubrication Engrs., Am. Filtration Soc., Soc. Mfg. Engrs., Am. Soc. Chem. Engrs. Avocations: skiing, vintage exotic sports cars. Fax: 707-562-1010. Office: Womack Internat Inc 700 Walnut Ave Vallejo CA 94592-1132

WONG, ASTRIA WOR, cosmetic business consultant; b. Hong Kong, Oct. 23, 1949; came to U.S., 1970; B in Vocat. Edn., Calif. State U., Long Beach, 1976. Cert. tchr., Calif. West coast sales trainer Revlon Inc., N.Y.C, 1975-82; nat. tng. dir. diReniel Internat., Palm Springs, Calif., 1982; dir. Beauty Cons. Svc. Agy., Long Beach, Calif., 1983—; pres. Boutique Astria, Scottsdale, Ariz., 1994—, Apricot House of Herbs, 1997—. Author: The Art of Femininity, 1971; editor (newsletter) So. Calif. Cosmetic, 1983-86. Chair Cmty. Involvement Paradise Rep. Woman's Club. Named Salesperson of Yr., Revlon, Inc., N.Y.C., 1978. Mem. So. Calif. Cosmetic Assn. (correspondence sec. 1982—), Women's Coun., Cosmetologist Tchr. Assn., Bus. and Profl. (ind. devel. chair.), Fashion Group Internat. Republican. Office: Beauty Cons Service Agy 7121 E 1st Ave Scottsdale AZ 85251-4305

WONG, CARRIE, executive. Ptnr. Niehaus Ryan Wong, South San Francisco. Office: 601 Gateway Blvd Ste 900 South San Francisco CA 94080-7009

WONG, CLEMENT PO-CHING, nuclear engineer; b. Hong Kong, Mar. 20, 1944; came to U.S., 1963; s. K Ng and Kum Sin (Shum) W.; m. Siu Yin, June 20, 1972; 1 child, Dong Ping. BS in Nuclear Engring., U. Wis., 1967, MSc in Nuclear Engring., 1969; PhD in Nuclear Engring., U. Tex., 1977. Prin. engr. General Atomics, San Diego, 1977—. Mem. ANS (sec., treas. 1996-98), APS. Office: General America PO Box 85608 San Diego CA 92186-5608

WONG, CORINNE HONG SLING, minister; b. Hong Kong, China, Nov. 24, 1930; came to U.S., 1940; d. William Hong Sling and Clara Grace (Low) Shen; m. Howard Marn Yung Wong, Sept. 16, 1953; children: Alison Marie Wong Noto, Mark David, Martin John. BS, Houghton Coll., 1951; MRE, N.Y. Theol. Sem., 1954; MDiv, Princeton Theol. Sem., 1986. ordained Am. Bapt. Chs., 1992. Asst. to pastor 1st Presbyn. Ch., Honolulu, 1986-87; min. Christian edn. Wahiawa (Hawaii) Korean Christian Ch., 1988-89; interim lay pastor St. Elizabeth's Episcopal Ch., Honolulu, 1989-90; min. adult ministries and outreach 1st Bapt. Ch. Honolulu, 1991-92; min. Diamond Head Fellowship, Honolulu, 1991—. Author: Studies in the Gospel of Mark, 1979, Studies in Colossians, 1984. Recipient grants for religious study Chinese Christian Assn., Honolulu, 1984-86, C.K. Ai Found., Honolulu, 1984-86, Presbyn. Ch. (U.S.A.), 1985-86. Office: 4203 Kaimanahila St Honolulu HI 96816-4751

WONG, DIANA SHUI IU, artist; b. Hong Kong, China, Apr. 14, 1938; came to U.S., 1970; d. Fut-Nom-Hong and Lai Kuen (Hui) W.; m. 1965 (dec. 1972); 1 child, Lia Tang. Student, Chinese U., Hong Kong; BA, Acad. Fine Arts, Rome; postgrad., Royal Sch. Arts, London. Artist Santa Monica, Calif., 1960—; guest on CNBC-TV News Hong Kong, 1997. One-women shows include Galleria Fontanella, Rome, 1960, City Hall Gallery, Hong Kong, 1962, Chatham Galleries, Kowloon, Hong Kong, 1964, Nat. Mus. History, Taipei, Taiwan, 1969, L.A. Mission Coll., San Fernando, Calif, 1976, M.M. Shinno Gallery, L.A., 1977, 82, 85-87, Pacific Asia Mus., Pasadena, Calif, 1983, Silpakom U. Art Gallery, Bangkok, 1987, Alison Fine Arts Gallery, 1988, Gallery Q 1, Tokyo, 1989, Filipin Gallery, Milan, 1992, LA Artcore Gallery, L.A., 1992, Seibu Art Gallery, Hong Kong, 1992, Merging One Gallery, Santa Monica, Calif., 1993, 96, Nat. Gallery, Beijing, 1994, Galleria Spazio Prospectiva, Milan, 1995, Trigram Gallery, Hong Kong, 1997, Robert V. Fullerton Art Mus., San Bernardino, Calif., 1997, Galleria Mazzocchi, Parma, Italy, 1998; exhibited in group shows includeBrand Libr. Art Galleries, Glendale, Calif., 1976, UCLA Group Invitational, 1978, L.A. County Mus. Art, 1982, LA Artcore Gallery, 1984, U. Hilo, Hawaii, 1986, Howard Salon, Taiwan, 1987, LA Artcore, Glendale, 1989, Korean Cultural Svcs., L.A., 1989, Onsten-Humrick House Mus., Ohio, 1990, Art LA, L.A., 1992, LaLit Kala Acad., New Dehli, 1996, David Lawrence Gallery, Beverly Hills, Calif., 1997, Alisan Fine Arts, Hong Kong, 1997, Pyong Tack (Korea) Internat. Art Festival, 1997, 98, Pao Galleries, Hong Kong, 1997, Gallery of the Rim, San Francisco, 1997, L.A. Internat. Art Festival, 1997, Merging One Gallery, Santa Monica, 1998, Gallery Blu, 1998, RTKL, Architects Gallery, L.A., 1998, represented in permanent collections Hong Kong Mus. Art, The Walker Art Collection, others. Recipient Black and White Composition award, Internat. Young Artists Competition, Gubbio, Italy, 1960, 6th Annual Juried Show, 3rd prize, N.J., 1970, 66th Nat. Orange Festival, 2nd place, San Bernardino, 1981. Mem. Am. I-Ching Soc. (pres.), Chinese Hist. Soc. So. Calif. (life).

WONG, HENRY LI-NAN, bank executive, economist; b. Rangoon, Burma, Nov. 3, 1940; s. Chew King and Jenny (Yu) W.; came to U.S., 1946. m. Laurie Yap, Apr. 11, 1968; children: Rachael S.Y., Remle S.W. BS, Waynesburg Coll., 1965; MS, U. Hawaii, 1968, PhD, 1969. Economist, Econ. Research Service U.S. Dept. Agr., Washington, 1969-70; economist Hawaii Dept. Budget and Fin., Honolulu, 1970-73; dir. Hawaii film office Hawaii Dept. Planning and Econ. Devel., Honolulu, 1973-84; exec. v.p. and chief adminstr., office of chmn. CB Bancshares Inc., Honolulu, 1984—; vice chmn., dir. Hawaii Strategic Devel. Corp., Honolulu, 1991-95; mem. coun. of revenue State of Hawaii, 1995—; v.p., bd. dirs. Friends of East West Ctr., Honolulu, 1983-84. NDEA fellow, 1965-69. Mem. Assn. Film Commrs. (pres. 1980), Am. Econ. Assn., Am. Agrl. Econs. Assn., Hawaii Internat. Film Festival, Chinese C. of C., Hawaii Soc. Corp. Planners, Lanakila Rehab. Ctr. (trustee), Alpha Kappa Psi, Theta Chi. Democrat. Presbyterian. Lodges: Elks, Masons (trustee), Shriners. Office: City Bank City Fin Tower 201 Merchant St Honolulu HI 96813-2992

WONG, JAMES BOK, economist, engineer, technologist; b. Canton, China, Dec. 9, 1922; came to U.S., 1938, naturalized, 1962; s. Gen Ham and Chen (Yee) W.; m. Wai Ping Lim, Aug. 3, 1946; children: John, Jane Doris, Julia Ann. BS in Agr., U. Md., 1949, BS in Chem. Engring., 1950; MS, U. Ill., 1951, PhD, 1954. Rsch. asst. U. Ill., Champaign-Urbana, 1950-53; chem. engr. Standard Oil of Ind., Whiting, 1953-55; process design engr., rsch. engr. Shell Devel. Co., Emeryville, Calif., 1955-61; sr. planning engr., prin. planning engr. Chem. Plastics Group, Dart Industries, Inc. (formerly Rexall Drug & Chem. Co.), L.A., 1961-66, supr. planning and econs., 1966-67, mgr. long range planning and econs., 1967, chief economist, 1967-72, dir. econs. and ops. analysis, 1972-78, dir. internat. techs., 1978-81; pres. James B. Wong Assocs., L.A., 1981—; chmn. bd. dirs. United Pacific Bank, 1988—, tech. cons. various corps. Contbr. articles to profl. jours. Bd. dirs., pres. Chinese Am. Citizens Alliance Found.; mem. Asian Am. Edn. Commn., 1971-81. Served with USAAF, 1943-46. Recipient Los Angeles Outstanding Vol. Service award, 1977. Mem. Am. Inst. Chem. Engrs., Am. Chem. Soc., VFW (vice comdr. 1959), Commodores (named to exec. order 1982), Sigma Xi, Tau Beta Pi, Phi Kappa Phi, Pi Mu Epsilon, Phi Lambda Upsilon, Phi Eta Sigma. Home: 2400 Venus Dr Los Angeles CA [illegible]

WONG, JOHN WING HING, family practice physician; b. Hong Kong, Apr. 1, 1932; came to U.S., 1963; s. Arthur P.F. and Minor S.T. W.; m. Jacoba Margaretha Johanna Bongaards-Van Deuveren, June 4, 1960; children: Kendall, Kimberley, Kevane, Carol, Kellicia, Keenan. BSc, U. Manitoba, Winnipeg, Manitoba, Can., 1957, MD, 1959; MPA, U. San Francisco, 1979. Diplomate Am. Bd. Family Practice. Chief med. officer Project Concern, Hong Kong, 1963-65; acting chief of medicine Tulare (Calif.) County Gen. Hosp., 1973-77; lectr. in clin. medicine dept. family medicine Sch. Medicine, U. Calif., Davis, 1976-78; chief of medicine, dir. emergency med. svc. and clinics Tulare County Gen. Hosp., 1977-78; med. dir. Tularz County Gen. Hosp., 1978-81, Visalia (Calif.) Med. Clinic, 1981—; pvt. practice, 1981—. Author: Centralization of Various Health Services--The Key To Cost Effectiveness in Health Administration for Tulare County, 1979, The Wong Clan-Zongshau--Onwards from the 22d Generation, 1994; (music book) Songs I Used to Sing in My Youth--for Classical Guitar, 1996; music for guitar, Consolation, Melody, The Rooster, 1996. Fellow Am. Acad. Family Practice, Am. Coll. Physician Execs; mem. Med. Coun. Hong Kong, Tulare County Med. Soc., Calif. Med. Assn. Republican. Episcopalian. Avocations: piano, classic guitar, fencing, tennis, painting. Office: Visalia Med Clinic 5400 W Hillsdale Visalia CA 93291

WONG, KENNETH LEE, software engineer, import executive, consultant; b. L.A., Aug. 15, 1947; s. George Yut and Yue Sam (Lee) W.; m. Betty (Louie) Wong, June 29, 1975; children: Bradford Keith, Karen Beth. BS in Engring., UCLA, 1969, MS in Engring., 1972, postgrad., 1972-73, 76-78. Cert. community coll. instr., Calif. Engring. aide Singer Librascope, Glendale, Calif., 1972-73; computer system design engr. Air Force Avionics Lab., Wright-Patterson AFB, Ohio, 1973-75; mem. tech. staff Hughes Aircraft Co., various cities, Calif., 1976-78, 79-81, TRW Def. and Space Systems Group, Redondo Beach, Calif., 1975-76, 78-79; engring. specialist Northrop Corp., Hawthorne, Calif., 1981-84; mem. tech. staff Jet Propulsion Lab., Pasadena, Calif., 1984-87; software cons. EG&G Spl. Projects, Las Vegas, Nev., 1987, AT&T Bell Labs., Warren, N.J., 1987-88, Westinghouse Electric Corp., Linthicom, Md., 1988, E Systems, Inc., Greenville, Tex., 1988-89; prin. Wong Soft Works, L.A., 1987—; pres. Oriental Silk Co., L.A., 1989—. Author tech. reports. 1st lt. USAF, 1973-75. Mem. AIAA, IEEE, Assn. Computing Machinery, Upsilon Pi Epsilon. Republican. Avocations: basketball, photography. Home: 3385 Mclaughlin Ave Los Angeles CA 90066-2004 Office: Oriental Silk Co 8377 Beverly Blvd Los Angeles CA 90048-2633

WONG, MICHAEL HENRY, anesthesiologist; b. L.A., Feb. 10, 1965; s. Henry and Beulah (Chan) W.; m. Evelyn Wing Han Mark, Dec. 30, 1989; children: Bryce Michael, Kira Krishne. BS in Biol. Sci., U. So. Calif., 1987; DO, Coll. Osteo. Medicine Pacific, Pomona, Calif., 1991. Intern San Bernardino County Med. Ctr., San Bernardino, Calif., 1991; resident in anesthesiology Loma Linda (Calif.) U. Med. Ctr., 1991-95; dir. anesthesiology South Coast Surgery Ctr., Santa Ana, Calif., 1995—; pres., med. dir. Anesthetix Inc., Huntington Beach, Calif., 1995—, So. Calif. Pain Control Ctr., Inc., Garden Grove, Calif., 1995—. Recipient Alumni Meml. award Coll. Osteo. Medicine of Pacific, 1989. Mem. AMA, Am. Soc. Anesthesiologists, World Tae Kwon Do Fedn. (Dan instr.), Sigma Sigma Phi. Avocations: martial arts, skiing. Office: So Calif Pain Control Ctr 7077 Orangewood Ave Ste 150 Garden Grove CA 92841-1443

WONG, NANCY L., dermatologist; b. Chung King, China, Aug. 23, 1943; came to U.S., 1947; d. YinPao Harry and Alice Wang; m. Robert Lipshutz; children: Seth, Alison, David. BS magna cum laude, Pa. State U., 1963; MS in Physics, Columbia U., 1965; MD, Jefferson Med. Coll., Phila., 1971. Diplomate Am. Bd. Dermatology. Intern Wilmington Med. Ctr., 1972; resident Jackson Meml. Hosp., Miami, Mount Sinai Med. Ctr., Miami, 1977; pvt. practice Palo Alto, Calif., 1987—. Woodrow Wilson fellow 1963-64, NSF fellow, 1963-64, AEC fellow, 1963-64. Fellow Am. Acad. Dermatology. Avocations: music, writing, painting. Office: 1101 Welch Rd Ste C6 Palo Alto CA 94304-1904

WONG, OTTO, epidemiologist; b. Canton, China, Nov. 14, 1947; came to U.S., 1967, naturalized, 1976; m. Betty Yeung, Feb. 14, 1970; children: Elaine, Jonathan. BS, U. Ariz., 1970; MS, Carnegie Mellon U., 1972; MS, U. Pitts., 1973, ScD, 1975. Cert. epidemiologist, Am. Coll. Epidemiology, 1982. USPHS fellow U. Pitts., 1972-75; asst. prof. epidemiology Georgetown U. Med. Sch., 1975-78; mgr. epidemiology Equitable Environ. Health Inc., Rockville, Md., 1977-78; dir. epidemiology Tabershaw Occupational Med. Assocs., Rockville, 1978-80; dir. occupational rsch. Biometric Rsch. Inst., Washington, 1980-81; exec. v.p., chief epidemiologist, ENSR Health Scis., Alameda, Calif., 1981-90; chief epidemiologist, pres. Applied Health Scis., San Mateo, Calif., 1991—; adj. prof. epidemiology and biostats. Tulane U. Med. Ctr., New Orleans; vis. prof. epidemiology and occupl. health Nat. Def. Med. Ctr., Taipei, Taiwan; cons. WHO, Nat. Cancer Inst., Nat. Inst. Occupl. Safety and Health, Occupl. Safety and Health Adminstrn., Nat. Heart, Lung and Blood Inst., Internat. Agy. for Rsch. on Cancer, U.S. EPA, Ford Motors Co., Gen. Electric, Mobil, Chevron, Union Carbide, Fairfax (Va.) Hosp., Agy. for Toxic Substances and Disease Registry, U. Ariz. scholar, 1967-68. Fellow Am. Coll. Epidemiology, Human Biology Council; mem. Am. Pub. Health Assn., Biometric Soc., Soc. Epidemiologic Rsch., Phi Beta Kappa, Pi Mu Epsilon. Republican. Contbr. articles to profl. jours. Office: Applied Health Scis PO Box 2078 181 2nd Ave Ste 628 San Mateo CA 94401-3812

WONG, PATRICK SECK LAI, chemical engineer; b. Canton, China, Aug. 8, 1936; came to U.S., 1957; m. Helen Wai Lun Wong, 1969; children: Julian, Francis, Alex. BSChemE, U. Mich., 1960; MS, MIT, 1962; PhD, Imperial Coll., London, 1967. Rsch. chemist W.R. Grace, Clifton, N.J., 1962-64; rsch. assoc. MIT, Cambridge, Mass., 1967-73; head transport process Alza Corp., Palo Alto, Claif., 1973-79, prin. scientist, 1981-85, dir. product rsch., 1985-87, sr. dir. rsch., 1987-91, exec. dir. R & D, 1991-94, v.p. rsch., 1994—; v.p. R & D Collins Indls. Co., Hong Kong, 1979-81, Bio-Electro System, Palo Alto, 1988-91. Contbr. articles to Jour. Polymer Sci. (London), AIChemE Jour., Ency. Pharm. Tech. Recipient Founder's award ALZA Corp., 1996. Mem. Am. Chem. Soc., Am. Assn. Pharm. Scientists, Controlled Release Soc., Tau Beta Pi, Sigma Xi. Achievements include over 150 patents for Controlled Drug Delivery, Procardia XL. Office: Alza Corp 950 Page Mill Rd Palo Alto CA 94304-1080

WONG, SAMUEL, conductor; b. Hong Kong, Apr. 12, 1962; m. Hae-Young Ham, Oct. 27, 1991. AB, Harvard U., 1984, MD, 1988. Music dir. N.Y. Youth Symphony, N.Y.C., 1988-93, Ann Arbor (Mich.) Symphony, from 1992; asst. conductor N.Y. Philharm., N.Y.C., 1990-94; music dir. Honolulu Symphony, 1996—; internat. guest conductor various orchs., in Montreal, Toronto, Vancouver, Seattle, Oreg., New Orleans, Hong Kong, Singapore, Brussels, Budapest, Israel, Mex., and New Zealand, Houston; guest conductor Japan Philharm., Tokyo, KBS Orch., Seoul. Operas conducted include The Barber of Seville, Madame Butterfly, La Bohème, Rigoletto. Office: Honolulu Symphony Orchestra Castle Cook Bldg 650 Iwilei Rd Ste 202 Honolulu HI 96817*

WONG, SUN YET, engineering consultant; b. Honolulu, Dec. 6, 1932; s. Chip Tong and Shiu Inn (Chang) W.; m. Janet Siu Hung Lau; children: Cathleen, Bryan, Jonathan. BS in Civil Engring. with honors, U. Hawaii, 1954; MS in Civil Engring., Yale U., 1955. Engr. N.Am. Aviation, Downey, Calif., 1955-58; mem. tech. staff Ramo Woolridge Space Tech. Labs., Redondo Beach, Calif., 1958-64; exec. v.p., treas., tech. dir. Mechanics Rsch. Inc., El Segundo, Calif., 1964-77; treas. System Devel. Corp., Santa Monica, Calif., 1977-79; chmn. bd., pres., treas. Applied Rsch. Inc., El Segundo, 1979-81; ind. cons. Rolling Hills Estates, Calif., 1981—; cons. Acurex, Mountain View, Calif., 1983, Ampex, Redwood City, Calif., 1991, Applied Tech., Mountain View, 1983-85, Astron, Mountain View, 1983-85, E Systems, Garland, Tex., 1986-93, Electromech. Systems Inc., Anaheim, Calif., 1984, Hughes, El Segundo, 1992, 94, 96—, Intercon, Cerritos, Calif., 1982-84, J.H. Wiggins Co., Redondo Beach, 1982-84, Kodak Datatape, Pasadena, Calif., 1989, Lion Engring., Rancho Palos Verdes, Calif., 1994—, Measurement Analysis Corp., Torrance, Calif., 1984-96, MRJ, Fairfax, Va., 1984, NASA Goddard, Greenbelt, Md., 1997, Odectics, Anaheim, 1990, Swales & Assocs., Beltsville, Md., 1992-93, Statis. Scis., Inc., Beverly Hills, Calif., 1986, Tompkins and Assocs., Torrance, 1984—, TRW, Redondo Beach, [illegible] Club View Ln Rolling Hills Estates CA [illegible]

WONG, TIMOTHY C., Chinese language and literature educator; b. Hong Kong, Jan. 24, 1941; came to U.S., 1951; s. Patrick J. and Rose (Poon) W.; m. Elizabeth Ann Steffens, Dec. 18, 1970; children: Sharon Elizabeth, Rachel Margaret, Laura Katherine. BA, St. Mary's Coll., Moraga, Calif., 1963; MA, U. Hawaii, 1968; PhD, Stanford U., 1975. Vol. U.S. Peace Corps, Thailand, 1963-65; asst. prof. Ariz. State U., Tempe, 1974-79, assoc. prof., 1979-85; resident dir. Coun. on Internat. Ednl. Exchange Peking (People's Rep. China) Univ., 1984-85; assoc. prof. Ohio State U., Columbus, 1985-95; prof. Ariz. State U., Tempe, 1995—, dir. Ctr. for Asian Studies, 1995—. Author: Wu Ching-tzu, 1978. Mem. Chinese Lang. Tchrs. Assn., Assn. Asian Studies, Am. Oriental Soc. (dir.-at-large 1996—). Democrat. Roman Catholic. Office: Ariz State U Ctr for Asian Studies 109 West Hall Tempe AZ 85287-1702

WONG, WALLACE, medical supplies company executive, real estate investor; b. Honolulu, July 13, 1941; s. Jack Yung Hung and Theresa (Goo) W.; m. Amy Ju, June 17, 1963; children: Chris, Bradley, Jeffery. Student, UCLA, 1960-63. Chmn., pres. South Bay Coll., Hawthorne, Calif., 1965-86; chmn. Santa Barbara (Calif.) Bus. Coll., 1975—; gen. ptnr. W B Co., Redondo Beach, Calif., 1982—; CEO Cal Am. Med. Supplies, Rancho Santa Margarita, Calif., 1986-96, Cal Am. Exports, Inc., Rancho Santa Margarita, 1986-96, Pacific Am. Group, Rancho Santa Margarita, 1991-96; chmn., CEO Alpine, Inc., Rancho Santa Margarita, Calif., 1993-96; pres. Bayside Properties, Rancho Santa Margarita, 1993—, San Juan Capistrano, Calif., 1993—; bd. dirs. Metrobank, L.A. FFF Enterprises; chmn. bd. 1st Ind. Fin. Group., San Juan Capistrano, 1994—; chmn. Affinity Fin. Corp., 1996—. Acting sec. of state State of Calif., Sacramento, 1982; founding mem. Opera Pacific, Orange County, Calif., 1985; mem. Hist. and Cultural Found., Orange County, 1986; v.p. Orange County Chinese Cultural Club, Orange County, 1985. Named for Spirit of Enterprise Resolution, Hist. & Cultural Found., Orange Country, 1987; recipient resolution City of Hawthorne, 1973. Mem. Westren Accred Schs. & Colls. (v.p. 1978-79), Magic Castle (life), Singapore Club. Avocations: traveling, skiing. Office: Bayside Properties 24701 La Plz Ste 201 Dana Point CA 92629-2584

WONG, WALTER FOO, county official; b. San Francisco, Apr. 11, 1930; s. Harry Yee and Grace (Won) W. AA, Hartnell Coll., 1952; BS, U. Calif., Berkeley, 1955; MPH, U. Hawaii, 1968. Registered sanitarian, Calif. Sanitarian Stanislaus County Health Dept., Modesto, Calif., 1955-56; sanitarian Monterey County Health Dept., Salinas, Calif., 1956-67, sr. sanitarian, 1968-69, supervising sanitarian, 1969-70, dir. environ. health, 1971—; sec. Monterey County Solid Waste Mgmt. Com., 1976—, Monterey County Hazardous Waste Mgmt. Com., 1987—; coord. Monterey County Genetic Engring. Rev. Com., 1987—; mem. Monterey County Genetic Engring. Experiment Permit Rev. Panel, 1995; mem. Monterey County Hazardous Materials Response Task Force, 1988—; mem. tech. adv. com. Monterey Peninsula Water Mgmt. Dist., 1985—, Monterey Regional Water Pollution Control Agy., 1985—; chmn. task force Monterey Regional Wastewater Reclamation Study for Agr., EPA and State of Calif. Chmn. Salinas Bicentennial Internat. Day Celebration, 1974, Pollution Clean-up Com. of Fort Ord Task Force, 1992; mem. Calif. Bare Closure Environ. adv. com., 1993. Recipient Community Svc. award Monterey County Med. Soc., 1998. Mem. Calif. Conf. Dirs. Environ. Health (pres. 1982-83), Assn. Environ. Health Adminstrs. (pres. 1982-83), Salinas C. of C. (Mem. of Yr. award 1971), U. Calif. Berkeley Alumni Assn., U. Hawaii Alumni Assn. (Disting. Alumni award 1992), Monterey County Hist. Soc. (pres. 1995-96), Ethnic Cultural Coun. (chmn. 1995). Republican. Presbyterian. Avocations: sports, music, outdoor recreation. Home: 234 Cherry Dr Salinas CA 93901-2807 Office: Monterey County Health Dept 1270 Natividad Rd Rm 301 Salinas CA 93906-3198

WONG, WAYNE D., nutritionist; b. San Francisco, May 13, 1950; s. Chaney Noon and La Dean Maryan (Mah) W. m. Betty Lee, Oct. 16, 1977; children: Michael Gabriel, Elizabeth Catherine, Whitney Forbes, Ellesse Florence. BS in Dietetic Adminstrn., U. Calif., Berkeley, 1972; MS in Sch. Bus. Mgmt., Pepperdine U., 1976; student, Nikon Sch. Photography, San Francisco, 1969, Canyon Hills Bible Coll., Bakersfield, Calif., 1998. Cert. Food Svc. Dir., Calif. Community Coll. tchr.; Registered Dietitian, Sch. Bus. Official, Benefit specialist. Food svc. worker, lab. asst. U. Calif., Berkeley, 1968-69, 70-71; mgmt. intern Mich. State U., East Lansing, 1970; dietetic intern Milw. Pub. Schs., 1972-73; food svc. cons. Trader Vic's, San Francisco, 1973; dir. food svcs. Bakersfield (Calif.) City Sch. Dist., 1973—; instr. Bakersfield Coll., 1978—; cons. Wong, R.D., Bakersfield, 1978—; registered Benefit Specialist Investors Retirement Mgmt., Carpenteria, Calif., 1988—; mem. nat. child nutrition adv. coun. USDA, Washington, 1977-79; 1st v.p. Ptnrs. in Nutrition Coop., Lancaster, Calif., 1988-90; food svc. edn. task force Calif. Dept. Edn., Sacramento, 1979; project coord. nutrition edn. and tng. exemplary program adoption grant Bakersfield City Sch. Dist., 1982, webmaster food svcs. website; project dir. basic skills, basic foods course, curriculum and recipe devel. grant Calif. Dept. Edn., 1985, cons. tchg. course, 1985-88; mem. adv. coun. Calif. State U. Long Beach Child Nutrition Program Mgmt. Tng. Ctr., 1991; mem. Sch. Nutrition Adv. Coun., Bakersfield, 1990—; graphics and tech. writing cons. Cal-Pro-Net Ctr., Fresno City Coll., 1995—; program panelist Ptnrs. Nutrition Coop., Am. Sch. Food Svc. Assn., Am. Nat. Conf., 1995; curriculum cons. Cal-Pro-Net Ctr., San Jose State U. Author: Food Service Equipment-How Long Should It Last?, 1985; co-author (videotape) Bettermade Plastics, 1991, Recycle: Save Earth's Resources Now; programmer Food Svc. Pers. Database, 1988, Dishmachine Labor and Energy Matrix, 1991; contbr. articles to profl. jours. BBQ fund-raiser co-chmn. Citizens for Yes on Measure B, Bakersfield, 1989; legis. com. Child Nutrition Facilities Act 1975, Sacramento, 1973-76; expert witness State Senate Select Subcom. on Nutrition and Human Needs, Sacramento, 1973; asst. troop leader Boy Scouts Am., Troop 219, San Francisco, 1965-67; participant Chinese Family Life Study U. Calif., Berkeley; dir. polystyrene recycling project Bakersfield City Sch. Dist., 1990; team leader Healthy Kids, Healthy Calif. program Calif. Dept. Edn., 1985-87; sponsor Christian Broadcasting Network Satellite Comms. Ctr., 1978; world vision sponsor India Cmty. Devel. Program, 1974-92; guitarist Canyon Hills Assembly of God Ch. Orch., 1996—; publicity coord. Bakersfield Youth Symphony. Recipient Leadership award Calif. State Dept. Edn., 1987, Outstanding Sch. Lunch Program award USDA, 1989; 1st pl. Calif. Sch. Food Svc. Assn. Country Cook-off, 1983, 84; Toto Wizard nominee Sabatasso Foods, 1985, Best Practice award USDA, 1992. Mem. Am. Dietetic Assn. (Young Dietitian of Yr. 1976), Am. Sch. Food Svc. Assn. (child nutrition mktg. bike ride 1991, Cycle Across Am. for Child Nutrition and Fitness 1993), Calif. Assn. Sch. Bus. Ofcls. (photographer 1985, food svc. R&D chmn. 1985-87, recognition 1987, food and nutrition R&D com. 1984), Calif. Sch. Food Svc. Assn. (edn. tng. chmn. 1975-76, wellness awareness bike ride 1990-91, child nutrition bike ride 1991, 1st pl. photo contest 1993, cover photographer assn. jour. Poppyseeds 1992), Sports and Cardiovasc. Nutritionists, Kern County Sch. Food Svc. Assn. (pres. 1987-90, Golden Poppy award 1990), Kern Wheelmen (v.p. 1992), Hour of Power Sparrows Club, Pi Alpha Phi, Omicron Nu. Republican. Mem. Assemblies of God Ch. Avocations: long distance bicycling, tennis, photography, classical guitar, bible study, classical guitar. Home: 4901 University Ave Bakersfield CA 93306-1773

WONG-DIAZ, FRANCISCO RAIMUNDO, lawyer, educator; b. Havana, Cuba, Oct. 29, 1944; came to U.S., Nov. 1961; s. Juan and Teresa (Diaz de Villegas) Wong; m. Elena Wong, 1997; 1 child, Richard Alan. BA with honors, No. Mich. U., 1963; MA with highest honors, U. Detroit, 1967; PhD, MA, U. Mich., 1974; JD, U. Calif.-Berkeley, 1976. Bar: Calif. 1980, U.S. Dist. Ct. (no. dist.) Calif. 1990, Fla. 1987. Adj. asst. prof. San Francisco State U., 1977; vis. scholar U. Calif. Berkeley Sch. Bus., Berkeley, 1983-84; prof. City Coll. San Francisco, 1975—, dept. chmn., 1978-85; rsch. atty. Marin Superior Ct., 1980-81; ct. arbitrator Marin Mcpl. Ct., 1985; solo practice, Kentfield, Calif., 1980—; assoc. dean Miami-Dade Coll., 1986; dir. Cutcliffe Consulting, Inc., Hawthorne, LaFamila Ctr., Inc., San Rafael, Calif., 1980-85, Small Bus. Inst., Kentfield, 1982-86; cons. ICC Internat., San Francisco, 1980-82. Bd. editors Indsl. Relations Law Jour., 1975-76; mem. editl. bd. California Lawyer, 1991-93; lector St. Sebastian's Ch., 1984—, Parish Coun., 1995. Diplomat-scholar U.S. Dept. State, Washington, 1976; Horace C. Rackham fellow U. Mich., 1970, Summer fellow U. Calif., Berkeley, 1995, Nat. Security Law Ctr. U. Va., 1996. Mem. Am. Polit. Sci. Assn., Latino Ednl. Assn. (treas. 1985), Cuban Am. Nat. Coun., World Affairs Coun. (seminar leader San Francisco 1980). Roman Catholic. Club: Commonwealth.

WOO, VERNON YING-TSAI, lawyer, real estate developer, judge; b. Honolulu, Aug. 7, 1942; s. William Shu-Bin and Hilda Woo; m. Arlene Gay Ischar, Feb. 14, 1971; children: Christopher Shu-Bin, Lia Gay. BA, U. Hawaii, 1964, MA, 1966; JD, Harvard U., 1969. Pres. Woo Kessner Duca & Maki, Honolulu, 1972-87; pvt. practice law Honolulu, 1987—; judge per diem Honolulu Dist. Family Ct., 1978-84, 95—. Bd. dirs. Boys and Girls Club of Honolulu,. 1985—, pres., 1990-92. Mem. ABA, Hawaii Bar Assn., Honolulu Bd. Realtors, Pacific Club. Home: 2070 Kalawahine Pl Honolulu HI 96822-2518 Office: 1019 Waimanu St Ste 205 Honolulu HI 96814-3409

WOOD, BENJAMIN CARROLL, JR., safety professional; b. Leonardtown, Md., June 16, 1956; s. Benjamin C. Sr. and Ethel M. (Cole) W.; m. Sheilaann P. Manibog; May 26, 1977; children: Dreamer K., Cinnamon K.; stepchildren: Reynaldo K. Yumul, Angelica K. Yumul. AGS, Chaminade U., Honolulu, 1984; BS in Fire Sci., U. Md., 1997; BA in environmental studies, U. Nev., Las Vegas. Cert. criminal justice instr., food svc./sanitation mgr., environ. health and safety law profl., Va.; notary pub., Va. Aviation ordnanceman USMC, 1974-90; non-nuclear safety officer USMC, El Toro, Calif., 1990-94; safety spec. Office of the Sheriff, Arlington, Va., 1995-98; safety coord. Monte Carlo Resort & Casino, Las Vegas, Nev., 1998—. Recipient Excellence in Pub. Svc. award, Arlington (Va.) County Govt., 1997, 98, Naval Commendation medal, Sec. Navy, Washington, 1982, Humanitarian Svc. medal CMA, Washington, 1984. Mem. Am. Soc. Safety Engrs., Soc. for Advancement of Safety and Health, Am. Jail Assn., Nat. Safety. Coun., Va. Safety Coun., Nev. Safety Coun., Am. Legion. Home: 7305 Hospitality Pl Las Vegas NV 89131-4588 Office: Monte Carlo Resort & Casino 3770 Las Vegas Blvd S Las Vegas NV 89109-4323

WOOD, CATHY LORRAINE, flight attendant; b. Lewiston, Idaho, Mar. 22, 1965; d. Gregory Elwood Collins and Lynne Adene Atteberry. AA, Kapi'olani C.C., 1998. Receptionist Latah County Prosecuting Atty., Moscow, Idaho, 1983; past-up artist, with sales dept. Am. Speedy Printing, Denver, 1984-85; receptionist Haddon Morgan & Foreman, Denver, 1985-86; internat. flight attendant Northwest Airlines, Honolulu, 1986—; assoc. editor Horizons, Honolulu, 1997-98. Contbr. articles to jours. Mem. Urasenke Found., Japan, 1995—; vol. Honolulu Acad. Art, 1998—. Kapi'olani C.C. Acad. scholar, 1995, Albert Simone Presdl. scholar U. Hawaii, 1998, Guistwhite scholar, 1998. Mem. Japan-Am. Soc., The Way of Tea Club, Regents and Presdl. Scholars, Golden Key Hon. Soc., Phi Theta Kappa. Avocations: Chanoyu Japanese tea ceremony, PADI master scuba diver, tennis. Address: PO Box 29934 Honolulu HI 96820-2334

WOOD, DAVID BRUCE, naturopathic physician; b. Fayetteville, N.C., Jan. 21, 1954; s. Marvin James and Rachel Elenor (Thom) W.; m. Wendy Ann McKiernan, Aug. 1974 (div. Aug. 1976); m. Cheryl Lynn Garbarino, Aug. 17, 1980. BS in Microbiology, U. Wash., 1977; D in Naturopathic Medicine, Bastyr U., Seattle, 1983. Pres., co-founder Trinity Family Health Clinic, Inc., P.S., Lynnwood, Wash., 1984—; Spkr. local and nat. TV programs. Singer Sound of Praise Choir, Overlake Christian Ch., Kirkland, Wash., 1987-92; narrator Easter Pagent, 1989; mem. Cedar Park Assembly of God, Bothel, Wash. Mem. Am. Assn. Nutritional Cons., Nat. Health Fedn., Am. Assn. Naturopathic Physicians, Wash. Assn. Naturopathic Physicians (trustee, exec. bd. 1989-92). Avocations: singing, snow skiing, snorkeling, bicycling, travel. Home: 13721 Cascadian Way Everett WA 98208-7345

WOOD, DAVID GLENN, lobbyist; b. Tacoma, Wash., Feb. 1, 1930; s. Harvey Glenn and Ellen Mae (Davis) W.; m. Joyce Elaine Hunter; children: Marcie Newton, Linda Wood, Janet Dukich, Glenda Wood, Kyle Wood, Kaysie Noll. BA in journalism, U. Wash., 1952. Pub. rels. rep. Bethlehem Steel Corp., Seattle, San Francisco, 1952-64; dir. devel. U. Wash., Seattle, 1964-68; polit. campaign mgmt. Seattle, 1969; instr. Sch. Comm. U. Wash., 1969-72; spl. asst. to Mayor City of Seattle, 1969-74; asst. dir. fed. affairs United Airlines, Wash., 1974-76; fundraising and pub. rels. cons. Seattle, 1977-85; lobbyist Olympia, Wash., 1986—; Dem. nominee for Congress, 1st dist. Wash., 1976; press sec., media advisor at various times to Gov. Albert D. Rosellini, Congressman (later Sen.) Brock Adams, Mayor Wes Uhlman, others. Pres. Seattle Urban League, 1972-73, People for Fair Taxes, 1983, 89; chmn. bd. dirs. Wash. State Protection & Advocacy Sys. for the Mentally Retarded and Mentally Ill, 1985-88. Life mem. Soc. Profl. Journalists, U. Wash. Alumni Assn.; mem. Mason County Econ. Devel. Coun. Home: 623 S 13th St Shelton WA 98584-2625 Office: People for Fair Taxes 1063 Capitol Way S Olympia WA 98501-1263

WOOD, FERGUS JAMES, geophysicist, consultant; b. London, Ont., Can., May 13, 1917; came to U.S., 1924, naturalized, 1932; s. Louis Aubrey and Dora Isabel (Elson) W.; student U. Oreg., 1934-36; AB, U. Calif., Berkeley, 1938, postgrad., 1938-39; postgrad. U. Chgo., 1939-40, U. Mich., 1940-42, Calif. Inst. Tech., 1946; m. Doris M. Hack, Sept. 14, 1946; children: Kathryn Celeste Wood Madden, Bonnie Patricia Wood Ward. Teaching asst. U. Mich., 1940-42; instr. in physics and astronomy Pasadena City Coll., 1946-48, John Muir Coll., 1948-49; asst. prof. physics U. Md., 1949-50; assoc. physicist Johns Hopkins U. Applied Physics Lab., 1950-55; sci. editor Ency. Americana, N.Y.C., 1955-60; aero. and space rsch. scientist, sci. asst. to dir. Office Space Flight Programs, Hdqrs., NASA, Washington, 1960-61; program dir. fgn. sci. info. NSF, Washington, 1961-62; phys. scientist, chief sci. and tech. info. staff U.S. Coast and Geodetic Survey, Rockville, Md., 1962-66, phys. scientist Office of Dir., 1967-73, rsch. assoc. Office of Dir., 1973-77, Nat. Ocean Svc.; cons. tidal dynamics, Bonita, Calif., 1978—; mem. Am. Geophys. Union, ICSU-UNESCO Internat. Geol. Correlation Project 274, Working Group #1-Crescendo Events in Coastal Environments, Past and Future (The Millennium Project), 1988—. Capt. USAAF, 1942-46. Recipient Spl. Achievement award Dept. Commerce, NOAA, 1970, 74, 76, 77. Mem. Sigma Pi Sigma, Pi Mu Epsilon, Delta Phi Alpha. Democrat. Presbyterian. Author: The Strategic Role of Perigean Spring Tides in Nautical History and North American Coastal Flooding, 1635-1976, 1978; Tidal Dynamics: Coastal Flooding, and Cycles of Gravitational Force, 1986, Synergetic Gravitational Forces in Tides and the Solar System, 2 vols., 1997; contbr. numerous articles to encys., reference sources, profl. jours.; writer, tech. dir. documentary film: Pathfinders from the Stars, 1967; editor-in-chief: The Prince William Sound, Alaska, Earthquake of 1964 and Aftershocks, vols. 1-2A and sci. coordinator vols. 2B, 2C and 3, 1966-69. Home: 3103 Casa Bonita Dr Bonita CA 91902-1735

WOOD, GINA ELEANE, state agency program administrator; b. Springfield, Mo., Aug. 29, 1959; d. George Henry and Emma (Cook) W. BA in Comm., U. Mo., 1983. With pub. rels. and sales Portland (Oreg.) Observer Newspaper, 1983-85; legis. asst. State Rep. Margaret Carter, Salem, Oreg., 1985-86; exec. dir. Highland Cmty. Svcs./Yaun Youth Care Ctr., Portland, 1986; legis./ops. mgr. Adult and Family Svcs., Salem, 1987-88; mem. gov. staff Gov. Neil Goldschmidt, Salem, 1988-89; regional coord. Child & Youth Commn., Salem, 1989-94; fed. program dir. Commn. Child and Families, Salem, 1994—; cons. Cmty. Rsch. Assocs., Champaign, Ill., 1993—. Precinct com. person Washington County, Portland, Oreg., 1992—; active Oreg. Women's Polit. Caucus, Portland, 1985—, Gov. Task Force on Family Law, Salem, 1993—. Mem. Am. Corrections Assn., Nat. Assn. Blacks in Criminal Justice, Pvt. Industry Coun. (past chair youth com.), Urban League Portland (past chairperson). Democrat. Avocations: reading, theatre, travelling, cooking, jazz music.

WOOD, GLADYS BLANCHE, retired secondary education educator, journalist; b. Sanborn, N.D., Aug. 12, 1921; d. Charles Kershaw and Mina Blanche (Kee) Crowther; m. Newell Edwin Wood, June 13, 1943 (dec. 1990); children: Terry N., Lani, Brian R., Kevin C.; m. F.L. Stutzman, Nov. 30, 1991. BA in Journalism, U. Minn., 1943; MA in Mass Comm., San Jose State U., 1972. Cert. secondary tchr., Calif. Reporter St. Paul Pioneer-Dispatch, 1943-45; editor J.C. Penney Co., N.Y.C., 1945-46; tchr. English and journalism Willow Glen H.S., San Jose, Calif., 1968-87; freelance writer, photographer, 1947—; cons. in field. Named Secondary Journalism Tchr. of Yr. Calif. Newpaper Pubs. Assn., 1977. Mem. AAUW, Soc. Profl. Journalists, Journalism Edn. Assn., Calif. Ret. Tchrs. Assn., Women in Comm., Santa Clara County Med. Assn. Aux., Friends of Libr., Delta Kappa Gamma, Alpha Omicron Pi. Republican. Methodist. Avocations: music, journalism, photography, travel. Home: 14161 Douglass Ln Saratoga CA 95070-5535

WOOD, HAROLD WILLIAM, lawyer; b. Whittier, Calif., Nov. 21, 1950; s. Harold William and Eva Imes W.; m. Jane Stunt, Dec. 29, 1979. BS in Natural Resources, U. Calif., Davis, 1973; MS in Forest Resources, U. Wash., 1976; JD, Seattle U., 1980. Bar: Calif. 1985. Atty. Tulare County Counsel, Visalia, Calif., 1985—. Editor: (website) John Muir Exhibit, 1994. Mem. Calif. Bar Assn., Sierra Club (chair environ. edn. 1997—), Universal Pantheist Soc. (editor 1973—). Democrat. Avocations: swimming, weightlifting, computers, reading, hiking. Office: Universal Pantheist Soc PO Box 265 Big Pine CA 93513

WOOD, JAMES MICHAEL, lawyer; b. Oakland, Calif., Mar. 22, 1948; s. Donald James and Helen Winifred (Reiman) W.; div.; children: Nathan, Sarah, Ruth. BA, St. Mary's Coll., 1970; JD, U. San Francisco, 1973. Bar: Calif. 1973, U.S. Dist. Ct. (no., cen. and so. dists.) Calif. 1973. Rsch. atty. Alameda County Superior Ct., Oakland, 1973-76; ptnr. Crosby, Heafey, Roach & May, Oakland, 1976—; mem. adv. com. Food Drug Law Inst., 1999—; presenter profl. confs. Contbr. articles to profl. jours. Chair alumni-faculty devel. fund St. Mary's Coll. Alumni Bd. Dirs., 1990-94. Mem. ABA (litigation sect., health law litigation com., litigation products liability com.), ATLA (assoc.), State Bar Calif., Calif. Trial Lawyers Assn. (assoc.), No. Calif. Assn. Def. Counsel, Alameda County Bar Assn., Def. Rsch. and Trial Lawyers Assn., Am. Acad. Hosp. Attys., Am. Soc. Pharmacy Law, Nat. Health Lawyers Assn., Drug Info. Assn. Office: Crosby Heafey Roach & May 1999 Harrison St Ste 2100 Oakland CA 94612-3572

WOOD, JEANNINE KAY, state official; b. Dalton, Nebr., Apr. 22, 1944; d. Grover L. and Elsie M. (Winkelman) Sanders; m. Charles S. Wood, Dec. 7, 1968; children: Craig C., Wendi L. Wood Armstrong. Exec. sec. Idaho Hosp. Assn., Boise, 1966-71; com. sec. Idaho State Senate, Boise, 1976-81, jour. clk., 1981-85, asst. to sec. of senate, 1985-91, sec. of senate, 1991—; pvt. practice typing svc. Boise, 1979-86. Mem. Am. Soc. Legis. Clks. and Secs. Methodist. Home: 3505 S Linder Rd Meridian ID 83642-6837 Office: Idaho State Capitol PO Box 83720 Boise ID 83720-3720

WOOD, JOHN MORTIMER, retired aerospace executive, aeronautical engineer; b. New Orleans, July 7, 1934; s. John Mortimer Sr. and Annie Jeff (Gates) W.; m. Bonnie Ann Blanchette, June 6, 1958 (div. Oct. 1977); m. Barbara Lee Butler, Aug. 12, 1978; 1 child, Mark Douglas. BA in Aero. Engring., U. Tex., 1957. Project engr. Gen. Dynamics/Convair, San Diego, 1957-58, Rocket Power, Inc., Mesa, Ariz., 1961-64; sales mgr. S.E. region Rocket Power, Inc., Huntsville, Ala., 1964-67; dir. mktg. Quantic Industries, San Carlos, Calif., 1967-70; sr. mktg. mgr. Talley Industries of Ariz., Mesa, 1970-77; dir. mktg. Universal Propulsion Co., Inc., Phoenix, 1977-85, v.p. mktg., 1985-91, v.p. contract mgmt., 1992-94, v.p. mktg., 1994-96, ret., 1997. 1st lt. USAF, 1958-61. Mem. Am. Def. Preparedness Assn., Assn. for Unmanned Vehicle Sytsems, Tech. Mktg. Soc. of Am., Survival and Flight Equipment Assn. Republican. Home: 111 W Canterbury Ln Phoenix AZ 85023-6252

WOOD, LARRY (MARY LAIRD), journalist, author, university educator, public relations executive, environmental consultant; b. Sandpoint, Idaho; d. Edward Hayes and Alice (McNeel) Small; children: Mary, Marcia, Barry. BA summa cum laude, U. Wash., 1939, MA summa cum laude, with highest honors, 1940; postgrad., Stanford U., 1940-43, U. Calif., Berkeley, 1946-47; cert. in photography, U. Calif., Berkeley, 1971; postgrad. journalism, U. Wis., 1971-72, U. Minn., 1971-72, U. Ga., 1972-73; postgrad. in art, architecture and marine biology, U. Calif., Santa Cruz, 1974-76, Stanford Hopkins Marine Sta., Santa Cruz, 1977-80. Lifetime secondary and jr. coll. teaching cert., Wash., Calif. Feature writer and columnist Oakland Tribune and San Francisco Chronicle, Calif., 1939—; archtl. and environ. feature and travel writer and columnist San Jose (Calif.) Mercury News (Knight Ridder), 1972-90; teaching fellow Stanford U., 1940-43; dir. pub. rels. 2-counties, 53-parks East Bay Regional Park Dist., No. Calif., 1948-68; pres. Larry Wood Pub. Rels., 1946—; pub. rels. dir. Calif. Children's Home Soc., 1947-58; prof. (tenure) pub. rels., mag. writing, journalism, investigative reporting San Diego State U., 1974, 75; disting. vis. prof. journalism San Jose State U., 1976; assoc. prof. journalism Calif. State U., Hayward, 1978; prof. sci. and environ. journalism U. Calif. Berkeley Ext. grad. divsn., 1979—; press del. nat. convs. Am. Geophys. Union Internat. Conf., 1986—, AAAS, 1989—, Nat. Park Svc. VIP Press Tour, Yellowstone after the fire, 1989—, Nat. Assn. Sci. Writers, 1989—, George Washington U./Am. Assn. Neurol. Surgeons Sci. Writers Conf., 1990, Am. Inst. Biol. Scis. Conf., 1990, Nat. Conf. Sci. Writers, Am. Heart Assn., 1995, Internat. Cardiologists Symposium for Med./Sci. Writers, 1995, Annenberg Program Electronic Media Symposium, Washington, 1995; EPA del. to USSR and Ea. Europe; expert witness on edn., pub. rels., journalism and copyright; cons. sci. writers interne project Stanford U., 1989—; spl. media guest Sigma Xi, 1990—; mem. numerous spl. press corps; selected White House Spl. Media, 1993—; selected mem. Duke U. 14th Ann. Sci. Reporters Conf., 1995; internat. press guest Can. Consulate Gen. Dateline Can., 1995—, French Govt. Tourist Office, 1996—, Ministerio delle Risorse Agricole Alimentari e Forestali and Assocs. Conf., 1995; appeared in TV documentary Larry Wood Covers Visit of Queen Elizabeth II. Contbr. over 5,000 articles on various topics for newspapers, nat. mags., nat. and internat. newspaper syndicates including L.A. Times-Mirror Syndicate, Knight-Ridder Syndicate, Washington Post, Phila. Inquirer, Chgo. Tribune, Miami Herald, Oakland Tribune, Seattle Times, San Francisco Chronicle, Parade, San Jose Mercury News (Nat. Headliner award), Christian Sci. Monitor, L.A. Times/Christian Sci. Monitor Worldwide News Syndicate, Washington Post, Phila. Inquirer, Hawaiian Airlines In Paradise and other in-flight mags., MonitoRadio, Donnelly Pubs., Sports Illus., Life, Mechanix Illus., Popular Mechanics, Parents (contbg. editor), House Beautiful, Am. Home (awards 1988, 89), Archl. Digest, Better Homes and Gardens, Sunset, Architectural Digest, National Geographic World, Travel & Leisure, Chevron USA/Odyssey (Calif. Pub.'s award 1984), Xerox Edn. Publs., Europe's Linguapress, PSA Mag., Off Duty, Oceans, Sea Frontiers, AAA Westways, AAA Motorland, Travelin', others. Significant works include home and garden columnist and editor, 5-part series Pacific Coast Ports, 5-part series Railroads of the West, series Immigration, Youth Gangs, Endangered Species, Calif. Lighthouse Chain, Lighthouses of the World, Pacific Coast Wetlands, Elkhorn Slough Nat. Estuarine Res., Ebey's Landing Nat. Hist. Island Res., Calif. Water Wars, BLM's Adopt a Horse Program, Mt. St. Helen's Eruption, Oreg's Covered Bridges, Loma Prieta Earthquake, Oakland Firestorm, Missing Children, Calif. Prison Reform, Columbia-Alaska's Receding Glacier, Calif. Underwater Parks, and many others; author: Wonderful U.S.A.: A State-by-State Guide to Its Natural Resources, 1989; co-author over 21 books including: McGraw-Hill English for Social Living, 1944, Fawcett Boating Books, 1956-66, Fodor's San Francisco, Fodor's California, 1982-89, Bell and Howell/Charles Merrill Focus on Life Science, Focus on Physical Science, Focus on Earth Science, 1983, 87, State of California's Golden State Travel Guide, 1998; contbr. Earth Science 1987; 8 works selected for use by Europe's Woltors-Nordoff-Longman English Language Texts, U.K., Netherlands, 1988; author: (with others) anthology West Winds, 1989; reviewer Charles Merrill texts, 1983-84; book reviewer Profl. Communicator, 1987—; selected writings in permanent collections Oakland Pub. Libr., U. Wash. Main Libr.; environ. works included in Dept. Edn. State of Md. textbook; contbr., author Journalism Quar.; author script PBS/AAA America series, 1992; contbg. editor: Parents, Fashion Showcase, Spokane Mag. Nat. chmn. travel writing contest for U.S. univ. journalism students Assn. for Edn. in Journalism/Soc. Am. Travel Writers, 1979-83; judge writing contest for Nat. Assn. Real Estate Editors, 1982—; press del. 1st Internat. Symposium Volcanism and Aviation Safety, 1991, Coun. for Advancement of Sci. Writing, 1977—, Rockefeller Media Seminar Feeding the World-Protecting the Earth, 1992, Global Conf. on Mercury as Pollutant, 1992, Earth Summit Global Forum, Rio de Janeiro, 1992; invited Nat. Park Svc. Nat. Conf. Sci. Writers, 1985, Postmaster Gen.'s 1992 Stamps, 1991, Internat. Geophys. Union Conf., 1982—, The Conf. Bd., 1995—, Corp. Comm. Conf., Calif. Inst. Tech.'s Media and Sci. Seminar, 1995—, Medical Writers Delegation to Russia and Estonia, 1997, N.Y. Times Opinion Rsch. Co. Corp. Image Conf., 1999, EPA and Dept. Energy Tech. Conf., 1992, Am. Soc. Photogrammetry and Remote Sensing Internat. Conv. Mapping Global Change, 1992, U.S. Conf. on Oceans, 1998, N.Y. Mus. Modern Art Matisse Retrospective Press Rev. and all media previews, 1992—, celebration 150th anniversary Oreg. Trail, 1993, Coun. Advancement Sci. Writing, 1993-96, Sigma Xi Nat. Conf., 1988-98, Nat. Sci. Writers Confs., 1996, PRSA Travel and Tourism Conf., 1993—, Internat. Conf. Environment, 1994, 95, Quality

Life Europe, Prague, 1994, Calif. Sesquicentennial, 1996, 14th Ann. Sci. Writers Conf., 1996, Picasso Retrospective, 1996, many others; mem. Gov.'s Conf. Tourism N.C., 1993-98, Calif., 1976—, Fla., 1987—; press guest 14 U.S. states and 12 fgn. countries' Depts. Tourism, 1986—. Recipient numerous awards, honors, citations, speaking engagements, including induction into Broadway Hall of Fame, U. Wash., 1984, Broadway Disting. Alumnus award, 1995; citations for environ. writing Nat. Park Svc., U.S. Forest Svc., Bur. Land Mgmt., Oakland Mus. Assn., Oakland C. of C., Chevron USA, USN plaque and citation, best mag. articles citation Calif. Pubs. Assn., 1984, U.S. Treasury award, 1946; co-recipient award for best Sunday newspaper mag. Nat. Headliners, citation for archtl. features Oakland Mus., 1983; honoree for achievements in journalism Nat. Mortar Bd., 1988, 89; selected as one of 10 V.I.P. press for Yellowstone Nat. Park field trip on "Let Burn" rsch., 1989; named one of Calif.'s top 40 contemporary authors for writings on Calif. underwater parks, 1989, nat. honoree Social Issues Resources Series, 1987, Gov.'s Calif. Women of Achievement award, 1988, 89, 90; invited V.I.P. press, spl. press guest numerous events worldwide. Mem. Am. Bd. Forensic Examiners, Calif. Acad. Scis., San Francisco Press Club, Nat. Press Club, Pub. Rels. Soc. Am. (charter mem. travel, tourism, environment and edn. divs.), Nat. Sch. Pub. Rels. Assn., Environ. Cons. N.Am., Am. Assn. Edn. in Journalism and Comm. (exec. bd. nat. mag. div. 1978, panel chmn. 1979, 80, author Journalism Quar. jour.), Women in Comm. (nat. bd. officer 1975-77, book reviewer Prof. Communicator), Soc. Profl. Journalists (nat. bd. for hist. sites 1980—), Nat. Press Photographers Assn. (hon. life, cons. Bay Area interne project 1989—, honoree 1995), Investigative Reporters and Editors (charter), Bay Area Advt. and Mktg. Assn., Nat. Assn. Sci. Writers, Calif. Writers Club (state bd., Berkeley bd. 1989—, honoree ann. conv. Asilomar, Calif. 1990), Am. Assn. Med. Writers, Internat. Assn. Bus. Communicators, Soc. Environ. Journalists (charter), Am. Film Inst., Am. Heritage Found. (citation 1986, 87, 88), Soc. Am. Travel Writers, Internat. Oceanographic Found., Oceanic Soc., Calif. Acad. Environ. News Writers, Seattle Advt. and Sales Club (former officer), Nature Conservancy, Smithsonian Audubon Soc., Nat. Wildlife Fedn., Nat. Parks and Conservation Assn., Calif. State Parks Found., Calif. Environ. Leadership Roundtable (trustee), Fine Arts Mus., San Francisco, Seattle Jr. Advt. Club (charter), U. Wash. Comm. Alumni (Sch. Comm. alumni, life, charter mem. ocean scis. alumni, Disting. Alumni 1987), U. Calif., Berkeley Alumni (life, v.p., scholarship chmn. 1975-81), Stanford Alumni (life), Mortar Board Alumnae Assn. (life, honoree 1988, 89), Am. Mgmt. Assn., Nat. Soc. Environ. Journalists (charter), Calif. Environ. Leadership Roundtable, Phi Beta Kappa (v.p., bd. dirs. Calif. Alumni Assn., statewide chmn. scholarship awards 1975-81), Purple and Gold Soc. (planning com., charter, 1995—), Pi Lambda Theta, Theta Sigma Phi. Home: Piedmont Pines 6161 Castle Dr Oakland CA 94611-2737

WOOD, LINCOLN JACKSON, aerospace engineer; b. Lyons, N.Y., Sept. 30, 1947; s. William Hulbert and Sarah Brock (Strumsky) W. BS with distinction, Cornell U., 1968; MS in Aeronautics and Astronautics, Stanford U., 1969, PhD, 1972. Staff engr. Hughes Aircraft Co., El Segundo, Calif., 1974-77; mem. tech. staff Jet Propulsion Lab. Calif. Inst. Tech., Pasadena, 1977-81, tech. group supr. Jet Propulsion Lab., 1981-89, tech. mgr., 1989-91, dep. tech. section mgr., 1991—; Bechtel instr. engring. Calif. Inst. Tech., Pasadena, 1972-74, lectr. in systems engring., 1975-76, vis. asst. prof., 1976-78, vis. assoc. prof., 1978-84; cons. in field. Contbr. articles on space navigation and optimal control theory to profl. jours. Bd. dirs. Boys Republic, Chino Hills, Calif., 1991, 97—. Assoc. fellow AIAA (tech. com. on astrodynamics 1985-86, chmn. 1986-88, assoc. editor Jour. Guidance, Control and Dynamics 1983-89); sr. mem. Am. Astro. Soc. (space flight mechanics com. 1980-97, chmn. 1993-95, assoc. editor Jour. of Astro. Scis. 1980-83, gen. chmn. AAS/AIAA Space Flight Mechanics Meeting, 1993), IEEE (sr. mem.), AAAS, Los Solteros (pres. 1991, 97—), Sigma Xi. Office: Jet Propulsion Lab 4800 Oak Grove Drive Mail Stop 301-125L Pasadena CA 91109

WOOD, LINDA MAY, librarian; b. Fort Dodge, Iowa, Nov. 6, 1942; d. John Albert and Beth Ida (Riggs) Wiley; m. C. James Wood, Sept. 15, 1964 (div. Oct. 1984). BA, Portland State U., 1964; M in Librarianship, U. Wash., 1965. Reference libr. Multnomah County Libr., Portland, Oreg., 1965-67, br. libr., 1967-72, adminstrv. asst. to libr., 1972-73, asst. libr., asst. dir., 1973-77; asst. city libr. L.A. Pub. Libr., 1977-80; libr. dir. Riverside (Calif.) City and County Pub. Libr., 1980-91; county libr. Alameda County Libr., Fremont, Calif., 1991—; adminstrv. coun. mem. Bay Area Libr. and Info. Svcs., Oakland, Calif., 1991—. Chair combined charities campaign County of Alameda, Oakland, 1992; bd. dirs. Inland AIDS Project, Riverside, Calif., 1990-91; vol. United Way of Inland Valleys, Riverside, 1986-87, Bicentennial Competition on the Constitution, 36th Congl. Dist., Colton, Calif., 1988-90. Mem. ALA (CLA chpt. councilor 1992-95), Calif. Libr. Assn. (pres. 1985, exec. com., ALA chpt. councilor 1992-95), Calif. County Librs. Assn. (pres. 1984), League of Calif. Cities (cmty. svcs. policy com. 1985-90), OCLC Users Coun. (Pacific Network del. 1986-89). Democrat. Avocations: folk dancing, opera, reading. Office: Alameda County Libr 2450 Stevenson Blvd Fremont CA 94538-2326

WOOD, MARCUS ANDREW, lawyer; b. Mobile, Ala., Jan. 18, 1947; s. George Franklin and Helen Eugenia (Fletcher) W.; m. Sandra Lee Pellonari, July 25, 1971; children: Edward Alan, Melinda Janel. BA cum laude, Vanderbilt U., 1969; JD, Yale U., 1974. Bar: Oreg. 1974, U.S. Dist. Ct. Oreg. 1974, U.S. Ct. Appeals (9th cir.) 1982. Assoc., then ptnr. Rives, Bonihadi & Smith, Portland, Oreg., 1974-78; ptnr. Stoel Rives LLP and predecessor firms, Portland, 1974—. Pres., bd. dirs. Indochinese Refugee Ctr., Portland, 1980, Pacific Ballet Theatre, Portland, 1986-87; bd. dirs. Outside In, Portland, 1989—. Lt. USNR, 1969-71. Mem. ABA, Phi Beta Kappa. Home: 9300 NW Finzer Ct Portland OR 97229-8035 Office: Stoel Rives 900 SW 5th Ave Ste 2300 Portland OR 97204-1235

WOOD, NATHANIEL FAY, editor, writer, public relations consultant; b. Worcester, Mass., June 23, 1919; s. Henry Fletcher and Edith (Fay) W.; m. Eleanor Norton, Dec. 19, 1945; children: Gary Nathaniel, Janet Ann. BS in Journalism, Bus. Adminstrn., Syracuse U., 1946. Editor, writer various publs., various cities, 1946-51; mng. editor Butane-Propane News, L.A., 1951-52; editor Western Metalworking Mag., L.A., 1952-62; western editorial mgr. Penton Pub. Co. Cleve., L.A., 1962-70; editor Orange County Illustrated, Orange County Bus., Newport Beach, Calif., 1970-71; western editor Hitchcock Pub., L.A., 1972-75; co-owner, mgr. Norton-Wood Pub. Rels. Svcs., Pasadena, Calif., 1975—; editorial dir. Security World, SDM and SCA Mags., Culver City, Calif., 1975-80; mgr. trade show Cahners Pub. and Expo Group, L.A., 1979-82; sr. editor Alarm Installer Dealer Mag., L.A., 1982-89; editor CNC West Mag., Westminster and Pasadena, Calif., 1982-98, sr. cons. editor, 1998—. Freelance indsl. writer miscellaneous bus. pubs. Organizer Willkie Presdl. Campaign, Syracuse, N.Y., 1940; advisor various GOP campaigns, L.A., Washington, 1940-96; charter mem. Rep. Nat. Com., 1995, del.-at-large GOP conv., 1996, mem. Pres.' Club, 1996, 97, 98, conv. guest, 1996; nat. adv. bd. Am. Security Coun.; donor L.A. Civic Light Opera and Ctr. Theatre Group; mem., donor L.A. Mus. Art, 1989—, Pasadena Playhouse; founding mem. Western Heritage Mus., L.A., 1989—; active Met. Opera Guild, Colonial Williamsburg Found., Mus. Natural History L.A. 2nd lt. U.S. Army, 1943-45, PTO. Decorated Purple Heart; recipient Silver, Bronze and Gold medals for Editorial Excellence Gov. of Calif., 1959, 60, 62. Mem. VFW, Am. Legion, Am. Film Inst., Scabbard and Blade, L.A. World Affairs Coun., Smithsonian Instn., The Nat. Air and Space Soc., Soc. Profl. Journalists, Alpha Epsilon Rho, Tau Theta Upsilon. Avocations: swimming, boating, travel, photography, gardening. Home and Office: 7116 Cross Creek Cir Apt B Dublin CA 94568

WOOD, PRUDY TALLMAN, writer; b. Orange, N.J.; d. Frank Gifford and Inez Evelyn (Foster) Tallman; (div.); children: Anne Slattery Howard, Duard Geis Slattery, Robin Tallman Babcock, Jody Tallman Racanelli. Student, Conn. Coll., 1948, U. Calif. San Diego, 1968-91. Freelance writer Calif. Press Women, 1983—. Contbr. articles to mags. Mem. Calif. Press Women (first place for feature article 1997, second place for feature article 1997), San Diego Writers/Editors Guild (first place for travel 1982), La Jolla Shores Assn. (bd. mem., ocean pollution monitor), League of Conservation Voters, Nat. Resources Def. Coun., Amnesty Internat., Common Cause, Humane Soc. U.S., Fund for Animals, World Soc. for the Protection Animals, People for the Ethical Treatment Animals, Performing Animals Welfare Soc., Last Chance for Animals. Avocations: aquariums, swimming, rock collecting, photography. Home and Office: 8368 Paseo Del Ocaso La Jolla CA 92037-3021

WOOD, ROBERT CLARK, neurosurgeon; b. Valley City, N.D., Mar. 24, 1936; s. Chester W. and Mary G. (McMillan) W.; m. Barbara Johnson, Dec. 20, 1961 (div. June 1972); children: Paul, Dan; m. Linda S. Osterholm, Dec. 29, 1980. BS, U. Minn., Duluth, 1958; MD, U. Minn., 1962. Diplomate Am. Bd. Neurosurgery. Resident in neurosurgery Mayo Med. Sch., Rochester, Minn., 1965-70; chmn. dept. neurosurgery Billings (Mont.) Clinic, 1971—. Capt. USAF Med. Corps, 1963-65. Mem. Yellowstone County Med. Soc. (pres. 1995), Alpha Omega Alpha. Avocations: hunting, fishing. Office: Billings Clinic Billings MT 59102

WOOD, ROBERT WARREN, lawyer; b. Des Moines, July 5, 1955; s. Merle Warren and Cecily Ann (Sherk) W.; m. Beatrice Wood, Aug. 4, 1979; 1 child, Bryce Mercedes. Student, U. Sheffield, Eng., 1975-76; AB, Humboldt State U., 1976; JD, U. Chgo., 1979. Bar: Ariz. 1979, Calif. 1980, U.S. Tax Ct. 1980, N.Y. 1989, D.C. 1993, Mont. 1998; Roll of Solicitors of Eng. and Wales, 1998. Assoc. Jennings, Strouss, Phoenix, 1979-80, McCutchen, Doyle, San Francisco, 1980-82, Broad, Khourie, San Francisco, 1982-85; assoc. Steefel, Levitt & Weiss, San Francisco, 1985-87, ptnr., 1987-91; ptnr. Bancroft & McAlister, San Francisco, 1991-93; prin. Robert W. Wood, P.C., San Francisco, 1993—; instr. in law U. Calif. San Francisco, 1981-82. Author: Taxation of Corporate Liquidations: A Complete Planning Guide, 1987, 2nd edit., 1994, The Executive's Complete Guide to Business Taxes, 1989, Corporate Taxation: Complete Planning and Practice Guide, 1989, S Corporations, 1990, The Ultimate Tax Planning Guide for Growing Companies, 1991, Taxation of Damage Awards and Settlement Payments, 1st edit., 1991, 2nd edit., 1998, Tax Strategies in Hiring, Retaining and Terminating Employees, 1991, The Home Office Tax Guide, 1991; co-author: (with others) California Closely Held Corporations: Tax Planning and Practice Guide, 1987, Legal Guide to Independent Contractor Status, 2nd edit., 1996; editor: California Small Busines Guide, 4 vols., 1998, Home Office Money & Tax Guide, 1992, Tax Aspects of Settlements and Judgements, 1993, 2d edit., 1998; editor-in-chief The M & A Tax Report; editor: Limited Liability Companies: Formation, Operation and Conversion, 1994, Limited Liability Partnerships: Formation, Operation and Taxation, 1996; mem. editl. bd. Real Estate Tax Digest, The Practical Accountant, Jour. Real Estate Taxation. Fellow Am. Coll. Tax Counsel; mem. Calif. Bd. Legal Specialization (cert. specialist taxation), Candian Bar Assn., Bohemian Club. Republican. Office: 477 Pacific Ave #300 San Francisco CA 94133

WOOD, STUART KEE, retired engineering manager; b. Dallas, Mar. 8, 1925; s. William Henry and Harriet (Kee) Wood; m. Loris V. Poock, May 17, 1951 (dec. June 1990); children: Linda S. Kuehl, Thomas N., Richard D.; m. Lois H. Morton, Nov. 25, 1994. BS in Aero. Engring., Tex. A&M U., 1949. Aircraft sheet metal worker USAF SAC, Kelly Field, San Antonio, Tex., 1942-45; structural design engr. B-52, 367-80, KC-135, 707 Airplanes Boeing, Seattle and Renton, Wash., 1949-55; thrust reverser design engr. 707 and 747 Airplanes Boeing, Renton, 1955-66; supr. thrust reverser group 747 Airplane Boeing, Everett, Wash., 1966-69; supr. rsch. basic engine noise 727 airplane FAA, NASA, 1969-74; supr. jetfoil propulsion Jetfoil Hydrofoil Boeing, Renton, 1974-75; supr. rsch. basic engine performance loss JT9D Pratt & Whitney, 1975-79; supr. propulsion systems 757 Airplane Boeing, Renton, 1979-90; supr., propulsion systems thrust reverser 737, 747, 757, 767 Boeing, Kent, Wash., 1990-94, ret., 1994. Patentee in field. Recipient Ed Wells award AIAA, N.W. chpt., Bellevue, Wash., 1992. Republican. Presbyterian. Avocations: photography, computers, travel. Home: 3831 46th Ave SW Seattle WA 98116-3723

WOOD, WILLIAM RANSOM, retired university president, city official, corporate executive; b. nr. Jacksonville, Ill., Feb. 3, 1907; s. William James and Elizabeth (Ransom) W.; m. Margaret Osborne, 1930 (dec. 1942); 1 son, William Osborne (dec. 1978); m. Dorothy Jane Irving, Mar. 18, 1944; children: Mark Irving, Karen Jane Parrish. A.B., Ill. Coll., 1927, LL.D., 1960; M.A., U. Iowa, 1936, Ph.D., 1939; LLD, U. Alaska, 1989. Tchr., coach pubs. schs. Mich., Iowa, Ill., 1928-46; asst. Supt. Evanston Twp. Schs., Ill., 1948-50; specialist jr. colls. and lower divs. U.S. Office Edn., 1950-53, program planning officer, 1953; dean statewide devel. higher edn. U. Nev., 1954-55, acting chmn. dept. English, 1955-56, acad. v.p., 1955-60, acting pres., 1958-60; pres. U. Alaska, 1960-73; mayor Fairbanks, Alaska, 1978-80; pres. Pacific Alaska Assocs., Ltd.; exec. v.p. Fairbanks Indsl. Devel. Corp., Festival Fairbanks '84, mem. staff study needs and resources higher edn. FAO, Libya, 1955; mem. study group off-duty ednl. program armed forces in Europe, U.S. Dept. Def., 1955; del. Am. Assembly Rgn. Rels., 1957-58; chmn. Nev. com. Fulbright scholarships, 1957-58; mem. chancellor's panel SUNY; mem. sci. group traveling to Antarctica, New Zealand, Australia; presenter sesquicentennial address Sigma Pi Literary Soc. of Ill. Coll., 1993. Editor: Looking Ahead, 1953, From Here On, 1954, All Around the Land, 1954, Youth and The World, 1955, To Be an American, 1957; author, editor: On Your Own, 1953; co-editor: Short Stories as You Like Them, 1940, Youth Thinks It Through, 1941, Just for Sport, 1943, Fact and Opinion, 1945, Short Stories, 1951, Study of Financing of Higher Education in Asia, 1968; author (verse): Not From Stone, 1983, Legacy of Dreams, 1993. Chmn. Alaska Am. Cancer Soc.; v.p. Alaska council Boy Scouts Am.; mem. bd. Rampart Dam adv. com.; mem. Gen. Med. Scis. Nat. Adv. Council, Alaska Higher Edn. Facilities Commn., 1967, Alaska Small Bus. Adv. Council, 1968, Satellite Communications Task Force; spl. asst. to mayor for trade and devel., Fairbanks North Star borough, 1984—; chmn. Greater Fairbanks Community Hosp. Found.; mem. White House Fellows Selection Panel, Nat. Adv. Council on Edn. Professions Devel.; chmn. Alaska Heart Assn.; mem. Alaskan Command Civilian Adv. Bd., 1962—; bd. dirs. U. Alaska Found., exec. dir. Fest. Fairbanks '84, 1981—. Served to lt. USNR, 1943-46; capt. USNR, ret. 1968. Recipient Outstanding Alaskan award, 1984, Alaskan of Yr. award, 1985, Centennial award Alexis de Tocqueville Soc., 1987, Disting. Citizen award Alaska coun. Boy Scouts Am., 1992; named to Ill. Coll. Athletic Hall of Fame, 1993, laureate Alaska Bus. Hall of Fame, 1996. Fellow Arctic Inst. N. Am.; mem. Am. Geog. Soc., Assn. Higher Edn. (exec. com.), Nat. Univ. Extension Assn., N.W. Assn. Secondary and Higher Schs., Western Assn. Colls., Navy League, AAAS, Assn. Applied Solar Energy (adv. council 1959), Am. Assn. Land-grant Colls. and State Univs., Internat. Assn. Univ. Presidents (exec. com.). Methodist. Clubs: Explorers, Fairbanks Petroleum, Washington Athletic. Lodge: Rotary (gov. dist. 503 1985-86). Home: 665 10th Ave Apt 305 Fairbanks AK 99701-4664

WOOD, WILLIS BOWNE, JR., retired utility holding company executive; b. Kansas City, Mo., Sept. 15, 1934; s. Willis Bowne Sr. and Mina (Henderson) W.; m. Dixie Gravel, Aug. 31, 1955; children: Bradley, William, Josh. BS in Petroleum Engring., U. Tulsa, 1957; grad. advanced mgmt. program, Harvard U., 1983; JD (hon.), Pepperdine U., 1996. With So. Calif. Gas Co., L.A., 1960-74, from v.p. to sr. v.p., 1975-80, exec. v.p., 1983-84; pres., CEO Pacific Lighting Gas Supply Co., L.A., 1981-83; from sr. v.p. to chmn., pres., CEO, Pacific Enterprises, L.A., 1984-93, chmn., CEO, 1993-98; ret., 1998; bd. dirs. Washington Mut., Seattle, Automobile Club Soc. Calif.; trustee U. So. Calif. Trustee, vice-chmn. Harvey Mudd Coll., Claremont, Calif., 1984—; trustee, past chmn. Calif. Med. Ctr. Found., L.A., 1983—; trustee, past pres. S.W. Mus., L.A., 1983—; trustee John and Dora Haynes Found., 1998—; past bd. dirs. L.A. World Affairs Coun.; dir., past chmn. bus. coun. for Sustainable Energy Future, 1994—; dir. Pacific Coun. for Internat. Affairs. Recipient Disting. Alumni U. Tulsa, 1995. Mem. Soc. Petroleum Energy Engrs., Am. Gas Assn., Pacific Coast Gas Assn. (past bd. dirs.), Pacific Energy Assn., Calif. State C. of C. (past bd. dirs.), Nat. Assn. of Mfrs. (past bd. dirs.), Hacienda Golf CLub, Ctr. Club, Calif. Club. Republican.

WOODARD, ALVA ABE, business consultant; b. Roy, N.Mex., June 28, 1928; s. Joseph Benjamin and Emma Luvenia (Watkins) W.; m. Esther Josepha Kaufmann, Apr. 5, 1947 (div. Sept. 1991); children: Nannette, Gregory, Loreen, Arne, Mark, Kevin, Steven, Curtis, Marlee, Julie, Michelle; m. Margaret Adele Evenson, Oct. 1, 1994. Student, Kinman Bus. U., 1948-49, Whitworth Coll., 1950, Wash. State U., 1953-54. Sec.-treas., dir. Green Top Dairy Farms, Inc., Clarkston, Wash., 1948-52; v.p., treas., sec., dir. ASC Industries, Inc. (subs. Gifford-Hill and Co.), Spokane, Wash., 1952-75; dir. Guenther Irrigation, Inc., Pasco, Wash., 1965-71; [illegible] Inc., Pasco, 1968-75, Rain Chief Irrigation Co., Grand Island, Nebr., 1968-75; sec., dir. Keeling Supply Co., Little Rock, 1969-72; pres., dir. Renters, Inc., Salt Lake City, 1971-75, Woodard Western Corp., Spokane, 1976-86, Woodard Industries, Inc., Auburn, Wash., 1987-90; cons. Woodard Assocs., Spokane, Wash., 1985—; pres., dir. TFI Industries, inc., Post Falls, Idaho, 1989-90; v.p., sec., treas., dir. Trans-Force, Inc., Post Falls, 1989-90, TFI Computer Scis., Inc., Post Falls, 1989-90. Newman Lake (Wash.) Rep. precinct committeeman, 1964-80; Spokane County del. Wash. Rep. Conv., 1968-80. Mem. Adminstrv. Mgmt. Soc. (bd. dirs. 1966-68), Optimists. Avocations: fishing, theater, golf, reading, dancing. Home and Office: 921 E 39th Ave Spokane WA 99203-3034

WOODARD, DOROTHY MARIE, insurance broker; b. Houston, Feb. 7, 1932; d. Gerald Edgar and Bessie Katherine (Crain) Floeck; student N.Mex. State U., 1950; m. Jack W. Woodard; June 19, 1950 (dec. May 1972); m. Norman W. Libby, July 19, 1982 (dec. Dec. 1991). Ptnr. Western Oil Co., Tucumcari, N.Mex., 1950—; owner, mgr. Woodard & Co., Las Cruces, N.Mex., 1959-67; agt., dist. mgr. United Nations Ins. Co., Denver, 1968-74; agt. Western Nat. Life Ins. Co., Amarillo, Tex., 1976—. Exec. dir. Tucumcari Indsl. Commn., 1979—; dir. Bravo Dome Study Com., 1979—; owner Libby Cattle Co., Libby Ranch Co.; regional bd. dirs. N.Mex., Eastern Plains Council Govts., 1979—. Mem. NAFE, Tucumcari C. of C., Mesa Country Club. Home: PO Box 823 Tucumcari NM 88401-0823

WOODARD, JOHN HENRY, quality control professional; b. Alameda, Calif., Mar. 25, 1948; s. Charles A. and Louise E. (Fick) W.; m. Nancy L. Smith, Apr. 8, 1972; 1 child, Victoria A. BA in Psychology, Calif. State Coll., Hayward, 1970. Quality control supr. Hunt Wesson Foods, Hayward, Calif., 1969-75; quality control mgr. Hunt Wesson Foods, Davis, Calif., 1975-92; quality control and bulk paste mgr. Hunt Wesson Foods, Davis, 1992—. Mem. Woodland (Calif.) Davis Rail Study, 1993-94. Mem. Inst. Food Technologists, Alpha Phi Omega (historian, treas., pres.). Republican. Episcopalian. Avocations: history, backpacking. Home: 614 Ashley Ave Woodland CA 95695-3671 Office: Hunt Wesson Foods 1111 E Covell Blvd Davis CA 95616-1299

WOODARD, LARRY L., college official; b. Lebanon, Oreg., Apr. 16, 1936; s. Hugh Frank and Ima Ellen (Bilyeu) W.; m. Bette Jeanette Brown, Aug. 10, 1956; children: Perry, Craig, Stacy. BS in Forestry, Oreg. State U., 1957. Forester Bur. of Land Mgmt., Oreg., 1957-69, Washington, 1969-72; dist. mgr. Bur. of Land Mgmt., Coeur d'Alene, Idaho, 1972-76; assoc. state dir. Bur. of Land Mgmt., Boise, Idaho, 1976-78, Santa Fe, 1978-82, Boise, 1982-86; state dir. Bur. of Land Mgmt., Santa Fe, 1987-93; dir. devel. Boise Bible Coll., 1993—. Author: A to Z, The Biography of Arthur Zimmerman, 1988, Before the First Wave, 1994. Bd. dirs. Boise Bible Coll., 1977-87; trustee N.Mex. Nature Conservancy, 1987-90. Recipient Disting. Svc. award U.S. Dept. Interior, 1986, Sec.'s Stewardship award U.S. Dept. Interior, 1989, Pres.'s Meritorious Exec. award, 1991. Republican. Avocations: teaching history, writing, hunting, gardening. Home: PO Box 365 Meridian ID 83680-0365 Office: Boise Bible Coll 8695 Marigold St Boise ID 83714-1220

WOODBURY, LAEL JAY, theater educator; b. Fairview, Idaho, July 3, 1927; s. Raymond A. and Wanda (Dawson) W.; m. Margaret Lillian Swenson, Dec. 19, 1949; children: Carolyn Inez (Mrs. Donald Hancock), Shannon Margaret (Mrs. J. Michael Busenbark), Jordan Ray, Lexon Dan. BS, Utah State U., 1952; MA, Brigham Young U., 1953; PhD (Univ. fellow), U. Ill., 1954. Teaching asst. U. Ill., 1953; assoc. prof. Brigham Young U., 1954-61; guest prof. Colo. State Coll., 1962; asst. prof. Bowling Green State U., 1961-62; asso. prof. U. Iowa, 1962-65; producer Ledges Playhouse, Lansing, Mich., 1963-65; prof. speech and dramatics, chmn. dept. Brigham Young U., 1966-70, assoc. dean Coll. Fine Arts and Communications, 1969-73, dean Coll. Fine Arts and Communications, 1973-82; vis. lectr. abroad; bd. dirs. Eagle Systems Internat.; bd. dir. workshop Fedn. for Asian Cultural Promotion, Republic of China; dir. European study tour. Author: Play Production Handbook, 1959, Mormon Arts, vol. 1, 1972, Mosaic Theatre, 1976, also articles, original dramas; profl. actor PBS and feature films. Chmn. gen. bd. drama com. Young Men's Mut. Improvement Assn., 1958-61; bd. dirs. Repertory Dance Theatre; bd. dirs., chmn. greater ctrl. Utah ARC; chmn. Utah Alliance for Arts Edn.; mem. adv. coun. Utah Arts Festival; missionary LDS Ch., N.Y.C., 1994. With USN, 1942-46. Recipient Creative Arts award Brigham Young U., 1971, Disting. Alumni award, 1975, Tchr. of Yr. award, 1988, Excellence in Rsch. award, 1992, Disting. Svc. award, 1992. Mem. Rocky Mountain Theatre Conf. (past pres.), Am. Theatre Assn. (chmn. nat. com. royalties 1972—, mem. fin. com. 1982—), NW Assn. Univs. and Colls. (accrediting officer), Am. Theatre Assn. (v.p. Univ. and Coll. Theatre Assn.), Theta Alpha Phi, Phi Kappa Phi. Home: 1303 Locust Ln Provo UT 84604-3651

WOODBURY, MARDA LIGGETT, librarian, writer; b. N.Y.C., Sept. 20, 1925; d. Walter W. and Edith E. (Fleischer) Liggett; m. Philip J. Evans, Sept. 1948 (div. 1950); 1 child, Mark W. Evans; m. Mark Lee Woodbury, 1956 (div. 1969); children: Brian, Heather. Student, Bklyn. Coll., 1942-44; BA in Chemistry and Polit. Sci., Bard Coll., 1946; BS in L.S., Columbia U., 1948; postgrad., U. Calif., Berkeley, 1955-56, 60-61, MJ, 1995. Cert. tchr. Libr. various spl., med. and pub. librs., San Francisco, 1946-60, Coll. Pk. High Sch., Mt. Diablo, Calif., 1962-67; elem. sch. libr. Oakland and Berkeley, Calif., 1967-69; libr. dir. Far West Lab. Ednl. Rsch. & Devel., San Francisco, 1969-73; libr., editor Gifted Resource Ctr., San Mateo, Calif., 1973-75; libr. cons. Rsch. Ventures, Berkeley, Calif., 1975—; libr. dir. Life Chiropractic Coll., San Lorenzo, Calif., 1980-95. Author: A Guide to Sources of Educational Information, 1976, 2d edit., 1982, Selecting Instructional Materials, 1978, Selecting Materials for Instruction, Vol. I: Issues and Policies, 1979, Vol. II: Media and the Curriculum, 1980, Vol. III: Subject Areas and Implementation, 1980, Childhood Information Resources, 1985 (Outstanding Ref. Work, Assn. Ref. Librs. 1985), Youth Information Resources, 1987, Stopping the Presses: The Murder of Walter W. Liggett, 1998; mem. editorial bd. Ref. Libr., 1980-95. Mem. Med. Libr. Assn. (editor Chiropractic Librs. 1990-92), Minn. Hist. Soc., Investigative Reporters and Editors. Home: 145 Monte Cresta Ave Apt 402 Oakland CA 94611-4809

WOODEN, JOHN ROBERT, former basketball coach; b. Martinsville, Ind., Oct. 14, 1910; s. Joshua Hugh and Roxie (Rothrock) W.; m. Nellie C. Riley, Aug. 8, 1932; children: Nancy Anne, James Hugh. B.S., Purdue U., 1932, M.S., Ind. State U., 1947. Athletic dir., basketball and baseball coach Ind. State Tchrs. Coll., 1946-48; head basketball coach UCLA, 1948-75; lectr. to colls., coaches, business. Author: Practical Modern Basketball, 1966, They Call Me Coach, 1972; Contbr. articles to profl. jours. Served to lt. USNR, 1943-46. Named All-Am. basketball player Purdue U., 1930-32, Coll. Basketball Player of Yr., 1932, to All-Time All-Am. Team Helms Athletic Found., 1943, Nat. Basketball Hall of Fame, Springfield (Mass.) Coll., as player, 1960, as coach, 1970, Ind. State Baksetball Hall of Fame, 1962, Calif. Father of Yr., 1964, 75, Coach of Yr. U.S. Basketball Writers Assn., 1964, 67, 69, 70, 72, 73, Sportsman of Yr. Sports Illustrated, 1973, GTE Acad. All-Am., 1994; recipient Whitney Young award Urban League, 1973, 1st ann. Velvet Covered Brick award Layman's Leadership Inst., 1974, 1st ann. Dr. James Naismith Peachbasket award, 1974, medal of excellence Bellarmine Coll., 1985, Sportslike Pathfinder award to Hoosier with extraordinary svc. on behalf of Am. youth, 1993, GET All Am. Acad. Hall of Fame, 1994, 40 for the Age award Sports Illustrated, 1994, the 1st Frank G. Wells Disney award for role model to youth, 1995, Disting. Am. award Pres. Reagan, 1995, Svc. to Mankind award Lexington Theol. Sem., 1995, NCAA Theodore Roosevelt Sportsman award, 1995.

WOODFIN, MARTHA, interior designer; b. Georgetown, Tex., Mar. 26, 1939; d. John Edward and Lenora (Beckmann) Cloud, m. Ronald L. Woodfin, Jan. 28, 1962; children; Alfred John, Edward Claude. BS in Interior Design, U. Tex., 1961. Instr. interior design Seattle C.C., 1966-70, Corro Coso C.C., Ridgecrest, Calif., 1972-78; interior designer Wm. L. Davis and Sons Co., Seattle, 1965-71, Leishman-Taack Interiors, Albuquerque, 1986-91, Martha Woodfin Interiors, Sandia Park, N.Mex., 1991—. Mem. Am. Soc. Interior Designers (1st place residential design award 1993, various offices, bd. dirs.). Baptist. Office: Martha Woodfin Interiors PO Box 55 Sandia Park NM 87047-0055

WOODFORD, MARY IMOGENE STEELE, secondary school educator; b. Balt., Jan. 7, 1919; d. [illegible] Steele; m. Hackley Elbridge Woodford, June 7, 1940; children: Peggy, John, Joan,

Barbara. BA, Howard U., 1940; MA, U. Chgo., 1960. Tchr. Benton Harbor (Mich.) Schs., 1960-70; tchr. Jr. and Sr. H.S., Pasadena, Calif., 1971-75, L.A., 1975-84. Bd. dirs. Girl Scouts of U.S., Benton Harbor, Mich., 1947-50; mem. Ys Neighbors, YWCA, Benton Harbor, St. Joseph, Mich., 1947-70. Recipient scholarship Lotta Crabtree Estate, Wayland, Boston 1936; named Mother of Yr. Mem. AAUW, Tuskegee Airmen Inc. (membership chair 1995, 96), The Links, Inc. (Mothr of Yr. 1994), Delta Sigma Theta Sorority Inc. Democrat. Presbyterian. Avocations: reading, crossword puzzles, sewing, swimming, tennis. Home: 16071 Avenida Lamego San Diego CA 92128-3151

WOODHOUSE, GAY VANDERPOEL, state attorney general, lawyer; b. Torrington, Wyo., Jan. 8, 1950; d. Wayne Gaylord and Sally (Rouse) Vanderpoel; m. Randy Woodhouse, Nov. 26, 1983; children: Dustin Ross, Houston. BA with honors, U. Wyo., 1972, JD, 1977. Bar: Wyo. 1978, U.S. Dist. Ct. Wyo., U.S. Supreme Ct. Dir. student Legal Services, Laramie, Wyo., 1976-77; assoc. Donald Jones Law Offices, Torrington, Wyo., 1977-78; asst. atty. gen. State of Wyo., Cheyenne, 1978-84, sr. asst. atty. gen., 1984-89, spl. U.S. atty., 1987-89, atty. gen., 1998—. Chmn. bd. Pathfinder, 1987; bd. dirs. S.E. Wyo. Mental Health; chmn. Wyo. Telephone Consumer Panel, Casper, 1982—; spl. projects cons. N.Am. Securities Adminstrs. Assn., 1987; advisor Cheyenne Halfway House, 1984—. Mem. ABA, Laramie County Bar Assn. Republican. Avocation: inline speed skating, stained glass. Office: 123 Capitol Bldg Cheyenne WY 82002*

WOODHULL, JOHN RICHARD, electronics company executive; b. LaJolla, Calif., Nov. 5, 1933; s. John Richard Woodhull and Mary Louise (Fahey) Hostetler; m. Barbara Adams; children: Elizabeth A., John A. BS in Engring. Physics, U. Colo., 1957, MS in Applied Math., 1960. Engr. Space Tech. Labs. (now TRW Systems), Redondo Beach, Calif., 1960-63; mgr., engr. Northrop Corp., Hawthorne, Calif., 1964; mem. tech. staff Logicon, Inc., San Pedro, Calif., 1964-69, pres., chief exec. officer, Torrance, Calif., 1969—, also bd. dirs.; instr. physics U. Colo., 1959-60; bd. dirs. 1st Fed. Fin. Corp. Bd. mgrs. San Pedro (Calif.) and Peninsula YMCA; bd. dirs. Los Angeles YMCA, 1985—, Sunrise Med., Torrance, 1986—. With USN, 1956-59. Mem. Chief Execs.' Orgn., World Bus. Coun., Nat. Indsl. Security Assn. (bd. dirs. 1986—). Avocations: sailboat racing, tennis, skiing. Office: Logicon Inc 3701 Skypark Dr Ste 200 Torrance CA 90505-4794

WOODROOF, ROBERT HARDING, educator, consultant; b. Nashville, July 31, 1950; s. Dan Harding and Francis Jane (Harris) W.; m. Sherry Jeanine Lemaster, Feb. 1, 1974. BA, Abilene (Tex.) Christian U., 1972; MEd, Ohio U., 1982; PhD, UCLA, 1993. Ptr. Jon Wood Assocs., Dallas, Tex., 1974-75; agent N.Y. Life Insurance, Dallas, Tex., 1975-76; dir. coll. rels. Ohio Valley Coll., Parkersburg, W. Va., 1976-85; from mgr. direct mktg. to assoc. prof. pub. rels. Pepperdine U., Malibu, Calif., 1985-94, assoc. prof. pub. rels., 1994—; cons. various colls. and univs., Pa., Calif., 1984—, Malibu (Calif.) C. of C., 1989—. Producer Going for the Gold The Bicentennial of Parkersburg, W. Va., 1985 (best of show 1985), Challenged to Lead Pepperdine U., 1994; editor New Directions for Cmty. Colls., 1990. Mem. Ch. of Christ. Avocations: sailing, cooking, ship modeling, wines. Home: 24223 Baxter Dr Malibu CA 90265-4754 Office: Pepperdine U 24255 Pacific Coast Hwy Malibu CA 90263-0002

WOODRUFF, FAY, paleoceanographer, geological researcher; b. Boston, Jan. 23, 1944; d. Lorande Mitchell and Anne (Fay) W.; m. Alexander Whitehill Clowes, May 20, 1972 (div. Oct. 1974); m. Robert G. Douglas, Jan. 27, 1980; children: Ellen, Katerina. RN, Mass. Gen. Hosp. Sch. Nursing, Boston, 1966; BA, Boston U., 1971; MS, U. So. Calif., 1979. Rsch. assoc. U. So. Calif., L.A., 1978-81, rsch. faculty, 1981-96; keynote spkr. 4th Internat. Symposium on Benthic Foraminifera, Sendai, Japan, 1990. Contbg. author: Geological Society of America Memoir, 1985; contbr. articles to profl. jours. Life mem. The Nature Conservancy, Washington, 1992; bd. dirs. Friends of Friendship Park, Inc., 1995-99; co-founder Resources Families Adopted Ea. European Children, Inc., L.A., 1996—. NSF grantee, 1986-94. Mem. Am. Geophys. Union, Geol. Soc. Am., Internat. Union Geol. Scis. (internat. commn. on stratigraphy, subcommn. on Neogene stratigraphy 1991-97), Soc. Woman Geographers (sec. So. Calif. chpt. 1990-96), Soc. Econ. Paleontologists and Mineralogists (sec., editor N.Am. Micropaleontology sect. 1988-90), Sigma Xi. Office: U So Calif Earth Scis Los Angeles CA 90089-0740

WOODRUFF, KATHRYN ELAINE, English language educator; b. Ft. Stockton, Tex., Oct. 12, 1940; d. James Arthur and Catherine H. (Stevens) Borron; m. Thomas Charles Woodruff, May 18, 1969; children: Robert Borron, David Borron. BA, Our Lady of the Lake U., San Antonio, 1963; MFA, U. Alaska, 1969; PhD, U. Denver, 1987. Cert. tchr., Tex., Colo. English and journalism tchr. Owensboro (Ky.) Cath. High Sch., 1963-64, Grand Junction (Colo.) Dist. 12, 1964-66; English tchr. Monroe High Sch., Fairbanks, Alaska, 1966-67; teaching asst. U. Alaska, Fairbanks, 1967-69, instr., 1969-70; instr. U. Colo., Boulder, 1979, Denver, 1988-89; instr. Regis Coll., Denver, 1987-89; asst. prof. Econs. Inst., Boulder, 1989-92; assoc. prof. English Colo. Christian U., Lakewood, 1993—; tchr. Upward Bound, Fairbanks, 1968; instr. ethnic and women writers course U. Colo., Denver, 1988-93; mem. Assoc. Writing Programs; soprano Boulder Chorale, Cantabile Singers; mem. Women's Studies Delegation to South Africa, 1998; active in missionary work in Ecuador, 1998, European Singing Tour, 1998. Author: (poetry) Before the Burning, 1994; poetry readings in Colo., Tex. and Paris; poems publ. in Denver Quarterly, The Incliner, Southwestern Am. Lit. Friend Chautauqua Music Festival, Boulder, 1985—; dir. 12th Annual Arts Festival, Fairbanks, 1969. Recipient Poet's Choice award Internat. Soc. Poetry, 1997; named one of Outstanding Young Women Am., 1966; nominated for Poet Laureate of Colo., 1996; NEH grantee, 1996. Mem. AAUW, MLA, Assoc. Writing Programs, Soc. Internat. Devel. UN Assn., Nat. Women's Hall of Fame, Acad. of Am. Poets. Democrat. Mem. Christian Ch. Avocations: singing, tennis, skiing, volleyball, travel. Office: Colo Christian U 180 S Garrison St Lakewood CO 80226-1053

WOODRUFF, SCOTT WILLIAM, cosmetic, reconstructive and maxillofacial surgeon; b. Pomaona, Calif., Mar. 6, 1961; s. Edwin Bruce and Mary Robbins (Bowen) W.; m. Susan White Woodruff, Aug. 31, 1996; 1 child, Parker Anne. BA, U. Washington, 1983, DDS, 1988; MD, Ea. Va. Med. Sch., 1996. Intern in surgery Brigham & Women's Hosp., Boston, 1988-89; fellow in maxillofacial surgery Emory U., Atlanta, 1989-90; resident in maxillofacial surgery U. Miami, Fla., 1990-94; pvt. practice Greenbelt, Md., 1994-96; resident in gen. surgery Swedish Med. Ctr., Seattle, 1996-97, fellowship in cosmetic/reconstructive surgery, 1997-98, pvt. practice in cosmetic/reconstructive and maxillofacial surgery, 1998—; cons. dental medicine Harvard Sch. Dental Medicine, 1988-89; cons. surgeon Dana Farber Cancer Inst., Boston, 1988-89. Editor, author: Coders Desk Reference, 1995. Big brother United Way, Seattle, 1982-88. Mem. AMA, ADA, Am. Assn. Oral Maxillofacial Surgeons (cert. of merit 1994), Am. Soc. Plastic and Reconstructive Surgeons, Am. Acad. Cosmetic Surgery. Republican. Avocations: sports, skiing, scuba, photography, literature. Home: 9754 45th Ave NE Seattle WA 98115-2606 Office: 3500 188th St SW Ste 670 Lynnwood WA 98037-4716

WOODS, BOBBY JOE, transportation executive; b. Frederick, Okla., June 20, 1935; s. Vivin Richard and Mattie Marie (Malone); m. Sherry Summers; children: Donald B., Kathryn M., David R., Lynda J. Student, U. Calif., Berkeley, 1955-56; AA, Phoenix Coll., 1955; student, Glendale (Ariz.) Coll., 1968, 75. Pres. Southwest Prorate Inc., Phoenix, 1967-95, TCAB Registration Cons., Inc., 1993—; dist. exec. Boy Scouts Am., Phoenix, 1968-76; pres. Facing E's Enterprises, Inc., Yarnell, Ariz., 1991-93. Mem. Profl. Trucking Svcs. Assn. (pres. 1989-90), Lions Club (dist. gov. 1992-93, zone chmn. 1983-84, dep. dist. gov. 1984-85, lt. gov. 1991-92, dist. sight and hearing chmn. 1985-91, Sight and Hearing Found. bd. mem. 1987—, state hearing chmn. 1985-89). Republican. Avocations: hiking, camping, stamp collecting, computers, collecting 78 RPM records. Home: 915 E Annette Dr Phoenix AZ 85022-1101 Office: TCAB Registration Cons 2045 W Glendale Ave Phoenix AZ 85021-7841

WOODS, DONALD PETER, real estate executive, marketing professional; b. Seneca Falls, N.Y., Oct. 14, 1911; s. James Henry and Isabell Teresa (McDonald) W.; m. June 17, 1935; children: Donald Peter Jr., Richard, Terrence, Lynn, Thomas. PhB, Niagara U., Niagara Falls, N.Y., 1933; postgrad., Bklyn. Law Sch., 1933-36. Law clk. N.Y. State Ins. Dept., N.Y.C., 1933-36; title examiner Abstract Title and Mortgage, Rochester, N.Y., 1936-38; title officer Monroe Abstract & Title, Rochester, 1938-43; pres., chief exec. officer D.P. Woods, Inc., Rochester, 1945-54, Don Woods Realty, Phoenix, 1954-82; assoc. v.p. Colliers Internat., Phoenix, 1982—. Lt. USNR, 1943-45, PTO. Mem. Internat. Coun. of Shopping Ctrs., Camelback Racquet Club (pres. Phoenix chpt. 1959—), Phi Delta Phi. Republican. Roman Catholic. Avocations: tennis, golf. Home: 3819 E Camelback Rd Apt 171 Phoenix AZ 85018-2649 Office: Colliers Internat 3636 N Central Ave Ste 600 Phoenix AZ 85012-1935

WOODS, DONNA MARIA, artist; b. L.A., June 10, 1957; d. Foy Cortez and Willie Catherine (Bizzell) W. AA, L.A. City Coll., 1985; student, Antioch U., 1985, Otis Sch Art, Coll. Design, 1996, 97. Graphic artist Shack & Assocs., L.A., 1980-81; prodn. photographer Arne Sign & Decal, San Jose, Calif., 1981-82; instr. art St. Elmo Village, L.A., 1983-92; owner Graphic Seed, L.A., 1983-97; tchrs. and art dept. asst. Otis Sch. Art, L.A., 1997; co-owner DaB Creative Endeavers, L.A., 1997—. Author: (poetry books) A Voyage to Remember, 1996, Portraits of Life, 1996, Best of Poems, 1997, The Isle of View, 1997. Mem. Nat. Water Color Soc., Calif. State Parks Found. Democrat. Avocations: yoga, nature walks, music, singing. Home and office: 1316 W 59th Pl Los Angeles CA 90044

WOODS, GURDON GRANT, sculptor; b. Savannah, Ga., Apr. 15, 1915; s. Frederick L. and Marion (Skinner) W. Student, Art Student's League N.Y.C., 1936-39, Bklyn. Mus. Sch., 1945-46; Ph.D. (hon.), Coll. San Francisco Art Inst., 1966. exec. dir. San Francisco Art Inst., 1955-64; dir. Calif. Sch. Fine Arts, 1955-65; prof. Adlai E. Stevenson Coll., U. Calif. at Santa Cruz, 1966-74; dir. Otis Art Inst., Los Angeles, 1974-77; asst. dir. Los Angeles County Mus. Natural History, 1977-80; Sculptor mem. San Francisco Art Commn., 1954-56; mem. Santa Cruz County Art Commn., Regional Arts Council of Bay Area. Exhibited: N.A.D., 1948, 49, San Francisco Art Assn. anns., 1952-54, Denver Mus. Anns., 1952, 53, Whitney Mus. Ann., 1953, Sao Paulo Biennial, 1955, Bolles Gallery San Francisco, 1969, 70, 72, L.A. Mcpl. Gallery, 1977, San Jose Inst. Contemporary Art (Calif.), Washington Project for the Arts retrospective, 1968-85, Washington, 1985, Retrospective Art Mus. Santa Cruz County, Calif., 1987, d.p. Fong Gallery, 1993, 94, Michael Angelo Gallery, Santa Cruz, 1995; commns. include: cast concrete reliefs and steel fountain, IBM Ctr., San Jose, Calif., fountain, Paul Masson Winery, Saratoga, Calif., McGraw Hill Pubs. (now Birkenstock), Novato, Calif.; work in permanent collection Oakland (Calif.) Mus.; papers in Archives of Am. Art, Smithsonian Instn., Washington. Recipient citation N.Y.C., 1948; prize N.A.D., 1949; Chapelbrook Found. research grantee, 1965-66; Sequoia Fund grantee, 1967; Research grantee Creative Arts Inst., U. Calif., 1968; grantee Carnegie Corp., 1968-69. Mem. Artists Equity Assn (pres. No. Calif. chpt. 1950-52, nat. dir. 1952-55). Address: 133 Seascape Dr Aptos CA 95003

WOODS, JAMES C., museum director. Dir. Herrett Ctr. Arts and Sci. and Faulkner Planetarium, Twin Falls, Idaho. Office: Coll Southern Idaho Herrett Ctr Arts and Sci 315 Falls Ave Twin Falls ID 83301-3367

WOODSIDE, GEORGE ROBERT, computer software developer; b. Meadville, Pa., Oct. 29, 1949; s. William Clinton and Bernadette Lorena (Greene) W.; m. Diane Claire Hickenlooper, June 14, 1980 (div. 1996). Grad. h.s., Fairview, Pa. Program GE Co., Erie, Pa., 1967-69; programmer-analyst Lovell Mfg. Co., Erie, 1969-70; mgr. data processing Eriez Mfg. Co., Erie, 1970-74; owner Woodside-Benson Assocs., Fairview, 1974-78; prin. mem. tech. staff Transaction Tech. Inc. (now Citicorp/TTI), Santa Monica, Calif., 1978-92; owner GRW Sys. and Programming, Sparks, Nev., 1993—. Contbr. articles to mags.; developer software to detect and eliminate computer viruses. Mem. IEEE. Avocations: photography, woodworking.

WOODWARD, CLINTON BENJAMIN, JR., civil engineering educator; b. El Paso, Tex., Mar. 4, 1943; s. Clinton Benjamin and Iris Elizabeth (Zant) W.; m. Willie Ann Shollenbarger, June 14, 1969 (div. June 1976); m. Deon Bennett Speir, Nov. 22, 1979; 1 child, Clinton Benjamin III. BSET, N.Mex. State U., 1976; MS, Colo. State U., 1978; MSCE, N.Mex. State U., 1984, PhD, 1986. Registered profl. engr., N.Mex. From asst. mgr. to pres. Woodward Enterprises Co., Inc., Las Cruces, N.Mex., 1968-82; assoc. prof. N.Mex. State U., 1987—. Contbr. articles to profl. jours. With USN, 1962-66.. Mem. ASCE, Am. Soc. for Engring. Edn., Soc. for Exptl. Mechanics, Forest Products Soc., Soc. Wood Sci. and Tech., Tau Beta Phi, Chi Epsilon, Phi Kappa Phi, Sigma Xi. Avocations: camping, fly fishing.

WOODWARD, JOHN RUSSELL, motion picture production executive; b. San Diego, July 10, 1951; s. Melvin C. and Dora M. (Rorabaugh) W. BA in Visual Arts, U. Calif., San Diego, 1973; MA in Cinema Prodn., U. So. Calif., 1978. V.p. prodn. World Wide Motion Pictures Corp., 1982—. Asst. prodr. The Manitou, 1977; 1st asst. dir. Mortuary, 1981, They're Playing with Fire, 1983, Prime Risk, 1984, Winners Take All, 1986, Kidnapped, 1986, Slam Dance, 1986, Honor Betrayed, 1986, The Hidden, 1987, New Monkees, 1987, Bad Dreams, 1987, Night Angel, 1988, Disorganized Crime, 1988, UHF, 1988, The Horror Show, 1988, Fear, 1989, Tremors, 1989, Young Guns II, 1990, Shattered, 1990, Tales from the Crypt, 1990, Two-Fisted Tales, 1990, Buried Alive, 1990, Dream On, 1991, Strays, 1991, Universal Soldier, 1991, An Army of One, 1992, The Vanishing, 1992, Ghost in the Machine, 1992, The Shawshank Redemption, 1993, City Slickers II, 1993, Breach of Conduct, 1994, The Craft, 1995, Broken Arrow, 1995, The Rich Man's Wife, 1995, Gattaca, 1996, Liar, Liar, 1996, Wild Things, 1997, Dennis the Menace 2, 1997, The 13th Warrior, 1998, BASEketball, 1998, Swing Vote, 1999; location mgr. Star Chamber, 1982, To Be or Not to Be, 1983, Flashdance, 1983, Two of a Kind, 1983, Touch and Go, 1984, Explorers, 1984, Sweet Dreams, 1985, The Long Shot, 1985, The Running Men, 1985, A Different Affair, 1985, Walk Like a Man, 1986. Avocations: fishing, camping, hunting.

WOODWARD, PHIL LLOYD, business educator; b. Newport Beach, Calif., July 25, 1956; s. Thomas Earl Woodward and Vivian Fallis; m. Camela Woodward, May 16, 1987; children: Thomas, Andrew. BS, U. So. Calif., L.A., 1978; MBA, Calif. State U., Fullerton, 1981; MBT, U. So. Calif., L.A., 1985. CPA, Calif. Sr. tax acct. Deloitte & Touche, Costa Mesa, Calif., 1981-84; asst. v.p. Butterfield Savs., Santa Ana, Calif., 1984-86; tax mgr. IDS, Corona, Calif., 1987, RealEcon, Santa Ana, 1987-98; lectr. Calif. State U., Fullerton, 1987-90; assoc. prof. Biola U., La Mirada, Calif., 1990—. Mem. Am. Acctg. Assn. Office: Biola U 13800 Biola Ave La Mirada CA 90639-0001

WOODWORTH, KATE, novelist; b. Stamford, Conn., May 28, 1953; d. Arthur Vernon and Mary (Ringwalt) W.; m. Timothy Claypool Houpt, Aug. 18, 1979; Joseph W., David W., Daniel M. BA in English, Trinity Coll., Hartford, Conn., 1975. Pub. rels. dir. Stein Eriksen Lodge, Deer Valley, Utah, 1986-88; alumni dir. U. Utah Med. Sch., Salt Lake City, 1990-97, U. Utah, Salt Lake City, 1997—. Author: (novel) Racing into the Dark, 1988 (Utah Arts Coun. Literary award 1987). Home: 573 Perry's Hollow Rd Salt Lake City UT 84103

WOODWORTH, STEPHEN DAVIS, investment banker; b. Stillwater, Okla., Nov. 4, 1945; s. Stanley Davis and Elizabeth (Webb) W.; m. Robin Woodworth; children: Lisa Alexander, Ashley Ives. BA, Claremont McKenna Coll., 1967; MBA, Calif. Lutheran U., 1975; grad. Mgmt. Policy Inst., U. So. Calif., 1981. Div. mgr. Security Pacific Bank, L.A., 1970-86; pres. Channel Island Equities, Oxnard, Calif., 1988—; chmn. Cen. Coast MIT Enterprise Forum, Santa Barbara, Calif., 1992-94; moderator The White House Conf. on Small Bus., 1995; exec. com., dir. World Affairs Coun. of Ventura County, 1995-98; dir. Greater Oxnard Econ. Devel. Corp., 1996—; vice chair Santa Barbara chpt. Am. Inst. Wine and Food, 1996-98; instr. fin. and banking Calif. Luth. U., 1978-79; active Calif. CPA Edn. Found., 1996; mem. adv. bd. Hanson Lab Furniture Ind., Inc., Newbury Park, Calif., 1995—, H.K. Canning, Inc., 1996—, Blois Constrn., 1997—; co-founder Calif. Family Bus. Inst., 1996. Contbr. articles to profl. jours. Chmn. Alliance for the Arts, Thousand Oaks, Calif., 1988-95. Ret. Lt. Col. U.S. Army Res., 1970-96, Korea. Recipient Outstanding Alumnus Calif. Lutheran U., 1986. Mem. Res. Officers Assn. of the U.S., Ventura County Econ. Devel. Assn., Tower Club, Santa Barbara Vintners Assn., James Beard Found., Marine Meml. Club, Spanish Hills Country Club. Republican. Roman Catholic. E-mail: swoodworth@ciequities.com. Home: 661 Corte De Quintero Camarillo CA 93010-8340 Office: Channel Islands Equities 300 E Esplanade Dr Ste 900 Oxnard CA 93030-1275

WOODY, WILLIAM EDWARD, software developer; b. San Luis Obispo, Calif., Oct. 3, 1965; s. William Claude and Toni Jean (Pierce) W.; m. Deborah Jenne Hollins, Dec. 10, 1994. BS in Math, Calif. Inst. Tech., Pasadena, 1988. Mem. tech. staff NASA/Jep Propulsion Lab., Pasadena, Calif., 1988-90; software design engr. Cheshire Engring. Corp., Pasadena, Calif., 1990-92; software engr. JBL Profl., Northridge, Calif., 1992-94; ptnr. In Phase Consulting, Glendale, Calif., 1994. Campaign mgr. Com. To Elect Michael Erin Woody, Fresno, Calif., 1992. Avocations: taekwondo, photography. Home and Office: In Phase Consulting 1545 Ard Eevin Ave Glendale CA 91202-1221

WOOLDRIDGE, SUSAN GOLDSMITH, author; b. Corning, N.Y., Jan. 30, 1946; d. Julian Royce and Ethel Juliette (Frank) Goldsmith; m. Kent Ernest Wooldridge, Aug. 25, 1968; children: Daniel Kent, Elisabeth Ann. BA, Barnard Coll., 1968; MA, Calif. State Univ., Chico, 1988. Asst. editor Univ. Chgo. Sch. Review, Chgo., 1967-68; copywriter Univ. Ill. Press, Urbana, 1968-74; photo journalist Chico News & Review, Chico, Calif., 1989-88; editor, writer Butte County Schs. News, Oroville, Calif., 1988-94; poet, tchr. Calif. Poets in the Schs., Chico, 1980-98, area coord., 1984-96; author Clarkson Potter, Random House, N.Y., 1996—; speaker workshop leader, 1996-98. Author: Poemcrazy: Freeing Your Life With Words, 1996; contbr. articles to profl. jours. Bd. dirs. 1078 Art Gallery, 1986-92, Calif. Poets in the Schs. (v.p.), 1992-94, Chico Creek Theater Festival, 1994-97, Chico H.S. PTA, 1991-95. Recipient Annie award for Advancement of Lit. Chico Annie's Arts Com., 1998. Mem. Calif. Poets in the Schs. Avocations: photography, pottery, collage, yoga, hiking. Home: 1991 Wild Oak Ln Chico CA 95928

WOOLF, MICHAEL E., lawyer; b. Phoenix, Mar. 17, 1949. BS, Ariz. State U., 1971, JD cum laude, 1974. Bar: ariz. 1974. Ptnr. O'Connor, Cavanagh, Anderson, Killingsworth & Beshears, P.A., Phoenix, 1977—. Mem. ABA, Maricopa County Bar Assn., State Bar Ariz. Office: O'Connor Cavanagh Anderson Killingsworth & Beshears PA 1 E Camelback Rd Ste 1100 Phoenix AZ 85012-1691*

WOOLLEY, DONNA PEARL, timber and lumber company executive; b. Drain, Oreg., Jan. 3, 1926; d. Chester A. and Mona B. (Cheever) Rydell; m. Harold Woolley, Dec. 27, 1952 (dec. Sept. 1970); children: Daniel, Debra, Donald. Diploma, Drain High Sch. Sec. No. Life Ins. Co., Eugene, Oreg., 1943-44; sec., bookkeeper D & W Lumber Co., Sutherlin, Oreg., 1944, Woolley Logging Co. & Earl Harris Lumber Co., Drain, 1944-70; pres. Woolley Logging Co., 1970—, Smith River Lumber Co., 1970—, Mt. Baldy Mill, 1970-81, Drain Plywood Co., 1970-81, Woolley Enterprises, Inc., Drain, 1973—, Eagle's View Mgmt. Co., Inc., Eugene, 1981—. Bd. dirs. Wildlife Safari, Winston, 1991, Oreg. Cmty. Found., Portland, Oreg., 1990—, chairperson, 1997-98; bd. dirs. Wildlife Safari, Winston, Oreg.; bd. trustees Linfield Coll., McMinnville, U. Oreg. Found., Eugene. Recipient Pioneer award U. Oreg., 1982, Econ. and Social Devel. award Soroptimist Club, 1991. Mem. Oreg. Women's Forum, Pacific Internat. Trapshooting Assn., Amateur Trapshooting Assn., Eugene C. of C. (bd. dirs. 1989-92), Arlington Club, Town Club (bd. dirs., pres.), Sunnydale Grange, Cottage Grove/Eugene Rod & Gun Club. Republican. Avocations: golf, travel. Office: Eagle's View Mgmt Co Inc 1399 Franklin Blvd Eugene OR 97403-1979

WOOLLIAMS, KEITH RICHARD, arboretum and botanical garden director; b. Chester, Eng., July 17, 1940; s. Gordon Frank and Margaret Caroline W.; m. Akiko Narita, Apr. 11, 1969; children: Frank Hiromi, Angela Misako. Grad., Cely Agrl. and Hort. Inst., North Wales, 1955; student, U. Liverpool, various horticultural insts., 1956-59; Kew Cert., Royal Bot. Gardens, Kew, U.K., 1963. Cert. Horticulture Union Cheshire and Lancs. Insts., 1955, Royal Hort. Soc., 1956, 57, 58, Nat. Cert. Horticulture, 1958, Cert. Arboriculture, 1962. Supt. field sta. U. London Queen Mary Coll., Brentwood, Essex, Eng., 1963-65; horticulturist Horizons Ltd., Bermuda, 1965-67; dept. forests, supt. botanic gardens Papua, New Guinea, 1967-68; instr. Eng. staff indsl. cos., Japan, 1968-71; supt., horticulturist Nat. Tropical Bot. Garden, Kauai, Hawaii, 1971-74; horticulturist Waimea Arboretum and Botanical Garden, Haleiwa, Hawaii, 1974-80, dir., 1980—; mem. Pacific islands plant recovery coordinating com. U.S. Fish and Wildlife Svc., 1993—; mem. Hawaii Rare Plant Restoration Group, 1991—. Contbr. articles to profl. jours., New Royal Hort. Soc. Dictionary of Gardening, 1992. Field assoc. botany Bishop Mus., Honolulu, 1981—; bd. dirs. Friends of Honolulu Bot. Gardens, 1980-96; v.p., founder Waimea Arboretum Found., 1977—; bd. dirs. Condominium Estate, Wahiawa, Hawaii, 1990—. Mem. Am. Assn. Botanical Gardens and Arboreta, Am. Hort. Soc., Hawaii Audubon Soc., Hawaiian Botanical Soc. (pres. 1979), Internat. Assn. Plant Taxonomists, Royal Hort. Soc., Kew Guild. Avocations: fishing, home repairs, music, reading, travel. Office: Waimea Arboretum & Bot Garden 59-864 Kamehameha Hwy Haleiwa HI 96712-9406

WOOLSEY, LYNN, congresswoman; b. Seattle, Nov. 3, 1937. BS, U. San Francisco, 1980. Mem. 103rd-105th Congresses from 6th Calif. dist., 1993 ; mem. Ho. Reps. com. on budget, edn. and the workforce. Office: US House of Reps 439 Cannon Bldg Washington DC 20515-0506*

WOOLSEY, ROBERT EUGENE DONALD, mineral economics, mathematics and business administration educator; b. Fort Worth, Oct. 31, 1936; s. Eugene Ralph W. and Ruby Ruth (White) Binder Woolsey; m. Ronita Elaine Packer, Sept. 17, 1958; children: Wysandria W.W., Darrell E. B.A., U. Tex., 1959, M.A., 1967, Ph.D., 1969. Staff mem. Sandia Corp., Albuquerque, 1966-68; assoc. dir. Computer Center U. Tex., Austin, 1968-69; assoc. prof. math. Colo. Sch. Mines, Golden, 1969-72, prof. math., 1972-74, prof. mineral econs., 1974-79, prof., head dept., 1979-81, MAPCO Found. prof., 1981-84, prof., program dir. Ops. Rsch./Mgmt. Sci. program divsn. econs. & bus., 1988—; vis. coll. Colo. Women's Coll., Denver, 1979-81; adj. prof. U. Waterloo, Ont., Can., 1972—, Instituto Technologico de Monterrey, Nuevo Leon, Mexico, 1974—, U. Witwatersrand, Johannesburg, S. Africa, 1984—; vis. prof. dept. engring. U.S. Mil. Acad., West Point, N.Y., 1986-87; prof. core faculty Walden U., 1990—; bd. dirs. Southland Energy Corp., Tulsa, New Tech. Devel. Co., Inc., Vancouver, B.C., Can. Author: Operations Research for Immediate Application, 1975, Applied Management Science, 1980; editor: Transactions of the Institute of Industrial Engineering, 1981-84, Production and Inventory Management, 1984—, Interfaces, 1975-82, Jour. Ops. Mgmt., 1986-87; contbr. articles to profl. jours. Pres. Rocky Mountain Fire Brigade, Inc., Golden, Colo., 1972-83. Served to capt. USAF, 1959-62. Named tchr. of yr. Standard Oil Ind., 1972, 96; recipient 1st Harold Larnder Meml. prize Can. Operational Rsch. Soc., 1986, Disting. Civilian Svc. medal U.S. Dept. Army, 1987, Comdrs. medal, 1991, Outstanding Civilian Svc. medal, 1995; named Hon. Col. 115 Engr. Regiment U.S. Army, 1987. Fellow Am. Inst. Decision Sci. (v.p. 1981-83); mem. Inst. Mgmt. Scis. (council 1976-78, pres. 1986-87), Inst. Indsl. Engrs. (sr. mem., editor 1981-84), Ops. Rsch. Soc. Am. (editor 1975-82), Newcomen Soc. Republican. Episcopalian. Home: 1826 Smith Rd Golden CO 80401-1756 Office: Colo Sch Mines Divsn Econs & Bus Golden CO 80401

WOOLSEY, ROY BLAKENEY, electronics company executive; b. Norfolk, Va., June 12, 1945; s. Roy B. and Louise Stookey (Jones) W.; m. Patricia Bernadine Elkins, Apr. 17, 1988. Student, Calif. Inst. Tech., 1962-64; BS with distinction, Stanford U., 1966, MS, 1967, PhD, 1970. Sr. physicist Tech. for Communications Internat., Mountain View, Calif., 1970-75; mgr. radio direction finding systems Tech. for Communications Internat., Mountain View, 1975-80, program mgr., 1980-83, dir. strategic systems, 1983-88, dir. research and devel., 1988-91, v.p. engring., 1991-92; v.p. programs Tech. for Communications Internat., Sunnyvale, Calif., 1992—; bd. dirs. Merit Software Corp., Menlo Park, 1990-96. Author: (with others) Applications of Artificial Intelligence to Command and Control Systems, 1988, Antenna Engineering Handbook, 1993; contbr. articles to profl. jours. Active YMCA, Palo Alto, Calif., Los Altos Hills com. rels. com., 1994—. Fellow NSF, 1966-70. Mem. AFCEA, Stanford Club, Sequoia Yacht Club, Sigma Xi, Phi Beta Kappa. Republican. Presbyterian. Avocations: sailing, tennis, racquetball, skiing, contract bridge, travel. Home: 26649 Snell Ln

Los Altos Hills CA 94022-2039 Office: Tech for Communications Internat 222 Caspian Dr Sunnyvale CA 94089-1014

WOOSLEY, ANNE I., cultural organization administrator. Dir. The Amerind Found., Inc., Dragoon, Ariz. Office: The Amerind Found Inc PO Box 400 2100 N Amerind Rd Dragoon AZ 85609*

WOOTEN, MICHAEL ERIC, career officer; b. San Diego, June 12, 1959; s. James Willis and Elease (Lewis) W.; m. D'Andrea Michele Wilson, Feb. 1, 1988; children: John Michael Christopher, Sarah Mary Elizabeth. AA, DeKalb C.C., 1981; BA in Psychology, Chapman U., 1986; MA in Leadership and Orgnl. Mgmt., Norwich U., 1996; MS in Acquisition and Contract Mgmt., Naval Postgrad. Sch., 1997. Cert. tower operator. Air traffic controller Hdqs. & Hdqs. Squadron, Tustin, Calif., 1983-86; commd. 2nd lt. USMC, 1987, advanced through grades to maj., 1997; officer student, 1987-88; asst. supply officer Second Maintenance Battalion, Camp LeJeune, N.C., 1988-89; supply officer Second Landing Support Battalion, Camp LeJeune, N.C., 1989-90; protocol officer Marine Corps Logistics Base, Albany, Ga., 1990; asst. br. head Mgmt. Br. Integrated Logistics Support, Albany, Ga., 1990-91; aide-de-camp Marine Corps Logistics Base, Albany, Ga., 1991-92; logistics officer Hdqs. Battalion, Albany, Ga., 1992-93; supply officer First sLight Anti Aircraft Missile Battalion, Yuma, Ariz., 1993-96; student Naval Postgrad. Sch., 1996-97; nonresident dir. Navy Mut. Aid Assn., Arlington, Va., 1994. Recipient Navy Commendation medal. Mem. Nat. Naval Officer Assn., NAACP, Toastmasters Internat., Masons, Phi Beta Sigma. Episcopalian. Avocations: writing, tae kwon do (1st degree black belt). Office: Contracting Officer Hdqrs USMC (ARDB) 2 Navy Anx Rm 1209 Washington DC 20370-0002

WORD, INETTA LOUISE, sewing educator, designer, writer; b. Colusa, Calif., June 5, 1949; d. Emery Grant and Neoma Clarice (Quick) Dowden; m. Calvin Hugh Word, Aug. 14, 1964; children: Wendy Lee, Calvin Hugh II. Sewing tchr. Fabric Fair, Colusa, Calif., 1989-97; free lance sewing tchr. Sewing Studio, Durham, Calif., 1990—, Concord (Calif.) Sewing, 1994—, Sew Tech - Internet, Vacaville, Calif., 1997—; sewing tchr. Viking Sewing Machine Co., Internat. Conv., Las Vegas, 1994, designer Embroidery Card #30 software for Viking #1 Plus sewing machine Viking Sewing Machine Co., 1998. Author: (books) Ynellas Machine Embroidery, 1991, Stitch Combinations, 1991, Snowflakes, 1991, Beadings and Borders, 1992, Baby Flakes, 1993, Victorian Heart, 1993, Viking 500 Stitch and Embroidery, 1996. Recipient award Viking Sewing Machine Co., L.A., 1990. E-mail: ynellas@mako.com.

WORDEN, KATHERINE A., osteopath, educator; b. Burton Wood AFB, Eng., Apr. 20, 1955; parents Am. citizens; d. Richard C. and Elizabeth A. (Bennett) W. BS in Microbiology, Purdue U., 1977; MS in virology, U. Chgo., 1979; postgrad., St. Joseph's Coll., Rensselaer, Inc., 1982; DO, Mich. State U., 1988. Diplomate Am. Bd. Family Practice. Assoc. prof. biology St. Joseph's Coll., 1979-84; intern Riverside Osteo. Hosp./Detroit Osteo. Hosp. Corp., 1988-90; resident in family practice Tucson Gen. Hosp., 1989-91; clin. instr. Mich. State U., East Lansing, 1989—; pvt. practice family practice and obstetrics, Tucson, 1997—; clin. instr. U. Ariz., Tucson, 1997—; splty. practice osteo. manipulative medicine, Tucson, 1997—; instr. postgrad. courses in manual medicine Mich. State U., East Lansing, 1992—; mem. family practice dept. Tucson Gen. Hosp., chair, 1995-97. Contbr. articles to profl. jours. NSF fellow, 1978-79; U. Ariz. grantee, 1996-97; recipient scholarships, awards. Mem. Am. Coll. Osteo. Family Physicians, Am. Acad. Osteopathy, Cranial Acad., Nat. Osteo. Women Physicians Assn., Ariz. Osteo. Med. Assn., Pima County Med. Soc., Tucson Soc. Women Physicians, N.W. Cmty. Women Physicians Group. Avocations: retreat work with college students, folk singing, biking, backpacking. Office: Kate Care Osteo Ctr 3333 N Campbell Ave Ste 10 Tucson AZ 85719-2362

WORRELL, RICHARD VERNON, orthopedic surgeon, college dean; b. Bklyn., June 4, 1931; s. John Elmer and Elaine (Callender) W.; BA, NYU, 1952; MD, Meharry Med. Coll., 1958; m. Audrey Frances Martiny, June 14, 1958; children: Philip Vernon, Amy Elizabeth. Intern Meharry Med. Coll., Nashville, 1958-59; resident gen. surgery Mercy-Douglass Hosp., Phila., 1960-61; resident orthopedic surgery State U. N.Y. Buffalo Sch. Medicine Affiliated Hosps., 1961-64; resident in orthopedic pathology Temple U. Med. Ctr., Phila., 1966-67; pvt. practice orthopedic surgery, Phila., 1964-68; asst. prof. acting head div. orthopedic surgery U. Conn. Sch. Medicine 1968-70; attending orthopedic surgeon E.J. Meyer Meml. Hosp., Buffalo, Millard Fillmore Hosp., Buffalo, VA Hosp., Buffalo, Buffalo State Hosp.; clin. instr. orthopedic surgery SUNY, Buffalo, 1970-74; chief orthopedic surgery VA Hosp., Newington, Conn., 1974-80; asst. prof. surgery (orthopedics) U. Conn. Sch. Medicine, 1974-77, assoc. prof., 1977-83, asst. dean student affairs, 1980-83; prof. clin. surgery SUNY Downstate Med. Ctr., Bklyn., 1983-86; dir. orthopedic surgery Brookdale Hosp. Med. Ctr., Bklyn., 1983-86; prof. of orthopedics U. N.Mex. Sch. of Medicine, 1986—, prof., vice chmn. dept. orthopaedics, 1997—; dir. orthopedic oncology U. N.Mex. Med. Ctr., 1987—; mem. med. staff U. N.Mex. Cancer Ctr., 1987—; chief orthopedic surgery VA Med. Ctr., Albuquerque, 1987-97; cons. in orthopedic surgery Newington (Conn.) Children's Hosp., 1968-70; mem. sickle cell disease adv. com. NIH, 1982-86. Bd. dirs. Big Bros. Greater Hartford. Served to capt. M.C., U.S. Army Res., 1962-69. Diplomate Am. Bd. Orthopedic Surgery, Nat. Bd. Med. Examiners. Fellow ACS, Am. Acad. Orthopedic Surgeons, Royal Soc. Medicine, London; mem. AMA, Am. Orthopaedic Assn., Am. Soc. Clin. Pathologists, Am. Soc. Clin. Oncology, Orthopedic Rsch. Soc., Internat. Soc. Orthopedic Surgery and Traumatology, N.Mex. Soc. Clin. Oncology, Internat. Fedn. Surg. Colls. (assoc.), Alpha Omega Alpha. Office: U NMex Sch Medicine Albuquerque NM 87131-5296

WORTH, MARK EDWARD, political journalist, media analyst; b. Hollywood, Fla., Jan. 20, 1964; s. Robert Charles and Phyllis Corlett (Judge) W. BSc in Journalism, U. Fla., 1986. Political writer N.Y. Times Co., Atlanta, 1986-89; co-pub. Moon Mag., Gainesville, Fla., 1990-91; assoc. editor N.W. Energy Markets, Seattle, 1991-92; assoc. editor, staff rschr. In Context/Context Inst., Bainbridge Island, Wash., 1992-93; pub. Wash. Free Press, Seattle, 1993-95; contributing writer Microsoft Corp., Redmond, Wash., 1994—; media columnist, political writer Seattle Weekly, 1997—; cons. KCMU-FM Pub. Radio, Seattle, 1993-94. Contbr. monographs to profl. jours. Exec. dir. Corporate Welfare Action Group, Seattle, 1996—, Puget Sound Media Watch, Seattle, 1997—; pub. policy com. Green Party of Seattle, 1998; bd. dirs. Cmty. Powered Radio, Seattle, 1994-95. Recipient Top 10 In-Depth News Story award William Randolph Hearst Found., San Francisco, 1986, Best Coverage Emerging Issues award UTNE Reader, Mpls., 1993, Best Non-Daily Newspaper Editor and Best Non-Daily Newspaper award Wash. Press Assn., Seattle, 1995. Mem. Soc. Profl. Journalists, Investigative Reporters and Editors (Nation's Best Mag. Story award 1995). Avocations: world travel, blues harmonica, Asian cooking. Home and Office: 514 Prospect Seattle WA 98109

WORTHEY, CAROL, composer; b. Worcester, Mass., Mar. 1, 1943; d. Bernard Krieger and Edith Lilian (Cramer) Symonds; m. Eugene Worthey III, June 1969 (div. 1980); 1 child, Megan; m. Raymond Edward Korns, Sept. 21, 1980. BA in Music Composition, Columbia U., 1965; grad., Dick Grove Sch. Music., L.A., 1979; grad. filmscoring prog., UCLA, 1978; music studies with Darius Milhaud, Walter Piston, Elliot Carter, Vincent Persichetti, Grant Beglarian, Karl Korte, Otto Luening, Eddy Lawrence Manson, Dick Grove; studied, RISD, 1948-54, Columbia U., 1965. Sr. composer, arranger Celebrity Ctr. Internat. Choir, Hollywood, Calif., 1985—. Composer, arranger The Hollywood Chorale; composer ballets Athena, 1963, The Barren, 1965, piano works performed in France, Italy, Germany, Canada, U.S., Eng. by Mario Feninger, 1992, Pastorale, performed in Mex., 1994, Neighborhood of the Heart, 1994, (choir) Unquenchable Light, 1993, (film score) The Special Visitor, 1992; compositions performed at Aspen Music Festival, 1963, Carnegie Hall, 1954, Dorothy Chandler Pavilion, 1986-89; appeared as singer-songwriter L.A. Songwriter's Showcase, 1977; arranger Merv Griffin Show, 1981, The Night Before Christmas, L.A. Children's Theater, 1988-91, Capistrano Valley Symphony, 1994, Very Old Merry Old Christmas, Dorothy Chandler Pavilion, 1994, Judge, 1994; (CD) David Arkenstone Return of the Guardian, 1996, Celtic Book of Days, 1998; composer, lyricist, librettist full-length musical The Envelope Please, 1988; author: Treasury of Holiday Music, 1992, (poems) The Lonely Wanderer Comes Home, 1994; art work exhibited RISD, 1952, Folk and Art Mus., L.A., 1975, 1st Internat. Art Exhibit Celebrity Ctr. Pavilion, 1992; cable tv show: Neighborhood of the Heart, 1995, 96. Vol. performer various childcare ctrs., old folks homes, etc.; judge Composer's Competition, Inner City Cultural Ctr., 1995-97. Recipient Silver Poet award World of Poetry, 1987, 2nd place winner, 1st BarComposers and Songwriters Competition for "Fanfare for Joy & Wedding March", 1990, Golden Poet award World of Poetry, 1992. Mem. Nat. Assn. Composers, USA, Broadcast Music Inc., Nat. Acad. Songwriters, Film Music Network, Songwriters and Composers Assn., Toastmasters Internat. (Advanced Toastmaster Bronze 1998), Film Adv. Bd. Jewish. Avocations: gourmet cooking, films, macrame, creative writing, calligraphy.

WORTZEL, GARY, artist, filmmaker; b. East Orange, N.J., Sept. 26, 1962; s. Donald Gilbert and Lillian (Salofsky) W.; m. Judith Kaufman, Nov. 11, 1989. BS, U. Del., 1984. Owner, dir. Gary Wortzel Fine Arts, Boston, 1988-90; prodr., dir. Alligator Films, N.Y.C., 1991-96; web page designer wortzelgrafix, Seattle, 1996—; cons. Driscoll Robbins Fine Oriental Carpets, Seattle, 1998—, 1919 Design Team, Seattle, 1998—. Prodr., dir. films Painted Sun, 1997, The Left Side of My Brain, 1994; artist etching South African, 1996; exhibited at Provincetown (Mass.) Art Mus., 1994. Mem. 911 Media Arts, Seattle, 1996—; prodr. Montague (Mass.) Cmty. T.V., 1994-96. Recipient Purchase award Time Warner Inc., N.Y.C., 1991. Mem. Provincetown Art Assn. Avocations: basketball, dancing, guitar, gardening. E-mail: garyw@speakeasy.org.

WOSK, MIRIAM, artist; b. Vancouver, B.C., Can., Aug. 17, 1947; d. Morris J. and Dena W.; 1 child, Adam. Student, U. B.C., Can., 1966; AAS, Fashion Inst. Tech., N.Y.C., 1969; postgrad., Sch. Visual Arts, New Sch. Social Rsch., N.Y.C., 1969-74. lectr. Fashion Inst. Tech., N.Y.C., Sch. Visual Arts, N.Y.C., Art Ctr. Sch. Design, Pasadena, Calif., Woman's Bldg. Graphic Ctr., L.A., Otis Parsons Sch. Design, L.A., Ctr. Early Edn., L.A., Crossroads Sch., Santa Monica, Calif., UCLA Ext., L.A., Folk Art Soc., L.A.; freelance illustrator N.Y.C. mags., 1970s-1980s, including 1st cover of Ms., Mademoiselle, N.Y. Times, Esquire, Vogue, N.Y. Mag., Viva, McCalls, Saturday Rev., Sesame St., New West, Psychology Today, 1969-79; curator group show The Inner Lives of Women: Psyche, Spirit and Soul, Spring St. Gallery, L.A., 1996. One woman shows include Transam. Ctr., L.A., 1983, West Beach, L.A., 1988, Wilshire Pacific Bldg., L.A., 1990, Robert Berman Gallery, Santa Monica, Calif., 1991, Drago, Santa Monica, 1992, Jazz, Pacific Design Ctr., West Hollywood, Calif., 1995; exhibited in group shows at Harkness House Gallery, N.Y.C., 1978, Steps into Space, L.A., 1979-80, Dist. 1199 Cultural Ctr. Inc., N.Y., 1981, Smithsonian Inst., Washington, 1981, China Club, L.A., 1981, Biltmore Hotel, L.A., 1982, Transam. Pyramid, San Francisco, 1983, Barnsdall Art Gallery, L.A., 1983, Functional Art Gallery, L.A., 1985, One Market Plaza, San Francisco, 1986, Laforet Mus., Tokyo, 1986, Art et Industrie Gallery, N.Y.C., 1986, Otis Parsons Sch. Design, L.A., 1987, B1 Gallery, Santa Monica, 1987, Katharina Rich Perlow Gallery, N.Y.C., 1988, Deborah Schiller Hadl Art, Culver City, Calif., 1988, L.A., 1993, Sam Francis Studio, Santa Monica, 1988, Gallery Functional Art, Santa Monica, 1989, 91, Art Store Gallery, L.A., Santa Monica, 1990, Santa Monica Mus. Art, 1990, Getty Mus., Malibu, Calif., 1990, James Corcoran Gallery, Santa Monica, 1990, Joan Robey Gallery, Denver, 1992, Cultural Ctr., Eureka, Calif., Calif. State U., Long Beach, 1992, Pacific Design Ctr., L.A., 1992, U. Art Mus., Long Beach, 1992, L.A. County Mus. Art, 1992, 96, Helander Gallery, Palm Beach, Fla., 1993, Spring Street Gallery, L.A., 1994, 96, Anderson Ranch Art Ctr., Aspen, Colo., 1995, Park Ave. Armory, N.Y.C., 1997, 98, Adam Baumgold Gallery, N.Y.C., 1997, Pub. Corp. Arts, Long Beach, 1998; pub. in nat. and internat. mags., books and newspapers. Recipient Merit award Art Dirs. Club N.Y., cert. of merit Soc. Illustrators, cert. excellence Am. Inst. Graphic Artists; named guest editor Maedmoiselle Mag. Home: 440 S Roxbury Dr Beverly Hills CA 90212-4102

WOTT, JOHN ARTHUR, arboretum and botanical garden executive, horticulture educator; b. Fremont, Ohio, Apr. 10, 1939; s. Arthur Otto Louis and Esther Wilhelmina (Werth) W.; children: Christopher, Timothy, Holly. BS, Ohio State U., 1961; MS, Cornell U., 1966, PhD, 1968. Mem. staff Ohio State Coop. Extension Svc., Bowling Green, 1961-64; rsch. asst. Cornell U., Ithaca, N.Y., 1964-68; prof. Purdue U., West Lafayette, Ind., 1968-81; prof. Ctr. Urban Horticulture U. Wash., Seattle, 1981—; assoc. dir. Ctr. Urban Horticulture U. Wash., Seattle, 1990-93; dir. arboreta Washington Park Arboretum, Seattle, 1993—. Writer columns for Nursery Mgmt. Profession, Balls and Burlap, Am. Nurseryman, The Arboretum Found.; contbr. articles to profl. jours. and papers including Nursery Mgr. Profl., Balls and Burlap, Arbreteum Found. Bull., Am. Nurseryman. Mem. Am. Soc. Hort. Sci. (com. chmn. 1967-82), Am. Assn. Bot. Gardens and Arboreta, Internat. Plant Propagators Soc. (pres. 1984, sec.-treas. 1985—). Avocations: music, antiques. Office: Internat Plant 2300 Arboretum Dr E Seattle WA 98112-2300

WOUDENBERG, TIMOTHY MARK, systems engineer; b. N.Y.C., Sept. 24, 1957; s. Richard William Woudenberg and Patricia Jean (Jordan) Wood; m. Liane Brookhart, May 2, 1981; children: Carina Ellen, Raina Eve, Cherissa Kay. BS, Purdue U., 1980; PhD, Tufts U., 1988. Sr. engr. Perkin-Elmer Corp., Norwalk, Conn., 1987-93; sr. staff engr. applied biosys. Perkin-Elmer Corp., Foster City, Calif., 1993—. 4 patents in field. Mem. Am. Chem. Soc. Avocations: hiking, bicycling, sailing, skiing. Home: PO Box 4 120 Arbor Ln Moss Beach CA 94038-9702 Office: Perkin Elmer Corp 850 Lincoln Centre Dr Foster City CA 94404-1128

WOWKOWYCH, PETER DMYTRO, architect; b. Rochester, N.Y., Jan. 28, 1963; s. Michael and Marion Wowkowych. BArch, U. Notre Dame, 1986; MArch, So. Calif. Inst. Architecture, 1997. Registered arch., N.Y., Calif. Arch. Edward Durell Stone Assocs., N.Y.C., 1986-88, Karen Van Lengen Archs., N.Y.C., 1988-91; asst. curator post WWII Italian artists show Peggy Guggenheim Mus., Venice, Italy, 1988; asst. curator Am. Pavilion Venice Bienalle, 1990; project designer Bahram Shirdel Architecture, L.A., 1991-92; project arch., urban planner Hardy Holzman Pfeiffer Assocs., L.A., 1992-95; project mgr. Sony Pictures, L.A., 1995—; mem. jury Columbia U., N.Y.C., 1989, 90, N.Y. Inst. Tech., Old Westbury, 1990. Editor Notre Dame Jour. Architecture, 1986; exhibited in group show at Mus. Modern Art, N.Y.C., 1992. Vol., arch. Cal-Earth Inst., Hesperia, Calif., 1996-97. Mem. AIA (docent), L.A. Forum Architecture and Urban Design. Avocations: painting, metal sculpture, rock climbing, mountaineering. Home: 1698 Electric Ave Venice CA 90291-4804 Office: Wowkowych Architecture 1698 Electric Ave Venice CA 90291-4804

WOYSKI, MARGARET SKILLMAN, retired geology educator; b. West Chester, Pa., July 26, 1921; d. Willis Rowland and Clara Louise (Howson) Skillman; m. Mark M. Woyski, June 19, 1948; children: Nancy Elizabeth, William Bruno, Ronald David, Wendelin Jane. BA in Chemistry, Wellesley (Mass.) Coll., 1943; MS in Geology, U. Minn., 1945, PhD in Geology, 1946. Geologist Mo. Geol. Survey and Water Resources, Rolla, 1946-48; instr. U. Wis., Madison, 1948-52; lectr. Calif. State U., Long Beach, 1963-67; lectr. to prof. Calif. State U., Fullerton, 1966-91, assoc. dean Sch. Natural Sci. and Math., 1981-91, emeritus prof., 1991—. Contbr. articles to profl. jours.; author lab. manuals; editor guidebooks. Fellow Geol. Soc. Am. (program chmn. 1982); mem. South Coast Geol. Soc. (hon. pres. 1974), Mineral Soc. Am. Home: 1843 Kashlan Rd La Habra CA 90631-8423

WOYTAK, LIDIA T., editor; b. Poznan, Poland, Sept. 26, 1946; d. Zygmunt and Alexandra (Kobus) Butlewski; m. Richard Andrew Woytak, July 15, 1968 (dec. Mar. 1998); children: Adele, Lillian, John, Stacy. MA, A. Mickiewicz U., 1968, PhD, 1981; MA, Monterey (Calif.) Inst., 1971. Editor Applied Lang. Learning Def. Lang. Inst. Fng. Lang. Ctr., Monterey, 1971—. Author manual and articles on linguistics and fgn. lang. edn.

WOZNIAK, CURTIS S., electronics company executive. Various positions in mfg., mktg. and ops. Gen. Motors Corp.; prodn. engring. mgr. Hewlett-Packard Co.; v.p. Desktop Graphics devel. Sun Microsys. Computer Corp., v.p., gen. mgr. Ednl. Products divsn., v.p. engring., v.p. worldwide mktg.; pres., COO Xilinx Inc.; CEO Electroglas Inc., 1996—, also chmn., 1997—; bd. dirs. SEMI/SEMATECH consortium, Mgmt. Inst. Office: Electroglas 2901 Coronado Dr Santa Clara CA [illegible]

WRIGHT, BERNARD, artist; b. Pitts., Feb. 23, 1938; s. Garfield and Emma (Jefferson) W.; m. Corrine Westley, Mar. 7, 1964; 1 son, Jeffrey. Student Otis Art Inst., Los Angeles, 1969-70, Los Angeles Trade Tech. Coll., 1971-73. Exhibited traveling art show Moscow, Baku, Leningrad, Alma Alta, USSR, European capitals, 1966, Los Angeles City Hall Rotunda Gallery, 1967, Calif. Lutheran Coll., Thousand Oaks, 1967, Compton (Calif.) C.C., 1967, 89, Alley Gallery, Beverly Hills, 1968, Florenz Art Gallery, Los Angeles, 1969, San Diego Mus., 1969, Phillip E. Freed Gallery of Fine Arts, Chgo., 1969, Playboy Club, Century City, Calif., 1971, Diplomat Hotel, Emerald Gallery, Hollywood Beach, Fla., 1971, Art West Gallery, Los Angeles, 1973, N.J. State Mus., Trenton, Detroit Inst. Arts, Mich., 1974, U. So. Calif., Calif. Mus. Sci. and Industry, 1974, City Art Mus., St. Louis, 1976, N.Y.C. Pub. Library, 1977, Pitts. City Hall Rotunda, 1982, The Mus. of African Am. Art, Los Angeles, 1982, Main Bridge Art Gallery, Los Angeles City Hall, 1983, Howard U. Art Gallery, Washington, 1983, L.A. Pub. Libr., Baldwin Hills Br., 1984, Morgan State U., James E. Lewis Mus. Art, Balt., 1984, Fisk U. Mus. Art, U. Galleries, Nashville, 1984, U.S. Amada, Ltd., Buena Park, Calif., 1985, L.A. Southwest Coll., 1986, Prairie View A&M U., Tex., 1987, Louis Newman Galleries, Beverly Hills, Calif., 1989, Mus. African & African Am. Art Antiquities, Buffalo, 1989, Griffon's Light Gallery, Denver, 1990, Sheraton Hotel, Akron/Cuyahoga Falls, Ohio, 1992, Hyatt Regency Hotel, Washington, 1992, U. Utah, Salt Lake City, 1993, many others; represented in pvt. and pub. collections including Howard U., Library of Congress. collections past pres. co-founder Wright's & Westley Prodns., furniture and garment designers. Cited by U.S. Rep. Cardiss Collins, Ill., 1978, state senator Bill Greene, Calif. 1981, Mayor Richard S. Callguiri, Pitts., 1981, Mayor Coleman A. Young, Detroit, 1981, Mayor Tom Bradley, Los Angeles. bd. supr. Kenneth Hahn, Los Angeles, 1981; active community involvement Sta. KHJ-TV, 1982. Mem. Art West Assn. (bd. dirs.). Home: PO Box 76169 Los Angeles CA 90076-0169

WRIGHT, C. T. ENUS, former academic administrator; b. Social Circle, Ga., Oct. 4, 1942; s. George and Carrie Mae (Enus) W.; m. Mary Stephens, Aug. 9, 1974. B.S., Fort Valley State U. (Ga.), 1964; M.A., Atlanta U., 1967; Ph.D., Boston U., 1977. Tchr., Ga. Pub. Schs., Social Circle, 1965-67; mem. faculty Morris Brown Coll., Atlanta, 1967-73, div. chmn., 1973-77; program dir., asst. provost Eastern Wash. U., Cheney, 1977-81; v.p. academic affairs Talladega Coll. (Ala.), 1981-82; pres. Cheyney U. Pa., Cheyney, 1982-85; v.p. and provost Fla. Meml. Coll., 1985-89; exec. dir. Internat. Found. and Coord. African-African Am. Summit, 1989—; cons. and lectr. in field. Author: (booklet) The History of Black Historical Mythology, 1980; contbr. articles to profl. jours. Commnr., Wash. Pub. Broadcasting, Olympia, 1980-84; exec. com. Boy Scouts Am., Phila., 1982—. Human Relations scholar, 1969, Nat. Teaching fellow Boston U., 1971. Mem. Am. Assn. Colls. and Univs. (coms. 1982—), Am. Hist. Assn. (coms. 1970—), Assn. Study Afro-Am. Life & History (coms. 1965—), Nat. Assn. Equal Opportunity in Higher Edn. (coms. 1982—), NEA (coms. 1965—). Am. Baptist. Clubs: Lions (Cheyney, Wash. (v.p. 1979-81)); Tuscan; Atlanta Constitution. Office: Intl Found 5122 E Shea Blvd Apt 2098 Scottsdale AZ 85254-4679

WRIGHT, CAROLE YVONNE, chiropractor; b. Long Beach, Calif., July 12, 1932; d. Paul Burt and Mary Leoan (Staley) Fickes; 1 child, Morgan Michelle. D. Chiropractic, Palmer Coll., Davenport, Iowa, 1976. Instr. Palmer Coll., 1975-76; dir., owner Wright Chiropractic Clinic, Rocklin, Calif., 1978-88, Woodland, Calif., 1980-81; co-owner Ft. Sutter Chiropractic Clinic, Sacramento, 1985-89; owner Wright Chiropractic Health Ctr., Sacramento, 1989—, Capitol Chiropractic, Sacramento, 1993—; cons. in field; lectr., speaker on radio and TV programs, at seminars. Contbr. articles to profl. jours. Co-chmn. Harold Michaels for Congress campaign, Alameda, Calif., 1972; dist. dir. 14th Congl. Dist., 1983—. Mem. Internat. Chiropractic Assn. Calif. (bd. dirs. 1978-81, pres. 1983-85), Palmer Coll. Alumni Assn. (Calif. state pres. 1981-83), Rocklin C. of C. (bd. dirs. 1979-81). Republican. Avocations: reading, travel. Home: 1404 Stonebridge Way Roseville CA 95661-5456

WRIGHT, CHARLES LEE, information systems consultant; b. Dalton, Ga., Dec. 18, 1949; s. Charlie William and Catherine Christine (Quarles) W.; children: Charles Lee, Christina, Leana. AA in Bus., Dalton Jr. Coll., 1971; BS in Bus., U. Tenn., Chattanooga, 1977; student, IBM classes. Trainee Ludlow Carpets, Dalton, 1971, EDP supr., 1971-73, EDP mgr., 1973-77; ops. mgr. Walter Carpet Mills, Industry, Calif., 1977-80; ptnr., cons. TCT Systems, San Dimas, Calif., 1978-92; ptnr., CEO Williams, Wright and Assocs., Upland, Calif., 1978-92; v.p. ops. Roland Corp., U.S., 1993—. Served as sgt. U.S. Army, 1969-71; Vietnam, Cambodia. Decorated Bronze Star, Army Commendation medal with oak leaf and oak leaf cluster, Air medal. Mem. Data Processing Mgmt. Assn., Am. Mgmt. Assn., Small Systems User Group, COMMON. Home and Office: 3708 Palamino Place Ontario CA 91761-5107

WRIGHT, CHATT GRANDISON, academic administrator; b. San Mateo, Calif., Sept. 17, 1941; s. Virgil Tandy and Louise (Jeschien) W.; children from previous marriage: Stephen Brook, Jon David, Shelley Adams; m. Janice Teply, Nov. 28, 1993. Student, U. Calif., Berkeley, 1960-62; BA in Polit. Sci., U. Calif., Davis, 1964; MA in Econs., U. Hawaii, 1968. Instr. econs. U. Hawaii, Honolulu, 1968-70; mgr. corp. planning Telecheck Internat., Inc., Honolulu, 1969-70; economist State of Hawaii, Honolulu, 1970-71; adminstr. manpower City & County of Honolulu, 1971-72; bus. adminstr., dean. Hawaii Pacific U., Honolulu, 1972-74, v.p., 1974-76, pres., 1976—. Mem. City and County of Honolulu Manpower Area Planning Commn., 1976-82; mem. Mayor's Salary Commn. City of County of Honolulu, 1977-80; mem. Honolulu City Ethics Commn., 1978-84; em. City and County of Honolulu Labor Market Adv. Coun., 1982-84; bd. dirs. Hawaii Econ. Devel. Corp., 1980-84; trustee Queen's Med. Ctr., Honolulu, 1986-92, Honolulu Armed Svcs. YMCA, 1984-86, Hawaii Maritime Ctr., 1990-92; chmn. bd. trustees Hist. Hawaii Found., 1995-96, mem., 1990-96; mem. adv. bd. Cancer Rsch. Ctr. Hawaii, 1987; trustee St. Andrew's Priory Sch., 1994-98; bd. dirs. Hawaii Visitors Bur., 1995-97; mem. adv. bd. HCEE, 1996—; bd. dirs. Downtown Improvement Assn., 1988-96, Outrigger Duke Kahanamoku Found., 1996-98, Hawaii Opera Theatre, 1997—; trustee Oceanic Inst., 1998—; mem. Hawaii Execs. Coun., 1996—, chmn. 1999; bd. govs. Hawaii Med. Libr., 1989-92; mem. adv. bd. Aloha coun. Boy Scouts Am., 1991—; trustee Molokai Gen. Hosp., 1991-92; mem. Pacific Asian Affairs Coun., 1998—. With USN, 1967-80. Recipient Pioneer award Pioneer Fed. Savs. Bank, 1982, Stephen L. Jackstadt award Hawaii Coun. on Econ. Edn., 1998; Paul Harris fellow Rotary, 1986. Mem. Am. Assn. Higher Edn., Assn. Governing Bds. Univs. and Colls., Japan-Am. Soc. Honolulu, Social Sci. Assn., Nat. Assn. Intercollegiate Athletics (vice chair NAIA coun. of pres. 1994, mem. 1985-98), Hawaii Joint Coun. Econ. Edn. (bd. dirs. 1982-88, Stephen L. Jackstadt award 1998), Western Coll. Assn. (exec. com. 1989-92), Hawaii Assn. Ind. Colls. and Univs. (chmn. 1986), Hawaii C. of C., Sales and Mktg. Execs. Club Honolulu, Outrigger Canoe Club, Pacific Club (Honolulu), Plaza Club (bd. govs. 1992-97), Waialae Country Club. Republican. Episcopalian. Avocations: hunting, fishing, reading, travel. Office: Hawaii Pacific U Office Pres 1166 Fort St Mall Honolulu HI 96813-2785

WRIGHT, DONALD FRANKLIN, newspaper executive; b. St. Paul, July 10, 1934; s. Floyd Franklin and Helen Marie (Hansen) W.; m. Sharon Kathleen Fisher, Dec. 30, 1960; children: John, Dana, Kara, Patrick. BME, U. Minn., 1957, MBA, 1958. With Mpls. Star & Tribune Co., 1958-77, research planning dir., then ops. dir., 1971-75, exec. editor, 1975-77; exec. v.p., gen. mgr. Newsday, Inc., L.I., 1977-78, pres., chief operating officer, 1978-81; pres., chief operating officer L.A. Times, 1981-87; sr. v.p. Times Mirror Co., L.A., from 1988; now pres., CEO L.A. Times; exec. v.p. Times Mirror Co., L.A., 1998—. Hon. mem., former vice chmn. bd. trustees Claremont Grad. Sch. and Univ. Ctr.; vice chmn., past chmn. L.A. Area coun. Boy Scouts Am., 1989—, v.p. western region, past pres. area IV; bd. dirs. Assocs. Calif. Inst. Tech., U. Minn. Found.; past bd. dirs. United Way Long Island, Calif.;. Mem. Am. Newspaper Pubs. Assn. (past chmn. telecom. com. and prodn. mgmt. com.), U. Minn. Alumni Assn., City Club Bunker Hill. Presbyterian. Office: Times Mirror Co Times Mirror Sq Los Angeles CA 90053*

WRIGHT, ERIC R., physician assistant; b. Fremont, Mich., Apr. 8, 1952; s. Owen Aaron and Ethlyn Emily (Crandall) W.; m. Teresa Christine Harrison, May 3, 1978; 1 child, Natalie Ann. Grad., Hackley Hosp. Sch. Radiol. Tech.,

Muskegon, Mich., 1975; AS in Physician Assisting with honors, Kettering (Ohio) Coll. Med.Art, 1984. Diplomate Colo. Bd. Med. Examiners; cert. graphoanalyst. Physician asst. Peak Nine Med. Ctr./Family & Emergency Med. Assocs., Breckenridge, Colo., 1984-85, Richard Wageman, M.D., Monument, Colo., 1985-86, Dennis Caldwell, M.D., Colorado Springs, Colo., 1986-88, Sheldon Ravin, D.O., Skyway Family Practice, Colorado Springs, 1988-90, The People's Clinic, Boulder, Colo., 1990-95, Columbine Family Practice Ctr., Loveland, Colo., 1991-93, Alpine Ear, Nose and Throat, Ft. Collins, Colo., 1993—. Author: Acute Mountain Sickness, 1988, Practice Guidelines for Physician Assistants, rev. edit., 1997. Mem. Internat. Graphoanalysis Soc., Am. Registry of Radiologic Technologists, Beaven-Black Student Soc. Physician Assts. (v.p. 1982-83), Am. Acad. Physician Assts., Colo. Assn. Physician Assts. (membership chmn. 1990-92), Soc. Physician Assts. in Otolaryngology. SDA. Avocations: guitar, bicycling, hiking, coin collecting, gardening. Home: 3411 N Douglas Loveland CO 80538-2574

WRIGHT, FRANCES JANE, educational psychologist; b. Los Angeles, Dec. 22, 1943; d. step-father John David and Evelyn Jane (Dale) Brinegar. BA, Long Beach State U., 1965, secondary tchr. cert., 1966; MA, Brigham Young U., 1968, EdD, 1980; postgrad. U. Nev., 1970, U. Utah, 1972-73; postdoctoral Utah State U., 1985-86. Cert. tchr., adminstr. Utah. Asst. dir. Teenpost Project, San Pedro, Calif., 1966; caseworker Los Angeles County, 1966-67; self-care inservice dir. Utah State Tng. Sch., American Fork, Utah, 1968, vocat. project designer, 1968; tchr. mentally handicapped Santa Ana Unified Schs., Calif., 1968-69; state specialist intellectually handicapped State Office Edn., Salt Lake City, 1969-70; vocat. counselor Manpower, Salt Lake City, 1970-71; tchr. severely handicapped Davis County Schs., Farmington, Utah, 1971-73, diagnostician, 1973-74, resource elem. tchr., 1974-78; instr. Brigham Young U., Salt Lake City, 1976-83; resource tchr. jr. high Davis County Schs., Farmington, 1978-90; ednl. cons., Murray, Utah, 1973-90; chief ednl. diagnostician Ctr. for Evaluation of Learning and Devel., Layton, Utah, 1989-90; clin. dir. assessment and observation program Idaho Youth Ranch, 1990-95, clin. dir. intake program, 1992-94, supr. family preservation svc./aftercare teams, 1993-95, co-ranch treatment dir. and placement officer, 1995; cons. juvenile correctional dist. 5, 1996—; clin. cons. Magic Hot Springs Youth Camp, 1996-97; mem. cmty. accountability bd. McNeil Assn., 1996—, Dist. 5 Juvenile Justice Commn., 1997—; lectr. in field. Author curriculums in spl. edn., tng. programs prision intervention with juveniles; contbr. articles to profl. jours. Named Profl. of Yr., Utah Assn. for Children with Learning Disabilities, 1985. Mem. Assn. Children/Adults with Learning Disabilities (del. 1979-85, 87, nat. nominating com. 1985-86, nat. bd. dirs. 1988-91), Utah Assn. Children/Adults with Learning Disabilities (exec. bd. 1978-84, profl. adv. bd. 1985-90, coord. LDA orgn. Idaho 1991—), Coun. Exceptional Children (div. learning disabilities, ednl. diagnostics, behavioral disorders), Coun. Learning Disabilities, ASCD (regional adv.), Windstar Found., Nat. Wildlife Found., World Wildlife Fedn., Best Friends Animal Sanctuary, Cousteau Soc., Nat. Assn. Sch. Adminstrs. Democrat. Mormon. Lodge: Job's Daughters. Avocations: geneology research, horseback riding, sketching, crafts, reading. Home: 2176 Julie Ln Twin Falls ID 83301-8361 Office: Youth Ctr Juvenile Corrections 2469 Wright Ave Twin Falls ID 83301-7972

WRIGHT, FREDERICK HERMAN GREENE, II, computer systems engineer; b. Quincy, Mass., Feb. 23, 1952; s. Frederick Herman Greene and Dorothy Louise (Harrold) W. Student, MIT, 1968-69. Test and measurement technician The Foxboro (Mass.) Co., 1968; hardware and software designer MIT Project MAC, Cambridge, Mass., 1969, Info. Internat., Brookline, Mass., 1969, Stanford Artificial Intelligence Lab, Palo Alto, Calif., 1971-73, Systems Concepts, San Francisco, 1970, 73-74, 1976-90; hardware and software designer, then pres. Resource One, San Francisco, 1974-76; pvt. cons. San Rafael, Calif., 1991—; computer cons. Langley-Porter Neuropsychiatric Inst., San Francisco, 1976. Membership chmn. Pacific Soaring Coun., San Francisco, 1983-85, bd. dirs., 1984-85; active Mayflower Cmty. Chorus, 1993—. Recipient Gold Soaring Badge Fed. Aeronautique Internat., 1983. Mem. Digital Equipment Corp. Users Soc., Bay Area Soaring Assn. Avocations: soaring, flying, singing. Home and Office: 251 C St San Rafael CA 94901-4916

WRIGHT, IAN SPENCER M., media production educator; b. Sydney, Australia, Mar. 1, 1951; s. Spencer Gibson and Dora Constance (Lane) W.; m. Sharon A. Schnakenberg, Feb. 23, 1986; children: Julie, Emily, Michael. M of Creative Arts, U. Wollongong, Australia, 1991, postgrad., 1996—. Trainee TCN-9, Sydney, Australia, 1963-73; video tape editor ATN-7, Sydney, Australia, 1975-79; ops. mgr. WIN-TV, Wollongong, Australia, 1979-89; lectr. U. Wollongong, Australia, 1984-90, Charles Sturt U., Bathurst, Australia, 1991-96. Author of short stories. Pres. Bush Fire Brigade, Perthville, Australia, 1996-97, Sch. Coun., Lagoon, 1995-96; media officer S.E.S., Bathurst, 1996. Mem. Australian Cinematographers Soc., Journalism Edn. Assn. Soc. Motion Pictures & Television Engrs. Avocations: swimming, car races, reading, travel, writing short stories. Office: PO Box 1104 Weldon CA 93283-1104

WRIGHT, JOAN L., artist; b. Dayton, Ohio, Mar. 24, 1933; d. William Henry and Elsie Christina (Motzer) Harrison; m. Barry Duane Wright, Aug. 20, 1953; children: Stephen Craig, Michael Alan, Jeffrey Lynn. Student, Art League of L.A., 1964-68, Valley Coll., 1966-69. Designer, sculpture, glazer Al Hardy, Burbank, Calif., 1951-53; budget coord. L.A. County, North Hollywood, Calif., 1953; writer Intermountain Contractor, Salt Lake City, 1954-56; artist, instr. Art League of L.A., Van Nuys, Calif., 1966—, Sylmar, Calif., 1966—; rep. for State of Calif., Presdl. Arts Program, Washington, 1980s. Artist collector plates, Danbury Mint, Norwalk, Conn., 1995—; contbr. to art publs.; illustrator/author films and children's book. Mem. Women Artists of the West (bd. dirs. 1971-73, pres. 1974-77, v.p. 1978—), Internat. Art and Culture Assn., Oil Painters Am. Avocations: birding and environ. activities, sports, stained glass, stamp collecting.

WRIGHT, JOHN MACNAIR, JR., retired career officer; b. L.A., Apr. 14, 1916; s. John MacNair and Ella (Stradley) W.; m. Helene Tribit, June 28, 1940; children: John MacNair III, Richard Kenneth. B.S., U.S. Mil. Acad., 1940; grad., Airborne Sch., 1947, Strategic Intelligence Sch., 1948; advanced course, Inf. Sch., 1951, Command and Gen. Staff Coll., 1953; M.B.A., U. So. Calif., 1956; grad., Army Logistics Mgmt. Sch., 1957, Advanced Mgmt. Program, U. Pitts., 1959, Nat. War Coll., 1961, Army Aviation Sch., 1965; M.S. in Internat. Affairs, George Washington U., 1973. Enlisted U.S. Army, 1935, comd. 2d. lt., 1940, advanced through grades to lt. gen., 1970; comdr. Battery Wright Corregidor, P.I., 1942; with intelligence div. War Dept. Gen. Staff, 1946-48; mil. attache Am. embassy, Paraguay, 1948-50; bn. comdr. 508th Airborne Regtl. Combat Team, 1951-52; asst. chief of staff for pers. 7th Inf. Div., Korea, 1953, asst. chief staff logistics, 1954; assigned office U.S. Army Chief of Staff, 1956-60; chief staff 8th Inf. Div., 1961-62, asst. chief staff plans and ops. 7th Corps, 1962-63, asst. chief staff plans and ops. 7th Army, 1963-64, asst. div. comdr. 11th Air Assault Div., 1964-65; asst. div. comdr. 1st Cav. Div. (Airmobile) Vietnam, 1965-66; assigned office asst. Chief Staff Force Devel., 1966-67; comdg. gen. U.S. Army Inf. Ctr., 1967-69; comdt. U.S. Army Inf. Sch., 1967-69; comdg. gen. 101st Airborne Div. (Airmobile), Vietnam, 1969-70; controller of the Army Washington, 1970-72; ret., 1973. Dir. R&D Boy Scouts Am., 1973, nat. dir. program, 1974-77, nat. dir. program support, 1977-78; nat. dir. exploring, 1978-81, mem. nat. exploring com., 1981—; pres. Chattahoochee (Ga.) coun. Boy Scouts Am., 1968-69, mem. exec. bd. region 5, 1967-69; mem. nat. coun., 1964-73; tech. adviser Vietnamese Boy Scout Assn., 1965-66; Regent for Life Nat. Eagle Scout Assn., 1988—; exploring chmn. five nations dist. Calif. Inland Empire Coun., 1992-96, mem.-at large 1996—. Decorated D.S.M. with 2 oak leaf clusters, Silver Star with oak leaf cluster, Legion of Merit with oak leaf cluster, D.F.C., Bronze Star with oak leaf cluster, Air medal with 59 oak leaf clusters, Army Commendation medal, Prisoner of War medal, Purple Heart with oak leaf cluster, Combat Inf. badge, Master Parachutist, Sr. Army Aviator, numerous area and campaign ribbons, fgn. decorations; recipient Silver Beaver award Boy Scouts Am., 1961, Silver Antelope award, 1969, Distinguished Eagle Scout award, 1971, Disting. Svc. award Founders and Patriots Am., 1988, Freedoms Found. at Valley Forge Hon. medal, 1992; elected Army Aviation Hall of Fame, 1986. Mem. Am. Defenders Bataan and Corregidor, Am. Ex-Prisoners of War, Nat. Eagle Scout Assn. (regent for life), Hon. Order Ky. Cols., Assn. U.S. Army, Army Aviation Assn Am., (pres. 1974-76), 101st Airborne Divsn. Assn., 1st Cavalry Divsn. Assn., SAR (pres. Tex. Soc. 1987-88, pres. Inland Empire chpt. 1992-93, Silver Good Citizenship medal 1984, 87, Meritorious Svc. medal 1986, Patriot, Liberty and Gold Good Citizenship medals 1988), Ret. Officers Assn., West Point Soc., Mil. Order World Wars (Patrick Henry award 1986, 90, comdr. Dallas chpt. 1985-86, vice comdr. dept. ctrl. Calif. 1991-92, comdr. Inland Empire chpt. 1992-93), Nat. Gavel Soc., Nat. Order Founders and Patriots of Am. (sec.-gen. 1986-88, gov. gen. 1988-90, councillor gen. Calif. Soc. 1990-95), Soc. Descendants of Colonial Clergy, Flagon and Tchr. Soc., Soc. Colonial Wars (lt. gov. Calif. soc. 1992-93, gov. 1997-98), Sons of the Revolution in State of Calif. (pres. 1993-94), Soc. War of 1812 (dist. dep. pres. gen. 1991-93, v.p. Calif. soc. 1993-94, pres. 1994-95), Nat. Huguenot Soc., Soc. Sons and Daus. of Pilgrims, Order Ams. Armorial Ancestry, Soc. Descs. Founders of Hartford, Old Plymouth Colony Descs., Mil. Order of the Loyal Legion of the U.S., Mil. Order Fgn. Wars of the U.S. (pres. Calif. Soc. 1996-97), Mil. Order of Purple Heart, Hereditary Order of First Families of Mass., Order of Crown Charlemagne, Baronial Soc. Magna Charta, DFC Soc., Order of Daedalians, Mil. Order of Carabao, Masons, Shriners, Sojourner, Phi Kappa Phi, Beta Gamma Sigma, Alpha Kappa Psi. Prisoner of war of Japanese, 1942-45. Home: 21227 George Brown Ave Riverside CA 92518-2881

WRIGHT, KENNETH WESTON, pediatric ophthalmologist; b. L.A., Oct. 25, 1950; s. Harvey Weston and Mary Jo W.; m. Donna Marie; children: Jamie, Matthew, Michael, Lisa, Andrew. BA, Calif. Lutheran Coll., 1972; MD, Boston U., 1977. Intern Harbor Gen. Hosp./UCLA, 1978; resident Doheny Eye Inst., L.A., 1978-81; fellow in pediat. ophthalmology Johns Hopkins Hosp., Balt., 1981, Children's Hosp. Nat. Medicine, Washington, 1982; assoc. prof. U. So. Calif., L.A., 1982-92; pvt. practice, 1992-94; head pediat. ophthalmology/strabismus Cleve. Clinic Found., 1994-97; pvt. practice L.A., 1997—. Author, editor: Textbook of Ophthalmology, 1996; editor: Pediatric Ophthalmology & Strabismus, 1995; contbr. articles to profl. jours. NIH grantee. Fellow Am. Acad. Pediatrics, Am. Acad. Ophthalmology (com.); mem. Am. Assn. Pediat. Ophthalmology/Strabismus, Wilmer Resident Assn. Avocations: surfing, tennis. Office: Am Eye Inst 8635 W 3rd St Los Angeles CA 90048-6101

WRIGHT, KIRBY MICHAEL, writer, editor; b. Honolulu, Sept. 1, 1955; s. Harold Stanley and June Gertrude (McCormack) W.; m. Darcy Laureen Mobraaten, Dec. 28, 1991. BA, U. Calif., San Diego, 1983; MFA, San Francisco State U., 1994. Pub. rels. dir. Winners Circle Resorts, Carlsbad, Calif., 1987-90; instr. Palo Alto (Calif.) Adult Sch., 1994-95; writer GT Prodn. Co., Palo Alto, 1995-96, editor, 1997—. Author: The Rainbow Warrior, 1998; (screenplay) Gordon & Al, 1996; (dramatic monologue) Blue Mesa Review, 1994 (1st pl. award Browning Soc. 1993, 94); (play) Houdini, 1999. Rschr. Ctr. for Auto Safety, Washington, 1980; advisor SAT Success, Palo Alto, 1998. Recipient Poetry prize Ann Fields Trust, San Francisco, 1993, 1st pl. Poets award Acad. Am. Poets, San Francisco, 1993. Fellow Arts Coun. Santa Clara County, Arts Coun. Silicon Valley. Democrat. Roman Catholic. Avocations: boxing, surfing, gourmet cooking. Office: GT Prodn Co 3259 Alma St Palo Alto CA 94306-2925

WRIGHT, MALCOLM STURTEVANT, nuclear facility manager, retired career officer; b. Orange, N.J., Sept. 2, 1941; s. Malcolm Everett and Margaret Sommer (Kohler) W.; m. Barbara Jean Larsen, June 5, 1963 (div. Aug., 1988); children: Tracy Ann, Karen Elizabeth; m. Lya Hanfri Baughman, Nov. 5, 1988; children: Zachary Seth, Sara Ann. BS in Engring., U.S. Naval Acad., 1963; MA in Polit. Sci., Villanova U., 1974. Commd. ensign USN, 1963, advanced through grades to capt., 1983, retired, 1993; dir. tactical tng. dept. US Naval Submarine Sch., Groton, Conn., 1982-84; commanding officer USS Alabama, Silverdale, Wash., 1984-87; planner polit.-mil. strategy Staff of Chmn. Joint Chiefs of Staff, Pentagon, Washington, 1987-90; comdr. Submarine Squadron Seventeen, Silverdale, Wash., 1990-92; chief of staff to comdr. Naval Base Seattle, 1992-93; mgr. waste and decontamination plant Westinghouse Hanford Co., Richland, Wash., 1993-96; mgr. 324/327 facility stabilization project Babcock and Wilcox Hanford Co., Richland, 1996—; tech. advisor Disney Studios, Burbank, Calif., 1994-95. Vol. ARC, East Orange, N.J., 1957-59. Decorated Legion of Merit, USN, 1982, 86, 92, 93, Meritorious Svc. medal 1984, Defense Superior Svc. medal, 1990. Mem. U.S. Naval Inst., U.S. Naval Submarine League, U.S. Naval Acad. Alumni Assn. Republican. Presbyterian. Avocations: military history, civil war, Scottish culture, golf. Home: 3512 W 30th Ave Kennewick WA 99337-2500 Office: B&W Hanford Co PO Box 1200 MSIN L1-02 Richland WA 99352

WRIGHT, MARY ROSE, state park superintendent; b. Hartford, Conn., Jan. 12, 1949; d. J. William and Eileen J. (Walsh) Bigoness; m. Roy C. Gunter III, June 24, 1972 (div. Feb. 1988); m. Kenneth Ross Wright, Dec. 1, 1988. BA, Marquette U., 1970; MS, U. Mo., 1972. Prgram analyst State Calif. Dept. Health, Sacramento, 1972-76; tng. ctr. dir. State Calif. Dept. Parks and Recreation, Pacific Grove, 1976-81; visitor svcs. mgr. State Calif. Dept. Parks and Recreation, Monterey, 1981-83, Monterey dist. supr., 1983-92, dep. dir., 1992-93; Monterey dist. supt. Calif. Dept. Parks and Recreation, 1993—; hist. preservation commr. City of Monterey, 1984-92. Bd. dirs. Big Sur Health Ctr., 1993—; bd. govs. Santa Lucia Conservancy, 1995-99. Office: Monterey Dist Calif State Parks 2211 Garden Rd Monterey CA 93940-5317

WRIGHT, RICHARD OSCAR, III, pathologist, educator; b. La Junta, Colo., Aug. 9, 1944; s. Richard O. Sr. and Frances R. (Curtiss) W.; m. Bernale Trout, May 31, 1969; children: Lauren Diane, Richard O. IV. BS in Biology, Midwestern State U., 1966; MS in Biology, U. Houston, 1968; DO, U. Health Sci., 1972. Cert. anatomic pathology and lab. medicine Am. Osteo. Bd. Pathology. Sr. attending pathologist Normandy Met. Hosps., St. Louis, 1977-81; sr. attending pathologist Phoenix (Ariz.) Gen. Hosps., 1981-97, dir. med. edn., 1989-92, 96—; clin. asst. prof. pathology Coll. Osteo. Medicine, Western U., Pomona, Calif., 1985—; dir. labs., chmn. dept. John C. Lincoln Hosp., Deer Valley, 1997—; dir. med. edn., dir. labs. John C. Lincoln Hosp., Deer Valley, Ariz., 1997—; v.p. Osteo. Postdoctoral Tng. Inst., Kirksville, Mo., 1998—; clin. instr. pathology Ohio U. Coll. Osteo. Medicine, Athens, 1976-77; clin. asst. prof. pathology Kirksville Coll. Osteo. Medicine, 1985-87; vis. lectr. pathology New Eng. Coll. Osteo. Medicine, Biddeford, Maine, 1989-92; clin. asst. prof. pathology Midwestern U. Ariz. Coll. Osteo. Medicine, 1997—; cons. pathologist Phoenix Indian Med. Ctr., 1992-94; adv. bd. Inter Soc. Coun. Pathology, Chgo., 1992—; sec. med. staff John C. Lincoln Hosp.-Deer Valley, 1997—. Active Ariz. Rep. Party, Phoenix, Rep. Nat. Coun., Washington; precinctman Dist. 18 Maricopa County, Ariz., 1996, Madison Heights Precinct, 1996; chmn. bd. trustees Phoenix (Ariz.) Gen. Hosp., 1994-95; ex-occicio, trustee, 1995-97; dir. John C. Lincoln Health Network Guild, 1997—; mem. found. adv. coun. Lincoln Health Found.-Phoenix Gen. Hosp. Osteo. Endowment Fund. Recipient Mead-Johnson award Nat. Osteo. Assn., 1975. Fellow Am. Osteo. Coll. Pathologists (disting., pres. 1989-90, bd. govs. 1984-91), Coll. Pathologists, Coll. Am. Pathologists, Am. Soc. Clin. Pathologists; mem. Ariz. Osteo. Med. Assn. (del. dist. 2 ho. of dels. 1998), Ariz. Soc. Pathologists, Century Club Alumni Assn., AAAS, Alpha Phi Omega, Rho Sigma Chi, Psi Sigma Alpha. Presbyterian. Office: Anatomic Pathology Assoc 19829 N 27th Ave Phoenix AZ 85027-4001

WRIGHT, THEODORE OTIS, forensic engineer; b. Gillette, Wyo., Jan. 17, 1921; s. James Otis and Gladys Mary (Marquiss) W.; m. Phyllis Mae Reeves, June 21, 1942 (div. 1968); children: Mary Suzanne, Theodore Otis Jr., Barbara Joan; m. Edith Marjorie Jewett, May 22, 1968; children: Marjorie Jane, Elizabeth Carter. BSEE, U. Ill., 1951, MS in Engring., 1952; postgrad., Air Command and Staff Coll., 1956-57, UCLA, 1958. Registered profl. engr. Wash. 2d lt. U.S. Air Force, 1942-65, advanced through grades to lt. col., 1957, ret., 1965; dep. for engring. Titan SPO, USAF Sys. Command, L.A., 1957-65; rsch. engr. The Boeing Co., Seattle, 1965-81; pres. The Pretzelwich, Inc., Seattle, 1981—; cons., forensic engr. in pvt. practice Bellevue, Wash., 1988—; adj. prof. U. Wash., Greenriver Jr. Coll., both 1967-68. Contbr. articles to nat. and internat. profl. jours. Decorated Purple Heart, Air medal. Mem. NSPE (v.p. western region 1985-87), ASTM (com. E-43 metric practice 1988—), Nat. Coun. Weights and Measures, Wash. Soc. Profl. Engrs. (state pres. 1981-82, Disting. Svc. award 1980, Engr. of Yr. 1996, Columbia award 1996), U.S. Metric Assn. (life, cert. advanced metrication speciallist), Am. Nat. Metric Coun. (bd. dirs. 1978-94), Air Force Assn. (charter life, state pres. 1974-76, 90-91, Jimmy Doolittle fellow 1975), Order of Daedalians (life), Eta Kappa Nu, Pi Mu Epsilon, Tau Beta Pi. Democrat. Presbyterian. Avocations: flying, photography, classical music, archaeology. Home: 141 140th Pl NE Bellevue WA 98007-6939

WRIGHT, THOMAS EDWARD, electronics production control specialist; b. L.A., May 29, 1958; s. Timothy and Lillian Alma Marie (Meinardus) W.; m. Debra Denise Sorvig; 1 child, David; step children (Rochanna Scott, Tsiska Clements. Student, L.A. Pierce Coll., Woodland Hills; student electronics, W. Valley Occupational Ctr., Woodland Hills, 1978. Electronic technician pvt. practive, Woodland Hills, Calif., 1978-80; prodn. control planner Litton Guidance & Control Divsn., Woodland Hills, 1980-88; sr. planner Litton Aero Products, Moor Park, Calif., 1988-89; prodn. control specialist Litton Aero Products, Woodland Hills, Calif., 1989—. Avocations: motorcycling, camping, fishing, carpentry. Home: 22943 Arminta St West Hills CA 91304-4501 Office: Litton Aero Products 21050 Burbank Blvd Woodland Hills CA 91367-6602

WRIGHT, TIM EUGENE, packaging development executive; b. Weed, N.Mex., Oct. 13, 1943; s. Clyde Everett and Juanita Delores (Barrett) W.; m. Nancy Ann Ausenbaugh, Oct. 2, 1965 (div. 1975); 1 child, Ramsey Jordan. Diploma, Dayton Art Inst., 1967, M.F.A., U. Idaho, 1969. Designer, Lawson Mfg. Co., Troy, Idaho, 1968-70, Boise Cascade, Burley, Idaho, 1970-72; project coord. Boise Cascade, Golden, Colo., 1972-76, product devel. mgr., Wallula, Wash., 1976-84; mng. ptnr. Matrix Applications Co., Pasco, Wash., 1984—. Patentee folding carton, spacer for rolls, collapsible pallet. Recipient Silver award for packaging, 1978. Mem. Inst. Packaging Profls., Western Packaging Assn. (bd. dirs., past pres. Columbia chpt.), Soc. Plastics Engrs., TAPPI. Office: Matrix Applications Co PO Box 3668 Pasco WA 99302-3668

WRITER, SHARON LISLE, secondary education educator; b. L.A., Aug. 29, 1939; d. Harlan Lawerance and Emma Mae (Cordery) Lisle; m. Robert Vincent Writer, Dec. 30, 1961; children: Martin Carl, Cynthia Louise, Brian Robert, Scott Andrew. BS, Mt. St. Marys Coll., 1961; MS in Sci. Edn., Calif. State U., Fullerton, 1989; postgrad., U. Calif., Irvine, 1987, Colo. Sch. Mines, 1994. Cert. secondary tchr., Calif. Tchr. St. Mary's Acad., L.A., 1961-62, Escambia High Sch., Pensacola, Fla., 1962-63; rsch. asst. U. So. Calif., L.A., 1964-65, U. Calif., Irvine, 1965-66; tchr. aide Cerro Villa Jr. High Sch., Villa Park, Calif., 1975-76, tchr., 1976-88; tchr. Villa Park High Sch., 1988—, mentor tchr., 1990—; tchr. of yr. com. Orange (Calif.) Unified Sch. Dist., 1992, supt. adv. coun., 1990—, curriculum sci. com., 1991—. Active Villa Park Womens League, 1975—, Assistance League of Orange, 1991—; project leader, county coord. Orange County 4-H Assn., Anaheim, Calif., 1975-84; bd. sec. Orange County Sci. Fair, 1986-91, awards chmn., 1991-94, pres., 1994—; mem. judging policy adv. com. Calif. State Sci. Fair, 1996—. Recipient Outstanding Sci. Tchr. award Orange County Sci. Tchrs. Assn., 1993; named Tchr. of Yr. Villa Park High Sch., 1990, 94, Outstanding Coach Orange County Sci. Olympiad, 1990, 92, 94, 96, Calif. State Sci. Olympiad, 1987. Mem. NSTA (conv. hospitality com. 1989, 90, hospitality co-chair 1994 nat. conv.), Am. Chem. Soc., Calif. Sci. Tchr. Assn., Orange County Sci. Educators Assn. (Disting. Sci. Tchr. award 1993). Roman Catholic. Avocations: tennis, swimming, water skiing, needlepoint. Home: 18082 Rosanne Cir Villa Park CA 92861-6431 Office: Villa Park High School 18042 Taft Ave Villa Park CA 92861-4186

WROAN, DOUGLAS BRADFORD, lawyer; b. Glendale, Calif., Aug. 22, 1967; s. Lyle Lee and Patricia Ann (Yeager) W. AA, Golden West Coll., 1987; BA, Calif. State U., Long Beach, 1991; JD, Western State U., 1994. Prin., owner L.A., 1995—; v.p. bus., legal affairs Arama Entertainment, Encino, Calif., 1997; gen. counsel The Malibu Ice Cream Co., Cresskill, N.J., 1996—, The Best Svc. Co., L.A., 1997—. Mem. Beverley Hills Bar Assn. Avocations: athletics, reading, writing. Home: 400 Thirty Third St Manhattan Beach CA 90266 Office: Law Offices of Douglas B Wroan 10960 Wilshire Blvd Ste 960 Los Angeles CA 90024-3712

WU, DAVID, congressman; b. Taiwan, Apr. 8, 1955; came to U.S., 1961; m. Michelle Wu; 1 child, Matthew. BS, Stanford U., 1977; student, Harvard Med. Sch.; JD, Yale U., 1982. Ptnr. Cohen & Wu, 1988-98; mem. 106th Congress from 1st Oreg. dist., 1999—. Mem. Congl. Asian Pacific Caucus (vice chair), New Democrat Coalition. Office: 510 Cannon House Office Bldg Washington DC 20515-2701 also: 620 NW Main Ste 606 Portland OR 97205*

WU, DONGDONG, optical engineer; b. Zhengzhou, Henan, China, Aug. 18, 1959; came to U.S., 1992; d. Xuemin Wu and Qi Wang; m. Ying Tao, Feb. 14, 1985; 1 child, Phillip Tao. BS in Physics, Zhengzhou U., 1982; MS in Optics, Shanxi U., Taiyuan, China, 1987; MS in Physics, Miss. State U., 1996. Tchg. asst. Henan U. Agr., Zhengzhou, 1982-84; asst. prof. S.W. Jiaotong U., Chengdu, China, 1987-92; cons. Gates Rubber Co., Denver, 1997; info. tech. engr. Broadbase Info. Sys., Inc., Menlo Park, Calif., 1997—; rsch. asst. Shanxi U., Taiyuan, 1984-87, Miss. State U., 1994-96. Contbr. articles to Applied Optics, Acta Optica Sinica. Recipient 2nd award Sci. Tech., Govt. Shanxi, 1991. Mem. China Soc. Computer Sci., Chengdu Soc. Laser, Sigma Xi (assoc.). Achievements include first to experimentally observe self-defocusing optical bistability and establish theoretical model to explain experimental results, demonstrate laser photofragmentation-laser induced fluorescence can be used to detect and measure TNT concentration in soil. Home: 672 Kodiak Ct Apt 6 Sunnyvale CA 94087-5519

WU, DONGPING (DON WU), optical and electrical engineer; b. Shi-jiazhuang, Hebei, China, Apr. 21, 1960; came to U.S., 1992; s. Hongquan and Shujian Wu; m. Helen Hongwei Zhu, July 30, 1988; children: Yue, Eric Z. BS, Harbin Inst. Elec. Tech., Heilongjiang, China, 1982; MS, Beijing U. Posts & Telecomms., 1987, U. Cin., 1996. Nat. profl. tng. in integrated optics, China. Tchr. Ma'anshan 2d H.S., Anhui, China, 1977-78; asst. engr. Shanghai Electric. Cable Rsch. Inst., 1982-84; asst. prof. S.E. U., Nanjing, Jiangsu, China, 1987-92; engr. Nanometrics, Inc., Sunnyvale, Calif., 1996-98; sr. engr. Uniphase Lasers, San Jose, Calif., 1998—; vice-sec. gen. Jiangsu Inst. Electronics, Nanjing, 1989-91; dept. sec. for rsch. and acad. affairs S.E. U., Nanjing, 1989-91. Contbr. articles to Beijing U. of Posts and Telecomms. jour., Procs. of IEEE-EMC Symposium, others. Recipient 2d prize sci. and tech. progress China Ministry Machinery Industry, 1986. Mem. IEEE Electromagnetic Compatibility Soc., Electron Devices Soc., China Inst. Electronics, Jiangsu Inst. Electronics. Achievements include E-M theory of anisotropic optical fibers; unified formula for E-M effects of power lines on telecommunication lines; processing and characterization of PCD and DLC semiconductor materials; anisotropic ellipsometry and reflectometry; optical characterization of copolymers; semiconductor lasers with waveguide-cavity combined structure; Argon Laser manufacturing; correction to Marcatili's model of channel waveguides, precision cleaning chemistry and precious metal brazing. Avocations: American history, reading, classical music, Chinese classical literature, language learning. Office: Uniphase Lasers 163 Baypointe Pkwy San Jose CA 95134-1622

WU, HAROLD POWAN, financial analyst; b. Hong Kong, July 3, 1969; came to the U.S., 1982; s. Clarence Wun Tuen and Catherine Hau Ying (Fung) W.; m. York Ping Chen, Sept. 29, 1993. BBA in Fin., Seattle U., 1991. Performance analyst Wurts, Johnson & Co., Seattle, 1991-95; sr. analyst Wurts & Assoc., Inc., Seattle, 1995—. Avocations: fishing, travel, movies. Fax: (206) 622-0548. E-mail: hpwu@aol.com. Office: Wurts & Assoc Inc 999 3rd Ave Ste 3650 Seattle WA 98104-4021

WU, INA ZHIQING, art educator; b. Tianjin, China; came to U.S., 1987; d. Wenjin Wu and June (Yuru) Ao. Student, Tianjin Art Inst., 1978-80; BFA, U. Wash., 1994, MFA, 1997. Artistic designer Printers and Plastics Manufactory, Tianjin, 1974-78; import-export adminstr. Linda Garment Manufactory, Hong Kong, 1980-87; art instr. Seattle Ctrl. C.C., 1997—. Works exhibited at Wismer Ctr. Gallery Seattle U., Art Ctr. Gallery Seattle Pacific U., Wash. State Conv. Trade Ctr., Seattle (honorable mention award), Kinsey Art Gallery Seattle U., Art Gallery Seattle Ctrl. C.C., Art Gallery North Seattle C.C., Is Is Collectibles Gallery, Seattle, Judith Schorr Gallery, Seattle, Jacob Lawrence Gallery, Seattle, Henry Art Gallery, Seattle, Van de Griff Gallery, Santa Fe, Heping Art Gallery, China, Tianjin Art Mus., China. Recipient curricular grant Seattle Ctrl. C.C., 1998, pres.'s fund, 1998, faculty devel. grant, 1997, Nordstrom scholarship, 1996, Gonzales scholarship. Mem. Coll. Art Assn. Avocations: painting, drawing, reading, golf. Office: Seattle Ctrl C C 1701 Broadway Seattle WA 98122-2413

WU, KESHENG (JOHN) (JOHN WU), computer scientist; b. Hefei, Anhui, China, Aug. 4, 1966; came to U.S., 1988; s. Mingde Wu and Shuying

Yu; m. Qi Ye, Sept. 3, 1994. BS, Nanjing (China) U., 1988; MS, U. Wis., 1990, PhD, U. Minn., 1997. Rsch. asst. U. Minn., Mpls., 1992-96; software engr. Guidant/CPI, St. Paul, 1996-97; computer scientist Lawrence Berkeley Lab., Berkeley, Calif., 1997—. Mem. IEEE, Assn. for Computing Machinery, Soc. Indsl. and Applied Math. Office: MS50F 1 Cyclotron Rd Berkeley CA 94720

WU, MARGARET MEI-LING KAN, pharmacist; b. Shanghai, Feb. 14, 1952; came to U.S., 1971; d. Hing Kwan and Winnie (Tsu) Kan; m. Cho Wu, Dec. 20, 1975; children: Jamie chi, Jonathan A. BS in Pharmacy, Oreg. State U., 1975. Lic. pharmacist, Calif. Staff pharmacist Pavilion Pharmacy, South Pasadena, Calif., 1980—. Home: PO Box 3154 South Pasadena CA 91030

WU, MICHAEL YICK-KUEN, minister; b. Kowloon, Hong Kong, Oct. 8, 1952; came to U.S., 1990; s. Yock Kwan and Lai Sheung (Leung) W.; m. Michelle Mei-Siu Jong, Aug. 10, 1975; children: Jeremy John, Nathaniel Joseph, Joanna Michelle. BSc, U. Calgary, Alta., Can., 1976; ThM, Dallas Theol. Sem., 1983. Cert. tchr., Alta., Sask.; ordained min. Christian and Missionary Alliance, 1986. Tchr. Calgary Bd. Edn., 1977-78, Rossignol Sch., Ile-a-la-Crosse, Sask., 1979; pastor Cantonese ministry Chinese Chapel, 1st Bapt. Ch., Dallas, 1981-83; pastor Calgary Chinese Alliance Ch., 1983-90; lectr. New Testament studies, registrar Gt. Commn. Theol. Sem.-A Sch. of Gordon-Conwell Theol. Sem., Pasadena, Calif., 1990-93; sr. pastor L.A. Chinese Alliance Ch., 1993—; chmn. regional coun. Chinese Coordination Ctr. of World Evangelism, Hong Kong and Can., 1987-90; mem. dist. exec. com. South Pacific dist. Chinese and Missionary Alliance, L.A., 1995-98. Trustee Simpson Coll., Redding, Calif., 1998—. Mem. Calgary Chinese Ministerial Assn. (chmn. 1985-90), Greater L.A. Chinese Ministerial Assn. (mem. exec. com. 1993-96, 98—), Sermon Prep Group (coord. 1998—). Avocations: music, reading, jogging. Office: L A Chinese Alliance Ch 2828 Glendale Blvd Los Angeles CA 90039

WU, QIONG JOAN, hydrologist; b. Hulin, China, July 25, 1964; came to U.S., 1990; d. De Di Wu and Zhong Qi Yang; m. Markus Flury, June 2, 1997; 1 child, Anna G. Flury. BS, Tongji U., Shanghai, China, 1986, MS, 1989; PhD, Ohio State U., 1994. Postdoctoral rschr. Ohio State U., Columbus, 1994-95; asst. prof. U. Calif., Riverside, 1995-98, Wash. State U., 1998—. Mem. Agronomy Soc. Am., Am. Geophys. Union.

WU, RAO-HSIEN RAY, engineering consultant; b. Tai-Chung, Taiwan, July 9, 1963; came to U.S., 1970; s. I-Chen and Hsiao-Hua W. BSME, U. Calif., Berkeley, 1986. Frame layout designer Peterbilt Motors, Newark, Calif., 1987-89; engring. aide Lockheed Aeronautics, Burbank, Calif., 1989-90; tech. staff II Hughes Missiles, Canoga Park, Calif., 1990-91, Hughes Space and Comm., El Segundo, Calif., 1991-94; cons. Allied Signal, Torrance, Calif., 1995—. Mem. Highland Club (life), Calif. Alumni Assn. (life). Republican. Avocations: memorizing scriptures, gynmastics, body building, piano, guitar.

WU, WILLIAM LUNG-SHEN (YOU-MING WU), aerospace medical engineering design specialist, foreign intelligence analyst; b. Hangchow, Chekiang Province, China, Sept. 1, 1921; came to U.S., 1941, naturalized, 1955; s. Sing-Chih and Mary (Ju-Mei) Wu. AB in Biochemistry, Stanford U., 1943, MD, 1946; MS in Chemistry and Internal Medicine, Tulane U., 1955; diploma, U.S. Naval Sch. Aviation Medicine, Pensacola, Fla., 1956, USAF Sch. Aviation Medicine, USAF Aerospace Med. Ctr., 1961; cert. of tng. in aviation medicine, U. Calif., Berkeley, 1962, 1964. Diplomate Am. Bd. Preventive Medicine, Am. Bd. Internal Medicine, Am. Bd. Psychiatry, Am. Bd. Pathology. Gen. rotating intern U. Iowa Hosps., Iowa City, 1945-46; resident Lincoln (Nebr.) Gen. Hosp., 1946-47, resident in pathology, 1947-48; resident in pathology Bryan Meml. Hosp., Lincoln, 1947-48; fellow, instr. in internal medicine Tulane U., New Orleans, 1948-54; asst. vis. physician Charity Hosp. and Hutchinson Meml. Teaching and Diagnostic and Cancer Detection Clinics, New Orleans, 1948-51, vis. physician, 1951-54; staff physician Holderman (Army) Hosp., Napa, Calif., 1958; staff physician Aviation Space and Radiation Med. Group Gen. Dynamics/Convair, San Diego, 1958-61; aerospace med. specialist, med. monitor for Life Sciences Sect. Gen. Dynamics/Astronautics, San Diego, 1961-65; aerospace med. and bioastronautics specialist Lovelace Found. for Med. Edn. and Rsch., Albuquerque, 1965-68; staff physician Laguna Honda Hosp., San Francisco, 1968-74; ret.; staff physician Kaiser-Permanente Hosp. all-night med. clinic, San Francisco, 1971-73; safety rep. and med. examiner U.S. Civil Aeronaut. Adminstrn., 1959; med. examiner Fed. Aviation Adminstrn., 1961; expert witness in forensic medicine and/or medicolegal jurisprudence for cts. Author 8 books and 100 tech. papers in field. Active mem. Planning, Rsch. and Devel. Commn. Redwood City; bd. dirs. Legal Aid Soc. Santa Clara County, U.S. Congl. Adv. Bd., Am. Security Coun. Found., Little House Sr. Multipurpose Ednl. Ctr.; Life Fellow Royal Soc. of Lichtenstein, Zurich, Switzerland, Oxford Club (N.Y. and Fla.), Royal Coll. of Heraldry. Comdr., flight surgeon M.C., USN, 1954-57. Recipient Gold medal Internat. Inst. Cmty. Svc., 1976, J. Edgar Hoover Gold Disting. Pub. Svc. award Am. Police Hall of Fame, 1991, Albert Einstein Bronze medal Universal Intelligence Data Bank Am., 1986, Cambridge Gold medal, Dedication Insignia. Fellow San Diego Biomed. Rsch. Inst. (bd. dirs. 1961-65, sec. of fellows 1961-62, chmn. of fellows 1963), Inst. Environ. Scis. (chmn. specifications and standards com.), AIAA (mem. nominating com. San Diego sect., plant rep. life sci. sect. 1963-65); mem. IEEE (vice chmn. San Diego chpt. profl. tech. group on biomed. electronics 1962-65), N.Y. Acad. Scis., Internat. Univ. Found. (hon. pres.), Internat. Acad. Found. (hon. registrar-sec.), Computer Club, Sigma Xi, U.S. Naval Inst. (life), Naval League of U.S. West-pac (life), Conss. Nat. Resource Ctr. Network. Achievements include research of theoretical aspects of cold catalyzed hydrogen fusion nuclear-rocket warm super-conductor hyper-magnetic, hydrogen-fusion space stations; patentee S(RAM-PANT)S. Home: 250 Budd Ave Apt 219 Campbell CA 95008-4061

WU, ZHAOMING, artist, educator; b. Guangzhou, Guangdong, China, Dec. 18, 1955; came to U.S., 1991; s. Fenli and Shicun (Chen) W.; m. Quizhen Wei, Aug. 22, 1984; 1 child, Dongyi. Cert., Shanghai Light Industry Coll., 1979; BA, Guangzhou Acad. Fine Art, 1983; MFA, Acad. Art Coll., San Francisco, 1996. Cert. coll. art prof., Bd. Higher Edn., Guangdong Province. Designer Guangzhou Light Industry Graphic Design Co., 1972-79; prof. art Guangzhou Acad. Fine Art, 1983-91, Acad. Art Coll., San Francisco, 1996—; freelance artist, 1983—; judge spring show Acad. Art Coll., 1997, 98; judge Duan Woo Festival Sketch Art Competition, Christine Art Ctr., San Jose, Calif., 1998. Recipient Gustafson Fund award Nat. Oil and Acrylic Painter's Soc., 1998, Lifeline '97 1st pl. award 9th Biennial Nat. Figure Drawing Exhbn., Calif., 1997, 1st prize Art of Human Body competition, Calif., 1995, Outstanding award 6th Nat. Fine Arts Exhbn., Beijing, 1984; winner Artist Showcase award Manhattan Arts Internat., N.Y. Mem. Nat. Chinese Artist Assn., Oil Painters Am. Avocations: poetry, movies, gymnastics, music, reading. Home: 529 42nd St # B Oakland CA 94609-2413 Office: Acad Art Coll 79 New Montgomery St San Francisco CA 94105-3410

WUEHLE, EDWIN EVERETT, association executive; b. Hettinger, N.D., Aug. 24, 1925; s. Edwin Herman and Alma Charlotte (Buehler) W.; m. Helen Jean, Aug. 21, 1971; children: Michele, Martin. BSE, Concordia Coll., River Forest, Ill., 1948; MA, DePaul U., 1952. Cert. elem., secondary sch. tchr. Tchr. St. John's Luth. Sch., Ventura, Iowa, 1943-44, Walz, Mich., 1944-45; tchr. Morton Grove (Ill.) Pub. Schs., 1949-53, prin., 1954-57; tchr. Lake Zurich (Ill.) Pub. Schs., 1953-54; supt. Bark River-Harris (Mich.) Schs., 1957-71, Manistique (Mich.) Area Schs., 1968-71; pres. Bay of Noc Community Com., Escanaba, Mich., 1971-85, Internat. Home and Pvt. Poker Player's Assn., Manistique, 1985—. Author: Poker Small Limit Game, 1980, Poker Record System, 1983. Mem. Rotary (past pres.), Elks. Lutheran. Avocations: poker, tennis. Home and Office: IH3PA 220 E Flamingo Rd Apt 127 Las Vegas NV 89109-0304

WUNSCH, KATHRYN SUTHERLAND, lawyer; b. Tipton, Mo., Jan. 30, 1935; d. Lewis Benjamin and Norene Marie (Wolf) Sutherland; m. Charles Martin Wunsch, Dec. 22, 1956 (div. May 1988); children: Debra Kay, Laura Ellen. AB, Ind. U., 1958, JD summa cum laude, 1977; postgrad., Stanford [illegible] Founder Wunsch and George, San Francisco, 1989-93, Kathryn Wunsch and Assoc. Counsel, San Francisco, 1993—. Articles editor Ind. U. Law Rev., 1975-76. Mem. ABA, Calif. Bar Assn. (bus. law prof., real property and trusts sect.), San Mateo County Bar Assn., Nat. Assn. Women Bus. Owners (pres. San Francisco chpt. 1992-93), San Francisco Opera Guild, City Club, Phi Beta Kappa (v.p. no. calif. 1995—), Psi Chi. Republican. Avocations: collecting fine art and antiques, theater, opera, gardening, hiking. Office: Ste 3320 701 Welch Rd Bldg 3320 Palo Alto CA 94304-1705

WUNSTELL, ERIK JAMES, non-profit organization administrator, communications consultant; b. Fresno, Calif., Dec. 24, 1951; s. John Wunstell and Rose Soldorian. Grad. comml. law, Dept. U.S. Treas., 1976; grad., N.Am. Sch. Acctg., 1978. Owner Camden Comm., Fresno, Calif., 1974—; founder, dir. Earth Ecology Found., Fresno, Calif., 1980—. Author: Earthology - The Physics of Solar Relativity, 1990, The Geometric Progression of Space and Time, 1979, The Binary Duality of the Universe, 1996, Ecological Civilization 2020, 1985, Earth's Unified Solar Field Pattern, 1998. Office: Earth Ecology Found 6120 W Tropicana Ave # A16-303 Las Vegas NV 89103-4694

WÜSTNER, MICHAEL FRANCIS, film producer; b. Williston, N.D., Oct. 17, 1940; s. Lorenz Josef and Ruby Marie (Ward) W.; m. Susan M. Davis; children: Lorenz Michael, Marie Caroline. BA, Am. U., 1968; MA in Cultural Anthropology, New Sch. Social Rsch., 1970. Pres., founder Touchstone Restoration; pres. No. Plains Prodn., Wolf Point Prodns.; adj. prof. Am. U., 1970. Creator, co-producer (movie) Montana, 1990; producer Métis Rebellion. Home and office: Wolf Point Prodns 21750 Nine Mile Rd Huson MT 59846-9504

WYATT, EDITH ELIZABETH, elementary education educator; b. San Diego, Aug. 13, 1914; d. Jesse Wellington and Elizabeth (Fultz) Carne; m. Lee Ora Wyatt, Mar. 30, 1947 (dec. Jan. 1966); children: Glenn Stanley (dec.), David Allen. *Grandparents John and Elizabeth Carne along with Elizabeth's two brothers and one sister left Cornwall, England in 1866 to join an older brother Joseph Barron who had arrived in California three years earlier. They came to work in the gold mines of Northern California because there was little employment in Cornwall. Transportation was by ship around the tip of South America which took several weeks. One cousin recently wrote a genealogy covering the descendants of these people who came to California between 1863 and 1866.* BA, San Diego State Coll., 1936. Elem. tchr. Nat. Sch. Dist., National City, Calif., 1938-76. Sec. San Diego County Parks Soc., 1986-96; librarian Congl. Ch. Women's Fellowship, Chula Vista, Calif., 1980—; active Boy Scouts Am, 1959—. Recipient Who award San Diego County Tchrs. Assn., 1968, Silver Fawn award Boy Scouts Am. Mem. AAUW (sec. 1978-80, pub. rels. 1985—), Calif. Ret. Tchrs. Assn. (scholarship com. 1985-90, 92-95, treas. South Shores divsn. # 60 1996—), Starlite Hiking Club (sec.-treas. 1979—). Avocation: hiking. Home: 165 E Millan St Chula Vista CA 91910-6255

WYATT, LENORE, civic worker; b. N.Y.C., June 12, 1929; d. Benedict S. Rosenfeld and Ora (Copel) Kanner; m. Bernard D. Copeland, May 17, 1953 (dec. March 1968); children: Harry (dec.), Robert (dec.); m. C. Wyatt Unger, Mar. 26, 1969 (dec. Feb. 1992); 1 child, Amy Unger; m. F. Lowry Wyatt, Sept. 12, 1992 (dec. Nov. 1996). Student, Mills Coll., 1946-48; BA, Stanford U., 1950, MA, 1952; postgrad., NYU, 1952-53. Instr. Stanford U., Palo Alto, Calif., 1952, Hunter Coll., N.Y.C., 1952-53, Calif. State U., Sacramento, 1956-60, U. Calif., Davis, 1965-69; property mgr. Unger, Demas & Markakis, Sacramento, 1974-83; former actress and model; fin. com. Charles Wright Acad. Pres. Sacramento Opera Assn., 1972-73; treas. Sacramento Children's Home, 1990-92, v.p., 1992—; former mem. bd. dirs. Sutter Hosp. Aux., Sutter Hosp. Med. Rsch. Found., Sacramento Symphony League, Temple B'nai Israel Sisterhood, Sacramento chpt. Hadassah, Sacramento Children's Home Guild; formerly active Sacramento Opera Assn., Crocker Soc. of Crocker Art Gallery, Sacramento Symphony Assn., Sacramento Repertory Theater Assn.; founding mem. Tacoma Cmtys. Art Sch.; mem. Temple Beth El of Tacoma; bd. dirs. Tacoma Art Mus.; mem. fin. com. Charles Wright Acad. Mem. Am. Contract Bridge League, Sacramento Pioneer Assn., Stanford U. Alumni Assn. (past bd. dirs. Sacramento) Sutter Club, Kandahar Ski Club, Sutter Lawn Tennis Club, DelPaso Country Club (capt. women's golf 1983), Tacoma Country and Golf Club, Maui Country Club, Wash. Athletic Club, Tacoma Club. Republican. Jewish. Avocations: golf, duplicate bridge.

WYCOFF, CHARLES COLEMAN, writer, retired anesthesiologist; b. Glazier, Tex., Sept. 2, 1918; s. James Garfield and Ada Sharpe (Braden) W.; m. Gene Marie Henry, May 16, 1942; children: Michelle, Geoffrey, Brian, Roger, Daniel, Norman, Irene, Teresa. AB, U. Calif., Berkeley, 1941; MD, U. Calif., San Francisco, 1943; postgrad., U. London, 1954-55. Diplomate Am. Bd. Anesthesiology. Intern San Francisco County Hosp., 1943-44; resident in anesthesiology U. Calif. Hosp., San Francisco, 1944-45; tng. in anesthesiology Walter Reed Genl. Hosp., 1945; founder The Wycoff Group of Anesthesiology, San Francisco, 1947-53; chief of anesthesia St. Joseph's Hosp., San Francisco, 1947-52, organizer residency tng. program in anesthesiology, 1950; organizer residency tng. program in anesthesiology San Francisco County Hosp., 1954, chief anesthesia, 1953-54; tchr. practice anesthesiology Presbyn. Med. Ctr., N.Y.C., 1955-63; asst. prof. anesthesiology Columbia U., N.Y.C., 1955-63; clin. practice anesthesiology St. Francis Meml. Hosp., San Francisco, 1963-84. Producer, dir. films on regional anesthesia; contbr. articles to sci. jours. Scoutmaster Boy Scouts Am., San Francisco, 1953-55. Capt. M.C., U.S. Army, 1945-47. Mem. Alumni Faculty Assn. Sch. Medicine U. Calif.-San Francisco (councilor-at-large 1979-80). Democrat. Avocations: research in evolution of human behavior, freelance writing, Sierra hiking, gardening, pigeon breeding. Home: 394 Cross St Napa CA 94559-3840

WYDEN, RON, senator; b. Wichita, Kans., May 3, 1949; s. Peter and Edith W.; m. Laurie Oseran, Sept. 5, 1978; 1 child, Adam David. Student, U. Santa Barbara, 1967-69; A.B. with distinction, Stanford U., 1971; J.D., U. Oreg., 1974. Campaign aide Senator Wayne Morse, 1972, 74; co-founder, co-dir. Oreg. Gray Panthers, 1974-80; dir. Oreg. Legal Services for Elderly, 1977-79; instr. gerontology U. Oreg., 1976, U. Portland, 1980, Portland State U., 1979; mem. 97th-104th Congresses from 3d Oreg. dist., Washington, D.C., 1981-96; U.S. Senator from Oreg., 1996—, mem. aging com., mem. budget com., mem. commerce sci. and transp. com., mem. energy and natural resources com., mem. environ. and pub. works com. Recipient Service to Oreg. Consumers award Oreg. Consumers League, 1978, Citizen of Yr. award Oreg. Assn. Social Workers, 1979, Significant Service award Multnomah County Area Agy. on Aging, 1980; named Young Man of Yr. Oreg. Jr. C. of C., 1980. Mem. Am. Bar Assn., Iowa Bar Assn. Democrat. Jewish. Office: 717 Hart Senate Office Bldg Washington DC 20510-3702*

WYLE, EWART HERBERT, clergyman; b. London, Sept. 12, 1904; s. Edwin and Alice Louise (Durman) W.; B.A., U. Louisville, 1930; B.D., Lexington Theol. Sem., 1933; postgrad. Louisville Presbyn. Theol. Sem., Temple U., 1933-35; D.D., Tex. Christian U., 1953; m. Prudence Harper, June 12, 1959; 1 son, Ewart Herbert. Ordained to ministry Christian Ch., 1935; pastor First Ch., Palestine, Tex., 1935-37, First Ch., Birmingham, Ala., 1937-41, First Ch., Tyler, Tex., 1944-54, Country Club Ch., Kansas City, Mo., 1954-59; minister Torrey Pines Ch., La Jolla, Calif., 1959-79, minister emeritus, 1979—. Bd. dirs. Scripps Meml. Hosp., pres., 1980-81. Served as chaplain, maj., AUS, 1941-44. Mem. Mil. Order World Wars, Am. Legion, Tau Kappa Epsilon, Pi Kappa Delta. Clubs: Masons (32 deg.), Shriners, Rotary, LaJolla Beach and Tennis. Home: 8850 N La Jolla Scenic Dr La Jolla CA 92037-1608

WYLIE, RICHARD THORNTON, aerospace engineer; b. Long Beach, Calif., July 11, 1956; s. Howard Hance and Marcella Dart (Metcalf) W. BS, Calif. State Poly. U., Pomona, 1978; MS, U. Calif., Berkeley, 1979. Registered profl. engr., Calif. Engr. Aerocraft Heat Treating, Paramount, Calif., 1991-94, TRW, Inc., Redondo Beach, Calif., 1980-91, 94—. Vol. tutor TRW Bootstrap, 1981—. Mem. Mensa (scholarship chmn. Harbor area 1995—, editor Harbor area newsletter 1996—). Avocation: Graphoanalysis. Home: 1005 Kornblum Ave Torrance CA 90503-5113

WYNKOOP, DONAL BROOKE, electric power company executive; b. Denver, July 10, 1943; s. Francis Yates and Marylynn Frances (Koogle) W.; m. Sheila Ann Bell, Dec. 17, 1961; children: Donal B. Jr., David Brian, Cheryl Lynn. Grad. high sch., Denver; cert. electric meter course, I.C.S., 1970, cert. electrical distrbn. engr., 1980. Journeyman Pub. Svc. Co. Colo., Denver, 1971-79, sr. meterman, 1979-86, unit mgr., 1986—. Avocations: camping, fishing, travel. Office: Pub Svc Co Colo 1123 W 3rd Ave Denver CO 80223-1351

WYNN, KARLA WRAY, artist, agricultural products company executive; b. Idaho Falls, Idaho, Oct. 1, 1943; d. Wiliam and Elma (McCowin) Lott; m. Russell D. Wynn, June 7, 1963 (div. 1996); children: Joseph, Jeffrey, Andrea. Student, Coll. of Holy Names, 1962-63, Providence Coll. Nursing, 1962-63; BFA, Idaho State U., 1989; postgrad., Alfred U., 1993. Co-owner R.D. Wynn Farms, American Falls, Idaho, 1963-96, office mgr., 1975-84; co-owner Redi-Gro Fertilizer Co., American Falls, 1970-96, office mgr., 1980-84; pres. Lakeside Farms, Inc. (name now Redi-Gro Fertilitzer Inc.), American Falls, 1975-96; artist, 1990—; owner Blue Heron, Pocatello, Idaho, 1991-96. Watercolor paintings and ceramic clay sculptures exhibited at various art shows and galleries. Buddhist.

WYNN, ROBERT RAYMOND, retired engineer, consultant; b. Omaha, Mar. 4, 1929; s. Horace Oscar and Yvonne Cecil (Witters) W.; m. Joann Elizabeth Swicegood, June 28, 1974; children: Kay, William, Frederick, Andrew, Emma, Lawrence, Robert. Diploma in Nuclear Engring., Capitol Radio Engring. Inst., 1964; BSEE, Pacific Internat. Coll. Arts and Scis., 1964; AA in Bus. Adminstrn., Allen Hancock Coll., 1969; MSEE, Pacific Internat. Coll. Arts and Scis., 1971; MSMS, West Coast U., 1975, ASCS, 1985; BSCS, U. State of N.Y., 1985. Registered profl. engr., Calif. Meteorologist United Air Lines, Calif., 1949-53; engring. planner Aircraft Tools Inc., Inglewood, Calif., 1953-55; field service engr. N. Am. Aviation, Inglewood, Calif., 1955-59; R&D engr. Carstedt Research Inc., N. Long Beach, Calif., 1959-60; test engr. Martin Marrietta Corp., Vandenburg AFB, Calif., 1960-64; project engr. Fed. Electric Corp., Vandenburg AFB, Calif., 1965-69; systems engr. Aeronutronic Ford Corp., Pasadena, Calif., 1970-75; MTS Jet Propulsion Lab., Pasadena, Calif., 1975-83; engring. mgr. Space Com., Redondo Beach, Calif., 1983-84; engring. specialist Boeing Service Inc., Pasadena, 1984-86; cons., mem. tech. staff Jet Propulsion Lab., Pasadena, 1986-96; ret., 1996; instr. computer sci. and CAD, Jet Propulsion Lab., 1980-82. With USAAF, 1946. Mem. Calif. Soc. Profl. Engrs., Exptl. Aircraft Assn. (pres. Lompoc chpt. 1968), Am. Legion Rep. (life), W. Coast U. Alumni Assn. Republican. Avocations: model airplane design and constrn., flying, camping. Home: PO Box 26316 Prescott Valley AZ 86312-6316

XIONG, TOUSU SAYDANGNMVANG, minister; b. Xieng Khouang, Laos, June 23, 1966; came to U.S., 1976; s. Nhialue Saydang and May (Vang) X.; m. Zoua Pahoua Moua, Sept. 14, 1993; children: Chivkeeb Genesis Toupa, Naamonunas Ruth, Nujsimloob Hebrews. BA in Bibl. Studies, Simpson Coll., San Francisco, 1989; MA in Theology, Mennonite Brethren Bibl. Sem., Fresno, Calif., 1991; AS in Computerized Acctg., Phillips Jr. Coll., Fresno, Calif., 1993. Ordained to ministry Christian and Missionary Alliance, 1991. Assoc. min. Hmong San Raphael (Calif.) Bapt. Ch., 1986-88; youth min. Hmong Alliance Ch. of Santa Barbara, Goleta, Calif., 1984-85, Hmong Alliance Ch. of Fresno, 1989—. Scoutmaster Boy Scouts Am., 1984-85. Home: 910 Orienta Ave # A Altamonte Springs FL 32701 Office: Hmong Alliance Ch Fresno 8234 E Belmont Ave Fresno CA 93727-9725

XU, WEI, scientist, engineer; b. Jiaxing, Zhejing, China, Aug. 5, 1958; came to U.S., 1992; s. Zhennian Xu and Tingzhou Chen; m. Gong Beilan, April 23, 1989; 1 child, Zhili. BEng., China U. Geoscis., Wuhan, 1982; MS, Hangzhou U., China, 1988; PhD, Miami U., Oxford, Ohio, 1997. Tchr. Xu-Wang Elem. Sch., Jiaxing, China, 1976-78; asst. lectr. China U. Geoscis., Wuhan, 1982-85; rsch. asst. Hangzhou U., China, 1985-88, lectr., 1988-92; rsch. asst. Miami U., Oxford, Ohio, 1992-97; scientist Boeing Co., Seattle, 1997—. Contbr. articles to profl. jours. Recipient 2nd place award for sci. tech. China Nat. Min. Aviation Industry, 1993, 2nd place award for sci. tech. Govt. Province of Zhejiang, 1993. Mem. Human Factors and Ergonomics Soc., Assn. Computing Machinery. Avocations: music, playing violin. Home: 8911 NE 151st Pl Bothell WA 98011-4589

YACCO, RICHARD A., television producer, educator; b. San Jose, Calif., Aug. 23, 1951; s. Samuel and Rose Yacco; 1 child, Cole. AA in Liberal Arts, DeAnza Coll., 1971; BA in Radio-TV, San Jose State U., 1974. Program/prodn. mgr. Sunnyvale (Calif.) Cablevision, 1970-74; program mgr. TelePrompTer of Los Gatos, Calif., 1974; dist. dir. programming TelePrompTer Corp., Santa Clara, Calif., 1974-79; prodn. mgr. Bay Area Interconnect, San Jose, Calif., 1979-89; v.p., mgr. Mktg. Video Prodns., Milpitas, Calif., 1989-92; adj. instr. Cogswell Poly. Coll., Sunnyvale, 1992-97; exec. prodr. Yacco Creative Svcs., San Jose, 1992—. Office: Yacco Creative Svcs 1767 Valhalla Ct San Jose CA 95132

YACK, PATRICK ASHLEY, editor; b. Little Rock, Oct. 25, 1951; s. Leo Patrick and Sarah Ann (Dew) Y.; m. Susan Marie Courtney, June 7, 1980; children: Alexander Ryan, Kendall Elizabeth. BFA, So. Meth. U., 1974. Staff asst. U.S. Rep. Alan Steelman, Washington, 1975-76; press aide U.S. Senator Charles Percy, Chgo., 1977-78; reporter Fla. Times-Union, Jacksonville, 1979-80; regional reporter Fla. Times-Union, Atlanta, 1981-82; reporter The Denver Post, 1983-85, Washington bur. chief, 1985-87; nat. editor Atlanta Constitution, 1987-89; mng. editor The Register-Guard, Eugene, Oreg., 1989-94; editor News & Record, Greensboro, N.C., 1994-98, Fla. Times-Union, Jacksonville, 1998—. Mem. Am. Soc. Newspaper Editors (past membership com. chair), AP Mng. Editors Assn.

YACKLE, ALBERT REUSTLE, aeronautical engineer; b. Willow Grove, Pa., May 13, 1922; s. Albert J. and Marion D. (Reustle) Y.; m. Ruth E. Everett, Sept. 18, 1948; children: Linda McCann, Tom, Brad. BS in Mech. Engring. Aeronautical Option, Pa. State U., 1943. Registered profl engr., Calif. Structures engr. Ea. Aircraft, 1944; structures engr. Kellett Aircraft Corp., 1946-48, chief structures engr., 1950-60; structures engr. Chase Aircraft, 1948-50; advanced design and program mgr. Lockheed Aircraft Corp., 1960-91; ret., 1991; cons. Huntington Med. Rsch. Inst., Pasadena, Calif., 1991-96. Contbr. tech. papers to profl. jours. Lt. (j.g.) USN, 1944-46. Recipient Lockheed Spl. Achievement awards, 1976, 77, 79, 87; inducted into H.S. Hall of Fame, 1996. Fellow (assoc.) AIAA; mem. Am. Helicopter Soc. Achievements include 2 patents in rigid rotor helicopters. Home: 5105 Quakertown Ave Woodland Hills CA 91364-3538

YACOB, YOSEF, lawyer, economist; b. Dire Dawa, Harar, Ethiopia, Nov. 12, 1947; s. Yacob and Egziaraya (Osman) Zanios; m. Betsy Ann Boynton; children: Sarah Ann, Matthew Yosef, Ezra Yosef, Jarred Yosef, Rachel Helen. BA, Linfield Coll., 1971; JD, Lewis and ClarkU., 1974. Bar: Oreg. 1975, U.S. Dist. Ct. Oreg. 1979, U.S. Ct. Appeals (9th cir.) 1980. Rschr. criminal justice State of Oreg., Salem, 1974, sr. administrv. analyst, 1974-76; adjudications specialist, legal counsel, law enforcement coun. Office of the Gov. State of Oregon, Salem, 1976-78; chief administrv. law judge State of Oregon, Milwaukie, 1978-83, dir. hearings, appeals, 1982-84; mng. atty. Hyatt Legal Services, Clakamas, Oreg., 1984-86; pres., sr. ptnr. Yacob & Assocs. P.C., Clackamas, 1986-93; dir. gen. for legal affairs, gen. counsel Ministry of Fgn. Affairs, Govt. of Ethiopia, 1993—. Co-author: Evaluation of Multwomah County District Attorney's High Impact Project, 1978. Avocations: alpine skiing, nordic skiing, water skiing, reading. Office: Yacob & Assocs PC Northwest Legal Svcs 6885 SW Montgomery Way Wilsonville OR 97070-6739

YAFFE, JAMES, author; b. Chgo., Mar. 31, 1927; s. Samuel and Florence (Scheinman) Y.; m. Elaine Gordon, Mar. 1, 1964; children: Deborah Ann, Rebecca Elizabeth, Gideon Daniel. Grad., Fieldston Sch., 1944; B.A. summa cum laude, Yale U., 1948. Prof. Colo. Coll., Colo. Springs, 1968—; dir. gen. studies Colo. Coll., 1981—. Author: Poor Cousin Evelyn, 1951, The Good-for-Nothing, 1953, What's the Big Hurry?, 1954, Nothing But the Night, 1959, Mister Margolies, 1962, Nobody Does You Any Favors, 1966, The American Jews, 1968, The Voyage of the Franz Joseph, 1970, So Sue Me!, 1972, Saul and Morris, Worlds Apart, 1982, A Nice Murder for Mom, 1988, Mom Meets Her Maker, 1990, Mom Doth Murder Sleep, 1991, Mom Among the Liars, 1992, My Mother the Detective, 1997; play The Deadly Game, 1960, (with Jerome Weidman) Ivory Tower, 1967, Cliffhanger, 1985; also TV plays, stories, essays, revs. Served with USNR, 1945-46. Recipient [illegible]

Guild of Am., Dramatists Guild, A.A.U.P., Mystery Writers of Am., Phi Beta Kappa. Jewish. Club: Elizabethan (Yale). Avocations: music, bridge, movies. Address: 1215 N Cascade Ave Colorado Springs CO 80903-2303 Office: Colo Coll Off Dir Gen Studies Colorado Springs CO 80903

YAGER, WALTER STUART, aerospace engineer; b. Calmar, Iowa, Mar. 31, 1936; s. Walter Douglas and Eldie Charolette (Grundland) Y.; m. Elizabeth Lee Sunbarger, Aug. 31, 1958; children: Ellen Denise Yager Brandon, Douglas Lee. BS in Aero. Engring., U. Okla., 1959; MS in Aerospace Mech. Engring., Air Force Inst. Tech., 1967. Engr. Northrup Aircraft, Hawthorne, Calif., 1959; commd. 2d lt. USAF, 1959, advanced through grades to col., 1979, ret., 1985; engr., dir. Martin Marietta, Denver, 1985—; mem. Titan II Mishap Investigation, Little Rock, 1978; pres. Def. Meteorol. Satellite Mishap Investigation, L.A., 1980. Active Civilian/Mil. Coun., Cape Canaveral, Fla., 1978-81. Decorated Legion of Merit. Mem. AIAA (sr.), Air Force Assn. Avocations: golf, bridge. Home: 811 Appleby Pl Castle Rock CO 80104-5312

YAKICH, DAVID ELI, international sales executive; b. Denver, May 31, 1957; s. Eli and Josephine (Goodnough) Y. Jr.; m. Carrie Elizabeth. BS, Colo. State U., 1979; postgrad., U. Minn., 1980-82; BA, U. Colo., 1984. Geophys. tech. Amoco Prodn. Corp., Denver, 1980-81; cons. geophysicist Lear Petroleum, Denver, 1982-84; computer svc. mgr. Daniel Geophys., Denver, 1984-87; nat. sales mgr. Graphics Info. Inc., Denver, 1987-89; area mgr. Far East Auto-trol Tech., Denver, 1989-91; v.p. sales and support GeoGraphix Inc., Denver, 1991; dir. internat. sales Visual Numerics Inc., 1992-93; Japan mktg. mgr. Xilinx, Inc., Boulder, Colo., 1994—; computer cons. Daniel Geophysical, Denver, 1983. Mem. Soc. Exploration Geophysics, Denver C. of C. Republican. Roman Catholic. Avocations: skiing, softball, tennis, golf, fishing.

YALAM, ARNOLD ROBERT, allergist, immunologist, consultant; b. N.Y.C., Apr. 1, 1940; s. Herman and Sylvia (Taber) Y.; m. Carol Ann Strocker, June 16, 1964; children: John, Matthew. AB, Johns Hopkins U., 1960; MD, U. Md., Balt., 1964. Diplomate Am. Bd. Internal Medicine, Am. Bd. Allergy and Immunology. Intern Jackson Meml. Hosp., Miami, Fla., 1964-65; resident in internal medicine SUNY Downstate Med. Ctr., Bklyn., 1965-67; fellow Scripps Clinic and Rsch. Found., La Jolla, Calif., 1967-68; cons. allergist and immunologist San Diego, 1970—. Maj. US Army, 1968-70. Fellow Am. Acad. Allergy and Immunoloy; mem. Am. Soc. Addiction Medicine (cert.), San Diego Allergy Soc. Office: 8929 University Center Ln San Diego CA 92122-1006

YAMAGATA, LESLIE CRAIG, realty specialist; b. Sacramento, Calif., Aug. 15, 1961; s. Mitsuru and Dorothy Tsuyumi (Toyota) Y. BA in History magna cum laude, San Diego State U., 1984; postgrad., Calif. State U., Sacramento, 1983-86. Exec. intern State of Calif., Sacramento, 1979; asst. forensic coach, 1980; life ins. analyst CalFarm Life Ins. Co., Sacramento, 1988-90, life/annuity specialist, 1989-90; contract specialist intern Gen. Svcs. Adminstrn., San Francisco, 1990-92, contract specialist, 1993-96, contracting officer, 1993-96, realty specialist, 1996-97. Mem. Japanese-Am. Citizens League, San Francisco, 1990, Very Spl. Arts Calif., 1991, Commonwealth Club San Francisco, 1992, World Affairs Coun., 1996, Federal Asian Pacific Am. Coun., 1997. Mem. Am. Mgmt. Assn., Nat. Contract Mgmt. Assn. (cert. assoc. contracts mgr., cert. profl. contracts mgr.), Fed. Mgrs. Assn., Nat. Forensic League, Profl. Mgrs. Assn., San Diego State U. Alumni Assn., Phi Alpha Theta, Phi Beta Kappa. Avocations: classical pianist, composer.

YAMAKAWA, DAVID KIYOSHI, JR., lawyer; b. San Francisco, Jan. 25, 1936; s. David and Shizu (Negishi) Y. BS, U. Calif., Berkeley, 1958, JD, 1963. Bar: Calif. 1964, U.S. Supreme Ct. 1970. Prin. Law Offices David K. Yamakawa Jr., San Francisco, 1964—; dep. dir. Cmty. Action Agy., San Francisco, 1968-69; dir. City Demonsration Agy., San Francisco, 1969-70; mem. adv. coun. Calif. Senate Subcom. on the Disabled, 1982-83, Ctr. for Mental Health Svcs., Substance Abuse and Mental Health Svcs. Adminstrn. U.S. Dept. Health and Human Svcs., 1995—; chmn. cmty. residential treatment system adv. com. Calif. Dept. Mental Health, 1980-85, San Francisco Human Rights Commn., 1977-80; pres. Legal Assistance to the Elderly, 1981-83; 2d v.p. Nat. Conf. Social Welfare, 1983—; v.p. Region IX Nat. Mental Health Assn., 1981 83. Vice chmn. Mt. Zion Hosp. and Med. Ctr., 1986-88; bd. dirs. United Neighborhood Ctrs. of Am., 1977-83, ARC Bay Area, 1988-91, Goldman Inst. on Aging, 1993—, v.p. 1994-96, vice-chmn. 1996—; trustee Mt. Zion Med. Ctr. U. Calif., San Francisco, 1993-97, UCSF/Mt. Zion, UCSF Stanford Health Care, 1997—; chmn. bd. trustees United Way Bay Area, 1983-85; CFO Action for Nature, Inc., 1987—; v.p. Friends of Legal Assistance to the Elderly, 1984—; bd. dirs. ind. sector, 1986-92. Friends of the San Francisco Human Rights Commn., 1980—, CFO, 1980-85, 94—, vice chmn. 1985-94, Father Alfred Boeddeker's La Madre Found., 1982—, v.p. 1994—, Nat. Concilio Am., 1987—, legal coun., 1996—, Hispanic Cmty. Found. of the Bay Area, 1989-98, legal coun., 1989-98; bd. dirs. Non-Profit Svcs., Inc., 1987—, sec. 1987-90, chmn. 1990—; pres. Coun. Internat. Programs, San Francisco, 1987-89, Internat. Inst. San Francisco, 1990-93; mem. citizens adv. com. San Francisco Hotel Tax Fund Grants for the Arts Program, 1991—. Recipient John B. Williams Outstanding Planning and Agy. Rels. vol. award United Way of the Bay Area, 1980, Mortimer Fleishhacker Jr. Outstanding Vol. award Unied Way, 1985, Spl. Recognition award Legal Assistance to the Elderly, 1983, Commendation award Bd. Suprs. City and County of San Francisco, 1983, cert. Honor, 1985, San Francisco Found. award, 1985, 1st Mental Health Awareness award Mental Health Assn., San Francisco, 1990, David Yamakawa Day proclaimed in San Francisco, 1985. Mem. ABA (Liberty Bell award 1986). Office: 582 Market St San Francisco CA 94104-5305

YAMAMOTO, IRWIN TORAKI, editor, publisher investment newsletter; b. Wailuku, Maui, Hawaii, Apr. 5, 1955; s. Torao and Yukie (Urata) Y. B in Bus. Adminstrn., Mktg., Chaminade U., 1977. Pres., editor, publisher The Yamamoto Forecast, Kahului, Hawaii, 1977—. Author: (book) Profit Making in the Stock Market, 1983; columnist The Hawaii Herald, 1978—. Named Top Market Timer, Top Gold Timer, and to Timer Digest Honor Roll by Timer Digest, also honored by Select Info. Exchange and Rating the Stock Selectors. Avocations: exercise, music, reading, philosophy. Home and Office: PO Box 573 Kahului HI 96733-7073

YAMAMOTO, MICHAEL TORU, journalist; b. San Francisco, July 9, 1960; s. Harry Naoto and Noriko (Yoshitomi) Y.; m. Marianne Chin, Oct. 9, 1993. BA Psychology, San Francisco State U., 1981, BA Journalism, 1981. Editor San Francisco State U. Phoenix, 1980; news editor Hayward (Calif.) Daily Rev., 1979-80, Long Beach (Calif.) Press-Telegram, 1981; nat. desk editor L.A. Times, 1981-85; night news editor L.A. Times, Washington, 1986-87, investigative projects editor, 1988; dep. city editor San Francisco Chronicle, 1989-92, exec. projects editor, 1993, city editor, 1993-95; mng. editor news CNET, San Francisco, 1996—; adj. prof. Am. U., Washington, 1987, Calif. State U. at Northridge, Calif., 1984-85; vis. faculty mem. Am. Press Inst., Reston, Va., 1994, Poynter Inst. for Media Studies, St. Petersburg, Fla., 1995, San Francisco Unified Sch. Dist., 1994; fellow Coro Found., San Francisco, 1990-91. Recipient Dow Jones Newspaper Fund scholarship, Princeton, N.J., 1980. Mem. Asian Am. Journalism Assn., White House Corr. Assn., Soc. Profl. Journalists., World Affairs Coun. Office: CNET 150 Chestnut St San Francisco CA 94111-1004*

YAMANAKA, WENDI SUZUKO, pharmacist; b. Stockton, Calif., July 27, 1957; d. Noboru and Dorothy Chisato (Kaneko) Y. AA in Natural Scis., San Joaquin Delta Coll., 1977; BS in Chemistry and Biology, U. Pacific, 1980, D in Pharmacy, 1983. Lic. pharmacist Calif., Nev. Intern Campus Pharmacy, Stockton, 1981; clin. intern in pharmacy San Joaquin Gen. Hosp., Stockton, 1982; intern pharmacist Drs. Med. Ctr., Modesto, Calif., 1983; pharmacist Payless Drug Stores, San Jose, Calif., 1984—. Mem. Calif. Pharm. Assn., Am. Soc. Hosp. Pharmacists. Buddhist. Avocations: music, photography, travel, softball, swimming. Home: 5015 Moss Creek Cir Stockton CA 95219-8075

YAMASHITA, FRANCIS ISAMI, magistrate judge; b. Hilo, Hawaii, May 14, 1949; s. Yuji and Sadako (Hirayama) Y.; m. Alexa D. M. Fujise, Feb. 26, 1983. BA, Pacific U., 1971; JD, U. Chgo., 1974. Bar: Hawaii 1974. Law clk. 1st Cir. Ct., Hawaii, 1975-76; dep. pros. atty. City/County of Honolulu, 1976-79, 82-87; assoc. Ikazaki, Devens, Lo, Youth & Nakano, Honolulu, 1979-82; dist. judge State of Hawaii, Honolulu, 1987-92, U.S. magistrate judge, 1992—. Office: US Dist Ct of Hawaii Room C-244 300 Ala Moana Blvd Rm C-244 Honolulu HI 96850-0001

YAMASHITA, KENNETH AKIRA, library administrator, librarian; b. Topaz, Utah, Sept. 11, 1945; s. Susumu and Kiyoko (Kitano) Y. BA, Rutgers U., 1967, MLS, 1972; ArtsD, Simmons Coll., 1982. Ref. libr. Montclair (N.J.) Free Pub. Libr., 1970-73; ext. svcs. libr. Decatur (Ill.) Pub. Libr., 1973-75; asst. to commr. Chgo. Pub. Libr., 1975-78; mktg. rep. Computer Libr. Sys., Inc., Newtonville, Mass., 1978-79; asst. to dir. Mass. Bd. Libr. Commrs., Boston, 1979-81; supervising libr. Stockton (Calif.)-San Joaquin County Pub. Libr., 1982-90, libr. divsn. mgr., 1990—; guest lectr. Sch. Libr. Sci., U. Mich., Ann Arbor, 1978; bldg. program cons. Lakeland (Fla.) Pub. Libr., Calaveras County (Calif.) Pub. Libr., 1982—; advisor to prof. publs. U. Wis., Madison, Calif. State Libr., Sacramento, Gale Pub., Detroit, 1989—; state, fed. grant writer Calaveras County Libr., San Andreas, Calif., 1991; mem. rev. com. multi-ethnic recruitment scholarship program Calif. State Libr., 1990, 95; mem. design com. Libr. Edn. Funding Program Calif. State Libr., 1998. Co-author: (chpt.) Opportunities for Minorities in Librarianship, 1977; contbr.: Problems in Library Management, 1981; assoc. editor: (reference) Guide to Multicultural Resources, 1995-97. Sec., bd. dirs. Stockton Shelter for Homeless, 1993-96; mem. diversity awareness team City of Stockton, 1994-98; mem. citizen rev. team United Way San Joaquin County, 1994, 95; participant Leadership Stockton, 1995. Asian Studies Com. fellow Ind. U., 1967-69, Carnegie Grant fellow Ind. U., 1969-70, Friends of the Montclair Free Pub. Libr. fellow Rutgers U., 1971, HEA Title II B fellow Simmons Coll., 1979-80. Mem. ALA (chair, adv. com. Office for Libr. Outreach Svcs. 1987-90, councilor 1995-98, 99—, nominating com. 1995, com. on coms. 1997-98, spectrum initiative steering com. 1997—), Asian/Pacific ALA (pres. 1996-97), Calif. Libr. Assn. (coun., assembly mem. 1987-93, pres. pub. libr. sect. 1998), Beta Phi Mu. Democrat. Avocations: videos/films, music, aerobics, cooking, travel. Home: 1209 W Downs St Stockton CA 95207-6913 Office: Stockton San Joaquin County Pub Libr 605 N El Dorado St Stockton CA 95202-1907

YAN, HONG-CHENG, electrical engineer educator; b. Fuzhou, Fujian, China, May 28, 1947; came to U.S., 1983; s. Ziqi Yan and Ruiting Xu; m. Meijie Xiang; 1 child, Qijia. BS in Elec. Phys. Engring., Harbin Poly. U., China, 1970; MSc in Control Theory, Chinese Acad. Scis. Grad. Sch., 1981; PhD in Engring. Sci., Clarkson U., 1986; PhD in Elec. Engring., Purdue U., 1993. Cert. of tng. for patent examiner World Intellectual Property Orgn., UN, 1981. Elec. engr. Fujian Longyan Iron and Steel Co., 1970-82; trainee, practitioner U.K. Patent Office, London, 1980-81; applied software engr. Inst. Petroleum Exploration and Devel., Beijing, 1982-83; tchg. asst. Clarkson U., Potsdam, N.Y., 1983-85; rsch. asst. Purdue U., West Lafayette, Ind., 1986-88; asst. prof. elec. engring. Mo. Western State Coll., St. Joseph, 1989-95; product engr. Astec Semiconductor, San Jose, 1995—. Contbr. articles to profl. jours. Fellowship World Intellectual Property Orgn., 1980. Mem. IEEE. Avocations: sports, travel. Address: 1748 Maysong Ct San Jose CA 95131-2727

YANAI, MICHIO, meteorologist, educator; b. Jan. 16, 1934; came to U.S., 1970; s. Kin (Watanabe) Y.; m. Yoko Miyazaki, Apr. 25, 1965; children: Takashi, Satoshi. BS, U. Tokyo, 1956, MS, 1958, DSc, 1961. Rsch. meteorologist Meteorol. Rsch. Inst. Japan Meteorol. Agy., Tokyo, 1961-65; asst. prof. U. Tokyo, 1965-70; from assoc. prof. to prof. UCLA, 1971—. Fellow Am. Meteorol. Soc. (awards com. 1992, assoc. editor Jour. Atmos. Scis. 1988-90, Jule Charney award 1986); mem. Am. Geophys. Union, Royal Meteorol. Soc., Meteorol. Soc. Japan (Soc. award 1962, Fujiwara award 1993). Achievements include discovery of a large-scale wave in the equatorial stratosphere called the Yanai wave; formulated a method of diagnosing mass flux in cumulus ensemble called Q1-Q2 diagnosis; revealed the role of the Tibetan Plateua in the onset of the Asian summer monsoon. Office: UCLA Dept Atmos Scis 405 Hilgard Ave Los Angeles CA 90095-9000

YANCEY, GARY, electronics company executive. Pres., CEO Applied Signal Tech., Sunnyvale, Calif. Office: Applied Signal Tech 400 W California Ave Sunnyvale CA 94086-5148*

YANG, BINGEN, mechanical engineering educator; b. Beijing, China, Mar. 4, 1955; came to U.S., 1984; m. Haiyan Wang; children: Sonia, Tanya. BS, Dalian Inst. of Tech., China, 1982; MS, Mich. State U., 1985; PhD, U. Calif., Berkeley, 1989. Asst. prof. U. So. Calif., Los Angeles, 1989-95, assoc. prof., 1995—; hon. prof. Dalian U. of Tech., China, 1994—; tech. program chmn. ASME 16th Biennial Conf. on Mechan. Vibration and Noise, Sacramento, 1997. Tech. assoc. editor ASME Jour. Vibration and Acoustics, 1996—; contbr. articles to profl. jours.; presenter in field. Regent fellow U. Calif., Berkeley, 1985; recipient Rsch. award Charles Lee Powell Found., 1989, U.S. Army Rsch. Office, 1993, Northrop Grumman Corp., 1995. Mem. ASME, AIAA. Achievements include pioneered the Distributed Transfer Function Method, a technique for modeling, analysis and control of complex distributed parameter systems; discovered the Eigenvalue Inclusion Principles for gyroscopic dynamic systems; developed innovative time-delay approach for non-colocated control of flexible mech. sys.; invented distributed vibration dampers for intelligent control of structures and machines. Avocations: reading, volleyball, classical music, travel. Office: USC Dept of Mech Engr OHE430 Los Angeles CA 90089-1453

YANG, BING-LIANG, educator, researcher; b. Yunan, Guangdong, China, Dec. 26, 1946; s. Jin-Tang and Yimei (Li) Y.; m. Miao-Yong Li, Feb. 4, 1972; children: Xi, Ying. BS, South China U. Tech., 1969; PhD, City U. Hong Kong, 1996. Asst. lectr. South China U. Tech., Guangzhou, 1969-78, lectr., 1979-92; sr. rsch. asst. U. Hong Kong, 1988-89; reviewer Acta Optica Sinica, China, 1991; rsch. assoc. City U. Hong Kong, 1992-95; assoc. prof. South China U. Tech., 1993—; vis. scholar U. Calif., Berkeley, 1996—. Contbr. articles to profl. jours. Mem. IEEE, Chinese Inst. Elecs., Chinese Inst. Physics. Avocation: swimming. Home: South China U Tech, Dept Applied Physics, Guangzhou 510641, China Office: U Calif Dept Elec Engring 231 Cory Hall Berkeley CA 94720-1771

YANG, HENRY T., university chancellor, educator; b. Chungking, China, Nov. 29, 1940; s. Chen Pei and Wei Gen Yang; m. Dilling Tsui, Sept. 2, 1966; children: Maria, Martha. BSCE, Nat. Taiwan U., 1962; MSCE, W.Va. U., 1965; PhD, Cornell U., 1968; D honoris causa, Purdue U., 1996. Rsch. engr. Gilbert Assocs., Reading, Pa., 1968-69; asst. prof. Sch. Aeros. and Astronautics, Purdue U., West Lafayette, Ind., 1969-72, assoc. prof., 1972-76, prof., 1976-94, Neil A. Armstrong Disting. prof., 1988-94, sch. head, 1979-84; dean engring. Purdue U., 1984-94; chancellor U. Calif., Santa Barbara, 1994—; mem. sci. adv. bd. USAF, 1985-89; mem. aero. adv. com. NASA, 1985-89; mem. engring. adv. com. NSF, 1988-91; mem. mechanics bd. visitors ONR, 1990-93; mem. def. mfg. bd. DOD, 1988-89, def. sci. bd., 1989-91; mem. acad. adv. bd. Nat. Acad. Engring., 1991-94; mem. tech. adv. com. Pratt & Whitney, 1993-95; bd. dirs. Allied Signal; mem. Naval Rsch. Adv. Com., 1996-98. Recipient 12 Best Tchg. awards Purdue U., 1971-94. Fellow AIAA, Am. Soc. Engring. Edn. (Centennial medal 1993, Benjamin Garver Lamme award 1998); mem. NAE, Academia Sinica. Office: U California Chancellors Office Santa Barbara CA 93106*

YANG, HSIN-MING, immunologist; b. Taipei, Taiwan, Dec. 2, 1952; came to U.S., 1980; s. Sze Piao and Yun-Huan (Chang) Y.; m. Yeasing Yeh, June 28, 1980; children: Elaine, Albert. BS, Nat. Taiwan U., 1976, MS, 1983; PhD, U. Wash., 1985. Rsch. assoc. Tri-Svc. Gen. Hosp., Taipei, 1979-80; fellow Scripps Clinic and Rsch. Found., La Jolla, Calif., 1986-88, sr. rsch. assoc., 1988-90; asst. prof. U. Nebr. Med. Ctr., Omaha, 1990-91; sr. rsch. scientist Pacific Biotech, Inc., San Diego, 1991-95; mgr. Scantibodies Lab., Inc., Santee, Calif., 1995-99; dir. Scantibodies Lab., Inc., 1999—; lectr. Yun-Pei Coll. Med. Tech., Shinchiu, Taiwan, 1979-80. Contbr. articles to profl. jours., chpt. to book; inventor in field; patentee on analyte detection device including a hydrophobic barrier for improved fluid flow. Joseph Drown Found. fellow, 1986, Nat. Cancer Ctr. fellow, 1987-88. Mem. Am. Assn. for Cancer Rsch., Am. Assn. Clin. Chemistry, N.Y. Acad. Scis. Avocations: tennis, swimming, table tennis. Office: Scantibodies Lab Inc 9336 Abraham Way Santee CA 92071-2861

YANG, LIN, chemist; b. Shenyang, China, Sept. 6, 1963; s. Chengxiang and Yushan (Li) Y.; m. Xiaoyun Zhu, June 20, 1988; 1 child, Mu. BS, East China U. Sci. and Tech., 1985, MS, 1988; PhD, U. Ariz., 1996. Rsch. scientist Pacific Corp., Shanghai, 1988-90; R&D engr. Integrated Process Equipment Corp., Phoenix, 1995—. Contbr. articles to profl. jours. Teaching fellow Boston U., 1990. Mem. Am. Chem. Soc. (Marvel award So. Ariz. sect. 1995). Achievements include inventions in ultra-low loss planar waveguides by a sol-gel method, sol-gel derived planar waveguide sensor, sol-gel based planar waveguide sensor for iodine. Office: Integrated Process Equip Co 4717 E Hilton Ave Phoenix AZ 85034-6402

YANG, ROBERT MENHSIU, healthcare system administrator; b. Madison, Wis., Jan. 29, 1971; s. Sweson and Chien-tai (Lin) Y. BSc, U. Notre Dame, 1993; M in Health Adminstrn., U. So. Calif., L.A., 1995. Asst. dir. bus. devel. APX Health Sys., Downey, Calif., 1993-94; dir. bus. devel. Latino Health Care, Santa Fe Springs, Calif., 1994-95; contracts adminstr. MedPartners, L.A., 1995-96; payer rels. mgr. Cedars-Sinai Health Sys., L.A., 1996-98, adminstrv. mgr. pediatrics, 1998—; cons. CEO adv., Irvine, Calif., 1994—. Creator web pages. Mem. Med. Group Mgmt. Assn., Notre Dame Club L.A. (bd. dirs. 1998—), U. So. Calif. Health Svcs. Adminstrn. Alumni Assn. (v.p. membership 1996). E-mail: yangrm@cshs.org. Home: 12 Faircliff Ct Glendale CA 91206-1723 Office: Cedars-Sinai Health System 8700 Beverly Blvd Los Angeles CA 90048-1804

YANKEE, MARIE, educator, publishing executive; m. J.R. Yankee, June 6, 1956; children: Michael, David, Stephen, Jennifer. Diploma Montessori edn., Montessori Inst. Am., 1968; MS, Southeastern U., Greenville, S.C., 1980, PhD, 1981. Chief exec. officer The Fernhaven Studio, Los Angeles, 1966—, Montessori Ednl. Environment, Los Angeles, 1974—, Yankee Montessori Mfg., L.A., 1980-86; pres. Internat. Montessori Inst. Tchr. Ednl. Programs, Sage, Calif., 1980—; rsch. editor Edn. Systems Pub., L.A., 1982—; dir. EEI, Inc., L.A., 1987—; cons. Calif. pub. schs., 1976; prof. Univ. Coll. Vancouver. Author: Montessori Curriculum, 1985, Reading Program, 1981, Science for Preschool, 1981, Geography for Preschool, 1982. Mem. Am. Montessori Soc., Montessori Inst. Am. Home: 38395 Trifone Rd Hemet CA 92544-9693 Office: PO Box 890944 Temecula CA 92589-0944

YANSOUNI, CYRIL J., executive. CEO, chmn. Read-Rite, Milpitas, Calif. Office: 345 Los Coches St Milpitas CA 95035*

YAO, HILDA MARIA HSIANG, banker, strategic planner; b. Honolulu, Sept. 11, 1956; d. Hsin-Nung and Dorothy Wen (Wu) Y. BA cum laude, U. Pacific, 1975; MA, U. Wis., 1976. Ops. analyst Visa Internat., San Mateo, Calif., 1977-80; sr. product mgr. Bank of Am., San Francisco, 1980-81, asst. v.p., strategic planner Calif. electronic banking div., 1981-84, v.p., div. strategic planner U.S. wholesale svcs. world banking div., 1984-85, v.p., head dealer corp. svcs., 1985-89, v.p., dir. retail banking adminstrn., 1989-90, v.p., CFO internat. pvt. banking divsn., 1990-92, v.p., dir., deputy mgr. internat. investment svcs., 1992-93, v.p., head fiduciary policy, 1993-95, sr. v.p., dir. pvt. banking, trust and investment mgmt., 1995-97, sr. v.p., dep. mng. dir. internat. pvt. banking, 1997—. Bd. regents U. Pacific, Stockton, Calif., 1984-85, 91—; treas. pres.'s jr. adv. coun. Bank of Am., 1982-83; active exec. com. Campaign for Wis., 1991—; bd. dirs. U. Wis. Found., 1995—; bd. visitors Coll. of Letters and Sci. U. Wis., Madison, 1995—; mem. adv. bd. program in medicine and philosophy Calif. Pacific Med. Ctr., San Francisco, 1993—; mem. Pacific Coun. on Internat. Policy, 1996—; mem. China study group Pacific Coun. on Internat. Policy and Rand Corp., 1996—; hon. advisor China Soc. for People's Friendship Studies, 1992—. U. Wis. fellow, 1975-76, alumni fellow U. Pacific, 1983, Outstanding Young Alumna award U. Pacific, 1989. Mem. Nat. Vehicle Leasing Assn. (treas. 1988-89), World Affairs Counc., Calif. Acad. Scis., Commonwealth Club Calif., Bank Am. Club, Bankers Club San Francisco, World Trade Club, Univ. Club, The Mus. Soc., Calif. Legion of Honor, Bascom Hill Soc. U. Wis., President's Circle U. Pacific, Nat. Soc. Hist. Preservation, 1841 Club-Punahou Sch., Odyssey Club. Avocations: Shakespeare, opera, languages, swimming, golf. Home: Gramercy Towers 1177 California St San Francisco CA 94108-2212 Office: Bank of Am 50 California St Ste 233 San Francisco CA 94111-4624

YAO, XIAOTIAN STEVE, electrical engineer, optical scientist; b. Hongzhou, Zhejiang, China, July 29, 1960; came to U.S., 1985; s. Dunli and Xianrong Yao; m. Yuanyuan Fang; 1 child, Leon. BS in Physics, Hebei U., China, 1982; MS in Applied Physics, N.W. Telecom. Engring. Inst., China, 1984; MSEE, U. So. Calif., 1989, PhD in Elec. Engring., 1992. Researcher N. China Electro-Optic Rsch. Inst., Beijing, 1982-84; optical engr. ADC Fiber Optics, Westboro, Mass., 1985-87; rsch. asst. U. So. Calif., L.A., 1987-90; mem. tech. staff Jet Propulsion Lab., Pasadena, Calif., 1990-96, sr. mem. tech. staff, 1996—; mem. adv. bd. Nat. Network Electro-Optic Mfg. Tech., Vandergrift, Pa., 1996—; mem. tech. com. Optical Fiber Comm. Conf., Washington, 1997—. Contbr. more than 20 articles to profl. jours.; patentee in field. Recipient 13 NASA Tech Innovations award; rsch. grantee NASA, 1992-, USAF, 1996—. Mem. IEEE, Optical Soc. Am. Achievements include invention of opto-electronic oscillator, brillouin microwave oscillator, dual microwave and optical wave oscillator, brillouin selective sideband amplification technique, index-switched variable optical delay device, Polarite polarization controller, polarization independent electro-optic modulator. Office: Jet Propulsion Lab 4800 Oak Grove Dr Pasadena CA 91109-8001

YARBROUGH, STEPHANY LANE, actress; b. San Francisco, Jan. 3, 1961; d. Glenn Robertson and Margaret Ellen (Goodhart) Y.; m. Paul Anthony Sutin, May 17, 1985 (div. 1991). BA, Dominican Coll., 1985; PhD, Union Inst., Cin., 1991. Freelance pub. rels. San Francisco, 1980-81; event organizer Dinemec, Geneva, Switzerland, 1985-87; pvt. practice psychology Geneva, 1987-89; lectr. Am. Inst. Advanced Med. Edn., Madrid, Athens, 1987-88; freelance actress L.A., 1991—. Vol. Terre des Hommes, Lausanne, Switzerland, 1986; theatrical prodr. UN 50th Anniversary, San Francisco, 1995. Mem. SAG, AFTRA, Am. Film Inst., Women in Film, Women in Theatre. Avocations: tennis, marksmanship, scuba diving, travel, dancing. Office: PO Box 1322 Studio City CA 91614-0322

YARLAGADDA, RAMBABU VENKATA, financial manager; b. Vijayawada, Andhra, India, July 16, 1959; came to U.S., 1982; s. Bhagat Singh and Kumdwati (Machineni) Y.; m. Rama Devi Ratakonda, May 21, 1987; children: Jay Kiran, Tara. BSChemE, Regional Engring., Rourkela, India, 1981; MSChemE, Ill. Inst. Tech., 1983; MBA, U. Chgo., 1988. Fin. ops. analyst Beatrice U.S. Food Corp., Chgo., 1984-86; cons. Beatrice Splty. Products, Inc., Chgo., 1986-87; acting controller E-II Food Splty s., Inc., Oakbrook Terrace, Ill., 1987-88, cons., 1988-89; zone fin. mgr. Taco Bell Corp., Elmhurst, Ill., 1989-90; mgr. planning Pepsi-Cola Co., Somers, N.Y., 1990-91, group mgr. planning, 1991-94; controller Sara Lee Meat Group, Sara Lee Corp., Memphis, 1994-95; v.p. fin., CFO Living Books, San Francisco, 1995-96; v.p. svcs. bus., CFO Narrative Comm. Corp., Los Altos, Calif., 1996—. Mem. Am. Inst. Chem. Engrs. Hindu. Avocations: horseback riding, reading, camping. Home: 109 Secluded Pl Lafayette CA 94549-6245

YARNELL, ELIZABETH GAIL, writer, journalist; b. N.Y.C., Feb. 4, 1969; d. Philip Robert Yarnell and Susan Swatzburg (Becker) Rutherford. AB, Bowdoin Coll., 1991; M in Liberal Studies, U. Denver, 1997. TV prodr. Pomegranate Consulting, Denver, 1991-94, multimedia writer, tech. writer, journalist, 1995—. Writer (CD-ROM) Peter Norton's PC Guru, 1997, Sports Illustrated Online, 1997, Microsoft's Denver-sidewalk.com., 1998. Founding chair Am. Cancer Soc. New Directions, Denver, 1994-95. Mem. Colo. Authors' League (newsletter editor 1997-98). Avocations: travel, languages, writing fiction, hiking. E-mail: eyarnell@aol.com. Home: 1236 Emerson St Apt 10 Denver CO 80218-4203

YASNYI, ALLAN DAVID, communications company executive; b. New Orleans, June 22, 1942; s. Ben Z. and Bertha R. (Michalove) Y.; BBA, Tulane U., 1964; m. Susan K. Manders; children: Benjamin Charles, Evelyn Judith, Brian Mallut. Free-lance exec. producer, producer, writer, actor and designer for TV, motion picture and theatre, 1961-73; producer, performer The Second City; dir. fin. and adminstrn. Quinn Martin Prodns., Hollywood, Calif., 1973-76, v.p. fin., 1976-77, exec. v.p. fin. and corp. planning, 1977; vice chmn., CEO QM Prodns., Beverly Hills, Calif., 1977-78, chmn. bd., CEO, 1978-80; pres., CEO The Synapse Communications Group, Inc., 1981—, ASI Entertainment, 1998—; exec. dir., adj. prof. U. So. Calif.

Entertainment Tech. Ctr., 1994—; participant IC IS Forum, 1990-95; exec. prodr. first live broadcast combining Intelsat, Intersputnik, The Voice of Am., and The Moscow World Radio Svc., 1990; resource guest Aspen Inst. Exec. Seminars, 1990; chmn. bd. dirs. Found. of Global Broadcasting, Washington, 1987-93. Trustee Hollywood Arts Coun., 1980-83; exec. v.p., trustee Hollywood Hist. Trust, 1981-91; bd. dirs. Internat. Ctr. for Intergative Studies, N.Y.C., 1988-92; bd. dirs. Asthma and Allergy Foun. Am., 1981-85. Logistical combat officer U.S. Army, 1964-66, Viet Nam. Named to Tulane U. Hall of Fame. Mem. Acad. TV Arts and Scis., Inst. Noetic Scis., Hollywood Radio and TV Soc., Hollywood C. of C. (dir., vice-chmn. 1978-93), Screen Actors Guild, Assn. Transpersonal Pyschology (keynote speaker 1988). Office: 4132 Fulton Ave Sherman Oaks CA 91423-4340

YASSIN, ROBERT ALAN, museum administrator, curator; b. Malden, Mass., May 22, 1941; s. Harold Benjamin and Florence Gertrude (Hoffman) Y.; m. Marilyn Kramer, June 9, 1963; children: Fredric Giles, Aaron David. BA (Rufus Choate scholar), Dartmouth Coll., 1962; postgrad., Boston U., 1962-63; M.A., U. Mich., 1965, postgrad. (Samuel H. Kress Found. fellow), 1968-70, Ph.D. candidate, 1970; postgrad (Ford Found. fellow), Yale U., 1966-68. Asst. to dir. Mus. Art U. Mich., 1965-66, asst. dir., 1970-72, assoc. dir., 1972-73, acting dir., 1973, instr. dept. history of art, 1970-73; co-dir. Joint Program in Mus. Trng., 1970-73; chief curator Indpls. Mus. Art, 1973-75, 87-89, acting dir., 1975, dir., 1975-89; exec. dir. Tucson Mus. Art, 1990—; adj. prof. Herron Sch. Art Ind. U./Purdue U., 1975-89. Contbr. to mus. publications. Mem. Ariz. Hist. Soc., Ariz. Mus. Assn., Tucson Mus. Assn., Tucson Arts Coalition, Tucson Downtown Adv. Coun. Mem. Am. Assn. Mus. (bd. dirs. Internat Coun. Mus. 1986-89), Assn. Art Mus. Dirs., Coll. Art Assn. Am., Intermus. Conservation Assn. (chmn. exec. com. 1977-78), Tucson C. of C. (cultural affairs com., econ. devel. com.), Nat. Trust Historic Preservation, Rotary. Jewish. Home: 3900 N Calle Casita Tucson AZ 85718-7204 Office: Tucson Mus Art 140 N Main Ave Tucson AZ 85701-8290

YATES, ALAYNE, psychiatrist; b. Bklyn.. BA, Radcliffe; MD, U. Ill. Coll. Medicine, 1961. Diplomate Am. Bd. Psychiatry and Neurology, Am. Bd. Pediatrics; lic. MD, Ill., Minn., Calif., Ariz. Intern Michael Reese Hosp., Chgo., 1961-62, resident, 1962-64; resident U. Minn., Mpls., 1970-72; fellow child psychiatry U. Calif., Davis, 1972-74; asst. prof. psychiatry and pediatrics U. Calif. at Davis, 1972-75; asst. prof. psychiatry and pediatrics Loma linda Calif.) Univ. Med. Sch., 1975-76, assoc. prof. psychiatry and pediatrics, 1976-79; assoc. prof. psychiatry and pediatrics U. Ariz. Coll. Medicine, 1979-84, chief child psychiatry, chief consulatation-liaison svc., 1979-93, prof. psychiatry and pediatrics, 1984-93; prof. psychiatry U. Hawaii, Honolulu, 1993—, dir. divsn. child/adolescent psychiatry, 1994—; cons. in field; clin. dir. Adolescent Partial Care Program, Palo Verde (Calif.) Hosp., 1986-88, Therapeutic Preschool, Palo Verde Hosp., 1986-88; med. dir. Child Unit, Sonora-Desert Hosp., 1989-91, adolescent program, Sierra and Tucson, 1991—. Author: Sex Without Shame: Encouraging the Child's Health Sexual Development, 1982, Compulsive Exercise and The Eating Disorders, 1991; contbr. articles to profl. jours. and chpts. to books; grantee in field; mem. editorial bd. Internat. Jour. Child Abuse and Neglect, Bibliography in Child Psychiatry, Jour. Am. Acad. Child and Adolescent Psychiatry. Recipient Mead Johnson Fellowship in Pediatrics, 1963-64, Disting. Leadership award The Internat. Dir. Disting. Leadership, 1985, Disting. Alumni award U. Calif., Davis, 1997. Fellow Am. Psychiat. Assn.; mem. Am. Acad. Child Psychiatry, AMA, Ariz. Psychiat. Soc., Tucson Psychiat. Soc., Am. Acad. Child Psychiatry, Soc. Profs. Child Psychiatry, Am. Coll. Psychiatrists, AAAS. Office: Univ of HI 6th Flr 1319 Punahou St F 6 Honolulu HI 96826-1001

YATES, ALBERT CARL, academic administrator, chemistry educator; b. Memphis, Tenn., Sept. 29, 1941; s. John Frank and Sadie L. (Shell) Y.; m. Ann Young; children: Steven, Stephanie, Aerin Alessandra, Sara Elizabeth. B.S., Memphis State U., 1965; Ph.D., Ind. U. 1968. Research assoc. U. So. Calif., Los Angeles, 1968-69; prof. chemistry Ind. U., Bloomington, 1969-74; v.p. research, grad. dean U. Cin., 1974-81; exec. v.p., provost, prof. chemistry Washington State U., Pullman, 1981-90; pres. Colo. State U., Fort Collins, 1990—; chancellor Colo. State U. System, Fort Collins, 1990—; mem. grad. record exam. bd. Princeton (N.J.) U., 1977-80, undergrad. assessment program council, 1977-81; cons. NRC, 1975-82, Office End., HEW, 1978-80; mem. exec. council acad. affairs NASULGC, 1983-87, ACE, 1983-87,. nat adv. council gen. med. scis. NIH, 1987—. Contbr.: research articles to Jour. Chem. Physics; research articles to Phys. Rev.; research articles to Jour. Physics, Phys. Rev. Letters, Chem. Physics Letters. Served with USN, 1959-62. Recipient univ. and State honors and awards. Mem. Am. Phys. Soc., Am. Chem. Soc., AAAS, Nat. Assn. State Univs. and Land Grant Colls. (mem. exec. council academic affairs), Am. Council Edn. (mem. exec. com. academic affairs), Sigma Xi, Phi Lambda Upsilon. Home: 1744 Hillside Dr Fort Collins CO 80524-1965 Office: Colo State U 102 Administration Bldg Fort Collins CO 80523-0100*

YATES, KEITH LAMAR, retired insurance company executive; b. Bozeman, Mont., Oct. 29, 1927; s. Thomas Bryan and Altha (Norris) Y.; m. Dolores Hensel, Aug. 30, 1948; children: Thomas A., Molly Yates McIntosh, Richard A., Nancy Yates Sands, Penny Dannielle Yates, Pamela Yates Beeler. BA, Eastern Wash. State U., 1953. Salesman Ancient Order United Workmen, Spokane, Wash., 1952-53, sales mgr., 1953-56, corp. sec., 1956-73; corp. sec. Neighbors of Woodcraft, Portland, Oreg., 1973-89, pres., 1989-92; ret., 1992. Author: Life of Willie Willey, 1966, The Fogarty Years, 1972, History of The Woodcraft Home, 1975, An Enduring Heritage, 1992. Pres. Wash. State Christian Mens Fellowship, Seattle, 1965-67; pres. Met. Area Assn. Christian Chs., 1981-83; mem. regional bd. Christian Chs. Oreg., 1990-94. Command sgt.-maj., ret., 1987; served with USN, USAF, USANG, 1946-87. Mem. Wash. State Frat. Cong., (cert. Commendation 1969, sec. 1957-68, pres., mem. exec. bd., chmn. conv. program advt. com. 1960-73), Oreg. State Frat. Cong. (Outstanding Frat. 1975-76, Spl. Appreciation award 1984, Frat. Family of Yr. 1986, 98, sec. 1975-87, pres., mem. exec. bd. 1974—), Nat. Fraternal Congress Am. (conv. arrangement com. 1964, 90, publicity com. 1964, 65, 68, 90, credentials com. 1970, 77, 78, pres. press & pub. rels. sec. 1971-72, pub. rels. com. 1971-73, chmn. 1972, co-chmn. press and pub. rels. frat. seminar 1972, frat. monitor com. 1974-75, mem. com. 1975-76, family life com. 1978-80, constitution com. 1980, pres. state frat. congs. sec. 1981-82, historian 1987—, Washington County's Disting. Patriot, 1988), Portland Ins. Acctg. and Statis. Soc., Am. Records Mgrs. and Adminstrs. (Oreg. chpt.), Portland C. of C., Wash. Ins. Coun., Wash. Claims Assn., Seattle Underwriting Assn. Home: 29860 SW Buckhaven Rd Hillsboro OR 97123-8821

YATES, MARGERY GORDON, elementary education educator; b. Walton, N.Y., July 3, 1910; d. McClellan Gordon and Marcia Beulah (Ramsdell) Gordon-Strahl; m. James McKendree Yates, Aug. 11, 1933; 1 child, Sally. BS, U. Houston, 1943, MS, 1948; MA, Stanford U., 1952. Tchr. Baldwin (N.Y.) Sch. Dist., 1928-34, Houston Sch. Dist., 1943-48; supr. primary edn. Watsonville (Calif.) Sch. Dist., 1948-53; edn. cons. San Mateo County Office Edn., Redwood City, Calif., 1953-58; supr. primary edn. Jefferson Elem. Sch. Dist., Daly City, Calif., 1958-65; tchr. Hillsborough (Calif.) Sch. Dist., 1965-75; instr. U. Houston, 1956, San Jose State Coll. 1957. Mem. AAUW (edn. area rep. 1987-88, 89-90, 91-92, 92-93, 93-94, Fellowship award honoree 1991), Burlingame Music Club (pres. 1992-93, 93-94), Commonwealth Club Calif., Alpha Delta Kappa (corr. sec. Calif. state bd. 1981-82, Gamma Beta chpt. pres. 1971-74, treas. 1985-89, 94—). Republican. Mem. Ch. Christian Sci. Avocations: gardening, edn., community support, travel, music, dance, theater. Home: PO Box 1857 Burlingame CA 94011-1857

YATES, STEVEN A., artist, curator; b. Chgo., Nov. 14, 1949; s. Thomas A. and Phyllis E. (Wilson) Y.; m. Lynne A. Smith, Aug. 5, 1972; children: Kelsey Victoria, Mackenzie Phyllis. BFA, U. N.Mex., 1972; MA, U. N.Mex., 1975, DFA, 1978. Curatorial asst. Sheldon Meml. Art Gallery, 1972-73; U. Art Mus., U. N.Mex., 1973-75; faculty dept. art Claremont (Calif.) Coll. and Pomona, 1976; part-time faculty, U. N.Mex., Albuquerque, 1976-79; assoc. adj. prof. art and art history U. N.Mex.; curator prints, drawings and photographs, Mus. of N.Mex., Santa Fe, 1980-84, curator of photography Mus. Fine Arts, 1985—; frequent lectr. in contemporary history of photography; guest artist Tamarind Inst., Albuquerque, 1988. Sherman Foun. individual fellowship and Comm. Coun. for Creative Arts fellowship, 1996; Guggenheim fellow, 1999;

3, Moscow, 1996, Up and Down Gallery, Kharkov, Ukraine, 1997, U. Nebr. 1997, Mus. Photography, Riga, Latvia, 1998; group shows include: San Francisco Mus. Modern Art, 1980, 81, 84, 86, 96, Cinema Ctr., Moscow, 1991, St. Petersburg, Russia, 1997 ; represented in permanent collections: San Francisco Mus. Modern Art, Sheldon Art Gallery, Mint Mus., Art Mus. U. N.Mex. Editor: The Essential Landscape, The New Mexico Photographic Survey, 1985; guest editor spl. issue Contemporary Photography, 1987, El Palacio, 1987. Ford Found. fellow, 1977, Nat. Endowment Arts fellow, 1980; recipient Vreeland award U. Nebraska, 1972, Outstanding Alumni Achievement award U. Nebraska, 1994; Sr. Fulbright Scholars award USSR, 1991, Russian Federation, 1995.

YATVIN, JOANNE INA, school principal; b. Newark, Apr. 17, 1931; d. John and Mary Edna (Cohen) Goldberg; m. Milton Brian Yatvin, June 8, 1952; children: Alan, Bruce, Lillian, Richard. Ba, Douglass Coll., 1952; MA, Rutgers U., 1962; PhD, U. Wis., 1974. Cert. sch. adminstr. Tchr. Hamburg (N.J.) Pub. Schs., 1952-53, New Brunswick (N.J.) Pub. Schs., 1953-55, Mayaguez (P.R.) Schs., 1958-59, Milltown (N.J.) Pub. Schs. 1959-62, East Brunswick (N.J.) Pub. Schs., 1962-63; tchr., prin. Madison (Wis.) Met. Sch. Dist., 1963-88; supt. Cottrell Sch. Dist., Boring, Oreg., 1988-97, prin., 1997—; adv. bd. mem. Big Books Mag., 1990-91; cons. various sch. dists.; mem. nat. reading panel Nat. Inst. of Child Health and Devel., 1998. Author: Learning Language Through Communication, 1986, (monograph) A Whole Language Program for a Whole School, 1991; contbr. chpts. in books and articles to profl. jours. Recipient Excellence in Print award Washington Edpress, 1987, Disting. Elem. Edn. Alumni award U. Wis., 1988; named Elem. Prin. of Yr. Wis. Dept. Edn., 1985, Wis. State Reading Assn., 1985; appointed to Nat. Reading Panel-Nat. Inst. Child and Health Devel. Mem. ASCD, Internat. Reading Assn., Nat. Coun. Tchrs. English (chair com. on ctrs. excellence 1986-89), Nat. Middle Sch. Assn., Oreg. Reading Assn., Oreg. Coun. Tchrs. English, Phi Delta Kappa. Home: 5226 SW Northwood Ave Portland OR 97201-2832 Office: Cottrell Sch 36225 SE Proctor Rd Boring OR 97009-9719

YE, JUN, electrical engineer; b. Sichuan, China, 1966; came to U.S., 1987; m. Huiqing Wang, 1991. BS, Fudan U., Shanghai, 1987; MS, Iowa State U., 1991; PhD, Stanford U., 1995. Rsch. assoc. Ames (Iowa) Lab., U.S. Dept. Energy, 1988-91; engr., cons. Intel Corp., Santa Clara, Calif., 1993-94, Hewlett-Packard Labs., Palo Alto, Calif. 1994-95; staff software engr. KLA Instruments Corp., San Jose, Calif., 1995-96; sr. staff software engr. KLA Instruments Corp., San Jose, 1996, engring. mgr., 1996—; rsch. asst. Stanford (Calif.) U., 1991-95. Contbr. articles to Precision Engring., Jour. Vaccum Sci. B., IEEE Trans. Achievements include patent pending for exact algorithm for self-calibration of 2D Precision Stages. Office: KLA Instruments 160 Rio Robles San Jose CA 95134-1809

YEAKEY, MICHAEL AARON, II, minister; b. Elkhart, Ind., Apr. 26, 1960; s. Michael Aaron Yeakey and Patricia Frances (McMichael) Stiver; m. Christine Beth Juhnke, June 7, 1986 (div. Aug. 1993); m. Kathleen Faye Nofziger, Dec. 31, 1994; 1 child, Magdalena. BA, U. Mont., 1983; MDiv/ MA, Pacific Sch. of Religion, Berkeley, Calif., 1988. Ordained minister Gen. Conf. Mennonite Ch., 1991; cert. tchr., Colo., Ind. Tchr. Salina (Kans.) Pub. Schs., 1988-89; co-pastor Salina Mennonite Ch., 1988-93; tchr. Wawasee Mid. Sch., Syracuse, Ind., 1993-96, Cheraw (Colo.) Sch., 1996—; pastor East Holbrook Mennonite Ch., Cheraw, 1996—; adj. instr. Bethany Coll., Lindsborg, Kans., 1989-93, Marymount Coll., Salina, 1989. Bd. dirs. Kans. Sch. of Religion, Lawrence, 1991-93, Salina Peace Coalition, 1991-92; vol. police chaplain Salina Police Dept., 1990-93. Avocations: bicycling, running, outdoor activities. Home: 33526 Rd KK La Junta CO 81050 Office: East Holbrook Mennonite Ch PO Box 139 32723 Rd 33 Cheraw CO 81030

YEARLEY, DOUGLAS CAIN, mining and manufacturing company executive; b. Oak Park, Ill., Jan. 7, 1936; s. Bernard Cain and Mary Kenny (Howard) Y.; m. Elizabeth Anne Dunbar, Feb. 8, 1958; children: Sandra, Douglas Jr., Peter. Andrew. BMetE. Cornell U., 1958; postgrad., Harvard U., 1968. Engr. welding Gen. Dynamics, Groton, Conn., 1958-60; dir. rsch., project engr. Phelps Dodge Copper Products, Elizabeth, N.J., 1960-68; mgr. ops. Phelps Dodge Internat. Co., N.Y.C., 1968-71; v.p. ops. Phelps Dodge Tube Co., L.A., 1971-73; exec. v.p. Phelps Dodge Cable and Wire Co., Yonkers, N.Y., 1973-75; pres. Phelps Dodge Brass Co., Lyndhurst, N.J., 1975-79; pres. Phelps Dodge Sales Co., N.Y.C., 1979-82, v.p. mktg., 1979-82; sr. v.p. Phelps Dodge Corp., N.Y.C., 1982-87, exec. v.p., 1987-89, chmn., CEO, 1989-91; chmn., CEO Phelps Dodge Corp., Phoenix, 1991-97, 1997, also bd. dirs.; bd. dirs. USX Corp., Pitts., J.P. Morgan and Co., Inc. and Morgan Guaranty Trust Co., N.Y.C, Lockheed Martin Corp., Bethesda, Md., So. Peru Copper Co.; mem. exec. com. ICME. Mem. Ariz. Econs. Coun., 1989—, Conf. Bd., 1989—; bd. dirs. Am. Grad. Sch. Internat. Mgmt., 1990-92, Phoenix Symphony, 1988-94; chmn. Arts Coalition, 1989-90; trustee Phoenix Art Mus., 1994—. Mem. Nat. Elec. Mfrs. Assn. (bd. dirs. 1983-92), Internat. Copper Assn. (bd. dirs. 1987—, chmn. 1990—), Am. Mining Congress (vice chmn.), Nat. Mining Assn. (chmn.), Copper Devel. Assn. (chmn. 1989-93, dir. 1993—), Nat. Assn. Mfrs. (bd. dirs. 1988-94), Bus. Roundtable, Bus. Coun., Sky Club, Echo Lake Country Club, Ariz. Club, Blind Brook Country Club. Republican. Congregationalist. Avocations: tennis, golf, classical music. Home: 8201 N Via De Lago Scottsdale AZ 85258-4215 Office: Phelps Dodge Corp 2600 N Central Ave Fl 14 Phoenix AZ 85004-3089*

YEE, HSIAN CHIANG, science administrator; b. Hangzhou, Cheking, China, July 15, 1959; s. K.C. and P.C. (Cai) Y.; m. Bolena Long, Feb. 6, 1992; children: Philina S., Derek S. MD, Cheking Med. Sch., Hangehow, China, 1981; MS in Bioengring., U. Wash., 1987, PhD, 1991. Design engr. IHG, Inc., Seattle, 1988-93; dir., v.p. AmeriTek, Inc., Seattle, 1993—. Patent for immunodiagnostic technology. Mem. Am. Clin. Technology Assn. Avocation: work. Home: 7338 23rd Ave NE Seattle WA 98115-5806 Office: AmeriTek Inc 7030 35th Ave NE Seattle WA 98115-5917

YEE, HSIAN PEI, electrical engineering executive; b. Hangchow, Cheking, China, July 4, 1965; came to U.S., 1981; s. K.C. and P.C. (Cai) Y. BSEE, U. Wash., 1986, MSEE, 1988, PhD, 1992. Asst. prof. U. Wash., Seattle, 1992—; pres., CEO Semi Tech. Design, Inc., Seattle, 1994—; cons. Shindengen Electric Mfg. Co. Ltd., Japan, 1992—. 6 patents in field. Mem. IEEE. Home: 7338 23d Ave NE Seattle WA 98115 Office: Semi Tech Design Inc 7030 35th Ave NE Seattle WA 98115-5917

YEE, KEITH PHILIP, accountant; b. Luton, Eng., Apr. 26, 1958; came to the U.S., 1985; m. Ginny Sung, Feb. 9, 1985; children: Ashley, Brittany. BA in Acctg. with honors, Exeter (Eng.) U., 1979. CPA, Calif. Audit sr. Ernst & Whinney, London, 1979-83; investigation supr. Ernst & Whinney, Hong Kong, 1983-85; audit mgr. Ernst & Whinney, Memphis, 1985-86; audit sr. mgr. Ernst & Young, San Francisco, 1986-91; internat. resident Ernst & Young, 1991-93; audit sr. mgr. Ernst & Young, San Francisco, 1993-95, Price Waterhouse, San Jose, Calif., 1995-97, Adaptec, Milpitas, Calif., 1997-98, Synnex Info. Tech., Fremont, Calif., 1998—. Vice chmn. adv. coun. for svcs. to srs. Salvation Army, San Francisco, 1989. Grad. leadership San Francisco program San Francisco C. of C., 1990. Fellow Inst. Chartered Accts. in Eng. and Wales; mem. AICPA, Asian Am. CPAs (mem. adv. bd. 1994-95), Calif. Soc. CPAs, Inst. for Internat. Edn. (student programs com. 1990-95), San Francisco C. of C. (internat. bus. devel. com. 1993-95), Asian Am. Mfrs. Assn., Churchill Club. Avocations: internat. travel, music, sports. Office: Synnex Info Tech Inc 3797 Spinnaker Ct Fremont CA 94538-6523

YEE, KUO CHIANG, neuroscientist, neurologist; b. Shanghai, Jan. 18, 1935; came to U.S., 1981; s. Hun and Wang J. Yee; m. Pei Ching Cai, Oct. 1, 1954; children: Hsiao Chiang, Hsiao Pei. MD, Zuzhen Med. Sch., Chekiang, China, 1954; MS, U. Wash., 1983; PhD, U.B.C., Vancouver, Can., 1992. Prof. U. B.C., Vancouver, 1992-93; dir. Neurosci. Med. Ctr., Seattle, 1981—; pres. AmeriTek, Inc., Seattle, 1993—. Author: Biological Effects and Dosimetry of Nonionizing Radiation, 1982; contbr. numerous articles to profl. jours. Achievements include development of advanced rapid in-vitro immunodiagnostic and clinical chemical reagent systems diagnostic test kits. Home: 7338 23rd Ave NE Seattle WA 98115-5806 Office: Neurosci Med Ctr

YEE, STEPHEN, airport executive. Adminstrv. asst. health dept. City of L.A., 1958-63, sr. adminstrv. asst. dept. airports, 1963-72, fed. aid coord., 1972-75, project mgr., 2d level roadway and terminal improvements, airport facilities planner, 1975-83, staff asst. to bd. airport commrs., 1983-85, airport mgr. L.A. Internat. Airport, 1985—. Office: Los Angeles Intl Airport Los Angeles Dept of Airports 1 World Way Los Angeles CA 90045-5803

YEGGE, ROBERT BERNARD, law educator, dean; b. Denver, June 17, 1934; s. Ronald Van Kirk and Fairy (Hill) Y. A.B. magna cum laude, Princeton U., 1956; M.A. in Sociology, U. Denver, 1958, J.D., 1959. Bar: Colo. 1959, D.C. 1978. Ptnr. Yegge, Hall and Evans, Denver, 1959-78; with Harding Shultz & Downs successor to Nelson and Harding, 1979—; prof. U. Denver Coll. Law, 1965—, dean, 1965-77, 97—, dean emeritus, 1977—; asst. to pres. Denver Post, 1971-75; v.p.; exec. dir. Nat. Ctr. Preventive Law, 1986-91. Author: Colorado Negotiable Instruments Law, 1960, Some Goals; Some Tasks, 1965, The American Lawyer: 1976, 1966, New Careers in Law, 1969, The Law Graduate, 1972, Tomorrow's Lawyer: A Shortage and Challenge, 1974, Declaration of Independence for Legal Education, 1976. Mng. trustee Denver Ctr. for Performing Arts, 1972-75; chmn. Colo. Coun. Arts and Humanities, 1968-80, chmn. emeritus, 1980—; mem. scholar selection com. Henry Luce Found., 1975—; Active nat. and local A.R.C., chmn. Denver region, 1985-88; trustee Denver Symphony Soc., Inst. of Ct. Mgmt., Denver Dumb Friends League, 1992—, Met. Denver Legal Aid Soc., 1994—, Colo. Acad.; trustee, vice chmn. Nat. Assembly State Arts Agys.; vice chmn. Mexican-Am. Legal Edn. and Def. Fund, 1970-76. Recipient Disting. Svc. award Denver Jr. C. of C., 1965; Harrison Tweed award Am. Assn. Continuing Edn. Adminstrs., 1985, Alumni Faculty award U. Denver, 1993. Mem. ABA (chmn. lawyers conf. 1987-88, chmn. accreditation commn. for legal asst. programs 1980-90, 98—, standing com. legal assts. 1987-92, standing com. delivery legal svcs. 1992-95, com. on Gavel award 1995-98, del. to jud. adminstrn. coun. 1989-95, Robert B. Yegge award 1996), Law and Soc. Assn. (life, pres. 1965-70), Colo. Bar Assn. (bd. govs. 1965-77, 97—), Denver Bar Assn., D.C. Bar Assn., Am. Law Inst., Am. Judicature Soc. (bd. dirs. 1968-72, 75-85, Herbert Harley award 1985), Am. Acad. Polit. and Social Sci., Am. Sociol. Soc., Am. Assn. Law Schs., Order St. Ives, Phi Beta Kappa, Beta Theta Pi, Phi Delta Phi, Alpha Kappa Keta, Omicron Delta Kappa. Home: 3472 S Race St Englewood CO 80110-3138 Office: U Denver Coll Law 1900 Olive St Denver CO 80220-1857

YEN, DUEN HSI, corporate executive, physicist; b. Nyack, N.Y., Apr. 24, 1949; s. Ernest Chu and Louise (Loo) Y.; m. Linda Leiko Takai, June 22, 1989. BS in Physics, Rensselaer Polytech. Inst., 1971; MA in Biophysics, Johns Hopkins U., 1974; MSEE, U. Vt., 1978. Mem. tech. staff Bell Telephone Labs., Holmdel, N.J., 1978-83; pres. Multipath Systems, Inc., Honolulu, 1984—; Violinist Oahu Civic Orch. Inventor noise detector, electronic travel aids for blind; contbr. articles to profl. jours. Small Bus. Innovation Rsch. grantee, NSF grantee 1984, Nat. Eye Inst. grantee 1988, 89, 91. Mem. Acoustical Soc. Am., Audio Engring. Soc., Sigma Pi Sigma. Avocations: binaural recording, stereo photography, violinist. Home: 1255 Nuuanu Ave Apt 2315E Honolulu HI 96817-4012

YEN, PETER T., business educator, education foundation executive; b. Calif., Sept. 22, 1937; s. Paul and Mary (Han) Y.; m. Selina Yu, Sept. 2, 1967; 1 child, Vevey. MA, Calif. State U., Fullerton, 1976; PhD, U. Calif., Riverside, 1979; postgrad., UCLA, 1980; cert., MIT, 1983. Lectr. Asian studies program U. Calif., Riverside, 1970-74; asst. prof. mgmt. devel. dept. H.F. devel. Va. Poly. Inst. and State U., Blacksburg, 1974-75; vis. prof., chair dept. bus. adminstrn. N.C.U., 1975-77; exch. prof. internat. mktg. and mgmt. Coll. Bus., U. West Fla., 1978-79; prof. mktg. and internat. bus. SBU Sch. Bus., N.Y., 1980-95; chmn. dept. mktg. SBU Sch. Bus., 1990-95; vis. prof. mktg. and internat. bus. Grad. Sch. Mgmt. KPI, 1995-97; prof. mktg. and mgmt. AUI Sch. Bus., 1998—; pres. Multinational Edn. Found., Wash. 1996—; presenter in field. Author: The Modern Management: Organizational Behavior Theories, 1980, Business Strategies Planning, 1988, The New Concepts of Marketing Strategies, 1994, International Business Strategies, 1996; contbr. articles to profl. jours. Recipient Cultural Exch. award State of Fla., 1980, Disting. Bus. award Far East Exec. Devel. Taiwan, 1983; grantee UN, N.Y., 1987-92; fellow Switzerland Govt., Fribourg, 1961-65. Fellow Internat. Acad. Mgmt.; mem. Am. Mktg. Assn., Am. Mgmt. Assn., Mktg. Rsch. Assn., Acad. Internat. Bus., Delta Epsilon Sigma, Pi Omega Pi. Home: PO Box 60081 Renton WA 98058-3081

YES, PHYLLIS ANN, artist, video and filmmaker, educator; b. Red Wing, Minn., May 15, 1941; d. Eldon William Dankers and Doris Elaine (Wold) Mendel. BA, Luther Coll., Decorah, Iowa, 1963; MA, U. Minn., 1968; PhD, U. Oreg., 1978. Art curriculum coord. Columbia Heights (Minn.) Sch. System, 1968-73; asst. prof. art Oreg. Coll. Edn., Monmouth, Oreg., 1973-76, Oreg. State U., Corvallis, 1976-78; asst. prof. art Lewis & Clark Coll., Portland, Oreg., 1978-88, prof. art, 1988—; juror Puget Sound U., Seattle, 1990; cons. Oreg. Sch. Arts and Crafts, Portland, 1989. Exhibited prin. works in several shows including Nishiazabu Asacloth Gallery, Tokyo, 1991, 93, Charles Allis Mus., 1989, Bklyn. Mus. 1986, Bernice Steinbaum Gallery, 1986, Columbia Mus. 1988. Mem. publicity com. N.Y. Women's Found., 1989-90; contbr. Art AIDS, Portland, 1987-89, OMSI Auction, Portland, 1989; active Beth Israel, Portland, 1989—. NEA fellow, 1987; Barbara Deming grantee, 1987, Oreg. Arts Commn. grantee, 1986; recipient Disting. Alumnus award Luther Coll., 1988, Juror's award Internat. Banners, Flags, Kites Exhibit, 1977. Mem. Japan Soc., Princeton Club, Mus. Modern Art, Artists Equity, Oreg. Alliance for Arts (juror 1990), Portland Ctr. for Visual Arts (exec. bd. dirs. 1980-82), Women's Caucus for Art (bd. dirs. 1979). Avocations: micology, fly fishing, biking, photography. Home: 2414 NE 36th Ave Portland OR 97212-5241 Office: Lewis & Clark Coll 615 SW Palatine Hill Rd Portland OR 97219-7879

YESTADT, JAMES FRANCIS, music director, conductor; b. Harrisburg, Pa., Nov. 24, 1921; s. Frederic John and Emelie Josephine (Speer) Y.; m. Victoria Ann Turco; children: Gregory James, Frederic John II, James Francis Jr. MusB, Lebanon Valley Conservatory Music, Pa., 1947; MA in Music, Columbia U., 1952; postgrad., New Sch. Music, Pa.; cert. in performance, Lucerne (Switzerland) Conservatory, 1962. Assoc. music prof. Xavier U., New Orleans, 1947-58; music dir., condr. New Orleans Summer Pops, 1954-58; resident condr. New Orleans Philharm. Symphony Orch., 1960-63; condr., dir. Transylvania Symphony Orch., Brevard, N.C., 1963-66; music dir., condr. Mobile (Ala.) Symphony Orch., 1965-71; dir. orchestral studies U. So. Miss., Hattiesburg, 1971-76; music dir., condr. Baton Rouge Symphony Orch., 1976-82; dir. orchestral studies La. State U., Baton Rouge, 1976-88; music dir., condr. Sun Cities Symphony of the West Valley, Sun City, Ariz., 1988—; dir., condr. Mobile Opera Co. 1966-82; guest condr. Jackson (Miss.) Symphony Orch., 1986, Zurich Radio Orch., Orquesta Sinfonica de castillia y Leon, Spain, New Orleans Opera, numerous festivals, U.S., Europe. Numerous TV appearances and radio shows;. Served with U.S. Army, 1942-46, ETO. Mem. Music Educators Nat. Conf. (Performance award 1984), Coll. Music Soc., Am. Symphony Orch. League. Office: Sun Cities Symphony Orch Assn 10451 Palmeras Dr Ste 210 Sun City AZ 85373*

YETTO, JOHN HENRY, company executive; b. N.Y.C., Apr. 25, 1928; s. Michael and Josephine Yetto; m. Nancy A. Cagliostro, June 9, 1957; children: Sheryl, Kay, Michelle. BSChemE, CCNY, 1950; postgrad., Bklyn. Poly., 1951, Rutgers U., 1952. Devel. engr. Materials Lab., N.Y. Naval Shipyard, Bklyn., 1951-52; process engr. Bakelite Co. Div. UCC, Bound Brook, N.J., 1953-57; asst. plant engr. Revlon, Inc., Passaic, N.J., 1957-59; dept. mgr. Aerojet, Inc., Sacramento, 1959-71; pres. Systemedics, Sacramento, 1971-85, Proserv, Inc., Sacramento, 1975—. Chmn. YMCA Bd. of Mgrs., San Juan, Sacramento, Calif., 1964; pres. Fairway Pines Homeowners Assn., 1989—; Sunrise Knolls Townhouse Owners' Assn., 1995. 1st lt. USAF, 1952-53. Mem. Fair Oaks C. of C. (pres. 1984), Rotary (pres. Fair Oaks 1982). Avocations: computers, tennis.

YEUN, PAUL LORENZO, minister; b. Hong Kong, Apr. 14, 1944; came to U.S., 1960; s. Kaki Yeun and Carmen (Flores) Pio; m. Elisabeth Wendy Chan, June 19, 1971; children: Evangeline, Abigail. BA, Azusa Pacific U., 1968; MDiv, Asbury Sem., 1971, MA, 1974; DMin, Lexington Sem., 1977. Ordained to ministry Meth. Ch., 1973; cert. marriage and family therapist; lic. prof. counselor. Cert. prof. mental health clergy . Parish pastor Ashland (Ohio) United Meth. Ch., 1971 ; tchr. Ashton (Ohio) United Meth.

Ch., 1972-76, Albany (Ohio) United Meth. Ch., 1976-78, Oakland Park United Meth. Ch., Columbus, Ohio, 1978-81; group chaplain USAF, Rickenbacker AFB, Ohio, 1980-81; protestant chaplain USAF, George Air Force Base, Calif., 1981-84; installation chaplain USAF, Clark Air Base, Philippines, 1984-87; sr. protestant chaplain USAF, Davis Monthan AFB, Tucson, 1987—; counselor Pastoral Counseling Ctr., Columbus, 1979-81; advisor Asian Pacific Fellowship, Tucson, 1987—; chair ch. and soc. South Dist. United Meth. Ch., Tucson, 1989-90; bd. dirs. Ariz. Marriage and Family Therapy, Tucson Met. Ministries. Author: Dealing with the Psychological needs of Aged, 1985, Meaning of our Membership Vows, 1987. Mem. Task Force in Credentialing, State of Ariz., 1989—. Major USAF, 1980—. Decorated Air Force Commendation medal; recipient award Air Force Best Sermons, 1985, Man of Achievement award; named to Ky. Cols. Mem. Am. Assn. Marriage and Family Therapy (clin.), Internt. Acad. Behavior, Medicine and Psychotherapy (diplomate), Asian Pacific Fellowship, Tucson Chaplain Assn. (steering com. 1987-90), Lions. Democrat. Office: 836 CSG/HC Davis Monthan AFB Tucson AZ 85707

YEUNG, ANTHONY TONG, orthopedic surgeon; b. Wuchow, China, Dec. 12, 1940; came to U.S., 1949; s. Heng Wah and Violet Lee Yeung; m. Eileen Ong, June 29, 1969; children: Christopher Alan, Kimberley Anne. BS, U. Ariz., 1965; MD, U. N.M., 1970. Chief orthopedics U.S. Naval Regional Med. Ctr., Subic Bay, The Philippines, 1976-78; orthopedic surgeon Ariz. Orthopedic Surgeons, Phoenix, 1978—; chmn. cmty. adv. bd. KAET Channel 8, Phoenix, 1992; bd. dirs. Valley Commerce Bank, Phoenix. Lt. comdr. USN, 1976-78. Mem. Phoenix Rotary. Republican. Avocations: tennis, skiing, travel. Office: Ariz Orthopedic Surgeons 1635 E Myrtle Ave Ste 400 Phoenix AZ 85020-5556

YGUADO, ALEX ROCCO, economics educator; b. Lackawanna, N.Y., Jan. 17, 1939; s. Manuel and Rose (Barrillio) Y.; m. Patricia Ann Rieker; children: Gary Alexander, Melissa Rose, Charissa Ann. BA, San Fernando State Coll., Northridge, 1968; MA, Calif. State U., Northridge, 1970; MS, U. So. Calif., 1972. Contractor Los Angeles, 1962-69; instr. Calif. Poly. State U., San Luis Obispo, 1969-70, U. So. Calif., Los Angeles, 1970-74; prof. econs. L.A. Mission Coll., San Fernando, Calif., 1975—, acad. senate pres., 1992-93, cluster chair profl. studies, 1993—; cons. Community Service Orgn., Los Angeles, 1969-71. Author: Principles of Economics, 1978; contbr. chpts. to books. Served with U.S. Army, 1957-60. Recipient: Blue Ribbon landscape design City of Albuquerque, 1962, Cert. Appreciation Los Angeles Mission Coll., 1978; Fulbright scholar, 1986-87. Mem. Calif. Small Bus. Assn. Democrat. Roman Catholic. Clubs: Newman (Los Angeles), Sierra Retreat (Malibu, sponsor). Avocations: gardening, skiing, photography. Home: 30960 Romero Canyon Rd Castaic CA 91384-3449 Office: LA Mission Coll 13356 Eldridge Ave Sylmar CA 91342-3200

YIN, GERALD ZHEYAO, technology and business executive; b. Beijing, Jan. 29, 1944; came to U.S., 1980; s. Huaixing and Halumi Yin; m. Junling June Yen; 1 child, John Chengjian. BS in Chem. Physics, U. Sci. & Tech. China, Beijing, 1967; postgrad., Beijing U., 1978-80; PhD in Chemistry, UCLA, 1984. Process engr. Lanzhou Oil Refinery, Lanzhou, People's Republic of China, 1968-73; mgr. research staff Chinese Acad. Sciences, Lanzhou, 1973-78; sr. process engr. Intel Corp. Santa Clara TD, Santa Clara, Calif., 1984-86; mgr., staff engr. Lam Rsch. Corp., Rsch. & Devel., Fremont, Calif., 1986-91; mng. dir. Etch New Product, Santa Clara, Calif., 1991—; chief tech. officer Etch Group, gen. mgr. Silicon Etch divsn.; v.p. Applied Materials, Inc., Santa Clara, 1996—. Author: Introducing Orthogonal Design to Semiconductor Industry, 1985; inventor Rainbow oxide etcher, 200mm enhanced Electron Cyclotron Resonance reactor, High Density plasma source for Dielectric Etch (IPS) and Decoupled Plasma Source and reactors for Conductor Etches (DPS). Recipient Nat. Acad. award People's Republic of China, 1979, Nat. Acad. Invention award, People's Republic of China, 1980. Mem. Electrochem. Soc., Am. Chem. Soc., Am. Vacuum Soc., Silicon Valley Chinese Engring. Assn. (founder, first pres.). Achievements include 22 U.S., Japanese and German patents, 30 patent applications pending. Office: Applied Materials Inc 974 E Arques Ave M/S 81301 Sunnyvale CA 94086

YIN, HONG ZHEN, neuropathologist, researcher; b. Helong, Jilin, China, July 9, 1945; came to U.S., 1990; s. Zhong Zhou and Wun Be Y.; m. Xiu Zhen Zhu, Oct. 3, 1970; children: Yu, Ye. MD, Normal Bethune U., Changchun, China, 1969, MS in Pathology, 1982. Physician Med. Ctr. Hosp. Yaniban Med. Coll., China, 1976-79; tchr. pathology, physician asst., from asst. to assoc. prof. Norman Bethune U., China, 1970-90, pathology lectr., 1982-84, chmn. dept. pathology, 1986-90; postdoct. fellow Loma Linda (Calif.) U., 1984-85; internat. vis. scholar U. Calif., Irvine, 1990-92; researcher dept. neurology, 1992—. Author: Neurodegenerative Diseases, 1996; contbr. articles to profl. jours. Mem. Am. Soc. Neurosci., Pathology Soc. Bethune U. (officer, sec. 1986-90), Pathology Soc. (officer 1986-90), Chinese Soc. Med. Sci. Achievements include development monoclonol antibody to type 3 and type 7 adenovirus. Home: 102 Duranzo Aisle Irvine CA 92606-8356 Office: U Calif-Irvine Dept Neurology 2101 Gillespie Bldg Irvine CA 92697

YNDA, MARY LOU, artist, educator; b. Los Angeles, Apr. 4, 1936; d. Ernest Pastor Ynda and Mary Estella (Ruiz) Zapotocky, m. Gary Lynn Coleman, Sept. 1, 1956 (div. Feb. 1983); children: Debra Lynn, Lisa Annette, David Gary; m. Miles Ciletti, May 25, 1991. Student, Immaculate Heart Coll., Los Angeles, 1973-79; AA in Fine Arts, Los Angeles City Coll., 1976; BA, Calif. State U., L.A., 1993. Instr. Fashion Inst. Design, L.A., 1980-81; tchr. art to disabled First St. Gallery, Claremont, Calif., 1991-94; tchr. art Tierra Del Sol Found., Sunland, Calif., 1995-96. Exhibited in group shows at Double Rocking G Gallery, L.A., 1983, Improv Theater West, West Hollywood, Calif., 1983, Exposition Gallery Calif. State U., L.A., 1983, L.A. Art Core Gallery, 1985, Poly. Tech. Sch., Pasadena, Calif., 1986, Bad Eye Gallery, L.A., 1987, Art in the Hall VI West Hollywood City Hall, 1989, Echo Park Gallery, L.A., 1991, Art N Barbee Gallery, 1992, A Celebration of City Life, 1993, DADA Show-Downtown Lives, L.A., 1994, 96, Spirit Exhbn. for Women's Caucus for Art, Santa Ana, Calif., 1995; designer Spoken Word CD Long Days and Monster Nights, 1994; contbg. author poetry Spoken Word Voices of the Angels, 1982; book rev. Yesterday and Tomorrow: California Women Artists, 1989. Archetypes and Contemporary Images in The Hispanic World. The City of Lancaster Mus./Art Gallery, Lancaster Calif. Mem. Women's Caucus for Art. Democrat. Avocations: mask making, fetish art, study of animal behavior.

YOCAM, DELBERT WAYNE, software products company executive; b. Long Beach, Calif., Dec. 24, 1943; s. Royal Delbert and Mary Rose (Gross) Y.; m. Janet McVeigh, June 13, 1965; children—Eric Wayne, Christian Jeremy, Elizabeth Janelle. BA in Bus. Adminstrn., Calif. State U.-Fullerton, 1966; MBA, Calif. State U., Long Beach, 1971. Mktg.-supply changeover coordinator Automotive Assembly div. Ford Motor Co., Dearborn, Mich., 1966-72; prodn. control mgr. Control Data Corp., Hawthorne, Calif., 1972-74; prodn. and material control mgr. Bourns Inc., Riverside, Calif., 1974-76; corp. material mgr. Computer Automation Inc., Irvine, Calif., 1976-78; prodn. planning mgr. central staff Cannon Electric div. ITT, World hdqrs., Santa Ana, Calif., 1978-79; exec. v.p., COO Apple Computer, Inc., Cupertino, Calif., 1979-91; pres., COO, dir. Textronix Inc., Wilsonville, Oreg., 1992-95; chmn., CEO Borland Internat., Inc./Inprise Corp., Scotts Valley, Calif., 1996—; ,em. faculty Cypress Coll., Calif., 1972-79; bd. dirs. Adobe Sys Inc., San Jose, Calif., 1991—, Oracle Corp., Redwood Shores, Calif., 1992-97, AST Rsch., Inc., Irvine, Calif., 1992-95, Integrated Measurement Sys. Inc., Beaverton, Oreg., 1995-97, Castelle, Inc., Santa Clara, Calif., 1995-96, Sapiens Internat. Corp., 1995-96, Boomtown, Inc., Verdi, Nev., 1995-97, Raster Graphics, Inc., San Jose, Calif., 1995—, Xircom, Inc., Thousand Oaks, Calif., 1996—, Hollywood Park, Inc., Inglewood, Calif., 1997-98; vice chmn. Tech. Ctr. Innovation, San Jose, Calif., 1989-90. Mem. Am. Electronics Assn. (nat. bd. dirs. 1988-89), Control Data Corp. Mgmt. Assn. (cofounder 1974), L.A. County Heart Assn. (active 1966).

YOCHES, ELIOT ZACHARY (DENVER), small business owner; b. Denver, July 3, 1954; s. Marvin and Ruth Dvora (Spiegelman) Y.; children: Amanda, Jacob, Jenna. Pres. Marble Apple, Denver, 1972-75, Nickel Audio/Video, Denver, 1975-79; v.p. sales Rocky Mountain Video, Denver, 1979-81; sales mgr. Dyna Mark, Denver, 1981-87; pres. Prime Source, Inc., Denver, 1987—; cons. Electronic Rep. Assn., Colorado Springs, 1991-94. Vice-pres. C. of C., Nederland, Colo., 1975-76. Mem. ICIA. Avocations: skiing, bicycling, riding, leather making. Home: 150 Magnolia St Denver CO 80220-6000 Office: Prime Source 2236 S Albion St Denver CO 80222-4906

YODER, DONALD EUGENE, minister; b. Middlebury, Ind., Dec. 16, 1930; s. Quinton J. and Edith Elizabeth Yoder; m. Bonnie Lou Miller, Sept. 25, 1955; children: LuAnne Beth Yoder Hershberger, Ross Arlin. BA, Goshen Coll., 1953; Th.B., Goshen Bibl. Sem., 1954. Ordained to ministry Mennonite Ch., 1953. Pastor Forks Mennonite Ch., Middlebury, Ind., 1953-64, Trinity Mennonite Ch., Glendale, Ariz., 1964-76, Koinonia Mennonite Ch., Chandler, Ariz., 1976-82; sec. evangelism Gen. Conf. Mennonite Ch., Newton, Kans., 1979-89; pastor Koinonia Mennonite Ch., Chandler, 1989-97; minister PSMC Area-Ariz., 1995—; mem. devel. disabilities com. Mennonite Cen. Com., Reedley, Calif., 1988-92. Contbr. articles to religious publs. Bd. overseers Hesston (Kans.) Coll., 1982-90. Democrat. Office: PSMC 6010 S Clark Dr Tempe AZ 85283-3304

YOHALEM, HARRY MORTON, lawyer; b. Phila., Jan. 21, 1943; s. Morton Eugene and Florence (Mishnun) Y.; m. Martha Caroline Remy, June 9, 1967; children: Seth, Mark. BA with honors, U. Wis., 1965; JD cum laude, Columbia U., 1969, M in Internat. Affairs., 1969. Bar: N.Y. 1969, D.C. 1981, Calif. 1992, U.S. Supreme Ct. 1985. Assoc. Shearman & Sterling, N.Y.C., 1969-71; asst. counsel to gov. State of N.Y., Albany, 1971-73, counsel office planning svcs., 1973-75; asst. gen. counsel FEA, Washington, 1975-77; mem. staff White House Energy Policy and Planning Office, Washington, 1977; dep. gen. counsel for legal svcs. Dept. Energy, Washington, 1978-80, dep. under sec., 1980-81; ptnr. Rogers & Wells, Washington, 1981-91; gen. counsel Calif. Inst. Tech., Pasadena, 1991—. Editor comments Columbia Jour. Transnat. Law, 1967-68, rsch. editor, 1968-69. Prin. Coun. for Excellence in Govt., Washington, 1990—; pres. Opera Bel Canto, Washington, 1984-87; mem. Lawyers Com. for Arts, Washington, 1981-88. Harlan Fiske Stone scholar Columbia U., 1967, 69. Mem. ABA, Calif. Bar Assn., D.C. Bar Assn. Athenaeum, Phi Kappa Phi. Home: 1060 Stoneridge Dr Pasadena CA 91105-2844 Office: Calif Inst Tech JPL 180-305 4800 Oak Grove Dr Pasadena CA 91109

YOHE, JOHN SPENCER, financial analyst; b. Lawrence, Kans., Jan. 5, 1954; s. Delton Spencer and Betty Claire (Foster) Y.; m. Sherri Sue Kendall, Sept. 1, 1979; 1 child, Darrell. BS in Acctg., U. Kans., 1977, BSBA, 1977. CPA; cert. quality analyst. Cost acct. Greyhound Exposition Svcs., Kansas City, Mo., 1977-78; systems analyst Gates Learjet, Tucson, Ariz., 1978-82; supr., cost acctg. Hughes Aircraft Co., Tucson, 1982-84; supr. bus. practices Sperry Corp., Phoenix, 1984-86; supr. fin. systems Motorola, Inc., Scottsdale, Ariz., 1986—. Home: PO Box 54252 Phoenix AZ 85078-4252

YOKLEY, RICHARD CLARENCE, fire department administrator; b. San Diego, Dec. 29, 1942; s. Clarence Ralph and Dorothy Junese (Sackman) Y.; m. Jean Elizabeth Liddle, July 25, 1964; children: Richard Clarence II, Karin Denise Yokley Dillard. Student, San Diego City Coll., 1967; AS, Miramar Coll., 1975; student, London Fire Brig. Tng. Acad., 1994, Fire Svc. Coll., Eng., 1994. Cert. fire officer, fire instr., Calif. Disc jockey Sta. KSDS-FM, San Diego, 1966-67; bldg. engr. Consolidated Systems, Inc., San Diego, 1968-72; with Bonita-Sunnyside Fire Dept., Calif., 1972—; fire marshal Bonita-Sunnyside Fire Dept., 1981-91, ops. chief, 1991-93, maintenance officer, 1993—; med. technician Hartson Ambulance, San Diego, 1978-80, Bay Gen. Hosp. (now Scripps Hosp.), Chula Vista, Calif., 1980-83, EMT-D Sea World of San Diego, 1997—; chmn. South Bay Emergency Med. Svc., 1988; mem. firefighter adv. coun. to San Diego Burn Inst., 1989, 1999—, mem. Coun. of Courage, 1991—. Contbr. articles to jours., newspapers and mags. Asst. curator Firehouse Mus., San Diego, 1972-89, docent, 1990-93; scoutmaster troop 874 Boy Scouts Am., Bonita, Calif., 1978-79. With USAF, 1962-66. Recipient Heroism and Community Svc. award Firehouse Mag., N.Y.C., 1987, Star News Salutes award Chula Vista Star News, 1987, Golden Svc. award San Diego County Credit Union, 1988. Mem. Internat. Assn. Firefighters (pres. local chpt. 1981-82), Calif. State Firefighters Assn. (dep. dir. so. divsn. 1994-97), Calif. Fire Mechanics, San Diego County Fire Prevention Officers (v.p. 1984, pres. 1985), Bonita Bus. and Profl. Assn. (bd. dirs. 1991-93, Historian award 1987, Pioneer award 1997), Fire Mark Cir. of the Ams. (dir. 1994—), Smokey Bear Collectors Assn. (co-founder, dir. 1995-97, advisor 1998), South Bay Commn., Bonita Hist. Mus. (co-founder 1986, adv. bd. 1997, v.p. 1998, 99), Sport Chalet Dive Club (v.p. 1991). Republican. Methodist. Avocations: scuba diving, visit fire departments of foreign countries, collect fire memorabilia, snow skiing. Office: Bonita-Sunnyside Fire Dept 4900 Bonita Rd Bonita CA 91902-1725

YONOVER, ROBERT NORRIS, geochemist; b. Chgo., Apr. 29, 1959; s. David Leon and Elaine (Goldman) Y.; m. Cindy M. Gruder, July 7, 1984; children: Jesse Harris, Kera Lani Gold. BS cum laude, Fla. State U., 1981, MS in Geology, Geochemistry, 1984; PhD in Geochemistry, Volcanology, U.Hawaii, 1989. Assoc. geologist Exxon Corp., Kingsville, Tex., 1981; gen. mgr., rsch. devel. dir. Vision Safe, Poly-Tech USA, Kancohe, Hawaii, 1989-94; rsch assoc. East-West Ctr., Honolulu, 1990-91; field scientist, prodr. Rivers of Fire, New Explorers PBS, Volcano, Hawaii, 1992; adj. prof. Hawaii Pacific U., Honolulu, 1994-95; sr. scientist, geochemist Hawaii Inst. Environ. Svcs., Kailua, 1996-97; pres., founder SEE/RESCUE Corp., Honolulu, 1994—; Grad. Student Rsch. fellow, NASA, Houston, 1985-88. Patentee in field. Vol. Sci. tchr., Elem. Schs., Honolulu, 1993—. Avocations: surfing, skin diving, fishing, hiking, paddling.

YOOL, GEORGE RICHARD, consultant; b. Orange, Calif., Apr. 16, 1969; s. George Malcolm and Norma Susan (Cravey) Follette; m. Megan Tiffaney Jacksen, June 6, 1991 (div. Nov. 1997); children: Thor Alexander, Logan Anthony. BS in Criminal Justice, No. Ariz. U., Flagstaff, 1993, MEd in Ednl. Leadership, 1995. Cons. dir. Cons. Unltd., Apache Junction, Ariz., 1988—; co-founder Barbarian Corp., 1996. Author: The Blue Rose/Silence, 1986 (1st pl. art contest 1986), Silent Dreams, 1992, The Writer's Cookbook, 1992, An Introduction to Zen Thought, 1993, rünLi Ching (Classic of Ethic), 1994, LiJie Ching (Classic of Knowledge), 1997, Metamorphosis of the Flying Rose, 1997, Unified Field Theory, 1998; co-author: Handbook for Humanizing Higher Education, 1995; creator, author: (discovery) Problem Solving Using Paradology, 1995, Integrated Theory of Learning and Development, 1995; author, discoverer: (book, presentation, discovery) Mensonnomy: A New Unified Cosmology, 1994; inventor: Virtual Keyboard, 1995; contbr. articles to profl. jours. Recipient grad. scholarship No. Ariz. U., Flagstaff, 1995. Mem. Ariz. Grad. Student Assn. (del. 1995), Students and Tchrs. Instrnl. Needs Group (pres. 1995—), Grad. Student Assn. No. Ariz. U. (pres. 1995). Avocations: reading, research, writing, math, physics, guest lecturing. E-mail: god@barbaria. com.

YOON, E. YUL, retired career officer; b. Pyungyang, Korea, Feb. 10, 1927; s. Jung Soon and Jung Duk (Lee) Y.; m. Sun Sam Lee Yoon, Nov. 29, 1931; children: Kyung Ran, Kyung Im, Kwang Ho. Grad., Mil. Acad. Seoul, 1948; BS in Politics and Fgn. Policy, Dangook U., Seoul, Korea, 1955; grad., U.S. Air U., Montgomery, Ala., 1957. Squadron comdr. The 12th Fighter SQ F-51, Korea, 1952-53; armed force attache Korean Embassy, Paris, 1959-61; wing comdr. The 1st Combat Wing, The 10th Fighter Wing, Seoul, 1961-63; pres. Korean Air Force Coll., Seoul, 1963-64; supt. Korean Air Acad., Seoul, 1964-66; commanding gen. Combat Air Command, Korea, 1968-70; minister plenipotentiary Korean Embassy, France, Mexico, 1966-68; vice minister for def. devel. Ministry of Def., Seoul, 1970-73; pres., CEO Korea Tacoma Shipbuilding Indsl. Co., Korea, 1973-76, Buyeon Co., Ltd., Seoul, 1976-86; cons. United Tech./Martin Marieta, 1976-85. Mem. Korean Heavy Industrialization Com., Seoul, 1970-73. Recipient Eulchi and two Gold Stars, Chungmoo Meritorious Svc. medals, Korea, 1952, 53, Korean Disting. Svc. medal, 1955; decorated U.S. Disting. Flying Cross, U.S. Air medal, Repub. of China Disting. Svc. medal. Mem. The Disting. Flying Cross Soc. (life), U.C.S.D. Chancellor's Assoc., Ministry of Nat. Def. of Korea (rsch. assoc.). Avocations: photography, art collecting, golf.

YOON, JI-WON, virology, immunology and diabetes educator, research administrator; b. Kang-Jin, Chonnam, Korea, Mar. 28, 1939; came to U.S., 1965; s. Baek-In and Duck-Soon (Lee) Y.; m. Chungja Rhim, Aug. 17, 1968; children: John W., James W. MS, U. Conn., 1971, PhD, 1973. Sr. investigator NIH, Bethesda, Md., 1978-84; prof., chief div. virology U. Calgary, Alta., Can., 1984—, prof., assoc. dir. diabetes rsch. ctr., 1985-90, prof., dir. diabetes rsch. ctr., 1990—; mem. edit. bd. Annual Review Advances Present Rsch. Animal Diabetes, 1990—, Diabetes Rsch. Clin. Practice, 1989—, Jour. Biomed. Rsch., 1992—, Jour. Exptl. Molecular Medicine, 1996—, Diabetologia, 1977; sci. coord. 10th Internat. Workshop on Immunology Diabetes, Jerusalem, 1989-90. Contbr. articles to New England Jour. Medicine, Jour. Virology, Sci., Nature, The Lancet, Jour. Diabetes, Jour. Immunology, Jour. Biochemistry, Jour. Exptl. Medicine. Rsch. fellow Sloan Kettering Cancer Inst., 1973-74, Staff fellow, Sr. Staff fellow NIH, 1974-76, 76-78; recipient NIH Dir. award, 1984, Heritage Med. Scientist award, Alberta Heritage Found. Med. Rsch., 1984, Lectrship. award, 3d Asian Symposium Childhood Diabetes, 1989, 8th Annual Meeting Childhood Diabetes, Osaka, Japan, 1990, 9th Korean/Can. Heritage award, 1989, 1st Compatriot award Fedn. Korean-Can. Assn., 1996. Mem. Am. Soc. Immunologists, Am. Diabetes Assn., Am. Soc. Microbiology, N.Y. Acad. Sci., Soc. Virology, Internat. Diabetes Fedn. Baptist. Achievements include first isolation of diabetogenic virus from patients with recent onset of IDDM; first demonstration of prevention of virus-induced diabetes by vaccination with nondiabetogenic virus in animals; discovery that autoimmune IDDM can be prevented by depletion of macrophages in autoimmune diabetic NOD mice, certain viral glycoproteins (rubella virus E2 glycoprotein) can induce organ-specific autoimmune disease; research on molecular identification of diabetogenic viral gene in animal models, discovery of a nontoxic organic compound with no side effects that completely prevents type I diabetes in NOD mice, discovery that bacterial superantigens such as staphylococcal enterotozins (SEC1, SEC3) can prevent autoimmune type I diabetes by activation of CD4+ suppressor T cells in NOD mice; research on the role of cloned T-Cells in the pathogenesis of autoimmune Type I Diabetes at cellular and molecular level, molecular role TGFB in prevention of Autoimmune IDDM, molecular role of macrophages in pathogenesis of virus-induced diabetes. Home: 206 Edgeview Dr NW, Calgary, AB Canada T3A 4W9 Office: Julia McFarlane Diabetes Rsch Ctr, 3330 Hospital Dr NW, Calgary, AB Canada T2N 4N1

YOON, SEWANG, engineering executive; b. Chinhae, Korea, July 28, 1949; came to U.S., 1975; s. Jah Choon and In Soon (Chung) Y.; m. Youngok Byun, Mar. 12, 1975; children: Janice J., Stella J. BS, Seoul (Korea) Nat. U., 1971; MS, UCLA, 1977, PhD, 1980. Mgr. R&D M/A-COM, PHI, Torrance, Calif., 1980-89; v.p. tech. Amonix Inc., Torrance, 1989—. Recipient Meritorious Paper award GOMAC-86, 1986, R & D 100 award for silicon photovoltaic cell, R&D Mag., 1994. Mem. IEEE (assoc.), Sigma Xi. Achievements include design, manufacture and commercialization of a point focus type concentrator solar cell with a record efficiency of 25.5% at 250X concentration, using a point contact cell concept. Office: Amonix Inc 3425 Fujita St Torrance CA 90505-4018

YORK, DOUGLAS ARTHUR, manufacturing and construction company executive; b. Centralia, Ill., June 5, 1940; s. Harry Bernice and Violet Alvera (Johnstone) Y.; student San Diego State Jr. Coll., 1957; m. Linda Kay McIntosh, Sept. 13, 1958; children—Deborah Ann, Darren Anthony. With Meredith & Simpson Constrn. Co./DBA Pressure Cool Co., Indio, Calif., 1958—, v.p., 1968—, sec., gen. mgr., 1976-82, pres., 1982—. Mem. Bldg. and Housing Appeals Bd. City of Indio, City of Coachella, Calif.; bd. dirs. Coachella Valley wild Bird Ctr.; trustee Eisenhower Med. Ctr., Rancho Mirage, Calif. Mem. ASHRAE, Internat. Conf. Bldg. Officials. Republican. Office: 83-801 Ave 45 Indio CA 92201

YORK, GARY ALAN, lawyer; b. Glendale, Calif., Aug. 29, 1943; m. Lois York, 1987; 1 child, Jonathan Alan. BA, Pomona Coll., 1965; LLB, Stanford U., 1968. Bar: Calif. 1969. Ptnr. Dewey Ballantine, L.A., 1985-95, Buchalter, Nemer, Fields & Younger, L.A., 1995-98, Le Boeuf, Lamb, Greene & MacRae, L.A., 1998—; instr. law sch. UCLA, 1968-69. Bd. editors Stanford Law review, 1966-68. Mem. ABA (chmn. real estate fin. com., real property probate and trust sect. 1987-89, chmn. usury com. 1992-93), L.A. County Bar Assn. (chmn. real estate fin. sect. 1993-96, exec. com. 1995—), State Bar of Calif., Am. Coll. Real Estate Lawyers, Am. Coll. Mortgage Attys. Office: Le Boeuf Lamb Greene & MacRae 725 S Figueroa St Ste 3600 Los Angeles CA 90017-5436

YORK, SHIRLEY MARIE, artist; b. Aurora, Ill., Aug. 25, 1923; d. John Frederick and Beulah Mary (Noack) Vockrodt; m. Herman Maxwell Grimwood, 1947 (div. Feb. 1959); children: Sherry Lynn, Jon Frederick; m. John Garth York, June 12, 1959. Student, Chgo. Art Inst., 1943, U. Chgo., 1944; BAF, U. N.Mex., 1945; student, Inst. of Fine Arts, Mexico City, 1960. Mosaic glass artist; worked with archtl. firms in Tex. and Okla. Artist: Italian glass mosaics, 1960-78; commd. artist in Tex., Okla., Ill., N.Y., Costa Rica, Mexico; represented in pvt. collections in U.S., Mexico and Europe. Recipient purchase award N.Mex. Arts Divsn., Office of Cultural Affairs, Santa Fe, 1995. Mem. AAUW. Avocations: writing, poetry. Address: 254 Camino De La Tierra Corrales NM 87048-8562

YORK, THEODORE ROBERT, consulting company executive; b. Mitchel Field, N.Y., May 4, 1926; s. Theodore and Helen (Zierak) Y.; m. Clara Kiefer, Jan. 3, 1952; children: Theodore R. II, Sharon L., Scott K., Krista A. Miller. BS, U.S. Mil. Acad., 1950; MBA, George Washington U., 1964; MPA, Nat. U., 1984. Commd. 2d lt. USAF, 1950, advanced through grades to col., 1970, ret., 1974; pres. T. R. York Cons., Fairfax, Va., 1974-79, T. R. Cons., San Diego, 1979-85, ULTRAPLECS Intelligent Bldgs., Sandy, Utah, 1991—; dir. Software Productivity Consortium, Herndon, Va., 1985-90. Mem. Loudoun County Rep. Com., Leesburg, Va., 1990-91. Decorated DFC, Air medal (5), Meritorius Svc. medal, Joint Svcs. Commendation medal, Air Force Commendation medal (5). Mem. Internat. Facilities Mgmt. Assn., Intelligent Bldgs. Inst. (advisor), Instituto Mexicana Del Edificios Intelegente (hon.), Office Planners and Users Group, Shriners, Masons. Avocations: computers, electronics. Office: ULTRAPLECS Intelligent Bldg 12189 Bluff View Dr Sandy UT 84092-5922

YORK, TINA, painter; b. Germany, Feb. 9, 1951. Student, Sch. Mus. Fine Arts, Boston, 1967-71; studied with, George Dergalis, Wayland, Mass., 1967-75; BA cum laude, Brandeis U., 1978; postgrad., N.Y. Med. Coll., 1980-83. Solo exhbns. include Gallery of Contemporary Art, Provincetown, Mass., 1969, Springfield (Mass.) Art Assn., 1971, Copley Soc., Boston, 1972, 73, Boston U., 1974, Mendler Gallery, Rockport, Mass., 1974, Cambridge (Mass.) Art Assn., 1975, Ames Gallery, N.Y.C., 1976, Gallery Seven, Boston, 1977, Brandeis U., Waltham, Mass., 1978, Rue Oker Gallery of Art, Sturbridge, Mass., 1979, Art Collectors Gallery, N.Y.C., 1981, 153 Gallery, Inc., N.Y.c., 1982, Creative Concepts, L.A., 1984, Alpha Contemporary Exhibits, L.A., 1985, Darraby Gallery, L.A., 1986, 8th St. Gallery, L.A., 1986, Koplin Gallery, L.A., 1987, Galerie Beverly Hills, Calif., 1988, Convention Ctr., Rome, 1988, Merck, Sharpe & Dohme, Rahway, N.J., 1988, Erlgangen Kultur Borse, Germany, 1989, Arwell Gallery, Laguna, Calif., 1989, Deutsch-Amerikanisches Inst., Regensburg, Germany, 1990, Art in Pub. Bldgs., Nuremberg, Germany, 1990, Art Expo, N.Y.C., 1990, Amerikahaus, Nuremberg, 1990, Art 5, Nuremberg, 1990, Dresdner Bank, Nuremberg, 1990, Studio Gallery, North Hollywood, Calif., 1991, 92, La Foire Internat d'Art Contemporain, Paris, 1992, Herbstmesse, Frankfurt, Germany, 1992, Kunstforum Internat., Aachen, Germany, 1993, Ambiente, Frankfurt, 1993, NASA Ames Rsch. Ctr., Moffett Field, Calif., 1994, NASA Johnson Space Ctr., Houston, 1995, West Valley Mus. Art, Pheonix, 1998; represented in permanent collections Mus. of Art, Las Vegas, Downey (Calif.) Mus. Art, Mus. Fine Arts, Salt Lake City, Mcpl. Art Mus., Osaka, Japan, Regional Mus. Art, Bautzen, Germany, Carter Ctr., Atlanta, Kennedy Space Ctr., Fla., New Zealand Space*. E-mail: www.farpoint.com/artpoint. Studio: Tina York Studio PO Box 17161 Fountain Hls AZ 85269-7161

YOSHIDA, KAREN KAMIJO CATEEL, public relations professional; b. Honolulu, Sept. 18, 1964; d. William Francis and Masako (Kamijo) Cateel. BSBA in Mktg., Hawaii Pacific Coll., 1989. Jour. editorial asst. Univ. Press, U. Hawaii, Honolulu, 1983; customer svc. rep. GTE Hawaiian Tel, Honolulu, 1988; account coord. Ogilvy & Mather Hawaii, Honolulu, 1989; pub. rels. asst. McCormick Communications, Honolulu, 1989-90; account dir. Joyce Timpson & Assocs., Honolulu, 1989-90; mgr. communications and pub. rels. Hawaii State Bar Assn., Honolulu, 1990—; tchr. spl. edn. Kahi Mohala Sch., 1994-97, Kaleiopuu Elem., 1997—; mng. mag. editor, dir. membership benefits Hawaii State Bar Assn., 1990—; mem. Pub. Radio Community Adv. Bd., 1993; instr. Honolulu C.C., 1993. Vol. Easter Seal

Soc., Hawaiian Humane Soc., Lanakila Elem. Sch. State contest winner Exec. Women's Internat., 1982. Mem. Sons. and Daus. 442nd RCT (newsletter and membership coms. 1993), Hawaii Pacific U. Alumni Assn. (comm. com. 1993). Avocations: writing, travel, cooking, horseback riding. Home: 94-217 Lumiaina Pl # A202 Waipahu HI 96797-5010 Office: Kahi Mohala School 91-2301 Fort Weaver Rd Ewa Beach HI 96706-3602

YOSHIKI-KOVINICK, MARIAN TSUGIE, author; b. L.A., Feb. 17, 1941; d. Eddie Junichi and Teruko Ruth (Kawamoto) Yoshiki; m. Philip Peter Kovinick, June 17, 1973. BA, U. So. Calif., 1963; MA, Azusa Pacific U., 1980. Tchr. Pasadena (Calif.) Unified Sch. Dist., 1964-66, Centinela Valley Union H.S. Dist., Lawndale, Calif., 1966-83; freelance writer, rschr. L.A., 1983—. Rschr., cons. for various exhbns.: The Woman Artist in the American West, 1976, California Light, 1990, Guy Rose, American Impressionist, 1995; rschr. for books: Elsie Palmer Payne, 1990, American Scene Painting, 1991; co-author: An Encyclopedia of Women Artists of the American West, 1997, Publications in Southern California Art, Vol. 6, 1999; archivist Archives of Am. Art, Smithsonian Instn., 1996—. Democrat. Avocations: calligraphy, crocheting, needlepoint, gardening, photography. Home and Office: 4735 Don Ricardo Dr Los Angeles CA 90008-2812

YOSHINO, GEORGE, food products executive; b. Kennewick, Wash., June 25, 1928; s. Frank H. and Kazuye (Hada) Y.; m. Frances T. Kaku, Dec. 29, 1951 (div. 1979); children: Jean Frances, Frankie Jo, Michael Stanton, Harry Walter; m. Marguerite Shirley Mosley, Dec. 8, 1990. Grad. high sch., Weiser, Idaho. Owner Yoshino Farms, Quincy, Wash., 1948—; pres. Columbia Growers Inc, Quincy, 1956-62, Yoshino Western, Inc., Quincy, 1962-68, Wyco, Inc., Seattle, 1968-74; asst. sr. v.p. U & I Inc., Pasco, Wash., 1974-79; dir., gen. mgr. Spad Distributing, Inc., Pasco, 1979-86; pres. Century 21 Products, Inc., Pasco, 1987—; bd. dirs. Pacific One NA; exec. bd. Benton-Franklin Govtl. Conf., 1993—; dir. Assoc. Wash. Bus. Mem. City Coun. Quincy, 1964-66; bd. dirs. Columbia Basin Commn., Olympia, Wash., 1964-68; dir. Associated Wash. Bus., 1994—; dir. exec. com. Benton Franklin Regional Coun., 1993—. Mem. Produce Mktg. Assn., Associated Wash. Bus. Republican. Office: Century 21 Products Inc 1917 N 2nd Ave Pasco WA 99301-3791

YOSHIZUMI, DONALD TETSURO, dentist; b. Honolulu, Feb. 18, 1930; s. Richard Kiyoshi and Hatsue (Tanouye) Y.; BS, U. Hawaii, 1952; DDS, U. Mo., 1960, grad. cert. prosthodontics, 1962, MS, 1963; m. Barbara Fujiko Iwashita, June 25, 1955 (dec. Feb. 1998); children: Beth Ann E., Cara Leigh S., Erin Yuri. Clin. instr. U. Mo. Sch. Dentistry, Kansas City, 1960-63; pvt. practice, Santa Clara, Calif., 1963-70, San Jose, Calif., 1970—. With USAF, 1952-56. Mem. Am. Dental Assn., Calif. Dental Assn., Santa Clara County Dental Soc., Omicron Kappa Upsilon, Delta Sigma Delta. Contbr. articles to profl. jours. Home: 5054 Parkfield Ave San Jose CA 95129-3225 Office: 2011 Forest Ave San Jose CA 95128-4813

YOUM, KYU HO, journalism educator; b. Kochang, South Korea, Sept. 6, 1952; s. Son-seop and Dok-rye (Lee) Y.; m. Bokim Lee, May 2, 1980; children: Harry, Eugene. MA, So. Ill. U., 1982, PhD, 1985; MSL, Yale Law Sch., New Haven, 1998. Asst. prof. Loras Coll., Dubuque, Iowa, 1985-88, U. Miami, 1988-91; from assoc. prof. to prof. Ariz. State U., Tempe, AZ, 1992—; pres. Southeast Coun. Edn. in Journalism and Mass Comm., Jonesboro, Ark., 1995-96. Author: Press Law in South Korea, 1996; contbr. articles to profl. jours. Fellow Inst. Far Eastern Studies, Seoul, 1994. Mem. Korean-Am. Univ. Prof. Assn. (regional chair 1997—), Assn. Edn. in Journalism & Mass Comm., Internat. Comm. Assn. (publ. com. 1995-97). Avocations: reading, writing, cinema. Home: 4415 E Cathedral Rock Dr Phoenix AZ 85044-6810 Office: Ariz State U Cronkite Sch Journalism & Telecomm Tempe AZ 85287-1305

YOUNG, ARTHUR WILLIAM, dean, consultant, engineer; b. Rutherfordton, N.C., Sept. 1, 1945; s. Charles Arthur and Elizabeth (Fletcher) Y.; m. Margaret Mary Helling, Sept. 17, 1977; children: Amanda Ruth, Molly Austin. BSChemE, N.C. State U., 1967; MS in Engring., U. Denver, 1974. Staff chem. engr. Procter and Gamble Co., Cin., 1967-68, prodn. mgr., 1968-71; asst. to the dean U. Denver, 1971-73; project engr. McCall, Ellingson & Morrill, Denver, 1973-74; dir. admissions and enrollment mgmt. Colo. Sch. of Mines, Golden, 1974-85, assoc. dean of students, 1985—; cons., spkr. in field.; co-sponsor Summer Admissions Inst., Colorado Springs, Colo., 1982—; bd. dirs. Denver Den. Excellence Program. Mem. Nat. Assn. Coll. Admissions Officers, Colo. Coun. on High Sch. and Coll. Rels. (pres. 1976-77, various coms.). Republican. Lutheran. Avocations: reading, handball, hiking. Home: 11427 E Berry Dr Englewood CO 80111-3910 Office: Colo Sch of Mines Weaver Towers 1511 Elm St Golden CO 80401

YOUNG, C. CLIFTON, state supreme court justice; b. Nov. 7, 1922, Lovelock, Nev.; m. Jane Young. BA, U. Nev., 1943; LLB, Harvard U., 1949. Bar: Nev. 1949, U.S. Dist. Ct. Nev. 1950, U.S. Supreme Ct. 1955. Justice Nev. Supreme Ct., Carson City, 1985—, chief justice, 1989-90. Office: Nev Supreme Ct Capitol Complex 201 S Carson St Carson City NV 89701-4702

YOUNG, CHARLES EDWARD, university chancellor emeritus; b. San Bernardino, Calif., Dec. 30, 1931; s. Clayton Charles and Eula May (Walters) Y. AA, San Bernardino Coll., 1954; AB, U. Calif., Riverside, 1955; MA, UCLA, 1957, PhD, 1960; DHL (hon.), U. Judaism, L.A., 1969, Occidental Coll., L.A., 1997. Congl. fellow Washington, 1958-59; adminstrv. analyst Office of the Pres., U. Calif., Berkeley, 1959-60; asst. prof. polit. sci. U. Calif., Davis, 1960; asst. prof. polit. sci. UCLA, 1960-66, assoc. prof., 1966-69, prof., 1969—, asst. to chancellor, 1960-62, asst. chancellor, 1962-63, vice chancellor, adminstrn., 1963-68, chancellor, 1968-97; bd. dirs. Intel Corp., Acad. TV Arts and Sci. Found.; cons. Peace Corps., 1961-62, Ford Found. on Latin Am. Activities, 1964-66; mem. bd. govs. L.A. Met. Project. Mem. Knight Found. Commn. on Intercollegiate Athletics, Calif. Coun. on Sci. and Tech., Town Hall of Calif., Carnegie Commn. Task Force on Sci. and Tech. and the States, Pacific Coun. on Internat. Policy, NCAA Pres.'s Commn., Coun. for Govt.-Univ.-Industry Rsch. Roundtable and the Nat. Rsch. Coun. Adv. Bd.-Issues in Sci. and Tech., Nat. Com. on U.S.-China Rels., chancellor's assocs. UCLA, coun. trustees L.A. Ednl. Alliance for Restructuring Now; past chair. Assn. Am. Univs., Nat. Assn. State Univs. and Land-Grant Colls.; past co-chair Calif. Campus Compact; mem. adminstrv. bd. Internat. Assn. Univs.; bd. govs. Found. Internat. Exchange Sci. and Cultural Info. by Telecom.,; bd. dirs. L.A. Internat. Visitors Coun., Greater L.A. Energy Coalition, L.A. World Affairs Coun.; trustee UCLA Found. With USAF, 1951-52. Named Young Man of Year Westwood Jr. C. of C., 1962; recipient Inter-Am. U. Cooperaton award Inter-Am. Orgn. Higher Edn., Neil H. Jacoby Internat. award UCLA Student Ctr., 1987, Edward A. Dickson Alumnus of Yr. award UCLA Alumni Assn., 1994, Disting. Svc. award U. Calif. Riverside Alumni Assn., 1996, Treasure of L.A. award L.A. Ctrl. City Assn., 1996, Albert Schweitzer Leadership award Hugh O'Brien Youth Found., 1996; hon. fellow UCLA Coll. Letters and Sci., 1996. Fellow AAAS. Office: 10920 Wilshire Blvd Ste 1835 Los Angeles CA 90024-6520*

YOUNG, DONALD ALLEN, writer, consultant; b. Columbus, Ohio, June 11, 1931; s. Clyde Allen and Helen Edith (Johnston) Y.; m. Rosemary Buchholz, Feb. 26, 1955 (div. Nov. 1976); children: Kent Allen, Kelly Ann; m. Marjorie Claire Shapiro, Aug. 20, 1977; stepchildren: Jo Alene, Andrea Lynn, Beth Ellen. Student, Ohio State U., 1949-51, Columbia Coll., 1952, North Cen. Coll., Naperville, Ill., 1956, Coll. DuPage, 1978. Editor various newspapers, mags., Detroit, Chgo., Columbus, 1946-63, 1973-74, 1978-79; v.p. Frydenlund Assocs., Chgo., 1963; pub. relations mgr. info. systems divsn. Gen. Electric Co., Phoenix, 1963-70; publs. dir. Data Processing Mgmt. Assn., Park Ridge, Ill., 1970-72; pub. relations mgr. Addressograph-Multigraph Corp., Arlington Heights, Ill., 1975-76; acct. exec. John Ripley & Assocs., Glenview, Ill., 1977-78; editorial dir. Radiology/Nuclear Medicine mag., Des Plaines, Ill., 1979-81; pres. Young Byrum Inc., Hinsdale, Ill., 1982-83; writer, consultant Tucson, 1983—; cons. in field; sports reporter, Copley newspapers, 1975-83; mem. adv. council Oakton C.C., 1970-75. Author: Principles of Automatic Data Processing, 1965, Data Processing, 1967, Rate Yourself as a Manager, 1985, Nobody Gets Rich Working for Somebody Else, 1987, [illegible] 1987, Rate Your Executive Potential, 1988, If They Can...You Can, 1989, The Entrepreneurial Family, 1990, How to Export, 1990, Women in Balance, 1991, Sleep Disorders: America's Hidden Nightmare, 1992, Small Business Troubleshooter, 1994, Crime Wave: America Needs a New Get-Tough Policy, 1996, Popcorn Publications, 1996, Adventure Guide to Southern California, 1997, Romantic Weekends: America's Southwest, 1998, Adventure Guide to the Pacific Northwest, 1998, Momentum: How to Get It-How to Keep It, 1999. Arbitrator Better Bus. Bur., Tucson, 1987-92; docent Ariz. Sonora Desert Mus., 1988-92, Tucson/Pima Arts Coun., 1993-94. With USAF, 1952-56. Recipient Jesse Neal award Assn. of Bus. Pub., 1959, 61, Silver Anvil award Pub. Rels. Soc. of Am., 1976. Mem. Publicity Club of Chgo. (pres. 1978-79). Soc. Southwestern Authors (pres. 1992), Glen Ellyn (Ill.) Jaycees (bd. dirs., SPOKE award 1959, Outstanding Jaycee 1960), Young Reps. Club (v.p. 1960). Avocations: photography, travel, hiking, fishing. Home: 4866 N Territory Loop Tucson AZ 85750-5948

YOUNG, DONALD E., congressman; b. Meridian, Calif., June 9, 1933; m. Lula Fredson; children—Joni, Dawn. AA, Yuba Jr. Coll., 1952; BA ., Chico (Calif.) State Coll., 1958. Former educator, river boat capt.; mem. Fort Yukon City Council, 6 years, mayor, 4 years; mem. Alaska Ho. of Reps., 1966-70, Alaska Senate, 1970-73, 93rd-104th Congresses from Alaska, 1973—; mem. transp. & infrastructure com., chmn. resources com. With U.S. Army, 1955-57. Republican. Episcopalian. Office: US House of Reps 2111 Rayburn Bldg Ofc B Washington DC 20515-0201*

YOUNG, DOUGLAS RYAN, technology company executive; b. Bronxville, N.Y., Apr. 30, 1945; s. Harold Sydney and Edith Isabelle (Ryan) Y.; m. Anne Honora Sullivan, May 23, 1970 (div.); children: Amanda Jennings Young, Christina Crawford Young, Ryan Townsend Young, Kielley Kavanaugh Young. BA, Princeton (N.J.) U., 1967; MBA, NYU, 1978. Various sales, mktg. and planning positions IBM, N.Y., 1970-82; regional mgr. Storage Tech. Corp., N.Y., 1982-84; pres. Unilease Computer Corp., London and N.Y.C., 1984-87; v.p. sale, mktg. and svc. Data Switch Corp., Shelton, Conn., 1987-89; dir. ins. vertical Oracle Corp., N.Y.C., 1989-91; v.p. enterprise mktg. Data Gen. Corp., Westboro, Mass., 1991-94; gen. mgr. worldwide indirect sales Hitachi Data Sys., Santa Clara, Calif., 1995—. Lt. (j.g.) USN, 1967-70. Avocations: computers, motorcycles, sailing, photography, stunt kite exhibitions. Office: Hitachi Data Sys 750 Central Expy Santa Clara CA 95050-2638

YOUNG, ERNEST, park administrator. Park ranger Puukahola Nat. Hist. Site, Kamuela, Hawaii. Office: PO Box 44340 Kamuela HI 96743-4340*

YOUNG, J. LOWELL, soil chemist, biologist; b. Perry, Utah, Dec. 13, 1925; s. I.A. and Elzada (Nelson) Y.; m. Ruth Ann Jones, Sept. 15, 1950; children: Gordon, LoAnn, Colene, Kathryn. BS, Brigham Young U., 1953; PhD, Ohio State U., 1956. Rsch. asst. Ohio Agrl. Expt. Sta., Columbus, 1953-56, postdoctoral fellow, 1956-57; chemist Agrl. Research Service USDA, Corvallis, Oreg., 1957-64, rsch. chemist, 1964-78; asst. prof. Oreg. State U., Corvallis, 1957-63, assoc. prof., 1963-78, prof. soil sci., 1978-90, Courtesy prof. soil sci., 1990—; rsch. chemist Horticultural Crops Rsch. Unit USDA, Corvallis, 1978-88; collaborator Horticultural Crops Rsch. Unit U.S. Dept. Agrl., Corvallis, 1988-91. Contbr. articles to profl jours. Served with USAAF, 1944-46. Mem. AAAS, Internat. Soil Sci. Soc., Internat. Humic Substances Soc., Soil Sci. Soc. of Am. (officer 1972-75, assoc. editor jour. 1975-80), Am. Soc. Agronomy (officer western 1966-72), Western Soc. Soil Sci. (officer 1966-71), Inst. for Alternative Agrl. Office: Oreg State U Crops & Soil Sci Dept Corvallis OR 97331

YOUNG, JEFFREY LEE, electrical engineering educator, consultant; b. Barberton, Ohio, May 1, 1959; s. Bas Roberson and Marilyn Sue (Combest) Y.; m. Elizabeth Fay Brown, Nov. 26, 1988; children: Elisabeth Grace, Hannah Katherine. BSEE, Ohio No. U., 1981; MSEE, U. Ariz., 1984, PhD in Elec. Engring., 1989. Mem. tech. staff Hughes Aircraft Co., Tucson, 1982-89, staff engr., 1989-91; asst. prof. U. Idaho, Moscow, 1991-96, assoc. prof., 1996—. Editor IEEE AP Soc., 1993—; contbr. articles to profl. jours. Recipient Hughes Doctoral fellowship Hughes Aircraft Co., 1984-89. Mem. IEEE (mem. tech. program com. AP symposium, session chmn., 1994, 95, 97, 98, reviewer 1991—), Internat. Union Radio Scientists. Avocations: reading, woodworking, music, landscaping, walking. Office: Univ Idaho Dept Elec Engring Moscow ID 83844-1023

YOUNG, JOANN ELIZABETH, veterinarian; b. Ware, Mass., July 2, 1953; D. Gordon Charles and Barbara Ann (Robinson) Y.; m. Jerome Peter Lang, May 24, 1986. AAS, SUNY, 1973; BSN, Boston U., 1985; DVM, Wash. State U., 1994. Lic. Vet. Wash., Mont., Maine. Vet. tech. Westboro (Mass.) Animal Hosp., 1973-78, Berkshire Vet. Hosp., Pittsfield, Mass., 1979-82; admitting officer U. Mass. Med. Ctr., Worcester, Mass., 1978-79; RN Ruidoso (N. Mex.) Hondo Valley Hosp., 1985-86, Group Health Ctrl. Hosp., Seattle, 1986-87, SE Wash. Home Health and Hospice, Pullman, 1988-90; vet. Colfax (Wash.) Vet. Hosp., 1994—. Mem. AVMA, Wash. State Vet. Med. Assn. Democrat. Roman Catholic. Avocations: horseback riding, gardening, travel. Home: 302 Old Moscow Rd Pullman WA 99163-8832 Office: Colfax Vet Hosp 1715 N Oak St Colfax WA 99111-9704

YOUNG, JOHN ALAN, electronics company executive; b. Nampa, Idaho, Apr. 24, 1932; s. Lloyd Arthur and Karen Eliza (Miller) Y.; m. Rosemary Murray, Aug. 1, 1954; children: Gregory, Peter, Diana. BSEE, Oreg. State U., 1953; MBA, Stanford U., 1958. Various mktg. and fin. positions Hewlett Packard Co. Inc., Palo Alto, Calif., 1958-63, gen. mgr. microwave divsn., 1963-68, v.p. electronic products group, 1968-74, exec. v.p., 1974-77, COO, 1977-78, pres., 1977-92, CEO, 1978-92; ret., 1992; bd. dirs. Wells Fargo Bank, Wells Fargo and Co., Chevron Corp., SmithKline Beecham Plc. Affymetrix, Inc., Ciphergen, Internat. Integration Inc., Novell, Inc.; chmn. Lucent Technologies. Chmn. ann. fund Stanford U., 1966-73, nat. chmn. corp. gifts, 1973-77, mem. adv. coun. Grad. Sch. Bus., 1967-73, 75-80, Univ. trustee, 1977-87; bd. dirs. Mid-Peninsula Urban Coalition, 1971-80, co-chmn., 1983-85; chmn. Pres.'s Commn. on Indsl. Competitiveness, 1983-85, Nat. Jr. Achievement, 1983-84; pres. Found. for Malcolm Baldrige Nat. Quality Award; mem. Adv. Com. on Trade Policy and Negotiations, 1988-92. With USAF, 1954-56. Mem. Nat. Acad. Engring., Coun. on Competitiveness (founder, founding chair computer systems policy project 1986), Bus. Coun. (co-chair pres. com. of adcisors on sci. & tech. 1993—).

YOUNG, JOHN BYRON, retired lawyer; b. Bakersfield, Calif., Aug. 10, 1913; s. Lewis James and Gertrude Lorraine (Clark) Y.; m. Helen Beryl Stone, Dec. 26, 1937; children: Sally Jean, Patricia Helen, Lucia Robin. BA, UCLA, 1934; LLB, U. Calif., Berkeley, 1937. Pvt. practice law Hargreaves & Young, later Young Wooldridge, Bakersfield, 1937-40; dep. county counsel County of Kern, Bakersfield, 1940-42; dep. rationing atty. U.S. OPA, Bakersfield and Fresno, Calif., 1942; ptnr. firm Young Wooldridge and predecessors, Bakersfield, 1946-78, assoc. law firm, 1978-91; bd. dirs., legal counsel Kern County Water Assn., Bakersfield, 1953-76. Mem., chmn. Kern County Com. Sch. Dist. Orgn., Bakersfield, 1950s and 60s; mem. Estate Planning Coun. of Bakersfield, 1960-76, pres., 1965-66. Capt. JAGC, U.S. Army, 1943-46. Mem. Kern County Bar Assn. (prs. 1948, Bench and Bar award 1978). Home: 13387 Barbados Way Del Mar CA 92014-3501 Office: Young Wooldridge 1800 30th St Fl 4 Bakersfield CA 93301-1919

YOUNG, JON NATHAN, archeologist; b. Hibbing, Minn., May 30, 1938; s. Robert Nathan Young and Mary Elizabeth (Barrows) Roy; m. Karen Sue Johnson, June 5, 1961 (div. May 1980); children: Shawn Nathan, Kevin Leigh; m. Tucker Heitman, June 18, 1988 (div. Apr. 1996). BA magna cum laude, U. Ariz., 1960, PhD, 1967; MA, U. Ky., 1962. Archeologist Nat. Park Svc. Southwest Archeol. Ctr., Globe and Tucson, Ariz., 1967-75; exec., camp dir. YMCA of Metro. Tucson, 1976-77; asst. dir. Kit Carson Meml. Found., Taos, N.Mex., 1978; co-dir. Las Palomas de Taos, 1979; archeologist Nat. Forest Svc., Carson Nat. Forest, Taos, 1980—; exec. order cons. U.S. Sec. Interior, 1973-75. Author: The Salado Culture in Southwestern Prehistory, 1967; co-author: Excavation of Mound 7, 1981, First-Day Road Log in Tectonic Development of the Southern Sangre de Cristo Mountains, 1990, The Gila Pueblo Salado, 1997. Advisor Boy Scouts Am.; active YMCA White Rag Soc.; mem. Kit Carson Hist. Mus. Grantee NEH, 1978; Ariz. Wilson Found., NSF, Ky. Rsch. Found. fellow, 1960-62; Baird Found., Bausch and Lomb, Elks; recipient cert. merit USDA, 1987, 89. Fellow AAAS, Am. Anthrop. Assn., Explorers Club, Royal Anthrop. Inst.; mem. Current Anthropology (assoc.), Ariz. Archaeol. and Hist. Soc., Ariz. Hist. Soc., Ctr. Anthropol. Studies, Coun. on Am.'s Mil. Past, Friends of Taos Pub. Libr., Kit Carson Hist. Mus., New Mex. Heritage Preservation Alliance, Soc. Hist. Archaeology, Soc. Am. Archaeology, Harwood Found., Millicent Rogers Mus., Taos Archaeol. Soc., San Juan County Mus. Assn., Taos County Hist. Soc. (bd. dirs.), Sigma Xi, Phi Beta Kappa, Alpha Kappa Delta, Phi Kappa Phi, Delta Chi. Home: PO Box 2207 Taos NM 87571-2207 Office: Nat Forest Svc Suprs Office 208 Cruz Alta Rd Taos NM 87571-5983

YOUNG, JOYCE HENRY, adult education educator, consultant; b. Oak Park, Ill., July 3, 1930; d. Jesse Martin and Adelina Patti (Gillander) H.; m. James Edward Young, Apr. 26, 1958; children: Richard Allen, Patti Ann. BA, Calif. State U., Fresno, 1951; MA, Northwestern U., 1952; EdD, U. So. Calif., 1986. Tchr. Glencoe (Ill.) Pub. Schs., 1952-53, Hayward (Calif.) Schs., 1953-59, Honolulu Dept. Edn., 1969-83, Kamehameha Schs., Honolulu, 1987; instr. Hawaii Pacific Coll., Honolulu, 1987, Honolulu Community Coll., 1988, Chaminade U., Honolulu, 1990, Kansai Gaidai Hawaii Coll., 1991-93; instr. U. Hawaii, Manoa, 1994, instr. emeritus, 1994—; cons. Computer Lab., Honolulu, 1988. Mem. AAUW, Am. Ednl. Rsch. Assn., Educom, Delta Epsilon, Kappa Delta Pi, Pi Lambda Theta. Democrat. Presbyterian. Avocations: German Shepherds, exotic birds.

YOUNG, KELLY LEE, university administrator, accountant; b. Ft. Worth, Feb. 18, 1963; s. Edwin L. and W. Carolyn (Wren) Y.; m. JoAnn McKee, July 21, 1989. BBA, Abilene Christian U., 1985; MBA, Baylor U., 1988. CPA. Comml. loan adminstr. lst State Bank, Abilene, Tex., 1985; mem. trust spl. project Tex. Nat. Bank Waco, 1985-88, trust officer, 1988-90; asst. v.p. Tex. Nat. Bank, Waco, 1990-92; mgr. Planned Giving Pepperdine U., 1992-96, dir. planned giving ops. and sr. trust officer, 1996-98, assoc. treas., 1998—; adj. prof. acctg. Pepperdine U.; asst. treas. Wave Enterprises, Wave Properties, Inc., Rancho/Robles Properties, Inc., 1994-97; v.p. Wave Svcs., Inc., 1997—. Pat Dunigan scholar lst State Bank, 1985. Mem. AICPA, Planned Giving Round Table So. Calif., Blue Key. Avocations: tennis, theater, symphony. Office: Pepperdine U 24255 Pacific Coast Hwy Malibu CA 90263-0002

YOUNG, LESTER REX, engineering and construction company executive; b. Marion, Ind., Aug. 26, 1946; s. Harold Leroy and Willow Marie (May) Y.; m. Bonnie Darline Denison, Sept. 5, 1965; children: Tamara Lynn, Kelby Gene, Kadee Lynn. BSEE, Kans. State U., 1969; MBA, Wichita State U., 1979. Reg. engr. Colo., Kans., Ohio, Mont., Utah, La. Plant engr. Beech Aircraft Corp., Wichita, Kans., 1973-75; asst. to v.p. mfg. Beech Aircraft Corp., Wichita, 1975-77; sr. project mgr. Smith & Boucher, Inc., Overland Park, Kans., 1977-80; dir. engring. R.M. Henning, Inc., New Philadelphia, Ohio, 1980-82; mgr. indsl. engring. Williams Internat., Ogden, Utah, 1982-84; mgr. plant engring. Sundstrand Corp., Denver, 1984-86; pres. ECS Engrs. Inc., Arvada, Colo., 1986-90; dir. bus. devel. Morrison Knudsen Corp., Denver, 1990-96; v.p. western region R&R Internat., Inc., Denver, 1996—; cons. Compliance Recycling Industires, Denver, 1984-87. Author: (reference manuals) Selection of Reverse Osmosis for Boiler Applications, 1987, Applications for Enzyme Activated Carbon, 1989, Integrated Refinery Waste Management, 1992. Capt. U.S. Army, 1969-73, Europe. Republican. Nazarene. Avocation: winter sports. Office: R&R Internat 3333 Quebec St Ste 7800 Denver CO 80207-2329

YOUNG, LOWELL SUNG-YI, medical administrator, educator; b. Honolulu, Dec. 5, 1938. AB, Princeton U., 1960; MD, Harvard U., 1964. Diplomate Am. Bd. Internal Medicine with subspecialty in infectious diseases. Intern, jr. asst. resident, sr. asst. resident med. divsn. Bellevue Hosp. and Meml. Hosp., N.Y.C., 1964-67; fellow in medicine Cornell U. Med. Coll., 1965-67; epidemic intelligence officer bacterial diseases br. Nat. Communicable Disease Ctr., Atlanta, 1967-69, chief spl. pathogens sect., 1968-69; spl. postdoctoral rsch. fellow Nat. Inst. Allergy and Infectious Diseases, 1969-70; rsch. fellow in medicine Meml. Hosp./Cornell U. Med. Coll., 1969-70; clin. asst. physicisn infectious disease svc. dept. medicine Meml. Hosp., 1970-72, assoc. dir. microbiology lab., 1971-72; instr. in medicine Cornell U. Med. Coll., 1970-72; asst. clinician Sloan-Kettering Inst. for Cancer Rsch., 1971-72; chief divsn. infectious disease Calif. Pacific Med. Ctr., San Francisco, 1985—; dir. Kuzell Inst., San Francisco, 1985—; adj. prof. pharmacy U. of Pacific, San Francisco, 1989—; mem. microbiology and invectious diseases adv. com. Nat. Inst. Allergy and Infectious Diseases, 1981-85, mem. allergy and immunology rsch. com., 1975-79; mem. staff Calif. Pacific Med. Ctr., Mt. Zion Hosp. and Med. Ctr., U. Calif., San Francisco; mem. sci. adv. bd. Am. Found. for AIDS Rsch. Mem. editl. bd. Infection, Infectious Diseases in Clin. Practice, Diagnostic Microbiology and Infectious Diseases, Antomicrobial Agts. and Chemotherapy, Infection and Immunity; contbr. numerous articles to profl. jours., chpts. to books. Recipient Alexander D. Langmuir prize Epidemic Intelligence Svc., 1970, Garrod medal Brit. Soc., 1992. Fellow ACP (mem. med. self-assessment com.), Infectious Diseases Soc. Am. (councillor 1983-85); mem. Am. Soc. for Clin. Investigation, Am. Fedn. for Clin. Rsch., Am. Soc. for Microbiology, Western Soc. for Clin. Rsch., Internat. Immunocompromised Host Soc., Brit. Soc. Antimicrobial Chemotherapy. Office: Kuzell Inst 2200 Webster St Ste 305 San Francisco CA 94115-1821 also: Calif Pacific Med Ctr 2100 Webster St #326 San Francisco CA 94115*

YOUNG, LYNN MARIE, psychotherapist; b. Mpls., Nov. 4, 1954; d. Vernon Earle and Shirley Ann (Mitchell) Mollan; m. Benjamin Brock Young, Dec. 22, 1979; children: Patrick Whiting, Megan Amanda. BS in Social Work magna cum laude, U. Minn., 1977; MA in Counseling and Human Svcs., Colo. U., 1996. Tng. asst. Planned Parenthood Minn., St. Paul, 1977-79; health educator Health Start, St. Paul, 1981-89; case mgr., regional affairs coord. Myron Stratton Home, Colorado Springs, Colo., 1990-91; adolescent outreach specialist Chrysalis, A Ctr. For Women, Mpls., 1994; sr. health educator Minn. Dept. of Health, Mpls., 1994-95; pregnancy counselor Luth. Family Svcs., Colorado Springs, 1996-98; pvt. practice psychotherapist Colorado Springs, 1996—. Co-author: Human Sexuality: Values and Choices, 1986, also video (Cert. of Merit, Chgo. Film Festival 1986, AMA 1989), Understanding Sexuality: Making Healthy Choices, 1988. Sinclair scholar U. Minn., 1976. Mem. ACA, Colo. Counseling Assn. Democrat. Congregationalist. Avocations: spirituality, reading, cooking, skiing, art. Home: 10435 Marble Creek Cir Colorado Springs CO 80908-4501

YOUNG, MARK THOMAS, lawyer; b. Burbank, Calif., Sept. 3, 1955; s. William and Margaret Young; m. Sherril L. Dutton, Nov. 18, 1989; children: Katie, Becky. BA, UCLA, 1976; JD, U. Calif., Davis, 1979. Bar: Calif. 1979. Clk. Times Mirror Co., L.A., 1978-79; assoc. Layman, Hanson, Jones & Voss, Newport Beach, Calif., 1980-81, Mayer & Glassman, L.A., 1981-86; ptnr. Mayer, Glassman & Gaines, L.A., 1986-96; pvt. practice Encino, Calif., 1996—. V.p., bd. dirs. Santa Clarita (Calif.) Cmty. Devel. Corp., 1996—. Office: Law Offices 15910 Ventura Blvd Ste 1650 Encino CA 91436-2842

YOUNG, MARTIN RAY, JR., architect; b. Mancos, Colo., Aug. 11, 1916; s. Martin Ray and Cynthia Jane (Porter) Y.; m. Beth Taylor, Oct. 1, 1936 (dec. April 1977); m. Georgia Lortz, July 2, 1977 (dec. July 1995); m. Thelma L. Neamy, Aug. 3, 1996; children: Cynthia Marie Young Willis, Lurlyne Young Farr, Deann Young McCune, Jeanette Young Staudage, Ronald Ray. BA, Brigham Young U., 1936. Registered arch., Ariz., N.Mex, Utah, Calif., Wash., Idaho, Ohio, Maine, N.C., Tex., Okla., Mont., Minn., Nebr., Nev. Draftsman Frank Wallace-Arch., Phoenix, 1936-39, 1939-41; draftsman Leschr & Mahoney-Archs., Phoenix, 1945-47; pvt. practice Green & Young Archs., Phoenix, 1947-48; prin. Martin Ray Young Jr. Arch., Mesa, Ariz., 1948—. Recipient Scarab award Young Archs., 1948. Fellow Internat. Inst. Arts Letters; mem. AIA (pres. local chpt. 1988—, Kachnia award 1994), Constrn. Specifications Inst. (pres. 1949—). Republican. Mem. LDS Ch. Home and Office: 50 S Udall Mesa AZ 85204-1038

YOUNG, MICHAEL EDWARD, composer, music educator; b. San Francisco, June 25, 1939; s. John Davis and Mary Katherine (Polese) Y. BA in Music, U. Wash., 1964, MA in Music, 1966. Organist First Presbyn. Ch., Seattle, 1961-65, St. Paul's Episcopal Ch., Seattle, 1966-70; instr. music Cornish Sch. Allied Arts, Seattle, 1966-70; organist Sts. Peter and Paul Ch., Vancouver, B.C., 1970-74, Cathedral of Our Lady of Lourdes, Spokane, Wash., 1979-92, Messiah Luth. Ch., Spokane, 1988-92; asst. to assoc. prof. music Whitworth Coll., Spokane, [illegible]

Baritone and Piano, 1992, Give Glory, All Creation for Trumpet, Choir and Organ, 1991, A Mountain Symphony for Orchestra, 1987-88, Mountain Sketches, Set 5, 1988, Set 9 for piano, 1994, String Quartet No. 2, 1986, Northwest Images Horn, Cello, Piano, 1981, Serenade to the Mountains for orch., 1995. With U.S. Army, 1957-60. Mem. Am. Guild Organists (assoc.; 25th Creative Ann award 1983), Christian Fellowship of Art Music Composers, Glacier Mountaineering Soc. (charter mem.), Alpine Club of Canada. Orthodox. Avocations: hiking, photography, mountain climbing. Office: Whitworth Collge Station 1701 Spokane WA 99251

YOUNG, PAUL HOWARD, fiber optics communications engineer, educator; b. Chgo., Sept. 26, 1940; s. Theodore Howard and Dorothy Emma (Davis) Y.; m. Beryl Elaine Cole, July 6, 1981; children: John, James, Sara. BSEE, Calif. State U., San Diego, 1965; MSEE, Calif. State U., San Jose, 1981; PhD in Elec. Engring., LaSalle U., 1995. Cert. secondary and cmty. coll. tchr., Calif.; registered profl. engr., Ariz. Electronic engr. Cubic Corp., San Diego, 1964-70, sr. engr., 1970-74; engring. cons. San Diego, 1974-76; instr. engring. City Coll. San Francisco, 1976-81; assoc. prof. Ariz. State U., Tempe, 1981-90; fiber optics engr., tchr. TACAN Corp., Carlsbad, Calif., 1990—; cons. Hewlett-Packard Corp., Rolm Corp., Motorola, Scottsdale, Ariz., 1985. Author: (text) Electronic Communication Techniques, 1985, 3d edit., 1994; contbr. tech. articles, papers to profl. jours. With USNR, 1960-62. NASA fellow, 1983-84, 86, 87; recipient Grad. Teaching Excellence award, 1989. Mem. NSPE, IEEE (sr.), Am. Soc. for Engring. Edn., Internat. Soc. for Photonics Engring., Nat. Assn. Telecom Engrs. (master cert.), Sierra Club. Avocations: distance running, backpacking, travel. Home: 3523 Brookfield Way Carlsbad CA 92008-7017 Office: TACAN Corp 2330 Faraday Ave Carlsbad CA 92008-7216

YOUNG, ROBERT EDWARD, computer company executive; b. L.A., Nov. 28, 1943; s. David and Sue (Wise) Y. Student, E. Los Angeles Coll., 1973, Santa Monica Coll., 1975; BA, UCLA, 1978. Cert. securities analyst N.Y. Inst. Fin., 1972. Computer operator Rocketdyne Corp., Canoga Park, Calif., 1963-65; computer ops. supr. Hughes Aircraft Corp., El Segundo, Calif., 1965-67; with investment securities dept. Smith, Tilton & Co., Inc., Santa Ana, Calif., 1967-70, Morton Seidel & Co., Inc., L.A., 1970-78; sales mgr. of comml. interior constrn. NICO Constrn. Co., Inc., L.A., 1978-80; sales mgr. Strauss Constrn. Co., Inc., L.A., 1981-82; v.p., instl. investment officer FCA Asset Mgmt./Am. Savs., Los Angeles, 1982-87; pres., chief exec. officer Avalon Fin. Group, Inc., Los Angeles, 1988-90; prin. Robert Young & Co., 1991—; bd. dirs. RESA Prodns. 1973-80, Edu Care, L.A., 1981-90, ASC Edn. Svcs. Inc., L.A., chmn. fin. com.; mktg. cons. Shehata Enterprises, L.A., 1978-79; sales tng. cons. Versailles Gallery, L.A., Schwartz Constrn., L.A., 1982; cons. PC Etcetera, L.A., 1990-91. Photographer: prin. works include Man at Work or Play UN, Geneva, 1976, Cat of Yr. photo, 1977, Photomontage U. So. Calif. Early Childhood Edn. Ctr., 1977; producer weekly pub. affairs prog. for family fin. planning sta. KPOL Radio, 1974, Stocks and Bonds Show KWHY-TV, 1975-78, MacRadio show, Am. Radio Network, 1989, WinRadio Show, 1990, MacWin Radio, 1991-93. Fin. cons. Hofheinz Fund, Houston, 1988. Served with USCGR, 1964-70. Mem. Archtl. Hist. Soc. (life mem. So. Calif. chpt.), Reel Sports Club, Masons, Marine Venice Yacht Club. Avocations: fishing, computers, sailing. Home: 4531 Don Arturo Pl Los Angeles CA 90008-2803 Office: Robert Young & Co 8306 Wilshire Blvd Ste 499 Beverly Hills CA 90211-2382

YOUNG, ROBERT WENDELL, language specialist, tribal relations specialist; b. Chgo., May 18, 1912; s. James M. and Nellie S. (Stevenson) Y.; m. Olga L. Maloni, 1939; 1 child, Linda Sue. BA, U. Ill., 1935; LLD (hon.), U. N.Mex., 1970. Indian language specialist Bur. Indian Affairs, Window Rock, Ariz., 1940-51, asst. to area dir., 1951-62; area tribal ops. Bur. Indian Affairs, Gallup, N.Mex., 1962-66, Albuquerque, 1966-71; adj. prof. Navajo linguistics U. N.Mex., Albuquerque, 1971—. Prin. author: The Navajo Language, 1980, rev. edit., 1987, Analytical Lexicon of Navajo, 1992; author: Political History of Navajo, 1978; author, compiler The Navajo Yearbook, 1956-60. Sgt. USMC, 1944-46. Recipient Disting. Svc. award U.S. Dept. Interior, 1969. Mem. Soc. Study Indigenous Langs. of the Americas, Benevolent Protective Order of Elks, Internat. Jour. Am. Linguistics, Linguistic Soc. Am., Am. Soc. Ethnohistory, Am. Geog. Soc. Avocations: photogrpahy, target shooting, reading. Home: 2929 Indiana St NE Albuquerque NM 87110-3425 Office: Univ NMex Dept Linguistics Humanities 526 Albuquerque NM 87131

YOUNG, ROGER CARL, computer company executive; b. Clayton, Mo., Mar. 21, 1932; s. Gerald Lee Young and Bertha Augusta (Schlottach) McCulloh; m. Nadine Fay Basch, Apr. 27, 1952; children: Julia Allyn, David Ford. Student, Washington U., St. Louis, 1956-57, U. Calif., Berkeley, 1957-60, Contra Costa Coll., 1970. V.p. and div. mgr. Crocker Nat. Bank, San Francisco, 1967-75; nat. accts. mgr. Wang Labs., San Francisco, 1975-78; industry cons. Fortune 500, 1978-81; pres. ComTrak, Richmond, Calif., 1981-83; dir. mktg. Delphi Systems, Inc., Westlake Village, Calif., 1983-89; regional sales mgr. Applied Systems, Inc., Chgo., 1991-92; pres. YOUNG Tech., Vacaville, Calif., 1992—. Served with USAF, 1951-55. Mem. Data Processing Mgmt. Assn. (cert., bd. dirs., sec. San Francisco chpt. 1965-67), Am. Contract Bridge League (life master 1959), Green Tree Golf Club. Republican. Avocations: golf, computer product design, tournament bridge. Home and Office: 779 Arbor Oaks Dr Vacaville CA 95687-5252

YOUNG, SARAH MOSKOWITZ, educational and computer consultant, journalist; b. Galveston, Tex., June 10, 1947; d. Irving Leonard and Joyce (Schreiber) Moskowitz; children: Clement Clarke III, Leonard Arthur. B Tech. Edn., Nat. U., San Diego, 1984, postgrad., 1984; EdD, Calif. Coast U., San Diego, 1989, postgrad. Adult edn. and community coll. credentials, cert. vision and hearing tech., pers. cons., Calif.; cert. first aid and CPR instr. trainer. Tchr. Vista High Sch., San Diego, 1980-81; project dir. Robert Harrow Co., San Diego, 1981-82; instr. North County Coll., Eldorado Coll., San Diego County, 1982-84, Bangkok U., Kasesart U., 1985-86; assoc. dean, chmn. dept. edn. Phillips Coll., New Orleans, 1988-89; instr., radio performer Am. Lang. Tng., Jakarta, Indonesia, 1989-90; ednl. cons.,journalist various mags. and newspapers, 1980—; seminar speaker Sci. Rsch. Assocs., 1980; tng. officer Naval Sea Cadets, Monterey, Calif., 1988-89; mem. nat. curriculum com. Am. Assn. Med. Transcriptionists, 1978-88; med. instr. Kelsey-Jenney Coll., San Diego, 1990-91; founder Disabled Individuals Suggesting Computer Solutions. Mem., bd. dirs. Mira Mesa Town Coun., San Diego, 1980-84, sec., 1983-84; bd. dirs. Mira Mesa Community Coun., 1982-84; precinct chmn. San Diego Mayoral Election Com., 1982-84. Scholar Nat. U., 1984. Mem. NAFE, Leadership Edn. Awareness and Devel., San Diego Computer Soc., Mensa (chmn. mayor's adv. com. San Diego 1982-84, career day 1983), San Diego Press Club, Tetra Soc. San Diego (founder), Delta Omicron Epsilon. Avocations: artist, musician, world culturee, languages, animals. Home and Office: 10257 Trails End Cir San Diego CA 92126-3517

YOUNG, SCOTT THOMAS, business management educator; b. Oak Park, Ill., Dec. 28, 1949; s. Thomas Menzies and Grace (Butler) Y.; children: Reginald, Galen. BA, U. Ga., 1974; MBA, Ga. Coll., 1982; PhD, Ga. State U., 1987. Prof. U. Utah, Salt Lake City, 1987—, chmn. mgmt. dept., 1994-97, assoc. dean David Eccles Sch. Bus.; mgmt. cons. to numerous orgns.; lectr., speaker, cons. on ops., quality and project mgmt. Author: Managing Global Operations; contbr. numerous articles to profl. jours. With U.S. Army, 1971-73. Decorated Commendation medal; grantee Nat. Assn. Purchasing Mgmt., 1986. Mem. Decision Sci. Inst., Acad. Mgmt., Prodn. and Ops. Mgmt. Soc. Avocation: marathon running. Office: U Utah David Eccles Sch Bus Salt Lake City UT 84112

YOUNG, STEVEN, professional football player; b. Salt Lake City, Oct. 11, 1961. JD, Brigham Young, 1993. With L.A. Express, USFL, 1984-85, Tampa Bay Buccaneers, 1985-87; quarterback San Francisco 49ers, 1987—; NFL MVP, 1992, NFL Player of the Year, 1994. Organized, manages the Forever Young Found. benefitting Bay Area & Utah youth-oriented charities. Davey O'Brien Award, 1983, All-America team quarterback, The Sporting News, 1983; Named NFL's Top-rated quarterback, 1991, named NFL MVP The Sporting News, 1992, NFL All-Pro team quarterback, The Sporting News, 1992, Bay Area Sports Hall of Fame Profl. Athlete of the Year, 1992, Superbowl MVP, 1994. Played in Pro Bowl 1992, 93; highest rated passer NFL, 1991-93. Office: San Francisco 49ers 4949 Centennial Blvd Santa Clara CA 95054-1229*

YOUNG, TAYLOR LYNN, special education administrator, consultant; b. Evansville, Ind., Dec. 7, 1952; s. James Taylor and Luvenia (Welborn) Y.; 1 child, Virginia Melin. BS in Edn., Ea. Ill. U., 1975; MS in Edn., Ill. State U., 1980; PhD in Edn., U. Denver, 1988. Tchr. spl. edn. St. Joseph (Ill.)-Ogden High Sch. Dist. 305, 1975-80; dir. Mid-State Spl. Edn. Coop., Hillsboro, Ill., 1980-81; dir. spl. edn. Mountain Bd. Coop. Svcs., Leadville, Colo., 1981-87; sr. cons. on sch. fin., cons. on spl. edn. Colo. Dept. Edn., Denver, 1987-88; prin. Laremont Sch., Spl. Edn. Dist. Lake County, Gurnee, Ill., 1988-89; dir. edn. Colo. Christian Home, Denver, 1989-92; special edn. tchr. El Paso County Dist. 11, Colo. Springs, Colo., 1992-93, special edn. supr., 1993—; cons. Project Choice, Ill. Bd. Edn., Springfield, 1989-90. Mem. ASCD, Coun. for Exceptional Children, Phi Delta Kappa. Republican. Avocations: golf, travel. Home: 1522 Server Dr Colorado Springs CO 80910-2039 Office: Schl Dist 11 1115 N El Paso St Colorado Springs CO 80903-2599

YOUNG, WARREN DALE, II, software engineer, writer; b. Cedar City, Utah, Feb. 18, 1974; s. Warren Dale and Elaine Y. Grad., Farmington (N. Mex.) H.S., 1992; student, San Juan Coll., 1992. Software engr. Teradon Industries, Aztec, N. Mex., 1992-94, Ednl. Tech. Resources, Aztec, N. Mex., 1994—; Editor: (book revs.) Web Apps Mag., 1996—; contbr. articles to profl. jours. Mem. IEEE (Computer Soc. affiliate), Assn. Computing Machines. Office: Ednl Tech Resources 120 E Chaco St Aztec NM 87410-1910

YOUNGBLOOD, DEBORAH SUE, lawyer; b. Fairview, Okla., July 29, 1954; d. G. Dean and Beatrice J. (Hiebert) White. BS with honors, Okla. State U., 1976, MA with honors, 1979; JD cum laude, Boston Coll. Law Sch., 1991; MPH in Health Care Mgmt., Harvard U., 1992. Bar: Colo., N.Mex., U.S. Ct. Appeals (10th cir.). Judicial law clk. Colo. Supreme Ct., 1992-94; assoc. atty. Patton Boggs, L.L.P., Denver, 1994-97, Vaglica & Meinhold, Colorado Springs, 1997—. Mem. ABA, Colo. Bar Assn., N.Mex. Bar Assn., Minoru Yasui Am. Inns of Ct. (exec. coun. 1995-97), Phi Kappa Phi. Avocation: travel. Office: Vaglica & Meinhold 105 E Moreno Ave Ste 1oo Colorado Springs CO 80903-3917

YOUNGQUIST, WALTER LEWELLYN, consulting geologist; b. Mpls., May 5, 1921; s. Walter Raymond and Selma Regina (Knock) Y.; m. Elizabeth Salome Pearson, Dec. 11, 1943; children: John, Karen, Louise, Robert. BA, Gustavus Adolphus Coll., St. Peter, Minn., 1942; MSc, U. Iowa, 1943, PhD, 1948. Registered profl. geologist, Oreg. Jr. geologist U.S. Geol. Survey, 1943-44; rsch. assoc. U. Iowa, Iowa City, 1945-48; asst. prof. geology U. Idaho, Moscow, 1948-51; sr. geologist Internat. Petroleum Co., Talara, Peru, 1951-54; prof. geology U. Kans., Lawrence, 1954-57, U. Oreg., Eugene, 1957-66; cons. geologist Minerals dept. Exxon Corp., Houston, 1968-73; geothermal cons. Eugene Water & Electric Bd., 1973-92; ind. cons. Eugene, 1992—. Author: Investing in Natural Resources, 1980, Mineral Resources and the Destinies of Nations, 1990, GeoDestinies, 1997; co-author: Ordovician Cephalopod Fauna of Baffin Island, 1954. Ensign, USNR, 1944-45. Recipient Lowden Prize in Geology, U. Iowa, 1943. Fellow AAAS, Geol. Soc. Am.; mem. Am. Assn. Petroleum Geologists, Geothermal Resources Coun., N.W. Energy Assn., N.Y. Acad. Scis., Sigma Xi. Lutheran. Avocations: fly-tying, photography, fishing. Office: PO Box 5501 Eugene OR 97405-0501

YOUNGS, JACK MARVIN, cost engineer; b. Bklyn., May 2, 1941; s. Jack William and Virginia May (Clark) Y.; B in Engring., CCNY, 1964; MBA, San Diego State U., 1973; m. Alexandra Marie Robertson, Oct. 31, 1964; 1 child, Christine Marie. Mass properties engr. Gen. Dynamics Corp., San Diego, 1964-68, rsch. engr., 1968-69, sr. rsch. engr., 1969-80, sr. cost devel. engr., 1980-81, cost devel. engring. specialist, 1981-95; prin. estimator Martin Marietta Astronautics, 1994-95; estimating adminstr. Lockheed Martin Astronautics, 1995-96; prin., owner Youngs Group, 1996—. Dist. dir. Scripps Ranch Civic Assn., 1976-79; pres. Scripps Ranch Swim Team, 1980-82; dir., 1986-87; judge Greater San Diego Sci. and Engring. Fair, 1981-92. Mem. Princeton U. Parents Assn. Recipient 5th place award World Body Surfing Championships, 1987, 6th place award, 1988. Mem. AIAA, N.Y. Acad. Scis., Alumni Assn, CUNY, Bklyn. Tech. H.S. Alumni Assn., Inst. Cost Analysis (cert., charter mem., treas. Greater San Diego chpt. 1986-90), Soc. Cost Estimating and Analysis (cert. cost estimator/analyst, pres. San Diego chpt. 1990-91), Internat. Soc. Parametric Analysts (bd. dirs. San Diego chpt. 1987-90), Nat. Mgmt. Assn. (space systems divsn. charter mem. 1985, award of honor Convair chpt. 1975), Assn. MBA Execs., San Diego State U. Bus. Alumni Assn. (charter mem. 1986), Convair Alumni Assn., Scripps Ranch Swim and Racquet Club (dir. 1977-80, treas. 1978-79, pres. 1979-80), Beta Gamma Sigma, Chi Epsilon, Sigma Iota Epsilon. Lutheran. Research in life cycle costing and econ. analysis. Office: 11461 Tribuna Ave San Diego CA 92131-1907

YOUNT, BOBBY LON, financial planner; b. Valdese, N.C., Aug. 6, 1947; s. George Lonnie and Mary Helen (Foard) Y.; m. Charlotte Marie Roberts, Aug. 16, 1969 (div. Sept. 1980); m. Elizabeth Bonner Frye, May 14, 1988. BS, U. N.C., 1969; MBA, Pepperdine U., 1982. CFP. Sr. sales rep. SRA, Winston Salem, N.C., 1973-79; acquistions editor Bobbs-Merrill, San Jose, Calif., 1979-85; western regional mgr. Data Nat., San Jose, 1985-87; regional mgr. Olsen Svcs., San Jose, 1987-88; sr. account rep. Waddell & Reed, San Jose, 1988—. Editor: Retailing, 1981, Business Dynamics, 1982. Exec. bd. mem. Boy Scouts Am., San Jose, 1990-95. Pvt. USAR, 1969-75. Mem. Internat. Assn. Fin. Planners, Jaguar Assocs. Group, Boy Scouts Am., Nat. Assn. Life Underwriters, Williamsburg Found., Nat. Trust for Historic Preservation. Democrat. Mem. Soc. of Friends. Avocations: downhill skiing, fly fishing. Office: Waddell & Reed 100 N Winchester Blvd Ste 260 Santa Clara CA 95050-6568

YOUNT, DAVID EUGENE, physicist, educator; b. Prescott, Ariz., June 5, 1935; s. Robert Ephram and Jeannette Francis (Judson) Y.; m. Christel Marlene Notz, Feb. 22, 1975; children—Laura Christine, Gregory Gordon, Steffen Jurgen Robert, Sonja Kate Jeannette. B.S. in Physics, Calif. Inst. Tech., 1957; M.S. in Physics, Stanford U., 1959, Ph.D. in Physics, 1963. Instr. Princeton U., 1962-63, asst. prof. physics, 1963-64, Minn. Mining and Mfg. fellow, 1963; NSF postdoctoral fellow U. Paris, Orsay, France, 1964-65; rsch. assoc. Stanford Linear Accelerator Ctr. Stanford U., 1965-69; assoc. prof. U. Hawaii, 1969-73, prof., 1973—, chmn. dept. physics and astronomy, 1979-85, acting asst. v.p. for acad. affairs, 1985-86, v.p. rsch. and grad. edn., 1986-95. Author: Who Runs the University: The Politics of Higher Education in Hawaii, 1985-92, 96. Mem. Am. Phys. Soc., Undersea and Hyperbaric Med. Soc., Am. Chem. Soc., U.S. Tennis Assn., Sigma Xi. Republican. Lutheran. Achievements include development (with J. Pine) of first high-energy positron beam, (with others) of SLAC two-meter streamer chamber; discovery (with others) of rho (1600) and psi (3772) mesons; development and experimental verification of theoretical model describing the nuclei which initiate bubble formation in aqueous media, including blood and tissue. Home: 5468 Opihi St Honolulu HI 96821-1924 Office: U Hawaii 2505 Correa Rd Honolulu HI 96822-2219

YOUNT, GEORGE STUART, paper company executive; b. L.A., Mar. 4, 1949; s. Stanley George and Agnes (Pratt) Y.; m. Geraldine Marie Silvio, July 18, 1970; children: Trisha Marie, Christopher George. Postgrad., Harvard U., 1983-86. Mgmt. trainee Fortifiber Corp., L.A., 1969-71, asst. to v.p. ops., 1971-75, adminstrv. v.p., treas., sec., 1975-85, exec. v.p., sec., CFO, bd. dirs., 1985-90, chmn., CEO, 1991—; pres., dir. Fonzia Corp., 1993—; bd. dirs. Stanwall Corp., pres., 1989—; bd. dirs. Thompson & Co. Ins. Svcs., Pasadena, Calif., 1996—; past pres. Hollister Ranch Cattle Coop., Gaviota, Calif., 1986-88; bd. dirs. Consol. Media Corp., Pasadena, Calif. Team leader L.A. United Way, 1981-86; bd. dirs. Big Bros. Greater L.A., 1984-87, L.A. coun. Boy Scouts Am., 1992—; mem. Young Pres. Orgn., 1991, forum moderator, 1993-95, chpt. forum officer, 1997—. Mem. Am. Paper Inst. (dir. 1993—, splty. coaters and extrusion sect. 1990—), Nat. Assn. Corp. Dirs., Harvard Bus. Club So. Calif., Harvard Owner/Pres. Mgmt. Program Club, Jonathan Club (L.A.), Rotary (bd. dirs. L.A. club 1992-94), Internat. Wine and Food Soc., Chaine des Rotisseurs Food and Wine Soc. Avocations: scuba diving, electronics, cattle ranching, computers. Office: Fortifiber Corp 1001 Tahoe Blvd Incline Village NV 89451-9309

YOWELL, ROBERT LEE, theater and dance educator; b. St. Louis, July 16, 1941; s. Walter J. and Edna Mae (Standford) Y.; m. Marsha Adele Reissaus, May 28, 1965; children—Robert Lee, Patrick Edward. AB, S.E. Mo. State U., 1966; MA, St. Louis U., 1968; PhD, Bowling Green State U., 1971; postgrad. Northwestern U., 1974. Instr., Florissant Valley Coll., Mo., 1967-68; teaching fellow Bowling Green State U., Ohio, 1968-71; asst. prof. Western Carolina U., Cullowhee, N.C., 1971-73; assoc. prof., chmn. dept. theatre and dance U. Ark.-Little Rock, 1973-81, U. Ala.-Birmingham, 1981-88; prof., chair dept. theater Calif. State U., San Bernardino, 1988—; prof. theatre No. Ariz. U.; bd. dirs. Birmingham Edn. Film Festival. Editor: Stepping Out: An Introduction to the Arts, 1985. Contbr. articles to profl. jours.; dir. 70 play prodns.; actor various stage, film prodns., TV commls. and tng. films. Active Am. Coll. Theatre Festival. Served with U.S. Army, 1959-62. Recipient 2 Obelisks (best direction; mus. comedy) Greater Birmingham Arts Alliance, Ala., 1982, 84, League award Inland Empire Theatre, Kennedy ctr. award for play El Paso Blue, 1994. Mem. Ala. Theatre League (treas., v.p., pres.), SW Theatre Conf. (sec., v.p. 1977-80), Ark. Alliance/Arts Edn. (v.p., pres. 1976-77), Conf. on Ark. Theatre (pres. 1975-76), SE Theatre, Am. Theatre Assn., So. Calif. Theatre Assn., Kennedy Ctr. Am. Theatre Assn. (Ariz. state chair). Democrat. Home: 4510 Flintwood Ln Flagstaff AZ 86004-7533 Office: Calif State U Dept Theatre San Bernardino CA 92407

YU, BEN W., materials engineer; b. Yiyang, China, Oct. 3, 1957; came to U.S., 1986; s. Bennan and Bingxiang (Lai) Y.; m. Emity Q. Liu, July 7, 1983; 1 child, Linda. BS in Materials Sci. and Engring., Huazhong U. Sci. & Tech., Wuhan, China, 1982; MS in Materials Engring., U. Minn., 1989, PhD in Materials Engring., 1994. Rsch. engr. CFD Rsch. Corp., Huntsville, Ala., 1994-97; sr. TCAD engr. Intel Corp., Hillsboro, Oreg., 1997—. Mem. Am. Vacuum Soc. Home: 7746 SW 189th Ave Aloha OR 97007-7613 Office: Intel 5200 NE Elam Young Pkwy Hillsboro OR 97124-6497

YU, KITSON SZEWAI, computer science educator; b. Toishan, Kwangtung, China, Apr. 4, 1950; came to U.S., 1969; s. Ho Yee and Yin Sang (Chan) Y.; m. Mabel Griseldis Wong, July 15, 1972; 1 child, Robin Roberta Emily. BS, Troy State U., 1974, MS, 1977, BS, 1980. Cert. systems profl.; cert. data processing educator. V.p. Troy (Ala.) Computer Ctr., 1976-81; computer instr. Tory State U., 1980-81, Linn Benton Community Coll., Albany, Oreg., 1981—; dir. real estate program Linn Benton Community Coll., 1985—; mng. broker Kitson Realty, Corvallis, Oreg., 1975—. Vice pres. econ. devel. Daleville C. of C., Ala., 1976; dir. Corvalis Youth Symphony, 1990-93. Mem. Data Processing Mgmt. Assn. (bd. dirs. at large 1982-93, v.p. 1984-85, pres. 1985-86), Greater Albany Rotary (treas. 1985—), Corvallis Multiple Listing Exch. (bd. dirs. 1990-94), Gamma Beta Phi. Home: 4926 SW Corbett Ave Apt 204 Portland OR 97201-3920 Office: Linn Benton C C 6500 Pacific Blvd SW Albany OR 97321-3755

YU, NANCY YEN-HO, artist, educator; b. Yentai, Shandong, China, Sept. 8, 1937; came to U.S., 1972; d. Sheng-Chung and Li-Si Liu; m. Peter Jye-Wu Yu, July 7, 1965; 1 child, Lisa Sh-Chen Yu. Student, Labrea Arts Inst., Milan, 1959-60; BA in Fine Arts, Nat. Taiwan Normal U., Taipei, 1964. vis. prof. Shandong Coll. Arts and Design, 1998; tchr. Fu-Shing Shan-Gong Profl. Sch., 1964-67. One-person shows include Freedom Party Club, Milan, 1969, Milan Libr., 1970, Chinese Conv. Ctr., L.A., 1989, Chinese Broadcasting Sta., 1990, Orgn. of Am. State Art Gallery, Washington, 1991, Chiang Kai-Sheck Meml. Hall Nat. Art Gallery, Taipei, 1993, Shi-R-Shi Art Gallery Han-Hwa Gallery, Arcadia, Calif., 1994, Evergreen Bookstore, L.A., 1995; exhibited in group shows Chinese Cultural Ctr., L.A., 1989, Chinese Nat. Day Exhbns., Taipei, 1991, Calif. Art Club, L.A., 1996, Beijing Fine ArtMus., 1996; featured in publs. including The Dictionary of the Achievements of World Chinese Artists. Recipient award for advocate of oversea's Chinese cultural activites in U.S.A., Com. of Overseas Chinese Affairs, 1995, award for advocate of overseas Chinese cultural activities in L.A., Office of China to L.A., 1996, 2d pl. award in watercolor painting San Gabriel Fine Art Assn., 1980, 1st, 2d, and 3d pl. award in watercolor painting Calif. Art Club, 1981, 2d pl. in watercolor painting Imperial Valley Fine Art Assn., 1994, Japan Nagoya City Edn. Coun. award, 1995, Spkr. of State of Eiji County award Japan Academician Assn., 1995, Cert. of Honor, World Famous Chinese Artists Almanac, 1996, Beijing Internat. Fine Arts Expo Com., 1996, diploma and cert. of merit Internat. Drawing Contest, World of Art/Art Addiction Internat. Gallery, Stockholm. Mem. Chinese Arts Soc. South Calif. (adviser 1995), Chinese Calligraphy and Painting Assn. (adviser 1995), Calif. Chinese Calligraphy Assn. (adviser 1995), San Marino Chinese Sch. (Chinese art tchr. 1997), L.A. Artist Assn. (pres. 1995—). Home: 2405 Lorain Rd San Marino CA 91108-2820

YUAN, ROBIN TSU-WANG, plastic surgeon; b. Boston, July 2, 1954; s. Robert Hsun-Piao and Grace I. (Chen) Y. AB, Harvard U., 1974, MD, 1978. Diplomate Am. Bd. Plastic Surgery. Resident in gen. surgery UCLA Med. Ctr., 1978-80, Cedars-Sinai Med. Ctr., L.A., 1980-81, 83-84; resident in plastic surgery U. Miami (Fla.)-Jackson Meml. Hosp., 1985-87; pvt. practice L.A., 1987—; clin. instr. div. plastic surgery UCLA, 1987—; vice-chief div. plastic surgery Cedars-Sinai Med. Ctr., L.A., 1991—; pres., chief exec. officer, founder Family of Independent Reconstructive Surgery Teams (F.I.R.S.T.), 1990—. Author: Cheer Up...You're Only Half Dead!, Reflections at Mid-Life, 1996; contbr. numerous articles to med. jours. Mem. Am. Soc. Plastic and Reconstructive Surgery, Am. Cleft Palate Assn., Calif. Med. Assn. (del.), L.A. County Med. Assn. (bd. govs. dist. 1), Phi Lambda (co-mgr. 1991—). Avocations: tennis, skiing, golf, creative writing, violin. Office: 150 N Robertson Blvd Ste 315 Beverly Hills CA 90211-2145

YUAN TSEH LEE, chemistry educator; b. Hsinchu, Taiwan, China, Nov. 29, 1936; came to U.S., 1962, naturalized, 1974; s. Tsefan and Pei (Tasi) L.; m. Bernice Wu, June 28, 1963; children: Ted, Sidney, Charlotte. BS, Nat. Taiwan U., 1959; MS, Nat. Tsinghua U., Taiwan, 1961; PhD, U. Calif., Berkeley, 1965. From asst. prof. to prof. chemistry U. Chgo., 1968-74; prof. emeritus U. Calif., Berkeley, 1974—, also former prin. investigator Lawrence Berkeley Lab. Contbr. numerous articles on chem. physics to profl. jours. Recipient Nobel Prize in Chemistry, 1986, Ernest O. Lawrence award Dept. Energy, 1981, Nat. Medal of Sci., 1986, 90, Peter Debye award for Phys. Chemistry, 1986; fellow Alfred P. Sloan, 1969-71, John Simon Guggenheim, 1976-77; Camille and Henry Dreyfus Found. Tchr. scholar, 1971-74, Harrison Howe award, 1983. Fellow Am. Phys. Soc.; mem. NAS, AAAS, Am. Acad. Arts and Scis., Am. Chem. Soc. Office: Acad Sinica, Nankang, Taipei 11529, Taiwan

YUEN, ANDY TAK SING, electronics executive; b. Wanchai, Hong Kong, Aug. 26, 1952; came to U.S., 1984; s. Yan Chong and Chi Oi (Tse) Y.; m. Kathy Man Kwan Chan, Jan. 29, 1983; children Lambert Hann Shi, Robin Hann Lang. Higher Cert. in Elec. Engring., Hong Kong Poly., 1975; Diploma in Bus. Mgmt., Hong Kong Bapt. Coll., 1976; Diploma in Exec. Devel., Chinese U., Hong Kong, 1981; MBA, Chui Hai Coll., Hong Kong, 1981; PhD in Bus. Mgmt., Calif. Coast U., 1987; diploma in mgmt. High Tech. Cos., Stanford Univ., 1996. Supervising engr. Teledyne Semiconductor Ltd., Kowloon, Hong Kong, 1976-79; ops. mgr. Microsemi (Hong Kong) Ltd., Kowloon, 1979-81, gen. mgr., 1981-84; corp. mgr. Microsemi Corp., Santa Ana, Calif., 1984-89, corp. v.p., 1989—; corp. dir. Semcon Electronics Pvt. Ltd., Bombay, 1984—. Author (books): Can Quality Circles Bring the Breakthrough to Hong Kong Industrial Management, 1982, Harnessing Japanese Quality Circles in Hong Kong, 1987. Fellow Inst. Sales and Mktg. Mgmt., Brit. Inst. Mgmt., Inst. Elec. and Electronics Inc. Engrs. Office: Microsemi Corp PO Box 26890 Santa Ana CA 92799-6890

YURIST, SVETLAN JOSEPH, mechanical engineer; b. Kharkov, USSR, Nov. 20, 1931; came to U.S., 1979, naturalized, 1985; s. Joseph A. and Rosalia S. (Zoilman) Y.; m. Imma Lea Erlikh, Oct. 11, 1960; 1 child, Eugene. M.S. in Mech. Engring. with honors, Poly. Inst., Odessa, USSR, 1954. Engr. designer Welding Equipment Plant, Novaya Utka, USSR, 1954-56; sr. tech. engr. Heavy Duty Automotive Crane Plant, Odessa, 1956-60, asst. chief matallugist, 1971-78; supr. research lab. Inst. Spl. Methods in Foundry Industry, Odessa, 1960-66, project engr. sci. research, 1966-71; engr. designer Teledyne Cast Product, Pomona, Calif., 1979-81; sr. mech. engr. Walt Elliot Disney Enterprises, Glendale, Calif., 1981-83; foundry liaison engr. Pacific Pumps div. Dresser Industries, Inc., Huntington Park, Calif., 1984-86; casting engr. Superior Industries Internat., Inc., Van Nuys, Calif., 1986-89; mech. engr. TAMCO Steel, Rancho Cucamonga, Calif., 1989-96. Recipient award for design of automatic lines for casting electric motor parts USSR Ministry Machine Bldg. and Handtools Mfr., 1966, for

equipment for permanent mold casting All Union Exhbn. of Nat. Econ. Achievements, 1966-70. Mem. Am. Foundrymen's Soc. Contbr. reports, articles to collections All Union Confs. Spl. Methods in Foundry, USSR; USSR patentee permanent mold casting. Home: 184 W Armstrong Dr Claremont CA 91711-1701

YUTKIN, GERALD DAVID, cable television executive; b. Chgo., Sept. 27, 1943; s. Ira and Doris Y.; children: Michael G., Joshua A. BA, U. Ill., 1966; MA, No. Ill. U., 1971; MBA, U. Chgo., 1977. With prodn. dept. Sta. WTTW-TV, Chgo., 1967-71; producer, dir. Supt. Pub. Instrn., Springfield, Ill., 1971-74; dir. broadcasting Chgo. Bd. Rabbis, 1974-77; asst. regional mgr. Am. TV and Communications, Appleton, Wis., 1978-79; regional mgr. Am. TV and Communications, Council Bluffs, Iowa, 1979-83; v.p. Jones Intercable, Englewood, Colo., 1983-89; mng. dir. East London Telecommunications, 1989-91; fund v.p. Jones Intercable, Englewood, 1991; pres. Jones Satellite Programming, Inc., Englewood, 1991-93; ind. cons. Chgo., 1993-95; mng.dir. Bresnan Polska, Warsaw, 1995-96; pres. Coaxial Internat., Denver, 1996—. Recipient Emmy award Chgo. Acad. TV Arts and Scis., 1975. Mem. Cable TV Assn. U.K. (bd. dirs. 1990-91). Office: Coaxial Internat 4582 S Ulster St Denver CO 80237-2632

YUZEITIS, JAMES RICHARD, information specialist; b. Chgo., Nov. 11, 1942; s. Stanley J. and Amy B. (English) Y.; m. Susan C. London, Oct. 7, 1967; children: Timothy, David, Amy. BA in Econs., Loyola U., Chgo., 1965, MS in Personnel Mgmt., 1968. Personnel adminstr. Chgo. Police Dept., 1965-67; personnel asst. McDonald's Corp., Chgo., 1967-69; ops. trainee McDonald's Corp., Washington, 1969-70; personnel mgr. McDonald's Corp., Detroit, 1970-72; licensing mgr. McDonald's Corp., Columbus, Ohio, 1972-73; internat. personnel cons. McDonald's Corp., Oakbrook, Ill., 1973-80, dir. of human resources, 1980-86, dir. human resources devel., 1986-91; pres. Quality Surveys, Inc., Big Timber, Mont., 1991—; cons. Ronald McDonald Children's Charities, Chgo., 1986-88. Cons. and vol. Ronald McDonald Houses, Chgo., 1987; vol. Crazy Mont. Mus. Soc., Big Timber, 1991-92; bd. dirs. Pioneer Med. Ctr., Big Timber, 1993—. Recipient medal of Merit Cath. Youth Orgn., Chgo., 1960. Mem. Soc. for Human Resource Mgmt., Human Resource Planning Soc., Indsl. Rels. Rsch. Soc. Avocations: ranch mgmt., fishing, music. Home: PO Box 1244 Big Timber MT 59011-1244 Office: Quality Surveys Inc PO Box 1089 Big Timber MT 59011-1089

ZABINSKY, ZELDA BARBARA, operations researcher, industrial engineering educator; b. Tonawanda, N.Y., Oct. 31, 1955; d. Joseph Marvin and Helen Phyllis (Kava) Z.; m. John Clinton Palmer, July 15, 1979; children: Rebecca Ann Zabinsky, Aaron Zeff Palmer. BS, U. Puget Sound, Tacoma, 1977; MS, U. Mich., 1984, PhD, 1985. Tutor math. U. Puget Sound, 1975-77; programmer, analyst Nat. Marine Fisheries, Seattle, 1977, Boeing Computer Svcs., Seattle, 1977-78; sr. systems analyst Vector Rsch. Inc., Ann Arbor, Mich., 1980-84; asst. prof. indsl. engring. U. Wash., Seattle, 1985-93, assoc. prof. indsl. engring., 1993-98, affiliated prof. mech. engring., 1993—, affiliated prof. civil engring., 1996—, prof. indsl. engring., 1998—; cons. Boeing Corp., Seattle, 1987, Numerical Methods, Inc., Seattle, 1989-90, METRO, Seattle, 1992. Contbr. articles to tech. jours. Mem. faculty adv. bd. Women in Engring., U. Wash., 1990—. Recipient E. Goman Math. award, 1977, Rsch. Initiation award NSF, 1992-95; Howarth-Thompson scholar, 1973-77; Benton fellow, 1983-84, Erskine fellow 1998; rsch. grantee NSF, NASA-Langley, FAA, Nat. Forest Svc., NATO, Boeing, 1985—. Mem. Ops. Rsch. Soc. Am., Inst. Indsl. Engrs. (sr.), Math. Programming Soc., Mortar Board, Phi Kappa Phi. Jewish. Avocations: family activities, camping, skiing, windsurfing. Office: U Wash PO Box 352650 Seattle WA 98195-2650

ZABSKY, JOHN MITCHELL, engineering executive; b. Joplin, Mo., Apr. 18, 1933; s. Joseph Anthony and Joan (Lucas) Z. AS, Joplin Jr. Coll., 1953; BSME, U. Mo., 1956; MSME, U. Kans., 1965. Profl. engr., Mo. System engr. Bendix KCD, Kansas City, Mo., 1958-62; rsch. engr. Rocketdyne, Neosho, Mo., 1962-65, Boeing Co., Huntsville, Ala., 1965-66; prin. rsch. engr., scientist Honeywell Inc., St. Paul, 1966-71; chief engr. Pressure Tank & Pipe Fabrication Co., Nashville, 1971-72, Engring. for Industry, Danville, Va., 1972-73; area mgr. fluid machinery Dresser Adv. Tech. Ctr., Irvine, Calif., 1973-85; v.p. ops. ATI, Laguna Niguel, Calif., 1985-93; pres. Cytoprobe, San Diego, 1993-94, v.p. ops., 1994-95; cons. Oral Care Products, L.A., 1990-92, Kleenair Sys., Inc., Irvine, Calif., 1995—. Patentee in field. Pres. Mpls.-St. Paul Singletons, 1969-72. Mem. AIAA, ASME, Mo. Soc. Profl. Engrs., Soc. Mfg. Engrs. Home: 3640 S Main St Apt C Santa Ana CA 92707-5726

ZACH, ELIZABETH PIROSKA, journalist; b. Sacramento, Calif., Apr. 6, 1971; d. Joseph Laszlo and Lourdes Garcia (Sanchez) Z. BA in History magna cum laude, U. Portland, 1993; MS in Journalism, Columbia U., 1996. Staff writer Wing Tips, Sacramento, 1991, Space Maker, North Highlands, Calif., 1992; freelance writer, 1993-95; peace corps. vol. Poland, 1993-95; reporter Alexandria (La.) Daily Town Talk, 1996-97, Sacramento Bee/Neighbors, 1997-98, Vacaville (Calif.) Reporter, 1998—. Mem. LWV, Soc. Profl. Journalists. Home: 2806 Eel Ave Davis CA 95616-2914 Office: Vacaville Reporter 916 Cotting Ln Vacaville CA 95688-8710

ZACHER, EDWIN G., structural engineer; b. Austin, Mich., Feb. 23, 1920; s. Charles F. and Caroline (Mills) Z.; m. Rose McKomel, Aug. 24, 1943; children: Kristine, Kerilee. BS in Civil Engring., U. Calif., Berkeley, 1948. Cert. civil and structural engr., Calif., Nev., Hawaii. Plan check engr. Contra Costa County Bldg. Inspection Dept., Martinez, Calif., 1948-54; rate setting engr., investigator Pacific Fire Rating Bur., San Francisco, 1954-61; structural engr. H.J. Brunnier Assocs., San Francisco, 1961—, v.p., 1990-97, pres., 1997—. Chmn. Bldg. Code Appeals Bd., Berkeley, 1985—. Comdr. USNR, 1940-46, PTO. Recipient John Fies award Internat. Conf. Bldg. Ofcls., Whittier, Calif., 1993. Fellow ASCE, Structural Engrs. Assn. Calif. (dir. 1979-81); mem. Structural Engrs. No. Calif. (hon., pres. 1978-79, Edwin G. Zacher award 1996), Engrs. Earthquake Rsch. Inst. Office: HJ Brunnier Assocs 55 New Montgomery St Ste 608 San Francisco CA 94105-3433

ZACHER, VALERIE IRENE, interior designer; b. Woodland, Calif., Dec. 12, 1942; d. Albert Richard and Laura Ruth (Mast) Z.; m. William Robert Wallace, June 14, 1964 (div. Oct. 1968); 1 child, Jason Zachery Wallace. BA in Polit. Sci., Stanford U., 1964; AS in Interior Design, West Valley Coll., 1982; cert. TESL, U. Calif. Santa Cruz, Santa Clara, 1994. Owner, operator Artefactorage, Fresno, Calif., 1968-77; owner, designer Viz a Viz, Los Gatos, Calif., 1978-82; facilities project mgr. Nat. Semiconductor, Santa Clara, Calif., 1982-85; project supr. Mervyns, Hayward, Calif., 1985-86; interior designer, project mgr. Charles Schwab & Co., San Francisco, 1986-87; small bus. advisor US Peace Corps, Gaborone, Botswana, 1987-89, Swedish Coop. Ctr., Gaborone, 1989-90; English tchr. YCC Am. Club, Yokohama, Japan, 1992-93; interior design cons. Los Gatos, 1993—; design/facilities cons. Octel Comm. Corp., Milpitas, Calif., 1994-97; interior designer Am. Cancer Soc. Designers Showcase, 1994, 95, 96, San Jose Symphony Designers Showhouse, 1998. Mem. Internat. Facilities Mgrs. Assn. Avocations: gourmet cooking, gardening, travel. Home and Office: 16721 Madrone Ave Los Gatos CA 95030-4120

ZACK, JAMES G(ORDON), JR., construction claims executive, consultant; b. Springfield, Mass., Sept. 6, 1946; s. James Gordon and Marione Mildred (Langevin) Z.; m. Yvonne Eileen Beezley, Oct. 26, 1970; children: Jennifer Yvonne, Stacy Rebecca, James William, Trevor David. AB in Polit. Sci., Assumption Coll., 1968; MPA, U. S.C., 1975. Dir. budgets and grants adminstrn. S.C. Dept. Health and Environ. Control, Columbia, 1972-78; mgr. constrn. contracts group CH2M Hill, Inc., Milw., 1978-85; mgr. scheduling and claims dept. CH2M Hill, Inc., L.A., 1986-95; mng. dir. constrn. claims and litigation support svcs. High-Point Rendel, L.A., 1995-97; v.p. Pinnacle One, Irvine, Calif., 1997—; cons. EPA, 1977-88; reviewer Engring. Mgmt. Jour., 1987—; expert witness on constrn. litigation, tech. profl. devel. seminars. Contbr. articles to profl. jours. Commr. Pacifica dist. Boy Scouts Am., 1987-94, scoutmaster, 1994—; mem. Calif. Compact Com., Huntington Beach, 1988-97. Mem. ASCE, Am. Assn. Cost Engrs., Project Mgmt. Inst., Constrn. Mgmt. Assn. Am., Am. Arbitration Assn.,. Methodist. Avocations: camping, reading, Boy Scout activities. Home: 9531 Netherway Dr Huntington Beach CA 92646-6061 Office: Pinnacle One 1100 Campus Dr Ste 650 Irvine CA 92612-4696

ZAFIROPOULO, ARTHUR, executive. CEO, pres., chmn. Ultratech Stepper, San Jose, Calif. Office: 3050 Zanker Rd San Jose CA 95134-2126*

ZAHARIA, ERIC STAFFORD, developmental disabilities program administrator; b. Pomona, Calif., Aug. 24, 1948; s. Edgar A. and Dorothy (Stafford) Z.; m. Caryle Koentz, Dec. 23, 1967; children: Tye W., Tieg A. BA, Pomona Coll., 1970; MEd, U. Ariz.-Tucson, 1973; PhD, George Peabody Coll., 1978; postgrad., Govt. Execs. Inst. U. N.C., Chapel Hill, 1981. Mental retardation worker Ariz. Tng. Program, Tucson, 1970-71, unit dir., 1971-73; dir. residential svcs. Willmar State Hosp., (Minn.), 1973-76; rsch. asst. Inst. on Mental Retardation and Intellectual Devel., Nashville, 1976-78; dir. mental retardation program svcs. Dept. Mental Health/Mental Retardation, State of Tenn., Nashville, 1978-79; dir. Caswell Ctr., Kinston, N.C., 1979-86; program adminstr. Colo. Div. of Devel. Disabilities, Denver, 1986-90; dir. Utah divsn. Svcs. for People with Disabilities, Salt Lake City, 1990-95; ind. cons. Park City, Utah, 1995—; mem. adj. faculty East Carolina U., Greenville, 1979-86; bd. dirs. Neuse Enterprises Inc., Kinston. Chmn. Big Bros./Sisters Kinston Inc., 1980-83; mem. N.C. Coalition for Community Svc., 1982-85. Mem. Am. Assn. Mental Retardation, Nat. Assn. Supts., Pub. Residential Facilities, Assn. Retarded Citizens, Kinston C. of C. (bd. dirs. 1983-86). Home: 8010 Juniper Dr Park City UT 84098-5370 Office: 120 N 200 W Salt Lake City UT 84103-1550

ZAHN, KARL THEODORE, information systems specialist, computer educator; b. Balt., Mar. 14, 1951; s. Theodore D. and Ruth Zahn; m. Elaine Chizuko Morimoto; children: Rick, Maria, Matthew. BS in Edn., Towson State U., 1977; postgrad., Calif. State U., Long Beach, 1977-79. Sr. field engring. instr. Western Regional Tng. Ctr. Unisys, El Monte, Calif., 1978-83, sr. media developer, 1983-86; sys. analysis engr. Unisys Mfg. Plant, Mission Viejo, Calif., 1987-88; sr. v.p. advanced technologies Syndetic Tech., Huntington Beach, Calif., 1988-91; dir. worldwide edn. Inference Corp., Novato, Calif., 1991—; cons. Multimedia/Knowledge Sys., Westminster, Calif., 1990—; chmn. creative dir. Sa. WZMG, Garden Grove, Calif., 1996-97. Inventor Decision Power, B9494 Simulator, Z-Filter, and CBR Express Tester. With USNR, 1969-71. Recipient Excellence Achievement award N.Am. Consulting, 1995. Mem. NRA (life), Golden Eagles (charter).

ZAHNER, DOROTHY SIMKIN, elementary education educator; b. Chengdu, Szechuan, China, May 1; came to U.S. in the 1930s; d. Robert Louis and Margaret Isadore (Timberlake) Simkin; divorced; children: Mary de Avilan, Robert Louis. BA in Sociology, Whittier Coll.; MLS, U. So. Calif., L.A. Cert. tchr. Calif., Ariz. Tchr. L.A. and Pasadena (Calif.) Schs., 1969-93; dir., owner Betty Ingram Sch., North Hollywood, Calif., 1976-79; dir. Foothill Nursery Sch., La Crescenta, Calif., 1970s; tchr. L.A. Unified Sch. Dist.; guest tchr. Washington Unified Sch. Dist., Phoenix, 1994-97; guest tchr. Osborn Sch. Dist., 1998—. Author: (poetry) Yucca Poetry Workshop, 1993-94, Treasured Poems of America, 1993, internat. poetry publ., others. Bd. dirs. Ariz. Tenants Assn., Phoenix, 1994, 95; vol. Am. Friends Svc. Com., Phila., Calif., 1985—, Common Cause, L.A., 1990, Dem. Candidates, L.A. and Phoenix. Recipient award for a poem, Ariz. State Poetry Soc., Phoenix, 1995. Mem. Phoenix Poetry Soc. (com. mem., pres. 1998), Phoenix Writers Club (sec. 1998), Alameda Writers Group. Avocations: theatre, films, music, swimming, reading.

ZAHRT, WILLIAM DIETRICH, II, lawyer; b. Dayton, Ohio, July 12, 1944; s. Kenton William and Orpha Catharine (Wagner) Z.; m. Patricia Ann Marek, June 10, 1969; children—Justin William, Alitheia Patricia. BS in Physics, Yale U., 1966, JD, 1969, M of Pub. and Pvt. Mgmt., 1990. Bar: N.Y. 1970, Ohio 1972, Tex. 1982, N.C. 1992, U.S. Ct. Appeals (Fed. cir.) 1977. Assoc. Kenyon & Kenyon, N.Y.C., 1969-71; assoc. Biebel, French & Nauman, Dayton, Ohio, 1971-80; sr. patent atty. Schlumberger Well Svcs., Houston, 1980-82; sole practice, Kingwood, Tex., 1982-85, 88-90; patent atty. Shell Oil Co., Houston, 1985-88; sr. patent counsel Raychem Corp., Fuquay-Varina, N.C., 1990-97, asst. gen. counsel Advanced Micro Devices, Sunnyvale, Calif., 1997—. Mem. ABA, Am. Intellectual Property Law Assn., Tex. Bar Assn., Peninsula Intellectual Property Law Assn., Dayton Racquet Club, Masons. Anglican. Home: 629 Villa Centre Way San Jose CA 95128-5138 Office: PO Box 3453 One AMD Pl Sunnyvale CA 94088

ZAID, MEL, sculptor; b. San Francisco; s. Max and Rose (Cohan) Z.; m. Kena Hodge; children: Jonathan, Adam, Andrew, Tina. BSME, Stanford U., 1948, MS in Engring. Mechs., 1949; M of Engring., ScD, MIT, 1951. Cons. N.Y.C., 1957-60; pres., dir. rsch. Technik Inc., N.Y.C., 1960-68; dir. advanced rsch. Colt Industries, N.Y.C., 1968-71; cons. F.M. Industries, Inc., Mass., 1971-97. Prin works exhibited at New Sch., N.Y.C., Nausset Sch. Sculpture, Cape Cod, Mass. Coll. Art, Boston, Fla. U., Boca Raton, Perma Flex Corp., Columbus, Ohio, others. MIT fellow, Std. Oil Ind. fellow. Mem. Phi Beta Kappa, Sigma Xi, Tau Beta Phi. Home: PO Box 20148 Santa Barbara CA 93120-0148

ZAIDI, EMILY LOUISE, retired elementary school educator; b. Hoquiam, Wash., Apr. 20, 1924; d. Burdick Newton and Emily Caroline (Williams) Johnston; m. M. Baqar Abbas Zaidi, June 12, 1949 (dec. Dec. 1983). BA in Edn. and Social Studies, Ea. Wash. State U., 1948; MEd, U. Wash., 1964, EdD, 1974. Tchr. 4th grade Hoquiam Schs., 1948-49; tchr. grades 5-6 Lake Washington Sch. Dist., Kirkland, Wash., 1949-51; tchr. grades 2-3 Port Angeles (Wash.) Schs., 1951-54; tchr. grade 2 Seattle Schs., 1954-55; tchr., reading specialist Northshore sch. Dist., Bothell, Wash., 1955-69, Sacramento City Schs., 1969-87; ret.; mem. Calif. State Instructional Materials Panel, Sacramento, 1975. Mem. Sacramento Opera Assn., 1986—, Sacramento Ballet Assn., 1987—, Sacramento Symphony Assn., 1985—. Fulbright Commn. Exchange Tchr., 1961-62. Mem. Reading Club, Comstock Club. Democrat. Avocations: writing, children's literature, reading, travel. Home: 4230 N River Way Sacramento CA 95864-6055

ZAIDI, IQBAL MEHDI, biochemist, scientist; b. Bijnor, India, June 30, 1957; s. Iqbal Haider and Habib (Zehra) Z.; m. Nuzhat Shikoh, Jan. 2, 1993; 1 child, Shan Zehra. BS in Chemistry with honors, Aligarh M. U., 1976, MS in Biochemistry, 1978, PhD in Biochemistry, 1984. Cert. in radiation. Rsch. fellow Indsl. Toxicology Rsch. Ctr., Lucknow, India, 1979-83; rsch. affiliate N.Y. State Health Dept., Albany, 1984-91; scientist Applied Biosystems div. Perkin Elmer Corp., Foster City, Calif., 1991—. Contbr. articles to profl. jours. Mem. AAAS, Am. Chem. Soc. (biochem. tech. div. 1992—), Shia Assn. Bay Area, N.Y. Acad. Scis. Avocations: photography, swimming, travel, natural history. Office: Perkin Elmer Corp Applied Biosystems Divsn 850 Lincoln Centre Dr Foster City CA 94404-1128

ZAJAC, JOHN, semiconductor equipment company executive; b. N.Y.C., July 21, 1946; s. John Andrew and Catherine (Canepa) Z.; m. Vera Barbagallo, Jan. 13, 1973; children: Jennifer, Michelle. AAS, NYU, 1966; BEE, U. Ky., 1968. Project engr. B.C.D. Computing, N.Y.C., 1968-70; v.p. Beacon Systems, Commack, N.Y., 1970-73, E.T. Systems, Santa Clara, Calif., 1973-77; v.p. research and devel. Eaton Corp., Sunnyvale, Calif., 1977-81; pres. Semitech/Gen. Signal, Los Gatos, Calif., 1981-83; mgr. advanced product div. Tegal/Motorola Inc., Novato, Calif., 1983-86; v.p. research and devel. U.S.A. Inc., San Jose, Calif., 1986-94; staff scientist Mattson Tech., Fremont, Calif., 1994—. Author: Delicate Balance, 1988, Pyramids, Prophecy and 666, 1999; holder of 22 patents in field; guest TV and radio. Office: Mattson Tech 3550 W Warren Ave Fremont CA 94538-6499

ZALESKI, BRIAN WILLIAM, computer programmer, analyst; b. Trenton, N.J., Oct. 27, 1962; s. Joseph Rudolph and Roseline (Moore) Z.; m. Petra Gertrude Tucker, Apr. 10, 1983 (div.); children: Natasha Reneé, Tatyana Amber. Student, Def. Lang. Inst., Monterey, Calif., 1980-81; BS, Palmer Coll., 1992, D of Chiropractic, 1992; MS in Computer Info. Sys., U. Phoenix, 1999. Indsl. disability evaluator, Calif.; qualified med. evaluator, Calif. Grad. rschr. Palmer Coll. of Chiropractice, Davenport, Iowa, 1991-92; chiropractor Peninsula Spinal Care, Daly City, Calif., 1992; chiropractor Creekside Family Chiropractic, Vacaville, Calif., 1992-96, Suisun City, Calif., 1996-98; sr. programmer, analyst Co-op Comm. Inc., San Rafael, Calif., 1999—; prin. investigator, presenter Internat. Conf. on Spinal Manipulation, 1992. Editor Napa Solano Chiropractor, 1996-98. Baseball umpire Iowa High Schs., Davenport, 1989-92, Men's Sr. League, Davenport, 1989-91, No. Calif. Umpires Assn., San Mateo, Calif., 1992; mem. adv. bd. Solano Serve Our Sr. Recipient scholarship Internat. Chiropractors Assn. 1989, 90, Cecil M. Grogan scholarship Palmer Internat. Alumni Assn., 1991, Alma Nielsen scholarship Internat. Chiropractors Assn. Aux., 1991, Student Rsch. grant Palmer Coll. Chiropractic, 1992, Best State Assn. Page award Am. Chiropractic Assn.; named to Dean's List, 1991-92. Mem. Internat. Chiropractors Assn. (coun. on chiropractic pediatrics), Calif. Chiropractic Assn. (net masters com., ins. rels. com., webmaster home pages sect., dep. chair membership dept., co-chair tech. comm. com., scholarship com., distance learning com., Presdl. award), Assn. for History of Chiropractic, Palmer Internat. Alumni Assn., Napa/Solano Chiropractic Soc. (pres., editor), Cal Chiropractic Assn. (membership dept., dep. chair, co-chair tech. comm. com., scholarship com., distance learning com., Presdl. award, Won ACA's Best Chiropractic Assn. Web Page), Masons, Delta Sigma Chi, Chi Rho Theta. Republican. Office: Co-op Comm Inc 899 Northgate Ave Ste 104 San Rafael CA 94903

ZALEWSKI, WOJCIECH MARIA, curator; b. Gdynia, Poland, Mar. 20, 1937; s. Atanazy and Małgorzata (Sentkowska) Z.; m. Rosemarie Böhm, Aug. 31, 1968; children: Barbara, Marcus. MA in Theology, Cath. U., Lublin, Poland, 1965; Lic. Bible Studies, Pontifical Bibl. Inst., Rome, 1967; D of Theology, Gregorian U., Rome, 1968; MA in Libr. Sci., San Jose State U., 1971. Curator Slavic collections Stanford (Calif.) U., 1971—, lectr. Slavic langs. and lits., 1973—. Author: Russian-English Dictionaries, 1981, Czesław Miłosz Bibliography, 1983, Fundamentals of Russian Reference Works, 1985, Slavic Collections at Stanford History, 1987, Dealers of Polish and Russian Books, 1990; author numerous poems; contbr. articles to profl. jours. Rsch. grantee Internat. Rsch. and Exchanges Bd., 1992, 94, 95, 98. Mem. ALA (Slavic and east European chair 1980-81, 86-87), Am. Assn. Advancement Slavic Studies, Polish Inst. Arts and Scis. Home: 162 Highland Ave San Carlos CA 94070-1909 Office: Stanford U Librs Stanford CA 94305-6004

ZALTA, EDWARD, otorhinolaryngologist, physician; b. Houston, Mar. 2, 1930; s. Nouri Louis and Marie Zahde (Lizmi) Z.; m. Carolyn Mary Gordon, Oct. 8, 1971; 1 child, Ryan David; children by previous marriage: Nouri Allan, Lori Ann, Barry Thomas, Marci Louise. BS, Tulane U., 1952, MD, 1956. Diplomate Am. Bd. Quality Assurance and Utilization Rev. Physicians. Intern Brooke Army Hosp., San Antonio, 1956-57; resident in otolaryngology U.S. Army Hosp., Ft. Campbell, Ky., 1957-60; practice medicine specializing in otolaryngology Glendora, West Covina and San Dimas, Calif., 1960-82; ENT cons. City of Hope Med. Ctr., 1961-76; mem. staff Foothill Presbyn.; past pres. L.A. Found. Cmty. Svc., L.A. Poison Info. Ctr., So. Calif. Physicians Coun., Inc.; founder, chmn. bd. dirs. CAPP CARE, INC.; founder Inter-Hosp. Coun. Continuing Med. Edn.; trustee U.S. Pharmacopeial Conv., Inc.; mem. adv. bd. Global Health Sys., Inc. Author: (with others) Medicine and Your Money; mem. editl. staff Jour. Assn. Managed Healthcare Orgns., Managed Care Interface, Mng. Employee Health Benefits; mem. editl. adv. bd. Inside Medicaid Managed Care, Disease Mgmt. News, Managed Care Outlook; contbr. articles to profl. jours. Pres. bd. govs. Glendora Unified Sch. Dist., 1965-71; mem. Calif. Cancer Adv. Coun., 1967-71, Commn. of Californias, L.A. County Commn. on Economy and Efficiency. Served to capt. M.C. AUS, 1957-60. Recipient Award of Merit Order St. Lazarus, 1981. Mem. AMA, Calif. Med. Assn., Am. Acad. Otolaryngology, Am. Coun. Otolaryngology, Am. Assn. Preferred Provider Orgns. (past pres.), Am. Coll. Med. Quality, L.A. County Med. Assn. (pres. 1980-81), Kappa Nu, Phi Delta Epsilon, Glendora CountryClub, Centurion Club, Sea Bluff Beach and Racquet Club; Center Club (Costa Mesa, Calif.), Pacific Golf Club (San Juan, Capistrano). Republican. Jewish. Home: 3 Morning Dove Laguna Niguel CA 92677-5331 Office: West Tower 4000 Macarthur Blvd Ste 10000 Newport Beach CA 92660-2526

ZALUTSKY, MORTON HERMAN, lawyer; b. Schenectady, Mar. 8, 1935; s. Albert and Gertrude (Daffner) Z.; m. Audrey Englebardt, June 16, 1957; children: Jane, Diane, Samuel. BA, Yale U., 1957; JD, U. Chgo., 1960. Bar: Oreg. 1961. Law clk. to presiding judge Oreg. Supreme Ct., 1960-61; assoc. Hart, Davidson, Veazie & Hanlon, 1961-63, Veatch & Lovett, 1963-64, Morrison, Bailey, Dunn, Cohen & Miller, 1964-69; prin. Morton H. Zalutsky, P.C., 1970-76; ptnr. Dahl, Zalutsky, Nichols & Hinson, 1977-79, Zalutsky & Klarquist, P.C., Portland, Oreg., 1980-85, Zalutsky, Klarquist & Johnson, Inc., Portland, 1985-94; Zalutsky & Klarquist, P.C., Portland, 1994—; instr. Portland State U., 1961-64, Northwestern Sch. of Law, 1969-70; assoc. prof. U. Miami Law Sch.; lectr. Practising Law Inst., 1971—, Oreg. State Bar Continuing Legal Edn. Program, 1970, Am. Law Inst.-ABA Continuing Legal Edn. Program, 1973—, 34th, 37th NYU ann. insts. fed. taxation, So. Fed. Tax Inst., U. Miami Inst. Estate Planning, Southwestern Legal Found., Internat. Foun. Employee Benefit Plans, numerous other profl. orgns.; dir. A-E-F-C Pension Plan, 1994—, chair, 1998—. Author: (with others) The Professional Corporation in Oregon, 1970, 82; contbg. author: The Dentist and the Law, 3d edit.; editor-in-chief (retirement plans) Matthew Bender's Federal Tax Service, 1987—; contbr. to numerous publs. in field. Mem. vis. com. U. Chgo. Law Sch., 1986-88. Mem. ABA (vice chair profl. svcs. 1987-89, mem. coun. tax sect. 1985-87, spl. coord. 1980-85), Am. Law Inst., Am. Bar Retirement Assn. (trustee, bd. dirs., vice chair 1990-91, chair 1991-92), Multnomah County Bar Assn., Am. Tax Lawyers (charter mem.), Oreg. Estate Planning Coun. Jewish. Home: 3118 SW Fairmount Blvd Portland OR 97201-1466 Office: 3d Fl 215 SW Washington St Portland OR 97204-2636

ZAMBAI, ROBYN S., business owner, therapist; b. Coolville, Utah, July 1, 1950; d. Louis Otis and Ione (Baker) Stotts; m. Frank A. Zambai, Dec. 19, 1970 (dec. July 1994); children: Tori L., Mandi M., Clint F. Student, U. Wyo., 1968-69, Western Wyo. C.C., 1969. Cert. divorce and child custody mediator, conflict resoultions specialist; apprenticeship cert. therapeutic massage. Field exec. Wyo. Girl Scout Coun., Casper, 1981-87; funding chairperson Expo Experience, Rock Springs, Wyo., 1987-88; bus. mgr. Total Exposure, Rock Springs, Wyo., 1989-92; owner, corp. pres. Total Exposure Inc., Rock Springs, Wyo., 1992-98, Alpha Omega Inc., Rock Springs, 1998—. Vol. United Way, Rock Springs, 1985-95; mem. adv. bd. Sweetwater County Support and Safe House, Rock Springs, 1994-96; bd. dirs. YWCA Sweetwate County, 1991—. Recipient Appreciation award Wyo. Girl Scout Coun., 1987. Mem. Am. Massage Therapy Assn. Avocations: painting, boating. Office: Alpha Omega Inc 440 Bridger Ave Rock Springs WY 82901-5211

ZAMBETTI, DENIS EGAN, product specialist; b. Riverdale, N.Y., Oct. 18, 1953; s. Emil John and Teresa Veronica (McSherry) Z. BS, U.S. Mil. Acad., 1977; MBA, Golden Gate U., 1985; grad., Command and Gen. Staff Coll., 1993. Commd. 2d lt. U.S. Army, 1977, advanced through ranks to capt., 1977-81, resigned, 1985; platoon leader B Co. 2d/22d Inf., Wiesbaden, Fed. Republic Germany, 1977-78, mortar platoon leader, 1978-79, exec. officer, 1979-80; communications and electronics officer HHC Co. 2d/22d Inf., Wiesbaden, 1980-81; morale support fund custodian U.S. Mil. Command Activity Group, Bad Kreuznach, Fed. Republic Germany, 1981-82; equal opportunity staff officer HQ Presidio of San Francisco, 1982-83, chief reserve pay, 1983-85; peninsula area mgr. Beringer Wines/Wineworld, San Francisco, 1985-87; nat. accts. mgr. SW region Beringer Wines/Wineworld, Mission Viejo, Calif., 1987—; v.p. product devel. IQUEST Bus. Devel., Santa Clara, Calif., 1988—; nat. accts. mgr. Sutter Home Winery, 1988-92; mgr. sales Union Camp Corp., Stockton, Calif., 1992-95; bulk specialist Union Camp Corp., Hanford, Calif., 1995—. Lt. comdr. USAR, 1996. Named One of Outstanding Young Men of Am. Jaycees, 1983. Mem. Knights of the Vine, West Point Soc. of Bay Area (bd. govs. 1982-85), West Point Soc. Orange County (admissions rep. 1987—, mil. liaison officer 1991—). Democrat. Roman Catholic. Avocations: skiing, cooking, golf, travel. Home: 4843 Kimberly Common Livermore CA 94550-7707

ZANDVAKILI, KATAYOON, writer; b. Tehran, Iran, Oct. 7, 1967; came to U.S., 1976; d. Amir Hossein and Nahid (Farazian) Z. BA, U. Calif., Berkeley, 1988; MFA, Sarah Lawrence Coll., 1992. Editl./oral history asst. McKinsey & Co., San Francisco, 1994-97; West Coast assoc. Pubs. Weekly, Woodacre, Calif., 1997-98. Author: (poetry) Deer Table Legs, 1998; contbg. poet: A World Between, 1998; contbr. work to Five Fingers Rev., Hawai'i Rev., Mass. Rev. Home: 11 Sotelo Ave Piedmont CA 94611-3534

ZANETTA, JOSEPH MICHAEL, university administrator, lawyer; b. Jamestown, N.Y., Apr. 26, 1953; s. Joseph A. and Freda (Felanzo) Z.; m. Ellen L. Leggett, June 2, 1979; 1 child, Samuel Leggett Zanetta. BS, Cornell U., 1975, JD, 1978. Bar: N.Y. 1980. Mem. Hartley & Fessenden, Attys.,

Jamestown, 1978-79; devel. officer Cornell U., Ithaca, N.Y., 1979-82; assoc. dir. maj. gifts Tufts U., Medford, Mass., 1982-83; dir. devel. Belmont Hill Sch., Belmont, Mass., 1983-86; exec. dir. external affairs Sch. Bus. Adminstrn. U. So. Calif., L.A., 1986-93; v.p. advancement Whittier (Calif.) Coll., 1993—; chmn. Pasadena Enterprise Ctr. Sec.-treas. Lord Found. of Calif., L.A., 1988-93. Mem. Coun. for Advancement and Support of Edn. (chair nat. confs. 1990, 92), Univ. Club of L.A. (bd. dirs. 1991—), Phi Kappa Phi (bd. dirs. 1991—). Roman Catholic. Avocations: golf, swimming, travel. Home: 391 S Parkwood Ave Pasadena CA 91107-5037 Office: Whittier College 13406 Philadelphia St Whittier CA 90601-4413

ZANONE, JON A., career officer; b. Louisville, Feb. 4, 1963; s. Twyman Thomas and Nancy Mae (Booker) Z.; m. Bobbie Sharlene Burton, Mar. 3, 1988 (div. June 1994); 1 child, Zachary Steven; m. Carole Marie Cordova, Aug. 24, 1995; 1 child, Austin Thomas. Cert. in video prodn. and documentation, cert. in photoprocessing and quality assurance, USAF. Enlisted USAF, 1981, advanced through grades to sgt.; non-commd. officer in charge quality assurance 12th Tactical Reconaissance Squadron, USAF, Bergstrom AFB, Tex., 1985-89, 496th Reconaissance Tech. Squadron, RAF Alconbury, Eng., 1989-93; non-commd. officer in charge video prodn. 377th Comm. Squadron, Kirtland AFB, N.Mex., 1993-96; non-commd. officer in charge TV prodn. 10th Comm. Squadron, USAF Acad., Colorado Springs, Colo., 1996—. Camerman TV program Air Force Football with Fisher Deberry, 1997; editor, dir. TV program Broken Dreams, 1998. Named Best Photographer, Louisville Courier-Jour., 1980. Avocations: bicycling, screenwriting.

ZAPP, MARILYN J., artist; b. Appleton, Wis., June 6, 1929; d. Edward E. and Dorothy Augusta (Van Ryzin) Z; m. Frank M. Tauriello, 1960 (wid. 1990); children: Mark, Lea, Erika Tauriello. Student, Cleve. Art Inst., 1947-51. Artist, philosopher Soc. of Little Flower, Chgo. and Darien, Ill., Pictura Graphica, Karlstud, Sweden, Jerome's Magic World, Irvine, Calif., Art Image, L.A., Heisman Fine Art, King of Prussia, Pa., Nolseweg 132, Belgium; founder, coord. and pres. Sawdust Festival, Laguna Beach, 1960s; demonstrator Art Clubs and Orgns. Illustrator: (book) Song for a Night Season. Recipient numerous awards in field. Republican. Roman Catholic. Avocations: gardening, game inventor. Home: 27703 Ortegg Hwy # 97 San Juan Capistrano CA 92675

ZAPPE, JOHN PAUL, city editor, educator, newspaper executive; b. N.Y.C., July 30, 1952; s. John Paul and Carolyn (Pikor) Z.; m. Siobhan Bradshaw, May 30, 1982. AA, Dutchess Community Coll., Poughkeepsie, 1971; BA, Marist Coll., 1973; JD, Syracuse (N.Y.) U., 1978. Reporter Poughkeepsie Jour., 1973-75, Nev. State Jour., Reno, 1979-80; freelance reporter Am. Media Bold, Oakland, Calif., 1981-83; reporter Press-Telegram, Long Beach, Calif., 1983-88, city editor, 1988-97, webmaster PT Connect, 1995-97, mgr. new media, 1997-98; mgr. new media Riverside (Calif.) Press-Enterprise, 1998—; tchr. Syracuse U., 1976-78, Calif. State U., 1985-87; cons. Am. Media Bold, 1981-83. Chmn. Local 69 Newspaper Guild, Long Beach, 1984-87. Mem. Investigative Editors and Reporters. E-mail: jzappe@pe.net. Office: Riverside Press Enterprise 3512 14th St Riverside CA 92501-3814

ZARBIN, EARL ARTHUR, retired newspaper reporter, editor, historian, consultant; b. Chgo., Jan. 3, 1929; s. Richard Bell and Charlotte (Benensohn) Z.; m. Billie Jo Marks, Apr. 11, 1954 (div. 1972); children: Nicholas, Gregory (dec.), Cathryn, Elizabeth, Jennifer; m. Dorothy Louise Johnson Creeden, Oct. 6, 1973; 1 child, Denei Kelleen Anya Pace. BA, U. Ariz., 1954. Reporter The Ariz. Daily Star, Tucson, 1953-56, The Kansas City (Mo.) Times/Star, 1956, 57; reporter/editor The Ariz. Republic, Phoenix, 1958-88; part-time cons. Ctrl. Ariz. Water Conservation Dist., Phoenix, 1989—. Author: Roosevelt Dam: A History to 1911, 1984, Salt River Project: Four Steps Forward, 1902-1910, 1986, All the Time a Newspaper, 1990, The Bench and The Bar: A History of Maricopa County's Legal Professions, 1991, Two Sides of the River: Salt River Valley Canals, 1867-1902, 1997, (booklet) The Swilling Legacy; essayist The Freeman; contbr. articles to profl. jour. With U.S. Army, 1948-50. Mem. Ariz. Hist. Soc., Phoenix Mus. History, Westerners, Ariz. Town Hall, Heard Mus., Ariz. Zool. Soc. Libertarian. Home: 3803 E Saint Catherine Ave Phoenix AZ 85040-5013

ZARDOUZIAN, KAM, marketing executive; b. Tehran, Iran, Oct. 4, 1966; arrived in U.S., 1979; p. Mike and Bahia (Farahi) Z. AA, Santa Barbara City Coll., 1988; BBA, Univ. San Diego, 1990, MBA, 1991. Elec. mktg. & inter. sales mgr. PR Nutrition, Inc., San Diego, 1993-95; project mgr., elec. mktg. Electronic Data Systems, Plano, Tex., 1995-96; dir. of mktg. rsch. Matchlogic, Inc., Louisville, Colo., 1996—. Com. mem. The Local Spiritual Assembly of San Diego Bahais, 1998. Avocations: triathlete, tennis player. Home: 415 Sunnyside Ln Boulder CO 80302-7940

ZAVOROTNY, VALERY USTIMOVICH, physicist, researcher; b. Chernovtsy, Ukraine, Feb. 14, 1948; came to the U.S., 1990; s. Ustim Mikhailovich and Lubov Dmitrievna (Gruzda) Z.; m. Valentina Aleksandrovna Yakimova, Sept. 30, 1970; children: Maxim Valerievich, Dmitri Valerievich. MS in Radio Physics, Gorki (USSR) State U., 1971; PhD in Physics and Math., USSR Acad. Scis., Moscow, 1979. Jr. rsch. scientist Inst. Atmospheric Physics, USSR Acad. Scis., Moscow, 1971-79, rsch. scientist, 1979-84, sr. rsch. scientist, 1984-90; sr. rsch. scientist Lebedev Phys. Inst., USSR Acad. Scis., Moscow, 1990-91; rsch. scientist environ. tech. lab. Cooperative Inst. Rsch. in Eviron. Scis./Nat. Oceanic and Atmospheric Adminstrn., Boulder, Colo., 1991—; mem. organizing com. Internat. Meeting for Wave Propagation in Random Media, Seattle, 1992. Author, editor: Wave Propagation in Random Media, 1993; contbr. chpts. to books. Recipient Sr. Rsch. Associateship award NRC/NAS, Washington, 1990. Mem. Optical Soc. Am. Achievements include contributions to the theory of wave propagation in random media, imaging through the turbulent atmosphere, scattering from rough surfaces. Avocations: tennis, hiking, cross-country skiing. Office: NOAA/Environ Tech Lab 325 Broadway St Boulder CO 80303-3337

ZAVRAS, MARK ANDREW, controller; b. Stamford, Conn., Mar. 7, 1959; s. Arthur A. and Nancy (Sioles) Z.; m. Donna Lynn Morrison, July 31, 1982; children: Courney Lynne, Ashley Elizabeth. BS, Oral Roberts U., 1984. Staff acct. Ernst and Young, Stamford, 1984-86, sr. acct., 1986-87; supr. internal reporting Comp-U-Card Internat., Stamford, 1987-88, supr. fin. reporting, 1988-89; corp. controller, treas. Interwest Appliance Distributing Corp., Phoenix, 1989—, also bd. dirs.; ptnr., sec.-treas. Westar Contract Kitchen & Bath Corp., Scottsdale, Ariz., 1992—, also bd. dirs.; ptnr., sec.-treas. Pacific States Window & Door, Inc., Scottsdale, 1992—, also bd. dirs. Fellow Am. Mgmt. Assn., Nat. Assn. Accts. Republican. Avocations: travel, golf, tennis, music, biking. Home: 9819 E Topaz Dr Scottsdale AZ 85258-4744 Office: Interwest Appliance Distributing Corp 2625 S Wilson St # 105 Tempe AZ 85282-2025

ZAWODNY, LARAE JEAN, artist, secondary education educator; b. Chgo., Feb. 9, 1949; d. Raymond William and Dorothy (Hammersmith) Koppit; m. Janusz Kazimierz Zawodny, Sept. 18, 1971; 1 child, Roman Janusz. BA magna cum laude, U. Nebr., 1970; MFA, Claremont (Calif.) Grad. U., 1982. Artist Color on Edge, Vancouver, Wash., 1985—; secondary tchr. dept. visual and performing arts Vancouver Sch. Dist., 1992—; artist, instr. Vancouver Sch. of Arts and Academics, 1996—. Solo exhibits at Claremont Grad. Sch., 1982, U. Portland, 1984, Columbia Arts Ctr., Vancouver, 1985, City Hall, Beaverton, Oreg., 1989, Royal Durst Theatre, Vancouver, 1997; group exhbns. include Lang Gallery Scripps Coll., Claremont, Calif., 1978, Libra Gallery, Claremont, Calif., 1981, 82, Factory Place, L.A., 1982, U. Calif., Irvine, 1982, Portland Ctr. for the Visual Arts, 1983, Elizabeth Leach Gallery, 1983, 84, Coos Bay (Oreg.) Art Mus., 1985, Marianne Partlow Gallery, Olympia, Wash., 1986-87, Pacific N.W. Art Expo, Seattle, 1986, Abbott Hall Gallery, Portland, Oreg., 1990, Vancouver Sch. of Arts and Academics, Oreg., 1997, 98; represented in permanent collections: Mercedes Benz Corp., Frankfurt, Germany, Pomona Coll., Claremont, Calif. Home: 23703 NE Margaret Rd Brush Prairie WA 98606

ZAZURSKEY, JUDY KAY, secondary education educator; b. Quincy, Mich., Apr. 23, 1948; d. Glenn Sutton and Mariam Lois (Foorch) McCann; m. Michael Zazurkey, Aug. 8, 1970. BA, Cedarville Coll., 1970; MA, Fla. Atlantic U., 1984. Elem. tchr. Sugarcreek Schs., Bellbrook, Ohio, 1970-73; phys. edn. tchr., cheerleading coach Westminster Acad., Ft. Lauderdale, 1974-87; dir. devel. Success Motivation Internat., Waco, Tex., 1988; English tchr., associated student body advisor, dir. student Christian H.S., El Cajon, Calif., 1990—; mem. sch. improvement com. Christian H.S., El Cajon, 1996-98. Mem. Spredeels Organ Soc. Presbyterian. Avocations: teaching aerobics, weight-lifting, reading, biking. Home: 2255 Cambridge Cardiff-by-Sea CA 92007 Office: Christian HS 2210 Greenfield Dr El Cajon CA 92019

ZEAMER, RICHARD JERE, engineer, executive; b. Orange, N.J., May 13, 1921; s. Jay and Margery Lilly (Herman) Z.; m. Jean Catherine Hellens, July 8, 1944 (div. 1966); children: Audrie Dagna, Richard Warwick, Geoffrey Hellens; m. Theresa Elizabeth Taborsky, Mar. 27, 1969; children: Emily Elizabeth, Charlotte Anne. BSME, MIT, 1943, MSCE, 1948; PhD in Mech. Engring., U. Utah, 1975. Registered profl. engr., Utah. Civil engr. Morton C. Tuttle, Boston, 1949-53; process design engr. Nekoosa Edwards Paper Co., Port Edwards, Wis., 1953-55; process engr. W.Va. Pulp and Paper Co., Luke, Md., 1955-60; rocket engr., supr. Allegany Ballistics Lab., Rocket Ctr., W.Va., 1960-65; engring. supr. Hercules Powder Co., Magna, Utah, 1965-69; engr. structures, heat, flow, combustion & failure analysis Hercules Rocket Plant, Magna, 1969-83; project engring. mgr. Hercules Aerospace Div., Magna, 1983-89; pres., mgr. Applied Sci. Assocs., Salt Lake City, 1989—; chmn. policy studies UN Assn. Utah, 1990—; project leader world problem analyses, 1990—. Contbr. papers, articles, reports to profl. publs. Judge sci. fair, Salt Lake County, Utah, 1985—; chmn. citizens policy panel Utah chpt. UN Assn., U.S.A., N.Y.C., 1990—; mem. Utah State Hist. Soc., Salt Lake City, 1968-91, Mil. History Soc. Utah, Salt Lake City, 1990—. 1st lt. U.S. Army, 1943-46. Recipient commendation for presentation on world population problem Utah's Forum on Global Environ., 1992. Fellow AIAA (astronautics assoc.); mem. Cons. Engrs. Coun. Utah (article award 1992), League Utah Writers, Wasatch Mountain Club (hike leader 1987—). Achievements include patent for improved artillery ammunition, successful application of engineering approach to analysis of history. Home and Office: Applied Sci Assocs 843 13th Ave Salt Lake City UT 84103-3327

ZEHR, NORMAN ROBERT, association administrator; b. Niagara Falls, N.Y., May 19, 1930; s. George Andrew and Ina Kate (Morrell) Z.; Engr. of Mines, Colo. Sch. Mines, 1952, M.S., 1956; m. Janet Hutchinson, Apr. 24, 1976; children—Jeannette Ann, Leslie. Sales trainee Ingersoll-Rand Co., N.Y.C., 1955-56, sales engr., Lima, Peru, 1956-64, regional mgr. mining and constrn. sales, Lima, Peru and N.Y.C., 1964-68, gen. sales mgr. Latin Am., N.Y.C., 1968-69, gen. mgr. Latin Am. ops., N.Y.C., 1969-71, v.p. Ingersoll Rand Internat., Woodcliff Lake, N.J., 1971-72, pres., 1972-83, , v.p. Ingersoll-Rand Co., 1975-83; exec. dir. Colo. Sch. Mines Alumni Assn., 1984-95, ret. 1995. Served with AUS, 1952-54. Recipient Colo. Sch. Mines Disting. Achievement medal, 1977. Mem. AIME, Scabbard and Blade, Nat. Soc. Pershing Rifles, Mining Club , Sigma Nu.

ZEHRING, PEGGY JOHNSON, artist; b. Hutchinson, Kans., Jan. 4, 1941; d. Phillip E. and Bernice (Ashley) Johnson; m. R. David Zehring, July 27, 1963; children: Lisa, Geoff. BS, U. Kans., 1963; BA, U. Ill., 1977. Instr. Bellevue (Wash.) C.C., 1979-93, Sch. Visual Concepts, Seattle, 1985-86, Seattle Ctrl. C.C., 1987-97, North Seattle C.C., 1987-97, Coupeville (Wash.) Art Ctr., 1993—; juror and lectr. Eastside Assn. Fine Art, Mercer Island Visual Arts League, Nat. League Am. Artists & Pen Women; lectr. Women Painters of Washington, Bellevue Art Mus., N.W. Watercolor Soc., Hutchinson Art Assn., Kans. One-woman shows include King County Arts Commn., Seattle, Blake Gallery, Seattle, Bellevue (Wash.) C.C., PACCAR, Bellevue, Pacific N.W. Bell, Seattle, U. Ill., Chgo., Hutchinson Art Assn.; exhibited in group shows at COCA Annual, Seattle, Seattle Art Mus. Sales & Rental Gallery, LewAllen Fine Art, Santa Fe, Bellevue Art Mus., Diablo Valley Coll., Elizabeth Prince Gallery, Prescott, Ariz.; represented in selected collections City of Lynnwood, Wash., Pacific NW Bell, PACCAR, Delitte, Haskins & Sells, Opti-Copy, Kansas City, Harper & Assocs., Bellevue and numerous other pvt. collections; work published in The Artistic Touch I, II and III, The Encyclopedia of Living Artists. Recipient 1st pl. award Ariz. Internat., Snowgrass Art Inst., Cashmere, Wash., Kans. State Fair, Hutchinson, Honorable Mention award W. Wash. State Fair, 2d pl. award Ea. N.Mex. U., Portales, Snowgrass Art Inst., Cashmere, Wash., Merit award Mont. Inst. of the Arts, Butte; named finalist Pierce County Libr. Project, Gig Harbor, Wash. Home: PO Box 967 La Veta CO 81055-0967

ZEIGER, ROBERT S., allergist; b. Bklyn., July 31, 1942; s. Murray and Mildred (Oransky) Z.; m. Karen P. Zeiger, June 25, 1967; children: Joanna, Laurie. BA with honors, Tulane U., 1963; MD, PhD, SUNY, Bklyn., 1969. Diplomate Am. Bd. Pediatrics, Am. Bd. Allergy-Immunology. Intern pediatrics Harriet Lane Johns Hopkins Hosp., Balt., 1969-70; staff assoc. NIH, Bethesda, Md., 1970-72; resident pediatrics Boston Children's Hosp., 1972-73, allergy fellow, 1973-75; instr. Harvard Med. Sch., Boston, 1975-76; chief of allergy Kaiser Permanente, San Diego, 1976—; clin. assoc. prof. U. Calif., San Diego, 1980-87, clin. prof., 1987—. Editorial bd. Family Practice Survey, 1983-85, Jour. Allergy Clin. Immunology, 1985-91, Pediatric Allergy Immunology Jour., 1990—; author: Nasal Manifestations of Systemic Diseases, 1990; contbr. articles to profl. jours. Lt. comdr. USPHS, 1970-72. Phizer Honor scholar Phizer Corp., 1967-69, Charles A. Janeway scholar Harvard U., 1975; Hood Found. grantee, 1975-77. Fellow Am. Acad. Pediatrics, Am. Acad. Allergy Clin. Immunology (Travel award 1975), Phi Beta Kappa, Alpha Omega Alpha. Democrat. Avocations: tennis, travel, golf, cinema. Office: So Calif Permanente Med Group 7060 Clairemont Mesa Blvd San Diego CA 92111-1003

ZEILINGER, ELNA RAE, elementary educator, gifted-talented education educator; b. Tempe, Ariz., Mar. 24, 1937; d. Clayborn Eddie and Ruby Elna (Laird) Simpson; m. Philip Thomas Zeilinger, June 13, 1970; children: Shari, Chris. BA in Edn., Ariz. State U., 1958, MA in Edn., 1966, EdS, 1980. Bookkeeper First Nat. Bank of Tempe, 1955-56; with registrar's office Ariz. State U., 1956-58; piano tchr., recreation dir. City of Tempe; tchr. Thew Sch., Tempe, 1958-61; elem. tchr. Mitchell Sch., Tempe, 1962-74, intern prin., 1976, personnel intern, 1977; specialist gifted edn. Tempe Elem. Schs., Tempe, 1977-86; elem. tchr. Holdeman Sch., Tempe, 1986-89; tchr. grades 1-12 and adult reading, lang. arts, English Zeilinger Tutoring Svc., 1991—; grad. asst. ednl. adminstrn., Iota Workshop coordinator Ariz. State U., 1978; presenter Ariz. Gifted Conf., 1978-81; condr. survey of gifted programs, 1980; reporter public relations Tempe Sch. Dist., 1978-80, Access com. for gifted programs, 1981-83. Author: Leadership Role of the Principal in Gifted Programs: A Handbook, 1980; Classified Personnel Handbook, 1977, also reports, monographs and paintings. Mem. Tempe Hist. Assn., liaison, 1975; mem. Tempe Art League; mem. freedom train com. Ariz. Bicentennial Commn., 1975-76; bd. dirs. Maple Property Owners Assn., 1994—; storyteller Tempe Hist. Mus., 1997—. Named Outstanding Leader in Elem. and Secondary Schs., 1976' Ariz. Cattle Growers scholar, 1954-55; Elks scholar, 1954-55; recipient Judges award Tempe Art League, 1970, Best of Show, Scottsdale Art League, 1976. Democrat. Congregationalist.

ZEILINGER, PHILIP THOMAS, aeronautical engineer; b. David City, Nebr., Feb. 13, 1940; s. Thomas Leroy and Sylvia Dorothy Zeilinger; m. Elna Rae Simpson, June 13, 1970; children: Shari, Chris. AS, Wentworth Mil. Acad., Lexington, Mo., 1959; BSME, Kans. U., 1962. Estimator, engr. Reynolds Electronics and Engring. Co., El Paso, Tex., 1966-68; accessories coord. ITI Garrett, Phoenix, 1974-79, ctrl. access engr., 1968-98, controls coord. ITEC, 1983-84, integrated support specialist ITEC, 1984-86, mgr. systems software light helo turbine engring. co. div., 1986-91, FAA designated engr. rep. engine div., 1991-98; chmn. Light Helicopter Turbine Engine Company Computer Aided Acquistion and Logistics Working Group. V.p. Indsl. Devel. Authority, Tempe, Ariz., 1979-84; pres. Univ. Royal Garden Homes Assn., Tempe, 1984-90. 1st lt. U.S. Army, 1962-66. Recipient Vol. Svc. award City of Tempe, 1984, Grand Cross of Color, Internat. Order of Rainbow Girls, 1978. Mem. AIAA, Aircraft Owners and Pilots Assn., Explt. Aircraft Assn. (v.p. chpt. 228 1974-79), Masons (master 1990-92, chmn. statewide picnic 1992, Mason of the Yr. 1992). Democrat. Unitarian. Achievements include patent for Airesearch/Garrett. Home: 760 N Sycamore Pl Chandler AZ 85224-6925

ZEITLER, BILL LORENZ, aviation engineer; b. Columbus, Ohio, July 14, 1920; s. Walter Andrew and Naomi Lee (Limes) Z.; BSCE, Calif. State U., Long Beach, 1965; m. Betty Eileen Thomas, Nov. 8, 1942; children: Eddie, Naomi Lawrence. Cert. vocat. tchr., Calif. Loftsman, Curtiss Wright Corp., Columbus, 1941-44, 45; linesman Lockheed Corp., Burbank, Calif., 1946, N.Am. Rockwell and Boeing-N.Am. (and predecessor firms), Inglewood, Calif., 1946-58, airframe designer, 1958-62, supr. engring. coll. unit, 1962-65, project engr. life scis., health care delivery systems, 1965-68, project dir. health care delivery systems, Princeton, W.Va., 1968-69, mem. tech. staff, Downey, Calif., 1969-85; project engr. space shuttle design, 1971-75, shuttle alignment and mating, 1975-77, space shuttle design support extra vehicular stowage and testing, 1978-85; ret., 1985; mem. Space Shuttle Speakers Bur. Instr. 55 Alive-mature driving classes; former pres. Big Bear Valley Sr. Citizens; mem. Annual Mayor's Prayer Breakfast Com., Big Bear Lake, Calif.; chairperson Living Forest Task Force, Friends of Moonridge Zoo; bd. dir. Sr. Center. Mem. AIAA, Nat. Space Inst., Nat. Geog. Soc., Smith Instn. Assocs., Boeing-N.Am. Mgmt. Club, Toastmasters, Kiwanis, Big Bear Mcpl. Water Dist. Citizens Adv. Com., Erwin Lake Home Owners Assoc.

ZEITLIN, EUGENIA PAWLIK, librarian, educator, writer; b. N.Y.C., Jan. 29; d. Charles and Pauline (Klimowski) Pawlik; m. Herbert Zakary Zeitlin, July 3, 1949; children: Mark Clyde, Joyce Therese Zeitlin Harris, Ann Victoria, Clare Katherine. BA in English, Bklyn. Coll., 1945; MA in English, NYU, N.Y.C., 1951; MALS, Rosary Coll., 1968. Teaching credential N.Y., Ariz., Calif., Ill. English tchr. Sea Cliff, L.I., N.Y., 1945-47; English, math. tchr. Merrick (N.Y.) Sch. Dist., 1948-49; English tchr. Wilson Sch. Dist., Phoenix, 1949-50; counselor West Phoenix (Ariz.) High Sch., 1953-56; asst. prof. English Wright Coll., Chgo., 1965-66; asst. prof. English, asst. to v.p. curriculum and instrn. Oakton C.C., Des Plaines, Ill., 1970-76; libr. Pasadena City Coll., L.A. C.C. Dist., L.A., 1979-91, City of L.A., 1984—. Contbr. articles to profl. jours. Named Northridge City Employee of Yr., 1986. Mem. AAUW (br. pres. Lancaster, Calif. 1958-60), Thoreau Soc. (life), Beta Phi Mu. Avocations: freelance writing and editing, book collecting. Home: 20124 Phaeton Dr Woodland Hills CA 91364-5633

ZEITLIN, MARILYN AUDREY, museum director; b. Newark, July 14, 1941; d. Sidney M. and Theresa Feigenblatt) Litchfield; widowed; children: Charles C. Sweedler, Milo Sweedler. Student, Vanderbilt U., 1963-65; AB in Humanities, Harvard U., 1966, MA in Teaching of English, 1967; postgrad., Cornell U., 1971-74. Dir. Ctr. Gallery, Bucknell U., Lewisburg, Pa., 1975-78; Freedman Gallery, Albright Coll., Reading, Pa., 1978-81, Anderson Gallery, Va. Commonwealth U., Richmond, 1981-87; curator, acting co-dir. Contemporary Arts Mus., Houston, 1987-90; exec. dir. Washington Projects for the Arts, 1990-92; dir. Univ. Art Mus., Ariz. State U., Tempe, 1992—; juror Dallas Mus. of Arts, McKnight Awards, Mpls.; grant evaluator IMS; grant evaluator, panelist NEH; lectr., cons. in field. Editor, contbr. essays to art pubis. Bd. dirs. Cultural Alliance Washington; curator, commr. for U.S. for 1995 Venice Biennale. Samuel H. Kress fellow, 1972-73. Mem. Assn. Coll. and Univ. Mus. and Galleries (v.p. 1986-88), Am. Assn. Mus., Coll. Art Assn. (U.S. commr. Venice Biennale 1995). Office: Ariz State U Art Mus PO Box 872911 Tempe AZ 85287-2911*

ZEITLIN, MAURICE, sociology educator, author; b. Detroit, Feb. 24, 1935; s. Albert J. and Rose (Goldberg) Z.; m. Marilyn Geller, Mar. 1, 1959; children: Michelle, Carla, Erica. BA cum laude, Wayne State U., 1957; MA, U. Calif., Berkeley, 1960, PhD, 1964. Instr. anthropology and sociology Princeton (N.J.) U., 1961-64, research assoc. Ctr. Internat. Studies, 1962-64; asst. prof. sociology U. Wis.-Madison, 1964-67, assoc. prof., 1967-70, prof., 1970-77, dir. Ctr. Social Orgn., 1974-76; prof. sociology UCLA, 1977—, also research assoc. Inst. Indsl. Relations; vis. prof. polit. sci. and sociology Hebrew U., Jerusalem, 1971-72. Author: (with R. Scheer) Cuba: An American Tragedy, 1963, 1964, Revolutionary Politics and the Cuban Working Class, 1967, 1970, The Civil Wars in Chile, 1984, (with R.E. Ratcliff) Landlords and Capitalists, 1988, The Large Corporation and Contemporary Classes, 1989; (with J. Stepan-Norris) Talking Union, 1996; Latin Am. editor Ramparts mag., 1967-73; editor-in-chief: Political Power and Social Theory, 1980-90; mem. editorial adv. bd. The Progressive mag., 1985-96; editor: (with J. Petras) Latin America: Reform or Revolution?, 1968, American Society, Inc., 1970, 1977, Father Camilo Torres: Revolutionary Writings, 1972, Classes, Class Conflict, and the State, 1980, How Mighty a Force?, 1983, Insurgent Workers: The Origins of Industrial Unionism, 1987. Chmn. Madison Citizens for a Vote on Vietnam, 1967-68; chmn. Am. Com. for Chile, 1973-75; mem. exec. bd. U.S. Com. for Justice to Latin Am. Polit. Prisoners, 1977-84; mem. exec. com. Calif. Campaign for Econ. Democracy, 1983-86. Ford Found. fellow, 1965-67, 70-71; Guggenheim fellow, 1981-82; NSF grantee, 1981, 82, 98; recipient Project Censored award Top Censored Story, 1981; named to Ten Best Censored list, 1978; recipient Inaugural Disting. Publ. award in Labor Studies, Soc. for the Study of Social Problems, 1996. Mem. Am. Sociol. Assn. (governing council 1977-80, Disting. Contbn. Scholarship award in Pol. Sociology 1992, 96). Internat. Sociol. Assn. (editorial bd. 1977-81), Latin Am. Studies Assn., Orgn. Am. Historians. Democrat. Jewish. Office: UCLA Dept Sociology 2201 Hershey Los Angeles CA 90095-1551

ZEKMAN, TERRI MARGARET, graphic designer; b. Chgo., Sept. 13, 1950; d. Theodore Nathan and Lois (Bernstein) Z.; m. Alan Daniels, Apr. 12, 1980; children: Jesse Logan, Dakota Caitlin. BFA, Washington U., St. Louis, 1971; postgrad, Art Inst. Chgo., 1974-75. Graphic designer (on retainer) greeting cards and related products Recycled Paper Products Co., Chgo., 1970—, Jillson Roberts, Inc., Calif.; apprenticed graphic designer Helmuth, Obata & Kassabaum, St. Louis, 1970-71; graphic designer Container Corp., Chgo., 1971; graphic designer, art dir., photographer Cuerden Advt. Design, Denver, 1971-74; art dir. D'Arcy, McManus & Masius Advt., Chgo., 1975-76; freelance graphic designer Chgo., 1976-77; art dir. Garfield Linn Advt., Chgo., 1977-78; graphic designer Keiser Design Group, Van Noy & Co., Los Angeles, 1978-79; owner and operator graphic design studio Los Angeles, 1979—; art and photography tchr. Ctr. for Early Edn., L.A., 1996—, Buckley Sch., Sherman Oaks, 1996—. Recipient cert. of merit St. Louis Outdoor Poster Contest, 1970, Denver Art Dirs. Club, 1973.

ZEKOWSKI, ARLENE, writer, English educator; b. L.I., N.Y., May 13, 1922; d. Harry and Belle (Sargoy) Zee; m. Stanley Berne, May 17, 1953. BA in Romance Langs., Bklyn. Coll., 1944; MA in Romance Langs., Duke U., 1945; Licence es Lettres, U. Paris, 1948; postgrad., La. State U., 1958-62, Columbia U., So. Meth. U., Hunter Coll. Lectr. French lit. U. Bridgeport, Conn., 1946; instr. French and Spanish Associated Colls. Upper N.Y. State, Plattsburgh and Utica, 1947-48; tchr. Berlitz Sch., Paris, 1949; assoc. prof. English Ea. N.Mex. U., Portales, 1963-80, rsch. prof. English, 1980—; guest lectr. French lit. Queens Coll., N.Y., 1955; vis. prof. U. of the Americas, Mexico City, 1965, U. S.D., Vermillion, 1968, Styrian Hauptschulen Paedagogische Akademie, Graz, Austria; lectr. in field. Author: Gidian Standards of Literary Value, 1945, Thursday's Season: 49 Poems, 1950, (with S. Berne) A First Book of the Neo-Narrative: Grounds for Possibilities, 1954, Hemispheres, 1954, (with S. Berne) Cardinals and Saints: On the Aims and Purposes of the Arts in Our Time, 1958, (with S. Berne) Every Person's Little Book of Plutonium, 1992, Against the Disappearance of Literature: Essays, Interludes, Dialogues, Invocations on the Creating Word, 1998; including in various anthologies, New World Writing, 1957, Trace, 1965, Assembling, 1973, Breakthrough Fictioneers, 1973, American Writing Today, 1992, Dictionary of the Avant-Gardes, 1993, The Living Underground, 1998, American Renaissance, 1999; contbr. articles to profl. jours.; host, co-prodr. with Stanley Berne (tv series) Future Writing Today, 1984-85; numerous radio and TV interviews and guest appearances. Mem. PEN, Comm. Small Mag. Editors and Pubs., Western Ind. Pubs., New Eng. Small Press Assn., Rio Grande Writers Assn., Santa Fe Writers Coop. Avocations: fossil and driftwood collecting, shell and beadcraft treasure necklaces, drawing and collages, RV wilderness hiking and mountain camping, snorkelling. Office: Rising Tide Press PO Box 6136 Santa Fe NM 87502-6136

ZELEZNAK, SHIRLEY ANNE, psychotherapist; b. Ft. Dodge, Iowa; d. Melvin Peter and Illiah Mary (Olson) Hood; m. Donald John Zeleznak, June 14, 1969; children: Kristine Anne, Ryan John. BA, Briar Cliff Coll., 1967; MS in Clin. and Ednl. Psychology and Counseling, Winona State U., 1972. Cert. hypnotherapist, psychotherapist. Secondary tchr. Rochester, Minn., 1969-74; secondary tchr./counselor Mankato, Minn., 1974-77; task force dir. Heart Assn., Mankato, 1978-82; mental health counselor Scottsdale, Ariz., 1985—; tchr. Maricopa County C.C., Scottsdale, 1986-89; motivational speaker, Mankato, 1974-84; sch. cons. Paradise Valley/Scottsdale Sch. Dist., 1987—; bd. dirs. Home Base, Phoenix; psychotherapist St. Maria Goretti

Ch., Scottsdale, 1986—; crisis intervention counselor, police dept., Phoenix, 1993—. Author: Series for Junior High Students, 1981 (books), 1982-83 (software programs). Chef A'La Heart, Minn. Heart Assn., Mankato, 1979-81; motivational speaker Gang Awareness, Scottsdale, 1992—. Recipient Appreciation award Minn. Heart Assn., 1981. Mem. Mental Health Counselors, Nat. Ctr. for Learning Disabilities, Am. Counseling Assn., Phoenix Scottish Rite Found., Inst. for Developmental and Behavioral Neurology. Roman Catholic. Avocations: golf, tennis, power walking.

ZELEZNY, WILLIAM FRANCIS, retired physical chemist; b. Rollins, Mont., Sept. 5, 1918; s. Joseph Matthew and Birdie Estelle (Loder) Z.; m. Virginia Lee Scarcliff, Sept. 14, 1949. BS in Chemistry, Mont. State Coll., 1940; MS in Metallurgy, Mont. Sch. Mines, 1941; PhD in Phys. Chemistry, State U. Iowa, 1951. Scientist NACA, Cleve., 1951-54; metallurgist div. indsl. research Wash. State Coll., Pullman, 1954-57; scientist atomic energy div. Phillips Petroleum Co., Idaho Falls, Id., 1957-66, Idaho Nuclear Corp., Idaho Falls, 1966-70; mem. staff Los Alamos (N.Mex.) Nat. Lab., 1970-80; instr. metallurgy State U. Iowa, Iowa City, 1948-49; asst. prof. metallurgy Wash. State Coll., 1956-57; instr. U. Idaho, Idaho Falls, 1960-68. Contbr. articles to profl. jours.; patentee in field. Served with AUS, 1944-46. Mem. Am. Chem. Soc. (sec. N.Mex. sect. 1978-79), Microbeam Analysis Soc., Am. Soc. Metals, The Minerals, Metals & Materials Soc., Sigma Xi, Alpha Chi Sigma. Democrat. Methodist. Avocation: gardening. Home: PO Box 37 Rollins MT 59931-0037

ZELLER, KURT-ALEXANDER, vocalist, actor, stage director, voice educator; b. Portland, Oreg.; s. Norman K. and Johanna (Beckham) Z. BFA, MusB, So. Meth. U.; MusM, U. Cin., D in Musical Arts, 1990. Asst. prof. voice Willamette U., Salem, Oreg., 1993—. Vocal performances with orgns. including Salem (Oreg.) Chamber Orch., Opera Theatre South Bend, Ind., Portland Chamber Orch., at Brevard (N.C.) Music Ctr., Rogue Valley (Oreg.) Opera, Oreg. Shakespeare Festival, Ashland; editor jour. Cantus Firmus, Internat. Soc. Early Music singers, 1992-97; contbr. articles to mus. publs. Mabel Henderson grantee Mu Phi Epsilon Found., 1987, Merle Montgomery doctoral grantee, 1989. Mem. Nat. Assn. Tchrs. of Singing (treas. Cascade chpt. 1993-97, Oreg. dist. winner artist awards 1996), Early Music Guild Oreg. (bd. dirs. 1993—), Mu Phi Epsilon (dir. Pacific N.W. dist 3 1992-96, chmn. internat. standing rules 1995—). Methodist. Home: 7035 SW Gable Pkwy Portland OR 97225-2617 Office: Willamette Univ Dept Music 900 State St Salem OR 97301-3931

ZELON, LAURIE DEE, lawyer; b. Durham, N.C., Nov. 15, 1952; d. Irving and Doris Miriam (Baker) Z.; m. David L. George, Dec. 30, 1979; children: Jeremy, Daniel. BA in English with distinction, Cornell U., 1974; JD, Harvard U., 1977. Bar: Calif. 1977, U.S. Ct. Appeals (9th cir.) 1978, U.S. Supreme Ct. 1989. Assoc. Beardsley, Hufstedler & Kemble, L.A., 1977-81; assoc. Hufstedler, Miller, Carlson & Beardsley, L.A., 1981-82, ptnr., 1983-88; ptnr. Hufstedler, Miller, Kaus & Beardsley, L.A., 1988-90, Hufstedler, Kaus & Ettinger, L.A., 1990-91, Morrison & Foerster, L.A., 1991—. Contbg. author: West's California Litigation Forms: Civil Procedure Before Trial, 1996; editor-in-chief Harvard Civil Rights and Civil Liberties Law Rev., 1976-77;. Bd. dirs. N.Y. Civil Liberties Union, 1973-74. Mem. ABA (chmn. young lawyers divsn. pro bono project 1981-83, delivery and pro bono projects com. 1983-85, subgrant competition-subgrant monitoring project 1985-86, chair standing com. on lawyers pub. svc. responsibility 1987-90, chair law firm pro bono project 1989-91, standing com. legal aid and indigent defendants 1991-97, chmn. 1993-97, mem. ho. dels. 1993—, commn. on ethics 2000 1997—), Calif. Bar Assn. (bd. dirs. appellate project 1995—, chair commn. on access to justice 1997—), L.A. County Bar Assn. (trustee 1989-91, v.p. 1992-93, sr. v.p. 1993-94, pres.-elect 1994-95, pres. 1995-96, fed. cts. and practices com. 1984-93, vice chmn. 1987-88, chmn. 1988-89, chmn. judiciary com. 1991-92, chmn. real estate litigation subsect. 1991-92), Women Lawyers Assn. L.A., Calif. Women Lawyers Assn. Democrat. Office: Morrison & Foerster 555 W 5th St Ste 3500 Los Angeles CA 90013-1024

ZELUS, PAUL ROBERT, education researcher; b. Chgo., May 28, 1947; s. Robert J. and Olga C. (Antonacci) Z.; m. Kathryn E. Rehorst, Jan. 15, 1972; children: Jason P., Aaron M. BA, Loyola U., Chgo., 1969, MA, 1972; PhD, Northwestern U., 1975. Asst. prof. sociology SUNY, Geneseo, 1972-79; assoc. prof. sociology Capital U., Columbus, Ohio, 1979-83; asst. prof. sociology Idaho State U., Pocatello, 1983-88, dir. Ctr. for Bus. Rsch., 1988—; prin. cons. Zelus Assocs., Pocatello, 1995—. Co-author: I Just Went to Work: J.R. Simplot and His Business Career, 1995. Bd. dirs. Greater Pocetello C. of C., 1994-96, Idaho Rural Devel. Coun., Boise, 1995. Fellow Gerontol. Soc. Am.; mem. Rotary Internat. Lutheran. Avocation: genealogy. Office: Ctr for Bus Rsch 1651 Alvin Ricken Dr Pocatello ID 83201-2727

ZEMBRUSKI, SARAH ANN GUSTAFSON, elementary school educator; b. Jacksonville, Ill., Sept. 2, 1969; d. Howard Alvin and Lynda Jane (Van Laningham) G.; m. Hugh James Zembruski, Mar. 17, 1996. BA in Edn., Ariz. State U., 1991; MA in Edn. Adminstrn., No. Ariz. U., 1997. Cert. elem. edn. with ESL endorsement, Ariz. Tchr. math. and lang. arts McCray Jr. H.S., Coolidge, Ariz., 1991-95; tchr. math. Desert Sand Mid. Sch., Phoenix, 1995—, team leader, 1997—. Recipient 1st place Golden Bell Tchg. award Ariz. Sch. Bd. Assn., 1997. Mem. Assn. Supervision and Curriculum Devel., Cartwright Edn. Assn. (campus rep. 1998—), Ariz. Sch. Adminstrs., Phi Delta Kappa. Avocations: basketball, volleyball, swimming. Home: 4602 W Gumina Ave Laveen AZ 85339-9788 Office: Desert Sands Mid Sch 6308 W Campbell Ave Phoenix AZ 85033-2731

ZEMEL, NORMAN PAUL, orthopedic surgeon; b. Bklyn., Oct. 15, 1939; s. Nathan M. and Mary (Sklarevsky) Z.; m. Mary P. Kane. BSN, Rutgers U., 1961; MD, Thomas Jefferson Med. Sch., 1965. Bd. cert. orthopaedic surgery with added qualification in hand surgery Am. Bd. Orthopaedic Surgery. Orthopaedic surgery resident Northwestern U., Chgo., 1969-73; hand surgery fellow Boyes Hand Fellowship, L.A., 1973-74; hand surgery physician Boyes, Stark, Ashworth, L.A., 1974-88, Kerlan-Jobe Orthopaedic Clinic, Inglewood, Calif., 1989—; clin. assoc. prof. dept. orthopaedics U. So. Calif. Sch. Medicine, L.A., 1977—. Contbr. chpts. to books and articles to profl. jours. Lt. USNR, 1966-68, Vietnam. Mem. ACS, Am. Acad. Orthopaedic Surgery (bd. councilors), Am. Soc. for Surgery of the Hand, Western Orthopaedic Assn. (pres. L.A. chpt. 1993-94), Soc. Internat. de Orthopedique et de Traumatologie. Avocations: walking, reading, photography. Office: Kerlan-Jobe Orthopaedic Clinic 6801 Park Ter Los Angeles CA 90045-1539

ZENEV, IRENE LOUISE, museum curator; b. Albuquerque, Nov. 18, 1948; d. Stanley D. and Louise Marie (Risler) Z.; 1 child, Carson M. Bell. BA, U. N.Mex., 1971. Dir. Umpqua Valley Arts Assn., Roseburg, Oreg., 1978-82; edn. coord. Douglas County Mus., Roseburg, 1985-86, curator history, 1986-98; exhibits curator Benton County Mus., Philomath, Oreg., 1998—; editor Dispatch newsletter Oreg. Mus. Assn., 1995-98; publs. rschr. Oreg. Mus. Assn., Portland, 1989-92. Reviewer The Roseburg News-Review, 1989-93. Chmn. Douglas County Oreg. Trail Sesquicentennial Celebration Com., 1991-93; mem. Oreg. Coun. for Humanities, 1997— (bd. sec. 1998—). Mem. Nat. Assn. for Mus. Exhbn. (Oreg. State rep. 1995-98), Registrar's Com. Western Region (Oreg. state rep. 1995—), Mus. Assessment Program Peer Reviewer, Am. Assn. Mus., 1997—.

ZEPEDA, SUSAN GHOZEIL, county official; b. N.Y.C., Aug. 8, 1946; d. Harry S. and Anne (Golden) Kantor; m. Isaac Ghozeil, Jan. 29, 1967 (div. Oct. 1979); children: Daniel Jacob, Adam Leo; m. Fernando Zepeda, Jan. 2, 1983 (div. Feb. 1998); children: Paloma Andrea, Sofia Elisa. BA, Brown U., 1967; MA, U. Ariz., 1971, postgrad., 1971-75; PhD, Internat. Coll., 1985. Rsch. assoc. div. bus. and econ. rsch. U. Ariz., Tucson, 1971-73, rsch. assoc. Coll. Medicine, 1975-76; assoc. dir. Pima Alcoholism Consortium, Tucson, 1976-79, exec. dir., 1979-80; dep. dir. pub. health Orange County Health Care Agy., Santa Ana, Calif., 1980-89; dir. policy, planning Orange County Health Care Agy., Santa Ana, 1989-90; dir. pub. fin. Orange County, 1990-92; dir. San Luis Obispo County Health Agy., 1993—; cons. Tucson Sch. Dist. No. 1, 1973-75, U.S. Dept. Labor, Washington, 1976-79, Indian Health Svc., Rockville, Md., 1984-85; ptnr. Zepeda Assocs., Fullerton, Calif., 1987-93; presenter confs. Mem. Fullerton Planning Commn., 1984-91, chmn., 1990-91, mem. Calif. Task Force on Comparable Worth, 1984-85, Calif. Dist. Appeal Bd. No. 310, L.A., 1986—. Recipient Woman of Achievement award Orange County Bd. Suprs., 1988, Disting. Achievement awards Nat. Assn. Counties, 1985, 86, 87, 89. Mem. APHA, County Health Execs. Assn. Calif. (v.p. 1998—), Nat. Assn. County and City Health Ofcls. (bd. dirs.), Ctrl. Coast Hosp. Coun. (chair 1996), County Alcohol Program Adminstrs. Assn. Calif. (v.p. 1983, pres. 1984-85), Rotary (San Luis Obispo de Tolosa). Avocation: fiber arts. Home: 109 Cerro Romauldo San Luis Obispo CA 93405-1274 Office: San Luis Obispo County Health Agy 2191 Johnson Ave San Luis Obispo CA 93401-4534

ZERETZKE, FREDERICK FRANK H., artist, educator; b. Milw., July 4, 1919; s. Herman and Hertha Hildegarde (Riebow) Z.; m. Marian Louise Elfers, Dec. 7, 1942; children: Frederick J., David L., Mary J., John E. Student, Milw. Art Inst., 1938-39, Layton Sch. of Art, Milw., 1940-41, Rockford (Ill.) Coll., 1947. Art tchr. Burpee Art Gallery, Rockford, Ill., 1946-48; mural artist People's Real Estate Agy., Rockford, 1958, Grace Luth. Ch., Loves Park, Ill., 1960, Sweden House, Rockford, 1972; artist oil meml. young girl First United Presbyn. Ch., Greeley, Colo., 1963; mural artist Linos, Rockford, 1974; art tchr. pvt. studio, Rockford, Ill., 1968-78; art. tchr. pvt. studio, Burlington, Wash., 1978—; artist and tchr. art in nat. def. Camp Callan, San Diego, 1942-43, Rock Valley Coll., Rockford, Ill., 1970-77, Skagit Valley Coll., Mt. Vernon, Wash., 1978-80; water color instr. Daniel Smith Art, Seattle, 1994, 95. Exhibited in Z Studio, Burlington, Vt., Departures Gallery, Anacortes, Wash., 1996, 97; also group shows in art galleries, Wis., Calif., Wash., Ill., Elements Gallery, Bellingham, Wash., 1988-90, Fox Glove Art Gallery, Mt. Vernon, Wash., 1989—, 37th Ann. Anacortes Arts Festival, 1998, Twisted Willow Gallery, Mt. Vernon, 1993—, Arts and Frame Gallerie, Canyon Lake, Calif., 1993, Arts Coun. Snohomish County, Everett, Wash., 1993; executed mural in Hadamar, Germany, 1945, Lino's Italian Restaurant, Rockford, Ill.; pvt. collections include Joseph Stroyan 1978-91, North Whidbey Inn, Oak Harbor, Wash., Kenney Fellers 1990-95, Timbers Restaurant, Sedro-Woolley, Wash., Pastor Karsten Baalson 1983-95. Sec. Loves Park (Ill.) Zoning Bd., 1949-56; mem. Skagit Human Rights Task Force to Protect Fundamental Human Rights Guaranteed in Constitution of U.S., 1996; mem. Mus. of Northwest Art, Laconner, Wash., 1998-99. With U.S. Army, 1941-45, ETO. Scholar Milw. Art Inst., 1939, Layton Sch. Art, 1940; awarded commission for design for Swedish Tour of Sveas Soner Chorus of Rockford, 1965; named Artist of Yr. Winnebago County, 1974. Mem. Tamaroa Water Color Soc. Rockford (hon. lifetime, founder, pres. 1964), Skagit Art Assn. (pres. 1987-88). Mem. Unitarian Ch. Avocations: photography, psychology, travel, hiking, outdoor life. Home: 722 Peterson Rd Burlington WA 98233-2656

ZERI, MASSIMO, director of photography; b. Rome, May 20, 1954; s. Fernando and Giuliana (Sciommeri) Z. B in Cinematography, Istituto di Stato Cinematograf, Rome, 1974. Dir. of photography (films) A Bedfull of Foreigners, 1995, No Experience Necessary, 1996, The Good Bad Guy, 1996, Cyberdorm, 1996, Double-Cross, 1997, Wedding Band, 1997, The Puzzle in the Air, 1998, Stavro, 1999. Mem. Italian Assn. Cinematographers, Internat. Cinematographers Guild (local 600), European Fedn. Cenmatographers. Avocation: commercial airplane pilot. Home and Office: 12012 Mitchell Ave Apt 7 Los Angeles CA 90066-4535

ZERUNYAN, FRANK VRAM, lawyer; b. Istanbul, Turkey, Sept. 17, 1959; came to U.S., 1978; s. Jack Hagop and Ayda (Yagupyan) Z.; m. Jody Lynn Forman, May 18, 1986; children: Daniel, Nicole. French Bacalaureat, Coll. Samuel Moorat, Paris, 1978; BA, Calif. State U., Long Beach, 1982; JD, Western State U., Fullerton, Calif., 1985; postgrad., U. Southern Calif., 1988. Bar: Calif. 1989, D.C., 1995, U.S. Dist. Ct. (cen. dist.) Calif. 1989, U.S. Ct. Internat. Trade 1994. V.p. law Internat. Mktg. Alliance, Torrance, Calif., 1985-89; pvt. practice L.A., 1989-92; ptnr., shareholder, mng. mem. Yacoubian & Zerunyan, P.C., L.A., 1992-95; mem. Sulmeyer, Kupetz, Baumann & Rothman, L.A., 1995—; instr. law Alex Pilibos Sch., L.A., 1993—; judge pro tem, L.A. Mcpl. Ct. Editor SKB&R Newsletter, 1995—. Bd. dirs. Am. Youth Soccer Orgn., Palos Verdes, Calif., 1995—, referee adminstr., 1995—; bd. dirs. Daniel Freeman Hosps. Found., 1998—; chmn. scholarship com. Orgn. Istanbul Armenians, Van Nuys, Calif., 1992-94; legal counsel and polity adv. com. Armenian Nat. Com. of Am., Washington, 1993. Mem. ABA, Financial Lawyers Conf. Avocations: golf, soccer, tennis. E-mail: fzerunyan@skbr.com. Office: Sulmeyer, Kupetz et al 300 S Grand Ave Ste 1400 Los Angeles CA 90071-3110

ZERZAN, CHARLES JOSEPH, JR., retired gastroenterologist; b. Portland, Oreg., Dec. 1, 1921; s. Charles Joseph and Margaret Cecelia (Mahony) Z.; BA, Wilamette U., 1948; MD, Marquette U., 1951; m. Joan Margaret Kathan, Feb. 7, 1948; children: Charles Joseph, Michael, Kathryn, Paul, Joan, Margaret, Terrance, Phillip, Thomas, Rose, Kevin, Gregory. Commd. 2d. lt., U.S. Army, 1940, advanced through grades to capt., 1945, ret., 1946, re-enlisted, 1951, advanced through grades to lt. col., M.C., 1965; intern Madigan Gen. Hosp., Ft. Lewis, Wash., 1951-52; resident in internal medicine Letterman Gen. Hosp., San Francisco, 1953-56, Walter Reed Gen. Hosp., Washington, 1960-61; chief of medicine Rodriquez Army Hosp., 1957-60, U.S. Army Hosp., Fort Gordon, Calif., 1962-65; chief gastroenterology Fitzsimmons Gen. Hosp., Denver, 1965-66; chief profl. services U.S. Army Hosp., Ft. Carson, Colo., 1967-68; dir. continuing med. edn. U. Oreg., Portland, 1968-73; ptnr. Permanente Clinic, Portland, 1973-92, ret., 1992; assoc. clin. prof. medicine U. Oreg., 1973-97; individual practice medicine, specializing in gastroenterology, Portland, 1968-92; staff Northwest Permanente, P.C., ret., 1996, dir., 1980-83. Mem. Portland Com. Fgn. Rels., 1986—, bd. dirs., 1994-97. Decorated Legion of Merit, Army Commendation medal with oak leaf cluster; Meritorious Alumnus award Oreg. Health Scis. U., 1990. Diplomate Am. Bd. Internal Medicine. Fellow A.C.P.; mem. Am. Gastroenterol. Assn., Oreg. Med. Assn. (del. Clackamas County), Ret. Officers Assn. Republican. Roman Catholic. Home and Office: 6364 SE Mcnary Rd Portland OR 97267-5119

ZETIN, MARK I., psychiatrist; b. Seattle, June 19, 1948; m. Dawn Honeywell. BA, Pomona Coll., 1970; MS, Stanford U., 1971; MD, U. Calif., Irvine, 1975. Diplomate Am. Bd. Psychiatry & Neurology. Clin. prof. psychiatry U. Calif., Irvine, 1979-94; pvt. practive psychiatry Garden Grove, Calif., 1994—. Mem. APA. Office: PO Box 879 Orange CA 92856-6879

ZETTER, LOIS C., personal manager; b. Boston, Jan. 6, 1939; d. Oscar and Pauline (Krasnov) Z.; m. Walter S. Unterseher, Sept. 25, 1988. BA in Theatre Arts cum laude, Brandeis U., 1960. Prin. LeMond/Zetter Mgmt. Inc., L.A., Carson City, Nev., 1971—. Appeared in plays Fiddler on the Roof, How To Succeed in Business Without Really Trying, Ben Bagley's Cole Porter Revue; assoc. prodr. (film) Moment By Moment; co-prodr. (TV series) Cover Up, Dads; prodn. cons. (films) Grease, Blow Out, Urban Cowboy; managed careers of John Travolta, Patrick Swayze, Katherine Helmond, Mickey Rourke, Mark Harmon, etc. Donor Aid for AIDS, Brandeis U., Friendly Hand Found., The Pacific Ctr., Gaucher Disease Found. Recipient Spirit award Brandeis U., 1995. Mem. Acad. TV Arts and Scis., Conf. Personal Mgrs., Women in Film. Office: LeMond/Zetter Mgmt Inc 5570 Old Us Highway 395 N Carson City NV 89704-9584

ZHANG, GUOTAI, process engineer, researcher, ethylene furnace specialist; b. Shanghai, July 6, 1943; came to U.S., 1981; s. Yunsun and Yuyin Zhang; m. Huapei Chen, Apr. 30, 1973; 1 child, Yingwen. BSCE, East China Inst. Chem. Tech., Shanghai, 1965; MSCE, Oreg. State U., 1990. Instr. East China Inst. Chem. Tech., Shanghai, 1979-86, assoc. prof., 1986-88; vis. scholar Oreg. State U., Corvallis, 1981-83, vis. rschr., 1988-91; sr. devel. engr. KTI Corp., Monrovia, Calif., 1991-94; prin. process engr. KTI Corp., San Dimas, Calif., 1994—. Co-author: Catalyst Deactivation, 1989; chief editor: Catalytic Reaction Engineering, 1988; contbr. more than 30 articles to profl. jours. Mem. AIChE. Avocations: swimming, tennis. Home: 1319 Marquette Dr Walnut CA 91789-1253 Office: KTI Corp 650 W Cienega Ave San Dimas CA 91773-2933

ZHANG, JIANPING, computer science educator, consultant; b. Wuhan, Hubei, China, Mar. 18, 1956; s. Shichang and Yaoquan (Pan) Z.; m. Yilin Weng; children: Lorna Lei, Edwin Meng. BS, Wuhan U., 1982; PhD, U. Ill., 1990. Asst. prof. Utah State U., Logan, 1990-96, assoc. prof., 1996—; guest assoc. prof. S.E. Univ., Nanjing, China, 1997. Contbr. articles to profl. jours. Mem. IEEE, Assn. for Artificial Intelligence, Assn. for Advancement Computing Edn., Assn. Computing Machinery. Home: 1207 Eastridge Dr Logan UT 84321-4982 Office: Utah State Univ Dept Computer Sci Logan UT 84322-4205

ZHAO, LI, fine arts company executive, teacher, consultant; b. Tianjin, China, Mar. 16, 1958; came to U.S., 1984; d. Robert Yunnian Chao and Qizhen Cao; m. Shiyi Zhang, Aug., 1984 (div. 1987); m. Kenneth Lloyd Schoolland, Aug. 8, 1988 (div. 1994); 1 child, Kenli Dulcinea. BA, Foreign Lang. Inst., Tianjin, China, 1983; MA, U. Minn., 1987; Mgmt. Sci. (Japanese), Japan-Am. Inst. Mgmt. Sci., Honolulu, 1988; MS in Japanes Bus. Study, Chaminade U., Honolulu, 1988. Steel mill worker Guang Xi, China, 1969-78; tchr. Liu-Zhou Steel Mill High Sch., Guang Xi, 1978; translator, researcher China Dept. Transp., Beijing, 1983-84; teaching asst. U. Minn., Mpls., 1985-87; intern trainee Tobu Dept. Store, Tokyo, Japan, 1988; pres. Schoolland Internat., 1988—; sales mgr. trainee Duty Free Shops, Honolulu, 1989-92; gen. mgr. Double-Eye Hawaii, Honolulu, 1989-92, 1989—; gen. mgr. Tianjin Victor Entertainment Co. Ltd., Tianjin, China, 1994—. Editor: (newsletters) Double-Eye News, 1989-92, Libertarian Party Hawaii News, 1991-93. Chmn. membership com. U.S.-China People's Friendship Assn., 1988-89; mem. legis. com. Small Bus. Hawaii; bd. dirs. Libertarian Party Hawaii, 1992. Recipient Model Citizen award Mpls. Police Dept., 1992; named Outstanding Grad. Student, U. Minn., 1992. Mem. Am. Mktg. Assn. (bd. dirs.), Am. Soc. Interior Designers, Sales and Mktg. Execs. of Honolulu, Honolulu Japanese C. of C. (chair com.), Honolulu Acad. Art, Japan-Am. Assn. Hawaii, Assn. Hawaii Artists (corr. sec.), Chinese C. of C. Honolulu. Avocations: writing, reading, swimming, dancing, travel.

ZHAO, MINGJUN, physicist, research scientist; b. Shaanxi, China, July 13, 1957; came to U.S., 1994; s. Yong Zhao and Fengying Xue; m. Shihong Chen, July 31, 1984; 1 child, Bowen. BS, Shaanxi Normal U., Xian, 1982; PhD, Xian Inst. Optics/Prec. Mechs., Chinese Acad. Scis., Xian, 1989. Faculty Xian Inst. Petroleum, 1982-86; postdoctoral fellow Xian Inst. Optics & Precision Mechanics Academia Sinica, Xian, 1990-92; Internat. Ctr. for Theoretical Physics fellow Inst. Nat. Optics, Firenze, Italy, 1992-93; rsch. fellow Inst. Phys. and Chem. Rsch., Wako-shi, Japan, 1993-94; rsch. assoc. N.Mex. State U., Las Cruces, 1994-96; rsch. engr. U. Calif., Santa Barbara, 1996; rsch. scientist Phys. Optics Corp., Torrance, Calif., 1996—. Contbr. articles to profl. jours. including Chinese Physics-Letter, Optics Comm., Optics Letter. Recipient 2d pl. natural scis. award Shaanxi Province, 1992, Excellent award Chinese Acad. Scis., 1991, Excellent award of Pres. Scholarship, 1989. Mem. AAAS, Internat. Soc. for Optical Engring., N.Y. Acad. Scis. Achievements include main contribution to nonlinear optics, especially in field of photorefractive multi-wave mixing, phase conjugation, created pertubation approximation theory for analysis of phase distortion in degenerate four-wave mixing, developed photorefractive spatial light modulator base on home-made BSO crystal; realization of self-pumped phase conjugation of diffusely reflected light in a KNSBN crystal, and dynamics pattern formation and storage; demonstrated system which combined ultrasound generation and double phase conjugation for non-destrictive evaluation application, and micro-optical and liquid crystal for 3-D display, and laser plasma diagnostics. Home: 20903 Amie Ave Apt 8 Torrance CA 90503-4752 Office: Phys Optics Corp 20600 Gramercy Pl Bldg 100 Torrance CA 90501-1821

ZHAO, XIXI, geologist, geophysicist; b. Nanchang, Jiangxi, China, Apr. 17, 1954; came to U.S., 1981; s. Wentou Zhao and Xing Qiu; m. Yvonne Lu, June 8, 1991; 1 child, Janeva. BS, U. Sci. & Tech. China, 1978, MS, 1981; PhD, U. Calif. Santa Cruz, 1987. Asst. rsch. geologist Inst. Geology Acad. Sinica, Beijing, 1978-81; tchg., rsch. asst. Dept. Earth Scis. U. Calif. Santa Cruz, 1981-87, mgr. Paleomagnetism Lab., 1987—; postdoctoral rsch. assoc. dept. earth scis. U. Calif. Santa Cruz, 1988-89, lectr., postdoctoral rsch. scientist, 1990-92, rsch. geophysicist Inst. Tectonics, 1992—; vis. rsch. scientist dept. geophysics Tex. A&M U., College Station, 1989-90; adj. prof. Chengdu (Sichun) Inst. Tech., 1995—; shipboard scientist Ocean Drilling Program, College Station, 1990, 93, 94, 97; vis. fellow Nonlinear Scis. Inst., Santa Cruz, 1990, U. Minn., Mpls., 1995. Co-editor: The Crust Growth and Mantle Plume Tectonics of South China Continent, 1996; contbr. articles to profl. jours. Grantee NSF, 1992, 95, 97, U.S. Sci. Support Program, 1991, 93, 95, 97, Amoco Prodn. Co., 1990, 94. Mem. Internat. Assn. Geomagnetism and Aeronomy, Internat. Union Geodesy and Geophysics, Am. Geophys. Union, Sigma Xi. Achievements include development of an innovative tectonic model which has brought new insight into the geologic and tectonic history of China, Siberia, and East Asia. Avocations: running, stamp collecting, hiking. Office: Univ Calif Inst Tectonics 1156 High St Santa Cruz CA 95064-1077

ZHENG, ALICE RUNPING, university director; b. Shanghai, Oct. 23, 1957; came to U.S., 1986; d. Bingquan Zheng and Wenhsien Chen; m. Leigh Carrington Rhett, Aug. 24, 1993. BA in English Lang. and Lit., Shanghai Tchr.'s U., 1982; MA in Edn., UCLA, 1988, PhD in Edn., 1996. Cert. law Social Scis. Acad. Shanghai, 1982. Tchr. Xiang Ming Mid. Sch., Shanghai, 1982-86; bus. mgr. U. Humanistic Studies, Del Mar, Calif., 1988-93; campus dir. Kelsey-Jenney Coll., San Diego, 1996-98; learning ctr. dir. U. Phoenix, San Diego, 1998—; advisor U. Phoenix Alumni Network, 1998. Mem. AAUW. Avocations: singing, swimming, handicrafts, Tai-chi, photography. Home: 11670 Tierra Del Sur San Diego CA 92130-2613 Office: Univ Phoenix 3890 Murphy Canyon Rd San Diego CA 92123-4497

ZHOU, CHIPING, mathematician, educator; b. Shanghai, People's Republic of China, Jan. 21, 1957; s. Xingui Zhou and Qi Zhu; m. Xiaoyu He, June 22, 1986; children: Kevin K., Brandon K. BS, Fudan U., Shanghai, 1983, MS, 1986; PhD, U. Hawaii, 1990. Asst. prof. Fudan U., Shanghai, 1986; lectr. Chaminade U., Honolulu, 1990; asst. prof. U. Hawaii, Honolulu, 1990-. Author: Some Problems for Elliptic and Hyperbolic Equations, 1986, Maximum Principles and Liouville Theorems for Elliptic Partial Differential Equations, 1991, (3 dimensional graphics software) Math Graph 3D, 1998; contbr. articles to profl. jours. Recipient rsch. fellowship Rsch. Corp. of U. Hawaii, 1989. Mem. Am. Math. Soc., Math. Assn. Am. Achievements include research in partial differential equations and their applications, Clifford algebras in analysis; discovery of generalized maximum principles for elliptic and parabolic systems. Office: U Hawaii - HCC Math Dept 874 Dillingham Honolulu HI 96817

ZHOU, ZHENYU, electrical engineer; b. Shanghai, June 26, 1964; came to U.S., 1990; s. Ming De and Yuhua (Zhuang) Z.; m. Qing Xue, Feb. 22, 1990; children: Kenneth, Catherine. MS, Zhejiang U., Hangzhou, China, 1989, U. So. Calif., 1992; PhD, U. So. Calif., 1995. Rsch. asst., Signal and Image Processing Inst. U. So. Calif., L.A., 1990-94; rsch. assoc. U. So. Calif., 1994-95; sr. engr. Rockwell Internat., Newport Beach, Calif., 1995-97; engring. group leader Rockwell Internat., Newport Beach, 1997—; digital signal processing cons. Hersh Acoustic Engring., Westlake Village, Calif., 1992-95. Contbr. chpt. to book Information Processing in Medical Imaging, 1995, articles to profl. jours. Patentee in field. Mem. IEEE. Office: Rockwell Semiconductor Systems 4311 Jamboree Rd Newport Beach CA 92660-3007

ZHU, JUN, mathematics educator; b. Suzhou, Jiangsu, People's Republic of China, June 13, 1957; arrived in Can, 1989; s. Chengyan and Ronghua (Jiang) Z.; m. Yunfang Xu, Jan. 1, 1985; 1 child, Chenchong. Student, Suzhou U., 1982. Tchr. Suzhou (Peoples Republic of China) U., 1982-89; researcher U. B.C., Vancouver, 1989—. Contbr. articles to profl. jours. Avocations: Weiqi, table tennis, Sing ethu, basketball. Office: U BC Dept Math, 1984 Math Rd, Vancouver, BC Canada V6T 1Z2

ZHU, PETER CHAOQUAN, chemist; b. Jiashan, China, May 8, 1957; came to U.S., 1987; s. Sanguan and Mingbao (Shen) Z.; m. June Zhu, Aug. 7, 1998. BS, Jiangxi Coll. Chinese Medicine, Nanchang, China, 1981, MS, 1987; PhD, Miss. State U., 1993. Instr. Jiangxi Coll Chinese Medicine, Nanchang, China, 1981-85; rsch. scientist 1st Chem. Corp., Mississippi State, Miss., 1990-92; sr. rsch. chemist 3M Health Care, Tustin, Calif., 1994—; adj. chemistry prof. Irvine Valley Coll., 1997—; donor and rschr. in field. Postdoctoral fellow U. Calif., Santa Barbara, 1993-94. Mem. Am. Chem. Soc. (divsn. organic chemistry, divsn. polymer, divsn. medicinal chemistry, divsn. carbohydrate chemistry, divsn. analytical chemistry). Achievements include nanochemistry application, nanobeads chemistry, attachment chemistry, new chemistry application in molecular biology; development of new chemistry of cyclic ketene acetals, including synthetic procedures and new reactions; invented pure monoacetylation of diols via cyclic ketene

acetals; first cationically polymerized cyclic ketene acetals and obtained stable polymers and copolymers; development of new chemistry which led to a chemical oxygen sensor used for open-heart surgery, of new CO2 chemical sensor for medical use; invented several industrial processes of speciality chemicals; discovered a new silicone rection; isolated one anti-cancer agent from a plant; development of a new preparative TLC method, analytical methods of amine on organic and inorganic polymers of a synthetic procedure to introduce PhSe group. Avocations: walking, fishing, piano, pingpong. Office: 3M Health Care 1311 Valencia Ave Tustin CA 92780-6447

ZIADA, HASSAN HIGAZI, mechanical engineer, educator; b. Santa, Gharbia, Egypt, Oct. 12, 1941; came to U.S., 1968; s. Higazi Ziada and Monira Abdul-Gawad Salim; m. Salwa Ali Mostafa, Jan. 1, 1970 (dec. Aug., 1982) chldren: Ahmad, Eman; m. Zonia Coromoto Quero, May 13, 1983; children: Akram, Amirah. BSc in Mech. Engring., Alexandria (Egypt) U., 1963; MSc in Engring., Kans. State U., 1970, PhD in Mech. Engring., 1976. Rschr. and instr. Assiut (Egypt) U., 1963-68; tchg. asst., rschr. Kans. State U., Manhattan, 1968-74; sr. engr. Westinghouse Advanced Reactors Divsn., Madison, Pa., 1974-77; asst. prof. King Abdul-Aziz U., Jeddah, Saudi Arabia, 1977-80; assoc. prof. King Abdul-Aziz U., Jeddah, 1983-89; cons. Madison, Pa., 1978, 79 summer; lead analyst reactor internal design Westinghouse, Madison, Pa., 1980-83; prin. engr. Westinghouse Hanford, Richland, Wash., 1989-96; fellow engr. Lockheed Martin & Numatec Hanford, Richland, Wash., 1996—; cons. various cos. and instns., Saudi Arabia and U.S., 1983-89. Contbr. High Temp. Design and Simplified Analysis Methods, 1975—; author, reviewer Tech. Papers, Bolts, Breeder Reactors; developer (short tng. course) Failure Analysis and Fracture Mechanics, 1986, (tng. program) Inspection and Quality Control, 1989. Pres. Arab-Am. Assocs. Manhattan, Kans., 1970-72; Imam, Islamic Ctr. of Tri-Cities, Richland, Wash., 1990—. Recipient Recognition for Space and Defence Power Systems, Dept. Energy, 1994. Mem. ASME (mem. fatigue strenth subgroup 1994—). Avocations: reading, fishing, travel, comty. support and activities. Home and Office: 6104 W 6th Ave Kennewick WA 99336-9327

ZIAKA-VASILEIADOU, ZOE DIMITRIOS, chemical engineer; b. Larissa, Thessalia, Greece, Apr. 15, 1963; came to U.S., 1988; d. Dimitrios J. and Melpomeni D. (Sakellariou) Z.; m. Savvas P. Vasileiadis, Feb. 17, 1985; children: Eugenia-Melina, Artemis-Dimitria. Diploma in Chem. Engring., Aristotle U. Thessaloniki, Greece, 1987; MS in Chem. Engring., Syracuse U., 1990; PhD in Chem. Engring., U. So. Calif., 1994. Registered profl. engr., European Cmty. Scholar chem. engring. Aristotle U. Thessaloniki, 1982-87; rschr. chem. lab. Exxon Corp., Thessaloniki, 1984, engring. mgr., 1986; fellow Norwegian Ednl. Coun., 1988; scholar Ctr. Indsl. Devel., Greece, 1987-88; rsch. assoc., scholar Syracuse (N.Y.) U., 1988-90; rsch. assoc., fellow U. So. Calif., L.A., 1990-94, lectr., 1995; cons. engr. ZIVATECH, L.A., 1994—; lectr., rsch. scientist Univ. Calif., Los Angeles, 1996—; practical trainee Internat. Assn. Exch. Student Engring., Finland, 1985, Israel, 1986; engring. cons. Zivatech, 1994—; patentee in field. Author: Pollution Prevention Principles, 1999; contbr. articles to AIChE Jour., Chem. Engring. Sci, Jour. Membrane Sci., Separation Sci. and Tech., 5th World Congress Chem. Engring, Chem. Engring. Commn. NATO fellow Greek Govt., Thessaloniki, 1987-88, AXIOS Found. for Worthiness fellow, Torrance, Calif., 1994, CRESPE, COGPS-U. So. Calif. fellow, L.A., 1992, 93, 94. Mem. AIChE, Materials Rsch. Soc., N.Am. Catalysis Soc. (fellow R.J. Kokes 1994), Greek Inst. Chem. Engrs., Internat. Platform Assn. Orthodox Christian. Achievements include research and development of catalytic membrane reactors; design of new separation processes, catalytic and polymeric materials; research in mathematical modelling of transport and reaction systems, programming and computing processes, optimization.

ZIECKER, RUSSELL SCOTT, personal manager; b. Springville, N.Y., Oct. 14, 1962; s. Ronald James and Marlene Marie (Lux) Z.; m. Ann-Mari Snyder, May 27, 1989 (div. Mar. 1997); 1 child, Madeline Marie; m. Heide Ann Lindsey, Sept. 5, 1998. Dir. creative affairs Chrysalis Music Group, L.A., 1983-87, N.Y.C., 1988-90; v.p. creative affairs Virgin Music-Am., West Hollywood, Calif., 1990-94; owner, founder, pres. Urge Rec. Co./ Poundhouse Prodn., Portland, Oreg., 1992-94, Zero, Beverly Hills, Calif., 1994—; music cons. MGM Films, Santa Monica, Calif., 1994-95. Music supr.: (feature films) Circles, 1997 (awards 1997), Headless Body in Topless Bar, 1996 (awards 1996). Avocations: roller-blading, boating, old films, traveling. Office: Zero PO Box 17874 Beverly Hills CA 90209-3874

ZIEGAUS, ALAN JAMES, public relations executive; b. Bremerton, Wash., May 8, 1948; s. Alan Moon and Dorothy (Lamont) Z.; m. Constance Jean Carver, 1972; children: Jennifer, Ashley. BJ, San Diego State U., 1970. Staff writer San Diego Tribune, 1972-77; exec. asst. San Diego City Council, 1977-78; v.p. Gable Agy., San Diego, 1978-80; pres. Stoorza, Ziegaus & Metzger, San Diego, 1980—. Mem. planning com. County San Diego, 1980-82; mem. sewage task force City of San Diego, 1986-88, civil svc. com., 1992—; trustee armed forces YMCA, San Diego, 1984—. Recipient Best Investigative Series award AP, 1975. Mem. San Diego Press Club (Best News Story award 1973). Home: 12351 Brassica St San Diego CA 92129-4127 Office: Stoorza Ziegaus & Metzger 225 Broadway Fl 18 San Diego CA 92101-5005*

ZIEGLER, MICHAEL ALAN, executive; b. San Francisco, Feb. 4, 1945; s. Martin and Alice (Struass) Z.; m. Deborah Ann Zeek; children: Jesse James, Zeek. MBA, U. San Francisco, 1990. Gen. mgr. Frank More, Inc, San Francisco, 1967-71, Bootique Trends, Inc., L.A., 1971-74; owner Red Carpet Car Wash, Inc., San Francisco, 1975-79; pres., CEO Pride Industries, Roseville, Calif., 1983—. Bd. dirs. Sacramento Metro Chamber, 1996—, Child Abuse Prevention Coun. Placer County, Auburn, Calif., 1995—, Comstock's Editl. Bd., Sacramento, 1996—; com. mem. Sacramento United Way Fin. Com., 1994—; leader coun. Placer County United Way, Roseville, 1994—, co-chair campaign, 1994—; com. mem. McClellan Air Force Base Privatization & Reuse Adv. Com., Sacramento, 1996—. Recipient Ernst & Young & Inc. Mag. Not-for-Profit Entrepreneur of Yr. award, 1992, Sacramento Met. Chamber Businessman of Yr. award, 1994. Mem. Roseville C. of C. (bd. dirs. 1995—). Home: 9845 Los Lagos Cir N Granite Bay CA 95746 Office: Pride Industries 1 Sierra Gate Plz Ste 200A Roseville CA 95678-6603

ZIELINSKI, MELISSA L., museum director. BS, Coll. William an Mary, 1978; MS, N.C. State U., 1983. Park svc. ranger, interpreter Cape Hatteras Nat. Seashore, Buxton, N.C., 1980, 81; exhibits intern N.C. Mus. Natural Scis., Raleigh, 1980-81, 81-82, asst. curator pub. programs, 1984-92; vol. svcs. coord. N.C. State U., 1981-82, 82-83, lab. instr. vertebrate zoology lab., 1983; naturalist Durant Nature Park Raleigh (N.C.) Parks and Recreation Dept., 1983-84; mus. educator Humboldt State U. Natural History Mus., Arcata, Calif., 1992-93, dir., 1993—. Co-author, editor, illustrator vertebrate zoology lab. text, 1983-84. Sch. edn. program dir. Friends of the Dunes The Nature Conservancy, Arcata, Calif., 1993-94, mem. Mem. Am. Mus. Natural History, Nat. Assn. Interpretation, Nat. Marine Educators Assn., Guild of Natural Sci. Illustrators, Nat. Audubon Soc. Home: 1363 Mill Creek Rd Mckinleyville CA 95519-4448 Office: Humboldt State U Natural History Mus 1315 G St Arcata CA 95521-5820*

ZIEMANN, G. PATRICK, bishop; b. Pasadena, Calif., Sept. 13, 1941. Attended, St. John's Coll. and St. John's Sem., Camarillo, Calif., Mt. St. Mary's Coll., L.A. Ordained priest Roman Cath., 1967. Titular bishop, aux. bishop Diocese Santa Rosa, Obba, 1986-92; bishop Diocese Santa Rosa, Santa Rosa, Calif., 1992—. Office: Diocese of Santa Rosa 320 10th St Santa Rosa CA 95401-5219*

ZIERNICKI, RICHARD MIECZYSLAW, engineering firm executive; b. Krakow, Poland, Feb. 3, 1950; came to U.S., 1981; m. Mila Kristine Czarnecka, Apr. 1, 1952; children: Maciek, Daniel. BS in Mech. Design, U. Mining and Metallurgy, Krakow, 1973, MS in Mech. Engring., 1975, PhD in Tech. Sci. cum laude, 1979. Registered profl. engr., Colo., Calif., Tex. and Wyo. Asst. prof. engring. Inst. Vibrations and Acoustics, Krakow, 1975-80; mgr. rsch. and devel. Inst. Tech., Krakow, 1980-81; mgr. mech. engring. Over-Lowe Co., Denver, 1981-84; sr. cons., pres., chmn., CEO Knott Lab., Denver, 1984—; presenter, lectr. in field at internat. tech. confs. in U.S., Europe, and South Am; spkr. Johns Hopkins U., Balt., Tech. Inst., Vienna, Austria, U. Denver. Contbr. articles to profl. jours.; patentee in field. NSF grantee. Mem. ASME, NSPE, Soc. Automotive Engrs., Soc. for Exptl. Stress Analysis, Robotic Internat. Soc. Mfg. Engrs., Profl. Engrs. Colo., Nat. Assn. Profl. Accident Reconstruction Specialists, Nat. Forensic Ctr., Nat. Acad. Forensic Engrs. Home: 5751 S Beech Ct Littleton CO 80121-3912 Office: Knott Lab Inc 2727 W 2nd Ave Denver CO 80219-1605

ZIGMAN, PAUL EDMOND, environmental consultant, executive; b. L.A., Mar. 10, 1924; s. Fernand and Rose (Orlijan) Z.; m. children: Andrea, Eric. BS in Chemistry, UCLA, 1948. Supr., applied research U.S. Naval Radiol. Def. Lab., San Francisco, 1949-59, head tech. mgmt. office, 1961-69; supr., analytical chemistry Atomics Internat., Canoga Park, Calif., 1960-61; pres. Environ. Sci. Assocs., San Francisco, 1969-94, chmn., bd. dirs, 1969—. Contbr. articles to profl. jours. Served as pvt. U.S. Army, 1943. Recipient USN Meritorious Civilian Service award, 1968. Mem. Am. Chem. Soc., Nat. Assn. Environ. Profls. (v.p. 1977), Assn. Environ. Profls. (pres. 1974-76) (Outstanding Service award 1977, Cert. Appreciation 1984). Home: 2311 Crystal Downs Ct Oxnard CA 93030-7755

ZIL, J. S., psychiatrist, physiologist; b. Chgo., Oct. 8, 1947; s. Stephen Vincent and Marillyn Charlotte (Jackson) Zilius; 1 child, Charlene-Elena. BS magna cum laude, U. Redlands, 1969; MD, U. Calif., San Diego, 1973; MPH, Yale U., 1977; JD with honors, Jefferson Coll., 1985. Intern, resident in psychiatry and neurology U. Ariz., 1973-75; fellow in psychiatry, advanced fellow in social and community psychiatry, Yale community cons. to Conn. State Dept. Corrections, Yale U., 1975-77, instr. psychiatry and physiology, 1976-77; instr. physiology U. Mass., 1976-77; unit chief Inpatient and Day Hosp. Conn. Mental Health Ctr., Yale-New Haven Hosp. Inc., 1975-76, unit chief, 1976-77; asst. prof. psychiatry U. Calif., San Francisco, 1977-82, assoc. prof. psychiatry and medicine, 1982-86, vice-chmn. dept. psychiatry, 1983-86; adj. prof. Calif. State U., 1985-87; assoc. prof. bioengring. U. Calif., Berkely and San Francisco, 1982-92, clin. faculty, Davis, 1991—; chief psychiatry and neurology VA Med. Ctr., Calif., 1977-86, prin. investigator Sleep Rsch. & Physiology Lab., 1980-86; dir. dept. psychiatry and neurology U. Calif.-San Francisco, Cen. San Joaquin Valley Med. Edn. Program and Affiliated Hosps. and Clinics, 1983-86; chief psychiatrist State of Calif. Dept. Corrections, 1986—; chmn. State of Calif. Inter-Agy. Tech. Adv. com. on Mentally Ill Inmates & Parolees, 1986-92; mem. med. adv. com. Calif. State Personnel Bd., 1986-95; appointed councillor Calif. State Mental Health Plan, 1988-93; cons. Nat. Inst. Corrections, 1992-94; invited faculty contbr. and editor Am. Coll. Psychiatrist's Resident in Tng. Exam., 1981-86. Author: The Case of the Sleepwalking Rapist, 1992, Mentally Disordered Criminal Offenders, 5 vols., 1989, reprinted, 1991, Suicide Prevention Handbook, 1987, 2d edit., 1992, 3d edit., 1996; contbg. author: The Measurement Mandate: On the Road to Performance Improvement in Health Care, 1993; co-editor: Psychiatric Services in Jails and Prisons, 2nd edit., 1999; assoc. editor Corrective and Social Psychiatry Jour., 1978-97, referee, 1980—, reviewer, 1981—; co-editor: Psychiatric Svcs in Jails and Prisons, 2d edit., 1999; contbr. articles in field to profl. jours. Nat. Merit scholar, 1965; recipient Nat. Recognition award Bank of Am., 1965, Julian Lee Roberts award U. Redlands, 1969, Kendall award Internat. Symposium in Biochemistry Research, 1970, Campus-Wide Profl. Achievement award U. Calif., 1992, Career Achievement award U. Redlands, 1994. Fellow Royal Soc. Health, Am. Assn. Social Psychiatry; mem. Am. Assn. Mental Health Profls. in Corrections (nat. pres. 1978-97), Calif. Scholarship Fedn. (past pres.), AAUP, Am. Psychiat. Assn., Nat. Council on Crime and Delinquency, Am. Pub. Health Assn., Delta Alpha, Alpha Epislon Delta. Office: PO Box 160208 Sacramento CA 95816-0208

ZILLIGEN, JIL A., environmental director; b. Phila.; m. Christopher Schedler. BA, Wesleyan U. Legis. assoc. Conn. Waste Mgmt. Svc., Hartford, 1987; environ. educator Wetlands Inst., Stone Harbor, N.J., 1988; head tchg. counselor Project to Increase Mastery Math. and Sci., Middletown, Conn., 1989-90; pollution prevention assoc. Ctr. for Marine Conservation, Washington, 1990-92; mgr. pollution prevention Ctr. for Marine Conservation, San Francisco, 1992-94; dir. environ. programs Patagonia, Inc., Ventura, Calif., 1994—; Bd. dirs. Calif. Wilderness Com., Davis, Calif. Author: Citizen's Guide to Plastics in the Ocean, 1994; contbr. articles to profl. jours. Bd. dirs. Conservation Alliance, 1994-97, Wildlife Damage Rev., Tucson, 1996-98; vol. Environ. Def. Ctr., Santa Barbara, Calif., 1995—. Mem. Environ. Grantmakers Assn. (program com. 1996-97, mgmt. com. 1997—). Office: Patagonia Inc 259 W Santa Clara St Ventura CA 93001-2545

ZILLY, THOMAS SAMUEL, federal judge; b. Detroit, Jan. 1, 1935; s. George Samuel and Bernice M. (McWhinney) Z.; divorced; children: John, Peter, Paul, Luke; m. Jane Greller Noland, Oct. 8, 1988; stepchildren: Allison Noland, Jennifer Noland. BA, U. Mich., 1956; LLD, Cornell U., 1962. Bar: Wash. 1962, U.S. Ct. Appeals (9th cir.) 1962, U.S. Supreme Ct. 1976. Ptnr. Lane, Powell, Moss & Miller, Seattle, 1962-88; dist. judge U.S. Dist. Ct. (we. dist.) Wash., Seattle, 1988—; judge pro tem Seattle Mcpl. Ct., 1972-80. Contbr. articles to profl. jours. Mem. Cen. Area Sch. Council, Seattle, 1969-70; scoutmaster Thunderbird Dist. council Boy Scouts Am. Seattle, 1976-84; bd. dirs. East Madison YMCA. Served to lt. (j.g.) USN, 1956-59. Recipient Tuahku Dist. Service to Youth award Boy Scouts Am., 1983. Mem. ABA, Wash. State Bar Assn., Seattle-King County Bar Assn. (treas. 1979-80, trustee 1980-83, sec. 1983-84, 2d v.p. 1984-85, 1st v.p. 1985-86, pres. 1986-87). Office: US Dist Ct 410 US Courthouse 1010 5th Ave Seattle WA 98104-1189*

ZIMA, GORDON EVERETT, metallurgist; b. Mason City, Iowa, June 20, 1920; s. Albert Gordon and Agnes Elisabeth (Nolan) Z.; m. Phyllis Anne Main, July 10, 1942; children: Marguerite, Antonia, Paula. AB, Stanford U., 1942; MS, Calif. Inst. Tech., 1952, PhD, 1956. Sr. rsch. engr. Jet Propulsion Lab., Pasadena, Calif., 1946-50; sect. head propulsion Naval Ordnance Test Sta., Pasadena, 1950-55; sr. rsch. metallurgist Internat. Nickel Co., Bayonne, N.J., 1956-58; sr. rsch. specialist GE Hanford Atomic Products, Richland, Wash., 1958-62, Boeing Nuclear Power Divsn., Seattle, 1962-63; sr. rsch. engr. Lawrence Radiation Lab., Livermore, Calif., 1963-70; sr. devel. engr. Battelle Pacific NW Lab., Richland, 1974-83. Patentee on classified materials; contbr. articles to tech. jours including Am. Soc. Metals, Powder Metallurgy, Metal Progress of Am. Soc. Metallurgists. Author: (young readers book) Sun Birds and Evergreens, 1996. 1st lt. U.S. Army Air Corps, 1942-46 PTO. Mem. Sigma Xi, Phi Lamda Upsilon. Avocations: photography, fly fishing, golf, tennis, hiking. Home: 4675 San Anselmo Rd Atascadero CA 93422-2618

ZIMKAS, CHARLES PATRICK, JR., space foundation administrator; b. Scranton, Pa., Sept. 8, 1940; s. Charles Zimkas Sr. and Margaret (Bakunas) Sullick; m. Ursula Frediel Marten; children: Robert L., Uwe F., Michael P., Brian David. Enlisted USAF, advanced through grades to chief master sgt., 1958; dep. chief of staff, personnel adminstrv. div. Aerospace Def. Command, Colorado Springs, Colo., 1971-74; exec. to dep. chief of staff personnel Aerospace Def. Command, Colorado Springs, 1975-80; chief of adminstrn. Air Forces Iceland, Keflavik, 1974-75; first sr. enlisted advisor USAF Space Command, Colorado Springs, 1980-84; ret., 1984; dir. regional devel. Noncommissioned Officers Assn., San Antonio, 1984-86; chief operating officer U.S. Space Found., Colorado Springs, 1986—. Named Air Force Outstanding Airman of Yr., 1978; recipient Air Force Legion of Merit. Mem. Noncommd. Officers Assn. (bd. dirs. 1978-84, chmn. bd. dirs. 1982-84, Order of Sword award 1978, Excalibur award 1979), Air Force Assn. (pres. Lance P. Sijan chpt., medal of merit 1990, 94, exceptional svc. award 1996, presdl. citation 1998). Home: 729 Drew Dr Colorado Springs CO 80911-2606 Office: US Space Found 2860 S Circle Dr Ste 2301 Colorado Springs CO 80906-4184

ZIMMER, GEORGE, men's apparel executive. CEO Men's Wearhouse, Freemont, Calif. Office: Men's Wearhouse 40650 Encyclopedia Cir Fremont CA 94538*

ZIMMER, PAUL GERALD, II, community care licensing professional; b. Detroit, Oct. 2, 1946; s. Paul Gerald and Beatrice Mae (Mitchell) Z.; m. Shelly Mardell Hallier, May 23, 1980; children: Paul Gerald III, Carrie Lea. BA in Religion/Social Work, Azusa Pacific U., 1973. Ordained to ministry So. Bapt. Conf., 1985. Vocat. rehab. counselor dept. vocat. rehab. State of Calif., Riverside, 1986-88, intake specialist dept. social svc. cmty. care licensing, 1988-91, licensing program supr. dept. social svc. cmty. care licensing, 1991—; instr., bd. dirs. Riverside County Office Edn.-Family-to-Family, 1993—; mem. Riverside County Dept. Pub. Social Svcs. Child Advocacy Coun., 1994—; co-chair RICKI com. Riverside County Dept. Health-Immunizations, 1996—. Author (booklet) The Age of Becoming, 1977; author (music album) Day-A-Comin', 1989, (lyrics) Flashback Music, 1996. Dist. exec./scout leader Boy Scouts Am., Redlands/Victorville, Calif., 1981-83; mem./instr. Riverside County Office Edn. Child Indio Care Initiative Project for Spanish Speaking Care Providers, 1994—; appointed mem. State of Calif. Equal Employment Opportunity Adv. Com.-Disability Adv. Com., Sacramento, 1997. With U.S. Army, 1967-68. Recipient Youth Adv. of Yr. award Riverside County Office Edn., 1993. Mem. Inland Empire Parents Anonymous (group facilitator, crisis counselor 1990-93). Avocations: writing/performing Christian music, fitness walking, coin collecting. Home: 1188 Wilson Ave Perris CA 92571

ZIMMERER, KATHY LOUISE, university art gallery director; b. Whittier, Calif., Dec. 9, 1951. BA cum laude, U. Calif., Berkeley, 1974; MA, Williams Coll., 1976. From tour guide to curatorial asst. Sterling and Francine Clark Inst., Williamstown, Mass., 1975-76; spl. asst. dept. modern art L.A. County Mus. Art, 1976-77; mus. edn. fellow Fine Arts Mus. San Francisco, 1977-78; dir. coll. art gallery SUNY, New Paltz, 1978-80; cons. in field, 1980-81; dir. univ. art gallery Calif. State U., Dominguez Hills, 1982—. Mem. Internat. Assn. Art Critics, Art Table. Office: Univ Art Gallery Calif State U 1000 E Victoria St Carson CA 90747-0001

ZIMMERMAN, HAROLD SAMUEL, retired state senator, newspaper editor and publisher, state administrator; b. Valley City, N.D., June 1, 1923; s. Samuel Alwin and Lulu (Wylie) Z.; m. Julianne Williams, Sept. 12, 1946; children—Karen, Steven, Judi Jean (dec.). B.A., U. Wash., 1947. News editor Sedro-Woolley (Wash.) Courier-Times, 1947-50; editor, pub. Advocate, Castle Rock, Wash., 1950-57; pub. Post-Record, Camas, Wash., 1957-80; assoc. pub., columnist, 1980; assoc. pub., columnist, dir. Eagle Publs., Camas, 1980-88. Mem. Wash. Ho. of Reps., 1967-80; mem. Wash. Senate, 1981-88, Wash. State Environ. Hearings Bd., Lacey, 1988-93. Served with USAAF, 1943-46. Mem. Grange, Sigma Delta Chi, Sigma Chi. Republican. United Methodist. Clubs: Lions, Kiwanis.

ZIMMERMAN, LINDA, author, editor, residential real estate agent; b. Chgo., Sept. 30, 1946; d. Louis Joseph and Sydell Muriel (Lakowitz) Z.; m. Gerry Goffin (div.). Student, Roosevelt U., 1963-65, Santa Monica Coll., 1981-83. Prodn. asst. films, asst. video editor various features, 1970-81; freelance photographer, 1979-86, freelance writer, 1983—; editor, pub. The Food Yellow Pages, L.A., 1987-91; contbg. editor Food Arts mag., L.A.; dir. westside housing Bradbury & Co., Realtors, 1996—; creative svcs. dir. El Cholo Restaurants, L.A.; instr. food journalism UCLA and various colls.; speaker radio and TV; specialist food and restaurants L.A., So. Calif. real estate, 1979—. Author: Puddings, Custards and Flans, 1990, (with Peggy Mellody) Cobblers, Crumbles and Crisps, 1991, (with Gerri Gilliland) Grills & Greens, 1993, Chicken Soup, 1994; contbr. articles to mags. and newspapers. Mem. AFTRA, Internat. Assn. Cooking Profls., Calif. Assn. Realtors, Nat. Assn. Realtors, Southland Regional Assn. Realtors, Women's Culinary Alliance (bd. dirs. 1988-92), So. Calif. Culinary Guild (bd. dirs.), N.Y.C. Authors Guild, Ciao Italia (hon., ednl. bd.). Office: 12164 Ventura Blvd Studio City CA 91604-2514

ZIMMERMAN, LORETTA ELLEN, history educator; b. Metairie, La., Sept. 14, 1935; d. Harry Peter and Hilda Katie (Brondum) Z.; m. Howard J. Kuhnle, II. BA, Newcomb Coll., 1957; MA, Tulane U., 1961, PhD, 1964. Asst. prof. William Woods Coll., Fulton, Mo., 1964-65; instr. Augustana Coll., Sioux Falls, S.D., 1965-66, U. Tex., Arlington, 1966-67; prof. history U. Portland, Oreg., 1967—; mem. adv. bd. (ann. edit.) Race and Ethnic Rels., 1994—. Author (with C. Baydo and John Boun) History of U.S. With Topics, vol. I and II, 1994. Mem. Phi Beta Kappa, Kappa Delta Pi, Alpha Lambda Delta, Phi Alpha Theta. Roman Catholic. Home: PO Box 431 Washougal WA 98671 Office: Univ Portland 5000 N Willamette Portland OR 97203

ZIMMERMAN, MICHAEL DAVID, state supreme court justice; b. Chgo., Oct. 21, 1943; s. Elizabeth Porter; m. Lynne Mariani (dec. 1994); children: Evangeline Albright, Alessandra Mariani, Morgan Elisabeth; m. Diane Hamilton, 1998. BS, U. Utah, 1966, JD, 1969. Bar: Calif. 1971, Utah 1978. Law clk. to Chief Justice Warren Earl Burger U.S. Supreme Ct., Washington, 1969-70; assoc. O'Melveny & Myers, L.A., 1970-76; assoc. prof. law U. Utah, 1976-78, adj. prof. law, 1978-84, 89-93; of counsel Kruse, Landa, Zimmerman & Maycock, Salt Lake City, 1978-80; spl. counsel Gov. of Utah, Salt Lake City, 1978-80; ptnr. Watkiss & Campbell, Salt Lake City, 1980-84; assoc. justice Supreme Ct. Utah, Salt Lake City, 1984-93, 98—, chief justice, 1994-98; co-moderator Justice Soc. Program of Snowbird Inst. for Arts and Humanities, 1991, 92, 93, 94, 95, 97, 98; moderator, Tanner lecture panel dept. philosophy U. Utah, 1994; faculty Judging Sci. Program Duke U., 1992, 93; bd. dirs. Conf. of Chief Justices, 1995-98. Note editor: Utah Law Rev., 1968-69; contbr. numerous articles to legal publs. Mem. Project 2000, Coalition for Utah's Future, 1985-96; trustee Hubert and Eliza B. Michael Found., Rowland-Hall St. Mark's Sch.; bd. dirs. Summit Inst. for Arts and Humanities, 1998—. Named Utah State Bar Appellate Ct. Judge of Yr., 1988; recipient Excellence in Ethics award, Ctr. for Study of Ethics, 1994, Disting. Svc. award Utah State Bar, 1998, Individual Achievement award Downtown Alliance, 1998; participant Justice and Soc. Program of Aspen Inst. for Humanistic Studies, 1988, co-moderator, 1989. Fellow Am. Bar Found.; mem. ABA (faculty mem. appellate judges' seminar 1993), Am. Law Inst., Utah Bar Assn., Salt Lake County Bar Assn., Jud. Conf. U.S. (adv. com. civil rules 1985-91), Utah Jud. Coun. (supreme ct. rep. 1986-91, chair 1994-98), Utah Constnl. Revisions Commn., Snowbird Inst. for Arts and Humanities (bd. dirs., 1989—), Am. Inns of Ct. VII, Am. Judicature Soc. (bd. dirs. 1995—), Order of Coif, Phi Kappa Phi. Office: Utah Supreme Ct Box 140210 450 S State St Salt Lake City UT 84114-0210

ZIMMERMAN, STEPHEN, marketing executive. Pres., CE0 Paria Group, Orem, Utah. Office: Paria Group Central Park East 390 West 800 North Ste 104 Orem UT 84057*

ZIMMERMANN, GERHARDT, conductor; b. Van Wert, Ohio, June 22, 1945; s. Ervin and Ethel Jane (Allen) Z.; m. Sharon Marie Reher, Mar. 17, 1974; children: Anna Marie, Peter Karl Irum. MusB, Bowling Green State U.; MFA, U. Iowa; student, with James Dixon, Leopold Sipe, Flora Contino, Richard Lert. Tchr. in Genoa (Ohio) Pub. Schs., 1967-70; condr. orch. Augustana Coll., Rock Island, Ill., 1971-72; music dir. Clinton (Iowa) Symphony Orch., 1971-72; asst. prof. music, condr. orchs. Western Ill. U., Macomb, 1972-74; asst. condr. St. Louis Symphony Orch., 1974-78, assoc. condr., 1978-82; music dir., condr. St. Louis Youth Orch., 1975-82, Canton Symphony Orch., 1980—, N.C. Symphony Orch., Raleigh, 1982—; guest condr. Recipient 2d Prize Georg Solti Conducting Competition 1973. Mem. Am. Symphony Orch. League, Nat. Acad. Rec. Arts and Scis., Phi Mu Alpha Sinfonia. Office: NC Symphony Orch Meml Auditorium PO Box 28026 Raleigh NC 27611-8026*

ZIMMERMANN, JOHN, magazine editor, writer; b. Hollywood, Calif., July 21, 1946; s. John Levi and Doris Jane (Schultz) Z.; m. Kimberly Hintt, Nov. 7, 1969 (div. June 1976). BS in Math., Lakeland Coll., 1969. Mng. editor Racecar Mag., L.A., 1980; editor Sports Car Mag., Santa Ana, Calif., 1980-81; founding editor On Track Mag., Fountain Valley, Calif., 1981-84; freelance writer various mags., 1984-86; motorsports editor Auto Week Mag., Detroit, 1986-87; editor Sports Car Mag., Tustin, Calif., 1988-92; founding editor Racer Mag., Tustin, 1992—. Author: The Atlantic Championship, 1998. Avocations: athletics, hiking, exploring, cycling, woodworking. Office: Racer Comm 1371 Warner Ave Ste E Tustin CA 92780-6448

ZIMMERMANN, JOHN PAUL, plastic surgeon; b. Milw., Mar. 9, 1945; s. Paul August and Edith Josephine (Tutsch) Z.; m. Bianca Maria Schaldach, June 13, 1970; cbildren: Veronica, Jean-Paul. BS in Biology, Chemistry, Marquette U., 1966; MD, Med. Coll. Wis., 1970. Diplomate Am Bd. Plastic Surgery. Internship surgery Stanford U. Sch. of Medicine, Calif., 1970-71, residency in gen. surgery, plastic & reconstructive surgery, 1974-79; flight surgeon USAF, 1971-73; fellowship head & neck surgery Roswell Park Meml. Cancer Inst., Buffalo, N.Y., 1977; pvt. practice Napa, Calif., 1979—; dir. Aesthetic Surgery Ctr. of Napa Valley, Calif., 1993—; clinical asst. prof.

of plastic surgery Stanford U. Sch. of Medicine, Calif., 1993—; bd. dirs. Interplast, Palo Alto, Calif. (pres., bd. dirs. 1991-94, chmn. bd. dirs. 1994-95). Mem. Am. Soc. Plastic & Reconstructive Surgeons, Am. Soc. Aesthetic Plastic Surgeons, Lipoplasty Soc., Calif. Soc. Plastic Surgeons (bd. dirs.), Calif. Med. Assn., Napa County Med. Assn. Republican. Roman Catholic. Avocations: sailing, golf, direct care of indigent patientsthrough Interplast. Office: Plastic Reconstructive Surgery Ctr 3344 Villa Ln Ste 10 Napa CA 94558

ZIMMET, JESSIE VERELYNN, nurse, trust manager, home designer; b. Garden City, Kans., May 26, 1955; d. Vere Edward and Jessie Nina (Harmon) Z. A in Gen. Sci., Garden City Coll., 1975, ADN, 1977; BSN, Ft. Hays State U., 1982. CCRN; ACLS, instr.; trauma nurse core course provider; neonatal resuscitation program provider. Aide Garden Valley, Garden City, 1975; ICU technician St. Catherine's Hosp., Garden City, 1975-76; PRN flight nurse Life Watch, Wichita, Kans., Amarillo, Tex., 1985; instr. Ft. Hays (Kans.) State U., 1979-80; med. nurse Hadly Regional Med. Ctr., Hays, 1977-83; charge nurse, staff N.W. Tex. Hosp., Amarillo, 1984-94; unit mgr. med. specialty Integrated Health System, Amarillo, 1994-95; High Plains Bapt. Hosp.; house supr. Holy Cross Hosp., Taos, N.Mex., 1995—; PRN CCU High Plains Bapt. Hosp.; spkr. in field. Devel. ventilator wean unit. Mem. San Jacinto Bapt. Ch., Amarillo, 1994; mem. Ulysses (Kans.) 1st Bapt. Ch., 1966. Mem. AACN, NAFE, Emergency Nurses Assn., Intravenous Nurse Assn. Avocations: home designer, builder. Home: 6945 Ndcbu Taos NM 87571-6243

ZIMRING, STUART DAVID, lawyer; b. L.A., Dec. 12, 1946; s. Martin and Sylvia (Robinson) Z.; m. Eve Axelrad, Aug. 24, 1969 (div. 1981); m. Carol Grenert, May 24, 1981; children: Wendy Lynn Grenert, Joseph Noah, Matthew Kevin Grenert, Dov Shimon. BA in U.S. History, UCLA, 1968, JD, 1971. Bar: Calif. 1972, U.S. Dist. Ct. (cen. dist.) Calif. 1972, U.S. Dist. Ct. (no. dist.) Calif. 1984; U.S. Supreme Ct., 1994; cert. specialist in estate planning, probate and trust law. Assoc. Law Offices Leonard Smith, Beverly Hills, Calif., 1971-73; ptnr. Law Offices Smith & Zimring, Beverly Hills, Calif., 1973-76; assoc. Levin & Ballin, North Hollywood, Calif., 1976-77; prin. Levin, Ballin, Plotkin, Zimring & Goffin, A.P.C., North Hollywood, 1978-91, Law Offices Stuart D. Zimring, North Hollywood, 1991—; lectr. Los Angeles Valley Coll., Van Nuys, Calif., 1974-82. Author: Inter Vivos Trust Trustees Operating Manual, 1994, Durable Powers of Attorney for Health Care--A Practical Approach to an Intimate Document, 1995, Reverse Mortgages--An Update, 1996, Cultural and Religious Concerns in Drafting Advance Directives, 1996. Bd. dirs. Bet Tzedek, Jewish Legal Svcs., L.A. 1975-88, chmn. legal svcs. com., 1978-80; bd. dirs. Brandeis-Bardin Inst., Simi Valley, Calif., 1976-80; bd. dirs. Bur. Jewish Edn., L.A., 1973-88, chmn. com. on parent and family edn., 1985-87; trustee Adat Ari El Synagogue, L.A., 1982—; bd. dirs. Orgn. for the Needs of the Elderly, 1994, 1st v.p. 1995-97, pres., 1997—. Recipient Circle award Juvenile Justice Connection Project, L.A., 1989, Wiley W. Manuel award for pro bono legal svcs., 1994, 95, 96, 97, 98. Fellow Nat. Acad. Elder Law Attys. (pres. So. Calif. chpt. 1997, chair nat. tech. com., nat. bd. dirs. 1997—); mem. State Bar Calif., San Fernando Valley Bar Assn. (trustee 1979-86). Democrat. Avocations: music, collecting wine, travel, photography. Office: 12650 Riverside Dr North Hollywood CA 91607-3421

ZINMAN, DAVID, conductor; b. Bklyn., 1936. Grad., Oberlin Conservatory; LHD (hon.), U. Minn.; postgrad., Boston Symphony's Tanglewood Music Ctr. Music dir., condr. Balt. Symphony Orch.; guest condr. London Symphony Orch., 1963, Phila. Orch., 1967, Hollywood Bowl, Mostly Mozart, Ravinia, Tanglewood music festivals, Berlin Philharm., Royal Philharm., others; artistic dir. Minn. Orch. Viennese Sommerfest, 1994-96; music dir., chief condr. Aurich Tonhalle Orch., 1995; music dir. Rochester Philharm., Rotterdam Philharm., Netherlands Chamber Orch., Aspen Music Festival, 1997, Aspen Music Sch., 1997. Recordings include (with Balt. Symphony) The New York Album, 1994, (2 Grammy awards), (with London Sinfonietta) Henryk górecki's Symphony No. 3, (with Christian Zacharias) Mozart Piano Concdertos, (with Berlin Radio Symphony) The Jungle Book (Gramophone award 1994), Metropolis Symphony, others; programmar, condr. numerous radio stas. including Pub. Radio Internat. Recipient 3 Grammy awards, 1990, 2 Grand Prix Disque awards, 2 Edison prizes, Deutsche Schallplatten Preis award. Office: ICM c/o Jenny Vogel 8942 Wilshire Blvd Beverly Hills CA 90211*

ZINN, DENNIS BRADLEY, magician, actor, corporate skills trainer; b. Phoenix, Dec. 15, 1957; s. Clarence LaVern and Juanita Alice (Martin) Z.; m. Brenda Ann Puckett, May 25, 1982. Grad. high sch., Phoenix. Actor (movies) Nobody's Fool, To Find My Son, The American Girls, A Fire in the Sky, Assault on Paradise, A Star Is Born; actor (stage) Glendale Little Theatre, Mesa Little Theatre, Scottsdale Little Theatre, Phoenix Little Theatre, Children's Little Theatre, Alhambra High Sch. Drama Dept.; performer numerous commls., voice-overs, indsl. films; guest appearances on numerous TV programs; magician appearances at Hollywood Magic Castle and Las Vegas, magician/performer for over 20 talk shows; host, producer The New Variety Arts Show; contbg. author: The Snake Basket; writer Genii mag., Linking Ring mag., ABRA mag., Magician's Weekly. Performer, fundraiser Phoenix Breakfast Civitan Club, 1979-92; mem. Valley Cmty. Access TV, 1990-93; mem. Phoenix and Valley of Sun Visitors and Conv. Bur. Recipient Patrick Henry award for oratory Ariz. Congress for God & Country, 1974, Am. Legion Citizenship award Ariz. Am. Legion, 1975. Mem. AFTRA (treas. Ariz. local 1989-90, bd. dirs. 1993-95), SAG, Internat. Brotherhood Magicians (pres. local ring 55, 1979, tar. rep. 1979-80, Close-Up Magician of Yr. 1976, Internat. Order of Merlin 1997), Soc. Am. Magicians (v.p. assembly 248 1997-98), Profl. Magicians Assn., Magic Castle. Republican. Avocations: book collecting, golf, travel. Home and Office: Brad Zinn Entertainment Enterprises 4803 W Evans Dr Glendale AZ 85306-4434

ZINN, RAY, computer company executive. CEO Micrel, San Jose, Calif. Office: Micrel 1849 Fortune Dr San Jose CA 95131-1724*

ZITO, MICHAEL ANTHONY, advertising and graphic design typesetting company owner; b. San Diego, Feb. 25, 1957; s. Richard and Margaret Jane (Greggs) Z. Student, El Paso C.C., 1977-78, Grossmont Coll., 1977-78. Emergency med. technician E&E Ambulance Svc., Colorado Springs, Colo., 1972-73; psychiat. technician Alvarado Hosp., San Diego, 1975-78; surg. technician, orderly Eisenhower Osteopathic Hosp., Colorado Springs, 1973-75; mktg. mgr. Calif. Dept. Forestry Fire Fighters, San Diego, 1978-79; mktg. rep. Mort Fin. Svcs., San Diego, 1980-81, Mil.-Civil Svc. Yellow Pages, San Diego, 1983-84; nuclear technician San Onofre (Calif.) Nuclear Power Plant, 1982-83; mktg. rep. Stas. XPRS, XHRM, KMLO, 1982-84; pres. Discount Yellow Pages, San Diego, 1984-87, 3-D Advt. Graphics and Typesetting Co., San Diego, 1987—; nat. coord. Robbins Rsch. Internat., La Jolla, Calif., 1993-94. Actor TV documentary and movies, San Diego, 1987 (award Nat. Movie Arts Festival and Movies 1988). Instr. YMCA/USO, 1971-72. Recipient award Nat. Movie Arts Festival, 1988. Roman Catholic. Avocations: beekeeping, musician, snow skiing, swimming, photography.

ZIVELONGHI, KURT DANIEL, artist, painter, art director, designer; b. Barstow, Calif., Oct. 3, 1960; s. Vincent Otto and Beverly Dean (Schwind) Z. Student, Pasadena City Coll., 1984-85, Art Students League, N.Y.C., 1988-89; BFA, Art Ctr. Coll. of Design, 1993. Mgr. Foothill Airplane Washing Svc., Claremont, Calif., 1980-82; sales rep. Valley Group Fin. Svc., Claremont, 1986-88; loan rep. Pacific Group Funding, Claremont, 1989-90; self employed fine artist Alhambra, Calif., 1990—; art dir. movies Seagull's Journey, Aspno LLC, The Innocent Bystander, Mad Dogs Prodns., 1998. One-man show at Coll. of Design Art Ctr., Pasadena, Calif., 1993, two-man show at Flux Gallery, Eagle Rock, Calif., 1993, group show at Art Students League, N.Y.C., 1989. Mem. Ctr. for the Study of Popular Culture, Century City, Calif., 1994. Mem. Am. Soc. Portrait Artists. Avocations: pianist, weight lifter, theatre, cinema. Office: Local Colors Rep 16624 Marquez Ave Pacific Palisades CA 90272-0000 Representation The Print Merchants Pacific Design Ctr 8687 Melrose Ave West Hollywood CA 90069-5701

ZLAKET, THOMAS A., state supreme court justice; b. May 30, 1941. AB in Polit. Sci., U. Notre Dame, 1962; LLB, U. Ariz., 1965. Bar: Ariz. 1965, U.S. Dist. Ct. Ariz. 1965. Atty. Lesher Scruggs Rucker Kimble & Lindamood, Tucson, 1965-68, Maud &

Zlaket, 1968-70, Estes Browning Maud and Zlaket, 1970-73, Slutes Estes Zlaket Sakrison & Wasley, 1973-82, Zlaket & Zlaket, 1982-92; judge pro tempore Pima County (Ariz.) Superior Ct., 1983—; justice Ariz. Supreme Ct., 1992, vice chief justice, 1996, chief justice, 1997. Fellow Am. Coll. Trial Lawyers, Am. Bar Found.; mem. ABA, Pima County Bar Assn., Am. Bd. Trial Advocates, Ariz. Coll. Trial Advocacy, U. Ariz. Law Coll. Assn., Ariz. Law Rev. Assn. Office: Arizona Supreme Ct 1501 W Washington St Phoenix AZ 85007-3231*

ZOBEL, JAN A., tax consultant; b. San Francisco, 1947; d. Jerome Fremont and Louise Maxine Zobel. BA, Whittier Coll., 1968; MA, U. Chgo., 1970. Tchr. Chgo. Pub. Schs., 1969-70, San Francisco Pub. Schs., 1971-78; editor, pub. People's Yellow Pages, San Francisco 1971-81; pvt. practice tax cons. San Francisco, Oakland, 1978—; tchr. community coll. dist., San Francisco, 1986—; tax lectr. U. Hawaii, 1989—, U. Calif., San Francisco State U., Marin C.C. Author: Minding Her Own Business: The Self-Employed Woman's Guide to Taxes and Recordkeeping, 1997, 2d edit., 1998; editor People's Yellow Pages, 1971-81 (cert. of honor San Francisco Bd. Suprs. 1974), Where the Child Things Are, 1977-80. Com. mem. Bay Area Career Women's Fund. Named Acct. Adv. of Yr., SBA, 1987; presented Key to City of Buffalo, 1970. Mem. Nat. Assn. Enrolled Agts., Calif. Assn. Enrolled Agts., Nat. Assn. Tax Preparers, Bay Area Career Women. Office: 1197 Valencia St San Francisco CA 94110-3026

ZOBEL, LOUISE PURWIN, author, educator, lecturer, writing consultant; b. Laredo, Tex., Jan. 10, 1922; d. Leo Max and Ethel Catherine (Levy) Purwin; m. Jerome Fremont Zobel, Nov. 14, 1943; children: Lenore Zobel Harris, Janice A., Robert E., Audrey Zobel Dollinger. BA cum laude, Stanford U., 1943, MA, 1976. Cert. adult edn. and community coll. tchr., Calif. Freelance mag. writer and author Palo Alto, Calif., 1942—; writer, editor, broadcastor UP Bur., San Francisco, 1943; lectr. on writing, history, travel No. Calif., 1964—; lectr. educator U. Calif. campuses, other colls. and univs., 1969—; writing cons. to pvt. clients, 1969—; editorial asst. Assn. Coll. Unions Internat., Palo Alto, 1972-73; acting asst. prof. journalism San Jose State U., 1976; keynote speaker, seminar leader, prin. speaker at nat. confs.; cruise/shipboard enrichment lectr. and presenter of travel slide programs; coord. TV shows; TV personality publicity and public rels. campaigns. Author: (books) The Travel Writer's Handbook, 1980, (paperback), 1982, 83, 84, 85, rev. edits., 1992, 94, 97; author, narrator (90 minute cassette) Let's Have Fun in Japan, 1982; contbr. articles to anthologies, nat. mags. and newspapers; writer advertorials. Bd. dirs., publicity chair Friends of Palo Alto Libr., 1985—; officer Santa Clara County Med. Aux., Esther Clark Aux., others; past pres. PTA. Recipient award for excellence in journalism Sigma Delta Chi, 1943, awards Writers Digest, 1967-95, Armed Forces Writers League, 1972, Nat. Writers Club, 1976, All Nippon Airways and Japanese Nat. Tourist Orgn., 1997. Mem. Am. Soc. Journalists and Authors, Travel Journalists Guild, Internat. Food, Wine and Travel Writers Assn., Pacific Asia Travel Assn., Calif. Writers Club (v.p. 1988-89), AAUW (v.p. 1955-57, Nat. writing award 1969), Stanford Alumni Assn., Phi Beta Kappa. Avocations: travel, reading, writing, photography. Home and Office: 23350 Sereno Ct Unit 30 Cupertino CA 95014-6543

ZOBELL, CHARLES W., newspaper managing editor; b. Provo, Utah, Mar. 17, 1950; m. Marilyn M. Earl, May 5, 1978; children: David, Rebecca. BA in comm., Brigham Young U., 1974. Reporter Las Vegas Rev-Jour., 1975-78; dir. Office Intergovtl. Rels. City of Las Vegas, 1978-80; city editor Las Vegas Rev.-Jour., 1980-92, mng. editor, 1992—. Vol. rep. Mormon Ch., Argentina, 2 yrs. Office: Las Vegas Review-Journal/Donrey Med Grp PO Box 70 1111 W Bonanza Rd Las Vegas NV 89125*

ZODL, JOSEPH ARTHUR, international trade executive, consultant; b. Hackensack, N.J., Aug. 13, 1948; s. Joseph Frank and Edna Josephine (Hokanson) Z. BA in Polit. Sci., Fordham Coll., 1970; MA in Polit. Sci., New Sch. for Social Rsch., N.Y.C., 1991; MBA in Internat. Bus., Wester Internat. U., Phoenix, 1998. Lic. customs broker U.S. Treasury Dept. Export mgr. Savage Universal Corp., Tempe, Ariz., 1984-93; corp. transp. mgr. Nat. Media Corp., Phoenix, 1993—; adj. instr. internat. bus. Rio Salado C.C., 1989—, Keller Grad. Sch. Bus., 1995—, Scottsdale C.C., 1996—. Author: Export-Import: Everything You and Your Company Need To Know To Compete in World Markets, 1992, rev., 1995; contbr. articles to profl. jours. Vice chmn. Legis. Dist. 20 Dems., 1978-80, chmn., 1980-82; mem. Ariz. State Dem. Com., 1978-89; cand. Ariz. Ho. Reps., 1986. Named Eagle Scout, Boy Scouts Am., 1966. Mem. Am. Polit. Sci. Assn., Ariz. World Trade Ctr., Internat. Transp. Mgmt. Assn. (dir. 1990-91), Phoenix Traffic Club, Phoenix Customs Brokers Assn., Delta Nu Alpha (pres. 1980-81, Ariz. Transp. Man of Yr. 1980), Alpha Phi Omega, Phi Theta Kappa, Delta Mu Delta. Roman Catholic.

ZOELLNER, ROBERT WILLIAM, chemistry educator; b. Marshfield, Wis., May 30, 1956; s. Willard Rudolph and Marie Martha (Prihoda) Z.; m. Barbara Moore, Feb. 5, 1983; children: Joan Moore, Thaddeus Barak. BS, St. Norbert Coll., De Pere, Wis., 1978; PhD, Kans. State U., 1983. Postdoctoral assoc. Cornell U., Ithaca, N.Y., 1983-84; vis. scientist U. Aix-Marseille (France) III, 1984-85; asst. prof. No. Ariz. U., Flagstaff, 1986-92, assoc. prof., 1992-98; sabbatical assoc. Istituto per lo Studio della Stereochimica Consiglio Nazionale delle Ricerche, 1994-95; assoc. prof. Humboldt State U., Arcata, Calif., 1998—. Mem. Am. Chem. Soc., Internat. Coun. on Main Group Chemistry, N.Y. Acad. Scis., Wis. Acad. Sci., Arts and Letters, Sigma Xi, Alpha Chi Sigma, Phi Lambda Upsilon. Office: Humboldt State Univ Dept of Chemistry Arcata CA 95521-8299

ZONE, JANINE DENISE, elementary education educator; b. L.A., Sept. 15, 1953; d. Michael and Mildred (Heischuber) Z. AA, L.A. City Coll., 1975; diploma in Lang. Studies, U. Vienna, Austria, 1977; BA in Art History, UCLA, 1979. Multiple subject credential profl., Calif. Tchr. Alexandria Ave. Sch. L.A. Unified Sch. Dist., 1986—; bd. dirs. Jr. Arts Ctr.-Barnsdall Art Pk., L.A., 1988—; mem. adv. bd. Cotsen Art Fellowship, L.A., 1985—; coord. visual arts L.A. Unified Sch. Dist. Festivals of Achievement, 1987-88; participant Vassar Coll. Inst. for Publishing Children's Books, 1994; mem. instrnl. leadership team LEARN, 1995—. Author: David Hockney Is Coming to the Jr. Arts Center, 1988; artist, author: (gallery installations) The Teacher's Press, 1987—. Vol. outreach educator, fund raiser U.S. Com. for UNICEF, L.A., 1986-96; precinct leader Dem. Nat. Com.; conf. participant Children's Def. Fund, Washington, 1993. Recipient Award of Appreciation, Hollywood Arts Coun., L.A. Children's Mus. Mem. United Tchrs. Avocations: travel and study tours, collecting Mexican folk art, volunteer art workshops for children and families, water sports. Home: 3941 Veselich Ave Apt 151 Los Angeles CA 90039-1436 Office: Alexandria Avenue Sch 4211 Oakwood Ave Los Angeles CA 90004-3214

ZONGOLOWICZ, HELEN MICHAELINE, education and psychology educator; b. Kenosha, Wis., July 22, 1936; d. Edmund S. and Helen (Ostrowski) Z.; EdB, Dominican Coll., 1966; MA, Cardinal Stritch Coll., 1973; EdD, U. No. Colo., 1977. Tchr. elem. schs. Kenosha, 1956-58, Center Line, Mich., 1958-59, Taft, Calif. 1960-61, Lake Wales, Fla., 1962-63, Albuquerque, 1963-65; tchr., asst. prin. St. Mary's Sch., Taft, 1965-69; asst. supt. Diocese of Fresno, Calif., 1969-70; tchr. primary grades Greasewood Boarding Sch., Ganado, Ariz., 1970-72, coord. spl. projects, 1972-75, liaison to parent adv. coun., 1972-75, tchr. supr., 1972-76; ednl. specialist Ft. Defiance Agy., Navajo Area, Ariz., 1974-75, ednl. diagnostician, 1979-80; asst. prof. Auburn (Ala.) U., 1977-79; asst. prof. U. N.Mex.-Gallup, 1981-94, prof. edn. and psychology, 1994—; dir. child care ctr., pres. faculty senate, 1995-97; prin. Chuska Sch., 1980-93; chair dept. psychology/edn. CDA dir., 1995—; vis. prof. U. Colo., 1976; mem. N.Mex. State Articulation Task Force, 1994—. Recipient Spl. Achievement award U.S. Dept. Interior, 1971, 73, Points of Light award, 1990, Superior Performance award, 1982, Achievement award Navajo Nation, 1993; named Prin. of Yr. Bur. of Indian Affairs, 1990, named Fnd. of Yr. Navajo Area Sch. Bd. Assn., 1991. Mem. AAUW, Nat. Assn. Edn. of Young Children, Nat. Staff Devel. Coun., Am. Assn. Mental Deficiency, Assn. for Supervision and Curriculum, Reading Assn., NAFE, Internat. Reading Assn., Assn. for Children with Learning Disabilities, Nat. Coun. Tchrs. of English, Assn. Childhood Edn. Internat. Home: Box 76 Fruitland NM 87416-0076 Office: U NM Gallup 200 College Rd Gallup NM 87301-4830

ZORN, KATHLEEN JOANNE, marketing specialist; b. San Rafael, Calif., Oct. 17, 1954; d. Vernon Keith and Constance Elva (Jeffery) Madison; m. Mark Alan Zorn, Sept. 11, 1984; children: Samantha, Jocelyn. BS, U. Oreg., 1979, MBA, 1995. Adult recreation program dir. Pearl Buck Ctr., Eugene, Oreg., 1977-78; vocat. trainer Diversified Prodns. Systems, Eugene, Oreg., 1978-79; insp. Spectra-Physics, Eugene, Oreg., 1982-85, product auditor, 1985-89, process/systems auditor, 1987-91, ISO9000 project mgr., 1991-93; advt. dir. The Bus. News, Eugene, Oreg., 1995—. Avocations: fitness, writing, hiking, reading, travel. Office: Northwest Media 326 W 12th Ave Eugene OR 97401-3449

ZORNES, JEANNE IRENE, writer, speaker; b. Inglewood, Calif., July 10, 1947; d. John Mohr and Irene Marie (Berge) Doering; m. Richard V. Zornes, Aug. 15, 1981; children: Zachary, Inga. BA in Edn., Western Wash. U., 1969; Cert. in Bible, Multnomah Bible Coll., Portland, Oreg., 1977; MA in Comms., Wheaton (Ill.) Coll., 1980. Reporter, editor Wenatchee (Wash.) World, 1970-74; editl. asst. Wycliffe Bible Translators, Huntington Beach, Calif., 1974-76; asst. editor Multnomah Press, Portland, Oreg., 1977-78, Moody Mag., Chgo., 1979-80; freelance writer and speaker, Wenatchee, 1980—; spkr. for women's retreats in Northwest. Author: The Power of Encouragement, 1981, When I Prayed for Patience. . .God Let Me Have It, 1995, When I Got on the Highway to Heaven, I Didn't Expect Rocky Roads, 1998, When I Felt Like Ragweed, God Saw a Rose, 1999, (with Dan Miller) Living, Laughing and Loving Life, 1997. Active Wenatchee Free Meth. Ch.; participant Bible Study fellowship. Recipient 5th Place award for humor Evangelical Press Assn., 1982, awards in fiction contests. Avocations: violin, piano, sewing, participating in church music programs. Home: 1025 Meeks St Wenatchee WA 98801-1640

ZORNES, MILFORD, artist; b. Camargo, Okla., Jan. 25, 1908; s. James Francis and Clara Delphine (Lindsay) Z.; m. Gloria Codd, 1935; 1 son, Franz Milford; m. Patricia Mary Palmer, Nov. 8, 1942; 1 dau., Maria Patricia. Student, Otis Art Inst., Los Angeles, 1929, Pomona Coll., 1930-34. Instr. art Pomona Coll., 1946-50; art dir. Vortox and Padua Hills Theatre, Claremont, 1954-66. Exhibited, Calif. Watercolor Soc., Met. Mus., Am. Watercolor Soc., Corcoran Gallery, Bklyn. Mus., Denver Mus., Cleve. Mus., L.A. Mus., Brooks Gallery, London, Bombay Art Assn., Chgo. Art Inst., Butler Mus., Gallery Modern Masters, Washington, Santa Barbara (Calif.) Mus., Cin. Mus., Laguna (Calif.) Art Gallery, Oklahoma City Mus., Springville (Utah) Mus., Claremont (Calif.) Fine Arts, Anderson Art Gallery, Sunset Beach, Calif.; represented in permanent collections at L.A. Mus., White House Collection, Met. Mus., Pentagon Bldg., Butler Mus., UCLA, Nat. Acad., San Diego Mus., L.A. County Fair, Home Savs. and Loan Assn., L.A., Corcoran Gallery, Washington; mem. art com., Nat. Orange Show, San Bernardino, Calif., 1963-65; author: A Journey to Nicaragua, 1977, The California Style: California Watercolor Artists, 1925-1955, 1985; subject of book by Gordon McClelland: Milford Zornes, Hillcrest Press, 1991. Served with U.S. Army, 1943-45, CBI. Recipient Paul Prescott Barrow award Pomona Coll., 1987, David Prescott Burrows award, 1991, A Most Disting. Citizen award So. Utah State Coll., 1988, Am. Artist Achievement award Am. Artist Mag., 1994; named Nat. Academician. Mem. NAD, Am. Watercolor Soc., Southwestern Watercolor Soc., Watercolor West, Nat. Watercolor Soc., Utah Watercolor Soc. Address: 2136 Brescia Ave Claremont CA 91711-1804

ZOU, KE, English linguistics educator; b. Nanchang, Jiangxi, Republic of China, Oct. 30, 1956; m. Yiu-Feng and Shun-Gau (Cheng) Chau; m. Ying Liu, Dec. 26, 1985. MA in Theoretical Linguistics, Ohio State U., 1989; MA in Gen. Linguistics, U. So. Calif., 1991, PhD in Gen. Linguistics, 1995. English and Linguistics instr. Jiangxi Normal U., Nanchang, 1982-86; linguistics instr. Ohio State U., Columbus, 1988-89; English lectr. El Camino Coll., Torrance, 1996-98, Calif. State Polytech. U., Pomona, 1997, Chapman U., Orange, Calif., 1998, Calif. State U., Dominguez Hills, 1990-98; asst. prof. English Calif. State U., Hayward, 1998—. Editor: The Grammer Bible, 1998. Mem. Linguistic Soc. of Am., Internat. Assn. of Chinese Linguistics. Avocations: computers, sports, cooking, travelling, movies. Office: English Dept Calif State U Hayward 25800 Carlos Bee Blvd Hayward CA 94542-3001

ZUBER, LIANNE CAROL, elementary school educator; b. Independence, Mo., Nov. 23, 1968; d. Jeffry Lane and Carol Yukuko Glauner; m. Michael John Zuber, Dec., 1990; 1 child, Mikala Johoku. BA in Edn., Park Coll., 1990; MA in Edn., Ctrl. Mich. U., 1998. Lic. computer tchr. Hawaii. Summer program coord. Hawaii Preparatory Acad., Kamuela, Hawaii, 1989-97; art tchr. k-6 Hawaii Preparatory Acad., Kamuela, 1990-91; counselor Honoka'a (Hawaii) Elem. and H.S., 1991-92, career guidance tchr., remedial tchr., 1992-93, grade 2 tchr., 1993-94; grade 1 tchr. Waikoloa Elem. Sch., Waikoloa, Hawaii, 1994—; mem. tech. com., curriculum com. Waikoloa Elem. sch., 1994—, workshop presenter, at local schs. and to Nat. Coun. Tchrs. of English Conv., Detroit, 1997, mem. instructional tech. com., 1998—, Nat. Coun. Tchrs. of English-Testing and Evaluation Com. and Instructional Tech. Com., 1998—. Recipient Perkins award, 1987; grantee Good Idea, 1994, 95, 98, Environmental grant, 1996, Hawaiian Studies grant, 1996. Mem. Hawaii State Tchrs. Assn. (v.p. Hamakua chpt. 1994-95, state conv. del. 1994, 95, co-chair 1996-98, mem. tech. sub-com. 1996—, state chair 1998), Delta Kappa Gamma (sec. Nu chpt. 1998—, presenter, com. mem. fall workshop). Office: Waikoloa Elem Sch 68-1730 Ho'oko St Waikoloa HI 96743

ZUCAL, STEVEN JOSEPH, priest; b. Denver, Sept. 3, 1959. BA in Communications, Regis Coll. Ordained priest Western Orthodox Ch. in Am., 1983. Pastor St. Ignatius of Antioch Parish, Englewood, Colo., 1983—; resident dir. Adsum House, Englewood, 1984-86; dir. mktg. Diakonia Credit Union, Denver, 1981-89; regional dir. Servants of the Good Shepherd, 1982—; vol. chaplain Dept. Institutions Div. Youth Services, 1980—; mem. Commn. on Western Orthodox Liturgy, 1983-91, Commn. on Ecumenical Witness and Religious Dialogue, Colo. Coun. Chs., 1989-91, Commn. on Instl. Ministries, Colo. Coun. Chs., 1988—; co-dir. Info. Services Team, Englewood, 1983—. Co-author (calendar) Ecclesiastical Calendar, 1984, 85; editor: The Ch. Manual, 1984-85. Mem. ad hoc com. Juvenile Advocacy, Denver, 1985, bd. dirs Juvenile Advocacy Group, Golden, Colo., 1985—; advisor Colo. Teen. Inst., Denver, 1984, steering com., 1985; bd. dirs. Youth in Prison, Denver, 1984; mem. K.I.D.S. (Kids In-Transition Developing Spiritually); mem. standing adv. coun. SGS/WOCA. Named Outstanding Vol., Colo. Teen Inst., 1984, Outstanding Bd. Mem., Mile High Coun. on Alcoholism and Drug Abuse, 1990; recipient appreciation St. Luke's Hops. Addictions Recovery Unit, 1983. Mem. Nat. Chaplains Assn. Youth Rehab., Mile High Council on Alcoholism and Drug Abuse. Office and Home: St Ignatius of Antioch Parish 1918 S Raleigh St Denver CO 80219-5153

ZUCKER, ALFRED JOHN, English educator, academic adminstrator; b. Hartford, Sept. 25, 1940; s. Samuel and Rose (Zucker) Z.; AA, L.A. Valley Coll., 1960; AB in English, UCLA, 1962, AB in Speech, MA in English, 1962, MA in Speech, 1963, PhD, 1966, postgrad., UCLA, U. So. Calif., Harvard U.; m. Sallie Lea Friedheim, Dec. 25, 1966; children—Mary Anne, John James, Jr., James Patrick, Patrick Jonathan, Anne-Marie Kathleen, Kathleen Mary. Lectr. English, Los Angeles City Coll., 1963-68; prof. English, philosophy, other div. humanities Los Angeles Southwest Coll., 1968-72, chmn. English dept., 1972-74, asst. dean instruction, 1974—; prof. English El Camino Coll., 1985—; prof. English Calif. Valley Coll., 1989—, chmn. English dept., 1997—. Mem. Los Angeles Coll. Dist. Senate, 1969—. Mem. Los Angeles Coll. Tchrs. Assn. (dir.), Calif. Jr. Coll. Assn., Calif. Tchrs. Assn., AAUP, World Affairs Coun., Mensa, Phi Beta Kappa, Phi Delta Kappa (pres. U. Calif. at Los Angeles chpt. 1966-67, v.p. 1967-68), Tau Alpha Epsilon, Phi Theta Kappa. Lodge: KC. Contbr. articles to profl. jours. Office: 5800 Fulton Ave Van Nuys CA 91401-4062

ZUCKSCHWERDT, OTTO GALVATORD, counselor substance abuse specialist, chaplain; b. N.Y.C., Aug. 16, 1947; s. Kenneth and Jennis Z.; m. Karola Valerie Dec. 28, 1968 (div. 1994) 1974; children: Christina J. Brown, Julie; in Bibl. Studies, Lee Coll., Cleveland, Tenn., 1980; PhD, DLitt. in Counseling, Evangel Christian U., Monroe, La., 1990; MEd in Counseling and Calif. Coast U., Santa Anna, 1998. Nat. cert. counselor and master addic-

tions counselor Nat. Bd. Cert. Counselors; lic. profl. counselor, psychologist extended provider, driving under influence and substance abuse evaluator, examiner, Idaho; cert. clin. supr., drug and alcohol counselor Bd. Alcoholism Drug Counselor's Cert., Inc.; internat. cert. substance abuse specialist Internat. Cert. Reciprocity Consortium and other Drug Abuse, Inc.; ordained min. Internat. Ministerial Fellowship, 1994; dr. of addiction Nat. Bd. Addiction Examiners; cert. criminal justice specialist; cert. chaplain Full Gospel Chs., 1993. Youth svc. coord. Port of Hope, Nampa, Idaho, 1982-87; coord. Big Bros. and Big Sisters, Nampa, Idaho, 1985-87; staff psychologist Idaho Child Protection, Caldwell, 1988-89; resource officer Canyon County Sheriff Dept., Caldwell, 1989-94; sr. counselor, CAFS dir. New Life Counseling Ctr., Boise, Idaho, 1989-94; sr. counselor Rice Clinic, Boise, Idaho, 1994—; clinician and youth counselor Challenge, Inc., Boise, Idaho, 1994—; sr. counselor, dir. children and family svcs., Boise, 1989-94; dual diagnosis counselor and youth clinician Challenge, Inc., 1994—; owner Northwerdt Psychol. Svcs., 1996—; pastor Assemblies of God and Ch. of Brethren, throughout U.S., 1970-92. Contbr. articles on Christian living to various jours.; developer various youth svcs. programs. Chaplain, lt. col. USAF CAP, Caldwell, 1985—; co-founder Marine Christian Cadet Corps, N.Y.C., 1966; chief chaplain St. Joseph County Sheriff Dept., Centerville, Mich., 1975-78; developer, promoter Dial-A-Blessing Ministries, 1980&; mem. Idaho Gov.'s Commn. for Youth, 1993-94, Idaho Crime Commn. Mem. ACA, Law Enforcement Alliance Am., Internat. Assn. for Addictions and Offender Counselors. Avocations: travel, reading. Home: 134 Poplar St Nampa ID 83651-2068

ZUETEL, KENNETH ROY, JR., lawyer; b. L.A., Apr. 5, 1954; s. Kenneth Roy Sr. and Adelle Francis (Avant) Z.; m. Cheryl Kay Morse, May 29, 1976; children: Bryan, Jarid, Christopher, Lauren. BA, San Diego State U., 1974; JD, U. San Diego, 1978. Bar: Calif. 1978 U.S. Ct. Appeals (9th cir.) 1979, U.S. Dist. Ct. (ctrl. dist.) Calif. 1979, U.S. Dist. Ct. (so. and no. dists.) Calif. 1980, U.S. Dist. Ct. (ea. dist.) 1981. Clk. to fed. Judge Martin Pence U.S. Dist. Ct. Hawaii, Honolulu, 1978-79; assoc. litigation Buchalter, Nemer, L.A., 1979-83, Thelen, Marrin, L.A., 1983-88; ptnr. Zuetel & Tomlinson, Pasadena, Calif., 1988—; superior ct. arbitrator L.A. Superior Ct., 1982-90, superior ct. settlement officer, 1988-93; judge pro temp L.A. Mcpl. Ct., 1983—, L.A. Superior Ct., 1989—; guest lectr. Loyola U. Sch. Law, 1986-95; CEB lectr. Author: Civil Procedure Before Trial, 1992; cons. editor: Cal. Civ. Proc., 1992; contbr. articles to profl. jours. Recipient Recognition award L.A. (Calif.) Bd. Suprs., 1988. Mem. State Bar Calif. (mem. adv. com. continuing edn. 1985-88, trial practice subcom. 1985-88, disciplinary examiner 1986), Los Angeles County Bar Assn. (chair trial atty. project 1982-83, mem. L.A. del. conf. of dels. 1986-96, chair L.A. de. conf. of dels. 1995, exec. com. barristers 1984-88, superior ct. com. 1985-88, civil practice com. 1992-94, exec. com. litigation sect. 1989-90), Pasadena Bar Assn., Inns of Ct. (barrister L.A. chpt. 1991-92), Phi Beta Kappa, Phi Kappa Phi, Phi Alpha Theta, Pi Sigma Alpha. Republican. Presbyterian. Home: 567 Willow Springs Ln Glendora CA 91741-2974 Office: Zuetel & Tomlinson 180 S Lake Ave Ste 540 Pasadena CA 91101-2666

ZUSCHLAG, NANCY HANSEN, environmental science/nature resources educator; b. Montclair, N.J., Dec. 12, 1954; d. Irving Djalmar and Carmen (Del Grippo) Z.; m. Jeffrey Jon Miller, Sept. 21, 1991. BA in Biology cum laude, Coe Coll., 1977; MA in Biology, U. Kans., 1982. Regional conservation educator and coord. Mo. Conservation Dept., Jefferson City, 1982-84; coord. sch. programs Denver Mus. Natural History, 1986-87; program dir. dept. natural resources and environ. edn. Coop. Ext. Colo. State U., Golden, 1988-98; ops. and edn. mgr. Arvada Mad Sci. of Denver, 1998—; instr. environ. educator Mus. Natural History, U. Kans., Lawrence, 1976-82, assoc. pub. edn. dept. , 1986-89; lectr. William Woods Coll., 1982-84; mem. study, rsch. rev. group Canary Islands, 1985; cons. Kongskilde Field Study Edn. Ctr., Soro, Denmark, 1985; bd. dirs. Foothills Nature Ctr., Boulder, Colo., 1987-89; assoc. zool. Denver Mus. Natural History, 1988; cons. and educator Mus. Zool., U. Copenhagen, 1984-85, 95-96. Author, editor: Back to Ancient Egypt, 1987; (with others) Science - Natur/Teknik, Assessment and Learning Studies and Educational Theory Curriculum, Vol. 22, 1995; editor: (with others) Contributions to Vertebrate Ecology and Systematic; a Tribute to Henry S. Fitch, 1983; contbr. articles to profl. jours. state edn. coord. Colo. Earth Day is Every Day campaign, Boulder, 1990; bd. dirs. Colo. Found. Agr., Denver, 1992-95, mem. edn. bd., 1993; facilitator and presenter UN Program Youth in the Environment, U. Colo., Boulder, 1993; chair environ. and natural resources future's task force com., Colo. State U. Coop. Ext., 1993; mem. nat. natural resources and eviron. mgmt. support team coop. states, rsch. ext. edn. sys., USDA, 1993-96; mem. synthesis team and original document writing team, Colo. Environ. Edn. Master Plan, 1994; mem. state steering com. Denver Urban Resources Partnership, 1996—, Denver Youth Naturally Project, 1995. Recipient N.J. award AUW, County Achievement award Nat. Assn. Counties, 1989, Environ. Scholar award USEPA, 1990, region 8 Outstanding Women's Contbns. in Environ. Edn. award, 1992, Nat. Environ. Coun. award, 1992, 94, Celebrate Colo. Environ. Leadership award Colo. State Gov., 1993; scholar Coe Coll., 1973-74; Virginia Harkness-Sawtelle Found. scholar Coe Coll. and U. Kans., 1976-78; Fulbright scholar U. Copenhagen Zool. Mus., 1984-85, Fulbright scholar assoc. Royal Danish Sch. Edn., 1995-96. Mem. Am. Assn. Biol. Scis., Nat. Wildlife Fedn. (mem. steering com. Naturlink 1993), North Am. Assn. Environ. Edn., Alliance Environ. Edn., Nat. Assn. Interpreters, Am. Arachnological Assn., Colo. Alliance Environ. Edn. (bd. dirs. 1988-92, pres. 1990-91, adv. bd. 1997), Colo. Assn. Tchrs., Fulbright Alumni Soc., Phi Sigma, Epsilon Sigma Phi (State Early Career Excellence award 1990). Avocations: hiking, writing on myth, nature and culture , jewelry-making. Office: Green Triangle Assocs Internat # 224 4255 S Buckley Rd Aurora CO 80013

ZWAHLEN, FRED CASPER, JR., journalism educator; b. Portland, Oreg., Nov. 11, 1924; s. Fred and Katherine (Meyer) Z.; m. Grace Eleanor DeMoss, June 24, 1959; children: Molly, Skip. BA, Oreg. State U., 1949; MA, Stanford U., 1952. Reporter San Francisco News, 1949-50; acting editor Stanford Alumni Rev., Palo Alto, Calif., 1950; successively instr. journalism, news bur. asst., prof. journalism, chmn. journalism dept. Oreg. State U., Corvallis, 1950-91, prof. emeritus, 1991—; Swiss tour guide, 1991—; corres. Portland Oregonian, 1950-67. Author: (with others) Handbook of Photography, 1984. Coord. E.E. Wilson Scholarship Fund, 1964—; active budget com. Corvallis Sch. Dist., 1979. Recipient Achievement award Sch. Journalism U. Oregon, 1988. Mem. Assn. for Edn. in Journalism and Mass Communications (conv. chmn. 1983, pres.' award 1988), Oreg. Newspaper Pubs. Assn. (hon. life 1998, bd. dirs. 1980-85, student loan fund named in his honor 1988), Soc. Profl. Journalists (nat. svc. citation 1988), Corvallis Country Club, Shriners, Masons, Elks, Moose, Eagles, Delta Tau Delta. Republican. Presbyterian. Avocations: photography, sightseeing, travel. Home: 240 SW 7th St Corvallis OR 97333-4551 Office: Oreg State U Dept Student Activities Corvallis OR 97331

ZWEIFEL, TERRY L., aeronautical engineer, researcher; b. Phoenix, Oct. 24, 1942; s. Robert Rudy and Ruby Mae (Toliver) Z.; m. Carol Jean Vogt, June 2, 1965. BS in Aero. Engring., U. Ariz., 1965; student, L.A. Valley Coll., 1971-75. Cert. controls engr., Calif. Tech. mgr. Lockheed Aero. Systems Co., Burbank, Calif., 1965-79; chief engr. Simmonds Precision Products Inc., Vergennes, Vt., 1979-81; sr. fellow Honeywell Inc., Phoenix, 1981—; lectr. to profl. groups. Contbr. numerous articles to profl. jours.; patentee windshear detection, flight guidance in windshear, cruise airspeed control, numerous other patents in field. Mem. AIAA (Atmospheric Environment award 1989). Avocations: computer software, chess, travel. Home: 7250 N 30th Dr Phoenix AZ 85051-7513 Office: Honeywell Inc 21111 N 19th Ave Phoenix AZ 85027-2700

ZWICK, BARRY STANLEY, newspaper editor, speechwriter; b. Cleve., July 21, 1942; s. Alvin Albert and Selma Davidovna (Makofsky) Z.; m. Roberta Joan Yaffe, Mar. 11, 1972; children: Natasha Yvette, Alexander Anatol. BA in Journalism, Ohio State U., 1963; MS in Journalism, Columbia U., 1965. Copy editor Phila. Inquirer, 1964; night news editor Detroit Free Press, 1965-67; West Coast editor L.A. Times/Washington Post News Svc, 1967-77; makeup editor L.A. Times, 1978—; adj. prof. U. So. Calif., L.A., 1975-77. Author: Hollywood Tanning Secrets, 1980. NEH profl. journalism fellow Stanford U., 1977-78. Jewish. Avocations: photography, jet skiing, snowmobiling. Office: LA Times Times Mirror Sq Los Angeles CA 90012

Professional Index

AGRICULTURE

UNITED STATES

ARIZONA

Munds Park
Fox, Kelvin Morgan *rancher, writer*

Paradise Valley
Twist, Robert Lanphier *farmer, rancher, cattle feeder*

CALIFORNIA

Caliente
Rankin, Helen Cross *cattle rancher, guest ranch executive*

Gilroy
Donohoe, Joseph A., V *rancher, real estate investor*

La Jolla
Foxley, William Coleman *cattleman*

Modesto
Osterli, Philip P. *agricultural educator*

Morro Bay
MacElvaine, William Stephen *rancher, consultant*

Oxnard
Hansen, J. Woodford *agricultural products supplier*

Pacific Palisades
Jennings, Marcella Grady *rancher, investor*

Sacramento
Wightman, Thomas Valentine *rancher, researcher*

Salinas
Merrill, Thomas M. *produce executive*

San Diego
Caughlin, Stephenie Jane *organic farmer*

San Luis Obispo
McCorkle, Robert Ellsworth *agribusiness educator*

COLORADO

Denver
McFarlane, Willis McKee *buffalo company executive*

Pine
Dixon, Fred Somers *cattle rancher*

Springfield
Wessler, Melvin Dean *farmer, rancher*

IDAHO

Boise
Johnson, Ronald Douglas *business executive*

Challis
Green, Roberta Helen *rancher, writer, historian*

Moscow
Foltz, John Clark *agricultural economics educator*

MONTANA

Choteau
De Bruycker, Lloyd Henry *rancher, feedlot operator*

Pony
Anderson, Richard Ernest *agribusiness development executive, rancher*

Utica
Stevenson, Sarah Schoales *rancher, business owner*

NEVADA

Yerington
Scatena, Lorraine Borba *rancher, women's rights advocate*

NEW MEXICO

Silver City
White, Don William *rancher, minister*

OREGON

Grants Pass
Miller, Richard Alan *agricultural consultant, hypnotherapist*

Hermiston
Rutherford, Jean *rancher*

WASHINGTON

Toppenish
Hefflinger, LeRoy Arthur *agricultural manager*

WYOMING

Douglas
Sanford, Leroy Leonard *rancher*

Gillette
Daly, John Michael *rancher, lawyer*

Lander
Raynolds, David Robert *buffalo breeder, writer*

Wheatland
Bunker, John Birkbeck *cattle rancher, retired sugar company executive*

ADDRESS UNPUBLISHED

Fenn, David L. *farmer*
Hitchcock, Vernon Thomas *farmer, lawyer*
Kontny, Vincent L. *rancher, engineering executive*

ARCHITECTURE AND DESIGN

UNITED STATES

ALASKA

Anchorage
Maynard, Kenneth Douglas *architect*

ARIZONA

Carefree
Robbins, Conrad W. *naval architect*

Mesa
Young, Martin Ray, Jr. *architect*

Paradise Valley
Blumer, Harry Maynard *architect*

Phoenix
Schiffner, Charles Robert *architect*
Schroeder, Michael Craig *architect*

Scottsdale
Ball, Donald Edmon *architect*
Barron, Michael James *interior designer*
Brown, Shirley Margaret Kern (Peggy Brown) *interior designer*
Corona, Luis *interior designer, floral designer*
Hooker, Jo *interior designer*
Klien, Wolfgang Josef *architect*
Overstreet, Robert Kinnear *architect*
Rutes, Walter Alan *architect*

Sedona
Christensen, Lee Norse *architect*

Tempe
Kenyon, David Lloyd *architect, architectural firm executive*
Thums, Charles William *designer, consultant*
Underwood, Max *architect, educator*

Tucson
Dinsmore, Philip Wade *architect*
Rogers, Walter E. *landscape architect*
Smith, Paul Jay *interior designer*
Turrentine, Lynda Gayle *interior designer*
Wallach, Leslie Rothaus *architect*
Wielgus, Ronald Stanley *retired architect, entomologist, author*

CALIFORNIA

Bakersfield
McAlister, Michael H. *architect*

Belvedere
Gale, Daniel Bailey *architect*

Benicia
Passalacqua, Kristine Gay *interior designer*

Berkeley
Alexander, Christopher *architecture educator*
Brocchini, Ronald Gene *architect*
Burger, Edmund Ganes *architect*
Burk, Gary Maurice *architect*
Gray, Ralph Gareth *architect and structural engineer*

Burlingame
Sadilek, Vladimir *architect*
Tanzi, Carol Anne *interior designer*

Camarillo
Field, Jeffrey Frederic *designer*
Johnston, Toni Annette Sophia *interior designer, educator*

Cardiff By The Sea
Trauth, Patricia Mary *landscape architect*

Chula Vista
Quisenberry, Robert Max *architect, industrial designer*

City Of Industry
Dahlin, Elsie *architect*

Colma
Smither, James Cumming *landscape architect*

Corona Del Mar
Muller, David Webster *architectural designer*

Coronado
Kaufman, Linda Scott *interior designer*

Costa Mesa
Graham, Cary Mark *architect*
Renne, Janice Lynn *interior designer*

Culver City
Moss, Eric Owen *architect*

Dana Point
Millicker, George Henry *interior designer*

Danville
Callan, Gwen *interior designer*

Duncans Mills
Eddy, Thomas John *landscape architect*

Encino
Rance, Quentin E. *interior designer*

Escondido
Devine, Walter Bernard *naval architect, marine engineer*

Fallbrook
Lindemulder, Carol Ann *interior designer, artist*

Fountain Valley
Perng, Jessica *interior designer*

Fresno
Pings, Anthony Claude *architect*
Putman, Robert Dean *golf course architect*
Sorrick, Sonja H. *interior designer*

Hanford
Christensen, Donald J. *architectural design executive, planning consultant*

Highland
Hamerly, Randall Alan *architect*

Laguna Niguel
Axon, Donald Carlton *architect*
Robinson, Theodore Gould *golf course architect*

Long Beach
Salvador, Wendell Carpio *interior designer, design educator*

Los Angeles
Becket, Bruce David *architect*
Breisch, Kenneth Alan *architectural educator*
Dillard, Suzanne *interior designer*
Koenig, Pierre *architecture educator, architect*
Krag, Olga *interior designer*
Maltzan, Michael Thomas *architect*
Moe, Stanley Allen *architect, consultant*
Morgan, Paul Evan *architect*
Phelps, Barton Chase *architect, educator*
Rubell, Joel *interior designer*

Los Gatos
Zacher, Valerie Irene *interior designer*

Manhattan Beach
Blanton, John Arthur *architect*

Mill Valley
D'Amico, Michael *architect, urban planner*

Montrose
Greenlaw, Roger Lee *interior designer*

Morgan Hill
Halopoff, William Evon *industrial designer, consultant*

Mountain View
Kobza, Dennis Jerome *architect*

Newport Beach
Bauer, Jay S. *architect*
Brody, DeAnna Maureen *interior designer*
Gonzalez, Manuel George, IV *architect*
Viggayan, Roberto Almazan *architect*

Oakland
Nicol, Robert Duncan *architect*
Winslow, Thomas Scudder, III *naval architect, marine consultant*
Wolfe, Clifford Eugene *architect, writer*

Oxnard
O'Connell, Hugh Mellen, Jr. *retired architect*

Palm Desert
Chambers, Milton Warren *architect*

Palm Springs
Broderick, Harold Christian *interior designer*
Lynne, Judith *interior designer*

Pasadena
Goei, Bernard Thwan-Poo (Bert Goei) *architectural and engineering firm executive*
Morris, Karlene Ekstrum *interior design educator*
Osifeso, Godwin Sotilewa *architect*
Thomas, Joseph Fleshman *architect*

Placerville
Eaton, Marybeth Brendon *interior designer*

Pleasanton
Shutts, Peter Geoffrey *architect*

Redondo Beach
Eberting, Corwin H., Jr. *architect*
Shellhorn, Ruth Patricia *landscape architect*

Redwood City
Morrison, Murdo Donald *architect*

Sacramento
Dahlin, Dennis John *landscape architect, environmental consultant*
Hallenbeck, Harry C. *architect*
Lionakis, George *architect*
Schroeder, Jerry M. *architect*
Wasserman, Barry L(ee) *architect*

Salinas
Carleton, Thomas J. *architect*

San Bernardino
Murphy, Michael J. *architect*

San Carlos
Stewart, John L. *architect*

San Diego
Blevins, Leaford Leven, Jr. *architect, consultant*
Fuller, Michelle Costello *interior designer*
Holl, Walter John *architect, interior designer*
Hronek, David Edward *architect*
Khalafi, Habib *architect*
Paderewski, Clarence Joseph (Sir) *architect*
Teshima, Ronald S. *landscpae architect*

San Francisco
Brown, Joseph E. *landscape architecture executive*
Bull, Henrik Helkand *architect*
Chevalier, Barbara Lansburgh *interior designer*
Costa, Walter Henry *architect*
Day, Caroline Wolfe *interior designer, entrepreneur*
Del Campo, Martin Bernardelli *architect*
Dodge, Peter Hampton *architect*
Field, John Louis *architect*
Gutkin, Peter Alan *furniture designer, sculptor*
Judd, Bruce Diven *architect*
Kane, Brian J. *industrial designer*
Karwacki, Andrzej Michael *landscape architect, artist*
Keenan, Robert *architect*
Kim, Kyun *architect, educator*
Marshall, Richard Cedric *architect*
Matas, Myra Dorothea *interior architect and designer*
Minar, Paul G. *design consultant*
Raeber, John Arthur *architect, construction consultant*
Werner, William Arno *architect*

San Jose
Bamburg, Marvin A. *architect*
Mansour, Faten Spironous *interior designer, multimedia computer designer, realtor*
Tanaka, Richard Koichi, Jr. *architect, planner*

San Luis Obispo
Fraser, Bruce Douglas, Jr. *architect, artist*

San Mateo
Castleberry, Arline Alrick *architect*

San Pedro
Tseng, William Hing-Way *architect*

San Rafael
Badgley, John Roy *architect*
Clark, Charles Sutter *interior designer*

Thompson, Peter Layard Hailey, Sr. *golf course architect*

Santa Barbara
Kelley, John Dennis *architect*
Kruger, Kenneth Charles *architect*
Pochini, Judy Hay *interior designer*
Radditz, Joan Frances *landscape architect*

Santa Cruz
Carter, Hugh David *architect, graphic artist*

Santa Monica
Eizenberg, Julie *architect*
Gehry, Frank Owen *architect*
Koning, Hendrik *architect*
Takahashi, Edward Katsuaki *architect*

Santa Rosa
Gilger, Paul Douglass *architect*
Price, Martin Lloyd *architect*

Sebastopol
Raye, Don *furniture finish designer*

Sherman Oaks
Ponder, Suzanne Herskovic *designer, real estate consultant*

Somerset
Setzekorn, William David *retired architect, consultant, author*

South Pasadena
Girvigian, Raymond *architect*
Man, Lawrence Kong *architect*

Tarzana
Heimler, James Leonard *architect, consultant*
Smith, Mark Lee *architect*

Torrance
Ryniker, Bruce Walter Durland *industrial designer, manufacturing executive*

Van Nuys
Fenton, Bradly Nolan *architect*

Venice
Baldon, Cleo *interior designer*
Wowkowych, Peter Dmytro *architect*

Ventura
Andrews, LeRoy Miles *architect*
Okuma, Albert Akira, Jr. *architect*
Ruebe, Bambi Lynn *interior, environmental designer*

Victorville
Bergum, Christian Olson *architect, educator*

Villa Park
Buffington, Linda Brice *interior designer*

West Hollywood
Kim, Ammie Yongmi *interior designer*
Luckman, Charles *architect*

Westlake Village
Bonner, Kathleen Sheppard Cleary *interior designer*
Gould, Eileen Tracy *interior designer, general contractor*

Woodlake
Maynard, Wayne *landscape architect*

COLORADO

Aspen
Alstrom, Sven Erik *architect*
Ensign, Donald H. *landscape architect*

Aurora
Durkop, Georgia F. *interior designer*

Boulder
Hoffman, Charles Fenno, III *architect*

Canon City
Bellah, Linda Ruth *design consultant*

Colorado Springs
Guman, William F. *landscape architect, city councilman*
Taylor, Clifford Paul *architect*

Denver
Anderson, John David *architect*
Behrendsen, Arden Eugene *interior designer, history educator*
Brownson, Jacques Calmon *architect*
Falkenberg, William Stevens *architect, contractor*
Fuller, Robert Kenneth *architect, urban designer*
Miller, Gary Ivan *architect*
Nagel, Jerome Kaub *architect*
Pacheco, Carole Elizabeth *architect, educator*
Wilk, Diane Lillian *architect, educator*
Williams, John James, Jr. *architect*

Englewood
Eccles, Matthew Alan *golf course and landscape architect*

Glenwood Springs
Brenner, Charles Frederick *architect*

Lakewood
Hynek, Frederick James *architect*

Littleton
Williams, Sally *landscape designer*

Manitou Springs
Eriksson, Laura Kerstin *architect, artist*

Pueblo
Cherry, Richard Duane *architect*

Vail
Nelson, Nevin Mary *interior designer*
Vosbeck, Robert Randall *architect*

HAWAII

Aiea
Chang, Walter Tuck, Sr. *drafting and autoCAD educator, real estate agent*

Haiku
Cannon, Thomas R. *architect*

Honolulu
Botsai, Elmer Eugene *architect, educator, former university dean*
Hamada, Duane Takumi *architect*
Hwang, Alice Ya-Ping *architect*
Shimokawa, Colin H. *architect*
Tamura, Keith Aichi *architect, consultant*
Vidal, Alejandro Legaspi *architect*

Kaneohe
Fisette, Scott Michael *golf course designer*
Jackson, Jane W. *interior designer*

IDAHO

Boise
Turney, Steven Craig *architect*

Grangeville
Nielsen, Boje Turin *landscape architect*

Sun Valley
Bryant, Woodrow Wesley *architect*
McLaughlin, James Daniel *architect*

MONTANA

Bozeman
DeHaas, John Neff, Jr. *retired architecture educator*

Helena
Schlenker, Errol Rickland *architect*

NEVADA

Las Vegas
Anderson, Eric Edward *architect, planner*
Eggener, Keith Leopold *architectural historian*
Southwick, Stanton W. *landscape architect*
Thomas, Roger Parry *interior designer, art consultant*

North Las Vegas
Mayer, Edward Maximilian *architect*

Reno
Juchem, Robert Stanley, Jr. *product development manager, educator*

NEW MEXICO

Albuquerque
Campbell, C(harles) Robert *architect*
Hakim, Besim Selim *architecture and urban design educator, researcher*
McNamara, James Anthony *architect*
Sabatini, William Quinn *architect*
Smith, Jean *interior design firm executive*

Questa
Sharkey, Richard David *architectural artisan, inventor, musician*

Sandia Park
Woodfin, Martha *interior designer*

Santa Fe
Leon, Bruno *architect, educator*

OREGON

Beaverton
Anderson, Jon M. *architect*

Bend
Baer, Peter Eric *architect*
Simpson, John Douglas *landscape architect*

Corvallis
Sandoval, Eric Michael *architect*

Eugene
Poticha, Otto Paul *architect*

Medford
Skelton, Douglas H. *architect*

Portland
Gassman, Diane Lynne *interior designer*
Giffin, Herb Kent *architect*
Hacker, Thomas Owen *architect*
Harris, Nicholas Todd *architect*
Kilbourn, Lee Ferris *architect, specifications writer*
Miller, Jeffrey Latourette *architect*
Prothe, Michael Dean *architect*
Ritz, Richard Ellison *architect, architectural historian, writer*

Tigard
Devlin, Jamie L. *interior designer*

UTAH

Salt Lake City
Beall, Burtch W., Jr. *architect*
Hullet, Michael Craig *industrial designer, artist, educator*

WASHINGTON

Auburn
Collins, Sarah Helen Boli *landscape architect*

Bellevue
Flom, Robert Michael *interior designer*

Fircrest
Wilder, Jennifer Rose *interior designer*

Kent
Bermudez, Mari Paz Tiangco *interior designer*

Kirkland
Mitchell, Joseph Patrick *architect*
Steinmann, John Colburn *architect*

Mount Vernon
Hall, David Ramsay *architect*
Klein, Henry *architect*

Ocean Shores
Morgan, Audrey *architect*

Olympia
Moffett, Frank Cardwell *architect, civil engineer, real estate developer*

Redmond
King, Indle Gifford *industrial designer, educator*

Seattle
Baldwin, Emory Riegel *architect, woodworker*
Benson, Donald Edward *landscape designer*
Bosworth, Thomas Lawrence *architect, educator*
Buckley, Richard George *architect, educator*
Buursma, William F. *architect*
Ferrin, Allan Hogate *architect*
Hartnett, Gary J. *architect*
Hastings, L(ois) Jane *architect, educator*
Jones, Johnpaul *architect*
Kofranek, Jan Jaroslav *architect*
Kolb, Keith Robert *architect, educator*
Lee, Michael Charles *landscape architect*
Meyer, C. Richard *architect*
Miles, Don Clifford *architect*
Morse, John Moore *architect, planner*
Ochsner, Jeffrey Karl *architect, educator*

Shelton
McClelland, Craig Alexander *architect, educator, business owner*

Spokane
Stone, Michael David *landscape architect*

WYOMING

Jackson
Carney, John Otis, Jr. *architect*

CANADA

BRITISH COLUMBIA

Vancouver
Oberlander, Cornelia Hahn *landscape architect*
Patkau, John *architect*
Patkau, Patricia *architect, architecture educator*

SASKATCHEWAN

Saskatoon
Henry, Keith Douglas *architect*

ADDRESS UNPUBLISHED

Aaronson, Barbara Harlan *interior designer*
Armistead, Katherine Kelly (Mrs. Thomas B. Armistead, III) *interior designer, travel consultant, civic worker*
Austin, James W. *architect, artist*
Bilezikjian, Edward Andrew *architect*
Blair, Frederick David *interior designer*
Budzinski, James Edward *interior designer*
Carey, Audrey Lane *interior designer, motivational speaker, designer*
Chao, James Min-Tzu *architect*
Cohen, Sharleen Cooper *interior designer, writer*
Crowther, Richard Layton *architect, consultant, researcher, author, lecturer*
Deal, Lynn Hoffmann *interior designer*
Dobbel, Rodger Francis *interior designer*
Ely, Marica McCann *interior designer*
Gerou, Phillip Howard *architect*
Hagiwara-Nagata, Erik Sumiharu *landscape consultant and designer*
Hooper, Roger Fellowes *architect, retired*
Hunker, Kurt Christian *architect*
Jensen, Barbara Wood *interior design business owner*
Kliman, Susan Schaefer *architect*
Klope, Thomas Michael *landscape architect*
Logan, Patricia Jean *interior designer*
Pardini, Sharon Kay Brown *architectural and interior designer*
Peters, Robert Woolsey *architect*
Rubio, Ethel Griño *architect*
Salazar, Luis Adolfo *architect*
Sande, Barbara *interior decorating consultant*
Sullivan, Robert Scott *architect*
Sutton, Marcella French *interior designer*
Thomas, Patricia Sutton *dollhouse designer, educator, writer*

Tomasi, Donald Charles *architect*

ARTS: LITERARY. *See also* COMMUNICATIONS MEDIA.

UNITED STATES

ALASKA

Anchorage
Starratt, Patricia Elizabeth *writer, actress, composer*
Strohmeyer, John *writer, former editor*
Thomas, Lowell, Jr. *author, lecturer, former lieutenant governor, former state senator*
Todd, Alden *writer, editor*

Gambell
Walunga, Allen R. *writer, researcher*

Homer
Gill, Shelley R. *writer*
Rearden, Jim Douglas *writer*

Iliamna
Tretikoff, Elena Helen *writer*

Kotzebue
Magdanz, James Sidney *writer*

Tok
Blasor-Bernhardt, Donna Jo *screenwriter, poet, author, photographer*

ARIZONA

Ajo
McCormick, Alma Heflin *writer, retired educator, psychologist*

Chandler
Allen, Louise *writer, educator*

Flagstaff
Cline, Platt Herrick *author*
Shapiro, Robert Joseph *trance channel, writer*

Oracle
Prichard, E. Dean *writer*

Phoenix
Duyck, Kathleen Marie *poet, musician, retired social worker*
Ellison, Cyril Lee *literary agent, retired publisher*
Estes, Mark Wayne *corporate communications writer, editor*
Leo, Mabel Rae *writer, office manager*

Sedona
Frankel, Jennie Louise *writer, composer, playwright*
Frankel, Terrie Maxine *author, composer, playwright, publisher*
Thorne, Kate Ruland *writer, publisher, editor*
Whitten, Phillip *writer, editor in chief*

Sierra Vista
Johnson, Dellena Sharon *poet, educator*

Snowflake
Freyermuth, Gundolf S. *writer*

Sun City West
Ault, Phillip Halliday *author, editor*
Bowkett, Gerald Edson *editorial consultant, writer*

Tempe
Raby, William Louis *author*
Sylvester, Edward Joseph *science writer, journalism educator*

Tsaile
Walters, Anna Lee *writer, educational administrator, educator*

Tucson
Bruner, Richard Wallace *writer*
Elkington, Sandra Louise *writer*
Ingalls, Jeremy *poet, educator*
Nord, Myrtle Selma *writer, researcher*
Stoker, Eugenia Ellen Eide *writer, former pediatrician*
Vicker, Ray *writer*
Young, Donald Allen *writer, consultant*

Yuma
Carroll, Sibyl *writer*

CALIFORNIA

Alameda
Grzanka, Leonard Gerald *writer, consultant*

Antioch
Chu, Valentin Yuan-ling *author*

Aptos
Jones, Jon Sydney *writer, educator*

Arcadia
Sloane, Beverly LeBov *writer, consultant*

Bakersfield
Presley, Arthur Henry *writer, artist*

Bellflower
Kouns, Alan Terry *writer, consultant*

Westminster
Amato, Carol Joy *writer, anthropologist*

Woodland Hills
Jason, Sonya *writer*
Keenan, William John *writer*
Stillson, Alan *author*

Yorba Linda
Medland, Maurice Blue *writer, educator*

Yucca Valley
Drake, Russell Moore *writer*

COLORADO

Aurora
Bower, Donald Edward *author*
Peters, Dorothy Marie *writer, consultant*

Boulder
Coel, Margaret Speas *writer*
Dold, Catherine Anne *writer, editor*
Katz, Steve Robert *novelist, poet, educator*
Kaye, Evelyn Patricia (Evelyn Patricia Sarson) *author, publisher, travel expert*
Saner, Reginald Anthony *poet, essayist, educator*
Schelling, Andrew *poet, translator, educator*
Sukenick, Ronald *author, English educator*

Broomfield
Amdahl, Kenn *writer*
Whipple, Daniel Sawyer, Jr. *writer*

Colorado Springs
Hicks, David Earl *author, inventor*
Rhodes, Daisy Chun *writer, researcher, oral historian*
Vosevich, Kathi Ann *writer, editor, scholar*
Yaffe, James *author*

Conifer
Hrcek, Margaret N. *writer*

Cortez
Galin, Robert Barry *writer, park ranger*

Denver
Carlson, Robert Ernest *freelance writer, architect, lecturer*
Martinez, Marie E. *poet*
May, Katherine (Kaki Heinemann) *author*
Nemiro, Beverly Mirium Anderson *author, educator*
Yarnell, Elizabeth Gail *writer, journalist*

Durango
Korns, Leota Elsie *writer, mountain land developer, insurance broker*

Fort Collins
Crow, Mary *poet, educator*

Grand Junction
Armstrong, Linda Jean (Gene) *writer, artist*

Greeley
Wilmot, Marlene June *writer*

Littleton
Schanker, Harry H., Jr. *writer*

Lyons
Ferraris, Alfred Charles, Jr. *poet*

Telluride
Trommer, Rosemerry Wahtola *writer, poet, editor*

Trinidad
Tamez, Lorraine Diane *writer, nurse*

Vail
Knight, Constance Bracken *writer, realtor, corporate executive*

DISTRICT OF COLUMBIA

Washington
Cavnar, Samuel Melmon *author, publisher, activist*

HAWAII

Honolulu
Branson, Helen Kitchen *writer*
Carson, Meredith Shelton *poetess, homemaker*
Nakano, Roy Y. *writer*

Kihei
O'Leary, Brian Todd *writer*

Lihue
Stephens, Jack *writer, photographer*

IDAHO

Boise
Conley, James Cort *writer, literature director, publisher*

Grangeville
Gildner, Gary Theodore *writer*

Moscow
McFarland, Ronald Earl *educator, writer, literary critic*

MONTANA

Bigfork
Brynie, Faith Hickman *writer, educator*

Livingston
Clarke, Urana *writer, musician, educator*

Mc Leod
Hjortsberg, William Reinhold *author*

Missoula
Glynn, Gary J. *writer*
Smith, Jeffrey John *writer, publisher*

NEVADA

Carson City
Atkinson, Sally Jo *writer*

Henderson
Furimsky, Stephen, Jr. *freelance writer*

Las Vegas
Caro, Mike *writer, editor, publisher*
Eddington, Carole Ann *writer, artist*
Eikenberry, Arthur Raymond *writer, service executive, researcher*
Palmer, Lynne *writer, astrologer*

Reno
Coffman, Virginia E(dith) *writer*
Hohn, Hazel Marjorie *author*
Key, Wilson Bryan *author, lecturer*
Knorr, Marjorie S. *writer*

NEW MEXICO

Albuquerque
Durant, Penny Lynne Raife *author, educator*
Finlay, Alice Sullivan *writer, educator*
Meyer, Carolyn Mae *writer children's books*
Willson, Harry *writer*

Angel Fire
Shelton, Connie Lee *writer, publisher*

Chimayo
Glendinning, Chellis *author, psychologist*

Corrales
Page, Jake (James K. Page, Jr.) *writer, editor*

Deming
Williams, Enid Jo *writer*

Las Cruces
Medoff, Mark Howard *playwright, screenwriter, novelist*

Las Vegas
Martínez, Valerie Lynne *poet, educator*

Los Alamos
Mark, Kathleen Abbott *writer*

Ranchos De Taos
Dickey, Robert Preston *author, educator, poet*

Rio Rancho
Bray, Marian Louise *writer, secondary education educator*

Roswell
Rosemire, Adeline Louise *writer, publisher*
Watson, Marilyn Fern *writer, artist*

Santa Fe
Bergé, Carol *author*
Christ, Ronald *writer, translator, publisher, editor*
McCord, Richard Colson *writer, journalist*
Tarn, Nathaniel *poet, translator, educator*
Zekowski, Arlene *writer, English educator*

NEW YORK

Point Lookout
Hemp, William (Bill) Henry *writer, artist*

OREGON

Aloha
Herrington, Steve Eugene *writer, illustrator, publishing executive*

Enterprise
Hunter, Kathleen *writer, educator*

Eugene
Ailor, Karen Tana *writer, editor, proposal consultant*
Pavlish, Daniel Vincent *poet, novelist*
Raitt, Sherry Lee *writer, songwriter, home designer*

Grants Pass
Stafford, Patrick Purcell *poet, writer, management consultant*

Hillsboro
Cornish, Linda Sowa Young *children's books author and illustrator, educator*

Newport
Kennedy, Richard Jerome *writer*
Perry, Carla Leslie *writer, editor*

Otis
King, Frank William *writer*

Pleasant Hill
Kesey, Ken *writer*

Portland
[illegible], David *poet, educator*
Cunningham, Donna Rae *writer, astrologer*

de Lackner, Barbara Elizabeth *author, educator*
Reyes, Carlos *poet, educator*
Scherer, Alice E. *writer, researcher*

Prineville
Braly, David Duane *writer*

Salem
Benson, Steven Donald *sheet metal research and marketing executive, sheet metal mechanic, programmer, author*
Copeland, Ann (Virginia W. Furtwangler) *writer, educator*
Marsh, Katherine Cynthia *writer, journalist, poet*

The Dalles
Conner, William Angus, II *writer*

West Linn
Hamilton, Eleanor Leigh *writer, therapist*

UTAH

Bountiful
Flack, Dora Dutson *writer, performing artist, lecturer*

Park City
Schefter, James Loran *author*
Solomon, Dorothy Jeanne Allred *writer, communications executive*

Provo
Hart, Edward LeRoy *poet, educator*

Salt Lake City
Black, Rosa Vida *writer, educator*
Bowes, Florence (Mrs. William David Bowes) *writer*
Bushman-Carlton, Marilyn *poet*
Trimble, Stephen *writer, photographer*
Warenski, Marilyn Belle *writer*
Western, Carole Ann *literary agent*
Woodworth, Kate *novelist*

Springville
Hickman, Craig Ronald *author*

WASHINGTON

Bellevue
Habbestad, Kathryn Louise *writer*

Bremerton
Hanf, James Alphonso *poet, government official*
Vroman, Charles Alvin *technical writer, programmer*

Index
Harmony, Patricia Starr *writer, poet*

Issaquah
Trask, Robert Chauncey Riley *author, lecturer, foundation executive*

La Conner
Davies, Kent Richard *writer*

Lynnwood
Bear, Gregory Dale *writer, illustrator*

Mead
Eilerman, Darin Lee *writer*

Mercer Island
Porad, Francine Joy *poet, painter*

Mill Creek
Dubois, Christine *writer, educator*

Nordland
Kramnicz, Rosanne *freelance writer*

Port Orchard
Blake, Rachelle S. *writer, editor, medical transcription educator*
Stevens, April O'Dell *writer*

Roslyn
Brodine, Virginia Warner *writer*

Seattle
Davis, Scott Campbell *writer*
Eichhorn, Dennis Paul *writer*
Jenkinson, Edward Leroy *poet*
Strasbaugh, William Edward *writer, federal agency administrator, retired career officer*
Strickland, Ronald Gibson *writer*

Snohomish
De Clements, Barthe Faith *writer*

Spokane
Murphy, Claire Rudolf *author, consultant*

Touchet
Hastings, John Jacob *writer, lyricist, consultant*

Vancouver
Hamby, Barbara Jean *writer, poet*

Vashon
Wisechild, Louise Marie *writer, researcher*

Wenatchee
Zornes, Jeanne Irene *writer, speaker*

WYOMING

Encampment
Moulton, Candy Lee *writer*

Gillette
Wise, Kitty *writer, composer*

Laramie
Boresi, Arthur Peter *author, educator*
Wischmann, Lesley Brook *writer, researcher*

ADDRESS UNPUBLISHED

Abugov, Jeff *scriptwriter*
Alberghini, Christopher Robert *producer, writer, actor*
Alkana, Louis David *writer, editor*
Anderson, Kevin J. *writer*
Avery, Stephen Neal *playwright, author*
Baird, Alan C. *screenwriter*
Baker, Lucinda *writer*
Baranek, Robert R. *writer, dockworker*
Barnes, Joanna *author, actress*
Barreto, Kathleen Anne Coogan *technical writing consultant*
Bird, Margaret Duering *writer*
Birnbaum, Jane Ellen *writer*
Bower, Janet Esther *writer, educator*
Bradford, Lee Tyler *writer*
Buckstein, Caryl Sue *writer*
Burns, Kitty *playwright*
Burns, William David *technical writer, technical consultant*
Cable, Mary *writer*
Campbell, Addison James, Jr. *writer*
Carter, Steven Andrew *writer, consultant*
Christensen, Marilyn D. *writer*
Claes, Gayla Christine *writer, editorial consultant*
Colgin, Kevin Jon *poet*
Conlin, Catherine *writer, studio owner, designer*
Conrad, Jane Kathryn *writer*
Cory, Angelica Jo *author, spiritual consultant*
Dal Bello, Peter Thomas *writer*
Dardick, Geeta *writer, psychotherapist*
Davidson, Mark *writer, educator*
DeCristoforo, Mary A. *writer*
De Vries, Mary A. *writer*
DiPietro, Anthony Michael *director, writer*
Doenges, Judith Ann *writer*
Drucker, Peter Ferdinand *writer, consultant, educator*
Easton, Robert (Olney) *author, environmentalist*
Edmonson-Nelson, Gloria Jean *freelance writer*
Fell, Jennifer Anne *writer*
Filleman, Teresa Ellen *technical writer*
Franks, Donald Richard *writer, website designer*
Gardner, Sonia Kay *writer*
Garibotto-Minness, Carlos Fernando *writer, translator*
Goddart, Michael *writer*
Goldberg, Howard Alan *writer*
Green, Phyllis Hartman *writer, playwright*
Greenley, Kenneth J. *writer*
Halbrook, Jane *writer*
Hamit, Francis Granger *freelance writer*
Harris, David Jake *writer, educator*
Harshman, Virginia Robinson *writer, historical researcher*
Hayes, Cynthia Ann *administrative assistant, writer*
Hellebust, Karsten Gene *writer, retired business economist*
Herman, George Adam *writer*
Hilson, Phoenix *writer*
Houze, Herbert George *writer*
Humphries, Stephen Edward *writer*
Hyde, Elinor Godfrey *writer*
Isbell, Harold M(ax) *writer, investor*
Jacobs, Wilbur Ripley *writer, history educator*
Kaplan-Gillispie, Mylinda *writer*
Kase, John D. *writer*
Kass, Jerome Allan *writer*
Kearse, David Grier *stage and screen writer, journalist*
Kellerman, Faye Marder *novelist, dentist*
Kimbrell, Grady Ned *author, educator*
Korolev, Nicholas Alexander *writer, artist*
Kramer, Anne Pearce *writer, communications and film executive, educator, psychotherapist, research psychoanalyst*
Lawrence, Jerome *playwright, director, educator*
Lawson, Dennis Lee *plant broker, writer*
Lipscomb, Richard Henry *playwright, former museum administrator*
Lowitz, Leza *writer, editor*
Luchetti, Cathy Lee *writer, historian*
Luhn, Robert Kent *writer, magazine editor*
MacLean, Judith E. *writer, editor*
Madsen, Susan Arrington *writer*
Mandava, Bhargavi Chandra *novelist, poet*
Markie, Shane Robert *poet*
Marquand, Barbara K. *freelance writer*
Marsh, Stephen Seabrooke *writer, journalist*
McDade, Donna Marie *writer*
McKay, W. Colin *playwright, screenwriter, educator*
McMillan, Terry L. *writer, educator*
McMillon, Billy Joe *writer, educator*
Morang, Diane Judy *writer, television producer, business entrepreneur*
Newhall, Barbara Falconer *writer, journalist*
Novarro, Leonard Anthony *writer*
O'Morrison, Kevin *playwright*
Osteen, Heyward Lewis *writer*
Parker, Allene Marie *writer, educator*
Perry, Josephine *screen writer, playwright, educator*
Peters, Barbara Humbird *writer, editor*
Pike, Diane Kennedy *writer, educator*
Platt, Randall Beth *writer*
Proulx, (Edna) Annie *writer*
Reid, Constance *writer*
Resnicoff, Ethel *author*
Rider, Fae B. *freelance writer*
Roa (Burkhart), JoAnn Virginia *writer*
Rosenwein, Andrea Lynn *writer*
Rotcop, J. Kenneth *screenwriter, producer*
Rothman, Howard Michael *writer*
Sandford, Michael Patrick *poet, nurse*
Saroyan, Aram *writer, educator, editor*
Schenkkan, Robert Frederic *writer, actor*
Schickel, Richard *writer, film critic, producer*
Schiller, Gerald Alan *writer*
Sears, Steven Lee *screenwriter, consultant*
Shearer, Karen Marie *writer, producer, director*
Shep, Robert Lee *editor, publisher, textile book researcher*
Simmons, Ted Conrad *writer*
Skinner, Knute rumsey *poet, English educator*
Somerville, Diana Elizabeth *author*
Spencer, Tricia Jane *writer*
Spies, Karen Bornemann *writer, education consultant*
Stafford, Elsan Hugh *novelist, poet, retired deputy sheriff*
Stone, Jack *screenwriter, musician, songwriter*

Ulin, David Lawrence *writer, editor, educator*
Underhill, Louise Flynn *retired educator, poet*
Vice, Lisa *writer, educator*
Warady, Phylis Ann *novelist*
Watkins, Thomas Henry *writer, educator*
Webber, Marilyn Aspen Kay *writer*
Weir, Charlene Martha *writer*
Whelchel, Sandra Jane *writer*
White, Celeste (Emily) *writer, publisher*
Wilson, Mary Susan *writer, publisher*

ARTS: PERFORMING

UNITED STATES

ALASKA

Fairbanks
Cole-McCullough, Daniel *music educator, conductor, clinician*
Harbaugh, John Paul *music educator*
Riccio, Thomas Patrick *theater director*

Kenai
Means, Lane Lewis *entertainer*

ARIZONA

Chandler
Mansour, Yousef *video specialist*

Flagstaff
Aurand, Charles Henry, Jr. *music educator*
Gall, A. Philip *recording engineer*
Gooch, Michael Thomas *television production professional, writer*

Fountain Hills
Tyl, Noel Jan *baritone, astrologer, writer*

Glendale
Zinn, Dennis Bradley *magician, actor, corporate skills trainer*

Mesa
Mason, Marshall W. *theater director, educator*

Phoenix
Aschaffenburg, Walter Eugene *composer, music educator*
Long, Michael Alan *musician*
Shaw, Lillie Marie King *vocalist*
Speers, David *opera company director*
Uthoff, Michael *dancer, choreographer, artistic director*

Scottsdale
James, John Sullivan *film and radio producer, director*
Nemiroff, Paul Raphael *producer, director*
Peterson, John Willard *composer, music publisher*
Vanier, Jerre Lynn *art director*
Whittaker, Sue McGhee *music educator, pianist*
Wolfgang, Bonnie Arlene *musician, bassoonist*

Sedona
Gregory, James *retired actor*
Griffin, (Alva) Jean *entertainer*

Sun City
Musgrave, Charles Edward *retired music director, correctional official*
Yestadt, James Francis *music director, conductor*

Tempe
Benson, M. (Bob) *artist, drama educator*
Dreyfoos, Dale LeRoy *director, music educator, singer, actor*
Lombardi, Eugene Patsy *orchestra conductor, violinist, educator, recording artist*

Tucson
Armstrong, R(obert) Dean *entertainer*
Cutietta, Robert Alan *music school administrator, educator*
Hanson, George *music director, conductor*
Laughlin, Edward Vincent, III *drummer, recording artist, golfer*
Malmgren, René Louise *educational theater administrator*
Puente, Tito Anthony *orchestra leader, composer, arranger*
Reid, Edward Fraser *musician, music educator*
Rich, Bobby *broadcast personality, radio programmer*
Roe, Charles Richard *baritone*
Seaman, Arlene Anna *musician, educator*

CALIFORNIA

Agoura Hills
Healy, Kieran John Patrick *lighting designer, consultant*

Albany
Ginzberg, Abigail *video producer*

Apple Valley
Beller, Gerald Stephen *professional magician, former insurance company executive*
Lavallee, Charles Phillip *music educator, musician*

Aptos
Swenson, Kathleen Susan *music and art educator*

Bel Air
Salvin, Linda Carol *radio metaphysician*

Belmont
Flores, Vera Jacobson *theater arts educator*

Benicia
Allen, Rick (Frederick Allen Klycinski) *magician, advertising and publicity consultant*
Cummings, Barton *musician*

Berkeley
Carlin, Joy *actress, director*
Cox, Cindy Annice *composer, educator*
Kleiman, Vivian Abbe *filmmaker*
Stork, Susan Diana *musician, composer*

Beverly Hills
Atchity, Kenneth John *producer, literary manager/producer*
Becks, Ronald Arthur *film producer*
Bernhard, Harvey *producer*
Bernstein, Charles Harry *composer*
Brokaw, Norman Robert *talent agency executive*
Chritton, George A. *film producer*
Corman, Eugene Harold *motion picture producer*
Fetler, Daniel Gregory *cinematographer*
Foch, Nina *actress, creative consultant, educator, director*
Foster, Lawrence *concert and opera conductor*
Hurd, Gale Anne *film producer*
Jordan, Glenn *director*
Khaiat, Laurent E. *producer, films*
Kravitz, Lenny *singer, guitarist*
Kritzer, Eddie *television producer*
Linkletter, Arthur Gordon *radio and television broadcaster*
Martinson, Constance Frye *television program hostess, producer*
Matovich, Mitchel Joseph, Jr. *motion picture producer, executive*
Mischer, Donald Leo *television director and producer*
Pike, Brian *agent*
Rafkin, Alan *television and film director*
Riley, Jack *actor, writer*
Spielberg, Steven *motion picture director, producer*
Weideman, Warren Milo *producer*
White, Betty *actress, comedienne*
Zinman, David *conductor*

Buena Park
Mauriello, Brian Dominick *educational media and television producer, writer and director*

Burbank
Britton, Matt J. *special effects company manager*
Chierighino, Brianne Siddall *voice-over, actress, assistant location manager*
Dubuque, Cheryl Whitman *film and video producer, writer*
Ernst, Donald William *producer*
Fanaris, John Michael *motion picture producer*
Lonsdale, Peter N. *film editor*
McGee, Anastasia Guiniviere *visual effects coordinator*
Miziker, Ronald Dennis *television producer*
Pace, Frank Anthony *television producer*
Rivera, Miluka *actress, journalist, writer*
Schulz, Jason Douglas *filmmaker*
Tatum, Thomas Deskins *film and television producer, director*

Calabasas
Albrecht, Joie *television and film producer, director, writer*
Gordon, Mark James *film producer and director*
Joyce, Bernadette *producer*

Calistoga
Sassoon, Janet *ballerina, educator*

Camarillo
Brockett, Dan D. *video producer*

Canoga Park
Peirson, George Ewell *film producer, writer, art director, educator*

Cardiff By The Sea
Devoe, Rick Daniel *agent*

Carmel
McKee, Robin Melinda *theatre director*

Carmichael
Lehr, Lester Eugene *music educator*

Carson
Sudalnik, James Edward *educator, director, producer, writer*

Chatsworth
Hampton, Bret Douglas *videotape editor*

Chula Vista
Lea, Schmidt-Rogers *music educator, musician*

Claremont
Doty, Horace Jay, Jr. *theater administrator, arts consultant*
Kohn, Karl George *educator, composer*

Costa Mesa
Remington, Alan *music educator*

Culver City
Fay, William Frederick *film producer*
Holman, David Calvin *television production executive*
O'Keefe, Terence Michael *writer, producer, director feature films*
Orsi, Thomas William *television and film audio engineer*
Stark, Ray *motion picture producer*

Cupertino
Tavernetti, Susan Pisoni *film studies educator, film critic*

Downey
Collier, William Thayer *bandleader, musician, educator*

El Cerrito
Bell, William James *music educator*

Encino
Ehrlich, Kenneth James *television producer*
Williams, Roger *musician*

Escondido
Ehrhart, Joseph Edward *retired television broadcast engineer*
Rockwell, Elizabeth Goode *dance company director, consultant, educator*

Fresno
Harvey, Raymond Curtis *conductor*
Mulligan, Kathleen Ann *dancer, choreographer, educator*
Warkentin, Larry Ray *music educator, composer*

Fullerton
Lewis, R. David *music educator*
Linahon, James Joseph *music educator, musician*
Wiley, David Cole *producer*

Glendale
Barrera, Joe Oscar, Jr. *composer, music producer, music publisher*
Benson, Gregory Douglas *video engineer*
Grillo, Leo *actor, photographer, animal rescuer*
Morgenroth, Robert William *producer*
Sprosty, Joseph Patrick *weapons specialist, producer, writer, consultant*

Hemet
Bible, Frances Lillian *mezzo-soprano, educator*

Hidden Hills
Andrews, Ralph Herrick *television producer*

Hollywood
Devlin, Christopher Matthew *actor, writer, director, producer*
Graham, Bruce Edward *video specialist*
Neff, John *recording engineer, producer*
Roberts, Mel (Melvin Richard Kells) *retired film editor*
Rogers, James Curtis *movie producer, publisher, screenwriter*
Salzman, David Elliot *entertainment industry executive*
Sorrell, Rozlyn *singer, actress*

Huntington Beach
Carter, Henrietta McKee *educator*

Idyllwild
Davila, William *music educator*

Irvine
Davis, Clifton D. *actor, composer*
Deenen, Charles Paulus *audio director*
Ruyter, Nancy Lee Chalfa *dance educator*

Joshua Tree
Styles, Beverly *entertainer*

Kentfield
Montfort, Matthew Charles *musician, music educator, writer*

La Canada
Melendy, Richard Francis *entertainer, artist*

La Jolla
Corrigan, Mary Kathryn *theater educator*
Price, Betty Jeanne *choirchime soloist, writer*
Reynolds, Roger Lee *composer*
Wagner, Arthur *actor, director, educator*

La Quinta
Reistad, Robert Knut *video production editor*

Laguna Beach
Harvey, G. Cameron *drama educator, artistic director*
Stein, Richard Allen *theatre producer, director*

Laguna Hills
Herold, Ralph Elliott *motion picture arts educator*

Lake Hughes
La Mont, Tawana Faye *camera operator, video director*

Larkspur
Earley, Edward Joseph, Jr. *studio musician, composer, copyist, trombonist*

Los Altos
Collins, Gordon Dent *recording company executive*

Los Angeles
Banner, Bob *television producer, director*
Barker, Robert William *television personality*
Bataillard, Stephan Marc *film and commercial producer*
Bell, Lee Phillip *television personality, television producer*
Belzberg, Leslie Carol *film and television producer*
Blits, Stanley E. *television music director*
Bourland, Roger *music educator, composer*
Brown, Rayner *composer, educator, performer*
Burrows, James *television and motion picture director, producer*
Calman, Craig David *writer, actor, director*
Candela, Michael A. *producer, director*
Caryl, Naomi *artist*
Champlin, Charles Davenport *television host, book critic, writer*
Cohen, Ellis Avrum *producer, writer, investigative journalist*
Conner, Lindsay Andrew *screenwriter, producer*
Davidson, Gordon *theatrical producer, director*
Dergarabedian, Paul, Jr. *film analyst, box office tracker*
Diehl, Dolores *communication arts director*
Donenfeld, Alice R. Greenbaum *producer, broadcast executive*
Durkin, James Brendan *music publisher*
Eubanks, Rachel Amelia *music educator*
Ferrell, Conchata Galen *actress, acting teacher and coach*
Fleischmann, Ernest Martin *music administrator*

Follmer, John Scott *visual effects producer, supervisor*
Gavin, Delane Michael *television writer, producer, director*
Greenberg, Barry Michael *talent executive*
Griffithe, Todd Allen *television associate director*
Hemion, Dwight Arlington *television producer, director*
Hemmings, Peter William *orchestra and opera administrator*
Hickey, Michelle Ann *filmmaker, screenwriter*
Hirsch, Judd *actor*
Hunt, Peter Roger *film director, writer, editor*
Ibanez, Armando P(erez) *film maker, poet*
Jackson, Isaiah *conductor*
Josselyn, Johnny B. *artistic director, magazine writer*
Kahan, Sheldon Jeremiah (Christopher Reed) *musician, singer*
Katz, Leon *theatre and drama educator*
Kaufman, Jeff *television producer*
Kelly, Kurt (Joseph E. Cronan) *entertainment executive, producer, director*
Klausner, Willette Jean *theatrical/film producer, marketing consultant*
Klauss, Kenneth Karl *composer, educator*
Laudicina, Salvatore Anthony *film industry executive*
Lesser, Julian (Bud) *film producer, historian*
Levitow, Roberta Lynne *theater artist, educator*
Lindeman, Douglas Jay *film producer*
Lochen, Elisabeth Yvonne Marie-Laure *director, sound consultant*
London, Andrew Barry *film editor*
Maldonado, Gregory Matthew *music director, educator*
McVey, Gary James *film curator*
Mossman, Thomas Mellish, Jr. *television manager*
Mulkey, Karen Landry *actress, artist, educator, writer*
O'Connell, Taaffe Cannon *actress, publishing executive*
Padorr Nilles, Laila *musician, record producer*
Parker, William Hayes, Jr. *film director, writer, photographer*
Pavicevic, Goran *cinematographer*
Reiss, Jonathan Allen *filmmaker, legal and government researcher*
Rudnicki, Stefan *media director, producer*
Seidelman, Arthur Allan *director*
Sharma, Peter, III *actor, clergyman*
Sherman, Eric *director, writer, educator*
Stevenson, Robert Murrell *music educator*
Supérnaw, William Michael (W. M. Supérnaw) *actor*
Tierney, Michael *filmmaker*
Veitch, Patrick Lee *performing arts entrepreneur*
Webber, Peggy *actress, producer, director, writer*
Woessner, Frederick T. *composer, pianist*
Zeri, Massimo *director of photography*

Los Osos
Gibson, George *retired scenic art director*
Mehring, Margaret *filmmaker, retired educator*

Malibu
Larsen, Carter Lawrence *pianist, composer*

Marina Del Rey
Bergmann, Peter Jay *television director and producer, educator*
Hammer, John Levering, IV *film propmaster*

Menlo Park
Baez, Joan Chandos *folk singer*

Merced
Harvey, Robert Ballengee *retired music educator, administrator*

Mission Hills
Krieg, Dorothy Linden *soprano, performing artist, educator*

Modesto
Pratt, Brett LeRoy *organist*

Monrovia
Del Vecchio, Dawn Marie *theater manager*

Montara
Anderson, Barbara Jane *songwriter, singer*

Monterey
Weis, Andrew (Andy) Jerome *musician, educator*

Montrose
Twitchell, Theodore Grant *music educator and composer*

Moreno Valley
Johnson, Fannie Miriam Harris *performing company executive*

Mountain Center
De Forest, Edgar Lester *actor, poet, educator*

North Hollywood
Balmuth, Bernard Allen *retired film editor*
Carmony, Kevin Brackett *recording company executive*
Jordan, Steven Edward *special effects expert*
Kantor, Igo *film and television producer*
Kuter, Kay E. *writer, actor*
Levin, Alvin Irving *composer, educator*
Marchiano, Bruce Joseph *actor*
Null, Thomas Blanton *recording producer*
Powell, Stephanie *visual effects director, supervisor*
Purl, Mara Celeste *entertainment executive, radio producer, writer*

Novato
Miller, Lee Robert *video director*
Valentino, Stephen Eric (Il Conté Valentino) *production and entertainment company executive, actor, singer*

Oakland
Crocker, Joy Laksmi *concert pianist and organist, composer*
DeFazio, Lynette Stevens *dancer, choreographer, educator, chiropractor, author, actress, musician*
Duderstadt, Mack Henry, Jr. *arts educator*
Randle, Ellen Eugenia Foster *opera and classical singer, educator*

Simonds, Martha Muñoz *musician, educator*

Oceanside
Fischler, Sandy Lynn *event producer*

Oxnard
Sturges, Jeffery Alan *composer*

Pacific Palisades
Leiviska, Nancy Lynn *entertainment production company executive*
Sevilla, Enid N. *production company executive*

Palo Alto
Beckman, Kenneth Oren *film and video specialist, researcher*
Deussen, Nancy Bloomer *composer, music educator, arts organizer*

Palos Verdes Estates
Benson, Francis M. *production engineer, radio producer*

Pasadena
Blankenburg, Heinz Horst *vocalist, director*
Egeli, Arthur Bjorn *independent film director, scripwriter*
Halberstadt, Deb Lee *producer, photographer*
Hernandez, Robert Jose *film and video producer, multimedia marketing*
Marien, Robert *producer, director, naturalist, photographer*
Mrazek, David Anton *documentary producer*

Petaluma
Daniel, Gary Wayne *motivation and performance consultant*

Playa Del Rey
Dando, Howard Charles *theatre and television producer*

Poway
Burnworth, Randy James *video company executive*

Rancho Cucamonga
Robertson, Carey Jane *musician, educator*

Rancho Mirage
New, Debra Marie *choreographer*

Redding
Meyer, Jeffrey Thore *music educator*
Weber, Dennis Millard *music educator*

Redlands
Rehfeldt, Phillip Richard *music educator*

Redondo Beach
McCoy, Shawn Aloysious *musician*

Redwood City
Dechance, Yvonne René *music educator*
Easter, Stanley Eugene *musician, counselor, educator*

Riverside
Adams, Byron *composer, conductor*

Rohnert Park
Cahill, Andre G. *video producer, editor*

Sacramento
Gawthrop, Daphne Wood *performing company executive*
McCann, Kim Lou M. *theater educator, director*
Park, David Coates *agent, music industry consultant, educator*
T'Sani, Nolan *ballet company director*

Salinas
Rosen, Jacqueline I. *flutist, music educator*

San Bernardino
Yowell, Robert Lee *theater and dance educator*

San Diego
Alburger, James Reid *audio production specialist, director, entertainer*
Campbell, Ian David *opera company director*
Elaine, Karen *musician, educator*
Farrell, Peter Snow *musician, retired educator*
Gibson, Geof Charles *audio engineer*
Graham, Peter Mark *multimedia producer*
Hooper, Robert Alexander *producer, communications educator*
Pagan, Keith Areatus *music educator, academic administrator*
Peck, William Truman *retired court clerk, actor*
Schulze, Mark Levon *video producer, communications executive*

San Dimas
Peters, Joseph Donald *filmmaker*
Wolfe, Edward William, II *music educator, composer*

San Francisco
Davis, Bob *music educator, composer*
De Coteau, Denis *music director, conductor*
Eilenberg, Lawrence Ira *theater educator, artistic director*
Fulkerson, Christopher Allen Paul *composer, conductor*
George, Vance *conductor*
Getty, Gordon Peter *composer, philanthropist*
Hopkins, Pamela Jené *producer*
King, Alonzo *artistic director, choreographer*
Larsen, Michael F. *literary agent, writer*
Moon, Spencer *author, program consultant, educator*
Pangaro, David Lawrence *theatre educator*
Rostreich, Peter *orchestra executive director*
Peterson, Wayne Turner *composer, pianist*
Pippin, Donald Ferrell *musician, director, conductor*
Roberts, Wendy Hunter *producer, writer, psycho-spiritual counselor*
Runnicles, Donald *conductor*
Talbot, Stephen H. *television producer, writer*
Tomasson, Helgi *dancer, choreographer, dance company executive*
Walker, Philip Eugene *producer, educator*

San Gabriel
Keeling, Geraldine Ann *musicologist, educator*

San Jose
Archibeque, Charlene Paullin *music educator*
Dalis, Irene *mezzo-soprano, opera company administrator, music educator*
Grin, Leonid *conductor*
Herrold, Rebecca Munn *music educator, writer*
Near, Timothy *theater director*
Walker, Ethel Pitts *theatre arts educator*
Yacco, Richard A. *television producer, educator*

San Leandro
Prachar, Thomas Patrick *dancer, mechanic*

San Marino
Hicklin, Ronald Lee *music production company executive*

San Rafael
Currier, Robert Stephen *theater company artistic director*
Lucas, George W., Jr. *film director, producer, screenwriter*
Platek, Gary Joseph *special effects expert*
Sheldon, Gary *conductor, music director*

Santa Ana
Gomez, Roman I. *producer, cameraman, editor*
Leonard, Victoria Lee *ballet instructor*
St. Clair, Carl *conductor, music director*

Santa Barbara
Ben-Dor, Giséle *conductor, musician*
Howorth, David *producer, director*
Mortilla, Michael Daniel *composer*
Pope, Stephen Travis *composer, computer scientist*
Prettyman, Jane Wardlow *editor, writer, media critic*
Snyder, Allegra Fuller *dance educator*
Wayland, Newton Hart *conductor*

Santa Cruz
Miller, Leta Ellen *musicologist, flutist, educator*
Rosenbloom, Robert A. *audio engineer*
Schechter, John Mendell *music educator*

Santa Maria
Miller, Denis Robert *radio personality, broadcast executive*

Santa Monica
Angel, Steven *musician*
Black, Noel Anthony *television and film director*
Griffin, Merv Edward *former entertainer, television producer, entrepreneur*
Joel, J. Brandt *agent*
Kaplan, Mike *film and video producer, director, and distributor, marketing executive*
Kirkpatrick, David Paul *feature film producer*
Kosa, Frank *filmmaker*
Schroeder, William Robert *actor, graphic designer, linguist*
Ulrich, Robert Gustav *film editor*

Santa Rosa
Conway, Lois Lorraine *piano teacher*

Sausalito
Matthews, Jennifer Lee *music industry executive*

Sepulveda
Davis, Donald Romain *composer*

Sherman Oaks
Foldes, Lawrence David *film producer, director, writer*
Graham, Steven Piddington *entertainment production company executive*
Heffner, Daniel Jason *film producer*
Heimann, Jurgen Steffen *special make-up effects artist, director, writer*
Manasse, George H. *motion picture and television producer*
Marshall, Meryl C(orinblit) *television producer, lawyer*
Peterson, Lowell *cinematographer*
Prince, Richard Hudson *film producer*
Tesh, John *television talk show host, musician*
Williams, Spice *actress*
Wilson, Jim Harold *musician*

Simi Valley
Schied, David Eugene *producer, animator, stunt-man*

Sonoma
Pollack, Phyllis Addison *ballerina*

South Lake Tahoe
Hamilton, David Arthur *performing arts educator, actor*

Stanford
Martinez, Alma R. *actor, director*

Stockton
Tregle, Linda Marie *dance educator*

Studio City
Barrett, Dorothy *performing arts administrator*
Cockrell, Frank Boyd, II *film production company executive*
Ett, Alan Paul *composer*
Presley, David G. *video technician*
Waterbury, David A. *music producer, composer*
Yarbrough, Stephany Lane *actress*

Suisun City
Maguire, George *theater artistic director, actor, educator*

Sunset Beach
Bettis, John Gregory *songwriter*

Sylmar
Foster, Dudley Edwards, Jr. *musician, educator*

Tarzana
Brook, Winston Rollins *retired audio-video design consultant*
Stroller, Louis A. *film producer*

Topanga
Hallas-Gottlieb, Lisa *film and television assistant director*
Redgrave, Lynn *actress*

Torrance
Fornelli, Paul Kevin *video producer, educator*

Turlock
Everett, Michael A. *producer*
Klein, James Mikel *music educator*

Universal City
Cohen, Jerry Sanford *music editor*
Ewing, Michael *producer, film company executive*
Wilder, King *film director, computer consultant*

Upland
Harwich, David Curtis *video design and production specialist*

Valencia
Schrader, Barry Walter *composer, educator*
Windsor, William Earl *consulting engineer, sales representative*

Valley Village
Barkin, Elaine Radoff *composer, music educator*
Casey, Patricia Lee *film producer*

Van Nuys
Allen, Stephen Valentine Patrick William *television comedian, author, pianist, songwriter*
Mayeur, Robert Gordon *music educator, guitarist*
Morgan, Lanny *musician*
Moss, Steve Hoyle *television and film producer and director*

Venice
Gund, Jeffrey Rainier *composer, sound designer*
Wexler, Howard Adam *director of photography*
Williams, Charles (Chad) Madison, III *music company executive*

Ventura
Garey, Judith Freeman *theatre educator*

Verdugo City
LeBlanc, Michele Marie *video production consultant, electrical engineer*

Visalia
Laney, David Scott *video company executive*

Walnut Creek
Jekowsky, Barry *conductor, music director*

West Hollywood
Alenikov, Vladimir *motion picture director and writer*
Franklyn, Audrey Pozen *talent promoter, television personality*
Golchan, Frederic Alfred *film producer, director*
Guedel, John Bimel *radio and television writer, producer*
Laskus, Jacek Wojciech *photography director*
Sherman, Robert B(ernard) *composer, lyricist, screenwriter*
Wessler, Charles B. *film producer*
Wisnievitz, David *film producer*

Westlake Village
Suppa, Ronald Anthony *film producer, writer, entertainment lawyer*

Whittier
Aguilar, Scott Lee *producer, director, writer*

Winnetka
Ball, Curt *actor, writer*
Kessler, Ralph *composer, conductor, educator*

Woodland Hills
Giritlian, James Sarkis *film producer, director, editor*
Gonzalez, Michael Joe *multimedia producer*
Wester, Keith Albert *film and television recording engineer, television executive*

Yreka
Beary, Shirley Lorraine *retired music educator*

COLORADO

Aspen
Harth, Robert James *music festival executive*

Aurora
Racek, Jerrine Ann *producer, editor*

Avon
Billingsley, Michael J. *producer*

Boulder
Bernstein, Giora *artistic director*
Boydston, James Christopher *composer*
Brakhage, James Stanley *filmmaker, educator*
Duckworth, Guy *musician, pianist, educator*
Fink, Robert Russell *music theorist, former university dean*
Kuchar, Theodore *conductor, academic administrator, musician*
Lamon, JoAnne *theatre producer, writer, educator, director*
Sarson, John Christopher *television producer, director, writer*
Symons, James Martin *theater and dance educator*
Waters, Keith John *music educator, pianist*

Brighton
Fitzpatrick, Thomas David *videographer, educator*

Colorado Springs
Bergman, Yaacov *performing company executive*

Denver
Boyles, Peter Guthrie *radio talk show host*
Bryans, Richard Waldron, Jr. *musician, lawyer*
Ceci, Jesse Arthur *violinist*
Davis, Greg William *television producer*
Elbaum, Jonathan Martin *performing arts director*
Fredmann, Martin *ballet artistic director, educator, choreographer*
Keats, Donald Howard *composer, educator*
Maes, Kathryn Gonder *educator*
Ozaki, Nancy Junko *performance artist, educator*
Robinson, Cleo Parker *artistic director*
Schwartz, Cherie Anne Karo *storyteller, writer*

Durango
Penington, Gary Thomas *concert hall manager, video producer*

Fort Collins
Cavarra, Robert N *music educator, musician*
DeJournett, William N. *music educator*

Golden
Brailsford, June Evelyn *musician, educator*

Grand Junction
Gustafson, Kirk *performing company executive*
Rosenbaum, George Gene *music educator, musician*
Vernon, Brian Thomas *dancer, choreographer, dance educator*

Greeley
McNally, Thomas P. *theater educator*

La Jara
Hayes, Robert Bruce *musician*

Lakewood
Garcia, Don (Garce) *television and video producer, videographer*

HAWAII

Honolulu
Engle, Robert Irwin *music educator, musician, composer, writer*
Landovsky, John *artistic director*
Moulin, Jane Ann Freeman *ethnomusicology educator, researcher*
Salgado, Brenda *news director*
Smith, Barbara Barnard *music educator*
Wong, Samuel *conductor*

Kahului
French, James L. *performing company executive*

Kailua
Maltby, Joyce Paula *actress, educator*

Kamuela
Pang, Michael Pili *artistic director*

IDAHO

Boise
Baldassarre, Joseph Anthony *musician, musicologist, music educator*
Ogle, James *performing company executive*
Pimble, Toni *artistic director, choreographer, educator*

Burley
Little, Glen Gordon *retired circus clown, educator*

Idaho Falls
LoPiccolo, John *conductor, music director*

Lewiston
Perconti, William John *music educator, musician*

Moscow
Ney, Charles Stephen *theatre educator*

Pocatello
George, Thom Ritter *conductor, composer*
Redd, Sherrill Edna *music educator*

Rexburg
Nelson, Robert William *theater arts educator*

Sandpoint
Kramer, Remi Thomas *film director*

Twin Falls
Halsell, George Kay *music educator*

MINNESOTA

Minneapolis
Severinsen, Doc (Carl H. Severinsen) *conductor, musician*

MONTANA

Bozeman
Savery, Matthew *music conductor, director, educator*

Great Falls
Johnson, Gordon James *artistic director, conductor*

Huson
Wüstner, Michael Francis *film producer*

Missoula
Henry, Joseph *orchestra director*
Kaufmann, Karen A. *dance educator*
Knowles, William Leroy (Bill Knowles) *television news producer, journalism educator*

Roundup
Di Tonnio, Anthony Michael Philip *recording company executive, minister,*

NEVADA

Boulder City
Hertzog, Eugene Edward *video producer, editor*

Carson City
Bugli, David *conductor, arranger, composer*
Zetter, Lois C. *personal manager*

Las Vegas
Blanton, Walter James *composer, musician, educator*
Capelle, Madelene Carole *opera singer, educator, music therapist*
Castro, Joseph Armand *music director, pianist, composer, orchestrator*
Cervera, David Ray *television producer*
Gold, Hyman *cellist*
Gronemeier, Dean Warren *music educator, musician*
Hansen, Geoffrey *magician, actor, composer, journalist*
Kalb, Benjamin Stuart *television producer, director*
Schafer, Marianne Marks (Marianne Marks) *television production company executive, actress*
Sulich, Vassili *artistic director*
Wiemer, Robert Ernest *film and television producer, writer, director*

Reno
Daniels, Ronald Dale *conductor*

NEW MEXICO

Albuquerque
Bachman, Sallyanne *opera singer, educator, coach*
Mendelwager, Greg *video production company executive*
Smyer, Myrna Ruth *drama educator*

Hobbs
McKay, Glen (Glen Gummess) *audio-visual specialist*

Las Cruces
Chávez, Denise Elia *drama educator, writer, actress*

Santa Fe
Barnett, Charles Radcliffe *film writer, producer, director*
Beal, Mary Evelyn *radio show personality, foundation administrator*
Blakemore, Paul Russell *sound recording engineer, producer*
Crosby, John O'Hea *conductor, opera manager*
Miller, Dwight Richard *cosmetologist, corporate executive, hair designer*
Pratt, Sabrina Vittoria *arts administrator*
Reggio, Godfrey *film director*
Wilson, Bart Allen *media director, marketing consultant, educator*

Taos
Murphey, Michael Martin *country western singer, songwriter*

NEW YORK

New York
Falletta, Jo Ann *musician*
Johanos, Donald *orchestra conductor*
Mansouri, Lotfollah (Lotfi Mansouri) *opera stage director, administrator*
Nagano, Kent George *conductor*
Salonen, Esa-Pekka *conductor*
Tilson Thomas, Michael *symphony conductor*

NORTH CAROLINA

Raleigh
Zimmermann, Gerhardt *conductor*

OHIO

Cleveland
Topilow, Carl S. *symphony conductor*

Delta
Monahan, Leonard Francis *musician, singer, composer, publisher*

OREGON

Ashland
Hirschfeld, Gerald Joseph *cinematographer*
Shaw, Arthur E. *conductor*

Corvallis
MacCormack, Harry Dilts Probjaski *theater, stage production educator*

Eugene
Bailey, Exine Margaret Anderson *soprano, educator*
Benson, Joan *musician, music educator*
Beudert, Mark Christopher *opera singer, voice educator*
Graffeo, Francis *artistic director*
Harth-Bedoya, Miguel *conductor*
Riley, Grannan *performing company executive*
Scheuerell, Douglas Andrew *musician, educator*
Weinstein, Rachel *clown*

Klamath Falls
Mallory, Gorden *music educator*

Medford
Tevis, Barry Lee *television producer, marketing executive*

Portland
Bailey, Robert C. *opera company executive*
Cansler, Philip Trent *music educator*
DePreist, James Anderson *conductor*
Edwards, Eric Alan *director of photography*
Gonzalez, Trudy Ann *television producer*
Gorsline, Russell Elvin *production company executive*
Huggett, Monica *performing company executive*
Kuhns, Sally Nelson *trumpeter, music ensemble director, educator*
Leyden, Norman *conductor*
Murlin, William Ewell *audiovisual specialist*
Saul, Walter Biddle, II *music educator, composer*

Salem
Peel, John Milton *composer, educator*
Zeller, Kurt-Alexander *vocalist, actor, stage director, voice educator*

UTAH

Cedar City
Cook, Douglas Neilson *theater educator, producer, artistic director*

Draper
Aubery, Stephen R.E. *film producer*

Logan
Kadis, Jonathan Brynn *multimedia and distance learning services director*

Provo
Pratt, Rosalie Rebollo *harpist, educator*
Woodbury, Lael Jay *theater educator*

Salem
Hahn, Joan Christensen *retired drama educator, travel agent*

Salt Lake City
Andrews, Donald L. *performing arts company executive*
Belnap, Norma Lee Madsen *musician*
Gornik, Holly Lee *musician, educator*
Hayes, Elizabeth Roths *retired dance educator*
Kåge, Jonas *ballet company artistic director*
Markus, Thomas Benjamin *theatre director, actor*
Silverstein, Joseph Harry *conductor, musician*
Van Wagenen, Sterling *film producer, director*

South Jordan
Davis, Cliss Johnson *musician*

WASHINGTON

Bellevue
French, James Rowley *radio dramatist, writer*

Bellingham
Whyte, Nancy Marie *performing arts educator*

Bremerton
Bolstad, Rose Irene *singer, songwriter*
Cottrell-Adkins, Leone *opera company director*

Chelan
Kronschnabel, Alan James *musician, real estate agent*

Everett
Boushey, David L. *stunt coordinator, fight master, educator*
Dodson, Richard Lee *music educator*

Freeland
Short, Gregory Norman *composer, musician, educator*

Gig Harbor
Breneman, David Clinton, II *audio producer, director*

Issaquah
Hunt, Robert William *theatrical producer, data processing consultant*

Kenmore
Jensen, Helen *musical artists management company executive*

Olympia
Johnson, Jerome John, Jr. (Jay Johnson) *producer, photographer*
Wilson, Dierdre Lynn *theater and dance educator, director, choreographer, psychotherapist, drama therapist*

Seattle
Anang, Kofi *artistic director, educator, dancer*
Bernard, Jonathan Walter *music educator*
Card, Deborah Frances *orchestra administrator*
Carlson, Bruce William *production company executive*
Forbes, David Craig *musician*
Jenkins, Speight *opera company executive, writer*
Nishitani, Martha *dancer*
Russell, Francia *ballet director, educator*
Ryder, Hal *theater educator, director*
Sateren, Terry *theater technical production*
Stowell, Kent *ballet director*
Wolf, Hans *opera company director*

Snohomish
Philpott, Larry La Fayette *horn player*

Spokane
Bray, R(obert) Bruce *music educator*
Durham, Warren John *television and radio producer*
Graham, Bill *opera company director*
Halvorson, Marjory *opera director*
Pugh, Kyle Mitchell, Jr. *musician, retired music educator*
Schmitt, Reed Reese *television director, sports photographer*
Young, Michael Edward *composer, music educator*

Tacoma
Farrell, Anne *opera company administrator*
Schultz, Paul W. *music educator, conductor*

WYOMING

Casper
Williams, Charles Preston *sound effects storyteller, author*

Laramie
Blair, Damian J. W. *composer, guitarist*

Rock Springs
Beach, John Laurence *storyteller, writer*

Torrington
Hamer, Jeanne Huntington *soprano, educator*

CANADA

ALBERTA

Alberta
Nissinen, Mikko Pekka *dancer*

Calgary
Epton, Gregg *performing company executive*
Graf, Hans *conductor*

BRITISH COLUMBIA

Vancouver
Agler, David *conductor*
Garber, Anne Theresa *television and radio personality*
Hallam, Robert J. *performing company executive, consultant*
Washburn, Jon *artistic director*

Victoria
Devan, David *opera company director*
Vernon, Timothy *artistic director*

ADDRESS UNPUBLISHED

Aaron, Roy Henry *entertainment company executive*
Aasen-Hull, Audrey Avis *music educator*
Akerman, Joseph Lax, Jr. *film and television producer*
Alberts, David *artistic director, mime*
Aldag, Richard Jeffrey *composer, educator*
Aliotti, Gilli *singer, songwriter*
Allen, Crystal DeeAn *producer, actress*
Andermann, Greg *producer, director, consultant*
Andrews, Carol Lynn *producer, writer*
Baerwald, Susan Grad *television broadcasting company executive producer*
Becker, Wendy Jeanne *music and drama educator*
Behlmer, Rudy H., Jr. *director, writer, film educator*
Belgrader, Andrei *director, writer*
Belshe, Judy Bernice *casting director*
Bergen, Candice *actress, writer, photojournalist*
Berman, Sanford Solomon *motion picture sound designer, composer, arranger, artist*
Bows, Robert Alan *television producer, writer, director*
Brady, Mary Rolfes *music educator*
Brosnan, Peter Lawrence *documentary filmmaker*
Callas, John Peter *director, producer*
Canin, Stuart Victor *violinist*
Casey, Shannon Gloria *visual effects producer*
Chambers, Thomas Francis *classical vocalist, financial consultant*
Cheung, Vincent Hua-Sheng *television writer, producer*
Colmano, Marino Giovanni Augusto *director, cinematographer, producer, media executive*
Cone, Stephanie J. *producer*
Cunningham, Ron *choreographer, artistic director*
Dagort, Aida Mulieri *musician*
Dale, Virginia Mariposa *author, educator*
Davidson, LeRoy *musician*
Deats, Richard Warren (Dicky Deats) *key grip*
Debus, Eleanor Viola *retired business management company executive*
Elikann, Lawrence S. (Larry Elikann) *television and film director*
Epcar, Richard Michael *actor, writer, director*
Erkiletian, Alexander Todd *filmmaker, philantropist*
Ferzacca, John Barry *director, playwright*
Fong, Wei-Ming Nickson *film special effects expert*
Forster, Robert *actor, speaker*
Frankish, Brian Edward *film producer, director*
Fullenwider, Nancy Vrana *music composer, dance educator*
Giroux, Paul Henry *retired music educator, musician*
Grainger-Haynes, Leslie *foreign language video producer, translator*
Great, Don Charles *composer, music company executive*
Grover, Hank L. *motion picture producer*
Guttman, Irving Allen *opera stage director*
Hansen, Edward Alvin Charles *feature animation executive*
Harper, Richard Henry *film producer, director*
Harris, Fred Orin *retired director*
Harris, Harry H. *television director*
Hauger, Eleanor Prapion Kallejian *pianist, singer*
Heidt, Horace Hamilton, Jr. *music director, conductor, business executive*
Hill, William Elmer, III *producer*
Hokanson, Randolph *concert pianist, educator*
Horton, Julie *music company executive*
Horvath, Imre Gabor *television producer and director*
Huning, Devon Gray *actress, dancer, audiologist, photographer, video producer and editor*
Issari, M(ohammad) Ali *film producer, writer, consultant*
Jarmel, Marcia J. *documentary filmmaker*
Johnson, John Henry *film director, producer, photographer, educator*
Johnson, Peter Neils *motion picture producer, educator*
Kane, Michael Joseph *director*
Kaylan, Howard Lawrence *musical entertainer, composer*
Koenig, John M. *producer, musician, lawyer*
Koritan, Bruce (Van) Lee *entertainer, composer*
Kubsch, Christian *film producer*
LaFrance, Reginald Michael, Jr. *television producer and director, videographer*
Lee, Cynthia *television producer, playwright, filmmaker*
Leshne, Carla *videomaker, videographer, editor*
Lewitzky, Bella *choreographer*
Little, Loren Everton *musician, ophthalmologist*
Lucas, Beth Anne *television producer*
Luther, Jeffrey Henry *art director, production designer*
Macan, Edward L. *music educator*
Magee, Thomas Robert *musician*
Mangicaro, Richard Alan *musician*
Manina, Mitchell Ray *video production company executive, consultant*
Marin, Paul (Solomon Schneider) *actor, writer*
Martin, Leonard Austin, II *music educator*
Martin, Patricia Ann *music educator*
Marts, Albert Lee *choirmaster, rehabilitation counselor*
Matheson, James Hugh *musician, educator*
Matthau, Charles Marcus *film director*
McBain, Diane Jean *actress, writer, newspaper columnist*
McClain, Richard Stan *cinematographer*
McEuen, John *musician, guitarist*
McKenna, Suzanne *performing arts educator*
Mendelson, Braddon Leigh *film producer*
Mish, Michael *composer, writer, motivational speaker*
Molina, William H. *cinematographer, director*
Moses, Kim M *film producer, director*
Myerson, Alan *director, film and television writer*
Neary, Patricia Elinor *ballet director*
Newton, Eric C. *dance educator*
Nichols, David Lawrence *television writer, producer*
Numano, Allen Stanislaus Motoyuki *musician, writer*
Nuss, William Martin (Bill Nuss) *television producer, writer*
O'Brien, Jack George *artistic director*
Palagyi, Addyse Lane *educator*
Palileo, Hazel Valencia *videographer*
Palmieri, Robert Michael *music educator, researcher, pianist*
Panajotovic, Ilija Svetislav *producer, director, writer*
Parker, Norman *actor*
Perez, Tom *film director, writer*
Phillips, Florence Tsu *choreographer, dance educator, lawyer*
Porter, Richard Kane *audio engineer, consultant*
Rain, Rhonda L. *performing arts executive, counselor, educator*
Reed, Lynda Bernal *video producer, writer*
Reynolds, Karen Jeanne *musician*
Rook, Ayesha L *producer, writer*
Rosner, Rick *television producer*
Sandrich, Jay H. *television director*
Schwarz, Gerard *conductor, musician*
Ser, Randy Jay *production designer, director*
Shusterman, Melissa Lynn *television producer, educator*
Sikes, Cynthia Lee *actress, singer*
Sisemore, Claudia *educational films and videos producer, director*
Smith, C. Jay *radio talk show host, marketing professional*
Smith, Irby Jay *film producer*
Solow, Herbert Franklin *film producer, writer*
Spier, Luise Emma *film editor, director*
Stanfill, Shelton G. *performing arts administrator*
Steinke, Greg A *music educator, administrator, composer, oboist*
Sullivan, W. Kim *theatrical producer, actress*
Summers, Cathleen Ann *film producer*
Sutherland, Bruce *composer, pianist*
Symmes, Daniel Leslie *three-dimensional technology executive, producer, director*
Taylor, Guy Watson *symphonic conductor*
Thomas, John Gilbert *producer*
Timmons, William Milton *producer, freelance writer, retired cinema arts educator, publisher, film maker*
Todus, Gina Marie *filmmaker, media artist*
Tokofsky, Jerry Herbert *film producer*
Vannozzi, Thomas *cameraman*
Van Rellim, Tim *film producer*
Wax, Stephen Martin *personal manager*
Weiskopf, Kim Robert *television producer, writer*
Whitehead, Graham Grant Robin *theater director*
Wilson, Michael Gregg *film producer, writer*
Worthey, Carol *composer*
Zhao, Li *fine arts company executive, teacher, consultant*

ARTS: VISUAL

UNITED STATES

ALASKA

Anchorage
Reed, Fran Ann *artist*
Sexton Atkins, Jannah *artist*

Cordova
Bugbee-Jackson, Joan *sculptor*

Kenai
Willard, Thomas Kirt *artist*

Ketchikan
Kennedy, Peggy Boogaard *artist, writer*
McDermott, David (John) *artist, writer, photographer*

Nome
Sloan, Patrice S. *artist*

Soldotna
Freeburg, Gary L. *art educator*

ARIZONA

Ash Fork
Jarvis, James Rees *artist*

Cave Creek
Lyon, Dustin L. *artist*
Peters, Andrew David *artist*

Chandler
Dulla, Joan *artist*
Matus, Nancy Louise *artist*

Cottonwood
Carr, Betty Lee *artist, educator*

Flagstaff
Brookins, Jacob Boden *artist*
Edgerton, Debra *artist, educator*

Fort Mohave
Masters, Larry James, Sr. *lapidary educator*

Fountain Hls
York, Tina *painter*

Glendale
Golubic, Theodore Roy *sculptor, designer, inventor*
Stong, David Henry *artist*

Green Valley
Nasvik-Dennison, Anna *artist*

Lake Montezuma
Burkee, Irvin *artist*

Mesa
Copley, Ed *artist*

Oro Valley
Loeh, Corinne Rachow *artist*

Paradise Valley
Heller, Jules *artist, writer, educator*
Maxey, Diane Meadows *artist*
Mayberry, Patricia Ann Tinthoff *artist, educator, interior designer*
Swartz, Beth Ames *artist*

Peoria
Meldman, Margery Lynn *writer, photographer*
Willard, Garcia Lou *artist*

Phoenix
Arvin, Joanie Ida *artist, consultant*
Braverman, Donna Caryn *fiber artist*
Herranen, Kathy *artist, graphic designer*
Knauf, James Edward *artist*
Missal, Stephen Joseph *art educator, portraitist*
Richter, Hank Charles, Jr. *artist*
Schmieder, Carl *jeweler*
Stone, Hazel Anne Decker *artist*
Williams, Joyce Marilyn *artist, business owner*

Prescott
Miley, Douglas Henry *artist*
Willoughby, James Russell *artist*

Scottsdale
Afsary, Cyrus *artist*
Estrada, Luis Tomás *artist*
Hillmer, Mary Jane *interior designer*
Lang, Margo Terzian *artist*
Magenta, Muriel *artist*
Pitcher, Helen Ione *advertising director*
Rothschild, John D. *art dealer*
Schutzky, Marilyn Horsley *artist*
Taylor, Cheryal A. *artist, educator*

Sedona
Seronde, Adele Herter *artist*

Tempe
Bates, Mary Patricia *art educator*
Gibson, Mitchell Earl *painter, consultant, psychiatrist*
Kinney, Raleigh Earl *artist*
Meissinger, Ellen Murray *artist, educator*
Radford, Deioreta Lea Funte *designer*
Schoebel, Henry Leo *artist, educator*

Tucson
Doherty, Betty Jean *artist*
Flint, Willis Wolfschmidt (Willi Wolfschmidt) *artist, sculptor*
Goodman, Mary A. *photographer*
Grygutis, Barbara *sculptor*
He, Xuzheng *artist, scenic designer*
Lascelles, Susan *artist*
Matthew, Neil Edward *artist, educator*
Petrevan, Charles Carl *artist, educator*
Root, Nile *photographer, educator*
Sleigh, Emily Smith *artist, writer*

CALIFORNIA

Acampo
Eger, Marilyn Rae *artist*

Alameda
Parks, Neal Stuart *artist*

Alhambra
Ehrman, Valerie Ann *artist*

Altadena
Green, David Oliver, Jr. *sculptor, designer*
Peltzer, Eric Thomas *sculptor*

Anaheim
Bennett, Genevieve *artist*
Nelipovich, Sandra Grassi *artist*

Aptos
Seltz, Gay *artist, investor*
Woods, Gurdon Grant *sculptor*

Arcadia
Danziger, Louis *graphic designer, educator*

Arcata
Land-Weber, Ellen *photography educator*

Aromas
Nutzle, Futzie (Bruce John Kleinsmith) *artist, author, cartoonist*

Atascadero
McMahon, John William *sculptor*

Avalon
Burns, Denise Ruth *artist*

Bayside
Bettiga, Floyd H. *artist, painter, educator*

Belmont
Pava, Esther Shub *artist, educator*

Ben Lomond
Grauer, Ronald Gene *artist*

Benicia
Stern, Arthur I *architectural glass artist, sculptor, painter*

Berkeley
Brixey, Shawn Alan *digital media artist, media educator, director*
Carson, G(ary) B(enson) *art appraiser*
Casida, Kati *artist*
Davis, Virginia Whiteford *artist*
Genn, Nancy *artist*
Hartman, Robert Leroy *artist, educator*
Healy, Anne *sculptor*
Nanao, Kenjilo *artist, educator*
Siegesmund, Richard Evans *art educator, consultant*

Beverly Hills
De Anda, Alicia *artist*
Moses, Gloria Jean *artist*
Shishim, Francis G. *artist, performer*
Silver, David Lawrence *art dealer*
Wosk, Miriam *artist*

Big Sur
Hawthorne, Gregory Thomas *painter, sculptor, gallery owner*

Bolinas
Cornwall, Dora Jane *artist, painter, poet, songwriter*
O'Connor, Birgit Christel Helen *artist*

Boonville
Hanes, John Ward *sculptor, civil engineer consultant*

Brentwood
Peters, William Frank *art educator*

Burbank
Fryman, Cherie Marie *video graphic artist*
Harrison, Allen C. *artist, educator*
Mahady, Eric M. *artist, animator*
Merrill, Thomas St. John *medical photographer*
Polmanski, Ted Chester *lighting director*

Burlingame
Pollard, Jann Diann *fine artist, graphic artist, educator*
Shaw, Kurt *artist*

Calistoga
Thollander, Earl Gustave *artist, author*

Camarillo
Lacayo, Omar D'León *artist*

Canoga Park
Rosenfeld, Sarena Margaret *artist*

Capitola
Johnson, Gwenavere Anelisa *artist*

Carlsbad
Di Roma, Tom *graphic technician, writer*
Smirnoy, Igor Vasilevich *artist*

Carmel
Allan, David Lewis *artist, researcher, educator*
Andreason, Sharon Lee *sculptor*
Brodie, Howard *artist*
Jacobs, Ralph, Jr. *artist*
Kennedy, John Edward *art dealer, appraiser, curator*
Kleefeld, Carolyn Mary *artist, writer, poet*
Skalagard, Hans Martin *artist*

Carmel Valley
Payton, Ralph Reed *photographer*
Sands, Sharon Louise *graphic design executive, art publisher, artist*

Carpinteria
Rosas, Susan Jane *designer, graphic artist, illustrator, art director*

Carson
Hirsch, Gilah Yelin *artist, writer*

Chatsworth
Ly, Vi Kim *artist, educator*

Chico
Applegate, (Harold) Reed *retired graphic designer, advertising executive*
Javan, Joseph *art educator*
Snider, Karen Cecile *artist*

Chula Vista
Cannon-Wilson, Margaret Elizabeth *art educator, artist*
Wilson-Cannon, Margaret Elizabeth *artist, educator*

Claremont
Gonzales-Day, Kenneth Robert *artist, educator*

Arcadia *(continued columns)*

Sides, Elizabeth M. *artist, educator*
Zornes, Milford *artist*

Clarksburg
Couzens, Julia *artist*

Concord
Brandhorst, Curt W. *graphic designer*

Corning
Blomquist, Robin Alice *artist, elementary education educator*

Corona Del Mar
Anapol, Berte *artist*

Coronado
Hubbard, Donald *marine artist, writer*
McNary, Sue Tushingham *artist*
Salsig, Doyen *photographer, photography studio owner*

Costa Mesa
Muller, Jerome Kenneth *photographer, art director, editor*
Westerman, Donna Day *artist*

Covina
Owen, Carol Thompson *artist, educator, writer*

Crestline
Noble, Lawrence Alan *artist*

Culver City
Gordon, Florence Irene *graphic artist, illustrator*

Cupertino
Geisinger, William Louis *art educator*
Lee, Eric Tom *apparel business owner, designer*
Rodriguez, Eugene *art educator*

Cypress
Bloom, Julian *artist, editor*

Daggett
Bailey, Katherine Christine *artist, writer*

Daly City
Kennedy, Gwendolyn Debra *film animator, parapsychologist, artist, play and film writer*
Leong, Lam-Po (Lanbo Liang) *artist, educator*
Ma, Zach *artist*

Dana Point
Swimm, Thomas Steven *artist*

Davis
Keizer, Susan Jane *artist*

Desert Hot Springs
Beeson, Mary A. *sculptor*

Downey
McFarland, Willelyn Shaw *artist, educator*

Eagleville
Minto, Floran Kay *sculptor*

El Dorado Hills
Peeples, Maija Woof *artist*

Encinitas
Breitwieser-Stacey, Diane Louise *artist*
Gill, Nilly *artist*

Encino
Jones, John Harding *photographer*

Escondido
Costilow, Virginia Katherine *artist, sculptor, poet*
Spinn, Marian Rose *artist, retired realtor*

Fair Oaks
Potter, George Kenneth *artist*

Fairfax
Tchaicovsky, Beny *artist, musician*

Fallbrook
Roche, Joan I. *artist*

Flintridge
Johnston, Oliver Martin, Jr. *animator*
Thomas, Franklin Rosborough *retired animator*

Folsom
Campbell, Ann Marie *artist*
Farcnik, Alexander *commercial artist, portraitist*
Fredericks, Michael Karl *freelance artist, writer, magazine publisher*

Forest Ranch
Morrison, Martha Kaye *photolithography engineer, executive*

Fremont
Ammon, Mary Louise *artist*
Ko, Hyunok *artist, jeweler*

Fresno
Johnson, Edith Curtice *art education administrator*
Stuart, Dorothy Mae *artist*

Fullerton
Morgenthaler, Patricia B. *visual artist*

Galt
Dymond, Richardene C. *artist*

Garden Grove
Caron, James Edward *artist, musician*

Glen Ellen
Anderson, Catherine *artist*

Glendale
Ho, Pin *artist, consultant*
Sweet, Harvey *theatrical, scenic and lighting designer*

Glendora
Rachford, Maryann Kvietkauskas *graphic designer, multimedia educator*

Granite Bay
Welden, Larry Truman *artist*

Greenbrae
Blatt, Morton Bernard *medical illustrator*

Hacienda Heights
Guo, XuanChang *sculptor, educator*

Half Moon Bay
Harris, David Jack *artist, painter, educator*

Hawthorne
Acker, George *artist*
Palmer, Charles Ray *retired graphics specialist, investor*

Hayward
Ferentz, Tom Bart *photographer, photography workshop administrator*
Jordahl, Geir Arild *photographer, educator*
Leblow, G. Hagny *artist*
Perrizo, James David *art and sculpture educator, forestry pilot*
Van Deusen, Larry Milton *artist*

Healdsburg
Bernard, Timothy Henry *sculptor, designer*

Huntington Beach
Camp, Roger Ortho *fine arts educator, artist, photographer*
de Barcza, Gladys Mary *art educator*
Shuss, Jane Margaret *artist*

Inglewood
Vario, Joyce *graphic designer*

Irvine
Giannulli, Mossimo *designer, apparel business executive*
Hack, David Frank *art director*
Varo, Marton-Geza *sculptor*

Kelseyville
Fletcher, Leland Vernon *artist*

Kentfield
Galli, Stanley Walter *artist*

Kingsburg
Olson, Maxine Louise *artist, lecturer*

La Jolla
Cohen, Barbara Ann *artist*
Hester, Perrietta Burke *artist, educator*
Hsieh, Victor C. *artist*
Imana, Jorge Garron *artist*
Lozito, Carol L. *artist*
Merrim, Louise Meyerowitz *artist, actress*
Quint, Mark Harley *art dealer*
Welchman, John *art educator*

La Mesa
Harmening, Gail Joan *craft pattern designer*

Lafayette
Beaumont, Mona *artist*
Kapp, Eleanor Jeanne *impressionistic artist, writer, researcher*
Shurtleff, Akiko Aoyagi *artist, consultant*

Laguna Beach
Barnett, Fila *artist, executive recruiter*
Blacketer, James Richard *artist*
Foote, Kay Rebber *artist*
Powers, Runa Skötte *artist*

Laguna Hills
Saudek, Martha Folsom *artist, educator*

Lagunitas
Holman, Arthur Stearns *artist*

Lakewood
Barton, Billie Jo *artist, educator*

Lancaster
Swart, Bonnie Blount *artist*

Larkspur
Teller, Pauline Ivancovich *artist*

Little River
Greenlead, Judith Carol *artist, art educator*

Livermore
Johnson, Katharine Decker *artist*

Long Beach
Korogodsky, Danila Zinovy *theater set and costume designer, educator*
Roemer, Carol Kaluga *art educator*
Sanchez-H., Jose *fine arts educator, producer, director, media consultant*
Tecson, Herminigildo Lisarondo *sculptor, painter*

Los Altos
Rothwell, Elaine B. *artist*
Sharpe, Kathryn Peck *artist*
Vargas, Marsha Lynn *art dealer, appraiser*

Los Angeles
Aguilar, Leticia (Leticia R Ballestero) *artist, graphic designer*
Asano, Hisako *fine arts educator*
Blitman, Joe *doll dealer*
Butler, Eugenia Perpetua *artist*
Chen, Edna Lau *art educator, artist*

Valencia
Alexander, Amy Jill *computer-video artist, art educator*
Morrison, James R. *art educator, sculptor*
Tanaka, Janice *artist, educator*

Van Nuys
Cook, Jenik Esterm *artist, educator*

Venice
Charlot, Martin Day *painter, muralist, writer, filmmaker, educator*
Chipman, Jack *artist*
Greenberg, Richard Alan *film designer*
Hartley, Corinne *painter, sculptor, educator*
Nielsen, Niels Lawrence *visual effects design and production, art director*
Schwartzman, Glenda Joy *artist*

Ventura
Abul-Haj, Elizabeth *fine arts and antique appraiser*
Koch, Gerd Hermann *artist, educator*
Manny, Brian Scott *graphic designer*

Walnut
Nelson, Michael Richard *artist, designer, photographer*

Walnut Creek
Little, Jerry James *artist*
Reimann, Arline Lynn *artist*
Sustek, Ritamarie *fine arts appraiser*

West Covina
Shiershke, Nancy Fay *artist, educator, property manager*

West Hills
Freas, Frank Kelly *illustrator*
Mears, Linda Shaw *artist*

Westlake Village
Castrejon, Elizabeth Blackwell *artist*
Newman, Ruth Tantlinger *artist*
Richardson, Leatrice Joy *artist*

Whitethorn
Webster, Kenneth Fewings *painter, consultant*

Wilmington
Webber, Nancy Wildermuth *artist, educator*

Windsor
Baran, Shirley Walters *artist, sculptor*

Woodland Hills
Bonassi, Jodi *artist, marketing consultant*

Yucaipa
Jacka, Robert Emmett *printmaker*

COLORADO

Alamosa
Venne, Georgia Pacheco *artist*

Arvada
Clark, Bruce Woodruff *graphic designer*
Miller, Gregory Alan *artist, writer*

Boulder
Bierman, Sandra L. *artist*
Ecker, Robert Rodgers *fine arts educator, artist*
Lange, Vidie *artist*
Matthews, Eugene Edward *artist*

Brighton
Shaklee, Kimberly Lorraine *sculptor*

Colorado Springs
Brierre, Micheline *artist*
Goehring, Kenneth *artist*
Lee, Kang S. *artist, educator*
Owen, Thomas James *artist, educator*
Selk, Eleanor Hutton *artist*
Uphoff, Joseph Anthony, Jr. *artist*

Cortez
Winterer-Schulz, Barbara Jean *art designer, author*

Cotopaxi
French, Edward Glen *artist*

Denver
Alcott Tempest Temple, Leslie *artist*
Barker, Elver Amos *artist, educator, social change activist*
Bonath, John Paul *graphic designer, educator*
Burger, Paula *artist*
Carter, Melvin Whitsett (Mel Carter) *artist, educator*
Cunningham, Eldon Lloyd *artist, educator*
Enright, Cynthia Lee *illustrator*
Norman, John Barstow, Jr. *designer, educator*
Pickrell-Takata, Linda *artist*
Smilanic, Michael Jerome *art director*

Englewood
Kristin, Karen *artist*
Lamb, Darlis Carol *sculptor*

Evergreen
Schomberg, A. Thomas *sculptor*

Fort Collins
Haire, James *sculptor*
Weimer, Dawn *sculptor*

Gardner
Schneider, Kenny *artist, educator*

Golden
Fisher, Philip Condon *artist*

Granby
Rienhoff, Joanne Winkenwerder *artist*

Greeley
Lezhan, Erlene *artist*

Hotchkiss
Blackstock, Virginia Harriett *artist*

La Veta
Zehring, Peggy Johnson *artist*

Lakewood
Filson, Jay Gordon *art educator*

Larkspur
Bierbaum, Janith Marie *artist*

Littleton
Barnes, Cloyd Ray *sculptor, retired engineer*
Lowry, Linda Eleanor *artist, educator*
Schonberger, Clayton James *artist*

Longmont
King, Jane Louise *artist*

Louisville
Qualley, Charles Albert *fine arts educator*

Loveland
McDowell, Ronald Wiles *artist*

Manitou Springs
Darpino, Fred J. *sculptor*

Morrison
Erlund, Julia Elizabeth *artist*

New Castle
Lively, Ricky *artist*

Red Feather Lakes
Gadbois, Linda D. *artist*

Salida
Kerndt, Arthur Loraine *artist, advertising sales representative*

Snowmass Village
Beeman, Malinda Mary *artist, program administrator*

Telluride
Hadley, Paul Burrest, Jr. (Tabbit Hadley) *domestic engineer, photographer*
Smith, Samuel David *artist, educator*

HAWAII

Hanalei
Helder, David Ernest *artist, educator*

Honolulu
Amor, Simeon, Jr. *photographer*
Belknap, Jodi Parry *graphic designer, writer, business owner*
Betts, Barbara Stoke *artist, educator*
Chang, Rodney Eiu Joon *artist, dentist*
Guthrie, Edgar King *artist*
Levin, Lauren (Lo Levin) *artist, teacher, designer*
Uhl, Philip Edward *marine artist*

Kaneohe
Nash, Paul Leslie *ceramic art educator*

Kapaau
Ackerman, Gary Edward *artist*

Kihei
Swanson, Jane Bradley *artist, realtor*

Kula
Altman, Robert Charles *apparel designer*

Lahaina
Killingsworth, Kathleen Nola *artist, photographer, company executive*
Sato, Tadashi *artist*

Lihue
Lai, Waihang *art educator*

Volcano
Ono, Ira *artist*

IDAHO

Boise
Budde, James Alfred *art educator*
Killmaster, John Henry, III *artist, educator*
Williams, DeWayne Arthur, Jr. *artist, environmental resource specialist*

Ketchum
Wilson, Jan Elizabeth *art dealer*

Moscow
Panttaja, Dean *scenic design, theater design educator*

MONTANA

Billings
Massee, Robert Lewis *visual arts educator, freelance photographer*

Bozeman
Helzer, Richard Brian *artist, educator*
Selyem, Bruce Jade *photographer*
Volkersz, Willem Aldert *artist, educator*

Browning
Scriver, Robert Macfie *sculptor*

Great Falls
Gallagher, Sherry E. *artist*

Helena
Cleary, Shirley Jean *artist, illustrator*
Holmes, Tim *sculptor*

Kalispell
von Krenner, Walther G. *artist, writer, art consultant and appraiser*

Livingston
Chatham, Russell *landscape artist*

Missoula
Morin, Paula Marie Yvette (Maryan Morin) *photographer, artist, photo researcher*

Thompson Falls
Phillips, Craig Stewart *artist*

NEVADA

Boulder City
Siller, Garrett Frank *wood craftsman*

Henderson
Turner, Florence Frances *ceramist*

Las Vegas
Goldblatt, Hal Michael *photographer, accountant*
Newquist, Donald Stewart *designer, technical director, consultant*
Sullivan, Barbara Jean *artist*

Reno
Goin, Peter Jackson *art educator*
Harder, Kelsie T. *artist, educator*
Hilts, Ruth *artist*
Newberg, Dorothy Beck (Mrs. William C. Newberg) *portrait artist*
Waddell, Theodore *painter*

NEW MEXICO

Albuquerque
Adams, Clinton *artist, historian*
Antreasian, Garo Zareh *artist, lithographer, art educator*
Aubin, Barbara Jean *artist*
Barrow, Thomas Francis *artist, educator*
Cia, Manuel Lopez *artist*
Coleman, Barbara McReynolds *artist*
Culpepper, Mabel Claire *artist*
De Jong, Constance A. *artist, educator*
Easley, Loyce Anna *painter*
Feinberg, Elen Amy *artist, educator*
Grinnell, Christopher Wade *photographer, art educator*
Hahn, Betty *artist, photographer, educator*
Hovel, Esther Harrison *art educator*
Humphries, Sandra Lee Forger *artist, teacher*
Keating, David *photographer*
Moyers, William Taylor *artist*
Multhaup, Merrel Keyes *artist*
Nelson, Mary Carroll *artist, author*
Paulos, Daniel Thomas *artist, writer, college program director*
Peterson, Gwen Entz *artist*
Sowers, Miriam Ruth *painter*
Steider, Doris *artist*
Townsend, Alvin Neal *artist*
Weems, Mary Ann *business owner*
Witkin, Joel-Peter *photographer*

Cerrillos
Harnack, Barbara Wood *artist, sculptor*

Corona
Steen, Nancy *artist*

Corrales
Eaton, Pauline *artist*
York, Shirley Marie *artist*

Espanola
Jonker, Pamela Lynn *artist*
Seeger, Sondra Joan *artist*

Farmington
Peters, Evelyn Joan *artist*

Gallup
Brown, Chester D. *artist, educator*
Cattaneo, Jacquelyn Annette Kammerer *artist, educator*

Hobbs
Best, Mickey D. *educator*
Duke, Marilyn Ann *graphic designer, educator*

Hondo
Seely, Alice Warder *artist*

Las Cruces
Ritter, Sallie *painter, sculptor*

Las Vegas
Aeby, Kim *artist, educator*

Mesilla
Herbel, Carolene Cal *apparel designer, retailer*

Montezuma
Lopez, Peter Edward *artist*

Portales
Bryant, James Patrick *art educator, artist*
Senn, Gregory Paul *artist, educator*

Rio Rancho
Warder, William *artist*

Roswell
Avery, Keith Willette *artist, educator*

Hallenbeck, Pomona Juanita *artist*
Peterson, Dorothy Hawkins *artist, educator*
Wiggins, Kim Douglas *artist, art dealer*

San Lorenzo
Renner, Eric Payne *artist*

San Patricio
Meigs, John Ligget *artist*

Santa Fe
Brycelea, Clifford *artist*
Burk, Yvonne Turner *artist, educator*
Clift, William Brooks, III *photographer*
Crowley, Kim William *sculptor*
Dean, Nat *artist, educator*
Dechert, Peter *photographer, writer, foundation administrator*
Horndeski, Gregory Walter *artist*
Kortz, Dirk Andrew *artist*
La Lumia, Frank Munzueto *artist*
Lamunière, Caroline Parker *artist*
LeRose, Thomas M. *photographer*
Malone, Roxanne Enyeart *artist, educator*
McGuire, Michael Allen *artist, educator*
Orduno, Robert Daniel *artist, painter, sculptor*
Reyner, Nancy Cooper *artist*
Schabacker, Betty Barchet *artist*
Shubart, Dorothy Louise Tepfer *artist, educator*
Shugard, Owen Stephen *fine arts and antiques dealer*
Silverman, Sherri Lynn *artist, educator*
Steinke, Bettina *artist*

Silver City
McCray, Dorothy Westaby *artist and educator*

Taos
Becker, Elisabeth Maria *artist, educator*
Bell, Larry Stuart *artist*
Martin, Agnes *artist*
Trumble, Beverly Jane *artist*
Wilde, Teruko *artist*

NEW YORK

Montauk
Taylor Bardwell, Mary-Beth Anne *artist, sculptor*

Shore Island Heights
German, Katy *artist*

NORTH CAROLINA

Carrboro
Anderson, Arthur Lee *sculptor, writer*

OREGON

Applegate
Boyle, (Charles) Keith *artist, educator*

Ashland
Hay, Richard Laurence *theater scenic designer*

Bandon
Holland, Gay Willman *art educator*
Lindquist, Louis William *artist, writer*

Bend
Schulz, Suzon Louise *fine artist*

Brookings
Johnson, Richard Vernon *artist, educator*

Cannon Beach
Dahlsten, Shirley Annette *artist, educator*
Greaver, Harry *artist*

Coos Bay
Van Allen, Katrina Frances *painter*

Corvallis
Hiratsuka, Yuji *artist, educator*

Dayton
Gilhooly, David James, III *artist*

Eugene
Buckner, Paul Eugene *sculptor, educator*
Caprario, Kathleen Maria *artist, art educator*
O'Connell, Megan Gerard *visual designer, educator*

Falls City
Osman, Randolph E. *art appraiser, curator*

Grants Pass
Marchini, Claudia Cilloniz *artist*
Remington, Mary *artist, author*

Hillsboro
Hurley, Bruce Palmer *artist*

Lebanon
Hamilton, Earl *artist*

Medford
Johnson, Morgan Burton *artist, writer*
Morgan, James L. *artist*

Newberg
Keith, Pauline Mary *artist, illustrator, writer*

Pendleton
Harper, Gloria Janet *artist, educator*

Phoenix
Hoffman-Snodgrass, Lynda Louise *artist,*

Portland
Baker, Allison Paige *photographer, musician,*
Bell, Leslie Ann *sculptor, moldmaker*

Canfield, James *art director*
Fisher, Jeff *graphic designer, artist*
Gonsalves, Pamela Yvonne *artist, educator, graphic designer*
Grimes, Bryan Kelly *artist*
Haun, Gregory Cosmo *artist*
Lucas, Leslee Suzanne *artist*
Montone, Kenneth Alan *art director, creative director, consultant*
Ramsby, Mark Delivan *lighting designer and consultant*
Tower, Sue Warncke *artist*
Waddingham, John Alfred *artist, journalist*
Yes, Phyllis Ann *artist, video and filmmaker, educator*

Roseburg
Comerford, Susan Marie *artist*
Ramsey, Patricia Prusak *artist*

Salem
Baker, Pat Ellen *artist, educator*
Pierre, Joseph Horace, Jr. *commercial artist*
Visgatis, Charles Anthony *artist, gallery director*

Springfield
Light, Dotty Jean *artist*

Talent
Winding, Ezshwan Kraus *artist*

Waldport
Frankfort, James *artist*

Wallowa
Ray, Jenny *artist*

TEXAS

Houston
Visconti-Tilley, Vicki Lorraine *illustrator*

UTAH

Bountiful
Elmer, Stan *artist*

Heber City
Barber, William Harold (Bill) *artist, sculptor, motion picture producer*

Logan
Terry, Christopher Thomas *artist*

Midvale
Bergman, Raymond Louis *art supply executive*

Moab
Hagner, John Gilbert *artist*

Monroe
Kirby, Orville Edward *potter, painter, sculptor*

Price
Bergera, Clifford Hreinson *art educator, artist*

Provo
McClellan, Catherine Ann *costume designer, educator*

Salt Lake City
Card, Royden *artist*
Pierce, Diane Jean *artist*
Sarver, Linda Kay *costume designer, educator*
Wassmer, Theodore Milton *artist*

Sandy
Coleman, Garth John *painter, investor*

Smithfield
Rasmuson, Brent (Jacobsen) *photographer, graphic artist, lithographer*

Springville
Francis, Rell Gardner *artist, photographer, writer*

Vernal
Harrison, Garth Trevier *artist, retired social worker*

Woodland Hills
Conrad, Bonnie Lynn *artist*

WASHINGTON

Anacortes
Currier, Alfred Patrick *artist*

Bainbridge Island
Grisham, Jeannie *artist*

Battle Ground
Hansen, James Lee *sculptor*

Bothell
Rideout, Edna Baker *artist*

Brush Prairie
Zawodny, LaRae Jean *artist, secondary education educator*

Burlington
Zeretzke, Frederick Frank H. *artist, educator*

Castle Rock
Richey, Candace *photographer*

Coupeville
Canfield, Stella Stojanka *artist, art gallery owner*

Edmonds
Mahaffey, Kay P. *artist, interior designer, facilities planner*

Ellensburg
Arends, Vernonica Joan *artist, painter*
Housner, Jeanette Ann *artist, jeweler*
Lewis, Keith Allen *artist*
Parker-Fairbanks, Dixie *artist*

Everett
Cooper, Shirley Ruth *artist, illustrator*

Freeland
Kelzer, Kimberly Ann *artist, furniture designer*

Friday Harbor
Rock, Mary Ann *fine artist, educator, consultant*

Gig Harbor
Causin, Janis Eisenhower *artist*
Shinstine, Drucella Gayle *artist*

Mercer Island
Steinhardt, Henry *photographer*

Naches
Searles, Quentin *artist*

North Bend
Kaplan, Donna Elaine *artist, educator*

Ocean Park
Lee, Martha *artist, writer*

Olympia
Cox, Patricia Jean *artist, researcher*
John, Yvonne Maree *artist, designer*

Palouse
Duffy, Irene Karen *artist*

Pullman
Salusso, Carol Joy *apparel design educator, consultant*

Puyallup
Chalk, Earl Milton *retired art director*

Redmond
Rushmer, Estella Virginia Dix (Dixie Rushmer) *artist*

Seattle
Adelman, Carol *artist*
Arreguin, Alfredo Mendoza *artist*
Berger, Paul Eric *artist, photographer*
Bothell, Lisa Jean *graphic designer*
Brody, David *artist, educator*
Christenson, Charles Elroy *art educator*
DeCaro, Pat Elizabeth *artist, educator*
Dickey, Tina Anne *artist, consultant*
Du Pen, Everett George *sculptor, educator*
Gardiner, T(homas) Michael *artist*
Gault, Rosette Ford *artist, writer, inventor*
Hirondelle, Anne Elizabeth *ceramic artist*
Jordan, Lorna Pauley *artist*
Kosché, René *artist, entrepreneur*
Leong, James Chan *artist*
Lundin, Norman Kent *artist, educator*
Makuuchi, Munio Howard (Munio Howard Takahashi) *artist, poet, educator*
McDonnell, Joseph Anthony *sculptor, critic*
Nguyen, Giang Dai *artist, sculptor, graphic artist, muralist*
Pawula, Kenneth John *artist, educator*
Sommers, Larry Donald *artist, educator*
Spafford, Michael Charles *artist*
Susynski, Kenneth *illustrator*
Washington, James Winston, Jr. *artist, sculptor*
Wu, Ina Zhiqing *art educator*

Sequim
Belson, Patricia A. *artist*

Spokane
Wilson, Gordon Russel *art educator*

Tacoma
Harris, Robert Gaylen *art director, graphic designer, illustrator*
Osaka, Michi *artist, printmaking educator*
Ragan, Betty Sapp *artist, educator*
Wilson, Karen Louise *artist, educator*

Tenino
Orsini, Myrna J. *sculptor, educator*

Vancouver
Hulburt, Lucille Hall *artist, educator*

Vashon
Ingalls-Cox, Pamela Lynn *artist, educator*
Schwennesen, Carol Ann *artist, educator*

Walla Walla
Sawada, Ikune *artist*

WYOMING

Boulder
Thomas, Lynn Marie *artist, retired dude ranch owner, operator*

Casper
Tuma, Suzanne Tulloss *artist*

Centennial
Russin, Robert Isaiah *sculptor, educator*

Cheyenne
Craft, Robbie Wright *artist*
Moore, Mary French (Muffy Moore) *potter, community activist*

Cody
Jackson, Harry Andrew *artist*
Skenandore, Rodney Curtis *artist*

Laramie
Guzzo, Anthony Victor *sculptor*

Parkman
Holt, Jessica Dickinson *artist*

Powell
DeBoer, (Stewart) Brett *graphic design educator*

CANADA

ALBERTA

Calgary
Esler, John Kenneth *artist*

Edmonton
Jungkind, Walter *design educator, writer, consultant*

BRITISH COLUMBIA

Duncan
Hughes, Edward John *artist*

Victoria
Harvey, Donald *artist, educator*

SASKATCHEWAN

Saskatoon
Bornstein, Eli *artist, sculptor*

SPAIN

Seville
Sanchez, Leonedes Monarrize Worthington (His Royal Highness Duke de Leonedes of Spain Sicily Greece) *fashion designer*

ADDRESS UNPUBLISHED

Abeles, Kim Victoria *artist*
Adcock, Ronald Wade *artist, sculptor*
Altschiller, Ira Richard *artist, desktop publishing and Internet consultant*
Bain, Jennifer *artist*
Ballaine, Jerrold Curtis *artist*
Benton, Fletcher *sculptor*
Bertagnole, Suzanne Bonacci *customer service administrator, writer, artist*
Blinder, Janet *art dealer*
Blitt, Rita Lea *artist*
Bogdanowicz, Loretta Mae *artist*
Bowen-Forbes, Jorge Courtney *artist, author, poet*
Bowman, Fay Louise *artist*
Braudy, Dorothy McGahee *artist, educator*
Bryan, Sukey *artist*
Cabot, Hugh, III *painter, sculptor*
Campbell, Demarest Lindsay *artist, designer, writer*
Cannon, Kevin Francis *sculptor*
Carney, Kevin Hughes *animator*
Carraher, Mary Lou Carter *art educator*
Chaiet, Margaret Szego *artist, writer*
Chen, Sherry Xiaohong *artist, educator*
Cofer, Deborah End *artist*
Colbert, Margaret Matthew *artist*
Coover, Doris Dimock *artist*
Cowell, Ernest Saul *lighting designer, consultant*
Cox, Pat *artist*
Dahn, Richard F. *artist, designer*
Dal Poggetto, Sandra Hope *artist, writer*
Daniels, Gannon *artist, educator*
Deakins, Roger Alexander *photographer*
Deal, David Allen *illustrator, cartoonist*
Decil, Stella Walters (Del Decil) *artist*
Dentith, Henry *artist*
deVeuve, Suzanne *artist*
Dickau, Keith Michael (Mike Dickau) *artist, secondary school educator*
Dill, Laddie John *artist*
Dominguez, Eddie *artist*
Dopp, Susan Marie *artist, educator*
Farmer, Barry Wayne *artist, art educator*
Farnham, Mary Glade Siemer *artist*
Farrar, Elaine Willardson *artist*
Fasman, Marjorie Lesser *artist, writer*
Fe, Sonya *artist, consultant*
Fell, Katherine Christine *artist*
Fetter, William Allan *computer graphics executive*
Fillmore, John Dillon *fine artist*
Finn, Mary Ralphe *artist*
Friday, Katherine Orwoll *artist*
Garber, Helen Kolikow *photographer, artist*
Geis, Edward Michael *photographer, film producer*
George, Suzanne Helen *shoe designer, consultant*
Gimbolo, Aleksei Frank Charles (Cimbolo) *artist, philosopher, author*
Glen, Niki *artist*
Gold, Betty Virginia *artist*
Golden, Judith Greene *artist, educator*
Graves, Lennie Keith *animator*
Gregory, Eleanor Anne *artist, educator*
Groth, David Mikael *artist*
Gurwitz-Hall, Barbara Ann *artist*
Haley, Sally Fulton *artist*
Hallam, Juanita May *visual artist, poet, writer*
Hanan, Laura Molen *artist*
Hanson, Janice Crawford *artist, financial analyst*
Harris, Gwen Moyers *artist, homemaker*
Heilman, Marlin Grant *photographer*
Hertel, Howard Jay *photographer*
Horton, Patricia Mathews *artist, violist and violinist*
Huber, Colleen Adlene *artist*
Hughes, Michael Patrick *artist*
Jacob, Ted Manas *biomedical and forensic photographer*
Johnson, Mary Cady *artist*
Jones, Margie Raben *antiques dealer, educator*
Kehew, George Mansir *artist*
Kidd, Jeremy *artist*
Ko, Daniel *graphic designer*
Korn-Davis, Dottie *artist, educator, consultant*
Kwon, Teresa Eun Young *illustrator*
Ladewig Goodman, Jeanne Margaret *artist*

Laws, Joyce Davis *artist*
Le Clair, Laurie (Isabella Laurence Le Clair) *artist*
Lefranc, Margaret (Margaret Schoonover) *artist, illustrator, editor, writer*
Leist, Andrew John *artist, musician, composer, producer*
Levin, Morton D(avid) *artist, printmaker, educator*
Ling, Jiayi *artist*
Lipofsky, Marvin Bentley *art educator*
Liu, Katherine Chang *artist, art educator*
Lloyd, Ivan Graham *artist*
Lo, Waituck *artist*
Lockart, Barbetta *fabric designer, artist, jeweler, art educator*
Long, Margaret Karen *art educator*
Mabin, Ann Marie *artist management executive, consultant*
Mann, Joan Ellona *artist, editor*
Marberry, James Fredric *artist, graphic designer*
Marsden, Guy Talbot *light sculptor, electronics engineer, products design consultant*
McCargar, Eleanor Barker *portrait painter*
McCloskey, Robin Ann *artist, educator*
Mercer, Toby *artist*
Micco, Teri René *artist*
Miller, Vel *artist*
Minami, Robert Yoshio *artist, graphic designer*
Moore, Teresa Margaret *artist*
Morey, Melinda Grace *artist*
Morrison, Robert Clifton *artist*
Nemiroff, Maxine Celia *art educator, gallery owner, consultant*
Nemo, Fred *artist*
Nilles, Darrell LeRad *artist, inventor, architect*
Ottevanger, Susan Lee *artist*
Palmer, Katharine Anne *artist*
Pease, Ron Dean *artist, builder*
Pedder, Nancy Shank *artist, writer*
Phillips, Billy Saxton *artist, designer, painter*
Phillips, Demetria Nickole *graphic designer*
Pierce, Hilda (Hilda Herta Harmel) *painter*
Pinataro, Jean Eleanor *artist*
Poundstone, William Nicholas, Jr. *artist, author*
Pruner, Gary Lee *art educator*
Qian, Zifen *artist, researcher*
Radebaugh, Alan Paine *artist*
Rendal, Camille Lynn *artist*
Root, Doris Smiley *portrait artist*
Ross, Molly Owings *gold and silversmith, jewelry designer, small business owner*
Rothstein, Marjorie Hope *sculptor, landscape and environmental designer*
Rowe, Elizabeth Ann *artist*
Saylors, Jo Ann *sculptor*
Schaffner, Rivka Ann *art educator, artist*
Seiden, Sandra Mae *artist*
Seldon, Mervyn W. Adams *artist, editor*
Smith, Leonore Rae *artist*
Solomon, Amelia Kroll *artist*
Starkweather, Teresa Madery *artist, educator*
Steele, Joelle writer, *artist, photographer*
Stevens, Janet *illustrator*
Stuart, Signe Margaret *artist*
Sturgen, Winston *photographer, printmaker, artist*
Swigger, Nancy Duncan *photographer*
Taylor, Alex *painter, sculptor, exhibit designer*
Taylor-Brown, Cameron Ann *artist, educator, consultant*
Todaro, Patricia Anne *painter, singer*
Tormey, Carlotta Ann *artist*
Tresslar, Nola V. *artist, retired foundation administrator, marketing professional*
Turner, Bonese Collins *artist, educator*
Van Tamelen, Jane Elizabeth *artist, filmmaker*
Versch, Esther Marie *artist*
Williams, Louise Rae *artist, educator*
Wiseman, Jay Donald *photographer, mechanical designer and contractor*
Wolfchief-Ghidossi, Marie Antonette Vicario *artist*
Wong, Diana Shui Iu *artist*
Wortzel, Gary *artist, filmmaker*
Wright, Joan L. *artist*
Wynn, Karla Wray *artist, agricultural products company executive*
Yates, Steven A. *artist, curator*
Ynda, Mary Lou *artist, educator*
Zekman, Terri Margaret *graphic designer*

ASSOCIATIONS AND ORGANIZATIONS. *See also* **specific fields.**

UNITED STATES

ALASKA

Anchorage
Jones, Jewel Louise *social services administrator*
Jones, Mark Logan *educational association executive, educator*
Kaplan, Diane Susan *foundation executive, consultant*
McKay, Tom *political organization administrator*
O'Regan, Deborah *association executive, lawyer*

Juneau
Harder, Kristine *civic worker*

ARIZONA

Dewey
Burch, Mary Lou *organization consultant, housing advocate*

Dragoon
Woosley, Anne I. *cultural organization administrator*

Phoenix
Dorland, Byrl Brown *retired civic worker*
Hays, E. Earl *youth organization administrator*
Hoyt, Diana Vaughn *fundraising consultant, small business owner*
Rodriguez, Leonard *foundation administrator*
Smith, Stuart Robert *foundation executive*

Scottsdale
Ferree, John Newton, Jr. *fundraising specialist, consultant*
King, Pauline Urbano *developer*

Sedona
Stoufer, Ruth Hendrix *community volunteer*

Sierra Vista
Hessler, Thomas John *community activist*

Sun City West
Horton, Barbara Marion Deady *fund developer*

Tempe
Sullivan-Boyle, Kathleen Marie *association executive*

Tucson
Pack, Phoebe Katherine Finley *civic worker*
Powers, Stephen *educational researcher, consultant*
Sickel, Joan Sottilare *foundation administrator*

CALIFORNIA

Agoura Hills
Oettinger, Robert Allan *foundation executive, writer*

Alamo
Hardy, Lois Lynn *educational training company executive*

Altadena
Griswold, Martha Kerfoot *social worker*

Anaheim
Prusa, James Graham *association executive*

Arcadia
Day-Gowder, Patricia Joan *retired association executive, consultant*

Atherton
King, Jane Cudlip Coblentz *volunteer educator*

Bakersfield
Stanley, Forrest Edwin *fundraiser, university program director*

Berkeley
Buell, Evangeline Canonizado *consumer cooperative official*
Chew, Linda Lee *fundraising management executive*
Leon, Joan *development consultant, nonprofit company executive*
Nuveen, John Septimus *cultural affairs organization executive*
Welter, Linda Allaire *development executive*

Beverly Hills
Khaladjan, Mikhail Nikolaevich *educator, song writer*
Scott, John Nathaniel *foundation administrator*

Brea
Tamura, Cary Kaoru *fundraiser, consultant*

Burbank
Angele, Alfred Robert *police labor union executive*
Hackett, Suzanne F. *cultural organization administrator*

Burlingame
Mahoney, Ann Dickinson *fundraiser*

Calabasas
Lightfoot, Gretchen Graham *fundraiser*

Canoga Park
Lederer, Marion Irvine *cultural administrator*

Carmel Valley
Heimann, Janet Barbara *volunteer trail consultant*

Chico
Burks, Rocky Alan *social services executive, disability consultant*

Chula Vista
Todd, Richard Emerson *administrator*

City Of Industry
Ansell, Phil Barry *social services professional*

Claremont
Pendleton, Othniel Alsop *fundraiser, clergyman*

Culver City
Bradkin, Tania Szlavik *foundation administrator*
Cherry, Deanna Duelund *social services center administrator*
Imlay, Gordon Lake *development consultant*
Netzel, Paul Arthur *fundraising management executive, consultant*

Duarte
Bury, David Alfred *fundraising executive*

Fresno
Balbas, Christine *social services administrator*

Hawthorne
Fink, Mark Elliott *union representative*

Hayward
Archuleta, Keith Anthony *arts administrator, consultant, educational administrator*

Hollister
Sattler, Joan Lessing *consultant*

Irvine
Kim, Wayne H.S. *educational association administrator, consultant*

Kentfield
Blum, Joan Kurley *fundraising executive*

La Crescenta
Stubbs, Daniel Gaie *labor relations consultant*

La Jolla
Knox, Elizabeth Louise *community volunteer, travel consultant*

Loma Linda
Gibson, L. James *organization administrator, biology educator*

Los Altos
Farber, Geraldine Ossman *civic worker*

Los Angeles
Bloch, Doris Beryl *charitable organization administrator*
Caldwell-Portenier, Patty Jean Grosskopf *advocate, educator*
Gottlieb, Leonard *foundation administrator*
Harris, Barbara Hull (Mrs. F. Chandler Harris) *social agency administrator*
Headlee, Rolland Dockeray *professional society administrator*
Hubbs, Donald Harvey *foundation executive*
Kaplansky, Laura Shlaferman *non-profit fundraiser, community organizer*
Lindley, F(rancis) Haynes, Jr. *foundation president emeritus, lawyer*
Mack, J. Curtis, II *civic organization administrator*
Marrow, Deborah *foundation executive, art historian*
Marshall, Mary Jones *civic worker*
Munitz, Barry *foundation administrator*
Pickens, William H. *educational administrator, consultant*
Schine, Wendy Wachtell *foundation administrator*
Williams, Harold Marvin *foundation official, former government official, former university dean, former corporate executive*

Manhattan Beach
Devitt-Grasso, Pauline Virginia *civic volunteer, nurse*
King, Lea Ann *community volunteer and leader*

Menlo Park
Fairbank, Jane Davenport *editor, civic worker*
Pallotti, Marianne Marguerite *foundation administrator*

Modesto
Barnes, William David *non-profit charities consultant, publisher*
Richardson, Ernest Ray (Rocky Richardson) *housing program supervisor*

Moffett Field
Scott, Donald Michael *educational association administrator, educator*

Montclair
Grayson, Margaret Marion *association executive, anthropologist*

Monterey
Hastey, Shari Rose *nonprofit foundation administrator*

Mountain View
Bills, Robert Howard *political party executive*

Newbury Park
Stuart, Gregory M. *nonprofit organization administrator*

Newport Beach
Ford, Michael Q. *not-for-profit association administrator*
Poole, Thomas Richard *endowment capital campaign director, fund raising counsel*

North Hollywood
Delu, Helena O. *director social welfare organization*

Oakland
Dozier, Flora Grace *civil and human rights activist, entrepreneur*
Misner, Charlotte Blanche Ruckman *community organization administrator*
Odermatt, Diana B. *development officer*
Silzer, Mark Mitchell *educational technology executive, consultant*
Widener, Mary Lee *non-profit financial executive*

Oceanside
Blow, John Needham *social services educator*

Orinda
Fisher, Robert Morton *foundation administrator, university administrator*

Pacoima
Corkum, Betty Jean *foundation administrator, former nurse, author*

Palm Springs
Hearst, Rosalie *philanthropist, foundation executive*

Palo Alto
Lovell, Howell, Jr. *non profit organization executive*

Pasadena
Imhoff, Judith Lammers *civic volunteer*
Krueger, Virginia Carmichael *foundation administrator*

Pauma Valley
Magee, Dennis *cultural organization administrator*

Pleasanton
Whisnand, Rex James *housing association executive*

Porterville
Mullen, Rod *nonprofit organization executive*

Redwood City
McFarland, Kevin John *foundation administrator*
Postel, Mitchell Paul *association administrator*
Spangler, Nita Reifschneider *volunteer*

Riverside
Loya, Praxedes *social services administrator*

Sacramento
Hayward, Fredric Mark *social reformer*
Meyer, Rachel Abijah *foundation director, artist, theorist, poet*
Naglestad, Frederic Allen *legislative advocate*
Smith, Sally Elaine *association executive*

Salinas
Butler, Billie Rae *educational administrator*
Chester, Lynne *foundation executive, artist*

San Diego
Boersma, Lawrence Allan *animal welfare administrator*
DeForge, Michele *foundation executive*
Hinsvark, Don George *social services agency professional*
Krejci, Robert Harry *non-profit organizations development consultant*
Lane, Gloria Julian *foundation administrator*
Sabin, Scott Cullen *cultural organization administrator*

San Francisco
Collins, Dennis Arthur *foundation executive*
Duffy, Gloria Charmian *foundation administrator*
Eastham, Thomas *foundation administrator*
Grose, Andrew Peter *foundation executive*
Hickman, Maxine Viola *social services administrator*
Lim, Harrison Bing Cheung *social services administrator*
Lord, Mia W. *world peace and disarmament activist*
Madson, David John *fundraising executive*
McCuaig, Ian Carruthers *fundraising consultant*
Schmidt, Mary Margaret *non-profit company administrator, consultant*
Swenson, Erick Lee *fundraising administrator*

San Jose
Dargis, Jean Anthony *retired voluntary health agency executive*
Een, Trudell Elaine *organization administrator*
Lind, Terrie Lee *social services administrator*
McDonald, Douglas Robert *non profit agency executive*
Torrisi, Ralph Joseph *labor union executive*

San Luis Obispo
Jamieson, James Bradshaw *foundation administrator*

San Pedro
Gammell, Gloria Ruffner *professional association administrator*

Santa Barbara
Krieger, David Malcolm *peace foundation executive, lawyer*
Mc Coy, Lois Clark *emergency services professional, retired county official, magazine editor*
Shobe, Nancy *fundraising consultant, small business owner*

Santa Clara
Raygoza, Lynette Rosalind *educational administrator*

Santa Clarita
Boyer, Carl, III *non-profit organization executive, former mayor, city official, secondary education educator*

Santa Cruz
McLean, Hulda Hoover *volunteer, conservationist, naturalist, artist*
Mc Manus, Philip James *advocate, human rights, peace-building activist*

Santa Monica
Foley, Jane Deborah *foundation executive*
Michaud, Gerald Fredrick *media advocacy nonprofit executive*

Santa Rosa
Ingerman, Michael Leigh *development director*

Sherman Oaks
Lazar, John Edward *administrator non-profit organization*
Marckwardt, Harold Thomas *association executive*

Simi Valley
Bumgardner, Larry G. *foundation administrator, law and political science educator*

Sonora
Coffill, Marjorie Louise *civic leader*

South Lake Tahoe
Prescott, Barbara Lodwich *educational administrator*

Stockton
Blodgett, Elsie Grace *association executive*

Sun Valley
Harvey, Rufus William *nonprofit administrator*

Sylmar
Froelich, Beverly Lorraine *foundation director*

Tiburon
Cook, Lyle Edwards *retired fund raising executive, consultant*

Truckee
Johnston, Bernard Fox *author, foundation executive*

Tustin
Oliver, Barbara Jeanne *social services administrator*

Visalia
Taylor, Helen Shields *civic worker*

Watsonville
Cane, William Earl *nonprofit organization executive*

West Hollywood
Hoffenblum, Allan Ernest *political consultant*

Woodland
Beeman, Anna Marie *volunteer*

COLORADO

Aurora
Fish, Ruby Mae Bertram (Mrs. Frederick Goodrich Fish) *civic worker*

Boulder
Johnson, Myrna Ellen *government relations executive*

Colorado Springs
Bagg, Gerald David *health foundation administrator*
Hawley, Nanci Elizabeth *social services administrator*
MacLeod, Richard Patrick *foundation administrator*
Marsh, Paul Norton *non-profit executive*
Miller, Zoya Dickins (Mrs. Hilliard Eve Miller, Jr.) *civic worker*

Denver
Blish, Eugene Sylvester *trade association administrator*
Bryan, A(lonzo) J(ay) *service club official*
Cole, George William *foundation administrator*
Curtis, Steve *political organization administrator*
Dulles, John Foster, II *civil rights administrator*
Eisenman, Athena Joyce *association administrator*
Gloss, Lawrence Robert *fundraising executive*
Henry, Ernestyne Ethel Thatch *educational administrator*
Johnson, Christine *educational administrator*
Jones, Jean Correy *organization administrator*
Kamlet, Barbara Lynn *director of volunteers*
Krausz, Stephen *social services administrator, physiologist*
Lindsey, William Fussell *retired newspaper association executive*
Low, Merry Cook *civic worker*
Raughton, Jimmie Leonard *educational foundation administrator, urban planner*
Rocksted, Elaine Marti *association administrator*
Walker, Barbara Monika Ann *trade association executive, lawyer*

Englewood
Holck, Richard William *association executive*
Myers, Claudia Boles *educational foundation executive*
Reese, Monte Nelson *agricultural association executive*

Greeley
Schrenk, Gary Dale *foundation executive*

Greenwood Village
Walker, Eljana M. du Vall *civic worker*

Lakewood
Dion, Susan M. *education director, educator*

Littleton
Keogh, Heidi Helen Dake *advocate*

Manitou Springs
Eversole, Finley Traweek *arts foundation executive*

Steamboat Springs
Sutton, Dianna *foundation executive*

U S A F Academy
Coppock, Richard Miles *nonprofit association administrator*

DISTRICT OF COLUMBIA

Washington
Skaggs, David E. *association administrator, lawyer, educator*

HAWAII

Hawaii National Park
Nicholson, Marilyn Lee *arts administrator*

Honolulu
Alcantara, Donna L. *political organization administrator*
Blackfield, Cecilia Malik *civic volunteer, educator*
Botti, Richard Charles *association executive*
Lee, Beverly Ing *educational administrator*
Mirikitani, John Masa *foundation administrator*
Olmsted, Ronald David *non-profit organization consultant*
Schoenke, Marilyn Leilani *foundation administrator*

IDAHO

Boise
Petterson, Kenneth Charles *foundation director of development*

Coeur D Alene
Sanderson, Holladay Worth *domestic violence advocate*

Homedale
Patterson, Beverly Ann Gross *fund raising consultant, grant writer, federal grants administrator, social services administrator, poet*

Moscow
Samaniego, Pamela Susan *organization administrator*

MONTANA

Billings
Sample, Joseph Scanlon *foundation executive*

Bozeman
Sanddal, Nels Dodge *foundation executive, consultant*

Great Falls
Ebbinga, Crystalle Yvonne *social services administrator*

Harrison
Jackson, Peter Vorious, III *retired association executive*

Helena
Alecksich-Akey, Susan C. *political organization administrator*
Almond, Elizabeth Anne *professional association administrator*
Porter, Jeanne Smith *civic worker*
Ream, Bob *political organization administrator*

Missoula
Amundson, Eva Donalda *civic worker*
Kemmis, Daniel Orra *cultural organization administrator, author*

Park City
Abrams, Ossie Ekman *fundraiser*

NEVADA

Carson City
Ayres, Janice Ruth *social service executive*

Henderson
Freyd, William Pattinson *fund raising executive, consultant*

Las Vegas
Brown, Janice Anne *political organization executive*
Henry, Paul *political organization administrator*
Martin, Myron Gregory *foundation administrator*
Sobkowski, Nikki Taminen *executive director*
Wuehle, Edwin Everett *association executive*
Wunstell, Erik James *non-profit organization administrator, communications consultant*

Laughlin
Simmons, Joy Louise *activist*

Pahrump
Hersman, Marion Frank *professional administrator, lawyer*

Reno
Winzeler, Judith Kay *foundation administrator*

NEW MEXICO

Albuquerque
Cole, Terri Lynn *organization administrator*
Dendahl, John *political organization administrator*
Reynalds, Jeremy Graham *rescue mission administrator*
Roberts, Dennis William *association executive*

Espanola
Khalsa, Guru Roop Kaur *foundation administrator*

Las Cruces
Eriksson, Anne-Marie *social services executive, educator*

Ranchos De Taos
Patrick, Stephen Adam *non profit organization administrator*

Santa Fe
Charles, Cheryl *non-profit business executive*
Millard, Olivia *fundraiser*

OREGON

Beaverton
Atkinson, Perry *political organization administrator*

Eugene
Hale, Dean Edward *social services administrator*

Junction City
Humphry, Derek *association executive, writer*

Lake Oswego
Miller, Barbara Stallcup *development consultant*

Lincoln City
Decker, Mary Duryea *retired educator, community volunteer*

Portland
Edmunson, Jim *political organization administrator*
Eshbaugh, David Charles *society administrator*
Franz, Marcia Kay *foundation administrator*
Holt, Mavis Murial *parents group executive*
Hudson, Jerry E. *foundation administrator*
Orloff, Chet *cultural organization administrator*
Pine, William Charles *foundation executive*
Rooks, Charles S. *foundation administrator*

Redmond
Johnson, Elizabeth Hill *foundation administrator*

Sherwood
Stroemple, Ruth Mary Thomas *social welfare administrator*

UTAH

Cedar City
Weaver, Max Kimball *social worker, consultant*

Ogden
Pappas, Leah Aglaia *civic worker, political consultant, educator*

Provo
Lee, Blaine Nelson *executive consultant, educator, author*

Salt Lake City
Bishop, Rob *political party executive*
Cofield, Philip Thomas *educational association administrator*
Holbrook, Meghan Zanolli *fundraiser, public relations specialist, state pol*
Melich, Doris S. *public service worker*
Wheadon, Kathleen Rose *university development director*

WASHINGTON

Bainbridge Island
Rosner, Robert Allan *advocate*

Bellevue
Arnold, Ronald Henri *nonprofit organization executive, consultant*
Kiest, Alan Scott *social services administrator*

Bellingham
Foote, Barbara Austin *civic foundation executive*

Blaine
James, Herb Mark (Jay James) *foundation and insurance executive, free trade consultant*

Ellensburg
Legere, Diane J. *art association administrator, alpaca breeder*

Federal Way
Osmonson, Wade Lane *fundraising executive*

Olympia
Olson, Steven Stanley *social service executive*
Wood, David Glenn *lobbyist*

Redmond
Andrew, Jane Hayes *non-profit organization executive*

Seattle
Arthur, William Lynn *environmental foundation administrator*
Belyea, Pamela Jill *art association administrator*
Berendt, Paul *political party administrator*
Iglitzin, Lara *foundation administrator*
Okimoto, David *social welfare administrator*
Ray, Marianne Yurasko *social services administrator*
Thompson, Alan McFadden *institute administrator*

Spokane
Falkner, James George *foundation executive*
McGrath, Sheryl Lynnette *executive director non-profit organization*
Murphy, Mary Ann *human services administrator*
Rowe, Marjorie Douglas *retired social services administrator*

Tacoma
Myrick, Helen Estelle *civic worker*

Vancouver
Smith, Sam Corry *retired foundation executive, consultant*

Yakima
Nelson, Bryan H(erbert) *non-profit agency administrator*

WYOMING

Casper
Bilek, Wendy Holly *lobbyist*
Ulrich, Wallace *political organization administrator*

Cody
Coe, Margaret Louise Shaw *community service volunteer*

CANADA

ALBERTA

Grande Prairie
Harper, Donald Calvin *social services administrator*

BRITISH COLUMBIA

Vancouver
Saywell, William George Gabriel *foundation administrator*

TAIWAN

Taipei
Tong, Chiling *trade and commerce administrator*

ADDRESS UNPUBLISHED

Borgmann, Carol A. *fundraising executive*
Briscoe, Marianne Grier *development professional, educator*
Bruce, John Allen *foundation executive, educator*
Conran, James Michael *consumer advocate, public policy consultant*
Cooper, Bobbie (Minna Louise Morgan Cooper) *volunteer*
Eastman, Francesca Marlene *volunteer, art historian*
Eliot, Theodore Lyman, Jr. *international consultant*
Gigray, Margaret Elizabeth *foundation trustee*
Hicks, Dolores Kathleen (De De Hicks) *association executive*
Himes, Diane Adele *buyer, fundraiser, actress*
Ikeda, Tsuguo (Ike Ikeda) *social services center administrator, consultant*
Keith, Susan M. *fundraiser*
Kelley, Lois Elizabeth *arts administrator, consultant*
Kezlarian, Nancy Kay *social services administrator, family counselor*
Kinslow, Margie Ann *volunteer worker*
Lucas, Robert Anthony *academic consultant, educator*
Lyman, Jing *social activist*
Mack, Charles Daniel, III *labor union executive*
Magoon, Nancy Amelia *art association administrator, philanthropist*
McMurray, Ron *political association executive*
Migden, Chester L. *professional society administrator*
Miller, Harriet Sanders *art center director, retired*
Mogulof, Melvin Bernard *consultant*
Peck, Robert David *educational foundation administrator*
Ramo, Virginia M. Smith *civic worker*
Richards, Morris Dick *social work administrator, educator*
Seiff, Gloria Louise *volunteer*
Shakely, John Bower (Jack Shakely) *foundation executive*
Stewart, Paul Anthony, II *trade association executive, author*
Stout, Elizabeth West *foundation administrator*
Sweeney, Robert Frank *foundation administrator*
Throndson, Edward Warner *residential association administrator*
Uehling, Barbara Staner *educational administrator*
Uhde, Larry Jackson *joint apprentice administrator*
Vogel, Nadine Orsoff *foundation executive*
Wyatt, Lenore *civic worker*
Zehr, Norman Robert *association administrator*

ATHLETICS

UNITED STATES

ARIZONA

Holbrook
Rhyan, Jeanette Delores *physical education educator*

Phoenix
Ainge, Danny Ray *professional basketball coach*
Benes, Andrew Charles *professional baseball player*
Bidwill, William V. *professional football executive*
Colangelo, Jerry John *professional basketball team executive*
Fitzsimmons, (Lowell) Cotton *professional basketball executive, broadcaster, former coach*
Johnson, Kevin Maurice *professional basketball player*
Kidd, Jason *professional basketball player*
Manning, Daniel Ricardo *professional basketball player*
Nedney, Joe *football player*
Showalter, Buck (William Nathaniel Showalter, III) *major league baseball team manager*
Tkachuk, Keith *professional hockey player*
Tobin, Vincent Michael *professional sports team executive*

Scottsdale
Khabibulin, Nikolai *hockey player*
Schoenfeld, Jim *professional hockey coach*

Tempe
Moore, Rob *professional football player*

Tucson
Kearney, Joseph Laurence *retired athletic conference administrator*

CALIFORNIA

Alameda
Brown, Timothy Donell *professional football player*
Davis, Allen *professional football team executive*
Gruden, Jon *professional football coach*
Herrera, John *professional football team executive*
Jett, James *football player*
Wisniewski, Stephen Adam *professional football player*

Anaheim
Collins, Terry *professional baseball manager*
Edmonds, James Patrick (Jim Edmonds) *professional baseball player*
Green, Travis *professional hockey player*
Hartsburg, Craig William *professional hockey coach*
Herbert, Guy *hockey player*
Lachemann, Marcel *professional baseball manager*
Selanne, Teemu *hockey player*
Stark, Milton Dale *sports association executive*

Beverly Hills
Shoemaker, Bill (William Lee Shoemaker) *retired jockey, horse trainer*

Burbank
Reed, Rosalie *horse trainer*

Carmel
Epstein-Shepherd, Bee *mental skills golf coach, hypnotist, professional speaker*

Coronado
Axelson, Joseph Allen *professional athletics executive, publisher*

Cypress
Dorn, Marian Margaret *educator, sports management administrator*

Danville
Behring, Kenneth E. *professional sports team owner*

Fountain Valley
Treadway-Dillmon, Linda Lee *athletic trainer, actress, stuntwoman*

Inglewood
Bryant, Kobe *basketball player*
Ferraro, Ray *hockey player*
Fiset, Stephane *hockey player*
Harris, Del William *professional basketball coach*
Johnson, Earvin (Magic Johnson) *professional sports team executive, former professional basketball coach*
Jones, Eddie *basketball player*
O'Neal, Shaquille Rashaun *professional basketball player*
Robinson, Larry Clark *professional hockey coach*
Sharman, William *professional basketball team executive*
Vitti, Gary John *athletic trainer, business owner*
West, Jerry Alan *professional basketball team executive*

Irvine
Farrell, Dennis *sports association executive*

Lake Arrowhead
Barnett, Michael *sports agent, business manager*

Los Angeles
Abdul-Jabbar, Kareem (Lewis Ferdinand Alcindor) *retired professional basketball player, sports commentator*
Baylor, Elgin Gay *professional basketball team executive*
Claire, Fred *professional baseball team executive*
Ford, Chris *professional basketball coach*
Furuya, Daniel Kensho *aikido instructor, priest*
Johnson, Davey (David Allen Johnson) *baseball team manager*
Lasorda, Thomas Charles (Tommy Lasorda) *professional baseball team manager*
Martin, Derrick *basketball player*
O'Malley, Peter *professional baseball club executive*
Park, Chan Ho *professional baseball player*
Russell, Bill *coach*
Sterling, Donald T. *professional basketball team executive*
Vaught, Loy *basketball player*
White, Devon Markes *professional baseball player*

Malibu
Louganis, Greg E. *former Olympic athlete, actor*

Marina Del Rey
Selinger, Andrew Joseph *ice and roller rink development company executive*

Menlo Park
Walsh, William *former football coach*

Oakland
Bogues, Tyrone Curtis (Muggsy Bogues) *professional basketball player*
Carlesimo, P. J. (Peter J. Carlesimo) *former college basketball coach, professional basketball coach*
Cohan, Christopher *professional sports team executive*
Gambi, Jason Gilbert *baseball player*
Howe, Art (Arthur Henry Howe, Jr.) *professional baseball manager*

Oceanside
Lomelí, Refugio (Jesse Lomelí) *athletics educator*

Palm Springs
Jumonville, Felix Joseph, Jr. *physical education educator, realtor*

Palo Alto
Van Derveer, Tara *university athletic coach*

Redlands
Clapp, Carl Roger *physical education educator*

Sacramento
Adelman, Rick *professional basketball coach*
Benner, Rick *professional basketball team executive*
Polynice, Olden *basketball player*
Scott, Byron Alton *professional basketball player*
Thomas, Jim *professional basketball team executive*
Williamson, Corliss *basketball player*

Sacremento
Webber, Chris, III (Mayce Edward Christopher Webber) *professional basketball player*

San Diego
Bochy, Bruce *professional sports team manager, coach*
Davis, Greg *football player*
Gwynn, Anthony Keith (Tony Gwynn) *professional baseball player*
Hoffman, Trevor William *professional baseball player*
Means, Natrone Jermaine *professional football player*
Riley, Michael (Mike Riley) *professional football coach*
Seau, Junior (Tiana Seau, Jr.) *professional football player*
Spanos, Alexander Gus *professional football team executive*

San Francisco
Baker, Dusty (Johnnie B. Baker, Jr.) *professional baseball team manager*
Bonds, Barry Lamar *professional baseball player*
Estes, Shawn *baseball player*
Kent, Jeffrey Franklin *baseball player*
Magowan, Peter Alden *professional baseball team executive, grocery chain executive*

San Jose
Hrudey, Kelly *hockey player*

Nolan, Owen *professional hockey player*
Sutter, Darryl John *former professional hockey coach*

San Luis Obispo
Buccola, Victor Allan *physical education educator, sports association executive*

Santa Clara
Hanks, Merton Edward *professional football player*
Kirby, Terry *football player*
Mariucci, Steve *coach professional and college football*
McDonald, Tim *professional football player*
Rice, Jerry Lee *professional football player*
Young, Steven *professional football player*

Sausalito
Casals, Rosemary *professional tennis player*

Sherman Oaks
Hamilton, Scott Scovell *professional figure skater, former Olympic athlete*

Sierra Madre
Whittingham, Charles Edward *thoroughbred race horse owner and trainer*

Thousand Oaks
Steiner, Betsy Davies *equestrian, trainer, public speaker, commentator, author*

Walnut Creek
Hallock, C. Wiles, Jr. *athletic official*
Hansen, Thomas Carter *college athletics conference commissioner*

COLORADO

Boulder
Neinas, Charles Merrill *athletic association executive*

Colorado Springs
Evans, Janet *Olympic swimmer*
Schultz, Richard Dale *national athletic organizations executive*

Denver
Baylor, Don Edward *professional baseball manager*
Bichette, Alphonse Dante *professional baseball player*
D'Antoni, Mike *professional basketball coach*
Deadmarsh, Adam *hockey player*
DiPoto, Jerry *baseball player*
Garrett, Dean *basketball player*
Gebhard, Bob *professional baseball team executive*
Hartley, Bob *hockey coach*
Lemieux, Claude *professional hockey player*
Leyland, James Richard *professional baseball team manager*
Roy, Patrick *professional hockey player*
Sakic, Joseph Steve *professional hockey player*
Van Exel, Nickey Maxwell *professional basketball player*
Walker, Larry Kenneth Robert *professional baseball player*

Englewood
Bowlen, Patrick Dennis *holding company executive, lawyer, professional sports team executive*
Craw, Nicholas Wesson *motor sports association executive*
Davis, Terrell *football player*
Elam, Jason *football player*
Elway, John Albert *professional football player*
Shanahan, Mike *professional football coach*
Sharpe, Shannon *professional football player*

MONTANA

Billings
Hahn, Woody *sports association executive*

NEVADA

Incline Village
Groebli, Werner Fritz (Mr. Frick) *professional ice skater, realtor*

Las Vegas
Schneiter, George Malan *golfer, development company executive*

NEW MEXICO

Albuquerque
Unser, Al *professional auto racer*

Hobbs
Black, Ronald Ross *educator, basketball coach*

Maxwell
Alexander, James Enos *race horse trainer*

OHIO

Youngstown
DeBartolo, Edward John, Jr. *professional football team owner, real estate developer*

OREGON

Portland
Glickman, Harry *professional basketball team executive*
[illegible] *professional basketball team executive*
Whitsitt, Robert James *professional basketball team executive*

UTAH

Park City
Kelly, Thomas J. *sports association executive*

Salt Lake City
Addis, Thomas Homer, III *professional golfer*
Howells, R. Tim *professional sports team executive*
Layden, Francis Patrick (Frank Layden) *professional basketball team executive, former coach*
Malone, Karl *professional basketball player*
Miller, Larry H. *professional sports team executive, automobile dealer*
Russell, Bryon *basketball player*
Sloan, Jerry (Gerald Eugene Sloan) *professional basketball coach*
Stockton, John Houston *professional basketball player*

WASHINGTON

Auburn
Sundquist, Leah Renata *physical education specialist*

Kirkland
Erickson, Dennis *professional football coach, former university football coach*
Holmgren, Mike *professional football coach*
Moon, Harold Warren, Jr. *professional football player*
Watters, Richard James *professional football player*

Seattle
Ackerley, Barry *professional basketball team executive, communications company executive*
Baker, Vincent Lamont *basketball player*
Ellis, Dale *professional basketball player*
Ellis, John W. *professional baseball team executive, utility company executive*
Griffey, Ken, Jr. (George Kenneth Griffey, Jr.) *professional baseball player*
Johnson, Randall David (Randy Johnson) *professional baseball player*
Martinez, Edgar *professional baseball player*
Payton, Gary Dwayne *professional basketball player*
Piniella, Louis Victor *professional baseball team manager*
Swift, William Charles *professional baseball player, Olympic athlete*
Walker, Walter Frederick *professional basketball team executive*

CANADA

ALBERTA

Calgary
Hay, William Charles *professional hockey team executive*

BRITISH COLUMBIA

Vancouver
Griffiths, Arthur R. *professional hockey team executive*
Jackson, Stu *professional sports team executive, former university basketball coach*

ADDRESS UNPUBLISHED

Karl, George *professional basketball coach*
Rodriguez, Alexander Emmanuel *professional baseball player*
Santos, Robert David *health and fitness educator, consultant*
Schrempf, Detlef *professional basketball player*
Wagner, Richard *athletics consultant, former baseball team executive*
Wooden, John Robert *former basketball coach*

BUSINESS. *See* FINANCE; INDUSTRY.

COMMUNICATIONS. *See* COMMUNICATIONS MEDIA; INDUSTRY: SERVICE.

COMMUNICATIONS MEDIA. *See also* ARTS: LITERARY.

UNITED STATES

ALASKA

Anchorage
Cowell, Fuller A. *publisher*
Dougherty, Patrick *editor*
Tobin, William Joseph *newspaper editor*

Fairbanks
Massey, Paul J. *newspaper publisher*

Homer
O'Meara, Janet Virginia *publisher, author*

ARIZONA

Bisbee
Eppele, David Louis *columnist, author*

Casa Grande
Kramer, Donovan Mershon, Sr. *newspaper publisher*

Flagstaff
Helford, Paul Quinn *communications educator, academic administrator*
Parker, Lea Jane *communications educator*
Siegmund, Mark Alan *editor, publisher, business consultant, design scientist*

Fountain Hills
Trask, Karen Dale *publisher, artist*

Mesa
Fouliard, Paul Emile *journalism educator, author*
Moran, Robert Earl, Jr. *sports journalist*
Mueller, Frank John *retired editor*
Silver, Ben(jamin) *broadcast journalist, journalism educator*

Phoenix
Benson, Stephen R. *editorial cartoonist*
Early, Robert Joseph *magazine editor*
Edens, Gary Denton *broadcasting executive*
Frank, Gary Wayne *broadcast technician, broadcast station executive*
Gebert, Herman John *Christian radio station executive*
Genrich, Mark L. *newspaper editorial writer, columnist*
Godwin, Mary Jo *editor, librarian consultant*
Grafe, Warren Blair *cable television executive*
Gunty, Christopher James *newspaper editor*
Johnson, Pam *newspaper editor*
Karr, Daryl Kelly Paul James *film and video service executive*
Leach, John F. *newspaper editor, journalism educator*
Melton, Brad Ray *editor, researcher, writer, historian*
Murian, Richard Miller *book company executive*
Oppedahl, John Fredrick *publisher*
Schatt, Paul *newspaper editor*
Stahl, Richard G. C. *journalist, editor*
Steckler, Phyllis Betty *publishing company executive*
Wade, Judy Lee *journalist*
Weil, Louis Arthur, III *newspaper publishing executive*
Weill, Louis Arthur, III (Chip) *publishing executive*
Zarbin, Earl Arthur *retired newspaper reporter, editor, historian, consultant*

Prescott
Anderson, Parker Lynn *editorial columnist, playwright*
Neal, James Madison, Jr. *retired editor and educator*

Prescott Valley
Cohen, Sanford Barry *radio executive, consultant*

Scottsdale
Everingham, Harry Towner *editor, publisher*
Faer, A.M. *magazine publishing consultant, poet*
Fox, Kenneth L. *retired newspaper editor, writer*
Frischknecht, Lee Conrad *retired broadcasting executive*
Marra, Julie Mitchell *project administrator, editor*
Mc Knight, William Warren, Jr. *publisher*
Myers, Patricia Seitters *journalist, author, editor*
Reidy, Richard Robert *publishing company executive*
Searight, Patricia Adelaide *retired radio and television executive*
Walsh, Mason *retired newspaperman*

Sedona
Sasmor, James Cecil *publishing representative, educator*

Tempe
Luey, Beth Edelmann *editor, educator*
Rankin, William Parkman *communications educator, former publishing company executive*
Youm, Kyu Ho *journalism educator*

Tucson
Buel, Bobbie Jo *editor*
Hatfield, Charles Donald *newspaper executive*
Jacobson, Jack *television executive*
Martin, June Johnson Caldwell *journalist*
Roos, Nestor Robert *consultant*
Stein, Mary Katherine *writer, editor, photographer, communications executive*
Weber, Samuel *editor, retired*

Wickenburg
Dickinson, James Gordon *editor*

Yuma
Marries, Danny Don *news anchor, reporter*
Watson, Larry Sullivan *editor, educator*

CALIFORNIA

Agoura Hills
Chagall, David *journalist, author*
Teresi, Joseph *publishing executive*

Alpine
Greenberg, Byron Stanley *newspaper and business executive, consultant*

Anaheim
Kosht, Randy Michael *publishing executive*
Matisoff, Martin Allen *medical editor, writer*

Auburn
McCartney, Patrick Kevin *newspaper editor, writer*

Avila Beach
Kamm, Herbert *journalist*

Bakersfield
Beene, Richard Stuart *editor*

Ford, Maryellen *reporter*
Jenner, Mike *newspaper editor*

Bay Point
Shrivastava, Vinay Kumar *communication arts educator, film and video producer*

Benicia
Shaboy, Benny *editor, writer*

Berkeley
Bagdikian, Ben Haig *journalist, emeritus university educator*
Bensky, Lawrence Martin *journalist*
Drechsel, Edwin Jared *retired magazine editor*
Krooth, Richard *editor, sociology and political studies educator*
Lesser, Wendy *literary magazine editor, writer, consultant*
Levine, Stephen *journalist*
Witt, Melvin Sylvan *editor, publisher*

Beverly Hills
Bland, Janeese Myra *editor*
Farhat, Carol Sue *motion picture company executive*
Filosa, Gary Fairmont Randolph V., II *multimedia executive, financier, writer*
Lond, Harley Weldon *editor, publisher*
Schneider, Charles I. *newspaper executive*
Sklarewitz, Norman *journalist*
Spivak, Kenin M. *broadcast executive*

Borrego Springs
Stone, Charles Joseph (Joe) *columnist, law enforcement*

Burbank
Ancier, Garth Richard *television broadcast executive*
Beiman, Nancy Robin *animator*
Brogliatti, Barbara Spencer *television and motion picture executive*
Chavez, Manny *film company executive*
Chiolis, Mark Joseph *television executive*
Disney, Roy Edward *broadcasting company executive*
Eisner, Michael Dammann *entertainment company executive*
Guerra, Juan E. *news correspondent*
Kryczko, Thaddeus Walter *record producer*

Burlingame
Golding, George Earl *journalist*
Sharples, Thomas Davy, Jr. *engineering executive*

Campbell
Kinniburgh, Hugh MacKenzie *digital media specialist, television producer*

Carmel
Bohannon-Kaplan, Margaret Anne *publisher, lawyer*
Koeppel, Gary Merle *publisher, art gallery owner, writer*
Mollman, John Peter *book publisher, consultant electronic publishing*

Cedarville
Sykes, Michael *publishing executive*

Chico
Ducommun, Debbie Luella *writer, publisher*

Chula Vista
Blankfort, Lowell Arnold *newspaper publisher*
Moctezuma-Bender, Lisa Beth *book distributor executive, art agent*
Pasqua, Thomas Mario, Jr. *journalism educator*

Cobb
Kandanes, Andrew *recording industry executive, percussionist*

Concord
Brill, Jesse M. *publishing executive*
Sinha-Morey, Bobbi Ann *poetry editor, researcher, poet*

Corona Del Mar
Michaels, Patrick Francis *broadcasting company executive*

Costa Mesa
Coker, Matthew Tod *newspaper editor, magazine editor*
Gottlieb, Jeffrey Paul *journalist*

Cotati
Carroll, Bonnie *publisher, editor*

Cupertino
Malone, Laura Kay *multimedia developer*

Daly City
Cole, David Macaulay *journalist, consultant*

Del Mar
Faludi, Susan C. *journalist, scholarly writer*
Kaye, Peter Frederic *television editor*

Discovery Bay
Arnow, Edward *retired reporter*

Dublin
Wood, Nathaniel Fay *editor, writer, public relations consultant*

El Centro
Lokey, Frank Marion, Jr. *broadcast executive, consultant*

El Dorado Hills
Schlachter, Gail Ann *publishing company executive*

El Segundo
Kelley, William Eugene, Jr. *broadcast executive*
McKee, John Morrison *broadcast executive*

Encinitas
Newman, Katharine Dealy *author, consultant*

Fair Oaks
Douglas, Marion Joan *proofreader, editor, labor negotiator*

Fairfax
Comstock, Margot Mary *editor, writer, graphic designer, consultant, artist*

Fall River Mills
Caldwell, Walter Edward *editor, small business owner*

Foster City
Ball, John Paul *publishing company executive*

Frazier Park
Nelson, Harry *journalist, medical writer*

Fremont
Rockstroh, Dennis John *journalist, screenwriter*

Fresno
Hart, Russ Allen *telecommunications educator*
Moyer, J. Keith *newspaper editor*
Wilson, James Ross *communications educator, broadcasting executive*

Gardena
White, Ruth Bryant *media consultant, analyst, counselor, minister*

Glendale
Benner, Michael *broadcast journalist, consultant*
Dupuy, Pedro *film company executive*
Stayton, Richard Joseph *journalist, editor*

Glendora
Ross, Kathleen Ann *editor*

Guerneville
Church, Peter Dawson *publishing executive*

Hayward
Dalldorf, Thomas E. *publisher*
Funston, Gary Stephen *publishing and advertising executive*
Ripplinger-Costa, Virginia (Ginger) Patrice *television executive*

Hollywood
Cannizzaro, Gerry North *music producer*
Haenel, Hal H., Jr. *film and TV studio executive*
McAdams, Frank Joseph, III *communications educator*
Oken, Alan Irwin *record company executive*
Sarley, John G. *broadcast executive, writer*

Huntington Beach
De Massa, Jessie G. *media specialist*
Frye, Judith Eleen Minor *editor*
Sanchez, Heather Yvonne *editor*

Indio
Ellis, Lee *publisher, editor*

Inyokern
Stallknecht-Roberts, Clois Freda *publisher, publicist*

Irvine
Brennan, Peter Joseph *journalist*
Jensen, Gerald Randolph *editor, graphics designer*
Schwartz, John Leonard *publishing executive, psychiatrist*

La Habra
Oliver, Joyce Anne *journalist, editorial consultant, columnist*

La Habra Heights
Maxwell, Donald Stanley *retired publishing executive*

La Jolla
Copley, Helen Kinney *newspaper publisher*
Hall, TennieBee M. *editor*
Hornaday, Aline Grandier *publisher, independent scholar*

Laguna Hills
Chan, Paul D. *executive editor*

Laguna Niguel
Cabada, Jose Luis *publisher*

Linden
Smith, Donald Richard *editor, publisher*

Loma Linda
Bell, Denise Louise *newspaper reporter, photographer, librarian*

Long Beach
Archbold, Richard *newspaper editor*
Boyd, John Marvin *broadcasting executive*
Ellis, Harriette Rothstein *editor, writer*
Hutchinson, William Kinsey, III *broadcast executive*
Morgan, Byron Albert *filmmaker, writer*
Welch, Matthew Lee *journalist*

Los Altos
Burkhart, Dorothy P. *art critic, catalog essayist*
Larsen, Mary Elizabeth *magazine publisher*
Miller, Ronald Grant *journalist*

Los Angeles
Askin, Richard Henry, Jr. *entertainment company executive*
Bart, Peter Benton *newspaper editor, film producer, novelist*
Bell, Alan *publishing company executive*
Borin, Boris Michaylovitch *writer, publisher*
Bouknight, Robert Michael *television executive*
Brody, Florian Tobias *electronic publishing and new media consultant*
Byrne, Gerard Anthony *publishing company executive, marketing consultant*
Camron, Roxanne *editor*
Churchill, Sharal Tomiko *motion picture company executive*
Collins, Scott Edgar *magazine editor*
Corrick, David Lawrence *radio producer, editor, journalist*
Crippens, David Lee *broadcast executive*
Del Olmo, Frank *newspaper editor*
Delugach, Albert Lawrence *journalist*
Dolan, Mary Anne *journalist, columnist*
Dwyre, William Patrick *journalist, public speaker*
Estes, Richard D. *recording industry executive*
Firstenberg, Jean Picker *film institute executive*
Flanigan, James J(oseph) *journalist*
Florescu, John Maurice *broadcast executive*
Garza, Oscar *newspaper editor*
Goldstein, Ira Steven *publishing company executive, consultant*
Groves, Martha *newspaper writer*
Hamel, Bernard Henri *publisher*
Hamlin, Doug *publishing executive*
Hart, John Lewis (Johnny Hart) *cartoonist*
Hines, William Everett *publisher, producer, cinematographer, writer*
Hudson, Christopher John *publisher*
Iafrate, Gerald Carl *motion picture company executive, lawyer*
Jampol, Jeffrey *music industry executive*
Jancso, Susan Zsuzsa *newspaper editor, translator*
Jarmon, Lawrence *developmental communications educator*
Kelley, Lee *publishing executive*
Kemper, Troxey *magazine editor*
Knittle, William Joseph, Jr. *media executive, psychologist, religious leader, management and marketing consultant, educator*
Kuznetsky, Michelle Hope *recording industry executive, producer*
Laird, Jere Don *news reporter*
Langguth, A(rthur) J(ohn) *writer, journalism educator*
Laventhol, David Abram *newspaper editor*
Lehmkuhl, Lynn *publishing executive*
Li, Lilia Huiying *journalist*
Loehwing, Rudi Charles, Jr. *publicist, radio broadcasting executive, journalist*
Maltin, Leonard *television commentator, writer*
Mann, Wesley F. *newspaper editor*
Margulies, Lee *newspaper editor*
Marroquin, Patricia *newspaper editor*
Maslin, Harry *recording industry executive, producer*
Matsuda, Craig Shin *journalist*
Metzker, Gary Howard *executive news editor*
Monge, Roger Eduardo *writer*
Morgan, Dirck *broadcast journalist*
Mouser, Andrew Lee *film company executive*
Murphy, Philip Edward *broadcast executive*
Nava, Yolanda Margot *broadcast journalist, author*
Nelson, Bryce Eames *journalist, educator*
O'Neil, W. Scott *publishing executive*
Parks, Michael Christopher *journalist*
Perenchio, Andrew Jerrold *film and television executive*
Petersen, Robert E. *publisher*
Phillips, Geneva Ficker *editor*
Radloff, William Hamilton *editor, writer*
Reade, Chris *recording industry executive*
Ream, Debbie Lynn *media and information publishing executive*
Regan, Suzanne Elizabeth *film and television educator*
Rense, Paige *editor, publishing company executive*
Richmond, Ray S(am) *journalist*
Rojany, Lisa Adrienne *publishing company executive*
Scott, Kelly *newspaper editor*
Shaw, David Lyle *journalist, author*
Smith, Lane Jeffrey *automotive journalist, technical consultant*
Stevens, Rick Daryl *entertainment industry executive*
Trembly, Cristy *television executive*
Truman, James *editor*
Wieder, Judy Sara *editor-in-chief*
Wilkins, Amy P. *publishing executive*
Willes, Mark Hinckley *media industry executive*
Wilson, Charles Zachary, Jr. *newspaper publisher*
Wolinsky, Leo C. *newspaper editor*
Wright, Donald Franklin *newspaper executive*
Zwick, Barry Stanley *newspaper editor, speechwriter*

Los Gatos
Goss, Eileen Abel *editor*
Meyers, Ann Elizabeth *sports broadcaster*

Malibu
Blakemore, Paul Henry, Jr. *retired publishing executive*
Klevit, Alan Barre *publishing executive, motivational speaker, writer*
Walker, Juanie Natalie *communication educator*

Marina
Grenfell, Gloria Ross *freelance journalist*

Menlo Park
Hearst, William Randolph, III *newspaper publisher*

Mill Valley
Cohn, Bruce *film and television company executive*
Leslie, Jacques Robert, Jr. *journalist*
McNamara, Stephen *newspaper executive*
Sinberg, Stan *columnist, radio commentator*

Modesto
Vasche, Mark *editor*

Monterey
Britton, Eve Marchant *newspaper reporter*
Gotshall, Cordia Ann *publishing company executive, distributing executive*

Monterey Park
Stapleton, Jean *journalism educator*

Mountain View
Campbell, Arlene Marie *photojournalist*

Murrieta
Casserly, John Joseph *author, journalist*

National City
Kaloyán, Luis Rivas *broadcast executive*

Nevada City
Murray, Kathleen Ellen *writer*

Newport Beach
Bryant, Thomas Lee *magazine editor*
Cutler, David Horton *editor, publisher*
McMahon, Brian *publishing executive*
Van Mols, Brian *publishing executive*

North Hollywood
Horowitz, Zachary I. *entertainment company executive*
Koran, Dennis Howard *publisher*

Northridge
Leps, Ants Arvo *mass communication educator, consultant*

Oakland
Conway, Nancy Ann *editor*
Crumlish, Christian Thomas Spitznas *writer, editor, literary agent*
Powell, Lane Alan *editor*
Schrag, Peter *editor, writer*
Torrez, Naomi Elizabeth *editor, librarian*
Wood, Larry (Mary Laird) *journalist, author, university educator, public relations executive, environmental consultant*

Ontario
Ferguson, Michael Roger *newspaper executive, publisher*
McAfee, Ivan Paul, III *editor*
Wagner, Rob Leicester *newspaper editor, writer*

Orange
Bakke, Leslie Ronica (Cookie) *editor*
Fletcher, James Allen *video company executive*

Pacific Palisades
Griessman, Benjamin Eugene *author, professional speaker*
Hadges, Thomas Richard *media consultant*

Pacifica
Ring, Robert John *sound studio executive*

Pacoima
Schmidt, Byron Winfield *film company executive*

Palm Desert
Spirtos, Andrea C. *columnist*

Palm Springs
Browning, Norma Lee (Mrs. Russell Joyner Ogg) *journalist*
Mann, Zane Boyd *editor, publisher*
Matteson, Robert James *music company executive, talent agent*
Weiner, Stewart George *magazine editor, writer, book publisher*

Palo Alto
Hamilton, David Mike *publishing company executive*
Hellyer, Constance Anne (Connie Anne Hellyer) *writer, musician*
Stein, M(eyer) L(ewis) *journalist, magazine editor, writer*

Paradise
Payne, Jack Wellesley *author, publisher*

Pasadena
Bergholz, Richard Cady *political writer*
Diroll, Patricia Corrigan *newspaper columnist, community volunteer*
Hopkins, Philip Joseph *journalist, editor*
Spector, Phil *record company executive*
Strickler, Carolyn Jeanette *writer, historian*

Petaluma
de Lappe, Pele Phyllis *retired journalist, artist*

Portola Valley
Garsh, Thomas Burton *publisher*

Quincy
Bey, Everett Edward *newspaper editor, publisher*

Rancho Palos Verdes
Hillinger, Charles *journalist, writer*

Rancho Santa Fe
McNally, Connie Benson *editor, publisher, antiques dealer*

Redding
Walsh, Madge Richardson *editor, writer*

Riverside
Locke, Francis Philbrick *retired editorial writer*
MacQueen, Cher *newscaster, sportscaster*
McQuern, Marcia Alice *newspaper publishing executive*
Opotowsky, Maurice Leon *newspaper editor*
Robbins, Karen Diane *editor*
Zappe, John Paul *city editor, educator, newspaper executive*

Rolling Hills Estates
Bradford, Susan Anne *political consultant, writer*

Sacramento
Baker, James Bruce *publishing company executive, writer*
Baltake, Joe *film critic*
Bottel, Helen Alfea *columnist, writer*
Endicott, William F. *journalist*
Favre, Gregory *editor*
Grossman, Marc Richard *media consultant*
Haag, Janis Linn *journalism and creative writing educator, writer*
Heaphy, Janis D. *newspaper executive*
Jones, Mark Alan *broadcast technician*
Knudson, Thomas Jeffery *journalist*
LaMont, Sanders Hickey *journalist*
Lundstrom, Marjie *newspaper editor*
McClatchy, James B. *editor, newspaper publisher*
Prine, Stephen Brent *publisher*
Pruitt, Gary B. *newspaper executive*
Retallack, Alexia Elizabeth *editor, writer*
Rodriguez, Rick *newspaper executive editor*
Simien, Octavia Ruben *reporter, former educator, principal*
Tibbitts, John Codding *publisher*
Williams, Arthur Cozad *broadcasting executive*

San Bernardino
Page, LaVerta Willine *television executive*

San Carlos
Jones, Georgia Ann *publisher*

San Clemente
Dixon, Christopher Jobie *editor, publisher*
Singer, Kurt Deutsch *news commentator, author, publisher*

San Diego
Bell, Gene *newspaper publishing executive*
Bennett, Ronald Thomas *photojournalist*
Berke, William Michael *production editor, writer*
Freedman, Jonathan Borwick *journalist, author, lecturer*
Gibson, Laurie Ann *editor, freelance journalist*
Johnson, James R. II *multimedia developer*
Kaufman, Julian Mortimer *broadcasting company executive, consultant*
Klein, Herbert George *newspaper editor*
Krulak, Victor Harold *newspaper executive*
McDonald, John N., Jr. *retired reporter, copy editor, consultant*
Mickelson, Sig *broadcasting executive, educator*
Milner, Daniel Paul *publishing executive, composer, producer*
Morgan, Neil *author, newspaper editor, lecturer, columnist*
Muñoz, Monica *journalist*
Owen, Charles Theodore *journalist, publisher*
Ristine, Jeffrey Alan *reporter*
Sheldon, Deena Lynn *television camera operator*
Simms, Maria Kay *writer, non-profit organization executive*
Steen, Paul Joseph *retired broadcasting executive*
Winner, Karin *newspaper editor*
Young, Sarah Moskowitz *educational and computer consultant, journalist*

San Francisco
Baskin, Cathryn *magazine editor*
Blackwell, Savannah Rose *journalist*
Blakey, Scott Chaloner *journalist, writer*
Bloomfield, Arthur John *music critic, food writer*
Brown, Kathan *publisher*
Burress, Charles Richard *journalist*
Caine, Carolyn Moore *activist, publishing executive, author, consultant*
Carroll, Jon *newspaper columnist*
Close, Sandy *journalist*
Cohen, Paul Martin *magazine editor, writer*
Colopy, Cheryl Gene *reporter*
Dobbrow, Chris *publishing executive*
Donnally, Patricia Broderick *newspaper editor*
Duscha, Julius Carl *journalist*
Elmore, Matthew Bret *radio, television announcer*
Falk, Steven B. *newspaper publishing executive*
German, William *newspaper editor*
Gore, Andrew *editor-in-chief, periodical*
Hill, Greg *newspaper bureau chief*
Hoyem, Andrew Lewison *publisher*
Jawad, Said Tayeb (Said Tayeb Djawad) *political commentator, writer*
Jenkins, Bruce *sportswriter*
Johns, Roy (Bud Johns) *publisher, author*
Jones, Gregory Fay *publisher, sales professional*
Kingston, Timothy Mark W. *reporter, video producer*
Kinney, Jay MacNeal *editor, author, illustrator*
Klein, Marc S. *newspaper editor and publisher*
Klein, Richard Michael *publisher*
Knapp, (Mary) Gwen *columnist*
Kolden-Ramsey, Melanie Ann *journalist*
Lam, Andrew Quang *journalist*
Lara, Adair *columnist, writer*
Lefevre, Greg *broadcast executive*
Lemmons, Philip *editor*
Louie, David A. *television journalist*
Marino, Richard J. *publishing executive*
Martin, Michael *publisher*
Mason, Greg *publishing executive*
Morgan, Michael Brewster *publishing company executive*
Mycue, Edward *writer, publisher, editor, book seller*
Reed, Sandy *magazine editor*
Rice, Jonathan C. *retired educational television executive*
Rosenheim, Daniel Edward *journalist, television news director*
Saunders, Debra J. *columnist*
Schwarz, Glenn Vernon *editor*
Shank, Gregory Lloyd *journal editor*
Somerson, Paul *editor-in-chief*
Talbot, David Lyle *editor*
Wilner, Paul Andrew *journalist*
Wilson, Johnny Lee *editor-in-chief*
Wilson, Matthew Frederick *newspaper editor*
Wolaner, Robin Peggy *internet and magazine publisher*
Yamamoto, Michael Toru *journalist*

San Jose
Baseman, Sandra Libbie *editor, financial advisor*
Carey, Peter Kevin *reporter*
Ceppos, Jerome Merle *newspaper editor*
Doctor, Kenneth Jay *editor*
Edmonds, Charles Henry *publisher*
Frymer, Murry *columnist, theater critic, critic-at-large*
Harris, Jay Terrence *newspaper editor*
Ingle, Robert D. *newspaper editor, newspaper executive*
Love, Amy Dundon *business executive, marketing and sales executive*
Pulcrano, Dan Michael *newspaper and online services executive*
Trounstine, Philip John *editor, journalist*

San Juan Capistrano
Broida, Rebecca Erin *magazine editor*

San Luis Obispo
Carr, Peter Emile *publisher*

San Marcos
Branch, Robert Hardin *radio and television educator, broadcast executive*

San Mateo
Moylan, Steve *publishing executive*

San Pedro
Bowling, Lance Christopher *record producer, publisher*

San Rafael
Knell, Dora Marie *publishing executive*
Matthews, Scott *record producer*
Sansweet, Stephen Jay *journalist, author, marketing executive*

Santa Ana
Cheverton, Richard E. *newspaper editor*
Katz, Tonnie *newspaper editor*
Lawrence, David Norman *broadcasting executive, consultant*

Santa Barbara
Brown, J'Amy Maroney *journalist, media relations consultant, investor*
Gibney, Frank Bray *publisher, editor, writer, foundation executive*
Hernández Herrero, Isaac *editor, photojournalist*
Poynter, Dan *publishing executive, writer*
Stimson, Grace Heilman *editor*

Santa Clara
Charles, Mary Louise *newspaper columnist, photographer, editor*

Santa Clarita
Adams, Jack *film company executive, screenwriter, producer, educator*

Santa Cruz
Meredith, Thomas Kirkpatrick *publisher, inventor*
Reynolds, Margaret Maupin *activist, journalist*

Santa Monica
Grabowski, Marilyn *photo editor*
Olney, Warren, IV *journalist*
Palmatier, Malcolm Arthur *editor, consultant*
Renetzky, Alvin *publisher*
Sepetys, Ruta Elizabeth *entertainment company executive*
Vaughan, Alan *parapsychologist*
Vellutato, James Lee *music publisher*

Santa Rosa
Cummins, Erik Howcroft *newspaper editor*
Seligman, Adam Ward *writer, publisher*
Swofford, Robert Lee *newspaper editor, journalist*

Sebastopol
Sherick, Michael Jack *publisher, editor*

Sherman Oaks
Davidson, Bill (William John Davidson) *entertainment journalist, author*
Yasnyi, Allan David *communications company executive*

Sierra Madre
Dewey, Donald William *magazine publisher, editor, writer*

South Pasadena
Farrar, Dana Glad *journalist*
Kane, Perry W. *publisher, writer*

Stanford
Andreopoulos, Spyros George *writer*
Maharidge, Dale Dimitro *journalist, educator*
Salisbury, David Francis *science and technology writer*

Stockton
Fitzgerald, Michael L. *newspaper columnist*
Lovell, Emily Kalled *journalist*

Studio City
O'Connor, Michael Arthur *music publishing executive*
Zimmerman, Linda *author, editor, residential real estate agent*

Temecula
Yankee, Marie *educator, publishing executive*

Thousand Oaks
Ginell, Cary David *music historian, radio broadcaster*

Tiburon
Anderson-Gram, Janice *publishing executive*

Toluca Lake
Ebner, Roger Scott *film and television professional*
Ragan, Ann Talmadge *media and production consultant, actor*

Torrance
Adelsman, (Harriette) Jean *newspaper editor*
Milligan, Ronald E. *journalist*
Wafer, Thomas J., Jr. *newspaper publisher*

Tustin
Brownfield, Florence Elizabeth *periodical editor, genealogist*
Zimmermann, John *magazine editor, writer*

Ukiah
Toms, Michael Anthony *broadcast journalist, editor, writer, producer*

Universal City
Geffen, David *recording company executive, producer*
Wasserman, Lew R. *film, recording and publishing company executive*

Vacaville
Zach, Elizabeth Piroska *journalist*

Valencia
Gordon-Brown, Nicholas *editor, consultant author*

Ventura
Forrest, Nancy L. *journalist, writer*
Gallagher, Tim *editor, newspaper*
Howry, Joe *newspaper editor*

Walnut Creek
Armstrong, John *newspaper editor*

Weldon
Wright, Ian Spencer M. *media production educator*

West Los Angeles
Cahan, Christopher Sykes *journalist*

West Sacramento
Davis, Patti Lynn *news anchor*

Whittier
Dannenbaum, Robert Marcus *publisher, editor*
Loughrin, Jay Richardson *mass communications educator, consultant*

Wilton
Harrison, George Harry, III (Hank Harrison) *publishing executive, author*

Woodland Hills
Anastasi, Michael Anton *journalist*
DeWitt, Barbara Jane *journalist*
Mucica, Mary Ann *editor, educator*

Yreka
Smith, Vin *sports editor, business owner, novelist*

Yucaipa
Phillips, Anna *publisher, editor-in-chief newspaper*

COLORADO

Aspen
Hayes, Mary Eshbaugh *newspaper editor*

Aurora
Savage, Eric Wayne *multimedia developer*

Boulder
El Mallakh, Dorothea Hendry *editor, publishing executive*
Scott, Dagny *editor-in-chief*
Sorrells, Amy Hutchinson *book publisher*

Broomfield
Simmons, Marcia Ann *reporter*

Castle Rock
Henry, Frances Ann *journalist, educator*

Cherry Hills Village
Stapleton, Katharine Hall (Katie Stapleton) *food broadcaster, author*

Colorado Springs
Dennison, Daniel Wayne *television news executive*
Mansfield, Roger Leo *astronomy and space publisher*
May, Stephen James *communications educator, writer*
Merrill, Dean Roger *publishing executive*
Shafer, Elizabeth Jane *writer*
Smith, Steven A. *newspaper editor*

Denver
Ballentine, Lee Kenney *writer, publishing company executive*
Bates, James Robert *newspaper editor*
Britton, Dennis A. *newspaper editor, newspaper executive*
Brom, Libor *journalist, educator*
Burdick, Robert W. *newspaper editor*
Clarkson, Richard Clair *publisher, editor, photographer*
Dallas, Sandra *correspondent, writer*
Dance, Francis Esburn Xavier *communication educator*
Dimond, Michael Len *broadcast executive, director*
Dubroff, Henry Allen *newspaper editor*
Erbacher, Kathryn Anne *editor, art and design writer, marketing consultant*
Maher, John Frederic (Jack Maher) *TV news executive*
McKibben, Ryan Timothy *newspaper executive*
Miranda, Monty Mitchell *film director*
Morrow, Ronald Edward *editor, publisher*
Price, Kathleen McCormick *book editor, writer*
Saltz, Howard Joel *newspaper editor*
Seebach, Linda Anne *journalist*
Strutton, Larry D. *newspaper executive*
Weinberg, Hedy Leah *journalist*
Willbanks, Roger Paul *publishing and book distributing company executive*
Witzler, Suzanne Iliff *publishing executive*
Yutkin, Gerald David *cable television executive*

Dillon
Follett, Nancy Crouthamel *publishing executive*

Durango
Ballantine, Morley Cowles (Mrs. Arthur Atwood Ballantine) *newspaper editor*
Hansen, Leonard Joseph *author, journalist*

Eastlake
Roberts, David Lowell *journalist*

Englewood
Kerklo, Norma Jean *publications executive*

Evergreen
Blumberg, Nathaniel Bernard *journalist, educator, writer and publisher*

Fort Collins
Hollahan, Kirk Edward *journalism educator*
MacLauchlin, Robert Kerwin *communications artist, educator*

Golden
Baron, Robert Charles *publishing executive*

Granby
Johnson, William Potter *newspaper publisher*

Greeley
Cobler, Christopher Craig *editor*

Idaho Springs
Kelley, Louanna Elaine *newspaper columnist, researcher*

Lakewood
Dengerink, Don D. *media production specialist*

Littleton
Kline, Brent P. *editor*

Longmont
Davis, Donald Alan *author, news correspondent, lecturer*
Hibler, Jude Ann *photojournalist*

Pueblo
Gregory, Leonard *publishing executive*
Rawlings, Robert Hoag *newspaper publisher*

Silverton
Denious, Jon Parks *publishing executive*
Denious, Sharon Marie *publisher*

Steamboat Springs
Towler, Sureva *publisher, writer*

Westminster
Wirkkala, John Lester *cable company executive*

DISTRICT OF COLUMBIA

Washington
Fenwick, James H(enry) *editor*
Herman, Andrea Maxine *newspaper editor*
May, Clifford Daniel *newspaper editor, journalist*

HAWAII

Aiea
Walker, Welmon, Jr. (Rusty Walker) *publisher, consultant*

Ewa Beach
Lewis, Mary Jane *communication specialist, video producer, writer*

Haleiwa
Austen, Shelli Oetter *radio news anchor, consultant*

Honolulu
Baker, Kent Alfred *broadcasting company executive*
Correa, E. Shan *author, editor*
Flanagan, John Michael *publisher*
Jellinek, Roger *editor*
Kamemoto, Garett Hiroshi *reporter*
Kim, Joung-Im *communication educator, consultant*
Luis-Wells, Cynthia Jo *sports writer*
McCoy, James Joseph *journalist*
Parma, Florence Virginia *magazine editor*
Shapiro, David *newspaper editor*
Simonds, John Edward *newspaper editor*
Tehranian, Majid *political economy and communications educator*
Wiley, Bonnie Jean *journalism educator*

Kahului
Yamamoto, Irwin Toraki *editor, publisher investment newsletter*

Kaneohe
McGlaughlin, Thomas Howard *publisher, retired naval officer*

Lahaina
Knowles, Myles Mike *television broadcast engineer*

IDAHO

Boise
Baker, Karen *newspaper editor*
Evancho, Joseph Hamilton *editor, publisher, writer, fishing guide*
Gramer, Rod Eugene *journalist*

Moscow
Anderson, Clifton Einar *writer, communications consultant*
Hirzel, Robin Lynn *editor*

Rexburg
Bennett, Ronald V. *communications educator, writer*

Rupert
Barborka, Clifford Joseph, III *broadcaster, marketing consultant*

Sandpoint
Bowne, Martha Hoke *publishing consultant*

Twin Falls
Tario, Terry C(harles) *broadcasting executive*

MONTANA

Bigfork
Blumberg, Nathaniel Bernard *journalist, educator, writer and publisher*

Billings
Larsen, Rimbert E. *journalist*
Schile, Wayne *newspaper publishing executive*

Svee, Gary Duane *newspaper editor, author, journalist*

Bozeman
Nickum, Mary Josephine *journal editor*
O'Donnell, Victoria Jean *communication educator*

Butte
van der Veur, Paul Roscoe *communication educator, researcher*

Conrad
Traxler, Buck *newspaper editor*

Havre
Gallus, Charles Joseph *journalist*

Kalispell
Ruder, Melvin Harvey *retired newspaper editor*

Poplar
Redelk, Bonnie Marie *editor*

Sidney
Degel, John William *journalist, photographer*

Superior
Davis, Deborah Johanna *newspaper editor*

Whitefish
Harrop, Thomas *publishing company executive*
James, Marion Ray *magazine founder, editor*

NEVADA

Boulder City
Hildebrand, Mary-Elizabeth *journal editor*
Kidd, Hillery Gene *educational publisher*

Carson City
Convis, Charles Lester *publisher*

Elko
Glass, Kristi Lyn *magazine publisher, writer*

Henderson
Martin, Donald Walter *author, publisher*

Incline Village
Diederich, J(ohn) William *internet publisher*
Scheller, Erin Linn *publishing company executive*

Las Vegas
Frederick, Sherman *publishing executive*
Herren, Rebecca Ann *editor*
Kelley, Michael John *newspaper editor*
Mitchell, Thomas *journal editor*
Mullen, Lawrence James *journalism educator*
Petrosino, James Michael *media consultant*
Scherf, Dietmar *publishing executive*
Zobell, Charles W. *newspaper managing editor*

Reno
Clark-Johnson, Susan *publishing executive*
Cunning, Tonia *newspaper managing editor*
Shur, Edward H. *newspaper editor*

NEW MEXICO

Alamogordo
Bass, Kenneth Lee *radio broadcast consultant*

Albuquerque
Brooks, Jimmy Alan *editor, writer*
Dahl, Donald Douglas *newswriter*
Davidson, Juli *creativity consultant*
Gentry, Sharon L. *journalism educator*
Goldston, Barbara M. Harral *editor*
Hadas, Elizabeth Chamberlayne *publisher*
Jaffe, Ira Sheldon *film critic, educator*
Johnson, Robert Hersel *journalist*
Lang, Thompson Hughes *publishing company executive*
Spiegel, Robert Moore *publishing executive, writer*
Stutt, Marilyn Jean *publisher*
Whiddon, Carol Price *writer, editor, consultant*
Wilde, David *publisher, writer, biographer*

Las Cruces
Williamson, Chilton, Jr. *magazine editor*

Los Alamos
Mendius, Patricia Dodd Winter *editor, educator, writer*

Santa Fe
Atkinson, John Christopher *magazine editor, critic, writer*
Bowman, Jon Robert *editor, film critic*
Forsdale, (Chalmers) Louis *education and communication educator*
Hice, Michael *editor, marketing professional*
Mc Kinney, Robert Moody *newspaper editor and publisher*
Stieber, Tamar *journalist*

NEW YORK

Farmingdale
Steckler, Larry *publisher, editor, author*

New York
Lamm, Donald Stephen *publishing company executive*

OREGON

Beaverton
Challem, Jack Joseph *health, advertising/public relations writer*

Coquille
Taylor, George Frederick *newspaper publisher, editor*

Corvallis
Zwahlen, Fred Casper, Jr. *journalism educator*

Eugene
Baker, Bridget Downey *newspaper executive*
Baker, Edwin Moody *retired newspaper publisher*
Hess, Suzanne Harriet *newspaper administrator, photographer*
Sherriffs, Ronald Everett *communication and film educator*
Tykeson, Donald Erwin *broadcasting executive*

Lincoln City
Doud, Charles Packard *newspaper editor, printer*

Medford
Shinn, Duane K. *music publisher*

Portland
Bhatia, Peter K. *editor, journalist*
Carter, Bonnie Marie *publisher, advertising sales*
Crabbs, Roger Alan *publisher, consultant, small business owner, educator*
Giarelli, Andrew Lino *publisher, educator*
Graves, Earl William, Jr. *journalist*
Johnston, Richard C. *newspaper editor*
Johnston, Virginia Evelyn *editor*
Jones, Cary Dennis *broadcast executive*
Loewenthal, Nessa Parker *communications educator*
Loomis, James Arthur *broadcast technician, newsletter editor*
Mapes, Jeffrey Robert *journalist*
Melton, Robert W., Jr. *communications educator*
Murphy, Francis Seward *journalist*
Newhouse, Theodore *newspaper executive*
Perry, Richard John *book publisher*
Rowe, Sandra Mims *newspaper editor*
Sterling, Donald Justus, Jr. *retired newspaper editor*
Stickel, Frederick A. *publisher*
Thompson, Judith Ann *editor, educator, writer*

Salem
Bentley, Sara *newspaper publishing executive*
Frank, Gerald Wendel *civic leader, journalist*
Mainwaring, William Lewis *publishing company executive, author*
Mazza, David Anthony *communications and media professional*
Wallace, Julia Diane *newspaper editor*

Scappoose
Lundquist, Peggy Ann *editor, publisher*

Sunriver
Phillips, Robert Lee *editor, freelance writer*

Tigard
Nokes, John Richard *retired newspaper editor, author*

Waldport
Lemert, James Bolton *journalist, educator*

Wallowa
Wizard, Brian *publisher, author*

Wilsonville
Bacon, Ursula A. *publisher*

RHODE ISLAND

Portsmouth
Quint, Bert *journalist*

SOUTH CAROLINA

Charleston
Chaplin, George *newspaper editor*

TEXAS

Austin
McMillan, Monty Hayes *filmmaker, security analyst*

UTAH

Bountiful
Meitzler, Leland Keith *executive editor*

Cedar City
Evans, David Harold *film company executive*

Logan
Earl, Bryan Kent *radio development director*

Odgen Walla
Corliss, Bryan Charles *journalist*

Ogden
Larson, Brent T. *broadcasting executive*
Thornburg, Ron *newspaper editor*
Trundle, W(infield) Scott *publishing executive newspaper*

Provo
Hatch, Steven Graham *publishing company executive*
Nelson, George Darrell *theatre and film educator*
Reim, John L. *television executive*
Stubbs, Stanford Todd *multimedia designer*
Tata, Giovanni *publishing executive*

Salt Lake City
Anderson, Arthur Salzner *publishing company executive, marketing executive*
Brown, Carolyn Smith *communications educator, consultant*
Davis, Theran *photojournalist*
Fehr, J. Will *newspaper editor*
Gallivan, John William *publisher*
Goodman, Jack *journalist*
Gregersen, R(onald) George *newspaper publishing executive*
Hatch, George Clinton *television executive*
Hughes, (Robert) John *journalist, educator*
Paulsen, Vivian *magazine editor*
Shelledy, James Edwin, III *editor*
Smith, Donald E. *broadcast engineer, manager*
Tice, Carolyn Kay *magazine editor*
Trapp, Gerald Bernard *retired journalist*
Walton, Nephi A. *multimedia producer, consultant*
Welch, Dominic *publishing executive*

VERMONT

Saint Johnsbury
Mandelstein, Paul Stanley *book publishing executive*

WASHINGTON

Auburn
Overholt, Miles Harvard *cable television consultant*

Bellingham
Doerper, John Erwin *publisher, editor*
Meals, Pamela F. *publishing executive*

Bothell
Scannell, John R. *publishing consultant*

Bremerton
Stallcop, Brian Kirby *journalist*

Des Moines
Landgraf, Susan I *journalism educator, photographer, poet*

Edmonds
Decker, Sharyn Lynn *newspaper reporter*
Owen, John *retired newspaper editor*

Issaquah
Gifford, Arthur Roy *publishing executive*

Kirkland
Welke, Elton Grinnell, Jr. *publisher, writer*

Longview
Natt, Theodore McClelland *newspaper editor, publisher*

Lynnwood
Krause, Thomas Evans *record promotion and radio consultant*

Mill Creek
Fillbrook, Frederick J. *newspaper publisher*

Olympia
Moon, Matthew Elliott *record company executive*

Othello
Grim, Mark Robert *newspaper editor*

Port Orchard
MacDonald, Andrea Denyse *editor, publisher, genealogist*

Port Townsend
Buhler, Jill Lorie *editor, writer*

Prosser
Willard, Helen W. *newswriter, photographer*

Pullman
Johnson, Glenn Allister *communications educator, announcer*

Puyallup
Mowery, Gerald Eugene *publisher, writer*

Seattle
Alexander, Jasper D. *publishing executive*
Anderson, Ross *columnist*
Blethen, Frank A. *newspaper publisher*
Boardman, David *newspaper editor*
Bruner, Nancy J. *publishing executive*
Buckner, Philip Franklin *newspaper publisher*
Bunting, Kenneth Freeman *newspaper editor*
Cochran, Wendell *science editor*
Fancher, Michael Reilly *newspaper editor, newspaper publishing executive*
Fluke, Lyla Schram (Mrs. John M. Fluke) *publisher*
Gouldthorpe, Kenneth Alfred Percival *publisher, state official*
Gwinn, Mary Ann *newspaper reporter*
Henkel, Cathy *newspaper sports editor*
Hills, Regina J. *journalist*
Johnson, Wayne Eaton *writer, editor, former drama critic*
Kelly, Carolyn Sue *newspaper executive*
MacLeod, Alex *newspaper editor*
McClelland, Kamilla Kuroda *news reporter, proofreader, book agent*
Nalder, Eric Christopher *investigative reporter*
Payne, Ancil Horace *retired broadcasting executive*
Read, Thomas A. *editor, retired*
Scigliano, Eric Robert *writer, newspaper editor*
Shipman, Keith Bryan *sportscaster*
Sizemore, Herman Mason, Jr. *newspaper executive*
Slaton, Steven Charles *radio announcer*
Szeto, Hung *publisher*
Turner, Wallace L. *reporter*
Worth, Mark Edward *political journalist, media analyst*

Snohomish
Frohnen, Richard Gene *journalism educator*

Spokane
Cowles, William Stacey *publisher*
Grant, Thomas Arthur *television journalist*
Gray, Alfred Orren *retired journalism educator, communications specialist*
Peck, Christopher *editor*
Thomas, George Thorp *editor, publisher*
Whitehouse, N. Virginia *communications studies educator*

Toledo
Weber, Stephen Ross *broadcast technician*

Tukwila
Houde, John Michael *television engineer*
Lamb, Ronald Alfred *editor*

Vancouver
Campbell, Scott *newspaper publishing company executive*

Vashon
Mann, Claud Prentiss, Jr. *retired television journalist, real estate agent*

WYOMING

Casper
Eisenhauer, David Thomas *journalist*
Hipschman, David *editor*

Cody
Fritjofson, Sarah Marie *reporter, columnist*

Jackson
Ninnemann, Thomas George *broadcast educator*

Laramie
Guzzo, Sandra Elizabeth *newspaper columnist, writer*
Smith, Conrad Glenn Page *communications educator*

Pinedale
Montgomery, Janet K. *newspaper editor*

Powell
Killen, Judy Tipton *news editor*

CANADA

ALBERTA

Edmonton
Davis, Murdoch *editor-in-chief*
Hughes, Linda J. *newspaper publisher*
Stanway, Paul William *newspaper editor*

BRITISH COLUMBIA

Vancouver
Babick, Don *newspaper executive*
Cruickshank, John Douglas *newspaper editor*
Neumueller, Anders J.F. *newspaper editor, writer*

MEXICO

Mexico DF
Heyman, Matthew David *entertainment executive*

ADDRESS UNPUBLISHED

Adelson, Merv Lee *entertainment and communication industry executive*
Akiyama, Carol Lynn *motion picture industry executive*
Anderson, Linda (Lynn Anderson) *radio executive*
Baltz, Antone Edward, III *journalist, writer, academic administrator*
Barnhurst, Christine Louise *broadcast executive*
Barry, Rick (Richard Francis Dennis Barry, III) *sportscaster, retired professional basketball player, marketing professional*
Bartanen, Kristine Marie *communications educator*
Berke, Judie *publisher, editor*
Bernheimer, Martin *music critic*
Bernstein, Jack Barry *film company executive, producer*
Blackstock, Joseph Robinson *newspaper editor*
Bradley, Jean Eleanor *newspaper executive, public relations consultant*
Bratzler, Mary Kathryn *desktop publisher*
Brusaschetti, Marilee Marshall *media executive*
Byrne-Dempsey, Cecelia *journalist*
Cairns, Diane Patricia *motion picture executive*
Cheshire, William Polk *retired newspaper columnist*
Clark, Karen Sue *editor, communication educator*
Cooper, Jon Hugh *public television executive*
Crawford, Mia Louisa *television network operations coordinator*
Cullen, Robert John *publishing executive, financial consultant*
Curtin, David Stephen *newswriter*
Day, Anthony *newspaper writer*
DeSantis, Gregory Joseph *motion picture executive*
Dietrich, William Alan *author, journalist*
Draznin, Jules Nathan *journalism and public relations educator, consultant*
Duncan, James Richard *systems administrator*
Ewell, Miranda Juan *journalist*
Farnsworth, Elizabeth *broadcast journalist*
Fistell, Ira J. *newspaper editor, adult education educator, newswriter, radio and television personality*
Flood, James Tyrrell *broadcasting executive, public relations consultant*
Franklin, Jon Daniel *writer, journalist, educator*
Gebhart, Fred *journalist*
Gist, John Montfort *publishing executive*
Gorry, Conner Clough *writer*
Gray, Thomas Stephen *newspaper editor*
Guittar, Lee John *retired newspaper executive*
Hardcastle, Marcia E. (Marcia E. Temme) *newspaper editor*
Harvey, Nancy Melissa *media specialist, art teacher*
Higgins, Michael Leo *multimedia developer, educator, webmaster*
Holland, James Daniel *columnist*
Kayfetz, Victor Joel *writer, editor, translator*
Keller, Shelly B. *writer, editor, marketing consultant*
Kennedy, Orin *film company executive*
Kleiner, Harold J. *record company executive*
Kuri, John Anthony *film company executive*
Landes, William Alan *publishing executive*
Lawrie, Laura Anne *editor*
Lee, Simi *sportswriter, sports promoter*
Lloyd, Michael Jeffrey *recording producer*
Loper, James Leaders *broadcasting executive*
Lourie, Iven *editor, writer*
Love, Laurie Miller *science editor*
Lush, Pamela Grace Meine *international publishing company executive*
Main, Robert Gail *communications educator, training consultant, television and film producer, former army officer*
Marmion, Suzanne Michelle *reporter*
Marroquin, Art *reporter*
McWilliams, Beatriz Duran *communications educator*
Mead, Jerry Dale *wine expert, writer*
Miller, Carole Ann Lyons *editor, publisher, marketing specialist*
Miller, Norman Charles, Jr. *journalism educator*
Mills, Dale Douglas *journalist*
Morain, Claudia Mitchell *journalist*
Nicholson, Loren Lee *journalism educator, author*
Nish, Albert Raymond, Jr. *retired newspaper editor*
Noeth, Louise Ann *journalist*
Otanez, Andrea Kaye *editor*
Peterson, Kevin Bruce *newspaper editor, publishing executive*
Pudney, Gary Laurence *television executive*
Ramsey, Jerry Virgil *educator, financial planner, radio broadcaster*
Reiner, Eric Alan *business consultant, author, lecturer, producer*
Riggs, George E. *newspaper publishing executive*
Ryan, Cathrine Smith *publisher*
Ryan, Michael Thomas *music editor, composer*
Sapsowitz, Sidney H. *entertainment and media company executive*
Schooley, Jennifer Lynn *broadcasting executive*
Schweizer, Edward Sowers *television network executive*
Semilian, Julian Andrei *film editor, poet, translator*
Serling, Carolyn K. *editor*
Sery, Gil *reporter*
Sheridan, Guy Mitchell *retired journalist*
Slater, Ken G. *motion picture executive*
Smith, Carter Blakemore *broadcaster*
Smith, Chester *broadcasting executive*
Smith, Linda Wasmer *writer*
Smith, Martin Bernhard *journalist*
Spitaleri, Vernon Rosario *newspaper publisher, manufacturing company executive*
Stamper, Malcolm Theodore *publishing company executive*
Steiner, Shari Yvonne *publisher, editor, journalist*
Sturges, Sherry Lynn *recording industry executive*
Sublett, Scott W. *screenwriting and film history educator, playwright*
Suwinsky, Pam Pokorney *book publisher*
Talvi, Silja Joanna Aller *freelance journalist, writer*
Tazza, David Robert *editor*
Toldanes, Roni De Jesus *journalist*
Traylor, William Robert *publisher*
Vandenberg, Peter Ray *magazine publisher*
Voorhees, John Lloyd *columnist*
Weaver, Howard C. *newspaper executive*
Weiland, Dave Allen *broadcast engineer*
Welsome, Eileen *journalist*
Williams, Elisa Ann *journalist*
Witmer, Diane F. *communications educator*
Woodward, John Russell *motion picture production executive*
Woytak, Lidia T. *editor*
Yack, Patrick Ashley *editor*

EDUCATION. For postsecondary education, *See also* specific fields.

UNITED STATES

ALASKA

Anchorage
Behrend, Donald Fraser *university administrator*
Byrd, Milton Bruce *college president, former business executive*
Collins, Michael Paul *secondary school educator, earth science educator, consultant*
Gorsuch, Edward Lee *chancellor*
Matsui, Dorothy Nobuko *elementary education educator*
Mitchell, Michael Kiehl *elementary and secondary education educator, minister*
Reed-Jackson, Leona Mae *educational administrator*
Skladal, Elizabeth Lee *retired elementary school educator*

Eagle River
Mathewson, Judith Jeanne *special education educator*
Standley, Mark *school program administrator, consultant*

Fairbanks
Schlegel, James M. *educational administrator*
Wadlow, Joan Krueger *academic administrator*
Wood, William Ransom *retired university president, city official, corporate executive*

Haines
Haas, June F. *special education educator, consultant*

Homer
Swartz, Carol I. *academic administrator*

Juneau
Romesburg, Kerry D. *state education administrator*

North Pole
Vanasse, Deb Lynn *secondary education educator, writer*

ARIZONA

Arizona City
Donovan, Willard Patrick *retired elementary education educator*

Buckeye
Burton, Edward Lewis *retired industrial procedures and training consultant, educator*

Casa Grande
Davies, Harriett Marie (Lolly Davies) *secondary education educator*

Chandler
Barnard, Annette Williamson *elementary school educator*

Cottonwood
Parrott, Sharon Lee *retired elementary educator*

Flagstaff
Bacon, Roger Lee *English educator, consultant*
Gahungu, Athanase *education educator, researcher*
Hatch, Lynda Sylvia *education educator*
Lapan, Stephen D. *gifted education educator, consultant*
Ratzlaff, Vernon Paul *elementary education educator, consultant*
Rowland, Paul McDonald *education educator*

Fort Huachuca
Adams, Frank *education specialist*

Fountain Hills
Humes, Charles Warren *counselor, educator*

Glendale
Bret, Donna Lee *elementary education educator*
Voris, William *academic administrator emeritus*

Goodyear
Asadi, Robert Samir *high school principal*

Green Valley
Carpenter, John Everett *retired principal, educational consultant*

Holbrook
Kraai, Janice Kay *adult education educator*
Schicketanz, Dale Edwin *educator*

Kingman
Roddy, David Bruce *college program director*

Morristown
Rosehnal, Mary Ann *educational administrator*

Nogales
Roselle, Cathy Colman *kindergarten education, educational consultant*

Page
Hart, Marian Griffith *retired reading educator*
Tsinigine, Allen *educator*

Payson
Johnson, Dee Strickland *retired educator, poet, musician*

Peoria
Jesse, Sandra Elizabeth *special education educator*
Rebb, Karen Marlene *music educator*

Phoenix
Barela, Bertha Cicci *elementary education educator, artist*
Becket, Johanna Nina *special education educator*
Boyd, Chris M. *elementary educator, consultant, writer*
Cain, Robert Joseph *elementary school educator*
Daggett, Barbara Dalicandro *secondary education director*
Durham, Fleta Evelyn *educator, community volunteer*
Forshier, Richard Steven *physics and biology educator*
Malcolm, Richard Ward *academic administrator, consultant*
Neal, Sheila Dianne *university adminstrator*
Peabody, Debbie Kay *elementary school educator*
Zembruski, Sarah Ann Gustafson *elementary school educator*

Prescott
Haynes, Janice Jaques Elizabeth *educator, editor*
Rheinish, Robert Kent *university administrator*

Scottsdale
Abramson, Treva Thomasson *teacher*
Churchill, William DeLee *retired education educator, psychologist*
Esquer, Deborah Anne *elementary education educator*
Hokin, Jeanne *education educator*
Mayer, Robert Anthony *retired college president*
Spero, Diane Frances *school director*
Wright, C. T. Enus *former academic administrator*

Sedona
Richards, Wanda Jamie *education educator*

Snowflake
Dwornik, Lynda Bebee *elementary school educator*

Somerton
Reed, Frank Vern *principal*

Sun City
Mitchell, Lucille Anne *retired elementary school educator*

Sun Lakes
Johnson, Marian Ilene *education educator*

Tempe
Coor, Lattie Finch *university president*
de los Santos, Alfredo Guadalupe, Jr. *education administrator, consultant*
Forsyth, Ben Ralph *academic administrator, medical educator*
Guzzetti, Barbara Jean *education educator*
Luehrsen, Sandra Lee *former education administrator, artist*
Mayer, Elizabeth Billmire *educational administrator*
Richardson, Richard Colby, Jr. *leadership and policy studies educator, researcher*
Simmons, Howard Lee *education educator*

Tucson
Bowlan, Nancy Lynn *elementary and secondary school educator*
Chliwniak, Luba *higher education consultant, educator*
Fountain, Linda *secondary education educator*
Gottfredson, Michael Ryan *criminal justice educator*
Heins, Marilyn *college dean, pediatrics educator, author*
Humphrey, John Julius *university program director, historian, writer*
Hurt, Charlie Deuel, III *dean, educator*
Jagodowski, Richard Ben *elementary school educator*
Jolivet, Anna Mary *retired school system administrator, association executive*
Leavitt, Jerome Edward *childhood educator*
Likins, Peter William *university administrator*
Mewes, Jennifer Robyn *counselor*
Reavis, Susan Scott *elementary educator*
Starr, Melvin Lee *counseling organization executive*
White, Danny Levius *counselor, consultant, educator*

Whiteriver
Clark, John Munro *superintendent of schools*

Yuma
Florence, Linda Sue *secondary school educator*
Kuechel, Rebecca June *elementary education educator*
Thompson, Lynn Kathryn Singer *educational director*

CALIFORNIA

Aguanga
Mendoza, Peggy Ann Gilbert *elementary education educator, writer*

Alameda
Carter, Roberta Eccleston *therapist, counselor*
Sakamoto, Katsuyuki *retired college chancellor, psychology educator*

Albany
Chook, Edward Kongyen *university official, disaster medicine educator*

Alpine
Stiles, Joanne Mary *secondary education educator*

Anaheim
Guajardo, Elisa *counselor, educator*
Jackson, David Robert *school system administrator*

Apple Valley
Tishner, Keri Lynn *secondary education educator*

Arcadia
Soriano, Debbie Ann *educator*

Arcata
McCrone, Alistair William *university president*
Slinker, John Michael *academic director*

Atwater
Dickey, Daniel H. *elementary education educator*

Azusa
Gray, Paul Wesley *university dean*
McCormick, Lawrence Ray *adult education educator*

Bakersfield
Arciniega, Tomas Abel *university president*
Hess, Helen Elizabeth *retired secondary school educator, musician*
Neumann, Herman Ernest *elementary and special education educator*
Skillin, Therese Jeno *elementary school educator*

Belmont Shore
Fleming, Jane Williams *retired educator, author*

Ben Lomond
Sikora, James Robert *educational business consultant*

Benicia
Dunaway, Phillip Lee, Jr. *secondary school education educator*
Garrop, Barbara Ann *elementary education educator*

Berkeley
Berdahl, Robert Max *academic administrator, historian, educator*
Christ, Carol Tecla *academic administrator, English educator*
Freedman, Sarah Warshauer *education educator*
Geist, Karin Ruth Tammeus Mcphail *secondary education educator, realtor, musician*
Hyatt, James Armstrong *university administrator*
Kay, Herma Hill *dean*
Linn, Marcia Cyrog *education educator*
Lyman, Peter *librarian, educator*
Ralston, Lenore Dale *academic policy and program analyst*
Shoemaker, Cameron David James *dean, educator*
Tien, Chang-Lin *engineer, educator*
Yang, Bing-Liang *educator, researcher*

Beverly Hills
Leeds, Margaret Ann *assistant principal*
Van de Kamp, Andrea Louise *academic administrator*

Bloomington
Llanusa, Steven Michael *elementary education educator*

Boulder Creek
Bevernick, Mary Bickert *school district administrator*

Boulevard
Charles, Blanche *retired elementary education educator*

Brentwood
Groseclose, Wanda Westman *retired elementary school educator*
Stillwell, Valorie Celeste *secondary school mathematics educator*

Burbank
Neumann, Nancy Ruth *studio educator*
Stokes, Gordon Arthur *educational company executive, author*
Walters, Kenneth C. *retired educator*

Burlingame
Raffo, Susan Henney *elementary education educator*
Yates, Margery Gordon *elementary education educator*

Calabasas
Margolis, Sylvia Ganz *retired secondary education educator*

Camarillo
Evans, James Handel *university administrator, architect, educator*

Cameron Park
Grubaugh, Karl David *secondary education educator*

Campo
Jermini, Ellen *educational administrator, philosopher*

Canyon Lake
Knight, Vick, Jr. *author, educator, counselor*

Carlsbad
Clark, Violet Cathrine *retired school administrator, volunteer*
Gardner, David Chambers *education educator, psychologist, business executive, author*

Carmichael
Brahms, Katheryn Ann *educator*
Marmaduke, Arthur Sandford *educational administrator*

Castro Valley
Shoptaw, Shauna Lynn *middle school educator*

Chatsworth
Miller, Robert Steven *secondary school educator*

Chico
Esteban, Manuel Antonio *university administrator, educator*
Waters, Anthony Edward *adult education educator, volunteer*

Chula Vista
Livziey, James Gerald *secondary school educator*
Steele, Nancy Eden Rogers *educator*
Wyatt, Edith Elizabeth *elementary education educator*

Claremont
Alexander, John David, Jr. *college administrator*
Bekavac, Nancy Yavor *academic administrator, lawyer*
Coray, Jeffrey Warren *assistant principal, instructor*
Douglass, Enid Hart *educational program director*
Faranda, John Paul *college administrator*
Hill, Brenda Barham *academic administrator*
Maguire, John David *academic administrator, educator, writer*
Monte, William David *education educator*
O'Kelly, Crystal Kathleen *secondary education educator, television producer*
Pitts, Sadie Turner *retired educator*
Platt, Joseph Beaven *former college president*
Riggs, Henry Earle *academic administrator, engineering management educator*
Stark, Jack Lee *academic administrator*
Strauss, Jon Calvert *academic administrator*

Clovis
Bitters, Conrad Lee *biological sciences educator*

Coalinga
Moreau, Joseph Anthony *educational administrator*

Colton
Slider, Margaret Elizabeth *elementary education educator*

Compton
Williams, Vivian Lewie *college counselor*

Concord
Thall, Richard Vincent *school system administrator*

Corcoran
Roberts, Alice Noreen *educational administrator*

Corte Madera
Lillig, Margo Andrea *child development professional*

Costa Mesa
Lavrakas, Lefteris *educator, researcher, consultant*

Covina
Aguilar, Gladys Maria *counselor, educator*

Culver City
Manwell Dragdon, Florence Moroney *school administrator, educational adviser*
Novick, Michael *adult education educator, author*

Davis
Ginosar, D. Elaine *elementary education educator*
Grey, Robert Dean *academic administrator, biology educator*
Hendrix, Louise Butts *retired educator, author*
Macleod, Dianne Sachko *educator*
Springer, Sally Pearl *university administrator*
Vanderhoef, Larry Neil *academic administrator*
Wick, Daniel Lewis *educator, writer*
Wolk, Bruce Alan *professor*

Diamond Bar
Domeño, Eugene Timothy *elementary education educator, principal*

Downey
Brooks, Lillian Drilling Ashton *adult education educator*
Gogolin, Marilyn Tompkins *educational administrator, language pathologist*
Ruecker, Martha Engels *retired special education educator*
Thompson, Rena Louise *elementary education educator*

Duarte
Tse, Man-Chun Marina *special education educator*

El Cajon
Thomas, Esther Merlene *elementary education educator*
Zazurskey, Judy Kay *secondary education educator*

El Cerrito
Herzberg, Dorothy Crews *secondary education educator*

Elk Grove
De Luca, Rodney John, Jr. *secondary educator*
Sparks, Jack Norman *college dean*

Encino
Bach, Cynthia *educational program director, writer*
Green, Kenneth Charles *education educator, researcher*

Escondido
Sanders, Adrian Lionel *educational consultant*

Fair Oaks
Lemke, Herman Ernest Frederick, Jr. *retired elementary education educator, consultant*

Fairfield
Kirkorian, Donald George *college official, management consultant*

Fallbrook
Evans, Anthony Howard *university president*

Fontana
Rynearson, Patricia Heaviside *elementary school educator*

Forestville
Kielsmeier, Catherine Jane *school system administrator*

Fortuna
Fisher, Bruce David *elementary school educator*
Mathews, Caroline Marie *secondary education educator*

Fountain Valley
Ecker, Marc Avery *school system administrator, educator*

Fremont
Brown, David Richard *school system administrator, minister*
Lapiroff, Jerry *secondary school educator*
Sousa, Joseph Philip *secondary education educator*

Fresno
Chesemore, David Lee *adult education educator, biologist*
Graves, Melissa June *elementary school educator*
Klassen, Peter James *academic administrator, history educator*
Staton, Angela Renee *educator, counselor*
Welty, John Donald *academic administrator*

Fullerton
Beers, Susan Alice *dean*
Donoghue, Mildred Ransdorf *education educator*
Gordon, Milton Andrew *academic administrator*
Smith, Ephraim Philip *academic administrator, former university dean, educator*

Galeta
Thompson, Beverly Pifford *vice-principal*

Gilroy
Dunham, Judith Ann *school administrator, education educator*

Glendale
Case, Lee Owen, Jr. *retired academic administrator*
DeVincintis, Lani *adult education educator*
Leeds-Horwitz, Susan Beth *school system administrator, speech-language pathology educator*
Vandermey, Herman Ronald *dean, religion educator*

Glendora
Konovnitzine, Elena *secondary school educator*
Schiele, Paul Ellsworth, Jr. *educational business owner, writer*

Grass Valley
Finocchiaro, Penny Morris *secondary school educator*

Guerneville
Pevehouse, Dolores Ferrell *educator, consultant, publisher, writer, artist*

Hacienda Heights
[illegible]

Hayward
McCune, Ellis E. *retired university system chief administrator, higher education consultant*
Rees, Norma S. *academic administrator*

San Leandro
Dolgin, Stephen Mark *teacher, social worker*
Loeffler, Garry Antone *principal, municipal official*

San Luis Obispo
Baker, Warren J(oseph) *university president*
Kintzer, Frederick C. *educator, researcher*

San Marcos
Boggs, George Robert *academic administrator*
Luna, James Alexander *counselor*

San Marino
Footman, Gordon Elliott *educational administrator*
Mothershead, J. Leland, III *dean*

San Pablo
Colfack, Andrea Heckelman *elementary education educator*

San Rafael
Cloud, James Merle *university and hospital administrator, learning specialist*
Lakritz, Bradley William *educational director*

Santa Barbara
Adair-Verbais, Trudy May *early childhood educator*
Allaway, William Harris *retired university official*
O'Dowd, Donald Davy *retired university president*
Rowe, James Arnold *retired education administrator, real estate agent*
Tettegah, Sharon Yvonne *education educator*
Yang, Henry T. *university chancellor, educator*

Santa Clara
Locatelli, Paul Leo *academic administrator*
Marelick, Lin *graphic arts educator, artist*
Nordmeyer, Mary Betsy *retired vocational educator*
Shin, Helen Hyun *academic administrator, educator*

Santa Clarita
Lavine, Steven David *academic administrator*

Santa Cruz
Mirk, Judy Ann *retired elementary educator*

Santa Fe Springs
Janowicz, Frank Dominic *correctional educator*

Santa Monica
Tigue, William Bernard *adult education educator*

Santa Rosa
Wilson, Margie (Marjorie) Jean *elementary education educator, writer*

Saratoga
Houston, Elizabeth Reece Manasco *correctional education consultant*
Whalen, Margaret Cavanagh *retired secondary school educator*
Wood, Gladys Blanche *retired secondary education educator, journalist*

Seal Beach
Melton, Cheryl Ann *educator, small business owner*

Sherman Oaks
Fortuna, Anthony Frank *retired educator, consultant*
Horner, Sandra Marie Groce (Sandy Heart) *educator, poet, songwriter, lyricist*
O'Neill, Sallie Boyd *educational consultant, business owner, sculptor*

Simi Valley
Bullock, Donald Wayne *elementary education educator, educational computing consultant*
Jackson, Thirston Henry, Jr. *retired adult education educator*

Soquel
Weston, Idanthea Beyette *school director*

Stanford
Bridges, Edwin Maxwell *education educator*
Raisian, John *university institute director, economist*
Selfridge-Field, Eleanor *educator*
Snow, Richard Eric *education educator*
Spence, Andrew Michael *dean, finance educator*
Strober, Myra Hoffenberg *education educator, consultant*

Stockton
Fung, Rosaline Lee *educator*
Jantzen, J(ohn) Marc *retired education educator*
Mahoney, Sandra Lea *program coordinator*
Washburn, Harriet Caroline *secondary education educator*

Sun Valley
Cinnamon, William, III *elementary and special education educator*
Sipus, Ronald G. *school administrator*

Sunnyvale
Knopf, Karl Gordon *educator*

Sylmar
Lisalda, Sylvia Ann *primary education educator*

Temecula
Raftery, Scott Robert *secondary education educator, athletic director*

Thousand Oaks
Cipriano, Patricia Ann *secondary education educator, consultant*

Torrance
Culton, Paul Melvin *retired counselor, educator, interpreter*
McNamara, Brenda Norma *secondary education educator*
Roney, Raymond G. *educator*

Trinidad
Conant, Ralph Wendell *educator, consultant, author*

Tujunga
Mayer, George Roy *educator*

Turlock
Antoniuk, Verda JoAnne *secondary school educator*

Twentynine Palms
Clemente, Patrocinio Ablola *psychology educator*
Huffman, Donald Gerald *special education educator*

Upland
Doyle, Michael James *educator, organist*

Vallejo
Baker, Christine Marie *secondary education educator*
Marshall, Roberta Navarre *middle school educator*

Van Nuys
Altshiller, Arthur Leonard *secondary education educator*

Venice
Dixon, Neil Edward *elementary school educator, paleoanthropologist*

Victorville
Ceseña, Carmen *education educator, education administrator*
Kurtz, Terry Cecil *secondary education educator, news anchorman*
Peterson, Leroy *retired secondary education educator*

Villa Park
Writer, Sharon Lisle *secondary education educator*

Visalia
Alkhalili, Oussama Ahmad *adult education educator, consultant, director*

Walnut
Spencer, Constance Marilyn *secondary education educator*
Wicker, Marjorie Arlene *elementary education educator*

Walnut Creek
Carver, Dorothy Lee Eskew (Mrs. John James Carver) *retired secondary education educator*
Lilly, Luella Jean *academic administrator*
Mackay, Patricia McIntosh *counselor*

Wawona
Horner, Michelle *elementary school educator, principal*

Weimar
Kerschner, Lee R(onald) *academic administrator, political science educator*

West Covina
Perez, Mary Angelica *bilingual specialist, educational administrator*

Westlake Village
Doerr, Patricia Marian *elementary and special education educator*

Whittier
De Lorca, Luis E. *educational administrator, educator, speaker*
Drake, E. Maylon *academic administrator*
Silvestri, Patti Marie *elementary education educator*
Tunison, Elizabeth Lamb *education educator*
Zanetta, Joseph Michael *university administrator, lawyer*

Wilmington
Menzies, Leila Kay *college official*

Woodland
Perry, Glen Joseph *educator*

Woodland Hills
Hernandez, Arthur *college administrator, labor arbitrator, artist*

Yorba Linda
Lunde, Dolores Benitez *retired secondary education educator*

Yuba City
Higdon, Bernice Cowan *retired elementary education educator*

Yucaipa
Gomez, Louis Salazar *college president*
Marks, Sharon Lea *primary school educator, nurse*

COLORADO

Alamosa
Jolly, Michael John *college administrator*

Arvada
Hammond-Blessing, DiAnn A. *elementary education educator*
Jamra, Ellen G. *college programs director*
Lucas, Theresa Eileen *elementary education educator*

Aurora
Fain, Karen Kellogg *retired history and geography educator*
Fair, Mary Louise *retired elementary school educator*
Fedak, Barbara Kingry *technical center administrator*
Gibson, Elisabeth Jane *principal*
Hartenbach, David Lawrence *school system administrator*
Verniero, Joan Evans *special education educator*
Walker, Joyce Marie *secondary school educator*
Zuschlag, Nancy Hansen *environmental science/nature resources educator*

Boulder
Buechner, John C. *academic administrator*

Byyny, Richard Lee *academic administrator, physician*
Healy, James Bruce *cooking school administrator, writer*
Kim, Jean *academic administrator*
Marshall, James Kenneth *academic administrator*
Sharan, Farida Jeannine *writer, natural medicine professional*
Snyder, Sherry Ann *university administrator*
Vigil, Daniel Agustin *academic administrator*

Broomfield
Little, Mark Douglas *secondary school educator*

Brush
Biren, Richard Lee *elementary school counselor, writer*

Calhan
Fuller, Janice Marie *secondary school educator*

Canon City
Baumann, Ernst Frederick *college president*

Castle Rock
Dickinson, Susan Joan *deaf studies educator, consultant*

Colorado Springs
Garcia, Roberto Ayala *college admissions director*
Grady, Dolores Anne *academic administrator, educator, consultant*
Guy, Mildred Dorothy *retired secondary school educator*
Louden, Suzanne Lois *educational consultant*
Nolte, Sylvia Ann Poe *education educator, program director*
Reddel, Carl Walter *education adminstration*
Rothenberg, Harvey David *educational administrator*
Ruch, Marcella Joyce *retired educator, biographer*
Shade, Linda Bunnell *university chancellor*
Spicer, Ronald L. *education educator*
Thompson, William Joseph *secondary school educator, coach*
Van Scotter, Richard Dale *education policy executive*
Wilcox, Rhoda Davis *elementary education educator*
Young, Taylor Lynn *special education administrator, consultant*

Deer Trail
Malson, Verna Lee *special education educator*

Denver
Black, Lavonne Patricia *special education educator*
Bosworth, Bruce Leighton *school administrator, educator, consultant*
Cannon, Elizabeth Anne *special education educator*
Cohrs, Marlin E. *academic facility administrator*
Comer, Lori Ann *secondary educator*
DePew, Marie Kathryn *retired secondary school educator*
Drake, Lucius Charles, Jr. *school administrator, university consultant, educator*
Driggs, Margaret *educator*
Fielden, C. Franklin, III *early childhood education consultant*
Fulkerson, William Measey, Jr. *college president*
Goss, Patricia Elizabeth *secondary education educator*
Heckler, Mark Alan *dean*
Hill, Kathleen Lois *performing art school executive*
Kao, Fa-Ten *education researcher*
Lehman, Patricia *adult education educator*
Lofthouse, Russ Wilbert *school administrator*
Lutes, Natalie K. *budget analyst*
Marion, Susan Felice *educator*
Miller, Clara Burr *education educator*
Mirich, David Gage *secondary education language educator*
Montgomery, Nancy Vincent *English as a second Language educator*
Ritchie, Daniel Lee *academic administrator*
Sather, Sylvia Carolyn *science educator, consultant*

Durango
Jones, Joel Mackey *academic administrator*

Englewood
James, William Earl *academic administrator, medical educator*
Leo, Mary Gaye *school administrator*

Estes Park
Stanton, Lea Kaye *elementary school educator, counselor*

Evergreen
Rogers, Spencer Thomas *education company director, consultant, writer*

Fort Collins
Cook, Dierdre Ruth Goorman *school administrator, secondary education educator*
Fotsch, Dan Robert *elementary education educator*
Rewerts, Milan Alvin *university program director*
Switzer, Teri Reynolds *education educator, librarian*
Yates, Albert Carl *academic administrator, chemistry educator*

Glenwood Springs
Rice, Steve E. *college dean*

Golden
Bickart, Theodore Albert *university president*
Klug, John Joseph *secondary education educator, director of dramatics*
Truly, Richard H. *academic administrator, former federal agency administrator, former astronaut*
Young, Arthur William *dean, consultant, engineer*

Grand Junction
Moberly, Linden Emery *educational administrator*
Thomas, Richard McKennon, II *college administrator*

Greeley
Duff, William Leroy, Jr. *university dean emeritus, business educator*
Skinner, Howard Morse *college dean, educator*

Hotchkiss
Perry, Jeanne Elyce *principal*

Hudson
Starks, Elizabeth Vial *gifted/talented education educator*

Lafayette
Baker, Carolyn Elizabeth Elliott *educator, writer*
London, Douglas *English educator*

Lakewood
Forrest, Kenton Harvey *science educator, historian*
Kolch, Zelma Trujillo *elementary education educator*
Milan, Marjorie Lucille *early childhood education educator*
Perito, Joseph Gerald, Jr. *educator, musician, counselor, consultant*
Spraggs, Laurence Dale *educator*

Littleton
Bush, Stanley Giltner *secondary school educator*
Pearlman, Mitzi Ann *elementary education educator*
Rockwell, Kay Anne *elementary education educator*
Wallisch, Carolyn E. *principal*

Longmont
Wetzbarger, Donna Kay *secondary education educator*

Monte Vista
Gabaldon, Paul James *high school principal*
Tillman, John Lee *principal*

Northglenn
Argys, Richard James *secondary education English and social studies educator*
Shaeffer, Thelma Jean *primary school educator*

Parker
Nelson, Paula Morrison Bronson *educator*

Pueblo
Griffith, Mary C. *community college vice president*
Lindskog, Marjorie Otilda *elementary school educator*
Shirley, Robert Clark *retired university president, strategic planning consultant, educator*
Tipton, Karen *middle school educator*
Vest, Rosemarie Lynn Torres *secondary school educator*

Salida
Rouse, Delmar Leon *school principal*

San Luis
Maldonado, Epifanio Mike *school counselor*

Trinidad
Evans, Gregory *college program administrator*
Palovich, Marilyn Lee *elementary education educator*
Sandoval, Mona Lisa *daycare provider, educator*

Westminster
Eaves, Stephen Douglas *educator, vocational administrator*
Hartman, Susan P(atrice) *adult education administrator*

DISTRICT OF COLUMBIA

Washington
Sullivan, Charles *university dean, educator, author*

HAWAII

Honolulu
Bauer, Mark David *educator*
Blumhardt, Jon Howard *college official*
Eppling, Jacqueline Quon *elementary school educator*
Masters, Elaine *educator, writer*
Mortimer, Kenneth P. *academic administrator*
Pacific, Joseph Nicholas, Jr. *educator*
Pickens, Alexander Legrand *education educator*
Pottenger, Francis Marion, III *education educator*
Souza, Joan of Arc *educational administrator*
Wright, Chatt Grandison *academic administrator*

Kailua Kona
Diama, Benjamin *retired educator, artist, composer, writer*

Kaneohe
Ing, Grace Sachiko Nakamura *elementary education educator*

Kula
Moore, Rosemary Kuulei *headmaster*

Lihue
Shigemoto, April Fumie *English educator secondary school*

Pearl City
Lee, Kenneth *secondary education educator*

Waikoloa
Zuber, Lianne Carol *elementary school educator*

IDAHO

Boise
Andrus, Cecil Dale *academic administrator*
Crane, Charles Arthur *college president*
Ellis-Vant, Karen McGee *elementary and special education educator, consultant*
Griffin, Gloria Jean *elementary school educator*
Griffin, Sylvia Gail *reading specialist*
Hackett, James Albert *university program administrator*
Kaupins, Gundars Egons *education educator*
MacGregor, Sharon Evonne *university official*

Maloof, Giles Wilson *academic administrator, educator, author*
Ruch, Charles P. *academic administrator*
Woodard, Larry L. *college official*

Caldwell
Buzza, Bonnie Wilson *academic administrator*
Hendren, Robert Lee, Jr. *academic administrator*

Coeur D Alene
Dunnigan, Mary Ann *former educational administrator*

Glenns Ferry
Reed, Beverly Jean *special education educator*

Homedale
Bernal, Jolene Christine *education educator*

Idaho Falls
Duncan, Ellen *media generalist*

Lewiston
Duley, Charlotte Dudley *vocational counselor*
Feathers, Elizabeth Kellogg *retired secondary education educator*
Venditti, Phillip Norris *institute president*

Moscow
Hoover, Robert Allan *university president*
Krings, Axel Werner *educator*
Willis, Barry *education educator, writer*

Mountain Home
Graves, Karen Lee *high school counselor*

Mountain Home AFB
Borchert, Warren Frank *elementary education educator*

New Plymouth
Horton, Nadine Rose *school system administrator*

Pocatello
Bowen, Richard Lee *academic administrator, political science educator*
Harris, Larry B. *academic administrator, dean*
Zelus, Paul Robert *education researcher*

Twin Falls
Anderson, Marilyn Nelle *elementary education educator, librarian, counselor*
Arrossa, Molly *middle school educator*

Wallace
Paroni, Genevieve Marie Swick *retired secondary education educator*

MONTANA

Antelope
Olson, Betty Jean *retired elementary education educator*

Bigfork
Keller, Ray B. *counselor*

Billings
Abbott, Patti Marie *middle school educator*
Bryngelson, Jim *educational administrator*
May, Michael Wayne *technical school executive*

Box Elder
Stamper, Edward Zene *foundations and research director*

Bozeman
Malone, Michael Peter *academic administrator, historian*
Monaco, Paul *academic administrator, educator, artist, writer*
Rogstad, Mark Roland *secondary school educator*

Crow Agency
Pease-Pretty On Top, Janine B. *community college administrator*

Great Falls
Gray, Chris Hables *adult education educator, writer*

Hardin
Alvarado, Rebecca Jane *secondary education educator*

Havre
Daehling, William A. *retired academic administrator*
Lanier, William Joseph *college program director*
Verploegen, Lorraine Jean *elementary school educator*

Helena
Crofts, Richard A. *academic administrator*
Duff, Gary Nolan *secondary education educator*
Morton, Claudette *education administrator*
O'Reilly, Frances Louise *academic administrator*

Kalispell
Supola, Susan Lenora *secondary education educator, artist*

Miles City
Emilsson, Elizabeth Maykuth *special education educator*

Missoula
Dennison, George Marshel *academic administrator*

NEVADA

Boulder City
Holmes, BarbaraAnn Krajkoski *secondary education educator*

Carson City
Wadman, William Wood, III *educational director, technical research executive, consulting company executive*

Hawthorne
Graham, Lois Charlotte *retired educator*

Henderson
Burnett, Sandra Jo *primary education educator*

Las Vegas
Gelfer, Jeffrey Ian *early childhood education educator*
Gerye, Robert Allen *secondary school administrator*
Hair, Kittie Ellen *secondary educator*
Harter, Carol Clancey *university president, English language educator*
Joyce, Phyllis Norma *educational administrator*
Pierce, Thresia (Tish) *primary school educator*
Russo, Angela Brown *assistant principal*
Shuman, R(obert) Baird *academic program director, writer, English language educator, educational consultant*

Lovelock
Rowe, Patricia Gene *elementary education educator, recreation director*

North Las Vegas
Moore, Richard *academic administrator*
Sullivan, Debra Kae *elementary education educator*

Reno
Crowley, Joseph Neil *university president, political science educator*
Dale, Debra Eileen *elementary school educator*
Jarvis, Richard S. *academic administrator*
Lord, Jacklynn Jean *student services representative*
McKay, Alice Vitalich *academic administrator*
Walen, Joanne Michele *secondary education educator, consultant*
Whiting, Judith A. *education educator*

NEW MEXICO

Albuquerque
Eastham, Sondra Lee *educational consultant*
Edwards, Louise Wiseman *career counselor, educator*
Howard, Jane Osburn *educator*
Lassen, Betty Jane *educator*
Lattman, Laurence Harold *retired academic administrator*
Miller, Mickey Lester *retired school administrator*
Peck, Richard Earl *academic administrator, playwright, novelist*
Van Why, Rebecca Rivera *retired guidance counselor*

Artesia
Sarwar, Barbara Duce *educational consultant*

Bluewater
Marquez, Martina Zenaida *retired elementary education educator*

Carlsbad
Vuk, Melvin Marvin *college director, educator*

Farmington
Kaul, Emil William (Bill) *director of youth development, educator*

Gallup
Lewis, Lorena Iona *elementary guidance counselor, educator*
Zongolowicz, Helen Michaeline *education and psychology educator*

Las Cruces
Boykin, William Edward *principal*
Devall, Esther Lynn *family and consumer sciences educator*
Gale, Thomas Martin *university dean*
Thayer, Michael J. *secondary education educator*

Las Vegas
Duxler, Michael *educator*

Pecos
Vigil, M(aria) Dolores *secondary education educator*

Portales
Byrnes, Lawrence William *dean*

Rehoboth
Evilsizor, Douglas E. *development director*

Rio Rancho
Meyerson, Barbara Tobias *elementary school educator*
Weber, Alois Hughes *principal*

Santa Fe
Harcourt, Robert Neff *educational administrator, journalist, genealogist*
Kluck, Linda Ann *academic administrator*
Wise, Janet Ann *college official*

Silver City
French, Laurence Armand *social science educator, psychology educator*

Socorro
Lopez, Daniel Heraldo *academic administrator*
Wagoner, Nancy Ann *university admissions executive, writer*

NEW YORK

Buffalo
Riepe, Charleine Williams *educator*

OREGON

Albany
Cazort, Barney Douglas *college counselor*
Link-Jobe, Jannice Louise *education educator*

Ashland
Baird, Susan Elizabeth *secondary education educator, writer*
Brown, James Chandler *college administrator*
Gorne, Ivan LeRoy *academic administrator*
Reno, Stephen Jerome *academic administrator*

Beaverton
Duncan, Richard Fredrick, Jr. *secondary education educator, travel consultant*

Boring
Schlaht, Kimber Lee *childcare provider*
Yatvin, Joanne Ina *school principal*

Corvallis
Arnold, Roy Gary *academic administrator, food science and technology educator*
Byrne, John Vincent *higher education consultant*
Hendricks, Jon Albert *college dean, educator*
Risser, Paul Gillan *academic administrator, botanist*
Verts, Lita Jeanne *university administrator*

Eugene
Barr, Sue *secondary education educator*
Bartlett, Thomas Alva *educational administrator*
Cox, Joseph William *academic administrator*
Frohnmayer, David Braden *university president*
Hawk, Norman Ray *academic administrator, retired*
Mallchok, Jeanne *special education educator*
Matthews, Esther Elizabeth *education educator, consultant*
Metltzoff, Nancy Jean *education educator*
Moseley, John Travis *university administrator, research physicist*
Moskus, Jerry Ray *academic administrator, educator*
Warpinski, Terri L. *academic administrator, artist*

Fairview
Deeder, John Dean *school system administrator*

Florence
Devereux, Barbara L. *elementary school educator*

Lake Oswego
Lenderman, Joanie *elementary education educator*
Meltebeke, Renette *career counselor*

Mcminnville
Howland, Peter McKinnon *academic administrator*

Medford
Weiss, Robert Mark *education administrator*

Newport
Fitzpatrick, Al W. *educator*

North Bend
de Sa e Silva, Elizabeth Anne *secondary school educator*

Portland
Bennett, Charles Leon *vocational and graphic arts educator*
Braun, Stephen Baker *academic administrator*
Campbell, William Joseph *academic director*
Casey, Ann Louise *college administrator*
Fan, Lee Siu *business executive and vocational training program administrator*
Hawkins, Ronald E. *academic administrator, counselor*
Kliewer, Stephen Paul *educator*
Kreinberg, Penelope Pettit *counselor*
Lawrence, Sally Clark *academic administrator*
Leupp, Edythe Peterson *retired education educator, administrator*
Lynch, Nita Marie Smith *vocational curriculum developer*
Martin, Ernest Lee *academic administrator, historian, theologian, writer*
Shaff, Beverly Gerard *educational administrator*
Williams, Evan Thomas *college dean, chemistry educator*
Wilson, Catherine Phillips *elementary education educator*

Roseburg
Johnson, Doris Ann *educational administrator*
Lee, Geraldine Hostetler *retired elementary education educator, shop owner*
Tilson, Daniel *elementary education educator*

Salem
Kearns, Homer H. *school system administrator*
Ray, Brian Daniel *education and science educator*

Siletz
Casey, Darla Diann *elementary school educator*

Sutherlin
Ohm, David Lee *school principal*

Terrebonne
Smith, Janice Alfreda *secondary school educator*

Wilsonville
Talus, Donna J. *educator*

Yachats
Robeck, Mildred Coen *educator, writer*

UTAH

Delta
Nielson, Barbara Broadhead *special education administrator*

Farmington
Flygare, Kathleen Tiffeni *elementary education educator, piano educator*

Hooper
Cornia, Ivan Edward *art educator, curriculum supervisor*

Ivins
McConnell, Dana Lou *middle school educator*

Kearns
De Wreede, Clarice Evans *retired special education educator*

Logan
Smith, Nathan McKay, Jr. *university administrator*

Mount Pleasant
Schade, Wilbert Curtis *educational administrator*

Nephi
Wallace, Lorraine D. *secondary school educator*

Ogden
Eisler, David L. *provost*
Jolovich-Motes, Sondra Lea *principal*
Protzman, Grant Dale *university administrator, state legislator*
Thompson, Paul Harold *university president*

Payson
Burdick, Brenda Lynn *secondary education educator*

Provo
Bateman, Merrill Joseph *university president*
Bowie, George Henry *university official, public relations consultant*
Peterson, Erlend Dean *dean*
Tolman, Marvin Nelson *education educator*
Tunnell, Michael O'Grady *education educator*

Salt Lake City
Bennion, John Warren *urban education educator*
Campbell, Holly Victoria Pink *university administrator*
Henderson, Sharlene Ottesen *special education educator*
Markham, Reed B. *education educator, consultant*
McIntyre, Jerilyn Sue *academic administrator*
Nielsen, Cherie Sue *elementary educator*
Peterson, Chase N. *university president*
Pickering, AvaJane *specialized education facility executive*
Teitelbaum, Lee E. *dean*
Trujillo, Augustine *university administrator*

Sandy
Beckman, Patty Zoe *special education educator, consultant*
Sabey, J(ohn) Wayne *academic administrator, consultant*

South Jordan
Voorhies, Janice Leavitt *secondary education educator*

Vernal
Phillips, Teresa Rae *elementary education educator, researcher*

WASHINGTON

Bellevue
Boxleitner, Linda Schraufnagel *secondary education educator*
Mitchell, Gloria Jean *elementary school principal, educator*

Bellingham
Masland, Lynne S. *university official*
Morse, Karen Williams *academic administrator*
Mueller, Pamela Sue *secondary school educator*
Pierce, George Adams *university administrator, educator*

Bothell
Banks, Cherry Ann McGee *education educator*
Dietzen, Edith Jane *school counselor, educator*
Fortier, Sharon Murphy *special education educator*

Bremerton
Garrison, Eva Heim *school counselor*

Buckley
Wickizer, Cindy Louise *elementary school educator*

Cheney
Carlson, Laurie Marie Winn *educator, writer*

Chimacum
Hollenbeck, Dorothy Rose *special education educator*

College Place
Cross, Nancy Kay *educator*

Edmonds
Carlstrom, R. William *retired special education educator*

Ellensburg
Jones, Gail Kathleen *educational administrator*
Nelson, Ivory Vance *academic administrator*

Elma
Dunn, Jeffrey Scott *secondary education educator*

Everett
Thunder, Spencer K. *retired elementary school principal*

Gig Harbor
Minnerly, Robert Ward *retired headmaster*

Harrah
Schilperoort, Sharon Ann *secondary education educator*

Kenmore
Pizzorno, Joseph Egidio, Jr. *college president*

Kennewick
Knight, Janet Ann *elementary education educator*
Thomas, Alta Parker *secondary school educator*

Kent
Chandler, Karen Regina *career guidance specialist*

Kirkland
Bentz, Penny Lennea *special education educator*
Campbell, Sandra Ruth *English as second language educator*
Stewart, James William *university administrator, minister*
Tyllia, Frank Michael *university official, educator*

Lakewood
Eastby, Ione Bernice *retired counselor*

Mountlake Terrace
Inman, Ana M. Jimenez *secondary education educator*

Oak Harbor
Porter, Edith Priscilla *elementary school educator*

Olympia
Geri, Laurance Rudolph *educator*
Hogan, Nancy Kay *elementary education educator*
Humphrey, Camilla Marie *retired special education educator*
Jervis, Jane Lise *college official, science historian*

Omak
Best, Susan Kimberly *gifted education educator*

Pullman
Bataille, Gretchen *academic administrator*
Smith, Samuel Howard *academic administrator, plant pathologist*

Renton
Walker, Roberta Smyth *school system administrator*

Richland
Haler, Lawrence Eugene *technology educator, councilman*

Seattle
Beaumonte, Phyllis Ilene *secondary school educator*
Brown, Lillie McFall *elementary school principal*
Hall, Wendy Lapic *program director*
Huntsman, Lee *university provost, academic administrator*
Leader, Alan Howard *college dean emeritus*
McCormick, Richard Levis *academic administrator*
Roberts, Helen Hoyt Randall *educator and writer*
Schulte, Henry Gustave *university administrator*
Simmons, George Michael *educational administrator*
Stringer, William Jeremy *university official*
Thompson, Dwight Alan *vocational rehabilitation expert*
Tschernisch, Sergei P. *academic administrator*
Wagness, Lorraine Melva *gifted education educator*

Silverdale
Taatgen, Henderikus Albert *university administrator, educator*

Spokane
Baker, Danial Edwin *director, consultant, pharmacy educator*
Herdrich, M. Susan *educator, writer*
Howell, Donald James *vocational school administrator*
Linn, Diana Patricia *elementary education educator*

Tacoma
Edwards, Lisa Simone *technical college administrator*
Ingram, Artonyon S. *adult basic skills educator*
King, Gundar Julian *retired university dean*
Maloney, Patsy Loretta *university official, nursing educator*
Reisberg, Leon Elton *education educator*

Toppenish
Ross, Kathleen Anne *college president*

Vancouver
Ghormley, William Frederick *elementary school educator, music educator*

Wenatchee
McKinley, Eileen Baldwin *elementary education educator*

White Salmon
Wells, Sally Ann *elementary education educator*

Yakima
Cook, Kay Ellen *remedial programs coordinator*

WEST VIRGINIA

Bethany
Balch, Pamela Mae *education educator*

WISCONSIN

Madison
Becker, Katharine Elizabeth *special education educator*

WYOMING

Casper
Agte, Lloyd Mark *adult education educator*
Matteson, Barbara Ann Vance *secondary education educator*

Centennial
Houston, Jane Hunt *retired educator*

Cheyenne
McDowell, Sherrie Lorraine *secondary education educator*
Rice, Wallace William *secondary education educator*
Weigner, Brent James *secondary education educator*

Cody
Fees, Nancy Fardelius *special education educator*
Soltero, Mary Ann *elementary education educator*

Laramie
Baldwin, Hugh John *dean*
Darnall, Roberta Morrow *academic administrator*
Forster, Bruce Alexander *dean*
Schmitt, Diana Mae *elementary education educator*
Simpson, Peter Kooi *university official*

Riverton
Davis, Pete Benton *vocational school educator, retired*

Rock Springs
Hall, Alice Averette *college administrator, counselor*
Kathka, David Arlin *director educational services*

CANADA

ALBERTA

Calgary
Samuels, Barbara Ann *university administrator, planner, educator, information architect*

BRITISH COLUMBIA

Abbotsford
Stronstad, Roger Jonathan *college administrator*

ADDRESS UNPUBLISHED

Allen, Floyd E. *secondary education educator*
Anderson, Carol Ruth *secondary school educator*
Anderson, Iris Anita *retired secondary education educator*
Apodaca, Michael *elementary educator*
Attig, John Clare *secondary education educator, consultant*
Bachtel, Ann Elizabeth *educational consultant, researcher, educator*
Baker, C. B. *retired day care director, organizer, communicator*
Baker, John Franklin, III *retired educational administrator, author*
Barber, Norma Ann *secondary education educator*
Bartel, Arthur Gabriel *educational administrator, city official*
Barville, Rebecca Penelope *elementary school educator*
Beel, Lorraine Kuhn *tutor*
Behle, J. Gregory *educator*
Beyersdorf, Marguerite Mulloy *educator*
Blummer, Kathleen Ann *counselor*
Boyle, Betsy H. *educational administrator*
Bracco, Gloria Jean *elementary education educator*
Brown, Linda M. *elementary education educator*
Bullock, Molly *retired elementary education educator*
Burroughs, Franklin Troy *academic administrator*
Caldwell, Jo Ann Kennedy *elementary educator*
Camerino, Jay Medina *assistant principal*
Campbell, Carolyn Evans *adult education educator*
Carlin, Betty *educator*
Casper, Gerhard *academic administrator, law educator*
Christensen, Caroline *vocational educator*
Christensen, Stephen D. *academic administrator, educational fund raiser*
Coates, E. Joyce *retired English educator*
Cohen, Shirley Mason *educator, writer, civic worker*
Davis, Jane Anne *preschool educator, writer, poet*
Dey, Carol Ruth *secondary education educator*
Dillard, Teresa Mary *school counselor*
Downey, Scheherazade Shula *academic administrator*
Edwards, Ardis Lavonne Quam *retired elementary education educator*
Esposito, Holly Tyler *secondary education educator*
Fair, Marcia Jeanne Hixson *retired educational administrator*
Fairham-Wheeler, Victoria Ruth Kuhns *secondary education educator*
Fairley, Peter Carlton *secondary education educator*
Fetters, Doris Ann *retired secondary education educator*
Fonoimoana, Roxann Puanani *school district education specialist*
Forney, Ronald Dean *elementary school educator, consultant, educational therapist*
Frey, Katie Manciet *educational administrator*
Frost, Everett Lloyd *academic administrator*
Galloway, Pamela Eilene *university official emeritus*
Garland, Robert Lee *educator, writer*
Giblett, Phylis Lee Walz *middle school educator*
Grabill, James R., Jr. *educator, writer*
Gray, Richard Moss *retired college president*
Griffin, Kenyon Neal *retired academic administrator*
Grishman, Lee Howard *college program administrator*
Haynes, Michael Scott, Sr. *resource specialist*
Hegarty, George John *university president, English educator*
Hill, Craig A. *English educator*
Hoagland, Pamela Redington *educational consultant, administrator*
Hoberecht, Reynotta *school system administrator*
Hughes, Eugene Morgan *university president*
Jerrytone, Samuel Joseph *trade school executive*
Jimmink, Glenda Lee *retired elementary school educator*
Johnson, Annette M. *arts administrator*
Johnson, Kirsten Denise *elementary education educator*
Johnson, Sylvia Sue *university administrator, educator*
Johnson, William Theodore *school system administrator*
Kapelovitz, Abbey Poze *academic administrator*
Keiper, Marilyn Morrison *elementary education educator*
Kilcullen, Carmen Solari *retired elementary education educator*
Kimbrough, Lorelei *elementary education educator*
Kirk, Rea Helene (Rea Helene Glazer) *special education educator*
Knapp, Lonnie Troy *elementary education educator*
Kolb, Dorothy Gong *elementary education educator*
Kormondy, Edward John *university official, biology educator*
Kretzmar, Mary Lynn *vocational education and sign language interpreter, educator*
Lantz, Anna Mae *secondary school educator*
Legington, Gloria R. *middle school educator*
Lindegren, Jack Kenneth *elementary and secondary education educator*
Lynch, Linda Lou *reading and language arts specialist, educator*
Lyne, Dorothy-Arden *educator*
Major, Patrick Webb, III *principal*
Marcus, H. Louise *educator, writer*
Marlatt, Dorothy Barbara *university dean*
Mason, Johanna Hendrika Anneke *retired secondary education educator*
Mastrolia, Lilyan Spitzer *educator*
Matera, Frances Lorine *elementary educator*
Matuszak, David F. *secondary education educator, writer*
McDonald, Mary Kathleen *secondary anatomy and physiology educator*
Meyer, Robert Lee *secondary education educator*
Milanovich, Norma JoAnne *educational company executive*
Miller, Richard Franklin *educational consultant, researcher*
Morales, Sandra Lee *educator*
Nakamoto, Carolyn Matsue *principal*
Naylor, Thomas Everett *account administrator*
Neff, Lester Leroy *administrator, minister*
Nielsen, Vera Bagley *retired teacher, librarian*
Olander, Helen Rinker *retired educator*
Oldham, Elaine Dorothea *retired elementary and middle school educator*
O'Malley, Thomas Patrick *academic administrator*
Polston, Barbara Jean *principal, educational psychologist*
Reece, Geraldine Maxine *elementary education educator*
Reeve, Edgar Gilbert *school counselor*
Reinalda, David Anthony *elementary education educator*
Rice, Condoleezza *academic administrator, political scientist*
Riggs, Lisa Anne *elementary school educator*
Ritchie, Anne *educational administrator*
Robison, Joanne Ahleen *elementary education educator*
Rogers, Marsha Scott *secondary education educator, poet*
Rooney, Peg (Margaret E. Rooney) *vocational education administrator*
Sanchez, Gilbert *retired academic administrator, microbiologist, researcher*
Sanders, Trisha Lynn *middle school educator*
Sasser, Teiko Takizawa *educator*
Schmoldt, Peggy Sue *cosmetology educator*
Sciaroni, Linda Gillingham *high school educator*
Scott, Patricia M. *educator*
Sestini, Virgil Andrew *retired biology educator*
Shagam, Marvin Hückel-Berri *private school educator*
Shaw, Valeen Jones *special education educator, elementary school educator*
Skaggs, Bebe Rebecca Patten *college dean, clergywoman*
Snow, W. Sterling *education educator, sports coach, science educator*
Steinberg, Joan Emily *retired middle school educator*
Striler, Ray *distance education consultant*
Szelenyi, Ivan *educator*
Tarbi, William Rheinlander *secondary education educator, curriculum consultant, educational technology researcher*
Terada, Alice Masae *retired elementary school teacher, writer*
Tonjes, Marian Jeannette Benton *education educator*
Weller, Debra Anne *elementary educator*
Wiebelhaus, Pamela Sue *school administrator, educator*
Wilkening, Laurel Lynn *academic administrator, planetary scientist*
Wilson, Robin Scott *university president, writer*
Young, Joyce Henry *adult education educator, consultant*
Zahner, Dorothy Simkin *elementary education educator*
Zeilinger, Elna Rae *elementary educator, gifted-talented education educator*

ENGINEERING

UNITED STATES

ALASKA

Anchorage
Jumao-as, Alex Baronda *civil engineer*
Pressley, James Ray *electrical engineer*
Thomas, Howard Paul *civil engineer, consultant*
Tompkins, Robert Walter *retired civil engineer*

ARIZONA

Chandler
Fordemwalt, James Newton *microelectronics engineering educator, consultant*
Leckman, Judith Ann *engineering executive*
Myers, Gregory Edwin *aerospace engineer*
Zeilinger, Philip Thomas *aeronautical engineer*

Fort Huachuca
Griswold, Douglas A. *engineer*
Weeks, Robert Lee *electronic engineer, program manager*

Glendale
Harris, Warren Lynn *development engineer*
Landrum, Larry James *computer engineer*

Goodyear
Rao, Jayanth Peechara *mechanical engineer, consultant*

Mesa
Baxter, Gene Kenneth *mechanical engineer, company executive*
Cousins, William Thomas *mechanical engineer*

Paradise Valley
Field, Charles William *metallurgical engineer, small business owner, consultant*

Phoenix
Amavisca, Edward Dean *electrical engineer*
Bachus, Benson Floyd *mechanical engineer, consultant*
Blevins, Willard Ahart *electrical engineer*
Cazier, Barry James *electrical engineer, software developer*
Chisholm, Tom Shepherd *environmental engineer*
Davis, Leo Russell *safety engineer*
Fullmer, Steven Mark *systems engineer*
Goldman, Charles *electromechanical engineer*
Hamilton, Darden Cole *flight test engineer*
Jorgensen, Gordon David *engineering company executive*
Kaliszek, Andrew Wojciech *mechanical engineer*
Leeland, Steven Brian *electronics engineer*
Nishioka, Teruo (Ted Nishioka) *electrical engineer*
Struble, Donald Edward *mechanical engineer*
Watson, Harold George *ordnance company executive, mechanical engineer*
Zweifel, Terry L. *aeronautical engineer, researcher*

Prescott Valley
Wynn, Robert Raymond *retired engineer, consultant*

Scottsdale
Bodensieck, Ernest Justus *mechanical engineer*
Eckelman, Richard Joel *engineering specialist*
Gookin, Thomas Allen Jaudon *civil engineer*
Kiehn, Mogens Hans *aviation engineer, consultant*
Lee, Dennis Turner *civil engineer, construction executive*
Newman, Marc Alan *electrical engineer*
Ngo, David Quat *electrical engineer*
Ragland, Samuel Connelly *industrial engineer, management consultant*
Roberts, Peter Christopher Tudor *engineering executive*

Sedona
Silvern, Leonard Charles *retired engineering executive*

Sun City West
Coté, Ralph Warren, Jr. *mining engineer, nuclear engineer*

Tempe
Burg, Jeffrey Howard *technology company executive*
Collins, Richard Augustine *mechanical engineer*
Doyle, Michael Phillip *civil engineer*
Passlack, Matthias *electrical engineer, researcher*
Rusnock, Karl Joseph *computer engineer*
Si, Jennie *engineering educator*
Stephenson, Frank Alex *engineer, consultant*
Tychowski, Christopher Roman *engineer*

Tucson
Arnell, Walter James William *mechanical engineering educator, consultant*
Brooks, Donald Lee *civil engineering and scientific consulting firm executive*
Brunton, Daniel William *mechanical engineer*
Buras, Nathan *hydrology and water resources educator*
Coates, Wayne Evan *agricultural engineer*
Davis, Roswita Beate *architectural engineer*
Eigel, James Anthony *environmental engineer*
Gill, Rebecca LaLosh *aerospace engineer*
Jones, Roger Clyde *retired electrical engineering educator*
Mitchell, Robert Campbell *nuclear consultant*
Oschmann, Jacobus Marinus, Jr. *optical systems engineer, consultant*
Roberts, Rollin Walter *metallurgical engineer, executive, consultant*
Sells, Kevin Dwayne *marine engineer*
Slack, Donald Carl *agricultural engineer, educator*

Vail
Hunnicutt, Robert William *engineer*

CALIFORNIA

Agoura Hills
Hokana, Gregory Howard *engineering executive*

Alpine
Doliber, Darrel Lee *consultant, design engineer*
Roberts, Dwight Loren *engineering consultant, novelist*

Alta Loma
Bordner, Gregory Wilson *chemical engineer*
Schwarz, Joseph Richard *engineering manager*

Altadena
Mizuki, Brian Todd *video engineer*

Anaheim
Kimme, Ernest Godfrey *communications engineer*
Schirm, Louis, IV *digital signal processing systems engineer*
Scott, Edward William *software engineer*
Watson, Oliver Lee, III *aerospace engineering manager*

Arcadia
Broderick, Donald Leland *electronics engineer*
Massier, Paul Ferdinand *mechanical engineer*

Auburn
Sun, Haiyin *optical engineer, educator*

Rancho Mirage
Copperman, William H. *value engineer, consultant*
Kramer, Gordon *mechanical engineer*

Rancho Palos Verdes
Serafini, Victor Renato *aerospace engineer*

Redondo Beach
Buchta, Edmund *engineering executive*
Hughes, James Arthur *electrical engineer*
Madden, James Gregory (Greg) *electrical engineer*
Tan, F. Dong *electronic engineer*

Redwood City
Herrin, Stephanie Ann *retired aerospace engineer*

Ridgecrest
Pearson, John *mechanical engineer*

Riverside
Miskus, Michael Anthony *electrical engineer*

Rocklin
Tovar, Nicholas Mario *mechanical engineer*

Rodeo
Emmanuel, Jorge Agustin *chemical engineer, environmental consultant*

Rohnert Park
Lord, Harold Wilbur *electrical engineer, electronics consultant*

Rolling Hills Estates
Diaz-Zubieta, Agustin *nuclear engineer, executive*
Wong, Sun Yet *engineering consultant*

Sacramento
Carleone, Joseph *aerospace executive*
Collins, William Leroy *telecommunications engineer*
Cross, Bryan Robert Kevin *software engineer*
Forsyth, Raymond Arthur *civil engineer*
Lathi, Bhagawandas Pannalal *electrical engineering educator*
Osborn, John Follett *engineer, editor*
Simeroth, Dean Conrad *chemical engineer*
Soriano, Bernard C. *engineering executive*

Salida
Munson, William Crawford, III *civil engineer*

San Bernardino
Bauer, Steven Michael *cost containment engineer*
French, Kirby Allan *transportation engineer, computer programmer*
Kirkland, Bertha Theresa *project engineer*

San Carlos
Symons, Robert Spencer *electronic engineer*

San Clemente
Cramer, Eugene Norman *nuclear power engineer, computer educator*
Slagle, Kenneth A. *engineering manager*

San Diego
Aleszka, James Charles *metallurgical and corrosion engineer*
Anderson, Karl Richard *aerospace engineer, consultant*
Arnold, Terry Sutton *security engineer executive*
Beyster, John Robert *engineering company executive*
Bhattacharjee, Subrata *mechanical engineering educator*
Burke, Arthur Thomas *engineering consultant*
Chen, Carlson S., Sr. *mechanical engineer*
Chen, Kao *consulting electrical engineer*
Crook, Sean Paul *aerospace systems program manager*
Dabiri, Ali *mechanical engineer, researcher*
Dutta, Partha *engineer*
Fay, Gerard William *quality assurance professional*
Geer, Derek Hunter *electronic engineer, musician*
Gray, Gavin Campbell, II *computer information engineer, computer consultant*
Hanna, Nabil *biomedical engineer*
Hills, Linda Launey *advisory systems engineer*
Huang, Chien Chang *electrical engineer*
Kropotoff, George Alex *civil engineer*
Lee, Long Chi *electrical engineering and chemistry educator*
Lutz, Jeffrey Christian *aerospace engineer*
McLeod, John Hugh, Jr. *mechanical and electrical engineer*
Paget, John Arthur *mechanical engineer*
Schryver, Bruce John *safety engineer*
Sell, Robert Emerson *electrical engineer*
Sheaffer, Richard Allen *electrical engineer*
Smith, Steven Cole *engineering process consultant*
Tom, Lawrence *engineering executive*
Tricoles, Gus Peter *electromagnetic engineer, physicist, consultant*
Wallace, Robert Joseph *systems engineer*
Wong, Clement Po-Ching *nuclear engineer*
Youngs, Jack Marvin *cost engineer*

San Dimas
Zhang, Guotai *process engineer, researcher, ethylene furnace specialist*

San Fernando
Bridges, Robert McSteen *mechanical engineer*

San Francisco
Barndollar, Donald Lee *engineering professional*
Bechtel, Riley Peart *engineering company executive*
Bechtel, Stephen Davison, Jr. *engineering company executive*
Brooks, William George *aeronautical engineer*
Engelmann, Rudolph Herman *electronics consultant*
Kam, James Ting *scientist, engineer, consultant*
Luft, Rene Wilfred *civil engineer*
Marshall, John Paul *broadcast technologist*
Shushkewich, Kenneth Wayne *structural engineer*
Smith, Bernard Joseph Connolly *civil engineer*
Tarakji, Ghassan *engineering educator*
Vreeland, Robert Wilder *electronics engineer*
Zacher, Edwin G. *structural engineer*

San Jose
Carlsen, John Richard *engineer*
Chandramouli, Ramamurti *electrical engineer*
Contos, Paul Anthony *engineer, investment consultant*
Dennison, Ronald Walton *engineer*
Duong, Tony *electrical engineer, consultant*
Erickson, Calvin Howard *computer systems engineer*
Gifford, Christopher Scott *electronic design engineer*
Gill, Hardayal Singh *electrical engineer*
Gopalakrishnan, Sudhakar *engineer*
Haque, Mohammed Shahidul *electrical engineer*
Hoang, Loc Bao *electrical engineer*
Hodgson, Gregory Bernard *software systems architect*
Huang, Francis Fu-Tse *mechanical engineering educator*
Israel, Paul Neal *computer design engineer, author*
Korsunsky, Mordko Isaakovitch *mechanical engineer*
Lewis, William Jeffrey *engineering executive*
Lin, Xi-Wei *electronics engineer*
Mittal, Manmohan *design and technology engineer*
Morimoto, Carl Noboru *computer system engineer, crystallographer*
Sankar, Subramanian Vaidya *aerospace engineer*
Shaw, Charles Alden *engineering executive*
Sin, Tommy Ka-Keung *engineering/business executive*
Tran, Jack Nhuan Ngoc *gas and oil reservoir engineer*
Wu, Dongping (Don Wu) *optical and electrical engineer*
Yan, Hong-Cheng *electrical engineer educator*
Ye, Jun *electrical engineer*

San Juan Capistrano
Chang, Zhao Hua *biomedical engineer*
Korb, Robert William *former materials and processes engineer*

San Leandro
Kint, Arne Tonis *industrial engineer, mechanical engineer*
Williams, Isabel Mafnas *computer systems engineer, computer consultant*

San Lorenzo
Thompson, Lyle Eugene *electrical engineer*

San Luis Obispo
Corovic, Michael M. *engineering educator, consultant*
Cummings, Russell Mark *aerospace engineer, educator*
Hoffmann, Jon Arnold *aeronautical engineer, educator*
Niku, Saeed Benjamin *engineering educator*

San Luis Rey
Melbourne, Robert Ernest *civil engineer*

San Marcos
Jeffredo, John Victor *aerospace engineer, manufacturing company executive, inventor*

San Pedro
Ellis, George Edwin, Jr. *chemical engineer*

San Rafael
Taylor, Irving *mechanical engineer, consultant*
Wright, Frederick Herman Greene, II *computer systems engineer*

San Ramon
Schlitt, William Joseph, III *metallurgical engineer*

Santa Ana
Bricken, Gordon Leonard *acoustical engineer*
Do, Tai Huu *mechanical engineer*
Zabsky, John Mitchell *engineering executive*

Santa Barbara
Crispin, James Hewes *engineering and construction company executive*
Duncan, Andrew Malcolm *engineer*
Gilbert, Paul Thomas *chemical development engineer*
Meriam, James Lathrop *mechanical engineering educator*
Mitra, Sanjit Kumar *electrical and computer engineering educator*
Ring, Christopher Lee *software engineer*

Santa Clara
Falgiano, Victor Joseph *electrical engineer, consultant*
Ghanti, Chandra Ratilal *engineering executive*
Jung, Henry Hung *mechanical engineer*
Kershaw, David Joseph *process engineer*
Olvera, Carlos Nelson *mechanical engineer, executive*
Philipossian, Ara *engineer, semiconductor process technologist*
Vu, Quat Thuong *electrical engineer*
Williams, Richard Kent *electrical engineer*

Santa Clarita
Granlund, Thomas Arthur *engineering executive, consultant*

Santa Monica
Martin, George *consulting engineer*
McGuire, Michael John *environmental engineer*
Thomas, Frank Joseph *retired nuclear engineer*

Saratoga
Brown, Paul Fremont *aerospace engineer, educator*
Dix, Gary Errol *engineering executive*
Sepehri, Ron Mehran *materials engineer*

Solana Beach
Bubien, M. Stanley *software engineer*

Sonoma
Sasaki, Yasunaga Tito *engineering executive*

South Pasadena
Glad, Dain Sturgis *retired aerospace engineer, consultant*

Stanford
Cox, Donald Clyde *electrical engineering educator*
[illegible]
Nelson, Drew Vernon *mechanical engineering educator*
Ott, Wayne Robert *environmental engineer*
Parkinson, Bradford Wells *astronautical engineer, educator*

Sunnyvale
Bercel, Danielle Suzanne *software engineer, artist*
Cao, Jie-Yuan *electronics engineer, researcher*
Chee, Uriel Hiram *biomedical engineer*
Laurance, Mark Rodney *applications engineer, entrepreneur*
Ma, Fengchow Clarence *agricultural engineering consultant*
Mulvey, Gerald John *telecommunication engineering administrator, meteorologist educator*
Peline, Val P. *engineering executive*
Petersen, Kurt Edward *electrical engineer, researcher, entrepreneur*
Poon, William Wai-Lik *industrial engineer, administrator*
Puckett, W. Greer *engineer*
Robbins, James Edward *electrical engineer*
Saluja, Sundar S. *international engineering consultant*
Venkateshwaran, Raghu *engineer*
Wu, Dongdong *optical engineer*
Yin, Gerald Zheyao *technology and business executive*

Sylmar
Madni, Asad Mohamed *engineering executive*

Tarzana
Portney, Joseph Nathaniel *aerospace executive*

Temecula
Petersen, Vernon Leroy *communications and engineering corporations executive*

Thousand Oaks
Attiyeh, Robert S. *retired biotechnology executive*
Deisenroth, Clinton Wilbur *electrical engineer*
Wiktorowicz, Andrew Charles *consultant technology-based business development*

Torrance
Gran, Robert *engineering company executive*
Liu, Gang Kevin *engineering executive*
Mende, Howard Shigeharu *mechanical engineer*
Sorstokke, Susan Eileen *systems engineer*
Wylie, Richard Thornton *aerospace engineer*
Yoon, Sewang *engineering executive*

Tracy
Nelson, Kenneth Arthur *electrical engineer*

Trona
Trujillo-Cuthrell, Loretta Marie *chemical engineer*

Tustin
Dorneman, Robert Wayne *manufacturing engineer*

Vacaville
Wilcox, Edward R. *engineering executive*

Van Nuys
Lagasse, Bruce Kenneth *structural engineer*

Ventura
Matley, Benvenuto Gilbert (Ben Matley) *computer engineer, educator, consultant*

Walnut
Caudron, John Armand *accident reconstructionist, technical forensic investigator*

Walnut Creek
Burgarino, Anthony Emanuel *environmental engineer, consultant*
Van Maerssen, Otto L. *aerospace engineer, consulting firm executive*

Warner Springs
Scott, Larry *electronics engineer*

Westminster
Armstrong, Gene Lee *systems engineering consultant, retired aerospace company executive*
Nguyen, Lan Kim *software engineer*

Woodland Hills
Amerine, Anne Follette *aerospace engineer*
Higginbotham, Lloyd William *mechanical engineer*
Kohl, Arthur L. *consulting chemical engineer, writer*
Yackle, Albert Reustle *aeronautical engineer*

COLORADO

Arvada
Loomis, Christopher Knapp *metallurgical engineer*
Wetch, Lyle Jeffrey *electrical engineer*

Aurora
Holien, David L. *engineering executive*

Boulder
Breddan, Joe *systems engineering consultant*
Jackson, William Charles *spacecraft systems engineer*
Kompala, Dhinakar Sathyanathan *chemical engineering educator, biochemical engineering researcher*
Uberoi, Mahinder Singh *aerospace engineering educator*
Waters, M. Bruce *engineering technician*

Broomfield
Fuhrman, Kendall Nelson *software engineer*

Castle Rock
Yager, Walter Stuart *aerospace engineer*

Colorado Springs
Borrego, Jesus Garcia *engineer*
Carroll, David Todd *computer engineer*
Chapman, Richard Grady *engineer*
Davis, Alan Mark *software engineering educator*
[illegible]
James, Wayne Edward *electrical engineer*
Keen, Ronald Lee *engineer, retired career officer*
Littlejohn, John Joseph *petroleum engineer*
McMillan, Larry Donald *engineering executive*
Sherman, Donald H. *civil engineer*
White, Gayle Clay *aerospace company executive*

Conifer
Powers, Edwin Malvin *consulting engineer*

Craig
Violette, Glenn Phillip *construction engineer*

Denver
Bogart, Frank Jeffrey *system and product planning engineer*
Colvis, John Paris *aerospace engineer, mathematician, scientist*
East, Donald Robert *civil engineer*
Ferguson, Lloyd Elbert *manufacturing engineer*
Mehring, Clinton Warren *engineering executive*
Riese, Arthur Carl *environmental engineering company executive, consultant*
Young, Lester Rex *engineering and construction company executive*
Ziernicki, Richard Mieczyslaw *engineering firm executive*

Durango
Langoni, Richard Allen *civil engineer*

Englewood
Adams, Shad Ardis *communication technician*
Beck, John Craig *industrial hygienist*
Bingham, Paris Edward, Jr. *electrical engineer, computer consultant*

Fort Collins
Jayasumana, Anura Padmananda *electrical engineering educator*
Mesloh, Warren Henry *civil and environmental engineer*
Rames, Douglas Dwight *civil engineer*

Golden
Bicknell, Barbara Ann *mechanical engineer, executive, consultant*
Chung, Jin Soo *ocean mining and offshore engineer*
Clausen, Bret Mark *industrial hygienist, safety professional*
Davenport, Roger Lee *research engineer*
Ervin, Patrick Franklin *nuclear engineer*
Gupta, Bimleshwar Prasad *mechanical engineer, manager*
Rozgonyi, Tibor George *mining engineer*

Grand Junction
Gardner, Arthur Speedie *engineering executive*

Greenwood Village
Peterson, Ralph R. *engineering executive*
Wallace, William Arthur, Jr. *environmental engineering executive*

Lafayette
Middlebrooks, Eddie Joe *environmental engineer*

Lakewood
Li, ChiaYang *environmental engineer*
Lu, Paul Haihsing *mining engineer, geotechnical consultant*

Lamar
Hourieh, Houssin Ali *electrical engineer*

Littleton
Brychel, Rudolph Myron *engineer, consultant*
Harney, Patricia Rae *nuclear analyst*
Montgomery, Robert Louis *chemical engineer*
Paredes, Bert (Norbert Paredes) *computer systems engineer*
Tom, Creighton Harvey *aerospace engineer, consultant*

Longmont
Muench, Lothar Wilhelm *electrical engineer, consultant*

Louisville
Donze, Jerry Lynn *electrical engineer*

Westminster
Dalesio, Wesley Charles *former aerospace educator*

Wheat Ridge
Scherich, Erwin Thomas *civil engineer, consultant*

HAWAII

Camp H M Smith
Harstad, Mark George *operations research analyst*

Honolulu
Saxena, Narendra K. *marine research educator*
Scofield, Norman William *civil engineer*
Toth, J. *engineering executive, consultant*
Wataru, Weston Yasuo *civil engineer*
White, Gary Richard *electrical engineer*

Kapolei
Manuel, Consorcio Don Cabatingan *mechanical engineer, energy conservationist*

Makawao
Lester, John James Nathaniel, II (Sean Lester) *engineer, environmental analyst, human rights activist*

Mountain View
Peterson, Gerald Joseph *aerospace executive, consultant*

Puunene
Tocho, Lee Frank *mechanical engineer*

Schofield Barracks
Chau, Hung *engineer, educator*

IDAHO

Boise
Nuttall, Michael Lee *engineer, educator*
Parry, Thad B. *process engineer*

Idaho Falls
Daniher, John M. *retired engineer*
Harvego, Edwin Allan *mechanical engineer*
Miller, Gregory Kent *structural engineer*
Paik, Seungho *mechanical engineer*
Williams, Ray Ralph *advisory engineer*

Moscow
Admassu, Wudneh *chemical engineering educator*
Sturgul, John Roman *mining engineering educator*
Young, Jeffrey Lee *electrical engineering educator, consultant*

Pocatello
Bennion, John Stradling *engineering educator, consultant*

Rigby
Peterson, Erle Vidaillet *retired metallurgical engineer*

KANSAS

Valley Falls
Shankland, Kenneth Carl *engineer*

MONTANA

Butte
Maloney, Patrick J. *petroleum engineer, saloon partner*

Helena
Johnson, David Sellie *civil engineer*
Johnson, Qulan Adrian *software engineer*

Missoula
Rice, Steven Dale *electronics educator*

NEVADA

Carson City
Hughes, Robert Merrill *control system engineer*
James, Daryl Norman *environmental engineer*

Las Vegas
Hall, William David *aerospace engineer*
Mulvihill, Peter James *fire protection engineer*
Peng, Zhong *electrical engineer*
Ramos, Albert A. *electrical engineer*
Schwichtenberg, Daryl Robert *drilling engineer*

Minden
Bently, Donald Emery *electrical engineer*
Goldman, Paul *mechanical engineer, researcher*

North Las Vegas
White, Jon McClendon *engineering educator, geologist*

Reno
Byars, Howard Marvin *construction executive, civil engineer, educator*
Whiting, Wallace Burton, II *chemical engineer, educator*

Silver City
Bloyd, Stephen Roy *environmental manager, educator, consultant*

Sparks
Byrd, Ronald Dallas *civil engineer*

NEW MEXICO

Albuquerque
Abdallah, Chaouki Tanios *electrical engineering educator*
Asher, Robert Bernard *aerospace engineer, educator, academic administrator*
Baum, Carl Edward *electromagnetic theorist*
Clark, Arthur Joseph, Jr. *mechanical and electrical engineer*
Eaton, George Wesley, Jr. *petroleum engineer, oil company executive*
Gruchalla, Michael Emeric *electronics engineer*
Haddad, Edward Raouf *civil engineer, consultant*
Hausner, Jerry *electronic engineer, consultant*
Henderson, Christopher Lee *electrical engineer*
Kraye, Sherwin Howard *engineering executive*
Orman, John Leo *software engineer, writer*
Owens, Phillip Reber *mechanical engineer*
Plough, Charles Tobias, Jr. *retired electronics engineering executive*
Prindle, Robert William *geotechnical engineer*
Reed, Ray Paul *engineering mechanics measurement consultant*
Robinett, Rush Daleth, III *robotics research manager*
Torres, Barbara Wood *technical services professional*

Belen
Toliver, Lee *mechanical engineer*

Bosque Farms
Kelly, Brian Matthew *industrial hygienist*

Embudo
Rogers, Benjamin Talbot *consulting engineer, solar energy consultant*

Farmington
Finch, Thomas Wesley *corrosion engineer*
Garretson, Owen Loren *chemical engineer*

Kirtland AFB
Singaraju, Bharadwaja Keshava *electronics engineer*

Las Cruces
Bell, Donald Ray *civil engineer*
Vick, Austin Lafayette *civil engineer*

Los Alamos
Lopez, Joe Jesus *safety engineer*
McDonald, Thomas Edwin, Jr. *electrical engineer*
Perry, Robert Terrell, Jr. *nuclear engineer, consultant*
Sicilian, James Michael *research engineer*
Tallerico, Paul Joseph *electrical engineer*
Van Tuyle, Gregory Jay *nuclear engineer*

Mayhill
Carter, Joy Eaton *electrical engineer, consultant*

Santa Fe
Dempster, William Fred *technical systems consultant*

White Sands Missile Range
Arthur, Paul Keith *electronic engineer*

OREGON

Beaverton
Chartier, Vernon Lee *electrical engineer*
Getreu, Ian E(dwin) *electronics engineer*

Brookings
Nolan, Benjamin Burke *retired civil engineer*

Clatskanie
Forrester, Stan *retired mechanical engineer, writer*

Cloverdale
Jortner, Julius *materials engineer, consultant*

Corvallis
Forbes, Leonard *engineering educator*
Rapier, Pascal Moran *chemical engineer, physicist*
Schlehuser, Todd Charles *industrial engineer*

Eugene
Martin, John Stewart *software engineer*
Ownbey, Pamela Jean *civil engineer, environmental engineer*
Richards, James William *electromechanical engineer*
Williams, Francis Leon *engineering executive*

Hillsboro
Calvert, James Donald, Jr. *civil engineer, researcher, consultant*
Yu, Ben W. *materials engineer*

Junction City
Sharples, Thomas Davy *retired mechanical engineer*

Klamath Falls
Buchanan, Walter Woolwine *electrical engineer, educator and administrator*
Lund, John William *civil engineering educator, researcher*

Lake Oswego
Kovtynovich, Dan *civil engineer*

Medford
Horton, Lawrence Stanley *electrical engineer, apartment developer*

Portland
Antoch, Zdenek Vincent *electrical engineering educator*
Bielagus, Joseph Bruce *mechanical engineer*
Cassidy, Richard Arthur *environmental engineer, governmental water resources specialist*
Couch, Robert G. *civil engineer*
Forsberg, Charles Alton *computer, information systems engineer*
Kennedy, R. Evan *retired structural engineer, executive*
Kocaoglu, Dundar F. *engineering management educator, industrial and civil engineer*
McCoy, Eugene Lynn *civil engineer*
McGarrigle, Roger William *civil and structural engineer*
Perkowski, Marek Andrzej *electrical engineering educator*
Pham, Kinh Dinh *electrical engineer, educator, administrator*
Tracht, David Adams *petroleum products consultant*

Salem
Butts, Edward Perry *civil engineer, environmental consultant*

Wilsonville
Knierim, Robert Valentine *electrical engineer, consultant*

TEXAS

Prairie View
Akujuobi, Cajetan Maduabuchukwu *systems engineer, electrical engineering educator, researcher*

UTAH

Brigham City
Krejci, Robert Henry *aerospace engineer*
Paxton, Ronald Brent *aerospace engineer*

Clearfield
Martin, Perry Clyde *electronic specialist, soil scientist*

Fort Duchesne
Cameron, Charles Henry *petroleum engineer*

Logan
Peralta, Richard Carl *groundwater engineer*

Orem
Nordgren, William Bennett *engineering executive*

Provo
Johnson, Daniel Leon *aeronautical engineer*

Salt Lake City
Anderson, Charles Ross *civil engineer*
De Vries, Kenneth Lawrence *mechanical engineer, educator*
Gandhi, Om Parkash *electrical engineer*
Hansen, Rex Cossey *mechanical engineer*
Hwu, Ruey-Jen Jennifer *electrical engineering educator, researcher*
Judd, Thomas Eli *electrical engineer*
Kopeček, Jindřich *biomedical scientist, biomaterials and pharmaceutics educator*
Lazzi, Gianluca *electronics engineer, researcher*
Ring, Terry Artjur *engineering educator*
Silver, Barnard Joseph Stewart *mechanical and chemical engineer, consultant, inventor*
Zeamer, Richard Jere *engineer, executive*

Sandy
Burchell, Paul William *petroleum engineer*

South Weber
Calder, Robert Mac *aerospace engineer*

WASHINGTON

Auburn
Duhnke, Robert Emmet, Jr. *retired aerospace engineer*
Westbo, Leonard Archibald, Jr. *electronics engineer*
Whitmore, Donald Clark *retired engineer*

Bainbridge Island
Whitener, Philip Charles *aeronautical engineer, consultant*

Bellevue
Erickson, Virginia Bemmels *chemical engineer*
Hibbard, Richard Paul *industrial ventilation consultant, lecturer*
Parks, Donald Lee *mechanical engineer, human factors engineer*
Wright, Theodore Otis *forensic engineer*

Bellingham
Albrecht, Albert Pearson *electronics engineer, consultant*
Johnstone, Kenneth Ernest *electronics and business consultant*

Black Diamond
Morris, David John *mining engineer, consultant, mining executive*

Blaine
Bacani, Nicanor-Guglielmo Vila *civil and structural engineer, consultant*

Bothell
Cao, Thai-Hai *industrial engineer*

Bremerton
Joseph, James Edward *mechanical engineering technician*

Colville
Jones, Randy Allen *electronic communications technician*

Edmonds
Peckol, James Kenneth *consulting engineer*

Federal Way
Studebaker, Irving Glen *mining engineering consultant*

Kelso
Vincent, Steve *environmental engineer*

Kennewick
Henager, Charles Henry *civil engineer*
Ziada, Hassan Higazi *mechanical engineer, educator*

Mercer Island
Bridgforth, Robert Moore, Jr. *aerospace engineer*

Mill Creek
Bloxom, David Megrath *electrical and control systems engineer*

Mukilteo
Bohn, Dennis Allen *electrical engineer, executive*

Olympia
Saari, Albin Toivo *electronics engineer*

Pullman
Guzman, Armando *electrical research engineer*
Scheer, Gary Werner *electrical engineer*

Redmond
Lane, James F. *software engineer*
Willard, H(arrison) Robert *electrical engineer*

Richland
Khaleel, Raziuddin *groundwater hydrologist*
Lutter, Delores Kay *environmental engineer*
Piper, Lloyd Llewellyn, II *engineer, government and service industry executive*
Schwinkendorf, Kevin Neil *nuclear engineer*
Vodopest, Edward L. *mechanical engineer*

Seattle
Addison, Wallace Lloyd *aerospace engineer*
Bates, Dwight Lee *mechanical engineer*
Bishop, Forrest Frederick *engineering executive*
Cal, Clarence Adam, Sr. *aerospace engineer*
Fay, Christopher Wayne *mechanical engineer, consultant*
Grisham, Andrew Fletcher *aerospace engineer, consultant*
Hom, Richard Yee *research engineer*
Hoyt, Robert Preis *astronautical engineer, glass artist*
Ii, Jack Morito *aerospace engineer*
Kim, Yongmin *electrical engineering educator*
Kinnison, Harry Austin *transportation engineer*
Kramlich, John Charles *chemical engineer, educator*
Lall, Vivek *aerospace engineer, educator*
Lewis, Mark Richard *aerospace engineer, educator*
Olson, Ronald Charles *aerospace executive*
Palao, Enrique Henry *electrical engineer*
Rudolph, Thomas Keith *aerospace engineer*
Scott, Amy Lynne *engineer*
Weidner, Mark *environmental research executive*
Wood, Stuart Kee *retired engineering manager*
Yee, Hsian Pei *electrical engineering executive*

Snohomish
Meister, John Edward, Jr. *consultant, technical educator, systems analyst*

South Bend
Heinz, Roney Allen *civil engineering consultant*

Spokane
Maus, John Andrew *computer systems engineer*
Nandagopal, Mallur R. *engineer*

Sunnyside
Capener, Regner Alvin *electronics engineer, minister, author, inventor*

Vancouver
Hofmann, Peter Ludwig *engineering executive, retired*

Woodinville
McGavin, Jock Campbell *airframe design engineer*

Woodland
Mairose, Paul Timothy *mechanical engineer, consultant*

Yakima
LaFontaine, Thomas E. *chemical engineer*

WYOMING

Casper
Hinchey, Bruce Alan *environmental engineering company executive*

Gillette
Sharp, Pamela Ann *quality assurance engineer*
Wagner, Ronald Dean *petroleum engineer*

Laramie
Stewart, Larry Ray *engineer, financial director, quality consultant*

Riverton
Pursel, Harold Max, Sr. *mining engineer, civil engineer, architectural engineer*

CANADA

ALBERTA

Calgary
Farries, John Keith *petroleum engineering company executive*

Edmonton
Morgenstern, Norbert Rubin *civil engineering educator*

BRITISH COLUMBIA

Victoria
Esmailzadeh, Ebrahim *mechanical engineering educator, consultant*

AUSTRALIA

Indoorpilly
Pohl, John Henning *chemical engineering educator*

SAUDI ARABIA

Jubail
Cross, Glenn Laban *engineering executive, development planner*

ADDRESS UNPUBLISHED

Alzofon, Frederick Ellis *retired optics engineer*
Ancell, William Joseph *civil and environmental engineer*
Ansell, George Stephen *retired metallurgical engineering educator, academic administrator*
Biggers, Walter David *mechanical engineer*
Bollinger, Kenneth John *aerospace engineer, computer and space scientist*
Brown, Ronald Malcolm *engineering corporation executive*
Carroll, Philip Joseph *engineering company executive*
Chance, Kenneth Donald *engineer*
Cheng, Wen-Hao *process engineer*
Coble, Hugh Kenneth *engineering and construction company executive*
Constant, Clinton *chemical engineer, consultant*
Cooper, Austin Morris *chemist, chemical engineer, consultant, researcher*
Cummins, Nancyellen Heckeroth *electronics engineer*
Dani, Ashay Arvind *materials engineer*
Dietz, Patricia Ann *engineering administrator*
Divine, Theodore Emry *electrical engineer*
Dong, Zhaoqin *materials and testing engineer, researcher*
Dycus, Terry Lee *engineer*

Ellington, James Willard *mechanical design engineer, retired*
Fowlkes, Donald Irwin *mechanical engineer*
Fritcher, Earl Edwin *civil engineer, consultant*
Goetzel, Claus Guenter *metallurgical engineer*
Gray, George Edward *transportation planner, engineer, consultant*
Holton, William Chester *engineer, consultant*
Johnson, Stewart Willard *civil engineer*
Kahn, Irwin William *industrial engineer*
Kersey, Terry L(ee) *astronautical engineer*
Ketchum, Milo Smith *civil engineer*
Kimbriel-Eguia, Susan *engineering planner*
Koltai, Stephen Miklos *mechanical engineer, consultant, economist, writer, educator*
Krause, Keith Winston *quality engineer*
Lara, Tony Richard *industrial engineer, consultant*
Lie, Yu-Chun Donald *electrical engineer*
MacDonough, Robert Howard *retired consulting engineer, tax consultant*
Meunier, Robert Raymond *research electrical engineer, optical engineer*
Moorman, Bridget Anne *clinical systems engineer*
Mortimer, David William *communications engineer*
Navickas, John *fluid dynamics engineer, researcher, consultant*
Niclas, Karl Bernhard *electronics engineer*
Nyman, David Harold *retired nuclear engineer*
Parker, William Elbridge *consulting civil engineer*
Peck, Joan Kay *systems engineer*
Peters, Douglas Cameron *mining engineer, geologist*
Pezeshki, Kambiz A. *metallurgical engineer*
Pi, Wen-Yi Shih *aircraft company engineer, researcher*
Ravichandran, Rajamiyer V. *structural engineer*
Rentz, William Oliphant *retired environmental engineer, consultant*
Salamon, Miklos Dezso Gyorgy *mining engineer, educator*
Savrun, Ender *engineering executive, researcher, engineer*
Seldner, Betty Jane *environmental engineer, consultant, aerospace company executive*
Siyan, Karanjit Saint Germain Singh *software engineer*
Skeels, Stephen Glenn *civil engineer*
Stavenger, Paul Lewis *chemical engineer*
Stiglich, Jacob John, Jr. *engineering consultant*
Stroud, John Franklin *engineering educator, scientist*
Sun, George Chi *chemical engineering executive, consultant*
Tellington, Wentworth Jordan *engineer*
Vobejda, William Frank *aerospace engineer*
Walasek, Otto Frank *chemical engineer, biochemist, photographer*
Wayman, Morris *chemical engineering educator, consultant*
White, Charles Olds *aeronautical engineer*
Williams, Howard Walter *aerospace engineer, executive*
Williams, Ronald Oscar *systems engineer*
Williams-Lohmar, Judith Ann *technical and engineering services company executive*
Willis, André Maurice *electrical engineer, computing service executive*
Willis, Selene Lowe *electrical engineer, software consultant*
Wilson, Gary Thomas *engineering executive*
Wilson, Melvin Edmond *civil engineer*
Wintle, Rosemarie *bio-medical electronic engineer*
Woodward, Clinton Benjamin, Jr. *civil engineering educator*
Wu, Rao-Hsien Ray *engineering consultant*
Zeitler, Bill Lorenz *aviation engineer*
Ziaka-Vasileiadou, Zoe Dimitrios *chemical engineer*

FINANCE: BANKING SERVICES. *See also* FINANCE: INVESTMENT SERVICES.

UNITED STATES

ALASKA

Anchorage
Harris, Roger J. *mortgage company executive, entrepreneur*
Rasmuson, Elmer Edwin *banker, former mayor*
Reed, Frank Metcalf *bank executive*

ARIZONA

Gilbert
Duran, Michael Carl *bank executive*

Phoenix
Wilson, Robert Sidney *banker*

Prescott
Moore, Elizabeth Jane *banker*

Scottsdale
Carpenter, Peter Rockefeller *bank executive*

Tucson
Barrios, John Anthony *bank official*
Pedolsky, Alan Robert *revenue officer*
Sniezek, Patrick William *real estate loan officer*

CALIFORNIA

Alhambra
Tang, Tom *banking executive*

Burlingame
Eckersley, Norman Chadwick *banker*

Crestline
Holloway, Cindy *mortgage company executive*

Covina
Morgan, Charles Edward Philip *bank executive*

Fairfax
Delaney, Marion Patricia *bank executive*

Glendale
Trafton, Stephen J. *bank executive*

Huntington Beach
MacCauley, Hugh Bournonville *banker*

Irvine
Kuhn, Robert Lawrence *investment banker, corporate financier, strategist, author, educator*

Irwindale
Rinehart, Charles R. *savings and loan association executive*

La Jolla
Angotti, Antonio Mario *international merchant, banker*

Laguna Hills
Pelton, Harold Marcel *mortgage broker*

Long Beach
Keller, J(ames) Wesley *credit union executive*

Los Angeles
Brown, Donald W. *banker*
Hilliard, Charles Stanley *investment banker*
McLarnan, Donald Edward *banker, corporation executive*
Van Asperen, Morris Earl *banker*

Monterey Park
Crawford, Philip Stanley *bank executive*

Oakland
Sandler, Herbert M. *savings and loan association executive*
Sandler, Marion Osher *savings and loan association executive*

Palo Alto
Cotsakos, Christos Michael *internet financial services company executive*

Pebble Beach
Burkett, William Andrew *banker*

Piedmont
Hoover, Robert Cleary *retired bank executive*

Playa Del Rey
Blomquist, Carl Arthur *medical and trust company executive, insurance executive*

Rancho Cordova
Ling, Robert Malcolm *banker, publishing executive*

Rancho Cucamonga
Horton, Michael L. *mortgage company executive, publishing executive*

Riverside
Watkin, Virginia Ruth *banker*

Sacramento
Waller, Larry Gene *mortgage banking executive*

San Diego
Sugihara, George *banker, oceanography educator*

San Francisco
Dinkelspiel, Paul Gaines *investment banking and public financial consultant*
Enslow, Robert Haven *merchant banker*
Gillette, Frankie Jacobs *retired savings and loan executive, social worker, government administrator*
Hazen, Paul Mandeville *banker*
Jackson, Ronald *bank examiner*
Lee, Pamela Anne *bank executive, accountant, business analyst*
Oliver, John Edward *bank strategic management and training consultant*
Peters, Raymond Robert *bank executive*
Rosenberg, Richard Morris *banker*
Rowe, David Mumford *commercial bank officer*
Trowbridge, Thomas, Jr. *mortgage banking company executive*
Vogt, Evon Zartman, III (Terry Vogt) *merchant banker*
Yao, Hilda Maria Hsiang *banker, strategic planner*

San Mateo
Douglass, Donald Robert *banker*

Santa Monica
Mortensen, William S. *banking executive*
Uberstine, Mitchell Neil *bank executive*

Stockton
Bonell, Paul Ian *credit union executive*

Tracy
Adams, Dianne F. *bank executive*

Turlock
Wallström, Wesley Donald *bank executive*

Woodland Hills
Floyd, Brett Alden *mortgage banker*

COLORADO

Denver
Grant, William West, III *banker*
Lerthson Blume T. *financial services executive*
Steitz, William Warren *bank executive*

Englewood
Corboy, James McNally *investment banker*

Hotchkiss
Fox, Maxine Randall *banker*

Greenwood Village
Davidson, John Robert (Jay) *banking executive*

Highlands Ranch
Hoover, Gary Lynn *banker*

HAWAII

Honolulu
Dods, Walter Arthur, Jr. *bank executive*
Hoag, John Arthur *retired bank executive*
Johnson, Lawrence M. *banker*
Keir, Gerald Janes *banker*
Stephenson, Herman Howard *retired banker*
Wong, Henry Li-Nan *bank executive, economist*

Kealakekua
Asam, Michael Evans *credit union administrator*

IDAHO

Eagle
Tschacher, Darell Ray *mortgage banking executive*

NEVADA

Las Vegas
Thomas, Keith Vern *bank executive*

Reno
Tuxon, Linda Louise *banking officer*

NEW MEXICO

Albuquerque
Constantineau, Constance Juliette *retired banker*
Frost, W. Gregory *mortgage company executive*

Deming
Rogers, Alice Louise *retired bank executive, writer, researcher*

OREGON

Eugene
Drennan, Michael Eldon *banker*

Portland
Jensen, Edmund Paul *retired bank holding company executive*

UTAH

Park City
Montgomery, James Fischer *savings and loan association executive*

Salt Lake City
Eccles, Spencer Fox *banker*
Simmons, Roy William *banker*

WASHINGTON

Mill Creek
Holmstrom, David Edwin Arthur *mortgage banking executive, consultant*

Oak Harbor
Piercy, Gordon Clayton *bank executive*

Seattle
Berg, Margarete Claire *banker*
Campbell, Robert Hedgcock *investment banker, lawyer*
Dierich, Darren Roger *controller*
Edgers, Tracy B. *mortgage banker*
Rice, Norman B. *bank executive, former mayor*
Taifel, Roman S. *retired mortgage company executive*
Williams, Walter Baker *mortgage banker*

Sequim
Laube, Roger Gustav *retired trust officer, financial consultant*

Spokane
Jones, D. Michael *banker*

Walla Walla
Oliver, Dan David *banker*

Yakima
Aldridge, Geanie Black *bank executive*

WYOMING

Cheyenne
Knight, Robert Edward *banker*

ADDRESS UNPUBLISHED

Clark, Raymond Oakes *banker*
Coleman, Lewis Waldo *bank executive*
Fielding, Harold Preston *bank executive*
Lankford, Duane Dall *investment banker, mountaineer*
McBratney, Timothy Michael *mortgage banker, researcher*
Stattin, Eric Laurentius *retired savings and loan company executive*
[illegible] *bank executive*

FINANCE: FINANCIAL SERVICES

UNITED STATES

ALASKA

Anchorage
Holfeld, Karl Bradford *accountant*
Illk, Serena Pearl *accountant*
Price, Margaret Ruth *financial services company executive*
Rylander, Robert Allan *financial service executive*

ARIZONA

Eagar
Saunders, James Harwood *accountant*

Gilbert
Larson, Dorothy Ann *business educator*

Lake Havasu City
Aldridge, Cynthia Lou *credit reporting agency executive*

Mesa
Tennison, William Ray, Jr. *financial planner, stockbroker, resort owner*

Peoria
Molinsky, Bert *tax consultant*

Phoenix
Atkins-Mersereau, James Marvin *accountant, educator*
Burg, Jerome Stuart *financial planning consultant*
Gibbs, William Harold *finance company executive*
Hockensmith, Robert Franklin, Jr. *accountant, consultant, financial planner*
Jungbluth, Connie Carlson *tax manager*
Khan, Ahmed Mohiuddin *finance, insurance executive*
Linxwiler, Louis Major, Jr. *retired finance company executive*
Miller, Rosemary Margaret *accountant*
Richardson, Judy McEwen *education administrator, consultant, cartoonist*
Robertson, Richard Curtis *credit union executive*
Ryan, Debbie Kaye *financial planner*
Schabow, John William *accountant*
Yohe, John Spencer *financial analyst*

Prescott
Lovell, Terry Jeffry *business educator*

Scottsdale
Rogers, William Cordell *financial executive*

Sun City
Cortright, Inga Ann *accountant*

Tempe
Brooke, Edna Mae *retired business educator*
Carlson, Paul Westlie *accountant*
Ger, Shaw-Shyong *accountant*
Kaufman, Herbert Mark *finance educator*
Zavras, Mark Andrew *controller*

Tucson
Hellon, Michael Thomas *tax consultant*
Nixon, Robert Obey, Sr. *business educator*
Schulman, Elizabeth Weiner *financial consultant*
Taveggia, Thomas Charles *management consultant*

CALIFORNIA

Aliso Viejo
Hamilton, Allen Philip *financial advisor*

Anaheim
Jurczyk, Joanne Monica *financial analyst*

Arnold
Puterbaugh, Kathryn Elizabeth *retired corporate executive*

Artesia
Lee, Jai Jung *accountant*

Bakersfield
Bacon, Leonard Anthony *accounting educator*

Belvedere Tiburon
Cook, Robert Donald *financial service executive*

Berkeley
Blume, James Beryl *financial advisor*
Bucklin, Louis Pierre *business educator, consultant*
Hotchkies, Barry *financial executive*
McKeever, Mike Pierce *economics and business educator*

Beverly Hills
Matzdorff, James Arthur *investment banker, financier*
Taggart, Sondra *financial planner, investment advisor*
Widaman, Gregory Alan *financial executive, accountant*

Brea
Barbas, Jeffrey Lawrence *finance company executive*

Burbank
Dene, Linda Jo *financial executive*
Gold, Stanley P. *diversified investments executive*
Sherbert, Sharon Debra *financial services executive*
Thornton, Cameron Mitchell *financial planner*

Camarillo
Smith, David Michael *financial planner*

Carlsbad
Peasland, Bruce Randall *financial executive*

Carmel
Bonfield, Andrew Joseph *tax practitioner*
Steele, Charles Glen *retired accountant*

Chico
O'Neill, Michael Foy *business educator*

Chula Vista
Scozzari, Albert *portfolio manager*

Claremont
Christian, Suzanne Hall *financial planner*

Concord
Boland, Margaret Camille *financial services administrator, consultant*

Coronado
Allen, Charles Richard *retired financial executive*
Baumer, Edward Ferdinand *financial services executive*

Costa Mesa
Goldfield, Emily Dawson *finance company executive, artist*
Kolanoski, Thomas Edwin *financial company executive*

Culver City
Richardson, John Edmon *marketing educator*

Cupertino
Supan, Richard Matthew *finance company executive*

Duarte
Fayad, Mike Samih *financial analyst*

El Segundo
Pettersen, Thomas Morgan *accountant, finance executive*

Escondido
Strong, James Thompson *management, security, human resources consultant*

Fairfax
Ackerman, Arlene Alice *accountant, business consultant, artist, writer*

Fountain Valley
Penderghast, Thomas Frederick *business educator*

Fremont
Jensen, Paul Edward Tyson *business educator, consultant*
Yee, Keith Philip *accountant*

Fresno
Pinkerton, Richard LaDoyt *management educator*
Shanafelt, Nancy Sue *quality consultant, career consultant*

Fullerton
Oh, Tai Keun *business educator*

Glendale
Sotomayor, Ivan J. *accountant, international consultant*
Tripoli, Masumi Hiroyasu *financial consultant and diplomat*

Harbor City
Lee, Grace Tze *controller*

Hayward
Doctors, Samuel Isaac *management educator, researcher director*

Hemet
Rowe, Mary Sue *accounting executive*

Huntington Beach
Strutzel, J(od) C(hristopher) *escrow company executive*

Irvine
Reguero, Melodie Huber *financial executive*

La Canada
Tookey, Robert Clarence *consulting actuary*

La Crescenta
Fisk, Irwin Wesley *financial investigator*

La Jolla
Genét, Barbara Ann *accountant, travel counselor*
Khamisa, Azim Noordin *financial consultant*

La Mirada
Woodward, Phil Lloyd *business educator*

Lafayette
Yarlagadda, Rambabu Venkata *financial manager*

Laguna Hills
Donahue, Mark Forrest *financial planner*

Larkspur
George, Wilfred Raymond *financial advisor, portfolio manager*

Long Beach
Brown, Pamela Sue *accountant*

Los Altos
Sanchez, Marla Rena *controller*

Los Angeles
Allison, Laird Burl *business educator*
Anderson, Kenneth Jeffery *family financial planner, accountant, lawyer*
Bennis, Warren Gameliel *business administration educator, author, consultant*
Broad, Eli *financial services executive*
Cooper, Gene Alfred *finance company executive*
Finie, Peter Henry *property tax manager*
Glazov, Beverly *controller*
Goedde, Alan George *financial company executive*
Gonzalez, Kimberly Regina *controller*
Gooch, Lawrence Boyd *accounting executive*
Kraus, Mitchell *financial planner*
Lin, Thomas Wen-shyoung *accounting educator, researcher, consultant*
Meloan, Taylor Wells *marketing educator*
Miller, Joan Wendy *financial advisor*
Moffatt, Robert Henry *accountant, publisher, writer, consultant*
More, Philip Harvey Birnbaum *business administration educator*
Morrow, Winston Vaughan *financial executive*
Murray Tuxill, Suzanne *accountant*
Porper, Mary *comptroller*
Siegel, David Aaron *accountant*
Stewart, David Wayne *marketing educator, psychologist, consultant*
Tanaka, Togo W(illiam) *retired real estate and financial executive*
Tiger, Peter Errol *controller*
Udvar-Hazy, Steven F. *leasing company financial executive*

Malibu
Baskin, Otis Wayne *business educator*

Manhattan Beach
Anderson, Charles Michael *accountant*

Menlo Park
Messmer, Harold Maximilian, Jr. *financial services executive*
Schleh, Edward Carl *business analyst*

Midway City
McCawley, William Dale, II *accountant, writer, ethnohistorian*

Mission Viejo
Rodrigues, Mark *financial executive, manpower consultant*

Modesto
Dunbar, Sharon Kay *controller, accountant*

Monterey Park
Lin, Lawrence Shuh Liang *accountant*
Tseng, Felix Hing-Fai *accountant*

Moraga
Coleman, Henry James, Jr. *management educator, consultant*

Napa
Harrison, E(rnest) Frank(lin) *management educator, consultant, author, former university president and chancellor*
Schunke, Hildegard Heidel *accountant*

Newbury Park
Koçen, Lorraine Ayral *accountant*

Newport Beach
Hoffman, George Bernard *estate planner*
Indiek, Victor Henry *finance corporation executive*
Randolph, Steven *insurance and estate planner*

Northridge
Lehtihalme, Larry (Lauri) K. *financial planner*
Li, Mingfang *educator*
Ruley, Stanley Eugene *cost analyst*

Oakland
Barlow, William Pusey, Jr. *accountant*
Lee, Jong Hyuk *accountant*
Prozan, Lawrence Ira *financial planner*
Randisi, Elaine Marie *accountant, educator, writer*

Oceanside
McIntyre, Louise S. *income tax consultant*
Taverna, Rodney Elward *financial services company executive*

Orange
Kathol, Anthony Louis *finance executive*

Orinda
Tracy, James Jared, Jr. *accountant, law firm administrator*

Palo Alto
Batinic, Maryanne Frances *accountant, volunteer*
Herrick, Tracy Grant *fiduciary*
Ivy, Benjamin Franklin, III *financial and real estate investment advisor*
Kohler, Fred Christopher *tax specialist*

Palos Verdes Estates
Hughs, Mary Geraldine *accountant, social service specialist*

Palos Verdes Peninsula
Barab, Marvin *financial consultant*

Pasadena
Walendowski, George Jerry *accounting educator*

Pittsburg
Williams Jones, Elizabeth *financial planner, business consultant*

Pleasanton
Vandenberghe, Ronald Gustave *accountant, real estate developer*

Poway
Gautier, Elizabeth Jolene *accountant, consultant*

Rancho Santa Fe
Garcia, Crisostomo Bautista *portfolio manager, management science educator*

Reseda
Chavez, Albert Blas *financial executive*

Riverside
Carpenter, Susan Ann *financial planner*
Harrison, Ethel Mae *financial executive*
Mc Cormac, Weston Arthur *retired educator, retired career officer*
Smith, Anita Bingham *accountant, tax preparer*

Sacramento
Doria, Robin Galian *financial consultant*
Gardner, Jerry Lee *financial consultant*
Ponder, Pearlie Mae *retired tax collector*
Truly, Diane Elizabeth *tax board administrator*

Salinas
Stevens, Wilbur Hunt *accountant*

San Clemente
Petruzzi, Christopher Robert *business educator, consultant*

San Diego
Disney, Michael George *financial services executive*
Gengor, Virginia Anderson *financial planning executive, educator*
Pelky, Lance A. *financial planner, educator*
Tennent, Valentine Leslie *accountant*

San Francisco
Been, Hans Henrik *finance executive*
Entriken, Robert Kersey *retired management educator*
Hahn, Jennifer Lynn *accountant*
Hallstrom, Robert Chris *government actuary*
Herringer, Frank Casper *diversified financial services company executive*
Jimenez, Josephine Santos *portfolio manager*
Kahn, Linda McClure *actuary, consultant*
Kahn, Paul Markham *actuary*
Kuhns, Craig Shaffer *business educator*
MacNab, JJ *financial planner, insurance analyst, consultant*
Mayer, Patricia Jayne *financial officer, management accountant*
Mumford, Christopher Greene *corporate financial executive*
Olshen, Abraham Charles *actuarial consultant*
Palmer, William Joseph *accountant*
Peterson, Harries-Clichy *financial adviser*
Rosenberg, Paul Henry *business analyst*
Rubin, Diane Marie *accountant*
Swett, Margaret Christine *finance executive*
Uri, George Wolfsohn *accountant*
Witter, Wendell Winship *financial executive, retired*
Zobel, Jan A. *tax consultant*

San Gabriel
Tadian, Luanne F. B. *financial analyst, consultant, researcher*

San Jose
Delucchi, George Paul *accountant*
Fort, Lee Earthmon *financial services representative*
Kertz, Marsha Helene *accountant, educator*
Morrison, William Fosdick *business educator, retired electrical company executive*

San Luis Obispo
Blakeslee, Diane Pusey *financial planner*

San Marino
Jariabka, Andrew John *financial consultant*

San Mateo
Hopkins, Cecilia Ann *business educator*
Johnson, Charles Bartlett *mutual fund executive*
Johnson, Rupert Harris, Jr. *finance company executive*
Wojno, Bradley Nelson *financial sales executive*

San Rafael
Bialik, Jeffrey Vincent *treasurer, academic administrator*

Santa Clara
Jo, Hoje *finance educator*
Yount, Bobby Lon *financial planner*

Santa Monica
Taylor, Nigel Brian *financial planner*

Santa Rosa
Adolph, Mary Rosenquist *financial company executive*
Harris, David Joel *financial planner*
Root, Charles Joseph, Jr. *finance executive, consultant*

Saratoga
McLaughlin, Glen *financial services company executive*

Sherman Oaks
Rich, Gareth Edward *financial planner*

Simi Valley
Rehart, Margaret Lee *controller*

Stanford
Serbein, Oscar Nicholas *business educator, consultant*

Stockton
Goldstrand, Dennis Joseph *business and estate planning executive*
Hoberg, Janet Lee *controller*
Hoverstad, Ronald Alan *marketing educator*

Sunnyvale
Li, Grace Chia-Chian *accountant, business planning manager*

Tarzana
Krivis, Scott Alan *accountant, limousine company executive*

Thousand Oaks
Allen, David Harlow *business educator, logistician, consultant*

Torrance
Kramer, Alexander Gottlieb *financial director*

Tustin
Roberts, Daniel John *financial advisor, educator*

Vallejo
Feil, Linda Mae *tax preparer*

Villa Park
Von Kaminsky, Elaine Isabelle *financier, congresswoman*

Vista
Babcock, Jeff Charles *financial planner*
Helmuth, Philip Alan *tax consultant*

Walnut Creek
Aghili, Shaun Shahriar *financial consultant, loan specialist*
Coit, R. Ken *financial planner*
Fridley, Saundra Lynn *internal audit executive*

West Hollywood
Santillan, Antonio *financial company executive*

Westlake Village
Cammalleri, Joseph Anthony *retired financial planner, air force officer*
Cucina, Vincent Robert *retired financial executive*
Detterman, Robert Linwood *financial planner*
Pollak, Norman L. *retired accountant*

Westminster
Amalsad, Meher Dadabhoy *financial consultant*

Whittier
Maxwell, Raymond Roger *accountant*

Willits
Akins, George Charles *accountant*

Woodbridge
Thames, Carroll Thomas *financial consultant*

Woodland Hills
Babayans, Emil *financial planner*

Woodside
Concannon, George Robert *business educator*

COLORADO

Arvada
Hancock, N(ewell) Les(lie) *accountant*
Laidig, Eldon Lindley *financial planner*
Wambolt, Thomas Eugene *financial consultant*

Boulder
Baugh, L. Darrell *financial executive*
Healy, Thomas E. *accountant*
Hyland, Laurie Zoe *financial planner*
Richardson, Donn Charles *business and marketing educator*
Stanton, William John, Jr. *marketing educator, author*

Brighton
Kersbergen, John Jay *financial management executive, consultant*

Broomfield
Affleck, Julie Karleen *accountant*

Colorado Springs
Bressan, Robert Ralph *accountant*
Fink, Kevin G. *finance executive*
Gagne, Margaret Lee *accounting educator*
Homan, Ralph William *finance company executive*
Vela, Steven Rene *portfolio manager*
Wheeler, Larry Richard *accountant*

Denver
Cook, Albert Thomas Thornton, Jr. *financial advisor*
Karras, Donald George *tax administrator*
Leraaen, Allen Keith *financial executive*
Lincoln, Alexander, III *financier, lawyer, private investor*
Lowman, Carl Darryl *financial executive*
Rankin, James Patrick *financial services company executive*
Steele, William Arthur *financial analyst, public utilities executive*

Englewood
Bondi, Bert Roger *accountant, financial planner*
Lager, Douglas Roy *property tax consultant*
Schwartz, Michael Lee *financial planner, consultant*
Shannon, Richard Stoll, III *financial executive*
Sprincz, Keith Steven *financial services company professional*

Fort Collins
Ewing, Jack Robert *accountant*
Kinnison, Robert Wheelock *retired accountant*
Thomas, Jeanette Mae *public accountant*

Golden
Gillis, Paul Leonard *accountant*
Weiskopf, William Harvard *accountant*

Grand Junction
Sewell, Beverly Jean *financial executive*

Greenwood Village
Barnard, Rollin Dwight *retired financial executive*

Jefferson
Maatsch, Deborah Joan *financial company executive, tax advisor*

Lakewood
Keller, Shirley Inez *accountant*
Szigethy, Nancy Sue *accountant*

Littleton
Newell, Michael Stephen *finance company executive, international finance, protective services consultant*

Northglenn
Eisele, Virginia A. *public accountant, investment professional*

Wheat Ridge
Leino, Deanna Rose *business educator*

DISTRICT OF COLUMBIA

Washington
Martin, Jane Everette *financial company executive*

HAWAII

Aiea
Tamura, Daniel Masanori *tax specialist*

Honolulu
Betts, James William, Jr. *financial analyst, consultant*
Ng, Wing Chiu *accountant, computer software consultant, educator, activist*
Palia, Aspy Phiroze *marketing educator, researcher, consultant*
Pilar, L. Prudencio R. *financial services executive*
Sterrett, James Melville *accountant, business consultant*

Kailua
Morrow, Cherylle Ann *accountant, bankruptcy, consultant*

IDAHO

Boise
Gray, Lonna Irene *indemnity fund executive*
Hedrick, Wallace Edward *business executive*

Burley
Westfall, Stephen Donald *accountant, small business owner*

Caldwell
Allen, Edward Raymond *retired business educator, accountant*

Coeur D Alene
Pinkerton, Daniel Walter *financial planner*

Idaho Falls
Riddoch, Hilda Johnson *accountant*

Pocatello
McClure, Robert Coke *financial consultant, minister*

Sun Valley
Hadley, Susan R. *accountant*

MONTANA

Billings
Elser, Danny Ray *financial planner*
O'Leary, Peggy René *accountant*

Cut Bank
McCormick, Betty Leonora *accountant*

Great Falls
Christiaens, Chris (Bernard Francis Christiaens) *financial analyst, state senator*

Missoula
Douglas, Patricia Pump *accounting and finance educator*

Stevensville
Laing-Malcolmson, Sally Anne *enrolled tax agent, tax consultant*

Troy
Sherman, Signe Lidfeldt *portfolio manager, former research chemist*

NEVADA

Carson City
Reid, Belmont Mervyn *brokerage house executive*

Las Vegas
Hobbs, Guy Stephen *financial executive*
Lentz, Constance Marchand *accountant*
Pierce, William A. *financial consultant, career officer*
Sevalstad, Suzanne Ada *accounting educator*
Wendt, Steven William *business educator*

North Las Vegas
Spiering, Nancy Jean *accounting executive*

Reno
Gilbert, Gregory L. *accountant*
Hurtado, Tracy Ellen *accountant*

NEW MEXICO

Albuquerque
Huffman, Nona Gay *financial consultant, retirement planning specialist*
Krahl, Bill L.
Royle, Anthony William *accountant*

Las Cruces
Bell, M. Joy Miller *financial planner, real estate broker*

OREGON

Beaverton
Herron, Carol Christine *financial planner, home economist*

Clackamas
Love, Susan Denise *accountant, consultant, small business owner*
Luchterhand, Ralph Edward *financial advisor*

Corvallis
Brown, Carol Elizabeth *management educator*

Eugene
Hamren, Nancy Van Brasch *bookkeeper*
Lindholm, Richard Theodore *economics and finance educator*

Lake Oswego
Mylnechuk, Larry Herbert *financial executive*
Pearson, Conrad E. *financial services executive*

Newport
Blackman-Buckout, Joann Louise *accountant*

Portland
Arnold, Ralph Leo, III *valuation analyst, consultant*
Beebe, Donald Paul *financial planner, consultant, editor*
Dow, Mary Alexis *auditor*
Hellenthal, S. Ronald *finance company executive*
Stewart, Marlene Metzger *financial planning practitioner, insurance agent*
Watne, Donald Arthur *accountant, educator*
Weber, George Richard *financial consultant, writer*

UTAH

Logan
Brackner, James Walter *accounting educator, consultant*

Provo
Hill, Ned Cromar *finance educator, consultant*

Saint George
Abel, James Calvin, Jr. *financial planner*

Salt Lake City
Apgood, Robert D. *financial consultant*
Bonny, Blaine Milan *retired accountant*
Creer, James Read *financial officer*
Furr, James William, Jr. *financial planner, consultant*
Johnson, Auston G. *auditor*
Shepherd, Karen *finance executive, former congresswoman*
Snell, Ned Colwell *financial planner*
Suniville, Harry Frederick *accountant*
Young, Scott Thomas *business management educator*

Sandy
Steensma, Michael Eric *controller*

WASHINGTON

Bellingham
Ross, Steven Charles *business administration educator, consultant*

Chelan
Lundberg, Larry Thomas *business executive*

Coulee Dam
Meyer, Barbara Ann *tax specialist*

Everett
Bartlett, Deborah Ann *financial management consultant*
Terwilliger, Robert Alan *auditor*

Medical Lake
Drummond, Marshall Edward *business educator, university administrator*

Mountlake Terrace
Rapp, Nina Beatrice *financial company executive*

Olympia
Christensen, Robert Wayne, Jr. *financial and leasing company executive*
Schlottmann, David Henry *accountant*

Redmond
Callinicos, Brent *assistant treasurer*

Renton
Yen, Peter T. *business educator, education foundation executive*

Seattle
Collett, Robert Lee *financial company executive*
Evans, Richard Lloyd *financial services company executive*
Feiss, George James, III *financial services company executive*
Gaskill, Herbert Leo *accountant, engineer*
Gorans, Gerald Elmer *accountant*
Kaminski, Charles Anthony *portfolio manager*
Kasama, Hideto Peter *accountant, business advisor, real estate consultant*
Tollett, Glenna Belle *accountant, mobile home park operator*
van der Werff, Terry Jay *management consultant, professional speaker, futurist*
Wu, Harold Powan *financial analyst*

Walker, Raymond Francis *business and financial consulting company executive*

Silverdale
Crane, Peter *financial consultant*

Spokane
Burton, Robert Lyle *accounting firm executive*
Teets, Walter Ralph *accounting educator*

Tacoma
Purdy, Jill *business management educator*

WYOMING

Afton
Hunsaker, Floyd B. *accountant*

Cheyenne
Day, Vaun Charles *accounting educator*
Ferrari, David Guy *auditor*
Price, Keith Glenn *accountant*
Spiegelberg, Emma Jo *business education educator, academic administrator*

Lusk
Denny, Carol Lee *financial officer*

Sheridan
Ryan, Michael Louis *controller*

Wheatland
Whitney, Ralph Royal, Jr. *financial executive*

CANADA

ALBERTA

Calgary
Schulz, Robert Adolph *management educator, management consultant*

SASKATCHEWAN

Saskatoon
Irvine, Vernon Bruce *accounting educator, administrator*

ADDRESS UNPUBLISHED

Abels, Robert Frederick *tax consultant*
Atcheson, Sue Hart *business educator*
Bagnull, Gary Lynn *accountant*
Barton, Ann Elizabeth *retired financial executive*
Belluomini, Frank Stephen *accountant*
Bishop, Betty Josephine *lawyer, expert witness mortgage banking*
Boxer, Alan Lee *accountant*
Brennan, Ciaran Brendan *accountant*
Cain, Patricia Jean *accountant*
Castle, Nancy Margaret Timma *accountant, banker*
Chiappelli, John Arthur *controller, accountant*
Coopersmith, Fredric S. *financial planning executive*
Davis, Robert H. *financial executive, arbitrator, mediator, educator*
Dibos, Dianne Louise *financial analyst*
Dunlap, James Riley, Sr. *former financial executive, credit manager*
Fagerberg, Dixon, Jr. *retired accountant, weather observer*
Frankel, Edward Irwin *financial consultant*
Gabriel, Rennie *financial planner*
Glyer, Michael Dale *tax specialist*
Harding, James George *financial executive*
Harlow, Charles Vendale, Jr. *finance educator, consultant*
Henne, Andrea Rudnitsky *business educator*
Hickson, Ernest Charles *financial executive*
Hutner, Herbert L. *financial consultant, lawyer*
Kaufman, Charles David *controller*
Larizadeh, M(ohammed) R(eza) *business educator*
Martin, Preston *financial services executive*
Norton, Karen Ann *accountant*
Oldshue, Paul Frederick *financial executive*
Pick, James Block *management and sociology educator*
Ray, Richard Stanley *accountant*
Rich, David Barry *financial executive, accountant, entertainer*
Roth, Suzanne Allen *financial services agent*
Schwyn, Charles Edward *accountant*
Sherwood, Gretchen Wieting *financial consultant, cosmetics company executive*
Smith, Clifford Neal *business educator, writer*
Spencer, Richard Prail *property management educator, job placement counselor*
Stewart, Scott Richard *financial consultant*
Wachbrit, Jill Barrett *accountant, tax specialist*
Whisner, Peggy Janelle *accountant*

FINANCE: INSURANCE

UNITED STATES

ALASKA

Anchorage
Trevithick, Ronald James *underwriter*

ARIZONA

Phoenix
Hacker, Kenneth Russell *insurance executive*
Healy, Barbara Anne *insurance company executive, financial planner*
Shpolnik, Robert Milton *insurance company executive*
Van Orden, Amanda Kay Mitchell *insurance consultant*

Scottsdale
LeClerc, Marc Gregory *insurance agent*

Prisbrey, Rex Prince *retired insurance agent, underwriter, consultant*

Tucson
Gerhart, Dorothy Evelyn *insurance executive, real estate professional*

CALIFORNIA

Alpine
Keller, Susan Agnes *insurance executive*

Arroyo Grande
Stenzel, Franz Robert, Jr. *insurance broker, financial consultant*

Bradbury
Christensen, Donn Wayne *insurance executive*

Brea
Radley, B.W. *insurance claims adjuster*
Spiegel, Ronald Stuart *insurance company executive*

Carlsbad
Haney, Robert Locke *retired insurance company executive*

Clayton
Distefano, Peter Andrew *insurance executive, entertainment photographer*

Costa Mesa
Palmer, Gilbert Charles *insurance company executive*

Dana Point
Lang, George Frank *insurance executive, consultant, lawyer*

Danville
Dyer, Richard Hutchins *risk management executive*

Downey
Lopez, Felix Bilgera *insurance company executive*

Fallbrook
Gonzales, Hilario Duran (Larry Gonzales) *insurance company executive, finance educator*

Folsom
Hopkins, Arlene Marie *insurance company executive*

La Habra
Melton, William Ray, Jr. *insurance company executive*

La Mesa
Schlador, Paul Raymond, Jr. *insurance agent*

Los Angeles
Boynton, Donald Arthur *title insurance company executive*
Holden, William Willard *insurance executive*
Inman, James Russell *claims consultant*
Johnson, E. Eric *insurance executive*
Lawrence, Dwight Timothy *insurance executive, consultant*
Milgrim, Darrow A. *insurance broker, recreation consultant*
Rinsch, Charles Emil *insurance company executive*
Winthrop, Kenneth Ray *insurance executive*

Mill Valley
Clark, Edgar Sanderford *insurance broker, consultant*

Monterey Park
Lim, Sally-Jane (SJ Lim) *insurance consultant*

Newport Beach
Cosgrove, Cameron *insurance executive*
Fitch, Edward M., Jr. *insurance company executive, retired*
Gerken, Walter Bland *insurance company executive*

Novato
Leaton, Marcella Kay *insurance representative, business owner*

Oakland
Ching, Eric San Hing *health care and insurance administrator*

Palm Springs
Lord, Jane Anne *insurance broker*

Pismo Beach
Brisbin, Robert Edward *insurance agency executive*

Pleasant Hill
Mansel, Charles Michael Longley *educational consultant, insurance specialist*

Sacramento
Basconcillo, Lindy *insurance and financial services company executive*

San Diego
Eichhoff, Darrell Dean *retired insurance company executive, consultant*

San Francisco
Enfield, D(onald) Michael *insurance executive*
Grove, Douglas David *insurance company executive*
Vuong, Frank Pheng *insurance executive*

San Jose
Jackson, Patrick Joseph *insurance executive*

San Mateo
MacCorkle, Emmett Wallace, III *insurance agent*

Santa Barbara
Reis, Edward Thomas, Jr. *insurance executive, educator*

Santa Rosa
Farrell, Thomas Joseph *insurance company executive, consultant*
Spikes, Barbra Jean *claims processor*

Sherman Oaks
Erickson, Richard Beau *insurance and financial company executive*

Sonoma
Bow, Stephen Tyler, Jr. *insurance and computer industry consultant*

Stockton
Ehlert, DeWayne Albert *underwriter*

Thousand Oaks
Gregory, Calvin *insurance service executive*

Tustin
Evans, Thomas Edgar, Jr. *title insurance agency executive*

Vista
Fuhlrodt, Norman Theodore *retired insurance executive*

COLORADO

Aurora
Kruger, Paul Robert *insurance broker*
Volpe, Richard Gerard *insurance accounts executive, consultant*

Breckenridge
Beery, Roger Lewis, II *risk management consultant*

Denver
Kelly, Jerome Bernard *insurance company executive*
Padilla, Philip K. *environmental health safety and risk specialist*
Rotherham, Larry Charles *insurance executive*
Walter, George Paul *insurance agency executive*

Englewood
Gunderman, William Jerome, III *insurance executive*
Hardy, Wayne Russell *insurance and investment broker*
Manley, Richard Walter *insurance executive*

Fort Collins
Schendel, Winfried George *insurance company executive*

Golden
Dunaway, John Allen *risk management professional*
Lott, Brenda Louise *insurance company executive*

Grand Junction
Mahoney, Brian Purcell *insurance agency executive*

Littleton
Moore, Dan Sterling *insurance executive, sales trainer*

Pueblo
Kelly, William Bret *insurance executive*

HAWAII

Honolulu
Kanehiro, Kenneth Kenji *insurance educator, risk analyst, consultant*
Lindsay, Karen Leslie *insurance company executive*
Matthews, Norman Sherwood, Jr. *insurance company executive*
Metcalf, Wayne C. *insurance commissioner*
Noguchi, Hideo *insurance agency executive*
Ronsman, Wayne John *insurance company executive*

IDAHO

Boise
Lowder, Robert Jackson *insurance agent*

Nampa
Heidt, Raymond Joseph *insurance company executive*

Twin Falls
Lewis, Frederick Thomas *insurance company executive*

NEVADA

Carson City
Marangi, Vito Anthony, Sr. *claim administrator*

NEW MEXICO

Albuquerque
Donato, Mary Eileen *risk management professional*
Wainio, Mark Ernest *insurance company consultant*

Tucumcari
Woodard, Dorothy Marie *insurance broker*

OREGON

Hillsboro
Yates, Keith Lamar *retired insurance company executive*

Lake Oswego
Atwood, Kelly Palmer *insurance agency executive*

Medford
Dvorak, Ray P. *insurance company official*

Portland
Atkins, William Theodore *insurance company executive*
Caradine, Linda Hildegard *contract analyst*

Salem
Rasmussen, Neil Woodland *insurance agent*
Schuster, Donald *insurance agency executive*

Tualatin
Chambers, Lois Irene *insurance automation consultant*

Waldport
Ginter, Carol(yn) Augusta Romtvedt *retired bond underwriter*

West Linn
Dunstan, Larry Kenneth *insurance company executive*

UTAH

Ogden
Breitweiser, James Russell *insurance company executive*

Salt Lake City
Allen, Brian R. *insurance company executive, state legislator*
Allen, Roy Verl *life insurance company executive*
Engar, Richard Charles *insurance executive, dentist, educator*
Poulton, Craig Kidd *insurance broker, consultant*

Sandy
Macumber, John Paul *insurance company executive*

WASHINGTON

Bellingham
Fullmer, Donald Kitchen *insurance executive*

Bremerton
Varga, Steven Carl *reinsurance company executive, consultant*

Kennewick
Stevens, Henry August *insurance agent, educator*

Kirkland
McDonald, Joseph Lee *insurance broker*

Mountlake Terrace
English, Donald Marvin *loss control representative*

Seattle
Duckworth, Tara Ann *insurance company executive*
Eigsti, Roger Harry *insurance company executive*
Kibble, Edward Bruce *insurance-investment advisory company executive*

WYOMING

Dubois
Furman, Melvin D. *insurance company executive*

Glenrock
Bennington, Leslie Orville, Jr. *insurance agent*

ADDRESS UNPUBLISHED

Bovey, Terry Robinson *insurance executive*
Clemens, Charles Joseph *insurance agent*
Dackow, Orest Taras *insurance company executive*
Fibiger, John Andrew *life insurance company executive*
Ipsen, Grant Ruel *insurance and investments professional*
Levine, Michael Joseph *insurance company executive*
McCaw, Bruce R. *insurance executive, airline and communications executive*
McGee, Craig Heslin *insurance company executive*
Mehdizadeh, Parviz *insurance company executive*
Porter, Dixie Lee *insurance executive, consultant*

FINANCE: INVESTMENT SERVICES

UNITED STATES

ALASKA

Anchorage
Hickel, Walter Joseph *investment firm executive, forum administrator*

ARIZONA

Phoenix
Hedberg, John Charles *investor*
Miller, Barbara Shaw *investment consultant, real estate appraiser*
Tribble, Richard Walter *brokerage executive*
Wallace, Kenneth Alan *investor*

Scottsdale
Gentry, Warren Miller *investment company executive*
Luke, David Kevin *investment company executive*
Rizzo, Mary Ann Frances *international trade executive, former educator*

Tucson
Shury, Vera *security services company executive, insurance agency executive*

Vail
Maierhauser, Joseph George *entrepreneur*

Yuma
Stuart, Gerard William, Jr. *investment company executive, city official*

CALIFORNIA

Arcadia
Berkus, David William *venture capitalist*

Beverly Hills
Balash, Jeffrey Linke *investment banker*
Dawson, Derek *investment company executive*
Evans, Louise *investor, retired psychologist, philanthropist*
Gambrell, Thomas Ross *investor, retired physician, surgeon*
Israel, Richard Stanley *investment banker*

Brea
Nizami, Tariq Ahmed *investment company executive*

Burbank
Henley, Richard Merle *business developer, marketing executive, producer, director*

Camarillo
Sullivan, Michael Evan *investment and management company executive*

Coronado
Smith, Albert Cromwell, Jr. *investments consultant*

Costa Mesa
Kiang, Assumpta (Amy Kiang) *brokerage house executive*

Covina
Colley, Janet Scritsmier *investment consultant*

Cupertino
Horn, Christian Friedrich *venture capital company executive*

Dana Point
Judson, Barbara Michael *business proposal manager, graphics director*

Dixon
Molina Villacorta, Rafael Antonio *investment company executive*

Escondido
Allen, Donald Vail *investment executive, writer, concert pianist*

Fawnskin
Garver, Richard Alvin *investment advisor*

Fresno
Armey, Douglas Richard *investment consultant*
Jolly, Steven Jon *brokerage house executive*

Glendale
Kinney, Paul William *investment company executive*

Granite Bay
Andrews, William Scott *investment advisor*

Guerneville
Salter, Tracy Lee *entrepreneur*

Hollywood
Marshall, Conrad Joseph *entrepreneur*

Irvine
Clabaugh, Matthew Martinsen *venture capitalist, real estate investor*
Le Bon, Douglas Kent *investment manager*

La Jolla
Stone, Donald D. *investment and sales executive*

La Mirada
Black, Lee Roy *investment professional, consultant*

Laguna Niguel
Heiden, William Mark *entrepreneur*

Lake Arrowhead
Fitzgerald, John Charles, Jr. *investment banker*

Los Angeles
Cochran, Jeri Lynn *entrepreneur*
DeBard, Roger *investment executive*
Emmeluth, Bruce Palmer *investment company executive, venture capitalist*
Gordy, Berry *entrepreneur, record company executive, motion picture executive*
Haytin, Harold Alexander *venture capital company executive*
Mann, Nancy Louise (Nancy Louise Robbins) *entrepreneur*
Paul, Laurence Edward *investment company executive*
Perry, Donald Lester, II *venture capitalist*
Reed, George Ford, Jr. *investment executive*
Tennenbaum, Michael Ernest *private investor*
Wiese, Kevin Glen *entrepreneur*

Menlo Park
Glynn, John W., Jr. *investment manager*
Lucas, Donald Leo *private investor*
Roberts, George R. *investment banking company executive*
Rosch, Thomas Lee *venture capitalist*
Walsh, William Desmond *investor*

Napa
Strock, David Randolph *brokerage house executive*

Newbury Park
Guggenheim-Boucard, Alan Andre Albert Paul Edouard *business executive, international consultant*

Newport Beach
Thorp, Edward Oakley *investment management company executive*

Oakland
Al Malek, Amir Isa *entrepreneur, business consultant, actor, musician*
Dominick, Anthony, Jr. *entrepreneur, Internet consultant*

Orinda
Bach, Martin Wayne *stockbroker, owner antique clock stores*

Oxnard
Woodworth, Stephen Davis *investment banker*

Pacific Palisades
Hagenbuch, Rodney Dale *stock brokerage house executive*

Palm Desert
Barnes, George E. *investment company executive*

Palm Springs
Lougheed, Arthur Lawrence *investment advisor, tax and pension consultant*

Palo Alto
Crawford, R. George *investment manager, educator*
Markkula, A. C., Jr. *entrepreneur, computer company executive*

Pasadena
Gold, Michael Nathan *investment banker, management consultant*
Liebau, Frederic Jack, Jr. *investment manager*

Point Richmond
Holman, John Foster *investment banker*

Porterville
Lindgren, Jennifer Goux *business executive, financial planner, educator*

Rancho Santa Fe
Polster, Leonard H. *investment company executive*

Ross
Rosenbaum, Michael Francis *securities dealer*

San Clemente
Tober, Mark Robert *investment representative, stockbroker*

San Diego
Bradley, Wade Harlow *acquisitions specialist*
Heath, Donald Wayne *securities wholesale executive, financial planner*
Martinez, John Stanley *entrepreneur*

San Francisco
Bass, Audrey *commodities trader*
Dellas, Robert Dennis *investment banker*
de Petra, Derek Guido *securities trader*
Dunn, Richard Joseph *retired investment counselor*
Greber, Robert Martin *financial investments executive*
Gund, George, III *financier, professional sports team executive*
Hagenbuch, John Jacob *investment banker*
Halliday, John Meech *investment company executive*
Hellman, F(rederick) Warren *investment advisor*
King, Jennifer Carolyn *marketing and promotions entrepreneur*
Miller, Corbin Russell *investment company executive*
Pottruck, David Steven *brokerage house executive*
Rebelein, Drew W. *entrepreneur*
Schwab, Charles R. *brokerage house executive*
Smelick, Robert Malcolm *investment bank executive*
Timmins, James Donald *venture capitalist*
Welsh, Stacey Lau *investment banker*

San Jose
Atwell, James D. *venture capitalist*
Hall, Robert Emmett, Jr. *investment banker, realtor*

San Leandro
Pansky, Emil John *entrepreneur*

San Rafael
Bibeault, Donald Bertrand *turnaround executive, investor*

Santa Barbara
Hansen, Robert Gunnard *philatelist, entrepreneur*

Santa Clara
Lynch, Charles Allen *investment executive, corporate director*

South Lake Tahoe
Diamond, Stephen Earle Michael *investor, consultant, inventor*

South San Francisco
Perkins, Thomas James *venture capital company executive*

Stockton
Kennedy, Thomas Edgar *investment banker*

Sun Valley
Salas, Edward Allen *securities trader*

Temecula
McKerahan, Karin E. *investment company executive*

Templeton
Guenther, Robert Stanley, II *investment and property executive*

Thousand Oaks
Horton, Kenneth *investor*

Vallejo
Muhammad, Khaleedah *entrepreneur, sales and marketing consultant, community activist*

Walnut Creek
Cervantez, Gil Lawrence *venture capital company executive*

West Covina
Tuck, Edward Fenton *business consultant, venture capitalist*

West Sacramento
Lipscomb, Jeffrey Jon *fund specialist*

Westlake Village
Fredericks, Ward Arthur *venture capitalist, food industry consultant*
Valentine, Gene C. *securities dealer*

Woodside
Isaacson, Robert Louis *investment company executive*

COLORADO

Boulder
Cooper, Daniel S. *securities trader, financial services executive*

Denver
Stephenson, Arthur Emmet, Jr. *corporate and investment company executive*
Wagner, Judith Buck *investment firm executive*

Durango
Pritchard, James Patrick *investment company executive*

Englewood
Moskowitz, Seymour *investment company executive, consultant, engineering executive, scientist*
Van Loucks, Mark Louis *venture capitalist, business advisor*

Evergreen
Jackson, William Richard *entrepreneur*

Grand Junction
Sewell, Ralph Byron *investment broker, financial planner, manager*
Skogen, Haven Sherman *investment company executive*

Idaho Springs
Ericson, Mark Frederick *investment analyst*

Kersey
Guttersen, Michael *ranching and investments professional*

Lakewood
Finnie, Doris Gould *investment company executive*

Snowmass Village
Bancroft, Paul, III *investment company executive*

DISTRICT OF COLUMBIA

Washington
Szekely, Deborah Beatrice *entrepreneur*

HAWAII

Honolulu
Haight, Warren Gazzam *investor*
Kagawa, Kathleen Hatsuyo *entrepreneur*

Kailua
Amos, Wally *entrepreneur*

IDAHO

Boise
Hendren, Merlyn Churchill *investment company executive*
Ling, Michael James *investment advisor*

Mountain Home
Bergh, David Morgan *entrepreneur*

MONTANA

Missoula
Liston, Albert Morris *investor, administrator, educator*
Williams, Susan Elaine *stockbroker, financial planner*

Polson
Marchi, Jon *cattle rancher, exporter, former investment brokerage executive*

NEVADA

Glenbrook
Jabara, Michael Dean *investment banker, entrepreneur*

Incline Village
James, Bruce Richard *investor*

Reno
Newberg, William Charles *stock broker, real estate broker, automotive engineer*

NEW MEXICO

Alamogordo
Green, Francis William *investment consultant, former missile scientist*

Albuquerque
Edenfield, T(homas) Keen, Jr. *music publishing and real estate investor*

Santa Fe
Dreisbach, John Gustave *investment banker*
Schuyler, Robert Len *investment company executive*

Taos
Lipscomb, Anna Rose Feeny *entrepreneur, arts organizer, fundraiser*

OREGON

Bend
Smith, Linda Zimbalist *investment research executive*

Chiloquin
Reed, David George *entrepreneur*

Portland
Hay, Andrew Mackenzie *merchant banking and commodities company executive*
Silver, Stephen Hal *stockbroker, financial planner*
Weller, Deborah Sue *investment company executive*

TEXAS

San Antonio
Colvin, Greta Wilmoth *entrepreneur*

UTAH

Salt Lake City
Brady, Rodney Howard *holding company executive, broadcast company executive, former college president, former government official*
Gilbert, Karen Ann *commodities trader*
Wallace, Matthew Walker *retired entrepreneur*

WASHINGTON

Bellevue
Jones, John Wesley *entrepreneur*

Kirkland
Ryles, Gerald Fay *private investor, business executive*

Seattle
Nelson, Allen F. *investor relations company executive*
Paup, Martin Arnold *real estate and securities investor*

Vancouver
Bilbruck, Daniel Wayne *investment company executive*

WYOMING

Jackson
Hirschfield, Alan James *entrepreneur*

CANADA

BRITISH COLUMBIA

Vancouver
Lyons, Terrence Allan *merchant banking, investment company executive*

ADDRESS UNPUBLISHED

Abboud, Sam *investor*
Balling, Christine *venture capitalist*
Birnbaum, Stevan Allen *investment company executive*
Black, Richard Bruce *business executive, consultant*
Browning, Jesse Harrison *entrepreneur*
Cockrum, William Monroe, III *investment banker, consultant, educator*
Colon, Richard Walter *retired stockbroker*
Fehribach, Ronald Steven *investment executive*
Friedlander, Charles Douglas *space consultant*
Gelpi, Michael Anthony *entrepreneur*
Graffis, Julie Anne *entrepreneur, retail consultant, interior designer*
Greene, Frank Sullivan, Jr. *investment management executive*
Groezinger, Leland Becker, Jr. *investment professional*
Hambrecht, William R. *retired venture capitalist*
Hapner, Mary Lou *securities trader and dealer*
Hermanson, Paul Douglas *investor*
Howard, James Webb *investment banker, lawyer, engineer*
Lynch, Phyllis Anne *stockbroker*
Marks, Leonard, Jr. *retired corporate executive*
Marler, Larry John *private investor, leadership consultant*
Merk, Elizabeth Thole *investment company executive*
Morgenroth, Earl Eugene *entrepreneur*
Paleji, Gregory Scott *venture capitalist*
Robinson, Annettmarie *entrepreneur*
Spangler, Scott Michael *retired private investor*
Stanfill, Dennis Carothers *business executive*
Svikhart, Edwin Gladdin *investment banker*
White-Vondran, Mary-Ellen *retired stockbroker*

FINANCE: REAL ESTATE

UNITED STATES

ALASKA

Anchorage
Faulkner, Sewell Ford *real estate executive*

Girdwood
Traunter, John James *real estate executive*

ARIZONA

Bullhead City
Jones, Vernon Quentin *surveyor*

Cottonwood
Izzo, Mary Alice *real estate broker*

Mesa
Bell, Daniel Carroll *realtor, community association, ranch and land manager*
Kegley, Joseph Edward *realtor*
McCollum, Alvin August *real estate company executive*

Phoenix
Clements, John Robert *real estate professional*
Donaldson, Wilburn Lester *property management corporation executive*
Montague, Sidney James *real estate developer*
Schrader, William P. *organization executive, farmer*
Snare, Carl Lawrence, Jr. *business executive*
Woods, Donald Peter *real estate executive, marketing professional*

Prescott
Martinez, Anthony Joseph *real estate appraiser*

Scottsdale
Bertiger, Karen Lee *real estate broker, asset manager, consultant*
Lennox, Gloria (Gloria Demeree) *real estate executive*
Spengeman, Edwin W. *real estate executive*

Sedona
Copeland, Suzanne Johnson *real estate executive*

Sun City
Lutin, David Louis *real estate development and finance consultant*
Meade, Kenneth John *realty company owner, broker*

Tempe
Berg, Linda Thoms *real estate broker*

Tucson
Stith, W(illiam) Mark *real estate executive*
Swihart, H. Gregg *real estate company executive*
Taylor, William Malcolm *environmentalist, educator, executive recruiter*

West Sedona
Lane, Margaret Anna Smith *property manager developer*

CALIFORNIA

Agoura Hills
Kaplan, Donald Sheldon *real estate developer and rehabilitator, property management company executive*

Alameda
Hirsch, Kathleen L. *realtor*

Alhambra
Perris, Andrew Arthur *real estate company official*

Anaheim
Naples, Susan Lorraine *property management company executive*

Apple Valley
Ledford, Gary Alan *real estate developer*

Arcadia
Freedman, Gregg *real estate appraisal company executive*

Atherton
Holvick, Patricia Valerie Jean *property manager, financial planner*

Beverly Hills
Diepholz, Daniel Ray *real estate consultant, accountant*
Josephson, Harold Allan *real estate developer*
Shank, Thom Lewis *real estate executive, entertainment consultant, author*
Tamkin, Curtis Sloane *real estate development company executive*

Big Sur
Cross, Robert Louis *realtor, land use planner, writer*
Owings, Margaret Wentworth *conservationist, artist*

Brentwood
Albers, Lucia Berta *land developer*

Capistrano Beach
Kurilchyk, Walter *real estate consultant, appraiser*

Carmel
Crowhurst Lennard, Suzanne Heather *organization executive*

CORONADO

Coronado
Stames, William Alexander *realtor, cost management executive*

Cypress
Osgood, Frank William *urban and economic planner, writer*

Dana Point
Lorenz, Timothy Carl *real estate agent*

Del Mar
Johnson, Hedy Bonder *real estate investor*

Elk Grove
Hull, Michael *estate planner*

Fremont
Jimenez, Tessie Casiano *realtor*

Fresno
Donaldson, George Burney *environmental consultant*

Glendale
Bitterman, Melvin Lee *real estate developer*

Goleta
Koart, Nellie Hart *real estate investor and executive*

Grand Terrace
Richens, Kimberlee Marie *real estate property manager, appraiser*

Grass Valley
Ozanich, Charles George *real estate broker*

Hemet
Coad, Dennis Lawrence *real estate broker*

Hermosa Beach
Williams, Jack Jeff *realtor, retired executive administrator*

Huntington Beach
Tillotson, Haydee Velazquez *real estate developer, property manager*

Inglewood
Buss, Jerry Hatten *real estate executive, sports team owner*

La Jolla
Anthony, Harry Antoniades *city planner, architect, educator*
Ripley, Stuart McKinnon *real estate consultant*

La Mesa
Jones, Darcy Glen Alan *land use planner, consultant*

Lancaster
Roths, Beverly Owen *organization executive*

Livermore
Nevin, David Wright *real estate broker, mortgage broker*

Long Beach
McGann, John Milton *real estate executive*
Reed, Norman Bruce *real estate developer*

Los Altos
Getreu, Sanford *city planner*

Los Angeles
Abernethy, Robert John *real estate developer*
Best, Roger Norman *real estate investment manager*
Furlotti, Alexander Amato *real estate development company executive*
Hunter, Diana Lynn *real estate consultant*
Kuraishi, Akari Luke *real estate company executive*
Levy, Alan David *real estate executive*
Montgomery, Robin Vera *realtor*
Schnebelen, Pierre *resort planner and developer, consultant*
Stark, Susan Marie *real estate agent*
Swartz, Roslyn Holt *real estate investment executive*

Los Osos
Polk, Emily DeSpain *conservationist, writer, designer*

Lynwood
Dove, Donald Augustine *city planner, educator*

Manhattan Beach
Krienke, Carol Belle Manikowske (Mrs. Oliver Kenneth Krienke) *realtor*
Schoenfeld, Lawrence Jon *real estate developer, asset lender*

Menlo Park
Fischer, Michael Ludwig *environmental executive*
Goodman, Beatrice May *real estate professional*

Moorpark
Bush, June Lee *real estate executive*

National City
Potter, J(effrey) Stewart *property manager*

Newbury Park
Fredericks, Patricia Ann *real estate executive*

Newport Beach
Fawcett, John Scott *real estate developer*
Matteucci, Dominick Vincent *real estate developer*
McClune, Michael Marlyn *real estate executive*

Oakland
Trimboli Blaine Margaret *real estate executive, interior designer*

Ontario
Ariss, David William, Sr. *real estate developer, consultant*

Oxnard
Narula, Mohan Lal *realtor*

Pacific Grove
Turrentine, Daniel Bruce *appraiser*

Palm Desert
Hilgenberg, Michael Charles *real estate agent*
Wiedle, Gary Eugene *real estate management company executive*

Palo Alto
McMillin, William Ray *real estate broker*

Pasadena
Crowley, John Crane *real estate developer*
Van Karnes, Kathleen Walker *realtor*

Placerville
Burnett, Eric Stephen *environmental consultant*

Rancho Palos Verdes
Randall, (Isaac) Eric *real estate broker*

Rancho Santa Fe
DeMarco, Ralph John *real estate developer*
Kessler, A. D. *business, financial, investment and real estate advisor, consultant, lecturer, author, broadcaster, producer*

Rolling Hills
Allbee, Sandra Moll *real estate broker*

Sacramento
Oliva, Stephen Edward *resource conservationist, lawyer*

San Bernardino
Willis, Harold Wendt, Sr. *real estate developer*

San Diego
Munson, Lucille Marguerite (Mrs. Arthur E. Munson) *real estate broker*
Oldham, Maxine Jernigan *real estate broker*

San Francisco
Barnes, William Anderson *real estate investment executive*
Brower, David Ross *conservationist*
Carmichael, Sharon Estelle *commercial real estate broker*
Frush, James Carroll, Jr. *real estate development company executive*
McIntyre, Robert Wheeler *conservation organization executive*
Ritchie, John Bennett *real estate executive*
Shorenstein, Walter Herbert *commercial real estate development company executive*
Williams, John Raymond, Jr. *real estate regional director*

San Marino
Doan, Larry Emery *real estate executive*

Santa Barbara
Arnold, Michael Neal *real property appraiser, consultant*
Smyth, Theodore Hilton *real estate developer*

Santa Cruz
Dilbeck, Charles Stevens, Jr. *real estate company executive*
Hersley, Dennis Charles *environmentalist, software systems consultant*

Santa Rosa
Brunner, Howard William *professional land surveyor*

Sausalito
Klingensmith, Arthur Paul *business and personal development consultant*

Seal Beach
Nesmith, Audrey Marie *retired military housing manager, writer*

Solana Beach
Jeske, Keith William *real estate and mortgage executive*

Sonora
Ogle, Madeline Ann Bright *realtor, investment counselor*

Spring Valley
Hillmann, Leo Charles *real estate company executive*

Torrance
Alter, Gerald L. *real estate executive*

Tracy
Dittman, Deborah Ruth *real estate broker*

Tustin
Prizio, Betty J. *property manager, civic worker*

West Hills
Struhl, Stanley Frederick *real estate developer*

Yorba Linda
Vilardi, Agnes Francine *real estate broker*

COLORADO

Aurora
Lochmiller, Kurtis L. *real estate entrepreneur*

Avon
Dunham, John Handy, II *real estate developer and broker*

Boulder
Hart, Michael John *environmental management consultant*
Morris, John Theodore *planning official*

Broomfield
Larson, Kenneth Gerard *real estate professional*

Colorado Springs
Beckett, Ted *commercial land developer*
Renneberger, Raymond Cecil *real estate professional*

Denver
Brown, Michael Gordon *design and real estate consultant, writer*
Mugler, Larry George *regional planner*
Norman, John Edward *petroleum landman*

Englewood
Smyth, David Shannon *real estate investor, commercial and retail builder and developer*

Golden
Sacks, Arthur Bruce *environmental and liberal arts educator*

Lakewood
Penwell, Jones Clark *real estate appraiser, consultant*
Weskamp, Kelley S. *account manager, real estate liquidation*
Williams, Ross Evans *planner, landscape architect*

Littleton
Grant, Newell M. *real estate investment manager*
Ward, Julie McDuff *real estate marketing specialist*

Pueblo
Neumayr, Sharon *land developer, writer*

Snowmass
Lovins, L. Hunter *public policy institute executive*

Telluride
Conner, Tom M. *real estate broker*

Vail
Kelton, Arthur Marvin, Jr. *real estate developer*

HAWAII

Honolulu
Adcock, Betty-Lee *real estate brokerage executive*
Albano, Andres, Jr. *real estate developer, real estate broker*
Chiu, Margaret Chi Yuan Liu *real estate broker*
Gillmar, Jack Notley Scudder *real estate company executive*
Lum, Jody Mae Kam Quon *real property appraiser*
Minerbi, Luciano Mario Lauro *urban and regional planning educator, consultant, community volunteer*
Mullahey, Ramona Kam Yuen *land use planner, educator*
Olsen, Harris Leland *real estate and international business executive, educator, diplomat*
Pedesky, Geraldine Golick *design project professional*
Vinton, Alice Helen *real estate company executive*
Walker, Margaret Smith *real estate company executive*

IDAHO

Boise
Clifton, Maurice S., III *real estate broker, real estate educator*
Fery, John Bruce *former real estate property manager*
Wilson, Carl Arthur *real estate broker*

Idaho Falls
Thorsen, Nancy Dain *real estate broker*

Payette
Jones, Donna Marilyn *real estate broker, legislator*

Pocatello
Hull, Lance Roland *real estate appraiser*

Stanley
Kimpton, David Raymond *natural resource consultant, writer*

Troy
Hepler, Merlin Judson, Jr. *real estate broker*

MONTANA

Sidney
Beagle, John Gordon *real estate broker*

NEVADA

Carson City
Empey, Gene F. *real estate executive*
McFadden, Robert Clyde *real estate broker*

Las Vegas
Broughton, James Walter *real estate development executive, consultant*
Dennis, Clinton Joel *property manager, small business owner*
Feldman, Robert Leon *real estate company officer, executive*
Griffin, James Edward *real estate consultant*
Maravich, Mary Louise *realtor*
Pulliam, Francine Sarno *real estate broker and developer*

Reno
Davenport, Janet Lee *real estate saleswomen, small business owner*
Jennison, Brian L. *environmental specialist*

West Wendover
Psenka, Robert Edward *real estate developer, behavioral scientist*

NEW MEXICO

Albuquerque
Davis, Betty Jean Bourbonia *real estate investment executive*
Godfrey, Richard George *real estate appraiser*
Kinney, Carol Naus Roberts *real estate broker*
Stahl, Jack Leland *real estate company executive*
Tinnin, Thomas Peck *real estate professional*

Hobbs
Seagrave, Janet Lee *economic developer*

Mora
Hanks, Eugene Ralph *land developer, cattle rancher, forester, retired naval officer*

OREGON

Lake Oswego
Morse, Lowell Wesley *banking and real estate executive*

Portland
Dickinson, Janet Mae Webster *relocation consulting executive*
Lilly, Elizabeth Giles *mobile park executive*
Miller, Ronald Edker *land use planner, artist*
Packard, Robert Goodale, III *planner*
Standring, James Douglas *real estate developer*

UTAH

Midvale
Teerlink, J(oseph) Leland *real estate developer*

Saint George
Tolbert, Beth Willden *real estate company owner, broker*

WASHINGTON

Bellevue
Edwards, Kirk Lewis *real estate company executive*

Edmonds
Soverel, Peter Wolcott *conservation executive, educator*

Ellensburg
Lathrop, F. Steven *commercial real estate developer, lawyer*

Friday Harbor
Padve, Martha Bertonneau *urban planning and arts consultant, fundraiser*

Mill Creek
Tovar, Carole L. *real estate management administrator*

Olympia
Stewart, Jeffree Robert *environmental planner, artist*

Renton
Kredlo, Thomas Andrew *real estate appraiser*

Rollingbay
Morris, Donald Charles *commercial real estate mergers and acquisitions*

Seabeck
Mjelde, Michael Jay *title company executive, writer*

Seattle
Dillard, Marilyn Dianne *property manager*
Flock, Roberta Rae *real estate executive*
Gerrodette, Charles Everett *real estate company executive, consultant*
McKinnon, James Buckner *real estate sales executive, writer, researcher*
Painter, Diana Jean *urban designer, artist, consultant*
Sander, Susan Berry *environmental planning engineering corporation executive*
Sasaki, Tsutomu (Tom Sasaki) *real estate company executive, international trading company executive, consultant*
Stevens, Clyde Benjamin, Jr. *property manager, retired naval officer*
Tu, Trang Dang *urban planner, fitness professional*

Tacoma
Wolf, Frederick George *environmentalist*

WYOMING

Evanston
Wheeler, Denice McIntire *real estate and investments professional, lecturer*

Rawlins
Pedersen, Martin Albert *consulting land surveyor*

CANADA

ALBERTA

Calgary
Milavsky, Harold Phillip *real estate executive*

BRITISH COLUMBIA

Vancouver
Chiavario, Nancy Anne *business and community relations executive*
Goldberg, Michael Arthur *land policy and planning educator*

ADDRESS UNPUBLISHED

Blog, Gloria DeLosh *retired property administrator*
Campbell, Jeff B. *realtor*
Dickey, Robert Marvin (Rick Dickey) *property manager*
Dreskin, Wendy *environmental educator*
Fischer, Zoe Ann *real estate and property marketing company executive, consultant*
Hentz, Marie Eva *real estate investor and developer*
Jordan, Lois Heywood *real estate developer*
Jungbluth, Kirk E. *real estate appraiser, mortgage banking executive*
Karakey, Sherry JoAnne *financial and real estate investment company executive, interior designer*
Kohn, Robert Samuel, Jr. *real estate investment consultant*
Latini, Henry Peter *real estate management consultant, journalist*
Lowe, Richard R. *real estate broker, pianist*
McCubbin, Susan Brubeck *real estate executive, lawyer*
Meyer, Daniel Kramer *real estate executive*
Moses, Stephen David *real estate investment professional*
Nakahata, Tadaka *retired consulting engineer, land surveyor*
Richman, Marvin Jordan *real estate developer, investor, educator*
Svidor, Rhona Beverly *real estate broker, elementary education educator*
Testa, Gabriel *real estate broker*
Yamagata, Leslie Craig *realty specialist*

GOVERNMENT: AGENCY ADMINISTRATION

UNITED STATES

ALASKA

Anchorage
Lacy, Gregory Lawrence *protective services official*
Nolan, James Michael *fire chief*
Scott, John Wayne *state manager*
Spaman, Morgan Patrick *fire and safety specialist*
Udland, Duane S. *protective services official*

Fairbanks
Davis, Charles Lee *fire marshal*

Juneau
Burke, Marianne King *state agency administrator, financial executive*

ARIZONA

Flagstaff
Madden, Edward P. *protective services official*

Glendale
Dobrotka, David A. *protective services official*
Goforth, Nathan Dan *police officer*

Grand Canyon
Arnberger, Robert *federal administrator*

Mesa
Ness, James Joseph *law enforcement educator*

Paradise Valley
Seal, Teddy Allen *police officer*

Peoria
Strope, Michael Lee *protective services official*

Phoenix
Bishop, C. Diane *state agency administrator, educator*
Brunacini, Alan Vincent *fire chief*
Houseworth, Richard Court *state agency administrator*
Meridith, Denise Patricia *government official*
Nielson, Theo Gilbert *law enforcement official, university official*
Simmons, Timothy Donald *fire service*
Travous, Kenneth E. *state agency administrator*

Scottsdale
Hill, Robert Martin *police detective, forensic document examiner, consultant, lecturer*

Sun City West
Eberling, George Gifford *federal agency administrator*

Tucson
Done, Robert Stacy *criminal investigation specialist, consultant*
Smith, David Mitchell *fire and explosion consultant*
Walker, Franklin Curtis *national park administrator*

CALIFORNIA

Anaheim
Bowman, Jeffrey R. *protective services official*
Gaston, Randall Wallace *police chief*

Bakersfield
Brummer, Steven E. *police chief*

Stepanek
Stepanek, Joseph Edward *industrial development consultant*

Benicia
von Studnitz, Gilbert Alfred *state official*

Berkeley
Butler, Daschel E. *protective services official*

Bonita
Yokley, Richard Clarence *fire department administrator*

Burbank
Chaffee, James Albert *protective services official*
Newsham, David P. *protective services official*

Castro Valley
Palmer, James Daniel *inspector*

Chico
Slaughter, Rodney Allen *firefighter, training consultant*

Costa Mesa
Snowden, David L. *protective services official*

El Centro
Steensgaard, Anthony Harvey *federal agent*

El Monte
Clayton, Wayne Charles *protective services official, educator*
George, Leslie Earl *protective services official*

Fremont
Steckler, Craig Theodore *law enforcement official*

Fresno
Winchester, Ed *protective services official*

Garden Grove
Sherrard, Raymond Henry *retired government official*

Indio
Hare, Paul DeHaven *public safety director*

Laytonville
Jones, Gilbert Leed *retired law enforcement officer, coroner, author*

Lodi
Landre, Rick Thomas *police officer*

Long Beach
Jeffery, James Nels *protective services official*
Luman, Robert M. *protective services official*

Los Angeles
Bangs, John Wesley, III *law enforcement administrator*
Fisher, Barry Alan Joel *protective services official*
Morten, Ralph Edward *police officer, bomb technician*

Modesto
Jefferson, Paul *police chief*

Moraga
Laye, John E(dward) *contingency planning and business continuity consulting executive*

Oakland
Samuels, Joseph, Jr. *police chief*

Ontario
Bernard, Alexander *airport police official*

Pasadena
Rivera, George *field investigator, security consultant*
Schander, Mary Lea *police official*

Placerville
Palmieri, Rodney August *state agency administrator, pharmacist*

Roseville
Simms, Thomas Haskell *police chief*

Sacramento
Callahan, Ronald *federal investigator, historian*
Coleman, Ronny Jack *fire chief*
Drown, Eugene Ardent *federal agency administrator*
Dunaway, Margaret Ann (Maggie Dunaway) *state agency consultant*
Edgerton, Lynne T. *state agency administrator, lawyer*
Pettite, William Clinton *public affairs consultant*

San Diego
Sanders, Jerry *protective services official*

San Francisco
Lau, Fred H. *protective services official*

Santa Ana
Walters, Paul *protective services official*

Santa Monica
Winchell, Robert Allen *government agency administrator, auditor*

Shingle Springs
Guay, Gordon Hay *postal service executive, marketing educator, consultant*

Sonora
Efford, Michael Robert *police administrator, educator*

Stockton
Chavez, Edward *police chief*
Jackson, Jewel *retired state youth authority executive*

Vacaville
Martinez, Gayle Frances *protective services official*

Westlake Village
Rogge, Richard Daniel *former government executive, security consultant, investigator*

Yuba City
Doscher, Richard John *protective services official*

COLORADO

Aurora
Barnes, Raymond Edward *fire department official*
Vincent, Verne Saint *protective services official*

Brighton
Otto, Thomas Joseph *criminal investigator, educator*

Colorado Springs
Kramer, Lorne C. *protective services official*
Linebaugh, David Eugene *fire marshal, educator*
Navarro, Manuel *protective services official*

Denver
Berger, John Milton *state agency administrator*
Gonzales, Richard L. *fire department chief*
Konrad, G. Gregory *protective services official*
Logan, James Scott, Sr. *federal agency administrator*
Smith, Waldo Gregorius *former government official*

Elizabeth
Rau, Randy J. *firefighter*

Englewood
Kirwin, Andrew Dean *protective services official*

Golden
Olson, Marian Katherine *emergency management executive, consultant, publisher*

Lakewood
Johnston, Charles *protective services official*

Littleton
Hayes, Roger Matthew *deputy sheriff*

Pueblo
Beurman, Albert Leroy *retired corrections officer*

Vail
McGee, Michael Jay *fire marshal, educator*

HAWAII

Hilo
Carvalho, Wayne G. *protective services official*

Honolulu
Dantsuka, Tracy Gail *police officer*
Devaney, David Everett *law enforcement official*
Kudo, Emiko Iwashita *former state official*
Roseberry, Edwin Southall *state agency administrator*

Kaneohe
Ikeda, Moss Marcus Masanobu *retired state education official, lecturer, consultant*

Paia
Kepani, Herman, Jr. *security officer*

IDAHO

Boise
Cory, Wallace Newell *state official, civil engineer*
Heitman, Gregory Erwin *state official*
McCambridge, Dennis *marshal*
Paulson, Larry A. *protective services official*
Turner, Hal Wesley *state agency administrator*
Wood, Jeannine Kay *state official*

MONTANA

Billings
Ballard, Lorren Lee *fire protection official*

NEVADA

Las Vegas
Chevers, Wilda Anita Yarde *probation officer*
Lally, Norma Ross *federal agency administrator, retired*
Martin, Michael Albert *surveillance agent*
Spencer, Carol Brown *association executive*
Wieting, Gary Lee *federal agency executive*
Wood, Benjamin Carroll, Jr. *safety professional*

NEW MEXICO

Albuquerque
Buelow, Grace Carlson *state agency surveyor, nurse*
Garcia y Griego, Renie C. *state agency administrator*
Maestas, Alex Walter *state agency clerk*
Williams, Marion Lester *government official*

Los Alamos
Griego, Juan Lawrence *federal agency administrator*

Santa Fe
McHenry, Patricia Rose *state agency administrator*
Mitio, John, III *state agency administrator*
Verant, William J. *state agency administrator*

OREGON

Medford
Cole, Richard George *public administrator*

Portland
Belille, Ronald *safety and security coordinator*

Salem
Myers, Walter E. *protective services official*

UTAH

Brigham City
McCullough, Edward Eugene *patent agent, inventor*

Provo
Cooper, Gregory M. *protective services official*

Salt Lake City
Gold, Rick L. *federal government executive*
Leary, G. Edward *state finance commisioner*

Springdale
Falvey, Donald *government official*

WASHINGTON

Enumclaw
Horlor, Ian Thomas *state official*

Fairchild Air Force Base
Sveen, James E. *state official*

Oakville
Accomando, Raymond Andrew *gambling commission executive, consultant*

Olympia
Mante, George Edward *tax administrator*

Redmond
Simpson, Linda Anne *retired police detective, municipal official*

Renton
Berkley, Robert John *federal agency professional*

Seattle
Harris, Claude *fire department chief*
Peddy, Julie Ann *admininstrative officer*
Stamper, Norman H. *police chief*
Williams, Clarence *protective services official*

Spokane
Dashiell, G. Ronald *marshal*
Mangan, Terence Joseph *police chief*
Williams, Robert Stone *protective services official*

Vancouver
Howsley, Richard Thornton *lawyer, regional government administrator*

Walla Walla
Andring, Ronald Paul *protective services official*

WYOMING

Casper
Reed, James Earl *fire department commander*

Jackson
Daily, John G. *protective services official*

CANADA

SASKATCHEWAN

Regina
Gordon, Hugh Sangster, Jr. *fire services administrator*

ADDRESS UNPUBLISHED

Clark, Thomas Ryan *retired federal agency executive, business and technical consultant*
Conway, James Valentine Patrick *forensic document examiner, former postal service executive*
Diamond, Robert Francis *federal agency administrator*
Flint, Lou Jean *retired state education official*
Hedrick, Basil Calvin *state agency administrator, ethnohistorian, educator, museum and multicultural institutions consultant*
Jiler, Linda Cerise *fire emergency dispatcher, consultant, researcher, writer*
Johnson, Rodney Dale *law enforcement officer, photographer*
Kelley, Kevin Patrick *security, safety, risk management administrator*
Le, Diana Lynn *county worker*
Nyquist, Maurice Otto *government agency administrator and scientist*
Parker, John Howard *state official*
Patino, Isidro Frank *law enforcement educator*
Pies, Ronald E. *retired city official*
Ramsey Lines, Sandra *forensic document examiner*
Rieder, Richard Walter *federal government official*
Ritchie, Catherine D. *correctional officer, deputy marshal*
Rushton, Clifford (Doug) *state water planner*
Shanahan, Michael George *police officer*
Shuman, Thomas Alan *correctional operations executive, consultant*
Silva, Robert Owen *retired protective service official*
Sorter, Bruce Wilbur *federal program administrator, educator, consultant*
Waggener, Theryn Lee *law enforcement professional*
Wood, Gina Eleane *state agency program administrator*

UNITED STATES

ALASKA

Anchorage
Selby, Jerome M. *mayor*

Fairbanks
Smith, Robert London, Sr. *commissioner, retired air force officer, political scientist, educator*

Juneau
Botelho, Bruce Manuel *state attorney general, mayor*
Knowles, Tony *governor*
Twomley, Bruce Clarke *commissioner, lawyer*
Ulmer, Frances Ann *state official*

ARIZONA

Florence
Griffis, Stanley Douglas *county manager*

Glendale
Scruggs, Elaine M. *mayor*

Mesa
Brown, Wayne J. *mayor*

Phoenix
Anthony, James Patrick *state program administrator, artist*
Bayless, Betsey *state official*
Cordova, Alexander M. *city clerk*
Curcio, Christopher Frank *city official*
Eaton, David E., II *city administrator*
Hull, Jane Dee *governor, former state legislator*
Kelly, John B. *state official*
McClennen, Miriam J. *former state official*
Miel, Vicky Ann *city official*
Rimsza, Skip *mayor*
Vanderheiden, Richard Thomas *government official, lawyer*
Welsh, John Richard *state official*
West, Tony *state official*

Prescott
Daly, Paul Sylvester *mayor, retired academic administrator*

Scottsdale
Dobronski, Mark William *judge, justice of the peace*
Warnas, Joseph John *municipal official*

Tucson
Crawford, Michael *city council*
Hutchinson, Edward Paul *city official*
Ibarra, Jose *city council*
Leal, Steve *city council*
Marcus, Janet *city council*
Miller, George *mayor*
Scott, Shirley *city council*

CALIFORNIA

Anaheim
Daly, Tom *mayor*
Hill, Harry David *city official, human resources professional*

Bakersfield
Price, Robert Otis *mayor*

Belmont
Roberts, Thomas Mulvihill *county official, lawyer*

Berkeley
Lambert, Bill *city official*
Sena, Robert Stephen *planner*

Brea
Georgino, Susan Martha *city redevelopment services administrator*

Century City
Wilson, Pete *former governor*

Chula Vista
Vaughan, Ralph Eugene *municipal administrator*

Coronado
Hostler, Charles Warren *international affairs consultant*

Covina
Sarver, Linda *mayor*

El Cajon
Pollock, Richard Edwin *former county administrator*
Thigpen, Mary Cecelia *city official, consultant*

El Monte
Wallach, Patricia *mayor*

Fall River Mills
Reed, Eva Silver Star *chieftain*

Fremont
Morrison, Gus (Angus Hugh Morrison) *mayor, engineer*

Fresno
Patterson, James *mayor*

Fullerton
Sa, Julie *council woman*

Glendale
Givens, Eileen Hadley *mayor*

Hayward
Cooper, Roberta *mayor*

Huntington Beach
Green, Peter *mayor, biological sciences educator*

La Verne
Cozad, Lyman Howard *city manager*

Lafayette
Hasseltine, Eric Hermon *government relations consultant*

Laguna Hills
Hussey, William Bertrand *retired foreign service officer*

Livermore
Brown, Cathie *city official*

Long Beach
Levi, Herbert A. *deputy city manager, consultant*
O'Neill, Beverly Lewis *mayor, former college president*
Topsy-Elvord, Doris Louise *municipal official*

Los Angeles
Blankenship, Juanita Chapman *court administrator*
Buichl, Anna Elizabeth *city official*
Davis, Michael Rico *county official*
Reagan, Nancy Davis (Anne Francis Robbins) *volunteer, wife of former President of United States*
Reagan, Ronald Wilson *former President of United States*
Riordan, Richard J. *mayor*

Mill Valley
Davis, Linda Jacobs *municipal official*

Mission Viejo
Wilson, Eleanor McElroy *county official*

Monterey
Wright, Mary Rose *state park superintendent*

Monterey Park
Smith, Betty Denny *county official, administrator, fashion executive*

Oakland
Brown, Edmund Gerald, Jr. (Jerry Brown) *mayor, former governor*
Harris, Elihu Mason *mayor*

Oceanside
L'Annunziata, Michael Frank *international official, nuclear scientist*
Lyon, Richard *mayor, retired naval officer*

Oroville
Curry, William Sims *county government administrator*

Rancho Mirage
Ford, Gerald Rudolph, Jr. *former President of United States*

Redlands
Hanson, Gerald Warner *retired county official*

Richmond
Corbin, Rosemary MacGowan *mayor*

Riverside
Loveridge, Ronald O. *mayor*

Roseville
Gray, Robert Donald *retired mayor*

Sacramento
Brooks, John Scott *county official*
Burton, John *state official*
Bustamante, Cruz M. *state official*
Corbett, Judith A. *municipal administrator*
Davis, Gray *governor*
Dunnett, Dennis George *state official*
Fong, Matthew Kipling *state official*
Hovious, Gregory Paul *municipal contract officer, contract consultant*
Hunter, Patricia Rae (Tricia) *state official*
Jones, Bill *state official, rancher*
Peck, Ellie Enriquez *retired state administrator*
Pernell, Robert *municipal official*
Serna, Joe, Jr. *mayor*
Villaraigosa, Antonio R. *state official*
Walston, Roderick Eugene *state government official*

Salinas
Wong, Walter Foo *county official*

San Bernardino
Lenz, Philip Joseph *municipal administrator*
Leuschen, Ronald James *county official*
Valles, Judith *mayor, former academic administrator*

San Diego
Bliesner, James Douglas *municipal/county official, consultant*
Golding, Susan *mayor*
Roberts, Ron *county board supervisor*
Walker, Lynn Cheryl *code compliance officer, consultant*

San Francisco
Brown, Willie Lewis, Jr. *mayor, former state legislator, lawyer*
Hewitt, Conrad W. *state superintendant of banks*
Islambouly, Hagar Abdel-Hamid *consul general*
Reilly, William Kane *former government official, educator, lawyer, conservationist*

San Jose
Gonzales, Ron *mayor, former county supervisor*
Hammer, Susan W. *mayor*

McHugh, Peter *mayor*
Winslow, Frances Edwards *city official*

San Luis Obispo
Zepeda, Susan Ghozeil *county official*

Santa Ana
Pulido, Miguel *mayor*

Santa Barbara
Conklin, Hal (Harold Conklin) *mayor*

Santa Monica
Rice, Donald Blessing *business executive, former secretary of air force*

Solana Beach
Beard, Ann Southard *government official, travel company executive*

South Gate
Mosby, Dorothea Susan *municipal official*

Stanford
Shultz, George Pratt *former government executive, economics educator*

Stockton
Podesto, Gary *mayor*
Simas, Edward Alfred *chairman county board supervisors*

Union City
Lewis, Mark Earldon *city manager*

West Covina
Manners, Nancy *retired mayor*

COLORADO

Aurora
Tauer, Paul E. *mayor, educator*

Boulder
Brooks, John Lanier, Jr. *county official*
Callen, Lon Edward *county official*
Trembour, Fred William *foreign service officer, metallurgist*

Colorado Springs
Makepeace, Mary Lou *mayor*

Denver
Brown, Keith Lapham *retired ambassador*
Buckley, Victoria *state official*
Feigin, Philip Alan *assistant commissioner*
Hackworth, Theodore James, Jr. *city official*
Howlett, John David *government relations*
Minger, Terrell John *public administration and natural resource institute executive*
Owens, Bill *governor*
Paramo, Patricia Ann *city/county official*
Rogero, Joe *state official*
Romer, Roy R. *former governor*
Salazar, Kenneth L. *state attorney general*
Walcher, Jennifer Lynne *city official*
Webb, Wellington E. *mayor*

Frisco
Phelps, Vada Jo *town official*

Grand Junction
Achen, Mark Kennedy *city manager*

Lakewood
Morton, Linda *mayor*

Pueblo
Occhiato, Michael Anthony *city official*

Silverton
Rich, Beverly Eileen *county official*

Sterling
Gustafson, Randall Lee *city manager*

DISTRICT OF COLUMBIA

Washington
Underwood, Robert Anacletus *congressional delegate, university official*

HAWAII

Honolulu
Bronster, Margery S *state attorney general*
Cayetano, Benjamin Jerome *governor, former state senator and representative*
Harris, Jeremy *mayor*
Hirono, Mazie Keiko *state official*
Marks, Robert Arthur *lawyer, attorney general*
Mizuguchi, Norman *state official*
Say, Calvin *state official*
Wakatsuki, Lynn Y. *commissioner*

Kapolei
Hao, Lawrence Kaholo *state official, clinical hypnotherapist*

Lihue
Kusaka, Maryanne Winona *mayor*

IDAHO

Boise
Benham, James H. *state official*
Cenarrusa, Pete T. *secretary of state*
Kempthorne, Dirk Arthur *governor*
Lance, Alan George *state attorney general*
Otter, Clement Leroy *lieutenant governor*
Williams, J. D. *state controller*

Donnelly
Edwards, Lydia Justice *state official*

Salmon
Sloan, Lanny Gene *municipal official*

MONTANA

Billings
Larsen, Richard Lee *former mayor and city manager, business, municipal and labor relations consultant, arbitrator*

Fairfield
Graf, Ervin Donald *municipal administrator*

Helena
Cooney, Mike *state official*
Hutchinson, Donald Wilson *state commissioner of financial institutions*
Mazurek, Joseph P. *state attorney general, former state legislator*
O'Keefe, Mark David *state official*
Racicot, Marc F. *governor*

Missoula
Brown, Horace Stuart *county surveyor*

NEVADA

Carson City
Del Papa, Frankie Sue *state attorney general*
Guinn, Kenny C. *governor*
Heller, Dean *state official*
Hunt, Lorraine T. *state official*
Krolicki, Brian Keith *state official*
Seale, Robert L. *state treasurer*
Walshaw, L. Scott *commissioner*

Las Vegas
Hammargren, Lonnie *former lieutenant governor*
Harvey, Ellen Mae *county official*
Hudgens, Sandra Lawler *retired state official*
Jones, Jan Laverty *mayor*
Miller, Robert Joseph *governor, lawyer*
Vandever, Judith Ann *county official*

NEW MEXICO

Albuquerque
Gonzales, Stephanie *state official*
Grossetete, Ginger Lee *retired gerontology administrator, consultant*
Haulenbeek, Robert Bogle, Jr. *government official*

Los Alamos
Weaver, Roy A. *national monument officer*

Raton
Quinn, William Francis *retired government executive, writer*

Santa Fe
Bradley, Walter D. *lieutenant governor, real estate broker*
Johnson, Gary Earl *governor*
Johnson, William Hugh, Jr. *state official, hospital administrator*
Madrid, Patricia Ann *state attorney general, lawyer*
Montoya, Michael A. *state treasurer, accountant*
Thompson, Jack Ernest *state official*
Vigil-Giron, Rebecca *state official*

OREGON

Dayton
Williams, Kenneth James *retired county official*

Eugene
Bascom, Ruth F. *retired mayor*
Collas-Dean, Angela G. *state commissioner, small business owner*

Lake Oswego
Campbell, Colin Herald *former mayor*

Portland
Burton, Mike *regional government administrator*
Church-Gaultier, Lorene Kemmerer *retired government official*
Katz, Vera *mayor, former college administrator, state legislator*
Moose, Charles A. *state official*
Stein, Beverly *chairperson county board supervisors*

Salem
Adams, Brady *state official*
Hill, Jim *state official*
Keisling, Phillip Andrew *state official*
Kitzhaber, John Albert *governor, physician, former state senator*
McMurdo, C(harles) Gregory *state official, lawyer*
Myers, Hardy *state attorney general, lawyer*
Tetzlaff, Karen Marie *state official*

UTAH

Ogden
Schow, Terry D. *state official*

Salt Lake City
Alter, Edward T. *state treasurer*
Corradini, Deedee *mayor*
Graham, Jan *state attorney general*
Johnson, Frank *retired state official, educator*
Leavitt, Michael Okerlund *governor, insurance executive*
Stephens, Martin R. *state official*
Walker, Olene S. *lieutenant governor*

WASHINGTON

Dayton
McFarland, Jon Weldon *retired county commissioner*

Edmonds
Thyden, James Eskel *diplomat, educator, lecturer*

Enumclaw
Krebs, Jennifer Amanda *city administrator*

Everett
Vaughn, Kathy *municipal official*

Olympia
Chopp, Frank *state official*
Hagens, William Joseph *state official, public health educator*
Locke, Gary *governor*
Mackie, Edward Buchanan *lawyer*
Munro, Ralph Davies *state government official*
Murphy, Michael Joseph *state official*
Owen, Bradley Scott *lieutenant governor*

Pullman
Halvorson, Alfred Rubin *retired mayor, consultant, education educator*

Seattle
Anderson, Dee *government relations and management consultant*
Lowry, Mike *former governor, former congressman*
Schell, Paul E. S. *mayor*
Skidmore, Donald Earl, Jr. *government official*
Smith, Le Roi Matthew-Pierre, III *municipal administrator*
Voget, Jane J. *city official, lawyer*

Sequim
Huston, Harriette Irene Otwell (Ree Huston) *retired county official*

Spokane
Talbott, John *mayor*

Sumas
Hemry, Larry Harold *former federal agency official, writer*

Tacoma
Vlasak, Walter Raymond *state official, management development consultant*

WYOMING

Cheyenne
Geringer, James E. *governor*
Ohman, Diana J. *state official, former school system administrator*
Smith, Stanford Sidney *state treasurer*
Woodhouse, Gay Vanderpoel *state attorney general*

Laramie
Meyer, Joseph B. *state official, former academic administrator*

CANADA

BRITISH COLUMBIA

Vancouver
Harcourt, Michael Franklin *retired premier of Province of British Columbia, lawyer, educator*

SASKATCHEWAN

Regina
Romanow, Roy John *provincial government official, barrister, solicitor*
Wiebe, J. E. N. *province official*

Saskatoon
Blakeney, Allan Emrys *Canadian government official, lawyer*
Hewitt, William James *municipal official*

ADDRESS UNPUBLISHED

Allen, Edgar Burns *records management professional*
Anderson, Ned, Sr. *Apache tribal chairman*
Batt, Philip E. *former governor*
Bradley, William Bryan *cable television regulator*
Denbrock, Kristie Ann *state official*
Eu, March Fong *ambassador, former state official*
Gregoire, Christine O. *state attorney general*
Hett, Joan Margaret *civic administrator*
Martz, Judy Helen *state official*
Peña, Federico Fabian *retired federal official*
Posey, James Madison *commissioner*
Ritter, Russell Joseph *mayor, college official*
Rudin, Anne Noto *former mayor, nurse*
Schoettler, Gail Sinton *former state official*
Tarkowski, Larry Michael *municipal official*
Whitney, Jane *foreign service officer*

GOVERNMENT: LEGISLATIVE ADMINISTRATION

UNITED STATES

ALASKA

Anchorage
Bunde, Con *state legislator, communication educator*

Porter, Brian Stanley *state legislator*
Sturgulewski, Arliss *state senator*

Homer
Phillips, Gail *state legislator*

Juneau
Kelly, Timothy Donahue *state senator*
Kohring, Victor H. *state legislator, construction executive*
Pearce, Drue *state legislator*

ARIZONA

Phoenix
Burns, Brenda *state legislator*
Eberhart, David L. *state legislator*
Groscost, Jeff *state legislator, small business owner*

Tucson
Richardson, Elaine *state legislator*

Window Rock
Henderson, James, Jr. *former senator*

CALIFORNIA

Danville
Baker, William P. (Bill Baker) *former congressman*

Garden Grove
Dornan, Robert Kenneth *former congressman*

Glendale
Moorhead, Carlos J. *former congressman*

Newport Beach
Cox, (Charles) Christopher *congressman*

Sacramento
Alpert, Deda Whittleton (Dede alpert) *state legislator*
Detwiler, Peter Murray *legislative consultant, educator*
Holmes, Robert Eugene *state legislative consultant, journalist*
Torres, Art *state senator*

COLORADO

Colorado Springs
Sinclair, William Donald *church official, fundraising consultant, political activist*

Denver
Bishop, Tilman Malcolm *state senator, retired college administrator*
Lamborn, Douglas L. *state legislator*
Meiklejohn, Alvin J., Jr. *state senator, lawyer, accountant*

Greeley
Brown, Hank *former senator, university administrator*

DISTRICT OF COLUMBIA

Washington
Abercrombie, Neil *congressman*
Akaka, Daniel Kahikina *senator*
Allard, A. Wayne *senator, veterinarian*
Baucus, Max S. *senator*
Becerra, Xavier *congressman, lawyer*
Bennett, Robert F. *senator*
Berkley, Shelley *congresswoman*
Berman, Howard Lawrence *congressman*
Bilbray, Brian P. *congressman*
Bingaman, Jeff *senator*
Blumenauer, Earl *congressman*
Boxer, Barbara *senator*
Brown, George Edward, Jr. *congressman*
Brown, Marta Macias *legislative staff member, executive assistant*
Bryan, Richard H. *senator*
Burns, Conrad Ray *senator*
Calvert, Ken *congressman*
Campbell, Ben Nighthorse *senator*
Campbell, Thomas J. *congressman*
Cannon, Christopher B. *congressman*
Capps, Lois Ragnhild Grimsrud *congresswoman, school nurse*
Chenoweth, Helen P. *congresswoman*
Condit, Gary Adrian *congressman*
Cook, Merrill A. *congressman, explosives industry executive*
Craig, Larry Edwin *senator*
Crapo, Michael Dean *senator, former congressman, lawyer*
Cubin, Barbara Lynn *congresswoman, former state legislator*
Cunningham, Randy *congressman*
DeFazio, Peter A. *congressman*
Dicks, Norman De Valois *congressman*
Dixon, Julian Carey *congressman*
Domenici, Pete V. (Vichi Domenici) *senator*
Dooley, Calvin Millard *congressman*
Doolittle, John Taylor *congressman*
Dreier, David Timothy *congressman*
Dunn, Jennifer Blackburn *congresswoman*
Enzi, Michael Bradley *senator, accountant*
Eshoo, Anna Georges *congresswoman*
Faleomavaega, Eni Fa'auaa Hunkin *congressman*
Farr, Sam *congressman*
Fazio, Vic *congressman*
Feinstein, Dianne *senator*
Filner, Robert *congressman*
Gallegly, Elton William *congressman*
Gibbons, James Arthur *congressman*
Hansen, James Vear *congressman*
Harman, Jane *congresswoman, lawyer*
Hastings, Doc *congressman*
Hayworth, John David, Jr. *congressman, sportscaster, commentator, broadcaster*
Hefley, Joel M. *congressman*

Hill, Rick Allan *congressman*
Hooley, Darlene *congresswoman, county commissioner*
Horn, Stephen *congressman, political science educator*
Inouye, Daniel Ken *senator*
Kolbe, James Thomas *congressman*
Kyl, Jon L. *senator*
Lantos, Thomas Peter *congressman*
Lewis, Charles Jeremy *congressman*
Lofgren, Zoe *congresswoman*
Martinez, Matthew Gilbert *congressman*
Matsui, Robert Takeo *congressman*
McCain, John Sidney, III *senator*
McDermott, James A. *congressman, psychiatrist*
McInnis, Scott Steve *congressman, lawyer*
McKeon, Howard P. (Buck McKeon) *congressman, former mayor*
Metcalf, Jack *congressman, retired state senator*
Millender-McDonald, Juanita *congresswoman, former school system administrator*
Miller, George *congressman*
Mink, Patsy Takemoto *congresswoman*
Murkowski, Frank Hughes *senator*
Murray, Patty *senator*
Nethercutt, George Rector, Jr. *congressman, lawyer*
Ose, Douglas *congressman*
Packard, Ronald C. *congressman*
Packwood, Bob *retired senator*
Pastor, Edward *congressman*
Pelosi, Nancy *congresswoman*
Pombo, Richard *congressman, rancher, farmer*
Radanovich, George P. *congressman*
Riggs, Frank *congressman*
Rohrabacher, Dana *congressman*
Roybal-Allard, Lucille *congresswoman*
Royce, Edward R. (Ed Royce) *congressman*
Salmon, Matt *congressman*
Sanchez, Loretta *congresswoman*
Schaefer, Dan L. *congressman*
Schroeder, Patricia Scott (Mrs. James White Schroeder) *former congresswoman*
Shadegg, John B. *congressman*
Skeen, Joseph Richard *congressman*
Smith, D. Adam *congressman*
Smith, Gordon Harold *senator*
Stark, Fortney Hillman (Pete Stark) *congressman*
Stevens, Theodore Fulton *senator*
Stump, Bob *congressman*
Tancredo, Thomas G. *congressman*
Thomas, Craig *senator*
Thomas, William Marshall *congressman*
Thompson, C. Michael *congressman*
Torres, Esteban Edward *congressman, business executive*
Waters, Maxine *congresswoman*
Waxman, Henry Arnold *congressman*
White, Rick *congressman*
Wilson, Heather Ann *congresswoman*
Woolsey, Lynn *congresswoman*
Wu, David *congressman*
Wyden, Ron *senator*
Young, Donald E. *congressman*

HAWAII

Honolulu
Fasi, Frank Francis *state senator*
Fong, Hiram Leong *former senator*

Wailuku
Baker, Rosalyn Hester *economic development administrator*

IDAHO

Boise
Ahrens, Pamela *state legislator*
Black, Pete *retired state legislator, educator*
McLaughlin, Marguerite P. *state senator, logging company executive*
Newcomb, Bruce *state legislator, farmer, rancher*

MARYLAND

Chevy Chase
Beilenson, Anthony Charles *former congressman*

MONTANA

Billings
Bowlinger, John C. *state senator*
Crippen, Bruce D. *senator, real estate manager*

Missoula
Williams, Pat *former congressman*

Polson
Mercer, John A. *state legislator*

NEVADA

Carson City
O'Connell, Mary Ann *state senator, business owner*
Tiffany, Sandra L. *state legislator*

Las Vegas
Vucanovich, Barbara Farrell *former congresswoman*
Wiener, Valerie *senator, communications consultant, positioning strategist, author*

Yerington
Dini, Joseph Edward, Jr. *state legislator*

NEW MEXICO

Albuquerque
Hall, Lois Riggs *former state senator, former symphony orchestra administrator*

Hobbs

Santa Fe
Sanchez, Raymond G. *state legislator*

OREGON

Bend
Cooley, Wes *former congressman*

Eugene
Hayden, Cedric L. *state legislator, dentist*

Portland
Hatfield, Mark Odem *former senator*

Salem
Brown, Kate *state legislator*
Oakley, Carolyn Le *state legislator, small business owner*

UTAH

Alpine
Tanner, Jordan *state legislator*

Bountiful
Burningham, Kim Richard *former state legislator*

Corinne
Ferry, Miles Yeoman *state official*

Hooper
Hull, Joseph L. *state senator*

Moroni
Blackham, Leonard Moyle *state senator*

Orem
Peterson, Craig Anton *former state senator*

Provo
Valentine, John Lester *state legislator, lawyer*

Salt Lake City
Orton, William H. (Bill Orton) *former congressman, lawyer*

Tooele
Mantes, George *state senator*

Tremonton
Kerr, Kleon Harding *former state senator, educator*

West Bountiful
Beattie, Lane *state senator*

WASHINGTON

Lake Stevens
Quigley, Kevin Walsh *state legislator, lawyer*

Olympia
Ballard, Clyde *state legislator*
Kohl-Welles, Jeanne Elizabeth *state senator, sociologist, educator*
Long, Jeanine Hundley *state legislator*
Neeld, Michael Earl *legislative staff administrator*
Thomas, Brian Chester *state legislator, engineer*

Ritzville
Schoesler, Mark Gerald *state legislator, farmer*

WYOMING

Douglas
Twiford, Jim *state legislator*

Gillette
Gilbertz, Larry E. *state legislator, entrepreneur*

Laramie
Hansen, Matilda *state legislator*

ADDRESS UNPUBLISHED

Aranda, Mary Kathryn *state legislator*
Baird, Brian N. *congressman*
Bilbray, James Hubert *former congressman, lawyer, consultant*
Cunningham, George *senator*
Hatch, Orrin Grant *senator*
Hickey, Winifred E(spy) *former state senator, social worker*
Hunter, Duncan Lee *congressman*
Pettis-Roberson, Shirley McCumber *former congresswoman*
Reid, Harry *senator*
Seastrand, Andrea H. *former congresswoman*
Simpson, Alan Kooi *former senator*
Sorensen, Sheila *state senator*
Zimmerman, Harold Samuel *retired state senator, newspaper editor and publisher, state administrator*

HEALTHCARE: DENTISTRY

UNITED STATES

ARIZONA

Flagstaff
Ririe, Craig Martin *periodontist*

Oro Valley

Phoenix
Fournier, Donald Frederick *dentist*
Sullivan, George Anerson *orthodontist*

Prescott
Lange, Gary David *periodontist*

Tucson
Davis, Richard Calhoun *dentist*
Kassman, Andrew Lance *orthodontist*
Oro, Robert John *dentist, consultant, writer*
Seklecki, Eugene Walter *retired oral surgeon*

CALIFORNIA

Antioch
Prowell, Roy Walters, Jr. *orthodontist*

Arcadia
Gamboa, George Charles *oral surgeon, educator*
Mak, Gilbert Kwok Kwong *pediatric dentist, researcher*

Arcata
Hise, Mark Allen *dentist*

Burbank
Bitting, Kevin Noel *pediatric craniofacial orthotist, researcher*

Burlingame
Truta, Marianne Patricia *retired oral and maxillofacial surgeon, educator, author*

Claremont
Valdez, Arnold *dentist, lawyer*

Costa Mesa
Aldrich, Dell Stanley *orthodontist*

El Centro
Barsan, Richard Emil *oral and maxillofacial surgeon*

Fullerton
Paik, Misung *dentist*

La Verne
Huigens, Daniel Dean *dentist*

Larkspur
Danielson, Gordon Douglas *dentist*

Long Beach
Gehring, George Joseph, Jr. *dentist*

Los Angeles
Etessami, Hirbod (Hiri Etessami) *endodontist, educator*

Manteca
Tonn, Elverne Meryl *pediatric dentist, dental benefits consultant*

Modesto
Boyd, J. Michael *dentist*

Northridge
Logan, Lee Robert *orthodontist*

Pebble Beach
Rossing, Catherine Barrett Schwab *dental hygienist*

San Francisco
Khosla, Ved Mitter *oral and maxillofacial surgeon, educator*

San Jose
Higgins, James Bradley *dentist*
Tanno, Ronald Louis *dentist*
Yoshizumi, Donald Tetsuro *dentist*

San Mateo
Wasserman, Bruce Arlen *dentist, mail order company executive*

Santa Monica
Gold, Steven *dentist*

Vacaville
Dedeaux, Paul J. *orthodontist*
Welton, Michael Peter *dentist*

Whittier
Lowe, Oariona *dentist*

COLORADO

Boulder
Schaffer, Joel Lance *dentist*

Denver
Patterson, Daniel William *dentist*

Golden
Christensen, Robert Wayne *oral maxillofacial surgeon, minister*

HAWAII

Honolulu
George, Peter T. *orthodontist*

Pearl City
Sue, Alan Kwai Keong *dentist*

IDAHO

Preston
Thompson, Mont Dean *retired dental hygienist*

MONTANA

Hardin
MacClean, Walter Lee *dentist*

NEVADA

Reno
DiGrazia, Peter Michael *dentist*
Waltz, Marcus Ernest *retired prosthodontist*

OREGON

Portland
Rosenthal, John David *dentist*

WASHINGTON

Bellevue
Carlson, Curtis Eugene *orthodontist, periodontist*

Lynnwood
Woodruff, Scott William *cosmetic, reconstructive and maxillofacial surgeon*

Seattle
Hollender, Lars Gösta *dental educator*
Lord, James Lorin *dentist*

Spokane
Foster, Ruth Mary *dental association administrator*
Kolsrud, Henry Gerald *dentist*
Steadman, Robert Kempton *oral and maxillofacial surgeon*

Vancouver
Tse, Dany Yui *dentist, dental administrator*

WYOMING

Casper
Keim, Michael Ray *dentist*

Jackson
Petersen, Richard Craig *dentist*

ADDRESS UNPUBLISHED

Cline, Darrell Eugene *dentist*
Schrumpf, Robyn Lynn *dentist*

HEALTHCARE: HEALTH SERVICES

UNITED STATES

ALASKA

Anchorage
Devens, John Searle *natural resources administrator*

Chugiak
Robinson, Thelma May *pediatrics nurse, researcher, writer*

Fairbanks
Stinson, Aviva Jochebed *psychosocial nurse*

Kodiak
Ackley, Marjorie Rose *health educator*

ARIZONA

Casa Grande
McGillicuddy, Joan Marie *psychotherapist, consultant*

Chandler
Boissoneau, Robert Allen *health management consultant, educator*
Graham, Anita Louise *correctional and community health nurse*
Shousha, Annette Gentry *critical care nurse*
Wall, Teresa Laurine *nursing and healthcare administrator*

Cottonwood
Peck, Donald Harvey *chiropractor*

Glendale
Jarnagin, Donald Edward *optometrist*

Mesa
Beck, Jerome Joseph *health care administrator, biomedical technologist*
Boyd, Leona Potter *retired social worker*
Fleisher, Mark *health care executive*

Paradise Valley
McKinley, Joseph Warner *health science facility executive*

Phoenix
Anderson, Christina Susanne *speech and language therapist*
Binnie, Nancy Catherine *retired nurse, educator*
Chan, Michael Chiu-Hon *chiropractor*
Fitzgerald-Verbonitz, Dianne Elizabeth *nursing educator*
Kern, Valarie Jean *medical technologist*
Levin, Linda Rose *mental health counselor*
Mitchell, Wayne Lee *health care administrator*
O'Donnell, Barbara Spence *nurse*
Sarten, Mary Ann *health facility administrator*

Seiler, Steven Lawrence *health facility administrator*
Todd, William Michael *counselor, educator*
Van Kilsdonk, Cecelia Ann *retired nursing administrator, volunteer*
Vermeer, Wanda Beth *healthcare consultant*
Welliver, Charles Harold *hospital administrator*

Pima
Shafer, James Albert *health care administrator*

Prescott
Goodman, Gwendolyn Ann *nursing educator*
Rindone, Joseph Patrick *clinical pharmacist, educator*

Prescott Valley
Campbell, Virginia Kolnick *retired rehabilitation counselor*

Scottsdale
Bagan-Prochelo, Barbara Ellen *psychotherapist*
Conlan, Irene Estelle *health care administrator*
Meyers, Marlene O. *hospital administrator*
Timmons, Evelyn Deering *pharmacist*
Troxell, Mary Theresa (Terry Troxell) *geriatrics services professional*

Sedona
Catterton, Marianne Rose *occupational therapist*

Sells
Enas, Lena Mae *research coordinator, consultant*

Sonoita
Scott, William Coryell *medical executive*

Sun City
DiDomizio, Robert Anthony *health facility administrator*

Tempe
Anchie, Toby Levine *health facility administrator*

Thatcher
Heaton, Debbie Ann *mental health services worker*

Tucson
Andersen, Luba *electrologist, electropigmentologist*
Avolio, Wendy Freedman *speech and language pathologist*
Harris, Emma Earl *nursing home executive*
Horan, Mary Ann Theresa *nurse*
Johnson, Elissa Sarah *speech pathologist, writer*
Kmet, Rebecca Eugenia Patterson *pharmacist*
Kopsco, Carol Jean *social worker, mental health psychotherapist, counselor*
McCabe, Monica Jane *oncological nurse*
Schussel, Alan Lewis *rehabilitation counselor*
Shropshire, Donald Gray *hospital executive*
Tong, Theodore G. *pharmacy educator, dean*

CALIFORNIA

Agoura Hills
Chabot, Gerri Louise *counselor, nurse*
Merchant, Roland Samuel, Sr. *hospital administrator, educator*

Alameda
Herrick, Sylvia Anne *health service administrator*

Alhambra
Liu, Zhong-Ping (Peter Liu) *natural medicine specialist, actor*

Aliso Viejo
Davidson, Melody Kay *critical care nurse, educator*

Alta Loma
Fenison, Eddie *health science educator*

Amador City
Evans-Shaw, Glenda *nursing administrator*

Anaheim
Lee, Donna Jean *retired hospice and respite nurse*

Arcadia
Anderson, Holly Geis *women's health facility administrator, commentator, educator*

Arcata
Janssen-Pellatz, Eunice Charlene *healthcare facility administrator*

Bakersfield
Decker, James Thomas *psychotherapist*
Murillo, Velda Jean *social worker, counselor*
Watkins, Judith Ann *nurse administrator*
Wong, Wayne D. *nutritionist*

Belmont
Schreiber, Andrew *psychotherapist*

Berkeley
Bondoc, Antonio C. *physician assistant*
Day, Lucille Lang *health facility administrator, educator, author*
Harris, Michael Gene *optometrist, educator, lawyer*
Poe, Lenora Madison *psychotherapist and author*
Tutashinda, A.K. Kweli (Brian P. Altheimer) *chiropractic physician, author*

Beverly Hills
Johnson, Patricia Diane *psychotherapist, consultant*
Mindell, Earl Lawrence *nutritionist, author*

Brea
Ramsey, Nancy Lockwood *nursing educator*
Schlose, William Timothy *health care executive*

Burbank
Ungerleider, Dorothy Fink *educational therapist*

Camarillo
Rieger, Elaine June *nursing administrator*

Canoga Park
Jourdan, Stephanie Carol *educator*

Carmel
Elmstrom, George P. *optometrist, writer*

Carson
Chan, Peter Wing Kwong *pharmacist*
Churchman, David Alan *conflict management educator*

Castro Valley
Bennett, Shoshana Stein *post partum counselor, consultant, lecturer*

Cedar Ridge
Bruno, Judyth Ann *chiropractor*

Cerritos
Sainer, Elliot A(rnold) *health care executive*

Chatsworth
Stephenson, Irene Hamlen *biorhythm analyst, consultant, editor, educator*

Chico
Clough, Saralyn Louise *speech and language pathologist*

Chula Vista
Kemery, William Elsworth *psychotherapist, hypnotherapist*

Claremont
Hartford, Margaret Elizabeth (Betty Hartford) *social work educator, gerontologist, writer*

Clovis
Lake, Ruth Elaine *optics technician*

Concord
Bouquin, James Richard *healthcare facility executive*

Costa Mesa
Hernandez, Jeffrey Scott, Sr. *counselor, administrator*
Klein, (Mary) Eleanor *retired clinical social worker*

Culver City
des Sagettes, Christiane Guillermin *pharmacist, biologist*

Cupertino
Byrd, Thomas Russell *health educator*

Downey
Hart-Duling, Jean Macaulay *clinical social worker*

Dublin
Ingram, Judith Elizabeth *counselor*

El Cerrito
Cooper, William Clark *physician*

El Monte
Glass, Jean Ann *special education services professional*

Emeryville
Finney, Lee *negotiator, social worker*

Encino
Bekey, Shirley White *psychotherapist*
House-Hendrick, Karen Sue *nursing consultant*

Escondido
Gentile, Robert Dale *optometrist, consultant*
Herron, Margaret Catherine *nursing administrator*

Fairfax
Neuharth, Daniel J., II *psychotherapist*

Fontana
DeGuire, Margaret Ann *nurse*

Forman Valley
Markel, Rex Allen *medical facility administrator*

Fountain Valley
Schweigert, Byron Frederick *health services administrator*

Fremont
Loarie, Thomas Merritt *healthcare executive*
Sahatjian, Manik *nurse, psychologist*

Fresno
Antrim, Minnie Faye *residential care facility administrator*
Connor, David John *health care executive, accountant*
Ezaki-Yamaguchi, Joyce Yayoi *renal dietitian*
Patton, Lynette Anne *nursing educator, consultant*
Schroeder, Rita Molthen *retired chiropractor*
Willems, Wally *health facility administrator*

Fullerton
Griffin, Kirsten Bertelsen *nursing educator*

Glendora
Rogers, Bryan Ross *health care facility administrator*

Guerneville
Kozlow, Beverly Kay *physical therapist, clinical psychologist, realtor*

Hayward
Hospy, Patricia L. *chiropractor, property management executive*

Healdsburg
McGinnis, Michael Patrick *psychotherapist*

Hemet
Hernandez, Lillian A. *health facility administrator*
Lawrence, Paula Denise *physical therapist*

Huntington Beach
Kanode, Carolyn Kerrigan *school nurse, pediatric nurse practitioner*
Olsen, Greg Scott *chiropractor*

Inglewood
Miller, Donna Jean *nursing educator*

La Canada
Kavin, Rebecca Jean *health science executive*

La Jolla
Castleman, Breaux Ballard *health management company executive*
Marshall, Sharon Bowers *nursing educator, director clinical trials*
Ruggeri, Zaverio Marcello *medical researcher*
Stephens, Stevie Marie *psychotherapist*

La Mesa
Boncher, JoAnne Barry *language, speech and hearing specialist*

Lafayette
Stoermer, Daphne Carol *physical therapist, consultant*

Laguna Hills
Banuelos, Betty Lou *rehabilitation nurse*
Henderson, Marsha Roslyn Thaw *clinical social worker*
Lindsay, Helen Mills *psychotherapist*
Shipley, Nancy Louise *health science association executive*

Lake Arrowhead
Keller, Sharon Pillsbury *speech pathologist*

Lake Elsinore
Riley, Sharell Denice *therapist, educator*

Lemoore
Davis, Cynthia Almarinez *nursing educator*

Lodi
Bernhoft, Franklin Otto *psychotherapist, psychologist*

Loma Linda
Bullock, Weldon Kimball *health facility administrator, pathologist, pathology educator*
Snyder, John Joseph *optometrist*

Long Beach
Brault, G(ayle) Lorain *healthcare executive*
Brown, Lester B. *social work educator*
Carlton-Adams, Dana Georgia Marie Anne *psychotherapist*
Ferreri, Michael Victor *optometrist*
Lulli, Bonnie Jean *medical group administrator*
Mullins, Ruth Gladys *nurse*
Russell, Joan Delight *hospital administrator, realtor, investor*

Los Alamitos
Anderson, Mitchell *chiropractor*
Ratliff, Leigh Ann *pharmacist*

Los Angeles
Ash, Lawrence Robert *public health educator, administrator*
Baron, Melvin Farrell *pharmacy educator*
Blitz-Weisz, Sally *speech pathologist*
Bourque, Linda Anne Brookover *public health educator*
Chen, Peter Wei-Teh *mental health services administrator*
Cohn, Daniel Howard *laboratory director*
Cottam, Calvin *retired chiropractor, author*
Dalzell, George Edward *social worker, author*
Donaldson, Mary Kendrick *nurse*
Dreyfuss, John Alan *health facility administrator*
Horowitz, Ben *medical center executive*
Hummel, Joseph William *hospital administrator*
Johnson, Leonidas Alexander *optometrist, minister*
Katzin, Carolyn F. *nutritionist, consultant*
Lopez-Navarro, Eduardo Luis *family therapist*
Meduski, Jerzy Wincenty *nutritionist, biochemist*
Neville-Harris, Alice Almeda (Alice Almeda Ahna) *retired critical care nurse*
Richardson, Winifred Lee *youth counselor, writer*
Schenkel, Felicia Ann *cardiothoracic transplant coordinator*
Shabot, Myron Michael *surgeon, critical care educator, informaticist*
Smith, Sheila Anne *nursing administrator, lecturer*
Somers, Leonora Patiño *psychotherapist*
Stevens, Eleanor Sandra *domestic services executive*
Thompson, Judith Kastrup *nursing researcher*
Utz, Sarah Winifred *nursing educator*
Ver Steeg, Donna Lorraine Frank *nurse, sociologist, educator*
Watkins, Gloria Thomas *health care worker*
Wells, Thelma M. *educator, educational administrator*
Whybrow, Peter Charles *psychiatrist, educator, author*
Yang, Robert Menhsiu *healthcare system administrator*

Los Gatos
Meyer, Judith Anne *health facility administrator*
Moore, Laurie Alison *expressive arts therapist, hypnotherapist*

Malibu
Kovner, Joel Wyatt *medical economist, banker*

Marina
Cornell, Annie Aiko *nurse, administrator, retired army officer*

Marina Del Rey
Nizze, Judith Anne *retired physician assistant*

Mariposa
Bryant, Carol Lee *public health educator, psychotherapist, consultant*

Harrison, Candace J. *physician assistant*

Marysville
Gray, Katherine *marriage and family counselor and support therapist*
Myers, Elmer *psychiatric social worker*

Menlo Park
McCreary, Deborah Dennis *oncology nurse*

Modesto
Lipomi, Michael Joseph *health facility executive*
Low, Marissa E. *health care administrator*

Monte Sereno
Jackson, Suzanne Elise *health education coordinator*

Monterey
Gustat, Matthew Peter, III *health care executive*

Moreno Valley
Gull, Paula Mae *renal transplant coordinator, nephrology nurse, medical-surgical nurse*

Mount Shasta
Mariner, William Martin *chiropractor*

Mountain View
Alameda, Russell Raymond, Jr. *radiologic technologist*

Napa
Lee, Margaret Anne *social worker, psychotherapist*
Sedlock, Joy *psychiatric social worker*

Newport Beach
Green, Melanie Jane *speech-language pathologist*
Johnson, Leayn Hutchinson *nursing educator, mental health nurse*
Stephens, Michael Dean *hospital administrator*

Oakland
Caulfield, W. Harry *health care industry executive, physician*
Hancock, Nannette Beatrice Finley *mental health educator, consultant*
Oberti, Sylvia Marie Antoinette *rehabilitation counselor and administrator, career advisor, textile consultant*
Pomper, Catherine Janice *health care administrator*
Wheatley, Barnarese P. (Bonnie Wheatley) *health services consultant*

Oceanside
Harbord, Anne Marie *consulting dietetics company executive*
Marlborough, Janet Lynn *healthcare consultant*

Orange
Brown, Lillian Eriksen *retired nursing administrator, consultant*
Meyer, Diana Lynn *clinical nurse specialist*
Price, Gail J. Goodman *marriage, family and child therapist, deaf and hearing impaired specialist*

Oroville
Strawn, Susan Heathcote *medical administrator*

Oxnard
Dimitriadis, Andre C. *health care executive*
Phillips, Dorothy Lowe *nursing educator*

Palm Springs
Boyajian, Timothy Edward *public health officer, educator, consultant*
Loya, Ranaldo *senior physician assistant*

Palo Alto
Kelsey, Edith Jeanine *psychotherapist, consultant*
Maiden, Eva Wenkart *psychotherapist, school psychologist*
Skeff, Kelley Michael *health facility administrator*
Ward-Shaw, Sheila Theresa *nurse*

Pasadena
Boytim, Michael J. *surgical nurse*

Perris
Zimmer, Paul Gerald, II *community care licensing professional*

Petaluma
James, Mary Spencer *nursing home health administrator*

Pico Rivera
Brotman, Richard Dennis *counselor*

Placerville
Wall, Sonja Eloise *nurse administrator*

Pleasanton
Shen, Mason Ming-Sun *medical center administrator*

Ramona
Cooper, James Melvin *healthcare executive, consultant*

Rancho Mirage
Doi, Lois *psychiatric social worker*
Ford, Betty Bloomer (Elizabeth Ford) *health facility executive, wife of former President of United States*
Kiser, Roberta Katherine *medical records administrator, education educator*

Rancho Santa Fe
Trout, Monroe Eugene *hospital systems executive*

Redlands
Coleman, Arlene Florence *nurse practitioner*

Redondo Beach
Diamonds, Blanca Maria *mental health counselor*
Kronenberg, Jacalyn (Jacki Kronenberg) *nurse administrator*

Redwood City
Behrens, Barbara Blauth *healthcare administrator*
Rothhammer, Craig Robert *social worker, consultant*

Richmond
Terrill, Karen Stapleton *retired medical planning consultant*

Riverside
Brandt, Blanch Marie *health care facility administrator*
Chang, Sylvia Tan *health facility administrator, educator*
Nieves, Carmen *emergency services coordinator*
Smith, Jeffry Alan *health administrator, physician, consultant*

Roseville
Wright, Carole Yvonne *chiropractor*

Sacramento
Beckwith, Charles Allan *healthcare administrator, consultant*
Bohnen, Mollyn Villareal *nurse, educator*
Headley, Nathan Leroy *laboratory executive*
Laronge, Lawrence Steven *health administrator, tax professional*
Manley, Barbara Lee Dean *occupational health nurse, hospital administrator, safety and health consultant*
Peck, Raymond Charles, Sr. *driver behavior research specialist and research administrator*
Roberts, Paul Dale *health services administrator*
Runfola, Sheila Kay *nurse*
Tyrrell, Eleanore Day *health program evaluation specialist*
Whitaker, Cynthia Ellen *nurse*

Salinas
Quick, Valerie Anne *sonographer*

San Bernardino
Corpuz, Sheila Mae *nurse*
Godager, Jane Ann *social worker*
Tacal, Jose Vega, Jr. *public health official, veterinarian*
Timmreck, Thomas C. *health sciences and health administration educator*

San Diego
Campbell, Raymond William *surgical nurse*
Cutright, Frances Larson *marriage and family therapist*
Donnelly, Edward James, Jr. *medical services company executive*
Dwyer, Lauraine Theresa *ambulatory care administrator, rehabilitation nurse*
Early, Ames S. *healthcare system executive*
Eimers, Jeri Anne *therapist*
Freeman-Zuniga, Rochelle Ellen Laskov *electrologist, medical technologist*
Maier-Lorentz, Madeline Marie *nurse educator*
Roberts-DeGennaro, Maria *social work educator*
Schmidt, Terry Lane *health care executive*
Smith, Raymond Edward *retired health care administrator*

San Francisco
Anargyros, Nedra Harrison *cytotechnologist*
Auerback, Sandra Jean *social worker*
Crear, Mildred Cleareatha *nursing administrator*
Dibble, Suzanne Louise *nurse, researcher*
Elias, Charles David *psychotherapist*
Facione, Noreen Carol *nursing educator, researcher*
Gaber, Jason Lee *social worker*
Howatt, Sister Helen Clare *human services director, former college library director*
Mannino, J. Davis *psychotherapist*
Noble, Susan Elvira *nurse*
Norbeck, Jane S. *nursing educator*
Rankin, Jimmie R. *neuroscience nurse*
Richmond, Rosalind *clinical social worker*
Stannard, Daphne Evon *critical care nurse*
Van Etten, Peter Walbridge *hospital administrator*
Young, Lowell Sung-yi *medical administrator, educator*

San Gabriel
Otaya, Michiko *nurse*

San Jose
Cunnane, Patricia S. *medical facility administrator*
Demers, Mary Adelaide *psychotherapist, educator*
Mayfield, Sandra Jeanne *recreational therapist, consultant*
Vieira, Linda Marie *administrative and technical coordinator, endoscopy technician*

San Leandro
Daniels, Lydia M. *health care administrator*

San Luis Obispo
Smith, Joey Spauls *mental health nurse, home health nurse, biofeedback therapist, consultant, educator, bodyworker, hypnotist*

San Mateo
Richens, Muriel Whittaker *AIDS therapist, counselor and educator*
Steiner, Mary Ann *nursing administrator, consultant*

San Rafael
Friesecke, Raymond Francis *health company executive*
Zaleski, Brian William *computer programmer, analyst*

San Ramon
Harman, Kenneth R. *counseling administrator*

Santa Ana
Oberstein, Marydale *geriatric specialist*

Santa Barbara
Barbakow, Jeffrey *health facility administrator*
Brown, Baillie Russell *health services administrator*
Focht, Michael Harrison *health care industry executive*
Narayanamurti, Venkatesh *research administrator*

Santa Cruz
Hilyard, David Franklin *optician*

Santa Monica
Levine, Peggy Aylsworth *psychotherapist, writer, poet*
Marei, Ibrahim *medical technologist*
McWaid-Harrah, Diana Megan *health service administrator*

Santa Rosa
Dempsey, Barbara Matthea *medical, surgical and critical care nurse*
Lewis, Marion Elizabeth *social worker*
Nickens, Catherine Arlene *retired nurse, freelance writer*
Pearson, Susan Rose *psychotherapist, fine arts educator, artist*
Searight, Mary Dell (Mrs. Paul James Searight) *nursing educator*

Santa Ynez
Walker, Burton Leith *engineering writer, psychotherapist*

Seal Beach
Stillwell, Kathleen Ann Swanger *healthcare consultant*

Sepulveda
Burton, Paul Floyd *social worker*

Sherman Oaks
Peplau, Hildegard Elizabeth *nursing educator*
Schumack, Maxine Lynne *community college counselor*
Silberman, Irwin Alan *retired public health physician*

Sonora
Cole, Barry Eliot *health science association administrator*

South Pasadena
Wu, Margaret Mei-Ling Kan *pharmacist*

Stockton
Hutchison, Loyal Dwayne *pharmacist*
Yamanaka, Wendi Suzuko *pharmacist*

Studio City
Herrman, Marcia Kutz *child development specialist*
Weiner, Sandra Samuel *critical care nurse, nursing consultant*

Tarzana
Rinsch, Maryann Elizabeth *occupational therapist*

Temecula
Gimbel, Hervey Willis *medical administrator*

Thousand Oaks
Emerson, Alton Calvin *retired physical therapist*
Mulkey, Sharon Renee *gerontology nurse*
Shirley, Courtney Dymally *nurse*

Torrance
Lemkin, Pamela Ayleen *health facility administrator, oncological nurse, consultant*
Prell, Joel James *medical group administrator*
Todd, Frances Eileen *pediatrics nurse*

Union City
Glueck, Mary A. *retired psychiatric and mental health nurse*

Vacaville
Dailey, Dawn Elaine *public health service official*

Vallejo
Emlet, Charles Arthur *social worker*

Van Nuys
Owens, Warner Barry *physical therapist*

Ventura
Bircher, Andrea Ursula *psychiatric-mental health nurse, educator, clinical nurse specialist*

Vista
Price-Tuma, Diane Lynette *nurse, business owner, educator*

Walnut
Cabrales, Luisita Katigbak *nurse administrator, consultant, entrepreneur*

Walnut Creek
Burns, Francis Raymond *biofeedback instructor, researcher*
Williams, Michael James *health care services consultant*

West Covina
Adams, Sarah Virginia *family counselor*

Westlake Village
Calhoun, Rose Taylor *health services administrator*

Westlake Vlg
Cole, Julie Parsons *social worker*

Woodland Hills
Kaysen, Max *clinical psychologist*
Williams, Beau Wilson *health services administrator*

Yountville
Jones, Thomas Robert *social worker*

Yucaipa
Mote, Gordon Edward *health facility administrator*

COLORADO

Aurora
Dunn, Karen K. *mental health center executive, psychotherapist*
Gardner, Sandra Lee *nurse, outreach consultant*

Boulder
Holdsworth, Janet Nott *women's health nurse*
Kelley, Bruce Dutton *pharmacist*
Middleton-Downing, Laura *psychiatric social worker, artist, small business owner*

Broomfield
Lybarger, Marjorie Kathryn *nurse*

Buena Vista
Herb, Edmund Michael *optometrist, educator*

Canon City
Honaker, Charles Ray *health facility administrator*
Romano, Rebecca Kay *counselor*

Colorado Springs
Cameron, Paul Drummond *research facility administrator*
Driscoll, David Lee *chiropractor*
Duston, Eldon Craig *nurse, educator*
Olson, Kenneth Paul *rehabilitation counselor*
Williams, Ruth Lee *clinical social worker*
Young, Lynn Marie *psychotherapist*

Denver
Allen, Robert Edward, Jr. *physician assistant*
Billings, Becky Leigh *nurse*
Bourg, Pamela Wilkinson *emergency nurse*
Brown, Linda Jean *nursing administrator*
Geiselhardt-Head, Barbara Theresa *nursing administrator*
Hand, Dale L. *pharmacist*
Jennett, Shirley Shimmick *home care management executive, nurse*
Mastrini, Jane Reed *social worker, consultant*
Miller, Jill Marie *psychoanalyst*
Nett, Louise Mary *nursing educator, consultant*
Parker, Catherine Susanne *psychotherapist*
Pepper, Norma Jean *mental health nurse*
Rael, Henry Sylvester *retired health administrator, financial and management consultant*
Rizzi, Teresa Marie *bilingual speech and language pathologist*
Wilkinson, Joan Kristine *nurse, pediatric clinical specialist*

Fort Collins
Ervin, Ardith Ann *psychiatric social worker*
Schatz, Mona Claire Struhsaker *social worker, educator, consultant, researcher*

Glenwood Springs
Reinisch, Nancy Rae *therapist, consultant*

Greeley
Engle, Cindy *medical transcriptionist*
Linde, Lucille Mae (Jacobson) *motor-perceptual specialist*

Highlands Ranch
Gehlmann, Sheila Cathleen *psychologist, research analyst*

Idledale
Brown, Gerri Ann *physical therapist*

Lakewood
Babel, Deborah Jean *social worker, paralegal*

Parker
Haas, Bradley Dean *pharmacy director, clinical pharmacist, consultant*
Lembeck, James Peter *nutritionist, writer, consultant*

Pueblo
Hawkins, Robert Lee *health facility administrator*

U S A F Academy
Grant, Laurie Louise *physician assistant, health educator, consultant, biofeedback and neurofeedback therapist*

Yuma
Hertneky, Randy Lee *optometrist*

HAWAII

Hanalei
Snyder, Francine *psychotherapist, registered nurse, writer*

Hilo
Braden, Warren Ramsey, Sr. *health administrator, educational consultant*
Clark, Janet *retired health services executive*
Werner, Marlin Spike *speech pathologist and audiologist*

Honolulu
Fischer, Joel *social work educator*
Flannelly, Laura T. *mental health nurse, nursing educator, researcher*
Gormley, Francis Xavier, Jr. *social worker*
Katz, Alan Roy *public health educator*
Loh, Edith Kwok-Yuen *oncology nurse, health education specialist*
Lum, Jean Loui Jin *nurse educator*
Mohrdick, Eunice Marie *nurse, consultant, health educator*
Roberson, Kelley Cleve *health care financial executive*
Tanaka, Stanley Katsuki *optometrist, consultant*
Thomas, Verneda Estella *retired perfusionist*
Toyomura, Akiko Charlotte *health administrator, nurse*

Kaneohe
Westerdahl, John Brian *nutritionist, health educator*

Kula
Miguel deSousa, Linda J. *critical care nurse, nursing educator*

Lahaina
Balog (Gillette), Dawn Lois *motivational therapist, nutritionist*
Vonderheid, Arda Elizabeth *nursing administrator*

Mililani
Kiley, Thomas *rehabilitation counselor*

Pearl Harbor
Godwin, Bruce Wayne *nurse corps officer*

Waipahu
Kuwabara, Dennis Matsuichi *optometrist*

IDAHO

Boise
Harper, Anthony *counselor, singer*
Kendrick, Beverly Ann *medical-surgical nurse, small business owner*
Robinson, Julia E. *health facility administrator*

Lewiston
Smith, Phyllis Mae *healthcare consultant, educator*

Nampa
Denney, Doris Elaine *pharmacist*
Doner, John Roland *hospital administrator*
Zuckschwerdt, Otto Salvatore *counselor, substance abuse specialist, chaplain*

Payette
Bragg, Darrell Brent *nutritionist, consultant*

Post Falls
Hamman, Steven Roger *vocational rehabilitation specialist*

MONTANA

Billings
Martinez, Bonnie Yvonne *retired social services worker*

Boulder
McCurdy, John *developmental caregiver*

Dillon
Hickcox, Leslie Kay *health educator, consultant, counselor*

Glendive
Bruno, Peter Jackson *counselor, consultant, pastor*

Helena
Venzke, Ray Frank *psychotherapist*

Missoula
Delaney, Sharon Eileen *nurse educator, consultant, family and child nurse*
Wemple, James Robert *psychotherapist*

Poplar
Gabrielson, Shirley Gail *nurse*

NEVADA

Carson City
Roelke, Ada (Knock-Leveen) *retired psychotherapist*

Hawthorne
Sortland, Trudith Ann *speech and language therapist, educator*

Las Vegas
Callender, Lorna Ophelia *nurse administrator*
Close, Jack Dean, Sr. *physical therapist*
Francis, Timothy Duane *chiropractor*
Israel, Joan *social worker*
Law, Flora Elizabeth (Libby Law) *retired community health and pediatrics nurse*
Leake, Brenda Gail *enterostomal therapist nurse practitioner*
Michel, Mary Ann Kedzuf *nursing educator*
Rose, Carol Denise *orthopedic unit nurse administrator, educator*
Van Noy, Terry Willard *health care executive*

Reno
Bramwell, Marvel Lynnette *nurse, social worker*
Graham, Denis David *retired education curriculum coordinator, marriage and family therapist, education consultant*
McGary, Rita Rose *social worker*

Schurz
Bolen, Terry Lee *optometrist*

NEW MEXICO

Albuquerque
Baca, Mary Frances *mental health therapist*
Exner, Jane Frances *nursing administrator*
Kroken, Patricia Ann *health science association administrator*
Pasternacki, Linda Lea *critical care nurse*
Sanderlin, Terry Keith *counselor*
Schetnan, Brenda *nurse*

Bernalillo
Koski, Charlene Weber *social worker*

Clovis
Rehorn, Lois M(arie) *nursing administrator*

Cordova
Kazmierski, Susan Hedwig *family nurse practitioner, nurse midwife*

Farmington
MacCallum, (Edythe) Lorene *pharmacist*

Gallup
Mulligan, Erlinda Rita *medical, surgical nurse*

Las Cruces
Welsh, Mary McAnaw *educator, family mediator*

Placitas
Simpson, Gary Lavern *public health medical executive*

Portales
Hilliard, William Kent *chiropractor*

Raton
Carter, Kathryn Ann *mental health nurse*

Rio Rancho
Beaton-Hollingsworth, Meredith *enterostomal therapy clinical nurse specialist*

Roswell
Brandt, LeVerne W. *healty facility administrator*
Faust, Marjorie Jaretta *nursing administrator*

Santa Fe
Melnick, Alice Jean (AJ Melnick) *counselor*
Moya, Rosemary Mercedes *mental health administrator*
Phipps, Claude Raymond *research scientist*
Pulitzer, Roslyn Kitty *social worker, psychotherapist*
Ruybalid, Louis Arthur *social worker, community development consultant*
Valdez, Joanne Marinda *critical care, medical and surgical nurse*
Wilson, Tish *children's services administrator*

Taos
Zimmet, Jessie Verelynn *nurse, trust manager, home designer*

Truth Or Consequences
Rush, Domenica Marie *health facilities administrator*

OREGON

Albany
Chowning, Orr-Lyda Brown *dietitian*

Coos Bay
Ballinger, Kathryn Annette (Phelps) *mental health counseling executive, consultant*

Cove
Kerper, Meike *family violence, sex abuse and addiction educator, consultant*

Dillard
Chism, Jenny Carol *nurse, sculptor*

Eugene
DuShane, Phyllis Miller *nurse*
Guardalabene, Jeannine Sue *marriage and family therapist*
Hibbard, Judith Hoffman *health services researcher*
Mihaloew, Donald Michael *marriage and family therapist, educator*
Vergamini, Judith Sharon Engel *counselor, educator*

Florence
Corless, Dorothy Alice *nurse educator*

Lake Oswego
Silbert, Amy Foxman *clinical art therapist*

Medford
Brown, Christopher Patrick *health care administrator, educator*
Linn, Carole Anne *dietitian*

Portland
Adams, Hilda Chaski *public health administrator, epidemiologist*
Artaud-Wild, Sabine Marie *retired research dietitian*
Baker, Timothy Alan *healthcare administrator, educator, consultant*
Christopherson, Burton G., Jr. *equal opportunity officer*
Elliott, Holly Hall *retired therapist for deaf*
Goldfarb, Timothy Moore *hospital administrator*
Hartnett, Kathleen Camblin *counselor*
Langslet, Careen Ann *occupational therapist*
Lemmon, Dianne *nurse researcher, nursing administrator*
Loveless, Peggy Ann *social work administrator*
McDaniel, Rickey David *senior living executive*
Meighan, Stuart Spence *hospital consultant, internist, writer*
Salibello, Cosmo *optometrist, medical products executive, industrial ergonomist*
Shireman, Joan Foster *social work educator*

Saint Helens
Van Horn, O. Frank *retired counselor, consultant*

Salem
Callahan, Marilyn Joy *social worker*
Fore, Ann *counselor, educator, country dance instructor*
Skeith, George Glenn *environmental health specialist, technologist*

Tualatin
Tyler, Darlene Jasmer *dietitian*

SOUTH CAROLINA

Greenville
Howe, Linda Arlene *nursing educator, writer*

UTAH

Bountiful
Rowland, Ruth Gailey *retired hospital official*

Kaysville
Ashmead, Allez Morrill *speech, hearing, and language pathologist, orofacial myologist, consultant*
McColley, Steven Richard *nurse anesthetist*

Ogden
Jones, Galen Ray *physician assistant*
Seager, Dauna Gayle Olson-Stokes *speech therapist*

Richfield
Murphy, Millene Freeman *psychiatric rehabilitation nurse, business executive*

Saint George
Chilow, Barbara Gail *social worker*
Violet, Woodrow Wilson, Jr. *retired chiropractor*

Salt Lake City
Barusch, Amanda Smith *social welfare educator, researcher*
Good, Rebecca Mae Wertman *learning and behavior counselor, grief and loss counselor, hospice nurse, therapeutic touch practitioner, educator*
Grabarz, Donald Francis *pharmacist*
Jones, Richard Nelson *clinical laboratory scientist, Arabist*
Jorgensen, Lou Ann Birkbeck *social worker*
Kelen, Joyce Arlene *social worker*
Lee, Glenn Richard *medical administrator, educator*
Morris, Elizabeth Treat *physical therapist*
Reeves, Bruce *social worker*
Sinclair, Sara Voris *health facility administrator, nurse*
White, Raymond *health facility administrator*
Zaharia, Eric Stafford *developmental disabilities program administrator*

Sandy
Evans, David Clark *medical systems analyst, pharmacist*

Smithfield
Berg, Fredericks *audiology educator*

WASHINGTON

Auburn
Sutter, Virginia Jean *health administrator, mental health specialist*

Bellevue
Nestler, Janice Rae *health facility administrator, educator*
Pinedo, Myrna Elaine *psychotherapist, educator*
Ridgway, Maureen Abbott *medical center administrator*

Covington
Malone, Kevin Craig *physical therapist*

Everett
Miller, Robert Scott *mental health administrator, social worker*
Sandahl, Bonnie Beardsley *pediatric nurse practitioner, clinical nurse specialist, nurse manager*

Everson
McGulpin, Elizabeth Jane *nurse*

Gig Harbor
Larson, Maureen Inez *rehabilitation consultant*

Issaquah
Cernak, Keith Patrick *health care and financial consultant*

Kennewick
Fann, Margaret Ann *counselor*

Lacey
Shkurkin, Ekaterina Vladimirovna (Katia Shkurkin) *social worker*

Longview
Moosburner, Nancy *nutritionist*

Mercer Island
Adams, Belinda Jeanette Spain *nursing administrator*

Mukilteo
Mead, Terry Eileen *practice management hospital consultant, CEO*

Olympia
Boruchowitz, Stephen Alan *health policy analyst*
Hattersley, Joseph Gilmore *research analyst*
Inverso, Marlene Joy *optometrist*
Reilly, Robert Joseph *counselor*

Port Angeles
Muller, Carolyn Bue *physical therapist, volunteer*

Poulsbo
Carle, Harry Lloyd *retired social worker, career development specialist*

Redmond
Oaks, Lucy Moberley *retired social worker*
Sasenick, Joseph Anthony *healthcare company executive*

Richland
Henry, Michael Fitzroy *psychotherapist*

Seattle
Benson, Karen A. *nursing educator*
Dear, Ronald Bruce *social work educator*
Everett, Virginia Sauerbrun *counselor*
Golston, Joan Carol *psychotherapist*
Harbaugh, James Michael *psychology educator*
Portuesi, Donna Rae *psychotherapist, consultant*
Schaller, Joanne F. *nursing consultant*
Temple, Patricia Collins *medical director*
Thompson, Arlene Rita *nursing educator*

Snohomish
Hill, Valerie Charlotte *nurse*

Spokane
Burkhead, Virginia Ruth *rehabilitation nurse*
Clark, Charlene Elizabeth *nursing educator*
Robinson, Herbert Henry, III *educator, psychotherapist*

Sultan
Canto, Diana Catherine *nurse practitioner*

Sumner
Nelson, Connie Rae *pharmacy education director, educator*

Tacoma
Reim, Ruthann *career and personal counselor, corporate trainer*

Vancouver
Simontacchi, Carol Nadine *nutritionist*

Walla Walla
Palmer, James W. *nurse*

Woodinville
Williams, Donna Reilly *counselor, writer, personnel consultant*

Yakima
McCown, Linda Jean *medical technology educator*
Simonson, Susan Kay *hospital administrator*

WYOMING

Cheyenne
Hardway, James Edward *vocational and rehabilitative specialist*
Laycock, Anita Simon *psychotherapist*

Green River
Thompson, Josie *nurse*

Hanna
Turner, Lillian Erna *nurse*

Pinedale
Margo, Kenneth Craig *counselor*

Rock Springs
O'Jack, Helen Margaret *clinical social worker*

Saratoga
Collamer, Sonja Mae Soreide *retired veterinary facility administrator*

Sundance
Peters, Roxanne Leigh *nurse practitioner, consultant*

Worland
Munsterteiger, Kay Diane *speech and language pathologist*

CANADA

ALBERTA

Edmonton
Fields, Anthony Lindsay Austin *health facility administrator, oncologist, educator*

ADDRESS UNPUBLISHED

Abernathy, Vicki Marie *nurse*
Allen, Bonnie Lynn *optometrist*
Allen, Sheila Hill *nursing executive, counselor, consultant*
Anderson, Dorothy Fisher *social worker, psychotherapist*
Barnhouse, Lillian May Palmer *retired medical surgical nurse, researcher, civic worker*
Belles, Donald Arnold *pastoral therapist, mental health counselor*
Bjorklund, Janet Vinsen *speech and language pathologist*
Blacher, Joan Helen *psychotherapist, educator*
Blomstrom, Bruce A. *healthcare executive*
Brame, Marillyn A. *hypnotherapist*
Callison, Nancy Fowler *nurse administrator*
Cash, Deanna Gail *nursing educator, retired*
Clecak, Dvera Vivian Bozman *psychotherapist*
Condry, Robert Stewart *retired hospital administrator*
Conrad, Diane *psychiatric nurse practitioner*
Craig, Carol Mills *marriage, family and child counselor*
Cunningham, Bridget Eugenia *medical records administrator*
Davidow, Jenny Jean *counselor, writer*
Davis, Gay Ruth *psychotherapist, social welfare educator, author, researcher, consultant*
DeShazer, Ruth Shomler *health information management professional*
DeStaffany, Sandra Russell *childbirth educator, author*
Diedrick, Geraldine Rose *retired nurse*
Dodge, Stephanie Lee *vocational rehabilitation counselor*
Dyer, Alice Mildred *psychotherapist*

Edelstein, Rosemarie *nurse educator, medical-legal consultant*
Ekong, Ruth J. *nursing administrator, author*
Faughnan, Margaret H. *nurse*
Frenzel, Frances Johnson *registered nurse, educator, lecturer*
Fryer, Gladys Constance *retired physician, medical director, educator*
Fuller, Ameenah Rashedah *medical record consultant*
Gaines, Jean Hunt *healthcare administrator*
Garvey, Evelyn Jewel *retired mental health nurse*
Garvey, Katherine Heston *gerontology nurse*
Gengler, Sue Wong *health educator, consultant, speaker, trainer*
Gerry, Debra Prue *psychotherapist*
Giles, Melva Theresa *nursing educator*
Giles, Walter Edmund *alcohol and drug treatment executive*
Gillett, Patricia *pulmonary nurse practitioner, clinical nurse specialist*
Giordano, Laura Ann *quality management professional*
Goetzke, Gloria Louise *social worker, income tax specialist*
Govan, Gladys Vernita Mosley *retired critical care and medical/surgical nurse*
Grant, Richard Earl *medical and legal consultant*
Gray, Barbara Bronson *nurse, writer, editor*
Green, Beth Ingber *intuitive practitioner, counselor, musician, composer*
Hansen-Kyle, Linda L. *managed health care nurse*
Hardy-Lee, Martha Maria *mental health nurse*
Harrigan, Rosanne Carol *nursing educator*
Healy, Sonya Ainslie *health facility administrator*
Henneman, Stephen Charles *counselor*
Higgins, Ruth Ann *social worker, family therapist*
Hofmann, Paul Bernard *healthcare consultant*
Hughes, W. James *optometrist*
Jacobs, Arthur Dietrich *educator, researcher, health services executive*
Juarez, Maretta Liya Calimpong *social worker*
Kaiser, Nina Irene *health care consultant*
Kellam, Norma Dawn *medical, surgical nurse*
Kepner, Jane Ellen *psychotherapist, educator, minister*
Klein, Fay Magid *health administrator*
Koleniak Gignoux, Barbara Donna *nurse*
Labins, Deborah Lynne *maternal women's health nurse*
Leigh, Vincenta M. *health administrator*
Lewis, Nancy Patricia *speech and language pathologist*
Lilly-Hersley, Jane Anne Feeley *nursing researcher*
Linton, LaVonne Evangeline *nurse*
Looft, Michelle Reneé *office manager, consultant*
Lovell, Joan Ellen *mental health professional*
Machanic, Mindy Robin *psychologist, educator, consultant, writer*
MacPherson, Shirley *clinical therapist*
Markham, Richard Glover *research executive*
Maroon, Mickey *clinical social worker*
Marshall, Donald Thomas *medical technologist*
Marshall, L. B. *clinical lab scientist*
McDougall, Jacquelyn Marie Horan *therapist*
Meyer, Roberta *mediator, communication consultant*
Mikel, Thomas Kelly, Jr. *laboratory administrator*
Mitchell, Geneva Brooke *hypnotherapist*
Moffatt, Hugh McCulloch, Jr. *hospital administrator, physical therapist*
Mosqueira, Charlotte Marianne *dietitian*
Muico-Mercurio, Luisa *critical care nurse*
Myers, Kathleen Anne *pediatrics nurse*
Nakagawa, Allen Donald *radiologic technologist*
Nusbaum, Geoffrey Dean *psychotherapist*
Parks, Richard Keith *clinical social worker*
Pilcher, Ellen Louise *rehabilitation counselor*
Piperno, Sherry Lynn *psychotherapist*
Pisciotta, Vivian Virginia *psychotherapist*
Plunkett, Lynda Leigh *pediatrics nurse*
Porter, Marie Ann *neonatal nurse, labor and delivery nurse*
Preszler, Sharon Marie *psychiatric home health nurse*
Reisch, Michael Stewart *social work educator*
Reith, Marianne *retired nurse, educator, researcher*
Robertshaw, Thomas Edward *social worker*
Romero, Elizabeth Rivera *public health nurse*
Rose, Joan Marie *medical-surgical nurse*
Sanders, Augusta Swann *retired nurse*
Schell, Merry L. *critical care and oncological nurse*
Simms, Maria Ester *health services administrator*
Sipos, Eva Magdalena *pharmacist*
Skarda, Richard Joseph *clinical social worker*
Skrocki, Edmund Stanley, II *health fair promoter, executive*
Sokol, Stewart *health services administrator*
Solomon, Julius Oscar Lee *pharmacist, hypnotherapist*
Splane, Richard Beverley *social work educator*
Stein, Ellyn Beth *mental health services professional*
Stickles, Bonnie Jean *nurse*
Suber, Robin Hall *former medical and surgical nurse*
Thomson, Grace Marie *nurse, minister*
Tyler, Gail Madeleine *nurse*
Valfre, Michelle Williams *nursing educator, administrator, author*
Voelker, Margaret Irene (Meg Voelker) *gerontology, medical, surgical nurse*
Walker, Gail Juanice *electrologist*
Wiese, Neva *critical care nurse*
Zeleznak, Shirley Anne *psychotherapist*

HEALTHCARE: MEDICINE

UNITED STATES

ALASKA

Fairbanks
Bergeson, Marvin Ernest *pediatrician*

ARIZONA

Gilbert
Labovitz, Earl A. *allergist*

Glendale
Michael, Cecil Francis, Jr. *pediatrician*

Mesa
Boren, Kenneth Ray *endocrinologist*
Bunchman, Herbert Harry, II *plastic surgeon*
Fiorino, John Wayne *podiatrist*
Thompson, Ronald MacKinnon *family physician, artist, writer*

Paradise Valley
Polson, Donald Allan *surgeon*

Phoenix
Allison, Rebecca Anne *cardiologist, writer*
Benach, Sharon Ann *physician assistant*
Borel, James David *anesthesiologist*
Butler, Byron Clinton *obstetrician, gynecologist*
Charlton, John Kipp *pediatrician*
England, David P. *anesthesiologist, educator*
Goldberg, Morris *internist*
Holman, Paul David *plastic surgeon*
Koep, Lawrence James *surgeon*
Kuivinen, Ned Allan *pathologist*
Kurth, Matthias C. *neurologist*
Le, Hung Duc *pediatrician*
Lee, Gilbert Brooks *retired ophthalmology engineer*
Lorenzen, Robert Frederick *ophthalmologist*
McLoone, James Brian *psychiatrist, educator*
Singer, Jeffrey Alan *surgeon*
Sonntag, Volker Karl Heinz *neurosurgeon, educator*
Stern, Stanley *psychiatrist*
Wright, Richard Oscar, III *pathologist, educator*
Yeung, Anthony Tong *orthopedic surgeon*

Scottsdale
Cawley, Leo Patrick *pathologist, immunologist*
DeHaven, Kenneth Le Moyne *retired physician*
Friedman, Shelly Arnold *cosmetic surgeon*
Lewis, John Christopher *allergist*
Lillo, Joseph Leonard *osteopath, family practice physician*
Muhm, John Robert *radiologist*
Stevens, John Clarke *neurologist*

Sedona
Hawkins, David Ramon *psychiatrist, writer, researcher*
Reno, Joseph Harry *retired orthopedic surgeon*

Sun City West
Anderson, Roger Banks *retired surgeon*
Calderwood, William Arthur *physician*
Forbes, Kenneth Albert Faucher *urological surgeon*
Roush, Dorothy Evelyn *medical laboratory educator, consultant*

Tempe
Anand, Suresh Chandra *physician*
Levin, Hal Alan *psychiatrist*

Tucson
Ahern, Geoffrey Lawrence *behavioral neurologist*
Ben-Asher, M. David *physician*
Colby, John Kingsbury, III *physician assistant*
Gallen, William Joseph *pediatrician, cardiologist*
Graham, Anna Regina *pathologist, educator*
Harris, David Thomas *immunology educator*
Hellman, Emanuel Scholem *physician*
Hess, Richard Neal *plastic surgeon*
Hildebrand, John G(rant) *neurobiologist, educator*
Hutter, John Joseph, Jr. *pediatric hematologist and oncologist, educator*
Kaszniak, Alfred Wayne *neuropsychologist*
Krasner, Scott Allan *physician, health facility administrator*
Marchalonis, John Jacob *immunologist, educator*
Martin, Loren Winston *physician*
Martinez, Maria Dolores *pediatrician*
Nichols, Andrew Wilkinson *public health physician, educator*
Reinmuth, Oscar MacNaughton *physician, educator*
Ricke, P. Scott *obstetrician, gynecologist*
Robles, Neopito de Leon *surgeon*
Salmon, Sydney Elias *medical educator, director*
Witten, Mark Lee *lung injury research scientist, educator*
Worden, Katherine A. *osteopath, educator*

Yuma
Solovay, Mark Lionel *cardiologist, educator*

CALIFORNIA

Agoura Hills
Bleiberg, Leon William *surgical podiatrist*

Anaheim
Carvajal, Jorge Armando *endocrinologist, internist*
Littlebird, Forrest Douglas *preventive medicine, tropical medicine physician*

Arcadia
Chinn, Douglas Owen *urologist, cryosurgeon*
Sleeter, John William Higgs *physician, health service administrator*

Aromas
Stubblefield, James Irvin *emergency medicine physician, health facility administrator*

Auburn
Hanowell, Ernest Goddin *physician*

Bakersfield
Prunes-Carrillo, Fernando *plastic surgeon, educator*

Baldwin Park
Barry(-Branks), Diane Dolores *podiatrist*

Barstow
Sutterby, Larry Quentin *internist*

Berkeley
[illegible], John William *health-research physician, educator*
Patterson, Lloyd Clifford *psychiatrist*
Poor, Clarence Alexander *retired physician*
Seitz, Walter Stanley *cardiovascular research consultant*
Taekman, Michael Seymour *neurological surgeon*

Beverly Hills
Allen, Howard Norman *cardiologist, educator*
Berkman, Samuel A. *internist*
Cambre, Athleo Louis, Jr. *plastic surgeon*
Catz, Boris *endocrinologist, educator*
Dennis, Karen Marie *plastic surgeon*
Dorman, Daniel *psychiatrist*
Fein, William *ophthalmologist*
Klein, Arnold William *dermatologist*
Kravitz, Hilard L(eonard) *physician*
Lesser, Gershon Melvin *physician, lawyer, medical and legal media commentator*
Marshak, Harry *physician, plastic surgeon*
Seiff, Stephen S. *ophthalmologist*
Semel, George Herbert *plastic surgeon*
Yuan, Robin Tsu-Wang *plastic surgeon*

Bodega Bay
Vecchio, Thomas James *medical researcher, consultant*

Bolinas
Remen, Rachel Naomi *pediatrician, psycho-oncologist*

Borrego Springs
Strong, John Oliver *plastic surgeon, educator*

Boulder Creek
Piazza, Duane Eugene *biomedical researcher*

Brawley
Jaquith, George Oakes *opthalmologist*

Burbank
Casey, William Carleton *physician, urologist, pschiatrist*

Burlingame
Beattie, George Chapin *orthopedic surgeon*
Preger, Leslie *radiologist*

Capo Beach
Roemer, Edward Pier *neurologist*

Carlsbad
Dziewanowska, Zofia Elizabeth *neuropsychiatrist, pharmaceutical executive, researcher, educator*

Carmel
Michel, James Wesley *family practice physician, nutritional consultant*

Carmel Valley
Chapman, Robert Galbraith *retired hematologist, administrator*

Cerritos
Goldsmith, Harry *podiatrist, practice management company executive*

Chula Vista
Hernandez-Fujigaki, Julio *urologist*
Kligerman, Morton *pediatrician*

Claremont
Gabriel, Earl A. *osteopathic physician*
Johnson, Jerome Linné *cardiologist*

Clovis
Terrell, Howard Bruce *psychiatrist*

Coronado
Considine, Kevin Charles *family physician*

Costa Mesa
Mera, Csaba Leslie *medical director, consultant*

Covina
Takei, Toshihisa *otolaryngologist*

Crockett
Oster, David Wayne *medical management executive*

Cypress
Tan, Mariano Buendia *physician*

Daly City
Shaw, Richard Eugene *cardiovascular researcher*

Davis
Hance, Anthony James *retired pharmacologist, educator*

Del Mar
Lesko, Ronald Michael *osteopathic physician*

Downey
Magnes, Harry Alan *physician*
Shapiro, Richard Stanley *physician*

Duarte
Comings, David Edward *physician, medical genetics scientist*

Encinitas
Jaffe, Charles J. *allergist*

Escondido
Edwards, Bruce George *ophthalmologist, naval officer*
Kelly, Jon Pembroke *orthopedic surgeon, medical association executive*
Weber, Richard Dean *physician, primary care practitioner, researcher*

Eureka
Newman, Harry Charles *family practice physician*

Fairfield
Martin, Clyde Verne *psychiatrist*
Munn, William Charles, II *psychiatrist*

Folsom
Ewing, Russell Charles, II *physician*

Fontana
Resch, Charlotte Susanna *plastic surgeon*

Fountain Valley
Dajee, Himmet *cardiothoracic surgeon*

Fremont
Sommer, John Lambert *retired surgeon*

Fresno
Chandler, Bruce Frederick *internist*
Glassheim, Jeffrey Wayne *allergist, immunologist, pediatrician*
Smith, V. Roy *neurosurgeon*

Fullerton
Macagba, Rufino L., Jr. *physician, international agency executive*

Garden Grove
Wong, Michael Henry *anesthesiologist*

Gilroy
Grisez, James Louis *physician, plastic surgeon*

Glendale
Dent, Ernest DuBose, Jr. *pathologist*

Glendora
Lasko, Allen Howard *pharmacist*

Half Moon Bay
Robertson, Abel L., Jr. *pathologist*

Hanford
Gamboa, Lucito G. *physician*

Harbor City
Kwan, Benjamin Ching Kee *ophthalmologist*

Hemet
Galletta, Joseph Leo *physician*

Huntington Beach
Appelbaum, Bruce David *physician*
Solmer, Richard *surgeon*

Inglewood
Sukov, Richard Joel *radiologist*

Irvine
Connolly, John Earle *surgeon, educator*
Gupta, Sudhir *immunologist, educator*
Quilligan, Edward James *obstetrician, gynecologist, educator*
Yin, Hong Zhen *neuropathologist, researcher*

La Canada Flintridge
Byrne, George Melvin *physician*

La Crescenta
Riccardi, Vincent Michael *pediatrician, researcher, educator, entrepreneur*

La Jolla
Covell, Ruth Marie *medical educator, medical school administrator*
Dalessio, Donald John *physician, neurologist, educator*
Hamburger, Robert N. *pediatrics educator, consultant*
Hench, Philip Kahler *physician*
Hofmann, Alan Frederick *biomedical educator, researcher*
Horner, Anthony Adam *pediatrician, educator*
Jaffer, Adrian Michael *physician*
Jorgensen, Judith Ann *psychiatrist*
Keeney, Edmund Ludlow *physician*
Lewis, Carson McLaughl *retired plastic surgeon*
Peebles, Carol Lynn *immunology researcher*
Rearden, Carole Ann *clinical pathologist, educator*
Reid, Robert Tilden *medical association administrator, internist*
Schneider, Gerald L. *plastic surgeon*
Singer, Robert *plastic surgeon*
Smith, Richard Alan *neurologist, medical association administrator*
Teirstein, Paul Shepherd *physician, health facility administrator*
Walker, Richard Hugh *orthopaedic surgeon*
Weigle, William Oliver *immunologist, educator*

La Mesa
Wohl, Armand Jeffrey *cardiologist*

Laguna Niguel
Strenger, George *surgeon*

Lakewood
Tong, Richard Dare *anesthesiologist*

Lodi
Albert, N. Erick *urologist*

Loma Linda
Alvarez, Ofelia Amparo *medical educator*
Behrens, Berel Lyn *physician, academic administrator*
Coggin, Charlotte Joan *cardiologist, educator*
Condon, Stanley Charles *gastroenterologist*
Green, Lora Murray *immunologist, researcher, educator*
Stilson, Walter Leslie *radiologist, educator*

Long Beach
Anderson, Garry Michael *diagnostic radiologist*
Bradley, William Guerin *radiologist, researcher, educator*
Burke, Donald Warren *anesthesiologist*
Fagan, Frederic *neurosurgeon*
Friis, Robert Harold *epidemiologist, health science administrator*
Macer, George Armen, Jr. *orthopedic hand surgeon*
Schoendorf, Judson Raymond *allergist*
Szabo, Sandor *pathologist*

Los Alamitos
DiSaia, John Philip *plastic surgeon, online author*

Los Altos
Martin, Leonardo San Juan *urologist, surgeon*

Los Angeles
Ahn, Samuel Seunghae *vascular surgeon, researcher, consultant*
Alkana, Ronald Lee *neuropsychopharmacologist, psychobiologist*
Anderson, Kathryn D. *surgeon*
Archie, Carol Louise *obstetrician and gynecologist, educator*
Aronowitz, Joel Alan *plastic and reconstructive surgeon*
Ashley, Sharon Anita *pediatric anesthesiologist*
Askanas-Engel, Valerie *neurologist, educator, researcher*
Beart, Robert W., Jr. *surgeon, educator*
Becker, Donald Paul *surgeon, neurosurgeon*
Bernstein, Sol *cardiologist, educator*
Bodey, Bela *immunomorphologist*
Brautbar, Nachman *physician, educator*
Cicciarelli, James Carl *immunology educator*
Cote, Richard James *pathologist, researcher*
Danoff, Dudley Seth *surgeon, urologist*
De Shazo, Billy W. *physician, plastic surgeon*
Dixit, Vivek *biomedical scientist, medical educator*
Edgerton, Bradford Wheatly *plastic surgeon*
Figlin, Robert Alan *physician, hematologist, oncologist*
Gambino, Jerome James *nuclear medicine educator*
Goin, Marcia Kraft *physician*
Grody, Wayne William *physician*
Hershman, Jerome Marshall *endocrinologist*
Hirsch, Anthony T. *physician*
Hoang, Duc Van *theoretical pathologist, educator*
Hsiao, Chie-Fang *neuroscientist*
Jacobson, Edwin James *medical educator*
Jensen, Dennis Michael *medical educator, researcher*
Jones, Neil Ford *surgeon*
Kahn, Fredrick Henry *internist*
Katz, Roger *pediatrician, educator*
Kerman, Barry Martin *ophthalmologist, educator*
Kilburn, Kaye Hatch *medical educator*
Kramer, Barry Alan *psychiatrist*
Lawrence, Sanford Hull *physician, immunochemist*
Levy, Michael Lee *neurosurgeon*
Liu, Don *ophthalmologist, medical researcher*
Markham, Charles Henry *neurologist*
Mekelburg, Brian Phillip *dermatologist*
Miles, Samuel I(srael) *psychiatrist, educator*
Miller, Timothy Alden *plastic and reconstructive surgeon*
Mockary, Peter Ernest *clinical laboratory scientist, researcher, medical writer*
Nathwani, Bharat Narottam *pathologist, consultant*
Newman, Anita Nadine *surgeon*
Nissenson, Allen Richard *physician, educator*
O'Neill, Ynez Violé *medical educator*
Parker, John William *pathology educator, investigator*
Quon, Wanda Ann *physician*
Rachelefsky, Gary S. *medical educator*
Raghavan, Derek *oncologist, medical researcher and educator*
Reynolds, Charles Patrick *pediatric oncologist, researcher*
Rimoin, David Lawrence *physician, geneticist*
Roven, Alfred Nathan *surgeon*
Schneider, Edward Lewis *medicine educator, research administrator*
Sherman, Randolph *plastic and reconstructive surgeon, educator*
Shi, Shan-Rong *research pathology educator*
Shtengold, Yefim Shelichovich *medical educator, researcher*
Siegel, Michael Elliot *nuclear medicine physician, educator*
Siegel, Sheldon C. *physician*
Sigman, Melvin Monroe *psychiatrist*
Sullivan, Stuart Francis *anesthesiologist, educator*
Titus, Edward Depue *psychiatrist, administrator*
Tourtellotte, Wallace William *neurologist, educator*
Tucker, Steven J. *oncologist*
Van Der Meulen, Joseph Pierre *neurologist*
Visscher, Barbara Ruth *epidemiologist, researcher*
Weiss, Martin Harvey *neurosurgeon, educator*
Wilson, Charles Lee *neuroscientist, epilepsy researcher, educator*
Wilson, Miriam Geisendorfer *retired physician, educator*
Wright, Kenneth Weston *pediatric ophthalmologist*
Zemel, Norman Paul *orthopedic surgeon*

Los Gatos
Naughten, Robert Norman *pediatrician*

Malibu
Lamers, William Matthias, Jr. *psychiatrist*

Manhattan Beach
Klaper, Michael Anthony *physician, nutrition educator*

Martinez
McKnight, Lenore Ravin *child psychiatrist*

Menlo Park
Barthold, Edward A. *physician*
Kovachy, Edward Miklos, Jr. *psychiatrist*

Merced
Maytum, Harry Rodell *retired physician*

Mill Valley
Harris, Jeffrey Saul *physician executive, consultant*
Wallerstein, Robert Solomon *psychiatrist*

Milpitas
Chiu, Peter Yee-Chew *physician*

Mission Hills
Quesada, Ramon S., Jr. *radiologist*
Tram, Kenneth Khai Kt *internist*

Mission Viejo
Caliendo, Theodore Joseph *pediatrician, neonatalogist*

Monterey
Burchard, Thomas Kirk *psychiatrist*
Lehr, Jeffrey Marvin *immunologist, allergist*

Mountain View
Lowen, Robert Marshall *plastic surgeon*
Snider, Paul Norman *psychiatrist*
Warren, Richard Wayne *obstetrician and gynecologist*

Napa
Zimmermann, John Paul *plastic surgeon*

Newport Beach
Chiu, John Tang *physician*
Zalta, Edward *otorhinolaryngologist, physician*

Novato
Franklin, Robert Blair *cardiologist*

Oakland
Burdick, Claude Owen *pathologist*
Collen, Morris Frank *physician*
Ng, Lawrence Ming-Loy *pediatrician*
Rowe, Richard *physician, consultant*
Weinmann, Robert Lewis *neurologist*

Oceanside
Curtin, Thomas Lee *ophthalmologist*
Folkerth, Theodore Leon *cardiovascular surgeon, educator*

Olympic Valley
Hsu, Shu-Dean *hematologist, oncologist*

Orange
Armentrout, Steven Alexander *oncologist*
Budner, Lawrence Jay *psychiatrist*
DiSaia, Philip John *gynecologist, obstetrician, radiology educator*
Fisher, Mark Jay *neurologist, neuroscientist, educator*
Furnas, David William *plastic surgeon*
Rowen, Marshall *radiologist*
Thompson, William Benbow, Jr. *obstetrician, gynecologist, educator*
Zetin, Mark I. *psychiatrist*

Oxnard
Niesluchowski, Witold S. *cardiovascular and thoracic surgeon*

Pacific Palisades
Claes, Daniel John *physician*
Love, Susan Margaret *surgeon, educator, medical administrator*

Palm Springs
Dulalia, Zosimo Garcia *physician*
Lunde, Donald Theodore *physician*
Schlesinger, Violet Murray *biomedical consultant*

Palmdale
Rubinoff, M. Lawrence *physician and surgeon*

Palo Alto
Adamson, Geoffrey David *reproductive endocrinologist, surgeon*
Bensch, Klaus George *pathology educator*
Blessing-Moore, Joann Catherine *physician*
Charlton, Randolph Seville *psychiatrist, educator*
Jamplis, Robert Warren *surgeon, medical foundation executive*
Lane, William Kenneth *physician*
Lobel, Charles Irving *physician*
Loveland, Jacqueline Jane *neuroscientist, biologist*
Roberts, James Allen *gynecologic oncologist*
Salvatierra, Oscar, Jr. *physician*
Weston, Jane Sara *plastic surgeon, educator*
Wong, Nancy L. *dermatologist*

Palos Verdes Peninsula
Thomas, Claudewell Sidney *psychiatry educator*

Panorama City
Bass, Harold Neal *pediatrician, medical geneticist*
Sue, Michael Alvin *physician*

Paramount
Cohn, Lawrence Steven *physician, educator*

Pasadena
Barnard, William Marion *psychiatrist*
Giem, Ross Nye, Jr. *surgeon*
Glovsky, Myron Michael *medical educator*
Morgan, Stanley Charles *plastic and reconstructive surgeon*
Opel, William *medical research administrator*
Pitts, Ferris Newcomb *physician, psychiatry educator*

Piedmont
Sharpton, Thomas *physician*

Placerville
Bonser, Quentin *surgeon*

Pleasanton
Hisaka, Eric Toru *plastic surgeon*

Pollock Pines
Knoll, Raymond L. *physician, surgeon, consultant*

Pomona
Vo, Huu Dinh *pediatrician, educator*

Rancho Mirage
Cone, Lawrence Arthur *research medicine educator*
Sofonio, Mark Vincent *plastic and reconstructive surgeon*

Redding
Renard, Ronald Lee *allergist*

Redlands
Adey, William Ross *physician*
Flores, John A. *internist*
Richardson, A(rthur) Leslie *former medical group consultant*
Skoog, William Arthur *former oncologist*
Smith, Dunbar Wallace *retired physician, clergyman*
Wang, Colleen Iona *medical association administrator, writer*

Redondo Beach
Davis, Lowell Livingston *cardiovascular surgeon*

Redway
Gruzalski, Marion May *health care administrator, artist*

Redwood City
Suba, Eric John *physician*

Riverside
Jukkola, George Duane *obstetrician, gynecologist*
Jung, Timothy Tae Kun *otolaryngologist*
Linaweaver, Walter Ellsworth, Jr. *physician*
Pena, Antonia Murillo *physician, radiologist*
Seyfert, Howard Bentley, Jr. *podiatrist*
Sparks, Dale Boyd *allergist, health facility administrator*
Stone, Herman Hull *internist*

Rolling Hills Estates
Bellis, Carroll Joseph *surgeon, educator*

Sacramento
Achtel, Robert Andrew *pediatric cardiologist*
Evrigenis, John Basil *obstetrician-gynecologist*
Lilla, James A. *plastic surgeon*
Lim, Alan Young *plastic surgeon*
Lippold, Roland Will *surgeon*
Nagy, Stephen Mears, Jr. *physician, allergist*
Reiber, Gregory Duane *forensic pathologist*
Shapero, Harris Joel *pediatrician*
Sharma, Arjun Dutta *cardiologist*
Tung, Prabhas *plastic surgeon*
Wolkov, Harvey Brian *radiation oncologist, researcher*
Zil, J. S. *psychiatrist, physiologist*

Salinas
Leighton, Henry Alexander *physician, consultant*
Phillips, John P(aul) *retired neurosurgeon*
Rever, Barbara L. *medical educator, consultant, researcher*

San Bernardino
Gorenberg, Alan Eugene *physician*
Kuehn, Klaus Karl Albert *ophthalmologist*

San Bruno
Bradley, Charles William *podiatrist, educator*

San Carlos
Ellis, Eldon Eugene *surgeon*

San Clemente
Kim, Edward William *ophthalmic surgeon*

San Diego
Brookler, Harry Aaron *retired physician*
Chambers, Henry George *orthopedic surgeon*
Cowen, Donald Eugene *retired physician*
Garland, Frank Caldwell *epidemiologist, educator*
Hunt, Robert Gary *medical consultant, oral and maxillofacial surgeon*
Intriere, Anthony Donald *physician*
Jones, Clyde William *anesthesiologist*
Kaweski, Susan *plastic surgeon, naval officer*
Kruggel, John Louis *plastic surgeon*
Levy, Jerome *dermatologist, retired naval officer*
Lewis, Gregory Williams *scientist*
Moossa, A. R. *surgery educator*
Mubarak, Scott J. *pediatric orthopedic surgeon*
Oliphant, Charles Romig *physician*
Pitt, William Alexander *cardiologist*
Rhein, Leroy Walker *ophthalmic surgeon*
Schmidt, Joseph David *urologist*
Schorr, Martin Mark *forensic examiner, psychologist, educator, screenwriter*
Teguh, Collin *osteopathic physician, educator*
Vreeland, Patricia Anne Martin *secondary education educator, teacher educator*
Wasserman, Stephen Ira *physician, educator*
Yalam, Arnold Robert *allergist, immunologist, consultant*
Zeiger, Robert S. *allergist*

San Francisco
Beebe, John E. *psychiatrist*
Benet, Leslie Zachary *pharmacokineticist*
Bishop, John Michael *biomedical research scientist, educator*
Blake-Inada, Louis Michael *cardiologist, researcher*
Brown, Donald Malcolm *plastic surgeon*
Capozzi, Angelo *surgeon*
Caputo, Gary Richard *radiology educator*
Debas, Haile T. *gastrointestinal surgeon, physiologist, educator*
Deicken, Raymond Friedrich *psychiatric physician, clinical neuroscientist*
Erskine, John Morse *surgeon*
Frick, Oscar Lionel *physician, educator*
German, Donald Frederick *physician*
Hering, William Marshall *medical organization executive*
Ikeda, Clyde Junichi *plastic and reconstructive surgeon*
Katzung, Bertram George *pharmacologist*
Kiprov, Dobri Dobrev *immunology researcher*
Kline, Howard Jay *cardiologist, educator*
Kramer, Steven G. *ophthalmologist*
Larsen, Loren Joseph *retired pediatric orthopedic surgeon*
Levin, Alan Scott *pathologist, allergist, immunologist, lawyer*
Mason, Dean Towle *cardiologist*
McAninch, Jack Weldon *urological surgeon, educator*
Mustacchi, Piero *physician, educator*
Pronove-Irreverre, Pacita *medical officer*
Ristow, Brunno *plastic surgeon*
Scholten, Paul *obstetrician, gynecologist, educator*
Shapiro, Larry Jay *pediatrician, scientist, educator*
Shumate, Charles Albert *retired dermatologist*
Simon, Joel Arthur *physician, medical educator*
Smith, David Elvin *physician*
Steinman, John Francis *psychiatrist*
Szabo, Zoltan *medical science educator, medical institute director*
Thompson, Charlotte Ellis *pediatrician, educator, author*
Wayburn, Edgar *internist, environmentalist*

San Gabriel
Chen, John Calvin *child and adolescent psychiatrist*

San Jose
Avakoff, Joseph Carnegie *medical and legal consultant*
Boldrey, Edwin Eastland *retinal surgeon, educator*
Gale, Arnold David *pediatric neurologist, consultant*
Lippe, Philipp Maria *physician, surgeon, neurosurgeon, educator, administrator*
Malish, David Marc *physician*
Mendenhall, Carrol Clay *physician*
Nelson, Randall Erland *surgeon*
Nguyen, Thinh Van *physician*
Shatney, Clayton Henry *surgeon*
Stein, Arthur Oscar *pediatrician*

San Juan Capistrano
Fisher, Delbert Arthur *physician, educator*

San Leandro
Noyes, Philip Patterson *ophthalmologist, retired*

San Marcos
Billing, Ronald James *immunologist, researcher*

San Marino
Sadun, Alfredo Arrigo *neuro-ophthalmologist, scientist, educator*

San Mateo
Adams, Robert Monroe *retired dermatologist, educator*
Bell, Leo S. *retired physician*
Van Kirk, John Ellsworth *cardiologist*
von Doepp, Christian Ernest *psychiatrist*
Wong, Otto *epidemiologist*

San Quentin
DeTata, Juan Carlos *forensic psychiatrist*

San Rafael
Hinshaw, Horton Corwin *physician*
Meecham, William James *ophthalmologist*

San Ramon
Ivani, Kristen Ann *embryologist*
Litman, Robert Barry *physician, author, television and radio commentator*
Novales-Li, Philipp *neuropharmacologist*

Santa Ana
Abbruzzese, Carlo Enrico *physician, writer, educator*
DeuPree, Robert Marshall *physician, minister, author*
Goodman, Matthew Mortensen *dermatologist, educator*

Santa Barbara
DePaoli, Alexander Mark *endocrinologist*
Ellis, Eugene Joseph *cardiologist*
Formby, Bent Clark *immunologist*
Klakeg, Clayton Harold *cardiologist*
Liebhaber, Myron I. *allergist*
Mathews, Barbara Edith *gynecologist*
Peus, Joseph Carl *orthopedic surgeon*
Rockwell, Don Arthur *psychiatrist*

Santa Cruz
Magid, Gail Avrum *neurosurgeon, neurosurgery educator*
Pletsch, Marie Eleanor *plastic surgeon*

Santa Fe Springs
Bao, Joseph Yue-Se *orthopedist, microsurgeon, educator*

Santa Monica
Bohn, Paul Bradley *psychiatrist, psychoanalyst*
Carr, Ruth Margaret *plastic surgeon*
Hoefflin, Steven M. *plastic surgeon*
Holve, Leslie Martin *pediatrician*
Katz, Robert Irwin *retired physician*
Kawamoto, Henry K. *plastic surgeon*
McGuire, Michael Francis *plastic and reconstructive surgeon*
Resnick, Jeffrey I. *plastic surgeon*
Thompson, Dennis Peters *plastic surgeon*

Santa Paula
Edwards, Samuel Roger *physician*

Santa Rosa
Leissring, John Cother *pathologist*
Leuty, Gerald Johnston *osteopathic physician and surgeon*
Trucker, Albert *plastic surgeon*

Santee
Yang, Hsin-Ming *immunologist*

Sherman Oaks
Fishman, Bruce Eliot *physician, surgeon, consultant*
Smith, Louis John *retired gynecologist*
Stein, Karl N. *plastic and reconstructive surgeon*

South San Francisco
Curd, John Gary *physician, scientist*

Stanford
Blumenkranz, Mark Scott *surgeon, researcher, educator*
Guiroy, Don Camance *psychiatrist*
Hentz, Vincent R. *surgeon*
Klima, Roger Radim *physiatrist*
Lee, Joselyn C.R. *physician, researcher*
Moss, Richard B. *pediatrician*
Reitz, Bruce Arnold *cardiac surgeon, educator*
Shortliffe, Edward Hance *internist, medical informatics educator*

Sylmar
Munro, Malcolm Gordon *obstetrician, gynecologist, educator*

Tehachapi
Melsheimer, Harold *obstetrician, gynecologist*

Temecula
Gill, Becky Lorette *addictionist, psychiatrist*

Templeton
Abernathy, Shields B. *allergist, immunologist, internist*
Carey, James C., Jr. *plastic surgeon*

Torrance
Hammer, Terence Michael *physician*
Krout, Boyd Merrill *psychiatrist*
Stern, David Howard *physician, journalist*
Tabrisky, Joseph *radiologist, educator*
Vargas, Hernan Isaac *surgeon*

Ventura
Abul-Haj, Suleiman Kahil *pathologist*
Armstrong, Dale P. *plastic surgeon*
Karlsberg, Paul *neurosurgeon*

Visalia
Riegel, Byron William *ophthalmologist*
Wong, John Wing Hing *family practice physician*

Volcano
Prout, Ralph Eugene *physician*

Walnut Creek
Chee, Lambert Hu-Kee *physician*
Sheen, Portia Yunn-ling *retired physician*

Watsonville
Alfaro, Felix Benjamin *physician*

West Covina
Schneider, Calvin *physician*

West Hollywood
Wilson, Myron Robert, Jr. *retired psychiatrist*

Whittier
Arcadi, John Albert *urologist*
Arenowitz, Albert Harold *psychiatrist*
Prickett, David Clinton *physician*

Willits
Williams, John Philip *osteopathic physician*

Woodland Hills
Herdeg, Howard Brian *physician*

COLORADO

Aspen
Oden, Robert Rudolph *surgeon*

Aurora
Stepp, Robert John *physician*

Castle Rock
Thornbury, John Rousseau *radiologist, physician*

Colorado Springs
Anderson, Paul Nathaniel *oncologist, educator*
Carollo, Bert Ross *radiologist*
Feiler, Frederic Charles *orthopedic surgeon*
Kinsey, Daniel L. *child and adolescent psychiatrist*
Todd, Harold Wade *association executive, retired air force officer*

Denver
Adler, Charles Spencer *psychiatrist*
Bunn, Paul A., Jr. *oncologist, educator*
Butterfield, Donald Gene *physician, gastroenterologist*
Campbell, David Neil *physician, educator*
Cochran, John Howard *plastic and reconstructive surgeon*
Eisenbarth, George Stephen *pediatrics educator*
Filley, Christopher Mark *neurologist*
Golitz, Loren Eugene *dermatologist, pathologist, clinical administrator, educator*
Harken, Alden Hood *surgeon, thoracic surgeon*
Hoehn, Robert J. *plastic surgeon, educator*
Huang, Linda Chen *plastic surgeon*
Kappy, Michael Steven *pediatrics educator*
Kluck, Clarence Joseph *physician*
Koyle, Martin Allan *surgeon, educator*
Lefkowitz, Jerry Bruce *pathology educator*
Lubeck, Marvin Jay *ophthalmologist*
Nelson, Nancy Eleanor *pediatrician, educator*
Pomerantz, Marvin *thoracic surgeon*
Roman-Unfer, Susan *hematologist, oncologist*
Wachtel, Thomas Lee *surgeon*
Washington, Reginald Louis *pediatric cardiologist*
Weatherley-White, Roy Christopher Anthony *surgeon, consultant*
Weiner, Norman *pharmacology educator*

Durango
Crue, Benjamin Lane, Jr. *retired neurosurgeon*
Wigton, Chester Mahlon *family physician*

Englewood
Vander Ark, Gary Duane *neurosurgeon*

Fort Garland
Leighninger, David Scott *cardiovascular surgeon*

Fort Morgan
Gibbs, Denis Laurel *radiologist*

Grand Junction
Janson, Richard Anthony *plastic surgeon*

Greeley
Cook, Donald E. *pediatrician*
Jaouen, Richard Matthie *plastic surgeon*

Greenwood Village
[illegible], Irving Kaufman Karchmer *ear surgeon, educator, entrepeneur*

Highlands Ranch
Bublitz, Deborah Keirstead *pediatrician*

Loveland
Fadhli, Hussam Abbas *retired cardiovascular surgeon, sculptor, painter*
Wright, Eric R. *physician assistant*

Pueblo
Mou, Thomas William *physician, medical educator and consultant*

Silverthorne
Rutherford, Robert Barry *surgeon*

Thornton
Langley, James Wallace *family practice physician, banker*

Wheat Ridge
Brown, Steven Brien *radiologist*

FLORIDA

Venice
Freibott, George August *physician, chemist, priest*

HAWAII

Hilo
Taniguchi, Tokuso *surgeon*

Honolulu
Brady, Stephen R.P.K. *physician*
Camara, Jorge de Guzman *ophthalmologist, educator*
Chee, Percival Hon Yin *ophthalmologist*
Chock, Clifford Yet-Chong *family practice physician*
Edwards, John Wesley, Jr. *urologist*
Fitz-Patrick, David *endocrinologist, educator*
Goldstein, Sir Norman *dermatologist*
Hay-Roe, Victor *plastic surgeon*
Ishii, Clyde Hideo *plastic surgeon*
Jim, Edward L.S. *surgeon*
Kane, Thomas Jay, III *orthopaedic surgeon, educator*
Kortvelesy, J. Scott *ophthalmologist, educator*
Lee, Yeu-Tsu Margaret *surgeon, educator*
Low, Lewis L. *physician, medical educator*
Matthews, Daryl Bruce *psychiatrist*
McCarthy, Laurence James *physician, pathologist*
Meagher, Michael *radiologist*
Meyer, Dennis Robert *physician*
Oda, Yoshio *physician, internist*
Oishi, Calvin Shizuo *orthopedic surgeon*
Pang, Herbert George *ophthalmologist*
Parsa, Fereydoun Don *plastic surgeon*
Shen, Edward Nin-Da *cardiologist, educator*
Stevens, Stephen Edward *psychiatrist*
Sugiki, Shigemi *ophthalmologist, educator*
Terminella, Luigi *critical care physician, educator*
Yates, Alayne *psychiatrist*

Kamuela
Bracher, George *radiologist*

Koloa
Donohugh, Donald Lee *physician*

Lihue
Kim, Peter M. *physician, internist*

Waikoloa
Copman, Louis *radiologist*

Wailuku
Savona, Michael Richard *physician*

IDAHO

Boise
Benavides, Mary Kathleen *anesthesiologist, nutritional consultant*
Clinkingbeard, Cynthia Lou *endocrinologist, educator, researcher*

Bonners Ferry
Kuhns, David Wallace *emergency physician*

Coeur D Alene
West, Robert Sumner *surgeon*

Nampa
Botimer, Allen Ray *retired surgeon, retirement center owner*

Saint Maries
Baines, David Ray *family physician, health education educator*

MONTANA

Billings
Glenn, Guy Charles *pathologist*
Wood, Robert Clark *neurosurgeon*

Bozeman
Rinker, Charles Frederick, II *surgeon*

Deer Lodge
Kidder, David Monroe *physician*

Helena
Reynolds, James Francis, Jr. *physician*

Missoula
Murray, Donald Eugene *plastic surgeon*

Wolf Point
Listerud, Mark Boyd *retired surgeon*

NEVADA

Carson City
Meyer, Roger Paul *physician*

Henderson
Perel, Michael Joseph *dermatologist, inventor*

Las Vegas
Bandt, Paul Douglas *physician*
Buchanan, Donald Edwin *nematologist*
Canada, William H. *plastic surgeon*
Hanson, Gerald Eugene *oral and maxillofacial surgeon*
Markewich, Gary Steven *dermatologist*
Matheis, Lawrence Paul *association executive, public health consultant*
Moritz, Timothy Bovie *psychiatrist*
Rodriguez, Benjamin John *plastic surgeon*
Trigiano, Lucien Lewis *physician*
Vanselow, Carl Robert, Jr. *physician assistant*
Venger, Benjamin Herschel *neurosurgeon, medical consultant*
Wax, Arnold *physician*

Reno
MacKintosh, Frederick Roy *oncologist*
Rahe, Richard Henry *psychiatrist, educator*
Rosenauer, Adolf Alois *neurosurgeon*

NEW MEXICO

Alamogordo
Ashdown, Franklin Donald *physician, composer*
Lindley, Norman Dale *physician*

Albuquerque
Abrums, John Denise *internist*
Baack, Bret Rolyn *plastic surgeon*
Goss, Jerome Eldon *cardiologist*
Hudson, Patrick A. *plastic surgeon*
Moneim, Moheb S. *orthopaedic surgeon, educator*
Stevenson, James Richard *radiologist, lawyer*
Summers, William Koopmans *neuropsychiatrist, researcher*
Tatum, Ronald Winston *physician, endocrinologist*
Worrell, Richard Vernon *orthopedic surgeon, college dean*

Gallup
Robertson, Gerald Rankin *physician, internist*

Hobbs
McLaughlin, Jerry DeWayne *obstetrician, gynecologist*
Vemula, Narasimharao *physician*

Las Cruces
Jacobs, Kent Frederick *dermatologist*
Talamantes, Roberto *developmental pediatrician*

Portales
Goodwin, Martin Brune *radiologist*

Tesuque
Balagura, Saul *neurosurgeon*

OREGON

Ashland
Kirschner, Richard Michael *naturopathic physician, speaker, author*

Beaverton
Swank, Roy Laver *physician, educator, inventor*

Corvallis
Hafner-Eaton, Chris *health services researcher, educator*

Eugene
Bascom, John Upton *surgeon*
Flanagan, Latham, Jr. *surgeon*
Nissel, Martin *radiologist, consultant*
Peat, Raymond Franklin *endocrinologist, reseracher, consultant*
Rose, Ann Wegener *physician assistant*
Stafl, Jan H. *physician*
Starr, Grier Forsythe *retired pathologist*

Grand Ronde
Mala, Theodore Anthony *physician, consultant*

Lebanon
Girod, Frank Paul *retired surgeon*

Portland
Benson, John Alexander, Jr. *physician, educator*
Berthelsdorf, Siegfried *psychiatrist*
Brummett, Robert Eddie *pharmacology educator*
Buist, Neil Robertson MacKenzie *medical educator, medical administrator*
Burry, Kenneth Arnold *physician, educator*
Butler, John Lowe, IV *psychiatrist, educator*
Collins, Michael Sean *obstetrician and gynecologist, educator*
English, Woodruff Jones, II *physician*
Guderian, Ronald Howard *pathologist*
Hagmeier, Clarence Howard *retired anesthesiologist*
Layman, Charles Donald *plastic surgeon*
Mozena, John Daniel *podiatrist*
Noonan, William Donald *physician, lawyer*
Nutt, John Gordon *neurologist, educator*
Prendergast, William John *ophthalmologist*
Schmidt, Waldemar Adrian *pathologist, educator*
Sklovsky, Robert Joel *naturopathic physician, pharmacist, educator*
Standage, Blayne Allan *surgeon*
Sutherland, Donald Wood *cardiologist*
Swan, Kenneth Carl *surgeon*
Szeto, Erik K. *family practice physician*
Takahashi, Gary Wayne *internist, hematologist oncologist*
Zerzan, Charles Joseph, Jr. *retired gastroenterologist*

Roseburg
Donahoo, Stanley Ellsworth *orthopedic surgeon*

Silverton
Centerwall, Willard Raymond *physician*

Springfield
Ehrmantraut, Harry Charles *medical consultant, researcher*

Wilsonville
Holmes, David M. *physician*

UTAH

Park City
Carmichael, Paul Louis *ophthalmic surgeon*

Salt Lake City
Bauer, A(ugust) Robert, Jr. *surgeon, educator*
Brandon, Kathryn Elizabeth Beck *pediatrician*
Davis, Brian Adam *physician*
Goates, Delbert Tolton *child psychiatrist*
Hill, Harry Raymond *medical educator*
Larsen, Lowell Don *retired pathologist*
Middleton, Anthony Wayne, Jr. *urologist, educator*
Osborn, Jeffrey Scott *cardiologist*
Petersen, Finn Bo *oncologist, educator*
Stanford, Joseph Barney *medical educator, physician*
Thomas, David Snow *plastic surgeon*
Vanderhooft, Jan Eric *orthopedic surgeon, educator*

WASHINGTON

Bellevue
Dunn, Jeffrey Edward *neurologist*

Bellingham
James, Helen Ann *plastic surgeon*

Chehalis
Faiola, Richard Louis *physician*
Neal-Parker, Shirley Anita *obstetrician and gynecologist*

Clarkston
Chinchinian, Harry *pathologist, educator*

Edmonds
Crone, Richard Allan *cardiologist, educator*

Everett
Beegle, Earl Dennis *family physician*
Wood, David Bruce *naturopathic physician*

Fort Lewis
Whittaker, Paul Emerson *physician, army officer*

Kennewick
Roach, John Michael *gastroenterologist*

Kirkland
Dundas, Dennis Franklin *plastic surgeon*
Norehad, Ernest A. *physician*
Strode, Gerald Marvin *physician assistant*

Longview
Kenagy, John Warner *surgeon*
Kirkpatrick, Richard Alan *internist*
Sandstrom, Robert Edward *physician, pathologist*

Mountlake Terrace
Imamura, Eugene Hachiro *osteopathic physician, surgeon*

Olympia
Fisher, Nancy Louise *pediatrician, medical geneticist, former nurse*
Smith, Sherwood Paul *plastic surgeon*

Seattle
Ballweg, Ruth Milligan *physician assistant, educator*
Chatard, Peter Ralph Noel, Jr. *aesthetic plastic surgeon*
Clarren, Sterling Keith *pediatrician*
Clowes, Alexander Whitehill *surgeon, educator*
Day, Robert Winsor *cancer researcher*
Florence, Michael Glenn *medical educator*
Giedt, Walvin Roland *epidemiologist, educator*
Han, Mao-Tang *surgeon, researcher*
Hargiss, James Leonard *ophthalmologist*
Kalina, Robert Edward *physician, educator*
Kraft, George Howard *physician, educator*
Krohn, Kenneth Albert *radiology educator*
Mangham, Charles Adley, Sr. *psychiatrist, psychoanalyst*
Merendino, K. Alvin *surgical educator*
Neppe, Vernon Michael *neuropsychiatrist, psychopharmacologist, author, educator*
Nishioka, Gary Jim *facial plastic surgeon*
Plorde, James Joseph *physician, educator*
Reade, C. Wight *physician*
Sale, George Edgar *physician*
Schimmelbusch, Werner Helmut *psychiatrist*
Scott, John Carlyle *retired gynecologist, oncologist*
Staheli, Lynn Taylor *pediatric orthopedist, educator*
Taft, David Allan *surgeon*
Thomas, Edward Donnall *physician, researcher*
Welk, Richard Andrew *plastic surgeon*
Williams, Joan Elaine *podiatric surgeon, educator*
Winn, H. Richard *surgeon*
Yee, Kuo Chiang *neuroscientist, neurologist*

Spokane
Gibson, Melvin Roy *pharmacognosy educator*
Lee, Sun Myung *physician*

Tacoma
Cheah, Keong-Chye *psychiatrist*
Irish, Thomas Judson *plastic surgeon*
Nazaire, Michel Harry *physician*
Nordby, Jon Jorgen *forensic scientist, educator*
Scarbrough, Michael Dean *anesthesiologist, photographer*
Verhey, Joseph William *psychiatrist, educator*

University Place
Flemming, Stanley Lalit Kumar *family practice physician, mayor, state legislator*

Wenatchee
Knecht, Ben Harrold *surgeon*
Sorom, Terry Allen *ophthalmic surgeon*

Yakima
Newstead, Robert Richard *urologist*

WYOMING

Buffalo
Watkins, Eugene Leonard *surgeon, educator*

Casper
Cole, Malvin *neurologist, educator*

Cheyenne
Darnell, Catherine Margaret *anatomy and physiology educator*
Flick, William Fredrick *surgeon*

Gillette
Naramore, James Joseph *family practice physician, educator*

Sheridan
Batty, Hugh Kenworthy *physician*

MILITARY ADDRESSES OF THE UNITED STATES

EUROPE

APO
Wilson, Robert McClain *plastic surgeon, educator*

CANADA

ALBERTA

Calgary
Leung, Alexander Kwok-Chu *pediatrician educator*

BRITISH COLUMBIA

New Westminster
Bishop, Rodney Philip *physician*

Vancouver
Roy, Chunilal *psychiatrist*

West Vancouver
Knauff, Hans Georg *physician, educator*

ADDRESS UNPUBLISHED

Altman, Adele Rosenhain *radiologist*
Angel, Armando Carlos *rheumatologist, internist*
Angelov, George Angel *pediatrician, anatomist, teratologist*
Boddie, Lewis Franklin *obstetrics and gynecology educator*
Bruggeman, Lewis LeRoy *radiologist*
Bussey, George Davis *psychiatrist*
Chen, Stephen Shau-tsi *retired psychiatrist, physiologist*
Clarke, Benjamin King *retired anethesiologist, state representative*
Cline, Carolyn Joan *plastic and reconstructive surgeon*
Cozen, Lewis *orthopedic surgeon*
Crues, John Vernon, III *radiologist, educator*
Dewhurst, William George *psychiatrist, educator, research director*
Di Salvo, Arthur Francis *physician, public health official*
Draur, Ronald Alvin *retired cardiologist*
Ford, Clynn Roberts *thoracic and cardiovascular surgeon, lab director*
Goldberg, Mark Arthur *neurologist*
Goodley, Paul Harvey *physician*
Greene, Laurence Whitridge, Jr. *surgical educator*
Groves, Sheridon Hale *orthopedic surgeon*
Heiner, Douglas Cragun *pediatrician, educator*
Iacono, Robert Paul *neurosurgeon, medical educator*
Iserson, Kenneth Victor *emergency medicine educator, bioethicist*
Jackman, Jay M. *psychiatrist*
Kandel, Joan Ellen *osteopath*
Kaplan, Melvin Raymond *physician, medical educator*
Karpilow, Craig *physician*
Kendall, Harry Ovid *internist*
Kern, Donald Michael *internist*
Kost, Gerald Joseph *physician, scientist*
Lunsford, Morlan Howard *toxicology laboratory technician*
Madlang, Rodolfo Mojica *retired urologic surgeon*
Makowski, Edgar Leonard *obstetrician and gynecologist*
Mathews, William Edward *neurological surgeon, educator*
Mays, James, Jr. *physician*
Mazzetti, Robert F. *real estate manager, retired orthopedic surgeon*
Metzner, Richard Joel *psychiatrist, psychopharmacologist, educator*
Meyer, George Wilbur *internist, health facility administrator*
Meyer, Greg Charles *psychiatrist*
Mould, Diane Renee *pharmacologist*
Mountain, Clifton Fletcher *surgeon, educator*
Nelson, William Rankin *surgeon, educator*
Nora, James Jackson *physician, author, educator*
Oates, Joyce Marie *psychiatrist*
Pardue, A. Michael *retired plastic and reconstructive surgeon*
Pomeroy, Kent Lytle *physical medicine and rehabilitation physician*
Ramos, Eleanor Lacson *transplant nephrologist*
Rebhun, Joseph *allergist, immunologist, medical educator*
Renson, Jean Felix *psychiatry educator*
Roberts, Alan Silverman *orthopedic surgeon*
Sachtleben, Thomas Ray *family and sports medicine physician*
Schmid, Lynette Sue *child and adolescent psychiatrist*
Shekter, William Bernard *ophthalmologist*
Silverberg, Stuart Owen *obstetrician, gynecologist*
Simmons, Geoffrey Stuart *physician*
Stewart, Stanford J. *oncologist, immunologist*
Stone, James Robert *surgeon*
Tan, Zhiqun *biomedical scientist*
Towers, Bernard Leonard *medical educator*
Toy, Pearl Tak-Chu Yau *transfusion medicine physician*
Van Brunt, Edmund Ewing *physician*
Watring, Watson Glenn *gynecologic oncologist, educator*
Werbach, Melvyn Roy *physician, writer*
Williams, Ronald Lee *pharmacologist*
Wilson, Almon Chapman *surgeon, physician, retired naval officer*

HUMANITIES: LIBERAL STUDIES

UNITED STATES

ALASKA

Anchorage
Haley, Michael Cabot *English educator, researcher*
Spatz, Ronald Marvin *English language educator, editor, filmmaker, writer*

Juneau
Ruotsala, James Alfred *historian, writer*

ARIZONA

Davis Monthan A F B
Miller, Charles Wallace *historian, environmental geologist*

Flagstaff
Marcus, Karen Melissa *foreign language educator*

Green Valley
Dmytryshyn, Basil *historian, educator*
Easton, Roger David *art history educator*
Elliott, Jeanne Bate *retired English educator, writer*

Lake Havasu City
Brydon, Ruth Vickery *history educator*

Mesa
Palmer, Patricia Ann *English language educator*

Phoenix
Benedict, Deborah Anklam *English language educator*
Cristiano, Marilyn Jean *speech communication educator*
Foxx, Daniel LeRoy, Jr. *history educator*
Maimon, Elaine Plaskow *English educator, university provost*
Scoggin, Daniel Paul *English educator*
Socwell, Margaret G. *reading and language arts educator, consultant*

Prescott
Moses, Elbert Raymond, Jr. *speech and dramatic arts educator*

Scottsdale
Bonner, Thomas Neville *history and higher education educator*
Mousseux, Renate *language educator*

Surprise
Clark, Lloyd *historian, educator*

Tempe
Major, Roy Coleman *language educator*
van Gelderen, Elly *English linguistics educator*
Wong, Timothy C. *Chinese language and literature educator*

Thatcher
Stevens, Susan Marie *English educator, poet, editor*

Tucson
Austin, John Norman *classics educator*
Birkinbine, John, II *philatelist*
Furlow, Mary Beverley *English language educator*
Kellogg, Frederick *historian*
Kleese, William Carl *genealogy research consultant*
Langendoen, Donald Terence *linguistics educator*
Martinson, Steven Delmar *German studies educator*
Mering, John Vollmer *retired history educator*
Milton, Corinne Holm *art history educator*
Negley, Floyd Rollin *genealogist, retired army officer and civilian military employee*
Rabuck, Donna Fontanarose *English writing educator*
Tao, Chia-lin Pao *humanities educator*

CALIFORNIA

Aptos
Dastagir, Zarmina *English as a second language educator*

Arcadia
Schwind, David Alan *historical researcher, writer*

Arcata
Gage, Thomas Evans *English language educator, author*
Martien, Norman Gerald (Jerry Martien) *creative writing and English educator, carpenter*

Bakersfield
Flachmann, Michael Charles *English language educator*
Schmidt, Joanne (Josephine Anne Schmidt) *language educator*

Bellflower
Hastings, Elisa Kipp *English language educator*

Belmont
Bazigos, Mary *English as a secong language speech and writing educator*

Berkeley
Baas, Jacquelynn *art historian, museum administrator*
Chiang, Yuet-Sim D. *English educator*
Lusheck, Catherine *art historian, consultant*
Mastronarde, Donald John *classicist, educator*
Nagler, Michael Nicholas *classics and comparative literature educator*
Rosenberg, Marvin *dramatic arts educator*
Shannon, Thomas Frederic *German language educator*

Beverly Hills
Kravitz, Ellen King *musicologist, educator*

Camarillo
Derr, Jeannie Combs *bilingual educator, anthropology educator*

Cambria
Salaverria, Helena Clara *foreign language educator*

Carmel
McGlynn, Betty Hoag *art historian*

Carmichael
Donaldson, Robert Charles *history educator*

Carson
Butler, Peter, Jr. *retired secondary education educator*

Chatsworth
Getz, Josephine Arlene *English educator*

Claremont
Elsbree, Langdon *English language educator*
Emerick, Judson Johnson *art historian*
Wheeler, Geraldine Hartshorn *historian*

Costa Mesa
Carlson, Lawrence Arvid *English language educator, real estate agent*
Parker, P. Kevin *English educator*
Prout, Carl Wesley *history educator*

Cotati
Castillo, Edward Daniel *humanities educator*

Cupertino
Tice, Bradley Scott *humanities educator*
Wassman, Rose Marie Madeline *English language educator*

Daly City
Gao, Luji *foreign language educator, columnist*

Davis
Manoliu, Maria *linguist*
Schaeffer, Peter Moritz-Friedrich *literature educator*
Taylor, Alan Shaw *history educator*
Vaz, Katherine Anne *English language educator, writer*

Del Mar
La Rosa, Frank Edward *retired English language and humanities educator*

El Cajon
Dana-Davidson, Laoma Cook *English language educator*

El Cerrito
Kuo, Ping-chia *historian, educator*

Escondido
McHenry, Anita Petei *historian, archaeologist*

Eureka
Ellis, Shelley Marie *English writing educator*

Fallbrook
Burns, Louis Francis *retired history educator*

Fresno
Clifton, Michael Edward *English language educator*
Genini, Ronald Walter *history educator, historian*
Kouymjian, Dickran *art historian, Orientalist, educator*

Fullerton
Castro, Donald Steven *history educator*

Glendale
di Santa Cristina, Leonardo de Grassi *art historian, educator*
Edelman, Bart *English literature educator, poet*
Plata, Armando Luis Carlos *Spanish voiceover artist and translator*

Grass Valley
Hotchkiss, Bill *author, educator*

Hayward
Warrin, Donald Ogden *retired foreign language educator*
Zou, Ke *English linguistics educator*

Huntington Beach
Barua, Dibakar *English language and literature educator, writer*
Cavanaugh, Jan Cathleen *art historian*

Imperial
McMullin, Linda Sue *English language educator*

Irvine
Fukui, Naoki *theoretical linguist*
Katrak, Ketu *English literature educator*
Lee, Meredith *German literature and language educator*
Lillyman, William John *German language educator, academic administrator*
Miles, Margaret Melanie *historian, educator*

Kingsburg
Garrigus, Charles Byford *retired literature educator*

La Jolla
George, Rosemary Marangoly *literature educator*
McDonald, Marianne *classicist*

La Verne
Werner, David Robert *English language educator*

Livermore
Hiskes, Dolores G. *educator*

Long Beach
Beebe, Sandra E. *retired English language educator, artist, writer*
Locklin, Gerald Ivan *language educator, poet, writer*
Lunderville, Gerald Paul *bilingual education educator*
Polakoff, Keith Ian *historian, university administrator*
Sater, William Frederick *history educator, writer*
Tang, Paul Chi Lung *philosophy educator*

Los Angeles
Alpers, Edward Alter *history educator*
Aoun, Joseph *linguistics educator, researcher*
Bahr, Ehrhard *Germanic languages and literature educator*
Behdad, Ali *English language educator*
Cherkin, Adina *interpreter, translator*
Clements, Ruth Loretta *humanities educator, writer, editor*
Cohen, Marshall *philosophy and law educator*
Cortinez, Veronica *literature educator*
Crecelius, Daniel Neil *history educator*
Darby, Joanne Tyndale (Jaye Darby) *arts and humanities educator*
Dumitrescu, Domnita *Spanish language educator, researcher*
Eckert, Geraldine Gonzales *language professional, educator, entrepreneur*
Giuliano, Cheryl Fallon *English educator*
Jorgensen, Paul Alfred *English language educator emeritus*
Klein, Snira L(ubovsky) *Hebrew language and literature educator*
Mellor, Ronald John *history educator*
Miles, Richard Robert *art historian, writer*
Nakanishi, Don Toshiaki *Asian American studies educator, writer*
Pecora, Vincent Pitt *English educator*
Quintero, Ruben David *English educator*
Schutz, John Adolph *historian, educator, former university dean*
See, Carolyn *English language educator, novelist, book critic*
Wilkie, James W. *history educator*
Wills, John Elliot, Jr. *history educator, writer*

Marina
Boldyrev, Peter Matveevich *Russian language and culture educator, writer*

Merced
Elliott, Gordon Jefferson *retired English language educator*

Millbrae
Palmer, Patricia Ann Texter *English language educator*

Mission Viejo
Bander, Carol Jean *German and English language educator*

Montclair
Haage, Robert Mitchell *retired history educator, organization leader*

Monterey
Aridi, Souhail Kamal *literature educator*
Franke, Jack Emil *foreign language educator*
Peet, Phyllis Irene *women's studies educator*
Shropshire, Helen Mae *retired historian*
Strolle, Jon Martin *language studies educator*

Monterey Park
Suntree, Susan Frances *English language educator, poet, playwright*

Moraga
Beran, Carol Louise Viertel *English language educator*

Northridge
Flores, William Vincent *Latin American studies educator*

Oakland
Matthews, Lydia Ann *art history educator*
Mehta, Brinda J. *foreign languages educator*

Orange
Barb Mingo, Arturo *romance literature and languages educator*

Pacific Grove
Shin, Ilsoon *foreign language educator*

Pacific Palisades
Popkin, Richard Henry *philosophy educator, writer, editor*

Palo Alto
Tsumura, Yumiko *Japanese language and culture educator, consultant*
Walker, Carolyn Peyton *English language educator*

Pasadena
Parr, James Allan *literature professor*
Stephans, Michael Lee *English language educator, musician, poet, author*

Placentia
Nettleship, Lois Ellen *history educator*

Placerville
Nesbitt, Paul Edward *historian, author, educator*

Pleasant Hill
Ashby, Denise Stewart *speech educator, communication consultant*

Pomona
Cook, Stanley Joseph *English language educator, poet*
Montgomery, Elizabeth Anne *English language educator*

Riverside
Brinkerhoff, Dericksen Morgan *art history educator*
Howe, Winona Ruth *English language educator*
Rudolph, Conrad *medieval art history educator*

Rohnert Park
Hester Williams, Kim Deatra *English educator*

Sacramento
Bloom, Linda Susan *art historian*
Madden, David William *English language educator*
Meindl, Robert James *English language educator*

San Bernardino
Pal, Anasuya *English educator*

San Diego
Chamberlin, Eugene Keith *historian, educator*
Davies, Thomas Mockett, Jr. *history educator*
González-Trujillo, César Augusto *Chicano studies educator, writer*
Huggins, Earl McClure *English language educator*
Moramarco, Fred Stephen *English writing educator, editor*
Peterson, Richard Hermann *history educator, retired*
Walsh, Sarah Elizabeth (Elizabeth Walsh) *English language educator*

San Dimas
Paige, Nancy Louise *genealogist*

San Francisco
Alayeto, Ofelia Luisa *writer, researcher, educator*
Batchelor, Karen Lee *English language educator*
Chirapravati, Pattaratorn *art historian, educator*
Hansen, Carol Louise *English language educator*
Jabbar, Abdul *English language educator*
Landar, Herbert Jay *linguistics educator, author*
Mann, Richard George *art history educator*
Needleman, Jacob *philosophy educator, writer*
Papakonstantino, Stacy *English language educator*
Sanazaro, Leonard Rocco *language educator, writer*
Schwartz, Stephen Alfred *historian, journalist*

San Jose
Gillett, Paula *humanities educator*
Leddy, Thomas Winter *philosophy educator*

San Luis Obispo
Gish, Robert Franklin *English language educator, writer*
Martinez, William, Jr. *Spanish langauge educator, multicultural issues consultant*
Miklowitz, Paul Stephen *philosophy educator*
Velasquez, Gloria Louise *language educator, writer*

San Marcos
Christman, Albert Bernard *historian*
Martinez, Marcos Louis *humanities educator*
Tanner, John Douglas, Jr. *history educator, writer*

San Marino
Karlstrom, Paul Johnson *art historian*

San Mateo
Fellows, Ward Jay *philosophy educator, minister*

Santa Ana
Mallory, Lee Wesley *English and French language educator, poet*

Santa Barbara
Abbott, H. Porter *English language educator*
Bazerman, Charles *English language educator, writing researcher*
Brownlee, Wilson Elliot, Jr. *history educator*
Mithun, Marianne *linguist, researcher, educator*
Scamahorn, Mark *English writing educator, artist*
Tobin, Ronald William *French language educator*

Santa Clara
Varona, Lucia Tarot *Spanish language educator, researcher*

Santa Cruz
Walker, T. Mike *creative writing and literature educator*

Santa Monica
Heimann-Hast, Sybil Dorothea *language arts and literature educator*
Hight, Mary Kathryn (Kay) *art historian*

Santa Rosa
Aman, Reinhold Albert *philologist, publisher*
Kuwabara, Lori Anne *educator, writer, consultant*
Van Gelder, Naneene Sue *English language educator*

Seaside
March, Annette Marie *English and literature educator*
Wang, Qun *English language educator*

Stanford
Carnochan, Walter Bliss *retired humanities educator*
Felstiner, John *literature educator, translator*
Guerard, Albert Joseph *retired modern literature educator, author*

Palumbo-Liu, David *literature educator*
Perry, John Richard *philosophy educator*
Saussy, Caleb Powell Haun *Asian language educator*

Stockton
Tedards, Douglas Manning *English language educator*

Studio City
Slide, Anthony Clifford *film historian, writer*

Suisun City
Bernier, Emily S. *English literature educator*

Sylmar
Suyama, Ruth Leiko *historian, educator*

Tarzana
Boyd, Jeanne Roswell *classic languages and literature educator*

Thousand Oaks
Tobias, Marilyn *historian, educator, writer*

Topanga
Waldron, Jill Genevieve *English language educator*

Torrance
Anderson, Marilyn Wheeler *English language educator*
Trejos, Charlotte Marie *humanities educator, consultant*

Turlock
Christopher, Renny Teresa *liberal studies educator*

Ukiah
Lohrli, Anne *retired English language educator, author*

Van Nuys
Zucker, Alfred John *English language educator, academic administrator*

Victorville
Basha, Claudia Ann *language and theater arts educator*

Walnut Creek
Judah, Jay Stillson *historian, educator*

Whittier
Barnstone, Tony Dimitrios *English writing educator*
Farmer, Ann Dahlstrom *English language professor*

Woodland Hills
Gani, Scarlett *language educator*
Pickard, Dean *philosophy and humanities educator*

Wrightwood
LaMay-Abner, Julie Ann *English educator*

Yorba Linda
Keating, Norma Storrs *professional genealogist, small business owner*

Yountville
Martin, Gilbert Edward *historian, writer*

Yucaipa
Acquistapace, Kris *English language and humanities educator*

COLORADO

Aurora
Kleinfeld, Elizabeth Anne *English literature educator, magazine editor*

Boulder
Minor, Vernon Hyde *art history educator*
Preston, Michael James *English and folklore educator, consultant*
Schütrumpf, Eckart Ernst *classical languages and philosophy educator*

Broomfield
Dilly, Marian Jeanette *humanities educator*

Colorado Springs
Anderson, Katheryn Lucille *language arts educator and author*
Bryson, Dorothy Printup *retired Latin educator*
Watkins, Lois Irene *English educator*

Denver
Black, Robert Clifford, III *history educator*
Dimmick, Lauretta *art historian, educator*
Dorhout, Marlene Sue *English language educator*
Espenlaub, Margo Linn *women's studies educator, artist*
Fleck, Richard Francis *English language educator, writer*
Kiteley, Brian Alan *English literature educator, writer*
Porter, Donna Jean *genealogist*
Ronning, Charlotte Jean *foreign language educator*
Storey, Brit Allan *historian*
Ward, Seth *history and Judaic studies educator*
Wetzel, Jodi (Joy Lynn Wetzel) *history and women's studies educator*

Durango
Jantzer-White, Marilee Joan *art history educator*

Englewood
Bardsley, Kay *historian, archivist, dance professional*
Benedict, Margaret Rose (Peggy Benedict) *English language and speech educator*
Sieveke-Pearson, Starla Jean *language educator*

Estes Park
Gibbs, Dorothy Scott *retired Latin educator*

Fort Collins
Becker, Leslee *English language and creative writing educator*
Schwartz, Steven *author, English language educator*

Golden
Iversen, Kristen D. *English language educator, editor, writer*

Grand Junction
Fay, Abbott Eastman *history educator*

Lakewood
Camy, Ann L. *English language educator*
Joy, Carla Marie *history educator*
Woodruff, Kathryn Elaine *English language educator*

Pueblo
Farwell, Hermon Waldo, Jr. *parliamentarian, educator, former speech communication educator*
Vorpagel, Wilbur Charles *historical consultant*

Sterling
Berns, Pamela Marie *English language and literature educator*
Christian, Roland Carl (Bud Christian) *retired English language and speech communications educator*

HAWAII

Honolulu
Aung-Thwin, Michael Arthur *history educator*
Fujita, James Hiroshi *history educator*
Hoffmann, Kathryn Ann *humanities educator*
Kasper, Gabriele *applied linguistics educator*
Marshall, William Gerald *English language educator*
Matson, Floyd William *humanities educator, writer*
Moore, Willis Henry Allphin *history and geography educator*
Nagtalon-Miller, Helen Rosete *humanities educator*
Peterson, Barbara Ann Bennett *history educator, television personality*
Rehbock, Philip Frederick *history educator*
Seidensticker, Edward George *Japanese language and literature educator*

Kailua Kona
Still, William Norwood, Jr. *retired history educator, researcher*

Pearl City
Perkins, Lily Leialoha *humanities educator*
Roberts, Norman Frank *English composition and linguistics educator*

IDAHO

Boise
Dayley, Jon Philip *linguistics educator*
Nguyen, King Xuan *language educator*
Wells, Merle William *historian, state archivist*

Coeur D Alene
McLeod, James Richard *English language educator*

Moscow
Burns-McCoy, Nancie E. *English literature educator*
Gier, Nicholas Francis *philosophy educator*
Greever, Janet Groff *history educator*
Harris, Robert Dalton *history educator, researcher, writer*
Passanante, Joy Cathey *English language educator*
Schwantes, Carlos Arnaldo *history educator, consultant*

MONTANA

Big Timber
Agnew, Kathleen Dianne Crosbie *language educator*

Great Falls
Weeks, Dennis LeRoy *English language educator*

Helena
Lambert, Richard Thomas *philosophy educator*

Missoula
Pape, Gregory Laurence *English language educator, poet*
Wigfied-Phillip, Ruth Genivea *genealogist, author, researcher*

NEVADA

Las Vegas
Abramson, Albert *television historian, consultant*
Buechler, Ralph Wolfgang *German language and literature educator*
Frasz, Geoffrey Bryce *philosophy educator*
Gajowski, Evelyn Jacqueline *English language educator*
Logsdon, Richard M. *English language educator, magazine editor*
Schmiedel, Donald Emerson *Spanish educator*

North Las Vegas
Miller, Eleanor *English language and literature educator*
Schmitt, Paul John *history and geography educator*

Reno
Casper, Scott E. *historian*

NEW MEXICO

Albuquerque
Houston, Gail Turley *English language educator*
Kutvirt, Duda Chytilova (Ruzena) [illegible] *translator*
Lamadrid, Enrique Russell *Spanish language educator, translator*

Pabisch, Peter Karl *German language educator*
Peña, Juan José *interpreter*
Robbins, Richard Gardner, Jr. *history educator*
White, Robert Rankin *writer and historian, hydrologist*
Young, Robert Wendell *language specialist, tribal relations specialist*

Aztec
Whitaker, Victoria Marie *English educator*

Carlsbad
Buckholz, Mark *language arts and theater educator, dramatist*
Burkhalter, Shelley *English language educator*

Las Cruces
Newman, Edgar Leon *historian, educator*

Las Vegas
Croxton, Dorothy Audrey Simpson *speech educator*

Roswell
Bowles, Nancy Rae *English language educator, registered nurse*

Santa Fe
Pfeiffenberger, Selma *art historian*

OREGON

Corvallis
Kesler, Roland Lincoln, Jr. *English language educator*
Sayre, Henry Marshall *art history educator, critic, writer*
Weaver, Roger Keys *retired English language educator*

Eugene
Lansdowne, Karen Myrtle *retired English language and literature educator*
Taylor, Donald Stewart *English literature educator*
White, David Olds *researcher, former educator*

Fossil
Lorts, Jack Edward *secondary education educator, poet*

Mcminnville
Mc Kaughan, Howard Paul *linguistics educator*

Netarts
Hartman-Irwin, Mary Frances *retired language professional*

North Bend
Shepard, Robert Carlton *English language educator*

Portland
Donovan, Thomas John *humanities educator*
Englert, Walter George *classics and humanities educator*
Harris, Frederick Philip *retired philosophy educator*
Manchester, Arthur Herschell *English and foreign language educator*
Schmidt, Stanley Eugene *retired speech educator*
Wadley, Stephen Alexander *foreign language educator*
Zimmerman, Loretta Ellen *history educator*

UTAH

Bountiful
Dollarhide, William Wiles *genealogist, writer*
Pedersen, Gaylen *genealogy organization administrator*

Ephraim
Parnell, Gary Lester *humanities educator, consultant*

Logan
Bame, James Edwin *English educator*
Lye, William Frank *history educator*
Milner, Clyde A., II *historian*
Robson, Kent E. *philosophy educator*

Ogden
LeTourneau, Mark Stephen *English language educator, researcher*

Orem
Bell, Elouise Mildred *English language educator, writer, speaker*
Coppersmith, Jo Ellen *English language educator*
Panina, Marina Petronna *Russian language educator*

Salt Lake City
Arrington, Harriet Ann Horne *historian, biographer, researcher, writer*
Hibbard, Charles Gustin *historian*
Justesen, Elaine Toomer *genealogist*
Lima, Marilynne *foreign language educator, consultant*
Nichols, Elizabeth L(uella) *genealogist, writer, publisher, researcher, consultant*
Olpin, Robert Spencer *art history educator*
Simpson, Linda Ann *English language educator*
Stensrud, Marene Hansen *English language educator*

WASHINGTON

Anacortes
Bertolino, James D. *English language educator*

Auburn
Sims, Marcie Lynne *English language educator, writer*

Bellingham
Highland, Frederick *writer, humanities educator*
Kaplan, Edward H. *history educator*
Tabor, Fred *philosophy educator*

Centralia
Foss, Linda Gray *English writing educator, writer*

Deer Park
Heydet, Sharon Lee Ford *English language educator*

Ellensburg
Schneider, Christian Immo *German language and literature educator*

Olympia
Beck, Gordon Eugene *art history educator, consultant*
Chang, Sheng-Tai *English language educator*

Seattle
Bentley, Judy *English educator, writer*
Bozarth, George S. *historian, musicologist, pianist*
Bultmann, William Arnold *historian*
Jones, Edward Louis *historian, educator*
Layton, Marilyn Smith *English language educator*
Pundt, Hermann G. *architectural historian*
Simeon, Estrella Balbas *educator*
VanArsdel, Rosemary Thorstenson *English studies educator*

Spokane
Carlson, Nancy Lee *English language educator*
Keeble, John Robert *English writing educator, writer*
Sen, Shusmita *English educator, researcher*
Stackelberg, John Roderick *history educator*

Tacoma
Collier, Richard Bangs *philosopher, foundation executive*
Curley, Michael Joseph *English language educator*
Davis, Albert Raymond *English language educator*
Krieger, William Carl *English language educator*
Potts, David Bronson *history educator*

Wenatchee
Berard, Stephen Alfred *foreign language educator*

WYOMING

Casper
Logan, Carolyn *English language educator*

Cody
Price, B. Byron *historian*

Kelly
Kreilkamp, Ann Renee *philosopher, magazine editor*

Laramie
Kohler, Eric Dave *history educator*
Nye, Eric William *English language and literature educator*
Roberts, Philip John *history educator, editor*

Sheridan
Aguirre-Batty, Mercedes *Spanish and English language and literature educator*

Torrington
Deahl, Wayne George *English language educator, communications and theater educator*

ADDRESS UNPUBLISHED

Addison, Alice Adams *international language educator*
Alcosser, Sandra *English language educator*
Alia, Valerie *humanities educator, writer*
Bailey, Charles-James Nice *linguistics educator*
Berry, Gregory Wayne *language arts educator*
Bordeaux, Jean-Luc *art expert, consultant, art historian*
Bosmajian, Haig Aram *speech communication educator*
Bush, Sarah Lillian *historian*
Caldwell, Howard Bryant *English language educator*
Cordell, R. Lewis *English educator, writer*
DesRoches, Diane Blanche *English language educator, writer, director, actor, editor*
Donelson, Kenneth LaVern *English language educator*
Duchow, Donna Prommas *English language educator*
Dunbar, Maurice Victor *English language educator*
Garcia, Mara Lucy *Spanish educator, researcher*
Ghymn, Esther Mikyung *English educator, writer*
Gilb, Corinne Lathrop *history educator*
Hadreas, Peter James *philosophy educator*
Harper, Jennifer Juanita *art historian*
Hidelson, Mark J. *art history educator*
Hilden, Patricia Penn *history educator*
Hutchinson, Joseph Candler *retired foreign language educator*
Ico, Lydia Malicdem *English language educator*
Irwin, Anna Mae *English language educator*
Johnson, Ben E. *English language educator*
Johnson, Hiroko *art history educator*
Lewis, Norman *retired English language educator, writer*
MacPike, Loralee *retired literature educator*
Maehl, William Harvey *historian, educator*
Matthews, Glenna Christine *historian*
McClure, Evelyn Susan *historian, photographer*
McEvoy-Jamil, Patricia Ann *English language educator*
McEwan, Angela *court interpreter*
Millbrooke, Anne *historian*
Moffitt, John Francis *art history educator, writer*
Nix, Nancy Jean *librarian, designer*
Nunis, Doyce Blackman, Jr. *historian, educator*
Parlante, Diane Goullard *interpreter, translator*
Partridge, Ernest *environmental philosopher, educator*
Paxton, Laura Belle-Kent *English language educator, management professional*
Porter, James B. *hieroglyphic specialist*
Powers, Rebecca Elizabeth *educator, writer*
Riasanovsky, Nicholas Valentine *historian, educator*
Robinson, Carmen Delores *educator*
Simmons, Marc Steven *historian*
Slatkin, Wendy *art historian, educator, researcher, writer*

Stafford, Kim R. *humanities educator, writer*
Strode, Deborah Lynn *English language educator*
Toso, Norman Erec *English language educator*
Walker-Hill, Helen Siemens *musicologist, piano instructor*
Walters, David Wayne *history and government educator, tennis coach*
Wilson, James Brian *English as a second language educator*

HUMANITIES: LIBRARIES

UNITED STATES

ALASKA

Fairbanks
Grigg, Susan Leslie *library administrator*

Juneau
Schorr, Alan Edward *librarian, publisher*

Ketchikan
Jenkinson, Judith Ellen *librarian*

ARIZONA

Chino Valley
Rothlisberg, Allen Peter *librarian, educator, deacon*

Mesa
Anderson, Herschel Vincent *librarian*

Phoenix
Fox, Frances Juanice *retired librarian, educator*
Norman, Nita Vegamora *librarian, educator, storyteller*

Prescott Valley
Beck, Doris Olson *retired library media director*

Scottsdale
Dalton, Phyllis Irene *library consultant*

Tempe
Maynard, Michael *librarian*
Weiler, Dorothy Esser *librarian*

Tucson
Grams, Theodore Carl William *librarian, educator*
Irwin, Mildred Lorine Warrick *library consultant, civic worker*
Wolfe, William Jerome *librarian, English language educator*

Winslow
Kaliher, Michael Dennis *librarian, historian*

CALIFORNIA

Alhambra
Harnsberger, Therese Coscarelli *librarian*

Altadena
Seward, Grace Evangeline *retired librarian*

Anaheim
Miller, Jean Ruth *librarian*

Bakersfield
Duquette, Diane Rhea *library director*

Berkeley
Bacon, Elizabeth Morrow *librarian, writer, editor, educator*
Minudri, Regina Ursula *librarian, consultant*
Snow, Maryly Ann *librarian, artist*

Camarillo
Kiser, Nagiko Sato *retired librarian*

Cupertino
Fletcher, Homer Lee *librarian*

Dana Point
Baird, Dorothy Scroggy *retired librarian, educator, consultant*

El Cerrito
Kao, Yasuko Watanabe *retired library administrator*

Fremont
Wood, Linda May *librarian*

Fresno
Kallenberg, John Kenneth *librarian*

Garden Grove
Moore, Richard Kenneth *high school librarian, columnist*

Huntington Beach
Halvorsen, Jan La Rayne *library services manager*
Hayden, Ron L. *library director*

La Jolla
Mirsky, Phyllis Simon *librarian*
Schiller, Anita Rosenbaum *librarian*

La Mesa
Freeland, Robert Frederick *retired librarian*

Lemoore
VanDerMolen, Susan Ann *library media specialist*

Livermore
Love, Sandra Rae *information specialist*

Los Angeles
Helgeson, Duane Marcellus *retired librarian*
Kent, Susan *library director, consultant*
O'Brian, Bonnie Jean *library services supervisor*
Szafran, Anita G. *research librarian*
Walters, Kim G. *librarian*
Wegner, Lucy Siefert *information specialist*

Menlo Park
White, Cecil Ray *librarian, consultant*

Mill Valley
Reese, Janet Isabella *library technician, music educator, researcher*

Mission Hills
Weber, Francis Joseph *archivist, museum director*

Modesto
Kreissman, Starrett *librarian*

Mountain View
Michalko, James Paul *library association administrator*

Napa
Cooper, William Patrick *library assistant*

Oakland
Ford, Gail *library administrator*
Lambrev, Garrett Ivan *librarian, writer*
Woodbury, Marda Liggett *librarian, writer*

Palmdale
Moore, Everett LeRoy *library administrator*

Palo Alto
Van Velzer, Verna Jean *retired research librarian*

Pleasant Hill
Gold, Anne Marie *library director*

Pollock Pines
Rickard, Margaret Lynn *library consultant, former library director*

Porter Ranch
Stump, D. Michael *librarian*

Redlands
Musmann, Klaus *librarian*

Sacramento
Killian, Richard M. *library director*

San Clemente
Stafford-Mann, Patricia Ann *library and textbook consultant, writer*

San Diego
Harvell, Tony Alan *librarian*
Ling, David Chang *international book dealer*
Sannwald, William Walter *librarian*

San Francisco
Carsch, Ruth Elizabeth *consulting librarian*
Cline, Fred Albert, Jr. *retired librarian, conservationist*
Dowlin, Kenneth Everett *librarian*
Fielden, Ned Lee *librarian*

Santa Ana
Adams, John M. *library director*

Santa Barbara
Fitch, Donald Everett *librarian*
Higgins, Isabelle Jeanette *librarian*

Santa Clara
Hopkinson, Shirley Lois *library and information science educator*

Santa Cruz
Nordquist, Joan Marie *bibliographer, indexer, researcher*

Santa Monica
Levin, Barry Raymond *rare book dealer*

Sebastopol
Sabsay, David *library consultant*

Stanford
Deken, Jean Marie *librarian, archivist*
Keller, Michael Alan *librarian, educator, musicologist*

Stockton
Yamashita, Kenneth Akira *library administrator, librarian*

Thousand Oaks
Brogden, Stephen Richard *library administrator*

Westminster
Gylseth, Doris (Lillian) Hanson *retired librarian*

Whittier
Topjon, Ann Johnson *librarian*

Woodland Hills
Zeitlin, Eugenia Pawlik *librarian, educator, writer*

COLORADO

Boulder
O'Brien, Elmer John *librarian, educator*

Colorado Springs
Chen, Lynn Chia-Ling *librarian*

Craig
Miller, Donna Pat *library administrator, consultant*

Denver
Ahern, Arleen Fleming *retired librarian*
Ashton, Rick James *librarian*

Golden
Mathews, Anne Jones *consultant, library educator and administrator*

Lakewood
Knott, William Alan *library director, library management and building consultant*

HAWAII

Honolulu
Lee, Pali Jae (Polly Jae Stead Lee) *retired librarian, writer*
Spencer, Caroline *library director*

IDAHO

Boise
Bolles, Charles Avery *librarian*

MONTANA

Belgrade
Beckman, Leeann Marie *researcher*

Helena
Schlesinger, Deborah Lee *librarian*

NEVADA

Carson City
Van Valkenburgh, Holly Viola *librarian, consultant*

Las Vegas
Hunsberger, Charles Wesley *library director*
Richardson, Jane *librarian*

NEW MEXICO

Albuquerque
Freeman, Patricia Elizabeth *library and education specialist*
Snell, Patricia Poldervaart *librarian, consultant*

Eunice
Suter, Peggy Jean *library director*

Gallup
Fellin, Octavia Antoinette *retired librarian*

Los Alamos
Sayre, Edward Charles *librarian*

OREGON

Ashland
Gaulke, Mary Florence *library administrator*

Astoria
Foster, Michael William *librarian*

Coos Bay
DePlois, Molly *library director*

Eugene
Edwards, Ralph M. *librarian*
Hildebrand, Carol Ilene *librarian*

Mcminnville
Chmelir, Lynn Kay *academic librarian*

Ontario
Edwards, Dale Leon *library director*

Portland
Browne, Joseph Peter *retired librarian*
Cooper, Ginnie *library director*

Salem
Kenyon, Carleton Weller *librarian*

UTAH

Logan
Anderson, Janet Alm *librarian*

Orem
Hall, Blaine Hill *retired librarian*

Riverside
Reveal, Arlene Hadfield *librarian, consultant*

WASHINGTON

Bellevue
Mutschler, Herbert Frederick *retired librarian*

Kennewick
Vickery, Byrdean Eyvonne Hughes (Mrs. Charles Everett Vickery, Jr.) *retired library services administrator*

Lacey
Smith, Donald Evans *library consultant*

Port Townsend
Hiatt, Peter *retired librarian studies educator*

Seattle
Bishop, Virginia Wakeman *retired librarian and humanities educator*
Blase, Nancy Gross *librarian*
Greggs, Elizabeth May Bushnell (Mrs. Raymond John Greggs) *retired librarian*
Stroup, Elizabeth Faye *librarian*

Spokane
Schwanz, Kathleen Ann *librarian*

Tacoma
Crisman, Mary Frances Borden *librarian*

WYOMING

Cheyenne
Johnson, Wayne Harold *librarian, county official*

CANADA

BRITISH COLUMBIA

Vancouver
Aalto, Madeleine *library director*

ADDRESS UNPUBLISHED

Anderson, Barbara Louise *retired library director*
Anderson, David Charles *librarian, writer*
Curley, Elmer Frank *librarian*
Dutton, Pauline Mae *fine arts librarian*
Eaton, Katherine Girton *retired library educator*
Felts, Margaret Davis *librarian, bibliographer*
Gould, Martha Bernice *retired librarian*
Gregor, Dorothy Deborah *librarian*
Hazekamp, Phyllis Wanda Alberts *library director*
Helfer, Doris Small *librarian*
Jones, Curley Cleveland *librarian*
Laslo, Laura Elizabeth *technical librarian, security manager, artist*
Lee, Harrison Hon *naval architecture librarian, consultant*
Nelson, Helen Martha *retired library director*
O'Brien, Betty Alice *theological librarian, researcher*
Pierik, Marilyn Anne *retired librarian*
Rafael, Ruth Kelson *archivist, librarian, consultant*
Silvia, Raymond Alan *librarian*
Thiele, Gloria Day *retired librarian, small business owner*
Wilson, Mark *library media specialist*
Wolf, Cynthia Tribelhorn *librarian, library educator*

HUMANITIES: MUSEUMS

UNITED STATES

ALASKA

Anchorage
Spencer, Ted *museum director*
Wolf, Patricia B. *museum director*

Denali National Park
Martin, Steve *national park service officer*

Fairbanks
Jonaitis, Aldona Claire *museum administrator, art historian*

Juneau
Kato, Bruce *curator*

ARIZONA

Bisbee
Gustavson, Carrie *museum director*

Flagstaff
Clark, Roger William *museum director, history educator*
Fox, Michael J. *museum director*

Grand Canyon
Richard, Carolyn Lee *curator, park ranger, fire fighter*

Mesa
Mead, Tray C. *museum director*

Petrified Forest Natl Park
Hillickson, Michele *national parks service official*

Phoenix
Ballinger, James K. *art museum executive*
Grinell, Sheila *museum director*
Keane, Melissa *museum director*
Lidman, Roger Wayne *museum director*
Myers, Cindy L. *museum director*
Rubin, David Stuart *curator, art critic*
Sullivan, Martin Edward *museum director*

Scottsdale
Jacobsen, Frank *museum official*

Tempe
Zeitlin, Marilyn Audrey *museum director*

Tucson
Dunn, B. museum director
Hancocks, David Morgan *museum director, architect*
Yassin, Robert Alan *museum administrator, curator*

Willcox
Catano, Lucy Baca *gallery manager*

CALIFORNIA

Arcata
Zielinski, Melissa L. *museum director*

Bakersfield
Enriquez, Carola Rupert *museum director*
Meyer, Charles G. *museum director*

Berkeley
Hirst, Robert H. *curator, English educator*

Beverly Hills
Berman, Jerome *museum director, curator*

Bodega Bay
Cohen, Daniel Morris *museum administrator, marine biology researcher*

Caliente
de Fonville, Paul Bliss *historic organization administrator*

Carson
Zimmerer, Kathy Louise *university art gallery director*

Costa Mesa
Botello, Troy James *arts administrator, educator*
Labbe, Armand Joseph *museum curator, anthropologist*

Death Valley
Martin, Richard H. *national park service executive*

Irvine
Botwinick, Michael *museum director*

La Jolla
Beebe, Mary Livingstone *curator*

Long Beach
Glenn, Constance White *art museum director, educator, consultant*
Nelson, Harold Bernhard *museum director*

Los Angeles
Barrett, Candice *museum administrator*
Beal, Graham William John *museum director*
Benson, Timothy Oliver *curator, educator*
Fontenote-Jamerson, Belinda *museum director*
Henderson, Jai *museum director*
Holo, Selma Reuben *museum director, educator*
Hopkins, Henry Tyler *museum director, art educator*
Kaye, Carole *museum director and curator*
Koshalek, Richard *museum director, consultant*
Laventhol, David *museum official*
Powell, James Lawrence *museum executive*
Rich, Andrea Louise *museum executive*
Rudolph, Jeffrey N. *museum director*
Teviotdale, Elizabeth Cover *museum curator*
Walsh, John *museum director*

Los Osos
Dorland, Frank Norton *art conservator, educator*

Northridge
Lewis, Louise Miller *gallery director, art history educator*

Oakland
Marx, Mary M. *museum director*
Power, Dennis Michael *museum director*
Reuther, Ronald Theodore *museum director*

Pacific Grove
Bailey, Stephen Fairchild *museum director and curator, ornithologist*
Penwell, Donna Carol *museum director*

Pebble Beach
Ramsey, Ray, Jr. *art gallery owner*

Redding
Gilmore, James Claus *museum curator*

Redlands
Griesemer, Allan David *retired museum director*

Riverside
Esparza, Richard R. *museum director*
Green, Jonathan William *museum administrator and educator, artist, author*
Warren, Katherine Virginia *art gallery director*

Sacramento
Gray, Walter P., III *archivist, consultant*

San Carlos
Schumacher, Henry Jerold *museum administrator, former career officer, business executive*

San Diego
Brezzo, Steven Louis *museum director*
Longenecker, Martha W. *museum director*
Maruyama, Tomoko *curator educator*
Ollman, Arthur Lee *museum director, photographer*
Petersen, Martin Eugene *museum curator*

San Francisco
Adler, Adrienne Edna-Lois *art dealer, gallery owner, publisher*
Aldrich, Michael Ray *library curator, health educator*
Delacote, Goery *museum director*
Israel, Michael L. *art gallery manager*
Killacky, John R. *museum administrator, educator, writer, filmmaker*
McKeon, Elaine *museum administrator*
Nash, Steven Alan *museum curator, art historian*
O'Neill, Brian *landmark administrator*
Parker, Harry S., III *art museum administrator*
Sano, Emily Joy *museum director*

San Jose
Callan, Josi Irene *museum director*

San Luis Obispo
Mette, Joe *museum director*

San Marino
Wark, Robert Rodger *art curator*

Santa Barbara
Karpeles, David *museum director*
Ruston, Shelly Smith *museum administrator*

Santa Clara
Schapp, Rebecca Maria *museum director*

Sausalito
Elliott, James Heyer *retired university art museum curator, fine arts consultant*

Stanford
Zalewski, Wojciech Maria *curator*

Tulare
Gorelick, Ellen Catherine *museum director, curator, artist, educator, civic volunteer*

Ukiah
Lee, Lila June *historical society officer, library director*

Walnut Creek
Becker, Stephen Arnold *museum administrator*

Watsonville
Hernandez, Jo Farb *museum curator, consultant*

Wilmington
O'Brien, Marge Ett *museum administrator*

Yosemite National Park
Bates, Craig Dana *curator, ethnographer, government official*

COLORADO

Aspen
Farver, Suzanne *museum administrator*

Boulder
Danilov, Victor Joseph *museum management program director, consultant, writer, educator*
Meier, Thomas Joseph *museum director, author*

Colorado Springs
Conway, Wallace Xavier, Sr. *retired curator*
Warner, Michael D. *museum director*

Denver
Decatur, Raylene *museum official*
Harrison, Carole Alberta *museum curator, restaurateur, civic worker*
O'Brien, Judy *art museum official*
Palovich, George Wesley *curator, artist, educator*
Sharp, Lewis I. *museum director*

HAWAII

Fort Shafter
Fairfull, Thomas McDonald *museum director*

Hilo
Dahlquist, Paul A. *museum director*

Honolulu
Billings, Kathy *national monument official*
de la Torre, David Joseph *art museum director*
Duckworth, Walter Donald *museum executive, entomologist*
Ellis, George Richard *museum administrator*
Klobe, Tom *art gallery director*

Kalaupapa
Alexander, Dean *museum director*

Kaneohe
Lagoria, Georgianna Marie *curator, writer, editor, visual art consultant*

Lihue
Lovell, Carol *museum director*

Puunene
Kubota, Gaylord *museum director*

IDAHO

Arco
Morris, James *national monument official*

Boise
Guerber, Stephen Craig *historical society director*
Revling, Michael *museum administrator*
Swanson, Kenneth J. *museum administrator*

Coeur D Alene
Dahlgren, Dorothy *museum director*

Lewiston
Bianchi, Robert Steven *author, lecturer, TV personality*

Pocatello
Jackson, Allen Keith *museum administrator*

Salmon
Wiederrick, Robert *museum director*

Twin Falls
Woods, James C. *museum director*

MONTANA

Billings
Moss, Lynda Bourque *museum director*
Towe, A. Ruth *museum director*

Bozeman
Davis, Leslie Beryl *curator archaeology, educator in anthropology*
Weaver, Judith A. *museum director*

Butte
Thompson, John *museum director*

Crow Agency
Deernose, Kitty *museum curator*

Deer Lodge
McWright, Michael J. *historic site administrator*

Dillon
Horst, Randy *museum director*

Great Falls
Abernathy, Charles C. *museum official*
Render, Lorne *museum director*

Helena
Cockhill, Brian Edward *historical society executive*

Missoula
Brown, Robert Munro *museum director*
Millin, Laura Jeanne *museum director*

NEVADA

Baker
Mills, Becky *park administrator*

Carson City
Stewart, Phillis *museum official*

Elko
Seymour, Lisa *museum director*

Las Vegas
Gillespie, Marilyn *museum administrator*
Le Blanc, Suzanne *museum director*
Lewis, Oli Parepa *curator*
Ruche, Tom *museum official*

Reno
Feinhandler, Edward Sanford *writer, photographer, art dealer, sports mentor, consultant, educator*

NEW MEXICO

Abiquiu
Martinez, Ray *museum director*

Alamogordo
Starkey, Don J. *museum director*

Albuquerque
Bawden, Garth Lawry *museum director*
Moore, James C. *museum director*
Smartt, Richard A. *museum director*
Stamm, Bob *museum official*

Las Cruces
Lovell, Charles Muir *museum curator, photographer*

Santa Fe
Ashman, Stuart *museum director*
Cerny, Charlene Ann *museum director*
Conley, Zeb Bristol *art gallery director*

OREGON

Bend
Wolf, Arthur Henry *museum administrator*

Crater Lake
Hendricks, Albert J. *national park service executive*

Portland
Buchanan, John E., Jr. *museum director*
Gilkey, Gordon Waverly *curator, artist*
Lacrosse, Patrick *museum administrator*
Mercer, William Earl *museum curator*
Roberts, Prudence Fenwick *curator, freelance*
Russo, Laura *gallery director*
Schnitzer, Arlene Director *art dealer*

UTAH

Salt Lake City
George, Sara B. *museum director*
Kohler, Dolores Marie *gallery owner*
Leonard, Glen M. *museum director*
Sanguinetti, Eugene Frank *art museum administrator, educator*

WASHINGTON

Bellevue
Douglas, Diane Miriam *museum director*
Hadrich, Gwen Elizabeth Pickel *curator*
Warren, James Ronald *retired museum director, author, columnist*

Longview
Freece, David Warren *museum director*

Marcus
DePaulo, Adygene Garrett *art gallery owner*

Redmond
Sobey, Edwin J. C. *museum director, oceanographer, consultant*

Seattle
Bufano, Ralph A. *museum director*
Gates, Mimi Gardner *museum administrator*
Sarkowsky, Herman *museum official*

Silverdale
Hess, Stanley William *curator, retired fine arts librarian*

WYOMING

Casper
Smith, Kay Pridgen *art museum officer*

Devils Tower
Cartwright, Chas *historic site administrator*

Kemmerer
Peternal, Nancy Farrell *museum director*

Laramie
Guerin, Charles Allan *museum director, artist*

CANADA

ALBERTA

Calgary
Janes, Robert Roy *museum executive, archaeologist*

Drumheller
Naylor, Bruce Gordon *museum director*

BRITISH COLUMBIA

Victoria
Barkley, William Donald *museum executive*
Finlay, James Campbell *retired museum director*

ADDRESS UNPUBLISHED

Butler, Kathleen Lois *museum administrator, independent scholar*
Friedman, Paula Naomi *museum public relations director*
Glad, Suzanne Lockley *retired museum director*
Mason, James Albert *retired museum director, former university dean*
Matelic, Candace Tangorra *museum studies educator, consultant, museum director*
Pal, Pratapaditya *museum curator*
Shimoda, Jerry Yasutaka *retired national historic park superintendent*
Swig, Roselyne Chroman *community art consultant*
Vroom, Steven Michael *director university gallery*
Welles, John Galt *retired museum director*
Whitchurch, Charles Augustus *art gallery owner, humanities educator*
Zenev, Irene Louise *museum curator*

INDUSTRY: MANUFACTURING. See also FINANCE: FINANCIAL SERVICES.

UNITED STATES

ALASKA

Anchorage
DeLoach, Robert Edgar *corporate executive*
Doran, Vincent James *steel fabricating company consultant*
Easley, George Washington *construction executive*

Fairbanks
Herning-Swaim, Shirley Ruth *general earthworks and utilities contractor*

Haines
Kaufman, David Graham *construction company executive*

Juneau
Lauber, Mignon Diane *food processing company executive*
Smith, Charles Anthony *businessman*

ARIZONA

Carefree
Galda, Dwight William *financial company executive*

Eagar
Gilliland, Thomas Joe *retired mining executive, educator*

Flagstaff
Giovale, Virginia Gore *medical products ecexutive, civic leader*

Glendale
Lopez, Steven Richard *small business owner, consultant*

Mesa
DeRosa, Francis Dominic *chemical company executive*
Frisk, Jack Eugene *recreational vehicle manufacturing company executive*

Stokes, Andrea G. *food service executive*

Phoenix
Crane, Frank Melvin *agricultural company executive*
Kopp, David Eugene *manufacturing company executive*
Logan, Richard Walter *bakery engineering mechanic*
Mardian, Daniel *construction company director*
Motsenbocker, Rex Alan *construction company executive*
Platt, James Robert *business executive*
Royer, Kenneth William *food consultant, business consultant*
Thompson, Herbert Ernest *tool and die company executive*
Van Horssen, Charles Arden *manufacturing executive*

Prescott
White, Brittan Romeo *manufacturing company executive*

Scottsdale
Francisco, Wayne M(arkland) *automotive executive*
Gans, Eugene Howard *cosmetic and pharmaceutical company executive*
Garrity, Thomas John *pharmaceutical executive*
Malohn, Donald A. *manufacturing executive, retired*
Wong, Astria Wor *cosmetic business consultant*

Sedona
Bolton, Robert Floyd *construction executive*

Tolleson
Etchart, Mike *agricultural products company executive*

Tucson
Acker, Loren Calvin *medical instrument company executive*
Bongarten, Harold *retired business executive, consultant*
Governal, Robert Andrew *technology executive*
Sundt, Harry Wilson *construction company executive*
Willoughby, Stuart Carroll *contractor*

Yuma
Curtis, Michael *food products executive*

CALIFORNIA

Alameda
Maurer, Robert Michael *medical company executive*

Alhambra
Fried, Elaine June *business executive*

Aliso Viejo
Baker, Susan Leigh *manufacturing company executive*
Baumgartner, Anton Edward *automotive sales professional*

Anaheim
Price, Richard Taft, Jr. *manufacturing company executive*
Valdez, James Gerald *automotive aftermarket executive*

Arcadia
Dodds, Dale Irvin *chemicals executive*

Atherton
Hogan, Clarence Lester *retired electronics executive*

Bakersfield
Barker, Douglas P. *food products executive*
Grimm, Bob *food products executive*

Beverly Hills
Brann, Alton Joseph *manufacturing company executive*
Colburn, Richard Dunton *business executive*
Hoch, Orion Lindel *corporate executive*
Winthrop, John *wines and spirits company executive*

Bishop
Naso, Valerie Joan *automotive dealership executive, travel company operator*

Buena Park
Okamura, Hideo *manufacturing executive*

Burbank
Altschul, David Edwin *record company executive, lawyer*
Beymer, Dale Allen *manufacturing executive*

Burlingame
Hepler, Kenneth Russel *manufacturing executive*

Calabasas
Broderick, Marsha *interior designer, general contractor*
Cohen, William *construction executive*

Campbell
Chan, Danny K.W. *construction inspector*
Crawford, Curtis J. *computer and electronics company executive*

Carlsbad
Bartok, Michelle *cosmetic company executive*
Crooke, Stanley Thomas *pharmaceutical company executive*
Randall, William B. *manufacturing company executive*

Carmel
McDowell, T.J. Rider *pharmaceutical executive*

Chatsworth
Schapira, Morey Rael *electronics sales executive*

Chula Vista
Manary, Richard Deane *manufacturing executive*

City Industry
Huck, Larry Ralph *manufacturing executive, sales consultant*

City Of Industry
Scritsmier, Jerome Lorenzo *manufacturing company executive*

Claremont
Forti, William Bell *sports products executive, inventor*

Colusa
Carter, Jane Foster *agriculture industry executive*

Compton
Golleher, George *food company executive*

Concord
Thompson, Jeremiah Beiseker *international medical business executive*

Costa Mesa
Brady, John Patrick, Jr. *electronics educator, consultant*
Hazewinkel, Van *manufacturing executive*

Cupertino
Mathias, Leslie Michael *electronic manufacturing company executive*

Cypress
Barman, Robert John *home electronics company executive*

Dana Point
Wong, Wallace *medical supplies company executive, real estate investor*

Delano
Caratan, Anton G. *food products executive*
Caratan, George *food products executive*

Duarte
Bres, Philip Wayne *automotive executive*

El Segundo
Amerman, John W. *toy company executive*

Emeryville
Nady, John *electronics company executive*

Encino
Davenport, Alfred Larue, Jr. *manufacturing company executive*

Fontana
De Tomaso, Ernest Pat *general building contractor, developer*

Fremont
Ciffone, Donald *electronics company executive*
Hsu, Gerald C. *electrical company executive*
Shah, Ajay *electronics company executive*
Zajac, John *semiconductor equipment company executive*
Zimmer, George *men's apparel executive*

Fresno
Baloian, Edward *food products executive*
Baloian, Timothy *food products executive*
Emigh, Mike *agricultural products company executive*

Gardena
Kanner, Edwin Benjamin *electrical manufacturing company executive*
Kuntz, David William *multimedia producer*

Glendale
Raval, Ruchika *regulatory affairs specialist*

Greenfield
Munoz, John Joseph *retired transportation company executive*

Gridley
Tanimoto, George *agricultural executive, farmer*

Hawthorne
Roberts, George Christopher *manufacturing executive*

Hayward
Hwang, Kou Mau *pharmaceutical executive*
Masterson, Linda Histen *medical company executive*
Minzner, Dean Frederick *aviation company executive*

Huntington Beach
Thomas-Cote, Nancy Denece *office products manufacturing company executive*

Indio
York, Douglas Arthur *manufacturing and construction company executive*

Irvine
Basler, Richard Alan *medical consultant*
Copeland, Lawrence R. *construction company executive*
Herbert, Gavin Shearer *health care products company executive*
Joseph, Ezekiel (Ed Joseph) *manufacturing company executive*
Salesky, William Jeffrey *corporate executive*
Schmidtkunz, James E. *chemical company executive*
Williams, Derek, Jr. *pharmaceutical professional*
Zack, James G(ordon), Jr. *construction claims executive, consultant*

King City
Giudici, Francis *food products executive*

La Mesa
Bourke, Lyle James *electronics company executive, small business owner*
Reiff, Theodore Curtis *construction executive*

Lafayette
Shurtleff, William Roy *food products executive*

Laguna Beach
Wild, Bonita Marie *healthcare company executive*

Laguna Hills
Trusiak, Jeffrey J. *electronics executive*

Laguna Niguel
Meyers, Theda Maria *textile company executive*

Lodi
Elkins, Carl *food products executive*

Long Beach
Bos, John Arthur *aircraft manufacturing executive*
Crane, Steven *financial company executive*
McGihon, Michael Edwin *sheet metal manufacturing executive*
McGuire, James Charles *aircraft company executive*
Roddy, Michael Vincent *construction executive*

Los Altos
Kao, Cheng Chi *electronics executive*

Los Angeles
Caldwell, Allan Blair *health services company executive*
Dalton, James Edward *aerospace executive, retired air force officer*
Gerstell, A. Frederick *aggregates and asphalt and concrete manufacturing executive*
Hourizadeh, Arash *espresso manufacturing company executive, physician*
Howard, Murray *manufacturing, real estate and property management executive, farmer, rancher*
Irani, Ray R. *oil and gas and chemical company executive*
Jones, Jerve Maldwyn *construction company executive*
Karatz, Bruce E. *business executive*
Leeds, Jeffrey L. *company executive*
Lesmez, Gwendolyn Billings *manufacturing company executive*
Perkins, William Clinton *company executive*
Ramer, Lawrence Jerome *corporation executive*

Los Gatos
Nitz, Frederic William *electronics company executive*

Malibu
Sherman, Richard S. *record and video company executive*

Manhattan Beach
Handschumacher, Albert Gustave *retired corporate executive*

Marina Del Rey
Brown, Anthony B. *aerospace executive*
Goldaper, Gabriele Gay *clothing executive, consultant*
Sylk, Robert F. *casino marketing executive*

Menlo Park
Carlson, Curtis R. *electronics research industry executive*
Cook, Paul Maxwell *technology company executive*
Harrell, Iris Faye *general contractor*
Kaplan, Jerry *electronics company executive*
Schnebly, F(rancis) David *aerospace and electronics company executive*
Westcott, Brian John *manufacturing executive*

Mill Valley
Winskill, Robert Wallace *manufacturing executive*

Milpitas
Berkley, Stephen Mark *computer peripherals manufacturing company executive*
Brown, Michael A. *computer hardware company executive*
Gray, Bruce *computer and electronics company executive*
Roddick, David Bruce *construction company executive*
Stephens, Bob *electronic executive*

Mission Viejo
Gilbert, Heather Campbell *manufacturing company executive*
Sheridan, George Edward *manufacturing company executive*

Mountain View
Cusumano, James Anthony *pharmaceutical company executive*

Murrieta
Stevens, Neal *construction executive, financing executive*

Newport Beach
Jones, Roger Wayne *electronics executive*
Rogers, Robert Reed *manufacturing company executive*

North Hollywood
Tushinsky, Fred Charles *manufacturing executive*

Northridge
dePaolis, Potito Umberto *food company executive*

Oakland
Koplin, Donald Leroy *health products executive, consumer advocate*
Sidney, William Wright *retired aerospace company executive*
Sullivan, G. Craig *household products executive*

Oceanside
Garruto, John Anthony *cosmetics executive*

Ojai
Weill, Samuel, Jr. *automobile company executive*

Orange
Gladney, Kenneth Edward *construction executive, consultant*
Kaempen, Charles Edward *manufacturing company executive*

Oxnard
Boskovich, George, Jr. *food products executive*
Gill, David *food products executive*
Gill, Steven *food products executive*
Poole, Henry Joe, Jr. *business executive*

Palo Alto
Chow, Winston *engineering research executive*
De Passe, Derrel Blauvelt *electronics industry executive*
Kennedy, W(ilbert) Keith, Jr. *electronics company executive*
Kung, Frank F. *biotechnology and life sciences venture capital investor*
Mario, Ernest *pharmaceutical company executive*
Smith, Pamela Iris *consulting company executive*
Sweitzer, Michael Cook *healthcare product executive*
Winfield, Roy A. *pharmaceutical company executive*

Palos Verdes Peninsula
Pfund, Edward Theodore, Jr. *electronics company executive*
Thomas, Hayward *manufacturing company executive*
Wilson, Theodore Henry *retired electronics company executive, aerospace engineer*

Pasadena
Caldwell, William Mackay, III *business executive*
Falick, Abraham Johnson *printing company executive*
McNulty, James F. *export company executive*
Miller, Charles Daly *self-adhesive materials company executive*
Neal, Philip Mark *diversified manufacturing executive*

Pomona
Puckett, Paul David *electronics company executive*

Poway
Aschenbrenner, Frank Aloysious *former diversified manufacturing company executive*

Rancho Mirage
Foster, David Ramsey *soap company executive*

Redlands
Skomal, Edward Nelson *aerospace company executive, consultant*

Redondo Beach
Dockstader, Jack Lee *retired electronics executive*
Sabin, Jack Charles *engineering and construction firm executive*

Redwood City
Hawkins, Trip *electronics company executive*
Muratore, Marilyn Ann *contractor*
Wang, Chen Chi *electronics company, real estate, finance company, investment services, and international trade executive*

Riverside
Kummer, Glenn F. *manufactured housing executive*

Salinas
Drever, Mark *food products executive*
Esquivel, Joe G. *food products executive*
Esquivel, Mary *agricultural products company executive*
Taylor, Steven Bruce *agriculture company executive*

San Clemente
Cate, Floyd Mills *electronic components executive*

San Diego
Allen, Russell Lawton *pharmaceutical executive*
Anjard, Ronald Paul, Sr. *business and industry executive, consultant, educator, technologist, importer, author*
Baird, Mellon Campbell, Jr. *electronics industry executive*
Bear, Jeffrey Warren *construction executive*
Carleton, David *consumer products executive*
Childs, John David *computer hardware and services company executive*
Cobianchi, Thomas Theodore *engineering and marketing executive, educator*
Jones, Ronald H. *computer information systems executive*
Keith, Norman Thomas *aerospace company administrator*
Khavari, Mike *construction company executive*
Nussbaum, Jon Kimbal *defense contractor executive*
Tidwell, Geoffrey Morgan *medical company executive*

San Francisco
Clark, Richard Ward *trust company executive, consultant*
Grubb, David H. *construction company executive*
Haas, Robert Douglas *apparel manufacturing company executive*
James, George Barker, II *apparel industry executive*
Kreitzberg, Fred Charles *construction management company executive*
Pulido, Mark A. *pharmaceutical and cosmetics company executive*
Satre, Rodrick Iverson *environmental consultant, business developer*
Wertheimer, Robert E. *paper company executive*

San Jose
Bell, W. Donald *electronics company executive*
Benzing, David Warren *semiconductor equipment company executive*
Carrabine, James *electronics company executive*
Cartwright, Peter *electronics company executive*
Chapman, Richard W. K. *electronics company executive*
Endriz, John Guiry *electronics executive*
Hill, Anna Marie *manufacturing executive*
Jacobson, Raymond Earl *electronics company entrepreneur and executive*
Johnson, Stephen C. *electric executive*
Kalkhoven, Kevin N. *electronics company executive*

Kissner, Charles D. *electrical company executive*
Marks, Michael E. *electronics company executive*
McDaniel, Roger D. *electrical company executive*
Newton, Paul E. *electrical company executive*
Perlegos, George *electronic company executive*
Schroeder, William John *electronics executive*

San Luis Obispo
Sullivan, Thomas James *retired manufacturing company executive*

San Marcos
Blackburn, Charles Edward *manufacturing executive*
Page, Leslie Andrew *disinfectant manufacturing company executive*

San Mateo
Aadahl, Jorg *business executive*
Grammater, Rudolf Dimitri *retired construction executive*
Grant, Kenneth Richard *technologist*

Sanger
Albertson, David *food products executive*

Santa Ana
Yuen, Andy Tak Sing *electronics executive*

Santa Clara
Dunlap, F. Thomas, Jr. *electronics company executive, engineer, lawyer*
Grove, Andrew S. *electronics company executive*
Halla, Brian *electronics company executive*
House, David L. *electronics components company executive*
Larson, William *electrical company executive*
Lee, Jimmy S.M. *electronic executive*
McCord, Vincent Abbott, Jr. *electronics industry executive*
Moore, Gordon E. *electronics company executive*
Wozniak, Curtis S. *electronics company executive*

Santa Cruz
Butterfield, Anthony Swindt *photographic oscillograph paper manufacturing company executive*
Marks, Peter Amasa *technical consulting company administrator*

Santa Maria
Ardantz, Henri *agricultural products executive*
Ferini, Robert Pat *agricultural products company executive*
Grames-Lyra, Judith Ellen *building engineering inspector, artist, educator*

Santa Monica
Deckter, Harlan Kennedy, Jr. *manufacturing company official*
Rive, Sarelle Roselyn *retired manufacturing company executive*

Santa Paula
Dillard, Michael L. *food products company executive*

Seal Beach
Beall, Donald Ray *multi-industry high-technology company executive*

Shasta Lake
Weissman, Shane Andrew *automobile accessories company owner*

Sherman Oaks
Gelnak, Leonard *electronics executive*

Soquel
Goodman, Charles Schaffner, Jr. *food product executive, consultant*

Stockton
Corkern, Robert J. *agricultural products company executive*
Guardino, Sal *food executive*

Sun Valley
Kamins, Philip E. *diversified manufacturing company executive*

Sunnyvale
Bowman, A. Blaine *electronics company executive*
Fairweather, Edwin Arthur *electronics company executive*
Kempf, Martine *voice control device manufacturing company executive*
Lewis, John Clark, Jr. *manufacturing company executive*
Lombard, George *electronics company executive*
St. Charles, David *electronics company executive*
Sanders, Walter Jeremiah, III *electronics company executive*
Woolsey, Roy Blakeney *electronics company executive*
Yancey, Gary *electronics company executive*

Tehachapi
Myers, Robert Gearold *developmental test executive, flight test engineer*

Thousand Oaks
Binder, Gordon M. *health and medical products executive*
Pope, Edward John Andrew *corporate executive, consultant*

Torrance
Bush, William Glenn *manufacturing company executive, engineer*
Grasser, Constance Udean *automotive industry executive*
Lee, James King *technology corporation executive*
Mann, Michael Martin *electronics company executive*
Woodhull, John Richard *electronics company executive*

Turlock
Arias, Joe *agricultural products executive*

Ukiah
Clausen, Barbara Ann *coatings company executive*

Upland
Porrero, Henry, Jr. *construction company executive*
Raymond, Lloyd W. *machinery company executive*

Vacaville
Castro, David Alexander *construction executive*

Vallejo
Barner, C. Henry *confectioner*
Womack, Thomas Houston *manufacturing company executive*

Walnut Creek
Palmer, Vincent Allan *construction consultant*

Watsonville
Costanzo, Patrick M. *construction executive*
Fields, Carl Victor *food company executive*
Repass, Randy *electrical company executive*
Solari, R. C. *heavy construction company executive*

Westlake Village
DeLorenzo, David A. *food products executive*
Weisman, Martin Jerome *manufacturing company executive*

Willits
Handley, Margie Lee *business executive*

Wilmington
Hamai, James Yutaka *business executive*

Woodland Hills
Wright, Thomas Edward *electronics production control specialist*

Woodside
Gates, Milo Sedgwick *retired construction company executive*
Skieller, Christian *manufacturing executive*

Yorba Linda
Forth, Kevin Bernard *beverage distributing industry consultant*

Yuba City
Giacolini, Earl L. *agricultural products company executive*

COLORADO

Arvada
Holden, George Fredric *brewing company executive, policy specialist, author*

Boulder
Johnston, David Ritchey *construction company executive*
Malone, Michael William *electronics executive, software engineer*

Castle Rock
Harper, Robert Levell *pharmaceutical company executive*

Colorado Springs
Tracy, George S. *healthcare service company executive*
Willis, Stephen C. *contractor*

Denver
Barry, Henry Ford *chemical company executive*
Bennett, James P. *construction executive*
Cook, Gary Morris *energy corporation executive*
Cooper, Larry S. *carpet industry consultant*
Gates, Charles Cassius *rubber company executive*
Gronning, Lloyd Joseph *engineering company executive, civil engineer*
Hohner, Kenneth Dwayne *retired fodder company executive*
Johnson, James Gibson, Jr. *community recycling specialist*
Onofrio, Joe Frederick, III *piano company executive*
Shreve, Theodore Norris *construction company executive*

Englewood
Runice, Robert E. *retired corporate executive*

Fort Collins
Watz, Martin Charles *brewery executive*

Golden
Coors, William K. *brewery executive*

Greeley
Morgensen, Jerry Lynn *construction company executive*

Henderson
Midyett, Michael Burton *contractor*

Highlands Ranch
Breuer, Werner Alfred *retired plastics company executive*

Kittredge
Freeman, Robin D. *manufacturers company executive, actress*

Lafayette
Barefoot, Linda *pharmaceutical company manager*

Lakewood
Heath, Gary Brian *manufacturing firm executive, engineer*
Markley, Richard Delbert *manufacturing company executive*
Rein, Fredric David *construction company executive*

Littleton
Gertz, David Lee *homebuilding company executive*

Price, Gayl Baader *residential construction company administrator*

Lone Tree
Bauer, Randy Mark *management training firm executive*

Monument
Karasa, Norman Lukas *home builder, developer, geologist*

Superior
Ripley, Dan *automotive executive, race car driver*

Wellington
Grant, Lewis O. *agricultural products executive, meteorology educator*

HAWAII

Honolulu
Buyers, John William Amerman *agribusiness and specialty foods company executive*
Couch, John Charles *diversified company executive*
Usui, Leslie Raymond *retired clothing executive*
Yen, Duen Hsi *corporate executive, physicist*

Kahului
Marrs, Linda Diane *manufacturing executive*
Viglione, Eugene Lawrence *automotive executive*

Keaau
Cole, Lecil *agricultural products company executive*

Papaikou
Andrasick, James Stephen *agribusiness company executive*

IDAHO

Boise
Appleton, Steven R. *electronics executive*
Harad, George Jay *manufacturing company executive*
Hennessey, Alice Elizabeth *forest products company executive*
McCain, Warren Earl *retired supermarket company executive*
McClary, James Daly *retired contractor*
Michael, Gary G. *retail supermarket and drug chain executive*
Sullivan, James Kirk *retired forest products company executive*

Hayden Lake
Wogsland, James Willard *retired heavy machinery manufacturing executive*

Idaho Falls
Hyde, William *automotive executive*

Salmon
Snook, Quinton *construction company executive*

MISSOURI

Saint Louis
Jansen, Evan Lee *pharmaceutical company manager*

MONTANA

Butte
Tuck, Michael Ray *technical services executive*

Helena
Warren, Christopher Charles *electronics executive*

Martinsdale
Gronli, John Victor *concrete manufacturing executive, college administrator, minister*

NEVADA

Carson City
Burns, Dan W. *manufacturing company executive*

Fallon
Tedford, Jack Nowlan, III *construction executive, small business owner*

Incline Village
Strack, Harold Arthur *retired electronics company executive, retired air force officer, planner, analyst, author, musician*
Yount, George Stuart *paper company executive*

Las Vegas
Albanese, Thomas *food industry executive, consultant*
Bernard, Thelma Rene *property management professional*
Gohres, Marc Phillip *construction company executive*
Opfer, Neil David *construction educator, consultant*
Peck, Gaillard Ray, Jr. *defense contractor, aerospace and business consultant, business owner*
Strahan, Julia Celestine *electronics company executive*

Reno
Schmidt, Baldwin Stephen *manufacturing company executive*

Sparks
Corbin, Krestine Margaret *manufacturing company executive, fashion designer, columnist*
Kramer, Gordon Edward *manufacturing executive*
Root, William Dixon *construction company executive*

NEW MEXICO

Albuquerque
Finley, Susie Quanstrom *solar energy company executive*

Carlsbad
Watts, Marvin Lee *minerals company executive, chemist, educator*

Gallup
Nelson, Barbara Jones *food service and theatre professional*

Roswell
Armstrong, Billie Bert *retired highway contractor*

Santa Fe
Bearwald, Jean Haynes *company executive*
Odell, John H. *construction company executive*
Robinson, Charles Wesley *energy company executive*

OREGON

Beaverton
Asiello, Robert Michael *manufacturing executive, retired military officer*
Donahue, Richard King *athletic apparel executive, lawyer*
Hayes, Delbert J. *athletic company executive*
Knight, Philip H(ampson) *shoe manufacturing company executive*

Bend
Babcock, Walter Christian, Jr. *membrane company executive*

Eugene
Woolley, Donna Pearl *timber and lumber company executive*

Hermiston
Betz, Richard *agricultural products executive*

Hood River
Garcia, David *agricultural products executive*
Girardelli, Ronald K. *food products executive*

Medford
Hannum, Gerald Luther (Lou Hannum) *retired tire manufacturing company official*

Oregon City
Danielson, Craig *wholesale grocery corporation executive*

Portland
Abbott, Robert Carl *management company executive*
Drinkward, Cecil W. *construction company executive*
Eberwein, Barton Douglas *construction company executive, consultant*
Gast, Nancy Lou *retired chemical company executive*
Leineweber, Peter Anthony *forest products company executive*
Nagel, Stanley Blair *retired construction and investment executive*
Russell, Marjorie Rose *manufacturing company executive*
Steinfeld, Ray, Jr. *food products executive*
Stott, Peter Walter *forest products company executive*
Swindells, William, Jr. *lumber and paper company executive*
Walker, Daphine Broadhead *construction executive*
Watkins, Charles Reynolds *medical equipment company executive*

Tualatin
Stott, James Charles *chemical company executive*

Wilsonville
Kimberley, A. G. *industrial products factory representative, management executive*
Meyer, Jerome J. *diversified technology company executive*
Subramanian, Gowri *business executive, web technologies consultant*

UTAH

Heber City
Day, Gerald W. *wholesale grocery company executive*

Logan
Arbuthnot, Jeanette Jaussaud *educator, researcher*

Ogden
Ehman, Michael Frederick *electronics executive*
Klepinger, John William *trailer manufacturing company executive*

Salt Lake City
Clark, Jeffrey Raphiel *research and development company executive*
Frank, Thomas *design, construction and management executive*
Holbrook, David Kroescher *general manager packaging manufacturer*
Huntsman, Jon Meade *chemical company executive*
Motter, Thomas Franklin *medical products executive*

Sandy
Robbins, Charles Dudley, III *manufacturing executive*

West Jordan
Bland, Dorothy Ann *construction executive, real estate agent*

WASHINGTON

Bainbridge Island
Blumenthal, Richard Cary *construction executive, consultant*

Bellevue
Hovind, David J. *manufacturing company executive*
Pigott, Charles McGee *transportation equipment manufacturing executive*
Pigott, Mark C. *automotive executive*

Brewster
Chapman, George J. *agricultural products executive*

Camas
Stuart, Robert D. *electronics executive*

Eastsound
Anders, William Alison *aerospace and defense manufacturing executive*

Federal Way
Creighton, John W., Jr. *retired forest products company executive*

Fife
Tracy, James Michael *building manufacturing executive*

Kirkland
Biggs, Thomas Wylie *chemical company executive*

Lake Stevens
Durden, Rome L. *aircraft manufacturing company executive*

Longview
Wollenberg, Richard Peter *paper manufacturing company executive*

Manson
Stager, Donald K. *construction company executive*

Pasco
Wright, Tim Eugene *packaging development executive*
Yoshino, George *food products executive*

Seattle
Bianchi, Richard *food products executive*
Braithwaite, Walt Waldiman *aircraft manufacturing company executive*
Mennella, Vincent Alfred *automotive manufacturing and airplane company executive*
Shrontz, Frank Anderson *airplane manufacturing executive*
Whitacre, John *apparel executive*

Spokane
Fosseen, Neal Randolph *business executive, former banker, former mayor*

Tacoma
Rogel, Steven R. *forest products company executive*
Sutherland, Douglass B. *former mayor, tent and awning company executive*
Tash, Graham Andrew, Jr. *automobile retail company executive*
Weyerhaeuser, George Hunt *forest products company executive*

Vancouver
Khormaei, Iranpour (Ron Khormaei) *electronics industry executive, educator*

Wenatchee
Birdsall, Brian *food products executive*
Chandler, Allen *food products executive*

Yakima
Grandy, Jay Franklin *fruit processing executive*

CANADA

ALBERTA

Calgary
Holman, J(ohn) Leonard *retired manufacturing corporation executive*
Jenkins, Kevin J. *technology and industrial company executive*

SASKATCHEWAN

Regina
Phillips, Roger *steel company executive*

TAIWAN

Hsinchu
Chang, Kuang-Yeh *microelectronics technologist*

ADDRESS UNPUBLISHED

Azarnoff, Daniel Lester *pharmaceutical company consultant*
Baker, Charles DeWitt *research and development company executive*
Barca, George Gino *winery executive, financial investor*
Bennett, Paul Grover *agribusiness executive*
Broadhurst, Norman Neil *foods company executive*
Buck, Linda Dee *recruiting company executive*
Carver, Juanita Ash *plastic company executive*
Cass, Lee H. *fashion industry consultant*
Castberg, Eileen Sue *construction company owner*
Chaykin, Robert Leroy *manufacturing and marketing executive*
Cureau, Frank Raymond *furniture company executive*
Dach, John Richard *manufacturing executive, farmer*
Diener, Royce *corporate director, retired healthcare services company executive*
Dobelis, George *manufacturing company executive*
Eissmann, Walter James *consulting company executive*
Fatzinger, James A. S. *construction educator, estimator*
Geisert, Otto *food products executive*
Goldberg, Lee Winicki *furniture company executive*
Gorman, Michael Stephen *construction executive*
Grass, George Mitchell, IV *pharmaceutical executive*
Hansen, Donald Curtis *retired manufacturing executive*
Hartwick, Thomas Stanley *technical management consultant*
Harvey, Joseph Emmett *construction executive*
Hoag, William Herbert *construction contractor*
Jackson, Robbi Jo *non-hazardous agricultural products company executive, lawyer*
Jordan, Michael (Rudy) *builder representative*
Kapcsandy, Louis Endre *building construction and manufacturing executive, chemical engineering consultant*
Kim, Dennis Kyle *software company executive*
Kostrikin, Marybeth Elaine *excavating company executive*
Lockwood, William Godfrey *free lance writer*
Macek, Anna Michaella *cosmetics executive*
Madden, Richard Blaine *forest products executive*
Madnick, Marc T. *software company executive*
Malson, Rex Richard *drug and health care corporation executive*
Marrington, Bernard Harvey *retired automotive company executive*
Maskell, Donald Andrew *contracts administrator*
Mason, Frank Henry, III *automobile company executive, leasing company executive*
McCann, Jack Arland *former construction and mining equipment company executive, consultant*
Miller, David Wayne *construction inspector, coordinator*
Moore, Joe Gilbert *manufacturing company executive*
Morita, Toshiyasu *technology professional*
Moylan, Jay Richard *medical products executive*
Pettigrew, Steven Lee *healthcare management consultant*
Platt, Lewis Emmett *electronics company executive*
Richter, James Lowell *plastics industry executive*
Rodgers, Nancy Lucille *corporate executive*
Romanos, Nabil Elias *business development manager*
Ross, Alvin *manufacturing executive*
Rymar, Julian W. *manufacturing company executive*
Sanders, Gordon C. *contractor owner*
Savin, Ronald Richard *chemical company executive, inventor*
Schilling, Dean William *manufacturing executive*
Singleton, Henry Earl *retired industrialist*
Smith, James Alexander *metal processing executive*
Stern, Arthur Paul *electronics company executive*
Wagner, Dana Eric *roofing company executive*
Wagner, John Lee *food products executive*
Warner, Walter Duke *corporate executive*
Wolf, Hans Abraham *retired pharmaceutical company executive*
Wolff, Brian Richard *metal manufacturing company executive*
Young, John Alan *electronics company executive*

INDUSTRY: SERVICE

UNITED STATES

ALASKA

Anchorage
Adams, Stephen Shawn *management consultant, hotel caterer*
Gottstein, Barnard Jacob *retail and wholesale food company executive, real estate executive*
King, Sidsel Elizabeth Taylor (Beth King) *hotel catering-hospitality professional*
Parker, Walter Bruce *arctic research specialist, consultant*
Porcaro, Michael Francis *advertising agency executive*
Schmitt, Nancy Cain *public and corporate relations executive, writer*
Schneibel, Vicki Darlene *public relations administrator*

Barrow
Helfferich, Merritt Randolph *industry and education consultant*

Wrangell
Kraft, Richard Joe *sales executive*

ARIZONA

Apache Junction
Cameron, Janice Carol *executive assistant*

Benson
Collmer, Russell Cravener *data processing executive, educator*

Chandler
Barrett, Craig R. *computer company executive*
Brunello-McCay, Rosanne *sales executive*
Harrison, Jeanette Kemchick *business executive*

Cortaro
Fossland, Joeann Jones *professional speaker, personal coach*

Flagstaff
Bolin, Richard Luddington *industrial development consultant*

Gilbert
Mitchell-Chavez, Bettianne (Ba Mitchell-Chavez) *franchise executive*

Glendale
Baum, Phyllis Gardner *travel management consultant*
Shimek, John Anton *legal investigation business owner, educator*

Kingman
Baker, Richard Earl *business management educator*

Mesa
Gottry, Steven Roger *communications executive, author, screenwriter*
Tindle, Charles Dwight Wood *broadcasting company executive*

Page
Leach, Shawna *food service director*

Paradise Valley
Denning, Michael Marion *entrepreneur, computer company executive*
Hawranek, Joseph Paul *computer company executive, consultant*
Kahn, Earl Lester *retired market research executive*
Shultz, Susan Kent Fried *executive search and international business consultant*

Peoria
Saunders, James *management and training consultant*

Phoenix
Bellus, Ronald Joseph *marketing and communications executive*
Booth, John Louis *service executive*
Brown, James Carrington, III (Bing Brown) *public relations and communications executive*
Collins, Dane H. *marketing executive*
DeWall-Owens, Karen Marie *marketing consultant*
DuMoulin, Diana Cristaudo *marketing professional*
Gall, Donald Alan *data processing executive*
Gossell, Terry Rae *advertising agency executive, small business owner*
Johnson, Elizabeth Misner *communications executive*
Koppenbrink, Joan Waisanen *semiconductor supplier executive*
Last, Dianna Linn Schneider *marketing company executive*
Lemon, Leslie Gene *retired diversified services company executive*
McCoy-Shay, Donna Carol *telecommunication manager*
McDowell, Robert Michael *management consultant*
Pastrone, Paul Nicolas *production manager*
Scott, Particia Jean *educational telecommunications administrator*
Simpson, Charles Robert *marketing professional*
Simunich, Mary Elizabeth Hedrick (Mrs. William A. Simunich) *public relations executive*
Snell, Richard *holding company executive*
Stewart, Sally *public relations practitioner*
Subach, James Alan *information systems company executive, consultant*
Sweet, Cynthia Kay *business administrator*
Teets, John William *retired diversified company executive*
Turner, William Cochrane *international management consultant*
West, Robert L., Jr. *marketing professional*
Wolfe, William Downing *public utility administrator*

Prescott
Mayol, Richard Thomas *advertising executive, political consultant*
Palmer, Robert Arthur *private investigator*

Queen Creek
Schnepf, Carrie Biggs *sales and marketing professional*

Scottsdale
Adams, Robert Granville *marketing professional*
Allen, Cynthia L. *personnel executive*
Blinder, Martin S. *business consultant, art dealer*
Boone, Earle Marion *business executive*
Dedera, Nancy Kovel *communications executive*
Doglione, Arthur George *data processing executive*
Grier, James Edward *hotel company executive, lawyer*
Gwinn, Mary Dolores *business developer, philosopher, writer, speaker*
Jensen, Cynthia Ann *marketing professional*
Joaquim, Richard Ralph *hotel executive*
Kain, Barbara Brown *communications executive*
Messinger, Cora R. *funeral director*
Millon, Jean-Pierre *health care executive*
O'Donnell, William Thomas *management consultant*
Parker, Charles Owen, II *energy company executive, consultant*
Pavlik, Nancy *convention services executive*
Perry, David Niles *public relations executive*
Press, Richard H. *sales executive, consultant*
Root, Laura Lee *personal care industry executive*
Swanson, Robert Killen *management consultant*

Sierra Vista
Reynolds, John Curby *sales representative*

Sun City West
Suttles, Virginia Grant *advertising executive*

Tempe
Dunbar, Richard Paul *sales manager*
Guinouard, Philip Andre *restaurant executive*
Haley, Arthur Joseph *recreation management educator, consultant*
Herbert, Christopher Jay *marketing professional, management consultant*
Huntsman, Edward Loyd *business consultant, marketing executive*
Jefferson, Myra LaVerne Tull *sales executive*
Sackton, Frank Joseph *public affairs educator*
Weissfeld, Amy M. *sales executive*

Tucson
Bryan, Judith Hager *travel consultant, educator*
Eberhardt, Marty Lampert *botanical garden administrator*
Gruenwald, T. Melissa *healthcare communications specialist*
Paley, Alfred Irving *value engineering and consulting company executive, lecturer*

Sankovich, Joseph Bernard *cemetery management consultant*
Sarlat, Gladys *public relations consultant*
Simpson, Warren Carl *information brokerage executive*
Sohnen-Moe, Cherie Marilyn *business consultant*
Toland, Florence Winifred *printing company executive, retired business educator*
Williams, John Charles, II *data processing executive*

Wickenburg
Kardinal, Royce Ann *hotel executive*

Window Rock
Etsitty, Sylvia Mae *administrator*

Yuma
Andrews, Aaron John *recreational facility executive*

CALIFORNIA

Adelanto
Carlson, Carl *waste water operator*

Agoura Hills
Patano, Patricia Ann *marketing and public relations specialist*
Powers, J. D., III *marketing executive*
Schmidt, Frank Broaker *executive recruiter*

Alameda
Billings, Thomas Neal *computer and publishing executive, management consultant*
Seamount, Philip James *retired machine operator*

Alamo
Shiffer, James David *retired utility executive*
Wallis, Wendy S. *sales and management consultant*

Alhambra
Sladoje, George *business executive*

Aliso Viejo
Stebbins, Elizabeth Joseph Hinton *management and statistics educator, researcher*

Altadena
Dobbins, Maggie Sonne *real estate investment company executive*
Fairbanks, Mary Kathleen *data analyst, researcher*

Anaheim
Jackson, Samuel John *scuba diving industry executive*
Kallay, Michael Frank, II *medical devices company official*
Keller, Kent Eugene *advertising and public relations executive*
Lefebvre, Peggy Anderson *advertising executive*
Murphy, Rondo A. *retired sales professional*
Noorda, Raymond J. *computer software company executive*
Nutter, William Scott *business consultant, real estate agent*
Stolrow, Gregory *computer company executive*

Aptos
Cecil, Paula Bernice *writer, management consultant, educator, publisher*
Jaffe, Jan Paynter *advertising and marketing consultant*

Atascadero
Stevenson, George Guilford *information systems specialist*

Atherton
Lowry, Larry Lorn *management consulting company executive*

Atwater
DeVoe, Kenneth Nickolas *food service executive*

Avila Beach
McLaren, Archie Campbell, Jr. *marketing executive*

Bakersfield
Weygand, Leroy Charles *service executive*

Benicia
Lantrip, Ivolue May *secretary*

Berkeley
Dost, Janice E.H. Burrows *human resources director*

Beverly Hills
Bismut, Alain Georges *video sales and international film licensing executive, writer, producer, editor*
Carlson, Gary Lee *public relations executive, director, producer*
Coury, Maryanne *advertising-marketing consultant*
Fickinger, Wayne Joseph *communications executive*
Florence, Verena Magdalena *business and computer consultant*
Gallagher, Thomas Edmund *hotel executive*
Hartman, Jeannette Marie *marketing specialist*
Hilton, Barron *hotel executive*
John, Joseph Robert *international business consultant, film producer*
Kardell, Maxine G. *jewelry and collectibles consultant, marketing professional*
Summerfield, Nan Drury *gemologist, estate jewelry specialist*
Young, Robert Edward *computer company executive*
Ziecker, Russell Scott *personal manager*

Bonita
Patel, Sudhir *service executive*

Brea
Herzing, Alfred Roy *computer executive*

Buena Park
Underwood, Thomas Woodbrook *communications company executive*

Burbank
Brankovich, Mark J. *restaurateur*

Collier, Neal Howard *sales professional*
Green, Judson C. *marketing agency executive*

Burlingame
Riach, Douglas Alexander *marketing and sales executive, retired military officer*

Camarillo
Carmi, Aviram *technology executive*

Cambria
Morse, Richard Jay *human resources and organizational development consultant, manufacturers' representative company executive*

Campbell
Roberts, George P. *computer company executive*
Shea, John Dwane *communications executive*

Carlsbad
Cheatham, David Todd *software company executive*
Houlgate, Deke *public relations consultant, writer*
Mitchell, Thomas Edward, Jr. *communications cabling executive*
Moore, Terry Wayne *high technology venture management consultant*
Withers, Richard Allen, Jr. *security firm executive, consultant*

Carmel
Allan, Robert Moffat, Jr. *corporate executive, educator*
Burns, Richard Leland *marketing consultant, columnist*
Creighton, John Wallis, Jr. *consultant, author, former management educator*
Smith, Gordon Paul *management consulting company executive*

Cathedral City
Schmidt, Jeanne Louise *retired sales specialist*

Cerritos
Rice, Barbara Pollak *advertising and marketing executive*

Chatsworth
Sklar, Louise Margaret *service executive*
Turner, Michael Seth *public relations and marketing executive*
Urmer, Diane Hedda *management firm executive, financial officer*

Chula Vista
Culbert, Michael Leon *communications executive*

Claremont
Kuenning, Geoffrey Houston *computer science educator*

Concord
Crocker, Kenneth Franklin *data processing consultant*
Jones, Gregory Taylor *human resources risk manager*
Padget, John E. *management professional*
Travers, Judith Lynnette *human resources executive*

Corona
Byrnes, Edward Richard, Jr. *sales and marketing executive*
Wetsch, Peggy A. *information systems specialist, publisher, educator, nurse*

Corona Del Mar
Terrell, A. John *university telecommunications director*

Costa Mesa
Damsky, Robert Philip *communications executive*
Smith, Sarah Kim Huey *training and development consultant*

Crescent City
Hight, Harold Philip *retired security company executive*

Culver City
Dutt, Birendra *research specialist*
Mehlman, Lon Douglas *information systems specialist*
Van Kirk, Richard Lee *management consultant*

Cupertino
Baab, Carlton *advertising executive*
Devlin, Mike *software company executive*
Eubanks, Gordon *software company executive*
Flynn, Ralph Melvin, Jr. *sales executive, marketing consultant*
Foley, Rita Virginia *computer company executive*
Geddes, Barbara Sheryl *communications executive, consultant*
Hall, Brenda *human resources executive*
Kvamme, Mark D. *marketing professional*
Mattathil, George Paul *communications specialist, consultant*
Suiter, Thomas *advertising executive*

Cypress
Hoover, Jeanne Kathryn *marketing and brand management executive*

Dana Point
Mardian, Robert Charles, Jr. *restaurateur*

Danville
da Roza, Victoria Cecilia *human resources administrator*
Gorman, Russell William *marketing executive, consultant*
Randolph, Kevin H. *marketing executive*

Davis
Woodard, John Henry *quality control professional*

Delano
Akagi, Leora Jean *marketing consultant*

Diamond Bar
Olson, Earle Oliver *marketing and sales executive, consultant*

Discovery Bay
Portway, Patrick Stephen *telecommunications consulting company executive, telecommunications educator*

Dublin
Payack, Paul JJ *marketing executive*

El Cajon
Granquist, Oskar Adam *sales professional*

El Dorado Hills
Davies, William Ralph *service executive*

El Segundo
Armstrong, Wallace Dowan, Jr. *data processor*
Autolitano, Astrid *consumer products executive*
Barad, Jill Elikann *toy company executive*
Cordner, Tom *advertising executive*
Gilbert, Scott *advertising executive*
Katz, Lew *advertising executive*
McQuillin, Richard Ross *management consultant*
Mooney, Roslyn Paula *computer company executive*

Eldridge
Chaplin, William Ratcliffe *cleaning service executive*

Elk Grove
Anderson, J. William *management consultant*
Bundesen, Faye Stimers *investment and management company owner, educator*
Crapo, Sheila Anne *telecommunications company professional, artist*
Mark, Arthur *information systems specialist*

Encinitas
Deuble, John L., Jr. *environmental science and engineering services consultant*

Escondido
Daniels, Richard Martin *public relations executive*
Hodgson, John Frederick, II *information systems specialist, photographer*
Kilmer, Maurice Douglas *marketing executive*

Fair Oaks
Church, Bryan P. *business owner, educator*
Nolan, Mark Gregory *advertising executive*

Fairfield
Muller, Lawrence George *communications consultant*

Fallbrook
Cralley, Lester Vincent *retired industrial hygienist, editor*

Fontana
Cory, Rolland Wayne *business administrator*

Fort Bragg
Galli, Darrell Joseph *management consultant*

Fort Jones
Weisberg, Maggie *public relations executive*

Foster City
Hunt, Leo *public relations executive*
McHenry, Julie *communications executive*
Wilson, Lerry *public relations executive*

Fountain Valley
Lonegan, Thomas Lee *retired restaurant corporation executive*

Fremont
Bagley, James W. *executive*
Chan, Fred S.L. *executive*
Hackworth, Michael L. *executive*
Harper, Ed *computer company executive*
McBride, Bonnie Tarbell *investor relations executive*
Parikh, Mihir *executive*
Schauer, Ronald L. *executive*
Shih, Andrew Han-Ting *marketing executive*

Fresno
Shmavonian, Gerald S. *entertainment executive*

Gardena
Sloan, Michael Dana *information systems specialist*

Gilroy
Katemopoulos, Mildred Josephine *executive secretary*

Glendale
Brunton, Donna Lee *secretarial services manager*
Dohring, Doug *marketing executive*
Dohring, Laurie *marketing executive*
Misa, Kenneth Franklin *management consultant*
Van Bebber, Annie *business developer*

Granada Hills
O'Connor, Betty Lou *service executive*
Shoemaker, Harold Lloyd *infosystem specialist*

Grass Valley
Hutcherson, Christopher Alfred *marketing, recruiting and educational fundraising executive*

Guerneville
Weese, Bruce Eric *pharmaceutical sales executive*

Hacienda Heights
Ittner, Perry Martin *sales and marketing consultant*

Half Moon Bay
Fennell, Diane Marie *marketing executive, process engineer*

Harbor City
Loggins, Paul Gregory [illegible]

Hawthorne
Perry, James Gregory *sales and marketing executive*

Healdsburg
Canfield, Grant Wellington, Jr. *management consultant*

Hermosa Beach
Le Veque, Matthew Kurt *public affairs and marketing consultant*

Hillsborough
West, Hugh Sterling *aircraft leasing company executive*

Hollywood
Rabun, Claude Lee *consumer products company executive, consultant*

Huntington Beach
Lopata, Martin Barry *business executive*
Sward, Jeffrey Edwin *information systems specialist*
Wing, Roger *management consultant*

Irvine
Alcone, Matt *advertising executive*
Barnhart, Jack Harmon *purchasing agent*
Dossett, Lawrence Sherman *professional services company official*
Huff, Dennis Lyle *marketing professional*
Kuhl, Ronald Webster *marketing executive*
Leber, Mike *advertising executive*
Leets, Peter J. *consulting firm executive*
Maybay, Duane Charles *recycling systems executive*
Oliver, Travis *advertising agency executive*
Schuetz, John Michael *sales executive*
Seller, Gregory Erol *marketing executive, writer*
Smith, Jon David *advertising executive*
Sowder, Kathleen Adams *marketing executive*
Stanton, Lewis Harris *software company executive*
von Tilsit, Heidemarie *information management specialist*

La Canada
MacNeal, Richard Henri *company executive, researcher*

La Crescenta
Sanders, David Clyde *management and marketing consultant*

La Habra
Hatai, Thomas Henry *international marketing professional*

La Jolla
Charlson, David Harvey *executive search company professional*
Cotter, John Joseph *management consultant, writer, educator*
Deal, Luisa *management consultant, trainer, former educator*
McNamara, Tom *scientific consulting corporation executive*
Reed, James Anthony *hotel industry executive, consultant*
Wadas, John W. *fundraiser, marketing executive*

La Mesa
Anders, Darrill James *sales professional*

La Mirada
Joseph, Mark Scott *entertainment company executive, television and radio personality*

La Puente
Ogden, Jean Lucille *sales executive*

La Quinta
Connerly, Dianna Jean *business official*
Peden, Lynn Ellen *marketing executive*

La Verne
Brueland, Clyde Eugene *advancement director*

Laguna Beach
Hafey, Edward Earl Joseph *precision tool company executive*
Smith, Patricia Jacquline *marketing executive*
Taylor, James Walter *marketing consultant*

Laguna Hills
Schulz, Raymond Alexander *medical marketing professional, consultant*

Laguna Niguel
Greenberg, Lenore *public relations professional*
Kursewicz, Lee Z. *marketing consultant*

Lake Almanor
Barca, Kathleen *marketing executive*

Lake Arrowhead
Bauer, Ralph Leroy *business executive*

Livermore
Williams, David Michael *manufacturing executive*
Zambetti, Denis Egan *product specialist*

Loma Linda
Huff, Dale Eugene *retired environmental services executive*
Maurice, Don *personal care industry executive*
Schmidt, Wallace Alan *communications executive*

Long Beach
Aldrich, David Lawrence *public relations executive*
Brown, (Jerene) Roxanne *sales executive*
Dostourian, Dick *computer systems executive*
Farnum, Nancy Alyson *communications executive*
Hantusch, Mark John *traffic administrator*
Johnson, William Harry *international management consultant*
Do, Nguyen Minh *computer company executive*
Lewis, Ralph Jay, III *management and human* [illegible]

Stoorza Gill, Gail *corporate professional*
Vallbona, Marisa *public relations counselor*
Ziegaus, Alan James *public relations executive*

San Fernando
Douglass, Ramona Elizabeth *medical sales professional*

San Francisco
Amidei, L. Neal *public relations counselor*
Bernstein, Gerald William *management consultant, researcher*
Bierly, Shirley Adelaide *communications executive*
Blanc, Maureen *public relations executive*
Bliss, Marian Alice *information systems professional*
Boyle, Antonia Barnes *audio producer, writer*
Buchanan, William Michaux, Jr. *electrical distribution executive*
Butenhoff, Susan *public relations executive*
Calvin, Dorothy Ver Strate *computer company executive*
Chaput, Eugene Michael *advertising executive*
Colton, Roy Charles *management consultant*
Connelly, Theodore Sample *communications executive*
Dehm, Scott M. *personnel specialist, consultant*
D'Errico, Didi *executive*
Edgar, James Macmillan, Jr. *management consultant*
Faron, Fay Cheryl *private investigator, writer*
Finkelstein, James Arthur *management consultant*
Fulmer, Lisa Michelle *marketing director, graphic arts consultant*
Galliani, Robert *marketing professional*
Gehb, Michael *public relations executive*
Goldberg, Fred Sellmann *advertising executive*
Gordon, Judith *communications consultant, writer*
Groth, Olaf Jonny *communications executive*
Haas, Peter E., Sr. *company executive*
Hallberg, Claudia Skye *marketing executive, consultant*
Hornbuckle, Michael *instructional technology consultant, writer*
Howarth, Susan Teer *management executive, consultant, association executive*
Jones, J. Gilbert *research consultant*
Jones, Stanton William *management consultant*
Kaufman, Jonathan Allan (Jon) *public relations executive*
Kemp, Jeanne Frances *office manager*
Kielarowski, Henry Edward *marketing executive*
Klammer, Joseph Francis *management consultant*
Landis, Richard Gordon *retired food company executive*
Magierek, Dylan Jay *marketing professional, consultant, producer*
Maneatis, George A. *retired utility company executive*
Marshall, Scott *advertising agency executive*
Massaro, Mike *advertising executive*
Messer, Angela *systems development executive*
Minor, Halsey M. *computer company executive*
Muegge, Lyn *advertising executive*
O'Rourke, Dennis *advertising executive*
Otus, Simone *public relations executive*
Parker, Diana Lynne *restaurant manager, special events director*
Probert, Colin *advertising executive*
Pullen, Nancy Ellen *marketing consultant*
Ramos, Dorothy Jo *information resource manager*
Riney, Hal Patrick *advertising executive*
Rutschke, Annamarie *administrative technician*
Sepetys, Kristina M. *economic and management consultant*
Sheeley, Ellen R. *marketing consultant, finance consultant*
Siegel, Patricia Ann *association management specialist*
Silverstein, Richard *advertising agency executive*
Sproul, John Allan *retired public utility executive*
Steel, Jon *advertising executive*
Tonini, Leon Richard *sales professional*
Weaver, Sara Lee *sales executive*
Wendle, Kevin *computer company executive*
Wentz, Jeffrey Lee *information systems consultant*
Wilson, Judith Faltysek *development executive*
Winter-Switz, Cheryl Donna *travel company executive*
Witherington, Jennifer Lee *sales and marketing executive, meeting planner*

San Jose
Beverett, Andrew Jackson *marketing executive*
Bolger, Brenna M. *executive*
Brough, Bruce Alvin *public relations and communications executive*
Byers, Charles Frederick *public relations executive, marketing executive*
Cade, Jack Carlton *marketing professional*
Chambers, John T. *computer company executive*
Connor, Gary Edward *manufacturing company marketing executive*
Der Torossian, Papken *executive*
Dietz, Russell Scott *communications company executive*
Emerson, Mark David *maternal products company executive*
Gharda, Laurent Kirk *software company executive*
Harding, Jack *executive*
Harkins, Craig *management consultant*
Harrus, Alain Simon *marketing professional*
Hawley, Kimra *software company executive*
Herson, Gene *computer company executive*
Highlander, Richard William *communications executive*
Hill, Richard *executive*
Hutcheson, Jerry Dee *manufacturing company executive*
Laskin, Barbara Virginia *marketing executive*
Levy, Kenneth *executive*
Lobo, Keith R. *executive*
Nguyen, Lam Duc *business executive, consultant*
Ostrom, Philip Gardner *computer company executive*
Palma, Michael Joseph *marketing professional*
Puette, Robert L. *executive*
Raghavan, Asuri *executive*
Roelandts, Willem P. *executive*
Simons, Steve *executive*
Smith, Charles Richard *high technology marketing executive*
Stegman, Charles Alexander (Chuck Alexander Stegman) *marketing professional*
Walklet, Judith Kyle *printing company executive*
Weinhardt, J. W. *computer company executive*
Zafiropoulo, Arthur *executive*
Zinn, Ray *computer company executive*

San Leandro
Polanco, J. Martin *field service technician, pastry artist*

San Luis Obispo
Vanderspek, Peter George *management consultant, writer*

San Mateo
Helfert, Erich Anton *management consultant, author, educator*
Jadallah, Charles I. *sales executive*
Jones, Louis Worth *retired management analyst, journalist*
Jung, Samson Pang *computer analyst, investment company executive, astrologer*
Leong, Carol Jean *electrologist*
Nazzaro, David Alfred *sales executive*
Siebel, Thomas M. *executive*
Wiefels, Paul Harold *management consultant*

San Pedro
Jezina, Carol Susan *secretary*

San Rafael
Gould, R(ichard) Martin (Richard Martin Goldman) *marketing consultant, researcher*
Thompson, John William *international management consultant*
Wilson, Ian Holroyde *management consultant, futurist*

San Ramon
Bloom, Michael Eugene *consulting executive*
Garcia, Michael Joseph *telecommunications company executive*
Moore, Justin Edward *data processing executive*

Santa Ana
Boynton, William Lewis *electronic manufacturing company official*
Holtz, Joseph Norman *marketing executive*
Kenney, Patti Marlene *sales executive*
Smith, Keith Larue *research company executive*

Santa Barbara
Amory, Thomas Carhart *management consultant*
Emmons, Robert John *corporate executive*
Hanley, Kevin Lance *maintenance manager*
Meyers, Diana Lee *public relations and fundraising consultant*

Santa Clara
Benhamou, Eric A. *computer company executive*
Beyer, Richard Michael *communications company executive*
Bottoms, Bill *executive*
Dickens, Thomas Paul *security executive*
Henry, Neil R. *data communications product manager*
Holdt, Terry *computer company executive*
Landa, Matthew *computer company executive*
Luongo, John R. *executive*
Martin, Norman Francis *public relations executive*
Menkin, Christopher (Kit Menkin) *leasing company executive*
Moore, Bruce *executive*
Mu, Xiao-chun *computer company executive*
Perham, Len *executive*
Reavis, Liza Anne *semiconductor executive*
Rudolph, Ronald Alvin *human resources executive*
Vincent, David Ridgely *management consulting executive*
Werning, Joseph Robert *computer company executive*
Young, Douglas Ryan *technology company executive*

Santa Cruz
Michels, Doug *executive*
Stilwill, Belle Jean *record company executive, printing company owner*

Santa Fe Springs
Hammond, Judy McLain *business services executive*
Loftis, James Madison *sales executive*
Morgan, Ronald William *sales executive*

Santa Monica
Bachrach, Charles Lewis *advertising agency executive*
Hagelstein, William C. *executive*
Janulaitis, M. Victor *consulting company executive*
Lucas, James Bruno *public relations consultant*
Mancuso, Vince *advertising executive*
Nakaki, Thomas *information systems specialist*
Postaer, Larry *advertising executive*
Remsing, Dennis *advertising agency executive*
Rubin, Gerrold Robert *advertising executive*
Salzman, Paul *social worker*
Seymour, Jeffrey Alan *governmental relations consultant*
Uretz, Michael Albert *health and fitness executive*

Santa Rosa
Howard, Victor *management consultant*

Santa Ynez
Palola, Harry Joel *international affairs executive, consultant*

Saugus
Hauenstein, Donald Herbert, Jr. *computer company executive*

Sausalito
Purdom, Paul Wakefield *public relations executive*

Scotts Valley
Delear, Richard Henry *personnel consultant*
Luczo, Stephen J. *executive*
Shugart, Alan F. *retired electronic computing equipment company executive*

Seal Beach
Burge, Willard, Jr. *software company executive*

Sherman Oaks
Boolootian, Richard Andrew *communications executive*

Di Massa, Ernani Vincenzo, Jr. *broadcast executive, television producer, writer*
Ellenberger, Allan Ralph *insurance company special projects assistant*
Krown, Seymour Richard *film production executive*

Signal Hill
Jarman, Donald Ray *retired public relations professional, minister*

Simi Valley
Ritacco, Patsy Richard *sales executive*

Sonora
Mathias, Betty Jane *communications and community affairs consultant, writer, editor, lecturer*

South Pasadena
Lowe, Richard Gerald, Jr. *computer programming manager*

South San Francisco
Lewis, Jason Alvert, Jr. *communications executive*
Niehaus, Ed *executive*
Ryan, Bill *executive*
Wong, Carrie *executive*

Stanford
Miller, William Frederick *research company executive, educator, business consultant*

Stockton
Dolgow, Allan Bentley *consulting company executive*
Klevan Neely, Jan Marie *communications executive*
Shebl, James Michael *communications executive*

Studio City
Chambers, Clytia Montllor *public relations consultant*
Linsteadt, Stephen Michael *health care executive*
Richman, Anthony E. *textile rental industry association executive*

Suisun City
Humphrey, Nancy Adele *employment and training specialist, consultant*

Sunnyvale
East, John *computer company executive*
Eufinger, Rosalie Rigg *public relations executive*
Harari, Eli *executive*
Lawrence, Frederick D. *executive*
Ratcliff, Mary Elizabeth *computer company executive*
Selvin, Neil *computer company executive*
Tsang, David D. *computer company executive*

Taft
Smith, Lee L. *hotel executive*

Temecula
Coram, David James *marketing professional*

Thousand Oaks
Cobb, Shirley Ann *public relations specialist, journalist*
Garcia, Cheryl Linda *sales professional*
Lopez, Justo Jose *sales executive*

Toluca Lake
Mracky, Ronald Sydney *marketing and promotion executive, travel consultant*

Torrance
Carey, Kathryn Ann *advertising and public relations executive, editor, consultant*
Drews, Joseph Harvey *administrator*
Kasari, Leonard Samuel *quality control professional, concrete consultant*
Signorovitch, Dennis James *communications executive*

Tracy
Green, Brian Gerald *marketing executive*

Truckee
Fitzpatrick, Michael Kieran *restaurant company executive*
Sanwick, James Arthur *international executive recruiter, management consultant*

Turlock
Kantz, Philip C. *executive*

Tustin
Bartlett, Arthur Eugene *franchise executive*
Jay, David Jakubowicz *management consultant*
Shelton, Jerrell Wilson *information company executive*

Twentynine Palms
Fultz, Philip Nathaniel *management analyst*
Ontek, Louis S. *retired utilities executive*

Upland
Deppisch, Paul Vincent *data communications executive*
Ward, Michael Alan *public information consultant*

Vacaville
Young, Roger Carl *computer company executive*

Valley Springs
Vitrac, Jean-Jacques Charles *international business consultant*

Valley Village
Mason, Dana Elaine *marketing manager*

Van Nuys
Josephs, Alice Ruth *retired executive secretary*

Venice
Hester, Gail *receptionist, writer*
Simon, Diane Meyer *environmental company executive*

Ventura
Zilligen, Jil A. *environmental director*

Victorville
Tate, Carl Roy *management consultant, real estate broker*

Villa Park
Britton, Thomas Warren, Jr. *management consultant*
Hawe, David Lee *consultant*

Walnut
Tan, Colleen Woo *communications educator*

Walnut Creek
Garlough, William Glenn *marketing executive*
Leftwich, James Stephen *management consultant*
Moore, John D. *management consultant*
Robles, Eliodoro Gonzales *consulting company executive, educator*

West Covina
Musich, Robert Lorin *motivational speaker*
West, Edward Alan *graphics communications executive*

West Hollywood
Einstein, Clifford Jay *advertising executive*
Holt, Dennis F. *media buying company executive*
Morris, Brian *advertising executive*
Pumpian, Betty Ann G. *advertising executive*
Sweeney, Vonny Hilton *promotion company executive*

Westlake Village
Agarwal, Steve (Sudhir) *software company executive*
Catrambone, Eugene Dominic *magazine editor*
Murdock, David H. *diversified company executive*
Reynolds, William George *insurance company executive*

Woodland Hills
Bellanich, Alice Marie *sales representative, minister*
Burke, Tamara Lynn *marketing professional*
Ennis, Thomas Michael *management consultant*
Maeda, J. A. *data processing executive*
Namkung, Xhana Marie *advertising executive*
Parrott, Dennis Beecher *sales executive*

Yucca Valley
Clay, Sean Cochrane *software development company executive*

COLORADO

Allenspark
Newman, Dean Gordon *business consultant*

Arvada
Hulse, Ralph Robert *management consultant*

Aspen
Bradford, Diane Goldsmith *multimedia marketing and product consultant*
Brendlinger, Jack Allen *broadcast executive*
Finster, Brent Edwin *public safety communications administrator*
McDade, James Russell *management consultant*

Aurora
Bobrick, Steven Aaron *marketing executive*
Harlan, Raymond Carter *communication executive*
Ivins, Orville Rush *marketing executive*
Pals, Brian Joseph *industrial hygiene company executive*
Peck, George Holmes *public relations executive*
Pohlman, David Lawrence *training systems consultant*
Reitan, Harold Theodore *management consultant*
Sexton, Jerry Lee *multimedia company executive, consultant*
Welch, Richard LeRoy *personal improvement company executive*

Bailey
Van Dusen, Donna Bayne *communication consultant, educator, researcher*

Boulder
Bryson, Gary Spath *cable television and telephone company executive*
Chimera, Donna Mae *marketing professional, writer*
Fisher, Joseph Stewart *management consultant*
Holbrook, William Francis *marketing executive*
McGehan, Frederick Parsons, Jr. *public affairs executive*
Volan, Wendy Tyson *marketing professional*
Zardouzian, Kam *marketing executive*

Colorado Springs
Deiotte, Charles Edward *computer software company executive*
Ford, James Carlton *human resources executive*
Fortune, James Michael *network analyst*
Guthrie, David Neal *marketing executive*
Loux, Jonathan Dale *business development consultant*
Midkiff, Donald Wayne *program manager*
Mitchell, John Henderson *management consultant, retired career officer*
Wainionpaa, John William *computer equipment company executive*

Denver
Arnold, Samuel P. *restauranteur, writer*
Berger, Robert Dale *communications company executive*
Charczenko, Peter *Internet development company executive*
Clinch, Nicholas Bayard, III *business executive*
Engel, Rachael Erin *management consultant*
Greenberg, Pamela Thayer *public policy specialist*
Hamrick, Joseph Eugene, Jr. *information services specialist*
Harris, Howard Jeffrey *marketing and printing company executive*
Haynes, Duane E. *recreation coordinator*
Heck, Gary L. *security management company executive*
Henry, David Allen *advertising executive*

Lindon
Best, Reed Wayne *quality assurance professional*

Logan
Wilkinson, Richard Francis, Jr. *marketing executive*

Midvale
Kitto, Franklin Curtis *computer systems specialist*
Phillips, Ted Ray *advertising agency executive*
Richardson, Alfred *food service executive, consultant*

Moab
Taylor, Lisa C. *marketing professional*

Ogden
Hardman, Sean Kevin *catering company executive*

Orem
Morey, Robert Hardy *communications executive*
Sawyer, Thomas Edgar *management consultant*
White, Ian Phillip *personal care facilitator*
Zimmerman, Stephen *marketing executive*

Provo
Buck, William Fraser, II *marketing executive*
Carter, Michael Dwayne *sales and marketing executive*
Clark, Loyal Frances *public affairs specialist*
Herrera, Shirley Mae *personnel and security executive*
Soter, Nicholas Gregory *advertising agency executive*

Saint George
Potwin, Juanita R. *marketing professional, dental hygienist*

Salt Lake City
Campbell, Stewart Clawson *retired sales executive, artist*
Fowles, Carl S. *human resources executive*
Fox, Harold Lavar *computer executive*
Hopson, Andy *public relations executive*
Johnson, Jon L. *advertising executive*
Lund, Victor L. *retail food company executive*
Maher, David L. *drug store company executive*
Mills, Carol Margaret *business consultant, public relations consultant*
Payne, Boyd Alan *marketing professional*
Scott, Howard Winfield, Jr. *temporary help services company executive*
Thomas, David G. *advertising executive*

Sandy
Mitchell, David Campbell *inventor, corporate executive*
York, Theodore Robert *consulting company executive*

West Valley City
Leibsla, Melvin Donald *data processing executive*

WASHINGTON

Anacortes
Spaulding, John Pierson *public relations executive, marine consultant*

Auburn
Howard, George Harmon *management consultant*

Bellevue
Cashman, Thomas Joseph *marketing executive*
Dunlap, Kathleen Jane *public relations executive*
Evans, Robert Vincent *sales and marketing executive*
Hall, Eleanor Williams *public relations executive*
Hertzog, Elwood W., III *directory and advertising consultant*
Johnson, Gary Kent *management education company executive*
Lauver, Lydia Monserrat Ollis *public relations executive*
O'Byrne, Michael *management consultant*
Robbins, Lynn Eileen *human resources specialist*

Burlington
Herbaugh, Roger Duane *computer and software company executive*

Carnation
Beshur, Jacqueline E. *pet training consultant, writer*

Edmonds
Brinton, Richard Kirk *marketing executive*

Everett
Koonce, Genio Cardwell *retired field engineer*

Kent
Cheung, John B. *research and development executive*

Littlerock
Gunderson, Cleon Henry *management consultant corporation executive*

Malaga
Nanto, Roxanna Lynn *marketing professional, management consultant*

Oak Harbor
Meaux, Alan Douglas *facilities technician, sculptor*

Olympia
Adkins, Ben Frank *management and engineering consultant*
Marcelynas, Richard Chadwick *management consultant*
Ogden, Valeria Munson *management consultant, state representative*
Reisman, Donald Felix *consultant*

Port Orchard
Teeters, Dorothy L. ... ... *administrator*

Poulsbo
Pfarrell, Linda Lee *technology management consultant*

Seteroff, Sviatoslav Steve *management and logistics company executive*

Redmond
Addams, Robert Jean *finance executive*
Bhela, Harvinder Singh *computer software company executive*
Davis, T. Ronald *marketing professional*
Gates, William Henry, III *software company executive*
Gilmore, A. Douglas *retail sales executive*
Ludin, Irwin Stevan *business/information technology consultant*

Renton
Bates, Charles Walter *human resources executive, lawyer*

Richland
Towner, Larry Edwin *consulting company executive*

Seattle
Andrews, Frederick M. *marketing analyst*
Beer, Joseph Ernest *telecommunications manager*
Bianco, James A. *research and development executive*
Chang, Taiping *marketing executive, magazine publisher*
D'Onofrio, Anthony *chef*
Duryea, David Anthony *management consultant*
Elgin, Ron Alan *advertising executive*
Gerwick-Brodeur, Madeline Carol *marketing and timing professional*
Gormèzano, Keith *arbitrator, writer, marketer*
Hansey, Renee Jeanne *retired communications executive*
Hawthorne, Nan Louise *internet resources consultant, web designer*
Kane, Karen Marie *public affairs consultant*
Kaperick, John Anthony *information specialist*
Kelly, Dennis Ray *sales executive*
MacDonald, Andrew Stephen *management consulting firm executive*
Miyata, Keijiro *culinary arts educator*
Murphy, Kelly *test and operations staff*
Patten, Richard E. *personnel company owner*
Porad, Laurie Jo *jewelry company official*
Reed, Stephen Gregory *sales executive*
Reis, Jean Stevenson *administrative secretary*
Santos, Joao Miguel *sales director*
Stark, Alan *sales and marketing administrator*
Stepherd, Michael R. *public relations executive*
Stumbles, James Rubidge *Washington multinational service company executive*
Wilson, Emily Marie *sales executive*

Spokane
Ballinger, Charles Kenneth *information specialist*
Geraghty, John Vincent *public relations consultant*
Moe, Orville Leroy *racetrack executive*
Nicolai, Eugene Ralph *public relations consultant, editor, writer*
Olson, William Thomas *business executive, educator, consultant*
Perry, Lois Wanda *safety and health administrator*
Ranck, John Stevens *human resources executive, consultant*
Storey, Francis Harold *business consultant, retired bank executive*
Tsutakawa, Edward Masao *management consultant*
Wilcox, Brent Keith *information systems specialist*
Woodard, Alva Abe *business consultant*

Tacoma
Forseth, Jon Edward *consultant*
Hudson, Edward Voyle *linen supply company executive*
Knudson, Melvin Robert *management consultant, business executive*
Licens, Lila Louise *administrative assistant*
Metsker, Thomas Charles *map company executive*
Robinson, Richard Allen, Jr. *human resources development trainer, consultant*
Taylor, Peter van Voorhees *advertising and public relations consultant*

Tonasket
Vawter, Donald *retired personnel management consultant*

Vancouver
Buchanan, Jerry Major *advertising executive*
Guenther, Sheila Walsh *sales and promotion executive*
Middlewood, Martin Eugene *technical communications specialist, writer, consultant*

Walla Walla
Potts, Charles Aaron *management executive, writer*

Woodinville
Mammoliti, Tony *executive*

Yakima
Myers, Elizabeth Rouse *management consultant*

WYOMING

Cheyenne
Twine, Bruce David *information services administrator*

Gillette
Berger, Duane W. (Dewey Berger) *technical coordinator*

Laramie
Hashimoto, Lloyd Ken *communications executive*

Mills
Kennerknecht, Richard Eugene *marketing executive*

Rock Springs
Zambai, Robyn S. *business owner, therapist*

Sheridan
Taylor, Judith Ann *marketing and sales executive*

CANADA

ALBERTA

Banff
Frey, Gerrard Rupert (Gary Frey) *management executive*

Calgary
Temple, Peter John Maskell *producer, communication consultant*

BRITISH COLUMBIA

Vancouver
Chu, Allen Yum-Ching *automation company executive, systems consultant*

GHANA

Accra
Ocansey, Aaron Akrofi *game designer*

ADDRESS UNPUBLISHED

Akbarian, Shah-Rokh *management consultant*
Allen, Paul *computer executive, professional sports team owner*
Ambrose, Thomas Cleary *communications executive*
Anderson, Jack Joe *retired communications and multimedia training consultant*
Anderson, Mark Robert *data processing executive, biochemist*
Anderson, Stuart *retired restaurant owner, retired rancher, writer*
Arnold, Severin Grundvig, Jr. *software company executive*
Baskerville, Tim *marketing executive*
Beck, Timothy Daniel *human resources specialist, consultant*
Bennett, Robert LeRoy *computer software development company executive*
Borda, Richard Joseph *management consultant*
Braden, George Walter, II (Barron of Carrigaline) *company executive*
Branting, Robert A., Sr. *marketing executive*
Brun, Margaret Ann Charlene *semiconductor industry buyer, planner*
Bruno, Cathy Eileen *management consultant, former state official*
Bueno, Ana *healthcare marketing and public relations executive, writer*
Camper, John Saxton *public relations and marketing executive*
Chamberlain, William Edwin, Jr. *management consultant*
Christy, Thomas Patrick *human resources executive, educator*
Cochran, Jacqueline Louise *management executive*
Collett, Merrill Judson *management consultant*
Collings, Celeste Louise (Shorty Vassalli) *marketing executive, professional artist*
Conto, Aristides *advertising agency executive*
Costa, Michael F. *multimedia communications executive*
Costello, Marcelle Welling *marketing consultant*
Cotter, Lawrence Raffety *management consultant*
Criswell, Kimberly Ann *public relations executive, dancer*
Crosson, John Albert *advertising executive*
Cruse, Denton W. *marketing and advertising executive, consultant*
Damaschino, Ann Toothman *development consultant*
Danner, Paul Kruger, III *telecommunications executive*
Dickerson, Cynthia Rowe *marketing firm executive, consultant*
Dolich, Andrew Bruce *sports marketing executive*
D'Onofrio, Mary Ann *medical transcription company executive*
Dorn, Natalie Reid *consultant*
Duke, William Edward *public affairs executive*
Dwight, Robert James *heavy equipment business owner*
Eggleston, Claud Hunt, III *company executive, venture capitalist*
Ellis, Robert Harry *retired television executive, university administrator*
Elsberry, Susan Davise *computer-aided manufacturing engineer*
Erb, Richard Louis Lundin *resort and hotel executive*
Farrell, William Edgar *sales executive, infosystems specialist, management consultant*
Fischer, Michele Elizabeth *screenwriter, actress*
Flagg, Norman Lee *retired advertising executive*
Frank, Debra Wilson *retail manager and trainer*
Frappia, Linda Ann *management executive*
Gilbertson, Robert G. *computer company executive*
Glatzer, Robert Anthony *marketing and sales executive*
Glenn, Beth *sales and marketing executive*
Glenn, Kathryn Irene (KK Glenn) *computer company professional*
Goodby, Jeffrey *advertising agency executive*
Gottlieb, Alan Merril *advertising, fundraising and broadcasting executive, writer*
Grant, John Carrington *advertising executive*
Green, James Craig *retired data systems company executive*
Greene, Richard Boyd, Jr. *marketing and sales executive*
Griggs, Emma *management executive*
Grindal, Mary Ann *former sales professional*
Grody, Mark Stephen *public relations executive*
Hamilton, Jody Ann *personal manager, film producer*
Hansen, Leland Joe *communications executive*
Hargitt, Rollin Jerry *retired telecommunications company executive*
Harlan, Kathleen Troy (Kay Harlan) *business consultant, professional speaker and seminar leader*
Hausdorfer, Gary Lee *management consultant*
Hemphill, William Alfred, III *marketing executive*
Herenda, William A. *executive*
Hirahara, Patti *public relations executive*
Ho, April Ahulani *sales professional, choreographer*

Hochschild, Carroll Shepherd *medical equipment and computer company executive, educator*
Hoffman, Mavis Wanda *business official*
Holland, Henry Norman *marketing consultant*
Jordan, Jeffrey Guy *marketing and marketing research consultant*
Karalis, John Peter *computer company executive, lawyer*
Kasulka, Larry Herman *management consultant*
Kelleher, Richard Cornelius *marketing and communications executive*
Kennedy, Debra Joyce *marketing professional*
Kline, Rory R. *regional marketing*
Koelmel, Lorna Lee *data processing executive*
Korec, Jacek *corporation executive*
Lampert, Eleanor Verna *retired human resources specialist*
LeBlanc, Laureen Alison *service company administrator*
Leger, Richard Roubine *public relations executive, writer*
Letcher, Naomi Jewell *quality engineer, educator, counselor*
Levitt, Irene Hansen *sales associate, writer, artist*
Loden, D. John *advertising executive*
Lommatsch, I. Lavon *retired business administration consultant*
Long, Bruce Alan *office automation specialist*
Loven, Charles John *human resource executive*
Lu, Ming Liang *software company executive, educator*
Macon, Carol Ann Gloeckler *micro-computer data base management company executive*
Malphurs, Roger Edward *biomedical marketing executive*
Maltin, Freda *retired university administrator*
Manion, Mary Patrice *recreation program director*
Marcus, Laura L. *remote control company executive, hypnotherapist*
Matthew, Lyn *sales and marketing executive consultant*
May, Robert *sales executive*
McCaw, Craig O. *communications executive*
McClendon, Irvin Lee, Sr. *company executive, computer consultant, writer and editor*
McDowell, Marcia Ann *security professional*
McInnis, Susan Musé *corporate communications manager*
McVeigh-Pettigrew, Sharon Christine *communications consultant*
Miller, Pamela Lynn *sales director*
Miller, Sean Jeffrey *information systems specialist*
Moore, Matthew Emerson *environmental program planning management specialist*
Nachman, Richard Joseph *management training executive*
Nason, Dolores Irene *computer company executive, counselor, eucharistic minister*
Niederman, Kim *marketing professional*
Nott, Carolyn Mary *water entertainment technology executive*
Novick, Stuart Allan *owner business consulting firm*
Olson, Floyd P. *service company executive*
Osborn, Susan Marie *management consultant*
Oviedo, Tamara Lenore *management consultant, photojournalist*
Parenti, Kathy Ann *sales professional*
Petrella, Ben Vincent *sales executive*
Philippi, Ervin William *mortician*
Pratt, Ronald Franklin *public relations executive*
Probasco, Dale Richard *management consultant*
Railsback, Sherrie Lee *adoption search and reunion consultant*
Rappaport, George Lee *communications executive, retired*
Rayl, India *marketing executive*
Rhyne, William J. *sales management consultant, musician*
Rini, William Anthony *communications company executive, multimedia engineer*
Rodrigues, Alfred Benjamin Kameeiamoku *marketing consultant*
Roiz, Myriam *foreign trade marketing executive*
Roller, Susan Lorrayne *industrial communications specialist, consultant*
Russell, Carol Ann *personnel service company executive*
Salzman, Marilyn B. Wolfson *service company executive*
Sanders, John Kenneth *marketing communications executive*
Saunders, Brian Keith *consulting company executive*
Scaglione, Cecil Frank *marketing executive, publisher*
Schultze, Ernst Eugene *marketing communications executive*
Sealing, Jeffery Alan *security officer, writer*
Simpson, Bob G. *retired quality assurance professional*
Smyth, Cornelius Edmonston *retired hotel executive*
Sommers, William Paul *management consultant, Research and development institute executive*
Sonntag, Martin Leroy *retired software company executive*
Spellman, Douglas Toby *advertising executive*
Spoor, James Edward *human resources executive, entrepreneur*
Springer, Gerald William *sales executive*
Srygley, Paul Dean *marketing manager*
Stangler, Greg Frank *infosystems executive*
Starkweather, Frederick Thomas *retired data processing executive*
Storozum, Steven Lee *marketing professional*
Terry, Richard Frank *data transcriber*
Thomas, Susan Duncan *fundraising consultant*
Thomas, Tom Edward *call center consultant*
Thompson, Craig Snover *corporate communications executive*
Thomson, Janyce K. *quality assurance administrator*
Tipton, Gary Lee *retired services company executive*
Toles, George Edward, Jr. *marketing communications executive*
Tooley, Charles Frederick *communications executive, consultant*
Tugend, Thomas Joseph *communications executive*
Underwood, Ralph Edward *computer systems engineer*
Unger, Stephen Alan *executive recruiter*
Valeskie-Hamner, Gail Yvonne *information systems specialist*
Vallerand, Philippe Georges *sales executive*
Verdiell, Jean-Marc *communications company executive*
von Linsowe, Marina Dorothy *information systems consultant*
... ... *computer company executive*
Weaver, Beth Ann *sales manager*
Werstiuk, Linda *hairstylist, photographic artist*
West, Billy Gene *public relations executive*

Wheaton, Alice Alshuler *administrative assistant*
White, Bonnie Yvonne *management consultant, retired educator*
White, Loray Betty *public relations executive, writer, actress, producer*
Wilkens, Steve *software marketing and sales executive*
Williams, Harry Edward *management consultant*
Wilton, Peter Campbell *marketing educator*
Winsor, David John *cost consultant*
Yakich, David Eli *international sales executive*
Yetto, John Henry *company executive*
Yocam, Delbert Wayne *software products company executive*
Yool, George Richard *consultant*
Zahn, Karl Theodore *information systems specialist, computer educator*
Zito, Michael Anthony *advertising and graphic design typesetting company owner*

INDUSTRY: TRADE

UNITED STATES

ALASKA

Anchorage
Schnell, Roger Thomas *business owner, state official, retired career officer*
Vandergriff, Jerry Dodson *retired computer store executive*

ARIZONA

Carefree
Adams, Sharron Ann Emanuel *business owner, educator*

Phoenix
Pasholk, Paul Douglas *retail executive, government official*
Weir, Jim Dale *small business owner*

Scottsdale
Boat, Ronald Allen *business executive*
Swenson, Susan Ann *engineering recruiting company executive*

Sun City
Thompson, Betty Jane *small business owner*

Tucson
Swanson, Cheryl Ann *small business owner, nurse*

ARKANSAS

Bentonville
Glass, David D. *department store company executive, professional baseball team executive*

CALIFORNIA

Alamo
Christoffersen, Susan Gray *small business owner*

Arcadia
Stangeland, Roger Earl *retail chain store executive*

Beverly Hills
Morris, Henry Arthur, Jr. *export company executive, consultant*
Orenstein, (Ian) Michael *philatelic dealer, columnist*
Rainey, Ron Paul *artist manager*

Burbank
Wise, Woodrow Wilson, Jr. *small business owner*

Burlingame
Wollega, Ras M. *small business owner, artist*

Chula Vista
Austin, Mary Jane *small business owner*

Danville
Ritchey, Samuel Donley, Jr. *retired retail store executive*

Emeryville
Weaver, Velather Edwards *small business owner*

Exeter
Pescosolido, Pamela Jane *legal research service owner, graphic designer*

Glendora
O'Hagan, William Gordon *state agency administrator*

Goleta
Winslow, Norman Eldon *business executive*

Grass Valley
Sjoberg, Jörgen Carl *business owner*

Harbor City
Briese, Leonard Arden *inventor*

Irvine
Webb, Lewis M. *retail executive*

La Quinta
Atkins, Honey Jean *retired business executive*

Lafayette
Koetser, David *export company executive*

Lancaster
Lawson, Marguerite Payne *small business owner*

Loomis
Keyston, Stephani Ann *small business owner*

Los Angeles
Blodgett, Julian Robert *small business owner*
Hawley, Philip Metschan *retired retail executive, consultant*
Lynch, Martin Andrew *retail company executive*
Player, Geraldine (Jeri Player) *small business executive*

Newark
Ferber, Norman Alan *retail executive*

Norwalk
Macon, Robin Jeffrey *small business owner*

Oakland
Little, William Paul *small business owner*
Spitzer, Matthew L. *retired retail store executive*

Orange
Underwood, Vernon O., Jr. *grocery stores executive*

Palo Alto
Carey, Theresa Wilkinson *small business owner, writer, editor*

Pleasant Hill
Dolan, Maryanne McLorn *small business owner, writer, educator, lecturer*

Redding
Streiff, Arlyne Bastunas *business owner, educator*

Riverside
Najjar, Tamara Litchfield *mail order business owner*

San Bernardino
Sagmeister, Edward Frank *business owner, hospitality industry executive, civic official, retired consultant, fund raiser, career officer*

San Diego
Saito, Frank Kiyoji *import-export firm executive*
Stoup, Thomas R. *bookstore owner, manager, retired educator*

San Francisco
Drexler, Millard S. *retail executive*
Fisher, Donald G. *casual apparel chain stores executive*
Seelenfreund, Alan *distribution company executive*
Sirdofsky, Katrina *personal manager, recording studio owner*
Ullman, Myron Edward, III *retail executive*

San Jacinto
Howard, Jo Ann *business owner*

San Jose
Pan, William Jiawei *import and export company executive, consultant*
Savage, Cynthia Gail *business owner*

Santa Ana
Fitzgerald, Robert Lynn *small business owner*
Shahin, Thomas John *dry cleaning wholesale supply company executive*

Santa Barbara
Bunn, Nadine *store owner*

Santa Cruz
Coonerty, Neal Patrick *small business owner*

Santa Fe Springs
Tripp, Susan Lynn *small business owner*

Santa Paula
Anderson, William *retail company executive, business education educator*

Sonoma
Morler, Edward Edwin *small business owner*

Stockton
Dornbush, Vicky Jean *medical billing systems executive*

Thousand Oaks
Knight, Jeffrey Richard *small business owner*

Upland
Graw, LeRoy Harry *purchasing-contract management company executive*

Walnut Creek
Bedsworth, O. Diane *retail executive*
Long, Robert Merrill *retail drug company executive*

Watsonville
Pye, David Thomas *specialty retail company executive*

West Sacramento
Teel, Joyce *supermarket and drugstore retail executive*

Westminster
Edwards, Charles Richard *retired printing equipment and supplies company executive*

COLORADO

Aurora
Magalnick, Elliott Ben *retail medical supply company executive*
Reynolds, Robert Harrison *retired export company executive*

Delta
Lowell, Lauretta Jane *craftsperson, poet*

Denver
Cashman, Michael Richard *small business owner*
Cheris, Elaine Gayle Ingram *business owner*
Etheridge, Clayton Dennis *small business owner*
Meyer, M. E. Joseph, III *small business owner*
Oakes, Terry Louis *retail clothing store executive*
Pracko, Bernard Francis, II *artist, business owner*
Yoches, Eliot Zachary (Denver) *small business owner*

Englewood
Tutt, Margaret Honnen *retail store owner*

Evergreen
Baxter, Millie McLean *business owner, educator*

Littleton
Bowe, Roger Lee *small business owner*

Loveland
Rodman, Alpine C. *arts and crafts company executive*
Rodman, Sue A. *wholesale Indian crafts company executive, artist, writer*

Pueblo
Pisciotta, Samuel James *small business owner*

Salida
Barnes, Robert James *small business owner, cosmetologist*

Westcliffe
Carson, Elizabeth Lorraine Neal *small business owner, civilian military employee*

HAWAII

Hanalei
Vogel, Richard Wiedemann *business owner, ichthyodynamicist, educator*

Honolulu
Lee, Candie Ching Wah *retail executive*
Miller, Georgia Ellen *business owner*
Nakabayashi, Nicholas Takateru *retired retail executive*

Kailua Kona
Luizzi, Ronald *wholesale distribution executive*

Waipahu
Matsui, Jiro *importer, wholesaler, small business owner*

IDAHO

Coeur D Alene
Jaeger, Ellen Louise *small business owner*

MONTANA

Gallatin Gateway
Johnson, Blanche Therese *small business owner*

NEVADA

Las Vegas
Danao, Danilo Gregorio *business owner*
Fitch, Bonnie Lynn *music store owner*

NEW MEXICO

Elephant Butte
Anton, Carol J. *small business owner, writer*

Farmington
Tucker, Janet Pike *employment agency owner*

Santa Fe
Furen, Shirley Ann *small business owner, art dealer*

Taos
Winslow, Bette Killingsworth *dance studio owner*

OREGON

Applegate
Pursglove, Betty Merle *computer-software quality assurance tester*

Bend
Nosler, Robert Amos *sports company executive*

Days Creek
Lassesen, Catherine Avery Clay *small business owner, manager, trainer*

Grants Pass
Lengwin, Emma Jean *small business owner*

Klamath Falls
Pastega, Richard Louis *retail specialist*

Medford
Stong, John Elliott *retail electronic company executive*

Myrtle Creek
Shirtcliff, John Delzell *business owner, oil jobber*

Portland
Greenstein, Merle Edward *import and export company executive*
Miller, Robert G. *retail company executive*
Paulson, Richard Guy *retail executive*

Ross, Moses Julian *wholesale distribution executive, publishing consultant*

Salem
Robertson, Marian Ella (Marian Ella Hall) *small business owner, handwriting analyst*
Snodgrass, Lynn *small business owner, state legislator*

TEXAS

Carrollton
Daily, John Scott, Sr. *small business owner, consumer products executive*

UTAH

Provo
Loflin, Andrea *small business owner*

Saint George
Day, John Denton *retired company executive, cattle and horse rancher, trainer, wrangler, actor, educator*

Salt Lake City
Cragun, Calvin *business owner*
Miller, Lorraine *business owner*

WASHINGTON

Bellingham
Olsen, Mark Norman *small business owner*

Elma
Sibbett, Gene *small business owner*

Everett
Olsen-Estie, Jeanne Lindell *golf course owner*

Issaquah
Brotman, Jeffrey H. *variety stores executive*
Sinegal, James D. *variety store wholesale business executive*

Lynnwood
Stocking, Sherl Dee *retail executive*

Redmond
Nagel, Daryl David *retail executive*

Seattle
Denniston, Martha Kent *business owner, author*
Fix, Wilbur James *department store executive*
Hagen, Larry William *manufacturing and retail executive*
Leale, Olivia Mason *import marketing company executive*
Nordstrom, Bruce A. *department store executive*
Nordstrom, John N. *department store executive*
Read, Charles Raymond, Sr. *business executive*
Stearns, Susan Tracey *lighting design company executive, lawyer*

Spokane
Sines, Randy Dwain *business executive*

Yakima
Newland, Ruth Laura *small business owner*

ADDRESS UNPUBLISHED

Busch, Joyce Ida *small business owner*
Card, Elizabeth Strobel *import company executive, journalist*
Debenham, Ray Gene *electric supply company executive*
Decker, Richard Kelsey *equipment distribution company executive*
Duffy, Harry Arthur *violin expert and dealer*
Edwards, Patricia Burr *small business owner, counselor, consultant*
Galvao, Louis Alberto *import and export corporation executive, consultant*
Green, Cyril Kenneth *retired retail company executive*
Kassner, Jay Edward *small business owner*
Kenna, Lawrence Allan *small business owner*
Martini, Robert Edward *wholesale pharmaceutical and medical supplies company executive*
Metz, Steven William *small business owner*
Phillips, Darrell *retail executive*
Thayer, Martha Ann *small business owner*
Tomkiel, Judith Irene *small business owner*
Williams, Leona Rae *lingerie shop owner, consultant*
Winfrey, Susan Carol *small business owner*
Winter, Richard Samuel, Jr. *computer training company owner, writer*
Zodl, Joseph Arthur *international trade executive, consultant*

INDUSTRY: TRANSPORTATION

UNITED STATES

ALASKA

Anchorage
Silverstein, Steven B. *railroad executive*

ARIZONA

Bullhead City
Hicks, Norm *airport operations executive*

Gilbert
Carrico, Donald Jefferson *public transit system manager*

Hayden
Jacobson, Lowell Steven (Jake Jacobson) *railroad executive*

Mesa
Aten, Fredrick Park *helicopter pilot, instructor, television engineer*

Phoenix
Amoako, James Kwaku *transportation services executive, financial analyst*
Bertholf, Neilson Allan, Jr. *aviation executive*
Mashalidis, Efstathios Steve *aeronautics educator, educational consultant*
Wood, John Mortimer *retired aerospace executive, aeronautical engineer*
Woods, Bobby Joe *transportation executive*

Scottsdale
Levy, Marian Muller *transportation executive*

Tucson
Burg, Walter A. *airport terminal executive*
Smith, Gordon Eugene *pilot*

CALIFORNIA

Bayside
Pierce, Lester Laurin *retired aviation consultant*

Burbank
Volk, Robert Harkins *aviation company executive*

Burlingame
Manit, Eddy C. *limousine company executive*

Camarillo
McConnel, Richard Appleton *aerospace company official*

Canoga Park
Hirschmann, Franz Gottfried *aerospace executive*

Corona Del Mar
Tether, Anthony John *aerospace executive*

Costa Mesa
Schooley, Otis Bryson, III *commercial airport executive*

Edwards
Smolka, James William *aerospace research pilot*

Encino
Gasich, Welko Elton *retired aerospace executive, management consultant*

Fountain Valley
Mauldin, Jean Humphries *aviation company executive*

Gardena
Hughes, Amber Lynn *parcel service company administrator*

Gilroy
Borton, George Robert *retired airline captain*

Hermosa Beach
Kokalj, James Edward *retired aerospace administrator*

Inyokern
Bass, Nancy Agnes *airport executive*

Irvine
MacDonnell, Kevin Michael *pilot*

Laguna Hills
Linhart, Eddie Gene *aerospace executive*

Lawndale
Warren, Stephan J. (Steve) *transportation executive*

Long Beach
Anderson, Gerald Verne *retired aerospace company executive*
Williams, David Alexander *pilot*

Los Altos
Stefanki, John X. *airline pilot*

Los Angeles
Anderson, Roy A. *aerospace company executive*
Coln, William Alexander, III *pilot*
Feldman, Nathaniel E. *aerospace engineering specialist*
Kresa, Kent *aerospace executive*
Moore, Walter Dengel *rapid transit system professional*
Puglisi, Davide Felice *rail transportation executive, consultant*
Williams, Walter David *aerospace executive, consultant*
Yee, Stephen *airport executive*

Mcclellan AFB
Dwyer, Roger Patrick *aviation executive, educator*

Menlo Park
Curry, Roger *trucking industry executive*
O'Brien, Raymond Francis *transportation executive*

Mission Viejo
LaRosa, Gianni *aerospace industry administrator*

Newbury Park
Lindsey, Joanne M. *flight attendant, poet*

Oakland
Reynolds, Kathleen Diane Foy (KDF Reynolds) *transportation executive*

Palo Alto
Moffitt, Donald Eugene *transportation company executive*

Palos Verdes Estates
Smith, Stephen Randolph *aerospace executive*

Rancho Palos Verdes
Slusser, Robert Wyman *aerospace company executive*

Redwood City
Waller, Stephen J *air transportation executive*

Sacramento
Engel, Thomas P. *airport executive*

San Diego
Williams, Douglas Arron *courier*

San Francisco
Anschutz, Philip F. *transportation executive*
Brice, Charles Steven *airline executive*
Freitag, Peter Roy *transportation specialist*
Takeuchi, Hajime Jim *airline executive, electrical engineer*

San Jose
Jackson, Douglas Leon *airline pilot*

San Mateo
Trabitz, Eugene Leonard *aerospace company executive*

Stockton
Biddle, Donald Ray *aerospace company executive*
DeAngelis, Dan *transportation executive*

Sunnyvale
Finnie, C(larence) Herbert (Herb Finnie) *aerospace company executive*

Temecula
Kinsler, Bruce Whitney *air traffic controller, consultant, air traffic control engineer, air defense engineer, air traffic control automation specialist*

Vallejo
Braxton, Bonnit D. *former transportation planner, music producer*

Van Nuys
Stender, Charles Frederick *test pilot*

COLORADO

Arvada
Childs, Donald Samuel *truck driver*

Aspen
Edwards, H. Boyd *air transportation executive*

Aurora
Minnich, Joseph Edward *tourist railway consultant*

Boulder
Stone, John Helms, Jr. *admiralty advisor*

Colorado Springs
Freeman, J. P. Ladyhawk *underwater exploration, security and transportation executive, educator, fashion model*

Denver
Rokosz, Richard Eugene *aerospace manager*

Englewood
Claussen, Bonnie Addison, II *aerospace company executive*

Georgetown
Ashby, Lindsey Gordon *railroad transportation executive*

Littleton
Burgess, Larry Lee *aerospace executive*

HAWAII

Honolulu
Pfeiffer, Robert John *business executive*
Wood, Cathy Lorraine *flight attendant*

IDAHO

Idaho Falls
Thorsen, James Hugh *aviation director, airport manager, retired*

MONTANA

Chester
LaSorte, Joseph John *rail transportation executive*

NEVADA

Las Vegas
Di Palma, Joseph Alphonse *airline company executive, lawyer*

Reno
White, Robert C. *air transportation executive*

NEW MEXICO

Albuquerque
Weh, Allen Edward *airline executive*

Farmington
Anderson, Mark Eugene *specialized truck driver, safety inspector*

OREGON

Aloha
Jones, Charles J. *transportation executive, firefighter*

Eugene
Phillips, Jane Banning *aviatrix, pilot examiner and flight instructor*

Mcminnville
Lane, Larry K. *air industry service executive*

Portland
Cheston, Michael Galloway *airport executive*

UTAH

Bountiful
Clement, Walter Hough *retired railroad executive*

Salt Lake City
Bouley, Joseph Richard *pilot*

West Jordan
Strasburg, Linda Ann *transportation executive, college official, clinical hypnotherapist*

WASHINGTON

Seattle
Cella, John J. *freight company executive*
Chittick, Arden Boone *steamship agency executive*
Clarkson, Lawrence William *airplane company executive*
Cline, Robert Stanley *air freight company executive*
Condit, Philip Murray *aerospace executive, engineer*
Miller, Paige *port executive*
Simmons, Newton Lester *aircraft company executive*

Spanaway
Loete, Steven Donald *pilot*

Sumner
Goodman, William Lee *commercial pilot*

Tacoma
Slater, Don Austin *shipyard executive, consultant*

CANADA

ALBERTA

Calgary
McCaig, Jeffrey James *transportation company executive*
Paquette, Richard *airport executive*

ONTARIO

Toronto
Turpen, Louis A. *airport terminal executive*

ADDRESS UNPUBLISHED

Ashley, LaDell Carol *transportation executive*
Boldon, Allifee *aerospace company executive*
Cassidy, Donald Lawrence *former aerospace company executive*
Cook, Stephen Champlin *retired shipping company executive*
Crowder, Richard Morgan *pilot*
Freitag, Kurt B. *trucking executive*
Gray, Richard Arden *transportation executive*
Hidalgo, Miguel *transportation company executive*
Kerbs, Wayne Allan *transportation executive*

INDUSTRY: UTILITIES, ENERGY, RESOURCES

UNITED STATES

ALASKA

Nikiski
Bumbaugh, Robert Warren, Sr. *oil industry executive*

ARIZONA

Cave Creek
LeNeau, Thomas Ervin *retired gas company executive*

Phoenix
LeonGuerrero, David Mesa *telecommunications company official*
St. Clair, Thomas McBryar *mining and manufacturing company executive*

Yearley, Douglas Cain *mining and manufacturing company executive*

Prescott
Bennett, Kenneth R. *oil company executive, school board executive*

Scottsdale
Baker, Jeffrey Charles *telecommunications executive*
Doyle, Michael Joseph *mining executive*

Sun City
Gustafson, Richard Paul *utilities administrator*

Tempe
Clevenger, Jeffrey Griswold *mining company executive*

Tucson
Davis, James Luther *retired utilities executive, lawyer*
Pillar, Charles Littlefield *retired mining consultant*

CALIFORNIA

Alameda
Lu, Wei *telecommunications executive*

Anaheim
Fenton, Donald Mason *retired oil company executive*

Camarillo
MacAlister, Robert Stuart *oil company executive*

El Segundo
Beach, Roger C. *oil company executive*
Imle, John F., Jr. *oil company executive*

Elk Grove
Prince, Terry *organizing consultant*

Folsom
Mine, Hilary Anne *telecommunications company executive, consultant*

Irvine
Hong, Ki Choong *oil recovery expert*

La Jolla
Rinaker, Samuel Mayo, Jr. *retired utilities executive*

La Puente
Dickerman, Robert N. *energy company executive*

Long Beach
Duarte, Luiz Guilherme *telecommunication consultant, journalist*

Los Angeles
Bowlin, Michael Ray *oil company executive*
Davis, Marvin *petroleum company executive, entrepreneur*
Foley, John V. *water company executive*
Jonker, Peter Emile *gas company executive*

Manteca
Talmage, Kenneth Kellogg *business executive*

Martinez
Meyer, Jarold Alan *oil company research executive*

Menlo Park
Quigley, Philip J. *telecommunications industry executive*

Monterey Park
Montag, David Moses *telecommunications company executive*

Newport Beach
Armstrong, Robert Arnold *petroleum company executive*

Rosemead
Bryson, John E. *utilities company executive*

Roseville
Rose, Sharon Marie *telecommunications professional*

San Diego
Alevy, Scott David *telecommunications company executive*

San Francisco
Blackburn, Frank Thomas *emergency water supply executive*
Bonney, John Dennis *retired oil company executive*
Clarke, Richard Alan *electric and gas utility company executive, lawyer*
Derr, Kenneth T. *oil company executive*
Ginn, Sam L. *telephone company executive*
Glynn, Robert D., Jr. *energy-based holding company*
Littlefield, Edmund Wattis *mining company executive*
Sullivan, James N. *fuel company executive*

San Jose
Juarez, Manuel J. *water company executive*

San Ramon
Grady, Cheryl Rae *telecommunications executive*

Stanford
Brinegar, Claude Stout *retired oil company executive*

Templeton
Gandsey, Louis John *petroleum and environmental consultant*

Van Nuys
Fisher, Earl Monty *utilities executive*

COLORADO

Colorado Springs
Russel, Richard Allen *telecommunications consultant, aerospace engineer, nuclear engineer, electrical engineer, retired naval officer*

Denver
Isaacs, Jonathan William *oil company executive*
Loucks, Thomas Alexander *mining industry executive*
McCormick, Richard *telecommunications company executive*
Morel, John A. *oil and gas consulting company owner, geologist*
Pepper, John Roy *oil and gas executive*
Taylor, Leslie George *mining and financial company executive*
Wynkoop, Donal Brooke *electric power company executive*

Durango
Thurston, William Richardson *oil and gas industry executive, geologist*

Englewood
Dreher, Richard Carl *telecommunications executive, educator*
Malone, John C. *telecommunications executive*
Teague, Don *telecommunications company executive*
Ward, Milton Hawkins *mining company executive*

Grand Junction
Pforzheimer, Harry, Jr. *oil consultant*

Lakewood
Hall, Larry D. *energy company executive, lawyer*

Littleton
Haley, John David *petroleum consulting company executive*
VanderLinden, Camilla Denice Dunn *telecommunications industry manager*

HAWAII

Honolulu
Bates, George E. *oil industry executive*
Clarke, Robert F. *utilities company executive*

Kaneohe
Amioka, Wallace Shuzo *retired petroleum company executive*

IDAHO

Boise
Stead, Jerre L. *telecommunications company executive*

Idaho Falls
Newman, Stanley Ray *oil refining company executive*

Mountain Home
Hiddleston, Ronal Eugene *drilling and pump company executive*

MONTANA

Billings
Nance, Robert Lewis *oil company executive*

Butte
Bishop, Robert Charles *architect, metals and minerals company executive*

NEVADA

Las Vegas
Garcia-Borras, Thomas *oil company executive*
Grace, John William *electrical company executive*

Reno
Busig, Rick Harold *mining executive*

NEW MEXICO

Hobbs
Garey, Donald Lee *pipeline and oil company executive*

Roswell
Robinson, Mark Leighton *oil company executive, petroleum geologist, horse farm owner*

Santa Fe
Reichman, Nanci Satin *oil company owner*
Shepard, Robert Henry *retired oil company executive*

OREGON

Bend
Miller, William Elwood *mining company executive*

Neskowin
Sifford, Benton Alexander, III *energy consultant*

Portland
Bacon, Vicky Lee *lighting services executive*
Frisbee, Don Calvin *retired utilities executive*
McCall, William Calder *oil and chemical company executive*
Reiten, Richard G. *natural gas industry executive*

Salem
Fischer, Rudolph F. *oil company chemical researcher*

UTAH

Magna
Albanese, Thomas *minerals company executive*

WASHINGTON

Bellevue
Weaver, William Schildecker *electric power industry executive*

Federal Way
Vaughan, Russell Fredric *internet executive*

Richland
Wright, Malcolm Sturtevant *nuclear facility manager, retired career officer*

Seattle
Beighle, Douglas Paul *electric power industry executive*
Smith, Andrew Vaughn *telephone company executive*

Sequim
Beaton, Roy Howard *retired nuclear industry executive*

Spokane
Ouellette, Reginald A. *oil industry executive*

Vancouver
Powell, Lee Gilbert, Jr. *petroleum company executive*

WYOMING

Casper
Smith, Dick Martin *oil field service company executive, owner*

Cheyenne
Weeks, William Rawle, Jr. *oil company executive*

Riverton
Bebout, Eli Daniel *oil executive*

CANADA

ALBERTA

Calgary
Furnival, George Mitchell *petroleum and mining consultant*
Isautier, Bernard François *business executive*
Maier, Gerald James *natural gas transmission and marketing company executive*
McIntyre, Norman F. *petroleum industry executive*
Mc Kee, John Angus *oil company executive*
Southern, Ronald D. *diversified corporation executive*

BRITISH COLUMBIA

Vancouver
Cecil. Robert Salisbury *telecommunications company executive*
Phelps, Michael Everett Joseph *energy company executive*

ADDRESS UNPUBLISHED

Ataie, Ata Jennati *oil products marketing executive*
Binder, James Kauffman *computer consultant*
Cashatt, Charles Alvin *retired hydro-electric power generation company executive*
Chen, George Chi-Ming *energy company executive*
Counsil, William Glenn *electric utility executive*
Eltringham, Thomas James Gyger *telecommunications professional*
Engel, Linda Jeanne *mining executive*
Hesse, Christian August *mining and underground construction consultant*
Krempel, Roger Ernest *public works management consultant*
Land, Kenneth Dean *test and balance agency executive, energy and environmental consultant*
McCready, Kenneth Frank *past electric utility executive*
Ormasa, John *retired utility executive, lawyer*
Osterhoff, James Marvin *retired telecommunications company executive*
Wharton, Thomas William *mining executive*
Wood, Willis Bowne, Jr. *retired utility holding company executive*

LAW: JUDICIAL ADMINISTRATION

UNITED STATES

ALASKA

Anchorage
Branson, Albert Harold (Harry Branson) *magistrate judge, educator*
Bryner, Alexander O. *state supreme court justice*
Compton, Allen T. *state supreme court justice*
Eastaugh, Robert L. *state supreme court justice*
Fabe, Dana Anderson *judge*
Holland, H. Russel *federal judge*
Singleton, James Keith *federal judge*

Bethel
Cooke, Christopher Robert *judge*
McMahon, Craig Roger *magistrate*

Fairbanks
Kleinfeld, Andrew Jay *federal judge*

ARIZONA

Phoenix
Canby, William Cameron, Jr. *federal judge*
Carroll, Earl Hamblin *federal judge*
Case, Charles G., II *federal bankruptcy judge*
Ehrlich, Susan Anne *judge*
Feldman, Stanley George *state supreme court justice*
Jones, Charles E. *state supreme court justice*
Martone, Frederick J. *state supreme court justice*
McGregor, Ruth Van Roekel *state supreme court justice*
McNamee, Stephen M. *federal judge*
Meyerson, Gregory Z. *judge, lawyer*
Rosenblatt, Paul Gerhardt *judge*
Schroeder, Mary Murphy *federal judge*
Strand, Roger Gordon *federal judge*
Weisenburger, Theodore Maurice *judge, poet, educator, writer*
Zlaket, Thomas A. *state supreme court justice*

Springerville
Geisler, Sherry Lynn *magistrate*

Tucson
Bilby, Richard Mansfield *federal judge*
Browning, William Docker *federal judge*
Roll, John McCarthy *judge*

CALIFORNIA

Berkeley
Schneider, Thomas *retired administrative law judge, mediator*

Fresno
Coyle, Robert Everett *federal judge*
Goodwin, Richard Cyrus *judge*
Wanger, Oliver Winston *federal judge*

Huntington Beach
Emerson, (Virgil) Leon *retired judge*

Imperial
Staton, Jack Warren *immigration judge*

Long Beach
Tucker, Marcus Othello *judge*

Los Angeles
Ahart, Alan M. *bankruptcy judge*
Alarcon, Arthur Lawrence *federal judge*
Armstrong, Orville *judge*
Baird, Lourdes G. *federal judge*
Bufford, Samuel Lawrence *federal judge*
Byrne, William Matthew, Jr. *federal judge*
Hatter, Terry Julius, Jr. *federal judge*
Hupp, Harry L. *federal judge*
Keller, William D. *federal judge*
Kenyon, David V. *federal judge*
Letts, J. Spencer *federal judge*
Lew, Ronald S. W. *federal judge*
Marshall, Consuelo Bland *federal judge*
Nelson, Rodney Ellsworth *judge*
Pfaelzer, Mariana R. *federal judge*
Rafeedie, Edward, Sr. *federal judge*
Rea, William J. *judge*
Real, Manuel Lawrence *federal judge*
Takasugi, Robert Mitsuhiro *federal judge*
Tevrizian, Dickran M., Jr. *federal judge*
Williams, David Welford *federal judge*
Wilson, Stephen Victor *federal judge*

Moraga
Harrington, Charles Lee *retired judge*

Oakland
Armstrong, Saundra Brown *federal judge*
Cline, Wilson Ettason *retired judge*
Jensen, D. Lowell *federal judge, lawyer, government official*

Pasadena
Boochever, Robert *federal judge*
Fernandez, Ferdinand Francis *federal judge*
Hall, Cynthia Holcomb *federal judge*
Klein, Earl H(yman) *judge*
Kozinski, Alex *federal judge*
Nelson, Dorothy Wright (Mrs. James F. Nelson) *federal judge*
Rymer, Pamela Ann *federal judge*
Tashima, Atsushi Wallace *federal judge*
Wardlaw, Kim A.M. *judge*

Redwood City
Harrington, Walter Howard, Jr. *judge*

Richmond
Herron, Ellen Patricia *retired judge*

Sacramento
Burrell, Garland E., Jr. *federal judge*
Garcia, Edward J. *federal judge*
Karlton, Lawrence K. *federal judge*
Levi, David F. *federal judge*

San Diego
Adler, Louise DeCarl *bankruptcy judge*
Brewster, Rudi Milton *federal judge*
Gilliam, Earl B. *federal judge*
Gonzalez, Irma Elsa *federal judge*
Huff, Marilyn L. *federal judge*
Keep, Judith N. *federal judge*
Lewis, Gerald Jorgensen *judge*
Thompson, David Renwick *federal judge*
Thompson, Gordon, Jr. *federal judge*
Wallace, J. Clifford *federal judge*

San Francisco
Baxter, Marvin Ray *state supreme court justice*
Brennan, Joan Stevenson *federal judge*
Brown, Janice Rogers *state supreme court justice*
Browning, James Robert *federal judge*
Carlson, Thomas E. *bankruptcy judge*
Chesney, Maxine M. *judge*

Chin, Ming *state supreme court justice*
George, Ronald M. *state supreme court chief justice*
Henderson, Thelton Eugene *federal judge*
Jarvis, Donald Bertram *judge*
Kennard, Joyce L. *state supreme court justice*
Legge, Charles Alexander *federal judge*
Mosk, Stanley *state supreme court justice*
Noonan, John T., Jr. *federal judge, legal educator*
Patel, Marilyn Hall *judge*
Schwarzer, William W *federal judge*
Walker, Vaughn R. *federal judge*
Werdegar, Kathryn Mickle *state supreme court justice*

San Jose
Ware, James W. *federal judge*
Whyte, Ronald M. *federal judge*

San Marino
Mortimer, Wendell Reed, Jr. *judge*

Santa Ana
Barr, James Norman *federal judge*
McLaughlin, Linda Lee Hodge *federal judge*
Rylaarsdam, William F. *judge*
Stotler, Alicemarie Huber *judge*
Taylor, Gary L. *federal judge*

Santa Barbara
Pattillo, James Louis *retired judge*

Santa Monica
Vega, Benjamin Urbizo *retired judge, television producer*

Stockton
Guiliani, Richard James *judge*

Studio City
Lasarow, William Julius *retired federal judge*

West Hollywood
Norris, William Albert *former federal judge*

Woodland Hills
Lax, Kathleen Thompson *bankruptcy judge*
Mund, Geraldine *judge*
Pregerson, Harry *federal judge*

COLORADO

Central City
Rodgers, Frederic Barker *judge*

Denver
Babcock, Lewis Thornton *federal judge*
Bender, Michael Lee *state supreme court justice, lawyer*
Brooks, Sidney B. *bankruptcy judge*
Brumbaugh, Roland John *bankruptcy judge*
Ebel, David M. *federal judge*
Hobbs, Gregory James, Jr. *state supreme court justice*
Kirshbaum, Howard M. *judge, arbitrator*
Kourlis, Rebecca Love *judge*
Martinez, Alex *state supreme court justice*
Matsch, Richard P. *judge*
Miller, Walker David *judge*
Mullarkey, Mary J. *state supreme court justice*
Nottingham, Edward Willis, Jr. *federal judge*
Porfilio, John Carbone *federal judge*
Rice, Nancy E. *state supreme court justice*
Rovira, Luis Dario *state supreme court justice*
Schlatter, O. Edward *judge*
Scott, Gregory Kellam *state supreme court justice*
Sparr, Daniel Beattie *federal judge*
Vollack, Anthony F. *former state supreme court justice*
Weinshienk, Zita Leeson *federal judge*

Englewood
Erickson, William Hurt *retired state supreme court justice*

HAWAII

Honolulu
Choy, Herbert Young Cho *federal judge*
Dannenberg, James Harry *lawyer, retired judge*
Ezra, David Alan *federal judge*
Gillmor, Helen *federal judge*
Heen, Walter Meheula *retired judge, political party executive*
Kay, Alan Cooke *federal judge*
King, Samuel Pailthorpe *federal judge*
Klein, Robert Gordon *state supreme court justice*
Levinson, Steven Henry *state supreme court justice*
Moon, Ronald T. Y. *state supreme court justice*
Nakayama, Paula Aiko *state supreme court justice*
Pence, Martin *federal judge*
Ramil, Mario R. *state supreme court justice*
Watanabe, Corinne Kaoru Amemiya *lawyer, judge, state official*
Yamashita, Francis Isami *magistrate judge*

IDAHO

Boise
Boyle, Larry Monroe *federal judge*
Hagan, Alfred Chris *federal judge*
Kidwell, Wayne L. *judge*
Lodge, Edward James *federal judge*
McDevitt, Charles Francis *state supreme court justice*
Nelson, Thomas G. *federal judge*
Pappas, Jim D. *chief bankruptcy judge*
Silak, Cathy R. *state supreme court justice*
Trott, Stephen Spangler *federal judge, musician*
Walters, Jesse Raymond, Jr. *judge*
Williams, Mikel H. *magistrate judge*
Winmill, B. Lynn *judge*

MONTANA

Billings
Shanstrom, Jack D. *federal judge*

Great Falls
Hatfield, Paul Gerhart *federal judge, lawyer*

Helena
Gray, Karla Marie *state supreme court justice*
Harrison, John Conway *state supreme court justice*
Hunt, William E., Sr. *state supreme court justice*
Leaphart, W. William *state supreme court justice*
Lovell, Charles C. *federal judge*
McDonough, Russell Charles *retired state supreme court justice*
Nelson, James C *state supreme court justice*
Regnier, James *state supreme court justice*
Trieweiler, Terry Nicholas *state supreme court justice*
Turnage, Jean A. *state supreme court justice*

NEVADA

Carson City
Agosti, Deborah *judge*
Becker, Nancy Anne *state supreme court justice*
Leavitt, Myron E *judge*
Maupin, Bill *state supreme court justice*
Rose, Robert E(dgar) *state supreme court justice*
Springer, Charles Edward *retired state supreme court chief justice*
Young, C. Clifton *state supreme court justice*

Las Vegas
George, Lloyd D. *federal judge*
Hunt, Roger Lee *judge*
Johnston, Robert Jake *federal magistrate judge*
Karau, Jon Olin *judge*
Pro, Philip Martin *judge*

Reno
Brunetti, Melvin T. *federal judge*
Gladstone, Arthur Abraham *judge, educator*
Hagen, David Warner *judge*
Hug, Procter Ralph, Jr. *federal judge*
McKibben, Howard D. *federal judge*
Reed, Edward Cornelius, Jr. *federal judge*

NEW MEXICO

Albuquerque
Conway, John E. *federal judge*
Hansen, Curtis LeRoy *federal judge*
Parker, James Aubrey *federal judge*

Las Cruces
Bratton, Howard Calvin *federal judge*

Los Lunas
Pope, John William *judge, law educator*

Roswell
Baldock, Bobby Ray *federal judge*

Santa Fe
Baca, Joseph Francis *state supreme court justice*
Campos, Santiago E. *federal judge*
Franchini, Gene Edward *state supreme court justice*
Kelly, Paul Joseph, Jr. *judge*
Maes, Petra Jimenez *state supreme court justice*
Minzner, Pamela B. *state supreme court justice*
Serna, Patricio *state supreme court justice*

OREGON

Eugene
Coffin, Thomas M. *federal magistrate judge*
Hogan, Michael R(obert) *judge*
Radcliffe, Albert E. *bankruptcy judge*

North Bend
Bechtold, Paula Miller *judge*

Portland
Frye, Helen Jackson *judge*
Graber, Susan P. *judge*
Jones, Robert Edward *federal judge*
Leavy, Edward *judge*
Marsh, Malcolm F. *federal judge*
O'Scannlain, Diarmuid Fionntain *judge*
Panner, Owen M. *federal judge*
Redden, James Anthony *federal judge*
Unis, Richard L. *judge*

Salem
Carson, Wallace Preston, Jr. *state supreme court justice*
Durham, Robert Donald, Jr. *state supreme court justice*
Kulongoski, Theodore Ralph *state supreme court justice*
Leeson, Susan M. *state judge*
Peterson, Edwin J. *retired supreme court justice, law educator*
Riggs, William *state judge*
Van Hoomissen, George Albert *state supreme court justice*

UTAH

Salt Lake City
Anderson, Stephen Hale *federal judge*
Benson, Dee Vance *federal judge*
Campbell, Tena *judge*
Clark, Glen Edward *judge*
Durham, Christine Meaders *state supreme court justice*
Greene, John Thomas *judge*
[illegible] *retired state supreme court chief justice*
Howe, Richard Cuddy *state supreme court chief justice*
Jenkins, Bruce Sterling *federal judge*
McKay, Monroe Gunn *federal judge*

Murphy, Michael R. *federal judge*
Rigtrup, Kenneth *state judge, arbitrator, mediator*
Russon, Leonard H. *state supreme court justice*
Sam, David *federal judge*
Stewart, Isaac Daniel, Jr. *state supreme court justice*
Winder, David Kent *federal judge*
Zimmerman, Michael David *state supreme court justice*

WASHINGTON

Olympia
Alexander, Gerry L. *state supreme court justice*
Durham, Barbara *state supreme court justice*
Guy, Richard P. *state supreme court justice*
Ireland, Faith *judge*
Johnson, Charles William *state supreme court justice*
Sanders, Richard Browning *state supreme court justice*
Smith, Charles Z. *state supreme court justice*

Seattle
Beezer, Robert Renaut *federal judge*
Coughenour, John Clare *federal judge*
Dimmick, Carolyn Reaber *federal judge*
Dwyer, William L. *federal judge*
Farris, Jerome *federal judge*
Fletcher, Betty B. *federal judge*
Mc Govern, Walter T. *federal judge*
Overstreet, Hon. Karen A. *federal bankruptcy judge*
Rothstein, Barbara Jacobs *federal judge*
Zilly, Thomas Samuel *federal judge*

Spokane
Bastine, Paul Arthur *judge*
Imbrogno, Cynthia *magistrate judge*
Nielsen, William Fremming *federal judge*
Quackenbush, Justin Lowe *federal judge*
Van Sickle, Frederick L. *federal judge*
Whaley, Robert Hamilton *judge*

Tacoma
Bryan, Robert J. *federal judge*

Yakima
McDonald, Alan Angus *federal judge*
Suko, Lonny Ray *judge*

WYOMING

Cheyenne
Brimmer, Clarence Addison *federal judge*
Brorby, Wade *federal judge*
Golden, T. Michael *state supreme court justice*
Hill, William U. *state supreme court justice*
Johnson, Alan Bond *federal judge*
Lehman, Larry L. *state supreme court justice*
Macy, Richard J. *state supreme court justice*
Schrader, Robert Wesley *judge*
Taylor, William Al *state supreme court justice*
Thomas, Richard Van *state supreme court justice*

Green River
Marty, Lawrence A. *magistrate*

TERRITORIES OF THE UNITED STATES

GUAM

Barrigada
Diaz, Ramon Valero *retired judge*

NORTHERN MARIANA ISLANDS

Saipan
Dela Cruz, Jose Santos *retired state supreme court chief justice*

CANADA

ALBERTA

Edmonton
Fraser, Catherine Anne *Canadian chief justice*

ADDRESS UNPUBLISHED

Boulden, Judith Ann *bankruptcy judge*
Burke, Edmond Wayne *retired judge, lawyer*
Dolliver, James Morgan *retired state supreme court justice*
Finesilver, Sherman Glenn *retired federal judge*
Gillette, W. Michael *state supreme court justice*
Linde, Hans Arthur *state supreme court justice*
Madsen, Barbara A *state supreme court justice*
Matthews, Warren Wayne *state supreme court justice*
McKee, Roger Curtis *retired federal magistrate judge*
Montgomery, Seth David *retired state supreme court chief justice*
Moore, Daniel Alton, Jr. *retired state supreme court justice*
Reinhardt, Stephen Roy *federal judge*
Rowen, Marvin David *judge*
Schroeder, Gerald F. *state supreme court justice*
Shearing, Miriam *state supreme court justice*
Shubb, William Barnet *judge*
Smith, Fern M. *judge*
Talmadge, Philip Albert *state [illegible] justice, former state senator*
Trout, Linda Copple *state supreme court justice*
Utter, Robert French *retired state supreme court justice*
[illegible], Fred J. *retired state supreme court justice*
Wiggins, Charles Edward *judge*

LAW: LAW PRACTICE AND ADMINISTRATION

UNITED STATES

ALASKA

Anchorage
Anderson, Kathleen Gay *mediator, hearing officer, arbitrator, educator*
Bundy, Robert Charles *prosecutor*
Butler, Rex Lamont *lawyer*
Fleischer, Hugh William *lawyer*
Fortier, Samuel John *lawyer*
Groh, Clifford John, Sr. *lawyer*
Hughes, Mary Katherine *lawyer*
Oesting, David W. *lawyer*
Owens, Robert Patrick *lawyer*
Reeves, James N. *lawyer*
Senungetuk, Vivian Ruth *lawyer*

Fairbanks
Rice, Julian Casavant *lawyer*

Juneau
Cole, Charles Edward *lawyer, former state attorney general*

Kodiak
Jamin, Matthew Daniel *lawyer, magistrate judge*
Ogg, R. Danforth *lawyer, commercial fishing administrator, fisherman*
Ott, Andrew Eduard *lawyer*

ARIZONA

Flagstaff
Pickett, A(lbert) Dean *lawyer*

Kingman
Basinger, Richard Lee *lawyer*

Mesa
Gainer, Michael Edward *legal assistant*
Hicks, Bethany Gribben *lawyer, commissioner*

Oro Valley
Robinson, Bernard Leo *retired lawyer*

Phoenix
Allen, Robert Eugene Barton *lawyer*
Beggs, Harry Mark *lawyer*
Brown, Jack Edward *lawyer*
Chanen, Steven Robert *lawyer*
Cohen, Ronald Jay *lawyer*
Comus, Louis Francis, Jr. *lawyer*
Condo, James Robert *lawyer*
Coppersmith, Sam *lawyer*
Corson, Kimball Jay *lawyer*
Dawson, John Joseph *lawyer*
Derdenger, Patrick *lawyer*
Derouin, James G. *lawyer*
Dunipace, Ian Douglas *lawyer*
Ehmann, Anthony Valentine *lawyer*
Evens, Timothy Walt *lawyer*
Forshey, Timothy Allan *lawyer*
Gaines, Francis Pendleton, III *lawyer*
Gallagher, Michael L. *lawyer*
Gauby, Karl Martin *lawyer, educator*
Gilbert, Donald Roy *lawyer*
Gilbert, Paul Ensign *lawyer*
Gladner, Marc Stefan *lawyer*
Hammond, Larry Austin *lawyer*
Hay, John Leonard *lawyer*
Hirsch, Steven A. *lawyer*
Holden, Michael John *lawyer*
Jakubczyk, John Joseph *lawyer*
James, Charles E., Jr. *lawyer*
Jirauch, Charles W. *lawyer*
Klahr, Gary Peter *lawyer*
Klausner, Jack Daniel *lawyer*
Klein, R. Kent *lawyer*
Knoller, Guy David *lawyer*
Koester, Berthold Karl *lawyer, educator, retired honorary German consul*
Kreutzberg, David W. *lawyer*
Le Clair, Douglas Marvin *lawyer, educator, judge*
Lindholm, Donald Wayne *lawyer*
Lundin, John E. *lawyer*
MacDonnell, Philip J. *lawyer*
Madden, Paul Robert *lawyer*
McDaniel, Joseph Chandler *lawyer*
McRae, Hamilton Eugene, III *lawyer*
Meschkow, Jordan Mark *patent lawyer*
Meyers, Howard Craig *lawyer*
Meyerson, Bruce Elliot *lawyer*
Napolitano, Janet Ann *prosecutor*
Norris, Raymond Michael *lawyer*
Olson, Robert Howard *lawyer*
Perry, Lee Rowan *retired lawyer*
Pietzsch, Michael Edward *lawyer*
Platt, Warren E. *lawyer*
Rose, Scott A. *lawyer*
Sherk, Kenneth John *lawyer*
Silverman, Alan Henry *lawyer*
Smith, Susan Kimsey *lawyer*
Stahl, Louis A. *lawyer*
Storey, Norman C. *lawyer*
Thompson, Joel Erik *lawyer*
Thompson, Terence William *lawyer*
Udall, Calvin Hunt *lawyer*
Ulrich, Paul Graham *lawyer, author, publisher, editor*
Walker, Richard K. *lawyer*
Wheeler, Steven M. *lawyer*
Woolf, Michael E. *lawyer*

Portal
[illegible], Henry Weber *lawyer*

Prescott
[illegible] *lawyer*

Scottsdale
[illegible] *lawyer*
Mybeck, Richard Raymond *lawyer*
Peshkin, Samuel David *lawyer*

Reisdorf, Edward Gary *lawyer, real estate executive*
Sears, Alan Edward *lawyer*
Simonson, Michael *lawyer, judge*

Sun City
Hauer, James Albert *lawyer*
Treece, James Lyle *lawyer*

Sun City West
Gillen, Arthur Fitzpatrick *retired lawyer*

Surprise
Hayes, Ray, Jr. *lawyer*

Tempe
Evans, Lawrence Jack, Jr. *lawyer*

Tucson
Betteridge, Frances Carpenter *retired lawyer, mediator*
Blackman, Jeffrey William *lawyer*
Boswell, Susan G. *lawyer*
Levitan, Roger Stanley *lawyer*
Meehan, Michael Joseph *lawyer*
Rollins, Michael F. *lawyer*
Simmons, Sarah R. *lawyer*
Waterman, David Moore *lawyer*

Yuma
Hossler, David Joseph *lawyer, law educator*

CALIFORNIA

Altadena
Vaughan, Audrey Judd *paralegal, musician*

Antioch
Richards, Gerald Thomas *lawyer, consultant, educator*

Auburn
Henry, Karen Hawley *lawyer*

Bakersfield
Kind, Kenneth Wayne *lawyer, real estate broker*
Martin, George Francis *lawyer*
Young, John Byron *retired lawyer*

Belvedere Tiburon
Buell, Edward Rick, II *lawyer*

Berkeley
Berring, Robert Charles, Jr. *law educator, law librarian, former dean*
Goldsmith, Donald William *lawyer, astronomer, writer*
Hetland, John Robert *lawyer, educator*
Hu, Chi-an *law educator*
Medak, Walter Hans *lawyer*
Ogg, Wilson Reid *lawyer, poet, retired judge, lyricist, curator, publisher, educator, philosopher, social scientist, parapsychologist*
Peterson, Andrea Lenore *law educator*
Reilley, Kathleen Patricia *lawyer*
Scheiber, Harry N. *law educator*

Beverly Hills
Bordy, Michael Jeffrey *lawyer*
Dickerson, William Roy *lawyer*
Donaldson, Michael Cleaves *lawyer*
Florence, Kenneth James *lawyer*
Genow, Richard Martin *lawyer*
Haile, Lawrence Barclay *lawyer*
Holmes, Henry W. *lawyer*
Horwin, Leonard *lawyer*
Jessup, W. Edgar, Jr. *lawyer*
Nicholas, Frederick M. *lawyer*
Ramer, Bruce M. *lawyer*
Rosen, Stuart Jay *defender*
Rosky, Burton Seymour *lawyer*
Russell, Irwin Emanuel *lawyer*
Schiff, Gunther Hans *lawyer*
Shacter, David Mervyn *lawyer*
Share, Mark Lowell *lawyer*
Shire, Harold Raymond *law educator, author, scientist*
Sobelle, Richard E. *lawyer*
Thompson, Richard Dickson *lawyer*

Big Pine
Wood, Harold William *lawyer*

Brea
Lounsbury, Steven Richard *lawyer*
Pearson, April Virginia *lawyer*

Burbank
Butler, Daniel Blake *lawyer*
Litvack, Sanford Martin *lawyer*
Oswald, Christina Metcalf *lawyer*

Burlingame
Cotchett, Joseph Winters *lawyer, author*
Spyros, Nicholas L., Jr. *lawyer*

Calabasas
Bozajian, James Robert *lawyer*

Camarillo
Hughes, Andrew Scott *lawyer*

Carmichael
Stassinos, Gail *lawyer*

Chula Vista
Santee, Dale William *lawyer, air force officer*

Claremont
Sweeney, Marvin A. *religious studies educator*
Taylor, Elenor Rita *law educator, director*

Coalinga
Frame, Ted Ronald *lawyer*

Concord
Dye, Alan *lawyer*
Romeo, Peter *lawyer*

Kleinberg, James P. *lawyer*
Klott, David Lee *lawyer*
La Vine, Robert L. *lawyer*
Lee, John Jin *lawyer*
Lopes, James Louis *lawyer*
Lynch, Timothy Jeremiah-Mahoney *lawyer, educator, theologian, realtor, writer*
Mattes, Martin Anthony *lawyer*
Miles, Donald F. *lawyer*
Morrissey, John Carroll, Sr. *lawyer*
Peritore, Laura *law librarian*
Philipsborn, John Timothy *lawyer, author*
Pickett, Donn Philip *lawyer*
Preuss, Charles F. *lawyer*
Raven, Robert Dunbar *lawyer*
Reding, John Anthony *lawyer*
Reese, John Robert *lawyer*
Riley, William L. *lawyer*
Rogan, Richard A. *lawyer*
Roman, Stan G. *lawyer*
Roosevelt, Michael A. *lawyer*
Rosch, John Thomas *lawyer*
Rossmann, Antonio *lawyer, educator*
Saxe, Steven Louis *lawyer*
Scarlett, Randall H. *lawyer*
Schaffer, Jeffrey L. *lawyer*
Seabolt, Richard L. *lawyer*
Sevier, Ernest Youle *lawyer*
Shepherd, John Michael *lawyer*
Shiffman, Michael A. *lawyer*
Sibley, Peter Edward *lawyer*
Siniscalco, Gary Richard *lawyer*
Smegal, Thomas Frank, Jr. *lawyer*
Sochynsky, Yaroslav *lawyer, mediator, arbitrator*
Sorensen, Linda *lawyer*
Staring, Graydon Shaw *lawyer*
Stephenson, Charles Gayley *lawyer*
Sutcliffe, Eric *lawyer*
Thompson, Robert Charles *lawyer*
Thornton, Charles Victor *lawyer*
Truett, Harold Joseph, III (Tim Truett) *lawyer*
Walsh, Francis Richard *law educator, lawyer, arbitrator*
Weber, Arnold I. *lawyer*
Weiner, Peter H. *lawyer*
Wilson, John Pasley *law educator*
Wolfe, Cameron Withgot, Jr. *lawyer*
Wood, Robert Warren *lawyer*
Yamakawa, David Kiyoshi, Jr. *lawyer*

San Jose
Alexander, Richard *lawyer*
Anderson, Edward Virgil *lawyer*
Beizer, Lance Kurt *lawyer*
Bohn, Robert Herbert *lawyer*
Denver, Thomas H R *lawyer*
Jensen, Lawrence Robert *lawyer*
King, Ellen McGinty *lawyer*
Kraw, George Martin *lawyer, essayist*
Liccardo, Salvador A. *lawyer*
McManis, James *lawyer*
Nopar, Alan Scott *lawyer*
Simpson, Mary Kathleen *lawyer*
Terry, Michael Joseph *courtroom clerk*

San Leandro
Newacheck, David John *lawyer*

San Mateo
Kenney, William Fitzgerald *lawyer*
Mandel, Martin Louis *lawyer*

San Rafael
Drexler, Kenneth *lawyer*
Freitas, David Prince *lawyer*

Santa Ana
Dillard, John Martin *lawyer, pilot*
Dunn, Edward Thomas, Jr. *lawyer, educator*
Eisenberg, Jonathan Michael *lawyer*
Fay-Schmidt, Patricia Ann *paralegal*
Harley, Robison Dooling, Jr. *lawyer, educator*
Mei, Tom Y. K. *lawyer*
Schroeder, Michael John *lawyer*

Santa Barbara
McKinley, Patrick *prosecutor*
Puzder, Andrew F. *lawyer*
Reed, Frank Fremont, II *retired lawyer*
Willey, Charles Wayne *lawyer*

Santa Clara
Blawie, James Louis *law educator*
Kaner, Cem *lawyer, computer software consultant*
Toman, Jiří *law educator, institute director*

Santa Monica
English, Charles Royal *lawyer*
Genego, William Joseph *lawyer*
Hughes, Jeffrey John *lawyer, small business owner*
Loo, Thomas S. *lawyer*
McGovern, David Carr *lawyer*
Roberts, Virgil Patrick *lawyer, business executive*
Schwertfeger, Frank Dennis *lawyer*
Weatherup, Roy Garfield *lawyer*

Santa Rosa
Henderson, Joe H. *lawyer, mediator, arbitrator, college dean*
Lanahan, Daniel Joseph *lawyer*
Olsen, Stephen Raymond *lawyer*

Saratoga
Stephens, Lawrence Keith *lawyer*

Seaside
Weingarten, Saul Myer *lawyer*

Sherman Oaks
Joyce, Stephen Michael *lawyer*

South Lake Tahoe
Marshall, William Patrick *lawyer, croupier*

South Pasadena
Gary, Karl *law educator*

Stanford
Brest, Paul A. *law educator*
Mann, J. Keith *arbitrator, law educator, lawyer*
Sofaer, Abraham David *lawyer, legal advisor, federal judge, law educator*

Sunnyvale
Zahrt, William Dietrich, II *lawyer*

Temecula
Thompson, James Avery, Jr. *legal assistant, consumer credit consultant*

Thousand Oaks
Dougherty, Gerard Michael *lawyer*
Trover, Ellen Lloyd *lawyer*

Tiburon
Bauch, Thomas Jay *lawyer, educator, former apparel company executive*

Torrance
Kohan, Betsy Burns *lawyer*
Matsunaga, Geoffrey Dean *lawyer*
Moore, Christopher Minor *lawyer*
Van Emburgh, Joanne *lawyer*
Ward, Anthony John *lawyer*

Ukiah
Sager, Madeline Dean *lawyer*

Universal City
Peter, Arnold Philimon *lawyer, business executive*

Upland
Fabrick, Olga *lawyer*

Van Nuys
Arabian, Armand *arbitrator, mediator, lawyer*

Ventura
Bysshe, Frederick Herbert, Jr. *lawyer*
English, Woodrow Douglas *lawyer*
Gartner, Harold Henry, III *lawyer*

Vernon
Smith, Lawrence Ronald *lawyer*

Villa Park
Dougherty, William Andersen *lawyer*

Visalia
Crowe, John T. *lawyer*
Hart, Timothy Ray *lawyer, dean*

Vista
Rigby, Amanda Young *paralegal firm executive*

Walnut
McKee, Catherine Lynch *law educator, lawyer*

Walnut Creek
Miller, Eugene H. *lawyer*
Ney, Michael James *lawyer*
Nolan, David Charles *lawyer, mediator*
Schreiber, John T. *lawyer*

West Hollywood
Tansey, Roger Kent *lawyer*

Woodland Hills
Even, Randolph M. *lawyer*
Strote, Joel Richard *lawyer*

Woodside
Martin, Joseph, Jr. *retired lawyer, former ambassador*

Yorba Linda
Ward, Robert Richard *lawyer*

COLORADO

Boulder
Dubofsky, Jean Eberhart *lawyer, retired state supreme court justice*
Gray, William R. *lawyer*
Porzak, Glenn E. *lawyer*
Purvis, John Anderson *lawyer*

Colorado Springs
Campbell, Frederick Hollister *retired lawyer, historian*
Evans, Paul Vernon *lawyer*
Rowan, Ronald Thomas *lawyer*
Salley, George Henry, III *lawyer*
Youngblood, Deborah Sue *lawyer*

Commerce City
Trujillo, Lorenzo A. *lawyer, educator*

Denver
Archibold, John Ewing *lawyer, consultant*
Arundel, James D. *lawyer*
Ash, Walter Brinker *lawyer*
Berardini, Jacqueline Hernandez *lawyer*
Bradley, Joseph *lawyer*
Bronesky, Joseph J. *lawyer*
Byrne, Thomas J. *lawyer*
Carrigan, Jim R. *arbitrator, mediator, retired federal judge*
Cassidy, Samuel H. *lawyer, lieutenant governor, state legislator*
Cohen, Brent Ross *lawyer*
Commander, Eugene R. *lawyer*
Conover, Frederic King *lawyer*
Daniel, Wiley Y. *lawyer*
De Gette, Diana Louise *lawyer, congresswoman*
Dempsey, Howard Stanley *lawyer, mining executive, investment banker*
DeMuth, Alan Cornelius *lawyer*
Dowdle, Patrick Dennis *lawyer*
Edwards, Daniel Walden *lawyer*
Eklund, Carl Andrew *lawyer*
Erisman, Frank *lawyer*
Finesilver, Jay Mark *lawyer*
Gehres, James *lawyer*
Gelt, Theodore Zvi *lawyer, director*
Grissom, Garth Clyde *lawyer*
Harris, Dale Ray *lawyer*
Hensen, Stephen Jerome *lawyer*
Hodges, Joseph Gilluly, Jr. *lawyer*
Houtsma, Peter C. *lawyer*
Imig, William Graff *lawyer, lobbyist*
Irwin, R. Robert *lawyer*
Jessop, Douglas Wayne *lawyer*
Jones, Peter F. *lawyer*
Jonsen, Eric R. *lawyer*
Kahn, Edwin S. *lawyer*
Kerwin, Mary Ann Collins *lawyer*
Krendl, Cathy Stricklin *lawyer*
Lerman, Eileen R. *lawyer*
Lutz, John Shafroth *lawyer*
Major, Alice Jean *lawyer*
Marquess, Lawrence Wade *lawyer*
Mauro, Richard Frank *lawyer, investment manager*
McKenna, Frederick Gregory *lawyer, consultant*
Meyer, Frederick G. *lawyer*
Murane, William Edward *lawyer*
Nelson, L. Bruce *lawyer*
O'Brien, Kevin E. *lawyer*
Otten, Arthur Edward, Jr. *lawyer, corporate executive*
Polumbus, Gary M. *lawyer*
Pringle, Edward E. *law educator, former state supreme court chief justice*
Quiat, Gerald M. *lawyer*
Rich, Ben Arthur *lawyer, educator*
Rich, Robert Stephen *lawyer*
Ritsema, Fredric A. *lawyer*
Rockwood, Linda Lee *lawyer*
Roy, Arthur Putnam *lawyer*
Sattler, Bruce Weimer *lawyer*
Sayre, John Marshall *lawyer, former government official*
Schindler, Ronald Irvin *lawyer*
Schmidt, L(ail) William, Jr. *lawyer*
Scott, Peter Bryan *lawyer*
Steefel, David Simon *lawyer*
Sterling, Harry Michael *lawyer, educator*
Tisdale, Douglas Michael *lawyer*
Welton, Charles Ephraim *lawyer*
Wheeler, Malcolm Edward *lawyer, law educator*
Williams, Michael Anthony *lawyer*
Yegge, Robert Bernard *law educator, dean*

Englewood
Bolocofsky, David N. *lawyer, psychology educator*
Harris, Robert W. *lawyer*
Karstaedt, Arthur R., III *lawyer*
Lidstone, Herrick Kenley, Jr. *lawyer*
McReynolds, Gregg Clyde *lawyer*
Syke, Cameron John *lawyer*
Wagner, David James *lawyer*

Evergreen
Coriden, Michael Warner *lawyer, consultant*

Fort Collins
Brown, Ronald Laming *lawyer*
Gilmore, Timothy Jonathan *paralegal*
Rogers, Garth Winfield *lawyer*

Golden
Boumann, Robert Lyle *lawyer*
Carney, T. J *lawyer*
Phillipson, Donald E. *lawyer*

Greenwood Village
Bowen, Peter Geoffrey *arbitrator, investment advisor, business management lecturer*
Poe, Robert Alan *lawyer*

Lakewood
Guyton, Samuel Percy *retired lawyer*
Isely, Henry Philip *association executive, integrative engineer, writer, educator*

Littleton
Eberhardt, Gretchen Ann *lawyer, hearing officer*
Keely, George Clayton *lawyer*
Ross, Jennifer Marie *paralegal*

Pueblo
Farley, Thomas T. *lawyer*
O'Conner, Loretta Rae *lawyer*
White, Rodney Curtis *paralegal, legal assistant*

Rifle
George, Russell Lloyd *lawyer, legislator*

DISTRICT OF COLUMBIA

Washington
Chandler, Vanessa Alison Yelvington *lawyer*
McClure, James A. *lawyer, retired senator*

HAWAII

Honolulu
Alm, Steve *prosecutor*
Bloede, Victor Carl *lawyer, academic executive*
Boas, Frank *lawyer*
Boggs, Steven Eugene *lawyer*
Chuck, Walter G(oonsun) *lawyer*
Cowan, Stuart Marshall *lawyer*
Dang, Marvin S. C. *lawyer*
Deaver, Phillip Lester *lawyer*
Devlin, Patricia *lawyer*
Dreher, Nicholas C. *lawyer*
Edmunds, John Sanford *lawyer*
Gebbia Pinetti, Karen Marie *lawyer, educator*
Gelber, Don Jeffrey *lawyer*
Geshell, Richard Steven *lawyer*
Hart, Brook *lawyer*
Hazlett, Mark A. *lawyer*
Heller, Ronald Ian *lawyer*
Jaffe, Edward A. *lawyer*
Kawachika, James Akio *lawyer*
Kotada, Kelly Kenichi *lawyer*
Lacy, John R. *lawyer*
Lilly, Michael Alexander *lawyer, author*
Miller, Clifford Joel *lawyer*
Miyasaki, Shuichi *lawyer*
Morry, G. Richard *retired lawyer*
Rinesmith, Steven Lee *lawyer*
Rohrer, Reed Beaver *lawyer*
Sato, Glenn Kenji *lawyer*
Schnack, Harold Clifford *lawyer*
Shigetomi, Keith Shigeo *lawyer*
Starshak, James L. *lawyer*
Woo, Vernon Ying-Tsai *lawyer, real estate developer, judge*

Kihei
Burns, Richard Gordon *retired lawyer, writer, consultant*

Kula
Rohlfing, Frederick William *lawyer, travel executive, political consultant, retired judge*

Makawao
Barrad, Catherine Marie *lawyer*

Wailuku
Luna, B. Martin *lawyer*

IDAHO

Boise
Klein, Edith Miller *lawyer, former state senator*
Luker, Lynn Michael *lawyer*
McGown, John, Jr. *lawyer*
Meyer, Christopher Hawkins *lawyer*
Minnich, Diane Kay *state bar executive*
Richardson, Betty H. *prosecutor*
Risch, James E. *lawyer*

Caldwell
Kerrick, David Ellsworth *lawyer*

Lewiston
Aherin, Darrel William *lawyer*

Pocatello
Nye, W. Marcus W. *lawyer*

Twin Falls
Hohnhorst, John Charles *lawyer*

MONTANA

Billings
Gannett, Damon L. *lawyer*
Haughey, James McCrea *lawyer, artist*
Matteucci, Sherry Scheel *lawyer*
Thompson, James William *lawyer*

Butte
Krueger, Kurt Donn *lawyer*

Helena
Wewer, William Paul *lawyer*

Kalispell
Heckathorn, I. James *lawyer*

Missoula
Bowman, Jean Louise *lawyer, civic worker*

NEVADA

Carson City
Ross, Donald Henry *lawyer*

Las Vegas
Cabot, Anthony Nathan *lawyer, educator*
Chesnut, Carol Fitting *lawyer*
Curran, William P. *lawyer*
Ecker, Howard *lawyer*
Faiss, Robert Dean *lawyer*
Galane, Morton Robert *lawyer*
Goodwin, John Robert *law educator, author*
Gray, Patricia Joyce *court administrator*
Hampton, Stephen Drew *law clerk*
Han, Ittah *lawyer, political economist, high technology and financial strategist, computer engineer*
Herch, Frank Alan *lawyer, law librarian*
Hilbrecht, Norman Ty *lawyer*
Hill, Judith Deegan *lawyer*
Kennedy, Dennis L. *lawyer*
Miley, Edward Randall *lawyer*
Parry, Stanley Warren *lawyer*
Schreiber, David M. *lawyer, judge*
Singer, Michael Howard *lawyer*
Solomon, Mark A. *lawyer*
Ventriglia, Phillip J. *lawyer*

Reno
Barkley, Thierry Vincent *lawyer*
Brill, Mark *lawyer*
Davenport, Brian Lynn *lawyer*
Elliot, Cameron Robert *legal administrator*
Hardy, Del *lawyer*
Hill, Earl McColl *lawyer*
Kent, Stephen Smiley *lawyer*
Richards, Paul A. *lawyer*
Walker, Etta L. *lawyer*

NEW MEXICO

Albuquerque
Addis, Richard Barton *lawyer*
Beach, Arthur O'Neal *lawyer*
DeLayo, Leonard J., Jr. *lawyer*
Farmer, Terry D(wayne) *lawyer*
Gill, Franklin Edward *law professor*
Kelly, John J. *prosecutor*
Lyon, Daniel Frank Southworth *lawyer*
Messinger, J. Henry *lawyer*
Miller, Gardner Hartmann *paralegal*
Miller, Ranne B. *lawyer*
Schwartz, Robert Lewis *law educator*
Thornton, J. Duke *lawyer*
Ussery, Albert Travis *lawyer, investment company executive*

Carlsbad
Wayman, Cooper Harry *lawyer*

Clovis
Byrnes, Peter *lawyer*

Farmington
Morgan, Jack M. *lawyer*

Titus, Victor Allen *lawyer*

Gallup
Allan, Robert Olav *lawyer*

Las Cruces
Lindley, Jearl Ray *lawyer*
Lutz, William Lan *lawyer*
Martin, Connie Ruth *lawyer*
Palacios, Pedro Pablo *lawyer*
Schweikart, Debora Ellen *lawyer*

Roswell
Bassett, John Walden, Jr. *lawyer*
Sabin, Robert Earl *lawyer*

Santa Fe
Bienvenu, John Charles *lawyer*
Brannen, Jeffrey Richard *lawyer*
Burton, John Paul (Jack Burton) *lawyer*
Casey, Patrick Anthony *lawyer*
Culbert, Peter V. *lawyer*
Cunningham, David Fratt *lawyer*
Schwarz, Michael *lawyer*
Shaw, Mark Howard *lawyer, business owner, entrepreneur*

OREGON

Ashland
Fine, J. David *lawyer*

Beaverton
Fulsher, Allan Arthur *lawyer*

Corvallis
Ringo, Robert Gribble *lawyer*

Eugene
Horn, John Harold *lawyer*
Scoles, Eugene Francis *law educator, lawyer*

Gold Beach
Specchio, Lisa Anna *lawyer*

Lake Oswego
Byczynski, Edward Frank *lawyer, financial executive*

Mcminnville
Thompson, Robert Samuel *lawyer*

Medford
O'Connor, Karl William (Goodyear Johnson) *lawyer*

Oregon City
Hill, Gary D. *lawyer*

Pendleton
Kottkamp, John Harlan *lawyer*
Williams, James David *lawyer*

Portland
Achterman, Gail Louise *lawyer*
Anderson, Mark Alexander *lawyer*
Bakkensen, John Reser *lawyer*
Bauer, Henry Leland *lawyer*
Blitz, Charles Akin *lawyer*
Brown, David W. *lawyer*
Canaday, Richard A. *lawyer*
Crooker, Constance Helen Emerson *lawyer*
Dailey, Dianne K. *lawyer*
DuBoff, Leonard David *lawyer*
Eakin, Margaretta Morgan *lawyer*
Edwards, Richard Alan *lawyer*
English, Stephen F. *lawyer*
Fell, James F. *lawyer*
Frank, Stephen Richard *lawyer*
Grossmann, Ronald Stanyer *lawyer*
Hammer, Susan M. *lawyer*
Harrell, Gary Paul *lawyer*
Helmer, M(artha) Christie *lawyer*
Jarvis, Peter R. *lawyer*
Jolles, Bernard *lawyer*
Josephson, Richard Carl *lawyer*
Jurinski, James John *law educator*
Knoll, James Lewis *lawyer*
Krahmer, Donald Leroy, Jr. *lawyer*
Lewis, Charles S., III *lawyer*
Livingston, Louis Bayer *lawyer*
Luedtke, Roger A. *lawyer*
Lusky, John A. *lawyer*
Matarazzo, Harris Starr *lawyer*
Moore, Thomas Scott *lawyer*
Nicolai, Thomas R. *lawyer*
Orth, Beverly Jean *lawyer*
Purcell, John F. *lawyer*
Rawlinson, Dennis Patrick *lawyer*
Rynerson, S(usan) Diane *lawyer*
Savage, John William *lawyer*
Schuster, Philip Frederick, II *lawyer, writer*
Shellan, Ronald A. *lawyer*
Shenker, Arden Earl *lawyer*
Sokol, Jan D. *lawyer*
Tomlinson, William M. *lawyer*
Weiler, Mary Pauline *lawyer, nurse*
Wood, Marcus Andrew *lawyer*
Zalutsky, Morton Herman *lawyer*

Roseburg
Cremer, Richard Anthony *lawyer*

Salem
Ferris, Evelyn Scott *lawyer*
Rosen, Steven O. *lawyer*
Tweedt, Anne Elizabeth *lawyer, legislative policy analyst*

Wilsonville
Yacob, Yosef *lawyer, economist*

UTAH

Logan
Hillyard, Lyle William *lawyer*

Ogden
Mecham, Glenn Jefferson *lawyer, mayor*

Richards, Richard *lawyer, political consultant*
Warner, Frank Shrake *lawyer*

Provo
Sutterfield, Kevin James *lawyer, consultant*

Salt Lake City
Callister, Louis Henry, Jr. *lawyer*
Clark, Scott H. *lawyer*
Cornaby, Kay Sterling *lawyer, former state senator*
Curtis, LeGrand R., Jr. *lawyer*
Detton, David K. *lawyer*
Doermann, David James *paralegal, writer*
Felt, Paul Schenk *lawyer*
Hedger, Cecil Raymond *lawyer*
Holbrook, James Russell *lawyer*
Leta, David Edward *lawyer*
Livsey, Herbert C. *lawyer*
Matsumori, Douglas *lawyer*
McCoy, Harry E., II *lawyer*
Mills, Lawrence *lawyer, business and transportation consultant*
Mooney, Jerome Henri *lawyer*
Moore, James R. *lawyer*
Ockey, Ronald J. *lawyer*
Rasmussen, Thomas Val, Jr. *lawyer, small business owner*
Reeder, F. Robert *lawyer*
Smith, Janet Hugie *lawyer*
Wangsgard, Chris Prince *lawyer*
Weiss, Loren Elliot *lawyer, law educator*
Wikstrom, Francis M. *lawyer*

Sandy
Bush, Rex Curtis *lawyer*

Spanish Fork
Ashworth, Brent Ferrin *lawyer*

WASHINGTON

Bellevue
Boespflug, John Francis, Jr. *lawyer*
Kimball, Mark Douglas *lawyer*
Sebris, Robert, Jr. *lawyer*

Bellingham
Packer, Mark Barry *lawyer, financial consultant, foundation official*

Hoquiam
Jones, Garth Lewis *lawyer*

Kirkland
Schultheis, Patrick Joseph *lawyer*
Wolff, Joel Henry *human factors engineer, lawyer*

Longview
Barlow, John Aden *lawyer*

Olympia
Coyne, Brian Joseph *lawyer*
Walker, Francis Joseph *lawyer*

Redmond
Burt, Thomas William *lawyer*

Renton
Thompson, George Lewis *lawyer*

Seattle
Alkire, John D. *lawyer, mediator, arbitrator*
Andreasen, Steven W. *lawyer*
Blais, Robert Howard *lawyer*
Cross, Bruce Michael *lawyer*
Cullen, Jack Joseph *lawyer*
Cunningham, Joel Dean *lawyer*
Dalton, Thomas George *paralegal, social worker, legal consultant*
Diggs, Bradley C. *lawyer*
Dolan, Andrew Kevin *lawyer*
Duris, Robert (Robert de Jong) *legal consultant, journalist*
Elliott, Clifton Langsdale *lawyer*
Freedman, Bart Joseph *lawyer*
Glover, Karen E. *lawyer*
Goeltz, Thomas A. *lawyer*
Graybeal, Lynne Elizabeth *lawyer*
Gunter, Robert L. *lawyer*
Guy, Andrew A. *lawyer*
Haggard, Joel Edward *lawyer*
Hansen, Wayne W. *lawyer*
Hazelton, Penny Ann *law librarian, educator*
Hermsen, James R. *lawyer*
Holtan, Ramer B., Jr. *lawyer*
Hopp, Richard A. *lawyer*
Huff, Gary D. *lawyer*
Jackson, Dillon Edward *lawyer*
Jaffe, Robert Stanley *lawyer*
Kaplan, Barry Martin *lawyer*
Katz, Charles J., Jr. *lawyer*
Keegan, John E. *lawyer*
Kellogg, Kenyon P. *lawyer*
Kelly, Kevin Francis *lawyer*
Linn, Brian James *lawyer*
Loftus, Thomas Daniel *lawyer*
Lopez, Carl A. Taylor *lawyer*
Lybeck, Kevin Lee *lawyer*
McKinstry, Ronald Eugene *lawyer*
Murray, Michael Kent *lawyer*
Mussehl, Robert Clarence *lawyer*
Nellermoe, Leslie Carol *lawyer*
Niemi, Janice *lawyer, former state legislator*
Noble, Phillip D. *lawyer*
Oles, Stuart Gregory *lawyer*
Palmer, Douglas S., Jr. *lawyer*
Perey, Ron *lawyer*
Peterson, Jan Eric *lawyer*
Pettigrew, Edward W. *lawyer*
Plotkin, Stacy Jo *lawyer*
Powers, Ragan Lewis *lawyer*
Pym, Bruce Michael *lawyer*
Rogers, James Steven *lawyer*
Schneidler, Jon Gordon *lawyer*
Scott, Brian David *lawyer*
Simburg, Melvyn Jay *lawyer*
Steers, George W. *lawyer*
Steinberg, Jack *lawyer*
Stoebuck, William Brees *law educator*
Strichartz, James Leonard *lawyer*
Tallman, Richard C. *lawyer*

Tessier, Dennis Medward *paralegal, lecturer, legal advisor, consultant*
Thorne, David W. *lawyer*
Veblen, John Elvidge *lawyer*
Vestal, Josephine Burnet *lawyer*
Wagner, Patricia Hamm *lawyer*
Wagoner, David Everett *lawyer*
Walter, Michael Charles *lawyer*
Wechsler, Mary Heyrman *lawyer*
Whitford, Joseph P. *lawyer*
Wilson, Richard Randolph *lawyer*

Shelton
Johansen, Ricky Lee, Jr. *paralegal investigator*

Spokane
Connelly, James P. *prosecutor*
Connolly, K. Thomas *lawyer*
Conrad, Charles Thomas *lawyer*
Harbaugh, Daniel Paul *lawyer*
Hayashi, Arthur *prosecutor*
Symmes, William Daniel *lawyer*
Weatherhead, Leslie R. *lawyer*

Tacoma
Frohmader, Frederick Oliver *lawyer*
George, Nicholas *criminal defense lawyer, entrepreneur*
Holt, William E. *lawyer*
Mungia, Salvador Alejo, Jr. *lawyer*
Nance, John Joseph *lawyer, writer, air safety analyst, broadcaster, consultant*
Sterbick, Peter Lawrence *lawyer*
Thompson, Ronald Edward *lawyer*

Tukwila
Gouras, Mark Steven *lawyer*

Wenatchee
Foreman, Dale Melvin *lawyer, state official*

Yakima
Larson, Paul Martin *lawyer*

WYOMING

Casper
Combs, W(illiam) Henry, III *lawyer*
Durham, Harry Blaine, III *lawyer*
Gray, Jan Charles *lawyer, business owner*
Hjelmstad, William David *lawyer*
Lowe, Robert Stanley *lawyer*
Miller, Corinne *lawyer*

Cheyenne
Freudenthal, David D. *prosecutor*
Hathaway, Stanley Knapp *lawyer*
Hickey, Paul Joseph *lawyer*
Palma, Jack D. *lawyer*
Scorsine, John Magnus *lawyer*

Douglas
Bunn, Dorothy Irons *court reporter*

Jackson
Goody, William Keith *lawyer*
Schuster, Robert Parks *lawyer*
Shockey, Gary Lee *lawyer*

Kemmerer
Sundar, Vijendra *lawyer educator*

Rawlins
DeHerrera, Juan Leo *lawyer*

Wheatland
Hunkins, Raymond Breedlove *lawyer, rancher*

CANADA

ALBERTA

Calgary
Lougheed, Peter *lawyer, former Canadian official*

ADDRESS UNPUBLISHED

Atkinson, Sheridan Earle *lawyer*
Bandy, Jack D. *lawyer*
Baughn, Alfred Fairhurst *lawyer*
Berry, Robert Worth *lawyer, educator, retired army officer*
Boorstyn, Neil *lawyer, educator*
Bouvier, Marshall Andre *lawyer*
Braun, Jerome Irwin *lawyer*
Brechbill, Susan Reynolds *lawyer, educator*
Carmack, Mildred Jean *retired lawyer*
Clabaugh, Elmer Eugene, Jr. *retired lawyer*
Cook, Glen André *lawyer*
Craig, Stephen Wright *lawyer*
Criscuolo, Wendy Laura *lawyer, interior design consultant*
Davey, Gerard Paul *lawyer*
Davis, Wanda Rose *lawyer*
De Concini, Dennis *lawyer, former United States senator, consultant*
Fortner, Hueston Gilmore *lawyer, writer, composer*
Frost, Sterling Newell *arbitrator, mediator, management consultant*
Gibb, Roberta Louise *lawyer, artist*
Gibson, Paula Lauren *lawyer*
Goldwater, Robert Williams, III *lawyer*
Gomez, David Frederick *lawyer*
Hall-Barron, Deborah *lawyer*
Harvey, Marc Sean *lawyer, consultant*
Hawes, Sue *lawyer*
Hybl, William Joseph *lawyer, foundation executive*
Jallins, Richard David *lawyer*
Jeffrey, John Orval *lawyer*
Jorgensen, Erik Holger *lawyer*
June, Roy Ethiel *lawyer*
Keister, Jean Clare *lawyer*
Kippur, Merrie Margolin *lawyer*
Kolodny, Stephen Arthur *lawyer*
Kubo, Edward Hachiro, Jr. *prosecutor*
Levinson, Kenneth Lee *lawyer*

Levy, David *lawyer, insurance company executive*
Lightstone, Ronald *lawyer*
Linde, Maxine Helen *lawyer, business executive, private investor*
Lowe, James Allen *lawyer*
Lundin, David Erik *lawyer*
Marker, Marc Linthacum *lawyer, investor*
Marks, Stanley Jacob *lawyer, historian, lecturer, author*
McCormick, Homer L., Jr. *lawyer*
McKay, John *lawyer*
Millard, Malcolm Stuart *retired lawyer*
Neece, Robert Barry *lawyer*
Orlebeke, William Ronald *retired lawyer, writer*
Paulus, Norma Jean Petersen *lawyer, state school system administrator*
Pear, Charles E., Jr. *lawyer*
Pereyra-Suarez, Charles Albert *lawyer*
Peterson, Howard Cooper *lawyer, accountant*
Rhodes, John Jacob *retired lawyer, former congressman*
Rosen, Martin Jack *lawyer*
Rubin, Edward *lawyer*
Salisbury, Robert Louis *lawyer, community activist*
Schor, Suzi *lawyer, psychologist*
Segel, Karen Lynn Joseph *lawyer*
Shambaugh, Stephen Ward *lawyer*
Sprung, Arnold *lawyer*
Stephenson, Barbera Wertz *lawyer*
Stott, Don Earl *family court mediator, educator*
Summe, Kimberly Anne *lawyer*
Tanaka, Jeannie E. *lawyer*
Taylor, Ruth Anne *lawyer*
Tolentino, Casimiro Urbano *lawyer*
Tso, Tom *law educator*
Turner, George Mason *lawyer*
von Sauers, Joseph F. *lawyer*
Walker, John Sumpter, Jr. *lawyer*
Wong-Diaz, Francisco Raimundo *lawyer, educator*

MEDICINE. *See* HEALTHCARE: MEDICINE.

MILITARY

UNITED STATES

ALASKA

Anchorage
Erving, Claude Moore, Jr. *career officer, pilot*
Overly, Frederick Dean *civilian military employee, entrepreneur*

Kodiak
Croyle, Douglas Eugene *career officer*

ARIZONA

Mesa
Boyd, Edward Hascal *retired career officer*

Phoenix
Beltrán, Anthony Natalicio *military non-commissioned officer, deacon*

Scottsdale
Coffinger, Maralin Katharyne *retired career officer, consultant*

Tucson
Bryan, Gordon Redman, Jr. *retired career officer*
Guice, John Thompson *retired career officer*
Huber, Linda Ruth *non-commissioned officer*

Yuma
Hudson, John Irvin *retired career officer*

CALIFORNIA

Edwards AFB
Bujold, David Alexis *career officer*

El Segundo
Hunt, Vanessa Ann *civilian military employee*

Healdsburg
Rawlins, Robert Daniel *career officer*

La Jolla
Greer, Howard Earl *retired career officer*

Lompoc
Walker, Duncan Edward *retired career officer*

Los Altos
Wheeler, Frank Knowles Blasdell *retired military officer, business consultant*

March Air Force Base
Dube'-Odell, Dorice Suzanne *career officer*

Monterey
Hoivik, Thomas Harry *military educator, international consultant*

Napa
Smith, Robert Bruce *former security consultant, retired career officer*

Pebble Beach
Fergusson, Robert George *retired career officer*

Point Mugu Nawc
Watkiss, Eric John *career officer*

Rancho Cordova
Meigel, David Walter *career officer, retired musician*

Riverside
Wright, John MacNair, Jr. *retired career officer*

San Diego
Allred, Keith Johns *naval officer*
Barnes, Larry Burdette *career officer*
Everett, Hobart Ray, Jr. *engineer, career officer, consultant, researcher, inventor*
Kirkbride, Max Verlyn *retired career officer*
Marburger, George Gerald *retired naval officer, educator*

Santa Maria
Everhart, Leon Eugene *retired career officer*
Roadarmel, Stanley Bruce *civilian military employee*

Santa Rosa
Andriano-Moore, Richard Graf *naval officer*

Seaside
Gales, Samuel Joel *retired civilian military employee, counselor*
Nussberger, Clint Joseph *career officer*

South Dos Palos
Hirohata, Derek Kazuyoshi *career officer*

Tustin
Rossel, Eugene David *career officer, electrical engineer*

COLORADO

Arvada
Eaves, Sally Ann *logistics director, research administrator*

Aurora
Dawes, Douglas Charles *retired career officer*

Colorado Springs
Allery, Kenneth Edward *air force officer*
Bailey, Paul Leroy *career officer*
Bowen, Clotilde Marion Dent *retired army officer, psychiatrist*
Forgan, David Waller *retired career officer*
Schaeffer, Reiner Horst *career officer, retired librarian, foreign language professional*

Englewood
Nuce, Madonna Marie *career officer*

Fort Collins
Roberts, Archibald Edward *retired career officer, author*

U S A F Academy
Krise, Thomas Warren *career officer, English language educator*

DISTRICT OF COLUMBIA

Washington
Wooten, Michael Eric *career officer*

HAWAII

Barbers Point N A S
Wheeler, Michael David *career officer, aviator, instructor*

Honolulu
Hays, Ronald Jackson *career officer*
Weyand, Frederick Carlton *retired military officer*

Pearl Harbor
Le Cain, Lloyd George *career officer*

MONTANA

Great Falls
Jimenez, Walter Anthony *career officer*
Loftin, Orrin Keith *retired career officer, poet, actor*
Taylor, Anthony Todd *career officer, pilot*

Hamilton
Stubblefield, Gary L. *retired career officer, consultant*

NEVADA

Henderson
Creech, Wilbur Lyman *retired career officer*

NEW MEXICO

Albuquerque
Kather, Gerhard *retired air force base administrator*
Schott, Marvin Arthur *military officer*

Belen
Smith, Helen Elizabeth *retired career officer*

Cedar Crest
Sheppard, Jack W. *retired career officer*

OREGON

Eagle Point
Largent, Regina Mary *military science educator*

UTAH

Highland
Baum, Kerry Robert *retired military officer*

Hill Air Force Base
Lohman, Arthur Grover *civilian military employee*

WASHINGTON

Lynnwood
Jenes, Theodore George, Jr. *retired career officer*

Yakima
Hill, Dale Richard *career officer*

ADDRESS UNPUBLISHED

Boyd, Herchell A. *career officer*
Bryant, Pamela Anne *career officer, retired, business owner*
Carter, William George, III *career officer*
DiCocco, Marc *career officer, flight test engineer*
Duvall, Lourdes M. *career officer*
Florie, Terry Lynn *career officer*
Glascoe, William Oliver, III *career officer*
Johnson, Brenda Faye *career officer*
Keene-Burgess, Ruth Frances *army official*
King, Charolette Elaine *retired career officer*
Marlow, Edward A. *career officer*
Newe, Ralph Axel *career officer, consultant*
Ninos, Nicholas Peter *retired career officer, physician*
Owens, William Arthur *career officer*
Robinson, David Brooks *retired naval officer*
Ryan, Mary Gene *career officer, occupational health nurse*
Smith, Charles Lewis *retired career officer and association executive*
Terrill, W(allace) Andrew *international security analyst, educator*
Troupe, Michael Eugene *career officer*
Walden, Joseph Lawrence *career officer*
Washington-Knight, Barbara J. *career officer, nurse*
Yoon, E. Yul *retired career officer*
Zanone, Jon A. *career officer*

RELIGION

UNITED STATES

ALASKA

Anchorage
Clary, William Victor *minister*
Hurley, Francis T. *archbishop*
Parsons, Donald D. *bishop*
Rosenfeld, Harry Leonard *rabbi*

Elmendorf AFB
Luckett, Byron Edward, Jr. *chaplain, career officer*

Fairbanks
Kaniecki, Michael Joseph *bishop*

Palmer
Guinotte, Henry Paul *clergyman*

ARIZONA

Arizona City
Ross, Lanson Clifford, Jr. *religion educator, author*

Duncan
Ouzts, Eugene Thomas *minister, secondary education educator*

Flagstaff
Castillo, Diana May *religious organization administrator*

Glendale
Chilton, Claude Lysias *minister, former career officer*

Mesa
Osman, Herbert Eugene *minister*
Simpson, John Berchman, Jr. *clergy member, chaplain, retired law enforcement officer, retired newspaper editor*

Paradise Valley
Kilgore, L(eRoy) Wilson *minister*
Sapp, Donald Gene *minister*

Phoenix
Darby, Wesley Andrew *minister, educator*
Dew, William Waldo, Jr. *bishop*
Fonville-Williams, Debra Marie *religious organization executive*
Humes, Linda Joyce *religious organization executive, editor*
Kuzma, George Martin *bishop*
Larkin, Ernest Eldon *priest, consultant, retired educator*
O'Brien, Thomas Joseph *bishop*
Whitlow, William La Fond *minister, theology school planter*

Pine
Pattison, Fred Lewis *minister, academic administrator*

Prescott
Winter, Peter John *religious minister*
Pence, James Roy *pastor*

Scottsdale
Freeman, William Taft, Jr. *minister*
Hoyt, James Edward *church administrator*
Jann, Donn Gerard *minister*
Mohler, James William *minister*
Mueller, Gerry Damon Adent *publisher, editor*
Stewart, Robert Ray *minister*

Sierra Vista
Ford, Frederick Jay *clergyman*

Sun City
Park, Francis Wood, III *minister*

Sun City West
Schmitz, Charles Edison *evangelist*

Tempe
Yoder, Donald Eugene *minister*

Tucson
Moreno, Manuel D. *bishop*
Stout, Arthur Paul *minister*
Warris, Anna Cummings *religious organization executive*
Yeun, Paul Lorenzo *minister*

Williams
Johnston, Lyle Wayne *minister*

Yuma
Phillips, Thomas H., Jr. *rector*

CALIFORNIA

Acton
Butman, Harry Raymond *clergyman, author*

Altadena
Willans, Jean Stone *religious organization executive*

Anaheim
Nguyen, Tai Anh *minister*
Reeves, Donald Buster *minister*
Settgast, Leland G. *religion educator, minister*

Antioch
Cakebread, Steven Robert *minister, chef*
Quattlebum, Donald Lee *minister*
Roper, Larry Lester *pastor, school administrator*

Apple Valley
Bray, James Wallace, II *minister*

Azusa
Grant, Earl E. *minister, educator*
Shoemaker, Melvin Hugh *religious educator*

Baldwin Park
Salazar, Arturo *deacon*

Barstow
Jones, Nathaniel *bishop*

Belmont
Sequeira, John Edward *deacon*

Berkeley
Lee, Young Ho (Jinwol) *Buddhist monk, educator*
Oliver, Mary Anne McPherson *religion educator*

Blythe
Bryant, Gary Jones *minister*

Bonita
Pitrone, Margo Rae *minister*

Burbank
Skelly, John Joshua *clergyman, fundraiser*
Teague, Jane Lorene *lay worker*

Canoga Park
Dickey, Gary Alan *minister*

Canyon Country
Chandler, Lois Jeanne *religious studies educator*

Capo Beach
Hallowell, John H *minister*

Carlsbad
Allen, Gary *association executive*

Castro Valley
Morrison, Glenn Leslie *minister*

Ceres
Neal, Albert Harvey *retired minister*

Chico
Rothe-Barneson, June Emma *lay worker*

Chula Vista
Harper, Kenneth Charles *clergyman*

Claremont
Kibler, Ray Franklin, III *minister*
Tengbom, Luverne Charles *religion educator*

Compton
Johnson, William R., Jr. *minister*
Vines, High, Jr. *minister, educator*

Costa Mesa
Hinkle, Jill Elaine *religion educator, counselor*
Regele, Michael Bruce *minister, information and marketing services executive*
Williams, William Corey *theology educator, consultant*

Covina
Casale, Francis Joseph *minister*
Sandstrom, Mark Rand *minister*

Crescent City
Irish, Terry Lee *minister*

Culver City
Ewing, James E. *priest*
Rooney-Ewing, Elisabeth Anne *priest*

Cupertino
Winslow, David Allen *chaplain, retired naval officer*

Daly City
Prym, Michael Leonard *pastoral counselor*

Davis
Brown, Arthur Carl, Jr. *retired minister*

Downey
Duarte, Harold Jorge *minister*

Duarte
Driskill, James Lawrence *minister*
Probst, John Elwin *chaplain, minister*

El Monte
Hwang, Tzu-Yang *minister*

Elk Grove
Talbert, Melvin George *bishop*

Escondido
Bergsma, Derke Peter *minister, religious studies educator*
Johnson, Stephen Randall *minister*
Jones, Peter Ronald *religious studies educator, author, speaker*
Raher, Richard Ray *minister*

Fair Oaks
Norvell, Thomas Vernon *minister*

Fallbrook
Snider, Ronald Albert *minister*

Fountain Valley
Einstein, Stephen Jan *rabbi*

Fresno
Howe, Ronald Evans *minister*
Steinbock, John Thomas *bishop*
Xiong, Tousu Saydangnmvang *minister*

Fullerton
Gorham, Daniel John *priest*

Garden Grove
Ballesteros, Juventino Ray, Jr. *minister*
Clarke, Gordon *clergyman*

Glendale
Cranch, Harold Covert *minister*
De Shay, William Leslie *minister*

Glendora
Richey, Everett Eldon *religion educator*

Goleta
Corbett, Gordon Leroy *minister*

Grass Valley
Robbins, Dale Alan *minister*

Hacienda Heights
Sim, John Kim-Chye *minister*

Hanford
Hetebrink, Darrow *pastor*

Inglewood
Reid, Benjamin Franklin *bishop*

Ione
Sparrowk, Cora Catherine *lay church leader*

Irvine
Christopher, Steven Lee *religious studies educator*
Sraon, Harbans Singh *temple executive, geneticist*

Julian
Stitt, Mari Leipper *writer*

La Habra Heights
Mulac, Pamela Ann *priest, pastoral counselor*

La Jolla
Freedman, David Noel *religion educator*
Wyle, Ewart Herbert *clergyman*

La Puente
Large, Timothy Wallace *religious organization administrator*

Lafayette
Fitterer, John Angus *priest, church administrator, author*

Laguna Beach
Gregg, Nadine Marie *pastor*

Laguna Hills
Faw, Duane Leslie *lay worker, law educator, retired career officer, author*
Wheatley, Melvin Ernest, Jr. *retired bishop*

Lake Forest
Hertweck, Galen Fredric *minister*

Lancaster
Runner, George Cyril, Jr. *minister, educational administrator*

Lindsay
Sanchez, Ruben Dario *minister, family counselor, parochial school educator, writer*

Littlerock
McDonald, Roscoe, Jr. minister, artist, writer

Long Beach
Booth, Leo W. priest, author
Lowentrout, Peter Murray religious studies educator
Mosby, Ralph Joseph minister

Los Angeles
Agbeja, Timothy Omolayo pastor
Behr, Ted Arthur religious organization administrator
Bermoy, Emiliano Simacio minister, church administrator
Blaire, Stephen E. bishop
Borsch, Frederick Houk bishop
Boyd, Malcolm minister, religious author
Breuer, Stephen Ernest temple administrator
Chedid, John G. bishop
Cook, Donald Ray pastor
Evans, Angela Marie religious organization executive
Fitzgerald, Tikhon (Lee R. H. Fitzgerald) bishop
Forman, Adine Oberlander religious organization administrator
Freehling, Allen Isaac rabbi
Hymers, Robert Leslie, Jr. pastor
Lotz, Linda A. religious organization administrator
Mahony, Cardinal Roger M. archbishop
Mc Pherson, Rolf Kennedy clergyman, church official
Ochoa, Armando bishop
O'Connor, Kevin Thomas archdiocese development official
Ogilvie, Lloyd John clergyman
Phillips, Keith Wendall minister
Pressman, Jacob rabbi
Robinson, Fisher Joseph priest
Sichol, Sister Marcia Winifred (Sister) nun, fund administrator
Stern, Seymour (Sholom) rabbi
Vasquez, Edmundo Eusebio religious organization administrator
Williams, Ronald Dean minister, religious organization executive
Wolf, Alfred rabbi
Wu, Michael Yick-Kuen minister

Malibu
Wilson, John Francis religion educator, archaeologist

Manhattan Beach
Dever, Thomas L. pastor

Mill Valley
Crews, William Odell, Jr. seminary administrator
DuBose, Francis Marquis clergyman
Stubblefield, Jerry Mason religious educator, minister

Modesto
Lindo, Edwin Thessalonians minister

Monrovia
Huffey, Vinton Earl clergyman

Monterey
Ryan, Sylvester D. bishop
Shimpfky, Richard Lester bishop

Moraga
Lu, Matthias priest, educator

Newbury Park
Marshall, Judy K. lay worker

Newport Beach
Huffman, John Abram, Jr. minister
Snow, Alan Albert religious studies writer

North Hollywood
Silverstein, David cantor, educator
Wannebo, Ode religious organization executive, opera-concert singer, educator

Northridge
Dart, John Seward religious material writer

Oakland
Cummins, John Stephen bishop
Jackson, Frank pastor
Jakubowsky, Frank Raymond author
Patten, Bebe Harrison minister, chancellor
Schomer, Howard retired clergyman, educator, social policy consultant

Oceanside
Peck, Paul Lachlan minister

Ojai
Pejza, John Philip priest, academic administrator
Springer, Karl Goerge religious organization administrator

Ontario
Willoughby, Jimmy Ray minister

Orange
Brown, Tod David bishop
Buhler, Richard Gerhard minister
Driscoll, Michael P. bishop
Mc Farland, Norman Francis bishop
Miller, Jay Anthony minister
Whan, Norman Wendell minister

Orangevale
Webb, Andrew Howard minister

Oxnard
Oncken, Ellen Lorraine minister, speaker

Pacoima
Tsai, Peter Ying-Shih minister

Palm Desert
Costa, Thomas Peter clergyman, writer, lecturer
Hunt, Barnabas John priest, religious order administrator

Palo Alto
Brown, Sally (Sarah Jane England) minister

Ching, Andy Kwok-yee minister
Forbes, Alfred Dean religious studies researcher, biomedical consultant

Palos Verdes Peninsula
Cubillos, Robert Hernan church administrator, philosophy educator

Pasadena
Gay, George Arthur religion educator, minister
Sano, Roy I. bishop
Shuster, Marguerite minister, educator
Torres, Ralph Chon minister
Warren, Judi Dell minister

Perris
Brown, Marvin Lee minister

Pittsburg
Schmalenberger, Jerry Lew pastor, seminary educator

Placerville
Robbins, Jo Ann minister

Pleasanton
Davis, Ron Lee clergyman, author
Ice, Richard Eugene retired minister, retirement housing company executive

Pomona
Kroll, C(harles) Douglas minister

Porterville
Eby, John Oliver minister

Poway
Wirt, Sherwood Eliot writer, minister

Rancho Cordova
Hayashida, Larry W. minister

Rancho Santa Fe
Denton, Rena Wilson religion educator

Redding
Potter, James Vincent educator

Redlands
DeRoulhac, Joseph Harold, Jr. minister

Redondo Beach
Hawkins, Harold Stanley pastor, police chaplain, school director
Sweeney, Dorothy Love minister, nurse

Reedley
Dick, Henry Henry minister
Shibata, George Eishin minister

Reseda
Gordon, Forrest Lyle minister

Riverside
Brodhead, Charles Nelson, III lay worker
Huang, Kai-Loo religion educator emeritus
Nichols, Vance Everett minister, principal
Storey, Arthur William minister
Webber, William Diderichsen clergyman

Sacramento
Bonner, Ethel Mae religious education educator, advocate
Clements, William Lewis, Jr. (Bill) minister
Cole, Glen David minister
Quinn, Francis A. bishop
Venema, Jon Roger educator, pastor
Weigand, William Keith bishop
Wells, George Henry minister

Salinas
Distler, Charles minister, administrator

San Anselmo
Lundeen, Ronald Arthur theology educator

San Bernardino
Barnes, Gerald R. bishop
Dixon, Barry Percy religion educator

San Bruno
Au, Lawrence minister

San Carlos
Pyne, Donald Eugene priest

San Diego
Brom, Robert H. bishop
Chavez, Gilbert Espinoza bishop
Downing, David Charles minister
Eaton, Kent Alexander theology educator
Hughes, Gethin B. bishop
Kraft, William Armstrong retired priest
McKinney, George D., Jr. pastor, bishop
Owen-Towle, Carolyn Sheets clergywoman
Savitripriya, Swami Hindu religious leader, author
Saylor, Dennis Elwood hospital chaplain
Siegel, Robert Irving Allen minister, writer

San Francisco
Brickner, David organization executive, consultant
Hurley, Mark Joseph bishop
Ilao, Tom Javate religious organization official, deacon
Kwong, Raymond minister
Levada, William Joseph archbishop
McGrath, Patrick Joseph bishop
Perlman, Susan Gail organization executive
Rosen, Moishe religious organization founder
Sevilla, Carlos A. bishop
Shreibman, Henry M. religious educator
Sparer, Malcolm Martin rabbi
Stuart, Laird James minister
Swing, William Edwin bishop
Tonsing, Cecilia Ann Degnan lay worker, foundation administrator

San Jose
Chae, Yoon Kwon minister, educator

Clemo, Ronald Carl (Rev.) priest
McCauley, Kevin Bruce minister
White, J(ob) Benton retired religion educator

San Juan Bautista
Fort, Robert Bradley minister

San Mateo
Dilenschneider, Anne Marie clergywoman

San Rafael
Tripp, Kevin Francis priest

Santa Ana
Connelly, Betty Fees lay ministries consultant
de Leon, Daniel Benitz minister
Vaughan, Paul Irvine minister

Santa Barbara
Campbell, Robert Charles minister, theology educator
Panikkar, Raimon priest
Sills, Deborah R. religious studies educator

Santa Clara
DuMaine, R. Pierre bishop
Soukup, Paul Arthur priest, educator

Santa Maria
Whiteaker, Linda Joyce minister, educational administrator

Santa Monica
Metoyer, Josep Phanor, Jr. minister, marketing executive
Soloff, Mordecai Isaac retired rabbi

Santa Rosa
Ziemann, G. Patrick bishop

Simi Valley
Kearns, Albert Osborn minister
O'Berg, Robert Myron minister

Solana Beach
Gilliam, Vincent Carver religion educator, minister, writer
Haynes, Olive Durham clergywoman, artist

Sonora
Patterson, Paul Edward minister

Spring Valley
Johnson, Arnold Hjalmer minister

Stockton
Mathre, Lawrence Gerhard minister, federal agency administrator
Schedler, Gilbert Walter religion educator

Sun Valley
Stitzinger, James Franklin religion educator, library director

Temple City
Perkins, Floyd Jerry retired theology educator

Thousand Oaks
Benedict, Monseigneur priest, religious researcher
Skeels, H(arry) Wilbur clergyman, composer
Wold, Margaret Barth religion educator

Turlock
Stensether, John Eldon minister

Upland
Chaney, Robert Galen religious organization executive
Winger, Walter Orval minister

Vallejo
McGowan, Thomas Randolph retired religious organization executive

Van Nuys
Chappell, Paul Gale religious studies educator, minister
Hayford, Jack W. minister

Victorville
Henry-John, Emmanuel Sylvester preacher, counselor

West Hills
Godsil, Richard William minister

West Hollywood
Eger, Denise Leese rabbi

Whittier
Price, Joseph Llewellyn religious educator

Wilmington
Moreno, Guillermo Fernandez minister

Windsor
Smith, Maynard Dwight minister

Yorba Linda
Carrington, James Donald minister

Yucaipa
Horn, Paul Ervin minister

COLORADO

Arvada
Pettit, Claud Martin religious organization administrator

Aurora
Stifel, Frederick Benton pastor, biochemist, nutritionist

Boulder
Rose, Herbert Herman rabbi

Buena Vista
Goddard, Hazel Bryan religious organization executive

Canon City
Williamson, Edward Henry chaplain, army officer

Cheraw
Yeakey, Michael Aaron, II minister

Colorado Springs
Bridges, Gerald Dean religious organization executive
Child, Joseph Alan minister
Evans, Anthony Lawrence minister, educator
Eyman, Roger Allen minister
Hanifen, Richard Charles bishop
Loux, Gordon Dale organization executive
Pickle, Joseph Wesley, Jr. religion educator

Denver
Barger, Louise Baldwin religious organization administrator
Borer, Anton Joseph priest
Brownlee, Judith Marilyn priestess, psychotherapist, psychic
Bukowiecki, Sister Angeline Bernadette nun
Burrell, Calvin Archie minister
Goldberg, Hillel rabbi, educator
Lewallen, Elinor Kirby organization executive, lay church worker
Meeks, Mark Anthony minister
Morgan, David Forbes minister
Sheeran, Michael John Leo priest, college administrator
Zucal, Steven Joseph priest

Englewood
Weissenbuehler, Wayne former bishop, pastor

Fort Collins
Pape, Arnis Weston minister
Rolston, Holmes, III theologian, educator, philosopher

Golden
Boulware, James L. minister

Lakewood
Hickman, Ruth Virginia Bible educator
Vogt, Hugh Frederick minister, college administrator

Las Animas
Davis, William Albert minister, educator

Littleton
Dungan, Shirley Ann religious organization administrator

Louisville
Marsh, Donald Pete hospital chaplain

Manitou Springs
Noebel, David Arthur minister, educator

Pueblo
Critchett, Hugh Adams minister
Tafoya, Arthur N. bishop

Wheat Ridge
Wilcox, Mary Marks Christian education consultant, educator

HAWAII

Honolulu
Amos, Stanley Edd minister
DiLorenzo, Francis X. bishop
Moody, John Henry minister
Tabrah, Ruth Milander minister, writer
Wong, Corinne Hong Sling minister

Kaneohe
Amber, Sharmai writer
Chappell, David Wellington religious studies educator

Kapaa
Subramuniya, Master (Satguru Sivaya Subramuniyaswami) spiritual leader, publisher

M C B H Kaneohe Bay
Travers, David Owens chaplain

Mililani
Ashpole, William Emory minister

Ocean View
Gilliam, Jackson Earle bishop

Waipahu
Eng, Christopher Kamuela minister, educator
Hiapo, Patricia Kamaka lay worker

IDAHO

Boise
Blewett, Patrick Alan clergyman
Caufield, Marie Celine religious organization administrator
Lawrence, Ralph Alan minister
Thornton, John S., IV bishop

Inkom
Houston, James Russell (Russ) retired minister

Jerome
Feiss, Hugh Bernard priest, religious educator

Nampa
Lyons, George religion educator

MONTANA

Great Falls
Milone, Anthony M. *bishop*

Helena
Hart, John William *theology educator*
Jones, Charles Irving *bishop*

Missoula
Patel, Bipinchandra Kantilal *clergy member, restauranteur*

Stevensville
Delancy, Michael Robinson *minister*

NEVADA

Boulder City
Ward, Herbert Arthur, Jr. *priest, child care executive*

Las Vegas
Flammang, Susann *author, publisher*
Walsh, Daniel Francis *bishop*

Minden
Jackson, John Jay *clergyman*

Reno
Chrystal, William George *minister*
Savoy, Douglas Eugene *bishop, religion educator, explorer, writer*
Shamlian, Barbara Sue *religion educator, biblical researcher*
Straling, Phillip Francis *bishop*
Walrath, Harry Rienzi *minister*

NEW MEXICO

Albuquerque
Barnhill, Kenneth Smaltz, Jr. *lay worker*
Butziger, Robert Anton *minister*
Davis, Otis Jay *chaplain*
George, Roy Kenneth *minister*
Griffin, W. C. *bishop*
Sanchez, Regina Star *minister*
Sheehan, Michael Jarboe *archbishop*
van Hudson, Mark Valentines *religion educator*

Artesia
Robinson, J. Kenneth *religious organization administrator, minister*

Farmington
Plummer, Steven Tsosie, Sr. *bishop*

Las Cruces
Egan, Phyllis Reitz *lay worker, educator*
Ramirez, Ricardo *bishop*

Los Alamos
Tracy, James Wayne *pastor, educator*

Portales
Overton, Edwin Dean *campus minister, educator*

Rio Rancho
Ove, Robert Stephen *clergyman, writer*

Roswell
Kennedy, Kirby Kenneth *minister*
Odom, George Cosby, Jr. *retired religion educator*

Silver City
Lewis, Alvin Thomas *minister, missionary*

OREGON

Beaverton
Mitchell, Bettie Phaenon *religious organization administrator*
Palau, Luis *evangelist*

Bend
Connolly, Thomas Joseph *bishop*

Coquille
Potter, Kenneth Roy *retired minister*

Corvallis
Borg, Marcus Joel *theologian, theology educator*
Dennis, John Davison *minister*
McCarthy, William Robert *minister*
Steiner, Kenneth Donald *bishop*

Hillsboro
Carpenter, Frank Robert *minister*
Rice, Richard Lee, Jr. *minister, office manager*

Lake Oswego
Ladehoff, Robert Louis *bishop*

Newberg
Tsohantaridis, Timotheos *minister, religion educator*

Oregon City
Clore, Frank Caldin *pastor, chaplain*

Pendleton
Nichols, Albert Myron *minister*

Philomath
Stensvad, Allan Maurice *minister*

Portland
Held, Jay Allen *pastor*
Powell, Charles William *coach, former minister*
Riddle, Earl Waldo *retired church official, small business owner*
Stedel, Yaeko *spiritual counselor*

West Linn
Bohrer, Richard William *religious writer, editor, educator*

UTAH

Bountiful
Carter, Richard Bert *retired church official, retired government official*

Ogden
Harrington, Mary Evelina Paulson (Polly Harrington) *religious journalist, writer, educator*

Salt Lake City
Brower, Maitland Dirk *church administrator, writer*
Hinckley, Gordon B. *church official*
Monson, Thomas Spencer *church official, former publishing company executive*
Niederauer, George H. *bishop*
Roberts, David Stone *bishop*
Smith, Eldred Gee *church leader*

Taylorsville
Greenwood, Val David *church administrator*

West Jordan
Mattson, Vernon Williams *theology educator*

WASHINGTON

Auburn
Dillon, Joseph Neil *pastor*

Bellevue
Leon, Richard Hayward *minister*

Bremerton
Bonar, Clayton Lloyd *minister*

Burlington
Carey, Preston Bradley *minister*

Camano Island
Blair, Edward Payson *theology educator*

Chehalis
Detrick, Donald Howard *minister*

Des Moines
Tuell, Jack Marvin *retired bishop*

Everett
Stanovsky, Elaine J.W. *minister, church organization administrator*

Federal Way
Holden, David Powell *minister*

Index
Davis, Peter (Peter Pathfinder Davis) *priest*

Lacey
Schaufler, Mark Sheridan *evangelist*
Suter, David Winston *religion educator, minister*

Langley
Le Roy, Robert Powell *minister, educator, writer*

Lynnwood
Curnutt, Brian Joe *religious studies educator*
Lee, Isaac *minister*

Marysville
Quintana, Ricardo E. *pastor*

Montesano
Clausel, Nancy Karen *minister*

Oak Harbor
Corey, Stuart Merton *minister*

Port Angeles
Jones, Douglas Michael *pastor*

Renton
Warren, Larry Michael *clergyman*

Seattle
Brunett, Alexander J. *bishop*
Burrows, Elizabeth MacDonald *religious organization executive, educator*
MacDonald, Harry Martin *Presbyterian minister, educator*
Stevens, Robert William *church denomination administrator*
Warner, Vincent W. *bishop*

Snohomish
Reese, Kerry David *minister*

Spokane
Keller, Robert M. *bishop*
Lee, Richard Francis James *evangelical clergyman, media consultant*
Polley, Harvey Lee *retired missionary and educator*
Shannon, Michael Thomas *priest*
Skylstad, William S. *bishop*
Terry, Frank Jeffrey *bishop*

Sumas
Labate, Frank Richard *minister*

Tacoma
Peterson, Thomas Charles *minister, pastoral counselor and therapist*
Rhoades, Freeman Sidney *pastor*
Wold, David C. *bishop*

Vancouver
Kingdom, Roger Douglass *theology educator, minister*

Yakima
Bishop, David Stewart *clergyman*

WYOMING

Cheyenne
Hart, Joseph H. *bishop*

Cody
Grimes, Daphne Buchanan *priest, artist*

Worland
Foster, William Silas, Jr. *minister*

TERRITORIES OF THE UNITED STATES

AMERICAN SAMOA

Pago Pago
Weitzel, John Quinn *bishop*

GUAM

Hagatna
Apuron, Anthony Sablan *archbishop*

CANADA

ALBERTA

Calgary
Curtis, John Barry *archbishop*

Camrose
Campbell, John D. *religious organization administrator*
Ingibergsson, Asgeir *minister, librarian*
Raaflaub, Vernon Arthur *religion educator*
Ritter, Walter Adolf *minister, educator*

Edmonton
Doyle, Wilfred Emmett *retired bishop*
Mac Neil, Joseph Neil *archbishop*

Sherwood Park
Johnson, Frank Arthur *minister*

BRITISH COLUMBIA

Abbotsford
Holdcroft, Leslie Thomas *clergyman, educator*

Clayburn
Van Kleek, Laurence McKee (Laurie Van Kleek) *minister, librarian, educator*

Kamloops
Sabatini, Lawrence *bishop*

Richmond
Plomp, Teunis (Tony Plomp) *minister*

Vancouver
Exner, Adam *archbishop*
Rothenberger, Victor Conrad Immanuel *minister*

Victoria
De Roo, Remi Joseph *bishop*

SASKATCHEWAN

Canora
Udod, Hryhory *priest, church official*

Prince Albert
Morand, Blaise E. *bishop*

Regina
Mallon, Peter *archbishop*

Saltcoats
Farquharson, Walter Henry *retired minister, church official*

Saskatoon
Jacobson, Sverre Theodore *retired minister*

YUKON TERRITORY

Whitehorse
Lobsinger, Thomas *bishop*

ENGLAND

London
Rader, Paul Alexander *minister, administrator*

ADDRESS UNPUBLISHED

Austin, David Leonard, II *bishop*
Baehr, Theodore *religious organization administrator, communications executive*
Barker, Verlyn Lloyd *retired minister, educator*
Black, Susan Easton *religious studies educator, writer*
Bond, Vernon Hugh *priest, Ph.D.*
Carter, Paul Dennis *pastor*
Crocker, J. A. Frazer, Jr. *minister, social worker*

Dawson, Martha Morgan *minister, writer*
Dornette, Ralph Meredith *church organization executive, educator, minister*
Emerson, R. Clark *priest, business administrator*
Ford, Alonzo Anthony *minister*
Hoops, William James *clergyman*
Johnson, Alice Elaine *retired academic administrator*
Johnson, Gordon Gilbert *religion educator, minister*
Jones, Elizabeth Selle *minister*
Kerr, Nancy Karolyn *pastor, mental health consultant*
Légaré, Henri Francis *archbishop*
McNabb, Robert Henry *minister*
Mobley, Patricia Ann (Trish Mobley) *lay church worker, church secretary*
Nelson, Alan Jan *minister, evangelist*
Norris, June Rudolph *minister*
Parsons, Elmer Earl *retired clergyman*
Pelotte, Donald Edmond *bishop*
Plastow, John Robert *religion writer, publisher, musician*
Roberts, Arthur Owen *religion and philosophy educator, clergyman*
Robinson, Clayton David *minister, educator*
Russell, Patrick James *priest*
Setchko, Edward Stephen *minister, theology educator*
Sherwood, John Martin *rabbi*
Swanson, Paul Rubert *minister*
Vreugdenhil, Ralph Lyle *minister*
Ward, John J. *bishop*
White, Lerrill James *clinical pastoral educator*
Williams, John Christopher Richard *bishop*

SCIENCE: LIFE SCIENCE

UNITED STATES

ALASKA

Anchorage
Keffer, Maria Jean *environmental auditor*
Kudenov, Jerry David *zoology educator*
Nielsen, Jennifer Lee *molecular ecologist, researcher*
Treacy, Stephen Delos *marine mammalogist, actor, playwright*

Fairbanks
White, Robert Gordon *research director, biology educator*

Palmer
Klebesadel, Leslie Joe *research agronomist*

Skagway
Barbee, Bob *administrator*

ARIZONA

Bisbee
Behney, Charles Augustus, Jr. *veterinarian*
Johnson, Heidi Smith *science educator*

Litchfield Park
Ollson, Mickey Louis *zoo owner*

Mesa
Ackerman, Lowell J. *veterinarian, writer*

Phoenix
Bolin, Vernon Spencer *microbiologist, consultant*
Papp, Harry *science association administrator*

Tempe
Meyer, Michael C. *diversified company executive*

Tucson
Blue, James Guthrie *retired veterinarian*
Gerba, Charles Peter *microbiologist, educator*
Lai, LiWen *molecular geneticist, educator*
McCormick, Floyd Guy, Jr. *agricultural educator, college administrator*
Shannon, Robert Rennie *optical sciences center administrator, educator*

Window Rock
Hathaway, Loline *zoo and botanic park curator*

CALIFORNIA

Antioch
Saho, S. Bamba *science educator, writer*

Arcadia
Morse, Judy *science foundation administrator*

Berkeley
Kohwi-Shigematsu, Terumi *research scientist*
Rao, Sulekha *molecular biologist, researcher*
Shank, Charles Vernon *science administrator, educator*
Wake, David Burton *biology educator*
Wohletz, Leonard Ralph *soil scientist, consultant*

Chino
Pfuntner, Allan Robert *entomologist*

Chula Vista
Neudecker, Stephen K. *marine ecologist, museum professional*

Citrus Heights
Brydon, Harold Wesley *entomologist, writer*

Costa Mesa
Visco, Frank Joseph *biology educator, consultant*
Visco, Kim Kelly *biologist, educator, financial consultant*

Cupertino
Cheeseman, Douglas Taylor, Jr. *wildlife tour executive, photographer, educator*

Davis
Bernoco, Domenico *immunogeneticist, educator*
Butler, Edward Eugene *plant pathology educator*
Chalupa, Leo M. *neurobiologist, educator, science administrator*
Klasing, Susan Allen *environmental toxicologist, consultant*
Kunkee, Ralph Edward *viticulture and enology educator*
Laidlaw, Harry Hyde, Jr. *entomology educator*

Duarte
Lundblad, Roger Lauren *research director*
Smith, Steven Sidney *molecular biologist*

El Centro
Flock, Robert Ashby *retired entomologist*

Encinitas
Duval, Julian J. *zoo executive*

Fairfield
Link, Julia Anne *urban horticulture educator*

Foothill Ranch
Courtney, Angela *veterinarian, researcher*

Gilroy
McGrogan, Michael Patrick *molecular and cell biologist*

Grass Valley
Pasten, Laura Jean *veterinarian*

Healdsburg
Vail, Michael Edward *viticulturist, agronomist*

Hopland
Timm, Robert Merle *wildlife specialist, administrator*

Irvine
Demetrescu, Mihai Constantin *research scientist, educator, computer company executive*
Lawton, Michael James *entomologist, pest management specialist*

Julian
Hirshberg, Jerilyn Burdette *biologist, naturalist*

La Jolla
Bayliff, William Henry *fishery biologist*
Blume-Jensen, Peter *molecular biologist*
Fishman, William Harold *cancer research foundation executive, biochemist*
Guillemin, Roger C. L. *physiologist*
McRee, Duncan Everett *molecular biologist, researcher*

Laguna Niguel
Coleman, Roger Dixon *bacteriologist*

Lake Arrowhead
Asher, James Edward *forestry consultant, engineer, arborist, forensic expert*

Lewiston
McColm, George Lester *international agricultural consultant, journalist*

Los Altos
Gale, Robert Martin *research scientist, consultant*

Los Angeles
Brown, Sally Ann *research scientist*
Burk, Maksymilian *retired scientist, writer*
Dell, Maria Margarita *anatomist*
Kaback, Howard Ronald *scientific research investigator, educator*
Kadner, Carl George *biology educator emeritus*
Korge, Paavo *cell physiologist*
Mattoni, Rudolf Heinrich Theodor *conservation biologist*
McClure, William Owen *biologist*
Mohr, John Luther *biologist, environmental consultant*
Plummer Cobb, Jewel *biologist, minority education advocate*
Rotter, Jerome Israel *medical geneticist*
Schopf, James William *paleobiologist*
Shi, Wenyuan *microbiologist*
Storms, Lester C. (C Storms) *retired veterinarian*
Teutsch, Champion Kurt *psycho-geneticist*

Magalia
Sincoff, Steven Lawrence *science administrator, scientist*

Manteca
Rainey, Barbara Ann *sensory evaluation consultant*

Menlo Park
Feder, John Nathan *molecular biologist*
Geibel, John Joseph *biologist*

Merced
Olsen, David Magnor *chemistry and astronomy educator*

Modesto
Moe, Andrew Irving *veterinarian*

Moffett Field
McDonald, Henry (Harry McDonald) *research center administrator*

Oakland
Firoozabady, Ebrahim *plant scientist*
Parrott, Joel *zoo director*
Whitsel, Richard Harry *biologist, entomologist*

Orinda
Borson, Daniel Benjamin *physiology educator, inventor, researcher, lawyer*

Palm Desert
Olsen, Deborah Andreé *agriculturist, researcher, consultant*

Palo Alto
Sanders, William John *research scientist*
Scoledes, Aristotle Georgius Michale *retired science and technology educator, research consultant*

Pasadena
Gruenwald, Oskar *research institute executive, consultant*
Lewis, Edward B. *biology educator*
Tappan, Janice Ruth Vogel *animal behavior researcher*

Riverside
Hamilton, Solomon Maximy *physiologist, educator*
Martins-Green, Manuela *cell biologist*

Sacramento
Baker, Maria *zoological park administrator*
Booze, Thomas Franklin *toxicologist*
Hackney, Robert Ward *plant pathologist, nematologist, parasitologist, molecular geneticist, commercial arbitrator*
Rosenberg, Dan Yale *retired plant pathologist*
Stoaks, Ralph Duval *science administrator*

San Bernardino
Mian, Lal Shah *entomologist, educator*

San Diego
Crick, Francis Harry Compton *science educator, researcher*
Donnelly, Tracy Ann *biological researcher*
Georgakakos, Konstantine Peter *research hydrologist*
Heuschele, Werner Paul *veterinary researcher*
Myers, Douglas George *zoological society administrator*
Nordt, Sean Patrick *clinical toxicologist*
Panetta, Joseph Daniel *biotechnology executive*
Risser, Arthur Crane, Jr. *zoo administrator*
Teng, Min *research scientist*
Wehrli, John Erich *biotechnology executive*
Weinrich, James Donald *psychobiologist, educator*

San Fernando
McCraven, Eva Stewart Mapes *health service administrator*

San Francisco
Anderson, David E. *zoological park administrator*
Brown, Walter Creighton *biologist*
Cappucci, Dario Ted, Jr. *veterinarian, scientist*
Furst, Arthur *toxicologist, educator*
Goldstein, Bernard *biology educator*
Handler, Evelyn *science administrator*
Nichols, Richard Alan *ecologist*
Turner, Paul Reginald *biologist*

San Jose
Bishop, James E. *biotechnologist, research scientist*
Khurshudov, Andrei *tribologist, researcher*
Taylor, Kendrick Jay *microbiologist*

San Juan Capistrano
White, Beverly Jane *cytogeneticist*

San Leandro
Pourfarzaneh, Mohammad-Taghi (Matt) *biotechnology*

San Luis Obispo
Piirto, Douglas Donald *forester, educator*

San Marcos
Liggins, George Lawson *microbiologist, diagnostic company executive*

San Marino
Hanson, George Peter *retired research botanist, real estate investor*

Santa Ana
Glazier, Ron *zoological park administrator*

Santa Barbara
Drapkin, Herbert *biology educator, consultant*
Jordan, Mary Ann *research biologist*
Schneider, Edward Lee *botanic garden administrator*

Santa Clara
Mansfield, Elaine Schultz *molecular geneticist, automation specialist*

Santa Monica
Lin, Hun-Chi *molecular biologist*

Santa Rosa
Heinberg, Richard William *science educator*

Santee
Hardy, Ben(son B.) *orchid nursery executive*
Morris, John David *research institute administrator, geology educator*

Stanford
Francke, Uta *medical geneticist, genetics researcher, educator*
Hsu, SheauYu *molecular physiologist*
Jettmar, Eva *research scientist, consultant*
Matin, A. *microbiology educator, consultant*
Strena, Robert Victor *university research laboratory manager*
Tiller, William Arthur *retired science educator, scientific researcher*

Stockton
Magness, Rhonda Ann *microbiologist*

Ventura
Arita, George Shiro *biology educator*

Vista
Winslow, Philip Charles *agriculturist, marketing consultant*

Walnut
Shannon, Cynthia Jean *biology educator*
Smith, Harry Mendell, Jr. *science educator*

Westminster
Allen, Merrill James *marine biologist*

Woodland Hills
Fox, Stuart Ira *physiologist*

COLORADO

Arvada
Dotson, Gerald Richard *retired biology educator*

Boulder
Armstrong, David Michael *biology educator*
Clifford, Steven Francis *science research director*
Knoelker, Michael *science observatory administrator*
Serafin, Robert Joseph *science center administrator, electrical engineer*
Staehelin, Lucas Andrew *cell biology educator*

Colorado Springs
Clifford, Walter Jess *microbiologist, immunologist*
Comes, Robert George *research scientist*
DuPee, Pamela Annette *fisheries biologist, educator, consultant*
Zimkas, Charles Patrick, Jr. *space foundation administrator*

Denver
Freiheit, Clayton Fredric *zoo director*
Heifets, Leonid *microbiologist, researcher*
Mitchell, Jerry Michael *biologist*
Salmon, Merlyn Leigh *laboratory executive*

Estes Park
Jones, A. Durand *park administrator*

Fort Collins
Burns, Denver P. *forestry research administrator*
Lameiro, Gerard Francis *corporate strategist*
Morgan, Jack Adrien *plant physiologist*
Seidel, George Elias, Jr. *animal scientist, educator*
Smith, Gary Chester *meat scientist, researcher*
Smith, Ralph Earl *virologist*

Golden
Bergeron, Sheila Diane *retired science educator, educational consultant*

Longmont
Ulrich, John August *microbiology educator*

Pueblo
Martínez, Lee Anne *aquatic ecologist, biology educator*

HAWAII

Ewa Beach
Chock, Alvin Keali'i *retired botanist*

Haleiwa
Woolliams, Keith Richard *arboretum and botanical garden director*

Honolulu
Donlon, Timothy A. *cytogeneticist*
Evenhuis, Neal Luit *entomologist*
Lamoureux, Charles Harrington *botanist, arboretum administrator*
Randall, Helen Au *biologist, researcher, editor*
Redman, Ken *zoo officer*
Siddiqi, Toufiq Aliuddin *science administrator, researcher, educator*
Stahl, Margo Schneebalg *marine biologist*

Kamuela
Young, Ernest *park administrator*

Kapaa
Chimoskey, John Edward *physiologist, medical educator*

Kihei
Skelton, Ray Beck *agriculture company administrator, consultant*

Lawai
Cox, Paul Alan *biologist, educator*

Pearl City
Hertlein, Fred, III *industrial hygiene laboratory executive*
Kanenaka, Rebecca Yae *microbiologist*

Tripler Army Medical Center
Uyehara, Catherine Fay Takako (Yamauchi) *physiologist, educator, pharmacologist*

IDAHO

Hayden Lake
Lehrer, William Peter, Jr. *animal scientist*

Idaho Falls
Blackman, Harold Stabler *research scientist*

Moscow
Mahler, Robert Louis *soil scientist, educator*

MONTANA

Bozeman
Costerton, John William Fisher *microbiologist*
Lavin, Matthew T. *horticultural educator*

Butte
Peoples, Donald R. *research scientist*

Great Falls
Paulson-Ehrhardt, Patricia Helen *sales executive*

Havre
Clouse, Vickie Rae *biology and paleontology educator*

Helena
Johnson, John Philip *geneticist, researcher*

Miles City
Bellows, Robert Alvin *research physiologist*

NEVADA

Fallon
Isidoro, Edith Annette *horticulturist*

Las Vegas
Alexander, John Bradfield *scientist, retired army officer*

Minden
Petchenev, Alex *scientist*

Reno
Johnson, Arthur William, Jr. *planetarium executive*
Luo, Yiqi *ecologist, researcher*

NEW MEXICO

Albuquerque
Darnell, Ray D. *zoo director*
Kuethe, Dean Otis *scientist*
Perez-Castro, Ana Veronica *developmental biology researcher*

Carlsbad
Deckert, Frank *park administrator*
Goldstein, Barry Bruce *biologist, food company executive, lawyer*

Cedar Crest
Rypka, Eugene Weston *microbiologist*

Las Cruces
Briggs, Dinus Marshall *agriculturist*
McElyea, Ulysses, Jr. *veterinarian*

Los Alamos
Freyer, James Paul *tumor biologist, educator*
Gupta, Goutam *biologist, biophysicist*

Rio Rancho
Bartels, Aloysia de Bessierés *mariculturist, seafood producer*

Santa Fe
Harding, Marie *ecological executive, artist*
Myers, Charlotte Will *biology educator*

OREGON

Ashland
Christianson, Roger Gordon *biology educator*

Clackamas
Wall, Brian Raymond *forest economist, business consultant, researcher, author, policy analyst, telemarketing sales executive*

Corvallis
Castellano, Michael Angelo *research forester*
Castle, Emery Neal *agricultural and resource economist, educator*
Ho, Iwan *research plant pathologist*
Rygiewicz, Paul Thaddeus *plant ecologist*
Young, J. Lowell *soil chemist, biologist*

Cottage Grove
Clark, Mary Eleanor *retired biology educator*

Elgin
Scott, Harlan Noel *tree farmer, writer*

Eugene
Grossen, Bonnie J. *research scientist*

Gresham
Arney, James Douglas *forestry biometrics consultant*

Hillsboro
Bhagwan, Sudhir *computer industry and research executive, consultant*

Newport
Weber, Lavern John *marine science administrator, educator*

Phoenix
Blackman, David Lee *research scientist*

Portland
Button, Jerry Edward *biologist*
Gillette, Richard Gareth *neurophysiology educator, researcher*
Grimsbo, Raymond Allen *forensic scientist*
Hagenstein, William David *forester, consultant*
Wilson, Thomas Woodrow, III *research scientist, consultant*

Salem
Douglas, Stephen Ross *scientist, physicist*

UTAH

Logan
Skujiņš, John Janis *soil biochemist, environmental consultant*
Vest, Hyrum Grant, Jr. *horticultural sciences educator*

Provo
Hansen, Ronald Gordon *retired research administrator, consultant*

Salt Lake City
Bloebaum, Roy Drake *biologist educator, bioengineering researcher*
Dinsmore, Craig *zoo director*
Opitz, John Marius *clinical geneticist, pediatrician*

WASHINGTON

Bothell
Xu, Wei *scientist, engineer*

Centralia
Kyte, Lydiane *retired botanist*

Colfax
Young, Joann Elizabeth *veterinarian*

Ellensburg
Ninnemann, John Louis *biology educator, college dean*

Friday Harbor
Brookbank, John W(arren) *retired microbiology educator*

Kent
Schneider, Eugene Saul *microbiologist, laboratory administrator*

Lakewood
Kennedy, Michael Leo *biology and chemistry educator*

Nespelem
Paris, Richard Wayne *forester*

Olympia
Raphael, Martin George *research wildlife biologist*

Pullman
Shen, Yongrong *research scientist*
Tang, Juming *food engineering educator*

Puyallup
Newcombe, Alan George *plant pathologist*

Richland
Anderson, James Arthur *research laboratory administrator*
Chikalla, Thomas David *retired science facility administrator*

Seattle
Disteche, Christine M. *geneticist*
Edmondson, W(allace) Thomas *retired limnologist, educator*
Iwasaki, Kouichi *molecular geneticist*
Lee, Qwihee Park *plant physiologist*
Miller, Robert Carmi, Jr. *microbiology educator, university administrator*
Motulsky, Arno Gunther *geneticist, physician, educator*
Ning, Xue-Han (Hsueh-Han Ning) *physiologist, researcher*
Schiffrin, Milton Julius *physiologist*
Wott, John Arthur *arboretum and botanical garden executive, horticulture educator*
Yee, Hsian Chiang *science administrator*

Sequim
Pearson, Walter Howard *marine biologist, researcher*

Tacoma
Otten, Thomas *zoological park director*

WYOMING

Jackson
Davis, Randy L. *soil scientist*

MILITARY ADDRESSES OF THE UNITED STATES

EUROPE

FPO
Haberberger, Richard Louis, Jr. *microbiologist, epidemiologist*

CANADA

ALBERTA

Calgary
Yoon, Ji-Won *virology, immunology and diabetes educator, research administrator*

BRITISH COLUMBIA

Vancouver
Newman, Murray Arthur *aquarium administrator*
Suzuki, David Takayoshi *geneticist, science*

Victoria
Bousfield, Edward Lloyd *biologist*
Finlay, Audrey Joy *environmental educator, consultant, naturalist*

ITALY

Milan
Dulbecco, Renato *biologist, educator*

ADDRESS UNPUBLISHED

Applehans, Troy Scot *animal scientist*
Baker, Joseph Roderick, III *aviculturist*
Bautista, Anthony Hernandez *biomedical company executive*
Cameron, Roy Eugene *scientist*
DeLuca, Thomas Henry *soil scientist, researcher*
Dubesa, Elaine J. *biotechnology company executive*
Fraker, Mark Arnott *environmental scientist*
Gennaro, Antonio L. *biology educator*
Gray, Nicolin Jane Plank *botanist, educator*
Herz, Michael Joseph *marine environmental scientist*
Jarvik, Gail Pairitz *medical geneticist*
Latham, James Richard *research scientist*
Lim, Hwa Aun *research geneticist, bioinformaticist, consultant*
Maslansky, Carol Jeanne *toxicologist*
Monary, Michael Anthony *horticulturist*
Palade, George Emil *biologist, educator*
Pettit, Ghery DeWitt *retired veterinary medicine educator*
Starr, Robert Irving *plant physiologist, chemist*
Thomas, Teresa Ann *microbiologist, educator*
Tung, Yeishin *research scientist*
van Hengel, Drusilla Ruth *social ecologist*
Weinstock, Ronald Jay *research and development company executive*

SCIENCE: MATHEMATICS AND COMPUTER SCIENCE

UNITED STATES

ALASKA

Elmendorf AFB
Carson, Gregory Donald *information scientist*

ARIZONA

Fort Huachuca
Clark, Brian Thomas *mathematical statistician, operations research analyst*

Phoenix
Doto, Irene Louise *statistician*
Heidmann, Paul Scott *software engineer*
Mandelin, Michael Forrest *computer scientist, consultant*
Nusbaum, Ellen Jane *technology professional*

Scottsdale
Loch, Patricia Ann *software company executive, consultant*

Sierra Vista
Sizemore, Nicky Lee *computer scientist*

Tucson
Barber, Kathleen Ann Starks *software developer, public relations consultant*
Ferko, Christopher Andrew *computer network engineering administrator*

CALIFORNIA

Albany
Depasquale, Donald L. *mathematics educator*

Antioch
Neimann, Albert Alexander *mathematician, business owner*

Banning
Swick, Sean Bowman *software developer*

Berkeley
Bailey, David H. *computer scientist*
Bickel, Peter John *statistician, educator*
Dimitrić, Radoslav Milan *mathematician, translator*
Frenkel, Edward Vladimir *mathematician, educator*
Khatri, Sunil Papanchand *computer engineer*
McKusick, Marshall Kirk *computer scientist*
Shvidler, Mark Joseph *mathematician*
Smith, Alan Jay *computer science educator, consultant*
Wahl, Bernt Rainer *mathematician, writer, software engineer*
Wu, Kesheng (John) (John Wu) *computer scientist*

Brea
de la Piedra, Xavier, III *computer and business systems analyst, programmer*

Burbank
Aylsworth, Wendy Lynn *technology executive*
Dickson, Stewart Price *graphics programmer*

Calabasas
Radin, Michael Ross *software company executive*

Camarillo
Vumix, C(ecil) Robert *programmer, systems analyst*

Campbell
Hales, Craig Paul *international systems mechanical engineer*

Sabram, Steve *software engineer, human resources specialist*

Carlsbad
Fairhurst, Jeffrey Thomas *software consultant*
Soltice, Caprice Ann *computer programmer*

Carmichael
Givant, Philip Joachim *mathematics educator, real estate investment executive*

Carson
Kowalski, Kazimierz *computer science educator, researcher*
Suchenek, Marek Andrzej *computer science educator*

Castroville
Guglielmo, Eugene Joseph *software engineer, consultant*

Concord
Fuld, Fred, III *computer consultant, financial consultant*

Corte Madera
Barker, Celeste Arlette *computer scientist*

Costa Mesa
Panaccione, Bruce Roy *system analyst, geographer*

Culver City
Hu, Lincoln *media technology executive, computer scientist*

Cupertino
Fleming, Laura Christine *software engineer*
Holmes, Richard Albert *software engineer, consultant*
Lu, Jian *computer scientist*
Sproule, Betty Ann *computer industry strategic planning manager*

Cypress
Cao, Dac-Buu *software engineer*

Davis
Mulase, Motohico *mathematics educator*
Olsson, Ronald Arthur *computer science educator*

El Segundo
Woike, Lynne Ann *computer scientist*

Elk Grove
McDavid, Douglas Warren *systems consultant*

Escondido
Collins, George Timothy *computer software consultant*

Folsom
Cross, Charley Bradford *software consultant*
Pederson, Carrie Ann *systems engineer, product trainer*

Foothill Ranch
Sperling, Scott Edward *software consultant*

Foster City
Scheer, Janet Kathy *mathematics educator*
Takara, Ken Takagi *software engineer, artist*

Fountain Valley
Berman, Steven Richard *software engineer*

Fremont
Dunn, Larry A. *computer engineer*

Fresno
Michael, James Daniel *computer scientist*

Gilroy
McCarty, Robert Clarke *mathematician*

Glendale
Nowitzky, Mark Albin *computer programmer*
Woody, William Edward *software developer*

Gonzales
Dunkle, Michael Joseph *mathematics and technology educator*

Hayward
Duncan, Doris Gottschalk *information systems educator*
Prada, Gloria Ines *mathematics and Spanish language educator*
Sabharwal, Ranjit Singh *mathematician*

Hermosa Beach
Trowe, Paul Biagio *computer scientist*

Huntington Beach
Willenborg, Jonathan Edward *computer specialist*

Irvine
Abu-Mostafa, Ayman Said *computer consultant*
Chacon, Michael Ernest *computer networking specialist*
Hoffman, Donald David *cognitive and computer science educator*
Juberg, Richard Kent *mathematician, educator*
Vibber, James Charles *software engineer*
Wan, Frederic Yui-Ming *mathematician, educator*

La Honda
Melvin, Jay Wayne *computer programmer*

La Jolla
Wallerstedt, James Douglas *information technology consultant*

La Mesa
Allen, David Charles *computer science educator*

Lancaster
Darr, David Carl *computer systems manager*

Livermore
Blattner, Meera McCuaig *computer science educator*
Haga, Enoch John *computer educator, author*

Long Beach
Palacios, Alana Sue *computer programmer*
Schroeder, Arnold Leon *mathematics educator*
Wollmer, Richard Dietrich *statistics and operations research educator*

Los Angeles
Abbott, Russell Joseph *computer scientist*
Cong, Jason Jingsheng *computer scientist, educator, consultant, researcher*
Delaney, Matthew Sylvester *mathematics educator, academic administrator*
Jacobsen, Laren *programmer, analyst*
Lyashenko, Nikolai Nikolaevich *mathematician, educator*
Maiocchi, Roberto *software engineer*
Malozemov, Leonid A. *mathematician*
Olsen, John David *computer consultant*
Pearl, Judea *computer scientist, educator*
Pottenger, Mark McClelland *computer programmer*
Requicha, Aristides Adelino Gualberto *computer scientist*
Stormes, John Max *instructional systems developer*
Symonds, Norman Leslie *computer programming specialist*
Wong, Kenneth Lee *software engineer, import executive, consultant*

Los Gatos
Vahur, Martin *systems analyst*

Malibu
Crawford, Natalie Wilson *applied mathematician*

Manhattan Beach
Lucas, Suzanne *statistician, entrepreneur*

Marina Del Rey
Touch, Joseph Dean *computer scientist, educator*

Martinez
Tong, Siu Wing *computer programmer*

Menlo Park
Neumann, Peter Gabriel *computer scientist*
Wilt, Adam Jay *engineering consultant, filmmaker, videographer*

Milpitas
Crain, Ray *statistician, consultant*

Mission Viejo
Srinivasan, Uppili R. *software engineer*

Moffett Field
Baldwin, Betty Jo *computer specialist*

Monterey
Lundy, Gilbert Moulton, Jr. *computer science educator*

Monterey Park
Hsieh, William Shen-chu *statistician, educator*

Morgan Hill
Mancini, Robert Karl *computer analyst, consultant*

Mountain View
Anton, Francis Matthew, Jr. *software engineer*

Northridge
Stratton, Gregory Alexander *computer specialist, administrator, mayor*

Oakland
Long, William Joseph *software engineer*
Onyeador, Emmanuel Osita *mathematics and computer educator*

Oceanside
Aaron, Alexander *systems analyst, consultant*

Orange
Smith, John LeRoy *mathematics educator*

Oxnard
Banner-Bacin, Linda Lenore *program analyst*

Palo Alto
Amin, Massoud *executive, systems science and mathematics educator*
Belalia, Abdelkader *computer consultant*
Beretta, Giordano Bruno *computer scientist, researcher*
Kolarov, Krasimir Dobromirov *computer scientist, researcher*
Mahmood, Aamer *computer system architect*
Shah, Devang Kundanlal *software engineer*

Pasadena
Patterson, Mark Jerome *computer software designer*

Pico Rivera
Donoghue, John Charles *software management consultant*

Pleasanton
Petersen, Ann Nevin *computer systems administrator, consultant*

Port Hueneme
Schilbrack, Karen Gail *systems analyst*

Portola Valley
Kuo, Franklin F. *computer scientist, electrical engineer*

Ramona
Bennett, James Chester *computer consultant, real estate developer*

Riverside
Bhanu, Bir *computer information scientist, educator, director university program*

SCIENCE: PHYSICAL SCIENCE

UNITED STATES

ARIZONA

Amado
Criswell, Stephen *astronomer*

Flagstaff
Millis, Robert Lowell *astronomer*

Glendale
Pearson, Keith Laurence *retired environmental scientist*

Kingman
Peterson, Claudette May *chemistry educator*

Page
Leus McFarlen, Patricia Cheryl *water chemist*

Peoria
Lichtenberg, Larry Ray *chemist, consultant, researcher*

Phoenix
Bolin, Vladimir Dustin *chemist*
Lovvik, Daryl Vaughn *consulting geologist*
McKeighen, Ronald Eugene *physicist*
Yang, Lin *chemist*

Prescott
Ayres, Jeffrey John *chemistry educator*

Rio Rico
Lowell, J(ames) David *geological consultant, cattle rancher*

Scottsdale
Hockmuth, Joseph Frank *physicist, psychotherapist*

Sedona
Cameron, Winifred Sawtell *astronomer*

Tempe
Comfort, Joseph Robert *physics educator*
Gulkarov, Ilia Semenovich *physicist, researcher*
Juvet, Richard Spalding, Jr. *chemistry educator*
McKelvy, Michael John *materials chemist, research scientist*
Moore, Carleton Bryant *geochemistry educator*
Sharma, Renu *educator, researcher*
Wehinger, Peter Augustus *astronomer, educator*

Tucson
Barrett, Bruce Richard *physics educator*
Clarke, Robert Francis *nuclear physicist, consultant*
Fink, James Brewster *geophysicist, consultant*
Grayeski, Mary Lynn *chemist, foundation administrator*
Green, Richard Frederick *astronomer*
Gruhl, James *energy scientist*
Kamilli, Robert Joseph *geologist*
Kiersch, George Alfred *geological consultant, retired educator*
Kippelen, Bernard *physicist, educator*
Lamb, Willis Eugene, Jr. *physicist, educator*
Osterkamp, Waite Robert *hydrologist*
Quigg, Richard John *metallurgist, lawyer*
Sewell, Charles Robertson *geologist, exploration company executive, investor*
Willis, Clifford Leon *geologist*

CALIFORNIA

Altadena
Mkryan, Sonya *geophysicist, researcher, educator*

Arcata
Zoellner, Robert William *chemistry educator*

Atascadero
Zima, Gordon Everett *metallurgist*

Bakersfield
Becerra, Augusto Antonio *geologist*

Belmont
Gombocz, Erich Alfred *biochemist*

Berkeley
Alpen, Edward Lewis *biophysicist, educator*
Birman, Alexander *physicist, researcher*
Chamberlain, Owen *nuclear physicist*
Fuhs, G(eorg) Wolfgang *environmental research manager*
Glaser, Donald Arthur *physicist*
Kurtzman, Ralph Harold *retired biochemist, researcher, consultant*
Lester, William Alexander, Jr. *chemist, educator*
Moore, C. Bradley *chemistry educator*
Seaborg, Glenn Theodore *chemistry educator*
Steiner, Herbert Max *physics educator*
Townes, Charles Hard *physics educator*
Weber, Eicke Richard *physicist*

Bonita
Wood, Fergus James *geophysicist, consultant*

Burlingame
Hotz, Henry Palmer *physicist*

Canyon Lake
Schilling, Frederick Augustus, Jr. *geologist, consultant*

Carmel
Clarke, Leo Creusot *retired meteorologist*
Vagnini, Livio Lee *chemist, forensic consultant*

Chino
Koestel, Mark Alfred *geologist, photographer*

Claremont
White, Kathleen Merritt *geologist*

Corona
Garrett, Thomas Monroe *chemist*

Costa Mesa
Bender, Edward Erik *geology educator, researcher*
Lattanzio, Stephen Paul *astronomy educator*
Lorance, Elmer Donald *organic chemistry educator*

Davis
Land, Donald Paul *chemistry educator*
Lee, Young Moo *protein chemist*
Stumpf, Paul Karl *biochemistry educator emeritus*

El Cerrito
Riddell, Robert James, Jr. *retired physicist*

El Segundo
Chien, Kuei-Ru *chemical physicist*
Kostoulas, Ioannis Georgiou *physicist*

Emeryville
Masri, Merle Sid *biochemist, consultant*

Encino
Thorpe, Gary Stephen *chemistry educator*

Escondido
Tomomatsu, Hideo *chemist*

Fallbrook
Tess, Roy William Henry *chemist*

Foothill Ranch
Testa, Stephen Michael *geologist, consultant*

Foster City
Banik, Gautam Gour *biochemical engineer*
Zaidi, Iqbal Mehdi *biochemist, scientist*

Fountain Valley
Davis, Jeremy Matthew *chemist*
Gittleman, Morris *consultant, metallurgist*

Fremont
Lee, Chan-Yun *physicist, process engineer, educator*

Fullerton
Evangelista, Ramon A. *chemist*
Perakh, Mark *physicst*

Glendale
Levy, Ezra Cesar *aerospace scientist, real estate broker*
Nercissiantz, Ara Z. *chemistry researcher*

Hollister
Smith, George Larry *analytical and environmental chemist*
Spencer, Douglas Lloyd *chemist, manufacturing executive*

Irvine
Bradshaw, Ralph Alden *biochemistry educator*
Cho, Zang Hee *physics educator*
Cicerone, Ralph John *geophysicist*
Rowland, Frank Sherwood *chemistry educator*

La Habra
Woyski, Margaret Skillman *retired geology educator*

La Jolla
Buckingham, Michael John *oceanography educator*
Burbidge, E. Margaret *astronomer, educator*
Edelman, Gerald Maurice *biochemist, neuroscientist, educator*
Goodman, Murray *chemistry educator*
Huntley, Mark Edward *biological oceanographer*
Kitada, Shinichi *biochemist*
Lobert, Jürgen Michael *research chemist*
Mullis, Kary Banks *biochemist*
Nierenberg, William Aaron *oceanography educator*
Patton, Stuart *biochemist, educator*
Ramanathan, Veerabhadran *oceanographer, educator*
Safonov, Vladimir Lazarevich *physicist, researcher*
Shih, Hsiencheng *medicinal chemist*

La Verne
Hwang, Cordelia Jong *chemist*

Livermore
Ellsaesser, Hugh Walter *retired atmospheric scientist*
Hooper, Edwin Bickford *physicist*
Saito, Theodore T. *physicist*
Tarter, Curtis Bruce *physicist, science administrator*
Wilson, James Ricker *physicist, consultant*

Los Altos
Hahn, Harold Thomas *physical chemist, chemical engineer*
Hall, Charles Frederick *space scientist, government administrator*

Los Angeles
Boado, Ruben Jose *biochemist*
Chester, Marvin *physics educator*
Coleman, Paul Jerome, Jr. *physicist, educator*
Cram, Donald James *chemistry educator*
Edwards, Kenneth Neil *chemist, consultant*
Kivelson, Margaret Galland *physicist*
Koga, Rokutaro *physicist*
Krupp, Edwin Charles *astronomer*
Lauer, George *environmental consultant*
Morrison, Jean *geochemist, geology educator*
Olah, George Andrew *chemist, educator*
Shapiro, Isadore *materials scientist, consultant*
Simkhovich, Boris Zalman *biochemist, researcher*
Smith, William Ray *retired biophysicist, engineer*
Woodruff, Fay *paleoceanographer, geological researcher*
Yanai, Michio *meteorologist, educator*

Los Osos
Topp, Alphonso Axel, Jr. *environmental scientist, consultant*

Malibu
Mataré, Herbert F. *physicist, consultant*
Pepper, David M. *physicist, educator, author, inventor*

Marina
Shane, William Whitney *astronomer*

Weaver, William Bruce *astronomer, operations analyst*

Menlo Park
Boyarski, Adam Michael *physicist*
Friend, David Robert *chemist*
Hodgen, Laurie Dee *geologist, editor*
Luepke, Gretchen *geologist*

Milpitas
Hines, Horace H., Jr. *physicist*

Modesto
Morrison, Robert Lee *physical scientist*

Moffett Field
Salama, Farid *astrophysicist, spectroscopist, research scientist*

Monrovia
Andary, Thomas Joseph *biochemist*

Montecito
Wheelon, Albert Dewell *physicist*

Monterey
Turner, Robert Elwood *physicist*

Morgan Hill
Kuster, Robert Kenneth *scientist*

Mountain View
Allamandola, Louis John *low temperature chemist/astrophysicist*

Northridge
Court, Arnold *climatologist*
Huebner, Albert Louis Charles *physics educator, writer*

Oak Park
Caldwell, Stratton Franklin *kinesiology educator*

Oakland
Brust, David *physicist*
Mikalow, Alfred Alexander, II *deep sea diver, marine surveyor, marine diving consultant*

Orange
Korb, Lawrence John *metallurgist*
Talbott, George Robert *physicist, mathematician, educator*

Orinda
Baker, Don Robert *chemist, inventor*

Pacific Grove
Lindstrom, Kris Peter *environmental consultant*

Pacific Palisades
Csendes, Ernest *chemist, corporate and financial executive*

Palmdale
Smith, Maureen McBride *laboratory administrator*

Palo Alto
Datlowe, Dayton Wood *space scientist, physicist*
Haisch, Bernhard Michael *astronomer*
Krishnamurthy, V.V. *chemist*
Panofsky, Wolfgang Kurt Hermann *physicist, educator*
Saxena, Arjun Nath *physicist*
Taimuty, Samuel Isaac *physicist*

Paradise
Wilder, James D. *geology and mining administrator*

Pasadena
Anderson, John David *astronomer, researcher*
Dressler, Alan Michael *astronomer*
Ferber, Robert Rudolf *physics researcher, educator*
Frautschi, Steven Clark *physicist, educator*
Frederickson, Arthur Robb *physicist*
Friedl, Randall Raymond *environmental scientist*
Heindl, Clifford Joseph *physicist*
Hughes, Emlyn Willard *physics educator*
Ingersoll, John Gregory *physicist, energy specialist, educator*
Koonin, Steven Elliot *physicist, educator, academic administrator*
Marcus, Rudolph Arthur *chemist, educator*
Oemler, Augustus, Jr. *astronomer*
Orton, Glenn Scott *astronomer, research scientist*
Schieldge, John Philip *physicist, researcher*
Stone, Edward Carroll *physicist, educator*
Tingay, Steven John *astronomer*
Tombrello, Thomas Anthony, Jr. *physics educator, consultant*

Penn Valley
Klohs, Murle William *chemist, consultant*

Placerville
Beneš, Norman Stanley *meteorologist*

Redondo Beach
Ball, William Paul *physicist, engineer*

Redwood City
Nacht, Sergio *biochemist*

Richmond
Barashkov, Nickolay Nickolayevich *polymer chemist, researcher*
Ward, Carl Edward *research chemist*

Ridgecrest
Bennett, Harold Earl *physicist, optics researcher*
Lepie, Albert Helmut *chemist, researcher*

Riverside
Orbach, Raymond Lee *physicist, educator*
White, Robert Stephen *physics educator*

Sacramento
Matanga, George Bwalya *hydrologist*

Salinas
Mercurio, Edward Peter *natural science educator*

San Diego
Clauson, Gary Lewis *chemist*
Fisher, Frederick Hendrick *oceanographer emeritus*
Funk, Clarence John *physicist*
Gillespie, George Hubert *physicist*
Hayes, Claude Quinten Christopher *research scientist*
Kraus, Pansy Daegling *gemology consultant, editor, writer*
Lapota, David *oceanographer, marine biologist*
Mogg, Donald Whitehead *chemist*
Morgan, Mark Quenten *astronomer, astrophysics educator*
Patel, Jasmin Rambhai *medicinal chemist, consultant, researcher*
Reeve, Lorraine Ellen *biochemist, researcher*
Roeder, Stephen Bernhard Walter *chemistry and physics educator*
Seegall, Manfred Ismar Ludwig *retired physicist, educator*
Shackelford, Gordon Lee, Jr. *physics educator*
Shneour, Elie Alexis *biochemist*
Tara *research chemist, publishing executive, writer*

San Francisco
Burri, Betty Jane *research chemist*
Gegeliya, Dmitriy Ilich *chemist, researcher*
Nguyen, Ann Cac Khue *pharmaceutical and medicinal chemist*
Raedeke, Linda Dismore *geologist*
Seibel, Erwin *oceanographer, educator*
Shapiro, Margaret Goodwin *astronomy educator*
Sussman, Brian Jay *meteorologist, weather broadcaster*

San Jose
Berkland, James Omer *geologist*
Eigler, Donald Mark *physicist*
Pitts, William Clarence *physicist*
Rao, Kameswara Kolla *physicist, electrical engineer*

San Luis Obispo
Grismore, Roger *physics educator, researcher*
Ludin, Roger Louis *physics educator*

Santa Ana
Dumdum, Josefina Martinez *chemist, researcher*

Santa Barbara
Gutsche, Steven Lyle *physicist*
Kennedy, John Harvey *chemistry educator*
Kohn, Walter *educator, physicist*
Kram, Mark Lenard *hydrogeologist, environmental geochemist*
Martzen, Philip D. *physicist, software developer*
Strahler, Arthur Newell *former geology educator, author*

Santa Clara
Gozani, Tsahi *nuclear physicist*

Santa Cruz
Anderson, Roger William *chemistry educator*
Bernasconi, Claude François *chemistry educator*
Brown, George Stephen *physics educator*
Kostic, Petar Jovan *physicist*
Zhao, Xixi *geologist, geophysicist*

Santa Maria
Ellis, Emory Leon *retired biochemist*

Santa Monica
Davies, Merton Edward *planetary scientist*
Intriligator, Devrie Shapiro *physicist*
Park, Edward Cahill, Jr. *retired physicist*

Saratoga
Shimazaki, Tatsuo *physicist*

Selma
Hushek, Joseph Charles *chemistry educator*

South San Francisco
Campos, Joaquin Paul, III *chemical physicist, regulatory affairs analyst*
Canova-Davis, Eleanor *biochemist, researcher*

Stanford
Berg, Paul *biochemist, educator*
Fetter, Alexander Lees *theoretical physicist, educator*
Kennedy, Donald *environmental science educator, former academic administrator*
Kornberg, Arthur *biochemist*
Mukerji, Tapan *geophysicist, researcher*
Osheroff, Douglas Dean *physicist, researcher*
Richter, Burton *physicist, educator*
Schawlow, Arthur Leonard *physicist, educator*
Taube, Henry *chemistry educator*
Taylor, Richard Edward *physicist, educator*
Trost, Barry Martin *chemist, educator*
Wang, Suwen *physicist, consultant*

Sunnyvale
Chang, William Zhi-Ming *physicist, researcher*
DeMello, Austin Eastwood *astrophysicist, concert artist, poet, writer*
Qian, Xueyu *physicist*

Tarzana
Nies, Kevin Allison *physics educator*

Thousand Oaks
Wang, I-Tung *atmospheric scientist*

Torrance
Manasson, Vladimir Alexandrovich *physicist*
Zhao, Mingjun *physicist, research scientist*

Tustin
Zhu, Peter Chaoquan *chemist*

Van Nuys
Duque, Ricardo German *analytical chemist*
[illegible], George E. *plasmaphysicist*

Weaverville
Hettich, Kay L. *wilderness advocate, mountaineer*

Woodland Hills
Harris, Sigmund Paul *physicist*
Michal, Ronald James *physicist*
Monteau, Norman Keith *gemologist*

Wrightwood
Haile, Marcus Alfred *retired chemistry educator*

COLORADO

Arvada
Downey, Joe S. *geohydrologist*

Aurora
Grace, William Pershing *petroleum geologist, real estate developer*

Boulder
Cech, Thomas Robert *chemistry and biochemistry educator*
Esposito, Larry Wayne *planetary astronomer*
Garstang, Roy Henry *astrophysicist, educator*
Goetz, Alexander Franklin Hermann *geophysicist, educator*
Koldewyn, William Almon *aerospace physicst*
Little, Charles Gordon *geophysicist*
MacDonald, Alexander Edward *meteorologist*
Miller, Harold William *nuclear geochemist*
Naugolnykh, Konstantin Aleksandrovich *physicist*
Rundle, John Belting *physicist, educator*
Schnell, Russell Clifford *atmospheric scientist, researcher*
Siewert, Thomas Allen *metallurgist*
Tatarskii, Valerian Il'Ich *physics researcher*
Trenberth, Kevin Edward *atmospheric scientist*
Whiteside, Lowell Stanley *seismologist*
Zavorotny, Valery Ustimovich *physicist, researcher*

Canon City
Fair, Annie May *geological computer specialist*

Colorado Springs
Gossard, Earl Everett *physicist*

Denver
Brown, Mark Steven *medical physicist*
Chaffee, Maurice Ahlborn *geologist*
Clark, Aaron Lee *environmental consulting executive*
Eaton, Gareth Richard *chemistry educator, university dean*
Hendrick, R. Edward *medical physicist, researcher, educator*
Johnson, Walter Earl *geophysicist*
Klipping, Robert Samuel *geophysicist*
Robinson, George Makenzia Lewis *mining services director*
Sherlin, Jerry Michael *retired hydro meteorological technician*
Smith, Dwight Morrell *chemistry educator*
Starkey, Harry Charles *retired geologist*

Englewood
Rosich, Rayner Karl *physicist*

Evergreen
Heyl, Allen Van, Jr. *geologist*

Golden
Corry, Charles Elmo *geophysicist, consultant*
Freeman, Val LeRoy *geologist*
Morrison, Roger Barron *geologist*
Trefny, John Ulric *academic administrator, dean*

Greeley
Fadner, Willard Lee *physics educator, researcher*

Lakewood
Mauter, Warren Eugene *chemist, business development manager*
Oakley, David Sterling *physics educator, consultant*
Parker, John Marchbank *consulting geologist*

Littleton
Eby, David Eugene *geologist*
Sjolander, Gary Walfred *physicist*

Westminster
Tohill, Bruce Owen *geologist*

HAWAII

Camp H M Smith
Surface, Stephen Walter *water treatment chemist, environmental protection specialist*

Hawaii National Park
Swanson, Donald Alan *geologist*

Hickam AFB
Miller, David Allen *physicist*

Honolulu
Kong, Laura S. L. *geophysicist*
Meech, Karen Jean *astronomer*
Ogburn, Hugh Bell *chemical engineer, consultant*
Yount, David Eugene *physicist, educator*

Kahului
Nishimoto, Marc Makoto *research chemist*

IDAHO

Deary
Cazeau, Charles Jay *geologist*

Emmett
Bennett, Gary Lee *physicist, consultant*

Idaho Falls
Jones, James Litton *nuclear scientist, research technologist*

Moscow
Goszczynski, Stefan *chemistry educator*
Miller, Maynard Malcolm *geologist, educator, research institute director, explorer, state legislator*
Shreeve, Jean'ne Marie *chemist, educator*
Stumpf, Bernhard Josef *physicist*

MONTANA

Billings
Darrow, George F. *natural resources company owner, consultant*

Bozeman
Rebane, Aleksander *physicist, educator*

Columbia Falls
Spade, George Lawrence *scientist*

Dayton
Volborth, Alexis von *geochemistry and geological engineering educator*

Rollins
Zelezny, William Francis *retired physical chemist*

Twin Bridges
Ruppel, Edward Thompson *geologist*

NEVADA

Carson City
Holmes, Richard Brooks *mathematical physicist*

Henderson
Holloway, Robert Wester *radiochemist*

Las Vegas
Kielhorn, Richard Werner *chemist*
Levich, Robert Alan *geologist*
Nacht, Steve Jerry *geologist*
Philip, Nixon Baldwin, Jr. *chemist*

Reno
Taranik, James Vladimir *geologist, educator*

Wellington
Drew, Charles Milton *chemist*

NEW MEXICO

Albuquerque
Cramer, James Dale *physicist, scientific company executive*
Evans, Pauline D. *physicist, educator*
Freiwald, David Allen *physicist, mechanical engineer*
Harrison, Charles Wagner, Jr. *applied physicist*
Hylko, James Mark *health physicist, certified quality auditor*
Johnson, Ralph Theodore, Jr. *physicist*
O'Donnell, Edward Earl *physicist*
Passman, Stephen Lee *theoretical mechanics scientist*
Robinson, Charles Paul *nuclear physicist, diplomat, business executive*
Romig, Alton Dale, Jr. *materials scientist, educator*
Seidel, Sally Carol *physicist, educator*
Weart, Wendell D. *nuclear waste management scientist*

Las Cruces
Lease, Jane Etta *environmental science consultant, retired librarian*
Mason, Paul Alexander *astronomer*

Los Alamos
Atcher, Robert Whitchill *chemist, educator*
Garvey, Doris Burmester *environmental administrator*
Grilly, Edward Rogers *physicist*
Hakkila, Eero Arnold *retired nuclear safeguards technology chemist*
Hansen, Glen Arthur *scientist, researcher*
Hirt, Cyril William *physicist*
Jagnow, David Henry *petroleum geologist*
Kwon, Chuhee *physics researcher*
Makaruk, Hanna Ewa *theoretical physicist*
Michaudon, André Francisque *physicist*
Mjolsness, Raymond Charles *retired physicist, researcher*
O'Brien, Harold Aloysius, Jr. *nuclear chemist, physics researcher, consultant*
Owczarek, Robert Michal *physicist*
Ramsay, John Barada *research chemist, educator*
Stratton, William Robert *physicist*
Trewhella, Jill *biophysicist*

Los Alanese
Ostrovsky, Lev Aronovich *physicist, oceanographer, educator*

Portales
Varela, Manuel Francisco *microbiologist*

Santa Fe
Cowan, George Arthur *chemist, bank executive, director*
Gell-Mann, Murray *theoretical physicist, educator*
Schoenborn, Benno P. *biophysicist, educator*
Wheeler, Charles Mervyn *retired chemistry educator*

Socorro
Broadhead, Ronald Frigon *petroleum geologist, geology educator*
Kottlowski, Frank Edward *geologist*

NORTH DAKOTA

Grand Forks
Gust, Gregory John *meteorologist, educator*

OREGON

Ashland
Abrahams, Sidney Cyril *physicist, crystallographer*
Grover, James Robb *chemist, editor*

Bend
Gustafson, Lewis Allan *engineering geologist*

Clackamas
Walters, Thomas Byron *metrology analyst*

Corvallis
Stevens, Jan Frederik *phytochemist, researcher, pharmacist*

Eugene
Diwu, Zhenjun *chemist*
Donnelly, Russell James *physicist, educator*
Girardeau, Marvin Denham *physics educator*
Hansen, Carl Frederick *chemistry educator*
Peticolas, Warner Leland *retired physical chemistry educator*
Youngquist, Walter Lewellyn *consulting geologist*

Monmouth
White, Donald Harvey *physics educator emeritus*

Otter Rock
Kassner, Michael Ernest *materials science educator, researcher*

Portland
Lincoln, Sandra Eleanor *chemistry educator*
Marsh, John Harrison *environmental planner, lawyer*

UTAH

Brigham City
Fife, Dennis Jensen *chemistry educator, career officer*

Garrison
Beeston, Joseph Mack *metallurgist*

Logan
Emert, George Henry *biochemist, academic administrator*
Scouten, William Henry *chemistry educator, academic administrator*

Provo
Bradshaw, Jerald Sherwin *chemistry educator, researcher*

Salt Lake City
Hardy, Byron Lynn *medical physicist*
Kenison, Lynn T. *chemist*
Mattis, Daniel Charles *physicist, educator*
Parry, Robert Walter *chemistry educator*
Taylor, Philip Craig *physics educator*
Wall, Lloyd L. *geological engineer*

WASHINGTON

Bellevue
Delisi, Donald Paul *fluid mechanic, geophysicist*
Fremouw, Edward Joseph *physicist*
Malik, Sohail *chemistry educator, researcher, consultant*
Rossi, Amadeo Joseph *chemist*
Watson, Mathew D. *optical scientist*

Bothell
Alvi, Khisal Ahmed *chemist*

Coupeville
Eaton, Gordon Pryor *geologist*

Ellensburg
Rosell, Sharon Lynn *physics and chemistry educator, researcher*

Everett
Punches, Howard Ki Neal *physicist, retired*

Independence
Feng, Xiangdong Shawn *chemist*

Manchester
Fearon, Lee Charles *chemist*

Oak Harbor
Daugherty, Kenneth Earl *research company executive, educator*

Olympia
Bloomquist, Rodney Gordon *geologist*
Schmidt, John Wesley *radiation health physicist, environmental scientist*

Port Ludlow
Dunning, Kenneth Laverne *research physicist*

Port Orchard
Chamberlain, Isabel Carmen (Isa Chamberlain) *environmental chemist*

Pullman
Banas, Emil Mike *physicist, educator*
Hamilton, Charles Howard *metallurgy educator*

Renton
Hu, John Chih-An *retired chemist, research engineer*

Richland
Fruchter, Jonathan Sewell *research scientist, geochemist*
Onishi, Yasuo *environmental researcher*
Stenner, Robert David *environmental and health research engineer, toxicologist*
Sundaram, Shanmugauelayutham Kamakshi *materials scientist, consultant*

Seattle
Dehmelt, Hans Georg *physicist*
El-Moslimany, Ann Paxton *paleoecologist, educator, writer*
Erdmann, Joachim Christian *physicist*
Evans, Bernard William *geologist, educator*
Fischer, Edmond Henri *biochemistry educator*
Gerhart, James Basil *physics educator*
Henley, Ernest Mark *physics educator, university dean emeritus*
Krebs, Edwin Gerhard *biochemistry educator*
Lackie, Kenneth William *physical scientist*
Lubatti, Henry Joseph *physicist, educator*
Walsh, Kenneth Andrew *biochemist*
Wasserman, William Jack *chemistry educator*

Spokane
Campbell, Harry Woodson *geologist, mining engineer*
Segal, Vladimir M. *metallurgist, researcher*

Tacoma
Ames, Kenneth Carl *hydrologist, geology educator*
Harding, Karen Elaine *chemistry educator and department chair*

Vancouver
Stockton, Roderick Alan *chemist*

WYOMING

Casper
Ptasynski, Harry *geologist, oil producer*

Laramie
Hausel, William Dan *economic geologist, martial artist*
Roark, Terry Paul *astronomer, educator*

Wapiti
Sowerwine, Elbert Orla, Jr. *chemist, chemical engineer*

CANADA

BRITISH COLUMBIA

Vancouver
Smith, Michael *biochemistry educator*

TAIWAN

Taipei
Yuan Tseh Lee *chemistry educator*

ADDRESS UNPUBLISHED

Ball, Lawrence *retired physical scientist*
Borges, William, III *environmental scientist*
Detert, Miriam Anne *chemical analyst*
Flor, Loy Lorenz *chemist, corrosion engineer, consultant*
Hatcher, Herbert John *biochemist, microbiologist*
Hubbard, Gregory Scott *physicist*
Hunt, Allen Gerhard *physicist, geologist*
Inlow, Rush Osborne *chemist*
Jones, Thornton Keith *research chemist*
Khattatov, Boris *geophysicist*
Levy, David Howard *astronomer, writer*
Lillegraven, Jason Arthur *paleontologist, educator*
Lloyd, Joseph Wesley *physicist, researcher*
Lowry, William Prescott *meteorologist, consultant*
Matossian, Jesse Nerses *physicist*
Mauzy, Michael Philip *environmental consultant, chemical engineer*
Mitkov, Igor *physicist*
Olsen, Clifford Wayne *retired physical chemist, consultant*
Pall-Pallant, Teri *paleontologist, inventor, behavioral scientist, design engineer, advertising agency executive*
Petersen, Arne Joaquin *chemist*
Price, Clifford Warren *retired metallurgist, researcher*
Procunier, Richard Werner *environmental scientist, administrator*
Pyper, James William *chemist*
Rigali, Louis Anthony *scientific instruments company executive*
Rosenkilde, Carl Edward *physicist*
Schelar, Virginia Mae *chemistry consultant*
Schmidt, Ruth A(nna) M(arie) *geologist*
Shariff, Asghar J. *geologist*
Sharon, Timothy Michael *physicist*
Shen, Jun *scientist*
Shockley, James Thomas *physics educator*
Steinlicht, Steven *astrologer, minister, educator*
Tartakovsky, Daniel Miron *hydrologist, applied mathematician*
Tedford, Charles Franklin *biophysicist*
West, Jack Henry *petroleum geologist*
Wu, Qiong Joan *hydrologist*
Yonover, Robert Norris *geochemist*

SOCIAL SCIENCE

UNITED STATES

ALASKA

Anchorage
Baker, Phillip Wilson *psychologist*
Gier, Karan Hancock *counseling psychologist*
Henderson, Karen Sue *psychologist*
Holland, Kathryn Marie *archaeologist, anthropologist*
Kernodle, Una Mae *home economics curriculum specialist, retired secondary education educator*
Risley, Todd Robert *psychologist, educator*
Suddock, Frances Suter Thorson *grief educator, writer*

Fairbanks
McBeath, Gerald Alan *political science educator, researcher*

Santa Cruz
Pratkanis, Anthony Richard *social psychologist, educator*
Rorer, Leonard George *psychologist, writer*

Santa Monica
Russell, Marlou *psychologist*
Wolf, Charles, Jr. *economist, educator*

Simi Valley
Whitley, David Scott *archaeologist*

Stanford
Abramovitz, Moses *economist, educator*
Anderson, Martin Carl *economist*
Arrow, Kenneth Joseph *economist, educator*
Bueno de Mesquita, Bruce James *political science educator*
Friedman, Milton *economist, educator emeritus, author*
Fuchs, Victor Robert *economics educator*
Krasner, Stephen David *political science educator*
Kreps, David Marc *economist, educator*
Lewis, John Wilson *political science educator*
Oksenberg, Michel Charles *political scientist, educator*
Paul, Benjamin David *anthropologist, educator*
Reynolds, Clark Winton *economist, educator*
Ricardo-Campbell, Rita *economist, educator*

Stockton
Phillips, John Chester *sociology educator*
Werner, Roger Harry *archaeologist*

Sun City
Fisher, Weston Joseph *economist*

Sylmar
Yguado, Alex Rocco *economics educator*

Tiburon
Harary, Keith *psychologist, researcher, writer*

Tustin
London, Ray William *clinical and forensic psychologist*

Upland
Rice, Sharon Margaret *clinical psychologist*

Ventura
Kent, Theodore Charles *psychologist*
Soper, Henry Victor *neuropsychologist*

Visalia
Fortier, Dana Suzanne *psychotherapist*

Vista
Beversdorf, Anne Elizabeth *astrologer, author, educator*

Walnut
Martin, George *psychologist, educator*

Walnut Creek
Keith, Bruce Edgar *political analyst, genealogist*

Whittier
Harvey, Richard Blake *political science educator*
McKenna, Jeanette Ann *archaeologist*

Woodland Hills
Blanchard, William Henry *psychologist*
Nierenberg, Norman *urban land economist, retired state official*

Yorba Linda
Kiley, Robert Ralph *governmental affairs consultant*

COLORADO

Boulder
Churchill, Ward L. *social sciences educator, writer*
Greenberg, Edward Seymour *political science educator, writer*
Harvey, O.J. *retired psychology educator*
Walker, Deward Edgar, Jr. *anthropologist, educator*

Canon City
Hubbell, Robert Newell *psychologist*

Colorado Springs
Plunkett, Michael C. *psychotherapist*

Denver
Adelman, Jonathan Reuben *political science educator, consultant*
Cortese, Charles Franklin *sociologist, educator, planning consultant*
Guyot, Gary Wayne *psychology educator*
Laird, Frank N. *political science educator*
Mills, Kathleen Claire *anthropology and mathematics educator*
Moeller, Richard Robert *political science educator*
Rosica, Karen *psychologist, psychoanalyst, writer*
Winters, Richard Allen *mineral economist*

Durango
Reddy, Mark Andrew *handwriting specialist, educator*

Estes Park
Moore, Omar Khayyam *experimental sociologist*

Fort Carson
Chomko, Stephen Alexander *archaeologist*

Fort Collins
Berry, Kenneth J. *sociology educator*
Hautaluoma, Jacob Edward *psychology educator, college associate dean*
Kling, Robert William *economist*
Phillips, Ronnie Jack *economics educator*
Standing Bear, Zugguelgeres Galafach *criminologist, forensic scientist, educator*
Suinn, Richard Michael *psychologist*

Fort Lupton
Stevenson, James Ralph *school psychologist, author*

Golden
Wellisch, William Jeremiah *social psychology educator*
Woolsey, Robert Eugene Donald *mineral economics, mathematics and business administration educator*

Greeley
Kelsey, Michael Loyal *geography educator*

La Junta
Strong, Mayda Nel *psychologist, educator*

Littleton
Drury, Doris Marie *economics educator, consultant, researcher*
Lohman, Loretta Cecelia *social scientist, consultant*
Milliken, John Gordon *research economist*

Longmont
Sorensen, Martha Stewart *psychologist*

Parker
James, Franklin Joseph, Jr. *public policy educator*

Pueblo
Kulkosky, Paul Joseph *psychology educator*
Vega, Jose Guadalupe *psychologist, clinical director*

DISTRICT OF COLUMBIA

Washington
Fata, Daniel Paul *foreign policy specialist*
Stiglitz, Joseph Eugene *economist*

HAWAII

Honolulu
Bitterman, Morton Edward *psychologist, educator*
Brennan, Jerry Michael *economics educator, statistician, researcher, clinical and forensic psychologist*
Cho, Lee-Jay *social scientist, demographer*
Corsini, Raymond Joseph *psychologist*
Cruthers, Mark Carroll Harold *social studies educator, religous instructor*
Flannelly, Kevin J. *psychologist, research analyst*
Fullmer, Daniel Warren *psychologist, educator, retired*
Gaydos, Gregory George *political scientist, educator*
Hatfield, Elaine Catherine *psychology educator*
Juarez, Carlos Edward *political scientist, researcher*
Laney, Leroy Olan *economist, banker, educator*
Levi, Werner *political science educator*
Morse, Richard *social scientist*
Riggs, Fred Warren *political science educator*
Weiner, Ferne *psychologist*

Kaneohe
Joshi-Peters, Karuna Laxmiprasad *psychologist*

Mililani
Kiyota, Heide P. *psychologist*

IDAHO

Boise
Overgaard, Willard Michele *retired political scientist, jurisprudent*

Caldwell
Lonergan, Wallace Gunn *economics educator, management consultant*

Sandpoint
Glock, Charles Young *sociologist*

Twin Falls
Wright, Frances Jane *educational psychologist*

KANSAS

Manhattan
Lemire, David Stephen *school psychologist, educator*

MONTANA

Bozeman
Gray, Philip Howard *retired psychologist, educator*
Spencer, Robert C. *retired political science educator*
Stroup, Richard Lyndell *economics educator, writer*

Helena
Seiler, Karen Peake *psychologist*

Missoula
Payne, (Orville) Thomas *political scientist, educator*
Watkins, John Goodrich *psychologist, educator*

NEVADA

Carson City
Brandenburg, Carlos Henry *clinical psychologist*

East Ely
Alderman, Minnis Amelia *psychologist, educator, small business owner*

Incline Village
Jones, Robert Alonzo *economist*

Las Vegas
Benbow, Richard Addison *psychological counselor*

North Las Vegas
Perlman, Seth Joseph *political risk analyst*

Reno
Chang, Maria Hsia *political science educator*
Chu, Shih-Fan (George Chu) *economics educator*
Cummings, Nicholas Andrew *psychologist*
Song, Shunfeng *economist, researcher*

NEW MEXICO

Albuquerque
Baker, Arnold Barry *economist*
Collins, Steven Thomas *archaeologist, educator*
Condie, Carol Joy *anthropologist, research facility administrator*
Heady, Ferrel *retired political science educator*
May, Philip Alan *sociology educator*
Stuart, David Edward *anthropologist, author, educator*
Tainter, Joseph Anthony *archaeologist*

Aztec
Moore, Roger Albert, Jr. *archaeologist*

Corrales
Adams, James Frederick *psychologist, educational administrator*

Las Cruces
Lease, Richard Jay *police science educator, former police officer*

Las Vegas
Riley, Carroll Lavern *anthropology educator*

Los Alamos
Thompson, Lois Jean Heidke Ore *psychologist*

Mesilla
Mather, E. Cotton *geography educator*

Santa Fe
Kingman, Elizabeth Yelm *anthropologist*

Taos
Pasternack, Robert Harry *school psychologist*
Young, Jon Nathan *archeologist*

OREGON

Ashland
Houston, John Albert *political science educator*

Corvallis
Gillis, John Simon *psychologist, educator*
Harter, Lafayette George, Jr. *economics educator emeritus*

Eugene
Aikens, C(lyde) Melvin *anthropology educator, archaeologist*

Gresham
Anderson, Michael Robert *computer forensics specialist*

Monmouth
Shay, Roshani Cari *political science educator*

Portland
Blodgett, Forrest Clinton *economics educator*
Broughton, Ray Monroe *economic consultant*
Goldy, Daniel Louis *economist, consultant*
Ricks, Mary F(rances) *archaeologist, anthropologist, consultant*

White City
Moore, Charles August, Jr. *psychologist*

UTAH

Ogden
Niklason, Lucille Viola *retired psychologist, marriage & family therapist*

Provo
Bahr, Howard Miner *sociologist, educator*
Bergin, Allen Eric *clinical psychologist, educator*
Cornwall, Marie *sociology educator*
Kunz, Phillip Ray *sociologist, educator*

Salt Lake City
Benjamin, Lorna Smith *psychologist*
Giles, Gerald Lynn *psychology, learning enhancement, computer educator*
Goodey, Ila Marie *psychologist*
Mangum, Garth Leroy *economist, educator*

Sandy
Smith, Willard Grant *psychologist*

WASHINGTON

Bellevue
Akutagawa, Donald *psychologist, educator*

Des Moines
Ortmeyer, Carl Edward *retired demographer*

Ellensburg
Collins, Fuji *mental health professional*
Jacobs, Robert Cooper *political scientist, consultant*

Everett
Van Ry, Ginger Lee *school psychologist*

Freeland
Helwing, Geraldine Marlene *psychologist, psychoanalyst, psychoneuroimmunologist*

Friday Harbor
MacGinitie, Walter Harold *psychologist*

Hansville
Blalock, Ann Bonar *policy analyst, evaluation researcher*

Pullman
Dunlap, Riley Eugene *sociologist*
McIntyre, Lisa Jean *sociologist, educator*

Richland
Roop, Joseph McLeod *economist*

Seattle
Beyers, William Bjorn *geography educator*
Butler, Keith Arnold *psychologist, software researcher*
Chirot, Daniel *sociology and international studies educator*
Cowhey, Peter Francis *international relations educator, consultant*
Downing, Douglas Allan *economics educator, writer*
Eliason, Leslie Carol *comparative public policy educator*
Ellings, Richard James *political and economic research institution executive*
Fox, Matthew Adrian *political campaign consultant, musician*
Herman-Dunn, Ruth Ann *psychologist*
Trippel, Stuart Andrew Thomas *economist, consultant*

Sequim
Mc Hugh, Margaret Ann Gloe *psychologist*

Tacoma
Guilmet, George Michael *cultural anthropologist, educator*

Vancouver
Craven, James Michael *economist, educator*

Walla Walla
Kaufman-Osborn, Timothy Vance *politics and leadership educator*

Wenatchee
Lehinger, Susan Elizabeth *school psychologist*

WYOMING

Cheyenne
Hirst, Wilma Elizabeth *retired psychologist*

Evanston
Faulkner, Theresa Anne *psychologist*

Laramie
Chai, Winberg *political science educator*
Gill, George Wilhelm *anthropologist*
Shaffer, Sherrill Lynn *economist*
Shogren, Jason Fredrick *economics educator*
Sprinkle, Ronald Leo *counseling psychologist, UFO researcher*

Powell
Brophy, Dennis Richard *psychology and philosophy educator, administrator, clergyman*

Wilson
Breitenbach, Mary Louise McGraw *psychologist, chemical dependency counselor*

CANADA

ALBERTA

Calgary
Forbis, Richard George *archaeologist*

Edmonton
Krotki, Karol Jozef *sociology educator, demographer*
Mardon, Austin Albert *geographer, writer, researcher*

BRITISH COLUMBIA

Vancouver
Aberle, David Friend *anthropologist, educator*
Feaver, George Arthur *political science educator*
Nemetz, Peter Newman *policy analysis educator, economics researcher*
Pearson, Richard Joseph *archaeologist, educator*

Victoria
Barber, Clarence Lyle *economics educator*

SASKATCHEWAN

Saskatoon
Randhawa, Bikkar Singh *psychologist, educator*

GERMANY

Wiesbaden
Choudhury, Raj Deo *economist*

PAPUA NEW GUINEA

Boroko
Pataki-Schweizer, Kerry Josef *behavioral scientist, medical anthropologist*

ADDRESS UNPUBLISHED

Anderson, Duane *anthropologist*
Anderson, Louise Stout *crime analyst*
Andress, Cathy *psychologist, educator*

Archer, Stephen Hunt *economist, educator*

Bandy, Amanda McNeill *anthropologist, educator*

Batson, Raymond Milner *retired cartographer*

Bonnell, Victoria Eileen *sociologist*

Bracey, Earnest Norton *political science educator*

Burkholder, Grace Eleanor *archeologist, educator*

Carden, Thom(as) Ray *psychologist*

Chapman, Richard LeRoy *public policy researcher*

Chatterji, Angana P. *anthropologist*

Crampton, Esther Larson *sociology and political science educator*

Debreu, Gerard *economics and mathematics educator*

Eckelkamp, Marylyn *psychologist*

Farah, Tawfic Elias *political scientist, educator*

Finnberg, Elaine Agnes *psychologist, editor*

Frantz, Gilda Gloria *Jungian analyst*

Grimm, Larry Leon *psychologist*

Haber, Ralph Norman *psychology consultant, researcher, educator*

Haining, Jeane *psychologist*

Hiller, Joan Vitek *sociologist*

Hirsch, Walter *economist, researcher*

Holmes, Paul Luther *political scientist, educational consultant*

Horan, Adel Edward *sociology and psychology educator*

Kealiinohomoku, Joann Wheeler *anthropologist, dance ethnologist, educator*

Keirsey, David West *psychologist, writer*

Kohan, Dennis Lynn *international trade educator, consultant*

Lee, Aldora G. *social psychologist*

Lewis, Robert Turner *retired psychologist*

Lonergan, Thomas Francis, III *criminal justice consultant*

Long, Barbara Ellis *psychologist*

Maquet, Jacques Jerome Pierre *anthropologist, writer*

Markovich, Patricia *economist*

Martin, Joy Anne *clinical psychologist, consultant*

Maxwell, Pamela Joy *clinical psychologist*

McHugh, Betsy Baldwin *sociologist, educator, journalist, business owner*

Pedersen, Knud George *economics educator, academic administrator*

Pine, Charles Joseph *clinical psychologist*

Potter, Anne Louise *political scientist*

Rainey, Marcella *sociology educator*

Richards, Ruth *psychiatrist, educational psychologist*

Sharpe, William Forsyth *economics educator*

Spinweber, Cheryl Lynn *psychologist, sleep specialist*

Stallone, Thomas Michael *clinical psychologist*

Steinhauser, Sheldon Eli *sociology and gerontology educator, consultant*

Stufano, Thomas Joseph *criminologist*

Tonello-Stuart, Enrica Maria *political economist*

Wallerstein, Judith Saretsky *marriage and divorce researcher*

Ward, Albert Eugene *research center executive, archaeologist, ethnohistorian*

Word, Inetta Louise *sewing educator, designer, writer*